# 2011
# College
# Handbook

# 2011 College Handbook

## CollegeBoard

Forty-Eighth Edition

The College Board, New York

**The College Board**

The College Board is a not-for-profit membership association whose mission is to connect students to college success and opportunity. Founded in 1900, the College Board is composed of more than 5,700 schools, colleges, universities and other educational organizations. Each year, the College Board serves seven million students and their parents, 23,000 high schools, and 3,800 colleges through major programs and services in college readiness, college admission, guidance, assessment, financial aid and enrollment. Among its widely recognized programs are the SAT®, the PSAT/NMSQT®, the Advanced Placement Program® (AP®), SpringBoard® and ACCUPLACER®. The College Board is committed to the principles of excellence and equity, and that commitment is embodied in all of its programs, services, activities and concerns.

For further information, visit www.collegeboard.com.

Editorial inquiries concerning this book should be directed to College Planning Services, The College Board, 45 Columbus Avenue, New York, NY 10023-6992; or telephone 212-713-8000.

Copies of this book are available from your local bookseller or may be ordered from College Board Publications, P.O. Box 8670, Reston, VA 20195. The book may also be ordered online through the College Board Store at www.collegeboard.com. The price is $29.99.

ISBN: 978-0-87447-903-4

Printed in the United States of America

The College Board is committed to publishing in a manner that both respects the environment and helps preserve the Earth's resources. We seek to achieve this through eco-friendly practices, including the use of FSC and recycled paper and biodegradable materials. When you see this symbol, be assured that we are working to reduce our ecological footprint. The interior of this book is made of 40% recycled/40% PCW paper.

# Contents

# Preface

When the *College Handbook* first appeared in 1941, students and parents had little access to college information of any kind. Now, in this Internet age, many find the amount of available information to be overwhelming.

What's needed is a single, trusted source where the key facts about colleges can be compared and contrasted on a consistent basis. From its inception, the *Handbook* has met this need by providing college-bound students and their advisers with the authoritative, reliable and up-to-date facts necessary to make informed college decisions.

This edition of the *Handbook* presents facts about 3,873 colleges, universities and technical schools. To be included, an institution must be accredited by a national or regional accrediting association recognized by the U.S. Department of Education and offer some undergraduate degree programs — at least an associate degree.

Throughout the *Handbook*, information is presented in accordance with the Common Data Set initiative, in which the College Board has taken a leading role. The goal of this collaborative effort with other publishers and college administrators is to provide students with the most accurate, consistently comparable data available.

The college descriptions are based primarily on information supplied by the colleges themselves in response to the College Board's Annual Survey of Colleges 2010, with some data supplied by federal and state agencies. The survey was completed by participating colleges in spring 2010. Several thousand college administrators across the country participated in this effort. Without their continued cooperation, publication of the *Handbook* would not be possible.

A staff of data editors verified the facts to be certain that all descriptions are as complete and accurate as possible. Although the College Board makes every effort to ensure that the information about colleges is correct and up to date, we urge students to confirm facts with the colleges themselves.

The enormous task of data collection, management and verification was directed by Connie Betterton and Stan Bernstein, with the assistance of Cathy Serico, Andrew Costello, Renée Gernand, Roger Harris and Doris Chow. Mary Anne Blazier, May Cooper, Marci Harman, Christina Latimer, Diana McDermott, Randy Peery, Leah Swaggerty, Jenny Xie and Katrina Kingdon compiled, edited and verified the data. Technical support was provided by Chris Dominic, Wayne Lau, Janis Linkov-Johnson, Jason Robertson, Elizabeth Shroyer, Sherry Chen, Sangeetha Nithilaselvan, James Gade, David Skrobela and Jim Clewley.

We thank our readers — you and the many students, parents and counselors whose comments and suggestions over the years have helped to make this the most widely used college directory in the nation. We welcome your suggestions on how the *Handbook* can continue to meet the ever-changing needs of future generations of college-bound students.


Tom Vanderberg
Senior Editor, College Planning Services


Michael Polizzi
Assistant Editor, College Planning Services

# What's in this book

If you're beginning your college search feeling a bit overwhelmed and intimidated by the sheer number of choices, you're not alone. Just about everyone starts out feeling that way. But even the most daunting job can be easily handled with the right tools and a plan, and the *College Handbook* gives you both.

## Getting Started

The *College Handbook* is the best place to begin your college search, and you will no doubt find yourself returning to this source as your search progresses and evolves. You should not, however, rely on this book exclusively. Take advantage of the other resources available to you — the Internet, campus visits and interviews, college fairs and viewbooks, your school counselor, family and friends — before you make your final decision. Don't be dismayed if you find that you must change directions more than once as you learn about the colleges. This only means that you are learning more about yourself as well.

The *Handbook* is divided into four major sections. The first (where you are now) contains guidance materials to help you plan for college. Four-year college descriptions are in the second section, two-year college descriptions are in the third, and the last section contains tables and indexes. Margin tabs help you to quickly move from section to section.

Although you might be eager to dive right into the college descriptions, it is far better to start your college search with a basic idea of what you want to look for. Take the time to go through the guidance materials in the first section to get on the right track. Read the articles, ranging from college admissions and placement tests to dorm life. The valuable insights you gain will give you confidence as you continue your college search.

Once you can identify your needs and preferences with regard to college size and type and have an idea of what other characteristics are important to you, the indexes at the end of the book will help you locate colleges that fit the bill.

**KNOW THE LINGO**

You'll find sidebars like this throughout the first part of this book highlighting and defining key terms. There's also a comprehensive glossary beginning on page 40.

For a complete explanation of the various index categories, see "Tables and Indexes" beginning on page 7.

The heart and soul of the *Handbook*, of course, are the descriptions of four-year and two-year colleges. These follow standard formats to make it easy to find a particular item of information in any description and to compare one college with another. Read "The College Descriptions" below to see what the descriptions contain and how the information is presented. If you are not sure of the meaning of a term found in the *Handbook* descriptions or guidance materials, check the glossary beginning on page 40.

# The College Descriptions

**The college.** Each description begins with the college's official name — which isn't always the one in popular use. The heading also includes the college's city, state and website address. Most colleges now have websites that are invaluable resources in your college search. The designation "CB member" after the college's name indicates that the college is a member of the College Board; the four-digit CB code should be used when requesting that SAT® scores or Advanced Placement® (AP®) grades be sent to the college.

**Key facts.** The bulleted list highlights information that you may want to compare across colleges and that you'll need if you decide to apply. This information includes:

- Type of institution (e.g., liberal arts college, university) and whether it has a religious affiliation.

- Whether the campus is urban, suburban or rural, and whether it is primarily a residential or a commuter campus.

- Total number of undergraduate students; profile of the undergraduate student body (percent part-time, women, minority breakdown, international); total number of graduate students on campus. *Two-year undergraduate data are included under Student Profile.*

- Percentage of applicants admitted to the freshman class, which gives you some idea of how competitive the college is. *Four-year colleges only.*

- Admissions requirements for fall 2011: tests, essay, interview (if required of all applicants).

- Percentage of students who graduate within six years (most students take more than four years to earn a bachelor's degree). Caveat: This figure is based on students who enrolled as freshmen and remained to graduate; it does not include students who transferred into or out of the college during that period.

**General information.** The date the college was founded, the type of institutional accreditation it has, the number and type of degrees awarded in 2008-09, and whether the college has an ROTC program will give you a sense of the academic life on campus. Whether the college organizes its calendar on a semester, trimester, quarter or some other schedule indicates the way the college structures its courses.

Pay particular attention to the faculty information. The total number of faculty and its makeup are important to your everyday experience at an institution. Class size information, showing percentages of classes with few or many students, is another indication of a college's learning environment. Colleges were also invited to provide a list of special facilities (from arboretums to zoos) or additional unique information about their institutions in this section.

*For two-year colleges only:* This is where you will find total enrollment figures for both degree-seeking and non-degree-seeking students, and information about partnerships with other schools or organizations.

**Freshman class profile.** (*Four-year colleges*) This provides a snapshot of the college's 2009 freshman class and is presented in tabular format to make it easily accessible. This is the best source of information about whether your own profile fits in with that of students currently attending the college, and whether you'd be comfortable if admitted.

- Number who applied, were admitted and enrolled.

- Mid-50 percent of enrolled freshmen's SAT/ACT test scores. This is the score range for half the freshman class. (Remember that 25 percent of enrolled freshmen scored below and 25 percent above the reported figures.)

- Information about high school GPA and class rank.

- Percentage who completed the year in good standing and returned as sophomores.

- Percentage who come from out of state, live on campus, are international students, and join fraternities or sororities.

**Student profile.** (*Two-year colleges*) This is similar to the freshman class profile for four-year colleges, but the data presented covers the entire undergraduate student body.

- Percentage enrolled in transfer or vocational programs. Number admitted and enrolled as first-time, first-year students. Percentage who already have a bachelor's degree or higher. Number who transferred from other institutions.

- Percentage of the total undergraduate student body who are part-time students, live on campus, are women, come from out of state, are minorities and are international students.

**Transfer out.** (*Two-year colleges*)

- Percentage of students in transfer programs who go on to four-year colleges.

- Colleges to which most students transferred in 2009.

**Basis for selection.** This is where you can find the details of a college's admissions policies, including factors the college considers most important in deciding whether or not to offer you admission. If it says "Open admission,"

---

## KNOW THE LINGO

**Campus** — The physical location of a college or university. Includes classroom buildings, libraries, research facilities, dormitories, dining halls and administration buildings.

**Branch campus** — A part of a college, university or community college that is geographically separate from the main campus, has its own faculty and administration, and may have separate admissions requirements and degree programs.

that means the college accepts anyone with a high school or GED diploma, space permitting. Special requirements for homeschooled and learning-disabled students are also reported here.

**High school preparation.** Almost all colleges listed in the *Handbook* require a high school diploma or its equivalent. Some colleges have very specific requirements in terms of education background and high school courses taken. The required and recommended number of course units that applicants should have taken in high school is listed here. Where a range is given, the lower number represents the required units; the higher number is a recommendation.

**2010-11 annual costs.** You should estimate and anticipate the total annual costs for each college you are considering. In doing so, the elements listed below need to be considered. Unless otherwise noted, the reported figures reflect the costs for the 2010-11 academic year.

- *Tuition/fees* include the cost of instruction and mandated fees for all students. For public colleges, both in-state and out-of-state costs are listed. If the college combines tuition, fees, and room and board expenses, that single figure is given as a comprehensive fee.

- *Room/board* figures are for a student living on campus in a double room with a full meal plan. Single rooms or rooms for three or more could cost a lot more or less than the figure reported here. Many colleges have a range of meal plans with fewer meals per week, which would lower your board cost.

- *Books/supplies* expenses can vary depending on the program you take. Some fields, such as art or architecture, may require more expensive supplies.

- *Personal expenses* include items such as clothing, laundry, entertainment and furnishings. Personal expenses will vary widely depending on your lifestyle. Transportation costs are not included.

- *Per-credit-hour tuition* (two-year colleges only) is of particular interest to students planning to attend college part time.

**Financial aid.** This information provides a summary of financial aid awarded for the academic year(s) indicated, and describes financial aid award policies for need-based and non-need-based aid. This information will give you an idea of how first-year and undergraduate student assistance has been awarded and will help you compare financial aid policies among the colleges. You should always contact the admissions or financial aid office for complete information and for answers to any questions you might have regarding eligibility and award policies.

**Application procedures.** This is where you can find out about the college's application procedures and deadlines for both admissions and financial aid.

- *Admissions.* Most colleges require an application fee, noted here, but will waive it for applicants with need. Take note of any "priority dates" — after which qualified applicants are considered on a first-come, first-served basis, and only for as long as slots are available.

**KNOW THE LINGO**

**College** — The generic term for an institution of higher education. Also a term used to designate divisions within a university.

**Liberal arts college** — A college that emphasizes the liberal arts in its core curriculum and academic offerings and does not offer vocational, professional or preprofessional programs.

**University** — An institution of higher education that is divided into several colleges, schools or institutes. Generally, university students take classes in the college to which they were accepted, but they may be allowed to take some courses offered by other colleges within the university, and can use shared facilities such as libraries and laboratories.

**KEEP IN MIND**

The "required" units listed under **"high school preparation"** are just that — the minimum requirement. **For your application to be competitive,** you should strive to complete the recommended units as well.

- *Financial aid.* Required forms plus priority, closing, notification and reply dates are listed for fall-term financial aid applications. The Free Application for Federal Student Aid (FAFSA) is required by every college offering federal financial aid. If the college requires the CSS/Financial Aid PROFILE® to determine your eligibility for nonfederal funds, it is noted here. "Institutional form" means the college has a form of its own. Pay special attention to priority dates and deadlines; if the college indicates "no deadline" for financial aid, it means it will continue to process requests as long as funds are available. You should always apply as early as possible to obtain the best consideration for financial aid awards.

**Academics.** Many colleges offer a range of special study options that can enrich or enhance your education experience. Special academic programs are listed in this section. Check the glossary for brief descriptions of each of the programs listed.

College policies on granting credit or advanced placement through the College Board's AP Program, College-Level Examination Program® (CLEP®), SAT Subject Tests™, and/or other placement programs and institutional tests are listed next. Most colleges have a maximum number of credit hours by examination that may be counted toward a degree, which is also listed.

Academic support services list the programs the college provides to assist students in succeeding academically. Preadmission summer programs, special counselors, tutoring, learning disabled programs and study skills assistance are some of the options offered.

**Honors college/program.** If a college has a separate undergraduate honors college or a program with different admissions and academic offerings from those available to regular students, this section will tell you what's available and how to apply.

**Majors.** Only majors leading to a bachelor's degree (for four-year colleges) or an associate degree (for two-year colleges) are included here. They are listed alphabetically by general category. The majors listed here are based on the U.S. Department of Education's Classification of Instructional Programs; colleges were asked to match the majors they offer to this list. Many colleges additionally offer concentrations within a major, which are not reflected here.

**Most popular majors.** This will give you an idea of whether a substantial number of students are completing a major in an area that is of interest to you. This list is based on the percentage of students who were awarded degrees in each of the general categories listed in the 2008-09 academic year.

**Computing on campus.** Whether you bring your own computer to campus, or plan on using college-provided workstations, you'll want to know what technological support the college provides for student use, and whether the college requires you to bring your own PC or laptop. This section lists the number of workstations available for student use and where they're located; whether dorms are wired for high-speed Internet access and/or linked to the campus network; if there is a wireless network; if there's online course registration, an online library or student Web hosting; and whether commuter students can link to the campus network.

**Student life.** If you attend the college, you will need to know if it requires enrollees to attend freshman orientation, and if it has policies and regulations governing student behavior.

If on-campus housing is available — whether it's in the form of dormitories, apartments, fraternity/sorority housing or cooperative housing — it will be indicated here. Most dormitories today are coeducational, but many colleges offer single-sex accommodations either in separate buildings or separate floors. Some colleges are now also offering "substance-free" or "wellness" dormitories, whose residents pledge not to use alcohol, tobacco or any illegal drugs. This section also indicates if on-campus housing is guaranteed for freshmen, or for all four years; and the policies and deadlines for deposits.

Most colleges have provided a selective list of student activities sponsored by the institution. Read the list carefully to see if it reflects the type of student organizations and opportunities of interest to you.

**Athletics.** Intercollegiate and intramural sports available at the college are listed here, along with the team name. Sports offered for men or women only are indicated by (M) or (W). The athletic association to which the college belongs also is indicated. If you want to know which colleges play in the NCAA and at what division level, see the index at the back of this book titled "NCAA sports by division," where you'll see each college listed by sport.

**Student services.** This section lists the college's basic range of services for students. Among these are health, personal counseling, services for adult students, student employment services, placement service for graduates, veterans' counseling and on-campus day care. This section also lists special services/facilities for learning disabled students and those with visual, speech or hearing impairments.

**Contact.** The last item in each description provides the admissions office's e-mail address, telephone and fax numbers, the name and/or title of the admissions director, and the mailing address of the college office to contact for further information and applications.

# Brief Descriptions

The 388 colleges that did not respond to our Annual Survey of Colleges are described in brief with the following information: name, city, state, college type, accreditation, location and calendar. Annual costs and financial aid information are provided, if available. The addresses to contact for further information are also listed.

---

**KNOW THE LINGO**

**NCAA** — The National Collegiate Athletic Association. This is the largest collegiate athletic association, and it oversees the most athletic scholarship money. The NCAA governs league play in 23 championship sports.

**NAIA** — The National Association of Intercollegiate Athletics. Its members are mostly small colleges, offering 13 sports.

**NJCAA** — The National Junior College Athletic Association. NJCAA members are all two-year community or junior colleges.

**USCAA** — United States Collegiate Athletic Association. USCAA's members are primarily very small colleges.

**NCCAA** — National Christian College Athletic Association. NCCAA sponsors league play among Bible colleges and other Christian-oriented institutions.

# Tables and Indexes

The tables and indexes in the back of this book are a useful tool to find colleges quickly and zero in on the schools that interest you.

## Early Application and Wait List Outcomes

If you are considering applying to a college early, the Early Decision and Early Action table on page 2083 shows application deadlines and notification dates for early application programs, as well as the number of students who applied and were admitted last year under those policies.

If you find that you have been placed on a college's wait list for acceptance, consult the wait list table on page 2095. It will give you a sense of your chances, by showing how many students were placed on the wait list last year, how many accepted their place on the list, and how many were eventually admitted from the list.

## College Indexes

You can use the college indexes to quickly find schools that interest you. In most of the indexes, colleges are listed alphabetically by state because, for many students, geographic location is a primary requirement. Colleges that are part of a system are listed alphabetically under the system name.

The following explanation of index terms may help you decide whether a certain type of college or a special program or policy interests you.

### College type

**Liberal arts.** Sometimes known as arts and sciences. The study of liberal arts is intended to develop general knowledge and reasoning ability as opposed to specific preparation for a career. Most liberal arts colleges are privately controlled. They generally don't offer as many majors in the technical or scientific disciplines as comprehensive colleges or universities.

**Upper-division.** Offer the last two years of undergraduate study (junior and senior courses only), usually in specialized programs leading to the bachelor's degree. Students generally transfer to upper-division colleges after completing an associate degree or after finishing their second year of study at a four-year college.

**Specialized.** Concentrate their offerings in one or two specific areas, such as business or engineering. Students who enroll at specialized colleges generally have a precise idea of what they want to study.

**KNOW THE LINGO**

There are so many **types of specialized colleges** that we didn't have room to describe them all here. If you'd like to know more about a specific type of college, see the glossary that begins on page 40.

## Special characteristics

**Colleges for men/women.** Some of these colleges may enroll a few women or men, but their student bodies are predominantly of one sex.

**Colleges with religious affiliations.** Lists each college under the official name of the denomination with which it is affiliated. Student life at some colleges is greatly influenced by the religious affiliation. At other colleges, the affiliation may be historic only, having little influence on college life.

**Historically black colleges.** Identifies historically or predominantly black colleges that are committed to educating African American students. The information was obtained from the National Association for Equal Opportunity in Higher Education and the U.S. government.

**Hispanic-serving colleges.** Identifies colleges where Hispanic students comprise at least 25 percent of the total full-time undergraduate enrollment. The information was obtained from the Hispanic Association of Colleges and Universities (HACU).

**Tribal colleges.** Identifies colleges committed to serving geographically isolated populations of Native Americans. The information was obtained from the Carnegie Classification of Institutions of Higher Education.

## Undergraduate enrollment size

The number of students at a college helps determine its environment.

**Very small.** Fewer than 750 undergraduates.

**Small.** 750 to 1,999 undergraduates.

**Medium to large.** 2,000 to 7,499 undergraduates.

**Large.** 7,500 to 14,999 undergraduates.

**Very large.** 15,000 or more undergraduates.

## Admission selectivity

**Admit under 50%, 50–75%, over 75%.** Colleges in three categories of selectivity that limit admission to applicants who meet specific requirements.

**Open admission.** Colleges that admit virtually all applicants with a high school diploma or its equivalent, as long as space is available.

Many public institutions offer open admissions to state residents but have selective admissions requirements for out-of-state students or to selected programs; check the college descriptions to see what applies.

## Admissions/placement policies

**No closing date.** These colleges will accept applications up to the time of registration.

**SAT Subject Test required/recommended.** These two indexes list colleges that require or recommend that applicants take one or more

SAT Subject Tests for admission. The college descriptions provide more detailed information.

## Colleges that offer ROTC

The U.S. armed forces offer Reserve Officers' Training Corps programs that prepare candidates for commissions in the Air Force, Army and Navy (Naval ROTC includes the Marine Corps). These programs are offered either at the colleges listed in the index or at cooperating institutions. ROTC programs may take either two or four years to complete. Use this index, organized by branch of service, to find colleges that offer the ROTC program of interest to you.

## Colleges with NCAA sports

Lists National Collegiate Athletic Association (NCAA) championship sports by division level and the colleges, state by state, that offer them. Also indicates whether each sport is available for men only or for women only. (Crew is an NCAA sport for women only; use the college search on collegeboard.com to find colleges that offer crew for men.) To be an NCAA member, colleges must offer at least four sports and have at least one in each season (fall, winter and spring).

## Alphabetical index of colleges

Lists the name and state abbreviation for every institution in the *Handbook*. If a name has changed, the old name is cross-referenced to the new name.

**KEEP IN MIND**

The **NCAA sports indexes** only list colleges that offer sports for which the NCAA holds a championship. There are NCAA sports that don't have a championship, such as men's rowing. And remember that many colleges offer sports through a different association (NAIA or NJCAA), or offer intramural play.

# About accreditation

Every college and university in this book is accredited by an agency recognized by the U.S. Department of Education. That means you can trust that any of them will give you an education that meets basic standards for college-level study, that your studies will qualify for federal need-based financial aid and/or federal education tax breaks, and that the degree you will earn at the end of your studies will be recognized by future employers.

## What Is Accreditation?

Accreditation is a voluntary process of peer review and self-regulation. The standards for each accrediting agency are slightly different but, generally, each agency ensures that its members meet basic standards in their administrative procedures, physical facilities and the quality of their academic programs.

The agencies listed on page 12 are *regional* and *national* agencies that accredit entire institutions. In majors that lead to a professional certification — such as nursing, engineering or teacher education — there may also be *specialized* agencies that accredit just one program, department or school at the college. For example, the Accreditation Board for Engineering and Technology (ABET) accredits engineering and engineering technology programs. In addition to guaranteeing the academic quality of programs, these specialized agencies often have a guidance component that helps university students make the transition to professional careers. You can find more information about specialized accrediting agencies in the College Board's *Book of Majors*, or at the Council for Higher Education Accreditation's website (www.chea.org).

**GOOD TO KNOW**

**Every college** contained in the *College Handbook* and collegeboard.com's College Search has been accredited by either a national or regional accrediting agency recognized by the U.S. Department of Education.

# What Does Accreditation Mean to Me?

If you attend an accredited college, you can be sure that:

- You will be able to use federal student aid (Title IV money) to help pay for your costs if you qualify based on financial need.

- Your tuition will qualify you for federal income tax deductions and/or credits (if you meet other conditions).

- Academic credits you earn there are eligible to transfer to another accredited college.

- Employers and professional licensing boards will recognize the degree you earn as an academic credential, as will graduate schools and other academic institutions to which you may apply.

You should, however, understand what accreditation *doesn't* mean:

- There's no guarantee that you will receive federal need-based financial aid just by attending any college, even if it's accredited.

- Regional and national accreditation ensures that every academic program at the college meets standards, but that doesn't mean that the quality of every program at the college is equal.

- If you're applying for transfer from one undergraduate institution to another, there's no guarantee that all your credits will count toward the graduation requirements of the college where you plan to finish your degree. If you plan to attend a lower-division college for your first two years of study and then go on to earn a bachelor's degree, be sure to talk to the transfer counselor there before enrolling in courses.

- Similarly, there's no guarantee that graduate schools or employers will see your undergraduate course of study as appropriate preparation for the demands of their program or job requirements.

# REGIONAL
## ACCREDITING ASSOCIATIONS

**Middle States Commission on Higher Education**
3624 Market Street
Philadelphia, PA 19104-2680
www.msche.org

Delaware, District of Columbia, Maryland, New Jersey, New York, Pennsylvania, Puerto Rico, Virgin Islands

**New England Association
of Schools and Colleges**
209 Burlington Road, Suite 201
Bedford, MA 01730-1433
www.neasc.org

Connecticut, Maine, Massachusetts, New Hampshire, Rhode Island, Vermont

**North Central Association
of Colleges and Schools**
30 North LaSalle Street, Suite 2400
Chicago, IL 60602-2504
www.ncahigherlearningcommission.org

Arizona, Arkansas, Colorado, Illinois, Indiana, Iowa, Kansas, Michigan, Minnesota, Missouri, Nebraska, New Mexico, North Dakota, Ohio, Oklahoma, South Dakota, West Virginia, Wisconsin, Wyoming

**Northwest Association of Accredited Schools**
1510 Robert Street, Suite 103
Boise, ID 83705-5194
www.northwestaccreditation.org

Alaska, Idaho, Montana, Nevada, Oregon, Utah, Washington

**Southern Association of Colleges and Schools**
1866 Southern Lane
Decatur, GA 30033-4097
www.sacs.org

Alabama, Florida, Georgia, Kentucky, Louisiana, Mississippi, North Carolina, South Carolina, Tennessee, Texas, Virginia

**Western Association of Schools and Colleges**
Accrediting Commission for Senior Colleges and Universities
985 Atlantic Avenue, Suite 100
Alameda, CA 94501
www.wascsenior.org

Accrediting Commission for Community and Junior Colleges
10 Commercial Boulevard, Suite 204
Novato, CA 94949
www.accjc.org

American Samoa, California, Guam, Hawaii, Trust Territory of the Pacific

**New York Board of Regents**
Office of College and University Evaluation
New York State Education Department
89 Washington Avenue
Albany, NY 12234
www.regents.nysed.gov

# NATIONAL
## ACCREDITING ASSOCIATIONS

**ACICS**   **Accrediting Council for Independent Colleges and Schools**
Washington, DC
www.acics.org

**ACCSC**   **Accrediting Commission of Career Schools and Colleges**
Arlington, VA
www.accsc.org

**ABHE**   **Association for Biblical Higher Education**
Orlando, FL
www.abhe.org

**AARTS**   **Association of Advanced Rabbinical and Talmudic Schools**
11 Broadway, Suite 405
New York, NY 10004

**ATS**   **Association of Theological Schools in the United States and Canada**
Pittsburgh, PA
www.ats.edu

**DETC**   **Distance Education and Training Council**
Washington, DC
www.detc.org

**TRACS**   **Transnational Association of Christian Colleges and Schools**
Forest, VA
www.tracs.org

# Selecting colleges

There are more than 3,800 accredited colleges in the United States. This book will help you get an idea of the types of colleges you're interested in attending and learn more about colleges that fall into those categories. From there, you can create a list of colleges you would like to learn more about, and start requesting information from them, visiting their websites, and (if you can) visiting their campuses. By December of your senior year, you should have your choices narrowed down to a final list of four to eight colleges to which you want to apply.

## KNOW THE LINGO

**"Target" school** — a college you'd like to attend that will be somewhat difficult for you to get in. Usually a college where your GPA and standardized test scores would be about average. Most students apply to between two and four target schools.

**"Reach" school** — a college you'd like to attend, but will be difficult for you to get in. Your GPA and test scores may be below average for this school, but some other aspect of your application may make up for that. You should apply to one or two reach schools.

**"Safety" school** — a college you'd like to attend that's also sure to accept you. You should apply to at least one safety school.

# Finding Your Fit

Every college is unique in some way. And everybody has different interests, ambitions and needs. When investigating colleges, you will probably look for different things than your friends, parents and siblings did when they applied. But there are some "big picture" elements that everyone, including you, should consider.

Colleges fall into broad categories — small and large, liberal arts and professionally oriented, academically selective, and open admissions. There are also personal criteria you need to consider, such as whether a college is in your hometown or a thousand miles away.

## Type of Institution

This will give you a sense of how the college organizes its academic departments. Different types of institutions include:

**Liberal arts colleges** offer a broad base of courses in the humanities, social sciences and natural sciences. Most are private and focus mainly on undergraduate students. Classes tend to be small, and personal attention is available. An education at a liberal arts college will prepare you for a broad range of career and graduate school options.

**Community and junior colleges** offer a degree after the completion of two years of full-time study. They frequently offer technical programs that prepare you for immediate entry into the job market. To learn more about the benefits of attending a community college, read "About Community Colleges" on page 20.

**Agricultural colleges, technical schools and professional institutes** emphasize preparation for specific careers. Examples include art institutes and music conservatories, Bible colleges, business colleges, schools of health science, seminaries and rabbinical yeshivas, and teachers colleges.

**Universities** are generally bigger than colleges and offer more majors and research facilities. Classes in introductory subjects may have hundreds of students, and some classes may be taught by graduate students.

Most universities are subdivided into colleges or schools. For example, a state university might have a large college of liberal arts, a school of engineering and applied sciences, a small school of nursing, a teachers college and several graduate schools all on the same campus.

Different universities have different rules for whether you can, for example, take a computer science course offered by the engineering school while enrolled in the liberal arts college. Generally, the different colleges of a university share campus facilities (such as dorms and dining halls) and some research facilities (such as libraries), and a university-wide administration handles admissions, financial aid and similar services for the various colleges.

## Size of the Student Body and Faculty

Size will affect many of your opportunities and experiences, including:

- the range of academic majors offered;
- the possibilities for extracurricular activities and athletics;
- the amount of personal attention you'll receive from faculty, administrators and other students; and
- the availability and size of academic facilities such as laboratories, libraries and art studios.

When considering size, be sure to look beyond the raw number of students attending. For example, perhaps you're considering a large university, but you'll be applying to its much smaller school of health sciences.

Also remember to investigate not just the number of faculty, but also how accessible faculty members are to students. You can get a rough sense of this from the "class size" entry in the *Handbook* descriptions, but if you are already interested in a particular major or department, it really helps to visit the campus and talk to students who are enrolled in that program.

## Location

Do you want to go home frequently, or do you see this as a time to experience a new part of the country? Perhaps you like an urban environment with access to museums, ethnic food or major league ball games. Or maybe you hope for easy access to the outdoors or the serenity of a small town.

# Academic Quality

The easiest way to measure a school's quality and the satisfaction of its students is to learn the percentage of students who return after the first year and the percentage of entering students who remain to graduate. Comparatively good retention and graduation rates are indicators that responsible academic, social and financial support systems exist for most students. These figures are reported in the *Handbook* descriptions. On average nationwide, 59 percent of four-year college students graduate from the same institution within six years or less.

One of the best ways to research a college's reputation is by talking to people who are familiar with colleges or the fields that interest you. Ask your parents if anyone they know went to one of the colleges on your short list. Talk to your school counselor — he or she probably knows quite a bit about local colleges and nationally known universities. Talk to your teachers — they might know the academic reputations of departments that relate to their teaching field. You can also research the reputations of colleges on the Internet, but beware — not everyone on the Internet is an expert, and sometimes rumors get passed along as fact.

If you already know what subjects you want to study, research the strengths of those schools or departments at the colleges and universities in which you're interested. One way to do this is to look at their departmental websites for the following:

- Are there a lot of courses offered, or just a few?

- Do the courses offered concentrate on one subfield within the major? This is not necessarily a bad thing, but it could tell you that the department is strong in some areas and weak in others.

- Do most of the professors have terminal degrees in their field? Usually the Ph.D. is the terminal degree, but in some fields, it's another graduate degree.

- The website may also tell you about research and scholarship that professors are doing, work that undergraduate students are doing, or the careers of recent alumni.

These are general questions that would apply to any department. For questions to ask colleges about a specific major, see the College Board's *Book of Majors*. It contains profiles of undergraduate majors, and each profile has a list of things to look for in a department offering that major.

**GOOD TO KNOW**

If you're still **undecided about your college major**, relax — just pick an academically balanced institution that offers a range of majors and programs, and take courses in subjects you find intriguing. Most colleges offer advising or mentoring to help you find a focus.

# Campus Life

Consider what your college life will be like beyond the classroom. Aim for a balance between academics, activities and social life. In your research, try to learn the answers to these questions:

- What extracurricular activities, athletics and special activities are available?
- Does the community around the college offer interesting outlets for students?
- Are students welcomed by the surrounding community?
- Is there a congregation of my faith on campus? Are there student groups based around my ethnic group or national culture?
- Is the college religiously affiliated? If so, how does that affiliation affect student life — for example, is attendance at services required?
- How do fraternities and sororities influence campus life?
- Is housing guaranteed? How are dorms assigned? (For more about housing options, see page 38.)

You can learn the answers to many of these questions by reading the college profiles in this book, but for others, you may have to do more in-depth research, such as visiting the college's website or its campus.

## Can I Afford This College?

Today's college price tags make cost an important consideration for most students. At the same time, most colleges work to ensure that academically qualified students from every economic circumstance can find financial aid. Be sure to look beyond the price tag in considering cost. The *Handbook* descriptions give you a general idea of the college's cost and its financial aid packages. For more detailed "cost profiles" of the colleges, and for general advice about financial aid, see the College Board's *Getting Financial Aid*, which is a companion volume to this book.

# Where Can I Get In?

Of course, finding a college that's the right fit for you is only half of the equation. Unless you're applying to a college with an open admissions policy, you also have to convince the admissions reviewers that you really are a good fit.

## What Are Colleges Looking For?

When they review your application, college admissions officers want to see, foremost, "students who have challenged themselves academically," says Martha Pitts, the director of admissions at the University of Oregon. But they don't just want to see good grades; they also want to make sure that candidates will add something positive to the campus community. Mike Sexton,

# Where to Find More Information

Once you've created a list of colleges you'd like to learn more about, you should try to get information from as many sources as possible. Different people will tell you different things about colleges, so the more the merrier!

✔ **Your school counselor** can tell you about colleges and let you know when college fairs or visits from admissions recruiters are coming to your school. He or she may also have a file of college course catalogs, viewbooks and other literature.

✔ **Visiting admissions staff** who come to your school — either by themselves or as part of a large college fair — can tell you more about the college they represent and its application process.

✔ **College websites and guidebooks** offer a wealth of information about majors offered, activities and life on campus.

✔ **Returning graduates** who went to your school and come home for breaks will probably be eager to tell you all about their experiences.

✔ **Campus visits** are a chance to see the campus and its dorms, libraries and other facilities in person; talk to admissions officers (whether informally or in an interview); observe classes and talk to students; and much more. Try to visit the campus while classes are in session. For tips on planning a visit, read the articles in the "Find a College" section of www.collegeboard.com, or get *Campus Visits & College Interviews* by Zola Dincin Schneider (College Board, 2002).

the dean of admissions at Lewis & Clark College, puts it this way: He looks at the applications for "a spark that tells us they'll be good roommates, good lab partners, good to have in class."

One thing you should never do is try to guess what the admissions committee is looking for and try to tailor your application to it. Admissions officers read thousands of applications every year, and they can almost instantly tell feigned interest in a college or a false presentation of oneself from the real thing.

## Your transcript is the most important thing

There it is, in large type, but it bears repeating: Your high school transcript is the most important thing for your application success. Colleges want to see that you've challenged yourself academically throughout high school and that you are willing to put academics first for the next two to four years.

Be aware that admissions staff won't just look at the grades on your transcript. They will look at which courses you took, and the grade trend over four years. For example, if you barely passed Intro to Biology as a freshman, but then turned around and got a B in AP Biology as a junior, colleges will consider that a plus. On the other hand, if you've been getting steady C's in English for the last three years, colleges may wonder why you haven't improved.

A related factor that admissions officers look for is an upward trend in the difficulty of your course work. Sexton says he becomes concerned when students "start taking a lighter load senior year. I can see why they would do it sometimes, but for some people, it's going to close doors." Don't feel you need to suffocate yourself with too many courses and extracurriculars, but don't try to cruise through your senior year either.

## Test scores are just part of the picture

Your scores on the admissions tests can be important, but generally they're not as important as your high school transcript. Most often, admissions officers will use your test scores to supplement your transcript or help them interpret it.

Although grades earned in high school courses are very important, they don't always mean the same thing. An A earned in the same course taught by different teachers in your school may not represent exactly the same amount of work, the same teaching or the same level of learning. Likewise, an A earned in the same course but in different schools and different parts of the country may not really be the same. That's where standardized tests can help.

If you've already taken an admissions test (e.g., the SAT), look at your scores the same way the admissions committee will look at them — objectively. They don't represent all that you've achieved or will achieve. The scores are one indicator of how far along you are right now in developing the skills you need for college and a career. In deciding where to apply to college, it's helpful to compare your scores to those of the mid-50 percent score range of freshmen who enrolled the previous year in the colleges you're considering. You'll find this information in the section titled "freshman class profile" of each four-year college description. If your scores compare favorably, you're on your way to finding the right match. But if your scores are higher or lower, it's not necessarily a mismatch. Only 50 out of every 100 freshmen had scores in that range, which means 25 had higher scores and 25 had lower scores. You may be well suited for this college in other important ways. You'll be better able to decide after reading the entire college description, visiting the college's website and (if possible) visiting the campus.

## Personality can go a long way

Very few colleges assess applications using just transcripts and test scores. Most will ask for information about your involvement in extracurricular activities, recommendations from your teachers, a recommendation from your counselor, and a brief application essay. Some will ask for an interview as well. A few will ask for recommendations from someone who is not on your school faculty, for example, a minister, employer or friend.

What all of these application components have in common is that they help admissions officers look "beyond the numbers" and see what kind of person you are, and how you might contribute to their campus community. They won't be the first, or most important, thing the college looks at, but they can

### EXPERT ADVICE

"**The first thing most colleges and universities will consider** will be the high school courses a student chose. Are they challenging? Are they college-prep, honors or AP courses?"

— *Mary Ellen Anderson, Director of Admissions, Indiana University-Bloomington* help round out your application and may help the admissions committee decide between you and several equally qualified candidates.

Here's a closer look at each of the personal factors colleges usually look at:

**Recommendations.** Recommendations will give the college a sense of your overall attitude toward learning, your character and the context for the grades on your transcript. Do you have a real passion for mathematics? Did you try really hard and improve over the year to get that "B" in U.S. History? Or could you have been an "A" student if you had taken the class more seriously? For tips on choosing which teachers to ask for recommendations, and how to ask them, see pages 27 and 28.

**Extracurriculars.** Your involvement in extracurricular activities — whether they're sports, a part-time job, volunteering in your community, the school play, the yearbook or something entirely different — will tell the college about how active you are in your community. From that, they'll have a good picture of your leadership potential and how likely you are to contribute to their own campus community. They'll also have a sense of how much time you spend on nonschool work, which gives them a context for reading your grades. Generally, it's best to dedicate yourself to a few extracurricular activities in which you're really interested. Making minor contributions to 10 different activities doesn't look as impressive as becoming a leader of one club that you're passionate about. Similarly, changing activities every semester makes you look fickle; it's better to show some consistency.

**Essays.** Admissions officers use application essays to learn how creative you are, how well you can write and, sometimes, whether you're truly interested in attending their college. They are the most subjective of all the components of an application, but they are also the one component over which you have total control. For more about how applications are used by admissions officials, and tips on writing your essays, read *The College Application Essay* by Sarah Myers McGinty (College Board, 2004).

**Interviews.** Interviews are rarely required and usually don't carry a great deal of weight in the overall application. If you are asked to come to an interview, you should look at it as an opportunity to put a personal face on your application, tell the college more about yourself, and learn more about whether the college would be a good fit for you. If you are shy, don't worry — no one ever gets rejected by a college because of a bad interview. For more about interviews, including checklists of questions to expect and questions you should ask, read *Campus Visits & College Interviews* by Zola Dincin Schneider (College Board, 2002).

## How "interested" are you?

As college admissions have become more competitive, colleges have begun to weigh an additional factor along with the other parts of the application: "demonstrated interest." What this means is that admissions officials try to determine whether, if they accept you, you will enroll at their college.

Interest in a college is not something you should try to fake — if you have to pretend to want to go to a college, you won't be happy going there, so your application is a waste of time. If you really want to go to a college, your interest will show itself naturally, and colleges will be able to tell. That said, here are some things that colleges usually look for when they try to gauge your level of interest:

- Is your application essay customized to the college, or does it seem like a generic essay that you could have sent to any college?

- Did you write the college asking for information about its programs?

- Have you talked to any admissions officers from the college — at your high school, via e-mail or when visiting the campus?

- If you interview with the college, do you ask basic questions that you could have answered by reading its website, or do you ask in-depth questions that show that you've already researched the college?

Like the personal factors, your level of interest in the college isn't nearly as important as the courses you've taken, your grades or your test scores. But if the admissions committee is trying to decide between you and another equally qualified candidate, it could tip your application one way or the other.

# About Community Colleges

Do you want a quick start to a career path? Do you need to cut the cost of a four-year college degree? Do you want to sharpen your study skills before enrolling at a university? Do you need to attend classes at night or on weekends? Do you want to attend a college close to home?

If you said yes to even one question above, check out your options at a community college (CC). You won't be alone — 45 percent of all first-time freshmen go to two-year colleges. One reason: These institutions offer two kinds of learning.

- If your goal is a four-year degree, you can earn a two-year associate degree at a low-cost community college, then transfer to a four-year college as a junior.

- If your goal is career training, you can earn an occupational degree or certificate in two years or less, then start working immediately in many high-demand fields (like health care or computer technology).

## Fit Your Education to Your Needs

A community college offers many advantages in terms of academic preparation for upper-division university work.

**If you need more academic preparation**, a community college can offer a leg up to achieving your goals. New students usually take placement tests in reading, writing and math. Those who need to build skills can take catch-up courses, then — over time — move into a regular academic program.

**A STUDENT'S STORY**

"I'm getting the basics out of the way at an inexpensive cost," says Samantha Mattioli, a freshman at Westchester Community College in Valhalla, N.Y. Sam, who is majoring in business management, says, **"I won't have a lot of debt** when I finish my associate degree." That will free up funds for her second degree, in massage therapy — step two toward Sam's goal of running her own massage therapy business.

**If your high school grades aren't the greatest**, but a four-year college is your goal, taking community college courses — and building a record of good grades — can polish your academic record. Then you can transfer. (But don't expect it to be easy — community college courses are no different than four-year college courses.)

**If you're achievement oriented**, community colleges offer challenging honors courses. Honors programs not only stimulate you but also offer mentoring and networking opportunities. They will also make you a strong candidate for transfer to a four-year college.

**If English is your second language**, community colleges have special programs that will help you build your English skills.

# Keep on Track at a Community College

If you go to a community college or junior college, it's important for you to keep your goals in mind as you choose courses.

### PLANNING TO TRANSFER TO A FOUR-YEAR COLLEGE?

✔ Talk to advisers at the community college. Most public CCs offer two-year course plans that fulfill requirements at nearby colleges. To transfer without losing credits, follow those plans!

✔ Talk to advisers at the four-year college you hope to attend, too. They may have inside info.

✔ Make sure you've fulfilled requirements to declare a major at the four-year college — not just the general admissions requirements. For example, Biology 101 at your CC may transfer, but might not be enough preparation for you to take the junior-level courses in the chemistry major.

✔ Don't self-advise! If you're not sure whether a course will transfer, ask. Wrong courses waste your time and money, and that's discouraging.

✔ Keep going. Don't "gap" your education, taking time out between semesters or colleges. Once you begin, keep at it — that's the path to getting your four-year degree.

### TRAINING FOR AN OCCUPATION?

Make sure your degree or certificate can lead to employment.

✔ Talk to advisers at your community college, but don't just accept claims that when you graduate, you'll get a job.

✔ Ask how many students have gone straight from the college to the workforce in recent years, what jobs they got, and with which employers.

✔ Before you enroll, talk to potential employers in the outside world, too.

# Learn on Your Schedule

Many CC students have jobs and family responsibilities. Scheduling classes may be a big challenge. So community colleges tend to offer day, night and weekend courses. They have pioneered new teaching methods, too. Some offer online courses (distance learning), combine Internet and classroom learning, give interactive TV courses, condense semester courses into a shorter time frame, and more.

# Community College Can Be a Ticket to Hot Job Markets

With two years or less of community college training, you can earn an occupational degree or certificate in

- Fast-growing health fields
- The computer world
- New and emerging fields

A community college may be the best route to many high-demand jobs that require two-year degrees not available at four-year colleges. Look for CC courses in construction technology, culinary arts, law enforcement and biotechnology. With homeland security in the news, colleges are training many first responders.

Many community colleges also have certificate options that provide intensive training in a specialized field like computer-assisted drafting, food service technology or paralegal studies. These certificates usually take six months to a year to complete.

## CCs often focus on preparing people to work in local industries.

Do you want work in your area? Look for programs like these in local community colleges:

**Joliet, Ill.** Joliet Junior College is nationally known for its agriculture and horticulture programs. Farming is big business in the Midwest, and Joliet grads have job offers waiting. Students learn at a 100-acre college farm and do paid internships for credit.

**Tucson, Ariz.** Home to many air-industry businesses, Pima Community College boasts an FAA-certified aviation tech program that prepares students to repair the structure, "airframe" and power plants of commercial jetliners. Pima's job placement record for successful grads of the program is over 95 percent.

Not bad! But also, not the case at every CC or in every field. So research your CC and your local job markets like crazy — just as you'd research a four-year college.

# Applying to colleges

After you've gone through some exploration and preliminary research, it's time to sit down and apply! In order to successfully apply, you'll need to budget and manage your time, follow each college's instructions to a T and, most important, take a good hard look at yourself and your interests.

## Managing Your Time

Most deadlines for regular admissions applications are due in early January or February, and most early application deadlines are in November. For any application, you'll need to fill out forms and request that your transcript and standardized test scores be sent to the college. For most applications to selective colleges, you'll also need to ask teachers and your counselor for recommendations, write an essay or personal statement, and maybe even schedule an interview with the admissions office. You may also want to take the SAT or SAT Subject Tests in November or December. Meanwhile, you'll be in the middle of your senior year, with academic, extracurricular and social commitments all over your calendar.

The first thing you should do once you decide to which colleges you're applying is to make a checklist of all the deadlines and tasks you'll have to accomplish for the applications. Remember to budget time for other people to do things. Teachers won't write recommendations overnight, and testing organizations will need a few weeks to send official score reports to colleges.

For some sample checklists and a college application calendar, read the articles in the "Apply to College" section of www.collegeboard.com. For more help, use the My Organizer feature of the site, which will help you plan and remind you of upcoming deadlines, or read *Get It Together for College: A Planner to Help You Get Organized and Get In* (College Board, 2008).

# JUNIOR YEAR CALENDAR

## THE SUMMER BEFORE

- **Read** interesting books — no matter what you select as a major in college, you'll need a good vocabulary and strong reading comprehension skills. Reading is also one of the best ways to get ready.
- **Get a Social Security number** if you don't already have one — you'll need it for your college applications.

- **Think about yourself.** What are you curious about — nature and animals? People and places? Math and science? What do you like to do — working with your hands or with computers? Helping people? Being outdoors? Knowing the basics about yourself will help you make the right college choices.
- **Talk to your family and friends** about college and your goals. They know you best and will have good insights.

## SEPTEMBER

- **Meet with your school counselor** to make sure you are taking the courses that colleges look for.
- **Resolve to get the best grades** you can this year. The payoff will be more colleges to choose from, and a better chance for scholarship money.
- **Pick up the *Official Student Guide to the PSAT/NMSQT®*** from your guidance office and take the practice test (you'll take the real test in October).
- Get involved in an **extracurricular activity**.
- Find out if your school will have a **college night**.

## OCTOBER

- Take the **PSAT/NMSQT**.
- Attend a **college fair**.
- Begin looking through the *College Handbook* — **start a preliminary list of colleges** that might interest you.
- Start to **learn about financial aid**. Use the College Board's *Getting Financial Aid* to learn how it works, and the financial aid calculators at **www.collegeboard.com** to estimate how much aid you might receive.

## NOVEMBER

- Begin to **research scholarships** — use the College Board's *Scholarship Handbook* to find out about deadlines and eligibility requirements.
- **Learn about the SAT.** Go to sat.collegeboard.com to learn how to get ready and when to register.
- If you are planning to major in the arts (drama, music, fine art), ask your teachers about requirements for a **portfolio or audition**.

## DECEMBER

- Review your **PSAT/NMSQT Score Report** with your school counselor. Sign up for your free My College QuickStart™ account on collegeboard.com/quickstart.
- Spend time over the holidays to **think about what kind of college** you want. Big or small? Far away or close to home? **Make a list** of the college features that are important to you.
- **Begin preparing for the SAT.** Learn more about SAT practice tools on **sat.collegeboard.com**.

## JANUARY

- **Meet with your school counselor** to talk about the colleges in which you are interested, what entrance exams you should take, and when you should take them.
- If English is not your primary language, decide when to take the **TOEFL** test.
- Start thinking about **what you want to study in college**. Use resources like the College Board's *Book of Majors* and My College QuickStart.
- **Register for the SAT** if you want to take it in **March**.

## FEBRUARY

- Think about which teachers you will ask to write **letters of recommendation**.
- If you're in AP courses, **register for AP Exams** given in May.
- Ask your counselor or teacher about taking the **SAT Subject Tests** in the spring. You should take them while course material is still fresh in your mind.

## MARCH

- **Register for the SAT and/or SAT Subject Tests** if you want to take them in **late spring**.
- **Narrow your college list** to a reasonable number. Explore the colleges' websites, read their brochures and catalogues, and talk to your family and friends.
- **Practice the SAT**. Try a full-length practice test and more at **sat.collegeboard.com**.

## APRIL

- **Register for the SAT and/or SAT Subject Tests** if you want to take them **before fall**.
- **Plan courses for your senior year.** Make sure you are going to meet the high school course requirements for your top-choice colleges.
- **Plan campus visits.** It's best to go when classes are in session. Start with colleges that are close by.

## MAY

- If you are considering **military academies or ROTC** scholarships, contact your counselor before leaving school for the summer.
- Talk to your counselor about **NCAA requirements** if you want to play Division I or II sports in college.
- Start looking for a **summer job or volunteer work** — the good ones go fast.

# SENIOR YEAR CALENDAR

## THE SUMMER BEFORE

- **Register for the SAT and/or SAT Subject Tests** if you want to take them in **the fall**.
- If you want to play a NCAA Division I or II sport in college, **register with the NCAA Eligibility Center (www.ncaaclearinghouse.net)**.
- **Visit colleges** on your list. Call ahead for the campus tour schedule.

- Begin working on your **college application essays**.
- Find out about **local scholarships** offered by church groups, civic associations and businesses in your area.
- **Write a résumé** (accomplishments, activities and work experiences) to help you later with your college applications.
- **Request college application forms** if you aren't going to apply online.

## SEPTEMBER

- Meet with your school counselor to **finalize your list of colleges**. Be sure your list includes "safety," "reach" and "target" schools.
- **Start a checklist** of all application requirements, deadlines, fees, etc.
- If you can't afford SAT or SAT Subject Test application fees, your counselor can help you request a **fee waiver**.
- Set up **final campus visits and interviews**; attend open houses at colleges that interest you.
- Find out if there will be a **family financial aid night** at your school or elsewhere in your area this fall, and put it on your calendar.

## OCTOBER

- **Register for the SAT and/or SAT Subject Tests** if you want to take them in **the winter**.
- If you are going to apply under an **Early Decision or Early Action** plan, get started now.
- **Ask for letters of recommendation** from your counselor, teachers, coaches or employers.
- Write **first drafts of your college essays** and ask your parents and teachers to review them.
- If you need to fill out the **CSS/Financial Aid PROFILE®**, you can do so on collegeboard.com starting Oct. 1.

## NOVEMBER

- **Finish your application essays**. Proofread them rigorously for mistakes.
- **Apply to colleges with rolling admission** (first-come, first-served) as early as possible. Keep hard copies.
- Make sure your **admissions test (e.g., SAT) scores** will be sent by the testing agency to each one of your colleges.
- Give your school counselor the proper **forms to send transcripts** to your colleges at least two weeks in advance.
- **Get PINs for the FAFSA** for both yourself and for one of your parents from **www.pin.ed.gov**.

## DECEMBER

- Try to **wrap up college applications** before winter break. Make copies for yourself and your school counselor.
- If you applied for **Early Decision**, you should have an answer by Dec. 15. If you are denied or deferred, submit applications now to other colleges.
- **Apply for scholarships** in time to meet application deadlines.
- Start gathering what you need to complete the FAFSA. **Visit FAFSA on the Web** for a list of needed documents.
- **Contact the financial aid office** at the colleges on your list to see if they require any **other financial aid forms**.

## JANUARY

- **Submit your FAFSA** as soon as you can. If a college to which you're applying has a financial aid priority date of Feb. 1, use estimates based on your end-of-year pay stubs and last year's tax returns.
- **Submit other financial aid forms** that may be required — such as PROFILE or the college's own forms. Keep copies.
- If a college wants to see your **midyear grades**, give the form to your school counselor.
- If you have any **new honors or accomplishments** that were not in your original application, let your colleges know.

## FEBRUARY

- **Contact your colleges** to confirm that all application materials have been received.
- Correct or update your **Student Aid Report (SAR)** that follows the FAFSA.
- If any **special circumstances** affect your family's financial situation, alert each college's financial aid office.
- **File income tax returns early.** Some colleges want copies of your family's returns before finalizing financial aid offers.
- **Register for AP Exams** you want to take. (If you are homeschooled or your school does not offer AP, you must contact AP Services by March 1.)

## MARCH

- **Admission decisions start arriving.** Read everything you receive carefully, as some documents may require prompt action on your part.
- **Revisit colleges** that accepted you if it's hard to make a choice.
- **Don't get senioritis!** Colleges want to see strong grades in the second half of your senior year.

## APRIL

- **Carefully compare financial aid award letters** from the colleges that accept you — it might not be clear which is the better offer. If you have questions, contact the college's financial aid office or talk to your school counselor.
- **If you don't get enough aid**, consider your options, which include appealing the award.
- Make a final decision, **accept the aid package, and mail a deposit check** to the college you select before May 1 (the acceptance deadline for most schools).
- **Notify the other colleges** that you won't be attending (so another student can have your spot).

## MAY

- AP Exams are given. Make sure your **AP score report** is sent to your college.
- **Study hard for final exams.** Most admissions offers are contingent on your final grades.
- **Thank everyone** who wrote you recommendations or otherwise helped with your college applications.
- If you plan on playing a Division I or II college sport, have your school counselor send your **final transcript to the NCAA Eligibility Center**.
- **If you weren't accepted** anywhere, don't give up — you still have options. Talk to your school counselor about them.

# Filling Out the Application

A typical application will ask you to provide some personal information; a list of schools you have attended; brief descriptions of your extracurricular activities, jobs and any academic honors you have earned; and standardized test scores. They will also ask for information about your family and their education background, which colleges may use to determine whether you merit special consideration as a first-generation college student or a "legacy" applicant. Finally, most applications give you the option of affiliating yourself with a race or ethnic group. If you choose to do so, colleges may take that into consideration when reviewing your application; however, your answer won't hurt your chances of admission.

Finally, all applications will ask whether and when you plan to file for financial aid. Checking this box does not mean you have applied for financial aid! It just lets the admissions office know that they should coordinate with the financial aid office later on. For more information on financial aid and how to apply for it, read the articles in the "Pay for College" section of www.collegeboard.com, or get the College Board's book, *Getting Financial Aid*.

## What Goes with Your Application

Besides the application form, there are several things that need to be included with your application. You will have to send some of them with the form; others will be sent to the college by other people.

### Application fee

The average college application fee is around $25. (Some colleges charge up to $60, while others don't have an application fee at all.) The fee is usually nonrefundable, even if you're not offered admission. Many colleges offer fee waivers for applicants from low-income families. If you need a fee waiver, call the college's admissions office for more information.

### High school transcript

This form is filled out by an official of your high school. If it comes with your admissions materials, you should give it to the guidance office to complete as early as possible. Some colleges send this form directly to your school after receiving your application.

### Admissions test scores

If you need to submit standardized test scores, you must make sure the testing agency itself sends an official score report. Writing your scores on your application or sending a photocopy of your own personal score report will not suffice. When you take the SAT, you are entitled to four free official score reports, which are sent to the colleges you choose. This service is included in the fee you pay to take the test.

**PLANNING AHEAD**

In addition to the traditional typed or handwritten application, many schools today accept **online applications** (if they do, it will say so in their *Handbook* description). You may also be able to fill out the **Common Application** and send it to several schools — though you should be aware that some Common Application subscribers also require a supplementary form of their own.

**KEEP IN MIND**

**If you apply online**, remember to print your applications and proofread them before you submit them, just as you would with a printed application. Also, be sure to tell your school counselor that you've applied online — your school will still need to send your transcript to the college.

In many cases, you'll be able to **reuse the same essay for several college applications** (and maybe even use it for a scholarship application or two as well). If you do this, be sure that the essay you want to use really does answer the question on each application, and that you change any references to the college from application to application.

## Letters of recommendation

Some colleges ask you to submit one or more letters of recommendation from a teacher, counselor or other adult who knows you well. Usually the person writing the letter will send it directly to the college, though sometimes your school counselor will assemble the letters and send them with your transcript.

## Essays short and long

If you're applying to selective colleges, your essay often plays a very important role. Whether you're writing an autobiographical statement or an essay on a specific theme, take the opportunity to express your individuality in a way that sets you apart from other applicants.

Some applications will ask you to attach a separate essay of one or two pages, others will ask you to fill in some one-paragraph short responses directly on the application form, and others will ask for both. Whichever type of question you're answering, give it some thought. Draft, revise and edit your response before putting it with the application, and be sure to type or (if you must) print legibly. (The "fun" fonts that came with your word processor are usually not legible.)

Your parents, school counselors and teachers may have some helpful insights into things you should talk about in your essays. For tips and strategies on how to approach different types of essay questions, general advice on the writing process, and information about how admissions officers evaluate essays, obtain a copy of Sarah Myers McGinty's *The College Application Essay* (College Board, 2004).

## Interview

An interview is required or recommended by some colleges. Even if it's not required, it's a good idea to set up an interview because it gives you a chance to make a personal connection with someone who will have a voice in deciding whether or not you'll be offered admission. If you're too far away for an on-campus interview, try to arrange to meet with an alumnus in your community.

Try to schedule interviews early in your senior year — if you wait until December you may not have time to make the appointment before the application is due. Also, scheduling an interview late in the year may make the college think that your decision to apply was an afterthought. Many students feel most comfortable scheduling their first interviews with colleges they feel confident about getting into. That way, they can experience interview situations and build their confidence before going to "high stakes" interviews with their "reach" schools.

For tips on preparing for interviews and getting the most out of them, obtain a copy of Zola Dincin Schneider's *Campus Visits & College Interviews* (College Board, 2002), or read the articles in the "Apply to College" section of the College Board website.

# How to ask for recommendations

The key to getting a great recommendation is to be a great student. But showing good manners helps.

✔ Be sure to *ask* for a recommendation — don't demand one.

✔ Respect the time constraints of those you're asking for this favor. Mary Lee Hoganson, a former counselor at Homewood-Flossmoor High School in Illinois, says that "teachers should always receive a minimum of two weeks' notice."

✔ Provide teachers and counselors with a deadline for each recommendation that you are requesting, especially noting the earliest deadline.

✔ Offer them a "brag sheet" or résumé reminding them of your accomplishments over the years. They might know your work in their classes very well, but they might not remember that you were also responsible for organizing the school talent show your junior year.

✔ Include addressed and stamped envelopes for each school to which you're applying.

✔ On the application form, waive your right to view recommendation letters. This makes the recommendation more credible in the eyes of the college.

✔ Follow up with your recommendation writers a week or so before your first deadline.

✔ Once you have decided which college to attend, write thank-you notes to everyone who provided a recommendation and tell them where you've decided to go to college. Be sure to do this before you leave high school.

## Auditions, portfolios and other supplementary materials

If you're applying for a fine or performing arts program in music, studio art or graphic design, you may have to document prior work by auditioning on campus or submitting an audiotape, slides or some other sample of your work to demonstrate your ability. Talk to a teacher or mentor in your subject for advice on both how to assemble a portfolio and which of your pieces to include. Be sure to check the deadlines for auditions — they are often different from the deadlines for applications.

In some cases, a college will ask all students to submit an academic writing sample, either instead of or in addition to a personal statement. You should send a graded essay, presentation or lab report that you did well on, preferably a copy that has your teacher's comments and the grade you received on it.

# Taking college admissions and placement tests

In your junior or senior year of high school, you will probably have to take a college admissions test to satisfy the admissions requirements at the colleges you are considering.

You may also want to take college-level exams in specific subjects in order to strengthen your application portfolio, place out of introductory college courses, get college credit for your high school work, or all three. At the end of this chapter, you'll find an introduction to the two most widely recognized college credit-by-exam programs.

## College Admissions Tests: Why You Should Take Them

This chapter will give you advice on how to get ready and register for the standardized tests that satisfy the admissions requirements at the colleges you are considering. You may also want to take the college-level exams in specific subjects in order to strengthen your application portfolio, place out of introductory college courses, get college credit for your high school work, or all three.

Some colleges also require one or more SAT Subject Tests. These requirements are all spelled out in the *Handbook* descriptions for each college.

# The SAT®

The SAT tests your knowledge of subjects that are necessary for success in college and beyond: reading, writing and mathematics. It shows you how well you use the skills and knowledge you have attained in and outside of the classroom — including how you think, solve problems and communicate. The SAT is an important resource for colleges, and it is the best predictor of how well you'll do in college when used with high school grades. The SAT is a fair and unbiased test that is geared to all students. Each question goes through a rigorous review to ensure that it's fair for students from all backgrounds. The SAT also allows you to connect to scholarship opportunities.

# What Are SAT Subject Tests™?

SAT Subject Tests are one-hour exams offered in 20 subjects that measure your achievement in foreign languages, mathematics, sciences, history and literature.

If your grades in college-preparatory courses are good, you may want to take one or several of these tests to demonstrate the content mastery you've achieved. The best time to take a Subject Test is after you have completed, or nearly completed, all the courses in that subject. A number of colleges use SAT Subject Test scores for various purposes:

**Admission:** Some colleges require Subject Tests for admission for all students. Others require them only for certain applicants, such as students who were homeschooled in high school. If they do, their *Handbook* descriptions will indicate this in the bulleted list of key facts and in the "Basis for selection" section. Even colleges that do not require Subjects Tests may use them if submitted in order to gauge achievement as part of an admissions review.

**Placement in honors programs:** A college might require Subject Tests for placement in an honors college or other special program.

**Scholarship awards:** Merit scholarships may be awarded partly on the basis of Subject Test scores. Information about each college's merit scholarships and their requirements is included in the College Board's *Getting Financial Aid*.

**Advanced placement:** Some colleges will allow you to skip introductory courses if your Subject Test score is sufficient.

For help practicing for your test(s), visit sat.collegeboard.com, or get *The Official Study Guide for all SAT Subject Tests*™, which is available in bookstores and libraries everywhere.

## KNOW THE LINGO

**The SAT** — A college entrance exam that measures the academic skills you'll need for success in college. The SAT assesses how well you analyze and solve problems — skills you learned in high school that you'll need in college. It consists of three sections: mathematics, critical reading and writing. The writing section includes both multiple-choice questions and a short essay.

**SAT Subject Tests** — Tests designed to measure mastery of specific subjects like English, history, mathematics, science and language for college admissions purposes. The tests are independent of any particular textbook or method of instruction. Depending on the subject, an SAT Subject Test may include multiple-choice questions, an essay or (for some foreign language tests) a listening section.

# 2010–2011 SAT® PROGRAM TEST CALENDAR

| Test Dates | Oct. 9* | Nov. 6 | Dec. 4 | Jan. 22† | Mar. 12 | May 7† | June 4 |
|---|---|---|---|---|---|---|---|
| **Registration Deadlines*** | | | | | | | |
| Regular | Sept. 10 | Oct. 8 | Nov. 5 | Dec. 23 | Feb. 11 | Apr. 8 | May 6 |
| Late | Sept. 24 | Oct. 22 | Nov. 19 | Jan. 7 | Feb. 25 | Apr. 22 | May 20 |
| **SAT** | ■ | ■ | ■ | ■ | ■ | ■ | ■ |
| **SAT Subject Tests** | | | | | | | |
| Literature | ■ | ■ | ■ | ■ | | ■ | ■ |
| United States (U.S.) History | ■ | ■ | ■ | ■ | | ■ | ■ |
| World History | | | ■ | | | | ■ |
| Mathematics Level 1†† | ■ | ■ | ■ | ■ | | ■ | ■ |
| Mathematics Level 2†† | ■ | ■ | ■ | ■ | | ■ | ■ |
| Biology E/M (Ecological/Molecular) | ■ | ■ | ■ | ■ | | ■ | ■ |
| Chemistry | ■ | ■ | ■ | ■ | | ■ | ■ |
| Physics | ■ | ■ | ■ | ■ | | ■ | ■ |
| **Languages: Reading Only** | | | | | | | |
| French | ■ | | ■ | ■ | | | ■ |
| German | | | | | | | ■ |
| Modern Hebrew | | | | | | | ■ |
| Italian | | | | | | | ■ |
| Latin | | | ■ | | | | ■ |
| Spanish | ■ | | ■ | | | ■ | ■ |
| **Languages: Reading and Listening** | | | | | | | |
| Chinese | | ■ | | | | | |
| French | | ■ | | | | | |
| German | | ■ | | | | | |
| Japanese | | ■ | | | | | |
| Korean | | ■ | | | | | |
| Spanish | | ■ | | | | | |

*Please note that all registration deadlines are subject to change. Visit sat.collegeboard.com for the most up-to-date listings.
†Question-and-Answer Service available.
††Calculator required.
*NOTE:* Sunday test dates follow each Saturday test date for students who cannot test on Saturday because of a religious observance.

## Services for Students with Disabilities

**Students may receive accommodations** (extended time, large print, etc.) on College Board exams if they submit an eligibility form and meet the eligibility requirements. **Students must: 1)** have a disability that requires testing accommodations; **2)** have documentation on file that supports the need for accommodations; **and 3)** receive and use the requested accommodations for school-based tests. (See program material regarding the Guidelines for Documentation, and for exceptions to the above requirements.)

### SSD Contacts
(all College Board programs):

| | |
|---|---|
| Voice | 609-771-7137 |
| TTY | 609-882-4118 |
| Fax | 609-771-7944 |
| E-mail | sat.ssd@ets.org |

www.collegeboard.com/ssd

# Getting Ready for the SAT

The best way to get ready for the SAT is to take challenging courses, study hard and familiarize yourself with the test. College admissions staff are more impressed by an academic record that shows real effort and achievement than they are by test scores alone.

Before taking the SAT, you should:

- Take the PSAT/NMSQT.

- Become familiar with the test's format, directions, answer sheet and question types.

- Understand the skills tested on the SAT using the Skills Insight™ tool on sat.collegeboard.com.

- Review algebra and geometry.

- Practice reading critically.

- Read and write as much as possible, in and out of school.

## The PSAT/NMSQT®

Taking the PSAT/NMSQT (Preliminary SAT/National Merit Scholarship Qualifying Test) is the best way to practice for the SAT. For many students, the PSAT/NMSQT is also the first official step on the road to college. It assesses skills developed through years of study in a wide range of courses as well as through experiences outside the classroom. Students taking the test in their junior year also may be eligible to enter National Merit Scholarship Corporation competitions and other scholarship programs.

All students who take the test receive free online access to My College QuickStart™ until they graduate from high school. This personalized planning kit, based on your test results, features:

- My Online Score Report — an enhanced score report that allows students to review each test question, their answers, and the correct answers with answer explanations

- My SAT Study Plan — a customized SAT study plan based on students' PSAT/NMSQT test performance, highlighting skills for review and practice

- My Personality — a detailed personality test that helps students learn about themselves and discover majors and careers that fit their strengths and interests

- My Major & Career Matches — extensive information about majors and careers, including insights about what to expect and what courses to take now

- My College Matches — a starter list of colleges based on students' home state and indicated choice of major

For more information about the PSAT/NMSQT, **visit www.collegeboard.com/psat.**

**PLANNING AHEAD**

**Most students take the SAT in the spring of their junior year** and again in the fall of their senior year. Students who take SAT Subject Tests usually do so near the end of the course taken in the subject area for each exam.

When you know which test(s) to take, you'll find a schedule of registration and administration dates on page 31. Your school counselor can tell you where the SAT will be administered close to your home and school. You can also find SAT information and practice tools at **www.sat.collegeboard.com**.

## Practice Materials

To help students get ready for the SAT and college success, the College Board offers many free and affordable online test practice tools. Available at collegeboard.com, these resources can help you get familiar with and practice for the SAT.

- **The Official SAT Question of the Day™:** Practice a different question each day with the College Board's popular SAT Question of the Day. Try it online, or sign up to receive free daily test questions via e-mail.

- **The Official SAT Practice Test:** Try the full-length test online. See how you score and get detailed answer explanations to help you better understand where you need to improve.

- **SAT Skills Insight:** A free online tool that shows you the skills you know and highlights those you need to know better, including:

  - Skills tested on the SAT.
  - Skills typical of students who score within a particular score band.
  - Suggestions for how to sharpen those skills.
  - Real SAT questions and answers.

- *The Official SAT Study Guide™:* This best-seller helps students practice for the SAT by providing:

  - 10 official practice tests, focused sets of practice questions and practice essay prompts.
  - A review of concepts and test-taking approaches.
  - Chapters on the PSAT/NMSQT and the SAT essay.
  - Exclusive access to free online practice-test score reports and answer explanations.

- **The Official SAT Online Course™:** This service is available anytime from any computer with Internet access. It features:

  - 18 interactive lessons that cover all SAT sections and the PSAT/NMSQT.
  - 10 practice tests and 600+ practice questions.
  - Powerful reporting tools for educators and detailed reports for students.
  - Answer explanations and immediate essay scoring.

# Taking the Test

## When should I take the test?

Many students decide that the end of their junior year is a logical point at which to take a college admissions test for the first time. By then, you've been studying English, math, science, social studies, and other courses for more than 11 years! You've been reading, studying and taking tests regularly during that time. And if you took the PSAT/NMSQT in October of your junior year, your memory will be fresh from the experience.

# How many times should I take the test?

Research shows that many students see modest increases in their score upon taking the test a second time. Most students who repeat the test take it once in the spring of their junior year and once in the fall of their senior year. Taking the test more than twice will probably not lead to significant gains.

Remember: All of the work you've done in school — including your reading, writing and math — is what really helps you do your best on the test and be better prepared for college.

# How to register

The best way to register is online. It's fast and easy, and it helps you avoid late fees or missed postmark deadlines. You can even register for next year's tests over the summer. SAT registration may be completed at sat.collegeboard.com.

To register for the SAT by mail, complete the paper registration form included with the *SAT Registration Guide* and send it with your test fee payment. You can get a *Registration Guide* in your school's guidance office. Registration deadlines are about four and a half weeks before the test date. There are also late registration deadlines, and it's possible to register on a standby basis. Both of these involve an additional fee.

# Score Choice™

Score Choice™ is a feature that gives you the option to choose the SAT scores you send to colleges by test date — in accordance with each college's or university's score-use practice. Designed to reduce your stress and improve the test-day experience, Score Choice gives you an opportunity to show colleges the scores you feel best represent your abilities.

Score Choice is optional, so if you don't actively choose to use it, all of your scores will be sent automatically. Since most colleges only consider your best scores, you should still feel comfortable reporting scores from all of your test dates.

Each college, university and scholarship program has different score-use practices. Our new easy-to-use score-reporting process displays score-use practices for each participating institution, but you should also check with colleges to ensure that you are following their score-reporting requirements. E-mail reminders will be sent to you if you have not sent SAT scores to any colleges by the typical deadlines.

Remember:

- Scores from an entire SAT test (critical reading, writing and mathematics sections) will be sent — scores of individual sections from different test dates cannot be selected independently.

- You can send any or all scores to a college on a single report — it will not cost more to send one, multiple or all test scores.

- You receive four free score reports with your registration. We continue to recommend that you take full advantage of these reports.

- Score Choice is available via the Web or by calling Customer Service (toll free within the United States).

# Earning College Credit by Examination

Most colleges allow you to place out of introductory courses in subject areas where you have already done college-level work, either in high school or through your own life experiences. For example, you might be able to skip the first year of college Spanish and go straight to intermediate-level courses. In order to demonstrate your knowledge, the college usually requires you to either take a nationally offered standardized test, such as an AP Exam, a CLEP exam, or an SAT Subject Test or to take an exam offered by the college on campus. (You often have a choice of doing either — that is, if you haven't taken the AP Spanish Language Exam, you can take the college's Spanish placement test as an alternative.)

If you take an AP Exam or CLEP exam, many colleges also allow you to earn credit based on your exam score. To use the same example as above, you wouldn't just place into second-year Spanish; you would also earn credits toward graduation as if you had taken first-year Spanish there on campus. If you have qualifying scores on enough exams, some colleges will even grant you "sophomore standing," meaning you are treated as a sophomore for academic purposes such as when you get to register for courses. (You still have to obey the college's other rules for freshmen, though, so don't expect to be given a single dorm room and a parking permit just because you have sophomore standing through AP.)

## KNOW THE LINGO

**Advanced placement** — The ability to skip an introductory course in a subject. Many colleges offer advanced placement in appropriate subjects for AP Exams, CLEP or SAT Subject Tests. You may also qualify for advanced placement by taking the college's own placement exam.

**Credit by exam** — College credit earned for prior knowledge, usually demonstrated on either an AP Exam or a CLEP exam.

**Sophomore standing** — If a college grants an incoming student the equivalent of 30 semester hours of credit by exam, they may allow the student to be considered a sophomore for academic purposes, such as when the student registers for courses or can declare a major.

## AP Course Calendar

| | |
|---|---|
| **Spring before starting an AP course** | Well ahead of time, you need to start thinking about what AP courses you might want to take. Discuss your plans with your parents, teachers and school counselor. |
| **Summer** | Some AP teachers require you to complete work (like reading) during the summer months to prepare for their courses. For example, for AP English Literature you may be given a reading list. Make sure you complete these assignments so that you're up to speed when the class begins. |
| **January** | Talk to your AP teachers and/or AP Coordinator about taking the exams. Contact the disabilities (SSD) coordinator at your school if you will need testing accommodations. |
| **February** | Deadlines for students with disabilities whose eligibility forms require Documentation Review. |
| **March** | Deadlines for homeschooled students and students whose schools do not offer AP to arrange for testing at a nearby school. Deadlines for students with disabilities whose eligibility forms do not require Documentation Review. |
| **May 2–6 and May 9–13, 2010** | Exam dates. |
| **June 15, 2010** | Deadline for receipt of requests for score withholding, score cancellation or a change in a college grade report recipient. |
| **July** | AP score reports released to designated colleges, and to students and their high schools. |

# More About AP®

AP offers a wide range of college-level courses that are taught in high schools by high school teachers; a national exam is given for each subject every May. AP courses give you a chance to do college-level work while still in high school. Research studies have shown that students with AP experience succeed in college at a rate significantly higher than the average student.

In all, there are more than 30 courses in a wide variety of subject areas. Even if an AP course is not offered at your school, you may still be able to take the exam if you make arrangements with your school's AP Coordinator (usually a school counselor or a teacher). If your school doesn't offer AP at all, or you are homeschooled, you can still make arrangements to take an AP Exam at a nearby school that offers AP.

AP courses are challenging — after all, you're doing college-level work in high school! They can also be very rewarding. If you're not sure whether you should take an AP course, talk to your teachers, your school counselor and your parents. You might also want to look at the College Board publications *Choose AP* or the bilingual *Get with the Program/Avanza con el Programa*. Your school should be able to order copies of these for you and your parents.

# More About the College-Level Examination Program® (CLEP®)

CLEP, as the program is familiarly known, is the most widely accepted college credit-by-examination program in the country. Approximately 2,900 accredited colleges and universities award credit for qualifying scores on CLEP exams.

Unlike AP Exams, CLEP exams do not correspond to courses that you take in high school. Rather, CLEP offers 33 exams in the areas of business, English composition and literature, foreign languages, history and social studies, and science and mathematics. You can take a CLEP exam at any time during your college career, and the exams are offered year-round. You can find out if your college grants credit for CLEP exams by using the CLEP college search at www.collegeboard.com/clepcolleges.

CLEP is computer based, allowing for instant score reports, so you know that day if you will be awarded credit for your performance. To find out more about CLEP exams, to see a list of suggested textbooks and online resources for each exam, and to download study guides, visit www.collegeboard.com/clep.

# Life on campus

A college isn't just a place where you'll take classes for two or four years. You'll also be spending most of your time there — and, if you're a residential student, you'll even be living there. When you're deciding where to go, academics should come first, but you should also consider how comfortable the campus feels. Some things to take into account are the housing options, local transit, whether the campus feels safe, and the social life of the campus.

# Housing Options

At most colleges, you'll have lots of choices about where to live. You may live in an on-campus dorm, an off-campus house or apartment building, or a fraternity/sorority house. At some colleges, you won't have as many choices your freshman year, but even then you may have a choice of several freshman dorms.

Typically, after you accept an offer of admission, the college's housing office will ask you to submit a form stating your housing preferences. You should use this form not only to state your preference of what dorm in which they will place you, but also to help them find you a roommate who will be compatible. Are you a quiet person? What times do you usually wake up and go to bed? Are you messy or neat? Do you smoke? The housing office will try to find someone whose answers to those questions were similar to your own.

## Living in Dorms

College dormitories have changed a lot over the years. While they were once bare-bones facilities that offered little more than a place to sleep, today most dorms offer a complete living and learning environment. It's not uncommon to find study areas, TV lounges, computer labs, small kitchens or even fast-food take-out restaurants built into modern dorms. While some dorms are still built on the traditional floor plan of a hallway of double rooms sharing a bathroom, others are based around suites or apartments.

Some colleges offer theme-related residences for both freshmen and upper-classmen. These programs give you the opportunity to live with other students who share similar interests in a field of study, culture, hobby or personal value. Students in theme residences not only live together, but often they also eat together and participate in social events related around the dorm's theme. Some theme residences will also have a member of the faculty who lives in the dorm and advises its students. Examples of theme residences include:

- *Diversity programs,* where the residents come from a wide variety of cultural backgrounds

- *Honors residences,* where all the students are on merit scholarships

- *Discipline-based residences,* such as a dorm for engineering and science majors

- *Foreign language immersion dorms,* where all the residents study and speak a particular foreign language

- *Substance-free housing* (a.k.a. "wellness" or "positive choice" housing), where all the residents pledge not to drink, smoke or do drugs

## Roommate issues

Most roommate situations work out OK; often, freshman roommates become good friends. But there are cases when roommates just don't get along.

The best way to avoid this is to communicate with your roommates. At the beginning of the semester, tell them what you expect in terms of when you'll go to bed, when you'll get up in the mornings, when it's OK to have friends visit the room, and whether you'll be able to sleep while they work on their computer. Remember that communication is a two-way street: You should also ask your roommates about their own expectations, and listen to what they tell you.

As the semester goes on, be sure to let your roommates know if something is bothering you. Don't ignore problems or obnoxious behavior — they will only get worse if you don't speak up. Similarly, if your roommate complains about your own habits, try to correct them.

If worse comes to worst, it's not unknown for colleges to reassign roommates in midsemester. But because of space issues, this isn't always possible, and when it is possible, it's not always ideal. You'll probably find yourself living in a new dorm, away from all the friends you've already made. You might also find yourself as the new third roommate who is squeezed into a room that had previously slept two.

**EXPERT ADVICE**

"**Be honest on your housing preferences form.** If you've been pretty quiet throughout high school and always go to bed at 10 p.m., don't say you party a lot and stay up past midnight. Random roommate placement is tricky enough without stacking the deck against yourself."

— *Caitlin, student, Puget Sound University*

# Glossary

Definitions of commonly used terms vary from college to college. Consult specific college catalogs or their websites for more detailed information.

**Accelerated study.** A college program of study completed in less time than is usually required, most often by attending classes in the summer or by taking extra courses during the regular academic terms. Completion of a bachelor's degree program in three years is an example of acceleration.

**Accreditation.** Recognition by an accrediting organization or agency that a college meets certain acceptable standards in its education programs, services and facilities. Regional accreditation applies to a college as a whole and not to any particular programs or courses of study. Accreditation of specific types of schools, such as Bible colleges or trade and technical schools, may also be determined by a national organization. Institutional accreditation by regional accrediting associations and by national accrediting organizations is included in the *Handbook*'s descriptions of colleges. See pages 10–12 for more information about accreditation and the names and addresses of the national and regional accrediting associations.

**ACT.** A college admissions examination given at test centers in the United States and other countries on specified dates. Please visit the organization's website for further information.

**Advanced placement.** Admission or assignment of a first-year student to an advanced course in a certain subject on the basis of evidence that the student has already completed the equivalent of the college's freshman course in that subject.

**Advanced Placement Program (AP).** An academic program of the College Board that provides high school students with the opportunity to study and learn at the college level. AP offers more than 30 courses and exams in a wide variety of subject areas. High schools offer the courses and administer the exams to interested students. Most colleges and universities in the United States accept qualifying AP Exam scores for credit, advanced placement or both.

**Agricultural college.** A college or university that primarily trains students in the agricultural sciences and agribusiness operations.

**Articulation agreement.** A formal agreement between two higher education institutions, stating specific policies relating to transfer and recognition of academic achievement in order to facilitate the successful transfer of students without duplication of course work.

**Associate degree.** A degree granted by a college or university after the satisfactory completion of the equivalent of a two-year, full-time program of study. In general, the associate of arts (A.A.) or associate of science (A.S.) degree is granted after completing a program of study similar to the first two years of a four-year college curriculum. The associate in applied science (A.A.S.) is awarded by many colleges on completion of technological or vocational programs of study.

**Bachelor's, or baccalaureate, degree.** A degree received after the satisfactory completion of a four- or five-year, full-time program of study (or its part-time equivalent) at a college or university. The bachelor of arts (B.A.), bachelor of science (B.S.) and bachelor of fine arts (B.F.A.) are the most common baccalaureates. Policies concerning their award vary from college to college.

**Bible college.** An undergraduate institution whose program, in addition to a general education in the liberal arts, includes a significant element of Bible study. Most Bible colleges seek to prepare their students for vocational or lay Christian ministry.

**Branch campus.** A part of a college, university or community college that is geographically separate from the main campus, has its own faculty and administration, and may have separate admissions requirements and degree programs.

**Business college.** A college that primarily prepares students to work in an office or entrepreneurial setting. The curriculum may focus on management, clerical positions or both.

**Campus.** The physical location of a college or university. Includes classroom buildings, libraries, research facilities, dormitories, dining halls and administration buildings.

**Calendar.** The system by which an institution divides its year into shorter periods for instruction and awarding credit. The most common calendars are those based on the semester, trimester, quarter and 4-1-4.

**Candidates Reply Date Agreement (CRDA).** A college subscribing to this College Board–sponsored agreement will not require any applicants offered admission as freshmen to notify the college of their decision to attend (or to accept an offer of financial aid) before May 1 of the year the applicants apply. The purpose of the agreement is to give applicants time to hear from all the colleges to which they have applied before having to make a commitment to any of them.

**CB code.** A four-digit College Board code number that students use to designate colleges or scholarship programs to receive their SAT score reports.

**Certificate.** An award for completing a particular program or course of study, usually given by two-year colleges or vocational or technical schools for nondegree programs of a year or less.

**College.** The generic term for an institution of higher education. Also a term used to designate divisions within a university.

**College-Level Examination Program (CLEP).** Thirty-three examinations in the subject areas of composition and literature, foreign languages, history and social sciences, science and mathematics, and business that provide students the opportunity to earn college credit by achieving a qualifying score. These exams are sponsored by the College Board and administered by 1,600 colleges year-round. More than 2,900 colleges grant credit for passing scores.

**College-preparatory subjects.** A term used to describe subjects required for admission to, or recommended as preparation for, college. It is usually understood to mean subjects from the fields of English, history and social studies, foreign languages, mathematics, science and the arts.

**College Scholarship Service (CSS).** A unit of the College Board that assists postsecondary institutions, state scholarship programs and private scholarship organizations in the equitable and efficient distribution of student financial aid funds.

**Combined bachelor's/graduate degree.** A program in which students complete a bachelor's degree and a master's degree or first-professional degree in less than the usual amount of time. In most programs, students apply to the graduate program during their first three years of undergraduate study, and begin the graduate program in their fourth year of college. Successful completion results in awarding of both a bachelor's degree and a graduate degree. At some colleges, this option is called a joint degree program.

**Common Application.** The standard application form distributed by the National Association of Secondary School Principals to colleges who are subscribers to the Common Application Group.

**Community/junior college.** A college that offers only the first two years of undergraduate study. Community colleges are public institutions, whereas junior colleges are privately operated on a not-for-profit basis. Both usually offer terminal (or "vocational") programs and transfer programs.

**Consortium.** A group of colleges and universities that share a common geographic location. Consortiums of colleges in the same town often allow students at one institution to take classes at other consortium colleges and use facilities (such as libraries) at the member colleges. Larger consortiums, on the state or regional level, may allow for "visiting semesters" or offer in-state tuition to out-of-state students.

**Cooperative education (co-op).** A program that provides for alternative class attendance and employment in business, industry or government. Students are typically paid for their work. Under a cooperative plan, five years are normally required to complete a bachelor's degree, but graduates have the advantage of about a year's practical work experience in addition to their studies.

**Cooperative housing.** College-owned, operated or affiliated housing in which students share room and board expenses and participate in household chores to reduce their living expenses.

**Credit hour.** A unit of measure representing an hour (50 minutes) of instruction over a 15-week period in a semester or trimester system, or over a 10-week period in a quarter system. It is applied toward the total number of hours needed for completing the requirements of a degree, diploma, certificate or other formal award.

**Credit/placement by examination.** Academic credit or placement out of introductory courses granted by a college to entering students who have demonstrated proficiency in college-level studies through examinations such as those administered by the College Board's AP and CLEP programs.

**Cross-registration.** The practice, through agreements between colleges, of permitting students enrolled at one college or university to enroll in courses at another institution without formally applying for admission to the second institution.

**CSS/Financial Aid PROFILE®.** An application and service offered by the College Board, which is used by some colleges, universities and private scholarship programs to award their own private financial aid funds. Students pay a fee to send reports to institutions and programs that use PROFILE. Students register for PROFILE on www.collegeboard.com. PROFILE provides a customized application for each registrant based on the individual's information and the requirements of the colleges and programs from which she or he is seeking aid. Students complete and submit the customized application to the College Board for processing and reporting to institutions. The PROFILE is not a federal form and may not be used to apply for federal student aid.

**Culinary school.** A vocational college that primarily prepares students to work as chefs or caterers.

**Deferred admission.** The practice of permitting students to postpone enrollment, usually for one year, after acceptance to the college.

**Degree.** An award given by a college or university certifying that a student has completed a course of study. *See* bachelor's degree, associate degree, graduate degree. *See also* Certificate.

**Distance learning.** An option for earning course credit off campus via cable television, the Internet, satellite classes, videotapes, correspondence courses or other means. *See also* Virtual university.

**Doctoral degree (doctorate).** *See* Graduate degree.

**Dormitory.** *See* Residence hall.

**Double major.** Any program in which a student concurrently completes the requirements of two majors.

**Dual enrollment.** The practice of students enrolling in college courses while still in high school.

**Early Action (EA).** Students who apply under a college's Early Action plan receive a decision earlier than the standard response date but are not required to accept the admissions offer or to make a deposit prior to May 1. See the Early Decision/Early Action table for a list of colleges that offer Early Action plans, including application deadlines and notification dates.

**Early admission.** The policy of some colleges of admitting certain students who have not completed high school — usually students of exceptional ability who have completed their junior year. These students are enrolled full-time in college.

**Early Decision (ED).** Students who apply under Early Decision make a commitment to enroll at the college if admitted and offered a satisfactory financial aid package. Application deadlines are usually in November or December with a mid-to-late-December notification date. Some colleges have two rounds of Early Decision. See the Early Decision/Early Action table for details.

**Engineering college/institute/school.** An institution of higher education that primarily prepares students for careers as licensed professional engineers or engineering technologists.

**Exchange student program.** Any arrangement that permits a student to study for a semester or more at another college in the United States without extending the amount of time required for a degree.

**External degree program.** A system of study whereby a student earns credit toward a degree through independent study, college courses, proficiency examinations and personal experience. External degree colleges generally have no campus or classroom facilities.

**FAFSA.** *See* Free Application for Federal Student Aid (FAFSA).

**For-profit college.** A private institution operated by its owners as a profit-making enterprise.

**4-1-4 calendar.** A variation of the semester calendar system, the 4-1-4 calendar consists of two terms of about 16 weeks each, separated by a one-month intersession used for intensive short courses, independent study, off-campus work or other types of instruction.

**Free Application for Federal Student Aid (FAFSA).** A form completed by all applicants for federal student aid. In many states, completion of the FAFSA is also sufficient to establish eligibility for state-sponsored aid programs. There is no charge to students for completing the FAFSA. The online form may be filed any time after Jan. 1 of the year for which one is seeking aid (e.g., after Jan. 1, 2011, for academic year 2011-12 assistance).

**General Educational Development (GED).** A series of tests that individuals who did not complete high school may take through their state education system to qualify for a high school equivalency certificate.

**Grade point average (GPA) or ratio.** A system used by many schools for evaluating the overall scholastic performance of students. Grade points are determined by first multiplying the number of hours given for a course by the numerical value of the grade and then dividing the sum of all grade points by the total number of hours carried. The most common system of numerical values for grades is A = 4, B = 3, C = 2, D = 1, and E or F = 0. Also called quality point average or ratio.

**Graduate degree.** A degree pursued after a student has earned a bachelor's degree. The master's degree, which requires one to three years of study, is usually the degree earned after the bachelor's. The doctoral degree requires further study. First-professional degrees are also graduate degrees.

**Health sciences college.** An institution of higher education that primarily prepares students to enter work in a clinic, hospital or private medical practice.

**Hispanic-serving college.** A college where Hispanic students comprise at least 25 percent of the total of full-time undergraduate enrollment.

**Historically black college.** An institution founded before 1964 whose mission was historically, and remains, the education of African Americans.

**Homeschooled.** For purposes of the application requirements described in the "basis for selection" entries of the college descriptions, this refers to homeschooling during the four years of secondary school (grades 9–12).

**Honors program.** Any special program for very able students that offers the opportunity for education enrichment, independent study, acceleration or some combination of these.

**Independent student.** For financial aid purposes, a student who is not dependent on financial support from his or her parents. Also called a self-supporting student.

**Independent study.** Academic work chosen or designed by the student under an instructor's supervision. This work is usually undertaken outside of the regular classroom structure.

**International Baccalaureate (IB).** A high school curriculum offered by some schools in the United States and other countries. Some colleges award credit for completion of this curriculum. Please visit the organization's website for further information.

**Internship.** A short-term, supervised work experience, usually related to a student's major field, for which the student earns academic credit. The work can be full or part time, on or off campus, paid or unpaid. Student teaching and apprenticeships are examples.

**Intersession term.** A short term offered between semesters. *See also* 4-1-4 calendar.

**Junior college.** *See* Community/junior college.

**Liberal arts.** The study of the humanities (literature, the arts and philosophy), history, foreign languages, social sciences, mathematics and natural sciences. Study of the liberal arts and humanities prepares students to develop general knowledge and reasoning ability rather than specific skills.

**Liberal arts/career combination.** A program of study in which a student typically completes three years of study in a liberal arts field followed by two years of professional/technical study (for example, engineering) at the end of which the student is awarded bachelor of arts and bachelor of science degrees. The combination is also referred to as a 3+2 program.

**Liberal arts college.** A college that emphasizes the liberal arts in its core curriculum and academic offerings and does not offer vocational or professional programs.

**Lower division.** The freshman and sophomore years of college study.

**Major.** A student's academic field of specialization. In general, most courses in the major are taken during the junior and senior years.

**Maritime college/institute/academy.** An institution of higher education that prepares students to operate commercial shipping or fishing vessels. Upon graduation, students of most maritime academies are commissioned as officers in the United States Merchant Marine, and simultaneously commissioned as officers in the U.S. Navy Reserve.

**Master's degree.** *See* Graduate degree.

**Military college/institute/academy.** An institution of higher education that prepares students (who are called "cadets" while enrolled) to become active-duty officers in the armed services. The curriculum usually combines a study of the liberal arts, military science and engineering. Cadets usually participate in military training assignments during the summer term in addition to attending the college in the fall and spring semesters.

**Minor.** Course work that is not as extensive as that in a major but gives students some specialized knowledge of a second field.

**NAIA.** The National Association of Inter-collegiate Athletics. NAIA members are mostly small colleges. Championships are offered in 13 sports.

**NCAA.** The National Collegiate Athletic Association. The largest collegiate athletic association, it oversees the most athletic scholarship money. The NCAA governs league play in 23 championship sports.

**NCCAA.** National Christian College Athletic Association. NCCAA sponsors league play among Bible colleges and other Christian-oriented institutions.

**NJCAA.** The National Junior College Athletic Association. NJCAA members are two-year junior or community colleges.

**Need-based financial aid.** Financial aid given to students who have demonstrated financial need, which is calculated by subtracting the student's expected family contribution from a college's total costs. The expected family contribution is derived from a need analysis of the family's overall financial circumstances.

**Nondegree study.** A college-level course of study that does not lead to a degree. Nondegree study may or may not be part of a program leading to a certificate.

**Nursing college.** An institution of higher education that primarily prepares students to become registered nurses (RNs) or licensed practical nurses (LPNs).

**Open admissions.** The college admissions policy of admitting high school graduates and other adults generally without regard to conventional academic qualifications, such as high school subjects, high school grades and admissions test scores. Virtually all applicants with high school diplomas or their equivalent are accepted, space permitting.

**Placement by examination.** *See* Credit/placement by examination.

**Private college.** Institutions described in this book as "private" are operated on a not-for-profit basis. They may be independent or church affiliated. *See also* Proprietary college.

**Professional degree.** A degree granted upon completion of academic requirements to become licensed in a recognized profession. The programs of study require at least two years of previous college work for entrance, and at least six years of total college work for completion. The medical doctorate (M.D.) is one kind of first-professional degree.

**PROFILE.** *See* CSS/Financial Aid PROFILE.

**Priority date.** The date by which an application, whether for admission, housing or financial aid, must be received to be given the strongest possible consideration. After that date, applicants are considered on a first-come, first-served basis.

**Proprietary college.** *See* For-profit college.

**PSAT/NMSQT (Preliminary SAT/National Merit Scholarship Qualifying Test).** A preparatory tool for the SAT that is administered by high schools to sophomores and juniors each year in October. The PSAT/NMSQT serves as the qualifying test for scholarships awarded by the National Merit Scholarship Corporation.

**Public college/university.** An institution that is supported by taxes and other public revenue and governed by a county, state or federal government agency.

**Quality point average.** *See* Grade point average (GPA) or ratio.

**Quarter.** An academic calendar period of about 12 weeks. Four quarters make up an academic year, but at colleges using the quarter system, students make normal academic progress by attending three quarters each year. In some colleges, students can accelerate their programs by attending all four quarters in one or more years.

**Rabbinical college.** *See* Seminary/rabbinical college.

**Regional accreditation.** *See* Accreditation.

**Regular admission.** Admission during the college's normal calendar for admissions, as opposed to Early Decision or Early Action admissions.

**Reserve Officers' Training Corps (ROTC).** Programs conducted by certain colleges in cooperation with the United States Air Force, Army and Navy. Navy ROTC includes the Marine Corps (the Coast Guard and Merchant Marine do not sponsor ROTC programs). Local recruiting offices of the services themselves can supply detailed information about these programs, as can participating colleges.

**Residence hall.** An on-campus living facility. Also known as a dormitory (or "dorm").

**Residency requirement.** The minimum number of terms that a student must spend taking courses on campus (as opposed to independent study, transfer credits from other colleges, or credit by examination) to be eligible for graduation. Can also refer to the minimum amount of time a student must have lived in-state in order to qualify for the in-state tuition rate at a public college or university.

**Rolling admissions.** An admissions procedure by which the college considers each student's application as soon as all the required credentials, such as school records and test scores, have been received. The college usually notifies an applicant of its decision without delay. At many colleges, rolling admissions allows for early notification and works much like nonbinding Early Action programs.

**Room and board.** The cost of housing and meals for students who reside on campus and/or dine in college-operated meal halls.

**The SAT.** A college entrance exam that tests critical reading, writing and mathematics skills, given on specified dates throughout the year at test centers in the United States and other countries. The SAT is used by most colleges and sponsors of financial aid programs.

**SAT Subject Tests.** Admissions tests in specific subjects given at test centers in the United States and other countries on specified dates throughout the year. The tests are used by colleges for help in both evaluating applicants for admission and determining course placement, and exemption of enrolled first-year students.

**Semester.** A period of about 16 weeks. Colleges on a semester system offer two semesters of instruction a year; there may be an additional summer session.

**Semester at sea.** A program for credit, usually for students with majors in oceanography or marine-related fields, in which students live on a ship, frequently a research vessel, for part of a semester. Academic courses are generally taken in conjunction with the sea experience.

**Seminary/rabbinical college.** An institution that prepares its student for professional religious ministry. Most seminaries are graduate-only institutions that offer first-professional degrees in divinity or rabbinical studies. The seminaries described in this book also offer undergraduate programs in philosophy, theology, Bible studies or other related liberal arts.

**Sophomore standing.** Consideration of a student as a sophomore for academic purposes such as registering for classes and declaring a major. A college may grant sophomore standing to incoming freshmen if they have enough credits from AP, CLEP or IB exams.

**Student Aid Report (SAR).** A report produced by the U.S. Department of Education and sent to students in response to their having filed the Free Application for Federal Student Aid (FAFSA). The SAR contains information the student provided on the FAFSA as well as the federally calculated result, which the financial aid office will use in determining the student's eligibility for a Federal Pell Grant and other federal student aid programs.

**Student-designed major.** An academic program that allows a student to construct a major field of study not formally offered by the college. Often nontraditional and interdisciplinary in nature, the major is developed by the student with the approval of a designated college officer or committee.

**Study abroad.** Any arrangement by which a student completes part of the college program — typically the junior year but sometimes only a semester or a summer — by studying in another country. A college may operate a campus abroad, or it may have a cooperative agreement with some other U.S. college or an institution of the other country.

**Teacher certification.** A college program designed to prepare students to meet the requirements for certification as teachers in elementary and secondary schools.

**Teachers college.** A college that specializes in preparing students to teach in elementary or secondary schools. Most teachers colleges offer a curriculum that combines a study of the liberal arts with the study of pedagogy.

**Technical college/school.** A college that offers a wide variety of vocational programs to students.

**Term.** The shorter period into which colleges divide the school year. *See* Calendar.

**Terminal degree.** The highest degree level attainable in a particular field. For most teaching faculty this is a doctoral degree. In certain fields, however, a master's degree is the highest level.

**Terminal program.** An education program designed to prepare students for immediate employment. These programs usually can be completed in less than four years beyond high school and are available in most community colleges and vocational-technical institutes.

**Test of English as a Foreign Language (TOEFL).** A test generally used by international students to demonstrate their English language proficiency at the advanced level required for study at colleges and universities in the United States. Please visit the organization's website for further information.

**Transcript.** A copy of a student's official academic record listing all courses taken and grades received.

**Transfer program.** An education program in a two-year college (or a four-year college that offers associate degrees), primarily for students who plan to continue their studies in a four-year college or university.

**Transfer student.** A student who has attended another college for any period, which may be defined by various colleges as any time from a single term up to three years. A transfer student may receive credit for all or some of the courses successfully completed before the transfer.

**Trimester.** An academic calendar period of about 15 weeks. Three trimesters make up one year. Students normally progress by attending two of the trimesters each year and in some colleges can accelerate their programs by attending all three trimesters in one or more years.

**Tuition.** The price of instruction at a college. Tuition may be charged per term or per credit hour.

**Two-year college.** *See* Community/junior college; Upper-division college.

**United Nations semester.** A program in which students take courses at a college in New York City while interning at the United Nations.

**University.** An institution of higher education that is divided into several colleges, schools or institutes. When applying to a university, students typically have to apply for admission to a specific college, which may have its own admissions requirements. Not all colleges within a university will admit applicants who are high school graduates — some may be for graduate study only, and some may be upper-division colleges. Generally, university students take classes in the college to which they were accepted, but they may be allowed to take some courses offered by other colleges within the university and can use shared facilities such as libraries and laboratories.

**Upper division.** The junior and senior years of study.

**Upper-division college.** A college offering bachelor's degree programs that begin with the junior year. Entering students must have completed their freshman and sophomore years at other colleges.

**Urban semester.** A program for credit in which students spend a semester in a major city and experience the complexities of an urban center through course work, seminars and/or internships related to their major.

**USCAA.** United States Collegiate Athletic Association. USCAA's members are primarily very small colleges.

**Virtual university.** A degree-granting, accredited institution wherein all courses are delivered by distance learning, with no physical campus.

**Vocational program.** *See* Terminal program.

**Wait list.** A list of students who meet the admissions requirements, but will only be offered a place in the class if space becomes available. See the wait-list table in the back of this book for a list of colleges that placed students on a wait list last year, along with the number of students who were eventually accepted from that list.

**Washington semester.** A program in which students intern with a government agency or department in the Washington, D.C., metropolitan area. Students earn field service credit for their work and frequently take courses at area colleges.

**Weekend college.** A program that allows students to take a complete course of study and attend classes only on weekends. These programs are generally restricted to a few areas of study at a college and require more than the traditional number of years to complete.

**Work-study.** An arrangement by which a student combines employment and college study. The employment may be an integral part of the academic program (as in cooperative education and internships) or simply a means of paying for college (as in the Federal Work-Study Program).

# Four-year colleges

## Alabama

### Alabama Agricultural and Mechanical University
Huntsville, Alabama     CB member
www.aamu.edu     CB code: 1003

- Public 4-year university and agricultural college
- Residential campus in small city
- 4,489 degree-seeking undergraduates: 8% part-time, 52% women
- 831 degree-seeking graduate students
- 47% of applicants admitted
- SAT or ACT (ACT writing optional) required

**General.** Founded in 1875. Regionally accredited. Campus located near Redstone Arsenal-Defense Research/Space Research Center. **Degrees:** 628 bachelor's awarded; master's, doctoral offered. **ROTC:** Army. **Location:** 2 miles from downtown, 95 miles from Birmingham. **Calendar:** Semester, extensive summer session. **Full-time faculty:** 314 total; 45% have terminal degrees, 55% minority, 40% women. **Part-time faculty:** 71 total; 20% have terminal degrees, 70% minority, 59% women. **Class size:** 49% < 20, 40% 20-39, 7% 40-49, 3% 50-99, less than 1% >100. **Special facilities:** State black archives research center and museum.

**Freshman class profile.** 5,697 applied, 2,696 admitted, 1,050 enrolled.

| Mid 50% test scores | | | |
|---|---|---|---|
| SAT critical reading: | 400-470 | SAT writing: | 380-460 |
| SAT math: | 380-470 | ACT composite: | 16-19 |
| | | Out-of-state: | 36% |

**Basis for selection.** 2.0 GPA required. Test scores important, but may be waived dependent upon evaluation of GPA and other achievements. Interview, essay recommended. **Homeschooled:** Must meet Alabama State Department of Education requirements.

**High school preparation.** Required units include English 4, mathematics 4 and science 2.

**2009-2010 Annual costs.** Tuition/fees: $5,322; $10,272 out-of-state. Room/board: $5,350.

**Financial aid.** **Non-need-based:** Scholarships awarded for athletics, minority status.

**Application procedures.** **Admission:** Priority date 5/1; deadline 7/15 (receipt date). $25 fee, may be waived for applicants with need. Admission notification on a rolling basis. **Financial aid:** FAFSA, institutional form required. Applicants notified on a rolling basis; must reply within 2 week(s) of notification.

**Academics.** Bachelor of Technical Studies available to adult learners in nontraditional fields. **Special study options:** Cooperative education, distance learning, double major, dual enrollment of high school students, exchange student, honors, independent study, internships, study abroad, teacher certification program, Washington semester, weekend college. **Credit/placement by examination:** AP, CLEP, SAT, ACT, institutional tests. 9 credit hours maximum toward bachelor's degree. Scores from DANTES, CLEP, ACE, and similar tests, and work experiences considered for credit toward degree. **Support services:** Learning center, reduced course load, remedial instruction, study skills assistance, tutoring.

**Honors college/program.** Second semester freshmen with 20-21 ACT (SAT 1030) may be considered with 3.5 college GPA, 12 credit hours completed at the university, and 3.3 high school GPA.

**Majors. Agriculture:** Economics. **Architecture:** Urban/community planning. **Biology:** General. **Business:** General, accounting, business admin, finance, marketing, office management, public finance. **Communications:** Journalism. **Communications technology:** General, graphic/printing. **Computer sciences:** General. **Education:** General, business, early childhood, elementary, music, physical, school counseling, secondary, special, speech impaired. **Engineering:** Civil, mechanical. **Engineering technology:** Civil. **Family/consumer sciences:** General. **Math:** General. **Physical sciences:** Chemistry, physics. **Psychology:** General. **Public administration:** Social work. **Social sciences:** Political science, sociology. **Visual/performing arts:** Art, conducting, music performance.

**Most popular majors.** Biology 12%, business/marketing 23%, education 12%, engineering/engineering technologies 12%, social sciences 6%.

**Computing on campus.** 928 workstations in dormitories, library, computer center, student center. Dormitories linked to campus network. Commuter students can connect to campus network. Helpline available.

**Student life. Freshman orientation:** Mandatory, $100 fee. Preregistration for classes offered. **Housing:** Guaranteed on-campus for all undergraduates. Single-sex dorms available. $100 deposit, deadline 8/1. **Activities:** Bands, choral groups, dance, drama, literary magazine, music ensembles, radio station, student government, student newspaper, TV station, Christian student organization, honor society, service clubs, NAACP, African-American political club, Baptist student union, Islamic association, Caribbean students association, International Association of Nigerian Students.

**Athletics.** NCAA. **Intercollegiate:** Baseball M, basketball, bowling W, cross-country, football (tackle) M, golf, soccer, softball W, tennis, track and field, volleyball W. **Intramural:** Basketball, football (tackle) M, soccer W, softball, volleyball. **Team name:** Bulldogs.

**Student services.** Adult student services, career counseling, student employment services, health services, personal counseling, placement for graduates, veterans' counselor. **Physically disabled:** Services for visually, speech, hearing impaired.

**Contact.** E-mail: juan.alexander@aamu.edu
Phone: (256) 372-5245 Toll-free number: (256) 372-5245
Fax: (256) 372-5249
Juan Alexander, Director of Admissions, Alabama Agricultural and Mechanical University, Box 908, Normal, AL 35762

### Alabama State University
Montgomery, Alabama     CB member
www.alasu.edu     CB code: 1006

- Public 4-year university
- Residential campus in small city
- 4,614 degree-seeking undergraduates: 9% part-time, 60% women, 98% African American
- 918 degree-seeking graduate students
- 53% of applicants admitted
- SAT or ACT with writing, interview required

**General.** Founded in 1867. Regionally accredited. **Degrees:** 497 bachelor's awarded; master's, doctoral, professional offered. **ROTC:** Army, Air Force. **Location:** 91 miles from Birmingham, 162 miles from Atlanta. **Calendar:** Semester, limited summer session. **Full-time faculty:** 241 total; 52% have terminal degrees, 54% women. **Part-time faculty:** 167 total; 6% have terminal degrees, 56% women. **Class size:** 47% < 20, 47% 20-39, 5% 40-49, less than 1% 50-99. **Special facilities:** Black history collection, E. D. Nixon papers from civil rights movement of 1960's.

**Freshman class profile.** 6,807 applied, 3,592 admitted, 1,221 enrolled.

| Mid 50% test scores | | | |
|---|---|---|---|
| SAT critical reading: | 360-440 | GPA 2.0-2.99: | 55% |
| SAT math: | 320-420 | Rank in top quarter: | 9% |
| ACT composite: | 13-17 | Rank in top tenth: | 2% |
| GPA 3.75 or higher: | 7% | Return as sophomores: | 52% |
| GPA 3.50-3.74: | 9% | Out-of-state: | 50% |
| GPA 3.0-3.49: | 29% | Live on campus: | 73% |

**Basis for selection.** School record and GPA very important; 2.2 GPA from accredited high school required. Interview and essay recommended. Audition required of music majors. Portfolio recommended for art majors. **Homeschooled:** Transcript of courses and grades required. 20 ACT required. **Learning Disabled:** Must submit appropriate documentation in order to be given special consideration.

**High school preparation.** College-preparatory program recommended. 15 units required. Required units include English 4, mathematics 3, social studies 3, science 3, foreign language 1, computer science 1 and visual/performing arts 1.

**2009-2010 Annual costs.** Tuition/fees: $6,132; $11,412 out-of-state. Room/board: $4,800. Books/supplies: $1,600. Personal expenses: $1,380.

**2009-2010 Financial aid. Need-based:** 1,159 full-time freshmen applied for aid; 1,136 were judged to have need; 1,088 of these received aid. Average need met was 60%. Average scholarship/grant was $5,011; average loan $3,263. 45% of total undergraduate aid awarded as scholarships/grants, 55% as loans/jobs. **Non-need-based:** Scholarships awarded for academics, alumni affiliation, art, athletics, job skills, leadership, minority status, music/drama, ROTC, state residency.

**Application procedures. Admission:** Closing date 7/30 (postmark date). $25 fee, may be waived for applicants with need. Admission notification on a rolling basis. **Financial aid:** Priority date 4/1; no closing date. FAFSA required. Applicants notified on a rolling basis starting 5/1.

**Academics. Special study options:** Combined bachelor's/graduate degree, cooperative education, cross-registration, distance learning, double major, honors, independent study, internships, teacher certification program. Enrollment with Auburn University Montgomery and Troy University Montgomery. **Credit/placement by examination:** AP, CLEP, SAT, ACT, institutional tests. 45 credit hours maximum toward bachelor's degree. Students must have approval of the academic advisor, department head, dean and vice president for academic affairs prior to taking CLEP exam. **Support services:** Learning center, remedial instruction, study skills assistance, tutoring, writing center.

**Honors college/program.** 3.3 GPA and 24 ACT or 1100 SAT required; 34 freshmen admitted.

**Majors. Biology:** General, marine. **Business:** Accounting, business admin, finance, marketing. **Communications:** General. **Computer sciences:** Computer science, information systems. **Education:** Early childhood, elementary, music, physical, secondary, special. **Health:** Medical records admin. **History:** General. **Math:** General. **Parks/recreation:** Facilities management. **Physical sciences:** Chemistry, physics. **Protective services:** Criminal justice. **Psychology:** General. **Public administration:** Social work. **Social sciences:** Political science, sociology. **Visual/performing arts:** Art, dramatic.

**Most popular majors.** Biology 10%, business/marketing 12%, communications/journalism 7%, computer/information sciences 7%, education 18%, psychology 7%, public administration/social services 6%, security/protective services 10%, visual/performing arts 6%.

**Computing on campus.** 405 workstations in library, computer center. Online course registration, online library, helpline, wireless network available.

**Student life. Freshman orientation:** Mandatory, $55 fee. Preregistration for classes offered. **Housing:** Single-sex dorms, special housing for disabled, apartments available. $200 fully refundable deposit, deadline 5/31. Living-learning communities available. **Activities:** Bands, campus ministries, choral groups, dance, drama, international student organizations, music ensembles, Model UN, musical theater, radio station, student government, student newspaper, Student Christian Association.

**Athletics.** NCAA. **Intercollegiate:** Baseball M, basketball, bowling W, cross-country, football (tackle) M, golf, soccer W, softball W, tennis, track and field, volleyball W. **Intramural:** Baseball M, basketball, softball, swimming, tennis, track and field, volleyball W. **Team name:** Hornets.

**Student services.** Adult student services, alcohol/substance abuse counseling, career counseling, services for economically disadvantaged, student employment services, financial aid counseling, health services, minority student services, personal counseling, placement for graduates, veterans' counselor. **Physically disabled:** Services for visually impaired. **Learning disabled:** Comprehensive services available.

**Contact.** E-mail: admissions@alasu.edu
Phone: (334) 229-4291 Toll-free number: (800) 253-5037
Fax: (334) 229-4984
Martha Pettway, Director of Admissions and Recruitment, Alabama State University, PO Box 271, Montgomery, AL 36101-0271

---

## Amridge University
### Montgomery, Alabama
www.amridgeuniversity.edu — **CB code: 7001**

- Private 4-year virtual university affiliated with Church of Christ
- Commuter campus in small city
- 385 degree-seeking undergraduates: 37% part-time, 52% women, 38% African American, 2% Asian American, 4% Hispanic American
- 372 degree-seeking graduate students

**General.** Founded in 1967. Regionally accredited. **Degrees:** 94 bachelor's, 6 associate awarded; master's, doctoral offered. **Location:** 100 miles from Birmingham, 150 miles from Atlanta. **Calendar:** Semester, extensive summer session. **Full-time faculty:** 58 total. **Part-time faculty:** 37 total.

**Basis for selection.** Open admission, but selective for some programs. Students admitted under conditional admission must earn a 2.0 during the first 24 semester hours attempted. **Homeschooled:** Transcript of courses and grades, interview required.

**High school preparation.** 15 units recommended.

**2009-2010 Annual costs.** $300 per-semester-hour charge; full-time students receive a $150 credit per semester. Books/supplies: $800. Personal expenses: $1,739.

**2008-2009 Financial aid. Non-need-based:** Scholarships awarded for academics, leadership.

**Application procedures. Admission:** No deadline. $75 fee. Admission notification on a rolling basis. **Financial aid:** Priority date 5/1, closing date 6/30. FAFSA, institutional form required. Must reply by 8/15 or within 2 week(s) of notification.

**Academics. Special study options:** Accelerated study, distance learning, double major, independent study, internships. Participant in the U.S. Department of Education's Distance Education Demonstration Program and in eArmyU and GoArmyEd initiatives. **Credit/placement by examination:** CLEP. 36 credit hours maximum toward bachelor's degree. **Support services:** Tutoring.

**Majors. Business:** Business admin. **Computer sciences:** General. **Liberal arts:** Arts/sciences. **Theology:** Bible.

**Most popular majors.** Liberal arts 44%, theological studies 52%.

**Computing on campus.** PC or laptop required. 25 workstations in library, computer center. Online course registration, online library, helpline available.

**Student life. Freshman orientation:** Available. Online orientation available at any time.

**Student services.** Financial aid counseling, placement for graduates, veterans' counselor.

**Contact.** E-mail: admissions@amridgeuniversity.edu
Phone: (334) 387-7524 Toll-free number: (800) 351-4040 ext. 7524
Fax: (334) 387-3878
Ora Davis, Admissions Officer, Amridge University, PO Box 240240, Montgomery, AL 36124-0240

---

## Andrew Jackson University
### Birmingham, Alabama
www.aju.edu — **CB code: 3877**

- For-profit 4-year virtual liberal arts college
- Very large city
- 540 degree-seeking undergraduates

**General.** Accredited by DETC. **Degrees:** 8 bachelor's, 12 associate awarded; master's offered. **Calendar:** Continuous, extensive summer session. **Part-time faculty:** 50 total.

**Basis for selection.** Open admission. **Homeschooled:** State high school equivalency certificate, letter of recommendation (nonparent) required.

**2009-2010 Annual costs.** Undergraduates pay $350 per semester for up to four courses; no tuition charged. Books/supplies: $750.

**Application procedures. Admission:** No deadline. $75 fee. Admission notification on a rolling basis. Must reply by May 1 or within 12 week(s) if notified thereafter.

**Academics. Special study options:** Accelerated study, distance learning, independent study. **Credit/placement by examination:** AP, CLEP. 15 credit hours maximum toward associate degree, 30 toward bachelor's. **Support services:** Reduced course load.

**Majors. Business:** General. **Communications:** General. **Protective services:** Criminal justice.

**Most popular majors.** Business/marketing 43%, security/protective services 43%.

**Computing on campus.** PC or laptop required.

**Student life. Freshman orientation:** Mandatory.

**Athletics. Team name:** Generals.

**Student services.** Adult student services, veterans' counselor.

**Contact.** E-mail: admissions@aju.edu
Phone: (205) 871-9288 ext. 107 Toll-free number: (800) 429-9300 ext. 107
Fax: (205) 871-9294
Tammy Kassner, Director of Admissions, Andrew Jackson University, 2919 John Hawkins Parkway, Birmingham, AL 35244

---

## Athens State University

Athens, Alabama
www.athens.edu                                      CB code: 0706

▸  Public two-year upper-division business, liberal arts and teachers college
▸  Commuter campus in large town

**General.** Founded in 1822. Regionally accredited. **Degrees:** 859 bachelor's awarded. **Articulation:** Agreements with state schools through the Alabama Articulation and General Studies Committee. **Location:** 14 miles from Decatur, 24 miles from Huntsville. **Calendar:** Semester, extensive summer session. **Full-time faculty:** 80 total; 12% minority, 45% women. **Part-time faculty:** 115 total; 10% minority, 57% women. **Class size:** 44% < 20, 44% 20-39, 4% 40-49, 3% 50-99, 5% >100.

**Student profile.** 3,276 degree-seeking undergraduates. 81% transferred from two-year, 19% transferred from four-year institutions.

| | | | |
|---|---|---|---|
| Women: | 67% | Native American: | 3% |
| African American: | 12% | Part-time: | 52% |
| Asian American: | 1% | Out-of-state: | 4% |
| Hispanic American: | 1% | 25 or older: | 90% |

**Basis for selection.** College transcript required. Transfer accepted as juniors, seniors.

**2009-2010 Annual costs.** Tuition/fees: $4,350; $7,950 out-of-state. Books/supplies: $800.

**Financial aid. Non-need-based:** Scholarships awarded for academics, alumni affiliation, art, athletics, leadership, minority status.

**Application procedures. Admission:** Rolling admission. $30 fee. **Financial aid:** FAFSA required.

**Academics. Special study options:** Cooperative education, distance learning, double major, dual enrollment of high school students, honors, independent study, internships, liberal arts/career combination, study abroad, teacher certification program, weekend college. **Credit/placement by examination:** AP, CLEP.

**Majors. Biology:** General. **Business:** Accounting, business admin, human resources, information resources management. **Computer sciences:** General. **Education:** General, biology, chemistry, early childhood, elementary,

---

English, history, mathematics, middle, physical, physics, science, secondary, social science, social studies, special, trade/industrial. **Engineering technology:** Instrumentation. **History:** General. **Interdisciplinary:** Behavioral sciences. **Liberal arts:** Arts/sciences. **Math:** General. **Philosophy/religion:** Religion. **Physical sciences:** Chemistry, physics. **Protective services:** Criminal justice. **Psychology:** General. **Social sciences:** Political science, sociology. **Visual/performing arts:** Art.

**Most popular majors.** Business/marketing 31%, computer/information sciences 6%, education 34%, interdisciplinary studies 6%, liberal arts 6%.

**Computing on campus.** 341 workstations in library, computer center, student center. Commuter students can connect to campus network. Online library available.

**Student life. Activities:** Campus ministries, drama, literary magazine, student government, student newspaper, African-American history association, Centurions, Athenian hosts/hostesses, TKE, Tau Kappa Epsilon, Wesley Fellowship campus ministries, Pi tau Chi, pre-law society, council for exceptional children.

**Student services.** Career counseling, student employment services, financial aid counseling, minority student services, placement for graduates, veterans' counselor. **Physically disabled:** Services for visually, speech, hearing impaired.

**Contact.** E-mail: admissions@athens.edu
Phone: (256) 233-8220 Toll-free number: (800) 522-0272
Fax: (256) 233-6565
Necedah Henderson, Coordinator of Admissions, Athens State University, 300 North Beaty Street, Athens, AL 35611

---

## Auburn University

Auburn, Alabama                                       CB member
www.auburn.edu                                        CB code: 1005

▸  Public 4-year university
▸  Commuter campus in large town
▸  19,916 degree-seeking undergraduates: 8% part-time, 48% women, 8% African American, 2% Asian American, 2% Hispanic American, 1% Native American, 1% international
▸  4,618 degree-seeking graduate students
▸  80% of applicants admitted
▸  SAT or ACT with writing, application essay required
▸  67% graduate within 6 years

**General.** Founded in 1856. Regionally accredited. **Degrees:** 3,942 bachelor's awarded; master's, doctoral, professional offered. **ROTC:** Army, Naval, Air Force. **Location:** 55 miles from Montgomery, 110 miles from Atlanta. **Calendar:** Semester, extensive summer session. **Full-time faculty:** 1,184 total; 16% minority, 33% women. **Part-time faculty:** 159 total; 6% minority, 45% women. **Class size:** 27% < 20, 52% 20-39, 6% 40-49, 9% 50-99, 5% >100. **Special facilities:** Nuclear science center, hybridoma facility, herbarium, art museum, hypervelocity impact facility, advanced microscopy and imaging laboratory, microelectronics science and technology center, water resources research institute, airport with aircraft and flight simulators, forest sustainability center, governmental services center, pharmacy operations and designs center, drug information and learning resources center, economic and community development institute, fish molecular genetics and biotechnology laboratory, forest policy center, forest products development center, fusion lab, early learning center, health behavior assessment center, highway research center, marriage and family therapy center, microfibrous materials manufacturing center, biomechanics lab, motor behavior center, plasma sciences lab, veterinary medicine radiology clinic, raptor rehabilitation center, animal health clinics.

**Freshman class profile.** 14,862 applied, 11,816 admitted, 3,918 enrolled.

| Mid 50% test scores | | GPA 2.0-2.99: | 5% |
|---|---|---|---|
| SAT critical reading: | 520-640 | Rank in top quarter: | 65% |
| SAT math: | 540-660 | Rank in top tenth: | 40% |
| SAT writing: | 510-620 | Return as sophomores: | 86% |
| ACT composite: | 23-29 | Out-of-state: | 43% |
| GPA 3.75 or higher: | 48% | Live on campus: | 68% |
| GPA 3.50-3.74: | 20% | Fraternities: | 25% |
| GPA 3.0-3.49: | 27% | Sororities: | 43% |

**Basis for selection.** Each student evaluated based on combination of standardized test scores, GPA, and additional information required on application.

**High school preparation.** College-preparatory program required. 12 units required; 15 recommended. Required and recommended units include English 4, mathematics 3, social studies 3, science 2 (laboratory 1-2) and foreign language 1. Math must include algebra I, algebra II, and either geometry, trigonometry, calculus or analysis. Science must include biology and a physical science.

**2009-2010 Annual costs.** Tuition/fees: $6,960; $19,440 out-of-state. Room/board: $8,972. Books/supplies: $1,100. Personal expenses: $2,398.

**2008-2009 Financial aid. Need-based:** 2,097 full-time freshmen applied for aid; 1,093 were judged to have need; 1,093 of these received aid. Average need met was 56%. Average scholarship/grant was $6,195; average loan $3,254. 35% of total undergraduate aid awarded as scholarships/grants, 65% as loans/jobs. **Non-need-based:** Awarded to 3,191 full-time undergraduates, including 1,204 freshmen. **Additional information:** State of Alabama has pre-paid college tuition plan for residents.

**Application procedures. Admission:** Priority date 2/1; deadline 6/1 (postmark date). $40 fee, may be waived for applicants with need. Admission notification on a rolling basis beginning on or about 10/15. Must reply by May 1 or within 4 week(s) if notified thereafter. **Financial aid:** Priority date 3/1; no closing date. FAFSA required. Applicants notified on a rolling basis starting 10/2.

**Academics. Special study options:** Accelerated study, cooperative education, distance learning, double major, dual enrollment of high school students, ESL, honors, independent study, internships, liberal arts/career combination, study abroad, teacher certification program, Washington semester. DVM-Master's in veterinary specialty, dual option program in education/subject areas. **Credit/placement by examination:** AP, CLEP, institutional tests. **Support services:** Learning center, reduced course load, study skills assistance, tutoring, writing center.

**Honors college/program.** 29 ACT/1280 SAT (exclusive of Writing) and 3.5 GPA required (3.4 GPA may be considered). Approximately 200 freshmen accepted last year.

**Majors. Agriculture:** Animal sciences, aquaculture, economics, horticultural science, poultry, soil science. **Architecture:** Architecture, environmental design, interior. **Biology:** General, bacteriology, biochemistry, botany, marine, molecular, zoology. **Business:** Accounting, business admin, finance, human resources, international, logistics, managerial economics, marketing, operations. **Communications:** Journalism, public relations, radio/tv. **Computer sciences:** General. **Conservation:** Environmental science, forest sciences, wildlife. **Education:** Adult/continuing, early childhood, elementary, English, foreign languages, health, mathematics, music, physical, science, social science, special, voc/tech. **Engineering:** Aerospace, agricultural, architectural, chemical, civil, computer, electrical, materials, mechanical, software, textile. **Family/consumer sciences:** Apparel marketing, family studies, food/nutrition, housing. **Foreign languages:** French, German, Spanish. **Health:** Audiology/speech pathology, communication disorders, health care admin, nursing (RN), premedicine. **History:** General. **Math:** General, applied. **Parks/recreation:** Exercise sciences. **Philosophy/religion:** Philosophy, religion. **Physical sciences:** Chemistry, geology, physics. **Psychology:** General. **Public administration:** General, social work. **Science technology:** Biological. **Social sciences:** Anthropology, economics, geography, political science, sociology. **Transportation:** Aviation management. **Visual/performing arts:** Design, dramatic, industrial design, studio arts.

**Most popular majors.** Biology 6%, business/marketing 24%, education 10%, engineering/engineering technologies 13%, social sciences 6%.

**Computing on campus.** 600 workstations in dormitories, library, computer center, student center. Dormitories linked to campus network. Commuter students can connect to campus network. Online course registration, online library, helpline, repair service available.

**Student life. Freshman orientation:** Available, $75 fee. Preregistration for classes offered. **Housing:** Coed dorms, single-sex dorms, special housing for disabled, apartments, fraternity/sorority housing, wellness housing available. Honors housing available. **Activities:** Bands, campus ministries, choral groups, dance, drama, film society, international student organizations, literary magazine, music ensembles, musical theater, opera, radio station, student government, student newspaper, symphony orchestra, TV station, over 300 organizations available.

**Athletics.** NCAA. **Intercollegiate:** Baseball M, basketball, cross-country, diving, equestrian W, football (tackle) M, golf, gymnastics W, soccer W, softball W, swimming, tennis, track and field, volleyball W. **Intramural:** Badminton, basketball, bowling, cheerleading, football (non-tackle), golf, gymnastics, lacrosse, racquetball, rugby, skiing, soccer, softball, swimming, table tennis, tennis, track and field, volleyball, wrestling M. **Team name:** Tigers.

**Student services.** Adult student services, alcohol/substance abuse counseling, career counseling, student employment services, financial aid counseling, health services, minority student services, personal counseling, placement for graduates, veterans' counselor, women's services. **Physically disabled:** Services for visually, speech, hearing impaired.

**Contact.** E-mail: admissions@auburn.edu
Phone: (334) 844-4080 Toll-free number: (800) 282-8769
Fax: (334) 844-6436
Cindy Singley, Director of University Recruitment, Auburn University, Quad Center, Auburn, AL 36849-5111

## Auburn University at Montgomery
**Montgomery, Alabama**     CB member
**www.aum.edu**     CB code: 1036

▶ Public 4-year university
▶ Commuter campus in small city
▶ 4,525 degree-seeking undergraduates: 31% part-time, 62% women, 32% African American, 2% Asian American, 1% Hispanic American, 1% Native American, 3% international
▶ 831 degree-seeking graduate students
▶ 95% of applicants admitted
▶ SAT or ACT (ACT writing optional) required

**General.** Founded in 1967. Regionally accredited. **Degrees:** 651 bachelor's awarded; master's offered. **ROTC:** Army, Air Force. **Location:** 100 miles from Auburn, 90 miles from Birmingham. **Calendar:** Semester, extensive summer session. **Full-time faculty:** 187 total; 19% minority, 46% women. **Part-time faculty:** 121 total; 13% minority, 56% women. **Class size:** 45% < 20, 50% 20-39, 3% 40-49, 3% 50-99.

**Freshman class profile.** 1,409 applied, 1,339 admitted, 872 enrolled.

| Mid 50% test scores | | | |
|---|---|---|---|
| ACT composite: | 18-23 | Rank in top quarter: | 36% |
| GPA 3.75 or higher: | 12% | Rank in top tenth: | 14% |
| GPA 3.50-3.74: | 12% | Return as sophomores: | 58% |
| GPA 3.0-3.49: | 29% | Out-of-state: | 6% |
| GPA 2.0-2.99: | 44% | Live on campus: | 24% |
| | | International: | 1% |

**Basis for selection.** GPA and ACT/SAT scores considered. Provisional admission may be available for students who do not meet requirements for regular admission. C average after 18 hours of academic courses required for provisional students to become regular students. **Learning Disabled:** Student must establish eligibility for services by providing documentation that meets institutional standards.

**High school preparation.** College-preparatory program recommended. 4 units recommended. Recommended units include English 3, mathematics 3, social studies 2, history 2, science 2 (laboratory 2), foreign language 2 and academic electives 2.

**2009-2010 Annual costs.** Tuition/fees: $5,970; $17,250 out-of-state. Room only: $3,720. Books/supplies: $900. Personal expenses: $1,170.

**2009-2010 Financial aid. Need-based:** Average scholarship/grant was $4,732; average loan $3,420. 26% of total undergraduate aid awarded as scholarships/grants, 74% as loans/jobs. **Non-need-based:** Scholarships awarded for academics, alumni affiliation, art, athletics, job skills, leadership, minority status, music/drama, religious affiliation, ROTC.

**Application procedures. Admission:** $25 fee. Admission notification on a rolling basis. **Financial aid:** Priority date 3/1; no closing date. FAFSA required. Applicants notified on a rolling basis starting 6/1; must reply within 2 week(s) of notification.

**Academics.** Interdisciplinary Master of Liberal Arts available. **Special study options:** Accelerated study, cooperative education, cross-registration, distance learning, double major, dual enrollment of high school students, ESL, honors, independent study, internships, liberal arts/career combination, study abroad, teacher certification program, weekend college. Joint Ph.D. in public administration with Auburn University; cooperative doctoral program in educational leadership with Auburn University (Ed.D.). **Credit/placement by examination:** AP, CLEP, IB, SAT, ACT, institutional tests. 64 credit hours maximum toward bachelor's degree. **Support services:** Learning center, reduced course load, remedial instruction, tutoring.

**Majors. Biology:** General. **Business:** General, accounting, business admin, finance, human resources, management information systems, managerial economics, marketing. **Communications:** General. **Education:** Elementary, secondary. **Foreign languages:** General. **Health:** Nursing (RN). **History:** General. **Liberal arts:** Arts/sciences. **Math:** General. **Physical sciences:** General. **Protective services:** Criminal justice. **Psychology:** General. **Social sciences:** Political science, sociology. **Visual/performing arts:** Art.

**Most popular majors.** Biology 10%, business/marketing 33%, education 13%, health sciences 11%, liberal arts 6%.

**Computing on campus.** 500 workstations in dormitories, library, computer center, student center. Dormitories wired for high-speed internet access and linked to campus network. Commuter students can connect to campus network. Online course registration, online library, helpline, repair service, student web hosting, wireless network available.

**Student life. Freshman orientation:** Mandatory, $50 fee. Preregistration for classes offered. Two sessions, 1 hour each, morning and evening. Programs held 2 days before start of each semester. **Policies:** Students required to conform to all policies and regulations by October registration. **Housing:** Coed dorms, special housing for disabled, apartments available. $100 nonrefundable deposit. **Activities:** Campus ministries, choral groups, drama, film society, international student organizations, musical theater, student government, student newspaper, American Humanics, S.A.L.T, Chinese association, Young African Americans Against Media Stereotypes.

**Athletics.** NAIA. **Intercollegiate:** Baseball M, basketball, soccer, softball W, tennis. **Intramural:** Baseball, basketball M, bowling, football (non-tackle), softball, tennis, volleyball. **Team name:** Senators.

**Student services.** Adult student services, career counseling, student employment services, financial aid counseling, health services, personal counseling, placement for graduates, veterans' counselor, women's services. **Physically disabled:** Services for visually, speech, hearing impaired.

**Contact.** E-mail: admitme@aum.edu
Phone: (334) 244-3615 Toll-free number: (800) 227-2649
Fax: (334) 244-3795
Valerie Crawford, Director of Admissions, Auburn University at Montgomery, 7400 East Drive, Room 139 Taylor Center, Montgomery, AL 36124-4023

## Birmingham-Southern College
**Birmingham, Alabama**
www.bsc.edu
**CB member**
**CB code: 1064**

- Private 4-year liberal arts college affiliated with United Methodist Church
- Residential campus in very large city
- 1,508 degree-seeking undergraduates: 2% part-time, 50% women, 8% African American, 4% Asian American, 2% Hispanic American, 1% Native American
- 41 degree-seeking graduate students
- 59% of applicants admitted
- SAT or ACT (ACT writing recommended), application essay required
- 72% graduate within 6 years; 43% enter graduate study

**General.** Founded in 1856. Regionally accredited. **Degrees:** 239 bachelor's awarded; master's offered. **ROTC:** Army, Air Force. **Location:** 3 miles from downtown. **Calendar:** 4-1-4, limited summer session. **Full-time faculty:** 111 total; 91% have terminal degrees, 2% minority, 42% women. **Part-time faculty:** 32 total; 9% have terminal degrees, 53% women. **Class size:** 63% < 20, 35% 20-39, 2% 40-49, less than 1% 50-99. **Special facilities:** Planetarium, Southern environmental center and interactive museum, urban environmental park.

**Freshman class profile.** 2,536 applied, 1,486 admitted, 424 enrolled.

| Mid 50% test scores | | | | |
|---|---|---|---|---|
| SAT critical reading: | 520-640 | Rank in top quarter: | | 53% |
| SAT math: | 510-630 | Rank in top tenth: | | 32% |
| ACT composite: | 23-28 | End year in good standing: | | 95% |
| GPA 3.75 or higher: | 33% | Return as sophomores: | | 81% |
| GPA 3.50-3.74: | 18% | Out-of-state: | | 43% |
| GPA 3.0-3.49: | 24% | Live on campus: | | 97% |
| GPA 2.0-2.99: | 25% | Fraternities: | | 43% |
| | | Sororities: | | 46% |

**Basis for selection.** High school record most important, followed by test scores, recommendations, and required essay. Interview required for early admission, recommended for borderline applicants. Auditions required for music, theatre, dance majors. **Homeschooled:** Interviews recommended.

**High school preparation.** College-preparatory program required. 16 units required. Required and recommended units include English 4, mathematics 4, social studies 2, history 2, science 4 (laboratory 2), foreign language 2 and academic electives 10.

**2009-2010 Annual costs.** Tuition/fees: $26,822. Room/board: $8,800. Books/supplies: $1,200. Personal expenses: $500.

**2009-2010 Financial aid. Need-based:** 328 full-time freshmen applied for aid; 263 were judged to have need; 263 of these received aid. Average need met was 98%. Average scholarship/grant was $8,792; average loan

$3,866. 52% of total undergraduate aid awarded as scholarships/grants, 48% as loans/jobs. **Non-need-based:** Awarded to 1,405 full-time undergraduates, including 417 freshmen. Scholarships awarded for academics, alumni affiliation, art, job skills, leadership, minority status, music/drama, religious affiliation, state residency. **Additional information:** Auditions required for music, theatre, dance applicants seeking scholarships. Portfolios required for art applicants seeking scholarships, and essays recommended for all applicants seeking scholarships.

**Application procedures. Admission:** Priority date 1/1; no deadline. $40 fee, may be waived for applicants with need. Admission notification on a rolling basis beginning on or about 7/1. **Financial aid:** Closing date 3/1. FAFSA required. Applicants notified on a rolling basis starting 3/1; must reply by 8/21.

**Academics. Special study options:** Combined bachelor's/graduate degree, cooperative education, cross-registration, double major, dual enrollment of high school students, exchange student, honors, independent study, internships, semester at sea, student-designed major, study abroad, teacher certification program, Washington semester. 4-1-4 in nursing with Vanderbilt; 3-2 in engineering with Washington University, Columbia University, University of Alabama, and Auburn University; 3-2 in environment studies with Duke University. **Credit/placement by examination:** AP, CLEP, IB, SAT, ACT, institutional tests. 64 credit hours maximum toward bachelor's degree. **Support services:** Learning center, pre-admission summer program, reduced course load, study skills assistance, tutoring, writing center.

**Majors. Biology:** General. **Business:** General, accounting, business admin, finance, international, marketing. **Computer sciences:** General, computer science. **Conservation:** Environmental studies. **Education:** General, art, early childhood, elementary, music, secondary, special. **Foreign languages:** French, German, Spanish. **History:** General. **Interdisciplinary:** Math/computer science. **Math:** General. **Philosophy/religion:** Philosophy, religion. **Physical sciences:** Chemistry, physics. **Psychology:** General. **Social sciences:** Economics, political science, sociology. **Theology:** Sacred music. **Visual/performing arts:** General, art, art history/conservation, dance, dramatic, drawing, music history, music theory/composition, painting, photography, piano/organ, sculpture, voice/opera.

**Most popular majors.** Biology 10%, business/marketing 21%, education 6%, English 10%, interdisciplinary studies 9%, psychology 10%, social sciences 8%, visual/performing arts 10%.

**Computing on campus.** 252 workstations in dormitories, library, computer center, student center. Dormitories wired for high-speed internet access and linked to campus network. Commuter students can connect to campus network. Online course registration, online library, helpline, student web hosting, wireless network available.

**Student life. Freshman orientation:** Mandatory. Preregistration for classes offered. One-day mini-session in June and 4-day session prior to beginning of fall classes. **Housing:** Guaranteed on-campus for all undergraduates. Single-sex dorms, special housing for disabled, apartments, fraternity/sorority housing, wellness housing available. $200 nonrefundable deposit, deadline 5/1. Handicapped students accommodated on individual basis. **Activities:** Bands, campus ministries, choral groups, dance, drama, international student organizations, literary magazine, music ensembles, musical theater, opera, student government, student newspaper, Fellowship of Christian Athletes, Young Republicans, Young Democrats, black student union, Allies, Students Offering Support, conservancy, Wesley Fellowship, Intervarsity Christian Fellowship.

**Athletics.** NCAA. **Intercollegiate:** Baseball M, basketball, cheerleading, cross-country, football (tackle) M, golf, lacrosse, rifle W, soccer, softball W, tennis, track and field, volleyball W. **Intramural:** Basketball, football (non-tackle), racquetball, soccer, softball, table tennis, volleyball, water polo. **Team name:** Panthers.

**Student services.** Alcohol/substance abuse counseling, chaplain/spiritual director, career counseling, student employment services, financial aid counseling, health services, personal counseling, placement for graduates, veterans' counselor.

**Contact.** E-mail: admission@bsc.edu
Phone: (205) 226-4696 Toll-free number: (800) 523-5793
Fax: (205) 226-3074
Sheri Salmon, Dean for Enrollment Management, Birmingham-Southern College, 900 Arkadelphia Road, Birmingham, AL 35254

## Columbia Southern University
**Orange Beach, Alabama**
www.columbiasouthern.edu
**CB code: 3878**

- For-profit 4-year virtual business college
- Commuter campus in small town
- 12,000 degree-seeking undergraduates

**General.** Accredited by DETC. **Degrees:** 786 bachelor's, 614 associate awarded; master's offered. **Location:** 60 miles from Mobile. **Calendar:** Continuous. **Full-time faculty:** 41 total. **Part-time faculty:** 205 total.

**Basis for selection.** Open admission.

**2009-2010 Annual costs.** Tuition/fees: $5,870.

**Application procedures. Admission:** No deadline. $25 fee. **Financial aid:** FAFSA, institutional form required.

**Academics. Special study options:** Distance learning. **Credit/placement by examination:** CLEP.

**Majors. Business:** Business admin, hospitality admin, human resources, marketing, tourism/travel. **Computer sciences:** Information technology. **Health:** Health care admin. **Protective services:** Firefighting, law enforcement admin. **Psychology:** General. **Other:** Occupational Safety and Health.

**Most popular majors.** Business/marketing 49%, health sciences 6%, natural resources/environmental science 6%, security/protective services 29%.

**Computing on campus.** PC or laptop required. Commuter students can connect to campus network. Online course registration, online library available.

**Student life. Freshman orientation:** Mandatory, $200 fee. Online course. **Activities:** Student newspaper.

**Student services.** Financial aid counseling.

**Contact.** E-mail: admissions@columbiasouthern.edu
Phone: (251) 981-3771 ext. 521 Toll-free number: (800) 977-8449 ext. 521
Fax: (251) 981-3815
Kathy Cole, Director of Admissions/Enrollments, Columbia Southern University, 21982 University Lane, Orange Beach, AL 36561

---

## Concordia College
### Selma, Alabama
**www.concordiaselma.edu**                    **CB code: 1989**

- Private 4-year liberal arts college affiliated with Lutheran Church - Missouri Synod
- Residential campus in large town

**General.** Founded in 1922. Regionally accredited. **Location:** 50 miles from Montgomery. **Calendar:** Semester.

**Annual costs/financial aid.** Tuition/fees (2009-2010): $7,370. Room/board: $3,700. Books/supplies: $600. Need-based financial aid available to full-time and part-time students.

**Contact.** Phone: (334) 874-5700
Director of Admissions, 1804 Green Street, Selma, AL 36701

---

## Faulkner University
### Montgomery, Alabama
**www.faulkner.edu**                    **CB code: 1034**

- Private 4-year university and liberal arts college affiliated with Church of Christ
- Residential campus in large city
- 2,753 degree-seeking undergraduates: 25% part-time, 64% women
- 510 degree-seeking graduate students
- 58% of applicants admitted
- SAT or ACT (ACT writing optional) required

**General.** Founded in 1942. Regionally accredited. Additional extended campuses (non-residential) in Birmingham, Huntsville and Mobile. **Degrees:** 779 bachelor's, 26 associate awarded; master's, professional offered. **ROTC:** Army, Air Force. **Location:** 10 miles from downtown. **Calendar:** Semester, limited summer session. **Full-time faculty:** 123 total; 65% have terminal degrees, 10% minority. **Part-time faculty:** 206 total; 30% have terminal degrees, 24% minority, 41% women. **Class size:** 76% < 20, 19% 20-39, 3% 40-49, 2% 50-99, less than 1% >100.

---

**Freshman class profile.** 999 applied, 582 admitted, 253 enrolled.

| Mid 50% test scores | | | |
|---|---|---|---|
| SAT critical reading: | 440-570 | Rank in top quarter: | 20% |
| SAT math: | 440-530 | Rank in top tenth: | 10% |
| ACT composite: | 18-22 | End year in good standing: | 75% |
| GPA 3.75 or higher: | 10% | Return as sophomores: | 53% |
| GPA 3.50-3.74: | 5% | Out-of-state: | 67% |
| GPA 3.0-3.49: | 20% | Live on campus: | 69% |
| GPA 2.0-2.99: | 60% | Fraternities: | 50% |
| | | Sororities: | 50% |

**Basis for selection.** Academic record, test scores, and personal or career goals most important. Interview and essay strongly recommended. **Learning Disabled:** After admission, students with disabilities are eligible to apply for services on campus.

**High school preparation.** College-preparatory program recommended. 15 units required. Required units include English 3, mathematics 3, history 3 and science 3.

**2010-2011 Annual costs.** Tuition/fees: $14,810. Room/board: $6,500. Books/supplies: $1,600. Personal expenses: $1,350.

**2009-2010 Financial aid. Need-based:** 316 full-time freshmen applied for aid; 247 were judged to have need; 247 of these received aid. Average need met was 60%. Average scholarship/grant was $2,650; average loan $3,500. 31% of total undergraduate aid awarded as scholarships/grants, 69% as loans/jobs. **Non-need-based:** Awarded to 1,116 full-time undergraduates, including 144 freshmen. Scholarships awarded for academics, alumni affiliation, art, athletics, leadership, music/drama, religious affiliation, ROTC, state residency.

**Application procedures. Admission:** Priority date 2/15; no deadline. $25 fee, may be waived for applicants with need. Admission notification on a rolling basis beginning on or about 8/15. **Financial aid:** Priority date 5/1; no closing date. FAFSA, institutional form required. Applicants notified on a rolling basis starting 6/1; must reply within 3 week(s) of notification.

**Academics.** Full-time students required to take Bible course each semester. **Special study options:** Accelerated study, cross-registration, distance learning, double major, dual enrollment of high school students, ESL, honors, independent study, internships, liberal arts/career combination, study abroad, teacher certification program, weekend college. **Credit/placement by examination:** AP, CLEP, IB, SAT, ACT, institutional tests. 16 credit hours maximum toward associate degree, 32 toward bachelor's. **Support services:** Learning center, pre-admission summer program, reduced course load, remedial instruction, study skills assistance, tutoring, writing center.

**Honors college/program.** 27 ACT English/640 SAT verbal and 3.0 GPA required. Students must take five Great Books courses and complete thesis.

**Majors. Biology:** General, biomedical sciences. **Business:** General, accounting/finance, business admin, human resources, management information systems, management science, marketing. **Communications:** Journalism. **Computer sciences:** General, computer science, information systems. **Education:** Biology, drama/dance, elementary, English, history, mathematics, multilevel teacher, physical, science, secondary, social science, social studies. **Family/consumer sciences:** Communication, family/community services. **Health:** Community health services, marriage/family therapy, mental health counseling, predental, premedicine, prenursing, prepharmacy, preveterinary. **History:** General. **Legal studies:** General, paralegal, prelaw. **Liberal arts:** Arts/sciences, humanities. **Math:** General. **Parks/recreation:** Health/fitness, sports admin. **Philosophy/religion:** Christian, religion. **Protective services:** Criminal justice. **Psychology:** General. **Social sciences:** General. **Theology:** Bible, missionary, theology, youth ministry. **Visual/performing arts:** Dramatic, theater arts management, theater design.

**Most popular majors.** Business/marketing 54%, public administration/social services 14%.

**Computing on campus.** 250 workstations in dormitories, library, computer center, student center. Dormitories wired for high-speed internet access and linked to campus network. Commuter students can connect to campus network. Online library, helpline, wireless network available.

**Student life. Freshman orientation:** Mandatory. Preregistration for classes offered. **Policies:** Religious observance required. **Housing:** Guaranteed on-campus housing for freshmen. Single-sex dorms, special housing for disabled, apartments, wellness housing available. $50 nonrefundable deposit, deadline 7/31. **Activities:** Bands, campus ministries, choral groups, drama, international student organizations, literary magazine, music ensembles, musical theater, student government, student newspaper, minister's club, service organizations, religious organizations.

**Athletics.** NAIA, NCCAA. **Intercollegiate:** Baseball M, basketball, cheerleading, cross-country, football (tackle) M, golf, softball W, volleyball W.

**Intramural:** Badminton, basketball, bowling, football (non-tackle), racquetball, softball, table tennis, tennis, track and field, volleyball. **Team name:** Eagles.

**Student services.** Adult student services, alcohol/substance abuse counseling, chaplain/spiritual director, career counseling, services for economically disadvantaged, student employment services, financial aid counseling, health services, personal counseling, placement for graduates, veterans' counselor. **Physically disabled:** Services for visually, speech, hearing impaired. **Learning disabled:** Comprehensive services available.

**Contact.** E-mail: admissions@faulkner.edu
Phone: (334) 386-7200 Toll-free number: (800) 879-9816 ext. 7200
Fax: (334) 386-7137
Keith Mock, Vice President of Enrollment Management, Director of Admissions, Faulkner University, 5345 Atlanta Highway, Montgomery, AL 36109-3398

## Heritage Christian University
**Florence, Alabama**
www.hcu.edu                                      CB code: 0805

- Private 4-year Bible college affiliated with Church of Christ
- Commuter campus in large town
- 83 degree-seeking undergraduates

**General.** Founded in 1971. Accredited by ABHE. **Degrees:** 6 bachelor's, 4 associate awarded; master's offered. **Location:** 125 miles from Birmingham, 50 miles from Huntsville. **Calendar:** Semester, limited summer session. **Full-time faculty:** 7 total. **Part-time faculty:** 11 total. **Class size:** 96% < 20, 4% 20-39.

**Freshman class profile.**

Out-of-state: 40%    Live on campus: 10%

**Basis for selection.** Religious affiliation and recommendations very important, school achievement considered. Interview recommended.

**2009-2010 Annual costs.** Tuition/fees: $10,620. Room only: $3,000. Books/supplies: $800. Personal expenses: $600.

**Application procedures. Admission:** No deadline. $25 fee. Admission notification on a rolling basis. **Financial aid:** Priority date 6/1; no closing date. FAFSA required. Applicants notified on a rolling basis starting 6/1; must reply by 7/28 or within 2 week(s) of notification.

**Academics. Special study options:** Accelerated study, distance learning, dual enrollment of high school students, independent study, internships. **Credit/placement by examination:** AP, CLEP, institutional tests. 24 credit hours maximum toward associate degree, 24 toward bachelor's. **Support services:** Reduced course load, remedial instruction, study skills assistance, tutoring.

**Majors. Theology:** Bible.

**Computing on campus.** 12 workstations in library, computer center. Wireless network available.

**Student life. Freshman orientation:** Mandatory. Preregistration for classes offered. **Housing:** Guaranteed on-campus for freshmen. Single-sex dorms, apartments, wellness housing available. **Activities:** Student government, Christian service program, mission club.

**Student services.** Career counseling, student employment services, personal counseling, placement for graduates, veterans' counselor.

**Contact.** E-mail: hcu@hcu.edu
Phone: (256) 766-6610 Toll-free number: (800) 367-3565
Fax: (256) 766-9289
Larry Davenport, Director of Enrollment Services, Heritage Christian University, 3625 Helton Drive, Florence, AL 35630

## Herzing University
**Birmingham, Alabama**
www.herzing.edu                                  CB code: 2851

- For-profit 4-year business and technical college
- Very large city
- 406 degree-seeking undergraduates

**General.** Regionally accredited. **Degrees:** 43 bachelor's, 19 associate awarded. **Calendar:** Semester, extensive summer session. **Full-time faculty:** 10 total. **Part-time faculty:** 26 total.

**Basis for selection.** Students must submit high school transcript or GED, interview with admissions representative, pass admissions exam or have 1275 SAT/17 ACT. TEAS test required for nursing applicants.

**2009-2010 Annual costs.** $340 to $490 per credit hour depending on program.

**Financial aid.** All financial aid based on need.

**Application procedures. Admission:** No deadline. No application fee. **Financial aid:** FAFSA required.

**Academics. Credit/placement by examination:** CLEP.

**Majors. Computer sciences:** General, information systems, LAN/WAN management. **Engineering technology:** Computer systems.

**Contact.** E-mail: admiss@bhm.herzing.edu
Phone: (205) 916-2800 Fax: (205) 916-2807
Tommy Dennis, Director of Admissions, Herzing University, 280 West Valley Avenue, Birmingham, AL 35209

## Huntingdon College
**Montgomery, Alabama**                          CB member
www.huntingdon.edu                               CB code: 1303

- Private 4-year liberal arts college affiliated with United Methodist Church
- Residential campus in small city
- 1,067 degree-seeking undergraduates: 20% part-time, 52% women, 16% African American, 1% Asian American, 1% Hispanic American, 1% international
- 67% of applicants admitted
- SAT or ACT (ACT writing optional) required
- 46% graduate within 6 years; 39% enter graduate study

**General.** Founded in 1854. Regionally accredited. Adult Degree Completion Program offered in Montgomery, Bay Minette, Brewton, Center Point, Clanton, Daphne, Enterprise, Huntsville, Pell City and Shelby. **Degrees:** 205 bachelor's awarded. **ROTC:** Army, Air Force. **Location:** 90 miles from Birmingham, 180 miles from Atlanta. **Calendar:** Semester, limited summer session. **Full-time faculty:** 45 total; 89% have terminal degrees, 7% minority, 40% women. **Part-time faculty:** 75 total; 39% have terminal degrees, 15% minority, 36% women. **Class size:** 63% < 20, 36% 20-39, 1% 40-49, less than 1% 50-99. **Special facilities:** Ecological center, recital hall with individual practice studios, sports medicine and athletic training facilities, United Methodist Church archives.

**Freshman class profile.** 1,138 applied, 757 admitted, 237 enrolled.

| Mid 50% test scores | | | |
|---|---|---|---|
| SAT critical reading: | 450-610 | Rank in top quarter: | 36% |
| SAT math: | 430-560 | Rank in top tenth: | 14% |
| SAT writing: | 450-560 | End year in good standing: | 91% |
| ACT composite: | 19-24 | Return as sophomores: | 63% |
| GPA 3.75 or higher: | 19% | Out-of-state: | 14% |
| GPA 3.50-3.74: | 16% | Live on campus: | 71% |
| GPA 3.0-3.49: | 41% | Fraternities: | 16% |
| GPA 2.0-2.99: | 24% | Sororities: | 29% |

**Basis for selection.** High school course selection and grades, entrance exam scores, individual achievements and interests, and other indications of ability to benefit important. Student should have 2.25 GPA and rank in top 50% of graduating class. Interview, essay recommended. Audition required of music majors; portfolio recommended for art majors. **Homeschooled:** Transcript of courses and grades required. **Learning Disabled:** Student must self-identify to Disabilities Intake Coordinator and provide appropriate and current documentation to verify disability. Documentation should include diagnosis and description of functional limitations that may affect student's academic performance.

**High school preparation.** College-preparatory program recommended. 14 units recommended. Recommended units include English 4, mathematics 3, social studies 3, science 2 and foreign language 2. Social studies units can be satisfied with history or social studies.

**2009-2010 Annual costs.** Tuition/fees: $20,990. Room/board: $7,500. Books/supplies: $1,000. Personal expenses: $1,045.

**2009-2010 Financial aid. Need-based:** 213 full-time freshmen applied for aid; 191 were judged to have need; 191 of these received aid. Average need met was 73%. Average scholarship/grant was $14,071; average loan $2,983. 69% of total undergraduate aid awarded as scholarships/grants, 31% as loans/jobs. **Non-need-based:** Awarded to 314 full-time undergraduates, including 70 freshmen. Scholarships awarded for academics, alumni affiliation, leadership, music/drama, religious affiliation, ROTC, state residency.

**Application procedures. Admission:** Priority date 5/15; deadline 8/15. No application fee. Admission notification on a rolling basis beginning on or about 9/7. Must reply by May 1 or within 2 week(s) if notified thereafter. **Financial aid:** Priority date 4/15; no closing date. Institutional form required. Applicants notified on a rolling basis starting 3/1; must reply by 5/1 or within 2 week(s) of notification.

**Academics. Special study options:** Combined bachelor's/graduate degree, cross-registration, double major, honors, independent study, internships, liberal arts/career combination, student-designed major, study abroad, teacher certification program, Washington semester. Dual engineering degree with Auburn University, exchange student program with universities Ireland. **Credit/placement by examination:** AP, CLEP, IB, SAT, ACT, institutional tests. **Support services:** Learning center, reduced course load, remedial instruction, study skills assistance, tutoring, writing center.

**Majors. Biology:** General, cellular/anatomical. **Business:** General, accounting, business admin. **Communications:** General. **Education:** Chemistry, elementary, English, history, mathematics, music. **Health:** Athletic training. **History:** General. **Math:** General. **Parks/recreation:** Exercise sciences, sports admin. **Philosophy/religion:** Religion. **Physical sciences:** Chemistry. **Psychology:** General. **Social sciences:** Political science. **Theology:** Religious ed. **Visual/performing arts:** Music performance, studio arts.

**Most popular majors.** Biology 11%, business/marketing 44%, education 6%, parks/recreation 8%.

**Computing on campus.** PC or laptop required. 12 workstations in library. Dormitories wired for high-speed internet access and linked to campus network. Commuter students can connect to campus network. Online library, repair service, student web hosting, wireless network available.

**Student life. Freshman orientation:** Mandatory. Preregistration for classes offered. 2 overnight programs held in June and July; Big Red Weekend in August following freshmen move-in. **Policies:** Students expected to conduct themselves according to Judeo-Christian values that reflect commitment of College community and to develop personal character and social attributes that reflect full maturity. **Housing:** Guaranteed on-campus for all undergraduates. Coed dorms, single-sex dorms available. **Activities:** Bands, campus ministries, choral groups, dance, drama, international student organizations, literary magazine, music ensembles, Model UN, student government, student newspaper, black student union, Students for Liberty, campus ministries, Fellowship of Christian Athletes.

**Athletics.** NCAA. **Intercollegiate:** Baseball M, basketball, cross-country, football (tackle) M, golf, soccer, softball W, tennis, volleyball W. **Intramural:** Basketball, bowling, football (non-tackle), soccer, softball, tennis, volleyball. **Team name:** Hawks.

**Student services.** Adult student services, alcohol/substance abuse counseling, chaplain/spiritual director, career counseling, student employment services, financial aid counseling, health services, personal counseling, placement for graduates.

**Contact.** E-mail: admiss@huntingdon.edu
Phone: (334) 833-4497 Toll-free number: (800) 763-0313
Fax: (334) 833-4347
Joseph Miller, Director, Office of Admission, Huntingdon College, 1500 East Fairview Avenue, Montgomery, AL 36106-2148

## Huntsville Bible College
**Huntsville, Alabama**
**www.hbc1.edu**

◗ Private 4-year Bible college
◗ Small city
◗ 72 degree-seeking undergraduates

**General.** Accredited by ABHE. **Degrees:** 3 bachelor's, 6 associate awarded. **Location:** 87 miles from Birmingham; 100 miles from Nashville, Tennessee. **Calendar:** Semester. **Part-time faculty:** 14 total.

**Freshman class profile.** 47 applied, 47 admitted, 33 enrolled.

**Basis for selection.** Open admission.

**2009-2010 Annual costs. Tuition/fees:** $3,080.

**Application procedures. Admission:** Closing date 9/1. $10 fee. **Financial aid:** Priority date 4/1, closing date 6/30.

**Academics. Credit/placement by examination:** CLEP.

**Majors. Theology:** Bible, theology.

**Student life. Freshman orientation:** Mandatory. Preregistration for classes offered.

**Contact.** E-mail: students@hbc1.edu
Phone: (256) 539-0834 Fax: (256) 539-0854
Jermaine Turner, Dean of Instruction, Huntsville Bible College, 904 Oakwood Avenue, Huntsville, AL 35811

## ITT Technical Institute: Birmingham
**Bessemer, Alabama**
**www.itt-tech.edu**                                **CB code: 2696**

◗ For-profit 4-year technical college
◗ Commuter campus in very large city

**General.** Accredited by ACICS. **Calendar:** Quarter.

**Contact.** Phone: (205) 991-5410
Director of Recruitment, 6270 Park South Drive, Bessemer, AL 35022

## Jacksonville State University
**Jacksonville, Alabama**
**www.jsu.edu**                                **CB code: 1736**

◗ Public 4-year university
◗ Commuter campus in small town
◗ 7,553 degree-seeking undergraduates: 22% part-time, 58% women
◗ 1,466 degree-seeking graduate students
◗ 88% of applicants admitted
◗ SAT or ACT (ACT writing optional) required
◗ 39% graduate within 6 years

**General.** Founded in 1883. Regionally accredited. **Degrees:** 1,137 bachelor's awarded; master's offered. **ROTC:** Army. **Location:** 75 miles from Birmingham, 100 miles from Atlanta. **Calendar:** Semester, extensive summer session. **Full-time faculty:** 322 total; 12% minority, 46% women. **Part-time faculty:** 141 total; 6% minority, 66% women. **Class size:** 38% < 20, 48% 20-39, 8% 40-49, 6% 50-99. **Special facilities:** Space observatory, Little River Canyon field school.

**Freshman class profile.** 2,919 applied, 2,559 admitted, 1,252 enrolled.

| Mid 50% test scores | | | |
|---|---|---|---|
| SAT critical reading: | 400-510 | Rank in top quarter: | 33% |
| SAT math: | 400-500 | Rank in top tenth: | 12% |
| ACT composite: | 17-22 | Return as sophomores: | 68% |
| GPA 3.75 or higher: | 11% | Out-of-state: | 25% |
| GPA 3.50-3.74: | 8% | Live on campus: | 57% |
| GPA 3.0-3.49: | 30% | International: | 2% |
| GPA 2.0-2.99: | 47% | Fraternities: | 9% |
| | | Sororities: | 9% |

**Basis for selection.** High school record and test scores very important. 17 ACT or 830 SAT (exclusive of Writing) required for conditional admission. 20 ACT or 950 SAT (exclusive of Writing) required for unconditional admission. SAT/ACT scores must be submitted by beginning of term.

**High school preparation.** 15 units required. Required units include English 3 and academic electives 4. 8 units required in math, science, foreign language, social studies/history.

**2009-2010 Annual costs. Tuition/fees:** $6,240; $12,480 out-of-state. Room/board: $5,000. Books/supplies: $1,204. Personal expenses: $3,178.

**2008-2009 Financial aid. Non-need-based:** Scholarships awarded for academics, alumni affiliation, art, athletics, music/drama, ROTC.

**Application procedures. Admission:** No deadline. $30 fee. Admission notification on a rolling basis. **Financial aid:** Priority date 3/15; no closing date. FAFSA, institutional form required. Applicants notified on a rolling basis starting 5/15; must reply within 2 week(s) of notification.

**Academics. Special study options:** Accelerated study, combined bachelor's/graduate degree, cooperative education, distance learning, double major, dual enrollment of high school students, ESL, honors, independent study, internships, teacher certification program. **Credit/placement by examination:** AP,

CLEP, SAT, ACT, institutional tests. 46 credit hours maximum toward bachelor's degree. Maximum credit hours awarded through CLEP examinations: 31 for general tests, 15 through subject tests. **Support services:** Learning center, pre-admission summer program, remedial instruction, tutoring.

**Majors. Biology:** General. **Business:** Accounting, business admin, finance, managerial economics, marketing. **Communications:** Radio/tv. **Computer sciences:** General. **Education:** Elementary, health, physical, secondary, special. **Engineering technology:** Electrical, manufacturing, occupational safety. **Family/consumer sciences:** General. **Foreign languages:** General. **Health:** Nursing (RN). **History:** General. **Liberal arts:** Arts/sciences. **Math:** General. **Parks/recreation:** General. **Physical sciences:** Chemistry, physics. **Protective services:** Criminal justice. **Psychology:** General. **Public administration:** Social work. **Social sciences:** Economics, geography, political science, sociology. **Visual/performing arts:** Art, dramatic.

**Most popular majors.** Business/marketing 16%, education 16%, health sciences 18%, public administration/social services 7%, security/protective services 7%.

**Computing on campus.** 330 workstations in library, student center. Dormitories linked to campus network. Commuter students can connect to campus network. Online course registration, online library, helpline, wireless network available.

**Student life. Freshman orientation:** Available, $40 fee. Preregistration for classes offered. **Housing:** Coed dorms, single-sex dorms, apartments, fraternity/sorority housing, wellness housing available. $100 deposit. **Activities:** Bands, choral groups, drama, international student organizations, music ensembles, musical theater, opera, radio station, student government, student newspaper, symphony orchestra, TV station, Panhellenic council, adult learners forum, peer counselors, African American association, book club.

**Athletics.** NCAA. **Intercollegiate:** Baseball M, basketball, cross-country, football (tackle) M, golf, rifle, soccer W, softball W, tennis, track and field, volleyball W. **Intramural:** Basketball, bowling, football (tackle) M, racquetball, rugby M, softball, tennis, track and field, volleyball. **Team name:** Gamecocks.

**Student services.** Career counseling, student employment services, financial aid counseling, health services, minority student services, on-campus daycare, personal counseling, placement for graduates, veterans' counselor. **Physically disabled:** Services for visually, speech, hearing impaired.

**Contact.** E-mail: info@jsu.edu
Phone: (256) 782-5268 Toll-free number: (800) 231-5291
Fax: (256) 782-5121
Martha Mitchell, Director of Admissions, Jacksonville State University, 700 Pelham Road North, Jacksonville, AL 36265-1602

## Judson College
**Marion, Alabama**
www.judson.edu                    CB code: 1349

- Private 4-year liberal arts college for women affiliated with Baptist faith
- Residential campus in small town
- 297 degree-seeking undergraduates: 16% part-time, 96% women, 13% African American, 1% Asian American, 2% Hispanic American, 1% Native American
- 82% of applicants admitted
- Interview required
- 37% graduate within 6 years; 19% enter graduate study

**General.** Founded in 1838. Regionally accredited. Men accepted for distance learning program only. **Degrees:** 44 bachelor's awarded. **ROTC:** Army. **Location:** 75 miles from Birmingham and Montgomery. **Calendar:** Semester, limited summer session. **Full-time faculty:** 19 total; 79% have terminal degrees, 37% women. **Part-time faculty:** 33 total; 46% have terminal degrees, 61% women. **Class size:** 82% < 20, 16% 20-39, less than 1% 40-49, less than 1% 50-99. **Special facilities:** Alabama Women's Hall of Fame, Baptist missionary memorabilia, equestrian facilities.

**Freshman class profile.** 269 applied, 221 admitted, 68 enrolled.

| Mid 50% test scores | | | |
|---|---|---|---|
| SAT critical reading: | 480-550 | GPA 2.0-2.99: | 17% |
| SAT math: | 470-550 | Rank in top quarter: | 51% |
| SAT writing: | 490-580 | Rank in top tenth: | 24% |
| ACT composite: | 18-28 | End year in good standing: | 84% |
| GPA 3.75 or higher: | 39% | Return as sophomores: | 64% |
| GPA 3.50-3.74: | 13% | Out-of-state: | 18% |
| GPA 3.0-3.49: | 29% | Live on campus: | 97% |

**Basis for selection.** Academic record, recommendations, test scores considered. Interview required.

**High school preparation.** College-preparatory program recommended. 16 units required; 20 recommended. Required and recommended units include English 4, mathematics 2-4, social studies 3-4, science 2-4, foreign language 2 and academic electives 5.

**2009-2010 Annual costs.** Tuition/fees: $12,890. Room/board: $7,970. Books/supplies: $1,200. Personal expenses: $1,600.

**2009-2010 Financial aid. Need-based:** 61 full-time freshmen applied for aid; 60 were judged to have need; 60 of these received aid. Average need met was 69%. Average scholarship/grant was $5,835; average loan $3,471. 63% of total undergraduate aid awarded as scholarships/grants, 37% as loans/jobs. **Non-need-based:** Scholarships awarded for academics, alumni affiliation, art, athletics, music/drama, religious affiliation, state residency.

**Application procedures. Admission:** Priority date 8/1; no deadline. $35 fee, may be waived for applicants with need. Admission notification on a rolling basis beginning on or about 8/1. **Financial aid:** Priority date 3/1; no closing date. FAFSA, institutional form required. Applicants notified on a rolling basis starting 3/1; must reply within 2 week(s) of notification.

**Academics. Special study options:** Accelerated study, cross-registration, distance learning, double major, dual enrollment of high school students, independent study, internships, student-designed major, study abroad, teacher certification program, Washington semester. **Credit/placement by examination:** AP, CLEP, IB, ACT, institutional tests. 30 credit hours maximum toward bachelor's degree. No student may receive more than 30 semester hours of non-attendance credit from all sources, or more than six semester hours in any one department. Maximum permitted from CLEP General Examinations is 15 of 30 hours. **Support services:** Reduced course load, remedial instruction, study skills assistance, tutoring, writing center.

**Majors. Biology:** General. **Business:** Business admin. **Education:** Elementary, English, mathematics, music, science, social science. **Foreign languages:** General. **History:** General. **Math:** General. **Philosophy/religion:** Religion. **Physical sciences:** Chemistry. **Protective services:** Law enforcement admin. **Psychology:** General. **Visual/performing arts:** Art.

**Most popular majors.** Biology 9%, business/marketing 11%, English 9%, history 16%, psychology 30%, social sciences 14%.

**Computing on campus.** 61 workstations in library, computer center. Commuter students can connect to campus network. Online library, helpline, wireless network available.

**Student life. Freshman orientation:** Available, $110 fee. Preregistration for classes offered. Orientation includes placement tests, academic registration. **Housing:** Guaranteed on-campus for all undergraduates. Wellness housing available. $110 nonrefundable deposit, deadline 8/15. **Activities:** Campus ministries, choral groups, drama, literary magazine, music ensembles, musical theater, student government, student newspaper, Students in Free Enterprise, College Democrats, College Republicans, psych-key club, Cahaba River society, Judson Ambassadors, campus ministries, student government, science club, art club.

**Athletics.** USCAA. **Intercollegiate:** Basketball W, equestrian W, soccer W, softball W, volleyball W. **Intramural:** Basketball W, field hockey W, football (non-tackle) W, soccer W, softball W, tennis W, volleyball W. **Team name:** Lady Eagles.

**Student services.** Adult student services, alcohol/substance abuse counseling, chaplain/spiritual director, career counseling, student employment services, financial aid counseling, health services, personal counseling.

**Contact.** E-mail: admissions@judson.edu
Phone: (334) 683-5110 Toll-free number: (800) 447-9472
Fax: (334) 683-5282
Charlotte Clements, Vice President for Admissions and Financial Aid, Judson College, 302 Bibb Street, Marion, AL 36756

## Miles College
**Birmingham, Alabama**
www.miles.edu                    CB code: 1468

▶ Private 4-year liberal arts college affiliated with Christian Methodist Episcopal Church
▶ Commuter campus in very large city
▶ 1,900 degree-seeking undergraduates

**General.** Founded in 1905. Regionally accredited. **Degrees:** 219 bachelor's awarded. **ROTC:** Army, Air Force. **Location:** 6 miles from downtown. **Calendar:** Semester, limited summer session. **Full-time faculty:** 95 total. **Part-time faculty:** 40 total. **Special facilities:** African-American materials center, learning research center.

**Basis for selection.** Open admission, but selective for some programs. 3 letters of recommendation required. Admission to education program based on 2.0 GPA, 16 ACT and recommendations.

**High school preparation.** 20 units recommended. Recommended units include English 4, mathematics 4, social studies 4, history 4 and science 4. 4 units math and science recommended, particularly, for natural science applicants.

**2009-2010 Annual costs.** Tuition/fees: $9,164. Room/board: $6,000. Books/supplies: $1,200. Personal expenses: $800.

**2008-2009 Financial aid.** All financial aid based on need.

**Application procedures. Admission:** Closing date 7/15. No application fee. Admission notification on a rolling basis. **Financial aid:** Priority date 4/15; no closing date. FAFSA required. Applicants notified on a rolling basis starting 7/15; must reply within 2 week(s) of notification.

**Academics. Special study options:** Cooperative education, cross-registration, double major, dual enrollment of high school students, exchange student, honors, independent study, internships, teacher certification program. **Credit/placement by examination:** CLEP, institutional tests. **Support services:** Reduced course load, remedial instruction, study skills assistance, tutoring, writing center.

**Majors. Biology:** General. **Business:** Accounting, business admin, purchasing. **Communications:** General. **Computer sciences:** General. **Conservation:** Environmental science. **Education:** Elementary, English, instructional media, mathematics, science, secondary, social science, social studies. **History:** General. **Math:** General. **Physical sciences:** Chemistry. **Public administration:** Social work. **Social sciences:** Political science. **Visual/performing arts:** Music pedagogy, music performance.

**Computing on campus.** 150 workstations in dormitories, library, computer center. Commuter students can connect to campus network.

**Student life. Freshman orientation:** Available, $100 fee. Preregistration for classes offered. Week-long program held week prior to start of classes. **Policies:** Students must maintain 2.0 GPA to participate in student activities that are not co-curricular on campus. **Housing:** Single-sex dorms, apartments, wellness housing available. $150 nonrefundable deposit. **Activities:** Marching band, choral groups, dance, drama, music ensembles, musical theater, radio station, student government, student newspaper, TV station, interdenominational ministerial association.

**Athletics.** NCAA. **Intercollegiate:** Baseball M, basketball, cross-country, football (tackle) M, softball W, volleyball. **Intramural:** Badminton, basketball, softball, tennis, volleyball. **Team name:** Golden Bears.

**Student services.** Adult student services, chaplain/spiritual director, career counseling, services for economically disadvantaged, student employment services, financial aid counseling, health services, personal counseling, placement for graduates.

**Contact.** E-mail: admissions@miles.edu
Phone: (205) 929-1655 Fax: (205) 923-9292
Christopher Robertson, Director of Admissions and Recruitment, Miles College, 5500 Myron-Massey Boulevard, Fairfield, AL 35064

## Oakwood University
**Huntsville, Alabama**                CB member
www.oakwood.edu                     CB code: 1586

▶ Private 4-year liberal arts college affiliated with Seventh-day Adventists
▶ Residential campus in small city
▶ 1,800 degree-seeking undergraduates
▶ 50 graduate students
▶ 51% of applicants admitted
▶ SAT or ACT (ACT writing optional) required

**General.** Founded in 1896. Regionally accredited. **Degrees:** 254 bachelor's, 3 associate awarded; master's offered. **Location:** 5 miles from Huntsville. **Calendar:** Semester, limited summer session. **Full-time faculty:** 105 total; 63% have terminal degrees, 46% women. **Part-time faculty:** 72 total; 50% women. **Class size:** 56% < 20, 36% 20-39, 6% 40-49, 3% 50-99.

**Freshman class profile.** 2,001 applied, 1,023 admitted, 394 enrolled.

| Mid 50% test scores | | | |
|---|---|---|---|
| SAT critical reading: | 400-530 | GPA 3.0-3.49: | 26% |
| SAT math: | 360-490 | GPA 2.0-2.99: | 44% |
| ACT composite: | 16-21 | Rank in top quarter: | 26% |
| GPA 3.75 or higher: | 13% | Rank in top tenth: | 8% |
| GPA 3.50-3.74: | 13% | Out-of-state: | 89% |
| | | Live on campus: | 90% |

**Basis for selection.** Applicants with 2.0 GPA considered for acceptance. Special consideration for exceptional applicants. **Homeschooled:** Transcript of courses and grades, letter of recommendation (nonparent) required.

**High school preparation.** 18 units recommended. Recommended units include English 4, mathematics 2, social studies 1, history 1, science 2 (laboratory 1) and foreign language 2.

**2009-2010 Annual costs.** Tuition/fees: $13,834. Room/board: $8,464.

**Financial aid. Non-need-based:** Scholarships awarded for academics, leadership, religious affiliation, state residency.

**Application procedures. Admission:** Priority date 6/30; no deadline. $25 fee, may be waived for applicants with need. Admission notification on a rolling basis beginning on or about 12/1. **Financial aid:** Priority date 3/31; no closing date. FAFSA required. Applicants notified on a rolling basis starting 4/1.

**Academics. Special study options:** Double major, honors, internships, study abroad, teacher certification program. **Credit/placement by examination:** AP, CLEP, SAT, ACT, institutional tests. **Support services:** Learning center, reduced course load, remedial instruction, study skills assistance, tutoring, writing center.

**Majors. Biology:** General, biochemistry, biomedical sciences. **Business:** Accounting, business admin, finance, marketing. **Communications:** General. **Computer sciences:** General, computer science, information technology. **Education:** Biology, business, chemistry, elementary, English, family/consumer sciences, history, mathematics, music, physical, science, social science. **Family/consumer sciences:** General, family studies, food/nutrition. **Foreign languages:** French, Spanish. **Health:** Cytotechnology. **History:** General. **Interdisciplinary:** Math/computer science, natural sciences. **Liberal arts:** Arts/sciences. **Math:** General, applied. **Parks/recreation:** Health/fitness. **Philosophy/religion:** Religion. **Physical sciences:** Chemistry. **Psychology:** General. **Public administration:** Social work. **Theology:** Religious ed, theology.

**Most popular majors.** Biology 16%, business/marketing 13%, communications/journalism 7%, education 7%, health sciences 7%, psychology 10%, theological studies 9%.

**Computing on campus.** 300 workstations in dormitories, library. Dormitories wired for high-speed internet access and linked to campus network. Commuter students can connect to campus network. Helpline, wireless network available.

**Student life. Freshman orientation:** Mandatory. **Policies:** Students sit on most faculty and administrative committees. Religious observance required. **Housing:** Single-sex dorms, apartments available. **Activities:** Choral groups, music ensembles, radio station, student government, student newspaper, Outreach, NAACP.

**Athletics. Intramural:** Baseball M, basketball, golf, gymnastics, soccer, softball, tennis, volleyball. **Team name:** Ambassadors.

**Student services.** Adult student services, chaplain/spiritual director, career counseling, student employment services, financial aid counseling, health services, on-campus daycare, personal counseling, placement for graduates, veterans' counselor.

**Contact.** E-mail: admission@oakwood.edu
Phone: (256) 726-7030 Toll-free number: (800) 824-5312
Fax: (256) 726-7154
Jason McCracken, Director of Enrollment Management, Oakwood University, 7000 Adventist Boulevard, NW, Huntsville, AL 35896

## Samford University

**Birmingham, Alabama**
www.samford.edu

**CB member**
**CB code: 1302**

- Private 4-year university affiliated with Southern Baptist Convention
- Residential campus in small city
- 2,879 degree-seeking undergraduates: 6% part-time, 64% women, 7% African American, 1% Asian American, 1% Hispanic American
- 1,716 degree-seeking graduate students
- 84% of applicants admitted
- SAT or ACT (ACT writing optional) required
- 74% graduate within 6 years

**General.** Founded in 1841. Regionally accredited. Students taught to integrate Christian faith with learning and living. **Degrees:** 558 bachelor's, 5 associate awarded; master's, doctoral, professional offered. **ROTC:** Army, Air Force. **Location:** 4 miles from downtown. **Calendar:** 4-1-4, extensive summer session. **Full-time faculty:** 282 total; 95% have terminal degrees, 9% minority, 46% women. **Part-time faculty:** 137 total; 64% have terminal degrees, 5% minority, 44% women. **Class size:** 65% < 20, 30% 20-39, 3% 40-49, 2% 50-99. **Special facilities:** Computer-assisted journalism laboratory, geographic information system, observatory, global center, planetarium, conservatory.

**Freshman class profile.** 2,288 applied, 1,911 admitted, 733 enrolled.

| Mid 50% test scores | | | |
|---|---|---|---|
| SAT critical reading: | 520-650 | Rank in top quarter: | 70% |
| SAT math: | 520-650 | Rank in top tenth: | 44% |
| ACT composite: | 21-28 | End year in good standing: | 94% |
| GPA 3.75 or higher: | 51% | Return as sophomores: | 83% |
| GPA 3.50-3.74: | 16% | Out-of-state: | 64% |
| GPA 3.0-3.49: | 24% | Live on campus: | 95% |
| GPA 2.0-2.99: | 9% | Fraternities: | 37% |
| | | Sororities: | 44% |

**Basis for selection.** High school GPA, courses selected and rigor, test scores, recommendations, essay, academic content and trend of high school grades important. Interview recommended. Audition required for music majors. Portfolio recommended for art and journalism majors. **Homeschooled:** Statement describing homeschool structure and mission, transcript of courses and grades, letter of recommendation (nonparent) required. Leadership resume required.

**High school preparation.** College-preparatory program recommended. 13 units required. Required units include English 4, mathematics 3, history 2, science 2 (laboratory 2) and foreign language 2.

**2009-2010 Annual costs.** Tuition/fees: $20,420. Room/board: $6,624.

**2008-2009 Financial aid. Need-based:** 511 full-time freshmen applied for aid; 329 were judged to have need; 329 of these received aid. Average need met was 80%. Average scholarship/grant was $11,672; average loan $4,402. 44% of total undergraduate aid awarded as scholarships/grants, 56% as loans/jobs. **Non-need-based:** Awarded to 1,472 full-time undergraduates, including 384 freshmen. Scholarships awarded for academics, alumni affiliation, art, athletics, leadership, music/drama, religious affiliation, ROTC, state residency.

**Application procedures. Admission:** Priority date 3/1; no deadline. $35 fee, may be waived for applicants with need. Admission notification on a rolling basis beginning on or about 10/1. Must reply by May 1 or within 2 week(s) if notified thereafter. **Financial aid:** Priority date 3/1; no closing date. FAFSA required.

**Academics. Special study options:** Accelerated study, cooperative education, cross-registration, distance learning, double major, honors, independent study, internships, liberal arts/career combination, study abroad, teacher certification program. **Credit/placement by examination:** AP, CLEP, IB, institutional tests. 30 credit hours maximum toward associate degree. **Support services:** Learning center, reduced course load, study skills assistance, tutoring, writing center.

**Majors. Area/ethnic studies:** Asian, Latin American. **Biology:** General, biochemistry, marine. **Business:** Accounting, business admin, entrepreneurial studies, finance, international, managerial economics, marketing, training/development. **Communications:** General, journalism. **Computer sciences:** Computer science. **Conservation:** Environmental science, environmental studies. **Education:** English, history, multi-level teacher, physical, social science. **Engineering:** Physics. **Family/consumer sciences:** Family studies. **Foreign languages:** General, ancient Greek, classics, French, German, Latin, Spanish. **Health:** Athletic training, nursing (RN). **History:** General. **Interdisciplinary:** Classical/archaeology, nutrition sciences, science/society. **Math:** General. **Parks/recreation:** Exercise sciences, health/fitness. **Philosophy/religion:** Philosophy, religion. **Physical sciences:** Chemistry, physics. **Psychology:** General, counseling. **Public administration:** General. **Social sciences:** Cartography, geography, international relations, political science, sociology. **Theology:** Sacred music. **Visual/performing arts:** Art, dramatic, graphic design, interior design, music pedagogy, music performance, music theory/composition, musical theater, piano/organ, voice/opera. **Other:** Counseling foundations, Manager/leadership development, Philosophy and religion, Sports medicine.

**Most popular majors.** Biology 9%, business/marketing 19%, communications/journalism 7%, education 6%, health sciences 14%, social sciences 6%, visual/performing arts 11%.

**Computing on campus.** Dormitories wired for high-speed internet access and linked to campus network. Commuter students can connect to campus network. Online library, helpline, repair service, wireless network available.

**Student life. Freshman orientation:** Mandatory, $150 fee. Preregistration for classes offered. Four sessions held in the summer for new students and parents. **Policies:** Student code of values observed. Religious observance required. **Housing:** Guaranteed on-campus for freshmen. Single-sex dorms, special housing for disabled, fraternity/sorority housing, wellness housing available. $250 nonrefundable deposit, deadline 5/1. **Activities:** Bands, campus ministries, choral groups, dance, drama, international student organizations, literary magazine, music ensembles, Model UN, musical theater, radio station, student government, student newspaper, symphony orchestra, TV station, Amnesty International, Circle K, Habitat for Humanity, Gamma Sigma Sigma, Alpha Phi Omega, College Republicans, international club, Samford Ambassadors, Beta Beta Beta, Ville Crew.

**Athletics.** NCAA. **Intercollegiate:** Baseball M, basketball, cross-country, football (tackle) M, golf, soccer W, softball W, tennis, track and field, volleyball W. **Intramural:** Basketball, bowling, cheerleading, football (nontackle) M, football (tackle), golf, racquetball, soccer, softball, table tennis, tennis, volleyball, water polo. **Team name:** Bulldogs.

**Student services.** Adult student services, alcohol/substance abuse counseling, chaplain/spiritual director, career counseling, student employment services, financial aid counseling, health services, personal counseling, placement for graduates. **Physically disabled:** Services for visually, speech, hearing impaired. **Learning disabled:** Comprehensive services available.

**Contact.** E-mail: admiss@samford.edu
Phone: (205) 726-3673 Toll-free number: (800) 888-7218
Fax: (205) 726-2171
Jason Black, Interim Dean of Admission, Samford University, 800 Lakeshore Drive, Birmingham, AL 35229

## Selma University

**Selma, Alabama**
www.selmauniversity.org

**CB code: 1792**

- Private 4-year university affiliated with Baptist faith
- Large town
- 127 degree-seeking undergraduates

**General.** Founded in 1878. Candidate for regional accreditation.; also accredited by ABHE. **Degrees:** 3 bachelor's awarded; master's offered. **Location:** 50 miles from Montgomery. **Calendar:** Semester, limited summer session. **Full-time faculty:** 3 total. **Part-time faculty:** 24 total.

**Basis for selection.** Open admission. Students with deficient high school record or low test scores must take remedial courses.

**2009-2010 Annual costs.** Tuition/fees: $4,587. Books/supplies: $600. Personal expenses: $600.

**Application procedures. Admission:** No deadline. $20 fee, may be waived for applicants with need. Admission notification on a rolling basis beginning on or about 8/1. **Financial aid:** Priority date 9/15; no closing date. FAFSA required. Applicants notified on a rolling basis starting 8/23; must reply within 2 week(s) of notification.

**Academics. Credit/placement by examination:** CLEP, institutional tests. **Support services:** Reduced course load, remedial instruction, tutoring.

**Majors. Theology:** Bible.

**Student life. Freshman orientation:** Mandatory. **Housing:** Single-sex dorms available. **Activities:** Campus ministries, choral groups, music ensembles, student government, Ministerial union.

**Athletics.** USCAA. **Intercollegiate:** Baseball M. **Team name:** Bulldogs.

**Student services.** Career counseling, financial aid counseling, personal counseling, veterans' counselor.

**Contact.** E-mail: selmau.adissions@yahoo.com
Phone: (334) 872-2533 ext. 18 Fax: (334) 872-7746
Leila Millhouse, Registrar, Selma University, 1501 Lapsley Street, Selma, AL 36701

## South University: Montgomery
### Montgomery, Alabama
www.southuniversity.edu                      CB code: 3947

- For-profit 4-year university
- Commuter campus in small city
- 598 degree-seeking undergraduates: 40% part-time, 75% women
- 58 graduate students
- Interview required

**General.** Founded in 1887. Regionally accredited. **Degrees:** 28 bachelor's, 64 associate awarded; master's offered. **Location:** 100 miles from Birmingham, 160 miles from Atlanta. **Calendar:** Quarter, extensive summer session. **Full-time faculty:** 18 total; 28% have terminal degrees, 17% minority, 50% women. **Part-time faculty:** 42 total; 26% have terminal degrees, 26% minority, 55% women.

**Basis for selection.** High school diploma or GED required. School-administered entrance test may be provided in place of SAT/ACT. SAT or ACT recommended. **Homeschooled:** Students must provide evidence that home schooling was conducted in accordance with state laws.

**2009-2010 Annual costs.** Tuition/fees: $14,985.

**2009-2010 Financial aid.** All financial aid based on need.

**Application procedures. Admission:** No deadline. $50 fee. Admission notification on a rolling basis. **Financial aid:** No deadline. FAFSA required. Applicants notified on a rolling basis starting 6/1.

**Academics. Special study options:** Distance learning, internships. **Credit/placement by examination:** CLEP, institutional tests. **Support services:** Remedial instruction, study skills assistance, tutoring.

**Majors. Business:** Business admin. **Computer sciences:** Information technology. **Health:** Health care admin, health services, nursing (RN). **Legal studies:** General. **Protective services:** Law enforcement admin. **Psychology:** General.

**Most popular majors.** Business/marketing 14%, computer/information sciences 25%, health sciences 11%, legal studies 46%.

**Computing on campus.** Online library, repair service, wireless network available.

**Student life. Freshman orientation:** Mandatory. Preregistration for classes offered.

**Student services.** Career counseling, financial aid counseling, placement for graduates, veterans' counselor.

**Contact.** E-mail: apearson@southuniversity.edu
Phone: (334) 395-8800 Fax: (334) 395-8859
Anna Pearson, Director of Admissions, South University: Montgomery, 5355 Vaughn Road, Montgomery, AL 36116-1120

## Southeastern Bible College
### Birmingham, Alabama
www.sebc.edu                      CB code: 1723

- Private 4-year Bible college affiliated with nondenominational tradition
- Commuter campus in very large city
- 203 degree-seeking undergraduates: 10% part-time, 37% women, 36% African American, 1% Hispanic American, 1% international
- 100% of applicants admitted
- SAT or ACT (ACT writing optional), application essay required

**General.** Founded in 1935. Accredited by ABHE. **Degrees:** 22 bachelor's, 2 associate awarded. **Calendar:** Semester, limited summer session. **Full-time faculty:** 8 total; 100% have terminal degrees, 12% women. **Part-time faculty:** 19 total; 32% have terminal degrees, 26% women. **Class size:** 82% <20, 13% 20-39, 1% 40-49, 3% 50-99.

**Freshman class profile.** 72 applied, 72 admitted, 33 enrolled.

| Mid 50% test scores | | | |
|---|---|---|---|
| ACT composite: | 18-22 | GPA 3.0-3.49: | 8% |
| GPA 3.75 or higher: | 4% | GPA 2.0-2.99: | 60% |
| GPA 3.50-3.74: | 20% | Return as sophomores: | 56% |
| | | Live on campus: | 55% |

**Basis for selection.** High school GPA and SAT or ACT test scores important. Christian character evaluated through 2 recommendations, one from church and the other a personal recommendation. Autobiography and statement of agreement with college's principle doctrines required. **Learning Disabled:** Students should meet with equity coordinator if desired.

**High school preparation.** College-preparatory program recommended. 24 units recommended. Recommended units include English 4, mathematics 4, social studies 4, science 4, computer science .5, academic electives 7.5.

**2009-2010 Annual costs.** Tuition/fees: $10,930. Room only: $2,450.

**2008-2009 Financial aid. Need-based:** 15 full-time freshmen applied for aid; 12 were judged to have need; 12 of these received aid. Average need met was 65%. Average scholarship/grant was $4,500; average loan $3,500. 19% of total undergraduate aid awarded as scholarships/grants, 81% as loans/jobs. **Non-need-based:** Awarded to 30 full-time undergraduates, including 7 freshmen. Scholarships awarded for academics, music/drama.

**Application procedures. Admission:** No deadline. $30 fee, may be waived for applicants with need. Admission notification on a rolling basis. **Financial aid:** Priority date 4/1; no closing date. FAFSA, institutional form required. Applicants notified on a rolling basis starting 1/1.

**Academics. Special study options:** Double major, internships. **Credit/placement by examination:** AP, CLEP, IB, ACT, institutional tests. **Support services:** Reduced course load, study skills assistance.

**Majors. Theology:** Bible. **Other:** Leadership ministries.

**Computing on campus.** 25 workstations in library, computer center. Dormitories wired for high-speed internet access. Wireless network available.

**Student life. Freshman orientation:** Mandatory. Preregistration for classes offered. One-day session held the day before registration. **Policies:** Religious observance required. **Housing:** Single-sex dorms available. $200 partly refundable deposit. **Activities:** Campus ministries, choral groups, music ensembles, student government, student missions fellowship.

**Athletics.** NCCAA. **Intercollegiate:** Basketball M. **Team name:** Sabers.

**Student services.** Adult student services, chaplain/spiritual director, financial aid counseling, personal counseling. **Physically disabled:** Services for speech, hearing impaired.

**Contact.** E-mail: info@sebc.edu
Phone: (205) 970-9210 Fax: (205) 970-9207
Lynn Gannett-Malick, Director of Enrollment Management, Southeastern Bible College, 2545 Valleydale Road, Birmingham, AL 35244-2083

## Spring Hill College
### Mobile, Alabama
www.shc.edu                      CB member
                                 CB code: 1733

- Private 4-year liberal arts college affiliated with Roman Catholic Church
- Residential campus in large city
- 1,304 degree-seeking undergraduates: 9% part-time, 62% women, 18% African American, 1% Asian American, 7% Hispanic American, 1% Native American, 1% international
- 196 degree-seeking graduate students
- 55% of applicants admitted
- SAT or ACT (ACT writing recommended), application essay required
- 60% graduate within 6 years; 32% enter graduate study

**General.** Founded in 1830. Regionally accredited. **Degrees:** 208 bachelor's awarded; master's offered. **ROTC:** Army, Air Force. **Location:** 140 miles from New Orleans. **Calendar:** Semester, limited summer session. **Full-time faculty:** 82 total; 85% have terminal degrees, 8% minority, 48% women. **Part-time faculty:** 51 total; 31% have terminal degrees, 4% minority, 49% women. **Class size:** 49% <20, 48% 20-39, 2% 40-49, less than 1% 50-99. **Special facilities:** National historic buildings, public radio broadcasting station, 450-acre wooded campus, 18-hole golf course.

**Freshman class profile.** 4,234 applied, 2,329 admitted, 358 enrolled.

| Mid 50% test scores | | | |
|---|---|---|---|
| SAT critical reading: | 480-600 | GPA 2.0-2.99: | 16% |
| SAT math: | 480-570 | Rank in top quarter: | 61% |
| SAT writing: | 480-590 | Rank in top tenth: | 27% |
| ACT composite: | 21-26 | End year in good standing: | 89% |
| GPA 3.75 or higher: | 36% | Return as sophomores: | 77% |
| GPA 3.50-3.74: | 22% | Out-of-state: | 57% |
| GPA 3.0-3.49: | 26% | Live on campus: | 89% |

**Basis for selection.** Grades, scores and achievements/accomplishments outside the classroom considered. Those students deemed unconditional admits are admitted by the admissions office. Those students deemed to have potential but who are considered to be at-risk are reviewed by the College's academic standards committee, which may admit students conditionally or unconditionally. Interview recommended; portfolio recommended of art majors. **Homeschooled:** Statement describing homeschool structure and mission, transcript of courses and grades, interview required. Comprehensive portfolio should be submitted and should include thorough explanation of all coursework, how it was graded, comprehensive reading list, documentation of any program affiliation, and personal assessments provided by both the student and the primary teacher. Information on any independent research project, community outreach, or unique experience that enriched the homeschooling experience may be included.

**High school preparation.** College-preparatory program recommended. 16 units recommended. Recommended units include English 4, mathematics 3, social studies 2, history 1, science 3 (laboratory 1), foreign language 2 and academic electives 1.

**2009-2010 Annual costs.** Tuition/fees: $25,450. Room/board: $9,730. Books/supplies: $1,300. Personal expenses: $1,250.

**2009-2010 Financial aid. Need-based:** 310 full-time freshmen applied for aid; 252 were judged to have need; 252 of these received aid. Average need met was 85%. Average scholarship/grant was $17,633; average loan $4,471. 72% of total undergraduate aid awarded as scholarships/grants, 28% as loans/jobs. **Non-need-based:** Awarded to 1,036 full-time undergraduates, including 308 freshmen. Scholarships awarded for academics, alumni affiliation, athletics, job skills, leadership, minority status, state residency.

**Application procedures. Admission:** Priority date 1/15; deadline 7/15 (postmark date). $25 fee, may be waived for applicants with need, free for online applicants. Admission notification on a rolling basis beginning on or about 11/1. Must reply by May 1 or within 2 week(s) if notified thereafter. **Financial aid:** Priority date 3/1; no closing date. FAFSA required. Applicants notified on a rolling basis starting 2/15; must reply by 5/1 or within 2 week(s) of notification.

**Academics. Special study options:** Accelerated study, distance learning, double major, dual enrollment of high school students, honors, independent study, internships, student-designed major, study abroad, teacher certification program, Washington semester. Marine biology courses at the Dauphin Island Sea Laboratory in conjunction with the Marine Environmental Sciences Consortium; 3-2 engineering with Auburn University, University of Alabama in Birmingham, Marquette University, University of Florida, and Texas A&M University. **Credit/placement by examination:** AP, CLEP, IB, SAT, ACT, institutional tests. 30 credit hours maximum toward bachelor's degree. **Support services:** Learning center, remedial instruction, study skills assistance, tutoring, writing center.

**Majors. Biology:** General, biochemistry. **Business:** Business admin. **Communications:** General. **Education:** Early childhood, elementary, secondary. **Engineering:** General. **Foreign languages:** Spanish. **Health:** Nursing (RN). **History:** General. **Interdisciplinary:** Biopsychology. **Liberal arts:** Humanities. **Math:** General. **Philosophy/religion:** Philosophy. **Physical sciences:** Chemistry. **Psychology:** General. **Social sciences:** General, international relations, political science. **Theology:** Theology. **Visual/performing arts:** Arts management, dramatic, graphic design, studio arts. **Other:** Writing.

**Most popular majors.** Biology 10%, business/marketing 32%, communications/journalism 7%, social sciences 9%, theological studies 6%.

**Computing on campus.** 200 workstations in library, computer center, student center. Dormitories wired for high-speed internet access and linked to campus network. Commuter students can connect to campus network. Online course registration, online library, helpline, student web hosting, wireless network available.

**Student life. Freshman orientation:** Mandatory, $200 fee. Preregistration for classes offered. 2-day program held in June for students and parents. **Housing:** Guaranteed on-campus for all undergraduates. Coed dorms, single-sex dorms, apartments available. $150 fully refundable deposit, deadline 6/1. **Activities:** Campus ministries, choral groups, dance, drama, literary magazine, student government, student newspaper, Amnesty International, College Democrats, College Republicans, Greenkeepers, Knights of

Columbus, multicultural student union, political and international studies club, Students for Life.

**Athletics.** NAIA. **Intercollegiate:** Baseball M, basketball, cross-country, golf, soccer, softball W, tennis, volleyball W. **Intramural:** Basketball, football (non-tackle), racquetball, soccer, softball, volleyball, weight lifting. **Team name:** Badgers.

**Student services.** Adult student services, alcohol/substance abuse counseling, chaplain/spiritual director, career counseling, student employment services, financial aid counseling, health services, minority student services, personal counseling, placement for graduates.

**Contact.** E-mail: admit@shc.edu
Phone: (251) 380-3030 Toll-free number: (800) 742-6704
Fax: (251) 460-2186
Steven Pochard, Dean of Admission and Financial Aid, Spring Hill College, 4000 Dauphin Street, Mobile, AL 36608-1791

## Stillman College
**Tuscaloosa, Alabama** — **CB member**
**www.stillman.edu** — **CB code: 1739**

- Private 4-year liberal arts college affiliated with Presbyterian Church (USA)
- Residential campus in small city
- 1,075 degree-seeking undergraduates
- 44% of applicants admitted
- SAT or ACT (ACT writing optional) required

**General.** Founded in 1876. Regionally accredited. **Degrees:** 110 bachelor's awarded. **ROTC:** Army, Naval, Air Force. **Location:** 60 miles from Birmingham. **Calendar:** Semester, limited summer session. **Full-time faculty:** 55 total. **Part-time faculty:** 10 total. **Class size:** 64% < 20, 24% 20-39, 5% 40-49, 7% 50-99.

**Freshman class profile.** 5,909 applied, 2,600 admitted, 390 enrolled.

| Mid 50% test scores | | | |
|---|---|---|---|
| SAT critical reading: | 380-450 | GPA 3.50-3.74: | 6% |
| SAT math: | 370-470 | GPA 3.0-3.49: | 25% |
| ACT composite: | 16-19 | GPA 2.0-2.99: | 65% |
| GPA 3.75 or higher: | 4% | Rank in top quarter: | 28% |
| | | Rank in top tenth: | 8% |

**Basis for selection.** School achievement record most important. Class rank, test scores, essay, extracurricular activities also important. **Homeschooled:** Students unable to present a high school transcript may enroll upon presentation of satisfactory passing score on GED.

**High school preparation.** 24 units required. Required units include English 4, mathematics 2, social studies 2 and science 1.

**2009-2010 Annual costs.** Tuition/fees: $13,430. Room/board: $6,336.

**2008-2009 Financial aid.** All financial aid based on need.

**Application procedures. Admission:** Priority date 5/1; no deadline. $50 fee, may be waived for applicants with need. Admission notification on a rolling basis. Admitted applicants must reply within 5 days of notification of acceptance. **Financial aid:** No deadline. FAFSA, institutional form required. Applicants notified on a rolling basis; must reply within 4 week(s) of notification.

**Academics. Special study options:** Combined bachelor's/graduate degree, cooperative education, double major, dual enrollment of high school students, honors, independent study, internships, study abroad, teacher certification program. **Credit/placement by examination:** CLEP, SAT, ACT, institutional tests. 30 credit hours maximum toward bachelor's degree. **Support services:** Learning center, reduced course load, remedial instruction, tutoring, writing center.

**Honors college/program.** High school average of A-, demonstrated success in arts, 1075 SAT (exclusive of Writing)/23 ACT, demonstrated leadership activity, strong performance in sciences, and original essay required.

**Majors. Biology:** General. **Business:** Business admin. **Computer sciences:** General. **Education:** Elementary, health. **History:** General. **Math:** General. **Visual/performing arts:** Art.

**Computing on campus.** PC or laptop required. 225 workstations in dormitories, library, computer center, student center. Dormitories wired for high-speed internet access and linked to campus network. Commuter students can connect to campus network. Online course registration, online library, helpline, student web hosting, wireless network available.

**Student life. Freshman orientation:** Available, $50 fee. Preregistration for classes offered. **Policies:** Religious observance required. **Housing:** Guaranteed on-campus for freshmen. Single-sex dorms available. $200 nonrefundable deposit, deadline 7/1. **Activities:** Bands, choral groups, drama, music ensembles, radio station, student government, student newspaper, Christian Student Association, Chancellorettes, Chancellors.

**Athletics.** NCAA. **Intercollegiate:** Baseball M, basketball, cross-country, football (tackle) M, softball W, tennis, track and field, volleyball W. **Intramural:** Basketball, softball, track and field W, volleyball. **Team name:** Tigers.

**Student services.** Chaplain/spiritual director, career counseling, student employment services, financial aid counseling, health services, personal counseling, placement for graduates, veterans' counselor.

**Contact.** E-mail: mfinch@stillman.edu
Phone: (205) 366-8814 Toll-free number: (800) 841-5722
Fax: (205) 366-8941
Monica Finch, Director of Admissions, Stillman College, 3600 Stillman Boulevard, Tuscaloosa, AL 35403

## Talladega College
### Talladega, Alabama
www.talladega.edu                     CB code: 1800

- Private 4-year liberal arts college affiliated with United Church of Christ
- Residential campus in large town
- 700 degree-seeking undergraduates
- Application essay required

**General.** Founded in 1867. Regionally accredited. **Degrees:** 42 bachelor's awarded. **ROTC:** Army. **Location:** 55 miles from Birmingham, 120 miles from Atlanta. **Calendar:** Semester, limited summer session. **Full-time faculty:** 33 total. **Part-time faculty:** 11 total. **Class size:** 33% < 20, 47% 20-39, 13% 40-49, 7% 50-99. **Special facilities:** Amistad murals.

**Freshman class profile.** 895 applied, 465 admitted, 261 enrolled.

**Basis for selection.** Open admission, but selective for some programs. SAT or ACT recommended for applicants to bachelor's degree program in education. Test scores considered for scholarships. Audition required of music majors. **Homeschooled:** Transcript of courses and grades, state high school equivalency certificate required.

**High school preparation.** 22 units required. Required units include English 4, mathematics 2, social studies 3, science 2 and academic electives 2. 2 units required in health/physical education.

**2009-2010 Annual costs.** Tuition/fees: $8,940. Room/board: $5,324. Books/supplies: $1,178. Personal expenses: $2,402.

**2009-2010 Financial aid.** All financial aid based on need.

**Application procedures. Admission:** No deadline. $25 fee, may be waived for applicants with need. Admission notification on a rolling basis. **Financial aid:** Priority date 4/15; no closing date. FAFSA, institutional form, CSS PROFILE required. Applicants notified on a rolling basis; must reply within 2 week(s) of notification.

**Academics. Special study options:** Combined bachelor's/graduate degree, cooperative education, double major, dual enrollment of high school students, independent study, internships, teacher certification program. Dual degree linkage programs with other colleges in nursing, engineering, pharmacy, veterinary sciences, geology, and allied health. **Credit/placement by examination:** AP, CLEP, institutional tests. 12 credit hours maximum toward bachelor's degree. **Support services:** Learning center, pre-admission summer program, reduced course load, remedial instruction, study skills assistance, tutoring, writing center.

**Majors. Area/ethnic studies:** African-American. **Biology:** General. **Business:** Accounting, business admin, finance, managerial economics, marketing. **Communications:** Journalism, media studies. **Computer sciences:** General. **Education:** Biology, chemistry, English, French, history, mathematics, music, secondary. **Foreign languages:** French, Spanish. **History:** General. **Legal studies:** Prelaw. **Math:** General. **Physical sciences:** Chemistry, physics. **Psychology:** General. **Public administration:** General, social work. **Social sciences:** Economics, sociology. **Visual/performing arts:** Piano/organ, studio arts, voice/opera.

**Most popular majors.** Biology 28%, computer/information sciences 8%, psychology 16%, social sciences 19%.

**Computing on campus.** 200 workstations in dormitories, library, computer center. Dormitories wired for high-speed internet access and linked to campus network. Commuter students can connect to campus network. Online library available.

**Student life. Freshman orientation:** Mandatory, $50 fee. Preregistration for classes offered. Held one week prior to school opening. **Policies:** Religious observance required. **Housing:** Guaranteed on-campus for freshmen. Single-sex dorms, wellness housing available. $200 deposit. Dorms for honors students, seniors, athletes. **Activities:** Concert band, choral groups, dance, drama, student government, Arna Bontemps Historical Society, biology club, business and economics club, chemistry club, debate club, Faith Outreach Campus Ministry, foreign language club, math club, National Association of Negro Musicians, psychology club.

**Athletics.** USCAA. **Intercollegiate:** Baseball M, basketball, cheerleading W, golf M, volleyball W. **Intramural:** Softball W, table tennis, tennis, volleyball W. **Team name:** Tornadoes.

**Student services.** Alcohol/substance abuse counseling, chaplain/spiritual director, career counseling, student employment services, financial aid counseling, health services, personal counseling, placement for graduates, veterans' counselor. **Physically disabled:** Services for visually, hearing impaired.

**Contact.** E-mail: admissions@talladega.edu
Phone: (205) 761-6235 Toll-free number: (800) 633-2440
Fax: (205) 362-0274
Floretta Dortch, Director of Admissions, Talladega College, 627 West Battle Street, Talladega, AL 35160

## Troy University
### Troy, Alabama                     CB member
www.troy.edu                          CB code: 1738

- Public 4-year university
- Residential campus in large town
- 22,029 degree-seeking undergraduates: 50% part-time, 60% women, 42% African American, 1% Asian American, 3% Hispanic American, 2% Native American, 2% international
- 7,064 degree-seeking graduate students
- 66% of applicants admitted
- SAT or ACT (ACT writing optional) required

**General.** Founded in 1887. Regionally accredited. **Degrees:** 2,940 bachelor's, 446 associate awarded; master's, professional offered. **ROTC:** Army, Air Force. **Location:** 50 miles from Montgomery. **Calendar:** Semester, extensive summer session. **Full-time faculty:** 516 total; 67% have terminal degrees, 16% minority, 41% women. **Part-time faculty:** 995 total; 37% have terminal degrees, 18% minority, 52% women. **Class size:** 44% < 20, 45% 20-39, 8% 40-49, 3% 50-99, less than 1% >100. **Special facilities:** Rosa Parks library and museum, planetarium, performing arts theatre.

**Freshman class profile.** 6,413 applied, 4,246 admitted, 3,322 enrolled.

| Mid 50% test scores | | | |
|---|---|---|---|
| ACT composite: | 18-23 | GPA 2.0-2.99: | 35% |
| GPA 3.75 or higher: | 16% | Rank in top quarter: | 45% |
| GPA 3.50-3.74: | 14% | Out-of-state: | 31% |
| GPA 3.0-3.49: | 35% | International: | 4% |

**Basis for selection.** 2.0 GPA and 18 ACT required. Audition required of music education majors.

**High school preparation.** 15 units required. Required units include English 3.

**2009-2010 Annual costs.** Tuition/fees: $6,400; $12,190 out-of-state. Room/board: $5,440. Books/supplies: $1,062. Personal expenses: $2,376.

**2009-2010 Financial aid. Need-based:** Average scholarship/grant was $4,591; average loan $3,607. 18% of total undergraduate aid awarded as scholarships/grants, 82% as loans/jobs. **Non-need-based:** Scholarships awarded for academics, alumni affiliation, art, athletics, leadership, minority status, music/drama, ROTC.

**Application procedures. Admission:** No deadline. $30 fee. Admission notification on a rolling basis. **Financial aid:** Closing date 5/1. FAFSA, institutional form required. Applicants notified on a rolling basis starting 5/1; must reply within 2 week(s) of notification.

**Academics. Special study options:** Combined bachelor's/graduate degree, distance learning, double major, dual enrollment of high school students, ESL, external degree, honors, independent study, internships, study abroad, teacher certification program, weekend college. **Credit/placement by examination:** AP, CLEP, SAT, ACT, institutional tests. 45 credit hours maximum toward associate degree, 90 toward bachelor's. **Support services:** Learning center, pre-admission summer program, reduced course load, remedial instruction, study skills assistance, tutoring, writing center.

**Majors. Biology:** General, marine. **Business:** General, accounting, business admin, finance, management information systems, marketing. **Communications:** Journalism, radio/tv. **Computer sciences:** General. **Conservation:** Environmental science. **Education:** Early childhood, elementary, multi-level teacher, secondary. **Engineering technology:** Electrical, surveying. **Foreign languages:** General, translation. **Health:** Athletic training, nursing (RN). **History:** General. **Liberal arts:** Arts/sciences. **Math:** General. **Parks/recreation:** Sports admin. **Physical sciences:** General, chemistry. **Protective services:** Criminal justice. **Psychology:** General. **Public administration:** Human services, social work. **Social sciences:** General, political science, sociology. **Visual/performing arts:** Art. **Other:** Rehabilitation, Resources and technology management.

**Most popular majors.** Business/marketing 40%, education 8%, psychology 12%, security/protective services 14%, social sciences 8%.

**Computing on campus.** 1,945 workstations in library, computer center, student center. Online course registration, online library, helpline available.

**Student life. Freshman orientation:** Mandatory, $55 fee. Preregistration for classes offered. 2-day sessions held during summer. **Housing:** Coed dorms, single-sex dorms, apartments, fraternity/sorority housing, wellness housing available. $100 partly refundable deposit. Substance-abuse-free housing, honor student housing available. **Activities:** Bands, choral groups, dance, drama, music ensembles, musical theater, student government, student newspaper, TV station, religious, service, and professional organizations; honor societies; Young Democrats; Young Republicans.

**Athletics. NCAA. Intercollegiate:** Baseball M, basketball, cheerleading, cross-country, football (tackle) M, golf, rodeo, soccer W, softball W, tennis, track and field, volleyball W. **Intramural:** Basketball, cross-country, diving, field hockey W, golf, softball, swimming, tennis, track and field, volleyball W. **Team name:** Trojans.

**Student services.** Chaplain/spiritual director, career counseling, student employment services, financial aid counseling, health services, on-campus daycare, personal counseling, placement for graduates, veterans' counselor, women's services. **Physically disabled:** Services for visually, hearing impaired.

**Contact.** E-mail: bstar@troy.edu
Phone: (334) 670-3179 Toll-free number: (800) 551-9716
Fax: (334) 670-3733
Buddy Starling, Dean of Enrollment Management, Troy University, University Avenue, Adams Administration 111, Troy, AL 36082

---

## Tuskegee University
**Tuskegee, Alabama**
www.tuskegee.edu

**CB member**
**CB code: 1813**

- Private 4-year university
- Residential campus in small town
- 965 degree-seeking undergraduates: 59% women
- 456 degree-seeking graduate students
- 58% of applicants admitted
- SAT or ACT (ACT writing optional) required
- 47% graduate within 6 years

**General.** Founded in 1881. Regionally accredited. **Degrees:** 347 bachelor's awarded; master's, doctoral, professional offered. **ROTC:** Army, Air Force. **Location:** 30 miles from Montgomery, 162 miles from Atlanta. **Calendar:** Semester, limited summer session. **Full-time faculty:** 276 total; 80% have terminal degrees, 73% minority, 33% women. **Part-time faculty:** 11 total; 73% have terminal degrees, 46% minority, 18% women. **Class size:** 55% <20, 27% 20-39, 8% 40-49, 10% 50-99, less than 1% >100. **Special facilities:** George Washington Carver museum, aerospace science and health education center.

**Freshman class profile.** 2,692 applied, 1,560 admitted, 689 enrolled.

| Mid 50% test scores | | | |
|---|---|---|---|
| SAT critical reading: | 390-500 | GPA 2.0-2.99: | 49% |
| SAT math: | 380-490 | Rank in top quarter: | 59% |
| ACT composite: | 17-21 | Rank in top tenth: | 20% |
| GPA 3.75 or higher: | 12% | Return as sophomores: | 65% |
| GPA 3.50-3.74: | 10% | Out-of-state: | 73% |
| GPA 3.0-3.49: | 29% | Live on campus: | 98% |

**Basis for selection.** School achievement record and test scores important. 800 SAT (exclusive of Writing) or equivalent ACT required for engineering and nursing applicants, 700 for other applicants. National League for Nursing Guidance Examination required of nursing applicants. Essay recommended; interview recommended for veterinary medicine majors.

**High school preparation.** College-preparatory program recommended. 16 units required. Required units include English 4, mathematics 3, social studies 3, science 2 and academic electives 4.

**2009-2010 Annual costs.** Tuition/fees: $16,280. Room/board: $7,350. Books/supplies: $949. Personal expenses: $1,596.

**2008-2009 Financial aid. Need-based:** 37% of total undergraduate aid awarded as scholarships/grants, 63% as loans/jobs. **Non-need-based:** Scholarships awarded for academics, athletics, ROTC, state residency.

**Application procedures. Admission:** Priority date 5/15; deadline 7/15. $25 fee. Admission notification on a rolling basis beginning on or about 3/1. Must reply by May 1 or within 2 week(s) if notified thereafter. **Financial aid:** Closing date 3/31. FAFSA, institutional form, CSS PROFILE required. Applicants notified on a rolling basis starting 5/15; must reply within 2 week(s) of notification.

**Academics. Special study options:** Combined bachelor's/graduate degree, cooperative education, double major, honors, independent study, internships, liberal arts/career combination, teacher certification program. Engineering program with 2-year colleges. **Credit/placement by examination:** AP, CLEP, SAT, ACT. Credit-by-examination policies determined individually by dean. **Support services:** Learning center, pre-admission summer program, reduced course load, remedial instruction, study skills assistance, tutoring.

**Majors. Agriculture:** Animal sciences, plant sciences, poultry, soil science. **Architecture:** Architecture. **Biology:** General, ecology. **Business:** Accounting, business admin, finance, hospitality admin, management science. **Computer sciences:** General. **Conservation:** General, forestry. **Education:** General, biology, early childhood, elementary, mathematics, mentally handicapped, physical, science, voc/tech. **Engineering:** Aerospace, chemical, electrical, mechanical. **Engineering technology:** Construction. **Family/consumer sciences:** Food/nutrition. **Health:** Clinical lab science. **History:** General. **Math:** General. **Physical sciences:** Chemistry, physics. **Psychology:** General. **Public administration:** Social work. **Social sciences:** Economics, political science, sociology.

**Most popular majors.** Agriculture 7%, biology 13%, business/marketing 16%, engineering/engineering technologies 16%, psychology 10%.

**Computing on campus.** 1,000 workstations in dormitories, library, computer center, student center. Dormitories wired for high-speed internet access and linked to campus network. Commuter students can connect to campus network. Online course registration, online library, helpline, repair service, wireless network available.

**Student life. Freshman orientation:** Available. **Housing:** Single-sex dorms, apartments available. $300 deposit. Honors dormitories available. Freshmen and sophomores not living with parents or guardians required to reside on campus. **Activities:** Bands, choral groups, dance, drama, film society, student government, student newspaper.

**Athletics. NCAA. Intercollegiate:** Baseball M, basketball, cross-country, football (tackle) M, softball W, tennis, track and field, volleyball W. **Intramural:** Basketball M, rifle. **Team name:** Golden Tigers.

**Student services.** Chaplain/spiritual director, career counseling, financial aid counseling, health services, on-campus daycare, personal counseling, placement for graduates, veterans' counselor.

**Contact.** E-mail: adm@tuskegee.edu
Phone: (334) 727-8500 Toll-free number: (800) 622-6531
Fax: (334) 724-4402
Robert Laney, Vice President/Director of Admissions and Enrollment Management, Tuskegee University, 102 Old Administration Building, Tuskegee, AL 36088

## United States Sports Academy
### Daphne, Alabama
### www.ussa.edu

- Private two-year upper-division university
- Large town
- Application essay required

**General.** Regionally accredited. **Degrees:** 21 bachelor's awarded; master's, doctoral offered. **Articulation:** Agreements with Alabama Southern CC, American River College, Andrew College, Barstow CC, Bishop State CC, Camden County College, City College of San Francisco, Columbus State CC, Consumes River College, Cuyahoga CC, Dakota County Technical College, Dallas County CC, East Mississippi CC, Eastern Iowa CC, Eastern Oklahoma State College, Faulkner State CC, Finger Lakes CC, Gadsden State CC, Hagerstown CC, Herkimer County CC, Hillsborough CC, Hiwassee College, Hudson Valley CC, Jamestown CC, Jones County Junior College, Jefferson Davis CC, Manatee CC, Monroe CC, Northern Virginia CC, Ocean County CC, Pensacola Junior College, Saddleback CC, Sufolk County CC. **Location:** 7 miles from Mobile. **Calendar:** Semester. **Full-time faculty:** 10 total. **Part-time faculty:** 20 total.

**Student profile.** 125 degree-seeking undergraduates.

**Basis for selection.** College transcript, application essay required. Transfer accepted as juniors, seniors.

**2009-2010 Annual costs.** Tuition/fees: $9,150. Books/supplies: $1,500.

**Application procedures. Admission:** Rolling admission. $50 fee. Application must be submitted online.

**Academics. Special study options:** Distance learning, internships, student-designed major. **Credit/placement by examination:** CLEP.

**Majors. Parks/recreation:** Sports admin. **Other:** Sports studies.

**Computing on campus.** PC or laptop required. Commuter students can connect to campus network. Online library, wireless network available.

**Student services.** Adult student services, financial aid counseling. **Physically disabled:** Services for visually, speech, hearing impaired. **Learning disabled:** Comprehensive services available.

**Contact.** E-mail: admissions@ussa.edu
Phone: (251) 626-3303 Toll-free number: (800) 223-2668
Fax: (251) 625-1035
Queint Higgins, Registrar, United States Sports Academy, One Academy Drive, Daphne, AL 36526

## University of Alabama
### Tuscaloosa, Alabama                    CB member
### www.ua.edu                             CB code: 1830

- Public 4-year university
- Residential campus in small city
- 23,296 degree-seeking undergraduates: 7% part-time, 52% women, 12% African American, 1% Asian American, 2% Hispanic American, 1% Native American, 1% international
- 4,848 degree-seeking graduate students
- 57% of applicants admitted
- SAT or ACT with writing required
- 66% graduate within 6 years; 6% enter graduate study

**General.** Founded in 1831. Regionally accredited. Services available for learning impaired students. **Degrees:** 3,713 bachelor's awarded; master's, doctoral, professional offered. **ROTC:** Army, Air Force. **Location:** 60 miles from Birmingham. **Calendar:** Semester, extensive summer session. **Full-time faculty:** 1,068 total; 88% have terminal degrees, 16% minority, 41% women. **Part-time faculty:** 369 total; 60% have terminal degrees, 10% minority, 50% women. **Class size:** 43% < 20, 34% 20-39, 7% 40-49, 9% 50-99, 7% >100. **Special facilities:** Museum of natural history, arboretum, marine science laboratory, archeological park, observatory, access to CRAY X-UP/24 supercomputer in Huntsville, simulated coal mine setting, concert hall.

**Freshman class profile.** 19,518 applied, 11,194 admitted, 5,116 enrolled.

| Mid 50% test scores | | Rank in top tenth: | 43% |
|---|---|---|---|
| SAT critical reading: | 500-600 | End year in good standing: | 84% |
| SAT math: | 500-620 | Return as sophomores: | 84% |
| ACT composite: | 21-28 | Out-of-state: | 38% |
| GPA 3.75 or higher: | 33% | Live on campus: | 91% |
| GPA 3.50-3.74: | 17% | International: | 1% |
| GPA 3.0-3.49: | 30% | Fraternities: | 43% |
| GPA 2.0-2.99: | 20% | Sororities: | 39% |
| Rank in top quarter: | 56% | | |

**Basis for selection.** Admissions based on ACT/SAT, GPA, and course schedule. Typically, students with 21 ACT or 1000 SAT (exclusive of Writing) and 3.0 GPA will be admitted. Interview required of any student who appeals admission type or rejection. Audition required for some performance programs. **Homeschooled:** Statement describing homeschool structure and mission, state high school equivalency certificate required. Students who do not present certified transcripts must submit GED and meet GED admission policy. **Learning Disabled:** Documentation concerning disability should be submitted to Office of Disability Services upon admission.

**High school preparation.** College-preparatory program required. 15 units required. Required units include English 4, mathematics 3, social studies 4, history 1, science 3 (laboratory 2), foreign language 1 and academic electives 5.

**2009-2010 Annual costs.** Tuition/fees: $7,000; $19,200 out-of-state. Room/board: $7,796. Books/supplies: $1,100. Personal expenses: $1,900.

**2008-2009 Financial aid. Need-based:** 2,309 full-time freshmen applied for aid; 1,702 were judged to have need; 1,702 of these received aid. Average need met was 55%. Average scholarship/grant was $7,063; average loan $3,621. 35% of total undergraduate aid awarded as scholarships/grants, 65% as loans/jobs. **Non-need-based:** Awarded to 8,461 full-time undergraduates, including 2,612 freshmen. Scholarships awarded for academics, alumni affiliation, art, athletics, leadership, minority status, music/drama, ROTC, state residency.

**Application procedures. Admission:** Priority date 2/1; no deadline. $40 fee, may be waived for applicants with need. Admission notification on a rolling basis beginning on or about 8/1. **Financial aid:** Priority date 3/1; no closing date. FAFSA required. Applicants notified on a rolling basis starting 4/1; must reply within 3 week(s) of notification.

**Academics. Special study options:** Accelerated study, combined bachelor's/graduate degree, cooperative education, cross-registration, distance learning, double major, dual enrollment of high school students, ESL, exchange student, external degree, honors, independent study, internships, liberal arts/career combination, student-designed major, study abroad, teacher certification program, Washington semester, weekend college. **Credit/placement by examination:** AP, CLEP, IB, institutional tests. **Support services:** Learning center, pre-admission summer program, remedial instruction, study skills assistance, tutoring, writing center.

**Honors college/program.** Students with 28 ACT/1250 SAT (exclusive of Writing) eligible to apply. Approximately 1100 first-time freshman enroll.

**Majors. Area/ethnic studies:** African-American, American, Latin American. **Biology:** General, marine, microbiology. **Business:** Accounting, business admin, finance, management information systems, management science, managerial economics, marketing, restaurant/food services. **Communications:** General, advertising, journalism, public relations, radio/tv. **Computer sciences:** General. **Conservation:** Environmental science. **Education:** Early childhood, elementary, music, physical, secondary, special. **Engineering:** Aerospace, chemical, civil, construction, electrical, mechanical, metallurgical. **Family/consumer sciences:** General, clothing/textiles, family resources, family studies. **Foreign languages:** General, Spanish. **Health:** Athletic training, audiology/speech pathology, dietetics, facilities admin, nursing (RN). **History:** General. **Math:** General. **Philosophy/religion:** Philosophy, religion. **Physical sciences:** Chemistry, geology, physics. **Protective services:** Criminal justice. **Psychology:** General. **Public administration:** Social work. **Social sciences:** Anthropology, geography, international relations, political science, sociology. **Visual/performing arts:** Art history/conservation, dance, dramatic, interior design, studio arts.

**Most popular majors.** Business/marketing 27%, communications/journalism 11%, education 7%, engineering/engineering technologies 6%, family/consumer sciences 8%, health sciences 9%.

**Computing on campus.** 2,200 workstations in dormitories, library, computer center, student center. Dormitories wired for high-speed internet access and linked to campus network. Commuter students can connect to campus network. Online course registration, online library, helpline, repair service, student web hosting, wireless network available.

**Student life. Freshman orientation:** Mandatory, $120 fee. Preregistration for classes offered. Two freshman Honors Express sessions, 15 freshman sessions available. **Policies:** Academic integrity policies guided by our Capstone Creed and administered through student honors council. Living/learning program offered. **Housing:** Guaranteed on-campus for freshmen. Coed dorms, single-sex dorms, special housing for disabled, apartments, fraternity/sorority housing available. $250 partly refundable deposit, deadline 3/1. Apartments for visiting scholars available. **Activities:** Bands, campus ministries, choral groups, dance, drama, film society, international student organizations, literary magazine, music ensembles, Model UN, musical theater, opera, radio station, student government, student newspaper, symphony orchestra, TV station, College Republicans, College Democrats, NAACP, African American association, Golden Key, National Society of Black Engineers.

**Athletics.** NCAA. **Intercollegiate:** Baseball M, basketball, cheerleading, cross-country, diving, football (tackle) M, golf, gymnastics W, rowing (crew) W, soccer W, softball W, swimming, tennis, track and field, volleyball W. **Intramural:** Badminton, basketball, bowling, football (non-tackle), golf, racquetball, soccer, softball, swimming, table tennis, tennis, volleyball. **Team name:** Crimson Tide.

**Student services.** Adult student services, alcohol/substance abuse counseling, chaplain/spiritual director, career counseling, services for economically disadvantaged, student employment services, financial aid counseling, health services, legal services, minority student services, on-campus daycare, personal counseling, placement for graduates, veterans' counselor, women's services. **Physically disabled:** Services for visually, speech, hearing impaired.

**Contact.** E-mail: admissions@ua.edu
Phone: (205) 348-5666 Toll-free number: (800) 933-2262
Fax: (205) 348-9046
Mary Spiegel, Executive Director of Undergraduate Admissions, University of Alabama, Box 870132, Tuscaloosa, AL 35487-0132

---

## University of Alabama at Birmingham

| Birmingham, Alabama | CB member |
| --- | --- |
| www.uab.edu | CB code: 1856 |

▶ Public 4-year university
▶ Residential campus in very large city
▶ 10,265 degree-seeking undergraduates: 23% part-time, 58% women, 26% African American, 4% Asian American, 2% Hispanic American, 2% international
▶ 5,623 degree-seeking graduate students
▶ 84% of applicants admitted
▶ SAT or ACT (ACT writing optional) required

**General.** Founded in 1969. Regionally accredited. **Degrees:** 1,916 bachelor's awarded; master's, doctoral, professional offered. **ROTC:** Army, Air Force. **Location:** Downtown. **Calendar:** Semester, extensive summer session. **Full-time faculty:** 845 total; 86% have terminal degrees, 20% minority, 43% women. **Part-time faculty:** 71 total; 82% have terminal degrees, 13% minority, 32% women. **Class size:** 41% < 20, 40% 20-39, 7% 40-49, 9% 50-99, 3% >100. **Special facilities:** Alabama Museum of Health Sciences.

**Freshman class profile.** 4,418 applied, 3,692 admitted, 1,517 enrolled.

| Mid 50% test scores | | End year in good standing: | 98% |
| --- | --- | --- | --- |
| ACT composite: | 21-27 | Return as sophomores: | 79% |
| GPA 3.75 or higher: | 38% | Out-of-state: | 8% |
| GPA 3.50-3.74: | 16% | Live on campus: | 63% |
| GPA 3.0-3.49: | 27% | International: | 2% |
| GPA 2.0-2.99: | 19% | Fraternities: | 17% |
| Rank in top quarter: | 55% | Sororities: | 12% |
| Rank in top tenth: | 27% | | |

**Basis for selection.** Admission decisions based on ACT/SAT, high school GPA, and college preparatory curriculum. **Homeschooled:** Statement describing homeschool structure and mission, transcript of courses and grades required.

**High school preparation.** 17 units required. Required units include English 4, mathematics 3, social studies 3, science 3 (laboratory 2), foreign language 1 and academic electives 3.

**2009-2010 Annual costs.** Tuition/fees: $6,152; $14,072 out-of-state. Room/board: $8,142. Books/supplies: $900. Personal expenses: $1,500.

**2008-2009 Financial aid. Need-based:** 817 full-time freshmen applied for aid; 564 were judged to have need; 554 of these received aid. Average

need met was 49%. Average scholarship/grant was $4,759; average loan $3,870. 37% of total undergraduate aid awarded as scholarships/grants, 63% as loans/jobs. **Non-need-based:** Awarded to 2,574 full-time undergraduates, including 722 freshmen. Scholarships awarded for academics, alumni affiliation, art, athletics, leadership, minority status, music/drama, ROTC.

**Application procedures. Admission:** Closing date 3/1 (receipt date). $35 fee, may be waived for applicants with need. Admission notification on a rolling basis beginning on or about 9/1. **Financial aid:** Priority date 4/1; no closing date. FAFSA, institutional form required. Applicants notified on a rolling basis starting 4/1; must reply within 4 week(s) of notification.

**Academics.** Combined bachelors/masters program also available in Biology. **Special study options:** Combined bachelor's/graduate degree, cooperative education, cross-registration, distance learning, double major, dual enrollment of high school students, honors, independent study, internships, student-designed major, study abroad, teacher certification program, weekend college. **Credit/placement by examination:** AP, CLEP, IB, SAT, ACT, institutional tests. 45 credit hours maximum toward bachelor's degree. **Support services:** Learning center, reduced course load, remedial instruction, study skills assistance, tutoring, writing center.

**Honors college/program.** Additional application required. Honors Academy comprised of University Honors Program, Science and Technology Honors Program, and Global and Community Leadership Honors Program. Each program enrolls 50 freshmen each year for a total of 150 entering freshmen, and either replaces the standard core curriculum with honors seminars or offers tailored curriculum based on program's theme.

**Majors. Area/ethnic studies:** African-American. **Biology:** General. **Business:** Accounting, business admin, finance, management information systems, managerial economics, marketing, sales/distribution. **Communications:** General. **Computer sciences:** General. **Education:** Early childhood, elementary, health, physical, secondary, special. **Engineering:** Biomedical, civil, electrical, materials, mechanical. **Foreign languages:** General. **Health:** Clinical lab science, cytotechnology, medical radiologic technology/radiation therapy, medical records admin, nuclear medical technology, nursing (RN), respiratory therapy technology. **History:** General. **Interdisciplinary:** Biological/physical sciences, global studies, natural sciences. **Math:** General. **Philosophy/religion:** Philosophy. **Physical sciences:** Chemistry, physics. **Protective services:** Criminal justice. **Psychology:** General. **Public administration:** Social work. **Social sciences:** Anthropology, political science, sociology. **Visual/performing arts:** Art, dramatic. **Other:** Health sciences, Industrial distribution.

**Most popular majors.** Biology 7%, business/marketing 16%, communications/journalism 7%, education 10%, health sciences 19%, psychology 8%.

**Computing on campus.** Dormitories wired for high-speed internet access and linked to campus network. Commuter students can connect to campus network. Online course registration, online library, helpline, student web hosting, wireless network available.

**Student life. Freshman orientation:** Mandatory, $150 fee. Preregistration for classes offered. 2-day program offered various times between May and August. **Housing:** Coed dorms, single-sex dorms, apartments available. $250 deposit, deadline 5/1. **Activities:** Bands, campus ministries, choral groups, dance, drama, international student organizations, literary magazine, music ensembles, musical theater, opera, radio station, student government, student newspaper, Young Democrats, College Republicans, campus civitan club, veterans student organization, Catholic student association, Muslim student association, Chinese student association, African student association.

**Athletics.** NCAA. **Intercollegiate:** Baseball M, basketball, cross-country W, football (tackle) M, golf, rifle, soccer, softball W, synchronized swimming W, tennis, track and field W, volleyball W. **Intramural:** Badminton, basketball, bowling, football (non-tackle), racquetball, skiing, soccer, softball, squash, swimming, table tennis, tennis, track and field, volleyball, water polo, wrestling M. **Team name:** Blazers.

**Student services.** Adult student services, career counseling, student employment services, financial aid counseling, health services, minority student services, on-campus daycare, personal counseling, placement for graduates, veterans' counselor, women's services. **Physically disabled:** Services for visually, speech, hearing impaired.

**Contact.** E-mail: undergradadmit@uab.edu
Phone: (205) 934-8221 Toll-free number: (800) 421-8743
Fax: (205) 975-7114
Chenise Ryan, Director of Admission, University of Alabama at Birmingham, HUC 260, 1530 Third Avenue South, Birmingham, AL 35294-1150

## University of Alabama in Huntsville
**Huntsville, Alabama**                                    **CB member**
**www.uah.edu**                                            **CB code: 1854**

- Public 4-year university
- Commuter campus in small city
- 5,956 degree-seeking undergraduates: 23% part-time, 47% women, 15% African American, 3% Asian American, 2% Hispanic American, 2% Native American, 3% international
- 1,412 degree-seeking graduate students
- 72% of applicants admitted
- SAT or ACT (ACT writing optional) required
- 48% graduate within 6 years

**General.** Founded in 1950. Regionally accredited. **Degrees:** 900 bachelor's awarded; master's, doctoral, professional offered. **ROTC:** Army. **Location:** 100 miles from Birmingham; 100 miles from Nashville, TN. **Calendar:** Semester, extensive summer session. **Full-time faculty:** 303 total; 90% have terminal degrees, 22% minority, 38% women. **Part-time faculty:** 154 total; 32% have terminal degrees, 7% minority, 48% women. **Class size:** 40% < 20, 37% 20-39, 9% 40-49, 13% 50-99, 2% >100. **Special facilities:** Applied optics center, micro-gravity research center, robotics center, solar research center, space plasma center, aeronomic research center, observatory with vector magnetograph.

**Freshman class profile.** 1,924 applied, 1,387 admitted, 802 enrolled.

| Mid 50% test scores | | | |
|---|---|---|---|
| SAT critical reading: | 500-630 | Rank in top tenth: | 34% |
| SAT math: | 520-640 | End year in good standing: | 79% |
| ACT composite: | 22-28 | Return as sophomores: | 76% |
| GPA 3.75 or higher: | 42% | Out-of-state: | 15% |
| GPA 3.50-3.74: | 17% | Live on campus: | 48% |
| GPA 3.0-3.49: | 28% | International: | 2% |
| GPA 2.0-2.99: | 13% | Fraternities: | 5% |
| Rank in top quarter: | 63% | Sororities: | 10% |

**Basis for selection.** School achievement record and test scores most important. Conditional admission may be available for applicants with evidence of serious commitment to academic pursuits who do not meet requirements for regular admission. **Homeschooled:** Official high school record should contain titles of courses, annotation of general content in academic courses, and textbooks used. Teaching credentials of home school teacher should be included with application.

**High school preparation.** College-preparatory program required. 20 units required. Required and recommended units include English 4, mathematics 3-4, social studies 4, science 3-4 (laboratory 2), foreign language 2 and academic electives 6. 4 credits required in either history or social studies.

**2009-2010 Annual costs.** Tuition/fees: $6,510; $15,628 out-of-state. Per-credit-hour rate decreases as number of hours registered increases. Room/board: $7,208. Books/supplies: $1,542. Personal expenses: $1,928.

**2009-2010 Financial aid. Need-based:** 707 full-time freshmen applied for aid; 364 were judged to have need; 363 of these received aid. Average need met was 62%. Average scholarship/grant was $6,236; average loan $5,340. 34% of total undergraduate aid awarded as scholarships/grants, 66% as loans/jobs. **Non-need-based:** Awarded to 1,098 full-time undergraduates, including 338 freshmen. Scholarships awarded for academics, art, athletics, leadership, minority status, music/drama, ROTC.

**Application procedures. Admission:** Closing date 8/15 (receipt date). $30 fee, may be waived for applicants with need. Admission notification on a rolling basis. **Financial aid:** Priority date 4/1, closing date 7/31. FAFSA required. Applicants notified on a rolling basis starting 4/1; must reply within 2 week(s) of notification.

**Academics. Special study options:** Combined bachelor's/graduate degree, cooperative education, cross-registration, distance learning, double major, dual enrollment of high school students, ESL, honors, independent study, internships, study abroad, teacher certification program. 3-2 program in engineering. Research centers employ undergraduate students on campus and in the community. Co-op program with U.S. Army Redstone Arsenal, NASA Marshall Space Flight Center, U.S. Army Missile Command, over 50 Fortune 500 companies. Intensive English Program (IEP) for nonnative speakers of English available prior to enrollment in a degree program. **Credit/placement by examination:** AP, CLEP, IB, SAT, ACT, institutional tests. 32 credit hours maximum toward bachelor's degree. **Support services:** Learning center, reduced course load, remedial instruction, study skills assistance, tutoring, writing center.

**Majors. Biology:** General. **Business:** Accounting, business admin, finance, management information systems, marketing, purchasing. **Computer sciences:** General. **Education:** Elementary. **Engineering:** Chemical, civil, computer, electrical, industrial, mechanical. **Foreign languages:** General. **Health:** Nursing (RN). **History:** General. **Math:** General. **Philosophy/religion:** Philosophy. **Physical sciences:** Chemistry, physics. **Psychology:** General. **Social sciences:** Political science, sociology. **Visual/performing arts:** Art. **Other:** Earth System Science, Optical engineering.

**Most popular majors.** Biology 7%, business/marketing 23%, engineering/engineering technologies 24%, health sciences 18%.

**Computing on campus.** 1,152 workstations in dormitories, library, computer center, student center. Dormitories wired for high-speed internet access and linked to campus network. Commuter students can connect to campus network. Online course registration, online library, helpline, repair service, student web hosting, wireless network available.

**Student life. Freshman orientation:** Mandatory, $95 fee. Preregistration for classes offered. Five 2-day sessions running from June to August for new students. **Housing:** Guaranteed on-campus for freshmen. Coed dorms, special housing for disabled, apartments, cooperative housing, fraternity/sorority housing available. $125 fully refundable deposit, deadline 6/1. Pets allowed in dorm rooms. Athletic team housing. **Activities:** Bands, campus ministries, choral groups, dance, drama, international student organizations, literary magazine, music ensembles, student government, student newspaper, black student association, Chargers for Christ, Chinese student & scholar association, Catholic student fellowship, College Republicans, Indian student organization, Invisible Children United, National Society of Black Engineers, Reformed University Fellowship.

**Athletics.** NCAA. **Intercollegiate:** Baseball M, basketball, cross-country, ice hockey M, soccer, softball W, tennis, track and field, volleyball W. **Intramural:** Badminton, basketball, football (non-tackle), golf, racquetball, soccer, softball, table tennis, volleyball. **Team name:** Chargers.

**Student services.** Adult student services, alcohol/substance abuse counseling, chaplain/spiritual director, career counseling, student employment services, financial aid counseling, health services, minority student services, personal counseling, veterans' counselor, women's services. **Physically disabled:** Services for visually, speech, hearing impaired.

**Contact.** E-mail: admitme@uah.edu
Phone: (256) 824-2773 Toll-free number: (800) 824-2255
Fax: (256) 824-6073
Sandra Patterson, Director of Admissions, University of Alabama in Huntsville, UAH Office of Undergraduate Admissions, Huntsville, AL 35899

## University of Mobile
**Mobile, Alabama**
**www.umobile.edu**                                        **CB code: 1515**

- Private 4-year university and liberal arts college affiliated with Baptist faith
- Commuter campus in small city
- 1,417 degree-seeking undergraduates: 11% part-time, 66% women, 22% African American, 1% Hispanic American, 2% Native American, 2% international
- 155 degree-seeking graduate students
- 78% of applicants admitted
- SAT or ACT (ACT writing optional) required
- 38% graduate within 6 years

**General.** Founded in 1961. Regionally accredited. **Degrees:** 269 bachelor's, 19 associate awarded; master's offered. **ROTC:** Army, Air Force. **Location:** 12 miles from downtown, 140 miles from New Orleans. **Calendar:** Semester, limited summer session. **Full-time faculty:** 84 total; 61% have terminal degrees, 5% minority, 45% women. **Part-time faculty:** 78 total; 18% have terminal degrees, 12% minority, 51% women. **Class size:** 54% < 20, 45% 20-39, less than 1% 40-49, less than 1% 50-99. **Special facilities:** Forest resource learning center, nature trails.

**Freshman class profile.** 796 applied, 618 admitted, 228 enrolled.

| Mid 50% test scores | | | |
|---|---|---|---|
| | | GPA 2.0-2.99: | 23% |
| SAT critical reading: | 470-590 | Rank in top quarter: | 55% |
| SAT math: | 430-540 | Rank in top tenth: | 27% |
| ACT composite: | 19-25 | Return as sophomores: | 77% |
| GPA 3.75 or higher: | 27% | Out-of-state: | 29% |
| GPA 3.50-3.74: | 21% | Live on campus: | 74% |
| GPA 3.0-3.49: | 26% | International: | 3% |

**Basis for selection.** Admission decisions based on test scores, high school record. SAT Subject Tests recommended. Interview recommended for nursing majors, audition recommended for music majors, portfolio recommended for art majors. **Homeschooled:** Statement describing homeschool structure and mission required.

**High school preparation.** College-preparatory program recommended. 22 units recommended. Recommended units include English 4, mathematics 3, social studies 3 and foreign language 2.

**2009-2010 Annual costs.** Tuition/fees: $15,000. Room/board: $7,570.

**2009-2010 Financial aid. Need-based:** 221 full-time freshmen applied for aid; 198 were judged to have need; 189 of these received aid. Average need met was 62%. Average scholarship/grant was $10,666; average loan $4,097. 67% of total undergraduate aid awarded as scholarships/grants, 33% as loans/jobs. **Non-need-based:** Scholarships awarded for academics, alumni affiliation, athletics, music/drama, religious affiliation, ROTC.

**Application procedures. Admission:** Closing date 8/1. $50 fee. Admission notification on a rolling basis. **Financial aid:** No deadline. FAFSA required. Applicants notified on a rolling basis starting 2/1; must reply within 2 week(s) of notification.

**Academics. Special study options:** Accelerated study, combined bachelor's/graduate degree, double major, honors, independent study, internships, teacher certification program. **Credit/placement by examination:** AP, CLEP, IB, SAT, ACT, institutional tests. 30 credit hours maximum toward associate degree, 30 toward bachelor's. **Support services:** Learning center, preadmission summer program, reduced course load, remedial instruction, study skills assistance, tutoring, writing center.

**Majors. Biology:** General, marine. **Business:** Accounting, business admin. **Communications:** General. **Computer sciences:** General. **Conservation:** Environmental science. **Education:** Biology, early childhood, elementary, English, history, mathematics, music, physical, social science. **Health:** Athletic training, nursing (RN). **History:** General. **Liberal arts:** Humanities. **Math:** General. **Parks/recreation:** Health/fitness. **Philosophy/religion:** Religion. **Psychology:** General. **Social sciences:** General, political science, sociology. **Theology:** Sacred music. **Visual/performing arts:** Art, dramatic, voice/opera.

**Most popular majors.** Business/marketing 21%, education 20%, health sciences 16%, liberal arts 8%, philosophy/religious studies 12%, visual/performing arts 6%.

**Computing on campus.** 110 workstations in library, computer center. Dormitories wired for high-speed internet access. Commuter students can connect to campus network. Online course registration, online library, helpline, wireless network available.

**Student life. Freshman orientation:** Mandatory, $100 fee. Preregistration for classes offered. **Policies:** Religious observance required. **Housing:** Guaranteed on-campus for freshmen. Single-sex dorms available. $250 non-refundable deposit, deadline 4/30. **Activities:** Bands, campus ministries, choral groups, drama, music ensembles, musical theater, opera, student government, campus activities board, student government association, ministerial association, honor societies, academic clubs, Fellowship of Christian Athletes.

**Athletics.** NAIA. **Intercollegiate:** Baseball M, basketball, cheerleading, cross-country, golf, soccer, softball W, tennis, volleyball W. **Intramural:** Basketball, football (non-tackle), softball, volleyball. **Team name:** Rams.

**Student services.** Adult student services, chaplain/spiritual director, career counseling, student employment services, financial aid counseling, health services, personal counseling, placement for graduates, veterans' counselor.

**Contact.** E-mail: adminfo@umobile.edu
Phone: (251) 442-2273 Toll-free number: (800) 946-7267
Fax: (251) 442-2498
Kim Leousis, Vice President for Enrollment Services and Campus Life, University of Mobile, 5735 College Parkway, Mobile, AL 36613-2842

## University of Montevallo
**Montevallo, Alabama**
www.montevallo.edu

**CB member**
**CB code: 1004**

- Public 4-year university and liberal arts college
- Residential campus in small town
- 2,547 degree-seeking undergraduates: 11% part-time, 67% women, 10% African American, 5% Asian American, 2% Hispanic American, 1% Native American, 2% international
- 446 degree-seeking graduate students

- 72% of applicants admitted
- SAT or ACT (ACT writing optional) required
- 52% graduate within 6 years

**General.** Founded in 1896. Regionally accredited. **Degrees:** 458 bachelor's awarded; master's offered. **ROTC:** Army, Air Force. **Location:** 35 miles from Birmingham. **Calendar:** Semester, extensive summer session. **Full-time faculty:** 137 total; 94% have terminal degrees, 12% minority, 51% women. **Part-time faculty:** 68 total; 9% have terminal degrees, 10% minority. **Class size:** 52% < 20, 43% 20-39, 4% 40-49, less than 1% 50-99. **Special facilities:** Glass-blowing studio, swamp, observatory, foreign language laboratory, child development center, mass communication production center, traffic safety center.

**Freshman class profile.** 1,350 applied, 976 admitted, 429 enrolled.

| Mid 50% test scores | | | |
|---|---|---|---|
| ACT composite: | 20-26 | Live on campus: | 73% |
| Return as sophomores: | 78% | International: | 3% |
| Out-of-state: | 4% | Fraternities: | 22% |
| | | Sororities: | 24% |

**Basis for selection.** High school record and test scores essential factors in individual evaluation. Interview recommended. Audition required of music majors; portfolio required of art majors. **Homeschooled:** Transcript of courses and grades required. **Learning Disabled:** Conditional admission may be granted if standard requirements not met. Reasonable accommodations will be provided as necessary. Enrolled students needing disability accommodations and services must provide current documentation and make requests through the Services for Students with Disabilities Office.

**High school preparation.** 16 units required. Required and recommended units include English 4, mathematics 2-3, social studies 2, history 2, science 2-3, foreign language 2 and academic electives 4.

**2009-2010 Annual costs.** Tuition/fees: $7,010; $13,550 out-of-state. Room/board: $4,440. Books/supplies: $900. Personal expenses: $1,980.

**2008-2009 Financial aid. Non-need-based:** Scholarships awarded for academics, art, athletics, job skills, leadership, minority status, music/drama, religious affiliation, ROTC.

**Application procedures. Admission:** Closing date 8/20. $25 fee, may be waived for applicants with need. Admission notification on a rolling basis. **Financial aid:** Priority date 4/1; no closing date. FAFSA required. Applicants notified on a rolling basis starting 4/20; must reply within 2 week(s) of notification.

**Academics.** Academic support programs available to all first-generation college students from low-income families and students with disabilities through the ASPIRE program. Tutoring, study-skills classes, academic counseling, career exploration, course advisement and registration, computer lab access, computer-assisted instruction, and cultural and social enrichment activities provided. **Special study options:** Accelerated study, combined bachelor's/graduate degree, cross-registration, double major, dual enrollment of high school students, exchange student, honors, independent study, internships, study abroad, teacher certification program. **Credit/placement by examination:** AP, CLEP, IB, institutional tests. 45 credit hours maximum toward bachelor's degree. **Support services:** Learning center, preadmission summer program, reduced course load, remedial instruction, study skills assistance, tutoring, writing center.

**Majors. Biology:** General. **Business:** Accounting, business admin, finance. **Communications:** Radio/tv. **Education:** Elementary. **Family/consumer sciences:** General. **Foreign languages:** General. **Health:** Audiology/hearing, speech pathology. **History:** General. **Math:** General. **Parks/recreation:** Health/fitness. **Physical sciences:** Chemistry. **Psychology:** General. **Public administration:** Social work. **Social sciences:** General, political science, sociology. **Visual/performing arts:** Art, dramatic.

**Most popular majors.** Business/marketing 17%, education 10%, English 7%, family/consumer sciences 11%, parks/recreation 6%, visual/performing arts 14%.

**Computing on campus.** 340 workstations in dormitories, library, computer center. Dormitories wired for high-speed internet access and linked to campus network. Commuter students can connect to campus network. Online course registration, online library, helpline, wireless network available.

**Student life. Freshman orientation:** Mandatory. Preregistration for classes offered. Two preregistration sessions during the summer and orientation immediately prior to beginning of fall semester. **Housing:** Guaranteed on-campus for freshmen. Coed dorms, single-sex dorms, apartments available. $100 fully refundable deposit. Several rooms are handicapped accessible. **Activities:** Bands, campus ministries, choral groups, dance, drama, international student organizations, literary magazine, music ensembles, Model UN, musical theater, student government, student newspaper, TV station, African American Society, Young Republicans, Young Democrats, campus outreach, Episcopal Student Fellowship, Feminine Majority Leadership Alliance.

**Athletics.** NCAA. **Intercollegiate:** Baseball M, basketball, cross-country W, golf, soccer, tennis W, volleyball W. **Intramural:** Basketball, soccer, softball, volleyball. **Team name:** Falcons.

**Student services.** Adult student services, alcohol/substance abuse counseling, chaplain/spiritual director, career counseling, student employment services, financial aid counseling, health services, minority student services, personal counseling, placement for graduates, veterans' counselor. **Physically disabled:** Services for visually, speech, hearing impaired.

**Contact.** E-mail: admissions@montevallo.edu
Phone: (205) 665-6030 Toll-free number: (800) 292-4349
Fax: (205) 665-6032
Ira Gurganus, Director of Admissions, University of Montevallo, Station 6030, Montevallo, AL 35115-6030

---

## University of North Alabama
**Florence, Alabama**  CB member
**www.una.edu**  CB code: 1735

- Public 4-year university
- Commuter campus in large town
- 5,814 degree-seeking undergraduates: 14% part-time, 56% women, 13% African American, 2% Hispanic American, 1% Native American, 6% international
- 953 degree-seeking graduate students
- 82% of applicants admitted
- SAT or ACT required
- 41% graduate within 6 years

**General.** Founded in 1830. Regionally accredited. **Degrees:** 894 bachelor's awarded; master's offered. **ROTC:** Army. **Location:** 116 miles from Birmingham. **Calendar:** Semester, extensive summer session. **Full-time faculty:** 236 total; 25% have terminal degrees, 36% minority, 46% women. **Part-time faculty:** 116 total; 21% have terminal degrees, 58% minority, 49% women. **Class size:** 38% < 20, 46% 20-39, 12% 40-49, 4% 50-99, less than 1% >100. **Special facilities:** Planetarium-observatory, laboratory school.

**Freshman class profile.** 2,583 applied, 2,128 admitted, 1,068 enrolled.

| Mid 50% test scores | | GPA 3.0-3.49: | 26% |
|---|---|---|---|
| SAT critical reading: | 400-490 | GPA 2.0-2.99: | 40% |
| SAT math: | 370-530 | Return as sophomores: | 70% |
| ACT composite: | 18-24 | Out-of-state: | 11% |
| GPA 3.75 or higher: | 14% | Live on campus: | 45% |
| GPA 3.50-3.74: | 9% | International: | 2% |

**Basis for selection.** 18 ACT or 700 SAT (exclusive of Writing), or rank in upper 50% of class required. If submitting GED, 35 on each section or average of 45 on all GED test sections required. Auditions required of music majors. Interviews recommended for education, nursing, social work, preprofessional programs. Portfolios recommended for art majors.

**High school preparation.** 13 units required. Required units include English 4, mathematics 2, social studies 3, science 2 and foreign language 2.

**2009-2010 Annual costs.** Tuition/fees: $6,018; $11,028 out-of-state. Room/board: $4,783. Books/supplies: $1,100.

**2008-2009 Financial aid. Need-based:** 689 full-time freshmen applied for aid; 522 were judged to have need; 505 of these received aid. Average need met was 61%. Average scholarship/grant was $4,060; average loan $2,115. 32% of total undergraduate aid awarded as scholarships/grants, 68% as loans/jobs. **Non-need-based:** Awarded to 3,409 full-time undergraduates, including 792 freshmen. Scholarships awarded for academics, art, athletics, leadership, minority status, music/drama, ROTC, state residency.

**Application procedures. Admission:** Priority date 8/1; no deadline. $25 fee. Admission notification on a rolling basis beginning on or about 6/15. **Financial aid:** Priority date 6/1; no closing date. FAFSA required. Applicants notified on a rolling basis starting 6/30; must reply within 2 week(s) of notification.

**Academics. Special study options:** Accelerated study, cooperative education, distance learning, double major, dual enrollment of high school students, ESL, honors, independent study, internships, student-designed major, study abroad, teacher certification program, weekend college. **Credit/placement by examination:** AP, CLEP, institutional tests. 34 credit hours maximum toward bachelor's degree. **Support services:** Learning center,

pre-admission summer program, reduced course load, remedial instruction, study skills assistance, tutoring, writing center.

**Majors. Biology:** General, marine. **Business:** Accounting, business admin, finance, management information systems, managerial economics, marketing. **Computer sciences:** General. **Education:** Elementary, multi-level teacher, secondary. **Family/consumer sciences:** General. **Foreign languages:** General. **Health:** Nursing (RN). **History:** General. **Math:** General. **Parks/recreation:** General. **Physical sciences:** Chemistry, geology, physics. **Protective services:** Law enforcement admin. **Psychology:** General. **Public administration:** Social work. **Social sciences:** Geography, political science, sociology. **Visual/performing arts:** Studio arts.

**Most popular majors.** Business/marketing 27%, education 10%, English 10%, health sciences 17%, social sciences 6%.

**Computing on campus.** 600 workstations in dormitories, library, computer center, student center. Dormitories wired for high-speed internet access and linked to campus network. Commuter students can connect to campus network. Online course registration, online library, helpline, wireless network available.

**Student life. Freshman orientation:** Mandatory, $25 fee. Preregistration for classes offered. Two-day sessions in June and July include academic advisement. **Housing:** Coed dorms, single-sex dorms, apartments, fraternity/sorority housing, wellness housing available. $100 nonrefundable deposit. **Activities:** Bands, choral groups, drama, international student organizations, literary magazine, music ensembles, musical theater, radio station, student government, student newspaper, Young Democrats, Young Republicans, Circle-K, Gold Triangle, black student alliance, Christian student fellowship.

**Athletics.** NCAA. **Intercollegiate:** Baseball M, basketball, cross-country, football (tackle) M, golf M, soccer W, softball W, tennis, volleyball W. **Intramural:** Badminton, baseball M, basketball, bowling, cross-country, football (tackle) M, golf M, racquetball, softball W, swimming, table tennis, tennis, volleyball. **Team name:** Lions.

**Student services.** Adult student services, alcohol/substance abuse counseling, chaplain/spiritual director, career counseling, student employment services, financial aid counseling, health services, minority student services, on-campus daycare, personal counseling, placement for graduates, veterans' counselor, women's services. **Physically disabled:** Services for visually, speech, hearing impaired.

**Contact.** E-mail: admissions@una.edu
Phone: (256) 765-4608 Toll-free number: (800) 825-5862
Fax: (256) 765-4329
Kim Mauldin, Director of Admissions, University of North Alabama, One Harrison Plaza, UNA Box 5011, Florence, AL 35632-0001

---

## University of South Alabama
**Mobile, Alabama**
**www.southalabama.edu**  CB code: 1880

- Public 4-year university
- Commuter campus in small city
- 11,250 degree-seeking undergraduates: 24% part-time, 57% women, 19% African American, 3% Asian American, 2% Hispanic American, 1% Native American, 4% international
- 3,114 degree-seeking graduate students
- 90% of applicants admitted
- 37% graduate within 6 years

**General.** Founded in 1963. Regionally accredited. **Degrees:** 1,654 bachelor's awarded; master's, doctoral, professional offered. **ROTC:** Army, Air Force. **Location:** 10 miles from downtown, 150 miles from New Orleans. **Calendar:** Semester, extensive summer session. **Full-time faculty:** 740 total; 80% have terminal degrees, 39% women. **Part-time faculty:** 304 total; 59% women. **Special facilities:** Sea laboratory.

**Freshman class profile.** 4,050 applied, 3,631 admitted, 1,841 enrolled.

| Mid 50% test scores | | Return as sophomores: | 67% |
|---|---|---|---|
| SAT critical reading: | 440-570 | International: | 2% |
| SAT math: | 430-550 | Fraternities: | 10% |
| ACT composite: | 18-24 | Sororities: | 10% |

**Basis for selection.** School achievement record and test scores important. Auditions required of music majors. **Learning Disabled:** Students should submit required documentation to special student services office if requesting services.

**High school preparation.** 16 units recommended. Recommended units include English 4, mathematics 3, social studies 2, science 2 and academic electives 2.

**2009-2010 Annual costs.** Tuition/fees: $5,962; $10,822 out-of-state. Room/board: $5,308. Books/supplies: $1,200.

**2008-2009 Financial aid. Non-need-based:** Scholarships awarded for academics, alumni affiliation, art, athletics, minority status, music/drama, ROTC, state residency.

**Application procedures. Admission:** Closing date 8/10. $35 fee. Application must be submitted on paper. Admission notification on a rolling basis. **Financial aid:** Priority date 5/1; no closing date. FAFSA, institutional form required. Applicants notified on a rolling basis starting 5/15.

**Academics.** Students in entry-level programming courses must own a laptop. **Special study options:** Accelerated study, combined bachelor's/graduate degree, cooperative education, distance learning, double major, ESL, honors, independent study, internships, student-designed major, study abroad, teacher certification program, weekend college. **Credit/placement by examination:** AP, CLEP, institutional tests. Maximum of 32 credit hours can be awarded under any combination of AP and CLEP examination credits. **Support services:** Learning center, remedial instruction, study skills assistance, tutoring, writing center.

**Majors. Biology:** General, biomedical sciences. **Business:** General, accounting, business admin, e-commerce, finance, marketing. **Communications:** General. **Computer sciences:** General. **Education:** Early childhood, elementary, health, physical, secondary, special. **Engineering:** Chemical, civil, computer, electrical, mechanical. **Foreign languages:** General. **Health:** Audiology/speech pathology, clinical lab science, EMT paramedic, medical radiologic technology/radiation therapy, nursing (RN), respiratory therapy technology. **History:** General. **Liberal arts:** Arts/sciences. **Math:** Statistics. **Parks/recreation:** General. **Philosophy/religion:** Philosophy. **Physical sciences:** Atmospheric science, chemistry, geology, physics. **Protective services:** Criminal justice. **Psychology:** General. **Public administration:** Social work. **Social sciences:** Anthropology, geography, political science, sociology. **Visual/performing arts:** Art, dramatic.

**Most popular majors.** Business/marketing 15%, education 14%, engineering/engineering technologies 6%, health sciences 22%.

**Computing on campus.** 500 workstations in library, computer center, student center. Dormitories wired for high-speed internet access and linked to campus network. Commuter students can connect to campus network. Online course registration, online library, helpline available.

**Student life. Freshman orientation:** Mandatory, $75 fee. **Housing:** Coed dorms, special housing for disabled, apartments, fraternity/sorority housing available. $150 deposit. **Activities:** Bands, choral groups, dance, drama, film society, literary magazine, music ensembles, musical theater, opera, student government, student newspaper, TV station.

**Athletics.** NCAA. **Intercollegiate:** Baseball M, basketball, cross-country, football (tackle) M, golf, soccer W, softball W, tennis, track and field, volleyball W. **Intramural:** Basketball, bowling, football (non-tackle), golf, racquetball, soccer, softball, table tennis, tennis, volleyball, water polo. **Team name:** Jaguars.

**Student services.** Adult student services, alcohol/substance abuse counseling, chaplain/spiritual director, career counseling, services for economically disadvantaged, student employment services, financial aid counseling, health services, minority student services, personal counseling, placement for graduates, veterans' counselor. **Physically disabled:** Services for visually, speech, hearing impaired.

**Contact.** E-mail: admiss@usouthal.edu
Phone: (251) 460-6141 Toll-free number: (800) 872-5247
Fax: (251) 460-7876
Norma Tanner, Director of Admissions, University of South Alabama, Meisler Hall, Suite 2500, Mobile, AL 36688-0002

## University of West Alabama
**Livingston, Alabama**
www.uwa.edu
CB code: 1737

- Public 4-year university
- Residential campus in small town
- 1,945 degree-seeking undergraduates: 21% part-time, 61% women
- 2,925 degree-seeking graduate students
- 61% of applicants admitted
- SAT or ACT (ACT writing optional) required
- 36% graduate within 6 years

**General.** Founded in 1835. Regionally accredited. **Degrees:** 859 bachelor's, 39 associate awarded; master's offered. **ROTC:** Air Force. **Location:** 60 miles from Tuscaloosa. **Calendar:** Semester, limited summer session. **Full-time faculty:** 116 total; 79% have terminal degrees, 16% minority, 47% women. **Part-time faculty:** 131 total; 95% have terminal degrees, 9% minority, 68% women. **Class size:** 58% < 20, 34% 20-39, 5% 40-49, 3% 50-99, less than 1% >100. **Special facilities:** Nature trail, herbarium, greenhouses, wildflower gardens, bluebird trail, lake.

**Freshman class profile.** 690 applied, 424 admitted, 310 enrolled.

| Mid 50% test scores | | Return as sophomores: | 70% |
|---|---|---|---|
| ACT composite: | 18-34 | Out-of-state: | 19% |

**Basis for selection.** School achievement record and test scores most important.

**High school preparation.** College-preparatory program recommended. 15 units required. Required units include English 3, mathematics 3, social studies 3, science 3 and academic electives 3.

**2009-2010 Annual costs.** Tuition/fees: $5,560; $10,620 out-of-state. Room/board: $4,416. Personal expenses: $1,200.

**2009-2010 Financial aid. Non-need-based:** Scholarships awarded for academics, alumni affiliation, athletics, leadership, music/drama, state residency.

**Application procedures. Admission:** No deadline. $50 fee. Admission notification on a rolling basis. **Financial aid:** Priority date 4/1; no closing date. FAFSA required. Applicants notified on a rolling basis starting 6/1; must reply within 2 week(s) of notification.

**Academics. Special study options:** Accelerated study, cooperative education, distance learning, double major, dual enrollment of high school students, honors, internships, teacher certification program. **Credit/placement by examination:** AP, CLEP, SAT, ACT, institutional tests. 15 credit hours maximum toward associate degree, 30 toward bachelor's. **Support services:** Learning center, reduced course load, remedial instruction, study skills assistance, tutoring, writing center.

**Majors. Biology:** General, marine. **Business:** Accounting, business admin, management information systems. **Conservation:** General. **Education:** Early childhood, elementary, physical, secondary, special. **Engineering technology:** Manufacturing. **Health:** Athletic training. **History:** General. **Math:** General. **Physical sciences:** Chemistry. **Psychology:** General. **Social sciences:** Sociology.

**Most popular majors.** Biology 11%, business/marketing 14%, education 30%, engineering/engineering technologies 6%, English 8%, psychology 7%, social sciences 12%.

**Computing on campus.** 310 workstations in dormitories, library, computer center, student center. Dormitories wired for high-speed internet access and linked to campus network. Commuter students can connect to campus network. Online course registration, online library, helpline, wireless network available.

**Student life. Freshman orientation:** Mandatory, $40 fee. Preregistration for classes offered. **Housing:** Guaranteed on-campus for all undergraduates. Coed dorms, single-sex dorms, apartments, wellness housing available. $100 partly refundable deposit. **Activities:** Bands, campus ministries, choral groups, drama, student government, student newspaper, TV station, Wesley Foundation, campus outreach, Fellowship of Christian Athletes, student support services club, African-American cultural association.

**Athletics.** NCAA. **Intercollegiate:** Baseball M, basketball, cross-country, football (tackle) M, rodeo, softball W, tennis, volleyball W. **Intramural:** Basketball, softball, table tennis, tennis, volleyball, wrestling M. **Team name:** Tigers.

**Student services.** Alcohol/substance abuse counseling, career counseling, student employment services, financial aid counseling, health services, personal counseling, placement for graduates, veterans' counselor. **Physically disabled:** Services for visually, hearing impaired.

**Contact.** E-mail: admissions@uwa.edu
Phone: (205) 652-3578 Toll-free number: (888) 636-8800
Fax: (205) 652-3708
Richard Hester, Director of Admissions, University of West Alabama, Station 4, Livingston, AL 35470

## Virginia College
**Birmingham, Alabama**
www.vc.edu
CB code: 2596

- For-profit 4-year technical college
- Commuter campus in very large city

**General.** Founded in 1975. Accredited by ACICS. **Calendar:** Quarter.

**Annual costs/financial aid.** Students taking 13-16 hours pay an average of $4,630 per quarter, fees included. Personal expenses: $100.

**Contact.** Phone: (205) 802-1200 .
Director of Admissions, Box 19249, Birmingham, AL 35219

## Virginia College at Huntsville
### Huntsville, Alabama
**www.vc.edu**                                              CB code: 3451

⯈ For-profit 4-year business and technical college
⯈ Small city

**General.** Accredited by ACICS. **Calendar:** Continuous.

**Annual costs/financial aid.** Students taking 13-16 hours pay an average of $4,630 per quarter, fees included. Personal expenses: $2,978. Need-based financial aid available to full-time and part-time students.

**Contact.** Phone: (256) 533-7387
Director of Admissions, 2800 Bob Wallace Avenue, Huntsville, AL 35805

# Alaska

## Alaska Bible College
### Glennallen, Alaska
### www.akbible.edu
**CB code: 1237**

◗ Private 4-year Bible college affiliated with nondenominational tradition
◗ Residential campus in rural community

**General.** Founded in 1966. Accredited by ABHE. **Location:** 187 miles from Anchorage, 250 miles from Fairbanks. **Calendar:** Semester.

**Annual costs/financial aid.** Tuition/fees: $7,230. Required fees, covering two semesters, include confirmation enrollment fees ($300) and facilities fees ($90). Room/board: $5,400. Books/supplies: $425. Personal expenses: $1,000. Need-based financial aid available for full-time students.

**Contact.** Phone: (907) 822-3201 ext. 224
Recruiting Specialist, Box 289, Glennallen, AK 99588-0289

## Alaska Pacific University
### Anchorage, Alaska
### www.alaskapacific.edu
**CB code: 4201**

◗ Private 4-year university and liberal arts college affiliated with United Methodist Church
◗ Commuter campus in large city
◗ 427 degree-seeking undergraduates: 41% part-time, 68% women, 4% African American, 2% Asian American, 5% Hispanic American, 17% Native American
◗ 247 graduate students
◗ 10% of applicants admitted
◗ SAT or ACT (ACT writing optional), application essay required

**General.** Founded in 1957. Regionally accredited. **Degrees:** 75 bachelor's, 5 associate awarded; master's offered. **ROTC:** Air Force. **Calendar:** Semester, limited summer session. **Full-time faculty:** 50 total; 64% have terminal degrees, 4% minority, 58% women. **Part-time faculty:** 46 total; 13% have terminal degrees, 2% minority, 59% women. **Class size:** 96% < 20, 4% 20-39. **Special facilities:** Climbing wall, walking trails, lake for canoeing and kayaking, Alaskana collection.

**Freshman class profile.** 1,588 applied, 162 admitted, 28 enrolled.

| Mid 50% test scores | | | |
|---|---|---|---|
| SAT critical reading: | 480-590 | GPA 3.50-3.74: | 16% |
| SAT math: | 480-590 | GPA 3.0-3.49: | 39% |
| SAT writing: | 460-570 | GPA 2.0-2.99: | 25% |
| ACT composite: | 21-26 | Out-of-state: | 75% |
| GPA 3.75 or higher: | 20% | Live on campus: | 93% |

**Basis for selection.** High school record, level of involvement in school and community activities, test scores, writing samples, recommendations most important. **Learning Disabled:** Documentation verifying the disability condition required.

**High school preparation.** 14 units recommended. Recommended units include English 4, mathematics 3, social studies 1, history 1, science 2 (laboratory 1) and foreign language 2.

**2010-2011 Annual costs.** Tuition/fees: $26,360. Room/board: $9,300. Books/supplies: $1,000. Personal expenses: $2,700.

**2009-2010 Financial aid. Need-based:** Average need met was 89%. Average scholarship/grant was $7,500; average loan $3,375. 58% of total undergraduate aid awarded as scholarships/grants, 42% as loans/jobs. **Non-need-based:** Scholarships awarded for academics, alumni affiliation, art, leadership, music/drama, religious affiliation, state residency.

**Application procedures. Admission:** Priority date 12/1; deadline 8/15. $25 fee, may be waived for applicants with need. Admission notification on a rolling basis beginning on or about 1/15. **Financial aid:** Priority date 4/15; no closing date. FAFSA required. Applicants notified on a rolling basis starting 2/1; must reply within 4 week(s) of notification.

**Academics. Special study options:** Accelerated study, distance learning, double major, exchange student, independent study, internships, semester at sea, student-designed major, study abroad, teacher certification program. Eco-League exchange program for Environmental Sciences with Prescott College, Northland College, College of the Atlantic, Antioch College, Green Mountain College. **Credit/placement by examination:** CLEP, IB, SAT, ACT, institutional tests. 22 credit hours maximum toward associate degree, 45 toward bachelor's. Sophomore standing available through AP and IB examinations by earning equivalent of 32 semester hours. **Support services:** Learning center, reduced course load, remedial instruction, study skills assistance, tutoring, writing center.

**Majors. Biology:** Marine. **Business:** Accounting/business management, business admin. **Conservation:** Environmental science, environmental studies, management/policy. **Education:** Elementary, middle. **Health:** Health care admin. **Liberal arts:** Arts/sciences. **Parks/recreation:** Facilities management. **Physical sciences:** Geology. **Psychology:** General. **Public administration:** Human services.

**Most popular majors.** Business/marketing 28%, education 9%, liberal arts 9%, natural resources/environmental science 14%, parks/recreation 16%, psychology 9%, public administration/social services 9%.

**Computing on campus.** 85 workstations in dormitories, library, computer center, student center. Dormitories wired for high-speed internet access. Online course registration, online library, helpline, student web hosting, wireless network available.

**Student life. Freshman orientation:** Mandatory. Usually 10 days long, includes outdoor camping events. **Policies:** Student representation on faculty committees and councils stressed. **Housing:** Guaranteed on-campus for freshmen. Coed dorms, cooperative housing available. $300 deposit, deadline 4/30. **Activities:** Campus ministries, choral groups, drama, international student organizations, literary magazine, music ensembles, student government, student newspaper, art club, business club, environmental club, photography club, psychology club, service club, soccer club, volleyball club.

**Athletics. Team name:** Moose.

**Student services.** Chaplain/spiritual director, career counseling, student employment services, financial aid counseling, minority student services, personal counseling.

**Contact.** E-mail: admissions@alaskapacific.edu
Phone: (907) 564-8248 Toll-free number: (800) 252-7528
Fax: (907) 564-8317
Jennifer Jensen, Director of Admissions, Alaska Pacific University, 4101 University Drive, Anchorage, AK 99508-3051

## Charter College
### Anchorage, Alaska
### www.chartercollege.edu
**CB code: 3453**

◗ Private 4-year junior and technical college
◗ Commuter campus in large city

**General.** Accredited by ACICS. **Calendar:** Continuous.

**Annual costs/financial aid.** Total cost for program resulting in an Associate degree ranges from $21,500 to $30,500; $43,500 to $59,500 for a Bachelor's degree. Costs vary by program and full- or part-time status; includes books and supplies. Books/supplies: $700. Need-based financial aid available to full-time and part-time students.

**Contact.** Phone: (907) 277-1000
Admissions Director, 2221 East Northern Lights Boulevard, Suite 120, Anchorage, AK 99508

## University of Alaska Anchorage
### Anchorage, Alaska
### www.uaa.alaska.edu
**CB member**
**CB code: 4896**

◗ Public 4-year university
◗ Residential campus in large city
◗ 11,878 degree-seeking undergraduates: 42% part-time, 59% women, 3% African American, 8% Asian American, 5% Hispanic American, 10% Native American, 1% international
◗ 970 degree-seeking graduate students

**General.** Founded in 1954. Regionally accredited. **Degrees:** 956 bachelor's, 684 associate awarded; master's offered. **ROTC:** Army, Air Force.

**Location:** 3 miles from downtown. **Calendar:** Semester, extensive summer session. **Full-time faculty:** 617 total; 52% have terminal degrees, 12% minority, 52% women. **Part-time faculty:** 661 total; 3% have terminal degrees, 9% minority, 57% women. **Class size:** 53% < 20, 38% 20-39, 6% 40-49, 4% 50-99, less than 1% >100. **Special facilities:** Centers of justice, rural health, supply chain integration; small business development center, alcohol and addiction studies, community engagement and learning, economic education, economic development, psychological services; institutes of environment and natural resources, circumpolar health studies, social and economic research; North Pacific Fisheries Observer Training Center, American Russian Center, CPISB Planetarium & Visualization Theater.

**Freshman class profile.** 4,259 applied, 3,274 admitted, 1,967 enrolled.

| Mid 50% test scores | | | |
|---|---|---|---|
| SAT critical reading: | 430-540 | GPA 3.0-3.49: | 28% |
| SAT math: | 420-560 | GPA 2.0-2.99: | 47% |
| ACT composite: | 17-24 | Rank in top quarter: | 29% |
| GPA 3.75 or higher: | 12% | Rank in top tenth: | 9% |
| GPA 3.50-3.74: | 9% | Return as sophomores: | 73% |
| | | Out-of-state: | 6% |

**Basis for selection.** Open admission, but selective for some programs. For acceptance into bachelor's program, applications must have high school GPA of at least 2.5 and either SAT, ACT or UAA-approved test scores; high school graduates with GPAs between 2.0 and 2.49 will be admitted on probation. Alternatively, applicants must have successful completion of the GED and either SAT, ACT or UAA-approved test scores. Interviews and essays vary according to program. **Homeschooled:** Transcript of courses and grades required. **Learning Disabled:** Make an appointment with DSS, provide current diagnostic and evaluative reports, and request reasonable accommodations that are supported by documentation.

**High school preparation.** Requirements vary by program.

**2009-2010 Annual costs.** Tuition/fees: $4,806; $14,706 out-of-state. Room/board: $8,605. Books/supplies: $990. Personal expenses: $1,427.

**Financial aid. Non-need-based:** Scholarships awarded for academics, athletics.

**Application procedures. Admission:** Closing date 7/1. $50 fee, may be waived for applicants with need. Application must be submitted online. Admission notification on a rolling basis. Freshman early admit plan allows students to apply early but wait as long as 2 years to enroll. **Financial aid:** Priority date 4/1, closing date 8/1. FAFSA, institutional form required. Applicants notified on a rolling basis starting 3/15; must reply within 4 week(s) of notification.

**Academics.** Many programs to assist nontraditional and/or at-risk students for college success. **Special study options:** Combined bachelor's/graduate degree, cooperative education, cross-registration, distance learning, double major, dual enrollment of high school students, ESL, exchange student, honors, independent study, internships, liberal arts/career combination, semester at sea, student-designed major, study abroad, teacher certification program, Washington semester. **Credit/placement by examination:** AP, CLEP, IB, institutional tests. Credit by examination is considered nonresident credit, and non-resident credit policies apply. **Support services:** Learning center, reduced course load, remedial instruction, study skills assistance, tutoring, writing center.

**Majors. Biology:** General. **Business:** Accounting, business admin, construction management, entrepreneurial studies, finance, hospitality admin, hospitality/recreation, logistics, management information systems, management science, marketing, restaurant/food services. **Communications:** Journalism. **Computer sciences:** Computer science. **Education:** Early childhood, elementary. **Engineering:** General, civil. **Engineering technology:** Electrical, surveying. **Family/consumer sciences:** General. **Foreign languages:** General, French, German, Japanese, Russian, Spanish. **Health:** Health services. **History:** General. **Interdisciplinary:** Biological/physical sciences, math/computer science, natural sciences. **Liberal arts:** Arts/sciences. **Math:** General. **Mechanic/repair:** Aircraft. **Parks/recreation:** Health/fitness. **Philosophy/religion:** Philosophy. **Physical sciences:** Chemistry. **Psychology:** General. **Public administration:** General. **Social sciences:** Anthropology, economics, political science, sociology. **Transportation:** General, air traffic control, airline/commercial pilot, aviation, aviation management. **Visual/performing arts:** Art, dramatic, studio arts.

**Most popular majors.** Business/marketing 19%, education 6%, engineering/engineering technologies 6%, health sciences 16%, psychology 8%, social sciences 6%.

**Computing on campus.** Dormitories wired for high-speed internet access and linked to campus network. Commuter students can connect to campus network. Online course registration, online library, helpline, repair service, student web hosting, wireless network available.

**Student life. Freshman orientation:** Available. Preregistration for classes offered. **Housing:** Coed dorms, special housing for disabled, apartments,

wellness housing available. $200 fully refundable deposit. Separate floors for Alaska natives studying engineering, nursing students, honor students, language and cultures, first-year students under age 20, healthy lifestyle, quiet lifestyle, WWAMI program, Far East exchange program. **Activities:** Jazz band, campus ministries, choral groups, dance, drama, film society, international student organizations, literary magazine, music ensembles, Model UN, musical theater, opera, radio station, student government, student newspaper, Alaska Native student organization, African American student associations, Baha'i club, College Republicans, Korean Campus Crusade for Christ, Intervarsity Christian Fellowship, disability awareness club, Student Organization Against Racism.

**Athletics.** NCAA. **Intercollegiate:** Basketball, cross-country, gymnastics W, ice hockey M, skiing, track and field, volleyball W. **Intramural:** Basketball, ice hockey, soccer, volleyball. **Team name:** Seawolves.

**Student services.** Adult student services, alcohol/substance abuse counseling, career counseling, services for economically disadvantaged, student employment services, financial aid counseling, health services, legal services, minority student services, on-campus daycare, personal counseling, veterans' counselor. **Physically disabled:** Services for visually, speech, hearing impaired. **Learning disabled:** Comprehensive services available.

**Contact.** E-mail: enroll@uaa.alaska.edu
Phone: (907) 786-1480 Fax: (907) 786-4888
Cecile Mitchell, Director of Admissions, University of Alaska Anchorage, PO Box 141629, Anchorage, AK 99514-1629

---

## University of Alaska Fairbanks

**Fairbanks, Alaska**                       CB member
**www.uaf.edu**                             CB code: 4866

- Public 4-year university
- Commuter campus in small city
- 5,273 degree-seeking undergraduates: 34% part-time, 57% women, 3% African American, 3% Asian American, 4% Hispanic American, 19% Native American, 2% international
- 1,113 degree-seeking graduate students
- 74% of applicants admitted
- SAT or ACT (ACT writing optional) required
- 33% graduate within 6 years; 38% enter graduate study

**General.** Founded in 1917. Regionally accredited. Public broadcasting TV and radio stations headquartered on UAF campus; extensive ski and multiuse trail system located on campus; University of the Arctic participating institution. **Degrees:** 483 bachelor's, 193 associate awarded; master's, doctoral offered. **ROTC:** Army. **Location:** 4 miles from downtown. **Calendar:** Semester, limited summer session. **Full-time faculty:** 341 total; 54% have terminal degrees, 43% women. **Part-time faculty:** 708 total; 38% have terminal degrees, 45% women. **Class size:** 62% < 20, 29% 20-39, 4% 40-49, 3% 50-99, less than 1% >100. **Special facilities:** Museum of the North, geophysical institute, bioscience library, institute of arctic biology, arctic region supercomputing center, international arctic research center, boreal forest research range, Alaska native language center, institute of marine sciences, institute of northern engineering, rocketry research range, agricultural and forestry experiment station, botanical garden.

**Freshman class profile.** 2,030 applied, 1,507 admitted, 1,008 enrolled.

| Mid 50% test scores | | | |
|---|---|---|---|
| SAT critical reading: | 450-600 | GPA 2.0-2.99: | 33% |
| SAT math: | 430-590 | Rank in top quarter: | 34% |
| SAT writing: | 420-550 | Rank in top tenth: | 15% |
| ACT composite: | 18-25 | End year in good standing: | 71% |
| GPA 3.75 or higher: | 21% | Return as sophomores: | 80% |
| GPA 3.50-3.74: | 14% | Out-of-state: | 8% |
| GPA 3.0-3.49: | 30% | Live on campus: | 32% |
| | | International: | 1% |

**Basis for selection.** GED not accepted. Minimum 2.5 high school GPA; 2.5 GPA in 16 core classes for bachelor's degree-seeking students. Open admissions for associate degree applicants over age 18. Some students may be required to take ASSET and/or COMPASS tests for additional course placement. Students with high school GPA of 2.5 or higher but less than 3.0 must have ACT composite score of at least 18 or total SAT score of at least 1290 for entry into baccalaureate program. Students with high school GPA below 3.0 and ACT composite score below 18 or total SAT score below 1290 are admitted as pre-majors. Regardless of GPA, ACT and SAT scores are used for placement in English and math classes. **Homeschooled:** Transcript of courses and grades, state high school equivalency certificate required. Students who have completed a state-recognized program and have a valid high school diploma may be admitted to a baccalaureate program. All others admitted via individual review by the UAF admissions office. **Learning Disabled:** Disability services program provides assistance for students with documented disabilities.

**High school preparation.** College-preparatory program required. 16 units required. Required and recommended units include English 4, mathematics 3, social studies 3, science 3 (laboratory 1) and foreign language 2. Mathematics should include 3 from algebra, geometry and trigonometry, precalculus or calculus.

**2009-2010 Annual costs.** Tuition/fees: $5,133; $15,033 out-of-state. Estimated course and lab fees: $500 per year. Room/board: $7,360. Books/supplies: $1,300. Personal expenses: $2,070.

**2008-2009 Financial aid. Need-based:** 577 full-time freshmen applied for aid; 353 were judged to have need; 338 of these received aid. Average need met was 55.8%. Average scholarship/grant was $5,574; average loan $8,377. 29% of total undergraduate aid awarded as scholarships/grants, 71% as loans/jobs. **Non-need-based:** Awarded to 1,115 full-time undergraduates, including 270 freshmen. Scholarships awarded for academics, art, athletics, leadership, minority status, music/drama, ROTC, state residency.

**Application procedures. Admission:** Priority date 2/15; deadline 7/1 (postmark date). $50 fee, may be waived for applicants with need. Admission notification 9/1. Admission notification on a rolling basis. **Financial aid:** Priority date 2/15, closing date 7/1. FAFSA required. Applicants notified on a rolling basis starting 3/1; must reply within 2 week(s) of notification.

**Academics.** Student support services program (federally funded) for students with qualified at-risk status. **Special study options:** Accelerated study, combined bachelor's/graduate degree, cooperative education, distance learning, double major, dual enrollment of high school students, exchange student, external degree, honors, independent study, internships, semester at sea, student-designed major, study abroad, teacher certification program. **Credit/placement by examination:** AP, CLEP, IB, SAT, ACT, institutional tests. Credit awarded for CEEB Advanced Placement Test scores of 3 or greater, International Baccalaureate scores of 4 or better, CLEP, DANTES-DSST, or local credit by exam. Credit by exam is not considered UAF residence credit and is not considered part of the semester course load for classification as a full-time student. For the baccalaureate degree, students are required to complete a minimum of 30 residence credits. **Support services:** Learning center, pre-admission summer program, remedial instruction, study skills assistance, tutoring, writing center.

**Honors college/program.** High school minimum GPA of 3.6 and minimum composite SAT of 1250 (or 1875 including Writing section) or composite ACT 29 for incoming freshmen. University GPA greater than 3.5 required for first-semester college sophomores.

**Majors. Area/ethnic studies:** Native American, Russian/Slavic. **Biology:** General. **Business:** Accounting, business admin, managerial economics. **Communications:** General, journalism. **Computer sciences:** General, computer science. **Conservation:** General, fisheries, forestry, management/policy, wildlife. **Education:** Elementary, music. **Engineering:** Civil, electrical, geological, mechanical, mining, petroleum. **Family/consumer sciences:** Child development. **Foreign languages:** General, Japanese, linguistics, Native American, Russian. **History:** General. **Interdisciplinary:** Biological/physical sciences. **Liberal arts:** Arts/sciences. **Math:** General, applied, statistics. **Philosophy/religion:** Philosophy. **Physical sciences:** Applied physics, chemistry, geology, physics. **Protective services:** Criminal justice. **Psychology:** General. **Public administration:** Community org/advocacy, social work. **Social sciences:** Anthropology, economics, geography, political science, sociology. **Visual/performing arts:** Art, dramatic, music performance, theater design. **Other:** Northern studies, Technology.

**Most popular majors.** Biology 9%, business/marketing 10%, engineering/engineering technologies 11%, psychology 9%, social sciences 8%, visual/performing arts 8%.

**Computing on campus.** 125 workstations in dormitories, library, computer center. Dormitories wired for high-speed internet access and linked to campus network. Commuter students can connect to campus network. Online course registration, online library, helpline, repair service, student web hosting, wireless network available.

**Student life. Freshman orientation:** Mandatory, $75 fee. Preregistration for classes offered. Held over the three days immediately proceeding start of classes each fall and spring term. **Policies:** Student organizations must be officially recognized on an annual basis by the Student Activities Office. **Housing:** Coed dorms, special housing for disabled, apartments, wellness housing available. $350 partly refundable deposit, deadline 8/1. Alaska native cultural housing. **Activities:** Bands, campus ministries, choral groups, dance, drama, international student organizations, literary magazine, music ensembles, Model UN, radio station, student government, student newspaper, symphony orchestra, TV station, Campus Bible Ministries, Baha'i Club, Hillel-Jewish Student Organization, Model United Nations Alliance, Coalition for Peace and Justice, American Indian Science and Engineering Society, Chinese Student Association, Inu-Yupiaq Dance Group, Alaska Native Social Workers Association, American Red Cross,

**Athletics.** NCAA. **Intercollegiate:** Basketball, cross-country, ice hockey M, rifle, skiing, swimming W, volleyball W. **Intramural:** Badminton, basketball, bowling, football (non-tackle), ice hockey, lacrosse, racquetball, soccer, table tennis, volleyball, water polo. **Team name:** Nanooks.

**Student services.** Alcohol/substance abuse counseling, chaplain/spiritual director, career counseling, services for economically disadvantaged, student employment services, financial aid counseling, health services, legal services, minority student services, on-campus daycare, personal counseling, placement for graduates, women's services. **Physically disabled:** Services for visually, speech, hearing impaired.

**Contact.** E-mail: admissions@uaf.edu
Phone: (907) 474-7500 Toll-free number: (800) 478-1823
Fax: (907) 474-5379
Mike Earnest, Director of Admissions, University of Alaska Fairbanks, PO Box 757480, Fairbanks, AK 99775-7480

---

## University of Alaska Southeast

| Juneau, Alaska | CB member |
| www.uas.alaska.edu | CB code: 4897 |

- Public 4-year university and liberal arts college
- Commuter campus in large town
- 1,503 degree-seeking undergraduates: 55% part-time, 68% women
- 351 degree-seeking graduate students
- 92% of applicants admitted

**General.** Founded in 1972. Regionally accredited. All campuses accessible only by ferry or air. **Degrees:** 88 bachelor's, 51 associate awarded; master's offered. **Location:** Downtown. **Calendar:** Semester, limited summer session. **Full-time faculty:** 107 total; 44% have terminal degrees, 6% minority, 46% women. **Part-time faculty:** 117 total; 3% have terminal degrees, 14% minority, 62% women. **Class size:** 76% < 20, 23% 20-39, less than 1% 40-49, less than 1% 50-99. **Special facilities:** Juneau ice field, Mendenhall glacier, Tongass national forest.

**Freshman class profile.** 279 applied, 257 admitted, 255 enrolled.

| Mid 50% test scores | | | |
|---|---|---|---|
| SAT critical reading: | 460-570 | GPA 3.0-3.49: | 31% |
| SAT math: | 450-550 | GPA 2.0-2.99: | 43% |
| SAT writing: | 410-530 | Rank in top quarter: | 24% |
| GPA 3.75 or higher: | 12% | Rank in top tenth: | 10% |
| GPA 3.50-3.74: | 7% | Return as sophomores: | 55% |
| | | Out-of-state: | 8% |

**Basis for selection.** High school record most important. Students not meeting BA requirements counseled to AA or certificate program with possibility of later transfer to BA program. Some BA programs admit students as pre-majors and upon satisfying prerequisites may be admitted to major. Financial statement and immunization records required of international applicants as well as a statement of educational equivalency written in English. SAT or ACT recommended. **Homeschooled:** Student must graduate from accredited home school program or obtain GED.

**High school preparation.** College-preparatory program recommended. Recommended units include English 4, mathematics 2, social studies 3, science 1 (laboratory 1).

**2009-2010 Annual costs.** Tuition/fees: $5,017; $14,917 out-of-state. Tuition reported is for lower division offerings. Room/board: $6,430. Books/supplies: $1,229. Personal expenses: $1,427.

**2008-2009 Financial aid. Need-based:** 155 full-time freshmen applied for aid; 72 were judged to have need; 69 of these received aid. Average need met was 46%. Average scholarship/grant was $1,177; average loan $1,682. 42% of total undergraduate aid awarded as scholarships/grants, 58% as loans/jobs. **Non-need-based:** Awarded to 172 full-time undergraduates, including 64 freshmen. Scholarships awarded for academics, job skills, leadership, music/drama, state residency. **Additional information:** Transfer, continuing, and freshman scholarship deadline March 1.

**Application procedures. Admission:** $40 fee. Admission notification on a rolling basis. Housing deposit refundable if written letter of cancellation provided prior to July 1. **Financial aid:** Priority date 4/15; no closing date. FAFSA required. Applicants notified on a rolling basis starting 3/1; must reply within 3 week(s) of notification.

**Academics. Special study options:** Combined bachelor's/graduate degree, distance learning, double major, dual enrollment of high school students, exchange student, independent study, internships, student-designed major, study abroad, teacher certification program. **Credit/placement by**

**examination:** AP, CLEP, SAT, ACT, institutional tests. 15 credit hours maximum toward associate degree, 30 toward bachelor's. **Support services:** Learning center, pre-admission summer program, remedial instruction, study skills assistance, tutoring, writing center.

**Majors. Biology:** General, marine. **Business:** General, accounting, management science, marketing. **Communications:** General. **Computer sciences:** Networking. **Conservation:** Environmental science. **Education:** Elementary. **Liberal arts:** Arts/sciences. **Math:** General. **Social sciences:** General, political science. **Visual/performing arts:** Art.

**Most popular majors.** Biology 17%, business/marketing 26%, education 8%, liberal arts 27%, social sciences 13%.

**Computing on campus.** 225 workstations in dormitories, library, computer center, student center. Dormitories wired for high-speed internet access and linked to campus network. Commuter students can connect to campus network. Online course registration, online library, helpline, repair service, student web hosting, wireless network available.

**Student life. Freshman orientation:** Mandatory, $75 fee. Preregistration for classes offered. Three-day orientation includes outdoor experiences. **Housing:** Coed dorms, apartments available. $200 deposit, deadline 4/1. **Activities:** International student organizations, student government, student newspaper, global connections club, Amnesty International, backcountry skiing club, gay organization, swing dancing club, rock climbing club, English club, Wooch Een Native student organization.

**Athletics. Intramural:** Badminton, basketball, football (non-tackle) M, racquetball, skiing, softball, tennis, volleyball, weight lifting.

**Student services.** Adult student services, alcohol/substance abuse counseling, career counseling, student employment services, financial aid counseling, health services, minority student services, personal counseling, placement for graduates, veterans' counselor. **Physically disabled:** Services for visually, hearing impaired.

**Contact.**   E-mail: admissions@uas.alaska.edu
Phone: (907) 796-6100 Toll-free number: (877) 465-4827
Fax: (907) 796-6365
Joe Nelson, Admissions Director, University of Alaska Southeast, 11120 Glacier Highway, Juneau, AK 99801-8681

# Arizona

## American Indian College of the Assemblies of God
**Phoenix, Arizona**
www.aicag.edu                                    CB code: 2597

- Private 4-year Bible and teachers college affiliated with Assemblies of God
- Residential campus in very large city
- 83 degree-seeking undergraduates
- 74% of applicants admitted
- SAT or ACT (ACT writing optional), application essay required

**General.** Founded in 1957. Regionally accredited. **Degrees:** 11 bachelor's, 5 associate awarded. **Location:** 15 miles from downtown. **Calendar:** Semester. **Full-time faculty:** 8 total; 38% have terminal degrees, 25% women. **Part-time faculty:** 12 total.

**Freshman class profile.** 43 applied, 32 admitted, 32 enrolled.

| Out-of-state: | 45% | Live on campus: | 78% |
|---|---|---|---|

**Basis for selection.** Applicants must show Christian commitment, willingness to abide by Student Handbook, favorable reference from home pastor, and ability to complete college-level instruction through SAT/ACT score and transcripts. ACT/SAT requirement may be waived by approval of Academic Dean when other evidence of student ability available. **Home-schooled:** Favorable pastoral reference required.

**2009-2010 Annual costs.** Tuition/fees: $7,874. Room/board: $5,232. Books/supplies: $500. Personal expenses: $2,570.

**Application procedures. Admission:** No deadline. No application fee. Admission notification on a rolling basis. Students admitted with proper paperwork through first week of semester. **Financial aid:** Priority date 4/1; no closing date. FAFSA required. Applicants notified on a rolling basis starting 7/15.

**Academics. Special study options:** Accelerated study, double major, ESL, independent study, internships, liberal arts/career combination, teacher certification program. **Credit/placement by examination:** CLEP, institutional tests. **Support services:** Learning center, pre-admission summer program, reduced course load, remedial instruction, study skills assistance, tutoring.

**Majors. Education:** Elementary. **Theology:** Theology.

**Most popular majors.** Education 27%, theological studies 73%.

**Computing on campus.** 39 workstations in library, computer center, student center.

**Student life. Freshman orientation:** Mandatory. Preregistration for classes offered. Pre-registration orientation session. **Policies:** Religious observance required. **Housing:** Guaranteed on-campus for freshmen. Single-sex dorms, special housing for disabled available. Pets allowed in dorm rooms. **Activities:** Choral groups, music ensembles, student government, associated student body, campus missions fellowship.

**Athletics. Intercollegiate:** Basketball. **Intramural:** Basketball. **Team name:** Warriors.

**Student services.** Adult student services, chaplain/spiritual director, career counseling, student employment services, financial aid counseling, personal counseling, placement for graduates.

**Contact.** E-mail: aicadm@aicag.edu
Phone: (602) 943-335 ext. 232 Toll-free number: (800) 933-3828 ext. 232
Fax: (602) 943-8299
Sandra Gonzales, Director of Enrollment Management, American Indian College of the Assemblies of God, 10020 North 15th Avenue, Phoenix, AZ 85021-2199

## Argosy University: Online
**Phoenix, Arizona**
www.online.argosy.edu

- For-profit 4-year virtual university
- 3,044 degree-seeking undergraduates

**General.** Regionally accredited. **Degrees:** 12 bachelor's awarded; master's, doctoral offered. **Calendar:** Continuous. **Full-time faculty:** 69 total. **Part-time faculty:** 519 total.

**Freshman class profile.** 822 enrolled.

**Basis for selection.** Open admission.

**Academics. Credit/placement by examination:** CLEP.

**Majors. Business:** Business admin. **Liberal arts:** Arts/sciences. **Protective services:** Police science. **Psychology:** General.

**Contact.** Phone: (866) 427-4679
Argosy University: Online, 2233 West Dunlap Avenue, Phoenix, AZ 85021

## Argosy University: Phoenix
**Phoenix, Arizona**
www.argosy.edu/phoenix

- For-profit 4-year university
- Very large city
- 109 degree-seeking undergraduates

**General.** Regionally accredited. **Degrees:** 23 bachelor's awarded; master's, doctoral, professional offered. **Calendar:** Continuous. **Full-time faculty:** 22 total. **Part-time faculty:** 51 total.

**Freshman class profile.** 8 enrolled.

**Basis for selection.** Open admission.

**Academics. Credit/placement by examination:** CLEP.

**Majors. Business:** Business admin. **Liberal arts:** Arts/sciences. **Protective services:** Police science. **Psychology:** General.

**Contact.** Phone: (602) 216-2600
Argosy University: Phoenix, 2233 West Dunlap Avenue, Phoenix, AZ 85021

## Arizona State University
**Tempe, Arizona**                                 CB member
www.asu.edu                                        CB code: 4007

- Public 4-year university
- Commuter campus in very large city
- 53,902 degree-seeking undergraduates: 16% part-time, 51% women, 5% African American, 6% Asian American, 16% Hispanic American, 2% Native American, 2% international
- 12,730 degree-seeking graduate students
- 91% of applicants admitted
- SAT or ACT (ACT writing recommended) required
- 56% graduate within 6 years

**General.** Founded in 1885. Regionally accredited. Flagship campus in Tempe; West campus, in northwest Phoenix; Polytechnic campus, located in the growing East Valley. **Degrees:** 11,229 bachelor's awarded; master's, doctoral, professional offered. **ROTC:** Army, Air Force. **Location:** Downtown Phoenix. **Calendar:** Semester, extensive summer session. **Full-time faculty:** 2,520 total; 86% have terminal degrees, 21% minority, 40% women. **Part-time faculty:** 382 total; 49% have terminal degrees, 15% minority, 48% women. **Special facilities:** Biodesign Institute, Global Institute of Sustainability.

**Freshman class profile.** 28,304 applied, 25,616 admitted, 9,344 enrolled.

| Mid 50% test scores | | | |
|---|---|---|---|
| SAT critical reading: | 470-590 | GPA 2.0-2.99: | 22% |
| SAT math: | 480-620 | Rank in top quarter: | 57% |
| ACT composite: | 20-26 | Rank in top tenth: | 31% |
| GPA 3.75 or higher: | 28% | Return as sophomores: | 81% |
| GPA 3.50-3.74: | 18% | Out-of-state: | 29% |
| GPA 3.0-3.49: | 32% | International: | 2% |

**Basis for selection.** Rank in top 25% of class, 3.0 GPA, 22 ACT/1040 SAT (exclusive of writing) required for in-state applicants. In-state requirements plus 24 ACT/1110 SAT (exclusive of Writing) required for out-of-state applicants. Additional requirements for some programs. Please review ASU undergraduate programs for descriptions and major requirements. Auditions, interviews and/or portfolios are required in certain majors. **Home-schooled:** Affidavit of Completion of Secondary School Education required.

**High school preparation.** College-preparatory program required. 16 units required. Required units include English 4, mathematics 4, social studies 1, history 1, science 3 (laboratory 3) and foreign language 2. 1 unit U.S. history recommended, 1 fine arts required. 2 of the same foreign languages recommended for College of Liberal Arts and Sciences. 1 each physics and chemistry required for nursing. 4 math, including calculus, recommended for engineering. Additional requirements vary by program.

**2009-2010 Annual costs.** Tuition/fees: $6,334; $18,919 out-of-state. Room/board: $9,210. Books/supplies: $1,270. Personal expenses: $2,170.

**2008-2009 Financial aid.** **Non-need-based:** Scholarships awarded for academics, art, athletics, leadership, music/drama, ROTC.

**Application procedures.** **Admission:** Priority date 12/1; deadline 2/1. $50 fee ($65 out-of-state). Admission notification on a rolling basis. **Financial aid:** Priority date 3/1; no closing date. FAFSA required. Applicants notified on a rolling basis.

**Academics.** ASU offers internships in many disciplines, study abroad in 60 countries, workstudy programs, accelerated degree programs and a variety of interdisciplinary undergraduate programs. Students may participate in educational programs supported by several institutes and centers. Also available are continuing education programs and summer programs for high school students. **Special study options:** Accelerated study, cooperative education, distance learning, double major, exchange student, honors, independent study, internships, semester at sea, study abroad, teacher certification program, Washington semester. **Credit/placement by examination:** AP, CLEP, IB, SAT, ACT, institutional tests. 60 credit hours maximum toward bachelor's degree. Http://catalog.asu.edu/credit_exam. **Support services:** Learning center, study skills assistance, tutoring, writing center.

**Majors.** **Agriculture:** Business. **Architecture:** Architecture, interior, landscape, urban/community planning. **Area/ethnic studies:** African-American, American, Chicano/Hispanic-American/Latino, Native American, women's. **Biology:** General, biochemistry, botany, conservation, microbiology, molecular. **Business:** Accounting, business admin, construction management, finance, international, management information systems, marketing, nonprofit/public, operations, purchasing, real estate, tourism/travel. **Communications:** General. **Communications technology:** Graphics. **Computer sciences:** General, computer science, systems analysis. **Education:** Early childhood, elementary, music, secondary, special. **Engineering:** General, aerospace, biomedical, chemical, civil, computer, electrical, environmental, industrial, materials, mechanical. **Engineering technology:** Computer, electrical, industrial, manufacturing, mechanical. **Family/consumer sciences:** Aging, family resources, food/nutrition. **Foreign languages:** East Asian, French, German, Italian, Russian, Spanish. **Health:** Communication disorders, music therapy, nursing (RN). **History:** General. **Interdisciplinary:** Global studies, science/society. **Liberal arts:** Arts/sciences, humanities. **Math:** General, applied, computational. **Parks/recreation:** General, exercise sciences. **Philosophy/religion:** Philosophy, religion. **Physical sciences:** Chemistry, geology, physics. **Protective services:** Criminal justice, law enforcement admin. **Psychology:** General. **Public administration:** Social work. **Social sciences:** General, anthropology, economics, geography, political science, sociology, urban studies. **Transportation:** Air traffic control, aviation. **Visual/performing arts:** General, art, dance, dramatic, graphic design, industrial design, music performance, music theory/composition.

**Most popular majors.** Business/marketing 17%, communications/journalism 7%, education 9%, engineering/engineering technologies 6%, interdisciplinary studies 9%, psychology 6%, social sciences 8%, visual/performing arts 6%.

**Computing on campus.** Dormitories wired for high-speed internet access and linked to campus network. Commuter students can connect to campus network. Online course registration, online library, helpline, wireless network available.

**Student life.** **Freshman orientation:** Available, $150 fee. Preregistration for classes offered. **Policies:** ASU has an expectation that first time freshmen live in ASU campus residential facilities. **Housing:** Guaranteed on-campus for freshmen. Coed dorms, special housing for disabled, apartments, fraternity/sorority housing available. $125 nonrefundable deposit. **Activities:** Bands, campus ministries, choral groups, dance, drama, film society, international student organizations, literary magazine, music ensembles, Model UN, musical theater, opera, radio station, student government, student newspaper, symphony orchestra, TV station, 675 organizations available.

**Athletics.** NCAA. **Intercollegiate:** Baseball M, basketball, cross-country, diving, football (tackle) M, golf, gymnastics W, soccer W, softball W, swimming, tennis W, track and field, volleyball W, water polo W, wrestling M. **Intramural:** Badminton, basketball, football (non-tackle), racquetball, soccer, table tennis, tennis, volleyball. **Team name:** Sun Devils.

**Student services.** Adult student services, career counseling, student employment services, health services, legal services, minority student services, on-campus daycare, personal counseling, placement for graduates, veterans' counselor. **Physically disabled:** Services for visually, speech, hearing impaired.

**Contact.** E-mail: ugradinq@asu.edu
Phone: (480) 965-7788 Fax: (480) 965-3610
Martha Byrd, Dean, Undergraduate Admissions, Arizona State University, Box 870112, Tempe, AZ 85287-0112

## Art Center Design College
Tucson, Arizona
www.theartcenter.edu                    CB code: 3037

- For-profit 4-year visual arts college
- Commuter campus in very large city
- 349 degree-seeking undergraduates: 32% part-time, 45% women
- SAT or ACT (ACT writing recommended), application essay, interview required

**General.** **Degrees:** 52 bachelor's, 6 associate awarded. **ROTC:** Army. **Calendar:** Semester, extensive summer session. **Full-time faculty:** 25 total. **Part-time faculty:** 32 total. **Class size:** 3% < 20, 97% 20-39.

**Freshman class profile.**

| Mid 50% test scores | | | |
|---|---|---|---|
| SAT critical reading: | 440-550 | ACT composite: | 16-22 |
| SAT math: | 360-540 | Out-of-state: | 3% |

**Basis for selection.** High school transcripts, ACT/SAT scores, essay, interview, personal statement form required. Admissions based on an evaluation of strengths, academic preparedness and communication skills. Art work required for illustration, fine arts, animation and graphic design programs.

**High school preparation.** College-preparatory program recommended.

**2009-2010 Annual costs.** Tuition/fees: $16,800. Books/supplies: $1,250. Personal expenses: $3,204.

**Financial aid.** All financial aid based on need.

**Application procedures.** **Admission:** No deadline. $25 fee. Admission notification on a rolling basis. **Financial aid:** No deadline. FAFSA required.

**Academics.** **Special study options:** Double major, independent study, internships, liberal arts/career combination. **Credit/placement by examination:** AP, CLEP, IB, SAT, ACT, institutional tests. **Support services:** Learning center, reduced course load, remedial instruction, study skills assistance, tutoring, writing center.

**Majors.** **Architecture:** Landscape. **Business:** Marketing. **Communications:** Advertising. **Communications technology:** Animation/special effects. **Visual/performing arts:** Graphic design, illustration, interior design, photography, studio arts.

**Computing on campus.** 125 workstations in library, computer center, student center. Online course registration, online library, helpline, student web hosting, wireless network available.

**Student life.** **Freshman orientation:** Mandatory. Preregistration for classes offered.

**Student services.** Adult student services, career counseling, student employment services, financial aid counseling, personal counseling, placement for graduates, veterans' counselor.

**Contact.** E-mail: inquire@theartcenter.edu
Phone: (520) 325-0123 Toll-free number: (800) 825-8753
Fax: (520) 325-5535
Sarah LaVetter, Director of Admissions, Art Center Design College, 2525
North Country Club Road, Tucson, AZ 85716

## Art Institute of Phoenix
### Phoenix, Arizona
### www.artinstitutes.edu/phoenix
**CB code: 4003**

- For-profit 3-year culinary school and visual arts college
- Commuter campus in very large city
- 1,125 degree-seeking undergraduates
- Application essay, interview required

**General.** Accredited by ACICS. **Degrees:** 235 bachelor's, 40 associate
awarded. **Calendar:** Quarter, extensive summer session. **Full-time faculty:**
50 total. **Part-time faculty:** 50 total. **Special facilities:** Culinary labs, video
studio, computer labs, editing suites, sound lab.

**Basis for selection.** High school diploma or GED required; high school
GPA considered.

**Application procedures. Admission:** Closing date 10/13 (receipt date).
$50 fee. Admission notification on a rolling basis. **Financial aid:** No dead-
line. FAFSA required.

**Academics. Special study options:** Distance learning, independent study,
internships, study abroad. **Credit/placement by examination:** AP, CLEP,
IB, SAT, ACT, institutional tests. **Support services:** Learning center, reduced course load, remedial instruction, tutoring.

**Majors. BACHELOR'S. Communications technology:** Animation/
special effects. **Computer sciences:** Web page design, webmaster. **Personal/
culinary services:** Culinary arts. **Visual/performing arts:** Cinematography, commercial/advertising art, graphic design, interior design. **ASSOCIATE.
Personal/culinary services:** Culinary arts. **Visual/performing arts:** Graphic
design.

**Student life. Freshman orientation:** Mandatory. Preregistration for classes
offered. **Housing:** Apartments available. $150 fully refundable deposit, dead-
line 10/13. **Activities:** Film society.

**Student services.** Adult student services, career counseling, student employment services, financial aid counseling, personal counseling, placement
for graduates.

**Contact.** E-mail: aipxadm@aii.edu
Phone: (602) 331-7500 Toll-free number: (800) 474-2479
Fax: (602) 331-5301
Denise Patterson, Director of Admissions, Art Institute of Phoenix, 2233
West Dunlap Avenue, Phoenix, AZ 85021-2859

## Art Institute of Tucson
### Tucson, Arizona
### www.artinstitutes.edu/tucson

- For-profit 4-year culinary school and visual arts college
- Commuter campus in very large city
- 353 degree-seeking undergraduates
- Application essay, interview required

**General.** Accredited by ACICS. Selected online courses offered through
consortium agreement with the Art Institute of Pittsburg online division.
**Degrees:** 1 bachelor's, 67 associate awarded. **Location:** 115 miles from
Phoenix. **Calendar:** Quarter, limited summer session. **Full-time faculty:** 7
total. **Part-time faculty:** 9 total. **Special facilities:** Fully equipped fashion
design lab with industrial sewing machines, sergers, dress forms, computer
pattern making software; fully stocked interior design resource room; MAC
lab; PC lab; digital video editing suite; green screen lab; audio lab; video
production, audio, and film editing suites; two kitchens and student-run dining labs.

**Basis for selection.** Open admission, but selective for some programs.
Artwork portfolio required. **Homeschooled:** Transcript of courses and grades,
interview required.

**2009-2010 Annual costs.** Tuition per-credit-hour charge, $467; cost of
starting kit (containing supplies and books) depends upon program.

**Application procedures. Admission:** No deadline. $50 fee. Applica-
tion must be submitted on paper. Admission notification on a rolling basis.

**Academics. Special study options:** Accelerated study. **Credit/
placement by examination:** AP, CLEP. **Support services:** Tutoring.

**Majors. Business:** Fashion. **Communications:** Advertising. **Communications technology:** Animation/special effects. **Computer sciences:** Web page
design. **Personal/culinary services:** Culinary arts. **Visual/performing arts:**
Cinematography, fashion design, graphic design, interior design, photography.

**Computing on campus.** Online library available.

**Student life. Freshman orientation:** Mandatory. Held the Saturday morning before classes begin. **Housing:** Apartments available. **Activities:** Film
society, international student organizations, American Society of Interior
Designers student chapter, fashion club.

**Student services.** Career counseling, student employment services, financial aid counseling, personal counseling, placement for graduates, veterans' counselor. **Learning disabled:** Comprehensive services available.

**Contact.** Phone: (520) 881-2900 Toll-free number: (866) 690-8850
Fax: (520) 881-4794
Gertrude Lomonaco, Senior Director of Admissions, Art Institute of
Tucson, 5099 East Grant Road, #100, Tucson, AZ 85712

## Brown Mackie College: Tucson
### Tucson, Arizona
### www.brownmackie.edu
**CB code: 3458**

- For-profit 4-year career college
- Commuter campus in very large city
- 650 degree-seeking undergraduates
- Interview required

**General.** Accredited by ACICS. **Degrees:** 68 bachelor's, 52 associate awarded.
**Location:** 117 miles from Phoenix. **Calendar:** Continuous. **Full-time faculty:** 20 total; 15% have terminal degrees, 55% minority, 50% women.
**Part-time faculty:** 19 total; 21% have terminal degrees, 63% minority, 74%
women. **Special facilities:** Labs for medical, surgical technology, computer
networking, and occupational therapy assistant programs.

**Basis for selection.** Open admission, but selective for some programs.
Additional admissions criteria for Occupational Therapy Assistant program.
**Homeschooled:** Transcript of courses and grades, state high school equiva-
lency certificate required.

**2009-2010 Annual costs.** Undergraduates in general curriculum pay $294
per credit hour; $310 per-credit-hour charge for surgical technology pro-
gram.

**Application procedures. Admission:** No deadline. No application fee.
Admission notification on a rolling basis.

**Academics. Special study options:** Internships. **Credit/placement by examination:** CLEP. **Support services:** Learning center, remedial instruction,
study skills assistance, tutoring, writing center.

**Majors. Business:** Accounting, business admin. **Computer sciences:** Computer science.

**Computing on campus.** 12 workstations in library. Online library, wireless network available.

**Student life. Freshman orientation:** Mandatory. Conducted prior to first
class.

**Student services.** Career counseling, financial aid counseling, personal
counseling, placement for graduates, veterans' counselor.

**Contact.** E-mail: kowens@brownmackie.edu
Phone: (520) 391-3300 Fax: (520) 325-0108
Karma Owens, Senior Director of Admissions, Brown Mackie College:
Tucson, 4585 East Speedway Boulevard, Tucson, AZ 85712

## College of the Humanities and Sciences
### Tempe, Arizona
### www.chumsci.edu/

- For-profit 4-year liberal arts college
- Small city
- 25 degree-seeking undergraduates: 48% women
- 90 graduate students

## Embry-Riddle Aeronautical University: Prescott Campus
**Prescott, Arizona**
www.embryriddle.edu                    CB code: 4305

- Private 4-year university
- Residential campus in large town
- 1,613 degree-seeking undergraduates: 7% part-time, 18% women
- 45 degree-seeking graduate students
- SAT or ACT (ACT writing optional) required

**General.** Founded in 1978. Regionally accredited. Eastern residential campus in Daytona Beach, Florida. More than 130 continuing education centers located throughout the United States and Europe. **Degrees:** 302 bachelor's awarded; master's offered. **ROTC:** Army, Air Force. **Location:** 100 miles from Phoenix. **Calendar:** Semester, extensive summer session. **Full-time faculty:** 98 total; 70% have terminal degrees, 8% minority, 18% women. **Part-time faculty:** 32 total; 22% have terminal degrees, 3% minority, 44% women. **Class size:** 52% < 20, 46% 20-39, 2% 40-49, less than 1% 50-99. **Special facilities:** Supersonic wind tunnel, fleet of 40 aircraft, engineering and technical center, aviation safety center.

**Freshman class profile.**

| | | | |
|---|---|---|---|
| Out-of-state: | 83% | Fraternities: | 9% |
| Live on campus: | 96% | Sororities: | 12% |

**Basis for selection.** High school GPA, class rank, test scores most important. Specific requirements vary by degree program. Flight program applicants must pass medical examination for Class I or II Federal Aviation Administration Medical Certificate at least 60 calendar days prior to enrollment. Interview and essay recommended.

**High school preparation.** College-preparatory program recommended. 16 units required; 18 recommended. Required and recommended units include English 4, mathematics 3-4, social studies 2, history 1, science 2-3 (laboratory 2-3), foreign language 2 and academic electives 4.

**2009-2010 Annual costs.** Tuition/fees: $27,744. Room/board: $8,212. Books/supplies: $1,200. Personal expenses: $1,448.

**2009-2010 Financial aid. Non-need-based:** Scholarships awarded for academics, alumni affiliation, athletics, leadership, ROTC.

**Application procedures. Admission:** Priority date 1/15; no deadline. $50 fee, may be waived for applicants with need. Admission notification on a rolling basis beginning on or about 11/1. Must reply by May 1 or within 2 week(s) if notified thereafter. Application closing date 60 days prior to start of term. Early application encouraged; available facilities limit enrollment in some programs. **Financial aid:** No deadline. FAFSA required. Applicants notified on a rolling basis starting 3/1; must reply within 4 week(s) of notification.

**Academics. Special study options:** Accelerated study, cooperative education, distance learning, double major, dual enrollment of high school students, ESL, exchange student, honors, independent study, internships. Flight training. **Credit/placement by examination:** AP, CLEP, IB, SAT, ACT, institutional tests. 15 credit hours maximum toward associate degree, 30 toward bachelor's. **Support services:** Remedial instruction, study skills assistance, tutoring, writing center.

**Majors. Engineering:** General, aerospace, computer, electrical, software. **Interdisciplinary:** Science/society. **Physical sciences:** Physics. **Social sciences:** International relations. **Transportation:** Airline/commercial pilot, aviation.

**Most popular majors.** Engineering/engineering technologies 27%, social sciences 13%, trade and industry 45%.

**Computing on campus.** 490 workstations in library, computer center, student center. Dormitories wired for high-speed internet access and linked to campus network. Commuter students can connect to campus network. Online library, helpline, wireless network available.

**Student life. Freshman orientation:** Available. Preregistration for classes offered. Held in August. **Policies:** Free tutoring available. **Housing:** Guaranteed on-campus for freshmen. Coed dorms, apartments available. $250 fully refundable deposit, deadline 7/15. **Activities:** Dance, literary magazine, music ensembles, radio station, student government, student newspaper, Rangers, student activities association, Angel Flight/Silver Wings, residence halls association, Arnold Air Society, Golden Eagles flight team, Greeks, aerobatic club, Japanese anime/manga.

**Athletics.** NAIA. **Intercollegiate:** Soccer, volleyball W, wrestling M. **Intramural:** Basketball, bowling, cross-country, football (non-tackle), golf,

racquetball, soccer, softball, swimming, table tennis, tennis, track and field, volleyball, weight lifting. **Team name:** Eagles.

**Student services.** Adult student services, career counseling, student employment services, health services, personal counseling, placement for graduates, veterans' counselor. **Physically disabled:** Services for visually, speech, hearing impaired.

**Contact.** E-mail: pradmit@erau.edu
Phone: (928) 777-6600 Toll-free number: (800) 888-3728
Fax: (928) 777-6606
Debra Cates-Foster, Director of Admissions, Embry-Riddle Aeronautical University: Prescott Campus, 3700 Willow Creek Road, Prescott, AZ 86301-3720

## Grand Canyon University
**Phoenix, Arizona**
www.gcu.edu/clgbrd                    CB code: 4331

- For-profit 4-year university
- Commuter campus in very large city
- 2,835 full-time, degree-seeking undergraduates
- 12,255 graduate students

**General.** Founded in 1949. Regionally accredited. **Degrees:** 956 bachelor's awarded; master's, doctoral offered. **ROTC:** Army. **Calendar:** Semester, limited summer session. **Full-time faculty:** 52 total; 14% minority, 62% women. **Part-time faculty:** 1,509 total; 1% minority, 56% women. **Class size:** 64% < 20, 35% 20-39, less than 1% 40-49, less than 1% 50-99. **Special facilities:** Cadaver laboratory.

**Basis for selection.** Admissions based on graduation from high school (or GED) and academic potential demonstrated by high school GPA of at least 2.25 or standardized test scores. Any student willing to uphold the University's vision and mission and open to the possibility of spiritual as well as intellectual development is encouraged to apply. **Homeschooled:** Transcript of courses and grades required.

**High school preparation.** College-preparatory program recommended. Recommended units include English 4, mathematics 4, social studies 2, science 3 (laboratory 1) and foreign language 1.

**2009-2010 Annual costs.** Tuition/fees: $17,050. Room/board: $12,400. Books/supplies: $1,200. Personal expenses: $2,400.

**2009-2010 Financial aid. Non-need-based:** Scholarships awarded for academics, alumni affiliation, athletics, leadership, religious affiliation, ROTC.

**Application procedures. Admission:** Closing date 8/22 (receipt date). $175 fee, may be waived for applicants with need. Admission notification on a rolling basis. **Financial aid:** No deadline. FAFSA required. Applicants notified on a rolling basis.

**Academics. Special study options:** Accelerated study, combined bachelor's/graduate degree, cooperative education, distance learning, double major, dual enrollment of high school students, exchange student, honors, independent study, internships, liberal arts/career combination, study abroad, teacher certification program. **Credit/placement by examination:** AP, CLEP, IB, institutional tests. 30 credit hours maximum toward bachelor's degree. **Support services:** Learning center, reduced course load, remedial instruction, tutoring, writing center.

**Majors. Biology:** General, biochemistry. **Business:** Accounting, business admin, entrepreneurial studies, marketing. **Communications:** General, public relations. **Education:** General, biology, chemistry, elementary, English, mathematics, physical, secondary, special. **Health:** Athletic training, nursing (RN). **History:** General. **Parks/recreation:** General, sports admin. **Philosophy/religion:** Religion. **Protective services:** Criminal justice, firefighting. **Psychology:** General. **Social sciences:** Sociology. **Theology:** Bible. **Other:** Medical imaging.

**Most popular majors.** Business/marketing 21%, education 8%, health sciences 53%.

**Computing on campus.** 65 workstations in library, computer center. Dormitories wired for high-speed internet access and linked to campus network. Commuter students can connect to campus network. Online course registration, online library, helpline, wireless network available.

**Student life. Freshman orientation:** Mandatory. Preregistration for classes offered. Held the week before classes. **Policies:** No alcohol and/or candles are allowed. Smoking allowed outdoors only. **Housing:** Guaranteed on-campus for all undergraduates. Coed dorms, special housing for disabled, apartments available. **Activities:** Concert band, campus ministries, choral groups, international student organizations, literary magazine, music ensembles, student government, student newspaper, international student organizations, honors organizations, professional clubs, Christ-purposed relationships, ethnic diversity in Christ, wildlife society, student health advocates.

**Athletics.** NCAA. **Intercollegiate:** Baseball M, basketball, bowling W, cheerleading M, cross-country, golf, lacrosse M, soccer, softball W, swimming, tennis, volleyball, water polo W, wrestling M. **Intramural:** Basketball, bowling, football (non-tackle), softball, volleyball. **Team name:** Lopes.

**Student services.** Alcohol/substance abuse counseling, chaplain/spiritual director, career counseling, student employment services, financial aid counseling, health services, personal counseling, placement for graduates, veterans' counselor, women's services. **Physically disabled:** Services for visually, speech, hearing impaired.

**Contact.** E-mail: admissionsonline@gcu.edu
Phone: (888) 261-2393 Toll-free number: (888) 261-2393
Fax: (602) 589-2017
Karilyn VanOosten, Director of Admissions, Grand Canyon University, 3300 West Camelback Road, Phoenix, AZ 85017

## International Baptist College
### Chandler, Arizona
### www.ibconline.edu

- Private 4-year Bible and seminary college affiliated with Independent Baptist
- Very large city
- 84 degree-seeking undergraduates
- 7 graduate students

**General.** Regionally accredited; also accredited by TRACS. **Degrees:** 12 bachelor's, 1 associate awarded; master's, doctoral offered. **Calendar:** 4-1-4, limited summer session. **Full-time faculty:** 7 total. **Part-time faculty:** 5 total.

**Basis for selection.** Open admission, but selective for some programs.

**2009-2010 Annual costs.** Tuition/fees: $9,660.

**Application procedures. Admission:** No deadline. **Financial aid:** Priority date 8/18; no closing date.

**Academics. Credit/placement by examination:** CLEP.

**Majors. Theology:** Missionary, pastoral counseling, religious ed, sacred music.

**Most popular majors.** Education 62%, theological studies 48%.

**Contact.** E-mail: info@ibconline.edu
Phone: (480) 245-7903 Toll-free number: (800) 422-4858 ext. 7970
Fax: (480) 245-7908
Chris Ball, Enrollment Manager, International Baptist College, 2211 West Germann Road, Chandler, AZ 85286

## ITT Technical Institute: Tempe
### Tempe, Arizona

- For-profit 4-year technical college
- Commuter campus in small city

**General.** Accredited by ACICS. **Calendar:** Quarter.

**Contact.** Phone: (602) 437-7500
Director of Recruitment, 5005 South Wendler Drive, Tempe, AZ 85282

## ITT Technical Institute: Tucson
### Tucson, Arizona
### www.itt-tech.edu
CB code: 3598

- For-profit 4-year technical college
- Commuter campus in large city

**General.** Founded in 1984. Accredited by ACICS. **Calendar:** Quarter.

**Contact.** Phone: (520) 408-7488
Director of Recruitment, 1455 West River Road, Tucson, AZ 85704

## Northcentral University
### Prescott Valley, Arizona
### www.ncu.edu
CB code: 3883

- For-profit 4-year virtual university
- Commuter campus in large town
- 451 degree-seeking undergraduates: 92% part-time, 54% women, 4% African American, 1% Asian American, 1% Hispanic American
- 7,959 degree-seeking graduate students

**General.** Regionally accredited. All courses and programs offered via distance education. **Degrees:** 52 bachelor's awarded; master's, doctoral offered. **Location:** 12 miles from Prescott, 92 miles from Phoenix. **Calendar:** Continuous, extensive summer session. **Full-time faculty:** 8 total. **Part-time faculty:** 411 total.

**Basis for selection.** Open admission.

**2010-2011 Annual costs.** Tuition/fees (projected): $10,470.

**Application procedures. Admission:** No deadline. $50 fee. Application must be submitted online. Admission notification on a rolling basis. **Financial aid:** No deadline. Must reply within 4 week(s) of notification.

**Academics.** Programs are 100% online, with one-on-one faculty mentoring and no residency requirement. **Special study options:** Distance learning. **Credit/placement by examination:** AP, CLEP, IB. **Support services:** Reduced course load, writing center.

**Majors. Business:** General, accounting, business admin, e-commerce, international, management science, marketing. **Computer sciences:** General. **Health:** Health care admin. **Protective services:** Emergency management/homeland security, law enforcement admin. **Psychology:** General. **Public administration:** General.

**Most popular majors.** Business/marketing 71%, psychology 29%.

**Computing on campus.** Commuter students can connect to campus network. Online course registration, online library, helpline available.

**Student life. Freshman orientation:** Available. Preregistration for classes offered.

**Student services.** Adult student services, financial aid counseling.

**Contact.** E-mail: info@ncu.edu
Phone: (928) 776-0331 Toll-free number: (866) 776-0331
Fax: (928) 541-7817
Kevin Lustig, Director of Admissions, Northcentral University, 10000 East University Drive, Prescott Valley, AZ 86314

## Northern Arizona University
### Flagstaff, Arizona
CB member
### www.nau.edu
CB code: 4006

- Public 4-year university
- Residential campus in small city
- 18,044 degree-seeking undergraduates: 15% part-time, 59% women, 3% African American, 3% Asian American, 14% Hispanic American, 5% Native American, 3% international
- 5,014 degree-seeking graduate students
- 73% of applicants admitted
- 50% graduate within 6 years

**General.** Founded in 1899. Regionally accredited. Additional 37 sites across Arizona. **Degrees:** 3,277 bachelor's awarded; master's, doctoral offered. **ROTC:** Army, Air Force. **Location:** 140 miles from Phoenix. **Calendar:** Semester, extensive summer session. **Full-time faculty:** 775 total. **Part-time faculty:** 725 total. **Class size:** 28% < 20, 50% 20-39, 12% 40-49, 8% 50-99, 2% >100. **Special facilities:** 400-acre forest, observatory, high altitude (7,000 feet) training center for athletes.

**Freshman class profile.** 26,334 applied, 19,200 admitted, 3,702 enrolled.

| Mid 50% test scores | | | |
|---|---|---|---|
| SAT critical reading: | 470-580 | GPA 3.0-3.49: | 36% |
| SAT math: | 470-590 | GPA 2.0-2.99: | 19% |
| SAT writing: | 450-560 | Return as sophomores: | 72% |
| ACT composite: | 20-25 | Out-of-state: | 32% |
| GPA 3.75 or higher: | 27% | Live on campus: | 89% |
| GPA 3.50-3.74: | 18% | International: | 2% |

**Basis for selection.** 3.0 GPA, class rank in top quarter; 22 ACT, 24 ACT out-of-state or 1040 SAT (exclusive of Writing), 1110 SAT out-of-state(exclusive of Writing), required for unconditional admission. Conditional admission with 2.5-2.99 GPA, class rank in upper half, and test scores below requirements for unconditional admission. Audition required of music, music education majors. **Homeschooled:** Transcript of courses and grades, state high school equivalency certificate required.

**High school preparation.** 16 units required. Required units include English 4, mathematics 4, social studies 1, history 1, science 3 (laboratory 1) and foreign language 2. Math must include 2 algebra, 1 geometry and 1 year of math after algebra II. One social science must be US history. 1 fine arts required.

**2009-2010 Annual costs.** Tuition/fees: $6,676; $17,902 out-of-state. Room/board: $7,872. Books/supplies: $916. Personal expenses: $2,778.

**2008-2009 Financial aid. Need-based:** 2,611 full-time freshmen applied for aid; 1,619 were judged to have need; 1,546 of these received aid. Average need met was 69%. Average scholarship/grant was $6,074; average loan $3,295. 46% of total undergraduate aid awarded as scholarships/grants, 54% as loans/jobs. **Non-need-based:** Awarded to 5,318 full-time undergraduates, including 1,616 freshmen. Scholarships awarded for academics, alumni affiliation, art, athletics, leadership, minority status, music/drama, ROTC, state residency.

**Application procedures. Admission:** Priority date 3/15; no deadline. $25 fee, may be waived for applicants with need. Admission notification on a rolling basis. **Financial aid:** Priority date 2/14; no closing date. FAFSA required. Applicants notified on a rolling basis starting 3/15.

**Academics. Special study options:** Accelerated study, cooperative education, distance learning, double major, dual enrollment of high school students, ESL, exchange student, honors, independent study, internships, study abroad, teacher certification program. **Credit/placement by examination:** AP, CLEP, IB, SAT, ACT, institutional tests. **Support services:** Learning center, pre-admission summer program, reduced course load, remedial instruction, study skills assistance, tutoring, writing center.

**Honors college/program.** Applicants must complete separate application and have 29 ACT, 1290 SAT (exclusive of Writing), or graduate in top 5% of high school class. Students who do not meet criteria can petition for admission to honors program by submitting completed application and unofficial high school transcript, letter of recommendation, and essay.

**Majors. Area/ethnic studies:** American, Native American, women's. **Biology:** General, animal behavior, aquatic, bacteriology, botany, cell/histology, cellular/molecular, ecology, microbiology, molecular, physiology, wildlife, zoology. **Business:** Accounting, business admin, construction management, fashion, finance, hospitality admin, hotel/motel admin, management information systems, managerial economics, marketing. **Communications:** General, advertising, broadcast journalism, digital media, journalism, public relations, radio/tv. **Computer sciences:** General, computer science. **Conservation:** Environmental science, environmental studies, forest sciences, forestry, wildlife. **Education:** General, art, biology, chemistry, drama/dance, elementary, English, French, German, health, history, mathematics, music, physical, physics, Spanish, special, speech, technology/industrial arts, trade/industrial, voc/tech. **Engineering:** General, civil, computer, electrical, environmental, mechanical, physics. **Engineering technology:** Computer systems, construction. **Foreign languages:** General, French, German, Spanish. **Health:** Athletic training, dental hygiene, health care admin, nursing (RN), premedicine, preveterinary. **History:** General. **Interdisciplinary:** Behavioral sciences, biological/physical sciences. **Legal studies:** Prelaw. **Liberal arts:** Arts/sciences, humanities. **Math:** General, probability. **Parks/recreation:** General, exercise sciences, facilities management, health/fitness. **Philosophy/religion:** Philosophy, religion. **Physical sciences:** General, astronomy, astrophysics, chemistry, geochemistry, geology, hydrology, paleontology, physics, planetary, theoretical physics. **Protective services:** Criminal justice, law enforcement admin. **Psychology:** General. **Public administration:** Policy analysis, social work. **Social sciences:** General, anthropology, cartography, economics, geography, international relations, political science, sociology, U.S. government. **Visual/performing arts:** General, art, art history/conservation, arts management, ceramics, design, dramatic, interior design, metal/jewelry, music history, music performance, painting, photography, printmaking, sculpture, studio arts, voice/opera.

**Most popular majors.** Business/marketing 20%, communications/journalism 6%, education 17%, health sciences 7%, liberal arts 8%, social sciences 8%.

**Computing on campus.** 1,000 workstations in dormitories, library, computer center, student center. Dormitories wired for high-speed internet access and linked to campus network. Commuter students can connect to campus network. Online course registration, online library, helpline, repair service, student web hosting, wireless network available.

**Student life. Freshman orientation:** Available, $150 fee. Preregistration for classes offered. **Policies:** Organizations required to register annually, have 12 or more members with 2.0 GPA to start club, have constitution and bylaws, be approved by ASNAU Senate and Office of Student Life, and officers must have 2.25 GPA. **Housing:** Guaranteed on-campus for all undergraduates. Coed dorms, single-sex dorms, apartments, fraternity/sorority housing available. $150 partly refundable deposit, deadline 5/1. Honor halls, floors for students 21 years of age and older available. **Activities:** Bands, campus ministries, choral groups, dance, drama, international student organizations, music ensembles, musical theater, opera, radio station, student government, student newspaper, symphony orchestra, TV station, Campus Crusade for Christ, Baptist student ministry, Holy Trinity Catholic Newman Center, Hillel at NAU, Episcopal Canterbury Fellowship, Hispanic honor society, African students organization, Asian Americans United, Japanese association.

**Athletics.** NCAA. **Intercollegiate:** Basketball, cross-country, diving W, football (tackle) M, golf W, soccer W, swimming W, tennis, track and field, volleyball W. **Intramural:** Archery, badminton, baseball M, basketball, bowling, cross-country, football (non-tackle), ice hockey M, lacrosse, racquetball, rugby, skiing, soccer, softball, swimming, table tennis, tennis, track and field, volleyball, water polo M. **Team name:** Lumberjacks.

**Student services.** Alcohol/substance abuse counseling, chaplain/spiritual director, career counseling, student employment services, financial aid counseling, health services, minority student services, personal counseling, placement for graduates, veterans' counselor. **Physically disabled:** Services for visually, speech, hearing impaired.

**Contact.** E-mail: undergraduate.admissions@nau.edu
Phone: (928) 523-5511 Toll-free number: (888) 628-2968
Fax: (928) 523-0226
Paul Orscheln, Director of Admissions, Northern Arizona University, PO Box 4084, Flagstaff, AZ 86011-4084.

---

### Prescott College
**Prescott, Arizona**
www.prescott.edu

**CB member**
**CB code: 0484**

- Private 4-year liberal arts college
- Commuter campus in large town
- 763 degree-seeking undergraduates: 17% part-time, 58% women, 2% African American, 1% Asian American, 7% Hispanic American, 2% Native American, 1% international
- 325 degree-seeking graduate students
- 81% of applicants admitted
- SAT or ACT (ACT writing optional), application essay required
- 42% graduate within 6 years

**General.** Founded in 1966. Regionally accredited. **Degrees:** 197 bachelor's awarded; master's, doctoral offered. **Location:** 100 miles from Phoenix. **Calendar:** Semester, limited summer session. **Full-time faculty:** 62 total; 50% have terminal degrees, 6% minority, 50% women. **Part-time faculty:** 23 total; 44% have terminal degrees, 9% minority, 56% women. **Class size:** 100% < 20. **Special facilities:** Marine studies center in Mexico, leadership services counseling & development center.

**Freshman class profile.** 342 applied, 278 admitted, 71 enrolled.

| Mid 50% test scores | | | |
|---|---|---|---|
| SAT critical reading: | 530-650 | GPA 2.0-2.99: | 42% |
| SAT math: | 470-580 | Rank in top quarter: | 32% |
| SAT writing: | 480-620 | Rank in top tenth: | 11% |
| ACT composite: | 19-26 | End year in good standing: | 74% |
| GPA 3.75 or higher: | 15% | Return as sophomores: | 67% |
| GPA 3.50-3.74: | 17% | Out-of-state: | 86% |
| GPA 3.0-3.49: | 20% | Live on campus: | 39% |
| | | International: | 1% |

**Basis for selection.** Essay and GPA most important. Letters of recommendation, any personal additions important. College visit, interview recommended. **Homeschooled:** Documentation consistent with requirements in state of residence.

**High school preparation.** 16 units recommended. Recommended units include English 4, mathematics 3, social studies 1, history 2, science 2 and foreign language 3. One arts unit recommended.

**2009-2010 Annual costs.** Tuition/fees: $23,643. Health insurance is required; cost of school's health insurance is $482 for fall term and $675 for spring term. Room only: $3,630. Books/supplies: $624. Personal expenses: $1,248.

**2009-2010 Financial aid. Need-based:** Average need met was 58%. Average scholarship/grant was $12,131; average loan $3,349. 45% of total undergraduate aid awarded as scholarships/grants, 55% as loans/jobs. **Non-need-based:** Scholarships awarded for academics, alumni affiliation, minority status, state residency.

**Application procedures. Admission:** Priority date 3/1; deadline 8/15 (postmark date). $25 fee, may be waived for applicants with need. Admission notification on a rolling basis beginning on or about 1/1. Must reply by May 1 or within 4 week(s) if notified thereafter. **Financial aid:** Priority date 3/1; no closing date. FAFSA required. Applicants notified on a rolling basis starting 3/15; must reply within 12 week(s) of notification.

**Academics. Special study options:** Cross-registration, distance learning, double major, dual enrollment of high school students, exchange student, external degree, independent study, internships, liberal arts/career combination, student-designed major, teacher certification program. Adult degree program designed for working adults to obtain degree on year-round, part-time basis. Master of arts self-study program available. Programs also available at center in Tucson. **Credit/placement by examination:** AP, CLEP, IB, institutional tests. 20 credit hours maximum toward bachelor's degree. **Support services:** Learning center, reduced course load, tutoring.

**Majors. Agriculture:** General, agronomy, food science, plant breeding, soil science. **Architecture:** Environmental design. **Area/ethnic studies:** Latin American, regional, women's. **Biology:** General, botany, conservation, ecology, environmental, marine, wildlife, zoology. **Business:** General, accounting, business admin, construction management, human resources, nonprofit/public, office management. **Communications:** General, journalism, media studies, photojournalism, radio/tv. **Computer sciences:** General, information systems. **Conservation:** General, environmental science, environmental studies, management/policy, wildlife. **Education:** General, adult/continuing, art, bilingual, biology, business, college student counseling, curriculum, drama/dance, early childhood, early childhood special, elementary, emotionally handicapped, English, foreign languages, history, learning disabled, mathematics, mentally handicapped, multi-level teacher, music, physical, school counseling, science, secondary, social science, social studies, Spanish, special, technology/industrial arts, voc/tech, Waldorf/Steiner teacher. **Family/consumer sciences:** Child development, family studies, family/community services. **Foreign languages:** Comparative lit, Spanish. **Health:** Art therapy, communication disorders, community health services, dance therapy, health care admin, health services, health services admin, mental health counseling, public health ed, recreational therapy. **History:** General. **Interdisciplinary:** Behavioral sciences, biological/physical sciences, global studies, natural sciences, peace/conflict. **Liberal arts:** Arts/sciences, humanities. **Math:** General. **Parks/recreation:** General, facilities management. **Philosophy/religion:** Religion. **Physical sciences:** Geology, planetary. **Psychology:** General, cognitive, community, counseling, developmental, educational, environmental, geropsychology, industrial, medical, social. **Public administration:** Community org/advocacy, human services, policy analysis, social work. **Social sciences:** General, anthropology, geography, international economic development, international relations, political science, sociology. **Visual/performing arts:** General, art, ceramics, cinematography, crafts, dance, dramatic, film/cinema, interior design, painting, photography, play/screenwriting, sculpture, studio arts. **Other:** Alpine geomorphology, Cultural studies, Ethnobotany, Integrated studies of culture, healing, and environment, Management in early childhood education, Natural history, Rehabilitation/therapeutic professions, Social justice, Somatic psychology, Sound arts.

**Most popular majors.** Biology 8%, education 38%, natural resources/environmental science 10%, psychology 14%, public administration/social services 7%.

**Computing on campus.** 50 workstations in dormitories, library, computer center, student center. Dormitories wired for high-speed internet access and linked to campus network. Online library, helpline, wireless network available.

**Student life. Freshman orientation:** Mandatory, $950 fee. Wilderness backpacking orientation offered. Water-based wilderness orientations and community-based orientations offered to those who cannot participate in backpacking session. **Housing:** Coed dorms available. $225 fully refundable deposit, deadline 4/1. **Activities:** Dance, drama, film society, international student organizations, literary magazine, radio station, student government, student newspaper, student environmental network, student chapter of Amnesty International, gender and sexuality alliance, peace and justice center, Aztlan center, service learning program, Maasai community project, student arts council, African-inspired dance gatherings.

**Student services.** Adult student services, career counseling, financial aid counseling, personal counseling, placement for graduates. **Physically disabled:** Services for visually, speech, hearing impaired.

**Contact.** E-mail: admissions@prescott.edu
Phone: (928) 350-2100 Toll-free number: (877) 350-2100
Fax: (928) 776-5242
Tim Robison, Dean of Enrollment Management, Prescott College, 220 Grove Avenue, Prescott, AZ 86301

## Southwestern College
**Phoenix, Arizona**
**www.swcaz.edu**                                              **CB code: 4736**

- Private 4-year Bible and liberal arts college affiliated with Baptist faith
- Residential campus in very large city
- 300 full-time, degree-seeking undergraduates
- 63% of applicants admitted
- SAT or ACT (ACT writing optional), application essay required

**General.** Founded in 1960. Regionally accredited; also accredited by ABHE. **Degrees:** 58 bachelor's, 1 associate awarded. **ROTC:** Naval, Air Force. **Calendar:** Semester, limited summer session. **Full-time faculty:** 10 total. **Part-time faculty:** 37 total.

**Freshman class profile.** 404 applied, 255 admitted, 143 enrolled.

| Mid 50% test scores | | | |
|---|---|---|---|
| SAT critical reading: | 430-640 | SAT writing: | 420-590 |
| SAT math: | 400-630 | ACT composite: | 17-24 |

**Basis for selection.** School achievement record and recommendations very important. Written testimony of conversion experience required for admission. **Homeschooled:** Transcript of courses and grades required. Must present ACT or SAT scores for admission.

**High school preparation.** Recommended units include English 4, mathematics 3, social studies 3, science 2 and foreign language 2.

**2009-2010 Annual costs.** Tuition/fees: $15,094. Room/board: $6,668. Books/supplies: $800. Personal expenses: $1,300.

**Financial aid. Non-need-based:** Scholarships awarded for academics, alumni affiliation, athletics, leadership, minority status, music/drama, religious affiliation.

**Application procedures. Admission:** Priority date 4/30; deadline 8/15. $30 fee, may be waived for applicants with need. Admission notification on a rolling basis. **Financial aid:** Priority date 3/15, closing date 8/31. FAFSA, institutional form required. Applicants notified on a rolling basis.

**Academics.** Off-campus, noncredit Christian internship work required during each semester. **Special study options:** Internships, teacher certification program. **Credit/placement by examination:** AP, CLEP, SAT, ACT. 30 credit hours maximum toward bachelor's degree. **Support services:** Reduced course load, remedial instruction, tutoring.

**Majors. Education:** Elementary, music, secondary. **Philosophy/religion:** Religion. **Psychology:** Family. **Theology:** Bible, missionary, religious ed, sacred music, theology. **Other:** Behavioral health.

**Computing on campus.** 60 workstations in dormitories, library, computer center. Dormitories wired for high-speed internet access. Online library available.

**Student life. Freshman orientation:** Mandatory. Preregistration for classes offered. **Policies:** Religious observance required. **Housing:** Guaranteed on-campus for all undergraduates. Single-sex dorms, apartments available. $100 nonrefundable deposit, deadline 4/30. **Activities:** Jazz band, choral groups, drama, music ensembles, musical theater, student government, student newspaper, symphony orchestra.

**Athletics.** NAIA, NCCAA. **Intercollegiate:** Basketball, cross-country, golf, soccer, volleyball W. **Intramural:** Football (tackle) M, table tennis, tennis, volleyball. **Team name:** Eagles.

**Student services.** Student employment services, financial aid counseling, health services, personal counseling, veterans' counselor.

**Contact.** E-mail: admissions@swcaz.edu
Phone: (602) 386-5300 ext. 100 Toll-free number: (800) 247-2697
Fax: (602) 404-2159
Heather Kim, Chief Enrollment Officer, Southwestern College, 2625 East
Cactus Road, Phoenix, AZ 85032-7042

## University of Advancing Technology
**Tempe, Arizona**
www.uat.edu                                             CB code: 3608

- For-profit 4-year university
- Residential campus in very large city
- 1,090 degree-seeking undergraduates: 10% women, 7% African
  American, 4% Asian American, 6% Hispanic American, 1% Native
  American
- 57 degree-seeking graduate students
- 45% graduate within 6 years

**General.** Founded in 1983. Accredited by ACICS. Bachelor's degree can
be earned in 2 2/3 years. **Degrees:** 163 bachelor's, 6 associate awarded;
master's offcred. **Location:** 7 miles from Phoenix. **Calendar:** Semester,
extensive summer session. **Full-time faculty:** 33 total; 18% have terminal
degrees, 36% women. **Part-time faculty:** 55 total; 6% have terminal degrees, 36% women. **Class size:** 68% < 20, 27% 20-39, 2% 40-49, 3% 50-
99. **Special facilities:** Technology lab, motion capture studio, robotics lab,
digital video studio.

**Freshman class profile.**

Return as sophomores:        63%        Out-of-state:        80%

**Basis for selection.** Academic achievements, leadership experience, career aspirations, hobbies and community and extra-curricular involvement
considered. Acceptance based on previous education, test scores (ACT/
SAT), the student's match with university culture and a passion for technology. SAT or ACT recommended. Test scores considered during admissions
process, but not required unless GPA is not satisfactory. **Homeschooled:**
Transcript of courses and grades, state high school equivalency certificate
required.

**2009-2010 Annual costs.** Tuition/fees: $17,900. Room/board: $10,348.
Books/supplies: $1,000. Personal expenses: $2,900.

**2008-2009 Financial aid. Need-based:** 58% of total undergraduate aid
awarded as scholarships/grants, 42% as loans/jobs.

**Application procedures. Admission:** No deadline. No application fee.
Admission notification on a rolling basis. **Financial aid:** Priority date 4/15;
no closing date. FAFSA required. Applicants notified on a rolling basis;
must reply within 2 week(s) of notification.

**Academics. Special study options:** Accelerated study, distance learning,
double major, independent study, internships, student-designed major. **Credit/
placement by examination:** AP, CLEP, IB, institutional tests. **Support services:** Learning center, tutoring.

**Majors. Communications technology:** Animation/special effects. **Computer sciences:** A.i./robotics, computer forensics, game design, LAN/WAN
management, networking, security, web page design, webmaster. **Engineering:** Software. **Engineering technology:** Robotics. **Other:** Technology management.

**Computing on campus.** 400 workstations in dormitories, library, computer center, student center. Dormitories wired for high-speed internet access and linked to campus network. Commuter students can connect to campus network. Online course registration, online library, helpline, student web
hosting, wireless network available.

**Student life. Freshman orientation:** Mandatory. Preregistration for classes
offered. **Housing:** Guaranteed on-campus for freshmen. Coed dorms, apartments available. $550 partly refundable deposit. **Activities:** Dance, film so-
ciety, student government, student newspaper, Bible study club.

**Athletics. Intercollegiate:** Fencing.

**Student services.** Career counseling, student employment services, financial aid counseling, personal counseling, placement for graduates.

**Contact.** E-mail: admissions@uat.edu
Phone: (602) 383-8228 Toll-free number: (800) 658-5744
Fax: (602) 383-8222
Michelle Wilcox, Manager of Enrollment, University of Advancing
Technology, 2625 West Baseline Road, Tempe, AZ 85283-1056

## University of Arizona
**Tucson, Arizona**                                        CB member
www.arizona.edu                                           CB code: 4832

- Public 4-year university
- Residential campus in very large city
- 30,333 degree-seeking undergraduates: 11% part-time, 52% women,
  4% African American, 7% Asian American, 18% Hispanic American,
  3% Native American, 3% international
- 7,636 degree-seeking graduate students
- 78% of applicants admitted
- Application essay required
- 58% graduate within 6 years

**General.** Founded in 1885. Regionally accredited. Sierra Vista campus
offers credit-bearing classes in general studies and education. **Degrees:** 5,914
bachelor's awarded; master's, doctoral, professional offered. **ROTC:** Army,
Naval, Air Force. **Location:** 111 miles from Phoenix. **Calendar:** Semester,
extensive summer session. **Full-time faculty:** 1,546 total; 91% have terminal degrees, 17% minority, 36% women. **Part-time faculty:** 407 total; 60%
have terminal degrees, 10% minority, 44% women. **Class size:** 39% < 20,
45% 20-39, 4% 40-49, 6% 50-99, 5% >100. **Special facilities:** Geological
museum, state anthropological museum, planetarium, observatory, center
for creative photography.

**Freshman class profile.** 24,625 applied, 19,207 admitted, 6,966 enrolled.

| Mid 50% test scores | | | |
|---|---|---|---|
| SAT critical reading: | 460-600 | GPA 2.0-2.99: | 25% |
| SAT math: | 490-620 | Rank in top quarter: | 62% |
| ACT composite: | 21-27 | Rank in top tenth: | 34% |
| GPA 3.75 or higher: | 23% | Return as sophomores: | 78% |
| GPA 3.50-3.74: | 17% | Out-of-state: | 39% |
| GPA 3.0-3.49: | 35% | Live on campus: | 81% |
| | | International: | 3% |

**Basis for selection.** Applicants must be in top 25% of class or have 3.0
GPA; 1110 SAT (exclusive of Writing), 1040 in-state (exclusive of Writing)
or 24 ACT (22 in-state). Conditional admission may be offered to in-state
applicants who meet 1 or more of following: top half of class or 2.5 GPA
and no more than 1 deficiency in any 2 required subjects, (deficiency not
allowed in both math and science). SAT or ACT recommended. Auditions
required of applied music and all performance majors. Portfolios required
for studio art majors. **Homeschooled:** Course work completion information
required. **Learning Disabled:** Separate application for fee-based program
(SALT).

**High school preparation.** College-preparatory program recommended.
16 units required. Required and recommended units include English 4, mathematics 3, social studies 1-2, history 1, science 3 (laboratory 3) and foreign
language 2. One unit fine arts required.

**2009-2010 Annual costs.** Tuition/fees: $6,855; $22,264 out-of-state. Room/
board: $8,614. Books/supplies: $1,000. Personal expenses: $2,368.

**2008-2009 Financial aid. Need-based:** 4,048 full-time freshmen applied for aid; 2,476 were judged to have need; 2,401 of these received aid.
Average need met was 65%. Average scholarship/grant was $7,794; average
loan $3,376. 54% of total undergraduate aid awarded as scholarships/grants,
46% as loans/jobs. **Non-need-based:** Awarded to 7,429 full-time undergraduates, including 2,550 freshmen. Scholarships awarded for academics, art,
music/drama. **Additional information:** Arizona Assurance Program: provides housing, books, and tuition for all new, incoming resident freshmen;
must be Pell-eligible with combined family income less than $42,500; fund-
ing provided as grants, scholarships, and federal work-study.

**Application procedures. Admission:** Closing date 5/1 (postmark date).
$50 fee ($65 out-of-state), may be waived for applicants with need. Admission notification on a rolling basis beginning on or about 11/1. Must reply
by May 1 or within 4 week(s) if notified thereafter. **Financial aid:** Priority
date 3/1; no closing date. FAFSA required. Applicants notified on a rolling
basis starting 4/1; must reply within 3 week(s) of notification.

**Academics. Special study options:** Accelerated study, combined bachelor's/
graduate degree, cooperative education, cross-registration, distance learning, double major, dual enrollment of high school students, ESL, exchange
student, external degree, honors, independent study, internships, liberal arts/
career combination, semester at sea, study abroad, teacher certification program, weekend college. **Credit/placement by examination:** AP, CLEP, IB,
SAT, ACT, institutional tests. 60 credit hours maximum toward bachelor's
degree. **Support services:** Learning center, pre-admission summer program, reduced course load, study skills assistance, tutoring, writing center.

**Majors. Agriculture:** General, agronomy, animal sciences, economics, plant sciences, soil science. **Architecture:** Architecture, urban/community planning. **Area/ethnic studies:** Chicano/Hispanic-American/Latino, East Asian, Latin American, Near/Middle Eastern, women's. **Biology:** General, animal physiology, bacteriology, biochemistry, cell/histology, ecology. **Business:** General, accounting, entrepreneurial studies, finance, human resources, management information systems, managerial economics, marketing, operations. **Communications:** General, journalism, radio/tv. **Computer sciences:** General. **Conservation:** General, environmental studies. **Education:** Art, biology, chemistry, drama/dance, elementary, English, family/consumer sciences, foreign languages, French, German, history, kindergarten/preschool, mathematics, music, physical, physics, science, secondary, social science, social studies, Spanish, special, speech. **Engineering:** General, aerospace, agricultural, chemical, civil, computer, electrical, geological, industrial, materials science, mechanical, mining, physics, systems, water resource. **Engineering technology:** Industrial management. **Family/consumer sciences:** Consumer economics, family studies. **Foreign languages:** Classics, French, German, Italian, linguistics, Russian, Spanish. **Health:** Clinical lab science, communication disorders, health care admin, nursing (RN), preveterinary, speech pathology. **History:** General. **Interdisciplinary:** Nutrition sciences. **Math:** General. **Philosophy/religion:** Judaic, philosophy, religion. **Physical sciences:** Astronomy, chemistry, geology, hydrology, optics, physics. **Protective services:** Law enforcement admin. **Psychology:** General. **Public administration:** General. **Social sciences:** Anthropology, applied economics, geography, political science, sociology. **Visual/performing arts:** General, art history/conservation, dance, dramatic, music performance, musical theater, studio arts, theater design. **Other:** Applied science, Engineering mathematics.

**Most popular majors.** Biology 10%, business/marketing 14%, communications/journalism 8%, education 7%, engineering/engineering technologies 7%, psychology 7%, social sciences 10%.

**Computing on campus.** 2,500 workstations in dormitories, library, computer center, student center. Dormitories wired for high-speed internet access and linked to campus network. Commuter students can connect to campus network. Online course registration, online library, helpline, repair service, student web hosting, wireless network available.

**Student life. Freshman orientation:** Mandatory, $100 fee. Preregistration for classes offered. 2-day program. **Housing:** Coed dorms, single-sex dorms, special housing for disabled, apartments, fraternity/sorority housing available. $300 partly refundable deposit, deadline 5/1. Special housing for honors students available. **Activities:** Bands, campus ministries, choral groups, dance, drama, international student organizations, literary magazine, music ensembles, Model UN, musical theater, opera, radio station, student government, student newspaper, symphony orchestra, TV station, over 400 clubs and organizations available.

**Athletics.** NCAA. **Intercollegiate:** Baseball M, basketball, cross-country, diving, football (tackle) M, golf, gymnastics W, lacrosse M, soccer W, softball W, swimming, tennis, track and field, volleyball W. **Intramural:** Badminton, basketball, bowling, cross-country, diving, football (non-tackle), golf, racquetball, soccer, softball, swimming, table tennis, tennis, track and field, volleyball. **Team name:** Wildcats.

**Student services.** Adult student services, alcohol/substance abuse counseling, chaplain/spiritual director, career counseling, services for economically disadvantaged, student employment services, financial aid counseling, health services, legal services, minority student services, personal counseling, placement for graduates, veterans' counselor, women's services. **Physically disabled:** Services for visually, speech, hearing impaired. **Learning disabled:** Comprehensive services available.

**Contact.** E-mail: appinfo@arizona.edu
Phone: (520) 621-3237 Fax: (520) 621-9799
Paul Kohn, Dean of Admissions, University of Arizona, Robert L. Nugent Building, Tucson, AZ 85721-0040

## University of Phoenix
**Phoenix, Arizona**
www.phoenix.edu
**CB member**
**CB code: 1024**

- For-profit 4-year virtual university
- Commuter campus in very large city
- 390,487 degree-seeking undergraduates: 68% women, 18% African American, 2% Asian American, 8% Hispanic American, 1% Native American, 2% international
- 84,704 degree-seeking graduate students

**General.** Founded in 1976. Regionally accredited. Classes offered in classroom environment and on-line in 39 states, Puerto Rico, Washington DC, Vancouver, British Columbia, Mexico and Europe. **Degrees:** 31,250 bachelor's, 23,828 associate awarded; master's, doctoral offered. **Calendar:** Continuous, extensive summer session. **Full-time faculty:** 1,472 total; 33% have terminal degrees, 18% minority, 47% women. **Part-time faculty:** 31,991 total; 19% have terminal degrees, 27% minority, 54% women.

**Freshman class profile.** 39,752 applied, 39,691 admitted, 39,419 enrolled.

**Return as sophomores:** 40% **International:** 1%

**Basis for selection.** Open admission, but selective for some programs.

**2009-2010 Annual costs.** Tuition/fees: $11,937. Books/supplies: $750.

**Application procedures. Admission:** No deadline. No application fee. Admission notification on a rolling basis. **Financial aid:** No deadline. FAFSA, institutional form required. Applicants notified on a rolling basis.

**Academics.** Online library. **Special study options:** Accelerated study, distance learning, independent study, internships, teacher certification program. **Credit/placement by examination:** AP, CLEP, IB. 30 credit hours maximum toward associate degree, 30 toward bachelor's. **Support services:** Remedial instruction, writing center.

**Majors. Business:** Accounting, accounting/business management, business admin, communications, e-commerce, entrepreneurial studies, finance, hospitality admin, international, logistics, management information systems, management science, marketing, nonprofit/public, office management, retailing. **Communications:** General, organizational. **Computer sciences:** General, database management, information technology, networking, programming, security, systems analysis, web page design, webmaster. **Education:** Elementary, secondary. **Engineering:** Software. **Health:** Facilities admin, health care admin, medical records technology, nursing (RN). **Interdisciplinary:** Behavioral sciences. **Protective services:** Law enforcement admin, security services. **Public administration:** Human services.

**Most popular majors.** Business/marketing 64%, computer/information sciences 9%, health sciences 12%, security/protective services 6%.

**Computing on campus.** Commuter students can connect to campus network. Online library, helpline, wireless network available.

**Student life. Freshman orientation:** Available. **Activities:** International student organizations.

**Student services.** Adult student services, financial aid counseling, personal counseling.

**Contact.** E-mail: chris.alvarado@phoenix.edu
Phone: (866) 766-0766 Toll-free number: (866) 766-0766
Mark Booker, Director of Admissions and Evaluation, University of Phoenix, 4035 South Riverpoint Parkway, Phoenix, AZ 85040-0723

## Western International University
**Phoenix, Arizona**
www.west.edu
**CB code: 1316**

- For-profit 4-year university and business college
- Commuter campus in very large city
- 1,957 degree-seeking undergraduates: 65% women, 10% African American, 2% Asian American, 13% Hispanic American, 3% Native American, 1% international
- 631 degree-seeking graduate students
- 78% of applicants admitted

**General.** Founded in 1978. Regionally accredited. Adult student body. Portfolio evaluation of relevant experience for course credit. **Degrees:** 403 bachelor's, 39 associate awarded; master's offered. **Calendar:** Semester, extensive summer session. **Part-time faculty:** 275 total; 14% have terminal degrees, 17% minority, 34% women.

**Freshman class profile.** 670 applied, 524 admitted, 387 enrolled.

**Basis for selection.** High school diploma or GED must be from regionally accredited or state licensed school. 2.5 GPA required. Interview and essay recommended.

**High school preparation.** Recommended units include English 4, mathematics 3, social studies 2 and science 2.

**2010-2011 Annual costs.** Tuition/fees (projected): $11,250. Books/supplies: $1,068.

**2008-2009 Financial aid.** All financial aid based on need.

**Application procedures. Admission:** No deadline. $25 fee. Admission notification on a rolling basis. **Financial aid:** No deadline. FAFSA, institutional form required. Applicants notified on a rolling basis.

**Academics. Special study options:** Accelerated study, distance learning, double major, honors, independent study, study abroad. **Credit/placement by examination:** AP, CLEP, IB, institutional tests. 24 credit hours maximum toward associate degree, 60 toward bachelor's. Maximum of 60 credits by examination and/or assessment may be counted toward degree; 36 hour residency requirement. **Support services:** Learning center, tutoring, writing center.

**Honors college/program.** Primarily for junior level students. Requirements include 18 credits (9 in residence), recommendation from employer, essay, 3.8 GPA, and good financial standing.

**Majors. Business:** General, accounting, business admin, finance, management information systems, marketing. **Computer sciences:** General. **Liberal arts:** Arts/sciences.

**Most popular majors.** Business/marketing 79%, computer/information sciences 6%, liberal arts 16%.

**Computing on campus.** 195 workstations in library, computer center. Commuter students can connect to campus network. Online course registration, online library, helpline, wireless network available.

**Student life. Freshman orientation:** Mandatory. Preregistration for classes offered. **Policies:** Cultural activities and special seminars/workshops available. **Activities:** International student organizations, Delta Mu Delta, Upsilon Pi Epsilon, Golden Key honor societies.

**Student services.** Adult student services, career counseling, financial aid counseling, veterans' counselor.

**Contact.** Phone: (602) 943-2311 Toll-free number: (866) 948-4636
Fax: (602) 371-8637
Jo Arney, Director of University Student Services, Western International University, 9215 North Black Canyon Highway, Phoenix, AZ 85021-2718

# Arkansas

## Arkansas Baptist College
**Little Rock, Arkansas**
www.arkansasbaptist.edu          CB code: 7301

▸ Private 4-year liberal arts college affiliated with American Baptist Churches in the USA
▸ Residential campus in small city
▸ 734 degree-seeking undergraduates: 19% part-time, 33% women

**General.** Founded in 1884. Regionally accredited. **Degrees:** 15 bachelor's, 16 associate awarded. **Calendar:** Semester, limited summer session. **Full-time faculty:** 20 total. **Part-time faculty:** 26 total. **Special facilities:** African American leadership institute, literacy writing center.

**Basis for selection.** Open admission. Applicants with test scores or GPA below our requirement may be admitted provisionally but must earn 2.0 GPA by end of first semester to continue in good academic standing. **Home-schooled:** Statement describing homeschool structure and mission, interview required.

**High school preparation.** 18 units recommended. Recommended units include English 4, mathematics 4, social studies 1 and science 2. Vocational and agriculture courses also recommended.

**2009-2010 Annual costs.** Tuition/fees: $7,018. Room/board: $7,606. Books/supplies: $700. Personal expenses: $850.

**Financial aid.** All financial aid based on need.

**Application procedures. Admission:** No deadline. $25 fee, may be waived for applicants with need. Admission notification on a rolling basis beginning on or about 6/30. **Financial aid:** Closing date 5/1. FAFSA required. Applicants notified on a rolling basis starting 6/15.

**Academics. Special study options:** Double major, independent study, internships. **Credit/placement by examination:** CLEP, institutional tests. **Support services:** Remedial instruction, tutoring, writing center.

**Majors. Business:** Business admin. **Education:** Elementary. **Social sciences:** General.

**Computing on campus.** Dormitories wired for high-speed internet access. Commuter students can connect to campus network. Helpline, wireless network available.

**Student life. Freshman orientation:** Mandatory, $10 fee. Preregistration for classes offered. Held in August and in January each year. **Policies:** Religious observance required. **Housing:** Single-sex dorms available. $150 nonrefundable deposit. **Activities:** Choral groups, student government, student newspaper, Baptist Student Union, student teacher organization.

**Athletics.** NJCAA. **Intercollegiate:** Basketball, cheerleading M, football (tackle) M. **Team name:** Buffaloes.

**Student services.** Career counseling, student employment services, health services, on-campus daycare, personal counseling, placement for graduates, veterans' counselor.

**Contact.** E-mail: admissions@arkansasbaptist.edu
Phone: (501) 244-5186 Toll-free number: (866) 920-4222
Fax: (501) 372-0321
Rosie Toney, Director of Admissions, Arkansas Baptist College, 1621 Dr. Martin Luther King Drive, Little Rock, AR 72202

## Arkansas State University
**State University, Arkansas**          CB member
www.astate.edu          CB code: 6011

▸ Public 4-year university
▸ Commuter campus in small city
▸ 9,441 degree-seeking undergraduates: 19% part-time, 58% women, 18% African American, 1% Asian American, 1% Hispanic American, 1% Native American, 2% international

▸ 2,078 degree-seeking graduate students
▸ 77% of applicants admitted
▸ SAT or ACT (ACT writing optional) required
▸ 37% graduate within 6 years; 14% enter graduate study

**General.** Founded in 1909. Regionally accredited. **Degrees:** 1,414 bachelor's, 284 associate awarded; master's, doctoral, professional offered. **ROTC:** Army. **Location:** 70 miles from Memphis. **Calendar:** Semester, extensive summer session. **Full-time faculty:** 482 total; 63% have terminal degrees, 18% minority, 50% women. **Part-time faculty:** 172 total; 6% have terminal degrees, 8% minority, 63% women. **Class size:** 37% < 20, 51% 20-39, 7% 40-49, 5% 50-99, less than 1% >100. **Special facilities:** Environmental ecotoxicology research facility, electron microscope facility, geographic information center facility, equine center, plantation, Donald Reynolds center for health sciences.

**Freshman class profile.** 4,118 applied, 3,156 admitted, 1,725 enrolled.

| Mid 50% test scores | | | |
|---|---|---|---|
| SAT critical reading: | 410-540 | Rank in top quarter: | 40% |
| SAT math: | 440-570 | Rank in top tenth: | 20% |
| SAT writing: | 390-520 | End year in good standing: | 80% |
| ACT composite: | 18-24 | Return as sophomores: | 68% |
| GPA 3.75 or higher: | 20% | Out-of-state: | 14% |
| GPA 3.50-3.74: | 14% | Live on campus: | 55% |
| GPA 3.0-3.49: | 24% | International: | 5% |
| GPA 2.0-2.99: | 39% | Fraternities: | 15% |
| | | Sororities: | 12% |

**Basis for selection.** For unconditional admission, must have: minimum of 18 on ACT scores composite, English, math, reading; or comparable scores on the SAT, ASSET, or COMPASS; or a minimum 2.35 high school GPA or minimum GED score of 500. Proof of immunization is required. Proof of registration with selective service is required for all males 18 to 25. Students with no ACT or SAT scores may submit ASSET scores. SAT, SAT Subject Tests, ACT scores must be received by first day of classes for fall term admission. Auditions required of music majors; portfolios required of art majors.

**High school preparation.** College-preparatory program recommended. 16 units recommended. Recommended units include English 4, mathematics 4, social studies 1, history 2, science 3 (laboratory 3) and foreign language 2.

**2009-2010 Annual costs.** Tuition/fees: $6,370; $14,290 out-of-state. Room/board: $5,856. Books/supplies: $1,000. Personal expenses: $3,800.

**2009-2010 Financial aid. Need-based:** 1,444 full-time freshmen applied for aid; 1,235 were judged to have need; 1,235 of these received aid. Average need met was 61%. Average scholarship/grant was $6,850; average loan $3,500. 55% of total undergraduate aid awarded as scholarships/grants, 45% as loans/jobs. **Non-need-based:** Awarded to 3,091 full-time undergraduates, including 694 freshmen. Scholarships awarded for academics, alumni affiliation, art, athletics, leadership, minority status, music/drama, ROTC, state residency.

**Application procedures. Admission:** Closing date 8/23 (receipt date). $15 fee. Admission notification on a rolling basis. **Financial aid:** Priority date 2/15, closing date 7/1. FAFSA, institutional form required. Applicants notified on a rolling basis starting 6/1; must reply within 2 week(s) of notification.

**Academics.** Of the first 59 hours completed in college, students allowed to repeat courses with final grade of less than C. No more than 18 semester hours of course work may be repeated. **Special study options:** Accelerated study, distance learning, double major, dual enrollment of high school students, ESL, exchange student, honors, independent study, internships, study abroad, teacher certification program, Washington semester. **Credit/placement by examination:** CLEP, SAT, ACT, institutional tests. 15 credit hours maximum toward associate degree, 30 toward bachelor's. **Support services:** Learning center, reduced course load, remedial instruction, study skills assistance, tutoring.

**Honors college/program.** Students must have a score of 27 or higher on the ACT or a high school GPA of 3.5 or higher.

**Majors. Agriculture:** General, agribusiness operations, animal sciences, plant sciences. **Biology:** General. **Business:** Accounting, business admin, finance, international, managerial economics, marketing. **Communications:** Digital media, journalism, radio/tv. **Communications technology:** Graphic/printing. **Computer sciences:** General, data processing. **Conservation:** Wildlife. **Education:** Agricultural, biology, business, chemistry, early childhood, English, ESL, foreign languages, mathematics, middle, music, physical, physics, social science, Spanish, special. **Engineering:** General, civil, electrical, mechanical. **Engineering technology:** General. **Foreign languages:** Linguistics. **Health:** Athletic training, audiology/speech pathology, clinical lab science, medical radiologic technology/radiation therapy, nursing (RN). **History:** General. **Math:** General. **Parks/recreation:** Exercise sciences, health/fitness, sports admin. **Philosophy/religion:** Philosophy. **Physical sciences:** Chemistry, physics. **Protective services:** Forensics. **Psychology:** General. **Public administration:** Social work. **Social sciences:** Criminology, economics, geography, political science, sociology. **Visual/performing arts:** Art, commercial/advertising art, dramatic, music performance. **Other:** Manufacturing technology.

**Most popular majors.** Business/marketing 18%, communications/journalism 6%, education 18%, health sciences 14%, liberal arts 7%.

**Computing on campus.** 510 workstations in dormitories, library, computer center, student center. Dormitories wired for high-speed internet access and linked to campus network. Commuter students can connect to campus network. Online course registration, online library, helpline, wireless network available.

**Student life. Freshman orientation:** Mandatory. Preregistration for classes offered. All-day session held on various dates. **Housing:** Coed dorms, single-sex dorms, apartments, fraternity/sorority housing, wellness housing available. $100 fully refundable deposit. Honors living/learning community available. **Activities:** Bands, campus ministries, choral groups, dance, drama, international student organizations, music ensembles, Model UN, musical theater, opera, radio station, student government, student newspaper, symphony orchestra, TV station, Habitat for Humanity, nontraditional student association, Colleges Against Cancer, Black student association, College Democrats, College Republicans, Arkansas State Student Activist, Campus Christian Fellowship.

**Athletics.** NCAA. **Intercollegiate:** Baseball M, basketball, bowling W, cross-country, football (tackle) M, golf, soccer W, tennis W, track and field, volleyball W. **Intramural:** Basketball, bowling, football (non-tackle), golf, racquetball, soccer, softball, table tennis, tennis, volleyball. **Team name:** Red Wolves.

**Student services.** Adult student services, alcohol/substance abuse counseling, career counseling, student employment services, financial aid counseling, health services, minority student services, on-campus daycare, personal counseling, placement for graduates, veterans' counselor. **Physically disabled:** Services for visually, speech, hearing impaired.

**Contact.** E-mail: admissions@astate.edu
Phone: (870) 972-3024 Toll-free number: (800) 382-3030
Fax: (870) 972-3406
Tammy Fowler, Director of Admissions, Arkansas State University, PO Box 1630, State University, AR 72467-1630

## Arkansas Tech University
**Russellville, Arkansas**
www.atu.edu                                    CB code: 6010

- Public 4-year university and liberal arts college
- Commuter campus in large town
- 7,331 degree-seeking undergraduates: 13% part-time, 53% women, 5% African American, 2% Asian American, 4% Hispanic American, 2% Native American, 3% international
- 545 degree-seeking graduate students
- 94% of applicants admitted
- SAT or ACT (ACT writing optional) required
- 42% graduate within 6 years

**General.** Founded in 1909. Regionally accredited. **Degrees:** 973 bachelor's, 165 associate awarded; master's offered. **ROTC:** Army. **Location:** 75 miles from Little Rock, 85 miles from Fort Smith. **Calendar:** Semester, extensive summer session. **Full-time faculty:** 293 total; 63% have terminal degrees, 8% minority, 47% women. **Part-time faculty:** 163 total; 8% have terminal degrees, 4% minority, 60% women. **Class size:** 32% < 20, 52% 20-39, 7% 40-49, 8% 50-99, less than 1% >100. **Special facilities:** Energy center, observatory, technology center.

**Freshman class profile.** 3,304 applied, 3,095 admitted, 1,841 enrolled.

| Mid 50% test scores | | | |
|---|---|---|---|
| SAT critical reading: | 370-530 | Rank in top quarter: | 45% |
| SAT math: | 460-620 | Rank in top tenth: | 19% |
| ACT composite: | 20-26 | Return as sophomores: | 71% |
| GPA 3.75 or higher: | 23% | Out-of-state: | 3% |
| GPA 3.50-3.74: | 17% | Live on campus: | 54% |
| GPA 3.0-3.49: | 27% | International: | 1% |
| GPA 2.0-2.99: | 31% | Fraternities: | 5% |
| | | Sororities: | 7% |

**Basis for selection.** Secondary school record and standardized test scores are very important; class rank is considered. **Homeschooled:** Documentation of home school completion with a composite ACT of 19 or greater.

**High school preparation.** College-preparatory program recommended. 4 units required; 20.5 recommended. Required and recommended units include English 4, mathematics 4, social studies 3, science 3 (laboratory 3), foreign language 2, visual/performing arts .5 and academic electives 4.

**2009-2010 Annual costs.** Tuition/fees: $5,610; $10,620 out-of-state. Room/board: $5,156. Books/supplies: $1,380. Personal expenses: $2,498.

**2008-2009 Financial aid. Need-based:** 1,170 full-time freshmen applied for aid; 896 were judged to have need; 870 of these received aid. Average need met was 73%. Average scholarship/grant was $4,064; average loan $2,835. 51% of total undergraduate aid awarded as scholarships/grants, 49% as loans/jobs. **Non-need-based:** Awarded to 2,290 full-time undergraduates, including 856 freshmen. Scholarships awarded for academics, athletics, leadership, music/drama, ROTC, state residency.

**Application procedures. Admission:** No deadline. No application fee. Admission notification on a rolling basis. Students can postpone their enrollment for one semester. **Financial aid:** Priority date 4/15; no closing date. FAFSA, institutional form required. Applicants notified on a rolling basis starting 5/1; must reply within 2 week(s) of notification.

**Academics. Special study options:** Distance learning, double major, dual enrollment of high school students, ESL, honors, independent study, internships, study abroad, teacher certification program. **Credit/placement by examination:** AP, CLEP, IB, SAT, ACT, institutional tests. 30 credit hours maximum toward associate degree, 30 toward bachelor's. **Support services:** Learning center, reduced course load, remedial instruction, study skills assistance, tutoring, writing center.

**Honors college/program.** Minimum GPA of 3.5 and ACT score of 23. Target of 23 students per year. Honors students required to take honors classes throughout their stay at ATU.

**Majors. Agriculture:** Agribusiness operations. **Biology:** General. **Business:** Accounting, business admin, hospitality admin. **Communications:** Journalism. **Computer sciences:** General, information technology, systems analysis. **Conservation:** General. **Education:** Art, biology, business, chemistry, early childhood, elementary, English, foreign languages, mathematics, middle, music, physical, science, social studies, speech. **Engineering:** Electrical, mechanical, physics. **Foreign languages:** General. **Health:** Clinical lab science, medical records admin, nursing (RN). **History:** General. **Interdisciplinary:** Global studies. **Math:** General. **Parks/recreation:** Facilities management. **Physical sciences:** General, chemistry, geology. **Protective services:** Emergency management/homeland security. **Psychology:** General. **Social sciences:** Economics, sociology. **Visual/performing arts:** Art.

**Most popular majors.** Business/marketing 12%, education 20%, English 6%, health sciences 13%.

**Computing on campus.** 700 workstations in dormitories, library, computer center, student center. Dormitories wired for high-speed internet access and linked to campus network. Commuter students can connect to campus network. Online course registration, online library, helpline, wireless network available.

**Student life. Freshman orientation:** Mandatory. Preregistration for classes offered. **Housing:** Guaranteed on-campus for freshmen. Coed dorms, single-sex dorms, special housing for disabled, apartments, fraternity/sorority housing available. $25 nonrefundable deposit. **Activities:** Bands, campus ministries, choral groups, dance, drama, international student organizations, literary magazine, music ensembles, musical theater, radio station, student government, student newspaper, TV station.

**Athletics.** NCAA. **Intercollegiate:** Baseball M, basketball, cross-country W, football (tackle) M, golf, softball W, tennis W, volleyball W. **Intramural:** Basketball, bowling, cheerleading, cross-country, football (tackle), golf, racquetball, soccer, softball, swimming, table tennis, tennis, volleyball. **Team name:** Wonder Boys, Golden Suns.

**Student services.** Adult student services, alcohol/substance abuse counseling, career counseling, services for economically disadvantaged, student employment services, financial aid counseling, health services, minority student services, personal counseling, placement for graduates, veterans' counselor. **Physically disabled:** Services for visually, speech, hearing impaired.

**Contact.** E-mail: tech.enroll@atu.edu
Phone: (479) 968-0343 Toll-free number: (800) 582-6953
Fax: (479) 964-0522
Shauna Donnell, Assistant Vice President for Enrollment Management, Arkansas Tech University, 1605 Coliseum Drive Suite 141, Russellville, AR 72801-2222

## Central Baptist College
Conway, Arkansas
www.cbc.edu                                    CB code: 0788

♦ Private 4-year Bible and junior college affiliated with Baptist faith
♦ Commuter campus in large town
♦ 621 degree-seeking undergraduates: 16% part-time, 46% women, 17% African American, 2% Hispanic American, 1% Native American, 3% international
♦ 75% of applicants admitted
♦ ACT (writing optional) required
♦ 35% graduate within 6 years

**General.** Founded in 1952. Regionally accredited. **Degrees:** 54 bachelor's, 35 associate awarded. **ROTC:** Army. **Location:** 30 miles from Little Rock. **Calendar:** Semester, limited summer session. **Full-time faculty:** 19 total; 42% have terminal degrees, 10% minority, 42% women. **Part-time faculty:** 37 total; 11% have terminal degrees, 14% minority, 43% women.

**Freshman class profile.** 183 applied, 138 admitted, 127 enrolled.

| Mid 50% test scores | | | |
|---|---|---|---|
| ACT composite: | 17-24 | GPA 3.0-3.49: | 28% |
| GPA 3.75 or higher: | 14% | GPA 2.0-2.99: | 35% |
| GPA 3.50-3.74: | 21% | International: | 2% |

**Basis for selection.** Religious commitment most important, followed by school achievement record. **Homeschooled:** Statement describing home-school structure and mission, transcript of courses and grades required.

**High school preparation.** College-preparatory program recommended. 15 units recommended. Recommended units include English 4, mathematics 2, social studies 2 and science 2.

**2009-2010 Annual costs.** Tuition/fees: $10,010. Room/board: $5,500. Books/supplies: $600. Personal expenses: $800.

**Financial aid. Non-need-based:** Scholarships awarded for academics, athletics, music/drama, religious affiliation.

**Application procedures. Admission:** Closing date 8/15 (postmark date). $25 fee. Admission notification on a rolling basis. **Financial aid:** Priority date 7/1, closing date 8/1. FAFSA required. Applicants notified on a rolling basis starting 4/1.

**Academics. Special study options:** Internships. **Credit/placement by examination:** AP, CLEP, ACT, institutional tests. 15 credit hours maximum toward associate degree, 27 toward bachelor's. **Support services:** Learning center, reduced course load, remedial instruction, study skills assistance, tutoring.

**Majors. Biology:** General, biotechnology. **Business:** Business admin, marketing, organizational behavior. **Computer sciences:** Data processing. **Health:** Health services. **Public administration:** Social work. **Theology:** Bible, sacred music.

**Most popular majors.** Business/marketing 35%, computer/information sciences 13%, liberal arts 7%, social sciences 7%, theological studies 38%.

**Computing on campus.** 52 workstations in library, computer center. Online library, wireless network available.

**Student life. Freshman orientation:** Mandatory, $50 fee. Preregistration for classes offered. **Policies:** Religious observance required. **Housing:** Guaranteed on-campus for freshmen. Single-sex dorms, wellness housing available. $100 partly refundable deposit, deadline 8/15. **Activities:** Choral groups, international student organizations, music ensembles, student government, student newspaper, Association of Baptist Students, College Republicans.

**Athletics.** NAIA, NCCAA. **Intercollegiate:** Baseball M, basketball, golf, soccer, softball W, volleyball W. **Intramural:** Basketball, football (non-tackle), softball, table tennis, tennis, volleyball. **Team name:** Mustangs.

**Student services.** Career counseling, financial aid counseling, health services, personal counseling, veterans' counselor.

**Contact.** E-mail: jwilson@cbc.edu
Phone: (501) 329-6872 Toll-free number: (501) 208-6872
Fax: (501) 329-2941
Jonathan Wilson, Director of Admissions, Central Baptist College, 1501 College Avenue, Conway, AR 72034

## Ecclesia College
Springdale, Arkansas
www.ecollege.edu

♦ Private 4-year Bible and liberal arts college affiliated with interdenominational tradition
♦ Residential campus in large town
♦ 123 degree-seeking undergraduates
♦ ACT (writing optional), application essay required

**General.** Accredited by ABHE. **Degrees:** 22 bachelor's, 2 associate awarded. **Location:** 10 miles from Fayetteville. **Calendar:** Semester, limited summer session. **Full-time faculty:** 1 total. **Part-time faculty:** 35 total.

**Freshman class profile.** 71 applied, 54 admitted, 45 enrolled.

Out-of-state:                25%        Live on campus:               75%

**Basis for selection.** Open admission, but selective for some programs. Recommendations and personal character very important. **Homeschooled:** Interview required.

**High school preparation.** College-preparatory program recommended. Recommended units include English 4, mathematics 3, social studies 3, science 3 and foreign language 1.

**2009-2010 Annual costs.** Tuition/fees: $15,050. Full-time students not living on campus may be subject to additional $750 nonresidents fee/semester. Room/board: $5,010. Books/supplies: $500. Personal expenses: $875.

**2009-2010 Financial aid. Non-need-based:** Scholarships awarded for academics, athletics, leadership, music/drama.

**Application procedures. Admission:** Closing date 8/22 (receipt date). $35 fee. Application must be submitted on paper. Admission notification on a rolling basis. **Financial aid:** No deadline. FAFSA required. Applicants notified on a rolling basis starting 7/1.

**Academics. Special study options:** Double major, dual enrollment of high school students, independent study, internships. **Credit/placement by examination:** CLEP, institutional tests. **Support services:** Remedial instruction, tutoring.

**Majors. Business:** Business admin. **Parks/recreation:** Sports admin. **Theology:** Bible, missionary, pastoral counseling, preministerial, religious ed, sacred music, theology, youth ministry. **Other:** Communication ministries.

**Most popular majors.** Theological studies 95%.

**Computing on campus.** 15 workstations in library, computer center. Dormitories wired for high-speed internet access. Online library, wireless network available.

**Student life. Freshman orientation:** Mandatory. Preregistration for classes offered. **Policies:** Religious observance required. **Housing:** Single-sex dorms, apartments, wellness housing available. **Activities:** Campus ministries, choral groups, drama, music ensembles, student government, Circle K.

**Athletics.** NCCAA. **Intercollegiate:** Baseball M, basketball. **Team name:** Royals.

**Student services.** Alcohol/substance abuse counseling, chaplain/spiritual director, career counseling, financial aid counseling, personal counseling, placement for graduates. **Physically disabled:** Services for visually impaired.

**Contact.** E-mail: admissions@ecollege.edu
Phone: (479) 248-7236 ext. 223 Fax: (479) 248-1455
Titus Hofer, Director of Admissions, Ecclesia College, 9653 Nations Drive, Springdale, AR 72762

## Harding University
Searcy, Arkansas
www.harding.edu                                CB code: 6267

♦ Private 4-year university affiliated with Church of Christ
♦ Residential campus in large town
♦ 4,052 degree-seeking undergraduates: 6% part-time, 53% women, 4% African American, 1% Asian American, 2% Hispanic American, 1% Native American, 6% international
♦ 1,170 degree-seeking graduate students

- 73% of applicants admitted
- SAT or ACT (ACT writing optional) required
- 61% graduate within 6 years

**General.** Founded in 1924. Regionally accredited. **Degrees:** 863 bachelor's awarded; master's, doctoral, professional offered. **Location:** 50 miles from Little Rock, 105 miles from Memphis. **Calendar:** Semester, extensive summer session. **Full-time faculty:** 248 total; 67% have terminal degrees, 3% minority, 31% women. **Part-time faculty:** 199 total; 28% have terminal degrees, 4% minority, 38% women. **Class size:** 50% < 20, 33% 20-39, 9% 40-49, 8% 50-99, less than 1% >100.

**Freshman class profile.** 1,970 applied, 1,430 admitted, 955 enrolled.

| Mid 50% test scores | | | |
|---|---|---|---|
| SAT critical reading: | 490-630 | Rank in top tenth: | 28% |
| SAT math: | 490-640 | End year in good standing: | 89% |
| ACT composite: | 21-28 | Return as sophomores: | 81% |
| GPA 3.75 or higher: | 39% | Out-of-state: | 75% |
| GPA 3.50-3.74: | 20% | Live on campus: | 96% |
| GPA 3.0-3.49: | 26% | International: | 6% |
| GPA 2.0-2.99: | 14% | Fraternities: | 40% |
| Rank in top quarter: | 50% | Sororities: | 42% |

**Basis for selection.** Test scores, academic record, references, interview important. Selective admission with limited openings, students must apply early. Students are encouraged to take rigorous classes in high school. Audition recommended for music majors, portfolio for art majors.

**High school preparation.** College-preparatory program recommended. 15 units required; 20 recommended. Required and recommended units include English 4, mathematics 3-4, social studies 3-4, science 2-4, foreign language 2 and academic electives 3.

**2009-2010 Annual costs.** Tuition/fees: $13,580. Room/board: $5,814. Books/supplies: $900. Personal expenses: $1,800.

**2008-2009 Financial aid. Need-based:** 732 full-time freshmen applied for aid; 516 were judged to have need; 514 of these received aid. Average need met was 83%. Average scholarship/grant was $7,557; average loan $4,163. 41% of total undergraduate aid awarded as scholarships/grants, 59% as loans/jobs. **Non-need-based:** Awarded to 843 full-time undergraduates, including 327 freshmen. Scholarships awarded for academics, alumni affiliation, art, athletics, leadership, music/drama, religious affiliation, ROTC, state residency. **Additional information:** Music scholarships available, audition required.

**Application procedures. Admission:** No deadline. $40 fee. Admission notification on a rolling basis. Early application encouraged. **Financial aid:** Priority date 4/15; no closing date. FAFSA required. Applicants notified on a rolling basis starting 2/15; must reply within 2 week(s) of notification.

**Academics. Special study options:** Accelerated study, combined bachelor's/graduate degree, cooperative education, distance learning, double major, dual enrollment of high school students, ESL, honors, independent study, internships, liberal arts/career combination, study abroad, teacher certification program. **Credit/placement by examination:** AP, CLEP, IB, SAT, ACT, institutional tests. 32 credit hours maximum toward bachelor's degree. **Support services:** Learning center, reduced course load, remedial instruction, study skills assistance, tutoring, writing center.

**Honors college/program.** ACT score of 27 or higher, or SAT of 1220 (exclusive of Writing) or higher. About 200 students admittedeach fall.

**Majors. Area/ethnic studies:** American. **Biology:** General, biochemistry, Biochemistry/biophysics and molecular biology. **Business:** Accounting, business admin, fashion, finance, human resources, international, marketing, sales/distribution. **Communications:** General, advertising, broadcast journalism, digital media, journalism, public relations. **Computer sciences:** Computer science, information technology, web page design. **Education:** Art, biology, chemistry, early childhood, early childhood special, elementary, English, family/consumer sciences, foreign languages, French, health, mathematics, middle, multi-level teacher, music, physical, science, social studies, Spanish, special, speech. **Engineering:** Computer, electrical, mechanical. **Family/consumer sciences:** General, housing. **Foreign languages:** French, Spanish. **Health:** Art therapy, athletic training, clinical lab science, communication disorders, dietetics, health care admin, nursing (RN), predental, premedicine, prepharmacy, preveterinary, speech pathology. **History:** General. **Interdisciplinary:** Global studies. **Legal studies:** Prelaw. **Liberal arts:** Humanities. **Math:** General. **Parks/recreation:** Exercise sciences, sports admin. **Physical sciences:** Chemistry, physics. **Protective services:** Criminal justice. **Psychology:** General. **Public administration:** General, social work. **Social sciences:** General, economics, political science. **Theology:** Bible, missionary, religious ed, theology, youth ministry. **Visual/performing arts:** Art, dramatic, graphic design, interior design, painting, studio arts.

**Most popular majors.** Business/marketing 21%, education 14%, health sciences 14%, liberal arts 8%.

**Computing on campus.** 470 workstations in library, computer center, student center. Dormitories wired for high-speed internet access and linked to campus network. Commuter students can connect to campus network. Online course registration, online library, helpline, repair service, wireless network available.

**Student life. Freshman orientation:** Available, $95 fee. Preregistration for classes offered. Three days of orientation immediately before the start of the fall semester. Includes all activities and meals, plus a t-shirt and academic planner. **Policies:** Religious observance required. **Housing:** Guaranteed on-campus for freshmen. Single-sex dorms, special housing for disabled, apartments, wellness housing available. $130 fully refundable deposit, deadline 5/1. Approved off-campus housing. **Activities:** Bands, campus ministries, choral groups, drama, international student organizations, music ensembles, radio station, student government, student newspaper, symphony orchestra, TV station, College Republicans, College Democrats, Good News Singers, Timothy Club, religious mission campaigns, Multi-cultural Student Action Committee, Harding Athletes as Role Models, Harding in Action.

**Athletics.** NCAA. **Intercollegiate:** Baseball M, basketball, cheerleading M, cross-country, football (tackle) M, golf, soccer, tennis, track and field, volleyball W. **Intramural:** Archery M, basketball, cross-country M, football (non-tackle), golf M, racquetball, soccer, softball, swimming, table tennis M, tennis, track and field, volleyball, weight lifting M. **Team name:** Bisons.

**Student services.** Adult student services, chaplain/spiritual director, career counseling, student employment services, financial aid counseling, health services, minority student services, personal counseling, placement for graduates. **Physically disabled:** Services for visually, speech, hearing impaired.

**Contact.** E-mail: admissions@harding.edu
Phone: (501) 279-4407 Toll-free number: (800) 477-4407
Fax: (501) 279-4129
Glenn Dillard, Assistant Vice President for Enrollment Management, Harding University, 915 East Market Avenue, Searcy, AR 72149-2255

---

## Henderson State University
**Arkadelphia, Arkansas**  CB member
**www.getreddie.com**  CB code: 6272

- Public 4-year university and liberal arts college
- Commuter campus in large town
- 3,073 degree-seeking undergraduates: 10% part-time, 54% women, 21% African American, 1% Asian American, 2% Hispanic American, 1% Native American, 2% international
- 400 degree-seeking graduate students
- 65% of applicants admitted
- SAT or ACT (ACT writing optional) required
- 32% graduate within 6 years

**General.** Founded in 1890. Regionally accredited. **Degrees:** 463 bachelor's awarded; master's offered. **ROTC:** Army. **Location:** 67 miles from Little Rock. **Calendar:** Semester, limited summer session. **Full-time faculty:** 170 total; 68% have terminal degrees, 17% minority, 42% women. **Part-time faculty:** 64 total; 20% have terminal degrees, 5% minority, 67% women. **Class size:** 60% < 20, 35% 20-39, 4% 40-49, 1% 50-99, less than 1% >100. **Special facilities:** Planetarium.

**Freshman class profile.** 2,555 applied, 1,659 admitted, 643 enrolled.

| Mid 50% test scores | | | |
|---|---|---|---|
| SAT critical reading: | 420-580 | GPA 2.0-2.99: | 33% |
| SAT math: | 470-580 | Rank in top quarter: | 42% |
| ACT composite: | 19-25 | Rank in top tenth: | 17% |
| GPA 3.75 or higher: | 17% | Return as sophomores: | 61% |
| GPA 3.50-3.74: | 16% | Out-of-state: | 16% |
| GPA 3.0-3.49: | 33% | Live on campus: | 81% |
| | | International: | 2% |

**Basis for selection.** Applicants must have ACT composite of 19 and minimum 2.5 GPA for unconditional admission. Those not meeting GPA requirement admitted conditionally. Applicants who do not meet minimum test score standards may be admitted through appeal process. Deadline for applying for appeal is July 15. ACT recommended. Test scores must be on file with Admissions prior to registering for classes. Audition recommended for music and theater arts majors. **Homeschooled:** Minimum ACT composite score of 18, transcript required. Completion of college prep curriculum encouraged. **Learning Disabled:** Student Support Disability Services assesses needs of students with learning disabilities.

**High school preparation.** 14 units required; 22 recommended. Required and recommended units include English 4, mathematics 4, social studies 2, history 1 and science 3. Required: 1/2 oral comm, 1/2 fine art, 6 career focus.

**2009-2010 Annual costs.** Tuition/fees: $6,204; $11,304 out-of-state. Room/board: $4,964. Books/supplies: $1,200. Personal expenses: $2,000.

**2009-2010 Financial aid. Need-based:** 593 full-time freshmen applied for aid; 478 were judged to have need; 475 of these received aid. Average need met was 83%. Average scholarship/grant was $11,558; average loan $3,500. 63% of total undergraduate aid awarded as scholarships/grants, 37% as loans/jobs. **Non-need-based:** Scholarships awarded for academics, alumni affiliation, art, athletics, leadership, minority status, music/drama, state residency.

**Application procedures. Admission:** Closing date 7/15 (receipt date). No application fee. Admission notification on a rolling basis. Application closing date July 15 for applicants with ACT score under 18. **Financial aid:** Priority date 4/15; no closing date. FAFSA required. Applicants notified on a rolling basis starting 3/1; must reply within 2 week(s) of notification.

**Academics. Special study options:** Cross-registration, distance learning, honors, internships, liberal arts/career combination, teacher certification program. **Credit/placement by examination:** AP, CLEP, SAT, ACT, institutional tests. 30 credit hours maximum toward bachelor's degree. **Support services:** Learning center, remedial instruction, study skills assistance, tutoring.

**Honors college/program.** Freshmen must have composite ACT of 26 or higher. Approximately 90 admitted. Sophomores must have cumulative GPA of 3.25 or higher to petition committee for admission.

**Majors. Biology:** General. **Business:** General, accounting, management information systems. **Communications:** Journalism. **Computer sciences:** General. **Education:** Art, biology, business, early childhood, middle, social science. **Family/consumer sciences:** General. **Foreign languages:** Spanish. **Health:** Athletic training, clinical lab science, nursing (RN). **History:** General. **Math:** General. **Parks/recreation:** Facilities management. **Physical sciences:** Chemistry, physics. **Psychology:** General. **Public administration:** General, social work. **Social sciences:** Political science, sociology. **Transportation:** Airline/commercial pilot. **Visual/performing arts:** Art, dramatic, music performance.

**Most popular majors.** Business/marketing 14%, education 23%, health sciences 10%, liberal arts 6%.

**Computing on campus.** 125 workstations in dormitories, library, computer center, student center. Dormitories linked to campus network. Commuter students can connect to campus network. Online library, helpline, wireless network available.

**Student life. Freshman orientation:** Mandatory. Preregistration for classes offered. Day-long program for students and parents includes preregistration, signing up for ID and e-mail address. Program held for week in June, again in July if necessary. **Housing:** Guaranteed on-campus for freshmen. Coed dorms, single-sex dorms, cooperative housing available. $50 deposit. Special hall for Honors College participants, special floor for freshman interest groups available. On-campus apartments leased by outside firm available. Two residence halls are co-ed. **Activities:** Bands, choral groups, dance, drama, literary magazine, music ensembles, radio station, student government, student newspaper, TV station, College Republicans, Young Democrats, Student Foundation, Heart & Key service organization, several religious organizations.

**Athletics.** NCAA. **Intercollegiate:** Baseball M, basketball, cross-country, football (tackle) M, golf, softball W, swimming, tennis W, volleyball W. **Intramural:** Soccer M. **Team name:** Reddies.

**Student services.** Career counseling, student employment services, health services, personal counseling, placement for graduates, veterans' counselor. **Physically disabled:** Services for visually, speech, hearing impaired.

**Contact.** E-mail: admissions@hsu.edu
Phone: (870) 230-5028 Toll-free number: (800) 228-7333
Fax: (870) 230-5066
Vikita Hardwrick, Director of Admissions, Henderson State University, 1100 Henderson Street, Arkadelphia, AR 71999-0001

---

## Hendrix College

**Conway, Arkansas**
www.hendrix.edu

**CB member**
**CB code: 6273**

- Private 4-year liberal arts college affiliated with United Methodist Church
- Residential campus in small city

- 1,454 degree-seeking undergraduates: 1% part-time, 56% women, 3% African American, 3% Asian American, 4% Hispanic American, 1% Native American, 3% international
- 7 degree-seeking graduate students
- 81% of applicants admitted
- SAT or ACT (ACT writing optional), application essay required
- 66% graduate within 6 years; 55% enter graduate study

**General.** Founded in 1876. Regionally accredited. **Degrees:** 200 bachelor's awarded; master's offered. **ROTC:** Army. **Location:** 30 miles from Little Rock. **Calendar:** Semester. **Full-time faculty:** 102 total; 95% have terminal degrees, 10% minority, 38% women. **Part-time faculty:** 33 total; 48% have terminal degrees, 6% minority, 58% women. **Class size:** 63% < 20, 34% 20-39, 2% 40-49, 1% 50-99. **Special facilities:** Teaching theater, two pipe organs, access to elephant farm for research and volunteer service, arboretum, ring laser, hybrid rocket lab, climbing wall.

**Freshman class profile.** 1,572 applied, 1,278 admitted, 412 enrolled.

| Mid 50% test scores | | | |
|---|---|---|---|
| SAT critical reading: | 580-700 | Rank in top quarter: | 77% |
| SAT math: | 560-680 | Rank in top tenth: | 49% |
| ACT composite: | 27-32 | End year in good standing: | 94% |
| GPA 3.75 or higher: | 59% | Return as sophomores: | 88% |
| GPA 3.50-3.74: | 16% | Out-of-state: | 52% |
| GPA 3.0-3.49: | 22% | Live on campus: | 99% |
| GPA 2.0-2.99: | 3% | International: | 5% |

**Basis for selection.** Academic competence, scholastic potential, motivation, character, and high school leadership important. High school transcript, application, and school report required. Interview may be required. **Homeschooled:** Interview required. Portfolio required.

**High school preparation.** College-preparatory program required. 14 units recommended. Recommended units include English 4, mathematics 3, social studies 3, science 2 and foreign language 2.

**2009-2010 Annual costs.** Tuition/fees: $30,270. Room/board: $8,664. Books/supplies: $900. Personal expenses: $1,225.

**2009-2010 Financial aid. Need-based:** 338 full-time freshmen applied for aid; 244 were judged to have need; 244 of these received aid. Average need met was 87%. Average scholarship/grant was $20,593; average loan $4,219. 76% of total undergraduate aid awarded as scholarships/grants, 24% as loans/jobs. **Non-need-based:** Awarded to 802 full-time undergraduates, including 256 freshmen. Scholarships awarded for academics, art, leadership, music/drama, religious affiliation.

**Application procedures. Admission:** Priority date 12/1; deadline 8/1 (postmark date). $40 fee, may be waived for applicants with need, free for online applicants. Admission notification on a rolling basis beginning on or about 11/1. Must reply by May 1 or within 4 week(s) if notified thereafter. **Financial aid:** Priority date 2/15; no closing date. FAFSA required. Applicants notified on a rolling basis starting 2/15; must reply by 5/1 or within 4 week(s) of notification.

**Academics. Special study options:** Combined bachelor's/graduate degree, cooperative education, double major, ESL, exchange student, independent study, internships, student-designed major, study abroad, teacher certification program, Washington semester. Hendrix-in-Brussels (Belgium), Hendrix-in-Costa Rica, Hendrix-in-Heilongjiang (China), Hendrix-in-Graz (Austria), Hendrix-in-London (UK), Hendrix-in-Madrid (Spain), Hendrix-in-Oxford (UK), Hendrix-in-Shangai, Hendrix-in-Uganda/Rwanda, Hendrix-in-Florence, Hendrix-in-Turkey, Academia dell 'Arte, other programs with 140 colleges and universities on 6 continents including countries such as Australia, Finland, France, Ghana, Japan. **Credit/placement by examination:** AP, CLEP, IB, SAT, ACT, institutional tests. 6 credit hours maximum toward bachelor's degree. **Support services:** Pre-admission summer program, study skills assistance, tutoring, writing center.

**Majors. Area/ethnic studies:** American. **Biology:** General, Biochemistry/biophysics and molecular biology. **Business:** Accounting. **Computer sciences:** Computer science. **Conservation:** Environmental studies. **Foreign languages:** Classics, French, German, Spanish. **Health:** Health services. **History:** General. **Math:** General. **Parks/recreation:** Exercise sciences. **Philosophy/religion:** Philosophy, religion. **Physical sciences:** Chemical physics, chemistry, physics. **Psychology:** General. **Social sciences:** Anthropology, economics, international relations, political science, sociology. **Visual/performing arts:** Art, dramatic. **Other:** Multi/Interdisciplinary studies, Philosophy/religious studies.

**Most popular majors.** Biology 9%, English 10%, history 8%, philosophy/religious studies 8%, physical sciences 7%, psychology 9%, social sciences 22%, visual/performing arts 7%.

**Computing on campus.** 75 workstations in dormitories, library, computer center, student center. Dormitories wired for high-speed internet access and linked to campus network. Commuter students can connect to campus network. Online course registration, helpline, repair service, student web hosting, wireless network available.

**Student life. Freshman orientation:** Mandatory. 7-day program prior to fall term. **Housing:** Guaranteed on-campus for freshmen. Coed dorms, single-sex dorms, special housing for disabled, apartments available. $350 nonrefundable deposit, deadline 5/1. Suite-style small houses. **Activities:** Bands, campus ministries, choral groups, dance, drama, film society, international student organizations, literary magazine, music ensembles, Model UN, radio station, student government, student newspaper, Students for Black Culture, College Republicans, Young Democrats, environmental group, Amnesty International, BACCHUS, Hendrix Peace Links, religious life council, volunteer action center, Students Promoting the Education of Asian Cultures.

**Athletics.** NCAA. **Intercollegiate:** Baseball M, basketball, cross-country, diving, field hockey W, golf, lacrosse M, soccer, softball W, swimming, tennis, track and field, volleyball W. **Intramural:** Badminton, basketball, cheerleading, football (non-tackle), football (tackle), racquetball, soccer, softball, table tennis, tennis. **Team name:** Warriors.

**Student services.** Alcohol/substance abuse counseling, chaplain/spiritual director, career counseling, student employment services, financial aid counseling, health services, minority student services, personal counseling, placement for graduates. **Physically disabled:** Services for visually impaired.

**Contact.** E-mail: adm@hendrix.edu
Phone: (501) 450-1362 Toll-free number: (800) 277-9017
Fax: (501) 450-3843
Laura Martin, Director of Admission, Hendrix College, 1600 Washington Avenue, Conway, AR 72032-3080

## ITT Technical Institute: Little Rock
**Little Rock, Arkansas**
www.itt-tech.edu                          CB code: 2721

▶ For-profit 4-year technical college
▶ Commuter campus in small city

**General.** Accredited by ACICS. **Calendar:** Quarter.

**Contact.** Phone: (501) 565-5550
Director of Recruitment, 4520 S. University Avenue, Little Rock, AR 72204

## John Brown University
**Siloam Springs, Arkansas**
www.jbu.edu                               CB code: 6321

▶ Private 4-year liberal arts college affiliated with interdenominational tradition
▶ Residential campus in large town
▶ 1,691 degree-seeking undergraduates: 19% part-time, 56% women
▶ 332 degree-seeking graduate students
▶ 73% of applicants admitted
▶ SAT or ACT (ACT writing optional), application essay required
▶ 64% graduate within 6 years

**General.** Founded in 1919. Regionally accredited. **Degrees:** 448 bachelor's awarded; master's offered. **ROTC:** Army, Air Force. **Location:** 30 miles from Fayetteville, 75 miles from Tulsa, Oklahoma. **Calendar:** Semester, limited summer session. **Full-time faculty:** 75 total; 72% have terminal degrees, 4% minority, 21% women. **Part-time faculty:** 55 total; 11% have terminal degrees, 9% minority, 44% women. **Class size:** 51% < 20, 43% 20-39, 6% 40-49. **Special facilities:** Cadaver lab, outdoor renewable energy lab, historical cathedral.

**Freshman class profile.** 846 applied, 616 admitted, 306 enrolled.

| Mid 50% test scores | | | |
|---|---|---|---|
| SAT critical reading: | 520-660 | | |
| SAT math: | 510-640 | | |
| SAT writing: | 510-640 | | |
| ACT composite: | 22-29 | | |
| GPA 3.75 or higher: | 47% | | |
| GPA 3.50-3.74: | 17% | | |
| GPA 3.0-3.49: | 25% | | |

| | |
|---|---|
| GPA 2.0-2.99: | 11% |
| Rank in top quarter: | 60% |
| Rank in top tenth: | 32% |
| Return as sophomores: | 77% |
| Out-of-state: | 69% |
| Live on campus: | 94% |
| International: | 7% |

**Basis for selection.** Test scores, secondary school record, recommendations, essay, interview most important. Special talents, class rank considered. Combined SAT score of 950 (exclusive of Writing), ACT score of 20 or above. Interview recommended. Audition required of music majors; portfolio recommended for art majors. **Homeschooled:** Transcript of courses and grades required.

**High school preparation.** College-preparatory program recommended. Recommended units include English 4, mathematics 3, social studies 2, history 1, science 2 (laboratory 1) and foreign language 2. 4 units of mathematics, 3 science for science and engineering majors; 2 foreign language recommended for home educated students.

**2010-2011 Annual costs.** Tuition/fees: $19,730. Room/board: $7,186. Books/supplies: $700. Personal expenses: $1,350.

**2009-2010 Financial aid. Need-based:** 245 full-time freshmen applied for aid; 126 were judged to have need; 126 of these received aid. Average need met was 50%. Average scholarship/grant was $7,061; average loan $3,042. 60% of total undergraduate aid awarded as scholarships/grants, 40% as loans/jobs. **Non-need-based:** Awarded to 733 full-time undergraduates, including 123 freshmen. Scholarships awarded for academics, alumni affiliation, art, athletics, leadership, music/drama.

**Application procedures. Admission:** Priority date 5/1; no deadline. $25 fee, may be waived for applicants with need. Admission notification on a rolling basis beginning on or about 12/1. Must reply by May 1 or within 2 week(s) if notified thereafter. **Financial aid:** Priority date 3/1; no closing date. FAFSA required. Applicants notified on a rolling basis starting 3/1; must reply within 4 week(s) of notification.

**Academics. Special study options:** Accelerated study, distance learning, double major, dual enrollment of high school students, ESL, exchange student, honors, independent study, internships, liberal arts/career combination, student-designed major, study abroad, teacher certification program, Washington semester. **Credit/placement by examination:** AP, CLEP, IB. 15 credit hours maximum toward associate degree, 30 toward bachelor's. **Support services:** Learning center, reduced course load, remedial instruction, study skills assistance, tutoring, writing center.

**Honors college/program.** Selected by admissions office/honors committee, requirements are high school GPA, SAT/ACT score and interview.

**Majors. Biology:** General, biochemistry. **Business:** Accounting, business admin, construction management, international, marketing. **Communications:** General, broadcast journalism, digital media, journalism, public relations. **Computer sciences:** Computer science. **Conservation:** General. **Construction:** Site management. **Education:** Biology, chemistry, early childhood, English, mathematics, middle, music, social studies. **Engineering:** General. **Family/consumer sciences:** Family/community services. **Foreign languages:** Spanish. **Health:** Athletic training. **History:** General. **Interdisciplinary:** Global studies. **Math:** General. **Parks/recreation:** Exercise sciences, sports admin. **Physical sciences:** Chemistry. **Psychology:** General. **Social sciences:** Political science. **Theology:** Missionary, sacred music, theology, youth ministry. **Visual/performing arts:** Graphic design, illustration, music performance, photography. **Other:** Leadership and management, Renewable energy.

**Most popular majors.** Business/marketing 50%, communications/journalism 6%, education 9%, theological studies 7%, visual/performing arts 7%.

**Computing on campus.** 200 workstations in dormitories, library, computer center, student center. Dormitories wired for high-speed internet access and linked to campus network. Commuter students can connect to campus network. Online course registration, online library, helpline, wireless network available.

**Student life. Freshman orientation:** Mandatory, $75 fee. Preregistration for classes offered. **Policies:** No alcohol, drugs, or tobacco allowed on campus; all applicants required to sign community covenant each year. Religious observance required. **Housing:** Guaranteed on-campus for freshmen. Coed dorms, single-sex dorms, special housing for disabled, apartments available. $200 deposit. **Activities:** Bands, campus ministries, choral groups, dance, drama, film society, international student organizations, literary magazine, music ensembles, musical theater, opera, radio station, student government, student newspaper.

**Athletics.** NAIA. **Intercollegiate:** Basketball, golf M, soccer, tennis, volleyball W. **Intramural:** Baseball M, basketball, football (non-tackle), football (tackle) M, racquetball, soccer, softball, tennis, volleyball. **Team name:** Golden Eagles.

**Student services.** Chaplain/spiritual director, career counseling, student employment services, financial aid counseling, health services, personal counseling, placement for graduates. **Physically disabled:** Services for visually, hearing impaired.

**Contact.** E-mail: jbuinfo@jbu.edu
Phone: (479) 524-7286 Toll-free number: (877) 528-4636
Fax: (479) 524-4196
Don Crandall, Vice President for Enrollment Management, John Brown University, 2000 West University Street, Siloam Springs, AR 72761-2121

## Lyon College
**Batesville, Arkansas**      **CB member**
**www.lyon.edu**      **CB code: 6009**

- Private 4-year liberal arts college affiliated with Presbyterian Church (USA)
- Residential campus in small town
- 592 degree-seeking undergraduates: 2% part-time, 55% women, 4% African American, 1% Asian American, 2% Hispanic American, 1% Native American, 2% international
- 67% of applicants admitted
- SAT or ACT (ACT writing optional) required
- 46% graduate within 6 years; 33% enter graduate study

**General.** Founded in 1872. Regionally accredited. **Degrees:** 83 bachelor's awarded. **Location:** 90 miles from Little Rock. **Calendar:** Semester, limited summer session. **Full-time faculty:** 41 total; 100% have terminal degrees, 10% minority, 24% women. **Part-time faculty:** 22 total; 4% have terminal degrees, 4% minority, 50% women. **Class size:** 76% < 20, 21% 20-39, 3% 40-49. **Special facilities:** Ozark Regional Studies Center.

**Freshman class profile.** 1,110 applied, 749 admitted, 217 enrolled.

| Mid 50% test scores | | | |
|---|---|---|---|
| SAT critical reading: | 470-630 | GPA 2.0-2.99: | 15% |
| SAT math: | 480-590 | Rank in top quarter: | 56% |
| SAT writing: | 440-570 | Rank in top tenth: | 26% |
| ACT composite: | 22-30 | End year in good standing: | 90% |
| GPA 3.75 or higher: | 36% | Return as sophomores: | 63% |
| GPA 3.50-3.74: | 18% | Out-of-state: | 25% |
| GPA 3.0-3.49: | 30% | Live on campus: | 94% |

**Basis for selection.** High school academic performance and standardized test scores are the most important. Personal essays and letters of recommendation are considered on a case by case basis. Math proficiency and placement are judged with ACT math subscores. Auditions or portfolios required for fine arts.

**High school preparation.** College-preparatory program recommended. 16 units required; 18 recommended. Required and recommended units include English 4, mathematics 3-4, social studies 1, history 2, science 3-4 (laboratory 2), foreign language 2 and academic electives 1.

**2009-2010 Annual costs.** Tuition/fees: $19,968. Room/board: $7,340. Books/supplies: $1,000. Personal expenses: $1,000.

**2009-2010 Financial aid. Need-based:** 198 full-time freshmen applied for aid; 165 were judged to have need; 165 of these received aid. Average need met was 84%. Average scholarship/grant was $14,519; average loan $3,166. 78% of total undergraduate aid awarded as scholarships/grants, 22% as loans/jobs. **Non-need-based:** Awarded to 645 full-time undergraduates, including 239 freshmen. Scholarships awarded for academics, art, athletics, leadership, minority status, music/drama, religious affiliation, state residency.

**Application procedures. Admission:** Priority date 1/15; no deadline. $25 fee, may be waived for applicants with need. Admission notification on a rolling basis. Must reply by May 1 or within 2 week(s) if notified thereafter. **Financial aid:** Priority date 3/15; no closing date. FAFSA required. Applicants notified on a rolling basis starting 3/1; must reply by 8/15.

**Academics.** Academic honor code administered by peer-elected student honor council. **Special study options:** Accelerated study, combined bachelor's/graduate degree, cross-registration, double major, dual enrollment of high school students, independent study, internships, student-designed major, study abroad, teacher certification program, Washington semester. **Credit/placement by examination:** AP, CLEP, IB, SAT, ACT, institutional tests. 33 credit hours maximum toward bachelor's degree. **Support services:** Learning center, study skills assistance, tutoring, writing center.

**Majors. Biology:** General, biochemistry. **Business:** Accounting, business admin. **Computer sciences:** Computer science. **Education:** Early childhood. **Foreign languages:** Spanish. **History:** General. **Math:** General. **Philosophy/religion:** Philosophy, religion. **Physical sciences:** Chemistry. **Psychology:** General. **Social sciences:** Economics, political science. **Visual/performing arts:** Art, dramatic.

**Most popular majors.** Biology 21%, business/marketing 27%, English 10%, psychology 16%, visual/performing arts 7%.

**Computing on campus.** 100 workstations in dormitories, library, computer center, student center. Dormitories wired for high-speed internet access and linked to campus network. Commuter students can connect to campus network. Online course registration, online library, helpline, repair service, wireless network available.

**Student life. Freshman orientation:** Mandatory, $150 fee. Preregistration for classes offered. **Policies:** Social code administered by peer-elected student social council. **Housing:** Guaranteed on-campus for all undergraduates. Coed dorms, single-sex dorms, apartments, wellness housing available. $100 fully refundable deposit. Limited college-owned off-campus housing is available. **Activities:** Concert band, campus ministries, choral groups, drama, international student organizations, literary magazine, music ensembles, Model UN, student government, student newspaper, Black students association, Fellowship of Christian Athletes.

**Athletics.** NAIA. **Intercollegiate:** Baseball M, basketball, cheerleading, cross-country, golf, soccer, softball W, volleyball W. **Intramural:** Badminton, basketball, football (non-tackle), softball, table tennis, tennis, volleyball. **Team name:** Scots (M), Pipers (W).

**Student services.** Chaplain/spiritual director, career counseling, financial aid counseling, health services, personal counseling, placement for graduates.

**Contact.** E-mail: admissions@lyon.edu
Phone: (870) 307-7250 Toll-free number: (800) 423-2542
Fax: (870) 307-7542
David Heringer, Vice President for Enrollment Services, Lyon College, PO Box 2317, Batesville, AR 72503-2317

## Ouachita Baptist University
**Arkadelphia, Arkansas**
**www.obu.edu**      **CB code: 6549**

- Private 4-year liberal arts college affiliated with Southern Baptist Convention
- Residential campus in large town
- 1,421 degree-seeking undergraduates: 1% part-time, 53% women, 7% African American, 1% Asian American, 2% Hispanic American, 1% Native American, 3% international
- 67% of applicants admitted
- SAT or ACT (ACT writing optional) required

**General.** Founded in 1886. Regionally accredited. **Degrees:** 296 bachelor's awarded. **ROTC:** Army. **Location:** 65 miles from Little Rock. **Calendar:** Semester, extensive summer session. **Full-time faculty:** 124 total; 74% have terminal degrees, less than 1% minority, 32% women. **Part-time faculty:** 27 total; 15% have terminal degrees, 78% women. **Class size:** 58% < 20, 40% 20-39, 2% 40-49.

**Freshman class profile.** 1,592 applied, 1,061 admitted, 390 enrolled.

| Mid 50% test scores | | | |
|---|---|---|---|
| SAT critical reading: | 470-590 | Rank in top quarter: | 61% |
| SAT math: | 490-610 | Rank in top tenth: | 32% |
| ACT composite: | 21-29 | Out-of-state: | 48% |
| GPA 3.75 or higher: | 43% | Live on campus: | 99% |
| GPA 3.50-3.74: | 17% | International: | 4% |
| GPA 3.0-3.49: | 25% | Fraternities: | 25% |
| GPA 2.0-2.99: | 15% | Sororities: | 40% |

**Basis for selection.** Test scores and school achievement record most important. Minimum high school GPA of 2.75 required, ACT score of 20 or higher. Interview recommended. Portfolio recommended for studio art majors.

**High school preparation.** College-preparatory program recommended. 15 units required; 19 recommended. Required and recommended units include English 4, mathematics 2-3, social studies 1, history 2, science 2-3, foreign language 2 and academic electives 4.

**2010-2011 Annual costs.** Tuition/fees (projected): $19,820. Room/board: $5,840. Books/supplies: $1,000. Personal expenses: $1,500.

**2008-2009 Financial aid. Need-based:** 333 full-time freshmen applied for aid; 269 were judged to have need; 269 of these received aid. Average need met was 88%. Average scholarship/grant was $13,230; average loan $4,456. 76% of total undergraduate aid awarded as scholarships/grants, 24% as loans/jobs. **Non-need-based:** Awarded to 794 full-time undergraduates,

including 210 freshmen. Scholarships awarded for academics, alumni affiliation, art, athletics, job skills, leadership, minority status, music/drama, religious affiliation, ROTC, state residency.

**Application procedures. Admission:** No deadline. No application fee. Admission notification on a rolling basis. **Financial aid:** Priority date 1/15, closing date 6/1. FAFSA required. Applicants notified on a rolling basis starting 11/1; must reply by 5/1.

**Academics.** Classes in Arkansas Folkways taught at Old Washington State Park. International exchange programs in Australia, Austria, China, Costa Rica, England, France, Germany, Hong Kong, Indonesia, Japan, Morocco, Russia, Scotland, and South Africa. **Special study options:** Cross-registration, distance learning, double major, ESL, honors, independent study, internships, study abroad, teacher certification program. **Credit/placement by examination:** AP, CLEP, IB, ACT, institutional tests. 24 credit hours maximum toward bachelor's degree. **Support services:** Learning center, reduced course load, remedial instruction, study skills assistance, tutoring, writing center.

**Majors. Biology:** General. **Business:** Accounting, business admin. **Communications:** Media studies. **Computer sciences:** Computer science. **Education:** Art, biology, business, chemistry, drama/dance, early childhood, English, foreign languages, French, health, history, mathematics, middle, music, physical, physics, science, secondary, social studies, Spanish, speech. **Foreign languages:** French, Russian, Spanish. **Health:** Athletic training, audiology/speech pathology, dietetics, predental, premedicine, prenursing, prepharmacy, preveterinary. **History:** General. **Math:** General. **Parks/recreation:** Exercise sciences. **Philosophy/religion:** Philosophy. **Physical sciences:** Chemistry, physics. **Psychology:** General. **Social sciences:** Political science, sociology. **Theology:** Bible, missionary, pastoral counseling, sacred music, theology, youth ministry. **Visual/performing arts:** Dramatic, graphic design, music history, music performance, music theory/composition, musical theater, piano/organ, studio arts, voice/opera. **Other:** Software engineering.

**Most popular majors.** Biology 9%, business/marketing 14%, communications/journalism 8%, education 6%, parks/recreation 6%, philosophy/religious studies 6%, psychology 6%, theological studies 14%, visual/performing arts 11%.

**Computing on campus.** 250 workstations in dormitories, library, computer center, student center. Dormitories wired for high-speed internet access and linked to campus network. Commuter students can connect to campus network. Online library, helpline, student web hosting, wireless network available.

**Student life. Freshman orientation:** Mandatory. Preregistration for classes offered. Three-part program: day-long pre-registration and orientation session for students and parents; 3-day weekend program prior to registration with one session for parents; optional 3-day summer retreat. **Policies:** Students under 22 years old must live in campus housing unless commuting. Only local fraternities and sororities are permitted. Religious observance required. **Housing:** Guaranteed on-campus for all undergraduates. Single-sex dorms, special housing for disabled, apartments, wellness housing available. $50 fully refundable deposit, deadline 6/1. **Activities:** Bands, campus ministries, choral groups, drama, international student organizations, literary magazine, music ensembles, Model UN, musical theater, opera, student government, student newspaper, Fellowship of Christian Athletes, Ouachita student foundation, Pew College Society, ROMS, Young Democrats, College Republicans.

**Athletics.** NCAA. **Intercollegiate:** Baseball M, basketball, cheerleading, cross-country W, diving, football (tackle) M, golf M, soccer, softball W, swimming, tennis, volleyball W. **Intramural:** Basketball, football (non-tackle), handball, racquetball, soccer, softball, table tennis, volleyball. **Team name:** Tigers.

**Student services.** Alcohol/substance abuse counseling, chaplain/spiritual director, career counseling, services for economically disadvantaged, student employment services, financial aid counseling, health services, minority student services, personal counseling, placement for graduates, veterans' counselor. **Physically disabled:** Services for visually, speech, hearing impaired.

**Contact.** E-mail: MOTLL@obu.edu
Phone: (870) 245-5110 Toll-free number: (800) 342-5628
Fax: (870) 245-5500
Lori Motl, Director of Admissions Counseling, Ouachita Baptist University, OBU Box 3776, Arkadelphia, AR 71998-0001

## Philander Smith College
**Little Rock, Arkansas** — **CB member**
www.philander.edu — **CB code: 6578**

- Private 4-year liberal arts college affiliated with United Methodist Church
- Commuter campus in small city

- 665 degree-seeking undergraduates
- 69% of applicants admitted
- SAT or ACT (ACT writing recommended) required

**General.** Founded in 1877. Regionally accredited. **Degrees:** 71 bachelor's awarded. **ROTC:** Army. **Calendar:** Semester, limited summer session. **Full-time faculty:** 55 total. **Part-time faculty:** 37 total.

**Freshman class profile.** 1,714 applied, 1,187 admitted, 159 enrolled.

| Mid 50% test scores | | | |
|---|---|---|---|
| SAT critical reading: | 400-480 | GPA 3.50-3.74: | 3% |
| SAT math: | 410-500 | GPA 3.0-3.49: | 29% |
| SAT writing: | 390-530 | GPA 2.0-2.99: | 58% |
| ACT composite: | 16-22 | Rank in top quarter: | 33% |
| GPA 3.75 or higher: | 6% | Rank in top tenth: | 14% |
| | | Out-of-state: | 27% |

**Basis for selection.** High school GPA of 2.5 and ACT Composite of 17 along with rigor of high school record. Students admitted without ACT scores are administered COMPASS test for placement purposes. Students who score below placement cut-off scores in writing, English, or math also required to take COMPASS test.

**High school preparation.** Recommended units include English 3, mathematics 3, social studies 2, science 3 (laboratory 1) and foreign language 2.

**2009-2010 Annual costs.** Tuition/fees: $9,000. Room/board: $6,850. Books/supplies: $1,000. Personal expenses: $1,554.

**2009-2010 Financial aid.** All financial aid based on need.

**Application procedures. Admission:** Priority date 5/1; no deadline. $25 fee, may be waived for applicants with need. Admission notification on a rolling basis. **Financial aid:** Priority date 3/1; no closing date. FAFSA, institutional form required. Applicants notified on a rolling basis starting 5/1; must reply within 2 week(s) of notification.

**Academics. Special study options:** Cooperative education, independent study, internships, liberal arts/career combination, study abroad, teacher certification program. **Credit/placement by examination:** AP, CLEP, SAT, ACT. 30 credit hours maximum toward bachelor's degree. **Support services:** Learning center, reduced course load, remedial instruction, tutoring.

**Majors. Biology:** General. **Business:** Administrative services, business admin. **Computer sciences:** Computer science. **Education:** Business. **Interdisciplinary:** Math/computer science. **Math:** General. **Philosophy/religion:** Philosophy, religion. **Physical sciences:** Chemistry. **Psychology:** General. **Public administration:** Social work. **Social sciences:** Political science, sociology.

**Computing on campus.** 72 workstations in dormitories, library, computer center. Dormitories wired for high-speed internet access and linked to campus network. Commuter students can connect to campus network. Online library, wireless network available.

**Student life. Freshman orientation:** Mandatory, $150 fee. **Housing:** Single-sex dorms available. $245 nonrefundable deposit, deadline 7/10. **Activities:** Choral groups, drama, student government, student newspaper.

**Athletics. Intercollegiate:** Baseball M, basketball, volleyball W. **Intramural:** Badminton, basketball, tennis. **Team name:** Panthers.

**Student services.** Career counseling, student employment services, health services, personal counseling, veterans' counselor. **Physically disabled:** Services for visually, hearing impaired.

**Contact.** E-mail: admissions@philander.edu
Phone: (501) 370-5221 Toll-free number: (800) 446-6772
Fax: (501) 370-5225
George Gray, Director of Admissions, Philander Smith College, 900 West Daisy Bates Drive, Little Rock, AR 72202-3718

## Southern Arkansas University
**Magnolia, Arkansas**
www.saumag.edu — **CB code: 6661**

- Public 4-year university
- Residential campus in large town
- 2,647 degree-seeking undergraduates: 10% part-time, 58% women
- 449 graduate students
- 74% of applicants admitted
- SAT or ACT (ACT writing optional) required
- 32% graduate within 6 years

**General.** Founded in 1909. Regionally accredited. **Degrees:** 370 bachelor's, 45 associate awarded; master's offered. **Location:** 53 miles from Texarkana, Texas, 70 miles from Shreveport, Louisiana. **Calendar:** Semester, extensive summer session. **Full-time faculty:** 162 total; 56% have terminal degrees, 18% minority, 44% women. **Class size:** 55% < 20, 35% 20-39, 6% 40-49, 4% 50-99. **Special facilities:** University farm.

**Freshman class profile.** 2,024 applied, 1,493 admitted, 619 enrolled.

| Mid 50% test scores | | GPA 3.0-3.49: | 31% |
|---|---|---|---|
| SAT critical reading: | 410-540 | GPA 2.0-2.99: | 35% |
| SAT math: | 470-560 | Return as sophomores: | 63% |
| ACT composite: | 18-24 | Out-of-state: | 27% |
| GPA 3.75 or higher: | 19% | Live on campus: | 80% |
| GPA 3.50-3.74: | 13% | | |

**Basis for selection.** For unconditional admission, applicants must have ACT of 19 or higher. ACT of 16 to 18 allows conditional admission. TOEFL required for non-native English speakers. Interview required of nursing majors.

**High school preparation.** Recommended units include English 4, mathematics 4, social studies 3, science 3 (laboratory 3) and foreign language 2. 0.5 computer science also recommended.

**2009-2010 Annual costs.** Tuition/fees: $6,056; $8,696 out-of-state. Room/board: $4,460. Books/supplies: $1,000. Personal expenses: $2,200.

**2008-2009 Financial aid.** **Need-based:** 41% of total undergraduate aid awarded as scholarships/grants, 59% as loans/jobs. **Non-need-based:** Scholarships awarded for academics, alumni affiliation, art, athletics, leadership, minority status, music/drama, state residency.

**Application procedures.** **Admission:** Closing date 8/30 (receipt date). No application fee. Admission notification on a rolling basis. **Financial aid:** Priority date 7/1; no closing date. FAFSA required. Applicants notified on a rolling basis starting 4/15; must reply within 2 week(s) of notification.

**Academics.** **Special study options:** Combined bachelor's/graduate degree, cross-registration, distance learning, double major, dual enrollment of high school students, honors, independent study, internships, teacher certification program. **Credit/placement by examination:** AP, CLEP, SAT, ACT. 15 credit hours maximum toward associate degree, 30 toward bachelor's. **Support services:** Learning center, reduced course load, remedial instruction, tutoring, writing center.

**Honors college/program.** Composite ACT score of 26 or higher.

**Majors. Agriculture:** Business. **Biology:** General. **Business:** General, accounting. **Communications:** Journalism. **Computer sciences:** General. **Education:** Agricultural, art, business, chemistry, early childhood, English, mathematics, middle, music, physical, science, social studies, Spanish. **Engineering technology:** Industrial. **Foreign languages:** Spanish. **Health:** Athletic training, clinical lab science, nursing (RN). **History:** General. **Interdisciplinary:** Biological/physical sciences. **Math:** General. **Parks/recreation:** Exercise sciences. **Physical sciences:** Chemistry, physics. **Protective services:** Criminal justice. **Psychology:** General. **Public administration:** Community org/advocacy, social work. **Social sciences:** General, political science, sociology. **Visual/performing arts:** Art, dramatic, studio arts. **Other:** Interdisciplinary studies.

**Most popular majors.** Biology 7%, business/marketing 36%, education 27%.

**Computing on campus.** 202 workstations in dormitories, library, computer center. Dormitories wired for high-speed internet access and linked to campus network. Commuter students can connect to campus network. Online library, helpline, wireless network available.

**Student life. Freshman orientation:** Mandatory, $25 fee. Preregistration for classes offered. **Policies:** Freshmen required to live on campus unless commuting or living with parents. **Housing:** Guaranteed on-campus for all undergraduates. Coed dorms, single-sex dorms, apartments, wellness housing available. $50 fully refundable deposit. **Activities:** Bands, choral groups, drama, international student organizations, music ensembles, musical theater, radio station, student government, student newspaper, More than 80 student organizations.

**Athletics.** NCAA. **Intercollegiate:** Baseball M, basketball, cross-country, football (tackle) M, golf M, softball W, tennis W, track and field, volleyball W. **Intramural:** Badminton, basketball, football (tackle) M, golf M, softball, table tennis, tennis, volleyball. **Team name:** Muleriders.

**Student services.** Alcohol/substance abuse counseling, career counseling, services for economically disadvantaged, student employment services, financial aid counseling, health services, minority student services, personal counseling, placement for graduates, veterans' counselor, women's services. **Physically disabled:** Services for visually, hearing impaired.

**Contact.** E-mail: sejennings@saumag.edu
Phone: (870) 235-4040 Toll-free number: (800) 332-7286
Fax: (870) 235-4931
Sarah Jennings, Dean of Enrollment Services, Southern Arkansas University, Box 9382, Magnolia, AR 71754-9382

## University of Arkansas
**Fayetteville, Arkansas**   CB member
**www.uark.edu**   CB code: 6866

- Public 4-year university
- Residential campus in small city
- 15,347 degree-seeking undergraduates: 12% part-time, 48% women, 5% African American, 3% Asian American, 4% Hispanic American, 2% Native American, 3% international
- 3,805 degree-seeking graduate students
- 56% of applicants admitted
- SAT or ACT (ACT writing optional) required
- 59% graduate within 6 years

**General.** Founded in 1871. Regionally accredited. Arkansas Center for Space and Planetary Sciences, GENESIS Technology Incubator program provides tech-based companies with research and development support. **Degrees:** 2,494 bachelor's awarded; master's, doctoral, professional offered. **ROTC:** Army, Air Force. **Location:** 192 miles from Little Rock, 120 miles from Tulsa, Oklahoma. **Calendar:** Semester, limited summer session. **Full-time faculty:** 897 total; 89% have terminal degrees, 12% minority, 34% women. **Part-time faculty:** 86 total; 56% have terminal degrees, 6% minority, 35% women. **Class size:** 31% < 20, 46% 20-39, 6% 40-49, 12% 50-99, 5% >100. **Special facilities:** Arts center, poultry science center, equine pavilion, animal science center.

**Freshman class profile.** 12,035 applied, 6,751 admitted, 2,919 enrolled.

| Mid 50% test scores | | Rank in top quarter: | 60% |
|---|---|---|---|
| SAT critical reading: | 500-620 | Rank in top tenth: | 30% |
| SAT math: | 520-640 | Return as sophomores: | 83% |
| ACT composite: | 23-29 | Out-of-state: | 36% |
| GPA 3.75 or higher: | 37% | Live on campus: | 87% |
| GPA 3.50-3.74: | 20% | International: | 2% |
| GPA 3.0-3.49: | 33% | Fraternities: | 24% |
| GPA 2.0-2.99: | 10% | Sororities: | 36% |

**Basis for selection.** Secondary school record, class rank, test scores, evidence of commitment to success most important. As mandated by state law, those with ACT subscore of 18 or less in English, Mathematics or Reading are assigned developmental coursework or required to take institutional placement test. University policies are more restrictive than the state of Arkansas' policies.

**High school preparation.** College-preparatory program required. 16 units required. Required and recommended units include English 4, mathematics 4, social studies 3, science 3 (laboratory 2), foreign language 2 and academic electives 2. Mathematics must include algebra I or 2 units applied math, and 3 units chosen from algebra II, geometry, calculus/trigonometry, and statistics. 2 foreign languages strongly recommended.

**2009-2010 Annual costs.** Tuition/fees: $6,459; $15,337 out-of-state. Room/board: $7,806. Books/supplies: $1,082. Personal expenses: $2,032.

**2008-2009 Financial aid.** **Need-based:** 1,856 full-time freshmen applied for aid; 1,211 were judged to have need; 1,187 of these received aid. Average need met was 68%. Average scholarship/grant was $6,550; average loan $3,458. 38% of total undergraduate aid awarded as scholarships/grants, 62% as loans/jobs. **Non-need-based:** Awarded to 2,983 full-time undergraduates, including 771 freshmen. Scholarships awarded for academics, alumni affiliation, art, athletics, leadership, minority status, music/drama, ROTC, state residency.

**Application procedures.** **Admission:** Priority date 11/15; deadline 8/1 (receipt date). $40 fee, may be waived for applicants with need. Admission notification on a rolling basis beginning on or about 9/15. **Financial aid:** Priority date 3/15; no closing date. FAFSA required. Applicants notified on a rolling basis starting 4/1; must reply within 4 week(s) of notification.

**Academics. Special study options:** Accelerated study, combined bachelor's/graduate degree, cooperative education, distance learning, double major, dual enrollment of high school students, ESL, honors, independent study, internships, liberal arts/career combination, student-designed major, study abroad, teacher certification program, United Nations semester. **Credit/placement**

**by examination:** AP, CLEP, IB, SAT, ACT, institutional tests. **Support services:** Learning center, reduced course load, remedial instruction, study skills assistance, tutoring, writing center.

**Honors college/program.** Minimum 28 ACT or SAT equivalent, minimum high school GPA of 3.5. Walton College of Business, minimum 28 ACT or SAT equivalent, minimum high school GPA of 3.75.

**Majors. Agriculture:** Agribusiness operations, agronomy, animal sciences, food science, ornamental horticulture, poultry. **Architecture:** Architecture, landscape. **Area/ethnic studies:** American. **Biology:** General, bacteriology. **Business:** General, accounting, business admin, finance, international, logistics, managerial economics, marketing. **Communications:** General, journalism. **Computer sciences:** General, data processing. **Conservation:** Environmental science. **Education:** Agricultural, elementary, kindergarten/preschool, middle, trade/industrial. **Engineering:** Agricultural, chemical, civil, computer, electrical, industrial, mechanical. **Family/consumer sciences:** Clothing/textiles, family studies, food/nutrition, housing. **Foreign languages:** Classics, French, German, Spanish. **Health:** Audiology/speech pathology, nursing (RN). **History:** General. **Math:** General. **Parks/recreation:** General, health/fitness. **Philosophy/religion:** Philosophy. **Physical sciences:** Chemistry, geology, physics. **Protective services:** Criminal justice. **Psychology:** General. **Public administration:** General, social work. **Social sciences:** Anthropology, economics, geography, international relations, political science, sociology. **Visual/performing arts:** Art, dramatic, music performance.

**Most popular majors.** Business/marketing 24%, communications/journalism 7%, education 6%, engineering/engineering technologies 9%, social sciences 7%.

**Computing on campus.** 2,859 workstations in dormitories, library, computer center, student center. Dormitories wired for high-speed internet access and linked to campus network. Commuter students can connect to campus network. Online course registration, online library, helpline, repair service, student web hosting, wireless network available.

**Student life. Freshman orientation:** Mandatory, $100 fee. Preregistration for classes offered. 2-day orientation held in summer for students and parents. Students stay overnight in a residence hall; fee $25; $50 for guest/parents. **Housing:** Coed dorms, single-sex dorms, special housing for disabled, apartments, fraternity/sorority housing available. $235 partly refundable deposit. Living/learning communities, suites with private bedrooms. Several residences remain open over holiday and winter breaks. **Activities:** Bands, campus ministries, choral groups, dance, drama, film society, international student organizations, literary magazine, music ensembles, musical theater, opera, radio station, student government, student newspaper, symphony orchestra, TV station, More than 200 organizations available.

**Athletics.** NCAA. **Intercollegiate:** Baseball M, basketball, cheerleading, cross-country, diving W, football (tackle) M, golf, gymnastics W, soccer W, softball W, swimming W, tennis, track and field, volleyball W. **Intramural:** Badminton, basketball, bowling, racquetball, soccer, softball, tennis, volleyball W. **Team name:** Razorbacks.

**Student services.** Adult student services, alcohol/substance abuse counseling, chaplain/spiritual director, career counseling, student employment services, financial aid counseling, health services, legal services, minority student services, personal counseling, placement for graduates, veterans' counselor. **Physically disabled:** Services for visually, speech, hearing impaired. **Learning disabled:** Comprehensive services available.

**Contact.** E-mail: uofa@uark.edu
Phone: (479) 575-5346 Toll-free number: (800) 377-8632
Fax: (479) 575-7515
Suzanne McCray, Vice Provost for Enrollment, University of Arkansas, 232 Silas Hunt Hall, Fayetteville, AR 72701

---

## University of Arkansas at Fort Smith
**Fort Smith, Arkansas**  **CB member**
www.uafortsmith.edu   CB code: 6220

- Public 4-year university
- Commuter campus in small city
- 6,582 degree-seeking undergraduates: 25% part-time, 58% women, 4% African American, 4% Asian American, 5% Hispanic American, 3% Native American

**General.** Founded in 1928. Regionally accredited. **Degrees:** 396 bachelor's, 471 associate awarded. **ROTC:** Army, Air Force. **Location:** 150 miles from Little Rock, 120 miles from Tulsa, Oklahoma. **Calendar:** Semester, limited summer session. **Full-time faculty:** 223 total; 47% have terminal degrees, 12% minority, 47% women. **Part-time faculty:** 176 total; 20% have terminal degrees, 3% minority, 48% women. **Class size:** 39% < 20, 51% 20-39, 5% 40-49, 5% 50-99. **Special facilities:** Art galleries.

**Freshman class profile.** 3,332 applied, 2,045 admitted, 1,306 enrolled.

| Mid 50% test scores | | | |
|---|---|---|---|
| ACT composite: | 19-24 | End year in good standing: | 67% |
| GPA 3.75 or higher: | 15% | Return as sophomores: | 69% |
| GPA 3.50-3.74: | 12% | Out-of-state: | 11% |
| GPA 3.0-3.49: | 31% | Live on campus: | 13% |
| GPA 2.0-2.99: | 38% | International: | 1% |
| Rank in top quarter: | 30% | Fraternities: | 2% |
| Rank in top tenth: | 10% | Sororities: | 4% |

**Basis for selection.** Open admission, but selective for some programs. Special criteria for health career and education programs. Pre-admission exams are required for all health science programs. Teacher education applicants must take PRAXIS I exam, have grade of C or B in specific English and Rhetoric courses. COMPASS required for placement if ACT/SAT not submitted, or if scores below acceptable minimum (18 on ACT). Interview required of nursing, radiology, surgical technology, paramedic, and dental hygiene majors, as well as teacher education programs. **Home-schooled:** Any private school, homeschool, or GED student who graduates after May 1, 2002, must have achieved a composite score of 19 on the ACT or the equivalent score on the SAT or COMPASS for unconditional admission. **Learning Disabled:** In order to be considered for accommodations, a student must first submit verification of his or her condition based on Student ADA Services' guidelines and meet with the Student ADA Services coordinator to discuss an accommodation request.

**High school preparation.** College-preparatory program recommended. 14 units recommended. Recommended units include English 4, mathematics 4, social studies 3, science 3 (laboratory 3).

**2009-2010 Annual costs.** Tuition/fees: $4,600; $10,000 out-of-state. Room only: $4,789. Books/supplies: $950. Personal expenses: $1,695.

**2008-2009 Financial aid. Need-based:** 938 full-time freshmen applied for aid; 777 were judged to have need; 759 of these received aid. Average need met was 69%. Average scholarship/grant was $4,403; average loan $3,018. 57% of total undergraduate aid awarded as scholarships/grants, 43% as loans/jobs. **Non-need-based:** Awarded to 1,415 full-time undergraduates, including 733 freshmen. Scholarships awarded for academics, athletics, job skills, leadership, music/drama.

**Application procedures. Admission:** No deadline. No application fee. Admission notification on a rolling basis. Early applications advised for financial aid. **Financial aid:** Priority date 6/15; no closing date. FAFSA required. Applicants notified on a rolling basis starting 3/1; must reply within 4 week(s) of notification.

**Academics. Special study options:** Distance learning, double major, dual enrollment of high school students, external degree, honors, independent study, internships, liberal arts/career combination, student-designed major, study abroad, teacher certification program, weekend college. Associate of Art through distance learning. **Credit/placement by examination:** AP, CLEP, institutional tests. 30 credit hours maximum toward associate degree, 30 toward bachelor's. Prior work/life experience credits awarded for military transcripts only; maximum 30 hours. **Support services:** Learning center, pre-admission summer program, reduced course load, remedial instruction, study skills assistance, tutoring, writing center.

**Majors. Biology:** General. **Business:** Business admin. **Computer sciences:** General. **Education:** Biology, chemistry, early childhood, English, history, mathematics, middle, music, Spanish. **Foreign languages:** Spanish. **Health:** Nursing (RN), radiologic technology/medical imaging. **History:** General. **Liberal arts:** Arts/sciences. **Math:** General. **Physical sciences:** Chemistry. **Protective services:** Law enforcement admin. **Psychology:** General. **Visual/performing arts:** Graphic design.

**Most popular majors.** Biology 6%, business/marketing 32%, education 26%, history 6%, interdisciplinary studies 6%, psychology 10%.

**Computing on campus.** 1,528 workstations in dormitories, library, computer center, student center. Dormitories wired for high-speed internet access and linked to campus network. Commuter students can connect to campus network. Online course registration, online library, helpline, wireless network available.

**Student life. Freshman orientation:** Available. Preregistration for classes offered. **Housing:** Apartments, wellness housing available. $300 fully refundable deposit. **Activities:** Bands, campus ministries, choral groups, drama, international student organizations, literary magazine, music ensembles, student government, student newspaper, symphony orchestra, Future Educators Organization, Students Together Effectively Progressing, First Generation, international club, drama club, Lions for Christ, math club, Sigma Tau Delta, Ozark Mountain Adventure club, organization for adult and returning students.

**Athletics.** NJCAA. **Intercollegiate:** Baseball M, basketball, golf, tennis, volleyball W. **Intramural:** Badminton, basketball, bowling, football (non-tackle), soccer, softball, table tennis, volleyball. **Team name:** Lions.

**Student services.** Adult student services, career counseling, services for economically disadvantaged, student employment services, financial aid counseling, health services, personal counseling, placement for graduates, veterans' counselor. **Physically disabled:** Services for visually, speech, hearing impaired.

**Contact.**   E-mail: information@uafortsmith.edu
Phone: (479) 788-7120 Toll-free number: (888) 512-5466
Fax: (479) 788-7402
Mark Lloyd, Director of Admissions, University of Arkansas at Fort Smith, PO Box 3649, Fort Smith, AR 72913-3649

## University of Arkansas at Little Rock
**Little Rock, Arkansas**                            **CB member**
**www.ualr.edu**                                     **CB code: 6368**

- Public 4-year university
- Commuter campus in small city
- 10,200 degree-seeking undergraduates
- 87% of applicants admitted
- ACT (writing optional) required

**General.** Founded in 1927. Regionally accredited. **Degrees:** 1,084 bachelor's, 244 associate awarded; master's, doctoral, professional offered. **ROTC:** Army. **Calendar:** Semester, limited summer session. **Full-time faculty:** 523 total. **Part-time faculty:** 318 total. **Special facilities:** Planetarium, observatory, government documents depository.

**Freshman class profile.** 2,120 applied, 1,851 admitted, 701 enrolled.

| Mid 50% test scores | ACT composite: | 17-24 |
|---|---|---|

**Basis for selection.** Unconditional admission based on minimum ACT score of 21 or above, or combined SAT score of 990 (exclusive of Writing) or above, high school GPA of 2.5 or above, and completion of college preparatory curriculum. Students must meet 2 of 3 basic criteria. All students born after January 1, 1957 required to show Arkansas Certificate of Immunization for Institutions of Higher Education. Interview recommended for academically weak applicants.

**High school preparation.** 15 units required. Required units include English 4, mathematics 3, social studies 3, science 2 (laboratory 2) and foreign language 2. Social studies should include 1 unit each of American history, world history, and civics or American government.

**2009-2010 Annual costs.** Tuition/fees: $6,332; $14,799 out-of-state. Room only: $3,100. Books/supplies: $1,000. Personal expenses: $800.

**Application procedures. Admission:** No deadline. $40 fee. Admission notification on a rolling basis. **Financial aid:** Closing date 8/1. FAFSA required. Applicants notified on a rolling basis starting 5/1.

**Academics. Special study options:** Accelerated study, cooperative education, distance learning, double major, dual enrollment of high school students, ESL, exchange student, honors, independent study, internships, student-designed major, study abroad, teacher certification program, weekend college. **Credit/placement by examination:** AP, CLEP, ACT, institutional tests. 30 credit hours maximum toward associate degree, 30 toward bachelor's. Credit obtained through examination is recorded as approved hours on the official permanent record without grade or grade points. **Support services:** Learning center, reduced course load, remedial instruction, tutoring, writing center.

**Majors. Biology:** General. **Business:** Accounting, business admin, finance, international, management information systems, managerial economics, marketing. **Communications:** General, advertising, journalism. **Computer sciences:** General, information systems. **Education:** Early childhood, elementary, middle. **Engineering:** Systems. **Engineering technology:** Construction. **Foreign languages:** French, German, sign language interpretation, Spanish. **Health:** Audiology/speech pathology, environmental health. **History:** General. **Interdisciplinary:** Biological/physical sciences. **Liberal arts:** Arts/sciences. **Math:** General, applied. **Philosophy/religion:** Philosophy. **Physical sciences:** Chemistry, geology, physics. **Protective services:** Criminal justice. **Psychology:** General. **Public administration:** Social work. **Social sciences:** Economics, international relations, political science, sociology. **Visual/performing arts:** Art, art history/conservation, dramatic. **Other:** Applied technology.

**Computing on campus.** 500 workstations in dormitories, library, computer center. Dormitories wired for high-speed internet access and linked to campus network. Commuter students can connect to campus network. Online course registration, online library, wireless network available.

**Student life. Freshman orientation:** Available. **Housing:** Coed dorms available. $100 fully refundable deposit. **Activities:** Bands, choral groups, dance, drama, literary magazine, music ensembles, musical theater, opera, radio station, student government, student newspaper, TV station, Baptist Student Union, University Republicans, Methodist student club, Muslim students association, Young Democrats, Association for Minority Students Education Needs and Development, Advocates for People with Disabilities.

**Athletics.** NCAA. **Intercollegiate:** Baseball M, basketball, cross-country, golf, soccer, swimming, tennis, track and field, volleyball W. **Intramural:** Badminton, basketball, bowling, football (tackle) M, golf, softball, swimming, table tennis M, tennis, volleyball. **Team name:** Trojans.

**Student services.** Adult student services, career counseling, student employment services, health services, personal counseling, placement for graduates, veterans' counselor. **Physically disabled:** Services for visually, speech, hearing impaired.

**Contact.**   Phone: (501) 569-3127 Toll-free number: (800) 482-8892
Fax: (501) 569-8956
Tammy Harrison, Director of Admissions and Financial Aid, University of Arkansas at Little Rock, 2801 South University Avenue, Little Rock, AR 72204

## University of Arkansas at Monticello
**Monticello, Arkansas**
**www.uamont.edu**                                   **CB code: 6007**

- Public 4-year university and technical college
- Commuter campus in large town
- 2,976 degree-seeking undergraduates: 17% part-time, 59% women, 33% African American, 1% Hispanic American, 1% Native American
- 107 degree-seeking graduate students
- 50% of applicants admitted
- 34% graduate within 6 years

**General.** Founded in 1909. Regionally accredited. **Degrees:** 265 bachelor's, 258 associate awarded; master's offered. **ROTC:** Army. **Location:** 100 miles from Little Rock, 50 miles from Pine Bluff. **Calendar:** Semester, extensive summer session. **Full-time faculty:** 168 total; 47% have terminal degrees, 13% minority, 47% women. **Part-time faculty:** 75 total; 11% have terminal degrees, 11% minority, 67% women. **Class size:** 58% < 20, 34% 20-39, 5% 40-49, 2% 50-99, less than 1% >100. **Special facilities:** Museum of natural history, extensive research forest, planetarium, farm.

**Freshman class profile.** 1,998 applied, 999 admitted, 795 enrolled.

| Mid 50% test scores | | End year in good standing: | 55% |
|---|---|---|---|
| ACT composite: | 16-22 | Return as sophomores: | 50% |
| GPA 3.75 or higher: | 12% | Out-of-state: | 10% |
| GPA 3.50-3.74: | 11% | Live on campus: | 38% |
| GPA 3.0-3.49: | 24% | Fraternities: | 10% |
| GPA 2.0-2.99: | 44% | Sororities: | 10% |

**Basis for selection.** Admissions based on entrance exam scores (ACT, SAT, ASSET, or COMPASS) and complete high school transcript. **Home-schooled:** Transcript of courses and grades required. ACT or SAT for placement and not for admission.

**High school preparation.** Recommended units include English 4, mathematics 4, social studies 3, science 3 and foreign language 2.

**2009-2010 Annual costs.** Tuition/fees: $4,750; $9,010 out-of-state. Room/board: $4,070. Books/supplies: $800. Personal expenses: $1,980.

**2008-2009 Financial aid. Non-need-based:** Scholarships awarded for academics, athletics, job skills, leadership, music/drama, ROTC, state residency.

**Application procedures. Admission:** Priority date 8/10; no deadline. No application fee. Admission notification on a rolling basis. **Financial aid:** Priority date 5/1; no closing date. FAFSA, institutional form required. Applicants notified on a rolling basis starting 4/1; must reply within 2 week(s) of notification.

**Academics. Special study options:** Combined bachelor's/graduate degree, cross-registration, distance learning, double major, dual enrollment of high school students, independent study, internships, liberal arts/career combination, study abroad, teacher certification program. **Credit/placement by examination:** AP, CLEP, IB, SAT, ACT, institutional tests. 9 credit hours maximum toward bachelor's degree. **Support services:** Learning center,

pre-admission summer program, reduced course load, remedial instruction, study skills assistance, tutoring, writing center.

**Majors. Agriculture:** Agribusiness operations. **Biology:** General. **Business:** General, accounting, business admin, management information systems. **Conservation:** Forestry, wildlife. **Education:** Kindergarten/preschool, middle, music, physical. **Engineering technology:** Surveying. **Health:** Nursing (RN). **History:** General. **Interdisciplinary:** Biological/physical sciences. **Math:** General. **Parks/recreation:** Health/fitness. **Physical sciences:** Chemistry. **Protective services:** Criminal justice. **Psychology:** General. **Public administration:** Social work. **Social sciences:** General, political science. **Visual/performing arts:** Art. **Other:** Applied science.

**Most popular majors.** Agriculture 7%, business/marketing 27%, education 8%, health sciences 10%, psychology 8%.

**Computing on campus.** 400 workstations in dormitories, library, computer center, student center. Dormitories wired for high-speed internet access and linked to campus network. Commuter students can connect to campus network. Online course registration, wireless network available.

**Student life. Freshman orientation:** Mandatory. Preregistration for classes offered. One day, beginning of semester. **Housing:** Guaranteed on-campus for all undergraduates. Single-sex dorms, special housing for disabled, apartments, wellness housing available. $60 fully refundable deposit, deadline 8/15. **Activities:** Bands, choral groups, drama, literary magazine, music ensembles, musical theater, student government, student newspaper, Baptist Student Union, Missionary Baptist Student Fellowship, Wesley Foundation, Christians in Action, Catholic Weevils, Chi Alpha.

**Athletics.** NCAA. **Intercollegiate:** Baseball M, basketball, cross-country, football (tackle) M, golf, rodeo, softball W, tennis W, volleyball W. **Intramural:** Archery, badminton, baseball M, basketball, bowling, boxing M, cross-country, football (tackle) M, golf, handball, racquetball, soccer, softball, swimming, table tennis, tennis, track and field, volleyball. **Team name:** Boll Weevils.

**Student services.** Alcohol/substance abuse counseling, chaplain/spiritual director, career counseling, student employment services, financial aid counseling, health services, personal counseling, placement for graduates, veterans' counselor. **Physically disabled:** Services for visually, speech, hearing impaired.

**Contact.** E-mail: whitingm@uamont.edu
Phone: (870) 460-1026 Toll-free number: (800) 844-1826
Fax: (870) 460-1926
Mary Whiting, Director of Admissions, University of Arkansas at Monticello, Box 3600, Monticello, AR 71656

## University of Arkansas at Pine Bluff
**Pine Bluff, Arkansas**
**www.uapb.edu**
**CB member**
**CB code: 6004**

- Public 4-year university
- Commuter campus in small city
- 3,624 degree-seeking undergraduates: 9% part-time, 58% women, 95% African American, 1% international
- 132 degree-seeking graduate students
- 33% of applicants admitted
- SAT or ACT (ACT writing optional) required
- 28% graduate within 6 years

**General.** Founded in 1873. Regionally accredited. **Degrees:** 401 bachelor's awarded; master's offered. **ROTC:** Army. **Location:** 42 miles from Little Rock. **Calendar:** Semester, limited summer session. **Full-time faculty:** 173 total; 61% have terminal degrees, 48% women. **Part-time faculty:** 85 total; 21% have terminal degrees, 45% women. **Class size:** 42% < 20, 47% 20-39, 6% 40-49, 5% 50-99. **Special facilities:** 220-acre farm, aquaculture fisheries.

**Freshman class profile.** 4,792 applied, 1,568 admitted, 977 enrolled.

| Mid 50% test scores | | | |
|---|---|---|---|
| SAT critical reading: | 370-490 | Return as sophomores: | 64% |
| SAT math: | 360-480 | Out-of-state: | 45% |
| SAT writing: | 370-490 | Live on campus: | 77% |
| ACT composite: | 14-18 | International: | 1% |

**Basis for selection.** Admission credentials for entering freshmen must include formal application, high school transcript, ACT test information and scores (SAT is accepted) and immunization record.

**High school preparation.** 21 units required. Required units include English 4, mathematics 3, social studies 1, history 2, science 3 (laboratory 2), foreign language 2 and academic electives 4.

**2009-2010 Annual costs.** Tuition/fees: $4,796; $9,476 out-of-state. Room/board: $6,168. Books/supplies: $800. Personal expenses: $800.

**2008-2009 Financial aid. Non-need-based:** Scholarships awarded for academics, alumni affiliation, art, athletics, leadership, minority status, music/drama, religious affiliation, ROTC, state residency.

**Application procedures. Admission:** Priority date 8/1; no deadline. No application fee. Admission notification on a rolling basis. **Financial aid:** Priority date 4/15; no closing date. FAFSA required. Applicants notified on a rolling basis starting 3/1.

**Academics. Special study options:** Cooperative education, cross-registration, distance learning, double major, dual enrollment of high school students, honors, internships, study abroad, teacher certification program. **Credit/placement by examination:** AP, CLEP, IB, SAT, ACT. **Support services:** Learning center, reduced course load, remedial instruction, study skills assistance, tutoring.

**Majors. Agriculture:** Agribusiness operations. **Biology:** General. **Business:** Accounting, business admin. **Communications:** Journalism. **Computer sciences:** General. **Conservation:** Fisheries. **Education:** Agricultural, art, business, early childhood, English, family/consumer sciences, mathematics, middle, physical, science, social science, special, trade/industrial. **Engineering technology:** Industrial. **Family/consumer sciences:** General, aging. **Health:** Nursing (RN). **History:** General. **Math:** General, applied. **Parks/recreation:** General. **Physical sciences:** Chemistry, physics. **Protective services:** Criminal justice. **Psychology:** General. **Public administration:** Social work. **Social sciences:** Political science, sociology. **Visual/performing arts:** Art. **Other:** Agricultural regulations, Rehabilitation services, Speech and drama.

**Most popular majors.** Business/marketing 18%, education 7%, English 6%, family/consumer sciences 10%, health sciences 8%, liberal arts 7%, security/protective services 9%.

**Computing on campus.** 1,000 workstations in dormitories, library, computer center, student center. Dormitories linked to campus network. Commuter students can connect to campus network. Online library, helpline, repair service available.

**Student life. Freshman orientation:** Mandatory. Preregistration for classes offered. **Housing:** Single-sex dorms available. $100 partly refundable deposit. **Activities:** Bands, campus ministries, choral groups, drama, international student organizations, music ensembles, radio station, student government, student newspaper, TV station, Baptist Student Union, political science/pre-law club, Church of God in Christ, Wesley Foundation, criminal justice club, accounting club, agriculture club, English club, Student Nurses Association, Students in Free Enterprise.

**Athletics.** NCAA. **Intercollegiate:** Baseball M, basketball, bowling W, cross-country, football (tackle) M, golf, soccer W, softball W, tennis, track and field, volleyball W. **Intramural:** Baseball M, basketball, bowling, cross-country M, football (tackle), golf, gymnastics, handball, racquetball, softball, swimming, table tennis, tennis, volleyball, weight lifting. **Team name:** Golden Lions.

**Student services.** Adult student services, alcohol/substance abuse counseling, chaplain/spiritual director, career counseling, services for economically disadvantaged, student employment services, financial aid counseling, health services, on-campus daycare, personal counseling, placement for graduates, veterans' counselor.

**Contact.** E-mail: jonesm@uapb.edu
Phone: (870) 575-8492 Toll-free number: (800) 264-6585
Fax: (870) 575-4607
Mary Jones, Director of Admissions, University of Arkansas at Pine Bluff, 1200 North University Drive, Mail Slot 4981, Pine Bluff, AR 71601-2799

## University of Arkansas for Medical Sciences
**Little Rock, Arkansas**
**www.uams.edu**
**CB code: 0424**

- Public 4-year university and health science college
- Commuter campus in large city

**General.** Founded in 1876. Regionally accredited. **Location:** One mile from downtown. **Calendar:** Semester.

**Annual costs/financial aid.** In-state students pay $200 per credit hour for the following programs: dental hygiene, diagnostic medical sonography, nuclear medicine imaging sciences and radiologic imaging sciences. In-state students pay $189 per credit hour for the following programs: cytotechnology, health information management, medical dosimetry, medical technology, ophthalmic medical technology, radiation therapy, respiratory care and surgical technology. All out-of-state students pay tuition of $458 per credit hour for programs on an undergraduate basis. Emergency medical sciences/paramedic students pay according to program: 4-semester program, $950 tuition; 5-semester program, $760 tuition. Additional required fees vary by program. Books/supplies: $500. Personal expenses: $1,800. Need-based financial aid available to full-time and part-time students.

**Contact.**  Phone: (501) 686-5000
4301 West Markham Street, Little Rock, AR 72205

## University of Central Arkansas
Conway, Arkansas                          CB member
www.uca.edu                               CB code: 6012

- Public 4-year university
- Residential campus in small city
- 9,224 degree-seeking undergraduates
- 94% of applicants admitted
- SAT or ACT (ACT writing optional) required

**General.** Founded in 1907. Regionally accredited. **Degrees:** 1,532 bachelor's, 35 associate awarded; master's, professional offered. **ROTC:** Army. **Location:** 30 miles from Little Rock. **Calendar:** Semester, extensive summer session. **Full-time faculty:** 510 total. **Part-time faculty:** 186 total. **Class size:** 50% < 20, 40% 20-39, 7% 40-49, 2% 50-99, less than 1% >100. **Special facilities:** Observatory, greenhouse, honors center, visual arts center, nature preserve, 24-hour study center, fitness center, human anatomy lab, herbarium, planetarium.

**Freshman class profile.** 3,821 applied, 3,595 admitted, 1,777 enrolled.

| Mid 50% test scores | | | |
|---|---|---|---|
| ACT composite: | 20-28 | GPA 3.0-3.49: | 29% |
| GPA 3.75 or higher: | 24% | GPA 2.0-2.99: | 30% |
| GPA 3.50-3.74: | 16% | Out-of-state: | 6% |
| | | Live on campus: | 77% |

**Basis for selection.** Test scores and high school GPA, along with class rank are important. **Learning Disabled:** Eligibility for services determined individually based on documentation of need. Prospective students encouraged to meet with DSS staff.

**High school preparation.** Recommended units include English 4, mathematics 4, social studies 1, history 2, science 3 and academic electives 10.

**2009-2010 Annual costs.** Tuition/fees: $6,450; $11,640 out-of-state. Room/board: $4,880. Books/supplies: $1,000. Personal expenses: $2,360.

**2008-2009 Financial aid.** **Non-need-based:** Scholarships awarded for academics, art, athletics, leadership, minority status, music/drama, ROTC, state residency. **Additional information:** Room and board may be paid monthly.

**Application procedures.** **Admission:** Priority date 5/1; no deadline. No application fee. Admission notification on a rolling basis. **Financial aid:** Priority date 4/15, closing date 7/1. FAFSA required. Applicants notified on a rolling basis starting 5/4.

**Academics.** **Special study options:** Accelerated study, combined bachelor's/graduate degree, cooperative education, distance learning, double major, dual enrollment of high school students, ESL, honors, independent study, internships, liberal arts/career combination, study abroad, teacher certification program. 5-year professional programs in physical therapy and occupational therapy. **Credit/placement by examination:** AP, CLEP, IB, SAT, institutional tests. 30 credit hours maximum toward associate degree, 30 toward bachelor's. **Support services:** Learning center, pre-admission summer program, remedial instruction, study skills assistance, tutoring, writing center.

**Honors college/program.** Special honors courses and minor in interdisciplinary studies offered. 27 ACT and 3.6 GPA minimum.

**Majors.** **Area/ethnic studies:** African-American. **Biology:** General. **Business:** General, accounting, business admin, finance, insurance, management information systems, marketing. **Communications:** Advertising, journalism, public relations. **Computer sciences:** General. **Conservation:** Environmental studies. **Education:** Business, family/consumer sciences, kindergarten/preschool, mathematics, middle, physical, science, social studies. **Family/consumer sciences:** General, food/nutrition. **Foreign languages:** French, Spanish. **Health:** Athletic training, audiology/speech pathology, clinical lab science, community health services, health services, medical radiologic technology/radiation therapy, nuclear medical technology, nursing (RN), substance abuse counseling. **History:** General. **Interdisciplinary:** Biological/physical sciences, global studies. **Liberal arts:** Arts/sciences. **Math:** General. **Parks/recreation:** Exercise sciences. **Philosophy/religion:** Philosophy, religion. **Physical sciences:** Chemistry, physics. **Psychology:** General. **Public administration:** General. **Social sciences:** Economics, geography, political science, sociology. **Visual/performing arts:** Art, cinematography, dramatic, interior design, music performance. **Other:** Leadership studies.

**Most popular majors.** Biology 6%, business/marketing 21%, education 12%, family/consumer sciences 6%, health sciences 22%.

**Computing on campus.** 608 workstations in dormitories, library, computer center, student center. Dormitories wired for high-speed internet access and linked to campus network. Commuter students can connect to campus network. Online course registration, online library, helpline, repair service, wireless network available.

**Student life.** **Freshman orientation:** Available. Preregistration for classes offered. **Housing:** Guaranteed on-campus for freshmen. Coed dorms, single-sex dorms, special housing for disabled, apartments, fraternity/sorority housing available. $100 deposit. **Activities:** Bands, campus ministries, choral groups, dance, drama, film society, international student organizations, literary magazine, music ensembles, Model UN, radio station, student government, student newspaper, symphony orchestra, TV station, Baptist student union, Methodist student union, Newman Club, Young Democrats, College Republicans, Students for Propagation of Black Culture, Association of Baptist Students, Catholic Campus Ministries, ORBIS.

**Athletics.** NCAA. **Intercollegiate:** Baseball M, basketball, cross-country, football (tackle) M, golf, soccer, softball W, tennis W, track and field, volleyball W. **Intramural:** Badminton, basketball, bowling, cross-country, football (non-tackle), golf, racquetball, soccer, softball, table tennis, tennis, volleyball. **Team name:** Bears.

**Student services.** Alcohol/substance abuse counseling, chaplain/spiritual director, career counseling, student employment services, financial aid counseling, health services, minority student services, on-campus daycare, personal counseling, placement for graduates, veterans' counselor, women's services. **Physically disabled:** Services for visually, speech, hearing impaired.

**Contact.**  E-mail: admissions@uca.edu
Phone: (501) 450-3128 Toll-free number: (800) 243-8245
Fax: (501) 450-5228
Penny Hatfield, Director of Admissions, University of Central Arkansas, 201 Donaghey Avenue, Conway, AR 72035

## University of the Ozarks
Clarksville, Arkansas
www.ozarks.edu                            CB code: 6111

- Private 4-year university and liberal arts college affiliated with Presbyterian Church (USA)
- Residential campus in small town
- 595 degree-seeking undergraduates: 1% part-time, 51% women, 5% African American, 1% Asian American, 5% Hispanic American, 3% Native American, 18% international
- 89% of applicants admitted
- SAT or ACT (ACT writing optional), application essay required
- 42% graduate within 6 years

**General.** Founded in 1834. Regionally accredited. **Degrees:** 118 bachelor's awarded. **Location:** 100 miles from Little Rock, 65 miles from Fort Smith. **Calendar:** Semester, limited summer session. **Full-time faculty:** 47 total; 79% have terminal degrees, 8% minority, 30% women. **Part-time faculty:** 34 total; 9% have terminal degrees, 53% women. **Class size:** 79% < 20, 21% 20-39.

**Freshman class profile.** 596 applied, 530 admitted, 152 enrolled.

| Mid 50% test scores | | | |
|---|---|---|---|
| SAT critical reading: | 430-530 | Rank in top quarter: | 41% |
| SAT math: | 460-560 | Rank in top tenth: | 14% |
| ACT composite: | 19-25 | End year in good standing: | 89% |
| GPA 3.75 or higher: | 26% | Return as sophomores: | 69% |
| GPA 3.50-3.74: | 18% | Out-of-state: | 36% |
| GPA 3.0-3.49: | 30% | Live on campus: | 86% |
| GPA 2.0-2.99: | 25% | International: | 9% |

**Basis for selection.** School achievement record and test scores most important. Interview required of those with marginal grades, recommended for all applicants.

**High school preparation.** College-preparatory program recommended. 18 units recommended. Recommended units include English 4, mathematics 4, social studies 1, history 2, science 3 (laboratory 2) and foreign language 2.

**2009-2010 Annual costs.** Tuition/fees: $18,900. Room/board: $6,050. Books/supplies: $800. Personal expenses: $2,901.

**2008-2009 Financial aid. Need-based:** 155 full-time freshmen applied for aid; 143 were judged to have need; 143 of these received aid. Average need met was 87%. Average scholarship/grant was $15,183; average loan $6,476. 66% of total undergraduate aid awarded as scholarships/grants, 34% as loans/jobs. **Non-need-based:** Awarded to 204 full-time undergraduates, including 44 freshmen. Scholarships awarded for academics, alumni affiliation, art, leadership, minority status, music/drama, religious affiliation, state residency. **Additional information:** Walton International Scholarship Program provides full scholarships to selected Central American and Mexican residents.

**Application procedures. Admission:** Priority date 4/1; no deadline. $30 fee, may be waived for applicants with need, free for online applicants. Admission notification on a rolling basis. **Financial aid:** Priority date 2/15; no closing date. FAFSA required. Applicants notified on a rolling basis starting 3/1; must reply within 2 week(s) of notification.

**Academics. Special study options:** Cooperative education, double major, dual enrollment of high school students, independent study, internships, liberal arts/career combination, study abroad, teacher certification program. **Credit/placement by examination:** AP, CLEP, SAT, ACT, institutional tests. 30 credit hours maximum toward bachelor's degree. **Support services:** Learning center, remedial instruction, study skills assistance, tutoring.

**Majors. Biology:** General. **Business:** Accounting, business admin, marketing. **Communications:** Broadcast journalism, media studies. **Conservation:** Environmental studies. **Education:** Biology, business, early childhood, elementary, middle, physical, science, special. **Health:** Predental, premedicine, prepharmacy, preveterinary. **History:** General. **Legal studies:** Prelaw. **Math:** General. **Parks/recreation:** Health/fitness. **Philosophy/religion:** Philosophy, religion. **Physical sciences:** Chemistry, physics. **Psychology:** General. **Public administration:** General. **Social sciences:** General, political science, sociology. **Visual/performing arts:** General, art, dramatic.

**Most popular majors.** Business/marketing 35%, communications/journalism 9%, education 10%, liberal arts 6%, social sciences 13%, visual/performing arts 9%.

**Computing on campus.** 150 workstations in dormitories, library, computer center, student center. Dormitories wired for high-speed internet access and linked to campus network. Commuter students can connect to campus network. Online course registration, online library, helpline, wireless network available.

**Student life. Freshman orientation:** Mandatory. Preregistration for classes offered. **Housing:** Guaranteed on-campus for freshmen. Coed dorms, single-sex dorms, apartments available. $100 partly refundable deposit, deadline 8/15. **Activities:** Campus ministries, choral groups, drama, film society, international student organizations, literary magazine, radio station, student government, TV station, Ozarks Area Mission, Alpha & Omega, other religious, ethnic, and social service organizations.

**Athletics.** NCAA. **Intercollegiate:** Baseball M, basketball, cheerleading, cross-country, soccer, softball W, tennis. **Intramural:** Badminton, basketball, bowling, football (non-tackle), racquetball, soccer, softball, tennis, volleyball. **Team name:** Eagles.

**Student services.** Chaplain/spiritual director, career counseling, student employment services, financial aid counseling, health services, personal counseling, placement for graduates, veterans' counselor. **Learning disabled:** Comprehensive services available.

**Contact.** E-mail: admiss@ozarks.edu
Phone: (479) 979-1227 Toll-free number: (800) 264-8636
Fax: (479) 979-1417
Kim Myrick, Dean of Enrollment, University of the Ozarks, 415 North College Avenue, Clarksville, AR 72830-2880

## Williams Baptist College
**Walnut Ridge, Arkansas**
www.wbcoll.edu
CB code: 6658

- Private 4-year liberal arts college affiliated with Southern Baptist Convention
- Residential campus in small town

- 509 degree-seeking undergraduates: 3% part-time, 55% women, 2% African American, 1% Native American, 1% international
- 64% of applicants admitted
- SAT or ACT (ACT writing optional) required
- 55% graduate within 6 years

**General.** Founded in 1941. Regionally accredited. **Degrees:** 75 bachelor's, 3 associate awarded. **ROTC:** Army. **Location:** 30 miles from Jonesboro, 100 miles from Memphis. **Calendar:** Semester, limited summer session. **Full-time faculty:** 28 total; 61% have terminal degrees, 39% women. **Part-time faculty:** 16 total; 6% have terminal degrees, 6% minority, 75% women. **Class size:** 52% < 20, 47% 20-39, less than 1% 40-49.

**Freshman class profile.** 550 applied, 353 admitted, 139 enrolled.

| Mid 50% test scores | | Out-of-state: | 10% |
|---|---|---|---|
| ACT composite: | 19-23 | Live on campus: | 85% |
| Return as sophomores: | 65% | | |

**Basis for selection.** Students must have a 19 composite ACT score and a 2.5 cumulative high school GPA in order to be admitted unconditionally.

**High school preparation.** Recommended units include English 4, mathematics 4, social studies 3, science 3 (laboratory 3) and foreign language 2.

**2009-2010 Annual costs.** Tuition/fees: $11,400. Room/board: $5,200. Books/supplies: $1,054. Personal expenses: $1,280.

**2008-2009 Financial aid. Need-based:** 112 full-time freshmen applied for aid; 64 were judged to have need; 64 of these received aid. Average scholarship/grant was $4,719; average loan $2,523. 49% of total undergraduate aid awarded as scholarships/grants, 51% as loans/jobs. **Non-need-based:** Awarded to 146 full-time undergraduates, including 67 freshmen. Scholarships awarded for academics, art, athletics, leadership, minority status, music/drama, religious affiliation, state residency. **Additional information:** Art scholarship applicants must submit portfolio.

**Application procedures. Admission:** No deadline. $20 fee. Admission notification on a rolling basis. **Financial aid:** Priority date 5/1; no closing date. FAFSA required. Applicants notified on a rolling basis starting 4/1; must reply within 2 week(s) of notification.

**Academics. Special study options:** Double major, dual enrollment of high school students, independent study, internships, study abroad. **Credit/placement by examination:** AP, CLEP, IB. 30 credit hours maximum toward bachelor's degree. **Support services:** Learning center, reduced course load, remedial instruction, study skills assistance, tutoring.

**Majors. Biology:** General. **Business:** Business admin, finance. **Computer sciences:** General. **Education:** General, art, early childhood, elementary, English, music, physical, secondary, social studies. **History:** General. **Psychology:** General. **Theology:** Bible, missionary, religious ed, sacred music, theology, youth ministry. **Visual/performing arts:** Studio arts.

**Most popular majors.** Business/marketing 11%, education 48%, psychology 15%, theological studies 20%.

**Computing on campus.** 70 workstations in library, computer center, student center. Dormitories wired for high-speed internet access and linked to campus network. Commuter students can connect to campus network. Online library, wireless network available.

**Student life. Freshman orientation:** Mandatory, $75 fee. 2-day program held at beginning of fall semester. **Policies:** Please see on-line Student Handbook. Religious observance required. **Housing:** Guaranteed on-campus for all undergraduates. Single-sex dorms, apartments available. $75 fully refundable deposit, deadline 5/1. All full-time students under 21 required to live in college housing, unless commuting. **Activities:** Campus ministries, choral groups, drama, international student organizations, music ensembles, student government, Fellowship of Christian Athletes, student activities board, student Ambassadors.

**Athletics.** NAIA. **Intercollegiate:** Baseball M, basketball, cheerleading, soccer M, softball W, volleyball W. **Intramural:** Baseball M, basketball, football (non-tackle), softball, volleyball. **Team name:** Eagles.

**Student services.** Alcohol/substance abuse counseling, chaplain/spiritual director, career counseling, financial aid counseling, health services, personal counseling, veterans' counselor.

**Contact.** E-mail: admissions@wbcoll.edu
Phone: (870) 759-4121 Toll-free number: (800) 722-4434
Fax: (870) 886-3924
Angela Flippo, Vice President for Enrollment, Williams Baptist College, PO Box 3665, Walnut Ridge, AR 72476

# California

## Academy of Art University
### San Francisco, California
### www.academyart.edu
**CB code: 1981**

- For-profit 4-year university and visual arts college
- Commuter campus in very large city
- 10,724 degree-seeking undergraduates: 40% part-time, 56% women, 6% African American, 10% Asian American, 8% Hispanic American, 1% Native American, 14% international
- 4,549 degree-seeking graduate students
- 32% graduate within 6 years; 7% enter graduate study

**General.** Founded in 1929. Equal emphasis on both fine and applied arts. **Degrees:** 750 bachelor's, 73 associate awarded; master's offered. **Calendar:** Semester, extensive summer session. **Full-time faculty:** 184 total; 23% have terminal degrees, 17% minority, 44% women. **Part-time faculty:** 758 total. **Class size:** 83% < 20, 16% 20-39, less than 1% 40-49, less than 1% 50-99. **Special facilities:** 3 nonprofit galleries, photography darkrooms, Bosch Telecen, green screen stage, interior design resource room, foundry, 50,000-square-foot sculpture center, Final Cut Pro, Media and Avid Express editing stations.

**Freshman class profile.** 4,716 applied, 4,716 admitted, 2,955 enrolled.

| | | | |
|---|---|---|---|
| End year in good standing: | 69% | Live on campus: | 35% |
| Return as sophomores: | 57% | International: | 10% |
| Out-of-state: | 47% | | |

**Basis for selection.** Open admission. Continuing education program offered. Interview recommended, and can be in person or over the phone. **Learning Disabled:** Reasonable accommodations made for students with disabilities.

**High school preparation.** Art and design courses recommended.

**2010-2011 Annual costs.** Tuition/fees (projected): $22,490. $500 tuition deposit (non-refundable) required for international applicants. Room/board: $13,400. Books/supplies: $1,638. Personal expenses: $2,250.

**2008-2009 Financial aid. Need-based:** 605 full-time freshmen applied for aid; 505 were judged to have need; 496 of these received aid. Average scholarship/grant was $4,649; average loan $2,647. 25% of total undergraduate aid awarded as scholarships/grants, 75% as loans/jobs. **Non-need-based:** Awarded to 198 full-time undergraduates, including 77 freshmen. Scholarships awarded for academics, art. **Additional information:** Numerous summer grant programs available.

**Application procedures. Admission:** No deadline. $100 fee. Admission notification on a rolling basis. Accepted applicants may preregister in mid March. **Financial aid:** Priority date 7/10; no closing date. FAFSA, institutional form required. Applicants notified on a rolling basis.

**Academics. Special study options:** Combined bachelor's/graduate degree, distance learning, ESL, honors, independent study, internships, student-designed major, teacher certification program. **Credit/placement by examination:** AP, CLEP, IB. Interview, essay recommended for placement. Portfolio recommended for bachelor of arts applicants. **Support services:** Learning center, pre-admission summer program, reduced course load, remedial instruction, study skills assistance, tutoring, writing center.

**Majors. Communications:** Advertising, media studies. **Communications technology:** Animation/special effects, desktop publishing. **Computer sciences:** Game design, web page design. **Education:** Art. **Visual/performing arts:** Cinematography, commercial photography, commercial/advertising art, design, drawing, fashion design, fiber arts, graphic design, illustration, industrial design, interior design, metal/jewelry, multimedia, painting, photography, printmaking, sculpture, studio arts. **Other:** Music for visual media.

**Most popular majors.** Communication technologies 27%, visual/performing arts 73%.

**Computing on campus.** 800 workstations in dormitories, library, computer center. Dormitories wired for high-speed internet access. Commuter students can connect to campus network. Online course registration, online library, helpline, student web hosting, wireless network available.

**Student life. Freshman orientation:** Mandatory. Preregistration for classes offered. 5-day session week before start of classes. **Housing:** Guaranteed on-campus for freshmen. Coed dorms, single-sex dorms, special housing for disabled, wellness housing available. $500 nonrefundable deposit. **Activities:** Dance, drama, film society, international student organizations, student government, student newspaper, Chinese society, Circle of Nations.

**Athletics. Intercollegiate:** Baseball M, basketball, cross-country, golf, soccer, softball W, tennis W, track and field, volleyball W. **Intramural:** Basketball, football (non-tackle), soccer, softball, table tennis, tennis, volleyball. **Team name:** Urban Knights.

**Student services.** Alcohol/substance abuse counseling, career counseling, student employment services, financial aid counseling, personal counseling. **Physically disabled:** Services for visually, hearing impaired.

**Contact.** E-mail: info@academyart.edu
Phone: (415) 274-2200 Toll-free number: (800) 544-2787
Fax: (415) 618-6287
Admissions, Academy of Art University, 79 New Montgomery Street, San Francisco, CA 94105-3410

## Alliant International University
### San Diego, California
### www.alliant.edu
**CB member**
**CB code: 4039**

- Private two-year upper-division university
- Commuter campus in very large city
- 92% of applicants admitted

**General.** Founded in 1952. Regionally accredited. Focuses on preparing students for professional careers in applied social sciences. Students may enter as transfers after 2 years of undergraduate study at San Diego, and as freshmen or transfers at Mexico City. A bachelor completion program in Forensic Behavioral Studies is scheduled to begin at Alliant's Fresno campus in Fall 2010. **Degrees:** 80 bachelor's awarded; master's, doctoral, professional offered. **Articulation:** Agreements with Cuyamaca College, Glendale College, Grossmont College, Imperial Valley College, MiraCosta College, Mt. San Antonio College, Mt. San Jacinto College, Palomar College, Pasadena College, Riverside Community College, Saddleback College, San Diego City College, San Diego Mesa College, San Diego Miramar College, Santa Monica College, Southwestern College, Ventura College. **Location:** 16 miles from downtown. **Calendar:** Semester, limited summer session. **Full-time faculty:** 161 total; 100% have terminal degrees, 17% minority, 43% women. **Part-time faculty:** 405 total; 93% have terminal degrees, 12% minority. **Class size:** 99% < 20, less than 1% 20-39.

**Student profile.** 151 degree-seeking undergraduates, 3,858 degree-seeking graduate students. 91 applied as first time-transfer students, 84 admitted, 44 enrolled. 45% transferred from two-year, 55% transferred from four-year institutions.

| | | | |
|---|---|---|---|
| Women: | 31% | International: | 8% |
| African American: | 4% | Part-time: | 68% |
| Asian American: | 5% | Out-of-state: | 14% |
| Hispanic American: | 21% | Live on campus: | 35% |
| Native American: | 1% | 25 or older: | 54% |

**Basis for selection.** High school transcript, college transcript required. Transfer accepted as sophomores, juniors, seniors.

**2009-2010 Annual costs.** Tuition/fees: $15,250. Room only: $7,000. Books/supplies: $1,566. Personal expenses: $2,214.

**Financial aid. Non-need-based:** Scholarships awarded for academics, alumni affiliation, athletics, leadership.

**Application procedures. Admission:** Priority date 3/2. $45 fee, may be waived for applicants with need. **Financial aid:** FAFSA required.

**Academics. Special study options:** Combined bachelor's/graduate degree, ESL, honors, independent study, internships, liberal arts/career combination, study abroad. **Credit/placement by examination:** AP, CLEP, IB, institutional tests. 27 credit hours maximum toward bachelor's degree.

**Majors. Area/ethnic studies:** Latin American. **Business:** Business admin, hospitality/recreation, international, management information systems, tourism promotion. **Communications:** Journalism. **Conservation:** Environmental studies. **Education:** ESL. **Protective services:** Law enforcement admin. **Psychology:** General, forensic. **Social sciences:** International relations.

**Most popular majors.** Business/marketing 52%, liberal arts 13%, psychology 17%, social sciences 15%.

**Computing on campus.** 100 workstations in library, computer center. Dormitories wired for high-speed internet access and linked to campus network. Commuter students can connect to campus network. Online library, student web hosting available.

**Student life. Housing:** Guaranteed on-campus for all undergraduates. Coed dorms available. $265 deposit. All dormitories made up of 2-bedroom suites with central living room. **Activities:** International student organizations, Model UN, student government, student newspaper, Indian student association, Latino student organization, Alliant Turk Society.

**Athletics. Intramural:** Basketball, bowling, soccer, softball, tennis, volleyball.

**Student services.** Adult student services, alcohol/substance abuse counseling, career counseling, student employment services, financial aid counseling, health services, personal counseling, placement for graduates, veterans' counselor, women's services. **Physically disabled:** Services for visually, speech, hearing impaired.

**Contact.** E-mail: admissions3@alliant.edu
Phone: (866) 825-5426 Toll-free number: (866) 825-5426
Fax: (858) 635-4555
Alliant International University, 10455 Pomerado Road, San Diego, CA 92131-1799

## American Jewish University
Los Angeles, California
www.ajula.edu                          CB code: 4876

- Private 4-year university and liberal arts college affiliated with Jewish faith
- Residential campus in very large city
- 112 degree-seeking undergraduates: 4% part-time, 54% women, 4% African American, 1% Asian American, 5% Hispanic American, 2% Native American, 2% international
- 22 degree-seeking graduate students
- 96% of applicants admitted
- SAT or ACT (ACT writing optional), application essay required
- 37% graduate within 6 years

**General.** Founded in 1947. Regionally accredited. **Degrees:** 25 bachelor's awarded; master's offered. **Location:** 5 miles from Los Angeles. **Calendar:** Semester. **Full-time faculty:** 13 total; 92% have terminal degrees, 38% women. **Part-time faculty:** 67 total; 24% have terminal degrees, 51% women. **Class size:** 100% < 20. **Special facilities:** Outdoor basketball court.

**Freshman class profile.** 49 applied, 47 admitted, 23 enrolled.

| Mid 50% test scores | | GPA 3.0-3.49: | 30% |
|---|---|---|---|
| SAT critical reading: | 450-530 | GPA 2.0-2.99: | 45% |
| SAT math: | 430-500 | Rank in top quarter: | 11% |
| SAT writing: | 420-540 | Return as sophomores: | 78% |
| ACT composite: | 18-20 | Out-of-state: | 48% |
| GPA 3.75 or higher: | 20% | Live on campus: | 91% |
| GPA 3.50-3.74: | 5% | | |

**Basis for selection.** An applicant's aspirations, goals, personal experience, ability to connect with others, interpersonal skills, and involvement with leadership activities weigh heavily in the application process. On-campus visit highly encouraged. If an applicant shows a lot of promise but has a truly low GPA and/or test scores, his/her file is brought to the Dean of the College of Arts and Sciences for further examination. Interview recommended.

**High school preparation.** College-preparatory program recommended.

**2010-2011 Annual costs.** Tuition/fees: $24,512. Room/board: $11,778. Books/supplies: $1,638. Personal expenses: $2,250.

**2009-2010 Financial aid. Need-based:** 23 full-time freshmen applied for aid; 23 were judged to have need; 23 of these received aid. Average need met was 87%. Average scholarship/grant was $13,220; average loan $3,070. 53% of total undergraduate aid awarded as scholarships/grants, 47% as loans/jobs. **Non-need-based:** Awarded to 128 full-time undergraduates, including 46 freshmen. Scholarships awarded for leadership, minority status, music/drama, state residency.

**Application procedures. Admission:** Closing date 5/31 (postmark date). $35 fee, may be waived for applicants with need. Application must be submitted online. Admission notification on a rolling basis beginning on or about 9/15. Varies due to rolling admissions. **Financial aid:** No deadline. FAFSA, institutional form required. Applicants notified on a rolling basis starting 1/1; must reply by 6/30.

**Academics.** In addition to majors and general education requirements, students take core curriculum of Jewish and Western Civilization classes. **Special study options:** Combined bachelor's/graduate degree, cross-registration, double major, independent study, internships, student-designed major, study abroad. **Credit/placement by examination:** AP, CLEP, IB, institutional tests. **Support services:** Reduced course load, study skills assistance, tutoring, writing center.

**Majors. Biology:** General. **Business:** General. **Communications:** Media studies. **Health:** Ethics. **Liberal arts:** Arts/sciences. **Philosophy/religion:** Judaic. **Social sciences:** Political science.

**Most popular majors.** Biology 11%, business/marketing 30%, communications/journalism 7%, philosophy/religious studies 7%, psychology 15%, social sciences 30%.

**Computing on campus.** 38 workstations in dormitories, library, computer center. Dormitories wired for high-speed internet access and linked to campus network. Commuter students can connect to campus network. Online library, helpline, wireless network available.

**Student life. Freshman orientation:** Mandatory. Held 1-2 weeks before the start of the traditional Fall semester. **Policies:** Kosher meals on campus. Students required to live on campus unless 21 or older. **Housing:** Guaranteed on-campus for all undergraduates. Coed dorms, special housing for disabled, apartments available. $100 nonrefundable deposit. **Activities:** Choral groups, drama, literary magazine, Model UN, student government, student newspaper, Team Shabbat, Hillel, Israel Action Committee, Giving Tree.

**Athletics. Team name:** Lions.

**Student services.** Alcohol/substance abuse counseling, chaplain/spiritual director, career counseling, student employment services, financial aid counseling, health services.

**Contact.** E-mail: admissions@ajula.edu
Phone: (310) 476-9777 ext. 247 Toll-free number: (877) 462-2585
Fax: (310) 471-3657
Matt Spooner, Director of Admissions, American Jewish University, Office of Undergraduate Admissions, Los Angeles, CA 90077

## Antioch University Los Angeles
Culver City, California
www.antiochla.edu                          CB code: 1862

- Private two-year upper-division branch campus and liberal arts college
- Commuter campus in very large city
- Application essay, interview required

**General.** Founded in 1972. Regionally accredited. Bachelor of Arts Degree Completion program offered on-campus with various attendance options available. **Degrees:** 33 bachelor's awarded; master's offered. **Articulation:** Agreements with UCLA Extension, Santa Monica College, West Los Angeles College, Compton City College. **Location:** 15 miles from Los Angeles. **Calendar:** Quarter, extensive summer session. **Full-time faculty:** 20 total. **Part-time faculty:** 40 total.

**Student profile.** 149 degree-seeking undergraduates.

**Basis for selection.** High school transcript, college transcript, application essay, interview required. Admission decision of full or provisional acceptance made by program chair. Transfer accepted as sophomores, juniors, seniors.

**2009-2010 Annual costs.** Tuition/fees: $16,666. Cost varies by program. Books/supplies: $1,500.

**Application procedures. Admission:** Deadline 8/1. $60 fee, may be waived for applicants with need. Must reply by 8/15. AULA does not accept freshman. Applicants are required to have at least 30 quarter/20 semester units of college-level learning from a regionally accredited institution of higher learning. **Financial aid:** FAFSA, institutional form required.

**Academics.** Prior experiential learning credits. **Special study options:** Accelerated study, combined bachelor's/graduate degree, cooperative education, cross-registration, double major, independent study, internships, liberal arts/career combination, student-designed major, study abroad, teacher

Four-Year Colleges

certification program, weekend college. **Credit/placement by examination:** AP, CLEP. 40 credit hours maximum toward bachelor's degree. DANTES examination scores accepted.

**Majors. Liberal arts:** Arts/sciences.

**Computing on campus.** 12 workstations in library, computer center. Commuter students can connect to campus network. Online library, helpline, wireless network available.

**Student life. Activities:** Student government, student newspaper, TV station.

**Athletics. Team name:** Radicals.

**Student services.** Adult student services, career counseling, student employment services, financial aid counseling, personal counseling, veterans' counselor. **Physically disabled:** Services for visually, speech, hearing impaired.

**Contact.** E-mail: admissions.aula@antioch.edu
Phone: (310) 578-1080 ext. 411 Toll-free number: (800) 726-8462
Fax: (310) 822-4824
Antioch University Los Angeles, 400 Corporate Pointe, Culver City, CA 90230-7615

## Antioch University Santa Barbara
### Santa Barbara, California
### www.antiochsb.edu
CB code: 3071

- Private two-year upper-division university and liberal arts college
- Commuter campus in small city
- Application essay, interview required

**General.** Founded in 1852. Regionally accredited. **Degrees:** 54 bachelor's awarded; master's, doctoral offered. **Articulation:** Agreements with Santa Barbara City College, University of California: Santa Barbara, Ventura Community College, Cuesta Community College, Allen Hancock Community College. **Location:** Downtown. **Calendar:** Quarter, extensive summer session. **Full-time faculty:** 17 total; 65% women. **Part-time faculty:** 53 total; 57% women.

**Student profile.** 48 degree-seeking undergraduates.

**Basis for selection.** Open admission. High school transcript, college transcript, application essay, interview required. Transfer accepted as juniors, seniors.

**2009-2010 Annual costs.** Tuition/fees: $15,876. Books/supplies: $1,600.

**Application procedures. Admission:** Rolling admission. $60 fee. **Financial aid:** Priority date 4/1, no deadline. FAFSA, institutional form required.

**Academics. Special study options:** Cross-registration, double major, independent study, internships, liberal arts/career combination, student-designed major, study abroad, teacher certification program, weekend college. **Credit/placement by examination:** CLEP, IB. **Support services:** Remedial instruction.

**Majors. Liberal arts:** Arts/sciences.

**Computing on campus.** 10 workstations in computer center. Online library, helpline available.

**Student services.** Adult student services, career counseling, financial aid counseling, personal counseling, veterans' counselor.

**Contact.** E-mail: admissions@antiochsb.edu
Phone: (805) 962-8179 Toll-free number: (866) 526-8464
Fax: (805) 962-4786
Antioch University Santa Barbara, 801 Garden Street, Suite 101, Santa Barbara, CA 93101-1581

## Argosy University: Inland Empire
### San Bernardino, California
### www.argosy.edu/inlandempire

- For-profit 4-year university
- Very large city
- 206 degree-seeking undergraduates

**General. Degrees:** 27 bachelor's awarded; master's, doctoral offered. **Calendar:** Continuous. **Full-time faculty:** 4 total. **Part-time faculty:** 54 total.

**Freshman class profile.** 29 enrolled.

**Basis for selection.** Open admission.

**Academics. Credit/placement by examination:** CLEP.

**Majors. Business:** Business admin. **Liberal arts:** Arts/sciences. **Protective services:** Police science. **Psychology:** General.

**Contact.** Phone: (909) 915-3800
Argosy University: Inland Empire, 636 East Brier Drive, Suite 120, San Bernardino, CA 92408

## Argosy University: Los Angeles
### Los Angeles, California
### www.argosy.edu/losangeles

- For-profit 4-year university
- Small city
- 116 degree-seeking undergraduates

**General.** Regionally accredited. **Degrees:** 5 bachelor's awarded; master's, doctoral offered. **Calendar:** Continuous. **Full-time faculty:** 5 total. **Part-time faculty:** 60 total.

**Freshman class profile.** 30 enrolled.

**Basis for selection.** Open admission.

**Academics. Credit/placement by examination:** CLEP.

**Majors. Business:** Business admin. **Liberal arts:** Arts/sciences. **Protective services:** Police science. **Psychology:** General.

**Contact.** E-mail: ausmadms@argosy.edu
Argosy University: Los Angeles, 5230 Pacific Concourse, Suite 200, Los Angeles, CA 90045

## Argosy University: Orange County
### Orange, California
### www.argosy.edu/orangecounty

- For-profit 4-year university
- Very large city
- 139 degree-seeking undergraduates

**General.** Regionally accredited. **Degrees:** 24 bachelor's awarded; master's, doctoral, professional offered. **Calendar:** Continuous. **Full-time faculty:** 12 total. **Part-time faculty:** 135 total.

**Freshman class profile.** 42 enrolled.

**Basis for selection.** Open admission.

**Academics. Credit/placement by examination:** CLEP.

**Majors. Business:** Business admin. **Liberal arts:** Arts/sciences. **Protective services:** Police science. **Psychology:** General.

**Contact.** Phone: (714) 620-3715 Toll-free number: (800) 716-9598
Argosy University: Orange County, 601 South Lewis Street, Orange, CA 92868

## Argosy University: San Diego
### San Diego, California
### www.argosy.edu/sandiego

- For-profit 4-year university
- Very large city
- 61 degree-seeking undergraduates

**General. Degrees:** 4 bachelor's awarded; master's, doctoral offered. **Calendar:** Continuous. **Full-time faculty:** 1 total. **Part-time faculty:** 40 total.

**Freshman class profile.** 15 enrolled.

**Basis for selection.** Open admission.

**Academics. Credit/placement by examination:** CLEP.

**Majors. Business:** Business admin. **Liberal arts:** Arts/sciences. **Protective services:** Police science. **Psychology:** General.

**Contact.** E-mail: ausdadmissions@argosy.edu
Argosy University: San Diego, 1615 Murray Canyon Road, San Diego, CA 92108

## Argosy University: San Francisco Bay Area
**Alameda, California**
**www.argosy.edu/sanfrancisco**

- For-profit 4-year university
- Small city
- 77 degree-seeking undergraduates

**General.** Regionally accredited. **Degrees:** 6 bachelor's awarded; master's, doctoral, professional offered. **Calendar:** Continuous. **Full-time faculty:** 17 total. **Part-time faculty:** 71 total.

**Freshman class profile.** 21 enrolled.

**Basis for selection.** Open admission.

**Academics. Credit/placement by examination:** CLEP.

**Majors. Business:** Business admin. **Liberal arts:** Arts/sciences. **Protective services:** Police science. **Psychology:** General.

**Contact.** E-mail: ausfadmissions@argosy.edu
Phone: (510) 217-4777
Argosy University: San Francisco Bay Area, 1005 Atlantic Avenue, Alameda, CA 94501

## Art Center College of Design
**Pasadena, California** — CB member
**www.artcenter.edu** — CB code: 4009

- Private 4-year visual arts college
- Commuter campus in small city
- 1,470 degree-seeking undergraduates: 9% part-time, 42% women
- 162 degree-seeking graduate students
- 69% of applicants admitted
- SAT or ACT, application essay required
- 94% graduate within 6 years

**General.** Founded in 1930. Regionally accredited. **Degrees:** 413 bachelor's awarded; master's offered. **Location:** 15 miles from Los Angeles. **Calendar:** Trimester, extensive summer session. **Full-time faculty:** 85 total. **Part-time faculty:** 369 total. **Class size:** 87% < 20, 12% 20-39, less than 1% 40-49, less than 1% 50-99. **Special facilities:** 3 galleries; 3-D modelling and industrial design facilities.

**Freshman class profile.** 1,110 applied, 767 admitted, 511 enrolled.

| Return as sophomores: | 90% | International: | 37% |
| Out-of-state: | 23% | | |

**Basis for selection.** Strength of specific portfolio for one major, academic record, standardized test scores. Interviews recommended for local applicants. **Homeschooled:** Transcript of courses and grades required.

**High school preparation.** College-preparatory program recommended. Art classes recommended.

**2010-2011 Annual costs.** Tuition/fees: $32,168. Books/supplies: $5,620. Personal expenses: $3,698.

**2008-2009 Financial aid. Need-based:** 255 full-time freshmen applied for aid; 240 were judged to have need; 231 of these received aid. Average scholarship/grant was $11,641; average loan $6,739. 56% of total undergraduate aid awarded as scholarships/grants, 44% as loans/jobs. **Non-need-based:** Awarded to 226 full-time undergraduates, including 42 freshmen. **Additional information:** Students may apply for scholarships after they enroll while progressing through the program.

**Application procedures. Admission:** Priority date 3/1; no deadline. $50 fee, may be waived for applicants with need. Admission notification on a rolling basis beginning on or about 1/1. **Financial aid:** Priority date 3/1; no

closing date. FAFSA required. Applicants notified on a rolling basis starting 5/15.

**Academics. Special study options:** Cross-registration, exchange student, independent study, internships, study abroad. **Credit/placement by examination:** AP, CLEP, IB, institutional tests. **Support services:** Tutoring, writing center.

**Majors. Architecture:** Environmental design. **Communications:** Advertising. **Communications technology:** Animation/special effects, graphics. **Visual/performing arts:** Cinematography, commercial photography, commercial/advertising art, graphic design, illustration, industrial design, interior design, painting, photography, sculpture, studio arts. **Other:** Entertainment design.

**Computing on campus.** 250 workstations in library, computer center. Commuter students can connect to campus network. Online library, wireless network available.

**Student life. Freshman orientation:** Mandatory. 3-day program including introduction to a mentor and testing. **Activities:** International student organizations, literary magazine, student government, Chroma Contraste, Eco Council, Women in Design, Out Network.

**Student services.** Career counseling, student employment services, financial aid counseling, personal counseling, placement for graduates. **Physically disabled:** Services for hearing impaired.

**Contact.** E-mail: admissions@artcenter.edu
Phone: (626) 396-2373 Fax: (626) 795-0578
Kit Baron, Vice President, Admissions, Art Center College of Design, 1700 Lida Street, Pasadena, CA 91103

## Art Institute of California: Hollywood
**North Hollywood, California**
**www.artinstitutes.edu/hollywood** — CB code: 3463

- For-profit 4-year culinary school and visual arts college
- Commuter campus in very large city
- 1,256 degree-seeking undergraduates: 50% part-time, 79% women
- Application essay, interview required

**General.** Accredited by ACICS. **Degrees:** 128 bachelor's, 46 associate awarded. **Location:** Downtown. **Calendar:** Quarter, extensive summer session. **Full-time faculty:** 19 total; 42% have terminal degrees, 10% minority, 53% women. **Part-time faculty:** 108 total; 44% have terminal degrees, 39% minority, 56% women. **Class size:** 68% < 20, 32% 20-39. **Special facilities:** Sewing and construction rooms, interior design resource room.

**Freshman class profile.** 255 applied, 196 admitted, 196 enrolled.

**Basis for selection.** Open admission.

**2009-2010 Annual costs.** Tuition/fees: $22,835. Cost for 7-quarter continuous enrollment associate degree program $56,486; cost for 12-quarter continuous enrollment bachelor's degree program $96,726. Fees vary by program. Room only: $9,285. Books/supplies: $1,692.

**Application procedures. Admission:** No deadline. $50 fee. Admission notification on a rolling basis.

**Academics. Special study options:** Distance learning, internships, study abroad, weekend college. **Credit/placement by examination:** AP, CLEP, institutional tests. **Support services:** Reduced course load, study skills assistance, tutoring, writing center.

**Majors. Business:** Fashion. **Communications technology:** Animation/special effects. **Computer sciences:** Web page design. **Personal/culinary services:** Chef training. **Visual/performing arts:** Fashion design, graphic design, industrial design, interior design, photography.

**Most popular majors.** Business/marketing 34%, visual/performing arts 66%.

**Computing on campus.** 162 workstations in library, computer center. Online library, helpline, wireless network available.

**Student life. Freshman orientation:** Mandatory. Preregistration for classes offered. **Housing:** Single-sex dorms available. $250 fully refundable deposit, deadline 10/5. **Activities:** Student newspaper.

**Student services.** Career counseling, student employment services, financial aid counseling, personal counseling, placement for graduates. **Physically disabled:** Services for hearing impaired.

**Contact.** E-mail: mromero@aii.edu
Phone: (818) 299-5100 Toll-free number: (877) 468-6232
Fax: (877) 299-5151
Melissa Huen, Senior Director of Admissions, Art Institute of California:
Hollywood, 5250 Lankershim Boulevard, North Hollywood, CA 91601

## Art Institute of California: Inland Empire
### San Bernardino, California
### www.artinstitutes.edu

- For-profit 4-year culinary school and visual arts college
- Large city
- 1,430 degree-seeking undergraduates

**General.** Regionally accredited; also accredited by ACCSC. **Degrees:** 26 bachelor's, 21 associate awarded. **Calendar:** Quarter. **Full-time faculty:** 22 total. **Part-time faculty:** 53 total.

**Academics. Credit/placement by examination:** CLEP.

**Majors. Communications technology:** Animation/special effects. **Computer sciences:** Game design. **Personal/culinary services:** Restaurant/catering. **Visual/performing arts:** Fashion design, graphic design, interior design, multimedia. **Other:** Fashion and retail management.

**Contact.** Toll-free number: (800) 353-0812
Art Institute of California: Inland Empire, 630 East Brier Drive, San Bernardino, CA 92408-2800

## Art Institute of California: Orange County
### Santa Ana, California
### www.artinstitutes.edu/orangecounty      CB code: 3831

- For-profit 3-year culinary school and visual arts college
- Commuter campus in very large city
- 1,873 degree-seeking undergraduates
- Application essay, interview required

**General.** Accredited by ACICS. **Degrees:** 295 bachelor's, 81 associate awarded. **Location:** 40 miles from Los Angeles, 90 miles from San Diego. **Calendar:** Quarter, extensive summer session. **Full-time faculty:** 60 total. **Part-time faculty:** 59 total. **Special facilities:** 4 professional skills kitchens, 11 computer labs, interior design resource library, interior design studio, industrial design workshop, student dining lab, fashion lab.

**Freshman class profile.** 1,151 applied, 424 admitted, 379 enrolled.

**Basis for selection.** Open admission, but selective for some programs. Proof of high school graduation, or equivalent from a foreign institution, required. International students require proof of English proficiency. Acceptance determined by committee of faculty members.

**2009-2010 Annual costs.** Tuition/fees: $24,344. Typical full-time load 16 credit hours per quarter. Culinary lab fee $315 per quarter, online fee $100 per class per quarter. Room only: $2,997. Books/supplies: $1,100. Personal expenses: $2,280.

**Financial aid. Non-need-based:** Scholarships awarded for academics, art, minority status.

**Application procedures. Admission:** No deadline. $50 fee. Admission notification on a rolling basis. **Financial aid:** No deadline. FAFSA required. Applicants notified on a rolling basis; must reply within 2 week(s) of notification.

**Academics. Special study options:** Cooperative education, distance learning, internships. Online courses. **Credit/placement by examination:** CLEP, IB, institutional tests. 3 credit hours maximum toward associate degree, 3 toward bachelor's. **Support services:** Learning center, pre-admission summer program, reduced course load, study skills assistance, tutoring.

**Majors. BACHELOR'S. Business:** Apparel. **Communications:** Digital media. **Communications technology:** Animation/special effects. **Computer sciences:** Computer graphics, web page design, webmaster. **Personal/culinary services:** Culinary arts, restaurant/catering. **Visual/performing arts:** Commercial/advertising art, fashion design, graphic design, industrial design, interior design. **ASSOCIATE. Communications:** Digital media. **Computer sciences:** Computer graphics, web page design, webmaster. **Personal/culinary services:** Chef training, culinary arts, restaurant/catering. **Visual/performing arts:** Commercial/advertising art, graphic design, interior design.

**Computing on campus.** 312 workstations in library, computer center, student center. Online course registration, online library, helpline, repair service, wireless network available.

**Student life. Freshman orientation:** Mandatory. **Housing:** Special housing for disabled, apartments available. School-sponsored housing available. **Activities:** Film society, student newspaper.

**Student services.** Career counseling, student employment services, financial aid counseling, personal counseling, placement for graduates, veterans' counselor. **Physically disabled:** Services for visually, speech, hearing impaired.

**Contact.** E-mail: aicaocadm@aii.edu
Phone: (888) 549-3055 Toll-free number: (888) 549-3055
Fax: (714) 556-1923
Timothy Hansen, Senior Director of Admissions, Art Institute of California: Orange County, 3601 West Sunflower Avenue, Santa Ana, CA 92704-7931

## Art Institute of California: Sacramento
### Sacramento, California
### www.artinstitutes.edu/sacramento

- For-profit 3-year culinary school and visual arts college
- Large city
- 781 degree-seeking undergraduates

**General.** Regionally accredited; also accredited by ACICS. **Calendar:** Quarter. **Full-time faculty:** 21 total. **Part-time faculty:** 30 total.

**2009-2010 Annual costs.** Tuition/fees: $22,635. Required fees vary by program. Room only: $6,525. Books/supplies: $1,692.

**Academics. Credit/placement by examination:** CLEP.

**Majors. BACHELOR'S. Communications technology:** Animation/special effects. **Computer sciences:** Game design. **Personal/culinary services:** Restaurant/catering. **Visual/performing arts:** Cinematography, graphic design, interior design, multimedia. **ASSOCIATE. Personal/culinary services:** General. **Visual/performing arts:** Graphic design, multimedia.

**Contact.** Phone: (800) 477-1957
Art Institute of California: Sacramento, 2850 Gateway Oaks Drive, Suite 100, Sacramento, CA 95833

## Art Institute of California: San Diego
### San Diego, California
### www.artinstitutes.edu/sandiego      CB code: 3036

- For-profit 3-year visual arts college
- Residential campus in very large city
- 2,053 degree-seeking undergraduates
- 33% of applicants admitted
- Application essay, interview required

**General.** Accredited by ACCSC. **Degrees:** 327 bachelor's, 141 associate awarded. **Calendar:** Quarter. **Full-time faculty:** 58 total. **Part-time faculty:** 75 total. **Special facilities:** Dining lab run by culinary students.

**Freshman class profile.** 956 applied, 315 admitted, 312 enrolled.

**Basis for selection.** High school record and general appropriateness of educational background to specific program applied for most important. Portfolio, interview, standardized test scores also important. **Learning Disabled:** Students requiring assistance should notify Assistant Director of Admissions.

**2009-2010 Annual costs.** Tuition/fees: $24,144.

**Application procedures. Admission:** No deadline. $50 fee. Admission notification on a rolling basis. **Financial aid:** No deadline. FAFSA required.

**Academics. Special study options:** Accelerated study, distance learning, internships. **Credit/placement by examination:** AP, CLEP. **Support services:** Study skills assistance, tutoring.

**Majors. BACHELOR'S. Communications:** Advertising. **Computer sciences:** Computer graphics, game design, web page design, webmaster. **Personal/culinary services:** Restaurant/catering. **Visual/performing arts:** Commercial/advertising art, fashion design, graphic design, interior design, multimedia. **Other:** Fashion marketing and management. **ASSOCIATE. Personal/**

**culinary services:** Chef training, restaurant/catering. **Visual/performing arts:** Commercial/advertising art, design, graphic design.

**Computing on campus.** 300 workstations in library, computer center. Online library, wireless network available.

**Student life. Freshman orientation:** Mandatory. Preregistration for classes offered. **Housing:** Single-sex dorms, apartments available. **Activities:** Student government, student newspaper.

**Student services.** Alcohol/substance abuse counseling, career counseling, services for economically disadvantaged, student employment services, financial aid counseling, personal counseling. **Physically disabled:** Services for visually, speech, hearing impaired. **Learning disabled:** Comprehensive services available.

**Contact.** E-mail: aicaadmin@aii.edu
Phone: (866) 275-2422 Toll-free number: (866) 275-2422
Melissa Garcia, Director of Admissions, Art Institute of California: San Diego, 7650 Mission Valley Road, San Diego, CA 92108-4423

## Art Institute of California: San Francisco
**San Francisco, California**
www.artinstitutes.edu/sanfrancisco          **CB code: 4421**

- For-profit 4-year culinary school and visual arts college
- Commuter campus in very large city
- 1,500 degree-seeking undergraduates
- Application essay required

**General.** Founded in 1939. Accredited by ACICS. **Degrees:** 249 bachelor's, 24 associate awarded; master's offered. **Location:** Downtown. **Calendar:** Quarter, extensive summer session. **Full-time faculty:** 34 total. **Part-time faculty:** 93 total.

**Basis for selection.** High school record and general appropriateness of educational background to specific program applied for most important. Portfolio, interview, standardized test scores also important. Interview and portfolio recommended.

**High school preparation.** Recommended units include English 1, mathematics 1, social studies 1 and history 1. One art class recommended.

**2009-2010 Annual costs.** Tuition/fees: $22,685. Supply Kits an additional $560-$1,485 estimate for all programs. Room/board: $11,490.

**Application procedures. Admission:** No deadline. $50 fee. Admission notification on a rolling basis. **Financial aid:** No deadline. FAFSA required. Applicants notified on a rolling basis.

**Academics. Special study options:** Combined bachelor's/graduate degree, distance learning, honors, internships, study abroad. **Credit/placement by examination:** AP, CLEP, IB. **Support services:** Reduced course load, remedial instruction, study skills assistance, tutoring.

**Majors. Business:** Fashion. **Communications technology:** Animation/special effects. **Computer sciences:** Computer graphics, web page design. **Personal/culinary services:** Chef training, restaurant/catering. **Visual/performing arts:** Commercial/advertising art, fashion design, film/cinema, graphic design, interior design.

**Computing on campus.** Wireless network available.

**Student life. Freshman orientation:** Mandatory. **Housing:** Coed dorms, apartments available. $300 deposit. **Activities:** International student organizations, student government, student newspaper, adLab, Society of Web Architects and Programmers, Design Innovation Club, Game Art & Design Club, Adventurous Appetites, Photo Club, Ai Production Workshop, Alpha Beta Kappa, Audio Club, Expressionz.

**Student services.** Career counseling, student employment services, financial aid counseling. **Physically disabled:** Services for hearing impaired.

**Contact.** E-mail: aisfadm@aii.edu
Phone: (415) 865-0198 Toll-free number: (888) 493-3261
Fax: (415) 863-6344
Louie Garcia, Senior Director of Admissions, Art Institute of California: San Francisco, 1170 Market Street, San Francisco, CA 94102

## Azusa Pacific University
**Azusa, California**                                **CB member**
www.apu.edu                                          **CB code: 4596**

- Private 4-year university affiliated with interdenominational tradition
- Residential campus in small city

- 4,874 degree-seeking undergraduates: 15% part-time, 64% women
- 3,630 degree-seeking graduate students
- 59% of applicants admitted
- SAT or ACT (ACT writing optional), application essay required
- 67% graduate within 6 years

**General.** Founded in 1899. Regionally accredited. **Degrees:** 1,245 bachelor's awarded; master's, doctoral, professional offered. **ROTC:** Army. **Location:** 30 miles from Los Angeles. **Calendar:** Semester, limited summer session. **Full-time faculty:** 339 total; 74% have terminal degrees, 22% minority, 47% women. **Part-time faculty:** 36 total; 61% have terminal degrees, 14% minority, 50% women. **Class size:** 64% < 20, 31% 20-39, 3% 40-49, 2% 50-99, less than 1% >100.

**Freshman class profile.** 5,262 applied, 3,090 admitted, 1,022 enrolled.

| Mid 50% test scores | | | |
|---|---|---|---|
| SAT critical reading: | 490-590 | Rank in top quarter: | 63% |
| SAT math: | 480-600 | Rank in top tenth: | 32% |
| ACT composite: | 21-27 | Return as sophomores: | 82% |
| GPA 3.75 or higher: | 44% | Out-of-state: | 27% |
| GPA 3.50-3.74: | 18% | Live on campus: | 93% |
| GPA 3.0-3.49: | 29% | | |
| GPA 2.0-2.99: | 9% | | |

**Basis for selection.** GPA, test scores, references, statement of agreement, essay important. Auditions required for music applicants. Interviews recommended for borderline applicants. **Homeschooled:** SAT or ACT and transcript from organization required.

**High school preparation.** College-preparatory program recommended. Recommended units include English 4, mathematics 3, social studies 1, history 2, science 2 and foreign language 3.

**2010-2011 Annual costs.** Tuition/fees: $27,750. Room/board: $8,314. Books/supplies: $1,638. Personal expenses: $2,250.

**2008-2009 Financial aid. Need-based:** 1,020 full-time freshmen applied for aid; 718 were judged to have need; 717 of these received aid. Average need met was 67%. Average scholarship/grant was $15,616; average loan $4,068. 67% of total undergraduate aid awarded as scholarships/grants, 33% as loans/jobs. **Non-need-based:** Awarded to 3,488 full-time undergraduates, including 915 freshmen. Scholarships awarded for academics, athletics, leadership, minority status, music/drama, religious affiliation, ROTC.

**Application procedures. Admission:** Priority date 2/15; deadline 6/1 (postmark date). $45 fee, may be waived for applicants with need. Admission notification 4/1. Must reply by 5/1. Students with 3.0 high school GPA or higher and 1000 SAT score or higher can apply at completion of junior year and/or before January 1 for admission consideration. Housing deposit due by move-in date. **Financial aid:** Priority date 3/2, closing date 7/1. FAFSA, institutional form required. Applicants notified on a rolling basis starting 3/1; must reply within 3 week(s) of notification.

**Academics.** More than 20 online masters and credential programs offered for library media teaching. All other online programs are part of individual face to face programs with exception of one course offered completely online. **Special study options:** Accelerated study, cooperative education, distance learning, double major, ESL, exchange student, honors, independent study, internships, study abroad, teacher certification program, urban semester, Washington semester. **Credit/placement by examination:** AP, CLEP, IB, institutional tests. 15 credit hours maximum toward bachelor's degree. Essays required for Analysis and Interpretation of Literature and Freshman College Composition. **Support services:** Learning center, reduced course load, remedial instruction, study skills assistance, tutoring, writing center.

**Majors. Biology:** General, biochemistry. **Business:** General, accounting, business admin, finance, management information systems, marketing. **Communications:** General, journalism. **Computer sciences:** General, computer science. **Education:** Art, business, elementary, middle, multi-level teacher, physical, secondary. **Foreign languages:** Spanish. **Health:** Nurse practitioner, nursing (RN), predental, premedicine. **History:** General. **Liberal arts:** Arts/sciences. **Math:** General. **Philosophy/religion:** Philosophy, religion. **Physical sciences:** General, chemistry, physics. **Psychology:** General. **Public administration:** Social work. **Social sciences:** General, international relations, political science, sociology. **Theology:** Bible, religious ed, sacred music, theology. **Visual/performing arts:** Art, dramatic, music performance, music theory/composition, studio arts.

**Most popular majors.** Business/marketing 20%, communications/journalism 8%, health sciences 17%, liberal arts 19%.

**Computing on campus.** 268 workstations in library, computer center, student center. Dormitories wired for high-speed internet access and linked to campus network. Commuter students can connect to campus network.

Online course registration, helpline, repair service, wireless network available.

**Student life. Freshman orientation:** Mandatory. Preregistration for classes offered. Class taken during first semester. **Policies:** Students will refrain from activities which may be spiritually or morally destructive. Religious observance required. **Housing:** Coed dorms, single-sex dorms, apartments available. $250 deposit, deadline 5/1. **Activities:** Bands, choral groups, drama, music ensembles, musical theater, opera, radio station, student government, student newspaper, symphony orchestra, TV station, minority student association.

**Athletics.** NAIA. **Intercollegiate:** Baseball M, basketball, cross-country, football (tackle) M, soccer, softball W, tennis M, track and field, volleyball W. **Intramural:** Basketball, football (tackle) M, skiing, volleyball. **Team name:** Cougars.

**Student services.** Chaplain/spiritual director, career counseling, student employment services, financial aid counseling, health services, minority student services, personal counseling, placement for graduates, veterans' counselor. **Physically disabled:** Services for visually, speech, hearing impaired.

**Contact.** E-mail: admissions@apu.edu
Phone: (626) 812-3016 Toll-free number: (800) 825-5278
Fax: (626) 812-3096
Dave Burke, Director of Undergraduate Admissions, Azusa Pacific University, 901 East Alosta Avenue, Azusa, CA 91702-7000

---

## Bethany University
### Scotts Valley, California
www.bethany.edu                                  CB code: 4021

- Private 4-year Bible and liberal arts college affiliated with Assemblies of God
- Residential campus in small town
- 421 degree-seeking undergraduates: 15% part-time, 61% women
- 74 degree-seeking graduate students
- 45% of applicants admitted
- SAT or ACT (ACT writing optional), application essay required
- 36% graduate within 6 years

**General.** Founded in 1919. Regionally accredited. Located in the Monterey Bay/Santa Cruz area. **Degrees:** 96 bachelor's, 1 associate awarded; master's offered. **ROTC:** Army. **Location:** 5 miles from Santa Cruz. **Calendar:** Semester, limited summer session. **Full-time faculty:** 25 total; 68% have terminal degrees, 40% women. **Part-time faculty:** 39 total; 59% women. **Class size:** 70% < 20, 25% 20-39, 2% 40-49, 3% 50-99. **Special facilities:** Early childhood learning center, wellness center, student individualized learning center.

**Freshman class profile.** 316 applied, 143 admitted, 79 enrolled.

| Mid 50% test scores | | | |
|---|---|---|---|
| SAT critical reading: | 440-510 | Return as sophomores: | 53% |
| SAT math: | 400-510 | Out-of-state: | 17% |
| ACT composite: | 16-21 | Live on campus: | 82% |

**Basis for selection.** Evaluation of academic records, and religious affiliation/commitment very important. Interviews recommended. **Homeschooled:** State high school equivalency certificate required. **Learning Disabled:** Students with learning disabilities are recommended to contact the Educational Support Services Offices during the admission's process.

**2009-2010 Annual costs.** Tuition/fees: $18,150. Room/board: $7,450. Books/supplies: $1,200. Personal expenses: $1,300.

**2009-2010 Financial aid. Non-need-based:** Scholarships awarded for academics, alumni affiliation, athletics, leadership, minority status, music/drama, religious affiliation.

**Application procedures. Admission:** Closing date 7/31 (postmark date). $35 fee. Admission notification on a rolling basis. **Financial aid:** Priority date 3/2; no closing date. FAFSA, institutional form required. Applicants notified on a rolling basis starting 4/15; must reply within 2 week(s) of notification.

**Academics. Special study options:** Accelerated study, combined bachelor's/graduate degree, distance learning, double major, external degree, independent study, internships, study abroad, teacher certification program. **Credit/placement by examination:** AP, CLEP, IB, SAT, ACT. 30 credit hours maximum toward associate degree, 30 toward bachelor's. **Support services:** Learning center, reduced course load, remedial instruction, study skills assistance, tutoring.

---

**Majors. Business:** General, business admin. **Communications:** General, organizational, public relations. **Education:** Early childhood. **Health:** Substance abuse counseling. **Liberal arts:** Arts/sciences. **Psychology:** General. **Social sciences:** General. **Theology:** Bible, missionary, pastoral counseling, sacred music, theology, youth ministry. **Visual/performing arts:** Dramatic.

**Most popular majors.** Business/marketing 17%, communications/journalism 10%, education 7%, psychology 13%, social sciences 12%, theological studies 44%.

**Computing on campus.** 25 workstations in library, computer center, student center. Dormitories wired for high-speed internet access and linked to campus network. Commuter students can connect to campus network. Online library, wireless network available.

**Student life. Freshman orientation:** Mandatory, $125 fee. Preregistration for classes offered. 5-day program before beginning of classes. **Policies:** Student ministry opportunities. Religious observance required. **Housing:** Guaranteed on-campus for all undergraduates. Single-sex dorms, apartments, wellness housing available. $100 nonrefundable deposit, deadline 7/31. **Activities:** Concert band, campus ministries, choral groups, drama, international student organizations, literary magazine, music ensembles, musical theater, student government, student newspaper, symphony orchestra.

**Athletics.** NAIA. **Intercollegiate:** Baseball M, basketball, cheerleading, cross-country, soccer, softball W, volleyball W. **Intramural:** Basketball, football (non-tackle). **Team name:** Bruins.

**Student services.** Adult student services, alcohol/substance abuse counseling, chaplain/spiritual director, career counseling, student employment services, financial aid counseling, health services, personal counseling, placement for graduates, veterans' counselor.

**Contact.** E-mail: info@fc.bethany.edu
Phone: (831) 438-3800 ext. 3900 Toll-free number: (800) 843-9410
Fax: (831) 461-1621
Dan Mooney, Director of Admission, Bethany University, 800 Bethany Drive, Scotts Valley, CA 95066-2898

---

## Bethesda Christian University
### Anaheim, California
www.bcu.edu                                  CB code: 3895

- Private 4-year university affiliated with Christian Church
- Commuter campus in large city
- 181 degree-seeking undergraduates
- Application essay, interview required

**General.** Accredited by ABHE. Extension office in South Korea. **Degrees:** 37 bachelor's awarded; master's offered. **Location:** 30 miles from Los Angeles. **Calendar:** Semester, limited summer session. **Full-time faculty:** 4 total. **Part-time faculty:** 44 total. **Class size:** 33% < 20, 64% 20-39, 3% 40-49.

**Basis for selection.** Open admission. GED not accepted. Admissions decision based on recommendations, essay and interview. Secondary school record also important. ESL placement test not required for students who have TOEFL score 550 or higher or have graduated from English-speaking high school. Auditions required for music majors. Portfolio required for design majors. Christian experience essay required. **Homeschooled:** Transcript of courses and grades, state high school equivalency certificate, letter of recommendation (nonparent) required.

**High school preparation.** College-preparatory program required.

**2010-2011 Annual costs.** Tuition/fees: $7,160. Room/board: $3,200. Books/supplies: $1,000.

**2009-2010 Financial aid.** All financial aid based on need.

**Application procedures. Admission:** Priority date 2/1; deadline 3/1 (receipt date). $35 fee ($80 out-of-state). Application must be submitted on paper. Admission notification on a rolling basis. **Financial aid:** Closing date 3/14. FAFSA, institutional form required. Applicants notified on a rolling basis starting 6/30.

**Academics. Special study options:** Combined bachelor's/graduate degree, distance learning, dual enrollment of high school students, ESL, external degree, independent study, liberal arts/career combination, study abroad, teacher certification program. **Credit/placement by examination:** CLEP, IB, institutional tests. **Support services:** Reduced course load.

**Majors. Computer sciences:** Information technology. **Education:** Early childhood. **Foreign languages:** Translation. **Philosophy/religion:** Religion.

**Theology:** Bible, missionary, religious ed, sacred music, theology. **Visual/performing arts:** Conducting, design, fashion design, metal/jewelry, music management, music performance, music theory/composition, piano/organ, stringed instruments, voice/opera.

**Computing on campus.** PC or laptop required. 30 workstations in dormitories, library, computer center, student center. Dormitories wired for high-speed internet access. Online course registration, helpline, repair service, wireless network available.

**Student life. Freshman orientation:** Mandatory. Preregistration for classes offered. **Policies:** Religious observance required. **Housing:** Off-campus housing available. **Activities:** Student government.

**Student services.** Chaplain/spiritual director, financial aid counseling, personal counseling.

**Contact.** E-mail: admission@bcu.edu
Phone: (714) 517-1945 Fax: (714) 517-1948
Jacqueline Ha, Director of Admissions, Bethesda Christian University, 730 North Euclid Street, Anaheim, CA 92801

## Biola University
### La Mirada, California
www.biola.edu                          CB code: 4017

- Private 4-year university and Bible college affiliated with interdenominational tradition
- Residential campus in large town
- 3,888 degree-seeking undergraduates: 9% part-time, 61% women, 3% African American, 12% Asian American, 12% Hispanic American, 1% Native American, 2% international
- 2,012 degree-seeking graduate students
- 82% of applicants admitted
- SAT or ACT (ACT writing recommended), application essay required
- 66% graduate within 6 years

**General.** Founded in 1908. Regionally accredited. Biola University is a Biblically centered Christian institution. Every undergraduate student graduates with a minor in Bible. **Degrees:** 894 bachelor's awarded; master's, doctoral, professional offered. **ROTC:** Army, Air Force. **Location:** 22 miles from downtown Los Angeles. **Calendar:** 4-1-4, extensive summer session. **Full-time faculty:** 220 total; 74% have terminal degrees, 27% women. **Part-time faculty:** 199 total; 42% women. **Class size:** 47% < 20, 44% 20-39, 4% 40-49, 3% 50-99, 2% >100. **Special facilities:** Concert hall, electron microscope, recording studio, film studio, MIDI lab for music composition, electronic piano lab, archaeological dig site.

**Freshman class profile.** 2,680 applied, 2,185 admitted, 792 enrolled.

| Mid 50% test scores | | | |
|---|---|---|---|
| SAT critical reading: | 500-620 | GPA 2.0-2.99: | 11% |
| SAT math: | 490-620 | Rank in top quarter: | 75% |
| SAT writing: | 500-610 | Rank in top tenth: | 43% |
| ACT composite: | 21-26 | Return as sophomores: | 83% |
| GPA 3.75 or higher: | 36% | Out-of-state: | 28% |
| GPA 3.50-3.74: | 22% | Live on campus: | 90% |
| GPA 3.0-3.49: | 31% | International: | 3% |

**Basis for selection.** Christian commitment most important; academic record, personal references, test scores next in importance. School, community, church activities helpful. Out-of-state and ethnic students encouraged to apply. Official transcripts, SAT/ACT, pastoral reference form required. No exceptions to SAT/ACT requirement. If more than one SAT score, the best combination of scores accepted. Auditions recommended for music applicants. Portfolios recommended for art applicants. Any body of work recommended for Cinema & Media Arts applicants. Some students asked for an interview. **Homeschooled:** Letter of recommendation (nonparent) required. Applicants advised to go through accreditation agency. **Learning Disabled:** Student must request the services of the ODS and provide documentation supporting the nature and limitations of a disability.

**High school preparation.** College-preparatory program recommended. 21 units recommended. Recommended units include English 4, mathematics 3, social studies 3, history 4, science 3 and foreign language 4. 1 algebra and 1 chemistry required of nursing applicants. 2 math, 1 physics, 1 chemistry required of biology applicants. Some deficiencies may be satisfied during freshman year.

**2009-2010 Annual costs.** Tuition/fees: $27,744. Room/board: $8,080. Books/supplies: $1,638. Personal expenses: $2,250.

**2008-2009 Financial aid. Non-need-based:** Scholarships awarded for academics, alumni affiliation, art, athletics, leadership, minority status, music/drama, state residency.

**Application procedures. Admission:** Priority date 12/1; deadline 3/1 (receipt date). $45 fee, may be waived for applicants with need. Admission notification on a rolling basis beginning on or about 4/1. Must reply by May 1 or within 4 week(s) if notified thereafter. **Financial aid:** Priority date 1/1; no closing date. FAFSA required. Applicants notified on a rolling basis starting 3/1.

**Academics. Special study options:** Combined bachelor's/graduate degree, double major, dual enrollment of high school students, ESL, exchange student, honors, independent study, internships, New York semester, student-designed major, study abroad, teacher certification program, Washington semester. 3-2 program with Los Angeles College of Chiropractic, 3-2 engineering program with University of Southern California. **Credit/placement by examination:** AP, CLEP, IB, SAT, ACT. Maximum of 32 credits from CLEP, AP, and IB can be counted toward degree. **Support services:** Learning center, reduced course load, remedial instruction, study skills assistance, tutoring, writing center.

**Honors college/program.** Admission to Torrey Honors Institute by invitation, after application to the university. Through the use of a classical learning style students are trained in rigorous discussion group format, learning high-level writing and critical thinking skills.

**Majors. Biology:** General, biochemistry. **Business:** Accounting, business admin, international, management information systems, marketing. **Communications:** General, broadcast journalism, journalism, public relations, radio/tv. **Computer sciences:** Computer science. **Education:** General, elementary, music, physical, secondary. **Engineering:** General. **Foreign languages:** Spanish. **Health:** Communication disorders, nursing (RN). **History:** General. **Interdisciplinary:** Intercultural. **Legal studies:** Prelaw. **Liberal arts:** Arts/sciences. **Math:** General. **Parks/recreation:** Exercise sciences, health/fitness. **Philosophy/religion:** Philosophy, religion. **Physical sciences:** Chemistry, physics. **Psychology:** General. **Social sciences:** General, anthropology, sociology. **Theology:** Bible, religious ed, theology. **Visual/performing arts:** Cinematography, commercial/advertising art, dramatic, drawing, music performance, music theory/composition, painting, sculpture, studio arts.

**Most popular majors.** Business/marketing 26%, communications/journalism 11%, education 9%, health sciences 6%, psychology 8%, social sciences 7%, theological studies 14%, visual/performing arts 8%.

**Computing on campus.** 225 workstations in library, computer center. Dormitories wired for high-speed internet access and linked to campus network. Commuter students can connect to campus network. Online course registration, online library, helpline, repair service, student web hosting, wireless network available.

**Student life. Freshman orientation:** Available, $75 fee. Week-long, held week before term begins. Students assigned to core group led by Biola student. **Policies:** All students encouraged to have Christian service assignment. Students adhere to code of conduct. Freshmen and sophomores under 21 required to live on campus unless living with relatives. Use and possession of drugs and/or alcohol is not permitted. All students (both on and off campus) sign a contract. Religious observance required. **Housing:** Guaranteed on-campus for freshmen. Coed dorms, single-sex dorms, special housing for disabled, apartments available. $250 partly refundable deposit, deadline 5/1. Flex-style dorms with single sex floors/wings available. **Activities:** Bands, campus ministries, choral groups, dance, drama, film society, international student organizations, music ensembles, musical theater, opera, radio station, student government, student newspaper, symphony orchestra, TV station, Student Missionary Union, Korean student association, evangelism team, International Justice Mission, theology club, Society of Christian Philosophy, Tijuana Ministry, Bas Bleu (women's issues), Naturally Diverse.

**Athletics.** NAIA. **Intercollegiate:** Baseball M, basketball, cross-country, diving, golf, soccer, softball W, swimming, tennis, track and field, volleyball W. **Intramural:** Basketball, football (non-tackle), soccer, softball, volleyball. **Team name:** Eagles.

**Student services.** Adult student services, chaplain/spiritual director, career counseling, student employment services, financial aid counseling, health services, minority student services, personal counseling, placement for graduates, veterans' counselor. **Physically disabled:** Services for speech, hearing impaired.

**Contact.** E-mail: admissions@biola.edu
Phone: (562) 903-4752 Toll-free number: (800) 652-4652
Fax: (562) 903-4709
Andre Stephens, Senior Director of Undergraduate Admissions, Biola University, 13800 Biola Avenue, La Mirada, CA 90639-0001

## Brooks Institute
### Santa Barbara, California
### www.brooks.edu
**CB code: 4228**

- For-profit 3-year visual arts college
- Commuter campus in small city
- 1,033 degree-seeking undergraduates: 46% women
- 56 degree-seeking graduate students
- 50% of applicants admitted
- Application essay, interview required
- 42% graduate within 6 years

**General.** Founded in 1945. Accredited by ACICS. **Degrees:** 390 bachelor's awarded; master's offered. **Location:** 90 miles from Los Angeles. **Calendar:** Semester, extensive summer session. **Full-time faculty:** 36 total. **Part-time faculty:** 65 total. **Special facilities:** 123,000 square feet of studio space for 40 set-ups, 90 cubicles for black and white enlarging, digital labs, design lab for visual communication program.

**Freshman class profile.** 1,425 applied, 714 admitted, 714 enrolled.

| | | | |
|---|---|---|---|
| Return as sophomores: | 72% | Out-of-state: | 53% |

**Basis for selection.** School achievement record most important. Photographic experience not required for entrance. Advanced standing may be offered to those with 4X5 view camera experience. Evaluation consists of written examination portfolio and review. TOEFL required of students whose first language is not English. Different standards exist based on paper vs. computer scores and for undergraduate and graduate applicants. At time of matriculation, institution will assess English and math proficiencies for students who have not demonstrated proficiency in both at the college level or by receiving minimum standard scores in national tests. Interviews can be conducted via telephone. Interview and photography portfolio required for advanced standing in core courses. **Homeschooled:** GED required if home schooling not recognized by state. **Learning Disabled:** Protocol for students seeking accommodation is mailed to accepted applicants with provisional acceptance letter.

**High school preparation.** College-preparatory program recommended. Recommended units include English 4, mathematics 2, social studies 1, science 1 and foreign language 2. College preparatory program recommended.

**2009-2010 Annual costs.** Tuition/fees: $17,840.

**Application procedures. Admission:** No deadline. $100 fee. Admission notification on a rolling basis. Students encouraged to apply at least 6 months in advance. **Financial aid:** Priority date 3/2; no closing date. FAFSA, institutional form required. Applicants notified on a rolling basis starting 5/1.

**Academics. Special study options:** Accelerated study, combined bachelor's/graduate degree, distance learning, double major, independent study, internships. Documentary courses in foreign countries, travel courses, water photography (for upper-division students). **Credit/placement by examination:** CLEP, institutional tests. 54 credit hours maximum toward bachelor's degree. **Support services:** Remedial instruction, tutoring.

**Majors. Communications:** Photojournalism. **Visual/performing arts:** Cinematography, graphic design, photography.

**Computing on campus.** 20 workstations in library, computer center. Online library, helpline, wireless network available.

**Student life. Freshman orientation:** Mandatory. Immediately prior to matriculation; normally 2-3 days of activities. **Policies:** Car necessary for travel between campuses and to assignment locations. **Activities:** Student government.

**Student services.** Career counseling, student employment services, financial aid counseling, personal counseling, placement for graduates.

**Contact.** E-mail: admissions@brooks.edu
Phone: (888) 304-3456 Toll-free number: (888) 304-3456
Fax: (805) 565-1386
Elmo Fraser, Vice President of Marketing and Admissions, Brooks Institute, 27 East Cota Street, Santa Barbara, CA 93101

## California Baptist University
### Riverside, California
### www.calbaptist.edu
**CB member**
**CB code: 4094**

- Private 4-year university and liberal arts college affiliated with Southern Baptist Convention
- Residential campus in large city

- 3,212 degree-seeking undergraduates: 14% part-time, 61% women
- 881 degree-seeking graduate students
- 74% of applicants admitted
- SAT or ACT (ACT writing optional), application essay required
- 59% graduate within 6 years; 52% enter graduate study

**General.** Founded in 1950. Regionally accredited. **Degrees:** 674 bachelor's awarded; master's offered. **ROTC:** Army, Air Force. **Location:** 60 miles from Los Angeles. **Calendar:** Semester. 4-4-1 semester system. Extensive summer session. **Full-time faculty:** 164 total; 52% have terminal degrees, 15% minority, 46% women. **Part-time faculty:** 175 total; 47% have terminal degrees, 19% minority, 54% women. **Class size:** 49% < 20, 41% 20-39, 4% 40-49, 5% 50-99, 1% >100. **Special facilities:** Hymnology collection, performance and recording studios, Nie Wieder! Holocaust collection, aquatic center, fitness center, digital design and photography studio, theater arts stage production workshop facility, prayer chapel.

**Freshman class profile.** 1,734 applied, 1,280 admitted, 576 enrolled.

| Mid 50% test scores | | | |
|---|---|---|---|
| SAT critical reading: | 450-570 | GPA 2.0-2.99: | 20% |
| SAT math: | 440-560 | Rank in top quarter: | 43% |
| SAT writing: | 440-560 | Rank in top tenth: | 16% |
| ACT composite: | 19-24 | End year in good standing: | 85% |
| GPA 3.75 or higher: | 29% | Return as sophomores: | 73% |
| GPA 3.50-3.74: | 16% | Out-of-state: | 11% |
| GPA 3.0-3.49: | 35% | Live on campus: | 89% |
| | | International: | 7% |

**Basis for selection.** School achievement record, test scores, essays, recommendations very important. Interviews recommended. Auditions required for music, drama applicants. **Homeschooled:** Transcript of courses and grades, letter of recommendation (nonparent) required.

**High school preparation.** College-preparatory program recommended. 15 units required; 19 recommended. Required and recommended units include English 4, mathematics 3-4, social studies 2, history 2, science 2-3 (laboratory 1-2), foreign language 2-3 and academic electives 3.

**2010-2011 Annual costs.** Tuition/fees: $24,654. Room/board: $8,370. Books/supplies: $1,638. Personal expenses: $2,250.

**2008-2009 Financial aid. Need-based:** 391 full-time freshmen applied for aid; 281 were judged to have need; 273 of these received aid. Average need met was 48%. Average scholarship/grant was $5,294; average loan $1,429. 45% of total undergraduate aid awarded as scholarships/grants, 55% as loans/jobs. **Non-need-based:** Awarded to 1,482 full-time undergraduates, including 318 freshmen. Scholarships awarded for academics, art, athletics, leadership, music/drama, religious affiliation, ROTC.

**Application procedures. Admission:** Priority date 2/1; no deadline. $45 fee, may be waived for applicants with need. Admission notification on a rolling basis beginning on or about 11/19. **Financial aid:** Priority date 3/2; no closing date. FAFSA required. Applicants notified on a rolling basis starting 3/2; must reply by 5/1 or within 3 week(s) of notification.

**Academics. Special study options:** Accelerated study, distance learning, double major, dual enrollment of high school students, ESL, exchange student, honors, internships, liberal arts/career combination, study abroad, teacher certification program, Washington semester, weekend college. **Credit/placement by examination:** AP, CLEP, IB, SAT, ACT, institutional tests. 30 credit hours maximum toward bachelor's degree. Portfolio course available to assist students in documenting work that may be counted for credit by prior learning experiences. **Support services:** Learning center, reduced course load, remedial instruction, study skills assistance, tutoring, writing center.

**Majors. Biology:** General, biochemistry, molecular. **Business:** Accounting, business admin, marketing. **Communications:** General, digital media, journalism, media studies. **Education:** General, early childhood, physical. **Engineering:** General, civil, electrical, mechanical. **Foreign languages:** Spanish. **Health:** Health services, nursing (RN). **History:** General. **Interdisciplinary:** Behavioral sciences, intercultural. **Liberal arts:** Arts/sciences. **Math:** General. **Parks/recreation:** Exercise sciences. **Philosophy/religion:** Christian, philosophy. **Physical sciences:** Chemistry. **Protective services:** Law enforcement admin, police science. **Psychology:** General. **Social sciences:** Political science, sociology. **Theology:** Bible, missionary. **Visual/performing arts:** Art, graphic design, music performance, music theory/composition, piano/organ, theater arts management, voice/opera. **Other:** Christian behavioral science, Foundational mathematics, Music education, Organizational leadership, Psychological anthropology.

**Most popular majors.** Business/marketing 18%, English 6%, health sciences 8%, liberal arts 19%, parks/recreation 7%, psychology 8%, social sciences 7%.

**Computing on campus.** 279 workstations in library, computer center. Dormitories wired for high-speed internet access and linked to campus network. Commuter students can connect to campus network. Online course registration, online library, helpline available.

**Student life. Freshman orientation:** Mandatory, $250 fee. Preregistration for classes offered. Held prior to beginning of semester. **Policies:** Students receiving institutional scholarships required to live in student housing. Religious observance required. **Housing:** Guaranteed on-campus for freshmen. Single-sex dorms, apartments, cooperative housing available. $300 fully refundable deposit, deadline 8/1. **Activities:** Bands, campus ministries, choral groups, drama, international student organizations, music ensembles, musical theater, student government, student newspaper, symphony orchestra, Young Republicans, Young Democrats, Fellowship of Christian Athletes, Black Student Union, Big Brother, Big Sister, active compassion, elderly ministry, homeless ministry.

**Athletics.** NAIA. **Intercollegiate:** Baseball M, basketball, cheerleading, cross-country, diving, golf, soccer, softball W, swimming, track and field, volleyball, water polo, wrestling M. **Intramural:** Basketball, bowling, football (non-tackle), golf, softball, table tennis, volleyball. **Team name:** Lancers.

**Student services.** Adult student services, chaplain/spiritual director, career counseling, student employment services, financial aid counseling, personal counseling, placement for graduates, veterans' counselor.

**Contact.** E-mail: admissions@calbaptist.edu
Phone: (951) 343-4212 Toll-free number: (877) 228-8866
Fax: (951) 343-4525
Allen Johnson, Associate Dean of Enrollment Services, California Baptist University, 8432 Magnolia Avenue, Riverside, CA 92504-3297

## California Coast University
### Santa Ana, California
### www.calcoast.edu

- For-profit 4-year virtual university
- Large city
- 3,675 degree-seeking undergraduates

**General.** Accredited by DETC. **Degrees:** 188 bachelor's, 28 associate awarded; master's, doctoral offered. **Calendar:** Continuous, extensive summer session. **Part-time faculty:** 26 total.

**Basis for selection.** Open admission.

**2009-2010 Annual costs.** Distance-learning undergraduate program total costs: $7,500 (associate degree) and $15,750 (bachelor's degree); international students pay $8,700 (associate degree) and $18,270 (bachelor's degree) in total costs per program.

**Application procedures. Admission:** No deadline. $75 fee.

**Academics. Special study options:** Accelerated study, cross-registration, distance learning, external degree, honors, independent study. **Credit/placement by examination:** CLEP.

**Majors. Business:** General, business admin. **Health:** Health care admin. **Psychology:** General. **Social sciences:** Criminology.

**Student life. Activities:** Student newspaper.

**Contact.** E-mail: admissions@calcoast.edu
Phone: (714) 547-9625
Admissions Director, California Coast University, 700 North Main Street, Santa Ana, CA 92701

## California College of the Arts
### San Francisco, California       CB member
### www.cca.edu                     CB code: 4031

- Private 4-year visual arts college
- Commuter campus in very large city
- 1,362 degree-seeking undergraduates: 7% part-time, 61% women, 4% African American, 17% Asian American, 11% Hispanic American, 1% Native American, 9% international
- 426 degree-seeking graduate students
- 75% of applicants admitted
- Application essay required
- 49% graduate within 6 years

**General.** Founded in 1907. Regionally accredited. 2 campuses located in San Francisco and Oakland. **Degrees:** 251 bachelor's awarded; master's offered. **Location:** 3 miles from downtown. **Calendar:** Semester, limited summer session. **Full-time faculty:** 81 total; 80% have terminal degrees, 18% minority, 48% women. **Part-time faculty:** 422 total; 64% have terminal degrees, 18% minority, 47% women. **Class size:** 89% < 20, 11% 20-39, less than 1% 40-49, less than 1% 50-99. **Special facilities:** Center for art and public life, contemporary arts institute, materials resource center.

**Freshman class profile.** 1,181 applied, 884 admitted, 212 enrolled.

| Mid 50% test scores | | | |
|---|---|---|---|
| SAT critical reading: | 460-630 | GPA 3.0-3.49: | 39% |
| SAT math: | 480-610 | GPA 2.0-2.99: | 35% |
| SAT writing: | 460-600 | Return as sophomores: | 73% |
| ACT composite: | 20-26 | Out-of-state: | 37% |
| GPA 3.75 or higher: | 11% | Live on campus: | 84% |
| GPA 3.50-3.74: | 15% | International: | 15% |

**Basis for selection.** High school achievement as evidenced by grade point average, portfolio of creative work, personal essay/statement of purpose, interview, and 2 letters of recommendation required. The college also reviews art/design activities and interests. SAT or ACT recommended. Test scores are primarily used for placement, but may be considered for admission. SAT or ACT scores with Writing highly recommended and used in English course placement. Portfolio of creative work and statement of artistic and professional goals required. **Homeschooled:** Transcript of courses and grades required. Detailed syllabus of courses (equivalent to grades 10-12) and details of curriculum, including community college transcripts (if applicable) required.

**High school preparation.** College-preparatory program recommended.

**2009-2010 Annual costs.** Tuition/fees: $33,254. No meal plan offered. Residence halls equipped with kitchens on each floor. Estimated food cost: $2,850. Room only: $6,870. Books/supplies: $1,500. Personal expenses: $2,200.

**2008-2009 Financial aid. Need-based:** 178 full-time freshmen applied for aid; 160 were judged to have need; 159 of these received aid. Average need met was 58%. Average scholarship/grant was $17,554; average loan $3,484. 62% of total undergraduate aid awarded as scholarships/grants, 38% as loans/jobs. **Non-need-based:** Awarded to 528 full-time undergraduates, including 168 freshmen. Scholarships awarded for academics, art. **Additional information:** Application deadline for merit scholarships February 1.

**Application procedures. Admission:** Priority date 2/1; no deadline. $60 fee, may be waived for applicants with need. Admission notification on a rolling basis beginning on or about 1/15. Must reply by May 1 or within 2 week(s) if notified thereafter. Maximum period of postponement is one semester. **Financial aid:** Priority date 3/1; no closing date. FAFSA required. Applicants notified on a rolling basis starting 3/15; must reply by 5/1 or within 3 week(s) of notification.

**Academics. Special study options:** Combined bachelor's/graduate degree, cross-registration, double major, ESL, exchange student, independent study, internships, student-designed major, study abroad. Sponsored studios, community engagement with project-based learning, community service fellowships, annual career expo, summer English second language (ESL) program for international students, pre-college program, disability services. **Credit/placement by examination:** AP, CLEP, IB, SAT, ACT, institutional tests. **Support services:** Learning center, pre-admission summer program, reduced course load, remedial instruction, study skills assistance, tutoring, writing center.

**Majors. Architecture:** Architecture. **Visual/performing arts:** Art, ceramics, cinematography, crafts, drawing, fashion design, fiber arts, graphic design, illustration, industrial design, interior design, metal/jewelry, painting, photography, printmaking, sculpture, studio arts.

**Most popular majors.** Architecture 14%, visual/performing arts 84%.

**Computing on campus.** 295 workstations in dormitories, library, computer center, student center. Dormitories wired for high-speed internet access and linked to campus network. Commuter students can connect to campus network. Online library, helpline, student web hosting, wireless network available.

**Student life. Freshman orientation:** Mandatory. Preregistration for classes offered. Educational and social programs are offered one week before classes start. **Housing:** Coed dorms, special housing for disabled, apartments, wellness housing available. $750 partly refundable deposit, deadline 5/15. First-year community, transfer community, multi-cultural community service theme halls available. **Activities:** Film society, international student organizations, literary magazine, student government, Quack, Students for Sustainability, Asian Student Association, Salon Collective, Chimera Council, Graduate

Student Alliance, Alliance for Multiculturalism in Architecture, Glass League, American Institute of Architecture Students, Ceramics Guild.

**Student services.** Alcohol/substance abuse counseling, career counseling, student employment services, financial aid counseling, personal counseling, placement for graduates. **Physically disabled:** Services for visually, speech, hearing impaired.

**Contact.**  E-mail: enroll@cca.edu
Phone: (415) 703-9523 Toll-free number: (800) 447-1278
Fax: (415) 703-9539
Robynne Royster, Director of Undergraduate Admission, California College of the Arts, 1111 Eighth Street, San Francisco, CA 94107-2247

## California College San Diego
### San Diego, California
**www.cc-sd.edu**                                    **CB code: 3354**

- For-profit 4-year business and health science college
- Very large city
- 817 degree-seeking undergraduates

**General.** Accredited by ACCSC. **Degrees:** 31 bachelor's, 130 associate awarded. **Calendar:** Continuous. **Full-time faculty:** 12 total. **Part-time faculty:** 22 total.

**Basis for selection.** Open admission.

**2009-2010 Annual costs.** Associate program: Respiratory Therapy $44,905; other Associate programs: $38,440. Bachelor program: Respiratory Therapy $75,459; other Bachelor programs: $70,080.

**Application procedures. Admission:** No deadline.

**Academics. Credit/placement by examination:** CLEP.

**Majors. Business:** Accounting, business admin. **Computer sciences:** Computer science. **Health:** Health care admin, nursing admin, respiratory therapy technology.

**Contact.**  Phone: (619) 680-4430 Toll-free number: (800) 622-3188
Fax: (619) 295-5762
Randy Wolford, Director of Admissions, California College San Diego, 2820 Camino del Rio South 300, San Diego, CA 92108

## California Institute of Integral Studies
### San Francisco, California
**www.ciis.edu**                                    **CB code: 3609**

- Private two-year upper-division liberal arts college
- Commuter campus in very large city
- 67% of applicants admitted
- Application essay required

**General.** Regionally accredited. Offers interdisciplinary, cross-cultural, and applied studies in psychology, philosophy, religion, cultural anthropology, transformative studies and leadership, integrative health, women's spirituality, counseling, community mental health, and the arts. **Degrees:** 60 bachelor's awarded; master's, doctoral offered. **Location:** Downtown. **Calendar:** Semester, extensive summer session. **Full-time faculty:** 71 total; 79% have terminal degrees, 21% minority, 49% women. **Part-time faculty:** 14 total. **Class size:** 54% < 20, 46% 20-39. **Special facilities:** Meditation room, roof garden.

**Student profile.** 70 degree-seeking undergraduates, 1,148 degree-seeking graduate students. 75 applied as first time-transfer students, 50 admitted, 39 enrolled.

| | | | |
|---|---|---|---|
| Women: | 66% | Part-time: | 13% |
| African American: | 14% | Out-of-state: | 5% |
| Asian American: | 1% | 25 or older: | 95% |
| Hispanic American: | 11% | | |

**Basis for selection.** College transcript, application essay required. Transfer accepted as juniors.

**2009-2010 Annual costs.** Tuition/fees: $14,460. Cost quoted for 2 semesters; 3-semester attendance mandatory. Books/supplies: $1,640.

**Financial aid. Need-based:** 188 applied for aid; 180 were judged to have need; 73 of these received aid. Average need met was 18%. 24% of total

undergraduate aid awarded as scholarships/grants, 76% as loans/jobs. **Non-need-based:** Awarded to 16 undergraduates. Scholarships awarded for academics, alumni affiliation, art, job skills, leadership, minority status, music/drama, ROTC, state residency.

**Application procedures. Admission:** Priority date 5/1. $65 fee, may be waived for applicants with need. Application priority dates differ by program. **Financial aid:** Priority date 4/15, no deadline.

**Academics. Special study options:** Distance learning, dual enrollment of high school students, independent study, internships, weekend college. **Credit/placement by examination:** AP, CLEP. 30 credit hours maximum toward bachelor's degree. **Support services:** Tutoring, writing center.

**Majors. Liberal arts:** Arts/sciences, humanities.

**Computing on campus.** 20 workstations in computer center. Commuter students can connect to campus network. Online library, helpline, wireless network available.

**Student life. Activities:** Choral groups, international student organizations, student government, People of Color, Queer at CIIS, Student Alliance, Interdisciplinary Dialog Group, UNITE!, AWARE (Awakening to Whiteness and Racism Everywhere), International Students & Friends, Zen Meditation Group, Theater for Change.

**Student services.** Career counseling, financial aid counseling, minority student services, personal counseling, placement for graduates.

**Contact.**  E-mail: admissions@ciis.edu
Phone: (415) 575-6150
Allyson Werner, Associate Director of Admissions, California Institute of Integral Studies, 1453 Mission Street, San Francisco, CA 94103

## California Institute of Technology
### Pasadena, California                              **CB member**
**www.caltech.edu**                                  **CB code: 4034**

- Private 4-year university
- Residential campus in small city
- 951 degree-seeking undergraduates: 38% women
- 1,179 degree-seeking graduate students
- 15% of applicants admitted
- SAT or ACT (ACT writing optional), SAT Subject Tests, application essay required

**General.** Founded in 1891. Regionally accredited. **Degrees:** 214 bachelor's awarded; master's, doctoral offered. **ROTC:** Army, Air Force. **Location:** 10 miles from downtown Los Angeles. **Calendar:** Quarter. **Full-time faculty:** 304 total; 98% have terminal degrees, 15% minority, 16% women. **Part-time faculty:** 23 total; 56% have terminal degrees, 26% minority, 39% women. **Class size:** 64% < 20, 23% 20-39, 4% 40-49, 5% 50-99, 4% >100. **Special facilities:** Jet Propulsion Laboratory, observatories, wind and water tunnels, radio observatory, seismological laboratory, marine biological laboratory.

**Freshman class profile.** 4,413 applied, 674 admitted, 252 enrolled.

| Mid 50% test scores | | Rank in top quarter: | 100% |
|---|---|---|---|
| SAT critical reading: | 690-770 | Rank in top tenth: | 98% |
| SAT math: | 770-800 | Out-of-state: | 65% |
| SAT writing: | 680-770 | Live on campus: | 100% |
| ACT composite: | 33-35 | | |

**Basis for selection.** High school preparation and record (particularly in mathematics and science), test scores, extracurricular activities (science and nonscience-related), counselors' and teachers' recommendations, and demonstrated interest in mathematics and science are major considerations. SAT Subject Test requirements: Math level IIC and one science, either biology (environmental or molecular), chemistry, or physics.

**High school preparation.** College-preparatory program required. Required and recommended units include English 3-4, mathematics 4, social studies 1-3, history 1, science 2-4 (laboratory 1).

**2010-2011 Annual costs.** Tuition/fees: $36,282. Room/board: $11,397. Books/supplies: $1,323. Personal expenses: $1,974.

**2009-2010 Financial aid. Need-based:** 176 full-time freshmen applied for aid; 144 were judged to have need; 144 of these received aid. Average need met was 100%. Average scholarship/grant was $28,991; average loan $2,900. 88% of total undergraduate aid awarded as scholarships/grants, 12%

as loans/jobs. **Non-need-based:** Awarded to 70 full-time undergraduates, including 29 freshmen.

**Application procedures. Admission:** Closing date 1/2 (postmark date). $65 fee, may be waived for applicants with need. Admission notification 4/1. Must reply by 5/1. **Financial aid:** Closing date 1/15. FAFSA, institutional form, CSS PROFILE required. Applicants notified by 4/1; must reply by 5/1.

**Academics.** Remedial services not formally offered. Remediation available for students deficient in basic scientific knowledge or technical skills. **Special study options:** Combined bachelor's/graduate degree, cooperative education, cross-registration, double major, ESL, exchange student, independent study, liberal arts/career combination, student-designed major, study abroad. **Credit/placement by examination:** CLEP, institutional tests. **Support services:** Reduced course load, tutoring.

**Majors. Biology:** General. **Business:** Managerial economics. **Computer sciences:** Computer science. **Engineering:** General, chemical, computer, electrical, environmental, materials science, mechanical, physics. **History:** General, science/technology. **Interdisciplinary:** Science/society. **Math:** General, applied. **Philosophy/religion:** Philosophy. **Physical sciences:** Astronomy, astrophysics, chemistry, geochemistry, geology, geophysics, physics, planetary. **Social sciences:** General, economics, political science. **Other:** Computational neural systems, Geobiology.

**Most popular majors.** Biology 13%, computer/information sciences 9%, engineering/engineering technologies 34%, mathematics 14%, physical sciences 29%.

**Computing on campus.** 112 workstations in dormitories, library, computer center. Dormitories wired for high-speed internet access and linked to campus network. Commuter students can connect to campus network. Online course registration, online library, helpline, repair service, student web hosting, wireless network available.

**Student life. Freshman orientation:** Mandatory, $500 fee. 3 day camp. **Policies:** Honor Code: "No member of the Caltech community shall take unfair advantage of any other member of the Caltech community.". **Housing:** Guaranteed on-campus for all undergraduates. Coed dorms, special housing for disabled, apartments available. Pets allowed in dorm rooms. Single-unit houses available. **Activities:** Bands, choral groups, dance, drama, film society, international student organizations, literary magazine, music ensembles, musical theater, opera, student government, student newspaper, symphony orchestra, Caltech Y, Christian fellowship, Newman Club, Hillel, Amnesty International, Caltech Center for Diversity.

**Athletics.** NCAA. **Intercollegiate:** Baseball M, basketball, cross-country, diving, fencing, soccer M, swimming, tennis, track and field, volleyball W, water polo. **Intramural:** Badminton, baseball M, basketball, cheerleading, cricket M, cross-country, football (tackle) M, soccer, softball, squash, swimming, table tennis, tennis, track and field, volleyball, water polo M. **Team name:** Beavers.

**Student services.** Alcohol/substance abuse counseling, chaplain/spiritual director, career counseling, student employment services, financial aid counseling, health services, minority student services, on-campus daycare, personal counseling, placement for graduates, women's services. **Physically disabled:** Services for visually, speech, hearing impaired.

**Contact.** E-mail: ugadmissions@caltech.edu
Phone: (626) 395-6341 Fax: (626) 683-3026
Ray Prado, Director of Admissions, California Institute of Technology, 1200 East California Boulevard, MC 1-94, Pasadena, CA 91125

---

## California Institute of the Arts

**Valencia, California**     CB member
**www.calarts.edu**          CB code: 4049

- Private 4-year visual arts and performing arts college
- Residential campus in small city
- 888 degree-seeking undergraduates: 1% part-time, 49% women, 8% African American, 12% Asian American, 12% Hispanic American, 1% Native American, 8% international
- 504 graduate students
- 33% of applicants admitted
- Application essay required
- 57% graduate within 6 years

**General.** Founded in 1961. Regionally accredited. Single complex of 6 professional schools: art, critical studies, dance, film/video, music and theater. **Degrees:** 196 bachelor's awarded; master's, doctoral offered. **Location:** 30 miles from Los Angeles. **Calendar:** Semester. **Full-time faculty:**

160 total; 66% have terminal degrees, 18% minority, 44% women. **Part-time faculty:** 143 total; 43% have terminal degrees, 20% minority, 32% women. **Class size:** 78% < 20, 20% 20-39, less than 1% 40-49, 2% 50-99. **Special facilities:** Art studios, galleries, animation studios, concert halls, 6 theaters (including a modular theater, a dance theater, and music pavillion).

**Freshman class profile.** 1,186 applied, 397 admitted, 160 enrolled.

| | | | |
|---|---|---|---|
| End year in good standing: | 91% | Live on campus: | 82% |
| Return as sophomores: | 75% | International: | 13% |
| Out-of-state: | 50% | | |

**Basis for selection.** Admission is talent based, evaluated by faculty via group review. Portfolio required for art/design, film/video, music composition majors, and theater design and production. Auditions required for acting, dance, music majors. Music applicants may submit audio tape recordings in lieu of live audition for some programs. Interview required for directing/performance/production studies majors. **Homeschooled:** Transcript of courses and grades, state high school equivalency certificate, letter of recommendation (nonparent) required.

**High school preparation.** College-preparatory program recommended. Recommended units include English 4, mathematics 3, social studies 3, science 3, foreign language 2, computer science 1, visual/performing arts 3 and academic electives 2.

**2010-2011 Annual costs.** Tuition/fees: $36,742. Room/board: $9,293. Books/supplies: $1,500. Personal expenses: $1,700.

**2009-2010 Financial aid. Need-based:** 132 full-time freshmen applied for aid; 108 were judged to have need; 105 of these received aid. Average need met was 71%. Average scholarship/grant was $14,771; average loan $4,502. 52% of total undergraduate aid awarded as scholarships/grants, 48% as loans/jobs. **Non-need-based:** Awarded to 80 full-time undergraduates, including 13 freshmen. Scholarships awarded for academics, art, minority status, music/drama.

**Application procedures. Admission:** Priority date 12/1; deadline 1/5 (receipt date). $70 fee, may be waived for applicants with need. Application must be submitted online. Admission notification on a rolling basis beginning on or about 4/1. Must reply by May 1 or within 2 week(s) if notified thereafter. Some programs remain open after January 5. Please contact the Office of Admissions for more information. **Financial aid:** Priority date 3/2; no closing date. FAFSA required. Applicants notified on a rolling basis starting 4/1; must reply by 5/1 or within 3 week(s) of notification.

**Academics.** Numerous special programs that cross traditional lines. **Special study options:** Independent study, internships, student-designed major, study abroad. **Credit/placement by examination:** CLEP, IB, institutional tests. 6 credit hours maximum toward bachelor's degree. **Support services:** Learning center, tutoring.

**Majors. Visual/performing arts:** Cinematography, dance, design, music performance, music theory/composition, photography, studio arts, theater design.

**Computing on campus.** 40 workstations in library, computer center. Dormitories wired for high-speed internet access. Helpline, wireless network available.

**Student life. Freshman orientation:** Mandatory. Held the week before classes begin each semester. **Housing:** Coed dorms, special housing for disabled, apartments available. $250 fully refundable deposit, deadline 4/27. **Activities:** Jazz band, dance, drama, film society, literary magazine, music ensembles, opera, radio station, student government, student newspaper, TV station, black student union, Latino student union, GLBT student union, Asian club, political issues club.

**Student services.** Career counseling, student employment services, financial aid counseling, health services, personal counseling, placement for graduates, veterans' counselor. **Physically disabled:** Services for visually, speech, hearing impaired.

**Contact.** E-mail: admiss@calarts.edu
Phone: (661) 255-1050 ext. 2185 Toll-free number: (800) 545-2787
Fax: (661) 253-7710
Molly Ryan, Director of Admissions, California Institute of the Arts, 24700 McBean Parkway, Valencia, CA 91355

---

## California Lutheran University

**Thousand Oaks, California**     CB member
**www.callutheran.edu**           CB code: 4088

- Private 4-year university and liberal arts college affiliated with Evangelical Lutheran Church in America
- Residential campus in small city

- 2,344 degree-seeking undergraduates: 3% part-time, 61% women, 4% African American, 5% Asian American, 16% Hispanic American, 1% Native American, 4% international
- 1,323 degree-seeking graduate students
- 62% of applicants admitted
- SAT or ACT (ACT writing optional), application essay required

**General.** Founded in 1959. Regionally accredited. **Degrees:** 499 bachelor's awarded; master's, professional offered. **ROTC:** Army, Air Force. **Location:** 45 miles from Los Angeles. **Calendar:** Semester, limited summer session. **Full-time faculty:** 144 total; 86% have terminal degrees, 17% minority, 46% women. **Part-time faculty:** 180 total; 48% have terminal degrees, 11% minority, 51% women. **Class size:** 68% < 20, 30% 20-39, 2% 40-49, less than 1% 50-99. **Special facilities:** Sports and fitness center with dance studio, Olympic-size pool, television studio with editing room.

**Freshman class profile.** 3,656 applied, 2,281 admitted, 464 enrolled.

| Mid 50% test scores | | | |
|---|---|---|---|
| SAT critical reading: | 490-600 | GPA 3.0-3.49: | 32% |
| SAT math: | 500-610 | GPA 2.0-2.99: | 15% |
| SAT writing: | 500-590 | Rank in top quarter: | 70% |
| ACT composite: | 22-27 | Rank in top tenth: | 31% |
| GPA 3.75 or higher: | 36% | Out-of-state: | 25% |
| GPA 3.50-3.74: | 17% | Live on campus: | 84% |
| | | International: | 2% |

**Basis for selection.** High school achievement record, rank in class, test scores, essay, letters of recommendation very important. Interview recommended. **Homeschooled:** Transcript of courses and grades, letter of recommendation (nonparent) required. Encouraged to submit passing score on GED and complete interview with Admission Counselor. Transcript must include: brief description of courses, textbook (title and author) information for each course, how foreign language verbal component and natural science laboratory requirements were met; official transcripts from other school(s) attended. **Learning Disabled:** Meeting with the Accessibility Resource Coordinator is recommended.

**High school preparation.** College-preparatory program recommended. Required units include English 4, mathematics 3, social studies 3, science 2 (laboratory 2) and foreign language 2. Math must be through algebra II and preferably 4 years; 2 years of foreign language must be same language; highly recommend 3 years of science.

**2010-2011 Annual costs.** Tuition/fees: $31,000. Room/board: $10,580. Books/supplies: $1,450. Personal expenses: $2,100.

**2009-2010 Financial aid. Need-based:** 455 full-time freshmen applied for aid; 323 were judged to have need; 323 of these received aid. Average need met was 88%. Average scholarship/grant was $17,600; average loan $3,400. 63% of total undergraduate aid awarded as scholarships/grants, 37% as loans/jobs. **Non-need-based:** Awarded to 1,021 full-time undergraduates, including 222 freshmen. Scholarships awarded for academics, alumni affiliation, art, leadership, minority status, music/drama, religious affiliation, state residency.

**Application procedures. Admission:** Priority date 11/15; deadline 3/15 (postmark date). $45 fee, may be waived for applicants with need. Admission notification 4/15. Must reply by May 1 or within 2 week(s) if notified thereafter. **Financial aid:** Priority date 3/1; no closing date. FAFSA required. Applicants notified on a rolling basis starting 3/15; must reply within 2 week(s) of notification.

**Academics. Special study options:** Accelerated study, cooperative education, double major, dual enrollment of high school students, exchange student, honors, independent study, internships, New York semester, semester at sea, student-designed major, study abroad, teacher certification program, Washington semester. **Credit/placement by examination:** AP, CLEP, IB, SAT, ACT, institutional tests. 30 credit hours maximum toward bachelor's degree. **Support services:** Learning center, reduced course load, study skills assistance, tutoring, writing center.

**Majors. Biology:** General, biochemistry, molecular. **Business:** General, accounting, business admin, finance, managerial economics, marketing. **Communications:** General, advertising, broadcast journalism, journalism, public relations. **Computer sciences:** General, computer graphics, computer science, information systems, programming. **Conservation:** Environmental science. **Education:** General, art, early childhood, elementary, English, foreign languages, mathematics, middle, music, physical, reading, science, secondary, social science, social studies, special. **Engineering:** Biomedical. **Foreign languages:** General, French, German, Spanish. **Health:** Athletic training, predental, premedicine, prepharmacy, preveterinary. **History:** General. **Interdisciplinary:** Biological/physical sciences, math/computer science. **Legal studies:** Prelaw. **Liberal arts:** Arts/sciences. **Math:** General. **Philosophy/religion:** Philosophy, religion. **Physical sciences:** Chemistry,

geology, physics. **Protective services:** Police science. **Psychology:** General. **Science technology:** Biological. **Social sciences:** Criminology, economics, international relations, political science, sociology. **Theology:** Religious ed, theology, youth ministry. **Visual/performing arts:** General, art, commercial/advertising art, dramatic.

**Most popular majors.** Biology 6%, business/marketing 30%, communications/journalism 14%, liberal arts 7%, psychology 6%, social sciences 7%.

**Computing on campus.** 172 workstations in library, computer center, student center. Dormitories wired for high-speed internet access and linked to campus network. Commuter students can connect to campus network. Online library, helpline, wireless network available.

**Student life. Freshman orientation:** Mandatory. Preregistration for classes offered. **Policies:** No alcohol on campus except in the chapel for communion, drug free campus. **Housing:** Coed dorms, special housing for disabled, apartments available. $195 fully refundable deposit, deadline 5/1. On campus houses available. **Activities:** Bands, campus ministries, choral groups, dance, drama, international student organizations, literary magazine, music ensembles, Model UN, musical theater, radio station, student government, student newspaper, symphony orchestra, TV station, Lutheran Church Congregation, multicultural and international clubs and organizations, Hillel, Habitat for Humanitiy.

**Athletics.** NCAA. **Intercollegiate:** Baseball M, basketball, cross-country, diving, football (tackle) M, golf M, soccer, softball W, swimming, tennis, track and field, volleyball W, water polo. **Intramural:** Basketball, football (non-tackle), soccer, softball, volleyball, water polo. **Team name:** Kingsmen/Regals.

**Student services.** Adult student services, alcohol/substance abuse counseling, chaplain/spiritual director, career counseling, services for economically disadvantaged, student employment services, financial aid counseling, health services, minority student services, personal counseling, placement for graduates, veterans' counselor, women's services. **Physically disabled:** Services for visually, hearing impaired. **Learning disabled:** Comprehensive services available.

**Contact.** E-mail: admissions@callutheran.edu
Phone: (805) 493-3135 Toll-free number: (877) 258-3678
Fax: (805) 493-3114
Matthew Ward, Vice President for Enrollment Management, California Lutheran University, 60 West Olsen Road #1350, Thousand Oaks, CA 91360-2787

---

## California Maritime Academy
**Vallejo, California**  **CB member**
**www.csum.edu**  **CB code: 4035**

- Public 4-year university and maritime college
- Residential campus in small city
- 825 degree-seeking undergraduates: 2% African American, 11% Asian American, 8% Hispanic American, 1% Native American
- 73% of applicants admitted

**General.** Founded in 1929. Regionally accredited. All students participate in at least one 2-month training cruise around Pacific Ocean geared toward their major. **Degrees:** 151 bachelor's awarded. **ROTC:** Naval. **Location:** 30 miles from San Francisco. **Calendar:** Semester, limited summer session. **Full-time faculty:** 50 total. **Part-time faculty:** 25 total. **Special facilities:** 500-foot training ship, computer-aided radar simulators, bridge simulator, steam simulator.

**Freshman class profile.** 910 applied, 667 admitted, 260 enrolled.

| Mid 50% test scores | | Out-of-state: | 17% |
|---|---|---|---|
| ACT composite: | 19-24 | Live on campus: | 90% |

**Basis for selection.** Applicants must meet California State University Eligibility Index requirements and have strong grades in mathematics and sciences. All accepted students must pass physical examination. Applicants must meet California State University Eligibility Index requirements and have strong grades in mathematics and sciences. All accepted students must pass physical examination.

**High school preparation.** Required and recommended units include English 4, mathematics 3-4, social studies 1, history 1, science 2 (laboratory 2), foreign language 2-3 and academic electives 1. One additional mathematics course recommended for mechanical engineering applicants. Chemistry or physics required. One visual or performing arts elective required.

**2009-2010 Annual costs.** Tuition/fees: $5,090; $16,250 out-of-state. Each student participates in at least one cruise and one internship prior to graduation. Some majors have additional cruise requirements. The cost for a cruise is $3,900. The cost for an internship/co-op is $225. Additionally, each incoming student must purchase a uniform. Prices range from $1,550-$1,785 depending on the major. Reduced out-of-state tuition for residents of AK, AZ, CO, HI, ID, MT, NV, NM, ND, OR, SD, UT, WA, WY available under the Western Undergraduate Exchange (WUE) program. WUE students pay one-and-a half the State University Fee ($3,354 this year), which is $5,031. Room/board: $9,360. Books/supplies: $1,656. Personal expenses: $2,826.

**2009-2010 Financial aid.** All financial aid based on need. **Additional information:** US Maritime Administration provides annual incentive payment of $3,000 per student, with certain conditions. Tuition waiver for children of deceased or disabled California veterans.

**Application procedures. Admission:** Closing date 11/30 (postmark date). $55 fee, may be waived for applicants with need. Admission notification on a rolling basis beginning on or about 2/1. Must reply by May 1 or within 2 week(s) if notified thereafter. **Financial aid:** Priority date 3/2; no closing date. FAFSA required. Applicants notified on a rolling basis starting 4/1.

**Academics.** Center for Excellence and Learning provides free tutoring/workshops hosted by professors. **Special study options:** Cooperative education, distance learning, double major, ESL, internships. International training cruise onboard ship "Golden Bear". **Credit/placement by examination:** CLEP. 24 credit hours maximum toward bachelor's degree. **Support services:** Learning center, remedial instruction, tutoring.

**Majors. Business:** Business admin, logistics. **Engineering:** Marine, mechanical. **Engineering technology:** General. **Interdisciplinary:** Global studies. **Social sciences:** Political science. **Other:** Marine transportation.

**Computing on campus.** 85 workstations in dormitories, library, computer center, student center. Dormitories wired for high-speed internet access and linked to campus network. Helpline, repair service available.

**Student life. Freshman orientation:** Mandatory, $200 fee. Preregistration for classes offered. Held last week of August. **Policies:** Students required to live on campus except those married or with children. **Housing:** Guaranteed on-campus for all undergraduates. Coed dorms available. $500 deposit, deadline 7/1. **Activities:** Student government, student newspaper.

**Athletics.** NAIA. **Intercollegiate:** Basketball, rowing (crew), rugby M, sailing, soccer, water polo. **Intramural:** Badminton, baseball M, basketball, boxing M, golf, racquetball, rowing (crew), rugby M, sailing, softball, tennis, volleyball, water polo. **Team name:** Keelhaulers.

**Student services.** Career counseling, student employment services, financial aid counseling, health services, minority student services, personal counseling, placement for graduates, veterans' counselor.

**Contact.** E-mail: admission@csum.edu
Phone: (707) 654-1330 Fax: (707) 654-1336
Marc McGee, Director of Admission, California Maritime Academy, 200 Maritime Academy Drive, Vallejo, CA 94590

## California National University for Advanced Studies
**Northridge, California**
**www.cnuas.edu**                    **CB code: 3894**

- For-profit 4-year virtual university
- Small city
- 137 degree-seeking undergraduates

**General.** Accredited by DETC. 100% distance learning university. **Degrees:** 8 bachelor's awarded; master's offered. **Calendar:** Continuous. **Part-time faculty:** 80 total.

**Basis for selection.** Application/portfolio important.

**2009-2010 Annual costs.** Domestic/Canada undergraduate tuition: $270/unit; international undergraduate tuition $300/unit.

**Application procedures. Admission:** No deadline. $75 fee.

**Academics. Special study options:** Distance learning. **Credit/placement by examination:** CLEP.

**Majors. Business:** Business admin. **Computer sciences:** Computer science. **Engineering:** General.

**Contact.** E-mail: cnuadms@mail.cnuas.edu
Phone: (818) 830-2411 Toll-free number: (800) 782-2422
Fax: (818) 830-2418
California National University for Advanced Studies, 8550 Balboa Boulevard, Suite 210, Northridge, CA 91325

## California Polytechnic State University: San Luis Obispo
**San Luis Obispo, California**          **CB member**
**www.calpoly.edu**                      **CB code: 4038**

- Public 4-year university
- Residential campus in large town
- 18,239 degree-seeking undergraduates: 4% part-time, 44% women, 1% African American, 11% Asian American, 12% Hispanic American, 1% Native American, 1% international
- 882 degree-seeking graduate students
- 37% of applicants admitted
- SAT or ACT (ACT writing optional) required
- 74% graduate within 6 years

**General.** Founded in 1901. Regionally accredited. **Degrees:** 3,824 bachelor's awarded; master's offered. **ROTC:** Army. **Location:** 200 miles from Los Angeles, 230 miles from San Francisco. **Calendar:** Quarter. **Full-time faculty:** 824 total; 82% have terminal degrees, 32% women. **Part-time faculty:** 411 total; 31% have terminal degrees, 44% women. **Class size:** 15% < 20, 58% 20-39, 14% 40-49, 9% 50-99, 4% >100. **Special facilities:** Printing press museum, university farm, dairy products technical center, architectural design institute.

**Freshman class profile.** 31,489 applied, 11,737 admitted, 3,908 enrolled.

| Mid 50% test scores | | | |
|---|---|---|---|
| SAT critical reading: | 530-630 | GPA 2.0-2.99: | 1% |
| SAT math: | 570-670 | Rank in top quarter: | 84% |
| ACT composite: | 24-29 | Rank in top tenth: | 48% |
| GPA 3.75 or higher: | 60% | Return as sophomores: | 91% |
| GPA 3.50-3.74: | 23% | Out-of-state: | 7% |
| GPA 3.0-3.49: | 16% | Live on campus: | 96% |
| | | International: | 1% |

**Basis for selection.** Course work, high school GPA, test scores most important. Extracurricular activities considered. Portfolio required for art, design majors.

**High school preparation.** College-preparatory program required. 15 units required; 22 recommended. Required and recommended units include English 4-5, mathematics 3-4, social studies 2, history 1, science 3-4 (laboratory 1-2), foreign language 2-3, visual/performing arts 1 and academic electives 1. History must be U.S. history/government.

**2009-2010 Annual costs.** Tuition/fees: $6,498; $17,658 out-of-state. Required fees vary by program. Room/board: $9,846. Books/supplies: $1,638. Personal expenses: $2,205.

**2008-2009 Financial aid. Need-based:** 2,401 full-time freshmen applied for aid; 1,168 were judged to have need; 1,055 of these received aid. Average need met was 66%. Average scholarship/grant was $2,050; average loan $3,149. 55% of total undergraduate aid awarded as scholarships/grants, 45% as loans/jobs. **Non-need-based:** Awarded to 1,094 full-time undergraduates, including 340 freshmen. Scholarships awarded for academics, alumni affiliation, art, athletics, job skills, leadership, music/drama, ROTC, state residency. **Additional information:** College-administered financial aid is not available for undergraduate international students.

**Application procedures. Admission:** Closing date 11/30 (postmark date). $55 fee, may be waived for applicants with need. Admission notification 4/1. Must reply by 5/1. Housing deposit due on first-come, first-served basis. **Financial aid:** Priority date 3/2; no closing date. FAFSA required. Applicants notified on a rolling basis starting 4/1.

**Academics. Special study options:** Combined bachelor's/graduate degree, cooperative education, distance learning, double major, ESL, exchange student, honors, internships, liberal arts/career combination, semester at sea, study abroad, teacher certification program. **Credit/placement by examination:** AP, CLEP, IB, SAT, ACT, institutional tests. 45 credit hours maximum toward bachelor's degree. **Support services:** Learning center, pre-admission summer program, reduced course load, remedial instruction, study skills assistance, tutoring, writing center.

**Majors. Agriculture:** Agribusiness operations, agronomy, animal sciences, dairy, food science, horticultural science, mechanization, ornamental horticulture, soil science. **Architecture:** Architecture, landscape, urban/

community planning. **Biology:** General, bacteriology, biochemistry. **Business:** Business admin. **Communications:** Journalism. **Communications technology:** Graphics. **Computer sciences:** Computer science, systems analysis. **Conservation:** Forestry. **Education:** Agricultural, kindergarten/preschool. **Engineering:** Aerospace, agricultural, architectural, biomedical, civil, computer, electrical, environmental, industrial, manufacturing, materials, mechanical, science. **Foreign languages:** General. **Health:** Dietetics. **History:** General. **Liberal arts:** Arts/sciences. **Math:** General, statistics. **Parks/recreation:** General, health/fitness. **Philosophy/religion:** Philosophy. **Physical sciences:** Chemistry, geology, physics. **Psychology:** General. **Social sciences:** General, economics, political science, sociology. **Visual/performing arts:** Dramatic, studio arts. **Other:** Business administration, management and operations, other, Civil engineering, other, Ethnic, cultural minority, and gender studies, other, Liberal arts and sciences, general studies and humanities, other, Multi-/interdisciplinary studies, other, Natural resources and conservation, other, Social sciences, other.

**Most popular majors.** Agriculture 13%, architecture 6%, business/marketing 18%, engineering/engineering technologies 22%.

**Computing on campus.** Dormitories wired for high-speed internet access and linked to campus network. Commuter students can connect to campus network. Online course registration, online library, helpline, student web hosting, wireless network available.

**Student life.** **Freshman orientation:** Available. Held week prior to start of fall term. **Housing:** Coed dorms, special housing for disabled, apartments available. $1,888 fully refundable deposit. **Activities:** Bands, campus ministries, choral groups, dance, drama, international student organizations, literary magazine, music ensembles, Model UN, musical theater, radio station, student government, student newspaper, symphony orchestra, TV station, MECHA, Society of Black Engineers and Scientists, Minority Engineering Program, Campus Crusade for Christ, Intervarsity Christian Fellowship, Engineering World Health.

**Athletics.** NCAA. **Intercollegiate:** Baseball M, basketball, cross-country, football (tackle) M, golf, soccer, softball W, swimming, tennis, track and field, volleyball W, wrestling M. **Intramural:** Basketball, equestrian, football (tackle), racquetball, soccer, softball, table tennis, tennis, volleyball. **Team name:** Mustangs.

**Student services.** Adult student services, alcohol/substance abuse counseling, chaplain/spiritual director, career counseling, student employment services, financial aid counseling, health services, minority student services, on-campus daycare, personal counseling, placement for graduates, women's services. **Physically disabled:** Services for visually, speech, hearing impaired.

**Contact.** E-mail: admissions@calpoly.edu
Phone: (805) 756-2311 Fax: (805) 756-5400
James Maraviglia, Assistant VP, Admissions, Recruitment & Financial Aid, California Polytechnic State University: San Luis Obispo, Admissions Office, Cal Poly, San Luis Obispo, CA 93407-0031

---

## California State Polytechnic University: Pomona

**Pomona, California**       **CB member**
**www.csupomona.edu**       **CB code: 4082**

- Public 4-year university
- Commuter campus in small city
- 20,136 degree-seeking undergraduates: 17% part-time, 43% women, 3% African American, 27% Asian American, 32% Hispanic American, 5% international
- 2,137 degree-seeking graduate students
- 61% of applicants admitted
- SAT or ACT (ACT writing optional) required
- 53% graduate within 6 years

**General.** Founded in 1938. Regionally accredited. **Degrees:** 3,570 bachelor's awarded; master's offered. **ROTC:** Army. **Location:** 30 miles from downtown Los Angeles. **Calendar:** Quarter, extensive summer session. **Full-time faculty:** 565 total; 35% minority, 41% women. **Part-time faculty:** 455 total; 29% minority, 36% women. **Class size:** 10% < 20, 57% 20-39, 18% 40-49, 13% 50-99, 2% >100. **Special facilities:** Electron microscope center, international center, small ruminant center, Arabian horse center, equine research center, land laboratory, ecological reserve, center for regenerative studies, center for community affairs.

**Freshman class profile.** 20,759 applied, 12,731 admitted, 2,913 enrolled.

| Mid 50% test scores | | | |
|---|---|---|---|
| SAT critical reading: | 450-560 | GPA 3.0-3.49: | 45% |
| SAT math: | 470-610 | GPA 2.0-2.99: | 18% |
| ACT composite: | 19-25 | Return as sophomores: | 87% |
| GPA 3.75 or higher: | 17% | Out-of-state: | 1% |
| GPA 3.50-3.74: | 20% | Live on campus: | 33% |
| | | International: | 3% |

**Basis for selection.** High school GPA, courses, and test scores important.

**High school preparation.** College-preparatory program required. 15 units required. Required and recommended units include English 4, mathematics 3-4, social studies 1, history 1, science 2 (laboratory 2), foreign language 2, visual/performing arts 1 and academic electives 1.

**2009-2010 Annual costs.** Tuition/fees: $4,551; $15,711 out-of-state. Room/board: $9,570. Books/supplies: $1,500. Personal expenses: $1,575.

**2009-2010 Financial aid.** Need-based: 2,122 full-time freshmen applied for aid; 1,485 were judged to have need; 1,338 of these received aid. Average need met was 79%. Average scholarship/grant was $9,318; average loan $3,036. 64% of total undergraduate aid awarded as scholarships/grants, 36% as loans/jobs. Non-need-based: Awarded to 586 full-time undergraduates, including 146 freshmen. Scholarships awarded for academics, alumni affiliation, athletics, leadership, state residency.

**Application procedures.** Admission: Closing date 11/30 (postmark date). $55 fee may be waived for applicants with need. Admission notification on a rolling basis beginning on or about 10/2. Must reply by May 1 or within 3 week(s) if notified thereafter. Applications for first time freshmen accepted October 1 through November 30. Financial aid: Priority date 3/2; no closing date. FAFSA required. Applicants notified on a rolling basis starting 4/1; must reply within 2 week(s) of notification.

**Academics.** Special study options: Cooperative education, cross-registration, distance learning, double major, dual enrollment of high school students, ESL, exchange student, external degree, honors, internships, study abroad, teacher certification program. Ocean studies institute, desert studies consortium. Credit/placement by examination: AP, CLEP, SAT, ACT, institutional tests. 36 credit hours maximum toward bachelor's degree. Support services: Learning center, pre-admission summer program, remedial instruction, study skills assistance, tutoring, writing center.

**Honors college/program.** Incoming freshmen invited to apply to Honors College if they have scores of 550 or higher on both math and critical reading SAT tests and GPA of 3.5 or higher. Incoming transfer students must have GPA of at least 3.5 at previous institution.

**Majors.** **Agriculture:** Animal sciences, business, food science, plant protection. **Architecture:** Architecture, landscape, urban/community planning. **Area/ethnic studies:** American. **Biology:** General, biotechnology, botany, environmental, microbiology, zoology. **Business:** Business admin, hospitality admin. **Communications:** General. **Computer sciences:** Computer science. **Education:** Agricultural. **Engineering:** General, aerospace, chemical, civil, computer, electrical, industrial, manufacturing, materials, mechanical. **Engineering technology:** General, construction, electrical. **Family/consumer sciences:** Clothing/textiles. **Foreign languages:** Spanish. **Health:** Dietetics. **History:** General. **Interdisciplinary:** Behavioral sciences. **Liberal arts:** Arts/sciences, humanities. **Math:** General. **Parks/recreation:** Health/fitness. **Philosophy/religion:** Philosophy. **Physical sciences:** Chemistry, geology, physics. **Psychology:** General. **Social sciences:** General, anthropology, economics, geography, political science, sociology. **Visual/performing arts:** Art, dramatic, graphic design. **Other:** Gender, ethnic, multicultural studies, Integrated earth studies.

**Most popular majors.** Business/marketing 29%, engineering/engineering technologies 20%, liberal arts 6%, psychology 6%.

**Computing on campus.** 280 workstations in library, computer center. Dormitories wired for high-speed internet access and linked to campus network. Commuter students can connect to campus network. Online course registration, helpline, student web hosting, wireless network available.

**Student life.** **Freshman orientation:** Mandatory, $40 fee. Preregistration for classes offered. Held between June to September (Freshman 3 days, 2 nights). **Housing:** Coed dorms, apartments available. $50 fully refundable deposit. **Activities:** Bands, campus ministries, choral groups, dance, drama, international student organizations, literary magazine, music ensembles, musical theater, opera, student government, student newspaper, symphony orchestra, Campus Crusade for Christ, black student union, Hawaiian club, MECHA, Studies of the World, Newman Club, Hillel, Bahai club, Coptic-Orthodox Christian club.

**Athletics.** NCAA. **Intercollegiate:** Baseball M, basketball, cross-country, soccer, tennis, track and field, volleyball W. **Intramural:** Badminton, basketball, football (non-tackle) M, golf, racquetball, softball, swimming, table tennis, tennis, track and field, volleyball. **Team name:** Broncos.

**Student services.** Adult student services, career counseling, student employment services, health services, on-campus daycare, personal counseling, placement for graduates, veterans' counselor. **Physically disabled:** Services for visually, speech, hearing impaired.

**Contact.** E-mail: admissions@csupomona.edu
Phone: (909) 869-3210 Fax: (909) 869-4529
Scott Duncan, Director of Admissions, California State Polytechnic University: Pomona, 3801 West Temple Avenue, Pomona, CA 91768-4019

## California State University: Bakersfield

| Bakersfield, California | CB member |
|---|---|
| www.csub.edu | CB code: 4110 |

- Public 4-year university and liberal arts college
- Commuter campus in small city
- 6,494 degree-seeking undergraduates
- 1,509 graduate students

**General.** Founded in 1965. Regionally accredited. **Degrees:** 1,309 bachelor's awarded; master's offered. **Location:** 112 miles from Los Angeles. **Calendar:** Quarter, limited summer session. **Full-time faculty:** 284 total; 14% have terminal degrees, 26% minority, 50% women. **Part-time faculty:** 157 total; 26% minority, 60% women. **Special facilities:** 40-acre facility for wild animal care, archaeological information center, center for business and economic research, center for economic education, well-sample repository, center for physiological research.

**Freshman class profile.**

| Mid 50% test scores | | | |
|---|---|---|---|
| SAT critical reading: | 380-490 | GPA 3.50-3.74: | 10% |
| SAT math: | 380-510 | GPA 3.0-3.49: | 43% |
| ACT composite: | 13-20 | GPA 2.0-2.99: | 34% |
| GPA 3.75 or higher: | 12% | Out-of-state: | 3% |
| | | Live on campus: | 12% |

**Basis for selection.** GPA, test scores, and certain honors courses must place applicant in upper third of California high school graduates (upper sixth for out-of-state applicants) using eligibility index table. Minimum test scores slightly higher for out-of-state students. GPA, test scores, and certain honors courses must place applicant in upper third of California high school graduates (upper sixth for out-of-state applicants) using eligibility index table. Minimum test scores slightly higher for out-of-state students.

**High school preparation.** Required units include English 4, mathematics 3, history 2, science 2 (laboratory 1), foreign language 2, visual/performing arts 1 and academic electives 1. Foreign language must be in same language; math must include algebra, geometry, and intermediate algebra; science must include biology and a physical science.

**2009-2010 Annual costs.** Tuition/fees: $5,091; $16,251 out-of-state. Reduced out-of-state tuition for residents of AK, AZ, CO, HI, ID, MT, NV, NM, ND, OR, SD, UT, WA, WY available under the Western Undergraduate Exchange (WUE) program. WUE students pay one-and-a half the State University Fees plus campus-based fees, which is $6,096 for the 2008/2009 academic year. Room/board: $6,678. Books/supplies: $1,638. Personal expenses: $2,562.

**2008-2009 Financial aid.** All financial aid based on need.

**Application procedures. Admission:** Priority date 3/1; no deadline. $55 fee, may be waived for applicants with need. Admission notification on a rolling basis beginning on or about 7/1. **Financial aid:** Priority date 3/2, closing date 4/1. FAFSA required. Applicants notified on a rolling basis; must reply within 2 week(s) of notification.

**Academics.** Most courses are 5 quarter units. Students enrolled in 3 courses are carrying full unit load. **Special study options:** Accelerated study, cooperative education, distance learning, double major, ESL, exchange student, external degree, honors, independent study, internships, liberal arts/career combination, student-designed major, study abroad, teacher certification program. 2+2 at specified locations for liberal studies (teaching) majors. **Credit/placement by examination:** AP, CLEP. Unlimited number of hours of credit by examination may be counted toward degree. **Support services:** Learning center, pre-admission summer program, reduced course load, remedial instruction, study skills assistance, tutoring.

**Majors. Biology:** General. **Business:** Business admin. **Communications:** General. **Computer sciences:** Computer science. **Conservation:** Land use planning. **Education:** Early childhood. **Foreign languages:** Spanish. **Health:**

Nursing (RN). **History:** General. **Liberal arts:** Arts/sciences. **Math:** General. **Philosophy/religion:** Philosophy, religion. **Physical sciences:** Chemistry, geology, physics. **Protective services:** Criminal justice. **Psychology:** General. **Public administration:** General. **Social sciences:** Anthropology, criminology, economics, political science, sociology. **Visual/performing arts:** General, art, dramatic.

**Most popular majors.** Business/marketing 15%, liberal arts 27%, psychology 10%, security/protective services 6%, social sciences 7%.

**Computing on campus.** 600 workstations in library, computer center, student center. Dormitories linked to campus network. Commuter students can connect to campus network. Online course registration, online library, helpline, student web hosting available.

**Student life. Freshman orientation:** Available, $35 fee. Preregistration for classes offered. **Housing:** Guaranteed on-campus for all undergraduates. Coed dorms, single-sex dorms available. $50 deposit. **Activities:** Jazz band, choral groups, dance, drama, literary magazine, music ensembles, musical theater, student government, student newspaper, black student union, Movimiento Estudiantil Chicano de Aztlan, Christian union, student nursing association, Circle-K, Latinos United for Education.

**Athletics.** NCAA. **Intercollegiate:** Basketball, cheerleading, cross-country W, golf M, soccer, softball W, swimming, tennis W, track and field, volleyball W, water polo W, wrestling M. **Intramural:** Badminton, basketball, golf, handball, racquetball, soccer, softball, tennis, volleyball. **Team name:** Roadrunners.

**Student services.** Adult student services, alcohol/substance abuse counseling, career counseling, services for economically disadvantaged, student employment services, financial aid counseling, health services, minority student services, on-campus daycare, personal counseling, placement for graduates, veterans' counselor. **Physically disabled:** Services for visually, speech, hearing impaired. **Learning disabled:** Comprehensive services available.

**Contact.** Phone: (661) 654-3036 Toll-free number: (800) 788-2782 Fax: (661) 654-3389
Jacqueline Mimms, Director of Admissions, California State University: Bakersfield, 9001 Stockdale Highway, Bakersfield, CA 93311-1099

## California State University: Channel Islands

| Camarillo, California | CB member |
|---|---|
| www.csuci.edu | CB code: 4128 |

- Public 4-year university
- Commuter campus in small city
- 3,575 degree-seeking undergraduates: 17% part-time, 63% women, 2% African American, 7% Asian American, 26% Hispanic American, 1% Native American
- 275 degree-seeking graduate students
- 45% of applicants admitted
- 50% graduate within 6 years

**General.** Regionally accredited. **Degrees:** 803 bachelor's awarded; master's offered. **Calendar:** Semester. **Full-time faculty:** 125 total; 84% have terminal degrees, 26% minority, 50% women. **Part-time faculty:** 157 total; 38% have terminal degrees, 18% minority, 55% women. **Class size:** 38% < 20, 53% 20-39, 5% 40-49, 4% 50-99, less than 1% >100.

**Freshman class profile.** 7,249 applied, 3,276 admitted, 732 enrolled.

| Mid 50% test scores | | | |
|---|---|---|---|
| SAT critical reading: | 440-540 | GPA 3.50-3.74: | 13% |
| SAT math: | 430-540 | GPA 3.0-3.49: | 47% |
| SAT writing: | 440-540 | GPA 2.0-2.99: | 31% |
| ACT composite: | 18-23 | End year in good standing: | 83% |
| GPA 3.75 or higher: | 9% | Return as sophomores: | 79% |
| | | Live on campus: | 42% |

**Basis for selection.** Academic GPA very important. Rigor of secondary school record and state residency important. Test scores required for students with less than 3.0 HS GPA.

**High school preparation.** College-preparatory program required. 15 units required. Required units include English 4, mathematics 3, social studies 1, history 1, science 2 (laboratory 2), foreign language 2, visual/performing arts 1 and academic electives 1.

**2009-2010 Annual costs.** Tuition/fees: $4,881; $16,041 out-of-state. Room/board: $10,780. Books/supplies: $1,700. Personal expenses: $3,000.

**2008-2009 Financial aid. Need-based:** 551 full-time freshmen applied for aid; 420 were judged to have need; 420 of these received aid. Average need met was 30%. Average scholarship/grant was $5,551; average loan

$3,212. 47% of total undergraduate aid awarded as scholarships/grants, 53% as loans/jobs. **Non-need-based:** Awarded to 183 full-time undergraduates, including 73 freshmen. Scholarships awarded for academics, leadership, state residency.

**Application procedures. Admission:** Priority date 11/30; deadline 1/15 (receipt date). $55 fee, may be waived for applicants with need. Admission notification on a rolling basis beginning on or about 1/2. Must reply by 5/1. **Financial aid:** Priority date 3/2; no closing date. FAFSA required. Applicants notified by 4/7.

**Academics. Special study options:** Double major, independent study, study abroad, teacher certification program. **Credit/placement by examination:** AP, CLEP, SAT, ACT, institutional tests. **Support services:** Preadmission summer program, remedial instruction, tutoring, writing center.

**Majors. Area/ethnic studies:** Chicano/Hispanic-American/Latino. **Biology:** General, biotechnology. **Business:** General. **Communications:** General. **Computer sciences:** General. **Conservation:** Environmental science, management/policy. **Education:** Early childhood. **Foreign languages:** Spanish. **History:** General. **Liberal arts:** Arts/sciences. **Math:** General. **Physical sciences:** Chemistry. **Psychology:** General. **Social sciences:** Economics, political science, sociology. **Visual/performing arts:** General, art.

**Most popular majors.** Biology 9%, business/marketing 24%, history 6%, liberal arts 14%, psychology 15%, social sciences 9%, visual/performing arts 9%.

**Computing on campus.** Dormitories wired for high-speed internet access. Commuter students can connect to campus network. Online course registration, online library, helpline, wireless network available.

**Student life. Freshman orientation:** Mandatory, $120 fee. Preregistration for classes offered. Two-day session in July. **Housing:** Coed dorms, wellness housing available. $1,000 fully refundable deposit, deadline 6/1. **Activities:** Choral groups, student government, student newspaper.

**Student services.** Alcohol/substance abuse counseling, career counseling, services for economically disadvantaged, student employment services, financial aid counseling, health services, personal counseling, women's services. **Physically disabled:** Services for visually, speech, hearing impaired. **Learning disabled:** Comprehensive services available.

**Contact.** E-mail: admissionsandrecords@csuci.edu
Phone: (805) 437-8400
Jane Sweetland, Dean of Enrollment, California State University: Channel Islands, One University Drive, Camarillo, CA 93012

---

## California State University: Chico

Chico, California                                    **CB member**
www.csuchico.edu                                     **CB code: 4048**

- Public 4-year university and liberal arts college
- Residential campus in small city
- 15,617 degree-seeking undergraduates: 8% part-time, 51% women, 1% African American, 2% Asian American, 6% Hispanic American, 3% international
- 885 degree-seeking graduate students
- 88% of applicants admitted
- SAT or ACT (ACT writing optional) required
- 54% graduate within 6 years

**General.** Founded in 1887. Regionally accredited. 119-acre campus. **Degrees:** 3,230 bachelor's awarded; master's offered. **Location:** 90 miles from Sacramento, 175 miles from San Francisco. **Calendar:** Semester, limited summer session. **Full-time faculty:** 504 total; 83% have terminal degrees, 18% minority, 42% women. **Part-time faculty:** 379 total; 28% have terminal degrees, 10% minority, 52% women. **Class size:** 28% < 20, 43% 20-39, 17% 40-49, 8% 50-99, 3% >100. **Special facilities:** 1,000-acre farm, planetarium, instructional media center, biology field station, anthropology museum, intercultural studies center, computer graphics lab, assistive technology center, media prep lab, recording arts studio, hydrotherapy pool, echocardiography system, gas displacement chamber, two ecological preserves with nearly 4,100 acres, forensics lab, archaeology lab and research center.

**Freshman class profile.** 12,881 applied, 11,298 admitted, 2,505 enrolled.

| Mid 50% test scores | | | |
|---|---|---|---|
| SAT critical reading: | 450-550 | Rank in top quarter: | 76% |
| SAT math: | 460-570 | Rank in top tenth: | 35% |
| ACT composite: | 19-24 | End year in good standing: | 73% |
| GPA 3.75 or higher: | 9% | Return as sophomores: | 82% |
| GPA 3.50-3.74: | 10% | Out-of-state: | 2% |
| GPA 3.0-3.49: | 43% | Live on campus: | 62% |
| GPA 2.0-2.99: | 38% | International: | 2% |

**Basis for selection.** Eligibility index derived from high school GPA and test scores. First-time freshmen applicants rank order based on characteristics of applicant pool. GPA determined from 10th, and 11th grade college prep courses only, excluding physical education. Nursing program open only to state residents. All freshmen applicants must submit SAT or ACT test scores regardless of high school GPA. SAT or ACT must be taken by the December test date for admission consideration. Portfolio required of fine arts majors. **Homeschooled:** Transcript of courses and grades required. Must be able to verify completion of required college preparatory subject requirements and meet institutional eligibility index. **Learning Disabled:** Students must meet established admission criteria.

**High school preparation.** College-preparatory program required. 15 units required. Required units include English 4, mathematics 3, social studies 2, science 2 (laboratory 2), foreign language 2 and visual/performing arts 1.

**2009-2010 Annual costs.** Tuition/fees: $5,336; $16,496 out-of-state. Reduced out-of-state tuition for residents of AK, AZ, CO. HI, ID, MT, NV, NM, ND, OR, SD, UT, WA, WY may be available under the Western Undergraduate Exchange (WUE) program. Room/board: $9,996. Books/supplies: $1,656. Personal expenses: $1,950.

**2009-2010 Financial aid. Non-need-based:** Scholarships awarded for academics, art, athletics, leadership, minority status, music/drama, religious affiliation.

**Application procedures. Admission:** Priority date 10/1; deadline 11/30 (postmark date). $55 fee, may be waived for applicants with need. Admission notification 3/1. Admission notification on a rolling basis. Must reply by May 1 or within 2 week(s) if notified thereafter. Applications for the following majors must be made during priority periods of October and August: nursing, media arts, graphic design, recording arts, and interior design. All first time freshmen fall applicants should apply between October 1 and November 30. **Financial aid:** Priority date 3/2; no closing date. FAFSA required. Applicants notified on a rolling basis starting 3/2.

**Academics. Special study options:** Cooperative education, cross-registration, distance learning, double major, dual enrollment of high school students, ESL, exchange student, external degree, honors, independent study, internships, student-designed major, study abroad, teacher certification program. **Credit/placement by examination:** AP, CLEP, IB, SAT, ACT, institutional tests. 30 credit hours maximum toward bachelor's degree. 6 semester hours awarded for each International Baccalaureate higher level exam passed with score of 4 to 7. **Support services:** Learning center, preadmission summer program, reduced course load, remedial instruction, study skills assistance, tutoring, writing center.

**Majors. Agriculture:** Agronomy, animal sciences, business, range science. **Architecture:** Urban/community planning. **Area/ethnic studies:** American, Asian, Latin American, women's. **Biology:** General, biochemistry, botany, ecology, microbiology. **Business:** Accounting, business admin, finance, human resources, management information systems, marketing. **Communications:** Journalism, organizational, public relations, radio/tv. **Computer sciences:** Computer graphics, computer science, information technology. **Conservation:** Environmental science, management/policy. **Education:** Agricultural, art, biology, chemistry, early childhood, English, ESL, French, German, health, instructional media, mathematics, music, physical, science, social science, Spanish. **Engineering:** Civil, computer, mechanical. **Engineering technology:** Construction. **Foreign languages:** French, German, linguistics, Spanish. **Health:** Clinical lab science, communication disorders, dietetics, health services, nursing (RN), predental, premedicine, prepharmacy, preveterinary, recreational therapy. **History:** General. **Interdisciplinary:** Accounting/computer science, gerontology, math/computer science. **Legal studies:** Paralegal. **Liberal arts:** Arts/sciences, humanities. **Math:** General, applied, statistics. **Parks/recreation:** General, exercise sciences, facilities management, health/fitness. **Philosophy/religion:** Judaic, philosophy, religion. **Physical sciences:** General, atmospheric science, chemistry, geology, hydrology, physics. **Protective services:** Criminal justice. **Psychology:** General. **Public administration:** General, social work. **Social sciences:** General, anthropology, economics, geography, international economics, international relations, political science, sociology. **Visual/performing arts:** Art, art history/conservation, design, dramatic, graphic design, interior design, music theory/composition, musical theater, piano/organ, studio arts.

**Other:** Concrete industry management, Ecological, evolutionary and organismal biology, Environmental economics, Mechatronics, Music industry and technology, Supply chain management systems.

**Most popular majors.** Business/marketing 16%, engineering/engineering technologies 8%, health sciences 7%, liberal arts 7%, parks/recreation 8%, psychology 6%, social sciences 10%, visual/performing arts 8%.

**Computing on campus.** 1,205 workstations in dormitories, library, student center. Dormitories wired for high-speed internet access and linked to campus network. Commuter students can connect to campus network. Online course registration, online library, helpline, repair service, student web hosting, wireless network available.

**Student life. Freshman orientation:** Available, $50 fee. Preregistration for classes offered. June and July sessions for students and parents. One-day session $50, two days $90. Free mini-orientation session in August, or online orientation also offered. **Housing:** Coed dorms, special housing for disabled, apartments, fraternity/sorority housing, wellness housing available. $1,000 fully refundable deposit, deadline 4/13. **Activities:** Bands, choral groups, dance, drama, film society, literary magazine, music ensembles, musical theater, opera, radio station, student government, student newspaper, symphony orchestra, over 200 organizations.

**Athletics.** NCAA. **Intercollegiate:** Baseball M, basketball, cross-country, golf, soccer, softball W, track and field, volleyball W. **Intramural:** Basketball, bowling, football (non-tackle), soccer, softball, volleyball. **Team name:** Wildcats.

**Student services.** Adult student services, alcohol/substance abuse counseling, career counseling, services for economically disadvantaged, student employment services, financial aid counseling, health services, legal services, minority student services, on-campus daycare, personal counseling, placement for graduates, veterans' counselor, women's services. **Physically disabled:** Services for visually, speech, hearing impaired. **Learning disabled:** Comprehensive services available.

**Contact.** E-mail: info@csuchico.edu
Phone: (530) 898-4428 Toll-free number: (800) 542-4426
Fax: (530) 898-6456
Allan Bee, Director of Admissions, California State University: Chico, 400 West First Street, Chico, CA 95929-0722

---

## California State University: Dominguez Hills

**Carson, California**　　　　　　　　**CB member**
**www.csudh.edu**　　　　　　　　　**CB code: 4098**

- Public 4-year university
- Commuter campus in small city
- 10,222 degree-seeking undergraduates: 34% part-time, 67% women, 27% African American, 9% Asian American, 40% Hispanic American, 2% international
- 2,636 degree-seeking graduate students
- 84% of applicants admitted
- 35% graduate within 6 years

**General.** Founded in 1960. Regionally accredited. **Degrees:** 1,941 bachelor's awarded; master's offered. **ROTC:** Army, Air Force. **Location:** 13 miles from Los Angeles. **Calendar:** Semester, extensive summer session. **Full-time faculty:** 284 total; 79% have terminal degrees, 24% minority, 49% women. **Part-time faculty:** 489 total; 36% have terminal degrees, 27% minority, 54% women. **Class size:** 20% < 20, 47% 20-39, 15% 40-49, 17% 50-99, 1% >100. **Special facilities:** Nature preserve, greenhouse, observatory, urban community research center, Japanese garden and theater complex.

**Freshman class profile.** 6,790 applied, 5,737 admitted, 1,135 enrolled.

| Mid 50% test scores | | | |
|---|---|---|---|
| SAT critical reading: | 370-460 | GPA 3.0-3.49: | 36% |
| SAT math: | 360-470 | GPA 2.0-2.99: | 54% |
| SAT writing: | 370-460 | End year in good standing: | 65% |
| ACT composite: | 15-19 | Return as sophomores: | 68% |
| GPA 3.75 or higher: | 3% | Out-of-state: | 1% |
| GPA 3.50-3.74: | 6% | Live on campus: | 17% |
| | | International: | 3% |

**Basis for selection.** Academic record and test scores are most important. SAT/ACT required of applicants who do not meet minimum requirement based on admissions eligibility index. Interview required of Educational Opportunity Program applicants. **Homeschooled:** Statement describing homeschool structure and mission, transcript of courses and grades, state high school equivalency certificate required. **Learning Disabled:** Student must show proof of learning disability to Office of Disability Services.

**High school preparation.** College-preparatory program required. 15 units required. Required units include English 4, mathematics 3, social studies 2, history 1, science 2 (laboratory 2), foreign language 2, visual/performing arts 1 and academic electives 1.

**2009-2010 Annual costs.** Tuition/fees: $4,645; $15,805 out-of-state. Reduced out-of-state tuition for residents of AK, AZ, CO, HI, ID, MT, NV, NM, ND, OR, SD, UT, WA, WY available under the Western Undergraduate Exchange (WUE) program. Room/board: $9,970. Books/supplies: $750. Personal expenses: $1,200.

**2008-2009 Financial aid. Non-need-based:** Scholarships awarded for academics, alumni affiliation, art, athletics, leadership, music/drama.

**Application procedures. Admission:** Priority date 11/30; no deadline. $55 fee, may be waived for applicants with need. Admission notification on a rolling basis beginning on or about 1/7. **Financial aid:** Priority date 3/2, closing date 4/15. FAFSA required. Applicants notified on a rolling basis starting 2/28; must reply within 4 week(s) of notification.

**Academics. Special study options:** Accelerated study, cross-registration, distance learning, double major, dual enrollment of high school students, external degree, honors, independent study, internships, student-designed major, study abroad, teacher certification program, weekend college. **Credit/placement by examination:** AP, CLEP, IB, SAT, ACT, institutional tests. **Support services:** Learning center, pre-admission summer program, reduced course load, remedial instruction, tutoring, writing center.

**Majors. Area/ethnic studies:** African-American, Chicano/Hispanic-American/Latino. **Biology:** General, biochemistry, cell/histology, ecology, microbiology. **Business:** General, accounting, business admin, entrepreneurial studies, international, labor studies, logistics, marketing, operations, real estate. **Communications:** General, digital media, journalism, public relations. **Computer sciences:** Computer science, information technology. **Engineering technology:** Quality control. **Foreign languages:** Spanish. **Health:** Clinical lab science, health care admin, health services, nursing (RN), physics/radiologic health. **History:** General. **Interdisciplinary:** Behavioral sciences, cultural resource management, natural sciences, peace/conflict. **Legal studies:** Prelaw. **Liberal arts:** Arts/sciences. **Math:** General. **Parks/recreation:** General, health/fitness. **Philosophy/religion:** Philosophy. **Physical sciences:** Chemistry, geology, physics. **Protective services:** Criminal justice. **Psychology:** General. **Public administration:** General, human services. **Social sciences:** Anthropology, geography, political science, sociology, urban studies. **Visual/performing arts:** Art, art history/conservation, dramatic, graphic design. **Other:** Interdisciplinary studies.

**Most popular majors.** Business/marketing 23%, communications/journalism 7%, health sciences 13%, liberal arts 14%, psychology 7%, public administration/social services 7%, social sciences 9%.

**Computing on campus.** 256 workstations in library, computer center. Dormitories wired for high-speed internet access and linked to campus network. Commuter students can connect to campus network. Online course registration, online library, helpline, student web hosting, wireless network available.

**Student life. Freshman orientation:** Available, $50 fee. Preregistration for classes offered. Offered eleven times a year to incoming admitted freshmen and transfer students. **Housing:** Special housing for disabled, apartments available. $300 fully refundable deposit. **Activities:** Bands, choral groups, dance, drama, international student organizations, literary magazine, music ensembles, musical theater, radio station, student government, student newspaper, TV station, Accounting Society, African-American Business Student Association, Dance Club, Literary Club, Phi Alpha Delta, Political Science Club, Science Society, Hispanic Association of Natural and Social Science, Campus Crusade for Christ.

**Athletics.** NCAA. **Intercollegiate:** Baseball M, basketball, cross-country W, golf M, soccer, softball W, track and field W, volleyball W. **Intramural:** Basketball, cross-country, football (non-tackle), golf, soccer, softball, swimming, tennis, track and field, volleyball, water polo, weight lifting. **Team name:** Toros.

**Student services.** Career counseling, services for economically disadvantaged, student employment services, financial aid counseling, health services, on-campus daycare, personal counseling, placement for graduates, veterans' counselor, women's services. **Physically disabled:** Services for visually, speech, hearing impaired.

**Contact.** Phone: (310) 243-3645 Fax: (310) 516-3609
Gayle Ball Parker, Director of University Outreach & Information Services, California State University: Dominguez Hills, 1000 East Victoria Street, Carson, CA 90747

## California State University: East Bay

**Hayward, California**

www.csueastbay.edu

**CB member**

**CB code: 4011**

- Public 4-year university
- Commuter campus in small city
- 11,086 degree-seeking undergraduates: 17% part-time, 60% women, 12% African American, 26% Asian American, 17% Hispanic American, 7% international
- 2,503 degree-seeking graduate students
- 48% graduate within 6 years

**General.** Founded in 1957. Regionally accredited. Branch campus in Concord and extensive online courses offered. **Degrees:** 2,400 bachelor's awarded; master's, doctoral offered. **Location:** 30 miles from San Francisco, 30 miles from San Jose. **Calendar:** Quarter, limited summer session. **Full-time faculty:** 366 total; 37% minority, 48% women. **Part-time faculty:** 454 total; 23% minority, 60% women. **Class size:** 38% < 20, 38% 20-39, 9% 40-49, 13% 50-99, 2% >100. **Special facilities:** Ecological field station, museum of anthropology, marine laboratory, geology summer field camp.

**Freshman class profile.** 8,722 applied, 6,388 admitted, 1,445 enrolled.

| Mid 50% test scores | | | |
|---|---|---|---|
| SAT critical reading: | 400-510 | GPA 3.50-3.74: | 10% |
| SAT math: | 400-520 | GPA 3.0-3.49: | 40% |
| SAT writing: | 400-510 | GPA 2.0-2.99: | 43% |
| ACT composite: | 16-22 | Return as sophomores: | 71% |
| GPA 3.75 or higher: | 7% | Out-of-state: | 1% |
| | | International: | 7% |

**Basis for selection.** Open admission, but selective for some programs. Eligibility index based on GPA, test results, and 15 units of subject requirements to yield students in top third of California high school graduates. Out-of-state applicants should be in top sixth of high school class. Test scores not required for residents with high school GPA above 3.0, nonresidents with high school GPA above 3.61.

**High school preparation.** College-preparatory program required. 15 units required. Required units include English 4, mathematics 3, history 2, science 2 (laboratory 2), foreign language 2 and academic electives 1. One visual and performing arts. Math must be algebra, geometry, and intermediate algebra. Science must be biology and a physical science. Foreign language units must be in same language.

**2009-2010 Annual costs.** Tuition/fees: $4,872; $16,032 out-of-state. Quoted freshman room-only charge is for suite shared by 6 to 8 students. Additional $3,200 advance purchase of flexible retail meal credits required. (Standard meal plans not available). Room/board: $10,029. Books/supplies: $1,734. Personal expenses: $3,114.

**2008-2009 Financial aid.** **Non-need-based:** Scholarships awarded for athletics, music/drama.

**Application procedures. Admission:** Closing date 8/31 (postmark date). $55 fee, may be waived for applicants with need. Admission notification on a rolling basis beginning on or about 10/1. **Financial aid:** Priority date 3/2; no closing date. FAFSA required. Applicants notified on a rolling basis; must reply within 3 week(s) of notification.

**Academics. Special study options:** Accelerated study, cooperative education, cross-registration, distance learning, double major, dual enrollment of high school students, ESL, exchange student, honors, independent study, internships, liberal arts/career combination, student-designed major, study abroad, teacher certification program. **Credit/placement by examination:** AP, CLEP, IB, SAT, ACT, institutional tests. 45 credit hours maximum toward bachelor's degree. 45-unit limitation excludes advanced placement. **Support services:** Learning center, pre-admission summer program, reduced course load, remedial instruction, study skills assistance, tutoring.

**Majors. Area/ethnic studies:** African-American, Asian-American, Chicano/Hispanic-American/Latino, Latin American, Native American. **Biology:** General, biochemistry, biomedical sciences. **Business:** General, accounting, business admin, entrepreneurial studies, finance, human resources, management information systems, managerial economics, marketing, purchasing, real estate. **Communications:** General, advertising, broadcast journalism, journalism, public relations. **Computer sciences:** General, computer science, information systems, networking. **Conservation:** General, environmental studies. **Education:** Mathematics, physical, speech. **Engineering:** Software. **Engineering technology:** Industrial management. **Foreign languages:** French, Spanish. **Health:** Athletic training, audiology/speech pathology, clinical lab technology, environmental health, prenursing, recreational therapy. **History:** General. **Liberal arts:** Arts/sciences. **Math:** General, applied, statistics. **Parks/recreation:** General, exercise sciences, facilities management, health/fitness. **Philosophy/religion:** Philosophy, religion. **Physical sciences:** Chemistry, geology, physics. **Protective services:** Corrections, law

enforcement admin. **Psychology:** General. **Public administration:** General, policy analysis, social work. **Social sciences:** Anthropology, archaeology, economics, geography, political science, sociology. **Visual/performing arts:** Art, art history/conservation, arts management, ceramics, commercial/advertising art, dance, dramatic, drawing, painting, photography, printmaking, sculpture, studio arts, theater design.

**Most popular majors.** Business/marketing 28%, health sciences 11%, liberal arts 10%, psychology 6%, social sciences 10%.

**Computing on campus.** 1,062 workstations in dormitories, library, computer center. Dormitories wired for high-speed internet access and linked to campus network. Commuter students can connect to campus network. Online course registration, helpline, student web hosting available.

**Student life. Freshman orientation:** Mandatory, $80 fee. Preregistration for classes offered. 2 day program with overnight lodging on campus optional. **Policies:** Community and campus-based volunteer programs available. **Housing:** Apartments available. $900 deposit, deadline 5/1. Private coeducational dormitory adjacent to campus. **Activities:** Bands, choral groups, dance, drama, literary magazine, music ensembles, musical theater, opera, radio station, student government, student newspaper, symphony orchestra, TV station, 90 campus organizations.

**Athletics.** NAIA, NCAA. **Intercollegiate:** Baseball M, basketball, cross-country, golf, soccer, softball W, swimming W, track and field, volleyball W, water polo W. **Intramural:** Badminton, basketball, golf, gymnastics M, racquetball, soccer, softball, swimming, tennis, volleyball. **Team name:** Pioneers.

**Student services.** Adult student services, career counseling, services for economically disadvantaged, student employment services, financial aid counseling, health services, legal services, minority student services, on-campus daycare, personal counseling, placement for graduates, veterans' counselor. **Physically disabled:** Services for visually, speech, hearing impaired.

**Contact.** E-mail: admissions@csueastbay.edu
Phone: (510) 885-2784 Fax: (510) 885-4059
Gregory Smith, Associate Vice President, Planning and Enrollment Management, California State University: East Bay, 25800 Carlos Bee Boulevard, Hayward, CA 94542-3095

## California State University: Fresno

**Fresno, California**

www.csufresno.edu

**CB member**

**CB code: 4312**

- Public 4-year university
- Commuter campus in very large city
- 18,216 degree-seeking undergraduates: 15% part-time, 57% women, 6% African American, 16% Asian American, 35% Hispanic American, 1% Native American, 1% international
- 3,284 degree-seeking graduate students
- 72% of applicants admitted
- SAT or ACT (ACT writing optional) required
- 48% graduate within 6 years

**General.** Founded in 1911. Regionally accredited. Designated as an arboretum in 1978. **Degrees:** 3,541 bachelor's awarded; master's, doctoral offered. **ROTC:** Army, Air Force. **Location:** 217 miles from Los Angeles, 192 miles from San Francisco. **Calendar:** Semester, limited summer session. **Full-time faculty:** 702 total; 76% have terminal degrees, 31% minority, 42% women. **Part-time faculty:** 496 total; 7% have terminal degrees, 26% minority, 54% women. **Class size:** 16% < 20, 56% 20-39, 18% 40-49, 8% 50-99, 3% >100. **Special facilities:** 1,190-acre university farm, planetarium.

**Freshman class profile.** 14,025 applied, 10,090 admitted, 2,765 enrolled.

| Mid 50% test scores | | | |
|---|---|---|---|
| SAT critical reading: | 400-520 | GPA 2.0-2.99: | 26% |
| SAT math: | 420-540 | End year in good standing: | 82% |
| ACT composite: | 17-22 | Return as sophomores: | 80% |
| GPA 3.75 or higher: | 19% | Live on campus: | 29% |
| GPA 3.50-3.74: | 16% | International: | 1% |
| GPA 3.0-3.49: | 39% | Fraternities: | 2% |
| | | Sororities: | 2% |

**Basis for selection.** Academic GPA, standardized test scores, and rigor of secondary school record very important. Tests recommended, but not required, if student has a high school GPA of 3.0 or higher. **Homeschooled:** Transcript of courses and grades required. **Learning Disabled:** Contact Services for Students with Disabilities after submitting application for consideration.

**High school preparation.** College-preparatory program required. 15 units required. Required units include English 4, mathematics 3, social studies 1, history 1, science 1 (laboratory 1), foreign language 2, visual/performing arts 1 and academic electives 1.

**2009-2010 Annual costs.** Tuition/fees: $4,672; $15,832 out-of-state. Room/board: $9,652. Books/supplies: $1,288. Personal expenses: $2,382.

**2009-2010 Financial aid. Need-based:** 2,153 full-time freshmen applied for aid; 1,771 were judged to have need; 1,699 of these received aid. Average need met was 74%. Average scholarship/grant was $9,888; average loan $2,944. 67% of total undergraduate aid awarded as scholarships/grants, 33% as loans/jobs. **Non-need-based:** Awarded to 1,552 full-time undergraduates, including 463 freshmen. Scholarships awarded for academics, art, athletics, leadership, music/drama, ROTC, state residency.

**Application procedures. Admission:** Closing date 10/1 (receipt date). $55 fee, may be waived for applicants with need. Application must be submitted online. Admission notification on a rolling basis. **Financial aid:** Priority date 3/3; no closing date. FAFSA required. Applicants notified on a rolling basis starting 4/1; must reply within 3 week(s) of notification.

**Academics. Special study options:** Accelerated study, combined bachelor's/graduate degree, cooperative education, cross-registration, distance learning, double major, dual enrollment of high school students, ESL, exchange student, honors, independent study, internships, student-designed major, study abroad, teacher certification program. **Credit/placement by examination:** AP, CLEP, IB, institutional tests. 30 credit hours maximum toward bachelor's degree. **Support services:** Learning center, pre-admission summer program, reduced course load, remedial instruction, study skills assistance, tutoring, writing center.

**Honors college/program.** Admits 50 students each year. Criteria include intellectual and creative potential and SAT of 1800 (Critical Reading/Math/Writing), upper 10 percent of graduating class, or minimum GPA of 3.6 (through the end of junior year). Students participate in 2 general education honors courses and honors colloquium each semester during first two years and 3 upper division honors courses during junior and senior years. 30 hours of community service required freshmen year with varying yearly requirement thereafter.

**Majors. Agriculture:** General, agronomy, animal health, animal sciences, business, dairy, food science, horticultural science, plant protection, plant sciences. **Area/ethnic studies:** African-American, Chicano/Hispanic-American/Latino, women's. **Biology:** General, anatomy, bacteriology, cell/histology, ecology, molecular. **Business:** Accounting, business admin, finance, human resources, international, logistics, management information systems, marketing, real estate. **Communications:** Media studies. **Computer sciences:** Computer science. **Conservation:** Environmental studies. **Education:** General, music. **Engineering:** Civil, computer, electrical, environmental, mechanical. **Engineering technology:** Construction, industrial, occupational safety, surveying. **Family/consumer sciences:** General, child development. **Foreign languages:** French, linguistics, Spanish. **Health:** Communication disorders, community health services, environmental health, nursing (RN), occupational health, prenursing, vocational rehab counseling. **History:** General. **Interdisciplinary:** Natural sciences. **Liberal arts:** Arts/sciences. **Math:** General. **Parks/recreation:** Exercise sciences, facilities management. **Philosophy/religion:** Philosophy, religion. **Physical sciences:** Chemistry, geology, physics. **Protective services:** Corrections, criminal justice. **Psychology:** General. **Public administration:** General, social work. **Social sciences:** Anthropology, criminology, economics, geography, political science, sociology. **Visual/performing arts:** Art, dramatic, interior design, music performance.

**Most popular majors.** Business/marketing 17%, health sciences 11%, liberal arts 10%, psychology 6%, social sciences 11%.

**Computing on campus.** 1,500 workstations in dormitories, library, computer center, student center. Dormitories linked to campus network. Commuter students can connect to campus network. Online course registration, online library, helpline, repair service, student web hosting, wireless network available.

**Student life. Freshman orientation:** Mandatory, $45 fee. One day program held during June and July for the fall semester and November and December for the spring semester. **Housing:** Coed dorms, single-sex dorms, fraternity/sorority housing available. $150 partly refundable deposit, deadline 4/1. **Activities:** Bands, choral groups, dance, drama, international student organizations, literary magazine, music ensembles, musical theater, radio station, student government, student newspaper, symphony orchestra, TV station, over 250 student organizations including religious and ethnic groups.

**Athletics.** NCAA. **Intercollegiate:** Baseball M, basketball, cross-country, equestrian W, football (tackle) M, golf, soccer W, softball W, tennis, track and field, volleyball W, wrestling M. **Intramural:** Basketball, football (non-tackle), racquetball, soccer, softball, tennis, volleyball. **Team name:** Bulldogs.

**Student services.** Adult student services, career counseling, services for economically disadvantaged, student employment services, financial aid counseling, health services, minority student services, on-campus daycare, personal counseling, placement for graduates, veterans' counselor, women's services. **Physically disabled:** Services for visually, speech, hearing impaired.

**Contact.** E-mail: admissions@csufresno.edu
Phone: (559) 278-2261 Fax: (559) 278-4812
Vivian Franco, Director, California State University: Fresno, 5150 North Maple Avenue, M/S JA 57, Fresno, CA 93740-8026

## California State University: Fullerton

Fullerton, California
www.fullerton.edu

CB member
CB code: 4589

- Public 4-year university
- Commuter campus in small city
- 30,670 degree-seeking undergraduates: 25% part-time, 58% women, 3% African American, 22% Asian American, 31% Hispanic American, 3% international
- 5,515 degree-seeking graduate students
- 55% of applicants admitted
- SAT or ACT required
- 52% graduate within 6 years

**General.** Founded in 1957. Regionally accredited. **Degrees:** 6,580 bachelor's awarded; master's, doctoral offered. **ROTC:** Army. **Location:** 30 miles from Los Angeles. **Calendar:** Semester, extensive summer session. **Full-time faculty:** 887 total; 82% have terminal degrees, 24% minority, 47% women. **Part-time faculty:** 965 total. **Class size:** 18% < 20, 52% 20-39, 17% 40-49, 10% 50-99, 3% >100. **Special facilities:** Wildlife sanctuary, arboretum, desert studies center, twin studies center, center for children who stutter, south central coastal information center, demographic research center, institute of gerontology, center for oral and public history, center for study of religion in American life, center for study of economics of aging.

**Freshman class profile.** 30,612 applied, 16,865 admitted, 4,065 enrolled.

| Mid 50% test scores | | | |
|---|---|---|---|
| SAT critical reading: | 440-540 | GPA 2.0-2.99: | 25% |
| SAT math: | 450-570 | End year in good standing: | 79% |
| ACT composite: | 18-23 | Return as sophomores: | 80% |
| GPA 3.75 or higher: | 12% | Out-of-state: | 1% |
| GPA 3.50-3.74: | 17% | Live on campus: | 7% |
| GPA 3.0-3.49: | 46% | International: | 2% |

**Basis for selection.** Eligibility index consisting of combination of high school GPA and SAT or ACT score. Audition required of music majors.

**High school preparation.** College-preparatory program required. 15 units required; 16 recommended. Required and recommended units include English 4, mathematics 3, social studies 1, history 1, science 2 (laboratory 2), foreign language 2-3, visual/performing arts 1 and academic electives 1. 1 unit U.S. history/government required.

**2009-2010 Annual costs.** Tuition/fees: $4,662; $15,622 out-of-state. Room/board: $9,082. Books/supplies: $1,638. Personal expenses: $2,700.

**2008-2009 Financial aid. Need-based:** 3,157 full-time freshmen applied for aid; 2,004 were judged to have need; 1,750 of these received aid. Average need met was 68%. Average scholarship/grant was $7,039; average loan $2,919. 69% of total undergraduate aid awarded as scholarships/grants, 31% as loans/jobs. **Non-need-based:** Awarded to 1,849 full-time undergraduates, including 605 freshmen. Scholarships awarded for academics. **Additional information:** Fee waiver for children of veterans killed in action or with service-connected disability whose annual income is $5,000 or less.

**Application procedures. Admission:** Closing date 11/30 (postmark date). $55 fee, may be waived for applicants with need. Application must be submitted online. Admission notification on a rolling basis beginning on or about 1/1. Must reply by 5/6. Reply date given on notification letter. **Financial aid:** Priority date 3/2; no closing date. FAFSA required. Applicants notified by 4/22; Applicants notified on a rolling basis starting 4/22; must reply within 4 week(s) of notification.

**Academics. Special study options:** Cross-registration, distance learning, double major, dual enrollment of high school students, honors, independent study, internships, study abroad, teacher certification program. Service Learning. **Credit/placement by examination:** AP, CLEP, IB, SAT, ACT, institutional tests. 30 credit hours maximum toward bachelor's degree. **Support**

services: Learning center, pre-admission summer program, reduced course load, remedial instruction, study skills assistance, tutoring, writing center.

**Majors. Area/ethnic studies:** African-American, American, Asian-American, Chicano/Hispanic-American/Latino, European, Latin American, women's. **Biology:** General, biochemistry. **Business:** Accounting, business admin, entrepreneurial studies, finance, international, managerial economics, marketing, tourism/travel. **Communications:** General, advertising, journalism, public relations, radio/tv. **Computer sciences:** Computer science, information technology. **Education:** Early childhood, music. **Engineering:** General, civil, computer, electrical, mechanical, operations research, science. **Foreign languages:** Comparative lit, French, German, Japanese, linguistics, Spanish. **Health:** Communication disorders, health services, nursing (RN), prenursing. **History:** General. **Liberal arts:** Arts/sciences. **Math:** General, applied, statistics. **Parks/recreation:** Health/fitness. **Philosophy/religion:** Philosophy, religion. **Physical sciences:** Chemistry, geology, physics. **Protective services:** Criminal justice. **Psychology:** General. **Public administration:** General, human services. **Social sciences:** Anthropology, economics, geography, political science, sociology. **Visual/performing arts:** Art, art history/conservation, dance, dramatic, music performance, studio arts.

**Most popular majors.** Business/marketing 26%, communications/journalism 14%, education 6%, psychology 6%, social sciences 6%, visual/performing arts 6%.

**Computing on campus.** 2,000 workstations in dormitories, library, computer center, student center. Dormitories wired for high-speed internet access and linked to campus network. Commuter students can connect to campus network. Online course registration, online library, helpline, repair service, wireless network available.

**Student life. Freshman orientation:** Mandatory. Preregistration for classes offered. **Housing:** Apartments, fraternity/sorority housing available. **Activities:** Bands, choral groups, dance, drama, international student organizations, music ensembles, Model UN, musical theater, radio station, student government, student newspaper, symphony orchestra, Chinese Christian Fellowship, Christian Student Association, Disabled Student Association, Fellowship of Christian Athletes, Human Services Student Association, Movimiento Estudiantil Chicano de Atlan, New Democratic Movement, Poltical Science Student Association, Asian, Hispanic, and African-American Faculty/Staff Associations.

**Athletics.** NCAA. **Intercollegiate:** Baseball M, basketball, cross-country, golf, gymnastics W, soccer, softball W, tennis W, track and field, volleyball W, wrestling M. **Intramural:** Badminton, basketball, bowling, football (non-tackle), gymnastics, handball M, racquetball, rugby M, skiing, soccer, softball, swimming, table tennis, tennis, volleyball, wrestling M. **Team name:** Titans.

**Student services.** Adult student services, career counseling, student employment services, financial aid counseling, health services, legal services, on-campus daycare, personal counseling, placement for graduates, veterans' counselor, women's services. **Physically disabled:** Services for visually, speech, hearing impaired.

**Contact.** E-mail: admissions@fullerton.edu
Phone: (657) 278-2370 Fax: (657) 278-2356
Jessica Wagoner, Director of Admissions, California State University: Fullerton, 800 North State College Boulevard, Langsdorf Hall-114, Fullerton, CA 92831-6900

## California State University: Long Beach

| Long Beach, California | CB member |
| --- | --- |
| www.csulb.edu | CB code: 4389 |

- Public 4-year university
- Commuter campus in large city
- 29,226 degree-seeking undergraduates: 19% part-time, 59% women, 5% African American, 24% Asian American, 29% Hispanic American, 1% Native American, 4% international
- 4,786 degree-seeking graduate students
- 32% of applicants admitted
- SAT or ACT (ACT writing optional) required
- 54% graduate within 6 years

**General.** Founded in 1949. Regionally accredited. **Degrees:** 6,685 bachelor's awarded; master's offered. **ROTC:** Army. **Location:** 25 miles from Los Angeles. **Calendar:** Semester, extensive summer session. **Full-time faculty:** 1,021 total; 85% have terminal degrees, 29% minority, 46% women. **Part-time faculty:** 963 total; 31% have terminal degrees, 26% minority, 55% women. **Class size:** 23% < 20, 54% 20-39, 12% 40-49, 6% 50-99, 5%

>100. **Special facilities:** Japanese garden, performing arts center, media center.

**Freshman class profile.** 45,771 applied, 14,543 admitted, 3,551 enrolled.

| Mid 50% test scores | | | |
| --- | --- | --- | --- |
| SAT critical reading: | 440-560 | GPA 2.0-2.99: | 13% |
| SAT math: | 460-590 | Rank in top quarter: | 82% |
| ACT composite: | 18-24 | End year in good standing: | 82% |
| GPA 3.75 or higher: | 23% | Return as sophomores: | 86% |
| GPA 3.50-3.74: | 23% | Out-of-state: | 1% |
| GPA 3.0-3.49: | 41% | Live on campus: | 30% |
| | | International: | 3% |

**Basis for selection.** Admission based on secondary school record and standardized test scores. Audition required of dance, music majors. Portfolio required of art, design majors.

**High school preparation.** College-preparatory program required. 15 units required. Required units include English 4, mathematics 3, social studies 1, history 1, science 2 (laboratory 2), foreign language 2 and academic electives 1. 1 unit fine arts required.

**2009-2010 Annual costs.** Tuition/fees: $4,370; $15,530 out-of-state. Room/board: $10,832.

**2009-2010 Financial aid. Non-need-based:** Scholarships awarded for academics, art, athletics, music/drama.

**Application procedures. Admission:** Closing date 11/30 (postmark date). $55 fee, may be waived for applicants with need. Admission notification on a rolling basis beginning on or about 12/1. **Financial aid:** Priority date 3/2; no closing date. FAFSA required. Applicants notified on a rolling basis starting 3/30; must reply within 3 week(s) of notification.

**Academics. Special study options:** Accelerated study, cross-registration, distance learning, double major, dual enrollment of high school students, ESL, honors, independent study, internships, student-designed major, study abroad, teacher certification program, Washington semester. Concurrent enrollment at other CSU campuses. **Credit/placement by examination:** AP, CLEP, IB, SAT, ACT, institutional tests. **Support services:** Learning center, pre-admission summer program, reduced course load, remedial instruction, study skills assistance, tutoring, writing center.

**Majors. Architecture:** Interior. **Area/ethnic studies:** African-American, Asian, Chicano/Hispanic-American/Latino, women's. **Biology:** General, bacteriology, biochemistry, botany, cell/histology, molecular. **Business:** General, accounting, fashion, finance, human resources, international, management science, managerial economics, operations, real estate. **Communications:** Broadcast journalism, journalism, public relations. **Computer sciences:** General, computer science, information systems. **Education:** Art, bilingual, elementary, English, family/consumer sciences, foreign languages, physical, science, social science. **Engineering:** General, aerospace, biomedical, chemical, civil, computer, electrical, materials, mechanical. **Engineering technology:** Civil, construction, electrical, manufacturing. **Family/consumer sciences:** General, clothing/textiles, food/nutrition. **Foreign languages:** Classics, comparative lit, French, German, Japanese, Spanish. **Health:** Medical illustrating, medical radiologic technology/radiation therapy, nursing (RN), public health ed. **History:** General. **Liberal arts:** Arts/sciences. **Math:** General, applied, statistics. **Parks/recreation:** Facilities management. **Philosophy/religion:** Philosophy, religion. **Physical sciences:** Chemistry, geology, physics. **Protective services:** Criminal justice. **Psychology:** General. **Public administration:** Social work. **Social sciences:** Anthropology, economics, geography, sociology. **Visual/performing arts:** Art, art history/conservation, ceramics, cinematography, commercial/advertising art, conducting, dance, design, dramatic, drawing, fiber arts, industrial design, interior design, jazz, metal/jewelry, music history, music performance, painting, photography, piano/organ, printmaking, sculpture, studio arts, theater design, voice/opera.

**Most popular majors.** Business/marketing 18%, English 9%, health sciences 7%, psychology 6%, social sciences 8%, visual/performing arts 8%.

**Computing on campus.** 1,200 workstations in dormitories, library, computer center. Dormitories linked to campus network. Commuter students can connect to campus network. Online course registration available.

**Student life. Freshman orientation:** Available, $45 fee. One-day pre-semester session. **Housing:** Coed dorms available. **Activities:** Bands, choral groups, dance, drama, film society, literary magazine, music ensembles, musical theater, opera, radio station, student government, student newspaper, symphony orchestra, TV station, more than 150 political, ethnic, and social service organizations.

**Athletics.** NCAA. **Intercollegiate:** Baseball M, basketball, cross-country, golf, soccer W, softball, tennis W, track and field, volleyball, water polo. **Intramural:** Basketball, handball, racquetball, rugby M, soccer, softball, tennis, volleyball. **Team name:** Forty-Niners.

**Student services.** Adult student services, alcohol/substance abuse counseling, chaplain/spiritual director, career counseling, services for economically disadvantaged, student employment services, financial aid counseling, health services, minority student services, on-campus daycare, personal counseling, placement for graduates, veterans' counselor, women's services. **Physically disabled:** Services for visually, speech, hearing impaired.

**Contact.** E-mail: eslb@csulb.edu
Phone: (562) 985-5471 Fax: (562) 985-4973
Thomas Enders, Assistant Vice President for Enrollment Services,
California State University: Long Beach, 1250 Bellflower Boulevard, Long Beach, CA 90840-0106

## California State University: Los Angeles

| Los Angeles, California | CB member |
|---|---|
| www.calstatela.edu | CB code: 4399 |

- Public 4-year university
- Commuter campus in very large city
- 15,734 degree-seeking undergraduates: 25% part-time, 60% women, 7% African American, 18% Asian American, 49% Hispanic American, 6% international
- 4,885 degree-seeking graduate students
- 68% of applicants admitted
- 34% graduate within 6 years

**General.** Founded in 1947. Regionally accredited. **Degrees:** 2,890 bachelor's awarded; master's offered. **ROTC:** Army, Air Force. **Location:** 5 miles from downtown. **Calendar:** Quarter, extensive summer session. **Full-time faculty:** 580 total; 41% minority, 47% women. **Part-time faculty:** 458 total; 37% minority, 49% women. **Class size:** 32% < 20, 53% 20-39, 9% 40-49, 5% 50-99, 1% >100. **Special facilities:** Baroque pipe organ, 4 megavolt Van de Graaff accelerator.

**Freshman class profile.** 21,365 applied, 14,536 admitted, 2,019 enrolled.

| Mid 50% test scores | | GPA 2.0-2.99: | 38% |
|---|---|---|---|
| SAT critical reading: | 350-500 | Rank in top quarter: | 3% |
| SAT math: | 380-490 | End year in good standing: | 86% |
| SAT writing: | 380-480 | Return as sophomores: | 74% |
| ACT composite: | 15-20 | Out-of-state: | 3% |
| GPA 3.75 or higher: | 4.3% | Live on campus: | 13% |
| GPA 3.50-3.74: | 11.5% | International: | 3% |
| GPA 3.0-3.49: | 45.8% | | |

**Basis for selection.** Secondary school record and standardized test scores important. SAT/ACT not required if GPA is 3.0 or above. EPT/ELM required for placement; may be waived based on SAT score. **Homeschooled:** Syllabi and written evaluation of courses completed may be required.

**High school preparation.** 15 units required. Required units include English 4, mathematics 3, social studies 1, history 1, science 2 (laboratory 2), foreign language 2 and academic electives 1. 1 visual and performing arts required.

**2009-2010 Annual costs.** Tuition/fees: $4,640; $15,800 out-of-state. Room/board: $13,179. Books/supplies: $1,638. Personal expenses: $2,892.

**2009-2010 Financial aid.** **Need-based:** 1,539 full-time freshmen applied for aid; 1,417 were judged to have need; 1,325 of these received aid. Average need met was 77%. Average scholarship/grant was $7,872; average loan $3,350. 61% of total undergraduate aid awarded as scholarships/grants, 39% as loans/jobs. **Non-need-based:** Awarded to 141 full-time undergraduates, including 5 freshmen.

**Application procedures.** **Admission:** Closing date 6/15 (postmark date). $55 fee, may be waived for applicants with need. Admission notification on a rolling basis beginning on or about 11/1. **Financial aid:** Priority date 3/1; no closing date. FAFSA required. Applicants notified on a rolling basis starting 4/1; must reply within 3 week(s) of notification.

**Academics.** **Special study options:** Accelerated study, combined bachelor's/graduate degree, cooperative education, cross-registration, distance learning, double major, dual enrollment of high school students, ESL, exchange student, honors, independent study, internships, student-designed major, study abroad, teacher certification program. **Credit/placement by examination:** AP, CLEP, institutional tests. **Support services:** Learning center, preadmission summer program, reduced course load, remedial instruction, tutoring.

**Majors.** **Area/ethnic studies:** African-American, Chicano/Hispanic-American/Latino, Latin American. **Biology:** General, biochemistry, microbiology. **Business:** Business admin. **Communications:** General, radio/tv. **Computer sciences:** General. **Education:** Kindergarten/preschool, physical, technology/industrial arts, trade/industrial. **Engineering:** General, civil, electrical, mechanical. **Engineering technology:** Industrial. **Family/consumer sciences:** Food/nutrition. **Foreign languages:** Chinese, French, Japanese, Spanish. **Health:** Communication disorders, nursing (RN). **History:** General. **Interdisciplinary:** Natural sciences. **Liberal arts:** Arts/sciences. **Math:** General. **Philosophy/religion:** Philosophy. **Physical sciences:** Chemistry, geology, physics. **Protective services:** Fire services admin, law enforcement admin. **Psychology:** General. **Public administration:** Social work. **Social sciences:** Anthropology, economics, geography, political science, sociology. **Visual/performing arts:** Art, commercial/advertising art, dramatic, music performance.

**Most popular majors.** Business/marketing 25%, health sciences 7%, liberal arts 6%, psychology 6%, public administration/social services 8%, security/protective services 7%, social sciences 8%.

**Computing on campus.** 1,500 workstations in dormitories, library, computer center, student center. Commuter students can connect to campus network. Online library, helpline, repair service, student web hosting, wireless network available.

**Student life.** **Freshman orientation:** Available, $35 fee. Preregistration for classes offered. **Housing:** Coed dorms, apartments available. $100 deposit, deadline 7/2. **Activities:** Jazz band, choral groups, dance, drama, literary magazine, music ensembles, musical theater, opera, student government, student newspaper, symphony orchestra, Chicanos for Creative Medicine, Hispanic business society, society of women engineers, Movimiento Estudiantil Chicanos de Aetlar, Asian student union, black student association, Sisters of the African Star, Vietnamese student association, Latin American society, Chinese American service club.

**Athletics.** NCAA. **Intercollegiate:** Baseball M, basketball, cross-country W, soccer, tennis W, track and field, volleyball W. **Intramural:** Basketball, bowling, gymnastics, handball, judo, racquetball, skiing, soccer, softball, swimming, synchronized swimming, tennis, track and field, volleyball, water polo, wrestling M. **Team name:** Golden Eagles.

**Student services.** Career counseling, student employment services, health services, on-campus daycare, personal counseling, placement for graduates, veterans' counselor. **Physically disabled:** Services for visually, speech, hearing impaired. **Learning disabled:** Comprehensive services available.

**Contact.** E-mail: admission@calstatela.edu
Phone: (323) 343-3901 Fax: (323) 343-3888
Joan Woosley, Director of Admissions and University Registrar, California State University: Los Angeles, 5151 State University Drive SA101, Los Angeles, CA 90032

## California State University: Monterey Bay

| Seaside, California | CB member |
|---|---|
| www.csumb.edu | CB code: 1945 |

- Public 4-year liberal arts and teachers college
- Residential campus in large town
- 4,278 degree-seeking undergraduates: 8% part-time, 59% women, 4% African American, 6% Asian American, 26% Hispanic American, 1% Native American, 1% international
- 197 degree-seeking graduate students
- 81% of applicants admitted
- 41% graduate within 6 years

**General.** Founded in 1995. Regionally accredited. Dedicated to serving low-income, adult learner, first-generation, and underrepresented populations. **Degrees:** 601 bachelor's awarded; master's offered. **Location:** 108 miles from San Francisco, 68 miles from San Jose. **Calendar:** Semester, limited summer session. **Full-time faculty:** 114 total; 90% have terminal degrees, 46% minority, 48% women. **Part-time faculty:** 163 total; 18% have terminal degrees, 24% minority, 56% women. **Class size:** 18% < 20, 61% 20-39, 12% 40-49, 8% 50-99, less than 1% >100. **Special facilities:** Watershed facilities to complement earth systems science and policy major, seafloor mapping lab.

**Freshman class profile.** 9,938 applied, 8,099 admitted, 949 enrolled.

| Mid 50% test scores | | | |
|---|---|---|---|
| SAT critical reading: | 440-550 | GPA 2.0-2.99: | 39% |
| SAT math: | 440-560 | Rank in top quarter: | 34% |
| SAT writing: | 440-540 | Rank in top tenth: | 9% |
| ACT composite: | 18-24 | End year in good standing: | 82% |
| GPA 3.75 or higher: | 7% | Return as sophomores: | 71% |
| GPA 3.50-3.74: | 12% | Out-of-state: | 1% |
| GPA 3.0-3.49: | 42% | Live on campus: | 89% |
| | | International: | 1% |

**Basis for selection.** Students must be high school graduates or GED equivalent, complete the 15-unit "a-g" course pattern of college preparatory study with grades of C or better and earn qualifying eligibility index. SAT/ACT test scores are not required for those students who earn a GPA of 3.00 or above in high school; 3.61 or above for non-residents. **Homeschooled:** Applicants may be asked to provide supplemental information to document completion of CSU eligibility requirements. **Learning Disabled:** Reviewed case-by-case by Student Disability Resources Department.

**High school preparation.** College-preparatory program required. 15 units required. Required units include English 4, mathematics 3, social studies 1, history 1, science 2 (laboratory 2), foreign language 2 and visual/performing arts 1. Science lab units must include 1 biological, 1 physical. Language must be the same language both years. History must include U.S. History.

**2009-2010 Annual costs.** Tuition/fees: $4,512; $15,672 out-of-state. Room/board: $8,290. Books/supplies: $1,386. Personal expenses: $2,520.

**2009-2010 Financial aid. Need-based:** 763 full-time freshmen applied for aid; 503 were judged to have need; 470 of these received aid. Average need met was 70%. Average scholarship/grant was $9,244; average loan $3,288. 68% of total undergraduate aid awarded as scholarships/grants, 32% as loans/jobs. **Non-need-based:** Awarded to 304 full-time undergraduates, including 92 freshmen. Scholarships awarded for academics, alumni affiliation, athletics, leadership, state residency.

**Application procedures. Admission:** Priority date 11/30; deadline 11/30 (postmark date). $55 fee, may be waived for applicants with need. Admission notification on a rolling basis beginning on or about 10/2. Must reply by 5/1. **Financial aid:** Priority date 3/2; no closing date. FAFSA required. Applicants notified by 3/1.

**Academics. Special study options:** Cross-registration, distance learning, double major, exchange student, independent study, internships, semester at sea, student-designed major, study abroad, teacher certification program. Service Learning. **Credit/placement by examination:** AP, CLEP, IB, SAT, ACT, institutional tests. 30 credit hours maximum toward bachelor's degree. **Support services:** Learning center, reduced course load, remedial instruction, study skills assistance, tutoring, writing center.

**Majors. Biology:** General. **Business:** Business admin. **Communications:** Radio/tv. **Computer sciences:** Computer science, networking. **Conservation:** Environmental science. **Foreign languages:** Linguistics. **Liberal arts:** Arts/sciences, humanities. **Math:** General. **Parks/recreation:** Health/fitness. **Psychology:** General. **Public administration:** Human services. **Social sciences:** General, international relations. **Visual/performing arts:** Art.

**Most popular majors.** Business/marketing 18%, communications/journalism 6%, liberal arts 25%, parks/recreation 7%, social sciences 11%.

**Computing on campus.** 980 workstations in library, computer center. Dormitories wired for high-speed internet access and linked to campus network. Commuter students can connect to campus network. Online course registration, online library, helpline, student web hosting, wireless network available.

**Student life. Freshman orientation:** Available, $65 fee. **Housing:** Coed dorms, special housing for disabled, apartments, wellness housing available. $250 fully refundable deposit, deadline 5/1. Six-person suite-style living available. **Activities:** Bands, campus ministries, choral groups, dance, drama, music ensembles, Model UN, radio station, student government, student newspaper, Business Club, Black Students United, First Year Council, M.E.Ch.A., and Electronic Music Culture (E=MC2), CAMP Club.

**Athletics.** NAIA, NCAA. **Intercollegiate:** Baseball M, basketball, cross-country, golf, sailing, soccer, softball W, volleyball W, water polo W. **Intramural:** Basketball, sailing, soccer, volleyball. **Team name:** Otters.

**Student services.** Adult student services, alcohol/substance abuse counseling, chaplain/spiritual director, career counseling, services for economically disadvantaged, student employment services, financial aid counseling, health services, minority student services, on-campus daycare, personal counseling, placement for graduates, veterans' counselor, women's services. **Physically disabled:** Services for visually, speech, hearing impaired.

**Contact.** E-mail: admissions@csumb.edu
Phone: (831) 582-3738 Fax: (831) 582-3783
David Linnevers, Director of Admissions & Recruitment, California State University: Monterey Bay, 100 Campus Center, Building 47, Seaside, CA 93955-8001

## California State University: Northridge
Northridge, California
www.csun.edu          CB code: 4707

- Public 4-year university
- Commuter campus in very large city
- 29,275 degree-seeking undergraduates: 26% part-time, 57% women, 8% African American, 12% Asian American, 32% Hispanic American, 6% international
- 5,923 degree-seeking graduate students
- 73% of applicants admitted
- SAT or ACT required
- 43% graduate within 6 years

**General. Founded** in 1958. Regionally accredited. University center in Ventura. **Degrees:** 6,416 bachelor's awarded; master's offered. **ROTC:** Army, Air Force. **Location:** 20 miles from Los Angeles. **Calendar:** Semester, limited summer session. **Full-time faculty:** 814 total; 32% minority, 44% women. **Part-time faculty:** 993 total; 22% minority, 52% women. **Class size:** 11% < 20, 60% 20-39, 16% 40-49, 9% 50-99, 4% >100. **Special facilities:** Anthropology museum, art botanical gardens, urban archives center, observatory, map library, center for the study of cancer and developmental biology, National Center on Deafness, planetarium.

**Freshman class profile.** 20,657 applied, 14,984 admitted, 4,203 enrolled.

| Mid 50% test scores | | | |
|---|---|---|---|
| SAT critical reading: | 410-520 | GPA 2.0-2.99: | 35% |
| SAT math: | 400-540 | Return as sophomores: | 71% |
| ACT composite: | 16-22 | Out-of-state: | 2% |
| GPA 3.0-3.49: | 65% | International: | 3% |

**Basis for selection.** Index using high school GPA and test scores, and completion of subject requirements. In-state applicants should rank in top third of class; out-of-state in the top sixth. Business administration, economics, engineering, computer science, and physical therapy open to California residents only. SAT scores can be used to meet English/Math proficiency requirements. Audition required of music majors.

**High school preparation.** College-preparatory program required. 15 units required. Required units include English 4, mathematics 3, social studies 1, history 1, science 2 (laboratory 2), foreign language 2, visual/performing arts 1 and academic electives 1.

**2009-2010 Annual costs.** Tuition/fees: $4,801; $15,961 out-of-state. Room/board: $10,872. Books/supplies: $1,638. Personal expenses: $3,920.

**2008-2009 Financial aid. Need-based:** 3,472 full-time freshmen applied for aid; 2,991 were judged to have need; 2,991 of these received aid. Average scholarship/grant was $7,804; average loan $3,565. 70% of total undergraduate aid awarded as scholarships/grants, 30% as loans/jobs. **Non-need-based:** Awarded to 6,431 full-time undergraduates, including 214 freshmen. Scholarships awarded for academics, athletics, state residency.

**Application procedures. Admission:** Closing date 11/30. $55 fee, may be waived for applicants with need. Admission notification on a rolling basis beginning on or about 3/1. Must reply by May 1 or within 2 week(s) if notified thereafter. Applications must be completed by November 30 for business administration, economics and physical therapy programs. **Financial aid:** Priority date 3/2; no closing date. FAFSA required. Applicants notified on a rolling basis starting 4/1.

**Academics. Special study options:** Cross-registration, distance learning, double major, dual enrollment of high school students, ESL, exchange student, independent study, internships, student-designed major, study abroad, teacher certification program. Evening degree program, Saturday classes, extended studies, open university, Program for Adult College Education (PACE) available. **Credit/placement by examination:** AP, CLEP, SAT, ACT, institutional tests. **Support services:** Learning center, pre-admission summer program, remedial instruction, tutoring.

**Majors. Area/ethnic studies:** African-American, Chicano/Hispanic-American/Latino. **Biology:** General, bacteriology, biochemistry, cell/histology, molecular. **Business:** Banking/financial services, business admin, human resources, management information systems, management science, managerial economics, real estate. **Communications:** Broadcast journalism, journalism. **Computer sciences:** General. **Education:** Art, business, English, family/consumer sciences, foreign languages, health, mathematics, music, physical, social science, social studies, speech impaired. **Engineering:** General, chemical, civil, computer, electrical, materials, mechanical, mechanics. **Family/consumer sciences:** General, business, child care, clothing/textiles, family studies, family/community services, food/nutrition, housing. **Foreign languages:** Comparative lit, French, German, linguistics, Spanish. **Health:** Nursing (RN), speech pathology. **History:** General. **Liberal arts:** Arts/sciences. **Math:** General, applied, statistics. **Parks/recreation:** General. **Philosophy/religion:** Philosophy, religion. **Physical sciences:** Chemistry, geology, geophysics, physics, planetary. **Psychology:** General. **Social sciences:** Anthropology, economics, geography, political science, sociology, urban studies. **Visual/performing arts:** Art, art history/conservation, ceramics, commercial/advertising art, crafts, dance, dramatic, drawing, metal/jewelry, music history, music performance, music theory/composition, painting, printmaking, sculpture.

**Most popular majors.** Business/marketing 21%, communications/journalism 9%, communication technologies 9%, English 6%, liberal arts 8%, psychology 9%, social sciences 13%, visual/performing arts 6%.

**Computing on campus.** 723 workstations in library, computer center. Dormitories wired for high-speed internet access and linked to campus network. Commuter students can connect to campus network. Online course registration, online library, helpline, student web hosting, wireless network available.

**Student life. Freshman orientation:** Mandatory. **Housing:** Apartments available. Off campus housing choices available. **Activities:** Bands, choral groups, dance, drama, music ensembles, musical theater, radio station, student government, student newspaper, women's center, communities, various clubs and organizations.

**Athletics.** NCAA. **Intercollegiate:** Baseball M, basketball, cross-country, diving, golf, soccer, softball W, swimming, tennis W, track and field, volleyball, water polo W. **Intramural:** Badminton, baseball M, basketball, bowling, cross-country, diving, handball, ice hockey M, racquetball, rugby, sailing, skiing, soccer, softball, swimming, table tennis, tennis, track and field, volleyball. **Team name:** Matadors.

**Student services.** Adult student services, alcohol/substance abuse counseling, career counseling, services for economically disadvantaged, student employment services, financial aid counseling, health services, minority student services, on-campus daycare, personal counseling, placement for graduates, veterans' counselor, women's services. **Physically disabled:** Services for visually, speech, hearing impaired.

**Contact.** E-mail: admissions.records@csun.edu
Phone: (818) 677-3700 Fax: (818) 677-3766
Eric Forbes, Director of Admissions and Records, California State
University: Northridge, 18111 Nordhoff Street, Northridge, CA 91328-8207

---

## California State University: Sacramento

**Sacramento, California**      **CB member**
**www.csus.edu**      **CB code: 4671**

❥ Public 4-year university

❥ Commuter campus in very large city

❥ 23,190 degree-seeking undergraduates: 18% part-time, 57% women, 7% African American, 20% Asian American, 16% Hispanic American, 1% Native American, 1% international

❥ 3,534 degree-seeking graduate students

❥ 80% of applicants admitted

❥ SAT or ACT (ACT writing optional) required

❥ 44% graduate within 6 years

**General.** Founded in 1947. Regionally accredited. **Degrees:** 5,075 bachelor's awarded; master's, doctoral offered. **ROTC:** Army, Air Force. **Location:** 100 miles from San Francisco. **Calendar:** Semester, extensive summer session. **Full-time faculty:** 688 total; 85% have terminal degrees, 30% minority, 46% women. **Part-time faculty:** 818 total; 31% have terminal degrees, 17% minority, 51% women. **Class size:** 18% < 20, 50% 20-39, 14% 40-49, 14% 50-99, 3% >100. **Special facilities:** Aquatic center, anthropology museum, Hellenic collection.

**Freshman class profile.** 14,460 applied, 11,570 admitted, 2,726 enrolled.

| Mid 50% test scores | | | |
|---|---|---|---|
| SAT critical reading: | 410-530 | GPA 3.0-3.49: | 44% |
| SAT math: | 430-550 | GPA 2.0-2.99: | 32% |
| ACT composite: | 17-23 | Return as sophomores: | 79% |
| GPA 3.75 or higher: | 10% | Out-of-state: | 1% |
| GPA 3.50-3.74: | 14% | Live on campus: | 25% |

**Basis for selection.** Student must meet admissions requirements.

**High school preparation.** College-preparatory program required. 15 units required. Required units include English 4, mathematics 3, history 2, science 2 (laboratory 2), foreign language 2, visual/performing arts 1 and academic electives 1. History must be U.S. history/government.

**2009-2010 Annual costs.** Tuition/fees: $4,900; $16,060 out-of-state. Room/board: $11,332. Books/supplies: $1,656. Personal expenses: $3,414.

**2008-2009 Financial aid. Need-based:** 2,608 full-time freshmen applied for aid; 2,274 were judged to have need; 1,554 of these received aid. Average need met was 53%. Average scholarship/grant was $3,871; average loan $1,716. 66% of total undergraduate aid awarded as scholarships/grants, 34% as loans/jobs. **Non-need-based:** Awarded to 1,106 full-time undergraduates, including 233 freshmen.

**Application procedures. Admission:** Priority date 11/30; deadline 3/1 (receipt date). $55 fee, may be waived for applicants with need. Admission notification on a rolling basis. Must reply by May 1 or within 2 week(s) if notified thereafter. **Financial aid:** FAFSA required. Applicants notified on a rolling basis starting 4/1; must reply within 4 week(s) of notification.

**Academics. Special study options:** Accelerated study, cooperative education, cross-registration, distance learning, double major, dual enrollment of high school students, ESL, honors, independent study, internships, student-designed major, study abroad, teacher certification program. **Credit/placement by examination:** AP, CLEP, IB, SAT, ACT, institutional tests. SAT/ACT may be used to exempt students from English/math placement tests. **Support services:** Learning center, remedial instruction, study skills assistance, tutoring, writing center.

**Majors. Architecture:** Interior. **Area/ethnic studies:** Asian. **Biology:** General, bacteriology, molecular. **Business:** Accounting, business admin, finance, human resources, insurance, international, marketing, operations, real estate. **Communications:** General, journalism. **Computer sciences:** General; information systems. **Conservation:** General, environmental studies. **Education:** General, kindergarten/preschool, mathematics. **Engineering:** Civil, computer, electrical, mechanical. **Engineering technology:** Construction, mechanical. **Family/consumer sciences:** General. **Foreign languages:** American Sign Language, French, Spanish. **Health:** Audiology/speech pathology, clinical lab technology, nursing (RN), prenursing. **History:** General. **Interdisciplinary:** Gerontology. **Liberal arts:** Arts/sciences, humanities. **Math:** General. **Parks/recreation:** General, health/fitness. **Philosophy/religion:** Philosophy, religion. **Physical sciences:** General, chemistry, geology, physics. **Protective services:** Corrections, law enforcement admin. **Psychology:** General. **Public administration:** Social work. **Social sciences:** General, anthropology, economics, geography, political science, sociology. **Visual/performing arts:** Art, cinematography, commercial/advertising art, dramatic, music management, music performance, music theory/composition, photography, voice/opera. **Other:** Ethnic, cultural minority, and gender studies, Teacher education.

**Most popular majors.** Business/marketing 22%, communication technologies 9%, health sciences 6%, psychology 6%, security/protective services 11%, social sciences 11%.

**Computing on campus.** 700 workstations in dormitories, library, computer center, student center. Dormitories wired for high-speed internet access and linked to campus network. Commuter students can connect to campus network. Online course registration, online library, helpline, repair service, student web hosting, wireless network available.

**Student life. Freshman orientation:** Mandatory, $50 fee. Preregistration for classes offered. **Housing:** Coed dorms, special housing for disabled, apartments available. $1,000 deposit, deadline 7/1. Suite style housing available. **Activities:** Bands, dance, drama, international student organizations, music ensembles, musical theater, radio station, student government, student newspaper, more than 250 clubs, organizations and special interest groups.

**Athletics.** NCAA. **Intercollegiate:** Baseball M, basketball, cross-country, football (tackle) M, golf, gymnastics W, rowing (crew) W, soccer, softball W, tennis, track and field, volleyball W. **Intramural:** Badminton, basketball, bowling, football (non-tackle), golf, racquetball, skiing, soccer, tennis, volleyball. **Team name:** Hornets.

**Student services.** Adult student services, alcohol/substance abuse counseling, career counseling, services for economically disadvantaged, student employment services, financial aid counseling, health services, legal services, on-campus daycare, personal counseling, placement for graduates, veterans' counselor, women's services. **Physically disabled:** Services for visually, speech, hearing impaired.

**Contact.** E-mail: outreach@csus.edu
Phone: (916) 278-7766 Fax: (916) 278-5603
Emiliano Diaz, Director of Outreach, Admissions & Records, California State University: Sacramento, 6000 J Street, Sacramento, CA 95819-6048

## California State University: San Bernardino

| San Bernardino, California | CB member |
|---|---|
| www.csusb.edu | CB code: 4099 |

- Public 4-year university and liberal arts college
- Commuter campus in small city
- 14,416 degree-seeking undergraduates: 15% part-time, 64% women, 11% African American, 8% Asian American, 43% Hispanic American, 1% Native American, 3% international
- 3,426 degree-seeking graduate students
- 70% of applicants admitted
- SAT or ACT (ACT writing optional) required
- 44% graduate within 6 years

**General.** Founded in 1962. Regionally accredited. Palm Desert satellite campus offers day and evening courses in degree and credential programs. **Degrees:** 2,702 bachelor's awarded; master's, professional offered. **ROTC:** Army, Air Force. **Location:** 60 miles from Los Angeles. **Calendar:** Quarter, limited summer session. **Full-time faculty:** 471 total; 29% minority, 46% women. **Part-time faculty:** 424 total; 27% minority, 52% women. **Class size:** 15% < 20, 54% 20-39, 10% 40-49, 15% 50-99, 6% >100. **Special facilities:** Animal house, greenhouse, desert studies center, college-operated museum.

**Freshman class profile.** 9,963 applied, 6,989 admitted, 2,017 enrolled.

| Mid 50% test scores | | | |
|---|---|---|---|
| SAT critical reading: | 400-500 | GPA 3.0-3.49: | 44% |
| SAT math: | 400-500 | GPA 2.0-2.99: | 37% |
| SAT writing: | 370-490 | Out-of-state: | 1% |
| ACT composite: | 16-21 | Live on campus: | 21% |
| GPA 3.75 or higher: | 9% | International: | 3% |
| GPA 3.50-3.74: | 10% | Fraternities: | 10% |
| | | Sororities: | 9% |

**Basis for selection.** High school GPA and test scores most important. SAT/ACT not required if high school GPA is 3.0 or higher. Entering undergraduates, except those who qualify for exemption, must take CSU entry-level mathematics (ELM) examination and CSU English placement test (EPT) after admission and before enrolling in classes.

**High school preparation.** 15 units required. Required units include English 4, mathematics 3, social studies 1, history 1, science 2 (laboratory 2), foreign language 2 and academic electives 1. One visual and performing arts unit also required. Students with disabilities may substitute alternate courses for specific subject requirements.

**2009-2010 Annual costs.** Tuition/fees: $4,839; $15,999 out-of-state. Substantial tuition reduction depending on SAT scores. Room/board: $9,432. Books/supplies: $1,638. Personal expenses: $2,400.

**2009-2010 Financial aid.** **Need-based:** 1,610 full-time freshmen applied for aid; 1,407 were judged to have need; 1,679 of these received aid. Average need met was 69%. Average scholarship/grant was $8,602; average loan $2,879. 62% of total undergraduate aid awarded as scholarships/grants, 38% as loans/jobs. **Non-need-based:** Awarded to 760 full-time undergraduates, including 153 freshmen.

**Application procedures.** **Admission:** No deadline. $55 fee, may be waived for applicants with need. Admission notification on a rolling basis. Students may apply as late as 3 weeks into quarter. **Financial aid:** Priority date 3/2; no closing date. FAFSA required. Applicants notified on a rolling basis starting 4/1.

**Academics.** **Special study options:** Accelerated study, cooperative education, cross-registration, distance learning, double major, dual enrollment of high school students, exchange student, honors, independent study, internships, study abroad, teacher certification program. School of Social and Behavioral Sciences offers master's in National Security Studies. **Credit/placement by examination:** AP, CLEP, IB, SAT, ACT, institutional tests. 40 credit hours maximum toward bachelor's degree. **Support services:** Learning center, pre-admission summer program, remedial instruction, tutoring, writing center.

**Majors.** **Area/ethnic studies:** African-American, American, Chicano/Hispanic-American/Latino. **Biology:** General, biochemistry. **Business:** Accounting, business admin, finance, human resources, international, management information systems, managerial economics, marketing, operations, organizational behavior, real estate. **Communications:** General, radio/tv. **Computer sciences:** Computer science, systems analysis. **Conservation:** Environmental studies. **Education:** Physical, trade/industrial. **Family/consumer sciences:** Child development, family studies, food/nutrition. **Foreign languages:** French, Spanish. **Health:** Environmental health, kinesiotherapy, nursing (RN), premedicine. **History:** General. **Interdisciplinary:** Museum. **Liberal arts:** Arts/sciences, humanities. **Math:** General. **Parks/recreation:** Exercise sciences. **Philosophy/religion:** Philosophy. **Physical sciences:** Chemistry, geology, physics. **Protective services:** Law enforcement admin. **Psychology:** General. **Public administration:** General, social work. **Social sciences:** General, anthropology, economics, geography, political science, sociology. **Visual/performing arts:** Art, art history/conservation, commercial/advertising art, dramatic, music history, music performance, musicology, studio arts, theater design, theater history.

**Most popular majors.** Biology 7%, business/marketing 23%, health sciences 7%, history 6%, liberal arts 11%, psychology 10%, security/protective services 6%, social sciences 12%.

**Computing on campus.** 600 workstations in dormitories, library, computer center, student center. Dormitories wired for high-speed internet access and linked to campus network. Commuter students can connect to campus network. Online course registration, online library, wireless network available.

**Student life. Freshman orientation:** Available. Preregistration for classes offered. **Housing:** Coed dorms, single-sex dorms, apartments, wellness housing available. $50 deposit. **Activities:** Jazz band, choral groups, dance, drama, music ensembles, musical theater, radio station, student government, student newspaper, symphony orchestra, TV station, more than 80 clubs and organizations.

**Athletics.** NCAA. **Intercollegiate:** Baseball M, basketball, cross-country W, golf M, soccer, softball W, swimming, tennis W, volleyball W, water polo. **Intramural:** Basketball, field hockey W, soccer, softball M, volleyball. **Team name:** Coyotes.

**Student services.** Adult student services, career counseling, student employment services, financial aid counseling, health services, legal services, minority student services, on-campus daycare, personal counseling, placement for graduates, veterans' counselor, women's services. **Physically disabled:** Services for visually, speech, hearing impaired.

**Contact.** E-mail: moreinfo@mail.csusb.edu
Phone: (909) 537-5188 Fax: (909) 537-7034
Olivia Rosas, Director of Admissions and Student Recruitment, California State University: San Bernardino, 5500 University Parkway, San Bernardino, CA 92407-2397

## California State University: San Marcos

| San Marcos, California | CB member |
|---|---|
| www.csusm.edu | CB code: 5677 |

- Public 4-year university
- Commuter campus in large town
- 8,686 degree-seeking undergraduates: 30% part-time, 61% women
- 542 degree-seeking graduate students
- 71% of applicants admitted
- SAT or ACT (ACT writing optional) required
- 46% graduate within 6 years

**General.** Founded in 1989. Regionally accredited. **Degrees:** 1,672 bachelor's awarded; master's offered. **ROTC:** Army, Naval, Air Force. **Location:** 30 miles from San Diego. **Calendar:** Semester, limited summer session. **Full-time faculty:** 314 total; 29% minority, 54% women. **Part-time faculty:** 143 total; 16% minority, 70% women. **Class size:** 15% < 20, 52% 20-39, 18% 40-49, 11% 50-99, 3% >100.

**Freshman class profile.** 9,734 applied, 6,953 admitted, 1,567 enrolled.

| Mid 50% test scores | | | |
|---|---|---|---|
| SAT critical reading: | 430-530 | GPA 3.0-3.49: | 50% |
| SAT math: | 430-540 | GPA 2.0-2.99: | 32% |
| GPA 3.75 or higher: | 7% | Return as sophomores: | 74% |
| GPA 3.50-3.74: | 11% | Out-of-state: | 1% |
| | | Live on campus: | 32% |

**Basis for selection.** Student eligibility index calculated on GPA and test score combination. **Learning Disabled:** C or better grades in all college preparatory classes -- Minimum GPA-2.0.

**High school preparation.** 15 units required; 16 recommended. Required and recommended units include English 4, mathematics 3-4, social studies 2, science 2 (laboratory 2), foreign language 2 and academic electives 1.

**2009-2010 Annual costs.** Tuition/fees: $4,650; $15,810 out-of-state. Room/board: $10,035. Books/supplies: $1,639. Personal expenses: $2,820.

**2008-2009 Financial aid. Non-need-based:** Scholarships awarded for academics, athletics, leadership, state residency.

**Application procedures. Admission:** $55 fee, may be waived for applicants with need. Admission notification on a rolling basis beginning on or about 12/1. Must reply by May 1 or within 3 week(s) if notified thereafter.

**Academics. Special study options:** Accelerated study, cross-registration, distance learning, double major, dual enrollment of high school students, ESL, independent study, internships, student-designed major, study abroad, teacher certification program, weekend college. Evening degree program, Program for Adult College Education (PACE), saturday classes, Air Force ROTC, extended studies, open university, special sessions, including winter. **Credit/placement by examination:** AP, CLEP, IB, institutional tests. 30 credit hours maximum toward bachelor's degree. **Support services:** Learning center, pre-admission summer program, study skills assistance, tutoring, writing center.

**Majors. Area/ethnic studies:** Women's. **Biology:** General, biochemistry, biotechnology. **Business:** Business admin. **Communications:** General. **Computer sciences:** General, computer science. **Family/consumer sciences:** Family studies. **Foreign languages:** Spanish. **History:** General. **Liberal arts:** Arts/sciences. **Math:** General. **Physical sciences:** Applied physics, chemistry, physics. **Psychology:** General. **Social sciences:** General, economics, political science, sociology. **Visual/performing arts:** General.

**Computing on campus.** 1,400 workstations in library, computer center. Dormitories wired for high-speed internet access and linked to campus network. Commuter students can connect to campus network. Online course registration, helpline, wireless network available.

**Student life. Freshman orientation:** Mandatory, $70 fee. One-day program. **Housing:** Special housing for disabled, apartments available. $50 nonrefundable deposit. **Activities:** Choral groups, drama, music ensembles, student newspaper, American Indian Science Engineering Society, Circle K, InterVarsity Christian Fellowship, Latter-day Saints student association, accounting society, Black Men on Campus, College Democrats, pre-health society, student housing association.

**Athletics.** NAIA. **Intercollegiate:** Baseball M, cross-country, golf, soccer, softball W, track and field. **Team name:** Cougars.

**Student services.** Adult student services, alcohol/substance abuse counseling, career counseling, services for economically disadvantaged, student employment services, financial aid counseling, health services, on-campus daycare, personal counseling, placement for graduates, veterans' counselor. **Physically disabled:** Services for visually, speech, hearing impaired.

**Contact.** E-mail: apply@csusm.edu
Phone: (760) 750-4848
Nathan Evans, Director of Admissions and Recruitment, California State University: San Marcos, 333 South Twin Oaks Valley Road, San Marcos, CA 92096-0001

## California State University: Stanislaus

Turlock, California     CB member
www.csustan.edu     CB code: 4713

- Public 4-year business and liberal arts college
- Commuter campus in small city
- 7,067 degree-seeking undergraduates: 31% part-time, 65% women, 3% African American, 12% Asian American, 32% Hispanic American, 1% Native American, 2% international
- 1,441 degree-seeking graduate students
- 66% of applicants admitted
- 50% graduate within 6 years; 79% enter graduate study

**General.** Founded in 1957. Regionally accredited. The University is composed of the College of the Arts, College of Business Administration, College of Education, College of Human and Health Sciences, College of Humanities and Social Sciences, and the College of Natural Sciences. Additional course offerings developed specifically for learners seeking professional or personal development are available through University Extended Education. **Degrees:** 1,429 bachelor's awarded; master's, doctoral offered. **Location:** 15 miles from Modesto. **Calendar:** 4-1-4, extensive summer session. **Full-time faculty:** 279 total; 88% have terminal degrees, 24% minority,

47% women. **Part-time faculty:** 111 total; 24% have terminal degrees, 14% minority, 47% women. **Special facilities:** Observatory, interactive television classrooms, laser laboratory, marine sciences station, greenhouse, mainstage theater, bio-ag eco building.

**Freshman class profile.** 4,751 applied, 3,136 admitted, 966 enrolled.

| Mid 50% test scores | | | |
|---|---|---|---|
| SAT critical reading: | 410-520 | GPA 3.50-3.74: | 16% |
| SAT math: | 420-540 | GPA 3.0-3.49: | 42% |
| SAT writing: | 410-520 | GPA 2.0-2.99: | 28% |
| ACT composite: | 17-22 | End year in good standing: | 76% |
| GPA 3.75 or higher: | 14% | Live on campus: | 31% |
| | | International: | 1% |

**Basis for selection.** High school GPA, courses taken, and test scores. Special consideration for veterans, low-income, and minority applicants. For non-native English speakers, ELPT can be substituted for TOEFL for placement. Exemptions result from scoring well on other specified tests or completion of appropriate courses. Test scores required if high school GPA is less than 3.0. Interview recommended for theatre arts and music majors. Audition recommended for music majors. Portfolio recommended for art majors. **Homeschooled:** Transcript of courses and grades, interview required. Applicant must submit SAT or ACT scores. **Learning Disabled:** Students with diagnosed learning disability or neurological disorder that significantly impairs academic performance in specified area may be eligible for waiver of General Education Breadth (GEB) requirement. Additional coursework required in lieu of GEB. Contact Disabled Student Services or submit documentation of disability.

**High school preparation.** College-preparatory program required. 15 units required. Required units include English 4, mathematics 3, social studies 1, history 1, science 2 (laboratory 2), foreign language 2, visual/performing arts 1 and academic electives 1. History units include history/social studies.

**2009-2010 Annual costs.** Tuition/fees: $4,840; $16,000 out-of-state. Room/board: $8,820. Books/supplies: $1,638. Personal expenses: $2,295.

**2009-2010 Financial aid. Non-need-based:** Scholarships awarded for academics, alumni affiliation, art, athletics, leadership, minority status, music/drama, state residency.

**Application procedures. Admission:** Priority date 10/1; no deadline. $55 fee, may be waived for applicants with need. Admission notification on a rolling basis beginning on or about 1/1. Must reply by May 1 or within 4 week(s) if notified thereafter. **Financial aid:** Priority date 3/2; no closing date. FAFSA required. Applicants notified on a rolling basis starting 3/15; must reply within 3 week(s) of notification.

**Academics.** First Year Programs, lecture series and cultural offerings, study abroad opportunities, University Honors Program, intensive learning experiences, ESL, community service and service learning opportunities, a variety of internships, and a Cooperative Learning Program. **Special study options:** Accelerated study, cooperative education, distance learning, double major, dual enrollment of high school students, ESL, exchange student, honors, independent study, internships, liberal arts/career combination, student-designed major, study abroad, teacher certification program. Executive MBA. **Credit/placement by examination:** AP, CLEP, IB, SAT, ACT, institutional tests. 24 credit hours maximum toward bachelor's degree. Credit by examination does not count toward residency requirement. **Support services:** Learning center, pre-admission summer program, reduced course load, remedial instruction, study skills assistance, tutoring, writing center.

**Majors. Agriculture:** General. **Biology:** General. **Business:** Business admin. **Communications:** General. **Computer sciences:** Computer science, information technology. **Education:** Early childhood. **Foreign languages:** Spanish. **Health:** Nursing (RN). **History:** General. **Liberal arts:** Arts/sciences. **Math:** General. **Parks/recreation:** Health/fitness. **Philosophy/religion:** Philosophy. **Physical sciences:** General, chemistry, geology, physics. **Protective services:** Criminal justice. **Psychology:** General, cognitive. **Social sciences:** General, anthropology, economics, geography, political science, sociology. **Visual/performing arts:** Art, dramatic, music performance, studio arts. **Other:** Gender studies.

**Most popular majors.** Business/marketing 23%, liberal arts 13%, psychology 10%, security/protective services 8%, social sciences 12%.

**Computing on campus.** 201 workstations in dormitories, library, computer center, student center. Dormitories wired for high-speed internet access and linked to campus network. Commuter students can connect to campus network. Online course registration, online library, helpline, wireless network available.

**Student life. Freshman orientation:** Available. Preregistration for classes offered. Held year-round. **Housing:** Coed dorms, special housing for disabled, apartments available. $200 partly refundable deposit, deadline 4/16. Summer housing available. **Activities:** Bands, choral groups, dance, drama, international student organizations, music ensembles, Model UN, musical theater, opera, radio station, student government, student newspaper, symphony orchestra, M.E.Ch.A., Fusion, Chi Alpha, Hunger Network, L.U-.L.A.C., Hmong Students Association, EcoWarriors, International Student Association, College Republicans.

**Athletics.** NCAA. **Intercollegiate:** Baseball M, basketball, cross-country, golf M, soccer, softball W, tennis W, track and field, volleyball W. **Intramural:** Basketball, football (non-tackle) M, soccer M, softball W, volleyball W. **Team name:** Warriors.

**Student services.** Adult student services, alcohol/substance abuse counseling, career counseling, services for economically disadvantaged, student employment services, financial aid counseling, health services, minority student services, on-campus daycare, personal counseling, placement for graduates, veterans' counselor, women's services. **Physically disabled:** Services for visually, speech, hearing impaired. **Learning disabled:** Comprehensive services available.

**Contact.** E-mail: outreach_help_desk@csustan.edu
Phone: (209) 667-3070 Toll-free number: (800) 300-7420
Fax: (209) 667-3788
Lisa Bernardo, Dean of Admissions, California State University: Stanislaus, One University Cirlce, Turlock, CA 95382-0256

## California University of Management and Sciences
### Anaheim, California
### www.calums.edu

- Private 4-year university
- Very large city
- 82 degree-seeking undergraduates: 49% women, 100% Asian American
- 45 degree-seeking graduate students
- Application essay, interview required

**General.** Regionally accredited; also accredited by ACICS. **Degrees:** 10 associate awarded; master's offered. **Location:** Downtown. **Calendar:** Quarter. **Full-time faculty:** 7 total; 86% have terminal degrees, 14% women. **Part-time faculty:** 18 total; 72% have terminal degrees, 11% women. **Special facilities:** Golf swing analysis room.

**Freshman class profile.**

| End year in good standing: | 60% | Return as sophomores: | 62% |
|---|---|---|---|

**Basis for selection.** GED not accepted. School record, GPA, interview most important followed by class rank, test scores, essay and recommendations. Completion of high school education is required among applicants for Associate and Bachelor degree programs. TOEFL test scores, EPAT test scores, and Wonderlic Test scores are used for admission. **Homeschooled:** Transcript of courses and grades, interview required.

**2009-2010 Annual costs.** Tuition/fees: $5,565.

**Application procedures. Admission:** No deadline. $100 fee.

**Academics. Special study options:** ESL, independent study. **Credit/placement by examination:** AP, CLEP, institutional tests. **Support services:** Remedial instruction, tutoring.

**Majors. Business:** Business admin. **Computer sciences:** General.

**Computing on campus.** 20 workstations in library, computer center. Online library, wireless network available.

**Student life. Freshman orientation:** Mandatory. Preregistration for classes offered.

**Contact.** E-mail: helenk@calums.edu
Phone: (714) 533-3946 Fax: (714) 533-7778
Lisa Lee, Director of Admissions, California University of Management and Sciences, 721 North Euclid Streeet, Anaheim, CA 92801

## Chapman University
### Orange, California          CB member
### www.chapman.edu            CB code: 4047

- Private 4-year university and liberal arts college affiliated with Christian Church (Disciples of Christ)
- Residential campus in very large city

- 4,437 degree-seeking undergraduates: 4% part-time, 58% women, 2% African American, 9% Asian American, 10% Hispanic American, 1% Native American, 3% international
- 1,912 degree-seeking graduate students
- 56% of applicants admitted
- SAT or ACT with writing, application essay required
- 73% graduate within 6 years

**General.** Founded in 1861. Regionally accredited. **Degrees:** 992 bachelor's awarded; master's, doctoral, professional offered. **ROTC:** Army, Air Force. **Location:** 35 miles from Los Angeles, 60 miles from San Diego. **Calendar:** 4-1-4, limited summer session. **Full-time faculty:** 356 total; 91% have terminal degrees, 14% minority, 37% women. **Part-time faculty:** 297 total; 39% women. **Class size:** 41% < 20, 55% 20-39, 3% 40-49, 1% 50-99, less than 1% >100. **Special facilities:** Albert Schweitzer collection of photographs, artifacts, and memorabilia, holocaust memorial library.

**Freshman class profile.** 6,159 applied, 3,468 admitted, 1,032 enrolled.

| Mid 50% test scores | | Rank in top quarter: | 90% |
|---|---|---|---|
| SAT critical reading: | 550-660 | Rank in top tenth: | 48% |
| SAT math: | 570-680 | End year in good standing: | 95% |
| SAT writing: | 560-670 | Return as sophomores: | 87% |
| ACT composite: | 25-29 | Out-of-state: | 37% |
| GPA 3.75 or higher: | 47% | Live on campus: | 89% |
| GPA 3.50-3.74: | 20% | International: | 3% |
| GPA 3.0-3.49: | 27% | Fraternities: | 12% |
| GPA 2.0-2.99: | 6% | Sororities: | 16% |

**Basis for selection.** Academic course work plus GPA and test scores most important. Recommendations, essay, extracurricular activities also considered. SAT Subject Tests recommended. Audition required for music, dance, theater majors. Portfolio required for art, film majors. Supplemental application required for all talent-based majors. **Homeschooled:** Statement describing homeschool structure and mission, state high school equivalency certificate, letter of recommendation (nonparent) required. Test scores required.

**High school preparation.** College-preparatory program required. 11 units required; 16 recommended. Required and recommended units include English 2-4, mathematics 2-3, social studies 3-4, science 2-3 (laboratory 1) and foreign language 2-3.

**2010-2011 Annual costs.** Tuition/fees: $38,524. Room/board: $12,957. Books/supplies: $1,200. Personal expenses: $1,600.

**2008-2009 Financial aid. Need-based:** 858 full-time freshmen applied for aid; 574 were judged to have need; 574 of these received aid. Average need met was 100%. Average scholarship/grant was $23,978; average loan $4,282. 74% of total undergraduate aid awarded as scholarships/grants, 26% as loans/jobs. **Non-need-based:** Awarded to 751 full-time undergraduates, including 163 freshmen. Scholarships awarded for academics, alumni affiliation, art, music/drama, religious affiliation, ROTC.

**Application procedures. Admission:** Closing date 1/15 (postmark date). $55 fee, may be waived for applicants with need. Application must be submitted online. Admission notification on a rolling basis beginning on or about 3/15. Must reply by May 1 or within 2 week(s) if notified thereafter. **Financial aid:** Priority date 3/2; no closing date. FAFSA required. Applicants notified on a rolling basis starting 3/15; must reply within 3 week(s) of notification.

**Academics. Special study options:** Combined bachelor's/graduate degree, distance learning, double major, ESL, honors, independent study, internships, liberal arts/career combination, semester at sea, student-designed major, study abroad, teacher certification program, Washington semester. **Credit/placement by examination:** AP, CLEP, IB, SAT, ACT, institutional tests. 32 credit hours maximum toward bachelor's degree. **Support services:** Learning center, reduced course load, remedial instruction, study skills assistance, tutoring, writing center.

**Majors. Biology:** General, biochemistry. **Business:** Accounting, business admin, managerial economics. **Communications:** General, broadcast journalism, public relations. **Computer sciences:** General, computer science. **Education:** General, music. **Foreign languages:** French, Spanish. **Health:** Athletic training, health services admin, predental, premedicine, preveterinary. **History:** General. **Interdisciplinary:** Peace/conflict. **Liberal arts:** Arts/sciences. **Math:** General. **Philosophy/religion:** Philosophy, religion. **Physical sciences:** Chemistry. **Psychology:** General. **Public administration:** Social work. **Social sciences:** Political science, sociology. **Visual/performing arts:** Acting, art, art history/conservation, cinematography, conducting, dance, dramatic, film/cinema, graphic design, music performance, music theory/composition, piano/organ, play/screenwriting, studio arts, voice/opera.

**Most popular majors.** Business/marketing 27%, communications/journalism 17%, social sciences 6%, visual/performing arts 21%.

**Computing on campus.** 453 workstations in dormitories, library, computer center. Dormitories wired for high-speed internet access and linked to campus network. Commuter students can connect to campus network. Online course registration, online library, helpline, repair service, student web hosting, wireless network available.

**Student life. Freshman orientation:** Mandatory, $145 fee. Preregistration for classes offered. 5-day summer program immediately preceding start of semester. **Housing:** Guaranteed on-campus for freshmen. Coed dorms, special housing for disabled, apartments, wellness housing available. $600 nonrefundable deposit, deadline 5/1. Housing for students with dependents available. **Activities:** Bands, campus ministries, choral groups, dance, drama, film society, international student organizations, literary magazine, music ensembles, Model UN, musical theater, opera, radio station, student government, student newspaper, symphony orchestra.

**Athletics.** NCAA. **Intercollegiate:** Baseball M, basketball, cross-country, football (tackle) M, golf M, rowing (crew) W, soccer, softball W, swimming W, tennis, track and field W, volleyball W, water polo. **Intramural:** Basketball, soccer, tennis, volleyball. **Team name:** Panthers.

**Student services.** Adult student services, alcohol/substance abuse counseling, chaplain/spiritual director, career counseling, student employment services, financial aid counseling, health services, on-campus daycare, personal counseling, placement for graduates, veterans' counselor. **Physically disabled:** Services for visually, speech, hearing impaired.

**Contact.** E-mail: admit@chapman.edu
Phone: (714) 997-6711 Toll-free number: (888) 282-7759
Fax: (714) 997-6713
Michael Drummy, Assistant Vice President and Chief Admission Officer, Chapman University, One University Drive, Orange, CA 92866

## Charles Drew University of Medicine and Science
**Los Angeles, California**
www.cdrewu.edu                          CB code: 4982

♦ Private 4-year university and health science college
♦ Commuter campus in very large city
♦ 226 degree-seeking undergraduates
♦ 30 degree-seeking graduate students
♦ Application essay, interview required
♦ 82% graduate within 6 years

**General.** Regionally accredited. **Degrees:** 33 bachelor's, 23 associate awarded; master's offered. **Location:** Downtown. **Calendar:** Semester, limited summer session. **Full-time faculty:** 23 total; 61% have terminal degrees, 52% minority, 65% women. **Part-time faculty:** 18 total; 33% have terminal degrees, 78% minority, 50% women. **Class size:** 77% < 20, 9% 20-39, 5% 40-49, 9% 50-99. **Special facilities:** Health sciences library, clinical and population-based research facilities.

**Freshman class profile.** 19 applied, 13 admitted, 13 enrolled.

End year in good standing:     86%     Return as sophomores:     87%

**Basis for selection.** Open admission, but selective for some programs. High school/college transcripts, performance on institutional examination if required by program, essay if required, all considered.

**2010-2011 Annual costs.** Tuition/fees (projected): $11,402. Books/supplies: $1,638.

**2008-2009 Financial aid. Need-based:** 18% of total undergraduate aid awarded as scholarships/grants, 82% as loans/jobs.

**Application procedures. Admission:** No deadline. $35 fee. Application deadlines vary by program.

**Academics. Special study options:** Combined bachelor's/graduate degree, cross-registration, distance learning, double major, dual enrollment of high school students, independent study, internships. **Credit/placement by examination:** AP, CLEP, IB, institutional tests. **Support services:** Learning center, pre-admission summer program, reduced course load, remedial instruction, study skills assistance, tutoring, writing center.

**Majors. Biology:** Biomedical sciences. **Health:** Health services, health services admin, nuclear medical technology, physician assistant, premedicine, radiologic technology/medical imaging, sonography.

**Computing on campus.** 100 workstations in library, computer center, student center. Commuter students can connect to campus network. Online course registration, online library, helpline, wireless network available.

**Student life. Freshman orientation:** Mandatory. Preregistration for classes offered. **Housing:** Off-campus housing available via California State University Dominguez Hills. **Activities:** Student government.

**Student services.** Career counseling, financial aid counseling, personal counseling.

**Contact.** E-mail: makaylahall@cdrewu.edu
Phone: (323) 563-5886 Fax: (323) 569-0597
Makayla Hall, Director of Admissions, Charles Drew University of Medicine and Science, 1731 East 120th Street, Los Angeles, CA 90059

## Claremont McKenna College
**Claremont, California**                  CB member
www.claremontmckenna.edu                   CB code: 4054

♦ Private 4-year liberal arts college
♦ Residential campus in large town
♦ 1,210 degree-seeking undergraduates: 45% women, 3% African American, 12% Asian American, 9% Hispanic American, 6% international
♦ 20 degree-seeking graduate students
♦ 18% of applicants admitted
♦ SAT or ACT with writing, application essay required
♦ 93% graduate within 6 years

**General.** Founded in 1946. Regionally accredited. One of a cluster of 5 undergraduate and 2 graduate schools on adjoining campuses. Campuses share some facilities. Cross-enrollment available at any of the 5 colleges, which include Claremont McKenna, Harvey Mudd, Pitzer, Pomona, and Scripps. **Degrees:** 282 bachelor's awarded; master's offered. **ROTC:** Army, Air Force. **Location:** 35 miles from downtown Los Angeles. **Calendar:** Semester. **Full-time faculty:** 128 total; 98% have terminal degrees, 21% minority, 30% women. **Part-time faculty:** 21 total; 81% have terminal degrees, 10% minority, 38% women. **Class size:** 76% < 20, 22% 20-39, 2% 40-49, less than 1% 50-99. **Special facilities:** 10 research institutes, athenaeum (center of intellectual, cultural, social activities), science center, leadership laboratory.

**Freshman class profile.** 3,856 applied, 697 admitted, 281 enrolled.

| Mid 50% test scores | | |
|---|---|---|
| SAT critical reading: | 630-730 | |
| SAT math: | 660-750 | |
| Rank in top quarter: | 98% | |
| Rank in top tenth: | 85% | |

| Return as sophomores: | 94% |
|---|---|
| Out-of-state: | 63% |
| Live on campus: | 99% |
| International: | 6% |

**Basis for selection.** School achievement record and test scores most important. Extracurricular activities, curriculum, recommendations, essays, interview, and motivation considered. Emphasis on leadership in high school career. Interviews recommended. Students can interview on campus or with alumni in their area. **Homeschooled:** Interview required. SAT Subject Tests required in 3 subjects (math, English, and one of choice).

**High school preparation.** College-preparatory program recommended. Required and recommended units include English 4, mathematics 3-4, social studies 1, history 1, science 2-3 (laboratory 2) and foreign language 3. Physics and chemistry required for management-engineering and science majors,.

**2009-2010 Annual costs.** Tuition/fees: $38,510. Room/board: $12,525. Books/supplies: $1,000. Personal expenses: $1,000.

**2009-2010 Financial aid. Non-need-based:** Scholarships awarded for academics.

**Application procedures. Admission:** Closing date 1/2 (postmark date). $60 fee, may be waived for applicants with need. Admission notification 4/1. Must reply by 5/1. **Financial aid:** Closing date 2/1. FAFSA, CSS PROFILE required. Applicants notified by 4/1; must reply by 5/1.

**Academics.** Philosophy, Politics and economics (PPE) major patterned after program at Oxford University available to 12-15 new students each year. Students accepted spring of sophomore year. Environment, economics, and politics (EEP) major also offered. **Special study options:** Combined bachelor's/graduate degree, cross-registration, double major, ESL, exchange student, independent study, internships, student-designed major, study abroad, Washington semester. **Credit/placement by examination:** AP, CLEP, IB, institutional tests. 16 credit hours maximum toward bachelor's degree. **Support services:** Tutoring, writing center.

**Majors. Area/ethnic studies:** African, African-American, American, Asian, Asian-American, Chicano/Hispanic-American/Latino, European, gay/

lesbian, Latin American, Pacific, regional, South Asian, Southeast Asian, Spanish/Iberian, Western European, women's. **Biology:** General, biochemistry, molecular. **Business:** Accounting, accounting/business management, managerial economics. **Communications:** Media studies. **Computer sciences:** Computer science. **Conservation:** Environmental science, environmental studies. **Engineering:** General. **Foreign languages:** Chinese, classics, French, German, Italian, Japanese, Russian, Spanish. **Health:** Premedicine. **History:** General. **Interdisciplinary:** Math/computer science, neuroscience. **Legal studies:** General, prelaw. **Math:** General. **Philosophy/religion:** Philosophy, religion. **Physical sciences:** Chemistry, physics. **Psychology:** General. **Social sciences:** Economics, international relations, political science. **Visual/performing arts:** Art, dance, dramatic.

**Most popular majors.** Business/marketing 6%, interdisciplinary studies 7%, psychology 13%, social sciences 45%.

**Computing on campus.** 169 workstations in dormitories, library, computer center, student center. Dormitories wired for high-speed internet access and linked to campus network. Commuter students can connect to campus network. Online library, helpline, repair service, student web hosting, wireless network available.

**Student life. Freshman orientation:** Mandatory. 5-day program. Parents invited for first day. **Policies:** Full-time rabbi, priest, and Protestant minister on campus. Also services for Mormon, Islamic, Christian Science, Quaker, and B'hai faiths. **Housing:** Guaranteed on-campus for all undergraduates. Coed dorms, special housing for disabled, apartments available. $500 fully refundable deposit, deadline 7/1. **Activities:** Pep band, campus ministries, choral groups, dance, drama, international student organizations, music ensembles, Model UN, radio station, student government, student newspaper, symphony orchestra, Debate/Forensics, Volunteer Service, Young Republicans, Young Democrats, Pan-African Students Association, MECHA, Asian American Student Alliance, Religious Activities Center, Intervarsity Faith Team (Christian nondenominational), Hillel.

**Athletics.** NCAA. **Intercollegiate:** Baseball M, basketball, cross-country, diving, football (tackle) M, golf, lacrosse W, soccer, softball W, swimming, tennis, track and field, volleyball W, water polo. **Intramural:** Archery, badminton, basketball, bowling, fencing, racquetball, rugby, sailing, skiing, soccer, softball, squash, swimming, tennis, track and field, volleyball, water polo, weight lifting. **Team name:** Stags (M), Athenas (W).

**Student services.** Alcohol/substance abuse counseling, chaplain/spiritual director, career counseling, student employment services, financial aid counseling, health services, minority student services, personal counseling, placement for graduates, women's services. **Physically disabled:** Services for visually, speech, hearing impaired. **Learning disabled:** Comprehensive services available.

**Contact.** E-mail: admission@claremontmckenna.edu
Phone: (909) 621-8088 Fax: (909) 621-8516
Richard Vos, Vice President and Dean of Admission & Financial Aid, Claremont McKenna College, 890 Columbia Avenue, Claremont, CA 91711-6425

## Cogswell Polytechnical College
**Sunnyvale, California**
**www.cogswell.edu**                    CB code: 4057

- Private 4-year visual arts, engineering and technical college
- Commuter campus in small city
- 199 degree-seeking undergraduates: 43% part-time, 16% women, 4% African American, 11% Asian American, 12% Hispanic American, 4% international
- 94% of applicants admitted
- Application essay required
- 35% graduate within 6 years

**General.** Founded in 1887. Regionally accredited. Program fusion of art and engineering. **Degrees:** 52 bachelor's awarded. **Location:** 45 miles from San Francisco, 4 miles from San Jose. **Calendar:** Semester, extensive summer session. **Full-time faculty:** 10 total; 60% have terminal degrees, 20% women. **Part-time faculty:** 31 total; 10% have terminal degrees, 19% women. **Class size:** 99% < 20, 1% 20-39. **Special facilities:** Electronic music laboratories, sound/recording studio, video studio, editing studio, computer imaging laboratories, SGI laboratory, MIDI laboratory, 2D and 3D animation laboratories.

**Freshman class profile.** 32 applied, 30 admitted, 21 enrolled.

| Mid 50% test scores | | | |
|---|---|---|---|
| SAT critical reading: | 550-650 | GPA 3.50-3.74: | 5% |
| SAT math: | 420-660 | GPA 3.0-3.49: | 55% |
| SAT writing: | 450-640 | GPA 2.0-2.99: | 35% |
| ACT composite: | 21-32 | End year in good standing: | 50% |
| GPA 3.75 or higher: | 5% | Return as sophomores: | 57% |
| | | Out-of-state: | 14% |

**Basis for selection.** Motivation, 2.7 GPA in academic subjects, test scores most important. Recommendations, art portfolio required for art programs, personal essay. SAT or ACT recommended. Portfolio required for all digital art programs. **Homeschooled:** Transcript of courses and grades, state high school equivalency certificate, letter of recommendation (nonparent) required. **Learning Disabled:** Must be documented by medical/psychological professional.

**High school preparation.** College-preparatory program recommended. 7 units required. Required units include English 3, mathematics 3, science 1 (laboratory 1), computer science 1 and visual/performing arts 1. 1 algebra, 1 geometry, 1 trigonometry required for engineering program; or 1 algebra, 1 geometry required for art programs.

**2009-2010 Annual costs.** Tuition/fees: $18,036.

**2008-2009 Financial aid. Non-need-based:** Scholarships awarded for academics.

**Application procedures. Admission:** Closing date 3/1 (postmark date). $55 fee, may be waived for applicants with need. Admission notification on a rolling basis. Must reply by 5/1. **Financial aid:** Priority date 3/2; no closing date. FAFSA required. Applicants notified on a rolling basis starting 4/30; must reply within 4 week(s) of notification.

**Academics. Special study options:** Distance learning, double major, exchange student, independent study, internships, student-designed major, study abroad. **Credit/placement by examination:** AP, CLEP, IB, institutional tests. 18 credit hours maximum toward bachelor's degree. **Support services:** Reduced course load, remedial instruction, tutoring.

**Majors. Engineering:** Software. **Protective services:** Fire safety technology, fire services admin. **Other:** Digital arts engineering, Digital audio technology.

**Most popular majors.** Security/protective services 37%, visual/performing arts 63%.

**Computing on campus.** 164 workstations in library, computer center. Commuter students can connect to campus network. Online course registration, online library, helpline, wireless network available.

**Student life. Freshman orientation:** Mandatory. Preregistration for classes offered. **Housing:** Apartments available. $300 fully refundable deposit, deadline 7/1. **Activities:** Radio station, student government.

**Athletics. Intramural:** Table tennis.

**Student services.** Alcohol/substance abuse counseling, career counseling, student employment services, financial aid counseling, personal counseling, placement for graduates.

**Contact.** E-mail: admissions@cogswell.edu
Phone: (408) 541-0100 Toll-free number: (800) 264-7955
Fax: (408) 747-0764
Andrew Hagedorn, Dean of Enrollment Management, Cogswell Polytechnical College, 1175 Bordeaux Drive, Sunnyvale, CA 94089-1299

## Coleman University
**San Diego, California**
**www.coleman.edu**                    CB code: 0955

- Private 4-year technical college
- Commuter campus in large city
- 417 degree-seeking undergraduates
- Interview required

**General.** Founded in 1963. Accredited by ACICS. **Degrees:** 74 bachelor's, 152 associate awarded; master's offered. **Calendar:** Continuous. **Full-time faculty:** 16 total. **Part-time faculty:** 47 total.

**Basis for selection.** Open admission, but selective for some programs. Institutional entrance exam important: math, spatial reasoning, and aptitude assessment tested. Test scores recommended for placement and credit. Institutionally administered aptitude test required. Skills test given during interview.

**2009-2010 Annual costs.** 13-month associate degree program in computer information science: $31,320. Bachelor degree program in computer information science: $52,200. Effective September 1, 2009. Costs vary depending on program. Personal expenses: $1,206.

**Financial aid.** All financial aid based on need.

**Application procedures. Admission:** No deadline. $100 fee. Admission notification on a rolling basis. **Financial aid:** Priority date 3/2; no closing date. FAFSA, institutional form required. Applicants notified on a rolling basis.

**Academics.** College uses inverted curriculum with major taken before general curriculum. Vast majority of students are transfers. **Special study options:** Accelerated study, cooperative education, distance learning, double major. **Credit/placement by examination:** AP, CLEP. 26 credit hours maximum toward associate degree, 36 toward bachelor's. **Support services:** Reduced course load, tutoring.

**Majors. Business:** Business admin. **Computer sciences:** General. **Engineering:** Computer. **Engineering technology:** Computer. **Visual/performing arts:** Graphic design.

**Most popular majors.** Computer/information sciences 95%.

**Computing on campus.** 365 workstations in library, computer center.

**Student life. Activities:** International student organizations, student government, student newspaper, student activities committee.

**Student services.** Career counseling, personal counseling, placement for graduates, veterans' counselor.

**Contact.** E-mail: admis@coleman.edu
Phone: (858) 499-0202 Toll-free number: (800) 430-2030
Fax: (858) 499-0233
Bobbie Strohm, Director of Admissions, Coleman University, 8888 Balboa Avenue, San Diego, CA 92123

## Concordia University
**Irvine, California**            **CB member**
**www.cui.edu**                   **CB code: 4069**

- Private 4-year university and liberal arts college affiliated with Lutheran Church - Missouri Synod
- Residential campus in small city
- 1,423 degree-seeking undergraduates: 4% part-time, 61% women, 2% African American, 4% Asian American, 13% Hispanic American, 1% Native American, 4% international
- 1,084 degree-seeking graduate students
- 62% of applicants admitted
- SAT or ACT (ACT writing optional), application essay required
- 64% graduate within 6 years

**General.** Founded in 1972. Regionally accredited. **Degrees:** 298 bachelor's awarded; master's offered. **ROTC:** Army. **Location:** 40 miles from Los Angeles, 80 miles from San Diego. **Calendar:** Semester, limited summer session. **Full-time faculty:** 65 total; 66% have terminal degrees, 8% minority, 34% women. **Part-time faculty:** 173 total; 22% have terminal degrees, 10% minority, 38% women. **Class size:** 56% < 20, 39% 20-39, 2% 40-49, 3% 50-99, less than 1% >100. **Special facilities:** Spectroscopy lab.

**Freshman class profile.** 1,915 applied, 1,192 admitted, 328 enrolled.

| Mid 50% test scores | | | |
|---|---|---|---|
| SAT critical reading: | 460-560 | End year in good standing: | 81% |
| SAT math: | 450-570 | Return as sophomores: | 74% |
| ACT composite: | 19-25 | Out-of-state: | 20% |
| GPA 3.75 or higher: | 27% | Live on campus: | 88% |
| GPA 3.50-3.74: | 24% | International: | 2% |
| GPA 3.0-3.49: | 36% | | |
| GPA 2.0-2.99: | 13% | | |

**Basis for selection.** Official secondary school transcript and standardized test scores are most important. Recommendations, involvement, and character/personal qualities are also important. **Homeschooled:** Each file is reviewed on an individual basis. Some documentation of home school structure, courses and grades, state high school equivalency, and/or personal recommendations may be requested.

**High school preparation.** College-preparatory program recommended. 14 units required. Required and recommended units include English 4, mathematics 3, social studies 2, history 2, science 3 (laboratory 2) and foreign language 4. Algebra I and II and geometry specifically required.

**2010-2011 Annual costs.** Tuition/fees: $26,000. Room/board: $8,380. Books/supplies: $1,600. Personal expenses: $2,200.

**2009-2010 Financial aid. Need-based:** 267 full-time freshmen applied for aid; 212 were judged to have need; 212 of these received aid. Average need met was 68%. Average scholarship/grant was $13,075; average loan $3,356. 76% of total undergraduate aid awarded as scholarships/grants, 24% as loans/jobs. **Non-need-based:** Awarded to 489 full-time undergraduates, including 122 freshmen. Scholarships awarded for academics, athletics, music/drama, religious affiliation.

**Application procedures. Admission:** Priority date 12/1; no deadline. $50 fee, may be waived for applicants with need, free for online applicants. Admission notification on a rolling basis beginning on or about 12/15. Must reply by May 1 or within 4 week(s) if notified thereafter. **Financial aid:** Priority date 3/2, closing date 2/1. FAFSA required. Applicants notified on a rolling basis starting 3/15; must reply within 4 week(s) of notification.

**Academics. Special study options:** Accelerated study, distance learning, double major, exchange student, honors, independent study, internships, student-designed major, study abroad, teacher certification program. **Credit/placement by examination:** AP, CLEP, IB, SAT, ACT. 32 credit hours maximum toward bachelor's degree. **Support services:** Learning center, reduced course load, study skills assistance, tutoring, writing center.

**Majors. Biology:** General. **Business:** Business admin. **Education:** Elementary. **Foreign languages:** Biblical. **History:** General. **Interdisciplinary:** Behavioral sciences, global studies. **Liberal arts:** Arts/sciences, humanities. **Math:** General. **Parks/recreation:** Exercise sciences. **Physical sciences:** Chemistry. **Psychology:** General. **Social sciences:** Political science. **Theology:** Theology. **Visual/performing arts:** Art, dramatic. **Other:** Christian education leadership, Communication.

**Most popular majors.** Business/marketing 25%, communications/journalism 7%, education 15%, liberal arts 17%, psychology 10%, visual/performing arts 6%.

**Computing on campus.** 100 workstations in dormitories, library, computer center, student center. Dormitories wired for high-speed internet access and linked to campus network. Commuter students can connect to campus network. Online course registration, online library, helpline, wireless network available.

**Student life. Freshman orientation:** Available, $75 fee. Preregistration for classes offered. **Housing:** Guaranteed on-campus for freshmen. Coed dorms, special housing for disabled, wellness housing available. $300 non-refundable deposit, deadline 6/30. **Activities:** Bands, campus ministries, choral groups, drama, international student organizations, literary magazine, music ensembles, musical theater, student government, student newspaper, Nuestra Voz, Improve Club, Republican Club, math club, sports medicine club, Fellowship of Christian Athletes, ethics club, Cross Cultural Link.

**Athletics.** NAIA. **Intercollegiate:** Baseball M, basketball, cross-country, soccer, softball W, swimming, tennis, track and field, volleyball W, water polo. **Intramural:** Basketball, bowling, football (non-tackle), soccer, softball, track and field, volleyball. **Team name:** Eagles.

**Student services.** Adult student services, alcohol/substance abuse counseling, chaplain/spiritual director, career counseling, financial aid counseling, health services, minority student services, personal counseling.

**Contact.** E-mail: admission@cui.edu
Phone: (949) 854-8002 ext. 1106 Toll-free
number: (800) 229-1200 ext. 1106 Fax: (949) 854-6894
Scott Rhodes, Executive Director, Admissions, Concordia University, 1530 Concordia West, Irvine, CA 92612-3203

## Design Institute of San Diego
**San Diego, California**
**www.disd.edu**                  **CB code: 3492**

- For-profit 4-year technical college
- Very large city
- 490 degree-seeking undergraduates
- 65% of applicants admitted
- Application essay, interview required

**General.** Accredited by ACICS. **Degrees:** 80 bachelor's awarded. **Calendar:** Semester. **Full-time faculty:** 6 total. **Part-time faculty:** 59 total.

**Freshman class profile.** 77 applied, 50 admitted, 41 enrolled.

**Basis for selection.** High school/college grades, 2 professional references considered.

**2009-2010 Annual costs.** Tuition/fees: $15,600. Books/supplies: $1,200.

**Application procedures.** **Admission:** No deadline. $25 fee. Admission notification on a rolling basis. **Financial aid:** No deadline. Applicants notified on a rolling basis.

**Academics.** **Credit/placement by examination:** CLEP.

**Majors.** **Visual/performing arts:** Interior design.

**Contact.** Phone: (858) 566-1200 Toll-free number: (800) 619-4337 Fax: (858) 566-2711
Paula Parrish, Director of Admissions, Design Institute of San Diego, 8555 Commerce Avenue, San Diego, CA 92121

## DeVry University: Fremont
### Fremont, California
### www.devry.edu
CB code: 0520

- For-profit 4-year university
- Commuter campus in small city
- 1,339 degree-seeking undergraduates: 44% part-time, 31% women, 10% African American, 22% Asian American, 22% Hispanic American, 1% Native American, 1% international
- 212 degree-seeking graduate students
- 39% graduate within 6 years

**General.** Regionally accredited. **Degrees:** 263 bachelor's, 18 associate awarded; master's offered. **Location:** 15 miles from San Jose. **Calendar:** Semester, extensive summer session. **Full-time faculty:** 35 total; 40% minority, 14% women. **Part-time faculty:** 196 total; 4% minority, 39% women.

**Freshman class profile.** 235 enrolled.

**Basis for selection.** Applicant must have high school diploma or equivalent, degree from accredited postsecondary institution, pass institutional placement examination, or submit acceptable test scores and be 17 years of age. New students may enter at beginning of any semester. SAT/ACT considered but not required for admission. If applicant chooses not to submit either, must take institution-administered admissions test.

**High school preparation.** College-preparatory program recommended.

**2009-2010 Annual costs.** Tuition/fees: $14,800. Books/supplies: $1,310. Personal expenses: $3,574.

**2008-2009 Financial aid.** All financial aid based on need.

**Application procedures.** **Admission:** No deadline. $50 fee. Admission notification on a rolling basis. **Financial aid:** No deadline. FAFSA required. Applicants notified on a rolling basis.

**Academics.** **Special study options:** Accelerated study, distance learning. **Credit/placement by examination:** CLEP, institutional tests. **Support services:** Learning center, remedial instruction, tutoring.

**Majors.** **Biology:** Bioinformatics. **Business:** Business admin. **Computer sciences:** Game design, networking, systems analysis. **Engineering technology:** Biomedical, computer, electrical. **Other:** Technical management.

**Most popular majors.** Business/marketing 60%, communication technologies 12%, engineering/engineering technologies 26%.

**Computing on campus.** 350 workstations in library, computer center. Online course registration, online library, helpline available.

**Student life.** **Freshman orientation:** Mandatory. **Housing:** Coed dorms available. Private apartments, student-plan housing, private rooms available. **Activities:** Institute of Electronic and Electrical Engineers, Hmong Organization on Technology, network communications club, Tau Alpha Pi national honor society for engineering technologies, women's organization, game development, Latino American student organization, Phi Beta Lambda national organization for business majors, chess club, self-defense club.

**Athletics.** **Intramural:** Soccer.

**Student services.** Career counseling, student employment services, financial aid counseling, placement for graduates, veterans' counselor. **Physically disabled:** Services for visually, hearing impaired.

**Contact.** Phone: (510) 574-1200 Toll-free number: (888) 393-3879
Marc Martin, Director of Admission, DeVry University: Fremont, 6600 Dumbarton Circle, Fremont, CA 94555-3615

## DeVry University: Long Beach
### Long Beach, California
### www.devry.edu
CB code: 2053

- For-profit 4-year university
- Commuter campus in large town
- 915 degree-seeking undergraduates: 56% part-time, 32% women, 15% African American, 17% Asian American, 41% Hispanic American
- 250 degree-seeking graduate students
- Interview required
- 32% graduate within 6 years

**General.** Regionally accredited. **Degrees:** 140 bachelor's, 30 associate awarded; master's offered. **Location:** 26 miles from Los Angeles. **Calendar:** Semester, extensive summer session. **Full-time faculty:** 20 total; 30% minority, 15% women. **Part-time faculty:** 81 total; 31% minority, 28% women.

**Freshman class profile.** 144 enrolled.

**Basis for selection.** Applicant must have high school diploma or equivalent, degree from an accredited postsecondary institution, or submit acceptable test scores and be at least 17 years of age on the first day of classes. New students may enter at beginning of any semester. SAT/ACT considered but not required for admission. If applicant chooses not to submit either, must take institution-administered admissions test.

**High school preparation.** College-preparatory program recommended.

**2009-2010 Annual costs.** Tuition/fees: $14,160. Books/supplies: $1,310. Personal expenses: $3,574.

**2008-2009 Financial aid.** All financial aid based on need.

**Application procedures.** **Admission:** No deadline. $50 fee. Admission notification on a rolling basis. **Financial aid:** No deadline. FAFSA required. Applicants notified on a rolling basis.

**Academics.** **Special study options:** Accelerated study, distance learning. **Credit/placement by examination:** CLEP. **Support services:** Learning center, remedial instruction, tutoring.

**Majors.** **Biology:** Bioinformatics. **Business:** Business admin, operations. **Computer sciences:** Game design, information technology, networking, systems analysis. **Engineering technology:** Computer, electrical. **Other:** Technical management.

**Most popular majors.** Business/marketing 61%, computer/information sciences 19%, engineering/engineering technologies 19%.

**Computing on campus.** 463 workstations in library, computer center. Online course registration, online library, helpline available.

**Student life.** **Freshman orientation:** Mandatory. **Housing:** Private apartments, student-plan housing, private rooms available. **Activities:** Associate Student Body Advocates, Society of Hispanic Professional Engineers, Epsilon Delta Pi, United Islands, Tau Alpha Pi, business and accounting association, National Society of Black Engineers (NSBE), Institute of Electronic and Electrical Engineers (IEEE).

**Student services.** Career counseling, student employment services, financial aid counseling, placement for graduates, veterans' counselor. **Physically disabled:** Services for visually, hearing impaired.

**Contact.** Phone: (562) 427-4162 Toll-free number: (800) 597-0444
Elaine Francisco, Director of Admissions, DeVry University: Long Beach, 3880 Kilroy Airport Way, Long Beach, CA 90806

## DeVry University: Pomona
### Pomona, California
### www.devry.edu
CB code: 4214

- For-profit 4-year university
- Commuter campus in small city
- 2,018 degree-seeking undergraduates: 56% part-time, 34% women, 12% African American, 14% Asian American, 41% Hispanic American, 1% Native American
- 303 degree-seeking graduate students
- Interview required

**General.** Founded in 1983. Regionally accredited. **Degrees:** 269 bachelor's, 35 associate awarded; master's offered. **Location:** 13 miles from Los Angeles. **Calendar:** Semester, extensive summer session. **Full-time faculty:** 25 total; 40% minority, 8% women. **Part-time faculty:** 138 total; 36% minority, 36% women.

**Freshman class profile.** 307 enrolled.

**Basis for selection.** Applicant must have high school diploma or equivalent, degree from an accredited postsecondary institution, or submit acceptable test scores and be at least 17 years of age on the first day of classes. New students may enter at beginning of any semester. SAT/ACT considered but not required for admission. If applicant chooses not to submit either, must take an institution-administered admissions test.

**High school preparation.** College-preparatory program recommended.

**2009-2010 Annual costs.** Tuition/fees: $14,160. Books/supplies: $1,310. Personal expenses: $3,574.

**2008-2009 Financial aid.** All financial aid based on need.

**Application procedures. Admission:** No deadline. $50 fee. Admission notification on a rolling basis. **Financial aid:** No deadline. FAFSA required. Applicants notified on a rolling basis.

**Academics. Special study options:** Accelerated study, distance learning. **Credit/placement by examination:** CLEP, institutional tests. **Support services:** Learning center, remedial instruction, tutoring.

**Majors. Business:** General. **Computer sciences:** General, game design, networking. **Engineering technology:** Biomedical, computer, electrical. **Other:** Technical management.

**Most popular majors.** Business/marketing 63%, computer/information sciences 22%, engineering/engineering technologies 15%.

**Computing on campus.** 517 workstations in library, computer center. Online course registration, online library, helpline available.

**Student life. Freshman orientation:** Mandatory. **Housing:** Private apartments, student-plan housing, private rooms available. **Activities:** Gaming association, Institute for Electrical and Electronic Engineers, Living in Truth, National Society of Black Engineers, Phi Beta Lambda, Society of Hispanic Professional Engineers, networking professional association, Toastmasters.

**Student services.** Career counseling, student employment services, financial aid counseling, placement for graduates, veterans' counselor. **Physically disabled:** Services for visually, hearing impaired.

**Contact.** Phone: (909) 622-8866
Jere Thrasher, Director of Admissions, DeVry University: Pomona, 901 Corporate Center Drive, Pomona, CA 91768-2642

## DeVry University: Sherman Oaks
Sherman Oaks, California
www.devry.edu                                CB code: 2800

- For-profit 4-year university
- Commuter campus in large city
- 728 degree-seeking undergraduates: 37% part-time, 34% women, 10% African American, 15% Asian American, 36% Hispanic American
- 202 degree-seeking graduate students
- Interview required
- 37% graduate within 6 years

**General.** Regionally accredited. **Degrees:** 85 bachelor's, 19 associate awarded; master's offered. **Location:** 30 miles from Los Angeles. **Calendar:** Semester, extensive summer session. **Full-time faculty:** 8 total; 25% minority, 12% women. **Part-time faculty:** 61 total; 18% minority, 25% women.

**Freshman class profile.** 129 enrolled.

| Out-of-state: | 1% | International: | 1% |
|---|---|---|---|

**Basis for selection.** Applicant must have high school diploma or equivalent, degree from an accredited postsecondary institution, or submit acceptable test scores and be at least 17 years of age on the first day of classes. New students may enter at beginning of any semester. SAT/ACT tests considered but not required for admission. If applicant chooses not to submit either, must take institution-administered admissions test.

**High school preparation.** College-preparatory program recommended.

**2009-2010 Annual costs.** Tuition/fees: $14,160. Books/supplies: $1,310. Personal expenses: $3,574.

**2008-2009 Financial aid.** All financial aid based on need.

**Application procedures. Admission:** No deadline. $50 fee. Admission notification on a rolling basis. **Financial aid:** No deadline. FAFSA required. Applicants notified on a rolling basis.

**Academics. Special study options:** Accelerated study, distance learning. **Credit/placement by examination:** CLEP, institutional tests. **Support services:** Learning center, remedial instruction, tutoring.

**Majors. Business:** Business admin. **Computer sciences:** Networking. **Engineering technology:** Computer, electrical. **Other:** Technical management.

**Most popular majors.** Business/marketing 64%, computer/information sciences 29%, engineering/engineering technologies 7%.

**Computing on campus.** 412 workstations in library, computer center. Online course registration, online library, helpline available.

**Student life. Freshman orientation:** Mandatory. **Housing:** Private apartments, student-plan housing, private rooms available. **Activities:** Student government, student newspaper, Institution of Electrical & Electronic Engineers, Society of Hispanic Professional Engineers, Students Under Mass Organization, Progressive Advancement in Life, Diverse National Alliance, bowling club, Omega Sigma Phi, Phi Theta Kappa, Epsilon Delta Pi, Japanese anime club.

**Athletics. Intramural:** Softball.

**Student services.** Career counseling, student employment services, financial aid counseling, placement for graduates, veterans' counselor. **Physically disabled:** Services for visually, hearing impaired.

**Contact.** Phone: (818) 587-6227 Toll-free number: (888) 610-0800
Dewey McGuirk, Director of Admissions, DeVry University: Sherman Oaks, 15301 Ventura Boulevard, D-100, Sherman Oaks, CA 91403

## Dominican University of California
San Rafael, California                       CB member
www.dominican.edu                            CB code: 4284

- Private 4-year university and liberal arts college
- Residential campus in small city
- 1,408 degree-seeking undergraduates: 17% part-time, 74% women, 6% African American, 24% Asian American, 17% Hispanic American, 1% Native American, 2% international
- 631 degree-seeking graduate students
- 56% of applicants admitted
- SAT or ACT with writing, application essay required
- 45% graduate within 6 years

**General.** Founded in 1890. Regionally accredited. **Degrees:** 299 bachelor's awarded; master's offered. **Location:** 12 miles from San Francisco. **Calendar:** Semester, limited summer session. **Full-time faculty:** 83 total; 76% have terminal degrees, 13% minority, 66% women. **Part-time faculty:** 272 total; 40% have terminal degrees, 15% minority, 65% women. **Class size:** 64% < 20, 33% 20-39, less than 1% 40-49, 2% 50-99.

**Freshman class profile.** 2,425 applied, 1,353 admitted, 289 enrolled.

| Mid 50% test scores | | GPA 2.0-2.99: | 17% |
|---|---|---|---|
| SAT critical reading: | 460-560 | Rank in top quarter: | 62% |
| SAT math: | 460-560 | Rank in top tenth: | 28% |
| SAT writing: | 460-560 | Return as sophomores: | 80% |
| ACT composite: | 20-25 | Out-of-state: | 16% |
| GPA 3.75 or higher: | 31% | Live on campus: | 87% |
| GPA 3.50-3.74: | 17% | International: | 2% |
| GPA 3.0-3.49: | 35% | | |

**Basis for selection.** School achievement record, test scores, rigor of secondary school record, character/qualities most important. Interview recommended for borderline applicants. Audition recommended for music majors. Portfolio recommended for art majors. **Homeschooled:** State high school equivalency certificate required.

**High school preparation.** College-preparatory program recommended. 11 units required; 15 recommended. Required and recommended units include English 4, mathematics 2-3, history 1-2, science 1-2 (laboratory 1) and foreign language 2.

**2009-2010 Annual costs.** Tuition/fees: $33,840. Room/board: $13,150. Books/supplies: $1,638. Personal expenses: $2,250.

**2008-2009 Financial aid. Need-based:** 246 full-time freshmen applied for aid; 217 were judged to have need; 217 of these received aid. Average need met was 67%. Average scholarship/grant was $20,065; average loan $3,837. 57% of total undergraduate aid awarded as scholarships/grants, 43% as loans/jobs. **Non-need-based:** Awarded to 395 full-time undergraduates, including 100 freshmen. Scholarships awarded for academics, alumni affiliation, athletics, leadership, minority status, music/drama. **Additional information:** 4-year guarantee program.

**Application procedures. Admission:** Priority date 2/1; no deadline. $40 fee, may be waived for applicants with need, free for online applicants. Admission notification on a rolling basis beginning on or about 10/15. Must reply by 5/1. **Financial aid:** Priority date 3/2; no closing date. FAFSA, institutional form required. Applicants notified on a rolling basis starting 3/15; must reply within 2 week(s) of notification.

**Academics. Special study options:** Accelerated study, combined bachelor's/graduate degree, cross-registration, distance learning, double major, dual enrollment of high school students, exchange student, honors, independent study, internships, student-designed major, study abroad, teacher certification program, weekend college. Pathways program (evening/weekend degree program for working adults), semester available at Aquinas College (MI), St. Thomas Aquinas College (NY), Barry University (FL), cross-registration with University of California, Berkeley, (4 + 1 humanities, occupational therapy, BA - MBA), liberal studies + multiple subject credential. **Credit/placement by examination:** AP, CLEP, IB, SAT, ACT, institutional tests. No more than 30 units from one of the following sources: CLEP/Regents College Exams, ACE/PONSI review courses, experiential learning portfolios. No more than 12 units from challenging courses. No more than 38 units from NLN exams. **Support services:** Learning center, reduced course load, remedial instruction, study skills assistance, tutoring, writing center.

**Majors. Area/ethnic studies:** Women's. **Biology:** General. **Business:** Business admin. **Communications:** General. **Health:** Health services, nursing (RN). **History:** General. **Liberal arts:** Arts/sciences, humanities. **Philosophy/religion:** Religion. **Psychology:** General. **Social sciences:** Political science. **Visual/performing arts:** Art, art history/conservation, dance, digital art. **Other:** Sustainable community studies.

**Most popular majors.** Biology 7%, business/marketing 22%, health sciences 29%, liberal arts 13%, psychology 12%.

**Computing on campus.** 260 workstations in library, computer center, student center. Dormitories wired for high-speed internet access and linked to campus network. Commuter students can connect to campus network. Helpline, repair service, wireless network available.

**Student life. Freshman orientation:** Available. Preregistration for classes offered. Fall program held week prior to start of classes. **Housing:** Coed dorms, wellness housing available. $500 fully refundable deposit, deadline 5/1. **Activities:** Jazz band, campus ministries, choral groups, dance, drama, international student organizations, literary magazine, music ensembles, musical theater, radio station, student government, student newspaper, STAND, Dominican Republican Women, ASDU, Black Student Union, Latinos of the Americas, Men's Bible Study, BASIC, Women's Bible Study.

**Athletics.** NAIA. **Intercollegiate:** Basketball, cheerleading M, golf, lacrosse M, soccer, softball W, tennis W, volleyball W. **Team name:** Penguins.

**Student services.** Adult student services, alcohol/substance abuse counseling, chaplain/spiritual director, career counseling, student employment services, financial aid counseling, health services, personal counseling, veterans' counselor, women's services. **Physically disabled:** Services for visually impaired.

**Contact.** E-mail: enroll@dominican.edu
Phone: (415) 485-3204 Toll-free number: (888) 323-6763
Fax: (415) 485-3214
Rebecca Finn Kenney, Director of Undergraduate Admissions, Dominican University of California, 50 Acacia Avenue, San Rafael, CA 94901-2298

## Everest College: Ontario Metro
Rancho Cucamonga, California
www.everest-college.com

- For-profit 4-year business college
- Commuter campus in small city

**General.** Accredited by ACICS. **Calendar:** Quarter.

**Contact.** Phone: (909) 484-4311
Director of Admissions, 9616 Archibald Avenue, Suite 100, Rancho Cucamonga, CA 91730-8525

## Ex'pression College for Digital Arts
Emeryville, California
www.expression.edu

- For-profit 4-year visual arts and technical college
- Large town
- 1,200 full-time, degree-seeking undergraduates

**General.** Accredited by ACCSC. **Degrees:** 314 bachelor's awarded. **Calendar:** Semester. **Full-time faculty:** 50 total. **Part-time faculty:** 100 total.

**Basis for selection.** Applicants to visual arts programs (animation and visual effects, game art & design and motion graphic design) required to complete either on-site drawing test, or submit 3 sketches of their hand holding an object of their choice.

**2009-2010 Annual costs.** Tuition/fees: $18,880.

**Application procedures. Admission:** No deadline. $95 fee.

**Academics. Credit/placement by examination:** CLEP.

**Majors. Communications technology:** Animation/special effects, graphics, photo/film/video. **Visual/performing arts:** Graphic design.

**Contact.** Phone: (510) 654-2934 Toll-free number: (877) 833-8800
Klint Schahrer, Director of Admissions, Ex'pression College for Digital Arts, 6601 Shellmound Street, Emeryville, CA 94608

## Fresno Pacific University
Fresno, California — CB member
www.fresno.edu — CB code: 4616

- Private 4-year university and liberal arts college affiliated with Mennonite Brethren Church
- Residential campus in large city
- 1,798 degree-seeking undergraduates: 15% part-time, 66% women
- 466 degree-seeking graduate students
- 72% of applicants admitted
- SAT and SAT Subject Tests or ACT (ACT writing optional) required

**General.** Founded in 1944. Regionally accredited. **Degrees:** 539 bachelor's awarded; master's offered. **Location:** 150 miles from San Francisco. **Calendar:** Semester, limited summer session. **Full-time faculty:** 78 total; 63% have terminal degrees, 12% minority, 35% women. **Part-time faculty:** 215 total; 6% have terminal degrees, 9% minority, 53% women. **Class size:** 72% < 20, 22% 20-39, 5% 40-49, less than 1% 50-99, less than 1% >100. **Special facilities:** Mennonite brethren studies center, conflict studies and peacemaking center.

**Freshman class profile.** 489 applied, 350 admitted, 172 enrolled.

| Mid 50% test scores | | | |
|---|---|---|---|
| SAT critical reading: | 420-540 | GPA 3.0-3.49: | 32% |
| SAT math: | 420-560 | GPA 2.0-2.99: | 20% |
| SAT writing: | 430-540 | Rank in top quarter: | 69% |
| ACT composite: | 18-24 | Rank in top tenth: | 32% |
| GPA 3.75 or higher: | 31% | Out-of-state: | 5% |
| GPA 3.50-3.74: | 16% | Live on campus: | 66% |

**Basis for selection.** School achievement record and test scores very important, minimum 3.1 high school GPA. Recommendations, autobiography also considered. Interview recommended for academically weak applicants. Auditions for music, English (with drama emphasis) majors.

**High school preparation.** 13 units required. Required units include English 4, mathematics 3, social studies 2, science 1 (laboratory 1) and foreign language 2. One year of visual or performing arts.

**2009-2010 Annual costs.** Tuition/fees: $23,898. Room/board: $6,180. Books/supplies: $1,638. Personal expenses: $2,250.

**2008-2009 Financial aid. Need-based:** 144 full-time freshmen applied for aid; 123 were judged to have need; 123 of these received aid. Average need met was 75%. Average scholarship/grant was $11,984; average loan $5,921. 40% of total undergraduate aid awarded as scholarships/grants, 60% as loans/jobs. **Non-need-based:** Awarded to 530 full-time undergraduates,

including 118 freshmen. Scholarships awarded for academics, athletics, music/drama.

**Application procedures. Admission:** Priority date 12/1; deadline 7/31 (postmark date). $40 fee, may be waived for applicants with need. Admission notification on a rolling basis beginning on or about 12/1. **Financial aid:** Priority date 3/2; no closing date. FAFSA, institutional form required. Applicants notified on a rolling basis starting 3/2; must reply by 7/30 or within 3 week(s) of notification.

**Academics. Special study options:** Accelerated study, distance learning, double major, dual enrollment of high school students, ESL, exchange student, independent study, internships, student-designed major, study abroad, teacher certification program, Washington semester. **Credit/placement by examination:** AP, CLEP, IB. 30 credit hours maximum toward associate degree, 30 toward bachelor's. **Support services:** Learning center, reduced course load, remedial instruction, study skills assistance, tutoring, writing center.

**Majors. Biology:** General. **Business:** General, accounting, business admin, human resources, international, management information systems, marketing, nonprofit/public, organizational behavior. **Communications:** General. **Computer sciences:** Computer science. **Conservation:** Environmental science, environmental studies. **Education:** Biology, business, elementary, English, mathematics, music, physical, science, social science. **Foreign languages:** Spanish. **Health:** Athletic training, premedicine. **History:** General. **Liberal arts:** Arts/sciences. **Math:** General, applied. **Parks/recreation:** Health/fitness, sports admin. **Philosophy/religion:** Philosophy. **Physical sciences:** Chemistry. **Protective services:** Criminalistics. **Psychology:** General. **Public administration:** Social work. **Social sciences:** General, political science, sociology. **Theology:** Bible. **Visual/performing arts:** Art, dramatic, music performance, music theory/composition.

**Most popular majors.** Business/marketing 38%, education 36%.

**Computing on campus.** 90 workstations in dormitories, library, computer center, student center. Dormitories wired for high-speed internet access and linked to campus network. Commuter students can connect to campus network. Online course registration, helpline, student web hosting, wireless network available.

**Student life. Freshman orientation:** Mandatory. Preregistration for classes offered. 4-day fall orientation, 1-day spring. **Housing:** Single-sex dorms, special housing for disabled, apartments, wellness housing available. $200 nonrefundable deposit, deadline 6/1. Several college-rented apartments available nearby. Resident freshmen under age 23 required to live on campus. **Activities:** Bands, choral groups, dance, drama, international student organizations, music ensembles, student government, student newspaper, Summer Harvest, Shalom Covenant, Kids Klub, Amigos Unidos, Students In Free Enterprise, student chaplains, Daughters of Christ, Faith Project, social work club.

**Athletics.** NAIA. **Intercollegiate:** Baseball M, basketball, cross-country, soccer, swimming, tennis, track and field, volleyball W, water polo. **Intramural:** Basketball, bowling, football (non-tackle), racquetball, soccer, table tennis, volleyball. **Team name:** Sunbirds.

**Student services.** Adult student services, alcohol/substance abuse counseling, chaplain/spiritual director, career counseling, student employment services, financial aid counseling, health services, personal counseling. **Physically disabled:** Services for visually, hearing impaired.

**Contact.** E-mail: ugadmis@fresno.edu
Phone: (559) 453-2039 Toll-free number: (800) 660-6089
Fax: (559) 453-2007
Rina Campbell, Director of Undergraduate Admissions, Fresno Pacific University, 1717 South Chestnut Avenue, Fresno, CA 93702-4709

## Golden Gate University
**San Francisco, California**
**www.ggu.edu** — CB code: 4329

- Private 4-year university
- Commuter campus in very large city
- 404 degree-seeking undergraduates: 81% part-time, 58% women
- 2,961 degree-seeking graduate students
- 88% of applicants admitted

**General.** Founded in 1853. Regionally accredited. Evening and weekend degree programs available in San Francisco, Silicon Valley, Los Angeles, and Seattle (WA). Program length differs by location. **Degrees:** 128 bachelor's awarded; master's, doctoral, professional offered. **Calendar:** Trimester, extensive summer session. **Full-time faculty:** 71 total; 35% women.

**Part-time faculty:** 313 total; 27% women. **Class size:** 83% < 20, 17% 20-39.

**Freshman class profile.** 8 applied, 7 admitted, 5 enrolled.

**Basis for selection.** School achievement record most important. Work history or military service factor in determining admission of adult students. SAT recommended. Interviews recommended for undecided major applicants.

**High school preparation.** 14 units recommended. Recommended units include English 4, mathematics 3, social studies 1, history 1, science 2 (laboratory 1) and foreign language 2.

**2010-2011 Annual costs.** Tuition/fees: $17,100.

**2009-2010 Financial aid.** All financial aid based on need.

**Application procedures. Admission:** Priority date 7/1; no deadline. $60 fee. Admission notification on a rolling basis. Students may be admitted up to 1 year (3 trimesters) before they intend to enroll. **Financial aid:** Priority date 1/2; no closing date. FAFSA, institutional form required. Applicants notified on a rolling basis starting 4/1; must reply within 3 week(s) of notification.

**Academics.** Professional degree, certification, and lifelong learning programs in business, law, tax, technology and related professions. **Special study options:** Accelerated study, distance learning, ESL, independent study, internships, study abroad. **Credit/placement by examination:** AP, CLEP, IB, institutional tests. **Support services:** Reduced course load, tutoring, writing center.

**Majors. Business:** Accounting, business admin, finance, human resources, information resources management, international, marketing, operations. **Computer sciences:** Information technology.

**Most popular majors.** Business/marketing 79%, computer/information sciences 20%.

**Computing on campus.** 300 workstations in library, computer center. Commuter students can connect to campus network. Online course registration, online library, wireless network available.

**Student life. Activities:** Student government, student newspaper, Phi Alpha Delta law fraternity, Chi Pi Alpha, Indonesian students organization, Malayan students association, Chinese students club, Indian student association, Korean student association, American Marketing Association, Toastmasters.

**Student services.** Adult student services, career counseling, student employment services, personal counseling, veterans' counselor. **Physically disabled:** Services for visually, speech, hearing impaired.

**Contact.** E-mail: info@ggu.edu
Phone: (415) 442-7800 Fax: (415) 442-7807
Louis Riccardi, Director of Enrollment Services, Golden Gate University, 536 Mission Street, San Francisco, CA 94105-2968

## Harvey Mudd College
**Claremont, California** — CB member
**www.hmc.edu** — CB code: 4341

- Private 4-year engineering and liberal arts college
- Residential campus in small city
- 757 degree-seeking undergraduates: 36% women, 1% African American, 20% Asian American, 7% Hispanic American, 1% Native American, 3% international
- 34% of applicants admitted
- SAT or ACT with writing, SAT Subject Tests, application essay required
- 91% graduate within 6 years; 47% enter graduate study

**General.** Founded in 1955. Regionally accredited. One of a cluster of 5 undergraduate and 2 graduate schools on adjoining campuses. Campuses share facilities and cross-enrollment is available within the 5 undergraduate colleges, which include Claremont-McKenna, Harvey Mudd, Pitzer, Pomona, and Scripps. **Degrees:** 164 bachelor's awarded. **ROTC:** Army, Air Force. **Location:** 35 miles from Los Angeles. **Calendar:** Semester, limited summer session. **Full-time faculty:** 81 total; 100% have terminal degrees, 15% minority, 28% women. **Part-time faculty:** 14 total; 93% have terminal degrees, 7% minority, 21% women. **Class size:** 60% < 20, 30% 20-39, 4% 40-49, 5% 50-99, 1% >100. **Special facilities:** Observatory, biological field station, high performance parallel processor.

**Freshman class profile.** 2,205 applied, 751 admitted, 207 enrolled.

| Mid 50% test scores | | | |
|---|---|---|---|
| SAT critical reading: | 680-770 | Rank in top tenth: | 94% |
| SAT math: | 740-790 | Return as sophomores: | 91% |
| SAT writing: | 660-750 | Out-of-state: | 62% |
| ACT composite: | 32-35 | Live on campus: | 100% |
| Rank in top quarter: | 100% | International: | 3% |

**Basis for selection.** School achievement record important, especially in mathematics and science. Test scores, recommendations, school and community activities important, interviews highly recommended. Students who take the SAT or ACT with writing must also submit SAT Subject Tests in Math Level 2 and in another subject of their choice. Interviews are not required but are highly recommended. **Homeschooled:** Portfolio suggested describing texts used, curriculum format, how instruction was given. Recommend lab science and foreign language courses be taken at high school or college.

**High school preparation.** College-preparatory program required. Required and recommended units include English 4, mathematics 3-4, social studies 2, history 1-2, science 3-4 (laboratory 2) and foreign language 2. 1 year of calculus, 1 year of chemistry, and 1 year of physics are required.

**2009-2010 Annual costs.** Tuition/fees: $38,567. Room and board expense covers 16-meal plan. Room/board: $12,570. Books/supplies: $800. Personal expenses: $900.

**2009-2010 Financial aid. Need-based:** 150 full-time freshmen applied for aid; 124 were judged to have need; 124 of these received aid. Average need met was 100%. Average scholarship/grant was $29,400; average loan $3,587. 79% of total undergraduate aid awarded as scholarships/grants, 21% as loans/jobs. **Non-need-based:** Awarded to 373 full-time undergraduates, including 84 freshmen. Scholarships awarded for academics.

**Application procedures. Admission:** Closing date 1/2 (postmark date). $60 fee, may be waived for applicants with need. Admission notification 4/1. Must reply by May 1 or within 2 week(s) if notified thereafter. **Financial aid:** Closing date 2/1. FAFSA, CSS PROFILE required. Applicants notified by 4/1; must reply by 5/1 or within 2 week(s) of notification.

**Academics.** Course work divided equally between technical core, major, and humanities and social sciences. **Special study options:** Combined bachelor's/graduate degree, cross-registration, double major, exchange student, independent study, internships, liberal arts/career combination, student-designed major, study abroad. Applied engineering, mathematics and computer science clinics, 4+1 BS/MBA with Claremont Graduate University. **Credit/placement by examination:** AP, CLEP, institutional tests. **Support services:** Learning center, pre-admission summer program, reduced course load, study skills assistance, tutoring, writing center.

**Majors. Biology:** General. **Computer sciences:** General. **Engineering:** General. **Interdisciplinary:** Math/computer science. **Math:** General, applied. **Physical sciences:** Chemistry, physics. **Other:** Mathematical biology.

**Most popular majors.** Biology 12%, computer/information sciences 15%, engineering/engineering technologies 36%, mathematics 12%, physical sciences 21%.

**Computing on campus.** 360 workstations in dormitories, library, computer center. Dormitories wired for high-speed internet access and linked to campus network. Commuter students can connect to campus network. Online course registration, online library, helpline, student web hosting, wireless network available.

**Student life. Freshman orientation:** Mandatory. 5-day residential introduction. **Policies:** Student-directed honor code governs academic and non-academic life on campus. **Housing:** Guaranteed on-campus for freshmen. Coed dorms, apartments available. $150 deposit, deadline 6/1. Pets allowed in dorm rooms. **Activities:** Bands, campus ministries, choral groups, dance, drama, film society, international student organizations, literary magazine, music ensembles, musical theater, radio station, student government, student newspaper, symphony orchestra, TV station, InterVarsity Christian Fellowship, Hillel, Society of Women Engineers, AIDS Awareness, Asian American student alliance, Korean student union, Muslim student association, Society of Hispanic Engineers, National Society of Black Engineers.

**Athletics.** NCAA. **Intercollegiate:** Baseball M, basketball, cross-country, diving, football (tackle) M, golf M, lacrosse W, soccer, softball W, swimming, tennis, track and field, volleyball W, water polo. **Intramural:** Basketball, football (tackle), soccer, softball, table tennis, tennis, volleyball, water polo. **Team name:** Athenas/Stags.

**Student services.** Alcohol/substance abuse counseling, chaplain/spiritual director, career counseling, student employment services, financial aid counseling, health services, minority student services, personal counseling, placement for graduates, women's services.

**Contact.** E-mail: admission@hmc.edu
Phone: (909) 621-8011 Fax: (909) 607-7046
Peter Osgood, Director of Admission, Harvey Mudd College, 301 Platt Boulevard, Claremont, CA 91711-5901

## Holy Names University
### Oakland, California
**www.hnu.edu**  CB code: 4059

- Private 4-year university affiliated with Roman Catholic Church
- Commuter campus in large city
- 578 degree-seeking undergraduates: 26% part-time, 71% women, 24% African American, 9% Asian American, 18% Hispanic American, 4% international
- 437 degree-seeking graduate students
- 77% of applicants admitted
- SAT or ACT (ACT writing optional), application essay required
- 17% graduate within 6 years

**General.** Founded in 1868. Regionally accredited. **Degrees:** 105 bachelor's awarded; master's offered. **ROTC:** Army, Air Force. **Location:** 14 miles from San Francisco. **Calendar:** Semester, limited summer session. **Full-time faculty:** 37 total; 84% have terminal degrees, 19% minority. **Part-time faculty:** 126 total; 29% have terminal degrees, 7% minority. **Class size:** 66% < 20, 34% 20-39. **Special facilities:** Folk music collection, institute for learning disabled.

**Freshman class profile.** 452 applied, 346 admitted, 127 enrolled.

| Mid 50% test scores | | | |
|---|---|---|---|
| SAT critical reading: | 390-480 | GPA 3.0-3.49: | 37% |
| SAT math: | 400-490 | GPA 2.0-2.99: | 46% |
| SAT writing: | 380-470 | End year in good standing: | 16% |
| ACT composite: | 16-20 | Return as sophomores: | 67% |
| GPA 3.75 or higher: | 8% | Out-of-state: | 11% |
| GPA 3.50-3.74: | 9% | Live on campus: | 83% |
| | | International: | 8% |

**Basis for selection.** Overall strength of high school preparation, SAT or ACT scores, personal essay, letter of recommendation, extracurricular activities and individual talents and achievements. For non-native English speakers, ESL Center proficiency report certifying completion of Level 107 or higher may be substituted for TOEFL. Proficiency exams in theory, sight-singing, dictation and piano are required of all students entering the music program. Exams offered during week prior to beginning of each semester. Music major applicant must also audition for faculty jury. **Homeschooled:** Transcript of courses and grades, letter of recommendation (nonparent) required. Transcript demonstrating completion of basic credit hours for high school along with short evaluation from primary instructor. May require additional portfolio or performance-based assessments to document competency.

**High school preparation.** College-preparatory program recommended. 15 units required. Required and recommended units include English 4, mathematics 3, history 1, science 1 (laboratory 1), foreign language 2-3 and academic electives 3. U.S. history or government required, plus 1 additional year of math, foreign language, or lab science.

**2010-2011 Annual costs.** Tuition/fees (projected): $28,350. Room/board: $9,780.

**2008-2009 Financial aid. Non-need-based:** Scholarships awarded for academics, athletics, leadership, music/drama, religious affiliation.

**Application procedures. Admission:** Priority date 3/2; deadline 8/15 (postmark date). No application fee. Admission notification on a rolling basis beginning on or about 10/1. Must reply by May 1 or within 2 week(s) if notified thereafter. **Financial aid:** Priority date 3/2, closing date 6/30. FAFSA required. Applicants notified on a rolling basis starting 9/1; must reply by 5/1 or within 2 week(s) of notification.

**Academics.** All undergraduate students must satisfy general education requirements. First component is Foundation in Critical Thinking and Communication. Remaining components use thematic and disciplinary approaches to learning. **Special study options:** Accelerated study, cross-registration, distance learning, double major, ESL, exchange student, independent study, internships, liberal arts/career combination, student-designed major, study abroad, teacher certification program, weekend college. **Credit/placement by examination:** AP, CLEP, IB, institutional tests. 6 credit hours maximum toward bachelor's degree. Maximum of 6 credit hours per general exam awarded. **Support services:** Learning center, reduced course load, remedial instruction, study skills assistance, tutoring.

**Majors. Biology:** General. **Business:** Business admin, communications, human resources, international, marketing. **Communications:** Digital media. **Foreign languages:** Spanish. **Health:** Nursing (RN). **History:** General. **Interdisciplinary:** Biopsychology. **Liberal arts:** Arts/sciences, humanities. **Philosophy/religion:** Philosophy, religion. **Psychology:** General, psychobiology. **Public administration:** Human services. **Social sciences:** Criminology, international relations, sociology. **Visual/performing arts:** Music pedagogy, music performance.

**Most popular majors.** Biology 6%, business/marketing 38%, health sciences 14%, liberal arts 8%, psychology 10%, social sciences 9%.

**Computing on campus.** 80 workstations in dormitories, library, computer center, student center. Dormitories wired for high-speed internet access and linked to campus network. Online course registration, online library, helpline, student web hosting, wireless network available.

**Student life. Freshman orientation:** Mandatory, $50 fee. Preregistration for classes offered. 2-3 day weekend event prior to start of term. **Housing:** Guaranteed on-campus for all undergraduates. Coed dorms, wellness housing available. $100 fully refundable deposit, deadline 8/18. **Activities:** Campus ministries, choral groups, drama, film society, music ensembles, Model UN, student government, symphony orchestra, Asian Pacific International, Black Student Union, drama club, speech and debate team, Holy Names Construction, Global Outlook, International Village, Latinos Unidos, social justice club.

**Athletics.** NAIA. **Intercollegiate:** Basketball, cross-country, golf M, soccer, softball W, volleyball. **Team name:** Hawks.

**Student services.** Adult student services, chaplain/spiritual director, career counseling, student employment services, financial aid counseling, personal counseling. **Physically disabled:** Services for visually impaired.

**Contact.** E-mail: admission@hnu.edu
Phone: (510) 436-1351 Toll-free number: (800) 430-1321
Fax: (510) 436-1325
Murad Dibbini, Dean of Enrollment Services, Holy Names University, 3500 Mountain Boulevard, Oakland, CA 94619-1699

## Hope International University
**Fullerton, California**
www.hiu.edu                                           CB code: 4614

▸ Private 4-year university and liberal arts college affiliated with Independent Christian Churches and Churches of Christ
▸ Residential campus in small city
▸ 690 degree-seeking undergraduates
▸ 37% of applicants admitted
▸ SAT or ACT (ACT writing optional), application essay required

**General.** Founded in 1928. Regionally accredited; also accredited by ABHE. In addition to the campus in Fullerton, CA, there is an extension site in Corona, CA. **Degrees:** 140 bachelor's, 8 associate awarded; master's offered. **Location:** 35 miles from Los Angeles. **Calendar:** 4-1-4, limited summer session. **Full-time faculty:** 31 total; 81% have terminal degrees, 10% minority. **Part-time faculty:** 92 total; 18% have terminal degrees, 5% minority. **Class size:** 56% < 20, 33% 20-39, 6% 40-49, 4% 50-99.

**Freshman class profile.** 419 applied, 157 admitted, 80 enrolled.

| Mid 50% test scores | | | |
|---|---|---|---|
| SAT critical reading: | 420-520 | GPA 3.0-3.49: | 37% |
| SAT math: | 430-540 | GPA 2.0-2.99: | 35% |
| SAT writing: | 420-510 | Rank in top quarter: | 38% |
| ACT composite: | 19-26 | Rank in top tenth: | 17% |
| GPA 3.75 or higher: | 20% | Out-of-state: | 20% |
| GPA 3.50-3.74: | 8% | Live on campus: | 77% |

**Basis for selection.** Prior academic achievement, standardized test scores, statement of purpose essays, commitment to the mission of the institution and recommendations are important. Extracurricular activities are also considered along with all other factors bearing on potential success. Interviews recommended for academically borderline applicants. **Homeschooled:** If schooled under the auspices of an organization that can offer transcripts, the university will accept these transcripts and SAT/ACT scores. If not, a GED score and SAT/ACT scores are required in the application process. **Learning Disabled:** All documentation must be recent, within the past three years of enrollment, and must have been completed by an appropriate professional, e.g., State licensed psychologist or school psychologist. Documentation shall include both appropriate tests of learning abilities as well as interview material.

**High school preparation.** College-preparatory program recommended. 13.5 units recommended. Recommended units include English 4, mathematics 2, history 1, science 1 (laboratory 1), foreign language 1, computer science .5 and academic electives 3. One half-unit speech and one-half unit computer science or literacy is recommended.

**2009-2010 Annual costs.** Tuition/fees: $22,520. Room/board: $8,800. Books/supplies: $1,638. Personal expenses: $2,250.

**2009-2010 Financial aid. Non-need-based:** Scholarships awarded for academics, job skills, leadership, music/drama, state residency.

**Application procedures. Admission:** Priority date 12/1; deadline 2/1. $40 fee, may be waived for applicants with need. Admission notification on a rolling basis. **Financial aid:** Closing date 3/2. FAFSA, institutional form required. Applicants notified on a rolling basis starting 3/15; must reply within 2 week(s) of notification.

**Academics.** Emphasis on field-based interactive learning combined with direct professional involvement with students. **Special study options:** Combined bachelor's/graduate degree, distance learning, double major, ESL, exchange student, external degree, internships, liberal arts/career combination, study abroad, teacher certification program. **Credit/placement by examination:** AP, CLEP, IB, institutional tests. The amount of credit for examinations depends upon the applicability of the exam(s) to the specific degree program requirements. **Support services:** Reduced course load, remedial instruction, study skills assistance, tutoring.

**Majors. Business:** Business admin. **Education:** Elementary, music, social science. **Family/consumer sciences:** Family studies. **Health:** Athletic training. **Psychology:** General. **Public administration:** Human services. **Social sciences:** General. **Theology:** Bible, missionary, sacred music, theology, youth ministry.

**Most popular majors.** Business/marketing 24%, education 7%, family/consumer sciences 33%, psychology 9%, social sciences 6%, theological studies 22%.

**Computing on campus.** 53 workstations in library, computer center. Dormitories wired for high-speed internet access. Online library, helpline, repair service, wireless network available.

**Student life. Freshman orientation:** Mandatory, $75 fee. Preregistration for classes offered. Fall and spring new student orientation held 3 days before beginning of term. **Policies:** No alcohol permitted, smoking discouraged. Religious observance required. **Housing:** Guaranteed on-campus for freshmen. Single-sex dorms, wellness housing available. $100 partly refundable deposit, deadline 7/1. Single students required to live on campus until age 21 or reaching junior standing, unless living at home or given special approval. **Activities:** Choral groups, drama, international student organizations, music ensembles, musical theater, student government, student newspaper, school outreach, minority students association, business club, counseling center, fitness center, University Praise.

**Athletics.** NAIA. **Intercollegiate:** Basketball, cheerleading, soccer, softball W, tennis, volleyball. **Intramural:** Badminton, basketball, football (nontackle) W, soccer, volleyball. **Team name:** Royals.

**Student services.** Adult student services, chaplain/spiritual director, career counseling, student employment services, financial aid counseling, health services, personal counseling, veterans' counselor.

**Contact.** E-mail: PCCAdmissions@hiu.edu
Phone: (714) 879-3901 ext. 2215 Toll-free number: (866) 722-4673
Fax: (714) 681-7423
Butch Ellis, Director of Undergraduate Admissions, Hope International University, 2500 East Nutwood Avenue, Fullerton, CA 92831-3199

## Horizon College of San Diego
**San Diego, California**
www.horizoncollege.org

▸ Private 4-year liberal arts college affiliated with Non-denominational
▸ Very large city
▸ 53 degree-seeking undergraduates: 81% part-time, 47% women

**General.** Candidate for regional accreditation.; also accredited by ABHE. **Degrees:** 7 bachelor's awarded. **Calendar:** Semester, limited summer session. **Part-time faculty:** 11 total; 73% have terminal degrees, 36% minority, 18% women.

**Freshman class profile.** 1 applied, 1 admitted, 1 enrolled.

**Basis for selection.** Open admission, but selective for some programs.

**2010-2011 Annual costs.** Tuition/fees: $4,800. Books/supplies: $500.

**Academics. Special study options:** Accelerated study, distance learning, independent study. **Credit/placement by examination:** CLEP.

**Majors. Theology:** Bible.

**Contact.** E-mail: info@horizoncollege.org
Phone: (858) 695-8587 Fax: (858) 695-9527
Horizon College of San Diego, 10625 Scripps Ranch Boulevard, Suite F, San Diego, CA 92131

## Humboldt State University
Arcata, California — CB member
www.humboldt.edu — CB code: 4345

- Public 4-year university and liberal arts college
- Residential campus in large town
- 7,093 degree-seeking undergraduates: 9% part-time, 54% women, 3% African American, 4% Asian American, 13% Hispanic American, 2% Native American, 1% international
- 776 degree-seeking graduate students
- 75% of applicants admitted
- 42% graduate within 6 years

**General.** Founded in 1913. Regionally accredited. **Degrees:** 1,187 bachelor's awarded; master's offered. **Location:** 275 miles from San Francisco. **Calendar:** Semester, limited summer session. **Full-time faculty:** 254 total; 99% have terminal degrees, 11% minority, 36% women. **Part-time faculty:** 254 total; 24% have terminal degrees, 13% minority, 60% women. **Class size:** 37% < 20, 42% 20-39, 9% 40-49, 8% 50-99, 3% >100. **Special facilities:** Marine lab, observatory, marsh and wildlife sanctuary, small lakes and ponds, 280-acre sand dune preserve, research vessel, freshwater fish hatchery, small-game animal pen, fungal genetic stock center, 360-acre experimental forest, 170,000 specimen herbarium, center for appropriate technology, energy research center.

**Freshman class profile.** 9,626 applied, 7,220 admitted, 1,385 enrolled.

| Mid 50% test scores | | GPA 2.0-2.99: | 35% |
|---|---|---|---|
| SAT critical reading: | 470-590 | Rank in top quarter: | 38% |
| SAT math: | 460-570 | Rank in top tenth: | 15% |
| SAT writing: | 450-570 | End year in good standing: | 72% |
| ACT composite: | 19-25 | Return as sophomores: | 74% |
| GPA 3.75 or higher: | 12% | Out-of-state: | 17% |
| GPA 3.50-3.74: | 13% | Live on campus: | 76% |
| GPA 3.0-3.49: | 40% | | |

**Basis for selection.** High school GPA and test scores most important. In-state residents with high school GPA of 3.0 or higher or out-of-state applicants with high school GPA over 3.61 do not have to submit test scores for admission. Essay recommended for academically weak, special consideration applicants.

**High school preparation.** College-preparatory program required. 15 units required. Required units include English 4, mathematics 3, social studies 1, history 1, science 2 (laboratory 2), foreign language 2, visual/performing arts 1 and academic electives 1.

**2009-2010 Annual costs.** Tuition/fees: $5,166; $16,326 out-of-state. Room/board: $9,510. Books/supplies: $1,528. Personal expenses: $2,246.

**2008-2009 Financial aid. Need-based:** 942 full-time freshmen applied for aid; 649 were judged to have need; 592 of these received aid. Average need met was 71%. Average scholarship/grant was $4,630; average loan $295. 57% of total undergraduate aid awarded as scholarships/grants, 43% as loans/jobs. **Non-need-based:** Awarded to 143 full-time undergraduates, including 31 freshmen. Scholarships awarded for academics, athletics.

**Application procedures. Admission:** Priority date 10/31; deadline 11/30. $55 fee, may be waived for applicants with need. Admission notification on a rolling basis beginning on or about 12/1. **Financial aid:** Priority date 3/2; no closing date. FAFSA required. Applicants notified on a rolling basis starting 4/15; must reply within 6 week(s) of notification.

**Academics.** Indian Teacher and Educational Personnel Program, Indian Natural Resources, Sciences and Engineering Program available. **Special study options:** Cooperative education, cross-registration, distance learning, double major, dual enrollment of high school students, ESL, exchange student, honors, independent study, internships, student-designed major, study abroad, teacher certification program. **Credit/placement by examination:** AP, CLEP, IB, SAT, ACT, institutional tests. 30 credit hours maximum toward bachelor's degree. Humboldt grants undergraduate degree credit for successful completion of non-collegiate instruction, either military or civilian, appropriate to the baccalaureate degree. Credit must be recommended by the Commission on Educational Credit and Credentials of the American Council on Education. **Support services:** Learning center, pre-admission summer program, reduced course load, remedial instruction, study skills assistance, tutoring, writing center.

**Majors. Agriculture:** Range science. **Area/ethnic studies:** Native American, women's. **Biology:** General, botany, zoology. **Business:** General, business admin. **Communications:** General, journalism. **Computer sciences:** General, information systems. **Conservation:** General, environmental studies, fisheries, forestry, management/policy, wildlife. **Education:** Early childhood, elementary, physical, trade/industrial. **Engineering:** Science. **Foreign languages:** French, Spanish. **Health:** Kinesiotherapy, nursing (RN). **History:** General. **Interdisciplinary:** Global studies, intercultural. **Liberal arts:** Arts/sciences. **Math:** General. **Parks/recreation:** Facilities management, health/fitness. **Philosophy/religion:** Philosophy, religion. **Physical sciences:** General, chemistry, geology, oceanography, physics. **Psychology:** General. **Public administration:** Social work. **Social sciences:** General, anthropology, economics, geography, political science, sociology. **Visual/performing arts:** Art, dance, dramatic.

**Most popular majors.** Biology 9%, English 6%, liberal arts 10%, natural resources/environmental science 11%, psychology 6%, social sciences 11%, visual/performing arts 10%.

**Computing on campus.** 1,098 workstations in dormitories, library, computer center, student center. Dormitories wired for high-speed internet access and linked to campus network. Commuter students can connect to campus network. Online course registration, online library, helpline, student web hosting, wireless network available.

**Student life. Freshman orientation:** Mandatory, $50 fee. Preregistration for classes offered. Student-directed program held June, July and August. **Housing:** Coed dorms, apartments, wellness housing available. $500 partly refundable deposit, deadline 4/16. **Activities:** Bands, choral groups, dance, drama, film society, literary magazine, music ensembles, musical theater, radio station, student government, student newspaper, symphony orchestra, Newman Club, Campus Crusade for Christ, Youth Educational Services, Black Students Union, MECHA, Gay, Lesbian and Bisexual Students Association, Native American Club, Jewish Student Union, Multicultural Center, Veterans Organization.

**Athletics.** NCAA. **Intercollegiate:** Basketball, cross-country, football (tackle) M, rowing (crew) W, soccer, softball W, track and field, volleyball W. **Intramural:** Badminton, basketball, football (tackle) M, soccer, softball, volleyball. **Team name:** Lumberjacks.

**Student services.** Adult student services, alcohol/substance abuse counseling, career counseling, student employment services, financial aid counseling, health services, minority student services, on-campus daycare, personal counseling, placement for graduates, veterans' counselor, women's services. **Physically disabled:** Services for visually, speech, hearing impaired.

**Contact.** E-mail: hsuinfo@humboldt.edu
Phone: (707) 826-4402 Toll-free number: (866) 850-9556
Fax: (707) 826-6190
Scott Hagg, Director of Admissions and Student Recruitment, Humboldt State University, One Harpst Street, Arcata, CA 95521-8299

## Humphreys College
Stockton, California
www.humphreys.edu — CB code: 4346

- Private 4-year business and liberal arts college
- Residential campus in large city
- 718 degree-seeking undergraduates
- Interview required

**General.** Founded in 1896. Regionally accredited. **Degrees:** 77 bachelor's, 49 associate awarded; master's, doctoral, professional offered. **Location:** 35 miles from Sacramento, California. **Calendar:** Quarter, extensive summer session. **Full-time faculty:** 18 total; 17% have terminal degrees, 28% minority, 44% women. **Part-time faculty:** 44 total; 14% have terminal degrees, 46% minority, 41% women. **Class size:** 80% < 20, 20% 20-39.

**Freshman class profile.** 107 applied, 107 admitted, 83 enrolled.

| Out-of-state: | 3% | Live on campus: | 25% |
|---|---|---|---|

**Basis for selection.** Open admission. ACT used for placement only. **Homeschooled:** State high school equivalency certificate required.

**2009-2010 Annual costs.** Tuition/fees: $9,648. School-controlled apartment housing cost quoted, not including utilities. Room only: $6,282. Books/supplies: $1,638. Personal expenses: $2,634.

**2009-2010 Financial aid. Non-need-based:** Scholarships awarded for academics, state residency.

**Application procedures. Admission:** No deadline. $35 fee, may be waived for applicants with need. Application must be submitted on paper. Admission notification on a rolling basis. **Financial aid:** Closing date 6/30. FAFSA required. Applicants notified on a rolling basis; must reply within 2 week(s) of notification.

**Academics. Special study options:** Combined bachelor's/graduate degree, cooperative education, cross-registration, double major, honors, independent study, internships. **Credit/placement by examination:** AP, CLEP, IB, institutional tests. 4 credit hours maximum toward associate degree, 45 toward bachelor's. **Support services:** Learning center, pre-admission summer program, remedial instruction, tutoring, writing center.

**Majors. Business:** General, accounting, administrative services, business admin, office technology, office/clerical. **Computer sciences:** General. **Education:** General. **Health:** Medical secretary. **Legal studies:** Court reporting, legal secretary, paralegal. **Liberal arts:** Arts/sciences. **Public administration:** Community org/advocacy. **Social sciences:** General.

**Computing on campus.** 25 workstations in library, computer center. Online library, helpline, wireless network available.

**Student life. Freshman orientation:** Available. Preregistration for classes offered. Held on campus the first week of each academic term. **Housing:** Apartments available. $200 partly refundable deposit, deadline 8/20. **Activities:** Student government, student newspaper, business club.

**Student services.** Career counseling, student employment services, financial aid counseling, on-campus daycare, personal counseling, placement for graduates, veterans' counselor.

**Contact.** E-mail: ugadmission@humphreys.edu
Phone: (209) 478-0800 Fax: (209) 478-8721
Santa Lopez-Minarte, Admissions Director, Humphreys College, 6650 Inglewood Avenue, Stockton, CA 95207-3896

## Interior Designers Institute
**Newport Beach, California**
www.idi.edu                    CB code: 2318

- For-profit 4-year visual arts college
- Large city
- 400 degree-seeking undergraduates

**General.** Accredited by ACCSC. **Degrees:** 23 bachelor's, 70 associate awarded; master's offered. **Calendar:** Continuous. **Part-time faculty:** 30 total.

**Basis for selection.** Open admission.

**2009-2010 Annual costs.** 12-week certificate program: $1,995. 2-year associate degree program: $15,950. Bachelor's degree program: $14,950. Books/supplies: $1,500.

**Application procedures. Admission:** No deadline. $95 fee. Application must be submitted on paper.

**Academics. Credit/placement by examination:** CLEP.

**Majors. Visual/performing arts:** Interior design.

**Contact.** E-mail: contact@idi.edu
Phone: (949) 675-4451 Fax: (949) 759-0667
Susan Bell, Office Manager, Interior Designers Institute, 1061 Camelback Road, Newport Beach, CA 92660-3228

## International Academy of Design and Technology: Sacramento
**Sacramento, California**
www.iadtsacramento.com

- For-profit 4-year liberal arts and technical college
- Very large city
- 429 degree-seeking undergraduates

**General.** Regionally accredited; also accredited by ACICS. **Degrees:** 7 associate awarded. **Calendar:** Continuous. **Full-time faculty:** 8 total. **Part-time faculty:** 38 total.

**Freshman class profile.** 26 enrolled.

**Basis for selection.** Open admission.

**Application procedures. Admission:** No deadline. $50 fee. **Financial aid:** No deadline.

**Academics. Credit/placement by examination:** CLEP.

**Majors. Visual/performing arts:** Fashion design, interior design. **Other:** Visual communications.

**Contact.** E-mail: aepperson@iadtsacramento.com
Phone: (916) 285-9468
Miguel Sanchez, Director of Admissions, International Academy of Design and Technology: Sacramento, 2450 Del Paso Road, Sacramento, CA 95834

## ITT Technical Institute: Anaheim
**Anaheim, California**
www.itt-tech.edu                    CB code: 3570

- For-profit 4-year technical college
- Commuter campus in small city

**General.** Founded in 1983. Accredited by ACICS. **Location:** 15 miles from Los Angeles. **Calendar:** Quarter.

**Contact.** Phone: (714) 535-3700
Director of Recruitment, 525 North Muller, Anaheim, CA 92801

## ITT Technical Institute: Lathrop
**Lathrop, California**
www.itt-tech.edu                    CB code: 2720

- For-profit 4-year technical college
- Commuter campus in small town

**General.** Accredited by ACICS. **Calendar:** Quarter.

**Contact.** Phone: (209) 858-0077
Director of Recruitment, 16916 South Harlan Road, Lathrop, CA 95330

## ITT Technical Institute: Oxnard
**Oxnard, California**
www.itt-tech.edu                    CB code: 2744

- For-profit 4-year technical college
- Commuter campus in small city

**General.** Accredited by ACICS. **Location:** 34 miles from Santa Barbara, 52 miles from Los Angeles. **Calendar:** Quarter.

**Contact.** Phone: (805) 988-0143
Director of Recruitment, 2051 Solar Drive, Building B, Oxnard, CA 93036

## ITT Technical Institute: Rancho Cordova
**Rancho Cordova, California**
www.itt-tech.edu                    CB code: 3597

- For-profit 4-year technical college
- Commuter campus in large city

**General.** Founded in 1954. Accredited by ACICS. **Location:** 11 miles from Sacramento, 87 miles from San Francisco. **Calendar:** Quarter.

**Contact.** Phone: (916) 366-3900
Director of Recruitment, 10863 Gold Center Drive, Rancho Cordova, CA 95670

## ITT Technical Institute: San Bernardino
San Bernardino, California
www.itt-tech.edu                    CB code: 7103

- For-profit 4-year technical college
- Commuter campus in very large city

**General.** Accredited by ACICS. **Location:** 60 miles from Los Angeles. **Calendar:** Quarter.

**Contact.** Phone: (800) 888-3801
Director of Recruitment, 670 East Carnegie Drive, San Bernardino, CA 92408-2800

## ITT Technical Institute: San Diego
San Diego, California
www.itt-tech.edu                    CB code: 0206

- For-profit 4-year technical college
- Commuter campus in very large city

**General.** Founded in 1981. Accredited by ACICS. **Calendar:** Quarter.

**Contact.** Phone: (858) 571-8500
Director of Recruitment, 9680 Granite Ridge Drive, San Diego, CA 92123

## ITT Technical Institute: Sylmar
Sylmar, California
www.itt-tech.edu                    CB code: 3571

- For-profit 4-year technical college
- Commuter campus in very large city

**General.** Founded in 1982. Accredited by ACICS. **Calendar:** Quarter.

**Contact.** Phone: (818) 364-5151
Director of Recruitment, 12669 Encinitas Avenue, Sylmar, CA 91342-3664

## ITT Technical Institute: Torrance
Torrance, California
www.itt-tech.edu                    CB code: 7104

- For-profit 4-year technical college
- Commuter campus in small city

**General.** Accredited by ACICS. **Calendar:** Quarter.

**Contact.** Phone: (310) 380-1555
Director of Recruitment, 20050 South Vermont Avenue, Torrance, CA 90502

## John F. Kennedy University
Pleasant Hill, California
www.jfku.edu                    CB code: 1362

- Private two-year upper-division university
- Commuter campus in large town
- Interview required

**General.** Founded in 1964. Regionally accredited. Undergraduate and graduate degree Linking program. **Degrees:** 39 bachelor's awarded; master's, professional offered. **Articulation:** Agreements with all California community colleges. **Location:** 35 miles from San Francisco. **Calendar:** Quarter, limited summer session. **Full-time faculty:** 55 total. **Part-time faculty:** 194 total. **Class size:** 81% < 20, 19% 20-39.

**Student profile.** 280 degree-seeking undergraduates.

Out-of-state:                    1%    **25 or older:**                    90%

**Basis for selection.** Open admission. College transcript, interview required. Deadlines for response to admissions decisions vary with programs. Interview required. Applicants must have 45 quarter hours. Transfer accepted as sophomores, juniors, seniors.

**2009-2010 Annual costs.** Tuition/fees: $16,401. Books/supplies: $1,100.

**Financial aid.** All financial aid based on need.

**Application procedures. Admission:** Rolling admission. $55 fee. **Financial aid:** Priority date 4/1. FAFSA, institutional form required.

**Academics. Special study options:** Combined bachelor's/graduate degree, cross-registration, independent study, internships, teacher certification program. **Credit/placement by examination:** AP, CLEP. 105 credit hours maximum toward bachelor's degree. Maximum of 105 units through combination of CLEP, DANTES, 2-year schools, and military training. **Support services:** Study skills assistance, writing center.

**Majors. Business:** Business admin. **Legal studies:** General, paralegal. **Liberal arts:** Arts/sciences. **Psychology:** General. **Visual/performing arts:** Studio arts. **Other:** Philosophy and religion.

**Most popular majors.** Business/marketing 26%, liberal arts 63%, psychology 11%.

**Computing on campus.** 25 workstations in library, computer center. Commuter students can connect to campus network.

**Student life. Activities:** Student government, student newspaper.

**Student services.** Career counseling, student employment services, veterans' counselor. **Physically disabled:** Services for visually, speech, hearing impaired.

**Contact.** E-mail: proginfo@jfku.edu
Phone: (925) 969-3535 Toll-free number: (800) 696-5358
Fax: (925) 969-3331
Jen Miller-Hogg, Director of Admissions, John F. Kennedy University, 100 Ellinwood Way, Pleasant Hill, CA 94523-4817

## The King's College and Seminary
Van Nuys, California
www.kingsseminary.edu                    CB code: 3896

- Private 4-year Bible and seminary college affiliated with nondenominational tradition
- Commuter campus in very large city
- 473 degree-seeking undergraduates
- 79% of applicants admitted
- Application essay required

**General.** Accredited by ABHE. Evangelical institution. **Degrees:** 20 bachelor's, 6 associate awarded; master's, professional offered. **Calendar:** Quarter, extensive summer session. **Full-time faculty:** 14 total. **Part-time faculty:** 39 total.

**Freshman class profile.** 14 applied, 11 admitted, 10 enrolled.

**Basis for selection.** Demonstration of commitment to Christian faith required, essays, references important. SAT or ACT recommended. **Home-schooled:** Statement describing homeschool structure and mission, transcript of courses and grades required.

**2010-2011 Annual costs.** Tuition/fees: $9,150. Books/supplies: $1,200.

**Financial aid. Non-need-based:** Scholarships awarded for academics. **Additional information:** Specific scholarships may require specific essays.

**Application procedures. Admission:** No deadline. $75 fee. Admission notification on a rolling basis. Must reply by May 1 or within 4 week(s) if notified thereafter. Must reply within 30 days. **Financial aid:** No deadline. FAFSA required. Applicants notified on a rolling basis; must reply within 4 week(s) of notification.

**Academics. Special study options:** Accelerated study, distance learning, external degree, independent study, internships, study abroad. **Credit/placement by examination:** AP, CLEP, IB, institutional tests. 45 credit hours maximum toward associate degree, 45 toward bachelor's. **Support services:** Pre-admission summer program, reduced course load, remedial instruction, study skills assistance.

**Majors. Theology:** Bible.

**Computing on campus.** Commuter students can connect to campus network. Online course registration, online library, helpline available.

**Student life. Freshman orientation:** Mandatory. Preregistration for classes offered. **Policies:** Drug- and alcohol-free campus. Religious observance required. **Activities:** Campus ministries, choral groups, music ensembles, student government, student newspaper, C.S. Lewis club, women in ministry group, Delta Epsilon, National Association of Evangelicals.

**Student services.** Adult student services, alcohol/substance abuse counseling, chaplain/spiritual director, career counseling, student employment services, financial aid counseling, personal counseling, placement for graduates, veterans' counselor, women's services.

**Contact.** E-mail: admissions@kingscollege.edu
Phone: (818) 779-8040 Toll-free number: (888) 779-8040
Fax: (818) 779-8429
Marilyn Chappell, Director of Admissions, The King's College and Seminary, 14800 Sherman Way, Van Nuys, CA 91405-2233

## LA College International
### Los Angeles, California
www.lac.edu  CB code: 3046

- For-profit 4-year business and technical college
- Commuter campus in very large city
- 600 degree-seeking undergraduates

**General.** Accredited by ACICS. **Degrees:** 35 associate awarded. **Calendar:** Continuous. **Part-time faculty:** 25 total.

**Basis for selection.** Open admission. ATB required if no high school diploma.

**2009-2010 Annual costs.** Tuition/fees: $12,512. Online tuition $325 per credit hour for AA and BS programs in business management. Books/supplies: $1,500.

**Application procedures. Admission:** No deadline. $35 fee. **Financial aid:** FAFSA, institutional form required.

**Academics. Credit/placement by examination:** CLEP.

**Majors. Business:** Business admin. **Computer sciences:** General.

**Student life. Freshman orientation:** Available. 4 days before start date. **Activities:** Student government.

**Contact.** Phone: (213) 381-3333 Toll-free number: (800) 574-6428
Fax: (213) 383-9369
Shavonne Turner, Admissions Director, LA College International, 3200 Wilshire Boulevard, Suite 400, Los Angeles, CA 90010-1308

## La Sierra University
### Riverside, California
CB member
www.lasierra.edu  CB code: 4380

- Private 4-year university affiliated with Seventh-day Adventists
- Residential campus in large city
- 1,455 degree-seeking undergraduates: 11% part-time, 56% women, 9% African American, 25% Asian American, 29% Hispanic American, 1% Native American, 12% international
- 329 degree-seeking graduate students
- 53% of applicants admitted
- SAT or ACT (ACT writing optional), application essay required
- 32% graduate within 6 years

**General.** Founded in 1922. Regionally accredited. **Degrees:** 210 bachelor's awarded; master's, doctoral offered. **Location:** 55 miles from Los Angeles. **Calendar:** Quarter, limited summer session. **Full-time faculty:** 93 total; 84% have terminal degrees, 42% minority, 43% women. **Part-time faculty:** 87 total; 29% minority, 45% women. **Class size:** 66% < 20, 26% 20-39, 5% 40-49, 3% 50-99, less than 1% >100. **Special facilities:** Museum of natural history with large freeze-dried collection (reptiles, mammals, birds), mineral spheres collection, arboretum, observatory, women's resource center.

**Freshman class profile.** 1,444 applied, 759 admitted, 348 enrolled.

| Mid 50% test scores | | | |
|---|---|---|---|
| SAT critical reading: | 420-560 | GPA 2.0-2.99: | 30% |
| SAT math: | 410-560 | Rank in top quarter: | 39% |
| ACT composite: | 17-22 | Rank in top tenth: | 13% |
| GPA 3.75 or higher: | 27% | Return as sophomores: | 74% |
| GPA 3.50-3.74: | 14% | Out-of-state: | 12% |
| GPA 3.0-3.49: | 29% | Live on campus: | 55% |
| | | International: | 9% |

**Basis for selection.** Secondary school record and GPA, test scores, recommendations, and religious affiliation or commitment important.

**High school preparation.** College-preparatory program required. 15 units required. Required and recommended units include English 4, mathematics 3-4, social studies 2, science 2-3 (laboratory 2-3), foreign language 2-3, visual/performing arts 1 and academic electives 1.

**2009-2010 Annual costs.** Tuition/fees: $24,573. Room/board: $6,990.

**2008-2009 Financial aid. Need-based:** 258 full-time freshmen applied for aid; 212 were judged to have need; 210 of these received aid. Average need met was 70%. Average scholarship/grant was $16,872; average loan $3,392. 56% of total undergraduate aid awarded as scholarships/grants, 44% as loans/jobs. **Non-need-based:** Awarded to 389 full-time undergraduates, including 88 freshmen. Scholarships awarded for academics, leadership, music/drama, religious affiliation.

**Application procedures. Admission:** Priority date 2/1; no deadline. $30 fee, may be waived for applicants with need. Admission notification on a rolling basis. **Financial aid:** Priority date 3/2; no closing date. FAFSA required. Applicants notified on a rolling basis starting 4/15; must reply by 9/1.

**Academics. Special study options:** Accelerated study, cross-registration, distance learning, double major, dual enrollment of high school students, ESL, honors, independent study, internships, student-designed major, study abroad, teacher certification program. **Credit/placement by examination:** AP, CLEP, IB, institutional tests. 24 credit hours maximum toward bachelor's degree. **Support services:** Learning center, pre-admission summer program, reduced course load, remedial instruction, study skills assistance, tutoring, writing center.

**Honors college/program.** High school GPA above 3.25 and ACT above 60th percentile. 25 freshmen admitted per year.

**Majors. Biology:** General, biochemistry, biometrics, biophysics. **Business:** Accounting, business admin, finance, human resources, marketing. **Communications:** General. **Computer sciences:** Computer science, information systems. **Foreign languages:** Spanish. **History:** General. **Interdisciplinary:** Global studies. **Liberal arts:** Arts/sciences. **Math:** General. **Parks/recreation:** Exercise sciences, health/fitness. **Philosophy/religion:** Religion. **Physical sciences:** General, chemistry. **Psychology:** General, psychobiology. **Public administration:** Social work. **Social sciences:** Economics, sociology. **Visual/performing arts:** Art, studio arts.

**Most popular majors.** Biology 18%, business/marketing 29%, liberal arts 10%, parks/recreation 11%, psychology 8%.

**Computing on campus.** 262 workstations in dormitories, library, computer center. Dormitories wired for high-speed internet access and linked to campus network. Commuter students can connect to campus network. Online course registration, helpline, wireless network available.

**Student life. Freshman orientation:** Mandatory, $200 fee. Preregistration for classes offered. **Policies:** Smoke- and alcohol-free campus. Religious observance required. **Housing:** Single-sex dorms, apartments, wellness housing available. $100 fully refundable deposit. Honors residence hall available. **Activities:** Bands, campus ministries, choral groups, drama, international student organizations, literary magazine, music ensembles, student government, student newspaper, symphony orchestra, black student association, Earth Awareness, Amnesty International, Korean club, Ole club, Students in Free Enterprise, South Asia student association.

**Athletics.** NCAA. **Intercollegiate:** Baseball M, basketball, golf M, soccer, softball W, tennis, volleyball W. **Intramural:** Badminton, basketball, football (tackle), softball. **Team name:** Golden Eagles.

**Student services.** Adult student services, chaplain/spiritual director, career counseling, student employment services, financial aid counseling, health services, personal counseling, placement for graduates, women's services.

**Contact.** E-mail: admissions@lasierra.edu
Phone: (951) 785-2176 Toll-free number: (800) 874-5587
Fax: (951) 785-2477
Faye Swayze, Director of Admissions & Registrar, La Sierra University, 4500 Riverwalk Parkway, Riverside, CA 92515-8247

## Laguna College of Art and Design
### Laguna Beach, California
www.lagunacollege.edu  CB code: 7248

- Private 4-year visual arts college
- Commuter campus in large town
- 371 degree-seeking undergraduates
- SAT or ACT (ACT writing optional) required

**General.** Founded in 1961. Regionally accredited. **Degrees:** 61 bachelor's awarded; master's offered. **Location:** 50 miles from Los Angeles, 75 miles from San Diego. **Calendar:** Semester, limited summer session. **Full-time faculty:** 10 total. **Part-time faculty:** 80 total.

**Basis for selection.** Selection based on academic record and overall merit of 10-piece portfolio which includes minimum of 4 observational drawings. Application fee waived for online applications. Portfolios required.

**High school preparation.** 14 units recommended. Recommended units include English 2, mathematics 2, social studies 2, history 2, science 2, foreign language 2 and academic electives 2. 3 units of studio art, drawing and painting recommended.

**2009-2010 Annual costs.** Tuition/fees: $21,600. Books/supplies: $2,400. Personal expenses: $2,826.

**Financial aid.** **Additional information:** Need- and merit-based scholarship deadline March 20.

**Application procedures.** **Admission:** Priority date 2/2; no deadline. $45 fee, may be waived for applicants with need, free for online applicants. Admission notification on a rolling basis. **Financial aid:** No deadline. FAFSA, institutional form required. Applicants notified on a rolling basis; must reply within 2 week(s) of notification.

**Academics.** **Special study options:** Cooperative education, double major, exchange student, independent study, internships, New York semester, study abroad. **Credit/placement by examination:** CLEP. **Support services:** Pre-admission summer program, reduced course load, remedial instruction, tutoring.

**Majors.** **Visual/performing arts:** Commercial/advertising art, drawing, painting.

**Computing on campus.** 26 workstations in library, computer center.

**Student life.** **Policies:** Very strong student government promoting activities on and off campus. Many art-related social gatherings. **Activities:** Student government, student newspaper, foreign student organization, cultural diversity organization.

**Student services.** Career counseling, personal counseling, veterans' counselor.

**Contact.** E-mail: admissions@lagunacollege.edu
Phone: (949) 376-6000 Toll-free number: (800) 255-0762
Fax: (949) 376-6009
Mike Rivas, Admissions Director, Laguna College of Art and Design, 2222 Laguna Canyon Road, Laguna Beach, CA 92651-1136

---

## Life Pacific College
### San Dimas, California
### www.lifepacific.edu
**CB code: 4264**

- Private 4-year Bible college affiliated with Christian - The Foursquare Church
- Residential campus in large town
- 400 degree-seeking undergraduates
- SAT or ACT with writing, application essay required

**General.** Founded in 1925. Candidate for regional accreditation.; also accredited by ABHE. **Degrees:** 82 bachelor's, 4 associate awarded. **Location:** 30 miles from Los Angeles. **Calendar:** Differs by program, limited summer session. **Full-time faculty:** 18 total; 22% have terminal degrees, 11% minority. **Part-time faculty:** 11 total; 54% have terminal degrees. **Class size:** 75% < 20, 20% 20-39, less than 1% 40-49, 5% 50-99.

**Freshman class profile.** 85 applied, 61 admitted, 44 enrolled.

| Mid 50% test scores | | ACT composite: | 18-21 |
|---|---|---|---|
| SAT critical reading: | 430-560 | Out-of-state: | 47% |
| SAT math: | 390-520 | Live on campus: | 81% |
| SAT writing: | 420-510 | | |

**Basis for selection.** Open admission, but selective for some programs. Christian character, motivation, and ability to accord with college's program most important. Cumulative GPA in last school attended and SAT or ACT scores also considered. **Homeschooled:** Must present official transcript with graduation date. SAT or ACT required. **Learning Disabled:** LIFE Challenges Program available to students with learning disabilities. Request information.

**2009-2010 Annual costs.** Tuition/fees: $12,250. Room/board: $6,000.

---

**2008-2009 Financial aid.** **Need-based:** 6 full-time freshmen applied for aid; 6 were judged to have need; 6 of these received aid. Average need met was 7%. Average scholarship/grant was $1,080; average loan $2,143. 43% of total undergraduate aid awarded as scholarships/grants, 57% as loans/jobs. **Non-need-based:** Scholarships awarded for academics, alumni affiliation.

**Application procedures.** **Admission:** Priority date 4/1; deadline 5/3 (postmark date). $35 fee. Application must be submitted on paper. Admission notification on a rolling basis. **Financial aid:** No deadline. FAFSA required. Applicants notified on a rolling basis starting 6/1.

**Academics.** Bible studies taught from Charismatic/Pentecostal perspective training leaders for ministry. **Special study options:** Cooperative education, distance learning, dual enrollment of high school students, external degree, independent study, internships, study abroad. **Credit/placement by examination:** AP, CLEP, SAT, ACT, institutional tests. 16 credit hours maximum toward associate degree, 16 toward bachelor's. Credit limited by the number of subjects accepted, course by course basis. **Support services:** Reduced course load, remedial instruction, study skills assistance, writing center.

**Majors.** **Theology:** Bible, pastoral counseling.

**Computing on campus.** 45 workstations in dormitories, library, computer center, student center. Dormitories wired for high-speed internet access and linked to campus network. Online course registration, online library, helpline, wireless network available.

**Student life.** **Freshman orientation:** Mandatory, $100 fee. Preregistration for classes offered. One full day (meal provided), includes testing. **Policies:** Religious observance required. **Housing:** Guaranteed on-campus for freshmen. Single-sex dorms, wellness housing available. $200 nonrefundable deposit, deadline 6/1. **Activities:** Choral groups, dance, drama, film society, music ensembles, student government, learning center (tutoring for junior high and high school).

**Athletics.** **Team name:** Warriors.

**Student services.** Adult student services, chaplain/spiritual director, career counseling, student employment services, financial aid counseling, minority student services, personal counseling, placement for graduates, veterans' counselor. **Physically disabled:** Services for speech, hearing impaired.

**Contact.** E-mail: admissions@lifepacific.edu
Phone: (909) 599-5433 ext. 314 Toll-free number: (877) 886-5433 ext. 314
Fax: (909) 706-3070
Dórienne Elston, Recruitment/Admissions Director, Life Pacific College, Attn: Admissions, San Dimas, CA 91773

---

## Lincoln University
### Oakland, California
### www.lincolnuca.edu
**CB code: 4386**

- Private 4-year university and business college
- Commuter campus in very large city
- 83 degree-seeking undergraduates: 28% part-time, 46% women
- 143 degree-seeking graduate students
- 63% of applicants admitted

**General.** Founded in 1919. Accredited by ACICS. Institution primarily serves international students. **Degrees:** 6 bachelor's, 10 associate awarded; master's offered. **Location:** 12 miles from San Francisco. **Calendar:** Semester, limited summer session. **Full-time faculty:** 9 total; 33% women. **Part-time faculty:** 16 total; 19% women.

**Freshman class profile.** 182 applied, 115 admitted, 69 enrolled.

**Basis for selection.** High school achievement record is most important. Prior to enrollment, students take following tests and procedures in English placement: 1) Michigan Test of English Language Proficiency (MTELP), 2) Comprehensive English Language Test Structure (CELT-SA), 3) Comprehensive English Language Test Listening (CELT-LA), 4) a writing sample, and 5) a personal interview. Interview recommended and personal statements encouraged. **Homeschooled:** Transcript of courses and grades, state high school equivalency certificate required.

**2009-2010 Annual costs.** Tuition/fees: $8,920. Tuition for Intensive English program $2,860 per 16 weeks. Books/supplies: $600. Personal expenses: $2,520.

**2008-2009 Financial aid.** All financial aid based on need. 7 full-time freshmen applied for aid; 7 were judged to have need; 7 of these received aid. Average need met was 100%. Average scholarship/grant was $5,350;

average loan $3,720. 10% of total undergraduate aid awarded as scholarships/grants, 90% as loans/jobs.

**Application procedures. Admission:** No deadline. $75 fee. Admission notification on a rolling basis. **Financial aid:** Priority date 3/22, closing date 8/22. FAFSA required. Applicants notified by 12/1; must reply by 1/2.

**Academics. Special study options:** Cross-registration, double major, ESL, internships. **Credit/placement by examination:** CLEP. **Support services:** Reduced course load, tutoring.

**Majors. Business:** Business admin, international, management information systems, managerial economics.

**Computing on campus.** 34 workstations in library, computer center. Online library, wireless network available.

**Student life. Freshman orientation:** Mandatory. Preregistration for classes offered. One hour discussion of procedures, event announcements. Student government provides information on banking, transportation and other related materials. **Activities:** Student government.

**Student services.** Career counseling, financial aid counseling, personal counseling.

**Contact.** E-mail: admissions@lincolnuca.edu
Phone: (510) 628-8010 Toll-free number: (888) 810-9998
Fax: (510) 628-8012
Peggy Au, Director of Admissions and Records, Lincoln University, 401 15th Street, Oakland, CA 94612

## Loma Linda University
**Loma Linda, California**
**www.llu.edu**                                    **CB code: 4062**

- Private 3-year university and health science college affiliated with Seventh-day Adventists
- Commuter campus in large town
- 1,054 degree-seeking undergraduates: 12% part-time, 71% women, 4% African American, 24% Asian American, 17% Hispanic American, 1% Native American, 10% international
- 2,990 degree-seeking graduate students

**General.** Founded in 1905. Regionally accredited. Two undergraduate schools: School of Allied Health and School of Nursing, offering sophomore, junior, senior year study. All LLU programs require previous college credit, thus no first-time freshman applicants accepted. Specific programs are applied to rather than generally to the university. **Degrees:** 293 bachelor's, 207 associate awarded; master's, doctoral, professional offered. **Location:** 60 miles from Los Angeles, 50 miles from Palm Springs. **Calendar:** Quarter, limited summer session. **Full-time faculty:** 377 total. **Part-time faculty:** 1,425 total. **Class size:** 59% < 20, 23% 20-39, 11% 40-49, 5% 50-99, less than 1% >100.

**Basis for selection.** LLU does not admit first-time freshman, only transfer students. A minimum amount of units are required for admissions.

**2009-2010 Annual costs.** Tuition/fees: $25,164. Tuition quoted for nursing program. Full-time tuition for dental hygiene program: $23,833 plus $1,590 fees. For allied health program $450/credit hour; for certificate programs, $338/credit. Application fee may vary by program; tuition may vary by grade level in program. Room only: $2,520.

**Application procedures. Admission:** No deadline. $60 fee. Application must be submitted online. Notification varies by program. Each program is applied to separately and has own requirements and dates. Student must give at least a two-week notice prior to housing entry date in order to receive a full refund; otherwise no refund will be given. **Financial aid:** FAFSA required.

**Academics. Special study options:** Combined bachelor's/graduate degree, cross-registration, distance learning, double major, independent study, internships, study abroad. **Credit/placement by examination:** AP, CLEP. **Support services:** Study skills assistance.

**Majors. BACHELOR'S. Conservation:** Environmental science. **Health:** Audiology/speech pathology, clinical lab science, cytotechnology, dental hygiene, dietetics, EMT paramedic, health care admin, health services, medical radiologic technology/radiation therapy, medical records admin, nursing (RN). **Physical sciences:** Geology. **Other:** Health geographics. **ASSOCIATE. Health:** Medical radiologic technology/radiation therapy, nursing (RN), occupational therapy assistant, physical therapy assistant.

**Computing on campus.** 482 workstations in library, computer center, student center. Dormitories wired for high-speed internet access and linked to campus network. Commuter students can connect to campus network. Online library, helpline, wireless network available.

**Student life. Policies:** Students are not allowed to smoke, use alcohol or drugs. Religious observance required. **Housing:** Guaranteed on-campus for all undergraduates. Single-sex dorms, apartments, wellness housing available. $145 fully refundable deposit. **Activities:** Campus ministries, choral groups, international student organizations, music ensembles, student government, student newspaper, Black Health Professional Student Association, Association of Latin American Students, Social Action Corps, Students for International Mission Service.

**Athletics. Intramural:** Basketball, football (non-tackle), soccer M, softball, tennis, volleyball.

**Student services.** Alcohol/substance abuse counseling, chaplain/spiritual director, financial aid counseling, health services, on-campus daycare, personal counseling. **Physically disabled:** Services for hearing impaired.

**Contact.** E-mail: admissions.app@llu.edu
Phone: (909) 651-5029 Toll-free number: (800) 422-4558
Fax: (909) 558-4879
Loma Linda University, Admissions Processing, Loma Linda, CA 92350

## Loyola Marymount University
**Los Angeles, California**                         **CB member**
**www.lmu.edu**                                    **CB code: 4403**

- Private 4-year university affiliated with Roman Catholic Church
- Residential campus in very large city
- 5,667 degree-seeking undergraduates: 3% part-time, 58% women, 8% African American, 13% Asian American, 19% Hispanic American, 1% Native American, 3% international
- 3,035 degree-seeking graduate students
- 59% of applicants admitted
- SAT or ACT (ACT writing recommended), application essay required
- 80% graduate within 6 years

**General.** Founded in 1911. Regionally accredited. **Degrees:** 1,415 bachelor's awarded; master's, doctoral, professional offered. **ROTC:** Army, Naval, Air Force. **Location:** 15 miles from downtown. **Calendar:** Semester, extensive summer session. **Full-time faculty:** 498 total; 100% have terminal degrees, 25% minority, 41% women. **Part-time faculty:** 444 total; 19% minority, 45% women. **Class size:** 47% < 20, 51% 20-39, less than 1% 40-49, 1% 50-99, less than 1% >100. **Special facilities:** Fine arts complex with recital hall and recording arts facilities, marine station.

**Freshman class profile.** 9,456 applied, 5,594 admitted, 1,385 enrolled.

| Mid 50% test scores | | Rank in top quarter: | 65% |
|---|---|---|---|
| SAT critical reading: | 530-630 | Rank in top tenth: | 29% |
| SAT math: | 550-650 | End year in good standing: | 96% |
| SAT writing: | 510-610 | Return as sophomores: | 88% |
| ACT composite: | 24-28 | Out-of-state: | 30% |
| GPA 3.75 or higher: | 42% | Live on campus: | 93% |
| GPA 3.50-3.74: | 25% | International: | 3% |
| GPA 3.0-3.49: | 28% | Fraternities: | 11% |
| GPA 2.0-2.99: | 5% | Sororities: | 33% |

**Basis for selection.** High school GPA, curriculum, test scores, recommendations, essays, activities important. Interview recommended for early admission, disabled, academically weak applicants. Portfolio required for animation major applicants.

**High school preparation.** College-preparatory program recommended. 18 units recommended. Recommended units include English 4, mathematics 3, social studies 3, science 2 (laboratory 2), foreign language 3 and academic electives 1. 4 math required of engineering, math, and science majors; physics and chemistry required of engineering and science majors; biology and chemistry required (physics recommended) of biology majors.

**2010-2011 Annual costs.** Tuition/fees: $36,404. Room/board: $13,930.

**2008-2009 Financial aid. Need-based:** 952 full-time freshmen applied for aid; 693 were judged to have need; 690 of these received aid. Average need met was 82%. Average scholarship/grant was $20,562; average loan $5,217. 60% of total undergraduate aid awarded as scholarships/grants, 40% as loans/jobs. **Non-need-based:** Awarded to 878 full-time undergraduates, including 312 freshmen. Scholarships awarded for academics, alumni affiliation, art, athletics, music/drama, religious affiliation, ROTC.

**Application procedures. Admission:** No deadline. $60 fee, may be waived for applicants with need. Admission notification on a rolling basis beginning on or about 11/1. Must reply by May 1 or within 2 week(s) if notified thereafter. Applicants who desire housing or financial aid should apply by January 15. **Financial aid:** Priority date 2/1, closing date 5/15. FAFSA, CSS PROFILE required. Applicants notified on a rolling basis starting 3/15; must reply by 5/1 or within 4 week(s) of notification.

**Academics. Special study options:** Accelerated study, combined bachelor's/graduate degree, cross-registration, distance learning, double major, dual enrollment of high school students, ESL, exchange student, honors, independent study, internships, liberal arts/career combination, semester at sea, student-designed major, study abroad, teacher certification program, Washington semester, weekend college. Encore program for adult students. **Credit/placement by examination:** AP, CLEP, IB, institutional tests. **Support services:** Learning center, reduced course load, study skills assistance, tutoring.

**Majors. Area/ethnic studies:** African-American, Asian, Chicano/Hispanic-American/Latino, European, women's. **Biology:** General, biochemistry. **Business:** General, accounting, business admin. **Communications:** General, radio/tv. **Communications technology:** Animation/special effects, recording arts. **Computer sciences:** General. **Engineering:** General, civil, electrical, mechanical, physics. **Foreign languages:** Ancient Greek, classics, French, German, Latin, modern Greek, Spanish. **Health:** Art therapy. **History:** General. **Interdisciplinary:** Ancient studies, natural sciences. **Liberal arts:** Arts/sciences, humanities. **Math:** General, applied. **Philosophy/religion:** Philosophy. **Physical sciences:** Chemistry, physics. **Psychology:** General. **Public administration:** General. **Social sciences:** Economics, political science, sociology, urban studies. **Theology:** Theology. **Visual/performing arts:** Art, art history/conservation, cinematography, dance, design, dramatic, film/cinema, play/screenwriting, studio arts.

**Most popular majors.** Business/marketing 30%, communications/journalism 8%, social sciences 12%, visual/performing arts 11%.

**Computing on campus.** 650 workstations in dormitories, library, computer center, student center. Dormitories wired for high-speed internet access and linked to campus network. Commuter students can connect to campus network. Online course registration, online library, helpline, repair service, student web hosting, wireless network available.

**Student life. Freshman orientation:** Available, $210 fee. Preregistration for classes offered. **Housing:** Guaranteed on-campus for freshmen. Coed dorms, single-sex dorms, special housing for disabled, apartments, wellness housing available. $400 nonrefundable deposit. **Activities:** Pep band, campus ministries, choral groups, dance, drama, international student organizations, literary magazine, music ensembles, radio station, student government, student newspaper, TV station, more than 130 student organizations, clubs, and associations.

**Athletics.** NCAA. **Intercollegiate:** Baseball M, basketball, cross-country, golf M, rowing (crew), soccer, softball W, swimming W, tennis, track and field, volleyball W, water polo. **Intramural:** Basketball, football (tackle), soccer, softball, table tennis, tennis, volleyball, water polo. **Team name:** Lions.

**Student services.** Adult student services, alcohol/substance abuse counseling, chaplain/spiritual director, career counseling, services for economically disadvantaged, student employment services, financial aid counseling, health services, minority student services, on-campus daycare, personal counseling, placement for graduates, veterans' counselor, women's services. **Physically disabled:** Services for visually, speech, hearing impaired.

**Contact.** E-mail: admissions@lmu.edu
Phone: (310) 338-2750 Toll-free number: (800) 568-4636
Fax: (310) 338-2797
Matthew Fissinger, Director of Admissions, Loyola Marymount University, Admissions, One LMU Drive, Los Angeles, CA 90045-8350

## The Master's College
### Santa Clarita, California
### www.masters.edu
**CB code: 4411**

- Private 4-year liberal arts and seminary college affiliated with Christian, Protestant, Conservative Evangelical
- Residential campus in small city
- 986 degree-seeking undergraduates: 11% part-time, 48% women
- 362 degree-seeking graduate students
- 83% of applicants admitted
- SAT or ACT with writing, application essay required

**General.** Founded in 1927. Regionally accredited. Branch campus in Israel; very strong overseas summer missions program. **Degrees:** 232 bachelor's awarded; master's, doctoral offered. **Location:** 40 miles from Los Angeles. **Calendar:** Semester, limited summer session. **Full-time faculty:** 66 total; 71% have terminal degrees, 11% minority, 17% women. **Part-time faculty:** 133 total; 16% have terminal degrees, 4% minority, 30% women. **Class size:** 76% < 20, 17% 20-39, 3% 40-49, 3% 50-99, less than 1% >100. **Special facilities:** Home economics - family and consumer sciences center.

**Freshman class profile.** 494 applied, 409 admitted, 209 enrolled.

| Mid 50% test scores | | | |
|---|---|---|---|
| SAT critical reading: | 480-630 | GPA 3.0-3.49: | 22% |
| SAT math: | 480-610 | GPA 2.0-2.99: | 8% |
| ACT composite: | 22-27 | Rank in top quarter: | 61% |
| GPA 3.75 or higher: | 51% | Rank in top tenth: | 33% |
| GPA 3.50-3.74: | 19% | Out-of-state: | 35% |
| | | Live on campus: | 90% |

**Basis for selection.** School achievement record, references, religious commitment most important. Applications from all individuals who have placed their faith in Jesus Christ as Lord and Savior are welcome. Audition required of music majors. **Homeschooled:** Transcript of courses and grades, letter of recommendation (nonparent) required. **Learning Disabled:** Must speak with human resources department before attending.

**High school preparation.** College-preparatory program recommended. Required and recommended units include English 4, mathematics 3, history 2, science 2 and academic electives 3.

**2009-2010 Annual costs.** Tuition/fees: $24,280. Room/board: $8,000. Books/supplies: $1,638. Personal expenses: $2,088.

**2008-2009 Financial aid. Non-need-based:** Scholarships awarded for academics, alumni affiliation, art, athletics, leadership, music/drama.

**Application procedures. Admission:** Priority date 3/2; no deadline. $40 fee, may be waived for applicants with need. Admission notification on a rolling basis beginning on or about 3/15. Must reply by May 1 or within 2 week(s) if notified thereafter. **Financial aid:** Priority date 3/2; no closing date. FAFSA, institutional form required. Applicants notified on a rolling basis starting 2/18; must reply by 5/1 or within 2 week(s) of notification.

**Academics.** Students who attend 4 years earn a minor in Biblical Studies upon graduation. **Special study options:** Accelerated study, cooperative education, distance learning, double major, independent study, internships, liberal arts/career combination, study abroad, teacher certification program, Washington semester, Israel semester. **Credit/placement by examination:** AP, CLEP, IB, SAT, ACT, institutional tests. 32 credit hours maximum toward bachelor's degree. **Support services:** Reduced course load, remedial instruction, study skills assistance, tutoring.

**Majors. Biology:** General, environmental. **Business:** Accounting, actuarial science, business admin, finance, management information systems. **Communications:** Media studies, public relations, radio/tv. **Computer sciences:** General. **Education:** General, elementary, ESL, middle, music, physical, science, secondary. **Family/consumer sciences:** General, food/nutrition. **Foreign languages:** Biblical. **Health:** Premedicine. **History:** General. **Interdisciplinary:** Biological/physical sciences, natural sciences. **Legal studies:** Pre-law. **Liberal arts:** Arts/sciences. **Math:** General, applied. **Parks/recreation:** Health/fitness. **Philosophy/religion:** Religion. **Physical sciences:** General. **Social sciences:** Political science, U.S. government. **Theology:** Bible, pastoral counseling, religious ed, sacred music, theology. **Visual/performing arts:** Music management, piano/organ, voice/opera.

**Most popular majors.** Biology 6%, business/marketing 17%, communications/journalism 9%, history 7%, liberal arts 10%, philosophy/religious studies 30%, visual/performing arts 7%.

**Computing on campus.** PC or laptop required. 57 workstations in library, computer center. Dormitories wired for high-speed internet access and linked to campus network. Commuter students can connect to campus network. Online course registration, online library, helpline, repair service, wireless network available.

**Student life. Freshman orientation:** Mandatory. Preregistration for classes offered. 5-day program before start of classes. **Policies:** Emphasis on Godly lifestyle, character and leadership development, service, learning, cross-cultural education. Religious observance required. **Housing:** Single-sex dorms, wellness housing available. $200 fully refundable deposit, deadline 5/2. **Activities:** Bands, campus ministries, choral groups, drama, music ensembles, opera, student government, symphony orchestra, summer missions, outreach team.

**Athletics.** NAIA, NCCAA. **Intercollegiate:** Baseball M, basketball, cross-country, golf M, soccer, tennis W, track and field, volleyball W. **Intramural:** Basketball, football (non-tackle), soccer, volleyball. **Team name:** Mustangs.

**Student services.** Adult student services, chaplain/spiritual director, career counseling, student employment services, financial aid counseling, health services, personal counseling, placement for graduates, veterans' counselor. **Physically disabled:** Services for visually, speech impaired.

**Contact.** E-mail: admissions@masters.edu
Phone: (661) 259-3540 ext. 3362 Toll-free
number: (800) 568-6248 ext. 3362 Fax: (661) 288-1037
Hollie Gorsh, Director of Admissions, The Master's College, 21726
Placerita Canyon Road, Santa Clarita, CA 91321-1200

## Menlo College
**Atherton, California**                                   **CB member**
**www.menlo.edu**                                          **CB code: 4483**

▸ Private 4-year business and liberal arts college
▸ Residential campus in small city
▸ 594 degree-seeking undergraduates: 4% part-time, 36% women, 4% African American, 12% Asian American, 14% Hispanic American, 12% international
▸ 52% of applicants admitted
▸ SAT or ACT (ACT writing optional), application essay required
▸ 62% graduate within 6 years

**General.** Founded in 1927. Regionally accredited. **Degrees:** 99 bachelor's awarded. **ROTC:** Army, Air Force. **Location:** 30 miles from San Francisco, 30 miles from San Jose. **Calendar:** Semester, limited summer session. **Full-time faculty:** 25 total; 92% have terminal degrees, 24% minority, 40% women. **Part-time faculty:** 49 total; 31% have terminal degrees, 22% minority, 49% women. **Class size:** 49% < 20, 51% 20-39.

**Freshman class profile.** 1,492 applied, 772 admitted, 133 enrolled.

| Mid 50% test scores | | | |
|---|---|---|---|
| SAT critical reading: | 420-540 | GPA 2.0-2.99: | 48% |
| SAT math: | 430-560 | Rank in top quarter: | 26% |
| SAT writing: | 420-520 | Rank in top tenth: | 13% |
| ACT composite: | 17-23 | End year in good standing: | 58% |
| GPA 3.75 or higher: | 15% | Return as sophomores: | 64% |
| GPA 3.50-3.74: | 13% | Out-of-state: | 33% |
| GPA 3.0-3.49: | 24% | Live on campus: | 89% |
| | | International: | 8% |

**Basis for selection.** High school record minimum GPA of 2.5, test scores (minimum 1200 SAT, exclusive of Writing, or16 ACT), 1 recommendation, essay, depth of achievement in cocurricular activities considered. **Homeschooled:** Statement describing homeschool structure and mission, transcript of courses and grades, state high school equivalency certificate, letter of recommendation (nonparent) required. **Learning Disabled:** Direct queries to Academic Success Center.

**High school preparation.** College-preparatory program recommended. 15 units required; 24 recommended. Required and recommended units include English 4, mathematics 3, social studies 3, science 3 and foreign language 2.

**2009-2010 Annual costs.** Tuition/fees: $32,120. Room/board: $11,330. Books/supplies: $1,566. Personal expenses: $2,214.

**2009-2010 Financial aid. Need-based:** 101 full-time freshmen applied for aid; 86 were judged to have need; 86 of these received aid. Average need met was 73%. Average scholarship/grant was $25,343; average loan $2,671. 75% of total undergraduate aid awarded as scholarships/grants, 25% as loans/jobs. **Non-need-based:** Awarded to 207 full-time undergraduates, including 48 freshmen. Scholarships awarded for academics.

**Application procedures. Admission:** Priority date 2/1; no deadline. $40 fee, may be waived for applicants with need. Admission notification on a rolling basis beginning on or about 10/1. Must reply by May 1 or within 4 week(s) if notified thereafter. **Financial aid:** Priority date 3/2, closing date 8/1. FAFSA required. Applicants notified on a rolling basis starting 12/15; must reply by 5/1 or within 2 week(s) of notification.

**Academics. Special study options:** Double major, dual enrollment of high school students, ESL, independent study, internships, student-designed major, study abroad. **Credit/placement by examination:** AP, CLEP, IB, institutional tests. 30 credit hours maximum toward bachelor's degree. **Support services:** Learning center, pre-admission summer program, reduced course load, remedial instruction, study skills assistance, tutoring, writing center.

**Majors. Business:** Business admin. **Communications:** General. **Liberal arts:** Arts/sciences.

**Most popular majors.** Business/marketing 68%, communications/journalism 14%, liberal arts 18%.

**Computing on campus.** 135 workstations in library, computer center. Dormitories wired for high-speed internet access and linked to campus network. Commuter students can connect to campus network. Online course registration, online library, helpline, repair service, wireless network available.

**Student life. Freshman orientation:** Mandatory. Preregistration for classes offered. Weekend before classes begin. Workshops for both parents and students. **Housing:** Guaranteed on-campus for all undergraduates. Coed dorms, single-sex dorms, special housing for disabled, wellness housing available. $300 fully refundable deposit, deadline 7/1. **Activities:** Film society, international student organizations, radio station, student government, student newspaper, TV station, International Club, African-American student union, Latino student union, Asia club, Rotaract, Chinese culture research club, Women's club, Alpha Chi Honor Society, French club, Gay Straight Alliance.

**Athletics.** NAIA, NCAA. **Intercollegiate:** Baseball M, basketball, cross-country, football (tackle) M, golf M, soccer, softball W, volleyball W, wrestling. **Intramural:** Basketball M. **Team name:** Oaks.

**Student services.** Career counseling, student employment services; financial aid counseling, personal counseling, placement for graduates, women's services. **Physically disabled:** Services for visually, hearing impaired.

**Contact.** E-mail: admissions@menlo.edu
Phone: (650) 543-3753 Toll-free number: (800) 556-3656
Fax: (650) 543-4496
David Placey, Dean of Enrollment Management, Menlo College, 1000 El Camino Real, Atherton, CA 94027

## Mills College
**Oakland, California**                                   **CB member**
**www.mills.edu**                                          **CB code: 4485**

▸ Private 4-year liberal arts college for women
▸ Residential campus in large city
▸ 914 degree-seeking undergraduates: 5% part-time, 100% women, 9% African American, 7% Asian American, 14% Hispanic American, 1% Native American, 3% international
▸ 580 degree-seeking graduate students
▸ 57% of applicants admitted
▸ SAT or ACT (ACT writing optional), application essay required
▸ 63% graduate within 6 years

**General.** Founded in 1852. Regionally accredited. Cross-registration program with University of California-Berkeley and California College of the Arts. Men admitted to graduate programs. **Degrees:** 236 bachelor's awarded; master's, doctoral offered. **ROTC:** Army. **Location:** 18 miles from San Francisco, 8 miles from Berkeley. **Calendar:** Semester, limited summer session. **Full-time faculty:** 93 total; 88% have terminal degrees, 25% minority, 62% women. **Part-time faculty:** 88 total; 68% have terminal degrees, 25% minority, 70% women. **Class size:** 74% < 20, 23% 20-39, 2% 40-49, 1% 50-99, less than 1% >100. **Special facilities:** Electronic collaborative learning center, center for contemporary music, laboratory children's school for student teachers, institute for civic leadership, center for the book.

**Freshman class profile.** 1,519 applied, 862 admitted, 162 enrolled.

| Mid 50% test scores | | | |
|---|---|---|---|
| SAT critical reading: | 530-650 | GPA 2.0-2.99: | 4% |
| SAT math: | 500-600 | Rank in top quarter: | 76% |
| SAT writing: | 530-630 | Rank in top tenth: | 44% |
| ACT composite: | 22-27 | End year in good standing: | 88% |
| GPA 3.75 or higher: | 45% | Return as sophomores: | 77% |
| GPA 3.50-3.74: | 29% | Out-of-state: | 27% |
| GPA 3.0-3.49: | 22% | Live on campus: | 96% |
| | | International: | 3% |

**Basis for selection.** Minimum 3.0 GPA required, school achievement record most important. All credentials considered. SAT Subject Tests recommended. Interview recommended. **Homeschooled:** Statement describing homeschool structure and mission, state high school equivalency certificate, letter of recommendation (nonparent) required. Must submit SAT Reasoning Test and two Subject Tests, or ACT.

**High school preparation.** Required and recommended units include English 4, mathematics 3-4, social studies 2-4, history 2-4, science 2-4 (laboratory 2), foreign language 2-4, visual/performing arts 2 and academic electives 2.

**2010-2011 Annual costs.** Tuition/fees: $37,605. Room/board: $10,924. Books/supplies: $1,400. Personal expenses: $2,000.

**2009-2010 Financial aid. Need-based:** 183 full-time freshmen applied for aid; 171 were judged to have need; 171 of these received aid. Average need met was 87%. Average scholarship/grant was $27,283; average loan $5,125. 72% of total undergraduate aid awarded as scholarships/grants, 28% as loans/jobs. **Non-need-based:** Awarded to 754 full-time undergraduates, including 166 freshmen. Scholarships awarded for academics, leadership, minority status, music/drama.

**Application procedures. Admission:** Priority date 2/1; deadline 8/1 (postmark date). $50 fee, may be waived for applicants with need. Admission notification on a rolling basis beginning on or about 11/1. Must reply by May 1 or within 2 week(s) if notified thereafter. **Financial aid:** Priority date 2/15; no closing date. FAFSA, institutional form required. Applicants notified on a rolling basis starting 3/1; must reply by 5/1 or within 2 week(s) of notification.

**Academics.** Cooperative bachelor of science in nursing program with Samuel Merritt College; pre-nursing students in this program receive a pre-nursing certificate from Mills upon completion of two years of study. Certificate pre-medicine program available to postbaccalaureate students. BA/MA in Infant Mental Health, BA/Teaching Credential/MA, and BA/MPP (Public Policy) offered. **Special study options:** Combined bachelor's/graduate degree, cross-registration, double major, exchange student, independent study, internships, liberal arts/career combination, student-designed major, study abroad, teacher certification program, Washington semester. **Credit/placement by examination:** AP, CLEP, IB, institutional tests. 8 credit hours maximum toward bachelor's degree. **Support services:** Learning center, pre-admission summer program, reduced course load, remedial instruction, study skills assistance, tutoring, writing center.

**Majors. Area/ethnic studies:** American, Chicano/Hispanic-American/Latino, French, Latin American, women's. **Biology:** General, biochemistry, molecular biochemistry. **Business:** General, managerial economics. **Computer sciences:** General, computer science. **Conservation:** Environmental science, environmental studies. **Engineering:** General. **Family/consumer sciences:** Child development. **Foreign languages:** Comparative lit, French, Spanish. **History:** General, American. **Interdisciplinary:** Biopsychology. **Legal studies:** General. **Liberal arts:** Arts/sciences. **Math:** General. **Philosophy/religion:** Philosophy. **Physical sciences:** Chemistry. **Psychology:** General. **Public administration:** Policy analysis. **Social sciences:** General, anthropology, economics, international relations, political science, sociology, U.S. government. **Visual/performing arts:** Art, art history/conservation, dance, multimedia, studio arts.

**Most popular majors.** Area/ethnic studies 6%, biology 6%, English 14%, foreign language 6%, interdisciplinary studies 11%, psychology 10%, social sciences 15%, visual/performing arts 13%.

**Computing on campus.** 341 workstations in dormitories, library, computer center, student center. Dormitories wired for high-speed internet access and linked to campus network. Commuter students can connect to campus network. Online course registration, online library, helpline, student web hosting, wireless network available.

**Student life. Freshman orientation:** Mandatory. Preregistration for classes offered. 5 days prior to the start of classes. **Policies:** Individual integrity and mutual respect are a foundation of the Mills College learning community. It is the responsibility of every Mills student to know and abide by the standards set forth in the Mills Honor Code. The code also obliges students to report any violations of any of its standards. **Housing:** Guaranteed on-campus for all undergraduates. Special housing for disabled, apartments, cooperative housing, wellness housing available. $150 fully refundable deposit, deadline 6/1. **Activities:** Campus ministries, choral groups, dance, literary magazine, music ensembles, Model UN, radio station, student government, student newspaper, Black Womens Collective, Mujeres Unidas, Asian Pacific Islander Sisterhood Alliance, Muslim Student Association, Pagan Alliance, Workers of Faith, Fem Dems, Vagina Friendly Club, Sisters Inspiring Sisters, Anime Alliance.

**Athletics.** NAIA, NCAA. **Intercollegiate:** Cross-country W, rowing (crew) W, soccer W, swimming W, tennis W, track and field W, volleyball W. **Intramural:** Badminton W, basketball W. **Team name:** Cyclones.

**Student services.** Adult student services, alcohol/substance abuse counseling, chaplain/spiritual director, career counseling, student employment services, financial aid counseling, health services, minority student services, personal counseling, placement for graduates, women's services. **Physically disabled:** Services for visually, speech, hearing impaired. **Learning disabled:** Comprehensive services available.

**Contact.** E-mail: admission@mills.edu
Phone: (510) 430-2135 Toll-free number: (800) 876-4557
Fax: (510) 430-3314
Giulietta Aquino, Dean of Undergraduate Admission, Mills College, 5000 MacArthur Boulevard, Oakland, CA 94613

## Mount St. Mary's College
Los Angeles, California     CB member
www.msmc.la.edu     CB code: 4493

- Private 4-year liberal arts college for women affiliated with Roman Catholic Church
- Residential campus in very large city
- 1,969 degree-seeking undergraduates: 25% part-time, 92% women, 9% African American, 20% Asian American, 48% Hispanic American
- 483 degree-seeking graduate students
- 79% of applicants admitted
- SAT or ACT (ACT writing optional), application essay required
- 62% graduate within 6 years

**General.** Founded in 1925. Regionally accredited. Mount St. Mary's College is primarily a women's college at the undergraduate level, although men are admitted to undergraduate nursing and music programs, graduate division, weekend college and some summer courses. **Degrees:** 327 bachelor's, 197 associate awarded; master's, professional offered. **Location:** 2 miles from Los Angeles. **Calendar:** Semester, limited summer session. **Full-time faculty:** 89 total; 61% have terminal degrees, 26% minority, 78% women. **Part-time faculty:** 263 total; 29% have terminal degrees, 38% minority, 70% women. **Class size:** 69% < 20, 31% 20-39, less than 1% 40-49.

**Freshman class profile.** 1,131 applied, 892 admitted, 371 enrolled.

| Mid 50% test scores | | | |
|---|---|---|---|
| SAT critical reading: | 470-560 | GPA 3.50-3.74: | 15% |
| SAT math: | 450-550 | GPA 3.0-3.49: | 32% |
| SAT writing: | 470-560 | GPA 2.0-2.99: | 35% |
| ACT composite: | 19-23 | Return as sophomores: | 78% |
| GPA 3.75 or higher: | 18% | Live on campus: | 51% |

**Basis for selection.** Primary emphasis on school academic record, then test scores, essay, and letters of recommendation. School and community activities also considered. Interview important. Admission requirements considered very competitive in baccalaureate program. Interviews recommended. Auditions recommended of music majors. Portfolios recommended of art majors. **Homeschooled:** Statement describing homeschool structure and mission, transcript of courses and grades, state high school equivalency certificate, letter of recommendation (nonparent) required. **Learning Disabled:** Documentation of learning disability required.

**High school preparation.** College-preparatory program recommended. 25 units required; 30 recommended. Required and recommended units include English 4, mathematics 2-3, social studies 1-3, history 2, science 2-3 (laboratory 2-3), foreign language 2-3 and academic electives 2-3. For associate degree applicants, required courses include algebra, geometry, American history/government, and 4 units English.

**2010-2011 Annual costs.** Tuition/fees: $30,303. Room/board: $9,830. Books/supplies: $1,638. Personal expenses: $2,500.

**2009-2010 Financial aid. Need-based:** 367 full-time freshmen applied for aid; 367 were judged to have need; 367 of these received aid. Average need met was 92%. Average scholarship/grant was $1,421; average loan $3,496. 59% of total undergraduate aid awarded as scholarships/grants, 41% as loans/jobs. **Non-need-based:** Awarded to 1,284 full-time undergraduates, including 373 freshmen. Scholarships awarded for academics, alumni affiliation.

**Application procedures. Admission:** Closing date 2/15 (postmark date). $40 fee, may be waived for applicants with need. Admission notification on a rolling basis beginning on or about 11/15. Must reply by May 1 or within 2 week(s) if notified thereafter. **Financial aid:** Priority date 2/15; no closing date. FAFSA required. Applicants notified on a rolling basis starting 3/15; must reply by 5/1.

**Academics. Special study options:** Accelerated study, combined bachelor's/graduate degree, cross-registration, double major, exchange student, honors, independent study, internships, student-designed major, study abroad, teacher certification program, United Nations semester, Washington semester, weekend college. **Credit/placement by examination:** CLEP, IB, institutional tests. 24 credit hours maximum toward associate degree, 30 toward bachelor's. **Support services:** Learning center, pre-admission summer program, reduced course load, remedial instruction, study skills assistance, tutoring, writing center.

**Majors. Area/ethnic studies:** American. **Biology:** General, biochemistry. **Business:** General, accounting, business admin, international. **Education:** Elementary, middle, secondary. **Foreign languages:** French, Spanish. **Health:**

Clinical lab technology, health care admin, nursing (RN), predental, premedicine, preveterinary. **History:** General. **Legal studies:** Prelaw. **Math:** General, applied. **Philosophy/religion:** Philosophy, religion. **Physical sciences:** Chemistry. **Psychology:** General. **Social sciences:** General, political science, sociology. **Theology:** Sacred music. **Visual/performing arts:** Music performance, music theory/composition, studio arts. **Other:** Film and social justice.

**Most popular majors.** Business/marketing 6%, education 11%, health sciences 35%, liberal arts 7%, psychology 9%, social sciences 19%.

**Computing on campus.** 168 workstations in dormitories, library, computer center, student center. Dormitories wired for high-speed internet access and linked to campus network. Commuter students can connect to campus network. Online course registration, helpline, student web hosting, wireless network available.

**Student life. Freshman orientation:** Available. Occurs during a weekend, typically in late June. **Policies:** Student resident life largely self-regulated under direction of Residence Council. **Housing:** Guaranteed on-campus for freshmen. $100 fully refundable deposit, deadline 5/1. **Activities:** Campus ministries, choral groups, dance, literary magazine, student government, student newspaper, symphony orchestra, various academic, service, cultural and greek organizations and student clubs available.

**Athletics. Intramural:** Badminton, basketball, golf, soccer, swimming, tennis, volleyball. **Team name:** Athenians.

**Student services.** Adult student services, chaplain/spiritual director, career counseling, student employment services, financial aid counseling, health services, personal counseling, placement for graduates.

**Contact.** E-mail: admissions@msmc.la.edu
Phone: (310) 954-4250 Toll-free number: (800) 999-9893
Fax: (310) 954-4259
Yvonne Berumen, Director of Admissions, Mount St. Mary's College, 12001 Chalon Road, Los Angeles, CA 90049

## Mt. Sierra College
### Monrovia, California
### www.mtsierra.edu
CB code: 3090

- For-profit 3-year visual arts and technical college
- Commuter campus in large city
- 467 degree-seeking undergraduates
- Application essay, interview required

**General.** Accredited by ACCSC. **Degrees:** 74 bachelor's awarded. **Location:** 20 miles from Los Angeles. **Calendar:** Quarter, extensive summer session. **Full-time faculty:** 12 total. **Part-time faculty:** 59 total. **Class size:** 98% < 20, 2% 20-39. **Special facilities:** Green-screen room for special effects video, sound room, mac and game arts computer labs.

**Basis for selection.** Open admission. High school graduates accepted upon the basis of writing, math, online assessments, and high school and/or college GPA. **Homeschooled:** Transcript of courses and grades, state high school equivalency certificate, interview required.

**2009-2010 Annual costs.** Tuition/fees: $14,840. Additional lab fees may apply. Fees vary by program. Books/supplies: $2,000.

**Application procedures. Admission:** No deadline. $50 fee, may be waived for applicants with need. Admission notification on a rolling basis. **Financial aid:** FAFSA required.

**Academics. Special study options:** Accelerated study, distance learning, independent study, weekend college. **Credit/placement by examination:** AP, CLEP, IB, institutional tests. **Support services:** Learning center, study skills assistance, tutoring.

**Majors. Business:** Business admin, entrepreneurial studies. **Computer sciences:** General, game design, information technology, networking, security, web page design. **Visual/performing arts:** Digital art, graphic design, multimedia.

**Most popular majors.** Business/marketing 14%, computer/information sciences 39%, visual/performing arts 47%.

**Computing on campus.** PC or laptop required. 35 workstations in library, computer center. Commuter students can connect to campus network. Online library, wireless network available.

**Student life. Freshman orientation:** Available. Preregistration for classes offered. Held prior to class start dates. Date of orientations are announced. **Activities:** Student newspaper.

**Student services.** Placement for graduates.

**Contact.** E-mail: pazadian@mtsierra.edu
Phone: (626) 873-2100 Toll-free number: (888) 828-8800
Fax: (626) 359-1378
Patrick Azadian, Director of Admissions, Mt. Sierra College, 101 East Huntington Drive, Monrovia, CA 91016

## National Hispanic University
### San Jose, California
### www.nhu.edu
CB code: 4593

- Private 4-year university
- Commuter campus in very large city
- 405 degree-seeking undergraduates
- 190 graduate students
- 37% of applicants admitted
- Application essay required
- 32% graduate within 6 years

**General.** Regionally accredited. **Degrees:** 29 bachelor's, 2 associate awarded. **Calendar:** Semester, limited summer session. **Full-time faculty:** 11 total; 46% have terminal degrees, 27% minority, 18% women. **Part-time faculty:** 65 total; 48% minority, 52% women. **Class size:** 67% < 20, 33% 20-39.

**Freshman class profile.** 312 applied, 114 admitted, 79 enrolled.

**Basis for selection.** High school GPA, transcript, two letters of recommendation required. **Homeschooled:** State high school equivalency certificate required.

**2009-2010 Annual costs.** Tuition/fees: $8,000. Books/supplies: $1,638. Personal expenses: $2,826.

**2008-2009 Financial aid. Non-need-based:** Scholarships awarded for academics.

**Application procedures. Admission:** No deadline. $50 fee, may be waived for applicants with need. Application must be submitted on paper. Admission notification on a rolling basis. **Financial aid:** No deadline. FAFSA required.

**Academics. Special study options:** Cross-registration, independent study, teacher certification program. **Credit/placement by examination:** CLEP, IB, institutional tests. **Support services:** Learning center, remedial instruction, study skills assistance, tutoring, writing center.

**Majors. Business:** Business admin. **Computer sciences:** General. **Liberal arts:** Arts/sciences.

**Most popular majors.** Business/marketing 41%, liberal arts 55%.

**Computing on campus.** 223 workstations in library, computer center, student center. Online library, wireless network available.

**Student life. Freshman orientation:** Mandatory. Preregistration for classes offered. **Activities:** Student government.

**Student services.** Financial aid counseling.

**Contact.** Phone: (408) 273-2696 Fax: (408) 254-1369
Pamela Bustillo, Director of Admissions/Registrar, National Hispanic University, 14271 Story Road, San Jose, CA 95127-3823

## National University
### La Jolla, California
### www.nu.edu
CB member
CB code: 0470

- Private 4-year university
- Commuter campus in very large city
- 7,756 degree-seeking undergraduates: 75% part-time, 61% women, 11% African American, 10% Asian American, 19% Hispanic American, 1% Native American, 2% international
- 17,634 degree-seeking graduate students
- Interview required
- 31% graduate within 6 years

**General.** Founded in 1971. Regionally accredited. Campuses in 11 major cities throughout California; courses offered both on-site and online. **Degrees:** 1,115 bachelor's, 86 associate awarded; master's offered. **ROTC:** Army, Naval, Air Force. **Calendar:** Continuous, limited summer session.

**Full-time faculty:** 235 total; 80% have terminal degrees, 25% minority, 47% women. **Part-time faculty:** 2,714 total; 23% have terminal degrees, 32% minority, 51% women. **Class size:** 71% < 20, 28% 20-39, less than 1% 40-49, less than 1% 50-99. **Special facilities:** Nursing labs, forensics labs, e-book collection.

**Freshman class profile.** 2,204 applied, 2,204 admitted, 865 enrolled.

**Out-of-state:** 11%    **International:** 6%

**Basis for selection.** Open admission, but selective for some programs. Interview, previous business and work experience, academic record considered.

**2009-2010 Annual costs.** Tuition/fees: $10,728. Books/supplies: $1,456. Personal expenses: $3,260.

**2008-2009 Financial aid. Need-based:** 30% of total undergraduate aid awarded as scholarships/grants, 70% as loans/jobs.

**Application procedures. Admission:** No deadline. $60 fee. Admission notification on a rolling basis. **Financial aid:** No deadline. FAFSA, institutional form required. Applicants notified on a rolling basis.

**Academics.** Agreements with over 950 public and private schools to place students earning teaching credentials in practicums. **Special study options:** Accelerated study, cross-registration, distance learning, double major, ESL, independent study, internships, liberal arts/career combination, teacher certification program. **Credit/placement by examination:** CLEP, institutional tests. 14 credit hours maximum toward associate degree, 23 toward bachelor's. **Support services:** Learning center, remedial instruction, tutoring, writing center.

**Majors. Area/ethnic studies:** Chinese, Near/Middle Eastern. **Business:** General, accounting, business admin, construction management, finance, hospitality admin, human resources, operations, organizational behavior. **Communications:** Broadcast journalism, digital media, journalism, media studies, radio/tv. **Computer sciences:** General, computer science, game design, information systems, information technology, security, system admin, systems analysis. **Conservation:** Environmental science, management/policy. **Education:** Early childhood, mathematics, multi-level teacher, secondary. **Engineering:** Construction, systems. **Engineering technology:** Civil drafting, industrial management. **Family/consumer sciences:** Child development. **Foreign languages:** American Sign Language, Arabic, Chinese, Persian. **Health:** Health care admin, nursing (RN), preop/surgical nursing. **History:** General. **Interdisciplinary:** Biological/physical sciences, global studies, intercultural. **Legal studies:** General. **Liberal arts:** Arts/sciences. **Math:** General. **Physical sciences:** General, geology. **Protective services:** Criminal justice, law enforcement admin, security services. **Psychology:** General. **Public administration:** General. **Social sciences:** Economics, sociology. **Visual/performing arts:** Multimedia.

**Most popular majors.** Business/marketing 24%, computer/information sciences 9%, education 12%, interdisciplinary studies 8%, legal studies 12%, liberal arts 8%, psychology 10%.

**Computing on campus.** 3,100 workstations in library, computer center, student center. Commuter students can connect to campus network. Online course registration, online library, helpline, wireless network available.

**Student life. Freshman orientation:** Available. Preregistration for classes offered.

**Student services.** Adult student services, career counseling, services for economically disadvantaged, student employment services, financial aid counseling, minority student services, placement for graduates, veterans' counselor. **Physically disabled:** Services for visually, speech, hearing impaired.

**Contact.** E-mail: advisor@nu.edu
Phone: (800) 628-8648 Toll-free number: (800) 628-8648
Fax: (858) 541-7792
Dominick Giovanniello, Associate Regional Dean - San Diego, National University, 11255 North Torrey Pines Road, La Jolla, CA 92037-1011

## NewSchool of Architecture & Design
**San Diego, California**
**www.newschoolarch.edu**    CB code: 2419

▶ For-profit 5-year visual arts and liberal arts college
▶ Commuter campus in very large city
▶ 352 degree-seeking undergraduates
▶ Interview required

**General.** Founded in 1980. Accredited by ACICS. **Degrees:** 38 bachelor's awarded; master's offered. **Location:** 90 miles from Los Angeles, 17 miles

from Tijuana, Mexico. **Calendar:** Quarter, extensive summer session. **Full-time faculty:** 17 total. **Part-time faculty:** 53 total. **Special facilities:** Design clinic.

**Freshman class profile.** 25 applied, 25 admitted, 25 enrolled.

**Basis for selection.** Open admission. Resume considered if submitted. Portfolio review required.

**2009-2010 Annual costs.** Tuition/fees: $21,225. Books/supplies: $2,775. Personal expenses: $2,754.

**2009-2010 Financial aid. Non-need-based:** Scholarships awarded for academics.

**Application procedures. Admission:** No deadline. $75 fee, may be waived for applicants with need. Admission notification on a rolling basis. Must reply by May 1 or within 4 week(s) if notified thereafter. **Financial aid:** No deadline. FAFSA required. Applicants notified on a rolling basis.

**Academics. Special study options:** Accelerated study, cooperative education, double major, internships, liberal arts/career combination. Cooperative program available at nearby U.S. International University, where students can take ESL and general education classes. **Credit/placement by examination:** CLEP. **Support services:** Pre-admission summer program, tutoring.

**Majors. Architecture:** Architecture.

**Computing on campus.** 17 workstations in library, computer center.

**Student life. Freshman orientation:** Available. Preregistration for classes offered. Held 1-2 days before start of classes in fall. **Housing:** Some housing through US International University. **Activities:** Literary magazine, student government, student newspaper, American Institute of Architects student chapter.

**Student services.** Career counseling, student employment services, health services, personal counseling, placement for graduates, veterans' counselor.

**Contact.** E-mail: admissions@newschoolarch.edu
Phone: (619) 235-4100 Fax: (619) 235-4651
Elizabeth O'Brien, Director of Admissions, NewSchool of Architecture & Design, 1249 F Street, San Diego, CA 92101

## Northwestern Polytechnic University
**Fremont, California**
**www.npu.edu**    CB code: 4335

▶ Private 4-year business and engineering college
▶ Commuter campus in small city
▶ 218 degree-seeking undergraduates: 4% part-time, 41% women, 98% Asian American
▶ 1,327 degree-seeking graduate students

**General.** Accredited by ACICS. **Degrees:** 18 bachelor's awarded; master's, doctoral offered. **Location:** 42 miles from San Francisco, 7 miles from San Jose. **Calendar:** Trimester, extensive summer session. **Full-time faculty:** 19 total. **Part-time faculty:** 58 total. **Class size:** 62% < 20, 38% 20-39.

**Basis for selection.** High school record, pre-calculus required. Recommendations and test scores as reference. Interview recommended. English placement exams are given to international students who do not provide standardized English test scores. On-campus English placement exam may replace TOEFL; on-campus freshman exam may replace SAT. Standardized test administered by ETS or on-campus equivalent assessment test acceptable. The test score does not affect the student's admission to the program.

**High school preparation.** College-preparatory program required. Required and recommended units include English 3, mathematics 2, social studies 1 and science 1. 1 math required for business programs.

**2010-2011 Annual costs.** Tuition/fees: $9,140. Books/supplies: $800.

**Financial aid. Additional information:** Work-study, co-op program, internships available. Employment opportunities with local engineering firms help defray costs.

**Application procedures. Admission:** Priority date 8/2; deadline 9/7 (postmark date). $60 fee. Admission notification on a rolling basis. Must reply by 9/7.

**Academics.** Curricula designed to meet needs of high-tech industries and global businesses. **Special study options:** ESL. **Credit/placement by examination:** AP, CLEP, IB, institutional tests. 15 credit hours maximum toward bachelor's degree. **Support services:** Learning center, tutoring.

**Majors. Business:** Business admin. **Engineering:** Electrical, software, systems.

**Most popular majors.** Business/marketing 63%, engineering/engineering technologies 37%.

**Computing on campus.** 250 workstations in library, computer center, student center. Dormitories wired for high-speed internet access. Commuter students can connect to campus network. Online library, helpline, repair service, student web hosting, wireless network available.

**Student life. Freshman orientation:** Mandatory. Preregistration for classes offered. One-day program before start of classes. **Policies:** Students are required to join student association, and encouraged to join student clubs. **Housing:** Apartments, wellness housing available. $300 fully refundable deposit, deadline 8/1. **Activities:** Dance, international student organizations, literary magazine, music ensembles, Model UN, student government.

**Athletics. Intercollegiate:** Table tennis. **Intramural:** Table tennis.

**Student services.** Adult student services, career counseling, services for economically disadvantaged, student employment services, personal counseling, placement for graduates, veterans' counselor.

**Contact.** E-mail: admission@npu.edu
Phone: (510) 592-9688 ext. 8 Fax: (510) 657-8975
Shilpa Eguvanti, Director of Admission, Northwestern Polytechnic University, 47671 Westinghouse Drive, Fremont, CA 94539

## Notre Dame de Namur University
**Belmont, California** — CB member
**www.ndnu.edu** — CB code: 4063

- Private 4-year university and liberal arts college affiliated with Roman Catholic Church
- Residential campus in large town
- 873 degree-seeking undergraduates: 40% part-time, 66% women, 8% African American, 15% Asian American, 25% Hispanic American, 1% Native American, 2% international
- 480 degree-seeking graduate students
- 79% of applicants admitted
- SAT or ACT with writing, application essay required
- 59% graduate within 6 years

**General.** Founded in 1851. Regionally accredited. **Degrees:** 189 bachelor's awarded; master's offered. **Location:** 19 miles from San Francisco. **Calendar:** Semester, limited summer session. **Full-time faculty:** 55 total; 91% have terminal degrees, 26% minority, 51% women. **Part-time faculty:** 113 total; 16% minority, 66% women. **Class size:** 70% < 20, 29% 20-39, 2% 40-49.

**Freshman class profile.** 998 applied, 791 admitted, 116 enrolled.

| Mid 50% test scores | | | |
|---|---|---|---|
| SAT critical reading: | 420-540 | GPA 3.0-3.49: | 21% |
| SAT math: | 420-520 | GPA 2.0-2.99: | 64% |
| SAT writing: | 410-510 | Return as sophomores: | 67% |
| ACT composite: | 17-21 | Out-of-state: | 25% |
| GPA 3.75 or higher: | 4% | Live on campus: | 92% |
| GPA 3.50-3.74: | 10% | International: | 5% |

**Basis for selection.** High school record and GPA most important; test scores also important. Essay, recommendation, and school and community activities considered. **Homeschooled:** Statement describing homeschool structure and mission, transcript of courses and grades, state high school equivalency certificate, interview, letter of recommendation (nonparent) required.

**High school preparation.** College-preparatory program recommended. 15 units required; 18 recommended. Required and recommended units include English 4, mathematics 2-3, social studies 2, history 1, science 1-2 (laboratory 1), foreign language 2-3 and academic electives 3. 3 additional units from fine arts, advanced laboratory science, advanced mathematics, or advanced foreign language also recommended.

**2010-2011 Annual costs.** Tuition/fees: $28,480. Room and board charges are based on Double Room/Triple Apartment and 19 meals per week for two semesters. Room/board: $11,720. Books/supplies: $1,560. Personal expenses: $3,150.

**2009-2010 Financial aid. Need-based:** 95 full-time freshmen applied for aid; 91 were judged to have need; 91 of these received aid. Average need met was 69%. **Non-need-based:** Awarded to 19 full-time undergraduates, including 4 freshmen. Scholarships awarded for academics, alumni affiliation, athletics, leadership, music/drama, religious affiliation.

**Application procedures. Admission:** Priority date 2/1; no deadline. $50 fee, may be waived for applicants with need. Admission notification on a rolling basis. Must reply by May 1 or within 3 week(s) if notified thereafter. **Financial aid:** Priority date 3/2; no closing date. FAFSA required. CSS PROFILE accepted but not required. Applicants notified on a rolling basis starting 1/15.

**Academics. Special study options:** Accelerated study, double major, ESL, exchange student, independent study, internships, liberal arts/career combination, student-designed major, study abroad, teacher certification program. **Credit/placement by examination:** AP, CLEP, IB, institutional tests. 30 credit hours maximum toward bachelor's degree. Units earned by examination cannot be used in satisfying the 30-unit residency requirement. **Support services:** Learning center, reduced course load, remedial instruction, study skills assistance, tutoring, writing center.

**Majors. Biology:** General, biochemistry. **Business:** Business admin. **Communications:** General. **Computer sciences:** General. **Health:** Predental, premedicine, prepharmacy, preveterinary. **History:** General. **Legal studies:** Prelaw. **Liberal arts:** Arts/sciences. **Parks/recreation:** Exercise sciences. **Philosophy/religion:** Philosophy, religion. **Psychology:** General. **Public administration:** Human services. **Social sciences:** General, political science, sociology. **Visual/performing arts:** Art, dramatic, graphic design, music performance, studio arts, voice/opera.

**Most popular majors.** Biology 8%, business/marketing 26%, English 7%, liberal arts 14%, psychology 8%, public administration/social services 13%, social sciences 7%, visual/performing arts 7%.

**Computing on campus.** 85 workstations in library, computer center. Dormitories wired for high-speed internet access and linked to campus network. Commuter students can connect to campus network. Helpline, student web hosting, wireless network available.

**Student life. Freshman orientation:** Mandatory, $160 fee. Preregistration for classes offered. 1 week preceding opening of classes. **Housing:** Guaranteed on-campus for freshmen. Coed dorms, apartments available. $200 nonrefundable deposit. **Activities:** Campus ministries, choral groups, dance, drama, international student organizations, literary magazine, music ensembles, musical theater, opera, student government, student newspaper, Hawaiian club, business/career club, Filipino club, Alianza Latina, Black Student Union, outdoor activities club, Amnesty International, science and medical careers club.

**Athletics.** NCAA. **Intercollegiate:** Basketball, cross-country, golf M, lacrosse M, soccer, softball W, tennis W, volleyball W. **Team name:** Argonauts.

**Student services.** Adult student services, alcohol/substance abuse counseling, chaplain/spiritual director, career counseling, student employment services, financial aid counseling, health services, personal counseling, placement for graduates. **Learning disabled:** Comprehensive services available.

**Contact.** E-mail: admiss@ndnu.edu
Phone: (650) 508-3600 Toll-free number: (800) 263-0545
Fax: (650) 508-3426
Rejeetha Gort, Director of Admissions, Notre Dame de Namur University, 1500 Ralston Avenue, Belmont, CA 94002-1908

## Occidental College
**Los Angeles, California** — CB member
**www.oxy.edu** — CB code: 4581

- Private 4-year liberal arts college affiliated with nondenominational tradition
- Residential campus in very large city
- 1,959 degree-seeking undergraduates: 1% part-time, 56% women, 6% African American, 16% Asian American, 13% Hispanic American, 1% Native American, 1% international
- 12 degree-seeking graduate students
- 44% of applicants admitted
- SAT or ACT with writing, application essay required
- 85% graduate within 6 years

**General.** Founded in 1887. Regionally accredited. **Degrees:** 440 bachelor's awarded; master's offered. **ROTC:** Army, Air Force. **Location:** 5 miles from downtown. **Calendar:** Semester. **Full-time faculty:** 163 total;

93% have terminal degrees, 31% minority, 47% women. **Part-time faculty:** 90 total; 27% minority, 40% women. **Class size:** 64% < 20, 34% 20-39, less than 1% 40-49, less than 1% 50-99. **Special facilities:** Film lab, print studio, marine biology with scuba access, plasma physics and fluid dynamics labs, ornithology collection, geological collection, astronomical instruments collection, vivarium, greenhouses.

**Freshman class profile.** 5,924 applied, 2,583 admitted, 576 enrolled.

| Mid 50% test scores | | | |
|---|---|---|---|
| SAT critical reading: | 600-700 | GPA 2.0-2.99: | 2% |
| SAT math: | 600-680 | Rank in top quarter: | 90% |
| SAT writing: | 610-700 | Rank in top tenth: | 59% |
| ACT composite: | 28-32 | Return as sophomores: | 91% |
| GPA 3.75 or higher: | 36% | Out-of-state: | 54% |
| GPA 3.50-3.74: | 31% | Live on campus: | 100% |
| GPA 3.0-3.49: | 31% | International: | 1% |

**Basis for selection.** Primary consideration given to academic credentials and holistic qualities such as intellectual curiosity, out-of-class interests, and personal character. SAT Subject Tests recommended. Interview recommended. **Homeschooled:** Statement describing homeschool structure and mission, transcript of courses and grades, state high school equivalency certificate, letter of recommendation (nonparent) required. At least 2 SAT Subject Tests recommended.

**High school preparation.** College-preparatory program required. 20 units recommended. Recommended units include English 4, mathematics 4, social studies 2, history 2, science 3 (laboratory 2), foreign language 3 and academic electives 2.

**2009-2010 Annual costs.** Tuition/fees: $38,922. Room/board: $10,780. Books/supplies: $1,054. Personal expenses: $1,397.

**2008-2009 Financial aid. Need-based:** 322 full-time freshmen applied for aid; 255 were judged to have need; 253 of these received aid. Average need met was 100%. Average scholarship/grant was $28,936; average loan $4,827. 77% of total undergraduate aid awarded as scholarships/grants, 23% as loans/jobs. **Non-need-based:** Awarded to 460 full-time undergraduates, including 124 freshmen. Scholarships awarded for academics, leadership, music/drama, state residency.

**Application procedures. Admission:** Closing date 1/10 (postmark date). $50 fee, may be waived for applicants with need. Admission notification 4/1. Must reply by May 1 or within 2 week(s) if notified thereafter. **Financial aid:** Closing date 2/1. FAFSA, CSS PROFILE required. Applicants notified by 4/1; must reply by 5/1.

**Academics. Special study options:** Combined bachelor's/graduate degree, cross-registration, double major, honors, independent study, internships, student-designed major, study abroad, United Nations semester. Richter Fellowships for international research, summer research program, endowment investment management program (Blyth Fund). **Credit/placement by examination:** AP, CLEP, IB, institutional tests. **Support services:** Learning center, pre-admission summer program, study skills assistance, tutoring, writing center.

**Majors. Area/ethnic studies:** American, Asian. **Biology:** General, biochemistry. **Foreign languages:** General, French, Spanish. **History:** General. **Interdisciplinary:** Cognitive science. **Math:** General. **Parks/recreation:** Exercise sciences. **Philosophy/religion:** Philosophy, religion. **Physical sciences:** Chemistry, geology, geophysics, physics. **Psychology:** General. **Social sciences:** Economics, international relations, political science, sociology. **Visual/performing arts:** Art, art history/conservation, dramatic. **Other:** Critical theory and social justice.

**Most popular majors.** Biology 11%, English 6%, physical sciences 7%, psychology 6%, social sciences 38%, visual/performing arts 8%.

**Computing on campus.** 300 workstations in dormitories, library, computer center. Dormitories linked to campus network. Commuter students can connect to campus network. Online course registration, online library, helpline, wireless network available.

**Student life. Freshman orientation:** Mandatory. Preregistration for classes offered. Held one week in August before the start of classes. Prior to Orientation, students can choose to participate in one of three experiences: a wilderness trip; community service program; or arts and culture in Los Angeles. **Policies:** All residence halls student-run; freshmen, sophomores and juniors are required to live on campus. **Housing:** Guaranteed on-campus for freshmen. Coed dorms, single-sex dorms, fraternity/sorority housing, wellness housing available. **Activities:** Bands, choral groups, dance, drama, film society, international student organizations, literary magazine, music ensembles, musical theater, radio station, student government, student newspaper, symphony orchestra, more than 80 clubs and organizations available.

**Athletics. NCAA. Intercollegiate:** Baseball M, basketball, cross-country, diving, football (tackle) M, golf, lacrosse W, soccer, softball W, swimming, tennis, track and field, volleyball W, water polo. **Intramural:** Basketball, football (non-tackle), volleyball. **Team name:** Tigers.

**Student services.** Adult student services, alcohol/substance abuse counseling, chaplain/spiritual director, career counseling, services for economically disadvantaged, financial aid counseling, health services, minority student services, on-campus daycare, personal counseling, women's services. **Physically disabled:** Services for hearing impaired.

**Contact.** E-mail: admission@oxy.edu
Phone: (323) 259-2700 Toll-free number: (800) 825-5262
Fax: (323) 341-4875
Vince Cuseo, Dean of Admission, Occidental College, 1600 Campus Road, Los Angeles, CA 90041

## Otis College of Art and Design

**Los Angeles, California**   CB member
**www.otis.edu**   CB code: 4394

- Private 4-year visual arts college
- Commuter campus in very large city
- 1,150 degree-seeking undergraduates: 1% part-time, 68% women, 3% African American, 32% Asian American, 13% Hispanic American, 16% international
- 68 degree-seeking graduate students
- 44% of applicants admitted
- SAT or ACT (ACT writing optional), application essay required
- 52% graduate within 6 years

**General.** Founded in 1918. Regionally accredited. **Degrees:** 221 bachelor's awarded; master's offered. **Calendar:** Semester, limited summer session. **Full-time faculty:** 56 total; 9% have terminal degrees, 16% minority, 57% women. **Part-time faculty:** 222 total; 4% have terminal degrees, 16% minority, 47% women. **Class size:** 78% < 20, 20% 20-39, less than 1% 40-49, less than 1% 50-99. **Special facilities:** Rare art books collection, full foundry and casting facilities, photographic darkroom, fully equipped print-making studio, fine art book press room, wood and metal working shops, toy design department, digital imaging studio.

**Freshman class profile.** 1,634 applied, 714 admitted, 171 enrolled.

| Mid 50% test scores | | | |
|---|---|---|---|
| SAT critical reading: | 450-560 | GPA 3.50-3.74: | 15% |
| SAT math: | 450-590 | GPA 3.0-3.49: | 31% |
| SAT writing: | 450-570 | GPA 2.0-2.99: | 41% |
| ACT composite: | 19-24 | Out-of-state: | 32% |
| GPA 3.75 or higher: | 12% | Live on campus: | 58% |
| | | International: | 15% |

**Basis for selection.** Portfolio most important, followed by school achievement record, essay and test scores. Activities, leadership, motivation also considered. Portfolio required. Interview recommended. **Homeschooled:** Documentation that student has solid academic foundation, is socially and intellectually mature, and has passion for the arts.

**High school preparation.** Required and recommended units include English 4, mathematics 3-4, social studies 1-2, history 2-3, science 2-4 (laboratory 1-4) and foreign language 2. Drawing and as much art as possible recommended.

**2009-2010 Annual costs.** Tuition/fees: $32,060. Books/supplies: $1,400. Personal expenses: $1,300.

**2009-2010 Financial aid. Need-based:** 149 full-time freshmen applied for aid; 121 were judged to have need; 121 of these received aid. Average need met was 49%. Average scholarship/grant was $15,662; average loan $3,351. 63% of total undergraduate aid awarded as scholarships/grants, 37% as loans/jobs. **Non-need-based:** Awarded to 325 full-time undergraduates, including 61 freshmen. Scholarships awarded for academics, art.

**Application procedures. Admission:** Priority date 2/15; no deadline. $50 fee, may be waived for applicants with need. Admission notification on a rolling basis beginning on or about 12/15. Must reply by May 1 or within 2 week(s) if notified thereafter. **Financial aid:** Priority date 2/15; no closing date. FAFSA required. Applicants notified by 3/1; Applicants notified on a rolling basis starting 3/1; must reply within 2 week(s) of notification.

**Academics.** Approximately one-third of curriculum consists of liberal arts classes. **Special study options:** Cooperative education, ESL, exchange student, honors, internships, study abroad, teacher certification program. **Credit/placement by examination:** AP, CLEP, IB, institutional tests. **Support services:** Pre-admission summer program, reduced course load, remedial instruction, study skills assistance, tutoring.

**Majors. Architecture:** Architecture, environmental design, interior, landscape. **Communications technology:** Animation/special effects. **Visual/performing arts:** Art, design, fashion design, graphic design, illustration, industrial design, interior design, multimedia, painting, photography, sculpture, studio arts.

**Most popular majors.** Visual/performing arts 95%.

**Computing on campus.** 350 workstations in library, computer center. Helpline, wireless network available.

**Student life. Freshman orientation:** Mandatory. Orientation held in January and August. **Housing:** Apartments available. $550 nonrefundable deposit, deadline 6/1. Otis sponsored off-campus apartments available. **Activities:** International student organizations, student government, literary organization, Campus Crusade.

**Student services.** Adult student services, alcohol/substance abuse counseling, career counseling, student employment services, financial aid counseling, personal counseling, placement for graduates. **Physically disabled:** Services for hearing impaired.

**Contact.** E-mail: admissions@otis.edu
Phone: (310) 665-6820 Toll-free number: (800) 527-6847
Fax: (310) 665-6821
Marc Meredith, Dean of Admissions, Otis College of Art and Design, 9045 Lincoln Boulevard, Los Angeles, CA 90045-9785

## Pacific Oaks College
**Pasadena, California**
www.pacificoaks.edu                                       CB code: 0482

- Private two-year upper-division teachers college
- Commuter campus in small city
- Application essay required

**General.** Founded in 1951. Regionally accredited. College and children's school founded by Quaker families as community education center. **Degrees:** 95 bachelor's awarded; master's offered. **Articulation:** Agreements with De Anza College, Glendale City College, College of the Canyons, Pasadena City College, Rio Hondo College, Santa Monica College, Santa Barbara College, East Los Angeles College, El Camino College, Mt. San Antonio College, Citrus College. **Location:** 10 miles from downtown Los Angeles. **Calendar:** Semester, limited summer session. **Full-time faculty:** 27 total; 52% have terminal degrees, 33% minority, 59% women. **Part-time faculty:** 101 total. **Class size:** 72% < 20, 28% 20-39.

**Student profile.** 84 degree-seeking undergraduates.

| Out-of-state: | 19% | 25 or older: | 94% |
|---|---|---|---|

**Basis for selection.** College transcript, application essay required. Must have completed equivalent of GED. Transfer accepted as juniors, seniors.

**2009-2010 Annual costs.** Tuition/fees: $26,100. Books/supplies: $1,638. Personal expenses: $3,096.

**Financial aid.** All financial aid based on need.

**Application procedures. Admission:** Priority date 4/15; deadline 6/1. $55 fee, may be waived for applicants with need. Application must be submitted on paper.

**Academics. Special study options:** Accelerated study, distance learning, independent study, internships, teacher certification program, weekend college. **Credit/placement by examination:** CLEP. 30 credit hours maximum toward bachelor's degree. Students age 30-35 without a bachelor's degree may earn credit based on life experience.

**Majors. Family/consumer sciences:** Family studies.

**Computing on campus.** 17 workstations in library, computer center. Online library available.

**Student life. Activities:** Teacher education student association; marriage, family therapy student association.

**Student services.** Adult student services, career counseling, financial aid counseling. **Physically disabled:** Services for visually, speech, hearing impaired.

**Contact.** E-mail: admissions@pacificoaks.edu
Phone: (626) 397-1349 Toll-free number: (800) 684-0900
Fax: (626) 666-1220
Augusta Pickens, Director of Admissions, Pacific Oaks College, 5 Westmoreland Place, Pasadena, CA 91103

## Pacific States University
**Los Angeles, California**
www.psuca.edu                                       CB code: 3547

- Private 4-year university
- Commuter campus in very large city
- 13 degree-seeking undergraduates: 54% women
- 160 degree-seeking graduate students

**General.** Accredited by ACICS. **Degrees:** 14 bachelor's awarded; master's, doctoral offered. **Location:** 5 miles from downtown. **Calendar:** Quarter, limited summer session. **Full-time faculty:** 7 total; 57% have terminal degrees, 100% minority, 14% women. **Part-time faculty:** 23 total; 44% have terminal degrees, 100% minority, 17% women.

**Freshman class profile.**

| Live on campus: | 10% | International: | 92% |
|---|---|---|---|

**Basis for selection.** Open admission, but selective for some programs. High school diploma and English proficiency required. TOEFL required of students whose native language is not English. **Homeschooled:** Transcript of courses and grades, state high school equivalency certificate required.

**2010-2011 Annual costs.** Tuition/fees (projected): $17,640. Books/supplies: $2,160.

**Financial aid. Non-need-based:** Scholarships awarded for academics.

**Application procedures. Admission:** No deadline. $100 fee. Application must be submitted on paper. Admission notification on a rolling basis. **Financial aid:** No deadline. FAFSA, institutional form required.

**Academics. Special study options:** Combined bachelor's/graduate degree, distance learning, double major, ESL, liberal arts/career combination. **Credit/placement by examination:** CLEP, IB. 8 credit hours maximum toward bachelor's degree.

**Majors. Business:** Accounting, management information systems, marketing. **Computer sciences:** General.

**Computing on campus.** 60 workstations in dormitories, library, computer center. Dormitories wired for high-speed internet access. Online library, wireless network available.

**Student life. Freshman orientation:** Available. Preregistration for classes offered. Held 2 weeks after each quarter starts, lasting 2 hours. **Housing:** Guaranteed on-campus for all undergraduates. Coed dorms, wellness housing available. **Activities:** Literary magazine, TV station.

**Student services.** Student employment services, financial aid counseling, personal counseling.

**Contact.** E-mail: admissions@psuca.edu
Phone: (323) 731-2383 ext. 203 Toll-free number: (888) 200-0383
Fax: (323) 731-7276
Seohee Yang, Admission Advisor, Pacific States University, 1516 South Western Avenue, Los Angeles, CA 90006

## Pacific Union College
**Angwin, California**
www.puc.edu                                       CB code: 4600

- Private 4-year liberal arts college affiliated with Seventh-day Adventists
- Residential campus in small town
- 1,515 degree-seeking undergraduates: 10% part-time, 56% women, 5% African American, 23% Asian American, 18% Hispanic American, 1% Native American, 5% international
- 71% of applicants admitted
- SAT or ACT (ACT writing recommended) required

**General.** Founded in 1882. Regionally accredited. **Degrees:** 196 bachelor's, 96 associate awarded; master's offered. **Location:** 30 miles from Napa, 75 miles from San Francisco. **Calendar:** Quarter, limited summer session. **Full-time faculty:** 81 total; 53% have terminal degrees, 24% minority, 41% women. **Part-time faculty:** 10 total; 40% have terminal degrees, 30% minority, 70% women. **Class size:** 69% < 20, 24% 20-39, 3% 40-49, 4% 50-99, less than 1% >100. **Special facilities:** Observatory, airport/flight training, biology museum, Pitcairn Island Study Center, 1500-acre nature preserve.

**Freshman class profile.** 824 applied, 586 admitted, 346 enrolled.

| Mid 50% test scores | | | | |
|---|---|---|---|---|
| SAT critical reading: | 460-580 | GPA 3.0-3.49: | | 31% |
| SAT math: | 440-570 | GPA 2.0-2.99: | | 29% |
| ACT composite: | 17-24 | Out-of-state: | | 18% |
| GPA 3.75 or higher: | 25% | Live on campus: | | 89% |
| GPA 3.50-3.74: | 14% | International: | | 6% |

**Basis for selection.** Minimum GPA of 2.3 and acceptable recommendations. **Homeschooled:** Transcript of courses and grades, state high school equivalency certificate, letter of recommendation (nonparent) required. **Learning Disabled:** Documentation if available.

**High school preparation.** 8 units required. Required and recommended units include English 4, mathematics 2-3, history 1-2, science 1-3 and foreign language 2. Computer literacy strongly recommended.

**2009-2010 Annual costs.** Tuition/fees: $23,979. Room/board: $6,750. Books/supplies: $1,427. Personal expenses: $2,206.

**2009-2010 Financial aid. Non-need-based:** Scholarships awarded for leadership, religious affiliation.

**Application procedures. Admission:** No deadline. $30 fee, may be waived for applicants with need, free for online applicants. Admission notification on a rolling basis beginning on or about 1/15. **Financial aid:** No deadline. FAFSA, institutional form required. Applicants notified on a rolling basis; must reply within 3 week(s) of notification.

**Academics. Special study options:** Combined bachelor's/graduate degree, double major, external degree, honors, independent study, internships, study abroad, teacher certification program. **Credit/placement by examination:** AP, CLEP, IB, SAT, ACT, institutional tests. 24 credit hours maximum toward associate degree, 45 toward bachelor's. **Support services:** Learning center, remedial instruction, study skills assistance, tutoring, writing center.

**Majors. Biology:** General, biochemistry, biophysics. **Business:** General, accounting, business admin, finance, international, management information systems, marketing. **Communications:** General, digital media, journalism, public relations. **Computer sciences:** Computer science. **Education:** Early childhood, elementary, English, mathematics, music, physical. **Foreign languages:** French, Spanish. **Health:** Nursing (RN). **History:** General. **Interdisciplinary:** Natural sciences. **Math:** General. **Parks/recreation:** Exercise sciences, health/fitness. **Philosophy/religion:** Religion. **Physical sciences:** Chemistry, physics. **Psychology:** General. **Public administration:** Social work. **Social sciences:** General. **Theology:** Bible, theology. **Transportation:** Aviation. **Visual/performing arts:** Cinematography, commercial/advertising art, music performance, photography, studio arts.

**Most popular majors.** Biology 17%, business/marketing 15%, education 10%, foreign language 8%, health sciences 8%, psychology 7%, visual/performing arts 7%.

**Computing on campus.** 178 workstations in dormitories, library. Dormitories wired for high-speed internet access and linked to campus network. Commuter students can connect to campus network. Online course registration, online library, helpline, repair service, wireless network available.

**Student life. Freshman orientation:** Mandatory. Preregistration for classes offered. **Policies:** Religious observance required. **Housing:** Guaranteed on-campus for freshmen. Single-sex dorms, apartments, wellness housing available. $150 deposit. **Activities:** Bands, choral groups, drama, film society, literary magazine, music ensembles, musical theater, radio station, student government, student newspaper, symphony orchestra, 20 clubs.

**Athletics.** NAIA. **Intercollegiate:** Basketball, cross-country, soccer, volleyball. **Intramural:** Basketball, football (non-tackle) M, softball, volleyball. **Team name:** Pioneers.

**Student services.** Adult student services, alcohol/substance abuse counseling, chaplain/spiritual director, career counseling, student employment services, financial aid counseling, health services, on-campus daycare, personal counseling, placement for graduates. **Physically disabled:** Services for visually, speech, hearing impaired.

**Contact.** E-mail: enroll@puc.edu
Phone: (707) 965-6336 Toll-free number: (800) 862-7080
Fax: (707) 965-6432
Darren Hagen, Director of Enrollment Services, Pacific Union College, One Angwin Avenue, Angwin, CA 94508

---

## Patten University
**Oakland, California**
www.patten.edu

**CB member**
**CB code: 4620**

- Private 4-year university and liberal arts college affiliated with interdenominational tradition
- Residential campus in large city
- 995 degree-seeking undergraduates
- SAT or ACT (ACT writing optional), application essay, interview required

**General.** Founded in 1944. Regionally accredited. **Degrees:** 50 bachelor's, 25 associate awarded; master's offered. **Location:** 18 miles from San Francisco, 30 miles from San Jose. **Calendar:** Semester, limited summer session. **Full-time faculty:** 20 total. **Part-time faculty:** 120 total.

**Freshman class profile.**

| Mid 50% test scores | | | |
|---|---|---|---|
| SAT critical reading: | 500-610 | ACT composite: | 18-25 |
| SAT math: | 460-590 | Out-of-state: | .5% |

**Basis for selection.** Christian commitment most important. High school record, interview, essay, test scores, recommendation important.

**High school preparation.** 22 units required. Required units include English 4, mathematics 2, social studies 4, history 2, science 2 (laboratory 1), foreign language 1 and academic electives 6.

**2010-2011 Annual costs.** Tuition/fees: $13,440. Room/board: $7,090. Books/supplies: $1,638. Personal expenses: $2,250.

**Financial aid. Non-need-based:** Scholarships awarded for academics, athletics, state residency.

**Application procedures. Admission:** Priority date 3/31; deadline 7/31. $30 fee, may be waived for applicants with need. Admission notification on a rolling basis. **Financial aid:** Priority date 3/31; no closing date. FAFSA, institutional form required. Applicants notified on a rolling basis starting 5/31.

**Academics. Special study options:** Accelerated study, double major, dual enrollment of high school students, independent study, teacher certification program, weekend college. **Credit/placement by examination:** AP, CLEP, institutional tests. **Support services:** Learning center, remedial instruction, tutoring, writing center.

**Majors. Business:** Business admin. **Education:** Adult/continuing, early childhood. **Liberal arts:** Arts/sciences. **Philosophy/religion:** Religion. **Psychology:** General. **Theology:** Religious ed, sacred music.

**Computing on campus.** 30 workstations in library, computer center. Dormitories wired for high-speed internet access. Online library, wireless network available.

**Student life. Freshman orientation:** Mandatory. Preregistration for classes offered. 3-day overview held week before start of classes. **Policies:** Christian service program designed to involve students in practical ministry. Religious observance required. **Housing:** Guaranteed on-campus for all undergraduates. Single-sex college, apartments available. $150 deposit, deadline 7/31. **Activities:** Concert band, choral groups, drama, music ensembles, student government, student newspaper, symphony orchestra, Community of Faith groups, prison ministry.

**Athletics.** NAIA. **Intercollegiate:** Baseball M, softball W. **Team name:** Lions.

**Student services.** Adult student services, career counseling, student employment services, personal counseling, placement for graduates, veterans' counselor.

**Contact.** E-mail: admissions@patten.edu
Phone: (510) 261-8500 ext. 7764 Toll-free number: (877) 472-8836
Fax: (510) 534-4344
Kim Guerra, Director of Admissions, Patten University, 2433 Coolidge Avenue, Oakland, CA 94601-2699

---

## Pepperdine University
**Malibu, California**
www.pepperdine.edu

**CB member**
**CB code: 4630**

- Private 4-year university and liberal arts college affiliated with Church of Christ
- Residential campus in small city

- 3,427 degree-seeking undergraduates: 11% part-time, 55% women, 7% African American, 10% Asian American, 12% Hispanic American, 1% Native American, 6% international
- 4,263 degree-seeking graduate students
- 41% of applicants admitted
- SAT or ACT with writing, application essay required
- 81% graduate within 6 years

**General.** Founded in 1937. Regionally accredited. Education, psychology, business graduate campuses in Los Angeles. Educational centers in Long Beach, Irvine, Encino, West Los Angeles, Westlake Village. Academic Year residential program offered in Heidelberg, Germany; London, United Kingdom; Florence, Italy; Buenos Aires, Argentina; Lausanne, Switzerland; and Shanghai, China. Part-time, evening, weekend classes for business undergrad programs. **Degrees:** 891 bachelor's awarded; master's, doctoral, professional offered. **ROTC:** Army, Air Force. **Location:** 14 miles from Santa Monica, 30 miles from Los Angeles. **Calendar:** Semester, limited summer session. **Full-time faculty:** 365 total; 90% have terminal degrees, 13% minority, 36% women. **Part-time faculty:** 271 total; 51% have terminal degrees, 11% minority, 47% women. **Class size:** 65% < 20, 30% 20-39, 2% 40-49, 2% 50-99, 1% >100.

**Freshman class profile.** 6,426 applied, 2,656 admitted, 729 enrolled.

| Mid 50% test scores | | | |
|---|---|---|---|
| SAT critical reading: | 560-660 | Rank in top quarter: | 76% |
| SAT math: | 560-680 | Rank in top tenth: | 42% |
| SAT writing: | 560-660 | Return as sophomores: | 90% |
| ACT composite: | 24-30 | Out-of-state: | 44% |
| GPA 3.75 or higher: | 51% | Live on campus: | 98% |
| GPA 3.50-3.74: | 21% | International: | 6% |
| GPA 3.0-3.49: | 25% | Fraternities: | 16% |
| GPA 2.0-2.99: | 3% | Sororities: | 27% |

**Basis for selection.** School achievement record and test scores most important. Special talents, school and community activities, letters of recommendation, personal qualities also considered. Audition required for music, theater majors. Portfolio recommended for art majors. **Homeschooled:** Transcript of courses and grades, state high school equivalency certificate required. **Learning Disabled:** Proper documentation from doctor diagnosing learning disability required.

**High school preparation.** College-preparatory program recommended. 28 units recommended. Recommended units include English 4, mathematics 4, social studies 3, history 3, (laboratory 3), foreign language 3 and academic electives 3. 1 speech recommended.

**2010-2011 Annual costs.** Tuition/fees: $39,080. Room/board: $11,390. Books/supplies: $1,200. Personal expenses: $900.

**2009-2010 Financial aid. Need-based:** 559 full-time freshmen applied for aid; 464 were judged to have need; 462 of these received aid. Average need met was 87%. Average scholarship/grant was $28,952; average loan $3,572. 76% of total undergraduate aid awarded as scholarships/grants, 24% as loans/jobs. **Non-need-based:** Awarded to 1,196 full-time undergraduates, including 283 freshmen. Scholarships awarded for academics, art, athletics, minority status, music/drama, religious affiliation.

**Application procedures. Admission:** Closing date 1/15 (postmark date). $65 fee, may be waived for applicants with need. Admission notification 4/1. Must reply by 5/1. **Financial aid:** Priority date 2/15, closing date 2/15. FAFSA required. Applicants notified by 4/15; must reply within 2 week(s) of notification.

**Academics.** Great books colloquium, freshman seminars and first year faculty mentor program for all students. **Special study options:** Double major, honors, independent study, internships, student-designed major, study abroad, teacher certification program, Washington semester. 3-2 engineering program with University of Southern California, Washington University, and Boston University. **Credit/placement by examination:** AP, CLEP, IB, institutional tests. 32 credit hours maximum toward bachelor's degree. IB credit awarded for higher level exams only: 4 credits for each score of 5 and above; maximum 16. **Support services:** Pre-admission summer program, remedial instruction, tutoring, writing center.

**Majors. Area/ethnic studies:** Asian, European, Latin American. **Biology:** General, biochemistry. **Business:** Accounting, business admin, finance, international, marketing. **Communications:** General, advertising, broadcast journalism, journalism, organizational, public relations, radio/tv. **Computer sciences:** General. **Education:** General, chemistry, English, music, physical, speech. **Engineering:** General. **Family/consumer sciences:** Food/nutrition. **Foreign languages:** French, German, Spanish. **Health:** Athletic training. **History:** General. **Interdisciplinary:** Global studies, math/computer science, natural sciences, nutrition sciences. **Liberal arts:** Arts/sciences, humanities. **Math:** General. **Parks/recreation:** Exercise sciences,

sports admin. **Philosophy/religion:** Philosophy, religion. **Physical sciences:** Chemistry, physics. **Psychology:** General. **Social sciences:** Economics, political science, sociology. **Visual/performing arts:** Acting, art, art history/conservation, dramatic, multimedia, music history, music theory/composition, studio arts, theater design.

**Most popular majors.** Business/marketing 30%, communications/journalism 25%, interdisciplinary studies 6%, social sciences 9%.

**Computing on campus.** 292 workstations in dormitories, library, computer center, student center. Dormitories wired for high-speed internet access and linked to campus network. Commuter students can connect to campus network. Online library, helpline, repair service, wireless network available.

**Student life. Freshman orientation:** Mandatory. Orientation held a week before the official start of the Fall semester. **Policies:** Students required to attend weekly convocation. Freshmen and sophomores live on campus or at home with parent or guardian if single and under 21. **Housing:** Guaranteed on-campus for freshmen. Single-sex dorms, special housing for disabled, apartments, cooperative housing available. **Activities:** Bands, campus ministries, choral groups, dance, drama, film society, international student organizations, literary magazine, music ensembles, Model UN, musical theater, opera, radio station, student government, student newspaper, symphony orchestra, TV station, Campus Crusade for Christ, College Republicans, Young Democrats, volunteer center, black student union, Latin student association, Hawaiian club, Korean student association, Japan club.

**Athletics.** NCAA. **Intercollegiate:** Baseball M, basketball, cross-country, golf, soccer W, swimming W, tennis, track and field W, volleyball, water polo M. **Intramural:** Basketball, football (non-tackle), handball, soccer, swimming, tennis, volleyball. **Team name:** Waves.

**Student services.** Alcohol/substance abuse counseling, chaplain/spiritual director, career counseling, student employment services, financial aid counseling, health services, personal counseling, placement for graduates, veterans' counselor. **Physically disabled:** Services for visually, hearing impaired.

**Contact.** E-mail: admission-seaver@pepperdine.edu
Phone: (310) 506-4392 Fax: (310) 506-4861
Mike Trushke, Director of Admission, Pepperdine University, 24255 Pacific Coast Highway, Malibu, CA 90263-4392

---

## Pitzer College
**Claremont, California**      **CB member**
www.pitzer.edu      **CB code: 4619**

- Private 4-year liberal arts college
- Residential campus in large town
- 1,043 degree-seeking undergraduates: 5% part-time, 59% women, 6% African American, 8% Asian American, 15% Hispanic American, 1% Native American, 3% international
- 20% of applicants admitted
- Application essay required
- 80% graduate within 6 years; 3% enter graduate study

**General.** Founded in 1963. Regionally accredited. One of a cluster of 5 undergraduate and 2 graduate institutions on adjoining campuses. Campuses share facilities. Cross-enrollment available at any of the 5 undergraduate colleges, which include Claremont-McKenna, Harvey Mudd, Pitzer, Pomona, and Scripps. Interdisciplinary curriculum with social responsibility requirement, intercultural education objective; no academic departments. **Degrees:** 241 bachelor's awarded. **ROTC:** Army, Air Force. **Location:** 35 miles from Los Angeles. **Calendar:** Semester, limited summer session. **Full-time faculty:** 73 total; 100% have terminal degrees, 37% minority, 47% women. **Part-time faculty:** 24 total; 79% have terminal degrees, 21% minority, 62% women. **Class size:** 67% < 20, 31% 20-39, 1% 40-49, less than 1% 50-99. **Special facilities:** Ecology center, nature reserve, arboretum, organic garden, women's studies center, restored arts and crafts home with poetry reading room.

**Freshman class profile.** 4,081 applied, 828 admitted, 256 enrolled.

| Mid 50% test scores | | | |
|---|---|---|---|
| SAT critical reading: | 610-690 | Rank in top quarter: | 89% |
| SAT math: | 590-680 | Rank in top tenth: | 47% |
| ACT composite: | 26-30 | Return as sophomores: | 90% |
| GPA 3.75 or higher: | 64% | Out-of-state: | 55% |
| GPA 3.50-3.74: | 17% | Live on campus: | 100% |
| GPA 3.0-3.49: | 19% | International: | 3% |

**Basis for selection.** School record, essays, 3 recommendations, test scores, leadership, community service, work experience, talent, involvement in sports considered. SAT/ACT not required of students graduating in top 10% of class, or those with an unweighted cumulative GPA of 3.50 or higher in academic subjects. Otherwise, one of the following required: ACT or SAT scores; 2 SAT Subject Tests (one in math); 2 or more AP test scores of at least 4 (one English or English Language and one math or science); 2 International Baccalaureate exams (one English 1A and one math); or one recent junior or senior year graded analytical writing sample from a humanities or social science course and one recent graded exam from an advanced math course. The samples must include the teacher's comments, grades, and the assignment. Interview recommended.

**High school preparation.** College-preparatory program recommended. 21 units required. Required units include English 4, mathematics 3, social studies 3, history 1, science 3 (laboratory 3), foreign language 3 and visual/performing arts 1.

**2009-2010 Annual costs.** Tuition/fees: $39,332. Room/board: $11,438. Books/supplies: $2,000. Personal expenses: $2,000.

**2009-2010 Financial aid. Need-based:** 130 full-time freshmen applied for aid; 104 were judged to have need; 104 of these received aid. Average need met was 100%. Average scholarship/grant was $32,831; average loan $2,614. 85% of total undergraduate aid awarded as scholarships/grants, 15% as loans/jobs. **Non-need-based:** Awarded to 49 full-time undergraduates, including 9 freshmen. Scholarships awarded for academics, leadership.

**Application procedures. Admission:** Closing date 1/1 (postmark date). $60 fee, may be waived for applicants with need. Admission notification 4/1. Must reply by 5/1. **Financial aid:** Closing date 2/1. FAFSA, CSS PROFILE required. Applicants notified by 4/1; must reply by 5/1.

**Academics.** Students may take up to one-third of courses at other Claremont campuses and must take 32 courses for graduation. Can create independent study courses and special majors. **Special study options:** Combined bachelor's/graduate degree, cooperative education, cross-registration, double major, ESL, exchange student, honors, independent study, internships, liberal arts/career combination, student-designed major, study abroad, urban semester. New Resources (for students over age 25 and nontraditional students), joint science program, joint BA/DO program. **Credit/placement by examination:** AP, CLEP, IB, institutional tests. **Support services:** Tutoring, writing center.

**Majors. Area/ethnic studies:** African-American, American, Asian, Asian-American, Caribbean, Chicano/Hispanic-American/Latino, European, Latin American, women's. **Biology:** General, biochemistry, biophysics, microbiology. **Business:** Organizational behavior. **Conservation:** Environmental science, environmental studies. **Foreign languages:** General, Chinese, classics, French, German, Italian, Japanese, linguistics, Russian, Spanish. **History:** General, American, European. **Interdisciplinary:** Biological/physical sciences, global studies, intercultural, natural sciences, neuroscience, science/society. **Math:** General. **Philosophy/religion:** Philosophy, religion. **Physical sciences:** Chemistry, organic chemistry, physics. **Psychology:** General. **Social sciences:** General, anthropology, economics, international relations, political science, sociology. **Visual/performing arts:** Art, art history/conservation, cinematography, dance, dramatic, film/cinema, studio arts.

**Most popular majors.** Communications/journalism 9%, foreign language 6%, interdisciplinary studies 9%, natural resources/environmental science 6%, psychology 20%, social sciences 25%, visual/performing arts 7%.

**Computing on campus.** 100 workstations in dormitories, library, computer center, student center. Dormitories wired for high-speed internet access and linked to campus network. Commuter students can connect to campus network. Online course registration, online library, helpline, student web hosting, wireless network available.

**Student life. Freshman orientation:** Mandatory. Held the week prior to start of fall semester. **Policies:** Strong philosophical framework of social responsibility and self-governance. **Housing:** Guaranteed on-campus for freshmen. Coed dorms, special housing for disabled, cooperative housing available. **Activities:** Campus ministries, choral groups, dance, drama, international student organizations, literary magazine, music ensembles, Model UN, radio station, student government, student newspaper, symphony orchestra, over 75 social service, religious, political, and ethnic organizations.

**Athletics.** NCAA. **Intercollegiate:** Badminton, baseball M, basketball, cross-country, diving, football (tackle) M, golf, lacrosse, soccer, softball W, swimming, tennis, track and field, volleyball W, water polo. **Intramural:** Archery, badminton, basketball, golf, racquetball, sailing, soccer, softball W, squash, tennis. **Team name:** Sagehens.

**Student services.** Adult student services, alcohol/substance abuse counseling, chaplain/spiritual director, career counseling, student employment services, financial aid counseling, health services, minority student services, personal counseling, women's services. **Physically disabled:** Services for visually, speech, hearing impaired.

**Contact.** E-mail: admission@pitzer.edu
Phone: (909) 621-8129 Toll-free number: (800) 748-9371
Fax: (909) 621-8770
Arnaldo Rodriguez, Vice President of Admission and Financial Aid, Pitzer College, 1050 North Mills Avenue, Claremont, CA 91711-6101

## Platt College: Ontario
Ontario, California
www.plattcollege.edu                    CB code: 3015

- For-profit 4-year branch campus and technical college
- Commuter campus in small city
- 385 degree-seeking undergraduates
- Application essay, interview required

**General.** Accredited by ACCSC. Branch of Los Angeles campus. **Degrees:** 54 bachelor's, 109 associate awarded. **Location:** 20 miles from Los Angeles. **Calendar:** Continuous. **Full-time faculty:** 10 total; 40% have terminal degrees, 30% minority. **Part-time faculty:** 25 total; 40% have terminal degrees, 48% minority. **Class size:** 71% < 20, 29% 20-39. **Special facilities:** Motion capture lab.

**Basis for selection.** Students admitted based on interview, high school diploma or GED, entrance test and essay, and completion of the admissions process. Math and English workshops available to students upon entrance if desired or recommended. **Learning Disabled:** Students with learning disabilities may request consideration for extra time to complete entrance test.

**2009-2010 Annual costs.** Cost varies by program. Associate degree cost ranges from $24,915 to $34,955. Bachelor's degree cost ranges from $69,930 to $73,930.

**Application procedures. Admission:** No deadline. $75 fee. Admission notification on a rolling basis. **Financial aid:** Priority date 3/2; no closing date. FAFSA, institutional form required. Applicants notified on a rolling basis starting 1/1.

**Academics. Special study options:** Accelerated study, cooperative education, internships. **Credit/placement by examination:** CLEP. 48 credit hours maximum toward associate degree, 48 toward bachelor's. **Support services:** Tutoring.

**Majors. Communications technology:** Animation/special effects, graphics. **Computer sciences:** Computer graphics, web page design. **Legal studies:** Legal secretary, paralegal. **Visual/performing arts:** General, commercial/advertising art, design.

**Computing on campus.** 12 workstations in library.

**Student life. Freshman orientation:** Mandatory. Preregistration for classes offered. Held on first day of classes. **Activities:** Various student clubs and activities available.

**Student services.** Adult student services, career counseling, student employment services, financial aid counseling, placement for graduates.

**Contact.** Phone: (909) 941-9410 Toll-free number: (866) 752-8846
Fax: (909) 941-9660
Admissions Director, Platt College: Ontario, 3700 Inland Empire Boulevard, Ontario, CA 91764

## Platt College: San Diego
San Diego, California
www.platt.edu                    CB code: 3020

- For-profit 4-year visual arts and technical college
- Commuter campus in very large city
- 292 degree-seeking undergraduates: 25% women, 5% African American, 10% Asian American, 22% Hispanic American, 1% Native American, 1% international
- Application essay, interview required
- 68% graduate within 6 years

**General.** Accredited by ACCSC. **Degrees:** 60 bachelor's, 77 associate awarded. **Calendar:** Continuous. **Full-time faculty:** 5 total. **Part-time faculty:** 34 total; 9% have terminal degrees, 18% minority, 59% women. **Class size:** 91% < 20, 9% 20-39.

**Freshman class profile.** 113 applied, 113 admitted, 113 enrolled.

**Basis for selection.** Open admission, but selective for some programs and for out-of-state students. Aptitude test used to measure academic preparedness to undertake college-level courses; SAT considered in lieu of test.

**2009-2010 Annual costs.** Tuition/fees: $15,310. Total program costs range from $17,910 to $36,310, depending on the program chosen. Books/supplies: $1,400.

**Application procedures. Admission:** No deadline. No application fee. Application must be submitted on paper. **Financial aid:** Closing date 3/2. FAFSA, institutional form required. Applicants notified on a rolling basis; must reply within 1 week(s) of notification.

**Academics. Special study options:** Accelerated study, internships, liberal arts/career combination. **Credit/placement by examination:** AP, CLEP, institutional tests. **Support services:** Study skills assistance, tutoring.

**Majors. Visual/performing arts:** General, commercial/advertising art.

**Computing on campus.** 200 workstations in library, computer center. Online library available.

**Student life. Freshman orientation:** Mandatory. Preregistration for classes offered.

**Student services.** Career counseling, services for economically disadvantaged, student employment services, financial aid counseling, personal counseling, placement for graduates.

**Contact.** E-mail: info@platt.edu
Phone: (619) 265-0107 Toll-free number: (866) 752-8826
Fax: (619) 308-0570
Al Medro, Vice President, Platt College: San Diego, 6250 El Cajon Boulevard, San Diego, CA 92115

---

## Point Loma Nazarene University
**San Diego, California**  CB member
**www.pointloma.edu**  CB code: 4605

- Private 4-year university and liberal arts college affiliated with Church of the Nazarene
- Residential campus in very large city
- 2,367 degree-seeking undergraduates: 3% part-time, 62% women, 3% African American, 7% Asian American, 12% Hispanic American, 1% Native American, 1% international
- 1,100 graduate students
- 74% of applicants admitted
- SAT or ACT (ACT writing optional), application essay, interview required
- 73% graduate within 6 years

**General.** Founded in 1902. Regionally accredited. **Degrees:** 585 bachelor's awarded; master's offered. **ROTC:** Army, Naval, Air Force. **Location:** 5 miles from downtown. **Calendar:** Semester, limited summer session. **Full-time faculty:** 159 total; 77% have terminal degrees, 13% minority, 40% women. **Part-time faculty:** 254 total; 9% minority, 53% women. **Class size:** 48% < 20, 39% 20-39, 10% 40-49, 3% 50-99. **Special facilities:** Historical Greek ampitheatre.

**Freshman class profile.** 2,490 applied, 1,852 admitted, 535 enrolled.

| Mid 50% test scores | | | |
|---|---|---|---|
| SAT critical reading: | 500-610 | Rank in top quarter: | 64% |
| SAT math: | 490-620 | Rank in top tenth: | 33% |
| ACT composite: | 21-27 | Return as sophomores: | 84% |
| GPA 3.75 or higher: | 47% | Out-of-state: | 21% |
| GPA 3.50-3.74: | 19% | Live on campus: | 94% |
| GPA 3.0-3.49: | 25% | | |
| GPA 2.0-2.99: | 9% | | |

**Basis for selection.** Moral character, maturity, intellectual ability, and academic achievement important. Preference given to self-directed applicants who appear to share ideals and objectives of college. SAT recommended.

**High school preparation.** College-preparatory program required. 18 units recommended. Recommended units include English 4, mathematics 3, social studies 2, history 1, science 2 (laboratory 2) and foreign language 2.

**2010-2011 Annual costs.** Tuition/fees: $27,100. Room/board: $8,600. Books/supplies: $1,638. Personal expenses: $2,250.

**2009-2010 Financial aid. Need-based:** 447 full-time freshmen applied for aid; 343 were judged to have need; 340 of these received aid. Average

need met was 65%. Average scholarship/grant was $13,188; average loan $4,226. 55% of total undergraduate aid awarded as scholarships/grants, 45% as loans/jobs. **Non-need-based:** Awarded to 622 full-time undergraduates, including 117 freshmen. Scholarships awarded for academics, athletics, leadership, music/drama.

**Application procedures. Admission:** Priority date 3/1; no deadline. $50 fee, may be waived for applicants with need. Admission notification on a rolling basis beginning on or about 4/1. Must reply by May 1 or within 2 week(s) if notified thereafter. **Financial aid:** Priority date 3/2; no closing date. FAFSA, institutional form required. Applicants notified on a rolling basis starting 3/1.

**Academics. Special study options:** Double major, honors, independent study, internships, semester at sea, study abroad, teacher certification program, United Nations semester, Washington semester. **Credit/placement by examination:** AP, CLEP, IB, SAT, institutional tests. 32 credit hours maximum toward bachelor's degree. Some restrictions apply in special majors. **Support services:** Learning center, reduced course load, remedial instruction, study skills assistance, tutoring, writing center.

**Majors. Biology:** General, biochemistry. **Business:** Accounting, business admin, communications, management information systems. **Communications:** General, broadcast journalism, journalism, media studies. **Computer sciences:** Computer science. **Conservation:** Environmental science. **Education:** Art, music. **Engineering:** Physics. **Family/consumer sciences:** General, child development, food/nutrition. **Foreign languages:** Romance, Spanish. **Health:** Athletic training, dietetics, nursing (RN). **History:** General. **Interdisciplinary:** Global studies. **Liberal arts:** Arts/sciences. **Math:** General. **Parks/recreation:** Exercise sciences, health/fitness. **Philosophy/religion:** Philosophy. **Physical sciences:** Chemistry, physics. **Psychology:** General, industrial. **Public administration:** Social work. **Social sciences:** General, political science, sociology. **Theology:** Bible, preministerial, sacred music, youth ministry. **Visual/performing arts:** Dramatic, fashion design, graphic design, interior design, music performance, music theory/composition, piano/organ, studio arts, voice/opera. **Other:** Philosophy and religious studies.

**Most popular majors.** Biology 7%, business/marketing 22%, communications/journalism 10%, health sciences 10%, liberal arts 6%, psychology 7%, social sciences 6%, visual/performing arts 7%.

**Computing on campus.** 485 workstations in dormitories, library, computer center, student center. Dormitories wired for high-speed internet access and linked to campus network. Commuter students can connect to campus network. Online course registration, online library, helpline, repair service, wireless network available.

**Student life. Freshman orientation:** Mandatory. **Policies:** Students are expected to exercise self-discipline, sound judgment and manage conduct both on and off campus consistent with agreements made upon application and with University catalog and Student Handbook. Religious observance required. **Housing:** Guaranteed on-campus for freshmen. Single-sex dorms, apartments, wellness housing available. $425 nonrefundable deposit, deadline 5/1. **Activities:** Bands, campus ministries, choral groups, drama, international student organizations, literary magazine, music ensembles, musical theater, opera, radio station, student government, student newspaper, symphony orchestra, TV station, Students for Social Justice, Social Work Club, College Democrats, College Republicans, Brothers and Sisters United, Association of Latin American Students.

**Athletics.** NAIA. **Intercollegiate:** Baseball M, basketball, cross-country, golf M, soccer, tennis, track and field, volleyball W. **Intramural:** Badminton, basketball, football (non-tackle), golf, soccer, softball, tennis, track and field, volleyball. **Team name:** Sea Lions.

**Student services.** Chaplain/spiritual director, career counseling, student employment services, financial aid counseling, health services, minority student services, on-campus daycare, personal counseling, veterans' counselor. **Physically disabled:** Services for visually, speech, hearing impaired.

**Contact.** E-mail: admissions@pointloma.edu
Phone: (619) 849-2273 Toll-free number: (800) 733-7770
Fax: (619) 849-2601
Eric Groves, Director of Undergraduate Admissions, Point Loma Nazarene University, 3900 Lomaland Drive, San Diego, CA 92106-2899

---

## Pomona College
**Claremont, California**  CB member
**www.pomona.edu**  CB code: 4607

- Private 4-year liberal arts college
- Residential campus in large town

◆ 1,531 degree-seeking undergraduates: 50% women, 9% African American, 14% Asian American, 11% Hispanic American, 4% international

◆ 16% of applicants admitted

◆ SAT and SAT Subject Tests or ACT (ACT writing recommended), application essay required

◆ 95% graduate within 6 years

**General.** Founded in 1887. Regionally accredited. One of a cluster of 5 undergraduate and 2 graduate schools on adjoining campuses. Campuses share facilities. Cross-enrollment available at any of the 5 colleges, which include Claremont-McKenna, Harvey Mudd, Pitzer, Pomona, and Scripps. Extensive overseas studies. **Degrees:** 371 bachelor's awarded. **ROTC:** Army, Air Force. **Location:** 35 miles from Los Angeles, 20 miles from Pasadena. **Calendar:** Semester. **Full-time faculty:** 188 total; 98% have terminal degrees, 27% minority, 43% women. **Part-time faculty:** 37 total; 62% have terminal degrees, 19% minority, 49% women. **Class size:** 66% < 20, 31% 20-39, less than 1% 40-49, 1% 50-99, less than 1% >100. **Special facilities:** Science center, center for modern language and international relations, observatory, biological field station, ecological preserve, botanic garden, social sciences center, Greek theater, multimedia labs, foreign language resource center, college-operated museum.

**Freshman class profile.** 6,149 applied, 992 admitted, 390 enrolled.

| Mid 50% test scores | | Rank in top tenth: | 92% |
|---|---|---|---|
| SAT critical reading: | 710-780 | Return as sophomores: | 97% |
| SAT math: | 690-770 | Out-of-state: | 70% |
| SAT writing: | 690-770 | Live on campus: | 100% |
| ACT composite: | 31-34 | International: | 4% |
| Rank in top quarter: | 100% | | |

**Basis for selection.** School achievement record, test scores, essays, 3 recommendations most important. Special skills in music, art, drama, or athletics; leadership, motivation, and diversity of background also important. Some preference to children of alumni; special consideration for underrepresented groups. School and community activities also considered. Students submitting SAT must also submit 2 SAT Subject Tests in different subject areas. Interview required for early admission applicants, strongly recommended for all applicants. Audition recommended for music, dance, theater majors. Portfolio recommended for studio art majors. **Homeschooled:** SAT and at least 3 SAT Subject Tests required, more recommended. Detailed description of curriculum required.

**High school preparation.** College-preparatory program required. 19 units required. Required and recommended units include English 4, mathematics 3-4, social studies 2, history 3, science 3-4 (laboratory 2-3) and foreign language 2-3. 3-4 laboratory science recommended for science applicants. Mathematics through calculus recommended for all applicants.

**2009-2010 Annual costs.** Tuition/fees: $37,017. Room/board: $12,651. Books/supplies: $900.

**2008-2009 Financial aid.** All financial aid based on need. 240 full-time freshmen applied for aid; 193 were judged to have need; 193 of these received aid. Average need met was 100%. Average scholarship/grant was $34,389. 96% of total undergraduate aid awarded as scholarships/grants, 4% as loans/jobs.

**Application procedures.** **Admission:** Closing date 1/2 (receipt date). $65 fee, may be waived for applicants with need. Must reply by May 1 or within 1 week(s) if notified thereafter. **Financial aid:** Closing date 2/1. FAFSA, CSS PROFILE required. Applicants notified by 4/1; must reply by 5/1.

**Academics.** **Special study options:** Combined bachelor's/graduate degree, cross-registration, double major, exchange student, independent study, internships, student-designed major, study abroad, Washington semester. 3-2 program in engineering with California Institute of Technology and Washington University (MO), 4-1 education certification program with Claremont Graduate University. **Credit/placement by examination:** AP, CLEP, IB, SAT, ACT, institutional tests. 2 credit hours maximum toward bachelor's degree. **Support services:** Tutoring, writing center.

**Majors.** **Area/ethnic studies:** African-American, American, Asian, Asian-American, Chicano/Hispanic-American/Latino, German, Latin American, women's. **Biology:** General, molecular. **Communications:** Media studies. **Computer sciences:** Computer science. **Conservation:** Environmental studies. **Foreign languages:** General, Chinese, classics, French, German, Japanese, linguistics, Russian, Spanish. **History:** General. **Interdisciplinary:** Cognitive science, global studies, math/computer science, neuroscience, science/society. **Math:** General. **Philosophy/religion:** Philosophy, religion. **Physical sciences:** Astronomy, chemistry, geology, physics. **Psychology:** General. **Public administration:** Policy analysis. **Social sciences:** General, anthropology, economics, international relations, political science, sociology. **Visual/**

**performing arts:** General, art, art history/conservation, dance, dramatic, studio arts.

**Most popular majors.** Area/ethnic studies 6%, biology 7%, interdisciplinary studies 8%, mathematics 6%, physical sciences 7%, psychology 8%, social sciences 24%, visual/performing arts 6%.

**Computing on campus.** 180 workstations in dormitories, library, computer center, student center. Dormitories wired for high-speed internet access and linked to campus network. Commuter students can connect to campus network. Online library, helpline, wireless network available.

**Student life.** **Freshman orientation:** Mandatory. Held immediately prior to fall semester. **Housing:** Guaranteed on-campus for all undergraduates. Coed dorms available. $500 nonrefundable deposit, deadline 5/1. **Activities:** Bands, campus ministries, choral groups, dance, drama, film society, international student organizations, literary magazine, music ensembles, Model UN, musical theater, radio station, student government, student newspaper, symphony orchestra, TV station, center for religious activities, international peace, Asian students association, Mortar Board (service organization), women's coalition, gay and lesbian student union, Office of Black Student Affairs, Chicano/Latino Student Association.

**Athletics.** NCAA. **Intercollegiate:** Baseball M, basketball, cross-country, diving, football (tackle) M, golf, lacrosse W, soccer, softball W, swimming, tennis, track and field, volleyball W, water polo. **Intramural:** Badminton, basketball, equestrian, handball, racquetball, skiing, soccer, softball, squash, table tennis, track and field, volleyball, water polo. **Team name:** Sagehens.

**Student services.** Chaplain/spiritual director, career counseling, services for economically disadvantaged, student employment services, financial aid counseling, health services, minority student services, personal counseling, placement for graduates. **Physically disabled:** Services for visually, hearing impaired.

**Contact.** E-mail: admissions@pomona.edu
Phone: (909) 621-8134 Fax: (909) 621-8952
Bruce Poch, Vice President and Dean of Admissions, Pomona College, 333 North College Way, Claremont, CA 91711-6312

### Remington College: San Diego
San Diego, California
www.remingtoncollege.edu                    CB code: 2574

◆ For-profit 4-year university

◆ Very large city

◆ 10 degree-seeking undergraduates

**General.** Accredited by ACICS. **Degrees:** 14 bachelor's, 37 associate awarded; master's offered. **Calendar:** Quarter. **Full-time faculty:** 20 total. **Part-time faculty:** 30 total.

**Basis for selection.** Open admission, but selective for some programs. Wonderlic exam used for admission.

**2009-2010 Annual costs.** Massage Therapy program $13,050; includes books and supplies.

**Financial aid.** **Additional information:** Application fee may be waived and applied toward tuition.

**Application procedures.** **Admission:** No deadline. $50 fee. **Financial aid:** FAFSA required.

**Academics.** **Credit/placement by examination:** CLEP.

**Majors.** **Business:** Business admin. **Protective services:** Criminal justice. **Psychology:** General.

**Student life.** **Freshman orientation:** Available. Held 1 week before start of classes.

**Contact.** Phone: (619) 686-8600 Toll-free number: (800) 214-7001
Fax: (619) 686-8684
April Webb, Director of Recruitment, Remington College: San Diego, 123 Camino de la Reina, Suite 100, North Building, San Diego, CA 92108-3002

### St. Mary's College of California
Moraga, California                          CB member
www.stmarys-ca.edu                          CB code: 4675

◆ Private 4-year liberal arts college affiliated with Roman Catholic Church

◆ Residential campus in large town

- 2,379 degree-seeking undergraduates: 4% part-time, 62% women, 7% African American, 11% Asian American, 22% Hispanic American, 1% Native American, 3% international
- 1,097 degree-seeking graduate students
- 79% of applicants admitted
- SAT or ACT (ACT writing optional), application essay required
- 58% graduate within 6 years; 25% enter graduate study

**General.** Founded in 1863. Regionally accredited. **Degrees:** 541 bachelor's, 39 associate awarded; master's, doctoral offered. **ROTC:** Army, Air Force. **Location:** 20 miles from San Francisco. **Calendar:** 4-1-4, limited summer session. **Full-time faculty:** 202 total; 95% have terminal degrees, 17% minority, 51% women. **Part-time faculty:** 201 total; 15% minority. **Class size:** 53% < 20, 47% 20-39, less than 1% 50-99. **Special facilities:** Observatory.

**Freshman class profile.** 3,241 applied, 2,555 admitted, 572 enrolled.

| Mid 50% test scores | | | |
|---|---|---|---|
| SAT critical reading: | 490-590 | GPA 2.0-2.99: | 25% |
| SAT math: | 490-600 | End year in good standing: | 78% |
| ACT composite: | 20-26 | Return as sophomores: | 82% |
| GPA 3.75 or higher: | 26% | Out-of-state: | 17% |
| GPA 3.50-3.74: | 13% | Live on campus: | 99% |
| GPA 3.0-3.49: | 36% | International: | 3% |

**Basis for selection.** School achievement record most important. Interview recommended. **Homeschooled:** Transcript of courses and grades, letter of recommendation (nonparent) required.

**High school preparation.** 16 units required; 19 recommended. Required and recommended units include English 4, mathematics 3-4, social studies 1, history 1, science 2-3 (laboratory 1), foreign language 2-3 and academic electives 2. One unit each of chemistry, physics, advanced algebra, and trigonometry required for applicants to school of science.

**2010-2011 Annual costs.** Tuition/fees: $35,430. Room/board: $12,350. Books/supplies: $1,512. Personal expenses: $2,250.

**2009-2010 Financial aid. Need-based:** 513 full-time freshmen applied for aid; 481 were judged to have need; 479 of these received aid. Average need met was 85%. Average scholarship/grant was $24,254; average loan $3,864. 70% of total undergraduate aid awarded as scholarships/grants, 30% as loans/jobs. **Non-need-based:** Awarded to 798 full-time undergraduates, including 218 freshmen. Scholarships awarded for academics, alumni affiliation, athletics, leadership.

**Application procedures. Admission:** Priority date 11/15; deadline 2/1 (postmark date). $55 fee, may be waived for applicants with need. Admission notification 3/15. Admission notification on a rolling basis. Must reply by May 1 or within 2 week(s) if notified thereafter. **Financial aid:** Priority date 2/15; no closing date. FAFSA required. Applicants notified on a rolling basis starting 3/15; must reply by 5/1 or within 2 week(s) of notification.

**Academics.** Academic support services are available by appointment. **Special study options:** Combined bachelor's/graduate degree, cross-registration, double major, exchange student, honors, independent study, internships, liberal arts/career combination, student-designed major, study abroad, teacher certification program. 4-year interdisciplinary program with Great Books orientation. **Credit/placement by examination:** AP, CLEP, IB, SAT, institutional tests. 30 credit hours maximum toward bachelor's degree. **Support services:** Learning center, study skills assistance, tutoring, writing center.

**Majors. Area/ethnic studies:** European, Latin American, women's. **Biology:** General, biochemistry. **Business:** General, accounting, business admin, finance, international. **Communications:** General. **Foreign languages:** General, classics, French, German, Italian, Japanese, Spanish. **Health:** Health care admin. **History:** General. **Interdisciplinary:** Biopsychology, math/computer science. **Liberal arts:** Arts/sciences. **Math:** General. **Parks/recreation:** Exercise sciences, health/fitness, sports admin. **Philosophy/religion:** Philosophy, religion. **Physical sciences:** Chemistry, physics. **Psychology:** General, developmental, experimental, industrial, social. **Social sciences:** Anthropology, archaeology, economics, political science, sociology. **Visual/performing arts:** General, art, dance, dramatic.

**Most popular majors.** Business/marketing 32%, communications/journalism 8%, English 6%, liberal arts 12%, psychology 8%, social sciences 9%.

**Computing on campus.** 244 workstations in dormitories, library, computer center. Dormitories wired for high-speed internet access and linked to campus network. Commuter students can connect to campus network. Online course registration, online library, helpline, student web hosting, wireless network available.

**Student life. Freshman orientation:** Mandatory, $250 fee. 4 day and one-half sessions. Freshmen attend 1 session plus 4-day weekend of welcome. **Housing:** Guaranteed on-campus for freshmen. Coed dorms, special housing for disabled, apartments available. $350 nonrefundable deposit, deadline 5/1. Honors, Science, Lasallian Community, and Santiago Community housing available. **Activities:** Bands, campus ministries, choral groups, dance, drama, film society, international student organizations, literary magazine, music ensembles, musical theater, radio station, student government, student newspaper, TV station, Catholic Institute for Lasallian Social Action, Habitat for Humanity, Amnesty International, Lasallian Collegians, Asian Pacific American Student Association, Black Student Union, Dante, Gay Straight Alliance, Hermanas Unidas, Humans Actively Practicing Aloha Club.

**Athletics.** NCAA. **Intercollegiate:** Baseball M, basketball, cross-country, golf M, lacrosse W, rowing (crew) W, soccer, softball W, tennis, volleyball W. **Intramural:** Basketball, bowling, football (non-tackle), golf, lacrosse, rowing (crew), skiing, soccer, softball, table tennis, tennis, volleyball, water polo. **Team name:** Gaels.

**Student services.** Alcohol/substance abuse counseling, chaplain/spiritual director, career counseling, services for economically disadvantaged, student employment services, financial aid counseling, health services, minority student services, personal counseling, placement for graduates, veterans' counselor, women's services. **Physically disabled:** Services for visually, speech, hearing impaired.

**Contact.** E-mail: smcadmit@stmarys_ca.edu
Phone: (925) 631-4224 Toll-free number: (800) 800-4762
Fax: (925) 376-7193
Dorothy Jones, Dean of Admissions, St. Mary's College of California, Box 4800, Moraga, CA 94575-4800

---

## Samuel Merritt University
**Oakland, California**
www.samuelmerritt.edu

**CB member**
**CB code: 4750**

- Private two-year upper-division health science and nursing college
- Commuter campus in large city
- 37% of applicants admitted
- Application essay required

**General.** Founded in 1909. Regionally accredited. Part of Alta Bates Summit Medical Center, a nonprofit, community-based health care organization. **Degrees:** 328 bachelor's awarded; master's, professional offered. **ROTC:** Army, Naval, Air Force. **Location:** 15 miles from San Francisco. **Calendar:** Differs by program, limited summer session. **Full-time faculty:** 119 total; 53% have terminal degrees, 19% minority, 71% women. **Part-time faculty:** 121 total; 19% have terminal degrees, 33% minority, 75% women. **Class size:** 8% < 20, 62% 20-39, 30% 40-49. **Special facilities:** Nursing resource laboratory, health education center, health science library, anatomy laboratory, therapeutic exercise laboratory, living skills laboratory, human occupations laboratory, health sciences simulation lab.

**Student profile.** 517 degree-seeking undergraduates, 820 degree-seeking graduate students. 179 applied as first time-transfer students, 66 admitted, 64 enrolled. 3% entered as juniors. 100% transferred from two-year institutions.

| | | | |
|---|---|---|---|
| Women: | 86% | Native American: | 1% |
| African American: | 3% | Part-time: | 1% |
| Asian American: | 22% | Out-of-state: | 2% |
| Hispanic American: | 9% | 25 or older: | 65% |

**Basis for selection.** College transcript, application essay required. Must have UC transferable college-level coursework in chemistry, anatomy, physiology, multicultural psychology, English (2) and humanities (2). Letter of recommendation and experience in health care environment required. Transfer accepted as juniors.

**2009-2010 Annual costs.** Tuition/fees: $35,398. $2,958 per semester health insurance mandatory unless student covered by existing insurance.

**Financial aid. Non-need-based:** Scholarships awarded for academics, leadership, minority status. **Additional information:** Ongoing private scholarships available. Students eligible to work in Medical Center (associated with college).

**Application procedures. Admission:** Priority date 3/1. $50 fee, may be waived for applicants with need. Application must be submitted on paper. Admission notification 4/1. Must reply by 5/1. **Financial aid:** Priority date 3/2, no deadline. Applicants notified on a rolling basis; must reply within 3 weeks of notification.

**Academics. Special study options:** Accelerated study, combined bachelor's/graduate degree, cooperative education, cross-registration, distance learning, ESL, independent study, internships, liberal arts/career combination. **Credit/placement by examination:** CLEP. 80 credit hours maximum toward bachelor's degree.

**Majors. Health:** Nursing (RN).

**Computing on campus.** 78 workstations in library, computer center. Online course registration, online library, helpline, wireless network available.

**Student life. Activities:** Student government, student newspaper, multicultural committee, American Physical Therapy Association, California Nursing Students Association, Christian Fellowship, American Occupational Therapy Association, Chi Eta Phi, gay, lesbian, bisexual and transgender group.

**Student services.** Career counseling, financial aid counseling, health services, personal counseling. **Physically disabled:** Services for visually, speech, hearing impaired.

**Contact.** E-mail: admission@samuelmerritt.edu
Phone: (510) 869-6576 Toll-free number: (800) 607-6377
Fax: (510) 869-6576
Anne Seed, Director of Admissions, Samuel Merritt University, 370 Hawthorne Avenue, Oakland, CA 94609-9954

## San Diego Christian College
**El Cajon, California**
**www.sdcc.edu**                              **CB code: 4150**

- Private 4-year liberal arts college affiliated with nondenominational tradition
- Residential campus in small city
- 420 degree-seeking undergraduates: 8% part-time, 47% women, 10% African American, 6% Asian American, 16% Hispanic American, 2% Native American, 2% international
- 18 degree-seeking graduate students
- 60% of applicants admitted
- SAT or ACT (ACT writing optional), application essay required
- 42% graduate within 6 years; 33% enter graduate study

**General.** Founded in 1970. Regionally accredited. **Degrees:** 90 bachelor's awarded. **ROTC:** Army, Naval, Air Force. **Location:** 15 miles from downtown San Diego. **Calendar:** Semester, limited summer session. **Full-time faculty:** 13 total; 38% have terminal degrees, 8% minority, 46% women. **Part-time faculty:** 42 total; 12% have terminal degrees, 17% minority, 38% women. **Class size:** 78% < 20, 20% 20-39, 3% 40-49. **Special facilities:** Museum supporting creationist view, flight school.

**Freshman class profile.** 255 applied, 152 admitted, 64 enrolled.

| Mid 50% test scores | | | |
|---|---|---|---|
| SAT critical reading: | 410-540 | Rank in top quarter: | 30% |
| SAT math: | 390-480 | Rank in top tenth: | 17% |
| SAT writing: | 400-540 | End year in good standing: | 81% |
| ACT composite: | 18-23 | Return as sophomores: | 60% |
| GPA 3.75 or higher: | 22% | Out-of-state: | 20% |
| GPA 3.50-3.74: | 23% | Live on campus: | 59% |
| GPA 3.0-3.49: | 33% | International: | 3% |
| GPA 2.0-2.99: | 19% | | |

**Basis for selection.** Academic abilities as indicated by school achievement record and test scores. Personal and spiritual qualities as indicated by essays, recommendations, and interview.

**High school preparation.** College-preparatory program recommended. 15 units recommended. Recommended units include English 4, mathematics 3, social studies 3, science 3 and foreign language 2.

**2009-2010 Annual costs.** Tuition/fees: $21,610. Room/board: $8,000. Books/supplies: $1,638. Personal expenses: $2,250.

**2009-2010 Financial aid. Need-based:** 54 full-time freshmen applied for aid; 48 were judged to have need; 48 of these received aid. Average need met was 52%. Average scholarship/grant was $8,957; average loan $2,493. 43% of total undergraduate aid awarded as scholarships/grants, 57% as loans/jobs. **Non-need-based:** Awarded to 440 full-time undergraduates, including 58 freshmen. Scholarships awarded for academics, alumni affiliation, athletics, leadership, music/drama, state residency.

**Application procedures. Admission:** Priority date 7/1; deadline 8/1 (postmark date). $25 fee, may be waived for applicants with need. Admission notification on a rolling basis. Must reply by May 1 or within 4 week(s) if notified thereafter. **Financial aid:** Priority date 3/2, closing date 7/15. FAFSA,

institutional form required. Applicants notified on a rolling basis starting 4/1; must reply by 5/1 or within 4 week(s) of notification.

**Academics. Special study options:** Accelerated study, distance learning, double major, ESL, honors, independent study, internships, liberal arts/career combination, student-designed major, study abroad, teacher certification program, Washington semester. **Credit/placement by examination:** AP, CLEP, IB, SAT, ACT, institutional tests. 9 credit hours maximum toward bachelor's degree. **Support services:** Learning center, reduced course load, remedial instruction, study skills assistance, tutoring, writing center.

**Majors. Biology:** General. **Business:** Business admin. **Communications:** General. **Education:** General, early childhood, elementary, English, history, mathematics, middle, music, physical, secondary, social science. **Family/consumer sciences:** Family studies. **Health:** Athletic training. **History:** General. **Math:** General. **Psychology:** General. **Social sciences:** General. **Theology:** Bible, missionary. **Visual/performing arts:** Dramatic, music performance.

**Most popular majors.** Business/marketing 11%, English 6%, family/consumer sciences 7%, interdisciplinary studies 12%, liberal arts 11%, parks/recreation 10%, psychology 8%, theological studies 9%.

**Computing on campus.** 48 workstations in library, computer center, student center. Dormitories wired for high-speed internet access and linked to campus network. Commuter students can connect to campus network. Online library, helpline, repair service, wireless network available.

**Student life. Freshman orientation:** Mandatory, $100 fee. Preregistration for classes offered. Takes place within 2 weeks of start of classes in fall. **Policies:** Religious observance required. **Housing:** Guaranteed on-campus for all undergraduates. Single-sex dorms available. $250 deposit, deadline 7/1. **Activities:** Concert band, campus ministries, choral groups, drama, music ensembles, musical theater, student government, student newspaper, student senate, flight team, missions club, art club.

**Athletics.** NAIA. **Intercollegiate:** Baseball M, basketball, cross-country, golf M, soccer, volleyball W. **Intramural:** Basketball, football (non-tackle) M, soccer, softball, tennis, volleyball. **Team name:** Hawks.

**Student services.** Adult student services, chaplain/spiritual director, career counseling, student employment services, financial aid counseling, health services, personal counseling, placement for graduates.

**Contact.** E-mail: admissions@sdcc.edu
Phone: (619) 588-7747 Toll-free number: (800) 676-2242
Fax: (619) 590-1739
Mitchell Fisk, Vice President for Enrollment & Marketing, San Diego Christian College, 2100 Greenfield Drive, El Cajon, CA 92019-1157

## San Diego State University
**San Diego, California**                        **CB member**
**www.sdsu.edu**                                **CB code: 4682**

- Public 4-year university
- Commuter campus in very large city
- 27,537 degree-seeking undergraduates: 16% part-time, 57% women, 4% African American, 15% Asian American, 26% Hispanic American, 1% Native American, 3% international
- 6,253 degree-seeking graduate students
- 36% of applicants admitted
- SAT or ACT (ACT writing optional) required
- 66% graduate within 6 years

**General.** Founded in 1897. Regionally accredited. Branch campus at Calexico in Imperial Valley. **Degrees:** 7,026 bachelor's awarded; master's, doctoral offered. **ROTC:** Army, Naval, Air Force. **Location:** 8 miles from downtown. **Calendar:** Semester, extensive summer session. **Full-time faculty:** 841 total; 92% have terminal degrees, 25% minority, 43% women. **Part-time faculty:** 689 total; 12% have terminal degrees, 21% minority, 52% women. **Class size:** 19% < 20, 47% 20-39, 9% 40-49, 18% 50-99, 7% >100. **Special facilities:** Observatory, electron microscope facility, open-air theater, aquatic center, international student center, American Language Institute, recital hall, field studies stations (off-campus), multimedia interactive fine arts lab.

**Freshman class profile.** 41,986 applied, 15,273 admitted, 4,273 enrolled.

| Mid 50% test scores | | | |
|---|---|---|---|
| SAT critical reading: | 450-570 | GPA 2.0-2.99: | 11% |
| SAT math: | 460-600 | Return as sophomores: | 81% |
| ACT composite: | 19-25 | Out-of-state: | 8% |
| GPA 3.75 or higher: | 25% | Live on campus: | 48% |
| GPA 3.50-3.74: | 27% | International: | 2% |
| GPA 3.0-3.49: | 37% | Fraternities: | 14% |
| | | Sororities: | 20% |

**Basis for selection.** High school GPA and test scores most important; 20% of those admitted selected using faculty-defined criteria, such as socioeconomic status and San Diego and Imperial County residency. **Homeschooled:** Transcript of courses and grades required. In cases where the Lab Science courses are not completed in at a regular high school or community college, we request course descriptions to ensure the lab component meets the CSU requirement for admission.

**High school preparation.** College-preparatory program recommended. 15 units required. Required and recommended units include English 4, mathematics 3-4, social studies 1, history 1, science 2 (laboratory 2), foreign language 2, visual/performing arts 1 and academic electives 1. One visual and performing arts required. History must be U.S. history or U.S. government. Science must be 1 biology, 1 physical science.

**2009-2010 Annual costs.** Tuition/fees: $4,902; $16,062 out-of-state. Room/board: $11,485. Books/supplies: $1,638. Personal expenses: $2,657.

**2009-2010 Financial aid. Need-based:** 3,200 full-time freshmen applied for aid; 2,000 were judged to have need; 2,000 of these received aid. Average need met was 71%. Average scholarship/grant was $7,900; average loan $3,000. 52% of total undergraduate aid awarded as scholarships/grants, 48% as loans/jobs. **Non-need-based:** Awarded to 4,020 full-time undergraduates, including 940 freshmen. Scholarships awarded for academics, alumni affiliation, art, athletics, leadership, music/drama, ROTC, state residency.

**Application procedures. Admission:** Closing date 11/30 (postmark date). $55 fee, may be waived for applicants with need. Application must be submitted online. Admission notification 3/1. Must reply by 5/1. **Financial aid:** Closing date 3/2. FAFSA required. Applicants notified on a rolling basis starting 2/14.

**Academics. Special study options:** Distance learning, double major, ESL, exchange student, external degree, honors, independent study, internships, liberal arts/career combination, study abroad, teacher certification program. **Credit/placement by examination:** AP, CLEP, IB, SAT, ACT, institutional tests. 30 credit hours maximum toward bachelor's degree. Must be registered in at least 1 course, matriculated and in good standing. Approval of department chair and dean of college required. Restricted to regular undergraduate courses. Does not count toward 30-unit minimum residency requirement. **Support services:** Pre-admission summer program, reduced course load, remedial instruction, tutoring.

**Majors. Agriculture:** Business. **Area/ethnic studies:** African-American, American, Asian, Central/Eastern European, Chicano/Hispanic-American/Latino, European, Latin American, Native American, Russian/Slavic, women's. **Biology:** General, microbiology. **Business:** General, accounting, business admin, finance, financial planning, hospitality admin, international, marketing, real estate. **Communications:** Advertising, journalism, public relations, radio/tv. **Computer sciences:** General, computer science, information systems, information technology. **Conservation:** General, environmental studies. **Education:** Early childhood, music, trade/industrial. **Engineering:** General, aerospace, civil, computer, electrical, environmental, mechanical. **Engineering technology:** Construction. **Family/consumer sciences:** Child development. **Foreign languages:** Classics, comparative lit, French, German, Japanese, linguistics, Russian, Spanish. **Health:** Communication disorders, health services, nursing (RN). **History:** General. **Interdisciplinary:** Gerontology. **Liberal arts:** Arts/sciences, humanities. **Math:** General, applied, statistics. **Parks/recreation:** General, health/fitness. **Philosophy/religion:** Judaic, philosophy, religion. **Physical sciences:** General, astronomy, chemistry, geology, molecular physics, physics, theoretical physics. **Protective services:** Law enforcement admin. **Psychology:** General. **Public administration:** General, social work. **Social sciences:** General, anthropology, economics, geography, international relations, political science, sociology, urban studies. **Visual/performing arts:** Art history/conservation, dance, design, dramatic, graphic design, interior design, music performance, studio arts. **Other:** Dietetics/food administration/nutrition, Modern Jewish studies, Telecommunications and film.

**Most popular majors.** Business/marketing 21%, English 7%, health sciences 6%, parks/recreation 6%, psychology 9%, security/protective services 6%, social sciences 12%.

**Computing on campus.** 400 workstations in dormitories, library, computer center, student center. Dormitories wired for high-speed internet access and linked to campus network. Commuter students can connect to campus network. Online course registration, online library, helpline, repair service, wireless network available.

**Student life. Freshman orientation:** Mandatory, $55 fee. Preregistration for classes offered. One-day academic orientation in July and August. Student life orientation held in August. **Housing:** Coed dorms, apartments, fraternity/sorority housing available. $800 partly refundable deposit. **Activities:** Bands, campus ministries, choral groups, dance, drama, film society, international student organizations, literary magazine, music ensembles, musical theater, opera, radio station, student government, student newspaper, symphony orchestra, TV station, more than 300 academic, recreational, sports, ethnic, political, honor, and service clubs on campus.

**Athletics.** NCAA. **Intercollegiate:** Baseball M, basketball, cross-country W, diving W, football (tackle) M, golf, rowing (crew) W, soccer, softball W, swimming W, tennis, track and field W, volleyball W, water polo W. **Intramural:** Basketball, bowling, football (non-tackle), golf, racquetball, soccer, softball, swimming, tennis, volleyball. **Team name:** Aztecs.

**Student services.** Alcohol/substance abuse counseling, chaplain/spiritual director, career counseling, services for economically disadvantaged, student employment services, financial aid counseling, health services, on-campus daycare, personal counseling, placement for graduates, veterans' counselor, women's services. **Physically disabled:** Services for visually, speech, hearing impaired. **Learning disabled:** Comprehensive services available.

**Contact.** E-mail: admissions@sdsu.edu
Phone: (619) 594-6336
Beverly Arata, Director of Admissions, San Diego State University, 5500 Campanile Drive, San Diego, CA 92182-7455

## San Francisco Art Institute
San Francisco, California — CB member
www.sfai.edu — CB code: 4036

- Private 4-year visual arts college
- Commuter campus in very large city
- 304 degree-seeking undergraduates: 9% part-time, 52% women, 5% African American, 10% Asian American, 10% Hispanic American, 2% Native American, 3% international
- 217 degree-seeking graduate students
- 94% of applicants admitted
- SAT or ACT (ACT writing optional), application essay required
- 22% graduate within 6 years

**General.** Founded in 1871. Regionally accredited. SFAI-sponsored lectures, film screenings, and symposium events with visiting artists available to students. **Degrees:** 89 bachelor's awarded; master's offered. **Location:** Downtown. **Calendar:** Semester, limited summer session. **Full-time faculty:** 48 total. **Part-time faculty:** 99 total. **Class size:** 81% < 20, 17% 20-39, 1% 40-49, less than 1% 50-99. **Special facilities:** EARS XXI high definition research lab, Diego Rivera gallery, digital media studio, digital imaging studio, studio production facilities in photography, printmaking, design/technology, and filmmaking, open studio spaces, graffiti art studio.

**Freshman class profile.** 417 applied, 390 admitted, 56 enrolled.

| Mid 50% test scores | | | |
|---|---|---|---|
| SAT critical reading: | 430-600 | GPA 3.50-3.74: | 10% |
| SAT math: | 450-580 | GPA 3.0-3.49: | 41% |
| SAT writing: | 450-600 | GPA 2.0-2.99: | 45% |
| ACT composite: | 21-25 | Return as sophomores: | 48% |
| GPA 3.75 or higher: | 4% | Live on campus: | 77% |

**Basis for selection.** Admission decisions based on evaluation of portfolio, academic credentials including transcripts and standardized test scores, letters of recommendation, and personal statement. Portfolio of artwork required. Interviews recommended, but not required. **Homeschooled:** State high school equivalency certificate, letter of recommendation (nonparent) required.

**High school preparation.** College-preparatory program recommended. Recommended units include English 4, mathematics 2, social studies 3, history 2, science 2, foreign language 2 and visual/performing arts 4. Strong background in English, humanities, and social sciences as well as extensive high school and extracurricular art education recommended.

**2010-2011 Annual costs.** Tuition/fees (projected): $32,894. Room/board: $10,300. Books/supplies: $1,620. Personal expenses: $2,250.

**2008-2009 Financial aid. Non-need-based:** Scholarships awarded for academics, art.

**Application procedures. Admission:** Priority date 2/15; no deadline. $65 fee, may be waived for applicants with need. Admission notification on a rolling basis. Must reply by May 1 or within 3 week(s) if notified thereafter. **Financial aid:** Priority date 3/1, closing date 5/31. FAFSA required. Applicants notified on a rolling basis starting 4/15; must reply within 3 week(s) of notification.

**Academics. Special study options:** Cross-registration, double major, ESL, exchange student, independent study, internships, New York semester, study abroad. **Credit/placement by examination:** AP, CLEP, IB, institutional tests. 20 credit hours maximum toward bachelor's degree. **Support services:** Learning center, remedial instruction, study skills assistance, tutoring, writing center.

**Majors. Social sciences:** Urban studies. **Visual/performing arts:** Art, art history/conservation, ceramics, cinematography, film/cinema, multimedia, painting, photography, printmaking, sculpture, studio arts. **Other:** Urban studies.

**Computing on campus.** 71 workstations in dormitories, library, computer center, student center. Dormitories wired for high-speed internet access. Wireless network available.

**Student life. Freshman orientation:** Mandatory. Preregistration for classes offered. **Housing:** Coed dorms, wellness housing available. $450 nonrefundable deposit, deadline 6/1. **Activities:** Film society, international student organizations, radio station, student government.

**Student services.** Career counseling, student employment services, financial aid counseling, personal counseling, placement for graduates, veterans' counselor. **Physically disabled:** Services for visually, speech, hearing impaired.

**Contact.** E-mail: admissions@sfai.edu
Phone: (415) 749-4500 Toll-free number: (800) 345-7324
Fax: (415) 749-4592
Director of Admissions, San Francisco Art Institute, 800 Chestnut Street, San Francisco, CA 94133-2299

## San Francisco Conservatory of Music
**San Francisco, California**
**www.sfcm.edu**                                    **CB code: 4744**

- Private 4-year music college
- Commuter campus in very large city
- 203 degree-seeking undergraduates: 2% part-time, 45% women, 4% African American, 13% Asian American, 7% Hispanic American, 1% Native American, 21% international
- 208 degree-seeking graduate students
- 57% of applicants admitted
- Application essay required
- 68% graduate within 6 years

**General.** Founded in 1917. Regionally accredited. A small school of 400 musicians, all conservatory students receive extensive performance opportunities, both on campus and in the San Francisco Bay area. **Degrees:** 55 bachelor's awarded; master's offered. **Location:** Downtown. **Calendar:** Semester. **Full-time faculty:** 32 total; 25% have terminal degrees, 16% minority, 31% women. **Part-time faculty:** 77 total; 18% have terminal degrees, 6% minority, 30% women. **Class size:** 66% < 20, 29% 20-39, 3% 40-49, 2% 50-99, 2% >100. **Special facilities:** Concert performance halls, recording studios, listening lab, music library.

**Freshman class profile.** 304 applied, 173 admitted, 72 enrolled.

| | | | |
|---|---|---|---|
| End year in good standing: | 88% | Live on campus: | 73% |
| Return as sophomores: | 78% | International: | 11% |
| Out-of-state: | 43% | | |

**Basis for selection.** Most important criterion is music audition, followed by school achievement record, letters of recommendation, and test scores. Musical needs of institution also influence admission decisions. Audition required. **Homeschooled:** Transcript of courses and grades, state high school equivalency certificate, letter of recommendation (nonparent) required. SAT or ACT required.

**High school preparation.** Recommended units include English 3 and foreign language 3.

**2009-2010 Annual costs.** Tuition/fees: $33,280. Room only: $7,000. Books/supplies: $580.

**2009-2010 Financial aid. Need-based:** 51 full-time freshmen applied for aid; 51 were judged to have need; 51 of these received aid. Average need met was 85%. Average scholarship/grant was $17,675; average loan

$3,132. 64% of total undergraduate aid awarded as scholarships/grants, 36% as loans/jobs. **Non-need-based:** Awarded to 87 full-time undergraduates, including 24 freshmen. Scholarships awarded for music/drama.

**Application procedures. Admission:** Closing date 12/1 (receipt date). $100 fee. Application must be submitted online. Admission notification on a rolling basis beginning on or about 4/1. Must reply by May 1 or within 2 week(s) if notified thereafter. **Financial aid:** Priority date 3/1; no closing date. FAFSA, institutional form required. Applicants notified by 4/1; must reply by 5/1 or within 2 week(s) of notification.

**Academics. Special study options:** Independent study, internships. **Credit/placement by examination:** AP, CLEP, institutional tests. 36 credit hours maximum toward bachelor's degree. **Support services:** Remedial instruction, study skills assistance, tutoring.

**Majors. Visual/performing arts:** Music performance, music theory/composition, piano/organ, stringed instruments, voice/opera.

**Computing on campus.** 25 workstations in library, computer center. Dormitories wired for high-speed internet access. Student web hosting, wireless network available.

**Student life. Freshman orientation:** Mandatory. **Housing:** Coed dorms available. **Activities:** Choral groups, music ensembles, musical theater, opera, student government, symphony orchestra.

**Student services.** Financial aid counseling, health services, personal counseling.

**Contact.** E-mail: admit@sfcm.edu
Phone: (415) 864-7326 Toll-free number: (800) 899-7326
Fax: (415) 503-6299
Melissa Cocco-Mitten, Director of Admission, San Francisco Conservatory of Music, 50 Oak Street, San Francisco, CA 94102

## San Francisco State University
**San Francisco, California**                        **CB member**
**www.sfsu.edu**                                    **CB code: 4684**

- Public 4-year university
- Commuter campus in very large city
- 25,001 degree-seeking undergraduates: 20% part-time, 59% women, 5% African American, 28% Asian American, 18% Hispanic American, 7% international
- 4,867 degree-seeking graduate students
- 73% of applicants admitted
- 44% graduate within 6 years

**General.** Founded in 1899. Regionally accredited. **Degrees:** 5,875 bachelor's awarded; master's, doctoral, professional offered. **ROTC:** Army, Naval, Air Force. **Location:** 10 miles from downtown. **Calendar:** Semester, limited summer session. **Full-time faculty:** 818 total; 74% have terminal degrees, 39% minority, 48% women. **Part-time faculty:** 748 total; 35% have terminal degrees, 32% minority, 56% women. **Class size:** 16% < 20, 43% 20-39, 15% 40-49, 18% 50-99, 8% >100. **Special facilities:** Marine laboratories, environmental studies center, Sierra Nevada field campus, anthropology museum, astronomy facility.

**Freshman class profile.** 28,218 applied, 20,465 admitted, 4,032 enrolled.

| Mid 50% test scores | | | |
|---|---|---|---|
| SAT critical reading: | 440-560 | GPA 3.0-3.49: | 44% |
| SAT math: | 450-570 | GPA 2.0-2.99: | 38% |
| SAT writing: | 440-560 | Return as sophomores: | 75% |
| ACT composite: | 19-24 | Out-of-state: | 1% |
| GPA 3.75 or higher: | 6% | Live on campus: | 50% |
| GPA 3.50-3.74: | 12% | International: | 4% |

**Basis for selection.** School achievement record and score on SAT or ACT most important. Students with GPA over 3.0 may be exempted from SAT/ACT. However, all applicants for admission are urged to take the SAT or ACT and provide the scores of such tests to each CSU to which they seek admission. Campuses use these test results for advising and placement purposes and may require them for admission to impacted majors or programs. Impacted CSU campuses require SAT or ACT scores of all applicants for freshman admission. SAT or ACT scores required if applicant's secondary school GPA is lower than 3.0 for California residents or 3.61 for nonresidents. **Homeschooled:** Local school district verification of completion of secondary schooling; SAT or ACT scores.

**High school preparation.** College-preparatory program required. 14 units required. Required and recommended units include English 4, mathematics 3, social studies 1, history 1, science 2 (laboratory 2), foreign language 2, visual/performing arts 1 and academic electives 1.

**2009-2010 Annual costs.** Tuition/fees: $4,740; $15,900 out-of-state. Room/board: $11,970. Books/supplies: $1,764. Personal expenses: $3,114.

**2009-2010 Financial aid.** All financial aid based on need. 2,895 full-time freshmen applied for aid; 2,174 were judged to have need; 2,067 of these received aid. Average need met was 65%. Average scholarship/grant was $9,357; average loan $2,567. 57% of total undergraduate aid awarded as scholarships/grants, 43% as loans/jobs.

**Application procedures. Admission:** Priority date 11/30; deadline 11/30. $55 fee, may be waived for applicants with need. Admission notification on a rolling basis beginning on or about 10/1. Must reply by May 1 or within 2 week(s) if notified thereafter. **Financial aid:** Priority date 3/2; no closing date. FAFSA required. Applicants notified on a rolling basis starting 2/1; must reply within 2 week(s) of notification.

**Academics. Special study options:** Cooperative education, cross-registration, distance learning, double major, dual enrollment of high school students, ESL, honors, independent study, internships, liberal arts/career combination, student-designed major, study abroad, teacher certification program, Washington semester. **Credit/placement by examination:** AP, CLEP, IB, SAT, ACT, institutional tests. 30 credit hours maximum toward bachelor's degree. **Support services:** Learning center, pre-admission summer program, remedial instruction, study skills assistance, tutoring, writing center.

**Majors. Area/ethnic studies:** African-American, American, Asian-American, Chicano/Hispanic-American/Latino, Native American, women's. **Biology:** General, biochemistry, botany, cell/histology, ecology, marine, microbiology, physiology, zoology. **Business:** Accounting, banking/financial services, business admin, e-commerce, finance, hospitality admin, international, labor studies, management science, marketing, small business admin. **Communications:** Journalism, radio/tv. **Computer sciences:** General, computer science. **Conservation:** Environmental studies. **Education:** Early childhood. **Engineering:** Civil, computer, electrical, mechanical. **Engineering technology:** Industrial. **Family/consumer sciences:** General, clothing/textiles. **Foreign languages:** Chinese, classics, comparative lit, French, German, Italian, Japanese, Spanish. **Health:** Clinical lab science, communication disorders, dietetics, nursing (RN), public health ed. **History:** General. **Liberal arts:** Arts/sciences, humanities. **Math:** General, applied, statistics. **Parks/recreation:** Exercise sciences, facilities management. **Philosophy/religion:** Judaic, philosophy. **Physical sciences:** Atmospheric science, chemistry, geology, physics. **Protective services:** Criminal justice. **Psychology:** General. **Public administration:** Social work. **Social sciences:** Anthropology, economics, geography, international relations, political science, sociology, urban studies. **Visual/performing arts:** Art, dance, dramatic, film/cinema, industrial design, interior design, music performance. **Other:** Philosophy and religion.

**Most popular majors.** Business/marketing 20%, communications/journalism 8%, psychology 9%, social sciences 10%, visual/performing arts 8%.

**Computing on campus.** 2,800 workstations in library, computer center. Dormitories wired for high-speed internet access and linked to campus network. Online course registration, online library, helpline, repair service, student web hosting, wireless network available.

**Student life. Freshman orientation:** Mandatory, $35 fee. Preregistration for classes offered. **Housing:** Coed dorms, special housing for disabled, apartments, wellness housing available. $200 fully refundable deposit. Women-only floors available. **Activities:** Bands, campus ministries, choral groups, dance, drama, film society, international student organizations, literary magazine, music ensembles, musical theater, opera, radio station, student government, student newspaper, symphony orchestra, TV station, College Democrats, College Republicans, Muslim Student Association, Hillel, Korean Student Association, Filipino American Collegiate Endeavor, Environmentally Concerned Organization of Students.

**Athletics.** NCAA. **Intercollegiate:** Baseball M, basketball, cross-country, soccer, softball W, track and field W, volleyball W, wrestling M. **Intramural:** Basketball, soccer, volleyball. **Team name:** Gators.

**Student services.** Adult student services, alcohol/substance abuse counseling, career counseling, services for economically disadvantaged, student employment services, financial aid counseling, health services, on-campus daycare, personal counseling, placement for graduates, veterans' counselor. **Physically disabled:** Services for visually, speech, hearing impaired.

**Contact.** E-mail: ugadmit@sfsu.edu
Phone: (415) 338-1113 Fax: (415) 338-7196
John Pliska, Director, Undergraduate Admissions, San Francisco State University, 1600 Holloway Avenue, San Francisco, CA 94132

## San Jose State University

San Jose, California — CB member
www.sjsu.edu — CB code: 4687

- Public 4-year university and liberal arts college
- Commuter campus in very large city
- 24,273 degree-seeking undergraduates: 25% part-time, 52% women, 5% African American, 34% Asian American, 19% Hispanic American, 4% international
- 7,007 degree-seeking graduate students
- 74% of applicants admitted
- 46% graduate within 6 years

**General.** Founded in 1857. Regionally accredited. **Degrees:** 4,730 bachelor's awarded; master's offered. **ROTC:** Army, Air Force. **Location:** 50 miles from San Francisco. **Calendar:** Semester, limited summer session. **Full-time faculty:** 710 total; 30% minority, 44% women. **Part-time faculty:** 1,178 total; 26% minority, 51% women. **Class size:** 24% < 20, 50% 20-39, 14% 40-49, 10% 50-99, 2% >100. **Special facilities:** Marine laboratory, natural history living museum, nuclear science lab, center for Beethoven studies, Chicano resource center, art metal foundry, deep-sea research ship, electro-acoustic and recording studio.

**Freshman class profile.** 21,836 applied, 16,251 admitted, 2,764 enrolled.

| Mid 50% test scores | | | |
|---|---|---|---|
| SAT critical reading: | 440-540 | GPA 3.0-3.49: | 46% |
| SAT math: | 460-580 | GPA 2.0-2.99: | 29% |
| SAT writing: | 430-540 | End year in good standing: | 81% |
| ACT composite: | 18-24 | Return as sophomores: | 81% |
| GPA 3.75 or higher: | 10% | Out-of-state: | 1% |
| GPA 3.50-3.74: | 15% | Live on campus: | 45% |

**Basis for selection.** High school record and test scores most important. SAT or ACT required for applicants with less than 3.0 GPA.

**High school preparation.** College-preparatory program recommended. 15 units required; 17 recommended. Required and recommended units include English 4, mathematics 3-4, social studies 2, history 1, science 2-3 (laboratory 2), foreign language 2, visual/performing arts 1 and academic electives 1. History is 2 units in history/social science.

**2009-2010 Annual costs.** Tuition/fees: $5,054; $16,214 out-of-state. Room/board: $10,438. Books/supplies: $1,656. Personal expenses: $2,786.

**2008-2009 Financial aid.** All financial aid based on need. 2,311 full-time freshmen applied for aid; 2,112 were judged to have need; 2,035 of these received aid. Average need met was 87%. Average scholarship/grant was $5,864; average loan $5,632. 47% of total undergraduate aid awarded as scholarships/grants, 53% as loans/jobs.

**Application procedures. Admission:** Closing date 11/30. $55 fee, may be waived for applicants with need. Application must be submitted online. Admission notification 10/1. Admission notification on a rolling basis. Must reply by May 1 or within 2 week(s) if notified thereafter. **Financial aid:** Priority date 3/2, closing date 6/12. FAFSA required. Applicants notified on a rolling basis starting 4/10; must reply within 2 week(s) of notification.

**Academics. Special study options:** Distance learning, double major, dual enrollment of high school students, honors, independent study, internships, student-designed major, study abroad, teacher certification program. **Credit/placement by examination:** AP, CLEP, institutional tests. **Support services:** Learning center, pre-admission summer program, remedial instruction, study skills assistance, tutoring, writing center.

**Majors. Area/ethnic studies:** African-American. **Biology:** General, biochemistry, conservation, marine, microbiology, molecular, physiology. **Business:** Accounting, business admin, finance, hospitality admin, human resources, international, marketing. **Communications:** Advertising, journalism, public relations, radio/tv. **Computer sciences:** Computer science, information systems, information technology, systems analysis. **Conservation:** Environmental studies. **Education:** Early childhood. **Engineering:** General, aerospace, chemical, civil, computer, electrical, industrial, materials, mechanical, software. **Engineering technology:** Quality control. **Foreign languages:** Chinese, French, German, Japanese, linguistics, Spanish. **Health:** Communication disorders, dietetics, health care admin, health services, nursing (RN). **History:** General. **Interdisciplinary:** Accounting/computer science, behavioral sciences, natural sciences. **Liberal arts:** Arts/sciences, humanities. **Math:** General, applied. **Parks/recreation:** General, health/fitness. **Philosophy/religion:** Philosophy, religion. **Physical sciences:** Chemistry, geology, physics. **Protective services:** Criminal justice, forensics. **Psychology:** General. **Public administration:** Social work. **Social sciences:** General, anthropology, economics, geography, international relations, political science, sociology. **Transportation:** Aviation. **Visual/performing arts:** General, art, art history/conservation, dance, dramatic, graphic design, industrial design, interior design, music performance, studio arts.

**Most popular majors.** Business/marketing 30%, engineering/engineering technologies 8%, health sciences 9%, psychology 6%, social sciences 6%, visual/performing arts 8%.

**Computing on campus.** Dormitories wired for high-speed internet access and linked to campus network. Commuter students can connect to campus network. Online course registration, online library, helpline, repair service, wireless network available.

**Student life. Freshman orientation:** Mandatory, $130 fee. Preregistration for classes offered. Mandatory overnight program for all first-time freshmen. **Housing:** Coed dorms, single-sex dorms, special housing for disabled, apartments, cooperative housing, fraternity/sorority housing available. $600 partly refundable deposit. **Activities:** Marching band, campus ministries, choral groups, dance, drama, film society, international student organizations, literary magazine, music ensembles, musical theater, radio station, student government, student newspaper, symphony orchestra, TV station.

**Athletics.** NCAA. **Intercollegiate:** Baseball M, basketball, cheerleading, cross-country, diving W, football (tackle) M, golf, gymnastics W, soccer, softball W, swimming W, tennis W, volleyball W, water polo W. **Intramural:** Archery, badminton, baseball M, basketball, bowling, field hockey W, football (non-tackle), lacrosse, racquetball, soccer, softball, swimming, table tennis, tennis, volleyball W, water polo. **Team name:** Spartans.

**Student services.** Adult student services, alcohol/substance abuse counseling, chaplain/spiritual director, career counseling, services for economically disadvantaged, student employment services, financial aid counseling, health services, legal services, minority student services, on-campus daycare, personal counseling, placement for graduates, veterans' counselor, women's services. **Physically disabled:** Services for visually, speech, hearing impaired.

**Contact.** E-mail: contact@sjsu.edu
Phone: (408) 283-7500
Deanna Gonzales, Director of Undergraduate/Graduate Admissions
Manager, San Jose State University, One Washington Square, San Jose, CA 95192-0011

---

### Santa Clara University

**Santa Clara, California**      CB member
**www.scu.edu**      CB code: 4851

- Private 4-year university affiliated with Roman Catholic Church
- Residential campus in small city
- 5,158 degree-seeking undergraduates: 2% part-time, 53% women, 4% African American, 17% Asian American, 15% Hispanic American, 1% Native American, 3% international
- 3,506 degree-seeking graduate students
- 59% of applicants admitted
- SAT or ACT with writing, application essay required
- 85% graduate within 6 years; 24% enter graduate study

**General.** Founded in 1851. Regionally accredited. **Degrees:** 1,254 bachelor's awarded; master's, doctoral, professional offered. **ROTC:** Army, Air Force. **Location:** 45 miles from San Francisco, 1 mile from San Jose. **Calendar:** Quarter, limited summer session. **Full-time faculty:** 436 total; 94% have terminal degrees, 19% minority, 41% women. **Part-time faculty:** 362 total; 58% have terminal degrees, 18% minority, 41% women. **Class size:** 35% < 20, 56% 20-39, 7% 40-49, 2% 50-99. **Special facilities:** Historic mission church with artifacts dating from California mission era, applied ethics center, observatory, tennis complex, de Saisset museum.

**Freshman class profile.** 10,226 applied, 6,057 admitted, 1,085 enrolled.

| Mid 50% test scores | | | |
|---|---|---|---|
| SAT critical reading: | 550-650 | Rank in top quarter: | 76% |
| SAT math: | 570-680 | Rank in top tenth: | 37% |
| ACT composite: | 25-30 | End year in good standing: | 95% |
| GPA 3.75 or higher: | 29% | Return as sophomores: | 92% |
| GPA 3.50-3.74: | 31% | Out-of-state: | 41% |
| GPA 3.0-3.49: | 36% | Live on campus: | 95% |
| GPA 2.0-2.99: | 4% | International: | 2% |

**Basis for selection.** GED not accepted. Rigor of high school curriculum and GPA most important, followed by test scores, teacher's recommendation, personal essay, and extracurricular activities. Ethnicity and alumni affiliations given special consideration. State Exam. Interviews not recommended. Audition recommended for music, theater arts majors. **Homeschooled:** Statement describing homeschool structure and mission required.

**High school preparation.** College-preparatory program required. 15 units required; 19 recommended. Required and recommended units include English 4, mathematics 3-4, social studies 3, science 2-3, foreign language 2-3, visual/performing arts 1 and academic electives 1. Social studies units include history.

**2010-2011 Annual costs.** Tuition/fees: $37,368. Room/board: $11,742. Books/supplies: $1,638. Personal expenses: $2,250.

**2009-2010 Financial aid. Need-based:** 714 full-time freshmen applied for aid; 506 were judged to have need; 489 of these received aid. Average need met was 74%. Average scholarship/grant was $22,031; average loan $3,289. 82% of total undergraduate aid awarded as scholarships/grants, 18% as loans/jobs. **Non-need-based:** Awarded to 2,359 full-time undergraduates, including 551 freshmen. Scholarships awarded for academics, alumni affiliation, athletics, music/drama, ROTC.

**Application procedures. Admission:** Closing date 1/7 (postmark date). $55 fee, may be waived for applicants with need. Application must be submitted online. Admission notification 4/1. Must reply by 5/1. **Financial aid:** Priority date 2/1; no closing date. FAFSA, CSS PROFILE required. Applicants notified by 4/1; must reply by 5/1 or within 2 week(s) of notification.

**Academics. Special study options:** Combined bachelor's/graduate degree, cooperative education, double major, honors, independent study, internships, student-designed major, study abroad, teacher certification program, Washington semester. **Credit/placement by examination:** AP, CLEP, IB, institutional tests. No credit by examination awarded to new students. Number of credit hours awarded for International Baccalaureate determined on case-by-case basis. **Support services:** Learning center, reduced course load, study skills assistance, tutoring, writing center.

**Majors. Area/ethnic studies:** Women's. **Biology:** General, biochemistry. **Business:** Accounting, accounting/business management, finance, management information systems, managerial economics, marketing, organizational behavior. **Communications:** General. **Computer sciences:** Web page design. **Conservation:** Environmental science, environmental studies. **Engineering:** General, agricultural, civil, computer, electrical, mechanical, physics. **Foreign languages:** Ancient Greek, classics, French, German, Italian, Latin, Spanish. **History:** General. **Interdisciplinary:** Ancient studies, math/computer science. **Liberal arts:** Arts/sciences. **Math:** General. **Philosophy/religion:** Philosophy, religion. **Physical sciences:** Chemistry, physics. **Psychology:** General. **Social sciences:** Anthropology, economics, political science, sociology. **Visual/performing arts:** Art history/conservation, dramatic, studio arts.

**Most popular majors.** Business/marketing 35%, communications/journalism 9%, engineering/engineering technologies 9%, psychology 7%, social sciences 13%.

**Computing on campus.** 640 workstations in dormitories, library, computer center, student center. Dormitories wired for high-speed internet access and linked to campus network. Commuter students can connect to campus network. Online course registration, online library, helpline, repair service, student web hosting, wireless network available.

**Student life. Freshman orientation:** Mandatory, $285 fee. Preregistration for classes offered. 2-day session in summer and 2-day session on weekend before school starts. Parents attend separate program. **Housing:** Guaranteed on-campus for freshmen. Coed dorms, apartments available. $250 nonrefundable deposit, deadline 5/1. **Activities:** Bands, campus ministries, choral groups, dance, drama, international student organizations, literary magazine, music ensembles, Model UN, musical theater, opera, radio station, student government, student newspaper, symphony orchestra, Asian Pacific Student Union, Ka Mana'o O Hawaii, community action program, Barkada, MECHA, Chinese student association, CORE Christian Fellowship, Engineers Without Borders, political science student association.

**Athletics.** NCAA. **Intercollegiate:** Baseball M, basketball, cross-country, golf, rowing (crew), soccer, tennis, track and field, volleyball W, water polo. **Intramural:** Badminton, baseball, football (non-tackle), soccer, softball, table tennis, tennis, volleyball. **Team name:** Broncos.

**Student services.** Alcohol/substance abuse counseling, chaplain/spiritual director, career counseling, student employment services, financial aid counseling, health services, legal services, minority student services, on-campus daycare, personal counseling, placement for graduates, veterans' counselor. **Physically disabled:** Services for visually, speech, hearing impaired.

**Contact.** Phone: (408) 554-4700 Fax: (408) 554-5255
Sandra Hayes, Dean of Undergraduate Admissions, Santa Clara University, 500 El Camino Real, Santa Clara, CA 95053

## School of Urban Missions: Oakland
### Oakland, California
### www.sum.edu

♦ Private 4-year Bible college affiliated with Assemblies of God
♦ Residential campus in very large city
♦ 139 degree-seeking undergraduates: 4% part-time, 43% women
♦ 18 degree-seeking graduate students
♦ 59% of applicants admitted
♦ Application essay, interview required

**General.** Regionally accredited; also accredited by ABHE. Extensive hands-on ministry training with 8 hours per week of ministry. Additional campus in New Orleans. **Degrees:** 15 bachelor's, 3 associate awarded. **Location:** Downtown. **Calendar:** Trimester, limited summer session. **Full-time faculty:** 4 total; 50% have terminal degrees, 25% women. **Part-time faculty:** 18 total; 17% have terminal degrees, 44% women. **Class size:** 37% < 20, 63% 20-39.

**Freshman class profile.** 111 applied, 65 admitted, 65 enrolled.

**Basis for selection.** Recommendations, interview, character/personal qualities are very important. Academic GPA and application essay are considered. Pastor's recommendation and one general recommendation required. **Homeschooled:** Transcript of courses and grades, state high school equivalency certificate, letter of recommendation (nonparent) required.

**High school preparation.** Required and recommended units include English 4, mathematics 3-4, history 2, science 2-3, foreign language 2-3, visual/performing arts 1 and academic electives 1. No academic requirement for high school diploma. Minimum 2.0 GPA preferred. If student is below 2.0, the student may be enrolled but with academic probation.

**2010-2011 Annual costs.** Tuition/fees: $7,830. Room only: $2,400. Books/supplies: $1,500.

**2008-2009 Financial aid. Non-need-based:** Scholarships awarded for academics, leadership, religious affiliation.

**Application procedures. Admission:** No deadline. $25 fee. Application must be submitted on paper. Admission notification on a rolling basis beginning on or about 1/1. **Financial aid:** No deadline. FAFSA required.

**Academics. Special study options:** Distance learning. **Credit/placement by examination:** AP, CLEP. No credit for life experience in the academic courses. Field ministry credits can be considered life experience. **Support services:** Reduced course load, remedial instruction, tutoring.

**Majors. Theology:** Bible.

**Computing on campus.** 5 workstations in library. Dormitories wired for high-speed internet access and linked to campus network. Online course registration, online library, wireless network available.

**Student life. Freshman orientation:** Mandatory. Preregistration for classes offered. **Policies:** 2 hours of Christian service required per week. Religious observance required. **Housing:** Guaranteed on-campus for all undergraduates. Single-sex dorms, apartments available. **Activities:** Campus ministries, student government.

**Student services.** Chaplain/spiritual director, financial aid counseling, health services, personal counseling.

**Contact.** E-mail: sum@sum.edu
Phone: (510) 567-6174 Toll-free number: (888) 567-6171
Fax: (510) 568-1024
Rev. Kenneth Searle, Academic Dean, School of Urban Missions: Oakland, 735 105th Avenue, Oakland, CA 94603

## Scripps College
### Claremont, California
### www.scrippscollege.edu
**CB member**
**CB code: 4693**

♦ Private 4-year liberal arts college for women
♦ Residential campus in large town
♦ 898 degree-seeking undergraduates: 100% women, 4% African American, 13% Asian American, 9% Hispanic American, 1% Native American, 2% international
♦ 15 graduate students
♦ 33% of applicants admitted
♦ SAT or ACT (ACT writing optional), application essay required
♦ 87% graduate within 6 years

**General.** Founded in 1926. Regionally accredited. One of cluster of 5 undergraduate and 2 graduate schools on adjoining campuses. Campuses share facilities. Cross-enrollment available at any of the Claremont colleges: Claremont-McKenna, Harvey Mudd, Pitzer, Pomona, and Scripps. **Degrees:** 226 bachelor's awarded. **ROTC:** Army, Air Force. **Location:** 35 miles from Los Angeles. **Calendar:** Semester, limited summer session. **Full-time faculty:** 81 total; 100% have terminal degrees, 21% minority, 56% women. **Part-time faculty:** 23 total; 70% have terminal degrees, 56% women. **Class size:** 81% < 20, 18% 20-39, less than 1% 40-49, less than 1% >100. **Special facilities:** Art slide library, biological field station, humanities museum.

**Freshman class profile.** 2,061 applied, 678 admitted, 203 enrolled.

| Mid 50% test scores | | | |
|---|---|---|---|
| SAT critical reading: | 640-730 | GPA 3.0-3.49: | 11% |
| SAT math: | 620-700 | Rank in top quarter: | 94% |
| SAT writing: | 640-730 | Rank in top tenth: | 69% |
| ACT composite: | 27-32 | Return as sophomores: | 88% |
| GPA 3.75 or higher: | 78% | Out-of-state: | 59% |
| GPA 3.50-3.74: | 11% | Live on campus: | 100% |
| | | International: | 5% |

**Basis for selection.** Rigor of high school curriculum, GPA, class rank, aptitude as reflected in standardized testing most important. Essays, recommendations, required graded writing assignment significant. SAT Subject Tests used for placement in language only; institutional language and math exam used for placement. Interviews recommended. Audition recommended for music, dance majors. Portfolio recommended for art majors. **Homeschooled:** Statement describing homeschool structure and mission, transcript of courses and grades, letter of recommendation (nonparent) required. Interview highly recommended. **Learning Disabled:** Documentation of learning disability required.

**High school preparation.** College-preparatory program recommended. 16 units required. Required units include English 4, mathematics 3, social studies 3, science 3 and foreign language 3.

**2010-2011 Annual costs.** Tuition/fees: $40,450. Room/board: $12,450. Books/supplies: $800. Personal expenses: $1,000.

**2008-2009 Financial aid. Need-based:** 104 full-time freshmen applied for aid; 73 were judged to have need; 73 of these received aid. Average need met was 100%. Average scholarship/grant was $30,601; average loan $2,313. 89% of total undergraduate aid awarded as scholarships/grants, 11% as loans/jobs. **Non-need-based:** Awarded to 202 full-time undergraduates, including 33 freshmen. Scholarships awarded for academics, leadership.

**Application procedures. Admission:** Closing date 1/1 (postmark date). $60 fee, may be waived for applicants with need. Admission notification 4/1. Must reply by 5/1. **Financial aid:** Priority date 2/1, closing date 2/1. FAFSA, CSS PROFILE required. Applicants notified by 4/1; must reply by 5/1.

**Academics.** Almost half of junior class elects to study abroad for semester or year. **Special study options:** Accelerated study, combined bachelor's/graduate degree, cross-registration, double major, dual enrollment of high school students, exchange student, independent study, internships, New York semester, student-designed major, study abroad, United Nations semester, Washington semester. Post-baccalaureate pre-medical certificate program, humanities internship program, 3-2 engineering program with Harvey Mudd College. **Credit/placement by examination:** AP, CLEP, IB, institutional tests. 32 credit hours maximum toward bachelor's degree. SAT Subject Tests recommended for placement. **Support services:** Reduced course load, tutoring, writing center.

**Majors. Area/ethnic studies:** African-American, American, Asian, Asian-American, Chicano/Hispanic-American/Latino, European, French, German, Italian, Latin American, Spanish/Iberian, women's. **Biology:** General, biochemistry, molecular. **Business:** Accounting, organizational behavior. **Computer sciences:** Computer science. **Conservation:** Environmental science, environmental studies. **Engineering:** General. **Foreign languages:** General, Chinese, classics, French, German, Italian, Japanese, linguistics, Russian, Spanish. **History:** General. **Interdisciplinary:** Biological/physical sciences, neuroscience, science/society. **Legal studies:** General. **Liberal arts:** Humanities. **Math:** General. **Philosophy/religion:** Judaic, philosophy, religion. **Physical sciences:** Chemistry, geology, physics. **Psychology:** General. **Public administration:** Policy analysis. **Social sciences:** Anthropology, econometrics, economics, political science, sociology. **Visual/performing arts:** Art history/conservation, dance, dramatic, film/cinema, studio arts. **Other:** Film/video and photographic arts.

**Most popular majors.** Area/ethnic studies 14%, biology 8%, English 8%, interdisciplinary studies 9%, psychology 10%, social sciences 15%, visual/performing arts 10%.

**Computing on campus.** 84 workstations in dormitories, library, computer center. Dormitories wired for high-speed internet access and linked to campus network. Commuter students can connect to campus network. Online library, helpline, repair service, student web hosting, wireless network available.

**Student life. Freshman orientation:** Mandatory. 5-day orientation begins last Thursday in August. **Housing:** Guaranteed on-campus for freshmen. Special housing for disabled, apartments, wellness housing available. Most sophomores, most juniors and all seniors have single rooms. Off-campus houses available to single students. **Activities:** Campus ministries, choral groups, dance, drama, international student organizations, literary magazine, music ensembles, Model UN, radio station, student government, student newspaper, symphony orchestra, Asian American Student Union, Cafe Con Leche, Claremont Colleges Ballroom Dance Team, Claremont Colleges Women's Rugby, Criminal Justice Network, Economic Society, International Club, Office of Black Student Affairs, On The Loose, and Scripps Associated Students.

**Athletics.** NCAA. **Intercollegiate:** Basketball W, cross-country W, diving W, golf W, lacrosse W, soccer W, softball W, swimming W, tennis W, track and field W, volleyball W, water polo W. **Intramural:** Basketball W, soccer W, softball W, volleyball W, water polo W. **Team name:** Athenas.

**Student services.** Adult student services, chaplain/spiritual director, career counseling, student employment services, financial aid counseling, health services, minority student services, personal counseling, placement for graduates, women's services.

**Contact.** E-mail: admission@scrippscollege.edu
Phone: (909) 621-8149 Toll-free number: (800) 770-1333
Fax: (909) 607-7508
Laura Stratton, Director of Admission, Scripps College, 1030 Columbia Avenue, Claremont, CA 91711-3905

## Shasta Bible College and Graduate School
Redding, California
www.shasta.edu

- Private 4-year Bible college affiliated with Baptist faith
- Residential campus in small city
- 47 degree-seeking undergraduates: 26% part-time, 60% women
- 10 degree-seeking graduate students
- 94% of applicants admitted
- Application essay required
- 44% graduate within 6 years; 10% enter graduate study

**General.** Regionally accredited; also accredited by TRACS. A strong emphasis on inductive Bible Study, hermeneutics (Bible Interpretation), biblical languages, evangelism, apologetics, and homiletics (preaching and teaching), along with general education requirements. **Degrees:** 9 bachelor's awarded; master's offered. **Calendar:** Semester, limited summer session. **Full-time faculty:** 7 total. **Part-time faculty:** 31 total. **Special facilities:** World class vernal pool (containing a variety of endangered species including slender orcutt grass, henderson bent blade grass, red bluff dwarf rush grass, fairy shrimp, tadpole shrimp), creation museum.

**Freshman class profile.** 18 applied, 17 admitted, 17 enrolled.

| | | | |
|---|---|---|---|
| End year in good standing: | 100% | Out-of-state: | 10% |
| Return as sophomores: | 33% | Live on campus: | 90% |

**Basis for selection.** An essay on Psalms 23, an autobiography, and 4 references required. All applicable transcripts from high school and colleges attended required. **Homeschooled:** Transcript of courses and grades required.

**2010-2011 Annual costs.** Tuition/fees: $8,870. Room/board: $2,400.

**2008-2009 Financial aid. Non-need-based:** Scholarships awarded for music/drama.

**Application procedures. Admission:** Closing date 8/29 (receipt date). $50 fee. Admission notification on a rolling basis. **Financial aid:** No deadline. FAFSA required. Applicants notified on a rolling basis.

**Academics. Special study options:** Distance learning, dual enrollment of high school students, independent study, teacher certification program. Association of Christian Schools International certificates standard and temporary. **Credit/placement by examination:** AP, CLEP, institutional tests. 30 credit hours maximum toward associate degree, 30 toward bachelor's.

**Majors. Theology:** Theology. **Other:** Christian teacher education.

**Computing on campus.** 10 workstations in library. Dormitories wired for high-speed internet access and linked to campus network. Commuter students can connect to campus network. Online course registration, online library, wireless network available.

**Student life. Freshman orientation:** Mandatory. Preregistration for classes offered. **Policies:** Lifestyle commitment must be signed annually by each student. Dress code. Religious observance required. **Housing:** Single-sex dorms available. $100 nonrefundable deposit. **Activities:** Campus ministries, choral groups, student government.

**Student services.** Chaplain/spiritual director, financial aid counseling, personal counseling.

**Contact.** E-mail: admissions@shasta.edu
Phone: (530) 221-4275
George Gunn, Dean of Admissions, Shasta Bible College and Graduate School, 2951 Goodwater Avenue, Redding, CA 96002

## Silicon Valley University
San Jose, California
www.svuca.edu

- Private 4-year university, business, engineering and technical college
- Commuter campus in very large city
- 17 degree-seeking undergraduates

**General.** Accredited by ACICS. **Degrees:** 3 bachelor's awarded; master's offered. **Calendar:** Trimester. **Full-time faculty:** 1 total. **Part-time faculty:** 28 total.

**Basis for selection. Homeschooled:** Transcript of courses and grades, state high school equivalency certificate, interview, letter of recommendation (nonparent) required.

**High school preparation.** College-preparatory program recommended.

**2009-2010 Annual costs.** Tuition/fees: $9,405. Books/supplies: $700.

**Application procedures. Admission:** Closing date 7/1. $75 fee. Application must be submitted online.

**Academics. Special study options:** Accelerated study, ESL, independent study, internships, weekend college. **Credit/placement by examination:** CLEP.

**Majors. Business:** Business admin. **Computer sciences:** Computer science.

**Computing on campus.** 12 workstations in library, computer center. Commuter students can connect to campus network. Online library, wireless network available.

**Student life. Freshman orientation:** Mandatory. Preregistration for classes offered. **Activities:** International student organizations, student government.

**Student services.** Minority student services, personal counseling.

**Contact.** E-mail: studentoffice@svuca.edu
Phone: (408) 435-8989 ext. 106
Silicon Valley University, 2160 Lundy Avenue Suite #110, San Jose, CA 95131

## Simpson University
Redding, California
www.simpsonu.edu                        CB code: 4698

- Private 4-year liberal arts college affiliated with Christian and Missionary Alliance
- Residential campus in small city
- 953 degree-seeking undergraduates: 3% part-time, 63% women, 4% African American, 8% Asian American, 6% Hispanic American, 1% Native American
- 187 graduate students

♦ 59% of applicants admitted
♦ Application essay required
♦ 45% graduate within 6 years

**General.** Founded in 1921. Regionally accredited. Christ-centered educational community. **Degrees:** 269 bachelor's awarded; master's offered. **ROTC:** Army. **Location:** 170 miles from Sacramento. **Calendar:** Semester, limited summer session. **Full-time faculty:** 39 total; 72% have terminal degrees, 10% minority, 26% women. **Part-time faculty:** 82 total; 33% have terminal degrees, 2% minority, 39% women. **Class size:** 71% < 20, 23% 20-39, 2% 40-49, 3% 50-99. **Special facilities:** Climbing wall, ropes course, outdoor recreation.

**Freshman class profile.** 662 applied, 392 admitted, 145 enrolled.

| Mid 50% test scores | | | |
|---|---|---|---|
| SAT critical reading: | 440-550 | Rank in top quarter: | 43% |
| SAT math: | 420-530 | Rank in top tenth: | 17% |
| SAT writing: | 440-530 | End year in good standing: | 85% |
| ACT composite: | 18-24 | Return as sophomores: | 73% |
| GPA 3.75 or higher: | 23% | Out-of-state: | 20% |
| GPA 3.50-3.74: | 24% | Live on campus: | 90% |
| GPA 3.0-3.49: | 33% | | |
| GPA 2.0-2.99: | 20% | | |

**Basis for selection.** Commitment to Jesus Christ as reflected in personal statement and required references, academic achievement, other recommendations, and standardized test scores important. SAT and SAT Subject Tests or ACT recommended. **Homeschooled:** Transcript of courses and grades required.

**High school preparation.** College-preparatory program recommended. Recommended units include English 4, mathematics 3, social studies 3, science 2 and foreign language 2. College-preparatory program highly recommended.

**2010-2011 Annual costs.** Tuition/fees (projected): $21,000. Room/board: $7,000. Books/supplies: $1,392. Personal expenses: $1,968.

**2009-2010 Financial aid. Need-based:** 144 full-time freshmen applied for aid; 134 were judged to have need; 134 of these received aid. 67% of total undergraduate aid awarded as scholarships/grants, 33% as loans/jobs. **Non-need-based:** Scholarships awarded for academics, alumni affiliation, athletics, leadership, minority status, music/drama, religious affiliation, state residency. **Additional information:** Work-study programs available.

**Application procedures. Admission:** No deadline. $50 fee, may be waived for applicants with need. Admission notification on a rolling basis. Must reply by May 1 or within 2 week(s) if notified thereafter. **Financial aid:** Priority date 3/2; no closing date. FAFSA, institutional form required. Applicants notified on a rolling basis starting 3/1; must reply within 4 week(s) of notification.

**Academics.** 34-semester-hour teacher credential program permits students to earn California Clear Credential for grades K-8 (multiple subjects) or for grades 7-12 (single subject). **Special study options:** Accelerated study, combined bachelor's/graduate degree, distance learning, double major, honors, independent study, internships, student-designed major, study abroad, teacher certification program, Washington semester, weekend college. **Credit/placement by examination:** AP, CLEP, SAT, ACT, institutional tests. 30 credit hours maximum toward bachelor's degree. Credit by examination granted only to enrolled students. Students may take challenge exam for particular course only once. **Support services:** Reduced course load, remedial instruction, study skills assistance, tutoring, writing center.

**Majors. Biology:** General. **Business:** Accounting, business admin, management information systems, organizational behavior. **Communications:** General. **Education:** Elementary, English, mathematics, music, social science. **Health:** Health care admin. **History:** General. **Liberal arts:** Arts/sciences. **Math:** General. **Parks/recreation:** General. **Philosophy/religion:** Christian, religion. **Psychology:** General. **Social sciences:** General. **Theology:** Bible, missionary, pastoral counseling, theology, youth ministry.

**Most popular majors.** Business/marketing 30%, health sciences 6%, liberal arts 21%, psychology 20%, theological studies 8%.

**Computing on campus.** 50 workstations in dormitories, library, computer center. Dormitories wired for high-speed internet access and linked to campus network. Commuter students can connect to campus network. Online course registration, online library, helpline, repair service, wireless network available.

**Student life. Freshman orientation:** Mandatory. Preregistration for classes offered. Sessions include placement tests. **Policies:** All single undergraduates under 22 required to live on campus. Request for off-campus living must be approved by Vice President for Student Development. Religious observance required. **Housing:** Guaranteed on-campus for all undergraduates. Single-sex dorms, special housing for disabled, apartments, wellness housing available. $100 fully refundable deposit, deadline 9/1. **Activities:** Jazz band, campus ministries, choral groups, dance, film society, music ensembles, student government, student newspaper, symphony orchestra, Asian Fellowship, Hispanic Fellowship, summer missions teams, chapel worship team, spiritual action committee, psychology club, Missionary Kids Association, commuter student association.

**Athletics.** NAIA, NCCAA. **Intercollegiate:** Baseball M, basketball, cross-country, golf, soccer, softball W, volleyball W. **Intramural:** Basketball, football (non-tackle), soccer. **Team name:** Red Hawks.

**Student services.** Adult student services, chaplain/spiritual director, career counseling, student employment services, financial aid counseling, health services, minority student services, personal counseling, veterans' counselor. **Physically disabled:** Services for visually, speech, hearing impaired.

**Contact.** E-mail: admissions@simpsonu.edu
Phone: (530) 226-4606 Toll-free number: (888) 974-6776
Fax: (530) 226-4861
Kendell Kluttz, Director of Undergraduate Admissions, Simpson University, 2211 College View Drive, Redding, CA 96003-8606

## Soka University of America
**Aliso Viejo, California**
www.soka.edu

**CB member**
**CB code: 4066**

♦ Private 4-year university and liberal arts college
♦ Residential campus in large town
♦ 439 degree-seeking undergraduates
♦ SAT or ACT with writing, application essay required

**General. Degrees:** 67 bachelor's awarded; master's offered. **Location:** 70 miles from Los Angeles, 75 miles from San Diego. **Calendar:** Semester. **Full-time faculty:** 38 total; 95% have terminal degrees, 32% minority, 45% women. **Part-time faculty:** 17 total; 53% have terminal degrees, 53% minority, 65% women. **Class size:** 100% < 20.

**Freshman class profile.**

| Mid 50% test scores | | | |
|---|---|---|---|
| SAT critical reading: | 440-660 | GPA 3.0-3.49: | 22% |
| SAT math: | 520-720 | GPA 2.0-2.99: | 3% |
| SAT writing: | 490-630 | Rank in top quarter: | 80% |
| ACT composite: | 23-24 | Rank in top tenth: | 43% |
| GPA 3.75 or higher: | 37% | Out-of-state: | 60% |
| GPA 3.50-3.74: | 38% | Live on campus: | 99% |

**Basis for selection.** GPA and courses most important. Test scores, essay, recommendations, extracurricular activities also important. **Homeschooled:** State high school equivalency certificate required. Program must be accredited by regional, state, or national agency. **Learning Disabled:** Admission decisions do not consider learning disabilities. Special needs discussed only after student has been admitted and has identified need.

**High school preparation.** 17 units recommended. Recommended units include English 4, mathematics 3, social studies 2, history 2, science 2 (laboratory 2) and foreign language 2.

**2009-2010 Annual costs.** Tuition/fees: $24,606. Room/board: $9,360. Books/supplies: $1,000. Personal expenses: $1,500.

**2008-2009 Financial aid. Non-need-based:** Scholarships awarded for academics, athletics.

**Application procedures. Admission:** Closing date 1/15 (postmark date). $45 fee. Admission notification 3/15. Must reply by 5/1. **Financial aid:** Closing date 3/1. FAFSA required. Applicants notified on a rolling basis starting 3/15; must reply within 4 week(s) of notification.

**Academics.** Study abroad required of all students during one semester of their junior year. **Special study options:** ESL, independent study, internships, study abroad. **Credit/placement by examination:** CLEP, SAT, ACT, institutional tests. **Support services:** Study skills assistance, tutoring, writing center.

**Majors. Liberal arts:** Arts/sciences.

**Computing on campus.** PC or laptop required. 100 workstations in dormitories, library, computer center. Dormitories wired for high-speed internet access and linked to campus network. Commuter students can connect to campus network. Online course registration, online library, helpline, repair service, wireless network available.

**Student life. Freshman orientation:** Mandatory. Preregistration for classes offered. 4-day orientation period before upperclassmen arrive. **Housing:** Guaranteed on-campus for all undergraduates. Coed dorms, wellness housing available. Students required to live on campus. **Activities:** Jazz band, choral groups, dance, film society, literary magazine, music ensembles, Model UN, student government, student newspaper, Amnesty International, Buena Vista social club, Chinese club, Green Planet, Humanism in Action, orchestra club, Activist Collective, French club.

**Athletics. NAIA. Intercollegiate:** Cross-country, soccer, swimming, track and field. **Intramural:** Badminton, basketball, racquetball, soccer, tennis, volleyball, weight lifting. **Team name:** Lions.

**Student services.** Alcohol/substance abuse counseling, career counseling, student employment services, financial aid counseling, health services, personal counseling, placement for graduates. **Physically disabled:** Services for visually, hearing impaired.

**Contact.** E-mail: admission@soka.edu
Phone: (949) 480-4150 Toll-free number: (888) 600-7652
Fax: (949) 480-4151
Christopher Brown, Director of Admission and Financial Aid, Soka University of America, One University Drive, Aliso Viejo, CA 92656-8081

## Sonoma State University
### Rohnert Park, California
**www.sonoma.edu**  **CB code: 4723**

- Public 4-year university and liberal arts college
- Commuter campus in large town
- 7,483 degree-seeking undergraduates: 12% part-time, 62% women, 1% African American, 4% Asian American, 12% Hispanic American, 1% Native American, 1% international
- 266 degree-seeking graduate students
- 77% of applicants admitted
- SAT or ACT (ACT writing optional) required
- 73% graduate within 6 years

**General.** Founded in 1960. Regionally accredited. **Degrees:** 1,656 bachelor's awarded; master's offered. **ROTC:** Army, Naval, Air Force. **Location:** 50 miles from San Francisco, 10 miles from Santa Rosa. **Calendar:** Semester, extensive summer session. **Full-time faculty:** 278 total; 91% have terminal degrees, 16% minority, 46% women. **Part-time faculty:** 263 total; 28% have terminal degrees, 12% minority, 57% women. **Class size:** 39% < 20, 45% 20-39, 9% 40-49, 5% 50-99, 2% >100. **Special facilities:** Observatory, performing arts center, nature preserves, information technology center.

**Freshman class profile.** 11,244 applied, 8,690 admitted, 2,215 enrolled.

| Mid 50% test scores | | | |
|---|---|---|---|
| SAT critical reading: | 450-560 | GPA 3.0-3.49: | 51% |
| SAT math: | 460-570 | GPA 2.0-2.99: | 26% |
| ACT composite: | 19-24 | Return as sophomores: | 75% |
| GPA 3.75 or higher: | 9% | Out-of-state: | 1% |
| GPA 3.50-3.74: | 14% | Live on campus: | 92% |
| | | International: | 2% |

**Basis for selection.** School GPA and test scores most important. SAT, ACT, SAT Subject Tests must be received before start of term. Audition required of music majors. Portfolio required of art majors. RN required for graduate nursing. **Learning Disabled:** Applicants with disabilities strongly encouraged to complete college preparatory course requirements if at all possible. If applicant judged unable to fulfill specific course requirement because of disability, alternative college preparatory courses may be substituted for specific subject requirements.

**High school preparation.** College-preparatory program required. 15 units required. Required units include English 4, mathematics 3, history 2, science 2 (laboratory 1), foreign language 2, visual/performing arts 1 and academic electives 1. One visual and performing arts, US government required.

**2009-2010 Annual costs.** Tuition/fees: $5,290; $16,450 out-of-state. Room/board: $10,418. Books/supplies: $1,732. Personal expenses: $2,928.

**2008-2009 Financial aid. Need-based:** 679 full-time freshmen applied for aid; 394 were judged to have need; 336 of these received aid. Average need met was 64%. Average scholarship/grant was $8,264; average loan $3,156. 56% of total undergraduate aid awarded as scholarships/grants, 44% as loans/jobs. **Non-need-based:** Awarded to 566 full-time undergraduates, including 101 freshmen. Scholarships awarded for academics, alumni affiliation, art, athletics, leadership, minority status, music/drama.

**Application procedures. Admission:** Priority date 11/30; deadline 11/30 (postmark date). $55 fee, may be waived for applicants with need. Admission notification 3/1. Admission notification on a rolling basis. Must reply by 5/1. **Financial aid:** Priority date 1/31; no closing date. FAFSA required. Applicants notified on a rolling basis starting 3/15; must reply within 2 week(s) of notification.

**Academics. Special study options:** Accelerated study, combined bachelor's/graduate degree, cross-registration, distance learning, double major, dual enrollment of high school students, ESL, exchange student, external degree, honors, independent study, internships, liberal arts/career combination, New York semester, semester at sea, student-designed major, study abroad, teacher certification program, United Nations semester, urban semester, Washington semester. Combined degree programs: bachelor's/MBA; bachelor's/MPA. **Credit/placement by examination:** AP, CLEP, SAT, ACT, institutional tests. 30 credit hours maximum toward bachelor's degree. **Support services:** Learning center, pre-admission summer program, reduced course load, remedial instruction, study skills assistance, tutoring, writing center.

**Majors. Area/ethnic studies:** African-American, Chicano/Hispanic-American/Latino, women's. **Biology:** General, biochemistry. **Business:** Business admin. **Communications:** General. **Computer sciences:** Computer science, programming. **Conservation:** General, environmental studies. **Engineering:** Computer. **Family/consumer sciences:** Family studies. **Foreign languages:** French, German, Spanish. **Health:** Nursing (RN). **History:** General. **Interdisciplinary:** Global studies. **Liberal arts:** Arts/sciences. **Math:** General. **Philosophy/religion:** Philosophy. **Physical sciences:** Chemistry, geology, physics. **Protective services:** Law enforcement admin. **Psychology:** General. **Social sciences:** Anthropology, economics, geography, political science, sociology. **Visual/performing arts:** General, art history/conservation, dramatic, studio arts.

**Most popular majors.** Business/marketing 22%, liberal arts 12%, psychology 12%, social sciences 9%.

**Computing on campus.** PC or laptop required. 400 workstations in library, computer center. Dormitories wired for high-speed internet access and linked to campus network. Commuter students can connect to campus network. Online course registration, online library, helpline, student web hosting, wireless network available.

**Student life. Freshman orientation:** Available. Preregistration for classes offered. 2-day residential program in June. Parents invited. **Housing:** Guaranteed on-campus for freshmen. Coed dorms, apartments, wellness housing available. $1,000 partly refundable deposit. Focus learning communities, freshman seminar, healthy living, women in math/science dorms available. **Activities:** Jazz band, choral groups, dance, drama, literary magazine, music ensembles, Model UN, musical theater, opera, radio station, student government, student newspaper, symphony orchestra, Student Advocates for Education, College Republicans, Asian Pacific Islander Organization, Raza Native American Council, El Movimiento Estudiantil Chicano/a de Aztlan, InterVarsity Christian Fellowship, Hillel, Best Buddies, Student Ambassadors.

**Athletics. NCAA. Intercollegiate:** Baseball M, basketball, golf, soccer, softball W, tennis, track and field W, volleyball W, water polo W. **Intramural:** Basketball, football (non-tackle), soccer, softball, volleyball. **Team name:** Sea Wolves.

**Student services.** Adult student services, alcohol/substance abuse counseling, career counseling, services for economically disadvantaged, student employment services, financial aid counseling, health services, minority student services, on-campus daycare, personal counseling, placement for graduates, veterans' counselor, women's services. **Physically disabled:** Services for visually, speech, hearing impaired.

**Contact.** Phone: (707) 664-2778 Fax: (707) 664-2060
Gustavo Flores, Director, Admissions, Sonoma State University, 1801 East Cotati Avenue, Rohnert Park, CA 94928-3609

## Southern California Institute of Architecture
### Los Angeles, California
**www.sciarc.edu**  **CB code: 1575**

- Private 5-year visual arts college
- Commuter campus in very large city
- 245 degree-seeking undergraduates: 27% women, 1% African American, 24% Asian American, 18% Hispanic American, 20% international
- 239 degree-seeking graduate students
- 91% of applicants admitted
- SAT or ACT (ACT writing optional), application essay required

**General.** Founded in 1972. Regionally accredited. **Degrees:** 48 bachelor's awarded; master's offered. **Location:** Downtown. **Calendar:** Semester, limited summer session. **Full-time faculty:** 36 total; 25% women. **Part-time faculty:** 31 total; 39% women. **Special facilities:** Wood and metal shop.

**Freshman class profile.** 70 applied, 64 admitted, 26 enrolled.

| | | | |
|---|---|---|---|
| End year in good standing: | 96% | Out-of-state: | 40% |
| Return as sophomores: | 93% | International: | 26% |

**Basis for selection.** School achievement record, test scores, portfolio, recommendations, and statement of purpose. Portfolio of creative work required.

**High school preparation.** Art, design or architecture courses recommended.

**2010-2011 Annual costs.** Tuition/fees: $27,850. Books/supplies: $4,094.

**2008-2009 Financial aid. Need-based:** 11% of total undergraduate aid awarded as scholarships/grants, 89% as loans/jobs. **Non-need-based:** Scholarships awarded for academics, state residency.

**Application procedures. Admission:** Closing date 2/1 (postmark date). $75 fee, may be waived for applicants with need. Application must be submitted on paper. Admission notification on a rolling basis beginning on or about 3/31. Must reply by 5/1. **Financial aid:** Priority date 3/1, closing date 5/2. FAFSA, institutional form required. Applicants notified on a rolling basis starting 4/15; must reply by 5/30.

**Academics.** Intensive summer session on introduction to architecture offered to graduates and high school students. **Special study options:** Exchange student, internships, study abroad. SCI-Arc study abroad programs in Switzerland and Japan; exchange programs in Japan, Australia, England, Israel, Netherlands, France, Mexico. **Credit/placement by examination:** CLEP, institutional tests. **Support services:** Pre-admission summer program.

**Majors. Architecture:** Architecture.

**Computing on campus.** PC or laptop required. 60 workstations in library, computer center. Commuter students can connect to campus network. Online course registration, online library, helpline, wireless network available.

**Student life. Freshman orientation:** Mandatory. Held for the three consecutive days prior to the first day of classes. **Policies:** Informal weekly gathering of entire school sponsored by student government. **Activities:** Student government, Architects, Designers, and Planners for Social Responsibility, American Institute of Architects student affiliation, Women in Architecture.

**Student services.** Career counseling, financial aid counseling, personal counseling, veterans' counselor. **Physically disabled:** Services for speech, hearing impaired.

**Contact.** E-mail: admissions@sciarc.edu
Phone: (213) 613-2200 ext. 320 Fax: (213) 613-2260
JJ Jackman, Director of Admissions, Southern California Institute of Architecture, 960 East Third Street, Los Angeles, CA 90013

## Southern California Institute of Technology
**Anaheim, California**
www.scitech.edu                               CB code: 3034

- For-profit 4-year business and engineering college
- Residential campus in large city
- 525 degree-seeking undergraduates
- Interview required

**General.** Accredited by ACCSC. Strong focus on applying theoretical concepts to real world projects and lab work. **Degrees:** 66 bachelor's, 15 associate awarded. **Calendar:** Continuous, extensive summer session. **Full-time faculty:** 16 total.

**Basis for selection.** Open admission, but selective for some programs. Interview required. High School Diploma, GED, official transcripts from other schools attended, standardized entrance exam required. Wonderlic required. **Homeschooled:** Transcript of courses and grades, interview required.

**2009-2010 Annual costs.** Electronic Engineering associate degree program tuition $27,170, fees $550; bachelor's degree program tuition $42,020, fees $660. Electrical Engineering bachelor's degree program tuition $40,700, fees $275. Accounting bachelor's program tuition $40,095, fees $700. Business Management bachelor's program tuition $40,535, fees $650. Books/supplies: $2,500.

**Application procedures. Admission:** No deadline. $100 fee. Application must be submitted on paper.

**Academics. Special study options:** Accelerated study, combined bachelor's/graduate degree, cooperative education, double major, ESL, liberal arts/career combination. **Credit/placement by examination:** CLEP. **Support services:** Tutoring.

**Majors. Business:** Business admin. **Engineering:** Electrical.

**Most popular majors.** Business/marketing 68%, engineering/engineering technologies 29%.

**Student life. Freshman orientation:** Available. Preregistration for classes offered.

**Student services.** Career counseling, financial aid counseling, placement for graduates.

**Contact.** E-mail: admissions@scitech.edu
Phone: (714) 300-0300 Fax: (714) 300-0310
Jodell Pinesett, Dean of Admissions, Southern California Institute of Technology, 222 South Harbor Boulevard, Suite 200, Anaheim, CA 92805-3758

## Southern California Seminary
**El Cajon, California**
www.socalsem.edu

- Private 4-year Bible and seminary college
- Commuter campus in small city
- 76 degree-seeking undergraduates: 57% part-time, 33% women
- 116 degree-seeking graduate students
- Application essay, interview required

**General.** Regionally accredited; also accredited by TRACS. **Degrees:** 5 bachelor's awarded; master's, professional offered. **Location:** 10 miles from San Diego. **Calendar:** Trimester, extensive summer session. **Full-time faculty:** 10 total. **Part-time faculty:** 34 total.

**Basis for selection.** Open admission, but selective for some programs. **Homeschooled:** Transcript of courses and grades, state high school equivalency certificate, letter of recommendation (nonparent) required. 2 essays on specific content.

**High school preparation.** College-preparatory program recommended.

**2009-2010 Annual costs.** Tuition/fees: $12,168. Room only: $5,110. Books/supplies: $1,700. Personal expenses: $1,700.

**Application procedures. Admission:** Closing date 8/15. $31 fee. **Financial aid:** Closing date 8/7.

**Academics. Credit/placement by examination:** CLEP, institutional tests.

**Majors. Theology:** Bible.

**Computing on campus.** Commuter students can connect to campus network. Online library, helpline, wireless network available.

**Student life. Freshman orientation:** Mandatory. **Housing:** Coed dorms, apartments available.

**Student services.** Chaplain/spiritual director, financial aid counseling, personal counseling, veterans' counselor.

**Contact.** E-mail: admissions@socalsem.edu
Phone: (619) 590-2129 Toll-free number: (888) 389-7244
Fax: (619) 590-2133
Thomas Pittman, Admissions Officer, Southern California Seminary, 2075 East Madison Avenue, El Cajon, CA 92019

## Stanford University
**Stanford, California**                        CB member
www.stanford.edu                               CB code: 4704

- Private 4-year university
- Residential campus in small city

- 6,564 degree-seeking undergraduates: 49% women, 10% African American, 23% Asian American, 13% Hispanic American, 3% Native American, 7% international
- 8,530 degree-seeking graduate students
- 8% of applicants admitted
- SAT or ACT with writing, application essay required
- 95% graduate within 6 years; 29% enter graduate study

**General.** Founded in 1885. Regionally accredited. Research university with seven schools: Business, Earth Sciences, Education, Engineering, Humanities and Sciences, Law, and Medicine. **Degrees:** 1,680 bachelor's awarded; master's, doctoral, professional offered. **ROTC:** Army, Naval, Air Force. **Location:** 29 miles from San Francisco. **Calendar:** Quarter, extensive summer session. **Full-time faculty:** 1,008 total; 99% have terminal degrees, 18% minority, 25% women. **Part-time faculty:** 15 total; 80% have terminal degrees. **Class size:** 51% < 20, 12% 20-39, 29% 40-49, 5% 50-99, 4% >100. **Special facilities:** Linear accelerator, 17 libraries, nature preserve, marine research center, Rodin sculpture garden, observatory, medical center.

**Freshman class profile.** 30,429 applied, 2,426 admitted, 1,694 enrolled.

| Mid 50% test scores | | | |
|---|---|---|---|
| SAT critical reading: | 660-760 | GPA 3.0-3.49: | 3% |
| SAT math: | 680-780 | Rank in top quarter: | 99% |
| SAT writing: | 670-760 | Rank in top tenth: | 91% |
| ACT composite: | 30-34 | Return as sophomores: | 98% |
| GPA 3.75 or higher: | 90% | Out-of-state: | 57% |
| GPA 3.50-3.74: | 7% | Live on campus: | 100% |
| | | International: | 8% |

**Basis for selection.** School achievement record, test scores, extracurricular activities, teacher and counselor evaluations, and personal qualifications most important. Rigor and variety of academic program very important. Personal qualities also considered. SAT Subject Tests recommended. Arts students may submit supplementary materials for review. Submissions should have previously received significant recognition at regional, state, national or international level. **Homeschooled:** Statement describing homeschool structure and mission required. Standardized test scores important. Subject tests recommended. **Learning Disabled:** Prospective students with disabilities are encouraged to meet with Disability Resource Center staff members.

**High school preparation.** 20 units recommended. Recommended units include English 4, mathematics 4, social studies 2, history 1, science 3 (laboratory 3) and foreign language 3.

**2010-2011 Annual costs.** Tuition/fees: $38,700. Room/board: $11,876. Books/supplies: $1,485. Personal expenses: $2,385.

**2008-2009 Financial aid.** All financial aid based on need. 1,051 full-time freshmen applied for aid; 863 were judged to have need; 859 of these received aid. Average need met was 100%. Average scholarship/grant was $38,037; average loan $2,614. 95% of total undergraduate aid awarded as scholarships/grants, 5% as loans/jobs. **Additional information:** For parents with total annual income below $60,000 and typical assets for this income range, Stanford will not expect a parent contribution toward educational costs. Students will still be expected to contribute toward their own expenses from their summer income, part-time work during the school year, and their own savings. For parents with total annual income below $100,000 and typical assets for this income range, Stanford will ensure that all tuition charges are covered with need-based scholarship, federal and state grants, and/or outside scholarship funds.

**Application procedures. Admission:** Closing date 1/1 (postmark date). $90 fee, may be waived for applicants with need. Admission notification 4/1. Must reply by 5/1. Early action candidates may not apply to other schools under any type of early action, early decision, or early notification program, but can apply under regular admissions. **Financial aid:** Priority date 2/15; no closing date. FAFSA, CSS PROFILE required. Applicants notified on a rolling basis starting 4/3; must reply by 5/1.

**Academics.** Undergraduate academic offerings stress access to senior faculty through small-group learning experiences and research opportunities. **Special study options:** Combined bachelor's/graduate degree, distance learning, double major, exchange student, honors, independent study, internships, student-designed major, study abroad, Washington semester. **Credit/placement by examination:** AP, CLEP, IB, institutional tests. 45 Advanced Placement units allowed. **Support services:** Learning center, pre-admission summer program, study skills assistance, tutoring, writing center.

**Majors. Area/ethnic studies:** African, African-American, American, Asian-American, Chicano/Hispanic-American/Latino, East Asian, German, Native American, women's. **Biology:** General. **Communications:** General. **Computer sciences:** General, computer science. **Conservation:** Environmental science. **Engineering:** General, chemical, civil, electrical, environmental,

materials, materials science, mechanical, petroleum. **Engineering technology:** Industrial management. **Foreign languages:** Chinese, classics, comparative lit, French, German, Italian, Japanese, linguistics, Slavic, Spanish. **History:** General. **Interdisciplinary:** Global studies, intercultural, math/computer science, science/society, systems science. **Liberal arts:** Humanities. **Math:** General. **Philosophy/religion:** Philosophy, religion. **Physical sciences:** Chemistry, geology, geophysics, physics. **Psychology:** General. **Public administration:** Policy analysis. **Social sciences:** Anthropology, archaeology, economics, international relations, political science, sociology, urban studies. **Visual/performing arts:** Art, dramatic, studio arts.

**Most popular majors.** Biology 7%, engineering/engineering technologies 17%, interdisciplinary studies 17%, social sciences 23%.

**Computing on campus.** 1,000 workstations in dormitories, library, computer center, student center. Dormitories wired for high-speed internet access and linked to campus network. Commuter students can connect to campus network. Online course registration, online library, helpline, repair service, student web hosting, wireless network available.

**Student life. Freshman orientation:** Mandatory, $438 fee. 6-day academically oriented program held in late September. **Policies:** Students are expected to abide by the Fundamental Standard and the Honor Code. **Housing:** Guaranteed on-campus for all undergraduates. Coed dorms, single-sex dorms, special housing for disabled, apartments, cooperative housing, fraternity/sorority housing available. **Activities:** Bands, campus ministries, choral groups, dance, drama, film society, international student organizations, literary magazine, music ensembles, Model UN, musical theater, opera, radio station, student government, student newspaper, symphony orchestra, TV station, approximately 600 student groups.

**Athletics.** NCAA. **Intercollegiate:** Baseball M, basketball, cross-country, diving, fencing, field hockey W, football (tackle) M, golf, gymnastics, lacrosse W, rowing (crew), sailing, soccer, softball W, squash W, swimming, synchronized swimming W, tennis, track and field, volleyball, water polo, wrestling M. **Intramural:** Badminton, basketball, football (non-tackle), golf, racquetball, soccer, softball, squash, table tennis, tennis, volleyball. **Team name:** Cardinal.

**Student services.** Alcohol/substance abuse counseling, chaplain/spiritual director, career counseling, student employment services, financial aid counseling, health services, legal services, minority student services, on-campus daycare, personal counseling, placement for graduates, women's services. **Physically disabled:** Services for visually, speech, hearing impaired. **Learning disabled:** Comprehensive services available.

**Contact.** E-mail: admission@stanford.edu
Phone: (650) 723-2091 Fax: (650) 723-6050
Richard Shaw, Dean of Undergraduate Admission and Financial Aid, Stanford University, Montag Hall, Stanford, CA 94305-6106

---

## Thomas Aquinas College
**Santa Paula, California**
www.thomasaquinas.edu

CB member
CB code: 4828

- Private 4-year liberal arts college affiliated with Roman Catholic Church
- Residential campus in rural community
- 345 degree-seeking undergraduates: 54% women, 2% Asian American, 8% Hispanic American, 1% Native American, 6% international
- 78% of applicants admitted
- SAT or ACT (ACT writing optional), application essay required
- 78% graduate within 6 years; 20% enter graduate study

**General.** Founded in 1971. Regionally accredited. **Degrees:** 69 bachelor's awarded. **Location:** 5 miles from Santa Paula, 20 miles from Ventura. **Calendar:** Semester. **Full-time faculty:** 28 total; 61% have terminal degrees, 7% women. **Part-time faculty:** 7 total; 57% have terminal degrees. **Class size:** 100% < 20. **Special facilities:** Walking trails, hiking trails into the Los Padres National Forest.

**Freshman class profile.** 184 applied, 144 admitted, 102 enrolled.

| Mid 50% test scores | | | |
|---|---|---|---|
| SAT critical reading: | 610-730 | GPA 2.0-2.99: | 6% |
| SAT math: | 550-640 | Rank in top quarter: | 75% |
| SAT writing: | 590-640 | Rank in top tenth: | 75% |
| ACT composite: | 25-30 | End year in good standing: | 91% |
| GPA 3.75 or higher: | 59% | Return as sophomores: | 79% |
| GPA 3.50-3.74: | 20% | Out-of-state: | 60% |
| GPA 3.0-3.49: | 14% | Live on campus: | 100% |
| | | International: | 3% |

**Basis for selection.** Faculty admission committee reviews each applicant for evidence of likely success in all parts of 4-year program. Required essays and 3 letters of reference supplement academic records and test scores. Test scores are accepted on a rolling basis throughout the year. Interview recommended for early admissions applicants, for those whose academic preparation is non-traditional, and for those who have been out of high school for a significant period of time. **Homeschooled:** Applicants not home schooled through formal programs must provide written records of all studies from grades 9 through 12.

**High school preparation.** College-preparatory program recommended. 13 units required; 16 recommended. Required and recommended units include English 4, mathematics 3-4, history 2, science 2-3 (laboratory 2), foreign language 2 and academic electives 3.

**2010-2011 Annual costs.** Tuition/fees: $22,400. Room/board: $7,400. Books/supplies: $450. Personal expenses: $2,250.

**2008-2009 Financial aid.** All financial aid based on need. 62% of total undergraduate aid awarded as scholarships/grants, 38% as loans/jobs.

**Application procedures. Admission:** No deadline. No application fee. Application must be submitted on paper. Admission notification on a rolling basis beginning on or about 10/1. Must reply by May 1 or within 1 week(s) if notified thereafter. **Financial aid:** Closing date 3/2. FAFSA, institutional form required. Applicants notified on a rolling basis starting 1/1; must reply by 5/1 or within 2 wcck(s) of notification.

**Academics.** Great Books curriculum. **Special study options:** Cross-disciplinary curriculum of liberal education through reading and analyzing the "Great Books," with special emphasis on theology, philosophy, math, laboratory science, and literature. **Credit/placement by examination:** CLEP. **Support services:** Tutoring.

**Majors. Liberal arts:** Arts/sciences.

**Computing on campus.** 17 workstations in dormitories, library, computer center, student center. Dormitories linked to campus network.

**Student life. Freshman orientation:** Mandatory. Preregistration for classes offered. 2-day program immediately before classes begin. **Housing:** Guaranteed on-campus for all undergraduates. Single-sex dorms available. **Activities:** Campus ministries, choral groups, dance, drama, literary magazine, music ensembles, musical theater, Pro-life group, Legion of Mary, Third Order Dominican, Habitat for Humanity.

**Athletics. Intramural:** Basketball, football (non-tackle) M, soccer, softball, table tennis, tennis, volleyball.

**Student services.** Alcohol/substance abuse counseling, chaplain/spiritual director, career counseling, financial aid counseling, health services, personal counseling, placement for graduates.

**Contact.** E-mail: admissions@thomasaquinas.edu
Phone: (805) 525-4417 Toll-free number: (800) 634-9797
Fax: (805) 421-5905
Jonathan Daly, Director of Admission, Thomas Aquinas College, 10000 North Ojai Road, Santa Paula, CA 93060-9621

## TUI University
**Cypress, California**
**www.tuiu.edu**

- Private 4-year virtual university
- Very large city

**General.** Regionally accredited. **Calendar:** Continuous.

**Contact.** Phone: (800) 375-9878
5665 Plaza Drive, 3rd Floor, Cypress, CA 90630

## University of California: Berkeley
**Berkeley, California**                               **CB member**
**www.berkeley.edu**                                   **CB code: 4833**

- Public 4-year university
- Residential campus in small city
- 25,530 degree-seeking undergraduates: 4% African American, 40% Asian American, 12% Hispanic American, 1% Native American, 5% international
- 10,313 graduate students
- 22% of applicants admitted

- SAT and SAT Subject Tests or ACT with writing, application essay required
- 90% graduate within 6 years

**General.** Founded in 1868. Regionally accredited. **Degrees:** 7,247 bachelor's awarded; master's, doctoral, professional offered. **ROTC:** Army, Naval, Air Force. **Location:** 10 miles from San Francisco. **Calendar:** Semester, extensive summer session. **Full-time faculty:** 1,575 total; 99% have terminal degrees, 21% minority, 32% women. **Part-time faculty:** 556 total; 99% have terminal degrees, 22% minority, 43% women. **Class size:** 61% < 20, 20% 20-39, 4% 40-49, 8% 50-99, 7% >100. **Special facilities:** Museums of art, anthropology, archaeology, paleontology and vertebrate zoology, film archive, science museum and research center for K-12 education, botanical garden, libraries of rare books, Western and Latin Americana, seismographic station, herbacia, performing arts facilities.

**Freshman class profile.** 48,650 applied, 10,561 admitted, 4,356 enrolled.

| Mid 50% test scores | | | |
|---|---|---|---|
| SAT critical reading: | 590-710 | GPA 3.0-3.49: | 4% |
| SAT math: | 640-760 | GPA 2.0-2.99: | 1% |
| SAT writing: | 610-720 | Rank in top quarter: | 100% |
| GPA 3.75 or higher: | 91% | Rank in top tenth: | 98% |
| GPA 3.50-3.74: | 4% | Out-of-state: | 8% |
| | | International: | 8% |

**Basis for selection.** Thorough review of academic performance; likely contribution to the intellectual and cultural vitality of the campus; diversity in personal background and experience; demonstrated qualities in leadership, motivation, concern for others and community; non-academic achievement in the performing arts, athletics or employment; demonstrated interest in major. All applicants must complete 2 SAT Subject Tests in different subject areas. If Math SAT Subject Test is taken, must be Level 2. Test scores must meet criteria determined by the applicant's residency and high school GPA.

**High school preparation.** College-preparatory program required. 15 units required; 18 recommended. Required and recommended units include English 4, mathematics 3-4, history 2, science 2-3 (laboratory 2-3), foreign language 2-3, visual/performing arts 1 and academic electives 1. 2 units in history or social sciences are required.

**2009-2010 Annual costs.** Tuition/fees: $8,325; $30,346 out-of-state. Room/board: $15,308. Books/supplies: $1,306. Personal expenses: $2,732.

**2009-2010 Financial aid. Non-need-based:** Scholarships awarded for academics.

**Application procedures. Admission:** Closing date 11/30. $60 fee, may be waived for applicants with need. Admission notification 3/31. Must reply by 5/1. **Financial aid:** Closing date 3/2. FAFSA required. Applicants notified by 4/15.

**Academics.** All students required to pass one American cultures class. **Special study options:** Accelerated study, cross-registration, double major, dual enrollment of high school students, ESL, exchange student, honors, independent study, internships, student-designed major, study abroad, teacher certification program. Freshman seminar, undergraduate research apprenticeship, university research expeditions. **Credit/placement by examination:** AP, CLEP, institutional tests. **Support services:** Learning center, pre-admission summer program, reduced course load, study skills assistance, tutoring.

**Majors. Architecture:** Architecture, landscape. **Area/ethnic studies:** African-American, American, Asian, Asian-American, Chicano/Hispanic-American/Latino, Latin American, Native American, Near/Middle Eastern, Southeast Asian, women's. **Biology:** General, botany, cellular/molecular, microbiology, toxicology. **Business:** Business admin. **Communications:** Media studies. **Computer sciences:** Computer science. **Conservation:** General, environmental science, environmental studies, forest management, forestry, management/policy. **Engineering:** Biomedical, chemical, civil, electrical, environmental, geological, manufacturing, materials science, mechanical, nuclear, operations research, physics, science. **Foreign languages:** Ancient Greek, Celtic, Chinese, classics, comparative lit, Dutch/Flemish, French, German, Italian, Japanese, Latin, linguistics, Scandinavian, Slavic, Spanish. **History:** General. **Interdisciplinary:** Classical/archaeology, cognitive science, nutrition sciences, peace/conflict. **Legal studies:** General. **Math:** General, applied, statistics. **Philosophy/religion:** Philosophy, religion. **Physical sciences:** General, astrophysics, atmospheric science, chemistry, geology, geophysics, oceanography, physics. **Psychology:** General. **Public administration:** Social work. **Social sciences:** Anthropology, economics, geography, political science, sociology, urban studies. **Visual/performing arts:** Art, art history/conservation, dance, dramatic, film/cinema.

**Most popular majors.** Biology 14%, engineering/engineering technologies 11%, English 6%, social sciences 21%.

**Computing on campus.** Dormitories wired for high-speed internet access and linked to campus network. Commuter students can connect to campus network. Online course registration, online library, helpline, repair service available.

**Student life. Freshman orientation:** Available, $50 fee. Preregistration for classes offered. **Housing:** Guaranteed on-campus for freshmen. Coed dorms, single-sex dorms, special housing for disabled, apartments, cooperative housing, fraternity/sorority housing available. $300 partly refundable deposit, deadline 5/25. **Activities:** Bands, choral groups, dance, drama, film society, international student organizations, literary magazine, music ensembles, Model UN, musical theater, radio station, student government, student newspaper, symphony orchestra, TV station, Asian American Christian fellowship, black recruitment and retention center, hiking and outdoor society, Americorps, forensics, Chabad, lesbian and gay alliance, Raza recruitment and retention center, College Democrats, College Republicans.

**Athletics.** NCAA. **Intercollegiate:** Baseball M, basketball, cross-country, diving, field hockey W, football (tackle) M, golf, gymnastics, lacrosse W, rowing (crew), rugby M, soccer, softball W, swimming, tennis, track and field, volleyball W, water polo. **Intramural:** Basketball, bowling, fencing, field hockey W, football (tackle), handball, ice hockey, lacrosse, racquetball, rowing (crew), sailing, skiing, soccer, softball, squash, tennis, volleyball M. **Team name:** Bears.

**Student services.** Adult student services, alcohol/substance abuse counseling, chaplain/spiritual director, career counseling, services for economically disadvantaged, student employment services, financial aid counseling, health services, legal services, minority student services, on-campus daycare, personal counseling, placement for graduates, veterans' counselor, women's services. **Physically disabled:** Services for visually, speech, hearing impaired.

**Contact.** Phone: (510) 642-3175
Walter Robinson, Director Undergraduate Admissions, University of California: Berkeley, 110 Sproul Hall, #5800, Berkeley, CA 94720-5800

---

## University of California: Davis

Davis, California  CB member
www.ucdavis.edu  CB code: 4834

- Public 4-year university
- Residential campus in small city
- 24,453 degree-seeking undergraduates: 1% part-time, 56% women, 3% African American, 40% Asian American, 14% Hispanic American, 1% Native American, 2% international
- 6,592 degree-seeking graduate students
- 47% of applicants admitted
- SAT or ACT with writing, SAT Subject Tests, application essay required
- 80% graduate within 6 years

**General.** Founded in 1905. Regionally accredited. **Degrees:** 5,762 bachelor's awarded; master's, doctoral, professional offered. **ROTC:** Army, Naval, Air Force. **Location:** 15 miles from Sacramento, 72 miles from San Francisco. **Calendar:** Quarter, extensive summer session. **Full-time faculty:** 1,586 total; 98% have terminal degrees, 19% minority, 33% women. **Part-time faculty:** 317 total; 98% have terminal degrees, 19% minority, 42% women. **Class size:** 34% < 20, 33% 20-39, 5% 40-49, 15% 50-99, 14% >100. **Special facilities:** 150-acre arboretum, equestrian center, craft center, marine laboratory, nuclear laboratory, California Regional Primate Research Center, natural reserves, raptor center.

**Freshman class profile.** 42,382 applied, 20,080 admitted, 4,413 enrolled.

| Mid 50% test scores | | GPA 2.0-2.99: | 1% |
|---|---|---|---|
| SAT critical reading: | 500-630 | Rank in top quarter: | 100% |
| SAT math: | 550-670 | Rank in top tenth: | 96% |
| SAT writing: | 510-640 | Return as sophomores: | 92% |
| ACT composite: | 22-28 | Out-of-state: | 3% |
| GPA 3.75 or higher: | 58% | Live on campus: | 92% |
| GPA 3.50-3.74: | 24% | International: | 2% |
| GPA 3.0-3.49: | 17% | | |

**Basis for selection.** Scholastic achievement most important, followed by school and community activities, academic interests, special circumstances, special achievements and awards. Two SAT Subject Tests in two different subject areas of student's choice required: history/social science, English literature, mathematics (Level 2), laboratory science or language other than English.

**High school preparation.** 15 units required; 18 recommended. Required and recommended units include English 4, mathematics 3-4, social studics 2, science 2-3 (laboratory 2-3), foreign language 2-3, visual/performing arts 1 and academic electives 1. History/social science (social studies above) requirement is one year of U.S. history, or one-half year of U.S. history and one-half year of civics or U.S. government; and one year of world history, cultures and geography. For academic elective ("g" requirement): two semesters chosen from the following areas: visual and performing arts (non-introductory-level courses), history, social science, English, advanced mathematics, laboratory science and language other than English.

**2009-2010 Annual costs.** Tuition/fees: $9,364; $32,033 out-of-state. Nonresident undergraduates pay an additional $648 in educational fees. Room/board: $12,361. Books/supplies: $1,590. Personal expenses: $1,347.

**2009-2010 Financial aid.** All financial aid based on need.

**Application procedures. Admission:** Closing date 11/30. $60 fee, may be waived for applicants with need. Admission notification 3/15. Must reply by 5/1. **Financial aid:** Priority date 3/2; no closing date. FAFSA required. Applicants notified on a rolling basis starting 3/12.

**Academics.** Seventy percent of undergraduates participate in full- and part-time internships. **Special study options:** Accelerated study, cross-registration, double major, dual enrollment of high school students, ESL, honors, independent study, internships, student-designed major, study abroad, teacher certification program, Washington semester. **Credit/placement by examination:** AP, CLEP. 10 credit hours maximum toward bachelor's degree. **Support services:** Learning center, pre-admission summer program, reduced course load, remedial instruction, study skills assistance, tutoring, writing center.

**Majors. Agriculture:** Agronomy, animal sciences, food science, international, range science, soil science. **Architecture:** Landscape, urban/community planning. **Area/ethnic studies:** African, African-American, American, Asian-American, Chicano/Hispanic-American/Latino, East Asian, Native American, women's. **Biology:** General, biotechnology, botany, cell/histology, entomology, environmental toxicology, evolutionary, exercise physiology, genetics, microbiology, molecular biochemistry, neurobiology/physiology, zoology. **Communications:** General. **Computer sciences:** Computer science. **Conservation:** General, environmental studies, urban forestry. **Engineering:** Aerospace, biomedical, chemical, civil, computer, electrical, materials, mechanical. **Engineering technology:** Laser/optical. **Family/consumer sciences:** Clothing/textiles, family studies. **Foreign languages:** Chinese, comparative lit, French, German, Italian, Japanese, linguistics, Russian, Spanish. **History:** General. **Interdisciplinary:** Classical/archaeology, medieval/Renaissance, natural sciences, nutrition sciences, science/society. **Math:** General, applied, computational, statistics. **Philosophy/religion:** Philosophy, religion. **Physical sciences:** Applied physics, atmospheric science, chemistry, geology, hydrology, physics. **Psychology:** General. **Social sciences:** Anthropology, economics, international relations, political science, sociology. **Visual/performing arts:** Art history/conservation, design, dramatic, film/cinema, studio arts. **Other:** Avian sciences, Computational applied science, Nature and culture, Technocultural studies, Wildlife, fish and conservation biology.

**Most popular majors.** Agriculture 9%, biology 21%, engineering/engineering technologies 8%, psychology 10%, social sciences 18%.

**Computing on campus.** 1,500 workstations in dormitories, library, computer center, student center. Dormitories wired for high-speed internet access and linked to campus network. Commuter students can connect to campus network. Online course registration, online library, helpline, repair service, wireless network available.

**Student life. Freshman orientation:** Available, $265 fee. Preregistration for classes offered. Summer advising June-August. **Policies:** Residents and visitors must abide by state and university regulations relating to alcohol. Alcohol delivery by outside vendors is prohibited. Behavioral problems while under the influence of alcohol or any other substance will not be tolerated and may be subject to disciplinary action. **Housing:** Guaranteed on-campus for freshmen. Coed dorms, single-sex dorms, special housing for disabled, apartments, cooperative housing, wellness housing available. $450 fully refundable deposit, deadline 6/9. Special interest housing available. **Activities:** Bands, campus ministries, choral groups, dance, drama, film society, international student organizations, literary magazine, music ensembles, Model UN, musical theater, radio station, student government, student newspaper, symphony orchestra, TV station, 316 student organizations.

**Athletics.** NCAA. **Intercollegiate:** Baseball M, basketball, cross-country, diving, field hockey W, football (tackle) M, golf, gymnastics W, lacrosse W, rowing (crew) W, soccer, softball W, swimming, tennis, track and field, volleyball W, water polo, wrestling M. **Intramural:** Badminton, basketball, bowling, golf, racquetball, soccer, softball, squash, table tennis, tennis, volleyball, water polo. **Team name:** Aggies.

**Student services.** Adult student services, alcohol/substance abuse counseling, chaplain/spiritual director, career counseling, services for economically disadvantaged, student employment services, financial aid counseling, health services, legal services, minority student services, on-campus daycare, personal counseling, placement for graduates, veterans' counselor, women's services. **Physically disabled:** Services for visually, speech, hearing impaired. **Learning disabled:** Comprehensive services available.

**Contact.** E-mail: undergraduateadmissions@ucdavis.edu
Phone: (530) 752-2971 Fax: (530) 752-1280
Pamela Burnett, Director of Undergraduate Admissions, University of California: Davis, One Shields Ave, Davis, CA 95616

## University of California: Irvine
**Irvine, California**        **CB member**
**www.uci.edu**        **CB code: 4859**

- Public 4-year university
- Residential campus in small city
- 22,226 degree-seeking undergraduates: 2% part-time, 53% women, 2% African American, 53% Asian American, 14% Hispanic American, 3% international
- 4,789 degree-seeking graduate students
- 44% of applicants admitted
- SAT and SAT Subject Tests or ACT with writing, application essay required
- 81% graduate within 6 years

**General.** Founded in 1965. Regionally accredited. **Degrees:** 5,948 bachelor's awarded; master's, doctoral, professional offered. **ROTC:** Army, Air Force. **Location:** 40 miles from Los Angeles. **Calendar:** Quarter, extensive summer session. **Full-time faculty:** 1,464 total; 98% have terminal degrees, 28% minority, 35% women. **Part-time faculty:** 428 total; 98% have terminal degrees, 24% minority, 39% women. **Class size:** 45% < 20, 31% 20-39, 4% 40-49, 8% 50-99, 12% >100. **Special facilities:** Outdoor laboratory, ecological preserve, freshwater marsh reserve, arboretum, center for art and technology, observatory.

**Freshman class profile.** 44,123 applied, 19,484 admitted, 4,030 enrolled.

| Mid 50% test scores | | | | |
|---|---|---|---|---|
| SAT critical reading: | 520-640 | Rank in top tenth: | | 96% |
| SAT math: | 570-680 | End year in good standing: | | 98% |
| SAT writing: | 530-640 | Return as sophomores: | | 94% |
| GPA 3.75 or higher: | 68% | Out-of-state: | | 2% |
| GPA 3.50-3.74: | 26% | Live on campus: | | 83% |
| GPA 3.0-3.49: | 5% | International: | | 2% |
| GPA 2.0-2.99: | 1% | Fraternities: | | 4% |
| Rank in top quarter: | 100% | Sororities: | | 7% |

**Basis for selection.** Demonstrated record of academic preparation, educational engagement, talent and skills important. Two SAT Subject Tests required: math and student's choice.

**High school preparation.** College-preparatory program required. 15 units required; 18 recommended. Required and recommended units include English 4, mathematics 3-4, history 2, science 2-3 (laboratory 2-3), foreign language 2-3, visual/performing arts 1 and academic electives 1.

**2009-2010 Annual costs.** Tuition/fees: $9,399; $32,068 out-of-state. Tuition not charged to in-state residents. Room/board: $11,291. Books/supplies: $1,645. Personal expenses: $1,592.

**2008-2009 Financial aid. Need-based:** 3,578 full-time freshmen applied for aid; 2,376 were judged to have need; 2,268 of these received aid. Average need met was 84%. Average scholarship/grant was $10,946; average loan $5,889. 74% of total undergraduate aid awarded as scholarships/grants, 26% as loans/jobs. **Non-need-based:** Awarded to 1,095 full-time undergraduates, including 230 freshmen. Scholarships awarded for academics, art, athletics, job skills, leadership, music/drama, state residency.

**Application procedures. Admission:** Closing date 11/30 (receipt date). $60 fee, may be waived for applicants with need. Application must be submitted online. Admission notification 3/31. Must reply by 5/1. **Financial aid:** Priority date 3/2, closing date 5/1. FAFSA required. Applicants notified by 4/1; must reply by 5/1.

**Academics. Special study options:** Accelerated study, combined bachelor's/graduate degree, distance learning, double major, dual enrollment of high school students, ESL, honors, independent study, internships, liberal arts/career combination, semester at sea, study abroad, teacher certification program, Washington semester. **Credit/placement by examination:** AP, CLEP, IB, institutional tests. **Support services:** Learning center, pre-admission summer program, reduced course load, remedial instruction, study skills assistance, tutoring, writing center.

**Majors. Area/ethnic studies:** African-American, Asian-American, Chicano/Hispanic-American/Latino, Chinese, East Asian, European, German, women's. **Biology:** General, Biochemistry/biophysics and molecular biology, bioinformatics, botany, cell/histology, ecology, evolutionary, genetics. **Business:** Business admin, managerial economics. **Communications:** Journalism. **Computer sciences:** General, computer science, information systems. **Conservation:** Environmental studies. **Engineering:** General, aerospace, biomedical, chemical, civil, computer, electrical, environmental, materials, mechanical. **Foreign languages:** Chinese, classics, comparative lit, French, Japanese, Korean, Latin, Spanish. **Health:** Pharmaceutical sciences. **History:** General. **Interdisciplinary:** Classical/archaeology, global studies, neuroscience. **Math:** General. **Philosophy/religion:** Philosophy, religion. **Physical sciences:** Chemistry, geology, physics. **Psychology:** General, social. **Social sciences:** General, anthropology, criminology, econometrics, economics, political science, sociology, urban studies. **Visual/performing arts:** Art history/conservation, dance, dramatic, film/cinema, music performance, studio arts. **Other:** Public health sciences.

**Most popular majors.** Biology 14%, engineering/engineering technologies 9%, interdisciplinary studies 8%, psychology 13%, social sciences 24%, visual/performing arts 7%.

**Computing on campus.** 1,500 workstations in dormitories, library, computer center, student center. Dormitories wired for high-speed internet access and linked to campus network. Commuter students can connect to campus network. Online course registration, online library, helpline, repair service, student web hosting, wireless network available.

**Student life. Freshman orientation:** Mandatory, $190 fee. Preregistration for classes offered. One or three-day program held during summer. **Housing:** Guaranteed on-campus for freshmen. Coed dorms, single-sex dorms, special housing for disabled, apartments, cooperative housing, fraternity/sorority housing, wellness housing available. $350 partly refundable deposit. **Activities:** Bands, choral groups, dance, drama, film society, international student organizations, literary magazine, music ensembles, Model UN, musical theater, opera, radio station, student government, student newspaper, symphony orchestra.

**Athletics.** NCAA. **Intercollegiate:** Baseball M, basketball, cross-country, golf, sailing, soccer, tennis, track and field, volleyball, water polo. **Intramural:** Basketball, bowling, football (non-tackle), racquetball, soccer, softball, swimming, tennis, track and field, volleyball, water polo, wrestling. **Team name:** Anteaters.

**Student services.** Alcohol/substance abuse counseling, career counseling, services for economically disadvantaged, student employment services, financial aid counseling, health services, minority student services, on-campus daycare, personal counseling, placement for graduates, veterans' counselor, women's services. **Physically disabled:** Services for visually, speech, hearing impaired.

**Contact.** E-mail: admissions@uci.edu
Phone: (949) 824-6703 Fax: (949) 824-2711
Brent Yunek, Director of Admissions, University of California: Irvine, 204 Aldrich Hall, Irvine, CA 92697-1075

## University of California: Los Angeles
**Los Angeles, California**        **CB member**
**www.ucla.edu**        **CB code: 4837**

- Public 4-year university
- Residential campus in very large city
- 26,687 degree-seeking undergraduates: 3% part-time, 56% women, 4% African American, 38% Asian American, 15% Hispanic American, 5% international
- 11,863 degree-seeking graduate students
- 22% of applicants admitted
- SAT or ACT with writing, SAT Subject Tests, application essay required
- 89% graduate within 6 years

**General.** Founded in 1919. Regionally accredited. Research, undergraduate instruction, and graduate training in more than 190 fields of study. **Degrees:** 7,193 bachelor's awarded; master's, doctoral, professional offered. **ROTC:** Army, Naval, Air Force. **Location:** Downtown. **Calendar:** Quarter, extensive summer session. **Full-time faculty:** 2,035 total; 98% have terminal degrees, 24% minority, 32% women. **Part-time faculty:** 676 total; 98% have terminal degrees, 30% minority, 40% women. **Class size:** 54% < 20, 22% 20-39, 3% 40-49, 10% 50-99, 11% >100. **Special facilities:**

Museums with specialized collections, centers for cancer research, plasma physics research labs, film and television archive, high power auroral simulation observatory, lab for embedded collaborative systems, research centers for molecular and neuroscience, graphic and animation labs, nanoscience research labs and centers, cell mimetic space exploration center, particle beam physics lab, southern California particle center, ranch for ecological studies, ethnomusicology archive.

**Freshman class profile.** 55,708 applied, 12,179 admitted, 4,472 enrolled.

| Mid 50% test scores | | | |
|---|---|---|---|
| SAT critical reading: | 570-680 | Rank in top quarter: | 100% |
| SAT math: | 600-730 | Rank in top tenth: | 97% |
| SAT writing: | 580-700 | Return as sophomores: | 97% |
| ACT composite: | 24-31 | Out-of-state: | 10% |
| GPA 3.75 or higher: | 92% | Live on campus: | 94% |
| GPA 3.50-3.74: | 4% | International: | 3% |
| GPA 3.0-3.49: | 3% | Fraternities: | 11% |
| GPA 2.0-2.99: | 1% | Sororities: | 11% |

**Basis for selection.** GPA, test scores, course work, number of and performance in honors and AP courses most important. Essay considered. Strong senior program important. Extracurricular activities, honors and awards also reviewed. SAT Subject Tests not required of Fall Quarter 2012, or later, freshmen applicants. Will review if submitted; certain SAT subject exams may be recommended for some majors. Audition required of music, dance, theater majors. Portfolio required of art majors.

**High school preparation.** College-preparatory program required. 15 units required; 18 recommended. Required and recommended units include English 4, mathematics 3-4, history 2, science 2-3 (laboratory 2-3), foreign language 2-3, visual/performing arts 1 and academic electives 1.

**2009-2010 Annual costs.** Tuition/fees: $9,151; $31,820 out-of-state. Room/board: $13,314. Books/supplies: $1,599. Personal expenses: $1,551.

**2008-2009 Financial aid. Non-need-based:** Scholarships awarded for academics, alumni affiliation, athletics, ROTC.

**Application procedures. Admission:** Closing date 11/30 (postmark date). $60 fee, may be waived for applicants with need. Admission notification 3/31. Must reply by 5/1. **Financial aid:** Priority date 3/2; no closing date. FAFSA required. Applicants notified on a rolling basis starting 3/15; must reply within 3 week(s) of notification.

**Academics. Special study options:** Accelerated study, double major, honors, independent study, internships, student-designed major, study abroad, urban semester, Washington semester. **Credit/placement by examination:** AP, CLEP. **Support services:** Learning center, study skills assistance, tutoring, writing center.

**Majors. Architecture:** Architecture. **Area/ethnic studies:** African-American, Asian, Asian-American, Chicano/Hispanic-American/Latino, East Asian, European, Latin American, Native American, Russian/Slavic, Southeast Asian, women's. **Biology:** General, bacteriology, biochemistry, biophysics, biotechnology, botany, cellular/molecular, ecology, immunology, marine, molecular genetics, physiology, systematic. **Business:** Managerial economics. **Computer sciences:** General. **Conservation:** Environmental science. **Engineering:** Aerospace, agricultural, chemical, civil, computer, electrical, geological, materials, materials science, mechanical. **Foreign languages:** African, ancient Greek, Arabic, Chinese, comparative lit, East Asian, French, German, Hebrew, Italian, Japanese, Korean, Latin, linguistics, Portuguese, Romance, Russian, Scandinavian, Slavic, Spanish. **History:** General. **Interdisciplinary:** Classical/archaeology, cognitive science, global studies, neuroscience. **Liberal arts:** Arts/sciences. **Math:** General, applied, computational, statistics. **Philosophy/religion:** Philosophy, religion. **Physical sciences:** Astrophysics, chemistry, geology, geophysics, physics. **Psychology:** General, psychobiology. **Social sciences:** Anthropology, economics, geography, international economic development, international economics, political science, sociology. **Visual/performing arts:** Art, art history/conservation, design, dramatic, film/cinema, music history, musicology. **Other:** Middle Eastern and North African studies.

**Most popular majors.** Biology 12%, engineering/engineering technologies 6%, English 6%, history 9%, interdisciplinary studies 6%, psychology 11%, social sciences 28%, visual/performing arts 6%.

**Computing on campus.** Dormitories wired for high-speed internet access and linked to campus network. Commuter students can connect to campus network. Online course registration, online library, helpline, repair service, student web hosting, wireless network available.

**Student life. Freshman orientation:** Available, $340 fee. Preregistration for classes offered. 3-day, 2-night program. **Housing:** Guaranteed on-campus for freshmen. Coed dorms, special housing for disabled, apartments, cooperative housing, fraternity/sorority housing, wellness housing

available. **Activities:** Bands, campus ministries, choral groups, dance, drama, film society, international student organizations, literary magazine, music ensembles, Model UN, musical theater, opera, radio station, student government, student newspaper, symphony orchestra, TV station.

**Athletics. NCAA. Intercollegiate:** Baseball M, basketball, cross-country, diving W, football (tackle) M, golf, gymnastics W, rowing (crew) W, soccer, softball W, swimming W, tennis, track and field, volleyball, water polo. **Intramural:** Badminton, basketball, football (non-tackle), golf, racquetball, soccer, squash, swimming, table tennis, tennis, track and field, volleyball. **Team name:** Bruins.

**Student services.** Alcohol/substance abuse counseling, chaplain/spiritual director, career counseling, services for economically disadvantaged, student employment services, financial aid counseling, health services, legal services, minority student services, on-campus daycare, personal counseling, placement for graduates, veterans' counselor, women's services. **Physically disabled:** Services for visually, speech, hearing impaired.

**Contact.** E-mail: ugadm@saonet.ucla.edu
Phone: (310) 825-3101 Fax: (310) 206-1206
Vu Tran, Director of Undergraduate Admissions, University of California: Los Angeles, 1147 Murphy Hall, Los Angeles, CA 90095-1436

---

## University of California: Merced
**Merced, California**                                   **CB member**
www.ucmerced.edu                                        **CB code: 4129**

- Public 4-year university
- Residential campus in small city
- 3,190 degree-seeking undergraduates: 1% part-time, 51% women, 7% African American, 33% Asian American, 32% Hispanic American, 1% Native American, 1% international
- 224 degree-seeking graduate students
- 91% of applicants admitted
- SAT or ACT with writing, SAT Subject Tests, application essay required

**General.** Candidate for regional accreditation. **Degrees:** 280 bachelor's awarded; master's, doctoral offered. **Location:** 120 miles from San Francisco, 60 miles from Fresno. **Calendar:** Semester, limited summer session. **Full-time faculty:** 185 total; 84% have terminal degrees, 31% minority, 38% women. **Part-time faculty:** 34 total; 41% have terminal degrees, 18% minority, 62% women. **Class size:** 40% < 20, 36% 20-39, 5% 40-49, 12% 50-99, 7% >100. **Special facilities:** Sierra Nevada research institute, Yosemite National Park research station, computational biology center, energy research center.

**Freshman class profile.** 20,851 applied, 19,042 admitted, 1,128 enrolled.

| Mid 50% test scores | | | |
|---|---|---|---|
| SAT critical reading: | 440-570 | GPA 3.0-3.49: | 52% |
| SAT math: | 460-600 | GPA 2.0-2.99: | 5% |
| SAT writing: | 450-560 | End year in good standing: | 73% |
| GPA 3.75 or higher: | 18% | Return as sophomores: | 83% |
| GPA 3.50-3.74: | 25% | Live on campus: | 76% |
| | | International: | 1% |

**Basis for selection.** Academic record and test scores determine eligibility. **Homeschooled:** If school is not accredited by a regional association, student must meet eligibility by examination alone.

**High school preparation.** College-preparatory program required. 15 units required; 18 recommended. Required and recommended units include English 4, mathematics 3-4, history 2, science 2-3 (laboratory 2-3), foreign language 2-3, visual/performing arts 1 and academic electives 1. History is 2 units in history/social science.

**2009-2010 Annual costs.** Tuition/fees: $8,411; $31,080 out-of-state. Room/board: $12,211. Books/supplies: $1,508. Personal expenses: $1,308.

**2009-2010 Financial aid. Non-need-based:** Scholarships awarded for academics.

**Application procedures. Admission:** Closing date 11/30 (postmark date). $60 fee, may be waived for applicants with need. Admission notification 3/31. Must reply by May 1 or within 3 week(s) if notified thereafter. **Financial aid:** Priority date 3/2; no closing date. FAFSA required. Applicants notified on a rolling basis starting 3/2.

**Academics. Special study options:** Accelerated study, double major, independent study, internships, study abroad, Washington semester. Research opportunities and internships at Lawrence Livermore National Laboratories and Yosemite National Park. **Credit/placement by examination:** AP, CLEP,

IB, institutional tests. Credit by examination with the approval of instructor giving examination and dean of school involved. Some courses may not be deemed appropriate for obtaining credit by examination. **Support services:** Learning center, study skills assistance, tutoring, writing center.

**Majors. Biology:** General. **Business:** Management science. **Engineering:** Biomedical, computer, environmental, materials, mechanical. **Foreign languages:** Comparative lit. **History:** General. **Interdisciplinary:** Cognitive science. **Math:** Applied. **Physical sciences:** Chemistry, geology, physics. **Psychology:** General. **Social sciences:** General, anthropology, economics, political science. **Other:** World cultures and history.

**Most popular majors.** Biology 31%, business/marketing 9%, engineering/engineering technologies 14%, psychology 26%, social sciences 6%.

**Computing on campus.** 157 workstations in dormitories, library, computer center. Dormitories wired for high-speed internet access and linked to campus network. Commuter students can connect to campus network. Online course registration, online library, helpline, wireless network available.

**Student life. Freshman orientation:** Available, $49 fee. Preregistration for classes offered. **Housing:** Coed dorms, special housing for disabled, wellness housing available. $300 partly refundable deposit, deadline 5/3. **Activities:** Marching band, choral groups, dance, film society, radio station, student government, student newspaper, African American student union, liberal activism club, student government advisory committee, Latino students alliance, Filipino student alliance, Circle K International, American Red Cross club, Jewish student union.

**Athletics. Intramural:** Basketball, football (non-tackle), racquetball, soccer, softball, tennis, volleyball. **Team name:** Golden Bobcats.

**Student services.** Alcohol/substance abuse counseling, career counseling, services for economically disadvantaged, student employment services, financial aid counseling, health services, minority student services, personal counseling, veterans' counselor, women's services. **Physically disabled:** Services for visually, hearing impaired. **Learning disabled:** Comprehensive services available.

**Contact.** E-mail: admissions@ucmerced.edu
Phone: (209) 228-4682 Toll-free number: (866) 270-7301
Fax: (209) 228-4244
Encarnacion Ruiz, Director, Admissions and Relations with Schools & Colleges, University of California: Merced, 5200 North Lake Road, Merced, CA 95343-5603

## University of California: Riverside

Riverside, California CB member
www.ucr.edu CB code: 4839

- Public 4-year university
- Residential campus in large city
- 16,996 degree-seeking undergraduates: 3% part-time, 52% women, 8% African American, 40% Asian American, 29% Hispanic American, 2% international
- 2,397 degree-seeking graduate students
- 80% of applicants admitted
- SAT or ACT with writing, SAT Subject Tests, application essay required
- 65% graduate within 6 years

**General.** Founded in 1954. Regionally accredited. **Degrees:** 3,055 bachelor's awarded; master's, doctoral offered. **ROTC:** Army, Air Force. **Location:** 60 miles from Los Angeles. **Calendar:** Quarter, limited summer session. **Full-time faculty:** 765 total; 98% have terminal degrees, 27% minority, 33% women. **Part-time faculty:** 154 total; 98% have terminal degrees, 29% minority, 51% women. **Class size:** 39% < 20, 38% 20-39, 4% 40-49, 10% 50-99, 10% >100. **Special facilities:** Botanical gardens, air pollution research center, photography museum, 8 nature preserves, citrus research center and agricultural experiment station, institute of geophysics and planetary physics, water resources center, salinity lab.

**Freshman class profile.** 24,969 applied, 19,916 admitted, 4,299 enrolled.

| Mid 50% test scores | | | |
|---|---|---|---|
| SAT critical reading: | 450-570 | GPA 3.0-3.49: | 52% |
| SAT math: | 480-620 | Rank in top quarter: | 100% |
| SAT writing: | 460-570 | Rank in top tenth: | 94% |
| ACT composite: | 19-25 | End year in good standing: | 80% |
| GPA 3.75 or higher: | 22% | Return as sophomores: | 87% |
| GPA 3.50-3.74: | 26% | Live on campus: | 73% |
| | | International: | 1% |

**Basis for selection.** A completed UC application with essay to include self reported secondary school courses and grades, and required examinations required. Students that meet UC eligibility will receive a comprehensive review that will culminate into an Academic Index Score (AIS). Applicants that meet the AIS cut-off will be admitted. SAT Subject Tests required from 2 different subject areas. SAT Math Subject Test must be Level 2. All required examinations must be taken by the month of December prior to the next fall term. **Homeschooled:** Transcript of courses and grades required. Portfolio describing subjects studied and methods of study is required.

**High school preparation.** College-preparatory program required. 15 units required; 19 recommended. Required and recommended units include English 4, mathematics 3-4, history 2, science 2-3 (laboratory 2-3), foreign language 2-3, visual/performing arts 1 and academic electives 1. One year of elective units from 1 of the following: visual/performing arts (non-introductory), history, English, advanced mathematics, laboratory science, foreign language, social science, arts. 2 social science units must include 1 U.S. history or .5 history and .5 civics, and 1 world history, cultures, or geography.

**2009-2010 Annual costs.** Tuition/fees: $8,507; $31,178 out-of-state. Room/board: $10,900. Books/supplies: $1,750. Personal expenses: $1,750.

**2009-2010 Financial aid. Need-based:** 3,717 full-time freshmen applied for aid; 3,014 were judged to have need; 2,957 of these received aid. Average need met was 91%. Average scholarship/grant was $14,081; average loan $4,761. 73% of total undergraduate aid awarded as scholarships/grants, 27% as loans/jobs. **Non-need-based:** Awarded to 418 full-time undergraduates, including 128 freshmen. Scholarships awarded for academics, art, athletics, job skills, leadership, music/drama, state residency.

**Application procedures. Admission:** Closing date 11/30 (postmark date). $60 fee, may be waived for applicants with need. Admission notification 3/31. Admission notification on a rolling basis. Must reply by 5/1. Must reply by May 1 or within 3 week(s) if notified thereafter. **Financial aid:** Closing date 3/2. FAFSA required. Applicants notified on a rolling basis starting 3/1; must reply by 5/1 or within 3 week(s) of notification.

**Academics. Special study options:** Accelerated study, cross-registration, distance learning, double major, ESL, honors, independent study, internships, study abroad, teacher certification program, Washington semester. **Credit/placement by examination:** AP, CLEP, IB, SAT, institutional tests. **Support services:** Learning center, pre-admission summer program, reduced course load, study skills assistance, tutoring, writing center.

**Majors. Area/ethnic studies:** African-American, Asian, Asian-American, Chicano/Hispanic-American/Latino, German, Latin American, Native American, Russian/Slavic, women's. **Biology:** General, biochemistry, botany, entomology. **Business:** Business admin, managerial economics. **Computer sciences:** Computer science. **Conservation:** Environmental science. **Engineering:** Biomedical, chemical, computer, electrical, environmental, materials science, mechanical. **Foreign languages:** General, classics, comparative lit, French, linguistics, Spanish. **History:** General. **Interdisciplinary:** Ancient studies, global studies, neuroscience. **Liberal arts:** Arts/sciences, humanities. **Math:** General, applied, statistics. **Philosophy/religion:** Philosophy, religion. **Physical sciences:** General, chemistry, geology, geophysics, physics. **Psychology:** General. **Public administration:** Policy analysis. **Social sciences:** Anthropology, economics, political science, sociology. **Visual/performing arts:** Art, art history/conservation, dramatic, studio arts. **Other:** Business informatics, Geoscience education, History/law and society, Law and society, Music and culture, Philosophy/law and society.

**Most popular majors.** Biology 13%, business/marketing 21%, psychology 10%, social sciences 19%.

**Computing on campus.** 1,072 workstations in dormitories, library, computer center, student center. Dormitories wired for high-speed internet access and linked to campus network. Commuter students can connect to campus network. Online course registration, online library, helpline, repair service, student web hosting, wireless network available.

**Student life. Freshman orientation:** Available. 2-day or 1-day summer programs. **Housing:** Guaranteed on-campus for freshmen. Coed dorms, special housing for disabled, apartments available. $250 deposit, deadline 5/10. **Activities:** Bands, campus ministries, choral groups, dance, drama, film society, international student organizations, literary magazine, music ensembles, musical theater, radio station, student government, student newspaper, 350 clubs and organizations available.

**Athletics. NCAA. Intercollegiate:** Baseball M, basketball, cross-country, golf, soccer, softball W, tennis, track and field, volleyball W. **Intramural:** Badminton, basketball, football (non-tackle), racquetball, soccer, softball, table tennis, tennis, volleyball. **Team name:** Highlanders.

**Student services.** Adult student services, alcohol/substance abuse counseling, career counseling, student employment services, financial aid counseling, health services, minority student services, on-campus daycare, personal counseling, placement for graduates, veterans' counselor, women's services. **Physically disabled:** Services for visually, speech, hearing impaired.

**Contact.** E-mail: admin@ucr.edu
Phone: (951) 827-3411 Fax: (951) 827-6344
Merlyn Campos, Director of Undergraduate Admissions, University of
California: Riverside, Admissions Office, Riverside, CA 92521

## University of California: San Diego

La Jolla, California — CB member
www.ucsd.edu — CB code: 4836

- Public 4-year university
- Residential campus in large town
- 24,817 degree-seeking undergraduates
- 42% of applicants admitted
- SAT or ACT with writing, SAT Subject Tests, application essay required
- 84% graduate within 6 years

**General.** Founded in 1959. Regionally accredited. Includes 6 small undergraduate cluster colleges, each with different housing and general education requirements. **Degrees:** 5,323 bachelor's awarded; master's, doctoral offered. **Location:** 12 miles from San Diego. **Calendar:** Quarter, extensive summer session. **Full-time faculty:** 943 total; 98% have terminal degrees, 24% minority. **Part-time faculty:** 219 total; 100% have terminal degrees, 17% minority. **Class size:** 44% < 20, 22% 20-39, 4% 40-49, 11% 50-99, 20% >100. **Special facilities:** Performing arts centers, student-run co-ops, supercomputer center, nature preserves, electron beam lithography facility, center for music experiment, structural engineering lab, aquarium, additional specialty research centers.

**Freshman class profile.** 47,365 applied, 19,717 admitted, 4,292 enrolled.

| Mid 50% test scores | | | |
|---|---|---|---|
| SAT critical reading: | 540-660 | Rank in top quarter: | 100% |
| SAT math: | 600-710 | Rank in top tenth: | 100% |
| SAT writing: | 560-670 | Return as sophomores: | 94% |
| ACT composite: | 24-30 | Out-of-state: | 4% |
| GPA 3.75 or higher: | 80% | Live on campus: | 92% |
| GPA 3.50-3.74: | 16% | International: | 4% |
| GPA 3.0-3.49: | 4% | Fraternities: | 10% |
| | | Sororities: | 10% |

**Basis for selection.** High school course pattern, GPA, essay and test scores most important. Admission for out-of-state applicants more selective than for residents. All applicants must take 2 SAT Subject Tests in different subject areas. If Math SAT Subject Test is taken, must be Level 2.

**High school preparation.** College-preparatory program required. 17 units required; 13 recommended. Required and recommended units include English 4, mathematics 3-4, history 2, science 2-3 (laboratory 2-3), foreign language 2-3, visual/performing arts 1 and academic electives 1. History is 2 units in history/social science.

**2009-2010 Annual costs.** Tuition/fees: $8,798; $31,467 out-of-state. Room/board: $11,057. Books/supplies: $1,560. Personal expenses: $1,526.

**2008-2009 Financial aid. Need-based:** 3,450 full-time freshmen applied for aid; 2,472 were judged to have need; 2,380 of these received aid. Average need met was 85%. Average scholarship/grant was $12,310; average loan $4,971. 69% of total undergraduate aid awarded as scholarships/grants, 31% as loans/jobs. **Non-need-based:** Awarded to 1,148 full-time undergraduates, including 280 freshmen. Scholarships awarded for academics, art, athletics, leadership, minority status, music/drama.

**Application procedures. Admission:** Closing date 11/30 (postmark date). $60 fee, may be waived for applicants with need. Application must be submitted online. Admission notification 3/31. Admission notification on a rolling basis. Must reply by 5/1. **Financial aid:** Priority date 3/2, closing date 6/1. FAFSA required. Applicants notified on a rolling basis starting 3/15; must reply within 3 week(s) of notification.

**Academics. Special study options:** Combined bachelor's/graduate degree, cross-registration, double major, dual enrollment of high school students, ESL, exchange student, honors, independent study, internships, liberal arts/career combination, semester at sea, student-designed major, study abroad, teacher certification program, Washington semester. In-depth academic assignments working in small groups or one-to-one with faculty; research programs. **Credit/placement by examination:** AP, CLEP, IB, SAT, institutional tests. **Support services:** Learning center, pre-admission summer program, reduced course load, study skills assistance, tutoring, writing center.

**Majors. Architecture:** Urban/community planning. **Area/ethnic studies:** Chinese, German, Italian, Japanese, Latin American, Russian/Slavic, women's. **Biology:** General, animal physiology, bacteriology, biochemistry, bioinformatics, biophysics, biotechnology, cell/histology, ecology, evolutionary, molecular. **Business:** Management science. **Communications:** General, digital media. **Computer sciences:** General, computer science, information systems, systems analysis. **Conservation:** Environmental science, environmental studies. **Engineering:** Aerospace, biomedical, chemical, computer, electrical, mechanical, mechanics, physics, science, structural, systems. **Engineering technology:** Aerospace. **Family/consumer sciences:** Family studies. **Foreign languages:** General, classics, French, German, Italian, Japanese, linguistics, Russian, Spanish. **History:** General. **Interdisciplinary:** Behavioral sciences, cognitive science, math/computer science, neuroscience. **Math:** General, applied. **Philosophy/religion:** Judaic, philosophy, religion. **Physical sciences:** Chemical physics, chemistry, molecular physics, physics, planetary. **Psychology:** General. **Public administration:** Policy analysis. **Social sciences:** Anthropology, archaeology, economics, political science, sociology, U.S. government, urban studies. **Visual/performing arts:** Art history/conservation, dance, dramatic, studio arts.

**Most popular majors.** Biology 17%, engineering/engineering technologies 14%, psychology 8%, social sciences 32%.

**Computing on campus.** 1,500 workstations in library, computer center, student center. Dormitories wired for high-speed internet access and linked to campus network. Commuter students can connect to campus network. Online course registration, online library, helpline, repair service, student web hosting, wireless network available.

**Student life. Freshman orientation:** Mandatory, $125 fee. Preregistration for classes offered. One- to two-day program for freshmen and transfers. **Housing:** Guaranteed on-campus for freshmen. Coed dorms, single-sex dorms, special housing for disabled, apartments, cooperative housing, fraternity/sorority housing available. $500 fully refundable deposit, deadline 5/3. Language, cultural interest and international houses available. **Activities:** Bands, campus ministries, choral groups, dance, drama, film society, international student organizations, literary magazine, music ensembles, Model UN, musical theater, opera, radio station, student government, student newspaper, symphony orchestra, TV station, 450 student organizations.

**Athletics.** NCAA. **Intercollegiate:** Baseball M, basketball, cross-country, diving, fencing, golf M, rowing (crew), soccer, softball W, swimming, tennis, track and field, volleyball, water polo. **Intramural:** Basketball, bowling, football (non-tackle), football (tackle), soccer, softball, tennis, volleyball, water polo. **Team name:** Tritons.

**Student services.** Alcohol/substance abuse counseling, career counseling, services for economically disadvantaged, student employment services, financial aid counseling, health services, legal services, minority student services, on-campus daycare, personal counseling, placement for graduates, veterans' counselor, women's services. **Physically disabled:** Services for visually, speech, hearing impaired. **Learning disabled:** Comprehensive services available.

**Contact.** E-mail: admissionsreply@ucsd.edu
Phone: (858) 534-4831 Fax: (858) 534-5629
Mae Brown, Assistant Vice Chancellor and Director of Admissions, University of California: San Diego, 9500 Gilman Drive, 0021, La Jolla, CA 92093-0021

## University of California: Santa Barbara

Santa Barbara, California — CB member
www.ucsb.edu — CB code: 4835

- Public 4-year university
- Residential campus in small city
- 19,793 degree-seeking undergraduates: 2% part-time, 54% women
- 3,054 degree-seeking graduate students
- 48% of applicants admitted
- SAT or ACT with writing, SAT Subject Tests, application essay required
- 80% graduate within 6 years

**General.** Founded in 1909. Regionally accredited. **Degrees:** 5,445 bachelor's awarded; master's, doctoral offered. **ROTC:** Army. **Location:** 10 miles from downtown, 100 miles from Los Angeles. **Calendar:** Quarter, extensive summer session. **Full-time faculty:** 919 total. **Part-time faculty:** 167 total. **Class size:** 49% < 20, 30% 20-39, 4% 40-49, 9% 50-99, 8% >100. **Special facilities:** Nature preserves with research facilities, seawater laboratories, robotics laboratory, free electron laser laboratory; institutes for polymers and organic solids, neuroscience research, quantum, nuclear particle astrophysics and cosmology, marine science, theoretical physics.

**Freshman class profile.** 44,707 applied, 21,540 admitted, 4,583 enrolled.

| Mid 50% test scores | | GPA 2.0-2.99: | 1% |
|---|---|---|---|
| SAT critical reading: | 540-660 | Return as sophomores: | 91% |
| SAT math: | 550-670 | Out-of-state: | 4% |
| SAT writing: | 540-660 | Live on campus: | 94% |
| ACT composite: | 24-30 | International: | 1% |
| GPA 3.75 or higher: | 66% | Fraternities: | 3% |
| GPA 3.50-3.74: | 21% | Sororities: | 9% |
| GPA 3.0-3.49: | 12% | | |

**Basis for selection.** Eligibility established by high school GPA, course requirement, and SAT scores. Special consideration for disadvantaged students. All applicants must take 2 SAT Subject Tests in different subject areas. If Math SAT Subject Test is taken, must be Level 2. Audition required of music, dance, drama majors. Portfolio required of art majors.

**High school preparation.** College-preparatory program required. Required and recommended units include English 4, mathematics 3-4, history 2, (laboratory 2-3), foreign language 2-3, visual/performing arts 1 and academic electives 1.

**2009-2010 Annual costs.** Tuition/fees: $9,077; $31,746 out-of-state. Room/board: $12,405. Books/supplies: $1,596. Personal expenses: $2,963.

**2008-2009 Financial aid. Need-based:** 3,389 full-time freshmen applied for aid; 2,361 were judged to have need; 2,202 of these received aid. Average need met was 82%. Average scholarship/grant was $14,219; average loan $4,935. 75% of total undergraduate aid awarded as scholarships/grants, 25% as loans/jobs. **Non-need-based:** Awarded to 625 full-time undergraduates, including 164 freshmen. Scholarships awarded for academics, athletics.

**Application procedures. Admission:** Closing date 11/30 (postmark date). $60 fee, may be waived for applicants with need. Admission notification 3/31. Must reply by 5/1. **Financial aid:** Priority date 3/2, closing date 5/31. Must reply within 2 week(s) of notification.

**Academics. Special study options:** Accelerated study, cross-registration, distance learning, double major, dual enrollment of high school students, ESL, exchange student, honors, independent study, internships, student-designed major, study abroad, teacher certification program, Washington semester. Graduate-level classes, off-campus study, freshman seminars, pre-professional programs and advising, academic minors, and undergraduate research, professional studies in school of environmental science and management and school of education. **Credit/placement by examination:** AP, CLEP, institutional tests. **Support services:** Learning center, pre-admission summer program, reduced course load, study skills assistance, tutoring, writing center.

**Majors. Area/ethnic studies:** African-American, Asian, Chicano/Hispanic-American/Latino, Latin American, women's. **Biology:** General, aquatic, bacteriology, biochemistry, cell/histology, ecology, marine, molecular, pharmacology, zoology. **Business:** Managerial economics. **Communications:** General. **Computer sciences:** General. **Conservation:** Environmental studies. **Engineering:** Chemical, computer, electrical, mechanical. **Foreign languages:** Chinese, classics, comparative lit, French, German, Italian, Japanese, linguistics, Portuguese, Russian, Slavic, Spanish. **History:** General. **Interdisciplinary:** Biological/physical sciences, biopsychology, global studies, medieval/Renaissance. **Legal studies:** General. **Math:** General, statistics. **Philosophy/religion:** Philosophy, religion. **Physical sciences:** Chemistry, geology, geophysics, physics. **Psychology:** General. **Social sciences:** Anthropology, economics, geography, political science, sociology. **Visual/performing arts:** General, art, art history/conservation, cinematography, dance, dramatic, film/cinema, studio arts.

**Most popular majors.** Biology 7%, business/marketing 12%, communications/journalism 6%, interdisciplinary studies 7%, psychology 7%, social sciences 18%, visual/performing arts 7%.

**Computing on campus.** 255 workstations in dormitories, library, computer center, student center. Dormitories wired for high-speed internet access and linked to campus network. Online library, repair service, student web hosting, wireless network available.

**Student life. Freshman orientation:** Available. Preregistration for classes offered. Two-day program; includes sessions for parents. **Housing:** Guaranteed on-campus for freshmen. Coed dorms, apartments, cooperative housing, fraternity/sorority housing, wellness housing available. $100 nonrefundable deposit, deadline 9/1. **Activities:** Bands, campus ministries, choral groups, dance, drama, film society, international student organizations, literary magazine, music ensembles, Model UN, musical theater, opera, radio station, student government, student newspaper, symphony orchestra, TV station, Hillel, Catholic Student Organization, Democratic and Republican student organizations, El Congreso, Persian Student Association, Habitat for Humanity.

**Athletics.** NCAA. **Intercollegiate:** Baseball M, basketball, cross-country, golf M, gymnastics, soccer, softball W, swimming, tennis, track and field, volleyball, water polo. **Intramural:** Badminton, basketball, bowling, cross-country, football (non-tackle), golf, gymnastics, racquetball, rowing (crew), soccer, softball, squash, tennis, volleyball, water polo. **Team name:** Gauchos.

**Student services.** Adult student services, alcohol/substance abuse counseling, career counseling, services for economically disadvantaged, student employment services, financial aid counseling, health services, minority student services, on-campus daycare, personal counseling, placement for graduates, veterans' counselor, women's services. **Physically disabled:** Services for visually, speech, hearing impaired. **Learning disabled:** Comprehensive services available.

**Contact.** E-mail: admissions@sa.ucsb.edu
Phone: (805) 893-2881 Fax: (805) 893-2676
Christine Van Gieson, Director of Admissions, University of California: Santa Barbara, 1210 Cheadle Hall, Santa Barbara, CA 93106-2014

---

### University of California: Santa Cruz

| Santa Cruz, California | CB member |
|---|---|
| www.ucsc.edu | CB code: 4860 |

- Public 4-year university
- Residential campus in small city
- 15,206 degree-seeking undergraduates: 1% part-time, 53% women, 3% African American, 22% Asian American, 18% Hispanic American, 1% Native American
- 1,432 degree-seeking graduate students
- 64% of applicants admitted
- SAT and SAT Subject Tests or ACT with writing, application essay required
- 74% graduate within 6 years

**General.** Founded in 1965. Regionally accredited. **Degrees:** 3,252 bachelor's awarded; master's, doctoral, professional offered. **ROTC:** Army, Naval, Air Force. **Location:** 75 miles from San Francisco, 30 miles from San Jose. **Calendar:** Quarter, limited summer session. **Full-time faculty:** 554 total; 95% have terminal degrees, 21% minority, 34% women. **Part-time faculty:** 237 total; 95% have terminal degrees, 13% minority, 53% women. **Class size:** 40% < 20, 33% 20-39, 5% 40-49, 9% 50-99, 14% >100. **Special facilities:** Observatories, arboretum, agroecology farm, campus preserve, nonlinear science center, music center, bilingual research center, institutes of marine sciences, tectonics, particle physics, center for adaptive optics.

**Freshman class profile.** 27,237 applied, 17,487 admitted, 3,214 enrolled.

| Mid 50% test scores | | GPA 2.0-2.99: | 2% |
|---|---|---|---|
| SAT critical reading: | 510-630 | Rank in top quarter: | 100% |
| SAT math: | 520-640 | Rank in top tenth: | 96% |
| SAT writing: | 520-630 | End year in good standing: | 89% |
| ACT composite: | 22-28 | Return as sophomores: | 89% |
| GPA 3.75 or higher: | 34% | Out-of-state: | 3% |
| GPA 3.50-3.74: | 34% | Live on campus: | 99% |
| GPA 3.0-3.49: | 30% | | |

**Basis for selection.** Test scores, GPA in required subjects most important. Personal statement very important. All applicants must take 2 SAT Subject Tests in different subject areas. If Math SAT Subject Test is taken, must be Level 2. For freshman applicants entering fall 2012 or later, SAT Subject Tests will no longer be required for admissions, although they may need to submit them for specific majors. Audition required for music majors. Portfolio recommended for art majors. **Homeschooled:** Eligibility appraised on basis of entrance examination or previous college-level work. **Learning Disabled:** Any extenuating circumstances should be included in the personal statement.

**High school preparation.** College-preparatory program required. 15 units required; 18 recommended. Required and recommended units include English 4, mathematics 3-4, social studies 1, history 1, science 2-3 (laboratory 2-3), foreign language 2-3, visual/performing arts 1 and academic electives 1. History is 2 units in history/social science. 2 semesters of approved arts courses from single visual and performing arts discipline: dance, drama/theater, music, or visual art. Required elective includes 2 semesters from following areas: visual and performing arts, history, social science, English, advanced mathematics, laboratory science, and language other than English.

**2009-2010 Annual costs.** Tuition/fees: $10,095; $22,071 out-of-state. Room/board: $13,641. Books/supplies: $1,392. Personal expenses: $1,512.

**2008-2009 Financial aid. Need-based:** 3,039 full-time freshmen applied for aid; 2,048 were judged to have need; 1,927 of these received aid. Average need met was 85%. Average scholarship/grant was $12,009; average loan $5,033. 66% of total undergraduate aid awarded as scholarships/grants, 34% as loans/jobs. **Non-need-based:** Awarded to 347 full-time undergraduates, including 79 freshmen. Scholarships awarded for academics, alumni affiliation, art, leadership, music/drama.

**Application procedures. Admission:** Closing date 11/30 (postmark date). $60 fee, may be waived for applicants with need. Admission notification 4/30. Must reply by 5/1. **Financial aid:** Closing date 3/2. FAFSA required. Applicants notified on a rolling basis starting 4/1; must reply within 4 week(s) of notification.

**Academics. Special study options:** Combined bachelor's/graduate degree, cooperative education, double major, dual enrollment of high school students, exchange student, independent study, internships, student-designed major, study abroad, teacher certification program, Washington semester. **Credit/placement by examination:** AP, CLEP, IB, institutional tests. **Support services:** Learning center, reduced course load, remedial instruction, study skills assistance, tutoring, writing center.

**Majors. Agriculture:** Plant sciences. **Area/ethnic studies:** American, German, Italian, women's. **Biology:** General, bioinformatics, cellular/molecular, ecology, marine, molecular biochemistry. **Business:** Managerial economics. **Computer sciences:** General, game design, web page design. **Conservation:** Environmental studies. **Engineering:** Biomedical, computer, electrical. **Foreign languages:** General, classics, linguistics. **History:** General. **Interdisciplinary:** Neuroscience. **Legal studies:** General. **Math:** General. **Philosophy/religion:** Philosophy. **Physical sciences:** Astrophysics, chemistry, geology, physics. **Psychology:** General. **Public administration:** Community org/advocacy. **Social sciences:** Anthropology, economics, political science, sociology. **Visual/performing arts:** Art, art history/conservation, dramatic. **Other:** Area, ethnic, cultural, and gender studies, Biological and biomedical sciences, Community studies, Computer and information sciences and support services, Film and digital media.

**Most popular majors.** Biology 15%, business/marketing 9%, English 7%, natural resources/environmental science 6%, psychology 10%, social sciences 15%, visual/performing arts 10%.

**Computing on campus.** Dormitories wired for high-speed internet access and linked to campus network. Commuter students can connect to campus network. Online course registration, online library, helpline, repair service, student web hosting, wireless network available.

**Student life. Freshman orientation:** Available, $110 fee. Preregistration for classes offered. One-day Orientation sessions held fall and winter terms for students and family. **Policies:** Student Organization Advising and Resources (SOARS) helps students create their own organizations. **Housing:** Guaranteed on-campus for freshmen. Coed dorms, single-sex dorms, apartments, cooperative housing, wellness housing available. $150 partly refundable deposit, deadline 5/1. **Activities:** Jazz band, choral groups, dance, drama, film society, international student organizations, literary magazine, music ensembles, Model UN, musical theater, opera, radio station, student government, student newspaper, symphony orchestra, TV station, more than 100 student organizations.

**Athletics.** NCAA. **Intercollegiate:** Basketball, cross-country W, diving, golf W, soccer, swimming, tennis, volleyball. **Intramural:** Basketball, football (non-tackle), soccer, softball, volleyball, water polo. **Team name:** Banana Slugs.

**Student services.** Adult student services, alcohol/substance abuse counseling, career counseling, services for economically disadvantaged, student employment services, financial aid counseling, health services, minority student services, on-campus daycare, personal counseling, veterans' counselor, women's services. **Physically disabled:** Services for visually, speech, hearing impaired.

**Contact.** E-mail: admissions@ucsc.edu
Phone: (831) 459-4008 Fax: (831) 459-4452
Michelle Whittingham, Director of Admissions, University of California: Santa Cruz, Cook House, 1156 High Street, Santa Cruz, CA 95064

## University of La Verne
**La Verne, California**      **CB member**
**www.laverne.edu**      **CB code: 4381**

- Private 4-year university and liberal arts college
- Commuter campus in large town
- 1,507 degree-seeking undergraduates: 5% part-time, 59% women, 7% African American, 4% Asian American, 39% Hispanic American, 1% Native American, 1% international

- 2,490 degree-seeking graduate students
- 68% of applicants admitted
- SAT or ACT with writing, application essay required
- 67% graduate within 6 years

**General.** Founded in 1891. Regionally accredited. Satellite campuses throughout California provide graduate and professional programs to adult students. **Degrees:** 364 bachelor's awarded; master's, doctoral, professional offered. **ROTC:** Army. **Location:** 35 miles from Los Angeles. **Calendar:** 4-1-4, limited summer session. **Full-time faculty:** 187 total; 82% have terminal degrees, 20% minority, 48% women. **Part-time faculty:** 202 total; 16% minority. **Class size:** 76% < 20, 23% 20-39, less than 1% 40-49, less than 1% 50-99. **Special facilities:** Natural science field station.

**Freshman class profile.** 1,452 applied, 989 admitted, 333 enrolled.

| Mid 50% test scores | | | |
|---|---|---|---|
| SAT critical reading: | 440-550 | GPA 2.0-2.99: | 25% |
| SAT math: | 440-560 | Rank in top quarter: | 55% |
| SAT writing: | 430-540 | Rank in top tenth: | 24% |
| ACT composite: | 17-23 | Return as sophomores: | 78% |
| GPA 3.75 or higher: | 21% | Out-of-state: | 4% |
| GPA 3.50-3.74: | 14% | Live on campus: | 50% |
| GPA 3.0-3.49: | 40% | International: | 1% |
| | | Sororities: | 8% |

**Basis for selection.** Secondary school record, recommendations, standardized test scores, and essay very important; extracurricular activities, character or personal qualities also important. Class rank, interview, special talents or abilities, alumni relationships, volunteer work, work experience may also be considered. Individual departments may require interview, audition, or portfolio.

**High school preparation.** College-preparatory program required. 14 units required; 19 recommended. Required and recommended units include English 4, mathematics 3-4, social studies 2, history 3, science 2 (laboratory 1-2), foreign language 2 and academic electives 2.

**2010-2011 Annual costs.** Tuition/fees: $29,800. Room/board: $10,440. Books/supplies: $1,638. Personal expenses: $2,400.

**2009-2010 Financial aid. Non-need-based:** Scholarships awarded for academics, alumni affiliation, art, leadership, minority status, music/drama, religious affiliation.

**Application procedures. Admission:** Priority date 2/1; no deadline. $50 fee, may be waived for applicants with need. Admission notification on a rolling basis beginning on or about 12/1. Must reply by May 1 or within 2 week(s) if notified thereafter. **Financial aid:** Priority date 3/2; no closing date. FAFSA required. Applicants notified on a rolling basis starting 3/17; must reply within 2 week(s) of notification.

**Academics.** Main Campus offers a traditional-age undergraduate program and an accelerated program for adults in school of continuing education. Off-campus centers available for degree-seeking students in selected majors. **Special study options:** Combined bachelor's/graduate degree, distance learning, double major, ESL, exchange student, honors, independent study, internships, liberal arts/career combination, student-designed major, study abroad, teacher certification program, weekend college. **Credit/placement by examination:** AP, CLEP, institutional tests. 44 credit hours maximum toward bachelor's degree. **Support services:** Learning center, reduced course load, study skills assistance, tutoring, writing center.

**Majors. Biology:** General, environmental. **Business:** Accounting, business admin, e-commerce, international, managerial economics. **Communications:** General, journalism, radio/tv. **Computer sciences:** General. **Conservation:** Environmental science. **Education:** General, early childhood, elementary, physical, secondary. **Family/consumer sciences:** Child care. **Foreign languages:** Comparative lit, French, German, Spanish. **Health:** Athletic training, health care admin. **History:** General. **Interdisciplinary:** Behavioral sciences, biological/physical sciences, natural sciences. **Legal studies:** General. **Liberal arts:** Arts/sciences. **Math:** General. **Philosophy/religion:** Philosophy, religion. **Physical sciences:** Chemistry, physics. **Psychology:** General. **Public administration:** General. **Social sciences:** General, anthropology, criminology, economics, international relations, political science, sociology. **Visual/performing arts:** Art, art history/conservation, dramatic.

**Most popular majors.** Business/marketing 20%, communications/journalism 12%, liberal arts 10%, psychology 11%, social sciences 17%.

**Computing on campus.** Dormitories wired for high-speed internet access and linked to campus network. Commuter students can connect to campus network. Online course registration, online library, helpline, student web hosting, wireless network available.

**Student life. Freshman orientation:** Available, $50 fee. Preregistration for classes offered. All-day events for both students and parents. Held primarily in August. **Policies:** Students must be in good academic standing to participate in clubs or organizations, including fraternities/sororities. Freshmen not permitted to join fraternities during the Fall term. **Housing:** Coed dorms, single-sex dorms, special housing for disabled available. $250 fully refundable deposit, deadline 5/1. **Activities:** Campus ministries, choral groups, dance, drama, international student organizations, literary magazine, music ensembles, Model UN, musical theater, radio station, student government, student newspaper, TV station, African American student alliance, Latino student forum, Brothers Forum, Sisters Circle, Rainbow Alliance.

**Athletics.** NCAA. **Intercollegiate:** Baseball M, basketball, cross-country, diving, football (tackle) M, golf M, soccer, softball W, swimming, tennis, track and field, volleyball W, water polo. **Intramural:** Basketball, soccer, softball, table tennis, volleyball. **Team name:** Leopards.

**Student services.** Adult student services, alcohol/substance abuse counseling, chaplain/spiritual director, career counseling, services for economically disadvantaged, student employment services, financial aid counseling, health services, minority student services, personal counseling, placement for graduates, veterans' counselor. **Physically disabled:** Services for visually, speech, hearing impaired.

**Contact.** E-mail: admissions@ulv.edu
Phone: (909) 392-2800 Toll-free number: (800) 876-4858
Fax: (909) 392-2714
Ana Liza Zell, Associate Dean of Undergraduate Admissions, University of La Verne, 1950 Third Street, La Verne, CA 91750

## University of Redlands

**Redlands, California**  **CB member**
**www.redlands.edu**  **CB code: 4848**

- Private 4-year university and liberal arts college
- Residential campus in small city
- 2,928 degree-seeking undergraduates: 23% part-time, 55% women, 4% African American, 5% Asian American, 15% Hispanic American, 1% Native American, 2% international
- 1,551 degree-seeking graduate students
- 70% of applicants admitted
- SAT or ACT (ACT writing recommended), application essay required
- 68% graduate within 6 years; 41% enter graduate study

**General.** Founded in 1907. Regionally accredited. NASM accredited School of Music within College of Arts & Sciences. **Degrees:** 445 bachelor's awarded; master's, doctoral offered. **ROTC:** Army, Naval, Air Force. **Location:** 65 miles from Los Angeles, 40 miles from Palm Springs. **Calendar:** 4-1-4, limited summer session. **Full-time faculty:** 221 total; 87% have terminal degrees, 45% minority, 47% women. **Part-time faculty:** 286 total. **Class size:** 70% < 20, 29% 20-39, 1% 40-49, less than 1% 50-99, less than 1% >100. **Special facilities:** Communicative disorders center, arts center, silver LEED certified facility for environmental studies, on-site co-generation plant, observatory.

**Freshman class profile.** 3,267 applied, 2,299 admitted, 561 enrolled.

| Mid 50% test scores | | | |
|---|---|---|---|
| SAT critical reading: | 520-620 | Rank in top quarter: | 67% |
| SAT math: | 540-630 | Rank in top tenth: | 31% |
| ACT composite: | 22-27 | End year in good standing: | 81% |
| GPA 3.75 or higher: | 37% | Return as sophomores: | 81% |
| GPA 3.50-3.74: | 21% | Out-of-state: | 39% |
| GPA 3.0-3.49: | 29% | Live on campus: | 94% |
| GPA 2.0-2.99: | 13% | International: | 2% |

**Basis for selection.** Course selection and grades important. Recommendations, test scores, essays, extracurricular activities are also considered. Interview required of Johnston Center for Integrated Studies applicants, strongly recommended for others. Audition required of music majors. Portfolio recommended of art (slides only), creative writing majors. **Homeschooled:** Statement describing homeschool structure and mission required. Common application homeschool supplement required.

**High school preparation.** College-preparatory program recommended. 15 units required; 17 recommended. Required and recommended units include English 4, mathematics 3, social studies 2, history 1, science 2-3 (laboratory 2) and foreign language 2.

**2010-2011 Annual costs.** Tuition/fees: $35,540. Room/board: $10,832. Books/supplies: $1,638. Personal expenses: $2,250.

**2009-2010 Financial aid. Need-based:** 491 full-time freshmen applied for aid; 455 were judged to have need; 449 of these received aid. Average need met was 71%. Average scholarship/grant was $25,240; average loan $4,979. 96% of total undergraduate aid awarded as scholarships/grants, 4%

as loans/jobs. **Non-need-based:** Awarded to 459 full-time undergraduates, including 165 freshmen. Scholarships awarded for academics, art, music/drama.

**Application procedures. Admission:** Priority date 12/15; deadline 6/1 (postmark date). $30 fee, may be waived for applicants with need. Admission notification on a rolling basis beginning on or about 12/1. Must reply by 5/1. **Financial aid:** Priority date 2/15; no closing date. FAFSA required. Applicants notified on a rolling basis starting 2/28; must reply by 5/1.

**Academics. Special study options:** Cross-registration, double major, exchange student, honors, independent study, internships, liberal arts/career combination, New York semester, student-designed major, study abroad, teacher certification program, United Nations semester, Washington semester. Nontraditional study programs available through Johnston Center for Integrated Studies and Schools of Business and Education. **Credit/placement by examination:** AP, CLEP, IB, SAT, ACT, institutional tests. 16 credit hours maximum toward bachelor's degree. **Support services:** Learning center, pre-admission summer program, reduced course load, study skills assistance, tutoring, writing center.

**Majors. Area/ethnic studies:** Asian, Latin American, women's. **Biology:** General, biochemistry. **Business:** General, accounting, business admin, management information systems, managerial economics. **Computer sciences:** General. **Conservation:** Environmental science, environmental studies, management/policy. **Education:** Elementary, middle, music, secondary, speech impaired. **Foreign languages:** French, German, Spanish. **Health:** Audiology/speech pathology. **History:** General. **Liberal arts:** Arts/sciences. **Math:** General. **Philosophy/religion:** Philosophy, religion. **Physical sciences:** Chemistry, physics. **Psychology:** General. **Social sciences:** Anthropology, economics, international relations, political science, sociology. **Visual/performing arts:** Art, art history/conservation, dramatic, music history, music performance, music theory/composition.

**Most popular majors.** Business/marketing 41%, health sciences 7%, psychology 6%, social sciences 9%.

**Computing on campus.** 655 workstations in dormitories, library, computer center, student center. Dormitories wired for high-speed internet access and linked to campus network. Commuter students can connect to campus network. Online library, helpline, repair service, student web hosting, wireless network available.

**Student life. Freshman orientation:** Mandatory. One full week preceding academic school year. **Housing:** Guaranteed on-campus for freshmen. Coed dorms, single-sex dorms, special housing for disabled, apartments, fraternity/sorority housing, wellness housing available. **Activities:** Bands, choral groups, dance, drama, literary magazine, music ensembles, musical theater, opera, radio station, student government, student newspaper, symphony orchestra, Associated Students, Intervarsity Christian Fellowship, African American association, Gay, Lesbian, Bisexual student union, women's center, College Republicans, College Democrats, Asian Pacific Islander Association, Theater Association, Students for Environmental Action.

**Athletics.** NCAA. **Intercollegiate:** Baseball M, basketball, cross-country, diving, football (tackle) M, golf, lacrosse W, soccer, softball W, swimming, tennis, track and field, volleyball W, water polo. **Intramural:** Basketball, football (non-tackle), racquetball, soccer, softball, table tennis, tennis, volleyball, water polo. **Team name:** Bulldogs.

**Student services.** Adult student services, alcohol/substance abuse counseling, chaplain/spiritual director, career counseling, student employment services, financial aid counseling, health services, minority student services, personal counseling, placement for graduates, veterans' counselor, women's services. **Physically disabled:** Services for visually, speech, hearing impaired.

**Contact.** E-mail: admissions@redlands.edu
Phone: (909) 748-8074 Toll-free number: (800) 455-5064
Fax: (909) 335-4089
Paul Driscoll, Dean of Admissions, University of Redlands, 1200 East Colton Avenue, Redlands, CA 92373-0999

## University of San Diego

**San Diego, California**  **CB member**
**www.sandiego.edu**  **CB code: 4849**

- Private 4-year university affiliated with Roman Catholic Church
- Residential campus in very large city
- 5,066 degree-seeking undergraduates: 4% part-time, 57% women, 3% African American, 11% Asian American, 15% Hispanic American, 2% Native American, 4% international
- 2,714 degree-seeking graduate students
- 49% of applicants admitted

♦ SAT or ACT with writing, application essay required
♦ 75% graduate within 6 years

**General.** Founded in 1949. Regionally accredited. **Degrees:** 1,264 bachelor's awarded; master's, doctoral, professional offered. **ROTC:** Army, Naval, Air Force. **Location:** 5 miles from downtown. **Calendar:** 4-1-4, extensive summer session. **Full-time faculty:** 381 total; 94% have terminal degrees, 18% minority, 45% women. **Part-time faculty:** 427 total; 59% have terminal degrees, 17% minority, 53% women. **Class size:** 42% < 20, 55% 20-39, 3% 40-49, less than 1% 50-99.

**Freshman class profile.** 11,000 applied, 5,434 admitted, 1,081 enrolled.

| Mid 50% test scores | | | |
|---|---|---|---|
| SAT critical reading: | 550-640 | Rank in top quarter: | 80% |
| SAT math: | 570-660 | Rank in top tenth: | 45% |
| SAT writing: | 550-650 | End year in good standing: | 93% |
| ACT composite: | 25-29 | Return as sophomores: | 85% |
| GPA 3.75 or higher: | 61% | Out-of-state: | 47% |
| GPA 3.50-3.74: | 21% | Live on campus: | 96% |
| GPA 3.0-3.49: | 17% | International: | 2% |
| GPA 2.0-2.99: | 1% | | |

**Basis for selection.** School achievement record, test scores, recommendations, and extracurricular activities important. Out-of-state and international applicants encouraged. Advanced Placement English examinations (language or literature) with grade of 4 or 5 may also be used for placement. Audition required of choral scholarship applicants. **Learning Disabled:** Must contact Director of Disability Services.

**High school preparation.** College-preparatory program recommended. 17 units required; 22 recommended. Required and recommended units include English 4, mathematics 3-4, social studies 3-4, science 3-4 (laboratory 2-3) and foreign language 2-3.

**2009-2010 Annual costs.** Tuition/fees: $36,292. Room/board: $12,602. Books/supplies: $1,638. Personal expenses: $2,250.

**2008-2009 Financial aid. Need-based:** 743 full-time freshmen applied for aid; 591 were judged to have need; 591 of these received aid. Average need met was 75%. Average scholarship/grant was $21,463; average loan $5,528. 67% of total undergraduate aid awarded as scholarships/grants, 33% as loans/jobs. **Non-need-based:** Awarded to 1,866 full-time undergraduates, including 581 freshmen. Scholarships awarded for academics, athletics, leadership, music/drama, religious affiliation, ROTC.

**Application procedures. Admission:** Priority date 1/15; deadline 3/1 (postmark date). $55 fee, may be waived for applicants with need. Admission notification 4/15. Must reply by May 1 or within 2 week(s) if notified thereafter. **Financial aid:** Priority date 3/2; no closing date. FAFSA required. Applicants notified on a rolling basis starting 3/1; must reply by 5/1 or within 3 week(s) of notification.

**Academics. Special study options:** Combined bachelor's/graduate degree, double major, ESL, honors, independent study, internships, liberal arts/career combination, semester at sea, study abroad, teacher certification program, Washington semester. **Credit/placement by examination:** AP, CLEP, IB, institutional tests. **Support services:** Pre-admission summer program, reduced course load, study skills assistance, tutoring, writing center.

**Majors. Biology:** General, biochemistry, marine. **Business:** Accounting, business admin, finance, managerial economics, marketing. **Communications:** General. **Computer sciences:** Computer science. **Engineering:** Electrical, industrial, mechanical. **Foreign languages:** French, Spanish. **Health:** Nursing (RN). **History:** General. **Interdisciplinary:** Intercultural. **Liberal arts:** Arts/sciences, humanities. **Math:** General. **Philosophy/religion:** Philosophy, religion. **Physical sciences:** Chemistry, physics. **Psychology:** General. **Social sciences:** Anthropology, economics, international relations, political science, sociology. **Visual/performing arts:** Art history/conservation, dramatic, studio arts.

**Most popular majors.** Biology 6%, business/marketing 41%, communications/journalism 10%, psychology 7%, social sciences 14%.

**Computing on campus.** Dormitories wired for high-speed internet access and linked to campus network. Commuter students can connect to campus network. Online course registration, helpline, repair service, student web hosting, wireless network available.

**Student life. Freshman orientation:** Mandatory. Preregistration for classes offered. 4-day program that starts at the beginning of the semester. **Policies:** Freshmen required to live on campus unless living with parents. **Housing:** Guaranteed on-campus for freshmen. Coed dorms, single-sex dorms, special housing for disabled, apartments, wellness housing available. $250 partly refundable deposit, deadline 5/1. **Activities:** Bands, campus ministries, choral groups, dance, drama, international student organizations, literary magazine, music ensembles, Model UN, musical theater, radio station, student government, student newspaper, symphony orchestra, TV station, Alcala Club, Amnesty International, Entrepreneurship Club, Filipino Student Organization, Founders Club, International Student Organization, Invisible Children, Mortar Board Society, Student Alumni Association, Students for Life.

**Athletics.** NCAA. **Intercollegiate:** Baseball M, basketball, cross-country, diving W, football (tackle) M, golf M, rowing (crew), soccer, softball W, swimming W, tennis, volleyball W. **Intramural:** Basketball, football (non-tackle), soccer, softball, tennis, volleyball. **Team name:** Toreros.

**Student services.** Alcohol/substance abuse counseling, chaplain/spiritual director, career counseling, services for economically disadvantaged, student employment services, financial aid counseling, health services, legal services, minority student services, on-campus daycare, personal counseling, placement for graduates, veterans' counselor, women's services. **Physically disabled:** Services for visually impaired.

**Contact.** E-mail: admissions@sandiego.edu
Phone: (619) 260-4506 Toll-free number: (800) 248-4873
Fax: (619) 260-6836
Stephen Pultz, Director of Admissions, University of San Diego, 5998 Alcala Park, San Diego, CA 92110

## University of San Francisco
San Francisco, California     CB member
www.usfca.edu     CB code: 4850

♦ Private 4-year university affiliated with Roman Catholic Church
♦ Residential campus in very large city
♦ 5,000 degree-seeking undergraduates: 3% part-time, 64% women
♦ 3,445 degree-seeking graduate students
♦ 71% of applicants admitted
♦ SAT or ACT with writing, application essay required
♦ 69% graduate within 6 years

**General.** Founded in 1855. Regionally accredited. **Degrees:** 1,281 bachelor's awarded; master's, doctoral, professional offered. **ROTC:** Army, Air Force. **Location:** 3 miles from downtown. **Calendar:** 4-1-4, extensive summer session. **Full-time faculty:** 386 total; 93% have terminal degrees, 22% minority, 47% women. **Part-time faculty:** 553 total; 21% minority, 58% women. **Class size:** 49% < 20, 40% 20-39, 8% 40-49, 2% 50-99, less than 1% >100. **Special facilities:** Rare book room, institute for Chinese western cultural history, electron microscope, law library available to all students.

**Freshman class profile.** 8,281 applied, 5,906 admitted, 1,073 enrolled.

| Mid 50% test scores | | | |
|---|---|---|---|
| SAT critical reading: | 500-610 | Rank in top quarter: | 61% |
| SAT math: | 510-610 | Rank in top tenth: | 24% |
| SAT writing: | 510-620 | Return as sophomores: | 84% |
| ACT composite: | 22-27 | Out-of-state: | 33% |
| GPA 3.75 or higher: | 28% | Live on campus: | 86% |
| GPA 3.50-3.74: | 21% | International: | 8% |
| GPA 3.0-3.49: | 43% | Fraternities: | 1% |
| GPA 2.0-2.99: | 8% | Sororities: | 1% |

**Basis for selection.** Require TOEFL for non-native speakers of English. Interviews required for nursing students. **Homeschooled:** Statement describing homeschool structure and mission, letter of recommendation (nonparent) required. Statement from parents on curriculum required if student not evaluated through high school homeschooling program or agency that evaluates home school programs. **Learning Disabled:** After acceptance, students with disabilities must contact Office of Disability Related Services to request accommodations.

**High school preparation.** 20 units required. Required units include English 4, mathematics 3, social studies 3, science 2 (laboratory 2), foreign language 2 and academic electives 6. One chemistry and 1 biology or physics required of nursing and science applicants.

**2010-2011 Annual costs.** Tuition/fees: $36,380. Room/board: $11,990. Books/supplies: $1,500. Personal expenses: $2,500.

**2009-2010 Financial aid. Non-need-based:** Scholarships awarded for academics, athletics, ROTC. **Additional information:** Individualized installment plans available.

**Application procedures. Admission:** Priority date 1/15; no deadline. $55 fee, may be waived for applicants with need. Notification begins approximately 4 weeks after all materials submitted including fall grades. Must reply by May 1 or within 2 week(s) if notified thereafter. **Financial aid:** Priority date 2/1; no closing date. FAFSA required. Applicants notified on a rolling basis starting 4/1; must reply within 4 week(s) of notification.

**Academics.** Pre-admission counseling, academic accommodations and counseling, alternative testing, alternate format/taped texts, auxiliary aids and services (including notetakers, laboratory assistants, readers and/or scribes , sign language/oral interpreters and captioning services). Alternative formats for printed material, such as e-text, RFB&D. Residential accommodations and counseling. Transportation and parking services. Information and referral source to University and community programs and service. **Special study options:** Combined bachelor's/graduate degree, cooperative education, cross-registration, double major, ESL, exchange student, external degree, honors, independent study, internships, liberal arts/career combination, study abroad, teacher certification program, Washington semester. College of Professional Studies for adult degree-seeking students coming back to school to earn undergraduate bachelor's degree; cooperative work study in Computer Science courses. **Credit/placement by examination:** AP, CLEP, IB, SAT, ACT, institutional tests. 30 credit hours maximum toward bachelor's degree. Credit for experiential learning limited to maximum of 30 undergraduate semester units for Professional Studies students in the School of Business and Professional Studies. **Support services:** Learning center, pre-admission summer program, reduced course load, study skills assistance, tutoring, writing center.

**Majors. Architecture:** Architecture. **Area/ethnic studies:** American. **Biology:** General. **Business:** General, accounting, business admin, entrepreneurial studies, finance, hotel/motel admin, international, marketing, organizational behavior, restaurant/food services. **Communications:** General, advertising, media studies. **Computer sciences:** General, information systems. **Conservation:** Environmental science, environmental studies. **Foreign languages:** Comparative lit, French, Japanese, Spanish. **Health:** Nursing (RN). **History:** General. **Liberal arts:** Arts/sciences. **Math:** General. **Parks/recreation:** Exercise sciences. **Philosophy/religion:** Philosophy. **Physical sciences:** Chemistry, physics. **Psychology:** General. **Public administration:** General. **Social sciences:** Economics, international economics, political science, sociology. **Theology:** Theology. **Visual/performing arts:** General, art history/conservation, arts management, commercial/advertising art, studio arts.

**Most popular majors.** Business/marketing 29%, communications/journalism 7%, computer/information sciences 6%, health sciences 8%, psychology 8%, social sciences 14%, visual/performing arts 6%.

**Computing on campus.** 320 workstations in dormitories, library, computer center, student center. Dormitories wired for high-speed internet access and linked to campus network. Commuter students can connect to campus network. Online course registration, online library, helpline, repair service, student web hosting, wireless network available.

**Student life. Freshman orientation:** Mandatory. Preregistration for classes offered. Two-day session including placement tests. **Policies:** Freshman and sophomores under 21 required to live in residence halls unless they have permanent address within 20-mile radius of campus. **Housing:** Guaranteed on-campus for freshmen. Coed dorms, single-sex dorms, special housing for disabled, apartments available. $300 nonrefundable deposit, deadline 5/1. **Activities:** Pep band, choral groups, dance, drama, international student organizations, literary magazine, music ensembles, musical theater, radio station, student government, student newspaper, TV station, St. Ignatius Institute, People Advocating Cultural Endeavors, Phelan multicultural community.

**Athletics.** NCAA. **Intercollegiate:** Baseball M, basketball, cross-country, golf, rifle, soccer, tennis, track and field, volleyball W. **Intramural:** Basketball, football (non-tackle), racquetball, soccer, softball, swimming, table tennis, tennis, volleyball. **Team name:** Dons.

**Student services.** Adult student services, alcohol/substance abuse counseling, chaplain/spiritual director, career counseling, student employment services, financial aid counseling, health services, minority student services, personal counseling, placement for graduates. **Physically disabled:** Services for visually, speech, hearing impaired. **Learning disabled:** Comprehensive services available.

**Contact.** E-mail: admissions@usfca.edu
Phone: (415) 422-6563 Toll-free number: (800) 225-5873
Fax: (415) 422-2217
Michael Hughes, Director of Admissions, University of San Francisco, 2130 Fulton Street, San Francisco, CA 94117-1046

## University of Southern California
**Los Angeles, California**
www.usc.edu

**CB member**
**CB code: 4852**

- Private 4-year university
- Residential campus in very large city
- 16,445 degree-seeking undergraduates: 3% part-time, 50% women, 6% African American, 24% Asian American, 13% Hispanic American, 1% Native American, 10% international

- 17,201 degree-seeking graduate students
- 24% of applicants admitted
- SAT or ACT with writing, application essay required
- 88% graduate within 6 years; 30% enter graduate study

**General.** Founded in 1880. Regionally accredited. Permanent facilities for study in Sacramento available. **Degrees:** 4,295 bachelor's awarded; master's, doctoral, professional offered. **ROTC:** Army, Naval, Air Force. **Location:** 3 miles from downtown. **Calendar:** Semester, limited summer session. **Full-time faculty:** 1,638 total; 89% have terminal degrees, 26% minority, 34% women. **Part-time faculty:** 1,133 total; 61% have terminal degrees, 33% minority, 39% women. **Class size:** 63% < 20, 20% 20-39, 6% 40-49, 7% 50-99, 4% >100. **Special facilities:** 3 art/architecture galleries, 2 museums, 2 sculpture gardens, marine science center, Gamble House designed by Greene and Greene, Freeman House designed by Frank Lloyd Wright, integrated media systems center, center for digital arts, technical theater laboratory, recording studio, cinematic arts complex.

**Freshman class profile.** 35,753 applied, 8,724 admitted, 2,869 enrolled.

| Mid 50% test scores | | Rank in top quarter: | 97% |
|---|---|---|---|
| SAT critical reading: | 620-710 | Rank in top tenth: | 86% |
| SAT math: | 650-740 | End year in good standing: | 97% |
| SAT writing: | 640-730 | Return as sophomores: | 96% |
| ACT composite: | 29-32 | Out-of-state: | 41% |
| GPA 3.75 or higher: | 50% | Live on campus: | 98% |
| GPA 3.50-3.74: | 31% | International: | 11% |
| GPA 3.0-3.49: | 18% | Fraternities: | 21% |
| GPA 2.0-2.99: | 1% | Sororities: | 26% |

**Basis for selection.** GED not accepted. Academic achievement, curriculum and test scores most important. Recommendations, activities, essays/writing samples are also very important. Audition required of music and theater majors. Portfolio required of fine arts and architecture majors. **Homeschooled:** 3 SAT Subject tests (1 must be in math) and detailed syllabi of courses, names of textbooks, names and applicable credentials of instructors, details of assistance received or curriculum followed through any public or private agency, and any additional information that may be helpful.

**High school preparation.** College-preparatory program required. 16 units required; 20 recommended. Required and recommended units include English 4, mathematics 3-4, social studies 2-3, science 2-3 (laboratory 2-3), foreign language 2-3 and academic electives 3.

**2009-2010 Annual costs.** Tuition/fees: $39,274. Room/board: $11,458. Books/supplies: $1,500. Personal expenses: $896.

**2009-2010 Financial aid. Need-based:** 1,761 full-time freshmen applied for aid; 1,185 were judged to have need; 1,185 of these received aid. Average need met was 100%. Average scholarship/grant was $25,657; average loan $3,757. 79% of total undergraduate aid awarded as scholarships/grants, 21% as loans/jobs. **Non-need-based:** Awarded to 6,460 full-time undergraduates, including 1,490 freshmen. Scholarships awarded for academics, alumni affiliation, art, athletics, leadership, music/drama, ROTC.

**Application procedures. Admission:** Priority date 12/1; deadline 1/10 (postmark date). $65 fee, may be waived for applicants with need. Admission notification 4/1. Must reply by 5/1. **Financial aid:** Priority date 2/2; no closing date. FAFSA, CSS PROFILE required. Applicants notified on a rolling basis starting 3/15; must reply by 5/1.

**Academics. Special study options:** Combined bachelor's/graduate degree, cooperative education, distance learning, double major, ESL, exchange student, honors, independent study, internships, liberal arts/career combination, student-designed major, study abroad, Washington semester. Learning communities, thematic option, undergraduate research, freshman seminars. **Credit/placement by examination:** AP, CLEP, IB, institutional tests. 32 credit hours maximum toward bachelor's degree. **Support services:** Learning center, reduced course load, study skills assistance, tutoring, writing center.

**Majors. Architecture:** Architecture, landscape. **Area/ethnic studies:** African-American, American, Asian-American, Chicano/Hispanic-American/Latino, East Asian, women's. **Biology:** General, biochemistry, biophysics. **Business:** Accounting, business admin, international. **Communications:** General, broadcast journalism, journalism, public relations, radio/tv. **Computer sciences:** Computer science. **Conservation:** Environmental science, environmental studies. **Engineering:** Aerospace, biomedical, chemical, civil, computer, construction, electrical, environmental, industrial, mechanical, petroleum, polymer, structural, systems. **Foreign languages:** Classics, comparative lit, East Asian, French, Italian, linguistics, Russian, Spanish. **Health:** Dental hygiene. **History:** General. **Interdisciplinary:** Classical/archaeology, gerontology, global studies, neuroscience. **Math:** General, applied. **Parks/recreation:** Exercise sciences. **Philosophy/religion:** Ethics, Judaic, philosophy, religion. **Physical sciences:** General, astronomy, chemistry, geology, physics. **Psychology:** General. **Public administration:** General. **Social sciences:** Anthropology, economics, geography, international relations, political science, sociology. **Visual/performing arts:** General, acting, art history/conservation, cinematography, dramatic, film/cinema, music management, music performance, music theory/composition, piano/organ, play/screenwriting, stringed instruments, studio arts, theater arts management, theater design, voice/opera. **Other:** Human performance, Literature and language, Narrative studies, Philosophy, politics and law.

**Most popular majors.** Business/marketing 27%, communications/journalism 9%, engineering/engineering technologies 9%, social sciences 14%, visual/performing arts 14%.

**Computing on campus.** 2,700 workstations in dormitories, library, computer center, student center. Dormitories wired for high-speed internet access and linked to campus network. Commuter students can connect to campus network. Online course registration, online library, helpline, repair service, student web hosting, wireless network available.

**Student life. Freshman orientation:** Available, $150 fee. Preregistration for classes offered. **Policies:** Every incoming student required to take online alcohol education course and pass final exam. **Housing:** Guaranteed on-campus for freshmen. Coed dorms, special housing for disabled, apartments, fraternity/sorority housing, wellness housing available. $400 fully refundable deposit. African-American, Jewish, Latino, LGBT, and Muslim floors, faculty-in-residence programs and residential colleges available. **Activities:** Bands, campus ministries, choral groups, dance, drama, film society, international student organizations, literary magazine, music ensembles, Model UN, musical theater, opera, radio station, student government, student newspaper, symphony orchestra, TV station, academic honors assembly, emerging leaders program, minority consortium, religious council, residential community council, student program board, student volunteer center.

**Athletics. NCAA. Intercollegiate:** Baseball M, basketball, cross-country, diving, football (tackle) M, golf, rowing (crew) W, soccer W, swimming, tennis, track and field, volleyball, water polo. **Intramural:** Baseball M, basketball, cross-country, football (non-tackle), golf, racquetball, soccer, softball, table tennis, tennis, track and field, volleyball, water polo. **Team name:** Trojans.

**Student services.** Alcohol/substance abuse counseling, chaplain/spiritual director, career counseling, services for economically disadvantaged, student employment services, financial aid counseling, health services, legal services, minority student services, on-campus daycare, personal counseling, placement for graduates, veterans' counselor, women's services. **Physically disabled:** Services for visually, speech, hearing impaired. **Learning disabled:** Comprehensive services available.

**Contact.** E-mail: admitusc@usc.edu
Phone: (213) 740-1111 Fax: (213) 821-0200
Timothy Brunold, Associate Dean and Director of Undergraduate Admission, University of Southern California, Office of Admission, Los Angeles, CA 90089-0911

---

## University of the Pacific
**Stockton, California**                             **CB member**
**www.pacific.edu**                                  **CB code: 4065**

▶ Private 4-year university
▶ Residential campus in large city
▶ 3,489 degree-seeking undergraduates: 3% part-time, 55% women
▶ 2,885 degree-seeking graduate students
▶ 42% of applicants admitted
▶ SAT or ACT (ACT writing optional), application essay required
▶ 68% graduate within 6 years

**General.** Founded in 1851. Regionally accredited. School of Dentistry in San Francisco. McGeorge School of Law in Sacramento. **Degrees:** 743 bachelor's awarded; master's, doctoral, professional offered. **ROTC:** Air Force. **Location:** 80 miles from San Francisco, 40 miles from Sacramento. **Calendar:** Semester, limited summer session. **Full-time faculty:** 434 total; 88% have terminal degrees, 20% minority, 40% women. **Part-time faculty:** 341 total; 50% have terminal degrees, 25% minority, 45% women. **Class size:** 62% < 20, 31% 20-39, 2% 40-49, 4% 50-99, less than 1% >100. **Special facilities:** Recital facilities, center for western studies, John Muir papers collection, music conservatory.

**Freshman class profile.** 14,970 applied, 6,218 admitted, 894 enrolled.

| Mid 50% test scores | | | |
|---|---|---|---|
| SAT critical reading: | 510-640 | GPA 3.0-3.49: | 35% |
| SAT math: | 540-680 | GPA 2.0-2.99: | 8% |
| SAT writing: | 500-640 | Rank in top quarter: | 76% |
| ACT composite: | 23-30 | Rank in top tenth: | 42% |
| GPA 3.75 or higher: | 28% | Out-of-state: | 12% |
| GPA 3.50-3.74: | 29% | Live on campus: | 87% |
| | | International: | 4% |

**Basis for selection.** Secondary school record, standardized test scores, recommendations, essay, extracurricular activities important. SAT Subject Tests recommended. Audition required of music/conservatory majors. **Homeschooled:** Standardized test scores weighted heavily.

**High school preparation.** College-preparatory program recommended. 16 units required. Required and recommended units include English 4, mathematics 3, social studies 2, history 1, (laboratory 2), foreign language 2, visual/performing arts 1 and academic electives 1. 1 fine/performing arts required.

**2009-2010 Annual costs.** Tuition/fees: $30,880. Room/board: $10,118. Books/supplies: $1,638. Personal expenses: $2,250.

**2009-2010 Financial aid. Need-based:** 786 full-time freshmen applied for aid; 665 were judged to have need; 664 of these received aid. Average scholarship/grant was $23,613; average loan $3,947. 72% of total undergraduate aid awarded as scholarships/grants, 28% as loans/jobs. **Non-need-based:** Awarded to 578 full-time undergraduates, including 174 freshmen. Scholarships awarded for academics, athletics, leadership, music/drama, religious affiliation.

**Application procedures. Admission:** Priority date 11/15; deadline 1/15. $60 fee, may be waived for applicants with need, free for online applicants. Admission notification on a rolling basis beginning on or about 3/15. Housing deposit refundable if canceled by May 1. **Financial aid:** Priority date 2/15; no closing date. FAFSA required. Applicants notified on a rolling basis starting 3/15.

**Academics. Special study options:** Accelerated study, combined bachelor's/graduate degree, cooperative education, double major, dual enrollment of high school students, ESL, exchange student, honors, independent study, internships, liberal arts/career combination, student-designed major, study abroad, teacher certification program, United Nations semester, Washington semester. Practicum, minors, undergraduate research, combination, ethnic studies, environmental science, gender studies, service learning, thematic minors. **Credit/placement by examination:** AP, CLEP, IB, SAT, ACT, institutional tests. 20 credit hours maximum toward bachelor's degree. **Support services:** Learning center, pre-admission summer program, reduced course load, remedial instruction, tutoring, writing center.

**Majors. Biology:** General, biochemistry. **Business:** Business admin. **Communications:** General. **Computer sciences:** General, computer science, information systems. **Conservation:** Environmental science, environmental studies. **Education:** General, elementary, multi-level teacher, music, secondary. **Engineering:** General, civil, computer, electrical, mechanical, physics. **Engineering technology:** Industrial management. **Foreign languages:** French, German, Japanese, Spanish. **Health:** Dental hygiene, music therapy, speech pathology. **History:** General. **Interdisciplinary:** Biological/physical sciences. **Liberal arts:** Arts/sciences. **Math:** General, applied. **Parks/recreation:** Health/fitness, sports admin. **Philosophy/religion:** Philosophy, religion. **Physical sciences:** Chemistry, geology, physics. **Psychology:** General. **Social sciences:** General, economics, international relations, political science, sociology. **Visual/performing arts:** Art, commercial/advertising art, dramatic, music history, music management, music performance, music theory/composition, piano/organ, studio arts, voice/opera. **Other:** Geosciences.

**Most popular majors.** Biology 15%, business/marketing 19%, engineering/engineering technologies 13%, health sciences 6%, parks/recreation 7%.

**Computing on campus.** 325 workstations in dormitories, library, computer center. Dormitories wired for high-speed internet access and linked to campus network. Commuter students can connect to campus network. Online course registration, online library, helpline, wireless network available.

**Student life. Freshman orientation:** Mandatory, $120 fee. Preregistration for classes offered. Offered in January, June, July & August, 2-4 days each. **Policies:** Freshmen and sophomores required to live on campus unless living with parents. **Housing:** Guaranteed on-campus for freshmen. Coed dorms, apartments, fraternity/sorority housing available. $250 fully refundable deposit. **Activities:** Bands, campus ministries, choral groups, dance, drama, film society, international student organizations, literary magazine, music ensembles, Model UN, musical theater, opera, radio station, student government, student newspaper, symphony orchestra, 100 student organizations and clubs.

**Athletics.** NCAA. **Intercollegiate:** Baseball M, basketball, cross-country W, field hockey W, golf M, soccer W, softball W, swimming, tennis, volleyball, water polo. **Intramural:** Badminton, basketball, bowling, football (tackle), golf, racquetball, soccer, softball, swimming, tennis, volleyball, water polo. **Team name:** Tigers.

**Student services.** Adult student services, alcohol/substance abuse counseling, chaplain/spiritual director, career counseling, services for economically disadvantaged, student employment services, financial aid counseling, health services, personal counseling, placement for graduates, veterans' counselor. **Physically disabled:** Services for visually, speech, hearing impaired.

**Contact.** E-mail: admission@pacific.edu
Phone: (209) 946-2211 Fax: (209) 946-2413
Rich Toledo, Director of Admissions, University of the Pacific, 3601 Pacific Avenue, Stockton, CA 95211-0197

## University of the West
### Rosemead, California
### www.uwest.edu

- Private 4-year business and liberal arts college affiliated with Buddhism
- Commuter campus in small city
- 54 degree-seeking undergraduates
- Application essay required

**General.** WASC-accredited, private, non-profit campus, Buddhist-founded institution. **Degrees:** 7 bachelor's awarded; master's, doctoral offered. **Location:** 5 miles from Pasadena, 10 miles from Los Angeles. **Calendar:** Semester, extensive summer session. **Full-time faculty:** 9 total. **Part-time faculty:** 21 total. **Special facilities:** Investment lab, meditation hall.

**Basis for selection.** Open admission. SAT scores are not required for admission, however a score does help in consideration for admission and for determination of scholarship awards. **Homeschooled:** Handled on case-by-case basis.

**2009-2010 Annual costs.** Tuition/fees: $10,060. Tuition is $300 per unit for all non-business courses; $320 per unit for all business courses. Room/board: $6,290. Books/supplies: $1,314. Personal expenses: $2,826.

**Application procedures. Admission:** Priority date 3/1; deadline 6/1 (postmark date). $50 fee, may be waived for applicants with need. Application must be submitted on paper. Admission notification on a rolling basis. **Financial aid:** No deadline.

**Academics. Special study options:** Combined bachelor's/graduate degree, ESL, exchange student, independent study, internships, study abroad. **Credit/placement by examination:** CLEP. 15 credit hours maximum toward bachelor's degree. **Support services:** Learning center, remedial instruction, study skills assistance, tutoring, writing center.

**Majors. Business:** Accounting, international. **History:** General. **Philosophy/religion:** Religion. **Psychology:** General.

**Most popular majors.** Business/marketing 40%, philosophy/religious studies 40%, psychology 8%.

**Computing on campus.** 30 workstations in dormitories, library, computer center. Dormitories wired for high-speed internet access and linked to campus network. Commuter students can connect to campus network. Online course registration, online library, student web hosting, wireless network available.

**Student life. Freshman orientation:** Mandatory. **Housing:** Guaranteed on-campus for all undergraduates. Coed dorms, apartments available. $200 fully refundable deposit. **Activities:** Campus ministries, international student organizations, literary magazine, student government.

**Student services.** Chaplain/spiritual director, career counseling, financial aid counseling.

**Contact.** E-mail: admission@uwest.edu
Phone: (626) 677-3311 Fax: (626) 571-1413
Grace Hsiao, Admissions Officer, University of the West, 1409 North Walnut Grove Avenue, Rosemead, CA 91770

## Vanguard University of Southern California
### Costa Mesa, California
### www.vanguard.edu                        CB code: 4701

- Private 4-year university and liberal arts college affiliated with Assemblies of God
- Residential campus in small city

- 1,565 degree-seeking undergraduates: 18% part-time, 60% women, 4% African American, 5% Asian American, 18% Hispanic American, 2% Native American, 1% international
- 272 degree-seeking graduate students
- 79% of applicants admitted
- SAT or ACT (ACT writing optional), application essay required
- 53% graduate within 6 years

**General.** Founded in 1920. Regionally accredited. **Degrees:** 517 bachelor's awarded; master's offered. **ROTC:** Army, Air Force. **Location:** 45 miles from Los Angeles, 70 miles from San Diego. **Calendar:** Semester, limited summer session. **Full-time faculty:** 66 total; 82% have terminal degrees, 11% minority, 44% women. **Part-time faculty:** 107 total; 36% have terminal degrees, 18% minority, 50% women. **Class size:** 57% < 20, 34% 20-39, 4% 40-49, 5% 50-99, less than 1% >100.

**Freshman class profile.** 787 applied, 625 admitted, 268 enrolled.

| Mid 50% test scores | | | |
|---|---|---|---|
| SAT critical reading: | 440-550 | GPA 2.0-2.99: | 21% |
| SAT math: | 420-530 | Rank in top quarter: | 29% |
| ACT composite: | 18-23 | Rank in top tenth: | 22% |
| GPA 3.75 or higher: | 26% | End year in good standing: | 88% |
| GPA 3.50-3.74: | 18% | Return as sophomores: | 73% |
| GPA 3.0-3.49: | 34% | Out-of-state: | 4% |
| | | Live on campus: | 90% |

**Basis for selection.** Priority given to students with GPA of 2.8 or higher, Christian commitment essay, academic reference, reference from pastor. Applications from Christian students who desire an education that integrates Christian faith with learning and living encouraged. Interview recommended for borderline applicants. Audition recommended for music, theater majors. **Homeschooled:** Should take GED to qualify for federal financial aid.

**High school preparation.** Recommended units include English 4, mathematics 2, social studies 3 and science 2.

**2010-2011 Annual costs.** Tuition/fees: $26,342. Room/board: $8,280. Books/supplies: $1,638. Personal expenses: $2,250.

**2008-2009 Financial aid. Need-based:** 248 full-time freshmen applied for aid; 206 were judged to have need; 206 of these received aid. Average need met was 73%. Average scholarship/grant was $9,424; average loan $3,864. 62% of total undergraduate aid awarded as scholarships/grants, 38% as loans/jobs. **Non-need-based:** Awarded to 1,108 full-time undergraduates, including 267 freshmen. Scholarships awarded for academics, athletics, music/drama, religious affiliation.

**Application procedures. Admission:** Priority date 12/1; no deadline. $45 fee, may be waived for applicants with need. Admission notification on a rolling basis beginning on or about 1/15. Must reply by May 1 or within 3 week(s) if notified thereafter. **Financial aid:** Priority date 3/2, closing date 3/2. FAFSA required. Applicants notified on a rolling basis starting 4/1; must reply within 3 week(s) of notification.

**Academics. Special study options:** Accelerated study, combined bachelor's/graduate degree, double major, liberal arts/career combination, study abroad, teacher certification program, Washington semester. **Credit/placement by examination:** AP, CLEP, IB, SAT, ACT. 24 credit hours maximum toward bachelor's degree. **Support services:** Learning center, reduced course load, study skills assistance, tutoring, writing center.

**Majors. Biology:** General, biochemistry. **Business:** General, accounting, business admin, finance, international, marketing. **Communications:** General, digital media. **Computer sciences:** Information technology. **Education:** Music, physical. **Family/consumer sciences:** Family studies. **Health:** Athletic training, nursing (RN), premedicine. **History:** General. **Interdisciplinary:** Biological/physical sciences, intercultural. **Legal studies:** Prelaw. **Liberal arts:** Arts/sciences. **Math:** General. **Parks/recreation:** Exercise sciences, health/fitness. **Philosophy/religion:** Christian, religion. **Physical sciences:** Chemistry. **Psychology:** General. **Social sciences:** General, anthropology, political science, sociology. **Theology:** Bible, missionary, pastoral counseling, religious ed, theology, youth ministry. **Visual/performing arts:** Cinematography, dramatic, music history, music performance, theater design. **Other:** Physical therapy/therapist.

**Most popular majors.** Business/marketing 24%, communications/journalism 11%, health sciences 9%, psychology 16%, social sciences 9%, theological studies 8%.

**Computing on campus.** 76 workstations in dormitories, library. Dormitories wired for high-speed internet access and linked to campus network. Commuter students can connect to campus network. Online course registration, online library, helpline, wireless network available.

**Student life. Freshman orientation:** Mandatory, $80 fee. Preregistration for classes offered. 4-day program prior to first day of fall semester. **Policies:** Students must be in good standing to live on campus. Religious observance required. **Housing:** Guaranteed on-campus for all undergraduates. Coed dorms, single-sex dorms, apartments, wellness housing available. $400 deposit, deadline 8/9. **Activities:** Bands, campus ministries, choral groups, drama, film society, international student organizations, literary magazine, music ensembles, musical theater, student government, student newspaper, Students for Social Action (SSA), Live 2 Free, Club Mosaic, El Puente, Students in Free Enterprise (SIFE), Invisible Children Club, Acting on AIDS, Prayer Movement, Hands Across the Border (HATB).

**Athletics.** NAIA. **Intercollegiate:** Baseball M, basketball, cross-country, soccer, softball W, swimming, tennis, track and field, volleyball W. **Intramural:** Basketball. **Team name:** Lions.

**Student services.** Adult student services, alcohol/substance abuse counseling, chaplain/spiritual director, career counseling, student employment services, financial aid counseling, health services, minority student services, personal counseling, placement for graduates, veterans' counselor, women's services.

**Contact.** E-mail: admissions@vanguard.edu
Phone: (714) 966-5496 ext. 3901 Toll-free number: (800) 722-6279
Fax: (714) 966-5471
Jessica Mireles, Vice President for Enrollment Management, Vanguard University of Southern California, 55 Fair Drive, Costa Mesa, CA 92626-9601

## West Coast University
### North Hollywood, California
### www.westcoastuniversity.edu
CB code: 4966

- For-profit 4-year health science college
- Commuter campus in very large city
- 1,709 degree-seeking undergraduates: 27% part-time, 77% women
- Interview required

**General.** Accredited by ACICS. **Degrees:** 21 bachelor's, 379 associate awarded. **Location:** Downtown. **Calendar:** Semester. **Full-time faculty:** 20 total. **Part-time faculty:** 35 total.

**Basis for selection.** Open admission, but selective for some programs. Incoming students must pass entrance exams for any program where it is required for entry. Academic record is important but not definitive. Interview with admissions and academic dean is required. **Learning Disabled:** Students with disabilities should make a request for accommodations through the Student Services Department.

**2009-2010 Annual costs.** Tuition/fees: $30,075. LVN to RN (associate degree in nursing), 4 semesters, $9,500/semester plus clinical course costs of $4,250 per clinical rotation, books and fees; RN to BSN Bridge Program, 4 semesters, $9,500/semester plus clinical course costs of $4,250 per clinical rotation, books and fees; bachelor of science in nursing, 8 semesters, $9,500/semester plus clinical course costs of $4,250 per clinical rotation, books and fees. Subject to change.

**Application procedures. Admission:** No deadline. $75 fee.

**Academics. Special study options:** Accelerated study, distance learning, internships. **Credit/placement by examination:** CLEP, institutional tests. May challenge test-out of 12 semester credits, maximum. Must achieve score of 75% or higher, one attempt only. Must be taken before enrolling in the course in which equivalency is sought. **Support services:** Study skills assistance, tutoring.

**Majors. Health:** Nursing (RN).

**Computing on campus.** 30 workstations in library. Online library available.

**Student life. Freshman orientation:** Mandatory. **Activities:** Student government.

**Student services.** Adult student services, career counseling, services for economically disadvantaged, student employment services, financial aid counseling, placement for graduates.

**Contact.** Phone: (877) 505-4928 Toll-free number: (877) 505-4928
Herman Whitaker, Admissions Director, West Coast University, 12215 Victory Boulevard, North Hollywood, CA 91606

## Western Career College: Emeryville
### Emeryville, California
### www.westerncollege.edu

- For-profit 4-year technical college
- Commuter campus in small town
- 204 degree-seeking undergraduates

**General.** Regionally accredited. **Degrees:** 22 associate awarded. **Calendar:** Continuous, extensive summer session. **Full-time faculty:** 15 total. **Part-time faculty:** 6 total.

**Basis for selection.** Open admission. CPAT required.

**2009-2010 Annual costs.** ASHS: tuition $11,748, fees $1,439; CJD: tuition $24,825, fees $2,326; GD: tuition $20,745, fees $382; GDD: tuition $29,289, fees $1,384; HCA: tuition $16,596, fees $796; HCAD: tuition $28,344, fees $2,235; HIT: tuition $16,596, fees $1,306; HITD: tuition $28,344, fees $2,745; MA: tuition $16,596, fees $411; MAD: tuition $28,344, fees $1,850; PTD: tuition $24,825, fees $1,825. Registration fee $100.

**Application procedures. Admission:** No deadline. $75 fee, may be waived for applicants with need. Admission notification on a rolling basis. **Financial aid:** FAFSA required. Applicants notified on a rolling basis.

**Academics. Credit/placement by examination:** CLEP. **Support services:** Learning center, tutoring.

**Majors. Communications technology:** Animation/special effects, desktop publishing. **Computer sciences:** Computer graphics.

**Student life. Freshman orientation:** Mandatory.

**Student services.** Student employment services, financial aid counseling.

**Contact.** Phone: (510) 601-0133 Toll-free number: (800) 750-5627
Western Career College: Emeryville, 6001 Shellmound, #145, Emeryville, CA 94608

## Westmont College
### Santa Barbara, California
### www.westmont.edu
CB member
CB code: 4950

- Private 4-year liberal arts college affiliated with nondenominational tradition
- Residential campus in small city
- 1,293 degree-seeking undergraduates: 62% women, 3% African American, 9% Asian American, 11% Hispanic American, 2% Native American, 1% international
- 4 graduate students
- 80% of applicants admitted
- SAT or ACT with writing, application essay required
- 80% graduate within 6 years

**General.** Founded in 1937. Regionally accredited. **Degrees:** 304 bachelor's awarded. **ROTC:** Army, Air Force. **Location:** 90 miles from Los Angeles. **Calendar:** Semester, limited summer session. **Full-time faculty:** 93 total; 91% have terminal degrees, 13% minority, 36% women. **Part-time faculty:** 40 total; 15% minority, 50% women. **Class size:** 61% < 20, 27% 20-39, 8% 40-49, 4% 50-99. **Special facilities:** Arts center with theater, observatory, electronic music lab, physiology lab.

**Freshman class profile.** 1,817 applied, 1,455 admitted, 320 enrolled.

| Mid 50% test scores | | |
|---|---|---|
| SAT critical reading: | 520-650 | |
| SAT math: | 530-650 | |
| SAT writing: | 530-650 | |
| ACT composite: | 23-29 | |
| GPA 3.75 or higher: | 34% | |
| GPA 3.50-3.74: | 18% | |
| GPA 3.0-3.49: | 32% | |
| GPA 2.0-2.99: | 16% | |
| Rank in top quarter: | 73% | |
| Rank in top tenth: | 40% | |
| Return as sophomores: | 84% | |
| Live on campus: | 100% | |

**Basis for selection.** Personal Christian statement, college preparatory high school curriculum, high school rank, test scores, 1 academic recommendation, and essay important. Personal interview, teacher, pastor, and other recommendations may enhance chances. Test scores must be received by November 1 for Early Action applicants. Personal interviews recommended. **Homeschooled:** Applicants encouraged. Evaluation based on individual merit as well as high school achievement. Greater emphasis may be given to SAT or ACT scores.

**High school preparation.** College-preparatory program required. 16 units required. Required and recommended units include English 4, mathematics 3, social studies 2, science 3 (laboratory 2), foreign language 2-3 and academic electives 4. Of 3 math credits recommended, 2 algebra, 1 geometry preferred. Applicants should take composition courses at least 1 semester per year.

**2009-2010 Annual costs.** Tuition/fees: $33,190. Room/board: $10,550. Books/supplies: $1,638. Personal expenses: $2,142.

**2009-2010 Financial aid. Need-based:** 252 full-time freshmen applied for aid; 206 were judged to have need; 206 of these received aid. Average need met was 71%. Average scholarship/grant was $20,396; average loan $4,070. 72% of total undergraduate aid awarded as scholarships/grants, 28% as loans/jobs. **Non-need-based:** Awarded to 466 full-time undergraduates, including 130 freshmen. Scholarships awarded for academics, art, athletics, leadership, minority status, music/drama.

**Application procedures. Admission:** Priority date 2/20; no deadline. $35 fee, may be waived for applicants with need. Admission notification on a rolling basis beginning on or about 3/1. Must reply by May 1 or within 2 week(s) if notified thereafter. Candidates not accepted for Early Action may be considered for admission under Regular Decision. This allows time for submission of additional materials that may strengthen overall application. **Financial aid:** Priority date 3/1; no closing date. FAFSA required. Applicants notified by 3/15; Applicants notified on a rolling basis starting 3/15; must reply by 5/1 or within 2 week(s) of notification.

**Academics. Special study options:** Accelerated study, double major, exchange student, honors, independent study, internships, New York semester, semester at sea, student-designed major, study abroad, teacher certification program, urban semester, Washington semester. Cross-cultural studies in Western and Eastern Europe, England, Africa, East Asia, Egypt; semester study available in San Francisco, Los Angeles, Mexico and at one of 12 other member colleges of the Christian College Consortium. **Credit/ placement by examination:** AP, CLEP, IB, SAT, ACT, institutional tests. 32 credit hours maximum toward bachelor's degree. **Support services:** Learning center, study skills assistance, tutoring, writing center.

**Majors. Area/ethnic studies:** European. **Biology:** General. **Business:** General. **Communications:** General. **Computer sciences:** Computer science. **Education:** General. **Engineering:** Physics. **Foreign languages:** French, Spanish. **Health:** Predental, premedicine, prenursing, prepharmacy, preveterinary. **History:** General. **Legal studies:** Prelaw. **Math:** General. **Parks/ recreation:** Exercise sciences. **Philosophy/religion:** Philosophy, religion. **Physical sciences:** Chemistry, physics. **Psychology:** General. **Social sciences:** General, anthropology, economics, political science, sociology. **Visual/ performing arts:** Art, dramatic. **Other:** English and modern languages.

**Most popular majors.** Biology 8%, business/marketing 14%, communications/journalism 9%, English 12%, parks/recreation 8%, philosophy/ religious studies 7%, social sciences 8%, visual/performing arts 9%.

**Computing on campus.** 100 workstations in library, computer center. Dormitories wired for high-speed internet access and linked to campus network. Commuter students can connect to campus network. Online course registration, online library, helpline, repair service, student web hosting, wireless network available.

**Student life. Freshman orientation:** Mandatory. Preregistration for classes offered. Held 4 days before Fall semester begins. **Policies:** Chapel attendance required on Mondays, Wednesdays, Fridays. Dry, tobacco-free campus. Men and women do not share hallways and bathrooms in dorms. Selected visiting hours for members of opposite sex. Religious observance required. **Housing:** Guaranteed on-campus for all undergraduates. Coed dorms, single-sex dorms, apartments, wellness housing available. $500 nonrefundable deposit, deadline 5/1. **Activities:** Jazz band, campus ministries, choral groups, dance, drama, film society, international student organizations, literary magazine, music ensembles, Model UN, musical theater, radio station, student government, student newspaper, symphony orchestra, Amnesty International, Habitat for Humanity, Leadership Development Program, political organizations, Fellowship of Christian Athletes, community service organizations.

**Athletics.** NAIA. **Intercollegiate:** Baseball M, basketball, cross-country, soccer, tennis, track and field, volleyball W. **Intramural:** Badminton, basketball, cross-country, field hockey W, football (non-tackle), golf, lacrosse W, racquetball, soccer, softball, swimming, table tennis, tennis, volleyball, water polo. **Team name:** Warriors.

**Student services.** Alcohol/substance abuse counseling, chaplain/ spiritual director, career counseling, student employment services, financial aid counseling, health services, minority student services, personal counseling, placement for graduates. **Physically disabled:** Services for visually, speech, hearing impaired.

**Contact.** E-mail: admissions@westmont.edu
Phone: (805) 565-6200 Toll-free number: (800) 777-9011
Fax: (805) 565-6234
Joyce Luy, Dean of Admission, Westmont College, 955 La Paz Road, Santa Barbara, CA 93108-1089

## Westwood College: Anaheim
### Anaheim, California
### www.westwood.edu

- For-profit 4-year technical college
- Very large city
- 1,216 degree-seeking undergraduates
- 37% of applicants admitted
- Interview required

**General.** Accredited by ACCSC. **Degrees:** 167 bachelor's, 9 associate awarded. **Calendar:** Continuous. **Full-time faculty:** 24 total. **Part-time faculty:** 64 total.

**Freshman class profile.** 896 applied, 332 admitted, 332 enrolled.

**Basis for selection.** Admissions decisions based on assessment test and interview.

**2009-2010 Annual costs.** Tuition/fees: $15,363. Personal expenses: $3,121.

**Application procedures. Admission:** No deadline. $25 fee. Admission notification on a rolling basis. **Financial aid:** FAFSA required. Applicants notified on a rolling basis.

**Academics. Credit/placement by examination:** AP, CLEP.

**Majors. Business:** Accounting/finance, business admin, marketing. **Computer sciences:** Networking, security, web page design, webmaster. **Visual/ performing arts:** Design.

**Contact.** Phone: (714) 938-6140 ext. 60100 Toll-free number: (877) 650-6050
Wes Camp, Director of Admissions, Westwood College: Anaheim, 1551 South Douglass Road, Anaheim, CA 92806

## Westwood College: Inland Empire
### Upland, California
### www.westwood.edu

- For-profit 3-year business and technical college
- Commuter campus in small city
- 1,200 degree-seeking undergraduates
- Interview required

**General.** Accredited by ACCSC. **Degrees:** 132 bachelor's, 19 associate awarded. **Location:** 45 miles from Los Angeles, 22 miles from Riverside. **Calendar:** Continuous, extensive summer session. **Full-time faculty:** 15 total. **Part-time faculty:** 70 total. **Class size:** 64% < 20, 36% 20-39.

**Basis for selection.** Interview required, documentation of prior education and proficiency in basic college-level skills required, English language proficiency required for applicants whose native language is not English. SAT or ACT recommended. If SAT or ACT scores are not submitted or do not meet minimum requirements, students must take campus-administered ACCUPLACER placement exam.

**2009-2010 Annual costs.** Tuition/fees: $14,763. Approximately 368 per unit for degree completers (transfer in 24.5 units or more). Books/supplies: $2,012. Personal expenses: $1,840.

**Financial aid. Non-need-based:** Scholarships awarded for academics.

**Application procedures. Admission:** Priority date 10/15; deadline 10/21 (receipt date). $25 fee. Admission notification on a rolling basis. **Financial aid:** No deadline. FAFSA, institutional form required. Must reply within 1 week(s) of notification.

**Academics. Special study options:** Cooperative education, distance learning, honors, independent study, liberal arts/career combination. Hybrid schedules: combination of both campus and online courses. **Credit/placement by examination:** AP, CLEP, IB, institutional tests. Students may test out of required courses by passing proficiency exams. **Support services:** Learning center, reduced course load, remedial instruction, study skills assistance, tutoring.

**Majors. BACHELOR'S. Business:** E-commerce, marketing. **Communications:** Digital media. **Communications technology:** Animation/special effects. **Computer sciences:** LAN/WAN management, web page design. **Protective services:** Police science. **Visual/performing arts:** Design, interior design. **ASSOCIATE. Communications:** Digital media. **Computer sciences:** Applications programming. **Engineering technology:** Architectural drafting, computer systems, drafting. **Visual/performing arts:** Commercial/advertising art, graphic design.

**Computing on campus.** 50 workstations in library. Online library available.

**Student life. Freshman orientation:** Mandatory. **Activities:** Student government, student newspaper.

**Student services.** Career counseling, services for economically disadvantaged, student employment services, financial aid counseling, placement for graduates, veterans' counselor.

**Contact.** E-mail: laiinternet@westwood.edu
Phone: (909) 931-7550 Toll-free number: (866) 288-9488
Fax: (909) 931-5962
Alma Salazar, Director of Admissions, Westwood College: Inland Empire, 20 West Seventh Street, Upland, CA 91786

## Westwood College: South Bay
### Torrance, California
### www.westwood.edu

- For-profit 4-year technical college
- Large city
- 712 degree-seeking undergraduates

**General.** Accredited by ACCSC. **Degrees:** 139 bachelor's, 15 associate awarded. **Calendar:** Continuous. **Full-time faculty:** 9 total; 44% women. **Part-time faculty:** 60 total.

**Basis for selection.** High school record and institutional assessment exam most important. Institutional assessment exam required if ACT/SAT not submitted.

**2009-2010 Annual costs.** Tuition/fees: $14,250. Books/supplies: $1,020.

**Application procedures. Admission:** No deadline. $100 fee.

**Academics. Credit/placement by examination:** CLEP.

**Majors. Communications technology:** Animation/special effects, graphics. **Computer sciences:** LAN/WAN management, security. **Construction:** General. **Protective services:** Criminal justice. **Visual/performing arts:** Interior design.

**Contact.** Phone: (310) 965-0888 Fax: (310) 516-8232
Fred Polk, Admissions Director, Westwood College: South Bay, 19700 South Vermont Avenue #100, Torrance, CA 90502

## Whittier College
### Whittier, California                    CB member
### www.whittier.edu                        CB code: 4952

- Private 4-year liberal arts college
- Residential campus in small city
- 1,361 degree-seeking undergraduates: 1% part-time, 53% women, 6% African American, 9% Asian American, 30% Hispanic American, 1% Native American, 2% international
- 610 degree-seeking graduate students
- 72% of applicants admitted
- SAT or ACT with writing, application essay required
- 61% graduate within 6 years

**General.** Founded in 1887. Regionally accredited. Historic affiliation with the Quakers. **Degrees:** 232 bachelor's awarded; master's offered. **ROTC:** Army. **Location:** 18 miles from Los Angeles. **Calendar:** 4-1-4, limited summer session. **Full-time faculty:** 96 total; 99% have terminal degrees, 27% minority, 47% women. **Part-time faculty:** 34 total; 47% have terminal degrees, 29% minority, 56% women. **Class size:** 59% < 20, 38% 20-39, 2% 40-49, less than 1% 50-99, less than 1% >100. **Special facilities:** Quaker books and materials collection, John Greenleaf Whittier collection including manuscripts, letters and furniture, collection of Richard M. Nixon gifts, Keck image processing laboratory.

**Freshman class profile.** 2,263 applied, 1,626 admitted, 358 enrolled.

| Mid 50% test scores | | GPA 2.0-2.99: | 46% |
|---|---|---|---|
| SAT critical reading: | 470-580 | Rank in top quarter: | 42% |
| SAT math: | 460-590 | Rank in top tenth: | 30% |
| SAT writing: | 470-570 | Return as sophomores: | 79% |
| ACT composite: | 19.25-25 | Live on campus: | 78% |
| GPA 3.75 or higher: | 9% | International: | 2% |
| GPA 3.50-3.74: | 7% | Fraternities: | 9% |
| GPA 3.0-3.49: | 38% | Sororities: | 19% |

**Basis for selection.** GPA, course selection, and class rank most important followed by essays, references, interviews, test scores, activities, and geographic considerations. Interview recommended. **Homeschooled:** Statement describing homeschool structure and mission, transcript of courses and grades, letter of recommendation (nonparent) required.

**High school preparation.** College-preparatory program required. Required and recommended units include English 3-4, mathematics 2-3, social studies 1-2, science 1-2 (laboratory 1) and foreign language 2-3.

**2010-2011 Annual costs.** Tuition/fees: $35,442. Room/board: $10,026. Books/supplies: $1,638. Personal expenses: $2,250.

**2009-2010 Financial aid. Need-based:** 355 full-time freshmen applied for aid; 256 were judged to have need; 256 of these received aid. Average need met was 89%. Average scholarship/grant was $12,698; average loan $9,384. 46% of total undergraduate aid awarded as scholarships/grants, 54% as loans/jobs. **Non-need-based:** Awarded to 1,090 full-time undergraduates, including 290 freshmen. Scholarships awarded for academics, alumni affiliation, art, leadership, minority status. **Additional information:** Auditions required for talent scholarship applicants in art, music, and theater.

**Application procedures. Admission:** Priority date 2/1; no deadline. $50 fee, may be waived for applicants with need. Admission notification on a rolling basis beginning on or about 12/30. Must reply by May 1 or within 2 week(s) if notified thereafter. **Financial aid:** Priority date 3/1, closing date 6/30. FAFSA, institutional form required. Applicants notified on a rolling basis starting 2/15; must reply within 2 week(s) of notification.

**Academics. Special study options:** Combined bachelor's/graduate degree, double major, independent study, internships, liberal arts/career combination, semester at sea, student-designed major, study abroad, teacher certification program, Washington semester. **Credit/placement by examination:** AP, CLEP, IB, SAT, ACT, institutional tests. 30 credit hours maximum toward bachelor's degree. **Support services:** Learning center, study skills assistance, tutoring, writing center.

**Majors. Area/ethnic studies:** Latin American. **Biology:** General. **Business:** General. **Conservation:** General. **Education:** General, early childhood. **Foreign languages:** General, comparative lit, French, Spanish. **Health:** Athletic training, predental, premedicine, prepharmacy, preveterinary, recreational therapy. **History:** General. **Legal studies:** Prelaw. **Liberal arts:** Arts/sciences. **Math:** General. **Philosophy/religion:** Philosophy, religion. **Physical sciences:** Chemistry, physics. **Psychology:** General. **Public administration:** Social work. **Social sciences:** Anthropology, international relations, political science, sociology, urban studies. **Visual/performing arts:** Art, art history/conservation, dramatic, music history, theater history.

**Most popular majors.** Biology 7%, business/marketing 17%, English 8%, family/consumer sciences 6%, parks/recreation 9%, psychology 6%, social sciences 25%, visual/performing arts 7%.

**Computing on campus.** 165 workstations in dormitories, library, computer center. Dormitories wired for high-speed internet access and linked to campus network. Online course registration, helpline, wireless network available.

**Student life. Freshman orientation:** Mandatory, $200 fee. Orientation begins over Labor Day weekend. **Housing:** Guaranteed on-campus for freshmen. Coed dorms, single-sex dorms, special housing for disabled, wellness housing available. $200 nonrefundable deposit, deadline 5/1. Multicultural hall, honors floor, living and learning community available. **Activities:** Jazz band, campus ministries, choral groups, dance, drama, film society, international student organizations, literary magazine, music ensembles, Model UN, musical theater, radio station, student government, student newspaper, national honor societies.

**Athletics.** NCAA. **Intercollegiate:** Baseball M, basketball, cross-country, diving, football (tackle) M, golf, lacrosse, soccer, softball W, swimming, tennis, track and field, volleyball W, water polo. **Intramural:** Basketball, softball, volleyball. **Team name:** Poets.

**Student services.** Career counseling, student employment services, health services, on-campus daycare, personal counseling, placement for graduates.

**Contact.** E-mail: admission@whittier.edu
Phone: (562) 907-4238 Fax: (562) 907-4870
Kieron Miller, Director of Admission, Whittier College, 13406 East
Philadelphia Street, Whittier, CA 90608-0634

## William Jessup University
### Rocklin, California
**www.jessup.edu**      **CB code: 4756**

◆ Private 4-year Bible and liberal arts college affiliated with nondenominational tradition

◆ Residential campus in small city

◆ 539 degree-seeking undergraduates: 24% part-time, 55% women, 7% African American, 4% Asian American, 8% Hispanic American, 3% Native American, 1% international

◆ 24 degree-seeking graduate students

◆ 76% of applicants admitted

◆ SAT or ACT (ACT writing optional), application essay required

**General.** Founded in 1939. Regionally accredited; also accredited by ABHE. **Degrees:** 151 bachelor's awarded. **Location:** 20 miles from Sacramento. **Calendar:** Semester, limited summer session. **Full-time faculty:** 18 total; 39% have terminal degrees, 6% minority, 44% women. **Part-time faculty:** 49 total; 67% have terminal degrees, 14% minority, 35% women. **Class size:** 76% < 20, 19% 20-39, 2% 40-49, 2% 50-99, 1% >100.

**Freshman class profile.** 205 applied, 155 admitted, 90 enrolled.

| Mid 50% test scores | | | |
|---|---|---|---|
| SAT critical reading: | 470-610 | GPA 3.0-3.49: | 33% |
| SAT math: | 460-570 | GPA 2.0-2.99: | 25% |
| SAT writing: | 450-580 | Rank in top quarter: | 38% |
| ACT composite: | 20-26 | Rank in top tenth: | 18% |
| GPA 3.75 or higher: | 28% | Return as sophomores: | 82% |
| GPA 3.50-3.74: | 14% | Out-of-state: | 9% |
| | | Live on campus: | 81% |

**Basis for selection.** Academic records, supporting documents, moral character, willingness to comply with standards and values of university strongly considered. Interview strongly recommended, may be required. Audition required for music scholarship (majors only). **Homeschooled:** Statement describing homeschool structure and mission required. Extra emphasis placed on SAT/ACT; professional/third-party home educators transcript provider preferred over in-home development of transcripts. **Learning Disabled:** Once voluntarily disclosed, student is asked to provide documentation of learning disability and to meet with academic support advisor regularly.

**High school preparation.** College-preparatory program recommended. 17 units required; 24 recommended. Required and recommended units include English 4, mathematics 3-4, social studies 1-2, history 2-3, science 2-3 (laboratory 1-2), foreign language 2-3, computer science 1, visual/performing arts 2 and academic electives 2-3. Religion taken for credit at accredited parochial/Christian high school may be given academic consideration.

**2010-2011 Annual costs.** Tuition/fees: $19,980. Room/board: $8,230. Books/supplies: $1,620. Personal expenses: $2,250.

**2009-2010 Financial aid. Need-based:** 79 full-time freshmen applied for aid; 70 were judged to have need; 70 of these received aid. Average need met was 77%. Average scholarship/grant was $16,199; average loan $2,605. 73% of total undergraduate aid awarded as scholarships/grants, 27% as loans/jobs. **Non-need-based:** Awarded to 264 full-time undergraduates, including 79 freshmen. Scholarships awarded for academics, athletics, leadership, minority status, music/drama, religious affiliation, state residency.

**Application procedures. Admission:** Priority date 4/1; deadline 8/25 (postmark date). $45 fee, may be waived for applicants with need. Admission notification on a rolling basis beginning on or about 11/1. Must reply by June 1 or within 2 weeks of notification of admission. $250 confirmation deposit is applied to housing and refundable until June 1 or within 2 weeks if notified thereafter. **Financial aid:** Priority date 3/2; no closing date. FAFSA required. Applicants notified on a rolling basis starting 3/2; must reply within 3 week(s) of notification.

**Academics.** All church vocation/ministry-based degrees offer dual major in Bible and Theology. Emphasis placed on pastoral training, missions, youth ministry, and family & children's ministry. **Special study options:** Double major, independent study, internships, study abroad, teacher certification program, Washington semester. Adult degree completion program (School of Professional Studies). **Credit/placement by examination:** AP, CLEP, IB, SAT, ACT, institutional tests. 16 credit hours maximum toward associate degree, 16 toward bachelor's. A maximum of 30 units will be awarded for

AP, IB, or CLEP. **Support services:** Reduced course load, study skills assistance, tutoring, writing center.

**Majors. Business:** Business admin. **Education:** Elementary. **History:** General. **Psychology:** General. **Theology:** Missionary, pastoral counseling, theology, youth ministry. **Other:** Family & children's ministry, Public policy.

**Most popular majors.** Business/marketing 11%, psychology 22%, theological studies 60%.

**Computing on campus.** 35 workstations in library, computer center. Dormitories wired for high-speed internet access and linked to campus network. Commuter students can connect to campus network. Online library, helpline, repair service, wireless network available.

**Student life. Freshman orientation:** Mandatory. Preregistration for classes offered. 2-day sessions in late spring and summer. **Policies:** Dry campus. Quiet hours, but no curfew. No formal dress code, but appropriate dress recommended. Chapel attendance required. Religious observance required. **Housing:** Guaranteed on-campus for freshmen. Coed dorms, single-sex dorms, apartments available. **Activities:** Jazz band, campus ministries, choral groups, film society, music ensembles, student government, student newspaper, spiritual formation groups, multicultural fellowship.

**Athletics.** NAIA. **Intercollegiate:** Basketball, cross-country, golf M, soccer, softball W, track and field, volleyball W. **Team name:** Warriors.

**Student services.** Chaplain/spiritual director, career counseling, financial aid counseling, personal counseling. **Physically disabled:** Services for visually, hearing impaired.

**Contact.** E-mail: admissions@jessup.edu
Phone: (916) 577-2222 Toll-free number: (800) 355-7522
Fax: (916) 577-2220
Vance Pascua, Director of Admission, William Jessup University, 333
Sunset Boulevard, Rocklin, CA 95765

## Woodbury University
### Burbank, California      **CB member**
**www.woodbury.edu**      **CB code: 4955**

◆ Private 4-year university

◆ Commuter campus in very large city

◆ 1,269 degree-seeking undergraduates: 17% part-time, 53% women, 5% African American, 10% Asian American, 33% Hispanic American, 10% international

◆ 313 degree-seeking graduate students

◆ 41% of applicants admitted

◆ SAT or ACT (ACT writing optional), application essay required

◆ 57% graduate within 6 years

**General.** Founded in 1884. Regionally accredited. **Degrees:** 290 bachelor's awarded; master's offered. **Location:** 15 miles from downtown Los Angeles. **Calendar:** Semester, limited summer session. **Full-time faculty:** 59 total; 83% have terminal degrees, 12% minority, 56% women. **Part-time faculty:** 221 total; 51% have terminal degrees, 38% women. **Class size:** 80% < 20, 20% 20-39. **Special facilities:** Design galleries.

**Freshman class profile.** 514 applied, 210 admitted, 128 enrolled.

| Mid 50% test scores | | | |
|---|---|---|---|
| SAT critical reading: | 390-520 | Return as sophomores: | 80% |
| SAT math: | 400-530 | International: | 19% |
| ACT composite: | 16-23 | Fraternities: | 12% |
| | | Sororities: | 8% |

**Basis for selection.** Primary emphasis placed on applicant's prior academic record and standardized test scores. Interview recommended. **Homeschooled:** State high school equivalency certificate required.

**High school preparation.** College-preparatory program recommended. 16 units recommended. Recommended units include English 4, mathematics 3, social studies 1, history 2, science 2 (laboratory 2) and foreign language 2.

**2010-2011 Annual costs.** Tuition/fees: $28,855. Room/board: $9,293. Books/supplies: $1,700. Personal expenses: $2,250.

**2008-2009 Financial aid. Need-based:** 113 full-time freshmen applied for aid; 107 were judged to have need; 107 of these received aid. Average need met was 58%. Average scholarship/grant was $15,303; average loan $3,792. 52% of total undergraduate aid awarded as scholarships/grants, 48% as loans/jobs. **Non-need-based:** Awarded to 153 full-time undergraduates, including 32 freshmen. Scholarships awarded for academics.

**Application procedures. Admission:** No deadline. $50 fee, may be waived for applicants with need. Admission notification on a rolling basis beginning on or about 11/1. Must reply by May 1 or within 4 week(s) if notified thereafter. **Financial aid:** Priority date 3/2; no closing date. FAFSA, institutional form required. Applicants notified on a rolling basis starting 3/15; must reply within 2 week(s) of notification.

**Academics.** Combines professional programs in design, architecture, and business with liberal arts components. **Special study options:** Accelerated study, double major, dual enrollment of high school students, ESL, exchange student, independent study, internships, liberal arts/career combination, student-designed major, study abroad, weekend college. **Credit/placement by examination:** AP, CLEP, IB, institutional tests. Institutional/departmental examinations used for placement or counseling. **Support services:** Learning center, reduced course load, remedial instruction, tutoring.

**Majors. Architecture:** Architecture, interior. **Business:** Accounting, business admin, fashion, marketing, organizational behavior. **Communications:** Media studies. **Computer sciences:** General. **Psychology:** General. **Visual/performing arts:** Commercial/advertising art, fashion design, graphic design. **Other:** Film/video and photographic arts, Politics and history.

**Most popular majors.** Architecture 41%, business/marketing 32%, visual/performing arts 17%.

**Computing on campus.** 135 workstations in library, computer center. Commuter students can connect to campus network. Online course registration, online library, helpline, wireless network available.

**Student life. Freshman orientation:** Mandatory, $75 fee. Preregistration for classes offered. **Housing:** Coed dorms available. $150 fully refundable deposit, deadline 5/1. Off-campus apartments available. **Activities:** Student government, Armenian student association, residence life council.

**Athletics. Intramural:** Basketball, soccer.

**Student services.** Adult student services, alcohol/substance abuse counseling, career counseling, services for economically disadvantaged, student employment services, financial aid counseling, health services, personal counseling, placement for graduates. **Physically disabled:** Services for visually, speech, hearing impaired.

**Contact.** E-mail: admissions@woodbury.edu
Phone: (818) 767-0888 ext. 221 Toll-free number: (800) 784-9663
Fax: (818) 767-7520
Ruth Lorenzana, Director of Admissions, Woodbury University, 7500 Glenoaks Boulevard, Burbank, CA 91510-7846

## World Mission University
### Los Angeles, California
### www.wmu.edu

- Private 4-year Bible and seminary college affiliated with nondenominational tradition
- Very large city
- 132 degree-seeking undergraduates

**General.** Accredited by ABHE. **Degrees:** 23 bachelor's awarded; master's, professional offered. **Location:** Downtown. **Calendar:** Semester, limited summer session. **Full-time faculty:** 5 total. **Part-time faculty:** 3 total.

**Basis for selection.** Admissions criteria include sense of calling for Christian ministry, participation in church community, academic performance, test results, recommendations. Audition and additional supplementary application required for music programs. **Homeschooled:** Statement describing homeschool structure and mission, transcript of courses and grades, letter of recommendation (nonparent) required.

**2010-2011 Annual costs.** Tuition/fees: $4,600.

**Application procedures. Admission:** No deadline. $50 fee. Application must be submitted on paper. Admission notification on a rolling basis.

**Academics. Special study options:** Distance learning, dual enrollment of high school students, ESL. **Credit/placement by examination:** CLEP, IB, institutional tests.

**Majors. Theology:** Bible.

**Computing on campus.** Online library, wireless network available.

**Student life. Freshman orientation:** Mandatory.

**Contact.** E-mail: wmuoffice@gmail.com
Phone: (213) 385-2322 Fax: (213) 385-2332
Edmund Rhee, Admissions Director, World Mission University, 500 Shatto Place, Los Angeles, CA 90020

## Yeshiva Ohr Elchonon Chabad/West Coast Talmudical Seminary
### Los Angeles, California
**CB code: 1331**

- Private 4-year rabbinical college for men affiliated with Jewish faith
- Residential campus in very large city
- 132 degree-seeking undergraduates: 8% international
- Interview required

**General.** Founded in 1953. Accredited by AARTS. Ordination available. **Degrees:** 23 bachelor's awarded. **Calendar:** Semester, limited summer session. **Full-time faculty:** 5 total; 100% have terminal degrees. **Part-time faculty:** 4 total.

**Freshman class profile.** 80 applied, 49 admitted, 49 enrolled.

| | | | |
|---|---|---|---|
| End year in good standing: | 100% | Live on campus: | 100% |
| Return as sophomores: | 42% | International: | 4% |
| Out-of-state: | 57% | | |

**Basis for selection.** Open admission, but selective for some programs. Interview, recommendations, religious affiliation or commitment, and test scores most important. Priority given to California residents. **Homeschooled:** Statement describing homeschool structure and mission, interview, letter of recommendation (nonparent) required.

**High school preparation.** Recommended units include English 3, mathematics 3, social studies 3, history 2, science 3 and foreign language 2.

**2010-2011 Annual costs.** Tuition/fees (projected): $11,500. $200 book fee. Room/board: $7,000. Books/supplies: $200. Personal expenses: $100.

**2008-2009 Financial aid.** All financial aid based on need.

**Application procedures. Admission:** No deadline. No application fee. Admission notification on a rolling basis. **Financial aid:** Priority date 1/15, closing date 6/30. FAFSA, institutional form required. Applicants notified by 5/1; must reply by 7/1.

**Academics. Special study options:** Independent study, weekend college. **Credit/placement by examination:** CLEP, institutional tests. 90 credit hours maximum toward bachelor's degree. For transfer students. **Support services:** Pre-admission summer program, remedial instruction, tutoring.

**Majors. Theology:** Religious ed, Talmudic.

**Most popular majors.** Liberal arts 50%, theological studies 50%.

**Computing on campus.** 18 workstations in dormitories, computer center.

**Student life. Freshman orientation:** Available. **Policies:** Religious observance required. **Housing:** Guaranteed on-campus for all undergraduates. $300 fully refundable deposit. **Activities:** Literary magazine, student government, student newspaper.

**Student services.** Career counseling, services for economically disadvantaged, financial aid counseling, minority student services, personal counseling. **Physically disabled:** Services for visually, speech impaired.

**Contact.** E-mail: MSpalter@yoec.edu
Phone: (323) 937-3763 Fax: (323) 937-9456
Rabbi Chaim Citron, Director of Admissions, Yeshiva Ohr Elchonon Chabad/West Coast Talmudical Seminary, 7215 Waring Avenue, Los Angeles, CA 90046

# Colorado

## Adams State College
Alamosa, Colorado
www.adams.edu
CB code: 4001

- Public 4-year liberal arts college
- Residential campus in small town
- 2,347 degree-seeking undergraduates: 18% part-time, 56% women, 5% African American, 2% Asian American, 29% Hispanic American, 2% Native American
- 698 degree-seeking graduate students
- 57% of applicants admitted
- SAT or ACT (ACT writing optional) required

**General.** Founded in 1921. Regionally accredited. Hispanic-serving institution. **Degrees:** 295 bachelor's, 24 associate awarded; master's offered. **Location:** 225 miles from Denver; 200 miles from Albuquerque, New Mexico. **Calendar:** Semester, limited summer session. **Full-time faculty:** 111 total; 68% have terminal degrees; 18% minority, 48% women. **Part-time faculty:** 55 total; 2% have terminal degrees, 7% minority, 67% women. **Class size:** 59% < 20, 30% 20-39, 8% 40-49, 3% 50-99. **Special facilities:** Observatory, planetarium, natural history museum, geology museum, cross-cultural center.

**Freshman class profile.** 2,332 applied, 1,335 admitted, 566 enrolled.

| Mid 50% test scores | | | |
|---|---|---|---|
| SAT critical reading: | 400-550 | GPA 3.0-3.49: | 29% |
| SAT math: | 420-550 | GPA 2.0-2.99: | 44% |
| SAT writing: | 400-510 | Rank in top quarter: | 20% |
| ACT composite: | 17-22 | Rank in top tenth: | 7% |
| GPA 3.75 or higher: | 9% | Return as sophomores: | 58% |
| GPA 3.50-3.74: | 14% | Out-of-state: | 10% |

**Basis for selection.** Open admissions for associate degree programs only. Bachelor's degree candidates must have either 2.0 GPA, or rank in top two-thirds of class with average or above average score on ACT or SAT. ACCUPLACER tests for math and English required if SAT or ACT not available. Audition required of music majors. Portfolio required of art majors. **Homeschooled:** Transcript of courses and grades required.

**High school preparation.** College-preparatory program recommended. 15 units required. Required and recommended units include English 4, mathematics 2, social studies 3, history 1, science 2 and foreign language 2. Computer applications: .5 units recommended. Math should include Algebra I and one advanced math course.

**2009-2010 Annual costs.** Tuition/fees: $4,454; $13,598 out-of-state. Room/board: $7,020.

**2008-2009 Financial aid.** **Need-based:** 436 full-time freshmen applied for aid; 345 were judged to have need; 341 of these received aid. Average need met was 51%. Average scholarship/grant was $50,844; average loan $2,841. 59% of total undergraduate aid awarded as scholarships/grants, 41% as loans/jobs. **Non-need-based:** Awarded to 598 full-time undergraduates, including 240 freshmen. Scholarships awarded for academics, alumni affiliation, art, athletics, leadership, minority status, music/drama, state residency.

**Application procedures.** **Admission:** Priority date 8/1; no deadline. $30 fee, may be waived for applicants with need. Admission notification on a rolling basis. **Financial aid:** Priority date 3/1, closing date 4/15. FAFSA required. Applicants notified on a rolling basis starting 4/30; must reply within 4 week(s) of notification.

**Academics.** **Special study options:** Accelerated study, distance learning, double major, dual enrollment of high school students, exchange student, external degree, independent study, internships, student-designed major, study abroad, teacher certification program, weekend college. **Credit/placement by examination:** AP, CLEP, IB, SAT, ACT, institutional tests. 15 credit hours maximum toward associate degree, 30 toward bachelor's. **Support services:** Learning center, pre-admission summer program, remedial instruction, study skills assistance, tutoring, writing center.

**Majors. Agriculture:** Business. **Biology:** General, bacteriology. **Business:** General, accounting, business admin, finance, management information systems, marketing, small business admin. **Communications:** General, advertising. **Computer sciences:** General. **Conservation:** Management/policy. **Education:** General, art, biology, business, chemistry, elementary, English, history, mathematics, middle, multi-level teacher, music, physical, science, secondary, social science, social studies, Spanish, special, speech. **Foreign languages:** Spanish. **Health:** Health care admin, health services, nursing (RN), predental, premedicine, prenursing, prepharmacy, preveterinary. **History:** General. **Legal studies:** Prelaw. **Liberal arts:** Arts/sciences. **Math:** General. **Parks/recreation:** Exercise sciences, health/fitness. **Physical sciences:** Chemical physics, chemistry, geology, physics. **Psychology:** General. **Social sciences:** Criminology, economics, sociology. **Visual/performing arts:** Art, ceramics, dramatic, drawing, metal/jewelry, music performance, music theory/composition, painting, photography, printmaking, sculpture, studio arts, voice/opera.

**Most popular majors.** Business/marketing 25%, liberal arts 28%, parks/recreation 7%, social sciences 12%, visual/performing arts 9%.

**Computing on campus.** 329 workstations in library, student center. Dormitories wired for high-speed internet access and linked to campus network. Commuter students can connect to campus network. Online course registration, online library, helpline, student web hosting, wireless network available.

**Student life.** **Freshman orientation:** Mandatory, $50 fee. Preregistration for classes offered. Program held weekend before start of semester. **Housing:** Guaranteed on-campus for freshmen. Coed dorms, single-sex dorms, special housing for disabled, apartments, wellness housing available. $150 partly refundable deposit. Learning community house, freshman interest-group housing, drug and alcohol-free learning community, outdoor adventure community, making the grade community (must maintain 3.5 GPA). **Activities:** Bands, campus ministries, choral groups, dance, drama, literary magazine, music ensembles, Model UN, musical theater, radio station, student government, student newspaper, Circle K, College Republicans, Newman club, student ambassadors, teacher education association, associated students and faculty, gay straight alliance, Semillas de la Tierra, El Parnaso.

**Athletics.** NCAA. **Intercollegiate:** Basketball, cross-country, football (tackle) M, golf, soccer, softball W, swimming W, track and field, volleyball W, wrestling M. **Intramural:** Basketball, bowling, football (non-tackle), racquetball, skiing, soccer, softball, swimming, volleyball, water polo. **Team name:** Grizzlies.

**Student services.** Adult student services, chaplain/spiritual director, career counseling, student employment services, financial aid counseling, health services, minority student services, on-campus daycare, personal counseling, placement for graduates, veterans' counselor. **Physically disabled:** Services for visually, hearing impaired.

**Contact.** E-mail: ascadmit@adams.edu
Phone: (719) 587-7712 Toll-free number: (800) 824-6494
Fax: (719) 587-7522
Eric Carpio, Director for Admissions, Adams State College, 208 Edgemont Boulevard, Alamosa, CO 81102

## American Sentinel University
Aurora, Colorado
www.americansentinel.edu
CB code: 3806

- For-profit 4-year virtual university
- Very large city
- 685 degree-seeking undergraduates

**General.** Accredited by DETC. **Degrees:** 126 bachelor's, 16 associate awarded; master's offered. **Calendar:** Continuous, extensive summer session. **Full-time faculty:** 4 total. **Part-time faculty:** 86 total.

**Basis for selection.** Open admission.

**2009-2010 Annual costs.** Cost of bachelor's program $8,850 to $35,400 depending on credits required to complete.

**Application procedures.** **Admission:** No deadline. No application fee. Admission notification on a rolling basis.

**Academics.** **Special study options:** Accelerated study, distance learning, honors, independent study, liberal arts/career combination. **Credit/placement by examination:** AP, CLEP. 45 credit hours maximum toward associate degree, 90 toward bachelor's. **Support services:** Learning center, reduced course load, tutoring.

**Majors. Business:** Business admin, e-commerce, human resources, management information systems, marketing. **Computer sciences:** General, computer science, game design, information systems, information technology, security, system admin, web page design. **Health:** Medical records technology, nursing (RN). **Protective services:** Law enforcement admin.

**Computing on campus.** PC or laptop required.

**Student life. Freshman orientation:** Mandatory. Preregistration for classes offered. **Activities:** Student newspaper.

**Contact.** E-mail: admissions@americansentinel.edu
Phone: (866) 922-5690 Toll-free number: (866) 922-5690
Fax: (866) 505-2450
Natalie Nixon, Director of Admissions, American Sentinel University, 500 Century Park South, Suite 202, Birmingham, AL 35226

## Argosy University: Denver
### Denver, Colorado
### www.argosy.edu/denver

- For-profit 4-year university
- Very large city
- 80 degree-seeking undergraduates

**General. Degrees:** 5 bachelor's awarded; master's, doctoral, professional offered. **Calendar:** Continuous. **Full-time faculty:** 6 total. **Part-time faculty:** 46 total.

**Freshman class profile.** 6 enrolled.

**Basis for selection.** Open admission.

**Academics. Credit/placement by examination:** CLEP.

**Majors. Business:** Business admin. **Liberal arts:** Arts/sciences. **Protective services:** Police science. **Psychology:** General.

**Contact.** Phone: (303) 248-2700
Argosy University: Denver, 1200 Lincoln Street, Denver, CO 80203

## Art Institute of Colorado
### Denver, Colorado
### www.artinstitutes.edu/denver          CB code: 7150

- For-profit 4-year culinary school and visual arts college
- Commuter campus in very large city
- 2,320 degree-seeking undergraduates: 37% part-time, 52% women
- SAT or ACT (ACT writing optional), application essay, interview required

**General.** Founded in 1952. **Degrees:** 274 bachelor's, 136 associate awarded. **Location:** Downtown. **Calendar:** Quarter, extensive summer session. **Full-time faculty:** 63 total. **Part-time faculty:** 68 total. **Special facilities:** Teaching restaurant open to the public at the International School of Culinary Arts.

**Basis for selection.** Commitment to career most important; essay, interview important; high school transcript considered with GPA. Portfolio required of advanced standing applicants. **Homeschooled:** Documentation of grades and official graduation date required.

**2010-2011 Annual costs.** Tuition/fees (projected): $24,796. Supply kit $565-$2,280 depending on program. Books/supplies: $3,487.

**2008-2009 Financial aid. Need-based:** 15% of total undergraduate aid awarded as scholarships/grants, 85% as loans/jobs.

**Application procedures. Admission:** No deadline. $150 fee. Admission notification on a rolling basis. **Financial aid:** No deadline. FAFSA, institutional form required. Applicants notified on a rolling basis.

**Academics. Special study options:** Distance learning, independent study, internships, study abroad. **Credit/placement by examination:** CLEP, IB, institutional tests. 30 credit hours maximum toward associate degree. **Support services:** Reduced course load, remedial instruction, study skills assistance, tutoring, writing center.

**Majors. Business:** Apparel. **Communications technology:** Animation/special effects. **Computer sciences:** Computer graphics, web page design. **Personal/culinary services:** Restaurant/catering. **Visual/performing arts:** Cinematography, graphic design, industrial design, interior design, multimedia, photography.

**Most popular majors.** Communication technologies 19%, computer/information sciences 9%, personal/culinary services 7%, visual/performing arts 65%.

**Computing on campus.** 500 workstations in dormitories, library, computer center. Dormitories wired for high-speed internet access. Online course registration, online library, helpline, repair service, wireless network available.

**Student life. Freshman orientation:** Mandatory. Preregistration for classes offered. **Housing:** Coed dorms, wellness housing available. $300 fully refundable deposit. **Activities:** Campus ministries, dance, literary magazine, student government, student newspaper.

**Student services.** Alcohol/substance abuse counseling, career counseling, student employment services, financial aid counseling, placement for graduates. **Physically disabled:** Services for visually, speech, hearing impaired.

**Contact.** E-mail: aicadm@aii.edu
Phone: (303) 837-0825 Toll-free number: (800) 275-2420
Fax: (303) 860-8520
Brian Parker, Senior Director of Admissions, Art Institute of Colorado, 1200 Lincoln Street, Denver, CO 80203-2983

## Aspen University
### Denver, Colorado
### www.aspen.edu

- For-profit 4-year virtual business college
- Very large city
- 520 degree-seeking undergraduates
- Application essay required

**General.** Accredited by DETC. **Degrees:** 2 bachelor's awarded; master's, doctoral offered. **Calendar:** Continuous.

**Basis for selection.** Open admission, but selective for some programs. Three letters of recommendation required. **Homeschooled:** State high school equivalency certificate required.

**2009-2010 Annual costs.** Tuition/fees: $7,500.

**Application procedures. Admission:** No deadline. $100 fee. Admission notification on a rolling basis. **Financial aid:** No deadline.

**Academics. Special study options:** Distance learning. **Credit/placement by examination:** CLEP. **Support services:** Remedial instruction.

**Majors. Business:** Business admin. **Education:** Early childhood. **Protective services:** Law enforcement admin. **Other:** Alternate energy, Medical management.

**Computing on campus.** PC or laptop required. Online library available.

**Contact.** E-mail: admissions@aspen.edu
Phone: (303) 333-4224 Toll-free number: (800) 441-4746
Amanda Hosking, Director of Admissions, Aspen University, 720 South Colorado Boulevard, Suite 1150N, Denver, CO 80246

## CollegeAmerica: Colorado Springs
### Colorado Springs, Colorado
### www.collegeamerica.edu

- For-profit 4-year career college
- Commuter campus in large city

**General.** Accredited by ACCSCT. **Calendar:** Continuous.

**Annual costs/financial aid.** Tuition ranges from $329 to $393 per quarter credit depending on program. First-year tuition for associates degree is $15,000 and $14,689 for bachelor's degree. Need-based financial aid available to full-time and part-time students.

**Contact.** Phone: (719) 637-0600
Director of Admissions, 3645 Citadel Drive South, Colorado Springs, CO 80909

## CollegeAmerica: Fort Collins
**Fort Collins, Colorado**
**www.collegeamerica.edu**

♦ For-profit 4-year business, health science and technical college
♦ Commuter campus in small city
♦ 255 degree-seeking undergraduates

**General.** Accredited by ACCSC. **Degrees:** 20 bachelor's, 37 associate awarded; master's offered. **Calendar:** Continuous, extensive summer session. **Full-time faculty:** 3 total; 100% women. **Part-time faculty:** 10 total; 40% women.

**Basis for selection.** Open admission. **Homeschooled:** Transcript of courses and grades required.

**2009-2010 Annual costs.** Tuition ranges from $329 to $393 per quarter credit depending on program.

**Application procedures. Admission:** No deadline. No application fee. **Financial aid:** No deadline.

**Academics. Special study options:** Accelerated study, combined bachelor's/graduate degree, distance learning, independent study. **Credit/placement by examination:** CLEP. **Support services:** Learning center, remedial instruction, study skills assistance, tutoring.

**Majors. Business:** General, accounting. **Computer sciences:** General. **Health:** Health services.

**Computing on campus.** 50 workstations in library, computer center, student center. Online library, helpline, repair service, wireless network available.

**Student life. Freshman orientation:** Mandatory. Preregistration for classes offered. **Activities:** Student government.

**Student services.** Adult student services, career counseling, services for economically disadvantaged, student employment services, financial aid counseling, personal counseling, placement for graduates, veterans' counselor. **Learning disabled:** Comprehensive services available.

**Contact.** Phone: (970) 223-6060 Toll-free number: (800) 622-2894 Kristy McNear, Director of Admissions, CollegeAmerica: Fort Collins, 4601 South Mason Street, Fort Collins, CO 80525

## Colorado Christian University
**Lakewood, Colorado**   **CB member**
**www.ccu.edu**   **CB code: 4659**

♦ Private 4-year university and liberal arts college affiliated with nondenominational tradition
♦ Residential campus in large city
♦ 2,031 degree-seeking undergraduates: 36% part-time, 62% women, 5% African American, 2% Asian American, 8% Hispanic American, 1% Native American
♦ 416 degree-seeking graduate students
♦ 28% of applicants admitted
♦ Application essay required
♦ 43% graduate within 6 years

**General.** Founded in 1914. Regionally accredited. Adult and graduate programs available online and at Colorado Springs, Grand Junction, Loveland, Denver (multiple locations), and Lakewood campuses. **Degrees:** 371 bachelor's, 30 associate awarded; master's offered. **ROTC:** Army, Air Force. **Location:** 10 miles from Denver. **Calendar:** Semester, extensive summer session. **Full-time faculty:** 41 total; 66% have terminal degrees, 5% minority, 42% women. **Part-time faculty:** 288 total; 28% have terminal degrees, 4% minority, 37% women. **Class size:** 82% < 20, 17% 20-39, less than 1% 40-49, less than 1% 50-99.

**Freshman class profile.** 5,552 applied, 1,558 admitted, 773 enrolled.

| Mid 50% test scores | | | |
|---|---|---|---|
| SAT critical reading: | 480-580 | GPA 3.0-3.49: | 29% |
| SAT math: | 450-570 | GPA 2.0-2.99: | 22% |
| SAT writing: | 460-570 | Rank in top quarter: | 45% |
| ACT composite: | 20-25 | Rank in top tenth: | 20% |
| GPA 3.75 or higher: | 31% | Return as sophomores: | 64% |
| GPA 3.50-3.74: | 18% | Out-of-state: | 53% |
| | | Live on campus: | 76% |

**Basis for selection.** Applicants should exemplify vital Christian experience. Decisions based on high academic ability, personal integrity, and desire for Christ-centered community. Applicant's course selection, academic performance, test scores, essays, spiritual recommendation, activities, and work experience carefully considered. Interviews encouraged. Audition required of music and theater majors.

**High school preparation.** College-preparatory program required. 19 units recommended. Recommended units include English 4, mathematics 3, social studies 3, history 2, science 2 (laboratory 2) and foreign language 2. Recommend 1 unit of computer science.

**2010-2011 Annual costs.** Tuition/fees: $22,040. Room/board: $9,120. Books/supplies: $1,300. Personal expenses: $825.

**2008-2009 Financial aid. Need-based:** 13% of total undergraduate aid awarded as scholarships/grants, 87% as loans/jobs. **Non-need-based:** Scholarships awarded for academics, athletics, leadership, music/drama.

**Application procedures. Admission:** Priority date 3/1; deadline 9/1 (receipt date). $30 fee, may be waived for applicants with need. Admission notification on a rolling basis beginning on or about 11/1. Must reply by May 1 or within 4 week(s) if notified thereafter. **Financial aid:** Priority date 3/15; no closing date. FAFSA required. Applicants notified on a rolling basis starting 4/1; must reply by 5/1 or within 4 week(s) of notification.

**Academics. Special study options:** Accelerated study, cooperative education, distance learning, double major, honors, independent study, internships, semester at sea, student-designed major, study abroad, teacher certification program, urban semester, Washington semester, weekend college. American studies program (Washington, D.C.), host university for Institute for Family Studies; China studies program at various sites in China, Latin American program (Costa Rica), Los Angeles film studies center, Middle East studies (Cairo, Egypt), Oxford honors program (University of Oxford, England), Russian studies program at various sites in Russia, Summer Institute of Journalism (Washington DC). **Credit/placement by examination:** AP, CLEP, IB, ACT, institutional tests. 15 credit hours maximum toward associate degree, 45 toward bachelor's. **Support services:** Learning center, reduced course load, remedial instruction, study skills assistance, tutoring, writing center.

**Majors. Biology:** General. **Business:** Accounting, business admin, human resources, management information systems, management science, organizational behavior. **Communications:** General. **Computer sciences:** General. **Education:** General, adult/continuing, early childhood, elementary, English, history, mathematics, music, science, secondary. **Health:** Nursing (RN). **History:** General. **Interdisciplinary:** Biological/physical sciences, global studies. **Liberal arts:** Arts/sciences. **Math:** General. **Psychology:** General. **Social sciences:** General. **Theology:** Bible, theology, youth ministry. **Visual/performing arts:** Music performance, studio arts. **Other:** Early childhood educational theory, Music ministry.

**Most popular majors.** Business/marketing 18%, computer/information sciences 8%, education 28%, psychology 6%, theological studies 6%.

**Computing on campus.** 186 workstations in dormitories, library, computer center, student center. Dormitories wired for high-speed internet access and linked to campus network. Commuter students can connect to campus network. Online course registration, online library, helpline, wireless network available.

**Student life. Freshman orientation:** Mandatory. Preregistration for classes offered. Seminars for students and parents held 4 days prior to beginning of classes. **Policies:** Use of alcoholic beverages, illegal drugs, and tobacco prohibited on campus and at college-sponsored activities. Premarital sexual relationships prohibited. Religious observance required. **Housing:** Guaranteed on-campus for freshmen. Coed dorms, single-sex dorms, special housing for disabled, apartments, wellness housing available. $200 fully refundable deposit, deadline 5/1. **Activities:** Bands, campus ministries, choral groups, drama, literary magazine, music ensembles, musical theater, student government, student newspaper, symphony orchestra, world missions, discipleship groups, Fat Boys, Footprints, prayer ministry, refugee family ministry, SALT, Snappers, Westside.

**Athletics.** NCAA, NCCAA. **Intercollegiate:** Baseball M, basketball, cross-country, golf, soccer, tennis, volleyball W. **Intramural:** Basketball, football (non-tackle), soccer, softball, tennis, volleyball. **Team name:** Cougars.

**Student services.** Adult student services, chaplain/spiritual director, career counseling, student employment services, financial aid counseling, health services, personal counseling, placement for graduates, veterans' counselor, women's services. **Physically disabled:** Services for visually, speech, hearing impaired.

**Contact.** E-mail: admission@ccu.edu
Phone: (303) 963-3200 Toll-free number: (800) 443-2484
Fax: (303) 963-3201
Jim McCormick, Vice President of Student Development, Colorado
Christian University, 8787 West Alameda Avenue, Lakewood, CO 80226

## Colorado College
**Colorado Springs, Colorado**                    **CB member**
**www.coloradocollege.edu**                       **CB code: 4072**

- Private 4-year liberal arts college
- Residential campus in large city
- 1,966 degree-seeking undergraduates: 53% women, 2% African American, 6% Asian American, 7% Hispanic American, 1% Native American, 4% international
- 29 degree-seeking graduate students
- 32% of applicants admitted
- SAT or ACT (ACT writing optional), application essay required
- 85% graduate within 6 years

**General.** Founded in 1874. Regionally accredited. Mountain cabin located about 35 minutes from campus for class and retreat use. Baca campus in Southern Colorado available for intensive study. **Degrees:** 510 bachelor's awarded; master's offered. **ROTC:** Army. **Location:** 70 miles from Denver. **Calendar:** Semester, extensive summer session. **Full-time faculty:** 164 total; 98% have terminal degrees, 20% minority, 42% women. **Part-time faculty:** 33 total. **Class size:** 60% < 20, 40% 20-39. **Special facilities:** Electronic music studio, telescope dome, multimedia computer lab, press, herbarium, environmental science van equipped for field research, petrographic microscopes, X-ray diffractometer, Fourier transform nuclear magnetic resonance spectrometer, sedimentology lab, metabolic equipment, hydrostatic weighing equipment, cadaver study in sports science, scanning electron microscope, transmission electron microscope.

**Freshman class profile.** 4,941 applied, 1,600 admitted, 526 enrolled.

| Mid 50% test scores | | End year in good standing: | 99% |
|---|---|---|---|
| SAT critical reading: | 620-710 | Return as sophomores: | 94% |
| SAT math: | 620-710 | Out-of-state: | 81% |
| SAT writing: | 610-710 | Live on campus: | 99% |
| ACT composite: | 28-31 | International: | 3% |
| Rank in top quarter: | 87% | Fraternities: | 4% |
| Rank in top tenth: | 63% | Sororities: | 7% |

**Basis for selection.** Personal essays, school achievement record most important. Counselor and teacher recommendations, extracurricular activities and test scores also important. Special talents, geographic, socioeconomic, ethnic diversity considered. Challenging curriculum, including honors/AP/IB courses if available, recommended. Interview optional. **Homeschooled:** Letter of recommendation (nonparent) required. Three letters of recommendation from people outside of the family who have some knowledge of student's academic capabilities and interests. Reading lists, curriculum information, teacher narratives about courses of study, and copies of papers or projects can be used in place of traditional transcript.

**High school preparation.** College-preparatory program recommended. 16 units required; 20 recommended. Required and recommended units include English 4.

**2009-2010 Annual costs.** Tuition/fees: $37,478. Room/board: $9,624.

**2009-2010 Financial aid. Non-need-based:** Scholarships awarded for academics, athletics. **Additional information:** Need-based financial aid available only to students enrolled half-time or more.

**Application procedures. Admission:** Closing date 1/15 (postmark date). $50 fee, may be waived for applicants with need. Admission notification 4/1. Must reply by May 1 or within 2 week(s) if notified thereafter. Campus visit recommended. Separate letter requesting early action and explaining reasons for applying early required for early action. **Financial aid:** Closing date 2/15. FAFSA, CSS PROFILE required. Applicants notified by 3/20; must reply by 5/1.

**Academics. Special study options:** Combined bachelor's/graduate degree, cooperative education, double major, ESL, independent study, internships, liberal arts/career combination, semester at sea, student-designed major, study abroad, urban semester, Washington semester. Teacher licensure program, urban studies, urban arts and urban education (Chicago); science semester (Oak Ridge, Tennessee); tropical field research (Costa Rica); wilderness field station (Wisconsin); ACM London-Florence program; ACM program in Tanzania and Zimbabwe. **Credit/placement by examination:** AP, CLEP, IB, institutional tests. 32 credit hours maximum toward bachelor's degree. **Support services:** Learning center, pre-admission summer program, study skills assistance, tutoring, writing center.

**Majors. Area/ethnic studies:** Asian, Chicano/Hispanic-American/Latino, French, Italian, regional, Russian/Slavic, women's. **Biology:** General, biochemistry. **Computer sciences:** Computer science. **Conservation:** Environmental science. **Foreign languages:** Classics, comparative lit, French, German, Italian, Russian, Spanish. **History:** General. **Interdisciplinary:** Math/computer science, neuroscience. **Liberal arts:** Arts/sciences. **Math:** General. **Philosophy/religion:** Philosophy, religion. **Physical sciences:** Chemistry, geology, physics. **Psychology:** General. **Social sciences:** Anthropology, econometrics, economics, international economics, political science, sociology. **Visual/performing arts:** Art history/conservation, dance, dramatic, film/cinema, studio arts. **Other:** Classics/history/politics.

**Most popular majors.** Biology 13%, English 8%, philosophy/religious studies 6%, physical sciences 6%, social sciences 30%, visual/performing arts 10%.

**Computing on campus.** 200 workstations in dormitories, library, computer center, student center. Dormitories wired for high-speed internet access and linked to campus network. Commuter students can connect to campus network. Online course registration, online library, helpline, student web hosting, wireless network available.

**Student life. Freshman orientation:** Mandatory. Preregistration for classes offered. One-week program prior to beginning of fall classes. Includes service trip. Parents welcome for first 3 days. **Housing:** Guaranteed on-campus for all undergraduates. Coed dorms, single-sex dorms, apartments, fraternity/sorority housing, wellness housing available. $200 nonrefundable deposit, deadline 6/29. Pets allowed in dorm rooms. **Activities:** Bands, campus ministries, choral groups, dance, drama, film society, international student organizations, literary magazine, music ensembles, musical theater, radio station, student government, student newspaper, Asian American students union, black student union, Chaverim/Hillel, gay/lesbian/bisexual alliance, community kitchen, environmental action, chapel council, Chicano/Latino organization, victim's assistance team.

**Athletics.** NCAA. **Intercollegiate:** Basketball, cross-country, ice hockey M, lacrosse, soccer, swimming, tennis, track and field, volleyball W. **Intramural:** Basketball, football (non-tackle), ice hockey, racquetball, soccer, softball, tennis, volleyball, water polo. **Team name:** Tigers.

**Student services.** Alcohol/substance abuse counseling, chaplain/spiritual director, career counseling, student employment services, financial aid counseling, health services, minority student services, on-campus daycare, personal counseling, women's services. **Physically disabled:** Services for visually, speech, hearing impaired.

**Contact.** E-mail: admission@coloradocollege.edu
Phone: (719) 389-6344 Toll-free number: (800) 542-7214
Fax: (719) 389-6816
Roberto Garcia, Director of Admission, Colorado College, 14 East Cache La Poudre Street, Colorado Springs, CO 80903-9854

## Colorado Heights University
**Denver, Colorado**
**www.chu.edu**                                    **CB code: 4878**

- Private 4-year business and liberal arts college
- Residential campus in very large city
- 360 full-time, degree-seeking undergraduates
- 20 graduate students
- Application essay required

**General.** Accredited by ACICS. Member of the Teikyo University Group of 50 campuses in Asia, Europe, and North America; all students complete part of their studies abroad. **Degrees:** 22 bachelor's awarded; master's offered. **Calendar:** Semester, limited summer session. **Full-time faculty:** 25 total. **Part-time faculty:** 8 total.

**Basis for selection.** High school record, class rank, GPA, recommendations, test scores, and essay most important.

**Application procedures. Admission:** No deadline. $50 fee, may be waived for applicants with need, free for online applicants. Admission notification on a rolling basis. International students who do not score an appropriate amount on the in-house English placement test must take English classes before attending the Degree Program. **Financial aid:** No deadline. FAFSA required.

**Academics. Special study options:** Combined bachelor's/graduate degree, double major, dual enrollment of high school students, ESL, independent study, internships, liberal arts/career combination, study abroad. **Credit/placement by examination:** AP, CLEP, IB.

**Majors. Business:** International. **Interdisciplinary:** Intercultural.

**Computing on campus.** PC or laptop required. Dormitories wired for high-speed internet access and linked to campus network. Online library available.

**Student life. Freshman orientation:** Available. **Policies:** Students under 21 required to live in dorms; exceptions may be made if living with a family member and for those who live on-campus for 1 year and then meet the waiver requirements to move off-campus. **Housing:** Guaranteed on-campus for all undergraduates. Coed dorms available. $230 nonrefundable deposit.

**Athletics. Team name:** Voyagers.

**Student services.** Career counseling, student employment services, financial aid counseling, placement for graduates.

**Contact.** E-mail: admissions@chu.edu
Phone: (303) 937-4280 Fax: (303) 937-4224
Ashley Henderson, Admissions Coordinator, Colorado Heights University, 3001 South Federal Boulevard, Denver, CO 80236

---

## Colorado School of Mines
**Golden, Colorado**      **CB member**
**www.mines.edu**      **CB code: 4073**

- Public 4-year university and engineering college
- Residential campus in large town
- 3,605 degree-seeking undergraduates: 4% part-time, 25% women, 2% African American, 6% Asian American, 7% Hispanic American, 1% Native American, 6% international
- 1,085 degree-seeking graduate students
- 63% of applicants admitted
- SAT or ACT (ACT writing recommended) required
- 69% graduate within 6 years

**General.** Founded in 1874. Regionally accredited. **Degrees:** 620 bachelor's awarded; master's, doctoral offered. **ROTC:** Army, Air Force. **Location:** 20 miles from Denver. **Calendar:** Semester, limited summer session. **Full-time faculty:** 235 total; 88% have terminal degrees, 19% minority, 19% women. **Part-time faculty:** 96 total; 24% have terminal degrees, 7% minority, 34% women. **Class size:** 46% < 20, 31% 20-39, 9% 40-49, 8% 50-99, 5% >100. **Special facilities:** Geology museum, US Geological Survey & Earthquake Center, Edar experimental mine, graduate research laboratory, center for technology and learning media.

**Freshman class profile.** 7,190 applied, 4,515 admitted, 880 enrolled.

| Mid 50% test scores | | | |
|---|---|---|---|
| SAT critical reading: | 550-650 | Rank in top quarter: | 85% |
| SAT math: | 620-700 | Rank in top tenth: | 52% |
| ACT composite: | 26-30 | Return as sophomores: | 90% |
| GPA 3.75 or higher: | 52% | Out-of-state: | 29% |
| GPA 3.50-3.74: | 25% | Live on campus: | 89% |
| GPA 3.0-3.49: | 21% | International: | 5% |
| GPA 2.0-2.99: | 2% | Fraternities: | 21% |
| | | Sororities: | 21% |

**Basis for selection.** Applicants should rank in top third of class, must complete 16 or more academic units, and submit test scores. Both scores and academic record considered with heavier weight given to academic record. **Homeschooled:** Transcript of courses and grades required. More weight given to ACT or SAT scores.

**High school preparation.** College-preparatory program required. 16 units required. Required and recommended units include English 4, mathematics 4, social studies 3, science 3 (laboratory 3), foreign language 1 and academic electives 2. Math units should include 2 algebra, 1 geometry, 1 advanced math (including trigonometry). Science units should include 1 chemistry and/or physics.

**2009-2010 Annual costs.** Tuition/fees: $12,244; $26,404 out-of-state. Room/board: $8,120. Books/supplies: $1,300. Personal expenses: $1,800.

**2008-2009 Financial aid. Need-based:** 689 full-time freshmen applied for aid; 443 were judged to have need; 443 of these received aid. Average need met was 84%. Average scholarship/grant was $7,357; average loan $4,471. 42% of total undergraduate aid awarded as scholarships/grants, 58% as loans/jobs. **Non-need-based:** Awarded to 1,228 full-time undergraduates, including 427 freshmen. Scholarships awarded for academics, athletics.

**Application procedures. Admission:** Priority date 4/1; deadline 5/1 (receipt date). $45 fee, may be waived for applicants with need, free for online applicants. Admission notification on a rolling basis beginning on or about

10/1. Must reply by May 1 or within 4 week(s) if notified thereafter. **Financial aid:** Priority date 2/1; no closing date. FAFSA required. Applicants notified on a rolling basis starting 3/1.

**Academics. Special study options:** Accelerated study, combined bachelor's/graduate degree, cooperative education, double major, dual enrollment of high school students, ESL, exchange student, honors, independent study, internships, study abroad. **Credit/placement by examination:** AP, CLEP, IB, institutional tests. **Support services:** Pre-admission summer program, reduced course load, study skills assistance, tutoring, writing center.

**Majors. Computer sciences:** General, computer science. **Engineering:** General, chemical, civil, electrical, environmental, geological, mechanical, metallurgical, mining, nuclear, petroleum, physics. **Interdisciplinary:** Math/computer science. **Math:** Applied, probability, statistics. **Physical sciences:** Chemistry, geology, geophysics, physics. **Social sciences:** Economics. **Other:** Chemical and biochemical engineering.

**Most popular majors.** Engineering/engineering technologies 87%, mathematics 8%.

**Computing on campus.** 400 workstations in dormitories, library, computer center, student center. Dormitories wired for high-speed internet access and linked to campus network. Commuter students can connect to campus network. Online course registration, online library, helpline, repair service, student web hosting, wireless network available.

**Student life. Freshman orientation:** Mandatory, $122 fee. Preregistration for classes offered. Held the weekend prior to start of fall semester; optional parent orientation offered on 4 separate days in the summer. **Housing:** Guaranteed on-campus for freshmen. Coed dorms, single-sex dorms, apartments, fraternity/sorority housing available. $150 partly refundable deposit, deadline 5/1. **Activities:** Bands, campus ministries, choral groups, dance, drama, international student organizations, literary magazine, music ensembles, musical theater, radio station, student government, student newspaper, symphony orchestra, Society of Women Engineers, American Indian Science and Engineering Society, Professional Asian Society of Engineers and Scientists, National Society of Black Engineers, Society of Hispanic Professional Engineers.

**Athletics.** NCAA. **Intercollegiate:** Baseball M, basketball, cross-country, diving, football (tackle) M, golf M, soccer, softball W, swimming, track and field, volleyball W, wrestling M. **Intramural:** Badminton, basketball, bowling, cross-country, diving, equestrian, field hockey, football (non-tackle), golf, handball, lacrosse, racquetball, rugby M, skiing, soccer, softball, swimming, table tennis, tennis, track and field, volleyball, water polo, wrestling M. **Team name:** Orediggers.

**Student services.** Alcohol/substance abuse counseling, career counseling, student employment services, financial aid counseling, health services, minority student services, personal counseling, placement for graduates, veterans' counselor. **Physically disabled:** Services for visually, hearing impaired.

**Contact.** E-mail: admit@mines.edu
Phone: (303) 273-3220 Toll-free number: (888) 446-9489
Fax: (303) 273-3509
Bruce Goetz, Director of Admissions, Colorado School of Mines, Undergraduate Admissions, Golden, CO 80401

---

## Colorado State University
**Fort Collins, Colorado**      **CB member**
**www.colostate.edu**      **CB code: 4075**

- Public 4-year university
- Residential campus in small city
- 21,204 degree-seeking undergraduates: 7% part-time, 51% women, 3% African American, 3% Asian American, 7% Hispanic American, 2% Native American, 2% international
- 4,209 degree-seeking graduate students
- 72% of applicants admitted
- SAT or ACT (ACT writing optional), application essay required
- 64% graduate within 6 years

**General.** Founded in 1870. Regionally accredited. Colorado State University is a Land Grant University. **Degrees:** 4,234 bachelor's awarded; master's, doctoral, professional offered. **ROTC:** Army, Air Force. **Location:** 60 miles from Denver. **Calendar:** Semester, extensive summer session. **Full-time faculty:** 944 total; 99% have terminal degrees, 13% minority, 32% women. **Part-time faculty:** 46 total; 98% have terminal degrees, 11% minority, 17% women. **Class size:** 37% < 20, 38% 20-39, 7% 40-49, 10% 50-99, 7% >100. **Special facilities:** Concert hall, thrust theatre, music hall, art museum, engineering research center, equine center, veterinary teaching hospital, environmental learning center, plant environmental research center.

**Freshman class profile.** 15,253 applied, 11,013 admitted, 4,322 enrolled.

| Mid 50% test scores | | | |
|---|---|---|---|
| SAT critical reading: | 500-610 | Rank in top quarter: | 50% |
| SAT math: | 510-640 | Rank in top tenth: | 22% |
| SAT writing: | 490-600 | Return as sophomores: | 83% |
| ACT composite: | 22-27 | Out-of-state: | 21% |
| GPA 3.75 or higher: | 35% | Live on campus: | 96% |
| GPA 3.50-3.74: | 24% | International: | 1% |
| GPA 3.0-3.49: | 36% | Fraternities: | 4% |
| GPA 2.0-2.99: | 5% | Sororities: | 8% |

**Basis for selection.** Priority consideration given to applicants with 3.25 GPA and successful completion of 18 recommended high school units. Applicants with a GPA below 3.25 and/or fewer than the 18 recommended high school units are encouraged to apply since many factors are considered in the holistic review process. Letter of recommendation required, preferably from teacher or school counselor.

**High school preparation.** College-preparatory program recommended. 17 units required; 18 recommended. Required and recommended units include English 4, mathematics 4, social studies 2, history 1, science 3 (laboratory 2), foreign language 1-2 and academic electives 2. Individual programs may have additional requirements.

**2009-2010 Annual costs.** Tuition/fees: $6,318; $22,240 out-of-state. Room/board: $8,378. Books/supplies: $1,126. Personal expenses: $2,232.

**2008-2009 Financial aid.** **Need-based:** 3,152 full-time freshmen applied for aid; 1,720 were judged to have need; 1,720 of these received aid. Average need met was 73%. Average scholarship/grant was $6,728; average loan $4,595. 43% of total undergraduate aid awarded as scholarships/grants, 57% as loans/jobs. **Non-need-based:** Awarded to 1,866 full-time undergraduates, including 545 freshmen. Scholarships awarded for academics, art, athletics, leadership, music/drama, ROTC, state residency.

**Application procedures. Admission:** Closing date 2/1 (receipt date). $50 fee, may be waived for applicants with need. Admission notification on a rolling basis. Must reply by May 1 or within 2 week(s) if notified thereafter. Early application (once 6th semester transcript is available) encouraged. **Financial aid:** Priority date 3/1; no closing date. FAFSA required. Applicants notified on a rolling basis starting 3/1.

**Academics. Special study options:** Accelerated study, combined bachelor's/graduate degree, cooperative education, cross-registration, distance learning, double major, dual enrollment of high school students, ESL, exchange student, external degree, honors, independent study, internships, liberal arts/career combination, semester at sea, study abroad, teacher certification program. **Credit/placement by examination:** AP, CLEP, IB, SAT, ACT, institutional tests. **Support services:** Learning center, study skills assistance, tutoring, writing center.

**Majors. Agriculture:** Agribusiness operations, agronomy, animal sciences, economics, education services, equestrian studies, horticultural science, horticulture, landscaping, nursery operations, range science, soil science. **Architecture:** Landscape. **Biology:** General, biochemistry, biomedical sciences, botany, microbiology, wildlife, zoology. **Business:** Accounting, business admin, construction management, finance, management information systems, marketing, real estate, restaurant/food services. **Communications:** General, journalism, public relations, radio/tv. **Computer sciences:** General, information systems, information technology. **Conservation:** General, economics, forest sciences, management/policy, water/wetlands/marine, wildlife. **Education:** General, agricultural, art, biology, business, chemistry, early childhood, English, family/consumer sciences, French, German, mathematics, music, physics, sales/marketing, science, social studies, Spanish, speech, technology/industrial arts, trade/industrial. **Engineering:** Chemical, civil, computer, electrical, environmental, mechanical, physics, science. **Engineering technology:** Computer systems, construction. **Family/consumer sciences:** General, apparel marketing, family studies, food/nutrition, human nutrition. **Foreign languages:** General, French, German, Spanish. **Health:** Athletic training, environmental health, music therapy. **History:** General. **Interdisciplinary:** Global studies, natural sciences. **Liberal arts:** Arts/sciences. **Math:** General, statistics. **Parks/recreation:** Exercise sciences, facilities management. **Philosophy/religion:** Philosophy. **Physical sciences:** General, chemistry, geology, physics. **Protective services:** Fire services admin. **Psychology:** General. **Public administration:** Social work. **Social sciences:** General, anthropology, economics, political science, sociology. **Visual/performing arts:** Art, art history/conservation, conducting, dance, dramatic, graphic design, interior design, music performance, music theory/composition, studio arts. **Other:** Applied computing technology, Fish, wildlife and conservation biology, Geology teacher education, Natural resources recreation and tourism, Range and forest management.

**Most popular majors.** Agriculture 6%, biology 8%, business/marketing 15%, communications/journalism 7%, engineering/engineering technologies 10%, family/consumer sciences 8%, parks/recreation 7%, social sciences 8%.

**Computing on campus.** 2,700 workstations in dormitories, library, computer center, student center. Dormitories wired for high-speed internet access and linked to campus network. Commuter students can connect to campus network. Online course registration, online library, helpline, repair service, student web hosting, wireless network available.

**Student life. Freshman orientation:** Available, $90 fee. Preregistration for classes offered. 21 sessions offered from mid-June to mid-July for incoming freshmen, family members, and guests. Charge includes lodging for student. **Housing:** Guaranteed on-campus for freshmen. Coed dorms, special housing for disabled, apartments, wellness housing available. $150 partly refundable deposit. Special interest floors, special floors for transfer students available. **Activities:** Bands, campus ministries, choral groups, dance, drama, international student organizations, literary magazine, music ensembles, musical theater, opera, radio station, student government, student newspaper, symphony orchestra, TV station, Asian/American student services, black student services, El Centro student services, GLBT student services, Native American student services, Campus Crusade for Christ, Chabad Jewish student alliance, Habitat for Humanity, College Republicans, Young Democrats.

**Athletics.** NCAA. **Intercollegiate:** Basketball, cross-country, diving W, football (tackle) M, golf, softball W, swimming W, tennis W, track and field, volleyball W, water polo W. **Intramural:** Basketball, bowling, football (non-tackle), golf, racquetball, soccer, softball, volleyball. **Team name:** Rams.

**Student services.** Adult student services, alcohol/substance abuse counseling, chaplain/spiritual director, career counseling, services for economically disadvantaged, student employment services, financial aid counseling, health services, legal services, minority student services, on-campus daycare, personal counseling, placement for graduates, veterans' counselor, women's services. **Physically disabled:** Services for visually, speech, hearing impaired.

**Contact.** E-mail: admissions@colostate.edu
Phone: (970) 491-6909 Fax: (970) 491-7799
James Rawlins, Executive Director of Admissions, Colorado State University, Office of Admissions/Colorado State University, Fort Collins, CO 80523-1062

## Colorado State University: Pueblo
**Pueblo, Colorado**
**www.colostate-pueblo.edu**                    CB code: 4611

- Public 4-year university
- Commuter campus in small city
- 4,735 degree-seeking undergraduates: 18% part-time, 54% women, 9% African American, 3% Asian American, 25% Hispanic American, 2% Native American, 1% international
- 290 degree-seeking graduate students
- 95% of applicants admitted
- SAT or ACT (ACT writing optional) required

**General.** Founded in 1933. Regionally accredited. **Degrees:** 722 bachelor's awarded; master's offered. **ROTC:** Army. **Location:** 42 miles from Colorado Springs, 100 miles from Denver. **Calendar:** Semester, extensive summer session. **Full-time faculty:** 192 total; 19% minority, 48% women. **Part-time faculty:** 226 total; 12% minority, 58% women. **Class size:** 42% < 20, 44% 20-39, 6% 40-49, 6% 50-99, 2% >100. **Special facilities:** 3 electron microscopes, golf course, river trail system, automotive service, ropes course, music amphitheater, 1+ megawatt solar system, 6 kilowatt solar system.

**Freshman class profile.** 2,758 applied, 2,614 admitted, 1,054 enrolled.

| Mid 50% test scores | | | |
|---|---|---|---|
| SAT critical reading: | 420-550 | Rank in top quarter: | 7% |
| SAT math: | 430-570 | Rank in top tenth: | 2% |
| ACT composite: | 18-23 | End year in good standing: | 60% |
| GPA 3.75 or higher: | 15% | Return as sophomores: | 65% |
| GPA 3.50-3.74: | 12% | Out-of-state: | 8% |
| GPA 3.0-3.49: | 25% | Live on campus: | 54% |
| GPA 2.0-2.99: | 48% | Fraternities: | 1% |
| | | Sororities: | 1% |

**Basis for selection.** High school achievement record and test scores most important. Auditions for music, portfolios for art required for scholarships.

**High school preparation.** College-preparatory program required. 17 units required. Required units include English 4, mathematics 4, social studies 2, history 1, science 3 (laboratory 2), foreign language 1 and academic electives 2.

**2009-2010 Annual costs.** Tuition/fees: $5,210; $15,602 out-of-state. WUE tuition is $2,551 less per semester than out-of-state rate (15 credits per semester). Differential tuition charged for business, nursing, computer information systems, and engineering courses at $18.65 more per-credit-hour. Room/board: $6,750. Books/supplies: $1,200. Personal expenses: $1,125.

**2009-2010 Financial aid. Need-based:** Average need met was 62%. Average scholarship/grant was $5,871; average loan $2,695. 48% of total undergraduate aid awarded as scholarships/grants, 52% as loans/jobs. **Non-need-based:** Scholarships awarded for academics, alumni affiliation, art, athletics, job skills, leadership, minority status, music/drama, ROTC, state residency.

**Application procedures. Admission:** Closing date 8/1 (receipt date). $25 fee, may be waived for applicants with need. Admission notification on a rolling basis beginning on or about 8/1. **Financial aid:** Priority date 3/1; no closing date. FAFSA, institutional form required. Applicants notified on a rolling basis starting 3/13; must reply within 3 week(s) of notification.

**Academics.** Tutoring center offers tutoring for all general education and developmental math courses. **Special study options:** Accelerated study, combined bachelor's/graduate degree, cooperative education, cross-registration, distance learning, double major, dual enrollment of high school students, ESL, exchange student, external degree, honors, independent study, internships, study abroad, teacher certification program, weekend college. **Credit/placement by examination:** AP, CLEP, IB, SAT, ACT, institutional tests. 30 credit hours maximum toward bachelor's degree. **Support services:** Learning center, reduced course load, remedial instruction, study skills assistance, tutoring, writing center.

**Majors. Biology:** General. **Business:** Accounting, managerial economics. **Communications:** Media studies. **Computer sciences:** Information systems. **Engineering:** General, industrial. **Engineering technology:** Automotive, civil. **Foreign languages:** General. **Health:** Nursing (RN). **History:** General. **Liberal arts:** Arts/sciences. **Math:** General. **Parks/recreation:** Exercise sciences. **Physical sciences:** Chemistry, physics. **Psychology:** General. **Public administration:** Social work. **Social sciences:** Political science, sociology. **Visual/performing arts:** Studio arts. **Other:** Mechatronics.

**Most popular majors.** Biology 6%, business/marketing 15%, communications/journalism 7%, engineering/engineering technologies 6%, health sciences 10%, parks/recreation 6%, social sciences 19%, visual/performing arts 6%.

**Computing on campus.** 702 workstations in dormitories, library, computer center, student center. Dormitories wired for high-speed internet access and linked to campus network. Commuter students can connect to campus network. Online library, helpline, student web hosting, wireless network available.

**Student life. Freshman orientation:** Mandatory, $50 fee. Preregistration for classes offered. 3-hour session held during summer. **Housing:** Guaranteed on-campus for all undergraduates. Coed dorms, special housing for disabled, apartments available. $250 partly refundable deposit, deadline 7/1. **Activities:** Bands, campus ministries, choral groups, dance, international student organizations, literary magazine, music ensembles, radio station, student government, student newspaper, symphony orchestra, TV station, Amnesty International, black students organization, Campus Crusade for Christ, College Republicans, Fellowship of Christian Athletes, Movimiento Estudiantil Chicano de Aztlan, political science club, Young Life, Students for Environmental Awareness.

**Athletics.** NCAA. **Intercollegiate:** Baseball M, basketball, cross-country W, football (tackle) M, golf, soccer, softball W, tennis, track and field W, volleyball W, wrestling M. **Intramural:** Basketball, football (non-tackle), golf, handball, judo, lacrosse, racquetball, rodeo, soccer, softball, squash, table tennis, volleyball. **Team name:** Thunderwolves.

**Student services.** Alcohol/substance abuse counseling, chaplain/spiritual director, career counseling, services for economically disadvantaged, student employment services, financial aid counseling, health services, minority student services, on-campus daycare, personal counseling, placement for graduates, veterans' counselor. **Physically disabled:** Services for visually, speech, hearing impaired.

**Contact.** E-mail: info@colostate-pueblo.edu
Phone: (719) 549-2461 Fax: (719) 549-2419
Dana Trujillo, Director of Admissions, Colorado State University: Pueblo, 2200 Bonforte Boulevard, Pueblo, CO 81001-4901

## Colorado Technical University
**Colorado Springs, Colorado**
**www.coloradotech.edu**                              CB code: 4133

- For-profit 4-year university and technical college
- Commuter campus in large city
- 1,400 degree-seeking undergraduates
- 465 graduate students
- Interview required

**General.** Founded in 1965. Regionally accredited. **Degrees:** 250 bachelor's, 80 associate awarded; master's, doctoral offered. **ROTC:** Army. **Location:** 63 miles from Denver. **Calendar:** Quarter, extensive summer session. **Full-time faculty:** 14 total. **Part-time faculty:** 250 total. **Class size:** 69% < 20, 31% 20-39. **Special facilities:** Extensive laboratories and computer facilities.

**Basis for selection.** Open admission, but selective for some programs. Certain programs require successful performance on one or more entrance assessments.

**2009-2010 Annual costs.** Tuition/fees: $13,340. Books/supplies: $1,300. Personal expenses: $1,215.

**Financial aid. Non-need-based:** Scholarships awarded for academics, ROTC.

**Application procedures. Admission:** No deadline. $50 fee. Admission notification on a rolling basis. **Financial aid:** No deadline. FAFSA required. Applicants notified on a rolling basis starting 6/30.

**Academics. Special study options:** Accelerated study, cooperative education, distance learning, double major, internships, weekend college. **Credit/placement by examination:** CLEP, institutional tests. 30 credit hours maximum toward associate degree, 60 toward bachelor's. Course challenge test offered. Credit for life experience based on evaluation by faculty. **Support services:** Learning center, reduced course load, remedial instruction, tutoring.

**Majors. Business:** Business admin, e-commerce, human resources, information resources management, logistics, management information systems. **Computer sciences:** General, computer science, information systems, information technology, system admin, systems analysis. **Engineering:** Computer, electrical, software. **Engineering technology:** Electrical.

**Most popular majors.** Business/marketing 34%, computer/information sciences 32%, engineering/engineering technologies 34%.

**Computing on campus.** 154 workstations in library, computer center. Commuter students can connect to campus network. Online library, helpline, wireless network available.

**Student life. Freshman orientation:** Mandatory. Preregistration for classes offered. **Policies:** Students must comply with university's standards of conduct. **Housing:** Apartments available. **Activities:** Student government.

**Student services.** Career counseling, student employment services, financial aid counseling, personal counseling, placement for graduates, veterans' counselor.

**Contact.** E-mail: cosadmissions@coloradotech.edu
Phone: (719) 598-0200 Fax: (719) 598-3740
Beth Braaten, Vice President of Admissions, Colorado Technical University, 4435 North Chestnut Street, Colorado Springs, CO 80907

## Denver School of Nursing
**Denver, Colorado**
**www.denverschoolofnursing.edu**

- For-profit 4-year nursing college
- Very large city

**General.** Regionally accredited. **Calendar:** Quarter.

**Contact.** Phone: (303) 292-0015
Director of Admissions, 1401 19th Street, Denver, CO 80202

## DeVry University: Westminster
**Westminster, Colorado**
**www.devry.edu**                                       CB code: 1327

- For-profit 4-year university
- Commuter campus in very large city

- 856 degree-seeking undergraduates: 63% part-time, 37% women, 6% African American, 4% Asian American, 14% Hispanic American, 1% Native American
- 81 degree-seeking graduate students
- Interview required

**General.** Founded in 1945. Regionally accredited. **Degrees:** 96 bachelor's, 15 associate awarded; master's offered. **Calendar:** Semester, extensive summer session. **Full-time faculty:** 13 total; 8% minority, 23% women. **Part-time faculty:** 87 total; 12% minority, 40% women.

**Freshman class profile.** 110 enrolled.

| Out-of-state: | 5% | International: | 1% |
|---|---|---|---|

**Basis for selection.** Applicants must have high school diploma or equivalent or a degree from an accredited postsecondary institution, demonstrate proficiency in basic college-level skills through SAT or ACT scores or institutional-administered placement exams, and be at least 17 years of age.

**High school preparation.** College-preparatory program recommended. Math unit must be algebra or higher.

**2009-2010 Annual costs.** Tuition/fees: $14,160. Books/supplies: $1,310. Personal expenses: $3,574.

**2008-2009 Financial aid.** All financial aid based on need.

**Application procedures. Admission:** No deadline. $50 fee. Admission notification on a rolling basis. **Financial aid:** No deadline. FAFSA required. Applicants notified on a rolling basis.

**Academics. Special study options:** Accelerated study, distance learning. **Credit/placement by examination:** CLEP, institutional tests. **Support services:** Learning center, tutoring.

**Majors. Business:** Business admin. **Computer sciences:** Networking, systems analysis, web page design. **Engineering:** Software. **Engineering technology:** Computer, electrical. **Other:** Technical management.

**Most popular majors.** Business/marketing 61%, computer/information sciences 23%, engineering/engineering technologies 16%.

**Computing on campus.** 308 workstations in library, computer center. Online course registration, online library, helpline available.

**Student life. Freshman orientation:** Mandatory.

**Athletics. Intramural:** Basketball, volleyball.

**Student services.** Career counseling, student employment services, financial aid counseling, placement for graduates, veterans' counselor.

**Contact.** E-mail: denver-admissions@den.devry.edu
Phone: (303) 280-7600 Toll-free number: (888) 212-1857
Fax: (303) 280-7606
Rick Rodman, Director of Admissions, DeVry University: Westminster, 1870 West 122 Avenue, Westminster, CO 80234-2010

## Fort Lewis College

**Durango, Colorado**
**www.fortlewis.edu**
**CB member**
**CB code: 4310**

- Public 4-year liberal arts college
- Residential campus in large town
- 3,571 degree-seeking undergraduates: 7% part-time, 48% women, 1% African American, 1% Asian American, 5% Hispanic American, 21% Native American, 1% international
- 68% of applicants admitted
- SAT or ACT (ACT writing optional) required
- 34% graduate within 6 years

**General.** Regionally accredited. **Degrees:** 696 bachelor's awarded. **Location:** 220 miles from Albuquerque, New Mexico; 342 miles from Denver. **Calendar:** Semester, extensive summer session. **Full-time faculty:** 171 total; 83% have terminal degrees, 10% minority, 45% women. **Part-time faculty:** 90 total; 32% have terminal degrees, 9% minority, 56% women. **Class size:** 57% < 20, 37% 20-39, 4% 40-49, 1% 50-99, less than 1% >100. **Special facilities:** Southwest studies center, nuclear magnetic resonance spectrometer, archaeological dig site, community concert hall, separations and spectroscopy lab, mass spectrometer facilities, tissue culture facility, atomic force microscope.

**Freshman class profile.** 2,722 applied, 1,845 admitted, 802 enrolled.

| Mid 50% test scores | | | |
|---|---|---|---|
| SAT critical reading: | 470-580 | GPA 3.0-3.49: | 39% |
| SAT math: | 460-570 | GPA 2.0-2.99: | 35% |
| SAT writing: | 450-570 | Rank in top quarter: | 30% |
| ACT composite: | 20-24 | Rank in top tenth: | 11% |
| GPA 3.75 or higher: | 12% | Out-of-state: | 36% |
| GPA 3.50-3.74: | 13% | Live on campus: | 90% |
| | | International: | 1% |

**Basis for selection.** Colorado Commission on Higher Education index score comprised of high school GPA and test scores utilized as part of admission criteria. Essay recommended. **Homeschooled:** Official copy of high school completion records; 1010 SAT (exclusive of Writing), 22 ACT.

**High school preparation.** College-preparatory program required. 17 units required. Required units include English 4, mathematics 4, social studies 2, history 1, science 3 (laboratory 2), foreign language 1 and academic electives 2.

**2009-2010 Annual costs.** Tuition/fees: $4,645; $17,615 out-of-state. Room/board: $7,444. Books/supplies: $1,698. Personal expenses: $2,508.

**2008-2009 Financial aid. Need-based:** 548 full-time freshmen applied for aid; 380 were judged to have need; 376 of these received aid. Average need met was 66%. Average scholarship/grant was $3,315; average loan $3,062. 49% of total undergraduate aid awarded as scholarships/grants, 51% as loans/jobs. **Non-need-based:** Awarded to 1,459 full-time undergraduates, including 588 freshmen. Scholarships awarded for academics, alumni affiliation, art, athletics, job skills, leadership, minority status, music/drama, state residency. **Additional information:** Tuition waived for Native Americans of federally recognized tribes; census number and Certificate of Indian Blood must accompany application.

**Application procedures. Admission:** Closing date 8/1 (postmark date). $40 fee, may be waived for applicants with need. Admission notification on a rolling basis beginning on or about 10/15. **Financial aid:** Priority date 2/15; no closing date. FAFSA required. Applicants notified on a rolling basis starting 3/15; must reply within 2 week(s) of notification.

**Academics. Special study options:** Accelerated study, cooperative education, distance learning, double major, dual enrollment of high school students, ESL, exchange student, honors, independent study, internships, liberal arts/career combination, student-designed major, study abroad, teacher certification program. **Credit/placement by examination:** AP, CLEP, IB, SAT, ACT, institutional tests. 24 credit hours maximum toward bachelor's degree. Up to 24 credits may be granted based on CLEP general exam scores. IB diploma holders will receive a minimum of 24 semester credits. **Support services:** Learning center, remedial instruction, study skills assistance, tutoring, writing center.

**Majors. Agriculture:** General, business, economics. **Area/ethnic studies:** Chicano/Hispanic-American/Latino, Native American, women's. **Biology:** General, ecology. **Business:** General, accounting, business admin, marketing, operations. **Computer sciences:** General. **Conservation:** Environmental studies. **Education:** Multicultural. **Foreign languages:** Spanish. **Health:** Athletic training. **History:** General. **Liberal arts:** Arts/sciences, humanities. **Math:** General. **Parks/recreation:** General, exercise sciences. **Philosophy/religion:** Philosophy. **Physical sciences:** Chemistry, geology, physics. **Psychology:** General, counseling, industrial. **Social sciences:** Anthropology, economics, political science, sociology. **Visual/performing arts:** Dramatic, studio arts.

**Most popular majors.** Business/marketing 27%, English 6%, liberal arts 11%, psychology 8%, social sciences 12%, visual/performing arts 8%.

**Computing on campus.** 672 workstations in dormitories, library, computer center, student center. Dormitories wired for high-speed internet access and linked to campus network. Commuter students can connect to campus network. Online course registration, online library, helpline, repair service, student web hosting, wireless network available.

**Student life. Freshman orientation:** Mandatory, $50 fee. Preregistration for classes offered. **Housing:** Guaranteed on-campus for all undergraduates. Coed dorms, special housing for disabled, apartments, wellness housing available. $100 partly refundable deposit, deadline 7/15. **Activities:** Bands, campus ministries, choral groups, drama, literary magazine, musical theater, radio station, student government, student newspaper, Newman Club, Circle-K International, international friendship club, business club, American Indian business leaders, American Indian science and engineering society, sociology club, Native American club, Habitat for Humanity.

**Athletics.** NCAA. **Intercollegiate:** Basketball, cross-country, football (tackle) M, golf M, soccer, softball W, volleyball W. **Intramural:** Badminton, basketball, football (tackle), racquetball, soccer, softball, volleyball. **Team name:** Skyhawks.

**Student services.** Adult student services, alcohol/substance abuse counseling, chaplain/spiritual director, career counseling, services for economically disadvantaged, student employment services, financial aid counseling, health services, legal services, minority student services, on-campus daycare, personal counseling, placement for graduates, veterans' counselor, women's services. **Physically disabled:** Services for visually, speech, hearing impaired.

**Contact.** E-mail: admission@fortlewis.edu
Phone: (970) 247-7184 Fax: (970) 247-7179
Andrew Burns, Director of Admission, Fort Lewis College, 1000 Rim Drive, Durango, CO 81301-3999

---

## ITT Technical Institute: Thornton
**Thornton, Colorado**
**www.itt-tech.edu**                    CB code: 3605

- For-profit 4-year technical college
- Commuter campus in large city

**General.** Founded in 1984. Accredited by ACICS. **Calendar:** Quarter.

**Contact.** Phone: (303) 288-4488
Director of Recruitment, 500 East 84th Avenue, Thornton, CO 80229

---

## Johnson & Wales University: Denver
**Denver, Colorado**
**www.jwu.edu**                          CB code: 3567

- Private 4-year university
- Residential campus in large city
- 1,461 degree-seeking undergraduates: 2% part-time, 55% women, 4% African American, 3% Asian American, 7% Hispanic American, 1% Native American, 1% international
- 72% of applicants admitted
- 49% graduate within 6 years

**General.** Regionally accredited. **Degrees:** 316 bachelor's, 237 associate awarded. **Calendar:** Quarter, limited summer session. **Full-time faculty:** 46 total; 28% women. **Part-time faculty:** 35 total; 54% women. **Class size:** 33% < 20, 57% 20-39, 10% 40-49. **Special facilities:** Community leadership institute.

**Freshman class profile.** 2,722 applied, 1,955 admitted, 400 enrolled.

| Mid 50% test scores | | | |
|---|---|---|---|
| SAT critical reading: | 420-540 | GPA 3.0-3.49: | 34% |
| SAT math: | 440-560 | GPA 2.0-2.99: | 40% |
| SAT writing: | 420-510 | Return as sophomores: | 67% |
| GPA 3.75 or higher: | 14% | Out-of-state: | 63% |
| GPA 3.50-3.74: | 11% | Live on campus: | 77% |
| | | International: | 1% |

**Basis for selection.** Academic record important, including secondary school curriculum, GPA, class rank, test scores. Student motivation and interest given strong consideration. SAT or ACT required for students entering honors program only. **Homeschooled:** Transcript of courses and grades, state high school equivalency certificate required. SAT or ACT required.

**High school preparation.** College-preparatory program recommended. Required units include English 4, mathematics 3, social studies 2 and science 3.

**2009-2010 Annual costs.** Tuition/fees: $23,490. Optional weekend meal plan available for $1,068. Room/board: $9,249. Books/supplies: $1,500. Personal expenses: $1,623.

**2009-2010 Financial aid. Non-need-based:** Scholarships awarded for academics, alumni affiliation, job skills, leadership, state residency.

**Application procedures. Admission:** No deadline. No application fee. Admission notification on a rolling basis beginning on or about 11/1. Must reply by May 1 or within 2 week(s) if notified thereafter. **Financial aid:** No deadline. FAFSA required. Applicants notified on a rolling basis starting 3/1; must reply within 2 week(s) of notification.

**Academics. Special study options:** Accelerated study, cooperative education, dual enrollment of high school students, ESL, exchange student, independent study, internships, study abroad. **Credit/placement by examination:** CLEP, institutional tests. **Support services:** Learning center, remedial instruction, study skills assistance, tutoring, writing center.

**Majors. Business:** Business admin, entrepreneurial studies, fashion, hospitality admin, hotel/motel admin, international, marketing. **Communications:** Advertising. **Family/consumer sciences:** Food/nutrition. **Parks/recreation:** Facilities management, sports admin. **Personal/culinary services:** Chef training, culinary arts, food service, restaurant/catering. **Protective services:** Law enforcement admin.

**Most popular majors.** Business/marketing 37%, family/consumer sciences 29%, parks/recreation 12%, personal/culinary services 17%.

**Computing on campus.** Dormitories wired for high-speed internet access and linked to campus network. Commuter students can connect to campus network. Online course registration, online library, helpline, repair service, wireless network available.

**Student life. Freshman orientation:** Mandatory, $250 fee. Preregistration for classes offered. **Housing:** Coed dorms available. $200 deposit. **Activities:** Drama, international student organizations, musical theater, student government, student newspaper.

**Athletics.** NAIA. **Intercollegiate:** Basketball, cross-country, volleyball. **Intramural:** Basketball, football (non-tackle), softball, volleyball. **Team name:** Wildcats.

**Student services.** Adult student services, alcohol/substance abuse counseling, career counseling, student employment services, financial aid counseling, health services, minority student services, personal counseling, placement for graduates. **Physically disabled:** Services for visually, speech, hearing impaired. **Learning disabled:** Comprehensive services available.

**Contact.** E-mail: admissions.den@jwu.edu
Phone: (303) 256-9300 Toll-free number: (877) 598-3368
Kim Ostrowski, Director of Admissions, Johnson & Wales University: Denver, 7150 Montview Boulevard, Denver, CO 80220

---

## Jones International University
**Centennial, Colorado**
**www.jiu.edu**                          CB code: 2785

- For-profit 4-year virtual college
- Large city
- 112 full-time, degree-seeking undergraduates
- 1,495 graduate students

**General.** Regionally accredited. **Degrees:** 55 bachelor's awarded; master's, doctoral offered. **Location:** 20 miles from Denver. **Calendar:** Continuous. **Full-time faculty:** 3 total; 100% have terminal degrees, 33% women. **Part-time faculty:** 136 total; 83% have terminal degrees, 48% women.

**Basis for selection.** Admissions based on students submitting requirements needed for each program and review by academic team for each program.

**High school preparation.** 16 units recommended. Recommended units include English 4, mathematics 4, social studies 1, history 1, science 3 (laboratory 3) and foreign language 2.

**2009-2010 Annual costs.** Tuition is $1,425 per course for bachelor's degrees. $65 technology fee per course. Books are approximately $170 per course. Books/supplies: $1,360.

**Financial aid. Additional information:** Loans available through Sallie Mae and PLATO. Most students have costs reimbursed by employers. GI Bill and VA benefits accepted.

**Application procedures. Admission:** No deadline. $60 fee. Application must be submitted online. Admission notification on a rolling basis. **Financial aid:** FAFSA required.

**Academics.** Online tutoring available around the clock. **Special study options:** Accelerated study, combined bachelor's/graduate degree, distance learning. **Credit/placement by examination:** CLEP, IB. 60 credit hours maximum toward bachelor's degree. **Support services:** Tutoring.

**Majors. Business:** General, business admin, communications, e-commerce, international, small business admin. **Communications:** General, digital media, journalism, organizational, public relations. **Communications technology:** General. **Computer sciences:** General, computer science, database management, programming, system admin, systems analysis. **Engineering:** Computer.

**Computing on campus.** PC or laptop required.

**Student life. Activities:** Student newspaper.

**Student services.** Career counseling, financial aid counseling.

**Contact.** E-mail: admissions@international.edu
Phone: (303) 784-8247 Toll-free number: (800) 811-5663 ext. 8247
Fax: (303) 799-0966
Joy Cadman, Director of Admissions and Records/Registrar, Jones
International University, 9697 East Mineral Avenue, Centennial, CO 80112

## Mesa State College
### Grand Junction, Colorado
**www.mesastate.edu**                    **CB code: 4484**

- Public 4-year community and liberal arts college
- Commuter campus in small city
- 6,375 degree-seeking undergraduates: 21% part-time, 56% women, 2% African American, 3% Asian American, 9% Hispanic American, 2% Native American
- 103 degree-seeking graduate students
- 81% of applicants admitted
- SAT or ACT (ACT writing optional) required

**General.** Founded in 1925. Regionally accredited. **Degrees:** 560 bachelor's, 171 associate awarded; master's offered. **Location:** 250 miles from Denver, 300 miles from Salt Lake City. **Calendar:** Semester, limited summer session. **Full-time faculty:** 230 total. **Part-time faculty:** 188 total. **Class size:** 49% < 20, 38% 20-39, 5% 40-49, 7% 50-99, 1% >100. **Special facilities:** Electron microscope laboratory, herbarium, computer-aided drafting laboratory, technical training facility, environmental restoration laboratory.

**Freshman class profile.** 4,275 applied, 3,466 admitted, 1,602 enrolled.

| Mid 50% test scores | | | |
|---|---|---|---|
| SAT critical reading: | 430-550 | GPA 2.0-2.99: | 44% |
| SAT math: | 430-560 | Rank in top quarter: | 22% |
| ACT composite: | 18-23 | Rank in top tenth: | 7% |
| GPA 3.75 or higher: | 13% | Return as sophomores: | 63% |
| GPA 3.50-3.74: | 11% | Out-of-state: | 13% |
| GPA 3.0-3.49: | 25% | Live on campus: | 51% |

**Basis for selection.** Admission based on GPA, ACT/SAT, class rank and satisfaction of HEAR requirements. Open admissions to most technical, associates and certificate programs. Audition required of music, music theater, theater majors. Interview recommended for nursing, allied health, teacher certification majors. **Homeschooled:** Statement describing homeschool structure and mission, transcript of courses and grades required.

**High school preparation.** College-preparatory program recommended. 17 units required. Required units include English 4, mathematics 4, social studies 3, science 3 (laboratory 2), foreign language 1 and academic electives 2.

**2009-2010 Annual costs.** Tuition/fees: $5,374; $14,340 out-of-state. Room/board: $7,507. Books/supplies: $1,698. Personal expenses: $1,942.

**2008-2009 Financial aid.** **Need-based:** 867 full-time freshmen applied for aid; 629 were judged to have need; 586 of these received aid. Average need met was 59%. Average scholarship/grant was $4,460; average loan $3,109. 49% of total undergraduate aid awarded as scholarships/grants, 51% as loans/jobs. **Non-need-based:** Awarded to 579 full-time undergraduates, including 165 freshmen. Scholarships awarded for academics, art, athletics, leadership, music/drama.

**Application procedures.** **Admission:** No deadline. $30 fee, may be waived for applicants with need. Admission notification on a rolling basis beginning on or about 9/1. **Financial aid:** Priority date 3/1; no closing date. FAFSA required. Applicants notified on a rolling basis starting 4/1; must reply within 5 week(s) of notification.

**Academics.** **Special study options:** Accelerated study, combined bachelor's/graduate degree, distance learning, double major, dual enrollment of high school students, exchange student, honors, independent study, internships, study abroad, teacher certification program. Area vocational school provides training in technical skills. **Credit/placement by examination:** AP, CLEP, IB, SAT, ACT, institutional tests. 12 credit hours maximum toward associate degree, 20 toward bachelor's. **Support services:** Learning center, pre-admission summer program, reduced course load, remedial instruction, study skills assistance, tutoring, writing center.

**Majors.** **Biology:** General. **Business:** General, accounting, management information systems. **Communications:** Media studies. **Computer sciences:** General. **Conservation:** Environmental science. **Engineering technology:** Architectural. **Foreign languages:** Spanish. **Health:** Athletic training, nursing (RN), radiologic technology/medical imaging. **History:** General.

**Liberal arts:** Arts/sciences. **Math:** General. **Parks/recreation:** Exercise sciences, sports admin. **Physical sciences:** General. **Protective services:** Criminal justice. **Psychology:** General. **Public administration:** General. **Social sciences:** General, political science, sociology. **Visual/performing arts:** Art, dramatic, graphic design.

**Most popular majors.** Biology 6%, business/marketing 22%, health sciences 12%, liberal arts 6%, parks/recreation 11%, psychology 7%, social sciences 6%, visual/performing arts 8%.

**Computing on campus.** 625 workstations in dormitories, library, computer center, student center. Dormitories wired for high-speed internet access and linked to campus network. Commuter students can connect to campus network. Online course registration, online library, helpline, student web hosting, wireless network available.

**Student life.** **Freshman orientation:** Available. Preregistration for classes offered. **Housing:** Coed dorms, single-sex dorms, special housing for disabled, apartments, wellness housing available. $150 partly refundable deposit. **Activities:** Bands, choral groups, dance, drama, film society, literary magazine, music ensembles, musical theater, radio station, student government, student newspaper, symphony orchestra, TV station, black student alliance, La Raza, Christian student fellowship, Native American student council, Polynesian club, cultral diversity board, dance society, drama society, sustainability council.

**Athletics.** NCAA. **Intercollegiate:** Baseball M, basketball, cross-country W, football (tackle) M, golf, lacrosse, soccer, softball W, swimming, tennis, track and field W, volleyball W, wrestling M. **Intramural:** Basketball, football (non-tackle), soccer, softball, volleyball. **Team name:** Mavericks.

**Student services.** Adult student services, alcohol/substance abuse counseling, chaplain/spiritual director, career counseling, services for economically disadvantaged, student employment services, financial aid counseling, health services, minority student services, on-campus daycare, personal counseling, veterans' counselor. **Physically disabled:** Services for visually, speech, hearing impaired.

**Contact.** E-mail: admissions@mesastate.edu
Phone: (970) 248-1875 Toll-free number: (800) 982-6372
Fax: (970) 248-1973
Jared Meier, Director of Admissions, Mesa State College, 1100 North Avenue, Grand Junction, CO 81501

## Metropolitan State College of Denver
### Denver, Colorado                    **CB member**
**www.mscd.edu**                    **CB code: 4505**

- Public 4-year liberal arts college
- Commuter campus in very large city
- 21,882 degree-seeking undergraduates
- SAT or ACT (ACT writing optional) required

**General.** Founded in 1963. Regionally accredited. Library, student center, physical education facilities, child care center shared with Community College of Denver and University of Colorado at Denver. Degree completion programs offered at off-campus sites in North Glen and Englewood. **Degrees:** 2,514 bachelor's awarded. **ROTC:** Army, Air Force. **Location:** Downtown. **Calendar:** Semester, extensive summer session. **Full-time faculty:** 516 total; 21% minority, 46% women. **Part-time faculty:** 732 total; 13% minority, 55% women. **Class size:** 35% < 20, 55% 20-39, 7% 40-49, 3% 50-99. **Special facilities:** Art galleries, CAD/CAM laboratory, world indoor airport.

**Freshman class profile.**

| Mid 50% test scores | | | |
|---|---|---|---|
| SAT critical reading: | 450-550 | GPA 3.0-3.49: | 28% |
| SAT math: | 420-550 | GPA 2.0-2.99: | 58% |
| ACT composite: | 18-22 | Rank in top quarter: | 8% |
| GPA 3.75 or higher: | 5% | Rank in top tenth: | 5% |
| GPA 3.50-3.74: | 7% | Out-of-state: | 4% |

**Basis for selection.** ACT/SAT, GPA, and class rank important. ACT/SAT not required of those submitting GED. Open admission for applicants 20 years of age and older who are high school graduates, have GED, or have 30 transferable credits.

**High school preparation.** College-preparatory program recommended. 15 units recommended. Recommended units include English 4, mathematics 3, social studies 2, history 1, science 3 and foreign language 2.

**2009-2010 Annual costs.** Tuition/fees: $3,639; $13,132 out-of-state. Books/supplies: $1,535. Personal expenses: $1,125.

**2008-2009 Financial aid. Non-need-based:** Scholarships awarded for academics, art, athletics, job skills, music/drama, state residency.

**Application procedures. Admission:** Closing date 8/25 (receipt date). $25 fee, may be waived for applicants with need. Admission notification on a rolling basis. **Financial aid:** Priority date 2/15; no closing date. FAFSA required. Applicants notified on a rolling basis starting 3/1.

**Academics. Special study options:** Accelerated study, cooperative education, cross-registration, distance learning, double major, dual enrollment of high school students, external degree, honors, independent study, internships, liberal arts/career combination, student-designed major, study abroad, teacher certification program, Washington semester. **Credit/placement by examination:** AP, CLEP, IB, SAT, ACT. 64 credit hours maximum toward bachelor's degree. **Support services:** Pre-admission summer program, study skills assistance, tutoring, writing center.

**Majors. Area/ethnic studies:** African-American, Chicano/Hispanic-American/Latino. **Biology:** General. **Business:** Accounting, business admin, finance, hospitality admin, hospitality/recreation, marketing, tourism promotion, tourism/travel. **Communications:** General, broadcast journalism, journalism. **Computer sciences:** General, computer science. **Conservation:** General, environmental studies, land use planning. **Education:** Art, music. **Engineering technology:** Civil, electrical, surveying. **Foreign languages:** General, Spanish. **Health:** Health care admin, nursing (RN). **History:** General. **Interdisciplinary:** Behavioral sciences. **Math:** General. **Parks/recreation:** General, exercise sciences. **Philosophy/religion:** Philosophy. **Physical sciences:** Atmospheric science, chemistry, physics. **Protective services:** Criminal justice, law enforcement admin. **Psychology:** General. **Public administration:** Human services, social work. **Social sciences:** Anthropology, economics, political science, sociology. **Transportation:** Air traffic control, aviation, aviation management. **Visual/performing arts:** Art, industrial design, music performance.

**Most popular majors.** Business/marketing 21%, English 8%, interdisciplinary studies 10%, psychology 7%, security/protective services 7%, visual/performing arts 6%.

**Computing on campus.** 700 workstations in library, computer center, student center. Commuter students can connect to campus network. Online course registration, online library, helpline, repair service, wireless network available.

**Student life. Freshman orientation:** Mandatory. Preregistration for classes offered. Several sessions held preceding each semester. **Housing:** Off-campus apartments in area. **Activities:** Bands, choral groups, dance, drama, international student organizations, literary magazine, music ensembles, musical theater, radio station, student government, student newspaper, TV station, Approximately 100 student organizations and clubs available.

**Athletics.** NCAA. **Intercollegiate:** Baseball M, basketball, cross-country, diving, soccer, swimming, tennis, volleyball W. **Intramural:** Basketball, handball, lacrosse M, racquetball, rugby M, skiing, softball W, tennis, volleyball. **Team name:** Roadrunners.

**Student services.** Adult student services, alcohol/substance abuse counseling, chaplain/spiritual director, career counseling, services for economically disadvantaged, student employment services, financial aid counseling, health services, legal services, on-campus daycare, personal counseling, placement for graduates, veterans' counselor, women's services. **Physically disabled:** Services for visually, speech, hearing impaired. **Learning disabled:** Comprehensive services available.

**Contact.** E-mail: askmetro@mscd.edu
Phone: (303) 556-3058 Fax: (303) 556-6345
Elena Sandoval-Lucero, Director of Admissions, Metropolitan State College of Denver, Campus Box 16, Denver, CO 80217

---

## Naropa University
**Boulder, Colorado**
**www.naropa.edu**

CB member
CB code: 0908

- Private 4-year university and liberal arts college
- Commuter campus in small city
- 464 degree-seeking undergraduates: 8% part-time, 61% women, 2% African American, 3% Asian American, 4% Hispanic American, 3% Native American, 3% international
- 592 degree-seeking graduate students
- 75% of applicants admitted
- Application essay, interview required
- 42% graduate within 6 years

**General.** Founded in 1974. Regionally accredited. Uses contemplative education, which is learning infused with the experience of awareness, insight and compassion for oneself and others, honed through the practice of sitting meditation and other contemplative disciplines. **Degrees:** 101 bachelor's awarded; master's offered. **Location:** 35 miles from Denver. **Calendar:** Semester, limited summer session. **Full-time faculty:** 51 total; 57% have terminal degrees, 16% minority, 59% women. **Part-time faculty:** 148 total; 26% have terminal degrees, 12% minority, 67% women. **Class size:** 90% < 20, 10% 20-39, less than 1% 50-99. **Special facilities:** Meditation halls, maitri rooms, consciousness laboratory, greenhouse, tea house, Chogyam Trungpa Rinpoche archives, performing arts center, dance studios, music studio, art studio, art exhibits, audio archives.

**Freshman class profile.** 152 applied, 114 admitted, 45 enrolled.

| | | | |
|---|---|---|---|
| GPA 3.75 or higher: | 20% | Return as sophomores: | 64% |
| GPA 3.50-3.74: | 13% | Out-of-state: | 71% |
| GPA 3.0-3.49: | 28% | Live on campus: | 83% |
| GPA 2.0-2.99: | 37% | International: | 2% |

**Basis for selection.** Assessment of academic background, community service, mission, and readiness important. Determination based on fit with unique mission, as well as academic background and readiness. Supplemental applications and/or art samples required for applicants to performance, environmental studies, interdisciplinary studies, music, visual arts, and writing and literature programs. **Homeschooled:** Portfolio of work completed during high school required, including subjects studied and modes of learning for each subject; extracurricular/community activities; academic achievements that support academic preparedness for college, such as internship positions; parent or teacher narrative; self-evaluation of work and how it contributed to intellectual growth; and transcripts from mainstream high schools or colleges (if applicable).

**High school preparation.** College-preparatory program recommended. 23 units recommended. Recommended units include English 4, mathematics 3, social studies 3, history 3, science 3 (laboratory 2), foreign language 3 and academic electives 4. Art, dance, theater and/or creative writing recommended.

**2009-2010 Annual costs.** Tuition/fees: $23,520. Room/board: $8,478.

**2009-2010 Financial aid.** All financial aid based on need. 32 full-time freshmen applied for aid; 29 were judged to have need; 29 of these received aid. Average need met was 86%. Average scholarship/grant was $16,225; average loan $7,547. 56% of total undergraduate aid awarded as scholarships/grants, 44% as loans/jobs.

**Application procedures. Admission:** Priority date 1/15; no deadline. $50 fee, may be waived for applicants with need. Admission notification on a rolling basis. Must reply by May 1 or within 3 week(s) if notified thereafter. **Financial aid:** Priority date 3/1; no closing date. FAFSA required. Applicants notified on a rolling basis starting 3/1; must reply within 3 week(s) of notification.

**Academics. Special study options:** Double major, dual enrollment of high school students, independent study, internships, student-designed major. Consortium agreement with University of Colorado allows degree-seeking students to take courses at University of Colorado at an in-state tuition rate. **Credit/placement by examination:** AP, CLEP, IB. 30 credit hours maximum toward bachelor's degree. **Support services:** Reduced course load, study skills assistance, tutoring, writing center.

**Majors. Conservation:** Environmental studies. **Education:** Early childhood. **Interdisciplinary:** Peace/conflict. **Philosophy/religion:** Religion. **Psychology:** General. **Visual/performing arts:** General, studio arts. **Other:** Interdisciplinary studies, Traditional Eastern arts.

**Most popular majors.** Education 8%, English 12%, interdisciplinary studies 12%, natural resources/environmental science 8%, parks/recreation 8%, psychology 32%, visual/performing arts 10%.

**Computing on campus.** 75 workstations in library, computer center. Online course registration, online library, wireless network available.

**Student life. Freshman orientation:** Mandatory. Preregistration for classes offered. Week-long session in August. One or 2-day orientations offered for parents and families. **Policies:** Code of Conduct enforced. **Housing:** Guaranteed on-campus for freshmen. Apartments, wellness housing available. $300 nonrefundable deposit, deadline 7/1. **Activities:** Jazz band, campus ministries, choral groups, dance, drama, international student organizations, literary magazine, music ensembles, musical theater, student government, Allies in Action, gender discussion group, students for peace and justice, healers, laughter club, Tibetan debate club, Reconnecting on Outer Terrain, Japanese tea ceremony club.

**Student services.** Alcohol/substance abuse counseling, chaplain/spiritual director, career counseling, financial aid counseling, minority student services, personal counseling. **Physically disabled:** Services for visually, hearing impaired.

**Contact.** E-mail: admissions@naropa.edu
Phone: (303) 546-3572 Toll-free number: (800) 772-6951
Fax: (303) 546-3583
Susan Boyle, Dean of Admissions, Naropa University, 2130 Arapahoe
Avenue, Boulder, CO 80302-6697

## National American University: Denver
### Denver, Colorado
www.national.edu                    CB code: 5354

- For-profit 4-year university and branch campus college
- Commuter campus in very large city

**General.** Founded in 1941. Regionally accredited. **Calendar:** Quarter.

**Annual costs/financial aid.** Books/supplies: $1,200.

**Contact.** Phone: (303) 876-7100
Director of Admissions, 1325 South Colorado Boulevard, Suite 100,
Denver, CO 80222-3308

## Nazarene Bible College
### Colorado Springs, Colorado
www.nbc.edu                    CB code: 0476

- Private 4-year Bible college affiliated with Church of the Nazarene
- Commuter campus in very large city
- 665 degree-seeking undergraduates: 68% part-time, 41% women
- Application essay required
- 30% graduate within 6 years; 20% enter graduate study

**General.** Founded in 1964. Accredited by ABHE. **Degrees:** 82 bachelor's,
3 associate awarded. **Location:** 60 miles from Denver. **Calendar:** Trimester, limited summer session. **Full-time faculty:** 9 total. **Part-time faculty:**
110 total.

**Freshman class profile.**

| | | | |
|---|---|---|---|
| End year in good standing: | 90% | Out-of-state: | 96% |
| Return as sophomores: | 65% | | |

**Basis for selection.** Open admission, but selective for some programs.
Essay, 2 recommendations required. **Homeschooled:** Transcript of courses
and grades, letter of recommendation (nonparent) required.

**2009-2010 Annual costs.** Tuition/fees: $9,600. Books/supplies: $900.

**2008-2009 Financial aid.** **Non-need-based:** Scholarships awarded for
religious affiliation. **Additional information:** Tuition waiver available to
students serving as student body officers.

**Application procedures.** **Admission:** No deadline. No application fee.
Admission notification on a rolling basis beginning on or about 5/1. **Financial aid:** Priority date 6/1; no closing date. FAFSA required. Applicants
notified on a rolling basis starting 6/15; must reply within 2 week(s) of
notification.

**Academics.** Full programs offered in evening classes, cater to adult students. Extensive online degree programs offered. Degree completion program offered online and on campus. **Special study options:** Accelerated
study, distance learning, double major, independent study, internships. **Credit/placement by examination:** AP, CLEP, institutional tests. 24 credit hours
maximum toward associate degree, 24 toward bachelor's. **Support services:** Learning center, reduced course load, remedial instruction, study skills
assistance, tutoring.

**Majors.** **Theology:** Bible, pastoral counseling, religious ed, sacred music.

**Computing on campus.** 20 workstations in library. Online library, wireless network available.

**Student life.** **Freshman orientation:** Mandatory. Preregistration for classes
offered. **Policies:** Religious observance required. **Activities:** Concert band,
campus ministries, choral groups, music ensembles, student government,
student newspaper.

**Student services.** Adult student services, alcohol/substance abuse counseling, chaplain/spiritual director, career counseling, services for economically disadvantaged, student employment services, financial aid counseling,
personal counseling, placement for graduates, women's services. **Physically disabled:** Services for visually, hearing impaired.

**Contact.** E-mail: campusadmissions@nbc.edu
Phone: (719) 884-5000 ext. 5096 Toll-free
number: (800) 873-3873 ext. 5096 Fax: (719) 884-5199
Jay Ott, Vice President for Campus Academic Services, Nazarene Bible
College, 1111 Academy Park Loop, Colorado Springs, CO 80910-3704

## Platt College: Aurora
### Aurora, Colorado
www.plattcolorado.edu                    CB code: 3012

- For-profit 4-year visual arts and nursing college
- Commuter campus in very large city
- 180 degree-seeking undergraduates
- Application essay, interview required

**General.** Accredited by ACCSC. **Degrees:** 20 bachelor's, 15 associate
awarded. **Calendar:** Quarter. **Full-time faculty:** 12 total. **Part-time faculty:** 21 total.

**Basis for selection.** Open admission, but selective for some programs.
Background check, letter of recommendation, Test of Essential Academic
Skills (TEAS) required for nursing applicants. Wonderlic required for graphic
arts applicants. **Homeschooled:** State high school equivalency certificate
required.

**High school preparation.** College-preparatory program recommended.

**2009-2010 Annual costs.** Visual and Performing Arts: associate program $34,000; bachelor's program $50,107. Nursing program (RN) $68,000.
Costs include tuition, registration fee, lab fees, supplies. Cost of books, art
kit vary with program.

**Financial aid.** All financial aid based on need.

**Application procedures.** **Admission:** No deadline. $75 fee. Admission
notification on a rolling basis. **Financial aid:** No deadline. FAFSA, institutional form required. Applicants notified on a rolling basis.

**Academics.** **Credit/placement by examination:** CLEP. **Support services:** Learning center, study skills assistance, writing center.

**Majors.** **Health:** Nursing (RN). **Visual/performing arts:** Commercial/advertising art.

**Computing on campus.** PC or laptop required.

**Student life.** **Freshman orientation:** Mandatory.

**Contact.** E-mail: admissions@plattcolorado.edu
Phone: (303) 369-5151 Toll-free number: (877) 369-5151
Fax: (303) 745-1433
Joni Aaron-Horton, Senior Admissions Coordinator, Platt College: Aurora,
3100 South Parker Road, Aurora, CO 80014-3141

## Regis University
### Denver, Colorado
www.regis.edu                    CB member    CB code: 4656

- Private 4-year university and liberal arts college affiliated with Roman
  Catholic Church
- Residential campus in very large city
- 1,503 degree-seeking undergraduates: 2% part-time, 63% women, 2%
  African American, 5% Asian American, 15% Hispanic American, 1%
  Native American, 1% international
- 95 degree-seeking graduate students
- 80% of applicants admitted
- SAT or ACT (ACT writing optional), application essay required
- 64% graduate within 6 years

**General.** Founded in 1877. Regionally accredited. **Degrees:** 341 bachelor's awarded; master's, professional offered. **ROTC:** Army, Naval, Air
Force. **Location:** 10 miles from downtown. **Calendar:** Semester, limited
summer session. **Full-time faculty:** 86 total; 80% have terminal degrees,
13% minority, 45% women. **Part-time faculty:** 30 total; 7% have terminal
degrees, 7% minority, 53% women. **Class size:** 66% < 20, 33% 20-39, less
than 1% 40-49, less than 1% 50-99. **Special facilities:** Center for the study
of war experience, Santos collection, recorder music center, arboretum.

**Freshman class profile.** 1,943 applied, 1,546 admitted, 377 enrolled.

| Mid 50% test scores | | | |
|---|---|---|---|
| SAT critical reading: | 470-590 | GPA 2.0-2.99: | 21% |
| SAT math: | 480-600 | Rank in top quarter: | 57% |
| ACT composite: | 21-26 | Rank in top tenth: | 26% |
| GPA 3.75 or higher: | 32% | Return as sophomores: | 80% |
| GPA 3.50-3.74: | 17% | Out-of-state: | 43% |
| GPA 3.0-3.49: | 30% | Live on campus: | 80% |

**Basis for selection.** High school record, test scores, recommendations, essay, school and community activities most important. Interview, campus visit recommended. Audition recommended of music majors.

**High school preparation.** 15 units required. Required and recommended units include English 4, mathematics 2, social studies 3, history 2, science 2 (laboratory 1) and foreign language 2.

**2009-2010 Annual costs.** Tuition/fees: $29,700. Tuition-free for any student who does not graduate in 4 years while maintaining required amount of credit hours. Room/board: $9,400. Books/supplies: $1,698. Personal expenses: $1,161.

**2008-2009 Financial aid. Need-based:** 24% of total undergraduate aid awarded as scholarships/grants, 76% as loans/jobs. **Non-need-based:** Scholarships awarded for academics, athletics, leadership, minority status, religious affiliation, ROTC, state residency.

**Application procedures. Admission:** Priority date 3/1; deadline 8/1 (postmark date). $40 fee, may be waived for applicants with need, free for online applicants. Admission notification on a rolling basis. Must reply by May 1 or within 2 week(s) if notified thereafter. **Financial aid:** Priority date 3/1; no closing date. FAFSA required. Applicants notified on a rolling basis starting 3/15.

**Academics.** School of Professional Studies offers part-time undergraduate, graduate, certificate and corporate education programs to adult students on 6 campuses and online. **Special study options:** Combined bachelor's/graduate degree, cross-registration, double major, exchange student, honors, independent study, internships, student-designed major, study abroad, teacher certification program. **Credit/placement by examination:** AP, CLEP, IB, institutional tests. 30 credit hours maximum toward bachelor's degree. Regis, CLEP, DANTES, Challenge exams offered. **Support services:** Learning center, pre-admission summer program, reduced course load, remedial instruction, study skills assistance, tutoring, writing center.

**Majors. Area/ethnic studies:** Women's. **Biology:** General, biochemistry. **Business:** General, accounting, business admin. **Communications:** General. **Computer sciences:** General, computer science. **Education:** General, biology, chemistry, elementary, English, history, mathematics, middle, physical, science, secondary, special. **Foreign languages:** French, Spanish. **Health:** Medical records admin, predental, premedicine, preveterinary. **History:** General. **Interdisciplinary:** Neuroscience. **Legal studies:** Prelaw. **Liberal arts:** Arts/sciences. **Math:** General. **Philosophy/religion:** Philosophy, religion. **Physical sciences:** Chemistry. **Psychology:** General. **Social sciences:** Criminology, economics, political science, sociology. **Visual/performing arts:** General.

**Most popular majors.** Biology 10%, business/marketing 28%, communications/journalism 6%, English 6%, interdisciplinary studies 12%, mathematics 6%, social sciences 12%.

**Computing on campus.** 337 workstations in dormitories, library, computer center, student center. Dormitories wired for high-speed internet access and linked to campus network. Commuter students can connect to campus network. Online course registration, online library, helpline, wireless network available.

**Student life. Freshman orientation:** Mandatory, $75 fee. Preregistration for classes offered. Held weekend before classes begin. **Policies:** Freshmen required to live on campus unless residing with parent, guardian or spouse in Denver metropolitan area. **Housing:** Guaranteed on-campus for freshmen. Coed dorms, single-sex dorms, special housing for disabled, apartments, cooperative housing, wellness housing available. $150 nonrefundable deposit, deadline 5/1. **Activities:** Bands, campus ministries, choral groups, dance, drama, literary magazine, music ensembles, musical theater, radio station, student government, student newspaper, peer education, environmental action program, Christian Fellowship, Jewish student group, Asian awareness association, black student alliance, Mi Gente, multicultural awareness committee, Romero House, Young Democrats and Republicans.

**Athletics.** NCAA. **Intercollegiate:** Baseball M, basketball, cross-country, golf, lacrosse W, soccer, softball W, volleyball W. **Intramural:** Basketball, bowling, football (non-tackle), soccer, softball, tennis, volleyball. **Team name:** Rangers.

**Student services.** Adult student services, alcohol/substance abuse counseling, chaplain/spiritual director, career counseling, student employment services, financial aid counseling, health services, minority student services, personal counseling, placement for graduates, veterans' counselor. **Physically disabled:** Services for visually, speech, hearing impaired. **Learning disabled:** Comprehensive services available.

**Contact.** E-mail: regisadm@regis.edu
Phone: (303) 458-4900 Toll-free number: (800) 388-2366 ext. 4900
Fax: (303) 964-5534
Victor Davolt, Director of Admissions, Regis College, Regis University, 3333 Regis Boulevard, Mail Code B20, Denver, CO 80221-1099

---

## Rocky Mountain College of Art & Design
**Denver, Colorado**
**www.rmcad.edu**                         **CB code: 1943**

- For-profit 4-year visual arts college
- Commuter campus in very large city
- 576 degree-seeking undergraduates: 9% part-time, 63% women, 2% African American, 3% Asian American, 10% Hispanic American, 1% Native American
- 99% of applicants admitted
- Interview required
- 55% graduate within 6 years; 20% enter graduate study

**General.** Founded in 1963. Regionally accredited. **Degrees:** 88 bachelor's awarded. **Calendar:** Semester, extensive summer session. **Full-time faculty:** 28 total; 39% have terminal degrees, 4% minority, 46% women. **Part-time faculty:** 61 total; 26% have terminal degrees, 7% minority, 46% women. **Class size:** 92% < 20, 8% 20-39. **Special facilities:** Fine arts center exhibition space.

**Freshman class profile.** 409 applied, 405 admitted, 137 enrolled.

| Mid 50% test scores | | | |
|---|---|---|---|
| SAT critical reading: | 460-570 | GPA 3.0-3.49: | 39% |
| SAT math: | 430-520 | GPA 2.0-2.99: | 33% |
| SAT writing: | 420-570 | End year in good standing: | 85% |
| ACT composite: | 19-24 | Return as sophomores: | 61% |
| GPA 3.75 or higher: | 12% | Out-of-state: | 34% |
| GPA 3.50-3.74: | 15% | Live on campus: | 40% |

**Basis for selection.** Applicants must show desire to pursue art career. Portfolio, essay, and recommendations required. Test scores required for all degree candidates. Portfolio required. **Homeschooled:** Statement describing homeschool structure and mission, transcript of courses and grades, state high school equivalency certificate required.

**2009-2010 Annual costs.** Tuition/fees: $24,840. Flat fee of $12,420 per term for students taking 12 to 18 credits. Books/supplies: $1,749. Personal expenses: $2,896.

**2009-2010 Financial aid. Need-based:** 120 full-time freshmen applied for aid; 113 were judged to have need; 113 of these received aid. Average need met was 71%. Average scholarship/grant was $4,462; average loan $3,353. 43% of total undergraduate aid awarded as scholarships/grants, 57% as loans/jobs. **Non-need-based:** Awarded to 479 full-time undergraduates, including 130 freshmen. Scholarships awarded for academics, art, state residency.

**Application procedures. Admission:** No deadline. $50 fee, may be waived for applicants with need. Admission notification on a rolling basis beginning on or about 9/1. **Financial aid:** Priority date 3/15; no closing date. FAFSA required. Applicants notified on a rolling basis starting 4/5; must reply within 2 week(s) of notification.

**Academics. Special study options:** Accelerated study, double major, honors, independent study, internships, teacher certification program. **Credit/placement by examination:** AP, CLEP, IB, SAT, ACT. 64 credit hours maximum toward bachelor's degree. **Support services:** Learning center, reduced course load, study skills assistance, tutoring, writing center.

**Majors. Communications technology:** Animation/special effects. **Computer sciences:** Computer graphics. **Education:** Art. **Visual/performing arts:** Design, graphic design, illustration, interior design, painting, photography, sculpture, studio arts. **Other:** Game art.

**Most popular majors.** Communication technologies 23%, visual/performing arts 73%.

**Computing on campus.** 300 workstations in library, computer center. Commuter students can connect to campus network. Online course registration, online library, helpline, student web hosting, wireless network available.

**Student life. Freshman orientation:** Mandatory. 3-day program held before start of term. **Housing:** Coed dorms available. **Activities:** Dance, film society, student government, student newspaper.

**Student services.** Career counseling, student employment services, financial aid counseling, personal counseling, placement for graduates, veterans' counselor. **Physically disabled:** Services for visually, speech, hearing impaired.

**Contact.** E-mail: admissions@rmcad.edu
Phone: (303) 753-6046 Toll-free number: (800) 888-2787
Fax: (303) 759-4970
Angela Carlson, Director of Marketing and Admissions, Rocky Mountain College of Art & Design, 1600 Pierce Street, Denver, CO 80214

## United States Air Force Academy

USAF Academy, Colorado        **CB member**
www.academyadmissions.com      **CB code: 4830**

- Public 4-year university and military college
- Residential campus in large city
- 4,620 degree-seeking undergraduates: 20% women, 5% African American, 8% Asian American, 8% Hispanic American, 1% Native American, 1% international
- 14% of applicants admitted
- SAT or ACT (ACT writing recommended), application essay, interview required
- 76% graduate within 6 years; 9% enter graduate study

**General.** Founded in 1954. Regionally accredited. **Degrees:** 1,062 bachelor's awarded. **Location:** 8 miles from Colorado Springs, 60 miles from Denver. **Calendar:** Semester, limited summer session. **Full-time faculty:** 506 total; 46% have terminal degrees, 8% minority, 22% women. **Part-time faculty:** 21 total; 86% have terminal degrees, 14% minority, 24% women. **Class size:** 64% < 20, 35% 20-39, less than 1% 40-49, less than 1% 50-99. **Special facilities:** 2 airfields; tri-sonic wind tunnel; aeronautics, instrumentation, research and radio-frequency systems laboratories; training facility; meteorology lab; engineering mechanics lab; laser optics center.

**Freshman class profile.** 9,897 applied, 1,362 admitted, 1,362 enrolled.

| Mid 50% test scores | | | |
|---|---|---|---|
| SAT critical reading: | 600-680 | GPA 2.0-2.99: | 1% |
| SAT math: | 630-700 | Rank in top quarter: | 81% |
| SAT writing: | 570-650 | Rank in top tenth: | 52% |
| ACT composite: | 28-32 | Return as sophomores: | 91% |
| GPA 3.75 or higher: | 67% | Out-of-state: | 93% |
| GPA 3.50-3.74: | 16% | Live on campus: | 100% |
| GPA 3.0-3.49: | 16% | International: | 1% |

**Basis for selection.** Must be a citizen of the United States, unmarried with no dependents, between the ages of 17 and not past the 23rd birthday on July 1 of the year of entry, and of good moral character. Legal nomination from member of Congress, US President or Vice President or other selected sources required. Secondary school record, test scores, leadership ability, extracurricular activities, character most important. Satisfactory completion of medical exam and fitness test, and personal interview required. Admissions counselors available to assist in the admission process.

**High school preparation.** College-preparatory program required. Recommended units include English 4, mathematics 4, social studies 3, history 3, science 4 (laboratory 4), foreign language 2 and computer science 1. English should include college preparatory composition and speech courses. Math should include algebra, geometry, trigonometry, calculus, and functional analysis (if available). Science should include biology, chemistry, physics, computers, and additional science courses. Foreign language instruction should be in a modern language.

**2009-2010 Annual costs.** Tuition, room, board, medical and dental care paid by U.S. Government. Each cadet receives monthly salary to pay for uniforms, supplies and personal expenses. A government loan is advanced to each member of the freshman class.

**Application procedures. Admission:** Closing date 2/15 (postmark date). No application fee. Admission notification on a rolling basis beginning on or about 10/15. Must reply by 5/1. Several stages of application process; begin junior year.

**Academics. Special study options:** Double major, ESL, exchange student, honors, independent study, student-designed major, study abroad. Academically at-risk, hospital instruction, extra instruction, and summer programs available. **Credit/placement by examination:** AP, CLEP, SAT, ACT, institutional tests. **Support services:** Learning center, study skills assistance, tutoring, writing center.

**Majors. Biology:** General. **Business:** Logistics, management science, travel services. **Computer sciences:** Computer science. **Engineering:** General, aerospace, civil, computer, electrical, environmental, mechanical, mechanics, operations research, systems. **History:** General. **Interdisciplinary:** Behavioral sciences, math/computer science. **Legal studies:** General. **Liberal arts:** Humanities. **Physical sciences:** Atmospheric science, chemistry, physics. **Social sciences:** General, economics, geography, political science. **Other:** Foreign area studies, Space operations, Systems engineering management.

**Most popular majors.** Business/marketing 11%, engineering/engineering technologies 36%, interdisciplinary studies 11%, physical sciences 10%, social sciences 12%.

**Computing on campus.** PC or laptop required. 200 workstations in library. Dormitories wired for high-speed internet access and linked to campus network. Online library, helpline, repair service, wireless network available.

**Student life. Freshman orientation:** Available. Three 2-day appointee orientation sessions held in April. **Housing:** Guaranteed on-campus for all undergraduates. Coed dorms available. **Activities:** Bands, campus ministries, choral groups, drama, Model UN, radio station, student government.

**Athletics.** NCAA. **Intercollegiate:** Baseball M, basketball, boxing M, cheerleading, cross-country, diving, fencing, football (tackle) M, golf M, gymnastics, ice hockey M, lacrosse M, rifle, soccer, swimming, tennis, track and field, volleyball W, water polo M, wrestling M. **Intramural:** Basketball, boxing M, cross-country, football (non-tackle), racquetball, rugby, soccer, softball, tennis, volleyball. **Team name:** Falcons.

**Student services.** Alcohol/substance abuse counseling, chaplain/spiritual director, health services, legal services, personal counseling, women's services.

**Contact.** E-mail: rr_webmail@usafa.edu
Phone: (719) 333-2520 Toll-free number: (800) 443-9266
Fax: (719) 333-3647
Col. Chevalier Cleaves, Director of Admissions, United States Air Force Academy, HQ USAF/RRS, 2304 Cadet Drive, Suite 2400, USAF Academy, CO 80840

## University of Colorado at Boulder

Boulder, Colorado        **CB member**
www.colorado.edu      **CB code: 4841**

- Public 4-year university
- Residential campus in small city
- 26,405 degree-seeking undergraduates: 6% part-time, 47% women, 2% African American, 6% Asian American, 6% Hispanic American, 1% Native American, 2% international
- 5,299 degree-seeking graduate students
- 84% of applicants admitted
- SAT or ACT (ACT writing optional), application essay required
- 67% graduate within 6 years; 21% enter graduate study

**General.** Founded in 1876. Regionally accredited. **Degrees:** 5,007 bachelor's awarded; master's, doctoral, professional offered. **ROTC:** Army, Naval, Air Force. **Location:** 30 miles from Denver. **Calendar:** Semester, extensive summer session. **Full-time faculty:** 1,392 total; 90% have terminal degrees, 16% minority, 37% women. **Part-time faculty:** 699 total; 32% have terminal degrees, 11% minority, 48% women. **Class size:** 46% < 20, 34% 20-39, 6% 40-49, 7% 50-99, 7% >100. **Special facilities:** Natural history museum, art museum and galleries, heritage center, observatory, planetarium and science center, electron microscope, outdoor theater, video interactive foreign language laboratory, mountain research station, centrifuge, engineering lab, multipurpose conference center, concert hall, multidisciplinary IT center.

**Freshman class profile.** 19,649 applied, 16,514 admitted, 5,555 enrolled.

| Mid 50% test scores | | | |
|---|---|---|---|
| SAT critical reading: | 520-630 | Rank in top tenth: | 25% |
| SAT math: | 550-650 | End year in good standing: | 90% |
| ACT composite: | 24-28 | Return as sophomores: | 83% |
| GPA 3.75 or higher: | 36% | Out-of-state: | 41% |
| GPA 3.50-3.74: | 21% | Live on campus: | 92% |
| GPA 3.0-3.49: | 36% | International: | 1% |
| GPA 2.0-2.99: | 7% | Fraternities: | 13% |
| Rank in top quarter: | 58% | Sororities: | 25% |

**Basis for selection.** Secondary school record (breadth and rigor of courses, grades, class rank) most important. Test scores and personal statement also very important. Recommendations and personal attributes and talents considered. Audition required of music majors.

**High school preparation.** College-preparatory program required. 17 units required. Required units include English 4, mathematics 4, social studies 2, history 1, science 3 (laboratory 2) and foreign language 3. English must include 2 composition for College of Arts and Science, School of Business. Math must include 2 algebra, 1 geometry, and 1 college preparatory math such as trigonometry, analytic geometry, or elementary functions for College of Arts and Sciences, School of Business, College of Engineering. 3 math required for Colleges of Music and Architecture and Planning. Physics or chemistry with lab required for College of Arts and Sciences, School of Business. For College of Engineering, science includes 1 of physics and 1 of chemistry or biology, or 2 of chemistry and 1 of physics or biology, or 2 of biology and 1 of chemistry or physics. Social Studies includes 1 of geography for College of Arts and Sciences, School of Business. 3 single foreign language required for College of Arts & Sciences, College of Engineering, School of Business; 2 single foreign language required for Colleges of Music and Architecture and Planning. 1 elective required for College of Architecture and Planning; 2 art electives required for College of Music.

**2009-2010 Annual costs.** Tuition/fees: $7,932; $28,186 out-of-state. One-time new student fee of $182. Room/board: $10,378. Books/supplies: $1,749. Personal expenses: $3,402.

**2009-2010 Financial aid.** **Need-based:** 4,941 full-time freshmen applied for aid; 2,181 were judged to have need; 2,177 of these received aid. Average need met was 92%. Average scholarship/grant was $7,508; average loan $5,715. 52% of total undergraduate aid awarded as scholarships/grants, 48% as loans/jobs. **Non-need-based:** Awarded to 6,916 full-time undergraduates, including 2,619 freshmen. Scholarships awarded for academics, alumni affiliation, art, athletics, leadership, music/drama, ROTC, state residency.

**Application procedures.** **Admission:** Priority date 12/1; deadline 1/15 (postmark date). $50 fee, may be waived for applicants with need. Admission notification 4/1. Must reply by May 1 or within 2 week(s) if notified thereafter. **Financial aid:** Priority date 4/1; no closing date. FAFSA required. Applicants notified on a rolling basis starting 3/1; must reply within 3 week(s) of notification.

**Academics.** Residential Academic Programs in leadership, natural or environmental sciences, humanities and service learning, the arts, honors, American West culture and society, international and global affairs, cultural diversity, business, or engineering available. **Special study options:** Accelerated study, combined bachelor's/graduate degree, cooperative education, cross-registration, distance learning, double major, dual enrollment of high school students, ESL, exchange student, honors, independent study, internships, liberal arts/career combination, semester at sea, student-designed major, study abroad, teacher certification program. Undergraduate research opportunities; concurrent bachelor's/master's programs; small group academic programs. **Credit/placement by examination:** AP, CLEP, IB, institutional tests. Policies vary by department. **Support services:** Learning center, preadmission summer program, reduced course load, study skills assistance, tutoring, writing center.

**Majors.** **Architecture:** Environmental design. **Area/ethnic studies:** Asian, Russian/Slavic, women's. **Biology:** Biochemistry, cellular/molecular, physiology. **Business:** Accounting, business admin, finance, international, management information systems, marketing, real estate, small business admin. **Communications:** General, journalism. **Computer sciences:** Computer science. **Conservation:** Environmental studies. **Education:** Music. **Engineering:** Aerospace, architectural, chemical, civil, computer, electrical, environmental, mechanical, physics. **Foreign languages:** Chinese, classics, French, Germanic, Italian, Japanese, linguistics, Spanish. **Health:** Communication disorders. **History:** General. **Interdisciplinary:** Global studies. **Liberal arts:** Humanities. **Math:** General, applied. **Philosophy/religion:** Philosophy, religion. **Physical sciences:** Astronomy, chemistry, geology, physics. **Psychology:** General. **Social sciences:** Anthropology, economics, geography, political science, sociology. **Visual/performing arts:** Art history/conservation, dance, dramatic, film/cinema, music performance, studio arts. **Other:** Chemical and biological engineering, Ecology and evolutionary biology.

**Most popular majors.** Biology 10%, business/marketing 14%, communications/journalism 9%, engineering/engineering technologies 8%, psychology 9%, social sciences 16%, visual/performing arts 6%.

**Computing on campus.** 1,842 workstations in dormitories, library, computer center, student center. Dormitories wired for high-speed internet access and linked to campus network. Commuter students can connect to campus network. Online course registration, online library, helpline, repair service, student web hosting, wireless network available.

**Student life.** **Freshman orientation:** Mandatory. Preregistration for classes offered. 2-day programs for students and parents held throughout summer. **Policies:** Honor code, lifestyle code of conduct, and 2-strikes disciplinary policy regarding alcohol violations. **Housing:** Guaranteed on-campus for freshmen. Coed dorms, special housing for disabled, apartments, fraternity/sorority housing, wellness housing available. $300 nonrefundable deposit. Residential academic programs within specific dorms. **Activities:** Bands, campus ministries, choral groups, dance, drama, film society, international student organizations, literary magazine, music ensembles, Model UN, musical theater, opera, radio station, student government, student newspaper, symphony orchestra, TV station, student outreach and retention center for equity, multicultural affairs center, volunteer clearing house, victim assistance, disability services, gay lesbian bisexual transgender resource center, ethical and civic engagement institute, College Democrats, College Republicans.

**Athletics.** NCAA. **Intercollegiate:** Basketball, cross-country, football (tackle) M, golf, skiing, soccer W, tennis W, track and field, volleyball W. **Intramural:** Basketball, football (non-tackle), ice hockey, soccer, tennis, volleyball, water polo. **Team name:** Colorado Buffaloes.

**Student services.** Adult student services, alcohol/substance abuse counseling, chaplain/spiritual director, career counseling, services for economically disadvantaged, student employment services, financial aid counseling, health services, legal services, minority student services, on-campus daycare, personal counseling, placement for graduates, veterans' counselor, women's services. **Physically disabled:** Services for visually, speech, hearing impaired.

**Contact.** E-mail: apply@colorado.edu
Phone: (303) 492-6301 Fax: (303) 492-7115
Kevin McLennan, Director of Admissions, University of Colorado at Boulder, 552 UCB, Boulder, CO 80309-0552

---

## University of Colorado at Colorado Springs
**Colorado Springs, Colorado**
www.uccs.edu                                    CB code: 4874

- Public 4-year university
- Commuter campus in large city
- 6,760 degree-seeking undergraduates: 20% part-time, 55% women, 4% African American, 5% Asian American, 10% Hispanic American, 1% Native American
- 1,841 degree-seeking graduate students
- 62% of applicants admitted
- SAT or ACT (ACT writing optional) required
- 46% graduate within 6 years; 34% enter graduate study

**General.** Founded in 1965. Regionally accredited. **Degrees:** 1,225 bachelor's awarded; master's, doctoral, professional offered. **ROTC:** Army. **Location:** 60 miles from Denver. **Calendar:** Semester, limited summer session. **Full-time faculty:** 367 total; 86% have terminal degrees, 12% minority, 52% women. **Part-time faculty:** 54 total; 7% minority, 63% women. **Class size:** 53% < 20, 30% 20-39, 8% 40-49, 8% 50-99, 1% >100.

**Freshman class profile.** 4,711 applied, 2,932 admitted, 1,097 enrolled.

| Mid 50% test scores | | | |
|---|---|---|---|
| SAT critical reading: | 480-590 | GPA 2.0-2.99: | 28% |
| SAT math: | 490-600 | Rank in top quarter: | 40% |
| SAT writing: | 460-580 | Rank in top tenth: | 14% |
| ACT composite: | 21-26 | End year in good standing: | 72% |
| GPA 3.75 or higher: | 18% | Return as sophomores: | 68% |
| GPA 3.50-3.74: | 17% | Out-of-state: | 14% |
| GPA 3.0-3.49: | 37% | Live on campus: | 46% |

**Basis for selection.** Priority given to applicants who rank in top 40% of graduating class, scored 1080 SAT (exclusive of Writing) or 24 ACT, 2.8 GPA, and completed all high school course units as required. Test of Standard Written English required of liberal arts applicants. **Homeschooled:** Transcript of courses and grades, state high school equivalency certificate required.

**High school preparation.** College-preparatory program recommended. 18 units required; 19 recommended. Required and recommended units include English 4, mathematics 3-4, social studies 2, science 3 (laboratory 3), foreign language 2 and academic electives 1.

**2009-2010 Annual costs.** Tuition/fees: $7,076; $16,973 out-of-state. Tuition varies by program. One-time matriculation fee of $25 required. Room/board: $7,490. Books/supplies: $700.

**2008-2009 Financial aid. Need-based:** 713 full-time freshmen applied for aid; 385 were judged to have need; 375 of these received aid. Average need met was 57%. Average scholarship/grant was $4,787; average loan $3,119. 42% of total undergraduate aid awarded as scholarships/grants, 58% as loans/jobs. **Non-need-based:** Awarded to 366 full-time undergraduates, including 138 freshmen. Scholarships awarded for academics, alumni affiliation, athletics, state residency.

**Application procedures. Admission:** Priority date 4/1; deadline 7/1. $50 fee. Admission notification on a rolling basis. **Financial aid:** Priority date 4/1; no closing date. FAFSA required. Applicants notified on a rolling basis starting 4/15.

**Academics. Special study options:** Accelerated study, cooperative education, distance learning, double major, dual enrollment of high school students, ESL, honors, independent study, internships, liberal arts/career combination, student-designed major, study abroad, teacher certification program. **Credit/placement by examination:** AP, CLEP, IB, institutional tests. 30 credit hours maximum toward bachelor's degree. **Support services:** Learning center, remedial instruction, study skills assistance, tutoring, writing center.

**Honors college/program.** 25 ACT or 1200 SAT (exclusive of Writing), 3.75 GPA and completion of Honors application (including the essay and statement of objectives).

**Majors. Area/ethnic studies:** Women's. **Biology:** General. **Business:** General, business admin. **Communications:** General. **Computer sciences:** General, computer graphics, game design, security. **Engineering:** General, computer, electrical, mechanical. **Foreign languages:** Spanish. **Health:** Health services, nursing (RN). **History:** General. **Math:** General. **Philosophy/religion:** Philosophy. **Physical sciences:** Chemistry, physics. **Protective services:** Law enforcement admin. **Psychology:** General. **Social sciences:** Anthropology, economics, geography, political science, sociology. **Visual/performing arts:** General. **Other:** Distributed studies.

**Most popular majors.** Biology 7%, business/marketing 20%, communications/journalism 9%, engineering/engineering technologies 6%, English 7%, health sciences 13%, history 6%, psychology 9%, social sciences 15%.

**Computing on campus.** 400 workstations in dormitories, library, computer center. Dormitories wired for high-speed internet access and linked to campus network. Commuter students can connect to campus network. Online course registration, online library, helpline, repair service, wireless network available.

**Student life. Freshman orientation:** Mandatory, $50 fee. One-day sessions throughout summer. **Housing:** Coed dorms, single-sex dorms, special housing for disabled, apartments available. $150 partly refundable deposit. **Activities:** Jazz band, choral groups, dance, drama, film society, international student organizations, literary magazine, music ensembles, musical theater, radio station, student government, student newspaper, advocating woman's assistance resources education, counseling honor society, math club, chemistry honor society, black student union, Latino student union, Inter-Varsity Christian Fellowship.

**Athletics. NCAA. Intercollegiate:** Basketball, cross-country, golf M, soccer M, softball W, track and field, volleyball W. **Intramural:** Basketball, football (non-tackle), soccer, table tennis, volleyball. **Team name:** Mountain Lions.

**Student services.** Adult student services, career counseling, student employment services, financial aid counseling, health services, minority student services, on-campus daycare, personal counseling, veterans' counselor. **Physically disabled:** Services for visually, speech, hearing impaired.

**Contact.** E-mail: admrec@uccs.edu
Phone: (719) 255-3383 Toll-free number: (800) 990-8227 ext. 3383
Fax: (719) 255-3116
Steve Ellis, Director of Admissions, University of Colorado at Colorado Springs, 1420 Austin Bluffs Parkway, Colorado Springs, CO 80933-7150

---

## University of Colorado at Denver
**Denver, Colorado**
www.ucdenver.edu
CB member
CB code: 4875

- Public 4-year university
- Commuter campus in very large city

---

- 9,060 degree-seeking undergraduates: 27% part-time, 56% women, 5% African American, 11% Asian American, 12% Hispanic American, 1% Native American, 4% international
- 7,476 degree-seeking graduate students
- 61% of applicants admitted
- SAT or ACT (ACT writing optional), application essay required
- 37% graduate within 6 years

**General.** Founded in 1912. Regionally accredited. Library, student center, and classrooms shared with Metropolitan State College and Community College of Denver. **Degrees:** 1,743 bachelor's awarded; master's, professional offered. **ROTC:** Army, Air Force. **Calendar:** Semester, extensive summer session. **Full-time faculty:** 2,420 total; 69% have terminal degrees, 11% minority, 50% women. **Part-time faculty:** 516 total; 31% have terminal degrees, 11% minority, 55% women. **Class size:** 32% < 20, 48% 20-39, 11% 40-49, 7% 50-99, 2% >100. **Special facilities:** Computational math centers, applied psychology center, environmental science center, transportation research center, Fourth World center for study of indigenous law and politics.

**Freshman class profile.** 4,850 applied, 2,941 admitted, 1,053 enrolled.

| Mid 50% test scores | | | |
|---|---|---|---|
| SAT critical reading: | 480-600 | GPA 2.0-2.99: | 26% |
| SAT math: | 490-610 | Rank in top quarter: | 40% |
| ACT composite: | 20-25 | Rank in top tenth: | 16% |
| GPA 3.75 or higher: | 20% | Return as sophomores: | 71% |
| GPA 3.50-3.74: | 16% | Out-of-state: | 8% |
| GPA 3.0-3.49: | 38% | Live on campus: | 28% |
| | | International: | 3% |

**Basis for selection.** Previous academic performance including high school course work and GPA; evidence of academic ability and accomplishments as indicated by test scores; and evidence of maturity, motivation, potential for academic success most important. Audition required of music majors.

**High school preparation.** College-preparatory program recommended. 15 units required. Required and recommended units include English 4, mathematics 3, social studies 2, history 1, science 3 (laboratory 2), foreign language 2 and academic electives 2. 4 math required for engineering and business students.

**2009-2010 Annual costs.** Tuition/fees: $6,657; $19,689 out-of-state. Tuition varies by program. One-time matriculation fee of $115 required. Books/supplies: $1,801. Personal expenses: $2,230.

**2008-2009 Financial aid. Need-based:** 688 full-time freshmen applied for aid; 555 were judged to have need; 555 of these received aid. Average need met was 59%. Average scholarship/grant was $6,292; average loan $3,074. 82% of total undergraduate aid awarded as scholarships/grants, 18% as loans/jobs. **Non-need-based:** Awarded to 859 full-time undergraduates, including 213 freshmen. Scholarships awarded for academics, alumni affiliation, art, job skills, leadership, music/drama, ROTC, state residency.

**Application procedures. Admission:** Priority date 7/22; deadline 9/1. $50 fee, may be waived for applicants with need. Admission notification on a rolling basis. **Financial aid:** Priority date 4/1; no closing date. FAFSA, institutional form required. Applicants notified on a rolling basis starting 5/1.

**Academics.** Learning opportunities through center for internships and cooperative education. **Special study options:** Accelerated study, combined bachelor's/graduate degree, cooperative education, cross-registration, distance learning, double major, ESL, honors, independent study, internships, liberal arts/career combination, student-designed major, study abroad, teacher certification program, weekend college. **Credit/placement by examination:** AP, CLEP, IB, institutional tests. 30 credit hours maximum toward bachelor's degree. **Support services:** Learning center, study skills assistance, tutoring, writing center.

**Majors. Biology:** General, biomedical sciences. **Business:** General, human resources. **Communications:** General. **Computer sciences:** General. **Engineering:** Civil, electrical, mechanical. **Foreign languages:** French, Spanish. **Health:** Dental hygiene, nursing (RN). **History:** General. **Interdisciplinary:** Global studies. **Math:** General. **Philosophy/religion:** Philosophy. **Physical sciences:** Chemistry, physics. **Psychology:** General. **Social sciences:** Anthropology, economics, geography, political science, sociology. **Visual/performing arts:** Dramatic, studio arts.

**Most popular majors.** Biology 8%, business/marketing 20%, communications/journalism 7%, engineering/engineering technologies 6%, health sciences 14%, psychology 9%, social sciences 11%, visual/performing arts 12%.

**Computing on campus.** 205 workstations in library, computer center, student center. Dormitories wired for high-speed internet access. Commuter students can connect to campus network. Online course registration, online library, helpline, student web hosting, wireless network available.

**Student life. Freshman orientation:** Mandatory. **Housing:** Coed dorms, wellness housing available. **Activities:** Jazz band, choral groups, dance, drama, music ensembles, musical theater, student government, student newspaper, more than 60 groups available.

**Athletics. Intramural:** Basketball, racquetball, tennis, volleyball.

**Student services.** Alcohol/substance abuse counseling, career counseling, student employment services, financial aid counseling, health services, legal services, minority student services, on-campus daycare, personal counseling, placement for graduates, veterans' counselor, women's services. **Physically disabled:** Services for visually, speech, hearing impaired.

**Contact.** E-mail: admissions@ucdenver.edu
Phone: (303) 556-2704 Fax: (303) 556-4838
Barbara Edwards, Director of Admissions, University of Colorado at Denver, Box 173364, Campus Box 167, Denver, CO 80217-3364

---

## University of Denver
Denver, Colorado                                    CB member
www.du.edu                                          CB code: 4842

▶ Private 4-year university affiliated with United Methodist Church
▶ Residential campus in very large city
▶ 5,314 degree-seeking undergraduates: 10% part-time, 56% women, 4% African American, 5% Asian American, 8% Hispanic American, 1% Native American, 6% international
▶ 6,104 degree-seeking graduate students
▶ 70% of applicants admitted
▶ SAT or ACT (ACT writing optional), application essay required
▶ 74% graduate within 6 years; 16% enter graduate study

**General.** Founded in 1864. Regionally accredited. **Degrees:** 1,319 bachelor's awarded; master's, doctoral, professional offered. **ROTC:** Army, Air Force. **Location:** 8 miles from downtown. **Calendar:** Quarter, limited summer session. **Full-time faculty:** 662 total; 83% have terminal degrees, 14% minority, 46% women. **Part-time faculty:** 644 total; 5% have terminal degrees, 8% minority, 48% women. **Class size:** 62% < 20, 29% 20-39, 5% 40-49, 5% 50-99, less than 1% >100. **Special facilities:** Observatory, high-altitude research laboratory, mechanical engineering testing facility, early learning center, center for gifted children.

**Freshman class profile.** 8,411 applied, 5,926 admitted, 1,207 enrolled.

| Mid 50% test scores | | Rank in top quarter: | 75% |
|---|---|---|---|
| SAT critical reading: | 540-640 | Rank in top tenth: | 45% |
| SAT math: | 550-650 | End year in good standing: | 99% |
| SAT writing: | 520-620 | Return as sophomores: | 86% |
| ACT composite: | 24-29 | Out-of-state: | 53% |
| GPA 3.75 or higher: | 52% | Live on campus: | 94% |
| GPA 3.50-3.74: | 23% | International: | 6% |
| GPA 3.0-3.49: | 21% | Fraternities: | 24% |
| GPA 2.0-2.99: | 4% | Sororities: | 19% |

**Basis for selection.** GPA, test scores and strength of curriculum most important. Interview, academic maturity, contributions to school and community activities, leadership also important. Recommendations from teacher and counselor, and personal essay considered. Interview strongly encouraged. Audition required of music majors. Portfolio recommended of art majors. **Homeschooled:** Letter of recommendation (nonparent) required.

**High school preparation.** College-preparatory program recommended. Recommended units include English 4, mathematics 4, social studies 2, history 2, science 4 (laboratory 2) and foreign language 4.

**2009-2010 Annual costs.** Tuition/fees: $35,481. Room/board: $9,900.

**2008-2009 Financial aid. Non-need-based:** Scholarships awarded for academics, art, athletics, leadership, music/drama, state residency.

**Application procedures. Admission:** Closing date 1/15 (postmark date). $50 fee, may be waived for applicants with need. Admission notification 3/15. Must reply by 5/1. **Financial aid:** Priority date 3/1; no closing date. FAFSA, CSS PROFILE required.

**Academics.** Special 3-week inter-term courses available for focused concentration. **Special study options:** Accelerated study, combined bachelor's/ graduate degree, cooperative education, distance learning, double major, dual

enrollment of high school students, ESL, honors, independent study, internships, semester at sea, student-designed major, study abroad, teacher certification program, Washington semester, weekend college. Learning disability services. **Credit/placement by examination:** AP, CLEP, IB, institutional tests. 45 credit hours maximum toward bachelor's degree. **Support services:** Learning center, reduced course load, study skills assistance, tutoring, writing center.

**Majors. Agriculture:** Animal sciences. **Area/ethnic studies:** Asian-American, women's. **Biology:** General, biochemistry, bioinformatics, ecology, molecular. **Business:** General, accounting, business admin, construction management, finance, hospitality admin, international, management information systems, managerial economics, marketing, organizational behavior, real estate, statistics. **Communications:** General, digital media, journalism. **Computer sciences:** Computer science, information technology, systems analysis. **Conservation:** Environmental science. **Engineering:** General, computer, electrical, mechanical. **Foreign languages:** French, German, Italian, Russian, Spanish. **History:** General. **Interdisciplinary:** Biological/ physical sciences, global studies, science/society. **Legal studies:** General. **Liberal arts:** Arts/sciences. **Math:** General. **Philosophy/religion:** Philosophy, religion. **Physical sciences:** General, chemistry, physics. **Psychology:** General. **Public administration:** Policy analysis. **Social sciences:** General, anthropology, criminology, economics, geography, international relations, political science, sociology. **Visual/performing arts:** Art, art history/ conservation, dramatic, graphic design, music performance, musicology. **Other:** Computer software and media applications, Ethnic, cultural, minority, gender studies.

**Most popular majors.** Biology 7%, business/marketing 46%, communications/journalism 8%, psychology 6%, social sciences 13%, visual/ performing arts 6%.

**Computing on campus.** PC or laptop required. 200 workstations in dormitories, library, computer center, student center. Dormitories wired for high-speed internet access and linked to campus network. Commuter students can connect to campus network. Online course registration, online library, helpline, repair service, student web hosting, wireless network available.

**Student life. Freshman orientation:** Mandatory. Preregistration for classes offered. Held first week of September for 5 days; includes programs for parents/families. **Policies:** Code of conduct, honor code in effect. **Housing:** Guaranteed on-campus for freshmen. Coed dorms, apartments, fraternity/ sorority housing, wellness housing available. $200 nonrefundable deposit, deadline 5/1. **Activities:** Bands, campus ministries, choral groups, dance, drama, film society, international student organizations, literary magazine, music ensembles, Model UN, musical theater, opera, radio station, student government, student newspaper, symphony orchestra, Campus Crusade for Christ, Chabad, Fellowship of Catholic University Students, Hillel, College Democrats, College Republicans, Students for a Democratic Society, Students for a Free Tibet, environmental team, volunteer club.

**Athletics. NCAA. Intercollegiate:** Basketball, diving, golf, gymnastics W, ice hockey M, lacrosse, skiing, soccer, swimming, tennis, volleyball W. **Intramural:** Basketball, football (non-tackle), ice hockey M, soccer, softball. **Team name:** Pioneers.

**Student services.** Adult student services, alcohol/substance abuse counseling, chaplain/spiritual director, career counseling, student employment services, financial aid counseling, health services, minority student services, personal counseling, placement for graduates, women's services. **Physically disabled:** Services for visually, speech, hearing impaired. **Learning disabled:** Comprehensive services available.

**Contact.** E-mail: admission@du.edu
Phone: (303) 871-2036 Toll-free number: (800) 525-9495
Fax: (303) 871-3301
Thomas Willoughby, Vice Chancellor, Enrollment, University of Denver, 2197 South University Boulevard, Denver, CO 80208

---

## University of Northern Colorado
Greeley, Colorado                                   CB member
www.unco.edu                                        CB code: 4074

▶ Public 4-year university
▶ Commuter campus in small city
▶ 9,710 degree-seeking undergraduates: 8% part-time, 61% women
▶ 1,876 degree-seeking graduate students
▶ 92% of applicants admitted
▶ SAT or ACT (ACT writing optional) required
▶ 48% graduate within 6 years

**General.** Founded in 1889. Regionally accredited. **Degrees:** 2,012 bachelor's awarded; master's, doctoral, professional offered. **ROTC:** Army, Air

Force. **Location:** 50 miles from Denver; 50 miles from Cheyenne, Wyoming. **Calendar:** Semester, limited summer session. **Full-time faculty:** 491 total; 11% minority, 50% women. **Part-time faculty:** 214 total; 6% minority, 68% women. **Class size:** 26% < 20, 52% 20-39, 8% 40-49, 13% 50-99, 2% >100. **Special facilities:** African-American cultural center, Hispanic cultural center, Native American and Asian Pacific cultural center.

**Freshman class profile.** 6,136 applied, 5,661 admitted, 2,351 enrolled.

| Mid 50% test scores | | | |
|---|---|---|---|
| SAT critical reading: | 470-590 | GPA 3.0-3.49: | 32% |
| SAT math: | 470-590 | GPA 2.0-2.99: | 37% |
| SAT writing: | 450-570 | Rank in top quarter: | 33% |
| ACT composite: | 20-25 | Rank in top tenth: | 11% |
| GPA 3.75 or higher: | 18% | End year in good standing: | 75% |
| GPA 3.50-3.74: | 13% | Return as sophomores: | 69% |
| | | Out-of-state: | 10% |

**Basis for selection.** Expected 2.9 GPA; 21 ACT or 970 SAT (exclusive of Writing). Higher ACT/SAT score can compensate for lower GPA and higher GPA can compensate for lower test score. Audition required of music majors.

**High school preparation.** College-preparatory program recommended. 15 units required. Required and recommended units include English 4, mathematics 3-4, social studies 3, science 3 (laboratory 2), foreign language 1 and academic electives 2. Math should include 2 algebra, additional higher level math unit.

**2009-2010 Annual costs.** Tuition/fees: $5,116; $15,364 out-of-state. Costs reflect student share of tuition after the Colorado College Opportunity Fund. Room/board: $8,370. Books/supplies: $1,300. Personal expenses: $2,854.

**2008-2009 Financial aid. Need-based:** 1,810 full-time freshmen applied for aid; 961 were judged to have need; 915 of these received aid. Average need met was 100%. Average scholarship/grant was $5,230; average loan $3,547. 49% of total undergraduate aid awarded as scholarships/grants, 51% as loans/jobs. **Non-need-based:** Awarded to 3,082 full-time undergraduates, including 1,157 freshmen. Scholarships awarded for academics, athletics, music/drama.

**Application procedures. Admission:** Priority date 8/1; no deadline. $45 fee, may be waived for applicants with need. Admission notification on a rolling basis. **Financial aid:** Priority date 3/1; no closing date. FAFSA required. Applicants notified on a rolling basis starting 4/15; must reply within 4 week(s) of notification.

**Academics. Special study options:** Cooperative education, cross-registration, distance learning, double major, ESL, exchange student, external degree, honors, independent study, internships, semester at sea, student-designed major, study abroad, teacher certification program. **Credit/placement by examination:** AP, CLEP, IB, institutional tests. 30 credit hours maximum toward bachelor's degree. **Support services:** Learning center, reduced course load, remedial instruction, study skills assistance, tutoring, writing center.

**Majors. Area/ethnic studies:** African-American, Chicano/Hispanic-American/Latino. **Biology:** General. **Business:** Business admin. **Communications:** General, journalism. **Education:** Music, special. **Family/consumer sciences:** Aging. **Foreign languages:** General, sign language interpretation, Spanish. **Health:** Audiology/hearing, audiology/speech pathology, dietetics, health care admin, health services, nursing (RN), public health ed, speech pathology, vocational rehab counseling. **History:** General. **Math:** General. **Parks/recreation:** Exercise sciences, facilities management. **Philosophy/religion:** Philosophy. **Physical sciences:** Chemistry, geology, physics. **Protective services:** Criminal justice. **Psychology:** General. **Public administration:** Human services. **Social sciences:** General, anthropology, economics, geography, political science, sociology. **Visual/performing arts:** Dramatic, studio arts.

**Most popular majors.** Business/marketing 14%, communications/journalism 10%, health sciences 11%, interdisciplinary studies 14%, parks/recreation 7%, psychology 7%, social sciences 7%, visual/performing arts 7%.

**Computing on campus.** 1,169 workstations in dormitories, library, computer center, student center. Dormitories wired for high-speed internet access and linked to campus network. Commuter students can connect to campus network. Online course registration, online library, helpline, repair service, wireless network available.

**Student life. Freshman orientation:** Available. Preregistration for classes offered. **Housing:** Guaranteed on-campus for all undergraduates. Coed dorms, single-sex dorms, special housing for disabled, apartments, fraternity/sorority housing, wellness housing available. $200 nonrefundable deposit. **Activities:** Bands, campus ministries, choral groups, dance, drama, film society, international student organizations, literary magazine, music ensembles, musical theater, opera, radio station, student government, student

newspaper, symphony orchestra, TV station, African-American student union, Hispanic students organization, Native American student services, Asian/Pacific American student services.

**Athletics.** NCAA. **Intercollegiate:** Baseball M, basketball, cross-country W, diving W, football (tackle) M, golf, soccer W, softball W, swimming W, tennis, track and field, volleyball W, wrestling M. **Intramural:** Basketball, football (non-tackle), golf, racquetball, soccer, softball, table tennis, tennis, volleyball, water polo. **Team name:** Bears.

**Student services.** Adult student services, alcohol/substance abuse counseling, chaplain/spiritual director, career counseling, student employment services, financial aid counseling, health services, legal services, minority student services, personal counseling, placement for graduates, veterans' counselor, women's services. **Physically disabled:** Services for visually, speech, hearing impaired.

**Contact.** E-mail: admissions.help@unco.edu
Phone: (970) 351-2881 Toll-free number: (888) 700-4862
Fax: (970) 351-2984
Director of Admissions, University of Northern Colorado, 1862 10th Avenue, Campus Box 10, Greeley, CO 80639

## Western State College of Colorado
**Gunnison, Colorado**
**www.western.edu**                                   CB code: 4946

- Public 4-year liberal arts college
- Residential campus in small town
- 2,193 degree-seeking undergraduates
- 72% of applicants admitted
- SAT or ACT (ACT writing optional) required

**General.** Founded in 1901. Regionally accredited. College-based mountain search and rescue team. **Degrees:** 406 bachelor's awarded. **Location:** 200 miles from Denver. **Calendar:** Semester, limited summer session. **Full-time faculty:** 107 total. **Part-time faculty:** 43 total. **Class size:** 49% < 20, 41% 20-39, 9% 40-49, 1% 50-99, less than 1% >100. **Special facilities:** Botanical gardens, archaeological site, dinosaur reconstruction lab.

**Freshman class profile.** 2,318 applied, 1,658 admitted, 499 enrolled.

| Mid 50% test scores | | | |
|---|---|---|---|
| SAT critical reading: | 450-550 | GPA 3.0-3.49: | 35% |
| SAT math: | 470-580 | GPA 2.0-2.99: | 48% |
| ACT composite: | 19-24 | Rank in top quarter: | 18% |
| GPA 3.75 or higher: | 8% | Rank in top tenth: | 7% |
| GPA 3.50-3.74: | 8% | Out-of-state: | 35% |
| | | Live on campus: | 94% |

**Basis for selection.** School achievement record, test scores very important; recommendations considered. Essay recommended. Interview recommended for academically weak applicants.

**High school preparation.** Required and recommended units include English 4, mathematics 3-4, social studies 2, history 2, science 3 (laboratory 2) and foreign language 2.

**2009-2010 Annual costs.** Tuition/fees: $4,064; $13,260 out-of-state. Room/board: $8,324. Books/supplies: $950. Personal expenses: $1,226.

**2009-2010 Financial aid. Non-need-based:** Scholarships awarded for academics, alumni affiliation, art, athletics, leadership, music/drama.

**Application procedures. Admission:** Priority date 3/15; deadline 6/1 (postmark date). $30 fee, may be waived for applicants with need. Admission notification on a rolling basis beginning on or about 11/1. Must reply by May 1 or within 2 week(s) if notified thereafter. **Financial aid:** Priority date 4/1; no closing date. FAFSA required. Applicants notified on a rolling basis starting 4/1; must reply within 4 week(s) of notification.

**Academics. Special study options:** Combined bachelor's/graduate degree, cooperative education, double major, dual enrollment of high school students, exchange student, honors, independent study, internships, liberal arts/career combination, semester at sea, study abroad, teacher certification program. **Credit/placement by examination:** AP, CLEP, IB, SAT, ACT, institutional tests. 30 credit hours maximum toward bachelor's degree. **Support services:** Study skills assistance, tutoring, writing center.

**Majors. Biology:** General. **Business:** Accounting, business admin, management information systems, resort management. **Communications:** General. **Conservation:** Environmental studies. **Education:** Art, elementary, English, foreign languages, mathematics, music, physical, science, social science, social studies, special. **Foreign languages:** Spanish. **History:** General. **Legal studies:** Prelaw. **Math:** General. **Parks/recreation:** Exercise sciences. **Physical sciences:** Chemistry, geology. **Protective services:** Criminal justice, police science. **Psychology:** General. **Social sciences:** Anthropology, economics, political science, sociology. **Visual/performing arts:** Art, music management, studio arts. **Other:** Outdoor leadership.

**Computing on campus.** 168 workstations in dormitories, library, student center. Dormitories linked to campus network. Commuter students can connect to campus network. Online course registration available.

**Student life. Freshman orientation:** Available, $65 fee. Preregistration for classes offered. Wilderness-based orientation available. **Housing:** Guaranteed on-campus for freshmen. Coed dorms, single-sex dorms, apartments available. $100 nonrefundable deposit. **Activities:** Bands, choral groups, dance, drama, literary magazine, music ensembles, radio station, student government, student newspaper, symphony orchestra, TV station, Hillel, black student alliance, Amigos, Campus Crusade, Hui-O-Ka-Aina, lesbian-gay-bisexual alliance, Newman club, Baptist student union, Christian athletes fellowship, women's action coalition.

**Athletics.** NCAA. **Intercollegiate:** Basketball, cross-country, football (tackle) M, skiing, track and field, volleyball W, wrestling M. **Intramural:** Baseball M, basketball, golf, ice hockey M, lacrosse, rugby, skiing, soccer, softball, swimming, tennis, track and field, volleyball, wrestling M. **Team name:** Mountaineers.

**Student services.** Adult student services, career counseling, health services, on-campus daycare, personal counseling, veterans' counselor. **Physically disabled:** Services for visually, hearing impaired. **Learning disabled:** Comprehensive services available.

**Contact.** E-mail: discover@western.edu
Phone: (970) 943-2119 Toll-free number: (800) 876-5309
Fax: (970) 943-2212
Tim Albers, Director of Admissions, Western State College of Colorado, 600 North Adams Street, Gunnison, CO 81231

## Westwood College: Denver North
Denver, Colorado
www.westwood.edu/locations/colorado/denver-north-campus
CB code: 3948

♦ For-profit 4-year technical college
♦ Commuter campus in very large city
♦ 4,215 full-time, degree-seeking undergraduates
♦ 35 graduate students
♦ Interview required

**General.** Founded in 1953. Accredited by ACCSC. **Degrees:** 159 bachelor's, 88 associate awarded. **Location:** 5 miles from downtown. **Calendar:** 5 ten-week terms per year. Extensive summer session. **Full-time faculty:** 50 total. **Part-time faculty:** 80 total.

**Basis for selection.** Institutional test (ACCUPLACER) and interview most important. Developmental courses may be required for those who do not pass entrance examination. SAT or ACT recommended. Accuplacer waived for students with sufficient scores on SAT or ACT.

**High school preparation.** At least 1 algebra required for electronics, drafting and surveying programs. General math required for all other programs.

**2009-2010 Annual costs.** Full-time tuition per 10-week term, $4,921 for most programs. Books/supplies: $370. Personal expenses: $2,000.

**Financial aid. Non-need-based:** Scholarships awarded for academics, state residency.

**Application procedures. Admission:** No deadline. $25 fee. Admission notification on a rolling basis. **Financial aid:** No deadline. FAFSA, institutional form required. Applicants notified on a rolling basis starting 1/1; must reply within 2 week(s) of notification.

**Academics.** Instruction and emphasis on laboratory work and practical application. **Special study options:** Accelerated study, cooperative education, distance learning, independent study, internships, liberal arts/career combination. **Credit/placement by examination:** CLEP, institutional tests. 69 credit hours maximum toward associate degree, 140 toward bachelor's. **Support services:** Learning center, remedial instruction, study skills assistance, tutoring.

**Majors. Architecture:** Interior. **Business:** General, accounting, business admin, e-commerce, management information systems, marketing. **Communications:** General. **Communications technology:** Graphic/printing. **Computer sciences:** General, computer graphics, information systems, networking, security, web page design, webmaster. **Engineering:** Electrical.

**Engineering technology:** Electrical. **Mechanic/repair:** Electronics/electrical. **Protective services:** Law enforcement admin. **Visual/performing arts:** Commercial/advertising art, design, graphic design.

**Most popular majors.** Business/marketing 20%, computer/information sciences 44%, engineering/engineering technologies 15%, visual/performing arts 21%.

**Computing on campus.** 50 workstations in library, computer center. Online library available.

**Student life. Freshman orientation:** Mandatory. Preregistration for classes offered. **Policies:** No-tolerance drug/alcohol policy.

**Student services.** Career counseling, student employment services, financial aid counseling, placement for graduates, veterans' counselor. **Physically disabled:** Services for visually impaired.

**Contact.** E-mail: rdejong@westwood.edu
Phone: (303) 650-5050 Fax: (303) 487-0214
Ron DeJong, Director of Admissions, Westwood College: Denver North, 7350 North Broadway, Denver, CO 80221

## Westwood College: Denver South
Denver, Colorado
www.westwood.edu/locations/colorado/denver-south-campus

♦ For-profit 4-year technical and career college
♦ Commuter campus in very large city
♦ 455 degree-seeking undergraduates
♦ Interview required

**General.** Accredited by ACCSC. **Degrees:** 104 bachelor's, 28 associate awarded. **Calendar:** Continuous, extensive summer session. **Full-time faculty:** 9 total. **Part-time faculty:** 24 total.

**Freshman class profile.** 257 applied, 257 admitted, 223 enrolled.

**Basis for selection.** Open admission. Admission based on ACT, SAT, or ACCUPLACER scores. Non-native English speakers must take ESL course. 475 TOEFL, high school diploma or GED, or proof of completion of accredited U.S. college program required.

**2009-2010 Annual costs.** Tuition/fees: $25,580. Tuition and fees may vary by program. Books/supplies: $1,250. Personal expenses: $2,534.

**Application procedures. Admission:** No deadline. $25 fee. Admission notification on a rolling basis. **Financial aid:** No deadline. FAFSA, institutional form required. Applicants notified on a rolling basis; must reply within 2 week(s) of notification.

**Academics. Special study options:** Accelerated study, distance learning, independent study, weekend college. **Credit/placement by examination:** CLEP, institutional tests. 67 credit hours maximum toward associate degree, 135 toward bachelor's. **Support services:** Reduced course load, remedial instruction, study skills assistance, tutoring, writing center.

**Majors. Architecture:** Interior. **Business:** E-commerce, fashion. **Communications technology:** Animation/special effects, desktop publishing, graphics. **Computer sciences:** Computer graphics, LAN/WAN management, networking, security, system admin, web page design, webmaster. **Protective services:** Law enforcement admin. **Visual/performing arts:** Commercial/advertising art, design, graphic design, interior design.

**Computing on campus.** 300 workstations in library, computer center, student center. Commuter students can connect to campus network. Online course registration, online library, wireless network available.

**Student life. Freshman orientation:** Mandatory. Preregistration for classes offered.

**Student services.** Adult student services, career counseling, student employment services, financial aid counseling, placement for graduates.

**Contact.** Phone: (303) 934-1122 Fax: (303) 934-2583
Michael Rushak, Director of Admissions, Westwood College: Denver South, 3150 South Sheridan Boulevard, Denver, CO 80227-5507

## Yeshiva Toras Chaim Talmudical Seminary
Denver, Colorado
CB code: 7008

♦ Private 4-year rabbinical college for men affiliated with Jewish faith
♦ Very large city

**General.** Accredited by AARTS. **Calendar:** Trimester.

**Contact.**   Phone: (303) 629-8200
1555 Stuart Street PO Box 40067, Denver, CO 80204

# Connecticut

## Albertus Magnus College

New Haven, Connecticut — **CB member**
www.albertus.edu — **CB code: 3001**

- Private 4-year liberal arts college affiliated with Roman Catholic Church
- Residential campus in small city
- 1,635 degree-seeking undergraduates: 8% part-time, 69% women, 28% African American, 1% Asian American, 11% Hispanic American
- 385 degree-seeking graduate students
- 82% of applicants admitted
- SAT or ACT (ACT writing optional), application essay required
- 58% graduate within 6 years

**General.** Founded in 1925. Regionally accredited. Majority of students enrolled in adult education and graduate programs. Approximately 500 undergraduates are traditional age and are able to live on campus. **Degrees:** 401 bachelor's, 111 associate awarded; master's offered. **Location:** 90 miles from New York City. **Calendar:** Semester, limited summer session. **Full-time faculty:** 43 total; 81% have terminal degrees, 5% minority, 44% women. **Part-time faculty:** 26 total; 50% have terminal degrees, 12% minority, 65% women. **Class size:** 69% < 20, 31% 20-39.

**Freshman class profile.** 654 applied, 538 admitted, 154 enrolled.

| Mid 50% test scores | | | |
|---|---|---|---|
| SAT critical reading: | 490-540 | GPA 2.0-2.99: | 62% |
| SAT math: | 470-520 | Rank in top quarter: | 28% |
| SAT writing: | 400-500 | Rank in top tenth: | 10% |
| GPA 3.75 or higher: | 4% | End year in good standing: | 91% |
| GPA 3.50-3.74: | 6% | Return as sophomores: | 79% |
| GPA 3.0-3.49: | 26% | Out-of-state: | 16% |

**Basis for selection.** School achievement record most important. Recommendations, test scores, interview, school and community activities also considered. **Homeschooled:** Letter of recommendation (nonparent) required. GED preferred.

**High school preparation.** 16 units required. Required and recommended units include English 4, mathematics 2-3, social studies 2-3, science 2-3 (laboratory 1) and foreign language 3.

**2009-2010 Annual costs.** Tuition/fees: $23,126. Room/board: $9,914. Books/supplies: $620. Personal expenses: $940.

**2008-2009 Financial aid. Need-based:** 665 full-time freshmen applied for aid; 443 were judged to have need; 399 of these received aid. Average need met was 52%. Average scholarship/grant was $12,529; average loan $3,416. 43% of total undergraduate aid awarded as scholarships/grants, 57% as loans/jobs. **Non-need-based:** Awarded to 74 full-time undergraduates, including 36 freshmen. Scholarships awarded for academics, art, job skills, leadership, music/drama, religious affiliation, state residency.

**Application procedures. Admission:** No deadline. $35 fee, may be waived for applicants with need. Admission notification on a rolling basis beginning on or about 12/1. Must reply by May 1 or within 4 week(s) if notified thereafter. **Financial aid:** Priority date 2/28; no closing date. FAFSA required. Applicants notified on a rolling basis starting 3/1; must reply within 2 week(s) of notification.

**Academics. Special study options:** Accelerated study, double major, honors, independent study, internships, liberal arts/career combination, student-designed major, teacher certification program. **Credit/placement by examination:** AP, CLEP, SAT, institutional tests. 21 credit hours maximum toward associate degree, 45 toward bachelor's. **Support services:** Learning center, reduced course load, study skills assistance, tutoring, writing center.

**Majors. Biology:** General. **Business:** Accounting, business admin, finance, international, management information systems, managerial economics. **Communications:** General, advertising, media studies. **Computer sciences:** Information systems. **Education:** General, art, biology, business, chemistry, English, history, mathematics, middle, science, secondary, social studies, Spanish. **Foreign languages:** Spanish. **Health:** Art therapy, premedicine. **History:** General. **Legal studies:** Prelaw. **Liberal arts:** Arts/sciences. **Math:**

General. **Philosophy/religion:** Philosophy, religion. **Physical sciences:** Chemistry. **Protective services:** Criminal justice. **Psychology:** General. **Public administration:** Human services, social work. **Social sciences:** General, economics, political science, sociology. **Visual/performing arts:** General, art, art history/conservation, commercial/advertising art, dramatic, photography, studio arts. **Other:** Performance communications.

**Most popular majors.** Business/marketing 51%, education 7%, psychology 7%, social sciences 10%.

**Computing on campus.** 175 workstations in library, computer center, student center. Dormitories wired for high-speed internet access and linked to campus network. Commuter students can connect to campus network. Repair service, wireless network available.

**Student life. Freshman orientation:** Mandatory. Preregistration for classes offered. **Housing:** Guaranteed on-campus for all undergraduates. Coed dorms, single-sex dorms, wellness housing available. $400 nonrefundable deposit, deadline 7/1. **Activities:** Campus ministries, choral groups, dance, drama, literary magazine, musical theater, student government, Outspoken Alliance, multicultural student union, Students United for a Better World.

**Athletics.** NCAA. **Intercollegiate:** Baseball M, basketball, cross-country, soccer, softball W, tennis, volleyball W. **Team name:** Falcons.

**Student services.** Adult student services, chaplain/spiritual director, career counseling, student employment services, financial aid counseling, health services, personal counseling, placement for graduates, veterans' counselor.

**Contact.** E-mail: admissions@albertus.edu
Phone: (203) 773-8501 Toll-free number: (800) 578-9160
Fax: (203) 773-5248
Richard LoLatte, Dean of Admissions and Enrollment Management, Albertus Magnus College, 700 Prospect Street, New Haven, CT 06511-1189

## Central Connecticut State University

New Britain, Connecticut — **CB member**
www.ccsu.edu — **CB code: 3898**

- Public 4-year university
- Commuter campus in small city
- 9,570 degree-seeking undergraduates: 18% part-time, 49% women, 8% African American, 3% Asian American, 7% Hispanic American, 1% international
- 2,150 degree-seeking graduate students
- 54% of applicants admitted
- SAT or ACT (ACT writing optional), application essay required
- 49% graduate within 6 years

**General.** Founded in 1849. Regionally accredited. **Degrees:** 1,660 bachelor's awarded; master's, professional offered. **ROTC:** Army, Air Force. **Location:** 9 miles from Hartford. **Calendar:** Semester, extensive summer session. **Full-time faculty:** 433 total; 82% have terminal degrees, 17% minority, 44% women. **Part-time faculty:** 491 total; 13% have terminal degrees, 8% minority, 41% women. **Class size:** 40% < 20, 57% 20-39, less than 1% 40-49, 1% 50-99, less than 1% >100. **Special facilities:** Observatory, planetarium.

**Freshman class profile.** 6,791 applied, 3,697 admitted, 1,288 enrolled.

| Mid 50% test scores | | | |
|---|---|---|---|
| SAT critical reading: | 460-550 | End year in good standing: | 84% |
| SAT math: | 470-560 | Return as sophomores: | 79% |
| SAT writing: | 460-550 | Out-of-state: | 4% |
| Rank in top quarter: | 30% | Live on campus: | 62% |
| Rank in top tenth: | 8% | International: | 1% |

**Basis for selection.** High school record, class rank, SAT scores most important. Letters of recommendation, optional student essay, and resume of activities to assess applicant's attitude toward future success considered. School of Business, social work program, communication program, and School of Education programs require acceptance into majors after admission to the university. Interview optional but would be considered. Audition required for music. **Homeschooled:** Statement describing homeschool structure and mission, transcript of courses and grades, state high school equivalency certificate required.

**High school preparation.** College-preparatory program recommended. 13 units required. Required and recommended units include English 4, mathematics 3, social studies 2, history 1, science 2 (laboratory 1) and foreign language 3. Social science should include US history; math should include algebra I and II and geometry.

**2009-2010 Annual costs.** Tuition/fees: $7,414; $17,106 out-of-state. Room/board: $9,122. Books/supplies: $1,100. Personal expenses: $1,920.

**2008-2009 Financial aid. Non-need-based:** Scholarships awarded for academics, athletics, minority status.

**Application procedures. Admission:** Priority date 10/1; deadline 6/1 (receipt date). $50 fee, may be waived for applicants with need. Admission notification on a rolling basis beginning on or about 12/1. Must reply by May 1 or within 2 week(s) if notified thereafter. **Financial aid:** Priority date 3/1, closing date 9/15. FAFSA required. Applicants notified on a rolling basis starting 3/30; must reply within 2 week(s) of notification.

**Academics. Special study options:** Cooperative education, cross-registration, distance learning, double major, dual enrollment of high school students, ESL, exchange student, honors, independent study, internships, student-designed major, study abroad, teacher certification program. Undergraduates may take graduate classes. **Credit/placement by examination:** AP, CLEP, IB, SAT, institutional tests. 30 credit hours maximum toward bachelor's degree. **Support services:** Learning center, pre-admission summer program, reduced course load, remedial instruction, study skills assistance, tutoring, writing center.

**Majors. Biology:** General, biochemistry, molecular. **Business:** Accounting, business admin, construction management, finance, management information systems, marketing, organizational behavior, travel services. **Communications:** General, journalism. **Computer sciences:** General. **Construction:** General. **Education:** Art, music, secondary, technology/industrial arts. **Engineering:** Civil, electrical, mechanical. **Engineering technology:** Civil, computer, industrial, manufacturing, mechanical. **Foreign languages:** French, German, Italian, Spanish. **Health:** Athletic training, nursing (RN). **History:** General. **Interdisciplinary:** Global studies. **Math:** General. **Philosophy/religion:** Philosophy. **Physical sciences:** Chemistry, geology, physics. **Psychology:** General. **Public administration:** Social work. **Social sciences:** General, anthropology, criminology, economics, geography, political science, sociology. **Visual/performing arts:** Art, design, dramatic. **Other:** Interdisciplinary science, Special studies.

**Most popular majors.** Business/marketing 30%, education 11%, engineering/engineering technologies 7%, English 6%, psychology 9%, social sciences 12%.

**Computing on campus.** 400 workstations in dormitories, library, computer center, student center. Dormitories wired for high-speed internet access and linked to campus network. Commuter students can connect to campus network. Online course registration, online library, helpline, repair service, wireless network available.

**Student life. Freshman orientation:** Available, $65 fee. Preregistration for classes offered. One-day program in late June or early July. **Housing:** Coed dorms, single-sex dorms available. $250 nonrefundable deposit, deadline 5/1. **Activities:** Bands, campus ministries, choral groups, dance, drama, film society, international student organizations, literary magazine, music ensembles, musical theater, radio station, student government, student newspaper, TV station, Newman Club, Union of Jewish Students, Christian Fellowship, Christian Science Organization, Afro-American and African students, Latin American student association.

**Athletics.** NCAA. **Intercollegiate:** Baseball M, basketball, cross-country, diving W, football (tackle) M, golf, lacrosse W, soccer, softball W, swimming W, track and field, volleyball W. **Intramural:** Badminton, basketball, field hockey W, football (tackle) M, gymnastics W, lacrosse M, rugby, soccer, softball W, tennis, volleyball, water polo M. **Team name:** Blue Devils.

**Student services.** Adult student services, alcohol/substance abuse counseling, chaplain/spiritual director, career counseling, student employment services, financial aid counseling, health services, minority student services, on-campus daycare, personal counseling, placement for graduates, veterans' counselor, women's services. **Physically disabled:** Services for visually, speech, hearing impaired.

**Contact.** E-mail: admissions@ccsu.edu
Phone: (860) 832-2278 Fax: (860) 832-2295
Lawrence Hall, Director of Admissions, Central Connecticut State University, 1615 Stanley Street, New Britain, CT 06050

## Charter Oak State College
**New Britain, Connecticut** — **CB member**
**www.charteroak.edu** — **CB code: 0870**

- Public 4-year virtual liberal arts college
- Commuter campus in small city
- 1,685 degree-seeking undergraduates: 91% part-time, 60% women, 14% African American, 2% Asian American, 8% Hispanic American, 1% Native American

**General.** Founded in 1973. Regionally accredited. Nearly all courses are on-line. **Degrees:** 424 bachelor's, 59 associate awarded. **Location:** 5 miles from Hartford. **Calendar:** Continuous, limited summer session. **Part-time faculty:** 97 total; 40% have terminal degrees, 9% minority, 50% women. **Class size:** 66% < 20, 31% 20-39, 3% 40-49.

**Basis for selection.** 9 college-level credits must be completed before enrolling. May be earned through college courses, testing, or ACE/PONSI recommendations for noncollege-sponsored instruction.

**2009-2010 Annual costs.** Academic Services Fee: In-state associate degree or bachelor's degree, $1,055; out-of-state $1,390. Books and supplies $1,000. Cost of education varies due to students having option to take courses at other institutions.

**2008-2009 Financial aid.** All financial aid based on need. 30% of total undergraduate aid awarded as scholarships/grants, 70% as loans/jobs.

**Application procedures. Admission:** No deadline. $75 fee, may be waived for applicants with need. Admission notification on a rolling basis. **Financial aid:** No deadline. FAFSA, institutional form required. Applicants notified on a rolling basis starting 8/23.

**Academics.** Tutoring and writing center available online free to students. **Special study options:** Accelerated study, distance learning, dual enrollment of high school students, external degree, independent study, liberal arts/career combination, student-designed major. Students can take courses at any regionally accredited institution. **Credit/placement by examination:** AP, CLEP, institutional tests. 60 credit hours maximum toward associate degree, 120 toward bachelor's. Unlimited number of hours of credit by examination may be counted toward degree. **Support services:** Tutoring, writing center.

**Majors. Liberal arts:** Arts/sciences.

**Computing on campus.** Online library, helpline, wireless network available.

**Student life. Activities:** Student government.

**Student services.** Adult student services, financial aid counseling, veterans' counselor.

**Contact.** E-mail: info@charteroak.edu
Phone: (860) 832-3800 Fax: (860) 832-3999
Lori Pendleton, Director of Admission, Charter Oak State College, 55 Paul Manafort Drive, New Britain, CT 06053-2150

## Connecticut College
**New London, Connecticut** — **CB member**
**www.conncoll.edu** — **CB code: 3284**

- Private 4-year liberal arts college
- Residential campus in large town
- 1,777 degree-seeking undergraduates: 61% women, 4% African American, 5% Asian American, 6% Hispanic American, 4% international
- 5 degree-seeking graduate students
- 37% of applicants admitted
- Application essay required
- 85% graduate within 6 years; 25% enter graduate study

**General.** Founded in 1911. Regionally accredited. **Degrees:** 437 bachelor's awarded; master's offered. **Location:** 105 miles from Boston, 124 miles from New York City. **Calendar:** Semester, limited summer session. **Full-time faculty:** 177 total; 91% have terminal degrees, 23% minority, 46% women. **Part-time faculty:** 65 total; 26% have terminal degrees, 9% minority, 51% women. **Special facilities:** 750-acre arboretum, greenhouse, ion accelerator, refracting telescope and observatory, scanning and transmission electron microscopes, nuclear magnetic resonance spectrometer, tunable diode laser spectroscopy laboratory, center for electronic and digital sound, neuroscience and animal behavior laboratories, clinical and social psychology research observation suites.

**Freshman class profile.** 4,733 applied, 1,738 admitted, 502 enrolled.

| Mid 50% test scores | | | |
|---|---|---|---|
| SAT critical reading: | 610-700 | Rank in top tenth: | 56% |
| SAT math: | 610-690 | Return as sophomores: | 90% |
| SAT writing: | 620-710 | Out-of-state: | 88% |
| ACT composite: | 25-30 | Live on campus: | 100% |
| Rank in top quarter: | 93% | International: | 5% |

**Basis for selection.** School achievement record most important. Recommendations, personal qualities, personal essay, special talents, extracurricular activities also significant. Interview recommended. Audition recommended for dance or music majors. Portfolio recommended for art majors. **Homeschooled:** State high school equivalency certificate, letter of recommendation (nonparent) required. Extracurricular activities encouraged.

**High school preparation.** College-preparatory program recommended.

**2010-2011 Annual costs.** Tuition/fees: $43,990. Room/board: $9,120. Books/supplies: $1,000. Personal expenses: $500.

**2009-2010 Financial aid.** All financial aid based on need. 297 full-time freshmen applied for aid; 237 were judged to have need; 237 of these received aid. Average need met was 100%. Average scholarship/grant was $31,051; average loan $2,961. 85% of total undergraduate aid awarded as scholarships/grants, 15% as loans/jobs.

**Application procedures. Admission:** Closing date 1/1 (postmark date). $60 fee, may be waived for applicants with need. Admission notification 3/31. Must reply by 5/1. **Financial aid:** Closing date 2/1. FAFSA, CSS PROFILE required. Applicants notified by 4/1; must reply by 5/1.

**Academics.** 4 interdisciplinary centers through which students may earn a certificate to complement their major; competitive application process for acceptance into these programs. **Special study options:** Cross-registration, double major, dual enrollment of high school students, exchange student, independent study, internships, student-designed major, study abroad, teacher certification program, Washington semester. 12-college exchange, National Theater Institute, Mystic Seaport Program in American Maritime Studies, Institute for Architecture and Urban Studies, American Academy in Rome, Associated Kyoto Program, cross-registration with U.S. Coast Guard Academy, Trinity College and Wesleyan University, study away-teach away opportunities, specially funded student research opportunities. **Credit/placement by examination:** AP, CLEP, IB, institutional tests. 32 credit hours maximum toward bachelor's degree. Students may use AP credit to repair credit deficiencies that arise from voluntary course withdrawals or failing grades, or to accelerate. **Support services:** Pre-admission summer program, reduced course load, study skills assistance, tutoring, writing center.

**Majors. Architecture:** Architecture. **Area/ethnic studies:** African, American, Chicano/Hispanic-American/Latino, East Asian, Latin American, Slavic, women's. **Biology:** General, biochemistry, Biochemistry/biophysics and molecular biology, botany, cellular/molecular, molecular. **Computer sciences:** Computer science. **Conservation:** Environmental studies. **Engineering:** Physics. **Family/consumer sciences:** Family studies. **Foreign languages:** Chinese, classics, French, German, Italian, Japanese, Slavic, Spanish. **History:** General. **Interdisciplinary:** Neuroscience. **Math:** General. **Philosophy/religion:** Philosophy, religion. **Physical sciences:** Astrophysics, chemistry, physics. **Psychology:** General. **Social sciences:** Anthropology, economics, international relations, political science, sociology, urban studies. **Visual/performing arts:** Art history/conservation, dance, dramatic, film/cinema, studio arts.

**Most popular majors.** Area/ethnic studies 8%, biology 10%, English 6%, foreign language 6%, social sciences 32%, visual/performing arts 13%.

**Computing on campus.** 500 workstations in library, computer center, student center. Dormitories wired for high-speed internet access and linked to campus network. Commuter students can connect to campus network. Online course registration, online library, helpline, student web hosting, wireless network available.

**Student life. Freshman orientation:** Mandatory. Preregistration for classes offered. Held week prior to start of classes. Optional outdoor orientation prior to full orientation (additional charge). **Policies:** Student-adjudicated honor code that governs both academic and social activities and behavior. **Housing:** Guaranteed on-campus for all undergraduates. Coed dorms, special housing for disabled, apartments, wellness housing available. $500 nonrefundable deposit, deadline 5/1. Quiet housing, men's and women's floors, living-and-learning housing (students in a particular class live near each other), gender-neutral housing. **Activities:** Bands, campus ministries, choral groups, dance, drama, film society, international student organizations, literary magazine, music ensembles, radio station, student government, student newspaper, symphony orchestra, College Democrats, College Republicans, Hillel, Intervarsity Christian Fellowship, multi-faith student council, Muslim student association, Asian/Asian American student association, Latino American student association, Sexual Orientations United for Liberation, African/African American student association.

**Athletics.** NCAA. **Intercollegiate:** Basketball, cross-country, diving, field hockey W, ice hockey, lacrosse, rowing (crew), sailing, soccer, squash, swimming, tennis, track and field, volleyball W, water polo. **Intramural:** Baseball M, basketball, football (non-tackle) M, racquetball, soccer, softball, squash, tennis, volleyball. **Team name:** Camels.

**Student services.** Adult student services, alcohol/substance abuse counseling, chaplain/spiritual director, career counseling, services for economically disadvantaged, student employment services, financial aid counseling, health services, minority student services, personal counseling, placement for graduates, women's services. **Physically disabled:** Services for visually, speech, hearing impaired. **Learning disabled:** Comprehensive services available.

**Contact.** E-mail: admission@conncoll.edu
Phone: (860) 439-2200 Fax: (860) 439-4301
Martha Merrill, Dean of Admission and Financial Aid, Connecticut College, 270 Mohegan Avenue, New London, CT 06320-4196

## Eastern Connecticut State University
**Willimantic, Connecticut** — **CB member**
**www.easternct.edu** — **CB code: 3966**

- Public 4-year university and liberal arts college
- Residential campus in large town
- 5,025 degree-seeking undergraduates: 14% part-time, 54% women
- 332 degree-seeking graduate students
- 62% of applicants admitted
- SAT or ACT (ACT writing optional) required
- 50% graduate within 6 years

**General.** Founded in 1889. Regionally accredited. Connecticut's public liberal arts college. **Degrees:** 926 bachelor's, 13 associate awarded; master's offered. **ROTC:** Army, Air Force. **Location:** 30 miles from Hartford, 90 miles from Boston. **Calendar:** Semester, extensive summer session. **Full-time faculty:** 198 total; 97% have terminal degrees, 22% minority. **Part-time faculty:** 253 total; 40% have terminal degrees, 10% minority, 47% women. **Class size:** 40% < 20, 51% 20-39, 8% 40-49, less than 1% 50-99. **Special facilities:** Child and family development complex, sustainable energy institute, free enterprise institute, arboretum, planetarium, farm, 2 electron microscopes, bell carillon.

**Freshman class profile.** 3,785 applied, 2,355 admitted, 981 enrolled.

| Mid 50% test scores | | | |
|---|---|---|---|
| SAT critical reading: | 470-550 | Rank in top quarter: | 26% |
| SAT math: | 480-560 | Rank in top tenth: | 5% |
| GPA 3.75 or higher: | 5% | Return as sophomores: | 78% |
| GPA 3.50-3.74: | 9% | Out-of-state: | 10% |
| GPA 3.0-3.49: | 36% | Live on campus: | 89% |
| GPA 2.0-2.99: | 48% | International: | 1% |

**Basis for selection.** Applicants should be in top half of class and recommended by high school. Quality of course work very important; 2.5 GPA in college preparatory program required. SAT score also important. Extracurricular activities considered. Interview and essay recommended.

**High school preparation.** College-preparatory program recommended. Required and recommended units include English 4, mathematics 3-4, social studies 2, science 2 (laboratory 1) and foreign language 2-3.

**2009-2010 Annual costs.** Tuition/fees: $7,813; $17,505 out-of-state. Room/board: $9,620. Books/supplies: $1,412. Personal expenses: $2,974.

**2008-2009 Financial aid. Non-need-based:** Scholarships awarded for academics. **Additional information:** Tuition waiver for veterans and members of National Guard.

**Application procedures. Admission:** Priority date 5/1; no deadline. $50 fee, may be waived for applicants with need. Admission notification on a rolling basis beginning on or about 12/1. Must reply by May 1 or within 2 week(s) if notified thereafter. **Financial aid:** Priority date 3/15; no closing date. FAFSA required. Applicants notified on a rolling basis starting 2/15; must reply within 2 week(s) of notification.

**Academics.** Life learning portfolio class available. **Special study options:** Accelerated study, cooperative education, cross-registration, distance learning, double major, dual enrollment of high school students, exchange student, external degree, honors, independent study, internships, student-designed major, study abroad, teacher certification program, weekend college. **Credit/placement by examination:** CLEP, institutional tests. 30 credit hours maximum toward associate degree, 60 toward bachelor's. Institutional placement test required for all entering freshmen. **Support services:** Learning center, pre-admission summer program, reduced course load, remedial instruction, study skills assistance, tutoring, writing center.

**Majors. Biology:** General, biochemistry. **Business:** Accounting, business admin, management information systems. **Communications:** General. **Computer sciences:** General. **Conservation:** Environmental science. **Education:** Early childhood, elementary, middle, physical, secondary. **Foreign languages:** Spanish. **History:** General. **Math:** General. **Parks/recreation:** Sports admin. **Psychology:** General. **Public administration:** Social work. **Social sciences:** Economics, political science, sociology. **Visual/performing arts:** General, studio arts.

**Most popular majors.** Business/marketing 15%, communications/journalism 7%, education 6%, English 7%, liberal arts 9%, psychology 11%.

**Computing on campus.** 637 workstations in dormitories, library, computer center. Dormitories wired for high-speed internet access and linked to campus network. Commuter students can connect to campus network. Online library, helpline, repair service, student web hosting, wireless network available.

**Student life. Freshman orientation:** Mandatory. Preregistration for classes offered. **Policies:** No alcohol permitted on campus; all halls are smoke-free; sign-in guest policy for all first-year halls from 7pm-12am. **Housing:** Coed dorms, apartments available. $250 nonrefundable deposit, deadline 5/1. **Activities:** Bands, choral groups, dance, drama, international student organizations, literary magazine, music ensembles, musical theater, radio station, student government, student newspaper, TV station, over 60 organizations.

**Athletics. NCAA. Intercollegiate:** Baseball M, basketball, cheerleading M, cross-country, field hockey W, lacrosse, soccer, softball W, swimming W, track and field, volleyball W. **Intramural:** Badminton, basketball, bowling, cross-country, football (tackle) M, gymnastics W, racquetball, rugby, skiing, soccer, softball, swimming, tennis, track and field, volleyball, water polo. **Team name:** Warriors.

**Student services.** Adult student services, alcohol/substance abuse counseling, chaplain/spiritual director, career counseling, services for economically disadvantaged, student employment services, financial aid counseling, health services, minority student services, on-campus daycare, personal counseling, placement for graduates, veterans' counselor, women's services. **Physically disabled:** Services for visually, speech, hearing impaired. **Learning disabled:** Comprehensive services available.

**Contact.** E-mail: admissions@easternct.edu
Phone: (860) 465-5286 Toll-free number: (877) 353-3278
Fax: (860) 465-5544
Kimberly Crone, Director of Admissions and Enrollment Planning, Eastern Connecticut State University, 83 Windham Street, Willimantic, CT 06226-2295

---

### Fairfield University
**Fairfield, Connecticut**
www.fairfield.edu

**CB member**
**CB code: 3390**

- Private 4-year university affiliated with Roman Catholic Church
- Residential campus in small city
- 3,623 degree-seeking undergraduates: 9% part-time, 58% women
- 1,157 degree-seeking graduate students
- 65% of applicants admitted
- Application essay required
- 85% graduate within 6 years

**General.** Founded in 1942. Regionally accredited. **Degrees:** 935 bachelor's, 2 associate awarded; master's offered. **ROTC:** Army, Air Force. **Location:** 55 miles from New York City. **Calendar:** Semester, limited summer session. **Full-time faculty:** 253 total; 92% have terminal degrees, 49% women. **Part-time faculty:** 229 total; 45% women. **Class size:** 43% < 20, 55% 20-39, less than 1% 40-49, 1% 50-99. **Special facilities:** Fine arts center containing 2 theaters, campus ministry center, art galleries, Japanese meditation garden, business experimental center, simulation and trading floor, nursing simulation lab.

**Freshman class profile.** 8,316 applied, 5,376 admitted, 1,414 enrolled.

| Mid 50% test scores | | | |
|---|---|---|---|
| SAT critical reading: | 520-610 | GPA 2.0-2.99: | 17% |
| SAT math: | 530-630 | Rank in top quarter: | 78% |
| SAT writing: | 530-630 | Rank in top tenth: | 41% |
| GPA 3.75 or higher: | 25% | Return as sophomores: | 88% |
| GPA 3.50-3.74: | 20% | Out-of-state: | 77% |
| GPA 3.0-3.49: | 38% | Live on campus: | 96% |
| | | International: | 2% |

**Basis for selection.** GED not accepted. School achievement record, recommendations, school activities, personal statement important. Special consideration given to children/siblings of alumni and students with special talents, diverse or unique backgrounds. Interview recommended. Portfolio highly recommended for music majors, resume for theater majors. **Homeschooled:** Statement describing homeschool structure and mission, transcript of courses and grades required.

**High school preparation.** College-preparatory program required. 16 units required; 20 recommended. Required and recommended units include English 4, mathematics 3-4, social studies 2, history 2, science 2-3 (laboratory 2), foreign language 2-4 and academic electives 1. 1 additional math and 2 science recommended for math, business and science.

**2009-2010 Annual costs.** Tuition/fees: $37,490. Standard meal plan covers 12 meals per week; 14-meal plan available with "dining dollars" (i.e., cash value added by deposit to student ID). Proof of health insurance required in order to waive health insurance fee. Room/board: $11,270. Books/supplies: $900. Personal expenses: $900.

**2009-2010 Financial aid. Need-based:** 624 full-time freshmen applied for aid; 493 were judged to have need; 484 of these received aid. Average need met was 92%. Average scholarship/grant was $24,000; average loan $4,012. 76% of total undergraduate aid awarded as scholarships/grants, 24% as loans/jobs. **Non-need-based:** Awarded to 908 full-time undergraduates, including 257 freshmen. Scholarships awarded for academics, alumni affiliation, art, athletics, leadership, music/drama. **Additional information:** Free tuition to any eligible student from Bridgeport with family income below $50,000. Enhanced financial aid available for veterans.

**Application procedures. Admission:** Closing date 1/15 (postmark date). $60 fee, may be waived for applicants with need. Admission notification 4/1. Must reply by 5/1. **Financial aid:** Closing date 2/15. FAFSA, CSS PROFILE required. Applicants notified by 4/1; must reply by 5/1.

**Academics. Special study options:** Combined bachelor's/graduate degree, cross-registration, double major, exchange student, honors, independent study, internships, liberal arts/career combination, student-designed major, study abroad, teacher certification program, Washington semester. 3-2 engineering program with University of Connecticut, Rensselaer Polytechnic Institute, Columbia University, and Stevens Institute of Technology. **Credit/placement by examination:** AP, CLEP, IB, institutional tests. 15 credit hours maximum toward bachelor's degree. **Support services:** Reduced course load, study skills assistance, tutoring, writing center.

**Majors. Area/ethnic studies:** American. **Biology:** General, biochemistry. **Business:** Accounting, business admin, finance, international, management information systems, marketing. **Communications:** General. **Computer sciences:** General. **Engineering:** Computer, electrical, mechanical, software. **Foreign languages:** French, German, Italian, Spanish. **Health:** Nursing (RN). **History:** General. **Math:** General. **Philosophy/religion:** Philosophy, religion. **Physical sciences:** Chemistry, physics. **Psychology:** General. **Social sciences:** Economics, international relations, political science, sociology. **Visual/performing arts:** General, art history/conservation, dramatic, studio arts. **Other:** Individual design major, New media film/televison/radio.

**Most popular majors.** Business/marketing 32%, communications/journalism 8%, English 7%, health sciences 9%, psychology 9%, social sciences 14%.

**Computing on campus.** 220 workstations in dormitories, library, computer center, student center. Dormitories wired for high-speed internet access and linked to campus network. Commuter students can connect to campus network. Online course registration, online library, helpline, repair service, student web hosting, wireless network available.

**Student life. Freshman orientation:** Available, $230 fee. Preregistration for classes offered. 2-day program in late June/early July for students and parents. **Policies:** Juniors and seniors may enter lottery to move off-campus. **Housing:** Guaranteed on-campus for all undergraduates. Coed dorms, special housing for disabled, apartments available. $300 nonrefundable deposit, deadline 5/1. Extensive theme based living-learning options for sophomores. **Activities:** Bands, campus ministries, choral groups, dance, drama, film society, international student organizations, literary magazine, music ensembles, Model UN, radio station, student government, student newspaper, TV station, College Democrats, College Republicans, Circle K, Asian student association, Jewish cultural organization, Spanish and Latino student association, African-American and Caribbean student association, Colleges Against Cancer, student environmental association.

**Athletics. NCAA. Intercollegiate:** Baseball M, basketball, cross-country, diving, field hockey W, golf, lacrosse, rowing (crew), soccer, softball W, swimming, tennis, volleyball W. **Intramural:** Basketball, field hockey W, football (non-tackle) M, golf, lacrosse, racquetball, soccer, softball, table tennis, tennis, volleyball. **Team name:** Stags.

**Student services.** Adult student services, alcohol/substance abuse counseling, chaplain/spiritual director, career counseling, student employment services, financial aid counseling, health services, minority student services, on-campus daycare, personal counseling, placement for graduates. **Physically disabled:** Services for visually, hearing impaired.

**Contact.** E-mail: admis@fairfield.edu
Phone: (203) 254-4100 Fax: (203) 254-4199
Karen Pellegrino, Director of Admission, Fairfield University, 1073 North
Benson Road, Fairfield, CT 06824-5195

## Holy Apostles College and Seminary
### Cromwell, Connecticut
**www.holyapostles.edu**      **CB code: 0921**

- Private 4-year liberal arts and seminary college affiliated with Roman Catholic Church
- Commuter campus in large town
- 46 degree-seeking undergraduates: 30% part-time, 35% women, 11% Hispanic American, 13% international
- 237 degree-seeking graduate students
- 100% of applicants admitted
- SAT, interview required

**General.** Founded in 1956. Regionally accredited. 75% of students are lay students, 25% are seminarians. **Degrees:** 10 bachelor's awarded; master's offered. **Location:** 13 miles from Hartford. **Calendar:** Semester, limited summer session. **Full-time faculty:** 13 total; 100% have terminal degrees, 8% minority, 31% women. **Part-time faculty:** 16 total; 100% have terminal degrees, 6% minority, 38% women.

**Freshman class profile.** 10 applied, 10 admitted, 10 enrolled.

| | | | |
|---|---|---|---|
| End year in good standing: | 80% | Out-of-state: | 9% |
| Return as sophomores: | 50% | International: | 20% |

**Basis for selection.** Interview, level of interest and recommendations most important. 1050 SAT and 3.0 GPA in high school core courses required. **Homeschooled:** State high school equivalency certificate, interview, letter of recommendation (nonparent) required.

**2009-2010 Annual costs.** Tuition/fees: $9,360. Books/supplies: $630. Personal expenses: $580.

**2009-2010 Financial aid.** All financial aid based on need. 4% of total undergraduate aid awarded as scholarships/grants, 96% as loans/jobs.

**Application procedures. Admission:** Priority date 8/15; no deadline. $50 fee, may be waived for applicants with need. Application must be submitted on paper. Admission notification on a rolling basis. Applications accepted up to one week before beginning of semester in which the applicant plans to enroll. **Financial aid:** Priority date 7/11; no closing date. FAFSA, institutional form required. Applicants notified on a rolling basis starting 8/25; must reply within 2 week(s) of notification.

**Academics.** 54-credit core curriculum required of all undergraduates. **Special study options:** Distance learning, ESL, independent study. **Credit/placement by examination:** AP, CLEP. 30 credit hours maximum toward bachelor's degree. **Support services:** Reduced course load, remedial instruction, tutoring.

**Majors. Liberal arts:** Humanities. **Philosophy/religion:** Philosophy, religion. **Social sciences:** General.

**Most popular majors.** Liberal arts 8%, philosophy/religious studies 92%.

**Computing on campus.** 10 workstations in library.

**Student life. Freshman orientation:** Available. Preregistration for classes offered. **Policies:** Men's dorms are for seminarians only; other students must commute. **Housing:** Single-sex dorms available. **Activities:** Choral groups, Life League, Toastmasters.

**Student services.** Chaplain/spiritual director, financial aid counseling, personal counseling.

**Contact.** E-mail: registrar@holyapostles.edu
Phone: (860) 632-3033 Toll-free number: (800) 330-7272
Fax: (860) 632-3075
Very Rev. Douglas Mosey, President-Rector, Holy Apostles College and Seminary, 33 Prospect Hill Road, Cromwell, CT 06416-2005

## Lyme Academy College of Fine Arts
### Old Lyme, Connecticut
**www.lymeacademy.edu**      **CB code: 1791**

- Private 4-year visual arts college
- Residential campus in small town
- 75 degree-seeking undergraduates: 15% part-time, 64% women, 1% African American, 1% Asian American, 3% Native American
- 1 degree-seeking graduate students
- 91% of applicants admitted
- Application essay, interview required
- 67% graduate within 6 years

**General.** Founded in 1976. Regionally accredited. **Degrees:** 25 bachelor's awarded. **Location:** 40 miles from Hartford. **Calendar:** Semester, limited summer session. **Full-time faculty:** 7 total; 43% women. **Part-time faculty:** 19 total; 5% have terminal degrees, 32% women. **Class size:** 89% < 20, 11% 20-39.

**Freshman class profile.** 35 applied, 32 admitted, 9 enrolled.

| Mid 50% test scores | | | |
|---|---|---|---|
| SAT critical reading: | 460-610 | GPA 3.0-3.49: | 33% |
| SAT math: | 430-570 | GPA 2.0-2.99: | 23% |
| SAT writing: | 450-620 | End year in good standing: | 91% |
| GPA 3.75 or higher: | 11% | Return as sophomores: | 82% |
| GPA 3.50-3.74: | 33% | Out-of-state: | 56% |

**Basis for selection.** Admissions based on portfolio, interview, essay, GPA. SAT or ACT recommended. Portfolio, two letters of recommendation required. Campus visit highly recommended. **Homeschooled:** Statement describing homeschool structure and mission, transcript of courses and grades, state high school equivalency certificate, interview, letter of recommendation (nonparent) required. **Learning Disabled:** Students should disclose their disabilities to Student Services so that modifications and assistance can be offered.

**2010-2011 Annual costs.** Tuition/fees: $24,684. Books/supplies: $1,500. Personal expenses: $500.

**2009-2010 Financial aid. Non-need-based:** Scholarships awarded for academics, art, leadership.

**Application procedures. Admission:** Priority date 2/15; no deadline. $55 fee. Admission notification on a rolling basis beginning on or about 2/15. Must reply by May 1 or within 2 week(s) if notified thereafter. **Financial aid:** Priority date 2/15, closing date 4/15. FAFSA required. Applicants notified on a rolling basis starting 3/1; must reply by 5/1 or within 2 week(s) of notification.

**Academics. Special study options:** Cross-registration, independent study. **Credit/placement by examination:** CLEP. **Support services:** Pre-admission summer program, reduced course load, remedial instruction, study skills assistance, tutoring.

**Majors. Visual/performing arts:** Drawing, illustration, painting, sculpture.

**Computing on campus.** 6 workstations in library. Online library, wireless network available.

**Student life. Freshman orientation:** Mandatory. Preregistration for classes offered. Usually one day before start of Fall classes. **Activities:** Film society, literary magazine, student government.

**Athletics. Intramural:** Badminton, basketball, table tennis, volleyball. **Team name:** The Ticks.

**Student services.** Alcohol/substance abuse counseling, career counseling, financial aid counseling, personal counseling, veterans' counselor, women's services.

**Contact.** E-mail: Jrenko@lymeacademy.edu
Phone: (860) 434-5232 ext. 120 Fax: (860) 434-8725
Jennifer Renko, Assistant Dean of Admissions, Lyme Academy College of Fine Arts, 84 Lyme Street, Old Lyme, CT 06371

## Mitchell College
### New London, Connecticut
**www.mitchell.edu**      **CB member**
     **CB code: 3528**

- Private 4-year liberal arts college
- Residential campus in small city
- 872 degree-seeking undergraduates: 6% part-time, 50% women, 12% African American, 1% Asian American, 8% Hispanic American, 2% Native American, 1% international
- 83% of applicants admitted

▶ Application essay, interview required

▶ 37% graduate within 6 years

**General.** Founded in 1938. Regionally accredited. **Degrees:** 119 bachelor's, 42 associate awarded. **Location:** 100 miles from New York City and Boston. **Calendar:** Semester, limited summer session. **Full-time faculty:** 35 total; 77% have terminal degrees, 9% minority, 51% women. **Part-time faculty:** 72 total; 22% have terminal degrees, 3% minority, 44% women. **Class size:** 77% < 20, 23% 20-39. **Special facilities:** Two beaches, dock with sailboat fleet, learning resource center for students with learning disabilities, hiking trails, nature preserve.

**Freshman class profile.** 802 applied, 663 admitted, 260 enrolled.

| | | | |
|---|---|---|---|
| GPA 3.75 or higher: | 2% | Return as sophomores: | 66% |
| GPA 3.50-3.74: | 4% | Out-of-state: | 51% |
| GPA 3.0-3.49: | 23% | Live on campus: | 83% |
| GPA 2.0-2.99: | 71% | International: | 1% |

**Basis for selection.** High school achievement, recommendations, motivation and interview very important. **Learning Disabled:** Students applying to Learning Resource Center should submit results of complete psycho-educational evaluation, testing accommodation recommendations made by professional who completed the evaluation, definitive diagnosis of learning disability or ADHD, and standardized achievement testing (reading, writing and math). All documentation should be less than 3 years old; testing must be administered by certified or licensed psychologist.

**High school preparation.** College-preparatory program recommended. 16 units required. Required units include English 4, mathematics 3, social studies 2, history 1, science 2 (laboratory 1) and academic electives 3.

**2009-2010 Annual costs.** Tuition/fees: $25,627. Room/board: $11,548. Books/supplies: $1,500. Personal expenses: $1,200.

**2009-2010 Financial aid. Need-based:** 213 full-time freshmen applied for aid; 186 were judged to have need; 186 of these received aid. Average need met was 66%. Average scholarship/grant was $11,474; average loan $3,607. 74% of total undergraduate aid awarded as scholarships/grants, 26% as loans/jobs. **Non-need-based:** Awarded to 650 full-time undergraduates, including 210 freshmen. Scholarships awarded for academics, alumni affiliation, art, leadership.

**Application procedures. Admission:** Priority date 4/1; no deadline. $35 fee, may be waived for applicants with need, free for online applicants. Admission notification on a rolling basis beginning on or about 12/15. Must reply by May 1 or within 2 week(s) if notified thereafter. **Financial aid:** Priority date 3/1; no closing date. FAFSA required. Applicants notified on a rolling basis starting 2/15; must reply within 3 week(s) of notification.

**Academics.** Free professional tutoring offered in most disciplines. **Special study options:** Independent study, internships, liberal arts/career combination, student-designed major, study abroad, teacher certification program. **Credit/placement by examination:** AP, CLEP, institutional tests. 30 credit hours maximum toward associate degree. **Support services:** Learning center, pre-admission summer program, reduced course load, study skills assistance, tutoring, writing center.

**Majors. Biology:** Environmental. **Business:** Accounting/business management, business admin, hospitality admin, hotel/motel admin, restaurant/food services, small business admin, tourism/travel. **Communications:** Broadcast journalism, digital media, journalism, media studies, organizational, public relations, radio/tv. **Communications technology:** Graphics. **Conservation:** Environmental studies. **Education:** Early childhood, kindergarten/preschool. **Family/consumer sciences:** Child care, family studies. **Interdisciplinary:** Behavioral sciences, global studies. **Legal studies:** General, prelaw. **Liberal arts:** Arts/sciences, humanities. **Parks/recreation:** Sports admin. **Protective services:** Criminal justice, emergency management/homeland security, juvenile corrections. **Psychology:** General, community, developmental. **Public administration:** Human services. **Social sciences:** Criminology, international economic development. **Visual/performing arts:** Graphic design.

**Most popular majors.** Business/marketing 27%, education 9%, liberal arts 29%, parks/recreation 8%, security/protective services 13%.

**Computing on campus.** 155 workstations in dormitories, library, computer center, student center. Dormitories wired for high-speed internet access and linked to campus network. Commuter students can connect to campus network. Helpline, repair service available.

**Student life. Freshman orientation:** Available. Held in September prior to start of classes; concurrent program specific to parent issues. **Housing:** Guaranteed on-campus for all undergraduates. Coed dorms, single-sex dorms, apartments available. **Activities:** Campus ministries, choral groups, dance, drama, literary magazine, music ensembles, musical theater, radio station, student government, student newspaper, multicultural club, Hillel, spirituality club, African American alliance, communication club, improv club, Bible study club, peer educators, gay straight alliance.

**Athletics.** NCAA. **Intercollegiate:** Baseball M, basketball, cross-country, golf, lacrosse M, sailing, soccer, softball W, tennis, volleyball W. **Intramural:** Basketball, sailing, soccer, softball, tennis, volleyball. **Team name:** Mariners.

**Student services.** Adult student services, career counseling, services for economically disadvantaged, student employment services, financial aid counseling, health services, minority student services, on-campus daycare, personal counseling, veterans' counselor. **Physically disabled:** Services for visually, speech, hearing impaired. **Learning disabled:** Comprehensive services available.

**Contact.** E-mail: admissions@mitchell.edu
Phone: (860) 701-5037 Toll-free number: (800) 443-2811
Fax: (860) 444-1209
Kimberly Hodges, Director of Admissions, Mitchell College, 437 Pequot Avenue, New London, CT 06320-4498

## Paier College of Art
**Hamden, Connecticut**
**www.paiercollegeofart.edu**          CB code: 3699

▶ For-profit 4-year visual arts college

▶ Commuter campus in small city

▶ 204 degree-seeking undergraduates: 27% part-time, 71% women, 2% African American, 2% Asian American, 5% Hispanic American

▶ 68% of applicants admitted

▶ SAT or ACT, interview required

▶ 72% graduate within 6 years; 17% enter graduate study

**General.** Founded in 1946. Accredited by ACCSC. **Degrees:** 37 bachelor's, 3 associate awarded. **Location:** 2 miles from New Haven. **Calendar:** Semester. **Full-time faculty:** 10 total; 40% have terminal degrees, 10% women. **Part-time faculty:** 29 total; 45% have terminal degrees, 28% women. **Class size:** 85% < 20, 15% 20-39.

**Freshman class profile.** 135 applied, 92 admitted, 69 enrolled.

| | | | |
|---|---|---|---|
| Mid 50% test scores | | Rank in top quarter: | 18% |
| SAT critical reading: | 430-520 | End year in good standing: | 88% |
| SAT math: | 400-530 | Return as sophomores: | 89% |

**Basis for selection.** Artistic ability, interest, and potential, as demonstrated in admission interview and portfolio review most important elements. Portfolio of 8 to 10 works of art required; essay recommended. **Homeschooled:** Statement describing homeschool structure and mission, transcript of courses and grades, interview, letter of recommendation (nonparent) required. Notification from school district required stating that student is being home-schooled.

**High school preparation.** Required units include English 4, mathematics 3, social studies 3, science 2, computer science 1 and visual/performing arts 4. Art classes recommended. All students must pass all state requirements.

**2010-2011 Annual costs.** Tuition/fees (projected): $12,965. Books/supplies: $1,000. Personal expenses: $600.

**2008-2009 Financial aid. Need-based:** 13 full-time freshmen applied for aid; 10 were judged to have need; 10 of these received aid. Average need met was 70%. Average scholarship/grant was $3,561; average loan $3,506. 46% of total undergraduate aid awarded as scholarships/grants, 54% as loans/jobs.

**Application procedures. Admission:** No deadline. $25 fee, may be waived for applicants with need. Application must be submitted on paper. Admission notification on a rolling basis beginning on or about 2/15. **Financial aid:** Priority date 4/15; no closing date. FAFSA required. Applicants notified on a rolling basis starting 6/1; must reply within 3 week(s) of notification.

**Academics.** Academics required for BFA degrees include: 4 art histories, English I and II, 1 requirement each in the humanities, math, physical and social sciences, and 1 academic elective. **Special study options:** Independent study. **Credit/placement by examination:** CLEP, IB, SAT, ACT. 6 credit hours maximum toward associate degree, 12 toward bachelor's. **Support services:** Reduced course load, remedial instruction, study skills assistance, tutoring.

**Majors. Visual/performing arts:** Commercial photography, commercial/advertising art, design, graphic design, illustration, interior design, painting, photography, studio arts.

**Computing on campus.** 75 workstations in library, computer center. Wireless network available.

**Student life. Freshman orientation:** Available. Preregistration for classes offered. Open to incoming students and their parents/guardians. Separate 1-hour library orientation. **Activities:** Student government.

**Student services.** Career counseling, student employment services, financial aid counseling, personal counseling, placement for graduates, veterans' counselor.

**Contact.** E-mail: paier.admission@snet.net
Phone: (203) 287-3031 Fax: (203) 287-3021
Daniel Paier, Dean of Admissions, Paier College of Art, 20 Gorham Avenue, Hamden, CT 06514-3902

---

## Post University

| Waterbury, Connecticut | CB member |
|---|---|
| www.post.edu | CB code: 3698 |

- For-profit 4-year university and business college
- Residential campus in small city
- 670 degree-seeking undergraduates: 6% part-time, 55% women, 30% African American, 1% Asian American, 12% Hispanic American, 3% international
- 361 degree-seeking graduate students
- 59% of applicants admitted
- SAT or ACT with writing required

**General.** Founded in 1890. Regionally accredited. **Degrees:** 120 bachelor's, 29 associate awarded; master's offered. **ROTC:** Army. **Location:** 32 miles from Hartford, 80 miles from New York City. **Calendar:** Semester, limited summer session. **Full-time faculty:** 30 total; 43% have terminal degrees, 13% minority, 47% women. **Class size:** 75% < 20, 24% 20-39, less than 1% 40-49.

**Freshman class profile.** 1,965 applied, 1,152 admitted, 248 enrolled.

| Mid 50% test scores | | | |
|---|---|---|---|
| SAT critical reading: | 390-500 | GPA 2.0-2.99: | 70% |
| SAT math: | 390-520 | Rank in top quarter: | 10% |
| SAT writing: | 400-510 | Rank in top tenth: | 5% |
| ACT composite: | 17-24 | End year in good standing: | 80% |
| GPA 3.75 or higher: | 1% | Return as sophomores: | 55% |
| GPA 3.50-3.74: | 4% | Out-of-state: | 30% |
| GPA 3.0-3.49: | 24% | Live on campus: | 71% |
| | | International: | 4% |

**Basis for selection.** Secondary school transcript, results of SAT/ACT most important. Guidance counselor's recommendation required. School and community activities and test scores also reviewed and considered. Interview recommended. **Homeschooled:** Statement describing homeschool structure and mission, transcript of courses and grades, interview, letter of recommendation (nonparent) required. **Learning Disabled:** Students must submit documentation once enrolled to receive services; documentation not used for admissions.

**High school preparation.** College-preparatory program recommended. 13 units required. Required and recommended units include English 4, mathematics 3, social studies 1, history 2, science 3 (laboratory 1) and foreign language 2.

**2009-2010 Annual costs.** Tuition/fees: $24,200. Room/board: $9,400. Books/supplies: $1,000. Personal expenses: $1,200.

**2009-2010 Financial aid. Need-based:** 251 full-time freshmen applied for aid; 251 were judged to have need; 251 of these received aid. Average need met was 71%. Average scholarship/grant was $4,310; average loan $3,561. 64% of total undergraduate aid awarded as scholarships/grants, 36% as loans/jobs. **Additional information:** Academic merit scholarships available based on GPA and test scores. Renewable contingent upon maintaining specific GPA.

**Application procedures. Admission:** Priority date 3/1; no deadline. $40 fee, may be waived for applicants with need, free for online applicants. Admission notification on a rolling basis beginning on or about 11/15. Must reply by May 1 or within 2 week(s) if notified thereafter. **Financial aid:** Priority date 3/15; no closing date. FAFSA required. Applicants notified on a rolling basis starting 4/15; must reply by 5/1 or within 3 week(s) of notification.

**Academics. Special study options:** Accelerated study, cooperative education, cross-registration, distance learning, double major, dual enrollment of high school students, ESL, independent study, internships, liberal arts/career combination, student-designed major, study abroad, weekend college. **Credit/placement by examination:** AP, CLEP, IB, institutional tests. 15 credit hours maximum toward associate degree, 30 toward bachelor's. **Support services:** Learning center, pre-admission summer program, reduced course load, remedial instruction, study skills assistance, tutoring, writing center.

**Majors. Agriculture:** Equestrian studies. **Biology:** General. **Business:** General, accounting, business admin, finance, marketing. **Computer sciences:** General. **Conservation:** General, environmental studies. **Legal studies:** Prelaw. **Protective services:** Law enforcement admin. **Psychology:** General. **Public administration:** Human services. **Social sciences:** Sociology.

**Computing on campus.** 94 workstations in library, computer center, student center. Dormitories wired for high-speed internet access and linked to campus network. Commuter students can connect to campus network. Online course registration, online library, helpline available.

**Student life. Freshman orientation:** Mandatory, $150 fee. Preregistration for classes offered. **Policies:** Student leadership opportunities encouraged and supported throughout student's experience. **Housing:** Guaranteed on-campus for all undergraduates. Coed dorms available. $150 fully refundable deposit, deadline 5/1. **Activities:** Dance, drama, international student organizations, literary magazine, musical theater, student government, Phi Theta Kappa, student ambassadors, peer advisors.

**Athletics.** NCAA. **Intercollegiate:** Baseball M, basketball, cross-country, golf M, lacrosse W, soccer, softball W, swimming, tennis, volleyball W. **Intramural:** Basketball, lacrosse W, tennis. **Team name:** Eagles.

**Student services.** Adult student services, alcohol/substance abuse counseling, career counseling, student employment services, financial aid counseling, health services, minority student services, personal counseling, placement for graduates, veterans' counselor. **Physically disabled:** Services for visually impaired.

**Contact.** E-mail: admissions@post.edu
Phone: (203) 596-4520 Toll-free number: (800) 345-2562
Fax: (203) 756-5810
Jay Murray, Director of Admissions, Post University, 800 Country Club Road, Waterbury, CT 06723-2540

---

## Quinnipiac University

| Hamden, Connecticut | CB member |
|---|---|
| www.quinnipiac.edu | CB code: 3712 |

- Private 4-year university
- Residential campus in small city
- 5,888 degree-seeking undergraduates: 3% part-time, 62% women, 3% African American, 3% Asian American, 5% Hispanic American, 1% international
- 1,754 degree-seeking graduate students
- 69% of applicants admitted
- SAT or ACT (ACT writing recommended), application essay required
- 74% graduate within 6 years; 40% enter graduate study

**General.** Founded in 1929. Regionally accredited. Three campuses include the Mount Carmel campus (academic, residential, athletic and recreational space for undergraduates), York Hill campus (residence facilities for juniors and seniors, parking garage and sports complex), North Haven campus (4 building complex for graduate programs and upper level courses in the School of Health Sciences). **Degrees:** 1,330 bachelor's awarded; master's, professional offered. **ROTC:** Army, Air Force. **Location:** 8 miles from New Haven. **Calendar:** Semester, limited summer session. **Full-time faculty:** 304 total; 85% have terminal degrees, 12% minority, 48% women. **Part-time faculty:** 541 total; 7% minority, 52% women. **Class size:** 46% < 20, 51% 20-39, 3% 40-49. **Special facilities:** Financial technology center, polling institute, community health education institute, diagnostic imaging suite, critical care simulation laboratories, motion analysis laboratory, Irish Famine museum, fully-digital high-definition production TV studio, audio production studio, news technology center.

**Freshman class profile.** 13,847 applied, 9,616 admitted, 1,588 enrolled.

| Mid 50% test scores | | | |
|---|---|---|---|
| SAT critical reading: | 540-610 | Rank in top quarter: | 68% |
| SAT math: | 560-630 | Rank in top tenth: | 26% |
| ACT composite: | 23-27 | End year in good standing: | 95% |
| GPA 3.75 or higher: | 13% | Return as sophomores: | 88% |
| GPA 3.50-3.74: | 31% | Out-of-state: | 75% |
| GPA 3.0-3.49: | 48% | Live on campus: | 95% |
| GPA 2.0-2.99: | 8% | International: | 1% |

**Basis for selection.** Primary emphasis placed on high school transcript, grades, grade pattern, level of difficulty. Test scores, essay and recommendation(s) also important. Interview recommended, extracurricular activities, evidence of leadership, and employment also considered. Must send official test scores for all SAT and/or ACT tests taken. Highest SAT (individual scores) or ACT (composite) scores used when reviewing applications for admission and for scholarships. Campus visit recommended. **Homeschooled:** Statement describing homeschool structure and mission, transcript of courses and grades, letter of recommendation (nonparent) required. Evaluation of completed education required.

**High school preparation.** College-preparatory program required. 16 units required. Required and recommended units include English 4, mathematics 3, social studies 2, science 3 (laboratory 2), foreign language 2-3 and academic electives 2. 4 lab science and 4 math required for students applying to physical therapy, occupational therapy, nursing and physician assistant programs. Physics highly recommended for physical therapy applicants.

**2010-2011 Annual costs.** Tuition/fees (projected): $34,250. Room/board: $12,730. Books/supplies: $800. Personal expenses: $900.

**2009-2010 Financial aid.** **Need-based:** 1,263 full-time freshmen applied for aid; 975 were judged to have need; 972 of these received aid. Average need met was 68%. Average scholarship/grant was $15,499; average loan $3,515. 51% of total undergraduate aid awarded as scholarships/grants, 49% as loans/jobs. **Non-need-based:** Awarded to 2,469 full-time undergraduates, including 746 freshmen. Scholarships awarded for academics, athletics.

**Application procedures. Admission:** Priority date 11/30; deadline 2/1 (postmark date). $45 fee, may be waived for applicants with need. Admission notification on a rolling basis beginning on or about 12/15. Must reply by May 1 or within 2 week(s) if notified thereafter. Students encouraged to apply early since applications are reviewed in the order they're received. Students applying for Nursing, BS/DPT in Physical Therapy or BS/MHS in Physician Assistant programs should apply by November 1. **Financial aid:** Priority date 3/1; no closing date. FAFSA required. Applicants notified on a rolling basis starting 2/15; must reply by 5/1 or within 2 week(s) of notification.

**Academics.** Incoming students must purchase a university recommended laptop computer. **Special study options:** Combined bachelor's/graduate degree, distance learning, double major, honors, independent study, internships, liberal arts/career combination, semester at sea, student-designed major, study abroad, teacher certification program, Washington semester. **Credit/placement by examination:** AP, CLEP, IB, institutional tests. 32 credit hours maximum toward bachelor's degree. **Support services:** Learning center, study skills assistance, tutoring.

**Majors. Biology:** General, biochemistry, biomedical sciences, biotechnology, molecular. **Business:** General, accounting, business admin, communications, entrepreneurial studies, finance, human resources, international, international marketing, management information systems, management science, managerial economics, marketing, nonprofit/public, office management. **Communications:** General, advertising, broadcast journalism, digital media, journalism, public relations. **Computer sciences:** General, applications programming, computer graphics, computer science. **Education:** Biology, chemistry, elementary, English, foreign languages, history, mathematics, middle, multi-level teacher, science, secondary, social studies, Spanish. **Foreign languages:** Spanish. **Health:** Athletic training, health care admin, nursing (RN), physician assistant, predental, premedicine, preveterinary, radiologic technology/medical imaging. **History:** General. **Interdisciplinary:** Biopsychology, gerontology, math/computer science. **Legal studies:** General, paralegal, prelaw. **Math:** General. **Physical sciences:** Chemistry. **Protective services:** Criminal justice. **Psychology:** General. **Science technology:** Biological. **Social sciences:** General, criminology, economics, political science, sociology. **Visual/performing arts:** Digital art, dramatic. **Other:** Biomedical marketing.

**Most popular majors.** Business/marketing 22%, communications/journalism 17%, health sciences 25%, psychology 8%, social sciences 6%.

**Computing on campus.** PC or laptop required. 500 workstations in library, computer center. Dormitories wired for high-speed internet access and linked to campus network. Commuter students can connect to campus network. Online course registration, online library, helpline, repair service, student web hosting, wireless network available.

**Student life. Freshman orientation:** Mandatory. Preregistration for classes offered. Three Friday-Saturday weekend sessions offered in June; 2-day session offered prior to start of classes. **Policies:** Housing guaranteed for 3 years to incoming freshmen, 2 years to incoming transfer students. **Housing:** Guaranteed on-campus for freshmen. Coed dorms, apartments, wellness housing available. $550 partly refundable deposit, deadline 5/1. **Activities:** Pep band, campus ministries, choral groups, dance, drama, international student organizations, literary magazine, radio station, student government, student newspaper, TV station, Hillel House, Hillel organization, Catholic services, black student union, Latino cultural society, Greenpeace, Amnesty International, SADD, women's center, Asian and Pacific Islander club, Christian Fellowship.

**Athletics.** NCAA. **Intercollegiate:** Baseball M, basketball, cheerleading M, cross-country, field hockey W, ice hockey, lacrosse, soccer, softball W, tennis, track and field W, volleyball W. **Intramural:** Archery, badminton, baseball M, basketball, bowling, field hockey W, soccer, softball, tennis, volleyball. **Team name:** Bobcats.

**Student services.** Adult student services, alcohol/substance abuse counseling, chaplain/spiritual director, career counseling, student employment services, financial aid counseling, health services, minority student services, personal counseling, placement for graduates.

**Contact.** E-mail: admissions@quinnipiac.edu
Phone: (203) 582-8600 Toll-free number: (800) 462-1944
Fax: (203) 582-8906
Carla Knowlton, Director of Admissions, Quinnipiac University, 275 Mount Carmel Avenue, Hamden, CT 06518-1908

## Sacred Heart University
**Fairfield, Connecticut** — CB member
**www.sacredheart.edu** — CB code: 3780

- Private 4-year university and liberal arts college affiliated with Roman Catholic Church
- Residential campus in large town
- 4,123 degree-seeking undergraduates: 14% part-time, 61% women, 4% African American, 2% Asian American, 7% Hispanic American, 1% international
- 1,831 degree-seeking graduate students
- 66% of applicants admitted
- Application essay required
- 66% graduate within 6 years; 43% enter graduate study

**General.** Founded in 1963. Regionally accredited. **Degrees:** 868 bachelor's, 26 associate awarded; master's, professional offered. **ROTC:** Army. **Location:** 55 miles from New York City. **Calendar:** Semester, extensive summer session. **Full-time faculty:** 204 total; 76% have terminal degrees, 12% minority, 51% women. **Part-time faculty:** 363 total; 31% have terminal degrees, 10% minority, 47% women. **Class size:** 41% < 20, 57% 20-39, 2% 40-49. **Special facilities:** Performing arts center, multipurpose communication studios, 36-hole golf course, rehabilitation clinics for occupational and physical therapies, contemporary art gallery, chapel.

**Freshman class profile.** 7,343 applied, 4,864 admitted, 909 enrolled.

| Mid 50% test scores | | | |
|---|---|---|---|
| SAT critical reading: | 460-570 | Rank in top tenth: | 18% |
| SAT math: | 490-580 | End year in good standing: | 95% |
| GPA 3.75 or higher: | 24% | Return as sophomores: | 82% |
| GPA 3.50-3.74: | 17% | Out-of-state: | 71% |
| GPA 3.0-3.49: | 36% | Live on campus: | 92% |
| GPA 2.0-2.99: | 23% | International: | 1% |
| Rank in top quarter: | 54% | Fraternities: | 7% |
| | | Sororities: | 14% |

**Basis for selection.** High school record and college preparatory curriculum most important. Standardized tests optional for all applicants except homeschooled students. Applicants may submit SAT/ACT scores if they want scores evaluated as part of their overall academic profile. SAT/ACT scores required upon deposit to the University for course placement purposes. Interview required for early decision candidates, recommended for all others. **Homeschooled:** SAT/ACT required.

**High school preparation.** College-preparatory program required. 22 units required; 30 recommended. Required and recommended units include English 4, mathematics 3-4, social studies 3-4, history 3-4, science 3-4 (laboratory 1-2), foreign language 2-4 and academic electives 3-4.

**2009-2010 Annual costs.** Tuition/fees: $30,298. Room/board: $11,684. Books/supplies: $1,000. Personal expenses: $1,000.

**2009-2010 Financial aid. Non-need-based:** Scholarships awarded for academics, alumni affiliation, art, athletics, leadership, minority status, music/drama. **Additional information:** Financial aid covers 100% tuition for first-year, full-time students from Fairfield County, CT who have family income at or below $50,000.

**Application procedures. Admission:** Priority date 2/1; no deadline. $50 fee, may be waived for applicants with need. Admission notification on a rolling basis beginning on or about 1/1. Must reply by May 1 or within 2 week(s) if notified thereafter. **Financial aid:** Priority date 2/15; no closing date. FAFSA, CSS PROFILE required. Applicants notified on a rolling basis starting 3/1; must reply within 2 week(s) of notification.

**Academics. Special study options:** Accelerated study, combined bachelor's/graduate degree, cooperative education, cross-registration, distance learning, double major, dual enrollment of high school students, ESL, honors, independent study, internships, liberal arts/career combination, student-designed major, study abroad, teacher certification program, United Nations semester, Washington semester, weekend college. Luxembourg semester, study abroad program in Ireland. **Credit/placement by examination:** AP, CLEP, IB, SAT, ACT, institutional tests. 30 credit hours maximum toward bachelor's degree. **Support services:** Learning center, reduced course load, remedial instruction, study skills assistance, tutoring, writing center.

**Honors college/program.** Holistic review of applicant is conducted. Recommended eligibility requirements: 3.4 GPA, 1250 SAT (exclusive of Writing) with 600 Critical Reading, rank in top 10% of high school class.

**Majors. Biology:** General, biochemistry. **Business:** General, accounting, fashion, finance, managerial economics, marketing. **Communications:** General, media studies. **Communications technology:** General. **Computer sciences:** General, computer science, game design, information technology. **Conservation:** General. **Foreign languages:** Spanish. **Health:** Athletic training, health services, kinesiotherapy, nursing (RN), predental, premedicine, preop/surgical nursing, prepharmacy, preveterinary. **History:** General. **Liberal arts:** Arts/sciences. **Math:** General. **Parks/recreation:** Sports admin. **Philosophy/religion:** Philosophy, religion. **Physical sciences:** Chemistry. **Protective services:** Law enforcement admin. **Psychology:** General. **Public administration:** Social work. **Social sciences:** Economics, political science, sociology. **Visual/performing arts:** Art, commercial/advertising art, design, fashion design. **Other:** Pre-occupational therapy.

**Most popular majors.** Business/marketing 31%, health sciences 15%, psychology 16%.

**Computing on campus.** PC or laptop required. 78 workstations in dormitories, library, computer center, student center. Dormitories wired for high-speed internet access and linked to campus network. Commuter students can connect to campus network. Online course registration, online library, helpline, repair service, student web hosting, wireless network available.

**Student life. Freshman orientation:** Mandatory. Preregistration for classes offered. Overnight 2-day program in late spring for both parents and students. **Policies:** Freshman Convocation required for all first-year students; held in September. **Housing:** Guaranteed on-campus for all undergraduates. Coed dorms, special housing for disabled, apartments, wellness housing available. $1,500 nonrefundable deposit, deadline 5/1. Living and learning communities available for specific academic programs, honors floors. **Activities:** Bands, campus ministries, choral groups, dance, drama, film society, international student organizations, literary magazine, music ensembles, musical theater, radio station, student government, student newspaper, TV station, ONE Campaign, La Hispanidad, Habitat for Humanity, Circle K, Read Aloud, UMOJA, Active Minds, gay/straight alliance, College Democrats, College Republicans.

**Athletics.** NCAA. **Intercollegiate:** Baseball M, basketball, bowling W, cross-country, equestrian W, fencing, field hockey W, football (tackle) M, golf, ice hockey, lacrosse, rowing (crew) W, soccer, softball W, swimming W, tennis, track and field, volleyball, wrestling M. **Intramural:** Basketball, bowling, cheerleading W, field hockey W, football (non-tackle), golf, skiing, soccer, softball, table tennis, tennis, volleyball. **Team name:** Pioneers.

**Student services.** Adult student services, alcohol/substance abuse counseling, chaplain/spiritual director, career counseling, services for economically disadvantaged, student employment services, financial aid counseling, health services, minority student services, personal counseling, placement for graduates, women's services. **Physically disabled:** Services for visually, speech, hearing impaired.

**Contact.** E-mail: enroll@sacredheart.edu
Phone: (203) 371-7880 Fax: (203) 365-7607
Karen Guastelle, Dean of Undergraduate Admissions, Sacred Heart University, 5151 Park Avenue, Fairfield, CT 06825

---

## Saint Joseph College
**West Hartford, Connecticut**  ·  **CB member**
www.sjc.edu  ·  **CB code: 3754**

- Private 4-year liberal arts and career college for women affiliated with Roman Catholic Church
- Residential campus in small city
- 947 degree-seeking undergraduates: 19% part-time, 99% women, 11% African American, 2% Asian American, 10% Hispanic American
- 825 degree-seeking graduate students
- 84% of applicants admitted
- SAT or ACT (ACT writing optional) required
- 46% graduate within 6 years

**General.** Founded in 1932. Regionally accredited. Men admitted to adult undergraduate degree-completion program and graduate school. **Degrees:** 228 bachelor's awarded; master's offered. **Location:** 3 miles from Hartford. **Calendar:** Semester, limited summer session. **Full-time faculty:** 78 total; 82% have terminal degrees, 13% minority, 72% women. **Part-time faculty:** 140 total. **Class size:** 72% < 20, 26% 20-39, 1% 40-49, less than 1% 50-99.

**Freshman class profile.** 1,150 applied, 961 admitted, 184 enrolled.

| Mid 50% test scores | | | |
|---|---|---|---|
| SAT critical reading: | 440-520 | Rank in top quarter: | 47% |
| SAT math: | 440-520 | Rank in top tenth: | 19% |
| GPA 3.75 or higher: | 16% | Return as sophomores: | 75% |
| GPA 3.50-3.74: | 17% | Out-of-state: | 15% |
| GPA 3.0-3.49: | 37% | Live on campus: | 79% |
| GPA 2.0-2.99: | 30% | International: | 1% |

**Basis for selection.** Decisions based on application, transcripts, SAT/ACT scores. **Homeschooled:** Statement describing homeschool structure and mission, letter of recommendation (nonparent) required.

**High school preparation.** College-preparatory program required. 16 units required. Required and recommended units include English 4, mathematics 3, social studies 3, science 3 and foreign language 3.

**2009-2010 Annual costs.** Tuition/fees: $27,202. Room/board: $12,437.

**2009-2010 Financial aid. Need-based:** 178 full-time freshmen applied for aid; 164 were judged to have need; 164 of these received aid. Average need met was 79%. Average scholarship/grant was $18,987; average loan $3,332. 75% of total undergraduate aid awarded as scholarships/grants, 25% as loans/jobs. **Non-need-based:** Awarded to 116 full-time undergraduates, including 27 freshmen. Scholarships awarded for academics.

**Application procedures. Admission:** No deadline. $50 fee, may be waived for applicants with need, free for online applicants. Admission notification on a rolling basis. **Financial aid:** Priority date 2/15; no closing date. FAFSA required. Applicants notified on a rolling basis starting 3/1.

**Academics. Special study options:** Accelerated study, combined bachelor's/graduate degree, distance learning, double major, honors, independent study, internships, liberal arts/career combination, student-designed major, study abroad, teacher certification program, weekend college. **Credit/placement by examination:** CLEP, institutional tests. **Support services:** Learning center, pre-admission summer program, reduced course load, study skills assistance, tutoring, writing center.

**Majors. Area/ethnic studies:** American, women's. **Biology:** General, biochemistry. **Business:** Accounting, business admin. **Education:** Special. **Family/consumer sciences:** General, child development, food/nutrition. **Foreign languages:** Spanish. **Health:** Nursing (RN). **History:** General. **Interdisciplinary:** Global studies. **Liberal arts:** Arts/sciences. **Math:** General. **Philosophy/religion:** Philosophy, religion. **Physical sciences:** Chemistry. **Psychology:** General. **Public administration:** Social work. **Visual/performing arts:** Art history/conservation.

**Most popular majors.** Biology 7%, business/marketing 7%, family/consumer sciences 10%, health sciences 27%, psychology 12%, public administration/social services 10%.

**Computing on campus.** Dormitories wired for high-speed internet access and linked to campus network. Online course registration, online library, helpline, wireless network available.

**Student life. Freshman orientation:** Mandatory. Preregistration for classes offered. **Housing:** Special housing for disabled, wellness housing available. $250 nonrefundable deposit, deadline 6/15. Single rooms available for nontraditional students. Medical singles with private bathrooms available on a limited basis. **Activities:** Campus ministries, choral groups, dance, drama, international student organizations, music ensembles, student government, student newspaper.

**Athletics.** NCAA. **Intercollegiate:** Basketball W, cross-country W, diving W, lacrosse W, soccer W, softball W, swimming W, tennis W, volleyball W. **Team name:** Blue Jays.

**Student services.** Adult student services, alcohol/substance abuse counseling, chaplain/spiritual director, career counseling, student employment services, financial aid counseling, health services, personal counseling, placement for graduates, women's services. **Physically disabled:** Services for visually, hearing impaired.

**Contact.**  E-mail: admissions@sjc.edu
Phone: (860) 231-5216 Toll-free number: (866) 442-8752
Nancy Wunderly, Director of Admissions, Saint Joseph College, 1678 Asylum Avenue, West Hartford, CT 06117

## Southern Connecticut State University

**New Haven, Connecticut** — **CB member**
**www.southernct.edu** — **CB code: 3662**

- Public 4-year university
- Residential campus in small city
- 8,594 degree-seeking undergraduates: 14% part-time, 63% women, 12% African American, 2% Asian American, 5% Hispanic American
- 3,221 degree-seeking graduate students
- 71% of applicants admitted
- SAT or ACT with writing, application essay required
- 42% graduate within 6 years

**General.** Founded in 1893. Regionally accredited. **Degrees:** 1,422 bachelor's awarded; master's, doctoral offered. **ROTC:** Army, Air Force. **Location:** 75 miles from New York City. **Calendar:** Semester, extensive summer session. **Full-time faculty:** 407 total; 86% have terminal degrees, 16% minority, 49% women. **Part-time faculty:** 678 total; 37% have terminal degrees, 12% minority, 55% women. **Class size:** 40% < 20, 53% 20-39, 5% 40-49, 1% 50-99, less than 1% >100. **Special facilities:** Planetarium, photonics laboratory, geospatial technology laboratory.

**Freshman class profile.** 5,596 applied, 3,993 admitted, 1,244 enrolled.

| Mid 50% test scores | | | |
|---|---|---|---|
| SAT critical reading: | 440-520 | Rank in top quarter: | 24% |
| SAT math: | 430-530 | Rank in top tenth: | 5% |
| SAT writing: | 440-530 | Return as sophomores: | 80% |
| GPA 3.75 or higher: | 3% | Out-of-state: | 11% |
| GPA 3.50-3.74: | 7% | Live on campus: | 68% |
| GPA 3.0-3.49: | 36% | Fraternities: | 1% |
| GPA 2.0-2.99: | 54% | Sororities: | 1% |

**Basis for selection.** School achievement record, test scores most important. Special consideration to culturally disadvantaged students. **Homeschooled:** Statement describing homeschool structure and mission, transcript of courses and grades, letter of recommendation (nonparent) required.

**High school preparation.** College-preparatory program required. 16 units required. Required and recommended units include English 4, mathematics 3-4, social studies 2-3, history 2-3, science 2-3 (laboratory 1) and foreign language 2-4. One unit of algebra II required.

**2009-2010 Annual costs.** Tuition/fees: $7,428; $17,120 out-of-state. Room/board: $9,469. Books/supplies: $1,300. Personal expenses: $250.

**Application procedures. Admission:** Closing date 4/1 (postmark date). $50 fee, may be waived for applicants with need. Admission notification on a rolling basis beginning on or about 12/1. Must reply by May 1 or within 2 week(s) if notified thereafter. **Financial aid:** Priority date 3/6; no closing date. Must reply within 2 week(s) of notification.

**Academics. Special study options:** Accelerated study, cooperative education, cross-registration, distance learning, double major, dual enrollment of high school students, exchange student, external degree, honors, independent study, internships, liberal arts/career combination, student-designed major, study abroad, teacher certification program. **Credit/placement by examination:** AP, CLEP, SAT, institutional tests. 30 credit hours maximum toward associate degree, 30 toward bachelor's. **Support services:** Learning center, pre-admission summer program, reduced course load, remedial instruction, study skills assistance, tutoring, writing center.

**Majors. Biology:** General. **Business:** Accounting, business admin, finance, management science, managerial economics, marketing. **Communications:** General, journalism. **Computer sciences:** General. **Education:** General, art,

biology, chemistry, elementary, English, history, mathematics, physical, physics, science, secondary, social science, social studies, Spanish. **Foreign languages:** General, French, German, Italian, Spanish. **Health:** Nursing (RN), predental, premedicine, prepharmacy, preveterinary. **History:** General. **Legal studies:** Prelaw. **Liberal arts:** Arts/sciences, library science. **Math:** General. **Parks/recreation:** General, exercise sciences. **Philosophy/religion:** Philosophy. **Physical sciences:** Chemistry, geology, physics. **Psychology:** General. **Public administration:** Social work. **Social sciences:** Geography, political science, sociology. **Visual/performing arts:** Art, art history/conservation, dramatic.

**Most popular majors.** Business/marketing 14%, communications/journalism 8%, education 12%, health sciences 11%, liberal arts 10%, psychology 12%, social sciences 7%.

**Computing on campus.** 750 workstations in dormitories, library, computer center, student center. Dormitories wired for high-speed internet access and linked to campus network. Commuter students can connect to campus network. Online course registration, online library, helpline, student web hosting, wireless network available.

**Student life. Freshman orientation:** Mandatory. Preregistration for classes offered. **Housing:** Coed dorms, special housing for disabled, apartments available. $250 nonrefundable deposit, deadline 3/30. Students must be 19 or older to live in upper-classmen apartments. **Activities:** Bands, campus ministries, choral groups, drama, literary magazine, music ensembles, radio station, student government, student newspaper, Christian Fellowship, Newman club, Latin American students organization, black student union, People to People, students for disability rights, veterans club.

**Athletics.** NCAA. **Intercollegiate:** Baseball M, basketball, cross-country, field hockey W, football (tackle) M, gymnastics W, lacrosse W, soccer, softball W, swimming, track and field, volleyball M. **Intramural:** Basketball, football (non-tackle), soccer, softball, tennis, volleyball. **Team name:** Owls.

**Student services.** Adult student services, alcohol/substance abuse counseling, chaplain/spiritual director, career counseling, student employment services, financial aid counseling, health services, personal counseling, placement for graduates, veterans' counselor, women's services. **Physically disabled:** Services for visually, speech, hearing impaired.

**Contact.**  Phone: (203) 392-5644 Toll-free number: (888) 500-7278
Fax: (203) 392-5727
James Williams, Admissions and Enrollment Management, Southern Connecticut State University, 131 Farnham Avenue, New Haven, CT 06515-1202

## Trinity College

**Hartford, Connecticut** — **CB member**
**www.trincoll.edu** — **CB code: 3899**

- Private 4-year liberal arts college
- Residential campus in large city
- 2,234 degree-seeking undergraduates: 2% part-time, 49% women, 6% African American, 6% Asian American, 6% Hispanic American, 5% international
- 144 degree-seeking graduate students
- 41% of applicants admitted
- SAT or ACT (ACT writing recommended), application essay required
- 86% graduate within 6 years; 18% enter graduate study

**General.** Founded in 1823. Regionally accredited. **Degrees:** 567 bachelor's awarded; master's offered. **ROTC:** Army. **Location:** 125 miles from New York City, 100 miles from Boston. **Calendar:** Semester, limited summer session. **Full-time faculty:** 195 total; 92% have terminal degrees, 20% minority, 40% women. **Part-time faculty:** 72 total; 65% have terminal degrees, 14% minority, 44% women. **Class size:** 66% < 20, 28% 20-39, 3% 40-49, 3% 50-99, less than 1% >100. **Special facilities:** Library collections on Native Americans, maritime history, early American texts, nuclear magnetic spectrometer, mass spectrometer, electronic microscope, plasma spectrometer, optical diagnostics and communications laboratory, natural science field station.

**Freshman class profile.** 4,532 applied, 1,874 admitted, 573 enrolled.

| Mid 50% test scores | | | |
|---|---|---|---|
| | | Rank in top tenth: | 68% |
| SAT critical reading: | 590-680 | End year in good standing: | 87% |
| SAT math: | 610-690 | Return as sophomores: | 91% |
| SAT writing: | 610-710 | Out-of-state: | 83% |
| ACT composite: | 26-30 | Live on campus: | 99% |
| Rank in top quarter: | 93% | International: | 6% |

**Basis for selection.** School record and recommendations most important. Test scores used for math and writing placement. SAT Subject Tests recommended. One of the following required: SAT, ACT, or 2 SAT Subject Tests. Interview recommended.

**High school preparation.** College-preparatory program recommended. 16 units required. Required units include English 4, mathematics 3, history 2, science 2 (laboratory 2) and foreign language 3.

**2009-2010 Annual costs.** Tuition/fees: $40,840. One-time $25 transcript fee for new students only. Room/board: $10,560. Books/supplies: $1,000. Personal expenses: $900.

**2009-2010 Financial aid. Need-based:** 279 full-time freshmen applied for aid; 247 were judged to have need; 247 of these received aid. Average need met was 100%. Average scholarship/grant was $33,695; average loan $3,691. 89% of total undergraduate aid awarded as scholarships/grants, 11% as loans/jobs. **Non-need-based:** Awarded to 213 full-time undergraduates, including 61 freshmen. Scholarships awarded for academics, leadership.

**Application procedures. Admission:** Closing date 1/1 (postmark date). $60 fee, may be waived for applicants with need. Admission notification 4/1. Must reply by May 1 or within 2 week(s) if notified thereafter. **Financial aid:** Priority date 2/1, closing date 3/1. FAFSA, CSS PROFILE required. Applicants notified by 4/1; must reply by 5/1 or within 2 week(s) of notification.

**Academics.** Math center available. **Special study options:** Accelerated study, combined bachelor's/graduate degree, cross-registration, double major, exchange student, honors, independent study, internships, liberal arts/career combination, New York semester, semester at sea, student-designed major, study abroad, teacher certification program, United Nations semester, urban semester, Washington semester. Community Learning Initiative (courses with community-based components) available. **Credit/placement by examination:** AP, CLEP, IB, SAT, ACT, institutional tests. **Support services:** Study skills assistance, tutoring, writing center.

**Majors. Area/ethnic studies:** African, African-American, American, Asian, gay/lesbian, Latin American, Near/Middle Eastern, Russian/Slavic, women's. **Biology:** General, biochemistry. **Computer sciences:** General, computer science. **Conservation:** Environmental science. **Education:** General. **Engineering:** General, biomedical, electrical, mechanical. **Foreign languages:** General, Chinese, classics, comparative lit, French, German, Italian, Japanese, Russian, Spanish. **Health:** Premedicine. **History:** General. **Interdisciplinary:** Neuroscience. **Legal studies:** Prelaw. **Math:** General. **Philosophy/religion:** Judaic, philosophy, religion. **Physical sciences:** Chemistry, physics. **Psychology:** General. **Public administration:** Policy analysis. **Social sciences:** General, anthropology, economics, international relations, political science, sociology, urban studies. **Visual/performing arts:** General, art, art history/conservation, dance, dramatic, film/cinema, studio arts.

**Most popular majors.** Area/ethnic studies 12%, English 7%, history 8%, interdisciplinary studies 6%, psychology 8%, social sciences 27%, visual/performing arts 6%.

**Computing on campus.** 327 workstations in library, computer center. Dormitories wired for high-speed internet access and linked to campus network. Commuter students can connect to campus network. Online course registration, online library, helpline, student web hosting, wireless network available.

**Student life. Freshman orientation:** Available. Preregistration for classes offered. 4-day session beginning Thursday before Labor Day. Advising days held in June to begin registration process; optional outdoor challenge program in early August. **Policies:** All dorms are non-smoking. **Housing:** Guaranteed on-campus for freshmen. Coed dorms, special housing for disabled, apartments, fraternity/sorority housing, wellness housing available. Community service dorm, quiet dorm, alternative social programming dorm, cooking units available. **Activities:** Jazz band, campus ministries, choral groups, dance, drama, film society, international student organizations, literary magazine, Model UN, musical theater, radio station, student government, student newspaper, Asian-American student association, Intervarsity Christian Fellowship, Encouraging Respect of Sexualities, Friends Active in Civic Engagement and Service, Hillel, Imani, La Voz Latina, Promoting Healthy Awareness of the Body, Promoting Respect for Inclusive Diversity in Education, black women's organization.

**Athletics.** NCAA. **Intercollegiate:** Baseball M, basketball, cross-country, diving, field hockey W, football (tackle) M, golf M, ice hockey, lacrosse, rowing (crew), soccer, softball W, squash, swimming, tennis, track and field, volleyball W, wrestling M. **Intramural:** Badminton, basketball, football (non-tackle), ice hockey, soccer, softball, squash, tennis. **Team name:** Bantams.

**Student services.** Adult student services, alcohol/substance abuse counseling, chaplain/spiritual director, career counseling, services for economically disadvantaged, student employment services, financial aid counseling, health services, minority student services, on-campus daycare, personal counseling, placement for graduates, women's services.

**Contact.** E-mail: admissions.office@trincoll.edu
Phone: (860) 297-2180 Fax: (860) 297-2287
Larry Dow, Dean of Admissions and Financial Aid, Trinity College, 300 Summit Street, Hartford, CT 06106

## United States Coast Guard Academy
**New London, Connecticut**       **CB member**
**www.uscga.edu**       **CB code: 5807**

▶ Public 4-year engineering and maritime college
▶ Residential campus in small city
▶ 973 degree-seeking undergraduates: 27% women, 3% African American, 4% Asian American, 7% Hispanic American, 1% Native American, 2% international
▶ 25% of applicants admitted
▶ SAT or ACT with writing, application essay required
▶ 77% graduate within 6 years

**General.** Founded in 1876. Regionally accredited. As a federal military service academy, The Coast Guard Academy is a tuition-free degree-granting institution. All students earn a modest stipend while enrolled, and receive medical and dental benefits at no charge. **Degrees:** 222 bachelor's awarded. **Location:** 120 miles from New York City, 130 miles from Boston. **Calendar:** Semester, limited summer session. **Full-time faculty:** 139 total; 48% have terminal degrees, 7% minority, 26% women. **Part-time faculty:** 2 total; 50% minority. **Class size:** 71% < 20, 29% 20-39. **Special facilities:** Museum, research and development center, 295-foot-tall ship, ship navigation simulation facilities with bridge simulator, 10,000 gallon circulating water channel, ship model towing tank, observatory with reflector telescope.

**Freshman class profile.** 1,672 applied, 411 admitted, 288 enrolled.

| Mid 50% test scores | | Rank in top quarter: | 83% |
|---|---|---|---|
| SAT critical reading: | 560-660 | Rank in top tenth: | 49% |
| SAT math: | 600-680 | End year in good standing: | 90% |
| ACT composite: | 24-30 | Return as sophomores: | 90% |
| GPA 3.75 or higher: | 51% | Out-of-state: | 94% |
| GPA 3.50-3.74: | 25% | Live on campus: | 100% |
| GPA 3.0-3.49: | 18% | International: | 2% |
| GPA 2.0-2.99: | 6% | | |

**Basis for selection.** Test scores, high school class rank, recommendations, essay, leadership potential as demonstrated by extracurricular activities, athletics, community affairs, and part-time employment considered. Congressional nomination not required. Applicants required to pass medical and physical fitness exams. Interview recommended. **Homeschooled:** AP and SAT Subject Tests recommended. Application should include detailed account of curriculum and course content. Students advised to take courses in math and science at a local college and have professor submit a recommendation. Recommendations from other adults required. Essay should include reasons for undertaking homeschooling, benefits realized, and how experience prepared student to succeed in college.

**High school preparation.** College-preparatory program recommended. Required units include English 4, mathematics 4, science 3 (laboratory 3). Math units should include algebra, quadratics, plane or coordinate geometry, or equivalent. Calculus and pre-calculus recommended. Sciences should include chemistry and physics.

**2010-2011 Annual costs.** All tuition, room and board for U.S. residents paid for by U.S. Government. Students make one-time entrance deposit of $3,000 to help defray the cost of uniforms, books, supplies and personal computer. All students paid a monthly stipend of $929.40. Cost of instruction for non-resident alien cadets is $71,349 per year. Before an international cadet is enrolled at the Academy, sponsoring country must agree to reimburse the U.S. Coast Guard for cost of instruction. Countries not listed on World Bank list would be eligible for partial tuition costs of $16,300 annually.

**Application procedures. Admission:** Priority date 11/1; deadline 2/1 (postmark date). No application fee. Application must be submitted online. Admission notification 4/15. Admission notification on a rolling basis. Must reply by May 1 or within 2 week(s) if notified thereafter. Application by 11/01 recommended to allow time to complete essays and supplemental forms, obtain teacher recommendations, and schedule required physical. **Financial aid:** No deadline.

**Academics.** Each student issued a laptop computer. Summers involve introductory and advanced Coast Guard/professional training including opportunities to sail aboard Eagle, fly Coast Guard aircraft, become small arms qualified (rifle and pistol), learn basic shipboard fire fighting and flooding control, and perform actual search and rescue coordination at Coast Guard units. Summer between junior and senior years typically involves piloting and navigation of Coast Guard Cutters and integration into all aspects of operational afloat Coast Guard missions. All graduates commissioned as officers in U.S Coast Guard with a 5-year obligatory military service after graduation. **Special study options:** Double major, exchange student, honors, independent study, internships. **Credit/placement by examination:** AP, CLEP, institutional tests. **Support services:** Learning center, pre-admission summer program, reduced course load, remedial instruction, study skills assistance, tutoring, writing center.

**Majors. Business:** Business admin. **Engineering:** Civil, electrical, marine, mechanical. **Physical sciences:** Oceanography. **Social sciences:** Political science. **Other:** Operations research.

**Most popular majors.** Biology 13%, business/marketing 12%, engineering/ engineering technologies 41%, mathematics 12%, social sciences 22%.

**Computing on campus.** PC or laptop required. 325 workstations in dormitories, library, computer center. Dormitories wired for high-speed internet access and linked to campus network. Online course registration, online library, helpline, repair service, student web hosting, wireless network available.

**Student life. Freshman orientation:** Mandatory. 7-week "swab summer," including one week onboard the Coast Guard Cutter Eagle. **Policies:** Students part of corps of cadets. On-campus residence mandatory. **Housing:** Guaranteed on-campus for all undergraduates. Coed dorms, wellness housing available. **Activities:** Bands, campus ministries, choral groups, dance, drama, international student organizations, music ensembles, Model UN, musical theater, student government, student newspaper, Officers Christian Fellowship, multicultural club, Fellowship of Christian Athletes, Big Brothers and Big Sisters, Boy Scouts, Genesis club.

**Athletics.** NCAA. **Intercollegiate:** Baseball M, basketball, cheerleading M, cross-country, diving, football (tackle) M, rifle, rowing (crew), sailing, soccer, softball W, swimming, tennis M, track and field, volleyball W, wrestling M. **Intramural:** Basketball, football (non-tackle), golf, racquetball, soccer, softball, tennis, volleyball. **Team name:** Bears.

**Student services.** Alcohol/substance abuse counseling, chaplain/ spiritual director, career counseling, health services, legal services, minority student services, on-campus daycare, personal counseling, placement for graduates.

**Contact.** E-mail: admissions@uscga.edu
Phone: (860) 444-8500 Toll-free number: (800) 883-8724
Fax: (860) 701-6700
Capt. Susan Bibeau, Director of Admissions, United States Coast Guard Academy, 31 Mohegan Avenue, New London, CT 06320

## University of Bridgeport
**Bridgeport, Connecticut** — CB member
www.bridgeport.edu — CB code: 3914

- Private 4-year university
- Residential campus in small city
- 2,248 degree-seeking undergraduates: 33% part-time, 68% women, 37% African American, 3% Asian American, 15% Hispanic American, 11% international
- 2,855 degree-seeking graduate students
- 55% of applicants admitted
- SAT or ACT (ACT writing optional), application essay required
- 43% graduate within 6 years; 50% enter graduate study

**General.** Founded in 1927. Regionally accredited. Off-campus facilities in Stamford and Waterbury. **Degrees:** 270 bachelor's, 40 associate awarded; master's, professional offered. **ROTC:** Army. **Location:** 60 miles from New York City. **Calendar:** Semester, extensive summer session. **Full-time faculty:** 125 total; 75% have terminal degrees, 23% minority, 37% women. **Part-time faculty:** 368 total; 14% minority, 43% women. **Class size:** 61% < 20, 37% 20-39, 1% 40-49, 1% 50-99. **Special facilities:** Theater, recital halls, studios, exhibit rooms.

**Freshman class profile.** 8,165 applied, 4,510 admitted, 440 enrolled.

| Mid 50% test scores | | | |
|---|---|---|---|
| SAT critical reading: | 400-490 | Rank in top quarter: | 29% |
| SAT math: | 410-500 | Rank in top tenth: | 7% |
| SAT writing: | 400-480 | End year in good standing: | 59% |
| ACT composite: | 16-20 | Return as sophomores: | 52% |
| GPA 3.75 or higher: | 7% | Out-of-state: | 66% |
| GPA 3.50-3.74: | 7% | Live on campus: | 74% |
| GPA 3.0-3.49: | 24% | International: | 7% |
| GPA 2.0-2.99: | 60% | Fraternities: | 1% |
| | | Sororities: | 1% |

**Basis for selection.** School achievement record most important, followed by test scores, activities, trend of grades and curriculum in high school. Audition required of music majors. Portfolio required of fine and applied arts majors. Interview recommended of dental hygiene, basic studies majors.

**High school preparation.** College-preparatory program recommended. 16 units required. Required units include English 4, mathematics 3, social studies 2, science 2 (laboratory 2) and academic electives 5. 4 math required for math, science, computer science and engineering applicants. Chemistry required for dental hygiene.

**2009-2010 Annual costs.** Tuition/fees: $25,465. Room/board: $11,080. Books/supplies: $1,500. Personal expenses: $3,007.

**2009-2010 Financial aid. Need-based:** 405 full-time freshmen applied for aid; 390 were judged to have need; 390 of these received aid. Average need met was 65%. Average scholarship/grant was $8,261; average loan $5,294. 72% of total undergraduate aid awarded as scholarships/grants, 28% as loans/jobs. **Non-need-based:** Awarded to 1,565 full-time undergraduates, including 421 freshmen. Scholarships awarded for academics, athletics, leadership, music/drama, state residency.

**Application procedures. Admission:** Priority date 4/1; no deadline. $25 fee, may be waived for applicants with need. Admission notification on a rolling basis. Must reply by May 1 or within 2 week(s) if notified thereafter. **Financial aid:** Priority date 4/1; no closing date. FAFSA required. Applicants notified on a rolling basis starting 4/1; must reply within 4 week(s) of notification.

**Academics. Special study options:** Accelerated study, combined bachelor's/ graduate degree, cooperative education, cross-registration, distance learning, double major, dual enrollment of high school students, ESL, exchange student, honors, independent study, internships, liberal arts/career combination, New York semester, semester at sea, student-designed major, study abroad, teacher certification program, United Nations semester, Washington semester, weekend college. **Credit/placement by examination:** AP, CLEP, IB, SAT, ACT, institutional tests. 30 credit hours maximum toward associate degree, 30 toward bachelor's. **Support services:** Learning center, pre-admission summer program, reduced course load, remedial instruction, study skills assistance, tutoring, writing center.

**Majors. Area/ethnic studies:** East Asian. **Biology:** General. **Business:** General, accounting, fashion, finance, international, labor relations, management information systems, marketing. **Communications:** General, advertising, journalism, media studies, public relations. **Computer sciences:** General. **Engineering:** Computer. **Health:** Clinical lab science, dental hygiene. **Liberal arts:** Arts/sciences, humanities. **Math:** General. **Philosophy/religion:** Religion. **Physical sciences:** General. **Psychology:** General. **Public administration:** Community org/advocacy. **Social sciences:** General, criminology, international relations, political science, sociology. **Visual/performing arts:** Graphic design, illustration, industrial design, interior design.

**Most popular majors.** Business/marketing 23%, health sciences 13%, liberal arts 21%, psychology 12%, public administration/social services 9%, visual/performing arts 10%.

**Computing on campus.** 600 workstations in dormitories, library, computer center, student center. Dormitories wired for high-speed internet access and linked to campus network. Commuter students can connect to campus network. Online library, helpline, repair service, student web hosting, wireless network available.

**Student life. Freshman orientation:** Mandatory, $100 fee. Preregistration for classes offered. Placement listing, registration, and orientation held during the summer with final program just prior to class. **Policies:** Student and dormitory governments plan student life activities. **Housing:** Guaranteed on-campus for all undergraduates. Coed dorms, wellness housing available. $200 deposit, deadline 5/1. Dormitories have special facilities. **Activities:** Choral groups, film society, international student organizations, literary magazine, music ensembles, Model UN, student government, student newspaper, interfaith center, black student alliance, social service sorority, Protestant fellowship, community service project.

**Athletics.** NCAA. **Intercollegiate:** Baseball M, basketball, cross-country, gymnastics W, lacrosse W, soccer, softball W, swimming, volleyball W. **Intramural:** Basketball, racquetball, soccer, softball, tennis, volleyball. **Team name:** Purple Knights.

**Student services.** Adult student services, alcohol/substance abuse counseling, chaplain/spiritual director, career counseling, student employment services, financial aid counseling, health services, minority student services, personal counseling, placement for graduates, veterans' counselor. **Physically disabled:** Services for visually, speech, hearing impaired.

**Contact.** E-mail: admit@bridgeport.edu
Phone: (203) 576-4552 Toll-free number: (800) 392-3582
Fax: (203) 576-4941
Bryan Gross, Dean of Admissions, University of Bridgeport, 126 Park Avenue, Bridgeport, CT 06604

## University of Connecticut
**Storrs, Connecticut**  **CB member**
**www.uconn.edu**  **CB code: 3915**

- Public 4-year university
- Residential campus in large town
- 16,691 degree-seeking undergraduates: 3% part-time, 50% women, 5% African American, 8% Asian American, 5% Hispanic American, 1% international
- 7,329 degree-seeking graduate students
- 50% of applicants admitted
- SAT or ACT with writing, application essay required
- 78% graduate within 6 years; 31% enter graduate study

**General.** Founded in 1881. Regionally accredited. Students may take courses at nonresidential campuses in Groton, Hartford, Stamford, Waterbury, and Torrington. **Degrees:** 4,610 bachelor's, 19 associate awarded; master's, doctoral, professional offered. **ROTC:** Army, Air Force. **Location:** 26 miles from Hartford, 80 miles from Boston. **Calendar:** Semester, extensive summer session. **Full-time faculty:** 1,003 total; 94% have terminal degrees, 20% minority, 36% women. **Part-time faculty:** 330 total; 29% have terminal degrees, 7% minority, 49% women. **Class size:** 43% < 20, 30% 20-39, 9% 40-49, 9% 50-99, 9% >100. **Special facilities:** Museum of natural history, research center, ice hockey/skating rink, dairy bar.

**Freshman class profile.** 21,999 applied, 10,931 admitted, 3,221 enrolled.

| Mid 50% test scores | | | |
|---|---|---|---|
| SAT critical reading: | 550-640 | Return as sophomores: | 92% |
| SAT math: | 570-670 | Out-of-state: | 32% |
| SAT writing: | 550-650 | Live on campus: | 97% |
| ACT composite: | 24-29 | International: | 2% |
| Rank in top quarter: | 83% | Fraternities: | 7% |
| Rank in top tenth: | 44% | Sororities: | 7% |

**Basis for selection.** Curriculum, grades, rank in class most important, followed by test scores. Particular consideration given to first generation college and/or socio-economically disadvantaged applicants and applicants with special talents. Audition required of music, acting, puppetry majors. Portfolio required for art major. Interview required for design/technical theater and theater studies majors. **Homeschooled:** Statement describing homeschool structure and mission, transcript of courses and grades required. **Learning Disabled:** Students may submit disability documentation to Center for Students with Disabilities upon admission.

**High school preparation.** College-preparatory program required. 16 units required. Required and recommended units include English 4, mathematics 3, social studies 2, science 2 (laboratory 2), foreign language 2-3 and academic electives 3. Some programs may require additional units.

**2010-2011 Annual costs.** Tuition/fees: $10,416; $26,880 out-of-state. Room/board: $10,782. Books/supplies: $800. Personal expenses: $1,640.

**2009-2010 Financial aid. Non-need-based:** Scholarships awarded for academics, art, athletics, leadership, minority status, music/drama. **Additional information:** Institution offers variety of need-based financial aid programs. Financial assistance packages may include grants, loans and work-study awards.

**Application procedures. Admission:** Closing date 2/1. $70 fee, may be waived for applicants with need. Admission notification on a rolling basis beginning on or about 1/1. Must reply by May 1 or within 2 week(s) if notified thereafter. **Financial aid:** Priority date 3/1; no closing date. FAFSA required. Applicants notified on a rolling basis starting 3/1; must reply within 4 week(s) of notification.

**Academics.** 5-year Eurotech Program program combining engineering and German language, including 6-month internship in Germany. **Special study options:** Accelerated study, combined bachelor's/graduate degree, cooperative education, distance learning, double major, dual enrollment of high school students, ESL, exchange student, honors, independent study, internships, liberal arts/career combination, New York semester, semester at sea, student-designed major, study abroad, teacher certification program, urban semester, Washington semester. Winter inter-session, summer session, urban semester. **Credit/placement by examination:** AP, CLEP, IB, SAT, institutional tests. 30 credit hours maximum toward bachelor's degree. **Support services:** Learning center, pre-admission summer program, study skills assistance, tutoring, writing center.

**Majors. Agriculture:** General, agronomy, animal sciences, economics, horticultural science. **Architecture:** Landscape. **Area/ethnic studies:** American, Latin American, Near/Middle Eastern, women's. **Biology:** General, animal physiology, biophysics, cellular/molecular, ecology, marine, pathology. **Business:** General, accounting, actuarial science, business admin, finance, insurance, management information systems, marketing, real estate. **Communications:** General, journalism. **Computer sciences:** Computer science. **Conservation:** General, environmental studies. **Education:** Agricultural, elementary, music, physical, special. **Engineering:** Biomedical, chemical, civil, computer, electrical, environmental, industrial, materials, materials science, mechanical, physics. **Family/consumer sciences:** Family studies. **Foreign languages:** Classics, French, German, Italian, linguistics, Spanish. **Health:** Clinical lab science, cytotechnology, dietetics, gene therapy, health care admin, health services, nursing (RN), prepharmacy. **History:** General. **Interdisciplinary:** Cognitive science, nutrition sciences. **Math:** General, applied, statistics. **Parks/recreation:** Facilities management. **Philosophy/religion:** Philosophy. **Physical sciences:** Chemistry, geology, physics. **Psychology:** General, cognitive. **Social sciences:** Anthropology, economics, geography, political science, sociology, urban studies. **Visual/performing arts:** Acting, art history/conservation, dramatic, studio arts, theater design. **Other:** Puppetry.

**Most popular majors.** Biology 7%, business/marketing 14%, communications/journalism 6%, engineering/engineering technologies 7%, English 6%, health sciences 9%, liberal arts 7%, psychology 7%, social sciences 15%.

**Computing on campus.** 1,318 workstations in dormitories, library, computer center, student center. Dormitories wired for high-speed internet access and linked to campus network. Commuter students can connect to campus network. Online course registration, online library, helpline, repair service, wireless network available.

**Student life. Freshman orientation:** Available, $60 fee. Preregistration for classes offered. Twelve 2-day sessions extending from late May to early July. **Housing:** Coed dorms, single-sex dorms, special housing for disabled, apartments, fraternity/sorority housing available. $150 nonrefundable deposit, deadline 5/1. Special interests; honors; foreign languages; older-student housing; freshmen year experience housing; global house; women in math, science, and engineering; other learning communities. **Activities:** Bands, campus ministries, choral groups, dance, drama, film society, international student organizations, literary magazine, music ensembles, Model UN, musical theater, opera, radio station, student government, student newspaper, symphony orchestra, TV station, over 300 organizations available.

**Athletics.** NCAA. **Intercollegiate:** Baseball M, basketball, cross-country, diving, field hockey W, football (tackle) M, golf M, ice hockey, lacrosse W, rowing (crew) W, soccer, softball W, swimming, tennis, track and field, volleyball W. **Intramural:** Badminton, baseball M, basketball, bowling, cross-country, diving, equestrian, fencing, football (non-tackle), football (tackle) M, ice hockey, lacrosse, racquetball, rowing (crew), rugby, sailing, skiing, soccer, softball, squash, swimming, table tennis, tennis, track and field, volleyball, water polo, weight lifting M. **Team name:** Huskies.

**Student services.** Adult student services, alcohol/substance abuse counseling, chaplain/spiritual director, career counseling, student employment services, financial aid counseling, health services, minority student services, on-campus daycare, personal counseling, placement for graduates, veterans' counselor, women's services. **Physically disabled:** Services for visually, speech, hearing impaired.

**Contact.** E-mail: beahusky@uconn.edu
Phone: (860) 486-3137 Fax: (860) 486-1476
Lee Melvin, Director of Admission, University of Connecticut, 2131 Hillside Road, Unit 3088, Storrs, CT 06269-3088

## University of Hartford
**West Hartford, Connecticut**  **CB member**
**www.hartford.edu**  **CB code: 3436**

- Private 4-year university
- Residential campus in small city

- 5,229 degree-seeking undergraduates: 11% part-time, 53% women
- 1,604 degree-seeking graduate students
- 69% of applicants admitted
- SAT or ACT with writing required
- 63% graduate within 6 years

**General.** Founded in 1877. Regionally accredited. **Degrees:** 964 bachelor's, 147 associate awarded; master's, professional offered. **ROTC:** Army, Air Force. **Location:** 4 miles from downtown. **Calendar:** Semester, extensive summer session. **Full-time faculty:** 344 total; 86% have terminal degrees, 13% minority, 38% women. **Part-time faculty:** 542 total; 4% minority. **Class size:** 62% < 20, 36% 20-39, less than 1% 40-49, less than 1% 50-99, less than 1% >100. **Special facilities:** Engineering applications center, humanities center.

**Freshman class profile.** 11,900 applied, 8,253 admitted, 1,394 enrolled.

| Mid 50% test scores | | | |
|---|---|---|---|
| SAT critical reading: | 450-550 | Return as sophomores: | 72% |
| SAT math: | 450-570 | Out-of-state: | 65% |
| ACT composite: | 19-24 | Live on campus: | 89% |
| | | International: | 2% |

**Basis for selection.** Quality of academic program, school achievement record, class rank important. Test scores secondary. Employment, extracurricular activities, and community service considered. Writing samples and interview also considered. Admission committee can offer admission to alternative program. Interview and essay recommended. Audition required of music, dance, acting majors. Portfolio required of art majors. **Home-schooled:** Statement describing homeschool structure and mission, transcript of courses and grades required.

**High school preparation.** 16 units required. Required and recommended units include English 4, mathematics 2-3, social studies 2, history 2, science 2-3, foreign language 3 and academic electives 4. Physics, chemistry, and 3.5 math (including trigonometry) recommended for engineering and science applicants.

**2010-2011 Annual costs.** Tuition/fees (projected): $29,852. Room/board: $11,572. Books/supplies: $860. Personal expenses: $1,350.

**2008-2009 Financial aid. Need-based:** 1,072 full-time freshmen applied for aid; 1,072 were judged to have need; 1,072 of these received aid. Average need met was 79%. Average scholarship/grant was $14,465; average loan $6,561. 60% of total undergraduate aid awarded as scholarships/grants, 40% as loans/jobs. **Non-need-based:** Awarded to 2,276 full-time undergraduates, including 722 freshmen. Scholarships awarded for academics, art, athletics, music/drama.

**Application procedures. Admission:** No deadline. $40 fee, may be waived for applicants with need. Admission notification on a rolling basis beginning on or about 10/1. Must reply by May 1 or within 2 week(s) if notified thereafter. **Financial aid:** Priority date 2/1; no closing date. FAFSA, institutional form required. Applicants notified on a rolling basis starting 3/1; must reply by 5/1.

**Academics. Special study options:** Combined bachelor's/graduate degree, cooperative education, cross-registration, distance learning, double major, dual enrollment of high school students, ESL, exchange student, honors, independent study, internships, liberal arts/career combination, student-designed major, study abroad, teacher certification program, Washington semester, weekend college, Saturday term. **Credit/placement by examination:** AP, CLEP, SAT, institutional tests. 30 credit hours maximum toward associate degree, 60 toward bachelor's. **Support services:** Learning center, reduced course load, tutoring, writing center.

**Majors. Architecture:** Architecture. **Area/ethnic studies:** Women's. **Biology:** General. **Business:** Accounting, business admin, entrepreneurial studies, finance, insurance, management information systems, marketing. **Communications:** General. **Computer sciences:** General, information systems. **Education:** Early childhood, elementary, music, secondary, special. **Engineering:** General, civil, computer, electrical, mechanical. **Engineering technology:** General, architectural, computer, electrical, environmental, mechanical. **Foreign languages:** General. **Health:** Clinical lab science, health services, medical radiologic technology/radiation therapy, nursing (RN), respiratory therapy technology. **History:** General. **Legal studies:** General, paralegal. **Liberal arts:** Arts/sciences. **Math:** General. **Philosophy/religion:** Judaic, philosophy. **Physical sciences:** Chemistry, physics. **Protective services:** Police science. **Psychology:** General. **Public administration:** Community org/advocacy. **Social sciences:** Economics, international economics, political science, sociology. **Theology:** Sacred music. **Visual/performing arts:** General, acting, art history/conservation, ceramics, cinematography, commercial/advertising art, dance, design, dramatic, drawing, film/cinema, jazz, music history, music management, music performance, music theory/composition, painting, photography, printmaking, sculpture.

**Most popular majors.** Business/marketing 16%, communications/journalism 7%, education 8%, engineering/engineering technologies 12%, health sciences 12%, psychology 6%, visual/performing arts 20%.

**Computing on campus.** 300 workstations in dormitories, library, computer center. Dormitories wired for high-speed internet access and linked to campus network. Commuter students can connect to campus network. On-line course registration, online library, helpline, repair service, student web hosting, wireless network available.

**Student life. Freshman orientation:** Mandatory. **Housing:** Guaranteed on-campus for freshmen. Coed dorms, single-sex dorms, special housing for disabled, apartments available. $200 deposit, deadline 5/1. Dormitories with resident faculty members, international residential college, residential college for the arts available. **Activities:** Bands, choral groups, dance, drama, international student organizations, literary magazine, music ensembles, musical theater, opera, radio station, student government, student newspaper, symphony orchestra, TV station, Hillel, Protestant student organization, Newman club, African American students association, academic department clubs, prelaw and premedical societies, Brothers and Sisters United, Global Friends Association, Malaysian student association, Turkish student association.

**Athletics.** NCAA. **Intercollegiate:** Baseball M, basketball, cross-country, golf, lacrosse M, soccer, softball W, tennis, track and field, volleyball W. **Intramural:** Basketball, football (non-tackle), handball, racquetball, soccer, softball, tennis, volleyball, water polo. **Team name:** Hawks.

**Student services.** Chaplain/spiritual director, career counseling, student employment services, financial aid counseling, health services, minority student services, personal counseling, placement for graduates, veterans' counselor.

**Contact.** Phone: (860) 768-4296 Fax: (860) 768-4961
Richard Zeiser, Dean of Admission, University of Hartford, Bates House, West Hartford, CT 06117-1599

## University of New Haven
**West Haven, Connecticut**   **CB member**
**www.newhaven.edu**   **CB code: 3663**

- Private 4-year university
- Residential campus in small city
- 3,972 degree-seeking undergraduates: 11% part-time, 50% women, 9% African American, 2% Asian American, 8% Hispanic American, 2% international
- 1,731 degree-seeking graduate students
- 61% of applicants admitted
- SAT or ACT (ACT writing optional), application essay required
- 51% graduate within 6 years

**General.** Founded in 1920. Regionally accredited. Experiential learning emphasized. **Degrees:** 612 bachelor's, 53 associate awarded; master's offered. **ROTC:** Army, Air Force. **Location:** 3 miles from downtown New Haven, 75 miles from New York City. **Calendar:** 4-1-4, limited summer session. **Full-time faculty:** 200 total; 83% have terminal degrees, 16% minority, 30% women. **Part-time faculty:** 362 total; 38% women. **Class size:** 51% < 20, 45% 20-39, 2% 40-49, 2% 50-99, less than 1% >100. **Special facilities:** Theater, music and sound recording studio, shoreline environmental study preserve, institute of forensic science, learning center for finance and technology.

**Freshman class profile.** 6,105 applied, 3,753 admitted, 1,271 enrolled.

| Mid 50% test scores | | | |
|---|---|---|---|
| SAT critical reading: | 450-550 | Rank in top quarter: | 20% |
| SAT math: | 450-570 | Rank in top tenth: | 7% |
| SAT writing: | 450-550 | Return as sophomores: | 70% |
| ACT composite: | 19-25 | Out-of-state: | 59% |
| GPA 3.75 or higher: | 12% | Live on campus: | 79% |
| GPA 3.50-3.74: | 22% | International: | 1% |
| GPA 3.0-3.49: | 37% | Fraternities: | 1% |
| GPA 2.0-2.99: | 29% | Sororities: | 1% |

**Basis for selection.** Academic record, recommendations, test scores, personal essay, advanced placement or honor courses, and extracurricular activities reviewed. **Learning Disabled:** Students required to meet with Disability Services Office to receive accommodations and/or services.

**High school preparation.** College-preparatory program recommended. Required units include English 4, mathematics 3, social studies 2, science 2 (laboratory 2), foreign language 2, computer science 1 and visual/performing arts 1.

**2009-2010 Annual costs.** Tuition/fees: $29,470. Room/board: $12,372. Books/supplies: $1,000. Personal expenses: $1,340.

**2009-2010 Financial aid. Need-based:** 1,145 full-time freshmen applied for aid; 1,035 were judged to have need; 1,035 of these received aid. Average need met was 68%. Average scholarship/grant was $17,221; average loan $3,464. 80% of total undergraduate aid awarded as scholarships/grants, 20% as loans/jobs. **Non-need-based:** Awarded to 745 full-time undergraduates, including 300 freshmen. Scholarships awarded for academics, alumni affiliation, athletics, leadership.

**Application procedures. Admission:** No deadline. $75 fee, may be waived for applicants with need. Admission notification on a rolling basis beginning on or about 12/1. Must reply by May 1 or within 2 week(s) if notified thereafter. **Financial aid:** Closing date 3/1. FAFSA required. Applicants notified on a rolling basis starting 3/1; must reply by 5/1 or within 2 week(s) of notification.

**Academics. Special study options:** Accelerated study, combined bachelor's/graduate degree, cooperative education, distance learning, double major, ESL, honors, independent study, internships, study abroad, teacher certification program, weekend college. **Credit/placement by examination:** AP, CLEP, IB, SAT, ACT, institutional tests. **Support services:** Learning center, reduced course load, remedial instruction, study skills assistance, tutoring, writing center.

**Majors. Architecture:** Interior. **Biology:** General, ecology, marine. **Business:** Accounting, business admin, finance, hospitality admin, hotel/motel admin, international, managerial economics, marketing. **Communications:** General. **Computer sciences:** General, information systems. **Conservation:** General. **Engineering:** General, chemical, civil, computer, electrical, mechanical. **Engineering technology:** Occupational safety. **Health:** Dental hygiene, dietetics. **History:** General. **Interdisciplinary:** Global studies, nutrition sciences. **Legal studies:** General. **Liberal arts:** Arts/sciences. **Math:** General, applied. **Parks/recreation:** Sports admin. **Physical sciences:** Chemistry. **Protective services:** Fire safety technology, firefighting, forensics, law enforcement admin. **Psychology:** General. **Public administration:** General. **Science technology:** Biological. **Social sciences:** Political science. **Visual/performing arts:** Graphic design, interior design, music management, studio arts.

**Most popular majors.** Business/marketing 15%, engineering/engineering technologies 7%, health sciences 6%, security/protective services 42%, visual/performing arts 11%.

**Computing on campus.** Dormitories wired for high-speed internet access and linked to campus network. Online course registration, helpline, repair service, wireless network available.

**Student life. Freshman orientation:** Mandatory. **Housing:** Coed dorms, special housing for disabled, apartments available. $200 nonrefundable deposit, deadline 5/1. Living/learning communities available for freshmen majoring in business, engineering, forensic science, or music. Some dorm rooms are handicapped accessible. **Activities:** Bands, campus ministries, choral groups, dance, drama, international student organizations, literary magazine, Model UN, radio station, student government, student newspaper, symphony orchestra.

**Athletics.** NCAA. **Intercollegiate:** Baseball M, basketball, cross-country, football (tackle), golf M, lacrosse W, soccer, softball W, tennis W, track and field, volleyball W. **Intramural:** Basketball, cricket, football (non-tackle), racquetball, soccer, softball, swimming, table tennis, volleyball. **Team name:** Chargers.

**Student services.** Career counseling, student employment services, financial aid counseling, health services, minority student services, personal counseling, placement for graduates, veterans' counselor, women's services. **Physically disabled:** Services for visually, speech, hearing impaired.

**Contact.** E-mail: adminfo@newhaven.edu
Phone: (203) 932-7319 Toll-free number: (800) 342-5864
Fax: (203) 931-6093
Kevin Phillips, Director of Undergraduate Admissions, University of New Haven, 300 Boston Post Road, West Haven, CT 06516

---

## Wesleyan University
**Middletown, Connecticut**
www.wesleyan.edu

CB member
CB code: 3959

- Private 4-year university and liberal arts college
- Residential campus in large town
- 2,766 degree-seeking undergraduates: 50% women, 7% African American, 10% Asian American, 9% Hispanic American, 1% Native American, 7% international

- 267 degree-seeking graduate students
- 22% of applicants admitted
- SAT and SAT Subject Tests or ACT (ACT writing recommended), application essay required
- 93% graduate within 6 years

**General.** Founded in 1831. Regionally accredited. **Degrees:** 735 bachelor's awarded; master's, doctoral offered. **ROTC:** Air Force. **Location:** 15 miles from Hartford, 25 miles from New Haven. **Calendar:** Semester, limited summer session. **Full-time faculty:** 330 total; 94% have terminal degrees, 18% minority, 42% women. **Part-time faculty:** 31 total; 45% have terminal degrees, 39% minority, 52% women. **Class size:** 67% < 20, 24% 20-39, 4% 40-49, 3% 50-99, 2% >100. **Special facilities:** 11-building arts center, observatory, science center with electron microscopes and nuclear magnetic resonance spectrometers, film studies center, center for humanities, East Asian studies center, African-American studies center.

**Freshman class profile.** 10,068 applied, 2,218 admitted, 745 enrolled.

| Mid 50% test scores | | |
|---|---|---|
| SAT critical reading: | 640-750 | |
| SAT math: | 650-750 | |
| SAT writing: | 640-740 | |
| ACT composite: | 29-33 | |
| GPA 3.75 or higher: | 64% | |
| GPA 3.50-3.74: | 23% | |
| GPA 3.0-3.49: | 12% | |
| GPA 2.0-2.99: | 1% | |

| | |
|---|---|
| Rank in top quarter: | 90% |
| Rank in top tenth: | 70% |
| Return as sophomores: | 95% |
| Out-of-state: | 93% |
| Live on campus: | 100% |
| International: | 6% |
| Fraternities: | 1% |
| Sororities: | 1% |

**Basis for selection.** High school transcript, class rank, test scores, extracurricular activities, 2 teacher evaluations, personal statement, and other evidence of outstanding accomplishments are considered. 2 SAT Subject Test scores required with SAT score. Interview recommended. **Home-schooled:** Campus interview, statement describing home school structure and mission, transcript of courses and grades, third-party recommendation, and home-school instructor recommendation strongly recommended. Financial aid applicants should be prepared to submit GED.

**High school preparation.** College-preparatory program recommended. Recommended units include English 4, mathematics 4, social studies 4, history 4, science 4 (laboratory 3) and foreign language 4.

**2009-2010 Annual costs.** Tuition/fees: $40,392. Room/board: $11,040. Books/supplies: $1,333. Personal expenses: $1,332.

**2008-2009 Financial aid.** All financial aid based on need. 405 full-time freshmen applied for aid; 335 were judged to have need; 335 of these received aid. Average need met was 100%. Average scholarship/grant was $32,975; average loan $2,496. 81% of total undergraduate aid awarded as scholarships/grants, 19% as loans/jobs.

**Application procedures. Admission:** Closing date 1/1 (postmark date). $55 fee, may be waived for applicants with need. Admission notification 4/1. Must reply by May 1 or within 2 week(s) if notified thereafter. **Financial aid:** Closing date 2/15. FAFSA, CSS PROFILE required. Applicants notified by 4/1; must reply by 5/1.

**Academics.** Students expected to complete 3 classes in each of following areas before graduation: natural sciences and math, arts and humanities, social and behavioral sciences. **Special study options:** Combined bachelor's/graduate degree, cross-registration, double major, dual enrollment of high school students, exchange student, honors, independent study, semester at sea, student-designed major, study abroad, urban semester, Washington semester. 12-college exchange, semester in environmental science at the Marine Biological Laboratory-Woods Hole, Wesleyan-Trinity-Connecticut College Consortium, 3-2 program in science and engineering, teaching apprentice program. **Credit/placement by examination:** AP, CLEP, IB, institutional tests. 2 credit hours maximum toward bachelor's degree. **Support services:** Reduced course load, tutoring, writing center.

**Majors. Area/ethnic studies:** African-American, American, Central/Eastern European, East Asian, French, gay/lesbian, German, Latin American, Russian/Slavic. **Biology:** General, biochemistry, molecular, molecular biochemistry. **Computer sciences:** General. **Conservation:** Environmental science. **Foreign languages:** Chinese, classics, East Asian, French, German, Italian, Japanese, Romance, Russian, Spanish. **History:** General. **Interdisciplinary:** Ancient studies, medieval/Renaissance, neuroscience, science/society. **Liberal arts:** Arts/sciences. **Math:** General. **Philosophy/religion:** Philosophy, religion. **Physical sciences:** Astronomy, chemistry, geology, physics, planetary. **Psychology:** General. **Social sciences:** Anthropology, archaeology, economics, political science, sociology. **Visual/performing arts:** Art history/conservation, dance, dramatic, film/cinema, studio arts.

**Most popular majors.** Area/ethnic studies 17%, biology 8%, English 9%, psychology 11%, social sciences 24%, visual/performing arts 11%.

**Computing on campus.** 300 workstations in library, computer center, student center. Dormitories wired for high-speed internet access and linked to campus network. Commuter students can connect to campus network. Online course registration, online library, helpline, repair service, student web hosting, wireless network available.

**Student life. Freshman orientation:** Mandatory. Preregistration for classes offered. Held one week before start of fall classes. **Housing:** Guaranteed on-campus for all undergraduates. Coed dorms, special housing for disabled, apartments, fraternity/sorority housing, wellness housing available. **Activities:** Bands, campus ministries, choral groups, dance, drama, film society, international student organizations, literary magazine, music ensembles, Model UN, musical theater, radio station, student government, student newspaper, symphony orchestra, more than 230 organizations.

**Athletics.** NCAA. **Intercollegiate:** Baseball M, basketball, cross-country, diving, field hockey W, football (tackle) M, golf M, ice hockey, lacrosse, rowing (crew), soccer, softball W, squash, swimming, tennis, track and field, volleyball W, wrestling M. **Intramural:** Basketball, ice hockey M, soccer, softball, squash, volleyball. **Team name:** Cardinals.

**Student services.** Adult student services, alcohol/substance abuse counseling, chaplain/spiritual director, career counseling, student employment services, financial aid counseling, health services, minority student services, on-campus daycare, personal counseling, placement for graduates, women's services. **Physically disabled:** Services for visually, speech, hearing impaired.

**Contact.** E-mail: admissions@wesleyan.edu
Phone: (860) 685-3000 Fax: (860) 685-3001
Nancy Meislahn, Dean of Admission and Financial Aid, Wesleyan University, 70 Wyllys Avenue, Middletown, CT 06459-0260

## Western Connecticut State University
### Danbury, Connecticut
**www.wcsu.edu**  CB code: 3350

- Public 4-year university
- Commuter campus in small city
- 5,521 degree-seeking undergraduates: 14% part-time, 55% women, 7% African American, 3% Asian American, 8% Hispanic American
- 676 degree-seeking graduate students
- 62% of applicants admitted
- SAT or ACT with writing required
- 40% graduate within 6 years

**General.** Founded in 1903. Regionally accredited. **Degrees:** 807 bachelor's, 20 associate awarded; master's, professional offered. **ROTC:** Army, Air Force. **Location:** 65 miles from New York City, 50 miles from Hartford. **Calendar:** Semester, extensive summer session. **Full-time faculty:** 218 total; 86% have terminal degrees, 14% minority, 48% women. **Part-time faculty:** 364 total; 6% minority, 43% women. **Class size:** 30% < 20, 67% 20-39, 2% 40-49, less than 1% 50-99, less than 1% >100. **Special facilities:** Weather station, observatory, nature preserve.

**Freshman class profile.** 4,175 applied, 2,596 admitted, 1,019 enrolled.

| Mid 50% test scores | | Rank in top quarter: | 21% |
|---|---|---|---|
| SAT critical reading: | 450-540 | Rank in top tenth: | 4% |
| SAT math: | 440-540 | Return as sophomores: | 70% |
| SAT writing: | 440-540 | Out-of-state: | 9% |
| GPA 3.75 or higher: | 2% | Live on campus: | 60% |
| GPA 3.50-3.74: | 7% | Fraternities: | 5% |
| GPA 3.0-3.49: | 34% | Sororities: | 5% |
| GPA 2.0-2.99: | 54% | | |

**Basis for selection.** Limited freshman class spaces given to students with strongest academic and extracurricular backgrounds, including test results. Essay and interview recommended. Audition required of music majors. Portfolio recommended of graphic design majors. **Homeschooled:** Transcript of courses and grades required. **Learning Disabled:** To receive services or accommodations, students must provide appropriate documentation by contacting the coordinator of disability services.

**High school preparation.** College-preparatory program required. 13 units required. Required and recommended units include English 4, mathematics 3, social studies 1, history 1, science 2 (laboratory 2) and foreign language 2-3. Additional credits in fine arts and computer science recommended. Academic course work in computer science, visual arts, theater, music or dance may be substituted for one of the required areas.

**2010-2011 Annual costs.** Tuition/fees (projected): $7,909; $16,906 out-of-state. Room/board: $10,130. Books/supplies: $1,300. Personal expenses: $2,325.

**2008-2009 Financial aid. Need-based:** 758 full-time freshmen applied for aid; 675 were judged to have need; 572 of these received aid. Average need met was 57%. Average scholarship/grant was $2,362; average loan $9,230. 34% of total undergraduate aid awarded as scholarships/grants, 66% as loans/jobs. **Non-need-based:** Awarded to 441 full-time undergraduates, including 133 freshmen. Scholarships awarded for academics.

**Application procedures. Admission:** Priority date 4/1; no deadline. $50 fee, may be waived for applicants with need. Admission notification on a rolling basis beginning on or about 12/1. Must reply by May 1 or within 2 week(s) if notified thereafter. **Financial aid:** Priority date 3/15, closing date 4/15. FAFSA, institutional form required. Applicants notified on a rolling basis starting 4/15; must reply by 5/1 or within 2 week(s) of notification.

**Academics. Special study options:** Cooperative education, cross-registration, distance learning, dual enrollment of high school students, honors, independent study, internships, student-designed major, study abroad, teacher certification program. **Credit/placement by examination:** AP, CLEP, IB, SAT, institutional tests. 30 credit hours maximum toward associate degree, 60 toward bachelor's. **Support services:** Learning center, pre-admission summer program, reduced course load, remedial instruction, study skills assistance, tutoring, writing center.

**Majors. Area/ethnic studies:** American. **Biology:** General. **Business:** Accounting, business admin, finance, management information systems, marketing. **Communications:** General, media studies. **Computer sciences:** General. **Education:** Elementary, health, music, secondary. **Foreign languages:** Spanish. **Health:** Clinical lab science, community health services, nursing (RN). **History:** General. **Liberal arts:** Arts/sciences. **Math:** General. **Physical sciences:** Atmospheric science, chemistry, geology. **Protective services:** Police science. **Psychology:** General. **Public administration:** Social work. **Social sciences:** General, economics, political science, sociology. **Visual/performing arts:** Art, dramatic, music theory/composition.

**Most popular majors.** Business/marketing 25%, communications/journalism 7%, education 10%, health sciences 9%, psychology 8%, security/protective services 9%, visual/performing arts 7%.

**Computing on campus.** 1,021 workstations in dormitories, library, computer center, student center. Dormitories wired for high-speed internet access and linked to campus network. Commuter students can connect to campus network. Online course registration, online library, helpline, student web hosting, wireless network available.

**Student life. Freshman orientation:** Available. Preregistration for classes offered. 2-day program for students and parents held the weekend before classes start. **Policies:** Hazing and smoking inside all buildings prohibited. Honor code applies. **Housing:** Coed dorms, single-sex dorms, apartments available. $250 nonrefundable deposit. **Activities:** Bands, campus ministries, choral groups, dance, drama, international student organizations, literary magazine, music ensembles, musical theater, opera, radio station, student government, student newspaper, symphony orchestra, black student alliance, Habitat for Humanity, justice and law club, Newman club, College Republicans, College Democrats,.

**Athletics.** NCAA. **Intercollegiate:** Baseball M, basketball, field hockey W, football (tackle) M, lacrosse, soccer, softball W, swimming W, tennis, volleyball W. **Intramural:** Basketball M, football (non-tackle) M. **Team name:** Colonials.

**Student services.** Adult student services, alcohol/substance abuse counseling, chaplain/spiritual director, career counseling, student employment services, financial aid counseling, health services, minority student services, on-campus daycare, personal counseling, placement for graduates, veterans' counselor, women's services. **Physically disabled:** Services for visually, speech, hearing impaired.

**Contact.** E-mail: admissions@wcsu.edu
Phone: (203) 837-9000 Toll-free number: (877) 837-9278
Fax: (203) 837-8338
Steven Goetsch, Director, Admissions, Western Connecticut State University, 181 White Street, Danbury, CT 06810-6826

## Yale University
### New Haven, Connecticut
**www.yale.edu**  CB member / CB code: 3987

- Private 4-year university
- Residential campus in small city

♦ 5,258 degree-seeking undergraduates: 50% women, 9% African American, 14% Asian American, 9% Hispanic American, 1% Native American, 9% international

♦ 6,248 degree-seeking graduate students

♦ 8% of applicants admitted

♦ SAT and SAT Subject Tests or ACT with writing, application essay required

♦ 98% graduate within 6 years; 24% enter graduate study

**General.** Founded in 1701. Regionally accredited. **Degrees:** 1,309 bachelor's awarded; master's, doctoral, professional offered. **ROTC:** Army, Air Force. **Location:** 75 miles from New York City. **Calendar:** Semester, limited summer session. **Full-time faculty:** 1,158 total; 91% have terminal degrees, 18% minority, 33% women. **Part-time faculty:** 495 total; 70% have terminal degrees, 11% minority, 39% women. **Class size:** 79% < 20, 13% 20-39, 2% 40-49, 5% 50-99, 2% >100. **Special facilities:** Natural history museum, clean room, wind tunnel, engine testing facility, graphic workstations, robotics labs, crystal growth, nuclear accelerators, nuclear magnetic resonance spectrometers, optical spectroscopy instruments, high-resolution mass spectrometer, x-ray diffraction instruments, electron microscopes, observatories, marine studies field station, Institute for Biospheric Studies, 10,000 acres of forest.

**Freshman class profile.** 26,003 applied, 1,958 admitted, 1,307 enrolled.

| Mid 50% test scores | | Rank in top tenth: | 96% |
|---|---|---|---|
| SAT critical reading: | 700-800 | Return as sophomores: | 99% |
| SAT math: | 700-780 | Out-of-state: | 93% |
| SAT writing: | 700-790 | Live on campus: | 100% |
| ACT composite: | 30-34 | International: | 9% |
| Rank in top quarter: | 100% | | |

**Basis for selection.** First criterion is evidence of ability to do successful academic work. Diversity of interests, background and special talents also sought. Successful candidates usually will have done honors work at secondary level, have high standardized test scores, and present high degree of accomplishment in one or more nonacademic areas. Interview recommended. Music and art submissions accepted digitally via Yale web portal. **Homeschooled:** Require 2 recommendations from teachers of courses taken outside home, such as community college courses.

**High school preparation.** College-preparatory program recommended. Students recommended to take richest possible mix of demanding academic offerings.

**2009-2010 Annual costs.** Tuition/fees: $36,500. Room/board: $11,000. Books/supplies: $3,000. Personal expenses: $2,050.

**2008-2009 Financial aid.** All financial aid based on need. **Additional information:** All scholarships based on demonstrated need.

**Application procedures. Admission:** Closing date 12/31 (postmark date). $75 fee, may be waived for applicants with need. Admission notification 4/1. Must reply by 5/1. **Financial aid:** Closing date 3/1. FAFSA, CSS PROFILE required. Applicants notified by 4/1; must reply by 5/1 or within 1 week(s) of notification.

**Academics. Special study options:** Accelerated study, combined bachelor's/graduate degree, double major, ESL, honors, independent study, internships, liberal arts/career combination, student-designed major, study abroad, teacher certification program. **Credit/placement by examination:** AP, CLEP, IB, institutional tests. **Support services:** Study skills assistance, tutoring, writing center.

**Majors. Architecture:** Architecture. **Area/ethnic studies:** African, African-American, American, East Asian, European, Latin American, Russian/Slavic, women's. **Biology:** General, biochemistry, Biochemistry/biophysics and molecular biology, molecular. **Computer sciences:** General. **Conservation:** Environmental studies. **Engineering:** Biomedical, chemical, electrical, environmental, mechanical, physics, science. **Foreign languages:** Ancient Greek, Biblical, Chinese, classics, French, German, Italian, Japanese, Latin, linguistics, Portuguese, Russian, Spanish. **History:** General, science/technology. **Interdisciplinary:** Ancient studies, cognitive science, math/computer science, medieval/Renaissance. **Liberal arts:** Humanities. **Math:** General, applied, statistics. **Philosophy/religion:** Judaic, philosophy, religion. **Physical sciences:** Astronomy, astrophysics, chemistry, geology, physics. **Psychology:** General. **Social sciences:** Anthropology, archaeology, economics, political science, sociology. **Visual/performing arts:** Art, art history/conservation, dramatic, film/cinema.

**Most popular majors.** Biology 8%, English 6%, history 12%, interdisciplinary studies 10%, psychology 7%, social sciences 25%, visual/performing arts 6%.

**Computing on campus.** 400 workstations in dormitories, library, computer center, student center. Dormitories wired for high-speed internet access and linked to campus network. Commuter students can connect to campus network. Online course registration, online library, helpline, student web hosting, wireless network available.

**Student life. Freshman orientation:** Mandatory. **Housing:** Guaranteed on-campus for freshmen. Coed dorms, special housing for disabled available. **Activities:** Bands, choral groups, dance, drama, film society, literary magazine, music ensembles, musical theater, opera, radio station, student government, student newspaper, symphony orchestra, TV station, over 135 organizations available.

**Athletics.** NCAA. **Intercollegiate:** Baseball M, basketball, cross-country, diving, fencing, field hockey W, football (tackle) M, golf, gymnastics W, ice hockey, lacrosse, rowing (crew), soccer, softball W, squash, swimming, tennis, track and field, volleyball W. **Intramural:** Baseball M, basketball, bowling, cross-country, field hockey W, football (tackle) M, golf, ice hockey, racquetball, rowing (crew), soccer, softball, squash, swimming, table tennis, tennis, volleyball, water polo, wrestling M. **Team name:** Bulldogs.

**Student services.** Alcohol/substance abuse counseling, chaplain/spiritual director, career counseling, student employment services, financial aid counseling, health services, minority student services, personal counseling, placement for graduates, women's services. **Physically disabled:** Services for visually, speech, hearing impaired.

**Contact.** E-mail: student.questions@yale.edu
Phone: (203) 432-9300 Fax: (203) 432-9392
Margit Dahl, Director of Undergraduate Admissions, Yale University, Box 208234, New Haven, CT 06520-8234

# Delaware

## Delaware State University
**Dover, Delaware** — CB member
www.desu.edu — CB code: 5153

- Public 4-year university
- Residential campus in large town
- 3,222 degree-seeking undergraduates: 13% part-time, 60% women, 70% African American, 1% Asian American, 2% Hispanic American, 1% international
- 387 graduate students
- 37% of applicants admitted
- SAT or ACT (ACT writing optional) required

**General.** Founded in 1891. Regionally accredited. University has its own fleet of planes. **Degrees:** 506 bachelor's awarded; master's, doctoral offered. **ROTC:** Army, Air Force. **Location:** 46 miles from Wilmington, 100 miles from Washington DC. **Calendar:** Semester, extensive summer session. **Full-time faculty:** 192 total; 90% have terminal degrees, 53% minority, 41% women. **Part-time faculty:** 149 total. **Class size:** 50% < 20, 41% 20-39, 6% 40-49, 3% 50-99. **Special facilities:** Science center, observatory, herbarium.

**Freshman class profile.** 8,075 applied, 2,999 admitted, 757 enrolled.

| Mid 50% test scores | | | |
|---|---|---|---|
| SAT critical reading: | 400-480 | GPA 3.0-3.49: | 21% |
| SAT math: | 390-480 | GPA 2.0-2.99: | 67% |
| ACT composite: | 15-19 | Rank in top quarter: | 22% |
| GPA 3.75 or higher: | 4% | Rank in top tenth: | 7% |
| GPA 3.50-3.74: | 6% | Out-of-state: | 67% |
| | | Live on campus: | 87% |

**Basis for selection.** High school curriculum and GPA most important. Test scores only used in conjunction with GPA. Class rank considered. Interviews upon invitation; band students audition for scholarships.

**High school preparation.** 16 units required. Required units include English 4, mathematics 3, social studies 2, science 3 (laboratory 3) and academic electives 4. Math units must include 2 algebra and 1 geometry.

**2009-2010 Annual costs.** Tuition/fees: $6,481; $13,742 out-of-state. Room/board: $9,386. Books/supplies: $1,500. Personal expenses: $1,600.

**2008-2009 Financial aid.** All financial aid based on need. **Additional information:** Students must file FAFSA by March 17 every year.

**Application procedures.** Admission: Priority date 4/1; no deadline. $25 fee, may be waived for applicants with need. Admission notification on a rolling basis beginning on or about 9/1. May enroll in an Early Bird program. **Financial aid:** Priority date 3/1, closing date 7/1. FAFSA required. Applicants notified on a rolling basis starting 4/1; must reply by 8/20.

**Academics. Special study options:** Accelerated study, combined bachelor's/graduate degree, cooperative education, distance learning, double major, dual enrollment of high school students, ESL, exchange student, honors, independent study, internships, semester at sea, study abroad, teacher certification program, weekend college. **Credit/placement by examination:** AP, CLEP, SAT, ACT, institutional tests. 30 credit hours maximum toward bachelor's degree. **Support services:** Learning center, pre-admission summer program, reduced course load, remedial instruction, study skills assistance, tutoring, writing center.

**Majors. Agriculture:** General, business, food science, plant sciences, poultry, soil science. **Biology:** General. **Business:** Accounting, business admin, finance, hospitality admin, nonprofit/public. **Communications:** Broadcast journalism, journalism, media studies, radio/tv. **Computer sciences:** General, computer science, data processing, systems analysis. **Conservation:** Environmental science, fisheries, forestry, management/policy, wildlife. **Education:** General, art, biology, business, chemistry, early childhood, elementary, English, French, gifted/talented, health, mathematics, middle, music, physical, physics, science, Spanish, special, trade/industrial. **Engineering:** Aerospace, electrical, geotechnical. **Engineering technology:** Architectural, civil, drafting, electrical, electromechanical, industrial, mechanical. **Family/consumer sciences:** Clothing/textiles, consumer economics, food/nutrition. **Foreign languages:** French, German, Spanish. **Health:** Nursing (RN), prenursing, preveterinary, public health nursing. **History:** General.

**Interdisciplinary:** Historic preservation, math/computer science. **Math:** General. **Parks/recreation:** Health/fitness, sports admin. **Philosophy/religion:** Philosophy. **Physical sciences:** Chemistry, forensic chemistry, physics. **Protective services:** Criminal justice, fire safety technology. **Psychology:** General. **Public administration:** Social work. **Science technology:** Biological. **Social sciences:** Criminology, political science, sociology, urban studies. **Transportation:** Aviation, aviation management. **Visual/performing arts:** General, arts management, studio arts. **Other:** Chemical lab technology, Engineering design, Fitness promotions, Natural resources technology, Physics pre-engineering, Political science business administration.

**Most popular majors.** Business/marketing 18%, communications/journalism 13%, education 6%, health sciences 9%, parks/recreation 6%, psychology 11%, public administration/social services 9%, social sciences 13%.

**Computing on campus.** 400 workstations in library, computer center, student center. Dormitories wired for high-speed internet access and linked to campus network. Commuter students can connect to campus network. Online course registration, online library, helpline, wireless network available.

**Student life. Freshman orientation:** Mandatory, $125 fee. Two-day program during June, July and August. **Policies:** First-time, first-year freshmen must submit written request for parking permit. **Housing:** Guaranteed on-campus for freshmen. Coed dorms, single-sex dorms, special housing for disabled, apartments, wellness housing available. $200 nonrefundable deposit, deadline 4/15. Suite style accommodations available for upper class students and honor students; residence hall available for honors students. **Activities:** Bands, campus ministries, choral groups, dance, drama, international student organizations, music ensembles, musical theater, radio station, student government, student newspaper, TV station, Wesley Foundation, commuters club, NAACP, black studies club, honor societies, Greek letter organizations, student ambassadors.

**Athletics.** NCAA. **Intercollegiate:** Baseball M, basketball, bowling W, cheerleading W, cross-country, equestrian W, football (tackle) M, soccer W, softball W, tennis, track and field, volleyball W, wrestling M. **Intramural:** Basketball, football (non-tackle), soccer, softball, swimming, table tennis, tennis, track and field, volleyball. **Team name:** Hornets.

**Student services.** Adult student services, alcohol/substance abuse counseling, chaplain/spiritual director, career counseling, health services, on-campus daycare, personal counseling, placement for graduates, veterans' counselor. **Physically disabled:** Services for visually, speech, hearing impaired.

**Contact.** E-mail: admissions@desu.edu
Phone: (302) 857-6351 Toll-free number: (800) 845-2544
Fax: (302) 857-6352
L Germaine Scott-Cheatham, Director of Admissions, Delaware State University, 1200 North DuPont Highway, Dover, DE 19901

## Goldey-Beacom College
**Wilmington, Delaware** — CB member
www.gbc.edu — CB code: 5255

- Private 4-year business college
- Commuter campus in small city
- 709 degree-seeking undergraduates: 31% part-time, 56% women, 21% African American, 7% Asian American, 6% Hispanic American
- 543 degree-seeking graduate students
- SAT required

**General.** Founded in 1886. Regionally accredited. **Degrees:** 148 bachelor's, 31 associate awarded; master's offered. **ROTC:** Air Force. **Location:** 15 miles from Wilmington, 36 miles from Philadelphia. **Calendar:** Semester, extensive summer session. **Full-time faculty:** 20 total; 100% have terminal degrees. **Part-time faculty:** 32 total. **Special facilities:** Nondenominational chapel, athletic facilities and fields, fitness center, computer lab.

**Basis for selection.** Bachelor degree candidates must submit SAT scores and official transcripts from high school(s) and or college(s) attended. High school performance is evaluated. When necessary, interviews are requested. Interview recommended. **Homeschooled:** Statement describing home-school structure and mission, transcript of courses and grades, state high school equivalency certificate, interview required. **Learning Disabled:** Evaluation of disability and submission of documentation regarding disability.

**High school preparation.** 16 units recommended. Recommended units include English 4, mathematics 3 and science 3. 3 math units required for bachelor's degree applicants.

**2010-2011 Annual costs.** Tuition/fees: $18,660. Room only: $5,021. Books/supplies: $887. Personal expenses: $2,506.

**2009-2010 Financial aid. Need-based:** Average need met was 40%. Average scholarship/grant was $8,205; average loan $4,243. 66% of total undergraduate aid awarded as scholarships/grants, 34% as loans/jobs. **Non-need-based:** Scholarships awarded for academics.

**Application procedures. Admission:** No deadline. No application fee. Admission notification on a rolling basis. SAT not required but recommended for associate degree applicants for placement and counseling. **Financial aid:** Priority date 4/1; no closing date. FAFSA required. Applicants notified on a rolling basis starting 3/1; must reply within 2 week(s) of notification.

**Academics. Special study options:** Accelerated study, combined bachelor's/ graduate degree, cooperative education, double major, dual enrollment of high school students, honors, internships. **Credit/placement by examination:** AP, CLEP, SAT, ACT, institutional tests. **Support services:** Learning center, pre-admission summer program, reduced course load, remedial instruction, study skills assistance, tutoring, writing center.

**Majors. Business:** General, accounting, business admin, international, management information systems, management science, marketing. **Computer sciences:** General. **Psychology:** General. **Social sciences:** Economics.

**Most popular majors.** Business/marketing 72%, computer/information sciences 6%.

**Computing on campus.** 150 workstations in library, computer center, student center. Dormitories linked to campus network. Commuter students can connect to campus network. Online library, wireless network available.

**Student life. Freshman orientation:** Mandatory. Preregistration for classes offered. **Housing:** Guaranteed on-campus for all undergraduates. Coed dorms, special housing for disabled, apartments, wellness housing available. $400 fully refundable deposit. Apartment-style residence halls. **Activities:** International student organizations, student government, student newspaper.

**Athletics.** NCAA. **Intercollegiate:** Basketball, cross-country, golf M, soccer, softball W, tennis W, volleyball W. **Team name:** Lightning.

**Student services.** Career counseling, student employment services, financial aid counseling, placement for graduates. **Physically disabled:** Services for visually, speech, hearing impaired.

**Contact.** E-mail: admissions@gbc.edu
Phone: (302) 225-6248 Toll-free number: (800) 833-4877
Fax: (302) 996-5408
Larry Eby, Director of Admissions, Goldey-Beacom College, 4701 Limestone Road, Wilmington, DE 19808

---

## University of Delaware
**Newark, Delaware** **CB member**
**www.udel.edu** **CB code: 5811**

- Public 4-year university
- Residential campus in large town
- 15,757 degree-seeking undergraduates: 5% part-time, 58% women, 5% African American, 5% Asian American, 6% Hispanic American, 2% international
- 3,527 degree-seeking graduate students
- 57% of applicants admitted
- SAT or ACT with writing, application essay required
- 75% graduate within 6 years

**General.** Founded in 1743. Regionally accredited. **Degrees:** 3,569 bachelor's, 195 associate awarded; master's, doctoral offered. **ROTC:** Army, Air Force. **Location:** 12 miles from Wilmington, 30 miles from Philadelphia. **Calendar:** 4-1-4, limited summer session. **Full-time faculty:** 1,159 total; 85% have terminal degrees, 17% minority, 39% women. **Part-time faculty:** 281 total; 37% have terminal degrees, 14% minority, 54% women. **Class size:** 40% < 20, 40% 20-39, 7% 40-49, 8% 50-99, 4% >100. **Special facilities:** Science development center, human performance laboratory, greenhouse, preschool lab, nutrition clinic, engineering research centers, 400-acre agriculture research complex, center for composites manufacturing and research, apparel design laboratory, simulated hospital rooms for nursing, physical therapy clinic, applied coastal research, Delaware biotechnology institute.

**Freshman class profile.** 24,744 applied, 14,109 admitted, 4,223 enrolled.

| Mid 50% test scores | | | |
|---|---|---|---|
| SAT critical reading: | 520-630 | GPA 2.0-2.99: | 10% |
| SAT math: | 540-650 | Rank in top quarter: | 74% |
| SAT writing: | 520-640 | Rank in top tenth: | 37% |
| ACT composite: | 24-28 | Return as sophomores: | 91% |
| GPA 3.75 or higher: | 35% | Out-of-state: | 69% |
| GPA 3.50-3.74: | 23% | Live on campus: | 93% |
| GPA 3.0-3.49: | 32% | International: | 3% |

**Basis for selection.** High school record, program of study, test scores most important. References, essay, extracurricular accomplishments considered. SAT Subject Tests recommended. Audition or portfolio required for music or art. **Homeschooled:** Transcript of courses and grades required. Students should provide reading lists for courses they have completed. Sample portfolio of work or sample research paper recommended. Applicants should submit at least 2 SAT Subject Tests of their choice. In lieu of SAT and SAT Subject Tests, students may submit ACT with Writing score.

**High school preparation.** 18 units required; 22 recommended. Required and recommended units include English 4, mathematics 3-4, social studies 2, history 2, science 3-4 (laboratory 2-3), foreign language 2-4 and academic electives 2. 4 math strongly recommended for engineering, business, science or math applicants. 4 laboratory science strongly recommended for science, nursing, and engineering applicants.

**2009-2010 Annual costs.** Tuition/fees: $9,486; $23,186 out-of-state. Room/board: $9,436. Books/supplies: $800. Personal expenses: $1,500.

**2008-2009 Financial aid.** All financial aid based on need. 3,319 full-time freshmen applied for aid; 1,872 were judged to have need; 1,793 of these received aid. Average need met was 78%. Average scholarship/grant was $7,156; average loan $6,075. 40% of total undergraduate aid awarded as scholarships/grants, 60% as loans/jobs. **Additional information:** December 15 application deadline to receive scholarship consideration. Sibling/parent tuition credit plan. Senior citizen tuition credit for state residents over 60.

**Application procedures. Admission:** Priority date 12/1; deadline 1/15 (postmark date). $75 fee, may be waived for applicants with need. Admission notification 3/15. Must reply by May 1 or within 3 week(s) if notified thereafter. **Financial aid:** Priority date 2/1, closing date 3/15. FAFSA required. Applicants notified on a rolling basis starting 3/15; must reply by 5/1 or within 3 week(s) of notification.

**Academics. Special study options:** Accelerated study, cooperative education, distance learning, double major, dual enrollment of high school students, ESL, honors, independent study, internships, liberal arts/career combination, student-designed major, study abroad, teacher certification program, Washington semester. Research program, minors in 68 disciplines, five-year engineering/liberal arts option. **Credit/placement by examination:** AP, CLEP, IB, SAT, institutional tests. For credit/placement to be awarded for International Baccalaureate, applicant must have taken higher level courses and have minimum score of 4 on exams. **Support services:** Pre-admission summer program, reduced course load, remedial instruction, study skills assistance, tutoring, writing center.

**Honors college/program.** Program emphasizes small classes, undergraduate research, honors housing, special scholarship opportunities. Special application required.

**Majors. Agriculture:** Agribusiness operations, agronomy, animal sciences, business, economics, food science, ornamental horticulture, plant sciences, soil science. **Area/ethnic studies:** Latin American, women's. **Biology:** General, biochemistry, biotechnology, entomology, plant pathology. **Business:** Accounting, business admin, fashion, finance, management information systems, operations. **Communications:** General, journalism. **Computer sciences:** General. **Conservation:** General, management/policy, wildlife. **Education:** General, agricultural, biology, chemistry, early childhood, elementary, English, ESL, family/consumer sciences, foreign languages, French, geography, German, health, history, mathematics, middle, music, physical, physics, psychology, science, secondary, social science, Spanish, special. **Engineering:** Aerospace, agricultural, biomedical, chemical, civil, computer, electrical, environmental, mechanical, operations research. **Family/consumer sciences:** General, child care, family studies, family/community services, food/nutrition. **Foreign languages:** General, Biblical, classics, comparative lit, French, German, Italian, Latin, Russian, Spanish. **Health:** Athletic training, clinical lab science, clinical lab technology, nursing (RN), predental, premedicine, prepharmacy, preveterinary. **History:** General. **Interdisciplinary:** Historic preservation, nutrition sciences. **Legal studies:** Prelaw. **Liberal arts:** Arts/sciences. **Math:** General, statistics. **Parks/recreation:** Exercise sciences, facilities management, health/fitness, sports admin. **Philosophy/religion:** Philosophy. **Physical sciences:** Astronomy, chemistry, geology, geophysics, physics, planetary. **Protective services:** Criminal justice. **Psychology:** General. **Social sciences:** Anthropology, economics, geography, international relations, political science, sociology. **Visual/ performing arts:** Art, art history/conservation, commercial/advertising art, fashion design, music performance, music theory/composition, piano/organ, studio arts, theater design, theater history, voice/opera.

**Most popular majors.** Business/marketing 20%, education 10%, engineering/engineering technologies 8%, health sciences 7%, social sciences 13%.

**Computing on campus.** 900 workstations in dormitories, library, computer center. Dormitories wired for high-speed internet access and linked to campus network. Commuter students can connect to campus network. Online course registration, online library, helpline, repair service, student web hosting, wireless network available.

**Student life. Freshman orientation:** Mandatory, $65 fee. Preregistration for classes offered. One-day summer program, plus 3-day program before start of classes. **Housing:** Guaranteed on-campus for all undergraduates. Coed dorms, single-sex dorms, special housing for disabled, apartments, fraternity/sorority housing, wellness housing available. $200 partly refundable deposit, deadline 5/1. **Activities:** Bands, campus ministries, choral groups, dance, drama, film society, international student organizations, literary magazine, music ensembles, Model UN, musical theater, opera, radio station, student government, student newspaper, symphony orchestra, TV station, Black student union, Asian student association, Cosmopolitan Club, Hillel, Hispanic student association, Indian student association, lesbian/gay/ bisexual student union, returning adult student association.

**Athletics.** NCAA. **Intercollegiate:** Baseball M, basketball, cheerleading, cross-country, diving, field hockey W, football (tackle) M, golf M, lacrosse, rowing (crew) W, soccer, softball W, swimming, tennis, track and field, volleyball W. **Intramural:** Badminton, basketball, cross-country, fencing, field hockey W, golf, lacrosse, racquetball, soccer, softball, table tennis, tennis, volleyball, water polo M. **Team name:** Fightin' Blue Hens.

**Student services.** Adult student services, alcohol/substance abuse counseling, chaplain/spiritual director, career counseling, services for economically disadvantaged, student employment services, financial aid counseling, health services, minority student services, personal counseling, placement for graduates, veterans' counselor, women's services. **Physically disabled:** Services for visually, speech, hearing impaired.

**Contact.** E-mail: admissions@udel.edu
Phone: (302) 831-8123 Fax: (302) 831-6905
Louis Hirsh, Director of Admission, University of Delaware, 210 South College Avenue, Newark, DE 19716

## Wesley College
Dover, Delaware
www.wesley.edu
CB member
CB code: 5894

- Private 4-year liberal arts college affiliated with United Methodist Church
- Residential campus in large town
- 2,030 degree-seeking undergraduates
- 196 graduate students
- SAT or ACT (ACT writing optional) required

**General.** Founded in 1873. Regionally accredited. **Degrees:** 268 bachelor's, 45 associate awarded; master's offered. **ROTC:** Army. **Location:** 75 miles from Philadelphia, 90 miles from Washington, DC. **Calendar:** Semester, limited summer session. **Full-time faculty:** 71 total. **Part-time faculty:** 91 total. **Class size:** 55% < 20, 43% 20-39, less than 1% 40-49, 1% 50-99.

### Freshman class profile.

| Mid 50% test scores | | | |
|---|---|---|---|
| SAT critical reading: | 400-490 | GPA 2.0-2.99: | 58% |
| SAT math: | 400-500 | Rank in top quarter: | 56% |
| SAT writing: | 390-490 | Rank in top tenth: | 24% |
| GPA 3.75 or higher: | 6% | Out-of-state: | 66% |
| GPA 3.50-3.74: | 9% | Live on campus: | 87% |
| GPA 3.0-3.49: | 27% | Sororities: | 6% |

**Basis for selection.** High school performance most important. Campus interview very important. Extracurricular activities important.

**High school preparation.** 20 units recommended. Recommended units include English 4, mathematics 4, social studies 2, history 2, science 4, foreign language 2 and academic electives 2.

**2009-2010 Annual costs.** Tuition/fees: $19,830. Room/board: $9,000. Books/supplies: $1,000. Personal expenses: $750.

**2008-2009 Financial aid.** All financial aid based on need.

**Application procedures. Admission:** Priority date 4/1; no deadline. $25 fee. Admission notification on a rolling basis. Must reply by May 1 or within 4 week(s) if notified thereafter. **Financial aid:** Priority date 2/1; no closing date. FAFSA, institutional form required. Applicants notified on a rolling basis starting 1/1; must reply within 2 week(s) of notification.

**Academics.** Credit requirement for bachelor's degree varies according to program. **Special study options:** Double major, ESL, exchange student, independent study, internships, liberal arts/career combination, study abroad, teacher certification program. **Credit/placement by examination:** AP, CLEP, institutional tests. 15 credit hours maximum toward associate degree, 33 toward bachelor's. **Support services:** Learning center, reduced course load, remedial instruction, study skills assistance, tutoring, writing center.

**Majors. Area/ethnic studies:** American. **Biology:** General. **Business:** Accounting, business admin, sales/distribution. **Communications:** General. **Conservation:** Environmental studies. **Education:** General, elementary, physical. **Health:** Clinical lab science, nursing (RN). **History:** General. **Legal studies:** Paralegal. **Liberal arts:** Arts/sciences. **Math:** General. **Parks/ recreation:** Health/fitness. **Psychology:** General. **Social sciences:** Economics, political science. **Other:** Biology/chemistry.

**Most popular majors.** Business/marketing 30%, communications/ journalism 7%, education 16%, parks/recreation 6%, psychology 16%, social sciences 8%.

**Computing on campus.** 225 workstations in library. Dormitories wired for high-speed internet access and linked to campus network. Commuter students can connect to campus network. Online course registration, online library, helpline, repair service available.

**Student life. Freshman orientation:** Mandatory. Preregistration for classes offered. **Housing:** Coed dorms, single-sex dorms, apartments, wellness housing available. $175 fully refundable deposit, deadline 5/1. Floors in coed dorms are single-sex. **Activities:** Jazz band, choral groups, drama, literary magazine, music ensembles, student government, student newspaper, TV station, community action, Christian student associations, student activity board, National Coed Community Service Organization, black student union.

**Athletics.** NCAA. **Intercollegiate:** Baseball M, basketball, cheerleading, cross-country, field hockey W, football (tackle) M, golf, lacrosse, soccer, softball W, tennis, volleyball W. **Intramural:** Basketball, cross-country, soccer M, volleyball. **Team name:** Wolverines.

**Student services.** Chaplain/spiritual director, career counseling, student employment services, financial aid counseling, health services, personal counseling, placement for graduates. **Physically disabled:** Services for speech impaired.

**Contact.** E-mail: admissions@wesley.edu
Phone: (302) 736-2400 Toll-free number: (800) 937-5398
Fax: (302) 736-2400
William Firman, Director of Admissions, Wesley College, 120 North State Street, Dover, DE 19901-3875

## Wilmington University
New Castle, Delaware
www.wilmu.edu
CB member
CB code: 5925

- Private 4-year liberal arts college
- Commuter campus in large town
- 6,000 degree-seeking undergraduates: 46% part-time, 64% women, 19% African American, 1% Asian American, 3% Hispanic American
- 5,007 graduate students
- 40% graduate within 6 years

**General.** Founded in 1967. Regionally accredited. Two 7-week sessions within each trimester in addition to regular trimester sessions and weekend modules. **Degrees:** 1,086 bachelor's, 51 associate awarded; master's, professional offered. **ROTC:** Army, Air Force. **Location:** 7 miles from Wilmington. **Calendar:** Trimester, limited summer session. **Full-time faculty:** 95 total. **Part-time faculty:** 880 total. **Class size:** 76% < 20, 24% 20-39.

### Freshman class profile.

| | | | |
|---|---|---|---|
| End year in good standing: | 67% | Out-of-state: | 15% |
| Return as sophomores: | 69% | | |

**Basis for selection.** Open admission. Interview recommended. **Homeschooled:** GED recommended for nonaccredited programs.

**2009-2010 Annual costs.** Tuition/fees: $9,030. Books/supplies: $1,000. Personal expenses: $165.

**Financial aid. Non-need-based:** Scholarships awarded for academics, athletics.

**Application procedures. Admission:** No deadline. $25 fee, may be waived for applicants with need. Admission notification on a rolling basis. **Financial aid:** Priority date 4/30; no closing date. FAFSA required. Applicants notified on a rolling basis starting 8/5; must reply within 2 week(s) of notification.

**Academics.** Mentoring program for all interested incoming freshmen. **Special study options:** Accelerated study, distance learning, double major, independent study, internships, liberal arts/career combination, teacher certification program, weekend college. **Credit/placement by examination:** AP, CLEP, institutional tests. 15 credit hours maximum toward associate degree, 15 toward bachelor's. **Support services:** Learning center, remedial instruction, tutoring, writing center.

**Majors. Business:** Accounting, finance, human resources, information resources management, marketing. **Computer sciences:** General, programming, web page design. **Education:** Early childhood, elementary. **Engineering technology:** Software. **Health:** Preop/surgical nursing. **Interdisciplinary:** Behavioral sciences. **Legal studies:** Prelaw. **Liberal arts:** Arts/sciences. **Protective services:** Criminal justice. **Psychology:** General. **Transportation:** Aviation, aviation management.

**Most popular majors.** Business/marketing 29%, computer/information sciences 12%, education 13%, liberal arts 18%, psychology 11%, social sciences 10%.

**Computing on campus.** 516 workstations in library, computer center.

**Student life. Freshman orientation:** Available. Videotaped orientation distributed to all new students. Two new student orientations offered in the fall. **Policies:** Adherence to student handbook expected. **Activities:** Student government, professional fraternities/organizations, Sigma Theta Tau Nursing Society, Business Professionals of America, Alpha Delta Chi, criminal justice club.

**Athletics.** NCAA. **Intercollegiate:** Baseball M, basketball, cross-country, golf M, lacrosse W, soccer, softball W, volleyball W. **Team name:** Wildcats.

**Student services.** Career counseling, student employment services, financial aid counseling, placement for graduates.

**Contact.** E-mail: inquire@wilmu.edu
Phone: (302) 356-4636 Toll-free number: (877) 967-5464
Fax: (302) 328-5902
Christopher Ferguson, Director of Admissions, Wilmington University, 320 Dupont Highway, New Castle, DE 19720

# District of Columbia

## American University
**Washington, District of Columbia**    CB member
**www.american.edu**    CB code: 5007

- Private 4-year university affiliated with United Methodist Church
- Residential campus in very large city
- 6,430 degree-seeking undergraduates: 3% part-time, 61% women, 4% African American, 6% Asian American, 5% Hispanic American, 6% international
- 5,428 degree-seeking graduate students
- 53% of applicants admitted
- SAT or ACT with writing, application essay required
- 77% graduate within 6 years

**General.** Founded in 1893. Regionally accredited. **Degrees:** 1,384 bachelor's, 1 associate awarded; master's, doctoral, professional offered. **ROTC:** Army, Air Force. **Location:** 2 miles from downtown. **Calendar:** Semester, extensive summer session. **Full-time faculty:** 626 total; 96% have terminal degrees, 18% minority, 47% women. **Part-time faculty:** 549 total; 9% minority, 46% women. **Class size:** 45% < 20, 47% 20-39, 5% 40-49, 2% 50-99, less than 1% >100. **Special facilities:** Arts center, museum, theater, spiritual life center, national arboretum.

**Freshman class profile.** 14,935 applied, 7,950 admitted, 1,533 enrolled.

| Mid 50% test scores | | | |
|---|---|---|---|
| SAT critical reading: | 590-700 | GPA 2.0-2.99: | 3% |
| SAT math: | 580-670 | Rank in top quarter: | 83% |
| SAT writing: | 580-690 | Rank in top tenth: | 50% |
| ACT composite: | 25-30 | Return as sophomores: | 91% |
| GPA 3.75 or higher: | 37% | Out-of-state: | 85% |
| GPA 3.50-3.74: | 29% | Live on campus: | 96% |
| GPA 3.0-3.49: | 31% | International: | 5% |

**Basis for selection.** High school record, GPA, test scores, writing sample, recommendations very important. Academic interests and demonstrated time commitments outside classroom of interest. Motivation and seriousness of purpose taken into consideration, often revealed in level and rigor of courses taken. Extracurricular activities, class rank, leadership roles considered. SAT Subject Tests recommended. Interview optional, nonevaluative and informational in scope. Audition/interview required of music and music theater majors. **Homeschooled:** Should submit at least 3 SAT Subject Test scores. **Learning Disabled:** Supplementary application, diagnostic reports, and high school transcript required for freshman learning services program.

**High school preparation.** College-preparatory program recommended. 16 units required; 18 recommended. Required and recommended units include English 4, mathematics 3-4, social studies 2-4, science 3-4 (laboratory 2), foreign language 2-3 and academic electives 3-4.

**2010-2011 Annual costs.** Tuition/fees (projected): $36,697. Room/board: $13,468.

**2009-2010 Financial aid.** All financial aid based on need. 1,144 full-time freshmen applied for aid; 849 were judged to have need; 849 of these received aid. Average need met was 93%. Average scholarship/grant was $17,325; average loan $4,180. 61% of total undergraduate aid awarded as scholarships/grants, 39% as loans/jobs. **Additional information:** Early decision applicants must submit estimated AU institutional financial aid application by 11/15 and a FASFA as soon as possible after Jan 1.

**Application procedures. Admission:** Closing date 1/15 (postmark date). $60 fee, may be waived for applicants with need. Admission notification 4/1. Must reply by May 1 or within 4 week(s) if notified thereafter. **Financial aid:** Closing date 2/15. FAFSA, institutional form required. Applicants notified by 4/1; must reply by 5/1 or within 4 week(s) of notification.

**Academics. Special study options:** Accelerated study, combined bachelor's/graduate degree, cooperative education, cross-registration, double major, exchange student, honors, independent study, internships, student-designed major, study abroad, teacher certification program, Washington semester, weekend college. One-semester, full-year, alternative spring break and language-immersion options are available. **Credit/placement by examination:** CLEP, IB, institutional tests. 30 credit hours maximum toward bachelor's degree. Credit awarded for some international high school learning programs such as British A Levels or German Arbitur; Advanced Placement, International Baccalaureate higher level tests only. **Support services:** Learning center, pre-admission summer program, reduced course load, study skills assistance, tutoring, writing center.

**Majors. Area/ethnic studies:** American, French, German, Latin American, Russian/Slavic, women's. **Biology:** General, biochemistry, environmental, marine. **Business:** Accounting, business admin, finance, management information systems. **Communications:** Journalism, media studies, public relations, radio/tv. **Communications technology:** Animation/special effects, recording arts. **Computer sciences:** General, computer graphics, computer science. **Conservation:** Environmental studies. **Education:** Elementary, secondary. **Foreign languages:** French, German, Russian, Spanish. **Health:** Predental, premedicine, prenursing, prepharmacy, preveterinary. **History:** General. **Interdisciplinary:** Biological/physical sciences, global studies. **Legal studies:** General, prelaw. **Liberal arts:** Arts/sciences. **Math:** General, applied, statistics. **Parks/recreation:** Health/fitness, sports admin. **Philosophy/religion:** Judaic, philosophy. **Physical sciences:** Acoustics, chemistry, physics. **Protective services:** Criminal justice, police science. **Psychology:** General. **Social sciences:** Anthropology, economics, international relations, political science, sociology. **Visual/performing arts:** General, art, art history/conservation, cinematography, design, dramatic, film/cinema, graphic design, multimedia, music history, music performance, music theory/composition, studio arts.

**Most popular majors.** Business/marketing 16%, communications/journalism 10%, social sciences 41%, visual/performing arts 7%.

**Computing on campus.** 650 workstations in dormitories, library, computer center, student center. Dormitories wired for high-speed internet access and linked to campus network. Commuter students can connect to campus network. Online course registration, online library, helpline, repair service, student web hosting, wireless network available.

**Student life. Freshman orientation:** Available, $140 fee. Preregistration for classes offered. 2-day programs in late June and early July. Students take placement exams and meet advisors. Parents may attend. **Policies:** Academic integrity code. **Housing:** Guaranteed on-campus for freshmen. Coed dorms, special housing for disabled, wellness housing available. $200 nonrefundable deposit, deadline 5/1. Housing for handicapped students handled individually; community service floor available. Some single-sex floors in coed dorms. **Activities:** Bands, campus ministries, choral groups, dance, drama, film society, international student organizations, literary magazine, music ensembles, musical theater, opera, radio station, student government, student newspaper, symphony orchestra, TV station, NAACP, Kennedy Political Union, Amnesty International, Habitat for Humanity, Asian students association, concert choir, Hillel, Latin American student organization.

**Athletics.** NCAA. **Intercollegiate:** Basketball, cross-country, diving, field hockey W, lacrosse W, soccer, swimming, track and field, volleyball W, wrestling M. **Intramural:** Basketball, football (non-tackle), soccer, softball, tennis, volleyball, weight lifting M. **Team name:** Eagles.

**Student services.** Alcohol/substance abuse counseling, chaplain/spiritual director, career counseling, student employment services, financial aid counseling, health services, minority student services, on-campus daycare, personal counseling, placement for graduates, women's services. **Physically disabled:** Services for visually, speech, hearing impaired.

**Contact.** E-mail: admissions@american.edu
Phone: (202) 885-6000 Fax: (202) 885-6014
Greg Grauman, Director of Admissions, American University, 4400 Massachusetts Avenue NW, Washington, DC 20016-8001

## Catholic University of America
**Washington, District of Columbia**    CB member
**www.cua.edu**    CB code: 5104

- Private 4-year university affiliated with Roman Catholic Church
- Residential campus in very large city
- 3,422 degree-seeking undergraduates: 6% part-time, 54% women, 5% African American, 3% Asian American, 7% Hispanic American, 3% international
- 3,188 degree-seeking graduate students
- 86% of applicants admitted
- SAT or ACT with writing, application essay required
- 71% graduate within 6 years; 66% enter graduate study

**General.** Founded in 1887. Regionally accredited. Strong orientation toward service-based activities; internship and study opportunities with Congress, federal agencies, and international embassies. **Degrees:** 721 bachelor's, 15 associate awarded; master's, doctoral, professional offered. **ROTC:**

Army, Naval, Air Force. **Calendar:** Semester, extensive summer session. **Full-time faculty:** 352 total; 98% have terminal degrees, 12% minority, 36% women. **Part-time faculty:** 342 total; 7% minority, 45% women. **Class size:** 57% < 20, 33% 20-39, 3% 40-49, 7% 50-99, less than 1% >100. **Special facilities:** Rare book collection, on-campus nuclear reactor, vitreous state laboratory.

**Freshman class profile.** 5,044 applied, 4,336 admitted, 814 enrolled.

| Mid 50% test scores | | | |
|---|---|---|---|
| SAT critical reading: | 510-610 | Return as sophomores: | 81% |
| SAT math: | 500-600 | Out-of-state: | 99% |
| ACT composite: | 21-26 | Live on campus: | 94% |
| GPA 3.75 or higher: | 18% | International: | 2% |
| GPA 3.50-3.74: | 22% | Fraternities: | 1% |
| GPA 3.0-3.49: | 31% | Sororities: | 1% |

*Note: GPA 2.0-2.99 header appears top-right with 29%.*

**Basis for selection.** School achievement record, including strength of curriculum and SAT or ACT scores. Recommendations and extracurricular activities, including leadership and service are also important. SAT Subject Tests recommended. Students admitted to School of Arts and Sciences or School of Philosophy are asked to submit SAT Subject Test scores in foreign languages for placement purposes. Audition required for music. **Homeschooled:** Statement describing homeschool structure and mission, transcript of courses and grades, letter of recommendation (nonparent) required. **Learning Disabled:** Matriculated students with learning disabilities are asked to submit documentation to Office of Disability Support Services.

**High school preparation.** College-preparatory program recommended. 17 units recommended. Recommended units include English 4, mathematics 3, social studies 4, science 3 (laboratory 1) and foreign language 2. 1 fine arts or humanities recommended.

**2009-2010 Annual costs.** Tuition/fees: $32,315. Full-time tuition for School of Engineering is $32,000. Full-time tuition for School of Architecture is $32,470. Part-time tuition for School of Architecture is $1,180 per credit hour. Room/board: $12,134. Books/supplies: $1,200. Personal expenses: $1,500.

**2009-2010 Financial aid. Need-based:** 659 full-time freshmen applied for aid; 525 were judged to have need; 525 of these received aid. Average need met was 86%. Average scholarship/grant was $16,752; average loan $3,416. 59% of total undergraduate aid awarded as scholarships/grants, 41% as loans/jobs. **Non-need-based:** Awarded to 1,010 full-time undergraduates, including 230 freshmen. Scholarships awarded for academics, alumni affiliation, music/drama, religious affiliation.

**Application procedures. Admission:** Closing date 2/15 (postmark date). $55 fee, may be waived for applicants with need. Admission notification on a rolling basis beginning on or about 3/15. Must reply by May 1 or within 2 week(s) if notified thereafter. **Financial aid:** Priority date 2/15, closing date 4/10. FAFSA required. Applicants notified on a rolling basis starting 4/1; must reply by 5/1 or within 2 week(s) of notification.

**Academics. Special study options:** Accelerated study, combined bachelor's/graduate degree, cross-registration, distance learning, double major, dual enrollment of high school students, ESL, honors, independent study, internships, study abroad, teacher certification program, Washington semester. **Credit/placement by examination:** AP, CLEP, IB, institutional tests. All credit-by-examination awarded on case-by-case basis. No credit by outside examination given to matriculated students. **Support services:** Learning center, reduced course load, study skills assistance, tutoring, writing center.

**Honors college/program.** Applicants with a combined SAT score of 1300 exclusive of Writing and a high school GPA of 3.5 or above are offered admission; students not meeting these requirements may petition for admission after their first semester. About 1 in 10 matriculated students belong to the University Honors Program.

**Majors. Architecture:** Architecture. **Biology:** General, biochemistry. **Business:** General, accounting, finance, human resources, international, international finance, management science. **Communications:** General. **Computer sciences:** General. **Education:** General, biology, chemistry, drama/dance, early childhood, elementary, English, ESL, French, history, mathematics, music, secondary, Spanish. **Engineering:** Biomedical, civil, electrical, mechanical. **Foreign languages:** Classics, French, German, Latin, Spanish. **Health:** Clinical lab science, nursing (RN). **History:** General. **Interdisciplinary:** Medieval/Renaissance. **Liberal arts:** Arts/sciences. **Math:** General. **Philosophy/religion:** Philosophy, religion. **Physical sciences:** Chemistry, physics. **Psychology:** General. **Public administration:** Social work. **Social sciences:** Anthropology, economics, political science, sociology. **Visual/performing arts:** Art, art history/conservation, dramatic, music history, music performance, music theory/composition, piano/organ, voice/opera.

**Most popular majors.** Architecture 13%, business/marketing 8%, engineering/engineering technologies 7%, health sciences 8%, psychology 7%, social sciences 16%, visual/performing arts 10%.

**Computing on campus.** 500 workstations in dormitories, library, computer center, student center. Dormitories wired for high-speed internet access and linked to campus network. Commuter students can connect to campus network. Online course registration, online library, helpline, repair service, student web hosting, wireless network available.

**Student life. Freshman orientation:** Available. Preregistration for classes offered. Held Thursday-Sunday before start of fall semester. **Policies:** Code of Student Conduct is the guiding behavioral document; medical insurance is required for all full-time students and all full and part-time international students; immunization requirement for students under 26 years of age. **Housing:** Guaranteed on-campus for freshmen. Coed dorms, single-sex dorms, special housing for disabled, apartments, wellness housing available. **Activities:** Jazz band, campus ministries, choral groups, dance, drama, film society, international student organizations, literary magazine, music ensembles, musical theater, opera, radio station, student government, student newspaper, symphony orchestra, College Republicans, College Democrats, Filipino Organization of Catholic University Students, Alpha Phi Omega service fraternity, Habitat for Humanity, Latin Alliance.

**Athletics.** NCAA. **Intercollegiate:** Baseball M, basketball, cross-country, field hockey W, football (tackle) M, lacrosse, soccer, softball W, swimming, tennis, track and field, volleyball W. **Intramural:** Basketball, football (non-tackle), racquetball, soccer, softball, tennis, volleyball. **Team name:** Cardinals.

**Student services.** Adult student services, alcohol/substance abuse counseling, chaplain/spiritual director, career counseling, student employment services, financial aid counseling, health services, legal services, minority student services, personal counseling, placement for graduates, veterans' counselor. **Physically disabled:** Services for visually, speech, hearing impaired.

**Contact.** E-mail: cua-admissions@cua.edu
Phone: (202) 319-5305 Toll-free number: (800) 673-2772
Fax: (202) 319-6533
Christine Mica, Dean, University Admissions, Catholic University of America, 102 McMahon Hall, Washington, DC 20064

## Corcoran College of Art and Design

**Washington, District of Columbia**      CB member
**www.corcoran.edu**      CB code: 5705

- Private 4-year visual arts college
- Commuter campus in very large city
- 350 degree-seeking undergraduates
- 53% of applicants admitted
- SAT or ACT (ACT writing optional) required

**General.** Founded in 1890. Regionally accredited. Member, Washington Consortium of Colleges. **Degrees:** 66 bachelor's, 6 associate awarded; master's offered. **Location:** Downtown. **Calendar:** Semester, limited summer session. **Full-time faculty:** 30 total. **Part-time faculty:** 112 total. **Class size:** 98% < 20, 2% 20-39. **Special facilities:** Full partnership to Corcoran Gallery of Art, Student Exhibition space within museum.

**Freshman class profile.** 435 applied, 229 admitted, 73 enrolled.

| Mid 50% test scores | | | |
|---|---|---|---|
| | | GPA 3.50-3.74: | 15% |
| SAT critical reading: | 470-610 | GPA 3.0-3.49: | 30% |
| SAT math: | 450-530 | GPA 2.0-2.99: | 40% |
| SAT writing: | 460-560 | Rank in top quarter: | 20% |
| ACT composite: | 20-26 | Out-of-state: | 94% |
| GPA 3.75 or higher: | 15% | Live on campus: | 90% |

**Basis for selection.** School achievement record, art portfolio, interview, and motivation important. Letters of recommendation and personal statement encouraged. School and community activities, test scores considered. Portfolio required (CD may replace original portfolio). Essay required. Interview required of applicants living within 200 miles of the school. **Homeschooled:** Statement describing homeschool structure and mission, transcript of courses and grades required.

**High school preparation.** College-preparatory program recommended. Recommended units include English 4, history 4 and visual/performing arts 4. Advanced art courses recommended.

**2009-2010 Annual costs.** Tuition/fees: $27,960. Room only: $9,700. Books/supplies: $2,580. Personal expenses: $1,334.

**2008-2009 Financial aid. Non-need-based:** Scholarships awarded for academics, art.

**Application procedures. Admission:** Priority date 3/1; no deadline. $45 fee, may be waived for applicants with need. Admission notification on a rolling basis. Must reply by May 1 or within 2 week(s) if notified thereafter. **Financial aid:** Priority date 3/15; no closing date. FAFSA, institutional form required. Applicants notified on a rolling basis starting 4/15; must reply by 5/1 or within 2 week(s) of notification.

**Academics. Special study options:** Combined bachelor's/graduate degree, cross-registration, exchange student, independent study, internships, liberal arts/career combination, New York semester, study abroad, teacher certification program. Mobility programs with members of Association of Independent Art Colleges, Washington Consortium Member. **Credit/ placement by examination:** AP, CLEP, IB. **Support services:** Reduced course load, study skills assistance, tutoring, writing center.

**Majors. Education:** Art. **Visual/performing arts:** General, art, graphic design, interior design, photography, studio arts.

**Computing on campus.** 110 workstations in library, computer center, student center. Dormitories wired for high-speed internet access. Commuter students can connect to campus network. Online library, helpline, student web hosting, wireless network available.

**Student life. Freshman orientation:** Mandatory. Preregistration for classes offered. Mandatory session introducing college, museum, faculty, majors, city. **Housing:** Guaranteed on-campus for freshmen. Coed dorms, apartments available. $400 fully refundable deposit, deadline 5/15.

**Student services.** Alcohol/substance abuse counseling, career counseling, student employment services, financial aid counseling, personal counseling, placement for graduates, veterans' counselor.

**Contact.** E-mail: admissions@corcoran.org
Phone: (202) 639-1814 Toll-free number: (888) 267-2672
Fax: (202) 639-1830
Robert Garcia, Director of Admissions, Corcoran College of Art and Design, 500 17th Street, NW, Washington, DC 20006-4804

## Gallaudet University
**Washington, District of Columbia**
www.gallaudet.edu                                    CB code: 5240

- Private 4-year university and liberal arts college
- Residential campus in very large city
- 1,053 degree-seeking undergraduates: 5% part-time, 53% women, 11% African American, 4% Asian American, 9% Hispanic American, 2% Native American, 5% international
- 407 degree-seeking graduate students
- 68% of applicants admitted
- SAT or ACT (ACT writing recommended), application essay required
- 39% graduate within 6 years

**General.** Founded in 1857. Regionally accredited. Only liberal arts university in the world designed exclusively for deaf and hard of hearing students. Bilingual (English/American Sign Language), multicultural environment, assistive devices (TTY's or campus phones, closed captioned television and campus films), specially-designed classrooms and dormitories available. **Degrees:** 201 bachelor's awarded; master's, doctoral offered. **Location:** Downtown. **Calendar:** Semester, limited summer session. **Full-time faculty:** 230 total. **Class size:** 94% < 20, 6% 20-39. **Special facilities:** Gallaudet Interpreting Services provides interpreters for university-related events.

**Freshman class profile.** 413 applied, 282 admitted, 211 enrolled.

| Mid 50% test scores | | GPA 2.0-2.99: | 13% |
|---|---|---|---|
| ACT composite: | 15-20 | Return as sophomores: | 75% |
| GPA 3.50-3.74: | 23% | Out-of-state: | 99% |
| GPA 3.0-3.49: | 64% | International: | 7% |

**Basis for selection.** Applicants with hearing loss who show evidence of academic ability and motivation considered. Test scores, grades, class rank, essay, recommendation important. Interview recommended. **Learning Disabled:** Untimed tests, psychological evaluations confirming disabilities required.

**High school preparation.** College-preparatory program recommended. 16 units recommended. Recommended units include English 4, mathematics 4, social studies 4, history 4, science 4 (laboratory 2).

**2010-2011 Annual costs.** Tuition/fees (projected): $11,226. Room/board: $9,660. Books/supplies: $942. Personal expenses: $4,672.

**2008-2009 Financial aid. Need-based:** 169 full-time freshmen applied for aid; 138 were judged to have need; 138 of these received aid. Average need met was 84%. Average scholarship/grant was $16,069; average loan $2,788. 84% of total undergraduate aid awarded as scholarships/grants, 16%

as loans/jobs. **Non-need-based:** Awarded to 310 full-time undergraduates, including 65 freshmen. Scholarships awarded for academics, leadership, minority status. **Additional information:** Institution receives substantial aid from state vocational rehabilitation agencies, supplemented by institutional grants when needed.

**Application procedures. Admission:** No deadline. $50 fee, may be waived for applicants with need. Admission notification on a rolling basis. **Financial aid:** Priority date 7/1; no closing date. FAFSA, institutional form required. Applicants notified on a rolling basis starting 3/1; must reply within 4 week(s) of notification.

**Academics.** Undergraduate degree program open to deaf and hard of hearing students and a limited number of hearing students; visiting and exchange student programs available to any qualified student. **Special study options:** Accelerated study, combined bachelor's/graduate degree, cross-registration, distance learning, double major, ESL, honors, independent study, internships, student-designed major, study abroad, teacher certification program. Experiential programs off-campus including orientation program for employers of deaf students and paraprofessional jobs on campus, programs for interpreter-assisted mainstreaming of students into area colleges such as Georgetown University, George Mason University, Catholic University, Howard University. **Credit/placement by examination:** AP, CLEP, ACT, institutional tests. **Support services:** Learning center, pre-admission summer program, reduced course load, remedial instruction, study skills assistance, tutoring, writing center.

**Majors. Biology:** General. **Business:** General, accounting, business admin, entrepreneurial studies, management information systems. **Communications:** General, broadcast journalism. **Computer sciences:** General, computer science, information systems. **Education:** General, art, Deaf/hearing impaired, early childhood, elementary, family/consumer sciences, multiple handicapped, physical, secondary. **Family/consumer sciences:** General, child care, food/nutrition. **Foreign languages:** American Sign Language, French, Spanish. **Health:** Recreational therapy. **History:** General. **Math:** General. **Parks/recreation:** Facilities management. **Philosophy/religion:** Philosophy. **Physical sciences:** Chemistry, physics. **Psychology:** General. **Public administration:** Social work. **Social sciences:** Criminology, economics, political science, sociology. **Visual/performing arts:** General, art history/conservation, commercial/advertising art, dramatic, studio arts.

**Most popular majors.** Business/marketing 10%, communications/journalism 8%, education 18%, psychology 6%, public administration/social services 8%, social sciences 8%, visual/performing arts 11%.

**Computing on campus.** 352 workstations in dormitories, library, computer center, student center. Dormitories wired for high-speed internet access and linked to campus network. Commuter students can connect to campus network. Online course registration, online library, helpline, repair service, student web hosting, wireless network available.

**Student life. Freshman orientation:** Mandatory. Preregistration for classes offered. Held 1 week before beginning of semester. **Policies:** No alcohol allowed in freshman dorms; no smoking in residence halls. Only full-time students may reside in dorms. All dormitories equipped for deaf and hard of hearing students. **Housing:** Guaranteed on-campus for freshmen. Coed dorms, special housing for disabled, apartments available. $150 fully refundable deposit, deadline 7/18. **Activities:** Campus ministries, dance, drama, film society, international student organizations, literary magazine, student government, student newspaper, Asian Pacific association, black deaf student union, Hispanic student association, literary society.

**Athletics.** NCAA. **Intercollegiate:** Baseball M, basketball, cross-country, football (tackle) M, soccer, softball W, swimming, tennis, track and field, volleyball, wrestling M. **Intramural:** Basketball, football (non-tackle) M, softball, volleyball. **Team name:** Bisons.

**Student services.** Adult student services, alcohol/substance abuse counseling, chaplain/spiritual director, career counseling, student employment services, health services, minority student services, on-campus daycare, personal counseling, placement for graduates. **Physically disabled:** Services for visually, speech, hearing impaired.

**Contact.** E-mail: admissions@gallaudet.edu
Phone: (202) 651-5750 Toll-free number: (800) 995-0550
Fax: (202) 651-5774
Charity Reedy-Hines, Director of Admissions, Gallaudet University, 800 Florida Avenue, NE, Washington, DC 20002

## George Washington University
**Washington, District of Columbia**                 CB member
www.gwu.edu/explore/                                 CB code: 5246

- Private 4-year university
- Residential campus in very large city

♦ 10,225 degree-seeking undergraduates: 6% part-time, 56% women, 7% African American, 11% Asian American, 7% Hispanic American, 1% Native American, 6% international
♦ 14,503 graduate students
♦ 37% of applicants admitted
♦ SAT or ACT (ACT writing recommended), application essay required
♦ 81% graduate within 6 years

**General.** Founded in 1821. Regionally accredited. **Degrees:** 2,428 bachelor's, 214 associate awarded; master's, doctoral, professional offered. **ROTC:** Army, Naval, Air Force. **Calendar:** Semester, extensive summer session. **Full-time faculty:** 903 total; 92% have terminal degrees, 20% minority, 37% women. **Part-time faculty:** 1,510 total; 30% have terminal degrees, 14% minority, 43% women. **Class size:** 56% < 20, 28% 20-39, 6% 40-49, 6% 50-99, 4% >100. **Special facilities:** Observatory.

**Freshman class profile.** 19,842 applied, 7,292 admitted, 2,592 enrolled.

| Mid 50% test scores | | | |
|---|---|---|---|
| SAT critical reading: | 600-690 | Return as sophomores: | 91% |
| SAT math: | 600-690 | Out-of-state: | 99% |
| SAT writing: | 600-690 | Live on campus: | 98% |
| ACT composite: | 27-30 | International: | 6% |
| Rank in top quarter: | 93% | Fraternities: | 22% |
| Rank in top tenth: | 67% | Sororities: | 21% |

**Basis for selection.** GED not accepted. Strong college-preparatory program, 3.0 GPA and class rank in top third important. Teacher and counselor recommendation and personal statement required. SAT Subject Tests recommended. SAT Subject Tests required for applicants to 7-year BA/MD and integrated engineering/MD programs (any math and any science); early admission applicants (any math, student's choice); and recommended for all for admission and placement. Interview recommended for all, required of early admission applicants. Audition required of bachelor of music applicants.

**High school preparation.** College-preparatory program required. Required and recommended units include English 4, mathematics 2-4, social studies 2-4, science 2-4 (laboratory 1) and foreign language 2-4. One physics, 1 chemistry, and additional 1 unit in math required for School of Engineering and Applied Science.

**2009-2010 Annual costs.** Tuition/fees: $41,655. Tuition stays fixed until student graduates, for a maximum of five years. Room/board: $10,120. Books/supplies: $1,200. Personal expenses: $1,400.

**2009-2010 Financial aid. Need-based:** Average need met was 94%. Average scholarship/grant was $25,467; average loan $4,649. 74% of total undergraduate aid awarded as scholarships/grants, 26% as loans/jobs. **Non-need-based:** Scholarships awarded for academics, art, athletics, music/drama, ROTC. **Additional information:** Auditions required for performing arts scholarships.

**Application procedures. Admission:** Closing date 1/10. $65 fee, may be waived for applicants with need. Admission notification 4/1. Admission notification on a rolling basis. Must reply by May 1 or within 2 week(s) if notified thereafter. Applications received after 2/1 reviewed on space-available basis. Supplemental applications required for honors program, 7-year integrated engineering/law program, integrated engineering/MD program. **Financial aid:** Closing date 2/1. FAFSA, CSS PROFILE required. Applicants notified on a rolling basis starting 3/24; must reply by 5/1.

**Academics. Special study options:** Accelerated study, cooperative education, cross-registration, distance learning, double major, dual enrollment of high school students, honors, independent study, internships, liberal arts/career combination, student-designed major, study abroad. 7-year integrated BA/MD liberal arts program, 8-year integrated engineering/JD and engineering/MD programs. **Credit/placement by examination:** AP, CLEP, IB, institutional tests. 30 credit hours maximum toward bachelor's degree. **Support services:** Pre-admission summer program, reduced course load, tutoring.

**Majors. Area/ethnic studies:** American, European, Latin American, Near/Middle Eastern. **Biology:** General, biomedical sciences, biophysics, pharmacology. **Business:** Accounting, business admin, finance, international, management information systems, tourism promotion. **Communications:** General, journalism, political. **Computer sciences:** General, information systems. **Conservation:** General, environmental studies. **Education:** Physical. **Engineering:** General, biomedical, civil, computer, electrical, mechanical. **Foreign languages:** General, Arabic, Chinese, classics, French, German, Hebrew, Italian, Japanese, Latin, Portuguese, Romance, Russian, Spanish. **Health:** Audiology/speech pathology, clinical lab technology, cytotechnology, physician assistant, sonography. **History:** General. **Liberal arts:** Arts/sciences.

**Math:** General, applied, statistics. **Parks/recreation:** Exercise sciences. **Philosophy/religion:** Judaic, philosophy, religion. **Physical sciences:** Chemistry, geology, physics. **Protective services:** Criminal justice, police science. **Psychology:** General. **Public administration:** Human services, policy analysis. **Social sciences:** Anthropology, archaeology, economics, geography, international relations, political science, sociology. **Visual/performing arts:** General, art history/conservation, dance, dramatic, interior design, studio arts, theater history.

**Most popular majors.** Business/marketing 19%, psychology 7%, social sciences 37%.

**Computing on campus.** 600 workstations in dormitories, library, computer center, student center. Dormitories linked to campus network. Commuter students can connect to campus network. Repair service available.

**Student life. Housing:** Guaranteed on-campus for freshmen. Coed dorms, apartments, fraternity/sorority housing, wellness housing available. $800 nonrefundable deposit, deadline 5/1. **Activities:** Bands, choral groups, dance, drama, film society, international student organizations, literary magazine, music ensembles, Model UN, musical theater, radio station, student government, student newspaper, TV station, religious groups, national political party organizations, ethnic, social action, public affairs groups.

**Athletics.** NCAA. **Intercollegiate:** Baseball M, basketball, cross country, diving, golf M, gymnastics W, lacrosse W, rowing (crew), soccer, softball W, squash W, swimming, tennis, volleyball W, water polo. **Intramural:** Basketball, football (tackle) M, golf, racquetball, soccer, softball, table tennis, tennis, volleyball. **Team name:** Colonials.

**Student services.** Alcohol/substance abuse counseling, career counseling, student employment services, financial aid counseling, health services, on-campus daycare, personal counseling, placement for graduates, veterans' counselor. **Physically disabled:** Services for visually, speech, hearing impaired.

**Contact.** E-mail: gwadm@gwu.edu
Phone: (202) 994-6040 Toll-free number: (800) 447-3765
Fax: (202) 994-0325
Kathryn Napper, Executive Dean for Undergraduate Admissions, George Washington University, 2121 I Street NW, Suite 201, Washington, DC 20052

## Georgetown University
**Washington, District of Columbia**     **CB member**
www.georgetown.edu     **CB code: 5244**

♦ Private 4-year university affiliated with Roman Catholic Church
♦ Residential campus in very large city
♦ 7,092 degree-seeking undergraduates: 3% part-time, 55% women, 7% African American, 9% Asian American, 6% Hispanic American, 7% international
♦ 8,684 degree-seeking graduate students
♦ 20% of applicants admitted
♦ SAT or ACT (ACT writing optional), application essay, interview required
♦ 94% graduate within 6 years

**General.** Founded in 1789. Regionally accredited. **Degrees:** 2,201 bachelor's awarded; master's, doctoral, professional offered. **ROTC:** Army, Naval, Air Force. **Location:** 1.5 miles from downtown. **Calendar:** Semester, extensive summer session. **Full-time faculty:** 873 total; 88% have terminal degrees, 14% minority, 39% women. **Part-time faculty:** 904 total; 60% have terminal degrees, 11% minority, 38% women. **Special facilities:** Observatory, language learning technology lab with satellite link, library with special collections including archives, rare books, prints, manuscripts dealing with medieval and early modern periods, and American history.

**Freshman class profile.** 18,616 applied, 3,682 admitted, 1,555 enrolled.

| Mid 50% test scores | | | |
|---|---|---|---|
| SAT critical reading: | 650-750 | Return as sophomores: | 96% |
| SAT math: | 650-750 | Out-of-state: | 99% |
| | | Live on campus: | 100% |
| ACT composite: | 27-33 | International: | 5% |

**Basis for selection.** School academic record most important, in addition to test scores, essays, extracurricular activities, interview, and recommendations. Special consideration given to qualified minorities, athletes, internationals, and alumni relatives. SAT Subject Tests recommended. Interview required unless not possible to assign based on geographic area; portfolio recommended for fine arts majors.

**High school preparation.** Required units include English 4, mathematics 2, social studies 2, history 2, science 1 and foreign language 2. Additional units in science, math, and foreign language recommended for some programs.

**2009-2010 Annual costs.** Tuition/fees: $39,036. Room/board: $13,125. Books/supplies: $1,060. Personal expenses: $1,620.

**2008-2009 Financial aid. Need-based:** 850 full-time freshmen applied for aid; 632 were judged to have need; 632 of these received aid. Average need met was 100%. Average scholarship/grant was $28,100; average loan $3,000. 82% of total undergraduate aid awarded as scholarships/grants, 18% as loans/jobs. **Non-need-based:** Awarded to 800 full-time undergraduates, including 200 freshmen. Scholarships awarded for athletics.

**Application procedures. Admission:** Closing date 1/10 (receipt date). $65 fee, may be waived for applicants with need. Application must be submitted on paper. Admission notification 4/1. Must reply by May 1 or within 2 week(s) if notified thereafter. Early Action plan limits students from applying to binding Early Decision programs. **Financial aid:** Closing date 2/1. FAFSA, CSS PROFILE required. Applicants notified by 4/1; must reply by 5/1 or within 2 week(s) of notification.

**Academics.** Early assurance program to university's medical and law schools. **Special study options:** Combined bachelor's/graduate degree, cross-registration, double major, ESL, honors, independent study, internships, student-designed major, study abroad, Washington semester. **Credit/placement by examination:** AP, CLEP, IB, institutional tests. **Support services:** Learning center, pre-admission summer program, study skills assistance, tutoring, writing center.

**Majors. Area/ethnic studies:** American, women's. **Biology:** General, biochemistry, biomedical sciences, neurobiology/physiology. **Business:** Accounting, business admin, finance, international, marketing. **Computer sciences:** Computer science. **Foreign languages:** Arabic, Chinese, classics, comparative lit, French, German, Italian, Japanese, linguistics, Portuguese, Russian, Spanish. **Health:** Health care admin, international public health, nursing (RN). **History:** General. **Interdisciplinary:** Biological/physical sciences, medieval/Renaissance, peace/conflict, science/society. **Liberal arts:** Arts/sciences. **Math:** General. **Philosophy/religion:** Philosophy, religion. **Physical sciences:** Chemistry, physics. **Psychology:** General. **Social sciences:** Anthropology, economics, international relations, political science, sociology. **Visual/performing arts:** Art, art history/conservation, studio arts.

**Most popular majors.** Business/marketing 27%, English 7%, foreign language 6%, health sciences 6%, social sciences 31%.

**Computing on campus.** Dormitories wired for high-speed internet access and linked to campus network. Commuter students can connect to campus network. Online course registration, online library, helpline, repair service, student web hosting, wireless network available.

**Student life. Freshman orientation:** Mandatory, $160 fee. Preregistration for classes offered. Student volunteer-led program. **Policies:** Freshmen and sophomores required to live on campus. Upperclass students obtain housing via lottery process. **Housing:** Guaranteed on-campus for freshmen. Coed dorms, special housing for disabled, apartments, wellness housing available. **Activities:** Bands, campus ministries, choral groups, dance, drama, film society, international student organizations, literary magazine, music ensembles, musical theater, radio station, student government, student newspaper, symphony orchestra, TV station, over 170 student organizations available.

**Athletics.** NCAA. **Intercollegiate:** Baseball M, basketball, cross-country, diving, field hockey W, football (tackle) M, golf, lacrosse, rowing (crew), sailing, soccer, softball W, swimming, tennis, track and field, volleyball W. **Intramural:** Basketball, cross-country, football (non-tackle), golf, handball, racquetball, skiing, soccer, softball, squash, table tennis, tennis, volleyball. **Team name:** Hoyas.

**Student services.** Alcohol/substance abuse counseling, chaplain/spiritual director, career counseling, student employment services, financial aid counseling, health services, minority student services, on-campus daycare, personal counseling, placement for graduates, women's services. **Physically disabled:** Services for visually, hearing impaired.

**Contact.** E-mail: guadmiss@georgetown.edu
Phone: (202) 687-3600 Fax: (202) 687-5084
Charles Deacon, Dean of Admissions, Georgetown University, 103 White-Gravenor, Washington, DC 20057-1002

## Howard University
**Washington, District of Columbia**    CB member
www.howard.edu    CB code: 5297

- Private 4-year university
- Residential campus in very large city

- 7,029 degree-seeking undergraduates
- 54% of applicants admitted
- SAT or ACT with writing required

**General.** Founded in 1867. Regionally accredited. 5 campuses. 25 major research centers and several campus programs. **Degrees:** 1,402 bachelor's awarded; master's, doctoral, professional offered. **ROTC:** Army, Air Force. **Location:** 38 miles from Baltimore, 105 miles from Richmond, Virginia. **Calendar:** Semester, extensive summer session. **Full-time faculty:** 986 total. **Part-time faculty:** 223 total. **Class size:** 62% < 20, 29% 20-39, 5% 40-49, 3% 50-99, less than 1% >100. **Special facilities:** Research center, including museum and archives, with collections on Africa and persons of African descent; international affairs center.

**Freshman class profile.** 9,209 applied, 4,976 admitted, 1,603 enrolled.

| Mid 50% test scores | | | |
|---|---|---|---|
| SAT critical reading: | 460-660 | GPA 3.0-3.49: | 42% |
| SAT math: | 440-660 | GPA 2.0-2.99: | 26% |
| SAT writing: | 430-660 | Rank in top quarter: | 55% |
| ACT composite: | 19-29 | Rank in top tenth: | 26% |
| GPA 3.75 or higher: | 14% | Out-of-state: | 98% |
| GPA 3.50-3.74: | 18% | Live on campus: | 92% |

**Basis for selection.** High school achievement record, test scores most important. Requirements vary from college to college. SAT Subject Tests recommended. Dental Hygiene Aptitude Test required of dental hygiene applicants. Essay recommended; required of Early Action applicants. Audition required of music, drama majors. Portfolio required of art, architecture majors. Interview recommended for pharmacy and pharmaceutical programs, physician assistant majors. **Homeschooled:** Must have GED.

**High school preparation.** 16 units required; 21 recommended. Required and recommended units include English 4, mathematics 2-3, social studies 2, science 2, foreign language 2 and academic electives 4. Academic electives must count toward graduation.

**2009-2010 Annual costs.** Tuition/fees: $16,075. Room/board: $7,966. Books/supplies: $1,300. Personal expenses: $1,800.

**2008-2009 Financial aid. Non-need-based:** Scholarships awarded for academics, art, athletics, music/drama.

**Application procedures. Admission:** Priority date 11/1; deadline 2/15 (receipt date). $45 fee. Admission notification on a rolling basis beginning on or about 4/15. Must reply by May 1 or within 4 week(s) if notified thereafter. Fall term procedures for applicants does not differ from the spring, however spring term applicants stand a better chance of acceptance. **Financial aid:** Priority date 2/15, closing date 8/15. FAFSA, institutional form required. Applicants notified on a rolling basis starting 4/1; must reply by 8/1 or within 4 week(s) of notification.

**Academics. Special study options:** Accelerated study, combined bachelor's/graduate degree, cooperative education, cross-registration, distance learning, double major, dual enrollment of high school students, exchange student, honors, independent study, internships, student-designed major, study abroad, teacher certification program. **Credit/placement by examination:** AP, CLEP, IB, SAT, ACT, institutional tests. 60 credit hours maximum toward bachelor's degree. **Support services:** Learning center, pre-admission summer program, reduced course load, remedial instruction, study skills assistance, tutoring, writing center.

**Majors. Architecture:** Architecture. **Area/ethnic studies:** African, African-American. **Biology:** General. **Business:** Accounting, business admin, fashion, finance, hospitality admin, hospitality/recreation, insurance, international, management information systems, market research. **Communications:** General, broadcast journalism, journalism, radio/tv. **Computer sciences:** Information systems, systems analysis. **Education:** Art, English, health, music, physical. **Engineering:** Chemical, civil, computer, electrical, mechanical, systems. **Foreign languages:** Ancient Greek, classics, French, German, modern Greek, Russian, Spanish. **Health:** Clinical lab science, medical radiologic technology/radiation therapy, music therapy, physician assistant, recreational therapy. **History:** General. **Interdisciplinary:** Nutrition sciences. **Math:** General. **Parks/recreation:** General. **Philosophy/religion:** Philosophy. **Physical sciences:** Chemistry, physics. **Psychology:** General. **Social sciences:** Anthropology, economics, political science, sociology. **Visual/performing arts:** General, art, art history/conservation, arts management, conducting, dance, design, interior design, jazz, music history, music management, music theory/composition, piano/organ, theater arts management, theater design, theater history, voice/opera.

**Most popular majors.** Biology 7%, business/marketing 18%, communications/journalism 16%, health sciences 22%, psychology 6%, social sciences 6%.

**Computing on campus.** 7,006 workstations in dormitories, library, computer center, student center. Dormitories wired for high-speed internet access and linked to campus network. Commuter students can connect to campus network. Online course registration, online library, helpline, student web hosting, wireless network available.

**Student life. Freshman orientation:** Mandatory. Preregistration for classes offered. Held during the summer. **Housing:** Guaranteed on-campus for freshmen. Coed dorms, single-sex dorms, apartments, wellness housing available. $200 nonrefundable deposit, deadline 4/1. **Activities:** Bands, campus ministries, choral groups, dance, drama, film society, international student organizations, literary magazine, music ensembles, musical theater, opera, radio station, student government, student newspaper, symphony orchestra, TV station, Absalom Jones student association, Adventist committee, Baptist student union, Christian Science organization, Christian Fellowship-Igbimo Otito, Lutheran student organization, Muslim students, Wesley Foundation Methodist Fellowship, William J. Seymour Pentacostal Fellowship, academic honorary societies.

**Athletics.** NCAA. **Intercollegiate:** Baseball M, basketball, bowling, cross-country, diving, football (tackle) M, golf W, gymnastics, lacrosse W, soccer, softball W, swimming, tennis, track and field, volleyball W, wrestling M. **Intramural:** Badminton W, basketball, bowling, soccer W, softball, table tennis. **Team name:** Bison.

**Student services.** Alcohol/substance abuse counseling, chaplain/spiritual director, career counseling, student employment services, financial aid counseling, health services, on-campus daycare, personal counseling, placement for graduates, veterans' counselor, women's services. **Physically disabled:** Services for visually, speech impaired.

**Contact.** E-mail: admissions@howard.edu
Phone: (202) 806-2700 Toll-free number: (800) 469-2738
Fax: (202) 806-4467
Linda Saunders-Hawkins, Associate Director of Admissions, Howard University, 2400 Sixth Street NW, Washington, DC 20059

### Potomac College
**Washington, District of Columbia**
www.potomac.edu — CB code: 3569

- For-profit 3-year business college
- Commuter campus in very large city
- 450 degree-seeking undergraduates
- Interview required

**General.** Regionally accredited. Additional campus in Herndon, Va. **Degrees:** 65 bachelor's, 10 associate awarded. **Calendar:** Continuous, extensive summer session. **Full-time faculty:** 8 total. **Part-time faculty:** 30 total.

**Basis for selection.** Open admission.

**2009-2010 Annual costs.** Tuition/fees: $13,480. Books/supplies: $630.

**Application procedures. Admission:** No deadline. $50 fee. Admission notification on a rolling basis beginning on or about 2/1. **Financial aid:** No deadline. FAFSA, institutional form required. Applicants notified on a rolling basis; must reply within 4 week(s) of notification.

**Academics.** Credit earned for work-related research projects. **Special study options:** Accelerated study, distance learning, independent study, internships, weekend college. **Credit/placement by examination:** CLEP, institutional tests. 30 credit hours maximum toward bachelor's degree. **Support services:** Learning center, remedial instruction, tutoring.

**Majors. BACHELOR'S. Business:** Accounting, management science, purchasing. **Computer sciences:** General. **ASSOCIATE. Business:** Accounting, management science.

**Computing on campus.** 30 workstations in library, computer center, student center. Online course registration, online library available.

**Student life. Freshman orientation:** Mandatory. Preregistration for classes offered. **Activities:** Student government.

**Student services.** Adult student services, financial aid counseling.

**Contact.** E-mail: admissions@potomac.edu
Phone: (202) 686-0876 Fax: (202) 686-0818
Joseph Mure, Director of Admissions, Potomac College, 4000 Chesapeake Street NW, Washington, DC 20016

### Strayer University
**Washington, District of Columbia** — CB member
www.strayer.edu — CB code: 5632

- For-profit 4-year university
- Commuter campus in very large city

**General.** Founded in 1892. Regionally accredited. **Location:** Downtown. **Calendar:** Quarter.

**Annual costs/financial aid.** Tuition/fees (2009-2010): $13,635. Tuition $1,515/course (3 or more courses), $1,590/course (less than 3 courses), $2,050/course (graduate courses). Application fee $50. Books/supplies: $1,200.

**Contact.** Phone: (202) 408-2400
Vice President, 1133 15th Sreet NW, Washington, DC 20005

### Trinity Washington University
**Washington, District of Columbia** — CB member
www.trinitydc.edu — CB code: 5796

- Private 4-year liberal arts college affiliated with Roman Catholic Church
- Residential campus in very large city
- 1,127 degree-seeking undergraduates
- 55% of applicants admitted
- Application essay required

**General.** Founded in 1897. Regionally accredited. **Degrees:** 6 bachelor's awarded; master's offered. **ROTC:** Army. **Calendar:** Semester, extensive summer session. **Full-time faculty:** 56 total. **Part-time faculty:** 138 total. **Class size:** 70% < 20, 30% 20-39.

**Freshman class profile.** 1,131 applied, 622 admitted, 255 enrolled.

**Out-of-state:** 50% **Live on campus:** 53%

**Basis for selection.** School achievement record, essay, recommendations, interview, school and community activities important. 3.0 GPA preferred. Test scores considered. SAT and SAT Subject Tests or ACT recommended. Interview recommended. **Homeschooled:** Transcript of courses and grades required.

**High school preparation.** 16 units required. Required and recommended units include English 4, mathematics 3-4, social studies 3-4, history 2, science 2-3 (laboratory 1-2) and foreign language 2.

**2009-2010 Annual costs.** Tuition/fees: $19,520. Mandatory health insurance. Room/board: $8,850. Books/supplies: $1,000. Personal expenses: $1,500.

**2009-2010 Financial aid. Non-need-based:** Scholarships awarded for academics, alumni affiliation, leadership.

**Application procedures. Admission:** Priority date 2/1; deadline 9/1 (receipt date). $40 fee, may be waived for applicants with need, free for online applicants. Admission notification 9/1. Admission notification on a rolling basis. Must reply by May 1 or within 3 week(s) if notified thereafter. After August 1, must reply within 1 week. **Financial aid:** Priority date 3/1; no closing date. FAFSA required. Applicants notified on a rolling basis starting 2/1; must reply within 2 week(s) of notification.

**Academics. Special study options:** Accelerated study, cross-registration, distance learning, double major, dual enrollment of high school students, honors, independent study, internships, student-designed major, study abroad, teacher certification program, Washington semester, weekend college. **Credit/placement by examination:** AP, CLEP, institutional tests. **Support services:** Learning center, pre-admission summer program, reduced course load, remedial instruction, tutoring.

**Majors. Biology:** General, biochemistry. **Business:** Business admin. **Communications:** General. **Conservation:** Environmental science. **Foreign languages:** General. **History:** General. **Liberal arts:** Arts/sciences. **Math:** General. **Physical sciences:** General, chemistry. **Protective services:** Law enforcement admin. **Psychology:** General. **Public administration:** Human services. **Social sciences:** Economics, international relations, political science, sociology. **Visual/performing arts:** Art history/conservation. **Other:** Languages and cultural studies.

**Most popular majors.** Biology 7%, business/marketing 17%, communications/journalism 10%, English 6%, psychology 34%, social sciences 13%.

**Computing on campus.** 70 workstations in dormitories, library, computer center.

**Student life. Freshman orientation:** Available. Preregistration for classes offered. **Policies:** Student life mostly self-governed. Honor code exists. **Housing:** Guaranteed on-campus for all undergraduates. Single-sex dorms available. $100 fully refundable deposit. **Activities:** Choral groups, dance, drama, film society, international student organizations, literary magazine, student government, student newspaper, Young Democrats, Young Republicans, Black Student Alliance, Inter-American Club, peer ministry.

**Athletics.** NCAA. **Intercollegiate:** Basketball W, lacrosse W, soccer W, tennis W, volleyball W. **Team name:** Tigers.

**Student services.** Adult student services, alcohol/substance abuse counseling, chaplain/spiritual director, career counseling, student employment services, financial aid counseling, health services, on-campus daycare, personal counseling, placement for graduates, veterans' counselor. **Physically disabled:** Services for visually, speech, hearing impaired.

**Contact.**  E-mail: admissions@trinitydc.edu
Phone: (202) 884-9400 Toll-free number: (800) 492-6882
Fax: (202) 884-9229
Kelly Gosnell, Director of Admissions, Trinity Washington University, 125 Michigan Avenue, NE, Washington, DC 20017

## University of the District of Columbia

**Washington, District of Columbia**　　　　**CB member**
**www.udc.edu**　　　　**CB code: 5929**

▶ Public 4-year university and liberal arts college
▶ Commuter campus in very large city
▶ 4,918 degree-seeking undergraduates: 53% part-time, 60% women
▶ 190 degree-seeking graduate students

**General.** Founded in 1976. Regionally accredited. **Degrees:** 377 bachelor's, 196 associate awarded; master's offered. **ROTC:** Army, Naval, Air Force. **Location:** Downtown. **Calendar:** Semester, limited summer session. **Full-time faculty:** 247 total; 64% have terminal degrees, 42% women. **Part-time faculty:** 58 total.

**Freshman class profile.** 2,567 applied, 2,403 admitted, 1,100 enrolled.

| | | | |
|---|---|---|---|
| Out-of-state: | 21% | Sororities: | 2% |
| Fraternities: | 1% | | |

**Basis for selection.** Open admission, but selective for some programs. Special requirements for nursing, art, and music programs. Interview recommended for nursing majors. Audition recommended for music majors. Portfolio recommended for art majors. **Homeschooled:** Transcript of courses and grades, state high school equivalency certificate required.

**High school preparation.** College-preparatory program required. Recommended units include English 4, mathematics 2, social studies 2, history 1, science 2, foreign language 2 and academic electives 3.

**2009-2010 Annual costs.** Tuition/fees: $3,899; $12,300 out-of-state. Books/supplies: $1,100. Personal expenses: $1,900.

**Financial aid.** All financial aid based on need.

**Application procedures. Admission:** Closing date 6/14 (postmark date). $75 fee ($100 out-of-state). Admission notification on a rolling basis. **Financial aid:** Priority date 3/15; no closing date. FAFSA required. Applicants notified on a rolling basis starting 5/1; must reply within 2 week(s) of notification.

**Academics. Special study options:** Cooperative education, cross-registration, double major, dual enrollment of high school students, ESL, honors, independent study, internships, teacher certification program, weekend college. **Credit/placement by examination:** CLEP, IB, institutional tests. Upon successful completion of the examination, the credit must be approved by the department chairperson and the dean. Credit earned by examination will apear on the students' transcripts as 'CR" and will not be included in computing the grade point average. **Support services:** Learning center, pre-admission summer program, remedial instruction, tutoring.

**Majors. Architecture:** Architecture, urban/community planning. **Biology:** General. **Business:** Accounting, business admin, finance, office management. **Communications technology:** Graphic/printing. **Computer sciences:** General, computer science. **Conservation:** General. **Education:** Art, business, early childhood, elementary, health, physical. **Engineering:** Civil, electrical, mechanical. **Family/consumer sciences:** General, family studies, food/nutrition. **Foreign languages:** French, Spanish. **Health:** Nursing (RN),

speech pathology. **History:** General. **Math:** General. **Philosophy/religion:** Philosophy. **Physical sciences:** Chemistry, physics. **Protective services:** Fire services admin. **Psychology:** General. **Public administration:** Social work. **Social sciences:** Anthropology, economics, geography, political science, sociology, urban studies. **Transportation:** Aviation. **Visual/performing arts:** Dramatic, studio arts.

**Most popular majors.** Biology 8%, business/marketing 16%, engineering/engineering technologies 9%, health sciences 8%, public administration/social services 15%, visual/performing arts 14%.

**Computing on campus.** PC or laptop required. 2 workstations in library, computer center. Helpline, repair service, wireless network available.

**Student life. Freshman orientation:** Mandatory. Preregistration for classes offered. **Activities:** Bands, choral groups, dance, drama, music ensembles, student government, student newspaper, symphony orchestra, TV station.

**Athletics.** NCAA. **Intercollegiate:** Basketball, cross-country, soccer, tennis, track and field, volleyball W. **Intramural:** Basketball, softball, swimming, tennis, volleyball W. **Team name:** Firebirds.

**Student services.** Career counseling, student employment services, financial aid counseling, health services, on-campus daycare, personal counseling, placement for graduates, veterans' counselor. **Physically disabled:** Services for visually, speech, hearing impaired.

**Contact.**  E-mail: www@udc.edu
Phone: (202) 274-6110 Fax: (202) 274-5552
LaVerne Hill-Flannigan, Director of Enrollment Services, University of the District of Columbia, 4200 Connecticut Avenue NW, Washington, DC 20008

# Florida

## Argosy University: Sarasota
**Sarasota, Florida**
**www.argosy.edu/sarasota**

- For-profit 4-year university
- Small city
- 64 degree-seeking undergraduates

**General.** Regionally accredited. **Degrees:** 5 bachelor's awarded; master's, doctoral, professional offered. **Calendar:** Continuous. **Full-time faculty:** 23 total. **Part-time faculty:** 95 total.

**Freshman class profile.** 18 enrolled.

**Basis for selection.** Open admission.

**Academics. Credit/placement by examination:** CLEP.

**Majors. Business:** Business admin. **Liberal arts:** Arts/sciences. **Protective services:** Police science. **Psychology:** General.

**Contact.** E-mail: ausradmissions@argosy.edu
Phone: (877) 331-4480 Toll-free number: (800) 331-5995
Argosy University: Sarasota, 5250 17th Street, Sarasota, FL 34235

## Argosy University: Tampa
**Tampa, Florida**
**www.argosy.edu/tampa**

- For-profit 4-year university
- Large city
- 74 degree-seeking undergraduates

**General.** Regionally accredited. **Degrees:** 13 bachelor's awarded; master's, doctoral, professional offered. **Calendar:** Continuous. **Full-time faculty:** 18 total. **Part-time faculty:** 74 total.

**Freshman class profile.** 11 enrolled.

**Basis for selection.** Open admission.

**Academics. Credit/placement by examination:** CLEP.

**Majors. Business:** Business admin. **Liberal arts:** Arts/sciences. **Protective services:** Police science. **Psychology:** General.

**Contact.** E-mail: autaadmis@argosy.edu
Phone: (866) 357-4426 Toll-free number: (800) 850-6488
Argosy University: Tampa, 1403 North Howard Avenue, Tampa, FL 33607

## Art Institute of Fort Lauderdale
**Fort Lauderdale, Florida**
**www.aifl.edu**                    CB code: 5040

- For-profit 4-year visual arts and technical college
- Commuter campus in large city
- 3,063 degree-seeking undergraduates: 42% part-time, 55% women, 21% African American, 2% Asian American, 34% Hispanic American, 1% international
- 39% of applicants admitted
- Application essay, interview required
- 42% graduate within 6 years

**General.** Founded in 1968. Accredited by ACICS. **Degrees:** 364 bachelor's, 219 associate awarded. **Location:** 25 miles from Miami, 30 miles from West Palm Beach. **Calendar:** Quarter, extensive summer session. **Full-time faculty:** 83 total; 36% have terminal degrees, 12% minority, 47% women. **Part-time faculty:** 58 total; 48% have terminal degrees, 34% minority, 34% women. **Special facilities:** Broadcasting studio, silicon graphics lab, full culinary kitchens.

**Freshman class profile.** 1,811 applied, 715 admitted, 689 enrolled.

| | | | |
|---|---|---|---|
| **Out-of-state:** | 23% | **International:** | 1% |
| **Live on campus:** | 12% | | |

**Basis for selection.** Interview, essay important. Portfolio recommended; required for game art design and illustration majors. **Homeschooled:** State high school equivalency certificate required. **Learning Disabled:** Documentation must be submitted if student needs accommodations.

**2010-2011 Annual costs.** Tuition/fees (projected): $22,505. Books/supplies: $1,275. Personal expenses: $1,980.

**2008-2009 Financial aid. Need-based:** 23% of total undergraduate aid awarded as scholarships/grants, 77% as loans/jobs. **Non-need-based:** Scholarships awarded for academics. **Additional information:** Internal scholarships available. Financial planning program allows personalized service to budget and meet college costs through individualized payment plans.

**Application procedures. Admission:** No deadline. $50 fee. Admission notification on a rolling basis. **Financial aid:** No deadline. FAFSA required.

**Academics.** Academic program designed to simulate working environment. After completion of associate degree, students may continue to earn bachelor of science. **Special study options:** Distance learning, ESL, honors, independent study, internships, study abroad. **Credit/placement by examination:** CLEP, IB, SAT, ACT. SAT or ACT preferred for placement but ACCUPLACER accepted. **Support services:** Remedial instruction, tutoring, writing center.

**Majors. Business:** Fashion. **Communications:** Advertising. **Communications technology:** Animation/special effects. **Computer sciences:** Computer graphics, programming, web page design. **Personal/culinary services:** Restaurant/catering. **Visual/performing arts:** Cinematography, fashion design, graphic design, illustration, industrial design, interior design, photography.

**Most popular majors.** Communication technologies 9%, computer/information sciences 16%, visual/performing arts 62%.

**Computing on campus.** Dormitories wired for high-speed internet access and linked to campus network. Online course registration, online library, helpline, repair service, student web hosting, wireless network available.

**Student life. Freshman orientation:** Mandatory. Preregistration for classes offered. Held at the beginning of each quarter and midquarter. **Housing:** Guaranteed on-campus for all undergraduates. Coed dorms, special housing for disabled available. $275 deposit. **Activities:** Campus ministries, drama, film society, international student organizations, radio station, student government, Industrial Design Society of America, American Society of Interior Design, Gay Straight Alliance, fashion club, Future Video Producers and Broadcasters, hip hop club, culinary club, photography club.

**Student services.** Adult student services, alcohol/substance abuse counseling, career counseling, services for economically disadvantaged, student employment services, financial aid counseling, personal counseling, placement for graduates. **Physically disabled:** Services for visually, speech, hearing impaired.

**Contact.** E-mail: kmoss@aii.edu
Phone: (954) 463-3000 ext. 2148 Toll-free number: (800) 275-7603 ext. 2148 Fax: (954) 728-8637
Kim Moss, Senior Director of Admissions, Art Institute of Fort Lauderdale, 1799 Southeast 17th Street, Fort Lauderdale, FL 33316

## Ave Maria University
**Ave Maria, Florida**
**www.avemaria.edu**                    CB code: 4249

- Private 4-year university and liberal arts college affiliated with Roman Catholic Church
- Residential campus in small town
- 669 degree-seeking undergraduates: 53% women, 4% African American, 3% Asian American, 15% Hispanic American, 7% international
- 146 degree-seeking graduate students
- SAT or ACT (ACT writing optional), application essay required

**General.** Candidate for regional accreditation. **Degrees:** 62 bachelor's awarded; master's, doctoral offered. **Location:** 30 miles from Naples. **Calendar:** Semester, limited summer session. **Full-time faculty:** 54 total; 100% have terminal degrees. **Part-time faculty:** 10 total. **Class size:** 70% < 20, 29% 20-39, less than 1% 40-49.

### Freshman class profile.

| Mid 50% test scores | | | |
|---|---|---|---|
| SAT critical reading: | 510-640 | Return as sophomores: | 86% |
| SAT math: | 500-620 | Out-of-state: | 53% |
| SAT writing: | 500-630 | Live on campus: | 94% |
| ACT composite: | 21-28 | International: | 5% |

**Basis for selection.** For regular admission, 2.8 GPA and 1580 SAT or 22 ACT required. Students who do not meet all requirements may attain admission by special recommendation of the Admissions Committee. **Home-schooled:** Transcript of courses and grades, letter of recommendation (non-parent) required.

**High school preparation.** College-preparatory program recommended. 15 units required; 17 recommended. Required and recommended units include English 3-4, mathematics 3-4, social studies 1, history 1-3, science 3 and foreign language 2.

**2010-2011 Annual costs.** Tuition/fees: $18,850. Room/board: $8,125.

**Application procedures. Admission:** No deadline. No application fee. Admission notification on a rolling basis.

**Academics. Special study options:** Double major, dual enrollment of high school students, internships, study abroad. **Credit/placement by examination:** AP, CLEP, IB, SAT, ACT, institutional tests. **Support services:** Pre-admission summer program, reduced course load, study skills assistance, tutoring, writing center.

**Majors. Biology:** General. **Foreign languages:** Classics. **History:** General. **Math:** General. **Philosophy/religion:** Philosophy. **Social sciences:** Economics, political science. **Theology:** Sacred music, theology.

**Most popular majors.** Biology 10%, English 13%, history 8%, philosophy/religious studies 15%, social sciences 16%, theological studies 34%.

**Computing on campus.** 150 workstations in dormitories, library, computer center, student center. Dormitories wired for high-speed internet access and linked to campus network. Commuter students can connect to campus network. Online library, helpline, wireless network available.

**Student life. Freshman orientation:** Mandatory. Preregistration for classes offered. Three-day program held at beginning of semester. **Policies:** Policies and procedures aligned with Catholic moral teaching. Students required to live on campus unless living with a parent or legal guardian, are 23 years of age or older, or receive special permission in certain unusual cases. **Housing:** Guaranteed on-campus for all undergraduates. Single-sex dorms available. **Activities:** Campus ministries, choral groups, dance, drama, film society, international student organizations, music ensembles, Model UN, musical theater, student government, student newspaper, Knights of Columbus, College Republicans, Global Awareness and Activism in Politics, World Youth Alliance, Students for Life, Faith in Action Today, Chastity Team, Communion and Liberation University.

**Athletics.** NAIA. **Intercollegiate:** Baseball M, basketball, golf, soccer, softball W, volleyball W. **Intramural:** Basketball, football (non-tackle), soccer, volleyball. **Team name:** Gyrene.

**Student services.** Alcohol/substance abuse counseling, chaplain/spiritual director, career counseling, student employment services, financial aid counseling, health services, personal counseling. **Physically disabled:** Services for visually, hearing impaired.

**Contact.** E-mail: admissions@avemaria.edu
Phone: (239) 280-2556 Toll-free number: (877) 283-8648
Fax: (239) 280-2559
Brett Ormandy, Director of Admissions, Ave Maria University, 5050 Ave Maria Boulevard, Ave Maria, FL 34142-9505

---

## Baptist College of Florida
**Graceville, Florida**
www.baptistcollege.edu                **CB code: 7322**

♦ Private 4-year Bible and teachers college affiliated with Southern Baptist Convention
♦ Residential campus in small town
♦ 546 degree-seeking undergraduates: 24% part-time, 38% women, 3% African American, 1% Asian American, 2% Hispanic American
♦ 73% of applicants admitted
♦ SAT or ACT (ACT writing optional), application essay required

---

**General.** Founded in 1943. Regionally accredited. **Degrees:** 108 bachelor's, 11 associate awarded. **Location:** 90 miles from Tallahassee, 60 miles from Panama City. **Calendar:** Semester, limited summer session. **Full-time faculty:** 23 total; 65% have terminal degrees, 22% women. **Part-time faculty:** 41 total; 90% have terminal degrees, 17% women. **Class size:** 76% < 20, 18% 20-39, 4% 40-49, 2% 50-99.

**Freshman class profile.** 295 applied, 215 admitted, 43 enrolled.

| Mid 50% test scores | | | |
|---|---|---|---|
| | | ACT composite: | 16-22 |
| SAT critical reading: | 470-480 | Out-of-state: | 21% |
| SAT math: | 420-540 | Live on campus: | 90% |

**Basis for selection.** Applicant must be member in good standing of church affiliated with Southern Baptist Convention or other evangelical body. Special program for non-high school graduates. Recommendations very important. Affirmation of faith required. Audition required of music applicants. Interview recommended. **Homeschooled:** Transcript of courses and grades required. 2.5 GPA; 20 academic units with at least 14 units from fields of English, math, social and natural sciences required.

**High school preparation.** Recommended units include English 4, mathematics 4, social studies 1, history 2 and science 3.

**2009-2010 Annual costs.** Tuition/fees: $8,450. Room/board: $4,066. Books/supplies: $900. Personal expenses: $400.

**2008-2009 Financial aid. Need-based:** 74 full-time freshmen applied for aid; 57 were judged to have need; 49 of these received aid. Average need met was 49%. Average scholarship/grant was $4,808; average loan $2,752. 54% of total undergraduate aid awarded as scholarships/grants, 46% as loans/jobs. **Non-need-based:** Awarded to 30 full-time undergraduates, including 11 freshmen. Scholarships awarded for academics, minority status, music/drama, religious affiliation.

**Application procedures. Admission:** Closing date 8/15 (receipt date). $20 fee, may be waived for applicants with need. Admission notification on a rolling basis. **Financial aid:** Priority date 4/1, closing date 4/15. FAFSA, institutional form required. Applicants notified on a rolling basis starting 6/15; must reply within 4 week(s) of notification.

**Academics. Special study options:** Distance learning, double major, independent study, internships, liberal arts/career combination, teacher certification program. **Credit/placement by examination:** AP, CLEP, IB, SAT, ACT, institutional tests. **Support services:** Learning center, reduced course load, remedial instruction, study skills assistance, tutoring, writing center.

**Majors. Education:** Elementary, history, music. **Philosophy/religion:** Religion. **Theology:** Bible, pastoral counseling, religious ed, sacred music, theology. **Other:** History and Social Studies Secondary Education.

**Most popular majors.** Education 10%, theological studies 90%.

**Computing on campus.** 25 workstations in library, computer center. Commuter students can connect to campus network. Online course registration, online library, wireless network available.

**Student life. Freshman orientation:** Mandatory. Preregistration for classes offered. Held week before classes begin for 1-2 days depending on major. **Policies:** Religious observance required. **Housing:** Single-sex dorms, apartments available. $100 fully refundable deposit. **Activities:** Bands, campus ministries, choral groups, drama, music ensembles, radio station, Baptist Collegiate Ministry.

**Athletics.** NCCAA. **Intercollegiate:** Golf M, volleyball W. **Intramural:** Basketball, football (non-tackle), golf, soccer, softball, table tennis, volleyball. **Team name:** Eagles.

**Student services.** Career counseling, student employment services, financial aid counseling, personal counseling, veterans' counselor. **Physically disabled:** Services for visually, speech, hearing impaired.

**Contact.** E-mail: admissions@baptistcollege.edu
Phone: (850) 263-3261 ext. 460 Toll-free number: (800) 328-2660 ext. 460
Fax: (850) 263-9026
Sandra Richards, Director of Marketing, Baptist College of Florida, 5400 College Drive, Graceville, FL 32440-3306

---

## Barry University
**Miami Shores, Florida**
www.barry.edu
**CB member**
**CB code: 5053**

♦ Private 4-year university affiliated with Roman Catholic Church
♦ Residential campus in large town

- 4,990 degree-seeking undergraduates: 17% part-time, 69% women, 20% African American, 1% Asian American, 25% Hispanic American, 6% international
- 3,748 graduate students
- 62% of applicants admitted
- SAT or ACT (ACT writing optional) required
- 39% graduate within 6 years

**General.** Founded in 1940. Regionally accredited. 22 off-campus sites for adult and continuing education and some graduate degrees. Center for Dominican Studies. **Degrees:** 1,311 bachelor's awarded; master's, doctoral, professional offered. **ROTC:** Army, Air Force. **Location:** 14 miles from Fort Lauderdale, 7 miles from Miami. **Calendar:** Semester, limited summer session. **Full-time faculty:** 325 total; 73% have terminal degrees, 28% minority, 54% women. **Part-time faculty:** 311 total; 29% minority, 49% women. **Class size:** 68% < 20, 31% 20-39, less than 1% 40-49, less than 1% 50-99, less than 1% >100. **Special facilities:** Human performance laboratory, athletic training room, cell biology/biotechnology lab, classroom of tomorrow, photography facilities, lighting studio, dark room, imaging lab, performing arts center, biomechanics lab.

**Freshman class profile.** 4,326 applied, 2,696 admitted, 648 enrolled.

| Mid 50% test scores | | | |
|---|---|---|---|
| SAT critical reading: | 440-520 | GPA 3.0-3.49: | 36% |
| SAT math: | 420-520 | GPA 2.0-2.99: | 38% |
| ACT composite: | 18-22 | Out-of-state: | 41% |
| GPA 3.75 or higher: | 12% | Live on campus: | 63% |
| GPA 3.50-3.74: | 14% | International: | 6% |

**Basis for selection.** Test scores and school record important. Higher test score, GPA, and course requirements for certain majors. Interviews highly recommended. **Homeschooled:** Statement describing homeschool structure and mission, transcript of courses and grades, state high school equivalency certificate required. Academic portfolio or GED, copy of home school rules of the state which home school is chartered required. **Learning Disabled:** Students must apply directly to comprehensive service program.

**High school preparation.** 13 units required; 16 recommended. Required and recommended units include English 4, mathematics 3, social studies 3 and science 3. For nursing program, 1 chemistry, 1 biology, algebra II required. For biology and allied health programs, 2 laboratory science including biology and chemistry, 3.5 math required. For math program, 4 math including algebra, geometry, trigonometry, required. For chemistry program, 3 math, 1 chemistry with lab required.

**2010-2011 Annual costs.** Tuition/fees: $27,200. Room/board: $9,002. Books/supplies: $800. Personal expenses: $1,500.

**2008-2009 Financial aid. Need-based:** 582 full-time freshmen applied for aid; 556 were judged to have need; 549 of these received aid. Average need met was 72%. Average scholarship/grant was $9,435; average loan $3,494. 45% of total undergraduate aid awarded as scholarships/grants, 55% as loans/jobs. **Non-need-based:** Awarded to 3,871 full-time undergraduates, including 644 freshmen. Scholarships awarded for academics, art, athletics, music/drama.

**Application procedures. Admission:** No deadline. $30 fee. Admission notification on a rolling basis beginning on or about 9/8. Students are allowed to postpone enrollment after admissions for up to 1 year. **Financial aid:** No deadline. FAFSA required. Applicants notified on a rolling basis starting 1/25.

**Academics. Special study options:** Accelerated study, combined bachelor's/graduate degree, double major, ESL, honors, internships, study abroad, teacher certification program. **Credit/placement by examination:** AP, CLEP, IB, SAT, ACT, institutional tests. 30 credit hours maximum toward bachelor's degree. All credit by examination should be completed prior to junior status. **Support services:** Learning center, reduced course load, remedial instruction, study skills assistance, tutoring, writing center.

**Majors. Biology:** General. **Business:** Accounting, business admin, finance, international, marketing. **Communications:** General, advertising, public relations, radio/tv. **Computer sciences:** General, computer science, information technology. **Education:** Early childhood, elementary, physical, special. **Foreign languages:** French, Spanish. **Health:** Athletic training, cardiovascular technology, clinical lab science, cytotechnology, health care admin, nuclear medical technology, nursing (RN), predental, premedicine, prepharmacy, preveterinary, sonography. **History:** General. **Interdisciplinary:** Global studies. **Legal studies:** General, prelaw. **Liberal arts:** Arts/sciences. **Math:** General. **Parks/recreation:** Exercise sciences, health/fitness, sports admin. **Philosophy/religion:** Philosophy. **Physical sciences:** Chemistry. **Psychology:** General. **Public administration:** General, social work. **Social sciences:** Criminology, political science, sociology. **Theology:** Theology. **Visual/performing arts:** Art, dramatic, photography.

**Most popular majors.** Business/marketing 17%, computer/information sciences 9%, education 20%, health sciences 14%, liberal arts 14%, public administration/social services 9%.

**Computing on campus.** 165 workstations in dormitories, library, computer center. Dormitories wired for high-speed internet access and linked to campus network. Commuter students can connect to campus network. On-line library, helpline, repair service, wireless network available.

**Student life. Freshman orientation:** Mandatory. Preregistration for classes offered. **Housing:** Coed dorms, single-sex dorms, special housing for disabled available. $200 nonrefundable deposit. **Activities:** Choral groups, dance, drama, literary magazine, music ensembles, musical theater, radio station, student government, student newspaper, TV station, Jamaican association, black student union, Habitat for Humanity, Caribbean student organization, Haitian intercultural association, Jewish/Christian/Muslim interfaith group, Latter-Day Saints student association, Best Buddies, Spanish club, Baptist dialogue group.

**Athletics.** NCAA. **Intercollegiate:** Baseball M, basketball, golf, rowing (crew) W, soccer, softball W, tennis, volleyball W. **Intramural:** Basketball, football (non-tackle), golf, skin diving, soccer, softball, volleyball. **Team name:** Buccaneers.

**Student services.** Adult student services, alcohol/substance abuse counseling, chaplain/spiritual director, career counseling, student employment services, financial aid counseling, health services, personal counseling, placement for graduates. **Physically disabled:** Services for visually, speech, hearing impaired. **Learning disabled:** Comprehensive services available.

**Contact.** E-mail: admissions@mail.barry.edu
Phone: (305) 899-3100 Toll-free number: (800) 695-2279
Fax: (305) 899-2971
Magda Castineyra, Director of Undergraduate Admissions, Barry University, 11300 Northeast Second Avenue, Miami Shores, FL 33161-6695

---

## Beacon College
### Leesburg, Florida
**www.beaconcollege.edu**　　　　　　　　　　**CB code: 3611**

- Private 4-year liberal arts college
- Residential campus in large town
- 125 degree-seeking undergraduates: 36% women
- 92% of applicants admitted
- Application essay required
- 77% graduate within 6 years; 8% enter graduate study

**General.** Regionally accredited. College solely for students with learning disabilities. **Degrees:** 31 bachelor's, 3 associate awarded. **Location:** 50 miles from Orlando. **Calendar:** Semester, limited summer session. **Full-time faculty:** 19 total; 63% have terminal degrees, 5% minority, 58% women. **Part-time faculty:** 1 total. **Class size:** 100% < 20.

**Freshman class profile.** 53 applied, 49 admitted, 29 enrolled.

| | | | |
|---|---|---|---|
| GPA 3.0-3.49: | 50% | Live on campus: | 100% |
| GPA 2.0-2.99: | 45% | Fraternities: | 32% |
| Return as sophomores: | 88% | Sororities: | 27% |
| Out-of-state: | 72% | | |

**Basis for selection.** Selective but noncompetitive process. Recommendations, interview, character, level of interest very important; followed by rigor of secondary school record, GPA, test scores, essay, extracurricular activities, ability, volunteer work. Class rank, work experience considered. SAT or ACT recommended. Scores used noncompetitively for informational purposes only. Interview may be required. **Homeschooled:** State high school equivalency certificate required. **Learning Disabled:** Students accepted by committee decision based on psychoeducational evaluation documenting learning disability, academic potential, evaluation of high school records, references, and campus interviews with assessments as part of admissions process. Students must provide current psychoeducational report (within 3 years) documenting learning disability as primary handicapping condition, including WAIS score.

**High school preparation.** College-preparatory program recommended. 12 units required. Required and recommended units include English 4, mathematics 1-2, social studies 1, history 2-3, science 1-2 and academic electives 3.

**2009-2010 Annual costs.** Tuition/fees: $27,400. Room/board: $8,150. Books/supplies: $900. Personal expenses: $2,565.

**2008-2009 Financial aid.** All financial aid based on need. **Additional information:** Work-study programs offered based on financial need.

**Application procedures. Admission:** Priority date 5/1; deadline 8/1 (receipt date). $50 fee. Application must be submitted on paper. Admission notification on a rolling basis. Must reply by May 1 or within 2 week(s) if notified thereafter. **Financial aid:** Priority date 4/1; no closing date. FAFSA, institutional form required. Applicants notified on a rolling basis starting 4/1; must reply within 2 week(s) of notification.

**Academics.** Provides remedial coursework in writing, reading, and math. **Special study options:** Double major, independent study, internships, liberal arts/career combination, study abroad. **Credit/placement by examination:** AP, CLEP, institutional tests. **Support services:** Learning center, reduced course load, remedial instruction, study skills assistance, tutoring, writing center.

**Majors. Computer sciences:** General. **Liberal arts:** Arts/sciences. **Public administration:** Human services.

**Most popular majors.** Computer/information sciences 20%, liberal arts 44%, public administration/social services 36%.

**Computing on campus.** 32 workstations in library, computer center, student center. Dormitories wired for high-speed internet access and linked to campus network. Commuter students can connect to campus network. Online library, helpline, repair service, student web hosting, wireless network available.

**Student life. Freshman orientation:** Mandatory. Preregistration for classes offered. **Housing:** Guaranteed on-campus for all undergraduates. Apartments, wellness housing available. $750 nonrefundable deposit, deadline 5/1. **Activities:** Dance, literary magazine, student government, student newspaper.

**Athletics. Team name:** Bull Dogs.

**Student services.** Alcohol/substance abuse counseling, career counseling, student employment services, financial aid counseling, personal counseling, placement for graduates. **Physically disabled:** Services for visually, speech, hearing impaired. **Learning disabled:** Comprehensive services available.

**Contact.** E-mail: admissions@beaconcollege.edu
Phone: (352) 787-7249 Fax: (352) 787-0721
Mary Bruck, Vice President of Enrollment Management and Academic Programs, Beacon College, 105 East Main Street, Leesburg, FL 34748

---

## Bethune-Cookman University

**Daytona Beach, Florida**      **CB member**
www.cookman.edu      **CB code: 5061**

- Private 4-year liberal arts college affiliated with United Methodist Church
- Residential campus in small city
- 3,587 degree-seeking undergraduates: 4% part-time, 60% women, 94% African American, 2% Hispanic American, 2% international
- 20 degree-seeking graduate students
- 69% of applicants admitted
- SAT or ACT (ACT writing optional), application essay required
- 40% graduate within 6 years; 20% enter graduate study

**General.** Founded in 1904. Regionally accredited. **Degrees:** 453 bachelor's awarded; master's offered. **ROTC:** Army, Air Force. **Location:** 60 miles from Orlando. **Calendar:** Semester, limited summer session. **Full-time faculty:** 210 total; 48% have terminal degrees, 57% minority, 50% women. **Part-time faculty:** 28 total; 61% minority, 54% women. **Class size:** 47% < 20, 50% 20-39, 1% 40-49, 1% 50-99. **Special facilities:** Observatory.

**Freshman class profile.** 5,188 applied, 3,587 admitted, 1,027 enrolled.

| Mid 50% test scores | | | |
|---|---|---|---|
| SAT critical reading: | 360-460 | GPA 2.0-2.99: | 73% |
| SAT math: | 360-460 | Rank in top quarter: | 15% |
| ACT composite: | 14-18 | Rank in top tenth: | 5% |
| GPA 3.75 or higher: | 3% | End year in good standing: | 90% |
| GPA 3.50-3.74: | 5% | Return as sophomores: | 63% |
| GPA 3.0-3.49: | 18% | Out-of-state: | 30% |
| | | Live on campus: | 72% |

**Basis for selection.** School achievement record most important. Test scores and letters of recommendation important. Interview required of music majors.

**High school preparation.** 19 units required. Required and recommended units include English 4, mathematics 3, social studies 1, history 2, science 3 (laboratory 1), foreign language 2 and academic electives 6. 1 unit computer literacy.

**2009-2010 Annual costs.** Tuition/fees: $12,936. Room/board: $7,672. Books/supplies: $1,000. Personal expenses: $2,800.

**2009-2010 Financial aid.** All financial aid based on need.

**Application procedures. Admission:** Priority date 6/30; no deadline. $25 fee, may be waived for applicants with need. Application must be submitted on paper. Admission notification on a rolling basis. **Financial aid:** Priority date 4/1; no closing date. FAFSA required. Applicants notified on a rolling basis starting 4/1; must reply within 3 week(s) of notification.

**Academics. Special study options:** Accelerated study, combined bachelor's/graduate degree, cooperative education, distance learning, double major, honors, independent study, internships, study abroad, teacher certification program, weekend college. **Credit/placement by examination:** AP, CLEP, IB, SAT, ACT, institutional tests. 30 credit hours maximum toward bachelor's degree. **Support services:** Learning center, reduced course load, remedial instruction, study skills assistance, tutoring, writing center.

**Majors. Biology:** General. **Business:** Accounting, business admin, hotel/motel admin, international. **Communications:** Journalism. **Computer sciences:** Computer science, information systems. **Conservation:** Environmental science. **Education:** General, biology, business, chemistry, elementary, English, learning disabled, music, physical, social studies. **Engineering:** Computer. **Health:** Nursing (RN). **History:** General. **Interdisciplinary:** Gerontology. **Math:** General. **Philosophy/religion:** Christian. **Physical sciences:** Chemistry, physics. **Protective services:** Law enforcement admin. **Psychology:** General. **Social sciences:** International relations, political science, sociology. **Visual/performing arts:** Music performance.

**Most popular majors.** Business/marketing 23%, communications/journalism 7%, education 14%, health sciences 7%, psychology 8%, security/protective services 14%, social sciences 6%.

**Computing on campus.** 567 workstations in dormitories, library, computer center, student center. Dormitories wired for high-speed internet access and linked to campus network. Commuter students can connect to campus network. Online course registration, online library, helpline, wireless network available.

**Student life. Freshman orientation:** Mandatory. Preregistration for classes offered. One-week program in beginning of fall and spring semster. **Housing:** Guaranteed on-campus for freshmen. Single-sex dorms, wellness housing available. $200 nonrefundable deposit, deadline 8/15. Scholarship housing available for honor students. **Activities:** Bands, choral groups, dance, drama, international student organizations, music ensembles, Model UN, radio station, student government, student newspaper, YM/YWCA, Religious Life fellowship, pre-seminarian club, Greek letter organization, Gamma Sigma Sigma national service sorority, Kappa Kappa Psi national band fraternity, Alpha Chi honor sorority, Alpha Kappa Mu honor sorority.

**Athletics.** NCAA. **Intercollegiate:** Baseball M, basketball, bowling W, cross-country, football (tackle) M, golf, softball W, tennis, track and field, volleyball W. **Intramural:** Basketball, football (tackle) M. **Team name:** Wildcats.

**Student services.** Adult student services, chaplain/spiritual director, career counseling, student employment services, financial aid counseling, health services, personal counseling, placement for graduates, veterans' counselor.

**Contact.** E-mail: admissions@cookman.edu
Phone: (386) 481-2600 Toll-free number: (800) 448-0228
Fax: (386) 481-2601
Aixa Melendez, Executive Director of Admissions, Bethune-Cookman University, Dr. Mary McLeod Bethune Boulevard, Daytona Beach, FL 32114-3099

---

## Carlos Albizu University

**Miami, Florida**
www.albizu.edu      **CB code: 2102**

- Private 4-year university
- Commuter campus in very large city
- 425 degree-seeking undergraduates
- 744 graduate students
- Application essay, interview required

**General.** Founded in 1980. Regionally accredited. **Degrees:** 133 bachelor's awarded; master's, professional offered. **Calendar:** Semester, extensive summer session. **Full-time faculty:** 24 total. **Part-time faculty:** 94 total. **Class size:** 39% < 20, 61% 20-39.

**Basis for selection.** Open admission, but selective for some programs. 2.0 GPA required. **Homeschooled:** State high school equivalency certificate required. **Learning Disabled:** Students requiring special accommodation must submit written request to Director of Student Affairs and attach documentary support.

**2009-2010 Annual costs.** Tuition/fees: $14,469. Reported tuition, fees and per credit hour charge are for bachelor's degree program in business. Other programs individually priced. Books/supplies: $690. Personal expenses: $1,800.

**Financial aid.** All financial aid based on need.

**Application procedures. Admission:** No deadline. $25 fee, may be waived for applicants with need. Admission notification on a rolling basis. **Financial aid:** Priority date 6/1; no closing date. FAFSA, institutional form required. Applicants notified on a rolling basis starting 2/1.

**Academics. Special study options:** Accelerated study, cooperative education, cross-registration, distance learning, double major, dual enrollment of high school students, ESL, honors, independent study, internships, study abroad, teacher certification program, weekend college. **Credit/placement by examination:** CLEP, IB, institutional tests. 12 credit hours maximum toward bachelor's degree. 6 for foreign language, 6 for other foundation courses. **Support services:** Learning center, remedial instruction, study skills assistance, tutoring, writing center.

**Majors. Business:** General. **Education:** Elementary. **Psychology:** General.

**Computing on campus.** 50 workstations in library, computer center, student center. Commuter students can connect to campus network. Online course registration, online library, wireless network available.

**Student life. Freshman orientation:** Mandatory. Preregistration for classes offered. Two-hour program held before session. **Activities:** Student government, student newspaper.

**Student services.** Adult student services, career counseling, services for economically disadvantaged, student employment services, financial aid counseling, minority student services, placement for graduates.

**Contact.** E-mail: webmaster@albizu.edu
Phone: (305) 593-1223 ext. 137 Toll-free number: (888) 468-6228
Fax: (305) 593-1854
Carmen Roca, Chancellor, Carlos Albizu University, 2173 NW 99th
Avenue, Miami, FL 33172

## Chipola College
**Marianna, Florida**
www.chipola.edu
CB code: 5106

◗ Public 4-year community and junior college
◗ Commuter campus in small town
◗ 1,647 degree-seeking undergraduates: 42% part-time, 63% women

**General.** Founded in 1947. Regionally accredited. **Degrees:** 16 bachelor's, 319 associate awarded. **Location:** 70 miles from Tallahassee. **Calendar:** Semester, limited summer session. **Full-time faculty:** 43 total; 30% have terminal degrees, 5% minority, 58% women. **Part-time faculty:** 89 total; 15% minority, 35% women.

**Basis for selection.** Open admission, but selective for some programs.

**High school preparation.** Recommended units include English 4, mathematics 3, social studies 3 and science 3.

**2009-2010 Annual costs.** Tuition/fees: $2,550; $7,314 out-of-state. Books/supplies: $800. Personal expenses: $1,500.

**2008-2009 Financial aid. Need-based:** 92% of total undergraduate aid awarded as scholarships/grants, 8% as loans/jobs. **Non-need-based:** Scholarships awarded for academics, alumni affiliation, art, athletics, job skills, leadership, minority status, music/drama.

**Application procedures. Admission:** Priority date 8/1; no deadline. No application fee. Admission notification on a rolling basis. **Financial aid:** Priority date 5/1; no closing date. FAFSA, institutional form required. Applicants notified on a rolling basis starting 1/2; must reply within 2 week(s) of notification.

**Academics. Special study options:** Accelerated study, cooperative education, distance learning, dual enrollment of high school students, honors, independent study, internships, liberal arts/career combination, teacher certification program. **Credit/placement by examination:** AP, CLEP, IB. 45 credit hours maximum toward associate degree, 45 toward bachelor's. **Support services:** Remedial instruction, study skills assistance, tutoring, writing center.

**Majors. Biology:** General. **Business:** Business admin. **Education:** Elementary, mathematics, middle, science, secondary, special. **Health:** Nursing (RN). **Math:** General.

**Computing on campus.** 150 workstations in library. Dormitories linked to campus network. Online library available.

**Student life. Freshman orientation:** Mandatory. Preregistration for classes offered. **Housing:** Only men's and women's athletic dorms available. **Activities:** Jazz band, campus ministries, choral groups, dance, drama, musical theater, student government, student newspaper, Black Student Union, Baptist Campus Ministry, Fellowship of Christian Athletes.

**Athletics.** NJCAA. **Intercollegiate:** Baseball M, basketball, softball W. **Team name:** Indians.

**Student services.** Career counseling. **Physically disabled:** Services for visually, hearing impaired.

**Contact.** Phone: (850) 526-2761 Fax: (850) 718-2287
Jayne Roberts, Dean of Enrollment Services, Chipola College, 3094 Indian Circle, Marianna, FL 32446

## City College: Fort Lauderdale
**Fort Lauderdale, Florida**
www.citycollege.edu
CB code: 3578

◗ For-profit 4-year business and technical college
◗ Commuter campus in very large city
◗ 572 degree-seeking undergraduates
◗ Application essay, interview required

**General.** Accredited by ACICS. **Degrees:** 25 bachelor's, 165 associate awarded. **Calendar:** Quarter. **Full-time faculty:** 12 total. **Part-time faculty:** 66 total.

**Basis for selection.** Open admission, but selective for some programs. **Homeschooled:** Statement describing homeschool structure and mission, transcript of courses and grades required.

**2009-2010 Annual costs.** Tuition/fees: $13,680. Books/supplies: $1,044. Personal expenses: $2,931.

**Application procedures. Admission:** No deadline. $40 fee, may be waived for applicants with need. Admission notification on a rolling basis.

**Academics. Special study options:** Distance learning, independent study, internships. **Credit/placement by examination:** CLEP, IB, institutional tests. 15 credit hours maximum toward associate degree, 30 toward bachelor's. **Support services:** Remedial instruction, tutoring.

**Majors. Business:** Business admin.

**Computing on campus.** 70 workstations in library. Online library available.

**Student life. Freshman orientation:** Mandatory. Preregistration for classes offered.

**Student services.** Adult student services, alcohol/substance abuse counseling, career counseling, student employment services, financial aid counseling, personal counseling, placement for graduates.

**Contact.** Phone: (954) 492-5353 Fax: (954) 491-1965
Judy Hernandez, Director of Admissions, City College: Fort Lauderdale, 2000 West Commercial Boulevard, Fort Lauderdale, FL 33309

## Clearwater Christian College
**Clearwater, Florida**
www.clearwater.edu
CB code: 5142

◗ Private 4-year liberal arts college affiliated with nondenominational tradition
◗ Residential campus in small city

- 561 degree-seeking undergraduates: 1% part-time, 49% women, 5% African American, 2% Asian American, 4% Hispanic American, 1% international
- 4 degree-seeking graduate students
- 89% of applicants admitted
- SAT or ACT, application essay required
- 44% graduate within 6 years; 25% enter graduate study

**General.** Founded in 1966. Regionally accredited. **Degrees:** 125 bachelor's, 2 associate awarded; master's offered. **ROTC:** Army, Naval, Air Force. **Location:** 15 miles from Tampa, 15 miles from St. Petersburg. **Calendar:** Semester, limited summer session. **Full-time faculty:** 32 total; 69% have terminal degrees, 3% minority, 34% women. **Part-time faculty:** 17 total; 41% have terminal degrees, 24% women. **Class size:** 69% < 20, 23% 20-39, 6% 40-49, 3% 50-99.

**Freshman class profile.** 278 applied, 247 admitted, 157 enrolled.

| Mid 50% test scores | | | |
|---|---|---|---|
| SAT critical reading: | 470-600 | Return as sophomores: | 68% |
| SAT math: | 450-560 | Out-of-state: | 52% |
| ACT composite: | 19-25 | Live on campus: | 95% |
| End year in good standing: | 84% | Fraternities: | 100% |
| | | Sororities: | 100% |

**Basis for selection.** 2.0 GPA, 870 SAT (exclusive of Writing) or 18 ACT, recommendations, and Christian testimony important. Interview recommended. Audition recommended for music majors. **Homeschooled:** Transcript of courses and grades required. GED required if transcript not available; liberal arts/college preparatory program recommended; academic placement testing may be administered.

**High school preparation.** Recommended units include English 4, mathematics 3, social studies 3, science 3 and foreign language 2. Math units should include geometry; English units should emphasize grammar and writing.

**2009-2010 Annual costs.** Tuition/fees: $14,710. Room/board: $6,740. Books/supplies: $900. Personal expenses: $2,050.

**2009-2010 Financial aid. Need-based:** 61% of total undergraduate aid awarded as scholarships/grants, 39% as loans/jobs. **Non-need-based:** Scholarships awarded for academics, alumni affiliation, leadership, music/drama, religious affiliation, ROTC. **Additional information:** Special consideration given to children of Christian service workers; need-based scholarships available to first-generation students; scholarships up to $3,000 available to dual-enrolled students.

**Application procedures. Admission:** Closing date 8/1 (receipt date). $35 fee, may be waived for applicants with need. Admission notification on a rolling basis. **Financial aid:** Priority date 3/15; no closing date. FAFSA, institutional form required. Applicants notified on a rolling basis starting 4/15; must reply within 2 week(s) of notification.

**Academics.** All students completing a bachelor's degree earn the equivalent of 20-credit minor in Bible. **Special study options:** Distance learning, double major, dual enrollment of high school students, honors, independent study, internships, liberal arts/career combination, student-designed major, study abroad, teacher certification program. International missions trips. **Credit/placement by examination:** AP, CLEP, IB, institutional tests. 24 credit hours maximum toward associate degree, 24 toward bachelor's. **Support services:** Reduced course load, remedial instruction, study skills assistance, tutoring.

**Majors. Biology:** General. **Business:** Accounting, business admin, office management. **Communications:** General. **Computer sciences:** Information systems. **Education:** Biology, elementary, English, mathematics, music, physical, social studies, special. **Health:** Premedicine. **History:** General. **Legal studies:** Prelaw. **Liberal arts:** Arts/sciences, humanities. **Math:** General. **Parks/recreation:** Exercise sciences, sports admin. **Psychology:** General. **Theology:** Bible, pastoral counseling, sacred music. **Other:** Church ministries, Interdisciplinary studies.

**Most popular majors.** Biology 6%, business/marketing 16%, education 18%, history 6%, liberal arts 15%, psychology 10%, theological studies 9%.

**Computing on campus.** 38 workstations in dormitories, library, computer center. Dormitories wired for high-speed internet access and linked to campus network. Commuter students can connect to campus network. Online library, helpline, repair service, wireless network available.

**Student life. Freshman orientation:** Mandatory. Preregistration for classes offered. 2-day program held prior to start of fall semester. **Policies:** Convocation and Christian Life Conference; chapel 4 days per week; evening Bible studies and prayer meetings required of students in the residence halls.

Religious observance required. **Housing:** Guaranteed on-campus for all undergraduates. Single-sex dorms available. $100 deposit. **Activities:** Bands, campus ministries, choral groups, drama, film society, music ensembles, musical theater, student government, student newspaper, symphony orchestra, political club, College Republicans, Fellowship of Preministerial Students, student missionary fellowship, China team, music ministry team, joy club.

**Athletics.** NCCAA. **Intercollegiate:** Baseball M, basketball, golf, soccer, softball W, volleyball W. **Intramural:** Basketball, football (non-tackle) M, soccer, table tennis, tennis, volleyball. **Team name:** Cougars.

**Student services.** Chaplain/spiritual director, career counseling, student employment services, financial aid counseling, personal counseling, placement for graduates. **Physically disabled:** Services for speech impaired.

**Contact.** E-mail: admissions@clearwater.edu
Phone: (727) 726-1153 ext. 220 Toll-free number: (800) 348-4463
Fax: (727) 726-8597
Keith Hutchison, Director of Admissions, Clearwater Christian College, 3400 Gulf-to-Bay Boulevard, Clearwater, FL 33759-4595

## DeVry University: Miramar
**Miramar, Florida**
www.devry.edu                CB code: 4134

- For-profit 4-year university
- Commuter campus in large town
- 1,099 degree-seeking undergraduates: 53% part-time, 40% women, 30% African American, 1% Asian American, 43% Hispanic American, 9% international
- 160 degree-seeking graduate students
- Interview required

**General. Degrees:** 173 bachelor's, 23 associate awarded; master's offered. **Calendar:** Semester, extensive summer session. **Full-time faculty:** 21 total; 43% minority, 14% women. **Part-time faculty:** 70 total; 44% minority, 37% women.

**Freshman class profile.**

| Out-of-state: | 5% | International: | 11% |
|---|---|---|---|

**Basis for selection.** Applicants must have high school diploma or equivalent, or degree from accredited postsecondary institution; demonstrate proficiency in basic college-level skills through SAT, ACT or institution-administered placement exams; and be at least 17. New students may enter at beginning of any semester.

**2009-2010 Annual costs.** Tuition/fees: $14,160. Books/supplies: $1,100. Personal expenses: $1,816.

**2008-2009 Financial aid.** All financial aid based on need.

**Application procedures. Admission:** No deadline. $50 fee. Admission notification on a rolling basis. **Financial aid:** No deadline. FAFSA required. Applicants notified on a rolling basis.

**Academics. Special study options:** Accelerated study, distance learning. **Credit/placement by examination:** CLEP. **Support services:** Learning center, remedial instruction, tutoring.

**Majors. Business:** Business admin. **Computer sciences:** Networking, systems analysis, web page design. **Engineering technology:** Biomedical, computer, electrical. **Other:** Technical management.

**Most popular majors.** Business/marketing 72%, computer/information sciences 18%, engineering/engineering technologies 10%.

**Computing on campus.** Online course registration, online library, helpline available.

**Student life. Activities:** Student government, student newspaper.

**Student services.** Career counseling, student employment services, financial aid counseling, placement for graduates, veterans' counselor. **Physically disabled:** Services for visually, hearing impaired.

**Contact.** E-mail: openhouse@mir.devry.edu
Phone: (954) 499-9700 Toll-free number: (866) 793-3879
Fax: (954) 499-9723
Aaron McCardell, Director of Admission, DeVry University: Miramar, 2300 Southwest 145th Avenue, Miramar, FL 33027

## DeVry University: Orlando
Orlando, Florida
www.devry.edu                                    CB code: 2881

- For-profit 4-year university
- Commuter campus in very large city
- 1,727 degree-seeking undergraduates: 48% part-time, 36% women, 22% African American, 3% Asian American, 24% Hispanic American, 1% international
- 200 degree-seeking graduate students
- Interview required
- 31% graduate within 6 years

**General.** Regionally accredited. **Degrees:** 207 bachelor's, 23 associate awarded; master's offered. **Calendar:** Semester, extensive summer session. **Full-time faculty:** 27 total; 7% minority, 30% women. **Part-time faculty:** 181 total; 25% minority, 41% women.

**Basis for selection.** Applicants must have high school diploma or equivalent, or degree from an accredited postsecondary institution. New students may enter at the beginning of any semester. SAT or ACT or institution-administered placement examination used to determine proficiency in basic college-level skills.

**High school preparation.** Required units include mathematics 1. Math unit must be algebra or higher.

**2009-2010 Annual costs.** Tuition/fees: $14,160. Books/supplies: $1,300. Personal expenses: $3,152.

**2008-2009 Financial aid.** All financial aid based on need.

**Application procedures. Admission:** No deadline. $50 fee. Admission notification on a rolling basis. **Financial aid:** No deadline. FAFSA required. Applicants notified on a rolling basis.

**Academics. Special study options:** Accelerated study, distance learning. **Credit/placement by examination:** CLEP, institutional tests. **Support services:** Learning center, remedial instruction, tutoring.

**Majors. Business:** Business admin. **Computer sciences:** Networking, systems analysis, web page design. **Engineering:** Software. **Engineering technology:** Biomedical, computer, electrical. **Other:** Technical management.

**Most popular majors.** Business/marketing 70%, computer/information sciences 12%, engineering/engineering technologies 18%.

**Computing on campus.** 303 workstations in library, computer center. Online course registration, online library, helpline available.

**Student life. Freshman orientation:** Mandatory. **Activities:** Student newspaper, student activities council, National Society of Black Engineers, association for IT professionals, chess club, technology forum, Millennia Engineering Students Association.

**Student services.** Career counseling, student employment services, financial aid counseling, placement for graduates, veterans' counselor. **Physically disabled:** Services for visually, hearing impaired.

**Contact.** Phone: (407) 370-3131 Toll-free number: (866) 353-3879 Fax: (407) 370-3198
Jody Wasmer, Director of Admissions, DeVry University: Orlando, 4000 Millennia Boulevard, Orlando, FL 32839-2426

## Eckerd College
St. Petersburg, Florida                          CB member
www.eckerd.edu                                   CB code: 5223

- Private 4-year liberal arts college affiliated with Presbyterian Church (USA)
- Residential campus in large city
- 1,847 degree-seeking undergraduates: 1% part-time, 58% women, 4% African American, 2% Asian American, 4% Hispanic American, 3% international
- 72% of applicants admitted
- SAT or ACT (ACT writing optional), application essay required
- 65% graduate within 6 years

**General.** Founded in 1958. Regionally accredited. **Degrees:** 377 bachelor's awarded. **ROTC:** Army, Air Force. **Location:** 25 miles from Tampa. **Calendar:** 4-1-4, limited summer session. **Full-time faculty:** 110 total; 94%

have terminal degrees, 11% minority, 41% women. **Part-time faculty:** 52 total; 31% have terminal degrees, 17% minority, 50% women. **Class size:** 35% < 20, 62% 20-39, 2% 40-49, 1% 50-99. **Special facilities:** Marine science laboratory, waterfront program.

**Freshman class profile.** 3,200 applied, 2,293 admitted, 505 enrolled.

| Mid 50% test scores | | | |
|---|---|---|---|
| SAT critical reading: | 520-630 | GPA 2.0-2.99: | 26% |
| SAT math: | 500-610 | Rank in top quarter: | 45% |
| SAT writing: | 500-610 | Rank in top tenth: | 15% |
| ACT composite: | 22-28 | Return as sophomores: | 80% |
| GPA 3.75 or higher: | 14% | Out-of-state: | 80% |
| GPA 3.50-3.74: | 17% | Live on campus: | 95% |
| GPA 3.0-3.49: | 43% | International: | 3% |

**Basis for selection.** School achievement record, school/community involvement, essay, student's character, test scores most important. Interview recommended. Audition tapes for music and theater majors accepted, portfolios accepted for art majors. **Homeschooled:** Statement describing home-school structure and mission, transcript of courses and grades, state high school equivalency certificate, letter of recommendation (nonparent) required. **Learning Disabled:** Students should provide proper documentation for any disability they wish to inform the college about.

**High school preparation.** College-preparatory program recommended. 18 units recommended. Recommended units include English 4, mathematics 3, social studies 2, history 1, science 3 (laboratory 2), foreign language 2 and academic electives 3.

**2010-2011 Annual costs.** Tuition/fees: $33,228. Room/board: $9,326. Books/supplies: $1,200. Personal expenses: $1,400.

**2009-2010 Financial aid. Non-need-based:** Scholarships awarded for academics, art, athletics, music/drama.

**Application procedures. Admission:** No deadline. $35 fee, may be waived for applicants with need. Admission notification on a rolling basis beginning on or about 10/1. Must reply by May 1 or within 2 week(s) if notified thereafter. **Financial aid:** Priority date 3/1; no closing date. FAFSA required. Applicants notified on a rolling basis starting 2/1.

**Academics. Special study options:** Accelerated study, combined bachelor's/graduate degree, double major, honors, independent study, internships, liberal arts/career combination, semester at sea, student-designed major, study abroad, United Nations semester, Washington semester. Winter term exchange with other 4-1-4 colleges, 3-2 in engineering with Columbia University, Washington University (MO). **Credit/placement by examination:** AP, CLEP, IB, institutional tests. 32 credit hours maximum toward bachelor's degree. **Support services:** Reduced course load, tutoring, writing center.

**Majors. Area/ethnic studies:** American, East Asian, women's. **Biology:** General, biochemistry, environmental, marine. **Business:** Business admin, international, management science. **Communications:** General. **Computer sciences:** General. **Conservation:** Environmental studies. **Foreign languages:** Classics, comparative lit, French, Spanish. **History:** General. **Interdisciplinary:** Global studies. **Liberal arts:** Humanities. **Math:** General. **Philosophy/religion:** Philosophy, religion. **Physical sciences:** Chemistry, physics. **Psychology:** General, developmental. **Social sciences:** Anthropology, economics, international relations, political science, sociology. **Visual/performing arts:** Art history/conservation, dramatic, studio arts.

**Most popular majors.** Biology 17%, business/marketing 15%, communications/journalism 6%, natural resources/environmental science 10%, psychology 10%, social sciences 15%.

**Computing on campus.** 300 workstations in dormitories, library. Dormitories wired for high-speed internet access and linked to campus network. Commuter students can connect to campus network. Online course registration, online library, helpline, repair service, student web hosting, wireless network available.

**Student life. Freshman orientation:** Mandatory. Preregistration for classes offered. 3-week session held in fall. **Housing:** Guaranteed on-campus for freshmen. Coed dorms, single-sex dorms, apartments, wellness housing available. Pets allowed in dorm rooms. **Activities:** Concert band, campus ministries, choral groups, dance, drama, international student organizations, literary magazine, music ensembles, Model UN, radio station, student government, student newspaper, TV station, Phi Beta Kappa, Afro-American society, search and rescue team, Circle-K, honor societies, Earth society.

**Athletics.** NCAA. **Intercollegiate:** Baseball M, basketball, golf, sailing, soccer, softball W, tennis, volleyball W. **Intramural:** Baseball M, basketball, bowling, sailing, soccer, softball, swimming, table tennis, tennis, volleyball. **Team name:** Tritons.

**Student services.** Adult student services, alcohol/substance abuse counseling, chaplain/spiritual director, career counseling, student employment services, financial aid counseling, health services, minority student services, personal counseling, placement for graduates, veterans' counselor, women's services.

**Contact.** E-mail: admissions@eckerd.edu
Phone: (727) 864-8331 Toll-free number: (800) 456-9009
Fax: (727) 866-2304
John Sullivan, Dean of Admissions and Financial Aid, Eckerd College, 4200 54th Avenue South, St. Petersburg, FL 33711-4700

## Edison State College
**Fort Myers, Florida**                      **CB member**
**www.edison.edu**                           **CB code: 5191**

- Public 4-year liberal arts college
- Commuter campus in very large city
- 16,034 undergraduates

**General.** Founded in 1961. Regionally accredited. Additional campus sites: Charlotte, Hendry Glades, Collier. **Degrees:** 2 bachelor's, 1,545 associate awarded. **Location:** 35 miles from Naples, 120 miles from Tampa. **Calendar:** Semester, limited summer session. **Full-time faculty:** 124 total; 41% have terminal degrees. **Part-time faculty:** 390 total. **Class size:** 31% < 20, 35% 20-39, 3% 40-49, 1% 50-99. **Special facilities:** Performing arts hall, observatory, 3-hole instructional golf course.

**Basis for selection.** Open admission, but selective for some programs. Special requirements for allied health programs. **Homeschooled:** Applicants must submit affidavit of completion.

**High school preparation.** 21 units required. Required units include English 4, mathematics 3, social studies 3 and science 3.

**2009-2010 Annual costs.** Tuition/fees: $2,636; $9,942 out-of-state. Books/supplies: $626. Personal expenses: $1,060.

**Financial aid.** **Non-need-based:** Scholarships awarded for art, music/drama.

**Application procedures.** **Admission:** Closing date 8/15 (receipt date). $25 fee, may be waived for applicants with need. Application must be submitted on paper. Admission notification on a rolling basis. **Financial aid:** Priority date 5/1; no closing date. FAFSA required. Applicants notified on a rolling basis starting 6/1; must reply within 2 week(s) of notification.

**Academics.** **Special study options:** Accelerated study, cooperative education, cross-registration, distance learning, double major, dual enrollment of high school students, ESL, honors, independent study, internships, liberal arts/career combination. **Credit/placement by examination:** AP, CLEP, IB, institutional tests. 45 credit hours maximum toward associate degree. Credit by exam not available. **Support services:** Learning center, reduced course load, remedial instruction, tutoring.

**Majors.** **Protective services:** Criminal justice.

**Computing on campus.** 80 workstations in library, computer center. Online course registration, online library, helpline available.

**Student life.** **Freshman orientation:** Mandatory. Preregistration for classes offered. **Activities:** Bands, choral groups, drama, music ensembles, student government, black student union, Intervarsity Christian Fellowship, Young Republicans, environmental club, foreign student club, Young Democrats, Rotaract, Latin American student association, student nurses association.

**Student services.** Career counseling, services for economically disadvantaged, student employment services, financial aid counseling, minority student services, on-campus daycare, placement for graduates, veterans' counselor. **Physically disabled:** Services for visually, speech, hearing impaired.

**Contact.** E-mail: registrar@edison.edu
Phone: (239) 489-9121 Toll-free number: (800) 749-2322
Fax: (239) 489-9094
Billee Silva, District Registrar, Edison State College, Box 60210, Fort Myers, FL 33906-6210

## Edward Waters College
**Jacksonville, Florida**                    **CB member**
**www.ewc.edu**                              **CB code: 5182**

- Private 4-year liberal arts college affiliated with African Methodist Episcopal Church
- Commuter campus in very large city

- 812 degree-seeking undergraduates
- 24% of applicants admitted
- SAT or ACT (ACT writing optional) required

**General.** Founded in 1866. Regionally accredited. **Degrees:** 85 bachelor's awarded. **Location:** 150 miles from Orlando; 90 miles from Savannah, Georgia. **Calendar:** Semester, extensive summer session. **Full-time faculty:** 34 total; 56% have terminal degrees, 91% minority, 50% women. **Part-time faculty:** 31 total; 6% have terminal degrees, 97% minority, 48% women. **Class size:** 52% < 20, 48% 20-39, less than 1% 40-49. **Special facilities:** African art collection, community resource center.

**Freshman class profile.** 1,689 applied, 405 admitted, 247 enrolled.

| | | | |
|---|---|---|---|
| GPA 3.75 or higher: | 4% | GPA 2.0-2.99: | 72% |
| GPA 3.50-3.74: | 3% | Out-of-state: | 22% |
| GPA 3.0-3.49: | 17% | Live on campus: | 82% |

**Basis for selection.** GPA and recommendations very important. **Homeschooled:** Statement describing homeschool structure and mission, transcript of courses and grades, state high school equivalency certificate, interview, letter of recommendation (nonparent) required.

**High school preparation.** College-preparatory program recommended. 13 units recommended. Recommended units include English 4, mathematics 3, social studies 3 and science 3.

**2009-2010 Annual costs.** Tuition/fees: $9,990. Room/board: $6,439. Books/supplies: $500. Personal expenses: $750.

**Application procedures.** **Admission:** Priority date 4/15; no deadline. $25 fee, may be waived for applicants with need. Admission notification on a rolling basis. Must reply by May 1 or within 4 week(s) if notified thereafter. **Financial aid:** Closing date 4/15. FAFSA required. Applicants notified on a rolling basis starting 5/1; must reply within 2 week(s) of notification.

**Academics.** **Special study options:** Accelerated study, cooperative education, cross-registration, double major, dual enrollment of high school students, independent study, internships, liberal arts/career combination, teacher certification program. **Credit/placement by examination:** AP, CLEP, institutional tests. 30 credit hours maximum toward bachelor's degree. **Support services:** Learning center, pre-admission summer program, remedial instruction, study skills assistance, tutoring.

**Majors.** **Biology:** General. **Business:** Business admin. **Communications:** General. **Computer sciences:** Computer science. **Education:** General, physical. **Liberal arts:** Arts/sciences. **Math:** General. **Protective services:** Law enforcement admin. **Psychology:** General. **Social sciences:** Sociology.

**Most popular majors.** Business/marketing 31%, communications/journalism 9%, education 11%, psychology 9%.

**Computing on campus.** 120 workstations in dormitories, library, computer center. Dormitories wired for high-speed internet access and linked to campus network. Repair service, wireless network available.

**Student life.** **Freshman orientation:** Mandatory. Preregistration for classes offered. **Policies:** Smoke-free campus. Religious observance required. **Housing:** Guaranteed on-campus for freshmen. Coed dorms, single-sex dorms, wellness housing available. $100 deposit, deadline 7/31. **Activities:** Bands, campus ministries, choral groups, dance, drama, international student organizations, music ensembles, student government, NAACP, ministerial alliance, debate club, Circle K.

**Athletics.** NAIA. **Intercollegiate:** Baseball M, basketball, cheerleading, cross-country M, football (tackle) M, golf, softball W, track and field M, volleyball W. **Intramural:** Table tennis, volleyball. **Team name:** Fighting Tigers.

**Student services.** Adult student services, career counseling, student employment services, financial aid counseling, health services, personal counseling, placement for graduates, veterans' counselor.

**Contact.** E-mail: admissions@ewc.edu
Phone: (904) 470-8000 Toll-free number: (888) 898-3191
Fax: (904) 470-8041
Edward Alexander, Director of Admissions, Edward Waters College, 1658 Kings Road, Jacksonville, FL 32209

## Embry-Riddle Aeronautical University
**Daytona Beach, Florida**
**www.embryriddle.edu**                      **CB code: 5190**

- Private 4-year university
- Residential campus in small city

- 4,430 degree-seeking undergraduates: 6% part-time, 17% women, 6% African American, 6% Asian American, 8% Hispanic American, 13% international
- 505 degree-seeking graduate students
- 81% of applicants admitted
- SAT or ACT (ACT writing optional) required
- 57% graduate within 6 years; 31% enter graduate study

**General.** Founded in 1926. Regionally accredited. Over 130 teaching centers across United States and Europe. **Degrees:** 846 bachelor's, 15 associate awarded; master's offered. **ROTC:** Army, Naval, Air Force. **Location:** 50 miles from Orlando. **Calendar:** Semester, extensive summer session. **Full-time faculty:** 242 total; 66% have terminal degrees, 9% minority, 19% women. **Part-time faculty:** 82 total; 12% have terminal degrees, 11% minority, 45% women. **Class size:** 29% < 20, 64% 20-39, 5% 40-49, 2% 50-99, less than 1% >100. **Special facilities:** Airway science simulation lab.

**Freshman class profile.** 3,536 applied, 2,851 admitted, 318 enrolled.

| Mid 50% test scores | | Rank in top quarter: | 44% |
|---|---|---|---|
| SAT critical reading: | 460-580 | Rank in top tenth: | 20% |
| SAT math: | 490-630 | Return as sophomores: | 71% |
| ACT composite: | 21-27 | Out-of-state: | 69% |
| GPA 3.75 or higher: | 17% | Live on campus: | 92% |
| GPA 3.50-3.74: | 17% | International: | 9% |
| GPA 3.0-3.49: | 36% | Fraternities: | 22% |
| GPA 2.0-2.99: | 30% | Sororities: | 33% |

**Basis for selection.** High school GPA, rank in class, and test scores important. Specific requirements vary by degree program. Interview and essay recommended.

**High school preparation.** 15 units required; 19 recommended. Required and recommended units include English 4, mathematics 3-4, social studies 2, history 1-2, science 2-3 (laboratory 2), foreign language 1 and academic electives 3.

**2010-2011 Annual costs.** Tuition/fees: $29,720. Room/board: $10,320. Books/supplies: $1,040. Personal expenses: $1,392.

**2009-2010 Financial aid. Need-based:** 699 full-time freshmen applied for aid; 604 were judged to have need; 601 of these received aid. Average scholarship/grant was $9,119; average loan $3,432. 51% of total undergraduate aid awarded as scholarships/grants, 49% as loans/jobs. **Non-need-based:** Awarded to 159 full-time undergraduates, including 27 freshmen. Scholarships awarded for academics, alumni affiliation, athletics, leadership, ROTC.

**Application procedures. Admission:** No deadline. $50 fee, may be waived for applicants with need. Admission notification on a rolling basis beginning on or about 11/1. Must reply by May 1 or within 4 week(s) if notified thereafter. Early application encouraged since available facilities limit enrollment in some programs. **Financial aid:** No deadline. FAFSA required. Applicants notified on a rolling basis starting 3/1; must reply within 4 week(s) of notification.

**Academics. Special study options:** Accelerated study, combined bachelor's/graduate degree, cooperative education, distance learning, double major, dual enrollment of high school students, ESL, honors, independent study, internships, student-designed major, study abroad. **Credit/placement by examination:** AP, CLEP, IB, SAT, ACT, institutional tests. 30 credit hours maximum toward bachelor's degree. **Support services:** Pre-admission summer program, remedial instruction, study skills assistance, tutoring, writing center.

**Majors. Business:** Business admin. **Communications:** General. **Computer sciences:** General, computer science. **Engineering:** General, aerospace, civil, computer, electrical, mechanical, physics, software. **Engineering technology:** Electrical, occupational safety. **Mechanic/repair:** Aircraft powerplant. **Physical sciences:** Atmospheric science, physics. **Protective services:** Emergency management/homeland security. **Transportation:** Air traffic control, airline/commercial pilot, aviation, aviation management. **Other:** Aerospace studies.

**Most popular majors.** Business/marketing 8%, engineering/engineering technologies 35%, trade and industry 47%.

**Computing on campus.** 1,013 workstations in library, computer center. Dormitories wired for high-speed internet access and linked to campus network. Commuter students can connect to campus network. Online library, helpline, student web hosting, wireless network available.

**Student life. Freshman orientation:** Mandatory. Preregistration for classes offered. **Housing:** Guaranteed on-campus for freshmen. Coed dorms available. $300 nonrefundable deposit, deadline 11/1. Special units available in regular coed dorms. **Activities:** Pep band, campus ministries, choral groups, dance, drama, international student organizations, music ensembles, Model UN, radio station, student government, student newspaper, more than 150 clubs and organizations available.

**Athletics.** NAIA. **Intercollegiate:** Baseball M, basketball M, cheerleading, cross-country, golf, soccer, tennis, track and field, volleyball W. **Intramural:** Badminton, basketball, bowling, football (non-tackle), golf, racquetball, soccer, table tennis, volleyball. **Team name:** Eagles.

**Student services.** Alcohol/substance abuse counseling, chaplain/spiritual director, career counseling, student employment services, financial aid counseling, health services, personal counseling, placement for graduates, veterans' counselor, women's services. **Physically disabled:** Services for visually, speech, hearing impaired.

**Contact.** E-mail: dbadmit@erau.edu
Phone: (386) 226-6100 Toll-free number: (800) 862-2416
Fax: (386) 226-7070
Robert Adams, Director of Admissions, Embry-Riddle Aeronautical University, 600 South Clyde Morris Boulevard, Daytona Beach, FL 32114-3900

## Embry-Riddle Aeronautical University: Worldwide Campus
Daytona Beach, Florida
www.embryriddle.edu                CB code: 5036

- Private 4-year university
- Commuter campus in small city
- 10,988 degree-seeking undergraduates: 81% part-time, 11% women, 10% African American, 4% Asian American, 10% Hispanic American, 1% Native American
- 4,112 degree-seeking graduate students

**General.** Regionally accredited. Campus is network of more than 130 centers and teaching sites in United States and Europe, with virtual presence via distance learning covering every continent. **Degrees:** 2,291 bachelor's, 693 associate awarded; master's offered. **Calendar:** Semester, extensive summer session. **Full-time faculty:** 122 total; 47% have terminal degrees, 9% minority, 18% women. **Part-time faculty:** 2,762 total; 18% have terminal degrees, 25% minority, 23% women.

**Basis for selection.** High school GPA, rank in class, and test scores important. Specific requirements vary by degree program.

**2010-2011 Annual costs.** Per credit hour charges range from $230 - $321.

**2009-2010 Financial aid. Need-based:** 20 full-time freshmen applied for aid; 17 were judged to have need; 17 of these received aid. Average scholarship/grant was $5,310; average loan $3,291. 13% of total undergraduate aid awarded as scholarships/grants, 87% as loans/jobs. **Non-need-based:** Scholarships awarded for academics.

**Application procedures. Admission:** No deadline. $50 fee, may be waived for applicants with need. **Financial aid:** Priority date 4/15; no closing date. FAFSA required. Applicants notified on a rolling basis starting 3/1; must reply within 4 week(s) of notification.

**Academics. Special study options:** Distance learning. **Credit/placement by examination:** AP, CLEP.

**Majors. Business:** Business admin. **Mechanic/repair:** Aircraft powerplant. **Transportation:** Aviation, aviation management.

**Most popular majors.** Business/marketing 15%, trade and industry 85%.

**Contact.** E-mail: ecinfo@erau.edu
Phone: (386) 225-6910 Toll-free number: (800) 522-6787
Fax: (386) 226-6984
Linda Dammer, Director of Admissions, Embry-Riddle Aeronautical University: Worldwide Campus, 600 South Clyde Morris Boulevard, Daytona Beach, FL 32114-3900

## Everest University: Brandon
Tampa, Florida
www.everest.edu                CB code: 3585

- For-profit 4-year university and business college
- Commuter campus in very large city

**General.** Accredited by ACICS. **Calendar:** Quarter.

**Annual costs/financial aid.** Tuition/fees (2009-2010): $16,740. Books/supplies: $1,200. Personal expenses: $1,799. Need-based financial aid available to full-time and part-time students.

**Contact.**  Phone: (813) 621-0041
Director of Admissions, 3924 Coconut Palm Drive, Tampa, FL 33619

## Everest University: Jacksonville
Jacksonville, Florida
www.fmu.edu                         CB code: 3801

- For-profit 4-year business college
- Commuter campus in large city

**General.** Accredited by ACICS. **Calendar:** Quarter.

**Annual costs/financial aid.** Tuition/fees: $16,740.

**Contact.**  Phone: (904) 731-4949
Director of Admissions, 8226 Phillips Highway, Jacksonville, FL 32256

## Everest University: Lakeland
Lakeland, Florida
www.everest.edu                     CB code: 3584

- For-profit 4-year university and branch campus college
- Small city

**General.** Accredited by ACICS. **Calendar:** Quarter.

**Annual costs/financial aid.** Tuition/fees (2009-2010): $16,740. Tuition and fees may vary by program. Need-based financial aid available to full-time and part-time students.

**Contact.**  Phone: (863) 686-1444
Registrar, 995 East Memorial Boulevard, Suite 110, Lakeland, FL 33801-1919

## Everest University: Largo
Largo, Florida
www.everest.edu                     CB code: 3583

- For-profit 4-year university and business college
- Commuter campus in large city

**General.** Accredited by ACICS. **Location:** 15 miles from Tampa. **Calendar:** Quarter.

**Annual costs/financial aid.** Tuition/fees (2009-2010): $16,740. Tuition and fees may vary by program. Books/supplies: $500. Need-based financial aid available to full-time and part-time students.

**Contact.**  Phone: (727) 725-2688
Director of Admissions, 1199 East Bay Drive Largo, Largo, FL 33770

## Everest University: Melbourne
Melbourne, Florida
www.cci.edu                         CB code: 3586

- For-profit 4-year business college
- Commuter campus in small city

**General.** Accredited by ACICS. **Calendar:** Quarter.

**Annual costs/financial aid.** Tuition/fees: $16,740.

**Contact.**  Phone: (321) 253-2929
Director of Admission, 2401 North Harbor City Boulevard, Melbourne, FL 32935

## Everest University: North Orlando
Orlando, Florida
www.everest.edu                     CB code: 0742

- For-profit 4-year business college
- Commuter campus in very large city

**General.** Founded in 1918. Accredited by ACICS. **Location:** 2 miles from downtown. **Calendar:** Quarter.

**Annual costs/financial aid.** Tuition/fees (2009-2010): $16,740. Tuition and fees may vary by program. Books/supplies: $700. Personal expenses: $1,764. Need-based financial aid available to full-time and part-time students.

**Contact.**  Phone: (407) 628-5870
Director of Admissions, 5421 Diplomat Circle, Orlando, FL 32810

## Everest University: Orange Park
Orange Park, Florida
www.fmu.edu

- For-profit 4-year business college
- Commuter campus in small city

**General.** Accredited by ACICS. **Calendar:** Quarter.

**Annual costs/financial aid.** Tuition/fees: $16,740. Tuition and fees vary by program.

**Contact.**  Phone: (904) 264-9122
805 Wells Road, Orange Park, FL 32073

## Everest University: Pompano Beach
Pompano Beach, Florida
www.everest.edu                     CB code: 5171

- For-profit 4-year business college
- Small city

**General.** Founded in 1940. Accredited by ACICS. **Location:** 35 miles from Miami. **Calendar:** Quarter.

**Annual costs/financial aid.** Tuition/fees (2009-2010): $16,740. Tuition may vary by program. Books/supplies: $600. Personal expenses: $1,584. Need-based financial aid available to full-time and part-time students.

**Contact.**  Phone: (954) 783-7339
Director of Admissions, 225 North Federal Highway, Pompano Beach, FL 33062

## Everest University: South Orlando
Orlando, Florida
www.everest.edu                     CB code: 3587

- For-profit 4-year university and business college
- Very large city

**General.** Accredited by ACICS. **Calendar:** Quarter.

**Annual costs/financial aid.** Tuition/fees (2009-2010): $16,935. Tuition and fees may vary according to program. Books/supplies: $1,200. Personal expenses: $1,764.

**Contact.**  Phone: (407) 851-2525
Director of Admissions, 9200 Southpark Center Loop, Orlando, FL 32819

## Everest University: Tampa
Tampa, Florida
www.everest.edu                     CB code: 0428

- For-profit 4-year university and business college
- Commuter campus in large city

**General.** Founded in 1890. Accredited by ACICS. **Location:** 85 miles from Orlando. **Calendar:** Quarter.

**Annual costs/financial aid.** Tuition/fees (2009-2010): $16,740. Tuition and fees vary by program. Books/supplies: $540. Personal expenses: $1,710. Need-based financial aid available to full-time and part-time students.

**Contact.**  Phone: (813) 879-6000
Director of Admissions, 3319 West Hillsborough Avenue, Tampa, FL 33614

## Everglades University: Boca Raton
Boca Raton, Florida
www.EvergladesUniversity.edu          CB code: 3191

♦ Private 4-year university
♦ Commuter campus in small city
♦ 1,000 degree-seeking undergraduates
♦ 100 graduate students

**General.** Accredited by ACCSC. **Degrees:** 164 bachelor's awarded; master's offered. **Calendar:** Semester, extensive summer session. **Full-time faculty:** 64 total. **Part-time faculty:** 54 total.

**Basis for selection.** University's entrance examination or SAT/ACT required. Score of 40 on the university's entrance exam, or 1200 SAT or 17 ACT required. Florida's CLAST exam is also acceptable with passing scores in computation and reading. Students entering with earned college degree not required to take entrance exam.

**2009-2010 Annual costs.** $1,600 education fee for online students. Books/supplies: $1,125.

**Application procedures. Admission:** No deadline. $50 fee. Admission notification on a rolling basis. **Financial aid:** No deadline. FAFSA required. Applicants notified on a rolling basis.

**Academics. Special study options:** Distance learning. **Credit/placement by examination:** CLEP. **Support services:** Study skills assistance, tutoring.

**Majors. Business:** Business admin, construction management. **Transportation:** Aviation, aviation management. **Other:** Alternative Medicine.

**Computing on campus.** 25 workstations in library, computer center. Online library, helpline, wireless network available.

**Student life. Freshman orientation:** Available. **Housing:** The Student Services Department is available to assist students in locating housing. **Activities:** Student government.

**Student services.** Adult student services, alcohol/substance abuse counseling, career counseling, student employment services, financial aid counseling, placement for graduates, veterans' counselor.

**Contact.** E-mail: admissions-boca@evergladesuniversity.edu
Phone: (561) 912-1211 Toll-free number: (888) 772-6077
Fax: (561) 912-1191
Jean Graham, Director of Admissions, Everglades University: Boca Raton, 5002 T-REX Avenue, Suite 100, Boca Raton, FL 33431

## Everglades University: Orlando
Altamonte Springs, Florida
www.evergladesuniversity.edu

♦ Private 4-year branch campus and liberal arts college
♦ Very large city

**General.** Regionally accredited. **Calendar:** Continuous.

**Contact.** Phone: (407) 277-0311
887 East Altamonte Drive, Altamonte Springs, FL 32701

## Flagler College
Saint Augustine, Florida                    CB member
www.flagler.edu                              CB code: 5235

♦ Private 4-year liberal arts college
♦ Residential campus in large town
♦ 2,706 degree-seeking undergraduates: 3% part-time, 60% women, 2% African American, 4% Hispanic American, 2% international
♦ 44% of applicants admitted
♦ SAT or ACT (ACT writing optional), application essay required
♦ 69% graduate within 6 years; 5% enter graduate study

**General.** Founded in 1968. Regionally accredited. Historic St. Augustine Research Institute is a joint partnership of St. Augustine Foundation, Flagler College and the University of Florida. **Degrees:** 589 bachelor's awarded. **Location:** 35 miles from Jacksonville. **Calendar:** Semester, limited summer session. **Full-time faculty:** 95 total; 57% have terminal degrees, 50% minority, 46% women. **Part-time faculty:** 102 total; 18% have terminal

degrees, 4% minority, 48% women. **Class size:** 36% < 20, 62% 20-39, 2% 40-49, less than 1% 50-99.

**Freshman class profile.** 2,585 applied, 1,149 admitted, 573 enrolled.

| Mid 50% test scores | | | |
|---|---|---|---|
| SAT critical reading: | 520-590 | GPA 2.0-2.99: | 19% |
| SAT math: | 510-590 | Rank in top quarter: | 56% |
| SAT writing: | 500-570 | Rank in top tenth: | 18% |
| ACT composite: | 21-24 | End year in good standing: | 85% |
| GPA 3.75 or higher: | 19% | Return as sophomores: | 76% |
| GPA 3.50-3.74: | 18% | Out-of-state: | 38% |
| GPA 3.0-3.49: | 44% | Live on campus: | 94% |
| | | International: | 3% |

**Basis for selection.** Academic record, including pattern of courses most important, followed by test scores. Extracurricular activities, recommendations, and intended major also considered. Education applicants must score at or above 45th percentile on SAT or ACT. Interview required for early admission applicants; recommended for all others.

**High school preparation.** College-preparatory program required. 16 units required; 24 recommended. Required and recommended units include English 4, mathematics 3-4, social studies 3, history 1-2, science 2-3 (laboratory 1-2), foreign language 2, computer science 1, visual/performing arts 1 and academic electives 2.

**2010-2011 Annual costs.** Tuition/fees: $13,860. Room/board: $7,590. Books/supplies: $1,000. Personal expenses: $2,400.

**2009-2010 Financial aid. Need-based:** 460 full-time freshmen applied for aid; 333 were judged to have need; 333 of these received aid. Average need met was 61%. Average scholarship/grant was $5,378; average loan $3,213. 53% of total undergraduate aid awarded as scholarships/grants, 47% as loans/jobs. **Non-need-based:** Awarded to 1,403 full-time undergraduates, including 290 freshmen. Scholarships awarded for academics, art, athletics, job skills, leadership, minority status, music/drama, state residency.

**Application procedures. Admission:** Priority date 1/15; deadline 3/1 (postmark date). $40 fee, may be waived for applicants with need. Admission notification 3/30. Must reply by May 1 or within 3 week(s) if notified thereafter. **Financial aid:** Priority date 4/1; no closing date. FAFSA, institutional form required. Applicants notified on a rolling basis starting 4/1; must reply within 2 week(s) of notification.

**Academics.** Freshmen must earn at least 24 semester hours credit for good academic standing. **Special study options:** Double major, external degree, independent study, internships, liberal arts/career combination, study abroad, teacher certification program. Deaf education majors work directly with faculty and students at nearby Florida School for the Deaf and Blind. **Credit/placement by examination:** AP, CLEP, IB, SAT, ACT. 30 credit hours maximum toward bachelor's degree. **Support services:** Learning center, reduced course load, study skills assistance, tutoring, writing center.

**Majors. Area/ethnic studies:** Latin American. **Business:** Accounting, business admin. **Communications:** General. **Education:** Art, Deaf/hearing impaired, drama/dance, elementary, English, social science, social studies, special. **Foreign languages:** Spanish. **History:** General. **Liberal arts:** Arts/sciences. **Parks/recreation:** Sports admin. **Philosophy/religion:** Philosophy. **Psychology:** General. **Public administration:** General. **Social sciences:** Economics, political science, sociology. **Visual/performing arts:** General, dramatic, studio arts.

**Most popular majors.** Business/marketing 24%, communications/journalism 11%, education 11%, English 7%, psychology 9%, social sciences 6%, visual/performing arts 11%.

**Computing on campus.** 250 workstations in library, computer center, student center. Dormitories wired for high-speed internet access and linked to campus network. Commuter students can connect to campus network. Online course registration, online library, helpline, student web hosting, wireless network available.

**Student life. Freshman orientation:** Mandatory. Preregistration for classes offered. 3-day program held each semester prior to classes; additional optional summer session. **Policies:** Male-female interdorm visitation not allowed in residence halls. Alcohol prohibited on campus. No smoking in buildings, including residence halls. **Housing:** Guaranteed on-campus for freshmen. Single-sex dorms available. $200 nonrefundable deposit, deadline 5/1. **Activities:** Campus ministries, choral groups, dance, drama, literary magazine, radio station, student government, student newspaper, Rotaract, Intervarsity Christian Fellowship, Catholic College Fellowship, Society for Advancement of Management, Students in Free Enterprises, deaf awareness club, sport management club, Club Unity.

**Athletics.** NCAA. **Intercollegiate:** Baseball M, basketball, cross-country, golf, soccer, softball W, tennis, volleyball W. **Intramural:** Badminton, basketball, bowling, football (non-tackle), golf, soccer, softball, table tennis, tennis, volleyball, weight lifting. **Team name:** Saints.

**Student services.** Career counseling, student employment services, financial aid counseling, health services, personal counseling, veterans' counselor. **Physically disabled:** Services for visually, speech, hearing impaired.

**Contact.** E-mail: admiss@flagler.edu
Phone: (904) 829-6220 Toll-free number: (800) 304-4208
Fax: (904) 829-6838
Marc Williar, Director of Admissions, Flagler College, 74 King Street, St. Augustine, FL 32084

## Florida Agricultural and Mechanical University

| | |
|---|---|
| Tallahassee, Florida | **CB member** |
| www.famu.edu | **CB code: 5215** |

◗  Public 4-year university
◗  Residential campus in small city
◗  10,097 degree-seeking undergraduates: 8% part-time, 59% women, 94% African American, 1% Asian American, 1% Hispanic American, 1% international
◗  1,990 degree-seeking graduate students
◗  61% of applicants admitted
◗  SAT or ACT (ACT writing optional) required
◗  41% graduate within 6 years; 35% enter graduate study

**General.** Founded in 1887. Regionally accredited. **Degrees:** 1,443 bachelor's, 47 associate awarded; master's, doctoral, professional offered. **ROTC:** Army, Naval, Air Force. **Location:** 169 miles from Jacksonville. **Calendar:** Semester, limited summer session. **Full-time faculty:** 590 total; 74% have terminal degrees, 80% minority, 44% women. **Part-time faculty:** 140 total; 70% minority, 49% women. **Class size:** 30% < 20, 41% 20-39, 10% 40-49, 17% 50-99, 1% >100. **Special facilities:** Black archives research center, observatory.

**Freshman class profile.** 7,952 applied, 4,824 admitted, 2,447 enrolled.

| Mid 50% test scores | | | |
|---|---|---|---|
| SAT critical reading: | 410-500 | GPA 3.0-3.49: | 34% |
| SAT math: | 410-500 | GPA 2.0-2.99: | 52% |
| SAT writing: | 400-490 | End year in good standing: | 74% |
| ACT composite: | 17-21 | Return as sophomores: | 78% |
| GPA 3.75 or higher: | 6% | Out-of-state: | 19% |
| GPA 3.50-3.74: | 8% | Live on campus: | 96% |

**Basis for selection.** School achievement record, test scores, recommendations, and essay very important. Essay required of nursing, architecture, and pharmacy applicants. Audition required of music major applicants. **Homeschooled:** Statement describing homeschool structure and mission, transcript of courses and grades, letter of recommendation (nonparent) required. Applicant may be asked to complete GED. **Learning Disabled:** Applicants who do not meet standard admissions criteria due to disability may seek admission under alternate criteria, by requesting it in writing when applying. Current and appropriate documentation required.

**High school preparation.** College-preparatory program required. 18 units required. Required units include English 4, mathematics 3, social studies 3, science 3 (laboratory 1), foreign language 2 and academic electives 3.

**2009-2010 Annual costs.** Tuition/fees: $4,120; $15,513 out-of-state. Room/board: $6,976. Books/supplies: $1,078. Personal expenses: $1,872.

**2008-2009 Financial aid. Need-based:** 1,006 full-time freshmen applied for aid; 994 were judged to have need; 975 of these received aid. Average need met was 75%. Average scholarship/grant was $5,812; average loan $3,166. 53% of total undergraduate aid awarded as scholarships/grants, 47% as loans/jobs. **Non-need-based:** Awarded to 1,016 full-time undergraduates, including 313 freshmen. Scholarships awarded for academics, art, athletics, leadership, music/drama.

**Application procedures. Admission:** Closing date 5/15 (receipt date). $30 fee. Admission notification on a rolling basis. **Financial aid:** Priority date 3/1; no closing date. FAFSA required. Applicants notified by 4/15.

**Academics. Special study options:** Accelerated study, combined bachelor's/graduate degree, cooperative education, distance learning, double major, dual enrollment of high school students, honors, independent study, internships, study abroad, teacher certification program, weekend college. **Credit/placement by examination:** AP, CLEP, IB, SAT, ACT. 30 credit hours maximum toward bachelor's degree. Student must have passing scores (determined by state) for AP and CLEP exams. **Support services:** Learning center, pre-admission summer program, remedial instruction, study skills assistance, tutoring, writing center.

**Majors. Agriculture:** General, agribusiness operations, international, landscaping. **Architecture:** Architecture. **Area/ethnic studies:** African-American. **Biology:** General. **Business:** Accounting, business admin, managerial economics. **Communications:** Journalism, public relations. **Computer sciences:** General. **Conservation:** Environmental science. **Education:** Art, business, early childhood, elementary, English, mathematics, music, physical, science, social science, trade/industrial. **Engineering:** Agricultural, chemical, civil, computer, electrical, industrial, mechanical. **Engineering technology:** Civil, construction, electrical, manufacturing. **Foreign languages:** French, Spanish. **Health:** Health care admin, health services, medical records admin, nursing (RN), respiratory therapy technology. **History:** General. **Math:** General. **Physical sciences:** Chemistry, physics. **Protective services:** Criminal justice. **Psychology:** General. **Public administration:** Social work. **Social sciences:** Economics, political science, sociology. **Visual/performing arts:** Dramatic, graphic design, jazz, music performance, studio arts. **Other:** Design and applied arts, Philosophy and religious studies.

**Most popular majors.** Business/marketing 21%, education 6%, health sciences 17%, psychology 6%, security/protective services 10%, social sciences 8%.

**Computing on campus.** 3,000 workstations in dormitories, library, computer center, student center. Dormitories wired for high-speed internet access and linked to campus network. Commuter students can connect to campus network. Online course registration, online library, helpline, repair service, wireless network available.

**Student life. Freshman orientation:** Mandatory, $35 fee. Preregistration for classes offered. 2.5 day session in fall. Cost contingent on whether student stays on campus. **Policies:** 2.5 GPA required for membership in social, service, honorary, and professional fraternities and sororities. 2.0 GPA and current enrollment required for active membership status in student organizations. **Housing:** Guaranteed on-campus for freshmen. Coed dorms, single-sex dorms, special housing for disabled, apartments available. $350 partly refundable deposit. **Activities:** Bands, campus ministries, choral groups, dance, drama, international student organizations, literary magazine, music ensembles, musical theater, radio station, student government, student newspaper, symphony orchestra, TV station.

**Athletics.** NCAA. **Intercollegiate:** Baseball M, basketball, bowling W, cheerleading, cross-country, football (tackle) M, golf, softball W, swimming, tennis, track and field, volleyball W. **Intramural:** Badminton, basketball, bowling, cheerleading W, football (non-tackle), football (tackle) M, golf, gymnastics, racquetball, skiing, soccer, softball, swimming, table tennis, tennis, track and field, volleyball, weight lifting, wrestling. **Team name:** Rattlers.

**Student services.** Alcohol/substance abuse counseling, career counseling, student employment services, financial aid counseling, health services, on-campus daycare, personal counseling, placement for graduates, veterans' counselor. **Physically disabled:** Services for visually, speech, hearing impaired.

**Contact.** E-mail: ugrdadmissions@famu.edu
Phone: (850) 599-3796 Toll-free number: (866) 642-1198
Fax: (850) 599-3069
Barbara Cox, Director of Admissions, Florida Agricultural and Mechanical University, FHAC, G-9, Tallahassee, FL 32307-3200

## Florida Atlantic University

| | |
|---|---|
| Boca Raton, Florida | **CB member** |
| www.fau.edu | **CB code: 5229** |

◗  Public 4-year university
◗  Commuter campus in small city
◗  21,620 degree-seeking undergraduates: 40% part-time, 58% women, 18% African American, 5% Asian American, 20% Hispanic American, 3% international
◗  4,148 degree-seeking graduate students
◗  46% of applicants admitted
◗  SAT or ACT (ACT writing optional), application essay required
◗  39% graduate within 6 years

**General.** Founded in 1961. Regionally accredited. Courses and degree programs offered at additional sites in Palm Beach, Broward, and St. Lucie counties. **Degrees:** 4,468 bachelor's, 157 associate awarded; master's, doctoral, professional offered. **ROTC:** Army, Air Force. **Location:** 17 miles from Fort Lauderdale. **Calendar:** Semester, extensive summer session. **Full-time faculty:** 785 total; 86% have terminal degrees, 22% minority, 42% women. **Part-time faculty:** 498 total; 10% minority, 51% women. **Class size:** 29% < 20, 51% 20-39, 7% 40-49, 8% 50-99, 6% >100. **Special facilities:** Environmental center, native fish research center, ocean engineering laboratory, marine research facility, robotics laboratory.

**Freshman class profile.** 14,532 applied, 6,745 admitted, 2,569 enrolled.

| Mid 50% test scores | | Rank in top quarter: | 39% |
|---|---|---|---|
| SAT critical reading: | 480-570 | Rank in top tenth: | 12% |
| SAT math: | 450-540 | End year in good standing: | 79% |
| SAT writing: | 470-550 | Out-of-state: | 6% |
| ACT composite: | 21-25 | Live on campus: | 66% |
| GPA 3.75 or higher: | 21% | International: | 1% |
| GPA 3.50-3.74: | 18% | Fraternities: | 1% |
| GPA 3.0-3.49: | 44% | Sororities: | 1% |
| GPA 2.0-2.99: | 17% | | |

**Basis for selection.** Secondary school record, standardized test scores most important. Recommendation, talent, ability also important. Top 20% of state high school graduates guaranteed admission. Audition recommended for theater majors. Portfolio recommended for art majors. **Homeschooled:** State high school equivalency certificate required.

**High school preparation.** College-preparatory program required. 18 units required; 19 recommended. Required and recommended units include English 4, mathematics 3-4, social studies 3, science 3 (laboratory 2), foreign language 2 and academic electives 3.

**2009-2010 Annual costs.** Tuition/fees: $4,187; $17,532 out-of-state. Room/board: $9,582. Books/supplies: $724. Personal expenses: $1,458.

**2008-2009 Financial aid. Need-based:** 1,736 full-time freshmen applied for aid; 1,179 were judged to have need; 1,156 of these received aid. Average need met was 85%. Average scholarship/grant was $6,740; average loan $2,929. 65% of total undergraduate aid awarded as scholarships/grants, 35% as loans/jobs. **Non-need-based:** Scholarships awarded for academics, athletics, music/drama, state residency.

**Application procedures. Admission:** Closing date 6/1 (receipt date). $30 fee, may be waived for applicants with need. Admission notification on a rolling basis beginning on or about 9/15. **Financial aid:** Priority date 3/1; no closing date. FAFSA required. Applicants notified on a rolling basis starting 4/1; must reply within 3 week(s) of notification.

**Academics. Special study options:** Accelerated study, combined bachelor's/graduate degree, cooperative education, cross-registration, distance learning, double major, dual enrollment of high school students, ESL, honors, independent study, internships, liberal arts/career combination, student-designed major, study abroad, teacher certification program, weekend college. **Credit/placement by examination:** AP, CLEP, IB. 45 credit hours maximum toward bachelor's degree. **Support services:** Learning center, pre-admission summer program, reduced course load, study skills assistance, tutoring, writing center.

**Honors college/program.** Most applicants will have 3.5 GPA, 1280 SAT (exclusive of Writing) or 29 on Enhanced ACT. Exceptional applicants who do not meet these criteria may be admitted on individual basis by Admissions Committee.

**Majors. Architecture:** Architecture, urban/community planning. **Biology:** General. **Business:** Accounting, business admin, finance, hospitality admin, human resources, international, management information systems, marketing, real estate. **Communications:** General, digital media. **Computer sciences:** General. **Education:** General, elementary, English, mathematics, music, science, social science, special. **Engineering:** Civil, computer, electrical, mechanical, ocean, surveying. **Engineering technology:** Computer systems. **Foreign languages:** French, German, linguistics, Spanish. **Health:** Health care admin, health services, nursing (RN). **History:** General. **Liberal arts:** Arts/sciences. **Math:** General. **Parks/recreation:** Exercise sciences. **Philosophy/religion:** Judaic, philosophy. **Physical sciences:** Chemistry, geology, physics. **Protective services:** Criminal justice. **Psychology:** General, psychobiology, social. **Public administration:** General, social work. **Social sciences:** General, anthropology, economics, geography, political science, sociology. **Visual/performing arts:** Art, dramatic, music management.

**Most popular majors.** Business/marketing 26%, education 11%, health sciences 7%, psychology 6%, security/protective services 6%, social sciences 8%.

**Computing on campus.** 1,000 workstations in dormitories, library, computer center, student center. Dormitories wired for high-speed internet access and linked to campus network. Commuter students can connect to campus network. Online course registration, online library, helpline, repair service, wireless network available.

**Student life. Freshman orientation:** Mandatory, $75 fee. Preregistration for classes offered. Held 2 different dates before semester starts. **Housing:** Guaranteed on-campus for freshmen. Coed dorms, single-sex dorms, apartments available. $200 partly refundable deposit, deadline 8/1. **Activities:**

Bands, campus ministries, choral groups, dance, drama, film society, international student organizations, literary magazine, music ensembles, Model UN, musical theater, opera, radio station, student government, student newspaper, symphony orchestra, TV station, Circle K, College Democrats, College Republicans, B'nai B'rith Hillel, Neumann Club, Christian College Fellowship, Human Rights Organization, European Student Association, NAACP, Peace Finders.

**Athletics.** NCAA. **Intercollegiate:** Baseball M, basketball, cheerleading, cross-country, football (tackle) M, golf, soccer, softball W, swimming, tennis, track and field W, volleyball W. **Intramural:** Basketball, diving, football (non-tackle), rugby, soccer M, softball, table tennis, volleyball M. **Team name:** Owls.

**Student services.** Adult student services, alcohol/substance abuse counseling, chaplain/spiritual director, career counseling, student employment services, financial aid counseling, health services, minority student services, on-campus daycare, personal counseling, placement for graduates, veterans' counselor, women's services. **Physically disabled:** Services for visually, speech, hearing impaired. **Learning disabled:** Comprehensive services available.

**Contact.** E-mail: Admissions@fau.edu
Phone: (561) 297-3040 Toll-free number: (800) 299-4328
Fax: (561) 297-2758
Barbara Pletcher, Director of Admissions, Florida Atlantic University, 777 Glades Road, Boca Raton, FL 33431

## Florida Career College: Lauderdale Lakes
### Lauderdale Lakes, Florida
### lauderdalelakes.college-Info.com

▶ For-profit 4-year technical and career college
▶ Large town

**General.** Accredited by ACICS. **Calendar:** Quarter.

**Annual costs/financial aid.** Tuition varies by length of program and is $445 per credit hour; which leads to certificate, associate or bachelor degree.

**Contact.** Phone: (954) 535-8700
Director of Admissions, 3383 North State Road 7, Lauderdale Lakes, FL 33319

## Florida Christian College
### Kissimmee, Florida
### www.fcc.edu
CB code: 2167

▶ Private 4-year Bible and teachers college affiliated with Christian Churches and Churches of Christ
▶ Residential campus in small city
▶ 226 degree-seeking undergraduates: 28% part-time, 42% women, 9% African American, 1% Asian American, 10% Hispanic American
▶ SAT or ACT (ACT writing optional), application essay required
▶ 43% graduate within 6 years

**General.** Founded in 1975. Candidate for regional accreditation.; also accredited by ABHE. **Degrees:** 52 bachelor's, 9 associate awarded. **Location:** 20 miles from Orlando. **Calendar:** Semester, limited summer session. **Full-time faculty:** 11 total; 100% have terminal degrees, 9% minority, 27% women. **Part-time faculty:** 18 total; 100% have terminal degrees, 6% minority. **Class size:** 79% < 20, 19% 20-39, 1% 40-49, 1% 50-99.

**Freshman class profile.**

| | | | |
|---|---|---|---|
| End year in good standing: | 66% | Out-of-state: | 10% |
| Return as sophomores: | 66% | Live on campus: | 84% |

**Basis for selection.** Autobiographical essays, personal recommendation, and church references required. **Homeschooled:** State high school equivalency certificate, letter of recommendation (nonparent) required.

**2009-2010 Annual costs.** Tuition/fees: $11,170. Room only: $2,520. Books/supplies: $850. Personal expenses: $895.

**2009-2010 Financial aid. Non-need-based:** Scholarships awarded for academics, alumni affiliation, leadership, music/drama, religious affiliation, state residency.

**Application procedures. Admission:** Priority date 7/15; deadline 8/1 (postmark date). $35 fee, may be waived for applicants with need. Admission notification on a rolling basis. **Financial aid:** Priority date 5/1, closing date 7/15. FAFSA, institutional form required. Applicants notified on a rolling basis starting 3/1.

**Academics. Special study options:** Accelerated study, distance learning, dual enrollment of high school students, independent study, internships, student-designed major, teacher certification program. **Credit/placement by examination:** AP, CLEP, IB. 15 credit hours maximum toward associate degree, 30 toward bachelor's. **Support services:** Reduced course load, study skills assistance, tutoring.

**Majors. Education:** Elementary. **Philosophy/religion:** Philosophy, religion. **Theology:** Bible, missionary, pastoral counseling, sacred music, theology.

**Computing on campus.** 8 workstations in library, student center. Dormitories wired for high-speed internet access and linked to campus network. Online course registration, online library, helpline, repair service, student web hosting, wireless network available.

**Student life. Freshman orientation:** Mandatory. **Policies:** Religious observance required. **Housing:** Special housing for disabled, apartments, wellness housing available. $100 fully refundable deposit, deadline 7/15. **Activities:** Choral groups, drama, music ensembles, student government, student newspaper, Christian service activities, mission group.

**Athletics.** NCCAA. **Intercollegiate:** Basketball M, volleyball W. **Intramural:** Football (non-tackle), soccer, softball, table tennis. **Team name:** Suns.

**Student services.** Career counseling, financial aid counseling, personal counseling, veterans' counselor. **Physically disabled:** Services for visually impaired.

**Contact.** E-mail: admissions@fcc.edu
Phone: (407) 569-1172 Toll-free number: (877) 468-6322
Fax: (321) 206-2007
Jake Deer, Director of Admission, Florida Christian College, 1011 Bill Beck Boulevard, Kissimmee, FL 34744-4402

## Florida College
### Temple Terrace, Florida
### www.floridacollege.edu                    CB code: 5216

- Private 4-year liberal arts college
- Residential campus in large town
- 467 degree-seeking undergraduates: 3% part-time, 53% women, 4% African American, 1% Asian American, 6% Hispanic American, 1% Native American, 2% international
- 61% of applicants admitted
- SAT or ACT (ACT writing optional) required

**General.** Founded in 1944. Regionally accredited. **Degrees:** 41 bachelor's, 132 associate awarded. **ROTC:** Army, Air Force. **Location:** 2 miles from Tampa. **Calendar:** Semester, limited summer session. **Full-time faculty:** 37 total; 38% have terminal degrees, 22% women. **Part-time faculty:** 17 total; 6% have terminal degrees, 47% women. **Class size:** 70% < 20, 23% 20-39, 4% 40-49, 2% 50-99.

**Freshman class profile.** 349 applied, 213 admitted, 213 enrolled.

| Mid 50% test scores | | | |
|---|---|---|---|
| SAT critical reading: | 460-570 | GPA 3.50-3.74: | 11% |
| SAT math: | 440-570 | GPA 3.0-3.49: | 23% |
| SAT writing: | 440-580 | GPA 2.0-2.99: | 24% |
| ACT composite: | 20-25 | Out-of-state: | 65% |
| GPA 3.75 or higher: | 42% | Live on campus: | 96% |
| | | International: | 2% |

**Basis for selection.** 2 recommendations, 2.0 GPA required. Test scores, moral character important. Interview and essay recommended. Portfolio required for art majors. Essay required for international students. **Homeschooled:** Homeschool completion certification required. **Learning Disabled:** Provide voluntary declaration of disability form and documentation.

**High school preparation.** 16 units required. Required and recommended units include English 4, mathematics 3, social studies 2-3, science 2 (laboratory 2) and foreign language 2.

**2009-2010 Annual costs.** Tuition/fees: $12,150. Room/board: $6,440. Books/supplies: $1,300. Personal expenses: $2,500.

**2008-2009 Financial aid. Need-based:** 92 full-time freshmen applied for aid; 87 were judged to have need; 87 of these received aid. Average need met was 27%. Average scholarship/grant was $4,972; average loan $3,294. 53% of total undergraduate aid awarded as scholarships/grants, 47%

as loans/jobs. **Non-need-based:** Awarded to 353 full-time undergraduates, including 121 freshmen. Scholarships awarded for academics, athletics, music/drama, state residency.

**Application procedures. Admission:** Priority date 4/1; deadline 8/1 (postmark date). $30 fee, may be waived for applicants with need. Admission notification on a rolling basis. **Financial aid:** FAFSA, institutional form required. Applicants notified on a rolling basis starting 3/1; must reply within 2 week(s) of notification.

**Academics. Special study options:** Cross-registration, double major, independent study, teacher certification program. **Credit/placement by examination:** AP, CLEP, IB, SAT, ACT, institutional tests. 30 credit hours maximum toward associate degree, 30 toward bachelor's. **Support services:** Reduced course load, remedial instruction, study skills assistance, tutoring, writing center.

**Majors. Business:** Business admin. **Education:** Elementary. **Liberal arts:** Arts/sciences. **Theology:** Bible.

**Most popular majors.** Business/marketing 14%, education 26%, liberal arts 33%, philosophy/religious studies 21%, visual/performing arts 6%.

**Computing on campus.** 85 workstations in library, computer center. Dormitories wired for high-speed internet access and linked to campus network. Online library, wireless network available.

**Student life. Freshman orientation:** Mandatory. **Policies:** All campus residents expected to attend Sunday worship services. **Housing:** Guaranteed on-campus for all undergraduates. Single-sex dorms, special housing for disabled, wellness housing available. $150 partly refundable deposit, deadline 8/1. **Activities:** Bands, choral groups, drama, literary magazine, music ensembles, musical theater, student government, honor society, social clubs.

**Athletics.** USCAA. **Intercollegiate:** Basketball M, cheerleading M, cross-country, soccer, volleyball W. **Intramural:** Basketball, football (non-tackle), soccer, softball, volleyball. **Team name:** Falcons.

**Student services.** Financial aid counseling, health services, personal counseling, veterans' counselor.

**Contact.** E-mail: admission@floridacollege.edu
Phone: (813) 899-6716 Toll-free number: (800) 326-7655
Fax: (813) 899-1799
Matthew Qualls, Director of Admissions, Florida College, 119 North Glen Arven Avenue, Temple Terrace, FL 33617

## Florida Gulf Coast University
### Ft. Myers, Florida                        CB member
### www.fgcu.edu                              CB code: 5221

- Public 4-year university
- Residential campus in small city
- 9,493 degree-seeking undergraduates: 17% part-time, 56% women, 5% African American, 2% Asian American, 14% Hispanic American, 1% Native American, 2% international
- 1,050 degree-seeking graduate students
- 66% of applicants admitted
- SAT or ACT required
- 39% graduate within 6 years

**General.** Regionally accredited. **Degrees:** 1,343 bachelor's, 226 associate awarded; master's, professional offered. **Location:** 100 miles from Tampa, 125 miles from Miami. **Calendar:** Semester, extensive summer session. **Full-time faculty:** 348 total; 76% have terminal degrees, 17% minority, 47% women. **Part-time faculty:** 208 total; 12% minority, 50% women. **Class size:** 22% < 20, 56% 20-39, 10% 40-49, 10% 50-99, 2% >100. **Special facilities:** Natural wetlands, observatory.

**Freshman class profile.** 8,298 applied, 5,441 admitted, 1,991 enrolled.

| Mid 50% test scores | | | |
|---|---|---|---|
| SAT critical reading: | 480-560 | GPA 2.0-2.99: | 23% |
| SAT math: | 470-550 | Rank in top quarter: | 39% |
| SAT writing: | 460-540 | Rank in top tenth: | 13% |
| ACT composite: | 19-24 | Return as sophomores: | 76% |
| GPA 3.75 or higher: | 21% | Out-of-state: | 9% |
| GPA 3.50-3.74: | 15% | Live on campus: | 70% |
| GPA 3.0-3.49: | 41% | International: | 1% |

**Basis for selection.** Grades in academic units, test scores very important. **Homeschooled:** Transcript of courses and grades required. 1010 SAT (exclusive of Writing) or 21 ACT required.

**High school preparation.** 18 units required. Required units include English 4, mathematics 3, social studies 3, science 3 (laboratory 2), foreign language 2 and academic electives 3.

**2009-2010 Annual costs.** Tuition/fees: $4,427; $19,768 out-of-state. Room/board: $7,950. Books/supplies: $1,200. Personal expenses: $1,700.

**2008-2009 Financial aid. Need-based:** 1,579 full-time freshmen applied for aid; 586 were judged to have need; 586 of these received aid. Average need met was 63%. Average scholarship/grant was $4,456; average loan $3,912. 43% of total undergraduate aid awarded as scholarships/grants, 57% as loans/jobs. **Non-need-based:** Scholarships awarded for academics, alumni affiliation, athletics, leadership, minority status, music/drama, religious affiliation, state residency.

**Application procedures. Admission:** Priority date 2/15; deadline 6/2 (postmark date). $30 fee, may be waived for applicants with need. Admission notification on a rolling basis. **Financial aid:** Priority date 3/1, closing date 6/30. FAFSA required. Applicants notified on a rolling basis starting 2/15.

**Academics. Special study options:** Accelerated study, combined bachelor's/graduate degree, cross-registration, distance learning, double major, dual enrollment of high school students, honors, independent study, internships, student-designed major, study abroad, teacher certification program, Washington semester. **Credit/placement by examination:** AP, CLEP, IB, SAT, ACT, institutional tests. 45 credit hours maximum toward bachelor's degree. Credit received from one exam program may not be duplicated by another, nor duplicated through dual enrollment credit. **Support services:** Learning center, reduced course load, remedial instruction, study skills assistance, tutoring, writing center.

**Majors. Biology:** General, biotechnology. **Business:** Accounting, business admin, finance, management information systems, marketing, resort management. **Communications:** Media studies. **Computer sciences:** General. **Conservation:** Environmental studies, water/wetlands/marine. **Education:** General, early childhood, elementary, special. **Engineering:** General, biomedical, civil, environmental. **Foreign languages:** Spanish. **Health:** Athletic training, clinical lab science, community health, health care admin, health services, nursing (RN). **History:** General. **Legal studies:** Paralegal. **Liberal arts:** Arts/sciences. **Math:** General. **Parks/recreation:** Exercise sciences. **Philosophy/religion:** Philosophy. **Physical sciences:** Chemistry. **Protective services:** Criminal justice, criminalistics. **Psychology:** General. **Public administration:** Social work. **Social sciences:** Anthropology, political science, sociology. **Visual/performing arts:** Art, dramatic, music performance.

**Most popular majors.** Business/marketing 29%, communications/journalism 8%, education 13%, health sciences 11%, liberal arts 8%, security/protective services 9%.

**Computing on campus.** 302 workstations in dormitories, library, computer center. Dormitories wired for high-speed internet access and linked to campus network. Commuter students can connect to campus network. Online course registration, online library, helpline, student web hosting, wireless network available.

**Student life. Freshman orientation:** Mandatory, $35 fee. Preregistration for classes offered. Two-day summer program prior to fall semester; families invited. **Policies:** Student code of conduct in effect. **Housing:** Coed dorms, special housing for disabled, apartments, wellness housing available. **Activities:** Campus ministries, dance, drama, film society, international student organizations, literary magazine, Model UN, student government, student newspaper, College Republicans, College Democrats, Christian Campus Fellowship, Intervarsity Christian Fellowship, Navigators, Colleges Against Cancer, American Association of University Women Student Affiliates, human services student organization.

**Athletics.** NCAA. **Intercollegiate:** Baseball M, basketball, cross-country, golf, softball W, tennis, volleyball W. **Intramural:** Basketball, cross-country, football (non-tackle), soccer, softball, table tennis, tennis, volleyball, water polo. **Team name:** Eagles.

**Student services.** Adult student services, alcohol/substance abuse counseling, career counseling, student employment services, financial aid counseling, health services, minority student services, on-campus daycare, personal counseling, placement for graduates, veterans' counselor, women's services. **Physically disabled:** Services for visually, speech, hearing impaired.

**Contact.** E-mail: admissions@fgcu.edu
Phone: (239) 590-7878 Toll-free number: (888) 889-1095
Fax: (239) 590-7894
Marc Laviolette, Director of Admissions and Records, Florida Gulf Coast University, 10501 FGCU Boulevard South, Ft. Myers, FL 33965-6565

## Florida Hospital College of Health Sciences
**Orlando, Florida**
**www.FHCHS.edu**                                    **CB code: 3614**

▶ Private 4-year health science and nursing college affiliated with Seventh-day Adventists
▶ Commuter campus in large city

**General.** Regionally accredited. **Calendar:** Trimester.

**Annual costs/financial aid.** Fees vary according to program. Books/supplies: $1,950. Personal expenses: $1,296. Need-based financial aid available to full-time and part-time students.

**Contact.** Phone: (407) 303-7742
Director of Admissions, 671 Winyah Drive, Orlando, FL 32803

## Florida Institute of Technology
**Melbourne, Florida**                               **CB member**
**www.fit.edu**                                      **CB code: 5080**

▶ Private 4-year university
▶ Residential campus in small city
▶ 4,839 degree-seeking undergraduates: 19% part-time, 45% women, 14% African American, 2% Asian American, 7% Hispanic American, 1% Native American, 14% international
▶ 3,135 degree-seeking graduate students
▶ 74% of applicants admitted
▶ SAT or ACT (ACT writing optional) required
▶ 58% graduate within 6 years; 28% enter graduate study

**General.** Founded in 1958. Regionally accredited. **Degrees:** 449 bachelor's, 1 associate awarded; master's, doctoral offered. **ROTC:** Army. **Location:** 76 miles from Orlando. **Calendar:** Semester, limited summer session. **Full-time faculty:** 240 total; 89% have terminal degrees, 14% minority, 23% women. **Part-time faculty:** 338 total; 54% have terminal degrees, 9% minority, 29% women. **Class size:** 55% < 20, 38% 20-39, 4% 40-49, 3% 50-99. **Special facilities:** Center for aviation training, center for textile arts, center for autism treatment, center for science and engineering, microelectronics lab, research vessel, infectious diseases lab, laser optics and instrumentation lab, robotics and spatial systems lab, synoptic meteorology lab, Vero Beach marine lab.

**Freshman class profile.** 3,340 applied, 2,477 admitted, 539 enrolled.

| Mid 50% test scores | | | |
|---|---|---|---|
| SAT critical reading: | 500-610 | Rank in top tenth: | 27% |
| SAT math: | 540-660 | End year in good standing: | 75% |
| ACT composite: | 23-28 | Return as sophomores: | 75% |
| GPA 3.75 or higher: | 40% | Out-of-state: | 60% |
| GPA 3.50-3.74: | 15% | Live on campus: | 91% |
| GPA 3.0-3.49: | 32% | International: | 19% |
| GPA 2.0-2.99: | 13% | Fraternities: | 16% |
| Rank in top quarter: | 52% | Sororities: | 16% |

**Basis for selection.** Applications reviewed with reference to specific degree programs or for admission to first-year programs in engineering, science and general studies. High school curriculum, GPA, class rank, SAT/ACT, teachers' recommendations, experiential essay, special classes, clubs or teams that involve research projects/opportunities, and advanced problem-solving techniques important. Interview recommended. **Homeschooled:** Transcript of courses and grades required. Self-descriptive 1-page essay, proof of research project participation required. SAT Subject Test strongly recommended (English composition, Math Level II, any sciences related to desired area of study).

**High school preparation.** College-preparatory program recommended. 20 units required; 26 recommended. Required and recommended units include English 4, mathematics 3-4, social studies 1-3, history 2, science 3-4 (laboratory 3-4), foreign language 2, computer science 2 and academic electives 7.

**2010-2011 Annual costs.** Tuition/fees: $32,294. Room/board: $11,210. Books/supplies: $1,200. Personal expenses: $1,500.

**2009-2010 Financial aid. Need-based:** 417 full-time freshmen applied for aid; 374 were judged to have need; 374 of these received aid. Average need met was 83%. Average scholarship/grant was $20,802; average loan $3,501. 65% of total undergraduate aid awarded as scholarships/grants, 35% as loans/jobs. **Non-need-based:** Scholarships awarded for academics, alumni affiliation, athletics, ROTC, state residency.

**Application procedures. Admission:** Priority date 1/15; no deadline. $50 fee, may be waived for applicants with need, free for online applicants. Admission notification on a rolling basis beginning on or about 7/1. Must reply by May 1 or within 4 week(s) if notified thereafter. **Financial aid:** Priority date 3/1; no closing date. FAFSA required. Applicants notified on a rolling basis starting 2/15; must reply by 5/1 or within 4 week(s) of notification.

**Academics. Special study options:** Accelerated study, cooperative education, distance learning, double major, dual enrollment of high school students, ESL, independent study, internships, study abroad, teacher certification program. Dual degrees in computer engineering/electrical engineering, chemical engineering/chemistry, molecular/marine biology. **Credit/placement by examination:** AP, CLEP, IB, institutional tests. **Support services:** Learning center, pre-admission summer program, remedial instruction, study skills assistance, tutoring.

**Majors. Biology:** General, aquatic, biochemistry, biomedical sciences, ecology, marine, molecular. **Business:** Accounting, accounting/business management, business admin, e-commerce, information resources management, international, management information systems, marketing. **Communications:** General. **Computer sciences:** Computer science, information systems. **Conservation:** Environmental science. **Education:** Biology, chemistry, mathematics, middle, physics, science. **Engineering:** General, aerospace, chemical, civil, computer, electrical, mechanical, ocean, software. **Engineering technology:** Construction. **Health:** Health care admin. **Interdisciplinary:** Biological/physical sciences. **Liberal arts:** Humanities. **Math:** General, applied. **Physical sciences:** Analytical chemistry, chemistry, meteorology, oceanography, physics, planetary. **Psychology:** General, forensic. **Transportation:** Aviation, aviation management. **Other:** Aviation science and human factors, Biomathematics, Criminal justice, Interdisciplinary science/military science, Preprofessional physics.

**Most popular majors.** Biology 13%, engineering/engineering technologies 41%, physical sciences 9%, trade and industry 18%.

**Computing on campus.** 400 workstations in library, computer center, student center. Dormitories wired for high-speed internet access and linked to campus network. Commuter students can connect to campus network. Online course registration, online library, helpline, repair service, student web hosting, wireless network available.

**Student life. Freshman orientation:** Mandatory. Preregistration for classes offered. Three-day program in late August. **Policies:** Function in accordance with written constitution and bylaws approved by Dean of Students. **Housing:** Guaranteed on-campus for freshmen. Coed dorms, apartments, wellness housing available. $200 fully refundable deposit. **Activities:** Pep band, campus ministries, choral groups, dance, drama, international student organizations, literary magazine, radio station, student government, student newspaper, TV station, Newman Club, InterVarsity Christian Fellowship, Taiwanese student association, Saudi student house, National Society of Black Engineers, Society of Women Engineers, Latin American student association, Caribbean students organization, College Republican, Muslim student association.

**Athletics.** NCAA. **Intercollegiate:** Baseball M, basketball, cross-country, golf, rowing (crew) W, soccer, softball W, tennis, volleyball W. **Intramural:** Badminton, basketball, bowling, football (non-tackle), racquetball, soccer, softball, tennis, volleyball, water polo. **Team name:** Panthers.

**Student services.** Alcohol/substance abuse counseling, career counseling, student employment services, financial aid counseling, health services, personal counseling, veterans' counselor. **Physically disabled:** Services for visually, speech, hearing impaired.

**Contact.** E-mail: admission@fit.edu
Phone: (321) 674-8030 Toll-free number: (800) 888-4348
Fax: (321) 674-8004
Michael Perry, Director, Undergraduate Admissions, Florida Institute of Technology, 150 West University Boulevard, Melbourne, FL 32901-6975

---

### Florida International University
Miami, Florida
www.fiu.edu

CB member
CB code: 5206

- Public 4-year university
- Commuter campus in very large city

---

- 30,936 degree-seeking undergraduates: 28% part-time, 56% women, 12% African American, 3% Asian American, 65% Hispanic American, 5% international
- 7,272 degree-seeking graduate students
- 35% of applicants admitted
- SAT or ACT (ACT writing optional) required
- 49% graduate within 6 years

**General.** Founded in 1965. Regionally accredited. **Degrees:** 6,005 bachelor's, 51 associate awarded; master's, doctoral, professional offered. **ROTC:** Army, Air Force. **Location:** 10 miles from downtown. **Calendar:** Semester, extensive summer session. **Full-time faculty:** 854 total. **Part-time faculty:** 700 total. **Class size:** 24% < 20, 42% 20-39, 13% 40-49, 16% 50-99, 5% >100. **Special facilities:** Nature preserve, art museum.

**Freshman class profile.** 15,978 applied, 5,591 admitted, 2,013 enrolled.

| Mid 50% test scores | | | |
|---|---|---|---|
| SAT critical reading: | 540-620 | GPA 3.0-3.49: | 23% |
| SAT math: | 530-610 | GPA 2.0-2.99: | 4% |
| SAT writing: | 530-610 | End year in good standing: | 90% |
| ACT composite: | 24-27 | Return as sophomores: | 81% |
| GPA 3.75 or higher: | 50% | Out-of-state: | 4% |
| GPA 3.50-3.74: | 23% | Live on campus: | 24% |
| | | International: | 3% |

**Basis for selection.** 3.0 GPA required. Lower GPA considered with higher test score. SAT Subject Tests recommended. Audition required of music performance and theater majors. Portfolio required of art and architecture majors. Interview and essay recommended for academically marginal applicants. **Homeschooled:** State high school equivalency certificate required. GED required if equivalency certificate is not available.

**High school preparation.** College-preparatory program required. 18 units required. Required units include English 4, mathematics 3, social studies 3, science 3 (laboratory 2), foreign language 2 and academic electives 3.

**2009-2010 Annual costs.** Tuition/fees: $4,580; $16,980 out-of-state. Room/board: $11,946. Books/supplies: $1,048. Personal expenses: $2,216.

**2008-2009 Financial aid. Non-need-based:** Scholarships awarded for academics, art, athletics, minority status, music/drama, state residency.

**Application procedures. Admission:** Priority date 12/1; no deadline. $30 fee, may be waived for applicants with need. Admission notification on a rolling basis beginning on or about 12/1. **Financial aid:** Priority date 3/1, closing date 5/15. FAFSA required. Applicants notified on a rolling basis; must reply by 5/1 or within 4 week(s) of notification.

**Academics. Special study options:** Accelerated study, combined bachelor's/graduate degree, cooperative education, distance learning, double major, dual enrollment of high school students, ESL, exchange student, honors, independent study, internships, study abroad, teacher certification program, weekend college. **Credit/placement by examination:** CLEP, IB, SAT, ACT, institutional tests. 45 credit hours maximum toward bachelor's degree. **Support services:** Learning center, pre-admission summer program, study skills assistance, tutoring.

**Honors college/program.** 3.5 weighted GPA and commensurate SAT/ACT scores required. Students may pursue any major while completing honors curriculum.

**Majors. Area/ethnic studies:** Asian, women's. **Biology:** General, marine. **Business:** Accounting, business admin, finance, hospitality admin, human resources, international, management information systems, marketing, real estate. **Communications:** General. **Computer sciences:** General, information technology. **Conservation:** General. **Education:** Art, early childhood, elementary, physical, special. **Engineering:** Biomedical, civil, computer, electrical, environmental, mechanical. **Engineering technology:** Construction. **Foreign languages:** French, Portuguese, Spanish. **Health:** Health care admin, nursing (RN). **History:** General. **Liberal arts:** Arts/sciences. **Math:** General, statistics. **Parks/recreation:** Facilities management. **Philosophy/religion:** Philosophy, religion. **Physical sciences:** Chemistry, geology, physics. **Protective services:** Criminal justice. **Psychology:** General. **Public administration:** General, social work. **Social sciences:** Economics, geography, international relations, political science, sociology. **Visual/performing arts:** Art history/conservation, dramatic, studio arts.

**Most popular majors.** Business/marketing 33%, education 6%, engineering/engineering technologies 6%, health sciences 10%, psychology 8%, social sciences 8%.

**Computing on campus.** 1,900 workstations in library, computer center, student center. Dormitories wired for high-speed internet access and linked to campus network. Commuter students can connect to campus network.

Online course registration, online library, repair service, wireless network available.

**Student life. Freshman orientation:** Mandatory, $90 fee. Preregistration for classes offered. 2-day overnight program. **Housing:** Coed dorms, apartments, fraternity/sorority housing available. $100 nonrefundable deposit. **Activities:** Bands, choral groups, drama, film society, music ensembles, Model UN, opera, radio station, student government, student newspaper, symphony orchestra, over 150 student organizations available.

**Athletics.** NCAA. **Intercollegiate:** Baseball M, basketball M, cross-country, football (tackle) M, golf W, soccer, softball W, swimming, tennis W, track and field, volleyball W. **Intramural:** Basketball W, cross-country, golf W, sailing, soccer, softball W, swimming, tennis W, volleyball W. **Team name:** Golden Panthers.

**Student services.** Adult student services, alcohol/substance abuse counseling, career counseling, student employment services, financial aid counseling, health services, minority student services, on-campus daycare, personal counseling, placement for graduates, veterans' counselor. **Physically disabled:** Services for visually, speech, hearing impaired.

**Contact.** E-mail: admiss@fiu.edu
Phone: (305) 348-2363 Fax: (305) 348-3648
Renee Peterson, Associate Director of Admissions, Florida International University, University Park Campus, PC 140, Miami, FL 33199

## Florida Memorial University
Miami Gardens, Florida — CB member
www.fmuniv.edu — CB code: 5217

- Private 4-year liberal arts college affiliated with American Baptist Churches in the USA
- Residential campus in very large city
- 1,933 degree-seeking undergraduates
- Application essay required

**General.** Founded in 1879. Regionally accredited. 4 branch campuses. **Degrees:** 190 bachelor's awarded; master's offered. **ROTC:** Army. **Location:** 15 miles from downtown Miami. **Calendar:** Semester, limited summer session. **Full-time faculty:** 95 total. **Part-time faculty:** 65 total. **Class size:** 70% < 20, 28% 20-39, 1% 40-49, less than 1% 50-99. **Special facilities:** Black archives, airway science building with simulator and air traffic control tower.

**Freshman class profile.**

| | | | |
|---|---|---|---|
| GPA 3.75 or higher: | 1% | GPA 2.0-2.99: | 71% |
| GPA 3.50-3.74: | 5% | Out-of-state: | 20% |
| GPA 3.0-3.49: | 15% | Live on campus: | 80% |

**Basis for selection.** 2.0 GPA required. School achievement record, test scores, interview, recommendations, and alumni affiliation considered. SAT or ACT recommended. Interview recommended.

**High school preparation.** 15 units recommended. Recommended units include English 4, mathematics 4, social studies 2, science 3 and foreign language 2. College-preparatory program strongly recommended.

**2009-2010 Annual costs.** Tuition/fees: $13,181. Room/board: $5,554. Books/supplies: $1,500. Personal expenses: $3,500.

**Financial aid. Additional information:** Need-based financial aid available to part-time students taking 6 credits or more per semester.

**Application procedures. Admission:** No deadline. $15 fee, may be waived for applicants with need. Admission notification on a rolling basis. **Financial aid:** No deadline. Applicants notified on a rolling basis; must reply within 2 week(s) of notification.

**Academics. Special study options:** Combined bachelor's/graduate degree, cooperative education, double major, dual enrollment of high school students, honors, independent study, internships, liberal arts/career combination, study abroad, teacher certification program, weekend college. **Credit/placement by examination:** AP, CLEP, institutional tests. 30 credit hours maximum toward bachelor's degree. **Support services:** Learning center, pre-admission summer program, remedial instruction, study skills assistance, tutoring, writing center.

**Majors. Biology:** General. **Business:** Accounting, business admin, management information systems. **Computer sciences:** General, computer science. **Education:** Elementary, physical. **Health:** Clinical lab science. **Math:** General. **Psychology:** General. **Public administration:** General. **Social sciences:** Sociology. **Transportation:** Aviation.

**Most popular majors.** Biology 9%, business/marketing 17%, computer/information sciences 11%, education 21%, psychology 9%, social sciences 16%.

**Computing on campus.** 300 workstations in dormitories, library, computer center, student center. Dormitories wired for high-speed internet access and linked to campus network. Commuter students can connect to campus network. Online library, helpline, repair service, wireless network available.

**Student life. Freshman orientation:** Mandatory. Preregistration for classes offered. **Housing:** Guaranteed on-campus for freshmen. Single-sex dorms available. **Activities:** Jazz band, choral groups, international student organizations, music ensembles, musical theater, student government, student newspaper, TV station, Christian student union, broadcasting club, Junior NAACP, Toastmasters, Professional Women of Tomorrow.

**Athletics.** NAIA. **Intercollegiate:** Baseball M, basketball, track and field, volleyball W. **Intramural:** Baseball M, basketball, soccer M, softball W, swimming, tennis, volleyball. **Team name:** Figthing lions.

**Student services.** Chaplain/spiritual director, career counseling, student employment services, health services, minority student services, personal counseling, placement for graduates.

**Contact.** E-mail: admit@fmuniv.edu
Phone: (305) 626-3750 Fax: (305) 623-1462
Peggy Martin, Director of Admissions, Florida Memorial University, 15800 Northwest 42 Avenue, Miami Gardens, FL 33054

## Florida Southern College
Lakeland, Florida — CB member
www.flsouthern.edu — CB code: 5218

- Private 4-year liberal arts college affiliated with United Methodist Church
- Residential campus in small city
- 1,881 degree-seeking undergraduates: 3% part-time, 58% women, 6% African American, 2% Asian American, 8% Hispanic American, 1% Native American, 3% international
- 148 degree-seeking graduate students
- 69% of applicants admitted
- SAT or ACT (ACT writing optional), application essay required
- 55% graduate within 6 years; 27% enter graduate study

**General.** Founded in 1885. Regionally accredited. **Degrees:** 550 bachelor's awarded; master's offered. **ROTC:** Army, Air Force. **Location:** 30 miles from Tampa, 50 miles from Orlando. **Calendar:** Semester, limited summer session. **Full-time faculty:** 109 total; 87% have terminal degrees, 9% minority, 40% women. **Part-time faculty:** 107 total; 20% have terminal degrees, 5% minority, 49% women. **Class size:** 47% < 20, 49% 20-39, 3% 40-49. **Special facilities:** Planetarium, Frank Lloyd Wright visitor center, boathouse, water dome.

**Freshman class profile.** 2,437 applied, 1,692 admitted, 553 enrolled.

| Mid 50% test scores | | | |
|---|---|---|---|
| SAT critical reading: | 490-580 | Rank in top quarter: | 48% |
| SAT math: | 480-580 | Rank in top tenth: | 21% |
| SAT writing: | 470-570 | End year in good standing: | 92% |
| ACT composite: | 21-25 | Return as sophomores: | 79% |
| GPA 3.75 or higher: | 26% | Out-of-state: | 31% |
| GPA 3.50-3.74: | 17% | Live on campus: | 70% |
| GPA 3.0-3.49: | 34% | International: | 2% |
| GPA 2.0-2.99: | 23% | Fraternities: | 33% |
| | | Sororities: | 23% |

**Basis for selection.** School achievement record most important, followed by test scores and recommendations. Character and motivation, demonstrated leadership and/or service, and extracurricular activities also important. No deadline for submitting SAT or ACT scores. Interview recommended. Audition required for music; audition recommended (required for scholarship consideration) for theater majors. Portfolio recommended (required for scholarship consideration) for art majors. **Homeschooled:** Transcript of courses and grades required.

**High school preparation.** College-preparatory program required. 18 units required. Required and recommended units include English 4, mathematics 3, social studies 3, history 3, science 2 (laboratory 2), foreign language 2 and academic electives 2.

**2010-2011 Annual costs.** Tuition/fees (projected): $24,662. Room/board: $8,310. Books/supplies: $1,150. Personal expenses: $1,050.

**2009-2010 Financial aid. Need-based:** 489 full-time freshmen applied for aid; 423 were judged to have need; 421 of these received aid. Average

need met was 68%. Average scholarship/grant was $6,470; average loan $3,325. 83% of total undergraduate aid awarded as scholarships/grants, 17% as loans/jobs. **Non-need-based:** Scholarships awarded for academics, alumni affiliation, art, athletics, job skills, leadership, minority status, music/drama, religious affiliation, ROTC, state residency.

**Application procedures. Admission:** Priority date 3/1; no deadline. $30 fee, may be waived for applicants with need. Admission notification on a rolling basis beginning on or about 1/15. Must reply by May 1 or within 2 week(s) if notified thereafter. Housing deposit refundable only through May 1. **Financial aid:** Priority date 3/1, closing date 7/1. FAFSA, institutional form required. Applicants notified on a rolling basis starting 3/1; must reply within 3 week(s) of notification.

**Academics. Special study options:** Combined bachelor's/graduate degree, double major, dual enrollment of high school students, external degree, honors, independent study, internships, liberal arts/career combination, New York semester, student-designed major, study abroad, teacher certification program, United Nations semester, Washington semester. **Credit/placement by examination:** AP, CLEP, IB, SAT, ACT. 60 credit hours maximum toward bachelor's degree. **Support services:** Reduced course load, study skills assistance, tutoring, writing center.

**Majors. Agriculture:** Business, horticultural science, ornamental horticulture, turf management. **Biology:** General, Biochemistry/biophysics and molecular biology, environmental. **Business:** Accounting, business admin, finance, international, management information systems, marketing. **Communications:** Advertising, broadcast journalism, journalism, public relations. **Education:** General, art, elementary, music, physical. **Foreign languages:** Spanish. **Health:** Athletic training, nursing (RN), predental, premedicine, preveterinary. **History:** General. **Interdisciplinary:** Math/computer science. **Liberal arts:** Humanities. **Math:** General. **Parks/recreation:** Sports admin. **Philosophy/religion:** Philosophy, religion. **Physical sciences:** Chemistry. **Psychology:** General. **Social sciences:** General, criminology, economics, political science, sociology. **Theology:** Youth ministry. **Visual/performing arts:** Art history/conservation, dramatic, graphic design, music management, music theory/composition, studio arts, theater design.

**Most popular majors.** Biology 6%, business/marketing 29%, communications/journalism 7%, education 16%, health sciences 8%, social sciences 10%, visual/performing arts 7%.

**Computing on campus.** 425 workstations in dormitories, library, computer center. Dormitories wired for high-speed internet access and linked to campus network. Commuter students can connect to campus network. Online course registration, online library, helpline, wireless network available.

**Student life. Freshman orientation:** Mandatory, $100 fee. Preregistration for classes offered. 4-days prior to classes for fall semester. **Housing:** Guaranteed on-campus for all undergraduates. Coed dorms, single-sex dorms, special housing for disabled, apartments, fraternity/sorority housing, wellness housing available. $500 fully refundable deposit, deadline 5/1. **Activities:** Bands, campus ministries, choral groups, dance, drama, international student organizations, literary magazine, music ensembles, musical theater, opera, student government, student newspaper, symphony orchestra, Wesley Fellowship, Fellowship of Christian Athletes, Upper Room Ministries, Antioch 2, Beyond Campus Ministries, Newman Club, social justice ministry, Jewish student opportunities, Sandwich Ministry to the homeless.

**Athletics.** NCAA. **Intercollegiate:** Baseball M, basketball, cross-country, golf, lacrosse M, soccer, softball W, swimming, tennis, track and field, volleyball W. **Intramural:** Basketball, bowling, cross-country, football (non-tackle), golf, soccer, softball, swimming, table tennis, tennis, volleyball. **Team name:** Moccasins.

**Student services.** Adult student services, alcohol/substance abuse counseling, chaplain/spiritual director, career counseling, student employment services, financial aid counseling, health services, minority student services, personal counseling, placement for graduates.

**Contact.** E-mail: fscadm@flsouthern.edu
Phone: (863) 680-4131 Toll-free number: (800) 274-4131
Fax: (863) 680-4120
Bill Langston, Director of Admission, Florida Southern College, 111 Lake Hollingsworth Drive, Lakeland, FL 33801-5698

## Florida State University
**Tallahassee, Florida**                              CB member
**www.fsu.edu**                                      CB code: 5219

- Public 4-year university
- Residential campus in small city

- 30,251 degree-seeking undergraduates: 9% part-time, 55% women, 10% African American, 4% Asian American, 13% Hispanic American, 1% Native American
- 8,536 degree-seeking graduate students
- 61% of applicants admitted
- SAT or ACT with writing, application essay required

**General.** Founded in 1851. Regionally accredited. **Degrees:** 7,630 bachelor's awarded; master's, doctoral, professional offered. **ROTC:** Army, Naval, Air Force. **Location:** 191 miles from Pensacola, 163 miles from Jacksonville. **Calendar:** Semester, extensive summer session. **Full-time faculty:** 1,407 total. **Part-time faculty:** 291 total. **Special facilities:** Marine laboratory/aquarium, institute of molecular biophysics, national high magnetic field laboratory, music research center, accelerator, oceanographic institute, planetarium, reservation, golf course, Middle East center, institute of science and public affairs, center for the advancement of human rights.

**Freshman class profile.** 23,439 applied, 14,308 admitted, 5,967 enrolled.

| Mid 50% test scores | | GPA 2.0-2.99: | 2% |
|---|---|---|---|
| SAT critical reading: | 550-640 | Rank in top quarter: | 61% |
| SAT math: | 560-650 | Rank in top tenth: | 34% |
| SAT writing: | 540-630 | Out-of-state: | 11% |
| ACT composite: | 24-28 | Live on campus: | 71% |
| GPA 3.75 or higher: | 45% | Fraternities: | 5% |
| GPA 3.50-3.74: | 29% | Sororities: | 8% |
| GPA 3.0-3.49: | 24% | | |

**Basis for selection.** Most Florida residents accepted have B+ average in academic subjects and 1100 SAT (exclusive of Writing) or 24 ACT. Out-of-state students must meet higher standards. Audition required of music, dance, BFA theater majors. Portfolio required of BFA art, interior design majors. Departmental application required for motion picture, television, and recording art programs. **Homeschooled:** Statement describing homeschool structure and mission, transcript of courses and grades required. Must provide detailed course syllabi with complete course description and names of textbooks used.

**High school preparation.** 19 units required; 23 recommended. Required and recommended units include English 4, mathematics 4, social studies 1-2, history 2, science 3-4 (laboratory 2), foreign language 2-4 and academic electives 3. Math courses must be algebra I and above; 2 units of same foreign language required; at least 3 units English with substantial writing requirements; social studies must include history. Additional consideration given for completion of higher level courses (AP, IB, honors, calculus and/or foreign language IV or V) and for completion of 4 or more senior academic courses.

**2009-2010 Annual costs.** Tuition/fees: $4,566; $19,011 out-of-state. Room/board: $8,730. Books/supplies: $1,000. Personal expenses: $3,462.

**2009-2010 Financial aid. Non-need-based:** Scholarships awarded for academics, athletics, state residency.

**Application procedures. Admission:** Priority date 10/15; deadline 1/19 (receipt date). $30 fee. Application must be submitted online. Notification on 12/8 and 3/16. Must reply by May 1 or within 2 week(s) if notified thereafter. Those applying before 10/15 who are denied admission are given additional opportunities to improve application standing. **Financial aid:** No deadline. FAFSA required. Applicants notified on a rolling basis starting 3/15.

**Academics.** 2+2 distance learning available in cooperation with selected Florida community colleges includes programs in computer science, interdisciplinary social sciences, and nursing (RN to BSN). **Special study options:** Accelerated study, combined bachelor's/graduate degree, cooperative education, cross-registration, distance learning, double major, dual enrollment of high school students, ESL, honors, independent study, internships, study abroad, teacher certification program. Cooperative programs with Florida Agricultural and Mechanical University and Tallahassee Community College; degree in three years; International year abroad, year-round study abroad in England, Italy, Panama, Spain; summer study abroad in Australia, Brazil, China, Costa Rica, Croatia, Czech Republic, Ecuador, England, France, Ireland, Italy, Japan, Netherlands, Russia, Switzerland. **Credit/placement by examination:** AP, CLEP, IB, SAT, ACT, institutional tests. 30 credit hours maximum toward associate degree, 45 toward bachelor's. English AP credit not awarded for more than 1 exam. **Support services:** Learning center, reduced course load, study skills assistance, tutoring, writing center.

**Majors. Area/ethnic studies:** American, Asian, Caribbean, Central/Eastern European, Latin American, Russian/Slavic. **Biology:** General, biochemistry. **Business:** Accounting, actuarial science, finance, hospitality admin, human resources, insurance, international, management information systems, marketing, real estate. **Communications:** Advertising, public relations. **Computer sciences:** General, computer science, information technology. **Conservation:** Environmental studies. **Education:** Early childhood, elementary, English, foreign languages, mathematics, music, physical, physics, science, social science. **Engineering:** Chemical, civil, computer, electrical, environmental, industrial, materials, mechanical, software. **Family/consumer sciences:** General, child development, clothing/textiles, family studies, food/nutrition, merchandising. **Foreign languages:** Ancient Greek, Chinese, French, German, Italian, Japanese, Latin, Russian, Spanish. **Health:** Athletic training, audiology/speech pathology, dietetics, music therapy, nursing (RN), predental, premedicine, prepharmacy, preveterinary. **History:** General. **Interdisciplinary:** Nutrition sciences. **Legal studies:** Prelaw. **Liberal arts:** Humanities. **Math:** General, applied, computational, statistics. **Parks/recreation:** Exercise sciences, facilities management, health/fitness, sports admin. **Philosophy/religion:** Philosophy, religion. **Physical sciences:** Atmospheric science, chemistry, physics. **Psychology:** General. **Public administration:** Social work. **Social sciences:** General, applied economics, criminology, economics, geography, international relations, political science, sociology. **Visual/performing arts:** Acting, art history/conservation, cinematography, dance, dramatic, interior design, jazz, music history, music performance, music theory/composition, piano/organ, stringed instruments, studio arts, theater design, voice/opera. **Other:** Computational biology, Computer Criminology.

**Most popular majors.** Business/marketing 19%, education 7%, English 6%, family/consumer sciences 6%, social sciences 18%, visual/performing arts 6%.

**Computing on campus.** PC or laptop required. 2,958 workstations in dormitories, library, computer center, student center. Dormitories wired for high-speed internet access and linked to campus network. Commuter students can connect to campus network. Online course registration, online library, helpline, repair service, student web hosting, wireless network available.

**Student life. Freshman orientation:** Mandatory, $90 fee. Preregistration for classes offered. Held during Summer. **Housing:** Coed dorms, single-sex dorms, special housing for disabled, apartments, fraternity/sorority housing, wellness housing available. $225 partly refundable deposit. Honor residences and living and learning communities available. **Activities:** Bands, campus ministries, choral groups, dance, drama, film society, literary magazine, music ensembles, musical theater, opera, radio station, student government, student newspaper, symphony orchestra, TV station, Hillel, Christian student association, Catholic student union, Campus Crusade for Christ, College Democrats, College Republicans, black student union, Hispanic student union, American civil liberties union.

**Athletics.** NCAA. **Intercollegiate:** Baseball M, basketball, cheerleading, cross-country, diving, football (tackle) M, golf, soccer W, softball W, swimming, tennis, track and field, volleyball W. **Intramural:** Basketball, bowling, field hockey, football (non-tackle), golf, racquetball, soccer, softball, swimming, table tennis, tennis, volleyball, wrestling. **Team name:** Seminoles.

**Student services.** Adult student services, alcohol/substance abuse counseling, career counseling, student employment services, financial aid counseling, health services, legal services, minority student services, on-campus daycare, personal counseling, placement for graduates, veterans' counselor, women's services. **Physically disabled:** Services for visually, speech, hearing impaired.

**Contact.** E-mail: admissions@admin.fsu.edu
Phone: (850) 644-6200 Fax: (850) 644-0197
Janice Finney, Director of Admissions, Florida State University, PO Box 3062400, Tallahassee, FL 32306-2400

## Full Sail University
**Winter Park, Florida**
**www.fullsail.edu**  CB code: 3164

- For-profit 4-year visual arts and technical college
- Commuter campus in very large city
- 7,379 degree-seeking undergraduates
- 1,297 graduate students

**General.** Accredited by ACCSC. **Degrees:** 3,955 bachelor's, 1,620 associate awarded; master's offered. **Location:** 8 miles from Orlando. **Calendar:** Continuous. **Full-time faculty:** 723 total. **Special facilities:** Recording studios, production suites, sound stages, green screen facility, motion capture production studio, game studio.

**Basis for selection.** Open admission, but selective for some programs. Applicants for game design and development bachelor's degree program must have A average in Algebra II. Geometry, physics and programming

experience also recommended. **Homeschooled:** Diplomas recognized if applicant's state board of education recognizes them. **Learning Disabled:** Require documentation, not more than 3 years old, describing learning disabilities.

**2010-2011 Annual costs.** Degree programs leading to an associate and bachelor range from $36,775 - $75,775. Includes books and supplies.

**Application procedures. Admission:** No deadline. $75 fee. Admission notification on a rolling basis. **Financial aid:** No deadline. FAFSA required. Applicants notified on a rolling basis; must reply within 2 week(s) of notification.

**Academics.** Cognitive development course offered at no charge. Tutoring offered through federal work study program. **Special study options:** Accelerated study, combined bachelor's/graduate degree, cooperative education, internships. **Credit/placement by examination:** CLEP, institutional tests. Students may take test-out exam in each course for which credit is being sought. If credit earned, tuition and program hours reduced accordingly. Minimum of 25% of degree program's semester hours or equivalent must be earned in residence to receive degree. **Support services:** Study skills assistance, tutoring, writing center.

**Majors. Communications technology:** Animation/special effects. **Computer sciences:** Game design, web page design. **Visual/performing arts:** Cinematography. **Other:** Entertainment business.

**Computing on campus.** 56 workstations in library, computer center. Online library, helpline, repair service, wireless network available.

**Student life. Freshman orientation:** Mandatory. **Policies:** Alcohol and drug free facility. **Activities:** Student government.

**Student services.** Career counseling, financial aid counseling, placement for graduates.

**Contact.** E-mail: admissions@fullsail.com
Phone: (407) 679-6333 Toll-free number: (800) 226-7625
Mary Beth Plank, Vice President of Admissions, Full Sail University, 3300 University Boulevard, Winter Park, FL 32792-7429

## Hobe Sound Bible College
**Hobe Sound, Florida**
**www.hsbc.edu**  CB code: 5306

- Private 4-year Bible college affiliated with interdenominational tradition
- Residential campus in small town
- 234 degree-seeking undergraduates
- SAT or ACT (ACT writing optional) required

**General.** Founded in 1960. Accredited by ABHE. **Degrees:** 23 bachelor's, 7 associate awarded. **Location:** 25 miles from West Palm Beach. **Calendar:** 4-1-4, limited summer session. **Full-time faculty:** 10 total. **Part-time faculty:** 10 total.

**Freshman class profile.**

| Mid 50% test scores | | | |
|---|---|---|---|
| SAT critical reading: | 450-680 | SAT math: | 430-570 |
| | | ACT composite: | 14-23 |

**Basis for selection.** Recommendations, essay, religious commitment important. **Homeschooled:** Must submit official transcripts from reputable organizations documenting completion of all academic coursework required for high school diploma.

**2009-2010 Annual costs.** Tuition/fees: $5,200. Room/board: $4,680. Books/supplies: $450. Personal expenses: $2,000.

**2009-2010 Financial aid. Non-need-based:** Scholarships awarded for academics, leadership.

**Application procedures. Admission:** Closing date 8/25. $25 fee, may be waived for applicants with need. Admission notification on a rolling basis beginning on or about 3/1. **Financial aid:** Closing date 8/1. FAFSA required.

**Academics.** Double major required of all students in 4-year programs. All students complete major in Bible as well as major in Christian vocational field. **Special study options:** Distance learning, double major, dual enrollment of high school students, ESL, external degree, internships, teacher certification program. **Credit/placement by examination:** CLEP, institutional tests. **Support services:** Reduced course load, remedial instruction.

**Majors. Education:** Elementary, English, mathematics, music. **Philosophy/religion:** Religion. **Theology:** Bible, missionary, sacred music, theology. **Visual/performing arts:** Music performance, piano/organ. **Other:** Child Evangelism.

**Computing on campus.** 10 workstations in computer center.

**Student life. Freshman orientation:** Mandatory. **Policies:** Religious observance required. **Housing:** Guaranteed on-campus for all undergraduates. Single-sex dorms, apartments available. Unmarried students under 25 required to live in campus dormitories or with parents. **Activities:** Concert band, choral groups, music ensembles, student government, Christian service organizations.

**Athletics. Intramural:** Basketball, football (tackle) M, racquetball, soccer, softball, tennis, volleyball.

**Student services.** Health services, personal counseling.

**Contact.** E-mail: admissions@hsbc.edu
Phone: (772) 546-5534 ext. 1015 Toll-free number: (800) 881-5534
Fax: (772) 545-1422
Judy Fay, Director of Admissions, Hobe Sound Bible College, Box 1065, Hobe Sound, FL 33475

## Hodges University
### Naples, Florida
www.hodges.edu    CB code: 7113

- Private 4-year university and business college
- Commuter campus in small city
- 2,032 degree-seeking undergraduates: 22% part-time, 69% women, 17% African American, 2% Asian American, 27% Hispanic American
- 254 degree-seeking graduate students
- 91% of applicants admitted

**General.** Founded in 1990. Regionally accredited. **Degrees:** 307 bachelor's, 127 associate awarded; master's offered. **Location:** 110 miles from Miami, 180 miles from Tampa. **Calendar:** Trimester, extensive summer session. **Full-time faculty:** 58 total; 59% have terminal degrees, 14% minority, 41% women. **Part-time faculty:** 57 total; 37% have terminal degrees, 7% minority, 56% women. **Class size:** 68% < 20, 28% 20-39, 2% 40-49, 2% 50-99.

**Freshman class profile.** 331 applied, 300 admitted, 287 enrolled.

**Out-of-state:** 5%    **International:** 1%

**Basis for selection.** Essay and interview important; level of interest very important.

**2009-2010 Annual costs.** Tuition/fees: $14,330. Books/supplies: $1,000. Personal expenses: $530.

**2009-2010 Financial aid. Need-based:** 246 full-time freshmen applied for aid; 214 were judged to have need; 214 of these received aid. Average need met was 66%. Average scholarship/grant was $2,600; average loan $2,800. 56% of total undergraduate aid awarded as scholarships/grants, 44% as loans/jobs. **Non-need-based:** Awarded to 598 full-time undergraduates, including 135 freshmen. Scholarships awarded for academics.

**Application procedures. Admission:** No deadline. $20 fee. Admission notification on a rolling basis. **Financial aid:** Priority date 9/7; no closing date. FAFSA required. Applicants notified on a rolling basis starting 7/7.

**Academics. Special study options:** Accelerated study, combined bachelor's/graduate degree, cooperative education, distance learning, double major, ESL, independent study, internships, weekend college. **Credit/placement by examination:** AP, CLEP, IB, institutional tests. **Support services:** Remedial instruction, tutoring.

**Majors. Business:** Accounting, business admin. **Computer sciences:** Information technology. **Health:** Health care admin. **Legal studies:** Paralegal. **Protective services:** Criminal justice.

**Most popular majors.** Business/marketing 46%, computer/information sciences 7%, health sciences 12%, interdisciplinary studies 23%.

**Computing on campus.** 500 workstations in library, computer center. Wireless network available.

**Student life. Freshman orientation:** Mandatory. **Activities:** Literary magazine.

**Student services.** Career counseling, financial aid counseling, personal counseling, placement for graduates.

**Contact.** E-mail: admit@hodges.edu
Phone: (239) 513-1122 Toll-free number: (800) 466-8017
Fax: (239) 513-9071
Rita Lampus, Vice President of Student Enrollment Management, Hodges University, 2655 Northbrooke Drive, Naples, FL 34119

## International Academy of Design and Technology: Orlando
### Orlando, Florida
www.iadt.edu    CB code: 4366

- For-profit 4-year career college
- Very large city

**General.** Accredited by ACICS. **Location:** Downtown. **Calendar:** Quarter.

**Contact.** Phone: (407) 857-2300
Vice President Admissions and Marketing, 5959 Lake Ellenor Drive, Orlando, FL 32809

## International Academy of Design and Technology: Tampa
### Tampa, Florida
www.academy.edu    CB code: 7114

- For-profit 4-year visual arts and technical college
- Commuter campus in very large city
- 2,561 degree-seeking undergraduates
- Interview required

**General.** Accredited by ACICS. **Degrees:** 271 bachelor's, 194 associate awarded; master's offered. **Calendar:** Quarter, extensive summer session. **Full-time faculty:** 12 total. **Part-time faculty:** 118 total.

**Basis for selection.** Open admission. Essay recommended. **Learning Disabled:** Submit Auxiliary Aid Application.

**2009-2010 Annual costs.** Tuition/fees: $18,780. Required fees vary from $300-$600.

**2008-2009 Financial aid. Non-need-based:** Scholarships awarded for academics.

**Application procedures. Admission:** No deadline. $50 fee, may be waived for applicants with need. Admission notification on a rolling basis. **Financial aid:** No deadline. FAFSA required.

**Academics. Special study options:** Accelerated study, cooperative education, internships, study abroad. **Credit/placement by examination:** AP, CLEP, institutional tests. 67 credit hours maximum toward associate degree, 135 toward bachelor's. **Support services:** Learning center, study skills assistance, tutoring.

**Majors. Business:** Merchandising. **Communications technology:** Animation/special effects. **Computer sciences:** Web page design. **Visual/performing arts:** Digital art, fashion design, interior design. **Other:** Audio production.

**Computing on campus.** Wireless network available.

**Student life. Freshman orientation:** Mandatory. Preregistration for classes offered.

**Student services.** Adult student services, student employment services, financial aid counseling, placement for graduates, veterans' counselor.

**Contact.** E-mail: admissions@academy.edu
Phone: (813) 881-0007 Toll-free number: (800) 222-3369
Fax: (813) 881-0008
Melissa Clark, Director of Admissions, International Academy of Design and Technology: Tampa, 5104 Eisenhower Boulevard, Tampa, FL 33634

## ITT Technical Institute: Ft. Lauderdale
### Ft. Lauderdale, Florida
www.itt-tech.edu    CB code: 2700

- For-profit 4-year technical college
- Commuter campus in small city

**General.** Accredited by ACICS. **Calendar:** Quarter.

**Contact.** Phone: (954) 476-9300
Director of Recruitment, 3401 South University Drive, Ft. Lauderdale, FL 33328

---

## ITT Technical Institute: Jacksonville
Jacksonville, Florida
www.itt-tech.edu                    CB code: 2716

▸ For-profit 4-year technical college
▸ Commuter campus in very large city

**General.** Accredited by ACICS. **Calendar:** Quarter.

**Contact.** Phone: (904) 573-9100
Director of Recruitment, 6600-10 Youngerman Circle, Jacksonville, FL 32244

---

## ITT Technical Institute: Lake Mary
Lake Mary, Florida
www.itt-tech.edu

▸ For-profit 4-year technical college
▸ Commuter campus in large town

**General.** Accredited by ACICS. **Calendar:** Quarter.

**Contact.** Phone: (407) 660-2900
Director of Recruitment, 1400 International Parkway South, Lake Mary, FL 32746

---

## ITT Technical Institute: Miami
Miami, Florida
www.itt-tech.edu                    CB code: 2733

▸ For-profit 4-year technical college
▸ Commuter campus in large city

**General.** Accredited by ACICS. **Calendar:** Quarter.

**Contact.** Phone: (305) 477-3080
Director of Recruitment, 7955 12th Street, Suite 119, Miami, FL 33126

---

## ITT Technical Institute: Tampa
Tampa, Florida
www.itt-tech.edu                    CB code: 2145

▸ For-profit 4-year technical college
▸ Commuter campus in large city

**General.** Founded in 1981. Accredited by ACICS. **Calendar:** Quarter.

**Contact.** Phone: (813) 885-2244
Director of Recruitment, 4809 Memorial Highway, Tampa, FL 33634

---

## Jacksonville University
Jacksonville, Florida                    CB member
www.ju.edu                               CB code: 5331

▸ Private 4-year university and liberal arts college
▸ Residential campus in very large city
▸ 3,084 degree-seeking undergraduates: 25% part-time, 60% women, 19% African American, 3% Asian American, 6% Hispanic American, 1% Native American, 2% international
▸ 356 degree-seeking graduate students
▸ 54% of applicants admitted
▸ SAT or ACT (ACT writing optional) required
▸ 41% graduate within 6 years

**General.** Founded in 1934. Regionally accredited. **Degrees:** 694 bachelor's awarded; master's offered. **ROTC:** Naval. **Calendar:** Semester, limited summer session. **Full-time faculty:** 166 total; 81% have terminal degrees, 10% minority, 45% women. **Part-time faculty:** 105 total. **Class size:** 58% < 20, 41% 20-39, less than 1% 40-49, less than 1% 50-99. **Special facilities:** Marine science research vessels, observatory, cybercafe.

**Freshman class profile.** 6,854 applied, 3,668 admitted, 669 enrolled.

| Mid 50% test scores | | | |
|---|---|---|---|
| SAT critical reading: | 470-560 | GPA 2.0-2.99: | 23% |
| SAT math: | 470-560 | Return as sophomores: | 63% |
| ACT composite: | 19-25 | Out-of-state: | 36% |
| GPA 3.75 or higher: | 28% | Live on campus: | 83% |
| GPA 3.50-3.74: | 15% | Fraternities: | 21% |
| GPA 3.0-3.49: | 34% | Sororities: | 16% |

**Basis for selection.** GPA and test scores very important, followed by rigor of secondary school record. Audition required of music, dance, theater majors. Portfolio required for art, computer art and design. **Homeschooled:** Transcript of courses and grades, interview required. 2 letters of recommendation evaluating academic potential from qualified educator or evaluator outside of homeschool environment, portfolio that includes 2 writing samples of at least 100 words, bibliography of reading completed and texts used, and description of curriculum required.

**High school preparation.** 13 units required; 16 recommended. Required and recommended units include English 4, mathematics 3-4, social studies 3, science 3 (laboratory 2) and foreign language 2. History units may be included for satisfaction of social studies requirement.

**2009-2010 Annual costs.** Tuition/fees: $25,300. $540 mandatory health insurance fee charged unless proof of other coverage is provided. Room/board: $9,060. Books/supplies: $800. Personal expenses: $816.

**2009-2010 Financial aid.** **Non-need-based:** Scholarships awarded for academics, art, athletics, job skills, leadership, music/drama, ROTC, state residency.

**Application procedures.** **Admission:** No deadline. No application fee. Admission notification on a rolling basis beginning on or about 10/1. Must reply by May 1 or within 2 week(s) if notified thereafter. **Financial aid:** Priority date 3/15; no closing date. FAFSA, institutional form required. Applicants notified on a rolling basis starting 2/15.

**Academics.** **Special study options:** Accelerated study, combined bachelor's/graduate degree, cooperative education, distance learning, double major, dual enrollment of high school students, honors, independent study, internships, liberal arts/career combination, semester at sea, student-designed major, study abroad, teacher certification program, Washington semester. **Credit/placement by examination:** AP, CLEP, IB, SAT, ACT, institutional tests. 30 credit hours maximum toward associate degree, 30 toward bachelor's. **Support services:** Learning center, remedial instruction, study skills assistance, tutoring, writing center.

**Majors.** **Biology:** General, marine. **Business:** General, accounting, business admin, finance, international, marketing. **Communications:** General. **Computer sciences:** General. **Education:** General, drama/dance, elementary, music, physical, secondary. **Engineering:** Electrical, mechanical, physics. **Foreign languages:** French, Spanish. **Health:** Nursing (RN), predental, premedicine, prenursing, preveterinary. **History:** General. **Legal studies:** Prelaw. **Liberal arts:** Arts/sciences, humanities. **Math:** General. **Parks/recreation:** Exercise sciences. **Philosophy/religion:** Philosophy. **Physical sciences:** Chemistry, physics. **Psychology:** General. **Social sciences:** Economics, geography, political science, sociology. **Theology:** Sacred music. **Transportation:** Airline/commercial pilot, aviation management. **Visual/performing arts:** Art, art history/conservation, dance, design, dramatic, music management, music performance, music theory/composition, studio arts, voice/opera.

**Most popular majors.** Business/marketing 19%, health sciences 43%, social sciences 10%, visual/performing arts 6%.

**Computing on campus.** 400 workstations in dormitories, library, computer center. Dormitories wired for high-speed internet access and linked to campus network. Commuter students can connect to campus network. Online course registration, online library, helpline, wireless network available.

**Student life.** **Freshman orientation:** Mandatory. Preregistration for classes offered. Spring program available for pre-registration; formal freshmen orientation occurs in the few days preceding first day of class. **Housing:** Guaranteed on-campus for freshmen. Coed dorms, single-sex dorms, special housing for disabled, apartments, fraternity/sorority housing available. $200 deposit, deadline 5/1. **Activities:** Bands, campus ministries, choral groups, dance, drama, international student organizations, literary magazine, music ensembles, musical theater, radio station, student government, student newspaper, symphony orchestra, TV station, political science society, black student union, Baptist campus ministry, Hillel, Circle-K, Rotaract, Caribbean student group, Dolphin Diversity.

**Athletics.** NCAA. **Intercollegiate:** Baseball M, basketball, cross-country, football (tackle) M, golf, rowing (crew) W, soccer, softball W, tennis, track and field W, volleyball W. **Intramural:** Basketball, bowling, football (non-tackle), soccer, softball, table tennis, tennis, volleyball. **Team name:** Dolphins.

**Student services.** Adult student services, alcohol/substance abuse counseling, career counseling, student employment services, financial aid counseling, health services, minority student services, personal counseling, placement for graduates. **Physically disabled:** Services for visually, speech, hearing impaired.

**Contact.** E-mail: admissions@ju.edu
Phone: (904) 256-7000 Toll-free number: (800) 225-2027
Fax: (904) 256-7012
Yvonne Martel, Director of First Year Admissions and Enrollment, Jacksonville University, 2800 University Boulevard North, Jacksonville, FL 32211-3394

## Johnson & Wales University: North Miami
**North Miami, Florida**
www.jwu.edu                                    CB code: 3441

- Private 4-year university
- Residential campus in large city
- 2,033 degree-seeking undergraduates: 3% part-time, 55% women, 22% African American, 1% Asian American, 17% Hispanic American, 8% international
- 60% of applicants admitted
- 49% graduate within 6 years

**General.** Regionally accredited. **Degrees:** 267 bachelor's, 400 associate awarded. **Calendar:** Quarter, extensive summer session. **Full-time faculty:** 60 total; 65% women. **Part-time faculty:** 32 total; 34% women. **Class size:** 47% < 20, 41% 20-39, 11% 40-49, less than 1% 50-99. **Special facilities:** University-operated hotel.

**Freshman class profile.** 6,253 applied, 3,765 admitted, 595 enrolled.

| Mid 50% test scores | | Return as sophomores: | 72% |
|---|---|---|---|
| SAT critical reading: | 390-510 | Out-of-state: | 46% |
| SAT math: | 410-510 | Live on campus: | 74% |
| SAT writing: | 410-500 | International: | 4% |

**Basis for selection.** Academic record, secondary school curriculum, GPA, class rank, and test scores important. Student motivation and interest given strong consideration. SAT/ACT required for honors program. **Homeschooled:** Transcript of courses and grades, state high school equivalency certificate required. SAT or ACT required.

**High school preparation.** College-preparatory program recommended. Required units include English 4, mathematics 3, social studies 2 and science 3.

**2010-2011 Annual costs.** Tuition/fees: $24,429. Room/board: $8,904. Books/supplies: $1,500.

**2009-2010 Financial aid. Non-need-based:** Scholarships awarded for academics, alumni affiliation, job skills, leadership, state residency.

**Application procedures. Admission:** No deadline. No application fee. Admission notification on a rolling basis beginning on or about 11/1. Must reply by May 1 or within 2 week(s) if notified thereafter. **Financial aid:** No deadline. FAFSA required. Applicants notified on a rolling basis starting 3/1; must reply within 2 week(s) of notification.

**Academics. Special study options:** Accelerated study, cooperative education, dual enrollment of high school students, ESL, exchange student, honors, independent study, internships, study abroad. **Credit/placement by examination:** CLEP, institutional tests. **Support services:** Learning center, pre-admission summer program, reduced course load, remedial instruction, study skills assistance, tutoring, writing center.

**Majors. Business:** Business admin, fashion, hospitality admin, hotel/motel admin, marketing, tourism/travel. **Family/consumer sciences:** Institutional food production. **Parks/recreation:** Facilities management, sports admin. **Personal/culinary services:** Chef training, culinary arts, food service, restaurant/catering. **Protective services:** Law enforcement admin.

**Most popular majors.** Business/marketing 50%, family/consumer sciences 18%, parks/recreation 13%, personal/culinary services 10%, security/protective services 9%.

**Computing on campus.** 60 workstations in library, computer center, student center. Dormitories wired for high-speed internet access and linked to campus network. Commuter students can connect to campus network.

Online course registration, online library, helpline, repair service, wireless network available.

**Student life. Freshman orientation:** Mandatory, $255 fee. Preregistration for classes offered. **Housing:** Guaranteed on-campus for freshmen. Coed dorms available. $200 nonrefundable deposit. All housing accessible for disabled students. **Activities:** Pep band, campus ministries, dance, international student organizations, music ensembles, student government, student newspaper.

**Athletics.** NAIA. **Intercollegiate:** Basketball, cheerleading, cross-country, golf M, soccer, track and field. **Intramural:** Basketball M, football (non-tackle), soccer, softball, volleyball. **Team name:** Wildcats.

**Student services.** Adult student services, alcohol/substance abuse counseling, career counseling, student employment services, financial aid counseling, health services, personal counseling, placement for graduates, veterans' counselor. **Physically disabled:** Services for visually, speech, hearing impaired.

**Contact.** E-mail: admissions.mia@jwu.edu
Phone: (305) 892-7600 Toll-free number: (866) 598-3567
Fax: (305) 892-7020
Jeff Greenip, Director of Admissions, Johnson & Wales University: North Miami, 1701 Northeast 127th Street, North Miami, FL 33181

## Jones College
**Jacksonville, Florida**
www.jones.edu                                    CB code: 5343

- Private 4-year business and teachers college
- Commuter campus in very large city
- 724 degree-seeking undergraduates: 66% part-time, 81% women
- Interview required

**General.** Founded in 1918. Accredited by ACICS. Branch campus in Miami. 2 campuses in Jacksonville. **Degrees:** 72 bachelor's, 13 associate awarded. **Calendar:** Trimester, extensive summer session. **Full-time faculty:** 10 total. **Part-time faculty:** 50 total. **Class size:** 91% < 20, 9% 20-39.

**Basis for selection.** Open admission. **Homeschooled:** State high school equivalency certificate required.

**2009-2010 Annual costs.** Tuition/fees: $8,340. Books/supplies: $1,500. Personal expenses: $1,312.

**Financial aid.** All financial aid based on need.

**Application procedures. Admission:** No deadline. No application fee. Admission notification on a rolling basis. **Financial aid:** No deadline. FAFSA required. Applicants notified on a rolling basis.

**Academics. Special study options:** Accelerated study, distance learning, double major, dual enrollment of high school students, independent study, internships, student-designed major, weekend college. **Credit/placement by examination:** AP, CLEP, institutional tests. 15 credit hours maximum toward associate degree, 15 toward bachelor's. Life experience: 21 hours if in bachelor's degree programs, 9 hours if in associate degree programs. **Support services:** Reduced course load, remedial instruction, study skills assistance, tutoring.

**Majors. Business:** Business admin. **Computer sciences:** General. **Education:** Elementary. **Health:** Medical assistant. **Legal studies:** Paralegal.

**Most popular majors.** Business/marketing 64%, computer/information sciences 20%, health sciences 10%, legal studies 6%.

**Computing on campus.** 166 workstations in library, computer center. Commuter students can connect to campus network. Online library, wireless network available.

**Student life. Freshman orientation:** Mandatory. Preregistration for classes offered. **Activities:** Radio station.

**Student services.** Career counseling, student employment services, financial aid counseling, personal counseling, placement for graduates, veterans' counselor.

**Contact.** E-mail: lvaughn@jones.edu
Phone: (904) 743-1122 ext. 112 Toll-free number: (800) 331-0176 ext. 112
Fax: (904) 743-4446
Linda Vaughn, Director of Admissions, Jones College, 5353 Arlington Expressway, Jacksonville, FL 32211

## Lynn University
**Boca Raton, Florida**
www.lynn.edu

CB member
CB code: 5437

- Private 4-year university
- Residential campus in small city
- 1,737 degree-seeking undergraduates: 9% part-time, 49% women, 3% African American, 7% Hispanic American, 15% international
- 438 degree-seeking graduate students
- 72% of applicants admitted
- SAT or ACT (ACT writing recommended), application essay required
- 35% graduate within 6 years

**General.** Founded in 1962. Regionally accredited. **Degrees:** 453 bachelor's awarded; master's offered. **ROTC:** Air Force. **Location:** 20 miles from Fort Lauderdale, 20 miles from Palm Beach. **Calendar:** Semester, extensive summer session. **Full-time faculty:** 103 total; 69% have terminal degrees, 23% minority, 42% women. **Part-time faculty:** 57 total; 37% have terminal degrees, 35% minority, 33% women. **Class size:** 61% < 20, 39% 20-39, less than 1% 50-99. **Special facilities:** University club (private dining room that serves as laboratory for hotel and restaurant management students), flight simulator, conservatory of music.

**Freshman class profile.** 2,454 applied, 1,773 admitted, 477 enrolled.

| Mid 50% test scores | | | |
|---|---|---|---|
| SAT critical reading: | 420-520 | GPA 2.0-2.99: | 54% |
| SAT math: | 420-530 | Rank in top quarter: | 23% |
| ACT composite: | 17-22 | Rank in top tenth: | 7% |
| GPA 3.75 or higher: | 4% | Return as sophomores: | 58% |
| GPA 3.50-3.74: | 10% | Out-of-state: | 73% |
| GPA 3.0-3.49: | 27% | Live on campus: | 83% |
| | | International: | 15% |

**Basis for selection.** School achievement record, high school counselor's recommendation, test scores important; class rank, school and community activities considered. Special consideration given to foreign and minority applicants. Interview and essay recommended. Portfolio recommended for art and graphic design majors. **Learning Disabled:** Submit psychological testing in addition to other admission documents.

**High school preparation.** 16 units required. Required units include English 4, mathematics 4, social studies 2, history 2 and science 4. Mathematics must include algebra I, algebra II, and either geometry, trigonometry, calculus, or analysis. Science must include biology and a physical science.

**2010-2011 Annual costs.** Tuition/fees: $30,900. Room/board: $11,950. Books/supplies: $1,200. Personal expenses: $1,600.

**2009-2010 Financial aid. Need-based:** 237 full-time freshmen applied for aid; 161 were judged to have need; 158 of these received aid. Average need met was 64%. Average scholarship/grant was $15,484; average loan $4,497. 60% of total undergraduate aid awarded as scholarships/grants, 40% as loans/jobs. **Non-need-based:** Awarded to 1,138 full-time undergraduates, including 253 freshmen. Scholarships awarded for academics, athletics, leadership, music/drama, religious affiliation, state residency.

**Application procedures. Admission:** No deadline. $35 fee, may be waived for applicants with need. Admission notification on a rolling basis beginning on or about 9/1. Must reply by May 1 or within 2 week(s) if notified thereafter. **Financial aid:** Priority date 3/1; no closing date. FAFSA, institutional form required. Applicants notified on a rolling basis starting 2/1; must reply within 2 week(s) of notification.

**Academics. Special study options:** Accelerated study, cooperative education, distance learning, double major, dual enrollment of high school students, ESL, honors, independent study, internships, liberal arts/career combination, study abroad, teacher certification program, Washington semester. **Credit/placement by examination:** AP, CLEP, IB, institutional tests. 30 credit hours maximum toward associate degree, 30 toward bachelor's. **Support services:** Learning center, reduced course load, tutoring, writing center.

**Majors. Area/ethnic studies:** American. **Biology:** General. **Business:** Business admin, hospitality admin, tourism promotion. **Communications:** Advertising, digital media, journalism, media studies, public relations. **Education:** Elementary. **Liberal arts:** Arts/sciences. **Protective services:** Law enforcement admin. **Psychology:** General. **Public administration:** Human services. **Social sciences:** International relations. **Visual/performing arts:** Arts management, dramatic, graphic design, music performance.

**Most popular majors.** Business/marketing 43%, communication technologies 16%, psychology 13%, security/protective services 9%, visual/performing arts 8%.

**Computing on campus.** 220 workstations in dormitories, library, computer center. Dormitories wired for high-speed internet access and linked to campus network. Online library, helpline, repair service, wireless network available.

**Student life. Freshman orientation:** Mandatory. **Housing:** Guaranteed on-campus for all undergraduates. Coed dorms, single-sex dorms, special housing for disabled, wellness housing available. **Activities:** Campus ministries, choral groups, dance, drama, film society, international student organizations, literary magazine, music ensembles, radio station, student government, student newspaper, symphony orchestra, TV station, Black student union, debate team, gay-straight alliance, Hillel, honors colloquium, hospitality club, Knights of the Roundtable.

**Athletics.** NCAA. **Intercollegiate:** Baseball M, basketball, cross-country, golf, rowing (crew) M, soccer, softball W, tennis, volleyball W. **Intramural:** Basketball, bowling, cross-country, equestrian, golf, handball, ice hockey, lacrosse, rugby M, soccer, softball, swimming, table tennis, tennis, volleyball, water polo. **Team name:** Fighting Knights.

**Student services.** Adult student services, chaplain/spiritual director, career counseling, student employment services, health services, personal counseling, placement for graduates, veterans' counselor.

**Contact.** E-mail: admissions@lynn.edu
Phone: (561) 237-7900 Toll-free number: (800) 888-5966 ext. 1
Fax: (561) 237-7100
Juan Tamayo, Director of Admissions, Lynn University, 3601 North Military Trail, Boca Raton, FL 33431-5598

## Miami International University of Art and Design
**Miami, Florida**
www.mymiu.com

CB code: 5327

- For-profit 3-year university and visual arts college
- Commuter campus in very large city
- 2,448 degree-seeking undergraduates: 23% part-time, 64% women, 9% African American, 1% Asian American, 34% Hispanic American, 3% international
- 66 graduate students
- Application essay, interview required

**General.** Founded in 1965. Regionally accredited. **Degrees:** 261 bachelor's, 87 associate awarded; master's offered. **Location:** 2 miles from downtown. **Calendar:** Quarter, extensive summer session. **Full-time faculty:** 80 total. **Part-time faculty:** 215 total.

**Basis for selection.** Keen interest in fashion, merchandising, art, interior design, or related areas required. Secondary school record, recommendations, and essay important. Placement test or SAT/ACT determines need for transitional studies (developmental/remedial) courses. Portfolio recommended. **Learning Disabled:** Students who require accommodations should advise the Student Affairs department during application process.

**2009-2010 Annual costs.** Fees vary according to program. Books/supplies: $1,500. Personal expenses: $1,200.

**Application procedures. Admission:** No deadline. $50 fee. Admission notification on a rolling basis. **Financial aid:** Priority date 7/1; no closing date. FAFSA, CSS PROFILE required. Applicants notified on a rolling basis starting 8/1.

**Academics. Special study options:** Distance learning, ESL, internships. **Credit/placement by examination:** AP, CLEP, IB, SAT, ACT, institutional tests. 28 credit hours maximum toward associate degree, 48 toward bachelor's. **Support services:** Learning center, reduced course load, remedial instruction, tutoring.

**Majors. BACHELOR'S. Business:** Fashion. **Communications:** Advertising. **Communications technology:** Animation/special effects, recording arts. **Computer sciences:** Web page design. **Visual/performing arts:** General, cinematography, commercial photography, fashion design, graphic design, interior design. **ASSOCIATE. Business:** Fashion. **Visual/performing arts:** Fashion design.

**Most popular majors.** Business/marketing 23%, communication technologies 11%, visual/performing arts 59%.

**Computing on campus.** 87 workstations in library, computer center. Online library, student web hosting, wireless network available.

**Student life. Freshman orientation:** Mandatory. Preregistration for classes offered. Held week before each quarter starts for approximately 4 hours.

Four-Year Colleges

**Housing:** Coed dorms available. **Activities:** International student organizations, student government, student newspaper.

**Student services.** Career counseling, student employment services, financial aid counseling.

**Contact.** E-mail: admissions@aii.edu
Phone: (305) 428-5700 Toll-free number: (800) 225-9023
Fax: (305) 374-7946
Kevin Ryan, Senior Director of Admissions, Miami International University of Art and Design, 1501 Biscayne Boulevard, Suite 100, Miami, FL 33132-1418

## New College of Florida
**Sarasota, Florida**                                    **CB member**
**www.ncf.edu**                                          **CB code: 5506**

◗ Public 4-year liberal arts college
◗ Residential campus in small city
◗ 825 degree-seeking undergraduates: 62% women, 2% African American, 3% Asian American, 11% Hispanic American, 1% Native American
◗ 53% of applicants admitted
◗ SAT or ACT with writing, application essay required
◗ 60% graduate within 6 years; 57% enter graduate study

**General.** Founded in 1960. Regionally accredited. State legislatively-designated honors college for liberal arts and sciences. **Degrees:** 158 bachelor's awarded. **Location:** 50 miles from Tampa, 2 miles from Sarasota. **Calendar:** 4-1-4. **Full-time faculty:** 71 total; 99% have terminal degrees, 16% minority, 48% women. **Part-time faculty:** 23 total; 87% have terminal degrees, 9% minority, 65% women. **Class size:** 64% < 20, 32% 20-39, less than 1% 40-49, 3% 50-99. **Special facilities:** High-field nuclear magnetic resonance spectrometer, hardware/software system for brain function analysis, scanning electron microscope, UV-visible and infrared spectrophotometer, inert atmosphere glove box, fine arts center, laboratories for environmental studies, anthropology, psychology, marine biology research facility and laboratories, academic resource center.

**Freshman class profile.** 1,403 applied, 739 admitted, 218 enrolled.

| Mid 50% test scores | | GPA 2.0-2.99: | 1% |
|---|---|---|---|
| SAT critical reading: | 630-730 | Rank in top quarter: | 84% |
| SAT math: | 590-680 | Rank in top tenth: | 49% |
| SAT writing: | 600-690 | End year in good standing: | 91% |
| ACT composite: | 27-30 | Return as sophomores: | 87% |
| GPA 3.75 or higher: | 75% | Out-of-state: | 21% |
| GPA 3.50-3.74: | 16% | Live on campus: | 96% |
| GPA 3.0-3.49: | 8% | International: | 1% |

**Basis for selection.** Challenging courses, strong grades, test scores, recommendations, and writing ability important. Class rank, extracurricular activities considered. Level of interest and availability of limited guaranteed scholarship funds may be considered. Optional portfolios and interview considered. **Homeschooled:** Transcript of courses and grades required. List of length and levels of study completed or planned for completion, textbook information and reading lists required. **Learning Disabled:** Documentation of disability must be provided. Applicant should submit evidence that any unmet requirement is due to disability, and would not constitute fundamental alteration of academic program.

**High school preparation.** College-preparatory program required. 18 units required; 20 recommended. Required and recommended units include English 4, mathematics 4, social studies 3-4, science 3-4 (laboratory 2), foreign language 2-4 and academic electives 2-5.

**2009-2010 Annual costs.** Tuition/fees: $4,784; $26,386 out-of-state. Room/board: $7,783. Books/supplies: $800. Personal expenses: $2,600.

**2009-2010 Financial aid. Need-based:** 172 full-time freshmen applied for aid; 108 were judged to have need; 108 of these received aid. Average need met was 96%. Average scholarship/grant was $11,297; average loan $2,942. 68% of total undergraduate aid awarded as scholarships/grants, 32% as loans/jobs. **Non-need-based:** Awarded to 465 full-time undergraduates, including 136 freshmen. Scholarships awarded for academics, state residency.

**Application procedures. Admission:** Priority date 2/15; deadline 4/15 (postmark date). $30 fee, may be waived for applicants with need. Admission notification 4/25. Admission notification on a rolling basis. Must reply by 5/1. **Financial aid:** Priority date 2/15; no closing date. FAFSA required. Applicants notified on a rolling basis starting 10/1; must reply by 5/1 or within 4 week(s) of notification.

**Academics.** All students required to complete three 4-week independent study projects, senior thesis, and oral baccalaureate exam before committee of faculty. **Special study options:** Cross-registration, double major, exchange student, honors, independent study, internships, semester at sea, student-designed major, study abroad, Washington semester. Academic contract, January Interterm (independent study), narrative evaluation/pass-fail, senior thesis, tutorials, undergraduate research. **Credit/placement by examination:** AP, CLEP, institutional tests. AP exam scores, IB higher-level exam scores, Advanced Certificate of Education A-level exam scores of E or higher and CLEP scores at certain levels may be used toward exemptions from Liberal Arts Curriculum requirements in subjects that are areas of study at New College. **Support services:** Learning center, study skills assistance, tutoring, writing center.

**Majors. Area/ethnic studies:** European, French, German, Latin American, Spanish/Iberian. **Biology:** General, biochemistry, marine. **Conservation:** Environmental studies. **Foreign languages:** General, Chinese, classics, French, German, Russian, Spanish. **History:** General. **Interdisciplinary:** Global studies, medieval/Renaissance, natural sciences. **Liberal arts:** Arts/sciences, humanities. **Math:** General, applied. **Philosophy/religion:** Philosophy, religion. **Physical sciences:** Chemistry, physics. **Psychology:** General. **Public administration:** Policy analysis. **Social sciences:** General, anthropology, economics, international relations, political science, sociology, urban studies. **Visual/performing arts:** Art history/conservation, studio arts.

**Computing on campus.** 41 workstations in library, computer center, student center. Dormitories wired for high-speed internet access and linked to campus network. Commuter students can connect to campus network. Online course registration, online library, helpline, student web hosting, wireless network available.

**Student life. Freshman orientation:** Mandatory, $120 fee. 7-day program. **Policies:** First-year students required to live on campus unless granted waiver by office of residential life. **Housing:** Guaranteed on-campus for freshmen. Coed dorms, special housing for disabled, apartments available. Specialized housing options may be arranged in response to student interest. **Activities:** Campus ministries, choral groups, dance, drama, film society, literary magazine, music ensembles, musical theater, radio station, student government, student newspaper, Amnesty International, China club, climate justice, origami club, Jesus club, service club, Best Buddies, Africa club, Food not Bombs, Hillel.

**Athletics. Intercollegiate:** Sailing. **Intramural:** Basketball, fencing, football (non-tackle), lacrosse, racquetball, swimming, table tennis, tennis, volleyball, weight lifting, wrestling.

**Student services.** Alcohol/substance abuse counseling, chaplain/spiritual director, career counseling, student employment services, financial aid counseling, health services, minority student services, on-campus daycare, personal counseling, women's services. **Physically disabled:** Services for visually, hearing impaired.

**Contact.** E-mail: admissions@ncf.edu
Phone: (941) 487-5000 Fax: (941) 487-5010
Kathleen Killion, Dean of Admissions and Financial Aid, New College of Florida, 5800 Bay Shore Road, Sarasota, FL 34243-2109

## Northwest Florida State College
**Niceville, Florida**
**www.nwfsc.edu**                                        **CB code: 5526**

◗ Public 4-year business and community college
◗ Commuter campus in large town
◗ 7,556 undergraduates

**General.** Founded in 1963. Regionally accredited. Additional teaching centers at Ft. Walton Beach, Eglin Air Force Base, Hurlburt Field, DeFuniak Springs and Crestview. **Degrees:** 78 bachelor's, 1,355 associate awarded. **ROTC:** Army. **Location:** 55 miles from Pensacola. **Calendar:** Semester, extensive summer session. **Full-time faculty:** 95 total; 42% have terminal degrees. **Part-time faculty:** 180 total. **Class size:** 3% < 20, 97% 20-39. **Special facilities:** Fine and performing arts center with 2 theaters and 2 art galleries.

**Basis for selection.** Open admission. Applicants without high school diploma may be admitted to credit-bearing certificate programs.

**High school preparation.** Recommended units include English 4, mathematics 3, social studies 3 and science 3.

**2009-2010 Annual costs.** Tuition/fees: $2,272; $9,197 out-of-state. Books/supplies: $974.

**2008-2009 Financial aid. Non-need-based:** Scholarships awarded for academics, art, athletics, leadership, minority status, music/drama.

**Application procedures. Admission:** Priority date 7/25; no deadline. No application fee. Admission notification on a rolling basis. **Financial aid:** Priority date 4/1; no closing date. FAFSA, institutional form required. Applicants notified on a rolling basis starting 2/1; must reply within 2 week(s) of notification.

**Academics. Special study options:** Combined bachelor's/graduate degree, cooperative education, cross-registration, distance learning, dual enrollment of high school students, ESL, independent study, internships, student-designed major. **Credit/placement by examination:** AP, CLEP, institutional tests. 32 credit hours maximum toward associate degree. **Support services:** Learning center, remedial instruction, study skills assistance, tutoring.

**Majors. Education:** Elementary, mathematics, science. **Health:** Nursing assistant.

**Computing on campus.** 900 workstations in library, computer center. Commuter students can connect to campus network. Online course registration, online library, wireless network available.

**Student life. Freshman orientation:** Mandatory. Preregistration for classes offered. Orientation can be completed online. **Activities:** Bands, campus ministries, choral groups, dance, drama, literary magazine, music ensembles, musical theater, student government, symphony orchestra, Student Christian Fellowship, African American student association, Circle K, College Republicans, environmental club.

**Athletics.** NJCAA. **Intercollegiate:** Baseball M, basketball, softball W. **Intramural:** Softball, volleyball. **Team name:** Raiders.

**Student services.** Adult student services, career counseling, student employment services, on-campus daycare, personal counseling, placement for graduates, veterans' counselor. **Physically disabled:** Services for visually, speech, hearing impaired.

**Contact.** E-mail: registrar@nwfsc.edu
Phone: (850) 729-5373 Fax: (850) 729-5215
Christine Bishop, Registrar, Northwest Florida State College, 100 College Boulevard, Niceville, FL 32578-1295

## Northwood University: Florida
**West Palm Beach, Florida**
**www.northwood.edu**     CB code: 5162

- Private 4-year university and business college
- Residential campus in small city
- 575 degree-seeking undergraduates: 4% part-time, 37% women, 10% African American, 1% Asian American, 10% Hispanic American, 34% international
- 55% of applicants admitted
- SAT or ACT (ACT writing optional), application essay required
- 40% graduate within 6 years; 10% enter graduate study

**General.** Regionally accredited. Specialty university offering only business degrees in professional management. Additional residential campuses in Michigan and Texas; 48 program centers; library center in Maine. **Degrees:** 174 bachelor's, 57 associate awarded; master's offered. **Location:** 75 miles from Miami. **Calendar:** Semester, limited summer session. **Full-time faculty:** 16 total; 38% have terminal degrees, 12% minority, 44% women. **Part-time faculty:** 36 total; 17% have terminal degrees, 6% minority, 33% women. **Class size:** 63% < 20, 36% 20-39, 1% 40-49.

**Freshman class profile.** 857 applied, 468 admitted, 99 enrolled.

| Mid 50% test scores | | | |
|---|---|---|---|
| SAT critical reading: | 410-490 | GPA 2.0-2.99: | 45% |
| SAT math: | 410-510 | Rank in top quarter: | 21% |
| SAT writing: | 400-500 | Rank in top tenth: | 10% |
| ACT composite: | 17-21 | End year in good standing: | 62% |
| GPA 3.75 or higher: | 9% | Return as sophomores: | 56% |
| GPA 3.50-3.74: | 7% | Out-of-state: | 42% |
| GPA 3.0-3.49: | 31% | Live on campus: | 49% |
| | | International: | 17% |

**Basis for selection.** 2.0 GPA and strong interest in business or related field required. Test scores considered. Interview recommended. **Homeschooled:** Transcript of courses and grades, state high school equivalency certificate required.

**High school preparation.** College-preparatory program recommended. 17 units recommended. Recommended units include English 4 and mathematics 3.

**2009-2010 Annual costs.** Tuition/fees: $18,429. Room/board: $8,562. Books/supplies: $1,581.

**2009-2010 Financial aid. Need-based:** 69 full-time freshmen applied for aid; 58 were judged to have need; 58 of these received aid. Average need met was 60%. Average scholarship/grant was $6,941; average loan $3,181. 58% of total undergraduate aid awarded as scholarships/grants, 42% as loans/jobs. **Non-need-based:** Awarded to 286 full-time undergraduates, including 38 freshmen. Scholarships awarded for academics, athletics, leadership, minority status, state residency.

**Application procedures. Admission:** No deadline. $25 fee, may be waived for applicants with need, free for online applicants. Admission notification on a rolling basis beginning on or about 10/1. **Financial aid:** No deadline. FAFSA required. Applicants notified on a rolling basis starting 3/1.

**Academics.** Writing, math and accounting labs available. **Special study options:** Accelerated study, combined bachelor's/graduate degree, distance learning, double major, dual enrollment of high school students, external degree, honors, independent study, internships, study abroad, weekend college. **Credit/placement by examination:** AP, CLEP, IB, SAT, ACT, institutional tests. 12 credit hours maximum toward associate degree, 12 toward bachelor's. **Support services:** Learning center, reduced course load, remedial instruction, study skills assistance, tutoring.

**Majors. Business:** Accounting, banking/financial services, business admin, hotel/motel admin, international, management information systems, marketing, vehicle parts marketing. **Communications:** Advertising. **Computer sciences:** General. **Parks/recreation:** Sports admin.

**Most popular majors.** Business/marketing 93%.

**Computing on campus.** 89 workstations in dormitories, library, computer center, student center. Dormitories wired for high-speed internet access and linked to campus network. Commuter students can connect to campus network. Online course registration, online library, helpline, student web hosting, wireless network available.

**Student life. Freshman orientation:** Mandatory, $125 fee. Preregistration for classes offered. 3-day program in early September. **Policies:** Adheres to all federal and state laws concerning alcohol and drugs. Freshmen and sophomores not living at home must live on campus. **Housing:** Guaranteed on-campus for freshmen. Single-sex dorms, wellness housing available. $100 nonrefundable deposit, deadline 5/1. **Activities:** International student organizations, student government, residence hall association, ambassador club.

**Athletics.** NAIA. **Intercollegiate:** Baseball M, basketball, golf, soccer, softball W, tennis, volleyball W. **Intramural:** Basketball, bowling, football (non-tackle), racquetball, tennis. **Team name:** Seahawks.

**Student services.** Adult student services, alcohol/substance abuse counseling, career counseling, student employment services, financial aid counseling, health services, personal counseling, placement for graduates. **Physically disabled:** Services for hearing impaired.

**Contact.** E-mail: fladmit@northwood.edu
Phone: (561) 478-5500 Toll-free number: (800) 458-8325
Fax: (561) 640-3328
Jack Letvintchuk, Director of Admissions, Northwood University: Florida, 2600 North Military Trail, West Palm Beach, FL 33409-2911

## Nova Southeastern University
**Fort Lauderdale, Florida**     CB member
**www.nova.edu**     CB code: 5514

- Private 4-year university
- Commuter campus in small city
- 5,868 degree-seeking undergraduates
- 45% of applicants admitted
- SAT or ACT (ACT writing optional) required
- 42% graduate within 6 years

**General.** Founded in 1964. Regionally accredited. Field-based programs offered throughout the nation and at selected international sites. **Degrees:** 1,390 bachelor's, 14 associate awarded; master's, doctoral, professional offered. **Location:** 10 miles from Fort Lauderdale. **Calendar:** Trimester, limited summer session. **Full-time faculty:** 712 total; 82% have terminal degrees, 25% minority, 46% women. **Part-time faculty:** 1,001 total; 74% have terminal degrees, 28% minority, 50% women. **Class size:** 79% < 20, 20% 20-39, less than 1% 40-49, less than 1% 50-99. **Special facilities:** Oceanographic center, university school (K-12).

**Freshman class profile.** 4,124 applied, 1,849 admitted, 579 enrolled.

**Basis for selection.** Test scores, GPA important. Career Development applicants (adult and evening/weekend) exempt from test score requirement; high school diploma or GED required. Interviews and essays recommended. **Homeschooled:** Information about home school program of study and GED score to demonstrate high school equivalence required.

**High school preparation.** College-preparatory program recommended. Recommended units include English 4, mathematics 3, social studies 3 and science 3.

**2009-2010 Annual costs.** Tuition/fees: $21,100. Room/board: $8,634. Books/supplies: $1,500. Personal expenses: $2,246.

**2008-2009 Financial aid. Non-need-based:** Scholarships awarded for academics, athletics, leadership, music/drama.

**Application procedures. Admission:** No deadline. $50 fee, may be waived for applicants with need. Admission notification on a rolling basis. **Financial aid:** Priority date 4/15; no closing date. FAFSA required. Applicants notified on a rolling basis starting 3/15.

**Academics.** 2 undergraduate programs: professional and liberal studies for traditional daytime students, career development for adult evening and weekend students. Core curriculum of liberal arts-based courses plus general education required. **Special study options:** Combined bachelor's/graduate degree, distance learning, double major, honors, independent study, internships, study abroad, teacher certification program. Dual admission with NSU graduate/professional programs. **Credit/placement by examination:** AP, CLEP, IB, SAT, ACT, institutional tests. 90 credit hours maximum toward bachelor's degree. **Support services:** Learning center, reduced course load, remedial instruction, study skills assistance, tutoring, writing center.

**Majors. Area/ethnic studies:** American. **Biology:** General, marine. **Business:** General, accounting, business admin, finance, marketing. **Communications:** General. **Computer sciences:** General, computer science. **Conservation:** Environmental science, environmental studies. **Education:** Early childhood, elementary, kindergarten/preschool, secondary, special. **Health:** Athletic training, health services, nursing (RN), premedicine, sonography. **History:** General. **Legal studies:** General, paralegal, prelaw. **Liberal arts:** Arts/sciences, humanities. **Parks/recreation:** Sports admin. **Protective services:** Criminal justice. **Psychology:** General. **Social sciences:** Economics, international relations, sociology. **Visual/performing arts:** Dance, studio arts, theater arts management. **Other:** Arts administration, Exercise and sport management.

**Most popular majors.** Biology 18%, business/marketing 31%, education 9%, health sciences 20%, psychology 10%.

**Computing on campus.** 2,708 workstations in dormitories, library, computer center, student center. Dormitories wired for high-speed internet access and linked to campus network. Commuter students can connect to campus network. Online course registration, online library, helpline, student web hosting, wireless network available.

**Student life. Freshman orientation:** Mandatory. Preregistration for classes offered. 2-day sessions offered 3 times in summer. **Housing:** Guaranteed on-campus for freshmen. Coed dorms, special housing for disabled, apartments, fraternity/sorority housing, wellness housing available. $500 partly refundable deposit. **Activities:** Bands, choral groups, dance, drama, film society, international student organizations, literary magazine, music ensembles, musical theater, radio station, student government, student newspaper, symphony orchestra, black student association, psychology club, Hillel, pre-med society, Alpha Phi Omega, Salsa, Indian student association, international Muslim association.

**Athletics.** NCAA. **Intercollegiate:** Baseball M, basketball, cheerleading M, cross-country, golf, rowing (crew) W, soccer, softball W, tennis W, track and field, volleyball W. **Intramural:** Basketball, football (non-tackle), golf, racquetball, soccer, softball, volleyball. **Team name:** Sharks.

**Student services.** Adult student services, career counseling, student employment services, financial aid counseling, health services, personal counseling, veterans' counselor, women's services. **Physically disabled:** Services for visually, speech, hearing impaired.

**Contact.** E-mail: admissions@nova.edu
Phone: (954) 262-8000 Toll-free number: (800) 338-4723 ext. 8000
Fax: (954) 262-3811
Maria Dillard, Director of Undergraduate Admissions, Nova Southeastern University, 3301 College Avenue, Fort Lauderdale, FL 33314

## Palm Beach Atlantic University
**West Palm Beach, Florida**
www.pba.edu                                 CB code: 5553

- Private 4-year university and liberal arts college affiliated with nondenominational tradition
- Residential campus in large city

- 2,419 degree-seeking undergraduates: 7% part-time, 64% women, 17% African American, 1% Asian American, 14% Hispanic American, 2% international
- 826 degree-seeking graduate students
- 69% of applicants admitted
- SAT or ACT (ACT writing optional), application essay, interview required
- 52% graduate within 6 years

**General.** Founded in 1968. Regionally accredited. Distinctly Christian university with emphasis on student community service. University offers mission trips around the world, weekly worship services, and student-led prayer groups. **Degrees:** 564 bachelor's, 12 associate awarded; master's, professional offered. **Location:** 60 miles from Miami, 180 miles from Orlando. **Calendar:** Semester, limited summer session. **Full-time faculty:** 156 total; 77% have terminal degrees, 13% minority, 46% women. **Part-time faculty:** 173 total; 38% have terminal degrees, 13% minority, 47% women. **Class size:** 60% < 20, 36% 20-39, 3% 40-49, less than 1% 50-99.

**Freshman class profile.** 1,401 applied, 965 admitted, 422 enrolled.

| Mid 50% test scores | | | |
|---|---|---|---|
| SAT critical reading: | 470-580 | GPA 2.0-2.99: | 20% |
| SAT math: | 450-550 | Rank in top quarter: | 54% |
| SAT writing: | 450-570 | Rank in top tenth: | 25% |
| ACT composite: | 20-26 | Return as sophomores: | 69% |
| GPA 3.75 or higher: | 32% | Out-of-state: | 40% |
| GPA 3.50-3.74: | 17% | Live on campus: | 86% |
| GPA 3.0-3.49: | 30% | International: | 3% |

**Basis for selection.** Secondary school record, recommendations, test scores, interview, autobiographical essay important. Audition required of music, theater and dance majors.

**High school preparation.** Required and recommended units include English 4, mathematics 3, social studies 3, science 4 (laboratory 2).

**2009-2010 Annual costs.** Tuition/fees: $22,700. Room/board: $8,220. Books/supplies: $1,200. Personal expenses: $1,650.

**2008-2009 Financial aid. Need-based:** 351 full-time freshmen applied for aid; 287 were judged to have need; 287 of these received aid. Average need met was 28%. Average scholarship/grant was $2,775; average loan $3,195. 43% of total undergraduate aid awarded as scholarships/grants, 57% as loans/jobs. **Non-need-based:** Awarded to 1,622 full-time undergraduates, including 338 freshmen. Scholarships awarded for academics, alumni affiliation, athletics, minority status, music/drama, state residency.

**Application procedures. Admission:** No deadline. $30 fee, may be waived for applicants with need. Admission notification on a rolling basis beginning on or about 9/1. **Financial aid:** Priority date 2/1, closing date 8/1. FAFSA required. Applicants notified on a rolling basis starting 2/15; must reply within 4 week(s) of notification.

**Academics. Special study options:** Accelerated study, combined bachelor's/graduate degree, distance learning, double major, dual enrollment of high school students, honors, independent study, internships, student-designed major, study abroad, teacher certification program, Washington semester. **Credit/placement by examination:** AP, CLEP, IB, SAT, ACT, institutional tests. 32 credit hours maximum toward bachelor's degree. If enrolled in one of undergraduate evening adult programs, aggregate of credit by examination or Professional Education Credit may not exceed 45 semester hours. **Support services:** Study skills assistance, tutoring, writing center.

**Honors college/program.** Students must rank in top 10 percent of the nation according to national test scores.

**Majors. Biology:** General. **Business:** Accounting/finance, business admin, entrepreneurial studies, international, marketing, nonprofit/public. **Communications:** General, broadcast journalism, journalism, organizational, radio/tv. **Education:** General, art, biology, drama/dance, English, history, mathematics, music, physical, social science. **Health:** Athletic training, nursing (RN). **History:** General. **Legal studies:** Prelaw. **Math:** General. **Philosophy/religion:** Philosophy, religion. **Psychology:** General. **Social sciences:** Political science. **Theology:** Bible, sacred music, theology. **Visual/performing arts:** General, acting, dance, dramatic, graphic design, music performance, music theory/composition, piano/organ, play/screenwriting, studio arts, voice/opera.

**Most popular majors.** Business/marketing 46%, communications/journalism 9%, health sciences 7%, psychology 7%, theological studies 7%, visual/performing arts 6%.

**Computing on campus.** 550 workstations in dormitories, library, computer center, student center. Dormitories wired for high-speed internet access and linked to campus network. Commuter students can connect to campus network. Online course registration, online library, helpline, wireless network available.

**Student life. Freshman orientation:** Mandatory, $40 fee. Preregistration for classes offered. **Policies:** Undergraduate students required to donate 45 hours of community service for each year of attendance. Religious observance required. **Housing:** Guaranteed on-campus for freshmen. Coed dorms, single-sex dorms, apartments available. $200 fully refundable deposit, deadline 5/1. **Activities:** Bands, campus ministries, choral groups, dance, drama, international student organizations, literary magazine, music ensembles, musical theater, radio station, student government, student newspaper, symphony orchestra, TV station, Students in Free Enterprise, Newman club, Kappa Delta Epsilon, Kappa Psi, Lambda Pi Eta, Theta Alpha Kappa, American Society of Health System Pharmacists, American Association of Christian Counselors, Alpha Psi Omega, campus programming association.

**Athletics.** NCAA, NCCAA. **Intercollegiate:** Baseball M, basketball, cheerleading, cross-country, golf, soccer, softball W, tennis, volleyball W. **Intramural:** Basketball, bowling, football (non-tackle), golf, racquetball, soccer, softball, table tennis, volleyball. **Team name:** Sailfish.

**Student services.** Career counseling, student employment services, financial aid counseling, health services, personal counseling, veterans' counselor.

**Contact.** E-mail: admit@pba.edu
Phone: (561) 803-2000 Toll-free number: (888) 468-6722
Fax: (561) 803-2115
Rod Sullivan, Director of Admission, Palm Beach Atlantic University, PO Box 24708, West Palm Beach, FL 33416-4708

## Rasmussen College: Fort Myers
**Fort Myers, Florida**
**www.rasmussen.edu**

- For-profit 4-year technical college
- Small city
- 510 degree-seeking undergraduates

**General.** Regionally accredited. **Calendar:** Quarter. **Full-time faculty:** 5 total. **Part-time faculty:** 43 total.

**Basis for selection.** Open admission, but selective for some programs.

**2009-2010 Annual costs.** Per credit hour charges vary from $365 to $450 leading to degree programs.

**Application procedures. Admission:** No deadline. $20 fee. **Financial aid:** No deadline.

**Academics. Credit/placement by examination:** CLEP.

**Majors. Business:** Accounting, business admin. **Communications technology:** Animation/special effects. **Computer sciences:** Game design. **Health:** Health care admin. **Protective services:** Police science.

**Contact.** Phone: (239) 477-2100
Carmen Cordisco, Director of Admissions, Rasmussen College: Fort Myers, 9160 Forum Corporate Parkway, Suite 100, Fort Myers, FL 33905-7805

## Rasmussen College: Ocala
**Ocala, Florida**
**www.rasmussen.edu**                    CB code: 3502

- For-profit 4-year career college
- Commuter campus in small city
- 1,212 degree-seeking undergraduates

**General.** Regionally accredited. **Degrees:** 17 bachelor's, 120 associate awarded. **Calendar:** Quarter, extensive summer session. **Full-time faculty:** 15 total. **Part-time faculty:** 365 total.

**Basis for selection.** Open admission, but selective for some programs. Some programs require entrance examinations and additional information. COMPASS used for placement.

**2009-2010 Annual costs.** Per credit hour charges vary from $365 to $450 leading to degree programs.

**Application procedures. Admission:** No deadline. $60 fee. Admission notification on a rolling basis. **Financial aid:** No deadline. FAFSA, institutional form required. Applicants notified on a rolling basis.

**Academics. Special study options:** Distance learning, double major, honors, independent study, internships. **Credit/placement by examination:** AP, CLEP, IB, institutional tests. 45 credit hours maximum toward associate degree, 90 toward bachelor's. Limited to specific programs, and to courses for which programs are available. **Support services:** Learning center, remedial instruction, study skills assistance, tutoring, writing center.

**Majors. Business:** Accounting, business admin. **Computer sciences:** Web page design. **Protective services:** Law enforcement admin.

**Computing on campus.** 100 workstations in library, computer center, student center. Online course registration, online library, helpline, wireless network available.

**Student life. Freshman orientation:** Mandatory.

**Student services.** Adult student services, career counseling, services for economically disadvantaged, student employment services, financial aid counseling, placement for graduates.

**Contact.** E-mail: miguel.ramos@rasmussen.edu
Phone: (352) 629-1941 Fax: (352) 629-0926
Miguel Ramos, Director of Admissions, Rasmussen College: Ocala, 2221 Southwest 19th Avenue Road, Ocala, FL 34471

## Rasmussen College: Pasco County
**Holiday, Florida**
**www.rasmussen.edu**                    CB code: 3503

- For-profit 4-year career college
- Commuter campus in small city
- 883 degree-seeking undergraduates

**General.** Regionally accredited. **Degrees:** 13 bachelor's, 41 associate awarded. **Location:** 30 miles from Tampa. **Calendar:** Quarter, extensive summer session. **Full-time faculty:** 10 total. **Part-time faculty:** 26 total.

**Basis for selection.** Open admission, but selective for some programs. Some programs require entrance examinations and additional information. COMPASS used for placement.

**2009-2010 Annual costs.** Per credit hour charges vary from $365 to $450 leading to degree programs.

**Application procedures. Admission:** No deadline. $20 fee. Admission notification on a rolling basis. **Financial aid:** No deadline. FAFSA, institutional form required. Applicants notified on a rolling basis.

**Academics. Special study options:** Distance learning, double major, honors, independent study, internships. **Credit/placement by examination:** AP, CLEP, IB, institutional tests. 45 credit hours maximum toward associate degree, 90 toward bachelor's. Limited to specific programs, and to courses. **Support services:** Learning center, remedial instruction, study skills assistance, tutoring, writing center.

**Majors. Business:** Accounting, business admin. **Computer sciences:** Web page design. **Health:** Health care admin. **Other:** Graphic technology.

**Computing on campus.** 100 workstations in library, computer center, student center. Online course registration, online library, helpline, wireless network available.

**Student life. Freshman orientation:** Mandatory.

**Student services.** Adult student services, career counseling, services for economically disadvantaged, student employment services, financial aid counseling, placement for graduates.

**Contact.** E-mail: staceyann.sinclair@rasmussen.edu
Phone: (727) 942-0069 Fax: (727) 938-5709
Staceyann Sinclair, Director of Admissions, Rasmussen College: Pasco County, 2127 Grand Boulevard, Holiday, FL 34690

## Remington College: Tampa
**Tampa, Florida**
**www.remingtoncollege.edu**                    CB code: 0123

- For-profit 4-year technical college
- Commuter campus in very large city

**General.** Founded in 1948. Accredited by ACCSCT. **Calendar:** Quarter.

**Annual costs/financial aid.** Costs of entire programs leading to diploma, associate degree, and bachelor's degree range from $13,950 to $39,950; include books and supplies. Personal expenses: $1,200. Need-based financial aid available for full-time students.

**Contact.** Phone: (813) 935-5700
Director of Recruiting, 6302 East Dr. Martin Luther King, Jr., Boulevard, Tampa, FL 33619

---

## Ringling College of Art and Design
**Sarasota, Florida**
www.ringling.edu
CB member
CB code: 5573

- Private 4-year visual arts college
- Residential campus in small city
- 1,318 degree-seeking undergraduates: 4% part-time, 57% women, 4% African American, 7% Asian American, 12% Hispanic American, 1% Native American, 6% international
- 73% of applicants admitted
- Application essay required
- 63% graduate within 6 years; 7% enter graduate study

**General.** Founded in 1931. Regionally accredited. **Degrees:** 225 bachelor's awarded. **Location:** 50 miles from Tampa. **Calendar:** Semester. **Full-time faculty:** 83 total; 66% have terminal degrees, 6% minority, 30% women. **Part-time faculty:** 65 total; 34% have terminal degrees, 2% minority, 43% women. **Class size:** 64% < 20, 35% 20-39, less than 1% 40-49, less than 1% 50-99. **Special facilities:** Art library, art center, art galleries.

**Freshman class profile.** 1,147 applied, 842 admitted, 319 enrolled.

| | | | |
|---|---|---|---|
| GPA 3.75 or higher: | 13% | Return as sophomores: | 81% |
| GPA 3.50-3.74: | 18% | Out-of-state: | 47% |
| GPA 3.0-3.49: | 38% | Live on campus: | 87% |
| GPA 2.0-2.99: | 31% | International: | 10% |
| End year in good standing: | 90% | | |

**Basis for selection.** Portfolio, school achievement record, statement of purpose, and recommendations important. Interview recommended. Portfolio required. **Homeschooled:** State high school equivalency certificate required. **Learning Disabled:** Students seeking special accommodations for learning disabilities must provide documentation of disability.

**High school preparation.** College-preparatory program recommended.

**2009-2010 Annual costs.** Tuition/fees: $28,924. Required fees may vary according to program. Room/board: $10,470.

**2009-2010 Financial aid. Need-based:** Average need met was 41%. Average scholarship/grant was $9,020; average loan $7,393. 38% of total undergraduate aid awarded as scholarships/grants, 62% as loans/jobs. **Non-need-based:** Scholarships awarded for academics, art.

**Application procedures. Admission:** Priority date 3/1; no deadline. $70 fee, may be waived for applicants with need. Admission notification on a rolling basis beginning on or about 9/1. **Financial aid:** Priority date 3/1; no closing date. FAFSA required. Applicants notified on a rolling basis starting 4/1; must reply within 2 week(s) of notification.

**Academics. Special study options:** Dual enrollment of high school students, exchange student, independent study, internships, New York semester, study abroad. **Credit/placement by examination:** AP, CLEP, IB. 30 credit hours maximum toward bachelor's degree. **Support services:** Learning center, pre-admission summer program, remedial instruction, study skills assistance, tutoring, writing center.

**Majors. Communications technology:** Animation/special effects. **Visual/performing arts:** Arts management, commercial/advertising art, graphic design, illustration, interior design, painting, photography, printmaking, sculpture, studio arts.

**Most popular majors.** Communication technologies 30%, visual/performing arts 70%.

**Computing on campus.** 850 workstations in dormitories, library, computer center, student center. Dormitories wired for high-speed internet access and linked to campus network. Commuter students can connect to campus network. Online course registration, helpline, repair service, student web hosting, wireless network available.

**Student life. Freshman orientation:** Mandatory. Held the week prior to start of classes. **Housing:** Coed dorms, single-sex dorms, special housing

for disabled, apartments, wellness housing available. $100 fully refundable deposit. All housing accommodations are ADA compliant. **Activities:** Campus ministries, dance, drama, international student organizations, student government.

**Athletics. Intramural:** Basketball, soccer, softball, table tennis, volleyball.

**Student services.** Career counseling, student employment services, financial aid counseling, health services, minority student services, personal counseling, placement for graduates, veterans' counselor, women's services. **Physically disabled:** Services for visually, hearing impaired.

**Contact.** E-mail: admissions@ringling.edu
Phone: (941) 351-5100 Toll-free number: (800) 255-7695
Fax: (941) 359-7517
James Dean, Dean of Admissions, Ringling College of Art and Design, 2700 North Tamiami Trail, Sarasota, FL 34234-5895

---

## Rollins College
**Winter Park, Florida**
www.rollins.edu
CB member
CB code: 5572

- Private 4-year liberal arts college
- Residential campus in large town
- 1,773 degree-seeking undergraduates: 58% women, 4% African American, 4% Asian American, 10% Hispanic American, 1% Native American, 4% international
- 713 degree-seeking graduate students
- 62% of applicants admitted
- Application essay required
- 66% graduate within 6 years

**General.** Founded in 1885. Regionally accredited. **Degrees:** 377 bachelor's awarded; master's offered. **Location:** 5 miles from Orlando. **Calendar:** Semester, limited summer session. **Full-time faculty:** 196 total; 93% have terminal degrees, 11% minority, 41% women. **Part-time faculty:** 40 total; 48% have terminal degrees, 18% minority, 55% women. **Class size:** 69% < 20, 31% 20-39, less than 1% 40-49. **Special facilities:** 2 theaters, child development center, center for psychology, greenhouse, high tech classrooms.

**Freshman class profile.** 2,999 applied, 1,847 admitted, 472 enrolled.

| | | | |
|---|---|---|---|
| Mid 50% test scores | | GPA 2.0-2.99: | 27% |
| SAT critical reading: | 560-650 | Rank in top quarter: | 65% |
| SAT math: | 560-650 | Rank in top tenth: | 39% |
| ACT composite: | 24-29 | Return as sophomores: | 82% |
| GPA 3.75 or higher: | 22% | Out-of-state: | 52% |
| GPA 3.50-3.74: | 11% | Live on campus: | 94% |
| GPA 3.0-3.49: | 40% | International: | 4% |

**Basis for selection.** School achievement record most important, followed by test scores, activities, essay, recommendations, interview. Audition recommended for music, theater arts majors.

**High school preparation.** College-preparatory program recommended. 17 units required; 24 recommended. Required and recommended units include English 4, mathematics 3-4, social studies 2-3, history 2-3, science 2-4, foreign language 2-3 and academic electives 2-3.

**2009-2010 Annual costs.** Tuition/fees: $36,220. Room/board: $11,320. Books/supplies: $750. Personal expenses: $3,005.

**2009-2010 Financial aid. Need-based:** 293 full-time freshmen applied for aid; 246 were judged to have need; 246 of these received aid. Average need met was 89%. Average scholarship/grant was $21,550; average loan $3,982. 60% of total undergraduate aid awarded as scholarships/grants, 40% as loans/jobs. **Non-need-based:** Awarded to 365 full-time undergraduates, including 92 freshmen. Scholarships awarded for academics, art, athletics, leadership, music/drama, state residency. **Additional information:** Audition required for theater arts and music scholarship applicants. Portfolio required for art scholarships.

**Application procedures. Admission:** Closing date 2/15 (postmark date). $40 fee, may be waived for applicants with need. Admission notification 4/1. Must reply by May 1 or within 3 week(s) if notified thereafter. **Financial aid:** Closing date 3/1. FAFSA, institutional form required. Applicants notified on a rolling basis starting 3/1.

**Academics.** International business major featuring language training, internships and study abroad available; pre-professional support services. **Special study options:** Accelerated study, combined bachelor's/graduate degree, cross-registration, double major, dual enrollment of high school students, exchange student, honors, independent study, internships, semester at sea, student-designed major, study abroad, teacher certification program, Washington semester. **Credit/placement by examination:** AP, CLEP, IB, institutional tests. 76 credit hours maximum toward bachelor's degree. **Support services:** Learning center, reduced course load, study skills assistance, tutoring, writing center.

**Honors college/program.** Top 10% of entering freshman class admitted.

**Majors. Area/ethnic studies:** Latin American. **Biology:** General, Biochemistry/biophysics and molecular biology, marine. **Business:** International. **Communications:** Media studies. **Computer sciences:** General. **Conservation:** Environmental studies. **Education:** General. **Foreign languages:** Classics, French, Spanish. **History:** General. **Math:** General. **Philosophy/religion:** Philosophy, religion. **Physical sciences:** Chemistry, physics. **Psychology:** General. **Social sciences:** Anthropology, economics, international relations, political science, sociology. **Visual/performing arts:** Art, art history/conservation, dramatic.

**Most popular majors.** Biology 6%, business/marketing 12%, psychology 15%, social sciences 32%, visual/performing arts 10%.

**Computing on campus.** 205 workstations in dormitories, library, computer center, student center. Dormitories wired for high-speed internet access and linked to campus network. Commuter students can connect to campus network. Online course registration, online library, helpline, repair service, student web hosting, wireless network available.

**Student life. Freshman orientation:** Mandatory. Preregistration for classes offered. Held just prior to fall semester. **Housing:** Guaranteed on-campus for freshmen. Coed dorms, single-sex dorms, special housing for disabled, apartments, fraternity/sorority housing available. $500 nonrefundable deposit, deadline 5/15. **Activities:** Bands, campus ministries, choral groups, dance, drama, film society, international student organizations, literary magazine, music ensembles, musical theater, radio station, student government, student newspaper, symphony orchestra, TV station, ally alliance, Muslim student association, Hillel, Rollins, Habitat for Humanity, 5 Stones, cultural action committee, College Republicans, College Democrats, Black Student Union.

**Athletics.** NCAA. **Intercollegiate:** Baseball M, basketball, cross-country, golf, lacrosse, rowing (crew), sailing, skiing, soccer, softball W, swimming, tennis, volleyball W. **Intramural:** Basketball M, football (non-tackle), soccer, softball, table tennis, tennis, volleyball. **Team name:** Tars.

**Student services.** Alcohol/substance abuse counseling, chaplain/spiritual director, career counseling, student employment services, financial aid counseling, health services, personal counseling, placement for graduates, veterans' counselor. **Physically disabled:** Services for visually, speech, hearing impaired.

**Contact.** E-mail: admission@rollins.edu
Phone: (407) 646-2161 Fax: (407) 646-1502
Mike Lynch, Director of Admission, Rollins College, 1000 Holt Avenue, Winter Park, FL 32789

## St. John Vianney College Seminary
**Miami, Florida**
www.sjvcs.edu                                    CB code: 5650

- Private 4-year liberal arts and seminary college for men affiliated with Roman Catholic Church
- Residential campus in very large city
- 61 degree-seeking undergraduates: 2% women, 3% African American, 3% Asian American, 40% Hispanic American, 17% international
- 15 degree-seeking graduate students
- 100% of applicants admitted
- Interview required

**General.** Founded in 1959. Regionally accredited. **Degrees:** 10 bachelor's awarded. **Location:** 12 miles from downtown. **Calendar:** Semester, limited summer session. **Full-time faculty:** 7 total. **Part-time faculty:** 12 total. **Class size:** 100% < 20.

**Freshman class profile.** 12 applied, 12 admitted, 12 enrolled.

| | | | |
|---|---|---|---|
| End year in good standing: | 100% | Live on campus: | 100% |
| Out-of-state: | 2% | | |

**Basis for selection.** Interview, academic record, recommendations required. Those to be formed for priesthood should present evidence of vocation for priesthood and submit psychological and physical evaluations. Applicants referred by home (church) Diocesan Offices of Vocations.

**High school preparation.** 20 units required. Required units include English 4, mathematics 2, social studies 2, history 2, science 2, foreign language 2 and academic electives 6.

**2009-2010 Annual costs.** Tuition/fees: $17,000. Room/board: $9,500. Books/supplies: $600.

**Application procedures. Admission:** Priority date 6/30; deadline 7/15 (receipt date). No application fee. Admission notification on a rolling basis. **Financial aid:** No deadline. FAFSA required. Applicants notified on a rolling basis.

**Academics.** Fluency in both English and Spanish must be achieved. Students required to take at least 1 course in alternate language each semester. **Special study options:** Cross-registration, ESL, independent study. **Credit/placement by examination:** AP, CLEP, institutional tests. **Support services:** Pre-admission summer program, reduced course load, remedial instruction, study skills assistance, tutoring.

**Majors. Philosophy/religion:** Philosophy.

**Computing on campus.** 12 workstations in library, computer center. Online library, wireless network available.

**Student life. Freshman orientation:** Mandatory, $2,000 fee. Preregistration for classes offered. 3 weeks during August. **Policies:** All sophomores and upperclassmen assigned weekly apostolic work at various locations. Religious observance required. **Housing:** Guaranteed on-campus for all undergraduates. **Activities:** Choral groups, drama, music ensembles, student government, student newspaper, apostolic works program.

**Athletics. Intramural:** Baseball M, basketball M, handball M, racquetball M, soccer M, softball M, swimming M, table tennis M, tennis M, volleyball M, weight lifting M.

**Student services.** Adult student services, career counseling, financial aid counseling, health services, personal counseling.

**Contact.** Phone: (305) 223-4561 ext. 115 Fax: (305) 223-0650
Ramon Santos, Academic Dean, St. John Vianney College Seminary, 2900 Southwest 87 Avenue, Miami, FL 33165-3244

## Saint Leo University
**Saint Leo, Florida**                             **CB member**
www.saintleo.edu                                   **CB code: 5638**

- Private 4-year university affiliated with Roman Catholic Church
- Residential campus in rural community
- 1,735 degree-seeking undergraduates: 5% part-time, 51% women, 10% African American, 1% Asian American, 11% Hispanic American, 8% international
- 2,373 degree-seeking graduate students
- 76% of applicants admitted
- SAT or ACT (ACT writing optional), application essay required
- 43% graduate within 6 years

**General.** Founded in 1889. Regionally accredited. **Degrees:** 278 bachelor's, 15 associate awarded; master's offered. **ROTC:** Army, Air Force. **Location:** 25 miles from Tampa. **Calendar:** Semester, limited summer session. **Full-time faculty:** 106 total; 87% have terminal degrees, 11% minority, 36% women. **Part-time faculty:** 51 total; 33% have terminal degrees, 8% minority, 37% women. **Class size:** 49% < 20, 51% 20-39. **Special facilities:** Center for Catholic and Jewish studies.

**Freshman class profile.** 2,074 applied, 1,586 admitted, 489 enrolled.

| Mid 50% test scores | | | |
|---|---|---|---|
| SAT critical reading: | 440-530 | GPA 2.0-2.99: | 37% |
| SAT math: | 450-550 | Rank in top quarter: | 33% |
| SAT writing: | 430-520 | Rank in top tenth: | 11% |
| ACT composite: | 20-24 | Return as sophomores: | 68% |
| GPA 3.75 or higher: | 21% | Out-of-state: | 39% |
| GPA 3.50-3.74: | 14% | Live on campus: | 89% |
| GPA 3.0-3.49: | 28% | International: | 5% |

**Basis for selection.** Test scores, GPA, guidance counselor's recommendation, high school curriculum important. Interview recommended. **Home-schooled:** Transcript of courses and grades, interview, letter of recommendation (nonparent) required. Bibliography of all high school reading material, 2 letters of recommendation, portfolio of sample work required.

**High school preparation.** College-preparatory program recommended. 16 units recommended. Recommended units include English 4, mathematics 3, social studies 3, science 2, foreign language 2 and academic electives 2. Algebra I and II, geometry strongly recommended. Those planning to study science should complete courses in biology and chemistry.

**2009-2010 Annual costs.** Tuition/fees: $17,646. Room/board: $8,724. Books/supplies: $1,200. Personal expenses: $1,330.

**2009-2010 Financial aid. Need-based:** 455 full-time freshmen applied for aid; 379 were judged to have need; 379 of these received aid. Average need met was 80%. Average scholarship/grant was $12,865; average loan $3,327. 63% of total undergraduate aid awarded as scholarships/grants, 37% as loans/jobs. **Non-need-based:** Awarded to 200 full-time undergraduates, including 47 freshmen. Scholarships awarded for academics, alumni affiliation, athletics, leadership, minority status, music/drama, religious affiliation, state residency.

**Application procedures. Admission:** Priority date 3/1; deadline 8/15 (postmark date). $35 fee, may be waived for applicants with need. Admission notification on a rolling basis beginning on or about 10/15. Must reply by May 1 or within 2 week(s) if notified thereafter. **Financial aid:** Priority date 3/1; no closing date. FAFSA required. Applicants notified on a rolling basis starting 1/31.

**Academics. Special study options:** Combined bachelor's/graduate degree, distance learning, double major, honors, independent study, internships, liberal arts/career combination, study abroad, teacher certification program, weekend college. Opportunity to study abroad in Italy, Switzerland, France, Ecuador, Spain, United Kingdom, Ireland, Australia, Germany, and Scotland. **Credit/placement by examination:** AP, CLEP, IB, SAT, ACT, institutional tests. 40 credit hours maximum toward associate degree, 40 toward bachelor's. **Support services:** Learning center, pre-admission summer program, reduced course load, remedial instruction, study skills assistance, tutoring, writing center.

**Honors college/program.** 3.5 GPA and 1060 SAT (exclusive of Writing) or 23 ACT required. Full honors curriculum consists of integrated sequence of 6 courses plus 2 research courses.

**Majors. Biology:** General. **Business:** Accounting, business admin, entrepreneurial studies, hospitality admin, human resources, international, management science, marketing. **Communications:** Media studies. **Computer sciences:** General. **Conservation:** Environmental studies. **Education:** Elementary, middle. **Health:** Clinical lab science, facilities admin, health care admin. **History:** General. **Math:** General. **Parks/recreation:** Sports admin. **Philosophy/religion:** Religion. **Protective services:** Criminal justice. **Psychology:** General. **Public administration:** Community org/advocacy, social work. **Social sciences:** International relations, political science, sociology.

**Most popular majors.** Biology 9%, business/marketing 32%, education 7%, parks/recreation 6%, psychology 10%, security/protective services 10%, social sciences 6%.

**Computing on campus.** 1,243 workstations in dormitories, library, student center. Dormitories wired for high-speed internet access and linked to campus network. Commuter students can connect to campus network. Online course registration, online library, helpline, repair service, student web hosting, wireless network available.

**Student life. Freshman orientation:** Mandatory, $300 fee. Preregistration for classes offered. 4-day program in August includes team-building, personal responsibility activities. Advising, testing, introduction to student life in mid-July. **Policies:** Fish aquariums allowed. **Housing:** Guaranteed on-campus for all undergraduates. Coed dorms, single-sex dorms, special housing for disabled, apartments, wellness housing available. $150 nonrefundable deposit, deadline 8/15. Freshmen-only housing available. **Activities:** Concert band, campus ministries, choral groups, dance, drama, film society, international student organizations, literary magazine, music ensembles, musical theater, student government, student newspaper, TV station, Circle-K, Samaritans, intercultural student association, Saint Leo Ambassadors, Best Buddies, student chaplain program, Pi Sigma Alpha, Brothers and Sisters United, social work club, Latino club.

**Athletics.** NCAA. **Intercollegiate:** Baseball M, basketball, cross-country, golf, lacrosse M, soccer, softball W, swimming, tennis, volleyball W. **Intramural:** Basketball, football (non-tackle), racquetball, soccer, softball, table tennis, tennis, volleyball. **Team name:** Lions.

**Student services.** Adult student services, alcohol/substance abuse counseling, chaplain/spiritual director, career counseling, student employment services, financial aid counseling, health services, personal counseling. **Physically disabled:** Services for visually impaired.

**Contact.** E-mail: admission@saintleo.edu
Phone: (352) 588-8283 Toll-free number: (800) 334-5532
Fax: (352) 588-8257
Martin Smith, Assistant Vice President of Enrollment, Saint Leo University, Office of Admission, Saint Leo, FL 33574-6665

---

## Saint Thomas University
**Miami Gardens, Florida**
www.stu.edu                                    CB code: 5076

- Private 4-year university affiliated with Roman Catholic Church
- Commuter campus in very large city
- 1,176 degree-seeking undergraduates: 6% part-time, 56% women, 25% African American, 1% Asian American, 48% Hispanic American, 9% international
- 1,300 degree-seeking graduate students
- 59% of applicants admitted
- SAT or ACT (ACT writing optional) required
- 36% graduate within 6 years

**General.** Founded in 1961. Regionally accredited. Multilocation institution. Affiliated with Archdiocese of Miami. **Degrees:** 287 bachelor's awarded; master's, doctoral, professional offered. **Location:** 10 miles from Miami. **Calendar:** Semester, extensive summer session. **Full-time faculty:** 100 total; 83% have terminal degrees, 29% minority, 43% women. **Part-time faculty:** 131 total; 47% have terminal degrees, 47% minority, 44% women. **Class size:** 65% < 20, 35% 20-39, less than 1% 40-49, less than 1% 50-99.

**Freshman class profile.** 674 applied, 400 admitted, 238 enrolled.

| Mid 50% test scores | | | |
|---|---|---|---|
| SAT critical reading: | 390-480 | Rank in top quarter: | 20% |
| SAT math: | 380-480 | Rank in top tenth: | 6% |
| SAT writing: | 380-470 | Return as sophomores: | 69% |
| ACT composite: | 16-19 | Out-of-state: | 16% |
| GPA 3.75 or higher: | 7% | Live on campus: | 31% |
| GPA 3.50-3.74: | 9% | International: | 9% |
| GPA 3.0-3.49: | 29% | | |
| GPA 2.0-2.99: | 55% | | |

**Basis for selection.** High school grades, test scores primary factors. Class rank, interview, school, community activities, recommendations also considered. Interview recommended.

**High school preparation.** College-preparatory program recommended. 18 units required. Required units include English 4, mathematics 3, social studies 3, science 2 and academic electives 6.

**2009-2010 Annual costs.** Tuition/fees: $21,690. Room/board: $6,516. Books/supplies: $1,000. Personal expenses: $1,870.

**2009-2010 Financial aid. Need-based:** 215 full-time freshmen applied for aid; 198 were judged to have need; 198 of these received aid. Average scholarship/grant was $2,411; average loan $3,528. 81% of total undergraduate aid awarded as scholarships/grants, 19% as loans/jobs. **Non-need-based:** Awarded to 1,084 full-time undergraduates, including 269 freshmen. Scholarships awarded for academics, athletics, leadership, music/drama, religious affiliation, state residency.

**Application procedures. Admission:** No deadline. $40 fee, may be waived for applicants with need. Admission notification on a rolling basis. Must reply by May 1 or within 2 week(s) if notified thereafter. Applicants needing on-campus housing strongly encouraged to apply before May 15. **Financial aid:** Priority date 4/1; no closing date. FAFSA required. Applicants notified on a rolling basis starting 3/1.

**Academics. Special study options:** Combined bachelor's/graduate degree, distance learning, double major, dual enrollment of high school students, honors, independent study, internships, liberal arts/career combination, teacher certification program. **Credit/placement by examination:** AP, CLEP, SAT, ACT, institutional tests. 45 credit hours maximum toward bachelor's degree. **Support services:** Learning center, pre-admission summer program, reduced course load, remedial instruction, study skills assistance, tutoring, writing center.

**Majors. Biology:** General. **Business:** Accounting, business admin, finance, hospitality admin, international, organizational behavior, tourism/travel. **Communications:** General, media studies. **Computer sciences:** General, computer science. **Conservation:** Environmental studies. **Education:** Elementary, secondary, social studies. **Health:** Health care admin, premedicine, preveterinary. **History:** General. **Legal studies:** Prelaw. **Liberal arts:** Arts/sciences. **Parks/recreation:** Sports admin. **Philosophy/religion:** Religion. **Physical sciences:** Chemistry. **Protective services:** Criminal justice. **Psychology:** General. **Public administration:** Human services. **Social sciences:** Political science. **Theology:** Religious ed.

**Most popular majors.** Business/marketing 51%, education 9%, psychology 8%, security/protective services 9%.

**Computing on campus.** 123 workstations in library, computer center. Dormitories linked to campus network. Online course registration, helpline, wireless network available.

**Student life. Freshman orientation:** Mandatory. **Housing:** Single-sex dorms available. $225 fully refundable deposit. **Activities:** Campus ministries, choral groups, international student organizations, literary magazine, music ensembles, student government, TV station, political action club, Students for Global Preservation, prelaw society, premedicine club, accounting club.

**Athletics.** NAIA. **Intercollegiate:** Baseball M, cross-country, golf, soccer, softball W, tennis, volleyball W. **Intramural:** Golf, soccer M, softball, tennis, volleyball. **Team name:** Bobcats.

**Student services.** Adult student services, alcohol/substance abuse counseling, career counseling, student employment services, financial aid counseling, health services, personal counseling, placement for graduates. **Physically disabled:** Services for visually, hearing impaired.

**Contact.** E-mail: signup@stu.edu
Phone: (305) 628-6546 Toll-free number: (800) 367-9010
Fax: (305) 628-6591
Lydia Amy, Dean, Enrollment Services, Saint Thomas University, 16401 Northwest 37th Avenue, Miami Gardens, FL 33054-6459

## Schiller International University
**Largo, Florida**
**www.schiller.edu**                    CB code: 0601

- For-profit 4-year university
- Residential campus in small city
- 110 degree-seeking undergraduates
- 410 graduate students

**General.** Founded in 1964. Accredited by ACICS. Campuses located in Florida, Paris, London, Madrid, Heidelberg, as well as Schiller Online. Students may transfer between campuses without loss of time or credit. **Degrees:** 20 bachelor's awarded; master's offered. **Location:** 20 miles from Tampa. **Calendar:** Semester, extensive summer session. **Full-time faculty:** 25 total. **Part-time faculty:** 168 total.

**Basis for selection.** Open admission. Interviews recommended.

**2009-2010 Annual costs.** Books/supplies: $1,250.

**2008-2009 Financial aid. Non-need-based:** Scholarships awarded for academics, alumni affiliation, leadership, minority status, state residency. **Additional information:** Special scholarship program for US students studying abroad at European campuses of Schiller. Work-study available to students taking 2 or more courses.

**Application procedures. Admission:** No deadline. $20 fee. Application must be submitted on paper. Admission notification on a rolling basis. **Financial aid:** Closing date 4/1. FAFSA, institutional form required. Applicants notified on a rolling basis starting 5/1; must reply within 3 week(s) of notification.

**Academics.** Completion of intermediate level of at least one foreign language required for most undergraduate degree programs. **Special study options:** Accelerated study, cooperative education, distance learning, double major, ESL, honors, independent study, internships, liberal arts/career combination, study abroad. **Credit/placement by examination:** AP, CLEP, IB, institutional tests. 16 credit hours maximum toward associate degree, 16 toward bachelor's. **Support services:** Learning center, reduced course load, study skills assistance, tutoring.

**Majors. Business:** General, banking/financial services, business admin, finance, hotel/motel admin, international, international marketing, management information systems, marketing, tourism/travel. **Foreign languages:** French, German. **Interdisciplinary:** Global studies. **Social sciences:** International economics, international relations.

**Most popular majors.** Business/marketing 77%.

**Computing on campus.** Online library, wireless network available.

**Student life. Freshman orientation:** Mandatory. **Housing:** Coed dorms available. **Activities:** Model UN, student government.

**Student services.** Adult student services, career counseling, services for economically disadvantaged, student employment services, financial aid counseling, minority student services, personal counseling, placement for graduates.

**Contact.** E-mail: admissions@schiller.edu
Phone: (727) 736-5082 Toll-free number: (800) 261-9751
Fax: (727) 734-0359
Phil Krebs, Director of Admissions, Schiller International University, 300 East Bay Drive, Largo, FL 33770-3716

## South University: Tampa
**Tampa, Florida**
**www.southuniversity.edu**

- For-profit 4-year university
- Commuter campus in large city
- 542 degree-seeking undergraduates: 25% part-time, 79% women
- Interview required

**General.** Regionally accredited. **Degrees:** 72 bachelor's awarded; master's offered. **Calendar:** Quarter, extensive summer session. **Full-time faculty:** 21 total; 48% have terminal degrees, 14% minority, 48% women. **Part-time faculty:** 39 total; 28% have terminal degrees, 33% minority, 80% women.

**Basis for selection.** Test scores most important followed by rigor of secondary school record. SAT or ACT recommended. **Homeschooled:** Students must provide evidence that home schooling was conducted in accordance with state laws. A certificate of attendance or completion is not sufficient.

**2009-2010 Annual costs.** Tuition/fees: $14,985.

**Application procedures. Admission:** No deadline. $50 fee. Admission notification on a rolling basis.

**Academics. Special study options:** Distance learning, internships. **Credit/placement by examination:** CLEP.

**Majors. Business:** Business admin. **Health:** Health care admin, health services, nursing (RN). **Psychology:** General.

**Computing on campus.** Commuter students can connect to campus network. Online library available.

**Student life. Freshman orientation:** Mandatory. Preregistration for classes offered.

**Student services.** Career counseling, student employment services, financial aid counseling, placement for graduates.

**Contact.** Phone: (813) 393-3800
Michele D'Alessio, Director of Admissions, South University: Tampa, 4401 North Himes Avenue, Tampa, FL 33614

## South University: West Palm Beach
**West Palm Beach, Florida**
**www.southuniversity.edu**          CB code: 5321

- For-profit 4-year university
- Commuter campus in large city
- 814 degree-seeking undergraduates: 29% part-time, 79% women
- 49 graduate students
- Interview required

**General.** Regionally accredited. **Degrees:** 83 bachelor's, 41 associate awarded; master's offered. **Location:** 3 miles from downtown, 29 miles from Fort Lauderdale. **Calendar:** Quarter, extensive summer session. **Full-time faculty:** 24 total; 25% minority, 62% women. **Part-time faculty:** 72 total; 36% minority, 56% women.

**Basis for selection.** Test scores most important, followed by rigor of secondary school record. SAT or ACT recommended. **Homeschooled:** Students must provide evidence that homeschooling was conducted in accordance with state laws. A certificate of attendance or completion is not sufficient.

**2009-2010 Annual costs.** Tuition/fees: $14,985.

**Application procedures. Admission:** No deadline. $50 fee. Admission notification on a rolling basis. **Financial aid:** No deadline. FAFSA required. Applicants notified on a rolling basis; must reply within 2 week(s) of notification.

**Academics. Special study options:** Distance learning, internships. **Credit/ placement by examination:** AP, CLEP, SAT, ACT, institutional tests. **Support services:** Remedial instruction, study skills assistance, tutoring.

**Majors. Business:** Business admin. **Computer sciences:** Information technology. **Health:** Health care admin, health services, nursing (RN). **Legal studies:** General. **Protective services:** Police science. **Psychology:** General.

**Most popular majors.** Business/marketing 10%, health sciences 78%, legal studies 11%.

**Computing on campus.** Commuter students can connect to campus network. Online library available.

**Student life. Freshman orientation:** Mandatory. Preregistration for classes offered.

**Student services.** Career counseling, student employment services, financial aid counseling, placement for graduates, veterans' counselor.

**Contact.** Phone: (561) 697-9200 Fax: (561) 697-9944
Gary Malisos, Director of Admissions, South University: West Palm Beach, 1760 North Congress Avenue, West Palm Beach, FL 33409-5178

## Southeastern University
Lakeland, Florida
www.seuniversity.edu                     CB code: 5621

- Private 4-year liberal arts and teachers college affiliated with Assemblies of God
- Residential campus in small city
- 2,497 degree-seeking undergraduates: 6% part-time, 58% women, 9% African American, 1% Asian American, 12% Hispanic American
- 251 degree-seeking graduate students
- Application essay required
- 48% graduate within 6 years

**General.** Founded in 1935. Regionally accredited. **Degrees:** 529 bachelor's awarded; master's offered. **ROTC:** Army. **Location:** 40 miles from Tampa, 50 miles from Orlando. **Calendar:** Semester, limited summer session. **Full-time faculty:** 83 total; 65% have terminal degrees, 17% minority, 28% women. **Part-time faculty:** 71 total; 20% have terminal degrees, 13% minority, 39% women. **Class size:** 53% < 20, 36% 20-39, 5% 40-49, 5% 50-99, less than 1% >100.

**Freshman class profile.** 1,163 applied, 882 admitted, 569 enrolled.

| Mid 50% test scores | | GPA 3.50-3.74: | 16% |
|---|---|---|---|
| SAT critical reading: | 440-560 | GPA 3.0-3.49: | 27% |
| SAT math: | 430-570 | GPA 2.0-2.99: | 24% |
| SAT writing: | 430-560 | Return as sophomores: | 65% |
| ACT composite: | 18-24 | Out-of-state: | 42% |
| GPA 3.75 or higher: | 31% | Live on campus: | 94% |

**Basis for selection.** Open admission, but selective for some programs. SAT or ACT used for placement in Math, English; also used to determine scholarship eligibility. Accuplacer may be used in lieu of SAT/ACT. Interview recommended for academically weak applicants.

**High school preparation.** College-preparatory program recommended. Recommended units include English 4, mathematics 4, social studies 4, science 4 and foreign language 2.

**2010-2011 Annual costs.** Tuition/fees (projected): $15,000. Room/board: $7,566. Books/supplies: $1,000.

**2008-2009 Financial aid. Need-based:** 473 full-time freshmen applied for aid; 397 were judged to have need; 397 of these received aid. Average need met was 62%. Average scholarship/grant was $10,191; average loan $3,450. 51% of total undergraduate aid awarded as scholarships/grants, 49% as loans/jobs. **Non-need-based:** Awarded to 432 full-time undergraduates, including 126 freshmen. Scholarships awarded for academics, athletics, leadership, music/drama, ROTC.

**Application procedures. Admission:** Closing date 5/1 (postmark date). $40 fee, may be waived for applicants with need. Admission notification on a rolling basis. Must reply by 6/1. **Financial aid:** Priority date 4/15; no

closing date. FAFSA, institutional form required. Applicants notified on a rolling basis starting 1/1; must reply within 6 week(s) of notification.

**Academics. Special study options:** Distance learning, double major, dual enrollment of high school students, honors, independent study, internships, study abroad, teacher certification program, weekend college. **Credit/ placement by examination:** AP, CLEP, IB, institutional tests. 45 credit hours maximum toward bachelor's degree. **Support services:** Reduced course load, remedial instruction, study skills assistance, tutoring, writing center.

**Majors. Biology:** General. **Business:** General, accounting, finance, international, management information systems, marketing. **Communications:** General, journalism, organizational, radio/tv. **Education:** Biology, elementary, English, mathematics, music, science, social science, special. **Health:** Premedicine. **History:** General. **Math:** General. **Parks/recreation:** Sports admin. **Protective services:** Law enforcement admin. **Psychology:** General. **Public administration:** Human services, social work. **Theology:** Missionary, preministerial, sacred music, youth ministry. **Visual/performing arts:** Dramatic, film/cinema, music performance, piano/organ, voice/opera. **Other:** Church leadership.

**Most popular majors.** Business/marketing 21%, communications/ journalism 9%, education 6%, psychology 6%, public administration/social services 13%, theological studies 23%.

**Computing on campus.** 145 workstations in library, computer center, student center. Dormitories wired for high-speed internet access and linked to campus network. Commuter students can connect to campus network. Online course registration, online library, helpline, wireless network available.

**Student life. Freshman orientation:** Mandatory. Preregistration for classes offered. **Policies:** Religious observance required. **Housing:** Guaranteed on-campus for freshmen. Single-sex dorms available. $200 fully refundable deposit, deadline 6/1. **Activities:** Bands, campus ministries, choral groups, drama, international student organizations, music ensembles, musical theater, opera, radio station, student government, student newspaper, TV station, College Republicans, Habitat for Humanity, International Justice Mission, Social Work Club, Christian Medical and Dental Association, Student Missions Organization.

**Athletics.** NAIA, NCCAA. **Intercollegiate:** Baseball M, basketball, cheerleading, golf M, soccer, tennis W, volleyball W. **Intramural:** Basketball, football (non-tackle), soccer, softball, tennis, volleyball. **Team name:** Fire.

**Student services.** Adult student services, chaplain/spiritual director, career counseling, student employment services, financial aid counseling, health services, personal counseling, placement for graduates.

**Contact.** E-mail: admission@seuniversity.edu
Phone: (863) 667-5018 Toll-free number: (800) 500-8760
Fax: (863) 667-5200
Chris Diaz, Director of Admission, Southeastern University, 1000 Longfellow Boulevard, Lakeland, FL 33801-6034

## State College of Florida, Manatee-Sarasota
Bradenton, Florida                        CB member
www.mccfl.edu                             CB code: 5427

- Public 4-year nursing and community college
- Commuter campus in small city
- 10,113 degree-seeking undergraduates: 49% part-time, 62% women

**General.** Founded in 1957. Regionally accredited. **Degrees:** 1,684 associate awarded. **Location:** 40 miles from Tampa, 20 miles from St. Petersburg. **Calendar:** Semester, extensive summer session. **Full-time faculty:** 169 total; 21% have terminal degrees, 11% minority, 62% women. **Part-time faculty:** 356 total; 4% have terminal degrees, 11% minority, 54% women.

**Freshman class profile.**

| End year in good standing: | 45% | International: | 1% |
|---|---|---|---|
| Out-of-state: | 4% | | |

**Basis for selection.** Open admission, but selective for some programs. Limited enrollment in health programs. Interview recommended for nursing, radiologic technology, respiratory therapy, occupational therapy assistant, physical therapist assistant, dental hygiene majors.

**High school preparation.** Recommended units include English 4, mathematics 3, social studies 2, history 1, science 3 and foreign language 2.

**2009-2010 Annual costs.** Tuition/fees: $2,636; $9,942 out-of-state. Books/ supplies: $1,202. Personal expenses: $1,910.

**2009-2010 Financial aid. Need-based:** 983 full-time freshmen applied for aid; 803 were judged to have need; 803 of these received aid. Average scholarship/grant was $483. **Non-need-based:** Scholarships awarded for academics, art, athletics, music/drama, state residency.

**Application procedures. Admission:** No deadline. No application fee. Admission notification on a rolling basis. **Financial aid:** Priority date 6/1, closing date 7/28. FAFSA required. Applicants notified on a rolling basis starting 3/15.

**Academics. Special study options:** Accelerated study, combined bachelor's/ graduate degree, cooperative education, distance learning, dual enrollment of high school students, honors, independent study, teacher certification program. **Credit/placement by examination:** CLEP. 30 credit hours maximum toward associate degree. SAT, ACT or CPT (Florida Placement Test) used for placement only. **Support services:** Learning center, remedial instruction, study skills assistance, tutoring.

**Computing on campus.** 2,275 workstations in library, computer center. Commuter students can connect to campus network. Online course registration, online library, helpline, repair service, wireless network available.

**Student life. Freshman orientation:** Mandatory. Preregistration for classes offered. **Activities:** Bands, drama, film society, literary magazine, music ensembles, musical theater, opera, student government, student newspaper, symphony orchestra, African-American Student Union, multicultural student club, art club, student Bible club, Manasota Geographic and Anthropological Society, American Chemical Society, student film club, Hispanic-American club.

**Athletics.** NJCAA. **Intercollegiate:** Baseball M, basketball M, softball W, volleyball W. **Intramural:** Basketball, golf, soccer, softball, volleyball, weight lifting. **Team name:** Manatees.

**Student services.** Chaplain/spiritual director, career counseling, student employment services, financial aid counseling, health services, personal counseling, placement for graduates, veterans' counselor. **Physically disabled:** Services for visually, speech, hearing impaired.

**Contact.** E-mail: admissions@scf.edu
Phone: (941) 752-5031 Fax: (941) 727-6380
Marilynn Lewy, Registrar, State College of Florida, Manatee-Sarasota, Box 1849, Bradenton, FL 34206-1849

---

## Stetson University
**DeLand, Florida**
www.stetson.edu

**CB member**
**CB code: 5630**

- Private 4-year university
- Residential campus in large town
- 2,151 degree-seeking undergraduates: 4% part-time, 57% women, 6% African American, 2% Asian American, 11% Hispanic American, 3% international
- 433 degree-seeking graduate students
- 53% of applicants admitted
- SAT or ACT (ACT writing optional), application essay required
- 62% graduate within 6 years; 60% enter graduate study

**General.** Founded in 1883. Regionally accredited. **Degrees:** 487 bachelor's awarded; master's, professional offered. **ROTC:** Army. **Location:** 20 miles from Daytona Beach, 40 miles from Orlando. **Calendar:** Semester, limited summer session. **Full-time faculty:** 229 total; 95% have terminal degrees, 11% minority, 42% women. **Part-time faculty:** 124 total; 68% have terminal degrees, 5% minority, 39% women. **Class size:** 61% < 20, 38% 20-39, less than 1% 40-49, less than 1% 50-99. **Special facilities:** Geological museum, greenhouse with growth chambers, digital arts laboratory.

**Freshman class profile.** 4,640 applied, 2,479 admitted, 502 enrolled.

| Mid 50% test scores | | | |
|---|---|---|---|
| SAT critical reading: | 500-610 | Rank in top quarter: | 64% |
| SAT math: | 500-600 | Rank in top tenth: | 29% |
| SAT writing: | 490-590 | End year in good standing: | 83% |
| ACT composite: | 21-26 | Return as sophomores: | 77% |
| GPA 3.75 or higher: | 53% | Out-of-state: | 15% |
| GPA 3.50-3.74: | 18% | Live on campus: | 86% |
| GPA 3.0-3.49: | 22% | International: | 3% |
| GPA 2.0-2.99: | 7% | Fraternities: | 25% |
| | | Sororities: | 25% |

**Basis for selection.** High school record most important, followed by class rank, standardized test scores, and secondary school's recommendation. Extracurricular activities and particular talents or abilities also important. Interview recommended. Audition required of music majors. Portfolio recommended for art majors.

**High school preparation.** College-preparatory program required. 14 units required. Required units include English 4, mathematics 3, social studies 2, science 3 and foreign language 2.

**2010-2011 Annual costs.** Tuition/fees: $33,424. Room/board: $9,805.

**2009-2010 Financial aid. Need-based:** 420 full-time freshmen applied for aid; 358 were judged to have need; 358 of these received aid. Average need met was 85%. Average scholarship/grant was $23,402; average loan $4,159. 73% of total undergraduate aid awarded as scholarships/grants, 27% as loans/jobs. **Non-need-based:** Awarded to 843 full-time undergraduates, including 188 freshmen. Scholarships awarded for academics, alumni affiliation, art, athletics, leadership, minority status, music/drama, religious affiliation, ROTC, state residency.

**Application procedures. Admission:** Priority date 3/15; no deadline. $40 fee, may be waived for applicants with need. Admission notification on a rolling basis beginning on or about 12/1. Must reply by May 1 or within 3 week(s) if notified thereafter. **Financial aid:** Priority date 3/15; no closing date. FAFSA, institutional form required. Applicants notified on a rolling basis starting 2/15.

**Academics. Special study options:** Accelerated study, combined bachelor's/ graduate degree, double major, honors, independent study, internships, liberal arts/career combination, student-designed major, study abroad, teacher certification program, Washington semester, weekend college. **Credit/ placement by examination:** AP, CLEP, IB, SAT, ACT, institutional tests. **Support services:** Reduced course load, study skills assistance, tutoring, writing center.

**Majors. Area/ethnic studies:** American, Latin American, Russian/Slavic. **Biology:** General, aquatic, biochemistry, molecular. **Business:** Accounting, business admin, entrepreneurial studies, finance, international, management information systems, management science, managerial economics, marketing. **Communications:** General. **Computer sciences:** General, computer science. **Conservation:** Environmental science. **Education:** Biology, elementary, English, foreign languages, French, German, mathematics, music, secondary, social science, Spanish. **Foreign languages:** French, German, Spanish. **Health:** Health services. **History:** General. **Liberal arts:** Humanities. **Math:** General. **Parks/recreation:** Sports admin. **Philosophy/religion:** Philosophy, religion. **Physical sciences:** Chemistry, physics. **Psychology:** General. **Social sciences:** General, economics, geography, international relations, political science, sociology. **Visual/performing arts:** Art, digital art, dramatic, music performance, music theory/composition, piano/organ, stringed instruments, voice/opera. **Other:** Music technology, orchestral instrument.

**Most popular majors.** Business/marketing 38%, education 7%, psychology 8%, social sciences 9%, visual/performing arts 6%.

**Computing on campus.** 473 workstations in dormitories, library, computer center, student center. Dormitories wired for high-speed internet access and linked to campus network. Commuter students can connect to campus network. Online course registration, online library, helpline, repair service, student web hosting, wireless network available.

**Student life. Freshman orientation:** Mandatory, $100 fee. Preregistration for classes offered. Held 4 days prior to first day of classes. **Housing:** Guaranteed on-campus for all undergraduates. Coed dorms, single-sex dorms, apartments, fraternity/sorority housing, wellness housing available. $200 nonrefundable deposit. Pets allowed in dorm rooms. **Activities:** Bands, campus ministries, choral groups, dance, drama, film society, literary magazine, music ensembles, musical theater, opera, radio station, student government, student newspaper, symphony orchestra, Black Student Association, Caribbean Student Organization, Habitat for Humanity, Indian Student Association, Jewish Student Organization, Roots and Shoots, Multicultural Student Council, College Democrats, College Republicans.

**Athletics.** NCAA. **Intercollegiate:** Baseball M, basketball, cross-country, golf, rowing (crew), soccer, softball W, tennis, volleyball W. **Intramural:** Baseball M, basketball, bowling, cross-country, football (non-tackle), golf, lacrosse, soccer, softball, swimming, table tennis, tennis, volleyball, water polo. **Team name:** Hatters.

**Student services.** Career counseling, student employment services, financial aid counseling, health services, minority student services, personal counseling, placement for graduates, women's services. **Physically disabled:** Services for visually, speech impaired.

**Contact.** E-mail: admissions@stetson.edu
Phone: (386) 822-7100 Toll-free number: (800) 688-0101
Fax: (386) 822-7112
Deborah Thompson, Vice President for Enrollment Management and
Campus Life, Stetson University, Campus Box 8378, DeLand, FL 32723

## Talmudic College of Florida
### Miami Beach, Florida
www.talmudicu.edu                                    CB code: 0514

- Private 4-year rabbinical college for men affiliated with Jewish faith
- Very large city

**General.** Founded in 1974. Accredited by AARTS. **Location:** 3 miles from
downtown. **Calendar:** Semester.

**Annual costs/financial aid.** Books/supplies: $900. Need-based finan-
cial aid available to full-time and part-time students.

**Contact.** Phone: (305) 534-0750
Dean of Students, 1910 Alton Road, Miami Beach, FL 33139

## Trinity Baptist College
### Jacksonville, Florida
www.tbc.edu

- Private 4-year Bible and teachers college
- Very large city
- 267 degree-seeking undergraduates

**General.** Regionally accredited; also accredited by TRACS. **Degrees:** 33
bachelor's, 9 associate awarded; master's offered. **Calendar:** Semester. **Full-
time faculty:** 15 total. **Part-time faculty:** 40 total.

**Basis for selection.** Meets school's high standard of Christian faith and
academic rigor.

**2009-2010 Annual costs.** Tuition/fees: $8,050. Room/board: $5,040.

**Application procedures. Admission:** $30 fee.

**Academics. Credit/placement by examination:** CLEP.

**Majors. Education:** Elementary, secondary, special. **Theology:** Missionary, pastoral counseling. **Other:** Church ministries.

**Contact.** E-mail: admissions@tbc.edu
Phone: (800) 786-2206
Director of Enrollment Management, Trinity Baptist College, 800
Hammond Boulevard, Jacksonville, FL 32221

## Trinity College of Florida
### Trinity, Florida
www.trinitycollege.edu                               CB code: 3975

- Private 4-year Bible college affiliated with interdenominational
  tradition
- Commuter campus in small city
- 210 degree-seeking undergraduates: 12% part-time, 39% women, 18%
  African American, 16% Hispanic American, 1% international
- 85% of applicants admitted
- SAT or ACT (ACT writing optional), application essay required
- 34% graduate within 6 years

**General. Degrees:** 33 bachelor's, 2 associate awarded. **Location:** 25 miles
from Tampa. **Calendar:** Semester, limited summer session. **Full-time faculty:** 6 total; 83% have terminal degrees, 17% women. **Part-time faculty:**
20 total; 25% have terminal degrees, 10% minority, 15% women. **Class
size:** 55% < 20, 38% 20-39, 8% 40-49.

**Freshman class profile.** 79 applied, 67 admitted, 33 enrolled.

| Mid 50% test scores | | | |
|---|---|---|---|
| SAT critical reading: | 460-550 | GPA 3.0-3.49: | 26% |
| SAT math: | 370-480 | GPA 2.0-2.99: | 63% |
| ACT composite: | 19-23 | End year in good standing: | 100% |
| GPA 3.75 or higher: | 7% | Return as sophomores: | 67% |
| | | Out-of-state: | 6% |

**Basis for selection.** Applicants must provide evidence of Christian character and witness, as well as academic ability largely based upon GPA and

SAT/ACT scores. **Homeschooled:** GED may be required if student is not
registered with local superintendent or umbrella school.

**High school preparation.** 18 units required. Required units include English 4, mathematics 4, social studies 2, history 2, science 4 and foreign
language 2.

**2010-2011 Annual costs.** Tuition/fees: $11,824. Room/board: $6,656.
Books/supplies: $1,185. Personal expenses: $2,614.

**2008-2009 Financial aid. Need-based:** 27 full-time freshmen applied
for aid; 24 were judged to have need; 24 of these received aid. Average
need met was 73%. Average scholarship/grant was $2,273; average loan
$1,750. 39% of total undergraduate aid awarded as scholarships/grants, 61%
as loans/jobs. **Non-need-based:** Awarded to 109 full-time undergraduates,
including 28 freshmen. Scholarships awarded for academics.

**Application procedures. Admission:** Closing date 8/2 (receipt date).
$25 fee, may be waived for applicants with need, free for online applicants.
Admission notification on a rolling basis. **Financial aid:** Priority date 3/15,
closing date 8/26. FAFSA, institutional form required. Applicants notified
on a rolling basis; must reply within 2 week(s) of notification.

**Academics. Special study options:** Accelerated study, double major, dual
enrollment of high school students, honors, independent study, internships,
weekend college. **Credit/placement by examination:** AP, CLEP, SAT, ACT,
institutional tests. 24 credit hours maximum toward associate degree, 24
toward bachelor's. **Support services:** Reduced course load, remedial instruction, tutoring, writing center.

**Majors. Business:** General. **Education:** Elementary. **Psychology:** Counseling. **Theology:** Missionary, pastoral counseling, preministerial, youth ministry. **Other:** Theological amd ministerial studies.

**Most popular majors.** Education 28%, theological studies 68%.

**Computing on campus.** 14 workstations in library, computer center.
Dormitories wired for high-speed internet access and linked to campus network. Online library, repair service, wireless network available.

**Student life. Freshman orientation:** Mandatory. Preregistration for classes
offered. Held 4 days before classes begin. Includes social gathering, vehicle
registration, student IDs, and assessment testing. **Policies:** Religious observance required. **Housing:** Guaranteed on-campus for all undergraduates.
Single-sex dorms, special housing for disabled, apartments, wellness housing available. $150 fully refundable deposit, deadline 7/1. **Activities:** Cam-
pus ministries, choral groups, drama, student government.

**Athletics.** NCCAA. **Intercollegiate:** Basketball M, volleyball W. **Intramural:** Basketball M, bowling, soccer M, softball M. **Team name:** Tigers.

**Student services.** Chaplain/spiritual director, career counseling, financial aid counseling, personal counseling.

**Contact.** E-mail: admissions@trinitycollege.edu
Phone: (727) 569-1411 Toll-free number: (800) 388-0869
Fax: (727) 569-1410
Mark Sawyer, Director of Admissions, Trinity College of Florida, 2430
Welbilt Boulevard, Trinity, FL 34655-4401

## Universidad FLET
### Miami, Florida
www.flet.edu

- Private 4-year university and Bible college
- Large city
- 265 degree-seeking undergraduates

**General.** Accredited by DETC. **Degrees:** 30 bachelor's awarded; master's
offered. **Calendar:** Continuous. **Full-time faculty:** 5 total. **Part-time faculty:** 15 total.

**Basis for selection.** Open admission. **Homeschooled:** Letter of recommendation (nonparent) required.

**Application procedures. Admission:** No deadline. $20 fee, may be
waived for applicants with need. **Financial aid:** No deadline.

**Academics. Special study options:** Distance learning. **Credit/placement
by examination:** CLEP.

**Majors. Theology:** Bible, theology.

**Student life. Freshman orientation:** Available. Preregistration for classes
offered.

**Contact.** E-mail: admisiones@flet.edu
Phone: (305) 378-8700 Toll-free number: (888) 376-3538
Fax: (305) 232-5832
Robert Bromley, Dean of Admission, Universidad FLET, 14540 SW 136th
Street, Suite 108, Miami, FL 33186

## University of Central Florida
**Orlando, Florida**                           CB member
**www.ucf.edu**                              CB code: 5233

- Public 4-year university
- Residential campus in very large city
- 45,048 degree-seeking undergraduates: 24% part-time, 55% women, 9% African American, 6% Asian American, 15% Hispanic American, 1% international
- 7,547 degree-seeking graduate students
- 47% of applicants admitted
- SAT or ACT with writing required
- 63% graduate within 6 years

**General.** Founded in 1963. Regionally accredited. **Degrees:** 9,468 bachelor's, 202 associate awarded; master's, doctoral, professional offered. **ROTC:** Army, Air Force. **Location:** 13 miles from downtown. **Calendar:** Semester, extensive summer session. **Full-time faculty:** 1,240 total; 78% have terminal degrees, 23% minority, 39% women. **Part-time faculty:** 467 total; 35% have terminal degrees, 14% minority, 52% women. **Class size:** 27% < 20, 38% 20-39, 10% 40-49, 18% 50-99, 7% >100. **Special facilities:** Solar energy center, simulation and training institute, research/education in optics and lasers center, space education and research center, biomolecular sciences center, forensic science center, arboretum, observatory.

**Freshman class profile.** 32,335 applied, 15,125 admitted, 6,397 enrolled.

| Mid 50% test scores | | | |
|---|---|---|---|
| SAT critical reading: | 530-620 | Rank in top quarter: | 77% |
| SAT math: | 560-650 | Rank in top tenth: | 35% |
| SAT writing: | 510-600 | End year in good standing: | 97% |
| ACT composite: | 23-28 | Return as sophomores: | 87% |
| GPA 3.75 or higher: | 45% | Out-of-state: | 7% |
| GPA 3.50-3.74: | 28% | Live on campus: | 70% |
| GPA 3.0-3.49: | 26% | International: | 1% |
| GPA 2.0-2.99: | 1% | Fraternities: | 8% |
| | | Sororities: | 6% |

**Basis for selection.** Two-thirds of admission offers made via review of GPA and standardized test scores. One-third made via review of factors such as grades, strength of coursework, essays, letters of recommendation, special talents. Essay recommended. Audition required of music majors. Portfolio recommended for art majors. **Homeschooled:** Provide detail about coursework and teaching process.

**High school preparation.** 18 units required. Required units include English 4, mathematics 4, social studies 3, science 3 (laboratory 2), foreign language 2 and academic electives 2.

**2009-2010 Annual costs.** Tuition/fees: $4,526; $20,005 out-of-state. Room/board: $8,574. Books/supplies: $924. Personal expenses: $2,276.

**2008-2009 Financial aid. Need-based:** 4,441 full-time freshmen applied for aid; 2,540 were judged to have need; 2,510 of these received aid. Average need met was 71%. Average scholarship/grant was $5,018; average loan $3,379. 50% of total undergraduate aid awarded as scholarships/grants, 50% as loans/jobs. **Non-need-based:** Awarded to 10,650 full-time undergraduates, including 3,102 freshmen. Scholarships awarded for academics, alumni affiliation, athletics, leadership, ROTC, state residency.

**Application procedures. Admission:** Priority date 1/1; deadline 5/1 (postmark date). $30 fee, may be waived for applicants with need. Admission notification on a rolling basis beginning on or about 10/1. Must reply by May 1 or within 3 week(s) if notified thereafter. **Financial aid:** Priority date 3/1, closing date 6/30. FAFSA required. Applicants notified on a rolling basis starting 3/15; must reply within 3 week(s) of notification.

**Academics. Special study options:** Accelerated study, combined bachelor's/graduate degree, cooperative education, distance learning, double major, dual enrollment of high school students, ESL, honors, independent study, internships, study abroad, teacher certification program. Lead Scholars program. **Credit/placement by examination:** AP, CLEP, IB, SAT, ACT, institutional tests. 45 credit hours maximum toward bachelor's degree. **Support services:** Learning center, pre-admission summer program, reduced course load, study skills assistance, tutoring, writing center.

**Honors college/program.** Requires separate application, admission based on GPA, test scores, and class rank. Small general and specialized honors

courses, honors building, and residence hall available. Accepts approximately 700 freshmen in the fall.

**Majors. Architecture:** Architecture. **Biology:** General, bacteriology, biotechnology. **Business:** General, accounting, business admin, finance, golf management, hospitality admin, managerial economics, marketing, real estate, restaurant/food services, tourism/travel. **Communications:** General, advertising, journalism, radio/tv. **Computer sciences:** General, information technology. **Education:** Art, early childhood, elementary, English, foreign languages, mathematics, music, physical, science, social science, special, trade/industrial. **Engineering:** Aerospace, civil, computer, electrical, environmental, industrial, mechanical, structural. **Foreign languages:** General, French, Spanish. **Health:** Athletic training, audiology/speech pathology, clinical lab science, health care admin, health services, medical records admin, nursing (RN), predental, premedicine, prepharmacy, preveterinary. **History:** General. **Interdisciplinary:** Global studies. **Legal studies:** Paralegal. **Liberal arts:** Arts/sciences, humanities. **Math:** General, statistics. **Philosophy/religion:** Philosophy, religion. **Physical sciences:** Chemistry, physics. **Protective services:** Criminal justice, forensics. **Psychology:** General. **Public administration:** General, social work. **Social sciences:** General, anthropology, economics, political science, sociology. **Visual/performing arts:** Art, cinematography, dramatic, multimedia, music performance, photography, studio arts.

**Most popular majors.** Business/marketing 26%, communications/journalism 6%, education 11%, engineering/engineering technologies 6%, health sciences 10%, liberal arts 6%, psychology 8%.

**Computing on campus.** 3,200 workstations in library, computer center, student center. Dormitories wired for high-speed internet access and linked to campus network. Commuter students can connect to campus network. Online course registration, online library, helpline, repair service, student web hosting, wireless network available.

**Student life. Freshman orientation:** Mandatory, $35 fee. Preregistration for classes offered. Ten sessions offered throughout spring and summer. 2-day event includes financial aid presentation, advising. **Housing:** Coed dorms, apartments, fraternity/sorority housing available. $250 nonrefundable deposit, deadline 3/1. Affiliated student residence housing. Students under guidance of university housing resident assistants considered part of on-campus housing. **Activities:** Bands, campus ministries, choral groups, drama, film society, international student organizations, literary magazine, music ensembles, Model UN, musical theater, radio station, student government, student newspaper, symphony orchestra, TV station, campus activities board, African American student union, orientation team, Hispanic American student association, Korean student association, Indian student association, Christian student association, Jewish student union.

**Athletics.** NCAA. **Intercollegiate:** Baseball M, basketball, cheerleading, cross-country, football (tackle) M, golf, rowing (crew) W, soccer, softball W, tennis, track and field W, volleyball W. **Intramural:** Badminton, baseball M, basketball, bowling, football (non-tackle), golf, racquetball, soccer, softball, tennis, volleyball, weight lifting, wrestling M. **Team name:** Knights.

**Student services.** Adult student services, alcohol/substance abuse counseling, career counseling, student employment services, financial aid counseling, health services, legal services, minority student services, on-campus daycare, personal counseling, placement for graduates, veterans' counselor, women's services. **Physically disabled:** Services for visually, speech, hearing impaired.

**Contact.** E-mail: admission@mail.ucf.edu
Phone: (407) 823-3000 Fax: (407) 823-5625
Gordon Chavis, Assistant Vice President, University of Central Florida, Box 160111, Orlando, FL 32816-0111

## University of Florida
**Gainesville, Florida**                        CB member
**www.ufl.edu**                              CB code: 5812

- Public 4-year university
- Residential campus in small city
- 33,038 degree-seeking undergraduates: 6% part-time, 55% women, 10% African American, 9% Asian American, 16% Hispanic American, 1% Native American, 1% international
- 12,118 degree-seeking graduate students
- 39% of applicants admitted
- SAT or ACT with writing, application essay required

**General.** Founded in 1853. Regionally accredited. **Degrees:** 9,207 bachelor's awarded; master's, doctoral, professional offered. **Location:** 70 miles from Jacksonville. **Calendar:** Semester, limited summer session. **Full-time faculty:** 1,937 total; 85% have terminal degrees, 20% minority, 31% women. **Part-time faculty:** 52 total; 77% have terminal degrees, 8% minority, 36%

women. **Class size:** 40% < 20, 31% 20-39, 7% 40-49, 12% 50-99, 10% >100. **Special facilities:** Natural history museum, marine laboratory, wildlife sanctuary, citrus research center, bell carillon, pipe organ, center for performing arts, hyperbaric chamber, microkelvin laboratory, brain institute, art museum, nuclear reactor.

**Freshman class profile.** 27,612 applied, 10,897 admitted, 6,382 enrolled.

| Mid 50% test scores | | | |
|---|---|---|---|
| SAT critical reading: | 570-680 | Rank in top quarter: | 92% |
| SAT math: | 590-700 | Rank in top tenth: | 76% |
| ACT composite: | 25-30 | Out-of-state: | 3% |
| GPA 3.75 or higher: | 88% | Live on campus: | 81% |
| GPA 3.50-3.74: | 8% | International: | 1% |
| GPA 3.0-3.49: | 3% | Fraternities: | 20% |
| GPA 2.0-2.99: | 1% | Sororities: | 21% |

**Basis for selection.** High school grades, academic course selection, SAT/ACT scores, extracurricular activities, awards, honors, recognitions, special talents and recommendations considered. SAT Subject Tests used strictly for placement except for applicants from non-regionally accredited schools. **Homeschooled:** Statement describing homeschool structure and mission, state high school equivalency certificate, letter of recommendation (nonparent) required. SAT Subject Test in math (level II-C) and letter from principal or guidance counselor required. **Learning Disabled:** Optional disclosure; students receive extra review by disability office.

**High school preparation.** 18 units required. Required units include English 4, mathematics 3, social studies 3, science 3 (laboratory 2) and foreign language 2. English must include substantial writing. Math must include algebra I and II, and geometry. Foreign language must be 2 units of same language.

**2009-2010 Annual costs.** Tuition/fees: $4,373; $23,744 out-of-state. Room/board: $7,500. Books/supplies: $990. Personal expenses: $3,320.

**2008-2009 Financial aid. Non-need-based:** Scholarships awarded for academics, art, athletics, leadership, minority status, music/drama, ROTC, state residency.

**Application procedures. Admission:** Closing date 11/1 (postmark date). $30 fee, may be waived for applicants with need. Application must be submitted online. Admission notification on a rolling basis beginning on or about 2/15. Must reply by May 1 or within 3 week(s) if notified thereafter. $200 tuition deposit required by May 1. **Financial aid:** Priority date 3/15; no closing date. FAFSA required. Applicants notified on a rolling basis starting 4/1.

**Academics. Special study options:** Accelerated study, cooperative education, cross-registration, distance learning, double major, dual enrollment of high school students, ESL, exchange student, external degree, honors, independent study, internships, liberal arts/career combination, semester at sea, student-designed major, study abroad, teacher certification program, Washington semester, weekend college. **Credit/placement by examination:** AP, CLEP, IB, SAT, ACT, institutional tests. 45 credit hours maximum toward bachelor's degree. **Support services:** Learning center, reduced course load, study skills assistance, tutoring, writing center.

**Majors. Agriculture:** Agronomy, animal sciences, dairy, economics, food science, horticultural science, plant sciences, poultry, soil science. **Architecture:** Architecture, landscape. **Area/ethnic studies:** Asian. **Biology:** Bacteriology, botany, entomology, plant pathology, zoology. **Business:** General, accounting, finance, insurance, management science, marketing, real estate. **Communications:** Advertising, journalism, public relations. **Computer sciences:** General. **Conservation:** Forestry. **Education:** Agricultural, art, elementary, middle, music, special. **Engineering:** Aerospace, agricultural, chemical, civil, computer, electrical, environmental, materials, mechanical, nuclear, science, systems. **Engineering technology:** Construction, surveying. **Family/consumer sciences:** Family/community services. **Foreign languages:** Classics, French, German, linguistics, Portuguese, Russian, Spanish. **Health:** Audiology/speech pathology, health services, nursing (RN). **History:** General. **Math:** General, statistics. **Parks/recreation:** Exercise sciences, facilities management. **Philosophy/religion:** Judaic, philosophy, religion. **Physical sciences:** Astronomy, chemistry, geology, physics. **Protective services:** Criminalistics. **Psychology:** General. **Social sciences:** Anthropology, economics, geography, political science, sociology. **Visual/performing arts:** Art history/conservation, dance, dramatic, interior design, studio arts.

**Most popular majors.** Agriculture 6%, business/marketing 15%, communications/journalism 8%, engineering/engineering technologies 12%, health sciences 7%, social sciences 14%.

**Computing on campus.** 1,000 workstations in library, student center. Dormitories wired for high-speed internet access and linked to campus network. Commuter students can connect to campus network. Online course registration, online library, helpline, student web hosting, wireless network available.

**Student life. Freshman orientation:** Mandatory, $120 fee. Preregistration for classes offered. 2-day program held various dates in May, June and July. **Policies:** Student code of conduct and honor code enforced. **Housing:** Coed dorms, special housing for disabled, apartments, fraternity/sorority housing available. $200 partly refundable deposit. Pets allowed in dorm rooms. Undergraduate honor halls, quiet/study floors, faculty-in-residence program, first-year experience program, wellness floor, no-visitation by opposite sex floor available. **Activities:** Bands, choral groups, dance, drama, film society, literary magazine, music ensembles, musical theater, radio station, student government, student newspaper, symphony orchestra, TV station, over 850 student groups available.

**Athletics.** NCAA. **Intercollegiate:** Baseball M, basketball, cheerleading, cross-country, diving, football (tackle) M, golf, gymnastics W, lacrosse W, soccer W, softball W, swimming, tennis, track and field, volleyball W. **Intramural:** Basketball, bowling, football (non-tackle), golf, racquetball, soccer, softball, swimming, tennis, track and field, volleyball, weight lifting, wrestling. **Team name:** Gators.

**Student services.** Adult student services, alcohol/substance abuse counseling, chaplain/spiritual director, career counseling, services for economically disadvantaged, student employment services, financial aid counseling, health services, legal services, minority student services, on-campus daycare, personal counseling, placement for graduates, veterans' counselor, women's services. **Physically disabled:** Services for visually, speech, hearing impaired.

**Contact.**   Phone: (352) 392-1365
Zina Evans, Assistant Provost and Director of Admissions, University of Florida, 201 Criser Hall-PO Box 114000, Gainesville, FL 32611-4000

---

## University of Miami
**Coral Gables, Florida**                                    CB member
**www.miami.edu**                                            CB code: 5815

- Private 4-year university
- Residential campus in small city
- 9,855 degree-seeking undergraduates: 6% part-time, 52% women, 8% African American, 5% Asian American, 24% Hispanic American, 9% international
- 5,029 degree-seeking graduate students
- 44% of applicants admitted
- SAT or ACT (ACT writing optional), application essay required
- 79% graduate within 6 years; 33% enter graduate study

**General.** Founded in 1925. Regionally accredited. **Degrees:** 2,575 bachelor's awarded; master's, doctoral, professional offered. **ROTC:** Army, Air Force. **Location:** 7 miles from downtown. **Calendar:** Semester, extensive summer session. **Full-time faculty:** 961 total; 87% have terminal degrees, 28% minority, 36% women. **Part-time faculty:** 335 total; 58% have terminal degrees, 30% minority, 41% women. **Class size:** 52% < 20, 36% 20-39, 6% 40-49, 5% 50-99, 2% >100. **Special facilities:** Cinema, observatory, palmetum, marine science research vessels, broadcasting studios, concert hall, arboretum, performing arts theater, film studios, sound stage, museum, art gallery.

**Freshman class profile.** 21,844 applied, 9,700 admitted, 2,006 enrolled.

| Mid 50% test scores | | | |
|---|---|---|---|
| SAT critical reading: | 570-680 | GPA 2.0-2.99: | 1% |
| SAT math: | 600-700 | Rank in top quarter: | 87% |
| SAT writing: | 570-670 | Rank in top tenth: | 63% |
| ACT composite: | 27-31 | End year in good standing: | 94% |
| GPA 3.75 or higher: | 74% | Return as sophomores: | 90% |
| GPA 3.50-3.74: | 13% | Out-of-state: | 56% |
| GPA 3.0-3.49: | 12% | Live on campus: | 84% |
| | | International: | 12% |

**Basis for selection.** Secondary school record, test scores, recommendations, and essay very important. SAT Subject Tests in math and science required for dual degree honors medical programs. Auditions required for music and theater arts. Portfolio required for art BFA program and architecture. **Homeschooled:** Statement describing homeschool structure and mission, transcript of courses and grades, interview required.

**High school preparation.** College-preparatory program recommended. 20 units recommended. Recommended units include English 4, mathematics 4, social studies 3, history 2, science 3 (laboratory 2), foreign language 2, computer science 1 and visual/performing arts 1.

**2010-2011 Annual costs.** Tuition/fees: $37,836. Room/board: $11,062. Books/supplies: $1,250. Personal expenses: $2,456.

**2009-2010 Financial aid. Need-based:** 1,223 full-time freshmen applied for aid; 924 were judged to have need; 924 of these received aid. Average need met was 83%. Average scholarship/grant was $23,904; average loan $3,934. 70% of total undergraduate aid awarded as scholarships/grants, 30% as loans/jobs. **Non-need-based:** Awarded to 3,457 full-time undergraduates, including 683 freshmen. Scholarships awarded for academics, athletics, music/drama, ROTC.

**Application procedures. Admission:** Closing date 1/15 (postmark date). $65 fee, may be waived for applicants with need. Admission notification 4/15. Must reply by May 1 or within 2 week(s) if notified thereafter. **Financial aid:** Priority date 2/1; no closing date. FAFSA required. Applicants notified on a rolling basis starting 3/1.

**Academics. Special study options:** Accelerated study, combined bachelor's/graduate degree, distance learning, double major, dual enrollment of high school students, ESL, honors, independent study, internships, liberal arts/career combination, student-designed major, study abroad, teacher certification program, Washington semester, weekend college. **Credit/placement by examination:** AP, CLEP, IB, SAT, institutional tests. **Support services:** Learning center, pre-admission summer program, reduced course load, remedial instruction, study skills assistance, tutoring, writing center.

**Majors. Architecture:** Architecture. **Area/ethnic studies:** African-American, American, Latin American, women's. **Biology:** General, bacteriology, biochemistry, marine. **Business:** Accounting, business admin, entrepreneurial studies, finance, human resources, international, management science, managerial economics, marketing, real estate. **Communications:** General, advertising, broadcast journalism, digital media, journalism, media studies, photojournalism, public relations, radio/tv. **Computer sciences:** Computer graphics, computer science, data processing, information systems, security. **Conservation:** Management/policy. **Education:** General, elementary, music. **Engineering:** General, aerospace, architectural, biomedical, civil, computer, electrical, environmental, industrial, mechanical, science. **Family/consumer sciences:** Family/community services. **Foreign languages:** Ancient Greek, classics, French, German, Latin, Spanish. **Health:** Athletic training, health services, music therapy, nursing (RN), predental, premedicine, preveterinary. **History:** General. **Interdisciplinary:** Ancient studies, neuroscience. **Legal studies:** General, prelaw. **Liberal arts:** Arts/sciences. **Math:** General, applied, probability. **Parks/recreation:** Exercise sciences, health/fitness, sports admin. **Philosophy/religion:** Judaic, philosophy, religion. **Physical sciences:** Atmospheric science, chemistry, geology, meteorology, oceanography, physics. **Psychology:** General, community. **Social sciences:** Anthropology, criminology, economics, geography, international relations, political science, sociology. **Visual/performing arts:** Acting, art, art history/conservation, ceramics, cinematography, design, dramatic, graphic design, jazz, music performance, music theory/composition, painting, photography, piano/organ, printmaking, sculpture, studio arts, theater arts management, theater design, voice/opera.

**Most popular majors.** Biology 9%, business/marketing 21%, communications/journalism 8%, health sciences 6%, psychology 8%, social sciences 13%, visual/performing arts 9%.

**Computing on campus.** Dormitories wired for high-speed internet access and linked to campus network. Commuter students can connect to campus network. Online course registration, online library, helpline, repair service, student web hosting, wireless network available.

**Student life. Freshman orientation:** Mandatory. Preregistration for classes offered. 3-day program held in August. **Policies:** Student initiated and administered honor code. **Housing:** Guaranteed on-campus for all undergraduates. Coed dorms, special housing for disabled, apartments, fraternity/sorority housing, wellness housing available. $250 nonrefundable deposit, deadline 5/1. **Activities:** Bands, campus ministries, choral groups, dance, drama, film society, international student organizations, literary magazine, music ensembles, Model UN, musical theater, opera, radio station, student government, student newspaper, symphony orchestra, TV station, 275 clubs and organizations.

**Athletics.** NCAA. **Intercollegiate:** Baseball M, basketball, cheerleading, cross-country, diving W, football (tackle) M, golf W, rowing (crew) W, soccer W, swimming W, tennis, track and field, volleyball W. **Intramural:** Badminton, basketball, bowling, football (non-tackle), golf, racquetball, soccer, softball, table tennis, tennis, volleyball. **Team name:** Hurricanes.

**Student services.** Adult student services, alcohol/substance abuse counseling, career counseling, services for economically disadvantaged, student employment services, financial aid counseling, health services, minority student services, on-campus daycare, personal counseling, placement for graduates, veterans' counselor, women's services. **Physically disabled:** Services for visually, speech, hearing impaired.

**Contact.** E-mail: admission@miami.edu
Phone: (305) 284-4323 Fax: (305) 284-2507
Edward Gillis, Assistant Vice President/Executive Director of Admission, University of Miami, 132 Ashe Building, Coral Gables, FL 33124-4616

## University of North Florida
Jacksonville, Florida     **CB member**
www.unf.edu     **CB code: 5490**

▸ Public 4-year university
▸ Residential campus in very large city
▸ 14,216 degree-seeking undergraduates: 27% part-time, 56% women, 11% African American, 6% Asian American, 7% Hispanic American, 1% international
▸ 1,779 degree-seeking graduate students
▸ 64% of applicants admitted
▸ SAT or ACT with writing required
▸ 46% graduate within 6 years

**General.** Founded in 1965. Regionally accredited. **Degrees:** 2,892 bachelor's, 476 associate awarded; master's, doctoral, professional offered. **ROTC:** Army, Naval. **Location:** 12 miles from downtown. **Calendar:** Semester, extensive summer session. **Full-time faculty:** 495 total; 79% have terminal degrees, 14% minority, 47% women. **Part-time faculty:** 246 total; 24% have terminal degrees, 13% minority, 57% women. **Class size:** 20% < 20, 53% 20-39, 15% 40-49, 7% 50-99, 5% >100. **Special facilities:** Nature trails, designated bird sanctuary, fine arts center.

**Freshman class profile.** 10,159 applied; 6,459 admitted, 2,227 enrolled.

| Mid 50% test scores | | | |
|---|---|---|---|
| SAT critical reading: | 510-610 | GPA 2.0-2.99: | 16% |
| SAT math: | 510-600 | Rank in top quarter: | 53% |
| ACT composite: | 21-24 | Rank in top tenth: | 22% |
| GPA 3.75 or higher: | 31% | Return as sophomores: | 83% |
| GPA 3.50-3.74: | 16% | Out-of-state: | 4% |
| GPA 3.0-3.49: | 37% | Live on campus: | 59% |

**Basis for selection.** SAT or ACT score and high school GPA based on 19 academic units very important. High school academic courses (not including electives) used for calculating GPA. Summer program available for some students who do not meet fall admissions criteria; students admitted on probation. Audition required for music majors. **Homeschooled:** Required to pass all sections of GED. **Learning Disabled:** Register with Disability Resource Center.

**High school preparation.** College-preparatory program required. 19 units required. Required units include English 4, mathematics 3, social studies 3, science 3 (laboratory 1), foreign language 2 and academic electives 4.

**2009-2010 Annual costs.** Tuition/fees: $4,193; $17,582 out-of-state. Room/board: $7,872. Books/supplies: $900. Personal expenses: $1,030.

**2009-2010 Financial aid. Need-based:** 1,416 full-time freshmen applied for aid; 922 were judged to have need; 909 of these received aid. Average need met was 91%. Average scholarship/grant was $1,080; average loan $1,609. 51% of total undergraduate aid awarded as scholarships/grants, 49% as loans/jobs. **Non-need-based:** Awarded to 4,088 full-time undergraduates, including 966 freshmen. Scholarships awarded for academics, athletics, leadership, minority status, music/drama, state residency.

**Application procedures. Admission:** Priority date 11/13; deadline 6/11 (receipt date). $30 fee, may be waived for applicants with need. Admission notification on a rolling basis beginning on or about 11/13. Must reply by 7/31. **Financial aid:** Priority date 4/1; no closing date. FAFSA required. Applicants notified on a rolling basis starting 3/15; must reply within 2 week(s) of notification.

**Academics. Special study options:** Accelerated study, combined bachelor's/graduate degree, cooperative education, distance learning, double major, dual enrollment of high school students, ESL, exchange student, honors, independent study, internships, student-designed major, study abroad, teacher certification program, Washington semester, weekend college. Learning Communities. **Credit/placement by examination:** AP, CLEP, IB, SAT, ACT, institutional tests. 30 credit hours maximum toward bachelor's degree. **Support services:** Learning center, pre-admission summer program, reduced course load, study skills assistance, tutoring, writing center.

**Majors. Area/ethnic studies:** French. **Biology:** General. **Business:** Accounting, banking/financial services, business admin, finance, international, managerial economics, marketing, transportation. **Communications:** Media studies. **Computer sciences:** General. **Education:** Art, early childhood, elementary, mathematics, middle, music, physical, science, secondary, special. **Engineering:** Civil, electrical, mechanical. **Engineering technology:** Construction. **Foreign languages:** Sign language interpretation, Spanish. **Health:** Athletic training, health services, nursing (RN). **History:** General. **Interdisciplinary:** Global studies. **Liberal arts:** Arts/sciences. **Math:** General, statistics. **Parks/recreation:** Sports admin. **Philosophy/religion:** Philosophy. **Physical sciences:** Chemistry, physics. **Protective services:** Criminal justice. **Psychology:** General. **Social sciences:** Anthropology, economics, political science, sociology. **Visual/performing arts:** Art, jazz, music performance, studio arts.

**Most popular majors.** Business/marketing 23%, communications/journalism 9%, education 11%, engineering/engineering technologies 7%, health sciences 14%, psychology 7%.

**Computing on campus.** 850 workstations in library, computer center, student center. Dormitories wired for high-speed internet access and linked to campus network. Commuter students can connect to campus network. Online course registration, online library, helpline, student web hosting, wireless network available.

**Student life. Freshman orientation:** Mandatory, $35 fee. Preregistration for classes offered. One-and-one-half day program held several times during summer. **Policies:** Students must abide by drug/alcohol policy, student code of conduct, model bill of rights and responsibilities. **Housing:** Coed dorms, special housing for disabled, apartments, fraternity/sorority housing available. $300 partly refundable deposit. Suite style housing available. **Activities:** Bands, campus ministries, choral groups, dance, drama, international student organizations, literary magazine, music ensembles, radio station, student government, student newspaper, TV station, African American student union, Jewish student union, InterVarsity Christian Fellowship, College Republicans, Jeffersonian Society, The New Left, Muslim student association, Filipino student association, Golden Key international honor society.

**Athletics.** NCAA. **Intercollegiate:** Baseball M, basketball, cross-country, diving W, golf M, soccer, softball W, swimming W, tennis, track and field, volleyball W. **Intramural:** Basketball, football (non-tackle), racquetball, soccer, softball, tennis, track and field, volleyball. **Team name:** Ospreys.

**Student services.** Adult student services, alcohol/substance abuse counseling, career counseling, student employment services, financial aid counseling, health services, minority student services, on-campus daycare, personal counseling, placement for graduates, veterans' counselor, women's services. **Physically disabled:** Services for visually, speech, hearing impaired.

**Contact.** E-mail: admissions@unf.edu
Phone: (904) 620-2624 Fax: (904) 620-2414
John Yancey, Director of Admissions, University of North Florida, 1 UNF Drive, Jacksonville, FL 32224-7699

## University of South Florida
Tampa, Florida  **CB member**
www.usf.edu  **CB code: 5828**

◗ Public 4-year university

◗ Commuter campus in very large city

◗ 35,750 degree-seeking undergraduates: 28% part-time, 57% women, 12% African American, 6% Asian American, 14% Hispanic American, 1% international

◗ 9,293 degree-seeking graduate students

◗ 43% of applicants admitted

◗ SAT or ACT with writing required

◗ 48% graduate within 6 years; 21% enter graduate study

**General.** Founded in 1956. Regionally accredited. Regional campuses in St. Petersburg, Sarasota/Manatee, and Lakeland Polytechnic. **Degrees:** 7,465 bachelor's, 219 associate awarded; master's, doctoral, professional offered. **ROTC's:** Army, Naval, Air Force. **Location:** 10 miles from downtown. **Calendar:** Semester, extensive summer session. **Full-time faculty:** 1,292 total; 79% have terminal degrees, 24% minority, 42% women. **Part-time faculty:** 127 total; 62% have terminal degrees, 20% minority, 49% women. **Class size:** 25% < 20, 52% 20-39, 9% 40-49, 11% 50-99, 3% >100. **Special facilities:** Art museum, weather station, botanical garden, anthropology museum.

**Freshman class profile.** 29,631 applied, 12,767 admitted, 4,368 enrolled.

| Mid 50% test scores | | | |
|---|---|---|---|
| SAT critical reading: | 510-620 | Rank in top quarter: | 59% |
| SAT math: | 520-630 | Rank in top tenth: | 26% |
| SAT writing: | 500-600 | Return as sophomores: | 86% |
| ACT composite: | 22-28 | Out-of-state: | 5% |
| GPA 3.75 or higher: | 44% | Live on campus: | 75% |
| GPA 3.50-3.74: | 21% | International: | 1% |
| GPA 3.0-3.49: | 30% | Fraternities: | 7% |
| GPA 2.0-2.99: | 5% | Sororities: | 6% |

**Basis for selection.** GPA and test scores most important. On sliding scale, higher grades compensate for lower test scores. Requirements higher for several degree programs. Audition required of music majors. Portfolio required of art majors. **Homeschooled:** State high school equivalency certificate required.

**High school preparation.** College-preparatory program required. 21 units required. Required and recommended units include English 4, mathematics 4, social studies 3, science 3-4 (laboratory 2-3), foreign language 2-4 and academic electives 3. Foreign language units must be in 1 language.

**2009-2010 Annual costs.** Tuition/fees: $4,577; $16,708 out-of-state. Room/board: $8,750. Books/supplies: $1,500. Personal expenses: $4,100.

**2008-2009 Financial aid. Need-based:** 3,372 full-time freshmen applied for aid; 2,479 were judged to have need; 2,462 of these received aid. Average need met was 49%. Average scholarship/grant was $6,451; average loan $2,949. 43% of total undergraduate aid awarded as scholarships/grants, 57% as loans/jobs. **Non-need-based:** Awarded to 5,118 full-time undergraduates, including 3,515 freshmen. Scholarships awarded for academics, alumni affiliation, art, athletics, job skills, leadership, minority status, music/drama, religious affiliation, ROTC, state residency. **Additional information:** Deferred tuition payment plan available for late financial aid recipients.

**Application procedures. Admission:** Priority date 3/1; deadline 4/15 (postmark date). $30 fee, may be waived for applicants with need. Admission notification on a rolling basis beginning on or about 10/1. Must reply by May 1 or within 2 week(s) if notified thereafter. **Financial aid:** Priority date 3/1; no closing date. FAFSA required. Applicants notified on a rolling basis starting 3/15.

**Academics. Special study options:** Accelerated study, combined bachelor's/graduate degree, cooperative education, cross-registration, distance learning, double major, dual enrollment of high school students, exchange student, honors, internships, study abroad, teacher certification program, Washington semester, weekend college. **Credit/placement by examination:** AP, CLEP, IB, SAT, ACT, institutional tests. **Support services:** Learning center, pre-admission summer program, tutoring.

**Majors. Area/ethnic studies:** African-American, American, women's. **Biology:** General, bacteriology, biomedical sciences. **Business:** General, accounting, business admin, finance, hospitality admin, international, management information systems, managerial economics, marketing. **Communications:** General. **Computer sciences:** General, information systems, information technology. **Conservation:** General. **Education:** General, art, business, drama/dance, early childhood, elementary, emotionally handicapped, English, foreign languages, learning disabled, mathematics, mentally handicapped, music, physical, science, social science, special, trade/industrial. **Engineering:** General, chemical, civil, computer, electrical, manufacturing, mechanical. **Foreign languages:** Classics, French, German, Italian, Russian, Spanish. **Health:** Athletic training, audiology/speech pathology, clinical lab science, nursing (RN). **History:** General. **Interdisciplinary:** Biological/physical sciences, gerontology. **Liberal arts:** Arts/sciences, humanities. **Math:** General. **Philosophy/religion:** Philosophy, religion. **Physical sciences:** Chemistry, geology, physics. **Protective services:** Criminal justice. **Psychology:** General. **Public administration:** Social work. **Social sciences:** General, anthropology, criminology, economics, geography, international relations, political science, sociology. **Visual/performing arts:** Art, art history/conservation, dance, dramatic, music performance, studio arts.

**Most popular majors.** Biology 9%, business/marketing 23%, education 10%, English 7%, psychology 8%, social sciences 16%.

**Computing on campus.** 500 workstations in dormitories, library, computer center, student center. Dormitories wired for high-speed internet access and linked to campus network. Commuter students can connect to campus network. Online course registration, helpline, wireless network available.

**Student life. Freshman orientation:** Mandatory, $35 fee. Preregistration for classes offered. **Housing:** Coed dorms, single-sex dorms, special housing for disabled, apartments, cooperative housing, fraternity/sorority housing, wellness housing available. $225 partly refundable deposit, deadline 8/1. **Activities:** Bands, choral groups, dance, drama, film society, international student organizations, literary magazine, music ensembles, musical theater, opera, radio station, student government, student newspaper, symphony orchestra, TV station, approximately 300 student organizations available.

**Athletics.** NCAA. **Intercollegiate:** Baseball M, basketball, cross-country, football (tackle) M, golf, sailing, soccer, softball W, tennis, track and field, volleyball W. **Intramural:** Badminton, basketball, bowling, cross-country, fencing, football (tackle) M, golf, handball, ice hockey, lacrosse, racquetball, rugby, sailing, soccer, softball W, swimming, table tennis, tennis, track and field, volleyball, wrestling M. **Team name:** Bulls.

**Student services.** Adult student services, career counseling, student employment services, financial aid counseling, health services, legal services, on-campus daycare, personal counseling, placement for graduates, veterans' counselor. **Physically disabled:** Services for visually, speech, hearing impaired.

**Contact.** E-mail: admissions@admin.usf.edu
Phone: (813) 974-3350 Fax: (813) 974-9689
J. Robert Spatig, Director of Admissions, University of South Florida, 4202 East Fowler Avenue, SVC 1036, Tampa, FL 33620-9951

---

## University of Tampa

Tampa, Florida — CB member
www.ut.edu — CB code: 5819

- Private 4-year university and liberal arts college
- Residential campus in large city
- 5,518 degree-seeking undergraduates: 6% part-time, 57% women, 5% African American, 2% Asian American, 10% Hispanic American, 9% international
- 740 degree-seeking graduate students
- 62% of applicants admitted
- SAT or ACT (ACT writing optional) required
- 57% graduate within 6 years; 46% enter graduate study

**General.** Founded in 1931. Regionally accredited. **Degrees:** 1,057 bachelor's, 2 associate awarded; master's offered. **ROTC:** Army, Naval, Air Force. **Location:** 20 miles from St. Petersburg, 70 miles from Orlando. **Calendar:** Semester, extensive summer session. **Full-time faculty:** 238 total; 91% have terminal degrees, 9% minority, 42% women. **Part-time faculty:** 293 total; 33% have terminal degrees, 17% minority, 57% women. **Class size:** 35% < 20, 64% 20-39, less than 1% 40-49, less than 1% 50-99. **Special facilities:** Art and furniture museum, dance studio, art studio, marine science research vessel, marine science research laboratory.

**Freshman class profile.** 9,929 applied, 6,109 admitted, 1,419 enrolled.

| Mid 50% test scores | | | |
|---|---|---|---|
| SAT critical reading: | 480-570 | Rank in top quarter: | 43% |
| SAT math: | 490-580 | Rank in top tenth: | 15% |
| SAT writing: | 480-570 | End year in good standing: | 89% |
| ACT composite: | 21-25 | Return as sophomores: | 74% |
| GPA 3.75 or higher: | 10% | Out-of-state: | 69% |
| GPA 3.50-3.74: | 18% | Live on campus: | 88% |
| GPA 3.0-3.49: | 46% | International: | 6% |
| GPA 2.0-2.99: | 26% | Fraternities: | 4% |
| | | Sororities: | 9% |

**Basis for selection.** Secondary school record, test scores most important. Recommendations, talent/ability, character/personal qualities considered. Interview recommended. Auditions required of music and performing arts majors. Portfolio recommended for art majors. **Homeschooled:** Submit a copy of the 11th year annual pupil's educational progress evaluation or annual assessment test results, if available. **Learning Disabled:** Documentation required.

**High school preparation.** College-preparatory program required. 18 units required. Required units include English 4, mathematics 3, social studies 3, science 3 (laboratory 2), foreign language 2 and academic electives 3.

**2009-2010 Annual costs.** Tuition/fees: $22,482. Room/board: $8,296. Books/supplies: $988. Personal expenses: $1,311.

**2009-2010 Financial aid.** **Need-based:** 1,085 full-time freshmen applied for aid; 838 were judged to have need; 838 of these received aid. Average need met was 71%. Average scholarship/grant was $6,679; average loan $3,875. 68% of total undergraduate aid awarded as scholarships/grants, 32% as loans/jobs. **Non-need-based:** Awarded to 2,852 full-time undergraduates, including 1,026 freshmen. Scholarships awarded for academics, alumni affiliation, art, athletics, leadership, music/drama, ROTC, state residency. **Additional information:** Early aid estimator service.

**Application procedures. Admission:** Priority date 11/15; no deadline. $40 fee, may be waived for applicants with need. Admission notification on

---

a rolling basis beginning on or about 10/1. Must reply by May 1 or within 4 week(s) if notified thereafter. **Financial aid:** No deadline. FAFSA required. Applicants notified on a rolling basis starting 2/1; must reply within 3 week(s) of notification.

**Academics. Special study options:** Combined bachelor's/graduate degree, double major, dual enrollment of high school students, exchange student, honors, independent study, internships, liberal arts/career combination, semester at sea, study abroad, teacher certification program, Washington semester. Certificate of International Studies. **Credit/placement by examination:** AP, CLEP, IB, SAT, ACT, institutional tests. 30 credit hours maximum toward associate degree, 30 toward bachelor's. **Support services:** Learning center, reduced course load, study skills assistance, tutoring, writing center.

**Majors. Biology:** General, biochemistry, marine. **Business:** Accounting, business admin, entrepreneurial studies, finance, international, managerial economics, marketing. **Communications:** General, digital media. **Computer sciences:** General, computer graphics. **Conservation:** Environmental science. **Education:** Biology, elementary, English, mathematics, music, secondary. **Foreign languages:** Spanish. **Health:** Athletic training, community health services, nursing (RN). **History:** General. **Interdisciplinary:** Math/computer science. **Liberal arts:** Arts/sciences. **Math:** General. **Parks/recreation:** Exercise sciences, sports admin. **Philosophy/religion:** Philosophy. **Physical sciences:** Chemistry, forensic chemistry. **Psychology:** General. **Social sciences:** Criminology, economics, political science, sociology. **Visual/performing arts:** General, art, dramatic, film/cinema, graphic design, music performance. **Other:** Advertising and public relations, Financial and operations systems.

**Most popular majors.** Biology 7%, business/marketing 27%, communications/journalism 12%, health sciences 8%, parks/recreation 6%, psychology 6%, social sciences 12%.

**Computing on campus.** 795 workstations in dormitories, library, computer center, student center. Dormitories wired for high-speed internet access and linked to campus network. Commuter students can connect to campus network. Online course registration, online library, helpline, student web hosting, wireless network available.

**Student life. Freshman orientation:** Mandatory, $75 fee. Preregistration for classes offered. **Housing:** Coed dorms, special housing for disabled, apartments available. $200 fully refundable deposit, deadline 5/1. **Activities:** Bands, campus ministries, choral groups, dance, drama, film society, international student organizations, literary magazine, music ensembles, Model UN, musical theater, radio station, student government, student newspaper, symphony orchestra, TV station, over 140 student organizations.

**Athletics.** NCAA. **Intercollegiate:** Baseball M, basketball, cross-country, golf M, rowing (crew) W, soccer, softball W, swimming, tennis W, volleyball W. **Intramural:** Basketball, field hockey W, football (non-tackle) W, football (tackle) M, golf, soccer, softball, swimming, table tennis W, tennis, track and field, volleyball. **Team name:** Spartans.

**Student services.** Adult student services, career counseling, student employment services, financial aid counseling, health services, minority student services, personal counseling, placement for graduates, veterans' counselor. **Physically disabled:** Services for visually, hearing impaired.

**Contact.** E-mail: admissions@ut.edu
Phone: (813) 253-6211 Toll-free number: (888) 646-2738
Fax: (813) 258-7398
Dennis Nostrand, Vice President for Enrollment, University of Tampa, 401 West Kennedy Boulevard, Tampa, FL 33606-1490

---

## University of West Florida

Pensacola, Florida
www.uwf.edu — CB code: 5833

- Public 4-year university
- Commuter campus in small city
- 8,718 degree-seeking undergraduates: 26% part-time, 59% women, 10% African American, 5% Asian American, 6% Hispanic American, 1% Native American, 1% international
- 1,607 degree-seeking graduate students
- 70% of applicants admitted
- SAT or ACT (ACT writing optional) required
- 43% graduate within 6 years

**General.** Founded in 1963. Regionally accredited. **Degrees:** 1,927 bachelor's, 122 associate awarded; master's, doctoral offered. **ROTC:** Army,

Air Force. **Location:** 10 miles from downtown. **Calendar:** Semester, extensive summer session. **Full-time faculty:** 312 total; 81% have terminal degrees, 15% minority, 41% women. **Part-time faculty:** 197 total; 22% have terminal degrees, 8% minority, 48% women. **Class size:** 31% < 20, 49% 20-39, 12% 40-49, 7% 50-99, 2% >100. **Special facilities:** Archaeology museum, nature preserve.

**Freshman class profile.** 4,513 applied, 3,154 admitted, 1,110 enrolled.

| Mid 50% test scores | | GPA 2.0-2.99: | 19% |
|---|---|---|---|
| SAT critical reading: | 490-590 | Rank in top quarter: | 43% |
| SAT math: | 470-570 | Rank in top tenth: | 18% |
| ACT composite: | 21-25 | Out-of-state: | 10% |
| GPA 3.75 or higher: | 31% | Live on campus: | 63% |
| GPA 3.50-3.74: | 16% | International: | 1% |
| GPA 3.0-3.49: | 34% | | |

**Basis for selection.** School achievement record, test scores, and school curriculum most important. **Homeschooled:** Transcript of courses and grades required. **Learning Disabled:** If requesting special consideration due to disability, student must provide documentation.

**High school preparation.** College-preparatory program recommended. 19 units required. Required units include English 4, mathematics 3, social studies 3, science 3 (laboratory 2), foreign language 2 and academic electives 4. 4 academic electives includes courses chosen from list above. Social science includes history, economics, government, psychology, sociology and geography.

**2009-2010 Annual costs.** Tuition/fees: $4,190; $16,478 out-of-state. Room/board: $7,576. Books/supplies: $1,200. Personal expenses: $2,300.

**2008-2009 Financial aid. Need-based:** 46% of total undergraduate aid awarded as scholarships/grants, 54% as loans/jobs. **Non-need-based:** Scholarships awarded for academics, alumni affiliation, art, athletics, minority status, music/drama, ROTC.

**Application procedures. Admission:** Closing date 6/30 (postmark date). $30 fee, may be waived for applicants with need. Admission notification on a rolling basis beginning on or about 10/1. Must apply by January 1 for scholarship consideration. **Financial aid:** Priority date 3/1; no closing date. FAFSA, institutional form required. Applicants notified on a rolling basis starting 2/1.

**Academics.** Weekend program in nursing (BSN) available. **Special study options:** Cooperative education, distance learning, double major, dual enrollment of high school students, exchange student, honors, independent study, internships, study abroad, teacher certification program. Joint electrical engineering and computer engineering with University of Florida. **Credit/placement by examination:** AP, CLEP, IB, SAT, ACT, institutional tests. 30 credit hours maximum toward associate degree, 30 toward bachelor's. Up to 60 hours can be accepted, but academic department determines how credit counts toward degree. **Support services:** Learning center, remedial instruction, study skills assistance, tutoring, writing center.

**Majors. Biology:** General, marine. **Business:** Accounting, business admin, finance, hospitality admin, management information systems, managerial economics, marketing. **Communications:** Media studies. **Computer sciences:** General, information technology. **Conservation:** Environmental science. **Education:** Art, early childhood, elementary, English, mathematics, mentally handicapped, middle, special, trade/industrial. **Engineering:** Computer, electrical. **Engineering technology:** General. **Health:** Community health services, nursing (RN). **History:** General. **Interdisciplinary:** Biological/physical sciences. **Legal studies:** Paralegal. **Liberal arts:** Humanities. **Math:** General. **Parks/recreation:** Health/fitness. **Philosophy/religion:** Philosophy. **Physical sciences:** Chemistry, oceanography, physics. **Protective services:** Criminal justice. **Psychology:** General. **Public administration:** Social work. **Social sciences:** General, anthropology, international relations, political science, sociology. **Visual/performing arts:** Art, dramatic, music performance, studio arts.

**Most popular majors.** Business/marketing 19%, communications/journalism 8%, education 18%, psychology 6%, social sciences 7%.

**Computing on campus.** 200 workstations in dormitories, library, computer center, student center. Dormitories wired for high-speed internet access and linked to campus network. Commuter students can connect to campus network. Online course registration, online library, helpline, student web hosting, wireless network available.

**Student life. Freshman orientation:** Mandatory, $92 fee. Preregistration for classes offered. Two-day programs held throughout summer; includes parents. **Housing:** Coed dorms, apartments, fraternity/sorority housing, wellness housing available. $225 partly refundable deposit. **Activities:** Bands, campus ministries, choral groups, dance, drama, international student organizations, music ensembles, musical theater, radio station, student government, student newspaper, symphony orchestra, TV station, black student union, CLOVE, College Republicans.

**Athletics.** NCAA. **Intercollegiate:** Baseball M, basketball, cross-country, golf, soccer, softball W, tennis, track and field, volleyball W. **Intramural:** Badminton, bowling, fencing, football (non-tackle), handball, racquetball, soccer, swimming, table tennis, volleyball, water polo, weight lifting. **Team name:** Argonauts.

**Student services.** Alcohol/substance abuse counseling, career counseling, student employment services, financial aid counseling, health services, minority student services, on-campus daycare, personal counseling, placement for graduates, veterans' counselor. **Physically disabled:** Services for visually, speech, hearing impaired.

**Contact.** E-mail: admissions@uwf.edu
Phone: (850) 474-2230 Toll-free number: (800) 263-1074
Fax: (850) 474-3360
Steve McKellips, Director of Admissions, University of West Florida, 11000 University Parkway, Pensacola, FL 32514-5750

## Warner University
Lake Wales, Florida
www.warner.edu                                   CB code: 5883

- Private 4-year liberal arts college affiliated with Church of God
- Commuter campus in large town
- 946 degree-seeking undergraduates: 11% part-time, 57% women, 23% African American, 1% Asian American, 11% Hispanic American, 2% international
- 114 degree-seeking graduate students
- 44% of applicants admitted
- SAT or ACT (ACT writing optional), application essay required
- 41% graduate within 6 years

**General.** Founded in 1968. Regionally accredited. Off-site locations including Lakeland Learning Center, Space Coast Learning Center in Melbourne, teaching site in Titusville. **Degrees:** 284 bachelor's, 46 associate awarded; master's offered. **Location:** 60 miles from Tampa, 55 miles from Orlando. **Calendar:** Semester, limited summer session. **Full-time faculty:** 33 total; 64% have terminal degrees, 9% minority, 33% women. **Part-time faculty:** 106 total; 28% have terminal degrees, 58% women. **Class size:** 72% < 20, 28% 20-39. **Special facilities:** Natural scrub brush preserve.

**Freshman class profile.** 579 applied, 254 admitted, 131 enrolled.

| Mid 50% test scores | | GPA 2.0-2.99: | 28% |
|---|---|---|---|
| SAT critical reading: | 370-550 | Rank in top quarter: | 27% |
| SAT math: | 350-570 | Rank in top tenth: | 6% |
| ACT composite: | 16-23 | Out-of-state: | 18% |
| GPA 3.75 or higher: | 22% | Live on campus: | 79% |
| GPA 3.50-3.74: | 13% | International: | 2% |
| GPA 3.0-3.49: | 37% | | |

**Basis for selection.** Two of the following required: 2.25 GPA, top 50% of class, or 18 ACT/870 SAT (exclusive of Writing). ACT Residual test administered to those without scores or with scores too low. Interview recommended. Audition required of music majors. **Homeschooled:** Statement describing homeschool structure and mission, transcript of courses and grades, interview, letter of recommendation (nonparent) required. GED or portfolio required of applicants without transcripts.

**High school preparation.** College-preparatory program recommended. Recommended units include English 4, mathematics 3, social studies 1, history 1, science 2, foreign language 2 and academic electives 2.

**2009-2010 Annual costs.** Tuition/fees: $15,320. One-time $50 security deposit for incoming freshmen living on campus. Room/board: $6,815. Books/supplies: $1,000. Personal expenses: $1,792.

**2008-2009 Financial aid. Non-need-based:** Scholarships awarded for academics, alumni affiliation, art, athletics, leadership, music/drama, religious affiliation, state residency.

**Application procedures. Admission:** No deadline. $20 fee, may be waived for applicants with need. Admission notification on a rolling basis beginning on or about 9/15. **Financial aid:** Priority date 5/1; no closing date. FAFSA required. Applicants notified on a rolling basis starting 3/15; must reply within 2 week(s) of notification.

**Academics. Special study options:** Accelerated study, combined bachelor's/graduate degree, distance learning, double major, dual enrollment of high school students, ESL, independent study, internships, study abroad, teacher certification program, Washington semester. Online distance learning opportunities available for those interested in Organizational Management or Church Ministry. **Credit/placement by examination:** AP, CLEP, IB, SAT, ACT, institutional tests. **Support services:** Learning center, remedial instruction, study skills assistance, tutoring.

**Majors. Biology:** General. **Business:** Business admin. **Communications:** General, journalism. **Education:** Elementary, English, music, physical, science, social science, special. **History:** General. **Parks/recreation:** Exercise sciences, sports admin. **Psychology:** General. **Public administration:** Social work. **Social sciences:** General. **Theology:** Bible, sacred music, theology.

**Most popular majors.** Business/marketing 63%, education 18%.

**Computing on campus.** 69 workstations in library, computer center, student center. Dormitories wired for high-speed internet access. Commuter students can connect to campus network. Online library, helpline, repair service, wireless network available.

**Student life. Freshman orientation:** Mandatory. Preregistration for classes offered. Three-day program at start of fall semester. **Policies:** Student lifestyle agreement keeping with the moral and spiritual nature of the institution required. Religious observance required. **Housing:** Guaranteed on-campus for all undergraduates. Single-sex dorms, wellness housing available. $50 nonrefundable deposit, deadline 8/15. **Activities:** Campus ministries, choral groups, drama, music ensembles, student government, student newspaper, star throwers, missions, Young Americans.

**Athletics.** NAIA. **Intercollegiate:** Baseball M, basketball, cheerleading, cross-country, golf, soccer, softball W, tennis, track and field, volleyball. **Intramural:** Basketball, football (non-tackle), soccer, volleyball W. **Team name:** Royals.

**Student services.** Alcohol/substance abuse counseling, career counseling, student employment services, financial aid counseling, health services, personal counseling, placement for graduates.

**Contact.** E-mail: admissions@warner.edu
Phone: (863) 638-7212 Toll-free number: (800) 309-9563
Fax: (863) 638-7290
Jason Roe, Director of Admissions, Warner University, 13895 Highway 27, Lake Wales, FL 33859

## Webber International University
**Babson Park, Florida**
**www.webber.edu**    **CB code: 5893**

- Private 4-year university and business college
- Residential campus in rural community
- 603 degree-seeking undergraduates: 8% part-time, 35% women, 26% African American, 9% Hispanic American, 17% international
- 64 degree-seeking graduate students
- 78% of applicants admitted
- SAT or ACT (ACT writing recommended) required

**General.** Founded in 1927. Regionally accredited. **Degrees:** 105 bachelor's, 5 associate awarded; master's offered. **Location:** 50 miles from Orlando, 60 miles from Tampa. **Calendar:** Semester, limited summer session. **Full-time faculty:** 19 total; 74% have terminal degrees, 16% minority, 42% women. **Part-time faculty:** 22 total; 9% have terminal degrees, 23% minority, 54% women. **Class size:** 49% < 20, 50% 20-39, less than 1% 50-99. **Special facilities:** Nature preserve.

**Freshman class profile.** 412 applied, 321 admitted, 173 enrolled.

| Mid 50% test scores | | | |
|---|---|---|---|
| SAT critical reading: | 420-510 | Rank in top quarter: | 27% |
| SAT math: | 430-530 | Rank in top tenth: | 8% |
| ACT composite: | 18-21 | End year in good standing: | 56% |
| GPA 3.75 or higher: | 17% | Return as sophomores: | 48% |
| GPA 3.50-3.74: | 12% | Out-of-state: | 5% |
| GPA 3.0-3.49: | 26% | Live on campus: | 87% |
| GPA 2.0-2.99: | 45% | International: | 17% |

**Basis for selection.** GPA and standardized test scores very important, followed by school record. Interview recommended. **Homeschooled:** Transcript of courses and grades required. Proof of graduation with 2.0 GPA required. **Learning Disabled:** Documentation of disability required in order to adequately assist student in studies.

**High school preparation.** College-preparatory program recommended. 15 units recommended. Required and recommended units include English 4, mathematics 2-3, social studies 2, history 2, science 1-3, foreign language 1 and academic electives 4. 2 business courses recommended.

**2009-2010 Annual costs.** Tuition/fees: $17,850. Room/board: $6,822. Books/supplies: $800. Personal expenses: $3,168.

**2009-2010 Financial aid. Need-based:** 54% of total undergraduate aid awarded as scholarships/grants, 46% as loans/jobs. **Non-need-based:** Scholarships awarded for academics, alumni affiliation, athletics, leadership, state residency.

**Application procedures. Admission:** Priority date 5/1; deadline 8/1 (postmark date). $35 fee, may be waived for applicants with need. Admission notification on a rolling basis beginning on or about 12/1. Must reply by May 1 or within 4 week(s) if notified thereafter. **Financial aid:** Priority date 5/1, closing date 8/1. FAFSA required. Applicants notified on a rolling basis starting 4/1; must reply within 4 week(s) of notification.

**Academics. Special study options:** Combined bachelor's/graduate degree, cooperative education, cross-registration, distance learning, double major, dual enrollment of high school students, ESL, exchange student, internships, study abroad, weekend college. **Credit/placement by examination:** AP, CLEP, IB, institutional tests. 30 credit hours maximum toward associate degree, 30 toward bachelor's. No more than 6 semester hours credit awarded in each of 5 areas (English, humanities, science, social science, mathematics). **Support services:** Reduced course load, remedial instruction, study skills assistance, tutoring.

**Majors. Business:** General, accounting, business admin, finance, hospitality admin, marketing. **Communications:** General. **Computer sciences:** General. **Legal studies:** Prelaw. **Parks/recreation:** Facilities management. **Protective services:** Security management.

**Most popular majors.** Business/marketing 80%, parks/recreation 16%.

**Computing on campus.** 92 workstations in library, computer center. Dormitories wired for high-speed internet access. Commuter students can connect to campus network. Online library, helpline available.

**Student life. Freshman orientation:** Mandatory. Five-day program immediately preceding semester opening. **Housing:** Guaranteed on-campus for freshmen. Single-sex dorms available. $205 fully refundable deposit, deadline 8/28. **Activities:** Bands, student government, student newspaper, Fellowship of Christian Athletes, fishing club, international club, marketing club, Phi Beta Lambda, photography club, Society of Hosteurs.

**Athletics.** NAIA. **Intercollegiate:** Baseball M, basketball, bowling, cross-country, football (tackle) M, golf, soccer, softball W, tennis, track and field, volleyball W. **Intramural:** Basketball, bowling, football (non-tackle), soccer, softball, table tennis, tennis. **Team name:** Warriors.

**Student services.** Adult student services, alcohol/substance abuse counseling, career counseling, student employment services, financial aid counseling, health services, personal counseling, placement for graduates, veterans' counselor, women's services.

**Contact.** E-mail: admissions@webber.edu
Phone: (863) 638-2910 Toll-free number: (800) 741-1844
Fax: (863) 638-1591
Julie Ragans, Director of Admission, Webber International University, 1201 North Scenic Highway, Babson Park, FL 33827-0096

## Yeshiva Gedolah Rabbinical College
**Miami Beach, Florida**

- Private 4-year rabbinical college for men affiliated with Jewish faith
- Very large city

**General.** Accredited by AARTS. **Calendar:** Semester.

**Contact.** Phone: (305) 673-5664
1140 Alton Road, Miami Beach, FL 33139

# Georgia

## Agnes Scott College

**Decatur, Georgia**                          **CB member**
**www.agnesscott.edu**                        **CB code: 5002**

- Private 4-year liberal arts college for women affiliated with Presbyterian Church (USA)
- Residential campus in very large city
- 784 degree-seeking undergraduates: 1% part-time, 100% women, 25% African American, 4% Asian American, 5% Hispanic American, 7% international
- 25 degree-seeking graduate students
- 46% of applicants admitted
- Application essay required
- 67% graduate within 6 years; 32% enter graduate study

**General.** Founded in 1889. Regionally accredited. **Degrees:** 185 bachelor's awarded; master's offered. **ROTC:** Army, Air Force. **Location:** 6 miles from downtown Atlanta. **Calendar:** Semester, limited summer session. **Full-time faculty:** 82 total; 98% have terminal degrees, 20% minority, 61% women. **Part-time faculty:** 26 total; 73% have terminal degrees, 12% minority, 62% women. **Class size:** 80% < 20, 19% 20-39, less than 1% 40-49. **Special facilities:** Observatory, planetarium, art collection, electron microscope, 30-inch Beck telescope, center for writing and speaking, interactive learning center, multi-media classrooms.

**Freshman class profile.** 1,984 applied, 918 admitted, 237 enrolled.

| Mid 50% test scores | | | |
|---|---|---|---|
| SAT critical reading: | 520-650 | GPA 2.0-2.99: | 5% |
| SAT math: | 490-620 | Rank in top quarter: | 66% |
| SAT writing: | 520-640 | Rank in top tenth: | 33% |
| ACT composite: | 22-28 | End year in good standing: | 92% |
| GPA 3.75 or higher: | 34% | Return as sophomores: | 86% |
| GPA 3.50-3.74: | 27% | Out-of-state: | 41% |
| GPA 3.0-3.49: | 34% | Live on campus: | 96% |
| | | International: | 11% |

**Basis for selection.** High school record, class rank, test scores, counselor recommendation, personal qualities, and extracurricular activities considered. SAT/ACT, interview, or graded writing sample required. Interview recommended. Audition required for music scholarship. **Homeschooled:** Statement describing homeschool structure and mission, interview required. SAT Subject Test required.

**High school preparation.** College-preparatory program recommended. 16 units recommended. Recommended units include English 4, mathematics 3, social studies 2, history 2, science 2 (laboratory 2) and foreign language 2.

**2010-2011 Annual costs.** Tuition/fees: $31,283. Room/board: $9,850. Books/supplies: $1,000. Personal expenses: $1,000.

**2009-2010 Financial aid. Need-based:** 200 full-time freshmen applied for aid; 182 were judged to have need; 182 of these received aid. Average need met was 91%. Average scholarship/grant was $54,448; average loan $3,293. 81% of total undergraduate aid awarded as scholarships/grants, 19% as loans/jobs. **Non-need-based:** Awarded to 336 full-time undergraduates, including 109 freshmen. Scholarships awarded for academics, leadership, minority status, music/drama, religious affiliation, state residency. **Additional information:** Middle Income Assistance Grants available. Auditions required for music scholarship applicants.

**Application procedures. Admission:** $35 fee, may be waived for applicants with need, free for online applicants. Admission notification on a rolling basis. Must reply by May 1 or within 2 week(s) if notified thereafter. Scholarship applicants must apply for regular admission by 1/15. **Financial aid:** Priority date 2/15, closing date 5/1. FAFSA required. Applicants notified on a rolling basis starting 3/1; must reply within 3 week(s) of notification.

**Academics. Special study options:** Accelerated study, combined bachelor's/graduate degree, cross-registration, double major, dual enrollment of high school students, exchange student, independent study, internships, semester at sea, student-designed major, study abroad, teacher certification program, United Nations semester, Washington semester. Global Awareness and Global Connections programs offer opportunities to visit other regions of the world. Internship opportunities guaranteed; over 250 internships and externships available in Atlanta and other cities. Atlanta Semester focuses on women, leadership and social change. Language Across the Curriculum links foreign languages to other disciplines. Opportunities to study at over 123 universities in 33 countries. **Credit/placement by examination:** AP, CLEP, IB, SAT, ACT, institutional tests. 32 credit hours maximum toward bachelor's degree. **Support services:** Learning center, reduced course load, study skills assistance, tutoring, writing center.

**Majors. Area/ethnic studies:** African, women's. **Biology:** General, biochemistry. **Foreign languages:** Classics, French, German, Spanish. **History:** General. **Math:** General. **Philosophy/religion:** Philosophy, religion. **Physical sciences:** Astrophysics, chemistry, physics. **Psychology:** General. **Social sciences:** Anthropology, applied economics, economics, international relations, political science, sociology. **Visual/performing arts:** Art, dance, dramatic, studio arts.

**Most popular majors.** Biology 8%, English 10%, foreign language 7%, history 11%, philosophy/religious studies 7%, psychology 13%, social sciences 22%, visual/performing arts 8%.

**Computing on campus.** 458 workstations in dormitories, library, computer center, student center. Dormitories wired for high-speed internet access and linked to campus network. Commuter students can connect to campus network. Online library, helpline, repair service, wireless network available.

**Student life. Freshman orientation:** Mandatory. Held five days prior to start of semester; includes signing of honor code, breakfast with college president, introduction to Big/Little Sister program. **Housing:** Guaranteed on-campus for all undergraduates. Apartments, wellness housing available. $350 nonrefundable deposit, deadline 5/1. College-owned houses for nontraditional students, CHOICE housing (Choosing Healthy Options in a Community Environment) available. **Activities:** Bands, campus ministries, choral groups, dance, drama, international student organizations, literary magazine, music ensembles, Model UN, musical theater, student government, student newspaper, symphony orchestra, TV station, religious life council, conservative forum, College Democrats, green Earth organization, Circle-K, African American student group, Asian cultural awareness association, Amnesty International.

**Athletics.** NCAA. **Intercollegiate:** Basketball W, lacrosse W, soccer W, softball W, tennis W, volleyball W. **Intramural:** Basketball W, cheerleading W, fencing W, field hockey W, football (non-tackle) W, soccer W, swimming W, tennis W, track and field W, volleyball W, weight lifting W. **Team name:** Scotties.

**Student services.** Adult student services, alcohol/substance abuse counseling, chaplain/spiritual director, career counseling, student employment services, financial aid counseling, health services, minority student services, personal counseling, placement for graduates, women's services. **Physically disabled:** Services for visually, speech, hearing impaired.

**Contact.**  E-mail: admission@agnesscott.edu
Phone: (404) 471-6285 Toll-free number: (800) 868-8602
Fax: (404) 471-6414
Lee Ann Afton, Dean of Admission, Agnes Scott College, 141 East College Avenue, Decatur, GA 30030-3797

## Albany State University

**Albany, Georgia**                           **CB member**
**www.asurams.edu/**                          **CB code: 5004**

- Public 4-year university and liberal arts college
- Residential campus in small city
- 3,988 degree-seeking undergraduates: 16% part-time, 66% women
- 427 degree-seeking graduate students
- 42% of applicants admitted
- SAT or ACT (ACT writing optional) required
- 50% graduate within 6 years

**General.** Founded in 1903. Regionally accredited. **Degrees:** 520 bachelor's, 3 associate awarded; master's offered. **ROTC:** Army. **Location:** 190 miles from Atlanta. **Calendar:** Semester, limited summer session. **Full-time faculty:** 152 total; 40% women. **Part-time faculty:** 132 total; 58% women. **Class size:** 44% < 20, 43% 20-39, 10% 40-49, 3% 50-99. **Special facilities:** Health and physical education complex.

**Freshman class profile.** 4,773 applied, 1,993 admitted, 732 enrolled.

| Mid 50% test scores | | GPA 3.50-3.74: | 4% |
|---|---|---|---|
| SAT critical reading: | 420-480 | GPA 3.0-3.49: | 28% |
| SAT math: | 410-480 | GPA 2.0-2.99: | 66% |
| ACT composite: | 17-19 | Out-of-state: | 4% |
| GPA 3.75 or higher: | 2% | | |

**Basis for selection.** Academic record, GPA and test scores very important. **Homeschooled:** Statement describing homeschool structure and mission, transcript of courses and grades required. School must be accredited. **Learning Disabled:** Students with documented disabilities should register with Office of Counseling, Testing, and Disabled Student Services.

**High school preparation.** College-preparatory program required. 16 units required. Required units include English 4, mathematics 4, social studies 3, science 3 (laboratory 2) and foreign language 2. 2 foreign language units must be same language.

**2009-2010 Annual costs.** Tuition/fees: $4,786; $16,400 out-of-state. Room/board: $5,290.

**2008-2009 Financial aid. Non-need-based:** Scholarships awarded for academics, alumni affiliation, art, athletics, music/drama, ROTC.

**Application procedures. Admission:** Priority date 5/1; deadline 7/1. $20 fee, may be waived for applicants with need. Admission notification on a rolling basis. Early admission high school students must have permission from their high school to attend; must also meet certain GPA and SAT/ACT test requirement. **Financial aid:** Priority date 4/15, closing date 4/30. FAFSA required. Applicants notified on a rolling basis; must reply within 2 week(s) of notification.

**Academics. Special study options:** Combined bachelor's/graduate degree, cooperative education, cross-registration, distance learning, double major, dual enrollment of high school students, honors, independent study, internships, liberal arts/career combination, study abroad, teacher certification program, weekend college. 3+2 and 2+2 engineering program with Georgia Institute of Technology. **Credit/placement by examination:** AP, CLEP, institutional tests. 45 credit hours maximum toward bachelor's degree. **Support services:** Learning center, remedial instruction, study skills assistance, tutoring, writing center.

**Majors. Biology:** General. **Business:** Accounting, business admin, logistics, management information systems, marketing. **Communications:** Journalism. **Computer sciences:** General, information systems. **Education:** Early childhood, elementary, mathematics, middle, music, physical, science, social science, special. **Foreign languages:** Spanish. **Health:** Nursing (RN). **History:** General. **Math:** General. **Parks/recreation:** Health/fitness. **Physical sciences:** Chemistry. **Protective services:** Criminal justice, forensics. **Psychology:** General. **Public administration:** Social work. **Social sciences:** Political science, sociology. **Visual/performing arts:** Drawing. **Other:** Technology management.

**Most popular majors.** Business/marketing 28%, education 24%, psychology 7%, public administration/social services 6%, security/protective services 9%, social sciences 6%.

**Computing on campus.** 400 workstations in dormitories, library, computer center, student center. Dormitories wired for high-speed internet access and linked to campus network. Commuter students can connect to campus network. Online course registration, online library, helpline, student web hosting, wireless network available.

**Student life. Freshman orientation:** Mandatory, $120 fee. Preregistration for classes offered. Held in January, May, June and August. **Housing:** Coed dorms, single sex dorms, special housing for disabled, apartments, wellness housing available. $150 partly refundable deposit. **Activities:** Bands, choral groups, dance, drama, music ensembles, musical theater, opera, radio station, student government, student newspaper, TV station, Annointed ASU Gospel Choir, Annointed Students in Unity Fellowship Fraternity & Sorority, Inc., Divine Visions Outreach, Young Democrats, NAACP, Habitat for Humanity, BAACHUS & GAMMA Peer Educators, Relay for Life, HIV Aids Peer Educator.

**Athletics.** NCAA. **Intercollegiate:** Baseball M, basketball, cheerleading M, cross-country, football (tackle) M, softball W, tennis W, track and field, volleyball W. **Intramural:** Basketball M, football (tackle) M, track and field. **Team name:** Rams.

**Student services.** Alcohol/substance abuse counseling, career counseling, student employment services, financial aid counseling, health services, personal counseling, placement for graduates, veterans' counselor. **Learning disabled:** Comprehensive services available.

**Contact.** E-mail: admissions@asurams.edu
Phone: (229) 430-4646 Toll-free number: (800) 822-7267
Fax: (229) 430-3936
Ronnie Jackson, Director of Recruitment and Admissions, Albany State University, 504 College Drive, Albany, GA 31705-2796

## American InterContinental University
**Atlanta, Georgia**
**www.buckhead.aiuniv.edu/**
CB code: 2486

- For-profit 4-year virtual university
- Commuter campus in very large city
- 1,952 degree-seeking undergraduates
- Application essay, interview required

**General.** Founded in 1977. Regionally accredited. Additional campuses in Dunwoody, South Florida, Houston, London, Dubai, online. **Degrees:** 276 bachelor's, 84 associate awarded; master's offered. **Calendar:** Quarter, extensive summer session. **Full-time faculty:** 27 total. **Part-time faculty:** 63 total. **Special facilities:** Sewing laboratories, darkroom laboratories, interior design library, video production studios, learning center.

**Basis for selection.** Essay, results of personal interview, portfolio, high school GPA and references important. SAT or ACT recommended. Prefer that test scores be received prior to beginning of term since they are used for placement. **Homeschooled:** State high school equivalency certificate required.

**2009-2010 Annual costs.** Costs vary by program. Books/supplies: $1,500. Personal expenses: $960.

**Application procedures. Admission:** No deadline. $50 fee. Admission notification on a rolling basis. **Financial aid:** Priority date 6/1; no closing date. FAFSA, institutional form required. Applicants notified on a rolling basis.

**Academics. Special study options:** Accelerated study, distance learning, double major, independent study, internships, study abroad. **Credit/placement by examination:** CLEP, IB, SAT, ACT, institutional tests. **Support services:** Learning center, pre-admission summer program, reduced course load, remedial instruction, study skills assistance, tutoring, writing center.

**Majors. Business:** Business admin, fashion. **Computer sciences:** Game design, information technology. **Protective services:** Law enforcement admin. **Visual/performing arts:** Design, fashion design, interior design. **Other:** Media production.

**Computing on campus.** Online library, helpline available.

**Student life. Freshman orientation:** Mandatory. Preregistration for classes offered. **Housing:** Apartments available. **Activities:** Student government, student newspaper, American Society of Interior Designers, fashion association, marketing association, graphic arts association, dressers club, portfolio club, cultural club.

**Student services.** Career counseling, student employment services, health services, personal counseling, placement for graduates, veterans' counselor.

**Contact.** E-mail: info@aiuniv.edu
Phone: (404) 965-5700 Toll-free number: (800) 955-2120
Fax: (404) 965-5701
Director of Admissions, American InterContinental University, 6600 Peachtree Dunwoody Road, 500 Embassy Row, Atlanta, GA 30328

## Argosy University: Atlanta
**Atlanta, Georgia**
**www.argosy.edu/atlanta**

- For-profit 4-year university
- Very large city
- 233 degree-seeking undergraduates

**General.** Regionally accredited. **Degrees:** 26 bachelor's awarded; master's, doctoral, professional offered. **Calendar:** Continuous. **Full-time faculty:** 39 total. **Part-time faculty:** 200 total.

**Freshman class profile.** 44 enrolled.

**Basis for selection.** Open admission.

**Academics. Credit/placement by examination:** CLEP.

**Majors. Business:** Business admin. **Liberal arts:** Arts/sciences. **Protective services:** Police science. **Psychology:** General.

**Contact.** E-mail: auaadmissions@argosy.edu
Phone: (770) 671-1200 Toll-free number: (888) 671-4777
Argosy University: Atlanta, 980 Hammond Drive, Suite 100, Atlanta, GA 30328

## Armstrong Atlantic State University
**Savannah, Georgia**
**www.armstrong.edu**                          **CB code: 5012**

- Public 4-year university
- Commuter campus in small city
- 6,587 degree-seeking undergraduates: 30% part-time, 65% women, 21% African American, 2% Asian American, 4% Hispanic American, 1% Native American, 4% international
- 920 degree-seeking graduate students
- 60% of applicants admitted
- SAT or ACT (ACT writing optional) required
- 30% graduate within 6 years

**General.** Founded in 1935. Regionally accredited. Regional center for health professions. **Degrees:** 898 bachelor's, 84 associate awarded; master's, professional offered. **ROTC:** Army, Naval. **Location:** 250 miles from Atlanta; 150 miles from Jacksonville, FL. **Calendar:** Semester, extensive summer session. **Full-time faculty:** 289 total; 53% women. **Part-time faculty:** 145 total; 56% women. **Class size:** 37% < 20, 49% 20-39, 9% 40-49, 5% 50-99, less than 1% >100.

**Freshman class profile.** 2,638 applied, 1,593 admitted, 1,091 enrolled.

| Mid 50% test scores | | End year in good standing: | 63% |
|---|---|---|---|
| SAT critical reading: | 450-550 | Return as sophomores: | 68% |
| SAT math: | 440-550 | Out-of-state: | 12% |
| ACT composite: | 18-23 | Live on campus: | 32% |
| GPA 3.75 or higher: | 11% | International: | 3% |
| GPA 3.50-3.74: | 11% | Fraternities: | 3% |
| GPA 3.0-3.49: | 36% | Sororities: | 4% |
| GPA 2.0-2.99: | 42% | | |

**Basis for selection.** 430 SAT math, 460 SAT verbal and 2.0 GPA required for regular admissions. Conditional admission possible with 1.8 GPA and lower test scores. **Homeschooled:** Applicants who do not complete an accredited program must pass SAT Subject Tests to satisfy college prep requirements.

**High school preparation.** College-preparatory program required. Required units include English 4, mathematics 4, social studies 3, science 3 (laboratory 2) and foreign language 2.

**2009-2010 Annual costs.** Tuition/fees: $4,802; $16,416 out-of-state. Declining balance meal plans available. Room only: $5,350. Books/supplies: $1,000.

**2008-2009 Financial aid. Non-need-based:** Scholarships awarded for academics, alumni affiliation, art, athletics, leadership, minority status, music/drama, state residency.

**Application procedures. Admission:** Priority date 6/1; deadline 8/1. $25 fee, may be waived for applicants with need. Admission notification on a rolling basis beginning on or about 10/1. **Financial aid:** Priority date 3/15; no closing date. FAFSA required. Applicants notified on a rolling basis starting 2/1; must reply by 4/15 or within 2 week(s) of notification.

**Academics. Special study options:** Combined bachelor's/graduate degree, cooperative education, distance learning, double major, dual enrollment of high school students, honors, independent study, internships, study abroad, teacher certification program, weekend college. **Credit/placement by examination:** AP, CLEP, IB, SAT, ACT, institutional tests. 30 credit hours maximum toward associate degree, 30 toward bachelor's. **Support services:** Learning center, reduced course load, remedial instruction, study skills assistance, tutoring, writing center.

**Majors. Biology:** General. **Computer sciences:** General, information technology. **Education:** Art, business, early childhood, elementary, English, health, learning disabled, mathematics, middle, music, physical, science, secondary, social science, special, speech impaired. **Foreign languages:** Spanish. **Health:** Clinical lab science, communication disorders, dental hygiene, health services, medical radiologic technology/radiation therapy, nuclear medical

technology, nursing (RN), respiratory therapy technology, sonography. **History:** General. **Math:** Applied. **Physical sciences:** Chemistry, physics. **Protective services:** Police science. **Psychology:** General. **Social sciences:** Economics, political science. **Visual/performing arts:** Art, dramatic.

**Most popular majors.** Education 21%, health sciences 35%, liberal arts 10%.

**Computing on campus.** Dormitories wired for high-speed internet access and linked to campus network. Commuter students can connect to campus network. Online course registration, online library, helpline, wireless network available.

**Student life. Freshman orientation:** Available, $45 fee. Preregistration for classes offered. One-day event prior to registration. **Housing:** Coed dorms, apartments available. $250 partly refundable deposit, deadline 7/16. **Activities:** Bands, choral groups, dance, drama, international student organizations, literary magazine, music ensembles, Model UN, musical theater, student government, student newspaper, symphony orchestra, NAACP, Baptist student union, Hispanic outreach and leadership, Cercle Francais, Newman Club, Wesley Foundation, College Democrats, College Republicans.

**Athletics.** NCAA. **Intercollegiate:** Baseball M, basketball, cross-country M, golf, softball W, tennis, volleyball W. **Intramural:** Badminton, basketball, bowling, cheerleading, football (non-tackle), golf, racquetball, soccer, softball, swimming, table tennis, tennis, volleyball. **Team name:** Pirates.

**Student services.** Adult student services, alcohol/substance abuse counseling, career counseling, student employment services, financial aid counseling, health services, minority student services, personal counseling, placement for graduates, veterans' counselor. **Physically disabled:** Services for visually, speech, hearing impaired.

**Contact.** E-mail: adm-info@armstrong.edu
Phone: (912) 344-2503 Toll-free number: (800) 633-2349
Fax: (912) 344-3470
Stephanie Whaley, Director of Admissions, Armstrong Atlantic State University, 11935 Abercorn Street, Savannah, GA 31419-1997

## Art Institute of Atlanta
**Atlanta, Georgia**                          **CB member**
**www.artinstitutes.edu/atlanta/**            **CB code: 5429**

- For-profit 4-year culinary school and visual arts college
- Commuter campus in very large city
- 3,839 degree-seeking undergraduates: 16% part-time, 44% women
- Application essay, interview required

**General.** Founded in 1949. Regionally accredited. **Degrees:** 250 bachelor's, 161 associate awarded. **Location:** 12 miles from city center. **Calendar:** Quarter, extensive summer session. **Full-time faculty:** 131 total; 48% have terminal degrees, 21% minority, 45% women. **Part-time faculty:** 107 total; 39% have terminal degrees, 31% minority, 55% women. **Class size:** 58% < 20, 42% 20-39. **Special facilities:** Camera video studios, video editing suites, digital audio studio, professional photography studios, traditional darkroom, digital darkroom, digital image capture systems, motion capture lab, color-calibrated monitors, scanners, printers.

**Basis for selection.** GPA or GED transcript; ACT, SAT, ASSET or COMPASS; and essay most important. Applicants for associate degree should have 2.0 GPA; 2.5 GPA for bachelor's degree. Test scores or life experience may be considered if GPA requirement not met. Students exempt from placement testing if one of the following apply: transfer credit in both English & math; 21 ACT; 500 SAT critical reading and math subscores. Portfolio required for national scholarship competition. **Homeschooled:** Transcript of courses and grades, state high school equivalency certificate required. State or accreditation-issued credential for high school graduation is required along with transcript. If credential not available, students must have GED. **Learning Disabled:** Students should submit current documentation of disability to disability services coordinator at least 6 weeks before accommodations will be needed.

**High school preparation.** College-preparatory program required.

**2010-2011 Annual costs.** Tuition/fees: $23,535. Room only: $9,984. Books/supplies: $1,700. Personal expenses: $7,692.

**Financial aid. Non-need-based:** Scholarships awarded for academics, art, state residency.

**Application procedures. Admission:** No deadline. $50 fee. Admission notification on a rolling basis. **Financial aid:** No deadline. FAFSA required. Applicants notified on a rolling basis starting 3/15.

**Academics. Special study options:** Accelerated study, distance learning, dual enrollment of high school students, honors, independent study, internships, study abroad, weekend college. **Credit/placement by examination:** CLEP, IB, SAT, ACT, institutional tests. **Support services:** Learning center, pre-admission summer program, reduced course load, remedial instruction, study skills assistance, tutoring, writing center.

**Majors. Communications:** Advertising, digital media. **Communications technology:** Animation/special effects, graphic/printing, graphics, photo/film/video, recording arts. **Computer sciences:** Web page design, webmaster. **Personal/culinary services:** Chef training, culinary arts, food service, restaurant/catering. **Visual/performing arts:** Cinematography, commercial photography, commercial/advertising art, fashion design, graphic design, illustration, interior design, multimedia, photography.

**Most popular majors.** Communication technologies 10%, computer/information sciences 24%, personal/culinary services 6%, visual/performing arts 56%.

**Computing on campus.** 385 workstations in dormitories, library, computer center. Dormitories wired for high-speed internet access. Online course registration, online library, helpline, student web hosting, wireless network available.

**Student life. Freshman orientation:** Available. Preregistration for classes offered. One day at beginning of each quarter. **Housing:** Guaranteed on-campus for all undergraduates. Coed dorms available. $250 fully refundable deposit. **Activities:** International student organizations, student government, Student Leadership Council.

**Student services.** Career counseling, student employment services, financial aid counseling, personal counseling, placement for graduates. **Physically disabled:** Services for visually, speech, hearing impaired.

**Contact.** E-mail: aia-admis@aii.edu
Phone: (770) 394-8300 Toll-free number: (800) 275-4242
Fax: (770) 394-0008
Joy McClure, Senior Director of Admissions, Art Institute of Atlanta, 6600 Peachtree Dunwoody Road, NE, Atlanta, GA 30328

## Atlanta Christian College
**East Point, Georgia**
www.acc.edu                           CB code: 5029

- Private 4-year Bible and liberal arts college affiliated with Christian Church
- Residential campus in small city
- 683 degree-seeking undergraduates: 3% part-time, 57% women, 54% African American, 1% Asian American, 4% Hispanic American
- 57% of applicants admitted
- SAT or ACT (ACT writing optional) required

**General.** Founded in 1937. Regionally accredited. **Degrees:** 69 bachelor's awarded. **Location:** 10 miles from Atlanta. **Calendar:** Semester, limited summer session. **Full-time faculty:** 24 total. **Part-time faculty:** 31 total.

**Freshman class profile.** 180 applied, 102 admitted, 72 enrolled.

| Mid 50% test scores | | ACT composite: | 18-23 |
|---|---|---|---|
| SAT critical reading: | 410-540 | Out-of-state: | 4% |
| SAT math: | 400-500 | | |

**Basis for selection.** Recommendations, scholastic ability, and test scores are most important. **Homeschooled:** Statement describing homeschool structure and mission, transcript of courses and grades, letter of recommendation (nonparent) required.

**High school preparation.** College-preparatory program recommended. 18 units required; 22 recommended. Required and recommended units include English 4, mathematics 3-4, history 3, science 3 (laboratory 3), foreign language 2 and academic electives 2.

**2009-2010 Annual costs.** Tuition/fees: $15,150. Room/board: $5,580. Books/supplies: $400. Personal expenses: $500.

**2008-2009 Financial aid. Need-based:** 44% of total undergraduate aid awarded as scholarships/grants, 56% as loans/jobs.

**Application procedures. Admission:** Priority date 7/1; deadline 8/1 (receipt date). $25 fee, may be waived for applicants with need. Admission notification on a rolling basis. **Financial aid:** Priority date 6/1, closing date 8/1. FAFSA required. Applicants notified on a rolling basis starting 3/1; must reply within 3 week(s) of notification.

**Academics. Special study options:** Accelerated study, distance learning, double major, dual enrollment of high school students, independent study, internships, liberal arts/career combination, study abroad, teacher certification program. **Credit/placement by examination:** AP, CLEP, IB, SAT, ACT, institutional tests. 16 credit hours maximum toward associate degree, 32 toward bachelor's. **Support services:** Reduced course load, remedial instruction, study skills assistance, tutoring, writing center.

**Majors. Business:** General, business admin. **Education:** Business, early childhood, elementary. **Interdisciplinary:** Intercultural. **Liberal arts:** Arts/sciences, humanities. **Psychology:** General. **Theology:** Bible, theology.

**Computing on campus.** 30 workstations in library, computer center, student center. Dormitories wired for high-speed internet access and linked to campus network. Commuter students can connect to campus network. Online library, helpline, repair service, wireless network available.

**Student life. Freshman orientation:** Mandatory. Preregistration for classes offered. **Policies:** Religious observance required. **Housing:** Guaranteed on-campus for freshmen. Single-sex dorms, special housing for disabled, apartments, wellness housing available. **Activities:** Campus ministries, choral groups, dance, drama, literary magazine, music ensembles, student government, student newspaper, religious organizations, Christian service clubs, service-oriented fraternities and sororities.

**Athletics.** NCCAA. **Intercollegiate:** Baseball M, basketball, soccer, volleyball W. **Intramural:** Basketball, football (non-tackle), softball W, volleyball, weight lifting. **Team name:** Chargers.

**Student services.** Adult student services, alcohol/substance abuse counseling, chaplain/spiritual director, career counseling, services for economically disadvantaged, student employment services, financial aid counseling, health services, personal counseling, placement for graduates, veterans' counselor. **Physically disabled:** Services for hearing impaired. **Learning disabled:** Comprehensive services available.

**Contact.** E-mail: admissions@acc.edu
Phone: (404) 669-3202 Toll-free number: (800) 776-8861
Fax: (404) 460-2451
Stacy Bartlett, Director of Admission, Atlanta Christian College, 2605 Ben Hill Road, East Point, GA 30344

## Augusta State University
**Augusta, Georgia**                    CB member
www.aug.edu                            CB code: 5336

- Public 4-year liberal arts and teachers college
- Commuter campus in small city
- 5,394 degree-seeking undergraduates
- SAT or ACT (ACT writing optional) required

**General.** Founded in 1925. Regionally accredited. **Degrees:** 608 bachelor's, 117 associate awarded; master's offered. **ROTC:** Army. **Location:** 145 miles from Atlanta. **Calendar:** Semester, extensive summer session. **Full-time faculty:** 236 total. **Part-time faculty:** 166 total. **Class size:** 41% < 20, 55% 20-39, 4% 40-49, less than 1% 50-99. **Special facilities:** History walk and museum, 18-hole golf course.

**Freshman class profile.**

| Mid 50% test scores | | GPA 3.0-3.49: | 28% |
|---|---|---|---|
| SAT critical reading: | 440-540 | GPA 2.0-2.99: | 52% |
| SAT math: | 430-540 | Out-of-state: | 7% |
| ACT composite: | 17-21 | Live on campus: | 16% |
| GPA 3.75 or higher: | 7% | Fraternities: | 1% |
| GPA 3.50-3.74: | 11% | Sororities: | 1% |

**Basis for selection.** 430 SAT Verbal or 17 ACT English, and 400 SAT Math or 17 ACT Math required. SAT Subject Tests required of GED recipients or graduates of non-accredited high schools.

**High school preparation.** 18 units required. Required units include English 4, mathematics 4, social studies 3, science 3, foreign language 2 and academic electives 2.

**2009-2010 Annual costs.** Tuition/fees: $4,634; $16,248 out-of-state. Books/supplies: $1,000. Personal expenses: $1,980.

**2008-2009 Financial aid. Non-need-based:** Scholarships awarded for academics, art, athletics, leadership, minority status, music/drama, ROTC, state residency.

**Application procedures. Admission:** Priority date 7/1; no deadline. $30 fee, may be waived for applicants with need. Application must be submitted on paper. Admission notification on a rolling basis. **Financial aid:** Closing date 6/1. FAFSA, institutional form required. Applicants notified on a rolling basis starting 3/1; must reply within 4 week(s) of notification.

**Academics. Special study options:** Cooperative education, cross-registration, distance learning, double major, dual enrollment of high school students, ESL, honors, independent study, internships, study abroad, teacher certification program. Paralegal certificate. **Credit/placement by examination:** AP, CLEP, institutional tests. 30 credit hours maximum toward associate degree, 30 toward bachelor's. **Support services:** Learning center, preadmission summer program, reduced course load, remedial instruction, study skills assistance, tutoring, writing center.

**Majors. Biology:** General. **Business:** Accounting, business admin, finance, management information systems, marketing. **Communications:** General. **Computer sciences:** General. **Education:** Elementary, mentally handicapped, middle, music, physical, special. **Foreign languages:** French, Spanish. **Health:** Clinical lab science. **History:** General. **Math:** General. **Physical sciences:** Chemistry, physics. **Protective services:** Criminal justice. **Psychology:** General. **Public administration:** Social work. **Social sciences:** Political science, sociology. **Visual/performing arts:** Multimedia, music performance.

**Most popular majors.** Biology 6%, business/marketing 22%, education 24%, psychology 8%, social sciences 8%.

**Computing on campus.** 300 workstations in library, computer center, student center. Commuter students can connect to campus network. Online course registration, online library, helpline, student web hosting, wireless network available.

**Student life. Freshman orientation:** Available. Preregistration for classes offered. **Housing:** Apartments available. **Activities:** Bands, choral groups, drama, international student organizations, literary magazine, radio station, student government, student newspaper, black student union, Los Amigos Hispanos, Le Cercle Francais, Muslim student association, Circle K, chess club, anime club, College Conservatives, Baptist student union.

**Athletics.** NCAA. **Intercollegiate:** Baseball M, basketball, cross-country, golf, softball W, tennis, volleyball W. **Intramural:** Basketball M. **Team name:** Jaguars.

**Student services.** Adult student services, alcohol/substance abuse counseling, career counseling, student employment services, financial aid counseling, minority student services, personal counseling, placement for graduates, veterans' counselor. **Physically disabled:** Services for visually, hearing impaired.

**Contact.** E-mail: admissio@aug.edu
Phone: (706) 737-1632 Toll-free number: (800) 341-4373
Fax: (706) 667-4355
Katherine Sweeney, Registrar and Director of Admissions, Augusta State University, 2500 Walton Way, Augusta, GA 30904-2200

## Bauder College
**Atlanta, Georgia**
www.bauder.edu                                    CB code: 5070

- For-profit 4-year career college
- Commuter campus in very large city

**General.** Founded in 1964. Regionally accredited. **Location:** Downtown. **Calendar:** Quarter.

**Annual costs/financial aid.** Additional book fee of $1280. Books/supplies: $900. Personal expenses: $1,100. Need-based financial aid available to full-time and part-time students.

**Contact.** Phone: (404) 237-7573
Director of Admissions, 384 Northyards Boulevard NW, Ste 190, Atlanta, GA 30313

## Berry College
**Mount Berry, Georgia**                           CB member
www.berry.edu                                      CB code: 5059

- Private 4-year liberal arts college
- Residential campus in large town
- 1,756 degree-seeking undergraduates: 1% part-time, 69% women, 5% African American, 2% Asian American, 3% Hispanic American, 2% international
- 136 degree-seeking graduate students
- 67% of applicants admitted

- SAT or ACT (ACT writing optional), application essay required
- 60% graduate within 6 years; 27% enter graduate study

**General.** Founded in 1902. Regionally accredited. **Degrees:** 336 bachelor's awarded; master's offered. **Location:** 72 miles from Atlanta; 75 miles from Chattanooga, TN. **Calendar:** Semester, limited summer session. **Full-time faculty:** 145 total; 90% have terminal degrees, 4% minority, 39% women. **Part-time faculty:** 59 total; 29% have terminal degrees, 3% minority, 39% women. **Class size:** 65% < 20, 33% 20-39, 1% 40-49, less than 1% 50-99. **Special facilities:** Museum, waterwheel, wildlife management area and refuge, equine center with boarding facilities, dairy and beef cattle research center, on-campus elementary and middle schools, child development center, science center with 60-foot Foucault pendulum, student campsites.

**Freshman class profile.** 2,412 applied, 1,616 admitted, 569 enrolled.

| Mid 50% test scores | | | |
|---|---|---|---|
| SAT critical reading: | 520-640 | GPA 2.0-2.99: | 8% |
| SAT math: | 510-610 | Rank in top quarter: | 66% |
| SAT writing: | 510-620 | Rank in top tenth: | 32% |
| ACT composite: | 22-28 | End year in good standing: | 72% |
| GPA 3.75 or higher: | 45% | Return as sophomores: | 74% |
| GPA 3.50-3.74: | 20% | Out-of-state: | 21% |
| GPA 3.0-3.49: | 27% | Live on campus: | 95% |
| | | International: | 1% |

**Basis for selection.** School achievement record and test scores most important. Class rank, recommendations and essays considered. Interview recommended; auditions required of music and theater majors; portfolio recommended for art majors. **Homeschooled:** Transcript of courses and grades, letter of recommendation (nonparent) required. Must meet or exceed academic profile of previous freshman class.

**High school preparation.** College-preparatory program required. 20 units required. Required units include English 4, mathematics 4, social studies 3, science 3 and foreign language 2. Algebra I, geometry or trigonometry, algebra II and fourth year higher than algebra II required.

**2010-2011 Annual costs.** Tuition/fees: $24,620. Room/board: $8,724. Books/supplies: $1,200. Personal expenses: $1,800.

**2009-2010 Financial aid. Need-based:** 528 full-time freshmen applied for aid; 416 were judged to have need; 416 of these received aid. Average need met was 85%. Average scholarship/grant was $16,818; average loan $2,968. 67% of total undergraduate aid awarded as scholarships/grants, 33% as loans/jobs. **Non-need-based:** Awarded to 802 full-time undergraduates, including 239 freshmen. Scholarships awarded for academics, art, athletics, leadership, minority status, music/drama, state residency. **Additional information:** Students are encouraged to work on-campus up to 20 hours per week.

**Application procedures. Admission:** Priority date 2/1; deadline 7/23 (receipt date). $50 fee, may be waived for applicants with need, free for online applicants. Admission notification on a rolling basis beginning on or about 11/1. Must reply by May 1 or within 4 week(s) if notified thereafter. **Financial aid:** Priority date 4/1; no closing date. FAFSA required. Applicants notified on a rolling basis starting 2/1.

**Academics. Special study options:** Combined bachelor's/graduate degree, cooperative education, cross-registration, double major, dual enrollment of high school students, honors, independent study, internships, student-designed major, study abroad, teacher certification program. 3-2 nursing with Emory University, 3-2 engineering with Georgia Institute of Technology. **Credit/placement by examination:** AP, CLEP, IB, SAT, ACT, institutional tests. No limit to credit by examination that may be applied to degree. **Support services:** Remedial instruction, study skills assistance, tutoring, writing center.

**Majors. Agriculture:** Animal sciences. **Biology:** General. **Business:** Accounting, finance, marketing. **Communications:** General. **Computer sciences:** Computer science. **Conservation:** Environmental science. **Education:** Early childhood, mathematics, middle, music, physical. **Engineering technology:** General. **Foreign languages:** French, German, Spanish. **Health:** Nursing (RN). **History:** General. **Math:** General. **Parks/recreation:** Exercise sciences. **Philosophy/religion:** Religion. **Physical sciences:** Chemistry, physics. **Psychology:** General. **Social sciences:** General, economics, international relations, political science. **Visual/performing arts:** Art, music management, theater arts management.

**Most popular majors.** Agriculture 7%, biology 10%, business/marketing 18%, communications/journalism 11%, education 11%, psychology 7%, social sciences 6%.

**Computing on campus.** 140 workstations in library, computer center, student center. Dormitories wired for high-speed internet access and linked to campus network. Commuter students can connect to campus network. Online library, helpline, repair service, wireless network available.

**Student life. Freshman orientation:** Mandatory, $90 fee. Preregistration for classes offered. Sessions for students and parents in June based on date of prepayment. Additional orientation 4 days prior to start of classes. **Policies:** Limited visitation hours. Dry campus. **Housing:** Guaranteed on-campus for freshmen. Coed dorms, single-sex dorms, apartments, wellness housing available. $100 fully refundable deposit, deadline 5/1. Special-interest houses for women in math and science available. **Activities:** Bands, campus ministries, choral groups, dance, drama, international student organizations, literary magazine, music ensembles, Model UN, musical theater, student government, student newspaper, symphony orchestra, Amnesty International, Baptist collegiate ministries, Wesley Foundation, Catholic student association, Habitat for Humanity, Canterbury club, campus outreach, Presbyterian student fellowship, Young Democrats, Republican club.

**Athletics.** NCAA. **Intercollegiate:** Baseball M, basketball, cross-country, diving, equestrian W, golf, lacrosse, soccer, softball W, swimming, tennis, volleyball W. **Intramural:** Badminton, basketball, bowling, cross-country, football (non-tackle), golf, racquetball, soccer, softball, swimming, table tennis, tennis, volleyball, water polo, weight lifting. **Team name:** Vikings.

**Student services.** Alcohol/substance abuse counseling, career counseling, student employment services, financial aid counseling, health services, minority student services, on-campus daycare, personal counseling, placement for graduates, veterans' counselor, women's services. **Physically disabled:** Services for visually, hearing impaired.

**Contact.** E-mail: admissions@berry.edu
Phone: (706) 236-2215 Toll-free number: (800) 237-7942
Fax: (706) 290-2178
Brett Kennedy, Director of Admissions, Berry College, PO Box 490159, Mount Berry, GA 30149-0159

## Beulah Heights University
**Atlanta, Georgia**
www.beulah.org                                    **CB code: 5082**

▸ Private 5-year university and Bible college affiliated with International Pentecostal Church of Christ
▸ Commuter campus in very large city
▸ 662 degree-seeking undergraduates
▸ Application essay required

**General.** Accredited by ABHE. **Degrees:** 60 bachelor's, 29 associate awarded; master's offered. **Location:** Downtown Atlanta. **Calendar:** Semester, extensive summer session. **Full-time faculty:** 11 total. **Part-time faculty:** 46 total.

**Basis for selection.** Open admission. Applicants must have accepted Christ, although personal denomination not considered. Pastoral and personal references required. Applicants pursuing GED may be accepted prior to completion, but must complete GED before college graduation. **Home-schooled:** Program must be approved by state of Georgia; 16 ACT or 900 SAT (exclusive of Writing) required.

**2009-2010 Annual costs.** Tuition/fees: $7,180. Room only: $3,200. Books/supplies: $150.

**Application procedures. Admission:** No deadline. $35 fee. Admission notification on a rolling basis.

**Academics. Special study options:** Cross-registration, distance learning, double major, ESL, independent study, internships, weekend college. **Credit/placement by examination:** CLEP. **Support services:** Learning center, reduced course load, study skills assistance, tutoring, writing center.

**Majors. Theology:** Bible.

**Computing on campus.** Dormitories wired for high-speed internet access. Commuter students can connect to campus network. Online course registration, online library, student web hosting, wireless network available.

**Student life. Freshman orientation:** Mandatory. **Policies:** Religious observance required. **Housing:** Single-sex dorms, apartments, wellness housing available. **Activities:** Campus ministries, choral groups, international student organizations, student government, student newspaper.

**Student services.** Adult student services, chaplain/spiritual director, career counseling, financial aid counseling, minority student services, personal counseling.

**Contact.** E-mail: admissions@beulah.org
Phone: (404) 627-2681 ext. 104 Toll-free number: (888) 777-2422
Fax: (404) 627-0702
John Dreher, Director of Admissions, Beulah Heights University, 892 Berne Street SE, Atlanta, GA 30316

## Brenau University
**Gainesville, Georgia**                           **CB member**
www.brenau.edu                                     **CB code: 5066**

▸ Private 4-year liberal arts college for women
▸ Residential campus in small city
▸ 794 degree-seeking undergraduates: 4% part-time, 100% women, 21% African American, 3% Asian American, 5% Hispanic American, 6% international
▸ 58 degree-seeking graduate students
▸ 38% of applicants admitted
▸ SAT or ACT (ACT writing optional) required
▸ 50% graduate within 6 years

**General.** Founded in 1878. Regionally accredited. Composed of 4 educational units: the Women's College (main campus), the Academy (women's secondary school), the Evening and Weekend College (coeducational), and the Online College. Performing arts and nursing daytime programs are coeducational. Some evening and weekend programs available to male students. **Degrees:** 162 bachelor's awarded; master's offered. **Location:** 45 miles from Atlanta, GA. **Calendar:** Semester, limited summer session. **Full-time faculty:** 73 total; 82% have terminal degrees, 12% minority, 71% women. **Part-time faculty:** 89 total; 32% have terminal degrees, 10% minority, 58% women. **Class size:** 74% < 20, 23% 20-39, less than 1% 40-49, 2% 50-99. **Special facilities:** Regional history museum, visual arts center, performing arts center, vintage clothing museum.

**Freshman class profile.** 3,493 applied, 1,329 admitted, 159 enrolled.

| Mid 50% test scores | | Out-of-state: | 12% |
|---|---|---|---|
| SAT critical reading: | 450-540 | Live on campus: | 80% |
| SAT math: | 420-510 | International: | 3% |
| End year in good standing: | 70% | Sororities: | 24% |
| Return as sophomores: | 68% | | |

**Basis for selection.** Course selection most important, followed by GPA and standardized test scores. Admission policies for Evening/Weekend College differ from Women's College. SAT or ACT used for placement into math courses. Auditions required of performing arts majors. **Home-schooled:** Transcript of courses and grades, interview required. **Learning Disabled:** Learning disability must be professionally diagnosed.

**High school preparation.** College-preparatory program recommended.

**2009-2010 Annual costs.** Tuition/fees: $19,356. Room/board: $9,772. Books/supplies: $900. Personal expenses: $1,300.

**2009-2010 Financial aid. Need-based:** 146 full-time freshmen applied for aid; 129 were judged to have need; 128 of these received aid. Average need met was .79%. Average scholarship/grant was $16,666; average loan $3,257. 80% of total undergraduate aid awarded as scholarships/grants, 20% as loans/jobs. **Non-need-based:** Awarded to 263 full-time undergraduates, including 50 freshmen. Scholarships awarded for academics, art, athletics, leadership, minority status, music/drama.

**Application procedures. Admission:** No deadline. $35 fee, may be waived for applicants with need. Admission notification on a rolling basis beginning on or about 10/1. **Financial aid:** Priority date 3/15; no closing date. FAFSA required. Applicants notified on a rolling basis starting 3/1.

**Academics.** Leadership curriculum available. **Special study options:** Combined bachelor's/graduate degree, cross-registration, distance learning, double major, dual enrollment of high school students, ESL, honors, independent study, internships, student-designed major, study abroad, teacher certification program, weekend college. **Credit/placement by examination:** AP, CLEP, IB, SAT, ACT, institutional tests. 27 credit hours maximum toward bachelor's degree. Total of 27 hours for non-traditional students allowed. **Support services:** Learning center, pre-admission summer program, reduced course load, remedial instruction, study skills assistance, tutoring, writing center.

**Majors. Biology:** General. **Business:** Accounting, business admin, fashion, marketing, organizational behavior. **Communications:** Media studies. **Education:** Art, drama/dance, elementary, mentally handicapped, middle, music, special. **Health:** Health services, nursing (RN), physician assistant. **History:** General. **Legal studies:** General. **Liberal arts:** Arts/sciences. **Psychology:** General. **Social sciences:** International relations. **Visual/performing arts:** Arts management, dance, dramatic, fashion design, graphic design, interior design, music performance, studio arts.

**Most popular majors.** Business/marketing 10%, communications/journalism 6%, education 17%, health sciences 39%, visual/performing arts 14%.

**Computing on campus.** 130 workstations in dormitories, library, computer center, student center. Dormitories wired for high-speed internet access and linked to campus network. Online course registration, online library, helpline, student web hosting, wireless network available.

**Student life. Freshman orientation:** Mandatory. Preregistration for classes offered. **Policies:** Single students under 22 years of age required to live on campus unless living with family or legal guardian; alcohol-free campus; required convocation attendance. **Housing:** Guaranteed on-campus for all undergraduates. Special housing for disabled, apartments, cooperative housing, fraternity/sorority housing available. $350 nonrefundable deposit. **Activities:** Campus ministries, choral groups, dance, drama, international student organizations, literary magazine, music ensembles, musical theater, radio station, student government, student newspaper, TV station, Brenau Fellowhip Association, Eco-Friends, Fellowship of Christian Athletes, College Republicans, College Democrats, Silhouettes, volunteer center, student alumni council, Greek letter service organizations.

**Athletics.** NAIA. **Intercollegiate:** Basketball W, cross-country W, soccer W, softball W, swimming W, tennis W, volleyball W. **Team name:** Golden Tigers.

**Student services.** Alcohol/substance abuse counseling, career counseling, student employment services, financial aid counseling, health services, minority student services, personal counseling, placement for graduates, women's services. **Physically disabled:** Services for visually, speech, hearing impaired. **Learning disabled:** Comprehensive services available.

**Contact.** E-mail: wcadmissions@brenau.edu
Phone: (770) 534-6100 Toll-free number: (800) 252-5119
Fax: (770) 538-4701
Scott Briell, Vice President of Enrollment Management, Brenau University, 500 Washington Street SE, Gainesville, GA 30501

---

## Brewton-Parker College
**Mount Vernon, Georgia**     **CB member**
www.bpc.edu     **CB code: 5068**

- Private 4-year liberal arts college affiliated with Southern Baptist Convention
- Residential campus in small town
- 1,030 degree-seeking undergraduates: 26% part-time, 57% women, 28% African American, 3% Hispanic American, 2% international
- 55% of applicants admitted
- SAT or ACT (ACT writing optional) required

**General.** Founded in 1904. Regionally accredited. **Degrees:** 152 bachelor's, 21 associate awarded. **Location:** 90 miles from Macon and Savannah. **Calendar:** Semester, limited summer session. **Full-time faculty:** 52 total; 64% have terminal degrees, 10% minority, 44% women. **Part-time faculty:** 69 total. **Class size:** 79% < 20, 20% 20-39, less than 1% 40-49. **Special facilities:** Living history museum, recital hall, greenhouse, nature trail.

**Freshman class profile.** 677 applied, 369 admitted, 183 enrolled.

| Mid 50% test scores | | Rank in top tenth: | 16% |
|---|---|---|---|
| SAT critical reading: | 400-500 | Return as sophomores: | 53% |
| SAT math: | 410-500 | Out-of-state: | 8% |
| SAT writing: | 360-470 | Live on campus: | 50% |
| ACT composite: | 16-20 | International: | 2% |
| Rank in top quarter: | 32% | | |

**Basis for selection.** Students evaluated on SAT/ACT scores and high school performance. Audition and interview required of music and drama majors.

**High school preparation.** College-preparatory program recommended. 13 units required. Required units include English 4, mathematics 3, social studies 3 and science 3.

**2009-2010 Annual costs.** Tuition/fees: $15,250. Applied music surcharge of $150 per credit. Room/board: $6,323. Books/supplies: $1,800. Personal expenses: $1,700.

**2008-2009 Financial aid. Need-based:** 191 full-time freshmen applied for aid; 171 were judged to have need; 170 of these received aid. Average need met was 73%. Average scholarship/grant was $9,501; average loan $2,782. 59% of total undergraduate aid awarded as scholarships/grants, 41% as loans/jobs. **Non-need-based:** Awarded to 227 full-time undergraduates, including 66 freshmen. Scholarships awarded for academics, athletics, music/drama, religious affiliation, state residency.

**Application procedures. Admission:** No deadline. $25 fee. Admission notification on a rolling basis beginning on or about 9/1. **Financial aid:** Priority date 5/1; no closing date. FAFSA required. Applicants notified on a rolling basis starting 2/27; must reply within 2 week(s) of notification.

**Academics. Special study options:** Accelerated study, double major, dual enrollment of high school students, exchange student, external degree, honors, independent study, internships, teacher certification program. **Credit/placement by examination:** AP, CLEP, SAT, ACT. 30 credit hours maximum toward associate degree, 30 toward bachelor's. **Support services:** Learning center, reduced course load, remedial instruction, study skills assistance, tutoring, writing center.

**Majors. Biology:** General. **Business:** Accounting, business admin. **Communications:** General. **Computer sciences:** Information systems. **Education:** General, biology, early childhood, English, history, mathematics, middle, music, physical, science, secondary. **Foreign languages:** Spanish. **History:** General. **Math:** General. **Parks/recreation:** Health/fitness. **Philosophy/religion:** Religion. **Psychology:** General. **Social sciences:** General, political science, sociology. **Theology:** Theology. **Visual/performing arts:** Music performance.

**Most popular majors.** Business/marketing 18%, education 21%, liberal arts 13%, parks/recreation 6%, psychology 6%, public administration/social services 8%, social sciences 6%.

**Computing on campus.** 104 workstations in library, computer center. Dormitories wired for high-speed internet access. Online course registration, online library, helpline, wireless network available.

**Student life. Freshman orientation:** Available, $100 fee. Preregistration for classes offered. Orientation is held the week and/or weekend before classes start. **Policies:** All day students required to live on campus except seniors, students residing with parents, students 22 or older. Religious observance required. **Housing:** Guaranteed on-campus for freshmen. Single-sex dorms available. $110 nonrefundable deposit. **Activities:** Bands, campus ministries, choral groups, drama, film society, international student organizations, literary magazine, music ensembles, musical theater, student government, student newspaper, ministerial association, Fellowship of Christian Athletes, Rotaract, Circle K, student activities council.

**Athletics.** NAIA. **Intercollegiate:** Baseball M, basketball, cheerleading, cross-country, soccer, softball W, volleyball W. **Intramural:** Basketball, football (non-tackle), softball, table tennis, tennis, volleyball. **Team name:** Barons.

**Student services.** Alcohol/substance abuse counseling, chaplain/spiritual director, career counseling, student employment services, financial aid counseling, health services, personal counseling, placement for graduates, veterans' counselor. **Physically disabled:** Services for visually, speech, hearing impaired.

**Contact.** E-mail: admissions@bpc.edu
Phone: (912) 583-2241 ext. 265 Toll-free number: (800) 342-1087 ext. 265
Fax: (912) 583-3598
Mike Price, Director of Admissions, Brewton-Parker College, Brewton-Parker College # 2011, Mount Vernon, GA 30445

---

## Carver Bible College
**Atlanta, Georgia**
www.carver.edu

- Private 4-year Bible college
- Commuter campus in very large city
- 67 degree-seeking undergraduates
- 53% of applicants admitted

**General.** Accredited by ABHE. **Degrees:** 8 bachelor's, 4 associate awarded. **Calendar:** Semester, limited summer session. **Full-time faculty:** 4 total. **Part-time faculty:** 10 total.

**Freshman class profile.** 36 applied, 19 admitted, 19 enrolled.

**Basis for selection.** Applicants assessed for admittance based on academic record, moral character and personal testimony of faith. Students who cannot meet the general entrance requirements may be given conditional admittance for probationary period.

**2009-2010 Annual costs.** Tuition/fees: $7,420.

**Application procedures. Admission:** No deadline.

**Academics. Special study options:** Distance learning, independent study. **Credit/placement by examination:** CLEP. **Support services:** Learning center.

**Majors. Theology:** Bible.

**Computing on campus.** Wireless network available.

**Student life. Freshman orientation:** Mandatory.

**Contact.** Phone: (404) 527-4520 Fax: (404) 527-4524
Bertha Mack, Director of Admissions, Carver Bible College, 3837 Cascade Road, SW, Atlanta, GA 30313

---

## Clark Atlanta University
**Atlanta, Georgia**  **CB member**
**www.cau.edu**  **CB code: 5110**

- Private 4-year university affiliated with United Methodist Church
- Residential campus in very large city
- 3,202 degree-seeking undergraduates: 4% part-time, 73% women, 90% African American, 1% international
- 671 degree-seeking graduate students
- 59% of applicants admitted
- SAT or ACT (ACT writing optional), application essay required
- 43% graduate within 6 years; 28% enter graduate study

**General.** Founded in 1869. Regionally accredited. Member of Atlanta University Center, a consortium of black private education institutions. **Degrees:** 493 bachelor's awarded; master's, doctoral offered. **ROTC:** Army, Naval. **Location:** 2 miles from downtown. **Calendar:** Semester, limited summer session. **Full-time faculty:** 178 total; 77% have terminal degrees, 90% minority, 38% women. **Part-time faculty:** 98 total; 43% have terminal degrees, 88% minority, 51% women. **Class size:** 30% < 20, 53% 20-39, 10% 40-49, 7% 50-99. **Special facilities:** Exhibition gallery, research center for science and technology.

**Freshman class profile.** 6,681 applied, 3,954 admitted, 703 enrolled.

| Mid 50% test scores | | | |
|---|---|---|---|
| SAT critical reading: | 410-480 | Rank in top quarter: | 23% |
| SAT math: | 400-470 | Rank in top tenth: | 8% |
| ACT composite: | 18-20 | End year in good standing: | 80% |
| GPA 3.75 or higher: | 6% | Return as sophomores: | 65% |
| GPA 3.50-3.74: | 11% | Out-of-state: | 74% |
| GPA 3.0-3.49: | 33% | Live on campus: | 69% |
| | | GPA 2.0-2.99: | 50% |

**Basis for selection.** Secondary school record most important. Test scores, recommendations, essay also important. Audition recommended for music and drama majors. **Homeschooled:** Course work portfolio required.

**High school preparation.** College-preparatory program recommended. 18 units required. Required units include English 4, mathematics 3, social studies 3, science 3 (laboratory 1), foreign language 2 and academic electives 3.

**2010-2011 Annual costs.** Tuition/fees: $17,954. Room/board: $7,540. Books/supplies: $2,200. Personal expenses: $1,540.

**2009-2010 Financial aid. Non-need-based:** Scholarships awarded for academics, art, athletics, leadership, minority status, music/drama, religious affiliation, ROTC, state residency.

**Application procedures. Admission:** Priority date 3/1; deadline 6/1 (postmark date). $35 fee, may be waived for applicants with need. Admission notification on a rolling basis beginning on or about 1/1. **Financial aid:** Priority date 3/1; no closing date. FAFSA required. Applicants notified on a rolling basis starting 4/1.

**Academics. Special study options:** Accelerated study, combined bachelor's/graduate degree, cooperative education, cross-registration, double major, dual enrollment of high school students, exchange student, honors, independent study, internships, study abroad, teacher certification program, Washington semester, weekend college. **Credit/placement by examination:** AP, CLEP, IB, institutional tests. 45 credit hours maximum toward bachelor's degree. **Support services:** Learning center, pre-admission summer program, reduced course load, remedial instruction, study skills assistance, tutoring, writing center.

**Majors. Biology:** General. **Business:** Accounting, business admin, managerial economics. **Computer sciences:** General, computer science. **Education:** General, early childhood. **Foreign languages:** French, Spanish. **History:** General. **Math:** General. **Philosophy/religion:** Philosophy, religion. **Physical sciences:** Chemistry, physics. **Protective services:** Criminal justice. **Psychology:** General. **Public administration:** Social work. **Social sciences:** Political science, sociology. **Visual/performing arts:** Art, fashion design, theater history. **Other:** Radio, television, and digital communications.

**Most popular majors.** Biology 7%, business/marketing 22%, communications/journalism 26%, psychology 8%, security/protective services 7%, visual/performing arts 7%.

**Computing on campus.** 650 workstations in dormitories, library, computer center, student center. Dormitories wired for high-speed internet access and linked to campus network. Commuter students can connect to campus network. Online course registration, online library, helpline, repair service, wireless network available.

**Student life. Freshman orientation:** Mandatory, $150 fee. Preregistration for classes offered. **Policies:** Drug/alcohol policy, sanctions for violations, policies governing Greek and other student organizations. **Housing:** Guaranteed on-campus for freshmen. Coed dorms, single-sex dorms, apartments available. $325 partly refundable deposit, deadline 6/1. **Activities:** Bands, campus ministries, choral groups, dance, drama, film society, international student organizations, literary magazine, music ensembles, musical theater, opera, radio station, student government, student newspaper, symphony orchestra, TV station, NAACP, pan-Hellenic council, Anointed Students in Fellowship, Campus Crusade for Christ, Christian Fellowship, National Council of Negro Women, Forensic Society, Gamma Sigma Sigma, Caribbean-oriented student organization.

**Athletics.** NCAA. **Intercollegiate:** Baseball M, basketball, cross-country, football (tackle) M, softball W, tennis W, track and field, volleyball W. **Intramural:** Basketball, football (non-tackle), tennis W, track and field. **Team name:** Panthers.

**Student services.** Alcohol/substance abuse counseling, chaplain/spiritual director, career counseling, student employment services, financial aid counseling, health services, personal counseling, placement for graduates, veterans' counselor, women's services. **Physically disabled:** Services for visually, speech, hearing impaired.

**Contact.** E-mail: cauadmissions@cau.edu
Phone: (404) 880-8784 Toll-free number: (800) 688-3228
Fax: (404) 880-6174
Michelle Davis, Director of Admissions, Clark Atlanta University, 223 James P. Brawley Drive, SW, Atlanta, GA 30314-4391

---

## Clayton State University
**Morrow, Georgia**  **CB member**
**www.clayton.edu**  **CB code: 5145**

- Public 4-year liberal arts and technical college
- Commuter campus in small city
- 6,412 degree-seeking undergraduates: 43% part-time, 70% women, 63% African American, 4% Asian American, 3% Hispanic American, 1% international
- 174 degree-seeking graduate students
- 62% of applicants admitted
- SAT or ACT (ACT writing optional) required

**General.** Founded in 1969. Regionally accredited. **Degrees:** 871 bachelor's, 122 associate awarded; master's offered. **ROTC:** Army, Naval, Air Force. **Location:** 12 miles from Atlanta. **Calendar:** Semester, extensive summer session. **Full-time faculty:** 196 total; 86% have terminal degrees, 31% minority, 52% women. **Part-time faculty:** 172 total; 27% have terminal degrees, 46% minority, 50% women. **Class size:** 34% < 20, 54% 20-39, 6% 40-49, 6% 50-99, less than 1% >100. **Special facilities:** Concert hall.

**Freshman class profile.** 4,844 applied, 2,999 admitted, 1,587 enrolled.

| Mid 50% test scores | | | |
|---|---|---|---|
| SAT critical reading: | 440-550 | Return as sophomores: | 67% |
| SAT math: | 430-540 | Out-of-state: | 9% |
| ACT composite: | 18-22 | Live on campus: | 30% |
| GPA 3.75 or higher: | 8% | International: | 1% |
| GPA 3.50-3.74: | 11% | Fraternities: | 8% |
| GPA 3.0-3.49: | 32% | Sororities: | 2% |
| | | GPA 2.0-2.99: | 49% |

**Basis for selection.** 17 ACT or 400 SAT math and 430 verbal required. Secondary school record also very important for health sciences, music, teacher education, and business programs. Auditions recommended for music majors. **Homeschooled:** Must validate the completion of a college prep curriculum. SAT tests may be used to do so.

**High school preparation.** 16 units required; 22 recommended. Required and recommended units include English 4, mathematics 4, social studies 3, history 2, science 3-4 (laboratory 3), foreign language 2-3 and academic electives 2. Students not meeting college-preparatory requirements must take remedial classes before entering any program.

**2009-2010 Annual costs.** Tuition/fees: $4,848; $16,462 out-of-state. Room/board: $8,078. Books/supplies: $1,000.

**2008-2009 Financial aid. Need-based:** 288 full-time freshmen applied for aid; 246 were judged to have need; 245 of these received aid. Average need met was 18%. Average scholarship/grant was $4,424; average loan $3,342. 40% of total undergraduate aid awarded as scholarships/grants, 60% as loans/jobs. **Non-need-based:** Awarded to 969 full-time undergraduates, including 159 freshmen. Scholarships awarded for academics, athletics, music/drama.

**Application procedures. Admission:** Priority date 2/1; no deadline. $40 fee, may be waived for applicants with need. Admission notification on a rolling basis beginning on or about 1/1. **Financial aid:** Priority date 7/1; no closing date. FAFSA required. Applicants notified on a rolling basis starting 3/22.

**Academics. Special study options:** Cooperative education, cross-registration, distance learning, double major, dual enrollment of high school students, exchange student, honors, independent study, internships, liberal arts/career combination, student-designed major, study abroad, teacher certification program. **Credit/placement by examination:** AP, CLEP, IB, institutional tests. **Support services:** Learning center, reduced course load, remedial instruction, study skills assistance, tutoring, writing center.

**Majors. Biology:** General. **Business:** General, accounting, business admin, marketing, office management, operations. **Communications:** General. **Computer sciences:** General, data processing, information systems, information technology, programming, systems analysis. **Education:** Middle. **Health:** Dental assistant, dental hygiene, facilities admin, health care admin, nursing (RN), nursing admin. **History:** General. **Liberal arts:** Arts/sciences. **Math:** General. **Parks/recreation:** Sports admin. **Protective services:** Criminal justice. **Psychology:** Community. **Social sciences:** Political science. **Visual/performing arts:** Dramatic, music performance, music theory/composition.

**Most popular majors.** Business/marketing 22%, education 6%, health sciences 25%, liberal arts 12%, psychology 13%.

**Computing on campus.** PC or laptop required. Dormitories wired for high-speed internet access and linked to campus network. Online course registration, online library, helpline, repair service, student web hosting, wireless network available.

**Student life. Freshman orientation:** Mandatory, $40 fee. Preregistration for classes offered. **Housing:** Coed dorms available. **Activities:** Jazz band, choral groups, drama, film society, literary magazine, music ensembles, musical theater, opera, radio station, student government, student newspaper, Approximately 20 student groups.

**Athletics.** NAIA, NCAA. **Intercollegiate:** Basketball, cross-country, golf M, soccer, tennis W, track and field. **Team name:** Lakers.

**Student services.** Adult student services, alcohol/substance abuse counseling, career counseling, student employment services, financial aid counseling, health services, minority student services, personal counseling, placement for graduates, veterans' counselor. **Physically disabled:** Services for visually, speech, hearing impaired.

**Contact.** E-mail: ccsu-info@mail.clayton.edu
Phone: (678) 466-4115 Fax: (678) 466-4149
Betty Momayezi, Director of Admissions, Clayton State University, 2000 Clayton State Boulevard, Morrow, GA 30260-0285

---

## Columbus State University

| Columbus, Georgia | CB member |
|---|---|
| www.colstate.edu | CB code: 5123 |

◗ Public 4-year university and liberal arts college
◗ Commuter campus in large city
◗ 6,760 degree-seeking undergraduates: 28% part-time, 60% women, 34% African American, 2% Asian American, 5% Hispanic American, 1% Native American, 1% international
◗ 1,189 degree-seeking graduate students
◗ 64% of applicants admitted
◗ SAT or ACT (ACT writing optional) required
◗ 34% graduate within 6 years

**General.** Founded in 1958. Regionally accredited. **Degrees:** 846 bachelor's, 41 associate awarded; master's, professional offered. **ROTC:** Army. **Location:** 100 miles from Atlanta. **Calendar:** Semester, extensive summer session. **Full-time faculty:** 276 total; 78% have terminal degrees, 21% minority, 44% women. **Part-time faculty:** 201 total; 15% have terminal degrees, 15% minority, 47% women. **Class size:** 38% < 20, 51% 20-39, 7%

40-49, 4% 50-99, less than 1% >100. **Special facilities:** Environmental learning center, space science center, fine and performing arts center.

**Freshman class profile.** 3,445 applied, 2,204 admitted, 1,319 enrolled.

| Mid 50% test scores | | GPA 2.0-2.99: | 46% |
|---|---|---|---|
| SAT critical reading: | 430-550 | End year in good standing: | 73% |
| SAT math: | 420-540 | Return as sophomores: | 66% |
| ACT composite: | 17-22 | Out-of-state: | 10% |
| GPA 3.75 or higher: | 10% | Live on campus: | 39% |
| GPA 3.50-3.74: | 11% | Fraternities: | 2% |
| GPA 3.0-3.49: | 33% | Sororities: | 2% |

**Basis for selection.** GED not accepted. 2.5 GPA, 460 SAT math/19 ACT math, and 490 SAT verbal/20 ACT English required. Students must be on track to graduate with college preparatory seal. Students with college prep deficiencies will be considered on individual basis. Interviews and auditions required of music majors. Portfolio recommended for art majors. **Homeschooled:** Statement describing homeschool structure and mission, transcript of courses and grades required. 1000 SAT (exclusive of Writing), Home School Credit Evaluation Table, letter from primary teacher certifying completion of high school and date of graduation and two letters of recommendation from non-family members required.

**High school preparation.** College-preparatory program required. 16 units required. Required units include English 4, mathematics 4, social studies 3, science 3 (laboratory 2) and foreign language 2. Social studies units required include U.S. history and world studies.

**2009-2010 Annual costs.** Tuition/fees: $5,024; $16,638 out-of-state. Room/board: $7,090. Books/supplies: $974. Personal expenses: $1,831.

**2009-2010 Financial aid. Need-based:** 1,023 full-time freshmen applied for aid; 797 were judged to have need; 785 of these received aid. Average need met was 72%. Average scholarship/grant was $4,984; average loan $3,214. 51% of total undergraduate aid awarded as scholarships/grants, 49% as loans/jobs. **Non-need-based:** Awarded to 1,317 full-time undergraduates, including 499 freshmen. Scholarships awarded for academics, alumni affiliation, art, athletics, job skills, leadership, minority status, music/drama, ROTC.

**Application procedures. Admission:** Priority date 5/15; deadline 6/30 (receipt date). $30 fee, may be waived for applicants with need. Admission notification on a rolling basis beginning on or about 9/1. **Financial aid:** Priority date 5/1; no closing date. FAFSA required. Applicants notified on a rolling basis starting 5/15; must reply within 4 week(s) of notification.

**Academics. Special study options:** Accelerated study, cooperative education, distance learning, double major, dual enrollment of high school students, ESL, honors, independent study, internships, liberal arts/career combination, study abroad, teacher certification program. **Credit/placement by examination:** AP, CLEP, IB, institutional tests. 30 credit hours maximum toward associate degree, 60 toward bachelor's. **Support services:** Learning center, reduced course load, remedial instruction, study skills assistance, tutoring, writing center.

**Majors. Biology:** General. **Business:** General, accounting, business admin, finance, management information systems, marketing. **Computer sciences:** General, information technology. **Education:** Art, biology, chemistry, drama/dance, early childhood, emotionally handicapped, English, learning disabled, mathematics, mentally handicapped, middle, music, physical, science, secondary, social science, social studies. **Foreign languages:** French, Spanish. **Health:** Health services, nursing (RN). **History:** General. **Liberal arts:** Arts/sciences. **Math:** General. **Parks/recreation:** Exercise sciences. **Physical sciences:** Chemistry, geology. **Protective services:** Criminal justice. **Psychology:** General. **Social sciences:** Political science, sociology. **Visual/performing arts:** Art, dramatic, music performance.

**Most popular majors.** Business/marketing 27%, education 17%, English 8%, health sciences 13%, security/protective services 9%, visual/performing arts 7%.

**Computing on campus.** 1,135 workstations in dormitories, library, computer center, student center. Dormitories wired for high-speed internet access and linked to campus network. Commuter students can connect to campus network. Online course registration, online library, helpline, repair service, wireless network available.

**Student life. Freshman orientation:** Mandatory, $85 fee. Preregistration for classes offered. **Housing:** Special housing for disabled, apartments, fraternity/sorority housing, wellness housing available. $225 partly refundable deposit, deadline 5/1. Apartments take place of traditional dorms; weekday meals included in fee. **Activities:** Bands, choral groups, dance, drama, international student organizations, literary magazine, music ensembles, Model UN, musical theater, opera, student government, student newspaper, symphony orchestra, College Republicans, Islamic association, Freethought Society, Cougars for Christ, CSU Democrats, minority student union, student political awareness, Westminster Fellowship, Baptist student union.

**Athletics.** NCAA. **Intercollegiate:** Baseball M, basketball, cross-country, golf, rifle, soccer W, softball W, tennis. **Intramural:** Badminton, basketball, football (tackle) M, skiing, soccer, softball, table tennis, tennis, volleyball. **Team name:** Cougars.

**Student services.** Adult student services, alcohol/substance abuse counseling, career counseling, student employment services, financial aid counseling, health services, minority student services, personal counseling, placement for graduates, veterans' counselor, women's services. **Physically disabled:** Services for visually, speech, hearing impaired.

**Contact.** E-mail: admissions@colstate.edu
Phone: (706) 568-2035 Toll-free number: (866) 264-2035
Fax: (706) 568-5091
Susan Lovell, Director of Enrollment Management, Columbus State University, 4225 University Avenue, Columbus, GA 31907-5645

## Covenant College
### Lookout Mountain, Georgia
www.covenant.edu                    CB code: 6124

- Private 4-year liberal arts college affiliated with Presbyterian Church in America
- Residential campus in small city
- 976 degree-seeking undergraduates: 1% part-time, 56% women, 2% African American, 2% Asian American, 2% Hispanic American, 1% international
- 63 degree-seeking graduate students
- 60% of applicants admitted
- SAT or ACT with writing, application essay required
- 65% graduate within 6 years

**General.** Founded in 1955. Regionally accredited. **Degrees:** 173 bachelor's awarded; master's offered. **ROTC:** Army. **Location:** 120 miles from Atlanta; 5 miles from Chattanooga, TN. **Calendar:** Semester, limited summer session. **Full-time faculty:** 58 total; 88% have terminal degrees, 7% minority, 19% women. **Part-time faculty:** 28 total; 39% have terminal degrees, 7% minority, 25% women. **Class size:** 59% < 20, 39% 20-39, 1% 40-49, less than 1% 50-99.

**Freshman class profile.** 1,078 applied, 649 admitted, 277 enrolled.

| Mid 50% test scores | | | |
|---|---|---|---|
| SAT critical reading: | 540-660 | GPA 2.0-2.99: | 7% |
| SAT math: | 510-620 | Rank in top quarter: | 56% |
| SAT writing: | 520-660 | Rank in top tenth: | 31% |
| ACT composite: | 22-28 | Return as sophomores: | 75% |
| GPA 3.75 or higher: | 50% | Out-of-state: | 75% |
| GPA 3.50-3.74: | 24% | Live on campus: | 98% |
| GPA 3.0-3.49: | 19% | International: | 2% |

**Basis for selection.** 1500 SAT (exclusive of Writing) or 21 ACT, 2.5 GPA, academic evaluation, church evaluation, and personal testimony of faith important. Students that do not meet minimum scores may be asked to provide additional information. Auditions required for music and voice majors. **Homeschooled:** Transcript of courses and grades, letter of recommendation (nonparent) required.

**High school preparation.** College-preparatory program recommended. 16 units required. Required and recommended units include English 4, mathematics 3, social studies 2, science 2, foreign language 2 and academic electives 3.

**2010-2011 Annual costs.** Tuition/fees: $26,226. Room/board: $7,450. Books/supplies: $1,000. Personal expenses: $1,300.

**2008-2009 Financial aid. Need-based:** 226 full-time freshmen applied for aid; 178 were judged to have need; 178 of these received aid. Average need met was 83%. Average scholarship/grant was $12,928; average loan $4,830. 65% of total undergraduate aid awarded as scholarships/grants, 35% as loans/jobs. **Non-need-based:** Awarded to 295 full-time undergraduates, including 73 freshmen. Scholarships awarded for academics, alumni affiliation, art, athletics, job skills, leadership, minority status, music/drama, religious affiliation, state residency.

**Application procedures. Admission:** Priority date 4/1; no deadline. $35 fee. Application must be submitted on paper. Admission notification on a rolling basis beginning on or about 8/1. Must reply by May 1 or within 3 week(s) if notified thereafter. **Financial aid:** No deadline. FAFSA required. Applicants notified on a rolling basis starting 2/1; must reply within 3 week(s) of notification.

**Academics.** Organizational management program for adult students with minimum 5 years work experience who have completed at least 2 years college. All classes held evenings, with degree completion in just over 1 year. **Special study options:** Double major, dual enrollment of high school students, exchange student, independent study, internships, student-designed major, study abroad, teacher certification program, Washington semester. Dual engineering degree with Georgia Tech, cooperative nursing program with Emory University and Chattanooga State; bridge program for MSN with Vanderbilt University. **Credit/placement by examination:** AP, CLEP, IB, SAT, ACT, institutional tests. 30 credit hours maximum toward associate degree, 30 toward bachelor's. **Support services:** Reduced course load, remedial instruction, study skills assistance, tutoring, writing center.

**Majors. Biology:** General. **Business:** General. **Computer sciences:** General. **Education:** Elementary, English, history, mathematics, science. **History:** General. **Interdisciplinary:** Biological/physical sciences. **Math:** General. **Philosophy/religion:** Philosophy. **Physical sciences:** General, chemistry, physics. **Psychology:** General. **Social sciences:** General, sociology. **Theology:** Bible. **Visual/performing arts:** Dramatic, music performance. **Other:** Philosophy and religious studies.

**Most popular majors.** Business/marketing 6%, education 9%, English 7%, history 7%, interdisciplinary studies 12%, psychology 6%, social sciences 21%, theological studies 8%, visual/performing arts 12%.

**Computing on campus.** 133 workstations in dormitories, library, computer center. Dormitories linked to campus network. Commuter students can connect to campus network. Online library, helpline, repair service, wireless network available.

**Student life. Freshman orientation:** Mandatory, $355 fee. Preregistration for classes offered. Held the week prior to beginning of classes. **Policies:** Smoking, alcoholic beverages, and drugs prohibited. Students are to use wisdom and Christ-like discretion in the application of Biblical principles to decisions regarding all areas of life. Religious observance required. **Housing:** Guaranteed on-campus for freshmen. Single-sex dorms, apartments available. $300 nonrefundable deposit. **Activities:** Concert band, choral groups, drama, literary magazine, music ensembles, radio station, student government, student newspaper, Rotaract, Young Life, pre-law club, Psi Chi, reformed university fellowship, Evangelism club.

**Athletics.** NAIA. **Intercollegiate:** Baseball M, basketball, cross-country, golf, soccer, softball W, tennis W, volleyball W. **Intramural:** Basketball, football (non-tackle), football (tackle) M, soccer, volleyball. **Team name:** Scots.

**Student services.** Adult student services, career counseling, student employment services, financial aid counseling, health services, personal counseling, placement for graduates.

**Contact.** E-mail: admissions@covenant.edu
Phone: (706) 419-1148 Toll-free number: (888) 451-2683
Fax: (706) 820-0893
Wallace Anderson, Vice President of Enrollment Management, Covenant College, 14049 Scenic Highway, Lookout Mountain, GA 30750

## Dalton State College
### Dalton, Georgia
www.daltonstate.edu                    CB code: 5167

- Public 4-year liberal arts and teachers college
- Commuter campus in large town
- 5,722 degree-seeking undergraduates: 40% part-time, 60% women
- 60% of applicants admitted

**General.** Founded in 1963. Regionally accredited. **Degrees:** 163 bachelor's, 338 associate awarded. **Location:** 90 miles from Atlanta. **Calendar:** Semester, limited summer session. **Full-time faculty:** 150 total; 61% have terminal degrees, 8% minority, 55% women. **Part-time faculty:** 73 total; 16% have terminal degrees, 6% minority, 56% women.

**Freshman class profile.** 3,327 applied, 1,986 admitted, 1,623 enrolled.

**Basis for selection.** 2.0 GPA in high school college preparatory curriculum and 2.2 GPA in Tech Prep curriculum required. **Homeschooled:** State high school equivalency certificate required.

**High school preparation.** 16 units required. Required units include English 4, mathematics 4, social studies 3, science 3 and foreign language 2.

**2009-2010 Annual costs.** Tuition/fees: $2,900; $10,382 out-of-state.

**2009-2010 Financial aid. Non-need-based:** Scholarships awarded for academics, leadership, minority status, state residency.

**Application procedures. Admission:** No deadline. $30 fee, may be waived for applicants with need. Admission notification on a rolling basis. **Financial aid:** Priority date 7/1; no closing date. FAFSA, institutional form required. Applicants notified on a rolling basis starting 7/1.

**Academics. Special study options:** Cooperative education, double major, dual enrollment of high school students, ESL, external degree, honors, independent study, internships, liberal arts/career combination, study abroad, teacher certification program, weekend college. **Credit/placement by examination:** CLEP, institutional tests. Credit is awarded only to admitted students and recorded only for those who enroll for credit courses. Credit is awarded only for offered courses. **Support services:** Remedial instruction, study skills assistance, tutoring, writing center.

**Majors. Biology:** General. **Business:** Accounting, business admin, management information systems, management science, marketing, operations. **Computer sciences:** General. **Education:** Elementary. **Family/consumer sciences:** Work/family studies. **History:** General. **Liberal arts:** Arts/sciences. **Math:** General. **Physical sciences:** Chemistry. **Protective services:** Police science. **Public administration:** Social work.

**Computing on campus.** 800 workstations in library, computer center, student center. Commuter students can connect to campus network. Online library, helpline available.

**Student life. Freshman orientation:** Mandatory. Preregistration for classes offered. **Housing:** $200 partly refundable deposit. **Activities:** International student organizations, literary magazine, student government, student newspaper, social work club, LPN, Baptist student union, psychology club, black student alliance, Phi The Kappa, Young Democrats, progressive student union.

**Athletics. Intramural:** Badminton, basketball, football (non-tackle) M, softball, table tennis, tennis, volleyball.

**Student services.** Adult student services, career counseling, student employment services, financial aid counseling, personal counseling, placement for graduates, veterans' counselor. **Physically disabled:** Services for hearing impaired.

**Contact.** Phone: (706) 272-4436 Toll-free number: (800) 829-4436 Fax: (706) 272-2530
Jodi Johnson, Vice President for Enrollment Services, Dalton State College, 650 College Drive, Dalton, GA 30720

## DeVry University: Alpharetta
**Alpharetta, Georgia**
www.devry.edu                                        CB code: 0077

- For-profit 4-year university
- Commuter campus in large town
- 709 degree-seeking undergraduates: 52% part-time, 40% women, 38% African American, 4% Asian American, 5% Hispanic American, 1% Native American
- 180 degree-seeking graduate students
- Interview required

**General.** Regionally accredited. **Degrees:** 13 bachelor's, 9 associate awarded; master's offered. **Location:** 18 miles from Atlanta. **Calendar:** Semester, extensive summer session. **Full-time faculty:** 27 total; 37% minority, 44% women. **Part-time faculty:** 31 total; 36% minority, 32% women.

**Freshman class profile.** 89 enrolled.

**Basis for selection.** Applicants must have high school diploma or equivalent, or degree from accredited postsecondary institution, demonstrate proficiency in basic college-level skills through ACT, SAT, or institution-administered placement examinations, and be at least 17 years of age. New students may enter at the beginning of any semester. DeVry-administered admissions test required for applicants without SAT/ACT.

**High school preparation.** College-preparatory program recommended.

**2009-2010 Annual costs.** Tuition/fees: $14,160. Books/supplies: $1,310. Personal expenses: $3,574.

**2008-2009 Financial aid.** All financial aid based on need.

**Application procedures. Admission:** No deadline. $50 fee. Admission notification on a rolling basis. **Financial aid:** No deadline. FAFSA required. Applicants notified on a rolling basis.

**Academics. Special study options:** Accelerated study, distance learning. **Credit/placement by examination:** CLEP, institutional tests. **Support services:** Learning center, remedial instruction, tutoring.

**Majors. Business:** Business admin, operations. **Communications technology:** General. **Computer sciences:** Game design, information systems, networking, systems analysis, web page design. **Engineering:** Software. **Engineering technology:** Computer, electrical. **Other:** Technical management.

**Most popular majors.** Business/marketing 78%, computer/information sciences 15%, engineering/engineering technologies 7%.

**Computing on campus.** 218 workstations in library, computer center. Online course registration, online library, helpline available.

**Student life. Freshman orientation:** Mandatory. **Housing:** Private apartments, student-plan housing, private rooms available. **Activities:** Alpha Sigma Lambda, Toastmasters International, international student organization, National Society of Black Engineers, Alpha Beta Kappa, Delta Pi Chi, Epsilon Delta Pi, Tau Alpha Pi, Future Business Leaders of America.

**Athletics. Intramural:** Basketball, football (non-tackle), softball, volleyball.

**Student services.** Career counseling, student employment services, financial aid counseling, placement for graduates, veterans' counselor. **Physically disabled:** Services for visually, hearing impaired.

**Contact.** E-mail: admissions@devry.edu
Phone: (770) 664-9520 Toll-free number: (800) 346-5420
Fax: (770) 664-8824
Gerry Purcell, Director of Admissions, DeVry University: Alpharetta, 2555 Northwinds Parkway, Alpharetta, GA 30004

## DeVry University: Decatur
**Decatur, Georgia**
www.devry.edu                                        CB code: 5715

- For-profit 4-year university
- Commuter campus in large town
- 2,759 degree-seeking undergraduates: 53% part-time, 51% women, 63% African American, 2% Asian American, 3% Hispanic American
- 394 degree-seeking graduate students
- Interview required
- 23% graduate within 6 years

**General.** Founded in 1969. Regionally accredited. **Degrees:** 359 bachelor's, 58 associate awarded; master's offered. **Location:** 15 miles from Atlanta. **Calendar:** Semester, extensive summer session. **Full-time faculty:** 35 total; 40% minority, 37% women. **Part-time faculty:** 162 total; 48% minority, 43% women.

**Freshman class profile.** 441 enrolled.

| | | |
|---|---|---|
| **Out-of-state:** | 7% | **International:** 1% |

**Basis for selection.** Applicants must have high school diploma or equivalent, or degree from accredited post-secondary institution, demonstrate proficiency in basic college-level skills through SAT or ACT scores or institution-administered placement examinations, and be at least 17 years of age. New students may enter at beginning of any semester. Applicants may also take a DeVry administered admissions test.

**High school preparation.** College-preparatory program recommended.

**2009-2010 Annual costs.** Tuition/fees: $14,160. Books/supplies: $1,310. Personal expenses: $3,574.

**2008-2009 Financial aid.** All financial aid based on need.

**Application procedures. Admission:** No deadline. $50 fee. Admission notification on a rolling basis. **Financial aid:** No deadline. FAFSA required. Applicants notified on a rolling basis.

**Academics. Special study options:** Accelerated study, distance learning. **Credit/placement by examination:** CLEP, institutional tests. **Support services:** Learning center, remedial instruction, tutoring.

**Majors. Business:** Business admin, operations. **Computer sciences:** Information systems, networking, systems analysis. **Engineering:** Software. **Engineering technology:** Biomedical, computer, electrical. **Other:** Technical management.

**Most popular majors.** Business/marketing 75%, computer/information sciences 15%, engineering/engineering technologies 6%.

**Computing on campus.** 300 workstations in library, computer center. Online course registration, online library, helpline available.

**Student life. Freshman orientation:** Mandatory. **Activities:** International student organizations, Toastmasters International, National Society of Black Engineers, Delta Pi Chi, Tau Alpha Pi, Sigma Beta Delta, Alpha Beta Kappa.

**Athletics. Intramural:** Basketball, football (non-tackle), softball, volleyball.

**Student services.** Career counseling, student employment services, financial aid counseling, placement for graduates, veterans' counselor. **Physically disabled:** Services for visually, hearing impaired.

**Contact.** E-mail: dsilva@admin.atl.devry.edu
Phone: (404) 292-2645 Toll-free number: (800) 221-4771
Fax: (404) 292-7011
Barbara Silva, Director of Admissions, DeVry University: Decatur, One West Court Square, Suite 100, Decatur, GA 30030-2556

---

## Emmanuel College

**Franklin Springs, Georgia**
**www.ec.edu**

**CB member**
**CB code: 5184**

- Private 4-year liberal arts and teachers college affiliated with Pentecostal Holiness Church
- Residential campus in rural community
- 685 degree-seeking undergraduates: 4% part-time, 53% women, 21% African American, 1% Asian American, 6% Hispanic American, 1% international
- 32% of applicants admitted
- SAT or ACT (ACT writing optional) required
- 41% graduate within 6 years

**General.** Founded in 1919. Regionally accredited. **Degrees:** 116 bachelor's, 13 associate awarded. **Location:** 30 miles from Athens, 90 miles from Atlanta. **Calendar:** Semester, limited summer session. **Full-time faculty:** 36 total; 69% have terminal degrees, 3% minority, 44% women. **Part-time faculty:** 33 total; 18% have terminal degrees, 39% women. **Class size:** 59% < 20, 39% 20-39, 2% 40-49, less than 1% 50-99.

**Freshman class profile.** 912 applied, 295 admitted, 164 enrolled.

| Mid 50% test scores | | Out-of-state: | 23% |
|---|---|---|---|
| SAT critical reading: | 440-460 | Live on campus: | 54% |
| SAT math: | 420-440 | International: | 1% |
| Return as sophomores: | 71% | | |

**Basis for selection.** High school record and SAT/ACT scores important. Audition required and interview recommended for music majors. **Learning Disabled:** Must submit documentation of disability from professional.

**2009-2010 Annual costs.** Tuition/fees: $12,880. Room/board: $5,520. Books/supplies: $1,094. Personal expenses: $1,397.

**2009-2010 Financial aid. Need-based:** 150 full-time freshmen applied for aid; 138 were judged to have need; 138 of these received aid. Average need met was 89%. Average scholarship/grant was $9,024; average loan $3,178. 51% of total undergraduate aid awarded as scholarships/grants, 49% as loans/jobs. **Non-need-based:** Awarded to 171 full-time undergraduates, including 36 freshmen. Scholarships awarded for academics, art, athletics, job skills, leadership, music/drama, religious affiliation, state residency.

**Application procedures. Admission:** Closing date 8/1 (receipt date). $25 fee, may be waived for applicants with need, free for online applicants. Admission notification on a rolling basis beginning on or about 1/1. **Financial aid:** Priority date 5/1, closing date 7/1. FAFSA, institutional form required. Applicants notified on a rolling basis starting 3/1; must reply within 2 week(s) of notification.

**Academics. Special study options:** Dual enrollment of high school students, independent study, internships, teacher certification program. **Credit/placement by examination:** AP, CLEP, IB, institutional tests. 24 credit hours maximum toward associate degree, 24 toward bachelor's. **Support services:** Remedial instruction, study skills assistance, tutoring, writing center.

**Majors. Biology:** General. **Business:** Business admin. **Communications:** General. **Education:** Business, elementary, English, history, mathematics, middle, music. **Health:** Premedicine. **History:** General. **Legal studies:** Prelaw. **Math:** General. **Parks/recreation:** Exercise sciences, sports admin. **Psychology:** General. **Theology:** Pastoral counseling, sacred music.

**Most popular majors.** Biology 10%, business/marketing 16%, communications/journalism 6%, education 27%, psychology 6%, theological studies 12%.

---

**Computing on campus.** 50 workstations in library, computer center. Dormitories wired for high-speed internet access and linked to campus network. Commuter students can connect to campus network. Online course registration, online library, repair service, wireless network available.

**Student life. Freshman orientation:** Mandatory. Preregistration for classes offered. Held first 2 days of semester. **Policies:** Chapel attendance required for all full-time students. Students not living at home must reside in college housing through junior year. Religious observance required. **Housing:** Guaranteed on-campus for all undergraduates. Single-sex dorms, apartments, wellness housing available. $150 fully refundable deposit, deadline 8/1. **Activities:** Concert band, campus ministries, choral groups, dance, drama, international student organizations, literary magazine, music ensembles, musical theater, student government, student newspaper, ministerial fellowship, missions fellowship, Students in Free Enterprise.

**Athletics.** NAIA, NCCAA. **Intercollegiate:** Baseball M, basketball, soccer, softball W, tennis. **Intramural:** Basketball, soccer, softball, table tennis, tennis, track and field, volleyball. **Team name:** Lions.

**Student services.** Adult student services, chaplain/spiritual director, career counseling, financial aid counseling, personal counseling, veterans' counselor.

**Contact.** E-mail: admission@ec.edu
Phone: (706) 245-7226 ext. 2874 Toll-free number: (800) 860-8800
Fax: (706) 245-2876
Kevin Jones, Director of Admissions, Emmanuel College, 181 Spring Street, Franklin Springs, GA 30639-0129

---

## Emory University

**Atlanta, Georgia**
**www.emory.edu**

**CB member**
**CB code: 5187**

- Private 4-year university affiliated with United Methodist Church
- Residential campus in very large city
- 5,223 degree-seeking undergraduates
- 30% of applicants admitted
- SAT or ACT with writing, application essay required
- 90% graduate within 6 years; 41% enter graduate study

**General.** Founded in 1836. Regionally accredited. **Degrees:** 1,646 bachelor's, 341 associate awarded; master's, doctoral, professional offered. **ROTC:** Army, Air Force. **Location:** 5 miles from downtown. **Calendar:** Semester, limited summer session. **Full-time faculty:** 1,229 total; 99% have terminal degrees, 17% minority, 40% women. **Part-time faculty:** 332 total; 98% have terminal degrees, 10% minority, 40% women. **Class size:** 64% < 20, 24% 20-39, 3% 40-49, 7% 50-99, 2% >100. **Special facilities:** Art, architecture and archaeology museum, biological field station, primate research center, 185 acre park, planetarium, healthcare facilities, access to the Center for Disease Control, manuscript, archives and rare book library, Carter Center.

**Freshman class profile.** 15,599 applied, 4,627 admitted, 1,315 enrolled.

| Mid 50% test scores | | | |
|---|---|---|---|
| SAT critical reading: | 640-730 | Rank in top tenth: | 85% |
| SAT math: | 660-750 | End year in good standing: | 97% |
| SAT writing: | 650-740 | Return as sophomores: | 96% |
| ACT composite: | 29-33 | Out-of-state: | 73% |
| GPA 3.75 or higher: | 71% | Live on campus: | 99% |
| GPA 3.50-3.74: | 22% | International: | 11% |
| GPA 3.0-3.49: | 7% | Fraternities: | 22% |
| Rank in top quarter: | 98% | Sororities: | 26% |

**Basis for selection.** GED not accepted. Challenging curriculum and community involvement important. SAT/ACT important, but not deciding factor. Diversity, character and maturity, and indications of interest considered. Alumni interviews available in limited number of cities. Students may audition for music programs or scholarships on-campus or via recorded performance. Art and other portfolios should be sent directly to department of interest. **Homeschooled:** Letter of recommendation (nonparent) required. 3 SAT Subject Tests required (1 math and 2 of student's choice).

**High school preparation.** College-preparatory program recommended. 16 units required. Required and recommended units include English 4, mathematics 3-4, social studies 2, history 2, science 2-3 (laboratory 3), foreign language 2-3, visual/performing arts 1 and academic electives 2. History should include country/region other than U.S.

**2010-2011 Annual costs.** Tuition/fees: $39,158. Room/board: $11,198. Books/supplies: $1,100. Personal expenses: $1,200.

**2009-2010 Financial aid. Need-based:** Average need met was 100%. Average scholarship/grant was $30,448; average loan $3,288. 87% of total undergraduate aid awarded as scholarships/grants, 13% as loans/jobs. **Non-need-based:** Scholarships awarded for academics, art, leadership, music/drama, religious affiliation, state residency. **Additional information:** Loan replacement grant and loan cap program available to students from families with total annual incomes of $100,000 or less who demonstrate need for financial aid.

**Application procedures. Admission:** Closing date 1/15 (postmark date). $50 fee, may be waived for applicants with need. Admission notification 4/1. Must reply by 5/1. **Financial aid:** Priority date 2/15, closing date 3/1. FAFSA, CSS PROFILE required. Applicants notified by 4/1; must reply by 5/1 or within 4 week(s) of notification.

**Academics. Special study options:** Combined bachelor's/graduate degree, cooperative education, cross-registration, double major, dual enrollment of high school students, ESL, honors, independent study, internships, liberal arts/career combination, study abroad, teacher certification program, Washington semester. 3-2 dual-degree program in engineering with Georgia Institute of Technology. **Credit/placement by examination:** AP, CLEP, IB, institutional tests. **Support services:** Learning center, pre-admission summer program, remedial instruction, study skills assistance, tutoring, writing center.

**Majors. Area/ethnic studies:** African, African-American, American, Caribbean, Chinese, East Asian, French, German, Italian, Japanese, Latin American, Russian/Slavic, South Asian, women's. **Biology:** General. **Business:** Accounting, business admin, finance, management science, marketing. **Communications:** Journalism. **Computer sciences:** Computer science. **Conservation:** Environmental studies. **Education:** General. **Foreign languages:** Ancient Greek, Chinese, classics, comparative lit, French, German, Italian, Japanese, Latin, linguistics, Russian, Spanish. **Health:** Nursing (RN). **History:** General. **Interdisciplinary:** Math/computer science, medieval/Renaissance, neuroscience. **Math:** General, applied. **Philosophy/religion:** Judaic, philosophy, religion. **Physical sciences:** Applied physics, astronomy, chemistry, physics. **Psychology:** General. **Social sciences:** Anthropology, economics, international relations, political science, sociology. **Visual/performing arts:** Art history/conservation, dance, dramatic, film/cinema. **Other:** Classical civilizations studies.

**Most popular majors.** Biology 8%, business/marketing 17%, health sciences 7%, interdisciplinary studies 7%, psychology 9%, social sciences 25%.

**Computing on campus.** 1,000 workstations in dormitories, library, computer center, student center. Dormitories wired for high-speed internet access and linked to campus network. Commuter students can connect to campus network. Online course registration, online library, helpline, repair service, wireless network available.

**Student life. Freshman orientation:** Mandatory. 5-day program held prior to start of classes. **Policies:** 2-year residency requirement. **Housing:** Guaranteed on-campus for freshmen. Coed dorms, single-sex dorms, special housing for disabled, apartments, fraternity/sorority housing available. $100 non-refundable deposit, deadline 5/1. **Activities:** Bands, campus ministries, choral groups, dance, drama, film society, international student organizations, literary magazine, music ensembles, Model UN, musical theater, radio station, student government, student newspaper, symphony orchestra, TV station, over 220 student clubs and organizations available.

**Athletics.** NCAA. **Intercollegiate:** Baseball M, basketball, cross-country, diving, golf M, soccer, softball W, swimming, tennis, track and field, volleyball W. **Intramural:** Basketball, football (non-tackle), racquetball, soccer, softball, swimming, tennis, track and field, volleyball. **Team name:** Eagles.

**Student services.** Alcohol/substance abuse counseling, chaplain/spiritual director, career counseling, student employment services, financial aid counseling, health services, legal services, minority student services, on-campus daycare, personal counseling, placement for graduates, women's services. **Physically disabled:** Services for visually, speech, hearing impaired.

**Contact.** E-mail: admiss@emory.edu
Phone: (404) 727-6036 Toll-free number: (800) 727-6036
Fax: (404) 727-4303
Jean Jordan, Dean of Admission, Emory University, 200 Dowman Drive, B Jones Center, Atlanta, GA 30322

---

## Fort Valley State University
**Fort Valley, Georgia**
**www.fvsu.edu**
**CB member**
**CB code: 5220**

- Public 4-year liberal arts and teachers college
- Residential campus in small town
- 3,421 degree-seeking undergraduates: 12% part-time, 57% women

- 150 degree-seeking graduate students
- 40% of applicants admitted
- SAT or ACT (ACT writing optional) required
- 39% graduate within 6 years

**General.** Founded in 1895. Regionally accredited. 1890 land-grant institution. **Degrees:** 230 bachelor's, 12 associate awarded; master's offered. **ROTC:** Army. **Location:** 30 miles from Macon. **Calendar:** Semester, limited summer session. **Full-time faculty:** 153 total; 64% have terminal degrees, 71% minority, 46% women. **Part-time faculty:** 49 total; 24% have terminal degrees, 71% minority, 65% women. **Class size:** 48% < 20, 36% 20-39, 7% 40-49, 7% 50-99, 1% >100.

**Freshman class profile.** 5,343 applied, 2,161 admitted, 998 enrolled.

| Mid 50% test scores | | | |
|---|---|---|---|
| SAT critical reading: | 410-510 | GPA 3.0-3.49: | 26% |
| SAT math: | 410-510 | GPA 2.0-2.99: | 64% |
| SAT writing: | 390-500 | Rank in top quarter: | 13% |
| ACT composite: | 16-22 | Rank in top tenth: | 5% |
| GPA 3.75 or higher: | 4% | Return as sophomores: | 73% |
| GPA 3.50-3.74: | 5% | Out-of-state: | 3% |
| | | Live on campus: | 93% |

**Basis for selection.** High school transcript, test scores, physical examination important. Audition recommended for music education majors.

**High school preparation.** College-preparatory program required. 16 units required. Required units include English 4, mathematics 4, social studies 1, history 2, science 3 and foreign language 2.

**2009-2010 Annual costs.** Tuition/fees: $5,012; $16,626 out-of-state. Room/board: $6,538. Books/supplies: $1,200. Personal expenses: $400.

**2009-2010 Financial aid. Need-based:** Average need met was 97%. Average scholarship/grant was $2,300; average loan $2,500. 38% of total undergraduate aid awarded as scholarships/grants, 62% as loans/jobs. **Non-need-based:** Scholarships awarded for academics, alumni affiliation, athletics, ROTC. **Additional information:** Loans decreased and grant aid offered to make institution more affordable. Financial aid transcripts must be received from former institutions before application for aid will be considered complete and reviewed for awards.

**Application procedures. Admission:** Closing date 7/19. $30 fee. Admission notification on a rolling basis. **Financial aid:** Priority date 4/15, closing date 6/30. FAFSA required. Applicants notified on a rolling basis starting 7/1; must reply within 1 week(s) of notification.

**Academics. Special study options:** Cross-registration, distance learning, double major, honors, independent study, internships, teacher certification program. **Credit/placement by examination:** CLEP, SAT, ACT, institutional tests. 20 credit hours maximum toward associate degree, 45 toward bachelor's. **Support services:** Learning center, reduced course load, remedial instruction, tutoring, writing center.

**Majors. Agriculture:** Animal sciences, economics, farm/ranch, horticultural science, plant sciences. **Biology:** General. **Business:** General, accounting, business admin, marketing, office management. **Communications:** Journalism, public relations. **Computer sciences:** General, information systems. **Education:** Agricultural, elementary, English, family/consumer sciences, foreign languages, French, mathematics, middle, music, physical, secondary. **Engineering:** Agricultural. **Engineering technology:** Electrical. **Family/consumer sciences:** General, child care, child development, family studies, food/nutrition. **Health:** Medical assistant, veterinary technology/assistant. **Liberal arts:** Arts/sciences. **Math:** General. **Physical sciences:** Chemistry. **Psychology:** General. **Public administration:** Human services, social work. **Social sciences:** Economics, political science, sociology.

**Most popular majors.** Agriculture 7%, biology 12%, business/marketing 20%, computer/information sciences 6%, family/consumer sciences 9%, health sciences 6%, public administration/social services 7%, security/protective services 10%.

**Computing on campus.** Dormitories linked to campus network. Commuter students can connect to campus network. Helpline available.

**Student life. Freshman orientation:** Mandatory. Preregistration for classes offered. **Housing:** Coed dorms, single-sex dorms, apartments available. $200 fully refundable deposit, deadline 8/28. **Activities:** Bands, choral groups, drama, international student organizations, music ensembles, radio station, student government, student newspaper, TV station.

**Athletics.** NCAA. **Intercollegiate:** Basketball, cross-country, football (tackle) M, softball W, tennis, track and field, volleyball W. **Intramural:** Basketball, softball, swimming, tennis, track and field, volleyball. **Team name:** Wildcats.

**Student services.** Adult student services, career counseling, student employment services, health services, on-campus daycare, personal counseling, placement for graduates, veterans' counselor.

**Contact.** E-mail: admissap@fvsu.edu
Phone: (478) 825-6307 Toll-free number: (877) 462-3878
Fax: (478) 825-6394
Donovan Coley, Director of Admissions, Fort Valley State University, 1005 State University Drive, Fort Valley, GA 31030-4313

## Georgia College and State University

**Milledgeville, Georgia**
**www.gcsu.edu**

**CB member**
**CB code: 5252**

- Public 4-year university and liberal arts college
- Residential campus in large town
- 5,603 degree-seeking undergraduates: 9% part-time, 60% women, 6% African American, 1% Asian American, 3% Hispanic American, 2% international
- 964 degree-seeking graduate students
- 62% of applicants admitted
- SAT or ACT with writing, application essay required
- 48% graduate within 6 years

**General.** Founded in 1889. Regionally accredited. Branch campuses in Macon and Warner Robins offering junior, senior, and graduate level options. **Degrees:** 1,004 bachelor's awarded; master's offered. **ROTC:** Army. **Location:** 95 miles from Atlanta, 30 miles from Macon. **Calendar:** Semester, limited summer session. **Full-time faculty:** 301 total; 79% have terminal degrees, 15% minority, 52% women. **Part-time faculty:** 112 total. **Special facilities:** Art galleries, greenhouse, challenge/ropes course, former Governor's mansion, Flannery O'Connor collection, Georgia education museum and archives.

**Freshman class profile.** 4,080 applied, 2,520 admitted, 1,204 enrolled.

| Mid 50% test scores | | | |
|---|---|---|---|
| SAT critical reading: | 520-600 | GPA 3.0-3.49: | 52% |
| SAT math: | 520-600 | GPA 2.0-2.99: | 16% |
| SAT writing: | 510-600 | Return as sophomores: | 84% |
| ACT composite: | 22-25 | Out-of-state: | 2% |
| GPA 3.75 or higher: | 12% | Live on campus: | 99% |
| GPA 3.50-3.74: | 20% | International: | 2% |
| | | Sororities: | 34% |

**Basis for selection.** Admissions based on total student portfolio, demonstrated potential for contribution to the university and probability for success. Test scores used in academic advising for honors program consideration. Audition required of music and drama majors. **Homeschooled:** Transcript of courses and grades required. Admissions of homeschooled students from non-accredited schools will be made based on students having SAT/ACT score equal to or above average score of previous year's entering freshmen class; other documentation may be required. **Learning Disabled:** Students must identify themselves as disabled during admissions process.

**High school preparation.** College-preparatory program required. 16 units required. Required and recommended units include English 4, mathematics 4, social studies 3, science 3 (laboratory 2-3) and foreign language 2-3. Additional courses from the following areas strongly recommended: trigonometry, fine arts and computer technology.

**2009-2010 Annual costs.** Tuition/fees: $6,902; $23,940 out-of-state. Room/board: $8,228. Books/supplies: $1,000. Personal expenses: $2,304.

**2008-2009 Financial aid.** **Need-based:** 1,044 full-time freshmen applied for aid; 420 were judged to have need; 378 of these received aid. Average need met was 34%. Average scholarship/grant was $3,620; average loan $3,191. 34% of total undergraduate aid awarded as scholarships/grants, 66% as loans/jobs. **Non-need-based:** Awarded to 1,989 full-time undergraduates, including 416 freshmen. Scholarships awarded for academics, alumni affiliation, art, athletics, job skills, leadership, minority status, music/drama, religious affiliation, ROTC, state residency.

**Application procedures.** **Admission:** Closing date 4/1 (postmark date). $40 fee. Admission notification on a rolling basis beginning on or about 1/1. Students encouraged to apply early to be considered for admission, university housing, scholarship funding, and financial aid. **Financial aid:** Priority date 3/1; no closing date. FAFSA, institutional form required. Applicants notified on a rolling basis starting 3/1; must reply within 2 week(s) of notification.

**Academics.** **Special study options:** Accelerated study, distance learning, double major, ESL, external degree, honors, independent study, internships, liberal arts/career combination, semester at sea, student-designed major, study abroad, teacher certification program, Washington semester. 3-2 engineering program with Georgia Institute of Technology. **Credit/placement by examination:** CLEP, IB, SAT, ACT, institutional tests. 30 credit hours maximum toward bachelor's degree. **Support services:** Learning center, pre-admission summer program, reduced course load, study skills assistance, tutoring, writing center.

**Majors.** **Biology:** General. **Business:** General, accounting, business admin, management science, managerial economics, marketing. **Communications:** Journalism. **Computer sciences:** General. **Conservation:** Environmental science. **Education:** Early childhood, health, middle, music, special. **Foreign languages:** French, Spanish. **Health:** Music therapy, nursing (RN). **History:** General. **Liberal arts:** Arts/sciences. **Math:** General. **Parks/recreation:** General. **Philosophy/religion:** Philosophy. **Physical sciences:** Chemistry. **Protective services:** Law enforcement admin. **Psychology:** General. **Social sciences:** Political science, sociology. **Visual/performing arts:** Art, dramatic. **Other:** Athletic training.

**Most popular majors.** Business/marketing 27%, communications/journalism 6%, education 16%, English 7%, health sciences 9%, psychology 8%.

**Computing on campus.** 180 workstations in dormitories, library, computer center, student center. Dormitories wired for high-speed internet access and linked to campus network. Commuter students can connect to campus network. Online course registration, online library, helpline, wireless network available.

**Student life.** **Freshman orientation:** Available, $60 fee. Preregistration for classes offered. Several summer sessions with shorter programs held during the academic year. **Policies:** All first-year students required to live in university housing for minimum of 2 consecutive semesters. Meal plan required of incoming freshmen living in central campus housing. **Housing:** Guaranteed on-campus for freshmen. Coed dorms, apartments, wellness housing available. $235 partly refundable deposit, deadline 5/1. Living learning communities available. **Activities:** Bands, campus ministries, choral groups, dance, drama, international student organizations, literary magazine, music ensembles, musical theater, radio station, student government, student newspaper, TV station, Baptist student alliance, student political movement, Young Democrats, ANGELS (AIDS Now Grasps Every Living Soul).

**Athletics.** NCAA. **Intercollegiate:** Baseball M, basketball, cheerleading, cross-country, golf M, soccer W, softball W, tennis. **Intramural:** Archery, basketball, bowling, football (non-tackle), golf, racquetball, soccer, softball, table tennis, tennis, volleyball. **Team name:** Bobcats.

**Student services.** Adult student services, career counseling, student employment services, financial aid counseling, health services, minority student services, personal counseling, placement for graduates, veterans' counselor, women's services. **Physically disabled:** Services for visually, hearing impaired.

**Contact.** E-mail: info@gcsu.edu
Phone: (478) 445-2774 Toll-free number: (800) 342-0471
Fax: (478) 445-1914
Suzanne Pittman, Assistant Vice President for Enrollment Management, Georgia College and State University, Campus Box 23, Milledgeville, GA 31061-0490

## Georgia Gwinnett College

**Lawrenceville, Georgia**
**www.ggc.edu**

- Public 4-year liberal arts college
- Large town
- 2,856 degree-seeking undergraduates

**General.** Regionally accredited. **Calendar:** Semester. **Full-time faculty:** 124 total. **Part-time faculty:** 43 total.

**Freshman class profile.** 807 enrolled.

**Basis for selection.** Open admission.

**Application procedures.** **Admission:** Closing date 7/15. **Financial aid:** Closing date 5/1.

**Academics.** **Credit/placement by examination:** CLEP.

**Majors.** **Biology:** General. **Business:** Business admin. **Computer sciences:** Information technology. **Education:** General. **History:** General. **Math:** General. **Protective services:** Police science. **Psychology:** General. **Social sciences:** Political science.

**Contact.** E-mail: ggcadmissions@ggc.edu
Phone: (678) 407-5313
Tee Mitchell, Director of Admissions, Georgia Gwinnett College, 1000
University Center Lane, Lawrenceville, GA 30043

## Georgia Institute of Technology

**Atlanta, Georgia**  CB member
**www.gatech.edu**  CB code: 5248

- Public 4-year university
- Residential campus in very large city
- 12,942 degree-seeking undergraduates: 5% part-time, 30% women, 6% African American, 17% Asian American, 4% Hispanic American, 6% international
- 6,695 degree-seeking graduate students
- 59% of applicants admitted
- SAT or ACT with writing, application essay required
- 79% graduate within 6 years; 23% enter graduate study

**General.** Founded in 1885. Regionally accredited. **Degrees:** 2,695 bachelor's awarded; master's, doctoral offered. **ROTC:** Army, Naval, Air Force. **Location:** Downtown Atlanta. **Calendar:** Semester, extensive summer session. **Full-time faculty:** 939 total; 97% have terminal degrees, 27% minority, 20% women. **Part-time faculty:** 125 total; 65% have terminal degrees, 23% minority, 36% women. **Class size:** 38% < 20, 31% 20-39, 6% 40-49, 17% 50-99, 8% >100. **Special facilities:** Nuclear magnetic resonance spectroscopy center, research institute, ovarian cancer institute, paper museum, mechanical properties research laboratory with scanning electron microscope, virtual factory laboratory, trading floor, advanced technology development center, advanced computing building, electron microscope, nanotechnology research center, solar decathlon house, wind tunnel, smart house.

**Freshman class profile.** 11,432 applied, 6,721 admitted, 2,660 enrolled.

| Mid 50% test scores | | | |
|---|---|---|---|
| SAT critical reading: | 580-680 | Rank in top quarter: | 95% |
| SAT math: | 650-750 | Rank in top tenth: | 81% |
| SAT writing: | 580-680 | End year in good standing: | 93% |
| ACT composite: | 27-31 | Return as sophomores: | 93% |
| GPA 3.75 or higher: | 65% | Out-of-state: | 32% |
| GPA 3.50-3.74: | 21% | Live on campus: | 97% |
| GPA 3.0-3.49: | 13% | International: | 12% |
| GPA 2.0-2.99: | 1% | Fraternities: | 18% |
| | | Sororities: | 31% |

**Basis for selection.** School achievement record and SAT math score most important, followed by SAT verbal score. Activities, leadership, and personal statement required. Test scores accepted through November test dates for competition in President's Scholarship Program; accepted through December test date for admission consideration. **Homeschooled:** If homeschool not accredited by an approved Council for Higher Education organization, the following must be provided: official documentation of all subjects studied, credit earned per subject, time span of each unit, bibliography of all textbooks used, grades, verification of completion of college preparatory curriculum.

**High school preparation.** College-preparatory program required. 16 units required. Required units include English 4, mathematics 4, social studies 3, science 3 (laboratory 3) and foreign language 2.

**2009-2010 Annual costs.** Tuition/fees: $7,506; $25,916 out-of-state. Room/board: $8,204.

**2008-2009 Financial aid. Need-based:** 1,974 full-time freshmen applied for aid; 897 were judged to have need; 872 of these received aid. Average need met was 74%. Average scholarship/grant was $9,512; average loan $3,526. 51% of total undergraduate aid awarded as scholarships/grants, 49% as loans/jobs. **Non-need-based:** Awarded to 3,290 full-time undergraduates, including 961 freshmen. Scholarships awarded for academics, athletics, leadership, music/drama, ROTC, state residency. **Additional information:** Scholarships, grants, and job opportunities combined to help eliminate student loan debt. Available to Georgia residents whose families have an annual income of less than $33,300 and are pursuing their first undergraduate degree including incoming freshmen, transfer, and currently enrolled students who meet the eligibility requirements.

**Application procedures. Admission:** Priority date 10/1; deadline 1/15 (postmark date). $65 fee, may be waived for applicants with need. Admission notification 3/15. Must reply by May 1 or within 2 week(s) if notified thereafter. Nonresident applicants advised to apply early. **Financial aid:** Closing date 3/1. FAFSA, institutional form required. Applicants notified by 4/1; must reply by 5/1.

**Academics. Special study options:** Accelerated study, combined bachelor's/graduate degree, cooperative education, cross-registration, distance learning, double major, dual enrollment of high school students, ESL, honors, independent study, internships, student-designed major, study abroad. Dual degree program (3-2); Regent's Engineering Transfer Program with 14 colleges in the University System of Georgia; Georgia Tech Regional Engineering Program (GTREP) offers undergraduate and graduate engineering degrees in collaboration with Armstrong Atlantic State University, Georgia Southern University, and Savannah State University. **Credit/placement by examination:** AP, CLEP, IB, SAT, ACT, institutional tests. **Support services:** Learning center, pre-admission summer program, reduced course load, remedial instruction, tutoring, writing center.

**Majors. Architecture:** Architecture. **Biology:** General, biochemistry. **Business:** Business admin, managerial economics. **Communications:** Digital media. **Computer sciences:** General. **Engineering:** Aerospace, biomedical, chemical, civil, computer, electrical, environmental, industrial, materials, mechanical, nuclear, textile. **History:** Science/technology. **Interdisciplinary:** Global studies, science/society. **Math:** Applied. **Physical sciences:** Chemistry, geology, physics, polymer chemistry. **Psychology:** Industrial. **Public administration:** Policy analysis. **Social sciences:** International relations. **Visual/performing arts:** Industrial design. **Other:** Building construction, Discrete mathematics & algorithms, combinatorics, and optimization, Earth and atmospheric sciences, Global economics and modern languages/internationall affairs and modern language.

**Most popular majors.** Business/marketing 14%, computer/information sciences 6%, engineering/engineering technologies 57%.

**Computing on campus.** PC or laptop required. 2,000 workstations in dormitories, library, computer center, student center. Dormitories wired for high-speed internet access and linked to campus network. Commuter students can connect to campus network. Online course registration, online library, helpline, student web hosting, wireless network available.

**Student life. Freshman orientation:** Available, $160 fee. Preregistration for classes offered. Offered at the start of each semester. **Policies:** First-time, first-year students not allowed to have car on campus during first semester. **Housing:** Guaranteed on-campus for freshmen. Coed dorms, single-sex dorms, special housing for disabled, apartments, fraternity/sorority housing available. $600 partly refundable deposit, deadline 5/1. **Activities:** Bands, campus ministries, choral groups, dance, drama, film society, international student organizations, literary magazine, music ensembles, Model UN, musical theater, radio station, student government, student newspaper, symphony orchestra, TV station, Campus Crusade for Christ, Wesley Foundation, College Democrats, College Republicans, National Model UN Club, Environmental Alliance, National Society of Black Engineers, Society of Women Engineers, Society of Hispanic Professional Engineers.

**Athletics.** NCAA. **Team name:** Yellow Jackets.

**Student services.** Alcohol/substance abuse counseling, career counseling, student employment services, financial aid counseling, health services, legal services, minority student services, on-campus daycare, personal counseling, placement for graduates, women's services. **Physically disabled:** Services for visually, speech, hearing impaired. **Learning disabled:** Comprehensive services available.

**Contact.** E-mail: admission@gatech.edu
Phone: (404) 894-4154 Fax: (404) 894-9511
Rick Clark, Director of Undergraduate Admissions, Georgia Institute of Technology, Georgia Institute of Technology, Atlanta, GA 30332-0320

## Georgia Southern University

**Statesboro, Georgia**  CB member
**www.georgiasouthern.edu**  CB code: 5253

- Public 4-year university
- Residential campus in large town
- 15,626 degree-seeking undergraduates: 6% part-time, 48% women, 22% African American, 1% Asian American, 3% Hispanic American, 1% international
- 2,484 degree-seeking graduate students
- 56% of applicants admitted
- SAT or ACT with writing required
- 48% graduate within 6 years; 24% enter graduate study

**General.** Founded in 1906. Regionally accredited. Member of the University System of Georgia; Carnegie Doctoral Research University. **Degrees:** 2,378 bachelor's awarded; master's, doctoral offered. **ROTC:** Army. **Location:** 50 miles from Savannah, 200 miles from Atlanta. **Calendar:** Semester, extensive summer session. **Full-time faculty:** 728 total; 80% have terminal degrees, 17% minority, 48% women. **Part-time faculty:** 109 total;

32% have terminal degrees, 8% minority, 62% women. **Class size:** 25% < 20, 56% 20-39, 7% 40-49, 10% 50-99, 2% >100. **Special facilities:** Planetarium, electron microscope, woodland nature preserve, museum, eagle sanctuary, national tick collection, wildlife education center, raptor center, botanical garden, family life center, international studies center, institute for anthropology and parasitology, performing arts center, black box theater.

**Freshman class profile.** 9,214 applied, 5,154 admitted, 3,539 enrolled.

| Mid 50% test scores | | | |
|---|---|---|---|
| SAT critical reading: | 510-580 | Rank in top quarter: | 42% |
| SAT math: | 510-590 | Rank in top tenth: | 14% |
| SAT writing: | 480-570 | End year in good standing: | 79% |
| ACT composite: | 21-25 | Return as sophomores: | 81% |
| GPA 3.75 or higher: | 12% | Out-of-state: | 4% |
| GPA 3.50-3.74: | 14% | Live on campus: | 83% |
| GPA 3.0-3.49: | 39% | International: | 1% |
| GPA 2.0-2.99: | 35% | Fraternities: | 8% |
| | | Sororities: | 12% |

**Basis for selection.** GED not accepted. Test scores, high school GPA, and college preparatory curriculum considered. Audition required for music majors. **Homeschooled:** SAT/ACT must be at or above average scores of previous year's fall first-time freshman class. **Learning Disabled:** Admissions coordinated through student disability resource center.

**High school preparation.** College-preparatory program required. 16 units required. Required units include English 4, mathematics 4, social studies 3, science 3 (laboratory 2) and foreign language 2.

**2009-2010 Annual costs.** Tuition/fees: $5,440; $17,416 out-of-state. Room/board: $7,900. Books/supplies: $1,200. Personal expenses: $3,100.

**2008-2009 Financial aid. Need-based:** 2,842 full-time freshmen applied for aid; 1,640 were judged to have need; 1,601 of these received aid. Average need met was 60%. Average scholarship/grant was $6,145; average loan $3,287. 45% of total undergraduate aid awarded as scholarships/grants, 55% as loans/jobs. **Non-need-based:** Awarded to 949 full-time undergraduates, including 333 freshmen. Scholarships awarded for academics, alumni affiliation, art, athletics, leadership, minority status, music/drama, ROTC, state residency. **Additional information:** Majority of available scholarships are need-blind.

**Application procedures. Admission:** Closing date 5/1 (postmark date). $30 fee, may be waived for applicants with need. Admission notification on a rolling basis. **Financial aid:** Priority date 4/20; no closing date. FAFSA required. Applicants notified on a rolling basis starting 4/20.

**Academics. Special study options:** Accelerated study, cooperative education, distance learning, double major, ESL, honors, independent study, internships, student-designed major, study abroad, teacher certification program, Washington semester. **Credit/placement by examination:** AP, CLEP, IB, institutional tests. 30 credit hours maximum toward bachelor's degree. For AP exams, more credit hours will be awarded for higher-than-minimum scores. **Support services:** Learning center, pre-admission summer program, reduced course load, remedial instruction, study skills assistance, tutoring, writing center.

**Majors. Biology:** General, pharmacology. **Business:** Accounting, business admin, finance, hotel/motel admin, international, logistics, management information systems, managerial economics, marketing. **Communications:** General, digital media, journalism, public relations. **Communications technology:** Graphic/printing. **Computer sciences:** General, information systems. **Conservation:** Forestry. **Education:** Elementary, middle, music, physical, special. **Engineering:** General, civil, computer, electrical, mechanical. **Engineering technology:** Civil, construction, electrical, industrial management, mechanical, occupational safety. **Family/consumer sciences:** Clothing/textiles, family studies, food/nutrition. **Foreign languages:** French, German. **Health:** Athletic training, nursing (RN), predental, premedicine, prepharmacy, preveterinary, public health ed. **History:** General. **Math:** General. **Parks/recreation:** General, exercise sciences, health/fitness, sports admin. **Philosophy/religion:** Philosophy. **Physical sciences:** Chemistry, geology, physics. **Protective services:** Criminal justice. **Psychology:** General. **Social sciences:** Anthropology, economics, geography, international economic development, international relations, political science, sociology. **Visual/performing arts:** Art, dramatic, interior design, music performance, music theory/composition. **Other:** Modern languages.

**Most popular majors.** Business/marketing 25%, education 13%, engineering/engineering technologies 7%, health sciences 6%, parks/recreation 7%.

**Computing on campus.** 3,260 workstations in dormitories, library, student center. Dormitories wired for high-speed internet access and linked to campus network. Commuter students can connect to campus network. Online course registration, online library, helpline, repair service, student web hosting, wireless network available.

**Student life. Freshman orientation:** Mandatory, $70 fee. Preregistration for classes offered. Freshman/parent program held for 2 days. **Policies:** Freshmen required to live on-campus. **Housing:** Guaranteed on-campus for freshmen. Coed dorms, special housing for disabled, apartments available. $200 partly refundable deposit. **Activities:** Bands, campus ministries, choral groups, dance, drama, film society, international student organizations, literary magazine, music ensembles, musical theater, radio station, student government, student newspaper, symphony orchestra, TV station, Baptist collegiate ministries, campus outreach, Catholic Newman association, Chi Alpha Christian Fellowship, Chosen Generation college ministry, Christian campus fellowship, Episcopal campus ministry, Fellowship of Christian Athletes, Hillel.

**Athletics.** NCAA. **Intercollegiate:** Baseball M, basketball, cheerleading, cross-country W, diving W, football (tackle) M, golf M, soccer, softball W, swimming W, tennis, track and field W, volleyball W. **Intramural:** Basketball, bowling, football (non-tackle), golf, racquetball, soccer, softball, swimming, table tennis, tennis, volleyball, weight lifting. **Team name:** Eagles.

**Student services.** Alcohol/substance abuse counseling, career counseling, services for economically disadvantaged, student employment services, financial aid counseling, health services, legal services, minority student services, on-campus daycare, personal counseling, veterans' counselor, women's services. **Physically disabled:** Services for visually, speech, hearing impaired. **Learning disabled:** Comprehensive services available.

**Contact.** E-mail: admissions@georgiasouthern.edu
Phone: (912) 478-5391 Fax: (912) 478-1156
Sarah Smith, Director of Admission, Georgia Southern University, PO Box 8024, Statesboro, GA 30460

## Georgia Southwestern State University

| Americus, Georgia | CB member |
|---|---|
| www.gsw.edu | CB code: 5250 |

- Public 4-year university and liberal arts college
- Residential campus in large town
- 2,594 degree-seeking undergraduates: 26% part-time, 65% women, 30% African American, 1% Asian American, 2% Hispanic American, 3% international
- 241 degree-seeking graduate students
- 70% of applicants admitted
- SAT or ACT (ACT writing optional) required
- 35% graduate within 6 years

**General.** Founded in 1906. Regionally accredited. **Degrees:** 385 bachelor's awarded; master's offered. **Location:** 135 miles from Atlanta. **Calendar:** Semester, limited summer session. **Full-time faculty:** 95 total; 79% have terminal degrees, 20% minority, 55% women. **Part-time faculty:** 47 total; 21% have terminal degrees, 8% minority, 64% women. **Class size:** 45% < 20, 42% 20-39, 10% 40-49, 3% 50-99. **Special facilities:** Observatory, glass blowing studio, golf course, indoor climbing wall.

**Freshman class profile.** 1,347 applied, 944 admitted, 490 enrolled.

| Mid 50% test scores | | | |
|---|---|---|---|
| SAT critical reading: | 440-530 | Rank in top quarter: | 39% |
| SAT math: | 440-530 | Rank in top tenth: | 13% |
| SAT writing: | 430-510 | Return as sophomores: | 69% |
| ACT composite: | 18-21 | Out-of-state: | 4% |
| GPA 3.75 or higher: | 15% | Live on campus: | 65% |
| GPA 3.50-3.74: | 12% | International: | 7% |
| GPA 3.0-3.49: | 31% | Fraternities: | 20% |
| GPA 2.0-2.99: | 42% | Sororities: | 16% |

**Basis for selection.** School achievement record, test scores most important. **Homeschooled:** Statement describing homeschool structure and mission, transcript of courses and grades, letter of recommendation (nonparent) required. Must complete home schooled application or submit SAT along with 7 SAT Subject tests or a portfolio outlining work in 5 critical college preparatory areas.

**High school preparation.** College-preparatory program required. 16 units required. Required and recommended units include English 4, mathematics 4, social studies 1, history 2, science 3 (laboratory 2), foreign language 2 and academic electives 2.

**2009-2010 Annual costs.** Tuition/fees: $4,762; $16,376 out-of-state. Room/board: $5,950. Books/supplies: $1,000.

**2008-2009 Financial aid. Non-need-based:** Scholarships awarded for academics, athletics, leadership.

**Application procedures. Admission:** Closing date 7/21 (postmark date). $25 fee, may be waived for applicants with need. Admission notification on a rolling basis. Must reply by May 1 or within 3 week(s) if notified thereafter. **Financial aid:** Priority date 4/1, closing date 6/1. FAFSA, institutional form required. Applicants notified on a rolling basis starting 3/1.

**Academics. Special study options:** Accelerated study, distance learning, double major, dual enrollment of high school students, ESL, honors, independent study, internships, study abroad, teacher certification program. 3+2 program in engineering with Georgia Institute of Technology. **Credit/placement by examination:** AP, CLEP, institutional tests. 45 credit hours maximum toward bachelor's degree. **Support services:** Learning center, reduced course load, remedial instruction, study skills assistance, tutoring, writing center.

**Majors. Biology:** General. **Business:** Accounting, business admin, human resources, marketing. **Computer sciences:** General, computer science. **Education:** Elementary, middle, physical, special. **Engineering technology:** Computer. **Health:** Nursing (RN). **History:** General. **Math:** General. **Parks/recreation:** Facilities management. **Physical sciences:** Chemistry, geology. **Psychology:** General. **Social sciences:** Political science, sociology. **Visual/performing arts:** Art, dramatic.

**Most popular majors.** Business/marketing 38%, education 23%, health sciences 8%, history 7%, psychology 10%.

**Computing on campus.** 550 workstations in dormitories, library, computer center, student center. Dormitories wired for high-speed internet access and linked to campus network. Commuter students can connect to campus network. Online course registration, online library, wireless network available.

**Student life. Freshman orientation:** Mandatory, $70 fee. Preregistration for classes offered. Three sessions in summer; includes parents' program. **Housing:** Guaranteed on-campus for freshmen. Coed dorms, apartments, fraternity/sorority housing available. $250 deposit. **Activities:** Bands, campus ministries, choral groups, drama, international student organizations, literary magazine, music ensembles, musical theater, student government, student newspaper, TV station, Baptist Student Union, Wesley Foundation, Young Republicans, Young Democrats, SABU, Habitat for Humanity, campus activity board, ZEPHYR recruitment team, College Republicans.

**Athletics.** NCAA. **Intercollegiate:** Baseball M, basketball, cross-country W, golf M, soccer, softball W, tennis. **Intramural:** Badminton, basketball, football (non-tackle), racquetball, soccer, table tennis, tennis, volleyball, weight lifting, wrestling M. **Team name:** Hurricanes.

**Student services.** Career counseling, services for economically disadvantaged, student employment services, financial aid counseling, health services, personal counseling, veterans' counselor. **Physically disabled:** Services for visually, speech, hearing impaired.

**Contact.** E-mail: gswapps@canes.gsw.edu
Phone: (229) 928-1273 Toll-free number: (800) 338-0082
Fax: (229) 931-2059
Gaye Hayes, Vice President of Enrollment Management, Georgia Southwestern State University, 800 Georgia Southwestern State University Drive, Americus, GA 31709-9957

---

## Georgia State University
**Atlanta, Georgia**
www.gsu.edu

**CB member**
**CB code: 5251**

- Public 4-year university
- Commuter campus in very large city
- 21,727 degree-seeking undergraduates: 22% part-time, 60% women, 34% African American, 12% Asian American, 7% Hispanic American, 2% international
- 7,532 degree-seeking graduate students
- 41% of applicants admitted
- SAT or ACT with writing required
- 50% graduate within 6 years

**General.** Founded in 1913. Regionally accredited. Courses offered at Alpharetta and Brookhaven Centers. Distance learning and web courses available in College of Health and Human Sciences and College of Education. **Degrees:** 3,834 bachelor's awarded; master's, doctoral, professional offered. **ROTC:** Army, Naval, Air Force. **Location:** Downtown. **Calendar:** Semester, extensive summer session. **Full-time faculty:** 1,096 total; 87% have terminal degrees, 23% minority, 48% women. **Part-time faculty:** 407 total. **Class size:** 17% < 20, 47% 20-39, 20% 40-49, 11% 50-99, 5% >100. **Special facilities:** Viral immunology center, writing studio, advanced biotechnology center, Asian studies center, multi-media instructional lab, child

development center, performing arts center, language acquisition and research centers, military science leadership lab, music media center, learning disorders center, speech and language center, hearing center.

**Freshman class profile.** 11,913 applied, 4,827 admitted, 2,934 enrolled.

| Mid 50% test scores | | | |
|---|---|---|---|
| SAT critical reading: | 490-580 | GPA 2.0-2.99: | 11% |
| SAT math: | 490-590 | Return as sophomores: | 83% |
| ACT composite: | 20-24 | Out-of-state: | 3% |
| GPA 3.75 or higher: | 12% | Live on campus: | 54% |
| GPA 3.50-3.74: | 21% | International: | 1% |
| GPA 3.0-3.49: | 56% | Fraternities: | 2% |
| | | Sororities: | 2% |

**Basis for selection.** 430 SAT verbal and 400 SAT math or 17 ACT English and 17 ACT math required. Audition and interview required for music majors. Portfolio required for art majors. **Homeschooled:** Transcript of courses and grades required. 1090 SAT (exclusive of Writing) or 24 ACT required. SAT Subject Test option available: 520 English Writing, 530 Literature, 500 Math IC or 570 Math IIC, 520 Biology, 540 Chemistry or 590 Physics, 560 American History and Social Studies, and 540 World History required.

**High school preparation.** College-preparatory program required. 16 units required. Required units include English 4, mathematics 4, social studies 2, history 1, science 3 (laboratory 2) and foreign language 2. 1 life sciences lab, 1 physical sciences lab plus additional science unit; foreign language units must be same language; math units must be algebra I, geometry, algebra II, and higher.

**2009-2010 Annual costs.** Tuition/fees: $7,298; $25,508 out-of-state. Room only: $7,740. Books/supplies: $1,000. Personal expenses: $1,970.

**2008-2009 Financial aid. Need-based:** 2,541 full-time freshmen applied for aid; 2,412 were judged to have need; 2,412 of these received aid. Average need met was 27%. Average scholarship/grant was $2,684; average loan $2,438. 93% of total undergraduate aid awarded as scholarships/grants, 7% as loans/jobs. **Non-need-based:** Awarded to 12,178 full-time undergraduates, including 2,664 freshmen. Scholarships awarded for academics.

**Application procedures. Admission:** Priority date 11/1; deadline 3/1 (postmark date). $60 fee, may be waived for applicants with need. Admission notification 4/1. Must reply by May 1 or within 2 week(s) if notified thereafter. **Financial aid:** Priority date 4/1, closing date 11/1. FAFSA, institutional form required. Must reply by 4/1 or within 2 week(s) of notification.

**Academics. Special study options:** Accelerated study, cooperative education, cross-registration, distance learning, double major, dual enrollment of high school students, ESL, honors, independent study, internships, student-designed major, study abroad, teacher certification program. Freshman learning communities available. **Credit/placement by examination:** AP, CLEP, IB, institutional tests. 30 credit hours maximum toward bachelor's degree. Some credit awarded for DANTES subject examinations. **Support services:** Learning center, pre-admission summer program, reduced course load, remedial instruction, study skills assistance, tutoring, writing center.

**Honors college/program.** Applicants should have 3.5 GPA and 1200 SAT with 500 verbal and math subsections. Number of freshmen admitted increases each year; 223 freshmen admitted for Fall 2009.

**Majors. Area/ethnic studies:** African-American, Asian, regional, women's. **Biology:** General. **Business:** Accounting, actuarial science, business admin, finance, insurance, international, managerial economics, marketing, real estate. **Communications:** General, journalism. **Computer sciences:** General, computer science. **Education:** Art, physical. **Foreign languages:** General, classics, French, German, linguistics, Spanish. **Health:** Dietetics, nursing (RN), respiratory therapy technology. **History:** General. **Interdisciplinary:** Ancient studies, classical/archaeology, gerontology, global studies. **Math:** General. **Parks/recreation:** Exercise sciences, health/fitness. **Philosophy/religion:** Philosophy, religion. **Physical sciences:** Chemistry, geology, physics. **Protective services:** Criminal justice. **Psychology:** General. **Public administration:** Policy analysis, social work. **Social sciences:** Anthropology, economics, geography, international economics, political science, sociology, urban studies. **Visual/performing arts:** Art, art history/conservation, design, drawing, film/cinema, music management, music performance, theater history.

**Most popular majors.** Biology 6%, business/marketing 31%, education 6%, psychology 9%, social sciences 12%, visual/performing arts 7%.

**Computing on campus.** 1,000 workstations in library, computer center. Dormitories wired for high-speed internet access and linked to campus network. Commuter students can connect to campus network. Online course registration, online library, helpline, student web hosting, wireless network available.

**Student life. Freshman orientation:** Mandatory, $56 fee. Preregistration for classes offered. Various summer sessions offered. **Housing:** Coed dorms, special housing for disabled, apartments, wellness housing available. $525 nonrefundable deposit. **Activities:** Bands, campus ministries, choral groups, dance, drama, film society, international student organizations, literary magazine, music ensembles, musical theater, opera, radio station, student government, student newspaper, symphony orchestra, TV station, African students association, Amnesty International, Brazillian student association, Bridge Builders, Campus Civitan, Catholic student association, Chinese student union, College Republicans, Christian legal society.

**Athletics.** NCAA. **Intercollegiate:** Baseball M, basketball, cross-country, football (tackle) M, golf, soccer, softball W, tennis, track and field, volleyball W. **Intramural:** Basketball, bowling, football (non-tackle), golf, racquetball, soccer, softball, table tennis, tennis, volleyball. **Team name:** Panthers.

**Student services.** Adult student services, alcohol/substance abuse counseling, chaplain/spiritual director, career counseling, services for economically disadvantaged, student employment services, financial aid counseling, health services, minority student services, on-campus daycare, personal counseling, placement for graduates, veterans' counselor. **Physically disabled:** Services for visually, speech, hearing impaired.

**Contact.** E-mail: admissions@gsu.edu
Phone: (404) 413-2500 Fax: (404) 413-2002
Scott Burke, Director of Admissions, Georgia State University, Box 4009, Atlanta, GA 30302-4009

## Herzing University
**Atlanta, Georgia**
**www.herzing.edu**                                           **CB code: 2342**

> - For-profit 3-year business and technical college
> - Commuter campus in very large city
> - 609 degree-seeking undergraduates
> - Interview required

**General.** Founded in 1949. Regionally accredited. **Degrees:** 49 bachelor's, 31 associate awarded. **Location:** 120 miles from Birmingham, Alabama; 70 miles from Chattanooga, Tennessee. **Calendar:** Semester, extensive summer session. **Full-time faculty:** 7 total. **Part-time faculty:** 21 total. **Class size:** 84% < 20, 16% 20-39.

**Basis for selection.** Open admission, but selective for some programs. Entrance test and evaluation for all applicants. Competitive admission to some programs based on score. SAT/ACT scores may be used for academic advising.

**2009-2010 Annual costs.** Costs may vary by program.

**Financial aid. Non-need-based:** Scholarships awarded for academics.

**Application procedures. Admission:** No deadline. $25 fee. Admission notification on a rolling basis. **Financial aid:** No deadline. FAFSA, institutional form required. Applicants notified on a rolling basis.

**Academics.** Students train on types of equipment used in the field. **Special study options:** Distance learning, independent study, internships, liberal arts/career combination. **Credit/placement by examination:** CLEP, IB, institutional tests. **Support services:** Learning center, study skills assistance, tutoring.

**Majors. BACHELOR'S. Business:** Business admin. **Computer sciences:** Information systems, programming. **ASSOCIATE. Business:** Business admin. **Computer sciences:** Information systems, programming. **Engineering technology:** Electrical.

**Most popular majors.** Business/marketing 31%, computer/information sciences 41%.

**Computing on campus.** 157 workstations in library, computer center. Online library available.

**Student life. Freshman orientation:** Mandatory, $25 fee. Preregistration for classes offered. Orientation held beginning of each term for 2 hours. **Activities:** Student government.

**Student services.** Career counseling, student employment services, financial aid counseling, personal counseling, placement for graduates, veterans' counselor.

**Contact.** E-mail: info@atl.herzing.edu
Phone: (404) 816-4533 Toll-free number: (800) 573-4533
Fax: (404) 816-5576
Christina Ricks, Director of Admissions, Herzing University, 3393 Peachtree Road NE, Suite 1003, Atlanta, GA 30326

## ITT Technical Institute: Duluth
**Duluth, Georgia**

> - For-profit 4-year technical college
> - Commuter campus in large town

**General.** Accredited by ACICS. **Calendar:** Quarter.

**Contact.** Phone: (866) 489-8818
Director of Recruitment, 10700 Abbotts Bridge Road, Duluth, GA 30097

## Kennesaw State University
**Kennesaw, Georgia**                                     **CB member**
**www.kennesaw.edu**                                      **CB code: 5359**

> - Public 4-year university
> - Commuter campus in large town
> - 20,237 degree-seeking undergraduates: 23% part-time, 59% women
> - 1,958 degree-seeking graduate students
> - 64% of applicants admitted
> - SAT or ACT (ACT writing optional) required
> - 37% graduate within 6 years

**General.** Founded in 1963. Regionally accredited. **Degrees:** 3,021 bachelor's awarded; master's, doctoral offered. **ROTC:** Army, Air Force. **Location:** 25 miles from Atlanta. **Calendar:** Semester, limited summer session. **Full-time faculty:** 703 total; 75% have terminal degrees, 23% minority, 51% women. **Part-time faculty:** 533 total; 29% have terminal degrees, 15% minority, 58% women. **Class size:** 20% < 20, 57% 20-39, 9% 40-49, 12% 50-99, 2% >100. **Special facilities:** Educational technology center, presentation technology department, teacher resource and activity center, 2 art galleries.

**Freshman class profile.** 7,877 applied, 5,010 admitted, 2,749 enrolled.

| Mid 50% test scores | | | |
|---|---|---|---|
| SAT critical reading: | 500-580 | Rank in top quarter: | 53% |
| SAT math: | 490-580 | Rank in top tenth: | 21% |
| SAT writing: | 470-560 | End year in good standing: | 84% |
| ACT composite: | 20-24 | Return as sophomores: | 75% |
| GPA 3.75 or higher: | 9% | Out-of-state: | 3% |
| GPA 3.50-3.74: | 15% | Live on campus: | 49% |
| GPA 3.0-3.49: | 44% | Fraternities: | 5% |
| GPA 2.0-2.99: | 32% | Sororities: | 9% |

**Basis for selection.** GED not accepted. 2.5 GPA in college prep courses and 490 SAT verbal/460 SAT math or 20 ACT English/19 ACT math required. Applicants with test scores below minimum must take institutional placement exams in appropriate subject areas. Audition required of music majors. Portfolio required of art majors. **Homeschooled:** Students considered based on portfolio, standardized tests scores, extra-curricular activities, and recommendations.

**High school preparation.** College-preparatory program required. 16 units required. Required units include English 4, mathematics 4, social studies 3, science 3 (laboratory 3) and foreign language 2.

**2009-2010 Annual costs.** Tuition/fees: $5,142; $17,118 out-of-state. Room only: $5,100. Books/supplies: $1,250. Personal expenses: $1,659.

**2009-2010 Financial aid. Non-need-based:** Scholarships awarded for academics, alumni affiliation, art, athletics, job skills, leadership, minority status, music/drama, ROTC, state residency.

**Application procedures. Admission:** Closing date 5/14 (receipt date). $40 fee, may be waived for applicants with need. Admission notification on a rolling basis beginning on or about 1/1. **Financial aid:** Priority date 4/1, closing date 7/1. FAFSA required. Applicants notified on a rolling basis starting 5/15.

**Academics. Special study options:** Cooperative education, cross-registration, distance learning, double major, ESL, honors, internships, study abroad, teacher certification program, weekend college. **Credit/placement by examination:** CLEP, IB, institutional tests. 30 credit hours maximum toward bachelor's degree. **Support services:** Learning center, reduced course load, remedial instruction, study skills assistance, tutoring, writing center.

**Honors college/program.** 3.5 GPA and 1200 SAT (exclusive of Writing) required. Joint enrollment honors program for high school junior and seniors; requires 3.0 GPA, 1100 SAT with 530 SAT verbal and math subscores (exclusive of writing) or 25 ACT, with 24 English and 20 Math subscores.

**Majors. Area/ethnic studies:** African. **Biology:** General, biochemistry, biotechnology. **Business:** Accounting, business admin, finance, international, managerial economics, marketing, sales/distribution. **Communications:** General. **Computer sciences:** General, information systems, security. **Education:** Art, biology, elementary, English, mathematics, middle, music, physical, social studies. **Health:** Nursing (RN). **History:** General. **Math:** General. **Parks/recreation:** Exercise sciences, sports admin. **Physical sciences:** Chemistry. **Protective services:** Criminal justice. **Psychology:** General. **Public administration:** Human services. **Social sciences:** Anthropology, cartography, geography, international relations, political science, sociology. **Visual/performing arts:** Art, dance, dramatic, music performance. **Other:** Modern language and culture.

**Most popular majors.** Business/marketing 27%, communications/journalism 7%, education 17%, health sciences 7%, psychology 6%, social sciences 7%.

**Computing on campus.** 1,400 workstations in library, computer center, student center. Dormitories wired for high-speed internet access. Commuter students can connect to campus network. Online course registration, online library, helpline, wireless network available.

**Student life. Freshman orientation:** Mandatory, $25 fee. Preregistration for classes offered. Held prior to semester. **Housing:** Apartments available. $375 nonrefundable deposit. **Activities:** Bands, campus ministries, choral groups, dance, drama, international student organizations, literary magazine, music ensembles, Model UN, musical theater, radio station, student government, student newspaper, symphony orchestra, Baptist student union, Student Nurses Association, College Ambassadors, volunteer club, American Marketing Association, African American student alliance, Circle K, Catholic student association.

**Athletics.** NCAA. **Intercollegiate:** Baseball M, basketball, cheerleading M, cross-country, golf, soccer W, softball W, tennis, track and field. **Intramural:** Basketball, bowling, football (non-tackle), soccer, softball, table tennis, tennis, volleyball. **Team name:** Fighting Owls.

**Student services.** Adult student services, alcohol/substance abuse counseling, career counseling, student employment services, financial aid counseling, health services, minority student services, personal counseling, placement for graduates, veterans' counselor. **Physically disabled:** Services for visually, speech, hearing impaired.

**Contact.** E-mail: ksuadmit@kennesaw.edu
Phone: (770) 423-6300 Fax: (770) 423-6541
Angela Evans, Director of Admissions, Kennesaw State University, 1000 Chastain Road, Kennesaw, GA 30144-5591

## LaGrange College
**LaGrange, Georgia**
www.lagrange.edu

**CB member**
**CB code: 5362**

- Private 4-year liberal arts college affiliated with United Methodist Church
- Residential campus in large town
- 860 degree-seeking undergraduates: 10% part-time, 55% women, 22% African American, 1% Asian American, 2% Hispanic American, 2% international
- 161 degree-seeking graduate students
- 65% of applicants admitted
- SAT or ACT (ACT writing optional), application essay required
- 55% graduate within 6 years; 17% enter graduate study

**General.** Founded in 1831. Regionally accredited. **Degrees:** 197 bachelor's, 2 associate awarded; master's offered. **Location:** 70 miles from Atlanta, 45 miles from Columbus. **Calendar:** 4-1-4, limited summer session. **Full-time faculty:** 65 total; 83% have terminal degrees, 48% women. **Part-time faculty:** 82 total; 12% have terminal degrees, 48% women. **Class size:** 86% < 20, 13% 20-39, less than 1% 40-49, less than 1% 50-99. **Special facilities:** Performing arts auditorium, natatorium, art center.

**Freshman class profile.** 1,342 applied, 869 admitted, 231 enrolled.

| Mid 50% test scores | | | |
|---|---|---|---|
| SAT critical reading: | 460-570 | Rank in top quarter: | 54% |
| SAT math: | 460-570 | Rank in top tenth: | 25% |
| ACT composite: | 20-25 | Return as sophomores: | 71% |
| GPA 3.75 or higher: | 26% | Out-of-state: | 13% |
| GPA 3.50-3.74: | 24% | Live on campus: | 91% |
| GPA 3.0-3.49: | 43% | International: | 2% |
| GPA 2.0-2.99: | 7% | Fraternities: | 10% |
| | | Sororities: | 15% |

**Basis for selection.** School achievement record and test scores most important. Interview and recommendations considered. Separate application typically during sophomore year for nursing applicants. Students undergo a writing sample and math placement test prior to registration. **Home-schooled:** Bibliography of high school readings, including textbooks, letter of recommendation from outside the home required.

**High school preparation.** College-preparatory program recommended. 14 units required; 16 recommended. Required and recommended units include English 4, mathematics 4, social studies 3, science 3 and foreign language 2.

**2009-2010 Annual costs.** Tuition/fees: $21,094. Room/board: $8,576. Books/supplies: $1,000. Personal expenses: $1,975.

**2008-2009 Financial aid. Need-based:** 140 full-time freshmen applied for aid; 116 were judged to have need; 116 of these received aid. Average need met was 82%. Average scholarship/grant was $12,175; average loan $3,536. 62% of total undergraduate aid awarded as scholarships/grants, 38% as loans/jobs. **Non-need-based:** Awarded to 232 full-time undergraduates, including 63 freshmen. Scholarships awarded for academics, art, leadership, music/drama, religious affiliation, state residency.

**Application procedures. Admission:** Priority date 3/1; no deadline. $30 fee, may be waived for applicants with need, free for online applicants. Admission notification on a rolling basis beginning on or about 9/15. Early admission candidates must be highly recommended by counselors and parents. **Financial aid:** Priority date 3/1; no closing date. FAFSA required. Applicants notified on a rolling basis starting 3/15; must reply by 8/15 or within 2 week(s) of notification.

**Academics. Special study options:** Accelerated study, combined bachelor's/graduate degree, double major, dual enrollment of high school students, independent study, internships, liberal arts/career combination, student-designed major, study abroad, teacher certification program, Washington semester. **Credit/placement by examination:** AP, CLEP, IB, institutional tests. 6 credit hours maximum toward bachelor's degree. USAFI credit accepted. **Support services:** Study skills assistance, tutoring, writing center.

**Majors. Biology:** General, biochemistry. **Business:** Accounting, business admin, organizational behavior. **Computer sciences:** General, computer science. **Education:** Elementary. **Foreign languages:** Spanish. **Health:** Nursing (RN). **History:** General. **Math:** General. **Philosophy/religion:** Religion. **Physical sciences:** Chemistry. **Psychology:** General. **Public administration:** Social work. **Social sciences:** Political science, sociology. **Theology:** Religious ed. **Visual/performing arts:** General, dramatic.

**Most popular majors.** Biology 11%, business/marketing 21%, health sciences 16%, psychology 7%, public administration/social services 11%, social sciences 8%, visual/performing arts 10%.

**Computing on campus.** 141 workstations in dormitories, library, computer center. Dormitories wired for high-speed internet access and linked to campus network. Commuter students can connect to campus network. Online library, helpline, student web hosting, wireless network available.

**Student life. Freshman orientation:** Mandatory. Preregistration for classes offered. Three 2-day summer orientation sessions available. **Housing:** Guaranteed on-campus for freshmen. Coed dorms, single-sex dorms, apartments, fraternity/sorority housing available. $100 fully refundable deposit, deadline 4/9. **Activities:** Pep band, campus ministries, choral groups, drama, international student organizations, literary magazine, music ensembles, musical theater, student government, student newspaper, symphony orchestra, Wesley Fellowship, Baptist Student Union, Circle-K, Rotaract, Interfaith Council, volunteer corps, Habitat for Humanity, Catholic group.

**Athletics.** NCAA. **Intercollegiate:** Baseball M, basketball, cheerleading M, cross-country, football (tackle) M, golf M, lacrosse W, soccer, softball W, swimming, tennis, volleyball W. **Intramural:** Basketball, football (tackle) M, softball, tennis, volleyball. **Team name:** Panthers.

**Student services.** Adult student services, chaplain/spiritual director, career counseling, student employment services, financial aid counseling, health services, personal counseling, placement for graduates.

**Contact.** E-mail: admission@lagrange.edu
Phone: (706) 880-8005 Toll-free number: (800) 593-2885
Fax: (706) 880-8010
Dana Paul, Vice President for Enrollment Management, LaGrange College, 601 Broad Street, LaGrange, GA 30240-2999

## Life University
**Marietta, Georgia**
**www.life.edu**                               CB code: 7006

- Private 4-year university
- Very large city
- 726 degree-seeking undergraduates: 27% part-time, 48% women, 30% African American, 4% Asian American, 6% Hispanic American, 1% Native American
- 1,574 degree-seeking graduate students
- 82% of applicants admitted
- SAT or ACT with writing required

**General.** Regionally accredited. **Degrees:** 61 bachelor's awarded; master's, professional offered. **Location:** 10 miles from downtown Atlanta. **Calendar:** Quarter, limited summer session. **Full-time faculty:** 119 total; 85% have terminal degrees, 22% minority, 37% women. **Part-time faculty:** 47 total; 66% have terminal degrees, 15% minority, 43% women. **Class size:** 67% < 20, 28% 20-39, 3% 40-49, 1% 50-99.

**Freshman class profile.** 322 applied, 263 admitted, 208 enrolled.

| Mid 50% test scores | | | |
|---|---|---|---|
| SAT critical reading: | 410-490 | GPA 3.50-3.74: | 9% |
| SAT math: | 400-510 | GPA 3.0-3.49: | 26% |
| SAT writing: | 390-520 | GPA 2.0-2.99: | 46% |
| ACT composite: | 18-23 | Return as sophomores: | 73% |
| GPA 3.75 or higher: | 15% | Out-of-state: | 65% |

**Basis for selection.** Standardized test scores and high school record most important. 2.0 GPA and 1430 SAT (including Writing) or 18 ACT important. **Homeschooled:** Transcript of courses and grades required. **Learning Disabled:** Letter from doctor required.

**High school preparation.** College-preparatory program recommended.

**2009-2010 Annual costs.** Tuition/fees: $8,352. Books/supplies: $1,650. Personal expenses: $2,187.

**2009-2010 Financial aid. Need-based:** 112 full-time freshmen applied for aid; 99 were judged to have need; 94 of these received aid. Average scholarship/grant was $4,600; average loan $3,900. 51% of total undergraduate aid awarded as scholarships/grants, 49% as loans/jobs. **Non-need-based:** Awarded to 236 full-time undergraduates, including 91 freshmen. Scholarships awarded for academics.

**Application procedures. Admission:** Closing date 9/1 (postmark date). $50 fee, may be waived for applicants with need. Admission notification on a rolling basis. **Financial aid:** No deadline. FAFSA required. Applicants notified on a rolling basis starting 5/1.

**Academics. Special study options:** Accelerated study, double major, ESL, independent study, internships, study abroad. **Credit/placement by examination:** AP, CLEP, SAT, ACT. **Support services:** Learning center, reduced course load, remedial instruction, study skills assistance, tutoring, writing center.

**Majors. Biology:** General. **Business:** General, management information systems. **Health:** Dietetics. **Interdisciplinary:** Nutrition sciences. **Parks/recreation:** Exercise sciences.

**Most popular majors.** Biology 54%, business/marketing 13%, health sciences 26%.

**Computing on campus.** Dormitories linked to campus network. Commuter students can connect to campus network. Online course registration, online library, wireless network available.

**Student life. Freshman orientation:** Mandatory. Two-day program usually held on Thursday and Friday before quarter begins. **Housing:** Apartments available. $250 partly refundable deposit. **Activities:** International student organizations, student newspaper.

**Athletics. Intramural:** Basketball, football (tackle), volleyball. **Team name:** Eagles.

**Student services.** Alcohol/substance abuse counseling, financial aid counseling, personal counseling.

**Contact.** E-mail: admissions@life.edu
Phone: (770) 426-2884 Toll-free number: (800) 543-3202
Fax: (770) 426-2895
Rebecca Koche, Director of New Student Development, Life University, 1269 Barclay Circle, Marietta, GA 30060

## Luther Rice University
**Lithonia, Georgia**
**www.lru.edu**

- Private 4-year Bible and seminary college
- Very large city
- 348 degree-seeking undergraduates
- 640 graduate students
- Application essay required

**General.** Regionally accredited; also accredited by TRACS. **Degrees:** 77 bachelor's awarded; master's, doctoral offered. **Location:** Less than 20 miles from Atlanta, Georgia. **Calendar:** Semester, limited summer session. **Full-time faculty:** 12 total. **Part-time faculty:** 29 total.

**Basis for selection.** Open admission. **Homeschooled:** Transcript of courses and grades, state high school equivalency certificate, letter of recommendation (nonparent) required. Bible Knowledge Test Doctoral students must submit MAT scores.

**2009-2010 Annual costs.** Tuition/fees: $6,540.

**Application procedures. Admission:** No deadline. $50 fee, may be waived for applicants with need. **Financial aid:** Closing date 8/18.

**Academics. Credit/placement by examination:** CLEP.

**Majors. Other:** Christian worldview/apologetics.

**Contact.** E-mail: admissions@lru.edu
Toll-free number: (800) 442-1577
James Kinnebrew, Director of Admissions, Luther Rice University, 3038 Evans Mill Road, Lithonia, GA 30038

## Macon State College
**Macon, Georgia**                  CB member
**www.maconstate.edu**              CB code: 5439

- Public 4-year College of Information Technology
- Commuter campus in small city
- 6,537 degree-seeking undergraduates

**General.** Founded in 1968. Regionally accredited. **Degrees:** 465 bachelor's, 342 associate awarded. **Location:** 85 miles from Atlanta. **Calendar:** Semester, extensive summer session. **Full-time faculty:** 195 total. **Part-time faculty:** 111 total. **Special facilities:** Botanical gardens.

**Basis for selection.** Open admission. Interview required for respiratory therapy, health information technology, health information management, health services administration, and technology programs. Education and nursing may require interview. **Homeschooled:** SAT and portfolio with list of courses required.

**High school preparation.** 16 units recommended. Recommended units include English 4, mathematics 4, social studies 1, history 2, science 3 (laboratory 2) and foreign language 2.

**2009-2010 Annual costs.** Tuition/fees: $2,782; $10,264 out-of-state. Books/supplies: $1,040. Personal expenses: $5,168.

**2008-2009 Financial aid.** All financial aid based on need.

**Application procedures. Admission:** Closing date 7/23 (receipt date). $20 fee, may be waived for applicants with need. Admission notification on a rolling basis. **Financial aid:** Priority date 4/1; no closing date. FAFSA required. Applicants notified on a rolling basis starting 4/15; must reply within 2 week(s) of notification.

**Academics. Special study options:** Distance learning, dual enrollment of high school students, honors, internships, liberal arts/career combination, study abroad, teacher certification program. **Credit/placement by examination:** AP, CLEP, IB, institutional tests. 40 credit hours maximum toward associate degree, 40 toward bachelor's. **Support services:** Learning center,

pre-admission summer program, reduced course load, remedial instruction, study skills assistance, tutoring, writing center.

**Majors. Business:** General, accounting, business admin, marketing, operations. **Communications:** General. **Computer sciences:** Applications programming, information systems, programming. **Education:** Early childhood. **Health:** Health care admin, health services, medical records admin, nursing (RN). **Math:** General. **Public administration:** General, human services.

**Computing on campus.** 150 workstations in library, computer center, student center. Commuter students can connect to campus network. Online course registration, online library, helpline, wireless network available.

**Student life. Freshman orientation:** Mandatory, $25 fee. Preregistration for classes offered. **Activities:** Choral groups, drama, literary magazine, music ensembles, Model UN, musical theater, student government, student newspaper, TV station, black student unification, association of nursing students, Spanish club, Baptist student union, astronomy club, pre-med club, honors student association, Amnesty International, information technology club.

**Athletics. Intramural:** Basketball, bowling, golf, softball, swimming, table tennis, tennis, volleyball.

**Student services.** Career counseling, student employment services, financial aid counseling, health services, minority student services, personal counseling, veterans' counselor.

**Contact.** E-mail: admissions@maconstate.edu
Phone: (478) 471-2800 Toll-free number: (800) 272-7619
Fax: (478) 471-5343
Dee Minter, Associate Vice President for Enrollment Services, Macon State College, 100 College Station Drive, Macon, GA 31206-5145

## Medical College of Georgia
**Augusta, Georgia** — **CB member**
www.mcg.edu — **CB code: 5406**

- Public two-year upper-division health science college
- Commuter campus in large city
- 41% of applicants admitted
- Test scores, application essay required

**General.** Founded in 1828. Regionally accredited. **Degrees:** 281 bachelor's awarded; master's, professional offered. **Location:** 157 miles from Atlanta. **Calendar:** Semester. **Full-time faculty:** 688 total; 88% have terminal degrees, 30% minority, 36% women. **Part-time faculty:** 143 total; 87% have terminal degrees, 17% minority, 44% women. **Special facilities:** 600-bed teaching hospital, over 80 clinics.

**Student profile.** 533 degree-seeking undergraduates, 1,971 degree-seeking graduate students. 744 applied as first time-transfer students, 302 admitted, 251 enrolled.

| | | | |
|---|---|---|---|
| Women: | 87% | Out-of-state: | 10% |
| Part-time: | 6% | 25 or older: | 31% |

**Basis for selection.** College transcript, application essay, standardized test scores required. Admission based on GPA, math and science test scores, 3 references, and statement of purpose. SAT/ACT and personal interview required. 60 semester hours of transferable prescribed liberal arts courses required. Closing dates and score reports vary by program. Transfer accepted as juniors.

**2009-2010 Annual costs.** Tuition/fees: $6,782; $24,992 out-of-state. Declining balance account available for meals. Room only: $1,912.

**Financial aid. Non-need-based:** Scholarships awarded for academics, state residency. **Additional information:** State Hope scholarships only available to Georgia residents.

**Application procedures. Admission:** Rolling admission. $30 fee. **Financial aid:** Priority date 3/31, closing date 5/30. Applicants notified on a rolling basis; must reply within 2 weeks of notification. FAFSA, institutional form required.

**Academics. Special study options:** Combined bachelor's/graduate degree, distance learning, internships, liberal arts/career combination, study abroad. Cooperative program with Augusta State University. **Credit/placement by examination:** AP, CLEP.

**Majors. Health:** Clinical lab science, dental hygiene, medical radiologic technology/radiation therapy, medical records admin, nursing (RN), physician assistant, preop/surgical nursing, respiratory therapy technology, sonography.

**Computing on campus.** 323 workstations in library, student center. Commuter students can connect to campus network. Online library, wireless network available.

**Student life. Housing:** Coed dorms, apartments, wellness housing available. **Activities:** Student government, student newspaper, Christian Medical Society, Black Student Medical Alliance.

**Athletics. Intramural:** Badminton, basketball, football (non-tackle), golf, racquetball, soccer, softball, table tennis, volleyball, weight lifting.

**Student services.** Career counseling, student employment services, health services, minority student services, on-campus daycare, personal counseling.

**Contact.** E-mail: underadm@mcg.edu
Phone: (706) 721-2725 Toll-free number: (800) 519-3388
Fax: (706) 721-7279
Beverly Boggs, Executive Director of Academic Admissions & Student Financial Aid, Medical College of Georgia, Office of Academic Admissions, Room 170 Kelly Building, Augusta, GA 30912-7310

## Mercer University
**Macon, Georgia** — **CB member**
www.mercer.edu — **CB code: 5409**

- Private 4-year university affiliated with Baptist faith
- Residential campus in small city
- 2,295 degree-seeking undergraduates: 2% part-time, 53% women, 16% African American, 6% Asian American, 3% Hispanic American, 3% international
- 3,474 degree-seeking graduate students
- 62% of applicants admitted
- SAT or ACT (ACT writing optional) required
- 64% graduate within 6 years; 23% enter graduate study

**General.** Founded in 1833. Regionally accredited. Evening and weekend continuing education programs available at 4 regional academic centers and transfer degree programs offered at Atlanta campus. **Degrees:** 415 bachelor's awarded; master's, doctoral, professional offered. **ROTC:** Army. **Location:** 85 miles from Atlanta. **Calendar:** Semester, extensive summer session. **Full-time faculty:** 370 total; 88% have terminal degrees, 19% minority, 45% women. **Part-time faculty:** 264 total; 43% have terminal degrees, 21% minority, 50% women. **Class size:** 53% < 20, 41% 20-39, 3% 40-49, 3% 50-99.

**Freshman class profile.** 4,877 applied, 3,034 admitted, 616 enrolled.

| Mid 50% test scores | | Rank in top quarter: | 73% |
|---|---|---|---|
| SAT critical reading: | 540-630 | Rank in top tenth: | 43% |
| SAT math: | 550-640 | End year in good standing: | 87% |
| SAT writing: | 510-620 | Return as sophomores: | 85% |
| ACT composite: | 24-31 | Out-of-state: | 18% |
| GPA 3.75 or higher: | 46% | Live on campus: | 92% |
| GPA 3.50-3.74: | 28% | International: | 2% |
| GPA 3.0-3.49: | 22% | Fraternities: | 20% |
| GPA 2.0-2.99: | 4% | Sororities: | 19% |

**Basis for selection.** GED not accepted. Admissions based on academic merit. GPA, SAT and extracurricular activities important. Interview recommended. Audition recommended for music majors. **Homeschooled:** Interview required. 1100 SAT (exclusive of Writing) and certified transcript indicating college-preparatory curriculum including titles of textbooks required. SAT Subject Tests or AP exams may be substituted for certified transcript. **Learning Disabled:** Documentation from licensed professional required.

**High school preparation.** College-preparatory program required. 16 units required. Required units include English 4, mathematics 4, social studies 1, history 2, science 3 and foreign language 2.

**2009-2010 Annual costs.** Tuition/fees: $29,540. Room/board: $8,788. Books/supplies: $1,200. Personal expenses: $1,201.

**2009-2010 Financial aid. Need-based:** 542 full-time freshmen applied for aid; 475 were judged to have need; 474 of these received aid. Average need met was 88%. Average scholarship/grant was $21,619; average loan $6,956. 75% of total undergraduate aid awarded as scholarships/grants, 25% as loans/jobs. **Non-need-based:** Awarded to 1,202 full-time undergraduates, including 328 freshmen. Scholarships awarded for academics, art, athletics, job skills, leadership, music/drama, religious affiliation, ROTC, state residency.

**Application procedures. Admission:** Priority date 4/1; deadline 7/1 (postmark date). $50 fee, may be waived for applicants with need, free for online applicants. Admission notification on a rolling basis beginning on or about 9/1. Must reply by May 1 or within 4 week(s) if notified thereafter. **Financial aid:** Priority date 4/1; no closing date. FAFSA, institutional form required. Applicants notified on a rolling basis starting 3/15; must reply within 2 week(s) of notification.

**Academics. Special study options:** Accelerated study, combined bachelor's/graduate degree, cooperative education, cross-registration, double major, dual enrollment of high school students, honors, independent study, internships, liberal arts/career combination, student-designed major, study abroad, teacher certification program. Students may satisfy general education requirements by completing either the Great Books Program or the Distributional Program. **Credit/placement by examination:** AP, CLEP, IB, SAT, ACT, institutional tests. 32 credit hours maximum toward bachelor's degree. **Support services:** Learning center, pre-admission summer program, reduced course load, study skills assistance, tutoring.

**Majors. Area/ethnic studies:** African, African-American, regional, women's. **Biology:** General, biochemistry. **Business:** General. **Communications:** General, journalism, media studies. **Computer sciences:** Computer science, information systems. **Conservation:** Environmental science, environmental studies. **Education:** Elementary, middle, music. **Engineering:** General. **Foreign languages:** Classics, French, German, Latin, Spanish. **Health:** Nursing (RN), predental, premedicine, prepharmacy. **History:** General. **Liberal arts:** Arts/sciences. **Math:** General. **Philosophy/religion:** Christian, philosophy. **Physical sciences:** Chemistry, physics. **Protective services:** Criminal justice. **Psychology:** General. **Public administration:** Community org/advocacy. **Social sciences:** Economics, international relations, political science, sociology. **Visual/performing arts:** Art, dramatic, music performance. **Other:** Computational science, Technical communications.

**Most popular majors.** Biology 10%, business/marketing 24%, communications/journalism 10%, engineering/engineering technologies 9%, psychology 7%, social sciences 11%.

**Computing on campus.** Dormitories wired for high-speed internet access and linked to campus network. Commuter students can connect to campus network. Online course registration, online library, helpline, repair service, wireless network available.

**Student life. Freshman orientation:** Mandatory. Preregistration for classes offered. One-day summer orientation and 4-day program in fall before semester begins. **Policies:** Alcohol not permitted on campus. **Housing:** Guaranteed on-campus for freshmen. Coed dorms, single-sex dorms, special housing for disabled, apartments, fraternity/sorority housing available. **Activities:** Bands, campus ministries, choral groups, dance, drama, film society, international student organizations, literary magazine, music ensembles, musical theater, opera, radio station, student government, student newspaper, TV station, reformed university fellowship, Habitat for Humanity, Amnesty International, College Republicans, College Democrats, Engineers without Borders, housing center, Indian cultural exchange, organization of black students, students for environmental action.

**Athletics. NCAA. Intercollegiate:** Baseball M, basketball, cross-country, golf, lacrosse, rifle M, soccer, softball W, tennis, volleyball W. **Intramural:** Basketball, football (non-tackle), soccer, softball, tennis, volleyball. **Team name:** Bears.

**Student services.** Adult student services, alcohol/substance abuse counseling, chaplain/spiritual director, career counseling, services for economically disadvantaged, student employment services, financial aid counseling, health services, minority student services, personal counseling, placement for graduates. **Physically disabled:** Services for visually, speech, hearing impaired.

**Contact.** E-mail: admissions@mercer.edu
Phone: (478) 301-2650 Toll-free number: (800) 840-8577
Fax: (478) 301-2828
Brian Dalton, Senior Vice President, Enrollment Services, Mercer University, 1400 Coleman Avenue, Macon, GA 31207-0001

---

## Morehouse College

Atlanta, Georgia  **CB member**
www.morehouse.edu  **CB code: 5415**

- Private 4-year liberal arts college for men
- Residential campus in very large city
- 2,673 degree-seeking undergraduates: 6% part-time, 95% African American, 3% international
- 67% of applicants admitted
- SAT or ACT (ACT writing recommended), application essay required
- 58% graduate within 6 years

**General.** Founded in 1867. Regionally accredited. One of 4 members of Atlanta University Center sharing facilities including library. **Degrees:** 490 bachelor's awarded. **ROTC:** Army, Naval, Air Force. **Location:** 3 miles from downtown. **Calendar:** Semester, limited summer session. **Full-time faculty:** 158 total; 63% have terminal degrees, 78% minority, 37% women. **Part-time faculty:** 55 total. **Special facilities:** Chapels, meditation room.

**Freshman class profile.** 2,352 applied, 1,584 admitted, 642 enrolled.

| Mid 50% test scores | | |
|---|---|---|
| SAT critical reading: | 460-570 | |
| SAT math: | 470-580 | |
| SAT writing: | 450-560 | |
| ACT composite: | 19-25 | |
| GPA 3.75 or higher: | 22% | |
| GPA 3.50-3.74: | 12% | |
| GPA 3.0-3.49: | 41% | |

| | |
|---|---|
| GPA 2.0-2.99: | 25% |
| Rank in top quarter: | 10% |
| Rank in top tenth: | 2% |
| End year in good standing: | 88% |
| Return as sophomores: | 81% |
| Out-of-state: | 55% |
| International: | 2% |

**Basis for selection.** Academic record most important, followed by test scores, counselor recommendation(s), school and community activities, and student leadership. Interview recommended.

**High school preparation.** College-preparatory program recommended. 13 units required; 16 recommended. Required and recommended units include English 4, mathematics 3, social studies 2, science 2, foreign language 2 and academic electives 3.

**2010-2011 Annual costs.** Tuition/fees: $22,444. Room/board: $11,494. Books/supplies: $2,000. Personal expenses: $2,500.

**2008-2009 Financial aid. Need-based:** 685 full-time freshmen applied for aid; 653 were judged to have need; 653 of these received aid. Average need met was 25%. Average scholarship/grant was $9,250; average loan $3,500. 25% of total undergraduate aid awarded as scholarships/grants, 75% as loans/jobs. **Non-need-based:** Awarded to 560 full-time undergraduates, including 170 freshmen. Scholarships awarded for academics, alumni affiliation, art, athletics, leadership, music/drama, ROTC, state residency.

**Application procedures. Admission:** Priority date 11/1; deadline 2/15 (postmark date). $45 fee, may be waived for applicants with need. Application must be submitted on paper. Admission notification 4/1. Must reply by 5/1. $525 acceptance fee must be paid by 6/1; applied toward first semester tuition. **Financial aid:** Priority date 2/15, closing date 4/1. FAFSA, institutional form, CSS PROFILE required. Must reply by 5/1 or within 4 week(s) of notification.

**Academics. Special study options:** Combined bachelor's/graduate degree, cooperative education, cross-registration, double major, dual enrollment of high school students, exchange student, honors, internships, liberal arts/career combination, semester at sea, study abroad. Dual degree program in engineering and architecture with other institutions. **Credit/placement by examination:** AP, CLEP, SAT, ACT, institutional tests. 30 credit hours maximum toward bachelor's degree. **Support services:** Learning center, pre-admission summer program, reduced course load, remedial instruction, study skills assistance, tutoring, writing center.

**Majors. Area/ethnic studies:** African-American. **Biology:** General. **Business:** Business admin. **Computer sciences:** General. **Education:** General. **Engineering:** General. **Foreign languages:** Spanish. **History:** General. **Math:** General. **Parks/recreation:** Exercise sciences, health/fitness. **Philosophy/religion:** Philosophy, religion. **Physical sciences:** Applied physics, chemistry, physics. **Psychology:** General. **Social sciences:** Economics, international relations, political science, sociology, urban studies. **Visual/performing arts:** Art, dramatic. **Other:** General Science.

**Most popular majors.** Business/marketing 35%, English 7%, psychology 8%, social sciences 19%.

**Computing on campus.** 300 workstations in dormitories, library, computer center. Dormitories wired for high-speed internet access and linked to campus network. Commuter students can connect to campus network. Online course registration, online library, helpline, repair service, wireless network available.

**Student life. Freshman orientation:** Mandatory, $480 fee. Preregistration for classes offered. Held several days before class begins each fall. **Housing:** Guaranteed on-campus for freshmen. Apartments, wellness housing available. **Activities:** Bands, choral groups, drama, international student organizations, literary magazine, music ensembles, student government, student newspaper, Martin Luther King International Chapel Assistants, mentoring program, Frederick Douglass Tutorial Program, political science club, New Life Inspirational Gospel Choir, NAACP, Eagle Scout Association.

**Athletics. NCAA. Intercollegiate:** Baseball M, basketball M, cross-country M, football (tackle) M, golf M, tennis M, track and field M. **Intramural:** Baseball M, basketball M, football (non-tackle) M, soccer M, softball M, swimming M, table tennis M, tennis M, weight lifting M. **Team name:** Maroon Tigers.

**Student services.** Alcohol/substance abuse counseling, chaplain/spiritual director, career counseling, student employment services, financial aid counseling, health services, personal counseling, placement for graduates, veterans' counselor. **Physically disabled:** Services for visually, speech, hearing impaired.

**Contact.** E-mail: admissions@morehouse.edu
Phone: (404) 681-2800 ext. 2632 Toll-free number: (800) 851-1254
Fax: (404) 524-5635
Danny Bellinger, Associate Dean of Admissions and Recruitment, Morehouse College, 830 Westview Drive SW, Atlanta, GA 30314

## North Georgia College & State University
**Dahlonega, Georgia**　　　　　　　　　　**CB member**
**www.northgeorgia.edu**　　　　　　　　　**CB code: 5497**

- Public 4-year university and military college
- Commuter campus in small town
- 5,014 degree-seeking undergraduates: 18% part-time, 57% women, 2% African American, 1% Asian American, 4% Hispanic American, 1% international
- 392 degree-seeking graduate students
- 54% of applicants admitted
- SAT or ACT (ACT writing optional) required
- 58% graduate within 6 years

**General.** Founded in 1873. Regionally accredited. **Degrees:** 770 bachelor's, 115 associate awarded; master's, professional offered. **ROTC:** Army. **Location:** 70 miles from Atlanta. **Calendar:** Semester, extensive summer session. **Full-time faculty:** 218 total; 10% minority, 54% women. **Part-time faculty:** 121 total; 2% minority, 68% women. **Class size:** 35% < 20, 54% 20-39, 7% 40-49, 3% 50-99, less than 1% >100. **Special facilities:** Observatory, rappeling tower, planetarium, nature preserve.

**Freshman class profile.** 2,993 applied, 1,620 admitted, 822 enrolled.

| Mid 50% test scores | | | |
|---|---|---|---|
| SAT critical reading: | 510-590 | GPA 3.0-3.49: | 36% |
| SAT math: | 500-590 | GPA 2.0-2.99: | 13% |
| ACT composite: | 21-25 | Return as sophomores: | 77% |
| GPA 3.75 or higher: | 28% | Out-of-state: | 5% |
| GPA 3.50-3.74: | 23% | Live on campus: | 70% |
| | | International: | 1% |

**Basis for selection.** High school academic record, test scores important, disciplinary record considered. Students must provide certification of immunization against communicable diseases. Commuting students must apply for permission to commute. Audition recommended for music majors. Portfolio recommended for art majors. **Homeschooled:** SAT Subject Tests required.

**High school preparation.** College-preparatory program required. 17 units required. Required units include English 4, mathematics 4, social studies 3, science 3 (laboratory 1) and foreign language 2.

**2009-2010 Annual costs.** Tuition/fees: $5,036; $16,650 out-of-state. Room/board: $5,544. Books/supplies: $500. Personal expenses: $1,000.

**2008-2009 Financial aid. Non-need-based:** Scholarships awarded for academics, alumni affiliation, art, athletics, job skills, leadership, minority status, music/drama, religious affiliation, ROTC, state residency.

**Application procedures. Admission:** Closing date 7/1. $30 fee, may be waived for applicants with need. Admission notification on a rolling basis. **Financial aid:** Priority date 3/17; no closing date. FAFSA required. Applicants notified on a rolling basis starting 3/1; must reply within 3 week(s) of notification.

**Academics. Special study options:** Combined bachelor's/graduate degree, cooperative education, distance learning, double major, dual enrollment of high school students, external degree, honors, independent study, internships, liberal arts/career combination, study abroad, teacher certification program. Dual degree program in engineering with Georgia Institute of Technology and Clemson University. **Credit/placement by examination:** AP, CLEP, SAT, ACT, institutional tests. 30 credit hours maximum toward associate degree, 30 toward bachelor's. **Support services:** Learning center, pre-admission summer program, reduced course load, remedial instruction, study skills assistance, tutoring, writing center.

**Majors. Biology:** General. **Business:** Accounting, business admin, finance, marketing. **Computer sciences:** General. **Education:** Art, early childhood, middle, music, physical, special. **Foreign languages:** French, German, Spanish. **Health:** Athletic training, nursing (RN). **History:** General. **Math:** General. **Parks/recreation:** Health/fitness. **Physical sciences:** Chemistry, physics. **Protective services:** Law enforcement admin. **Psychology:** General. **Social sciences:** International relations, political science, sociology.

**Most popular majors.** Biology 6%, business/marketing 26%, education 22%, health sciences 6%, history 6%, psychology 6%, security/protective services 7%, social sciences 10%.

**Computing on campus.** 850 workstations in dormitories, library, computer center, student center. Dormitories linked to campus network. Commuter students can connect to campus network. Online course registration, online library, helpline, repair service, student web hosting, wireless network available.

**Student life. Freshman orientation:** Available. Preregistration for classes offered. Two and 1/2-day program held 4 times during June, July, August; students stay in residence halls. **Housing:** Coed dorms, single-sex dorms, apartments available. $250 fully refundable deposit, deadline 5/1. **Activities:** Bands, campus ministries, choral groups, dance, drama, international student organizations, literary magazine, music ensembles, Model UN, student government, student newspaper, TV station, Students for Social Awareness, Baptist student union, commuter council, Muslim student association, Newman Club, Habitat for Humanity.

**Athletics.** NCAA. **Intercollegiate:** Baseball M, basketball, cheerleading M, cross-country, rifle, soccer, softball W, tennis, track and field. **Intramural:** Basketball, football (non-tackle) W, football (tackle) M, golf, softball W, table tennis, volleyball, water polo. **Team name:** Saints.

**Student services.** Alcohol/substance abuse counseling, career counseling, student employment services, financial aid counseling, health services, minority student services, personal counseling, placement for graduates, veterans' counselor. **Physically disabled:** Services for visually, hearing impaired.

**Contact.** E-mail: admissions@northgeorgia.edu
Phone: (706) 864-1800 Toll-free number: (800) 498-9581
Fax: (706) 864-1478
Jennifer Chadwick, Director of Admissions, North Georgia College & State University, 82 College Circle, Dahlonega, GA 30597

## Oglethorpe University
**Atlanta, Georgia**　　　　　　　　　　　**CB member**
**www.oglethorpe.edu**　　　　　　　　　　**CB code: 5521**

- Private 4-year liberal arts college
- Residential campus in very large city
- 974 degree-seeking undergraduates: 9% part-time, 60% women, 23% African American, 4% Asian American, 5% Hispanic American, 3% international
- 69 degree-seeking graduate students
- 42% of applicants admitted
- SAT or ACT (ACT writing recommended) required
- 56% graduate within 6 years

**General.** Founded in 1835. Regionally accredited. Professional Shakespeare repertory theater on campus, integrated with theater program. **Degrees:** 196 bachelor's awarded; master's offered. **ROTC:** Air Force. **Location:** 10 miles from downtown. **Calendar:** Semester, extensive summer session. **Full-time faculty:** 61 total; 94% have terminal degrees, 11% minority, 35% women. **Part-time faculty:** 53 total; 47% have terminal degrees, 11% minority, 51% women. **Class size:** 73% < 20, 27% 20-39. **Special facilities:** Art museum, performing arts center.

**Freshman class profile.** 4,891 applied, 2,040 admitted, 230 enrolled.

| Mid 50% test scores | | | |
|---|---|---|---|
| | | GPA 2.0-2.99: | 13% |
| SAT critical reading: | 550-650 | Rank in top quarter: | 63% |
| SAT math: | 510-630 | Rank in top tenth: | 24% |
| SAT writing: | 510-620 | Return as sophomores: | 75% |
| ACT composite: | 23-27 | Out-of-state: | 27% |
| GPA 3.75 or higher: | 43% | Live on campus: | 87% |
| GPA 3.50-3.74: | 15% | International: | 2% |
| GPA 3.0-3.49: | 29% | | |

**Basis for selection.** High school GPA and general academic record most important, followed by test scores. Recommendations required. Activities considered. Interview recommended.

**High school preparation.** College-preparatory program recommended. Required and recommended units include English 4, mathematics 3, social studies 3, science 2 and foreign language 2. Honors, AP, IB recommended where available.

**2010-2011 Annual costs.** Tuition/fees: $27,950. Room/board: $9,990. Books/supplies: $900. Personal expenses: $2,000.

**2009-2010 Financial aid. Non-need-based:** Scholarships awarded for academics, music/drama.

**Application procedures. Admission:** No deadline. $40 fee, may be waived for applicants with need. Admission notification on a rolling basis beginning on or about 12/1. Must reply by May 1 or within 3 week(s) if notified thereafter. **Financial aid:** Priority date 2/1; no closing date. FAFSA, institutional form required. Applicants notified on a rolling basis starting 3/1; must reply by 5/1 or within 3 week(s) of notification.

**Academics. Special study options:** Accelerated study, cooperative education, cross-registration, double major, dual enrollment of high school students, honors, independent study, internships, liberal arts/career combination, student-designed major, study abroad. Dual engineering degree program with Auburn University, Georgia Institute of Technology, University of Florida, Auburn University, Mercer University, and University of Southern California; dual degree program in environmental studies with the Nicholas School of the Environment at Duke University; international partner degree program with the Université Catholique de Lille in France. **Credit/placement by examination:** AP, CLEP, IB, institutional tests. 32 credit hours maximum toward bachelor's degree. **Support services:** Learning center, tutoring, writing center.

**Majors. Area/ethnic studies:** American. **Biology:** General. **Business:** Accounting, business admin, managerial economics, organizational behavior, training/development. **Communications:** General. **Foreign languages:** French, Japanese, Spanish. **Health:** Predental, premedicine, prepharmacy, preveterinary. **History:** General. **Interdisciplinary:** Biopsychology. **Legal studies:** Prelaw. **Liberal arts:** Arts/sciences. **Math:** General. **Philosophy/religion:** Philosophy. **Physical sciences:** Chemistry, physics. **Psychology:** General. **Public administration:** Social work. **Social sciences:** Economics, international relations, political science, sociology. **Visual/performing arts:** Art, art history/conservation, studio arts, theater history.

**Most popular majors.** Business/marketing 23%, English 16%, history 6%, psychology 18%, social sciences 11%.

**Computing on campus.** 64 workstations in library, computer center. Dormitories wired for high-speed internet access and linked to campus network. Commuter students can connect to campus network. Helpline, wireless network available.

**Student life. Freshman orientation:** Available. Preregistration for classes offered. **Housing:** Guaranteed on-campus for freshmen. Coed dorms, fraternity/sorority housing available. $200 fully refundable deposit, deadline 5/1. **Activities:** Pep band, campus ministries, choral groups, dance, drama, international student organizations, literary magazine, music ensembles, musical theater, radio station, student government, student newspaper, Catholic student association, black student caucus, Christian fellowship, environmentally concerned students, Jewish student union, Students Against Homophobia, APO service organization, Circle K.

**Athletics.** NCAA. **Intercollegiate:** Baseball M, basketball, cross-country, golf, soccer, tennis, track and field, volleyball W. **Intramural:** Badminton, basketball, softball, tennis, volleyball. **Team name:** Stormy Petrels.

**Student services.** Adult student services, career counseling, financial aid counseling, health services, personal counseling. **Physically disabled:** Services for visually, speech, hearing impaired.

**Contact.** E-mail: admission@oglethorpe.edu
Phone: (404) 364-8307 Toll-free number: (800) 428-4484
Fax: (404) 364-8491
Lucy Leusch, Vice President for Enrollment and Financial Aid, Oglethorpe University, 4484 Peachtree Road NE, Atlanta, GA 30319-2797

## Paine College
**Augusta, Georgia**
**www.paine.edu**
**CB member**
**CB code: 5530**

- Private 4-year liberal arts college affiliated with Christian Methodist Episcopal Church and United Methodist Church
- Residential campus in large city
- 901 degree-seeking undergraduates: 5% part-time, 65% women
- 39% of applicants admitted
- SAT or ACT (ACT writing optional), application essay required

**General.** Founded in 1882. Regionally accredited. **Degrees:** 76 bachelor's awarded. **ROTC:** Army. **Location:** 72 miles from Columbia, SC; 150 miles from Atlanta. **Calendar:** Semester, limited summer session. **Full-time faculty:** 58 total; 64% have terminal degrees, 76% minority, 36% women. **Part-time faculty:** 20 total; 20% have terminal degrees, 90% minority, 75% women. **Class size:** 62% < 20, 38% 20-39.

**Freshman class profile.** 3,424 applied, 1,331 admitted, 274 enrolled.

| Mid 50% test scores | | | |
|---|---|---|---|
| SAT critical reading: | 350-440 | GPA 3.0-3.49: | 31% |
| SAT math: | 350-440 | GPA 2.0-2.99: | 48% |
| ACT composite: | 14-18 | Return as sophomores: | 57% |
| GPA 3.75 or higher: | 3% | Out-of-state: | 29% |
| GPA 3.50-3.74: | 8% | Live on campus: | 90% |

**Basis for selection.** School achievement record, test scores, and recommendations considered. 2.0 GPA required. Two letters of recommendation required. Essay must be typed. Interview recommended. **Learning Disabled:** Contact the Office of Disability Services to register with them and arrange an appointment.

**High school preparation.** College-preparatory program recommended. 16 units recommended. Recommended units include English 4, mathematics 3, social studies 2, history 1, science 3 (laboratory 2) and academic electives 3.

**2009-2010 Annual costs.** Tuition/fees: $11,794. Room/board: $5,748. Books/supplies: $800. Personal expenses: $1,940.

**2009-2010 Financial aid. Need-based:** 277 full-time freshmen applied for aid; 264 were judged to have need; 262 of these received aid. Average need met was 54%. Average scholarship/grant was $7,054; average loan $3,342. 44% of total undergraduate aid awarded as scholarships/grants, 56% as loans/jobs. **Non-need-based:** Awarded to 57 full-time undergraduates, including 21 freshmen. Scholarships awarded for academics, alumni affiliation, athletics, music/drama, religious affiliation, ROTC.

**Application procedures. Admission:** Closing date 8/1 (receipt date). $25 fee, may be waived for applicants with need. Admission notification on a rolling basis. **Financial aid:** Priority date 3/1; no closing date. FAFSA required. Applicants notified on a rolling basis starting 5/1; must reply within 2 week(s) of notification.

**Academics. Special study options:** Combined bachelor's/graduate degree, cooperative education, cross-registration, distance learning, dual enrollment of high school students, honors, independent study, internships, liberal arts/career combination, study abroad, teacher certification program. Dual degree in engineering and mathematics with Florida A & M University, Tuskegee University, Tennessee State University. **Credit/placement by examination:** AP, CLEP, SAT, ACT, institutional tests. **Support services:** Learning center, reduced course load, remedial instruction, study skills assistance, tutoring.

**Majors. Biology:** General. **Business:** Accounting, business admin, international, management information systems, marketing. **Communications:** Broadcast journalism, journalism, public relations. **Conservation:** Environmental science. **Education:** Biology, elementary, English, history, mathematics, middle. **History:** General. **Interdisciplinary:** Math/computer science. **Math:** General. **Philosophy/religion:** Philosophy, religion. **Physical sciences:** Chemistry. **Psychology:** General, counseling, experimental, social. **Social sciences:** Criminology, sociology. **Visual/performing arts:** Dramatic.

**Most popular majors.** Biology 7%, business/marketing 13%, communications/journalism 11%, education 9%, English 8%, psychology 24%, social sciences 18%.

**Computing on campus.** 225 workstations in dormitories, library, computer center, student center. Dormitories wired for high-speed internet access and linked to campus network. Commuter students can connect to campus network. Online course registration, online library, helpline, repair service, wireless network available.

**Student life. Freshman orientation:** Mandatory, $117 fee. Preregistration for classes offered. Pre-testing and orientation held 1 week at beginning of semester. **Housing:** Single-sex dorms, wellness housing available. $75 nonrefundable deposit, deadline 8/1. **Activities:** Campus ministries, choral groups, dance, drama, international student organizations, literary magazine, music ensembles, student government, student newspaper, NAACP, pre-alumni club, National Pan Hellenic Council, Wesley Fellowship.

**Athletics.** NCAA. **Intercollegiate:** Baseball M, basketball, cross-country, golf M, softball W, track and field, volleyball W. **Intramural:** Badminton, baseball M, basketball, cross-country, football (non-tackle) M, softball, table tennis, tennis, track and field, volleyball, weight lifting. **Team name:** Lions.

**Student services.** Alcohol/substance abuse counseling, chaplain/spiritual director, career counseling, student employment services, financial aid counseling, health services, personal counseling, placement for graduates, veterans' counselor.

**Contact.** E-mail: jtinsley@paine.edu
Phone: (706) 821-8320 Toll-free number: (800) 476-7703
Fax: (706) 821-8648
Joseph Tinsley, Director of Admissions, Paine College, 1235 15th Street, Augusta, GA 30901-3182

## Piedmont College
**Demorest, Georgia**      **CB member**
**www.piedmont.edu**      **CB code: 5537**

- Private 4-year liberal arts and teachers college affiliated with United Church of Christ
- Commuter campus in rural community
- 1,232 degree-seeking undergraduates: 9% part-time, 70% women, 10% African American, 1% Asian American, 2% Hispanic American
- 1,543 degree-seeking graduate students
- 60% of applicants admitted
- SAT or ACT required
- 40% graduate within 6 years

**General.** Founded in 1897. Regionally accredited. **Degrees:** 230 bachelor's awarded; master's, doctoral offered. **Location:** 30 miles from Gainesville, 75 miles from Atlanta. **Calendar:** Semester, limited summer session. **Full-time faculty:** 111 total. **Part-time faculty:** 157 total. **Class size:** 73% < 20, 27% 20-39, less than 1% >100. **Special facilities:** Performing arts and communication center, pipe organ, worship and music center, botanical center.

**Freshman class profile.** 1,321 applied, 788 admitted, 239 enrolled.

| Mid 50% test scores | | | |
|---|---|---|---|
| SAT critical reading: | 450-540 | GPA 3.0-3.49: | 39% |
| SAT math: | 430-550 | GPA 2.0-2.99: | 12% |
| ACT composite: | 18-23 | Rank in top quarter: | 41% |
| GPA 3.75 or higher: | 16% | Rank in top tenth: | 14% |
| GPA 3.50-3.74: | 32% | Return as sophomores: | 74% |
| | | Live on campus: | 74% |

**Basis for selection.** Test scores and GPA most important. Essay recommended. Interview recommended for academically weak. **Homeschooled:** Interview, letter of recommendation (nonparent) required. Transcript or portfolio detailing high school coursework completed, 2 letters of recommendation from sources outside home who have knowledge of student's academic/extracurricular achievements required. Interview with student and family may be required.

**High school preparation.** College-preparatory program recommended. 21 units recommended. Recommended units include English 4, mathematics 3, social studies 1, history 2, science 3 and foreign language 2.

**2010-2011 Annual costs.** Tuition/fees: $18,000. Room/board: $6,000. Books/supplies: $1,500. Personal expenses: $2,350.

**2009-2010 Financial aid.** **Need-based:** 183 full-time freshmen applied for aid; 151 were judged to have need; 143 of these received aid. Average need met was 62%. Average scholarship/grant was $1,024; average loan $3,546. 39% of total undergraduate aid awarded as scholarships/grants, 61% as loans/jobs. **Non-need-based:** Awarded to 788 full-time undergraduates, including 195 freshmen. Scholarships awarded for academics, art, leadership, music/drama, religious affiliation, state residency. **Additional information:** College meets 100% of unmet direct financial need for early applicants through grants, scholarships, and loan programs.

**Application procedures.** **Admission:** Closing date 7/1. No application fee. **Financial aid:** Priority date 5/1; no closing date. FAFSA, institutional form required. Applicants notified on a rolling basis; must reply within 2 week(s) of notification.

**Academics.** Experiential learning credit allows students to document work experience for college credit as appropriate. **Special study options:** Accelerated study, combined bachelor's/graduate degree, distance learning, double major, dual enrollment of high school students, honors, independent study, internships, student-designed major, study abroad, teacher certification program. **Credit/placement by examination:** AP, CLEP. 30 credit hours maximum toward bachelor's degree. **Support services:** Study skills assistance, tutoring.

**Majors. Biology:** General. **Business:** Business admin. **Communications:** Media studies. **Conservation:** Environmental science. **Education:** Biology,

chemistry, drama/dance, early childhood, English, history, middle, secondary, special. **Foreign languages:** Spanish. **Health:** Nursing (RN). **History:** General. **Interdisciplinary:** Math/computer science. **Math:** General. **Philosophy/religion:** Philosophy, religion. **Physical sciences:** Chemistry. **Protective services:** Criminal justice. **Psychology:** General. **Social sciences:** General, political science, sociology. **Visual/performing arts:** Art, dramatic, studio arts.

**Most popular majors.** Business/marketing 27%, education 33%, psychology 7%, social sciences 6%, visual/performing arts 6%.

**Computing on campus.** 240 workstations in dormitories, library, computer center, student center. Dormitories wired for high-speed internet access and linked to campus network. Commuter students can connect to campus network. Online library, wireless network available.

**Student life.** **Freshman orientation:** Mandatory. Preregistration for classes offered. Three-day weekend with activities for students, resident assistants, faculty and staff. **Policies:** Unmarried students under 21 must live in dormitories or with blood relatives. **Housing:** Guaranteed on-campus for all undergraduates. Coed dorms, single-sex dorms, special housing for disabled, apartments, wellness housing available. $100 deposit. **Activities:** Campus ministries, choral groups, drama, film society, literary magazine, music ensembles, radio station, student government, student newspaper, symphony orchestra, TV station, psychology club, Fellowhip of Christian Athletes, Green Giants, Student Association of Educators, literary society, science club, environmental club, Rotaract, history society.

**Athletics.** NCAA. **Intercollegiate:** Baseball M, basketball, cross-country, golf, soccer, softball W, tennis, volleyball W. **Intramural:** Basketball, football (non-tackle), soccer, softball, table tennis, volleyball. **Team name:** Lions.

**Student services.** Chaplain/spiritual director, career counseling, financial aid counseling, health services, personal counseling, placement for graduates, veterans' counselor.

**Contact.** E-mail: ugrad@piedmont.edu
Phone: (706) 776-0103 Toll-free number: (800) 277-7020
Fax: (706) 776-6635
Cynthia Peterson, Director of Admissions, Piedmont College, 165 Central Avenue, Demorest, GA 30535-0010

## Reinhardt College
**Waleska, Georgia**      **CB member**
**www.reinhardt.edu**      **CB code: 5568**

- Private 4-year business and teachers college affiliated with United Methodist Church
- Commuter campus in rural community
- 1,026 degree-seeking undergraduates: 7% part-time, 61% women, 9% African American, 1% Asian American, 5% Hispanic American
- 67 graduate students
- 68% of applicants admitted
- SAT or ACT (ACT writing optional) required
- 42% graduate within 6 years

**General.** Founded in 1883. Regionally accredited. Off-campus center in Alpharetta. **Degrees:** 164 bachelor's, 9 associate awarded; master's offered. **Location:** 50 miles from Atlanta. **Calendar:** Semester, extensive summer session. **Full-time faculty:** 60 total; 78% have terminal degrees, 12% minority, 50% women. **Part-time faculty:** 100 total; 24% have terminal degrees, 4% minority, 49% women. **Class size:** 81% < 20, 18% 20-39, less than 1% 40-49, less than 1% 50-99. **Special facilities:** Indian history museum, visual arts center, performing arts center.

**Freshman class profile.** 1,191 applied, 810 admitted, 239 enrolled.

| Mid 50% test scores | | | |
|---|---|---|---|
| SAT critical reading: | 430-540 | ACT composite: | 17-23 |
| SAT math: | 410-530 | Return as sophomores: | 62% |

**Basis for selection.** School achievement record most important, followed by test scores, recommendations. Interview recommended. Audition required of music majors. Portfolio required of art majors. **Homeschooled:** Transcript of courses and grades, state high school equivalency certificate required. **Learning Disabled:** Recommend that students be counseled by Academic Support Office.

**High school preparation.** College-preparatory program recommended. 14 units required. Required and recommended units include English 4, mathematics 4, social studies 3, science 3 and foreign language 2.

**2009-2010 Annual costs.** Tuition/fees: $16,670. Room/board: $6,496. Books/supplies: $850. Personal expenses: $3,450.

**2008-2009 Financial aid. Need-based:** 196 full-time freshmen applied for aid; 157 were judged to have need; 157 of these received aid. Average need met was 58%. Average scholarship/grant was $9,375; average loan $2,782. 77% of total undergraduate aid awarded as scholarships/grants, 23% as loans/jobs. **Non-need-based:** Awarded to 196 full-time undergraduates, including 128 freshmen. Scholarships awarded for academics, art, athletics, leadership, music/drama, religious affiliation, state residency.

**Application procedures. Admission:** No deadline. $25 fee, may be waived for applicants with need. Admission notification on a rolling basis beginning on or about 9/1. **Financial aid:** Priority date 5/1; no closing date. FAFSA required. Applicants notified on a rolling basis starting 2/1; must reply within 2 week(s) of notification.

**Academics. Special study options:** Accelerated study, combined bachelor's/graduate degree, distance learning, double major, dual enrollment of high school students, external degree, honors, independent study, internships, study abroad, teacher certification program, weekend college. **Credit/placement by examination:** AP, CLEP, SAT, ACT, institutional tests. 15 credit hours maximum toward associate degree, 30 toward bachelor's. **Support services:** Learning center, pre-admission summer program, reduced course load, remedial instruction, study skills assistance, tutoring, writing center.

**Majors. Biology:** General. **Business:** General, accounting, business admin. **Communications:** General. **Computer sciences:** Information systems. **Education:** Biology, early childhood, elementary, English, middle, music, physical. **History:** General. **Liberal arts:** Arts/sciences. **Parks/recreation:** Sports admin. **Philosophy/religion:** Religion. **Psychology:** General. **Social sciences:** Sociology. **Visual/performing arts:** Studio arts.

**Most popular majors.** Biology 8%, business/marketing 32%, education 26%, liberal arts 6%, visual/performing arts 9%.

**Computing on campus.** 165 workstations in dormitories, library, computer center, student center. Dormitories wired for high-speed internet access and linked to campus network. Commuter students can connect to campus network. Online course registration, online library, helpline, student web hosting, wireless network available.

**Student life. Freshman orientation:** Mandatory, $35 fee. Preregistration for classes offered. One- or 2-day program. **Housing:** Guaranteed on-campus for freshmen. Coed dorms, single-sex dorms, special housing for disabled, apartments, wellness housing available. $200 fully refundable deposit, deadline 8/15. Honors house available. **Activities:** Bands, campus ministries, choral groups, drama, film society, international student organizations, music ensembles, student government, student newspaper, TV station, Baptist Collegiate Ministry, Wesley Fellowship, Reinhardt Athletes for Christ Everyday (RACE), Phi Theta Kappa, Circle-K International, Habitat for Humanity, Breast Cancer Awareness Committee.

**Athletics.** NAIA. **Intercollegiate:** Baseball M, basketball, cheerleading, cross-country, golf M, lacrosse, soccer, softball W, tennis. **Intramural:** Basketball, football (non-tackle), soccer, softball, volleyball. **Team name:** Eagles.

**Student services.** Adult student services, alcohol/substance abuse counseling, chaplain/spiritual director, career counseling, student employment services, financial aid counseling, health services, personal counseling, placement for graduates, veterans' counselor. **Physically disabled:** Services for visually, speech, hearing impaired.

**Contact.** E-mail: admissions@mail.reinhardt.edu
Phone: (770) 720-5526 Toll-free number: (877) 343-4273
Fax: (770) 720-5602
Julie Fleming, Director of Admissions, Reinhardt College, 7300 Reinhardt College Circle, Waleska, GA 30183-2981

## Savannah College of Art and Design
**Savannah, Georgia**
**www.scad.edu**

CB member
CB code: 5631

- Private 4-year visual arts and performing arts college
- Commuter campus in small city
- 8,056 degree-seeking undergraduates: 11% part-time, 60% women, 4% African American, 1% Asian American, 3% Hispanic American, 9% international
- 1,714 degree-seeking graduate students
- 68% of applicants admitted
- SAT or ACT (ACT writing recommended) required
- 66% graduate within 6 years

**General.** Founded in 1978. Regionally accredited. Additional location in Atlanta. eLearning program available. Extensive study abroad program in France at Lacoste School of the Arts. **Degrees:** 1,567 bachelor's awarded; master's offered. **ROTC:** Army. **Location:** 250 miles from Atlanta; 150 miles from Jacksonville, FL. **Calendar:** Quarter, limited summer session. **Full-time faculty:** 491 total; 72% have terminal degrees, 11% minority, 40% women. **Part-time faculty:** 167 total; 68% have terminal degrees, 13% minority, 46% women. **Class size:** 84% < 20, 16% 20-39. **Special facilities:** Art museums, 2 vintage diners, amphitheater, restored 1943 theater.

**Freshman class profile.** 8,108 applied, 5,503 admitted, 1,682 enrolled.

| Mid 50% test scores | | | |
|---|---|---|---|
| SAT critical reading: | 490-600 | GPA 3.0-3.49: | 32% |
| SAT math: | 470-590 | GPA 2.0-2.99: | 20% |
| SAT writing: | 470-580 | Return as sophomores: | 82% |
| ACT composite: | 20-26 | Out-of-state: | 79% |
| GPA 3.75 or higher: | 27% | Live on campus: | 87% |
| GPA 3.50-3.74: | 21% | International: | 8% |

**Basis for selection.** Entrance test scores, 3 letters of recommendation, and high school transcript required. 540 SAT math/23 ACT math required for architecture regular acceptance; provisional status may be granted with lower scores. Interview, portfolio recommended. Essay recommended for historic preservation, art history, and architectural history programs. Portfolio or audition required for scholarship consideration. **Homeschooled:** Statement describing homeschool structure and mission, transcript of courses and grades, state high school equivalency certificate required. **Learning Disabled:** Documentation of specific nature of disability required.

**High school preparation.** College-preparatory program recommended.

**2010-2011 Annual costs.** Tuition/fees: $29,570. Room/board: $11,750. Books/supplies: $2,400. Personal expenses: $1,560.

**2009-2010 Financial aid. Non-need-based:** Scholarships awarded for academics, art, athletics, music/drama. **Additional information:** Degree-seeking students may be awarded maximum of one scholarship from college, but may receive additional scholarships from other sources, as well as additional forms of financial aid. Scholarships based on academic achievement are awarded through admission office.

**Application procedures. Admission:** Priority date 2/15; deadline 8/1 (receipt date). $50 fee. Admission notification on a rolling basis. Students encouraged to apply early to gain priority for housing. **Financial aid:** Priority date 2/15; no closing date. FAFSA, institutional form required. Applicants notified on a rolling basis starting 6/1.

**Academics.** Strong fine arts foundation along with strong liberal arts curriculum. **Special study options:** Distance learning, double major, dual enrollment of high school students, ESL, independent study, internships, New York semester, study abroad, teacher certification program, Washington semester. Off-campus programs in Europe and other art centers. Cross registration available at SCAD-Atlanta through membership in ARCHE. Teacher certification in art and drama available through MA in Teaching program. **Credit/placement by examination:** AP, CLEP, IB, SAT, ACT. 15 credit hours maximum toward bachelor's degree. **Support services:** Learning center, pre-admission summer program, reduced course load, study skills assistance, tutoring, writing center.

**Majors. Agriculture:** Equestrian studies. **Architecture:** Architecture, history/criticism. **Communications:** Digital media. **Communications technology:** Animation/special effects, recording arts. **Computer sciences:** Game design. **Family/consumer sciences:** Apparel marketing. **Interdisciplinary:** Historic preservation. **Visual/performing arts:** Art history/conservation, cinematography, commercial/advertising art, dramatic, fashion design, fiber arts, graphic design, illustration, industrial design, interior design, metal/jewelry, painting, photography, printmaking, sculpture, theater design. **Other:** Furniture design.

**Most popular majors.** Architecture 6%, communication technologies 19%, visual/performing arts 70%.

**Computing on campus.** 2,859 workstations in dormitories, library, computer center, student center. Dormitories wired for high-speed internet access and linked to campus network. Commuter students can connect to campus network. Online course registration, online library, helpline, repair service, student web hosting, wireless network available.

**Student life. Freshman orientation:** Available, $110 fee. Preregistration for classes offered. Held before start of classes at no charge. Optional 2-day summer program, which includes parents, carries a fee. **Housing:** Coed dorms, single-sex dorms, apartments available. $250 nonrefundable deposit, deadline 6/1. Some apartment-style residence halls with full kitchen facilities available. Students with disabilities accommodated on individual basis.

**Activities:** Campus ministries, choral groups, dance, drama, international student organizations, music ensembles, musical theater, radio station, student government, student newspaper, TV station, American Institute of Architecture Students, American Society of Interior Designers, united student forum, inter-club council, student activities council, intercultural student association, Society of Illustrators, art history society, Society for Collegiate Journalists.

**Athletics. NAIA. Intercollegiate:** Baseball M, basketball, cross-country, equestrian, golf, lacrosse, soccer, softball W, swimming, tennis, volleyball W. **Intramural:** Basketball, football (non-tackle), soccer, softball, tennis, volleyball. **Team name:** Bees.

**Student services.** Adult student services, alcohol/substance abuse counseling, career counseling, student employment services, financial aid counseling, health services, personal counseling, placement for graduates. **Physically disabled:** Services for visually, speech, hearing impaired.

**Contact.** E-mail: admission@scad.edu
Phone: (912) 525-5100 Toll-free number: (800) 869-7223
Fax: (912) 525-5986
Sara Malbrough, Executive Director of Admission, Savannah College of Art and Design, PO Box 2072, Savannah, GA 31402-2072

## Savannah State University
Savannah, Georgia — CB member
www.savannahstate.edu — CB code: 5609

- Public 4-year business and liberal arts college
- Commuter campus in small city
- 3,686 degree-seeking undergraduates: 14% part-time, 56% women, 94% African American, 1% international
- 130 degree-seeking graduate students
- 40% of applicants admitted
- SAT or ACT (ACT writing optional) required

**General.** Founded in 1890. Regionally accredited. **Degrees:** 326 bachelor's awarded; master's offered. **ROTC:** Army, Naval. **Location:** 250 miles from Atlanta; 120 miles from Jacksonville, FL. **Calendar:** Semester, extensive summer session. **Full-time faculty:** 151 total. **Part-time faculty:** 31 total. **Special facilities:** Marine biology dock, college archives, natural estuary.

**Freshman class profile.** 4,450 applied, 1,783 admitted, 870 enrolled.

| Mid 50% test scores | | | |
|---|---|---|---|
| SAT critical reading: | 400-470 | GPA 3.0-3.49: | 21% |
| SAT math: | 390-470 | GPA 2.0-2.99: | 72% |
| ACT composite: | 16-19 | End year in good standing: | 86% |
| GPA 3.75 or higher: | 1% | Return as sophomores: | 71% |
| GPA 3.50-3.74: | 5% | Out-of-state: | 9% |
| | | Live on campus: | 50% |

**Basis for selection.** Test scores and high school GPA very important. Students lacking complete college-preparatory requirements admitted on provisional basis.

**High school preparation.** College-preparatory program recommended. 16 units required. Required units include English 4, mathematics 4, social studies 3, science 3 and foreign language 2.

**2009-2010 Annual costs.** Tuition/fees: $4,774; $16,388 out-of-state. Room/board: $5,958. Books/supplies: $750. Personal expenses: $800.

**2009-2010 Financial aid. Non-need-based:** Scholarships awarded for academics, alumni affiliation, music/drama.

**Application procedures. Admission:** Closing date 7/1. $20 fee, may be waived for applicants with need. Admission notification on a rolling basis beginning on or about 3/1. **Financial aid:** Closing date 4/1. FAFSA required. Applicants notified on a rolling basis starting 4/15; must reply within 2 week(s) of notification.

**Academics. Special study options:** Cooperative education, cross-registration, double major, dual enrollment of high school students, exchange student, honors, independent study, internships, study abroad. **Credit/placement by examination:** AP, CLEP, institutional tests. 45 credit hours maximum toward bachelor's degree. **Support services:** Learning center, remedial instruction, tutoring.

**Majors. Area/ethnic studies:** African. **Biology:** General, marine. **Business:** Accounting, business admin, marketing. **Communications:** Media studies. **Computer sciences:** General, computer science, information systems. **Conservation:** Environmental studies. **Education:** Early childhood. **Engineering technology:** Civil, computer, electrical. **History:** General. **Math:**

General. **Physical sciences:** Chemistry. **Protective services:** Emergency management/homeland security, law enforcement admin. **Public administration:** Social work. **Social sciences:** Political science, sociology. **Visual/performing arts:** General. **Other:** Behavioral analysis.

**Most popular majors.** Biology 15%, business/marketing 21%, communications/journalism 11%, engineering/engineering technologies 8%, psychology 8%, security/protective services 6%, social sciences 10%.

**Computing on campus.** 300 workstations in library, computer center. Commuter students can connect to campus network. Wireless network available.

**Student life. Freshman orientation:** Available. Preregistration for classes offered. Available during various times leading up to fall semester. Private appointments available upon request. **Housing:** Single-sex dorms, apartments available. $100 deposit. **Activities:** Bands, campus ministries, choral groups, dance, drama, international student organizations, literary magazine, music ensembles, radio station, student government, student newspaper.

**Athletics. NCAA. Intercollegiate:** Baseball M, basketball, bowling W, cross-country, football (tackle) M, golf, softball W, tennis W, track and field, volleyball W. **Intramural:** Baseball M, bowling, softball W, table tennis. **Team name:** Tigers.

**Student services.** Student employment services, health services, on-campus daycare, personal counseling, placement for graduates, veterans' counselor.

**Contact.** E-mail: admissions@savannahstate.edu
Phone: (912) 356-2181 Toll-free number: (800) 788-0478
Fax: (912) 356-2256
Admissions Office, Savannah State University, Office of Admissions and Recruitment, Savannah, GA 31404

## Shorter College
Rome, Georgia — CB member
www.shorter.edu — CB code: 5616

- Private 4-year liberal arts college affiliated with Southern Baptist Convention
- Residential campus in large town
- 1,194 degree-seeking undergraduates: 3% part-time, 49% women, 14% African American, 1% Asian American, 2% Hispanic American, 5% international
- 65% of applicants admitted
- SAT or ACT (ACT writing optional), application essay required
- 54% graduate within 6 years

**General.** Founded in 1873. Regionally accredited. **Degrees:** 195 bachelor's awarded. **Location:** 70 miles from Atlanta; 65 miles from Chattanooga, TN. **Calendar:** Semester, limited summer session. **Full-time faculty:** 83 total; 74% have terminal degrees, 12% minority, 48% women. **Part-time faculty:** 66 total; 8% have terminal degrees, 2% minority, 56% women. **Class size:** 62% < 20, 35% 20-39, 3% 40-49, less than 1% 50-99, less than 1% >100. **Special facilities:** Music collection, local history microfilm archive.

**Freshman class profile.** 1,672 applied, 1,089 admitted, 333 enrolled.

| Mid 50% test scores | | | |
|---|---|---|---|
| SAT critical reading: | 430-570 | Rank in top quarter: | 50% |
| SAT math: | 430-550 | Rank in top tenth: | 23% |
| SAT writing: | 420-560 | End year in good standing: | 82% |
| ACT composite: | 18-23 | Return as sophomores: | 69% |
| GPA 3.75 or higher: | 31% | Out-of-state: | 9% |
| GPA 3.50-3.74: | 15% | Live on campus: | 71% |
| GPA 3.0-3.49: | 22% | International: | 4% |
| GPA 2.0-2.99: | 32% | Fraternities: | 12% |
| | | Sororities: | 33% |

**Basis for selection.** High school achievement, curriculum most important. Test scores, essay, counselor recommendation considered. Auditions required of music and drama majors. Portfolios required of art majors. **Homeschooled:** Interview may be required.

**High school preparation.** College-preparatory program required. 16 units required. Required units include English 4, mathematics 4, history 3, science 3 and foreign language 2. Math units should include 2 algebra, 1 geometry.

**2009-2010 Annual costs.** Tuition/fees: $16,300. Room/board: $7,800. Books/supplies: $1,000. Personal expenses: $1,770.

**2009-2010 Financial aid. Need-based:** 304 full-time freshmen applied for aid; 260 were judged to have need; 260 of these received aid. Average need met was 75%. Average scholarship/grant was $12,687; average loan $3,058. 66% of total undergraduate aid awarded as scholarships/grants, 34% as loans/jobs. **Non-need-based:** Awarded to 535 full-time undergraduates, including 144 freshmen. Scholarships awarded for academics, art, athletics, music/drama, religious affiliation. **Additional information:** Cost is reduced for all in-state students by state tuition equalization grant program. College matches for out-of-state full-time students.

**Application procedures. Admission:** Priority date 3/15; no deadline. $25 fee, may be waived for applicants with need. Application must be submitted on paper. Admission notification on a rolling basis beginning on or about 11/1. Must reply by May 1 or within 2 week(s) if notified thereafter. **Financial aid:** Priority date 4/1; no closing date. FAFSA, institutional form required. Applicants notified on a rolling basis starting 4/1; must reply within 2 week(s) of notification.

**Academics. Special study options:** Cross-registration, double major, dual enrollment of high school students, honors, independent study, internships, student-designed major, study abroad, teacher certification program. Annual extended seacoast field trips in natural science. **Credit/placement by examination:** AP, CLEP, IB, SAT, institutional tests. 30 credit hours maximum toward bachelor's degree. **Support services:** Learning center, pre-admission summer program, remedial instruction, study skills assistance, tutoring, writing center.

**Majors. Biology:** General. **Business:** Accounting, business admin, managerial economics. **Communications:** General, public relations. **Computer sciences:** General. **Conservation:** General, environmental studies. **Education:** Art, elementary, mathematics, middle, music. **Foreign languages:** French, Spanish. **History:** General. **Interdisciplinary:** Global studies. **Liberal arts:** Arts/sciences. **Math:** General. **Parks/recreation:** Sports admin. **Philosophy/religion:** Religion. **Physical sciences:** Chemistry. **Psychology:** General. **Social sciences:** General, sociology. **Theology:** Sacred music, theology. **Visual/performing arts:** Dramatic, piano/organ, studio arts, voice/opera.

**Most popular majors.** Biology 8%, business/marketing 26%, education 14%, history 6%, liberal arts 6%, visual/performing arts 12%.

**Computing on campus.** 50 workstations in library, computer center. Dormitories wired for high-speed internet access and linked to campus network. Online course registration, online library, helpline, wireless network available.

**Student life. Freshman orientation:** Mandatory, $175 fee. Preregistration for classes offered. Several summer overnight sessions from June to August during which freshmen take placement exams. **Policies:** All housing is alcohol, drug and smoke free. **Housing:** Guaranteed on-campus for freshmen. Single-sex dorms, apartments, wellness housing available. $200 fully refundable deposit, deadline 8/20. **Activities:** Bands, campus ministries, choral groups, dance, drama, film society, international student organizations, literary magazine, music ensembles, Model UN, musical theater, opera, radio station, student government, student newspaper, TV station, Baptist student union, Shorter Relations Society, Fellowship of Christian Athletes, optimist club.

**Athletics.** NAIA. **Intercollegiate:** Baseball M, basketball, cheerleading, cross-country, football (tackle) M, golf, soccer, softball W, tennis, track and field, volleyball W. **Intramural:** Basketball, bowling, football (non-tackle), soccer, softball, table tennis, tennis, track and field, volleyball. **Team name:** Hawks.

**Student services.** Adult student services, alcohol/substance abuse counseling, chaplain/spiritual director, career counseling, student employment services, financial aid counseling, health services, personal counseling, placement for graduates. **Physically disabled:** Services for visually, hearing impaired.

**Contact.** E-mail: admissions@shorter.edu
Phone: (706) 233-7319 Toll-free number: (800) 868-6980
Fax: (706) 233-7224
John Head, Vice President for Enrollment Management, Shorter College, 315 Shorter Avenue, Rome, GA 30165

---

## South University: Savannah
Savannah, Georgia
www.southuniversity.edu                    CB code: 5157

- For-profit 4-year university
- Commuter campus in small city
- 804 degree-seeking undergraduates: 32% part-time, 77% women
- 553 graduate students
- Interview required

---

**General.** Founded in 1899. Regionally accredited. **Degrees:** 327 bachelor's, 108 associate awarded; master's, professional offered. **Location:** 225 miles from Atlanta; 165 miles from Jacksonville, FL. **Calendar:** Quarter, extensive summer session. **Full-time faculty:** 136 total; 70% have terminal degrees, 15% minority, 59% women. **Part-time faculty:** 595 total; 55% have terminal degrees, 30% minority, 55% women.

**Basis for selection.** Test scores and school achievement record considered. SAT or ACT recommended. Computerized placement test may be submitted in place of test scores for admission. **Homeschooled:** Students must provide evidence that homeschooling was conducted in accordance with state laws (certificate of attendance or completion is not sufficient).

**2009-2010 Annual costs.** Tuition/fees: $14,985. Additional cost for nursing program.

**Application procedures. Admission:** No deadline. $50 fee. Admission notification on a rolling basis. **Financial aid:** No deadline. FAFSA required. Applicants notified on a rolling basis starting 9/1.

**Academics. Special study options:** Combined bachelor's/graduate degree, distance learning, internships. **Credit/placement by examination:** AP, CLEP, IB, SAT, ACT, institutional tests. **Support services:** Learning center, reduced course load, remedial instruction, study skills assistance, tutoring.

**Majors. Business:** Business admin. **Computer sciences:** Information technology. **Health:** Health care admin, health services, nursing (RN). **Legal studies:** General. **Protective services:** Law enforcement admin. **Psychology:** General.

**Most popular majors.** Business/marketing 18%, health sciences 69%.

**Computing on campus.** Commuter students can connect to campus network. Online library, helpline, repair service, wireless network available.

**Student life. Freshman orientation:** Mandatory. Preregistration for classes offered. **Housing:** Apartments available.

**Student services.** Career counseling, student employment services, financial aid counseling, placement for graduates, veterans' counselor.

**Contact.** Phone: (912) 201-8100 Toll-free number: (866) 629-2901
Fax: (912) 201-8070
Marie Neal, Senior Director of Admissions, South University: Savannah, 709 Mall Boulevard, Savannah, GA 31406

---

## Southern Polytechnic State University
Marietta, Georgia                          CB member
www.spsu.edu                               CB code: 5626

- Public 4-year university and engineering college
- Commuter campus in small city
- 4,450 degree-seeking undergraduates: 26% part-time, 19% women, 20% African American, 5% Asian American, 5% Hispanic American, 6% international
- 640 graduate students
- 75% of applicants admitted
- SAT or ACT with writing required

**General.** Founded in 1948. Regionally accredited. **Degrees:** 519 bachelor's, 2 associate awarded; master's offered. **ROTC:** Army, Naval, Air Force. **Location:** 15 miles from Atlanta. **Calendar:** Semester, extensive summer session. **Full-time faculty:** 177 total; 51% have terminal degrees, 25% minority, 29% women. **Part-time faculty:** 101 total; 31% have terminal degrees, 26% minority, 36% women. **Class size:** 42% < 20, 54% 20-39, 3% 40-49, less than 1% 50-99, less than 1% >100.

**Freshman class profile.** 1,289 applied, 961 admitted, 539 enrolled.

| Mid 50% test scores | | | |
|---|---|---|---|
| SAT critical reading: | 500-590 | GPA 2.0-2.99: | 31% |
| SAT math: | 530-630 | Return as sophomores: | 75% |
| SAT writing: | 470-560 | Out-of-state: | 1% |
| ACT composite: | 21-25 | Live on campus: | 51% |
| GPA 3.75 or higher: | 11% | International: | 3% |
| GPA 3.50-3.74: | 18% | Fraternities: | 20% |
| GPA 3.0-3.49: | 40% | Sororities: | 22% |

**Basis for selection.** GED not accepted. SAT/ACT test scores, high school college prep units, GPA considered. **Homeschooled:** Portfolio and 1120 SAT (exclusive of Writing) with 500 verbal and math subscores required.

**High school preparation.** College-preparatory program required. 18 units required. Required units include English 4, mathematics 4, social studies 3, science 3 (laboratory 2), foreign language 2 and academic electives 2. 2 history (1 U.S., 1 world); 2 algebra, 1 geometry; foreign language must include 2 years same language.

**2009-2010 Annual costs.** Tuition/fees: $5,374; $18,494 out-of-state. Room/board: $5,950. Books/supplies: $1,700. Personal expenses: $1,700.

**2008-2009 Financial aid. Need-based:** 469 full-time freshmen applied for aid; 469 were judged to have need; 460 of these received aid. Average need met was 76%. Average scholarship/grant was $2,893; average loan $3,095. 38% of total undergraduate aid awarded as scholarships/grants, 62% as loans/jobs. **Non-need-based:** Awarded to 764 full-time undergraduates, including 326 freshmen. Scholarships awarded for academics, athletics, minority status.

**Application procedures. Admission:** Closing date 7/1 (postmark date). $20 fee, may be waived for applicants with need. Admission notification on a rolling basis. **Financial aid:** Priority date 3/1; no closing date. FAFSA required. Applicants notified on a rolling basis starting 4/1.

**Academics. Special study options:** Cooperative education, cross-registration, distance learning, double major, dual enrollment of high school students, honors, independent study, internships, liberal arts/career combination, study abroad. **Credit/placement by examination:** AP, CLEP, IB, institutional tests. 20 credit hours maximum toward associate degree, 30 toward bachelor's. **Support services:** Learning center, reduced course load, study skills assistance, tutoring.

**Majors. Architecture:** Architecture. **Biology:** General. **Business:** Accounting, construction management, entrepreneurial studies. **Communications:** Media studies. **Computer sciences:** Applications programming, computer science, information technology. **Engineering:** Civil, construction, electrical, mechanical, software, systems. **Engineering technology:** Architectural, civil, computer, electrical, mechanical, surveying, telecommunications. **Math:** General. **Physical sciences:** Chemistry, physics. **Psychology:** General. **Social sciences:** International relations, political science.

**Most popular majors.** Architecture 9%, business/marketing 22%, computer/information sciences 13%, engineering/engineering technologies 46%.

**Computing on campus.** 850 workstations in dormitories, library, computer center, student center. Dormitories wired for high-speed internet access and linked to campus network. Commuter students can connect to campus network. Online course registration, online library, helpline, student web hosting, wireless network available.

**Student life. Freshman orientation:** Mandatory, $85 fee. Preregistration for classes offered. One-and-a-half day programs held twice prior to beginning of semester; includes 1 night in a dorm. Half-day sessions also available. **Housing:** Coed dorms, apartments available. $235 partly refundable deposit, deadline 8/1. **Activities:** Bands, choral groups, international student organizations, radio station, student government, student newspaper, campus activities board, National Society of Black Engineers, Baptist student union, African students association, Bahai club, Japanese Friendship Society, Muslim student association, Indian culture exchange, Chinese Friendship Association, Sexual Acceptance For Everyone, Caribbean student association.

**Athletics.** NAIA. **Intercollegiate:** Baseball M, basketball, soccer M. **Intramural:** Badminton, basketball, football (non-tackle), golf, racquetball, soccer, softball, table tennis, tennis, volleyball. **Team name:** Runnin' Hornets.

**Student services.** Alcohol/substance abuse counseling, career counseling, student employment services, financial aid counseling, health services, minority student services, personal counseling, placement for graduates, veterans' counselor. **Physically disabled:** Services for visually, speech, hearing impaired.

**Contact.** E-mail: admiss@spsu.edu
Phone: (678) 915-4188 Toll-free number: (800) 635-3204
Fax: (678) 915-7292
Gary Bush, Director of Admissions, Southern Polytechnic State University, 1100 South Marietta Parkway, Marietta, GA 30060-2896

## Spelman College
Atlanta, Georgia
www.spelman.edu

CB member
CB code: 5628

- Private 4-year liberal arts college for women
- Residential campus in very large city
- 2,229 degree-seeking undergraduates: 5% part-time, 100% women

- 41% of applicants admitted
- SAT or ACT (ACT writing optional), application essay required
- 83% graduate within 6 years

**General.** Founded in 1881. Regionally accredited. One of 6 members of Atlanta University Center sharing facilities, resources, and activities. Students may take courses at the other undergraduate schools in the Atlanta University Consortium. **Degrees:** 444 bachelor's awarded. **ROTC:** Army, Naval, Air Force. **Location:** 2 miles from downtown. **Calendar:** Semester. **Full-time faculty:** 171 total; 83% have terminal degrees, 64% women. **Part-time faculty:** 75 total. **Special facilities:** Women's research and resource center, fine art museum.

**Freshman class profile.** 5,452 applied, 2,259 admitted, 567 enrolled.

| Mid 50% test scores | | | |
|---|---|---|---|
| SAT critical reading: | 490-570 | GPA 2.0-2.99: | 8% |
| SAT math: | 470-550 | Rank in top quarter: | 65% |
| ACT composite: | 20-24 | Rank in top tenth: | 33% |
| GPA 3.75 or higher: | 31% | Return as sophomores: | 85% |
| GPA 3.50-3.74: | 24% | Out-of-state: | 79% |
| GPA 3.0-3.49: | 37% | International: | 4% |

**Basis for selection.** School achievement record, letters of recommendation, test scores, leadership, activities, essay important. Portfolio required of art majors.

**High school preparation.** College-preparatory program recommended. 16 units required; 20 recommended. Required and recommended units include English 4, mathematics 3-4, social studies 3-4, science 3-4 (laboratory 2-3) and foreign language 3-4. Mathematics units must include algebra and geometry. Must have 2 years of the same foreign language. Social studies units should include 2 years of history.

**2009-2010 Annual costs.** Tuition/fees: $20,926. Room/board: $10,062. Books/supplies: $1,150. Personal expenses: $2,100.

**2008-2009 Financial aid. Need-based:** 510 full-time freshmen applied for aid; 431 were judged to have need; 429 of these received aid. Average need met was 42%. Average scholarship/grant was $12,107; average loan $3,545. 65% of total undergraduate aid awarded as scholarships/grants, 35% as loans/jobs. **Non-need-based:** Awarded to 14 full-time undergraduates, including 2 freshmen. Scholarships awarded for academics, alumni affiliation, leadership, music/drama, state residency.

**Application procedures. Admission:** Closing date 2/1 (postmark date). $35 fee, may be waived for applicants with need. Admission notification 4/1. Admission notification on a rolling basis. Must reply by May 1 or within 2 week(s) if notified thereafter. **Financial aid:** Priority date 3/1; no closing date. FAFSA, institutional form required. Applicants notified on a rolling basis starting 2/15; must reply within 2 week(s) of notification.

**Academics. Special study options:** Cross-registration, double major, dual enrollment of high school students, exchange student, honors, independent study, internships, New York semester, student-designed major, study abroad, teacher certification program, Washington semester. **Credit/placement by examination:** AP, CLEP, IB, institutional tests. 16 credit hours maximum toward bachelor's degree. **Support services:** Learning center, pre-admission summer program, study skills assistance, tutoring, writing center.

**Majors. Area/ethnic studies:** Women's. **Biology:** General, biochemistry. **Computer sciences:** General. **Conservation:** Environmental science. **Education:** Early childhood. **Engineering:** General. **Family/consumer sciences:** Child care. **Foreign languages:** French, Spanish. **History:** General. **Interdisciplinary:** Biological/physical sciences, global studies. **Math:** General. **Philosophy/religion:** Philosophy, religion. **Physical sciences:** Chemistry, physics. **Psychology:** General. **Public administration:** Human services. **Social sciences:** Economics, political science, sociology. **Visual/performing arts:** Dramatic, studio arts.

**Most popular majors.** Biology 14%, English 14%, psychology 17%, social sciences 27%.

**Computing on campus.** 102 workstations in dormitories, library, computer center, student center. Dormitories wired for high-speed internet access and linked to campus network. Commuter students can connect to campus network. Online library, helpline, repair service, wireless network available.

**Student life. Freshman orientation:** Mandatory. 1-week program prior to registration. **Housing:** Guaranteed on-campus for freshmen. **Activities:** Jazz band, choral groups, dance, drama, music ensembles, student government, student newspaper, subject-related clubs, community services office.

**Athletics.** NCAA. **Intercollegiate:** Basketball W, cross-country W, soccer W, softball W, tennis W, track and field W, volleyball W. **Intramural:** Basketball W, bowling W, golf W, soccer W, softball W, swimming W, tennis W, track and field W, volleyball W. **Team name:** Jaguars.

**Student services.** Adult student services, chaplain/spiritual director, career counseling, student employment services, health services, on-campus daycare, personal counseling, placement for graduates, women's services. **Physically disabled:** Services for visually, speech, hearing impaired.

**Contact.** E-mail: admiss@spelman.edu
Phone: (404) 270-5193 Toll-free number: (800) 982-2411
Fax: (404) 270-5201
Ingrid Hayes, Associate Vice President, Enrollment Management, Spelman College, 350 Spelman Lane SW, Campus Box 277, Atlanta, GA 30314

---

## Thomas University
### Thomasville, Georgia
### www.thomasu.edu
**CB code: 5072**

- Private 4-year university and liberal arts college
- Commuter campus in large town

**General.** Founded in 1950. Regionally accredited. **Location:** 60 miles from Albany; 35 miles from Tallahassee, FL. **Calendar:** Semester.

**Annual costs/financial aid.** Tuition/fees (2009-2010): $12,339. Room: $2,766. Books/supplies: $1,100. Personal expenses: $1,500. Need-based financial aid available to full-time and part-time students.

**Contact.** Phone: (229) 226-1621 ext. 124
Executive Director for Enrollment Management and Student Affairs, 1501 Millpond Road, Thomasville, GA 31792-7499

---

## Toccoa Falls College
### Toccoa Falls, Georgia
### www.tfc.edu
**CB member**
**CB code: 5799**

- Private 4-year Bible and liberal arts college affiliated with Christian and Missionary Alliance
- Residential campus in large town
- 797 degree-seeking undergraduates: 4% part-time, 55% women, 4% African American, 8% Asian American, 1% Hispanic American, 3% international
- 53% of applicants admitted
- SAT or ACT (ACT writing recommended), application essay required
- 48% graduate within 6 years

**General.** Founded in 1907. Regionally accredited; also accredited by ABHE. **Degrees:** 177 bachelor's, 3 associate awarded. **Location:** 90 miles from Atlanta; 60 miles from Greenville, SC. **Calendar:** 4-1-4, limited summer session. **Full-time faculty:** 50 total; 58% have terminal degrees, 8% minority, 22% women. **Part-time faculty:** 20 total; 10% have terminal degrees, 10% minority, 40% women. **Class size:** 72% < 20, 22% 20-39, 4% 40-49, 1% 50-99, less than 1% >100. **Special facilities:** 186-foot waterfall, 1898 hydroelectric generator, nature trails.

**Freshman class profile.** 767 applied, 404 admitted, 174 enrolled.

| Mid 50% test scores | | | |
|---|---|---|---|
| SAT critical reading: | 460-570 | Return as sophomores: | 67% |
| SAT math: | 440-550 | Out-of-state: | 34% |
| ACT composite: | 16-22 | Live on campus: | 83% |
| | | International: | 3% |

**Basis for selection.** Evidence of Christian commitment, character, capacity and desire to learn considered. Index score calculated by multiplying unweighted GPA by best total standardized test score. Students with score of 48 on GED also considered. Personal statement of Christian faith required.

**High school preparation.** College-preparatory program recommended. 19 units recommended. Recommended units include English 4, mathematics 3, social studies 3, science 3 and academic electives 6.

**2009-2010 Annual costs.** Tuition/fees: $15,575. Room/board: $5,650. Books/supplies: $908. Personal expenses: $2,270.

**2008-2009 Financial aid. Non-need-based:** Scholarships awarded for academics, alumni affiliation, leadership, music/drama, religious affiliation, state residency.

**Application procedures. Admission:** Priority date 5/1; deadline 8/1 (postmark date). $20 fee, may be waived for applicants with need. Admission notification on a rolling basis beginning on or about 3/1. Must reply by May 1 or within 2 week(s) if notified thereafter. **Financial aid:** Priority date

5/1, closing date 8/1. FAFSA, institutional form required. Applicants notified on a rolling basis starting 3/1; must reply within 2 week(s) of notification.

**Academics.** All students complete at least 30 credit hours of Bible courses (18 credit hours for associate degrees). **Special study options:** Distance learning, double major, dual enrollment of high school students, independent study, internships, teacher certification program. **Credit/placement by examination:** AP, CLEP, SAT, ACT, institutional tests. 30 credit hours maximum toward associate degree, 45 toward bachelor's. **Support services:** Learning center, reduced course load, study skills assistance, tutoring.

**Majors. Biology:** General. **Business:** Business admin, international. **Communications:** Media studies, organizational. **Education:** Early childhood, English, history, middle, music, science. **History:** General. **Philosophy/religion:** Philosophy. **Psychology:** General. **Theology:** Bible, missionary, pastoral counseling, sacred music, youth ministry. **Visual/performing arts:** Music performance. **Other:** Family & children's ministries.

**Most popular majors.** Business/marketing 7%, communications/journalism 7%, education 14%, psychology 18%, theological studies 42%.

**Computing on campus.** 60 workstations in library, computer center. Dormitories wired for high-speed internet access and linked to campus network. Commuter students can connect to campus network. Online course registration, online library, helpline, student web hosting, wireless network available.

**Student life. Freshman orientation:** Mandatory. Preregistration for classes offered. Held 1 week in fall and throughout spring semester. **Policies:** Students attend weekly church services and participate in student ministry field assignments. Religious observance required. **Housing:** Guaranteed on-campus for freshmen. Single-sex dorms, apartments, wellness housing available. $200 fully refundable deposit. **Activities:** Bands, campus ministries, choral groups, drama, international student organizations, music ensembles, radio station, student government, student newspaper, over 50 different ministry opportunities.

**Athletics.** NCCAA. **Intercollegiate:** Baseball M, basketball, cross-country, golf, soccer, volleyball W. **Intramural:** Basketball, football (non-tackle), soccer, softball, volleyball. **Team name:** Eagles.

**Student services.** Chaplain/spiritual director, career counseling, student employment services, financial aid counseling, health services, personal counseling. **Physically disabled:** Services for visually impaired.

**Contact.** E-mail: admissions@tfc.edu
Phone: (706) 886-6831 ext. 5380 Toll-free number: (888) 785-5264
Fax: (706) 282-6012
Michael Davis, Director of Admissions, Toccoa Falls College, PO Box 800899, Toccoa Falls, GA 30598-0368

---

## Truett-McConnell College
### Cleveland, Georgia
### www.truett.edu
**CB member**
**CB code: 5798**

- Private 4-year liberal arts college affiliated with Southern Baptist Convention
- Residential campus in small town
- 373 degree-seeking undergraduates: 4% part-time, 51% women
- 62% of applicants admitted
- SAT or ACT (ACT writing optional) required

**General.** Founded in 1946. Regionally accredited. Associated with Baptist Convention of the State of Georgia. **Degrees:** 27 bachelor's, 37 associate awarded. **Location:** 75 miles from Atlanta, 25 miles from Gainesville. **Calendar:** Semester, limited summer session. **Full-time faculty:** 23 total; 65% have terminal degrees, 26% women. **Part-time faculty:** 41 total; 61% women. **Class size:** 78% < 20, 21% 20-39, 1% 50-99.

**Freshman class profile.** 534 applied, 329 admitted, 139 enrolled.

| Mid 50% test scores | | | |
|---|---|---|---|
| SAT critical reading: | 370-490 | GPA 3.75 or higher: | 13% |
| SAT math: | 380-490 | GPA 3.50-3.74: | 16% |
| SAT writing: | 380-490 | GPA 3.0-3.49: | 31% |
| ACT composite: | 15-20 | GPA 2.0-2.99: | 37% |
| | | Return as sophomores: | 45% |

**Basis for selection.** 2.0 GPA in core classes and 720 SAT (exclusive of Writing) or 15 ACT required. Students with lower scores may apply and are reviewed by an appeal committee. Audition required of music majors. **Homeschooled:** Transcript of courses and grades required. Letter from local school board stating that student has completed homeschool program requirements and placement exams required. **Learning Disabled:** Students may request accommodations upon presentation of appropriate documentation of disability. Determination of reasonable accommodations made on individual basis.

**High school preparation.** College-preparatory program recommended. Recommended units include English 4, mathematics 3, social studies 3, science 3 and foreign language 2.

**2009-2010 Annual costs.** Tuition/fees: $14,000. Room/board: $5,700. Books/supplies: $1,000. Personal expenses: $3,500.

**Financial aid. Non-need-based:** Scholarships awarded for academics, athletics, music/drama, religious affiliation, state residency.

**Application procedures. Admission:** Closing date 8/1 (receipt date). $25 fee, may be waived for applicants with need. Admission notification on a rolling basis. Must reply by May 1 or within 1 week(s) if notified thereafter. **Financial aid:** Priority date 6/1; no closing date. FAFSA, institutional form required. Applicants notified on a rolling basis starting 4/1; must reply within 2 week(s) of notification.

**Academics. Special study options:** Distance learning, double major, dual enrollment of high school students, independent study, teacher certification program. **Credit/placement by examination:** CLEP, SAT, ACT, institutional tests. 30 credit hours maximum toward associate degree, 30 toward bachelor's. **Support services:** Remedial instruction, tutoring.

**Majors. Business:** General. **Education:** Early childhood. **History:** General. **Liberal arts:** Humanities. **Philosophy/religion:** Christian.

**Most popular majors.** Education 33%, history 15%, liberal arts 26%, philosophy/religious studies 11%, visual/performing arts 15%.

**Computing on campus.** 45 workstations in library, computer center, student center. Dormitories linked to campus network. Commuter students can connect to campus network. Online course registration, wireless network available.

**Student life. Freshman orientation:** Mandatory, $25 fee. Preregistration for classes offered. Several one-day sessions held during summer prior to fall classes beginning. **Policies:** Tobacco-free campus. Religious observance required. **Housing:** Single-sex dorms, apartments, wellness housing available. $100 fully refundable deposit. **Activities:** Bands, choral groups, music ensembles, student government, Baptist Student Union, Phi Theta Kappa, Impact Teams and Majesty, Phi Beta Lambda, Ministerial Association, Student Professional Association of Georgia Educators, Fellowship of Christian Athletes.

**Athletics.** NAIA, NCCAA. **Intercollegiate:** Baseball M, basketball, cross-country, golf, soccer, softball W. **Intramural:** Basketball, football (non-tackle), soccer. **Team name:** Bears.

**Student services.** Chaplain/spiritual director, financial aid counseling, veterans' counselor. **Physically disabled:** Services for visually, speech, hearing impaired.

**Contact.** E-mail: admissions@truett.edu
Phone: (706) 865-2134 Toll-free number: (800) 226-8621
Fax: (706) 865-3110
Andrew Gailey, Director of Admissions, Truett-McConnell College, 100 Alumni Drive, Cleveland, GA 30528

## University of Georgia

| Athens, Georgia | |
|---|---|
| www.uga.edu | CB member |
| | CB code: 5813 |

- ▶ Public 4-year university
- ▶ Commuter campus in small city
- ▶ 25,882 degree-seeking undergraduates: 5% part-time, 57% women, 7% African American, 7% Asian American, 3% Hispanic American, 1% international
- ▶ 8,280 degree-seeking graduate students
- ▶ 54% of applicants admitted
- ▶ SAT or ACT with writing, application essay required
- ▶ 81% graduate within 6 years

**General.** Founded in 1785. Regionally accredited. **Degrees:** 6,316 bachelor's awarded; master's, doctoral, professional offered. **ROTC:** Army, Air Force. **Location:** 60 miles from Atlanta. **Calendar:** Semester, extensive summer session. **Full-time faculty:** 1,775 total; 89% have terminal degrees, 17% minority, 35% women. **Part-time faculty:** 438 total; 57% have terminal degrees, 11% minority, 45% women. **Class size:** 36% < 20, 44% 20-39,

8% 40-49, 7% 50-99, 5% >100. **Special facilities:** Botanical garden, golf course, art museum.

**Freshman class profile.** 17,776 applied, 9,557 admitted, 4,684 enrolled.

| Mid 50% test scores | | | |
|---|---|---|---|
| SAT critical reading: | 560-660 | Rank in top quarter: | 89% |
| SAT math: | 570-670 | Rank in top tenth: | 54% |
| SAT writing: | 570-660 | Return as sophomores: | 94% |
| ACT composite: | 25-29 | Out-of-state: | 11% |
| GPA 3.75 or higher: | 67% | Live on campus: | 98% |
| GPA 3.50-3.74: | 22% | International: | 1% |
| GPA 3.0-3.49: | 10% | Fraternities: | 33% |
| GPA 2.0-2.99: | 1% | Sororities: | 28% |

**Basis for selection.** GPA in core academic courses, rigor of course selection, and best combination of SAT/ACT scores important. Applications reviewed for conduct issues, recommendations, and satisfactory completion of all courses including required college preparatory courses. Audition required of music majors.

**High school preparation.** College-preparatory program required. 16 units required; 18 recommended. Required and recommended units include English 4, mathematics 4, social studies 3, history 2, science 3 (laboratory 2), foreign language 2-3 and academic electives 1.

**2009-2010 Annual costs.** Tuition/fees: $7,530; $25,740 out-of-state. Room/board: $8,046. Books/supplies: $960. Personal expenses: $1,194.

**2009-2010 Financial aid. Need-based:** 3,359 full-time freshmen applied for aid; 1,659 were judged to have need; 1,648 of these received aid. Average need met was 83%. Average scholarship/grant was $9,976; average loan $2,834. 65% of total undergraduate aid awarded as scholarships/grants, 35% as loans/jobs. **Non-need-based:** Awarded to 2,975 full-time undergraduates, including 801 freshmen. Scholarships awarded for academics, athletics, ROTC, state residency.

**Application procedures. Admission:** Priority date 10/15; deadline 1/15 (postmark date). $60 fee, may be waived for applicants with need. Admission notification 4/1. Must reply by May 1 or within 2 week(s) if notified thereafter. **Financial aid:** Priority date 3/1; no closing date. FAFSA required. Applicants notified on a rolling basis starting 5/15; must reply within 2 week(s) of notification.

**Academics. Special study options:** Accelerated study, combined bachelor's/graduate degree, cooperative education, cross-registration, distance learning, double major, dual enrollment of high school students, exchange student, external degree, honors, independent study, internships, liberal arts/career combination, student-designed major, study abroad, teacher certification program, Washington semester. **Credit/placement by examination:** AP, CLEP, IB, institutional tests. Unlimited number of hours of credit by examination may be counted toward bachelor's degree. **Support services:** Learning center, pre-admission summer program, reduced course load, remedial instruction, study skills assistance, tutoring, writing center.

**Majors. Agriculture:** General, agribusiness operations, animal sciences, communications, dairy, economics, food science, horticulture, poultry, turf management. **Architecture:** Landscape. **Area/ethnic studies:** African-American, Latin American, women's. **Biology:** General, biochemistry, biotechnology, botany, cell/histology, ecology, entomology, genetics, microbiology. **Business:** General, accounting, business admin, fashion, finance, insurance, international, management information systems, managerial economics, marketing, real estate. **Communications:** Advertising, broadcast journalism, journalism, public relations. **Communications technology:** Radio/tv. **Computer sciences:** Computer science. **Conservation:** General, environmental science, environmental studies, fisheries, forestry, wildlife. **Education:** Agricultural, English, family/consumer sciences, foreign languages, health, kindergarten/preschool, mathematics, music, physical, science, social studies, special, voc/tech. **Engineering:** General, agricultural, chemical, computer, environmental. **Family/consumer sciences:** Child development, communication, consumer economics, family resources, food/nutrition, housing. **Foreign languages:** Ancient Greek, Arabic, Chinese, classics, comparative lit, French, German, Italian, Japanese, Latin, linguistics, Romance, Russian, Spanish. **Health:** Communication disorders, dietetics, environmental health, music therapy, public health ed. **History:** General. **Interdisciplinary:** Biological/physical sciences, cognitive science, nutrition sciences. **Liberal arts:** Arts/sciences. **Math:** General, statistics. **Parks/recreation:** Sports admin. **Philosophy/religion:** Philosophy, religion. **Physical sciences:** Astronomy, chemistry, geology, physics. **Protective services:** Criminal justice. **Psychology:** General, educational. **Public administration:** Social work. **Social sciences:** Anthropology, economics, geography, international relations, political science, sociology. **Visual/performing arts:** Art, art history/conservation, dance, dramatic, film/cinema, music performance, music theory/composition, studio arts.

**Most popular majors.** Biology 8%, business/marketing 23%, communications/journalism 6%, education 9%, family/consumer sciences 6%, psychology 6%, social sciences 10%.

**Computing on campus.** 3,190 workstations in dormitories, library, computer center, student center. Dormitories wired for high-speed internet access and linked to campus network. Commuter students can connect to campus network. Online course registration, online library, helpline, repair service, student web hosting, wireless network available.

**Student life. Freshman orientation:** Mandatory. Preregistration for classes offered. Two-day sessions offered during summer. **Housing:** Guaranteed on-campus for freshmen. Coed dorms, single-sex dorms, special housing for disabled, apartments, fraternity/sorority housing available. Honors and language focused housing available. **Activities:** Bands, campus ministries, choral groups, dance, drama, film society, international student organizations, literary magazine, music ensembles, Model UN, musical theater, opera, radio station, student government, student newspaper, symphony orchestra, TV station.

**Athletics.** NCAA. **Intercollegiate:** Baseball M, basketball, cross-country, diving, equestrian W, football (tackle) M, golf, gymnastics W, soccer W, softball W, swimming, tennis, track and field, volleyball W. **Intramural:** Basketball, football (non-tackle), football (tackle), golf, racquetball, soccer, softball, squash, tennis, track and field, volleyball. **Team name:** Bulldogs.

**Student services.** Adult student services, alcohol/substance abuse counseling, career counseling, student employment services, financial aid counseling, health services, legal services, minority student services, on-campus daycare, personal counseling, placement for graduates, veterans' counselor, women's services. **Physically disabled:** Services for visually, speech, hearing impaired. **Learning disabled:** Comprehensive services available.

**Contact.** E-mail: undergrad@admissions.uga.edu
Phone: (706) 542-8776 Fax: (706) 542-1466
Nancy McDuff, Associate Vice President for Admissions and Enrollment Management, University of Georgia, Office of Undergraduate Admissions, Athens, GA 30602-1633

---

## University of West Georgia

**Carrollton, Georgia** — **CB member**
**www.westga.edu** — **CB code: 5900**

- Public 4-year university
- Commuter campus in large town
- 9,622 degree-seeking undergraduates: 16% part-time, 60% women, 27% African American, 1% Asian American, 2% Hispanic American, 1% international
- 1,878 degree-seeking graduate students
- 58% of applicants admitted
- SAT or ACT (ACT writing optional) required
- 36% graduate within 6 years

**General.** Founded in 1906. Regionally accredited. Off-campus undergraduate sites in Newnan. Advanced Academy of Georgia for academically accelerated high school juniors and seniors. **Degrees:** 1,331 bachelor's awarded; master's, doctoral offered. **ROTC:** Army. **Location:** 50 miles from Atlanta. **Calendar:** Semester, extensive summer session. **Full-time faculty:** 431 total; 78% have terminal degrees, 16% minority, 50% women. **Part-time faculty:** 134 total; 50% have terminal degrees, 8% minority, 72% women. **Class size:** 35% < 20, 45% 20-39, 9% 40-49, 8% 50-99, 2% >100. **Special facilities:** Observatory, performing arts center, archaeological laboratory, technology enhanced learning center.

**Freshman class profile.** 5,981 applied, 3,444 admitted, 2,033 enrolled.

| Mid 50% test scores | | | |
|---|---|---|---|
| SAT critical reading: | 450-540 | GPA 2.0-2.99: | 45% |
| SAT math: | 450-530 | Return as sophomores: | 73% |
| SAT writing: | 440-520 | Out-of-state: | 3% |
| ACT composite: | 18-22 | Live on campus: | 68% |
| GPA 3.75 or higher: | 8% | International: | 2% |
| GPA 3.50-3.74: | 11% | Fraternities: | 12% |
| GPA 3.0-3.49: | 35% | Sororities: | 13% |

**Basis for selection.** GED not accepted. Freshman admission based on SAT/ACT, GPA in college preparatory subjects, and system-mandated college preparatory curriculum. **Homeschooled:** 430 SAT verbal and 410 SAT math or 17 ACT English and math required. Must submit academic portfolio booklets detailing all 16 high school college prep courses.

**High school preparation.** College-preparatory program required. 16 units required. Required and recommended units include English 4, mathematics 4, social studies 1, history 2, science 3-4 (laboratory 2) and foreign language 2. 1 math higher than algebra II required.

**2009-2010 Annual costs.** Tuition/fees: $5,382; $17,358 out-of-state. Room/board: $6,504. Books/supplies: $1,000. Personal expenses: $3,060.

**2009-2010 Financial aid. Need-based:** 1,686 full-time freshmen applied for aid; 1,269 were judged to have need; 1,248 of these received aid. Average need met was 65%. Average scholarship/grant was $6,614; average loan $3,232. 53% of total undergraduate aid awarded as scholarships/grants, 47% as loans/jobs. **Non-need-based:** Awarded to 1,364 full-time undergraduates, including 409 freshmen. Scholarships awarded for academics, alumni affiliation, art, athletics, leadership, minority status, music/drama, religious affiliation, state residency.

**Application procedures. Admission:** Priority date 5/1; deadline 6/1 (receipt date). $30 fee, may be waived for applicants with need. Admission notification on a rolling basis beginning on or about 8/1. **Financial aid:** No deadline. FAFSA required. Applicants notified on a rolling basis starting 6/1; must reply within 4 week(s) of notification.

**Academics. Special study options:** Accelerated study, cooperative education, distance learning, double major, dual enrollment of high school students, external degree, honors, independent study, internships, study abroad, teacher certification program. **Credit/placement by examination:** AP, CLEP, IB, SAT, ACT, institutional tests. 30 credit hours maximum toward bachelor's degree. **Support services:** Learning center, pre-admission summer program, reduced course load, remedial instruction, study skills assistance, tutoring, writing center.

**Honors college/program.** Open to entering freshmen who meet 2 of the following: 1200 SAT or 26 ACT; 610 SAT verbal or 27 ACT English; 3.5 GPA. Recommended entrance no later than beginning of sophomore year.

**Majors. Biology:** General. **Business:** Accounting, business admin, finance, management information systems, managerial economics, marketing, real estate. **Communications:** Journalism. **Computer sciences:** General. **Conservation:** Environmental science, environmental studies. **Education:** Biology, business, chemistry, elementary, kindergarten/preschool, middle, music, physical, physics, secondary, special. **Foreign languages:** General, French, German, Spanish. **Health:** Nursing (RN), speech pathology. **History:** General. **Math:** General. **Parks/recreation:** Facilities management. **Philosophy/religion:** Philosophy. **Physical sciences:** Chemistry, geology, physics. **Psychology:** General. **Social sciences:** Anthropology, criminology, economics, geography, international economics, international relations, political science, sociology. **Visual/performing arts:** Art, dramatic, music performance, music theory/composition. **Other:** Economics/secondary education.

**Most popular majors.** Biology 6%, business/marketing 25%, education 20%, health sciences 9%, psychology 7%, social sciences 12%.

**Computing on campus.** 1,000 workstations in dormitories, library, computer center, student center. Dormitories wired for high-speed internet access and linked to campus network. Online course registration, online library, helpline, repair service, student web hosting, wireless network available.

**Student life. Freshman orientation:** Mandatory, $85 fee. Preregistration for classes offered. Held beginning of semester; includes registration assistance and presentation of available services. **Policies:** All freshmen required to reside on-campus unless married or living with parents, relatives, or legal guardians. **Housing:** Guaranteed on-campus for freshmen. Coed dorms, single-sex dorms, special housing for disabled, fraternity/sorority housing available. $250 fully refundable deposit, deadline 7/1. **Activities:** Bands, choral groups, dance, drama, international student organizations, literary magazine, music ensembles, musical theater, opera, radio station, student government, student newspaper, TV station, Baptist Student Union, Catholic Student Life, Muslim student alliance, Latter-Day Saint student association, Jewish student group, Black Students Alliance, Democratic organization, Republican organization.

**Athletics.** NCAA. **Intercollegiate:** Baseball M, basketball, cheerleading, cross-country, football (tackle) M, golf, soccer W, softball W, volleyball W. **Intramural:** Basketball, football (non-tackle), golf, sailing, soccer, softball, table tennis, tennis, track and field, volleyball, weight lifting. **Team name:** Wolves.

**Student services.** Adult student services, career counseling, student employment services, financial aid counseling, health services, minority student services, on-campus daycare, personal counseling, placement for graduates, veterans' counselor. **Physically disabled:** Services for visually, speech, hearing impaired.

**Contact.** E-mail: admiss@westga.edu
Phone: (678) 839-4000 Fax: (678) 839-4747
Bobby Johnson, Director of Admissions, University of West Georgia, 1601 Maple Street, Carrollton, GA 30118

## Valdosta State University

**Valdosta, Georgia**
**www.valdosta.edu**

**CB member**
**CB code: 5855**

- Public 4-year university
- Commuter campus in small city
- 10,275 degree-seeking undergraduates: 12% part-time, 58% women, 31% African American, 1% Asian American, 1% Hispanic American, 2% international
- 1,999 degree-seeking graduate students
- 71% of applicants admitted
- SAT or ACT (ACT writing optional) required
- 43% graduate within 6 years

**General.** Founded in 1906. Regionally accredited. **Degrees:** 1,631 bachelor's, 57 associate awarded; master's, doctoral offered. **ROTC:** Air Force. **Location:** 228 miles from Atlanta; 124 miles from Jacksonville, FL. **Calendar:** Semester, extensive summer session. **Full-time faculty:** 456 total; 75% have terminal degrees, 10% minority, 48% women. **Part-time faculty:** 120 total; 18% have terminal degrees, 2% minority, 66% women. **Class size:** 34% < 20, 53% 20-39, 10% 40-49, 2% 50-99, 1% >100. **Special facilities:** Planetarium, herbarium, observatory, archives museum, pedestrian mall.

**Freshman class profile.** 6,703 applied, 4,744 admitted, 2,467 enrolled.

| Mid 50% test scores | | | |
|---|---|---|---|
| SAT critical reading: | 470-550 | GPA 2.0-2.99: | 45% |
| SAT math: | 460-540 | Return as sophomores: | 72% |
| SAT writing: | 450-540 | Out-of-state: | 3% |
| ACT composite: | 20-23 | Live on campus: | 75% |
| GPA 3.75 or higher: | 9% | International: | 2% |
| GPA 3.50-3.74: | 10% | Fraternities: | 7% |
| GPA 3.0-3.49: | 36% | Sororities: | 9% |

**Basis for selection.** GED not accepted. 440 SAT Verbal, 410 SAT Math or 18 ACT English, 17 ACT Math required. Freshmen Index of 2040 required, based on academic GPA multiplied by 500 added to SAT verbal and math scores. **Homeschooled:** 1050 SAT (exclusive of Writing) or 23 ACT, declaration of intent to homeschool filed with Board of Education, portfolio that demonstrates satisfactory completion of college prep curriculum, letter from primary teacher certifying completion of high school and date of graduation, 2 letters of recommendation from non-family members, certificate of immunization required. **Learning Disabled:** Untimed SAT/ACT accepted.

**High school preparation.** College-preparatory program required. 16 units required. Required units include English 4, mathematics 4, social studies 3, science 3 (laboratory 2) and foreign language 2.

**2009-2010 Annual costs.** Tuition/fees: $5,506; $17,482 out-of-state. Room/board: $6,670. Books/supplies: $1,200. Personal expenses: $2,740.

**2008-2009 Financial aid.** **Need-based:** 1,781 full-time freshmen applied for aid; 1,296 were judged to have need; 1,286 of these received aid. Average need met was 90%. Average scholarship/grant was $5,725; average loan $4,457. 37% of total undergraduate aid awarded as scholarships/grants, 63% as loans/jobs. **Non-need-based:** Awarded to 410 full-time undergraduates, including 127 freshmen. Scholarships awarded for academics, alumni affiliation, art, athletics, minority status, music/drama, ROTC, state residency.

**Application procedures.** **Admission:** Closing date 6/15 (receipt date). $40 fee, may be waived for applicants with need. Admission notification on a rolling basis beginning on or about 9/1. **Financial aid:** Priority date 5/1; no closing date. FAFSA required. Applicants notified on a rolling basis starting 5/15.

**Academics.** **Special study options:** Accelerated study, cooperative education, distance learning, double major, dual enrollment of high school students, ESL, external degree, honors, independent study, internships, study abroad, teacher certification program, weekend college. **Credit/placement by examination:** AP, CLEP, IB, SAT, ACT. 30 credit hours maximum toward associate degree, 30 toward bachelor's. **Support services:** Study skills assistance, tutoring, writing center.

**Majors. Biology:** General. **Business:** Accounting, administrative services, business admin, finance, managerial economics, marketing. **Communications:** Media studies. **Computer sciences:** General, information systems. **Conservation:** Environmental science. **Education:** Art, business, Deaf/hearing impaired, early childhood, French, middle, music, physical, secondary, Spanish, special, trade/industrial. **Foreign languages:** French, sign language interpretation, Spanish. **Health:** Athletic training, nursing (RN), speech pathology. **History:** General. **Legal studies:** Paralegal. **Liberal arts:** Arts/sciences. **Math:** General, applied. **Parks/recreation:** Health/fitness. **Philosophy/religion:** Philosophy. **Physical sciences:** Astronomy, chemistry, physics. **Protective services:** Criminal justice. **Psychology:** General. **Social sciences:** Political science, sociology. **Visual/performing arts:** General, art, dance, interior design, music performance.

**Most popular majors.** Business/marketing 19%, education 22%, English 9%, health sciences 9%, social sciences 7%.

**Computing on campus.** 1,225 workstations in dormitories, library. Dormitories wired for high-speed internet access and linked to campus network. Commuter students can connect to campus network. Online course registration, online library, helpline, repair service, student web hosting, wireless network available.

**Student life. Freshman orientation:** Available, $35 fee. Preregistration for classes offered. One-day programs held in May, June, July, and August. **Housing:** Coed dorms, special housing for disabled, apartments available. $300 fully refundable deposit, deadline 4/15. Honors floors available. **Activities:** Bands, campus ministries, choral groups, dance, drama, international student organizations, literary magazine, music ensembles, Model UN, radio station, student government, student newspaper, symphony orchestra, TV station, Black Student League, outdoor adventure club, Habitat for Humanity, other religious and social service organizations.

**Athletics.** NCAA. **Intercollegiate:** Baseball M, basketball, cross-country, football (tackle) M, golf M, softball W, tennis, volleyball W. **Intramural:** Badminton, basketball, bowling, football (non-tackle), soccer, softball, table tennis, tennis, volleyball, weight lifting. **Team name:** Blazers.

**Student services.** Alcohol/substance abuse counseling, career counseling, student employment services, financial aid counseling, health services, minority student services, personal counseling, placement for graduates, veterans' counselor. **Physically disabled:** Services for visually, speech, hearing impaired. **Learning disabled:** Comprehensive services available.

**Contact.** E-mail: admissions@valdosta.edu
Phone: (229) 333-5791 Toll-free number: (800) 618-1878
Fax: (229) 333-5482
Walter Peacock, Director of Admissions, Valdosta State University, 1500 North Patterson Street, Valdosta, GA 31698-0170

## Wesleyan College

**Macon, Georgia**
**www.wesleyancollege.edu**

**CB member**
**CB code: 5895**

- Private 4-year liberal arts college for women affiliated with United Methodist Church
- Residential campus in small city
- 610 degree-seeking undergraduates: 37% part-time, 100% women
- 96 degree-seeking graduate students
- 53% of applicants admitted
- SAT or ACT (ACT writing optional), application essay required

**General.** Founded in 1836. Regionally accredited. **Degrees:** 77 bachelor's awarded; master's offered. **Location:** 75 miles from Atlanta. **Calendar:** Semester, limited summer session. **Full-time faculty:** 47 total; 100% have terminal degrees, 8% minority, 55% women. **Part-time faculty:** 33 total; 21% have terminal degrees, 70% women. **Class size:** 91% < 20, 9% 20-39. **Special facilities:** Equestrian facilities, arboretum, lake.

**Freshman class profile.** 536 applied, 286 admitted, 100 enrolled.

| Mid 50% test scores | | | |
|---|---|---|---|
| SAT critical reading: | 500-610 | ACT composite: | 20-28 |
| SAT math: | 460-600 | Out-of-state: | 22% |
| SAT writing: | 480-630 | Live on campus: | 90% |

**Basis for selection.** Admission committee reviews applicants based on academic performance in college preparatory courses, standardized test scores, extra-curricular activities and recommendations. Interview recommended; required for scholarship competitions. Audition required of music or theater students interested in performance arts scholarship. Portfolio required of art majors. **Homeschooled:** Statement describing homeschool structure and mission, transcript of courses and grades, letter of recommendation (nonparent) required. Diplomas issued by parents are recognized. Student may provide biography of high school literature and essay to evaluate exposure and thinking skills. Extra-curricular activities, counselor interviews considered.

**High school preparation.** College-preparatory program recommended. 15 units required; 22 recommended. Required and recommended units include English 4, mathematics 3-4, social studies 3-4, science 3-4 (laboratory 2-3), foreign language 2-4 and academic electives 2.

**2010-2011 Annual costs.** Tuition/fees: $18,000. Room/board: $8,100. Books/supplies: $1,000. Personal expenses: $1,000.

**2009-2010 Financial aid. Need-based:** 81 full-time freshmen applied for aid; 72 were judged to have need; 72 of these received aid. Average need met was 83%. Average scholarship/grant was $14,881; average loan $3,471. 65% of total undergraduate aid awarded as scholarships/grants, 35% as loans/jobs. **Non-need-based:** Awarded to 178 full-time undergraduates, including 53 freshmen. Scholarships awarded for academics, alumni affiliation, art, job skills, leadership, minority status, music/drama, religious affiliation, state residency.

**Application procedures. Admission:** Priority date 3/1; deadline 6/1 (postmark date). $30 fee, may be waived for applicants with need. Admission notification on a rolling basis beginning on or about 10/1. Must reply by 7/1. **Financial aid:** Priority date 2/15, closing date 6/3. FAFSA, institutional form required. Applicants notified on a rolling basis starting 3/1; must reply by 5/1 or within 3 week(s) of notification.

**Academics. Special study options:** Accelerated study, combined bachelor's/graduate degree, cross-registration, double major, dual enrollment of high school students, exchange student, honors, independent study, internships, liberal arts/career combination, student-designed major, study abroad, teacher certification program, weekend college. **Credit/placement by examination:** AP, CLEP, IB, institutional tests. 30 credit hours maximum toward bachelor's degree. **Support services:** Learning center, reduced course load, study skills assistance, tutoring, writing center.

**Majors. Biology:** General. **Business:** Business admin, international. **Communications:** General, advertising. **Computer sciences:** General. **Education:** Early childhood. **Foreign languages:** French, Spanish. **History:** General. **Liberal arts:** Arts/sciences. **Math:** General. **Philosophy/religion:** Philosophy, religion. **Physical sciences:** Chemistry, physics. **Psychology:** General. **Social sciences:** General, economics, international relations. **Theology:** Preministerial. **Visual/performing arts:** Art history/conservation, dramatic, studio arts.

**Most popular majors.** Business/marketing 8%, communications/journalism 13%, liberal arts 7%, psychology 17%, visual/performing arts 24%.

**Computing on campus.** PC or laptop required. 20 workstations in library, student center. Dormitories wired for high-speed internet access and linked to campus network. Commuter students can connect to campus network. Online course registration, online library, helpline, repair service, wireless network available.

**Student life. Freshman orientation:** Mandatory. Preregistration for classes offered. Summer orientation held in June; includes registration. Fall orientation held in August prior to start of classes. **Policies:** Students required to live on campus unless married or living with immediate family in the local area. Honor Code used. **Housing:** Guaranteed on-campus for all undergraduates. Special housing for disabled, apartments available. $150 deposit, deadline 7/1. **Activities:** Campus ministries, choral groups, dance, drama, international student organizations, literary magazine, music ensembles, Model UN, student government, student newspaper, honor council, Mortar board, Young Democrats, Circle K, College Republicans, Council on Religions Concerns, American Chemical Society, Wesleyan Disciples.

**Athletics.** NCAA. **Intercollegiate:** Basketball W, cross-country W, equestrian W, soccer W, softball W, tennis W. **Intramural:** Basketball W, cross-country W, soccer W, softball W, volleyball W. **Team name:** Pioneers.

**Student services.** Adult student services, alcohol/substance abuse counseling, chaplain/spiritual director, career counseling, student employment services, financial aid counseling, health services, minority student services, personal counseling, women's services.

**Contact.** E-mail: admission@wesleyancollege.edu
Phone: (478) 757-5206 Toll-free number: (800) 447-6610
Fax: (478) 757-4030
C. Stephen Farr, Vice President for Enrollment Services, Wesleyan College, 4760 Forsyth Road, Macon, GA 31210-4462

## Westwood College: Atlanta Midtown
Atlanta, Georgia
www.westwood.edu/locations/georgia/atlanta-midtown-campus

▶  For-profit 3-year technical college
▶  Commuter campus in very large city

**General.** Accredited by ACICS. **Calendar:** Differs by program.

**Contact.**  Phone: (404) 745-9096
Director of Admissions, 1100 Spring Street, Suite 200, Atlanta, GA 30309

## Westwood College: Northlake
Atlanta, Georgia
www.westwood.edu

▶  For-profit 4-year visual arts and technical college
▶  Very large city

**General.** Accredited by ACICS. **Calendar:** Differs by program.

**Contact.**  Phone: (404) 962-2998
2220 Parklake Drive, Suite 175, Atlanta, GA 30345

# Hawaii

## Argosy University: Hawaii
Honolulu, Hawaii
www.argosy.edu/hawaii

- For-profit 4-year university
- Large city
- 50 degree-seeking undergraduates

**General.** Regionally accredited. **Degrees:** 11 bachelor's awarded; master's, doctoral, professional offered. **Calendar:** Continuous. **Full-time faculty:** 17 total. **Part-time faculty:** 41 total.

**Freshman class profile.** 16 enrolled.

**Basis for selection.** Open admission.

**Academics. Credit/placement by examination:** CLEP.

**Majors. Business:** Business admin. **Liberal arts:** Arts/sciences. **Protective services:** Police science. **Psychology:** General.

**Contact.** E-mail: auhonadmissions@argosy.edu
Phone: (808) 791-5214 Toll-free number: (888) 323-2777
Argosy University: Hawaii, 400 ASB Tower, 1001 Bishop Street, Honolulu, HI 96813

## Brigham Young University-Hawaii
Laie, Hawaii
www.byuh.edu                                         CB code: 4106

- Private 4-year university and liberal arts college affiliated with Church of Jesus Christ of Latter-day Saints
- Residential campus in small town

**General.** Founded in 1955. Regionally accredited. **Location:** 38 miles from Honolulu. **Calendar:** Semester.

**Annual costs/financial aid.** Tuition/fees (2009-2010): $3,800. 100% higher tuition and per-credit-hour charges for students who are not members of The Church of Jesus Christ of Latter-day Saints. Room/board: $4,580. Books/supplies: $800. Personal expenses: $1,600. Need-based financial aid available to full-time and part-time students.

**Contact.** Phone: (808) 675-3738
Dean of Admissions and Records, 55-220 Kulanui Street, #1973, Laie, HI 96762-1294

## Chaminade University of Honolulu
Honolulu, Hawaii                                     CB member
www.chaminade.edu                                    CB code: 4105

- Private 4-year university affiliated with Roman Catholic Church
- Commuter campus in large city
- 1,013 degree-seeking undergraduates: 4% part-time, 66% women, 3% African American, 68% Asian American, 7% Hispanic American, 1% Native American, 3% international
- 727 degree-seeking graduate students
- 95% of applicants admitted
- SAT and SAT Subject Tests or ACT (ACT writing optional), application essay required
- 41% graduate within 6 years

**General.** Founded in 1955. Regionally accredited. Campus shared with St. Louis School. **Degrees:** 314 bachelor's, 102 associate awarded; master's offered. **ROTC:** Army, Air Force. **Location:** 2 miles from Waikiki. **Calendar:** Semester, limited summer session. **Full-time faculty:** 70 total; 71% have terminal degrees, 40% minority, 37% women. **Part-time faculty:** 50 total; 14% have terminal degrees, 32% minority, 50% women. **Class size:** 59% < 20, 41% 20-39. **Special facilities:** Montessori laboratory preschool, observatory, theater.

**Freshman class profile.** 1,037 applied, 989 admitted, 264 enrolled.

| Mid 50% test scores | | | |
|---|---|---|---|
| SAT critical reading: | 420-520 | GPA 2.0-2.99: | 35% |
| SAT math: | 420-520 | Rank in top quarter: | 34% |
| SAT writing: | 410-510 | Rank in top tenth: | 9% |
| ACT composite: | 18-22 | Return as sophomores: | 69% |
| GPA 3.75 or higher: | 14% | Out-of-state: | 42% |
| GPA 3.50-3.74: | 15% | Live on campus: | 73% |
| GPA 3.0-3.49: | 36% | International: | 2% |

**Basis for selection.** School achievement record, test scores, statement of purpose important. Interview recommended for marginal students.

**High school preparation.** Recommended units include English 4, mathematics 3, social studies 3, science 2 and academic electives 4.

**2010-2011 Annual costs.** Tuition/fees: $17,740. Room/board: $10,490. Books/supplies: $1,200. Personal expenses: $1,254.

**2009-2010 Financial aid. Non-need-based:** Scholarships awarded for academics, art, athletics, leadership, religious affiliation, ROTC, state residency. **Additional information:** For students whose eligibility for federal and institutional aid does not meet entire costs, alternative student loans may be secured for eligible applicants.

**Application procedures. Admission:** No deadline. $50 fee. Admission notification on a rolling basis. **Financial aid:** Priority date 2/15; no closing date. FAFSA required. Applicants notified on a rolling basis starting 2/15; must reply within 4 week(s) of notification.

**Academics. Special study options:** Accelerated study, distance learning, double major, exchange student, independent study, internships, semester at sea, student-designed major, teacher certification program. Accelerated sessions in evening division. **Credit/placement by examination:** AP, CLEP, IB, institutional tests. 30 credit hours maximum toward associate degree, 30 toward bachelor's. **Support services:** Learning center, pre-admission summer program, remedial instruction, study skills assistance, tutoring.

**Majors. Biology:** General. **Business:** Accounting, business admin, marketing. **Communications:** General, broadcast journalism, media studies, public relations. **Computer sciences:** General, computer science. **Conservation:** Environmental studies. **Education:** Early childhood, elementary, secondary. **History:** General. **Interdisciplinary:** Behavioral sciences. **Liberal arts:** Arts/sciences. **Philosophy/religion:** Religion. **Protective services:** Criminalistics, forensics. **Psychology:** General. **Social sciences:** General, international relations, political science. **Visual/performing arts:** Interior design.

**Most popular majors.** Business/marketing 11%, communications/journalism 6%, education 17%, English 6%, history 8%, psychology 15%, security/protective services 20%.

**Computing on campus.** 100 workstations in dormitories, library, computer center, student center. Dormitories wired for high-speed internet access and linked to campus network. Online library, helpline, repair service, wireless network available.

**Student life. Freshman orientation:** Mandatory, $140 fee. Preregistration for classes offered. **Housing:** Guaranteed on-campus for freshmen. Coed dorms, single-sex dorms, special housing for disabled, apartments, wellness housing available. $300 deposit, deadline 5/1. **Activities:** Choral groups, drama, literary magazine, musical theater, student government, student newspaper, symphony orchestra, Samoan club, Hawaiian club, Rotaract club, accounting club, Black Student Union, Filipino club, CJ Sleuths, communications club.

**Athletics.** NCAA. **Intercollegiate:** Basketball M, cross-country, golf, softball W, tennis, volleyball W. **Intramural:** Cheerleading. **Team name:** Silverswords.

**Student services.** Adult student services, alcohol/substance abuse counseling, chaplain/spiritual director, career counseling, services for economically disadvantaged, student employment services, financial aid counseling, health services, personal counseling, placement for graduates. **Physically disabled:** Services for visually, speech, hearing impaired.

**Contact.** E-mail: admissions@chaminade.edu
Phone: (808) 735-4735 Toll-free number: (800) 735-3733
Fax: (808) 739-4647
Dan Yoshitake, Associate Director of Admissions, Chaminade University of Honolulu, 3140 Waialae Avenue, Honolulu, HI 96816

## Hawaii Pacific University

**Honolulu, Hawaii**
**www.hpu.edu**

CB member
CB code: 4352

- Private 4-year university and liberal arts college
- Commuter campus in large city
- 6,342 degree-seeking undergraduates: 43% part-time, 58% women
- 1,167 degree-seeking graduate students
- 73% of applicants admitted
- SAT or ACT (ACT writing optional) required
- 39% graduate within 6 years

**General.** Founded in 1965. Regionally accredited. Three (3) main campuses connected by free shuttle service. Programs offered for military personnel and their dependents and for older students. Satellite campus on six (6) military installations on Oahu. Affiliated with the Oceanic Institute. **Degrees:** 1,045 bachelor's, 135 associate awarded; master's offered. **ROTC:** Army, Air Force. **Calendar:** Semester, extensive summer session. **Full-time faculty:** 253 total; 64% have terminal degrees, 22% minority, 45% women. **Part-time faculty:** 346 total; 30% have terminal degrees, 35% minority, 47% women. **Class size:** 63% < 20, 37% 20-39, less than 1% 40-49. **Special facilities:** Oceanic Institute, entrepreneurship center, research boat, theater.

**Freshman class profile.** 3,645 applied, 2,668 admitted, 637 enrolled.

| Mid 50% test scores | | | |
|---|---|---|---|
| SAT critical reading: | 430-560 | Rank in top quarter: | 49% |
| SAT math: | 450-570 | Rank in top tenth: | 24% |
| SAT writing: | 430-540 | End year in good standing: | 93% |
| ACT composite: | 18-24 | Return as sophomores: | 66% |
| GPA 3.75 or higher: | 22% | Out-of-state: | 53% |
| GPA 3.50-3.74: | 18% | Live on campus: | 24% |
| GPA 3.0-3.49: | 34% | International: | 6% |
| GPA 2.0-2.99: | 26% | | |

**Basis for selection.** Academic record, test scores most important. Interview also important, recommendations considered. Essay recommended. **Homeschooled:** Interview, letter of recommendation (nonparent) required.

**High school preparation.** 14 units recommended. Recommended units include English 4, mathematics 4, social studies 3, history 2, science 2 (laboratory 1) and foreign language 2. Additional science and mathematics required for nursing and marine science.

**2010-2011 Annual costs.** Tuition/fees: $15,820. Room/board: $11,648. Books/supplies: $1,300. Personal expenses: $800.

**2009-2010 Financial aid. Need-based:** 15% of total undergraduate aid awarded as scholarships/grants, 85% as loans/jobs. **Non-need-based:** Scholarships awarded for academics, alumni affiliation, athletics, job skills, leadership, music/drama, religious affiliation, ROTC.

**Application procedures. Admission:** Priority date 3/1; no deadline. $50 fee, may be waived for applicants with need. Admission notification on a rolling basis. Must reply by May 1 or within 4 week(s) if notified thereafter. **Financial aid:** Priority date 3/1; no closing date. FAFSA required. Applicants notified on a rolling basis starting 4/1; must reply within 3 week(s) of notification.

**Academics.** All students complete core requirements based on following themes: global systems, world cultures, communication skills, research/epistemology, values and choices. **Special study options:** Accelerated study, combined bachelor's/graduate degree, cooperative education, distance learning, double major, dual enrollment of high school students, ESL, honors, independent study, internships, liberal arts/career combination, student-designed major, study abroad, teacher certification program, weekend college, 3-2 engineering program with University of Southern California (CA), Washington University, St. Louis (MO). **Credit/placement by examination:** AP, CLEP, IB, SAT, ACT, institutional tests. 36 credit hours maximum toward associate degree, 36 toward bachelor's. **Support services:** Learning center, pre-admission summer program, reduced course load, remedial instruction, study skills assistance, tutoring.

**Majors. Biology:** General, marine. **Business:** General, accounting, banking/financial services, business admin, communications, finance, human resources, international, international finance, management information systems, managerial economics, marketing, tourism/travel. **Communications:** General, advertising, journalism, public relations. **Computer sciences:** General, computer science. **Conservation:** General, environmental science, environmental studies. **Education:** ESL. **Family/consumer sciences:** Family studies. **Foreign languages:** Comparative lit. **Health:** Nursing (RN), premedicine. **History:** General. **Interdisciplinary:** Behavioral sciences. **Liberal arts:** Arts/sciences. **Math:** Applied. **Physical sciences:** Oceanography. **Protective services:** Law enforcement admin. **Psychology:** General. **Public**

administration: General, human services, social work. **Social sciences:** General, anthropology, economics, international relations, political science, sociology.

**Most popular majors.** Business/marketing 35%, communications/journalism 9%, health sciences 24%, security/protective services 6%.

**Computing on campus.** 590 workstations in library, computer center, student center. Dormitories wired for high-speed internet access and linked to campus network. Commuter students can connect to campus network. Online course registration, online library, helpline, student web hosting, wireless network available.

**Student life. Freshman orientation:** Available, $80 fee. Preregistration for classes offered. Week of activities including on-campus sessions and off-campus activities. In fall, weekend (Friday, Saturday) including above. In spring, day activities that include on-campus sessions in summer. **Housing:** Coed dorms, apartments, wellness housing available. $500 nonrefundable deposit. **Activities:** Bands, campus ministries, choral groups, dance, drama, film society, international student organizations, literary magazine, music ensembles, musical theater, student government, student newspaper, Rotaract, President's Hosts, Christian Fellowship, American marketing association, hiking club, honors societies, computing club, Students In Free Enterprise.

**Athletics.** NCAA. **Intercollegiate:** Baseball M, basketball, cheerleading, cross-country, golf M, soccer, softball W, tennis, volleyball W. **Intramural:** Basketball, football (tackle), soccer, softball, table tennis, volleyball. **Team name:** Sea Warriors.

**Student services.** Adult student services, alcohol/substance abuse counseling, chaplain/spiritual director, career counseling, student employment services, financial aid counseling, personal counseling, placement for graduates, veterans' counselor.

**Contact.** E-mail: admissions@hpu.edu
Phone: (808) 544-0238 Toll-free number: (866) 225-5478
Fax: (808) 544-1136
Sara Sato, Director of Admissions, Hawaii Pacific University, 1164 Bishop Street, Suite 200, Honolulu, HI 96813

## University of Hawaii at Hilo

**Hilo, Hawaii**
**www.uhh.hawaii.edu**

CB member
CB code: 4869

- Public 4-year university
- Commuter campus in large town
- 3,317 degree-seeking undergraduates: 15% part-time, 59% women, 1% African American, 50% Asian American, 3% Hispanic American, 1% Native American, 5% international
- 472 degree-seeking graduate students
- 50% of applicants admitted
- SAT or ACT (ACT writing optional) required
- 33% graduate within 6 years

**General.** Founded in 1970. Regionally accredited. **Degrees:** 546 bachelor's awarded; master's offered. **Location:** 200 miles from Honolulu. **Calendar:** Semester, limited summer session. **Full-time faculty:** 262 total. **Part-time faculty:** 83 total. **Class size:** 50% < 20, 44% 20-39, 4% 40-49, 2% 50-99, less than 1% >100. **Special facilities:** Active volcanoes study center, space science center, small business development center, marine education center, 110-acre farm laboratory, fitness center/pool.

**Freshman class profile.** 2,165 applied, 1,093 admitted, 495 enrolled.

| Mid 50% test scores | | | |
|---|---|---|---|
| SAT critical reading: | 440-590 | Rank in top quarter: | 47% |
| SAT math: | 440-600 | Rank in top tenth: | 17% |
| ACT composite: | 17-24 | End year in good standing: | 81% |
| GPA 3.75 or higher: | 20% | Return as sophomores: | 69% |
| GPA 3.50-3.74: | 17% | Out-of-state: | 27% |
| GPA 3.0-3.49: | 40% | Live on campus: | 64% |
| GPA 2.0-2.99: | 23% | International: | 1% |

**Basis for selection.** High school GPA in academic subjects, SAT/ACT test scores, class rank, and school recommendation considered.

**High school preparation.** 17 units required. Required and recommended units include English 4, mathematics 3, social studies 2, history 2, science 3, foreign language 2 and academic electives 7. 3 mathematics beyond pre-algebra, 7 academic electives not including physical education or ROTC. 4 math and 4 science recommended for science and business majors.

**2009-2010 Annual costs.** Tuition/fees: $4,888; $14,392 out-of-state. Room/board: $7,014. Books/supplies: $1,017. Personal expenses: $1,166.

**2008-2009 Financial aid. Need-based:** 273 full-time freshmen applied for aid; 272 were judged to have need; 272 of these received aid. Average need met was 54%. Average scholarship/grant was $4,583; average loan $3,171. 44% of total undergraduate aid awarded as scholarships/grants, 56% as loans/jobs. **Non-need-based:** Awarded to 317 full-time undergraduates, including 74 freshmen. **Additional information:** Hawaii student incentive grants and tuition waivers (merit and need-based) available to Hawaii residents at participating institutions.

**Application procedures. Admission:** Priority date 3/1; deadline 7/1 (postmark date). $50 fee, may be waived for applicants with need. Admission notification on a rolling basis beginning on or about 10/1. Must reply by May 1 or within 2 week(s) if notified thereafter. **Financial aid:** Priority date 3/1; no closing date. FAFSA required. Applicants notified on a rolling basis starting 4/15; must reply within 2 week(s) of notification.

**Academics. Special study options:** Combined bachelor's/graduate degree, cross-registration, distance learning, double major, dual enrollment of high school students, exchange student, honors, independent study, internships, student-designed major, study abroad, teacher certification program. Marine sciences and astronomy summer programs. **Credit/placement by examination:** CLEP, IB, institutional tests. 30 credit hours maximum toward bachelor's degree. **Support services:** Learning center, tutoring, writing center.

**Majors. Agriculture:** Agribusiness operations, agronomy, animal sciences, horticultural science, plant protection, soil science. **Area/ethnic studies:** Native American. **Biology:** General, marine. **Business:** General, accounting, business admin, finance, marketing. **Communications:** General. **Computer sciences:** General. **Foreign languages:** Japanese, linguistics. **Health:** Premedicine. **History:** General. **Interdisciplinary:** Natural sciences. **Liberal arts:** Arts/sciences. **Math:** General. **Parks/recreation:** Facilities management, health/fitness. **Philosophy/religion:** Philosophy, religion. **Physical sciences:** Astronomy, chemistry, geology, physics. **Psychology:** General. **Public administration:** General. **Social sciences:** Anthropology, economics, geography, political science, sociology. **Visual/performing arts:** Art.

**Most popular majors.** Biology 12%, business/marketing 9%, communications/journalism 7%, health sciences 9%, psychology 16%, social sciences 14%.

**Computing on campus.** 600 workstations in dormitories, library, computer center, student center. Commuter students can connect to campus network. Online course registration, online library, helpline, repair service available.

**Student life. Freshman orientation:** Available, $25 fee. Preregistration for classes offered. 1-week program before start of classes. **Housing:** Coed dorms, special housing for disabled, apartments available. $20 deposit, deadline 7/15. Student housing units available for mobility-impaired students. **Activities:** Bands, choral groups, dance, drama, literary magazine, music ensembles, musical theater, student government, student newspaper, international student association, Samoan club, Delta Sigma Pi business fraternity, World Hope, Rotoract, Bayanihan club, Bahai Club, Chuukese Student Association, Earth Action, Nihon no kai.

**Athletics.** NCAA. **Intercollegiate:** Baseball M, basketball, cross-country, golf, soccer, softball W, tennis, volleyball W. **Intramural:** Archery, badminton, basketball, bowling, cross-country, golf, softball, table tennis, tennis, volleyball. **Team name:** Vulcans.

**Student services.** Career counseling, services for economically disadvantaged, student employment services, financial aid counseling, health services, minority student services, personal counseling, placement for graduates, women's services. **Physically disabled:** Services for visually, speech, hearing impaired.

**Contact.** E-mail: uhhadm@hawaii.edu
Phone: (808) 974-7414 Toll-free number: (800) 897-4456
Fax: (808) 933-0861
James Cromwell, Director of Admissions, University of Hawaii at Hilo, 200 West Kawili Street, Hilo, HI 96720-4091

---

## University of Hawaii at Manoa
**Honolulu, Hawaii**                          CB member
**www.manoa.hawaii.edu**                      CB code: 4867

- Public 4-year university
- Commuter campus in very large city
- 13,583 degree-seeking undergraduates: 18% part-time, 54% women, 1% African American, 67% Asian American, 3% Hispanic American, 1% Native American, 4% international

- 5,726 degree-seeking graduate students
- 67% of applicants admitted
- SAT or ACT with writing required
- 51% graduate within 6 years

**General.** Founded in 1907. Regionally accredited. **Degrees:** 2,933 bachelor's awarded; master's, doctoral, professional offered. **ROTC:** Army, Air Force. **Location:** 3 miles from downtown. **Calendar:** Semester, extensive summer session. **Full-time faculty:** 1,200 total; 87% have terminal degrees, 34% minority, 41% women. **Part-time faculty:** 70 total; 69% have terminal degrees, 47% minority, 51% women. **Class size:** 45% < 20, 39% 20-39, 5% 40-49, 6% 50-99, 4% >100. **Special facilities:** Institute for astronomy, observatories, arboretum, East-West center, Japanese tea house and garden, Hawaiian studies center, Korean studies center.

**Freshman class profile.** 7,196 applied, 4,837 admitted, 1,922 enrolled.

| Mid 50% test scores | | | |
|---|---|---|---|
| SAT critical reading: | 480-580 | Rank in top quarter: | 60% |
| SAT math: | 510-620 | Rank in top tenth: | 28% |
| SAT writing: | 480-570 | End year in good standing: | 97% |
| ACT composite: | 21-25 | Return as sophomores: | 77% |
| GPA 3.75 or higher: | 24% | Out-of-state: | 28% |
| GPA 3.50-3.74: | 22% | Live on campus: | 15% |
| GPA 3.0-3.49: | 38% | International: | 2% |
| GPA 2.0-2.99: | 16% | Fraternities: | 1% |
| | | Sororities: | 1% |

**Basis for selection.** School achievement record, test scores, class rank important. **Homeschooled:** State high school equivalency certificate required. In absence of official transcript from accredited school, students must submit GED results in addition to other requirements.

**High school preparation.** College-preparatory program required. 22 units required. Required units include English 4, mathematics 3, social studies 3, science 3 and academic electives 5.

**2009-2010 Annual costs.** Tuition/fees: $7,168; $19,216 out-of-state. Room/board: $8,493. Books/supplies: $1,123. Personal expenses: $1,474.

**2008-2009 Financial aid. Need-based:** 1,330 full-time freshmen applied for aid; 671 were judged to have need; 589 of these received aid. Average need met was 62%. Average scholarship/grant was $5,707; average loan $3,035. 50% of total undergraduate aid awarded as scholarships/grants, 50% as loans/jobs. **Non-need-based:** Awarded to 2,649 full-time undergraduates, including 502 freshmen. Scholarships awarded for academics, alumni affiliation, art, athletics, job skills, leadership, minority status, music/drama, religious affiliation, ROTC, state residency. **Additional information:** Hawaii student incentive grants and tuition waivers (merit and need-based) available to Hawaii residents at participating institutions.

**Application procedures. Admission:** Priority date 1/2; deadline 5/1 (receipt date). $50 fee, may be waived for applicants with need. Admission notification on a rolling basis beginning on or about 12/1. Must reply by May 1 or within 2 week(s) if notified thereafter. **Financial aid:** Priority date 3/1; no closing date. FAFSA required. Applicants notified on a rolling basis starting 3/15; must reply within 4 week(s) of notification.

**Academics. Special study options:** Cooperative education, distance learning, double major, ESL, exchange student, honors, independent study, internships, semester at sea, student-designed major, study abroad, teacher certification program. **Credit/placement by examination:** AP, CLEP, IB, SAT, ACT, institutional tests. 30 credit hours maximum toward bachelor's degree. **Support services:** Learning center, pre-admission summer program, remedial instruction, study skills assistance, tutoring, writing center.

**Majors. Agriculture:** Animal sciences, plant protection. **Area/ethnic studies:** American, Asian, Native American. **Biology:** General, botany, marine, microbiology, zoology. **Business:** General, accounting, business admin, finance, human resources, international, management information systems, marketing, tourism/travel. **Communications:** General, journalism. **Computer sciences:** General, computer science. **Conservation:** Environmental science, management/policy. **Education:** Elementary, ESL, secondary. **Engineering:** Agricultural, civil, electrical, mechanical. **Family/consumer sciences:** General, clothing/textiles. **Foreign languages:** Chinese, classics, Filipino/Tagalog, French, German, Japanese, Korean, Russian, Spanish. **Health:** Audiology/speech pathology, clinical lab science, dental hygiene, nursing (RN). **History:** General. **Interdisciplinary:** Nutrition sciences. **Liberal arts:** Arts/sciences. **Math:** General. **Parks/recreation:** Exercise sciences. **Philosophy/religion:** Philosophy, religion. **Physical sciences:** Chemistry, geology, meteorology, physics. **Psychology:** General. **Public administration:** Social work. **Social sciences:** Anthropology, economics, geography, political science, sociology. **Visual/performing arts:** Art, dance, dramatic. **Other:** Ethnobotany, Tropical plant and soil sciences.

**Most popular majors.** Biology 6%, business/marketing 21%, education 6%, engineering/engineering technologies 6%, psychology 6%, social sciences 11%.

**Computing on campus.** 1,400 workstations in dormitories, library, computer center, student center. Dormitories wired for high-speed internet access and linked to campus network. Commuter students can connect to campus network. Online course registration, online library, helpline, repair service, student web hosting, wireless network available.

**Student life. Freshman orientation:** Available, $80 fee. Preregistration for classes offered. 2-day program. **Housing:** Guaranteed on-campus for freshmen. Coed dorms, apartments, wellness housing available. $225 partly refundable deposit, deadline 5/1. **Activities:** Bands, campus ministries, choral groups, dance, drama, film society, international student organizations, literary magazine, music ensembles, musical theater, radio station, student government, student newspaper, symphony orchestra, TV station, over 150 registered organizations.

**Athletics.** NCAA. **Intercollegiate:** Baseball M, basketball, cheerleading, cross-country W, diving, football (tackle) M, golf, sailing, soccer W, softball W, swimming, tennis, track and field W, volleyball, water polo W. **Intramural:** Badminton, basketball, cross-country, golf, soccer, softball, table tennis, tennis, track and field W, volleyball, weight lifting. **Team name:** Warriors, Rainbow Warriors, Rainbows, Rainbow Wahine.

**Student services.** Adult student services, alcohol/substance abuse counseling, career counseling, services for economically disadvantaged, student employment services, financial aid counseling, health services, minority student services, on-campus daycare, personal counseling, placement for graduates, veterans' counselor, women's services. **Physically disabled:** Services for visually, speech, hearing impaired.

**Contact.** E-mail: ar-info@hawaii.edu
Phone: (808) 956-8975 Toll-free number: (800) 823-9771
Fax: (808) 956-4148
Jan Heu, Director of Admissions and Records, University of Hawaii at Manoa, 2600 Campus Road, QLC Rm 001, Honolulu, HI 96822

## University of Hawaii: West Oahu
**Pearl City, Hawaii**
www.uhwo.hawaii.edu
**CB member**
**CB code: 1042**

- Public 4-year liberal arts and teachers college
- Commuter campus in large town
- 1,253 degree-seeking undergraduates: 68% part-time, 71% women, 2% African American, 64% Asian American, 2% Hispanic American, 3% international
- 81% of applicants admitted
- 56% graduate within 6 years

**General.** Founded in 1976. Regionally accredited. **Degrees:** 211 bachelor's awarded. **ROTC:** Army, Air Force. **Location:** 10 miles from Honolulu. **Calendar:** Semester, limited summer session. **Full-time faculty:** 46 total; 96% have terminal degrees, 50% minority, 46% women. **Part-time faculty:** 28 total; 36% have terminal degrees, 32% minority, 46% women. **Class size:** 60% < 20, 37% 20-39, 3% 40-49.

**Freshman class profile.** 241 applied, 196 admitted, 77 enrolled.

| Mid 50% test scores | | | |
|---|---|---|---|
| ACT composite: | 17-22 | GPA 2.0-2.99: | 31% |
| GPA 3.75 or higher: | 6% | Return as sophomores: | 60% |
| GPA 3.50-3.74: | 13% | Out-of-state: | 1% |
| GPA 3.0-3.49: | 50% | International: | 6% |

**Basis for selection.** Students with 2.7 high school GPA and 22 credits of required high school coursework will be automatically accepted. **Homeschooled:** State high school equivalency certificate required.

**High school preparation.** 22 units required. Required units include English 4, mathematics 3, social studies 3, science 3 and academic electives 5. Math credits must include Algebra II and Geometry. 4 credits of college prep coursework ( language, fine arts, etc.) also required.

**2009-2010 Annual costs.** Tuition/fees: $4,186; $12,970 out-of-state. Foreign students pay out-of-state tuition rates. However, citizens of an eligible Pacific island district, commonwealth, territory or insular jurisdiction, state or nation which does not provide public institutions that grant baccalaureate degrees may be allowed to pay 150% of the resident tuition. Books/supplies: $1,123. Personal expenses: $1,265.

**2008-2009 Financial aid. Need-based:** 42% of total undergraduate aid awarded as scholarships/grants, 58% as loans/jobs. **Non-need-based:** Scholarships awarded for academics, alumni affiliation, leadership, state residency.

**Application procedures. Admission:** Priority date 4/1; deadline 8/1 (postmark date). $50 fee, may be waived for applicants with need. Application must be submitted on paper. Admission notification on a rolling basis beginning on or about 2/1. Must reply by May 1 or within 2 week(s) if notified thereafter. **Financial aid:** Priority date 4/1; no closing date. FAFSA required. Applicants notified on a rolling basis starting 4/1.

**Academics. Special study options:** Distance learning, double major, teacher certification program. **Credit/placement by examination:** AP, CLEP, IB, SAT, ACT, institutional tests. 42 credit hours maximum toward bachelor's degree. 21 lower division and 21 upper division credits may be earned through examination. **Support services:** Study skills assistance, tutoring, writing center.

**Majors. Area/ethnic studies:** Pacific. **Business:** Accounting, business admin. **Computer sciences:** LAN/WAN management. **Education:** Early childhood, elementary. **History:** General. **Personal/culinary services:** Restaurant/catering. **Philosophy/religion:** Philosophy. **Protective services:** Law enforcement admin. **Psychology:** General. **Public administration:** General. **Social sciences:** General, anthropology, economics, political science, sociology.

**Most popular majors.** Business/marketing 37%, psychology 18%, public administration/social services 20%, social sciences 14%.

**Computing on campus.** 18 workstations in computer center. Commuter students can connect to campus network. Online course registration, online library, helpline, student web hosting, wireless network available.

**Student life. Freshman orientation:** Available. Preregistration for classes offered. **Activities:** Student government, accounting club, anthropology/sociology club, business club, economics club, Hawaiian-Pacific Club, humanities club, political science club, psychology association, students in free enterprise.

**Student services.** Career counseling, student employment services, financial aid counseling, veterans' counselor. **Physically disabled:** Services for visually, hearing impaired.

**Contact.** E-mail: admissions@uhwo.hawaii.edu
Phone: (808) 454-4700 Fax: (808) 453-6075
Robyn Oshiro, Admissions Specialist, University of Hawaii: West Oahu, 96-129 Ala Ike, Pearl City, HI 96782

# Idaho

**Contact.** E-mail: boisebible@boisebible.edu
Phone: (208) 376-7731 Toll-free number: (800) 893-7755
Fax: (208) 376-7743
Martin Flaherty, Admissions Director, Boise Bible College, 8695 West
Marigold Street, Boise, ID 83714-1220

## Boise Bible College
### Boise, Idaho
www.boisebible.edu                     CB code: 0891

- Private 4-year Bible college affiliated with nondenominational tradition
- Residential campus in small city
- 173 degree-seeking undergraduates
- SAT or ACT (ACT writing optional), application essay required

**General.** Founded in 1945. Accredited by ABHE. **Degrees:** 20 bachelor's, 6 associate awarded. **Location:** 4 miles from downtown. **Calendar:** Semester. **Full-time faculty:** 8 total. **Part-time faculty:** 8 total.

### Freshman class profile.

| Mid 50% test scores | | | |
|---|---|---|---|
| SAT critical reading: | 380-570 | GPA 3.50-3.74: | 11% |
| SAT math: | 420-490 | GPA 3.0-3.49: | 39% |
| SAT writing: | 350-490 | GPA 2.0-2.99: | 33% |
| ACT composite: | 18-21 | Rank in top quarter: | 23% |
| GPA 3.75 or higher: | 15% | Rank in top tenth: | 3% |

**Basis for selection.** Christian conduct or ethical code standards based on signed student statement, recommendation of home church minister, 1 employment/school reference, and 1 personal reference required. School achievement important. **Homeschooled:** Transcript of courses and grades required. GED or transcripts from homeschooling agency recommended. Applicants submitting home-prepared transcripts advised to consult admissions office.

**High school preparation.** Recommended units include English 4, mathematics 2, history 2 and foreign language 1.

**2009-2010 Annual costs.** Tuition/fees: $8,750. Room/board: $5,832. Books/supplies: $605. Personal expenses: $1,210.

**Financial aid. Non-need-based:** Scholarships awarded for academics, leadership, music/drama, religious affiliation.

**Application procedures. Admission:** Priority date 5/1; deadline 8/1 (receipt date). $25 fee. Application must be submitted on paper. Admission notification on a rolling basis. Must reply by June 1 or 3 weeks after acceptance date if accepted after June 1. **Financial aid:** Priority date 5/1; no closing date. FAFSA, institutional form required. Applicants notified on a rolling basis starting 5/2; must reply by 8/1 or within 2 week(s) of notification.

**Academics. Special study options:** Distance learning, double major, independent study, internships. **Credit/placement by examination:** AP, CLEP, IB, SAT, ACT, institutional tests. ABHE Bible Knowledge Test. **Support services:** Reduced course load, remedial instruction.

**Majors. Theology:** Bible, missionary, pastoral counseling, religious ed, sacred music, theology, youth ministry.

**Computing on campus.** 7 workstations in library, computer center.

**Student life. Freshman orientation:** Mandatory, $50 fee. Preregistration for classes offered. 2 days of training and testing, followed by whitewater boat trip. **Policies:** Religious observance required. **Housing:** Guaranteed on-campus for freshmen. Single-sex dorms available. $150 deposit, deadline 7/1. Trailer hookups for married students. **Activities:** Choral groups, music ensembles, student government, student newspaper, Christian service missions club.

**Athletics. Intramural:** Basketball, football (non-tackle) M, soccer, volleyball. **Team name:** Lions.

**Student services.** Adult student services, career counseling, student employment services, financial aid counseling, health services, personal counseling, placement for graduates, veterans' counselor.

## Boise State University
### Boise, Idaho                     CB member
www.boisestate.edu                     CB code: 4018

- Public 4-year university
- Commuter campus in small city
- 15,997 degree-seeking undergraduates: 24% part-time, 54% women, 2% African American, 3% Asian American, 7% Hispanic American, 1% Native American, 2% international
- 1,924 degree-seeking graduate students
- 87% of applicants admitted
- SAT or ACT (ACT writing optional) required

**General.** Founded in 1932. Regionally accredited. **Degrees:** 2,063 bachelor's, 524 associate awarded; master's, doctoral offered. **ROTC:** Army. **Location:** Downtown. **Calendar:** Semester, extensive summer session. **Full-time faculty:** 542 total; 78% have terminal degrees, 9% minority, 45% women. **Part-time faculty:** 461 total; 18% have terminal degrees, 7% minority, 52% women. **Class size:** 40% < 20, 42% 20-39, 8% 40-49, 6% 50-99, 3% >100. **Special facilities:** Performing arts center, technology center, natural area and world center for birds of prey research.

### Freshman class profile. 4,127 applied, 3,606 admitted, 2,194 enrolled.

| Mid 50% test scores | | | |
|---|---|---|---|
| SAT critical reading: | 460-570 | Rank in top quarter: | 36% |
| SAT math: | 470-590 | Rank in top tenth: | 13% |
| SAT writing: | 440-560 | End year in good standing: | 93% |
| ACT composite: | 19-25 | Return as sophomores: | 69% |
| GPA 3.75 or higher: | 19% | Out-of-state: | 12% |
| GPA 3.50-3.74: | 19% | Live on campus: | 41% |
| GPA 3.0-3.49: | 39% | International: | 1% |
| GPA 2.0-2.99: | 23% | Fraternities: | 1% |
| | | Sororities: | 1% |

**Basis for selection.** Admission based on high school GPA and ACT or SAT score. Applicants without high school diploma or GED may petition for admission. Interview required for nursing majors. **Homeschooled:** State high school equivalency certificate required.

**High school preparation.** College-preparatory program recommended. 15 units required. Required and recommended units include English 4, mathematics 3, social studies 3, science 3 and foreign language 1. One unit foreign language, humanities, or fine arts and 1.5 units other college preparatory also recommended.

**2009-2010 Annual costs.** Tuition/fees: $4,865; $13,868 out-of-state. Out-of-state students (undergraduate and graduate) taking less than 8 credit hours pay in-state rate. Room/board: $5,114. Books/supplies: $1,168. Personal expenses: $2,270.

**2009-2010 Financial aid. Need-based:** Average need met was 19%. Average scholarship/grant was $3,807; average loan $4,902. 36% of total undergraduate aid awarded as scholarships/grants, 64% as loans/jobs. **Non-need-based:** Scholarships awarded for academics, athletics, music/drama, ROTC, state residency.

**Application procedures. Admission:** Closing date 6/30 (postmark date). $40 fee. Admission notification on a rolling basis beginning on or about 2/15. Strongly recommended that students apply January-March. **Financial aid:** Priority date 4/1; no closing date. FAFSA required. Applicants notified on a rolling basis starting 6/1; must reply within 2 week(s) of notification.

**Academics.** Basque studies program abroad. **Special study options:** Distance learning, double major, dual enrollment of high school students, exchange student, honors, independent study, internships, student-designed major, study abroad, teacher certification program, weekend college. **Credit/placement by examination:** AP, CLEP, SAT, ACT, institutional tests. 21 credit hours maximum toward associate degree, 42 toward bachelor's. **Support services:** Learning center, pre-admission summer program, reduced course load, remedial instruction, study skills assistance, tutoring, writing center.

**Honors college/program.** High School GPA minimum 3.5, ACT Composite 27 or higher or SAT Combined of 1200 or higher. Transfer students with 15 completed credits and GPA of 3.5 or higher.

**Majors. Biology:** General. **Business:** Accounting, construction management, finance, human resources, international, management information systems, managerial economics, market research, marketing, operations. **Communications:** General, journalism, media studies. **Computer sciences:** Computer science, information systems. **Conservation:** Environmental studies. **Education:** General, art, bilingual, biology, chemistry, elementary, French, German, history, music, physical, physics, science, social science, social studies, Spanish, special, speech. **Engineering:** Civil, electrical, materials science, mechanical. **Foreign languages:** French, German, Spanish. **Health:** Athletic training, environmental health, medical radiologic technology/radiation therapy, medical records admin, nursing (RN), predental, premedicine, preveterinary, respiratory therapy technology. **History:** General. **Liberal arts:** Arts/sciences. **Math:** General, applied. **Parks/recreation:** Exercise sciences, health/fitness. **Philosophy/religion:** Philosophy. **Physical sciences:** Chemistry, geology, geophysics, physics. **Protective services:** Law enforcement admin. **Psychology:** General. **Public administration:** Social work. **Social sciences:** General, anthropology, economics, political science, sociology. **Visual/performing arts:** Art, art history/conservation, commercial/advertising art, dramatic, music management, music performance, music theory/composition. **Other:** Geoarcheology.

**Most popular majors.** Business/marketing 22%, communications/journalism 8%, education 11%, health sciences 9%, psychology 6%, social sciences 8%.

**Computing on campus.** 900 workstations in dormitories, library, computer center. Dormitories wired for high-speed internet access and linked to campus network. Commuter students can connect to campus network. Online course registration, wireless network available.

**Student life. Freshman orientation:** Mandatory, $75 fee. Preregistration for classes offered. **Housing:** Coed dorms, single-sex dorms, special housing for disabled, apartments, fraternity/sorority housing, wellness housing available. $225 fully refundable deposit, deadline 7/1. **Activities:** Bands, choral groups, dance, drama, international student organizations, literary magazine, music ensembles, musical theater, radio station, student government, student newspaper, symphony orchestra, TV station, Black Student Union, Native American association, Organization de Estudiantes Latino-Americanos, Latter-day Saints student association, Alternative Mobility Adventure Seekers.

**Athletics.** NCAA. **Intercollegiate:** Basketball, cheerleading, cross-country, football (tackle) M, golf, gymnastics W, rodeo, soccer W, swimming W, tennis, track and field, volleyball W, wrestling M. **Intramural:** Basketball, bowling, handball, racquetball, soccer M, softball, swimming, tennis, volleyball. **Team name:** Broncos.

**Student services.** Adult student services, alcohol/substance abuse counseling, career counseling, student employment services, financial aid counseling, health services, legal services, minority student services, on-campus daycare, personal counseling, placement for graduates, veterans' counselor, women's services. **Physically disabled:** Services for visually, speech, hearing impaired. **Learning disabled:** Comprehensive services available.

**Contact.** E-mail: bsuinfo@boisestate.edu
Phone: (208) 426-1156 Toll-free number: (800) 824-7017
Fax: (208) 426-3765
Jenny Cerda, Director of Admissions, Boise State University, 1910 University Drive, Boise, ID 83725

---

## Brigham Young University-Idaho
**Rexburg, Idaho**
**www.byui.edu**                          CB code: 4657

- Private 4-year university affiliated with Church of Jesus Christ of Latter-day Saints
- Residential campus in large town
- 14,944 degree-seeking undergraduates
- 97% of applicants admitted
- ACT (writing optional), application essay required

**General.** Founded in 1888. Regionally accredited. **Degrees:** 3,424 bachelor's, 1,206 associate awarded. **ROTC:** Army. **Location:** 30 miles from Idaho Falls, 240 miles from Salt Lake City. **Calendar:** Semester, extensive summer session. **Full-time faculty:** 470 total. **Part-time faculty:** 165 total. **Class size:** 28% < 20, 49% 20-39, 8% 40-49, 13% 50-99, 1% >100. **Special facilities:** Observatory, planetarium, livestock center, off-campus outdoor educational facility, leadership and service institute.

**Freshman class profile.** 6,887 applied, 6,684 admitted, 3,951 enrolled.

| Mid 50% test scores | | | |
|---|---|---|---|
| SAT critical reading: | 470-570 | GPA 3.50-3.74: | 30% |
| SAT math: | 480-580 | GPA 3.0-3.49: | 40% |
| ACT composite: | 20-25 | GPA 2.0-2.99: | 7% |
| GPA 3.75 or higher: | 23% | Out-of-state: | 73% |
| | | Live on campus: | 21% |

**Basis for selection.** Religious affiliation, recommendations most important. High school record, test scores, personal essay, extracurricular activities also important. Interview with student's ecclesiastical leader required. Auditions required for music, dance, theater majors. **Homeschooled:** GED required; may be waived for homeschooled students with 24 ACT composite score.

**2009-2010 Annual costs.** Tuition/fees: $3,580. Tuition for students who are not members of The Church of Jesus Christ of Latter-day Saints is $6,560 for academic year. Room/board: $7,550. Books/supplies: $1,110. Personal expenses: $2,020.

**2008-2009 Financial aid. Non-need-based:** Scholarships awarded for academics, athletics, leadership. **Additional information:** Application deadline for merit scholarships 3/1.

**Application procedures. Admission:** Closing date 2/1 (receipt date). $35 fee. **Financial aid:** Priority date 5/1; no closing date. FAFSA required. Applicants notified on a rolling basis starting 2/1.

**Academics. Special study options:** Accelerated study, distance learning, double major, independent study, internships, student-designed major, study abroad, teacher certification program, urban semester. **Credit/placement by examination:** AP, CLEP, IB, institutional tests. **Support services:** Learning center, reduced course load, remedial instruction, study skills assistance, tutoring, writing center.

**Majors. Agriculture:** Agronomy, animal sciences, horticulture. **Biology:** General, zoology. **Business:** Accounting, business admin. **Communications:** General, advertising, broadcast journalism, journalism, public relations. **Computer sciences:** General, computer science. **Education:** Elementary. **Engineering:** Computer, mechanical. **Health:** Nursing (RN), predental, premedicine, prepharmacy, preveterinary. **History:** General. **Math:** General. **Parks/recreation:** General. **Physical sciences:** Geology, physics. **Psychology:** General. **Social sciences:** Economics, political science, sociology. **Visual/performing arts:** Art, interior design.

**Most popular majors.** Biology 6%, business/marketing 18%, communications/journalism 8%, education 18%, health sciences 9%, liberal arts 9%.

**Computing on campus.** 2,500 workstations in dormitories, library, computer center, student center. Dormitories wired for high-speed internet access and linked to campus network. Commuter students can connect to campus network. Online course registration, online library, helpline, student web hosting, wireless network available.

**Student life. Freshman orientation:** Available. **Policies:** Students encouraged to attend weekly devotional at which noted church leaders speak. Religious observance required. **Housing:** Single-sex dorms, apartments, wellness housing available. $175 deposit. **Activities:** Bands, choral groups, dance, drama, international student organizations, literary magazine, music ensembles, musical theater, radio station, student government, student newspaper, symphony orchestra, TV station, Lambda Delta Sigma, Sigma Gamma Chi, business club, married student association, outdoor club.

**Athletics. Intramural:** Archery, badminton, baseball, basketball, bowling, cheerleading, cross-country, diving, fencing, field hockey, football (non-tackle), football (tackle), golf, ice hockey, racquetball, skiing, skin diving, soccer, softball, swimming, table tennis, tennis, track and field, volleyball, water polo, wrestling M. **Team name:** Vikings.

**Student services.** Career counseling, student employment services, health services, personal counseling, placement for graduates, veterans' counselor. **Physically disabled:** Services for visually, hearing impaired.

**Contact.** E-mail: admissionser@byui.edu
Phone: (208) 496-1020 Fax: (208) 496-1185
Rob Garrett, Director of Admissions, Brigham Young University-Idaho, 120 Kimball Building, Rexburg, ID 83460-1615

---

## College of Idaho
**Caldwell, Idaho**                    CB member
**www.collegeofidaho.edu**             CB code: 4060

- Private 4-year liberal arts college
- Residential campus in large town
- 990 degree-seeking undergraduates: 5% part-time, 58% women

- 4 degree-seeking graduate students
- 62% of applicants admitted
- SAT or ACT with writing, application essay required
- 62% graduate within 6 years

**General.** Founded in 1891. Regionally accredited. **Degrees:** 171 bachelor's awarded; master's offered. **ROTC:** Army. **Location:** 30 miles from Boise. **Calendar:** 13-6-13. **Full-time faculty:** 74 total; 81% have terminal degrees, 7% minority, 43% women. **Part-time faculty:** 26 total; 12% have terminal degrees, 4% minority, 42% women. **Class size:** 61% < 20, 32% 20-39, 4% 40-49, 3% 50-99. **Special facilities:** Natural history museum, mineral and gem collection, planetarium, observatory, performing and fine arts center.

**Freshman class profile.** 1,214 applied, 758 admitted, 299 enrolled.

| Mid 50% test scores | | Rank in top quarter: | 64% |
|---|---|---|---|
| SAT critical reading: | 440-580 | Rank in top tenth: | 30% |
| SAT math: | 460-600 | End year in good standing: | 91% |
| SAT writing: | 430-560 | Return as sophomores: | 74% |
| ACT composite: | 22-27 | Out-of-state: | 21% |
| GPA 3.75 or higher: | 34% | Live on campus: | 94% |
| GPA 3.50-3.74: | 39% | International: | 14% |
| GPA 3.0-3.49: | 19% | Fraternities: | 3% |
| GPA 2.0-2.99: | 8% | Sororities: | 12% |

**Basis for selection.** Academic record, test scores, extracurricular activities, essay, teacher recommendation important. Interview and essay recommended. Audition required of music, theater majors. Portfolio required of art majors. **Homeschooled:** Transcript of courses and grades, letter of recommendation (nonparent) required. Course descriptions required. **Learning Disabled:** Student must submit a request for accommodations, submit appropriate documentation of the diagnosed disability from a qualified treatment provider completed within the last 3 years; provide a signed release of information form with contact information to the Student Disability Services Office; and schedule an appointment with the Disability Services Coordinator.

**High school preparation.** College-preparatory program recommended. 15 units required; 20 recommended. Required and recommended units include English 4, mathematics 3-4, social studies 2, history 3, science 2-4, foreign language 4 and academic electives 3.

**2010-2011 Annual costs.** Tuition/fees (projected): $21,380. Room/board: $7,700. Books/supplies: $1,200. Personal expenses: $700.

**2009-2010 Financial aid. Need-based:** Average need met was 86%. Average scholarship/grant was $6,165; average loan $3,727. 62% of total undergraduate aid awarded as scholarships/grants, 38% as loans/jobs. **Non-need-based:** Scholarships awarded for academics, alumni affiliation, art, athletics, leadership, minority status, music/drama, religious affiliation, ROTC.

**Application procedures. Admission:** Priority date 6/1; deadline 8/1 (postmark date). No application fee. Admission notification on a rolling basis beginning on or about 10/15. Must reply by 5/1. **Financial aid:** Priority date 2/15; no closing date. FAFSA, institutional form required. Applicants notified on a rolling basis starting 2/1; must reply within 3 week(s) of notification.

**Academics. Special study options:** Combined bachelor's/graduate degree, cross-registration, double major, dual enrollment of high school students, ESL, exchange student, honors, independent study, internships, student-designed major, study abroad, teacher certification program, Washington semester. BA/MBA with Boise State University and Gonzaga University (OR); BA/BS Dual-Degree Program in Engineering with Boise State University, University of Idaho, and Columbia University; BA/BS Dual-Degree Program in Engineering and Applied Science with Washington University; 3+3 BA or BS/JD with the University of Idaho College of Law; 3-2 BA or BS/MM Master of Management with Willamette University; Master of Natural Resources with the U of I; BS/BS Dual-Degree Program in Nursing with Idaho State University; BS/BS Dual-Degree in Clinical Laboratory Science with ISU; Coop Program in Speech-Language Pathology and Audiology with ISU; Coop Program in Occupational Therapy with ISU; Coop Program in Public Health with ISU; Master's of Physical Assistant Studies with ISU; BA or BS/DPT Coop Program in Physical Therapy with ISU; BS/Pharm.D. Coop Program in Pharmacy with ISU. **Credit/placement by examination:** AP, CLEP, IB, SAT, ACT. **Support services:** Learning center, reduced course load, study skills assistance, tutoring, writing center.

**Majors. Biology:** General. **Business:** Accounting, business admin, international. **Conservation:** Environmental studies. **Education:** Physical. **Engineering:** General. **Foreign languages:** Spanish. **Health:** Prenursing. **History:** General. **Liberal arts:** Arts/sciences. **Math:** General, applied. **Parks/recreation:** Exercise sciences, health/fitness, sports admin. **Philosophy/religion:** Philosophy, religion. **Physical sciences:** Chemistry. **Psychology:** General. **Social sciences:** Anthropology, economics, international relations, political science, sociology. **Visual/performing arts:** Art, dramatic.

**Most popular majors.** Biology 9%, business/marketing 22%, history 9%, psychology 12%, social sciences 12%, visual/performing arts 8%.

**Computing on campus.** 250 workstations in dormitories, library, computer center, student center. Dormitories wired for high-speed internet access and linked to campus network. Commuter students can connect to campus network. Online library, helpline, repair service, student web hosting, wireless network available.

**Student life. Freshman orientation:** Mandatory. Preregistration for classes offered. One-day sessions to assist students and parents. **Policies:** Freshmen and sophomores under age 21 must live on campus unless living with parents or relatives. All buildings smoke-free. Honor Code has been implemented for all students. **Housing:** Guaranteed on-campus for freshmen. Coed dorms, special housing for disabled, apartments, fraternity/sorority housing, wellness housing available. $300 fully refundable deposit, deadline 5/1. Academic communities (min GPA). **Activities:** Bands, campus ministries, choral groups, dance, drama, international student organizations, literary magazine, music ensembles, Model UN, musical theater, opera, radio station, student government, student newspaper, symphony orchestra, over 75 activities or organizations.

**Athletics.** NAIA. **Intercollegiate:** Baseball M, basketball, cross-country, golf, skiing, soccer, softball W, swimming, tennis, track and field, volleyball W. **Intramural:** Badminton, basketball, football (non-tackle), soccer, softball, volleyball. **Team name:** Coyotes.

**Student services.** Alcohol/substance abuse counseling, chaplain/spiritual director, career counseling, student employment services, financial aid counseling, health services, minority student services, personal counseling, placement for graduates, women's services. **Physically disabled:** Services for hearing impaired.

**Contact.** E-mail: admissions@collegeofidaho.edu
Phone: (208) 459-5305 Toll-free number: (800) 224-3246
Fax: (208) 459-5757
John Klockentager, Vice President of Enrollment Management, College of Idaho, 2112 Cleveland Boulevard, Caldwell, ID 83605-4432

---

## Idaho State University
**Pocatello, Idaho**
www.isu.edu

**CB member**
**CB code: 4355**

- Public 4-year university
- Commuter campus in small city
- 10,034 degree-seeking undergraduates: 24% part-time, 54% women, 1% African American, 2% Asian American, 6% Hispanic American, 2% Native American, 1% international
- 1,959 degree-seeking graduate students
- 73% of applicants admitted
- ACT (writing optional) required

**General.** Founded in 1901. Regionally accredited. Designated by State Board of Education as institution specializing in health-related programs. **Degrees:** 1,042 bachelor's, 293 associate awarded; master's, doctoral, professional offered. **ROTC:** Army. **Location:** 150 miles from Salt Lake City, 230 miles from Boise. **Calendar:** Semester, limited summer session. **Full-time faculty:** 618 total; 55% have terminal degrees, 7% minority, 44% women. **Part-time faculty:** 149 total; 9% have terminal degrees, 3% minority, 51% women. **Class size:** 59% < 20, 32% 20-39, 4% 40-49, 4% 50-99, 1% >100. **Special facilities:** Natural history museum, multi-purpose housing/classroom/meeting facility, accelerator center, geographical information systems center, performing arts center.

**Freshman class profile.** 3,889 applied, 2,856 admitted, 1,906 enrolled.

| Mid 50% test scores | | Rank in top tenth: | 13% |
|---|---|---|---|
| ACT composite: | 18-24 | Return as sophomores: | 60% |
| GPA 3.75 or higher: | 20% | Out-of-state: | 7% |
| GPA 3.50-3.74: | 15% | Live on campus: | 20% |
| GPA 3.0-3.49: | 28% | Fraternities: | 1% |
| GPA 2.0-2.99: | 34% | Sororities: | 1% |
| Rank in top quarter: | 31% | | |

**Basis for selection.** For general admissions, predicted GPA of 2.0 (based on core GPA and test scores). Students not meeting those standards can be admitted through various levels and by petition. TOEFL, IELTS, Compass English, and SAT Critical Reading required for international students. US High School graduates with an "A" or "B" in English and students who completed ELS Language Centers level 112 are exempted. Students from countries where English is the official language can be exempted based on academic performance. ACT preferred. Students 21 years or older are exempt from submitting ACT/SAT scores. Interview recommended. Audition recommended for music majors. Portfolio recommended for experiential credit-seeking applicants. **Homeschooled:** Students need to complete their GED along with taking the ACT or SAT test.

**High school preparation.** College-preparatory program required. 16 units required. Required and recommended units include English 4, mathematics 3-4, social studies 3, science 3 (laboratory 1) and foreign language 1. 1.5 Units in humanities and health also required.

**2009-2010 Annual costs.** Tuition/fees: $4,968; $14,770 out-of-state. $1,046 refundable health insurance. Room/board: $5,050. Books/supplies: $900. Personal expenses: $2,869.

**2008-2009 Financial aid. Non-need-based:** Scholarships awarded for academics, alumni affiliation, art, athletics, leadership, minority status, music/drama, ROTC, state residency.

**Application procedures. Admission:** No deadline. $40 fee, may be waived for applicants with need. Admission notification on a rolling basis beginning on or about 3/1. High school students who graduate early may petition admissions committee to enroll full time. **Financial aid:** Priority date 3/1; no closing date. FAFSA required. Applicants notified on a rolling basis starting 4/1.

**Academics. Special study options:** Accelerated study, combined bachelor's/graduate degree, cooperative education, cross-registration, distance learning, double major, dual enrollment of high school students, ESL, exchange student, honors, independent study, internships, liberal arts/career combination, student-designed major, study abroad, teacher certification program, weekend college. **Credit/placement by examination:** AP, CLEP, IB, ACT, institutional tests. 32 credit hours maximum toward associate degree, 64 toward bachelor's. A student is unable to receive credit by challenge exam for courses already taken, or for courses that are prerequisites to courses already completed. **Support services:** Learning center, remedial instruction, study skills assistance, tutoring, writing center.

**Majors. Area/ethnic studies:** American. **Biology:** General, biochemistry, botany, ecology, microbiology, zoology. **Business:** General, accounting, business admin, finance, human resources, insurance, marketing. **Communications:** General, media studies. **Computer sciences:** General, computer graphics, information systems. **Conservation:** Environmental science. **Education:** Early childhood, elementary, health, music, physical, secondary, special. **Engineering:** Civil, electrical, mechanical, nuclear. **Engineering technology:** Energy systems, mechanical, surveying, telecommunications. **Family/consumer sciences:** General. **Foreign languages:** French, German, sign language interpretation, Spanish. **Health:** Audiology/speech pathology, clinical lab science, dental hygiene, dietetics, health care admin, health services, medical radiologic technology/radiation therapy, nursing (RN). **History:** General. **Math:** General, statistics. **Mechanic/repair:** Business machine. **Philosophy/religion:** Philosophy. **Physical sciences:** Chemistry, geology, physics. **Protective services:** Firefighting. **Psychology:** General. **Public administration:** Social work. **Social sciences:** Anthropology, economics, international relations, political science, sociology. **Visual/performing arts:** Art, dramatic, music performance.

**Most popular majors.** Biology 6%, business/marketing 16%, education 16%, health sciences 24%, social sciences 7%.

**Computing on campus.** 697 workstations in dormitories, library, computer center, student center. Dormitories wired for high-speed internet access and linked to campus network. Commuter students can connect to campus network. Online course registration, online library, helpline, repair service, student web hosting, wireless network available.

**Student life. Freshman orientation:** Available, $35 fee. Preregistration for classes offered. Held several times before classes begin in both fall and spring semesters. **Policies:** In order for a student to be eligible for student housing he/she must be taking a minimum of 6 credits per semester and be working towards a degree. **Housing:** Coed dorms, single-sex dorms, special housing for disabled, apartments, fraternity/sorority housing, wellness housing available. $150 partly refundable deposit, deadline 8/23. Housing modified for disabled available on request, subject to waiting list. Graduate housing is also available. **Activities:** Bands, campus ministries, choral groups, dance, drama, international student organizations, literary magazine, music ensembles, musical theater, opera, radio station, student government, student newspaper, symphony orchestra, TV station, Newman Center, Latter-day Saints Institute, student ambassadors, Young Democrats, Young Republicans, Campus Crusade for Christ, Associated Black Students, Native Americans United, Cooperative Wilderness Handicapped Outdoor Group.

**Athletics.** NCAA. **Intercollegiate:** Basketball, cheerleading, cross-country, football (tackle) M, golf W, soccer W, softball W, tennis, track and field, volleyball W. **Intramural:** Badminton, basketball, bowling, fencing, football (non-tackle) M, judo, racquetball, soccer, softball, table tennis, tennis, volleyball, wrestling M. **Team name:** Bengals.

**Student services.** Adult student services, alcohol/substance abuse counseling, career counseling, student employment services, financial aid counseling, health services, legal services, minority student services, on-campus daycare, personal counseling, placement for graduates, veterans' counselor, women's services. **Physically disabled:** Services for visually, speech, hearing impaired.

**Contact.** E-mail: info@isu.edu
Phone: (208) 282-2475 Fax: (208) 282-4511
Laura McKenzie, Director, Idaho State University, 921 South 8th Stop 8270, Pocatello, ID 83209-8270

## ITT Technical Institute: Boise
**Boise, Idaho**
**www.itt-tech.edu**                          **CB code: 3596**

- For-profit 4-year technical college
- Commuter campus in small city

**General.** Founded in 1906. Accredited by ACICS. **Calendar:** Quarter.

**Contact.** Phone: (208) 322-8844
Director of Recruitment, 12302 West Explorer Drive, Boise, ID 83713-1529

## Lewis-Clark State College
**Lewiston, Idaho**
**www.lcsc.edu**                              **CB code: 4385**

- Public 4-year liberal arts and technical college
- Commuter campus in small city
- 3,239 degree-seeking undergraduates: 22% part-time, 60% women, 1% African American, 2% Asian American, 4% Hispanic American, 4% Native American, 3% international
- 98% of applicants admitted

**General.** Founded in 1893. Regionally accredited. Courses offered at outreach centers (Orofino, Grangeville, Coeur d'Alene, Kamiah, and Lapwai). **Degrees:** 400 bachelor's, 163 associate awarded. **ROTC:** Army, Naval, Air Force. **Location:** 300 miles from Boise, 100 miles from Spokane, Washington. **Calendar:** Semester, limited summer session. **Full-time faculty:** 172 total; 64% have terminal degrees, 5% minority, 55% women. **Part-time faculty:** 97 total; 28% have terminal degrees, 50% women. **Class size:** 25% < 20, 2% 20-39; 50% 50-99, 24% >100. **Special facilities:** Biodiversity museum and collection, geographical information systems center, observatory.

**Freshman class profile.** 1,273 applied, 1,252 admitted, 635 enrolled.

| Mid 50% test scores | | GPA 2.0-2.99: | 45% |
|---|---|---|---|
| SAT critical reading: | 450-540 | Rank in top quarter: | 18% |
| SAT math: | 440-540 | Rank in top tenth: | 5% |
| ACT composite: | 17-22 | Return as sophomores: | 52% |
| GPA 3.75 or higher: | 12% | Out-of-state: | 16% |
| GPA 3.50-3.74: | 12% | International: | 2% |
| GPA 3.0-3.49: | 26% | | |

**Basis for selection.** High school courses, GPA, test scores considered. Non-native speakers may be required to take ESL classes until they can pass TOEFL. ACT and SAT may be accepted for all students. Students may be asked to take COMPASS test under certain circumstances. **Homeschooled:** Must have predicted college GPA of 2.0 based on ACT or SAT. Must have acceptable performance on 2 testing indicators: GED score of 500 (50 if tested before 2002) or higher, or other standardized diagnostic test such as ACT, SAT, COMPASS, ASSET, or CPT.

**High school preparation.** College-preparatory program required. 15 units required. Required units include English 4, mathematics 3, social studies 2.5, science 3 (laboratory 2), academic electives 1.5.

**2009-2010 Annual costs.** Tuition/fees: $4,596; $12,874 out-of-state. Room/board: $5,900. Books/supplies: $1,520. Personal expenses: $1,960.

**2008-2009 Financial aid. Need-based:** 473 full-time freshmen applied for aid; 371 were judged to have need; 356 of these received aid. Average need met was 8%. Average scholarship/grant was $3,434; average loan $2,870. 43% of total undergraduate aid awarded as scholarships/grants, 57% as loans/jobs. **Non-need-based:** Awarded to 839 full-time undergraduates, including 393 freshmen. Scholarships awarded for academics, alumni affiliation, art, athletics, leadership, minority status, music/drama.

**Application procedures. Admission:** No deadline. $35 fee. Admission notification on a rolling basis. **Financial aid:** Priority date 3/1; no closing date. FAFSA required. Applicants notified on a rolling basis starting 4/15; must reply within 2 week(s) of notification.

**Academics.** Communications/speech lab to help students prepare for speeches and presentations. **Special study options:** Accelerated study, cooperative education, distance learning, dual enrollment of high school students, ESL, independent study, internships, study abroad, teacher certification program. **Credit/placement by examination:** AP, CLEP, IB, SAT, ACT, institutional tests. 16 credit hours maximum toward associate degree, 32 toward bachelor's. **Support services:** Learning center, reduced course load, remedial instruction, study skills assistance, tutoring, writing center.

**Majors. Biology:** General. **Business:** Accounting technology, administrative services, business admin, hospitality admin, small business admin. **Communications:** General. **Communications technology:** Graphic/printing. **Computer sciences:** General, computer science, webmaster. **Education:** Elementary, English, mathematics, physical, science, social science. **Engineering technology:** Drafting, manufacturing. **Family/consumer sciences:** Child development. **Health:** Management/clinical assistant, nursing (RN), office assistant. **Interdisciplinary:** Natural sciences. **Legal studies:** Legal secretary, paralegal. **Math:** General. **Mechanic/repair:** General, auto body, automotive, diesel, electronics/electrical, heating/ac/refrig, industrial electronics. **Parks/recreation:** Exercise sciences. **Physical sciences:** Chemistry. **Production:** Welding. **Protective services:** Corrections, criminal justice, firefighting. **Psychology:** General. **Public administration:** Social work. **Social sciences:** General.

**Most popular majors.** Business/marketing 26%, education 14%, health sciences 14%, public administration/social services 8%, security/protective services 7%.

**Computing on campus.** 455 workstations in dormitories, library, computer center, student center. Dormitories wired for high-speed internet access and linked to campus network. Commuter students can connect to campus network. Online course registration, helpline, student web hosting, wireless network available.

**Student life. Freshman orientation:** Available. Preregistration for classes offered. One-day session held in August. **Housing:** Coed dorms, apartments available. $200 partly refundable deposit. **Activities:** Jazz band, campus ministries, drama, international student organizations, literary magazine, radio station, student government, student newspaper, Native American Indian student organization, ambassadors' club, criminal justice society, Idaho student lobby, business students organization, Latter-day Saints student association, College Democrats, College Republicans.

**Athletics.** NAIA. **Intercollegiate:** Baseball M, basketball, cross-country, golf, tennis, track and field W, volleyball W. **Intramural:** Badminton, baseball, basketball, bowling, field hockey, football (non-tackle), golf, lacrosse, racquetball, rugby M, skiing, soccer, softball, table tennis, tennis, volleyball, weight lifting. **Team name:** Warriors.

**Student services.** Adult student services, alcohol/substance abuse counseling, career counseling, services for economically disadvantaged, student employment services, financial aid counseling, health services, minority student services, on-campus daycare, personal counseling, placement for graduates, veterans' counselor, women's services. **Physically disabled:** Services for visually, speech, hearing impaired.

**Contact.** E-mail: admissions@lcsc.edu
Phone: (208) 792-2210 Toll-free number: (800) 933-5272
Fax: (208) 792-2876
Diane Douglas, Registrar/Director of Admissions, Lewis-Clark State College, 500 Eighth Avenue, Lewiston, ID 83501-2698

## New Saint Andrews College
Moscow, Idaho
www.nsa.edu                                                CB code: 3855

- Private 4-year liberal arts college
- Residential campus in large town
- 203 degree-seeking undergraduates: 12% part-time, 51% women
- 9 degree-seeking graduate students
- 50% of applicants admitted
- SAT or ACT (ACT writing optional), application essay required

**General.** Regionally accredited; also accredited by TRACS. **Degrees:** 25 bachelor's, 10 associate awarded; master's offered. **Calendar:** Quarter. **Full-time faculty:** 7 total. **Part-time faculty:** 7 total.

**Freshman class profile.** 118 applied, 59 admitted, 42 enrolled.

| Mid 50% test scores | | | |
|---|---|---|---|
| SAT critical reading: | 600-690 | SAT writing: | 540-660 |
| SAT math: | 500-600 | ACT composite: | 25-31 |

**Basis for selection.** Academic achievement and test scores very important.

**2010-2011 Annual costs.** Tuition/fees: $9,945. Books/supplies: $1,200.

**Application procedures. Admission:** Priority date 12/1; deadline 8/1 (postmark date). $40 fee, may be waived for applicants with need. Admission notification on a rolling basis beginning on or about 12/10. **Financial aid:** Priority date 2/15; no closing date. Institutional form required.

**Academics. Credit/placement by examination:** CLEP.

**Majors. Liberal arts:** Arts/sciences.

**Computing on campus.** Online course registration, wireless network available.

**Student life. Freshman orientation:** Mandatory. **Housing:** Coed dorms available. **Activities:** Campus ministries, choral groups.

**Contact.** E-mail: admissions@nsa.edu
Phone: (208) 882-1566 Fax: (208) 882-4293
Brenda Schlect, Director of Admissions, New Saint Andrews College, PO Box 9025, Moscow, ID 83843

## Northwest Nazarene University
Nampa, Idaho
www.nnu.edu                                                CB code: 4544

- Private 4-year university affiliated with Church of the Nazarene
- Residential campus in small city
- 1,257 degree-seeking undergraduates: 6% part-time, 57% women
- 622 degree-seeking graduate students
- SAT or ACT (ACT writing optional), application essay required

**General.** Founded in 1913. Regionally accredited. **Degrees:** 280 bachelor's awarded; master's offered. **ROTC:** Army, Air Force. **Location:** 18 miles from Boise. **Calendar:** Semester, limited summer session. **Full-time faculty:** 98 total; 86% have terminal degrees, 44% women. **Part-time faculty:** 6 total; 17% women. **Class size:** 46% < 20, 40% 20-39, 9% 40-49, 5% 50-99. **Special facilities:** Depository for federal government publications.

**Freshman class profile.**

| Mid 50% test scores | | | |
|---|---|---|---|
| SAT critical reading: | 460-610 | GPA 3.50-3.74: | 23% |
| SAT math: | 460-590 | GPA 3.0-3.49: | 23% |
| ACT composite: | 19-26 | GPA 2.0-2.99: | 17% |
| GPA 3.75 or higher: | 37% | Rank in top quarter: | 47% |
| | | Rank in top tenth: | 24% |

**Basis for selection.** For unconditional admission 2 of following criteria must be met: minimum 2.5 high school GPA, class rank in top 50 percent, minimum ACT score of 18. Provisional admission available. Interview recommended for students with provisional admission.

**High school preparation.** College-preparatory program recommended. Recommended units include English 4, mathematics 3, history 3, science 3 and foreign language 2.

**2009-2010 Annual costs.** Tuition/fees: $22,250. Room/board: $5,830. Books/supplies: $1,000. Personal expenses: $900.

**2009-2010 Financial aid. Non-need-based:** Scholarships awarded for academics, alumni affiliation, art, athletics, leadership, minority status, music/drama, religious affiliation, ROTC.

**Application procedures. Admission:** Priority date 3/1; deadline 8/15. $25 fee, may be waived for applicants with need. Admission notification on a rolling basis. **Financial aid:** Priority date 3/1; no closing date. FAFSA, institutional form required. Applicants notified on a rolling basis starting 3/1; must reply within 3 week(s) of notification.

**Academics. Special study options:** Accelerated study, combined bachelor's/graduate degree, cooperative education, cross-registration, distance learning, double major, exchange student, honors, independent study, internships, liberal arts/career combination, student-designed major, study abroad, teacher certification program. **Credit/placement by examination:** AP, CLEP,

IB, SAT, ACT, institutional tests. 31 credit hours maximum toward bachelor's degree. **Support services:** Learning center, reduced course load, remedial instruction, study skills assistance, tutoring, writing center.

**Majors. Biology:** General, biochemistry, cellular/molecular, ecology. **Business:** Accounting, business admin. **Communications:** General, journalism, media studies. **Computer sciences:** Computer science. **Education:** General, art, biology, chemistry, computer, elementary, English, health, history, mathematics, music, physical, physics, psychology, secondary, social science, Spanish. **Engineering:** Aerospace, chemical, civil, electrical, physics. **Foreign languages:** Spanish. **Health:** Nursing (RN), physician assistant, predental, premedicine, prepharmacy, preveterinary. **History:** General. **Interdisciplinary:** Neuroscience. **Legal studies:** Prelaw. **Liberal arts:** Arts/sciences. **Math:** General. **Parks/recreation:** General, exercise sciences, health/fitness, sports admin. **Philosophy/religion:** Philosophy, religion. **Physical sciences:** Chemistry, physics. **Psychology:** General, industrial. **Public administration:** Social work. **Social sciences:** General, international relations, political science. **Theology:** Bible, missionary, pastoral counseling, religious ed, sacred music, youth ministry. **Visual/performing arts:** Ceramics, drawing, graphic design, music performance, music theory/composition, painting, piano/organ, printmaking, sculpture, voice/opera. **Other:** Environmental chemistry.

**Most popular majors.** Business/marketing 22%, education 11%, health sciences 18%, liberal arts 9%, theological studies 6%.

**Computing on campus.** 275 workstations in dormitories, library, computer center, student center. Dormitories wired for high-speed internet access and linked to campus network. Commuter students can connect to campus network. Online library, helpline, repair service, student web hosting, wireless network available.

**Student life. Freshman orientation:** Mandatory. Preregistration for classes offered. **Policies:** All students required to live on campus until senior year or age 21. Religious observance required. **Housing:** Guaranteed on-campus for all undergraduates. Single-sex dorms, apartments available. $50 fully refundable deposit. Some rental units available. **Activities:** Bands, campus ministries, choral groups, drama, international student organizations, literary magazine, music ensembles, musical theater, opera, student government, student newspaper, symphony orchestra, summer ministries, Circle-K, urban ministries club, social work clubs, Angels Ministry, PALS ministry, AIDS ministry, Fellowship of Christian Athletes, multicultural affairs club.

**Athletics.** NCAA. **Intercollegiate:** Baseball M, basketball, cross-country, golf M, soccer W, softball W, track and field, volleyball W. **Intramural:** Basketball, cross-country, football (non-tackle), softball, volleyball. **Team name:** Crusaders.

**Student services.** Adult student services, alcohol/substance abuse counseling, chaplain/spiritual director, career counseling, student employment services, financial aid counseling, health services, minority student services, personal counseling, placement for graduates. **Physically disabled:** Services for visually, hearing impaired.

**Contact.** E-mail: admissions@nnu.edu
Phone: (208) 467-8496 Toll-free number: (877) 668-4968
Fax: (208) 467-8645
Stacey Berggren, Director of Admissions, Northwest Nazarene University, 623 Holly Street, Nampa, ID 83686-5897

---

## University of Idaho
**Moscow, Idaho**
www.uidaho.edu

**CB member**
**CB code: 4843**

- Public 4-year university
- Residential campus in large town
- 8,757 degree-seeking undergraduates: 6% part-time, 47% women, 1% African American, 2% Asian American, 6% Hispanic American, 1% Native American, 2% international
- 2,359 degree-seeking graduate students
- 80% of applicants admitted
- SAT or ACT (ACT writing optional) required
- 56% graduate within 6 years

**General.** Founded in 1889. Regionally accredited. Residential land-grant university. **Degrees:** 1,670 bachelor's awarded; master's, doctoral, professional offered. **ROTC:** Army, Naval, Air Force. **Location:** 85 miles from Spokane, Washington. **Calendar:** Semester, extensive summer session. **Full-time faculty:** 601 total; 75% have terminal degrees, 10% minority, 30% women. **Part-time faculty:** 94 total; 24% have terminal degrees, 4% minority, 49% women. **Class size:** 49% < 20, 36% 20-39, 5% 40-49, 7% 50-99, 3% >100. **Special facilities:** Arboretum, 18-hole golf course, indoor climbing facility.

**Freshman class profile.** 5,099 applied, 4,069 admitted, 1,780 enrolled.

| Mid 50% test scores | | | |
|---|---|---|---|
| SAT critical reading: | 490-600 | GPA 3.0-3.49: | 34% |
| SAT math: | 490-610 | GPA 2.0-2.99: | 19% |
| SAT writing: | 460-570 | Rank in top quarter: | 46% |
| ACT composite: | 19-26 | Rank in top tenth: | 19% |
| GPA 3.75 or higher: | 26% | Return as sophomores: | 77% |
| GPA 3.50-3.74: | 20% | Out-of-state: | 40% |
| | | International: | 1% |

**Basis for selection.** Applicants must have 3.0 high school GPA, or 2.2 to 3.0 high school GPA with high SAT/ACT scores. Recommendations, essay required of applicants with nonstandard high school diploma and adults long out of high school. **Homeschooled:** Letter of recommendation (nonparent) required. Copy of GED test results, three signed letters of recommendation from individuals who know of and can attest to applicant's academic ability, a written statement from applicant including goals, education and/or professional objective, and explanation of past academic performance.

**High school preparation.** 15 units required. Required units include English 4, mathematics 3, social studies 3, science 3 (laboratory 1), foreign language 1 and academic electives 2. Up to 1 unit of history, literature, philosophy, or fine arts may be substituted for foreign language requirement, but foreign language strongly recommended.

**2009-2010 Annual costs.** Tuition/fees: $4,932; $15,012 out-of-state. Room/board: $6,850. Books/supplies: $1,474. Personal expenses: $3,066.

**2008-2009 Financial aid. Need-based:** 1,354 full-time freshmen applied for aid; 992 were judged to have need; 974 of these received aid. Average need met was 79%. Average scholarship/grant was $3,631; average loan $5,173. 41% of total undergraduate aid awarded as scholarships/grants, 59% as loans/jobs. **Non-need-based:** Awarded to 6,117 full-time undergraduates, including 1,454 freshmen. Scholarships awarded for academics, alumni affiliation, art, athletics, leadership, minority status, music/drama, ROTC, state residency.

**Application procedures. Admission:** Priority date 2/15; deadline 8/1 (receipt date). $40 fee. Admission notification on a rolling basis. **Financial aid:** Priority date 2/15; no closing date. FAFSA required. Applicants notified on a rolling basis starting 3/30; must reply within 4 week(s) of notification.

**Academics. Special study options:** Accelerated study, combined bachelor's/graduate degree, cooperative education, cross-registration, distance learning, double major, dual enrollment of high school students, ESL, exchange student, honors, independent study, internships, student-designed major, study abroad, teacher certification program. **Credit/placement by examination:** AP, CLEP, IB, SAT, ACT, institutional tests. 48 credit hours maximum toward bachelor's degree. **Support services:** Learning center, pre-admission summer program, reduced course load, remedial instruction, study skills assistance, tutoring, writing center.

**Majors. Agriculture:** General, agronomy, animal husbandry, animal sciences, business, communications, dairy, economics, equipment technology, food science, horticultural science, mechanization, plant protection, plant sciences, range science, soil science. **Architecture:** Architecture, interior, landscape. **Area/ethnic studies:** American, Latin American. **Biology:** General, bacteriology, biochemistry, botany, conservation, entomology, microbiology, molecular, zoology. **Business:** General, accounting, administrative services, business admin, finance, human resources, management information systems, managerial economics, marketing, operations. **Communications:** General, advertising, digital media, journalism, media studies, organizational, public relations, radio/tv. **Communications technology:** Animation/special effects. **Computer sciences:** Computer science. **Conservation:** General, environmental science, fisheries, forest management, forest resources, forest sciences, management/policy, wildlife, wood science. **Education:** General, agricultural, art, business, early childhood, elementary, English, family/consumer sciences, health, music, physical, secondary, special, technology/industrial arts, trade/industrial, voc/tech. **Engineering:** Agricultural, biomedical, chemical, civil, computer, electrical, environmental, geological, materials, mechanical, metallurgical, mining, water resource. **Family/consumer sciences:** General, clothing/textiles, family resources, family studies, food/nutrition. **Foreign languages:** General, classics, French, German, Latin, Spanish. **Health:** Athletic training, clinical lab science, nursing (RN), predental, premedicine. **History:** General. **Interdisciplinary:** Museum. **Math:** General, applied. **Parks/recreation:** Exercise sciences, facilities management, sports admin. **Philosophy/religion:** Philosophy. **Physical sciences:** Chemistry, geology, physics. **Protective services:** Criminal justice. **Psychology:** General. **Social sciences:** Anthropology, cartography, economics, geography, international relations, political science, sociology. **Visual/performing arts:** Art, dance, design, dramatic, interior design, music history, music management, music performance, music theory/composition, musical theater, photography, studio arts, voice/opera. **Other:** Applied music, Fire ecology and management, Naval science.

**Most popular majors.** Agriculture 10%, business/marketing 8%, education 9%, engineering/engineering technologies 8%, natural resources/environmental science 8%, visual/performing arts 6%.

**Computing on campus.** 604 workstations in dormitories, library, computer center, student center. Dormitories wired for high-speed internet access and linked to campus network. Commuter students can connect to campus network. Online course registration, online library, helpline, repair service, student web hosting, wireless network available.

**Student life. Freshman orientation:** Available. Preregistration for classes offered. **Housing:** Guaranteed on-campus for freshmen. Coed dorms, single-sex dorms, special housing for disabled, apartments, cooperative housing, fraternity/sorority housing available. $250 partly refundable deposit. **Activities:** Bands, campus ministries, choral groups, dance, drama, film society, international student organizations, literary magazine, music ensembles, musical theater, opera, radio station, student government, student newspaper, symphony orchestra, TV station, Amnesty International, Women of Color Alliance, Environmental Club, War on Hunger, Intervarsity Christian Fellowship, Habitat for Humanity, Sabor de la Raza, Soil Stewards, Society of Professional Journalists.

**Athletics.** NCAA. **Intercollegiate:** Basketball, cross-country, football (tackle) M, golf, soccer W, swimming W, tennis, track and field, volleyball W. **Intramural:** Badminton, basketball, golf, racquetball, rifle, skiing, soccer, softball, table tennis, tennis, wrestling M. **Team name:** Vandals.

**Student services.** Adult student services, alcohol/substance abuse counseling, chaplain/spiritual director, career counseling, student employment services, financial aid counseling, health services, legal services, minority student services, on-campus daycare, personal counseling, placement for graduates, veterans' counselor, women's services. **Physically disabled:** Services for visually, speech, hearing impaired.

**Contact.**  E-mail: admissions@uidaho.edu
Phone: (208) 885-6326 Toll-free number: (888) 884-3246
Fax: (208) 885-9119
Daniel Davenport, Director of Admissions and Student Financial Aid,
University of Idaho, PO Box 444264, Moscow, ID 83844-4264

# Illinois

## American Academy of Art
**Chicago, Illinois**
www.aaart.edu                                      CB code: 1013

- For-profit 4-year visual arts college
- Commuter campus in very large city

**General.** Founded in 1923. Accredited by ACCSCT. **Location:** Downtown. **Calendar:** Semester.

**Annual costs/financial aid.** Books/supplies: $800.

**Contact.** Phone: (312) 461-0600
Director of Admissions, 332 South Michigan Avenue, Suite 300, Chicago, IL 60604-4302

## Argosy University: Chicago
**Chicago, Illinois**
www.argosy.edu/chicago                             CB code: 3922

- For-profit 4-year university
- Very large city
- 164 degree-seeking undergraduates: 40% part-time, 74% women
- 1,184 degree-seeking graduate students

**General.** Regionally accredited. Additional campuses in Northwest Chicago, Washington, D.C., Atlanta, Seattle, Tampa, Minneapolis/St. Paul, San Francisco Bay area, Dallas, Honolulu, Nashville, Phoenix, Sarasota, and Orange County, CA. **Degrees:** 79 bachelor's awarded; master's, doctoral, professional offered. **Calendar:** Continuous, extensive summer session. **Full-time faculty:** 30 total. **Part-time faculty:** 113 total.

**Freshman class profile.** 2 enrolled.

**Basis for selection.** 18 ACT, 850 SAT (exclusive of Writing) or passing score on institution's entrance exam required. Other requirements vary by program. SAT or ACT recommended.

**2009-2010 Annual costs.** Tuition/fees: $15,612. Costs vary by program.

**Application procedures. Admission:** No deadline. $50 fee.

**Academics. Special study options:** Distance learning. **Credit/placement by examination:** CLEP.

**Majors. Business:** Business admin. **Psychology:** General.

**Most popular majors.** Psychology 96%.

**Computing on campus.** Online library available.

**Contact.** Phone: (312) 201-0200 Toll-free number: (800) 626-4123
Micki Pyszkowski, Director of Admissions, Argosy University: Chicago, 225 North Michigan Avenue, Suite 1300, Chicago, IL 60601

## Argosy University: Schaumburg
**Schaumburg, Illinois**
www.argosy.edu/schaumburg

- For-profit 4-year university
- Small city
- 145 degree-seeking undergraduates

**General.** Regionally accredited. **Degrees:** 27 bachelor's awarded; master's, doctoral, professional offered. **Calendar:** Continuous. **Full-time faculty:** 17 total. **Part-time faculty:** 77 total.

**Freshman class profile.** 17 enrolled.

**Basis for selection.** Open admission.

**Academics. Credit/placement by examination:** CLEP.

**Majors. Business:** Business admin. **Liberal arts:** Arts/sciences. **Protective services:** Police science. **Psychology:** General.

**Contact.** Phone: (847) 969-4910 Toll-free number: (866) 290-2777
Argosy University: Schaumburg, 999 North Plaza Drive, Suite 111, Schaumburg, IL 60173-5403

## Augustana College
**Rock Island, Illinois**                          CB member
www.augustana.edu                                  CB code: 1025

- Private 4-year liberal arts college affiliated with Evangelical Lutheran Church in America
- Residential campus in large city
- 2,457 degree-seeking undergraduates: 1% part-time, 57% women, 2% African American, 2% Asian American, 3% Hispanic American, 1% international
- 73% of applicants admitted
- 78% graduate within 6 years; 35% enter graduate study

**General.** Founded in 1860. Regionally accredited. **Degrees:** 555 bachelor's awarded. **Location:** 165 miles from Chicago. **Calendar:** Quarter, limited summer session. **Full-time faculty:** 174 total; 89% have terminal degrees, 18% minority, 43% women. **Part-time faculty:** 89 total; 38% have terminal degrees, 7% minority, 47% women. **Class size:** 61% < 20, 36% 20-39, 2% 40-49, 1% 50-99. **Special facilities:** Educational technology center, planetarium/observatory, map library, geology museum, Swedish immigration research center, research foundation, 500 acres of environmental laboratories, scanning electron microscope, high-field NMR, x-ray diffractometer, scanning tunneling microscope, HeliFlux station magnetometer.

**Freshman class profile.** 3,633 applied, 2,638 admitted, 616 enrolled.

| Mid 50% test scores | | Return as sophomores: | 82% |
|---|---|---|---|
| ACT composite: | 23-29 | Out-of-state: | 13% |
| Rank in top quarter: | 64% | Live on campus: | 95% |
| Rank in top tenth: | 35% | International: | 1% |

**Basis for selection.** GPA, class rank, test scores, high school curriculum most important. Extracurricular activities and essay important. Academic honors and special qualifications also considered. SAT or ACT recommended. Test optional for those who interview and submit a photocopy of a graded high school paper. Interview and essay required of freshman honors program applicants, recommended for all applicants. Essay required of academically marginal applicants and for certain departmental programs. Portfolio required of applicants to some art programs. Audition recommended for music and theater majors.

**High school preparation.** College-preparatory program recommended. 16 units recommended. Required and recommended units include English 3-4, mathematics 3-4, social studies 1-2, history 1, science 3-4 (laboratory 2), foreign language 1-2 and academic electives 4. Engineering, science, and math majors should have 3 units math (1.5 algebra, 1 plane geometry, .5 trigonometry).

**2009-2010 Annual costs.** Tuition/fees: $31,326. Room/board: $7,950. Books/supplies: $900. Personal expenses: $800.

**2008-2009 Financial aid. Need-based:** 548 full-time freshmen applied for aid; 431 were judged to have need; 431 of these received aid. Average need met was 86%. Average scholarship/grant was $15,396; average loan $6,025. 68% of total undergraduate aid awarded as scholarships/grants, 32% as loans/jobs. **Non-need-based:** Awarded to 922 full-time undergraduates, including 291 freshmen. Scholarships awarded for academics, alumni affiliation, art, leadership, music/drama, religious affiliation.

**Application procedures. Admission:** Priority date 2/1; no deadline. $35 fee, may be waived for applicants with need. Admission notification on a rolling basis. **Financial aid:** Priority date 4/1; no closing date. FAFSA, institutional form required. Applicants notified on a rolling basis.

**Academics.** Term-abroad programs in Asia, Europe, and South America. Internship programs in cities throughout United States and in South America, Europe, Asia, Africa, and Australia. Exchange programs with universities in People's Republic of China, Peru, and Sweden. Summer language study programs in Sweden, France, Ecuador and Israel. Team-taught, interdisciplinary honors sequence available. June registration for classes. **Special study options:** Accelerated study, combined bachelor's/graduate degree, double major, honors, independent study, internships, liberal arts/career combination, student-designed major, study abroad, teacher certification program. 3-2 forestry and environmental management program with Duke University,

3-2 landscape architecture program with University of Illinois at Urbana-Champaign, 3-2 engineering program with Washington University (MO), Iowa State University, University of Illinois at Urbana-Champaign, and Purdue University, 3-2 occupational therapy program with Washington University, early selection programs in dentistry with University of Iowa, study abroad programs in Asia, Europe, and South America. **Credit/placement by examination:** AP, CLEP, IB, ACT, institutional tests. More than 18 hours of credit by examination must be approved by the Dean of the College. **Support services:** Learning center, pre-admission summer program, reduced course load, study skills assistance, tutoring, writing center.

**Majors. Area/ethnic studies:** Asian, women's. **Biology:** General, biochemistry. **Business:** General, accounting, business admin, finance, international, management information systems, marketing. **Communications:** General. **Computer sciences:** Computer science. **Conservation:** General. **Education:** General, art, biology, chemistry, elementary, English, foreign languages, French, German, history, mathematics, middle, music, physical, physics, science, secondary, social science, Spanish, speech. **Engineering:** Physics. **Foreign languages:** Ancient Greek, classics, French, German, Latin, Scandinavian, Spanish. **Health:** Audiology/speech pathology, predental, premedicine. **History:** General. **Interdisciplinary:** Math/computer science. **Legal studies:** Prelaw. **Liberal arts:** Arts/sciences. **Math:** General. **Philosophy/religion:** Philosophy, religion. **Physical sciences:** Chemistry, geology, physics, planetary. **Psychology:** General. **Public administration:** General. **Social sciences:** Anthropology, economics, geography, political science, sociology. **Visual/performing arts:** Art, art history/conservation, dramatic, jazz, music performance, piano/organ, studio arts, voice/opera.

**Most popular majors.** Biology 16%, business/marketing 22%, foreign language 6%, health sciences 8%, psychology 7%, social sciences 10%, visual/performing arts 7%.

**Computing on campus.** 500 workstations in dormitories, library, computer center, student center. Dormitories wired for high-speed internet access and linked to campus network. Commuter students can connect to campus network. Online course registration, online library, helpline, repair service, student web hosting, wireless network available.

**Student life. Freshman orientation:** Mandatory. Preregistration for classes offered. Three-day program held before start of fall classes. **Policies:** Students represented on all major faculty/administrative committees and act as observers at Board of Trustees meetings. Student life governed by Bill of Student Rights and code of social conduct. Campus judiciary process includes student participation. Lower-division students not living with parents required to live on campus unless released to live off-campus by student services office. **Housing:** Guaranteed on-campus for all undergraduates. Coed dorms, single-sex dorms, apartments available. **Activities:** Bands, campus ministries, choral groups, dance, drama, international student organizations, literary magazine, music ensembles, Model UN, musical theater, opera, radio station, student government, student newspaper, symphony orchestra, Black student union, Asian student organization, Latinos Unidos, Latin American council, multicultural programming board, feminist forum, Global Affect, Intervarsity Christian Fellowship, Catholic organization, Muslim student association, Viking Volunteers, College Republicans/Democrats, Habitat for Humanity, Amnesty International.

**Athletics.** NCAA. **Intercollegiate:** Baseball M, basketball, cross-country, diving, football (tackle) M, golf, soccer, softball W, swimming, tennis, track and field, volleyball W, wrestling M. **Intramural:** Badminton, basketball, bowling, cross-country, fencing, football (non-tackle), golf, handball, racquetball, rowing (crew), skiing, soccer, softball, swimming M, table tennis, tennis, track and field, volleyball, water polo, wrestling M. **Team name:** Vikings.

**Student services.** Alcohol/substance abuse counseling, chaplain/spiritual director, career counseling, student employment services, financial aid counseling, health services, minority student services, personal counseling, placement for graduates, women's services. **Physically disabled:** Services for visually, speech, hearing impaired.

**Contact.** E-mail: admissions@augustana.edu
Phone: (309) 794-7341 Toll-free number: (800) 798-8100
Fax: (309) 794-8797
W. Kent Barnds, Vice President of Enrollment, Augustana College, 639 38th Street, Rock Island, IL 61201-2296

## Aurora University
**Aurora, Illinois**
**www.aurora.edu**                                   **CB code: 1027**

- Private 4-year university
- Commuter campus in small city
- 2,377 degree-seeking undergraduates: 13% part-time, 67% women, 10% African American, 3% Asian American, 14% Hispanic American

- 1,853 degree-seeking graduate students
- 71% of applicants admitted
- SAT or ACT (ACT writing optional) required
- 48% graduate within 6 years

**General.** Founded in 1893. Regionally accredited. George Williams College of Aurora University is a branch campus on shores of Geneva Lake in Williams Bay, Wisconsin offering undergraduate and graduate degree programs. **Degrees:** 496 bachelor's awarded; master's, doctoral offered. **ROTC:** Army. **Location:** 40 miles from Chicago. **Calendar:** Semester, limited summer session. **Full-time faculty:** 120 total; 82% have terminal degrees, 7% minority, 51% women. **Part-time faculty:** 298 total; 26% have terminal degrees, 12% minority, 57% women. **Class size:** 45% < 20, 55% 20-39. **Special facilities:** Museum of Native American history.

**Freshman class profile.** 1,620 applied, 1,151 admitted, 417 enrolled.

| Mid 50% test scores | | | |
|---|---|---|---|
| SAT critical reading: | 460-540 | GPA 2.0-2.99: | 28% |
| SAT math: | 480-550 | Rank in top quarter: | 40% |
| ACT composite: | 20-24 | Rank in top tenth: | 13% |
| GPA 3.75 or higher: | 19% | End year in good standing: | 84% |
| GPA 3.50-3.74: | 19% | Return as sophomores: | 75% |
| GPA 3.0-3.49: | 34% | Out-of-state: | 12% |
| | | Live on campus: | 71% |

**Basis for selection.** High school achievement record most important, followed by test scores. Recommendations considered. Interview and essay recommended. **Homeschooled:** State high school equivalency certificate, interview required. Writing sample (graded paper or personal statement) required.

**High school preparation.** College-preparatory program required. 16 units required. Required units include English 4, mathematics 3, social studies 3, science 3 and academic electives 3.

**2010-2011 Annual costs.** Tuition/fees: $18,700. Course laboratory/clinical fees in lab sciences, photography, nursing, physical education and student teaching. Tuition will vary for several adult degree completion programs. Room/board: $8,170. Books/supplies: $1,000. Personal expenses: $1,400.

**2009-2010 Financial aid. Need-based:** 395 full-time freshmen applied for aid; 352 were judged to have need; 352 of these received aid. Average need met was 90%. Average scholarship/grant was $7,450; average loan $3,301. 54% of total undergraduate aid awarded as scholarships/grants, 46% as loans/jobs. **Non-need-based:** Awarded to 1,919 full-time undergraduates, including 407 freshmen. Scholarships awarded for academics, alumni affiliation, art, music/drama, religious affiliation, ROTC, state residency.

**Application procedures. Admission:** Closing date 5/1 (receipt date). $25 fee, may be waived for applicants with need, free for online applicants. Admission notification on a rolling basis beginning on or about 9/1. Must reply by 6/20. Candidates may apply early and have until May 1 to have tuition and housing deposits refunded. **Financial aid:** Priority date 4/15; no closing date. FAFSA required. Applicants notified on a rolling basis starting 3/1; must reply by 5/1 or within 3 week(s) of notification.

**Academics. Special study options:** Accelerated study, cross-registration, double major, dual enrollment of high school students, honors, independent study, internships, liberal arts/career combination, student-designed major, study abroad, teacher certification program. **Credit/placement by examination:** AP, CLEP, SAT, ACT. 30 credit hours maximum toward bachelor's degree. **Support services:** Learning center, pre-admission summer program, reduced course load, remedial instruction, study skills assistance, tutoring, writing center.

**Majors. Biology:** General. **Business:** General, accounting, actuarial science, finance, management information systems, management science, marketing, operations. **Communications:** General. **Computer sciences:** General, computer science. **Education:** Elementary, physical, secondary, special. **Foreign languages:** Spanish. **Health:** Athletic training, clinical lab science, nursing (RN). **History:** General. **Legal studies:** Prelaw. **Liberal arts:** Arts/sciences. **Math:** General. **Parks/recreation:** General. **Philosophy/religion:** Religion. **Protective services:** Criminal justice. **Psychology:** General. **Public administration:** Social work. **Social sciences:** Political science, sociology. **Visual/performing arts:** Art, dramatic.

**Most popular majors.** Business/marketing 24%, education 19%, health sciences 22%, psychology 7%, public administration/social services 7%, security/protective services 6%.

**Computing on campus.** 90 workstations in library, computer center, student center. Dormitories wired for high-speed internet access and linked to campus network. Commuter students can connect to campus network. Online library, helpline, wireless network available.

**Student life. Freshman orientation:** Mandatory. Preregistration for classes offered. Day-long sessions held each May and June for admitted first-year students and their parents. **Housing:** Coed dorms, wellness housing available. $100 fully refundable deposit, deadline 5/1. **Activities:** Bands, campus ministries, choral groups, drama, literary magazine, Model UN, radio station, student government, student newspaper, Black student association, Latin American student organization, Native American club, Students for Wellness, Fellowship of Christian Athletes, Circle K International, Intervarsity Christian Fellowship, political science club, Future Leaders of the World, games club.

**Athletics.** NCAA. **Intercollegiate:** Baseball M, basketball, cross-country, football (tackle) M, golf, soccer, softball W, tennis, track and field, volleyball W. **Intramural:** Basketball, football (non-tackle), volleyball. **Team name:** Spartans.

**Student services.** Adult student services, alcohol/substance abuse counseling, chaplain/spiritual director, career counseling, student employment services, financial aid counseling, health services, personal counseling, placement for graduates. **Physically disabled:** Services for visually, speech, hearing impaired.

**Contact.** E-mail: admission@aurora.edu
Phone: (630) 844-5533 Toll-free number: (800) 742-5281
Fax: (630) 844-5535
James Lancaster, Director of Freshman Admission, Aurora University, 347 South Gladstone Avenue, Aurora, IL 60506-4892

## Benedictine University
Lisle, Illinois
www.ben.edu                                         CB code: 1707

- Private 4-year university and liberal arts college affiliated with Roman Catholic Church
- Commuter campus in large town
- 3,244 degree-seeking undergraduates: 31% part-time, 57% women
- 2,293 degree-seeking graduate students
- 79% of applicants admitted
- SAT or ACT (ACT writing optional), application essay required
- 62% graduate within 6 years

**General.** Founded in 1887. Regionally accredited. **Degrees:** 723 bachelor's, 90 associate awarded; master's, doctoral offered. **ROTC:** Army. **Location:** 25 miles from Chicago. **Calendar:** Semester, extensive summer session. **Full-time faculty:** 103 total; 88% have terminal degrees, 18% minority, 46% women. **Part-time faculty:** 467 total; 19% have terminal degrees, 16% minority, 54% women. **Class size:** 60% < 20, 38% 20-39, 2% 40-49, less than 1% 50-99. **Special facilities:** Nature museum, Benedictine abbey, arboretum, Fermi nuclear accelerator laboratories, Argonne national laboratories.

**Freshman class profile.** 1,667 applied, 1,317 admitted, 445 enrolled.

| Mid 50% test scores | | | |
|---|---|---|---|
| ACT composite: | 20-26 | Rank in top quarter: | 39% |
| GPA 3.75 or higher: | 26% | Rank in top tenth: | 15% |
| GPA 3.50-3.74: | 13% | Return as sophomores: | 74% |
| GPA 3.0-3.49: | 28% | Out-of-state: | 9% |
| GPA 2.0-2.99: | 32% | Live on campus: | 48% |
| | | International: | 1% |

**Basis for selection.** Require rank in top half of class and 21 ACT. Candidates falling below these criteria reviewed by admissions committee. Audition required of musical instrument and voice majors.

**High school preparation.** 16 units required. Required and recommended units include English 4, mathematics 3-4, social studies 3, history 1, science 2-3 (laboratory 1-2) and foreign language 2.

**2009-2010 Annual costs.** Tuition/fees: $22,310. Room/board: $6,945. Books/supplies: $1,260. Personal expenses: $2,220.

**2008-2009 Financial aid. Non-need-based:** Scholarships awarded for academics, alumni affiliation, minority status, music/drama, ROTC, state residency.

**Application procedures. Admission:** Priority date 8/30; no deadline. $40 fee, may be waived for applicants with need. Admission notification on a rolling basis. Must reply by May 1 or within 2 week(s) if notified thereafter. **Financial aid:** Priority date 4/15; no closing date. FAFSA required. Applicants notified on a rolling basis starting 2/15; must reply within 2 week(s) of notification.

**Academics. Special study options:** Accelerated study, combined bachelor's/graduate degree, cross-registration, distance learning, double major, dual

enrollment of high school students, ESL, honors, independent study, internships, liberal arts/career combination, study abroad, teacher certification program, weekend college. Engineering degree program with Illinois Institute of Technology. **Credit/placement by examination:** AP, CLEP, institutional tests. 30 credit hours maximum toward bachelor's degree. **Support services:** Learning center, reduced course load, remedial instruction, study skills assistance, tutoring, writing center.

**Majors. Biology:** General, biochemistry, molecular. **Business:** Accounting, finance, international, managerial economics, marketing, organizational behavior. **Communications:** General, publishing. **Computer sciences:** Computer science, information systems. **Conservation:** Environmental science. **Education:** Elementary, special. **Engineering:** Science. **Family/consumer sciences:** Food/nutrition. **Foreign languages:** Spanish. **Health:** Clinical lab science, health care admin, health services, nuclear medical technology, nursing (RN), sonography. **History:** General. **Interdisciplinary:** Global studies. **Math:** General. **Philosophy/religion:** Philosophy. **Physical sciences:** Chemistry, physics. **Psychology:** General. **Social sciences:** General, economics, international relations, political science, sociology. **Theology:** Theology. **Visual/performing arts:** Arts management, studio arts. **Other:** Bilingual journalism.

**Most popular majors.** Biology 9%, business/marketing 38%, education 8%, health sciences 16%, psychology 10%.

**Computing on campus.** 200 workstations in dormitories, library, computer center, student center. Dormitories wired for high-speed internet access and linked to campus network. Commuter students can connect to campus network. Online course registration, online library, helpline, wireless network available.

**Student life. Freshman orientation:** Mandatory, $75 fee. Preregistration for classes offered. Summer parent and student program. Student program 3 days prior to first day of classes. **Housing:** Coed dorms, single-sex dorms, apartments, wellness housing available. $125 deposit. **Activities:** Bands, campus ministries, choral groups, dance, drama, film society, international student organizations, literary magazine, music ensembles, Model UN, student government, student newspaper, symphony orchestra, TV station, Muslim student association, African-American student union, Knights of Columbus, Daughters of Isabella, Students for Life, Relay for Life, Best Buddies, South Asian student association, Democracy Matters, Hindu student association.

**Athletics.** NCAA. **Intercollegiate:** Baseball M, basketball, cross-country, football (tackle) M, golf, soccer, softball W, tennis W, track and field, volleyball W. **Intramural:** Basketball, bowling, football (non-tackle), softball, table tennis, volleyball. **Team name:** Eagles.

**Student services.** Adult student services, chaplain/spiritual director, career counseling, student employment services, financial aid counseling, health services, personal counseling, placement for graduates. **Physically disabled:** Services for visually, speech, hearing impaired. **Learning disabled:** Comprehensive services available.

**Contact.** E-mail: admissions@ben.edu
Phone: (630) 829-6300 Toll-free number: (888) 829-6363
Fax: (630) 829-6301
Kari Gibbons, Dean of Enrollment, Benedictine University, 5700 College Road, Lisle, IL 60532

## Blackburn College
Carlinville, Illinois                                CB member
www.blackburn.edu                                    CB code: 1065

- Private 4-year liberal arts college affiliated with Presbyterian Church (USA)
- Residential campus in small town
- 595 degree-seeking undergraduates
- SAT or ACT (ACT writing optional) required

**General.** Founded in 1837. Regionally accredited. **Degrees:** 110 bachelor's awarded. **Location:** 40 miles from Springfield, 60 miles from St. Louis. **Calendar:** Semester, limited summer session. **Full-time faculty:** 36 total. **Part-time faculty:** 28 total. **Class size:** 72% < 20, 25% 20-39, 2% 40-49, less than 1% 50-99.

**Freshman class profile.**

| Mid 50% test scores | | | |
|---|---|---|---|
| | | GPA 2.0-2.99: | 28% |
| ACT composite: | 19-25 | Rank in top quarter: | 43% |
| GPA 3.75 or higher: | 32% | Rank in top tenth: | 15% |
| GPA 3.50-3.74: | 15% | Out-of-state: | 9% |
| GPA 3.0-3.49: | 25% | Live on campus: | 87% |

**Basis for selection.** High school academic record, substantiated by test scores, most important. Interview recommended. Audition recommended for music majors. Portfolio recommended for art majors. **Homeschooled:** Statement describing homeschool structure and mission, transcript of courses and grades, state high school equivalency certificate required.

**High school preparation.** 16 units recommended. Recommended units include English 4, mathematics 3, social studies 2, history 2, science 3 and foreign language 2.

**2009-2010 Annual costs.** Tuition/fees: $14,286. All on-campus students participate in a work program which reduces net tuition costs. Room/board: $4,581. Books/supplies: $700. Personal expenses: $800.

**2009-2010 Financial aid. Non-need-based:** Scholarships awarded for academics, state residency. **Additional information:** Each resident student works 160 hours per semester.

**Application procedures. Admission:** No deadline. No application fee. Admission notification on a rolling basis beginning on or about 10/15. **Financial aid:** Priority date 4/1; no closing date. FAFSA required. Applicants notified on a rolling basis starting 3/1; must reply within 4 week(s) of notification.

**Academics. Special study options:** Accelerated study, cooperative education, double major, dual enrollment of high school students, independent study, internships, student-designed major, study abroad, teacher certification program, Washington semester. British studies semester, Mexico studies semester. **Credit/placement by examination:** AP, CLEP, SAT, ACT, institutional tests. 30 credit hours maximum toward bachelor's degree. **Support services:** Learning center, reduced course load, remedial instruction, study skills assistance, tutoring, writing center.

**Majors. Area/ethnic studies:** Latin American. **Biology:** General, biochemistry, environmental. **Business:** Accounting, marketing. **Communications:** General. **Computer sciences:** Computer science. **Education:** Art, biology, elementary, English, mathematics, physical, social science. **Foreign languages:** Spanish. **Health:** Clinical lab science. **History:** General. **Math:** General. **Parks/recreation:** Health/fitness. **Physical sciences:** Chemistry. **Protective services:** Criminal justice. **Psychology:** General. **Public administration:** General. **Social sciences:** Political science. **Visual/performing arts:** Art.

**Most popular majors.** Biology 9%, business/marketing 19%, communications/journalism 12%, education 24%, psychology 8%, security/protective services 7%.

**Computing on campus.** 75 workstations in library, computer center. Dormitories linked to campus network. Helpline available.

**Student life. Freshman orientation:** Mandatory. Preregistration for classes offered. One-day summer orientation and two day orientation prior to beginning of fall semester. **Policies:** Participation in student-managed work program required for all resident students. Resident students work 160 hours per semester to reduce costs and gain valuable career skills. Alcohol allowed for students 21 and older. All residence halls are smoke-free. **Housing:** Guaranteed on-campus for all undergraduates. Coed dorms, single-sex dorms, wellness housing available. $150 fully refundable deposit, deadline 7/31. Quiet study housing available. **Activities:** Concert band, choral groups, drama, literary magazine, student government, student newspaper, Cultural Expressions, Habitat for Humanity chapter, Catacombs, Newman Club, Common Ground, Republican club, health and wellness club, fishing club, Beavers Against Destructive Decisions, psychology club.

**Athletics.** NCAA. **Intercollegiate:** Baseball M, basketball, cross-country, football (tackle) M, golf M, soccer, softball W, tennis W, volleyball W. **Intramural:** Badminton, basketball, racquetball, softball, swimming, table tennis, tennis, volleyball, water polo. **Team name:** Beavers.

**Student services.** Adult student services, alcohol/substance abuse counseling, career counseling, student employment services, financial aid counseling, minority student services, personal counseling, placement for graduates. **Physically disabled:** Services for visually, hearing impaired.

**Contact.** E-mail: jmali@blackburn.edu
Phone: (217) 854-3231 Toll-free number: (800) 233-3550
Fax: (217) 854-3713
John Malin, Director of Admissions, Blackburn College, 700 College Avenue, Carlinville, IL 62626

## Blessing-Rieman College of Nursing
**Quincy, Illinois**
www.brcn.edu                                    CB code: 0139

- Private 4-year nursing college
- Commuter campus in small city

- 212 degree-seeking undergraduates: 12% part-time, 91% women, 4% African American, 2% Asian American, 2% Native American
- 10 degree-seeking graduate students
- 58% of applicants admitted
- SAT or ACT (ACT writing optional) required

**General.** Founded in 1891. Regionally accredited. Joint degree programs with Culver-Stockton College and Quincy University leading to Bachelor of Science in Nursing. General education classes held at partner campus, with nursing classes at BRCN campus and clinical experiences at Blessing Hospital, a regional medical center. **Degrees:** 50 bachelor's awarded; master's offered. **Location:** 120 miles from St. Louis, 100 miles from Springfield. **Calendar:** Semester, limited summer session. **Full-time faculty:** 20 total; 85% have terminal degrees, 100% women. **Part-time faculty:** 7 total; 100% women. **Class size:** 52% < 20, 48% 20-39.

**Freshman class profile.** 475 applied, 277 admitted, 104 enrolled.

| Mid 50% test scores | | | |
|---|---|---|---|
| ACT composite: | 21-29 | GPA 3.0-3.49: | 34% |
| GPA 3.75 or higher: | 14% | GPA 2.0-2.99: | 28% |
| GPA 3.50-3.74: | 20% | Out-of-state: | 39% |
| | | Live on campus: | 82% |

**Basis for selection.** 3.0 GPA and 22 ACT required. **Homeschooled:** Transcript of courses and grades required.

**High school preparation.** Required units include English 4, mathematics 2, social studies 3, science 4 (laboratory 2). Biology, chemistry, algebra required.

**2009-2010 Annual costs.** Tuition/fees: $22,290. Tuition and fees are average costs charged to freshman. Partnered with Quincy University and Culver-Stockton College. Freshmen and sophomores pay partnering school's tuition rate. Room/board: $7,890. Books/supplies: $1,000. Personal expenses: $1,775.

**2009-2010 Financial aid. Additional information:** Financial aid for freshmen and sophomores administered by Culver-Stockton College and Quincy University.

**Application procedures. Admission:** No deadline. No application fee. Admission notification on a rolling basis. **Financial aid:** No deadline. FAFSA required.

**Academics. Special study options:** Accelerated study, combined bachelor's/graduate degree, internships. **Credit/placement by examination:** CLEP, IB, SAT, ACT, institutional tests. **Support services:** Study skills assistance, tutoring.

**Majors. Health:** Nursing (RN).

**Computing on campus.** 25 workstations in dormitories, library, computer center. Dormitories wired for high-speed internet access and linked to campus network. Online library, wireless network available.

**Student life. Policies:** Immunization and background check required for sophomore level and up. **Housing:** Guaranteed on-campus for all undergraduates. Coed dorms, single-sex dorms, apartments, wellness housing available. Men's and women's dormitories available at Culver-Stockton College and Quincy University. **Activities:** Student government, student nurses organization.

**Student services.** Alcohol/substance abuse counseling, career counseling, student employment services, financial aid counseling, health services, on-campus daycare, personal counseling, placement for graduates.

**Contact.** E-mail: admissions@brcn.edu
Phone: (217) 228-5520 ext. 6949 Toll-free
number: (800) 877-9140 ext. 6949 Fax: (217) 223-4661
Ann O'Sullivan, Assistant Dean, Blessing-Rieman College of Nursing, PO Box 7005, Quincy, IL 62305-7005

## Bradley University
**Peoria, Illinois**                              CB member
www.bradley.edu                                 CB code: 1070

- Private 4-year university
- Residential campus in large city
- 5,049 degree-seeking undergraduates: 5% part-time, 54% women, 8% African American, 4% Asian American, 4% Hispanic American, 1% international
- 648 degree-seeking graduate students
- 74% of applicants admitted

- SAT or ACT (ACT writing recommended), application essay required
- 78% graduate within 6 years; 17% enter graduate study

**General.** Founded in 1897. Regionally accredited. **Degrees:** 1,169 bachelor's awarded; master's, professional offered. **ROTC:** Army. **Location:** 157 miles from Chicago, 164 miles from St. Louis. **Calendar:** Semester, limited summer session. **Full-time faculty:** 345 total; 83% have terminal degrees, 14% minority, 38% women. **Part-time faculty:** 204 total; 4% minority, 49% women. **Class size:** 49% < 20, 44% 20-39, 3% 40-49, 3% 50-99, less than 1% >100. **Special facilities:** Global communications center, 2 art galleries.

**Freshman class profile.** 6,221 applied, 4,573 admitted, 1,106 enrolled.

| Mid 50% test scores | | Rank in top quarter: | 60% |
|---|---|---|---|
| SAT critical reading: | 480-600 | Rank in top tenth: | 26% |
| SAT math: | 510-640 | End year in good standing: | 90% |
| ACT composite: | 22-27 | Return as sophomores: | 89% |
| GPA 3.75 or higher: | 35% | Out-of-state: | 12.6% |
| GPA 3.50-3.74: | 21% | Live on campus: | 92% |
| GPA 3.0-3.49: | 33% | Fraternities: | 42% |
| GPA 2.0-2.99: | 11% | Sororities: | 34% |

**Basis for selection.** High school curriculum and achievement, test scores, special talents, co-curricular activities, letters of recommendation, personal statement, educational goals important. Student's academic interest, motivational level, and quality of secondary school education also considered. Interview recommended. Audition required of music majors, recommended for theater majors. Portfolio recommended for art majors. **Homeschooled:** Transcript of courses and grades required. Record of courses taken, grades earned, personal statement, letter of recommendation and record of activities or club memberships required. Interview may be required and highly recommended.

**High school preparation.** College-preparatory program recommended. 16 units required. Required and recommended units include English 4-5, mathematics 3-4, social studies 2-3, science 2-3 (laboratory 2-3) and foreign language 2. Additional requirements for business, science, engineering, music, nursing, and health science majors.

**2009-2010 Annual costs.** Tuition/fees: $24,224. Room/board: $7,650. Books/supplies: $1,050. Personal expenses: $1,876.

**2008-2009 Financial aid. Need-based:** 876 full-time freshmen applied for aid; 708 were judged to have need; 708 of these received aid. Average need met was 78%. Average scholarship/grant was $12,430; average loan $3,669. 71% of total undergraduate aid awarded as scholarships/grants, 29% as loans/jobs. **Non-need-based:** Awarded to 1,522 full-time undergraduates, including 292 freshmen. Scholarships awarded for academics, alumni affiliation, art, athletics, leadership, music/drama.

**Application procedures. Admission:** Priority date 3/1; deadline 8/1 (postmark date). $35 fee, may be waived for applicants with need, free for online applicants. Admission notification on a rolling basis beginning on or about 10/1. Must reply by May 1 or within 2 week(s) if notified thereafter. **Financial aid:** Priority date 3/1; no closing date. FAFSA required. Applicants notified on a rolling basis starting 2/15.

**Academics.** Academic Exploration Program assists undergraduates in choosing major. **Special study options:** Accelerated study, combined bachelor's/graduate degree, cooperative education, double major, honors, independent study, internships, liberal arts/career combination, student-designed major, study abroad, teacher certification program, Washington semester. **Credit/placement by examination:** AP, CLEP, IB, institutional tests. 60 credit hours maximum toward bachelor's degree. **Support services:** Learning center, study skills assistance, tutoring, writing center.

**Majors. Biology:** General, biochemistry, cellular/molecular. **Business:** Accounting, actuarial science, business admin, entrepreneurial studies, finance, human resources, insurance, international, management information systems, managerial economics, marketing, selling, small business admin. **Communications:** General, advertising, journalism, organizational, photojournalism, public relations, radio/tv. **Communications technology:** Animation/special effects. **Computer sciences:** Computer science, information systems. **Conservation:** Environmental science. **Education:** Art, biology, chemistry, drama/dance, early childhood, elementary, English, family/consumer sciences, French, German, history, learning disabled, mathematics, mentally handicapped, music, physics, psychology, science, social science, social studies, Spanish, speech. **Engineering:** Civil, computer, construction, electrical, industrial, manufacturing, mechanical, physics. **Engineering technology:** Manufacturing. **Family/consumer sciences:** General, merchandising. **Foreign languages:** French, German, Spanish. **Health:** Clinical lab science, dietetics, health services, nursing (RN). **History:** General. **Liberal arts:** Arts/sciences, humanities. **Math:** General. **Philosophy/religion:** Philosophy, religion. **Physical sciences:** Chemistry, physics. **Protective services:**

Law enforcement admin. **Psychology:** General. **Public administration:** Social work. **Social sciences:** Economics, international relations, political science, sociology. **Visual/performing arts:** Acting, art, art history/conservation, ceramics, directing/producing, dramatic, drawing, graphic design, music management, music performance, music theory/composition, painting, photography, printmaking, sculpture, studio arts. **Other:** Biology-ecology & evolutionary biology, Civil engineering, environmental, Legal studies in business.

**Most popular majors.** Business/marketing 22%, communications/journalism 9%, education 8%, engineering/engineering technologies 12%, health sciences 12%, social sciences 8%.

**Computing on campus.** 900 workstations in dormitories, library, computer center. Dormitories wired for high-speed internet access and linked to campus network. Commuter students can connect to campus network. Online course registration, helpline, student web hosting, wireless network available.

**Student life. Freshman orientation:** Mandatory, $115 fee. Preregistration for classes offered. 13 sessions throughout summer. **Housing:** Guaranteed on-campus for freshmen. Coed dorms, single-sex dorms, apartments, fraternity/sorority housing, wellness housing available. $100 partly refundable deposit, deadline 5/1. **Activities:** Bands, campus ministries, choral groups, dance, drama, film society, international student organizations, literary magazine, music ensembles, Model UN, musical theater, opera, radio station, student government, student newspaper, symphony orchestra, TV station, Alpha Phi Omega, Lewis J. Burger Center for Student Leadership and Public Services, Hillel, InterVarsity Christian Fellowship, mock trial, Amnesty International, Habitat for Humanity, Beyond Prejudice.

**Athletics.** NCAA. **Intercollegiate:** Baseball M, basketball, cross-country, golf, soccer M, softball W, tennis, track and field W, volleyball W. **Intramural:** Badminton, basketball, bowling, fencing, football (tackle) M, golf, handball, racquetball, soccer, softball, swimming, table tennis, tennis, volleyball, water polo, wrestling M. **Team name:** Braves.

**Student services.** Alcohol/substance abuse counseling, career counseling, student employment services, financial aid counseling, health services, minority student services, personal counseling, placement for graduates, veterans' counselor.

**Contact.** E-mail: admissions@bradley.edu
Phone: (309) 677-1000 Toll-free number: (800) 447-6460
Fax: (309) 677-2797
Rodney San Jose, Director of Admissions, Bradley University, 1501 West Bradley Avenue, Peoria, IL 61625

## Chicago State University
**Chicago, Illinois**
**www.csu.edu**

CB member
CB code: 1118

- Public 4-year university
- Commuter campus in very large city
- 3,541 full-time, degree-seeking undergraduates
- 56% of applicants admitted
- ACT (writing optional) required

**General.** Founded in 1867. Regionally accredited. **Degrees:** 711 bachelor's awarded; master's, doctoral, professional offered. **ROTC:** Army. **Location:** 12 miles from downtown. **Calendar:** Semester, limited summer session. **Full-time faculty:** 310 total. **Part-time faculty:** 111 total. **Class size:** 48% < 20, 51% 20-39, less than 1% 40-49, less than 1% 50-99. **Special facilities:** Electron microscopy laboratory, video conference room, center of African heritage and culture.

**Freshman class profile.** 3,371 applied, 1,888 admitted, 642 enrolled.

| Mid 50% test scores | | Rank in top tenth: | 13% |
|---|---|---|---|
| ACT composite: | 16-19 | Out-of-state: | 6% |
| Rank in top quarter: | 35% | Live on campus: | 23% |

**Basis for selection.** High school GPA, standardized test scores, and subject/units completed important.

**High school preparation.** 15 units required. Required units include English 4, mathematics 3, social studies 3, science 3 and academic electives 2. 2 units foreign language, music, vocational education or art.

**2009-2010 Annual costs.** Tuition/fees: $9,712; $17,107 out-of-state. Rates guaranteed for 4 years. Room/board: $7,250. Books/supplies: $1,400. Personal expenses: $2,800.

**2008-2009 Financial aid. Non-need-based:** Scholarships awarded for academics, athletics, ROTC, state residency. **Additional information:** Freshmen of outstanding academic ability and talent eligible for Scholars Program full-tuition scholarship.

**Application procedures. Admission:** No deadline. $25 fee, may be waived for applicants with need. Admission notification on a rolling basis. **Financial aid:** Priority date 3/1; no closing date. FAFSA, institutional form required.

**Academics. Special study options:** Cooperative education, distance learning, double major, ESL, honors, independent study, internships, liberal arts/career combination, student-designed major, study abroad, teacher certification program. Programs for mature adults (University Without Walls, individualized curriculum, Board of Governors degree program). **Credit/placement by examination:** AP, CLEP, institutional tests. 60 credit hours maximum toward bachelor's degree. **Support services:** Learning center, remedial instruction, study skills assistance, tutoring, writing center.

**Majors. Area/ethnic studies:** African-American. **Biology:** General, bacteriology, biochemistry, environmental, molecular. **Business:** Accounting, business admin, fashion, finance, management information systems. **Communications:** Broadcast journalism. **Computer sciences:** General, data processing, information systems. **Education:** General, art, biology, business, chemistry, early childhood, elementary, English, health, history, mathematics, mentally handicapped, multi-level teacher, music, physical, secondary, technology/industrial arts. **Foreign languages:** Spanish. **Health:** Medical records admin, nursing (RN). **History:** General. **Math:** General. **Parks/recreation:** Health/fitness. **Physical sciences:** Chemistry, physics. **Psychology:** General. **Social sciences:** Anthropology, economics, geography, political science, sociology. **Visual/performing arts:** Art, commercial/advertising art.

**Most popular majors.** Business/marketing 14%, education 11%, health sciences 9%, liberal arts 30%, psychology 8%.

**Computing on campus.** 156 workstations in dormitories, library, computer center, student center. Dormitories wired for high-speed internet access. Commuter students can connect to campus network. Online course registration, online library available.

**Student life. Freshman orientation:** Mandatory. Preregistration for classes offered. One-day programs in July and August. **Housing:** Coed dorms available. $125 deposit, deadline 8/1. **Activities:** Bands, choral groups, dance, drama, literary magazine, music ensembles, radio station, student government, student newspaper, TV station, 47 clubs and organizations.

**Athletics.** NCAA. **Intercollegiate:** Baseball M, basketball, cross-country, golf, tennis, track and field, volleyball W. **Intramural:** Basketball, gymnastics, swimming, volleyball. **Team name:** Cougars.

**Student services.** Adult student services, alcohol/substance abuse counseling, chaplain/spiritual director, career counseling, student employment services, financial aid counseling, health services, minority student services, on-campus daycare, personal counseling, placement for graduates, veterans' counselor, women's services.

**Contact.** E-mail: ug-admissions@csu.edu
Phone: (773) 995-2513 Fax: (773) 995-3820
Addie Epps, Director of Admissions, Chicago State University, 9501 South King Drive, Chicago, IL 60628

---

## Columbia College Chicago

**Chicago, Illinois**          **CB member**
**www.colum.edu**             **CB code: 1135**

- Private 4-year visual arts and liberal arts college
- Commuter campus in very large city
- 11,465 degree-seeking undergraduates: 9% part-time, 52% women, 16% African American, 3% Asian American, 10% Hispanic American, 1% Native American, 1% international
- 534 degree-seeking graduate students
- Application essay required
- 37% graduate within 6 years

**General.** Founded in 1890. Regionally accredited. **Degrees:** 2,011 bachelor's awarded; master's offered. **Location:** Downtown. **Calendar:** Semester, limited summer session. **Full-time faculty:** 354 total; 15% minority, 46% women. **Part-time faculty:** 1,381 total. **Class size:** 74% < 20, 25% 20-39, 1% 40-49, less than 1% 50-99, less than 1% >100. **Special facilities:** Contemporary photography museum, photography studios, film/video sound stage, dance performance space, theater, audio technology center, psychoacoustic classroom, animation facilities, reverb chamber, book and paper arts center, black music research center, community media workshop, international Latino cultural center, community arts partnership center, concert hall.

**Freshman class profile.** 5,687 applied, 4,752 admitted, 2,158 enrolled.

| | | | |
|---|---|---|---|
| GPA 3.75 or higher: | 12% | Rank in top tenth: | 6% |
| GPA 3.50-3.74: | 10% | Return as sophomores: | 63% |
| GPA 3.0-3.49: | 25% | Out-of-state: | 40% |
| GPA 2.0-2.99: | 45% | International: | 1% |
| Rank in top quarter: | 22% | | |

**Basis for selection.** Open admission, but selective for some programs. Proof of high school graduation (or earned GED), letter of recommendation, and essay required for placement/counseling. Students with less than 2.0 GPA may be required to attend special summer program. All freshmen take COMPASS placement test on campus. Interview recommended. **Home-schooled:** Transcript of courses and grades required. **Learning Disabled:** Student must have regular earned GED or HS diploma and may have to complete BRIDGE program.

**High school preparation.** College-preparatory program recommended.

**2009-2010 Annual costs.** Tuition/fees: $18,970. Room/board: $12,000. Books/supplies: $1,346. Personal expenses: $1,760.

**2008-2009 Financial aid. Need-based:** 1,837 full-time freshmen applied for aid; 1,543 were judged to have need; 1,528 of these received aid. Average need met was 23%. Average scholarship/grant was $1,834; average loan $3,408. 19% of total undergraduate aid awarded as scholarships/grants, 81% as loans/jobs. **Non-need-based:** Awarded to 5,976 full-time undergraduates, including 1,430 freshmen. Scholarships awarded for academics, art, leadership, music/drama, state residency.

**Application procedures. Admission:** Priority date 5/1; no deadline. $35 fee, may be waived for applicants with need. Admission notification on a rolling basis beginning on or about 11/1. **Financial aid:** Priority date 5/1; no closing date. FAFSA, institutional form required. Applicants notified on a rolling basis.

**Academics. Special study options:** Cooperative education, distance learning, dual enrollment of high school students, ESL, independent study, internships, liberal arts/career combination, student-designed major, study abroad, teacher certification program. **Credit/placement by examination:** AP, CLEP, IB, institutional tests. 62 credit hours maximum toward bachelor's degree. **Support services:** Learning center, pre-admission summer program, reduced course load, remedial instruction, study skills assistance, tutoring, writing center.

**Majors. Architecture:** Interior. **Business:** Business admin, fashion, marketing. **Communications:** Advertising, broadcast journalism, journalism, public relations, radio/tv. **Communications technology:** Animation/special effects, recording arts. **Computer sciences:** Game design, web page design. **Education:** Early childhood, kindergarten/preschool. **Foreign languages:** Sign language interpretation. **Liberal arts:** Arts/sciences. **Visual/performing arts:** General, acting, art, art history/conservation, arts management, cinematography, commercial/advertising art, dance, design, directing/producing, dramatic, fashion design, film/cinema, graphic design, illustration, industrial design, interior design, jazz, multimedia, music management, music performance, photography, play/screenwriting, studio arts, theater design, voice/opera. **Other:** Cultural studies, Interdisciplinary arts.

**Most popular majors.** Business/marketing 11%, communications/journalism 13%, visual/performing arts 62%.

**Computing on campus.** 851 workstations in dormitories, library, computer center, student center. Dormitories wired for high-speed internet access and linked to campus network. Commuter students can connect to campus network. Online course registration, helpline, wireless network available.

**Student life. Freshman orientation:** Mandatory, $70 fee. Preregistration for classes offered. Parent orientation and parent weekend program available. **Housing:** Coed dorms, apartments available. $500 deposit. Student housing available at nearby colleges and universities. **Activities:** Bands, campus ministries, choral groups, dance, drama, film society, international student organizations, literary magazine, music ensembles, musical theater, radio station, student government, student newspaper, TV station, Association of Black Journalists, Umoja, Black Actor's Guild, Black Ink, Latino Alliance, environmental campus organization, Hillel, Not In Our Name.

**Athletics. Intramural:** Baseball, basketball, soccer.

**Student services.** Adult student services, alcohol/substance abuse counseling, career counseling, services for economically disadvantaged, student employment services, financial aid counseling, health services, minority student services, personal counseling, placement for graduates, veterans' counselor, women's services. **Physically disabled:** Services for visually, speech, hearing impaired.

**Contact.** E-mail: admissions@colum.edu
Phone: (312) 369-7130 Fax: (312) 369-8024
Murphy Monroe, Executive Director of Admissions, Columbia College
Chicago, 600 South Michigan Avenue, Chicago, IL 60605-1996

## Concordia University Chicago

| River Forest, Illinois | CB member |
|---|---|
| www.cuchicago.edu | CB code: 1140 |

- Private 4-year university and teachers college affiliated with Lutheran Church - Missouri Synod
- Residential campus in large town
- 1,232 degree-seeking undergraduates: 4% part-time, 57% women
- 3,278 graduate students
- 83% of applicants admitted
- ACT (writing optional) required

**General.** Founded in 1864. Regionally accredited. **Degrees:** 247 bachelor's awarded; master's, doctoral offered. **Location:** 10 miles from Chicago. **Calendar:** Semester, limited summer session. **Full-time faculty:** 122 total. **Part-time faculty:** 200 total. **Class size:** 58% < 20, 41% 20-39, less than 1% 40-49, less than 1% 50-99. **Special facilities:** Early childhood education laboratory school, curriculum center (teacher's resource), human performance laboratory.

**Freshman class profile.** 1,742 applied, 1,452 admitted, 363 enrolled.

| Mid 50% test scores | | | |
|---|---|---|---|
| SAT critical reading: | 460-580 | GPA 3.50-3.74: | 12% |
| SAT math: | 460-570 | GPA 3.0-3.49: | 32% |
| ACT composite: | 19-24 | GPA 2.0-2.99: | 42% |
| GPA 3.75 or higher: | 13% | Out-of-state: | 38% |

**Basis for selection.** School achievement record, character reference most important. 2.0 GPA in college preparatory classes and rank in top half of class with 20 ACT or 930 SAT (exclusive of Writing) required. Interview recommended. Essay and interview required for students who do not meet academic admission requirements. **Homeschooled:** Statement describing homeschool structure and mission, transcript of courses and grades required. Syllabus for each course, personal statement or essay describing an important event or individual, certificate of completion from home school (if available), official transcripts of any college work completed required.

**High school preparation.** College-preparatory program required. 15 units required. Required and recommended units include English 4, mathematics 3, social studies 2, history 1, science 2-4 (laboratory 1) and foreign language 2.

**2010-2011 Annual costs.** Tuition/fees: $24,581. Room/board: $8,000. Books/supplies: $1,200. Personal expenses: $800.

**2008-2009 Financial aid. Need-based:** 235 full-time freshmen applied for aid; 205 were judged to have need; 204 of these received aid. Average need met was 77%. Average scholarship/grant was $13,670; average loan $3,644. 75% of total undergraduate aid awarded as scholarships/grants, 25% as loans/jobs. **Non-need-based:** Awarded to 368 full-time undergraduates, including 81 freshmen. Scholarships awarded for academics, alumni affiliation, music/drama, religious affiliation, state residency.

**Application procedures. Admission:** No deadline. No application fee. Admission notification on a rolling basis beginning on or about 9/4. **Financial aid:** Priority date 4/1; no closing date. FAFSA required. Applicants notified on a rolling basis starting 3/1; must reply within 4 week(s) of notification.

**Academics. Special study options:** Combined bachelor's/graduate degree, cross-registration, distance learning, double major, exchange student, honors, independent study, internships, study abroad, teacher certification program. Adult degree completion program. **Credit/placement by examination:** AP, CLEP, IB, institutional tests. 12 credit hours maximum toward bachelor's degree. **Support services:** Learning center, reduced course load, study skills assistance, tutoring, writing center.

**Majors. Biology:** General. **Business:** General, accounting, business admin, marketing. **Communications:** General, advertising. **Computer sciences:** General, computer science. **Education:** General, biology, chemistry, computer, early childhood, elementary, English, history, multi-level teacher, music, physical, science, secondary, social science, social studies. **Foreign languages:** Ancient Greek, Hebrew, Latin. **Health:** Prenursing. **History:** General. **Interdisciplinary:** Natural sciences. **Math:** General. **Parks/recreation:** Exercise sciences. **Philosophy/religion:** Philosophy. **Physical sciences:** Chemistry. **Protective services:** Criminal justice, law enforcement admin, police science. **Psychology:** General. **Public administration:**

Social work. **Social sciences:** Geography, political science, sociology. **Theology:** Religious ed, sacred music, theology. **Visual/performing arts:** Art, music performance, music theory/composition.

**Most popular majors.** Business/marketing 18%, communications/journalism 7%, education 36%, health sciences 6%, psychology 8%, visual/performing arts 7%.

**Computing on campus.** 85 workstations in library, computer center, student center. Dormitories wired for high-speed internet access and linked to campus network. Commuter students can connect to campus network. Online course registration, helpline, repair service, student web hosting, wireless network available.

**Student life. Freshman orientation:** Mandatory. Preregistration for classes offered. **Housing:** Guaranteed on-campus for freshmen. Coed dorms, single-sex dorms available. $200 deposit, deadline 7/1. **Activities:** Bands, campus ministries, choral groups, drama, literary magazine, music ensembles, musical theater, radio station, student government, student newspaper, TV station, minority student alliance, Ambassadors for Christ, sociology/social service club, Fellowship of Christian Athletes, environmental awareness club, Pace Jail Ministries, Latin student union.

**Athletics.** NCAA. **Intercollegiate:** Baseball M, basketball, cross-country, football (tackle) M, soccer, softball W, tennis, track and field, volleyball W. **Intramural:** Badminton, basketball, bowling, cross-country, softball, swimming, tennis, track and field, volleyball. **Team name:** Cougars.

**Student services.** Career counseling, student employment services, financial aid counseling, health services, on-campus daycare, personal counseling, placement for graduates.

**Contact.** E-mail: crfadmis@cuchicago.edu
Phone: (708) 209-3100 Toll-free number: (866) 462-2873
Fax: (708) 209-3473
Gwen Kanelos, Assistant Vice President for Enrollment, Concordia University Chicago, 7400 Augusta Street, River Forest, IL 60305-1499

## DePaul University

| Chicago, Illinois | CB member |
|---|---|
| www.depaul.edu | CB code: 1165 |

- Private 4-year university affiliated with Roman Catholic Church
- Residential campus in very large city
- 15,821 degree-seeking undergraduates: 17% part-time, 55% women
- 8,689 degree-seeking graduate students
- 74% of applicants admitted
- SAT or ACT (ACT writing optional), application essay required
- 63% graduate within 6 years; 16% enter graduate study

**General.** Founded in 1898. Regionally accredited. Largest Catholic university in the United States. **Degrees:** 3,133 bachelor's awarded; master's, doctoral, professional offered. **ROTC:** Army. **Location:** Downtown. **Calendar:** Quarter, extensive summer session. **Full-time faculty:** 919 total; 88% have terminal degrees, 24% minority, 44% women. **Part-time faculty:** 904 total; 13% have terminal degrees, 12% minority, 42% women. **Class size:** 35% < 20, 52% 20-39, 12% 40-49, less than 1% 50-99, less than 1% >100. **Special facilities:** Environmental science & chemistry building, digital cinema laboratory with motion-capture system, green-screen studio, converged newsroom, welcome center, theatre, art museum, biological & environmental science building, fitness & recreational center, three-level student center.

**Freshman class profile.** 11,564 applied, 8,584 admitted, 2,531 enrolled.

| Mid 50% test scores | | | |
|---|---|---|---|
| SAT critical reading: | 520-640 | GPA 2.0-2.99: | 17% |
| SAT math: | 520-620 | Rank in top quarter: | 29% |
| SAT writing: | 520-630 | Rank in top tenth: | 22% |
| ACT composite: | 22-27 | End year in good standing: | 96% |
| GPA 3.75 or higher: | 32% | Return as sophomores: | 85% |
| GPA 3.50-3.74: | 17% | Out-of-state: | 31% |
| GPA 3.0-3.49: | 34% | Live on campus: | 70% |
| | | International: | 1% |

**Basis for selection.** Secondary school record most important; class rank, recommendations, test scores, essay, extracurricular activities, talent/ability, character, volunteer and work experience important. Interview, alumni/ae relation, geographical location, state residency, religious affiliation, racial or ethnic status considered. Interview required of acting, theater technologies, and recording sound technology majors. Auditions required of music and theater majors. Portfolios required of theater technology and design majors. **Homeschooled:** Transcript of courses and grades required. Official community college transcripts for any courses taken required. Listing of textbooks used, especially in math and science, recommended.

**High school preparation.** College-preparatory program required. 12 units required. Required and recommended units include English 4, mathematics 3, science 3 (laboratory 2) and foreign language 2. 2 units social science/history.

**2010-2011 Annual costs.** Tuition/fees: $28,858. Room/board: $10,955. Books/supplies: $1,005. Personal expenses: $1,704.

**2009-2010 Financial aid. Need-based:** 2,291 full-time freshmen applied for aid; 1,825 were judged to have need; 1,780 of these received aid. Average need met was 72%. Average scholarship/grant was $16,124; average loan $3,457. 51% of total undergraduate aid awarded as scholarships/grants, 49% as loans/jobs. **Non-need-based:** Awarded to 3,623 full-time undergraduates, including 1,144 freshmen. Scholarships awarded for academics, art, athletics, leadership, music/drama, ROTC, state residency.

**Application procedures. Admission:** Priority date 11/15; deadline 2/1 (postmark date). $40 fee, may be waived for applicants with need. Admission notification 3/15. Must reply by May 1 or within 2 week(s) if notified thereafter. Applications are accepted after 2/1 as space is available. Early action applicants receive early financial aid estimates, priority registration, priority housing and priority advising. **Financial aid:** Priority date 3/1; no closing date. FAFSA required. Applicants notified on a rolling basis starting 3/15.

**Academics.** Honors programs offered in arts and sciences, business. Conservatory program in theater and music provides professional training. **Special study options:** Accelerated study, combined bachelor's/graduate degree, cooperative education, distance learning, double major, dual enrollment of high school students, ESL, honors, independent study, internships, student-designed major, study abroad, teacher certification program, weekend college. **Credit/placement by examination:** AP, CLEP, IB, SAT, ACT, institutional tests. Senior year residency requirement excludes CLEP, AP or IB credits. For transfer students, CLEP, IB or AP credits combined with transfer credits from 2-year institutions may total no more than 99 hours, and combined with transfer credits from 4-year institutions may total no more than 132 hours. **Support services:** Learning center, pre-admission summer program, reduced course load, remedial instruction, study skills assistance, tutoring, writing center.

**Majors. Architecture:** History/criticism. **Area/ethnic studies:** African-American, American, East Asian, Latin American, women's. **Biology:** General. **Business:** General, accounting, business admin, e-commerce, finance, hospitality admin, human resources, management information systems, management science, managerial economics, marketing, organizational behavior, real estate. **Communications:** General. **Communications technology:** Animation/special effects. **Computer sciences:** General, applications programming, computer graphics, computer science, information systems, information technology, networking, programming, security, web page design. **Conservation:** Environmental science, environmental studies. **Education:** Art, early childhood, elementary, health, music, physical, secondary, special. **Foreign languages:** Arabic, Chinese, French, German, Italian, Spanish. **Health:** Art therapy, clinical lab science, nursing (RN). **History:** General. **Interdisciplinary:** Biological/physical sciences, math/computer science. **Liberal arts:** Humanities. **Math:** General. **Parks/recreation:** Health/fitness. **Philosophy/religion:** Islamic, Judaic, philosophy, religion. **Physical sciences:** Chemistry, physics. **Psychology:** General, educational. **Public administration:** Community org/advocacy, policy analysis. **Social sciences:** General, anthropology, economics, geography, international relations, political science, sociology, urban studies. **Visual/performing arts:** Acting, art, art history/conservation, arts management, cinematography, dramatic, jazz, music management, music performance, music theory/composition, play/screenwriting, theater design, theater history. **Other:** Media & cinema studies, Music - recording technology.

**Most popular majors.** Business/marketing 33%, communications/journalism 10%, computer/information sciences 7%, education 6%, liberal arts 9%, psychology 8%, social sciences 10%.

**Computing on campus.** 1,800 workstations in dormitories, library, computer center, student center. Dormitories wired for high-speed internet access and linked to campus network. Online course registration, online library, helpline, repair service, student web hosting, wireless network available.

**Student life. Freshman orientation:** Mandatory, $170 fee. Preregistration for classes offered. Two-day summer program for students and their families. **Policies:** Student organizations must have a minimum of 4 DePaul students, agree to the abide by applicable policies and procedures as well as applicable city, state and federal laws. Other policies that impact clubs include: travel, contracts, funding, guest speakers, casino/gambling policy. **Housing:** Coed dorms, special housing for disabled, apartments available. $200 fully refundable deposit. **Activities:** Bands, campus ministries, choral groups, dance, drama, film society, international student organizations, literary magazine, music ensembles, Model UN, musical theater, opera, radio station, student government, student newspaper, symphony orchestra, over 300 student organizations.

**Athletics.** NCAA. **Intercollegiate:** Basketball, cross-country, golf M, soccer, softball W, tennis, track and field, volleyball W. **Intramural:** Badminton, basketball, football (non-tackle), racquetball, soccer, softball, table tennis, tennis, volleyball, water polo. **Team name:** Blue Demons.

**Student services.** Adult student services, alcohol/substance abuse counseling, chaplain/spiritual director, career counseling, services for economically disadvantaged, student employment services, financial aid counseling, health services, legal services, minority student services, personal counseling, placement for graduates, veterans' counselor, women's services. **Physically disabled:** Services for visually, speech, hearing impaired. **Learning disabled:** Comprehensive services available.

**Contact.** E-mail: admission@depaul.edu
Phone: (312) 362-8300 Toll-free number: (800) 433-7285
Fax: (312) 362-5749
Carlene Kennelly, Dean of Undergraduate Admission, DePaul University, One East Jackson Boulevard, Chicago, IL 60604-2287

## DeVry University: Addison
**Addison, Illinois**
**www.devry.edu** CB code: 3204

- For-profit 4-year university
- Commuter campus in large town
- 1,504 degree-seeking undergraduates: 39% part-time, 27% women, 10% African American, 13% Asian American, 14% Hispanic American, 1% Native American, 3% international
- Interview required
- 36% graduate within 6 years

**General.** Founded in 1982. Regionally accredited. **Degrees:** 330 bachelor's, 40 associate awarded. **Location:** 20 miles from Chicago. **Calendar:** Semester, extensive summer session. **Full-time faculty:** 45 total; 27% minority, 24% women. **Part-time faculty:** 109 total; 18% minority, 37% women.

**Freshman class profile.** 205 enrolled.

**Basis for selection.** Applicants must have high school diploma or equivalent, or degree from an accredited postsecondary institution and demonstrate proficiency in basic college-level skills through test scores and/or institution-administered placement examinations, and be at least 17 years of age. New students may enter at the beginning of any semester. SAT/ACT or DeVry-administered admissions test required for all.

**High school preparation.** College-preparatory program recommended.

**2009-2010 Annual costs.** Tuition/fees: $14,160. Books/supplies: $1,310. Personal expenses: $3,574.

**2008-2009 Financial aid.** All financial aid based on need.

**Application procedures. Admission:** No deadline. $50 fee. Admission notification on a rolling basis. **Financial aid:** No deadline. FAFSA required. Applicants notified on a rolling basis.

**Academics. Special study options:** Accelerated study, distance learning. **Credit/placement by examination:** CLEP, institutional tests. **Support services:** Learning center, remedial instruction, tutoring.

**Majors. Business:** Business admin, e-commerce. **Computer sciences:** Game design, information systems, information technology, networking, systems analysis, web page design. **Engineering:** Biomedical, electrical, software. **Engineering technology:** Biomedical, computer, electrical. **Other:** Technical management.

**Most popular majors.** Business/marketing 65%, computer/information sciences 23%, engineering/engineering technologies 12%.

**Computing on campus.** 548 workstations in library, computer center. Online course registration, online library, helpline available.

**Student life. Freshman orientation:** Mandatory. **Housing:** Private apartments, student-plan housing, private rooms available. **Activities:** International student organizations, literary magazine, student government, student newspaper, Muslim student association, Alpha Sigma Lambda, Christian Fellowship, Chi Pi Alpha, Epsilon Delta Pi, Phi Theta Kappa, Institute of Electrical and Electronics Engineers, computer users group.

**Athletics. Intramural:** Basketball, soccer M, softball, tennis.

**Student services.** Career counseling, student employment services, financial aid counseling, placement for graduates, veterans' counselor. **Physically disabled:** Services for visually, hearing impaired.

**Contact.** Phone: (630) 953-2000 Toll-free number: (800) 346-5420 Fax: (630) 953-1236
Sandra Stack, Director of Admissions, DeVry University: Addison, 1221 North Swift Road, Addison, IL 60101-6106

## DeVry University: Chicago
### Chicago, Illinois
**www.devry.edu**                                   **CB code: 1171**

- For-profit 4-year university
- Commuter campus in very large city
- 2,063 degree-seeking undergraduates: 43% part-time, 43% women, 34% African American, 6% Asian American, 34% Hispanic American, 2% international
- Interview required
- 34% graduate within 6 years

**General.** Founded in 1931. Regionally accredited. **Degrees:** 310 bachelor's, 167 associate awarded. **Location:** 6 miles from downtown. **Calendar:** Semester, extensive summer session. **Full-time faculty:** 40 total; 20% minority, 30% women. **Part-time faculty:** 163 total; 28% minority, 39% women.

**Freshman class profile.** 423 enrolled.

**Basis for selection.** Applicants must have high school diploma or equivalent, or degree from an accredited postsecondary institution, demonstrate proficiency in basic college-level skills through ACT scores or institution-administered placement examinations, and be at least 17 years of age. New students may enter at beginning of any semester. SAT/ACT or DeVry-administered admissions test required for all.

**High school preparation.** College-preparatory program recommended.

**2009-2010 Annual costs.** Tuition/fees: $14,160. Books/supplies: $1,310. Personal expenses: $3,574.

**2008-2009 Financial aid.** All financial aid based on need.

**Application procedures. Admission:** No deadline. $50 fee. Admission notification on a rolling basis. **Financial aid:** No deadline. FAFSA required. Applicants notified on a rolling basis.

**Academics. Special study options:** Accelerated study, distance learning. **Credit/placement by examination:** CLEP, institutional tests. **Support services:** Learning center, remedial instruction, tutoring.

**Majors. Business:** Business admin. **Computer sciences:** Networking, systems analysis, web page design. **Engineering:** Biomedical, electrical. **Engineering technology:** Biomedical, computer, electrical. **Health:** Clinical lab science. **Other:** Technical management.

**Most popular majors.** Business/marketing 54%, computer/information sciences 25%, engineering/engineering technologies 20%.

**Computing on campus.** 600 workstations in library, computer center. Online course registration, online library, helpline available.

**Student life. Freshman orientation:** Mandatory. **Housing:** Private apartments, student-plan housing, private rooms available. **Activities:** Student government, student newspaper, Muslim student association, Alpha Beta Gamma, Alpha Chi, Bible club, National Society of Black Engineers, Tau Alpha Pi.

**Student services.** Career counseling, student employment services, financial aid counseling, placement for graduates, veterans' counselor. **Physically disabled:** Services for visually, hearing impaired.

**Contact.** E-mail: admissions2@devry.edu
Phone: (773) 929-6550 Toll-free number: (800) 383-3879
Fax: (773) 697-2710
Christine Hierl, Director of Admissions, DeVry University: Chicago, 3300 North Campbell Avenue, Chicago, IL 60618-5994

## DeVry University: Online
### Addison, Illinois
**www.devry.edu**

- For-profit 4-year virtual college
- Small city

- 16,994 degree-seeking undergraduates: 69% part-time, 53% women, 23% African American, 2% Asian American, 8% Hispanic American, 1% Native American
- 4,755 degree-seeking graduate students
- 23% graduate within 6 years

**General.** Regionally accredited. **Degrees:** 1,187 bachelor's, 239 associate awarded; master's offered. **Calendar:** Semester. **Full-time faculty:** 4 total. **Part-time faculty:** 3,062 total; 21% minority, 46% women.

**Freshman class profile.** 2,806 enrolled.

**Basis for selection.** Applicants must have high school diploma or equivalent, or degree from accredited post-secondary institution, demonstrate proficiency in basic college-level skills through SAT or ACT scores or institution-administered placement examinations, and be at least 17 years of age.

**High school preparation.** College-preparatory program recommended.

**2009-2010 Annual costs.** Tuition/fees: $14,800. Books/supplies: $1,300. Personal expenses: $3,574.

**2008-2009 Financial aid. Non-need-based:** Scholarships awarded for academics.

**Application procedures. Admission:** No deadline. $50 fee. Admission notification on a rolling basis. **Financial aid:** No deadline. FAFSA required. Applicants notified on a rolling basis.

**Academics. Special study options:** Accelerated study, distance learning. **Credit/placement by examination:** CLEP.

**Majors. Business:** Accounting/finance, business admin, e-commerce. **Computer sciences:** Game design, networking, systems analysis, web page design. **Engineering:** Software. **Engineering technology:** Computer, electrical. **Other:** Technical management.

**Most popular majors.** Business/marketing 88%, computer/information sciences 8%.

**Contact.** DeVry University: Online, One Tower Lane, Oakbrook Terrace, IL 60181

## DeVry University: Tinley Park
### Tinley Park, Illinois
**www.devry.edu**                                   **CB code: 2818**

- For-profit 4-year university
- Commuter campus in large town
- 1,131 degree-seeking undergraduates: 48% part-time, 34% women, 36% African American, 2% Asian American, 9% Hispanic American
- 329 degree-seeking graduate students
- Interview required
- 39% graduate within 6 years

**General.** Regionally accredited. **Degrees:** 153 bachelor's, 22 associate awarded; master's offered. **Location:** 20 miles from Chicago. **Calendar:** Semester, extensive summer session. **Full-time faculty:** 32 total; 6% minority, 25% women. **Part-time faculty:** 47 total; 32% minority, 38% women.

**Freshman class profile.** 149 enrolled.

**Basis for selection.** Applicants must have high school diploma or equivalent, or degree from an accredited postsecondary institution and demonstrate proficiency in basic college-level skills through test scores and/or institution-administered placement examinations, and be at least 17 years of age. New students may enter at the beginning of any semester. SAT/ACT or DeVry-administered admissions test required.

**High school preparation.** College-preparatory program recommended.

**2009-2010 Annual costs.** Tuition/fees: $14,160. Books/supplies: $1,310. Personal expenses: $3,574.

**2008-2009 Financial aid.** All financial aid based on need.

**Application procedures. Admission:** No deadline. $50 fee. Admission notification on a rolling basis. **Financial aid:** No deadline. FAFSA required. Applicants notified on a rolling basis.

**Academics. Special study options:** Accelerated study, distance learning. **Credit/placement by examination:** CLEP. **Support services:** Learning center, remedial instruction, tutoring.

**Majors. Business:** Business admin, management information systems. **Communications technology:** General. **Computer sciences:** Game design, information systems, networking, systems analysis, web page design. **Engineering:** Biomedical, computer, software. **Engineering technology:** Biomedical, computer, electrical. **Other:** Technical management.

**Most popular majors.** Business/marketing 52%, computer/information sciences 38%, engineering/engineering technologies 10%.

**Computing on campus.** 344 workstations in library, computer center. Online course registration, online library, helpline available.

**Student life. Freshman orientation:** Mandatory. **Activities:** Student activities association, student leadership group, women in technology.

**Student services.** Career counseling, student employment services, financial aid counseling, placement for graduates, veterans' counselor. **Physically disabled:** Services for visually, hearing impaired.

**Contact.** Phone: (708) 342-3100 Toll-free number: (877) 305-8184 Fax: (708) 342-3505
Bruce Jones, Director of Admissions, DeVry University: Tinley Park, 18624 West Creek Drive, Tinley Park, IL 60477-6243

---

## Dominican University

**River Forest, Illinois**　　　　　**CB member**
**www.dom.edu**　　　　　**CB code: 1667**

- Private 4-year university and liberal arts college affiliated with Roman Catholic Church
- Residential campus in large town
- 1,769 degree-seeking undergraduates: 7% part-time, 69% women, 6% African American, 2% Asian American, 26% Hispanic American, 2% international
- 1,703 degree-seeking graduate students
- 72% of applicants admitted
- SAT or ACT (ACT writing optional), application essay required
- 72% graduate within 6 years

**General.** Founded in 1901. Regionally accredited. **Degrees:** 292 bachelor's awarded; master's, doctoral offered. **Location:** 10 miles from downtown. **Calendar:** Semester, extensive summer session. **Full-time faculty:** 142 total; 84% have terminal degrees, 60% women. **Part-time faculty:** 298 total. **Class size:** 63% < 20, 37% 20-39, less than 1% 50-99. **Special facilities:** Food science laboratory.

**Freshman class profile.** 1,805 applied, 1,292 admitted, 405 enrolled.

| Mid 50% test scores | | Out-of-state: | 8% |
|---|---|---|---|
| ACT composite: | 20-25 | Live on campus: | 58% |
| Return as sophomores: | 81% | | |

**Basis for selection.** Rank in upper half of class, 2.75 GPA, have ACT or SAT at or above national average, and 16 units of college prep work required. Interview recommended. **Homeschooled:** Transcript of courses and grades required.

**High school preparation.** 16 units required. Required and recommended units include English 4, mathematics 3, social studies 1, history 2, science 3 (laboratory 2) and foreign language 2. 14 credits must be in English, math, social science, laboratory science, and foreign languages.

**2010-2011 Annual costs.** Tuition/fees: $25,810. Room/board: $8,000. Books/supplies: $1,200. Personal expenses: $1,000.

**2009-2010 Financial aid. Non-need-based:** Scholarships awarded for academics, alumni affiliation, leadership.

**Application procedures. Admission:** Priority date 6/1; no deadline. $25 fee, may be waived for applicants with need, free for online applicants. Admission notification on a rolling basis beginning on or about 10/1. Must reply by May 1 or within 2 week(s) if notified thereafter. **Financial aid:** Priority date 6/1; no closing date. FAFSA required. Applicants notified on a rolling basis starting 2/15; must reply within 2 week(s) of notification.

**Academics. Special study options:** Accelerated study, combined bachelor's/graduate degree, cross-registration, distance learning, double major, dual enrollment of high school students, ESL, honors, independent study, internships, liberal arts/career combination, study abroad, teacher certification program, Washington semester. 2+2 nursing with Rush University, 5-year BA/BS engineering program with Illinois Institute of Technology, license preparation in gerontology on-campus, 5 year program in occupational therapy with

Rush University leading to master's degree. **Credit/placement by examination:** AP, CLEP, IB, institutional tests. 28 credit hours maximum toward bachelor's degree. **Support services:** Learning center, pre-admission summer program, reduced course load, remedial instruction, study skills assistance, tutoring, writing center.

**Majors. Area/ethnic studies:** African-American, American. **Biology:** General, biochemistry. **Business:** Accounting, business admin, communications, fashion, international, organizational behavior. **Communications:** General, journalism, public relations. **Computer sciences:** General, computer science, information systems. **Conservation:** Environmental science, environmental studies. **Education:** Early childhood. **Engineering:** Architectural, chemical, civil, computer, electrical, mechanical. **Family/consumer sciences:** Food/nutrition, institutional food production. **Foreign languages:** French, Italian, Spanish. **Health:** Dietetics, predental, premedicine, prenursing, prepharmacy, preveterinary, substance abuse counseling. **History:** General. **Interdisciplinary:** Gerontology, math/computer science, neuroscience, nutrition sciences. **Math:** General. **Philosophy/religion:** Philosophy. **Physical sciences:** Chemistry. **Psychology:** General. **Social sciences:** General, criminology, economics, international relations, political science, sociology. **Theology:** Pastoral counseling, theology. **Visual/performing arts:** Art, art history/conservation, commercial/advertising art, dramatic, fashion design, photography, studio arts.

**Most popular majors.** Biology 7%, business/marketing 24%, health sciences 7%, physical sciences 6%, psychology 8%, social sciences 8%, visual/performing arts 10%.

**Computing on campus.** 309 workstations in dormitories, library, computer center, student center. Dormitories wired for high-speed internet access and linked to campus network. Commuter students can connect to campus network. Online course registration, online library, helpline, wireless network available.

**Student life. Freshman orientation:** Mandatory. Preregistration for classes offered. Two-day program with overnight on campus. **Housing:** Guaranteed on-campus for freshmen. Coed dorms, apartments, wellness housing available. $100 partly refundable deposit. Pets allowed in dorm rooms. **Activities:** Campus ministries, choral groups, dance, drama, international student organizations, literary magazine, musical theater, student government, student newspaper, Organization of Latino Americans, social service organization, business club, Italian club, black student union, psychology club, education club, gospel choir.

**Athletics.** NCAA. **Intercollegiate:** Baseball M, basketball, cross-country, soccer, softball W, tennis, volleyball W. **Intramural:** Basketball, bowling, cheerleading, racquetball, soccer, softball W, table tennis, volleyball, water polo. **Team name:** Stars.

**Student services.** Adult student services, alcohol/substance abuse counseling, career counseling, student employment services, financial aid counseling, health services, minority student services, on-campus daycare, personal counseling, placement for graduates, veterans' counselor. **Physically disabled:** Services for visually, hearing impaired.

**Contact.** E-mail: domadmis@dom.edu
Phone: (708) 524-6800 Toll-free number: (800) 828-8475
Fax: (708) 524-6864
Mary Ann Rowan, Vice President for Enrollment Management, Dominican University, 7900 West Division Street, River Forest, IL 60305-1099

---

## East-West University

**Chicago, Illinois**
**www.eastwest.edu**　　　　　**CB code: 0798**

- Private 4-year university
- Commuter campus in very large city
- 1,040 full-time, degree-seeking undergraduates
- Interview required

**General.** Founded in 1978. Regionally accredited. **Degrees:** 97 bachelor's, 67 associate awarded. **Calendar:** Quarter, limited summer session. **Full-time faculty:** 14 total. **Part-time faculty:** 72 total.

**Freshman class profile.** 3,100 applied, 1,550 admitted, 520 enrolled.

| Mid 50% test scores | | Out-of-state: | 10% |
|---|---|---|---|
| ACT composite: | 16-22 | | |

**Basis for selection.** Open admission, but selective for some programs. SAT or ACT recommended.

**2009-2010 Annual costs.** Tuition/fees: $15,795. Books/supplies: $1,200. Personal expenses: $2,100.

**Financial aid. Non-need-based:** Scholarships awarded for academics. **Additional information:** Foreign students eligible for institutional scholarship.

**Application procedures. Admission:** Priority date 5/1; no deadline. $40 fee, may be waived for applicants with need. Admission notification on a rolling basis. **Financial aid:** No deadline. FAFSA required. Applicants notified on a rolling basis starting 1/4; must reply within 4 week(s) of notification.

**Academics. Special study options:** Cooperative education, double major, ESL, honors, independent study, internships. **Credit/placement by examination:** CLEP, institutional tests. Interview recommended for placement. **Support services:** Tutoring.

**Majors. Business:** Business admin. **Communications:** General. **Computer sciences:** General. **Engineering technology:** Electrical. **Liberal arts:** Arts/sciences. **Math:** General.

**Most popular majors.** Business/marketing 32%, computer/information sciences 11%, engineering/engineering technologies 16%, liberal arts 40%.

**Computing on campus.** 10 workstations in computer center. Online library available.

**Student life. Freshman orientation:** Available. **Activities:** Drama, student government, student newspaper.

**Athletics. Team name:** Phantom.

**Student services.** Career counseling.

**Contact.** E-mail: seeyou@eastwest.edu
Phone: (312) 939-0111 Toll-free number: (877) 398-9376
Fax: (312) 939-0083
Ho Chung, Director of Admissions, East-West University, 816 South Michigan Avenue, Chicago, IL 60605

---

## Eastern Illinois University
**Charleston, Illinois**
**www.eiu.edu**                                    **CB code: 1199**

- Public 4-year university and teachers college
- Residential campus in large town
- 10,055 degree-seeking undergraduates: 10% part-time, 58% women, 12% African American, 1% Asian American, 3% Hispanic American, 1% Native American
- 1,635 degree-seeking graduate students
- 68% of applicants admitted
- SAT or ACT (ACT writing optional) required
- 56% graduate within 6 years

**General.** Founded in 1895. Regionally accredited. Off-campus sites in AIAI of Chicago, Arlington Heights, Bridgeview, Carterville, Centralia, Champaign, Danville, Decatur, Effingham, Olney, River Grove, Mattoon, Robinson and Vandalia. **Degrees:** 2,332 bachelor's awarded; master's offered. **ROTC:** Army. **Location:** 180 miles from Chicago, 125 miles from Indianapolis. **Calendar:** Semester, limited summer session. **Full-time faculty:** 629 total; 70% have terminal degrees, 10% minority, 46% women. **Part-time faculty:** 163 total; 9% have terminal degrees, 6% minority, 63% women. **Class size:** 32% < 20, 59% 20-39, 4% 40-49, 3% 50-99, 1% >100. **Special facilities:** Arts center, greenhouse, electron microscope, observatory.

**Freshman class profile.** 7,563 applied, 5,173 admitted, 1,654 enrolled.

| Mid 50% test scores | | Rank in top tenth: | 3% |
|---|---|---|---|
| ACT composite: | 19-24 | Return as sophomores: | 79% |
| GPA 3.75 or higher: | 10% | Out-of-state: | 2% |
| GPA 3.50-3.74: | 10% | Live on campus: | 99% |
| GPA 3.0-3.49: | 31% | Fraternities: | 24% |
| GPA 2.0-2.99: | 49% | Sororities: | 20% |
| Rank in top quarter: | 12% | | |

**Basis for selection.** Applicants must be in top quarter of class with 18 ACT, in top half of class with 19 ACT, or be in upper three-quarters of class with 22 ACT. Gateway admissions program for students with at least 14 ACT and 2.0 GPA. Audition required of music majors. **Homeschooled:** GED requirement may be waived with acceptable ACT score for students who present transcript of all courses completed with grades listed for each class.

**High school preparation.** College-preparatory program required. 15 units required. Required and recommended units include English 4, mathematics 3, social studies 3, science 3 (laboratory 3), foreign language 2 and academic electives 2. Significant science lab experience required.

**2009-2010 Annual costs.** Tuition/fees: $9,429; $23,769 out-of-state. Room/board: $8,078. Books/supplies: $120. Personal expenses: $1,600.

**2009-2010 Financial aid. Need-based:** 1,455 full-time freshmen applied for aid; 902 were judged to have need; 863 of these received aid. Average need met was 61%. Average scholarship/grant was $3,243; average loan $3,245. 44% of total undergraduate aid awarded as scholarships/grants, 56% as loans/jobs. **Non-need-based:** Awarded to 1,411 full-time undergraduates, including 297 freshmen. Scholarships awarded for academics, art, athletics, leadership, music/drama, ROTC.

**Application procedures. Admission:** No deadline. $30 fee, may be waived for applicants with need. Admission notification on a rolling basis. Consult university for possible early cut-off date. **Financial aid:** Priority date 3/1; no closing date. FAFSA required. Applicants notified on a rolling basis starting 3/1; must reply within 2 week(s) of notification.

**Academics. Special study options:** Distance learning, double major, dual enrollment of high school students, exchange student, external degree, honors, independent study, internships, study abroad, teacher certification program. Cooperative program in engineering with University of Illinois. **Credit/placement by examination:** AP, CLEP, ACT, institutional tests. **Support services:** Learning center, reduced course load, study skills assistance, tutoring, writing center.

**Majors. Area/ethnic studies:** African-American. **Biology:** General. **Business:** Accounting, business admin, finance, management information systems, management science, marketing. **Communications:** Journalism. **Education:** Elementary, health, kindergarten/preschool, science, social science, special, voc/tech. **Engineering:** General. **Engineering technology:** Industrial. **Family/consumer sciences:** General. **Foreign languages:** General. **Health:** Athletic training, clinical lab science, communication disorders, nursing (RN). **History:** General. **Interdisciplinary:** Math/computer science. **Liberal arts:** Arts/sciences. **Math:** General. **Parks/recreation:** Exercise sciences, facilities management. **Philosophy/religion:** Philosophy. **Physical sciences:** Chemistry, geology, physics. **Psychology:** General. **Social sciences:** Economics, geography, political science, sociology. **Visual/performing arts:** Art, dramatic. **Other:** Career and organizational studies.

**Most popular majors.** Business/marketing 13%, education 29%, English 9%, family/consumer sciences 7%, liberal arts 8%, social sciences 6%.

**Computing on campus.** 792 workstations in dormitories, library, computer center. Dormitories wired for high-speed internet access and linked to campus network. Commuter students can connect to campus network. Online course registration, helpline, student web hosting, wireless network available.

**Student life. Freshman orientation:** Mandatory. Preregistration for classes offered. All day sessions held on various dates from May-August. **Housing:** Guaranteed on-campus for freshmen. Coed dorms, single-sex dorms, special housing for disabled, apartments, fraternity/sorority housing available. $50 nonrefundable deposit. Quiet study floors available. **Activities:** Bands, campus ministries, choral groups, dance, drama, international student organizations, literary magazine, music ensembles, musical theater, opera, radio station, student government, student newspaper, symphony orchestra, TV station, College Democrats, Republicans, African Students Association, Christian Campus Fellowship, Newman Catholic center, Unity Gospel Choir, Epsilon Sigma Alpha, Students United for World Change, Association of International Students, minority leaders group.

**Athletics.** NCAA. **Intercollegiate:** Baseball M, basketball, cross-country, diving, football (tackle) M, golf, rugby W, soccer, softball W, swimming, tennis, track and field, volleyball W. **Intramural:** Badminton, basketball, bowling, football (non-tackle), racquetball, soccer, softball, table tennis, tennis, volleyball, weight lifting. **Team name:** Panthers.

**Student services.** Adult student services, alcohol/substance abuse counseling, career counseling, services for economically disadvantaged, student employment services, financial aid counseling, health services, legal services, minority student services, personal counseling, placement for graduates, veterans' counselor, women's services. **Physically disabled:** Services for visually, speech, hearing impaired.

**Contact.** E-mail: admissions@eiu.edu
Phone: (217) 581-2223 Toll-free number: (877) 581-2348
Fax: (217) 581-7060
Brenda Major, Director of Admissions, Eastern Illinois University, 600 Lincoln Avenue, Charleston, IL 61920-3011

## Elmhurst College

**Elmhurst, Illinois**
www.elmhurst.edu

**CB member**
**CB code: 1204**

- Private 4-year liberal arts college affiliated with United Church of Christ
- Commuter campus in large town
- 3,007 degree-seeking undergraduates: 6% part-time, 62% women
- 136 degree-seeking graduate students
- 70% of applicants admitted
- SAT or ACT (ACT writing optional) required

**General.** Founded in 1871. Regionally accredited. **Degrees:** 698 bachelor's awarded; master's offered. **ROTC:** Army, Air Force. **Location:** 16 miles from Chicago. **Calendar:** 4-1-4, limited summer session. **Full-time faculty:** 125 total; 84% have terminal degrees, 10% minority, 52% women. **Part-time faculty:** 215 total; 18% have terminal degrees, 5% minority, 51% women. **Class size:** 59% < 20, 41% 20-39, less than 1% 40-49. **Special facilities:** 2 nuclear accelerators, 4 electron microscopes, Impressionist art collection, computer science and technology center, media center, sound studio, greenhouse.

**Freshman class profile.** 2,762 applied, 1,935 admitted, 587 enrolled.

| Mid 50% test scores | | | |
|---|---|---|---|
| SAT critical reading: | 460-560 | Out-of-state: | 12% |
| SAT math: | 480-610 | Live on campus: | 61% |
| SAT writing: | 480-560 | International: | 1% |
| ACT composite: | 21-27 | Fraternities: | 17% |
| | | Sororities: | 20% |

**Basis for selection.** School achievement record, including grades and course levels, most important, followed by test scores. Applicants should rank in top half of class. Activities and counselor recommendations also important. Interview and essay recommended for all applicants, required of academically marginal applicants. Audition required of music majors. Portfolio recommended for art majors. **Homeschooled:** Interview strongly recommended.

**High school preparation.** College-preparatory program recommended. 16 units required; 21 recommended. Required and recommended units include English 4, mathematics 2-3, social studies 2-3, history 1-2, science 2-3 (laboratory 2-3), foreign language 1-2 and academic electives 4. Chemistry required for nursing applicants. 3 mathematics required for most business administration and computer-related specialties applicants.

**2009-2010 Annual costs.** Tuition/fees: $27,270. Room/board: $8,886. Books/supplies: $1,000. Personal expenses: $1,200.

**2008-2009 Financial aid. Need-based:** 487 full-time freshmen applied for aid; 409 were judged to have need; 409 of these received aid. Average need met was 82%. Average scholarship/grant was $15,062; average loan $3,859. 79% of total undergraduate aid awarded as scholarships/grants, 21% as loans/jobs. **Non-need-based:** Awarded to 852 full-time undergraduates, including 270 freshmen. Scholarships awarded for academics, alumni affiliation, art, minority status, music/drama, religious affiliation, ROTC, state residency. **Additional information:** Must apply for admission by 1/15 for priority consideration for scholarships.

**Application procedures. Admission:** Priority date 4/15; no deadline. No application fee. Admission notification on a rolling basis beginning on or about 11/1. Must reply by May 1 or within 2 week(s) if notified thereafter. **Financial aid:** Priority date 4/15; no closing date. FAFSA required. Applicants notified on a rolling basis starting 3/1; must reply within 3 week(s) of notification.

**Academics. Special study options:** Accelerated study, cooperative education, double major, dual enrollment of high school students, honors, independent study, internships, liberal arts/career combination, study abroad, teacher certification program, Washington semester. 3+2 engineering with Illinois Institute of Technology, University of Illinois at Urbana-Champaign, and Washington University (MO). **Credit/placement by examination:** AP, CLEP, IB, institutional tests. 48 credit hours maximum toward bachelor's degree. **Support services:** Learning center, pre-admission summer program, reduced course load, study skills assistance, tutoring.

**Majors. Area/ethnic studies:** American. **Biology:** General. **Business:** Accounting, business admin, finance, international, logistics, marketing. **Communications:** General. **Computer sciences:** Computer science, information systems. **Conservation:** Management/policy. **Education:** General, agricultural, art, biology, chemistry, early childhood, elementary, English, French, German, history, kindergarten/preschool, mathematics, music, physical, physics, secondary, Spanish, special. **Foreign languages:** French, German, Spanish. **Health:** Nursing (RN), predental, premedicine, prepharmacy, preveterinary, speech pathology. **History:** General. **Legal studies:** Prelaw. **Liberal arts:** Arts/sciences. **Math:** General. **Parks/recreation:** Exercise sciences, health/fitness, sports admin. **Philosophy/religion:** Philosophy. **Physical sciences:** Chemistry, physics. **Protective services:** Criminal justice, law enforcement admin. **Psychology:** General. **Social sciences:** Criminology, economics, geography, political science, sociology, urban studies. **Theology:** Preministerial, theology. **Visual/performing arts:** Art, dramatic, music management.

**Most popular majors.** Business/marketing 20%, education 20%, health sciences 11%, psychology 9%.

**Computing on campus.** 440 workstations in library, computer center, student center. Dormitories wired for high-speed internet access and linked to campus network. Commuter students can connect to campus network. Online library, helpline, repair service, wireless network available.

**Student life. Freshman orientation:** Mandatory. Three-day program held immediately prior to term. **Policies:** Each residence hall is self-governing. **Housing:** Coed dorms, apartments available. $300 nonrefundable deposit, deadline 4/1. **Activities:** Bands, campus ministries, choral groups, drama, literary magazine, music ensembles, musical theater, radio station, student government, student newspaper, over 90 organizations.

**Athletics.** NCAA. **Intercollegiate:** Baseball M, basketball, bowling W, cross-country, football (tackle) M, golf, soccer, softball W, tennis, track and field, volleyball W, wrestling M. **Intramural:** Basketball, football (tackle) M, golf, racquetball, softball, volleyball. **Team name:** Blue Jays.

**Student services.** Adult student services, career counseling, student employment services, financial aid counseling, health services, minority student services, on-campus daycare, personal counseling, placement for graduates.

**Contact.** E-mail: admit@elmhurst.edu
Phone: (630) 617-3400 Toll-free number: (800) 697-1871
Fax: (630) 617-5501
Stephanie Levenson, Director of Admission, Elmhurst College, 190 South Prospect Avenue, Elmhurst, IL 60126-3296

## Eureka College

**Eureka, Illinois**
www.eureka.edu

**CB member**
**CB code: 1206**

- Private 4-year liberal arts college affiliated with Christian Church (Disciples of Christ)
- Residential campus in small town
- 716 degree-seeking undergraduates
- SAT or ACT (ACT writing recommended) required

**General.** Founded in 1855. Regionally accredited. **Degrees:** 167 bachelor's awarded. **Location:** 140 miles from Chicago. **Calendar:** Semester, limited summer session. **Full-time faculty:** 44 total. **Part-time faculty:** 22 total. **Class size:** 64% < 20, 36% 20-39. **Special facilities:** Ronald Reagan Museum, peace garden, lilac arboretum, labyrinth, fitness center.

**Freshman class profile.**

| Mid 50% test scores | | | |
|---|---|---|---|
| ACT composite: | 19-27 | Rank in top tenth: | 23% |
| | | Out-of-state: | 4% |
| Rank in top quarter: | 56% | Live on campus: | 90% |

**Basis for selection.** Class rank, high school GPA, ACT scores, and high school curriculum most important. Recommendations and interviews also important. Audition required for music and drama scholarships. Portfolio required for art scholarship. **Homeschooled:** Interview required.

**High school preparation.** 14 units recommended. Recommended units include English 4, mathematics 3, social studies 3, science 2 and foreign language 2.

**2009-2010 Annual costs.** Tuition/fees: $17,390. Room/board: $7,440. Books/supplies: $1,000. Personal expenses: $510.

**2009-2010 Financial aid. Non-need-based:** Scholarships awarded for academics, alumni affiliation, art, leadership, music/drama, religious affiliation.

**Application procedures. Admission:** Priority date 5/1; deadline 8/10 (postmark date). No application fee. Admission notification on a rolling basis. Must reply by May 1 or within 3 week(s) if notified thereafter. **Financial aid:** Priority date 4/15; no closing date. FAFSA required. Applicants notified on a rolling basis starting 2/15; must reply by 5/1 or within 3 week(s) of notification.

**Academics. Special study options:** Cooperative education, double major, dual enrollment of high school students, honors, independent study, internships, liberal arts/career combination, student-designed major, study abroad, teacher certification program, Washington semester. Students who began as freshmen, have a record of leadership and service, and hold a 3.5 GPA at the end of their sophomore year qualify for a mentorship paid for by the college. **Credit/placement by examination:** AP, CLEP, institutional tests. **Support services:** Learning center, reduced course load, remedial instruction, study skills assistance, tutoring, writing center.

**Honors college/program.** Admitted by invitation, includes advanced and special classes, advanced general education requirements along with thesis preparation and presentation, honors seminars on special topics.

**Majors. Biology:** General, environmental. **Business:** General, accounting, business admin, finance, management information systems, marketing. **Communications:** General, media studies, public relations. **Computer sciences:** General, computer science. **Education:** General, elementary, middle, multilevel teacher, secondary, special. **Engineering:** General. **Health:** Predental, premedicine, prenursing, preveterinary. **History:** General. **Interdisciplinary:** Math/computer science. **Legal studies:** Prelaw. **Liberal arts:** Arts/sciences. **Math:** General. **Philosophy/religion:** Philosophy, religion. **Physical sciences:** Chemistry. **Protective services:** Law enforcement admin. **Psychology:** General. **Social sciences:** Political science. **Visual/performing arts:** Art, arts management, dramatic, music performance. **Other:** Leadership.

**Computing on campus.** 50 workstations in dormitories, library, computer center, student center. Dormitories wired for high-speed internet access and linked to campus network. Commuter students can connect to campus network. Online library, helpline, repair service available.

**Student life. Freshman orientation:** Mandatory. Preregistration for classes offered. Orientation for new students held at start of school year. **Policies:** All single students under 24 not living with parents required to live on campus. **Housing:** Guaranteed on-campus for all undergraduates. Coed dorms, single-sex dorms, special housing for disabled, fraternity/sorority housing, wellness housing available. $150 fully refundable deposit, deadline 8/14. **Activities:** Bands, choral groups, dance, drama, film society, literary magazine, music ensembles, musical theater, student government, student newspaper, Disciples on Campus, PRIDE, Young Republicans, Campus Democrats, Catholic Salve Regina Newman Center, Campus Crusade for Christ, Black student union, Habitat for Humanity, Student Foundation, International Healthcare Development Program.

**Athletics.** NCAA. **Intercollegiate:** Baseball M, basketball, cross-country, diving, football (tackle) M, golf, soccer, softball W, swimming, tennis, track and field, volleyball W. **Intramural:** Badminton, basketball, bowling, football (non-tackle), golf, softball, swimming, table tennis, tennis, volleyball. **Team name:** Red Devils.

**Student services.** Adult student services, alcohol/substance abuse counseling, chaplain/spiritual director, career counseling, student employment services, financial aid counseling, health services, personal counseling, placement for graduates.

**Contact.** E-mail: admissions@eureka.edu
Phone: (309) 467-6350 Toll-free number: (888) 438-7352
Fax: (309) 467-6576
Kurt Krile, Dean of Admissions and Financial Aid, Eureka College, 300 East College Avenue, Eureka, IL 61530-1500

---

## Governors State University
### University Park, Illinois
### www.govst.edu
CB code: 0807

▸ Public two-year upper-division university
▸ Commuter campus in large town
▸ 85% of applicants admitted

**General.** Founded in 1969. Regionally accredited. **Degrees:** 766 bachelor's awarded; master's, professional offered. **Articulation:** Agreements with Prairie State College, Joliet Junior College, Kankakee CC, Moraine Valley CC, South Suburban College of Cook County, College of DuPage, Morton College, City Colleges of Chicago, Waubonsee CC, Triton College, Parkland College, College of Lake County, Illinois Valley College, Ivy Tech State College (IN). **Location:** 30 miles from Chicago. **Calendar:** Trimester, extensive summer session. **Full-time faculty:** 202 total. **Part-time faculty:** 201 total. **Special facilities:** 750-acre campus, nature trails, 6 lakes, sculpture park, prairie restoration.

**Student profile.** 2,791 degree-seeking undergraduates, 2,883 degree-seeking graduate students. 2,430 applied as first time-transfer students, 2,073

---

admitted, 1,503 enrolled. 63% transferred from two-year, 37% transferred from four-year institutions.

| | | | |
|---|---|---|---|
| **Women:** | 68% | **Out-of-state:** | 5% |
| **Part-time:** | 63% | **25 or older:** | 61% |

**Basis for selection.** College transcript required. 60 semester hours or associate degree required. Transfer accepted as juniors, seniors.

**2009-2010 Annual costs.** Tuition/fees: $8,352; $18,432 out-of-state. Books/supplies: $1,200. Personal expenses: $800.

**Financial aid. Non-need-based:** Scholarships awarded for academics.

**Application procedures. Admission:** Priority date 5/15. $25 fee, may be waived for applicants with need.

**Academics. Special study options:** Distance learning, double major, dual enrollment of high school students, external degree, honors, independent study, internships, student-designed major, teacher certification program. Dual admission with several community colleges. **Credit/placement by examination:** AP, CLEP. 60 credit hours maximum toward bachelor's degree.

**Majors. Biology:** General. **Business:** Accounting, business admin, management information systems. **Communications:** General, broadcast journalism, journalism. **Computer sciences:** General, computer science. **Education:** Biology, chemistry, early childhood, elementary, English, mathematics. **Health:** Health care admin, nursing (RN), speech pathology. **Liberal arts:** Arts/sciences. **Math:** General. **Physical sciences:** Chemistry. **Protective services:** Criminal justice. **Psychology:** General. **Public administration:** General, social work. **Social sciences:** General. **Visual/performing arts:** Art.

**Computing on campus.** 280 workstations in library, computer center, student center. Commuter students can connect to campus network. Online library, helpline, wireless network available.

**Student life. Policies:** A minimum of seven students can seek chartering as a student club or organization through the Office of Student Life. All organizations must renew their charters each academic year. **Activities:** Drama, international student organizations, student government, student newspaper, TV station, Art Forum, Association of Latin American Students, Black Student Union, Chinese students association, Japanese philosophy, art and culture club, Spanish reading club, table tennis club, wellness club, over 30 co-curricular professional service organizations.

**Athletics. Intramural:** Table tennis.

**Student services.** Career counseling, financial aid counseling, minority student services, on-campus daycare, personal counseling. **Physically disabled:** Services for visually, speech, hearing impaired.

**Contact.** Phone: (708) 534-4490 Fax: (708) 534-1640
Sharon Evans, Director of Admissions & Student Recruitment, Governors State University, One University Parkway, University Park, IL 60484

---

## Greenville College
### Greenville, Illinois
### www.greenville.edu
CB code: 1256

▸ Private 4-year liberal arts college affiliated with Free Methodist Church of North America
▸ Residential campus in small town
▸ 1,360 degree-seeking undergraduates: 2% part-time, 55% women, 8% African American, 1% Asian American, 2% Hispanic American, 1% Native American, 2% international
▸ 194 degree-seeking graduate students
▸ 78% of applicants admitted
▸ SAT or ACT (ACT writing optional), application essay required
▸ 46% graduate within 6 years

**General.** Founded in 1892. Regionally accredited. Academic and Christian values emphasized. **Degrees:** 324 bachelor's awarded; master's offered. **Location:** 50 miles from St. Louis, 190 miles from Indianapolis. **Calendar:** 4-1-4, limited summer session. **Full-time faculty:** 61 total; 70% have terminal degrees, 3% minority, 34% women. **Part-time faculty:** 111 total; 52% women. **Class size:** 51% < 20, 40% 20-39, 5% 40-49, 4% 50-99. **Special facilities:** Sculpture collection, Frank Lloyd Wright architectural drawings, 140 acre field station and nature preserve, observatory, environmental education center.

**Freshman class profile.** 932 applied, 727 admitted, 252 enrolled.

| Mid 50% test scores | | GPA 2.0-2.99: | 26% |
|---|---|---|---|
| SAT critical reading: | 440-590 | Rank in top quarter: | 39% |
| SAT math: | 410-560 | Rank in top tenth: | 16% |
| SAT writing: | 410-550 | End year in good standing: | 77% |
| ACT composite: | 20-27 | Return as sophomores: | 66% |
| GPA 3.75 or higher: | 25% | Out-of-state: | 40% |
| GPA 3.50-3.74: | 17% | Live on campus: | 94% |
| GPA 3.0-3.49: | 32% | International: | 2% |

**Basis for selection.** Secondary school record, class rank, standardized test scores, essay, character/personal qualities, and religious affiliation or commitment all very important. Recommendations, extracurricular activities, talent/ability and alumni/ae relation considered. Interview required of academically weak applicants. Audition recommended for music majors. **Homeschooled:** Transcript of courses and grades required.

**High school preparation.** College-preparatory program recommended. 11 units recommended. Recommended units include English 4, mathematics 2, history 1, science 1 (laboratory 1) and foreign language 2. Math recommendation includes algebra and geometry.

**2010-2011 Annual costs.** Tuition/fees: $20,924. Room/board: $7,034.

**2008-2009 Financial aid. Need-based:** 279 full-time freshmen applied for aid; 258 were judged to have need; 256 of these received aid. Average need met was 83%. Average scholarship/grant was $13,266; average loan $3,767. 68% of total undergraduate aid awarded as scholarships/grants, 32% as loans/jobs. **Non-need-based:** Awarded to 261 full-time undergraduates, including 82 freshmen. Scholarships awarded for academics, alumni affiliation, art, leadership, minority status, music/drama, religious affiliation, state residency.

**Application procedures. Admission:** Closing date 8/15. $25 fee, may be waived for applicants with need. Admission notification on a rolling basis beginning on or about 10/15. Housing deposit is not refundable after May 1st. **Financial aid:** Priority date 4/1; no closing date. FAFSA required. Applicants notified on a rolling basis starting 3/1; must reply within 3 week(s) of notification.

**Academics. Special study options:** Accelerated study, cooperative education, cross-registration, double major, external degree, honors, independent study, internships, liberal arts/career combination, semester at sea, student-designed major, study abroad, teacher certification program, urban semester, Washington semester. **Credit/placement by examination:** AP, CLEP, IB, SAT, ACT, institutional tests. 32 credit hours maximum toward bachelor's degree. **Support services:** Learning center, reduced course load, remedial instruction, study skills assistance, tutoring.

**Majors. Biology:** General, environmental. **Business:** Accounting, business admin, management information systems, marketing, organizational behavior. **Communications:** Media studies, public relations. **Computer sciences:** General. **Education:** Biology, chemistry, early childhood, elementary, English, history, mathematics, music, physical, physics, Spanish, special. **Foreign languages:** Spanish. **Health:** Predental, premedicine, prenursing, preveterinary. **History:** General. **Interdisciplinary:** Global studies. **Liberal arts:** Arts/sciences. **Math:** General. **Parks/recreation:** General, exercise sciences, sports admin. **Philosophy/religion:** Philosophy, religion. **Physical sciences:** Chemistry, physics. **Protective services:** Law enforcement admin. **Psychology:** General. **Public administration:** Social work. **Social sciences:** Sociology. **Theology:** Pastoral counseling, youth ministry. **Visual/performing arts:** Art, dramatic, music management.

**Most popular majors.** Business/marketing 35%, education 22%, visual/performing arts 8%.

**Computing on campus.** 95 workstations in library, computer center. Dormitories wired for high-speed internet access and linked to campus network. Commuter students can connect to campus network. Online library, helpline, repair service, wireless network available.

**Student life. Freshman orientation:** Mandatory. Preregistration for classes offered. Service project conducted over orientation weekend. **Policies:** Signed statements of Christian values and academic honesty requested. Required chapel. All single students not living at home must live in college housing. Religious observance required. **Housing:** Guaranteed on-campus for all undergraduates. Single-sex dorms, apartments, wellness housing available. $200 deposit. Upper division students may live in college-owned houses. **Activities:** Bands, campus ministries, choral groups, drama, music ensembles, musical theater, radio station, student government, student newspaper, Habitat for Humanity, Fellowship of Christian Athletes, Campus Activities Board, student outreach, Agape music festival, Circle K, E-cafe, Mosaic, Young Republicans, Big Brother/Big Sister.

**Athletics.** NCAA, NCCAA. **Intercollegiate:** Baseball M, basketball, cross-country, football (tackle) M, soccer, softball W, tennis, track and field, volleyball W. **Intramural:** Badminton, basketball, football (non-tackle), soccer, softball, table tennis, tennis, volleyball. **Team name:** Panthers.

**Student services.** Adult student services, career counseling, student employment services, financial aid counseling, personal counseling, placement for graduates.

**Contact.** E-mail: admissions@greenville.edu
Phone: (618) 664-7100 Toll-free number: (800) 345-4440
Fax: (618) 664-9841
Michael Ritter, Assistant Vice President for Enrollment, Greenville College, 315 East College Avenue, Greenville, IL 62246-0159

## Harrington College of Design
### Chicago, Illinois
www.harringtoncollege.com                    CB code: 0940

- For-profit 4-year visual arts college
- Commuter campus in very large city
- 1,084 degree-seeking undergraduates
- Interview required

**General.** Founded in 1931. Accredited by ACICS. Accredited by Council for Interior Design Accreditation (CIDA), Accrediting Council for Independent Schools and Colleges (ACICS), in candidacy status for Regional Accreditation (NCA). **Degrees:** 173 bachelor's, 123 associate awarded; master's offered. **Location:** Downtown. **Calendar:** Semester, extensive summer session. **Full-time faculty:** 20 total. **Part-time faculty:** 89 total. **Class size:** 84% < 20, 16% 20-39. **Special facilities:** Access to Chicago Merchandise Mart's wholesale showroom.

**Basis for selection.** Open admission, but selective for some programs. Personal interview, commitment to career, 2.0 GPA most important.

**2009-2010 Annual costs.** Tuition/fees: $17,270. Required fees vary depending on program. Some programs require laptop computer purchase. Books/supplies: $850. Personal expenses: $2,500.

**Financial aid.** All financial aid based on need.

**Application procedures. Admission:** No deadline. $60 fee, may be waived for applicants with need. Admission notification on a rolling basis. **Financial aid:** Closing date 7/15. FAFSA required. Applicants notified on a rolling basis; must reply within 2 week(s) of notification.

**Academics.** Exchange program with Interior Architecture Department, Rotterdam College of Art and Design, The Netherlands. **Special study options:** Cooperative education, internships, study abroad. **Credit/placement by examination:** CLEP. **Support services:** Tutoring, writing center.

**Majors. Visual/performing arts:** Graphic design, interior design.

**Computing on campus.** 35 workstations in library, computer center.

**Student life. Freshman orientation:** Mandatory. Preregistration for classes offered. One-day program held 1 or 2 weeks before classes begin. **Housing:** Students may reside at Crown Center Residence at nearby Roosevelt University. **Activities:** Student government, American Society of Interior Design student chapter.

**Student services.** Career counseling, financial aid counseling, personal counseling, placement for graduates, veterans' counselor.

**Contact.** E-mail: admissions@interiordesign.edu
Phone: (312) 939-4975 Toll-free number: (877) 939-4975
Fax: (312) 939-8005
Wendi Franczyk, Vice President of Admissions, Harrington College of Design, 200 West Madison Avenue, Chicago, IL 60606

## Hebrew Theological College
### Skokie, Illinois
www.htc.edu                    CB code: 0817

- Private 4-year liberal arts and rabbinical college affiliated with Jewish Orthodox
- Residential campus in small city
- 394 degree-seeking undergraduates: 4% part-time, 85% women
- 16 degree-seeking graduate students
- 91% of applicants admitted
- SAT or ACT, application essay, interview required

**General.** Regionally accredited. Offers single-gender programs held on separate campuses. **Degrees:** 21 bachelor's awarded. **Location:** 15 miles from downtown. **Calendar:** Semester, limited summer session. **Full-time**

**faculty:** 11 total; 91% have terminal degrees, 27% women. **Part-time faculty:** 32 total; 59% have terminal degrees, 6% minority, 44% women. **Class size:** 94% < 20, 6% 20-39.

**Freshman class profile.** 300 applied, 272 admitted, 272 enrolled.

**2010-2011 Annual costs.** Tuition/fees (projected): $13,225. Room/board: $9,640.

**Application procedures. Admission:** No deadline. $75 fee, may be waived for applicants with need. Application must be submitted on paper.

**Academics. Special study options:** Combined bachelor's/graduate degree. **Credit/placement by examination:** AP, CLEP, institutional tests. **Support services:** Remedial instruction, tutoring, writing center.

**Majors. Business:** General, accounting. **Education:** Elementary, special. **Liberal arts:** Arts/sciences. **Philosophy/religion:** Judaic. **Psychology:** General.

**Student life. Freshman orientation:** Mandatory. Preregistration for classes offered. **Housing:** Single-sex dorms, apartments available.

**Contact.** E-mail: admissions@htt.edu
Phone: (847) 982-2500 Fax: (847) 674-6381
Rabbi. Joshua Zisook, Director of Admissions, Hebrew Theological College, 7135 North Carpenter Road, Skokie, IL 60077

## Illinois College
Jacksonville, Illinois
www.ic.edu
CB member
CB code: 1315

♦ Private 4-year liberal arts college affiliated with United Church of Christ and Presbyterian Church (USA)
♦ Residential campus in large town
♦ 854 degree-seeking undergraduates: 50% women, 5% African American, 1% Asian American, 2% Hispanic American, 1% Native American, 3% international
♦ 55% of applicants admitted
♦ 60% graduate within 6 years; 32% enter graduate study

**General.** Founded in 1829. Regionally accredited. New England style quad and architecture. **Degrees:** 176 bachelor's awarded. **Location:** 30 miles from Springfield, 90 miles from St. Louis. **Calendar:** Semester, limited summer session. **Full-time faculty:** 74 total; 84% have terminal degrees, 10% minority, 50% women. **Part-time faculty:** 17 total; 29% have terminal degrees, 12% minority, 41% women. **Class size:** 68% < 20, 30% 20-39, 1% 40-49, less than 1% 50-99. **Special facilities:** Biology station, observatory.

**Freshman class profile.** 1,313 applied, 719 admitted, 225 enrolled.

| Mid 50% test scores | | GPA 2.0-2.99: | 24% |
|---|---|---|---|
| SAT critical reading: | 510-580 | Rank in top quarter: | 56% |
| SAT math: | 490-640 | Rank in top tenth: | 26% |
| SAT writing: | 460-630 | End year in good standing: | 95% |
| ACT composite: | 21-27 | Return as sophomores: | 83% |
| GPA 3.75 or higher: | 29% | Out-of-state: | 12% |
| GPA 3.50-3.74: | 17% | Live on campus: | 96% |
| GPA 3.0-3.49: | 30% | International: | 4% |

**Basis for selection.** Core course GPA, rank in top half of class, test scores, 1 letter of recommendation from teacher, 1 letter of recommendation from guidance counselor are important. Interview recommended, essay considered. **Homeschooled:** Transcript of courses and grades, letter of recommendation (nonparent) required.

**High school preparation.** College-preparatory program recommended. 16 units required; 20 recommended. Required and recommended units include English 4, mathematics 3, social studies 1, history 1, science 2-3 (laboratory 2-3), foreign language 2 and academic electives 3.

**2010-2011 Annual costs.** Tuition/fees (projected): $21,300. Room/board: $7,600. Books/supplies: $900. Personal expenses: $1,010.

**2009-2010 Financial aid. Need-based:** 200 full-time freshmen applied for aid; 174 were judged to have need; 174 of these received aid. Average need met was 88%. Average scholarship/grant was $14,346; average loan $3,864. 69% of total undergraduate aid awarded as scholarships/grants, 31% as loans/jobs. **Non-need-based:** Awarded to 252 full-time undergraduates, including 71 freshmen. Scholarships awarded for academics, art, minority status, music/drama.

**Application procedures. Admission:** Priority date 12/1; no deadline. No application fee. Admission notification on a rolling basis beginning on or about 11/15. **Financial aid:** Priority date 3/1; no closing date. FAFSA required. Applicants notified on a rolling basis starting 3/1; must reply within 2 week(s) of notification.

**Academics. Special study options:** Combined bachelor's/graduate degree, cross-registration, double major, dual enrollment of high school students, independent study, internships, liberal arts/career combination, student-designed major, study abroad, teacher certification program, Washington semester. Intercultural exchange program with Ritsumeikan University, Japan. **Credit/placement by examination:** AP, CLEP, IB, SAT, ACT, institutional tests. 84 credit hours maximum toward bachelor's degree. **Support services:** Reduced course load, study skills assistance, tutoring, writing center.

**Majors. Area/ethnic studies:** American. **Biology:** General, environmental. **Business:** Accounting, finance, management information systems, managerial economics. **Computer sciences:** Computer science. **Education:** Early childhood, elementary, physical. **Foreign languages:** French, German, Spanish. **History:** General. **Interdisciplinary:** Global studies. **Math:** General. **Philosophy/religion:** Philosophy, religion. **Physical sciences:** Chemistry, physics. **Psychology:** General. **Social sciences:** Economics, political science, sociology. **Visual/performing arts:** Art, dramatic, studio arts. **Other:** Management and organizational leadership.

**Most popular majors.** Biology 16%, business/marketing 8%, education 12%, English 10%, interdisciplinary studies 14%, social sciences 16%.

**Computing on campus.** 125 workstations in library, computer center. Dormitories wired for high-speed internet access and linked to campus network. Commuter students can connect to campus network. Online course registration, online library, helpline, repair service, student web hosting, wireless network available.

**Student life. Freshman orientation:** Mandatory. Preregistration for classes offered. Overnight orientation program and several summer sessions are available. **Policies:** Student representation on faculty committees. **Housing:** Guaranteed on-campus for all undergraduates. Coed dorms, single-sex dorms, apartments available. $200 fully refundable deposit, deadline 5/1. **Activities:** Concert band, campus ministries, choral groups, drama, international student organizations, literary magazine, music ensembles, Model UN, student government, student newspaper, Young Republicans, Young Democrats, Alpha Phi Omega, men's and women's literary societies, debate club, Action Jacksonville.

**Athletics.** NCAA. **Intercollegiate:** Baseball M, basketball, cheerleading, cross-country, football (tackle) M, golf, soccer, softball W, tennis, track and field, volleyball W. **Intramural:** Basketball, cricket, football (non-tackle) M, handball, racquetball, softball, volleyball. **Team name:** Blueboys, Lady Blues.

**Student services.** Alcohol/substance abuse counseling, chaplain/spiritual director, career counseling, student employment services, financial aid counseling, health services, personal counseling, placement for graduates. **Physically disabled:** Services for visually, hearing impaired.

**Contact.** E-mail: admissions@ic.edu
Phone: (217) 245-3030 Toll-free number: (866) 464-5265
Fax: (217) 245-3034
Barb Lundberg, Vice President for Enrollment, Illinois College, 1101 West College Avenue, Jacksonville, IL 62650

## Illinois Institute of Art: Chicago
Chicago, Illinois
www.ilic.artinstitutes.edu
CB code: 2908

♦ For-profit 4-year visual arts college
♦ Commuter campus in very large city

**General.** Founded in 1916. Accredited by ACCSCT. **Calendar:** Semester.

**Annual costs/financial aid.** Tuition/fees (2009-2010): $21,372. Room/board: $10,197. Books/supplies: $1,000. Need-based financial aid available to full-time and part-time students.

**Contact.** Phone: (312) 280-3500
Senior Director of Admissions, 350 North Orleans Street, Chicago, IL 60654

## Illinois Institute of Art: Schaumburg
Schaumburg, Illinois
www.artinstitutes.edu/schaumburg
CB code: 3043

♦ For-profit 3-year visual arts and career college
♦ Commuter campus in small city

◆ 1,153 degree-seeking undergraduates

◆ Application essay, interview required

**General.** Accredited by ACCSC. **Degrees:** 290 bachelor's, 5 associate awarded. **Location:** 26 miles from Chicago. **Calendar:** Quarter, extensive summer session. **Full-time faculty:** 37 total. **Part-time faculty:** 48 total. **Special facilities:** Gallery, motion capture studio, lighting lab, sound lab, green room.

**Basis for selection.** Open admission, but selective for some programs. SAT or ACT recommended. Portfolios required for some majors. **Home-schooled:** Transcript of courses and grades required.

**2009-2010 Annual costs.** Tuition/fees: $21,600. Room/board: $7,080. Books/supplies: $987. Personal expenses: $1,788.

**Financial aid. Non-need-based:** Scholarships awarded for academics, art.

**Application procedures. Admission:** No deadline. $50 fee. Admission notification on a rolling basis. **Financial aid:** Priority date 3/1; no closing date. FAFSA required.

**Academics. Special study options:** Accelerated study, internships, liberal arts/career combination, study abroad. **Credit/placement by examination:** CLEP. **Support services:** Learning center, pre-admission summer program, reduced course load, remedial instruction, study skills assistance, tutoring.

**Majors. BACHELOR'S. Business:** Fashion, special products marketing. **Communications:** Advertising. **Communications technology:** Graphics, photo/film/video. **Computer sciences:** Game design, webmaster. **Visual/performing arts:** General, art, commercial/advertising art, design, interior design, multimedia. **ASSOCIATE. Communications technology:** Graphics. **Computer sciences:** Webmaster. **Visual/performing arts:** Design.

**Student life. Freshman orientation:** Mandatory. Preregistration for classes offered. Held the week before school begins. **Housing:** Single-sex dorms available. $200 deposit. Dormitory-style living in college-leased apartments. **Activities:** Literary magazine, student government, student newspaper.

**Student services.** Adult student services, career counseling, student employment services, financial aid counseling, personal counseling, placement for graduates, veterans' counselor.

**Contact.** E-mail: ilisadmissions@aii.edu
Phone: (847) 619-3450 Toll-free number: (800) 314-3450
Fax: (847) 619-3064
Jennifer Sorenson, Senior Director of Admissions, Illinois Institute of Art: Schaumburg, 1000 North Plaza Drive, Schaumburg, IL 60173

---

## Illinois Institute of Technology

| Chicago, Illinois | CB member |
| --- | --- |
| www.iit.edu | CB code: 1318 |

◆ Private 4-year university and engineering college

◆ Commuter campus in very large city

◆ 2,618 degree-seeking undergraduates: 5% part-time, 29% women, 4% African American, 13% Asian American, 8% Hispanic American, 1% Native American, 17% international

◆ 4,749 degree-seeking graduate students

◆ 60% of applicants admitted

◆ Application essay required

◆ 65% graduate within 6 years

**General.** Founded in 1890. Regionally accredited. **Degrees:** 471 bachelor's awarded; master's, doctoral, professional offered. **ROTC:** Army, Naval, Air Force. **Location:** 3 miles from downtown. **Calendar:** Semester, extensive summer session. **Full-time faculty:** 385 total; 89% have terminal degrees, 3% minority, 21% women. **Part-time faculty:** 270 total; 51% have terminal degrees, 4% minority, 24% women. **Class size:** 55% < 20, 35% 20-39, 4% 40-49, 5% 50-99, less than 1% >100. **Special facilities:** Engineering, design, scientific, and medical research centers.

**Freshman class profile.** 2,918 applied, 1,759 admitted, 459 enrolled.

| Mid 50% test scores | | | |
| --- | --- | --- | --- |
| SAT critical reading: | 540-670 | Rank in top quarter: | 72% |
| SAT math: | 630-720 | Rank in top tenth: | 41% |
| SAT writing: | 530-640 | Return as sophomores: | 89% |
| ACT composite: | 25-31 | Out-of-state: | 41% |
| GPA 3.75 or higher: | 41% | Live on campus: | 68% |
| GPA 3.0-3.49: | 55% | International: | 13% |
| GPA 2.0-2.99: | 4% | Fraternities: | 13% |
| | | Sororities: | 2% |

**Basis for selection.** Academic performance, strength of curriculum, test scores, counselor recommendations and essay most important. Class rank and interview, extracurricular activities, alumni relationship, volunteer and work experience also considered. Interview recommended. Portfolio optional for first-year freshmen entering College of Architecture. **Home-schooled:** Statement describing homeschool structure and mission, letter of recommendation (nonparent) required.

**High school preparation.** College-preparatory program recommended. 15 units required; 19 recommended. Required and recommended units include English 4, mathematics 4, social studies 2, history 2, science 3 (laboratory 2), foreign language 2, computer science 1 and visual/performing arts 1. Technology and other courses recommended but not required.

**2009-2010 Annual costs.** Tuition/fees: $29,362. Tuition and fees cover unlimited number of courses during academic year and include library and computer usage fees. Room/board: $9,940.

**2008-2009 Financial aid. Need-based:** 399 full-time freshmen applied for aid; 344 were judged to have need; 342 of these received aid. Average need met was 79%. Average scholarship/grant was $19,900; average loan $4,124. 70% of total undergraduate aid awarded as scholarships/grants, 30% as loans/jobs. **Non-need-based:** Awarded to 1,154 full-time undergraduates, including 256 freshmen. Scholarships awarded for academics, alumni affiliation, athletics, leadership, ROTC.

**Application procedures. Admission:** Priority date 2/1; no deadline. No application fee. Admission notification on a rolling basis beginning on or about 10/1. Must reply by May 1 or within 2 week(s) if notified thereafter. $300 enrollment deposit required. **Financial aid:** Priority date 4/15; no closing date. FAFSA required. Applicants notified on a rolling basis starting 3/5.

**Academics.** Interprofessional Projects Program provides team-based learning environment in which students from various concentrations and disciplines work together to solve real-world problems. Research opportunities for undergraduates in science, engineering, technology and mathematics. **Special study options:** Combined bachelor's/graduate degree, cooperative education, cross-registration, distance learning, double major, ESL, independent study, liberal arts/career combination, study abroad, teacher certification program. Joint enrollment at 2 institutions for 2 degrees. **Credit/placement by examination:** AP, CLEP, IB, SAT, ACT, institutional tests. 18 credit hours maximum toward bachelor's degree. No limit for advanced placement credit. **Support services:** Learning center, study skills assistance, tutoring, writing center.

**Majors. Architecture:** Architecture. **Biology:** General, biochemistry, Biochemistry/biophysics and molecular biology. **Business:** Business admin. **Communications:** Journalism. **Computer sciences:** General, computer science, information technology, web page design. **Engineering:** Aerospace, architectural, biomedical, chemical, civil, computer, electrical, materials, mechanical. **Engineering technology:** Industrial management. **Liberal arts:** Arts/sciences. **Math:** Applied. **Physical sciences:** Chemistry, physics. **Psychology:** General. **Social sciences:** Political science. **Other:** LL.M., M.C.L.

**Most popular majors.** Architecture 21%, biology 6%, computer/information sciences 9%, engineering/engineering technologies 50%.

**Computing on campus.** 500 workstations in dormitories, library, computer center, student center. Dormitories wired for high-speed internet access and linked to campus network. Online course registration, online library, helpline, student web hosting, wireless network available.

**Student life. Freshman orientation:** Mandatory, $150 fee. Preregistration for classes offered. Five summer sessions. Welcome Week held prior to start of classes. **Policies:** Student organizations register each semester, are nondiscriminatory and prohibit hazing. **Housing:** Coed dorms, fraternity/sorority housing available. Men's/women's floors in residence halls, university apartments available. **Activities:** Concert band, campus ministries, choral groups, dance, drama, film society, international student organizations, literary magazine, music ensembles, musical theater, radio station, student government, student newspaper, TV station, Red Cross Club, Engineers Without Borders, Greek Council, Haiti Outreach, InterVarsity Christian Fellowship, Latinos Involved in Further Education, National Society of Black Engineers, Society of Women Engineers, Union Board.

**Athletics.** NAIA. **Intercollegiate:** Baseball M, cross-country, diving, soccer, swimming, volleyball W. **Intramural:** Badminton, basketball, football (non-tackle), racquetball, table tennis, volleyball. **Team name:** Scarlet Hawks.

**Student services.** Alcohol/substance abuse counseling, career counseling, student employment services, financial aid counseling, health services, legal services, minority student services, personal counseling, placement for graduates, women's services. **Physically disabled:** Services for visually, hearing impaired.

**Contact.** E-mail: admission@iit.edu
Phone: (312) 567-3025 Toll-free number: (800) 448-2329
Fax: (312) 567-6939
Gerald Doyle, Vice Provost, Undergraduate Admission and Financial Aid, Illinois Institute of Technology, 10 West 33rd Street, Chicago, IL 60616

## Illinois State University
**Normal, Illinois**  CB member
**www.ilstu.edu**  CB code: 1319

- Public 4-year university
- Residential campus in small city
- 18,325 degree-seeking undergraduates: 6% part-time, 56% women, 6% African American, 2% Asian American, 5% Hispanic American
- 2,505 degree-seeking graduate students
- 62% of applicants admitted
- SAT or ACT (ACT writing optional), application essay required
- 69% graduate within 6 years

**General.** Founded in 1857. Regionally accredited. **Degrees:** 4,117 bachelor's awarded; master's, doctoral, professional offered. **ROTC:** Army. **Location:** 132 miles from Chicago, 168 miles from St. Louis. **Calendar:** Semester, limited summer session. **Full-time faculty:** 876 total; 83% have terminal degrees, 14% minority, 48% women. **Part-time faculty:** 304 total; 23% have terminal degrees, 7% minority, 53% women. **Class size:** 31% < 20, 54% 20-39, 4% 40-49, 7% 50-99, 4% >100. **Special facilities:** 310-acre farm, planetarium, museum of nations, laboratory school.

**Freshman class profile.** 14,114 applied, 8,711 admitted, 3,033 enrolled.

| Mid 50% test scores | | | |
|---|---|---|---|
| ACT composite: | 22-26 | Return as sophomores: | 85% |
| GPA 3.75 or higher: | 22% | Out-of-state: | 1% |
| GPA 3.50-3.74: | 20% | Live on campus: | 97% |
| GPA 3.0-3.49: | 41% | Fraternities: | 15% |
| GPA 2.0-2.99: | 17% | Sororities: | 17% |

**Basis for selection.** School achievement record and test scores most important. Interview required of special admission applicants. Audition recommended for music majors. Portfolio recommended for art majors.

**High school preparation.** College-preparatory program required. 15 units required. Required units include English 4, mathematics 3, social studies 2, science 2 (laboratory 2), foreign language 2 and academic electives 2. 2 units required in foreign language and/or fine arts, 2 units in social studies and/or history. Electives may include fundamentals of computing or vocational education courses.

**2009-2010 Annual costs.** Tuition/fees: $10,531; $16,561 out-of-state. Room/board: $7,782. Books/supplies: $1,084. Personal expenses: $2,337.

**2009-2010 Financial aid. Need-based:** 2,535 full-time freshmen applied for aid; 1,727 were judged to have need; 1,602 of these received aid. Average need met was 78%. Average scholarship/grant was $9,134; average loan $6,349. 46% of total undergraduate aid awarded as scholarships/grants, 54% as loans/jobs. **Non-need-based:** Awarded to 3,246 full-time undergraduates, including 1,013 freshmen. Scholarships awarded for academics, art, athletics, music/drama.

**Application procedures. Admission:** Priority date 11/15; deadline 3/1 (receipt date). $40 fee, may be waived for applicants with need. Admission notification on a rolling basis beginning on or about 9/1. **Financial aid:** Priority date 3/1; no closing date. FAFSA required. Applicants notified on a rolling basis starting 5/1; must reply within 2 week(s) of notification.

**Academics. Special study options:** Accelerated study, combined bachelor's/graduate degree, cooperative education, distance learning, double major, dual enrollment of high school students, ESL, exchange student, honors, independent study, internships, student-designed major, study abroad, teacher certification program, Washington semester. **Credit/placement by examination:** AP, CLEP, SAT, ACT, institutional tests. 26 credit hours maximum

toward bachelor's degree. **Support services:** Learning center, preadmission summer program, tutoring.

**Majors. Agriculture:** Agribusiness operations. **Biology:** General, biochemistry. **Business:** Accounting, business admin, finance, insurance, international, management science, marketing. **Communications:** Journalism, media studies, public relations. **Computer sciences:** Computer science, information technology, networking. **Education:** Business, early childhood, elementary, health, middle, music, physical, social studies, special, technology/industrial arts. **Engineering technology:** Energy systems, industrial. **Family/consumer sciences:** General. **Foreign languages:** General, French, German, Spanish. **Health:** Athletic training, audiology/speech pathology, clinical lab science, environmental health, medical records admin, nursing (RN), occupational health. **History:** General. **Liberal arts:** Arts/sciences. **Math:** General. **Parks/recreation:** Exercise sciences, facilities management. **Philosophy/religion:** Philosophy. **Physical sciences:** Chemistry, geology, physics. **Protective services:** Criminal justice. **Psychology:** General. **Public administration:** Social work. **Social sciences:** Anthropology, economics, geography, political science, sociology. **Visual/performing arts:** Art, dramatic, music history, music performance, studio arts.

**Most popular majors.** Business/marketing 18%, communications/journalism 6%, education 19%, health sciences 7%, social sciences 6%.

**Computing on campus.** PC or laptop required. 2,275 workstations in dormitories, library, computer center, student center. Dormitories wired for high-speed internet access and linked to campus network. Commuter students can connect to campus network. Online course registration, online library, helpline, repair service, student web hosting, wireless network available.

**Student life. Freshman orientation:** Mandatory, $50 fee. Preregistration for classes offered. Two-day sessions held each week from mid-June to end of July. **Housing:** Guaranteed on-campus for freshmen. Coed dorms, single-sex dorms, special housing for disabled, apartments, fraternity/sorority housing, wellness housing available. $300 partly refundable deposit. **Activities:** Bands, campus ministries, choral groups, dance, drama, film society, international student organizations, literary magazine, music ensembles, Model UN, musical theater, radio station, student government, student newspaper, symphony orchestra, TV station, over 250 student organizations.

**Athletics.** NCAA. **Intercollegiate:** Baseball M, basketball, cross-country, diving W, football (tackle) M, golf, gymnastics W, soccer W, softball W, swimming W, tennis, track and field, volleyball W. **Intramural:** Badminton, basketball, football (tackle), golf, racquetball, soccer, softball, volleyball. **Team name:** Redbirds.

**Student services.** Adult student services, alcohol/substance abuse counseling, career counseling, student employment services, financial aid counseling, health services, legal services, minority student services, on-campus daycare, personal counseling, placement for graduates, veterans' counselor. **Physically disabled:** Services for visually, speech, hearing impaired.

**Contact.** E-mail: admissions@ilstu.edu
Phone: (309) 438-2181 Toll-free number: (800) 366-2478
Fax: (309) 438-3932
Molly Arnold, Director of Admissions, Illinois State University, Campus Box 2200, Normal, IL 61790-2200

## Illinois Wesleyan University
**Bloomington, Illinois**  CB member
**www.iwu.edu**  CB code: 1320

- Private 4-year university and liberal arts college
- Residential campus in small city
- 2,059 degree-seeking undergraduates: 59% women, 5% African American, 5% Asian American, 3% Hispanic American, 4% international
- 54% of applicants admitted
- SAT or ACT (ACT writing optional), application essay required
- 86% graduate within 6 years; 34% enter graduate study

**General.** Founded in 1850. Regionally accredited. **Degrees:** 488 bachelor's awarded. **ROTC:** Army. **Location:** 125 miles from Chicago, 165 miles from St. Louis. **Calendar:** 4-4-1 (2 semesters plus May Term). **Full-time faculty:** 162 total; 92% have terminal degrees, 13% minority, 40% women. **Part-time faculty:** 67 total; 40% have terminal degrees, 4% minority, 61% women. **Class size:** 63% < 20, 35% 20-39, 1% 40-49, less than 1% 50-99, less than 1% >100. **Special facilities:** Observatory, natural sciences research labs, computerized music lab, social science research lab, visual anthropology lab, student-managed real-dollar investment portfolio program, nursing lab, lab theatre producing original works by undergraduates, Action Research Center (supporting community-based student research for academic credit).

**Freshman class profile.** 3,321 applied, 1,785 admitted, 518 enrolled.

| Mid 50% test scores | | | |
|---|---|---|---|
| SAT critical reading: | 570-680 | Return as sophomores: | 93% |
| SAT math: | 600-720 | Out-of-state: | 11% |
| ACT composite: | 26-30 | Live on campus: | 100% |
| Rank in top quarter: | 81% | International: | 4% |
| Rank in top tenth: | 45% | Fraternities: | 28% |
| End year in good standing: | 93% | Sororities: | 29% |

**Basis for selection.** Test scores, class rank, high school record, and essay or personal statement most important. Interview strongly recommended. Audition required for bachelor of music or BFA in theater or music theater. Portfolio review required for BFA in art. **Homeschooled:** Transcript of courses and grades required. **Learning Disabled:** Students welcome to submit information on learning disabilities as part of application review process.

**High school preparation.** College-preparatory program recommended. 15 units recommended. Recommended units include English 4, mathematics 3, social studies 2, science 3 (laboratory 2) and foreign language 3. Biology and chemistry are required for admission to nursing and biology.

**2010-2011 Annual costs.** Tuition/fees: $35,256. Room/board: $8,106. Books/supplies: $780. Personal expenses: $660.

**2009-2010 Financial aid.** **Need-based:** 417 full-time freshmen applied for aid; 347 were judged to have need; 347 of these received aid. Average need met was 92%. Average scholarship/grant was $19,231; average loan $3,951. 75% of total undergraduate aid awarded as scholarships/grants, 25% as loans/jobs. **Non-need-based:** Awarded to 777 full-time undergraduates, including 214 freshmen. Scholarships awarded for academics, art, music/drama, ROTC.

**Application procedures.** **Admission:** Priority date 11/1; no deadline. No application fee. Admission notification on a rolling basis beginning on or about 12/15. Must reply by May 1 or within 3 week(s) if notified thereafter. **Financial aid:** Closing date 3/1. FAFSA, institutional form required. Institution's own financial aid form or CSS PROFILE required. Applicants notified on a rolling basis starting 2/15; must reply by 5/1 or within 3 week(s) of notification.

**Academics.** Optional 3-week May Term provides opportunities for students to pursue experimental courses, travel courses, interships, or independent research projects. Fall Term in London and Spring Term in Madrid led by Illinois Wesleyan faculty members where students may earn General Education credit during these terms. **Special study options:** Combined bachelor's/graduate degree, double major, exchange student, honors, independent study, internships, New York semester, student-designed major, study abroad, teacher certification program, United Nations semester, urban semester, Washington semester. 3-2 cooperative program in engineering with Washington University, Case Western Reserve University, and Northwestern University; 3-2 program in forestry and environmental management with Duke University; 3-2 program in occupational therapy with Washington University, 2-2 program in engineering with the University of Illinois, and a non-guaranteed cooperative program in engineering with Dartmouth College. **Credit/placement by examination:** AP, CLEP, IB, institutional tests. 32 credit hours maximum toward bachelor's degree. Limit of 16 hours (equivalent to four courses) may count toward general education credit. Up to 16 additional hours (equivalent to four courses) can be awarded as elective credit. **Support services:** Reduced course load, study skills assistance, tutoring, writing center.

**Majors.** **Area/ethnic studies:** African, American, Asian, Central/Eastern European, Latin American, Western European, women's. **Biology:** General. **Business:** Accounting, business admin, insurance, international. **Computer sciences:** General. **Conservation:** Environmental studies. **Education:** General, biology, chemistry, elementary, English, French, history, mathematics, music, physics, Spanish. **Foreign languages:** Classics, French, German, Spanish. **Health:** Nursing (RN). **History:** General. **Math:** General. **Philosophy/religion:** Philosophy, religion. **Physical sciences:** Chemistry, physics. **Psychology:** General. **Social sciences:** Anthropology, economics, political science, sociology. **Visual/performing arts:** Acting, art, dramatic, music performance, music theory/composition, musical theater, piano/organ, stringed instruments, theater design, voice/opera.

**Most popular majors.** Business/marketing 23%, English 9%, psychology 7%, social sciences 14%, visual/performing arts 11%.

**Computing on campus.** 400 workstations in dormitories, library, computer center, student center. Dormitories wired for high-speed internet access and linked to campus network. Commuter students can connect to campus network. Online course registration, online library, helpline, repair service, student web hosting, wireless network available.

**Student life.** **Freshman orientation:** Mandatory. Preregistration for classes offered. Orientation for parents held in June. New student orientation held 5-6 days prior to start of classes. **Policies:** No smoking permitted in residence halls. Beer and wine permitted in designated areas for students of legal age. **Housing:** Guaranteed on-campus for freshmen. Coed dorms, special housing for disabled, apartments, fraternity/sorority housing, wellness housing available. **Activities:** Bands, campus ministries, choral groups, dance, drama, film society, literary magazine, music ensembles, Model UN, musical theater, opera, radio station, student government, student newspaper, symphony orchestra, TV station, black student union, InterVarsity Christian Fellowship, Alpha Phi Omega, Council of Latin American Student Enrichment, Habitat for Humanity, several environmental concerns organizations, Amnesty International, Pan-Asian student association, College Democrats, College Republicans.

**Athletics.** NCAA. **Intercollegiate:** Baseball M, basketball, cross-country, diving, football (tackle) M, golf, soccer, softball W, swimming, tennis, track and field, volleyball W. **Intramural:** Badminton, basketball, football (non-tackle), golf, soccer, softball, tennis, volleyball. **Team name:** Titans.

**Student services.** Alcohol/substance abuse counseling, chaplain/spiritual director, career counseling, student employment services, financial aid counseling, health services, minority student services, personal counseling, placement for graduates. **Physically disabled:** Services for visually, speech, hearing impaired.

**Contact.** E-mail: iwuadmit@iwu.edu
Phone: (309) 556-3031 Toll-free number: (800) 332-2498
Fax: (309) 556-3820
Tony Bankston, Dean of Admissions, Illinois Wesleyan University, PO Box 2900, Bloomington, IL 61702-2900

## International Academy of Design and Technology: Chicago
**Chicago, Illinois**
www.iadtchicago.edu                    CB code: 3363

- For-profit 4-year visual arts and technical college
- Commuter campus in very large city
- 1,574 degree-seeking undergraduates
- Interview required

**General.** Founded in 1977. Accredited by ACICS. **Degrees:** 265 bachelor's, 58 associate awarded. **Location:** Downtown. **Calendar:** Quarter, extensive summer session. **Full-time faculty:** 14 total. **Part-time faculty:** 99 total. **Class size:** 53% < 20, 44% 20-39, 3% 40-49.

**Freshman class profile.** 106 enrolled.

**Basis for selection.** Open admission. **Homeschooled:** Transcript of courses and grades required. Should be registered with state or accrediting agency.

**2009-2010 Annual costs.** Books/supplies: $1,800. Personal expenses: $1,596.

**2008-2009 Financial aid.** All financial aid based on need. **Additional information:** College work study programs available to day and evening students.

**Application procedures.** **Admission:** No deadline. $20 fee. Admission notification on a rolling basis. **Financial aid:** No deadline. FAFSA required. Applicants notified on a rolling basis.

**Academics.** **Special study options:** Distance learning, independent study, internships, study abroad, weekend college. **Credit/placement by examination:** AP, CLEP, IB, institutional tests. 40 credit hours maximum toward associate degree, 100 toward bachelor's. **Support services:** Learning center, reduced course load, remedial instruction, study skills assistance, tutoring.

**Majors.** **Business:** Fashion. **Communications technology:** Animation/special effects. **Computer sciences:** Computer forensics, game design, information technology. **Visual/performing arts:** Commercial/advertising art, fashion design, graphic design, interior design.

**Most popular majors.** Business/marketing 31%, communication technologies 14%, visual/performing arts 53%.

**Computing on campus.** 386 workstations in library, computer center, student center. Online course registration, online library, wireless network available.

**Student life.** **Freshman orientation:** Mandatory. **Activities:** Student newspaper, Fashion Council, merchandising management club, information technology club, video and animation club, Omega Pi Delta, International Interior Design Association, graphic design club, international club, chess club, movie club.

**Student services.** Adult student services, career counseling, student employment services, financial aid counseling, personal counseling, placement for graduates, veterans' counselor. **Physically disabled:** Services for visually impaired.

**Contact.** Phone: (312) 980-9200 Toll-free number: (877) 222-3369 Fax: (312) 541-3929
Ernest Cochran, Vice President of Admissions, International Academy of Design and Technology: Chicago, One North State Street, Suite 500, Chicago, IL 60602

## International Academy of Design and Technology: Schaumburg
**Schaumburg, Illinois**
**www.iadtschaumburg.com**

- For-profit 4-year visual arts and technical college
- Commuter campus in small city
- 258 degree-seeking undergraduates

**General.** Accredited by ACICS. **Degrees:** 37 bachelor's, 5 associate awarded. **Calendar:** Quarter. **Full-time faculty:** 3 total. **Part-time faculty:** 20 total.

**Basis for selection.** Open admission.

**2009-2010 Annual costs.** Tuition/fees: $17,100. Books/supplies: $1,800.

**Application procedures. Admission:** No deadline. $50 fee.

**Academics. Credit/placement by examination:** CLEP.

**Majors. Communications technology:** Animation/special effects. **Computer sciences:** Web page design. **Visual/performing arts:** Fashion design, interior design.

**Contact.** Phone: (847) 969-2800 Fax: (847) 969-0599
Cambria Padgett, Director of Admissions, International Academy of Design and Technology: Schaumburg, 915 National Parkway, Schaumburg, IL 60173

## ITT Technical Institute: Burr Ridge
**Burr Ridge, Illinois**
**www.itt-tech.edu**            CB code: 2698

- For-profit 4-year technical college
- Commuter campus in small town

**General.** Accredited by ACICS. **Calendar:** Quarter.

**Contact.** Phone: (630) 455-6470
Director of Recruitment, 7040 High Grove Boulevard, Burr Ridge, IL 60527

## ITT Technical Institute: Mount Prospect
**Mount Prospect, Illinois**
**www.itt-tech.edu**            CB code: 4271

- For-profit 4-year technical college
- Commuter campus in small city

**General.** Founded in 1986. Accredited by ACICS. **Location:** 20 miles from Chicago. **Calendar:** Quarter.

**Contact.** Phone: (847) 375-8800
Director of Recruitment, 1401 Feehanville Drive, Mount Prospect, IL 60056

## Judson University
**Elgin, Illinois**
**www.judsonu.edu**            CB code: 1351

- Private 4-year university and liberal arts college affiliated with American Baptist Churches in the USA
- Residential campus in small city
- 983 degree-seeking undergraduates: 14% part-time, 56% women, 4% African American, 2% Asian American, 7% Hispanic American, 5% international
- 117 degree-seeking graduate students

- 71% of applicants admitted
- SAT or ACT (ACT writing optional) required
- 54% graduate within 6 years

**General.** Founded in 1963. Regionally accredited. **Degrees:** 248 bachelor's awarded; master's offered. **ROTC:** Army, Naval, Air Force. **Location:** 40 miles from Chicago. **Calendar:** Semester, limited summer session. **Full-time faculty:** 53 total. **Class size:** 80% < 20, 20% 20-39, less than 1% 40-49. **Special facilities:** Green academic center.

**Freshman class profile.** 532 applied, 377 admitted, 174 enrolled.

| Mid 50% test scores | | | |
|---|---|---|---|
| SAT critical reading: | 490-600 | Rank in top quarter: | 44% |
| SAT math: | 520-610 | Rank in top tenth: | 15% |
| ACT composite: | 20-26 | End year in good standing: | 68% |
| GPA 3.75 or higher: | 28% | Return as sophomores: | 72% |
| GPA 3.50-3.74: | 18% | Out-of-state: | 28% |
| GPA 3.0-3.49: | 25% | Live on campus: | 80% |
| GPA 2.0-2.99: | 29% | International: | 1% |

**Basis for selection.** School achievement record and test scores important. Counselor's reference considered. Audition recommended for performing arts majors. Portfolio recommended for art majors. Essay required for architecture majors. **Homeschooled:** Transcript of courses and grades required.

**High school preparation.** College-preparatory program required. Recommended units include English 4, mathematics 3, social studies 2, science 2 (laboratory 2).

**2009-2010 Annual costs.** Tuition/fees: $23,500. Room/board: $8,200. Books/supplies: $1,500. Personal expenses: $2,000.

**2008-2009 Financial aid. Need-based:** 150 full-time freshmen applied for aid; 125 were judged to have need; 125 of these received aid. Average need met was 40%. Average scholarship/grant was $5,830; average loan $2,897. 37% of total undergraduate aid awarded as scholarships/grants, 63% as loans/jobs. **Non-need-based:** Awarded to 337 full-time undergraduates, including 139 freshmen. Scholarships awarded for academics, alumni affiliation, art, athletics, music/drama.

**Application procedures. Admission:** No deadline. $50 fee, may be waived for applicants with need. Admission notification on a rolling basis beginning on or about 7/1. **Financial aid:** Priority date 3/15, closing date 5/1. FAFSA required. Applicants notified on a rolling basis starting 3/1; must reply within 4 week(s) of notification.

**Academics. Special study options:** Accelerated study, combined bachelor's/graduate degree, distance learning, double major, honors, independent study, internships, student-designed major, study abroad, teacher certification program, urban semester, Washington semester. **Credit/placement by examination:** AP, CLEP, IB, ACT, institutional tests. 30 credit hours maximum toward bachelor's degree. **Support services:** Learning center, reduced course load, remedial instruction, study skills assistance, tutoring.

**Majors. Architecture:** Architecture. **Biology:** General, biochemistry. **Business:** Accounting, business admin, human resources, management information systems, management science. **Communications:** General, media studies. **Conservation:** Environmental studies. **Education:** Art, early childhood, elementary, music, physical, secondary. **History:** General. **Interdisciplinary:** Intercultural. **Math:** General. **Parks/recreation:** Sports admin. **Physical sciences:** Chemistry. **Protective services:** Criminal justice. **Psychology:** General. **Public administration:** Human services. **Social sciences:** Sociology. **Theology:** Bible, sacred music, youth ministry. **Visual/performing arts:** Art, graphic design, interior design, music performance, studio arts. **Other:** Science/mathematics, general, Worship arts.

**Most popular majors.** Architecture 8%, business/marketing 37%, education 7%, public administration/social services 15%.

**Computing on campus.** 200 workstations in dormitories, library, computer center, student center. Dormitories wired for high-speed internet access and linked to campus network. Online course registration, online library, helpline, wireless network available.

**Student life. Freshman orientation:** Mandatory. Preregistration for classes offered. **Policies:** Chapel services held 3 mornings a week. **Housing:** Guaranteed on-campus for all undergraduates. Coed dorms, single-sex dorms, special housing for disabled, apartments, wellness housing available. $175 fully refundable deposit, deadline 5/1. **Activities:** Concert band, campus ministries, choral groups, drama, music ensembles, student government, student newspaper, symphony orchestra.

**Athletics.** NAIA, NCCAA. **Intercollegiate:** Baseball M, basketball, cross-country, soccer, softball W, volleyball W. **Intramural:** Badminton, basketball, racquetball, soccer, softball, volleyball. **Team name:** Eagles.

**Student services.** Adult student services, career counseling, student employment services, financial aid counseling, health services, personal counseling, placement for graduates.

**Contact.** E-mail: admissions@judsonu.edu
Phone: (847) 628-2510 Toll-free number: (800) 879-5376
Fax: (847) 628-2526
William Dean, Director of Admissions, Judson University, 1151 North State Street, Elgin, IL 60123-1404

## Kendall College
**Chicago, Illinois**
**www.kendall.edu**                                    **CB code: 1366**

- Private 4-year culinary school and teachers college
- Commuter campus in very large city
- 2,159 degree-seeking undergraduates: 35% part-time, 70% women, 18% African American, 4% Asian American, 13% Hispanic American, 5% international
- 99% of applicants admitted
- Application essay, interview required
- 39% graduate within 6 years

**General.** Founded in 1934. Regionally accredited. Internships required in every major. **Degrees:** 185 bachelor's, 106 associate awarded. **Location:** Downtown. **Calendar:** Quarter, extensive summer session. **Full-time faculty:** 45 total; 13% have terminal degrees, 11% minority, 49% women. **Part-time faculty:** 158 total; 8% minority, 50% women. **Class size:** 56% < 20, 44% 20-39, less than 1% 40-49, less than 1% 50-99.

**Freshman class profile.** 442 applied, 438 admitted, 159 enrolled.

| | | | |
|---|---|---|---|
| GPA 3.75 or higher: | 2% | End year in good standing: | 57% |
| GPA 3.50-3.74: | 11% | Return as sophomores: | 60% |
| GPA 3.0-3.49: | 27% | Out-of-state: | 22% |
| GPA 2.0-2.99: | 46% | International: | 6% |

**Basis for selection.** High school record most important, followed by test scores, class rank, recommendations and interview. Placement test may be required. SAT or ACT recommended.

**High school preparation.** Recommended units include English 4, mathematics 2, social studies 2, science 2 and foreign language 2. Specific academic units required for certain majors.

**2010-2011 Annual costs.** Tuition costs range from $7,200 to $21,450 per academic year. Required fees: $825. Room/board: $10,485. Books/supplies: $1,800.

**2008-2009 Financial aid. Need-based:** 122 full-time freshmen applied for aid; 101 were judged to have need; 101 of these received aid. 29% of total undergraduate aid awarded as scholarships/grants, 71% as loans/jobs. **Non-need-based:** Awarded to 253 full-time undergraduates, including 33 freshmen. Scholarships awarded for academics, job skills.

**Application procedures. Admission:** No deadline. $50 fee, may be waived for applicants with need, free for online applicants. Admission notification on a rolling basis. Must reply by May 1 or within 4 week(s) if notified thereafter. **Financial aid:** Priority date 4/15; no closing date. FAFSA, institutional form required. Applicants notified on a rolling basis starting 1/1; must reply within 2 week(s) of notification.

**Academics. Special study options:** Accelerated study, combined bachelor's/graduate degree, distance learning, internships, study abroad, teacher certification program, weekend college. **Credit/placement by examination:** AP, CLEP, IB, institutional tests. 24 credit hours maximum toward associate degree, 48 toward bachelor's. **Support services:** Learning center, reduced course load, remedial instruction, study skills assistance, tutoring, writing center.

**Majors. Business:** Business admin, hospitality admin. **Education:** Early childhood. **Personal/culinary services:** Culinary arts. **Psychology:** General.

**Most popular majors.** Business/marketing 48%, education 41%, personal/culinary services 11%.

**Computing on campus.** 45 workstations in library, computer center, student center. Dormitories wired for high-speed internet access and linked to campus network. Commuter students can connect to campus network. Online library, helpline, wireless network available.

**Student life. Freshman orientation:** Mandatory. Preregistration for classes offered. One-day event held 1 week before start of quarter. **Housing:** Coed dorms, wellness housing available. $350 nonrefundable deposit. **Activities:** Student government, student newspaper.

**Athletics. Team name:** The Viking.

**Student services.** Adult student services, career counseling, student employment services, financial aid counseling, personal counseling, placement for graduates.

**Contact.** E-mail: admissions@kendall.edu
Phone: (312) 752-2020 Toll-free number: (866) 667-3344
Fax: (312) 752-2021
Lisa Marrello, Director of Admissions, Kendall College, 900 N North Branch Street, Chicago, IL 60642-4278

## Knox College
**Galesburg, Illinois**                                **CB member**
**www.knox.edu**                                       **CB code: 1372**

- Private 4-year liberal arts college
- Residential campus in large town
- 1,384 degree-seeking undergraduates: 60% women, 5% African American, 7% Asian American, 5% Hispanic American, 1% Native American, 7% international
- 74% of applicants admitted
- Application essay required
- 73% graduate within 6 years; 21% enter graduate study

**General.** Founded in 1837. Regionally accredited. **Degrees:** 306 bachelor's awarded. **Location:** 180 miles from Chicago, 200 miles from St. Louis. **Calendar:** Trimester. **Full-time faculty:** 108 total; 94% have terminal degrees, 14% minority, 40% women. **Part-time faculty:** 29 total; 62% have terminal degrees, 17% minority, 52% women. **Class size:** 66% < 20, 30% 20-39, 3% 40-49, less than 1% 50-99. **Special facilities:** Electron microscope, greenhouse, studio and large-scale production theaters, 760-acre biological field station, ceramics, sculpture, painting, and printmaking studios.

**Freshman class profile.** 2,427 applied, 1,788 admitted, 359 enrolled.

| Mid 50% test scores | | Rank in top quarter: | 67% |
|---|---|---|---|
| SAT critical reading: | 600-730 | Rank in top tenth: | 37% |
| SAT math: | 560-690 | End year in good standing: | 90% |
| SAT writing: | 560-680 | Return as sophomores: | 90% |
| ACT composite: | 26-31 | Out-of-state: | 53% |
| GPA 3.75 or higher: | 23% | Live on campus: | 96% |
| GPA 3.50-3.74: | 18% | International: | 6% |
| GPA 3.0-3.49: | 35% | Fraternities: | 30% |
| GPA 2.0-2.99: | 24% | Sororities: | 17% |

**Basis for selection.** Course of study, grades, essay, and recommendations most important. Class rank, extracurricular activities, special skills, talents and personal qualities, interview also considered. Preference given to students who have taken advantage of academic opportunities offered by high school (honors, Advanced Placement, International Baccalaureate and/or college level courses) if available. SAT or ACT submission optional for most applicants. Applicants from secondary schools that do not provide grades are asked to submit test scores. Interview strongly recommended. **Homeschooled:** Statement describing homeschool structure and mission, transcript of courses and grades, state high school equivalency certificate required. Applicants should provide detailed documentation of coursework completed, including course syllabi as appropriate. SAT/ACT scores required.

**High school preparation.** College-preparatory program required. 19 units recommended. Recommended units include English 4, mathematics 4, social studies 2, history 2, science 4 (laboratory 3) and foreign language 3.

**2010-2011 Annual costs.** Tuition/fees: $33,024. Room/board: $7,341. Books/supplies: $900. Personal expenses: $1,000.

**2009-2010 Financial aid. Need-based:** 345 full-time freshmen applied for aid; 293 were judged to have need; 293 of these received aid. Average need met was 92%. Average scholarship/grant was $21,625; average loan $4,289. 77% of total undergraduate aid awarded as scholarships/grants, 23% as loans/jobs. **Non-need-based:** Awarded to 391 full-time undergraduates, including 139 freshmen. Scholarships awarded for academics, art, music/drama.

**Application procedures. Admission:** Priority date 12/1; deadline 2/1 (postmark date). $40 fee, may be waived for applicants with need. Admission notification 3/31. Must reply by May 1 or within 2 week(s) if notified thereafter. **Financial aid:** Priority date 2/1; no closing date. FAFSA, institutional form required. Applicants notified on a rolling basis starting 3/15; must reply by 5/1 or within 2 week(s) of notification.

**Academics.** Academic work conducted under honor system, placing primary responsibility for academic honesty on student. Examinations not proctored. **Special study options:** Combined bachelor's/graduate degree, double major, dual enrollment of high school students, honors, independent study, internships, liberal arts/career combination, student-designed major, study abroad, teacher certification program, urban semester, Washington semester. Extensive overseas study centers with more than 30 international and off-campus study programs. Significant independent research opportunities with funding for projects. Repertory theater, psychology, and Green Oaks (environmental) terms. **Credit/placement by examination:** AP, CLEP, IB, SAT, ACT, institutional tests. 9 credit hours maximum toward bachelor's degree. Up to 25% of 36 required Knox credits may be obtained through examination. **Support services:** Learning center, reduced course load, study skills assistance, tutoring, writing center.

**Majors. Area/ethnic studies:** African-American, American, Asian, women's. **Biology:** General, biochemistry. **Computer sciences:** Computer science. **Conservation:** Environmental studies. **Education:** General, social science. **Foreign languages:** General, classics, French, German, Spanish. **History:** General. **Interdisciplinary:** Global studies, neuroscience. **Math:** General, applied. **Philosophy/religion:** Philosophy. **Physical sciences:** Chemistry, physics. **Psychology:** General. **Social sciences:** Anthropology, economics, international relations, political science, sociology. **Visual/performing arts:** Art history/conservation, dramatic, studio arts.

**Most popular majors.** Biology 8%, education 7%, English 10%, foreign language 9%, psychology 7%, social sciences 26%, visual/performing arts 7%.

**Computing on campus.** 335 workstations in library, computer center, student center. Dormitories wired for high-speed internet access and linked to campus network. Commuter students can connect to campus network. Online course registration, online library, helpline, student web hosting, wireless network available.

**Student life. Freshman orientation:** Mandatory. Preregistration for classes offered. 1 week before beginning of fall term. Additional orientation for international students. **Policies:** Students actively engaged in college governance. All students requred to live on campus. **Housing:** Coed dorms, single-sex dorms, special housing for disabled, apartments, fraternity/sorority housing, wellness housing available. $300 nonrefundable deposit, deadline 5/1. **Activities:** Jazz band, campus ministries, choral groups, dance, drama, international student organizations, literary magazine, music ensembles, Model UN, radio station, student government, student newspaper, symphony orchestra, InterVarsity Christian Fellowship, Amnesty International, Latin American Concerns, Allied Blacks for Liberty and Equality, Lo Nuestro, Habitat for Humanity, Common Ground.

**Athletics.** NCAA. **Intercollegiate:** Baseball M, basketball, cross-country, diving, football (tackle) M, golf, soccer, softball W, swimming, tennis, track and field, volleyball W, wrestling M. **Intramural:** Basketball, football (tackle), soccer, softball, volleyball. **Team name:** Prairie Fire.

**Student services.** Alcohol/substance abuse counseling, career counseling, services for economically disadvantaged, student employment services, financial aid counseling, health services, minority student services, personal counseling. **Physically disabled:** Services for visually, hearing impaired.

**Contact.** E-mail: admission@knox.edu
Phone: (309) 341-7100 Toll-free number: (800) 678-5669
Fax: (309) 341-7070
Paul Steenis, Dean of Admission, Knox College, Knox College - Campus Box 148, Galesburg, IL 61401-4999

---

## Lake Forest College
**Lake Forest, Illinois**
**www.lakeforest.edu**

CB member
CB code: 1392

- Private 4-year liberal arts college
- Residential campus in large town
- 1,375 degree-seeking undergraduates: 59% women, 5% African American, 4% Asian American, 7% Hispanic American, 11% international
- 17 degree-seeking graduate students
- 69% of applicants admitted
- Application essay required

---

**General.** Founded in 1857. Regionally accredited. **Degrees:** 305 bachelor's awarded; master's offered. **Location:** 30 miles from Chicago. **Calendar:** Semester, limited summer session. **Full-time faculty:** 95 total; 98% have terminal degrees, 12% minority, 40% women. **Part-time faculty:** 76 total; 47% have terminal degrees, 9% minority, 62% women. **Class size:** 63% < 20, 37% 20-39, less than 1% 40-49, less than 1% 50-99. **Special facilities:** Multimedia language laboratory, electronic music studio, technology resource center, rhetoric and production room, Center for Chicago Programs.

**Freshman class profile.** 2,026 applied, 1,398 admitted, 355 enrolled.

| Mid 50% test scores | | | |
|---|---|---|---|
| SAT critical reading: | 520-630 | GPA 2.0-2.99: | 14% |
| SAT math: | 530-640 | Rank in top quarter: | 62% |
| SAT writing: | 530-640 | Rank in top tenth: | 38% |
| ACT composite: | 23-29 | Return as sophomores: | 83% |
| GPA 3.75 or higher: | 34% | Out-of-state: | 53% |
| GPA 3.50-3.74: | 18% | Live on campus: | 94% |
| GPA 3.0-3.49: | 34% | International: | 10% |

**Basis for selection.** Holistic approach to candidate review with emphasis on academic preparedness and character. Copy of graded paper required. ACT/SAT optional except for applicants for the highest academic scholarships and international students. Interviews are required for certain scholarships and for students who do not submit standardized test scores; highly recommended for all applicants. Audition required for theater and music scholarships. Portfolio required for art, foreign language and writing scholarships. **Homeschooled:** Statement describing homeschool structure and mission, transcript of courses and grades, interview, letter of recommendation (nonparent) required. SAT/ACT required.

**High school preparation.** College-preparatory program required. 19 units required; 23 recommended. Required and recommended units include English 4, mathematics 3-4, social studies 2, history 2, science 3-4 (laboratory 3-4), foreign language 2-4 and academic electives 3. 1 honors or AP course recommended.

**2010-2011 Annual costs.** Tuition/fees: $35,525. Room/board: $8,327. Books/supplies: $800. Personal expenses: $1,736.

**2009-2010 Financial aid. Need-based:** 282 full-time freshmen applied for aid; 282 were judged to have need; 282 of these received aid. Average scholarship/grant was $26,800; average loan $4,300. 74% of total undergraduate aid awarded as scholarships/grants, 26% as loans/jobs. **Non-need-based:** Awarded to 229 full-time undergraduates, including 57 freshmen. Scholarships awarded for academics, alumni affiliation, leadership, music/drama, religious affiliation, state residency.

**Application procedures. Admission:** Closing date 2/15. $40 fee, may be waived for applicants with need. Admission notification 3/20. Must reply by May 1 or within 3 week(s) if notified thereafter. **Financial aid:** Priority date 2/15, closing date 5/1. FAFSA, institutional form required. Applicants notified on a rolling basis starting 3/1; must reply by 5/1 or within 2 week(s) of notification.

**Academics.** In freshman studies program, students select 1 of 4 fall courses from designated set with class size limit of 12 students. Faculty member teaching course serves as student's academic adviser. **Special study options:** Accelerated study, combined bachelor's/graduate degree, double major, honors, independent study, internships, liberal arts/career combination, semester at sea, student-designed major, study abroad, teacher certification program, urban semester, Washington semester. International internship program in Paris and Santiago, Chile; 3-2 engineering program with Washington University. **Credit/placement by examination:** AP, CLEP, IB, institutional tests. **Support services:** Learning center, study skills assistance, tutoring, writing center.

**Majors. Area/ethnic studies:** American, Asian, Latin American. **Biology:** General. **Business:** General. **Communications:** General. **Computer sciences:** Computer science. **Conservation:** Environmental studies. **Education:** General. **Foreign languages:** Comparative lit, French, Spanish. **History:** General. **Math:** General. **Philosophy/religion:** Philosophy, religion. **Physical sciences:** Chemistry, physics. **Psychology:** General. **Social sciences:** Economics, international relations, political science. **Visual/performing arts:** General, art. **Other:** Sociology and anthropology.

**Most popular majors.** Biology 7%, business/marketing 8%, communications/journalism 12%, English 7%, history 7%, psychology 6%, social sciences 28%, visual/performing arts 7%.

**Computing on campus.** 130 workstations in library, computer center, student center. Dormitories wired for high-speed internet access and linked to campus network. Commuter students can connect to campus network. Online library, helpline, repair service, student web hosting, wireless network available.

**Student life. Freshman orientation:** Mandatory, $100 fee. Preregistration for classes offered. **Housing:** Guaranteed on-campus for freshmen. Coed dorms, single-sex dorms, special housing for disabled, apartments, wellness housing available. $300 nonrefundable deposit, deadline 5/1. **Activities:** Bands, campus ministries, choral groups, dance, drama, film society, international student organizations, literary magazine, music ensembles, Model UN, musical theater, radio station, student government, student newspaper, Christian Fellowship, Interfaith Council, Amnesty International, Habitat for Humanity, League for Environmental Awareness and Protection, United Black Association, Latinos Unidos, Asian Interest Group, Diversity Advocates (ALLY), Hillel.

**Athletics.** NCAA. **Intercollegiate:** Basketball, cross-country, diving, football (tackle) M, handball, ice hockey, soccer, softball W, swimming, tennis, volleyball W. **Intramural:** Basketball, football (non-tackle), racquetball, soccer, softball, tennis, volleyball. **Team name:** Foresters.

**Student services.** Adult student services, alcohol/substance abuse counseling, career counseling, student employment services, financial aid counseling, health services, minority student services, personal counseling, placement for graduates, women's services. **Physically disabled:** Services for visually, hearing impaired.

**Contact.** E-mail: admissions@lakeforest.edu
Phone: (847) 735-5000 Toll-free number: (800) 828-4751
Fax: (847) 735-6271
William Motzer, Vice President for Admissions and Career Services, Lake Forest College, 555 North Sheridan Road, Lake Forest, IL 60045-2338

## Lakeview College of Nursing
**Danville, Illinois**
www.lakeviewcol.edu                          **CB code: 0149**

◗ Private two-year upper-division nursing college
◗ Commuter campus in large town
◗ Application essay required

**General.** Founded in 1894. Regionally accredited. **Degrees:** 104 bachelor's awarded. **Articulation:** Agreements with Danville Area Community College, Eastern Illinois University. **Location:** 35 miles from Urbana-Champaign, 130 miles from Chicago. **Calendar:** Semester, limited summer session. **Full-time faculty:** 20 total. **Part-time faculty:** 8 total. **Special facilities:** Free clinic, nature preserve.

**Student profile.** 278 degree-seeking undergraduates.

| Out-of-state: | 2% | 25 or older: | 83% |
|---|---|---|---|

**Basis for selection.** High school transcript, college transcript, application essay required. Based on interview, references, and transcripts. Applicant must have completed 33 credit hours of general course work with 2.5 GPA prior to admission. Transfer accepted as sophomores, juniors.

**2009-2010 Annual costs.** Tuition/fees: $11,850. Books/supplies: $582.

**Financial aid.** All financial aid based on need.

**Application procedures. Admission:** Rolling admission. $100 fee. Application must be submitted on paper. National League for Nursing examinations used to determine advanced placement for entering students who already have RN degree. **Financial aid:** Priority date 4/15, no deadline. FAFSA, institutional form required.

**Academics.** BS in nursing requires total of 125 credit hours. 95% of entering students complete degree in 5 years or less. **Special study options:** Distance learning, honors, independent study. **Credit/placement by examination:** CLEP. **Support services:** Reduced course load, study skills assistance, tutoring.

**Majors. Health:** Nursing (RN).

**Computing on campus.** 12 workstations in library, computer center.

**Student life. Activities:** Student government, student newspaper, Illinois Student Nurses Association, National Student Nurses Association.

**Student services.** Adult student services, career counseling, financial aid counseling, health services, personal counseling, veterans' counselor.

**Contact.** E-mail: admissions@lakeviewcol.edu
Phone: (217) 554-6899 Fax: (217) 477-2970
Connie Young, Director of Enrollment/Registrar, Lakeview College of Nursing, 903 North Logan Avenue, Danville, IL 61832

## Lewis University
**Romeoville, Illinois**                        **CB member**
www.lewisu.edu                              **CB code: 1404**

◗ Private 4-year university affiliated with Roman Catholic Church
◗ Commuter campus in large town
◗ 4,008 degree-seeking undergraduates: 19% part-time, 58% women, 9% African American, 4% Asian American, 11% Hispanic American, 3% international
◗ 1,768 degree-seeking graduate students
◗ 74% of applicants admitted
◗ SAT or ACT (ACT writing optional) required
◗ 59% graduate within 6 years

**General.** Founded in 1932. Regionally accredited. Sponsored by De La Salle Christian Brothers. **Degrees:** 918 bachelor's, 4 associate awarded; master's, doctoral offered. **ROTC:** Army, Air Force. **Location:** 30 miles from Chicago. **Calendar:** Semester, extensive summer session. **Full-time faculty:** 187 total; 68% have terminal degrees, 10% minority, 52% women. **Part-time faculty:** 384 total; 11% have terminal degrees, 14% minority, 44% women. **Class size:** 65% < 20, 34% 20-39, 1% 40-49, less than 1% 50-99. **Special facilities:** Campus airport, aeronautical training center, all digital radio station.

**Freshman class profile.** 2,674 applied, 1,991 admitted, 658 enrolled.

| Mid 50% test scores | | Rank in top quarter: | 39% |
|---|---|---|---|
| SAT critical reading: | 420-530 | Rank in top tenth: | 15% |
| SAT math: | 470-580 | Return as sophomores: | 79% |
| SAT writing: | 450-540 | Out-of-state: | 7% |
| ACT composite: | 20-25 | Live on campus: | 61% |
| GPA 3.75 or higher: | 20% | International: | 4% |
| GPA 3.50-3.74: | 12% | Fraternities: | 1% |
| GPA 3.0-3.49: | 32% | Sororities: | 2% |
| GPA 2.0-2.99: | 35% | | |

**Basis for selection.** Applicants must graduate from approved high school with 2.0 GPA. Class rank and ACT/SAT scores must indicate strong likelihood of success in university studies. 20 ACT required for admission to nursing program. Interview recommended. **Homeschooled:** Statement describing homeschool structure and mission required.

**High school preparation.** College-preparatory program recommended. 18 units required. Required and recommended units include English 3-4, mathematics 3, social studies 2, history 1, science 2 (laboratory 1), foreign language 2 and academic electives 4. 1 year chemistry and 2 years math at 2.0 level or above strongly recommended for nursing applicants.

**2010-2011 Annual costs.** Tuition/fees: $23,780. Room/board: $8,600. Books/supplies: $1,000. Personal expenses: $1,320.

**2009-2010 Financial aid. Need-based:** 602 full-time freshmen applied for aid; 512 were judged to have need; 510 of these received aid. Average need met was 81%. Average scholarship/grant was $8,121; average loan $3,378. 45% of total undergraduate aid awarded as scholarships/grants, 55% as loans/jobs. **Non-need-based:** Awarded to 2,291 full-time undergraduates, including 629 freshmen. Scholarships awarded for academics, alumni affiliation, art, athletics, music/drama, religious affiliation, ROTC.

**Application procedures. Admission:** Priority date 4/15; no deadline. $40 fee, may be waived for applicants with need. Admission notification on a rolling basis beginning on or about 10/1. Must reply by May 1 or within 2 week(s) if notified thereafter. **Financial aid:** Closing date 5/1. FAFSA required. Applicants notified on a rolling basis starting 2/1; must reply by 5/1 or within 2 week(s) of notification.

**Academics.** Accelerated degree completion program available to students 24 years and older. **Special study options:** Accelerated study, combined bachelor's/graduate degree, distance learning, double major, dual enrollment of high school students, ESL, exchange student, honors, independent study, internships, liberal arts/career combination, student-designed major, study abroad, teacher certification program. **Credit/placement by examination:** AP, CLEP, institutional tests. 60 credit hours maximum toward bachelor's degree. **Support services:** Learning center, pre-admission summer program, reduced course load, remedial instruction, study skills assistance, tutoring, writing center.

**Majors. Area/ethnic studies:** American. **Biology:** General, biochemistry, environmental. **Business:** General, accounting, business admin, finance, human resources, international, management information systems, management science, managerial economics, marketing. **Communications:** General, broadcast journalism, digital media, journalism, public relations, radio/tv. **Communications technology:** General, radio/tv. **Computer sciences:**

General, computer graphics, computer science, information systems. **Conservation:** General. **Education:** General, elementary, special. **Health:** Athletic training, chiropractic assistant, health care admin, health services, nursing (RN), pharmacy assistant, predental, premedicine, prenursing, prepharmacy, preveterinary. **History:** General. **Interdisciplinary:** Global studies. **Legal studies:** Prelaw. **Liberal arts:** Arts/sciences. **Math:** General. **Mechanic/repair:** Aircraft, avionics. **Parks/recreation:** Sports admin. **Philosophy/religion:** Philosophy, religion. **Physical sciences:** Chemistry, physics. **Protective services:** Correctional facilities, criminal justice, fire services admin, forensics, law enforcement admin, police science, security services. **Psychology:** General. **Public administration:** General, community org/advocacy, human services, social work. **Social sciences:** Economics, political science, sociology. **Transportation:** Air traffic control, airline/commercial pilot, aviation, aviation management. **Visual/performing arts:** Art, commercial/advertising art, dramatic, drawing, graphic design, illustration, music management, painting, studio arts, theater arts management. **Other:** Aviation security.

**Most popular majors.** Business/marketing 26%, education 7%, health sciences 19%, psychology 8%, security/protective services 12%.

**Computing on campus.** 350 workstations in library, computer center. Dormitories wired for high-speed internet access and linked to campus network. Commuter students can connect to campus network. Online course registration, online library, helpline, wireless network available.

**Student life. Freshman orientation:** Mandatory, $100 fee. Preregistration for classes offered. Two-day program includes transition seminars, assessment, and academic advising. Summer/winter orientations (overnight for Freshman only) available, includes parent orientations and welcome weekend before first day of classes. **Housing:** Guaranteed on-campus for all undergraduates. Coed dorms, special housing for disabled available. $100 nonrefundable deposit, deadline 5/1. Handicapped accessibility available in most residence halls. **Activities:** Jazz band, campus ministries, choral groups, dance, drama, international student organizations, literary magazine, music ensembles, musical theater, radio station, student government, student newspaper, TV station, Fellowship of Justice, Black student union, Latin American student organization, InterFraternity Council, National Panhellenic Council, American Association of Airport Executives, Coffey Aviation student organization, student nurses association, Teachers of Tomorrow.

**Athletics.** NCAA. **Intercollegiate:** Baseball M, basketball, cheerleading, cross-country, golf, soccer, softball W, swimming, tennis, track and field, volleyball. **Intramural:** Basketball, bowling, field hockey, football (nontackle), golf, handball, racquetball, soccer, softball, table tennis, tennis, volleyball. **Team name:** Flyers.

**Student services.** Adult student services, alcohol/substance abuse counseling, career counseling, student employment services, financial aid counseling, health services, minority student services, personal counseling, placement for graduates, veterans' counselor.

**Contact.** E-mail: admissions@lewisu.edu
Phone: (815) 836-5250 Toll-free number: (800) 897-9000
Fax: (815) 836-5002
Andrew Sison, Dean of Admission, Lewis University, One University Parkway, Romeoville, IL 60446-2200

## Lexington College
### Chicago, Illinois
### www.lexingtoncollege.edu
**CB code: 3843**

- Private 4-year hospitality management college for women affiliated with Roman Catholic Church
- Commuter campus in very large city
- 60 full-time, degree-seeking undergraduates
- 47% of applicants admitted
- SAT or ACT, application essay required

**General.** Founded in 1977. Regionally accredited. **Degrees:** 4 bachelor's, 4 associate awarded. **Location:** Downtown. **Calendar:** Semester. **Full-time faculty:** 6 total. **Part-time faculty:** 15 total. **Class size:** 100% < 20. **Special facilities:** Culinary demonstration laboratory, computer laboratory.

**Freshman class profile.** 49 applied, 23 admitted, 6 enrolled.

| Mid 50% test scores | | Out-of-state: | 8% |
|---|---|---|---|
| ACT composite: | 19-25 | | |

**Basis for selection.** School achievement record, essay, and interview most important. Work experience considered. **Homeschooled:** Letter of recommendation (nonparent) required. Must submit GED with scores.

**High school preparation.** 10 units recommended. Recommended units include English 4, mathematics 2, social studies 2 and science 2.

**2009-2010 Annual costs.** Tuition/fees: $23,800. Room/board: $8,000. Books/supplies: $750. Personal expenses: $400.

**2009-2010 Financial aid.** All financial aid based on need. **Additional information:** Work-study is available.

**Application procedures. Admission:** No deadline. $30 fee, may be waived for applicants with need. Admission notification on a rolling basis. **Financial aid:** Closing date 5/15. FAFSA required. Applicants notified on a rolling basis starting 7/1; must reply within 2 week(s) of notification.

**Academics. Special study options:** Cooperative education, independent study, internships, study abroad. **Credit/placement by examination:** AP, CLEP, institutional tests. **Support services:** Remedial instruction, study skills assistance, tutoring.

**Majors. Business:** Business admin, hotel/motel admin, restaurant/food services. **Family/consumer sciences:** Institutional food production.

**Computing on campus.** 30 workstations in library, computer center. Online library, wireless network available.

**Student life. Freshman orientation:** Mandatory. Preregistration for classes offered. 2-day program before classes begin. **Activities:** Student government, student newspaper, campus ministry.

**Student services.** Chaplain/spiritual director, career counseling, student employment services, financial aid counseling, personal counseling, placement for graduates.

**Contact.** E-mail: admissions@lexingtoncollege.edu
Phone: (312) 226-6294 Toll-free number: (866) 647-3093
Fax: (312) 226-6405
Carmen Larios, Enrollment Manager, Lexington College, 310 South Peoria Street, Suite 512, Chicago, IL 60607-3534

## Lincoln Christian University
### Lincoln, Illinois
### www.lincolnchristian.edu
**CB code: 1405**

- Private 4-year university and Bible college affiliated with Church of Christ
- Residential campus in large town
- 638 degree-seeking undergraduates: 16% part-time, 50% women
- 106 degree-seeking graduate students
- 65% of applicants admitted
- SAT or ACT with writing, application essay required
- 52% graduate within 6 years; 30% enter graduate study

**General.** Founded in 1944. Regionally accredited; also accredited by ABHE, ATS. **Degrees:** 125 bachelor's, 7 associate awarded; master's, doctoral offered. **Location:** 30 miles from Springfield. **Calendar:** Semester, limited summer session. **Full-time faculty:** 45 total; 58% have terminal degrees, 7% minority, 20% women. **Part-time faculty:** 54 total; 15% have terminal degrees, 44% women. **Class size:** 78% < 20, 14% 20-39, 3% 40-49, 3% 50-99, 2% >100.

**Freshman class profile.** 232 applied, 150 admitted, 115 enrolled.

| Mid 50% test scores | | GPA 2.0-2.99: | 28% |
|---|---|---|---|
| ACT composite: | 19-25 | End year in good standing: | 92% |
| GPA 3.75 or higher: | 24% | Return as sophomores: | 71% |
| GPA 3.50-3.74: | 23% | Out-of-state: | 20% |
| GPA 3.0-3.49: | 25% | Live on campus: | 85% |

**Basis for selection.** Recommendation of applicant's church leaders as to suitability for church-related vocations very important. High school record (core courses) and ACT scores also considered. Subscores of writing and English, application essay also important. Interview recommended. Audition required of music majors. **Homeschooled:** Transcript of courses and grades, interview, letter of recommendation (nonparent) required. List of involvement outside of education/academics required. **Learning Disabled:** Students with learning disabilities usually recommended to academic resource center.

**High school preparation.** 17 units recommended. Recommended units include English 4, mathematics 3, social studies 3, history 3, science 2 and foreign language 2.

**2009-2010 Annual costs.** Tuition/fees: $13,020. Room/board: $5,783. Books/supplies: $600. Personal expenses: $1,700.

**2008-2009 Financial aid. Need-based:** 84 full-time freshmen applied for aid; 64 were judged to have need; 63 of these received aid. Average need met was 60%. Average scholarship/grant was $6,000; average loan $3,368. 55% of total undergraduate aid awarded as scholarships/grants, 45% as loans/jobs. **Non-need-based:** Awarded to 229 full-time undergraduates, including 41 freshmen. Scholarships awarded for academics.

**Application procedures. Admission:** No deadline. $25 fee, may be waived for applicants with need. Admission notification on a rolling basis. **Financial aid:** Priority date 3/1; no closing date. FAFSA required. Applicants notified on a rolling basis starting 3/1; must reply within 2 week(s) of notification.

**Academics. Special study options:** Distance learning, double major, dual enrollment of high school students, honors, independent study, internships, study abroad, weekend college. Study abroad through the CCCU-BestSemester program. **Credit/placement by examination:** AP, CLEP, ACT, institutional tests. **Support services:** Learning center, reduced course load, remedial instruction, study skills assistance, tutoring, writing center.

**Majors. Business:** Business admin. **Philosophy/religion:** Religion. **Psychology:** General. **Theology:** Bible, missionary, religious ed, sacred music, theology, youth ministry.

**Most popular majors.** Business/marketing 9%, theological studies 81%.

**Computing on campus.** 51 workstations in library, computer center, student center. Dormitories wired for high-speed internet access and linked to campus network. Commuter students can connect to campus network. Online course registration, online library, helpline, repair service, wireless network available.

**Student life. Freshman orientation:** Mandatory, $250 fee. Preregistration for classes offered. **Policies:** Religious observance required. **Housing:** Guaranteed on-campus for all undergraduates. Single-sex dorms, apartments, wellness housing available. $150 fully refundable deposit, deadline 8/10. **Activities:** Campus ministries, choral groups, drama, international student organizations, music ensembles, musical theater, student government, student newspaper, volunteer groups in local health care institutions, missions interest groups, Christian service and outreach groups.

**Athletics.** NCCAA. **Intercollegiate:** Baseball M, basketball, soccer, volleyball W. **Intramural:** Badminton W, basketball M, football (non-tackle), soccer, volleyball. **Team name:** Red Lions.

**Student services.** Student employment services, financial aid counseling, health services, personal counseling. **Physically disabled:** Services for visually, hearing impaired. **Learning disabled:** Comprehensive services available.

**Contact.** E-mail: admissions@lincolnchristian.edu
Phone: (217) 732-3168 ext. 2251 Toll-free number: (888) 522-5228
Fax: (217) 732-4199
Palmer Muntz, Director of Admissions, Lincoln Christian University, 100 Campus View Drive, Lincoln, IL 62656-2167

## Loyola University Chicago

**Chicago, Illinois**          CB member
**www.luc.edu**               CB code: 1412

◗ Private 4-year university affiliated with Roman Catholic Church
◗ Residential campus in very large city
◗ 9,602 degree-seeking undergraduates: 5% part-time, 65% women, 5% African American, 12% Asian American, 10% Hispanic American, 1% international
◗ 5,606 degree-seeking graduate students
◗ 78% of applicants admitted
◗ SAT or ACT (ACT writing optional), application essay required
◗ 68% graduate within 6 years

**General.** Founded in 1870. Regionally accredited. Extensive degree program for returning adults. Lake Shore and Water Tower campuses in Chicago, and Medical Center campus in suburbs. **Degrees:** 2,601 bachelor's awarded; master's, doctoral, professional offered. **ROTC:** Army, Naval, Air Force. **Location:** Downtown. **Calendar:** Semester, extensive summer session. **Full-time faculty:** 629 total; 97% have terminal degrees, 10% minority, 44% women. **Part-time faculty:** 723 total; 10% minority, 53% women. **Class size:** 32% < 20, 48% 20-39, 11% 40-49, 7% 50-99, 2% >100. **Special facilities:** Theater, language learning resource center, wellness center, computer resource center, neuroscience labs, biodiesel lab, mock trial room, performance and specialized fine arts rooms, clinical nursing labs.

**Freshman class profile.** 17,383 applied, 13,583 admitted, 2,076 enrolled.

| Mid 50% test scores | | Rank in top quarter: | 67% |
|---|---|---|---|
| SAT critical reading: | 540-650 | Rank in top tenth: | 32% |
| SAT math: | 530-650 | End year in good standing: | 98% |
| SAT writing: | 540-640 | Return as sophomores: | 85% |
| ACT composite: | 24-29 | Out-of-state: | 42% |
| GPA 3.75 or higher: | 45% | Live on campus: | 86% |
| GPA 3.50-3.74: | 25% | International: | 1% |
| GPA 3.0-3.49: | 27% | Fraternities: | 4% |
| GPA 2.0-2.99: | 3% | Sororities: | 13% |

**Basis for selection.** High school GPA, rigor of high school curriculum, official test scores (ACT or SAT), recommendation letter and essay are important. Personal interviews recommended but not required.

**High school preparation.** College-preparatory program required. 15 units required; 20 recommended. Required and recommended units include English 4, mathematics 3-4, social studies 2, history 1-2, science 3, foreign language 2 and academic electives 3. Additional requirements for certain majors.

**2010-2011 Annual costs.** Tuition/fees: $31,846. Room/board: $11,220. Books/supplies: $1,200. Personal expenses: $1,600.

**2009-2010 Financial aid. Need-based:** 1,833 full-time freshmen applied for aid; 1,548 were judged to have need; 1,539 of these received aid. Average need met was 84%. Average scholarship/grant was $17,781; average loan $3,810. 61% of total undergraduate aid awarded as scholarships/grants, 39% as loans/jobs. **Non-need-based:** Awarded to 1,978 full-time undergraduates, including 541 freshmen. Scholarships awarded for academics, athletics, leadership, religious affiliation.

**Application procedures. Admission:** Priority date 4/1; no deadline. No application fee. Admission notification on a rolling basis beginning on or about 10/1. Must reply by May 1 or within 2 week(s) if notified thereafter. Separate application, recommendation and essay required for admission to Interdisciplinary Honors Program. Must apply by March 1. **Financial aid:** Priority date 3/1; no closing date. FAFSA required. Applicants notified on a rolling basis starting 2/15; must reply within 3 week(s) of notification.

**Academics. Special study options:** Accelerated study, combined bachelor's/graduate degree, distance learning, double major, dual enrollment of high school students, exchange student, honors, independent study, internships, study abroad, teacher certification program, Washington semester. School of professional studies offers part-time evening programs leading to bachelor's degrees; cooperative programs with Erikson Institute for Early Education and St. Joseph's Seminary; study abroad in Italy and Mexico available. **Credit/placement by examination:** AP, CLEP, IB, SAT, ACT, institutional tests. 24 credit hours maximum toward bachelor's degree. **Support services:** Learning center, pre-admission summer program, reduced course load, study skills assistance, tutoring, writing center.

**Majors. Area/ethnic studies:** African-American, women's. **Biology:** General, biochemistry, bioinformatics, biophysics. **Business:** Accounting, business admin, finance, human resources, international, management information systems, managerial economics, marketing, office management, operations, organizational behavior. **Communications:** General, journalism. **Computer sciences:** General, information technology, security. **Conservation:** Environmental science. **Education:** Bilingual, early childhood, elementary, mathematics, science, secondary, special. **Foreign languages:** Ancient Greek, classics, French, Italian, Latin, Spanish. **Health:** Clinical lab science, clinical nutrition, health care admin, nursing (RN). **History:** General. **Interdisciplinary:** Behavioral sciences, math/computer science. **Math:** General, statistics. **Parks/recreation:** Sports admin. **Philosophy/religion:** Philosophy. **Physical sciences:** Chemistry, physics. **Protective services:** Criminal justice, forensics. **Psychology:** General. **Public administration:** Human services, social work. **Social sciences:** Anthropology, international relations, political science, sociology. **Theology:** Religious ed, theology. **Visual/performing arts:** Art history/conservation, dramatic, studio arts. **Other:** Applied psychology, Health law, International cinema and video, Software Development, Visual communications.

**Most popular majors.** Biology 9%, business/marketing 21%, communications/journalism 7%, health sciences 12%, psychology 10%, social sciences 13%.

**Computing on campus.** 1,314 workstations in library, computer center, student center. Dormitories wired for high-speed internet access and linked to campus network. Commuter students can connect to campus network. Online course registration, online library, helpline, repair service, student web hosting, wireless network available.

**Student life. Freshman orientation:** Mandatory, $350 fee. Preregistration for classes offered. 2-day orientation program at Lake Shore campus.

**Housing:** Guaranteed on-campus for freshmen. Coed dorms, special housing for disabled, apartments, wellness housing available. $250 deposit, deadline 5/1. 24-hour quiet facility, honors floor, living learning community floors available. **Activities:** Bands, campus ministries, dance, drama, film society, international student organizations, literary magazine, music ensembles, Model UN, musical theater, radio station, student government, student newspaper, TV station, Agape Christian Fellowship, College Republicans, College Democrats, international club, student environmental alliance, Bible Fellowship, Black Cultural Center, Armed Forces Club, Model United Nations, Graduate Students of Color Alliance.

**Athletics.** NCAA. **Intercollegiate:** Basketball, cheerleading, cross-country, golf, soccer, softball W, track and field, volleyball. **Intramural:** Badminton, basketball, football (non-tackle), racquetball, soccer, table tennis, tennis, volleyball. **Team name:** Ramblers.

**Student services.** Adult student services, alcohol/substance abuse counseling, chaplain/spiritual director, career counseling, student employment services, financial aid counseling, health services, minority student services, on-campus daycare, personal counseling, placement for graduates, veterans' counselor. **Physically disabled:** Services for visually, speech, hearing impaired.

**Contact.** E-mail: admission@luc.edu
Phone: (312) 915-6500 Toll-free number: (800) 262-2373
Fax: (312) 915-7216
Lori Greene, Director of Admissions, Loyola University Chicago, 820 North Michigan Avenue, Chicago, IL 60611-9810

---

## MacMurray College

**Jacksonville, Illinois**
**www.mac.edu**
**CB member**
**CB code: 1435**

▶ Private 4-year liberal arts college affiliated with United Methodist Church
▶ Residential campus in large town
▶ 507 degree-seeking undergraduates: 7% part-time, 64% women
▶ 59% of applicants admitted
▶ SAT or ACT (ACT writing optional) required
▶ 49% graduate within 6 years

**General.** Founded in 1846. Regionally accredited. **Degrees:** 123 bachelor's, 1 associate awarded. **Location:** 30 miles from Springfield. **Calendar:** Semester, limited summer session. **Full-time faculty:** 31 total. **Part-time faculty:** 31 total. **Class size:** 59% < 20, 39% 20-39, 2% 40-49, 1% 50-99.

**Freshman class profile.** 492 applied, 291 admitted, 96 enrolled.

| Mid 50% test scores | |
|---|---|
| ACT composite: | 17-22 |

**Basis for selection.** ACT composite 20, high school or college transfer GPA 2.5 required for unconditional acceptance. Application reviewed for ACT composite between 15 and 19, high school or college transfer GPA less than 2.5. ACT of 20 required for nursing applicants. ACT composite less than 15 or GPA less than 1.5 is automatic denial. School, community, and church activities, and recommendations also considered. Interview recommended for academically deficient applicants. Portfolio recommended for art scholarship.

**2009-2010 Annual costs.** Tuition/fees: $18,390. Room/board: $7,278. Books/supplies: $1,000. Personal expenses: $960.

**2009-2010 Financial aid. Non-need-based:** Scholarships awarded for academics, alumni affiliation, art, leadership, religious affiliation. **Additional information:** Merit scholarships for accepted, enrolled freshman based on academic record. Need-based program meets 100% of direct tuition charges after family contribution and financial aid.

**Application procedures. Admission:** Priority date 4/9; no deadline. No application fee. Admission notification on a rolling basis beginning on or about 9/1. **Financial aid:** Priority date 5/1; no closing date. FAFSA required. Applicants notified on a rolling basis starting 2/1; must reply within 2 week(s) of notification.

**Academics. Special study options:** Combined bachelor's/graduate degree, cooperative education, distance learning, double major, dual enrollment of high school students, independent study, internships, liberal arts/career combination, student-designed major, study abroad, teacher certification program, weekend college. **Credit/placement by examination:** AP, CLEP, IB, institutional tests. 32 credit hours maximum toward bachelor's degree. **Support services:** Learning center, reduced course load, study skills assistance, tutoring, writing center.

---

**Majors. Biology:** General. **Business:** Accounting, business admin, finance, management information systems. **Communications:** Journalism. **Computer sciences:** General, computer science. **Education:** Biology, Deaf/hearing impaired, elementary, emotionally handicapped, English, history, learning disabled, mathematics, music, physical, secondary, Spanish, special. **Engineering:** General. **Foreign languages:** French, sign language interpretation, Spanish. **Health:** Predental, premedicine, preveterinary. **History:** General. **Math:** General. **Parks/recreation:** Sports admin. **Philosophy/religion:** Philosophy, religion. **Physical sciences:** Chemistry, physics. **Psychology:** General. **Public administration:** Social work. **Social sciences:** International relations, political science. **Visual/performing arts:** Art, dramatic. **Other:** Student personnel services.

**Most popular majors.** Business/marketing 16%, education 22%, health sciences 11%, psychology 6%, security/protective services 9%.

**Computing on campus.** 75 workstations in dormitories, library, computer center. Dormitories wired for high-speed internet access and linked to campus network. Online library, helpline, wireless network available.

**Student life. Freshman orientation:** Mandatory. Preregistration for classes offered. Two-day acclimation to campus life held prior to start of classes. **Housing:** Guaranteed on-campus for all undergraduates. Coed dorms, single-sex dorms, special housing for disabled available. $150 fully refundable deposit. **Activities:** Campus ministries, choral groups, drama, international student organizations, literary magazine, student government.

**Athletics.** NCAA. **Intercollegiate:** Baseball M, basketball, football (tackle) M, golf, soccer, softball W, volleyball W. **Intramural:** Basketball, soccer, softball, volleyball. **Team name:** Highlanders.

**Student services.** Alcohol/substance abuse counseling, chaplain/spiritual director, career counseling, student employment services, financial aid counseling, health services, personal counseling, placement for graduates, veterans' counselor. **Physically disabled:** Services for visually, hearing impaired.

**Contact.** E-mail: admissions@mac.edu
Phone: (217) 479-7056 Toll-free number: (800) 252-7485
Fax: (217) 291-0702
James Malley, Vice President for Admissions, MacMurray College, 447 East College Avenue, Jacksonville, IL 62650-2590

---

## McKendree University

**Lebanon, Illinois**
**www.mckendree.edu**
**CB code: 1456**

▶ Private 4-year university and liberal arts college affiliated with United Methodist Church
▶ Residential campus in small town
▶ 2,194 degree-seeking undergraduates: 30% part-time, 55% women, 13% African American, 2% Asian American, 3% Hispanic American, 2% international
▶ 1,013 degree-seeking graduate students
▶ 71% of applicants admitted
▶ SAT or ACT (ACT writing optional), application essay required
▶ 70% graduate within 6 years; 35% enter graduate study

**General.** Founded in 1828. Regionally accredited. **Degrees:** 516 bachelor's awarded; master's offered. **ROTC:** Army, Air Force. **Location:** 12 miles from Belleville, 23 miles from St. Louis. **Calendar:** Semester, limited summer session. **Full-time faculty:** 95 total; 77% have terminal degrees, 7% minority, 56% women. **Part-time faculty:** 243 total. **Class size:** 72% < 20, 28% 20-39. **Special facilities:** Networked faculty and classroom buildings, fine arts center with theatre.

**Freshman class profile.** 1,291 applied, 914 admitted, 307 enrolled.

| Mid 50% test scores | | | | |
|---|---|---|---|---|
| SAT critical reading: | 340-580 | GPA 2.0-2.99: | 31% |
| SAT math: | 380-600 | Rank in top quarter: | 35% |
| SAT writing: | 300-550 | Rank in top tenth: | 12% |
| ACT composite: | 18-27 | End year in good standing: | 85% |
| GPA 3.75 or higher: | 20% | Return as sophomores: | 88% |
| GPA 3.50-3.74: | 15% | Out-of-state: | 11% |
| GPA 3.0-3.49: | 33% | Live on campus: | 82% |
| | | International: | 4% |

**Basis for selection.** Holistic approach to admissions; variety of criteria considered including GPA, rigor of secondary school record, standardized test scores, and interview, when possible. RN required of Nursing Completion Program applicants. Interviews recommended. Audition required of music majors and minors. Portfolio recommended for art majors. **Home-schooled:** Statement describing homeschool structure and mission, letter of recommendation (nonparent) required. Applicants must submit description of courses studied, 3 letters of recommendation (not including that of parents).

**High school preparation.** College-preparatory program recommended. 14 units recommended. Recommended units include English 4, mathematics 3, social studies 2, history 1, science 3 and foreign language 1.

**2010-2011 Annual costs.** Tuition/fees: $23,130. Room/board: $8,240. Books/supplies: $1,200. Personal expenses: $1,000.

**2009-2010 Financial aid. Need-based:** 289 full-time freshmen applied for aid; 263 were judged to have need; 262 of these received aid. Average need met was 84%. Average scholarship/grant was $17,039; average loan $3,196. 68% of total undergraduate aid awarded as scholarships/grants, 32% as loans/jobs. **Non-need-based:** Awarded to 540 full-time undergraduates, including 100 freshmen. Scholarships awarded for academics, alumni affiliation, art, athletics, leadership, minority status, music/drama, religious affiliation.

**Application procedures. Admission:** No deadline. $40 fee, may be waived for applicants with need, free for online applicants. Admission notification on a rolling basis beginning on or about 9/15. **Financial aid:** Priority date 5/31; no closing date. FAFSA required. Applicants notified on a rolling basis starting 3/1; must reply within 4 week(s) of notification.

**Academics. Special study options:** Accelerated study, combined bachelor's/graduate degree, cooperative education, distance learning, double major, external degree, honors, independent study, internships, liberal arts/career combination, student-designed major, study abroad, teacher certification program. 3-2 and 3-3 occupational therapy program with Washington University. **Credit/placement by examination:** AP, CLEP, IB, SAT, ACT, institutional tests. 36 credit hours maximum toward associate degree, 64 toward bachelor's. **Support services:** Learning center, reduced course load, remedial instruction, study skills assistance, tutoring, writing center.

**Honors college/program.** 3.6 GPA, 27 ACT, top 10% of class required; approximately 20 freshmen admitted.

**Majors. Biology:** General. **Business:** Accounting, business admin, management science, marketing. **Communications:** General. **Computer sciences:** General, computer science, information systems, information technology. **Education:** General, art, business, elementary, health, history, music, physical, science. **Health:** Athletic training, nursing (RN). **History:** General. **Liberal arts:** Arts/sciences. **Math:** General. **Philosophy/religion:** Philosophy, religion. **Physical sciences:** Chemistry. **Psychology:** General. **Social sciences:** General, economics, international relations, political science, sociology. **Visual/performing arts:** Studio arts.

**Most popular majors.** Business/marketing 37%, computer/information sciences 9%, education 11%, health sciences 11%, psychology 6%.

**Computing on campus.** 220 workstations in library, computer center, student center. Dormitories wired for high-speed internet access and linked to campus network. Commuter students can connect to campus network. Online course registration, online library, helpline, repair service, student web hosting, wireless network available.

**Student life. Freshman orientation:** Mandatory, $50 fee. Preregistration for classes offered. Three day program held weekend before start of classes. **Policies:** Students are required to live on campus unless 21 years of age, of senior class standing, married, commuting from the home of a parent or legal guardian, or a veteran with at least two years active military duty. **Housing:** Guaranteed on-campus for all undergraduates. Coed dorms, special housing for disabled, apartments, wellness housing available. $200 fully refundable deposit. **Activities:** Bands, campus ministries, choral groups, dance, drama, film society, international student organizations, literary magazine, music ensembles, Model UN, musical theater, radio station, student government, student newspaper, Campus Christian Fellowship, Students Against Social Injustice, black student organization, service organizations, resident hall association, Intergreek Council, Community Service Fellows.

**Athletics.** NAIA. **Intercollegiate:** Baseball M, basketball, bowling, cheerleading, cross-country, football (tackle) M, golf, ice hockey, soccer, softball W, tennis, track and field, volleyball W, wrestling M. **Intramural:** Basketball, football (non-tackle), softball, volleyball. **Team name:** Bearcats.

**Student services.** Adult student services, alcohol/substance abuse counseling, chaplain/spiritual director, career counseling, student employment services, financial aid counseling, health services, minority student services, personal counseling, placement for graduates, veterans' counselor. **Physically disabled:** Services for visually, speech, hearing impaired.

**Contact.** E-mail: inquiry@mckendree.edu
Phone: (618) 537-6831 Toll-free number: (800) 232-7228 ext. 6831
Fax: (618) 537-6496
Chris Hall, Vice President for Admission and Financial Aid, McKendree University, 701 College Road, Lebanon, IL 62254

- For-profit 4-year business college
- Commuter campus in small city
- 548 degree-seeking undergraduates: 59% part-time, 81% women, 24% African American, 1% Asian American, 2% Hispanic American
- 99% of applicants admitted
- Application essay, interview required

**General.** Founded in 1888. Regionally accredited. **Degrees:** 60 bachelor's, 70 associate awarded. **Location:** 165 miles from Chicago. **Calendar:** Quarter, extensive summer session. **Full-time faculty:** 25 total; 12% have terminal degrees, 8% minority, 64% women. **Part-time faculty:** 38 total; 8% minority, 55% women.

**Freshman class profile.** 72 applied, 71 admitted, 45 enrolled.

**Basis for selection.** Rigorous secondary school program and quality of application essay and interview important. Extracurricular activities, character and relationships to alumnae considered. Entrance exam, including writing sample, and math placement tests administered to all applicants. Necessity for remedial support determined from results.

**2009-2010 Annual costs.** Tuition/fees: $12,600. Fees vary according to program.

**Application procedures. Admission:** No deadline. $25 fee. Admission notification on a rolling basis. **Financial aid:** No deadline. FAFSA, institutional form required. Applicants notified on a rolling basis; must reply within 4 week(s) of notification.

**Academics. Special study options:** Distance learning, double major, dual enrollment of high school students, internships. **Credit/placement by examination:** AP, CLEP, institutional tests. 24 credit hours maximum toward associate degree, 46 toward bachelor's. **Support services:** Learning center, reduced course load, remedial instruction, study skills assistance, tutoring.

**Majors. Business:** Accounting, business admin. **Computer sciences:** Information systems. **Health:** Medical records technology. **Legal studies:** Court reporting.

**Computing on campus.** 109 workstations in library, computer center. Commuter students can connect to campus network. Online library, helpline, repair service, wireless network available.

**Student life. Freshman orientation:** Mandatory. Preregistration for classes offered. Held first day of each quarter. **Activities:** Student government.

**Student services.** Career counseling, student employment services, financial aid counseling, personal counseling, placement for graduates, veterans' counselor.

**Contact.** E-mail: admissions@midstate.edu
Phone: (309) 692-4092 Toll-free number: (800) 251-4299
Fax: (309) 692-3893
Jessica Auer, Director of Admissions, Midstate College, 411 West Northmoor Road, Peoria, IL 61614-3558

- Private 4-year university affiliated with Presbyterian Church (USA)
- Residential campus in small city
- 2,214 degree-seeking undergraduates: 4% part-time, 60% women, 10% African American, 1% Asian American, 3% Hispanic American, 1% international
- 37 degree-seeking graduate students
- 60% of applicants admitted
- SAT or ACT (ACT writing optional) required
- 63% graduate within 6 years; 24% enter graduate study

**General.** Founded in 1901. Regionally accredited. **Degrees:** 609 bachelor's awarded; master's offered. **Location:** 180 miles from Chicago, 120 miles from St. Louis. **Calendar:** Semester, limited summer session. **Full-time faculty:** 154 total; 81% have terminal degrees, 10% minority, 51% women. **Part-time faculty:** 123 total; 26% have terminal degrees, 11% minority, 61% women. **Class size:** 67% < 20, 31% 20-39, less than 1% 40-49, 2% 50-99. **Special facilities:** Porcelain, glass and decorative arts museum,

32-track recording studio, computer imaging center, greenhouse, observatory, performance center, 24-hour computer labs, video-conferencing classroom, proscenium theater, science center, 3-D arts building, student-run art gallery, student-owned and operated publishing company, student-operated record label.

**Freshman class profile.** 3,167 applied, 1,905 admitted, 542 enrolled.

| Mid 50% test scores | | Rank in top quarter: | 40% |
|---|---|---|---|
| SAT critical reading: | 480-590 | Rank in top tenth: | 17% |
| SAT math: | 480-560 | End year in good standing: | 85% |
| SAT writing: | 460-560 | Return as sophomores: | 80% |
| ACT composite: | 20-25 | Out-of-state: | 18% |
| GPA 3.75 or higher: | 26% | Live on campus: | 87% |
| GPA 3.50-3.74: | 15% | Fraternities: | 20% |
| GPA 3.0-3.49: | 31% | Sororities: | 12% |
| GPA 2.0-2.99: | 28% | | |

**Basis for selection.** School achievement record most important. Class rank, GPA, recommendation, test scores important. Applicant should rank in top half of class. Character references considered. Interview recommended. Audition required of music, music/theater majors. Portfolio required of art majors.

**High school preparation.** College-preparatory program recommended. 16 units required. Required and recommended units include English 4, mathematics 3, social studies 2, history 2, science 3 and foreign language 2.

**2010-2011 Annual costs.** Tuition/fees: $27,425. Room/board: $8,291.

**2008-2009 Financial aid. Need-based:** 456 full-time freshmen applied for aid; 388 were judged to have need; 387 of these received aid. Average need met was 94%. Average scholarship/grant was $10,361; average loan $3,486. 67% of total undergraduate aid awarded as scholarships/grants, 33% as loans/jobs. **Non-need-based:** Awarded to 1,715 full-time undergraduates, including 455 freshmen. Scholarships awarded for academics, alumni affiliation, art, leadership, minority status, music/drama.

**Application procedures. Admission:** Priority date 5/1; no deadline. No application fee. Admission notification on a rolling basis beginning on or about 9/15. **Financial aid:** Priority date 3/15; no closing date. FAFSA required. Applicants notified on a rolling basis starting 3/15; must reply by 5/1 or within 4 week(s) of notification.

**Academics.** Small business consulting and accelerated adult education available. **Special study options:** Accelerated study, combined bachelor's/graduate degree, double major, exchange student, honors, independent study, internships, student-designed major, study abroad, teacher certification program, United Nations semester, urban semester, Washington semester. **Credit/placement by examination:** AP, CLEP, IB, ACT, institutional tests. 30 credit hours maximum toward bachelor's degree. To receive CLEP credit student must not have attended secondary school in the past 3 years; CLEP credit cannot count in the major and may not be used if the equivalent course has been attempted. **Support services:** Learning center, reduced course load, study skills assistance, tutoring, writing center.

**Majors. Biology:** General, molecular. **Business:** Accounting, business admin, entrepreneurial studies, finance, international, management information systems, marketing. **Communications:** General. **Education:** Art, biology, chemistry, early childhood, elementary, English, mathematics, music, physical, social science. **Foreign languages:** Spanish. **Health:** Art therapy, athletic training, nursing (RN), predental, premedicine, prepharmacy, preveterinary. **History:** General. **Interdisciplinary:** Global studies. **Legal studies:** Prelaw. **Math:** Applied. **Parks/recreation:** Sports admin. **Philosophy/religion:** Philosophy. **Physical sciences:** Chemistry, physics. **Psychology:** General. **Public administration:** Human services. **Social sciences:** Political science, sociology. **Visual/performing arts:** Commercial/advertising art, dramatic, music performance, musical theater, piano/organ, studio arts, theater design, voice/opera. **Other:** Management and organizational leadership, Multi-interdisciinary studies.

**Most popular majors.** Biology 6%, business/marketing 21%, education 14%, health sciences 11%, visual/performing arts 18%.

**Computing on campus.** 198 workstations in dormitories, library, computer center, student center. Dormitories wired for high-speed internet access and linked to campus network. Commuter students can connect to campus network. Online course registration, online library, helpline, student web hosting, wireless network available.

**Student life. Freshman orientation:** Mandatory, $100 fee. Held 5 days before beginning of classes. **Housing:** Guaranteed on-campus for freshmen. Coed dorms, single-sex dorms, special housing for disabled, apartments, fraternity/sorority housing, wellness housing available. $150 fully refundable deposit, deadline 5/1. Learning communities available. **Activities:** Bands,

choral groups, dance, drama, film society, international student organizations, literary magazine, music ensembles, Model UN, musical theater, opera, radio station, student government, student newspaper, symphony orchestra, Black student union, Latin American student organization, Amnesty International, Multicultural Voices of Praise, Multicultural Affairs Roundtable, Young Republicans, Inter-Varsity Christian Fellowship, Newman Catholic Community, pagan student association, Fellowship of Christian Athletes.

**Athletics. NCAA. Intercollegiate:** Baseball M, basketball, cheerleading, cross-country, football (tackle) M, golf, soccer, softball W, swimming, tennis W, track and field, volleyball W. **Intramural:** Basketball, bowling, football (non-tackle), soccer, softball, table tennis, volleyball. **Team name:** Big Blue.

**Student services.** Adult student services, alcohol/substance abuse counseling, career counseling, services for economically disadvantaged, student employment services, financial aid counseling, health services, minority student services, personal counseling, placement for graduates, women's services. **Physically disabled:** Services for visually, speech impaired.

**Contact.** E-mail: admis@millikin.edu
Phone: (217) 424-6210 Toll-free number: (800) 373-7733
Fax: (217) 425-4669
Stacey Hubbard, Dean of Admission and Financial Aid, Millikin University, 1184 West Main Street, Decatur, IL 62522-2084

| **Monmouth College** | |
|---|---|
| **Monmouth, Illinois** | **CB member** |
| **www.monm.edu** | **CB code: 1484** |

- Private 4-year liberal arts college affiliated with Presbyterian Church (USA)
- Residential campus in large town
- 1,362 degree-seeking undergraduates: 52% women, 6% African American, 1% Asian American, 5% Hispanic American, 1% Native American, 1% international
- 70% of applicants admitted
- SAT or ACT (ACT writing optional) required
- 64% graduate within 6 years; 25% enter graduate study

**General.** Founded in 1853. Regionally accredited. **Degrees:** 245 bachelor's awarded. **ROTC:** Army. **Location:** 180 miles from Chicago, 60 miles from Peoria. **Calendar:** Semester. **Full-time faculty:** 83 total; 83% have terminal degrees, 8% minority, 42% women. **Part-time faculty:** 43 total; 12% have terminal degrees, 7% minority, 54% women. **Class size:** 45% < 20, 53% 20-39, 2% 40-49, less than 1% 50-99. **Special facilities:** Ecological field station, biology field station, nature preserve, art and antiquities collection, collection of letters by U.S. First Ladies, Federal government documents repository.

**Freshman class profile.** 2,070 applied, 1,450 admitted, 440 enrolled.

| Mid 50% test scores | | Rank in top quarter: | 32% |
|---|---|---|---|
| SAT critical reading: | 510-590 | Rank in top tenth: | 9% |
| SAT math: | 430-570 | End year in good standing: | 86% |
| SAT writing: | 440-520 | Return as sophomores: | 77% |
| ACT composite: | 20-25 | Out-of-state: | 6% |
| GPA 3.75 or higher: | 17% | Live on campus: | 97% |
| GPA 3.50-3.74: | 13% | International: | 1% |
| GPA 3.0-3.49: | 30% | Fraternities: | 21% |
| GPA 2.0-2.99: | 40% | Sororities: | 20% |

**Basis for selection.** Record of academic achievement is most important, followed by the recommendations of counselor and teachers, test scores, and interview. An essay and an Interview are highly recommended.

**High school preparation.** College-preparatory program required. 14 units required; 22 recommended. Required and recommended units include English 4, mathematics 3-4, social studies 2-3, history 1-2, science 2-3 (laboratory 1-2) and foreign language 2-3.

**2010-2011 Annual costs.** Tuition/fees: $26,900. Room/board: $7,300. Books/supplies: $650. Personal expenses: $400.

**2009-2010 Financial aid. Need-based:** 373 full-time freshmen applied for aid; 337 were judged to have need; 337 of these received aid. Average need met was 87%. Average scholarship/grant was $18,189; average loan $3,226. 79% of total undergraduate aid awarded as scholarships/grants, 21% as loans/jobs. **Non-need-based:** Awarded to 369 full-time undergraduates, including 94 freshmen. Scholarships awarded for academics, art, leadership, music/drama, ROTC.

**Application procedures. Admission:** No deadline. No application fee. Admission notification on a rolling basis beginning on or about 9/15. Must reply by May 1 or within 2 week(s) if notified thereafter. **Financial aid:** Priority date 3/1; no closing date. FAFSA required. Applicants notified on a rolling basis starting 3/1; must reply by 8/15 or within 2 week(s) of notification.

**Academics. Special study options:** Combined bachelor's/graduate degree, double major, ESL, exchange student, honors, independent study, internships, semester at sea, student-designed major, study abroad, teacher certification program, urban semester, Washington semester. Off-campus (domestic and study abroad) programs available in cooperation with Associated Colleges of the Midwest and other study-abroad organizations, plus institutional off-campus programs and student-exchange agreements with universities in Ireland, France, Greece, Mexico, Morocco, Senegal, Scotland and Sweden. Monmouth College belongs to the International Student Exchange Program (ISEP). **Credit/placement by examination:** AP, CLEP, IB, SAT, ACT, institutional tests. 5 credit hours maximum toward bachelor's degree. **Support services:** Learning center, study skills assistance, tutoring, writing center.

**Majors. Biology:** General, biochemistry. **Business:** Accounting, business admin, international, managerial economics. **Communications:** General, public relations. **Computer sciences:** Computer science. **Conservation:** Environmental science. **Education:** General, elementary, physical. **Foreign languages:** Ancient Greek, classics, French, Latin, Spanish. **History:** General. **Interdisciplinary:** Biopsychology, global studies, math/computer science. **Liberal arts:** Arts/sciences. **Math:** General. **Philosophy/religion:** Philosophy, religion. **Physical sciences:** Chemistry, physics. **Psychology:** General. **Social sciences:** Anthropology, economics, international relations, political science, sociology. **Visual/performing arts:** Art, dramatic, studio arts.

**Most popular majors.** Business/marketing 26%, communications/journalism 7%, education 17%, English 9%, psychology 6%, social sciences 9%, visual/performing arts 7%.

**Computing on campus.** 140 workstations in dormitories, library, computer center, student center. Dormitories wired for high-speed internet access and linked to campus network. Commuter students can connect to campus network. Online course registration, online library, helpline, student web hosting, wireless network available.

**Student life. Freshman orientation:** Mandatory, $140 fee. Preregistration for classes offered. Before the start of the fall semester, includes activities, workshops, academic advising (group and individual) and matriculation ceremony. **Housing:** Guaranteed on-campus for all undergraduates. Coed dorms, single-sex dorms, special housing for disabled, apartments, cooperative housing, fraternity/sorority housing, wellness housing available. $150 partly refundable deposit. **Activities:** Bands, campus ministries, choral groups, dance, drama, film society, international student organizations, literary magazine, music ensembles, musical theater, radio station, student government, student newspaper, symphony orchestra, TV station, Coalition for Ethnic Awareness,interdenominational religious groups, Students Organized for Service, PRISM: People Respecting Individual Sexualities at Monmouth, Students for Environmental Awareness, Liberal Legion, Conservative Club, Art Alliance.

**Athletics.** NCAA. **Intercollegiate:** Baseball M, basketball, cross-country, diving, football (tackle) M, golf, soccer, softball W, swimming, tennis, track and field, volleyball W. **Intramural:** Badminton, basketball, cheerleading, football (non-tackle), golf, soccer, softball, tennis, volleyball. **Team name:** Fighting Scots.

**Student services.** Alcohol/substance abuse counseling, chaplain/spiritual director, career counseling, services for economically disadvantaged, student employment services, financial aid counseling, health services, minority student services, personal counseling, placement for graduates, veterans' counselor, women's services.

**Contact.** E-mail: admit@monm.edu
Phone: (309) 457-2131 Toll-free number: (800) 747-2687
Fax: (309) 457-2141
Christine Johnston, Dean of Admission, Monmouth College, 700 East Broadway, Monmouth, IL 61462-1998

## Moody Bible Institute
### Chicago, Illinois
### www.moody.edu
**CB code: 1486**

- Private 4-year Bible college affiliated with interdenominational tradition
- Residential campus in very large city
- 2,300 degree-seeking undergraduates
- 442 graduate students
- 75% of applicants admitted

- SAT or ACT with writing, application essay required
- 78% graduate within 6 years; 36% enter graduate study

**General.** Founded in 1886. Regionally accredited; also accredited by ABHE. **Degrees:** 380 bachelor's, 10 associate awarded; master's offered. **Location:** Downtown. **Calendar:** Semester, limited summer session. **Full-time faculty:** 85 total; 59% have terminal degrees, 11% minority, 24% women. **Part-time faculty:** 98 total; 26% have terminal degrees, 4% minority, 9% women. **Class size:** 33% < 20, 55% 20-39, 4% 40-49, 4% 50-99, 4% >100.

**Freshman class profile.** 1,056 applied, 794 admitted, 355 enrolled.

| Mid 50% test scores | | | |
|---|---|---|---|
| SAT critical reading: | 510-620 | End year in good standing: | 68% |
| SAT math: | 490-620 | Return as sophomores: | 73% |
| ACT composite: | 21-28 | Out-of-state: | 81% |
| | | Live on campus: | 98% |

**Basis for selection.** Rank in top half of graduating class and/or high school GPA above 2.0. Applicants must have been Christians for at least 1 year. Membership in Evangelical Protestant Church and recommendation from church leadership required. Interview recommended. Audition required of music majors. **Homeschooled:** ACT plus GED or SAT required.

**High school preparation.** College-preparatory program recommended. 12 units recommended.

**2009-2010 Annual costs.** Undergraduate students in the BA and BMus programs on main campus are not charged tuition. Courses through distance learning programs (ABS, BSBS) and in BSMAT (Bachelor of Science in Missionary Aviation) program cost $230 per credit hour. Required fees of $1,880 and room/board of $8,250 per year for full-time students. Books/supplies: $600. Personal expenses: $500.

**2009-2010 Financial aid.** All financial aid based on need. Average scholarship/grant was $2,305. 6% of total undergraduate aid awarded as scholarships/grants, 94% as loans/jobs. **Additional information:** Aid available to upperclassmen is based on private and not federal/state sources.

**Application procedures. Admission:** Priority date 12/1; deadline 3/1 (postmark date). $50 fee, may be waived for applicants with need. Admission notification 4/1. Must reply by May 1 or within 6 week(s) if notified thereafter. **Financial aid:** No deadline. Institutional form required. Applicants notified on a rolling basis; must reply by 7/1.

**Academics. Special study options:** Distance learning, double major, dual enrollment of high school students, external degree, independent study, internships, student-designed major, study abroad. International Studies Program partnerships with Adelaide College of Ministries, Bible College of Queensland, Bible College of Victoria, Sydney Bible and Missionary College (Australia); All Nations College, London School of Theology, Moorlands College (England); Institut Biblique de Nogent (France); Ambex (Germany); Greek Bible Institute (Greece); IBEX, Israel College of the Bible (Israel); Jerusalem Evangelical Theological Seminary (Jordan); Laidlaw College, Mueller Colleg of Ministries, Pathways College of Bible and Missions (New Zealand); International Christian College (Spain); Spanish Bible Institute (Spain); Odessa Theological Seminary (Ukraine). **Credit/placement by examination:** AP, CLEP, IB, institutional tests. 9 credit hours maximum toward associate degree, 12 toward bachelor's. **Support services:** Learning center, pre-admission summer program, reduced course load, study skills assistance, tutoring.

**Majors. Communications:** General. **Education:** General, ESL. **Foreign languages:** Ancient Greek, Hebrew, linguistics. **Mechanic/repair:** Aircraft. **Philosophy/religion:** Judaic. **Theology:** Bible, missionary, pastoral counseling, religious ed, sacred music, theology. **Visual/performing arts:** Music performance, music theory/composition, piano/organ, voice/opera.

**Most popular majors.** Communications/journalism 7%, education 15%, theological studies 74%.

**Computing on campus.** 50 workstations in dormitories, library, computer center. Dormitories wired for high-speed internet access and linked to campus network. Commuter students can connect to campus network. Online course registration, helpline, repair service, wireless network available.

**Student life. Freshman orientation:** Mandatory. Preregistration for classes offered. Orientation is held for main and regional campus students at the beginning of the fall term. **Policies:** Students are required to suscribe to and follow community life standards published in the student handbook. Religious observance required. **Housing:** Guaranteed on-campus for all undergraduates. Single-sex dorms, apartments available. $350 nonrefundable deposit, deadline 5/1. **Activities:** Concert band, campus ministries, choral groups, drama, international student organizations, music ensembles, radio station, student government, student newspaper, symphony orchestra, Student Missionary Fellowship, Gospel teams, Embrace, International Student Fellowship, Big Brother/Big Sister Program, married students fellowship, residence activities council, Hispanic Student Fellowship, student wives fellowship.

**Athletics.** NCCAA. **Intercollegiate:** Basketball, soccer M, volleyball. **Intramural:** Badminton, basketball, cross-country, football (non-tackle), racquetball, soccer, swimming, table tennis, tennis, volleyball, water polo. **Team name:** Archers.

**Student services.** Career counseling, student employment services, health services, minority student services, on-campus daycare, personal counseling, placement for graduates, veterans' counselor. **Physically disabled:** Services for visually impaired. **Learning disabled:** Comprehensive services available.

**Contact.** E-mail: admissions@moody.edu
Phone: (312) 329-4400 Toll-free number: (800) 967-4624
Fax: (312) 329-8987
Charles Dresser, Dean of Admissions, Moody Bible Institute, 820 North La Salle Boulevard, Chicago, IL 60610

## National University of Health Sciences
Lombard, Illinois
www.nuhs.edu                                   CB code: 1567

- Private 4-year university and health science college
- Commuter campus in large town
- 74 degree-seeking undergraduates
- 670 graduate students

**General.** Regionally accredited. **Degrees:** 35 bachelor's awarded; master's, professional offered. **Location:** 20 miles from Chicago. **Calendar:** Trimester, extensive summer session. **Full-time faculty:** 39 total; 26% women. **Part-time faculty:** 88 total; 52% women. **Special facilities:** Learning resource center, medical library, onsite clinic.

**Basis for selection.** Associate degree and certificate programs require 2.0 GPA or GED; bachelor's completion program in biomedical science requires minimum of 60 semester hours of prerequisite courses. Must be 18 years of age and of good moral character. Applicants to BS degree completion program may be considered for conditional acceptance as a non-degree student for one semester to determine academic eligibility.

**2009-2010 Annual costs.** $18,352 represents average tuition cost for academic year, plus "room only" charge of $4,660 to $7,400.

**2008-2009 Financial aid. Need-based:** 26% of total undergraduate aid awarded as scholarships/grants, 74% as loans/jobs. **Additional information:** Massage therapy certificate program is eligible for Title IV financial aid. Program is half-time and qualifies for half-time and less-than-half-time Pell grants, federal work-study and loan programs.

**Application procedures. Admission:** Closing date 8/1. $55 fee. **Financial aid:** No deadline.

**Academics.** College of Professional Studies offers doctor of chiropractic, with a doctor of naturopathy, and master's degrees in acupuncture and Oriental Medicine. Primary undergraduate enrollment is in certificate programs in massage therapy and chiropractic assistance. Accelerated prerequisite program available for students needing to complete science entrance requirements. Bachelor of science completion program available. **Special study options:** Internships. **Credit/placement by examination:** CLEP. **Support services:** Learning center, tutoring.

**Majors. Biology:** Biomedical sciences.

**Computing on campus.** 75 workstations in library, computer center. Online course registration, helpline, student web hosting, wireless network available.

**Student life. Freshman orientation:** Mandatory. Preregistration for classes offered. **Policies:** Must be 21 to live on campus. **Housing:** Coed dorms available. Pets allowed in dorm rooms. **Activities:** Student government, student newspaper, student chiropractic organizations, professional sororities and fraternities, christian chiropractic association.

**Athletics. Intramural:** Basketball, golf, soccer, softball, tennis, volleyball.

**Student services.** Financial aid counseling, health services.

**Contact.** E-mail: admissions@nuhs.edu
Phone: (630) 889-6566 Toll-free number: (800) 826-6285
Fax: (630) 889-6554
Victoria Sweeney, Director of Communications and Enrollment Services, National University of Health Sciences, 200 East Roosevelt Road, Lombard, IL 60148-4583

## National-Louis University
Chicago, Illinois                              CB member
www.nl.edu                                     CB code: 1551

- Private 4-year university and teachers college
- Commuter campus in small city
- 1,581 degree-seeking undergraduates: 35% African American, 2% Asian American, 14% Hispanic American
- 4,913 graduate students
- 33% of applicants admitted
- SAT or ACT required

**General.** Founded in 1886. Regionally accredited. Additional in-state locations in Skokie, Wheeling, Lisle and Elgin. Field programs available on and off campus. Out-of-state campuses located in Milwaukee/Beloit, McLean, Washington DC, and Tampa. **Degrees:** 645 bachelor's awarded; master's, doctoral offered. **Location:** 10 miles from Chicago. **Calendar:** Quarter, limited summer session. **Full-time faculty:** 254 total; 70% have terminal degrees. **Part-time faculty:** 448 total. **Special facilities:** Elementary demonstration school for practice teaching and observation.

**Freshman class profile.** 27 applied, 9 admitted, 1 enrolled.

| Mid 50% test scores | ACT composite: | 19-22 |
|---|---|---|

**Basis for selection.** Rank in top half of high school class, score 19 ACT, 750 SAT (exclusive of Writing) and 2 letters of recommendation from counselors or teachers. Interview and essay recommended.

**High school preparation.** Recommended units include English 4, mathematics 3, social studies 3, science 2 (laboratory 1) and foreign language 2. 1 unit U.S. government or U.S. history recommended.

**2009-2010 Annual costs.** Tuition/fees: $18,435.

**2008-2009 Financial aid. Non-need-based:** Scholarships awarded for academics.

**Application procedures. Admission:** No deadline. $40 fee, may be waived for applicants with need. Admission notification on a rolling basis. **Financial aid:** Priority date 4/15; no closing date. FAFSA, institutional form required. Applicants notified on a rolling basis starting 5/1; must reply within 2 week(s) of notification.

**Academics.** Degree-completion programs available in allied health leadership, management, and applied behavioral science. Field classes offered evenings/weekends. **Special study options:** Accelerated study, combined bachelor's/graduate degree, distance learning, double major, dual enrollment of high school students, ESL, honors, independent study, internships, liberal arts/career combination, teacher certification program. **Credit/placement by examination:** AP, CLEP. 132 credit hours maximum toward bachelor's degree. **Support services:** Learning center, pre-admission summer program, reduced course load, remedial instruction, study skills assistance, tutoring, writing center.

**Majors. Biology:** General. **Business:** Accounting, business admin. **Computer sciences:** Information systems. **Education:** Early childhood, elementary. **Health:** Clinical lab science, health care admin, medical radiologic technology/radiation therapy, respiratory therapy technology, substance abuse counseling. **Interdisciplinary:** Behavioral sciences, biological/physical sciences. **Liberal arts:** Arts/sciences. **Math:** General, applied. **Psychology:** General. **Public administration:** Human services. **Social sciences:** General, anthropology, economics. **Visual/performing arts:** Art, dramatic.

**Computing on campus.** 500 workstations in library, computer center. Commuter students can connect to campus network. Online course registration, online library, helpline, repair service available.

**Student life. Freshman orientation:** Available. **Housing:** Coed dorms available. $50 deposit, deadline 7/30. **Activities:** Drama, musical theater, student government, student newspaper, Chinese club, Polish club, educational club, social science club, school psychology club, drama club, educational honorary society.

**Student services.** Adult student services, career counseling, student employment services, health services, personal counseling, placement for graduates. **Physically disabled:** Services for visually, speech, hearing impaired.

**Contact.** E-mail: admissions@nl.edu
Phone: (847) 947-5718 Toll-free number: (800) 443-5522 ext. 5718
Fax: (847) 465-5730
Madeleine Waxman, Associate Registrar, National-Louis University, 122 South Michigan Avenue, Chicago, IL 60603

## North Central College
**Naperville, Illinois**
www.northcentralcollege.edu

CB member
CB code: 1555

- Private 4-year liberal arts college affiliated with United Methodist Church
- Residential campus in small city
- 2,423 degree-seeking undergraduates: 5% part-time, 57% women, 4% African American, 3% Asian American, 6% Hispanic American, 1% international
- 249 degree-seeking graduate students
- 67% of applicants admitted
- SAT or ACT (ACT writing optional) required
- 65% graduate within 6 years

**General.** Founded in 1861. Regionally accredited. **Degrees:** 505 bachelor's awarded; master's offered. **ROTC:** Army, Air Force. **Location:** 25 miles from Chicago. **Calendar:** Quarter, limited summer session. **Full-time faculty:** 118 total; 84% have terminal degrees, 13% minority, 46% women. **Part-time faculty:** 134 total; 39% have terminal degrees, 8% minority, 53% women. **Class size:** 39% < 20, 59% 20-39, 2% 40-49, less than 1% 50-99. **Special facilities:** Fermi accelerator laboratory, Argonne laboratory, arboretum.

**Freshman class profile.** 2,762 applied, 1,854 admitted, 543 enrolled.

| Mid 50% test scores | | | |
|---|---|---|---|
| ACT composite: | 22-27 | GPA 2.0-2.99: | 16% |
| GPA 3.75 or higher: | 32% | Return as sophomores: | 77% |
| GPA 3.50-3.74: | 19% | Out-of-state: | 12% |
| GPA 3.0-3.49: | 33% | Live on campus: | 83% |
| | | International: | 1% |

**Basis for selection.** Academic record, SAT or ACT scores, and personal character all considered important. Interview and essay recommended for marginal students. **Homeschooled:** Interview required. Review of the student's portfolio and curriculum, writing sample, interview with the Director of Freshman Admission, interview with a faculty member may be required. **Learning Disabled:** Students who self-identify are referred to the academic support center.

**High school preparation.** College-preparatory program required. 16 units required; 19 recommended. Required and recommended units include English 4, mathematics 3, social studies 2, history 1, science 3 (laboratory 1-3), foreign language 3 and academic electives 3.

**2010-2011 Annual costs.** Tuition/fees: $28,224. Room/board: $8,463. Books/supplies: $1,200. Personal expenses: $1,182.

**2009-2010 Financial aid.** **Need-based:** 502 full-time freshmen applied for aid; 440 were judged to have need; 439 of these received aid. Average need met was 82%. Average scholarship/grant was $17,228; average loan $3,530. 69% of total undergraduate aid awarded as scholarships/grants, 31% as loans/jobs. **Non-need-based:** Awarded to 700 full-time undergraduates, including 187 freshmen. Scholarships awarded for academics, art, leadership, minority status, music/drama, religious affiliation, ROTC, state residency.

**Application procedures.** **Admission:** Priority date 4/15; no deadline. $25 fee, may be waived for applicants with need, free for online applicants. Admission notification on a rolling basis beginning on or about 10/1. Must reply by May 1 or within 4 week(s) if notified thereafter. **Financial aid:** No deadline. FAFSA, institutional form required. Applicants notified on a rolling basis starting 3/1; must reply within 4 week(s) of notification.

**Academics.** **Special study options:** Accelerated study, combined bachelor's/graduate degree, cross-registration, double major, dual enrollment of high school students, ESL, exchange student, honors, independent study, internships, New York semester, student-designed major, study abroad, teacher certification program, United Nations semester, urban semester, Washington semester. Independent study project grants; 3-2 engineering program with Universities of Illiinois at Urbana-Champaign and Minnesota; 5-year bachelor's/master's degree programs. **Credit/placement by examination:** AP, CLEP, IB, SAT, ACT, institutional tests. 28 credit hours maximum toward bachelor's degree. Students must be tested or otherwise assessed in order for experiential credit to be awarded. **Support services:** Pre-admission summer program, reduced course load, remedial instruction, study skills assistance, tutoring, writing center.

**Majors.** **Area/ethnic studies:** East Asian. **Biology:** General, biochemistry. **Business:** Accounting, actuarial science, business admin, finance, human resources, international, management information systems, marketing, small business admin. **Communications:** General, journalism, organizational, radio/

tv. **Communications technology:** Animation/special effects. **Computer sciences:** General. **Education:** General, art, elementary, music, physical. **Foreign languages:** Classics, French, German, Japanese, Spanish. **Health:** Athletic training, medical radiologic technology/radiation therapy, nuclear medical technology. **History:** General. **Interdisciplinary:** Global studies. **Liberal arts:** Arts/sciences. **Math:** General, applied. **Parks/recreation:** Exercise sciences, health/fitness, sports admin. **Philosophy/religion:** Philosophy, religion. **Physical sciences:** Chemistry, physics. **Psychology:** General. **Social sciences:** General, anthropology, economics, political science, sociology. **Visual/performing arts:** Art, art history/conservation, dramatic, jazz, musical theater. **Other:** Interactive media: graphic arts.

**Most popular majors.** Business/marketing 29%, communications/journalism 7%, education 13%, foreign language 6%, psychology 6%, social sciences 14%.

**Computing on campus.** 310 workstations in dormitories, library, computer center, student center. Dormitories wired for high-speed internet access and linked to campus network. Commuter students can connect to campus network. Online library, helpline, repair service, student web hosting, wireless network available.

**Student life.** **Freshman orientation:** Available, $125 fee. Preregistration for classes offered. Three orientations held in June, one in August. Session also held the week before beginning of term. **Housing:** Guaranteed on-campus for all undergraduates. Coed dorms, single-sex dorms, special housing for disabled, wellness housing available. $100 nonrefundable deposit, deadline 5/1. **Activities:** Bands, campus ministries, choral groups, dance, drama, international student organizations, literary magazine, music ensembles, Model UN, musical theater, opera, radio station, student government, student newspaper, United Methodist Student Organization, Black student organization, Fellowship of Christian Athletes, Raza Unida, Cardinals in Action, Green Scene, commuter student organization, Students in Free Enterprise.

**Athletics.** NCAA. **Intercollegiate:** Baseball M, basketball, cross-country, football (tackle) M, golf, lacrosse W, soccer, softball W, swimming, tennis, track and field, volleyball W, wrestling M. **Intramural:** Basketball, bowling, cheerleading, football (tackle) M, golf, softball, table tennis, volleyball. **Team name:** Cardinals.

**Student services.** Adult student services, alcohol/substance abuse counseling, career counseling, student employment services, financial aid counseling, health services, minority student services, personal counseling, placement for graduates. **Physically disabled:** Services for visually, hearing impaired.

**Contact.** E-mail: admissions@noctrl.edu
Phone: (630) 637-5800 Toll-free number: (800) 411-1861
Fax: (630) 637-5819
Martin Sauer, Dean of Admission and Financial Aid, North Central College, PO Box 3063, Naperville, IL 60566-7063

## North Park University
**Chicago, Illinois**
www.northpark.edu

CB member
CB code: 1556

- Private 4-year university and liberal arts college affiliated with Evangelical Covenant Church
- Residential campus in very large city
- 2,131 degree-seeking undergraduates: 18% part-time, 61% women, 8% African American, 6% Asian American, 10% Hispanic American, 3% international
- 1,010 degree-seeking graduate students
- 71% of applicants admitted
- SAT or ACT (ACT writing recommended), application essay required
- 48% graduate within 6 years

**General.** Founded in 1891. Regionally accredited. **Degrees:** 481 bachelor's awarded; master's, professional offered. **ROTC:** Army, Air Force. **Location:** 8 miles from downtown. **Calendar:** Semester, limited summer session. **Full-time faculty:** 120 total; 96% have terminal degrees, 17% minority, 51% women. **Part-time faculty:** 165 total; 60% have terminal degrees, 16% minority, 50% women. **Class size:** 58% < 20, 35% 20-39, 4% 40-49, 2% 50-99, less than 1% >100.

**Freshman class profile.** 1,473 applied, 1,039 admitted, 363 enrolled.

| Mid 50% test scores | | | |
|---|---|---|---|
| SAT critical reading: | 490-600 | Rank in top quarter: | 34% |
| SAT math: | 460-550 | Rank in top tenth: | 10% |
| ACT composite: | 19-25 | End year in good standing: | 88% |
| GPA 3.75 or higher: | 13% | Return as sophomores: | 71% |
| GPA 3.50-3.74: | 15% | Out-of-state: | 45% |
| GPA 3.0-3.49: | 29% | Live on campus: | 77% |
| GPA 2.0-2.99: | 42% | International: | 2% |

**Basis for selection.** Admission based on full review of student's record, and considers courses taken, GPA, class rank, test scores, recommendations, essay or writing sample, co-curricular involvements, and community service. Nursing has an early admission option available to high achieving students. An interview may be required for some applicants. All students who visit campus are interviewed by an admission counselor. **Home-schooled:** Transcript of courses and grades, letter of recommendation (nonparent) required.

**High school preparation.** College-preparatory program recommended. Recommended units include English 4, mathematics 3, social studies 1, history 1, science 3 and foreign language 2.

**2010-2011 Annual costs.** Tuition/fees (projected): $19,900. Room/board: $8,330. Books/supplies: $1,000. Personal expenses: $1,450.

**2008-2009 Financial aid. Need-based:** 348 full-time freshmen applied for aid; 288 were judged to have need; 288 of these received aid. Average need met was 69%. Average scholarship/grant was $5,466; average loan $3,875. 57% of total undergraduate aid awarded as scholarships/grants, 43% as loans/jobs. **Non-need-based:** Scholarships awarded for academics, art, music/drama, religious affiliation.

**Application procedures. Admission:** Priority date 4/1; deadline 7/1 (receipt date). $40 fee, may be waived for applicants with need. Admission notification on a rolling basis beginning on or about 9/15. Must reply by May 1 or within 4 week(s) if notified thereafter. **Financial aid:** Priority date 5/1, closing date 8/1. FAFSA required. Applicants notified on a rolling basis starting 10/1; must reply by 5/1 or within 4 week(s) of notification.

**Academics. Special study options:** Accelerated study, combined bachelor's/graduate degree, distance learning, double major, ESL, exchange student, honors, independent study, internships, liberal arts/career combination, student-designed major, study abroad, teacher certification program, Washington semester. **Credit/placement by examination:** AP, CLEP, IB, SAT, ACT, institutional tests. **Support services:** Learning center, pre-admission summer program, reduced course load, remedial instruction, study skills assistance, tutoring, writing center.

**Majors. Biology:** General. **Business:** General, business admin, nonprofit/public, organizational behavior. **Communications:** General, advertising. **Computer sciences:** General. **Education:** Early childhood, elementary, middle, multi-level teacher. **Family/consumer sciences:** Family studies. **Foreign languages:** French, Scandinavian, Spanish. **Health:** Clinical lab science, nursing (RN). **History:** General. **Math:** General. **Philosophy/religion:** Philosophy. **Physical sciences:** Chemistry, physics. **Protective services:** Law enforcement admin. **Psychology:** General. **Public administration:** Human services. **Social sciences:** Political science, sociology. **Theology:** Bible, theology, youth ministry. **Visual/performing arts:** Art, commercial/advertising art, music performance.

**Most popular majors.** Biology 8%, business/marketing 18%, education 9%, family/consumer sciences 6%, health sciences 14%, psychology 6%, theological studies 6%.

**Computing on campus.** 100 workstations in dormitories, library, computer center, student center. Dormitories wired for high-speed internet access and linked to campus network. Commuter students can connect to campus network. Online course registration, online library, helpline, wireless network available.

**Student life. Freshman orientation:** Mandatory. Preregistration for classes offered. Begins 5 days before start of classes. **Policies:** Alcohol-free and smoke-free campus. Visiting hours in residence halls for persons of opposite sex. **Housing:** Guaranteed on-campus for all undergraduates. Single-sex dorms, apartments available. $250 nonrefundable deposit, deadline 5/1. **Activities:** Bands, campus ministries, choral groups, drama, literary magazine, music ensembles, musical theater, opera, student government, student newspaper, symphony orchestra, gospel teams, Black student association, Latino student organization, Korean student association, Catholic association, Middle Eastern student association, Scandinavian student association.

**Athletics.** NCAA. **Intercollegiate:** Baseball M, basketball, cross-country, football (tackle) M, golf, rowing (crew) W, soccer, softball W, track and field, volleyball W. **Intramural:** Basketball, cheerleading W, football (non-tackle), soccer, tennis, volleyball. **Team name:** Vikings.

**Student services.** Adult student services, alcohol/substance abuse counseling, chaplain/spiritual director, career counseling, services for economically disadvantaged, student employment services, financial aid counseling, health services, minority student services, personal counseling, placement for graduates.

**Contact.** E-mail: admission@northpark.edu
Phone: (773) 244-5500 Toll-free number: (800) 888-6728
Fax: (773) 244-5243
Shari Nordstrom, Director, Undergraduate Admission, North Park University, 3225 West Foster Avenue Box 19, Chicago, IL 60625-4895

## Northeastern Illinois University

| Chicago, Illinois | CB member |
|---|---|
| www.neiu.edu | CB code: 1090 |

- Public 4-year university
- Commuter campus in very large city
- 9,025 degree-seeking undergraduates: 42% part-time, 58% women, 10% African American, 10% Asian American, 30% Hispanic American, 4% international
- 1,936 degree-seeking graduate students
- 74% of applicants admitted
- SAT or ACT (ACT writing optional) required

**General.** Founded in 1961. Regionally accredited. Two extension centers serve Hispanic and African-American communities. **Degrees:** 1,615 bachelor's awarded; master's offered. **ROTC:** Army, Air Force. **Calendar:** Semester, limited summer session. **Full-time faculty:** 404 total; 73% have terminal degrees, 27% minority, 49% women. **Part-time faculty:** 295 total; 23% have terminal degrees, 27% minority, 51% women. **Class size:** 39% < 20, 54% 20-39, 5% 40-49, 2% 50-99, less than 1% >100.

**Freshman class profile.** 4,035 applied, 2,997 admitted, 1,070 enrolled.

| Mid 50% test scores | | | |
|---|---|---|---|
| | | GPA 3.0-3.49: | 20% |
| ACT composite: | 16-21 | GPA 2.0-2.99: | 49% |
| GPA 3.75 or higher: | 13% | Return as sophomores: | 67% |
| GPA 3.50-3.74: | 7% | International: | 4% |

**Basis for selection.** Rank in top half of graduating class or 19 ACT/equivalent SAT required. Audition recommended for dance and music majors. Portfolio recommended for art majors.

**High school preparation.** College-preparatory program required. 15 units required. Required units include English 4, mathematics 3, social studies 3 and science 3. 2 additional units in fine arts, music, art, foreign languages, or vocational education. (Only 1 vocational education course accepted.).

**2009-2010 Annual costs.** Tuition/fees: $8,590; $15,940 out-of-state.

**2009-2010 Financial aid. Non-need-based:** Scholarships awarded for academics, art, leadership, music/drama.

**Application procedures. Admission:** Closing date 7/1 (receipt date). $25 fee, may be waived for applicants with need. Admission notification on a rolling basis beginning on or about 9/1. **Financial aid:** Priority date 2/28; no closing date. FAFSA, institutional form required. Applicants notified on a rolling basis starting 4/1; must reply within 3 week(s) of notification.

**Academics. Special study options:** Cooperative education, distance learning, double major, dual enrollment of high school students, exchange student, honors, independent study, student-designed major, study abroad, teacher certification program. **Credit/placement by examination:** AP, CLEP, IB, ACT, institutional tests. 30 credit hours maximum toward bachelor's degree. **Support services:** Learning center, pre-admission summer program, remedial instruction, study skills assistance, tutoring, writing center.

**Majors. Area/ethnic studies:** Women's. **Biology:** General. **Business:** General, accounting, business admin, finance, marketing. **Computer sciences:** Computer science. **Conservation:** Environmental studies. **Education:** Bilingual, early childhood, elementary, physical, special. **Foreign languages:** French, linguistics, Spanish. **Health:** Community health services. **History:** General. **Liberal arts:** Arts/sciences. **Math:** General. **Philosophy/religion:** Philosophy. **Physical sciences:** Chemistry, geology, physics. **Protective services:** Criminal justice. **Psychology:** General. **Public administration:** Social work. **Social sciences:** General, anthropology, economics, geography, political science, sociology. **Visual/performing arts:** Art.

**Most popular majors.** Business/marketing 18%, education 15%, English 9%, liberal arts 12%, security/protective services 10%, social sciences 13%.

**Computing on campus.** 315 workstations in library, computer center, student center. Commuter students can connect to campus network. Online course registration, helpline, wireless network available.

**Student life. Freshman orientation:** Available. **Activities:** Bands, choral groups, dance, drama, literary magazine, music ensembles, musical theater, radio station, student government, student newspaper, Muslim student association, black heritage club, politics club, Chimexla student union, Indian student association, university bible association, program board, Union of Puerto Rican Students, Hillel, outdoor adventure club.

**Athletics. Intramural:** Badminton, basketball, cross-country, racquetball, soccer, softball, table tennis, tennis, volleyball, weight lifting. **Team name:** Eagles.

**Student services.** Adult student services, career counseling, student employment services, financial aid counseling, health services, minority student services, on-campus daycare, personal counseling, placement for graduates, veterans' counselor, women's services. **Physically disabled:** Services for visually, speech impaired.

**Contact.** E-mail: admerc@neiu.edu
Phone: (773) 442-4000 Fax: (773) 442-4020
Janice Harring-Hendon, Director of Admissions and Records, Northeastern Illinois University, 5500 North St. Louis Avenue, Chicago, IL 60625

---

## Northern Illinois University
### DeKalb, Illinois
**CB member**
### www.niu.edu
**CB code: 1559**

- Public 4-year university
- Residential campus in large town
- 18,229 degree-seeking undergraduates: 10% part-time, 51% women, 14% African American, 6% Asian American, 8% Hispanic American, 1% Native American, 1% international
- 4,993 degree-seeking graduate students
- 59% of applicants admitted
- SAT or ACT required
- 51% graduate within 6 years

**General.** Founded in 1895. Regionally accredited. Classes also held at Loredo Taft Field campus in Oregon. **Degrees:** 4,027 bachelor's awarded; master's, doctoral, professional offered. **ROTC:** Army. **Location:** 65 miles from Chicago. **Calendar:** Semester, extensive summer session. **Full-time faculty:** 922 total; 83% have terminal degrees, 13% minority, 45% women. **Part-time faculty:** 251 total; 38% have terminal degrees, 5% minority, 49% women. **Class size:** 41% < 20, 43% 20-39, 4% 40-49, 9% 50-99, 3% >100.

**Freshman class profile.** 17,787 applied, 10,409 admitted, 3,033 enrolled.

| Mid 50% test scores | | Return as sophomores: | 73% |
|---|---|---|---|
| ACT composite: | 19-24 | Out-of-state: | 3% |
| Rank in top quarter: | 33% | Live on campus: | 92% |
| Rank in top tenth: | 9% | International: | 1% |
| End year in good standing: | 90% | | |

**Basis for selection.** 19 ACT required of applicants who rank in top half of class, 23 ACT required of applicants in top two-thirds of class or with high school equivalency certificate. Interview required of CHANCE program applicants. Audition required of music majors. Portfolio recommended for art majors.

**High school preparation.** 15 units required. Required and recommended units include English 4, mathematics 2-4, social studies 2-3, history 1, science 2-4 (laboratory 1-2) and foreign language 1-2. One unit of art, film, music, theater, or foreign language required. Mathematics must include algebra and/or geometry. Social sciences must include US history or a combination of US history and government.

**2009-2010 Annual costs.** Tuition/fees: $9,394; $16,654 out-of-state. Room/board: $9,588. Books/supplies: $700. Personal expenses: $1,584.

**2008-2009 Financial aid. Non-need-based:** Scholarships awarded for academics, athletics, ROTC.

**Application procedures. Admission:** Priority date 3/1; deadline 8/1. No application fee. Admission notification on a rolling basis. **Financial aid:** Priority date 3/1; no closing date. FAFSA, institutional form required. Applicants notified on a rolling basis starting 4/15.

---

**Academics. Special study options:** Cooperative education, distance learning, double major, dual enrollment of high school students, honors, independent study, internships, student-designed major, study abroad, teacher certification program. **Credit/placement by examination:** AP, CLEP, institutional tests. Credit by examination not awarded for courses that are prerequisites for courses for which the student already has credit or is currently enrolled. **Support services:** Tutoring.

**Majors. Biology:** General. **Business:** General, accounting, finance, marketing, operations. **Communications:** General, journalism. **Computer sciences:** General, computer science. **Education:** General, art, elementary, family/consumer sciences, health, physical, special. **Engineering:** Electrical, industrial, mechanical. **Engineering technology:** Industrial. **Family/consumer sciences:** Clothing/textiles, family studies, food/nutrition. **Foreign languages:** French, German, Russian, Spanish. **Health:** Clinical lab science, communication disorders, nursing (RN), public health nursing. **History:** General. **Liberal arts:** Arts/sciences. **Math:** General, applied, computational, probability. **Philosophy/religion:** Philosophy. **Physical sciences:** Atmospheric science, chemistry, geology, physics. **Psychology:** General. **Social sciences:** Anthropology, economics, geography, political science, sociology. **Visual/performing arts:** Art, art history/conservation, dramatic, studio arts.

**Most popular majors.** Business/marketing 20%, communications/journalism 8%, education 11%, engineering/engineering technologies 6%, health sciences 10%, social sciences 12%.

**Computing on campus.** 550 workstations in dormitories, library, computer center, student center. Commuter students can connect to campus network. Helpline available.

**Student life. Freshman orientation:** Mandatory, $60 fee. **Housing:** Guaranteed on-campus for freshmen. Coed dorms, special housing for disabled, apartments, fraternity/sorority housing available. $150 deposit. Quiet and alcohol-free lifestyle floors, 21 and over student floors, honors floors available. **Activities:** Bands, campus ministries, choral groups, dance, drama, film society, opera, radio station, student government, student newspaper, symphony orchestra, TV station, numerous organizations available.

**Athletics. NCAA. Intercollegiate:** Baseball M, basketball, cross-country W, football (tackle) M, golf, gymnastics W, soccer, softball W, swimming, tennis, track and field W, volleyball W, wrestling M. **Intramural:** Badminton, baseball M, basketball, football (tackle) M, golf, ice hockey M, racquetball, sailing, soccer, softball, table tennis, tennis, volleyball, wrestling M. **Team name:** Huskies.

**Student services.** Career counseling, student employment services, health services, legal services, minority student services, on-campus daycare, personal counseling, placement for graduates, veterans' counselor, women's services. **Physically disabled:** Services for visually, speech, hearing impaired.

**Contact.** E-mail: admission-info@niu.edu
Phone: (815) 753-0446 Toll-free number: (800) 892-3050
Fax: (815) 753-8312
Brandon Lagana, Director of Admissions, Northern Illinois University, DeKalb, IL 60115-2854

---

## Northwestern University
### Evanston, Illinois
**CB member**
### www.northwestern.edu
**CB code: 1565**

- Private 4-year university
- Residential campus in small city
- 8,908 degree-seeking undergraduates: 5% part-time, 52% women, 6% African American, 19% Asian American, 7% Hispanic American, 6% international
- 8,595 degree-seeking graduate students
- 26% of applicants admitted
- SAT or ACT with writing, application essay required

**General.** Founded in 1851. Regionally accredited. **Degrees:** 2,037 bachelor's awarded; master's, doctoral, professional offered. **ROTC:** Army, Naval, Air Force. **Location:** 12 miles from downtown Chicago. **Calendar:** Quarter, limited summer session. **Full-time faculty:** 1,027 total. **Part-time faculty:** 126 total. **Class size:** 75% < 20, 14% 20-39, 3% 40-49, 4% 50-99, 3% >100. **Special facilities:** Nanotechnology center, fine-arts complex, dance center, observatory, engineering design center, tennis center.

**Freshman class profile.** 25,013 applied, 6,503 admitted, 2,081 enrolled.

| Mid 50% test scores | | Rank in top tenth: | 85% |
|---|---|---|---|
| SAT critical reading: | 670-750 | Out-of-state: | 80% |
| SAT math: | 690-780 | Live on campus: | 99% |
| SAT writing: | 670-750 | Fraternities: | 25% |
| ACT composite: | 30-33 | Sororities: | 34% |
| Rank in top quarter: | 96% | | |

**Basis for selection.** Academic record, essays, test scores, activity record, school recommendations important. SAT Subject Tests recommended. SAT Subject Tests in Math Level 2 and Chemistry required of all applicants for Honors Program in Medical Education. Applicants to Integrated Science Program must take SAT Subject Tests in Chemistry or Physics, Math Level 2, plus second science. Audition required for music majors. **Homeschooled:** 3 SAT Subject Tests required. Math Level 1 or 2 for students who plan to study sciences or engineering, Math Level 2 preferable, plus 2 other SAT Subject Tests of applicant's choice from different subject areas required.

**High school preparation.** College-preparatory program recommended. 16 units recommended. Recommended units include English 4, mathematics 3, social studies 2, science 2 (laboratory 2), foreign language 2 and academic electives 1. 4 units of mathematics recommended for engineering applicants. Applicants typically have 20 academic high school units.

**2009-2010 Annual costs.** Tuition/fees: $38,461. Room/board: $11,703. Books/supplies: $1,686. Personal expenses: $1,734.

**2009-2010 Financial aid. Non-need-based:** Scholarships awarded for academics, athletics, music/drama, ROTC.

**Application procedures. Admission:** Closing date 1/1 (postmark date). $65 fee, may be waived for applicants with need. Admission notification 4/15. Must reply by May 1 or within 2 week(s) if notified thereafter. **Financial aid:** Closing date 2/15. FAFSA, CSS PROFILE required. Applicants notified by 4/15; must reply by 5/1 or within 2 week(s) of notification.

**Academics.** One unit of credit awarded for each course; 45-48 units required for graduation. **Special study options:** Accelerated study, combined bachelor's/graduate degree, cooperative education, double major, honors, independent study, internships, liberal arts/career combination, student-designed major, study abroad, teacher certification program. 3-year integrated science program; 4-year mathematical methods in social sciences bachelor's program; honors programs in undergraduate research engineering, engineering and management, medical education; 7-year BA/MD program resulting in both an undergraduate degree and MD. **Credit/placement by examination:** AP, CLEP, IB, institutional tests. **Support services:** Study skills assistance, tutoring, writing center.

**Majors. Area/ethnic studies:** African-American, American, Asian, European, women's. **Biology:** General, ecology. **Business:** Organizational behavior. **Communications:** General, broadcast journalism, journalism, radio/tv. **Computer sciences:** General, computer science, information systems. **Conservation:** Environmental science, environmental studies. **Education:** General, learning disabled, mathematics, music, secondary. **Engineering:** General, biomedical, chemical, civil, computer, electrical, environmental, industrial, manufacturing, materials, materials science, mechanical, science. **Foreign languages:** Classics, comparative lit, East Asian, French, German, Italian, linguistics, Slavic, Spanish. **Health:** Communication disorders, premedicine. **History:** General. **Interdisciplinary:** Biological/physical sciences, neuroscience, science/society. **Legal studies:** General. **Liberal arts:** Arts/sciences. **Math:** General, applied, statistics. **Philosophy/religion:** Philosophy, religion. **Physical sciences:** Chemistry, geology, physics. **Psychology:** General, cognitive, community. **Public administration:** Community org/advocacy, policy analysis. **Social sciences:** Anthropology, economics, geography, international relations, political science, sociology, urban studies. **Visual/performing arts:** General, art, art history/conservation, dance, dramatic, jazz, music performance, music theory/composition, musicology, piano/organ, stringed instruments, theater history, voice/opera. **Other:** Area studies, Radio, television, and digital communication.

**Most popular majors.** Communications/journalism 20%, engineering/engineering technologies 15%, psychology 8%, social sciences 17%, visual/performing arts 10%.

**Computing on campus.** Dormitories wired for high-speed internet access and linked to campus network. Commuter students can connect to campus network. Online course registration, online library, helpline, repair service, student web hosting, wireless network available.

**Student life. Freshman orientation:** Mandatory. Held for 5 days prior to start of classes. **Housing:** Guaranteed on-campus for freshmen. Coed dorms, single-sex dorms, fraternity/sorority housing, wellness housing available. $200 nonrefundable deposit, deadline 5/25. Residential colleges available.

**Activities:** Bands, campus ministries, choral groups, dance, drama, film society, international student organizations, literary magazine, music ensembles, musical theater, opera, radio station, student government, student newspaper, symphony orchestra, TV station, over 300 organizations.

**Athletics. NCAA. Intercollegiate:** Baseball M, basketball, cheerleading, cross-country W, diving, fencing W, field hockey W, football (tackle) M, golf, lacrosse W, soccer, softball W, swimming, tennis, volleyball W, wrestling M. **Intramural:** Basketball, football (non-tackle), ice hockey, soccer, softball, volleyball. **Team name:** Wildcats.

**Student services.** Adult student services, alcohol/substance abuse counseling, chaplain/spiritual director, career counseling, student employment services, financial aid counseling, health services, minority student services, personal counseling, placement for graduates, women's services. **Physically disabled:** Services for visually, speech, hearing impaired.

**Contact.** E-mail: ug-admission@northwestern.edu
Phone: (847) 491-7271
Christopher Watson, Dean of Undergraduate Admissions, Northwestern University, 1801 Hinman Avenue, Evanston, IL 60204-3060

## Olivet Nazarene University
**Bourbonnais, Illinois**   CB member
**www.olivet.edu**   CB code: 1596

- Private 4-year university and liberal arts college affiliated with Church of the Nazarene
- Residential campus in small city
- 3,175 degree-seeking undergraduates
- 81% of applicants admitted
- ACT (writing optional) required

**General.** Founded in 1907. Regionally accredited. Evangelical liberal arts institution emphasizing Christian values. **Degrees:** 650 bachelor's, 40 associate awarded; master's offered. **ROTC:** Army. **Location:** 60 miles from Chicago. **Calendar:** Semester, extensive summer session. **Full-time faculty:** 118 total. **Part-time faculty:** 350 total. **Class size:** 39% < 20, 46% 20-39, 5% 40-49, 9% 50-99, 1% >100. **Special facilities:** Planetarium, observatory, science museum, distance learning classroom.

**Freshman class profile.** 2,898 applied, 2,347 admitted, 1,549 enrolled.

| Mid 50% test scores | | Out-of-state: | 52% |
|---|---|---|---|
| ACT composite: | 20-27 | Live on campus: | 90% |

**Basis for selection.** 2.0 GPA in college-preparatory subjects, ranking in top three-quarters of class, 18 ACT, 2 recommendations required. Interview recommended. Audition required of music majors. Portfolios required for art scholarship applicants.

**High school preparation.** 15 units required. Required and recommended units include English 4, mathematics 3, social studies 4, history 2, science 3 and foreign language 2.

**2010-2011 Annual costs.** Tuition/fees: $25,590. Room/board: $6,900. Books/supplies: $1,000. Personal expenses: $400.

**2008-2009 Financial aid. Non-need-based:** Scholarships awarded for academics, art, athletics, leadership, music/drama, religious affiliation, ROTC, state residency.

**Application procedures. Admission:** Closing date 5/15 (postmark date). $25 fee, may be waived for applicants with need, free for online applicants. Admission notification on a rolling basis. **Financial aid:** Priority date 3/1; no closing date. FAFSA, institutional form required. Applicants notified on a rolling basis starting 1/15; must reply within 2 week(s) of notification.

**Academics. Special study options:** Accelerated study, distance learning, double major, honors, independent study, internships, liberal arts/career combination, student-designed major, study abroad, teacher certification program, Washington semester. Council of Christian Colleges and Universities study programs, adult studies degree program. **Credit/placement by examination:** AP, CLEP, IB, ACT, institutional tests. **Support services:** Learning center, pre-admission summer program, reduced course load, remedial instruction, tutoring.

**Majors. Biology:** General, zoology. **Business:** General, accounting, business admin, fashion, finance, international, marketing. **Communications:** General, broadcast journalism, journalism. **Computer sciences:** General, computer science, information systems, programming. **Conservation:** Environmental studies. **Education:** Art, biology, chemistry, early childhood, elementary, English, family/consumer sciences, foreign languages, health, history, mathematics, music, physical, science, secondary, social science, social studies, Spanish. **Engineering:** General. **Family/consumer sciences:** General, family/community services, housing. **Foreign languages:** General, Spanish. **Health:** Athletic training. **History:** General. **Interdisciplinary:** Biological/physical sciences. **Liberal arts:** Arts/sciences. **Math:** General. **Parks/recreation:** Exercise sciences, sports admin. **Philosophy/religion:** Religion. **Physical sciences:** Chemistry, geology. **Protective services:** Criminal justice. **Psychology:** General. **Public administration:** Policy analysis, social work. **Social sciences:** General, economics, political science, sociology. **Theology:** Bible, religious ed, sacred music, theology. **Visual/performing arts:** Art, music performance, piano/organ, voice/opera.

**Most popular majors.** Business/marketing 20%, education 10%, health sciences 16%, social sciences 6%.

**Computing on campus.** 125 workstations in library, computer center, student center. Dormitories wired for high-speed internet access and linked to campus network. Commuter students can connect to campus network. Online library, helpline, repair service, student web hosting, wireless network available.

**Student life. Freshman orientation:** Mandatory. Preregistration for classes offered. Three-day program held on second and third weekends in June. Comprehensive for students and parents. **Policies:** Chapel convocations held twice weekly. Religious observance required. **Housing:** Guaranteed on-campus for all undergraduates. Single-sex dorms, special housing for disabled, apartments available. **Activities:** Bands, campus ministries, choral groups, drama, international student organizations, literary magazine, music ensembles, musical theater, radio station, student government, student newspaper, symphony orchestra, social service clubs, spiritual life groups.

**Athletics.** NAIA, NCCAA. **Intercollegiate:** Baseball M, basketball, cheerleading, cross-country, football (tackle) M, golf M, soccer, softball W, tennis, track and field, volleyball W. **Intramural:** Badminton, basketball, bowling, cross-country, football (non-tackle) W, golf, handball, racquetball, soccer, softball, table tennis, tennis, track and field, volleyball. **Team name:** Tigers.

**Student services.** Adult student services, alcohol/substance abuse counseling, chaplain/spiritual director, career counseling, services for economically disadvantaged, student employment services, financial aid counseling, health services, personal counseling, placement for graduates, veterans' counselor.

**Contact.** E-mail: admissions@olivet.edu
Phone: (815) 939-5203 Toll-free number: (800) 648-1463
Fax: (815) 939-5069
Susan Wolff, Director of Admissions, Olivet Nazarene University, One University Avenue, Bourbonnais, IL 60914

## Principia College
**Elsah, Illinois**
**www.principia.edu**
**CB member**
**CB code: 1630**

- Private 4-year liberal arts college affiliated with First Church of Christ, Scientist (Christian Science)
- Residential campus in rural community
- 526 degree-seeking undergraduates
- 67% of applicants admitted
- SAT or ACT with writing, application essay required

**General.** Founded in 1910. Regionally accredited. All faculty, staff, and students are Christian Scientists. **Degrees:** 129 bachelor's awarded. **Location:** 35 miles from St. Louis. **Calendar:** Quarter. **Full-time faculty:** 55 total. **Part-time faculty:** 11 total. **Class size:** 94% < 20, 6% 20-39. **Special facilities:** School of Nations museum, astronomical observatory telescope, media center, tropical aviary, on-site mammoth excavation, Christian Science practitioner's office, athletic center with natatorium, 3,069-pipe organ, 39 bronze bell carillon.

**Freshman class profile.** 234 applied, 157 admitted, 114 enrolled.

| Mid 50% test scores | | | |
|---|---|---|---|
| SAT critical reading: | 520-650 | ACT composite: | 22-29 |
| SAT math: | 490-620 | Out-of-state: | 90% |
| | | Live on campus: | 100% |

**Basis for selection.** School achievement record and essay or personal statement most important. Applicant must be practicing Christian Scientist. Test scores important. Foreign language SAT Subject Test required for placement purposes. Interview recommended. Portfolio recommended for art majors. **Homeschooled:** Must submit curricula program from accredited high school or accepted agency, plus GED.

**High school preparation.** 16 units required; 20 recommended. Required and recommended units include English 4, mathematics 3-4, social

studies 1, history 1-2, science 3-4 (laboratory 2), foreign language 2-3 and academic electives 2.

**2010-2011 Annual costs.** Tuition/fees: $23,955. Room/board: $9,000. Books/supplies: $900. Personal expenses: $750.

**2009-2010 Financial aid. Need-based:** 100 full-time freshmen applied for aid; 97 were judged to have need; 97 of these received aid. Average need met was 100%. Average scholarship/grant was $20,493; average loan $4,922. 84% of total undergraduate aid awarded as scholarships/grants, 16% as loans/jobs. **Non-need-based:** Awarded to 162 full-time undergraduates, including 32 freshmen. Scholarships awarded for academics, alumni affiliation, leadership. **Additional information:** Need-based tuition reduction work plan combines job with grant.

**Application procedures. Admission:** Priority date 11/15; deadline 3/1 (postmark date). No application fee. Application must be submitted online. Admission notification on a rolling basis beginning on or about 10/15. Must reply by May 1 or within 2 week(s) if notified thereafter. **Financial aid:** Closing date 3/1. Institutional form, CSS PROFILE required. Applicants notified by 4/1.

**Academics. Special study options:** Double major, independent study, internships, liberal arts/career combination, student-designed major, study abroad, teacher certification program. 3-2 engineering with Washington University, University of Southern California, Southern Illinois University at Edwardsville. **Credit/placement by examination:** AP, CLEP, IB, institutional tests. **Support services:** Learning center, study skills assistance, tutoring, writing center.

**Majors. Biology:** General. **Business:** Business admin. **Communications:** Media studies. **Computer sciences:** General, computer science. **Conservation:** General. **Education:** Elementary. **Engineering:** Science. **Foreign languages:** General, French, Spanish. **History:** General. **Interdisciplinary:** Global studies. **Liberal arts:** Arts/sciences, humanities. **Math:** General. **Parks/recreation:** Sports admin. **Philosophy/religion:** Philosophy, religion. **Physical sciences:** Chemistry, physics. **Social sciences:** General, anthropology, economics, political science, sociology. **Visual/performing arts:** Art history/conservation, dramatic, studio arts.

**Computing on campus.** 250 workstations in dormitories, library, computer center, student center. Dormitories wired for high-speed internet access and linked to campus network. Online course registration, online library, helpline, student web hosting, wireless network available.

**Student life. Freshman orientation:** Mandatory. Preregistration for classes offered. Writing and orientation program immediately precedes start of fall classes. **Policies:** Students required to comply with standards of Christian Science. No alcoholic beverages, smoking, drugs. High moral standards and behavior expected. Standards maintained regarding abstinence from premarital sex or homosexual activity. Religious observance required. **Housing:** Guaranteed on-campus for all undergraduates. Coed dorms, single-sex dorms, apartments, wellness housing available. $100 nonrefundable deposit, deadline 5/1. Single-sex wings, 8 person cottages for non-traditional students available. **Activities:** Jazz band, choral groups, dance, drama, international student organizations, music ensembles, musical theater, radio station, student government, student newspaper, symphony orchestra, TV station, Christian Science Organization, black student union, Latin American student organization, student volunteer program, public affairs conference.

**Athletics.** NCAA. **Intercollegiate:** Baseball M, basketball, cross-country, diving, golf M, soccer, swimming, tennis, track and field, volleyball W. **Intramural:** Basketball, soccer, softball, volleyball W. **Team name:** Panthers.

**Student services.** Adult student services, career counseling, student employment services, financial aid counseling, health services, on-campus daycare, personal counseling.

**Contact.** E-mail: collegeadmissions@principia.edu
Phone: (618) 374-5181 Toll-free number: (800) 277-4648 ext. 2802
Fax: (618) 374-4000
Brian McCauley, Dean of Enrollment Management, Principia College, One Maybeck Place, Elsah, IL 62028-9799

## Quincy University
**Quincy, Illinois**
**www.quincy.edu**
**CB code: 1645**

- Private 4-year university and liberal arts college affiliated with Roman Catholic Church
- Residential campus in large town
- 1,166 degree-seeking undergraduates: 6% part-time, 56% women, 10% African American, 1% Asian American, 4% Hispanic American, 1% international

♦ 480 degree-seeking graduate students
♦ 90% of applicants admitted
♦ SAT or ACT (ACT writing optional), application essay required
♦ 42% graduate within 6 years; 23% enter graduate study

**General.** Founded in 1860. Regionally accredited. **Degrees:** 208 bachelor's awarded; master's offered. **Location:** 300 miles from Chicago, 120 miles from St. Louis. **Calendar:** Semester, limited summer session. **Full-time faculty:** 53 total; 76% have terminal degrees, 9% minority, 30% women. **Part-time faculty:** 116 total; 22% have terminal degrees, 4% minority, 66% women. **Class size:** 70% < 20, 30% 20-39, less than 1% 40-49. **Special facilities:** National public radio station, 200-seat theater, multi-media and graphic design labs, environmental studies institute, TV broadcast studio, temperature-controlled rare books archive, hospital simulation lab, aviation facility with aviation simulator.

**Freshman class profile.** 986 applied, 892 admitted, 249 enrolled.

| Mid 50% test scores | | Rank in top quarter: | 35% |
|---|---|---|---|
| SAT critical reading: | 420-480 | Rank in top tenth: | 12% |
| SAT math: | 430-540 | Return as sophomores: | 69% |
| ACT composite: | 19-24 | Out-of-state: | 34% |
| GPA 3.75 or higher: | 20% | Live on campus: | 83% |
| GPA 3.50-3.74: | 12% | International: | 2% |
| GPA 3.0-3.49: | 32% | Fraternities: | 2% |
| GPA 2.0-2.99: | 35% | Sororities: | 15% |

**Basis for selection.** School achievement record and test scores most important. Applicants for BS in nursing must have minimum 22 ACT and 3.0 GPA and meet other requirements. All applicants must submit letter of recommendation and personal statement. Audition required of music majors. Portfolio recommended for art majors. **Homeschooled:** Transcript of courses and grades, letter of recommendation (nonparent) required. Required documentation may vary. **Learning Disabled:** Must submit documentation of disability.

**High school preparation.** College-preparatory program recommended. 16 units recommended. Recommended units include English 4, mathematics 3, science 3 and foreign language 2. 3 social sciences; courses in computers and the arts recommended.

**2010-2011 Annual costs.** Tuition/fees: $23,000. Room and board charges vary according to board plan and housing facility selected. Room/board: $8,960. Books/supplies: $1,250. Personal expenses: $1,500.

**2009-2010 Financial aid.** **Need-based:** 237 full-time freshmen applied for aid; 221 were judged to have need; 221 of these received aid. Average need met was 85%. Average scholarship/grant was $17,950; average loan $3,907. 71% of total undergraduate aid awarded as scholarships/grants, 29% as loans/jobs. **Non-need-based:** Awarded to 248 full-time undergraduates, including 71 freshmen. Scholarships awarded for academics, alumni affiliation, art, athletics, music/drama.

**Application procedures.** **Admission:** No deadline. $25 fee. Admission notification on a rolling basis beginning on or about 9/1. **Financial aid:** Priority date 3/1; no closing date, FAFSA required. Applicants notified on a rolling basis starting 2/15.

**Academics.** Associate degrees are offered in all majors by arrangement with institution. **Special study options:** Accelerated study, distance learning, double major, dual enrollment of high school students, honors, independent study, internships, student-designed major, study abroad, teacher certification program, Washington semester. 3-2 in engineering with Washington University; 3-1 program in medical technology with various hospitals. **Credit/placement by examination:** AP, CLEP, IB, institutional tests. 40 credit hours maximum toward bachelor's degree. Combined total of 40 semester hours of credit from nontraditional sources accepted toward a bachelor's degree. **Support services:** Learning center, pre-admission summer program, reduced course load, remedial instruction, study skills assistance, tutoring, writing center.

**Majors. Biology:** General. **Business:** Accounting, business admin, finance, management science, marketing. **Communications:** General. **Computer sciences:** Computer science, information systems. **Education:** Elementary, multi-level teacher, music, physical, special. **Foreign languages:** Sign language interpretation. **Health:** Clinical lab science, nursing (RN). **History:** General. **Liberal arts:** Arts/sciences, humanities. **Math:** General. **Parks/recreation:** Health/fitness, sports admin. **Physical sciences:** Chemistry. **Protective services:** Criminal justice. **Psychology:** General. **Public administration:** Human services. **Social sciences:** Political science. **Transportation:** Airline/commercial pilot, aviation management. **Visual/performing arts:** Graphic design. **Other:** Communication and music production, Theology/philosophy.

**Most popular majors.** Business/marketing 26%, communications/journalism 6%, education 13%, health sciences 12%, liberal arts 7%, public administration/social services 7%.

**Computing on campus.** 190 workstations in dormitories, library, computer center. Dormitories wired for high-speed internet access and linked to campus network. Commuter students can connect to campus network. Online library, helpline, wireless network available.

**Student life. Freshman orientation:** Mandatory, $120 fee. Preregistration for classes offered. Academic year begins with 1-2 week registration and advisement program and 1-week social program. **Housing:** Guaranteed on-campus for all undergraduates. Coed dorms, single-sex dorms, apartments, fraternity/sorority housing available. $150 nonrefundable deposit. Honors housing available. **Activities:** Bands, campus ministries, choral groups, dance, drama, literary magazine, music ensembles, musical theater, opera, radio station, student government, student newspaper, symphony orchestra, TV station, Circle K International, environmental club, minority student association, Peers 2 Peers, student senate, student programming board.

**Athletics.** NAIA, NCAA. **Intercollegiate:** Baseball M, basketball, football (tackle) M, golf, soccer, softball W, tennis, volleyball. **Intramural:** Basketball, bowling, football (non-tackle), golf, racquetball, soccer, softball, table tennis, volleyball. **Team name:** Hawks.

**Student services.** Alcohol/substance abuse counseling, chaplain/spiritual director, career counseling, student employment services, financial aid counseling, health services, minority student services, personal counseling, placement for graduates. **Physically disabled:** Services for visually, hearing impaired.

**Contact.** E-mail: admissions@quincy.edu
Phone: (217) 228-5210 Toll-free number: (800) 688-4295
Fax: (217) 228-5479
Syndi Peck, Director of Admissions, Quincy University, 1800 College Avenue, Quincy, IL 62301-2699

---

## Robert Morris University: Chicago

**Chicago, Illinois** — CB member
www.robertmorris.edu — CB code: 1670

♦ Private 4-year university
♦ Commuter campus in very large city
♦ 4,137 degree-seeking undergraduates: 5% part-time, 62% women, 35% African American, 2% Asian American, 23% Hispanic American, 1% international
♦ 469 degree-seeking graduate students
♦ 81% of applicants admitted
♦ 73% graduate within 6 years

**General.** Founded in 1913. Regionally accredited. Branch campuses in DuPage, Elgin, Lake County, Bensenville, Orland Park, Peoria, Springfield, and Schaumburg. **Degrees:** 945 bachelor's, 1,001 associate awarded; master's offered. **ROTC:** Army. **Location:** Downtown. **Calendar:** 5 10-week sessions. Extensive summer session. **Full-time faculty:** 113 total; 34% have terminal degrees, 24% minority, 51% women. **Part-time faculty:** 179 total; 19% have terminal degrees, 18% minority, 41% women. **Class size:** 44% < 20, 52% 20-39, 2% 40-49, 1% 50-99, less than 1% >100.

**Freshman class profile.** 2,982 applied, 2,404 admitted, 959 enrolled.

| GPA 3.75 or higher: | 4% | Rank in top tenth: | 5% |
|---|---|---|---|
| GPA 3.50-3.74: | 5% | End year in good standing: | 64% |
| GPA 3.0-3.49: | 19% | Return as sophomores: | 57% |
| GPA 2.0-2.99: | 60% | Out-of-state: | 8% |
| Rank in top quarter: | 20% | Live on campus: | 9% |

**Basis for selection.** Must submit high school transcript or GED for review. Secondary school record, class rank, GPA and interview most important. Extra curricular activities and level of interest considered. Meeting with admissions counselor and campus visit strongly recommended. **Homeschooled:** Transcript of courses and grades, state high school equivalency certificate required. Curriculum documentation, state certification, and standardized exam with acceptable achievement level required.

**High school preparation.** College-preparatory program recommended.

**2010-2011 Annual costs.** Tuition/fees (projected): $20,100. Room only: $8,100. Books/supplies: $1,500. Personal expenses: $2,190.

**2008-2009 Financial aid. Need-based:** 1,245 full-time freshmen applied for aid; 1,214 were judged to have need; 1,180 of these received aid. Average need met was 41%. Average scholarship/grant was $8,795; average loan $4,606. 44% of total undergraduate aid awarded as scholarships/grants, 56% as loans/jobs. **Non-need-based:** Awarded to 292 full-time undergraduates, including 66 freshmen. Scholarships awarded for academics, art, athletics, state residency.

**Application procedures. Admission:** No deadline. $30 fee, may be waived for applicants with need. Admission notification on a rolling basis. **Financial aid:** No deadline. FAFSA required. Applicants notified on a rolling basis.

**Academics. Special study options:** Accelerated study, combined bachelor's/ graduate degree, cooperative education, distance learning, honors, independent study, internships, study abroad. Master's Advantage. **Credit/ placement by examination:** AP, CLEP, institutional tests. 44 credit hours maximum toward associate degree, 44 toward bachelor's. **Support services:** Learning center, reduced course load, study skills assistance, tutoring, writing center.

**Majors. Business:** Business admin. **Computer sciences:** Information technology. **Visual/performing arts:** Graphic design. **Other:** Professional studies.

**Most popular majors.** Business/marketing 81%, computer/information sciences 10%, visual/performing arts 8%.

**Computing on campus.** 1,538 workstations in library, computer center, student center. Dormitories wired for high-speed internet access. Wireless network available.

**Student life. Freshman orientation:** Mandatory. Held 1-4 weeks prior to commencement of classes. Students required to attend one 2 1/2-hour session. **Policies:** Students required to comply with University's dress code, attendance policies, and housing rules and regulations. **Housing:** Coed dorms, apartments available. $300 fully refundable deposit, deadline 5/1. **Activities:** Bands, choral groups, dance, literary magazine, student newspaper.

**Athletics.** NAIA, USCAA. **Intercollegiate:** Baseball M, basketball, cross-country, diving W, golf, soccer, softball W, swimming W, tennis W, track and field W, volleyball. **Team name:** Eagles.

**Student services.** Adult student services, alcohol/substance abuse counseling, career counseling, services for economically disadvantaged, student employment services, financial aid counseling, personal counseling, placement for graduates. **Physically disabled:** Services for visually, speech, hearing impaired.

**Contact.** E-mail: ais@robertmorris.edu
Phone: (312) 935-4400 Toll-free number: (800) 762-5960
Fax: (312) 935-4440
Catherine Lockwood, Senior Vice President for Enrollment Management, Robert Morris University: Chicago, 401 South State Street, Chicago, IL 60605

## Rockford College
**Rockford, Illinois**      **CB member**
**www.rockford.edu**      **CB code: 1665**

- Private 4-year liberal arts college
- Residential campus in small city
- 857 degree-seeking undergraduates: 12% part-time, 61% women, 8% African American, 2% Asian American, 6% Hispanic American
- 207 degree-seeking graduate students
- 41% of applicants admitted
- SAT or ACT (ACT writing optional) required
- 47% graduate within 6 years

**General.** Founded in 1847. Regionally accredited. **Degrees:** 222 bachelor's awarded; master's offered. **Location:** 90 miles from Chicago. **Calendar:** Semester, limited summer session. **Full-time faculty:** 69 total; 68% have terminal degrees, 3% minority, 42% women. **Part-time faculty:** 87 total; 17% have terminal degrees, 6% minority, 46% women. **Class size:** 75% < 20, 24% 20-39, less than 1% 40-49. **Special facilities:** Black box theater, nursing lab, center for civic engagement, prairie conservation area, center for ethics and entrepreneurship.

**Freshman class profile.** 967 applied, 398 admitted, 92 enrolled.

| Mid 50% test scores | | | |
|---|---|---|---|
| **ACT composite:** | 19-24 | **Rank in top quarter:** | 31% |
| **GPA 3.75 or higher:** | 15% | **Rank in top tenth:** | 14% |
| **GPA 3.50-3.74:** | 13% | **End year in good standing:** | 85% |
| **GPA 3.0-3.49:** | 36% | **Return as sophomores:** | 65% |
| **GPA 2.0-2.99:** | 36% | **Out-of-state:** | 22% |
| | | **Live on campus:** | 60% |

**Basis for selection.** School achievement record and test scores are most important. Recommendations and activities also are considered. Auditions required of theater arts and musical theater performance majors. Personal statements required of students who fall below standard admission criteria.

**High school preparation.** College-preparatory program required. 15 units required. Required units include English 4, mathematics 3, social studies 3, science 3 (laboratory 3) and academic electives 2.

**2009-2010 Annual costs.** Tuition/fees: $24,250. Room/board: $6,750. Books/supplies: $1,200. Personal expenses: $2,250.

**2008-2009 Financial aid. Need-based:** 56% of total undergraduate aid awarded as scholarships/grants, 44% as loans/jobs. **Non-need-based:** Scholarships awarded for academics, alumni affiliation, leadership, minority status, music/drama, state residency.

**Application procedures. Admission:** No deadline. $35 fee, may be waived for applicants with need, free for online applicants. Admission notification on a rolling basis beginning on or about 9/15. **Financial aid:** Priority date 3/1; no closing date. FAFSA required. Applicants notified on a rolling basis starting 3/1; must reply within 4 week(s) of notification.

**Academics.** Community-based learning opportunities available. **Special study options:** Accelerated study, distance learning, double major, ESL, exchange student, honors, independent study, internships, study abroad, teacher certification program, United Nations semester, Washington semester. Tutorial classes, special studies courses. **Credit/placement by examination:** AP, CLEP, SAT, ACT, institutional tests. **Support services:** Learning center, reduced course load, remedial instruction, study skills assistance, tutoring, writing center.

**Majors. Biology:** General, biochemistry. **Business:** Accounting, business admin. **Computer sciences:** Computer science. **Education:** General, elementary, physical. **Foreign languages:** Classics, French, German, Latin, Romance, Spanish. **Health:** Nursing (RN). **History:** General. **Liberal arts:** Humanities. **Math:** General. **Philosophy/religion:** Philosophy. **Physical sciences:** Chemistry. **Psychology:** General. **Social sciences:** General, economics, international relations, political science. **Visual/performing arts:** Art, art history/conservation, dramatic, musical theater. **Other:** Anthropology/ sociology, Management studies, Science and mathematics.

**Most popular majors.** Business/marketing 22%, education 30%, health sciences 11%, psychology 8%.

**Computing on campus.** 80 workstations in library, computer center, student center. Dormitories wired for high-speed internet access and linked to campus network. Commuter students can connect to campus network. Helpline, repair service, wireless network available.

**Student life. Freshman orientation:** Mandatory. Preregistration for classes offered. Four-day program held the week prior to beginning of fall classes, includes introduction to college resources. **Policies:** Alcohol and guest policies, Academic Honor Code in place. **Housing:** Guaranteed on-campus for all undergraduates. Coed dorms, special housing for disabled, wellness housing available. $100 nonrefundable deposit. Special housing available for first-year students. **Activities:** Pep band, campus ministries, choral groups, dance, drama, international student organizations, literary magazine, music ensembles, musical theater, student government, Jane Adams Center for Civic Engagement, Intervarsity, multicultural club, Black student union, Democrats Encouraging and Motivating Students (DEMS), Rockford College Grand New Party, Rotoract.

**Athletics.** NCAA. **Intercollegiate:** Baseball M, basketball, cross-country, football (tackle) M, golf M, soccer, softball W, tennis, track and field, volleyball W. **Team name:** Regents.

**Student services.** Alcohol/substance abuse counseling, chaplain/ spiritual director, career counseling, student employment services, financial aid counseling, health services, personal counseling, veterans' counselor. **Physically disabled:** Services for visually impaired.

**Contact.** E-mail: rcadmissions@rockford.edu
Phone: (815) 226-4050 Toll-free number: (800) 892-2984
Fax: (815) 226-2822
Jennifer Nordstrom, Associate Vice President for Undergraduate Admission and Strategic Marketing, Rockford College, 5050 East State Street, Rockford, IL 61108-2393

## Roosevelt University
**Chicago, Illinois**      **CB member**
**www.roosevelt.edu**      **CB code: 1666**

- Private 4-year university
- Commuter campus in very large city
- 4,113 degree-seeking undergraduates: 31% part-time, 67% women
- 3,100 degree-seeking graduate students
- 50% of applicants admitted

- SAT or ACT (ACT writing optional) required
- 41% graduate within 6 years

**General.** Founded in 1945. Regionally accredited. Additional campus in Schaumburg. **Degrees:** 1,005 bachelor's awarded; master's, doctoral, professional offered. **Location:** Downtown. **Calendar:** Semester, extensive summer session. **Full-time faculty:** 219 total; 87% have terminal degrees, 17% minority, 41% women. **Part-time faculty:** 415 total; 46% women. **Class size:** 57% < 20, 40% 20-39, 2% 40-49, less than 1% 50-99, less than 1% >100.

**Freshman class profile.** 4,245 applied, 2,118 admitted, 597 enrolled.

| Mid 50% test scores | | | |
|---|---|---|---|
| SAT critical reading: | 510-630 | GPA 2.0-2.99: | 42% |
| SAT math: | 470-580 | Rank in top quarter: | 6% |
| ACT composite: | 19-25 | Rank in top tenth: | 2% |
| GPA 3.75 or higher: | 16% | Return as sophomores: | 52% |
| GPA 3.50-3.74: | 10% | Out-of-state: | 34% |
| GPA 3.0-3.49: | 32% | Live on campus: | 67% |

**Basis for selection.** Recent secondary school performance most crucial. Personal statement and recommended interview can be used to communicate special circumstances. Placement evaluation required for all admitted, degree-seeking undergraduate students. Test results must be submitted by first year or transfer applicants with scores less than 2 years old. Interview recommended for early admission and borderline applicants. Audition required of music and theater majors. Portfolio recommended for art and theater majors. **Homeschooled:** Statement describing homeschool structure and mission, letter of recommendation (nonparent) required.

**High school preparation.** College-preparatory program required. 15 units required; 19 recommended. Required and recommended units include English 4, mathematics 3-4, social studies 2, history 1, science 3 (laboratory 2), foreign language 2 and academic electives 2. Extensive work in English, history, mathematics, foreign language, and science recommended.

**2010-2011 Annual costs.** Tuition/fees: $23,000. Full time tuition for undergraduate students in the College of Performing Arts is $29,900. Room/board: $11,200. Books/supplies: $1,000. Personal expenses: $4,300.

**2008-2009 Financial aid. Non-need-based:** Scholarships awarded for academics, alumni affiliation, leadership, minority status, music/drama, state residency.

**Application procedures. Admission:** Priority date 8/1; deadline 9/1 (receipt date). $25 fee, may be waived for applicants with need. Admission notification on a rolling basis beginning on or about 10/15. Must reply by May 1 or within 4 week(s) if notified thereafter. **Financial aid:** Priority date 4/1; no closing date. FAFSA required. Applicants notified on a rolling basis starting 3/15; must reply within 2 week(s) of notification.

**Academics. Special study options:** Accelerated study, combined bachelor's/graduate degree, distance learning, double major, dual enrollment of high school students, ESL, honors, independent study, internships, study abroad, teacher certification program. **Credit/placement by examination:** AP, CLEP, SAT, ACT, institutional tests. 30 credit hours maximum toward bachelor's degree. **Support services:** Learning center, pre-admission summer program, reduced course load, remedial instruction, study skills assistance, tutoring, writing center.

**Majors. Area/ethnic studies:** African-American, women's. **Biology:** General, biotechnology. **Business:** General, accounting, actuarial science, communications, finance, financial planning, hospitality admin, human resources, insurance, management science, marketing, office management, organizational behavior. **Communications:** General, journalism, organizational. **Computer sciences:** Computer science, networking. **Education:** Early childhood, elementary, music, secondary, special. **Engineering technology:** Electrical. **Foreign languages:** General, comparative lit, Spanish. **Health:** Clinical lab science, medical radiologic technology/radiation therapy, nuclear medical technology. **History:** General. **Legal studies:** Paralegal. **Liberal arts:** Arts/sciences. **Math:** General. **Philosophy/religion:** Philosophy. **Physical sciences:** Chemistry. **Protective services:** Criminal justice. **Psychology:** General. **Social sciences:** Economics, international relations, political science, sociology. **Visual/performing arts:** Acting, art history/conservation, dramatic, jazz, music performance, music theory/composition, musical theater, piano/organ, stringed instruments, voice/opera. **Other:** Allied health, Integrated communication.

**Most popular majors.** Business/marketing 34%, communications/journalism 6%, education 7%, personal/culinary services 8%, psychology 14%, social sciences 6%, visual/performing arts 8%.

**Computing on campus.** 250 workstations in dormitories, library, computer center, student center. Dormitories wired for high-speed internet access and linked to campus network. Commuter students can connect to campus network. Online course registration, online library, helpline, repair service available.

**Student life. Freshman orientation:** Mandatory. Preregistration for classes offered. Ongoing from mid-Spring through the summer; 1-2 days in duration, with coverage of academic and non-academic elements of student life. **Housing:** Guaranteed on-campus for all undergraduates. Coed dorms, apartments available. $500 fully refundable deposit, deadline 8/1. High-rise residence hall in cooperation with University Center of Chicago available. **Activities:** Jazz band, dance, drama, international student organizations, literary magazine, music ensembles, musical theater, radio station, student government, student newspaper, Christian Bible groups, theater club, Black student union, Hispanic organization, residence hall council, Asociacion de Latinos Unidos.

**Athletics. Intercollegiate:** Baseball M, basketball, cross-country, golf M, soccer, softball W, tennis, volleyball W. **Intramural:** Badminton, baseball M, basketball, table tennis. **Team name:** Lakers.

**Student services.** Adult student services, alcohol/substance abuse counseling, career counseling, student employment services, financial aid counseling, personal counseling, placement for graduates, veterans' counselor. **Physically disabled:** Services for visually, hearing impaired.

**Contact.** E-mail: applyru@roosevelt.edu
Toll-free number: (877) 277-5978 Fax: (847) 619-8636
Elizabeth Gierach, Assistant Vice President for Admission, Roosevelt University, 430 South Michigan Avenue, Chicago, IL 60605-1394

---

## Rush University
### Chicago, Illinois
### www.rushu.rush.edu
**CB code: 3262**

- Private two-year upper-division health science and nursing college
- Commuter campus in very large city
- Application essay required

**General.** Founded in 1971. Regionally accredited. Educational component of Rush University Medical Center. Students use clinical and laboratory facilities of the medical center, affiliated hospitals, and community health centers. Based on teacher-practitioner model. **Degrees:** 128 bachelor's awarded; master's, doctoral, professional offered. **Articulation:** Agreements with College of DuPage, Triton College, Parkland College, Moraine Valley Community College, Oakton Community College, William Rainey Harper College, Kankakee Community College. **Location:** 2 miles from downtown. **Calendar:** Quarter, limited summer session. **Full-time faculty:** 450 total. **Part-time faculty:** 350 total. **Class size:** 37% < 20, 36% 20-39, 27% 50-99.

**Student profile.** 59 degree-seeking undergraduates. 100% entered as juniors.

| | | | |
|---|---|---|---|
| Out-of-state: | 15% | 25 or older: | 65% |
| Live on campus: | 20% | | |

**Basis for selection.** College transcript, application essay required. Admission based on GPA and letters of recommendation. Application closing dates: nursing April 1, clinical lab sciences/medical technology June 1, perfusion technology, March 1. Transfer accepted as juniors.

**2009-2010 Annual costs.** Tuition/fees: $23,022. Tuition costs vary by program. Room only: $9,000. Books/supplies: $700. Personal expenses: $2,313.

**Application procedures. Admission:** Rolling admission. $40 fee, may be waived for applicants with need. Application deadlines vary by program. **Financial aid:** Priority date 5/1, no deadline. Applicants notified on a rolling basis starting 4/1; must reply within 3 weeks of notification. FAFSA, institutional form required.

**Academics. Special study options:** Accelerated study, combined bachelor's/graduate degree, distance learning, liberal arts/career combination. Registered nurse completion program. **Credit/placement by examination:** CLEP, institutional tests. 45 credit hours maximum toward bachelor's degree.

**Majors. Health:** Clinical lab science, perfusion technology, respiratory therapy technology.

**Computing on campus.** 140 workstations in library, computer center, student center. Commuter students can connect to campus network. Online library, helpline, wireless network available.

**Student life. Policies:** Funds available for official student groups. **Housing:** Apartments available. $200 deposit. **Activities:** Student government, student newspaper, Christian Fellowship, rape victim advocate program, medical technicians club, National Student Nurses' Association chapter, Lesbian/Gay/Bisexual/Allies, Health Science Students for Choice.

**Student services.** Alcohol/substance abuse counseling, career counseling, student employment services, financial aid counseling, health services, on-campus daycare, personal counseling, veterans' counselor.

**Contact.** E-mail: rush_admissions@rush.edu
Phone: (312) 942-7100 Fax: (312) 942-2219
Hicela Woods, Director of College Admission Services, Rush University, College Admissions, Chicago, IL 60612

## Saint Anthony College of Nursing
Rockford, Illinois
www.sacn.edu                          CB code: 3923

- Private two-year upper-division nursing college affiliated with Roman Catholic Church
- Commuter campus in small city
- 49% of applicants admitted
- Application essay, interview required

**General.** Regionally accredited. MSN in Nurse Educator, Clinical Nurse Specialist (Adult Health) and Clinical Nurse Leader offered. **Degrees:** 70 bachelor's awarded; master's offered. **Articulation:** Agreements with Rock Valley College, McHenry County College, Sauk Valley Community College, Kishwaukee College, Elgin Community College, Blackhawk Technical College, Highland Community College. **Location:** 90 miles from of Chicago. **Calendar:** Semester, limited summer session. **Full-time faculty:** 11 total. **Part-time faculty:** 5 total; 80% women. **Class size:** 12% < 20, 62% 20-39, 25% 40-49. **Special facilities:** Nursing labs, hospital facility.

**Student profile.** 163 degree-seeking undergraduates, 17 degree-seeking graduate students. 117 applied as first time-transfer students, 57 admitted, 41 enrolled. 100% entered as juniors. 88% transferred from two-year, 12% transferred from four-year institutions.

| | | | |
|---|---|---|---|
| Women: | 94% | Part-time: | 19% |
| African American: | 4% | Out-of-state: | 6% |
| Asian American: | 9% | 25 or older: | 53% |
| Hispanic American: | 6% | | |

**Basis for selection.** College transcript, application essay, interview required. 64 credits required in specific pre-nursing and general education courses. Transfer accepted as juniors.

**2009-2010 Annual costs.** Tuition/fees: $19,086. Required fees may vary. Books/supplies: $2,200. Personal expenses: $1,785.

**Financial aid. Non-need-based:** Scholarships awarded for academics, leadership, state residency.

**Application procedures. Admission:** Deadline 9/15. $50 fee. Admission notification 10/31. Must reply by 11/30. **Financial aid:** No deadline. Applicants notified on a rolling basis starting 8/18. FAFSA required.

**Academics. Credit/placement by examination:** AP, CLEP.

**Majors. Health:** Adult health nursing.

**Computing on campus.** 37 workstations in library, computer center. Commuter students can connect to campus network. Online library, wireless network available.

**Student life. Activities:** Student government.

**Student services.** Alcohol/substance abuse counseling, chaplain/spiritual director, career counseling, financial aid counseling, health services, legal services, personal counseling, women's services.

**Contact.** E-mail: admissions@sacn.edu
Phone: (815) 227-2141 Fax: (815) 227-2730
Cheryl Delgado, Supervisor of Enrollment Management, Saint Anthony College of Nursing, 5658 East State Street, Rockford, IL 61108-2468

## St. Augustine College
Chicago, Illinois
www.staugustine.edu                   CB code: 0697

- Private 4-year liberal arts college affiliated with Episcopal Church
- Commuter campus in very large city
- 1,263 degree-seeking undergraduates: 19% part-time, 75% women, 5% African American, 11% Asian American, 82% Hispanic American

**General.** Founded in 1980. Regionally accredited. **Degrees:** 18 bachelor's, 209 associate awarded. **Calendar:** Semester, limited summer session. **Full-time faculty:** 22 total; 50% women. **Part-time faculty:** 112 total.

**Freshman class profile.** 389 enrolled.

**Basis for selection.** Open admission. Must demonstrate ability to benefit through high school diploma, GED or Ability to Benefit testing. **Home-schooled:** Placement test in English, math, and Spanish required.

**2009-2010 Annual costs.** Tuition/fees: $10,752. Books/supplies: $600.

**Application procedures. Admission:** No deadline. No application fee. Application must be submitted on paper. Admission notification on a rolling basis. **Financial aid:** No deadline. FAFSA, institutional form required. Applicants notified on a rolling basis.

**Academics. Special study options:** Cooperative education, double major, ESL, independent study, internships, liberal arts/career combination. **Credit/placement by examination:** CLEP, IB, institutional tests. **Support services:** Learning center, pre-admission summer program, remedial instruction, tutoring.

**Majors. Public administration:** Social work.

**Computing on campus.** 100 workstations in library, computer center. Online library available.

**Student life. Freshman orientation:** Mandatory. Preregistration for classes offered.

**Student services.** Adult student services, alcohol/substance abuse counseling, career counseling, services for economically disadvantaged, financial aid counseling, minority student services, on-campus daycare, personal counseling, placement for graduates.

**Contact.** Phone: (773) 878-8756 Fax: (773) 878-0937
St. Augustine College, 1345 West Argyle, Chicago, IL 60640-3501

## St. Francis Medical Center College of Nursing
Peoria, Illinois
www.sfmccon.edu                        CB code: 1756

- Private two-year upper-division nursing college affiliated with Roman Catholic Church
- Commuter campus in small city
- 50% of applicants admitted
- Application essay required

**General.** Founded in 1905. Regionally accredited. Located at large medical center. National League of Nursing accredited. NCA accredited. Offers experience at Tazewell County, Fulton County, Peoria City/County Health Departments, Human Service Center and various other community agencies. **Degrees:** 143 bachelor's awarded; master's, professional offered. **Location:** 180 miles from Chicago, 160 miles from St. Louis. **Calendar:** Semester, limited summer session. **Full-time faculty:** 32 total; 38% have terminal degrees, 100% women. **Part-time faculty:** 13 total; 92% women. **Class size:** 23% < 20, 37% 20-39, 33% 40-49, 7% 50-99.

**Student profile.** 363 degree-seeking undergraduates, 136 degree-seeking graduate students. 180 applied as first time-transfer students, 90 admitted, 90 enrolled. 100% entered as juniors. 92% transferred from two-year, 8% transferred from four-year institutions.

| | | | |
|---|---|---|---|
| Women: | 88% | 25 or older: | 75% |
| Part-time: | 22% | | |

**Basis for selection.** High school transcript, college transcript, application essay required. Enrollment depends on satisfactory completion of 62 semester hours of a specified prenursing curriculum. Applications may be submitted after satisfactory completion of 30 semester hours of required prenursing courses. Must include 8 semester hours of physical/life sciences. 2.5 GPA required. Transfer accepted as juniors.

**2010-2011 Annual costs.** Tuition/fees: $14,660. Room only: $2,400. Books/supplies: $1,532. Personal expenses: $3,105.

**Financial aid. Need-based:** 230 applied for aid; 204 were judged to have need; 204 of these received aid. Average need met was 56%. 38% of total undergraduate aid awarded as scholarships/grants, 62% as loans/jobs. **Non-need-based:** Awarded to 48 undergraduates. Scholarships awarded for academics, alumni affiliation. **Additional information:** OSF Saint Francis Medical Center Education student loan available to full-time students on a limited basis. Tuition waiver program for hospital employees available.

**Application procedures. Admission:** Deadline 9/1. $50 fee. Application must be submitted on paper. **Financial aid:** No deadline. Applicants notified on a rolling basis starting 5/15; must reply within 2 weeks of notification. FAFSA, institutional form required.

**Academics. Special study options:** Combined bachelor's/graduate degree, distance learning. **Credit/placement by examination:** CLEP.

**Majors. Health:** Nursing (RN).

**Computing on campus.** 31 workstations in library, computer center. Dormitories linked to campus network. Commuter students can connect to campus network. Online library, helpline, repair service available.

**Student life. Housing:** Guaranteed on-campus for all undergraduates. Coed dorms, wellness housing available. **Activities:** Student government, Christian fellowship, student nurses' association, minority association.

**Student services.** Adult student services, financial aid counseling, health services, personal counseling.

**Contact.** E-mail: janice.farquharson@osfhealthcare.org
Phone: (309) 655-2245 Fax: (309) 624-8973
Janice Farquharson, Director of Admissions and Recruitment, St. Francis Medical Center College of Nursing, 511 NE Greenleaf Street, Peoria, IL 61603-3783

## St. John's College
### Springfield, Illinois
### www.stjohnscollegespringfield.edu/index.html

- Private two-year upper-division nursing college affiliated with Roman Catholic Church
- Commuter campus in small city
- 38% of applicants admitted
- Test scores required

**General. Degrees:** 28 bachelor's awarded. **Location:** 220 miles from Chicago, 100 miles from St. Louis. **Calendar:** Semester. **Full-time faculty:** 7 total. **Part-time faculty:** 7 total.

**Student profile.** 79 degree-seeking undergraduates. 120 applied as first time-transfer students, 46 admitted, 36 enrolled.

| | | | |
|---|---|---|---|
| Women: | 95% | Out-of-state: | 2% |
| African American: | 1% | 25 or older: | 30% |
| Asian American: | 1% | | |

**Basis for selection.** High school transcript, college transcript, standardized test scores required. Transfer accepted as juniors.

**2009-2010 Annual costs.** Tuition/fees: $12,800. Books/supplies: $1,772. Personal expenses: $1,854.

**Financial aid. Need-based:** 71 applied for aid; 56 were judged to have need; 56 of these received aid. Average need met was 90%. 76% of total undergraduate aid awarded as scholarships/grants, 24% as loans/jobs. **Non-need-based:** Awarded to 50 undergraduates.

**Application procedures. Admission:** $60 fee.

**Academics. Credit/placement by examination:** CLEP.

**Majors. Health:** Nursing (RN).

**Computing on campus.** 23 workstations in library, computer center. Commuter students can connect to campus network. Online library, helpline, repair service, wireless network available.

**Contact.** E-mail: linda.quigley@stjohnscollegespringfield.edu
Phone: (217) 525-5628 Fax: (217) 757-6870
Linda Quigley, Admissions Officer, St. John's College, 729 East Carpenter Street, Springfield, IL 62702

## Saint Xavier University
### Chicago, Illinois
### www.sxu.edu

**CB member**
**CB code: 1708**

- Private 4-year university affiliated with Roman Catholic Church
- Commuter campus in very large city
- 3,060 degree-seeking undergraduates: 19% part-time, 70% women, 17% African American, 3% Asian American, 14% Hispanic American
- 1,943 degree-seeking graduate students
- 25% of applicants admitted
- SAT or ACT (ACT writing optional) required
- 53% graduate within 6 years

**General.** Founded in 1847. Regionally accredited. Affiliated with Sisters of Mercy. **Degrees:** 820 bachelor's awarded; master's offered. **ROTC:** Air Force. **Location:** 20 miles from downtown. **Calendar:** Semester, limited summer session. **Full-time faculty:** 180 total; 100% have terminal degrees, 14% minority, 56% women. **Part-time faculty:** 226 total; 23% have terminal degrees, 8% minority, 63% women. **Class size:** 46% < 20, 51% 20-39, 2% 40-49, 1% 50-99. **Special facilities:** Music performance studio, reading clinic, speech clinic, learning disabilities clinic, mathematics laboratory.

**Freshman class profile.** 12,175 applied, 3,008 admitted, 439 enrolled.

| Mid 50% test scores | | | |
|---|---|---|---|
| SAT critical reading: | 510-580 | GPA 3.0-3.49: | 28% |
| SAT math: | 490-600 | GPA 2.0-2.99: | 39% |
| SAT writing: | 460-590 | Rank in top quarter: | 44% |
| ACT composite: | 20-25 | Rank in top tenth: | 17% |
| GPA 3.75 or higher: | 19% | Return as sophomores: | 76% |
| GPA 3.50-3.74: | 13% | Out-of-state: | 9% |
| | | Live on campus: | 61% |

**Basis for selection.** GPA, test scores most important. Counselor recommendation, class rank considered. Interview recommended for borderline applicants. Audition required of music majors.

**High school preparation.** College-preparatory program recommended. 16 units recommended. Recommended units include English 4, mathematics 3, foreign language 2 and academic electives 3. 4 units of science and social studies combined.

**2009-2010 Annual costs.** Tuition/fees: $24,465. Room/board: $8,408. Books/supplies: $1,200. Personal expenses: $1,026.

**2008-2009 Financial aid. Need-based:** 510 full-time freshmen applied for aid; 470 were judged to have need; 470 of these received aid. Average need met was 82%. Average scholarship/grant was $14,870; average loan $3,404. 55% of total undergraduate aid awarded as scholarships/grants, 45% as loans/jobs. **Non-need-based:** Awarded to 704 full-time undergraduates, including 140 freshmen. Scholarships awarded for academics, athletics, music/drama.

**Application procedures. Admission:** No deadline. $25 fee, may be waived for applicants with need, free for online applicants. Admission notification on a rolling basis. Must reply by May 1 or within 4 week(s) if notified thereafter. **Financial aid:** Priority date 3/1; no closing date. FAFSA required. Applicants notified on a rolling basis starting 2/1; must reply by 5/1 or within 2 week(s) of notification.

**Academics. Special study options:** Accelerated study, combined bachelor's/graduate degree, cooperative education, distance learning, double major, dual enrollment of high school students, ESL, external degree, honors, independent study, internships, liberal arts/career combination, semester at sea, student-designed major, study abroad, teacher certification program. **Credit/placement by examination:** AP, CLEP, institutional tests. 27 credit hours maximum toward bachelor's degree. **Support services:** Learning center, pre-admission summer program, reduced course load, remedial instruction, study skills assistance, tutoring, writing center.

**Majors. Biology:** General, botany. **Business:** General, accounting, actuarial science, international. **Communications:** General, organizational. **Computer sciences:** General, computer science. **Education:** General, art, biology, history, mathematics, music, secondary, social science, Spanish. **Foreign languages:** Spanish. **Health:** Nursing (RN), premedicine, prepharmacy, speech pathology. **History:** General. **Interdisciplinary:** Biological/physical sciences, natural sciences. **Legal studies:** Prelaw. **Liberal arts:** Arts/sciences. **Math:** General. **Philosophy/religion:** Philosophy, religion. **Physical sciences:** Chemistry. **Protective services:** Criminal justice. **Psychology:** General, industrial. **Social sciences:** General, international relations, political science, sociology. **Theology:** Theology. **Visual/performing arts:** Studio arts, voice/opera.

**Most popular majors.** Biology 6%, business/marketing 24%, education 16%, health sciences 19%, liberal arts 8%, psychology 7%, social sciences 8%.

**Computing on campus.** 500 workstations in dormitories, library, computer center, student center. Dormitories wired for high-speed internet access and linked to campus network. Commuter students can connect to campus network. Online course registration, online library, helpline, student web hosting, wireless network available.

**Student life. Freshman orientation:** Mandatory, $125 fee. Preregistration for classes offered. Two-day overnight orientation held in summer. **Housing:** Coed dorms, special housing for disabled, apartments available. $100 nonrefundable deposit, deadline 5/1. **Activities:** Bands, campus ministries, choral groups, film society, international student organizations, literary magazine, music ensembles, radio station, student government, student newspaper, symphony orchestra, black student organization, Hispanic student organization, student activities board, student nurses association, Muslim student association, Celtic Connection, Fellowship of Christian Athletes, Xi Delta.

**Athletics.** NAIA. **Intercollegiate:** Baseball M, basketball, cross-country, football (tackle) M, soccer, softball W, volleyball W. **Intramural:** Basketball M, bowling, volleyball. **Team name:** Cougars.

**Student services.** Adult student services, alcohol/substance abuse counseling, chaplain/spiritual director, career counseling, services for economically disadvantaged, student employment services, financial aid counseling, health services, on-campus daycare, personal counseling, placement for graduates, veterans' counselor. **Physically disabled:** Services for speech impaired.

**Contact.** E-mail: admissions@sxu.edu
Phone: (773) 298-3050 Toll-free number: (800) 462-9288
Fax: (773) 298-3076
Anne Brennan, Assistant Vice President of Recruitment and Admission Enrollment, Saint Xavier University, 3700 West 103rd Street, Chicago, IL 60655

---

## School of the Art Institute of Chicago
**Chicago, Illinois**
www.saic.edu
**CB member**
**CB code: 1713**

- Private 4-year visual arts college
- Commuter campus in very large city
- 2,379 degree-seeking undergraduates: 7% part-time, 66% women, 4% African American, 12% Asian American, 9% Hispanic American, 1% Native American, 17% international
- 681 degree-seeking graduate students
- 81% of applicants admitted
- SAT or ACT (ACT writing optional), application essay required
- 63% graduate within 6 years

**General.** Founded in 1866. Regionally accredited. **Degrees:** 477 bachelor's awarded; master's offered. **Location:** Downtown Chicago. **Calendar:** Semester, extensive summer session. **Full-time faculty:** 135 total; 18% minority, 58% women. **Part-time faculty:** 462 total; 14% minority. **Class size:** 82% < 20, 15% 20-39, 1% 40-49, less than 1% 50-99, less than 1% >100. **Special facilities:** Art collection, film center, video data bank, poetry center, art galleries, fashion resource center, artists' book collection, Roger Brown house museum and study collection.

**Freshman class profile.** 3,114 applied, 2,533 admitted, 462 enrolled.

| Mid 50% test scores | | | |
|---|---|---|---|
| SAT critical reading: | 520-630 | Return as sophomores: | 75% |
| | | Out-of-state: | 81% |
| SAT math: | 490-610 | Live on campus: | 85% |
| ACT composite: | 21-27 | International: | 13% |

**Basis for selection.** Portfolio very important, statement of purpose, 500 SAT Critical Reading or 20 ACT English, academic credentials, and recommendations also considered. Interview recommended. Portfolio required.

**High school preparation.** Advanced-level study of art recommended.

**2009-2010 Annual costs.** Tuition/fees: $34,600. Students will be required to purchase a laptop through SAIC. Costs range from $2,000 to $2,200. Room only: $9,200. Books/supplies: $2,560. Personal expenses: $2,520.

**2008-2009 Financial aid. Need-based:** 281 full-time freshmen applied for aid; 245 were judged to have need; 245 of these received aid. Average need met was 73%. Average scholarship/grant was $12,315; average loan $3,740. 51% of total undergraduate aid awarded as scholarships/grants, 49% as loans/jobs. **Non-need-based:** Awarded to 638 full-time undergraduates, including 116 freshmen. Scholarships awarded for academics, art.

---

**Application procedures. Admission:** Priority date 2/15; deadline 6/1 (receipt date). $65 fee, may be waived for applicants with need. Application must be submitted online. Admission notification on a rolling basis beginning on or about 10/1. **Financial aid:** Priority date 3/15; no closing date. FAFSA required. Applicants notified on a rolling basis starting 3/1.

**Academics.** Interdisciplinary curriculum allows students to personalize education or concentrate on single discipline. **Special study options:** Cooperative education, cross-registration, double major, ESL, exchange student, independent study, internships, New York semester, student-designed major, study abroad, teacher certification program. Interdisciplinary curriculum with 6 credit off-campus study requirement, "credit/no-credit" grading system. **Credit/placement by examination:** AP, CLEP, IB. 18 credit hours maximum toward bachelor's degree. DANTES scores accepted. **Support services:** Learning center, pre-admission summer program, reduced course load, remedial instruction, study skills assistance, tutoring.

**Majors. Architecture:** Interior. **Communications:** Digital media. **Communications technology:** Animation/special effects, desktop publishing, graphics, photo/film/video, recording arts. **Education:** Art. **Visual/performing arts:** General, art, art history/conservation, ceramics, cinematography, design, digital art, drawing, fashion design, fiber arts, graphic design, industrial design, interior design, multimedia, painting, photography, printmaking, sculpture, studio arts. **Other:** Designed objects, Visual and critical studies.

**Computing on campus.** PC or laptop required. 350 workstations in dormitories, library, computer center. Dormitories wired for high-speed internet access and linked to campus network. Commuter students can connect to campus network. Online library, helpline, repair service, student web hosting, wireless network available.

**Student life. Freshman orientation:** Mandatory, $100 fee. Preregistration for classes offered. 4 days prior to beginning of class. First day open to parents, family and friends. **Housing:** Coed dorms, special housing for disabled, wellness housing available. $550 nonrefundable deposit. **Activities:** Campus ministries, dance, drama, film society, international student organizations, literary magazine, radio station, student government, student newspaper, TV station, Black at SAIC, Hillel, InterVarsity, Korean Student Association, Latin American Student Organization, Oxfam, Taiwanese Student Organization.

**Student services.** Alcohol/substance abuse counseling, career counseling, student employment services, financial aid counseling, health services, minority student services, personal counseling, veterans' counselor. **Physically disabled:** Services for visually, speech, hearing impaired.

**Contact.** E-mail: admiss@saic.edu
Phone: (312) 629-6100 Toll-free number: (800) 232-7242
Fax: (312) 629-6101
Scott Ramon, Director, Undergraduate Admissions, School of the Art Institute of Chicago, 36 South Wabash Avenue, Chicago, IL 60603

---

## Shimer College
**Chicago, Illinois**
www.shimer.edu
**CB code: 1717**

- Private 4-year liberal arts college
- Residential campus in very large city
- 104 degree-seeking undergraduates: 12% part-time, 49% women, 2% African American, 4% Asian American, 4% Hispanic American, 1% Native American
- 29% of applicants admitted
- Application essay, interview required
- 32% graduate within 6 years

**General.** Founded in 1853. Regionally accredited. Located on campus of Illinois Institute of Technology. **Degrees:** 18 bachelor's awarded. **Location:** 3 miles from downtown. **Calendar:** Semester, limited summer session. **Full-time faculty:** 9 total; 78% have terminal degrees, 11% minority, 44% women. **Part-time faculty:** 4 total; 75% have terminal degrees. **Class size:** 100% < 20.

**Freshman class profile.** 190 applied, 56 admitted, 17 enrolled.

| | | | |
|---|---|---|---|
| GPA 3.75 or higher: | 44% | Return as sophomores: | 72% |
| GPA 3.50-3.74: | 14% | Out-of-state: | 74% |
| GPA 3.0-3.49: | 21% | Live on campus: | 79% |
| GPA 2.0-2.99: | 14% | | |

**Basis for selection.** Essays and interviews most important. Test scores, GPA, recommendations, motivation, maturity considered. Demonstrated writing skills and interest in and enthusiasm about Great Books curriculum and discussion method important. Early entrants and other applicants who do not have high school diplomas may be required to submit GED; applicants without high school diplomas who are too young to take GED may be required to complete additional approved testing in order to comply with financial aid regulations. Applicants to early entrance program, who leave high school without graduating, must submit ACT or SAT scores.

**High school preparation.** College-preparatory program recommended. 20 units recommended. Recommended units include English 4, mathematics 3, social studies 3, history 2, science 3 (laboratory 1), foreign language 3 and visual/performing arts 1.

**2009-2010 Annual costs.** Tuition/fees: $25,960. Cost of 14 meal plan: $4,528. Room only: $6,907. Books/supplies: $1,400. Personal expenses: $1,020.

**2008-2009 Financial aid.** **Need-based:** 29 full-time freshmen applied for aid; 22 were judged to have need; 22 of these received aid. Average need met was 64%. Average scholarship/grant was $11,644; average loan $3,545. 47% of total undergraduate aid awarded as scholarships/grants, 53% as loans/jobs. **Non-need-based:** Awarded to 7 full-time undergraduates, including 6 freshmen. Scholarships awarded for alumni affiliation.

**Application procedures.** **Admission:** Priority date 3/1; deadline 7/31 (receipt date). $25 fee, may be waived for applicants with need. Admission notification on a rolling basis beginning on or about 9/15. Must reply by May 1 or within 3 week(s) if notified thereafter. **Financial aid:** Priority date 3/1; no closing date. FAFSA, institutional form required. Applicants notified on a rolling basis starting 4/1; must reply by 5/1 or within 3 week(s) of notification.

**Academics.** Curriculum is based on The Great Books of Western Culture. **Special study options:** Combined bachelor's/graduate degree, cross-registration, double major, dual enrollment of high school students, internships, study abroad, weekend college. **Credit/placement by examination:** CLEP, institutional tests. Shimer Institutional placement examinations may result in credit; no outside testing is accepted. **Support services:** Reduced course load, study skills assistance, tutoring, writing center.

**Majors.** **Interdisciplinary:** Natural sciences. **Liberal arts:** Arts/sciences, humanities. **Social sciences:** General.

**Most popular majors.** Interdisciplinary studies 15%, liberal arts 70%, social sciences 15%.

**Computing on campus.** 25 workstations in dormitories, library, computer center, student center. Dormitories wired for high-speed internet access and linked to campus network. Commuter students can connect to campus network. Helpline, wireless network available.

**Student life.** **Freshman orientation:** Mandatory, $100 fee. Held 3-4 days prior to start of classes. Includes demonstration class, placement exams, orientation to residence hall and Chicago. **Housing:** Guaranteed on-campus for freshmen. Coed dorms, single-sex dorms, apartments available. $300 partly refundable deposit, deadline 5/1. **Activities:** Jazz band, campus ministries, choral groups, dance, drama, film society, international student organizations, literary magazine, music ensembles, musical theater, radio station, student government, student newspaper, American Red Cross, Catholic campus ministry, gays/lesbians/allies and more, Hillel, Hindu student council, gospel choir, Muslim students association, chess club.

**Athletics.** **Intramural:** Basketball, football (non-tackle), soccer, softball, track and field, volleyball. **Team name:** Flaming Smelts.

**Student services.** Adult student services, alcohol/substance abuse counseling, career counseling, student employment services, financial aid counseling, health services, personal counseling, placement for graduates.

**Contact.** E-mail: admission@shimer.edu
Phone: (312) 235-3506 Toll-free number: (800) 215-7173
Fax: (312) 235-3501
Elaine Vincent, Director of Enrollment Services, Shimer College, 3424 South State Street, Chicago, IL 60616

## Southern Illinois University Carbondale

**Carbondale, Illinois** **CB member**
**www.siuc.edu** **CB code: 1726**

- Public 4-year university
- Residential campus in large town
- 15,524 degree-seeking undergraduates: 12% part-time, 43% women, 19% African American, 2% Asian American, 5% Hispanic American, 2% international
- 4,737 degree-seeking graduate students
- 69% of applicants admitted

- SAT or ACT (ACT writing optional) required
- 44% graduate within 6 years; 58% enter graduate study

**General.** Founded in 1869. Regionally accredited. **Degrees:** 4,130 bachelor's, 69 associate awarded; master's, doctoral, professional offered. **ROTC:** Army, Air Force. **Location:** 100 miles from St. Louis. **Calendar:** Semester, extensive summer session. **Full-time faculty:** 958 total; 81% have terminal degrees, 17% minority, 36% women. **Part-time faculty:** 136 total; 60% have terminal degrees, 12% minority, 46% women. **Class size:** 50% < 20, 41% 20-39, 4% 40-49, 3% 50-99, 1% >100. **Special facilities:** University press, coal research center, materials technology center, outdoor education laboratory, university farms, center for study of crime, electron microscopy center, cooperative wildlife research laboratory, cooperative fisheries research laboratory, vivarium, airport training facility, laboratory theater, child development laboratory, center for archaeological investigations, small business incubator, public policy institute, dental and medical clinics, environmental center, media center.

**Freshman class profile.** 11,509 applied, 7,900 admitted, 2,450 enrolled.

| Mid 50% test scores | | | |
|---|---|---|---|
| SAT critical reading: | 420-570 | Rank in top quarter: | 28% |
| SAT math: | 440-560 | Rank in top tenth: | 10% |
| SAT writing: | 410-520 | Return as sophomores: | 67% |
| ACT composite: | 19-24 | International: | 1% |

**Basis for selection.** High school class rank and ACT scores most important. Holistic approach using these two items along with GPA, and core unit courses. Interviews required for major scholarships only, not for admission. **Homeschooled:** Transcript of courses and grades required. **Learning Disabled:** Special requirements only apply for certain programs.

**High school preparation.** College-preparatory program required. 15 units required. Required units include English 4, mathematics 3, social studies 3, science 3 and academic electives 2.

**2009-2010 Annual costs.** Tuition/fees: $10,411; $21,346 out-of-state. Room/board: $7,673. Books/supplies: $900. Personal expenses: $1,218.

**2008-2009 Financial aid.** **Need-based:** 2,233 full-time freshmen applied for aid; 1,785 were judged to have need; 1,738 of these received aid. Average need met was 95%. Average scholarship/grant was $7,406; average loan $3,637. 47% of total undergraduate aid awarded as scholarships/grants, 53% as loans/jobs. **Non-need-based:** Awarded to 5,160 full-time undergraduates, including 1,116 freshmen. Scholarships awarded for academics, alumni affiliation, athletics, leadership, minority status, ROTC. **Additional information:** Need-based financial aid available to part-time students enrolled in minimum of 6 semester hours.

**Application procedures.** **Admission:** Priority date 5/1; no deadline. $30 fee, may be waived for applicants with need. Admission notification on a rolling basis beginning on or about 9/1. Must reply by May 1 or within 6 week(s) if notified thereafter. **Financial aid:** Priority date 4/1; no closing date. FAFSA required. Applicants notified on a rolling basis starting 5/1; must reply within 4 week(s) of notification.

**Academics.** Active production schedule in several theaters includes contemporary works, musicals, operas, original plays by faculty and students, and world drama from major periods in theater history. **Special study options:** Combined bachelor's/graduate degree, cooperative education, distance learning, double major, ESL, honors, independent study, internships, student-designed major, study abroad, teacher certification program. **Credit/placement by examination:** AP, CLEP, IB, ACT, institutional tests. 15 credit hours maximum toward associate degree, 30 toward bachelor's. **Support services:** Learning center, pre-admission summer program, reduced course load, remedial instruction, study skills assistance, tutoring, writing center.

**Majors.** **Agriculture:** General, animal sciences, economics, plant sciences. **Architecture:** Architecture. **Biology:** General, botany, microbiology, physiology, zoology. **Business:** Accounting, business admin, finance, hospitality admin, management science, managerial economics, marketing. **Communications:** Journalism, radio/tv. **Computer sciences:** Computer science, information systems. **Conservation:** Forestry. **Education:** Early childhood, elementary, health, physical, special, trade/industrial. **Engineering:** Civil, computer, electrical, mechanical, mining. **Engineering technology:** General, automotive, electrical, industrial. **Family/consumer sciences:** Clothing/textiles, food/nutrition. **Foreign languages:** Classics, French, German, linguistics, Spanish. **Health:** Athletic training, communication disorders, dental hygiene, health care admin, medical radiologic technology/radiation therapy, physician assistant. **History:** General. **Interdisciplinary:** Nutrition sciences. **Legal studies:** Paralegal. **Liberal arts:** Arts/sciences. **Math:** General. **Mechanic/repair:** Avionics. **Parks/recreation:** General, exercise sciences. **Personal/culinary services:** Mortuary science. **Philosophy/religion:** Philosophy. **Physical sciences:** Chemistry, geology, physics. **Protective services:** Fire services admin, law enforcement admin. **Psychology:** General.

**Public administration:** Social work. **Social sciences:** General, anthropology, economics, geography, political science, sociology. **Transportation:** Aviation management. **Visual/performing arts:** Art, cinematography, design, dramatic, interior design, musical theater, studio arts. **Other:** Electronics systems technologies, Foreign languages and international trade, Rehabilitation services, Technical resource management.

**Most popular majors.** Business/marketing 10%, education 20%, engineering/engineering technologies 11%, health sciences 8%, visual/performing arts 6%.

**Computing on campus.** 1,776 workstations in dormitories, library, computer center, student center. Dormitories wired for high-speed internet access and linked to campus network. Commuter students can connect to campus network. Online course registration, online library, helpline, student web hosting, wireless network available.

**Student life. Freshman orientation:** Mandatory, $75 fee. Preregistration for classes offered. Several 1-day seminars offered April through July. **Housing:** Guaranteed on-campus for freshmen. Coed dorms, single-sex dorms, special housing for disabled, apartments, fraternity/sorority housing available. $650 partly refundable deposit, deadline 6/1. Living/learning, residential college, freshman interest group housing available. **Activities:** Bands, campus ministries, choral groups, dance, drama, film society, international student organizations, literary magazine, music ensembles, musical theater, opera, radio station, student government, student newspaper, symphony orchestra, TV station, over 400 student organizations.

**Athletics.** NCAA. **Intercollegiate:** Baseball M, basketball, cheerleading, cross-country, diving, football (tackle) M, golf, softball W, swimming, tennis, track and field, volleyball W. **Intramural:** Badminton, basketball, cricket, cross-country, football (non-tackle), golf, handball, racquetball, soccer, softball, squash, swimming, table tennis, tennis, triathlon, volleyball, water polo, wrestling M. **Team name:** Salukis.

**Student services.** Adult student services, alcohol/substance abuse counseling, career counseling, services for economically disadvantaged, student employment services, financial aid counseling, health services, legal services, minority student services, on-campus daycare, personal counseling, placement for graduates, veterans' counselor, women's services. **Physically disabled:** Services for visually, speech, hearing impaired. **Learning disabled:** Comprehensive services available.

**Contact.** E-mail: admrec@siu.edu
Phone: (618) 453-4381 Fax: (618) 453-3250
Patsy Reynolds, Director, Admissions, Southern Illinois University Carbondale, Mailcode 4701, Carbondale, IL 62901-4701

---

## Southern Illinois University Edwardsville

**Edwardsville, Illinois**  **CB member**
**www.siue.edu**  **CB code: 1759**

- Public 4-year university
- Commuter campus in very large city
- 11,055 degree-seeking undergraduates: 14% part-time, 54% women, 11% African American, 2% Asian American, 2% Hispanic American, 1% international
- 2,796 degree-seeking graduate students
- 87% of applicants admitted
- 46% graduate within 6 years; 30% enter graduate study

**General.** Founded in 1957. Regionally accredited. **Degrees:** 2,162 bachelor's awarded; master's, professional offered. **ROTC:** Army, Air Force. **Location:** 18 miles from St. Louis. **Calendar:** Semester, extensive summer session. **Full-time faculty:** 622 total; 80% have terminal degrees, 15% minority, 49% women. **Part-time faculty:** 248 total; 11% minority, 45% women. **Class size:** 41% < 20, 40% 20-39, 9% 40-49, 9% 50-99, 1% >100. **Special facilities:** Museum collections, arboretum, greenhouse, engineering labs, clinical nursing facility, observatory, applied research and technology park, corn-to-ethanol research center, biotechnology laboratory incubator, pharmaceutical care lab.

**Freshman class profile.** 6,952 applied, 6,077 admitted, 1,950 enrolled.

| Mid 50% test scores | | | |
|---|---|---|---|
| ACT composite: | 20-25 | Return as sophomores: | 71% |
| Rank in top quarter: | 42% | Out-of-state: | 7% |
| Rank in top tenth: | 18% | Live on campus: | 69% |

**Basis for selection.** Students admitted with 2.5 GPA and 21 ACT (970-1000 SAT, exclusive of Writing), or with rank in top 25% of class. Applicants who do not meet requirements subject to additional review. SAT or

ACT recommended. Audition recommended for music majors; portfolio recommended for art majors.

**High school preparation.** 15 units required. Required and recommended units include English 4, mathematics 3, social studies 3, science 3 (laboratory 3), foreign language 2 and academic electives 2. At least 2 years of history or government required; 2 years foreign language, music, dance, theater, art, or vocational education (1 year maximum) electives required; 2 years of 1 foreign language and 1 year music and/or art recommended; 1 year chemistry and 1 year biology required.

**2009-2010 Annual costs.** Tuition/fees: $8,336; $17,638 out-of-state. Required fees include book rental. Room/board: $7,461. Books/supplies: $696. Personal expenses: $1,506.

**2008-2009 Financial aid.** All financial aid based on need.

**Application procedures. Admission:** Priority date 12/1; deadline 5/1 (postmark date). $30 fee, may be waived for applicants with need. Admission notification on a rolling basis beginning on or about 9/1. Application and all official documents required to be on file 3 weeks before beginning of term. **Financial aid:** Priority date 3/1, closing date 6/1. FAFSA required. Applicants notified on a rolling basis starting 3/15; must reply within 4 week(s) of notification.

**Academics.** Senior project required. **Special study options:** Accelerated study, combined bachelor's/graduate degree, cooperative education, cross-registration, distance learning, double major, ESL, honors, independent study, internships, student-designed major, study abroad, teacher certification program. **Credit/placement by examination:** AP, CLEP, institutional tests. 32 credit hours maximum toward bachelor's degree. Placement tests required for some students in reading, writing and/or math; determination based on test scores and GPA. **Support services:** Learning center, pre-admission summer program, reduced course load, remedial instruction, study skills assistance, tutoring, writing center.

**Majors. Biology:** General, biotechnology. **Business:** Accounting, business admin, management information systems, managerial economics. **Communications:** Media studies. **Computer sciences:** Computer science. **Education:** Early childhood, elementary, health, science, special. **Engineering:** Civil, computer, electrical, industrial, manufacturing, mechanical. **Engineering technology:** Construction. **Foreign languages:** General. **Health:** Audiology/speech pathology, nursing (RN). **History:** General. **Liberal arts:** Arts/sciences. **Math:** General. **Parks/recreation:** Exercise sciences, health/fitness. **Philosophy/religion:** Philosophy. **Physical sciences:** Chemistry, physics. **Protective services:** Criminal justice. **Psychology:** General. **Public administration:** Social work. **Social sciences:** Anthropology, economics, geography, political science, sociology. **Visual/performing arts:** Art, dramatic, studio arts.

**Most popular majors.** Biology 6%, business/marketing 20%, education 10%, engineering/engineering technologies 9%, English 6%, health sciences 10%, psychology 6%, social sciences 9%.

**Computing on campus.** 600 workstations in dormitories, library, computer center, student center. Dormitories linked to campus network. Commuter students can connect to campus network. Online course registration, online library, helpline available.

**Student life. Freshman orientation:** Available. Preregistration for classes offered. Offer summer pre-entry advisement and registration program in addition to freshman orientation. **Housing:** Coed dorms, special housing for disabled, apartments, fraternity/sorority housing, wellness housing available. $300 deposit, deadline 5/1. Focused-interest communities. **Activities:** Bands, campus ministries, choral groups, dance, drama, literary magazine, music ensembles, musical theater, opera, radio station, student government, student newspaper, symphony orchestra, TV station, 170 organizations and honor societies available.

**Athletics.** NCAA. **Intercollegiate:** Baseball M, basketball, cross-country, golf, soccer, softball W, tennis, track and field, volleyball W, wrestling M. **Intramural:** Badminton, basketball, bowling, fencing, football (non-tackle), golf, racquetball, soccer, softball, table tennis, tennis, volleyball, water polo. **Team name:** Cougars.

**Student services.** Alcohol/substance abuse counseling, career counseling, services for economically disadvantaged, student employment services, financial aid counseling, health services, legal services, on-campus daycare, personal counseling, placement for graduates, veterans' counselor. **Physically disabled:** Services for visually, speech, hearing impaired. **Learning disabled:** Comprehensive services available.

**Contact.** E-mail: admissions@siue.edu
Phone: (618) 650-3705 Toll-free number: (800) 447-7483
Fax: (618) 650-5013
Todd Burrell, Director of Admissions, Southern Illinois University Edwardsville, Campus Box 1600, Rendleman Hall, Rm 2120, Edwardsville, IL 62026-1600

## Telshe Yeshiva-Chicago
**Chicago, Illinois**

CB code: 7009

- Private 4-year rabbinical college for men affiliated with Jewish faith
- Very large city
- 77 degree-seeking undergraduates

**General.** Accredited by AARTS. **Degrees:** 4 bachelor's awarded; master's offered. **Calendar:** Continuous. **Full-time faculty:** 5 total. **Part-time faculty:** 1 total.

**Application procedures. Admission:** No deadline. No application fee.

**Academics. Credit/placement by examination:** CLEP.

**Majors. Theology:** Talmudic.

**Contact.** Phone: (773) 463-7738 Fax: (773) 463-2894
Director of Admissions, Telshe Yeshiva-Chicago, 3535 West Foster Avenue, Chicago, IL 60625

## Trinity Christian College
**Palos Heights, Illinois**
www.trnty.edu

CB code: 1820

- Private 4-year liberal arts college affiliated with Reformed (unaffiliated)
- Residential campus in very large city
- 1,345 degree-seeking undergraduates: 22% part-time, 69% women, 8% African American, 2% Asian American, 7% Hispanic American, 2% international
- 86% of applicants admitted
- SAT or ACT (ACT writing optional), application essay, interview required
- 58% graduate within 6 years

**General.** Founded in 1959. Regionally accredited. **Degrees:** 303 bachelor's awarded. **Location:** 20 miles from Chicago. **Calendar:** Semester, limited summer session. **Full-time faculty:** 79 total; 67% have terminal degrees, 11% minority, 40% women. **Part-time faculty:** 72 total; 49% have terminal degrees, 15% minority, 43% women. **Class size:** 58% < 20, 40% 20-39, 2% 40-49. **Special facilities:** Dutch heritage center archives.

**Freshman class profile.** 625 applied, 536 admitted, 201 enrolled.

| Mid 50% test scores | | | |
|---|---|---|---|
| SAT critical reading: | 440-640 | GPA 2.0-2.99: | 26% |
| SAT math: | 430-670 | Rank in top quarter: | 40% |
| ACT composite: | 17-29 | Return as sophomores: | 73% |
| GPA 3.75 or higher: | 33% | Out-of-state: | 43% |
| GPA 3.50-3.74: | 11% | Live on campus: | 84% |
| GPA 3.0-3.49: | 29% | International: | 3% |

**Basis for selection.** 3.0 GPA with 2.0 GPA in English and math, and 22 ACT or 950 SAT (exclusive of Writing) required. ACT recommended. Statement of religious faith recommended.

**High school preparation.** College-preparatory program recommended. 16 units required; 18 recommended. Required and recommended units include English 3-4, mathematics 3-4, social studies 2-3, history 2, science 2-3 and foreign language 2. One 3-year major in mathematics, science, or social studies, and 2 2-year minors in mathematics, science, social studies, or foreign language recommended.

**2009-2010 Annual costs.** Tuition/fees: $20,959. Room/board: $7,680. Books/supplies: $1,100. Personal expenses: $2,015.

**2009-2010 Financial aid. Need-based:** 192 full-time freshmen applied for aid; 153 were judged to have need; 153 of these received aid. Average need met was 39%. Average scholarship/grant was $4,287; average loan $3,710. 65% of total undergraduate aid awarded as scholarships/grants, 35% as loans/jobs. **Non-need-based:** Awarded to 966 full-time undergraduates, including 342 freshmen. Scholarships awarded for academics, alumni affiliation, art, athletics, leadership, minority status, music/drama, religious affiliation. **Additional information:** High school transcripts and ACT or SAT scores required for merit scholarships.

**Application procedures. Admission:** No deadline. $20 fee, may be waived for applicants with need. Admission notification on a rolling basis beginning on or about 9/1. Must reply by May 1 or within 2 week(s) if

notified thereafter. **Financial aid:** Priority date 2/15, closing date 4/15. FAFSA, institutional form required. Applicants notified on a rolling basis starting 4/1; must reply by 5/1 or within 2 week(s) of notification.

**Academics. Special study options:** Double major, ESL, honors, independent study, internships, liberal arts/career combination, study abroad, teacher certification program, urban semester, Washington semester. **Credit/placement by examination:** AP, CLEP, IB, SAT, ACT, institutional tests. 30 credit hours maximum toward bachelor's degree. **Support services:** Learning center, pre-admission summer program, reduced course load, remedial instruction, study skills assistance, tutoring, writing center.

**Honors college/program.** Must have 28 ACT, be in top 10% of high school class, and have 3.5 high school GPA. 13-19 semester hours of unique courses. Approximately 15 freshmen admitted each year.

**Majors. Biology:** General. **Business:** General, accounting, communications, management information systems. **Communications:** General. **Computer sciences:** Computer science, information systems. **Education:** General, art, biology, business, chemistry, elementary, English, history, mathematics, music, physical, science, Spanish, special. **Foreign languages:** Spanish. **Health:** Nursing (RN). **History:** General. **Math:** General. **Parks/recreation:** Exercise sciences, health/fitness. **Philosophy/religion:** Philosophy. **Physical sciences:** Chemistry. **Psychology:** General. **Public administration:** Social work. **Social sciences:** Political science, sociology. **Theology:** Theology. **Visual/performing arts:** Art, music performance, studio arts. **Other:** Church and ministry leadership, Sport and leisure studies.

**Most popular majors.** Business/marketing 17%, education 38%, health sciences 13%.

**Computing on campus.** 140 workstations in dormitories, library, computer center. Dormitories wired for high-speed internet access and linked to campus network. Commuter students can connect to campus network. Helpline, wireless network available.

**Student life. Freshman orientation:** Mandatory, $210 fee. Preregistration for classes offered. Two-day program in early July and two-week program in late August. **Housing:** Guaranteed on-campus for freshmen. Coed dorms, apartments available. $75 fully refundable deposit, deadline 9/1. **Activities:** Bands, campus ministries, choral groups, dance, drama, music ensembles, musical theater, student government, student newspaper, religious drama club, theology club, pro-life, Bread for the World, Inter-Varsity Fellowship, Big Brother/Big Sister, Association for Public Justice, PACE literacy program in Cook County jail.

**Athletics.** NAIA, NCCAA. **Intercollegiate:** Baseball M, basketball, cross-country, soccer, softball W, track and field, volleyball W. **Intramural:** Basketball, racquetball, soccer, volleyball. **Team name:** Trolls.

**Student services.** Adult student services, alcohol/substance abuse counseling, chaplain/spiritual director, career counseling, student employment services, financial aid counseling, health services, minority student services, personal counseling, placement for graduates, veterans' counselor. **Physically disabled:** Services for visually, speech, hearing impaired.

**Contact.** E-mail: admissions@trnty.edu
Phone: (708) 239-4708 Toll-free number: (866) 874-6463
Fax: (708) 239-4826
Jeremy Klyn, Director of Admissions, Trinity Christian College, 6601 West College Drive, Palos Heights, IL 60463

## Trinity College of Nursing and Health Sciences
**Rock Island, Illinois**
www.trinitycollegeqc.edu

CB code: 2555

- Private 4-year nursing college
- Commuter campus in very large city
- 264 degree-seeking undergraduates: 48% part-time, 80% women, 3% African American, 2% Asian American, 5% Hispanic American
- SAT or ACT (ACT writing recommended) required

**General. Degrees:** 16 bachelor's, 64 associate awarded. **Calendar:** Semester, limited summer session. **Full-time faculty:** 17 total; 94% women. **Part-time faculty:** 10 total; 90% women.

**Freshman class profile.**

| | | | |
|---|---|---|---|
| GPA 3.75 or higher: | 10% | GPA 3.0-3.49: | 50% |
| GPA 3.50-3.74: | 15% | GPA 2.0-2.99: | 25% |

**Basis for selection.** Requirements vary by program. **Homeschooled:** Transcript of courses and grades required.

**High school preparation.** Required units include English 4, mathematics 3, social studies 3, science 3 (laboratory 1).

**2009-2010 Annual costs.** Tuition/fees: $12,227. Students are required to have a uniform and other health equipment.

**2009-2010 Financial aid. Need-based:** 45% of total undergraduate aid awarded as scholarships/grants, 55% as loans/jobs.

**Application procedures. Admission:** Closing date 12/15 (postmark date). $50 fee, may be waived for applicants with need. Admission notification on a rolling basis beginning on or about 12/1.

**Academics. Special study options:** Accelerated study, combined bachelor's/graduate degree, cooperative education, distance learning. 15 month accelerated BSN program for students with a previous degree. Affiliated with Trinity Medical Center and the Iowa Health System. Offers license preparation for respiratory care and pharmacy, in addition to nursing, radiology and paramedic. **Credit/placement by examination:** CLEP, ACT. **Support services:** Study skills assistance, tutoring.

**Majors. Health:** Nursing (RN).

**Computing on campus.** 15 workstations in computer center. Commuter students can connect to campus network. Helpline, wireless network available.

**Student life. Freshman orientation:** Mandatory, $10 fee. Preregistration for classes offered. **Activities:** Student government.

**Student services.** Career counseling, financial aid counseling, minority student services, on-campus daycare, personal counseling. **Learning disabled:** Comprehensive services available.

**Contact.** E-mail: kimpeb@trinityqc.com
Phone: (309) 779-7814 Fax: (309) 779-7748
Joanne Cunningham, Dean of Enrollment, Student Affairs and Alumni, Trinity College of Nursing and Health Sciences, 2122 25th Avenue, Rock Island, IL 61201

## Trinity International University
**Deerfield, Illinois**                          CB member
**www.tiu.edu**                                  CB code: 1810

- Private 4-year university and liberal arts college affiliated with Evangelical Free Church of America
- Residential campus in large town
- 987 degree-seeking undergraduates
- 97% of applicants admitted
- SAT or ACT (ACT writing optional), application essay required

**General.** Founded in 1897. Regionally accredited. Off-campus programs available through Christian College Consortium. **Degrees:** 215 bachelor's awarded; master's, doctoral offered. **Location:** 25 miles from Chicago. **Calendar:** Semester, limited summer session. **Full-time faculty:** 43 total; 84% have terminal degrees, 14% minority, 42% women. **Part-time faculty:** 39 total; 13% have terminal degrees, 8% minority, 51% women. **Class size:** 41% < 20, 39% 20-39, 16% 40-49, 5% 50-99. **Special facilities:** Seminary facilities.

**Freshman class profile.** 384 applied, 372 admitted, 156 enrolled.

| Mid 50% test scores | | | |
|---|---|---|---|
| SAT critical reading: | 400-580 | GPA 3.0-3.49: | 27% |
| SAT math: | 450-580 | GPA 2.0-2.99: | 30% |
| ACT composite: | 19-25 | Rank in top quarter: | 43% |
| GPA 3.75 or higher: | 29% | Rank in top tenth: | 37% |
| GPA 3.50-3.74: | 14% | Out-of-state: | 51% |
| | | Live on campus: | 93% |

**Basis for selection.** School achievement record, test scores, recommendations, evidence of Christian commitment, essays most important. Interview recommended for borderline applicants. **Homeschooled:** Transcript of courses and grades required.

**High school preparation.** College-preparatory program required. Required units include English 4, mathematics 2, social studies 2, history 2, science 2 (laboratory 1), foreign language 2 and visual/performing arts 2.

**2009-2010 Annual costs.** Tuition/fees: $22,370. Room/board: $7,430. Books/supplies: $1,080. Personal expenses: $1,130.

**2009-2010 Financial aid. Non-need-based:** Scholarships awarded for academics, alumni affiliation, athletics, minority status, music/drama, religious affiliation.

**Application procedures. Admission:** No deadline. $25 fee, may be waived for applicants with need. Admission notification on a rolling basis beginning on or about 9/1. **Financial aid:** Priority date 4/1; no closing date. FAFSA required. Applicants notified on a rolling basis starting 2/15; must reply within 4 week(s) of notification.

**Academics. Special study options:** Accelerated study, cooperative education, cross-registration, distance learning, double major, dual enrollment of high school students, exchange student, honors, independent study, internships, liberal arts/career combination, student-designed major, study abroad, teacher certification program, urban semester, Washington semester. REACH (for nontraditional students with previous college credit), graduate courses available to undergraduates with junior or senior standing. **Credit/placement by examination:** AP, CLEP, IB, SAT, ACT, institutional tests. Permission and approval by department chair required. May not be used to satisfy senior residency requirement. **Support services:** Learning center, remedial instruction, study skills assistance, tutoring, writing center.

**Majors. Biology:** General. **Business:** General, accounting, human resources, management science, marketing, nonprofit/public, organizational behavior, training/development. **Communications:** General. **Education:** Biology, elementary, English, history, mathematics, music, physical, secondary. **Health:** Athletic training, premedicine. **History:** General. **Legal studies:** Prelaw. **Liberal arts:** Humanities. **Math:** General. **Parks/recreation:** Health/fitness. **Philosophy/religion:** Philosophy. **Physical sciences:** Chemistry. **Psychology:** General. **Social sciences:** General. **Theology:** Bible, pastoral counseling, preministerial, religious ed, sacred music, theology, youth ministry. **Visual/performing arts:** Music pedagogy, music performance, music theory/composition, piano/organ, voice/opera.

**Most popular majors.** Business/marketing 22%, education 26%, health sciences 7%, liberal arts 6%, psychology 10%, theological studies 17%.

**Computing on campus.** 100 workstations in library, computer center, student center. Dormitories wired for high-speed internet access and linked to campus network. Commuter students can connect to campus network. Online course registration, online library, helpline, repair service, student web hosting, wireless network available.

**Student life. Freshman orientation:** Mandatory, $30 fee. Preregistration for classes offered. Orientation held the week before classes each fall and spring. Generally lasts entire week. **Policies:** Community expectations, general patterns of Christian lifestyle, policy on drug and alcohol abuse. Religious observance required. **Housing:** Guaranteed on-campus for freshmen. Single-sex dorms, special housing for disabled, apartments, wellness housing available. $50 partly refundable deposit, deadline 5/1. **Activities:** Bands, campus ministries, choral groups, dance, drama, music ensembles, musical theater, student government, student newspaper, symphony orchestra, Association of Believers for Black America, Global Christian Movement, Kappa Tau, Discipleship Cabinet, FAT Thursdays, Chapel Cabinet, Kids on Kampus, Wives Fellowship, Men's Ministry.

**Athletics.** NAIA, NCCAA. **Intercollegiate:** Baseball M, basketball, football (tackle) M, soccer, softball W, volleyball W. **Intramural:** Baseball M, basketball, bowling, football (non-tackle) M, racquetball, rugby M, soccer, softball, volleyball. **Team name:** Trojans.

**Student services.** Alcohol/substance abuse counseling, chaplain/spiritual director, career counseling, student employment services, financial aid counseling, health services, minority student services, on-campus daycare, personal counseling, placement for graduates. **Physically disabled:** Services for visually impaired.

**Contact.** E-mail: tcadmissions@tiu.edu
Phone: (847) 317-7000 Toll-free number: (800) 822-3225
Fax: (847) 317-8097
Aaron Mahl, Director of Admissions, Trinity International University, 2065 Half Day Road, Deerfield, IL 60015

## University of Chicago
**Chicago, Illinois**                            CB member
**www.uchicago.edu**                             CB code: 1832

- Private 4-year university and liberal arts college
- Residential campus in very large city
- 5,063 degree-seeking undergraduates: 1% part-time, 49% women, 6% African American, 15% Asian American, 9% Hispanic American, 9% international
- 7,050 degree-seeking graduate students
- 27% of applicants admitted
- SAT or ACT (ACT writing optional), application essay required
- 91% graduate within 6 years

**General.** Founded in 1891. Regionally accredited. **Degrees:** 1,207 bachelor's awarded; master's, doctoral, professional offered. **ROTC:** Army, Air Force. **Location:** 7 miles from Chicago. **Calendar:** Quarter, extensive summer session. **Full-time faculty:** 1,082 total; 100% have terminal degrees, 19% minority, 29% women. **Part-time faculty:** 580 total; 67% have terminal degrees, 12% minority, 32% women. **Class size:** 78% < 20, 15% 20-39, 3% 40-49, 3% 50-99, 1% >100. **Special facilities:** Oriental institute, art museum, theater, modern art gallery, Argonne National Laboratory, library of sciences, Fermi National Accelerator Laboratory, film studies center, observatory.

**Freshman class profile.** 13,564 applied, 3,708 admitted, 1,335 enrolled.

| Mid 50% test scores | | | |
|---|---|---|---|
| SAT critical reading: | 690-780 | GPA 3.0-3.49: | 3% |
| SAT math: | 680-780 | GPA 2.0-2.99: | 1% |
| SAT writing: | 670-760 | Rank in top quarter: | 96% |
| ACT composite: | 28-32 | Rank in top tenth: | 85% |
| GPA 3.75 or higher: | 89% | Return as sophomores: | 98% |
| GPA 3.50-3.74: | 7% | Out-of-state: | 79% |
| | | International: | 10% |

**Basis for selection.** Secondary school record, recommendations, essay, talent/ability and character/personal qualities very important. Interview recommended.

**High school preparation.** Recommended units include English 4, mathematics 4, social studies 2, history 2, science 4 and foreign language 3.

**2010-2011 Annual costs.** Tuition/fees: $41,091. Room/board: $12,153. Books/supplies: $1,050. Personal expenses: $1,919.

**2009-2010 Financial aid.** **Non-need-based:** Scholarships awarded for academics, leadership.

**Application procedures.** Admission: Closing date 1/2 (postmark date). $65 fee, may be waived for applicants with need. Admission notification 4/1. Must reply by 5/1. **Financial aid:** Closing date 2/1. FAFSA, institutional form, CSS PROFILE required. Applicants notified by 4/15; must reply by 5/1.

**Academics.** **Special study options:** Accelerated study, combined bachelor's/graduate degree, cross-registration, double major, dual enrollment of high school students, ESL, exchange student, honors, independent study, internships, student-designed major, study abroad, teacher certification program, Washington semester. **Credit/placement by examination:** AP, CLEP, IB, institutional tests. **Support services:** Study skills assistance, tutoring.

**Majors.** **Area/ethnic studies:** African, African-American, East Asian, German, Latin American, Near/Middle Eastern, Russian/Slavic, Slavic, South Asian. **Biology:** General, biochemistry. **Computer sciences:** General. **Conservation:** Environmental studies. **Foreign languages:** Ancient Greek, Arabic, Biblical, classics, comparative lit, East Asian, French, German, Hebrew, Italian, Latin, linguistics, Portuguese, Russian, Scandinavian, Slavic, South Asian, Spanish. **History:** General. **Liberal arts:** Arts/sciences. **Math:** General, applied, statistics. **Philosophy/religion:** Judaic, philosophy, religion. **Physical sciences:** Chemistry, geophysics, physics. **Psychology:** General. **Public administration:** Policy analysis. **Social sciences:** Anthropology, economics, geography, international relations, political science, sociology. **Visual/performing arts:** General, art history/conservation, film/cinema.

**Most popular majors.** Biology 11%, English 6%, foreign language 8%, mathematics 7%, physical sciences 7%, psychology 6%, social sciences 34%.

**Computing on campus.** 1,000 workstations in dormitories, library, computer center, student center. Dormitories wired for high-speed internet access and linked to campus network. Commuter students can connect to campus network. Online course registration, online library, helpline, repair service, student web hosting, wireless network available.

**Student life.** **Freshman orientation:** Mandatory, $536 fee. Held 10 days before classes begin in the fall. **Housing:** Guaranteed on-campus for all undergraduates. Coed dorms, apartments, fraternity/sorority housing available. **Activities:** Bands, campus ministries, choral groups, dance, drama, film society, international student organizations, literary magazine, music ensembles, Model UN, musical theater, radio station, student government, student newspaper, symphony orchestra, over 300 organizations.

**Athletics.** NCAA. **Intercollegiate:** Baseball M, basketball, cross-country, football (tackle) M, soccer, softball W, swimming, tennis, track and field, volleyball W, wrestling M. **Intramural:** Archery, badminton, basketball, cross-country, fencing, handball, racquetball, soccer, softball, swimming, table tennis, tennis, track and field, volleyball. **Team name:** Maroons.

**Student services.** Adult student services, alcohol/substance abuse counseling, chaplain/spiritual director, career counseling, services for economically disadvantaged, student employment services, financial aid counseling,

health services, minority student services, personal counseling, placement for graduates, veterans' counselor, women's services. **Physically disabled:** Services for visually, speech, hearing impaired.

**Contact.** E-mail: collegeadmissions@uchicago.edu
Phone: (773) 702-8650 Fax: (773) 702-4199
James Nondorf, Vice President, Dean of Admissions and Financial Aid, University of Chicago, 1101 East 58th Street, Chicago, IL 60637

---

## University of Illinois at Chicago

**Chicago, Illinois**      **CB member**
**www.uic.edu**      **CB code: 1851**

▸ Public 4-year university
▸ Commuter campus in very large city
▸ 15,986 degree-seeking undergraduates: 7% part-time, 52% women, 8% African American, 22% Asian American, 18% Hispanic American, 1% international
▸ 9,876 degree-seeking graduate students
▸ 63% of applicants admitted
▸ SAT and SAT Subject Tests or ACT (ACT writing optional), application essay required
▸ 54% graduate within 6 years

**General.** Founded in 1946. Regionally accredited. Medical, dental, nursing and pharmacy colleges, and medical center within university complex. **Degrees:** 3,379 bachelor's awarded; master's, doctoral, professional offered. **ROTC:** Army, Naval, Air Force. **Location:** One mile from downtown. **Calendar:** Semester, limited summer session. **Full-time faculty:** 1,160 total; 80% have terminal degrees, 24% minority, 45% women. **Part-time faculty:** 380 total; 53% have terminal degrees, 21% minority, 50% women. **Class size:** 33% < 20, 41% 20-39, 7% 40-49, 10% 50-99, 9% >100. **Special facilities:** Jane Addams' Hull House museum, prairie preserve, health sciences center, software technologies research facility.

**Freshman class profile.** 14,661 applied, 9,244 admitted, 3,147 enrolled.

| Mid 50% test scores | | | |
|---|---|---|---|
| SAT critical reading: | 460-630 | Return as sophomores: | 81% |
| SAT math: | 510-660 | Out-of-state: | 2% |
| SAT writing: | 490-630 | Live on campus: | 45% |
| ACT composite: | 21-26 | International: | 1% |
| Rank in top quarter: | 62% | Fraternities: | 4% |
| Rank in top tenth: | 28% | Sororities: | 4% |

**Basis for selection.** Class rank, GPA, and test scores most important. High school course selection and personal statement strongly considered. Auditions required of music and theater majors. Portfolio required of art majors. **Homeschooled:** Transcript of courses and grades required. **Learning Disabled:** Students may add learning disability information to personal essay.

**High school preparation.** College-preparatory program required. 15 units required. Required and recommended units include English 4, mathematics 3-4, social studies 3, science 3 and foreign language 2. Additional course requirements vary with college and program.

**2009-2010 Annual costs.** Tuition/fees: $12,034; $24,424 out-of-state. Room/board: $9,435. Books/supplies: $1,200. Personal expenses: $2,096.

**2008-2009 Financial aid.** **Need-based:** 2,467 full-time freshmen applied for aid; 2,003 were judged to have need; 1,903 of these received aid. Average need met was 73%. Average scholarship/grant was $11,948; average loan $3,277. 56% of total undergraduate aid awarded as scholarships/grants, 44% as loans/jobs. **Non-need-based:** Awarded to 1,163 full-time undergraduates, including 299 freshmen. Scholarships awarded for academics, art, athletics, music/drama, ROTC.

**Application procedures.** Admission: Closing date 1/15 (postmark date). $40 fee, may be waived for applicants with need. Admission notification on a rolling basis beginning on or about 11/30. Must reply by May 1 or within 2 week(s) if notified thereafter. **Financial aid:** Priority date 3/1; no closing date. FAFSA required. Applicants notified on a rolling basis starting 3/15; must reply by 5/1.

**Academics.** **Special study options:** Accelerated study, cooperative education, distance learning, double major, dual enrollment of high school students, exchange student, honors, independent study, internships, student-designed major, study abroad, teacher certification program. **Credit/placement by examination:** AP, CLEP, IB, institutional tests. 30 credit hours maximum toward bachelor's degree. **Support services:** Learning center, pre-admission summer program, remedial instruction, study skills assistance, tutoring, writing center.

**Majors. Architecture:** Architecture. **Area/ethnic studies:** African-American, German, Latin American. **Biology:** General, biochemistry. **Business:** Accounting, business admin, entrepreneurial studies, finance, management science, marketing. **Communications:** General. **Computer sciences:** Computer science, information systems. **Education:** Art, biology, chemistry, elementary, English, French, German, history, mathematics, physics, Spanish. **Engineering:** Biomedical, chemical, civil, computer, electrical, industrial, mechanical, physics. **Engineering technology:** Industrial management. **Foreign languages:** Classics, French, Italian, Polish, Russian, Spanish. **Health:** Dietetics, medical records admin, nursing (RN), predental. **History:** General. **Interdisciplinary:** Classical/archaeology, neuroscience. **Liberal arts:** Arts/sciences. **Math:** General, statistics. **Parks/recreation:** Exercise sciences. **Philosophy/religion:** Philosophy. **Physical sciences:** Chemistry, geology, physics. **Protective services:** Criminal justice. **Psychology:** General. **Social sciences:** Anthropology, economics, political science, sociology, urban studies. **Visual/performing arts:** Art history/conservation, cinematography, dramatic, graphic design, industrial design, photography, studio arts. **Other:** Gender and women's studies, Mathematics and computer science, Performance.

**Most popular majors.** Biology 10%, business/marketing 20%, engineering/engineering technologies 9%, health sciences 7%, psychology 12%, social sciences 10%.

**Computing on campus.** 1,100 workstations in dormitories, library, computer center, student center. Dormitories wired for high-speed internet access and linked to campus network. Commuter students can connect to campus network. Online course registration, online library, helpline, student web hosting, wireless network available.

**Student life. Freshman orientation:** Mandatory, $75 fee. Preregistration for classes offered. Two-day, overnight offered 12 times from early June to mid-August. **Housing:** Coed dorms, single-sex dorms, apartments available. $150 partly refundable deposit, deadline 3/1. Honors floors, Presidential Award House available. **Activities:** Bands, campus ministries, choral groups, drama, international student organizations, music ensembles, radio station, student government, student newspaper, over 200 student groups available.

**Athletics.** NCAA. **Intercollegiate:** Baseball M, basketball, cheerleading, cross-country, diving, gymnastics, soccer M, softball W, swimming, tennis, track and field, volleyball W. **Intramural:** Badminton, basketball, bowling, cross-country, football (non-tackle), racquetball, soccer, softball, table tennis, tennis, volleyball. **Team name:** Flames.

**Student services.** Adult student services, alcohol/substance abuse counseling, career counseling, services for economically disadvantaged, student employment services, financial aid counseling, health services, legal services, minority student services, on-campus daycare, personal counseling, placement for graduates, veterans' counselor, women's services. **Physically disabled:** Services for visually, speech, hearing impaired.

**Contact.** E-mail: uicadmit@uic.edu
Phone: (312) 996-4350 Fax: (312) 413-7628
Thomas Glenn, Executive Director Admissions and Records, University of Illinois at Chicago, PO Box 5220, Chicago, IL 60680-5220

## University of Illinois at Urbana-Champaign
**Champaign, Illinois**   **CB member**
**www.illinois.edu**   **CB code: 1836**

- Public 4-year university
- Residential campus in small city
- 30,694 degree-seeking undergraduates
- SAT or ACT with writing, application essay required

**General.** Founded in 1867. Regionally accredited. **Degrees:** 7,313 bachelor's awarded; master's, doctoral, professional offered. **ROTC:** Army, Naval, Air Force. **Location:** 130 miles from Chicago, 125 miles from Indianapolis. **Calendar:** Semester, extensive summer session. **Full-time faculty:** 2,289 total. **Part-time faculty:** 393 total. **Class size:** 38% < 20, 38% 20-39, 5% 40-49, 10% 50-99, 9% >100. **Special facilities:** Natural history museum, museum of world history and culture, performing and visual arts centers, 37 public libraries, institute of genomic biology, institute for advanced science and technology, computer science center, national center for supercomputing applications, arboretum, observatory, hiking trails, Japanese house and gardens, ice arena.

**Freshman class profile.**

| Mid 50% test scores | | ACT composite: | 26-31 |
|---|---|---|---|
| SAT critical reading: | 540-660 | Out-of-state: | 17% |
| SAT math: | 660-770 | | |

**Basis for selection.** High school course work, personal essay, class rank, SAT/ACT test scores most important. Audition required of dance, music, theater (performance) majors. Professional interest statement required of all applicants. **Homeschooled:** Provide detailed information about home school environment/coursework; applicants should contact admissions office early in high school career with questions or concerns. **Learning Disabled:** Recommended that students address disability and any accommodations they receive in required personal statement section.

**High school preparation.** Required and recommended units include English 4, mathematics 3-4, social studies 2-4, science 2-4 (laboratory 2), foreign language 2-4 and academic electives 2. Specific subject requirements vary with college and program.

**2009-2010 Annual costs.** Tuition/fees: $12,528; $26,670 out-of-state. Room/board: $9,284. Books/supplies: $1,200. Personal expenses: $2,510.

**2009-2010 Financial aid. Non-need-based:** Scholarships awarded for academics, alumni affiliation, art, athletics, leadership, music/drama, ROTC, state residency.

**Application procedures. Admission:** Priority date 11/1; deadline 1/2 (postmark date). $40 fee, may be waived for applicants with need. Admission notification 2/19. Must reply by May 1 or within 2 week(s) if notified thereafter. **Financial aid:** Priority date 3/15; no closing date. FAFSA required.

**Academics.** Students generally declare a major upon enrollment. Students without a declared major may apply for the general curriculum option in the Division of General Studies. **Special study options:** Accelerated study, combined bachelor's/graduate degree, cooperative education, cross-registration, distance learning, double major, dual enrollment of high school students, ESL, exchange student, honors, independent study, internships, liberal arts/career combination, semester at sea, student-designed major, study abroad, teacher certification program, Washington semester. Honors programs, campus honors, Illinois Leadership & Entrepreneurial programs. **Credit/placement by examination:** AP, CLEP, IB, SAT, ACT, institutional tests. Unlimited credit hours may be counted toward a degree. **Support services:** Learning center, reduced course load, study skills assistance, tutoring, writing center.

**Majors. Agriculture:** Agronomy, animal husbandry, animal sciences, business, communications, economics, education services, food processing, food science, horticultural science, horticulture, international, mechanization, ornamental horticulture. **Architecture:** Architecture, landscape, urban/community planning. **Area/ethnic studies:** East Asian, Latin American, Russian/Slavic, women's. **Biology:** General, biochemistry, biophysics, biotechnology, botany, cell/histology, cellular/molecular, entomology, microbiology, physiology, plant molecular. **Business:** General, accounting, accounting/business management, actuarial science, auditing, banking/financial services, business admin, entrepreneurial studies, finance, financial planning, hospitality admin, human resources, insurance, logistics, management information systems, management science, market research, marketing, operations, organizational behavior, purchasing, real estate, sales/distribution. **Communications:** General, advertising, broadcast journalism, journalism, media studies, organizational. **Computer sciences:** General, computer science, programming, security. **Conservation:** General, environmental science, forest sciences, management/policy, urban forestry, wildlife. **Education:** Agricultural, art, biology, chemistry, early childhood, early childhood special, elementary, English, foreign languages, French, German, history, kindergarten/preschool, Latin, mathematics, multi-level teacher, multiple handicapped, music, physical, physics, science, secondary, social science, social studies, Spanish, special. **Engineering:** General, aerospace, agricultural, biomedical, ceramic, chemical, civil, computer, computer hardware, construction, electrical, environmental, geotechnical, industrial, manufacturing, materials, materials science, mechanical, mechanics, metallurgical, nuclear, operations research, physics, polymer, software, structural, transportation, water resource. **Family/consumer sciences:** Child development, consumer economics, family studies, human nutrition. **Foreign languages:** Classics, comparative lit, East Asian, French, German, Hebrew, Italian, linguistics, Portuguese, Russian, Spanish. **Health:** Athletic training, audiology/hearing, audiology/speech pathology, community health, dietetics, environmental health, health services admin, preveterinary, vocational rehab counseling. **History:** General. **Interdisciplinary:** Global studies, math/computer science, science/society. **Legal studies:** Prelaw. **Liberal arts:** Arts/sciences, humanities. **Math:** General, computational, statistics. **Parks/recreation:** General, exercise sciences, sports admin. **Philosophy/religion:** Philosophy, religion. **Physical sciences:** Astronomy, atmospheric science, chemistry, geology, physics. **Psychology:** General. **Social sciences:** Anthropology, economics, geography, political science, sociology. **Transportation:** Airline/commercial pilot, aviation management. **Visual/performing arts:** Acting, art history/

conservation, crafts, dance, directing/producing, dramatic, film/cinema, graphic design, jazz, music history, music performance, music theory/composition, painting, photography, sculpture, studio arts, theater history, voice/opera. **Other:** Biological and biomedical sciences, Human sciences business services, Plant protection and integrated pest management.

**Most popular majors.** Biology 8%, business/marketing 15%, engineering/ engineering technologies 14%, English 7%, psychology 7%, social sciences 10%.

**Computing on campus.** 4,420 workstations in dormitories, library, computer center, student center. Dormitories wired for high-speed internet access and linked to campus network. Commuter students can connect to campus network. Online course registration, online library, helpline, repair service, student web hosting, wireless network available.

**Student life. Freshman orientation:** Mandatory. Preregistration for classes offered. One-day program, held end of May through July. **Policies:** Freshmen required to live on campus unless over 21 years, married, or living with parents. **Housing:** Guaranteed on-campus for freshmen. Coed dorms, single-sex dorms, special housing for disabled, apartments, cooperative housing, fraternity/sorority housing, wellness housing available. $200 fully refundable deposit, deadline 5/1. Living/learning communities available. **Activities:** Bands, campus ministries, choral groups, dance, drama, film society, international student organizations, literary magazine, music ensembles, Model UN, musical theater, opera, radio station, student government, student newspaper, symphony orchestra, TV station, more than 1,000 registered student organizations.

**Athletics.** NCAA. **Intercollegiate:** Baseball M, basketball, cheerleading, cross-country, diving W, football (tackle) M, golf, gymnastics, soccer W, softball W, swimming W, tennis, track and field, volleyball W, wrestling M. **Intramural:** Badminton, basketball, cross-country, diving, football (nontackle), football (tackle) M, golf, racquetball, soccer, softball W, tennis, volleyball, wrestling M. **Team name:** Illini.

**Student services.** Alcohol/substance abuse counseling, career counseling, services for economically disadvantaged, student employment services, financial aid counseling, health services, legal services, minority student services, on-campus daycare, personal counseling, placement for graduates, veterans' counselor, women's services. **Physically disabled:** Services for visually, speech, hearing impaired. **Learning disabled:** Comprehensive services available.

**Contact.** E-mail: admissions@illinois.edu
Phone: (217) 333-0302 Fax: (217) 244-4614
Stacey Kostell, Director of Undergraduate Admissions, University of Illinois at Urbana-Champaign, 901 West Illinois, Urbana, IL 61801-3028

---

## University of Illinois: Springfield

**Springfield, Illinois**
**www.uis.edu**

CB member
CB code: 0834

- Public 4-year university and liberal arts college
- Commuter campus in small city
- 2,920 degree-seeking undergraduates: 34% part-time, 55% women, 13% African American, 3% Asian American, 3% Hispanic American, 1% Native American, 1% international
- 1,717 degree-seeking graduate students
- 58% of applicants admitted
- SAT or ACT (ACT writing recommended) required
- 67% graduate within 6 years

**General.** Founded in 1969. Regionally accredited. Third campus of University of Illinois system. **Degrees:** 618 bachelor's awarded; master's, doctoral offered. **Location:** 95 miles from St. Louis, 200 miles from Chicago. **Calendar:** Semester, extensive summer session. **Full-time faculty:** 211 total; 17% minority, 42% women. **Part-time faculty:** 147 total; 9% minority, 50% women. **Class size:** 46% < 20, 48% 20-39, 4% 40-49, 2% 50-99. **Special facilities:** Observatory, studio theater.

**Freshman class profile.** 1,349 applied, 777 admitted, 288 enrolled.

| Mid 50% test scores | | Rank in top tenth: | 18% |
|---|---|---|---|
| ACT composite: | 20-25 | End year in good standing: | 77% |
| GPA 3.75 or higher: | 22% | Return as sophomores: | 74% |
| GPA 3.50-3.74: | 14% | Out-of-state: | 2% |
| GPA 3.0-3.49: | 30% | Live on campus: | 83% |
| GPA 2.0-2.99: | 34% | International: | 2% |
| Rank in top quarter: | 43% | | |

**Basis for selection.** GPA, rank, record, completion of college-prepatory program, recommendations, admission test scores, and formal demonstration of competencies all fully considered. Personal or telephone interview may be required.

**High school preparation.** College-preparatory program required. Required units include English 4, mathematics 3, science 3 (laboratory 2) and foreign language 2. Fine arts can be substituted for foreign language.

**2009-2010 Annual costs.** Tuition/fees: $9,007; $18,157 out-of-state. Freshman costs reflect guaranteed tuition plan figures; tuition rate is fixed for 4 years. Room/board: $9,200.

**2008-2009 Financial aid. Need-based:** 289 full-time freshmen applied for aid; 219 were judged to have need; 217 of these received aid. Average need met was 76%. Average scholarship/grant was $8,356; average loan $3,172. 44% of total undergraduate aid awarded as scholarships/grants, 56% as loans/jobs. **Non-need-based:** Awarded to 450 full-time undergraduates, including 134 freshmen. Scholarships awarded for academics, alumni affiliation, art, athletics, job skills, leadership, minority status, music/drama, state residency.

**Application procedures. Admission:** Priority date 3/15; no deadline. $40 fee, may be waived for applicants with need. Admission notification on a rolling basis beginning on or about 9/15. It is requested that students reply as soon as possible after notification of admissions decision. **Financial aid:** Priority date 4/1, closing date 11/15. FAFSA required. Applicants notified on a rolling basis starting 1/1; must reply within 3 week(s) of notification.

**Academics. Special study options:** Distance learning, double major, ESL, honors, independent study, internships, study abroad, teacher certification program. **Credit/placement by examination:** AP, CLEP, IB, ACT, institutional tests. 30 credit hours maximum toward bachelor's degree. **Support services:** Learning center, reduced course load, remedial instruction, study skills assistance, tutoring, writing center.

**Majors. Biology:** General. **Business:** Accounting, business admin. **Communications:** General. **Computer sciences:** Computer science. **Health:** Clinical lab science. **History:** General. **Interdisciplinary:** Global studies. **Legal studies:** General. **Liberal arts:** Arts/sciences. **Math:** General. **Philosophy/ religion:** Philosophy. **Physical sciences:** Chemistry. **Protective services:** Criminal justice. **Psychology:** General. **Public administration:** Social work. **Social sciences:** General, economics, political science. **Visual/performing arts:** Studio arts.

**Most popular majors.** Business/marketing 26%, communications/ journalism 7%, computer/information sciences 9%, liberal arts 10%, psychology 11%, security/protective services 6%, social sciences 6%.

**Computing on campus.** 500 workstations in dormitories, library, computer center, student center. Dormitories wired for high-speed internet access and linked to campus network. Commuter students can connect to campus network. Online course registration, online library, helpline, student web hosting, wireless network available.

**Student life. Freshman orientation:** Mandatory. **Housing:** Guaranteed on-campus for freshmen. Coed dorms, special housing for disabled, apartments, wellness housing available. $250 partly refundable deposit. Family housing available. **Activities:** Bands, campus ministries, choral groups, dance, drama, film society, international student organizations, music ensembles, Model UN, student government, student newspaper, Christian student fellowship, ACLU, Indian student organization, Habitat for Humanity, Living Word Bible Study, College Democrats, College Republicans, Queer Straight Alliance.

**Athletics.** NAIA, NCAA. **Intercollegiate:** Baseball M, basketball, cheerleading M, golf, soccer, softball W, tennis, volleyball W. **Intramural:** Badminton, basketball, bowling, football (non-tackle), golf, racquetball, skiing, soccer, softball, squash, table tennis, volleyball. **Team name:** Prairie Stars.

**Student services.** Alcohol/substance abuse counseling, career counseling, student employment services, financial aid counseling, health services, minority student services, on-campus daycare, personal counseling, women's services. **Physically disabled:** Services for visually, speech, hearing impaired.

**Contact.** E-mail: admissions@uis.edu
Phone: (217) 206-4847 Toll-free number: (800) 977-4847
Fax: (217) 206-6620
Lori Giordano, Associate Director of Admissions, University of Illinois: Springfield, One University Plaza, MS UHB 1080, Springfield, IL 62703

---

## University of St. Francis

**Joliet, Illinois**
**www.stfrancis.edu**

CB code: 1130

- Private 4-year university and liberal arts college affiliated with Roman Catholic Church
- Commuter campus in small city

- 1,247 degree-seeking undergraduates: 3% part-time, 68% women, 7% African American, 4% Asian American, 12% Hispanic American, 1% international
- 837 degree-seeking graduate students
- 50% of applicants admitted
- SAT or ACT (ACT writing optional) required
- 59% graduate within 6 years

**General.** Founded in 1920. Regionally accredited. Affiliated with Argonne National Laboratories, Morton Arboretum, Will County Forest Preserve, Midewin Tallgrass Prairie, Shedd Aquarium. **Degrees:** 336 bachelor's awarded; master's, doctoral offered. **Location:** 35 miles from Chicago. **Calendar:** Semester, extensive summer session. **Full-time faculty:** 88 total; 68% have terminal degrees, 9% minority, 58% women. **Part-time faculty:** 147 total; 22% have terminal degrees, 10% minority, 58% women. **Class size:** 68% < 20, 31% 20-39, less than 1% 40-49, less than 1% 50-99. **Special facilities:** Performing arts center, greenhouse, health and wellness center operated by nursing faculty and students, arthouse for visual arts majors.

**Freshman class profile.** 1,274 applied, 632 admitted, 223 enrolled.

| Mid 50% test scores | | Rank in top quarter: | 50% |
|---|---|---|---|
| ACT composite: | 21-26 | Rank in top tenth: | 20% |
| GPA 3.75 or higher: | 16% | End year in good standing: | 89% |
| GPA 3.50-3.74: | 21% | Return as sophomores: | 76% |
| GPA 3.0-3.49: | 37% | Out-of-state: | 9% |
| GPA 2.0-2.99: | 26% | Live on campus: | 60% |

**Basis for selection.** High school GPA and rank, test scores important. Essay and letters of recommendation required and interview recommended for students who do not meet admissions requirements.

**High school preparation.** College-preparatory program required. 17 units required. Required units include English 4, mathematics 3, social studies 2, science 2 (laboratory 1) and academic electives 3. 3 units required from 2 areas: foreign language, music/art, or computer science.

**2009-2010 Annual costs.** Tuition/fees: $22,698. Room/board: $7,938.

**2009-2010 Financial aid. Need-based:** 209 full-time freshmen applied for aid; 178 were judged to have need; 178 of these received aid. Average need met was 78%. Average scholarship/grant was $7,734; average loan $3,676. 68% of total undergraduate aid awarded as scholarships/grants, 32% as loans/jobs. **Non-need-based:** Awarded to 1,191 full-time undergraduates, including 171 freshmen. Scholarships awarded for academics, alumni affiliation, art, athletics, leadership, music/drama, religious affiliation, state residency.

**Application procedures. Admission:** Priority date 5/1; deadline 8/1 (receipt date). $30 fee, may be waived for applicants with need. Admission notification on a rolling basis beginning on or about 9/15. Must reply by 5/1. **Financial aid:** Priority date 3/15; no closing date. FAFSA, institutional form required. Applicants notified on a rolling basis starting 2/15.

**Academics. Special study options:** Combined bachelor's/graduate degree, cross-registration, distance learning, double major, honors, independent study, internships, student-designed major, study abroad, teacher certification program, Washington semester. **Credit/placement by examination:** AP, CLEP, IB, SAT, ACT, institutional tests. 33 credit hours maximum toward bachelor's degree. **Support services:** Learning center, pre-admission summer program, reduced course load, remedial instruction, study skills assistance, tutoring, writing center.

**Majors. Biology:** General. **Business:** General, accounting, actuarial science, business admin, finance, human resources, management science, marketing, organizational behavior. **Communications:** Advertising, broadcast journalism, media studies, public relations, radio/tv. **Computer sciences:** Computer science, information technology, webmaster. **Conservation:** Environmental science. **Education:** Art, elementary, English, mathematics, music, science, social studies, special. **Health:** Clinical lab science, health care admin, medical radiologic technology/radiation therapy, nuclear medical technology, nursing (RN), predental, premedicine, prepharmacy, preveterinary, radiologic technology/medical imaging, recreational therapy. **History:** General. **Interdisciplinary:** Math/computer science. **Liberal arts:** Arts/sciences. **Math:** General. **Parks/recreation:** Facilities management. **Protective services:** Law enforcement admin. **Psychology:** General. **Public administration:** Social work. **Social sciences:** Political science. **Theology:** Theology. **Visual/performing arts:** General, music performance.

**Most popular majors.** Business/marketing 13%, education 20%, health sciences 35%.

**Computing on campus.** 382 workstations in dormitories, library, computer center, student center. Dormitories wired for high-speed internet access and linked to campus network. Commuter students can connect to campus network. Online course registration, online library, helpline, wireless network available.

**Student life. Freshman orientation:** Mandatory, $120 fee. **Policies:** Visitation between 9am and 2am. Marian Hall is alcohol-free. All halls close during major breaks (fall break, winter break, spring break) unless special permission received to remain in hall. **Housing:** Guaranteed on-campus for freshmen. Coed dorms, apartments, wellness housing available. $50 fully refundable deposit, deadline 5/1. **Activities:** Campus ministries, choral groups, dance, drama, international student organizations, literary magazine, music ensembles, musical theater, opera, radio station, student government, student newspaper, symphony orchestra, TV station, student activities board, black student association, student business association, Unidos Vamos a Alcanzar, student nurses organization, recreation club, council for environmental and scientific awareness, council for social activism, social work club, mock trial club.

**Athletics.** NAIA. **Intercollegiate:** Baseball M, basketball, cheerleading M, cross-country, football (tackle) M, golf, soccer, softball W, tennis, track and field, volleyball W. **Intramural:** Basketball, bowling, volleyball. **Team name:** Saints.

**Student services.** Adult student services, chaplain/spiritual director, career counseling, student employment services, financial aid counseling, health services, minority student services, personal counseling, placement for graduates. **Physically disabled:** Services for visually, speech, hearing impaired.

**Contact.** E-mail: admissions@stfrancis.edu
Phone: (815) 740-5037 Toll-free number: (800) 735-7500
Fax: (815) 740-5032
Julie Marlatt, Director Undergraduate Admissions, University of St. Francis, 500 Wilcox Street, Joliet, IL 60435

## VanderCook College of Music
**Chicago, Illinois**
**www.vandercook.edu**                     CB code: 1872

- Private 4-year music and teachers college
- Residential campus in very large city
- 140 degree-seeking undergraduates
- 98% of applicants admitted
- Application essay, interview required

**General.** Founded in 1909. Regionally accredited. Access to student services at Illinois Institute of Technology. **Degrees:** 21 bachelor's awarded; master's offered. **Location:** Central Chicago. **Calendar:** Semester. **Full-time faculty:** 13 total. **Part-time faculty:** 26 total. **Class size:** 64% < 20, 30% 20-39, 1% 50-99, 4% >100. **Special facilities:** MIDI/electronic music laboratory, library with music education collection.

**Freshman class profile.** 52 applied, 51 admitted, 31 enrolled.

| Mid 50% test scores | | Rank in top quarter: | 40% |
|---|---|---|---|
| SAT critical reading: | 510-650 | Rank in top tenth: | 20% |
| SAT math: | 480-620 | Out-of-state: | 12% |
| SAT writing: | 490-630 | Live on campus: | 54% |
| ACT composite: | 19-25 | | |

**Basis for selection.** Academic credentials, SAT or ACT scores and recommendations are weighed along with student's musical audition and interview. Institutional test required. Audition required. **Homeschooled:** Should obtain experience performing with a concert band or chorus.

**High school preparation.** 15 units recommended. Recommended units include English 3, mathematics 2, social studies 3, science 2, foreign language 2 and academic electives 3. Art may be substituted for foreign language.

**2009-2010 Annual costs.** Tuition/fees: $21,360. Room/board: $9,940. Books/supplies: $1,620. Personal expenses: $2,000.

**Financial aid. Non-need-based:** Scholarships awarded for academics, alumni affiliation, leadership, minority status, music/drama, state residency. **Additional information:** Musical talent considered for partial tuition waiver.

**Application procedures. Admission:** Priority date 4/1; no deadline. $35 fee. Admission notification on a rolling basis. **Financial aid:** Priority date 3/1, closing date 4/30. FAFSA required. Applicants notified on a rolling basis starting 5/15; must reply within 2 week(s) of notification.

**Academics. Special study options:** Teacher certification program. **Credit/placement by examination:** AP, CLEP, SAT, ACT, institutional tests.

**Majors. Education:** Music.

**Computing on campus.** 10 workstations in dormitories, library, computer center, student center.

**Student life. Freshman orientation:** Mandatory, $100 fee. **Policies:** Student life focuses around musical activities at VanderCook and on the Illinois Institue of Technology campus. **Housing:** Guaranteed on-campus for all undergraduates. Coed dorms, apartments, fraternity/sorority housing available. $100 deposit. Apartments for single students 23 and older available. **Activities:** Bands, choral groups, music ensembles, musical theater.

**Student services.** Career counseling, student employment services, health services, personal counseling, placement for graduates.

**Contact.** E-mail: admissions@vandercook.edu
Phone: (312) 225-6288 ext. 230 Fax: (312) 225-5211
Amy Lenting, Director of Recruiting and Retention, VanderCook College of Music, 3140 South Federal Street, Chicago, IL 60616-3731

## West Suburban College of Nursing
**Oak Park, Illinois**
**www.wscn.edu**                                 **CB code: 1927**

- Private two-year upper-division nursing college affiliated with Roman Catholic Church
- Commuter campus in very large city
- Test scores, application essay required

**General.** Founded in 1982. Regionally accredited. Facilities located in West Suburban Medical Center. **Degrees:** 82 bachelor's awarded; master's offered. **Location:** 10 miles from downtown Chicago. **Calendar:** Semester, limited summer session. **Full-time faculty:** 19 total; 21% have terminal degrees, 5% minority, 95% women. **Part-time faculty:** 14 total; 21% minority, 93% women. **Class size:** 20% < 20, 23% 20-39, 26% 40-49, 31% 50-99. **Special facilities:** In-hospital location, health sciences library, nursing clinical skills laboratory.

**Student profile.** 236 degree-seeking undergraduates.

**Basis for selection.** College transcript, application essay, standardized test scores required. Natural and behavioral science grades more heavily weighted. Recommendation and essay required. Must have 2.75 science GPA. Satisfactory score on TEAS required. Transfer accepted as juniors.

**2009-2010 Annual costs.** Tuition/fees: $21,526. Books/supplies: $1,400. Personal expenses: $2,116.

**Financial aid. Non-need-based:** Scholarships awarded for academics, alumni affiliation.

**Application procedures. Admission:** $30 fee. Application must be submitted online. **Financial aid:** Priority date 4/15, no deadline. Applicants notified on a rolling basis; must reply within 3 weeks of notification. FAFSA required.

**Academics. Special study options:** Accelerated study, independent study. Evening and weekend BS completion program for registered nurses. **Credit/placement by examination:** CLEP.

**Majors. Health:** Nursing (RN).

**Computing on campus.** 10 workstations in library, computer center. Online library, wireless network available.

**Student life. Activities:** Student government.

**Student services.** Career counseling, student employment services, health services, personal counseling.

**Contact.** E-mail: admissions@wscn.edu
Phone: (708) 763-6530 Fax: (708) 763-1531
Cindy Valdez, Director of Enrollment Management, West Suburban College of Nursing, Three Erie Court, Oak Park, IL 60302

## Western Illinois University
**Macomb, Illinois**
**www.wiu.edu**                                 **CB code: 1900**

- Public 4-year university
- Residential campus in large town
- 10,553 degree-seeking undergraduates: 9% part-time, 47% women, 9% African American, 1% Asian American, 5% Hispanic American, 1% international
- 2,020 degree-seeking graduate students
- 64% of applicants admitted

- SAT or ACT (ACT writing optional) required
- 59% graduate within 6 years

**General.** Founded in 1899. Regionally accredited. **Degrees:** 2,530 bachelor's awarded; master's, doctoral offered. **ROTC:** Army. **Location:** 83 miles from Rock Island, 78 miles from Peoria. **Calendar:** Semester, limited summer session. **Full-time faculty:** 679 total; 72% have terminal degrees, 14% minority, 43% women. **Part-time faculty:** 83 total; 18% have terminal degrees, 2% minority, 51% women. **Class size:** 43% < 20, 46% 20-39, 6% 40-49, 4% 50-99, less than 1% >100. **Special facilities:** Geology museum.

**Freshman class profile.** 8,331 applied, 5,301 admitted, 1,641 enrolled.

| Mid 50% test scores | | Rank in top tenth: | 7% |
|---|---|---|---|
| ACT composite: | 19-23 | End year in good standing: | 88% |
| GPA 3.75 or higher: | 10% | Return as sophomores: | 74% |
| GPA 3.50-3.74: | 9% | Out-of-state: | 6% |
| GPA 3.0-3.49: | 27% | Live on campus: | 93% |
| GPA 2.0-2.99: | 54% | International: | 1% |
| Rank in top quarter: | 24% | | |

**Basis for selection.** Standardized test scores, class rank very important. Audition required for music majors. **Homeschooled:** Transcript of courses and grades required.

**High school preparation.** College-preparatory program recommended. 15 units recommended. Recommended units include English 4, mathematics 3, social studies 3, science 3 and academic electives 2. 2 units of art, film, foreign language, music, speech, theater, journalism, religion, philosophy or vocational education also recommended.

**2009-2010 Annual costs.** Tuition/fees: $8,958; $12,347 out-of-state. Residents of nearby counties in Iowa and Missouri pay in-state tuition during first year. Room/board: $7,642.

**2009-2010 Financial aid. Need-based:** 1,370 full-time freshmen applied for aid; 1,115 were judged to have need; 1,099 of these received aid. Average need met was 58%. Average scholarship/grant was $8,498; average loan $3,333. 51% of total undergraduate aid awarded as scholarships/grants, 49% as loans/jobs. **Non-need-based:** Awarded to 730 full-time undergraduates, including 125 freshmen. Scholarships awarded for academics, alumni affiliation, art, athletics, leadership, minority status, music/drama, ROTC.

**Application procedures. Admission:** Priority date 5/15; no deadline. $30 fee. Admission notification on a rolling basis. **Financial aid:** Priority date 2/15; no closing date. FAFSA required. Applicants notified on a rolling basis starting 1/15.

**Academics. Special study options:** Distance learning, double major, dual enrollment of high school students, ESL, external degree, honors, independent study, internships, student-designed major, study abroad, teacher certification program, weekend college. **Credit/placement by examination:** AP, CLEP, IB. 30 credit hours maximum toward bachelor's degree. **Support services:** Remedial instruction, study skills assistance, tutoring, writing center.

**Honors college/program.** 28 ACT or upper 10% of class and 24 ACT.

**Majors. Agriculture:** General. **Area/ethnic studies:** African-American, women's. **Biology:** General. **Business:** Accounting, business admin, construction management, finance, human resources, logistics, management information systems, managerial economics, marketing. **Communications:** General, journalism, radio/tv. **Communications technology:** Graphic/printing. **Computer sciences:** General, networking. **Education:** Bilingual, elementary, health, instructional media, special. **Engineering:** Electrical. **Engineering technology:** Manufacturing. **Family/consumer sciences:** General. **Foreign languages:** French, Spanish. **Health:** Athletic training, clinical lab science, communication disorders, health care admin, nursing (RN). **History:** General. **Liberal arts:** Arts/sciences. **Math:** General. **Parks/recreation:** Exercise sciences, facilities management. **Philosophy/religion:** Philosophy, religion. **Physical sciences:** Chemistry, forensic chemistry, geology, meteorology, physics. **Protective services:** Emergency management/homeland security, law enforcement admin. **Psychology:** General. **Public administration:** Social work. **Social sciences:** Economics, geography, political science, sociology. **Visual/performing arts:** Art, dramatic, music performance, musical theater, studio arts.

**Most popular majors.** Business/marketing 15%, communications/journalism 8%, education 8%, liberal arts 10%, parks/recreation 7%, security/protective services 15%.

**Computing on campus.** 1,000 workstations in dormitories, library, computer center. Dormitories wired for high-speed internet access and linked to campus network. Commuter students can connect to campus network. Online course registration, online library, helpline, wireless network available.

**Student life. Freshman orientation:** Mandatory. Preregistration for classes offered. Held week prior to beginning of classes. **Housing:** Guaranteed on-campus for all undergraduates. Coed dorms, single-sex dorms, apartments, fraternity/sorority housing, wellness housing available. $100 partly refundable deposit. **Activities:** Bands, choral groups, dance, drama, music ensembles, musical theater, radio station, student government, student newspaper, symphony orchestra, TV station, 67 special-interest organizations, 5 service organizations, 14 religious organizations, 32 national honorary and professional fraternities.

**Athletics. NCAA. Intercollegiate:** Baseball M, basketball, cheerleading, cross-country, diving, football (tackle) M, golf, soccer, softball W, swimming, tennis, track and field, volleyball W. **Intramural:** Badminton, basketball, bowling, cross-country, football (non-tackle), football (tackle) M, golf, handball, lacrosse M, racquetball, rugby, skin diving, soccer, softball, swimming, table tennis, tennis, volleyball, water polo. **Team name:** Leathernecks.

**Student services.** Adult student services, alcohol/substance abuse counseling, career counseling, student employment services, financial aid counseling, health services, legal services, minority student services, on-campus daycare, personal counseling, placement for graduates, veterans' counselor, women's services. **Physically disabled:** Services for visually, speech, hearing impaired.

**Contact.** E-mail: wiuadm@wiu.edu
Phone: (309) 298-3157 Toll-free number: (877) 742-5948
Fax: (309) 298-3111
Eric Campbell, Director of Admissions, Western Illinois University, One University Circle, Macomb, IL 61455-1390

## Westwood College: Chicago Loop
### Chicago, Illinois
### www.westwood.edu/locations/illinois/chicago-loop-campus

- For-profit 4-year technical college
- Commuter campus in very large city
- 887 degree-seeking undergraduates

**General.** Accredited by ACICS. **Degrees:** 85 bachelor's, 20 associate awarded. **Calendar:** Continuous. **Full-time faculty:** 15 total. **Part-time faculty:** 63 total.

**Basis for selection.** Admission based on interview, applicant's level of interest and test scores. SAT or ACT recommended.

**High school preparation.** 4 units required.

**2009-2010 Annual costs.** $4,251 per term; 5 terms per year.

**Application procedures. Admission:** Priority date 8/6; deadline 8/9. $25 fee. **Financial aid:** No deadline.

**Academics. Special study options:** Independent study, internships. **Credit/placement by examination:** CLEP, SAT, ACT, institutional tests.

**Majors. Business:** Marketing. **Communications technology:** Animation/special effects. **Computer sciences:** Security. **Protective services:** Police science. **Visual/performing arts:** Design.

**Contact.** Phone: (312) 739-0850 Fax: (312) 739-1004
Jeff Hill, Director of Admissions, Westwood College: Chicago Loop, 17 North State Street, Suite 300, Chicago, IL 60602

## Westwood College: DuPage
### Woodridge, Illinois
### www.westwood.edu                    CB code: 5096

- For-profit 4-year technical college
- Commuter campus in large city
- 571 degree-seeking undergraduates
- Interview required

**General.** Accredited by ACICS. **Degrees:** 105 bachelor's, 15 associate awarded. **Location:** 20 miles from downtown Chicago. **Calendar:** Quarter. **Full-time faculty:** 5 total. **Part-time faculty:** 41 total.

**Basis for selection.** Successful completion of Accuplacer test required prior to admission; SAT/ACT scores may be used in lieu of Accuplacer. SAT or ACT recommended.

**2009-2010 Annual costs.** Expenses vary by program; however, average cost for academic year is $14,867, which includes tuition, fees and books.

**Application procedures. Admission:** No deadline. $50 fee.

**Academics. Special study options:** Accelerated study, independent study. **Credit/placement by examination:** CLEP, institutional tests.

**Majors. Business:** Business admin. **Computer sciences:** Game design, security, webmaster. **Construction:** Site management. **Protective services:** Criminal justice. **Visual/performing arts:** Interior design.

**Student life. Activities:** Student government.

**Contact.** Phone: (630) 434-8244 Toll-free number: (866) 721-7646
Fax: (630) 743-0667
Scott Kawall, Director of Admissions, Westwood College: DuPage, 7155 Janes Avenue, Woodridge, IL 60517

## Westwood College: O'Hare Airport
### Chicago, Illinois
### www.westwood.edu

- For-profit 4-year technical and career college
- Commuter campus in very large city

**General.** Accredited by ACICS. **Location:** Downtown. **Calendar:** Continuous.

**Annual costs/financial aid.** Tuition/fees (2009-2010): $15,273. Tuition varies by program. Room/board: $6,828. Books/supplies: $300. Need-based financial aid available to full-time and part-time students.

**Contact.** Phone: (773) 380-6800
Director of Admissions, 8501 West Higgins Road, Chicago, IL 60631

## Westwood College: River Oaks
### Calumet City, Illinois
### www.westwood.edu

- For-profit 4-year career college
- Commuter campus in very large city

**General.** Accredited by ACICS. **Calendar:** Continuous.

**Contact.** Phone: (708) 832-1988
80 River Oaks Center, Suite D-49, Calumet City, IL 60409

## Wheaton College
### Wheaton, Illinois                    CB member
### www.wheaton.edu                     CB code: 1905

- Private 4-year liberal arts college affiliated with nondenominational tradition
- Residential campus in small city
- 2,369 degree-seeking undergraduates: 2% part-time, 50% women, 4% African American, 8% Asian American, 4% Hispanic American, 1% international
- 429 degree-seeking graduate students
- 71% of applicants admitted
- SAT or ACT with writing, application essay required
- 88% graduate within 6 years; 32% enter graduate study

**General.** Founded in 1860. Regionally accredited. **Degrees:** 611 bachelor's awarded; master's, doctoral, professional offered. **ROTC:** Army, Air Force. **Location:** 25 miles from Chicago. **Calendar:** Semester, limited summer session. **Full-time faculty:** 202 total; 95% have terminal degrees, 10% minority, 29% women. **Part-time faculty:** 104 total; 38% have terminal degrees, 10% minority, 45% women. **Class size:** 57% < 20, 35% 20-39, 4% 40-49, 2% 50-99, 2% >100. **Special facilities:** Billy Graham museum, science station, Christian residential camp, collection of books and papers of 7 British authors, center for applied Christian ethics.

**Freshman class profile.** 1,950 applied, 1,390 admitted, 620 enrolled.

| Mid 50% test scores | | GPA 2.0-2.99: | 2% |
|---|---|---|---|
| SAT critical reading: | 600-710 | Rank in top quarter: | 83% |
| SAT math: | 600-700 | Rank in top tenth: | 59% |
| SAT writing: | 590-700 | End year in good standing: | 99% |
| ACT composite: | 27-31 | Return as sophomores: | 96% |
| GPA 3.75 or higher: | 52% | Out-of-state: | 77% |
| GPA 3.50-3.74: | 25% | Live on campus: | 100% |
| GPA 3.0-3.49: | 21% | International: | 2% |

**Basis for selection.** Evidence of a vital Christian experience, moral character, personal integrity, social concern, academic ability, and desire for a liberal arts education as defined by the college are most important. Interview recommended. Audition required of music majors. **Homeschooled:** Statement describing homeschool structure and mission required. Applicants advised to take the ACT to satisfy the "Ability to Benefit" requirements. **Learning Disabled:** Personal interview required. Student must contact Registrar to request services or equipment and provide documentation/diagnosis of disability.

**High school preparation.** College-preparatory program required. 18 units required. Required and recommended units include English 4, mathematics 4, social studies 4, science 4 and foreign language 3.

**2009-2010 Annual costs.** Tuition/fees: $26,520. Room/board: $7,770. Books/supplies: $800. Personal expenses: $2,000.

**2009-2010 Financial aid. Need-based:** 486 full-time freshmen applied for aid; 341 were judged to have need; 336 of these received aid. Average need met was 86%. Average scholarship/grant was $18,058; average loan $4,460. 72% of total undergraduate aid awarded as scholarships/grants, 28% as loans/jobs. **Non-need-based:** Awarded to 818 full-time undergraduates, including 212 freshmen. Scholarships awarded for academics, alumni affiliation, art, minority status, music/drama. **Additional information:** First $500 to $2,000 of need awarded as grant instead of loan.

**Application procedures. Admission:** Closing date 1/10 (receipt date). $50 fee, may be waived for applicants with need. Admission notification 4/1. Must reply by May 1 or within 3 week(s) if notified thereafter. **Financial aid:** Priority date 2/15; no closing date. FAFSA, institutional form required. Applicants notified on a rolling basis starting 3/1.

**Academics. Special study options:** Combined bachelor's/graduate degree, cross-registration, double major, exchange student, independent study, internships, liberal arts/career combination, student-designed major, study abroad, teacher certification program, urban semester, Washington semester. **Credit/placement by examination:** AP, CLEP, IB, SAT, ACT, institutional tests. 76 credit hours maximum toward bachelor's degree. **Support services:** Study skills assistance, writing center.

**Majors. Biology:** General. **Business:** Managerial economics. **Communications:** General. **Computer sciences:** Computer science. **Conservation:** Environmental studies. **Education:** Elementary, music, secondary. **Engineering:** General. **Foreign languages:** Classics, French, German, Spanish. **Health:** Health services, nursing (RN). **History:** General. **Math:** General. **Philosophy/religion:** Philosophy. **Physical sciences:** Chemistry, geology, physics. **Psychology:** General. **Social sciences:** Anthropology, archaeology, economics, international relations, political science, sociology. **Theology:** Bible, religious ed. **Visual/performing arts:** Art, music history, music performance, music theory/composition.

**Most popular majors.** Business/marketing 8%, communications/journalism 6%, education 7%, English 8%, foreign language 7%, psychology 6%, social sciences 18%, theological studies 10%, visual/performing arts 7%.

**Computing on campus.** 125 workstations in dormitories, library, computer center, student center. Dormitories wired for high-speed internet access and linked to campus network. Commuter students can connect to campus network. Online library, helpline, wireless network available.

**Student life. Freshman orientation:** Mandatory. Preregistration for classes offered. Four-day program during the week before classes begin. **Policies:** All college and college-related functions are alcohol and tobacco free. Religious observance required. **Housing:** Guaranteed on-campus for freshmen. Coed dorms, single-sex dorms, apartments, cooperative housing available. Housing for disabled provided as needed. **Activities:** Bands, campus ministries, choral groups, dance, drama, film society, international student organizations, literary magazine, music ensembles, Model UN, musical theater, opera, radio station, student government, student newspaper, symphony orchestra, TV station, Christian Service Council, Student Missionary Project, Youth Hostel Ministries, World Christian Fellowship, Students for Biblical Equality, Earthkeepers, Jonathan Blanchard Society, Unidad Christiana, Koinonia.

**Athletics.** NCAA. **Intercollegiate:** Baseball M, basketball, cross-country, football (tackle) M, golf, soccer, softball W, swimming, tennis, track and field, volleyball W, water polo W, wrestling M. **Intramural:** Badminton, basketball, bowling, football (non-tackle) M, golf, soccer, softball M, tennis, volleyball, water polo. **Team name:** Thunder.

**Student services.** Chaplain/spiritual director, career counseling, student employment services, financial aid counseling, health services, minority student services, personal counseling, placement for graduates, veterans' counselor. **Physically disabled:** Services for visually, speech, hearing impaired.

**Contact.** E-mail: admissions@wheaton.edu
Phone: (630) 752-5005 Toll-free number: (800) 222-2419
Fax: (630) 752-5285
Shawn Leftwich, Director of Undergraduate Admissions, Wheaton College, 501 College Avenue, Wheaton, IL 60187-5593

# Indiana

## Anderson University

**Anderson, Indiana**
www.anderson.edu

**CB member**
**CB code: 1016**

- Private 4-year liberal arts college affiliated with Church of God
- Residential campus in small city
- 2,097 degree-seeking undergraduates
- 73% of applicants admitted
- SAT or ACT with writing required

**General.** Founded in 1917. Regionally accredited. **Degrees:** 489 bachelor's, 2 associate awarded; master's offered. **Location:** 45 miles from Indianapolis. **Calendar:** Semester, limited summer session. **Full-time faculty:** 136 total. **Part-time faculty:** 179 total. **Class size:** 57% < 20, 37% 20-39, 4% 40-49, 3% 50-99, less than 1% >100. **Special facilities:** Religious art collection, museum of Bible and Near Eastern studies, glass studio, wellness center.

**Freshman class profile.** 2,109 applied, 1,548 admitted, 561 enrolled.

| Mid 50% test scores | | | |
|---|---|---|---|
| SAT critical reading: | 470-570 | GPA 3.0-3.49: | 26% |
| SAT math: | 470-580 | GPA 2.0-2.99: | 28% |
| ACT composite: | 22-26 | Rank in top quarter: | 47% |
| GPA 3.75 or higher: | 30% | Rank in top tenth: | 24% |
| GPA 3.50-3.74: | 16% | Out-of-state: | 31% |
| | | Live on campus: | 94% |

**Basis for selection.** GED not accepted. Rank in top half of class, test scores, reference important. School, church, and community activities also considered. Additional requirements for entry into nursing, athletic training, and educational programs. Essay recommended. Interview required of academically weak applicants. Audition required of music majors. Portfolio recommended for art majors. **Homeschooled:** Interview may be required.

**High school preparation.** 17 units required; 30 recommended. Required and recommended units include English 4, mathematics 3-4, social studies 1-2, history 1-2, science 3-4 (laboratory 3-4), foreign language 2-3, computer science 1, visual/performing arts 1 and academic electives 5.

**2009-2010 Annual costs.** Tuition/fees: $22,910. Room/board: $7,980. Books/supplies: $1,000. Personal expenses: $1,600.

**2009-2010 Financial aid. Non-need-based:** Scholarships awarded for academics, alumni affiliation, art, leadership, minority status, music/drama, religious affiliation.

**Application procedures. Admission:** Priority date 1/15; deadline 7/1. $25 fee, may be waived for applicants with need, free for online applicants. Admission notification on a rolling basis beginning on or about 9/1. Must reply by May 1 or within 2 week(s) if notified thereafter. **Financial aid:** Priority date 3/1; no closing date. FAFSA required. Applicants notified on a rolling basis starting 3/1.

**Academics. Special study options:** Accelerated study, combined bachelor's/graduate degree, cross-registration, double major, honors, independent study, internships, student-designed major, study abroad, teacher certification program, urban semester. **Credit/placement by examination:** AP, CLEP, IB, SAT, ACT, institutional tests. 30 credit hours maximum toward bachelor's degree. **Support services:** Learning center, pre-admission summer program, reduced course load, tutoring.

**Majors. Biology:** General, biochemistry. **Business:** Accounting, business admin, entrepreneurial studies, finance, international, managerial economics, marketing, organizational behavior. **Communications:** Media studies. **Computer sciences:** Computer science, information systems. **Education:** General, art, biology, chemistry, drama/dance, elementary, English, French, mathematics, music, physical, physics, social studies, Spanish. **Family/consumer sciences:** Family systems. **Foreign languages:** French, Spanish. **Health:** Athletic training, nursing (RN). **History:** General. **Interdisciplinary:** Math/computer science. **Legal studies:** Prelaw. **Math:** General. **Parks/recreation:** Exercise sciences. **Philosophy/religion:** Philosophy, religion. **Physical sciences:** Chemistry, physics. **Protective services:** Criminal justice. **Psychology:** General. **Public administration:** Social work. **Social sciences:** Political science, sociology. **Theology:** Bible, sacred music, theology. **Visual/performing arts:** Design, dramatic, music management, music performance, studio arts, voice/opera.

**Most popular majors.** Business/marketing 23%, education 15%, health sciences 9%.

**Computing on campus.** 225 workstations in dormitories, library, computer center, student center. Dormitories linked to campus network. Commuter students can connect to campus network. Wireless network available.

**Student life. Freshman orientation:** Mandatory. Preregistration for classes offered. **Policies:** Religious observance required. **Housing:** Coed dorms, single-sex dorms, apartments, wellness housing available. $100 nonrefundable deposit, deadline 5/1. **Activities:** Bands, campus ministries, choral groups, dance, drama, international student organizations, literary magazine, music ensembles, Model UN, musical theater, opera, radio station, student government, student newspaper, symphony orchestra, multicultural student union, Religious Life Council, business club, women's clubs, men's clubs, international student association.

**Athletics.** NCAA. **Intercollegiate:** Baseball M, basketball, cross-country, football (tackle) M, golf, soccer, softball W, tennis, track and field, volleyball W. **Intramural:** Basketball, bowling, football (tackle), soccer, softball, swimming, tennis, volleyball, water polo. **Team name:** Ravens.

**Student services.** Adult student services, chaplain/spiritual director, career counseling, student employment services, financial aid counseling, health services, minority student services, personal counseling, placement for graduates, veterans' counselor. **Physically disabled:** Services for visually, speech impaired.

**Contact.** E-mail: info@anderson.edu
Phone: (765) 641-4080 Toll-free number: (800) 428-6414
Fax: (765) 641-4091
Jim King, Director of Admissions, Anderson University, 1100 East Fifth Street, Anderson, IN 46012-3495

## Ball State University

**Muncie, Indiana**
www.bsu.edu

**CB member**
**CB code: 1051**

- Public 4-year university
- Residential campus in small city
- 17,403 degree-seeking undergraduates: 6% part-time, 52% women, 7% African American, 1% Asian American, 2% Hispanic American, 2% international
- 3,333 degree-seeking graduate students
- 74% of applicants admitted
- 61% graduate within 6 years

**General.** Founded in 1918. Regionally accredited. **Degrees:** 3,057 bachelor's, 371 associate awarded; master's, doctoral, professional offered. **ROTC:** Army. **Location:** 56 miles from Indianapolis. **Calendar:** Semester, extensive summer session. **Full-time faculty:** 940 total; 74% have terminal degrees, 14% minority, 43% women. **Part-time faculty:** 240 total; 23% have terminal degrees, 8% minority, 55% women. **Class size:** 32% < 20, 50% 20-39, 8% 40-49, 7% 50-99, 3% >100. **Special facilities:** Planetarium, nature preserves, wellness institute, art museum, media design center.

**Freshman class profile.** 13,022 applied, 9,592 admitted, 4,178 enrolled.

| Mid 50% test scores | | | |
|---|---|---|---|
| SAT critical reading: | 470-570 | GPA 2.0-2.99: | 28% |
| SAT math: | 470-580 | Rank in top quarter: | 45% |
| SAT writing: | 460-560 | Rank in top tenth: | 16% |
| ACT composite: | 19-24 | Return as sophomores: | 78% |
| GPA 3.75 or higher: | 18% | Out-of-state: | 10% |
| GPA 3.50-3.74: | 16% | Live on campus: | 92% |
| GPA 3.0-3.49: | 38% | Fraternities: | 10% |
| | | Sororities: | 8% |

**Basis for selection.** High school transcript, GPA, test scores most important. Credentials of non-traditional students (age 23 or older) evaluated for admission on individual basis. Personal statement required of all non-traditional students. Non-traditional applicants may not be required to submit scores. Audition required of music and theater majors; portfolio recommended for art and architecture majors. **Homeschooled:** Statement describing homeschool structure and mission, transcript of courses and grades required.

**High school preparation.** College-preparatory program required. Required and recommended units include English 4, mathematics 3, social studies 3, science 3 (laboratory 2) and foreign language 3. History included under Social Studies.

**2009-2010 Annual costs.** Tuition/fees: $7,830; $20,398 out-of-state. Room/board: $7,932. Books/supplies: $970. Personal expenses: $1,560.

**2009-2010 Financial aid.** **Need-based:** 3,759 full-time freshmen applied for aid; 2,747 were judged to have need; 2,725 of these received aid. Average need met was 56%. Average scholarship/grant was $7,145; average loan $3,543. 50% of total undergraduate aid awarded as scholarships/grants, 50% as loans/jobs. **Non-need-based:** Awarded to 4,949 full-time undergraduates, including 1,713 freshmen. Scholarships awarded for academics, athletics, leadership, minority status, music/drama, ROTC, state residency.

**Application procedures.** **Admission:** Priority date 3/1; deadline 8/15 (postmark date). $25 fee, may be waived for applicants with need. Admission notification on a rolling basis. Must reply by May 1 or within 2 week(s) if notified thereafter. **Financial aid:** Priority date 3/10; no closing date. FAFSA required. Applicants notified on a rolling basis starting 4/1.

**Academics.** Minimum credit hours in major for associate degree 30 to 45; for bachelor's, 45 to 65. All undergraduates must meet writing competency requirement. **Special study options:** Accelerated study, combined bachelor's/graduate degree, distance learning, double major, dual enrollment of high school students, ESL, exchange student, external degree, honors, independent study, internships, student-designed major, study abroad, teacher certification program, Washington semester. **Credit/placement by examination:** AP, CLEP, IB, SAT, ACT, institutional tests. 15 credit hours maximum toward associate degree, 63 toward bachelor's. **Support services:** Learning center, reduced course load, study skills assistance, tutoring, writing center.

**Honors college/program.** 344 freshmen students were admitted in Fall 2009.

**Majors.** **Architecture:** Architecture, environmental design, landscape, urban/community planning. **Area/ethnic studies:** Women's. **Biology:** General. **Business:** General, accounting, actuarial science, business admin, entrepreneurial studies, finance, human resources, management information systems, managerial economics, marketing, office management, operations. **Communications:** Journalism, radio/tv. **Computer sciences:** General. **Conservation:** General. **Education:** Business, elementary, health, kindergarten/preschool, multiple handicapped, physical, science, technology/industrial arts. **Engineering:** General. **Engineering technology:** Industrial. **Family/consumer sciences:** General. **Foreign languages:** Classics, French, German, Japanese, Latin, Spanish. **Health:** Audiology/speech pathology, clinical lab science, dietetics, medical radiologic technology/radiation therapy, nursing (RN), predental, premedicine, respiratory therapy technology. **History:** General. **Liberal arts:** Arts/sciences, library science. **Math:** General. **Philosophy/religion:** Philosophy, religion. **Physical sciences:** Chemistry, geology, physics. **Protective services:** Criminal justice. **Psychology:** General. **Public administration:** Social work. **Social sciences:** General, anthropology, economics, geography, political science, sociology, urban studies. **Visual/performing arts:** Art, dance, dramatic. **Other:** General arts, Graphic arts management, Legal administration.

**Most popular majors.** Business/marketing 16%, education 14%, health sciences 7%, liberal arts 12%, visual/performing arts 6%.

**Computing on campus.** PC or laptop required. 1,023 workstations in dormitories, library, computer center, student center. Dormitories wired for high-speed internet access and linked to campus network. Commuter students can connect to campus network. Online course registration, online library, helpline, repair service, student web hosting, wireless network available.

**Student life.** **Freshman orientation:** Mandatory, $100 fee. Preregistration for classes offered. 2-day program held in June and July. **Policies:** Freshmen and sophomore transfer students required to live on campus unless living with parents or guardian, or 21 years of age or older. **Housing:** Guaranteed on-campus for freshmen. Coed dorms, single-sex dorms, special housing for disabled, apartments, fraternity/sorority housing, wellness housing available. $125 nonrefundable deposit. Living/learning communities. **Activities:** Bands, campus ministries, choral groups, dance, drama, film society, literary magazine, music ensembles, musical theater, opera, radio station, student government, student newspaper, symphony orchestra, TV station, over 350 student organizations.

**Athletics.** NCAA. **Intercollegiate:** Baseball M, basketball, cheerleading, cross-country, diving, field hockey W, football (tackle) M, golf, gymnastics W, soccer W, softball W, swimming, tennis, track and field W, volleyball. **Intramural:** Badminton, baseball M, basketball, bowling, football (non-tackle), golf, racquetball, soccer, softball, swimming, tennis, track and field W, volleyball. **Team name:** Cardinals.

**Student services.** Adult student services, alcohol/substance abuse counseling, career counseling, services for economically disadvantaged, student employment services, financial aid counseling, health services, legal services, minority student services, on-campus daycare, personal counseling, placement for graduates, veterans' counselor, women's services. **Physically disabled:** Services for visually, speech, hearing impaired.

**Contact.** E-mail: askus@bsu.edu
Phone: (765) 285-8300 Toll-free number: (800) 482-4278
Fax: (765) 285-1632
Tom Taylor, Vice President of Enrollment, Marketing and Communications, Ball State University, 2000 West University Avenue, Muncie, IN 47306-1022

## Bethel College
**Mishawaka, Indiana**
**www.bethelcollege.edu**      **CB code: 1079**

◗ Private 4-year liberal arts college affiliated with Missionary Church
◗ Residential campus in small city
◗ 1,879 degree-seeking undergraduates: 21% part-time, 67% women, 13% African American, 1% Asian American, 3% Hispanic American, 1% Native American, 2% international
◗ 232 degree-seeking graduate students
◗ 78% of applicants admitted
◗ SAT or ACT (ACT writing optional) required
◗ 60% graduate within 6 years

**General.** Founded in 1947. Regionally accredited. **Degrees:** 397 bachelor's, 87 associate awarded; master's offered. **ROTC:** Army, Air Force. **Location:** 140 miles from Indianapolis, 90 miles from Chicago. **Calendar:** Semester, limited summer session. **Full-time faculty:** 91 total; 62% have terminal degrees, 7% minority, 44% women. **Part-time faculty:** 114 total; 8% have terminal degrees, 6% minority, 60% women. **Class size:** 69% < 20, 26% 20-39, 3% 40-49, 2% 50-99, less than 1% >100. **Special facilities:** Otis Bowen Museum & Archives, Missionary Church Archives.

**Freshman class profile.** 847 applied, 657 admitted, 309 enrolled.

| Mid 50% test scores | | | |
|---|---|---|---|
| SAT critical reading: | 450-580 | GPA 2.0-2.99: | 23% |
| SAT math: | 460-580 | Rank in top quarter: | 51% |
| SAT writing: | 440-560 | Rank in top tenth: | 24% |
| ACT composite: | 19-26 | Return as sophomores: | 82% |
| GPA 3.75 or higher: | 28% | Out-of-state: | 28% |
| GPA 3.50-3.74: | 18% | Live on campus: | 91% |
| GPA 3.0-3.49: | 30% | International: | 2% |

**Basis for selection.** School achievement record, test scores, character recommendations, personal statement important. Interview recommended for all applicants, required for some scholarship awards. Audition/portfolio required of art, music and theatre majors for scholarship consideration. Portfolio recommended for returning adults.

**High school preparation.** College-preparatory program recommended. 17 units recommended. Recommended units include English 4, mathematics 3, social studies 1, history 2, science 1 (laboratory 1), foreign language 2 and academic electives 3.

**2010-2011 Annual costs.** Tuition/fees: $21,990. Room/board: $6,670. Books/supplies: $1,600. Personal expenses: $1,400.

**2009-2010 Financial aid.** **Non-need-based:** Scholarships awarded for academics, art, athletics, job skills, leadership, minority status, music/drama, religious affiliation, ROTC, state residency.

**Application procedures.** **Admission:** Priority date 12/1; deadline 8/15 (postmark date). $25 fee, may be waived for applicants with need, free for online applicants. Admission notification on a rolling basis beginning on or about 10/1. Must reply by 5/1. **Financial aid:** Priority date 3/1, closing date 3/10. FAFSA, institutional form required. Applicants notified by 4/15; must reply within 3 week(s) of notification.

**Academics.** **Special study options:** Accelerated study, cross-registration, double major, ESL, exchange student, independent study, internships, student-designed major, study abroad, teacher certification program, urban semester, Washington semester. **Credit/placement by examination:** AP, CLEP, IB, SAT, ACT, institutional tests. 20 credit hours maximum toward bachelor's degree. **Support services:** Learning center, reduced course load, remedial instruction, study skills assistance, tutoring, writing center.

**Majors.** **Biology:** General. **Business:** Accounting, business admin, human resources. **Communications:** General. **Computer sciences:** Information systems. **Conservation:** General. **Education:** Art, business, early childhood, elementary, English, foreign languages, mathematics, music, physical, science, social studies. **Engineering:** General. **Foreign languages:** Sign language interpretation, Spanish. **Health:** Nursing (RN), predental, premedicine. **History:** General. **Liberal arts:** Arts/sciences, humanities. **Math:** General. **Parks/recreation:** Facilities management. **Philosophy/religion:** Philosophy, religion. **Physical sciences:** Chemistry. **Psychology:** General. **Public

**administration:** Human services. **Social sciences:** General, sociology. **Theology:** Bible, sacred music, theology. **Visual/performing arts:** Art, design, dramatic.

**Most popular majors.** Business/marketing 39%, education 6%, health sciences 11%, liberal arts 13%, theological studies 8%.

**Computing on campus.** 160 workstations in dormitories, library, computer center. Dormitories wired for high-speed internet access and linked to campus network. Helpline, wireless network available.

**Student life. Freshman orientation:** Mandatory, $600 fee. Preregistration for classes offered. **Policies:** Religious observance required. **Housing:** Guaranteed on-campus for freshmen. Single-sex dorms, special housing for disabled, apartments available. $100 fully refundable deposit, deadline 5/1. **Activities:** Bands, campus ministries, choral groups, drama, literary magazine, music ensembles, musical theater, opera, radio station, student government, student newspaper, symphony orchestra, Fellowship of Christian Athletes, ministerial association, interest clubs.

**Athletics.** NAIA, NCCAA. **Intercollegiate:** Baseball M, basketball, cheerleading, cross-country, golf, soccer, softball W, tennis, track and field, volleyball W. **Intramural:** Badminton, baseball M, basketball, football (tackle) M, soccer, softball, table tennis, tennis, volleyball. **Team name:** Pilots.

**Student services.** Adult student services, alcohol/substance abuse counseling, chaplain/spiritual director, career counseling, student employment services, financial aid counseling, health services, minority student services, personal counseling, placement for graduates. **Physically disabled:** Services for visually, hearing impaired.

**Contact.** E-mail: admissions@bethelcollege.edu
Phone: (574) 807-7600 Toll-free number: (800) 422-4101
Fax: (574) 807-7650
Krista Wong, Director of Admission, Bethel College, 1001 Bethel Circle, Mishawaka, IN 46545-5591

## Butler University
### Indianapolis, Indiana
CB member
www.butler.edu
CB code: 1073

- Private 4-year university
- Residential campus in very large city
- 3,715 degree-seeking undergraduates: 2% part-time, 60% women, 4% African American, 2% Asian American, 2% Hispanic American, 2% international
- 733 degree-seeking graduate students
- 79% of applicants admitted
- SAT or ACT with writing, application essay required
- 76% graduate within 6 years; 24% enter graduate study

**General.** Founded in 1855. Regionally accredited. **Degrees:** 619 bachelor's awarded; master's, professional offered. **ROTC:** Army, Air Force. **Location:** 5 miles from downtown. **Calendar:** Semester, limited summer session. **Full-time faculty:** 327 total; 83% have terminal degrees, 12% minority, 46% women. **Part-time faculty:** 139 total; 26% have terminal degrees, 10% minority, 39% women. **Class size:** 58% < 20, 37% 20-39, 1% 40-49, 2% 50-99, 1% >100. **Special facilities:** Observatory, planetarium, herbarium, performing arts auditorium, canal, nature preserve.

**Freshman class profile.** 6,246 applied, 4,928 admitted, 946 enrolled.

| Mid 50% test scores | | | |
|---|---|---|---|
| SAT critical reading: | 520-630 | GPA 2.0-2.99: | 6% |
| SAT math: | 540-650 | Rank in top quarter: | 79% |
| SAT writing: | 520-620 | Rank in top tenth: | 50% |
| ACT composite: | 25-30 | End year in good standing: | 94% |
| GPA 3.75 or higher: | 54% | Return as sophomores: | 90% |
| GPA 3.50-3.74: | 20% | Out-of-state: | 46% |
| GPA 3.0-3.49: | 20% | Live on campus: | 96% |
| | | International: | 2% |

**Basis for selection.** Test scores, high school record most important. Recommendations, activities considered. Audition required of dance, drama, music, and media arts majors. **Homeschooled:** Statement describing home-school structure and mission, transcript of courses and grades, letter of recommendation (nonparent) required.

**High school preparation.** College-preparatory program required. 16 units required. Required units include English 4, mathematics 3, social studies 2, history 2, science 3 (laboratory 2), foreign language 2 and academic electives 2. 4 math units required for business administration majors.

**2009-2010 Annual costs.** Tuition/fees: $29,246. Room/board: $9,740. Books/supplies: $800. Personal expenses: $1,450.

**2009-2010 Financial aid. Need-based:** 895 full-time freshmen applied for aid; 664 were judged to have need; 664 of these received aid. Average scholarship/grant was $17,486; average loan $4,512. 64% of total undergraduate aid awarded as scholarships/grants, 36% as loans/jobs. **Non-need-based:** Scholarships awarded for academics, athletics, music/drama.

**Application procedures. Admission:** Priority date 11/15; deadline 8/1 (postmark date). $35 fee, may be waived for applicants with need, free for online applicants. 3 separate notification plans. Must reply by May 1 or within 2 week(s) if notified thereafter. **Financial aid:** Priority date 3/1; no closing date. FAFSA required. Applicants notified on a rolling basis starting 3/15; must reply within 3 week(s) of notification.

**Academics. Special study options:** Combined bachelor's/graduate degree, cooperative education, cross-registration, double major, dual enrollment of high school students, exchange student, honors, independent study, internships, student-designed major, study abroad, teacher certification program, Washington semester. Dual-degree engineering program with Purdue University; cooperative program in Business. **Credit/placement by examination:** AP, CLEP, IB, SAT, ACT, institutional tests. **Support services:** Learning center, reduced course load, study skills assistance, tutoring, writing center.

**Majors. Biology:** General. **Business:** Accounting, actuarial science, finance, international, marketing. **Communications:** General, journalism, radio/tv. **Communications technology:** Recording arts. **Computer sciences:** General, information systems. **Education:** Early childhood, elementary, kindergarten/preschool, middle, music, secondary. **Engineering:** Physics. **Foreign languages:** French, German, Latin, modern Greek, Spanish. **Health:** Communication disorders, pharmaceutical sciences, physician assistant. **History:** General. **Interdisciplinary:** Science/society. **Liberal arts:** Arts/sciences. **Math:** General. **Philosophy/religion:** Philosophy, religion. **Physical sciences:** Chemistry, physics. **Protective services:** Criminal justice. **Psychology:** General. **Social sciences:** Anthropology, criminology, economics, international relations, political science, sociology, urban studies. **Visual/performing arts:** Arts management, dance, dramatic, music management, music pedagogy, music performance, music theory/composition, piano/organ, stringed instruments, voice/opera.

**Most popular majors.** Business/marketing 17%, communications/journalism 8%, education 9%, foreign language 7%, health sciences 24%, social sciences 7%, visual/performing arts 7%.

**Computing on campus.** 430 workstations in dormitories, library, computer center, student center. Dormitories wired for high-speed internet access and linked to campus network. Commuter students can connect to campus network. Online course registration, helpline, wireless network available.

**Student life. Freshman orientation:** Mandatory, $100 fee. Preregistration for classes offered. Three-day program held in August. Early registration for Fall classes held March through June. **Housing:** Guaranteed on-campus for all undergraduates. Coed dorms, single-sex dorms, apartments, fraternity/sorority housing available. $100 fully refundable deposit, deadline 5/1. **Activities:** Bands, campus ministries, choral groups, dance, drama, international student organizations, literary magazine, music ensembles, Model UN, musical theater, opera, student government, student newspaper, symphony orchestra, TV station, volunteer center, black student union, Campus Crusade for Christ, YMCA, College Republicans, Mortar Board, academic honoraries, Alpha Phi Omega.

**Athletics.** NCAA. **Intercollegiate:** Baseball M, basketball, cross-country, football (tackle) M, golf, soccer, softball W, swimming W, tennis, track and field, volleyball W. **Intramural:** Badminton, baseball M, basketball, bowling, football (tackle) M, golf, soccer, softball, swimming, table tennis, tennis, track and field, volleyball, weight lifting. **Team name:** Bulldogs.

**Student services.** Alcohol/substance abuse counseling, career counseling, student employment services, financial aid counseling, health services, minority student services, personal counseling, placement for graduates. **Physically disabled:** Services for visually, speech impaired.

**Contact.** E-mail: admission@butler.edu
Phone: (317) 940-8100 Toll-free number: (888) 940-8100
Fax: (317) 940-8150
Scott Ham, Director of Admissions, Butler University, 4600 Sunset Avenue, Indianapolis, IN 46208

## Calumet College of St. Joseph
### Whiting, Indiana
www.ccsj.edu
CB code: 1776

- Private 4-year liberal arts college affiliated with Roman Catholic Church
- Commuter campus in small city
- 1,088 degree-seeking undergraduates: 49% part-time, 48% women

- 177 degree-seeking graduate students
- 52% of applicants admitted
- Application essay required

**General.** Founded in 1951. Regionally accredited. **Degrees:** 258 bachelor's, 14 associate awarded; master's offered. **Location:** 20 miles from Chicago. **Calendar:** Semester, limited summer session. **Full-time faculty:** 34 total; 68% have terminal degrees, 15% minority, 32% women. **Part-time faculty:** 12 total; 17% have terminal degrees, 8% minority, 58% women. **Class size:** 71% < 20, 25% 20-39, 4% 40-49, less than 1% >100.

**Freshman class profile.** 454 applied, 234 admitted, 154 enrolled.

| | | | |
|---|---|---|---|
| GPA 3.75 or higher: | 2% | GPA 2.0-2.99: | 58% |
| GPA 3.50-3.74: | 2% | Rank in top quarter: | 25% |
| GPA 3.0-3.49: | 13% | Rank in top tenth: | 8% |

**Basis for selection.** High school record most important. ACT/ COMPASS Assessment Test, rank top half of class, 2.0 GPA required. Compass testing used for placement. Essay used to place students in English courses as part of placement exam. SAT or ACT recommended. Interview recommended. **Homeschooled:** State high school equivalency certificate required.

**High school preparation.** 15 units recommended. Recommended units include English 4, mathematics 3, social studies 3, science 2 (laboratory 1) and foreign language 1.

**2010-2011 Annual costs.** Tuition/fees: $14,000. Books/supplies: $1,500. Personal expenses: $1,140.

**2008-2009 Financial aid. Non-need-based:** Scholarships awarded for academics, alumni affiliation, athletics, religious affiliation. **Additional information:** Immediate computerized estimate of financial aid eligibility available to students applying in person.

**Application procedures. Admission:** No deadline. No application fee. Admission notification on a rolling basis. **Financial aid:** Priority date 3/1; no closing date. FAFSA required. Applicants notified on a rolling basis; must reply within 2 week(s) of notification.

**Academics. Special study options:** Accelerated study, cooperative education, double major, dual enrollment of high school students, ESL, honors, independent study, internships, liberal arts/career combination, student-designed major, teacher certification program, weekend college. **Credit/ placement by examination:** AP, CLEP, SAT, ACT, institutional tests. 30 credit hours maximum toward associate degree, 60 toward bachelor's. **Support services:** Learning center, reduced course load, remedial instruction, study skills assistance, tutoring, writing center.

**Majors. Business:** General, accounting, business admin, organizational behavior. **Communications:** General, media studies. **Computer sciences:** General. **Education:** General, elementary, science, secondary. **Health:** Health care admin. **Legal studies:** Paralegal. **Liberal arts:** Arts/sciences. **Philosophy/ religion:** Religion. **Protective services:** Police science. **Psychology:** General. **Public administration:** Human services. **Social sciences:** General. **Visual/ performing arts:** Studio arts.

**Most popular majors.** Business/marketing 21%, education 12%, legal studies 50%.

**Computing on campus.** 72 workstations in library, computer center. Online library, wireless network available.

**Student life. Freshman orientation:** Mandatory, $85 fee. Preregistration for classes offered. Held 1 week before classes begin, followed up by mentoring program. **Activities:** Pep band, campus ministries, choral groups, dance, drama, literary magazine, student government, student newspaper, Los Amigos, black student organization, criminal justice club, media and fine arts club, creative writing club, paralegal studies club, booster club, human services club, educators club.

**Athletics.** NAIA. **Intercollegiate:** Baseball M, basketball, bowling, cheerleading M, cross-country, golf, soccer, softball W, tennis, track and field, volleyball, wrestling M. **Team name:** Crimson Wave.

**Student services.** Adult student services, chaplain/spiritual director, career counseling, student employment services, financial aid counseling, on-campus daycare, personal counseling, placement for graduates, veterans' counselor.

**Contact.** E-mail: admissions@ccsj.edu
Phone: (219) 473-4215 Toll-free number: (877) 700-9100
Fax: (219) 473-4259
Gina Pirtle, Director of Admissions/Financial Aid, Calumet College of St. Joseph, 2400 New York Avenue, Whiting, IN 46394-2195

## DePauw University
**Greencastle, Indiana**
**www.depauw.edu**

**CB member**
**CB code: 1166**

- Private 4-year music and liberal arts college affiliated with United Methodist Church
- Residential campus in small town
- 2,354 degree-seeking undergraduates: 57% women
- 66% of applicants admitted
- SAT or ACT with writing, application essay required
- 83% graduate within 6 years

**General.** Founded in 1837. Regionally accredited. **Degrees:** 507 bachelor's awarded. **ROTC:** Army, Air Force. **Location:** 45 miles from Indianapolis. **Calendar:** 4-1-4. **Full-time faculty:** 224 total; 98% have terminal degrees, 20% minority, 43% women. **Part-time faculty:** 55 total; 62% have terminal degrees, 13% minority, 51% women. **Class size:** 61% < 20, 39% 20-39, less than 1% 40-49. **Special facilities:** Nature park and arboretum, ethnographic museums, closed circuit tv studio facilities, music instructional technology studio, digital media laboratory, visual resources library with digital image collection, digital video studio, observatory, 2 theaters, 2 music concert halls, concert pipe organ.

**Freshman class profile.** 4,347 applied, 2,877 admitted, 717 enrolled.

| Mid 50% test scores | | | |
|---|---|---|---|
| SAT critical reading: | 530-650 | Rank in top quarter: | 82% |
| SAT math: | 550-670 | Rank in top tenth: | 51% |
| SAT writing: | 530-640 | Return as sophomores: | 90% |
| ACT composite: | 24-29 | Out-of-state: | 59% |
| GPA 3.75 or higher: | 35% | Live on campus: | 100% |
| GPA 3.50-3.74: | 22% | International: | 9% |
| GPA 3.0-3.49: | 39% | Fraternities: | 70% |
| GPA 2.0-2.99: | 4% | Sororities: | 60% |

**Basis for selection.** Academic achievement and preparation, demonstrated verbal and quantitative skills, evidence of continuing commitment to learning most important. TOEFL recommended for international students. Interview strongly recommended. Audition required for School of Music candidates. **Homeschooled:** Transcript of courses and grades, interview required.

**High school preparation.** College-preparatory program recommended. 32 units recommended. Recommended units include English 4, mathematics 4, social studies 4, science 4 (laboratory 2), foreign language 4 and academic electives 10.

**2009-2010 Annual costs.** Tuition/fees: $33,250. Room/board: $8,740. Books/supplies: $750. Personal expenses: $1,000.

**2009-2010 Financial aid. Need-based:** 518 full-time freshmen applied for aid; 408 were judged to have need; 408 of these received aid. Average need met was 90%. Average scholarship/grant was $25,918; average loan $2,905. 81% of total undergraduate aid awarded as scholarships/grants, 19% as loans/jobs. **Non-need-based:** Awarded to 1,309 full-time undergraduates, including 396 freshmen. Scholarships awarded for academics, alumni affiliation, leadership, minority status, music/drama, ROTC.

**Application procedures. Admission:** Closing date 2/1 (postmark date). $40 fee, may be waived for applicants with need, free for online applicants. Admission notification 4/1. Must reply by May 1 or within 2 week(s) if notified thereafter. **Financial aid:** Closing date 3/1. FAFSA, institutional form required. Applicants notified by 3/27; must reply by 5/1.

**Academics.** Demonstrated competence in writing, quantitative reasoning, and oral communication required of all students. Seminar, thesis, project, or comprehensive examination in major also required. More than 700 students participate in off-campus winter term programs; 40% study off-campus. **Special study options:** Combined bachelor's/graduate degree, double major, dual enrollment of high school students, exchange student, honors, independent study, internships, student-designed major, study abroad, teacher certification program. **Credit/placement by examination:** AP, CLEP, IB, SAT, ACT, institutional tests. 32 credit hours maximum toward bachelor's degree. **Support services:** Learning center, study skills assistance, tutoring, writing center.

**Majors. Area/ethnic studies:** African-American, East Asian, women's. **Biology:** General, biochemistry. **Communications:** Media studies. **Computer sciences:** Computer science. **Conservation:** Environmental science. **Education:** Music. **Foreign languages:** Ancient Greek, classics, French, German, Latin, Romance, Spanish. **Health:** Athletic training. **History:** General. **Interdisciplinary:** Peace/conflict. **Math:** General. **Parks/recreation:** Exercise sciences. **Philosophy/religion:** Philosophy, religion. **Physical sciences:** Chemistry, geology, physics. **Psychology:** General. **Social sciences:**

Anthropology, economics, political science, sociology. **Visual/performing arts:** Art history/conservation, dramatic, film/cinema, music management, music performance, music theory/composition, studio arts.

**Most popular majors.** Biology 11%, communications/journalism 12%, English 12%, foreign language 7%, social sciences 19%, visual/performing arts 6%.

**Computing on campus.** PC or laptop required. 413 workstations in dormitories, library, computer center, student center. Dormitories wired for high-speed internet access and linked to campus network. Commuter students can connect to campus network. Online course registration, online library, helpline, repair service, student web hosting, wireless network available.

**Student life. Freshman orientation:** Mandatory. Preregistration for classes offered. Four-day program in August. **Housing:** Guaranteed on-campus for all undergraduates. Coed dorms, apartments, fraternity/sorority housing, wellness housing available. $400 nonrefundable deposit, deadline 5/1. **Activities:** Bands, campus ministries, choral groups, dance, drama, film society, international student organizations, literary magazine, music ensembles, musical theater, opera, radio station, student government, student newspaper, symphony orchestra, TV station, African American students association, international student association, union board, coalition for women's concerns, College Republicans, College Democrats, Habitat for Humanity, Christian fellowship, United DePauw, Latino concerns committee.

**Athletics.** NCAA. **Intercollegiate:** Baseball M, basketball, cheerleading, cross-country, diving, field hockey W, football (tackle) M, golf, soccer, softball W, swimming, tennis, track and field, volleyball W. **Intramural:** Badminton, basketball, bowling, football (non-tackle), golf, racquetball, soccer, softball, table tennis, tennis, volleyball. **Team name:** Tigers.

**Student services.** Alcohol/substance abuse counseling, chaplain/spiritual director, career counseling, student employment services, financial aid counseling, health services, minority student services, on-campus daycare, personal counseling, placement for graduates, women's services. **Physically disabled:** Services for visually, hearing impaired.

**Contact.** E-mail: admission@depauw.edu
Phone: (765) 658-4006 Toll-free number: (800) 447-2495
Fax: (765) 658-4007
Earl Macam, Director of Admission, DePauw University, 101 East Seminary Street, Greencastle, IN 46135-1611

## DeVry University: Indianapolis
**Indianapolis, Indiana**
**www.devry.edu**

- For-profit 4-year university
- Commuter campus in very large city
- 231 degree-seeking undergraduates: 57% part-time, 44% women, 30% African American, 2% Asian American, 2% Hispanic American
- 133 degree-seeking graduate students

**General. Degrees:** 26 bachelor's, 2 associate awarded; master's offered. **Calendar:** Semester. **Part-time faculty:** 33 total; 21% minority, 39% women.

**Freshman class profile.** 42 enrolled.

**Basis for selection.** Interview and GPA important; standardized test scores considered.

**High school preparation.** College-preparatory program recommended.

**2009-2010 Annual costs.** Tuition/fees: $14,160. Books/supplies: $1,310. Personal expenses: $3,270.

**2008-2009 Financial aid. Non-need-based:** Scholarships awarded for academics.

**Application procedures. Admission:** No deadline. $50 fee. Admission notification on a rolling basis. **Financial aid:** No deadline. FAFSA required. Applicants notified on a rolling basis.

**Academics. Special study options:** Accelerated study, distance learning. **Credit/placement by examination:** CLEP.

**Majors. Business:** Business admin. **Computer sciences:** Networking, security, systems analysis, web page design. **Other:** Technical management.

**Most popular majors.** Business/marketing 96%.

**Student life. Housing:** Private apartments, student-plan housing, private rooms.

**Contact.** Phone: (866) 513-3879
DeVry University: Indianapolis, 9100 Keystone Crossing, Suite 350, Indianapolis, IN 46240

## Earlham College
**Richmond, Indiana**  CB member
**www.earlham.edu**  CB code: 1195

- Private 4-year liberal arts and seminary college affiliated with Society of Friends (Quaker)
- Residential campus in large town
- 1,097 degree-seeking undergraduates: 1% part-time, 55% women, 6% African American, 3% Asian American, 2% Hispanic American, 1% Native American, 14% international
- 135 degree-seeking graduate students
- 76% of applicants admitted
- SAT or ACT with writing, application essay required
- 72% graduate within 6 years; 36% enter graduate study

**General.** Founded in 1847. Regionally accredited; also accredited by ATS. **Degrees:** 259 bachelor's awarded; master's offered. **Location:** 70 miles from Indianapolis; 45 miles from Dayton, Ohio. **Calendar:** Semester. **Full-time faculty:** 89 total; 98% have terminal degrees, 22% minority, 45% women. **Part-time faculty:** 9 total; 56% have terminal degrees, 44% women. **Class size:** 61% < 20, 30% 20-39, 5% 40-49, 4% 50-99, less than 1% >100. **Special facilities:** Natural history museum, observatory, planetarium, herbarium, working farm, biological field stations.

**Freshman class profile.** 1,668 applied, 1,272 admitted, 292 enrolled.

| Mid 50% test scores | | | |
|---|---|---|---|
| SAT critical reading: | 560-690 | GPA 2.0-2.99: | 11% |
| SAT math: | 530-640 | Rank in top quarter: | 59% |
| SAT writing: | 550-660 | Rank in top tenth: | 31% |
| ACT composite: | 24-29 | End year in good standing: | 85% |
| GPA 3.75 or higher: | 38% | Return as sophomores: | 81% |
| GPA 3.50-3.74: | 19% | Out-of-state: | 74% |
| GPA 3.0-3.49: | 32% | Live on campus: | 99% |
| | | International: | 19% |

**Basis for selection.** Combination of GPA, quality of high school program, SAT or ACT scores, recommendations, essay, and extracurricular activities important. Interview preferred. **Homeschooled:** Statement describing homeschool structure and mission, interview, letter of recommendation (nonparent) required. Portfolio or other evidence of learning, test scores, and essay.

**High school preparation.** College-preparatory program required. Required and recommended units include English 4, mathematics 3-4, social studies 4, history 2, science 3-4 (laboratory 2), foreign language 2-4 and visual/performing arts 1.

**2010-2011 Annual costs.** Tuition/fees: $36,694. Room/board: $7,400. Books/supplies: $850. Personal expenses: $1,000.

**2008-2009 Financial aid. Need-based:** 222 full-time freshmen applied for aid; 194 were judged to have need; 194 of these received aid. Average need met was 91%. Average scholarship/grant was $17,620; average loan $4,662. 78% of total undergraduate aid awarded as scholarships/grants, 22% as loans/jobs. **Non-need-based:** Awarded to 537 full-time undergraduates, including 152 freshmen. Scholarships awarded for academics, minority status, religious affiliation.

**Application procedures. Admission:** Priority date 1/1; deadline 2/15 (postmark date). No application fee. Admission notification 3/15. Must reply by May 1 or within 3 week(s) if notified thereafter. **Financial aid:** Closing date 3/1. FAFSA required. Applicants notified on a rolling basis starting 2/15; must reply by 5/1 or within 3 week(s) of notification.

**Academics. Special study options:** Accelerated study, combined bachelor's/graduate degree, cross-registration, double major, dual enrollment of high school students, ESL, independent study, internships, New York semester, student-designed major, study abroad, urban semester. Teacher certification at Master's level only. **Credit/placement by examination:** CLEP, IB, institutional tests. 18 credit hours maximum toward bachelor's degree. **Support services:** Learning center, pre-admission summer program, reduced course load, study skills assistance, tutoring, writing center.

**Majors. Area/ethnic studies:** African-American, Japanese, Latin American, women's. **Biology:** General, biochemistry. **Business:** Business admin. **Computer sciences:** General. **Conservation:** Environmental studies. **Foreign languages:** Classics, comparative lit, French, German, Spanish. **Health:**

Premedicine. **History:** General. **Interdisciplinary:** Peace/conflict. **Math:** General. **Philosophy/religion:** Philosophy, religion. **Physical sciences:** Chemistry, physics. **Psychology:** General, psychobiology. **Social sciences:** Economics, political science, sociology. **Visual/performing arts:** Art, dramatic. **Other:** Geosciences, International studies.

**Most popular majors.** Area/ethnic studies 7%, biology 13%, business/marketing 7%, English 7%, foreign language 9%, history 6%, interdisciplinary studies 11%, psychology 8%, social sciences 14%, visual/performing arts 8%.

**Computing on campus.** 164 workstations in library, computer center. Dormitories wired for high-speed internet access and linked to campus network. Commuter students can connect to campus network. Online course registration, online library, helpline, repair service, student web hosting, wireless network available.

**Student life. Freshman orientation:** Mandatory. Preregistration for classes offered. Five-day program held just prior to beginning of fall semester. **Policies:** Community and academic honor codes. **Housing:** Guaranteed on-campus for all undergraduates. Coed dorms, single-sex dorms, special housing for disabled, wellness housing available. Friendship houses. **Activities:** Bands, campus ministries, choral groups, dance, drama, film society, international student organizations, literary magazine, music ensembles, Model UN, radio station, student government, student newspaper, symphony orchestra, Young Friends, Questing Catholics, Christian Fellowship, Jewish student union, Muslim student union, Bahai club, Amnesty International, Model UN, Coalition for Racial Justice, Fellowship of Christian Athletes.

**Athletics.** NCAA. **Intercollegiate:** Baseball M, basketball, cross-country, field hockey W, football (tackle) M, soccer, tennis, track and field, volleyball W. **Intramural:** Basketball, bowling, football (non-tackle) M, racquetball, soccer, triathlon. **Team name:** Quakers.

**Student services.** Chaplain/spiritual director, career counseling, student employment services, financial aid counseling, health services, minority student services, on-campus daycare, personal counseling, placement for graduates, women's services. **Physically disabled:** Services for visually, speech, hearing impaired.

**Contact.** E-mail: admission@earlham.edu
Phone: (765) 983-1600 Toll-free number: (800) 327-5426
Fax: (765) 983-1560
Jeff Rickey, Vice Presdient and Dean of Admissions and Financial Aid, Earlham College, 801 National Road West, Richmond, IN 47374-4095

## Franklin College

**Franklin, Indiana**
www.franklincollege.edu

**CB member**
**CB code: 1228**

- Private 4-year liberal arts college affiliated with American Baptist Churches in the USA
- Residential campus in large town
- 1,271 degree-seeking undergraduates: 18% part-time, 52% women, 3% African American, 1% Asian American, 1% Hispanic American
- 67% of applicants admitted
- SAT or ACT with writing, application essay required
- 56% graduate within 6 years

**General.** Founded in 1834. Regionally accredited. **Degrees:** 183 bachelor's awarded. **ROTC:** Army. **Location:** 20 miles from Indianapolis. **Calendar:** 4-1-4, limited summer session. **Full-time faculty:** 67 total; 87% have terminal degrees, 6% minority, 45% women. **Part-time faculty:** 36 total; 11% have terminal degrees, 56% women. **Class size:** 70% < 20, 29% 20-39, less than 1% 40-49.

**Freshman class profile.** 1,734 applied, 1,156 admitted, 319 enrolled.

| Mid 50% test scores | | | |
|---|---|---|---|
| SAT critical reading: | 420-520 | GPA 2.0-2.99: | 15% |
| SAT math: | 460-570 | Rank in top quarter: | 56% |
| SAT writing: | 440-540 | Rank in top tenth: | 21% |
| ACT composite: | 19-24 | Return as sophomores: | 79% |
| GPA 3.75 or higher: | 25% | Live on campus: | 92% |
| GPA 3.50-3.74: | 22% | Fraternities: | 54% |
| GPA 3.0-3.49: | 37% | Sororities: | 66% |

**Basis for selection.** Class rank, test scores, essay and counselor recommendations important. Extracurricular activities considered. Interview recommended for all. **Homeschooled:** Transcript of courses and grades, interview, letter of recommendation (nonparent) required. Submit research paper(s), art work, community service projects, educational trip or programs, writing samples, other pertinent documents. Formal interview on campus required.

**Learning Disabled:** Students with learning disabilities asked to schedule meeting with Director of Academic Support Services.

**High school preparation.** Required and recommended units include English 4, mathematics 4, social studies 3, science 2 and foreign language 2.

**2009-2010 Annual costs.** Tuition/fees: $23,275. Room/board: $6,885. Books/supplies: $1,000. Personal expenses: $75.

**2008-2009 Financial aid. Need-based:** 312 full-time freshmen applied for aid; 265 were judged to have need; 265 of these received aid. Average need met was 82%. Average scholarship/grant was $14,379; average loan $4,024. 70% of total undergraduate aid awarded as scholarships/grants, 30% as loans/jobs. **Non-need-based:** Awarded to 313 full-time undergraduates, including 121 freshmen. Scholarships awarded for academics, alumni affiliation, art, leadership, minority status, religious affiliation, state residency.

**Application procedures. Admission:** Priority date 1/15; no deadline. $30 fee, may be waived for applicants with need. Admission notification on a rolling basis beginning on or about 9/1. **Financial aid:** Closing date 3/10. FAFSA, institutional form required. Applicants notified on a rolling basis; must reply by 5/1 or within 4 week(s) of notification.

**Academics. Special study options:** Cross-registration, double major, dual enrollment of high school students, exchange student, independent study, internships, semester at sea, study abroad, teacher certification program, United Nations semester, Washington semester. **Credit/placement by examination:** AP, CLEP, SAT, ACT, institutional tests. 30 credit hours maximum toward bachelor's degree. **Support services:** Learning center, remedial instruction, study skills assistance, tutoring, writing center.

**Majors. Area/ethnic studies:** American, Canadian. **Biology:** General. **Business:** General, accounting, finance, marketing. **Communications:** Broadcast journalism, journalism. **Computer sciences:** General, computer science. **Education:** Biology, chemistry, elementary, English, French, mathematics, physical, Spanish. **Foreign languages:** French, Spanish. **Health:** Athletic training. **History:** General. **Math:** General. **Parks/recreation:** General. **Philosophy/religion:** Philosophy, religion. **Physical sciences:** Chemistry. **Psychology:** General. **Social sciences:** Economics, political science, sociology. **Visual/performing arts:** Dramatic.

**Most popular majors.** Biology 10%, business/marketing 13%, communications/journalism 17%, education 13%, parks/recreation 6%, social sciences 6%.

**Computing on campus.** 250 workstations in dormitories, library, student center. Dormitories wired for high-speed internet access and linked to campus network. Online course registration, online library, helpline, repair service, wireless network available.

**Student life. Freshman orientation:** Mandatory, $50 fee. Preregistration for classes offered. Orientation for all students held 4 days prior to start of classes. **Policies:** All students must live on campus until senior year unless living with family. **Housing:** Guaranteed on-campus for all undergraduates. Coed dorms, single-sex dorms, special housing for disabled, fraternity/sorority housing, wellness housing available. $100 deposit, deadline 5/1. **Activities:** Pep band, choral groups, dance, drama, literary magazine, musical theater, radio station, student government, student newspaper, student association for the support of multiculturalism, Habitat for Humanity, college mentors for kids, Fellowship of Christian Athletes, ODK Leadership, international club.

**Athletics.** NCAA. **Intercollegiate:** Baseball M, basketball, cheerleading M, cross-country, diving, football (tackle) M, golf, soccer, swimming, tennis, track and field, volleyball W. **Intramural:** Basketball, football (non-tackle), racquetball, softball, volleyball. **Team name:** Grizzlies.

**Student services.** Alcohol/substance abuse counseling, chaplain/spiritual director, career counseling, student employment services, financial aid counseling, health services, minority student services, personal counseling, placement for graduates, veterans' counselor, women's services.

**Contact.** E-mail: admissions@franklincollege.edu
Phone: (317) 738-8062 Toll-free number: (800) 852-0232
Fax: (317) 738-8274
Jacqueline Acosta, Director of Admissions, Franklin College, 101 Branigin Boulevard, Franklin, IN 46131-2623

## Goshen College

**Goshen, Indiana**
www.goshen.edu
**CB code: 1251**

- Private 4-year liberal arts college affiliated with Mennonite Church
- Residential campus in large town

- 951 degree-seeking undergraduates: 5% part-time, 60% women, 4% African American, 2% Asian American, 7% Hispanic American, 4% international
- 43 degree-seeking graduate students
- 68% of applicants admitted
- SAT or ACT (ACT writing optional), application essay required
- 70% graduate within 6 years; 10% enter graduate study

**General.** Founded in 1894. Regionally accredited. 1,150 acre environmental study facility located 30 miles from campus. **Degrees:** 235 bachelor's awarded; master's offered. **Location:** 25 miles from South Bend, 120 miles from Chicago. **Calendar:** Semester, limited summer session. **Full-time faculty:** 68 total; 68% have terminal degrees, 6% minority, 47% women. **Part-time faculty:** 54 total; 28% have terminal degrees, 4% minority, 54% women. **Class size:** 56% < 20, 38% 20-39, 3% 40-49, 4% 50-99. **Special facilities:** Concert hall, X-ray precision laboratory, electron microscope, marine biology laboratory in Florida Keys, historical library and archives, laboratory kindergarten and child care center, media production studio, nature preserve, student-run coffee shop.

**Freshman class profile.** 788 applied, 532 admitted, 238 enrolled.

| Mid 50% test scores | | GPA 2.0-2.99: | 15% |
|---|---|---|---|
| SAT critical reading: | 470-640 | Rank in top quarter: | 58% |
| SAT math: | 490-630 | Rank in top tenth: | 30% |
| SAT writing: | 450-620 | End year in good standing: | 92% |
| ACT composite: | 21-29 | Return as sophomores: | 84% |
| GPA 3.75 or higher: | 50% | Out-of-state: | 48% |
| GPA 3.50-3.74: | 15% | Live on campus: | 82% |
| GPA 3.0-3.49: | 20% | International: | 3% |

**Basis for selection.** Admission review required for low GPA, class rank and/or test scores. Nursing and education programs require college GPA of 2.5 for entrance and continuation. Interview recommended. **Home-schooled:** Statement describing homeschool structure and mission, transcript of courses and grades required. **Learning Disabled:** Documentation of disability and special requirements dated within last 3 years required. Exit interview with high school special needs counselor, if working with one, required.

**High school preparation.** College-preparatory program recommended. 12 units required; 16 recommended. Required and recommended units include English 4, mathematics 2-3, social studies 2, history 2, science 2-3 and foreign language 2.

**2009-2010 Annual costs.** Tuition/fees: $23,400. Room/board: $7,900. Books/supplies: $890. Personal expenses: $1,100.

**2009-2010 Financial aid. Need-based:** 218 full-time freshmen applied for aid; 201 were judged to have need; 199 of these received aid. Average need met was 83%. Average scholarship/grant was $17,214; average loan $3,132. 76% of total undergraduate aid awarded as scholarships/grants, 24% as loans/jobs. **Non-need-based:** Awarded to 359 full-time undergraduates, including 96 freshmen. Scholarships awarded for academics, art, athletics, leadership, music/drama.

**Application procedures. Admission:** Priority date 2/1; deadline 8/1 (postmark date). $25 fee, may be waived for applicants with need. Admission notification on a rolling basis beginning on or about 9/15. Must reply by May 1 or within 2 week(s) if notified thereafter. **Financial aid:** Priority date 2/1; no closing date. FAFSA, institutional form required. Applicants notified on a rolling basis starting 3/1; must reply by 5/1 or within 2 week(s) of notification.

**Academics.** Practicum and senior seminar course required in all majors. International education through on-campus courses or study abroad required. Study abroad incorporates language study, academic and cultural learning and service. Students live in homes of country where studying for one semester. **Special study options:** Combined bachelor's/graduate degree, cross-registration, double major, dual enrollment of high school students, independent study, internships, liberal arts/career combination, student-designed major, study abroad, teacher certification program, urban semester, Washington semester. Adult degree completion program (one evening per week, concentrated study). **Credit/placement by examination:** AP, CLEP, IB, SAT, ACT, institutional tests. **Support services:** Learning center, reduced course load, remedial instruction, study skills assistance, tutoring, writing center.

**Majors. Biology:** General, molecular. **Business:** Accounting, business admin. **Communications:** General, broadcast journalism, journalism, public relations. **Computer sciences:** Computer science, information systems. **Conservation:** Environmental science. **Education:** General, art, biology, business, chemistry, elementary, English, ESL, mathematics, music, physical, physics, science, secondary, social studies, Spanish, special. **Foreign languages:** American Sign Language, sign language interpretation, Spanish. **Health:** Nursing (RN). **History:** General. **Interdisciplinary:** Peace/

conflict. **Math:** General, applied. **Parks/recreation:** Health/fitness. **Physical sciences:** Chemistry, physics. **Psychology:** General. **Public administration:** Social work. **Social sciences:** Sociology. **Theology:** Youth ministry. **Visual/performing arts:** Art, dramatic. **Other:** Bible and religion, History and investigative skills, Journalism education.

**Most popular majors.** Biology 6%, business/marketing 16%, education 9%, health sciences 14%, public administration/social services 7%, visual/performing arts 13%.

**Computing on campus.** 130 workstations in dormitories, library, computer center, student center. Dormitories wired for high-speed internet access and linked to campus network. Commuter students can connect to campus network. Online course registration, online library, helpline, student web hosting, wireless network available.

**Student life. Freshman orientation:** Mandatory. Preregistration for classes offered. 1 of 3 possible days in June, plus 3 days prior to fall semester in August. **Policies:** No smoking and no drinking alcoholic beverages on campus. **Housing:** Guaranteed on-campus for all undergraduates. Coed dorms, single-sex dorms, special housing for disabled, apartments, wellness housing available. $200 fully refundable deposit, deadline 5/1. **Activities:** Bands, campus ministries, choral groups, drama, film society, international student organizations, music ensembles, musical theater, opera, radio station, student government, student newspaper, symphony orchestra, black student union, Latino student union, international student club, women's association, Catholic student association, eco-pax club, Peace (Pax) club, fellowship of Christian athletes, social work action association.

**Athletics.** NAIA. **Intercollegiate:** Baseball M, basketball, cross-country, golf M, soccer, softball W, tennis, track and field, volleyball W. **Intramural:** Badminton, basketball, ice hockey M, racquetball, soccer, softball, table tennis, volleyball. **Team name:** Maple Leafs.

**Student services.** Adult student services, alcohol/substance abuse counseling, chaplain/spiritual director, career counseling, student employment services, financial aid counseling, health services, minority student services, on-campus daycare, personal counseling, placement for graduates, veterans' counselor, women's services. **Physically disabled:** Services for visually, speech, hearing impaired.

**Contact.** E-mail: admission@goshen.edu
Phone: (574) 535-7535 Toll-free number: (800) 348-7422
Fax: (574) 535-7609
Lynn Jackson, Executive Director of Enrollment Services, Goshen College, 1700 South Main Street, Goshen, IN 46526-4724

## Grace College
**Winona Lake, Indiana**
**www.grace.edu** — CB code: 1252

- Private 4-year liberal arts college affiliated with Brethren Church
- Residential campus in small town
- 1,384 degree-seeking undergraduates: 6% part-time, 53% women
- 164 degree-seeking graduate students
- 97% of applicants admitted
- SAT or ACT (ACT writing recommended) required
- 60% graduate within 6 years

**General.** Founded in 1948. Regionally accredited. **Degrees:** 210 bachelor's, 61 associate awarded; master's, doctoral offered. **Location:** 40 miles from Fort Wayne. **Calendar:** Semester, limited summer session. **Full-time faculty:** 57 total; 65% have terminal degrees, 4% minority, 16% women. **Part-time faculty:** 71 total; 14% have terminal degrees, 3% minority, 32% women. **Class size:** 54% < 20, 35% 20-39, 7% 40-49, 3% 50-99, less than 1% >100. **Special facilities:** Creation science center, Winona history museum.

**Freshman class profile.** 1,027 applied, 994 admitted, 233 enrolled.

| Mid 50% test scores | | GPA 2.0-2.99: | 15% |
|---|---|---|---|
| SAT critical reading: | 460-600 | Rank in top quarter: | 57% |
| SAT math: | 470-590 | Rank in top tenth: | 28% |
| ACT composite: | 21-28 | Return as sophomores: | 74% |
| GPA 3.75 or higher: | 39% | Out-of-state: | 46% |
| GPA 3.50-3.74: | 19% | Live on campus: | 87% |
| GPA 3.0-3.49: | 26% | | |

**Basis for selection.** References, religious affiliation/commitment, high school class rank, test scores most important. Interview recommended for music and art majors. Audition recommended for music majors. Portfolio recommended for art majors. **Homeschooled:** Transcript of courses and grades required.

**High school preparation.** College-preparatory program recommended. Required and recommended units include English 3-4, mathematics 2-4, social studies 2-3, history 2-3, science 2-3 (laboratory 2-3) and foreign language 2-4.

**2009-2010 Annual costs.** Tuition/fees: $21,100. Room/board: $6,880. Books/supplies: $800. Personal expenses: $800.

**2008-2009 Financial aid. Need-based:** 74% of total undergraduate aid awarded as scholarships/grants, 26% as loans/jobs. **Non-need-based:** Scholarships awarded for academics, art, athletics, leadership, minority status, music/drama, religious affiliation.

**Application procedures. Admission:** Priority date 12/1; deadline 8/1 (postmark date). $30 fee, may be waived for applicants with need, free for online applicants. Admission notification on a rolling basis beginning on or about 9/15. Must reply by May 1 or within 2 week(s) if notified thereafter. **Financial aid:** Closing date 3/1. FAFSA required. Applicants notified on a rolling basis starting 3/1; must reply by 5/1.

**Academics. Special study options:** Cooperative education, cross-registration, distance learning, double major, dual enrollment of high school students, exchange student, honors, independent study, internships, liberal arts/career combination, study abroad, teacher certification program. **Credit/placement by examination:** AP, CLEP, IB, SAT, ACT, institutional tests. 30 credit hours maximum toward associate degree, 30 toward bachelor's. **Support services:** Learning center, reduced course load, remedial instruction, study skills assistance, tutoring, writing center.

**Majors. Biology:** General, environmental. **Business:** General, accounting, business admin, finance, international, management information systems, marketing, nonprofit/public. **Communications:** General, journalism, public relations. **Education:** Art, business, elementary, English, French, mathematics, music, science, social studies, Spanish, special. **Foreign languages:** General, French, German, Spanish. **History:** General. **Math:** General, statistics. **Parks/recreation:** Health/fitness, sports admin. **Physical sciences:** General. **Protective services:** Criminal justice, law enforcement admin. **Psychology:** General. **Public administration:** Social work. **Social sciences:** Sociology. **Theology:** Bible, missionary, youth ministry. **Visual/performing arts:** Dramatic, drawing, film/cinema, graphic design, illustration, music management, music performance, music theory/composition, piano/organ, voice/opera. **Other:** Journalism education, Management, Social studies, non-teaching.

**Most popular majors.** Business/marketing 39%, education 16%, psychology 9%, theological studies 6%, visual/performing arts 6%.

**Computing on campus.** 160 workstations in dormitories, library, computer center, student center. Dormitories wired for high-speed internet access and linked to campus network. Commuter students can connect to campus network. Online course registration, helpline, wireless network available.

**Student life. Freshman orientation:** Mandatory. Preregistration for classes offered. Weekend program held at beginning of fall semester. **Policies:** Students are to refrain from use of alcoholic beverages, illegal drugs, tobacco, sexual misconduct, morally degrading media and literature, coarse or obscene language or any other conduct inconsistent with the goals and traditions of the college. Religious observance required. **Housing:** Guaranteed on-campus for all undergraduates. Single-sex dorms, apartments available. $200 nonrefundable deposit, deadline 5/1. **Activities:** Bands, campus ministries, choral groups, drama, literary magazine, music ensembles, musical theater, opera, student government, student newspaper, symphony orchestra, 20 Christian clubs and organizations.

**Athletics.** NAIA, NCCAA. **Intercollegiate:** Baseball M, basketball, cross-country, golf M, soccer, softball W, tennis, track and field, volleyball W. **Intramural:** Badminton, basketball, soccer, volleyball. **Team name:** Lancers.

**Student services.** Chaplain/spiritual director, career counseling, student employment services, financial aid counseling, health services, personal counseling, placement for graduates, veterans' counselor. **Physically disabled:** Services for visually impaired.

**Contact.** E-mail: admissions@grace.edu
Phone: (574) 372-5100 ext. 6008 Toll-free
number: (800) 544-7223 ext. 6008 Fax: (574) 372-5120
Cynthia Sisson, Dean of Admissions, Grace College, 200 Seminary Drive, Winona Lake, IN 46590

---

## Hanover College

**Hanover, Indiana**
**www.hanover.edu**

**CB member**
**CB code: 1290**

- Private 4-year liberal arts college affiliated with Presbyterian Church (USA)
- Residential campus in rural community

---

- 932 degree-seeking undergraduates: 54% women, 2% African American, 1% Asian American, 2% Hispanic American, 3% international
- 61% of applicants admitted
- SAT or ACT with writing, application essay required
- 63% graduate within 6 years; 27% enter graduate study

**General.** Founded in 1827. Regionally accredited. **Degrees:** 210 bachelor's awarded. **Location:** 45 miles from Louisville, 70 miles from Cincinnati. **Calendar:** 4-1-4. 4-4-1. **Full-time faculty:** 91 total; 100% have terminal degrees, 8% minority, 37% women. **Part-time faculty:** 4 total; 75% have terminal degrees, 75% women. **Class size:** 81% < 20, 19% 20-39, less than 1% 50-99. **Special facilities:** Geology museum, observatory.

**Freshman class profile.** 3,019 applied, 1,830 admitted, 293 enrolled.

| Mid 50% test scores | | | |
|---|---|---|---|
| SAT critical reading: | 490-600 | GPA 2.0-2.99: | 4% |
| SAT math: | 500-620 | Rank in top quarter: | 71% |
| SAT writing: | 470-570 | Rank in top tenth: | 32% |
| ACT composite: | 22-28 | End year in good standing: | 86% |
| GPA 3.75 or higher: | 41% | Return as sophomores: | 80% |
| GPA 3.50-3.74: | 18% | Out-of-state: | 31% |
| GPA 3.0-3.49: | 37% | Live on campus: | 97% |
| | | International: | 2% |

**Basis for selection.** GED not accepted. Selection of and performance in academic courses most important. Interview recommended. **Homeschooled:** Transcript of courses and grades required.

**High school preparation.** College-preparatory program required. 18 units required; 25 recommended. Required and recommended units include English 4, mathematics 3-4, social studies 2-3, history 2-3, science 3-4 (laboratory 2-3), foreign language 2-4 and academic electives 2-3.

**2009-2010 Annual costs.** Tuition/fees: $26,350. Room/board: $7,900. Books/supplies: $900. Personal expenses: $900.

**2008-2009 Financial aid. Need-based:** 322 full-time freshmen applied for aid; 239 were judged to have need; 238 of these received aid. Average need met was 85%. Average scholarship/grant was $18,947; average loan $2,654. 79% of total undergraduate aid awarded as scholarships/grants, 21% as loans/jobs. **Non-need-based:** Awarded to 354 full-time undergraduates, including 152 freshmen. Scholarships awarded for academics, alumni affiliation, art, leadership, minority status, music/drama, religious affiliation, state residency. **Additional information:** Academic Honors Diploma Scholarship is a grant program committed to meeting 100% of Indiana student's demonstrated need. Available to Indiana students who graduate with an Academic Honors Diploma (AHD), have completed their application for admission by January 15, and file a complete and valid FAFSA by March 10.

**Application procedures. Admission:** Closing date 3/1 (postmark date). $40 fee, may be waived for applicants with need, free for online applicants. Admission notification on a rolling basis beginning on or about 9/1. Must reply by May 1 or within 2 week(s) if notified thereafter. **Financial aid:** Priority date 3/1; no closing date. FAFSA required. Applicants notified on a rolling basis starting 3/31; must reply by 5/1 or within 2 week(s) of notification.

**Academics.** Students take only one course in the 4-week spring term. **Special study options:** Double major, dual enrollment of high school students, independent study, internships, student-designed major, study abroad, teacher certification program, Washington semester. Philadelphia Center, Washington Center internships, Business Scholars in the Center for Business Preparation. **Credit/placement by examination:** AP, CLEP, IB, institutional tests. **Support services:** Learning center, reduced course load, study skills assistance, tutoring, writing center.

**Majors. Biology:** General. **Communications:** General. **Computer sciences:** General. **Education:** Elementary. **Foreign languages:** Classics, French, German, Spanish. **History:** General. **Interdisciplinary:** Medieval/Renaissance. **Math:** General. **Parks/recreation:** Exercise sciences. **Philosophy/religion:** Philosophy. **Physical sciences:** Chemistry, geology, physics. **Psychology:** General. **Social sciences:** Anthropology, economics, political science, sociology. **Theology:** Theology. **Visual/performing arts:** Art history/conservation, dramatic, studio arts.

**Most popular majors.** Biology 6%, communications/journalism 7%, English 6%, foreign language 7%, history 7%, psychology 9%, social sciences 19%, visual/performing arts 7%.

**Computing on campus.** 195 workstations in library, computer center, student center. Dormitories wired for high-speed internet access and linked to campus network. Commuter students can connect to campus network. Online course registration, online library, helpline, student web hosting, wireless network available.

**Student life. Freshman orientation:** Available. Preregistration for classes offered. Six 1-day orientation sessions in April, May, June, and August. Additional orientation starts 1 week before classes begin. **Housing:** Guaranteed on-campus for all undergraduates. Coed dorms, single-sex dorms, apartments, fraternity/sorority housing, wellness housing available. $250 fully refundable deposit, deadline 5/1. **Activities:** Bands, campus ministries, choral groups, dance, drama, film society, international student organizations, literary magazine, music ensembles, musical theater, radio station, student government, student newspaper, symphony orchestra, TV station, Campus Fellowship, political and social service organizations, international club, academic clubs, Christian Life, Love Out Loud (GLBT group).

**Athletics.** NCAA. **Intercollegiate:** Baseball M, basketball, cross-country, football (tackle) M, golf, lacrosse M, soccer, softball W, tennis, track and field, volleyball W. **Intramural:** Basketball, football (non-tackle) W, football (tackle) M, racquetball, soccer, softball, table tennis, volleyball. **Team name:** Panthers.

**Student services.** Alcohol/substance abuse counseling, chaplain/spiritual director, career counseling, student employment services, financial aid counseling, health services, minority student services, personal counseling, placement for graduates.

**Contact.** E-mail: admission@hanover.edu
Phone: (812) 866-7021 Toll-free number: (800) 213-2178
Fax: (812) 866-7098
Jon Riester, Dean of Admission and Financial Assistance, Hanover College, PO Box 108, Hanover, IN 47243-0108

## Holy Cross College
**Notre Dame, Indiana**          **CB member**
**www.hcc-nd.edu**          **CB code: 1309**

- Private 4-year liberal arts college affiliated with Roman Catholic Church
- Residential campus in small city
- 441 degree-seeking undergraduates
- SAT or ACT (ACT writing recommended), application essay required

**General.** Founded in 1966. Regionally accredited. **Degrees:** 35 bachelor's, 10 associate awarded. **ROTC:** Army, Air Force. **Location:** 1 mile from South Bend, 90 miles from Chicago. **Calendar:** Semester, limited summer session. **Full-time faculty:** 31 total. **Part-time faculty:** 28 total. **Class size:** 66% < 20, 34% 20-39.

**Freshman class profile.**

| Mid 50% test scores | | | |
|---|---|---|---|
| | | **ACT composite:** | 18-24 |
| SAT critical reading: | 470-590 | **Out-of-state:** | 49% |
| SAT math: | 430-550 | **Live on campus:** | 49% |

**Basis for selection.** Academic GPA and school achievement most important. Interview recommended. **Homeschooled:** Statement describing homeschool structure and mission required.

**High school preparation.** College-preparatory program recommended. Required and recommended units include English 4, mathematics 3-4, social studies 2-4, science 2-4 and foreign language 2.

**2009-2010 Annual costs.** Tuition/fees: $18,700. Room/board: $8,000. Books/supplies: $1,200.

**2008-2009 Financial aid. Need-based:** 55% of total undergraduate aid awarded as scholarships/grants, 45% as loans/jobs. **Non-need-based:** Scholarships awarded for academics, leadership.

**Application procedures. Admission:** Priority date 3/1; deadline 8/15. $25 fee, may be waived for applicants with need, free for online applicants. Admission notification 5/3. Admission notification on a rolling basis. Must reply by May 1 or within 3 week(s) if notified thereafter. **Financial aid:** Closing date 3/1. FAFSA required. Applicants notified on a rolling basis starting 5/1; must reply within 2 week(s) of notification.

**Academics. Special study options:** Accelerated study, cross-registration, ESL, honors, independent study, internships, study abroad, teacher certification program. **Credit/placement by examination:** AP, CLEP, IB, SAT, ACT, institutional tests. 30 credit hours maximum toward associate degree, 30 toward bachelor's. **Support services:** Learning center, reduced course load, remedial instruction, study skills assistance, tutoring, writing center.

**Majors. Business:** General, business admin. **Communications:** General. **Communications technology:** Graphics. **Education:** Elementary. **History:** General. **Liberal arts:** Arts/sciences. **Psychology:** General. **Theology:** Theology. **Visual/performing arts:** General.

**Computing on campus.** 40 workstations in library, computer center, student center. Dormitories wired for high-speed internet access and linked to campus network. Commuter students can connect to campus network. Online course registration, online library, helpline, repair service, wireless network available.

**Student life. Freshman orientation:** Mandatory. Preregistration for classes offered. **Housing:** Coed dorms, single-sex dorms, special housing for disabled, apartments available. $200 partly refundable deposit, deadline 5/3. **Activities:** Marching band, campus ministries, choral groups, drama, literary magazine, music ensembles, student government, student newspaper, student advisory committee.

**Athletics.** NAIA. **Intercollegiate:** Cross-country M. **Intramural:** Basketball, cheerleading, football (non-tackle), football (tackle) M, golf, lacrosse M, soccer, volleyball. **Team name:** Saints.

**Student services.** Alcohol/substance abuse counseling, chaplain/spiritual director, career counseling, financial aid counseling, health services, personal counseling.

**Contact.** E-mail: admissions@hcc-nd.edu
Phone: (574) 239-8400 Fax: (574) 239-8323
Marie Bensman, Dean of Admissions and Enrollment Management, Holy Cross College, 54515 State Road 933 North, Notre Dame, IN 46556-0308

## Huntington University
**Huntington, Indiana**
**www.huntington.edu**          **CB code: 1304**

- Private 4-year university and liberal arts college affiliated with United Brethren in Christ
- Residential campus in large town
- 949 degree-seeking undergraduates
- 89% of applicants admitted
- SAT or ACT with writing, application essay required

**General.** Founded in 1897. Regionally accredited. **Degrees:** 185 bachelor's, 13 associate awarded; master's offered. **Location:** 20 miles from Fort Wayne. **Calendar:** 4-1-4, limited summer session. **Full-time faculty:** 62 total. **Part-time faculty:** 41 total. **Class size:** 73% < 20, 24% 20-39, 4% 40-49. **Special facilities:** Nature preserve, greenhouse, disc golf course.

**Freshman class profile.** 897 applied, 802 admitted, 260 enrolled.

| Mid 50% test scores | | GPA 3.0-3.49: | 44% |
|---|---|---|---|
| SAT critical reading: | 480-580 | GPA 2.0-2.99: | 16% |
| SAT math: | 480-560 | Rank in top quarter: | 26% |
| SAT writing: | 440-580 | Out-of-state: | 44% |
| ACT composite: | 20-26 | Live on campus: | 95% |
| GPA 3.75 or higher: | 19% | Sororities: | 1% |
| GPA 3.50-3.74: | 21% | | |

**Basis for selection.** Class rank in top half, satisfactory test scores, 2.3 GPA most important. Selected students with 860 SAT (exclusive of Writing), 2.0 GPA, or rank in top 50% of class may be admitted on a minimum load. Interview recommended. Audition required of music majors. Portfolio required for art scholarships. Essay required for presidential scholarships. Test required for journalism scholarships. **Learning Disabled:** Documentation of learning disability required in some cases where both GPA and standardized test results are below minimum requirement for admission.

**High school preparation.** College-preparatory program required. Required and recommended units include English 4, mathematics 3, social studies 2, history 2, science 2 (laboratory 1), foreign language 2, computer science 1, visual/performing arts 2 and academic electives 2.

**2009-2010 Annual costs.** Tuition/fees: $21,290. Room/board: $7,180. Books/supplies: $900. Personal expenses: $1,250.

**2009-2010 Financial aid. Non-need-based:** Scholarships awarded for academics, alumni affiliation, art, athletics, leadership, music/drama, religious affiliation.

**Application procedures. Admission:** Priority date 3/1; deadline 8/1 (receipt date). $20 fee, may be waived for applicants with need. Admission notification on a rolling basis beginning on or about 10/1. Education majors must apply separately to the Education Department before entering those major classes. Performance grants also require a separate application process for those majoring in music, theatre, art, and communication. **Financial aid:** Priority date 3/1; no closing date. FAFSA required. Applicants notified on a rolling basis starting 3/1; must reply by 5/1 or within 2 week(s) of notification.

**Academics.** Special study options: Cross-registration, double major, independent study, internships, study abroad, teacher certification program, Washington semester. **Credit/placement by examination:** AP, CLEP, SAT, ACT, institutional tests. 38 credit hours maximum toward bachelor's degree. **Support services:** Learning center, pre-admission summer program, reduced course load, remedial instruction, study skills assistance, tutoring, writing center.

**Majors.** **Biology:** General. **Business:** General, accounting, accounting/finance, business admin, entrepreneurial studies, managerial economics, nonprofit/public, small business admin. **Communications:** General, broadcast journalism, digital media, journalism, public relations, radio/tv. **Computer sciences:** General, computer science. **Education:** General, art, biology, business, chemistry, elementary, English, mathematics, music, physical, science, secondary, social studies, special. **Foreign languages:** Spanish. **Health:** Nursing (RN), premedicine. **History:** General. **Interdisciplinary:** Math/computer science. **Legal studies:** Prelaw. **Math:** General. **Parks/recreation:** Exercise sciences, facilities management, sports admin. **Philosophy/religion:** Philosophy, religion. **Physical sciences:** Chemistry. **Psychology:** General. **Public administration:** Social work. **Social sciences:** Sociology. **Theology:** Bible, missionary, religious ed, sacred music, youth ministry. **Visual/performing arts:** Art, dramatic, film/cinema, graphic design, music management, music performance, piano/organ, studio arts, theater design, voice/opera.

**Most popular majors.** Business/marketing 23%, communications/journalism 8%, education 20%, theological studies 14%.

**Computing on campus.** 164 workstations in dormitories, library, computer center, student center. Dormitories wired for high-speed internet access and linked to campus network. Commuter students can connect to campus network. Online library, helpline, student web hosting, wireless network available.

**Student life.** **Freshman orientation:** Mandatory. Three-day orientation held immediately before first semester. **Policies:** No social dancing. Chapel/convocation attendance required 2 out of 4 weekly programs. Use of alcohol, drugs, and tobacco prohibited. Religious observance required. **Housing:** Guaranteed on-campus for all undergraduates. Coed dorms, single-sex dorms, apartments available. $100 partly refundable deposit, deadline 8/15. College-owned houses available. Single-sex floors available. **Activities:** Bands, campus ministries, choral groups, drama, film society, international student organizations, literary magazine, music ensembles, musical theater, radio station, student government, student newspaper, symphony orchestra, TV station, Acting on AIDS, Alpha Gamma Pi Sorority, Global Vision, Habitat for Humanity, volunteer service center.

**Athletics.** NAIA, NCCAA. **Intercollegiate:** Baseball M, basketball, cross-country, golf M, soccer, softball W, tennis, track and field, volleyball W. **Intramural:** Basketball, football (non-tackle), racquetball, softball, volleyball. **Team name:** Foresters.

**Student services.** Adult student services, alcohol/substance abuse counseling, chaplain/spiritual director, career counseling, student employment services, financial aid counseling, health services, minority student services, on-campus daycare, personal counseling, placement for graduates, women's services. **Physically disabled:** Services for visually, speech, hearing impaired.

**Contact.** E-mail: admissions@huntington.edu
Phone: (260) 359-4000 Toll-free number: (800) 642-6493
Fax: (260) 358-3699
Jeffrey Berggren, Vice President of Enrollment Management & Marketing, Huntington University, 2303 College Avenue, Huntington, IN 46750-1237

---

## Indiana Institute of Technology

**Fort Wayne, Indiana**       **CB member**
**www.indianatech.edu**       **CB code: 1323**

- Private 4-year business and engineering college
- Residential campus in large city
- 3,592 degree-seeking undergraduates: 33% part-time, 56% women, 24% African American, 1% Asian American, 3% Hispanic American, 1% Native American, 1% international
- 372 degree-seeking graduate students
- 74% of applicants admitted
- SAT or ACT (ACT writing optional) required

**General.** Founded in 1930. Regionally accredited. ABET accreditation for electrical engineering and mechanical engineering. **Degrees:** 388 bachelor's, 201 associate awarded; master's, doctoral offered. **Location:** 120 miles from Indianapolis. **Calendar:** Semester, limited summer session. **Full-time faculty:** 37 total; 32% have terminal degrees, 14% minority, 27% women. **Part-time faculty:** 280 total; 4% have terminal degrees, 10% minority, 36% women. **Class size:** 62% < 20, 36% 20-39, 2% 40-49. **Special facilities:** Computer-aided design center, outdoor amphitheater, movie theater, bowling alley.

**Freshman class profile.** 1,823 applied, 1,346 admitted, 329 enrolled.

| Mid 50% test scores | | GPA 2.0-2.99: | 48% |
|---|---|---|---|
| SAT critical reading: | 400-510 | Rank in top quarter: | 20% |
| SAT math: | 430-560 | Rank in top tenth: | 5% |
| SAT writing: | 400-500 | End year in good standing: | 70% |
| ACT composite: | 17-22 | Return as sophomores: | 54% |
| GPA 3.75 or higher: | 6% | Out-of-state: | 45% |
| GPA 3.50-3.74: | 8% | Live on campus: | 71% |
| GPA 3.0-3.49: | 28% | International: | 2% |

**Basis for selection.** GPA, test scores most important, however each file is individually evaluated and given consideration based on other criteria. Interviews and essays or personal statements recommended. **Home-schooled:** For out-of-state students, require certification that homeschool organization is registered with that state.

**High school preparation.** Required and recommended units include English 4, mathematics 2-4, science 2-3 and academic electives 7. Engineering and computer science majors require 13.5 units including 4 English; 3.5 math; 2 physical science; 4 history, social studies, or language.

**2009-2010 Annual costs.** Tuition/fees: $21,400. Room/board: $8,040. Personal expenses: $3,000.

**2009-2010 Financial aid.** **Non-need-based:** Scholarships awarded for academics, alumni affiliation, athletics, leadership, minority status, music/drama, state residency.

**Application procedures.** **Admission:** No deadline. $50 fee, may be waived for applicants with need, free for online applicants. Admission notification on a rolling basis beginning on or about 10/15. **Financial aid:** Closing date 3/10. FAFSA, institutional form required. Applicants notified on a rolling basis starting 2/2; must reply within 2 week(s) of notification.

**Academics.** Special study options: Accelerated study, cross-registration, distance learning, double major, dual enrollment of high school students, external degree, independent study, internships, student-designed major. **Credit/placement by examination:** AP, CLEP, IB, SAT, ACT, institutional tests. 45 credit hours maximum toward associate degree, 90 toward bachelor's. **Support services:** Reduced course load, remedial instruction, study skills assistance, tutoring.

**Majors.** **Business:** General, accounting, business admin, human resources, management information systems, marketing, nonprofit/public, operations. **Computer sciences:** General, computer science, game design, information systems, networking, security. **Education:** Elementary, physical. **Engineering:** Biomedical, computer, electrical, industrial, mechanical, software. **Health:** Recreational therapy. **Parks/recreation:** Facilities management, sports admin. **Protective services:** Criminal justice, law enforcement admin. **Psychology:** General. **Public administration:** Human services. **Other:** Energy engineering, Public relations, advertising, and applied communication.

**Most popular majors.** Business/marketing 81%, engineering/engineering technologies 6%.

**Computing on campus.** 370 workstations in library, computer center. Dormitories wired for high-speed internet access and linked to campus network. Commuter students can connect to campus network. Online library, helpline, repair service, student web hosting, wireless network available.

**Student life.** **Freshman orientation:** Mandatory. Preregistration for classes offered. Two day program, mandatory for all new students. One day is an orientation to the university through the Freshman College, the second day is a community service project through Student Life. **Housing:** Guaranteed on-campus for freshmen. Coed dorms, special housing for disabled, apartments, fraternity/sorority housing available. $350 deposit. **Activities:** Bands, campus ministries, dance, student government, student newspaper, student board, black student association, Indiana Tech Gaming Society, Society for Women Engineers, American Society of Mechanical Engineers, Society for Human Resource Management, Society of Automotive Engineering, Collegiate Cyber Defense Team, Sport Recreation and Leisure Society.

**Athletics.** NAIA. **Intercollegiate:** Baseball M, basketball, bowling, cheerleading, cross-country, golf, lacrosse, soccer, softball W, tennis, track and field, volleyball W. **Intramural:** Badminton, basketball, bowling, football (non-tackle), golf, soccer, softball, table tennis, tennis, volleyball. **Team name:** Warriors.

**Student services.** Adult student services, chaplain/spiritual director, career counseling, student employment services, financial aid counseling, health services, personal counseling, placement for graduates.

**Contact.** E-mail: admissions@indianatech.edu
Phone: (260) 422-5561 ext. 2205 Toll-free
number: (800) 937-2448 ext. 2205 Fax: (260) 422-7696
Monica Chamberlain, Associate Vice President of Enrollment Management,
Indiana Institute of Technology, 1600 East Washington Boulevard, Fort
Wayne, IN 46803-1297

## Indiana State University
### Terre Haute, Indiana
www.indstate.edu

CB member
CB code: 1322

- Public 4-year university
- Residential campus in small city
- 8,405 degree-seeking undergraduates: 13% part-time, 51% women, 15% African American, 1% Asian American, 2% Hispanic American, 3% international
- 2,023 degree-seeking graduate students
- 68% of applicants admitted
- SAT or ACT with writing required
- 43% graduate within 6 years

**General.** Founded in 1865. Regionally accredited. **Degrees:** 1,456 bachelor's, 100 associate awarded; master's, doctoral offered. **ROTC:** Army, Air Force. **Location:** 70 miles from Indianapolis. **Calendar:** Semester, extensive summer session. **Full-time faculty:** 430 total; 85% have terminal degrees, 14% minority, 41% women. **Part-time faculty:** 213 total; 23% have terminal degrees, 4% minority, 52% women. **Class size:** 35% < 20, 47% 20-39, 9% 40-49, 7% 50-99, 2% >100. **Special facilities:** Observatory, museum, flight simulator.

**Freshman class profile.** 8,154 applied, 5,582 admitted, 2,035 enrolled.

| Mid 50% test scores | | | |
|---|---|---|---|
| SAT critical reading: | 410-510 | Rank in top quarter: | 29% |
| SAT math: | 420-520 | Rank in top tenth: | 9% |
| SAT writing: | 390-500 | End year in good standing: | 70% |
| ACT composite: | 17-22 | Return as sophomores: | 64% |
| GPA 3.75 or higher: | 10% | Out-of-state: | 9% |
| GPA 3.50-3.74: | 9% | Live on campus: | 68% |
| GPA 3.0-3.49: | 28% | International: | 2% |
| GPA 2.0-2.99: | 52% | Fraternities: | 11% |
| | | Sororities: | 10% |

**Basis for selection.** Students who rank in top 50% of high school class usually admitted. High school curriculum, GPA, test scores, class rank, type of high school, and interview all considered. Interview required of some scholarship applicants, recommended for applicants below 50th percentile of high school graduating class. Essay recommended. Audition required of music majors. Portfolio recommended for art majors.

**High school preparation.** 20 units recommended. Recommended units include English 4, mathematics 3, social studies 2, history 1, science 3 (laboratory 3), foreign language 1 and academic electives 1. 3 or more units recommended in career area.

**2009-2010 Annual costs.** Tuition/fees: $7,426; $16,002 out-of-state. Room/board: $7,463. Books/supplies: $1,170. Personal expenses: $1,670.

**2008-2009 Financial aid.** All financial aid based on need. 1,687 full-time freshmen applied for aid; 1,344 were judged to have need; 1,312 of these received aid. Average need met was 81%. Average scholarship/grant was $6,322; average loan $3,048. 54% of total undergraduate aid awarded as scholarships/grants, 46% as loans/jobs. **Additional information:** Financial aid application deadline March 1 for Indiana residents applying for state grant.

**Application procedures. Admission:** Priority date 7/1; deadline 8/15. $25 fee, may be waived for applicants with need. Admission notification on a rolling basis. Must reply by 5/1. **Financial aid:** Priority date 3/1; no closing date. FAFSA required. Applicants notified on a rolling basis starting 4/15.

**Academics. Special study options:** Accelerated study, cooperative education, distance learning, double major, dual enrollment of high school students, ESL, honors, independent study, internships, semester at sea, study abroad, teacher certification program. **Credit/placement by examination:** AP, CLEP, SAT, ACT, institutional tests. 31 credit hours maximum toward bachelor's degree. **Support services:** Learning center, pre-admission summer program, study skills assistance, tutoring, writing center.

**Majors. Architecture:** Interior. **Area/ethnic studies:** African-American. **Biology:** General. **Business:** Accounting, business admin, finance, human resources, insurance, management information systems, marketing, office

management. **Communications:** General. **Computer sciences:** General, information technology. **Education:** Art, business, elementary, physical, science, social studies, special, trade/industrial. **Engineering technology:** Architectural, automotive, computer, electrical, industrial, manufacturing, occupational safety, robotics. **Family/consumer sciences:** General, clothing/textiles, family studies, food/nutrition. **Health:** Athletic training, audiology/speech pathology, clinical lab science, community health services, nursing (RN). **History:** General. **Liberal arts:** Arts/sciences. **Math:** General. **Parks/recreation:** Facilities management. **Philosophy/religion:** Philosophy. **Physical sciences:** Chemistry, geology. **Psychology:** General. **Public administration:** Social work. **Social sciences:** Anthropology, criminology, economics, geography, political science. **Transportation:** Airline/commercial pilot, aviation management. **Visual/performing arts:** Art, dramatic, music performance, studio arts. **Other:** Language studies, Mechanical engineering technology, Operations marketing and analysis.

**Most popular majors.** Business/marketing 18%, education 16%, engineering/engineering technologies 7%, health sciences 11%, social sciences 12%.

**Computing on campus.** PC or laptop required. 395 workstations in library, computer center, student center. Dormitories wired for high-speed internet access and linked to campus network. Commuter students can connect to campus network. Online course registration, online library, helpline, repair service, student web hosting, wireless network available.

**Student life. Freshman orientation:** Mandatory. Preregistration for classes offered. Two-day program. **Housing:** Guaranteed on-campus for freshmen. Coed dorms, single-sex dorms, special housing for disabled, apartments, fraternity/sorority housing, wellness housing available. Apartments for students with dependent children and special housing for freshmen. **Activities:** Bands, campus ministries, choral groups, dance, drama, film society, international student organizations, literary magazine, music ensembles, musical theater, radio station, student government, student newspaper, symphony orchestra, over 170 student organizations available.

**Athletics.** NCAA. **Intercollegiate:** Baseball M, basketball, cross-country, football (tackle) M, golf W, soccer W, softball W, track and field, volleyball W. **Intramural:** Badminton, basketball, football (non-tackle), racquetball, soccer, softball, swimming, tennis, volleyball. **Team name:** Sycamores.

**Student services.** Adult student services, chaplain/spiritual director, career counseling, student employment services, financial aid counseling, health services, minority student services, on-campus daycare, personal counseling, placement for graduates, women's services. **Physically disabled:** Services for visually, speech, hearing impaired.

**Contact.** E-mail: admissions@indstate.edu
Phone: (812) 237-2121 Toll-free number: (800) 468-6478
Fax: (812) 237-8023
Richard Toomey, Director, Indiana State University, Office of Admissions, Erickson 114, Terre Haute, IN 47809-9989

## Indiana University Bloomington
### Bloomington, Indiana
www.iub.edu

CB member
CB code: 1324

- Public 4-year university
- Residential campus in small city
- 32,000 degree-seeking undergraduates: 3% part-time, 50% women, 5% African American, 4% Asian American, 3% Hispanic American, 6% international
- 9,375 degree-seeking graduate students
- 73% of applicants admitted
- SAT or ACT with writing required
- 74% graduate within 6 years

**General.** Founded in 1820. Regionally accredited. Big Ten research university. **Degrees:** 5,941 bachelor's, 23 associate awarded; master's, doctoral, professional offered. **ROTC:** Army, Air Force. **Location:** 50 miles from Indianapolis. **Calendar:** Semester, extensive summer session. **Full-time faculty:** 1,917 total; 78% have terminal degrees, 17% minority, 38% women. **Part-time faculty:** 368 total; 24% have terminal degrees, 10% minority, 48% women. **Class size:** 32% < 20, 43% 20-39, 6% 40-49, 12% 50-99, 8% >100. **Special facilities:** Cyclotron; 2 observatories; museum of anthropology, history, and folklore; rare book library; outdoor educational center; center for excellence in education; garden and nature center; arboretum; automated virtual environment.

**Freshman class profile.** 33,011 applied, 23,975 admitted, 7,327 enrolled.

| Mid 50% test scores | | GPA 2.0-2.99: | 6% |
|---|---|---|---|
| SAT critical reading: | 520-630 | Rank in top quarter: | 71% |
| SAT math: | 540-660 | Rank in top tenth: | 34% |
| ACT composite: | 24-29 | Return as sophomores: | 89% |
| GPA 3.75 or higher: | 42% | Out-of-state: | 32% |
| GPA 3.50-3.74: | 22% | Live on campus: | 98% |
| GPA 3.0-3.49: | 30% | International: | 5% |

**Basis for selection.** Strength of student's college preparatory program, senior year program, grade trends, class rank (if provided), and SAT or ACT test scores important. SAT Subject Tests recommended. Campus visit encouraged. Audition required for majority of music majors. **Learning Disabled:** Current and comprehensive documentation of disability required to receive services.

**High school preparation.** College-preparatory program required. 14 units required; 19 recommended. Required and recommended units include English 4, mathematics 3-4, social studies 2-3, science 1-3 (laboratory 1), foreign language 3 and academic electives 4. Indiana students expected to complete Core 40 state mandated requirements. Non-Indiana students expected to complete minimum of 32 semesters in required areas.

**2009-2010 Annual costs.** Tuition/fees: $8,613; $26,160 out-of-state. Room and board figure includes $2,900 standard meal plan. Room rate represents most common among new first-year students. Room/board: $7,546. Books/supplies: $792. Personal expenses: $2,348.

**2008-2009 Financial aid. Need-based:** 5,148 full-time freshmen applied for aid; 3,222 were judged to have need; 3,121 of these received aid. Average need met was 91%. Average scholarship/grant was $8,980; average loan $3,717. 53% of total undergraduate aid awarded as scholarships/grants, 47% as loans/jobs. **Non-need-based:** Awarded to 7,536 full-time undergraduates, including 2,431 freshmen. Scholarships awarded for academics, art, athletics, leadership, minority status, music/drama, religious affiliation, ROTC. **Additional information:** Majority of institutional gift aid merit-based. Some need-based grants go to merit winners with financial need.

**Application procedures. Admission:** $55 fee, may be waived for applicants with need. Admission notification on a rolling basis. Must reply by May 1 or within 3 week(s) if notified thereafter. **Financial aid:** Priority date 3/1; no closing date. FAFSA required. Applicants notified by 3/10; Applicants notified on a rolling basis starting 4/1.

**Academics. Special study options:** Accelerated study, combined bachelor's/graduate degree, cooperative education, distance learning, double major, dual enrollment of high school students, ESL, external degree, honors, independent study, internships, liberal arts/career combination, semester at sea, student-designed major, study abroad, teacher certification program, United Nations semester, Washington semester. **Credit/placement by examination:** AP, CLEP, IB, SAT, ACT, institutional tests. **Support services:** Learning center, preadmission summer program, reduced course load, remedial instruction, study skills assistance, tutoring, writing center.

**Honors college/program.** Top 5% of high school graduating class or 1350 SAT or 31 ACT required. Qualified students will receive application to Honors College Scholarship automatically. Completed applications reviewed by faculty panel. Honors College participants complete at least 3 approved honors courses during first 4 semesters on campus.

**Majors. Area/ethnic studies:** African-American, East Asian, women's. **Biology:** General, bacteriology, biochemistry. **Business:** General, accounting, business admin, finance, labor relations. **Communications:** General, digital media, journalism. **Communications technology:** Recording arts. **Computer sciences:** General. **Conservation:** General, environmental science. **Education:** General, art, biology, chemistry, early childhood, elementary, English, French, German, health, Latin, mathematics, multi-level teacher, music, physical, physics, science, secondary, social studies, Spanish, special, speech. **Family/consumer sciences:** Clothing/textiles. **Foreign languages:** General, African, ancient Greek, comparative lit, East Asian, French, German, Italian, Latin, linguistics, Portuguese, Slavic, Spanish. **Health:** Audiology/hearing, audiology/speech pathology, cytotechnology, dental hygiene, health care admin, medical radiologic technology/radiation therapy, medical records technology, nuclear medical technology, nursing (RN), respiratory therapy technology, sonography. **History:** General. **Interdisciplinary:** Science/society, systems science. **Liberal arts:** Arts/sciences. **Math:** General. **Parks/recreation:** General, facilities management. **Philosophy/religion:** Judaic, philosophy, religion. **Physical sciences:** Astronomy, astrophysics, chemistry, geology, physics. **Protective services:** Criminal justice. **Psychology:** General. **Public administration:** General. **Social sciences:** General, anthropology, economics, geography, political science, sociology. **Visual/performing arts:** General, art history/conservation, commercial/advertising art, conducting, dance, dramatic, interior design, jazz, music performance, music theory/composition, piano/organ, studio arts, voice/opera.

**Most popular majors.** Biology 6%, business/marketing 20%, communications/journalism 10%, education 16%, public administration/social services 6%, social sciences 7%, visual/performing arts 6%.

**Computing on campus.** 2,262 workstations in dormitories, library, computer center, student center. Dormitories wired for high-speed internet access and linked to campus network. Commuter students can connect to campus network. Online course registration, helpline, repair service, student web hosting, wireless network available.

**Student life. Freshman orientation:** Mandatory, $125 fee. Preregistration for classes offered. Two-day program held between June 14 and July 20. **Housing:** Guaranteed on-campus for freshmen. Coed dorms, single-sex dorms, special housing for disabled, apartments, cooperative housing, fraternity/sorority housing available. $200 deposit. Residential language houses, living/learning centers, wellness center, African-American living/learning center, honors college floors, first-year academic interest group housing available. **Activities:** Bands, campus ministries, choral groups, dance, drama, international student organizations, literary magazine, music ensembles, musical theater, opera, radio station, student government, student newspaper, symphony orchestra, TV station, College Democrats, College Republicans, Young Americans for Freedom, black student union, Latinos Unidos, Asian-American association, Alpha Phi Omega, volunteers student bureau, College Mentors for Kids, Golden Key.

**Athletics.** NCAA. **Intercollegiate:** Baseball M, basketball, cross-country, diving, field hockey W, football (tackle) M, golf, rowing (crew) W, soccer, softball W, swimming, tennis, track and field, volleyball W, water polo W, wrestling M. **Intramural:** Archery, badminton, basketball, bowling, cross-country, diving, equestrian, fencing, field hockey W, gymnastics, handball, ice hockey M, lacrosse, racquetball, rifle, rowing (crew), rugby, sailing, skiing, skin diving, soccer, softball, squash, swimming, table tennis, tennis, track and field, volleyball, water polo, wrestling M. **Team name:** Hoosiers.

**Student services.** Adult student services, alcohol/substance abuse counseling, chaplain/spiritual director, career counseling, services for economically disadvantaged, student employment services, financial aid counseling, health services, legal services, minority student services, on-campus daycare, personal counseling, placement for graduates, veterans' counselor, women's services. **Physically disabled:** Services for visually, speech, hearing impaired.

**Contact.** E-mail: iuadmit@indiana.edu
Phone: (812) 855-0661 Fax: (812) 855-5102
Mary Ellen Anderson, Director of Undergraduate Admissions, Indiana University Bloomington, 300 North Jordan Avenue, Bloomington, IN 47405

---

## Indiana University East
### Richmond, Indiana
www.iue.edu                                      CB code: 1194

- Public 4-year university and branch campus college
- Commuter campus in large town
- 2,444 degree-seeking undergraduates: 38% part-time, 68% women, 4% African American, 1% Asian American, 1% Hispanic American
- 49 degree-seeking graduate students
- 74% of applicants admitted
- SAT or ACT with writing required

**General.** Founded in 1971. Regionally accredited. **Degrees:** 250 bachelor's, 50 associate awarded; master's offered. **Location:** 70 miles from Indianapolis. **Calendar:** Semester, extensive summer session. **Full-time faculty:** 86 total; 56% have terminal degrees, 13% minority, 58% women. **Part-time faculty:** 119 total; 18% have terminal degrees, 5% minority, 56% women. **Class size:** 58% < 20, 38% 20-39, 3% 40-49, 2% 50-99.

**Freshman class profile.** 861 applied, 633 admitted, 400 enrolled.

| Mid 50% test scores | | GPA 3.0-3.49: | 32% |
|---|---|---|---|
| SAT critical reading: | 400-510 | GPA 2.0-2.99: | 46% |
| SAT math: | 420-510 | Rank in top quarter: | 24% |
| ACT composite: | 17-22 | Rank in top tenth: | 5% |
| GPA 3.75 or higher: | 7% | Return as sophomores: | 60% |
| GPA 3.50-3.74: | 12% | Out-of-state: | 15% |

**Basis for selection.** Traditional students (3 years or less after high school graduation) required to take SAT or ACT for placement. May attend 1 semester while waiting to take test. Additional admission criteria for nursing program. Interview recommended. **Homeschooled:** Must graduate from national accredited home school program or take GED.

**High school preparation.** College-preparatory program recommended. 14 units required; 16 recommended. Required and recommended units include English 4, mathematics 3, social studies 2, science 1 (laboratory 1) and academic electives 4. 4 additional mathematics, laboratory science, social science, computer science, or other courses of college preparatory nature recommended. Foreign language strongly recommended.

**2009-2010 Annual costs.** Tuition/fees: $5,801; $14,957 out-of-state. Books/supplies: $1,076. Personal expenses: $2,242.

**2008-2009 Financial aid. Need-based:** 273 full-time freshmen applied for aid; 232 were judged to have need; 227 of these received aid. Average need met was 95%. Average scholarship/grant was $5,264; average loan $2,797. 45% of total undergraduate aid awarded as scholarships/grants, 55% as loans/jobs. **Non-need-based:** Awarded to 75 full-time undergraduates, including 33 freshmen. Scholarships awarded for academics, alumni affiliation, leadership.

**Application procedures. Admission:** No deadline. $35 fee, may be waived for applicants with need. Admission notification on a rolling basis beginning on or about 9/1. **Financial aid:** Priority date 3/1; no closing date. FAFSA, institutional form required. Applicants notified on a rolling basis starting 5/1; must reply within 2 week(s) of notification.

**Academics. Special study options:** Cooperative education, cross-registration, distance learning, double major, dual enrollment of high school students, external degree, honors, independent study, internships, teacher certification program, weekend college. State-wide technology program with Purdue University. **Credit/placement by examination:** AP, CLEP, SAT, ACT, institutional tests. **Support services:** Remedial instruction, study skills assistance, tutoring, writing center.

**Majors. Biology:** General. **Business:** Accounting, business admin, management information systems, marketing. **Communications:** General. **Education:** Elementary, secondary. **Health:** Nursing (RN). **Interdisciplinary:** Biological/physical sciences, natural sciences. **Liberal arts:** Humanities. **Protective services:** Criminal justice. **Psychology:** General. **Public administration:** Social work. **Social sciences:** Sociology.

**Most popular majors.** Business/marketing 34%, education 10%, health sciences 12%, liberal arts 14%, public administration/social services 8%.

**Computing on campus.** 120 workstations in library, computer center.

**Student life. Freshman orientation:** Mandatory, $50 fee. Preregistration for classes offered. **Activities:** Drama, literary magazine, student government, student newspaper, TV station.

**Athletics. Intramural:** Basketball, softball, volleyball. **Team name:** Pioneers.

**Student services.** Adult student services, career counseling, student employment services, financial aid counseling, health services, on-campus daycare, personal counseling, placement for graduates. **Physically disabled:** Services for visually, speech, hearing impaired.

**Contact.** E-mail: eaadmit@indiana.edu
Phone: (765) 973-8208 Toll-free number: (800) 959-3278
Fax: (765) 973-8288
Molly Vanderpool, Director of Admissions, Indiana University East, 2325 Chester Boulevard, Richmond, IN 47374-1289

## Indiana University Kokomo
Kokomo, Indiana
www.iuk.edu                                    CB code: 1337

- Public 4-year university
- Commuter campus in large town
- 2,350 degree-seeking undergraduates: 34% part-time, 67% women, 5% African American, 1% Asian American, 2% Hispanic American
- 102 degree-seeking graduate students
- 81% of applicants admitted
- SAT or ACT with writing required

**General.** Founded in 1945. Regionally accredited. **Degrees:** 341 bachelor's, 87 associate awarded; master's offered. **ROTC:** Army. **Location:** 50 miles from Indianapolis. **Calendar:** Semester, limited summer session. **Full-time faculty:** 89 total; 63% have terminal degrees, 16% minority, 57% women. **Part-time faculty:** 86 total; 5% have terminal degrees, 7% minority, 57% women. **Class size:** 46% < 20, 41% 20-39, 10% 40-49, 3% 50-99, less than 1% >100. **Special facilities:** Observatory.

**Freshman class profile.** 758 applied, 615 admitted, 434 enrolled.

| Mid 50% test scores | | | |
|---|---|---|---|
| SAT critical reading: | 420-520 | GPA 3.0-3.49: | 29% |
| SAT math: | 430-530 | GPA 2.0-2.99: | 47% |
| ACT composite: | 17-22 | Rank in top quarter: | 32% |
| GPA 3.75 or higher: | 9% | Rank in top tenth: | 9% |
| GPA 3.50-3.74: | 11% | Return as sophomores: | 58% |
| | | Out-of-state: | 1% |

**Basis for selection.** Test scores, class rank, course work important. In-state applicants should be in top half of graduating class (top third for out-of-state applicants).

**High school preparation.** College-preparatory program required. 14 units required. Required and recommended units include English 4, mathematics 3, social studies 2, history 2, science 1 and foreign language 2.

**2009-2010 Annual costs.** Tuition/fees: $5,838; $14,527 out-of-state. Books/supplies: $858. Personal expenses: $3,840.

**2008-2009 Financial aid. Need-based:** 311 full-time freshmen applied for aid; 214 were judged to have need; 198 of these received aid. Average need met was 93%. Average scholarship/grant was $5,306; average loan $2,875. 45% of total undergraduate aid awarded as scholarships/grants, 55% as loans/jobs. **Non-need-based:** Awarded to 102 full-time undergraduates, including 36 freshmen. Scholarships awarded for academics.

**Application procedures. Admission:** $45 fee, may be waived for applicants with need. Application must be submitted on paper. Admission notification on a rolling basis. **Financial aid:** Closing date 3/1. FAFSA, institutional form required. Applicants notified on a rolling basis starting 5/1; must reply within 4 week(s) of notification.

**Academics. Special study options:** Accelerated study, cross-registration, distance learning, double major, dual enrollment of high school students, external degree, honors, independent study, internships, liberal arts/career combination, study abroad, teacher certification program. **Credit/placement by examination:** AP, CLEP, SAT, ACT, institutional tests. **Support services:** Learning center, reduced course load, remedial instruction, tutoring.

**Majors. Biology:** General. **Business:** General, accounting, business admin, labor relations, marketing. **Communications:** General. **Computer sciences:** General. **Education:** Elementary. **Health:** Nursing (RN). **Interdisciplinary:** Behavioral sciences, biological/physical sciences, gerontology. **Liberal arts:** Humanities. **Math:** General. **Physical sciences:** Chemistry. **Protective services:** Criminal justice. **Psychology:** General. **Public administration:** General. **Social sciences:** General, sociology.

**Most popular majors.** Business/marketing 14%, education 12%, health sciences 33%, liberal arts 24%.

**Computing on campus.** 100 workstations in library, computer center, student center. Online course registration, helpline available.

**Student life. Freshman orientation:** Available, $28 fee. Preregistration for classes offered. **Activities:** Choral groups, drama, music ensembles, student government, student newspaper.

**Athletics. Intramural:** Basketball M, soccer, softball, volleyball.

**Student services.** Adult student services, career counseling, student employment services, financial aid counseling, minority student services, on-campus daycare, personal counseling, placement for graduates, veterans' counselor. **Physically disabled:** Services for visually, hearing impaired.

**Contact.** E-mail: iuadmis@iuk.edu
Phone: (765) 455-9217 Toll-free number: (888) 875-4485
Fax: (765) 455-9537
Reeta Piirala-Skoglund, Assistant Director of Admissions, Indiana University Kokomo, Box 9003, KC 230A, Kokomo, IN 46904-9003

## Indiana University Northwest
Gary, Indiana
www.iun.edu                                    CB code: 1338

- Public 4-year university
- Commuter campus in small city
- 4,531 degree-seeking undergraduates: 32% part-time, 69% women, 21% African American, 2% Asian American, 13% Hispanic American
- 571 degree-seeking graduate students
- 79% of applicants admitted
- SAT or ACT with writing required

**General.** Founded in 1948. Regionally accredited. **Degrees:** 355 bachelor's, 165 associate awarded; master's offered. **ROTC:** Army. **Location:** 35 miles from Chicago. **Calendar:** Semester, limited summer session. **Full-time faculty:** 177 total; 72% have terminal degrees, 23% minority, 50% women. **Part-time faculty:** 182 total; 22% have terminal degrees, 19% minority, 56% women. **Class size:** 33% < 20, 52% 20-39, 8% 40-49, 6% 50-99, less than 1% >100.

**Freshman class profile.** 1,707 applied, 1,351 admitted, 954 enrolled.

| Mid 50% test scores | | | |
|---|---|---|---|
| SAT critical reading: | 400-500 | GPA 3.0-3.49: | 22% |
| SAT math: | 390-500 | GPA 2.0-2.99: | 52% |
| ACT composite: | 16-22 | Rank in top quarter: | 22% |
| GPA 3.75 or higher: | 5% | Rank in top tenth: | 7% |
| GPA 3.50-3.74: | 5% | Return as sophomores: | 69% |
| | | Out-of-state: | 1% |

**Basis for selection.** School achievement record and test scores most important. Applicants should be in top half of class and have 2.0 GPA.

**High school preparation.** College-preparatory program recommended. 16 units required. Required and recommended units include English 4, mathematics 3, social studies 2, science 1 (laboratory 1), foreign language 2 and academic electives 4.

**2009-2010 Annual costs.** Tuition/fees: $5,919; $15,024 out-of-state. Books/supplies: $1,100. Personal expenses: $3,562.

**2008-2009 Financial aid. Need-based:** 482 full-time freshmen applied for aid; 375 were judged to have need; 357 of these received aid. Average need met was 88%. Average scholarship/grant was $5,047; average loan $3,094. 41% of total undergraduate aid awarded as scholarships/grants, 59% as loans/jobs. **Non-need-based:** Awarded to 150 full-time undergraduates, including 58 freshmen. Scholarships awarded for academics, athletics.

**Application procedures. Admission:** Priority date 8/1; no deadline. $25 fee, may be waived for applicants with need. Admission notification on a rolling basis. **Financial aid:** Priority date 3/1; no closing date. FAFSA, institutional form required. Applicants notified on a rolling basis starting 5/1; must reply within 2 week(s) of notification.

**Academics. Special study options:** Accelerated study, cooperative education, distance learning, double major, dual enrollment of high school students, external degree, independent study, internships, liberal arts/career combination, student-designed major, study abroad, teacher certification program, Washington semester, weekend college. **Credit/placement by examination:** AP, CLEP, institutional tests. **Support services:** Learning center, pre-admission summer program, reduced course load, remedial instruction, tutoring.

**Majors. Area/ethnic studies:** African-American. **Biology:** General. **Business:** General, actuarial science, labor relations. **Communications:** General. **Computer sciences:** Data processing. **Education:** Elementary, English, mathematics, secondary, social studies, Spanish. **Foreign languages:** French, Spanish. **Health:** Health care admin, medical records admin, nursing (RN). **History:** General. **Math:** General. **Philosophy/religion:** Philosophy. **Physical sciences:** Chemistry, geology. **Protective services:** Criminal justice. **Psychology:** General. **Public administration:** General. **Social sciences:** Economics, political science, sociology. **Visual/performing arts:** Art, dramatic.

**Most popular majors.** Business/marketing 14%, education 9%, health sciences 25%, liberal arts 19%, security/protective services 11%.

**Computing on campus.** 170 workstations in library, computer center, student center. Commuter students can connect to campus network. Online course registration, helpline available.

**Student life. Freshman orientation:** Available. Preregistration for classes offered. **Activities:** Choral groups, dance, drama, international student organizations, literary magazine, musical theater, radio station, student government, student newspaper, Christian Student Fellowship, Young Republicans, Young Democrats, Women with a Challenge, student guide services, black student union.

**Athletics.** NAIA. **Intercollegiate:** Basketball, golf, volleyball W. **Intramural:** Baseball M, basketball M, bowling, cheerleading W, golf. **Team name:** Red Hawks.

**Student services.** Adult student services, career counseling, student employment services, financial aid counseling, on-campus daycare, personal counseling, placement for graduates, veterans' counselor, women's services. **Physically disabled:** Services for visually impaired.

**Contact.** E-mail: admit@iun.edu
Phone: (219) 980-6991 Toll-free number: (800) 968-7486
Fax: (219) 981-4219
Linda Templeton, Director of Admissions, Indiana University Northwest, 3400 Broadway, Gary, IN 46408

## Indiana University South Bend
**South Bend, Indiana**
www.iusb.edu                                    **CB code: 1339**

- Public 4-year university
- Commuter campus in small city
- 6,360 degree-seeking undergraduates: 32% part-time, 62% women, 8% African American, 1% Asian American, 5% Hispanic American, 2% international
- 724 degree-seeking graduate students
- 80% of applicants admitted
- SAT or ACT required

**General.** Founded in 1922. Regionally accredited. Off-campus course offerings in Elkhart, Warsaw, Plymouth. **Degrees:** 673 bachelor's, 130 associate awarded; master's offered. **ROTC:** Army, Naval, Air Force. **Location:** 90 miles from Chicago. **Calendar:** Semester, limited summer session. **Full-time faculty:** 292 total; 63% have terminal degrees, 20% minority, 51% women. **Part-time faculty:** 254 total; 21% have terminal degrees, 7% minority, 60% women. **Class size:** 41% < 20, 51% 20-39, 5% 40-49, 3% 50-99, less than 1% >100.

**Freshman class profile.** 2,272 applied, 1,816 admitted, 1,206 enrolled.

| Mid 50% test scores | | | |
|---|---|---|---|
| SAT critical reading: | 420-520 | GPA 2.0-2.99: | 52% |
| SAT math: | 420-530 | Rank in top quarter: | 22% |
| ACT composite: | 17-23 | Rank in top tenth: | 7% |
| GPA 3.75 or higher: | 5% | Return as sophomores: | 67% |
| GPA 3.50-3.74: | 9% | Out-of-state: | 2% |
| GPA 3.0-3.49: | 29% | International: | 2% |

**Basis for selection.** Rank in top half of class important. Core 40 completion with 2.0 or higher. Interview recommended for academically weak applicants or those with unusual circumstances. Audition required of music majors. Portfolios required for some art majors. **Homeschooled:** Applicants to degree-seeking programs must meet institution's requirement for college-prep courses.

**High school preparation.** College-preparatory program required. 13 units required. Required and recommended units include English 4, mathematics 3, social studies 2, science 1 (laboratory 1) and foreign language 2. Strong preparation in math and sciences recommended.

**2009-2010 Annual costs.** Tuition/fees: $6,015; $15,712 out-of-state. Room only: $5,200. Books/supplies: $1,200. Personal expenses: $2,242.

**2008-2009 Financial aid. Need-based:** 774 full-time freshmen applied for aid; 581 were judged to have need; 558 of these received aid. Average need met was 93%. Average scholarship/grant was $5,679; average loan $2,879. 47% of total undergraduate aid awarded as scholarships/grants, 53% as loans/jobs. **Non-need-based:** Awarded to 214 full-time undergraduates, including 70 freshmen. Scholarships awarded for academics, athletics.

**Application procedures. Admission:** Priority date 7/1; no deadline. $45 fee, may be waived for applicants with need. Admission notification on a rolling basis. **Financial aid:** Closing date 3/1. FAFSA, institutional form required. Applicants notified on a rolling basis starting 5/1.

**Academics.** Most allied health programs must be completed at Indianapolis campus. **Special study options:** Accelerated study, cross-registration, distance learning, double major, ESL, external degree, honors, internships, liberal arts/career combination, study abroad, teacher certification program, weekend college. Electrical, mechanical engineering, computer technology with Purdue University on Indiana University South Bend campus; Northern Indiana Consortium for Education (part of 6 member institutions sharing library resources, faculty expertise, and academic strengths). **Credit/placement by examination:** AP, CLEP, IB, institutional tests. 90 credit hours maximum toward bachelor's degree. **Support services:** Learning center, pre-admission summer program, reduced course load, remedial instruction, tutoring, writing center.

**Majors. Area/ethnic studies:** Women's. **Biology:** General. **Business:** General, actuarial science, business admin, finance, labor relations, labor studies, marketing. **Communications:** Media studies. **Computer sciences:** General. **Education:** Biology, chemistry, elementary, mathematics, music, physics, science, secondary, social studies, Spanish, special. **Foreign languages:** French,

German, Spanish. **Health:** Health care admin, nursing (RN). **History:** General. **Math:** General, applied. **Philosophy/religion:** Philosophy. **Physical sciences:** Chemistry, physics. **Protective services:** Criminal justice. **Psychology:** General. **Public administration:** General. **Social sciences:** Economics, political science, sociology. **Visual/performing arts:** Art, dramatic, music performance, studio arts.

**Most popular majors.** Business/marketing 16%, education 17%, health sciences 15%, liberal arts 17%, psychology 7%.

**Computing on campus.** 325 workstations in library, computer center. Commuter students can connect to campus network. Online library, helpline available.

**Student life. Freshman orientation:** Available, $35 fee. Preregistration for classes offered. Two and a half hour sessions held in May, June, July and August. **Housing:** Some housing for athletes and visiting scholars. **Activities:** Jazz band, campus ministries, choral groups, drama, film society, international student organizations, literary magazine, music ensembles, musical theater, opera, student government, student newspaper, symphony orchestra, student educational association, black student union, student council for exceptional children, Latino student union, Asian student union, women's student union, Habitat for Humanity, departmental clubs.

**Athletics.** NAIA. **Intercollegiate:** Basketball. **Intramural:** Badminton, basketball, bowling, football (tackle), racquetball, softball, table tennis, tennis, volleyball. **Team name:** Titans.

**Student services.** Adult student services, chaplain/spiritual director, career counseling, student employment services, on-campus daycare, personal counseling, placement for graduates, veterans' counselor. **Physically disabled:** Services for visually, speech, hearing impaired.

**Contact.** E-mail: admissio@iusb.edu
Phone: (574) 520-4480 Fax: (574) 520-4834
Jeff Johnston, Director Recruitment/Admissions, Indiana University South Bend, 1700 Mishawaka Avenue, South Bend, IN 46634-7111

## Indiana University Southeast
New Albany, Indiana — CB member
www.ius.edu — CB code: 1314

- Public 4-year university
- Commuter campus in large town
- 5,716 degree-seeking undergraduates: 32% part-time, 60% women, 6% African American, 2% Asian American, 2% Hispanic American
- 678 degree-seeking graduate students
- 85% of applicants admitted
- SAT or ACT with writing required
- 32% graduate within 6 years

**General.** Founded in 1941. Regionally accredited. **Degrees:** 662 bachelor's, 128 associate awarded; master's offered. **ROTC:** Army, Air Force. **Location:** 10 miles from Louisville. **Calendar:** Semester, limited summer session. **Full-time faculty:** 200 total; 72% have terminal degrees, 16% minority, 48% women. **Part-time faculty:** 265 total; 16% have terminal degrees, 9% minority, 52% women. **Class size:** 31% < 20, 64% 20-39, 4% 40-49, 1% 50-99. **Special facilities:** Cultural and community center.

**Freshman class profile.** 1,985 applied, 1,688 admitted, 1,094 enrolled.

| Mid 50% test scores | | GPA 3.0-3.49: | 29% |
|---|---|---|---|
| SAT critical reading: | 420-520 | GPA 2.0-2.99: | 49% |
| SAT math: | 420-520 | Rank in top quarter: | 27% |
| ACT composite: | 17-22 | Rank in top tenth: | 6% |
| GPA 3.75 or higher: | 7% | Return as sophomores: | 63% |
| GPA 3.50-3.74: | 12% | Out-of-state: | 23% |

**Basis for selection.** Rank in top half of class for in-state applicants. Interview recommended.

**High school preparation.** 14 units required; 19 recommended. Required and recommended units include English 3-4, mathematics 3-4, social studies 2, history 1, science 1-2 (laboratory 1-2), foreign language 2 and academic electives 4.

**2009-2010 Annual costs.** Tuition/fees: $5,890; $14,578 out-of-state. Room/board: $6,230. Books/supplies: $880.

**2008-2009 Financial aid. Need-based:** 810 full-time freshmen applied for aid; 580 were judged to have need; 550 of these received aid. Average need met was 91%. Average scholarship/grant was $5,760; average loan $2,918. 46% of total undergraduate aid awarded as scholarships/grants, 54% as loans/jobs. **Non-need-based:** Awarded to 244 full-time undergraduates,

including 74 freshmen. Scholarships awarded for academics, art, athletics, leadership, minority status, music/drama.

**Application procedures. Admission:** Priority date 7/15; no deadline. $30 fee, may be waived for applicants with need. Admission notification on a rolling basis. **Financial aid:** Priority date 3/1; no closing date. FAFSA required. Applicants notified on a rolling basis starting 5/1; must reply within 3 week(s) of notification.

**Academics. Special study options:** Accelerated study, cross-registration, double major, dual enrollment of high school students, external degree, independent study, internships, student-designed major, study abroad, teacher certification program, weekend college. Member of Metroversity consortium of institutions of higher education in Louisville area. **Credit/placement by examination:** AP, CLEP, IB, institutional tests. **Support services:** Reduced course load, remedial instruction, study skills assistance, tutoring, writing center.

**Majors. Biology:** General. **Business:** General, accounting, accounting technology, labor relations. **Communications:** General, journalism. **Computer sciences:** General. **Education:** General, biology, elementary, English, mathematics, science, secondary, social studies, special. **Foreign languages:** French, German, Spanish. **Health:** Clinical lab science, nursing (RN). **History:** General. **Math:** General. **Philosophy/religion:** Philosophy. **Physical sciences:** Chemistry, physics. **Psychology:** General. **Social sciences:** Economics, geography, international relations, political science, sociology. **Visual/performing arts:** Art, studio arts.

**Most popular majors.** Business/marketing 24%, communications/journalism 6%, education 13%, health sciences 8%, liberal arts 21%.

**Computing on campus.** 165 workstations in library, computer center, student center. Commuter students can connect to campus network. Online course registration, online library, helpline, student web hosting, wireless network available.

**Student life. Freshman orientation:** Mandatory, $50 fee. Preregistration for classes offered. One-day summer program. **Activities:** Concert band, choral groups, drama, literary magazine, music ensembles, student government, student newspaper, symphony orchestra, Christian fellowship, students for world peace, multicultural student union.

**Athletics.** NAIA. **Intercollegiate:** Baseball M, basketball, cross-country, tennis, volleyball W. **Intramural:** Basketball, bowling, softball, tennis, volleyball. **Team name:** Grenadier.

**Student services.** Adult student services, alcohol/substance abuse counseling, chaplain/spiritual director, career counseling, student employment services, financial aid counseling, minority student services, on-campus daycare, personal counseling, placement for graduates, veterans' counselor. **Physically disabled:** Services for visually, speech, hearing impaired.

**Contact.** E-mail: admissions@ius.edu
Phone: (812) 941-2212 Toll-free number: (800) 852-8835
Fax: (812) 941-2595
Anne Skuce, Assistant Vice Chancellor for Enrollment Management, Indiana University Southeast, 4201 Grant Line Road, New Albany, IN 47150-6405

## Indiana University-Purdue University Fort Wayne
Fort Wayne, Indiana — CB member
www.ipfw.edu — CB code: 1336

- Public 4-year university and branch campus college
- Commuter campus in large city
- 11,483 degree-seeking undergraduates: 27% part-time, 55% women, 7% African American, 2% Asian American, 3% Hispanic American, 1% international
- 697 degree-seeking graduate students
- 96% of applicants admitted
- SAT or ACT (ACT writing optional) required

**General.** Founded in 1964. Regionally accredited. Degrees awarded through Indiana University or Purdue University, depending on course of study. **Degrees:** 1,009 bachelor's, 466 associate awarded; master's offered. **ROTC:** Army. **Location:** 110 miles from Indianapolis. **Calendar:** Semester, limited summer session. **Full-time faculty:** 407 total; 85% have terminal degrees, 19% minority, 42% women. **Part-time faculty:** 405 total; 12% have terminal degrees, 7% minority, 56% women. **Class size:** 41% < 20, 52% 20-39, 4% 40-49, 3% 50-99, less than 1% >100. **Special facilities:** Lake biological research station.

**Freshman class profile.** 3,597 applied, 3,463 admitted, 2,222 enrolled.

| Mid 50% test scores | | | |
|---|---|---|---|
| SAT critical reading: | 420-530 | Rank in top quarter: | 30% |
| SAT math: | 430-550 | Rank in top tenth: | 10% |
| SAT writing: | 400-510 | End year in good standing: | 95% |
| ACT composite: | 18-24 | Return as sophomores: | 62% |
| GPA 3.75 or higher: | 12% | Out-of-state: | 2% |
| GPA 3.50-3.74: | 11% | Live on campus: | 19% |
| GPA 3.0-3.49: | 31% | International: | 1% |
| GPA 2.0-2.99: | 44% | Sororities: | 1% |

**Basis for selection.** In-state applicants should rank in top half of high school class, out-of-state in top third. Test scores important. TOEFL or Michigan Test may be used to assess English proficiency. Audition required of music majors. Portfolio required of visual arts majors. **Homeschooled:** Transcript of courses and grades required.

**High school preparation.** College-preparatory program required. 20 units required. Required units include English 4, mathematics 3, social studies 3, science 3, foreign language 2 and academic electives 5. Additional requirements vary by program.

**2009-2010 Annual costs.** Tuition/fees: $6,926; $16,478 out-of-state. Room only: $5,620. Books/supplies: $1,300. Personal expenses: $2,677.

**2008-2009 Financial aid. Need-based:** 1,671 full-time freshmen applied for aid; 1,290 were judged to have need; 1,220 of these received aid. Average need met was 52%. Average scholarship/grant was $5,890; average loan $3,104. 34% of total undergraduate aid awarded as scholarships/grants, 66% as loans/jobs. **Non-need-based:** Awarded to 1,384 full-time undergraduates, including 512 freshmen. Scholarships awarded for academics, athletics, state residency.

**Application procedures. Admission:** Closing date 8/1. $50 fee, may be waived for applicants with need. Admission notification on a rolling basis beginning on or about 11/1. **Financial aid:** Priority date 3/10; no closing date. FAFSA required. Applicants notified on a rolling basis starting 5/15; must reply within 3 week(s) of notification.

**Academics. Special study options:** Accelerated study, cooperative education, distance learning, double major, ESL, exchange student, honors, independent study, internships, liberal arts/career combination, student-designed major, study abroad, teacher certification program, Washington semester, weekend college. **Credit/placement by examination:** AP, CLEP, IB, institutional tests. Hours of credit awarded by examination varies by program. **Support services:** Learning center, pre-admission summer program, remedial instruction, study skills assistance, tutoring, writing center.

**Majors. Area/ethnic studies:** Women's. **Biology:** General. **Business:** Accounting, business admin, finance, hospitality admin, labor studies, managerial economics, marketing, operations. **Communications:** General, media studies, organizational. **Computer sciences:** Computer science, information systems. **Education:** Art, biology, chemistry, elementary, English, French, German, history, mathematics, music, physics, science, secondary, social studies, Spanish, speech. **Engineering:** Civil, computer, electrical, mechanical. **Engineering technology:** Computer, construction, electrical, industrial, mechanical. **Foreign languages:** French, German, Spanish. **Health:** Audiology/hearing, clinical lab science, clinical lab technology, community health services, health care admin, health services admin, mental health services, music therapy, nursing (RN), predental, premedicine, preveterinary, substance abuse counseling. **History:** General. **Interdisciplinary:** Math/computer science. **Math:** General, computational, statistics. **Philosophy/religion:** Philosophy. **Physical sciences:** Chemistry, geology, physics. **Protective services:** Law enforcement admin. **Psychology:** General. **Public administration:** General, policy analysis. **Social sciences:** Anthropology, economics, political science, sociology. **Visual/performing arts:** Commercial/advertising art, crafts, dramatic, drawing, graphic design, interior design, painting, photography, piano/organ, printmaking, sculpture, studio arts, voice/opera.

**Most popular majors.** Business/marketing 19%, education 14%, engineering/engineering technologies 7%, health sciences 6%, liberal arts 17%.

**Computing on campus.** 642 workstations in dormitories, library, computer center, student center. Dormitories wired for high-speed internet access and linked to campus network. Commuter students can connect to campus network. Online course registration, online library, helpline, repair service, student web hosting, wireless network available.

**Student life. Freshman orientation:** Mandatory, $30 fee. Preregistration for classes offered. 8-hour program; 15 dates available between June and August; Freshmen Fest held 2 days in late August. **Housing:** Apartments available. $150 fully refundable deposit. **Activities:** Bands, campus ministries, choral groups, dance, drama, film society, international student organizations, literary magazine, music ensembles, musical theater, opera, student government, student newspaper, symphony orchestra, TV station, Black

Collegian Caucus, Hispanos Unidos, InterVarsity Christian Fellowship, international student organization, Campus Crusade for Christ, campus ministry, Bangladesh student association.

**Athletics.** NCAA. **Intercollegiate:** Baseball M, basketball, cross-country, golf, soccer, softball W, tennis, track and field W, volleyball. **Intramural:** Badminton, basketball, bowling, football (non-tackle), golf, racquetball, table tennis, tennis, volleyball. **Team name:** Mastodons.

**Student services.** Adult student services, alcohol/substance abuse counseling, chaplain/spiritual director, career counseling, student employment services, financial aid counseling, health services, minority student services, on-campus daycare, personal counseling, placement for graduates, veterans' counselor, women's services. **Physically disabled:** Services for visually, speech, hearing impaired.

**Contact.** E-mail: ask@ipfw.edu
Phone: (260) 481-6812 Toll-free number: (800) 324-4739
Fax: (260) 481-6880
Carol Isaacs, Director of Admissions, Indiana University-Purdue University Fort Wayne, 2101 East Coliseum Boulevard, Fort Wayne, IN 46805-1499

## Indiana University-Purdue University Indianapolis

| Indianapolis, Indiana | CB member |
|---|---|
| www.iupui.edu | CB code: 1325 |

▸ Public 4-year university
▸ Commuter campus in very large city
▸ 20,926 degree-seeking undergraduates: 26% part-time, 58% women, 10% African American, 3% Asian American, 3% Hispanic American, 3% international
▸ 7,597 degree-seeking graduate students
▸ 67% of applicants admitted
▸ SAT or ACT with writing required

**General.** Founded in 1969. Regionally accredited. **Degrees:** 3,167 bachelor's, 377 associate awarded; master's, doctoral, professional offered. **ROTC:** Army, Naval, Air Force. **Calendar:** Semester, extensive summer session. **Full-time faculty:** 2,116 total; 83% have terminal degrees, 22% minority, 38% women. **Part-time faculty:** 980 total; 26% have terminal degrees, 11% minority, 50% women. **Class size:** 34% < 20, 48% 20-39, 8% 40-49, 9% 50-99, 1% >100.

**Freshman class profile.** 9,641 applied, 6,414 admitted, 3,019 enrolled.

| Mid 50% test scores | | | |
|---|---|---|---|
| SAT critical reading: | 440-550 | Rank in top quarter: | 44% |
| SAT math: | 450-560 | Rank in top tenth: | 15% |
| ACT composite: | 19-24 | Return as sophomores: | 72% |
| GPA 3.75 or higher: | 18% | Out-of-state: | 3% |
| GPA 3.50-3.74: | 14% | Live on campus: | 21% |
| GPA 3.0-3.49: | 40% | International: | 3% |
| GPA 2.0-2.99: | 27% | Fraternities: | 1% |
| | | Sororities: | 1% |

**Basis for selection.** Course curriculum, grades, trend in grades, and test scores are the factors used. Portfolio recommended for some art applicants.

**High school preparation.** College-preparatory program required. 21 units required; 26 recommended. Required and recommended units include English 4, mathematics 3-4, social studies 3, history 2, science 3-4 (laboratory 3), foreign language 3 and academic electives 4. Additional math and science units required for science, engineering and nursing programs. 4 additional units required in some combination of foreign language, laboratory science, math, social science, or computer science. Courses that develop writing composition skills strongly recommended.

**2009-2010 Annual costs.** Tuition/fees: $7,523; $22,420 out-of-state. Additional Residence Life Programming fee may be charged depending on dorm accommodations. Room only: $3,320. Books/supplies: $672. Personal expenses: $3,200.

**2008-2009 Financial aid. Need-based:** 2,354 full-time freshmen applied for aid; 1,797 were judged to have need; 1,731 of these received aid. Average need met was 89%. Average scholarship/grant was $7,393; average loan $2,987. 42% of total undergraduate aid awarded as scholarships/grants, 58% as loans/jobs. **Non-need-based:** Awarded to 1,571 full-time undergraduates, including 430 freshmen. Scholarships awarded for academics, ROTC.

**Application procedures. Admission:** Closing date 5/1. $50 fee, may be waived for applicants with need. Admission notification on a rolling basis. Application deadlines for nursing and allied health programs range from October 15 to February 1. **Financial aid:** Priority date 3/1; no closing date. FAFSA required. Applicants notified on a rolling basis starting 4/1.

**Academics. Special study options:** Accelerated study, cooperative education, cross-registration, distance learning, double major, dual enrollment of high school students, ESL, exchange student, external degree, honors, independent study, internships, student-designed major, study abroad, teacher certification program, weekend college. **Credit/placement by examination:** AP, CLEP, IB, SAT, ACT, institutional tests. Policy varies by school. **Support services:** Learning center, reduced course load, remedial instruction, tutoring, writing center.

**Majors. Biology:** General. **Business:** General, accounting, finance, human resources, international, labor relations, labor studies, management information systems, market research, nonprofit/public, tourism/travel. **Communications:** General, advertising, journalism, public relations. **Computer sciences:** General, computer graphics, information systems, system admin, web page design, webmaster. **Conservation:** Environmental science. **Education:** Art, biology, chemistry, elementary, English, ESL, French, German, health occupations, mathematics, physical, physics, secondary, social studies, Spanish, speech. **Engineering:** General, biomedical, computer, electrical, mechanical. **Engineering technology:** Computer, computer hardware, computer systems, construction, electrical, mechanical, robotics, software. **Foreign languages:** American Sign Language, French, German, Spanish. **Health:** Clinical lab science, cytotechnology, dental hygiene, medical informatics, medical radiologic technology/radiation therapy, medical records admin, nuclear medical technology, nursing (RN), predental, premedicine, prenursing, prepharmacy, preveterinary, radiologic technology/medical imaging, respiratory therapy assistant. **History:** General. **Legal studies:** Prelaw. **Liberal arts:** Arts/sciences. **Math:** General. **Parks/recreation:** Exercise sciences. **Philosophy/religion:** Philosophy, religion. **Physical sciences:** Chemistry, geology, physics. **Protective services:** Criminal justice, forensics. **Psychology:** General. **Public administration:** General, social work. **Social sciences:** Anthropology, economics, geography, political science, sociology. **Visual/performing arts:** Art, art history/conservation, ceramics, design, interior design, painting, photography, printmaking, sculpture, studio arts.

**Most popular majors.** Business/marketing 17%, education 10%, engineering/engineering technologies 7%, health sciences 16%, liberal arts 14%.

**Computing on campus.** 750 workstations in library, computer center, student center. Dormitories wired for high-speed internet access and linked to campus network. Commuter students can connect to campus network. Online course registration, helpline, repair service, wireless network available.

**Student life. Freshman orientation:** Mandatory, $110 fee. Preregistration for classes offered. **Policies:** Smoking policy, code of conduct. **Housing:** Coed dorms, apartments available. $100 deposit. **Activities:** Bands, campus ministries, choral groups, dance, drama, international student organizations, literary magazine, music ensembles, student government, student newspaper, black student union, international affairs club.

**Athletics.** NCAA. **Intercollegiate:** Basketball, cheerleading, cross-country, diving, golf, soccer, softball W, swimming, tennis, volleyball W. **Intramural:** Basketball, football (non-tackle), golf, ice hockey, racquetball, soccer, softball, tennis, volleyball. **Team name:** Jaguars.

**Student services.** Adult student services, chaplain/spiritual director, career counseling, student employment services, financial aid counseling, health services, minority student services, on-campus daycare, personal counseling, placement for graduates, veterans' counselor, women's services. **Physically disabled:** Services for visually, speech, hearing impaired. **Learning disabled:** Comprehensive services available.

**Contact.** E-mail: apply@iupui.edu
Phone: (317) 274-4591 Fax: (317) 278-1862
Chris Foley, Director of Admissions, Indiana University-Purdue University Indianapolis, 420 North University Boulevard, Cavanaugh Hall R129, Indianapolis, IN 46202-5143

## Indiana Wesleyan University
**Marion, Indiana**
www.indwes.edu                    CB code: 1446

- Private 4-year university and liberal arts college affiliated with Wesleyan Church
- Residential campus in large town
- 3,400 degree-seeking undergraduates
- SAT or ACT (ACT writing recommended), application essay required

**General.** Founded in 1920. Regionally accredited. Education centers in Indianapolis, Fort Wayne, Columbus (IN), Kokomo, Merrillville, Shelbyville, Cleveland, Cincinnati, Lexington, Louisville and Dayton. **Degrees:** 586 bachelor's, 11 associate awarded; master's offered. **ROTC:** Army. **Location:** 65 miles from Indianapolis. **Calendar:** Semester, limited summer session. **Full-time faculty:** 165 total. **Part-time faculty:** 145 total. **Class**

size: 54% < 20, 35% 20-39, 4% 40-49, 6% 50-99, 1% >100. **Special facilities:** History museum, nature preserve, museum of European oil paintings, photograph collection.

**Freshman class profile.**

| Mid 50% test scores | | | |
|---|---|---|---|
| SAT critical reading: | 480-600 | GPA 3.0-3.49: | 24% |
| SAT math: | 480-600 | GPA 2.0-2.99: | 18% |
| ACT composite: | 21-27 | Rank in top quarter: | 55% |
| GPA 3.75 or higher: | 41% | Rank in top tenth: | 28% |
| GPA 3.50-3.74: | 17% | Out-of-state: | 52% |
| | | Live on campus: | 96% |

**Basis for selection.** High school record, class rank, and test scores most important. Recommendations required. Standardized tests, institutional tests used to assist students in selecting appropriate level classes; designated scores determine placement in Math and English. Audition recommended for music majors. Portfolio recommended for art majors. **Homeschooled:** Transcript of courses and grades, letter of recommendation (nonparent) required. Transcript must have GPA on 4.0 scale. Recommendation from pastor required.

**High school preparation.** College-preparatory program recommended. 20 units recommended. Recommended units include English 4, mathematics 3, social studies 3, science 3, foreign language 2 and academic electives 5.

**2009-2010 Annual costs.** Tuition/fees: $20,496. Required fees vary by program. Room/board: $6,770. Books/supplies: $800. Personal expenses: $800.

**2009-2010 Financial aid. Non-need-based:** Scholarships awarded for academics, alumni affiliation, art, athletics, music/drama, ROTC.

**Application procedures. Admission:** Priority date 12/1; deadline 8/1 (receipt date). $25 fee, may be waived for applicants with need. Admission notification on a rolling basis beginning on or about 10/1. **Financial aid:** Closing date 3/1. FAFSA required. Applicants notified by 4/1.

**Academics. Special study options:** Accelerated study, cross-registration, distance learning, double major, dual enrollment of high school students, honors, independent study, internships, liberal arts/career combination, student-designed major, study abroad, teacher certification program. **Credit/placement by examination:** AP, CLEP, IB, SAT, ACT, institutional tests. Students must complete at least 30 hours in residence. **Support services:** Learning center, reduced course load, remedial instruction, study skills assistance, tutoring, writing center.

**Honors college/program.** 1250 SAT (exclusive of Writing) or 28 ACT, 3.6 GPA or class rank in the top 10%, and desire to participate in interdisciplinary community of committed learners required.

**Majors. Biology:** General, Biochemistry/biophysics and molecular biology. **Business:** Accounting, business admin, finance, management information systems, managerial economics, marketing. **Communications:** General, journalism, media studies, public relations. **Computer sciences:** General, applications programming, computer graphics, computer science, web page design, webmaster. **Education:** Art, business, elementary, English, mathematics, middle, music, physical, science, secondary, social studies. **Foreign languages:** Spanish. **Health:** Athletic training, nursing (RN), predental, premedicine, prepharmacy, preveterinary, substance abuse counseling. **History:** General. **Legal studies:** Prelaw. **Math:** General. **Parks/recreation:** Exercise sciences, facilities management, health/fitness, sports admin. **Philosophy/religion:** Philosophy, religion. **Physical sciences:** Chemistry. **Protective services:** Criminal justice. **Psychology:** General. **Public administration:** Social work. **Social sciences:** General, criminology, economics, international relations, political science, urban studies. **Theology:** Bible, religious ed, sacred music, theology. **Visual/performing arts:** Ceramics, dramatic, drawing, graphic design, illustration, interior design, music performance, music theory/composition, painting, photography, printmaking, studio arts.

**Most popular majors.** Business/marketing 13%, computer/information sciences 6%, education 17%, health sciences 17%, psychology 6%, theological studies 13%.

**Computing on campus.** 675 workstations in dormitories, library, computer center, student center. Dormitories wired for high-speed internet access and linked to campus network. Commuter students can connect to campus network. Online library, helpline, repair service, student web hosting, wireless network available.

**Student life. Freshman orientation:** Mandatory. Preregistration for classes offered. Held the weekend before school begins. **Policies:** No alcohol allowed on campus; students attend chapel services 3 times weekly. Religious observance required. **Housing:** Guaranteed on-campus for all undergraduates. Single-sex dorms, special housing for disabled, apartments, wellness housing available. $100 fully refundable deposit, deadline 8/15. **Activities:** Bands, campus ministries, choral groups, drama, film society, international student organizations, literary magazine, music ensembles, musical theater, opera, radio station, student government, student newspaper, symphony orchestra, TV station, World Christian Fellowship, Fellowship of Christian Athletes, Habitat for Humanity, Young Republicans, College Libertarians, IWU Democrats.

**Athletics.** NAIA, NCCAA. **Intercollegiate:** Baseball M, basketball, cross-country, golf M, soccer, softball W, tennis, track and field, volleyball W. **Intramural:** Badminton, basketball, bowling, football (non-tackle), golf, racquetball, soccer, softball, swimming, table tennis, tennis, volleyball, water polo, weight lifting. **Team name:** Wildcats.

**Student services.** Adult student services, alcohol/substance abuse counseling, chaplain/spiritual director, career counseling, services for economically disadvantaged, student employment services, financial aid counseling, health services, minority student services, personal counseling, placement for graduates. **Physically disabled:** Services for visually, speech, hearing impaired. **Learning disabled:** Comprehensive services available.

**Contact.** E-mail: admissions@indwes.edu
Phone: (765) 677-2138 Toll-free number: (800) 332-6901
Fax: (765) 677-2333
Daniel Solms, Director of Admissions, Indiana Wesleyan University, 4201 South Washington Street, Marion, IN 46953-4999

## International Business College
**Fort Wayne, Indiana**
www.ibcfortwayne.edu          CB code: 1330

- For-profit 4-year business and community college
- Small city
- 645 degree-seeking undergraduates
- Interview required

**General.** Founded in 1889. Accredited by ACICS. Branch campus located in Indianapolis. **Degrees:** 45 bachelor's, 156 associate awarded. **Location:** 4 miles from downtown. **Calendar:** Semester, extensive summer session. **Full-time faculty:** 15 total. **Part-time faculty:** 40 total.

**Freshman class profile.**

| | | | |
|---|---|---|---|
| Out-of-state: | 30% | Live on campus: | 40% |

**Basis for selection.** Open admission, but selective for some programs.

**2009-2010 Annual costs.** Tuition/fees: $12,760. Room/board: $5,840. Books/supplies: $900.

**Application procedures. Admission:** No deadline. $50 fee. Admission notification on a rolling basis. **Financial aid:** Closing date 5/1. Applicants notified by 9/15.

**Academics. Special study options:** Independent study, internships. **Credit/placement by examination:** CLEP. **Support services:** Tutoring.

**Majors. Business:** General.

**Computing on campus.** 146 workstations in library, computer center.

**Student life. Freshman orientation:** Available. **Housing:** Coed dorms, single-sex dorms available. **Activities:** Student government, accounting club, secretarial club.

**Student services.** Career counseling, student employment services, personal counseling, placement for graduates.

**Contact.** Phone: (260) 459-4500 Toll-free number: (800) 589-6363
Fax: (260) 436-1896
Steve Kinzer, Director of Admissions, International Business College, 5699 Coventry Lane, Fort Wayne, IN 46804

## ITT Technical Institute: Fort Wayne
**Fort Wayne, Indiana**
www.itt-tech.edu          CB code: 0650

- For-profit 4-year technical college
- Commuter campus in large city

**General.** Founded in 1967. Accredited by ACICS. **Location:** 122 miles from Indianapolis. **Calendar:** Quarter.

**Contact.** Phone: (260) 484-4107
Director of Recruitment, 2810 Dupont Commerce Court, Fort Wayne, IN 46825

## ITT Technical Institute: Indianapolis
**Indianapolis, Indiana**
www.itt-tech.edu          CB code: 0640

- For-profit 4-year technical college
- Commuter campus in very large city

**General.** Founded in 1956. Accredited by ACICS. **Location:** 10 miles from downtown. **Calendar:** Quarter.

**Contact.** Phone: (317) 875-8640
Director of Recruitment, 9511 Angola Court, Indianapolis, IN 46268-1119

## Manchester College
**North Manchester, Indiana**          CB member
www.manchester.edu          CB code: 1440

- Private 4-year liberal arts college affiliated with Church of the Brethren
- Residential campus in small town
- 1,187 degree-seeking undergraduates: 1% part-time, 50% women
- 77% of applicants admitted
- SAT or ACT with writing required
- 49% graduate within 6 years

**General.** Founded in 1889. Regionally accredited. **Degrees:** 187 bachelor's, 1 associate awarded; master's offered. **Location:** 35 miles from Fort Wayne, 100 miles from Indianapolis. **Calendar:** 4-1-4, limited summer session. **Full-time faculty:** 67 total; 82% have terminal degrees, 9% minority, 45% women. **Part-time faculty:** 26 total; 23% have terminal degrees, 46% women. **Class size:** 50% < 20, 46% 20-39, 3% 40-49, less than 1% 50-99. **Special facilities:** Observatory, 100-acre environmental studies and retreat center.

**Freshman class profile.** 2,991 applied, 2,292 admitted, 426 enrolled.

| Mid 50% test scores | | | |
|---|---|---|---|
| SAT critical reading: | 430-550 | GPA 2.0-2.99: | 31% |
| SAT math: | 450-570 | Rank in top quarter: | 54% |
| SAT writing: | 410-540 | Rank in top tenth: | 20% |
| ACT composite: | 18-25 | Return as sophomores: | 66% |
| GPA 3.75 or higher: | 19% | Out-of-state: | 11% |
| GPA 3.50-3.74: | 17% | Live on campus: | 95% |
| GPA 3.0-3.49: | 33% | International: | 2% |

**Basis for selection.** School achievement record most important, with emphasis on college-preparatory courses, followed by SAT or ACT scores, class rank, recommendations. Interview recommended. Essay recommended for academically borderline applicants. Audition recommended for music majors. **Homeschooled:** Provide full information in detailed cover letter with application. **Learning Disabled:** School reviews ability to meet student needs.

**High school preparation.** 14 units required; 17 recommended. Required and recommended units include English 4, mathematics 2-3, social studies 2, history 1-2, science 2-3 (laboratory 2-3), foreign language 2 and academic electives 1-2.

**2009-2010 Annual costs.** Tuition/fees: $23,790. Health insurance and other fees as required. Room/board: $8,050. Books/supplies: $1,000. Personal expenses: $900.

**2009-2010 Financial aid. Need-based:** 404 full-time freshmen applied for aid; 359 were judged to have need; 359 of these received aid. Average need met was 87%. Average scholarship/grant was $18,110; average loan $3,775. 72% of total undergraduate aid awarded as scholarships/grants, 28% as loans/jobs. **Non-need-based:** Awarded to 954 full-time undergraduates, including 404 freshmen. Scholarships awarded for academics, alumni affiliation, minority status, music/drama, religious affiliation. **Additional information:** Students automatically considered for all scholarship programs.

**Application procedures. Admission:** Priority date 5/1; no deadline. $25 fee, may be waived for applicants with need, free for online applicants. Admission notification on a rolling basis beginning on or about 9/1. Must reply by May 1 or within 2 week(s) if notified thereafter. **Financial aid:** Priority date 3/1; no closing date. FAFSA required. Applicants notified on a rolling basis starting 2/15; must reply within 2 week(s) of notification.

**Academics.** Students required to earn 2 credits in Values, Ideas and the Arts. **Special study options:** Accelerated study, cross-registration, double major, dual enrollment of high school students, exchange student, honors, independent study, internships, liberal arts/career combination, student-designed major, study abroad, teacher certification program, urban semester. Medical technology programs with area hospitals, 3-2 engineering dual-degree program with Washington University (MO) and others, 2-2 nursing program with Goshen College. **Credit/placement by examination:** CLEP, IB, SAT, ACT, institutional tests. First year students take college proficiency tests to place out of the first year of modern language. Unlimited credit hours by examination may be counted toward associate or bachelor's degree. **Support services:** Learning center, reduced course load, study skills assistance, tutoring, writing center.

**Majors.** **Area/ethnic studies:** Women's. **Biology:** General, biochemistry. **Business:** General, accounting, banking/financial services, business admin, marketing, nonprofit/public. **Communications:** General, broadcast journalism, journalism. **Computer sciences:** General, computer science. **Conservation:** General, environmental studies. **Education:** General, biology, chemistry, elementary, English, foreign languages, French, German, health, history, mathematics, mentally handicapped, middle, multi-level teacher, music, physical, physics, science, secondary, social science, social studies, Spanish, special. **Engineering:** Science. **Foreign languages:** General, French, German, Spanish. **Health:** Clinical lab science, predental, premedicine, prepharmacy, preveterinary. **History:** General. **Interdisciplinary:** Global studies, math/computer science, peace/conflict. **Legal studies:** Prelaw. **Liberal arts:** Arts/sciences. **Math:** General. **Philosophy/religion:** Philosophy, religion. **Physical sciences:** Chemistry, physics. **Psychology:** General. **Public administration:** Social work. **Social sciences:** General, economics, political science, sociology. **Theology:** Sacred music. **Visual/performing arts:** Art, music performance.

**Most popular majors.** Business/marketing 27%, education 17%, health sciences 12%, psychology 6%, social sciences 6%.

**Computing on campus.** 165 workstations in dormitories, library, computer center. Dormitories wired for high-speed internet access and linked to campus network. Helpline, student web hosting available.

**Student life.** **Freshman orientation:** Mandatory, $125 fee. Preregistration for classes offered. Held the 3 days prior to start of fall classes. **Policies:** Significant student involvement in governance, programming, activities, and administrative services such as security, health, and residence hall management. Students under 21 required to live on-campus unless living with family. **Housing:** Guaranteed on-campus for freshmen. Coed dorms, special housing for disabled, apartments, wellness housing available. **Activities:** Bands, campus ministries, choral groups, dance, drama, international student organizations, literary magazine, music ensembles, Model UN, musical theater, opera, radio station, student government, student newspaper, symphony orchestra, political clubs, black student union, Hispanos Unidos, Habitat for Humanity, volunteer corps, intercollegiate ministries, Amnesty International, environmental club.

**Athletics.** NCAA. **Intercollegiate:** Baseball M, basketball, cross-country, football (tackle) M, golf, soccer, softball W, tennis, track and field, volleyball W, wrestling M. **Intramural:** Badminton, basketball, bowling, cross-country, golf, racquetball, soccer, softball, swimming, table tennis, tennis, track and field, volleyball, wrestling M. **Team name:** Spartans.

**Student services.** Chaplain/spiritual director, career counseling, student employment services, financial aid counseling, health services, minority student services, personal counseling, placement for graduates, veterans' counselor. **Physically disabled:** Services for visually, hearing impaired.

**Contact.** E-mail: admitinfo@manchester.edu
Phone: (260) 982-5055 Toll-free number: (800) 852-3648
Fax: (260) 982-5239
Stuart Jones, Dean of Enrollment, Manchester College, 604 East College Avenue, North Manchester, IN 46962-0365

---

## Marian University
**Indianapolis, Indiana**
www.marian.edu

CB member
CB code: 1442

- Private 4-year liberal arts college affiliated with Roman Catholic Church
- Residential campus in very large city
- 1,947 degree-seeking undergraduates: 24% part-time, 64% women, 18% African American, 1% Asian American, 3% Hispanic American
- 218 degree-seeking graduate students
- 54% of applicants admitted
- SAT or ACT with writing required
- 47% graduate within 6 years; 18% enter graduate study

---

**General.** Founded in 1851. Regionally accredited. **Degrees:** 324 bachelor's, 114 associate awarded; master's offered. **ROTC:** Army. **Location:** 4 miles from downtown. **Calendar:** Semester, limited summer session. **Full-time faculty:** 86 total; 52% have terminal degrees, 5% minority, 54% women. **Part-time faculty:** 116 total; 13% have terminal degrees, 16% minority, 63% women. **Class size:** 62% < 20, 36% 20-39, less than 1% 40-49, less than 1% 50-99. **Special facilities:** Archives (materials on development of education in Archdiocese), 35 acre wetlands biology/ecology laboratory, Allison and Wheeler-Stokely mansions, Japanese tea house and garden, undergraduate seminary.

**Freshman class profile.** 1,858 applied, 1,002 admitted, 316 enrolled.

| Mid 50% test scores | | GPA 2.0-2.99: | 37% |
|---|---|---|---|
| SAT critical reading: | 450-540 | Rank in top quarter: | 34% |
| SAT math: | 450-560 | Rank in top tenth: | 10% |
| ACT composite: | 19-23 | End year in good standing: | 88% |
| GPA 3.75 or higher: | 13% | Return as sophomores: | 72% |
| GPA 3.50-3.74: | 12% | Out-of-state: | 11% |
| GPA 3.0-3.49: | 38% | Live on campus: | 82% |

**Basis for selection.** School achievement record, test scores, recommendations important. Interview recommended. Essay recommended for academically weak applicants.

**High school preparation.** College-preparatory program recommended. 20 units required. Required and recommended units include English 4, mathematics 2-3, social studies 1, history 1, science 2-3 (laboratory 2), foreign language 1-2 and academic electives 9.

**2009-2010 Annual costs.** Tuition/fees: $24,000. Room/board: $7,512. Books/supplies: $1,200. Personal expenses: $900.

**2009-2010 Financial aid.** **Non-need-based:** Scholarships awarded for academics, alumni affiliation, art, athletics, leadership, music/drama, religious affiliation.

**Application procedures.** **Admission:** Priority date 3/1; deadline 8/1 (receipt date). $35 fee, may be waived for applicants with need, free for online applicants. Admission notification on a rolling basis beginning on or about 9/1. Must reply by May 1 or within 2 week(s) if notified thereafter. **Financial aid:** Priority date 3/15; no closing date. FAFSA, institutional form required. Applicants notified on a rolling basis starting 3/15; must reply within 2 week(s) of notification.

**Academics.** **Special study options:** Accelerated study, cooperative education, cross-registration, distance learning, double major, dual enrollment of high school students, honors, independent study, internships, liberal arts/career combination, study abroad, teacher certification program. **Credit/placement by examination:** AP, CLEP, IB, SAT, ACT, institutional tests. 30 credit hours maximum toward associate degree, 60 toward bachelor's. **Support services:** Learning center, reduced course load, remedial instruction, study skills assistance, tutoring, writing center.

**Majors.** **Biology:** General. **Business:** General, accounting, finance, management information systems, marketing. **Communications:** General. **Education:** Elementary, music, physical. **Foreign languages:** French, Spanish. **Health:** Nursing (RN). **History:** General. **Math:** General. **Parks/recreation:** Sports admin. **Philosophy/religion:** Philosophy. **Physical sciences:** Chemistry. **Psychology:** General. **Social sciences:** Economics, political science, sociology. **Theology:** Religious ed, theology. **Visual/performing arts:** Art, art history/conservation, commercial/advertising art.

**Most popular majors.** Business/marketing 44%, education 7%, health sciences 20%.

**Computing on campus.** 300 workstations in dormitories, library, computer center, student center. Dormitories wired for high-speed internet access and linked to campus network. Online course registration, online library, helpline, wireless network available.

**Student life.** **Freshman orientation:** Mandatory. Preregistration for classes offered. Held weekend prior to start of school. Community service project required. **Policies:** Drinking under the age of 21 on campus prohibited. **Housing:** Guaranteed on-campus for freshmen. Coed dorms, special housing for disabled, apartments, cooperative housing, wellness housing available. $125 fully refundable deposit, deadline 5/1. College-owned apartments for students 21 or older, voluntary spiritual living community, nonsmoking areas, suite-style rooms, singles available. **Activities:** Bands, campus ministries, choral groups, dance, drama, international student organizations, literary magazine, music ensembles, musical theater, student government, student newspaper, service organization, Campus America Life League, BACCHUS, Project Earth, community ministries, union for black identity, Fellowship of Christian Athletes, Campus Crusade for Christ.

**Athletics.** NAIA. **Intercollegiate:** Baseball M, basketball, bowling, cheerleading, cross-country, football (tackle) M, golf, soccer, softball W, tennis, track and field, volleyball W. **Intramural:** Basketball, football (non-tackle), racquetball, softball W, volleyball W. **Team name:** Knights.

**Student services.** Adult student services, alcohol/substance abuse counseling, chaplain/spiritual director, career counseling, student employment services, financial aid counseling, health services, personal counseling, placement for graduates. **Physically disabled:** Services for visually, hearing impaired.

**Contact.** E-mail: admissions@marian.edu
Phone: (317) 955-6300 Toll-free number: (800) 772-7264
Fax: (317) 955-6401
Luann Brames, Director of Enrollment, Marian University, 3200 Cold Spring Road, Indianapolis, IN 46222-1997

## Martin University
### Indianapolis, Indiana
**www.martin.edu**     **CB code: 1379**

▶ Private 4-year university and liberal arts college
▶ Commuter campus in very large city

**General.** Founded in 1977. Regionally accredited. **Calendar:** Semester.

**Annual costs/financial aid.** Tuition/fees (2009-2010): $13,520. Books/supplies: $1,000. Personal expenses: $1,300.

**Contact.** Phone: (317) 917-3329
Vice President for Student Affairs, 2171 Avondale Place, Indianapolis, IN 46218

## Oakland City University
### Oakland City, Indiana
**www.oak.edu**     **CB code: 1585**

▶ Private 4-year university and liberal arts college affiliated with Baptist General Conference
▶ Commuter campus in small town
▶ 1,429 degree-seeking undergraduates: 10% part-time, 52% women
▶ 173 graduate students
▶ SAT or ACT required

**General.** Founded in 1885. Regionally accredited. Branches in Bedford and at Branchville Training Center. Accelerated degrees offered at several off-campus sites (National Guard bases and civilian locations), Rockville Training Center, Madison Correctional Facility, New Castle Correctional Facility, Miami Correctional Center, and Indiana Women's Prison. **Degrees:** 336 bachelor's, 136 associate awarded; master's, doctoral, professional offered. **Location:** 30 miles from Evansville. **Calendar:** Semester, limited summer session. **Full-time faculty:** 65 total. **Part-time faculty:** 19 total. **Class size:** 81% < 20, 19% 20-39, less than 1% 40-49.

### Freshman class profile.

| Mid 50% test scores | | GPA 3.50-3.74: | 14% |
|---|---|---|---|
| SAT critical reading: | 400-510 | GPA 3.0-3.49: | 31% |
| SAT math: | 420-530 | GPA 2.0-2.99: | 27% |
| SAT writing: | 400-500 | Rank in top quarter: | 16% |
| ACT composite: | 17-23 | Rank in top tenth: | 9% |
| GPA 3.75 or higher: | 16% | Out-of-state: | 10% |

**Basis for selection.** 2.5 high school GPA and SAT/ACT test scores most important. Recommendations considered. Interview and essay recommended. **Homeschooled:** Transcript of courses and grades required.

**High school preparation.** 12 units recommended. Recommended units include English 4, mathematics 3, social studies 2 and science 3.

**2009-2010 Annual costs.** Tuition/fees: $15,400. Room/board: $6,700. Books/supplies: $1,500. Personal expenses: $1,500.

**2009-2010 Financial aid.** **Non-need-based:** Scholarships awarded for academics, alumni affiliation, art, athletics, minority status, music/drama, religious affiliation.

**Application procedures.** **Admission:** Closing date 9/8 (receipt date). $35 fee, may be waived for applicants with need. Admission notification on a rolling basis. **Financial aid:** Closing date 3/1. FAFSA required. Applicants notified on a rolling basis starting 5/1.

**Academics.** **Special study options:** Accelerated study, combined bachelor's/graduate degree, cooperative education, distance learning, double major, dual

enrollment of high school students, external degree, honors, independent study, internships, liberal arts/career combination, teacher certification program. Combined bachelor's/graduate degree: M.S. in Management. **Credit/placement by examination:** AP, CLEP, IB, institutional tests. 16 credit hours maximum toward associate degree, 32 toward bachelor's. **Support services:** Learning center, pre-admission summer program, reduced course load, remedial instruction, tutoring.

**Majors.** **Biology:** General. **Business:** General, accounting, business admin, human resources, management information systems, organizational behavior. **Computer sciences:** General. **Education:** Art, biology, business, early childhood, elementary, English, health, history, mathematics, music, physical, reading, science, social science, social studies, special, voc/tech. **History:** General. **Liberal arts:** Arts/sciences, humanities. **Math:** Applied. **Parks/recreation:** Health/fitness. **Philosophy/religion:** Religion. **Protective services:** Criminal justice. **Psychology:** General. **Social sciences:** General, sociology. **Visual/performing arts:** Art, graphic design, industrial design, music performance.

**Most popular majors.** Business/marketing 59%, education 15%, liberal arts 7%.

**Computing on campus.** 92 workstations in library, computer center, student center. Dormitories wired for high-speed internet access and linked to campus network. Commuter students can connect to campus network. Online library, wireless network available.

**Student life.** **Freshman orientation:** Mandatory, $75 fee. Preregistration for classes offered. One day immediately before each semester. **Housing:** Guaranteed on-campus for all undergraduates. Single-sex dorms, apartments, wellness housing available. $100 fully refundable deposit, deadline 7/22. **Activities:** Pep band, choral groups, drama, music ensembles, student government, student newspaper, mental health assistance group, Circle-K, Student Christian Association, Fellowship of Christian Athletes, Theologs, student education association.

**Athletics.** NCAA, NCCAA. **Intercollegiate:** Baseball M, basketball, cheerleading M, cross-country, golf, soccer, softball W, tennis, volleyball W. **Intramural:** Basketball, bowling, football (non-tackle), softball, table tennis, tennis, volleyball. **Team name:** Oaks.

**Student services.** Adult student services, chaplain/spiritual director, career counseling, services for economically disadvantaged, student employment services, financial aid counseling, personal counseling, placement for graduates, veterans' counselor.

**Contact.** E-mail: ocuadmit@oak.edu
Phone: (812) 749-4781 ext. 222 Toll-free number: (800) 737-5125
Fax: (812) 749-1433
Kim Heldt, Director of Admissions, Oakland City University, 138 North Lucretia Street, Oakland City, IN 47660

## Purdue University
### West Lafayette, Indiana
**www.purdue.edu**     **CB member**     **CB code: 1631**

▶ Public 4-year university
▶ Residential campus in small city
▶ 30,932 degree-seeking undergraduates: 4% part-time, 42% women, 3% African American, 5% Asian American, 3% Hispanic American, 9% international
▶ 8,552 degree-seeking graduate students
▶ 73% of applicants admitted
▶ SAT or ACT with writing, application essay required
▶ 71% graduate within 6 years; 19% enter graduate study

**General.** Founded in 1869. Regionally accredited. **Degrees:** 6,139 bachelor's, 516 associate awarded; master's, doctoral, professional offered. **ROTC:** Army, Naval, Air Force. **Location:** 65 miles from Indianapolis. **Calendar:** Semester, limited summer session. **Full-time faculty:** 2,367 total; 82% have terminal degrees, 17% minority, 70% women. **Part-time faculty:** 353 total; 40% have terminal degrees, 6% minority, 50% women. **Class size:** 32% < 20, 41% 20-39, 7% 40-49, 11% 50-99, 8% >100. **Special facilities:** Linear accelerator, horticultural park, concert hall, 3 theaters, outdoor concert facility, 2 professional golf courses, on-campus airport, center for data perceptualization.

**Freshman class profile.** 27,213 applied, 19,905 admitted, 6,042 enrolled.

| Mid 50% test scores | | | |
|---|---|---|---|
| SAT critical reading: | 500-610 | GPA 2.0-2.99: | 9% |
| SAT math: | 540-670 | Rank in top quarter: | 72% |
| SAT writing: | 490-600 | Rank in top tenth: | 38% |
| ACT composite: | 23-29 | End year in good standing: | 89% |
| GPA 3.75 or higher: | 37% | Return as sophomores: | 87% |
| GPA 3.50-3.74: | 24% | Out-of-state: | 38% |
| GPA 3.0-3.49: | 30% | International: | 11% |

**Basis for selection.** Rigor of high school curriculum, standardized test scores, GPA and information provided by both applicant and high school counselor considered. Interview required for veterinary medicine, veterinary technology and pharmacy applicants.

**High school preparation.** College-preparatory program recommended. Required and recommended units include English 4, mathematics 3-4, social studies 3, science 3 (laboratory 3) and foreign language 2.

**2009-2010 Annual costs.** Tuition/fees: $8,638; $25,118 out-of-state. Differential general service fees: Engineering students pay additional $1,000 per academic year. Management undergraduate students pay additional $1,274 per academic year. School of Technology students pay an additional $500 per academic year. Degree-seeking students who are continuously enrolled prior to the summer 2009 term are not charged the $500 per academic year Strategic Plan fee. Effective fall 2009, undergraduate resident new to campus students will be rebated the Strategic Plan fee for the 2009-10 academic year only. Room/board: $8,710. Books/supplies: $1,050. Personal expenses: $1,690.

**2009-2010 Financial aid.** **Need-based:** 45% of total undergraduate aid awarded as scholarships/grants, 55% as loans/jobs. **Non-need-based:** Scholarships awarded for academics, athletics, job skills, leadership, music/drama, ROTC. **Additional information:** Cooperative work for credit available in many programs.

**Application procedures.** **Admission:** Priority date 11/15; deadline 3/1 (receipt date). $50 fee, may be waived for applicants with need. Admission notification on a rolling basis beginning on or about 12/5. Must reply by May 1 or within 3 week(s) if notified thereafter. November 15 deadline for flight technology program, veterinary technology program, preferential deadline for pre-pharmacy, health sciences and nursing, and scholarships. **Financial aid:** Priority date 3/1; no closing date. FAFSA required. Applicants notified by 4/15.

**Academics.** Minimal number of courses outside major allowed on pass/fail basis, not to exceed 20% of total credit hours required. **Special study options:** Accelerated study, combined bachelor's/graduate degree, cooperative education, cross-registration, distance learning, double major, dual enrollment of high school students, exchange student, honors, independent study, internships, liberal arts/career combination, New York semester, study abroad, teacher certification program, weekend college. **Credit/placement by examination:** AP, CLEP, IB, SAT, ACT, institutional tests. **Support services:** Learning center, pre-admission summer program, reduced course load, remedial instruction, study skills assistance, tutoring, writing center.

**Majors.** **Agriculture:** General, agronomy, animal sciences, communications, economics, farm/ranch, food science, horticultural science, horticulture, mechanization, production, products processing. **Architecture:** Landscape. **Area/ethnic studies:** African-American, Asian, French, German, Japanese, women's. **Biology:** General, biochemistry, Biochemistry/biophysics and molecular biology, botany, cellular/molecular, entomology, microbiology, molecular, plant genetics, zoology. **Business:** Accounting, accounting/business management, accounting/finance, actuarial science, business admin, fashion, financial planning, hospitality admin, hotel/motel admin, human resources, marketing, operations, tourism/travel. **Communications:** General, advertising, broadcast journalism, journalism, public relations. **Computer sciences:** General, computer graphics, computer science, networking. **Conservation:** General, environmental science, fisheries, forestry, wildlife. **Education:** General, agricultural, art, biology, chemistry, early childhood, early childhood special, elementary, family/consumer sciences, foreign languages, French, German, health, kindergarten/preschool, mathematics, multilevel teacher, physical, physics, secondary, social studies, Spanish, technology/industrial arts. **Engineering:** Aerospace, agricultural, biomedical, chemical, civil, computer, construction, electrical, industrial, materials, mechanical, nuclear, surveying. **Engineering technology:** Aerospace, architectural, computer, construction, electrical, industrial, industrial management, manufacturing, mechanical, mechanical drafting, robotics, surveying. **Family/consumer sciences:** General, clothing/textiles, family studies, family/community services, food/nutrition. **Foreign languages:** General, classics, East Asian, Japanese, Russian, Spanish. **Health:** Athletic training, audiology/hearing, audiology/speech pathology, clinical lab science, dietetic technician, dietetics, health services, nursing (RN), occupational health, predental,

premedicine, speech pathology, veterinary technology/assistant. **History:** General. **Interdisciplinary:** Biological/physical sciences, nutrition sciences. **Liberal arts:** Arts/sciences, humanities. **Math:** General, applied, statistics. **Parks/recreation:** Exercise sciences, health/fitness. **Philosophy/religion:** Philosophy, religion. **Physical sciences:** Atmospheric science, chemistry, geology, meteorology, physics. **Protective services:** Law enforcement admin. **Psychology:** General. **Public administration:** Social work. **Social sciences:** General, anthropology, political science, sociology. **Transportation:** Air traffic control, airline/commercial pilot, aviation, aviation management. **Visual/performing arts:** General, acting, art, art history/conservation, design, dramatic, fashion design, film/cinema, interior design, photography, studio arts.

**Most popular majors.** Business/marketing 16%, education 7%, engineering/engineering technologies 26%, family/consumer sciences 7%, health sciences 6%, social sciences 6%.

**Computing on campus.** 25,967 workstations in dormitories, library, computer center, student center. Dormitories wired for high-speed internet access and linked to campus network. Commuter students can connect to campus network. Online course registration, helpline, wireless network available.

**Student life. Freshman orientation:** Available, $320 fee. Preregistration for classes offered. Held the week before classes. **Policies:** Nondiscrimination, antiharassment, antihazing policies; bill of students' rights. **Housing:** Coed dorms, single-sex dorms, special housing for disabled, apartments, cooperative housing, fraternity/sorority housing, wellness housing available. $100 nonrefundable deposit, deadline 4/30. **Activities:** Bands, campus ministries, choral groups, dance, drama, international student organizations, literary magazine, music ensembles, radio station, student government, student newspaper, symphony orchestra, TV station, over 850 religious, political, ethnic, academic, hobby and social service organizations.

**Athletics.** NCAA. **Intercollegiate:** Baseball M, basketball, cross-country, diving, football (tackle) M, golf, soccer W, softball W, swimming, tennis, track and field, volleyball W, wrestling M. **Intramural:** Badminton, basketball, cross-country, football (non-tackle), golf, racquetball, soccer, softball, swimming, table tennis, tennis, track and field, volleyball. **Team name:** Boilermakers.

**Student services.** Adult student services, alcohol/substance abuse counseling, career counseling, services for economically disadvantaged, student employment services, financial aid counseling, health services, legal services, minority student services, on-campus daycare, personal counseling, placement for graduates, veterans' counselor, women's services. **Physically disabled:** Services for visually, speech, hearing impaired.

**Contact.** E-mail: admissions@purdue.edu
Phone: (765) 494-1776 Fax: (765) 494-0544
Pamela Horne, Dean of Admissions, Purdue University, 475 Stadium Mall Drive, West Lafayette, IN 47907-2050

---

**Purdue University Calumet**
Hammond, Indiana
www.calumet.purdue.edu

CB member
CB code: 1638

- Public 4-year university and branch campus college
- Commuter campus in small city
- 8,403 degree-seeking undergraduates: 31% part-time, 55% women, 19% African American, 1% Asian American, 15% Hispanic American, 3% international
- 913 degree-seeking graduate students
- 69% of applicants admitted
- SAT or ACT with writing required

**General.** Founded in 1943. Regionally accredited. Experiential learning curricular components required by all undergraduate students. **Degrees:** 856 bachelor's, 160 associate awarded; master's offered. **Location:** 20 miles from Chicago. **Calendar:** Semester, extensive summer session. **Full-time faculty:** 268 total; 69% have terminal degrees, 20% minority, 48% women. **Part-time faculty:** 250 total; 11% have terminal degrees, 15% minority, 47% women. **Class size:** 28% < 20, 63% 20-39, 4% 40-49, 5% 50-99, less than 1% >100.

**Freshman class profile.** 5,884 applied, 4,081 admitted, 1,359 enrolled.

| Mid 50% test scores | | | |
|---|---|---|---|
| SAT critical reading: | 410-510 | Rank in top quarter: | 28% |
| SAT math: | 410-520 | Rank in top tenth: | 10% |
| ACT composite: | 17-23 | Return as sophomores: | 69% |
| GPA 3.75 or higher: | 3% | Out-of-state: | 13% |
| GPA 3.50-3.74: | 3% | Live on campus: | 15% |
| GPA 3.0-3.49: | 16% | Fraternities: | 1% |
| GPA 2.0-2.99: | 61% | Sororities: | 1% |

**Basis for selection.** Class rank, grade average in subjects related to degree objectives, trends in achievement throughout high school, satisfactory high school subject matter requirements, strength of college preparatory program, and standardized test results most important. Graduation from high school with minimum of 15 units of credit required. **Homeschooled:** Transcript of courses and grades required.

**High school preparation.** College-preparatory program recommended. 14 units required. Required and recommended units include English 4, mathematics 2, social studies 1, history 1, science 1-2 and foreign language 2. Course requirements vary according to program.

**2009-2010 Annual costs.** Tuition/fees: $6,308; $14,116 out-of-state. Room only: $4,680. Books/supplies: $1,125.

**2008-2009 Financial aid. Need-based:** 967 full-time freshmen applied for aid; 747 were judged to have need; 681 of these received aid. Average need met was 12%. Average scholarship/grant was $2,947; average loan $1,908. 35% of total undergraduate aid awarded as scholarships/grants, 65% as loans/jobs. **Non-need-based:** Awarded to 898 full-time undergraduates, including 261 freshmen. Scholarships awarded for academics, athletics, minority status, state residency.

**Application procedures. Admission:** No deadline. No application fee. Admission notification on a rolling basis. **Financial aid:** Priority date 3/10, closing date 6/30. FAFSA required. Applicants notified on a rolling basis starting 4/15; must reply within 2 week(s) of notification.

**Academics. Special study options:** Accelerated study, combined bachelor's/graduate degree, cooperative education, distance learning, double major, dual enrollment of high school students, ESL, honors, independent study, internships, study abroad, teacher certification program, weekend college. **Credit/placement by examination:** AP, CLEP, SAT, ACT, institutional tests. **Support services:** Learning center, reduced course load, remedial instruction, study skills assistance, tutoring, writing center.

**Honors college/program.** 3.5 GPA, 27 ACT/1200 SAT (exclusive of Writing) required. Must maintain 3.5 GPA. Additional factors include outstanding academic achievement, strength of academic program, demonstrated leadership, creativity, community involvement, essay, and letter(s) of recommendation.

**Majors. Biology:** General. **Business:** General, accounting, business admin, entrepreneurial studies, finance, human resources, retailing, small business admin. **Communications:** General, broadcast journalism, journalism, public relations. **Computer sciences:** General, computer graphics, computer science, database management, information systems, networking, programming. **Education:** General, biology, chemistry, early childhood, elementary, English, French, multi-level teacher, physics, science, secondary, social science, social studies. **Engineering:** General, computer, electrical, mechanical, mechanics, software. **Engineering technology:** Construction, electrical, industrial management. **Foreign languages:** General, French, Spanish. **Health:** Clinical lab science, nursing (RN), premedicine, preop/surgical nursing, prepharmacy, preveterinary. **History:** General. **Interdisciplinary:** Gerontology, math/computer science. **Legal studies:** Prelaw. **Math:** General, applied. **Philosophy/religion:** Philosophy. **Physical sciences:** Chemistry, physics. **Protective services:** Law enforcement admin. **Psychology:** General. **Social sciences:** Political science, sociology.

**Most popular majors.** Business/marketing 25%, communications/journalism 8%, engineering/engineering technologies 14%, health sciences 12%, social sciences 9%.

**Computing on campus.** 1,500 workstations in library, computer center, student center. Dormitories wired for high-speed internet access and linked to campus network. Commuter students can connect to campus network. Online course registration, online library, helpline, wireless network available.

**Student life. Freshman orientation:** Mandatory. Preregistration for classes offered. **Housing:** Apartments, wellness housing available. **Activities:** Campus ministries, choral groups, dance, drama, international student organizations, literary magazine, student government, student newspaper, black student union, Los Latinos, Society of Professional Hispanic Engineers, InterVarsity Christian Fellowship, Muslim student association, New Life Ministries, National Society of Black Engineers, Indian students association, Korean student organization, social justice club.

**Athletics.** NAIA. **Intercollegiate:** Basketball, cheerleading. **Intramural:** Basketball, bowling, golf, racquetball, sailing, soccer, softball, table tennis, volleyball, weight lifting. **Team name:** Peregrines.

**Student services.** Adult student services, career counseling, student employment services, financial aid counseling, health services, on-campus daycare, personal counseling, placement for graduates, veterans' counselor. **Physically disabled:** Services for visually, speech, hearing impaired.

**Contact.** E-mail: adms@calumet.purdue.edu
Phone: (219) 989-2213 Toll-free number: (800) 447-76383 ext. 2213
Fax: (219) 989-2775
Paul McGuinness, Director of Admissions, Purdue University Calumet, 2200 169th Street, Hammond, IN 46323-2094

---

## Purdue University North Central
**Westville, Indiana**  **CB member**
www.pnc.edu   **CB code: 1640**

- Public 4-year branch campus college
- Commuter campus in rural community
- 3,814 degree-seeking undergraduates: 28% part-time, 56% women, 7% African American, 1% Asian American, 5% Hispanic American, 1% Native American
- 71 degree-seeking graduate students
- 86% of applicants admitted

**General.** Founded in 1943. Regionally accredited. **Degrees:** 324 bachelor's, 190 associate awarded; master's offered. **Location:** 10 miles from Michigan City, 13 miles from Laporte. **Calendar:** Semester, limited summer session. **Full-time faculty:** 121 total; 63% have terminal degrees, 18% minority, 43% women. **Part-time faculty:** 193 total; 17% have terminal degrees, 9% minority, 51% women. **Class size:** 51% < 20, 44% 20-39, 4% 40-49, 1% 50-99, less than 1% >100.

**Freshman class profile.** 1,563 applied, 1,341 admitted, 768 enrolled.

| Mid 50% test scores | | | |
|---|---|---|---|
| SAT critical reading: | 420-520 | GPA 3.0-3.49: | 24% |
| SAT math: | 420-540 | GPA 2.0-2.99: | 60% |
| SAT writing: | 400-500 | Rank in top quarter: | 16% |
| ACT composite: | 18-22 | Rank in top tenth: | 4% |
| GPA 3.75 or higher: | 4% | Return as sophomores: | 54% |
| GPA 3.50-3.74: | 5% | Out-of-state: | 2% |

**Basis for selection.** Class rank and test scores important. Admission requirements reduced for community college division. SAT or ACT recommended. Interview recommended for academically weak applicants.

**High school preparation.** College-preparatory program recommended. 15 units recommended. Recommended units include English 4, mathematics 3, social studies 1, history 1, science 3 (laboratory 3).

**2009-2010 Annual costs.** Tuition/fees: $6,384; $15,057 out-of-state. Books/supplies: $1,815.

**2008-2009 Financial aid. Need-based:** 565 full-time freshmen applied for aid; 445 were judged to have need; 406 of these received aid. Average need met was 35%. Average scholarship/grant was $3,730; average loan $3,014. 41% of total undergraduate aid awarded as scholarships/grants, 59% as loans/jobs. **Non-need-based:** Awarded to 865 full-time undergraduates, including 262 freshmen. Scholarships awarded for academics, athletics, leadership, state residency.

**Application procedures. Admission:** Priority date 8/1; no deadline. No application fee. Admission notification on a rolling basis. **Financial aid:** Priority date 3/10, closing date 6/30. FAFSA required. Applicants notified on a rolling basis starting 4/1; must reply by 8/1 or within 2 week(s) of notification.

**Academics. Special study options:** Combined bachelor's/graduate degree, distance learning, dual enrollment of high school students, independent study, internships, teacher certification program, weekend college. **Credit/placement by examination:** AP, CLEP, SAT, ACT, institutional tests. **Support services:** Learning center, reduced course load, remedial instruction, tutoring, writing center.

**Majors. Biology:** General. **Business:** General, accounting, human resources, labor relations, marketing, operations. **Communications:** General.

**Computer sciences:** Applications programming, data processing. **Education:** Early childhood, elementary. **Engineering:** Mechanical. **Engineering technology:** General, architectural, electrical, mechanical. **Health:** Nursing (RN). **Liberal arts:** Arts/sciences.

**Most popular majors.** Business/marketing 29%, education 12%, engineering/engineering technologies 11%, health sciences 6%, liberal arts 26%.

**Computing on campus.** 240 workstations in library, computer center. Commuter students can connect to campus network. Online course registration, online library, helpline, wireless network available.

**Student life. Freshman orientation:** Available. **Activities:** Campus ministries, drama, literary magazine, student government, student newspaper, Active Voices, Alpha Phi Alpha, Christian bible study, Rotaract club, TRIO service club.

**Athletics.** NAIA. **Intercollegiate:** Baseball M, basketball M, softball W, volleyball W. **Intramural:** Golf. **Team name:** Panthers.

**Student services.** Career counseling, student employment services, financial aid counseling, on-campus daycare, personal counseling, placement for graduates. **Physically disabled:** Services for visually, hearing impaired.

**Contact.** E-mail: admissions@pnc.edu
Phone: (219) 785-5505 Toll-free number: (800) 782-1231
Fax: (219) 785-5538
Anthony Cardenas, Assistant Dean of Enrollment and Outreach Recruitment, Purdue University North Central, 1401 South US Highway 421, Westville, IN 46391-9542

## Rose-Hulman Institute of Technology

| Terre Haute, Indiana | CB member |
|---|---|
| www.rose-hulman.edu | CB code: 1668 |

- Private 4-year engineering college
- Residential campus in small city
- 1,842 degree-seeking undergraduates: 20% women, 3% African American, 5% Asian American, 2% Hispanic American, 3% international
- 120 degree-seeking graduate students
- 70% of applicants admitted
- SAT or ACT (ACT writing optional) required
- 80% graduate within 6 years; 22% enter graduate study

**General.** Founded in 1874. Regionally accredited. **Degrees:** 367 bachelor's awarded; master's offered. **ROTC:** Army, Air Force. **Location:** 73 miles from Indianapolis. **Calendar:** Quarter, limited summer session. **Full-time faculty:** 160 total; 100% have terminal degrees, 11% minority, 22% women. **Part-time faculty:** 8 total; 88% have terminal degrees, 25% women. **Class size:** 38% < 20, 62% 20-39, less than 1% 40-49, less than 1% 50-99. **Special facilities:** Advanced learning center, observatory, center for technological research with industry.

**Freshman class profile.** 3,554 applied, 2,495 admitted, 465 enrolled.

| Mid 50% test scores | | | |
|---|---|---|---|
| SAT critical reading: | 560-670 | Rank in top tenth: | 61% |
| SAT math: | 630-720 | End year in good standing: | 87% |
| SAT writing: | 520-640 | Return as sophomores: | 89% |
| ACT composite: | 26-32 | Out-of-state: | 55% |
| Rank in top quarter: | 89% | Live on campus: | 99% |
| | | International: | 5% |

**Basis for selection.** GED not accepted. Primary consideration given to school achievement record and subjects taken. Applicants must rank in top quarter of graduating class. Test scores also very important. Recommendations important. Extracurricular and leadership activities, alumni ties considered. Interviews, although not required, can be determining factor. **Homeschooled:** Statement describing homeschool structure and mission, transcript of courses and grades, letter of recommendation (nonparent) required. Lab courses must have been taken at high school or community college.

**High school preparation.** College-preparatory program required. 16 units required. Required and recommended units include English 4, mathematics 4-5, social studies 2, science 2-3 (laboratory 2) and academic electives 4.

**2009-2010 Annual costs.** Tuition/fees: $34,560. Purchase of laptop computer (approximately $2,800) required of freshmen. Room/board: $9,441. Books/supplies: $1,500. Personal expenses: $1,500.

**2009-2010 Financial aid. Need-based:** 391 full-time freshmen applied for aid; 337 were judged to have need; 337 of these received aid. Average need met was 88%. Average scholarship/grant was $4,901; average loan $3,580. 50% of total undergraduate aid awarded as scholarships/grants, 50%

as loans/jobs. **Non-need-based:** Awarded to 631 full-time undergraduates, including 168 freshmen. Scholarships awarded for academics, minority status, ROTC.

**Application procedures. Admission:** Priority date 12/1; deadline 3/1 (postmark date). $40 fee, may be waived for applicants with need, free for online applicants. Admission notification on a rolling basis beginning on or about 10/1. Must reply by 5/1. **Financial aid:** Priority date 3/1; no closing date. FAFSA required. Applicants notified on a rolling basis starting 3/10.

**Academics.** Area minor programs in science, engineering, humanities and social sciences. Additional certificate and interdisciplinary programs available in imaging systems, technical translation, consulting engineering, semiconductor materials and devices, management studies, robotics and optical communications. **Special study options:** Accelerated study, cooperative education, cross-registration, double major, independent study, internships, study abroad. **Credit/placement by examination:** AP, CLEP, IB, institutional tests. **Support services:** Learning center, reduced course load, study skills assistance, tutoring, writing center.

**Majors. Biology:** General, biochemistry. **Computer sciences:** Computer science. **Engineering:** Biomedical, chemical, civil, computer, electrical, mechanical, physics, software. **Math:** General. **Physical sciences:** Chemistry, physics. **Social sciences:** Economics. **Other:** Optical Engineering.

**Most popular majors.** Engineering/engineering technologies 81%.

**Computing on campus.** PC or laptop required. 14 workstations in library. Dormitories wired for high-speed internet access and linked to campus network. Commuter students can connect to campus network. Online course registration, online library, helpline, repair service, student web hosting, wireless network available.

**Student life. Freshman orientation:** Mandatory. **Housing:** Guaranteed on-campus for freshmen. Coed dorms, single-sex dorms, apartments, fraternity/sorority housing available. $75 fully refundable deposit, deadline 6/7. **Activities:** Bands, choral groups, dance, drama, international student organizations, literary magazine, music ensembles, musical theater, radio station, student government, student newspaper, Inter-Varsity Christian Fellowship, Circle K, National Society of Black Engineers, Spanish club, student activities board, Society of Woman Engineers, Alpha Phi Omega Service Fraternity, Orthodox Christian Fellowship.

**Athletics.** NCAA. **Intercollegiate:** Baseball M, basketball, cross-country, diving, football (tackle) M, golf, rifle, soccer, softball W, swimming, tennis, track and field, volleyball W. **Intramural:** Basketball, cross-country, football (non-tackle), golf, racquetball, soccer, softball, swimming, table tennis, tennis, track and field, volleyball. **Team name:** Fightin' Engineers.

**Student services.** Alcohol/substance abuse counseling, career counseling, student employment services, financial aid counseling, health services, personal counseling, placement for graduates.

**Contact.** E-mail: admissions@rose-hulman.edu
Phone: (812) 877-8213 Toll-free number: (800) 248-7448
Fax: (812) 877-8941
Lisa Norton, Director of Admissions, Rose-Hulman Institute of Technology, Office of Admissions, Terre Haute, IN 47803-3999

## Saint Joseph's College

| Rensselaer, Indiana | CB member |
|---|---|
| www.saintjoe.edu | CB code: 1697 |

- Private 4-year liberal arts college affiliated with Roman Catholic Church
- Residential campus in small town
- 998 degree-seeking undergraduates: 5% part-time, 57% women, 10% African American, 1% Asian American, 5% Hispanic American, 1% international
- 1,011 graduate students
- 73% of applicants admitted
- SAT or ACT (ACT writing optional) required
- 58% graduate within 6 years; 15% enter graduate study

**General.** Founded in 1889. Regionally accredited. **Degrees:** 213 bachelor's awarded; master's offered. **Location:** 80 miles from Chicago, 90 miles from Indianapolis. **Calendar:** Semester, limited summer session. **Full-time faculty:** 57 total; 86% have terminal degrees, 4% minority, 42% women. **Part-time faculty:** 43 total; 7% have terminal degrees, 2% minority, 65% women. **Class size:** 78% < 20, 19% 20-39, 2% 40-49, 1% 50-99.

**Freshman class profile.** 1,218 applied, 886 admitted, 231 enrolled.

| Mid 50% test scores | | | |
|---|---|---|---|
| SAT critical reading: | 420-520 | GPA 2.0-2.99: | 46% |
| SAT math: | 420-550 | Rank in top quarter: | 38% |
| ACT composite: | 18-26 | Rank in top tenth: | 14% |
| GPA 3.75 or higher: | 16% | End year in good standing: | 84% |
| GPA 3.50-3.74: | 9% | Return as sophomores: | 55% |
| GPA 3.0-3.49: | 28% | Out-of-state: | 29% |
| | | Live on campus: | 89% |

**Basis for selection.** For applicants with requirement deficiencies, admissions decision may be deferred until additional requirements (which may include an interview, recommendations, further course work, or an essay) are evaluated. Limited number of these applicants will be admitted under the Freshman Academic Support Program. **Homeschooled:** Statement describing homeschool structure and mission, transcript of courses and grades required. **Learning Disabled:** Documentation of learning disability not considered in application process. After admission, documentation of learning disability must be submitted to Director of Counseling Services in order to receive academic accommodations.

**High school preparation.** College-preparatory program recommended. 15 units recommended. Recommended units include English 4, mathematics 3, social studies 3, science 3 (laboratory 2) and foreign language 2. 10 recommended units must be from English, foreign language, social studies, math, and natural science. 3 units distributed among social studies, history, and academic electives.

**2010-2011 Annual costs.** Tuition/fees (projected): $25,260. Room/board: $7,640. Books/supplies: $800. Personal expenses: $680.

**2008-2009 Financial aid. Need-based:** 272 full-time freshmen applied for aid; 229 were judged to have need; 229 of these received aid. Average need met was 85%. Average scholarship/grant was $15,789; average loan $3,757. 66% of total undergraduate aid awarded as scholarships/grants, 34% as loans/jobs. **Non-need-based:** Awarded to 324 full-time undergraduates, including 101 freshmen. Scholarships awarded for academics, alumni affiliation, athletics, minority status, music/drama.

**Application procedures. Admission:** Priority date 12/1; no deadline. $25 fee, may be waived for applicants with need. Admission notification on a rolling basis beginning on or about 12/1. Must reply by May 1 or within 2 week(s) if notified thereafter. **Financial aid:** Priority date 3/1; no closing date. FAFSA required. Applicants notified on a rolling basis starting 3/1; must reply by 5/1 or within 2 week(s) of notification.

**Academics.** Core program is a sequence of 10 interdisciplinary courses and seeks to integrate Christian humanism with critical appraisal of human condition. **Special study options:** Accelerated study, cross-registration, double major, dual enrollment of high school students, honors, independent study, internships, liberal arts/career combination, student-designed major, study abroad, teacher certification program, Washington semester. **Credit/placement by examination:** AP, CLEP, institutional tests. **Support services:** Learning center, reduced course load, study skills assistance, tutoring.

**Majors. Biology:** General, biochemistry. **Business:** General, accounting, management information systems. **Communications:** Media studies. **Computer sciences:** General. **Education:** Art, elementary, physical, secondary. **Health:** Clinical lab science, nursing (RN), predental, premedicine, preveterinary. **History:** General. **Legal studies:** Prelaw. **Math:** General. **Parks/recreation:** Health/fitness, sports admin. **Philosophy/religion:** Philosophy. **Physical sciences:** Chemistry. **Protective services:** Criminal justice. **Psychology:** General. **Social sciences:** Economics, international relations, political science, sociology. **Theology:** Pastoral counseling. **Visual/performing arts:** Directing/producing, music history, music management, studio arts. **Other:** Religion/philosophy.

**Most popular majors.** Biology 9%, business/marketing 17%, education 8%, health sciences 24%, visual/performing arts 7%.

**Computing on campus.** 69 workstations in library, computer center, student center. Dormitories wired for high-speed internet access and linked to campus network. Online course registration, helpline, student web hosting, wireless network available.

**Student life. Freshman orientation:** Mandatory. Preregistration for classes offered. One-day optional early registrations in April, June and July; 4-day required orientation in August. **Housing:** Guaranteed on-campus for all undergraduates. Coed dorms, single-sex dorms, special housing for disabled, apartments, wellness housing available. $200 nonrefundable deposit, deadline 5/1. Special dormitories available for non-traditional full-time students. **Activities:** Bands, campus ministries, choral groups, dance, drama, film society, literary magazine, music ensembles, musical theater, radio station, student government, student newspaper, TV station, charitable society, Habitat for Humanity, Kairos Team, College Republicans, College Democrats,

peer ministry, Right to Life, volunteer corps, diversity coalition, St. Thomas Aquinas Catholic society.

**Athletics.** NCAA. **Intercollegiate:** Baseball M, basketball, cross-country, football (tackle) M, golf, soccer, softball W, tennis, track and field, volleyball W. **Intramural:** Basketball, football (non-tackle), soccer, softball, volleyball. **Team name:** Pumas.

**Student services.** Chaplain/spiritual director, career counseling, financial aid counseling, health services, personal counseling, placement for graduates.

**Contact.** E-mail: admissions@saintjoe.edu
Phone: (219) 866-6170 Toll-free number: (800) 447-8781
Fax: (219) 866-6122
John Wadell, Assistant VP Enrollment Management, Saint Joseph's College, Box 890, Rensselaer, IN 47978

---

## St. Mary-of-the-Woods College

| St. Mary-of-the-Woods, Indiana | CB member |
|---|---|
| www.smwc.edu | CB code: 1704 |

- Private 4-year liberal arts college for women affiliated with Roman Catholic Church
- Residential campus in rural community
- 1,274 degree-seeking undergraduates: 56% part-time, 96% women
- 212 degree-seeking graduate students
- 82% of applicants admitted
- SAT or ACT with writing, application essay required
- 60% graduate within 6 years

**General.** Founded in 1840. Regionally accredited. The traditional campus program open to women only. External degree (distance education) undergraduate program and graduate programs open to men and women. **Degrees:** 132 bachelor's, 5 associate awarded; master's offered. **ROTC:** Army, Air Force. **Location:** 4 miles from Terre Haute, 70 miles from Indianapolis. **Calendar:** Semester, extensive summer session. **Full-time faculty:** 63 total; 59% have terminal degrees, 5% minority, 68% women. **Part-time faculty:** 73 total; 8% have terminal degrees, 1% minority, 80% women. **Class size:** 93% < 20, 7% 20-39. **Special facilities:** Equine indoor and outdoor arenas, wildlife habitat restoration areas.

**Freshman class profile.** 249 applied, 204 admitted, 90 enrolled.

| Mid 50% test scores | | | |
|---|---|---|---|
| SAT critical reading: | 430-540 | GPA 3.0-3.49: | 45% |
| SAT math: | 410-520 | GPA 2.0-2.99: | 27% |
| SAT writing: | 410-550 | End year in good standing: | 95% |
| ACT composite: | 18-25 | Return as sophomores: | 74% |
| GPA 3.75 or higher: | 20% | Out-of-state: | 25% |
| GPA 3.50-3.74: | 8% | Live on campus: | 70% |

**Basis for selection.** School achievement record, test scores most important. Recommendations, evaluation of potential for college success considered. Interview recommended. Audition required of music majors. Portfolio required of art and journalism majors. **Learning Disabled:** Meeting with Learning Resource Coordinator strongly recommended.

**High school preparation.** College-preparatory program required. 13 units required; 16 recommended. Required and recommended units include English 4, mathematics 3, social studies 3, science 3 (laboratory 3) and foreign language 2.

**2009-2010 Annual costs.** Tuition/fees: $23,060. Room/board: $8,450. Books/supplies: $1,500. Personal expenses: $1,000.

**2008-2009 Financial aid. Need-based:** 66% of total undergraduate aid awarded as scholarships/grants, 34% as loans/jobs. **Non-need-based:** Scholarships awarded for academics, alumni affiliation, art, athletics, leadership, minority status, music/drama, state residency. **Additional information:** Portfolio or audition required of applicants who wish to be considered for Creative Arts Scholarship.

**Application procedures. Admission:** Closing date 8/15 (receipt date). $30 fee, may be waived for applicants with need, free for online applicants. Admission notification on a rolling basis beginning on or about 10/1. Must reply by 5/1. **Financial aid:** Priority date 3/1; no closing date. FAFSA required. Applicants notified on a rolling basis starting 12/1; must reply within 6 week(s) of notification.

**Academics.** Distance education program available in over 20 majors. **Special study options:** Accelerated study, cross-registration, distance learning, double major, external degree, honors, independent study, internships, student-designed major, study abroad, teacher certification program, weekend college. Woods' External Degree Program: students throughout country visit campus 1 or 2 days twice a year and do course work at home. Exchange program with Providence University in Taiwan. Agreement with Regent's College, London. **Credit/placement by examination:** AP, CLEP, IB, SAT, ACT, institutional tests. 30 credit hours maximum toward associate degree, 60 toward bachelor's. We follow ACE guidelines for the awarding of credit by testing. **Support services:** Learning center, reduced course load, study skills assistance, tutoring, writing center.

**Honors college/program.** 1100 SAT, 24 ACT, 3.5 GPA, teacher recommendation and excellent writing skills required; 11 students admitted in Fall 2009.

**Majors. Agriculture:** Animal husbandry, equestrian studies, equine science. **Biology:** General. **Business:** General, accounting, business admin, communications, e-commerce, human resources, marketing, nonprofit/public. **Communications:** Journalism, media studies, public relations. **Communications technology:** General, graphics. **Computer sciences:** General, web page design. **Education:** General, art, biology, early childhood, elementary, English, foreign languages, kindergarten/preschool, mathematics, music, science, secondary, social science, social studies, Spanish, special. **Health:** Music therapy, predental, premedicine, prepharmacy, preveterinary. **Interdisciplinary:** Biological/physical sciences. **Legal studies:** Paralegal, pre-law. **Liberal arts:** Arts/sciences, humanities. **Math:** General. **Psychology:** General. **Public administration:** Human services. **Social sciences:** General, criminology. **Theology:** Theology. **Visual/performing arts:** Art, design, dramatic, graphic design, photography. **Other:** Women and theatre.

**Most popular majors.** Agriculture 6%, biology 6%, business/marketing 12%, education 37%, psychology 9%, visual/performing arts 8%.

**Computing on campus.** 90 workstations in dormitories, library, computer center, student center. Dormitories wired for high-speed internet access and linked to campus network. Commuter students can connect to campus network. Online library, helpline, wireless network available.

**Student life. Freshman orientation:** Mandatory. Preregistration for classes offered. 3-day program before classes start; requires service component. **Policies:** All students whose families do not live in contiguous county must live on-campus all 4 years. **Housing:** Guaranteed on-campus for all undergraduates. Wellness housing available. $100 nonrefundable deposit, deadline 8/15. **Activities:** Bands, campus ministries, choral groups, dance, drama, international student organizations, literary magazine, music ensembles, musical theater, student government, student newspaper, symphony orchestra, Habitat for Humanity, literacy volunteers, environmentalist activities, peace and justice committee, arts and issues committee, Race-for-the-Cure, United Way.

**Athletics.** USCAA. **Intercollegiate:** Basketball W, cross-country W, equestrian W, golf W, soccer W, softball W. **Team name:** Pomeroys.

**Student services.** Adult student services, alcohol/substance abuse counseling, chaplain/spiritual director, career counseling, student employment services, financial aid counseling, health services, on-campus daycare, personal counseling, placement for graduates. **Physically disabled:** Services for visually, hearing impaired.

**Contact.** E-mail: smwcadms@smwc.edu
Phone: (812) 535-5106 Toll-free number: (800) 926-7692
Fax: (812) 535-5010
Aaron Kelley, Director of Admission, St. Mary-of-the-Woods College, Rooney Library, SMWC, St. Mary of the Woods, IN 47876

---

## Saint Mary's College

Notre Dame, Indiana
www.saintmarys.edu

CB member
CB code: 1702

◆ Private 4-year liberal arts college for women affiliated with Roman Catholic Church

◆ Residential campus in small city

◆ 1,640 degree-seeking undergraduates: 100% women, 1% African American, 1% Asian American, 7% Hispanic American, 1% international

◆ 86% of applicants admitted

◆ SAT or ACT with writing, application essay required

◆ 78% graduate within 6 years; 33% enter graduate study

**General.** Founded in 1844. Regionally accredited. Campus in Rome, Italy and programs in Ireland, India, Spain, France and Australia. Summer European study tour. Co-exchange enrollment with the University of Notre Dame. Volunteer service opportunities in the United States and abroad. **Degrees:** 337 bachelor's awarded. **ROTC:** Army, Naval, Air Force. **Location:** 3 miles

from South Bend. **Calendar:** Semester, limited summer session. **Full-time faculty:** 129 total; 88% have terminal degrees, 8% minority, 65% women. **Part-time faculty:** 62 total; 31% have terminal degrees, 3% minority, 76% women. **Class size:** 57% < 20, 40% 20-39, less than 1% 40-49, 2% 50-99. **Special facilities:** Nature trail, performing arts center, greenhouse, galleries.

**Freshman class profile.** 1,357 applied, 1,162 admitted, 435 enrolled.

| Mid 50% test scores | | | |
|---|---|---|---|
| SAT critical reading: | 510-620 | GPA 2.0-2.99: | 4% |
| SAT math: | 510-600 | Rank in top quarter: | 58% |
| SAT writing: | 510-620 | Rank in top tenth: | 38% |
| ACT composite: | 23-28 | End year in good standing: | 94% |
| GPA 3.75 or higher: | 48% | Return as sophomores: | 87% |
| GPA 3.50-3.74: | 22% | Out-of-state: | 69% |
| GPA 3.0-3.49: | 26% | Live on campus: | 97% |
| | | International: | 1% |

**Basis for selection.** School achievement record, high school transcript, GPA, test scores, activities important. Essay, class rank, school recommendations considered. Students must submit at least one writing component; ACT with Writing required if applicant is not also taking SAT (with mandatory Writing); ACT with Writing recommended even if applicant is also taking SAT. Interview recommended. Audition recommended for music majors. Portfolio recommended for art majors. **Homeschooled:** Statement describing homeschool structure and mission required. Students are encouraged to apply. Candidate should contact the Admission Office for details.

**High school preparation.** College-preparatory program recommended. 16 units required; 20 recommended. Required and recommended units include English 4, mathematics 3-4, history 2, science 2-4 (laboratory 2), foreign language 2-4 and academic electives 2. Science and nursing programs require more science and math. All students must take additional 4 units distributed among English, math, science, foreign language, and social studies.

**2010-2011 Annual costs.** Tuition/fees: $31,020. Room/board: $9,480. Books/supplies: $1,200. Personal expenses: $1,000.

**2009-2010 Financial aid. Need-based:** 356 full-time freshmen applied for aid; 312 were judged to have need; 311 of these received aid. Average need met was 82%. Average scholarship/grant was $20,093; average loan $3,493. 66% of total undergraduate aid awarded as scholarships/grants, 34% as loans/jobs. **Non-need-based:** Awarded to 1,206 full-time undergraduates, including 333 freshmen. Scholarships awarded for academics, art.

**Application procedures. Admission:** Priority date 2/15; no deadline. $30 fee, may be waived for applicants with need, free for online applicants. Admission notification on a rolling basis beginning on or about 1/1. $400 housing deposit refunded if letter sent in by May 1. Housing deposit nonrefundable for early decision. **Financial aid:** Priority date 3/1; no closing date. FAFSA, CSS PROFILE required. Applicants notified on a rolling basis starting 12/15.

**Academics.** Department of Religious Studies coordinated with Department of Theology at University of Notre Dame. After first year, student can take courses in either department. **Special study options:** Accelerated study, combined bachelor's/graduate degree, cross-registration, double major, exchange student, independent study, internships, liberal arts/career combination, student-designed major, study abroad, teacher certification program, Washington semester. **Credit/placement by examination:** AP, CLEP, IB, institutional tests. 30 credit hours maximum toward bachelor's degree. **Support services:** Reduced course load, study skills assistance, tutoring, writing center.

**Majors. Biology:** General. **Business:** Accounting, business admin, management information systems. **Communications:** General. **Education:** Elementary. **Foreign languages:** French, Italian, Spanish. **Health:** Communication disorders, nursing (RN). **History:** General. **Interdisciplinary:** Math/computer science. **Liberal arts:** Humanities. **Math:** General, applied, statistics. **Philosophy/religion:** Philosophy, religion. **Physical sciences:** Chemistry. **Psychology:** General. **Public administration:** Social work. **Social sciences:** Economics, political science, sociology. **Visual/performing arts:** Art, dramatic, studio arts.

**Most popular majors.** Biology 8%, business/marketing 11%, communications/journalism 11%, education 10%, English 7%, health sciences 11%, history 7%, psychology 7%, social sciences 7%, visual/performing arts 6%.

**Computing on campus.** 288 workstations in dormitories, library, computer center, student center. Dormitories wired for high-speed internet access and linked to campus network. Commuter students can connect to campus network. Online course registration, online library, helpline, student web hosting, wireless network available.

**Student life. Freshman orientation:** Mandatory. Preregistration for classes offered. Held weekend prior to beginning of fall semester. Summer orientation sessions held for fall admits during June. **Policies:** Educational judicial system guaranteeing certain due process rights to all students involved in discipline situation; student judicial board provides opportunity for peer review system. **Housing:** Guaranteed on-campus for all undergraduates. Apartments available. $400 fully refundable deposit, deadline 5/1. Intercultural living floor. **Activities:** Bands, campus ministries, choral groups, dance, drama, international student organizations, literary magazine, music ensembles, musical theater, opera, radio station, student government, student newspaper, TV station, Neighborhood study help program, Community of International Lay Apostolate, Urban Plunge community program, Circle-K, World Hunger Coalition, Student Alliance for Women's Colleges, Right to Life, Women for the Environment, Sisters of Nefertiti, Fuerza y Union Entre las Razas.

**Athletics.** NCAA. **Intercollegiate:** Basketball W, cross-country W, diving W, golf W, soccer W, softball W, swimming W, tennis W, volleyball W. **Intramural:** Soccer W, softball W, tennis W, volleyball W. **Team name:** Belles.

**Student services.** Adult student services, chaplain/spiritual director, career counseling, student employment services, financial aid counseling, health services, minority student services, on-campus daycare, personal counseling, placement for graduates, women's services. **Physically disabled:** Services for visually, hearing impaired.

**Contact.** E-mail: admission@saintmarys.edu
Phone: (574) 284-4587 Toll-free number: (800) 551-7621
Fax: (574) 284-4841
Mona Bowe, Director of Admission, Saint Mary's College, Notre Dame, IN 46556-5001

## Taylor University
Upland, Indiana
www.taylor.edu
CB member
CB code: 1802

- Private 4-year university and liberal arts college affiliated with interdenominational tradition
- Residential campus in small town
- 1,938 degree-seeking undergraduates: 3% part-time, 55% women, 2% African American, 3% Asian American, 2% Hispanic American, 3% international
- 123 degree-seeking graduate students
- 83% of applicants admitted
- SAT or ACT (ACT writing recommended), application essay required
- 77% graduate within 6 years; 15% enter graduate study

**General.** Founded in 1846. Regionally accredited. Christ-centered, covenant community committed to service. **Degrees:** 422 bachelor's, 1 associate awarded; master's offered. **Location:** 20 miles from Muncie, 70 miles from Indianapolis. **Calendar:** 4-1-4, limited summer session. **Full-time faculty:** 129 total; 80% have terminal degrees, 6% minority, 26% women. **Part-time faculty:** 117 total; 3% minority, 45% women. **Class size:** 59% <20, 33% 20-39, 4% 40-49, 3% 50-99, less than 1% >100. **Special facilities:** Arboretum, environmental studies laboratory, NASA-approved clean room, particle accelerator, NASA project space research equipment, C.S. Lewis Collection of original manuscripts.

**Freshman class profile.** 1,975 applied, 1,643 admitted, 486 enrolled.

| Mid 50% test scores | | | |
|---|---|---|---|
| SAT critical reading: | 500-650 | GPA 2.0-2.99: | 10% |
| SAT math: | 510-640 | Rank in top quarter: | 66% |
| SAT writing: | 490-620 | Rank in top tenth: | 41% |
| ACT composite: | 24-31 | End year in good standing: | 89% |
| GPA 3.75 or higher: | 49% | Return as sophomores: | 85% |
| GPA 3.50-3.74: | 19% | Out-of-state: | 65% |
| GPA 3.0-3.49: | 22% | Live on campus: | 97% |
| | | International: | 3% |

**Basis for selection.** High school transcript, test scores important. Recommend rank in top 25% of graduating class with 3.3 GPA and 1000 SAT (exclusive of Writing). Recommendations from applicant's pastor and counselor required. Cocurricular activities considered. Audition required of music majors. Portfolio recommended for art majors. Interviews required for some financial and academic programs. **Homeschooled:** Letter of recommendation (nonparent) required.

**High school preparation.** College-preparatory program recommended. 15 units required. Required and recommended units include English 4, mathematics 3-4, social studies 2-3, science 3-4 (laboratory 3-4), foreign language 2, computer science 1, visual/performing arts 1 and academic electives 3.

**2009-2010 Annual costs.** Tuition/fees: $25,396. Room/board: $6,708. Books/supplies: $1,000. Personal expenses: $1,800.

**2009-2010 Financial aid. Need-based:** 400 full-time freshmen applied for aid; 312 were judged to have need; 312 of these received aid. Average need met was 75%. Average scholarship/grant was $13,910; average loan $4,429. 66% of total undergraduate aid awarded as scholarships/grants, 34% as loans/jobs. **Non-need-based:** Awarded to 633 full-time undergraduates, including 186 freshmen. Scholarships awarded for academics, alumni affiliation, art, athletics, leadership, minority status, music/drama, religious affiliation, state residency.

**Application procedures. Admission:** No deadline. $25 fee, may be waived for applicants with need, free for online applicants. Admission notification on a rolling basis beginning on or about 10/1. Must reply by May 1 or within 2 week(s) if notified thereafter. **Financial aid:** Closing date 3/10. FAFSA required. Applicants notified on a rolling basis starting 3/1; must reply by 5/1.

**Academics. Special study options:** Combined bachelor's/graduate degree, cooperative education, distance learning, double major, dual enrollment of high school students, exchange student, honors, independent study, internships, semester at sea, student-designed major, study abroad, teacher certification program, urban semester, Washington semester. **Credit/placement by examination:** AP, CLEP, IB, institutional tests. 30 credit hours maximum toward associate degree, 30 toward bachelor's. **Support services:** Learning center, remedial instruction, study skills assistance, tutoring, writing center.

**Majors. Biology:** General. **Business:** Accounting, business admin, finance, international, managerial economics, marketing. **Communications:** General, media studies. **Computer sciences:** General. **Conservation:** Environmental science. **Education:** Art, elementary, English, French, mathematics, music, physical, science, social studies, Spanish. **Engineering:** Computer, environmental, physics. **Foreign languages:** French, Spanish. **History:** General. **Interdisciplinary:** Biological/physical sciences. **Math:** General, applied. **Parks/recreation:** Exercise sciences, sports admin. **Philosophy/religion:** Philosophy. **Physical sciences:** Chemistry, geology, physics. **Psychology:** General. **Public administration:** Social work. **Social sciences:** General, economics, geography, international economic development, international relations, political science, sociology. **Theology:** Bible, religious ed. **Visual/performing arts:** General, art, dramatic. **Other:** Chemistry-environmental science, Communication arts education, Computer science-new media, Environmental biology, Mathematics-environmental science, Media communication, Professional writing, Visual arts-new media, Wellness.

**Most popular majors.** Business/marketing 12%, communications/journalism 8%, education 14%, psychology 10%, social sciences 6%, theological studies 10%, visual/performing arts 9%.

**Computing on campus.** 339 workstations in library, computer center. Dormitories wired for high-speed internet access and linked to campus network. Commuter students can connect to campus network. Online course registration, online library, helpline, repair service, student web hosting, wireless network available.

**Student life. Freshman orientation:** Available. Preregistration for classes offered. **Policies:** Students and faculty sign Life Together Covenant explaining expectations and responsibilities of living in Christian community where faith is integrated with academic progress. Religious observance required. **Housing:** Guaranteed on-campus for freshmen. Single-sex dorms, apartments, wellness housing available. $200 deposit, deadline 5/1. Some off-campus apartments available to upperclassmen with special permission. **Activities:** Bands, choral groups, drama, film society, international student organizations, literary magazine, music ensembles, musical theater, opera, radio station, student government, student newspaper, symphony orchestra, TV station, missions service program, multicultural society, missionary kids organizations, community outreach, Campus Life/Young Life, international student society, Habitat for Humanity, ReaLife Inner City Children's Ministry, high school youth conference, Acting on AIDS.

**Athletics.** NAIA, NCCAA. **Intercollegiate:** Baseball M, basketball, cross-country, football (tackle) M, golf M, soccer, softball W, tennis, track and field, volleyball W. **Intramural:** Badminton, basketball, football (non-tackle), golf, racquetball, soccer, softball, table tennis, tennis, volleyball. **Team name:** Trojans.

**Student services.** Chaplain/spiritual director, career counseling, student employment services, financial aid counseling, health services, minority student services, personal counseling, placement for graduates. **Physically disabled:** Services for visually, speech, hearing impaired.

**Contact.** E-mail: admissions@tayloru.edu
Phone: (765) 998-5511 Toll-free number: (800) 882-3456
Fax: (765) 998-4925
Stephen Mortland, Dean of Enrollment Management, Taylor University, 236 West Reade Avenue, Upland, IN 46989-1001

## Trine University

**Angola, Indiana**
www.trine.edu

CB member
CB code: 1811

- Private 4-year university and engineering college
- Residential campus in small town
- 1,535 degree-seeking undergraduates: 4% part-time, 34% women, 4% African American, 1% Asian American, 2% Hispanic American, 3% international
- 8 degree-seeking graduate students
- 75% of applicants admitted
- SAT or ACT (ACT writing optional) required
- 46% graduate within 6 years; 35% enter graduate study

**General.** Founded in 1884. Regionally accredited. **Degrees:** 225 bachelor's, 15 associate awarded; master's offered. **ROTC:** Air Force. **Location:** 40 miles from Fort Wayne; 80 miles from Toledo, Ohio. **Calendar:** Semester, limited summer session. **Full-time faculty:** 72 total; 60% have terminal degrees, 12% minority, 26% women. **Part-time faculty:** 30 total; 17% have terminal degrees, 3% minority, 30% women. **Class size:** 46% < 20, 54% 20-39, less than 1% 40-49. **Special facilities:** Educational media resource center, 18 hole championship golf course, student-operated radio station.

**Freshman class profile.** 2,340 applied, 1,760 admitted, 458 enrolled.

| Mid 50% test scores | | | |
|---|---|---|---|
| SAT critical reading: | 440-570 | Rank in top quarter: | 48% |
| SAT math: | 490-600 | Rank in top tenth: | 22% |
| ACT composite: | 20-25 | End year in good standing: | 92% |
| GPA 3.75 or higher: | 23% | Return as sophomores: | 72% |
| GPA 3.50-3.74: | 14% | Out-of-state: | 38% |
| GPA 3.0-3.49: | 35% | Live on campus: | 90% |
| GPA 2.0-2.99: | 27% | Fraternities: | 5% |
| | | Sororities: | 1% |

**Basis for selection.** School achievement, class rank, test scores, school and community activities, and recommendations important. Interview and essay recommended. **Homeschooled:** Statement describing homeschool structure and mission, transcript of courses and grades required. **Learning Disabled:** Must submit clinical evaluation of learning disability (completed within last 5 years prior to enrollment).

**High school preparation.** College-preparatory program required. 18 units required. Required units include English 4, mathematics 3, social studies 3, science 3 (laboratory 2) and academic electives 3. 3 1/2 years of math, physics, and chemistry required for engineering, math and computer science majors.

**2009-2010 Annual costs.** Tuition/fees: $24,200. Room/board: $8,300. Books/supplies: $1,500. Personal expenses: $3,300.

**2009-2010 Financial aid. Non-need-based:** Scholarships awarded for academics, alumni affiliation, minority status, music/drama, ROTC.

**Application procedures. Admission:** Priority date 6/1; deadline 8/1. No application fee. Application must be submitted online. Admission notification 8/1. Admission notification on a rolling basis. Must reply by 5/1. **Financial aid:** Priority date 3/10, closing date 3/10. FAFSA required. Applicants notified on a rolling basis starting 2/15; must reply by 5/1 or within 2 week(s) of notification.

**Academics. Special study options:** Combined bachelor's/graduate degree, cooperative education, distance learning, double major, dual enrollment of high school students, ESL, honors, internships, study abroad, teacher certification program. **Credit/placement by examination:** AP, CLEP, IB, institutional tests. **Support services:** Learning center, reduced course load, remedial instruction, study skills assistance, tutoring, writing center.

**Majors. Biology:** General. **Business:** Accounting, business admin, entrepreneurial studies, finance, operations. **Communications:** General. **Computer sciences:** General, computer science. **Education:** Elementary, English, health, mathematics, middle, physical, science, social studies. **Engineering:** Chemical, civil, computer, electrical, mechanical. **Engineering technology:** Drafting. **Health:** Premedicine. **Math:** General. **Parks/recreation:** Health/fitness, sports admin. **Physical sciences:** Chemistry. **Protective services:** Criminal justice, forensics. **Psychology:** General. **Social sciences:** General.

**Most popular majors.** Business/marketing 23%, education 19%, engineering/engineering technologies 36%, parks/recreation 9%, security/protective services 10%.

**Computing on campus.** 150 workstations in dormitories, library, computer center, student center. Dormitories wired for high-speed internet access and linked to campus network. Commuter students can connect to campus network. Online library, helpline, wireless network available.

**Student life. Freshman orientation:** Mandatory. Preregistration for classes offered. Held 3 days at start of fall semester. **Housing:** Guaranteed on-campus for all undergraduates. Coed dorms, single-sex dorms, apartments available. $150 nonrefundable deposit, deadline 5/1. Honors housing; independent fraternity/sorority housing available. **Activities:** Bands, choral groups, dance, drama, international student organizations, music ensembles, radio station, student government, student newspaper, Circle K, Newman Fellowship, InterVarsity Christian Fellowship, Christian campus house, international student association, multicultural student association, Students Against Destructive Decisions, Habitat for Humanity, SPEAK (environmental/ecological concerns).

**Athletics.** NCAA. **Intercollegiate:** Baseball M, basketball, cross-country, football (tackle) M, golf, lacrosse, soccer, softball W, tennis, track and field, volleyball W, wrestling M. **Intramural:** Badminton, basketball, cheerleading, football (non-tackle) M, golf, handball, racquetball, softball, table tennis, volleyball. **Team name:** Thunder.

**Student services.** Alcohol/substance abuse counseling, chaplain/spiritual director, career counseling, student employment services, financial aid counseling, personal counseling, placement for graduates, veterans' counselor.

**Contact.** E-mail: admit@trine.edu
Phone: (260) 665-4100 Toll-free number: (800) 347-4878
Fax: (260) 665-4578
Scott Goplin, Dean of Admission, Trine University, One University Avenue, Angola, IN 46703

## University of Evansville

**Evansville, Indiana**
www.evansville.edu

CB member
CB code: 1208

- Private 4-year university and liberal arts college affiliated with United Methodist Church
- Residential campus in small city
- 2,549 degree-seeking undergraduates: 3% part-time, 59% women, 2% African American, 1% Asian American, 2% Hispanic American, 6% international
- 168 degree-seeking graduate students
- 86% of applicants admitted
- SAT or ACT with writing required
- 64% graduate within 6 years; 23% enter graduate study

**General.** Founded in 1854. Regionally accredited. **Degrees:** 498 bachelor's, 14 associate awarded; master's, professional offered. **Location:** 170 miles from Indianapolis and St. Louis. **Calendar:** Semester, limited summer session. **Full-time faculty:** 172 total; 87% have terminal degrees, 8% minority, 35% women. **Part-time faculty:** 49 total; 24% have terminal degrees, 47% women. **Class size:** 40% < 20, 46% 20-39, 9% 40-49, 5% 50-99, less than 1% >100.

**Freshman class profile.** 3,012 applied, 2,593 admitted, 701 enrolled.

| Mid 50% test scores | | | |
|---|---|---|---|
| SAT critical reading: | 510-610 | Rank in top quarter: | 70% |
| SAT math: | 510-630 | Rank in top tenth: | 38% |
| SAT writing: | 490-600 | Return as sophomores: | 79% |
| ACT composite: | 22-28 | Out-of-state: | 42% |
| GPA 3.75 or higher: | 52% | Live on campus: | 89% |
| GPA 3.50-3.74: | 14% | International: | 2% |
| GPA 3.0-3.49: | 20% | Fraternities: | 30% |
| GPA 2.0-2.99: | 14% | Sororities: | 20% |

**Basis for selection.** Weighted GPA calculated using academic courses only. Extracurricular activities important. Interview recommended. Essay required for Physical Therapy applicants. Audition required of music and theater majors. **Homeschooled:** Letter of recommendation (nonparent) required. **Learning Disabled:** Students requesting accommodations must provide documentation of the disability and the significant impact of the disability on academic functioning.

**High school preparation.** College-preparatory program required. 11 units required; 15 recommended. Required and recommended units include English 4, mathematics 3-4, social studies 1, history 1, science 2-3 (laboratory 2) and foreign language 2. One or more years of physics, additional chemistry and math, and 2 or more years of a foreign language recommended for engineering programs.

**2009-2010 Annual costs.** Tuition/fees: $26,756. Room/board: $8,670. Books/supplies: $1,000. Personal expenses: $954.

**2009-2010 Financial aid. Need-based:** 654 full-time freshmen applied for aid; 553 were judged to have need; 550 of these received aid. Average need met was 92%. Average scholarship/grant was $22,648; average loan $3,753. 76% of total undergraduate aid awarded as scholarships/grants, 24% as loans/jobs. **Non-need-based:** Awarded to 2,144 full-time undergraduates, including 665 freshmen. Scholarships awarded for academics, alumni affiliation, art, athletics, leadership, minority status, music/drama, religious affiliation, ROTC, state residency. **Additional information:** Early financial planning service allows prospective students to get free estimate of available aid.

**Application procedures. Admission:** Priority date 12/1; deadline 2/1 (postmark date). $35 fee, may be waived for applicants with need. Admission notification 2/15. Admission notification on a rolling basis. Must reply by 5/1. **Financial aid:** Priority date 3/10; no closing date. FAFSA required. Applicants notified on a rolling basis starting 3/25; must reply by 5/1.

**Academics. Special study options:** Accelerated study, cooperative education, double major, dual enrollment of high school students, ESL, external degree, honors, independent study, internships, semester at sea, student-designed major, study abroad, teacher certification program, Washington semester. British Campus at Harlaxton College, the Washington Center for Internships, and undergraduate research. **Credit/placement by examination:** AP, CLEP, IB, SAT, ACT, institutional tests. 6 credit hours maximum toward associate degree, 6 toward bachelor's. **Support services:** Pre-admission summer program, study skills assistance, tutoring, writing center.

**Majors. Biology:** General, biochemistry. **Business:** Accounting, business admin, finance, international, management information systems, managerial economics, marketing. **Computer sciences:** General. **Conservation:** Environmental science, environmental studies. **Education:** General, art, biology, chemistry, drama/dance, elementary, English, French, German, mathematics, music, physical, physics, social science, social studies, Spanish, special. **Engineering:** Civil, computer, electrical, mechanical. **Foreign languages:** Classics, French, German, Spanish. **Health:** Athletic training, clinical lab science, health care admin, music therapy, nursing (RN), predental, premedicine, preveterinary. **History:** General. **Interdisciplinary:** Cognitive science, neuroscience. **Liberal arts:** Arts/sciences. **Math:** General, applied. **Parks/recreation:** Exercise sciences, sports admin. **Philosophy/religion:** Philosophy. **Physical sciences:** Chemistry, physics. **Psychology:** General. **Social sciences:** Archaeology, economics, international relations, political science, sociology. **Theology:** Bible, theology. **Visual/performing arts:** Art, art history/conservation, design, dramatic, music management, music performance, theater arts management. **Other:** Communication and media studies, Legal professions.

**Most popular majors.** Business/marketing 15%, education 9%, engineering/engineering technologies 7%, health sciences 8%, parks/recreation 8%, social sciences 9%, visual/performing arts 11%.

**Computing on campus.** 385 workstations in dormitories, library, computer center, student center. Dormitories wired for high-speed internet access and linked to campus network. Commuter students can connect to campus network. Online library, helpline, repair service, student web hosting, wireless network available.

**Student life. Freshman orientation:** Mandatory. Preregistration for classes offered. Two programs available: one in summer includes testing, advising, and registration; another 3 1/2 day program held prior to beginning of semester. **Housing:** Guaranteed on-campus for freshmen. Coed dorms, single-sex dorms, apartments, fraternity/sorority housing available. $100 partly refundable deposit, deadline 5/1. Honors program housing, global living and learning community. **Activities:** Bands, campus ministries, choral groups, dance, drama, film society, international student organizations, literary magazine, music ensembles, Model UN, musical theater, opera, radio station, student government, student newspaper, symphony orchestra, black student union, Hillel, Kappa Chi (service), Amnesty International, Habitat for Humanity, Circle K, College Democrats, College Republicans.

**Athletics.** NCAA. **Intercollegiate:** Baseball M, basketball, cross-country, diving, golf, soccer, softball W, swimming, tennis W, volleyball W. **Intramural:** Badminton, basketball, bowling, cross-country, diving, football (non-tackle), golf, racquetball, soccer, softball, swimming, table tennis, tennis, volleyball. **Team name:** Purple Aces.

**Student services.** Adult student services, alcohol/substance abuse counseling, chaplain/spiritual director, career counseling, student employment services, financial aid counseling, health services, minority student services, personal counseling, placement for graduates, veterans' counselor. **Physically disabled:** Services for visually, speech, hearing impaired.

**Contact.** E-mail: admission@evansville.edu
Phone: (812) 488-2468 Toll-free number: (800) 423-8633 ext. 2468
Fax: (812) 488-4076
Don Vos, Dean of Admissions, University of Evansville, 1800 Lincoln Avenue, Evansville, IN 47722

## University of Indianapolis
**Indianapolis, Indiana**　　　　　　　**CB member**
**www.uindy.edu**　　　　　　　　　**CB code: 1321**

- Private 4-year university and liberal arts college affiliated with United Methodist Church
- Residential campus in very large city
- 3,734 degree-seeking undergraduates: 23% part-time, 67% women, 11% African American, 1% Asian American, 2% Hispanic American, 5% international
- 1,163 degree-seeking graduate students
- 80% of applicants admitted
- SAT or ACT (ACT writing optional) required
- 50% graduate within 6 years

**General.** Founded in 1902. Regionally accredited. **Degrees:** 619 bachelor's, 74 associate awarded; master's, doctoral offered. **ROTC:** Army. **Location:** 5 miles from downtown. **Calendar:** Semester, limited summer session. **Full-time faculty:** 205 total. **Class size:** 58% < 20, 41% 20-39, 1% 40-49, less than 1% 50-99. **Special facilities:** Observatory, fine arts center.

**Freshman class profile.** 3,944 applied, 3,151 admitted, 743 enrolled.

| Mid 50% test scores | | | | |
|---|---|---|---|---|
| SAT critical reading: | 450-560 | GPA 3.0-3.49: | 32% |
| SAT math: | 460-570 | GPA 2.0-2.99: | 26% |
| SAT writing: | 440-550 | Rank in top quarter: | 59% |
| ACT composite: | 19-25 | Rank in top tenth: | 26% |
| GPA 3.75 or higher: | 25% | Return as sophomores: | 73% |
| GPA 3.50-3.74: | 17% | Out-of-state: | 7% |
| | | Live on campus: | 78% |

**Basis for selection.** Recommendations, GPA, SAT/ACT scores, class rank important. Involvement in extracurricular activities considered. Essay recommended. Interview recommended for borderline applicants. Audition required of music majors. Portfolio recommended for art majors. **Home-schooled:** Transcript of courses and grades required. **Learning Disabled:** Students with learning disabilities may apply to the BUILD program through separate application process.

**High school preparation.** 15 units required; 18 recommended. Required and recommended units include English 4, mathematics 3-4, social studies 1, history 1, science 2-3 (laboratory 1-2), foreign language 2 and academic electives 1-3.

**2009-2010 Annual costs.** Tuition/fees: $21,170. Room/board: $8,040. Books/supplies: $1,000. Personal expenses: $1,520.

**2009-2010 Financial aid. Non-need-based:** Scholarships awarded for academics, alumni affiliation, art, athletics, job skills, leadership, music/drama, religious affiliation, state residency.

**Application procedures. Admission:** No deadline. $25 fee, may be waived for applicants with need, free for online applicants. Admission notification on a rolling basis beginning on or about 9/1. Must reply by May 1 or within 2 week(s) if notified thereafter. **Financial aid:** Priority date 3/10; no closing date. FAFSA, institutional form required. Applicants notified on a rolling basis starting 3/1; must reply within 3 week(s) of notification.

**Academics. Special study options:** Accelerated study, combined bachelor's/graduate degree, cross-registration, double major, dual enrollment of high school students, ESL, honors, independent study, internships, liberal arts/career combination, student-designed major, study abroad, teacher certification program. Baccalaureate for University of Indianapolis Learning Disabled (BUILD). **Credit/placement by examination:** AP, CLEP, IB, SAT, ACT, institutional tests. 3-8 hours awarded for International Baccalaureate based on scores. **Support services:** Learning center, pre-admission summer program, reduced course load, remedial instruction, study skills assistance, tutoring, writing center.

**Majors. Biology:** General, cell/histology. **Business:** Accounting, business admin, international, management information systems, managerial economics, marketing, tourism/travel. **Communications:** General. **Computer sciences:** General, computer science, information systems. **Education:** General, art, biology, business, chemistry, elementary, English, foreign languages, French, history, mathematics, music, physical, physics, science, secondary, social studies, Spanish, speech. **Foreign languages:** French, German, Spanish. **Health:** Art therapy, athletic training, clinical lab technology, nursing

(RN), respiratory therapy technology. **History:** General. **Math:** General. **Parks/recreation:** Exercise sciences, sports admin. **Philosophy/religion:** Philosophy, religion. **Physical sciences:** Chemistry, geology, physics. **Protective services:** Law enforcement admin. **Psychology:** General. **Public administration:** Social work. **Social sciences:** Anthropology, archaeology, economics, international relations, political science, sociology. **Visual/performing arts:** Art, commercial/advertising art, design, dramatic, music performance.

**Most popular majors.** Biology 6%, business/marketing 29%, education 12%, health sciences 15%, liberal arts 7%, psychology 7%.

**Computing on campus.** 222 workstations in dormitories, library, computer center, student center. Dormitories wired for high-speed internet access and linked to campus network. Commuter students can connect to campus network. Online library, helpline, wireless network available.

**Student life. Freshman orientation:** Mandatory, $40 fee. Preregistration for classes offered. Student attends one of 6 summer registration programs. **Housing:** Coed dorms, single-sex dorms, apartments, wellness housing available. $50 partly refundable deposit, deadline 5/1. **Activities:** Bands, campus ministries, choral groups, dance, drama, literary magazine, music ensembles, musical theater, opera, radio station, student government, student newspaper, TV station, Young Democrats, Young Republicans, Fellowship of Christian Athletes, Circle-K, social service, honorary societies.

**Athletics.** NCAA. **Intercollegiate:** Baseball M, basketball, cross-country, diving, football (tackle) M, golf, soccer, softball W, swimming, tennis, track and field, volleyball W, wrestling M. **Intramural:** Basketball, football (nontackle) M, soccer, softball, volleyball. **Team name:** Greyhounds.

**Student services.** Adult student services, chaplain/spiritual director, career counseling, student employment services, health services, personal counseling, placement for graduates, veterans' counselor. **Physically disabled:** Services for visually, speech, hearing impaired. **Learning disabled:** Comprehensive services available.

**Contact.** E-mail: admissions@uindy.edu
Phone: (317) 788-3216 Toll-free number: (800) 232-8634
Fax: (317) 788-3300
Ron Wilks, Director of Admissions, University of Indianapolis, 1400 East Hanna Avenue, Indianapolis, IN 46227-3697

## University of Notre Dame
**Notre Dame, Indiana**
www.nd.edu
**CB member**
**CB code: 1841**

- Private 4-year university affiliated with Roman Catholic Church
- Residential campus in small city
- 8,367 degree-seeking undergraduates: 46% women, 4% African American, 7% Asian American, 10% Hispanic American, 1% Native American, 3% international
- 3,250 degree-seeking graduate students
- 29% of applicants admitted
- SAT or ACT (ACT writing optional), application essay required

**General.** Founded in 1842. Regionally accredited. Notre Dame Study Centers in Washington, DC; Dublin, Ireland; London, England; Rome, Italy; several other countries. **Degrees:** 2,102 bachelor's awarded; master's, doctoral, professional offered. **ROTC:** Army, Naval, Air Force. **Location:** 90 miles from Chicago. **Calendar:** Semester, extensive summer session. **Full-time faculty:** 947 total; 14% minority, 28% women. **Part-time faculty:** 108 total; 6% minority, 29% women. **Special facilities:** Germ-free research facility, radiation laboratory, nature preserve for biological research, wind-tunnel research facility, art museum.

**Freshman class profile.** 14,357 applied, 4,113 admitted, 2,064 enrolled.

| Mid 50% test scores | | ACT composite: | 31-34 |
|---|---|---|---|
| SAT critical reading: | 650-750 | Out-of-state: | 93% |
| SAT math: | 680-760 | Live on campus: | 100% |
| SAT writing: | 640-730 | International: | 3% |

**Basis for selection.** GED not accepted. Demonstrated academic achievement and test scores most important. Essay, teacher recommendations, extracurricular activities, and personal statement also important. Three SAT Subject Tests required for home schooled students. Audition recommended for music majors. Portfolio recommended for art majors.

**High school preparation.** College-preparatory program required. 16 units required; 20 recommended. Required and recommended units include English 4, mathematics 3-4, history 2-4, science 2-4 (laboratory 2), foreign language 2-4 and academic electives 3. Pre-calculus or calculus, chemistry

and physics recommended for architecture, engineering and science programs. Social studies requirement should include history.

**2009-2010 Annual costs.** Tuition/fees: $38,477. Room/board: $10,368. Books/supplies: $850. Personal expenses: $900.

**2009-2010 Financial aid. Non-need-based:** Scholarships awarded for athletics, ROTC.

**Application procedures. Admission:** Closing date 12/31 (postmark date). $65 fee, may be waived for applicants with need. Admission notification 4/10. Must reply by May 1 or within 2 week(s) if notified thereafter. **Financial aid:** Closing date 2/15. FAFSA, CSS PROFILE required. Applicants notified by 4/1; must reply by 5/1.

**Academics. Special study options:** Cross-registration, double major, dual enrollment of high school students, exchange student, honors, independent study, internships, liberal arts/career combination, student-designed major, study abroad, teacher certification program, Washington semester. Teacher certification available only through cross-registration with St. Mary's College; triple majors, quadruple majors, triple degrees, double majors within dual degrees. **Credit/placement by examination:** AP, CLEP, IB, institutional tests. Students with HL score of 6 or 7 eligible to receive credit in anthropology, biology, chemistry, English, French, German, Greek, American history, Latin, math, music, physics, psychology, and Spanish. **Support services:** Learning center, study skills assistance, tutoring, writing center.

**Majors. Architecture:** Architecture. **Area/ethnic studies:** African-American, American. **Biology:** General, biochemistry. **Business:** General, accounting, finance, management information systems, marketing. **Computer sciences:** General. **Conservation:** Environmental science. **Education:** Science. **Engineering:** Aerospace, chemical, civil, computer, electrical, environmental, mechanical. **Foreign languages:** Ancient Greek, Arabic, Chinese, classics, French, German, Italian, Japanese, Romance, Russian, Spanish. **Health:** Premedicine. **History:** General. **Interdisciplinary:** Biological/physical sciences, medieval/Renaissance. **Liberal arts:** Arts/sciences. **Math:** General. **Philosophy/religion:** Philosophy. **Physical sciences:** Chemistry, physics. **Psychology:** General. **Social sciences:** Anthropology, economics, political science, sociology. **Theology:** Theology. **Visual/performing arts:** Art history/conservation, design, dramatic, studio arts.

**Most popular majors.** Biology 6%, business/marketing 24%, engineering/engineering technologies 10%, psychology 6%, social sciences 16%.

**Computing on campus.** 261 workstations in dormitories, library, computer center, student center. Dormitories wired for high-speed internet access and linked to campus network. Commuter students can connect to campus network. Online course registration, helpline, repair service, wireless network available.

**Student life. Freshman orientation:** Mandatory. Preregistration for classes offered. **Housing:** Guaranteed on-campus for freshmen. Single-sex dorms available. $50 deposit, deadline 5/1. Requests for ground level housing or housing suitable for a disabled student will be honored. **Activities:** Bands, campus ministries, choral groups, dance, drama, film society, literary magazine, music ensembles, musical theater, opera, radio station, student government, student newspaper, symphony orchestra, More than 260 clubs and organizations available.

**Athletics.** NCAA. **Intercollegiate:** Baseball M, basketball, cross-country, diving, fencing, football (tackle) M, golf, ice hockey M, lacrosse, rowing (crew) W, soccer, softball W, swimming, tennis, track and field, volleyball W. **Intramural:** Badminton, baseball M, basketball, bowling, cross-country, football (non-tackle), football (tackle) M, golf, ice hockey M, lacrosse, racquetball, soccer, softball, table tennis, tennis, volleyball, water polo. **Team name:** Fighting Irish.

**Student services.** Alcohol/substance abuse counseling, chaplain/spiritual director, career counseling, student employment services, health services, minority student services, on-campus daycare, personal counseling, placement for graduates, women's services. **Physically disabled:** Services for visually, hearing impaired.

**Contact.** E-mail: admissions@nd.edu
Phone: (574) 631-7505 Fax: (574) 631-8865
Daniel Saracino, Director of Admissions, University of Notre Dame, 220 Main Building, Notre Dame, IN 46556

## University of St. Francis
**Fort Wayne, Indiana**
www.sf.edu
**CB code: 1693**

- Private 4-year university and liberal arts college affiliated with Roman Catholic Church
- Commuter campus in small city

- 1,780 degree-seeking undergraduates
- 50% of applicants admitted
- SAT or ACT (ACT writing optional) required

**General.** Founded in 1890. Regionally accredited. **Degrees:** 254 bachelor's, 150 associate awarded; master's offered. **Location:** 120 miles from Indianapolis, 150 miles from Chicago. **Calendar:** Semester, limited summer session. **Full-time faculty:** 115 total; 49% have terminal degrees, 5% minority, 61% women. **Part-time faculty:** 117 total; 9% have terminal degrees, 3% minority, 68% women. **Class size:** 60% < 20, 37% 20-39, 2% 40-49, 2% 50-99. **Special facilities:** Planetarium, nature preserve, cadaver lab.

**Freshman class profile.** 1,454 applied, 732 admitted, 312 enrolled.

| Mid 50% test scores | | | |
|---|---|---|---|
| SAT critical reading: | 430-550 | GPA 3.0-3.49: | 33% |
| SAT math: | 450-560 | GPA 2.0-2.99: | 28% |
| SAT writing: | 420-540 | Rank in top quarter: | 40% |
| ACT composite: | 19-24 | Rank in top tenth: | 14% |
| GPA 3.75 or higher: | 21% | Out-of-state: | 17% |
| GPA 3.50-3.74: | 16% | Live on campus: | 61% |

**Basis for selection.** School achievement record, rank in top half of class, and test scores most important. Additional requirements for health care majors, education majors. Admission procedures may vary among schools within the university. Essay and portfolio recommended. Interview recommended for underprepared applicants. **Homeschooled:** State high school equivalency certificate, letter of recommendation (nonparent) required. Bibliography of books read, extracurricular activities.

**High school preparation.** 20 units required; 26 recommended. Required and recommended units include English 4, mathematics 2-3, social studies 2-3, history 1, science 2-3 and academic electives 1-4.

**2009-2010 Annual costs.** Tuition/fees: $21,760. Room/board: $6,750. Books/supplies: $1,000. Personal expenses: $1,100.

**2008-2009 Financial aid.** **Need-based:** 301 full-time freshmen applied for aid; 259 were judged to have need; 259 of these received aid. Average need met was 80.72%. Average scholarship/grant was $13,010; average loan $3,181. 55% of total undergraduate aid awarded as scholarships/grants, 45% as loans/jobs. **Non-need-based:** Awarded to 459 full-time undergraduates, including 123 freshmen. Scholarships awarded for academics, alumni affiliation, art, athletics, music/drama.

**Application procedures.** **Admission:** Priority date 8/1; no deadline. $20 fee, may be waived for applicants with need, free for online applicants. Admission notification on a rolling basis beginning on or about 8/1. **Financial aid:** Priority date 3/10; no closing date. FAFSA required. Applicants notified on a rolling basis starting 3/1.

**Academics.** **Special study options:** Combined bachelor's/graduate degree, cross-registration, double major, dual enrollment of high school students, exchange student, honors, independent study, internships, liberal arts/career combination, teacher certification program. **Credit/placement by examination:** AP, CLEP, SAT, ACT, institutional tests. 16 credit hours maximum toward associate degree, 32 toward bachelor's. **Support services:** Learning center, reduced course load, remedial instruction, study skills assistance, tutoring, writing center.

**Majors.** **Area/ethnic studies:** American. **Business:** Accounting, business admin. **Communications:** General, public relations. **Conservation:** General, environmental studies. **Education:** Art, business, chemistry, elementary, English, health, science, social studies, special. **Health:** Clinical lab science, nursing (RN), physician assistant, predental, premedicine, prepharmacy. **History:** General. **Legal studies:** Prelaw. **Liberal arts:** Arts/sciences. **Math:** General. **Philosophy/religion:** Philosophy. **Physical sciences:** Chemistry, forensic chemistry. **Psychology:** General. **Public administration:** Social work. **Social sciences:** Political science, sociology. **Theology:** Theology. **Visual/performing arts:** Art, art history/conservation, commercial/advertising art, graphic design, studio arts.

**Most popular majors.** Business/marketing 14%, education 15%, health sciences 33%, interdisciplinary studies 6%, visual/performing arts 10%.

**Computing on campus.** 415 workstations in dormitories, library, computer center, student center. Dormitories wired for high-speed internet access and linked to campus network. Commuter students can connect to campus network. Online course registration, online library, helpline, repair service, wireless network available.

**Student life.** **Freshman orientation:** Mandatory, $32 fee. Three-day program held weekend prior to beginning of classes. **Policies:** No alcohol allowed in residence halls, no smoking in campus buildings. Full-time students under 21 not living at home or with adult relatives must live in residence halls. **Housing:** Guaranteed on-campus for freshmen. Coed dorms, apartments available. $200 fully refundable deposit. **Activities:** Bands, campus ministries, choral groups, dance, drama, film society, student government, student newspaper, Educators in Action, student nursing association, peer ministers, Fellowship of Christian Athletes.

**Athletics.** NAIA. **Intercollegiate:** Baseball M, basketball, cheerleading, cross-country, football (tackle) M, golf, soccer, softball W, tennis W, track and field, volleyball W. **Intramural:** Basketball, bowling, football (non-tackle), soccer, volleyball. **Team name:** Cougars.

**Student services.** Adult student services, chaplain/spiritual director, career counseling, student employment services, financial aid counseling, health services, personal counseling, placement for graduates. **Physically disabled:** Services for visually, hearing impaired.

**Contact.** E-mail: admiss@sf.edu
Phone: (260) 399-8000 Toll-free number: (800) 729-4732
Fax: (260) 434-7590
JP Spagnolo, Director of Admissions, University of St. Francis, 2701 Spring Street, Fort Wayne, IN 46808

## University of Southern Indiana
**Evansville, Indiana**
www.usi.edu
CB code: 1335

- Public 4-year university and liberal arts college
- Commuter campus in small city
- 9,442 degree-seeking undergraduates: 15% part-time, 58% women, 5% African American, 1% Asian American, 1% Hispanic American, 2% international
- 787 degree-seeking graduate students
- 88% of applicants admitted
- SAT or ACT (ACT writing recommended) required
- 37% graduate within 6 years

**General.** Founded in 1965. Regionally accredited. Credit courses offered at various off-campus sites in Evansville and surrounding areas. **Degrees:** 1,288 bachelor's, 113 associate awarded; master's, doctoral offered. **ROTC:** Army. **Location:** 150 miles from Indianapolis. **Calendar:** Semester, limited summer session. **Full-time faculty:** 338 total; 64% have terminal degrees, 6% minority, 54% women. **Part-time faculty:** 330 total; 19% have terminal degrees, 4% minority, 58% women. **Class size:** 36% < 20, 53% 20-39, 6% 40-49, 3% 50-99, 2% >100. **Special facilities:** Restored historic town managed by university.

**Freshman class profile.** 5,324 applied, 4,694 admitted, 2,093 enrolled.

| Mid 50% test scores | | | |
|---|---|---|---|
| SAT critical reading: | 420-530 | Rank in top quarter: | 31% |
| SAT math: | 430-540 | Rank in top tenth: | 12% |
| SAT writing: | 410-510 | End year in good standing: | 77% |
| ACT composite: | 18-23 | Return as sophomores: | 68% |
| GPA 3.75 or higher: | 12% | Out-of-state: | 8% |
| GPA 3.50-3.74: | 12% | Live on campus: | 62% |
| GPA 3.0-3.49: | 29% | International: | 1% |
| GPA 2.0-2.99: | 43% | Fraternities: | 5% |
| | | Sororities: | 3% |

**Basis for selection.** 2.0 GPA required for out-of-state applicants. 900 SAT (exclusive of Writing) required for applicants to health programs. Students accepted at 1 of 3 levels based on academic record and test scores. Placement test administered prior to registration. SAT/ACT used to place students at 1 of 3 levels within institution. **Homeschooled:** Transcript of courses and grades required.

**High school preparation.** College-preparatory program recommended. 18 units recommended. Recommended units include English 4, mathematics 4, social studies 2, history 2, science 2, foreign language 2 and academic electives 2. 2 units computer and/or art recommended.

**2009-2010 Annual costs.** Tuition/fees: $5,480; $12,770 out-of-state. Room/board: $6,750. Books/supplies: $1,000. Personal expenses: $2,800.

**2009-2010 Financial aid.** **Need-based:** 1,876 full-time freshmen applied for aid; 1,329 were judged to have need; 1,321 of these received aid. Average need met was 80%. Average scholarship/grant was $4,887; average loan $2,886. 39% of total undergraduate aid awarded as scholarships/grants, 61% as loans/jobs. **Non-need-based:** Awarded to 1,188 full-time undergraduates, including 385 freshmen. Scholarships awarded for academics, art, athletics, leadership, music/drama, state residency.

**Application procedures.** **Admission:** Closing date 8/15 (receipt date). $25 fee, may be waived for applicants with need. Admission notification on a rolling basis beginning on or about 7/1. Applicants accepted through first week of classes, but encouraged to apply by August 15 for fall and January 1 for spring. **Financial aid:** Closing date 3/1. FAFSA, institutional form required. Applicants notified on a rolling basis starting 3/15.

**Academics. Special study options:** Combined bachelor's/graduate degree, cooperative education, distance learning, double major, dual enrollment of high school students, ESL, honors, independent study, internships, study abroad, teacher certification program. **Credit/placement by examination:** AP, CLEP, SAT, ACT, institutional tests. 96 credit hours maximum toward bachelor's degree. **Support services:** Learning center, reduced course load, remedial instruction, study skills assistance, tutoring, writing center.

**Majors. Biology:** General, biophysics. **Business:** General, accounting, business admin, entrepreneurial studies, finance, marketing, office management, operations. **Communications:** Advertising, journalism, media studies, radio/tv. **Computer sciences:** General, data processing. **Education:** Business, early childhood, elementary, physical. **Engineering:** General. **Engineering technology:** Manufacturing. **Foreign languages:** French, German, Spanish. **Health:** Dental hygiene, health care admin, nursing (RN). **History:** General. **Interdisciplinary:** Biological/physical sciences, nutrition sciences. **Liberal arts:** Arts/sciences. **Math:** General. **Parks/recreation:** Exercise sciences. **Philosophy/religion:** Philosophy. **Physical sciences:** Chemistry, geology. **Protective services:** Criminal justice. **Psychology:** General. **Public administration:** Social work. **Social sciences:** General, economics, international relations, political science, sociology. **Visual/performing arts:** Art, dramatic.

**Most popular majors.** Business/marketing 21%, communications/journalism 10%, education 11%, health sciences 25%, social sciences 7%.

**Computing on campus.** 306 workstations in dormitories, library, computer center, student center. Dormitories linked to campus network. Commuter students can connect to campus network. Online course registration, online library, helpline, wireless network available.

**Student life. Freshman orientation:** Mandatory, $65 fee. Preregistration for classes offered. Two-day program, includes parent participation. **Housing:** Coed dorms, special housing for disabled, apartments, fraternity/sorority housing, wellness housing available. $200 partly refundable deposit, deadline 3/1. **Activities:** Bands, campus ministries, choral groups, dance, drama, international student organizations, literary magazine, Model UN, radio station, student government, student newspaper, black student union, Habitat for Humanity, Kappa Chi (Christian service fraternity), Baptist student ministry, Newman Catholic student organization, Collegiate Democrats, Collegiate Republicans.

**Athletics.** NCAA. **Intercollegiate:** Baseball M, basketball, cheerleading, cross-country, golf, soccer, softball W, tennis, track and field, volleyball W. **Intramural:** Badminton, basketball, bowling, cross-country, football (non-tackle), golf, soccer, softball, swimming, table tennis, tennis, volleyball. **Team name:** Screaming Eagles.

**Student services.** Adult student services, chaplain/spiritual director, career counseling, student employment services, financial aid counseling, health services, minority student services, on-campus daycare, personal counseling, placement for graduates, veterans' counselor. **Physically disabled:** Services for visually, speech, hearing impaired.

**Contact.** E-mail: enroll@usi.edu
Phone: (812) 464-1765 Toll-free number: (800) 467-1965
Fax: (812) 465-7154
Eric Otto, Director of Admission, University of Southern Indiana, 8600 University Boulevard, Evansville, IN 47712

## Valparaiso University
**Valparaiso, Indiana**
**www.valpo.edu**
**CB member**
**CB code: 1874**

 Private 4-year university affiliated with Lutheran Church
 Residential campus in large town
 2,823 degree-seeking undergraduates: 4% part-time, 52% women, 6% African American, 2% Asian American, 5% Hispanic American, 1% Native American, 3% international
 1,139 degree-seeking graduate students
 91% of applicants admitted
 SAT or ACT (ACT writing recommended), application essay required
 76% graduate within 6 years; 24% enter graduate study

**General.** Founded in 1859. Regionally accredited. **Degrees:** 622 bachelor's, 1 associate awarded; master's, doctoral, professional offered. **ROTC:** Army, Air Force. **Location:** 55 miles from Chicago. **Calendar:** Semester, limited summer session. **Full-time faculty:** 242 total; 92% have terminal degrees, 7% minority, 35% women. **Part-time faculty:** 114 total; 34% have terminal degrees, 12% minority, 56% women. **Class size:** 43% < 20, 48%

20-39, 3% 40-49, 4% 50-99, 1% >100. **Special facilities:** Electron microscope, observatory, storm chasing equipment, weather station, Doppler Radar facility, planetarium, center for learning and information resources, virtual nursing learning center, scientific visualization laboratory.

**Freshman class profile.** 2,932 applied, 2,674 admitted, 671 enrolled.

| Mid 50% test scores | | Rank in top quarter: | 58% |
|---|---|---|---|
| SAT critical reading: | 480-630 | Rank in top tenth: | 26% |
| SAT math: | 500-620 | End year in good standing: | 87% |
| SAT writing: | 480-610 | Return as sophomores: | 83% |
| ACT composite: | 22-29 | Out-of-state: | 62% |
| GPA 3.75 or higher: | 35% | Live on campus: | 88% |
| GPA 3.50-3.74: | 17% | International: | 2% |
| GPA 3.0-3.49: | 31% | Fraternities: | 26% |
| GPA 2.0-2.99: | 17% | Sororities: | 24% |

**Basis for selection.** High school record most important. Test scores next in importance, followed by recommendations and activities. Nature of high school program considered. Interview recommended. Audition required of music majors. Portfolio recommended for art majors. **Homeschooled:** Transcript of courses and grades required. Must specify primary educator and provide course description list or reading list. **Learning Disabled:** Student should submit suitable documentation to the Disability Support Services Office following admission into the University in order to determine eligibility of services.

**High school preparation.** College-preparatory program recommended. 16 units required; 19 recommended. Required and recommended units include English 4, mathematics 3-4, social studies 1, history 2, science 2-3 (laboratory 2-3), foreign language 2 and academic electives 3.

**2009-2010 Annual costs.** Tuition/fees: $28,320. Room/board: $7,960. Books/supplies: $1,200. Personal expenses: $890.

**2008-2009 Financial aid. Need-based:** 598 full-time freshmen applied for aid; 494 were judged to have need; 494 of these received aid. Average need met was 82%. Average scholarship/grant was $18,200; average loan $3,980. 70% of total undergraduate aid awarded as scholarships/grants, 30% as loans/jobs. **Non-need-based:** Awarded to 923 full-time undergraduates, including 219 freshmen. Scholarships awarded for academics, alumni affiliation, art, athletics, leadership, music/drama, religious affiliation, ROTC, state residency. **Additional information:** Financial assistance based on need, academic record, talent available through university.

**Application procedures. Admission:** Priority date 1/15; deadline 8/15 (receipt date). $30 fee, may be waived for applicants with need, free for online applicants. Admission notification on a rolling basis beginning on or about 10/1. Must reply by May 1 or within 4 week(s) if notified thereafter. **Financial aid:** Priority date 3/1; no closing date. FAFSA required. Applicants notified on a rolling basis starting 3/1; must reply by 5/1.

**Academics. Special study options:** Accelerated study, combined bachelor's/graduate degree, cooperative education, cross-registration, distance learning, double major, ESL, exchange student, honors, independent study, internships, liberal arts/career combination, student-designed major, study abroad, teacher certification program, United Nations semester, urban semester, Washington semester. **Credit/placement by examination:** AP, CLEP, IB, institutional tests. **Support services:** Learning center, reduced course load, study skills assistance, tutoring, writing center.

**Honors college/program.** Approximately 80 students enroll per year in Christ College, the Honors College. Must demonstrate academic excellence in high school, intellectual curiosity, and leadership skills. Program integrates history, literature, philosophy, religion, and art.

**Majors. Area/ethnic studies:** American, East Asian. **Biology:** General, biochemistry. **Business:** Accounting, actuarial science, finance, international, management science, marketing. **Communications:** Journalism, media studies, organizational, public relations, radio/tv. **Computer sciences:** Computer science. **Conservation:** Environmental science. **Education:** Art, biology, chemistry, drama/dance, elementary, English, foreign languages, French, geography, German, history, mathematics, middle, music, physical, physics, psychology, science, secondary, social science, Spanish. **Engineering:** Civil, computer, electrical, mechanical. **Foreign languages:** Classics, French, German, Spanish. **Health:** Nursing (RN). **History:** General. **Liberal arts:** Humanities. **Math:** General. **Parks/recreation:** Exercise sciences, health/fitness, sports admin. **Philosophy/religion:** Philosophy. **Physical sciences:** Astronomy, atmospheric science, chemistry, geology, physics. **Psychology:** General. **Public administration:** Social work. **Social sciences:** General, criminology, economics, geography, international economics, international relations, political science, sociology. **Theology:** Sacred music, theology. **Visual/performing arts:** Art, dramatic, music performance, music theory/composition, piano/organ, voice/opera. **Other:** Communication and expressive arts, Economics and computer analysis.

**Most popular majors.** Business/marketing 14%, communications/journalism 6%, education 8%, engineering/engineering technologies 9%, health sciences 11%, physical sciences 6%, social sciences 10%.

**Computing on campus.** 900 workstations in dormitories, library, computer center, student center. Dormitories wired for high-speed internet access and linked to campus network. Commuter students can connect to campus network. Online course registration, helpline, student web hosting, wireless network available.

**Student life. Freshman orientation:** Available, $95 fee. Preregistration for classes offered. Overnight program held in June. **Housing:** Guaranteed on-campus for all undergraduates. Coed dorms, single-sex dorms, apartments, fraternity/sorority housing, wellness housing available. $100 fully refundable deposit, deadline 5/1. **Activities:** Bands, campus ministries, choral groups, dance, drama, film society, international student organizations, literary magazine, music ensembles, musical theater, radio station, student government, student newspaper, symphony orchestra, Alpha Phi Omega, InterVarsity Christian Fellowship, St. Teresa of Avila, Black Student Organization, Habitat for Humanity, Asian American Association, Latinos in Valparaiso for Excellence, College Democrats.

**Athletics.** NCAA. **Intercollegiate:** Baseball M, basketball, bowling W, cross-country, diving, football (tackle) M, golf, soccer, softball W, swimming, tennis, track and field, volleyball W. **Intramural:** Badminton, basketball, bowling, football (non-tackle), golf, racquetball, soccer, softball M, swimming, table tennis, tennis, volleyball. **Team name:** Crusaders.

**Student services.** Adult student services, alcohol/substance abuse counseling, chaplain/spiritual director, career counseling, student employment services, financial aid counseling, health services, legal services, minority student services, personal counseling, placement for graduates. **Physically disabled:** Services for visually impaired.

**Contact.** E-mail: undergrad.admissions@valpo.edu
Phone: (219) 464-5011 Toll-free number: (888) 468-2576
Fax: (219) 464-6898
David Fevig, Director of Admission, Valparaiso University, Kretzmann Hall, 1700 Chapel Drive, Valparaiso, IN 46383-6493

---

## Wabash College
**Crawfordsville, Indiana**  **CB member**
**www.wabash.edu**  **CB code: 1895**

- Private 4-year liberal arts college for men
- Residential campus in large town
- 874 degree-seeking undergraduates: 1% part-time, 6% African American, 2% Asian American, 5% Hispanic American, 1% Native American, 7% international
- 49% of applicants admitted
- SAT or ACT with writing, application essay required
- 67% graduate within 6 years

**General.** Founded in 1832. Regionally accredited. **Degrees:** 196 bachelor's awarded. **Location:** 45 miles from Indianapolis, 125 miles from Chicago. **Calendar:** Semester. **Full-time faculty:** 90 total; 99% have terminal degrees, 8% minority, 36% women. **Part-time faculty:** 2 total; 50% have terminal degrees, 50% women. **Class size:** 77% < 20, 17% 20-39, 3% 40-49, 2% 50-99. **Special facilities:** Biology field station, qualitative and quantitative skills center, electron microscope, parallel computer, nature preserve, archival center.

**Freshman class profile.** 1,588 applied, 775 admitted, 247 enrolled.

| Mid 50% test scores | | | |
|---|---|---|---|
| SAT critical reading: | 500-600 | Rank in top quarter: | 70% |
| SAT math: | 530-660 | Rank in top tenth: | 31% |
| SAT writing: | 470-600 | End year in good standing: | 97% |
| ACT composite: | 21-27 | Return as sophomores: | 85% |
| GPA 3.75 or higher: | 31% | Out-of-state: | 28% |
| GPA 3.50-3.74: | 22% | Live on campus: | 99% |
| GPA 3.0-3.49: | 36% | International: | 9% |
| GPA 2.0-2.99: | 11% | Fraternities: | 59% |

**Basis for selection.** Class rank, school achievement, recommendation, essay and test scores important. Interview recommended. Character and personal qualities considered. **Learning Disabled:** All students considered on an individual basis.

**High school preparation.** College-preparatory program required. 17 units recommended. Recommended units include English 4, mathematics 4, social studies 2, science 2 (laboratory 2), foreign language 2 and academic electives 3.

**2009-2010 Annual costs.** Tuition/fees: $29,750. Room/board: $8,100. Books/supplies: $900. Personal expenses: $1,500.

**2009-2010 Financial aid. Need-based:** 233 full-time freshmen applied for aid; 202 were judged to have need; 202 of these received aid. Average need met was 98%. Average scholarship/grant was $19,459; average loan $5,674. 74% of total undergraduate aid awarded as scholarships/grants, 26% as loans/jobs. **Non-need-based:** Awarded to 411 full-time undergraduates, including 88 freshmen. Scholarships awarded for academics, art, leadership, music/drama, state residency.

**Application procedures. Admission:** Priority date 12/1; no deadline. $40 fee, may be waived for applicants with need. Admission notification on a rolling basis beginning on or about 11/15. Must reply by May 1 or within 2 week(s) if notified thereafter. **Financial aid:** Priority date 2/15, closing date 3/1. FAFSA, CSS PROFILE required. Applicants notified by 3/31.

**Academics. Special study options:** Combined bachelor's/graduate degree, double major, independent study, internships, liberal arts/career combination, New York semester, semester at sea, study abroad, teacher certification program, United Nations semester, urban semester, Washington semester. Cooperative law program with Columbia University, International and Domestic Study Program of Great Lakes Colleges Association, 3-2 engineering program with Columbia University and Washington University. **Credit/placement by examination:** AP, CLEP, SAT, institutional tests. AP credit based on AP exam scores and with in-house exams and subsequent coursework. **Support services:** Learning center, study skills assistance, tutoring, writing center.

**Majors. Biology:** General. **Foreign languages:** Ancient Greek, classics, French, German, Latin, Spanish. **History:** General. **Liberal arts:** Arts/sciences. **Math:** General. **Philosophy/religion:** Philosophy, religion. **Physical sciences:** Chemistry, physics. **Psychology:** General. **Social sciences:** Economics, political science. **Visual/performing arts:** Art, dramatic.

**Most popular majors.** Biology 9%, English 13%, foreign language 8%, history 9%, philosophy/religious studies 15%, psychology 12%, social sciences 20%.

**Computing on campus.** 360 workstations in dormitories, library, computer center, student center. Dormitories wired for high-speed internet access and linked to campus network. Commuter students can connect to campus network. Online library, helpline, repair service, student web hosting, wireless network available.

**Student life. Freshman orientation:** Mandatory. Preregistration for classes offered. **Policies:** The Gentleman's Rule is the college's only rule. **Housing:** Guaranteed on-campus for all undergraduates. Apartments, cooperative housing, fraternity/sorority housing, wellness housing available. $150 non-refundable deposit, deadline 6/25. **Activities:** Bands, campus ministries, choral groups, drama, film society, international student organizations, literary magazine, music ensembles, Model UN, musical theater, radio station, student government, student newspaper, symphony orchestra, political groups, Newman Center, Alpha Phi Omega, Fellowship of Christian Athletes, Muslim student association, Wabash Christian Fellowship, pre-law society, moot court competition, Sphinx club, Malcolm X Institute of Black Studies.

**Athletics.** NCAA. **Intercollegiate:** Baseball M, basketball M, cross-country M, diving M, football (tackle) M, golf M, soccer M, swimming M, tennis M, track and field M, wrestling M. **Intramural:** Badminton M, basketball M, bowling M, cross-country M, diving M, football (non-tackle) M, golf M, handball M, racquetball M, soccer M, softball M, swimming M, table tennis M, tennis M, track and field M, volleyball M, wrestling M. **Team name:** Little Giants.

**Student services.** Alcohol/substance abuse counseling, chaplain/spiritual director, career counseling, student employment services, financial aid counseling, health services, minority student services, personal counseling, placement for graduates. **Physically disabled:** Services for visually, hearing impaired.

**Contact.** E-mail: admissions@wabash.edu
Phone: (765) 361-6225 Toll-free number: (800) 345-5385
Fax: (765) 361-6437
Steven Klein, Dean of Admissions and Financial Aid, Wabash College, PO Box 352, Crawfordsville, IN 47933

# Iowa

## Allen College
**Waterloo, Iowa**
www.allencollege.edu                    CB code: 3610

- Private 4-year health science and nursing college
- Commuter campus in small city
- 314 degree-seeking undergraduates: 21% part-time, 93% women, 2% African American, 1% Native American
- 134 degree-seeking graduate students
- 40% of applicants admitted
- SAT or ACT (ACT writing optional), application essay required
- 56% graduate within 6 years; 10% enter graduate study

**General.** Regionally accredited. **Degrees:** 91 bachelor's, 11 associate awarded; master's offered. **ROTC:** Army. **Calendar:** Semester, limited summer session. **Full-time faculty:** 29 total; 24% have terminal degrees, 3% minority, 97% women. **Part-time faculty:** 9 total; 100% women. **Class size:** 56% < 20, 36% 20-39, 4% 40-49, 4% 50-99.

**Freshman class profile.** 40 applied, 16 admitted, 3 enrolled.

| Mid 50% test scores | | | |
|---|---|---|---|
| ACT composite: | 21-24 | Rank in top quarter: | 67% |
| GPA 3.75 or higher: | 33% | Rank in top tenth: | 33% |
| GPA 3.0-3.49: | 67% | End year in good standing: | 75% |
| | | Return as sophomores: | 75% |

**Basis for selection.** College and secondary school record, class rank, test scores important; recommendations, essay considered. Pre-requisite courses required prior to admission to BSN and health science degree programs.

**High school preparation.** 4 units required. Required units include English 4, mathematics 3, social studies 3, science 3 (laboratory 2).

**2010-2011 Annual costs.** Tuition/fees (projected): $14,995. Room/board: $7,157. Books/supplies: $1,063. Personal expenses: $3,248.

**2008-2009 Financial aid. Need-based:** 4 full-time freshmen applied for aid; 2 were judged to have need; 2 of these received aid. Average need met was 32%. Average scholarship/grant was $6,116; average loan $3,375. 38% of total undergraduate aid awarded as scholarships/grants, 62% as loans/jobs. **Non-need-based:** Awarded to 17 full-time undergraduates, including 2 freshmen. Scholarships awarded for academics, leadership, minority status, ROTC.

**Application procedures. Admission:** Priority date 3/1; deadline 8/1 (receipt date). $50 fee, may be waived for applicants with need. Admission notification on a rolling basis. Must reply by May 1 or within 4 week(s) if notified thereafter. **Financial aid:** Priority date 6/1; no closing date. FAFSA, institutional form required. Applicants notified on a rolling basis starting 4/1; must reply within 2 week(s) of notification.

**Academics. Special study options:** Accelerated study, combined bachelor's/graduate degree, cooperative education, distance learning, external degree, honors, independent study, internships, liberal arts/career combination. **Credit/placement by examination:** AP, CLEP, IB. **Support services:** Learning center, study skills assistance, tutoring, writing center.

**Majors. Health:** Clinical lab science, nuclear medical technology, nursing (RN).

**Computing on campus.** 29 workstations in dormitories, library, computer center. Dormitories wired for high-speed internet access. Online library, helpline, wireless network available.

**Student life. Freshman orientation:** Mandatory. Includes registration, assessment testing, and completion of mandatory health career training. **Housing:** Coed dorms, single-sex dorms, special housing for disabled, apartments, cooperative housing, wellness housing available. $200 nonrefundable deposit. On-campus suite housing available and dorm-style housing offered at cooperating institutions. **Activities:** Choral groups, student government, student newspaper.

**Student services.** Alcohol/substance abuse counseling, chaplain/spiritual director, career counseling, financial aid counseling, health services, on-campus daycare, personal counseling, placement for graduates, women's services. **Physically disabled:** Services for visually, speech, hearing impaired.

**Contact.** E-mail: allencollegeadmissions@ihs.org
Phone: (319) 226-2000 Fax: (319) 226-2051
Michelle Koehn, Admissions Counselor, Allen College, 1825 Logan Avenue, Waterloo, IA 50703

## Ashford University
**Clinton, Iowa**                    CB member
www.ashford.edu                    CB code: 6418

- For-profit 4-year university
- Commuter campus in large town

**General.** Founded in 1918. Regionally accredited. **Location:** 35 miles from Davenport, 138 miles from Chicago. **Calendar:** Semester.

**Annual costs/financial aid.** Tuition/fees (2009-2010): $15,900. Room/board: $5,800. Books/supplies: $1,000. Need-based financial aid available to full-time and part-time students.

**Contact.** Phone: (563) 242-4153
Director of Enrollment, 400 North Bluff Boulevard, Clinton, IA 52733-2967

## Briar Cliff University
**Sioux City, Iowa**                    CB member
www.briarcliff.edu                    CB code: 6046

- Private 4-year liberal arts college affiliated with Roman Catholic Church
- Residential campus in small city
- 1,018 degree-seeking undergraduates: 12% part-time, 56% women, 7% African American, 3% Asian American, 6% Hispanic American, 2% Native American
- 74 degree-seeking graduate students
- 62% of applicants admitted
- ACT (writing optional) required
- 47% graduate within 6 years; 23% enter graduate study

**General.** Founded in 1930. Regionally accredited. **Degrees:** 227 bachelor's awarded; master's offered. **ROTC:** Army. **Location:** 90 miles from Omaha, Nebraska. **Calendar:** Trimester, limited summer session. **Full-time faculty:** 60 total; 72% have terminal degrees, 3% minority, 53% women. **Part-time faculty:** 48 total; 4% have terminal degrees, 60% women. **Class size:** 74% < 20, 24% 20-39, less than 1% 40-49, 1% 50-99. **Special facilities:** Prairie nature preserve, human anatomy/cadaver laboratory, integrated media lab, nursing simulation lab, entrepreneurship lab, music lab.

**Freshman class profile.** 1,579 applied, 976 admitted, 223 enrolled.

| Mid 50% test scores | | | |
|---|---|---|---|
| SAT critical reading: | 430-490 | GPA 2.0-2.99: | 33% |
| SAT math: | 410-510 | Rank in top quarter: | 34% |
| ACT composite: | 19-25 | Rank in top tenth: | 11% |
| GPA 3.75 or higher: | 20% | End year in good standing: | 82% |
| GPA 3.50-3.74: | 14% | Return as sophomores: | 65% |
| GPA 3.0-3.49: | 33% | Out-of-state: | 54% |
| | | Live on campus: | 91% |

**Basis for selection.** 2.0 GPA and 18 ACT required for full acceptance. Students not meeting requirement may be accepted conditionally or may appeal admission decision if not accepted. Interview and essay recommended. **Homeschooled:** Transcript of high school work should be obtained from the school district where the student resides full time. **Learning Disabled:** Students should submit official documentation directly to Student Support Services office.

**High school preparation.** 16 units recommended. Recommended units include English 4, mathematics 3, social studies 3, science 3, foreign language 2 and academic electives 1.

**2009-2010 Annual costs.** Tuition/fees: $22,536. Room/board: $6,978. Books/supplies: $900. Personal expenses: $1,935.

**2009-2010 Financial aid. Need-based:** 220 full-time freshmen applied for aid; 178 were judged to have need; 178 of these received aid. Average need met was 87%. Average scholarship/grant was $6,300; average loan $3,900. 62% of total undergraduate aid awarded as scholarships/grants, 38% as loans/jobs. **Non-need-based:** Awarded to 1,309 full-time undergraduates, including 360 freshmen. Scholarships awarded for academics, alumni affiliation, art, athletics, leadership, music/drama, religious affiliation, state residency.

**Application procedures. Admission:** Priority date 4/1; no deadline. $20 fee, may be waived for applicants with need. Admission notification on a rolling basis beginning on or about 6/1. **Financial aid:** Priority date 3/15; no closing date. FAFSA required. Applicants notified on a rolling basis starting 3/15; must reply by 5/1 or within 2 week(s) of notification.

**Academics. Special study options:** Accelerated study, cross-registration, distance learning, double major, honors, independent study, internships, liberal arts/career combination, student-designed major, study abroad, teacher certification program, urban semester, weekend college. Radiologic technology 1-2-1 program, medical technology 3-1 program. **Credit/placement by examination:** AP, CLEP, IB, ACT, institutional tests. 45 credit hours maximum toward bachelor's degree. Examinations must be taken before student enters last 30 hours of study. **Support services:** Learning center, preadmission summer program, reduced course load, remedial instruction, study skills assistance, tutoring, writing center.

**Majors. Biology:** General. **Business:** Accounting, business admin, human resources, management information systems. **Communications:** Digital media, media studies. **Communications technology:** Graphics. **Computer sciences:** General, computer science. **Conservation:** Environmental science. **Education:** General, art, biology, chemistry, elementary, English, history, mathematics, music, physical, reading, science, secondary, social science. **Foreign languages:** Spanish. **Health:** Clinical lab science, medical radiologic technology/radiation therapy, nursing (RN). **History:** General. **Interdisciplinary:** Biological/physical sciences. **Math:** General. **Parks/recreation:** Exercise sciences, health/fitness, sports admin. **Physical sciences:** Chemistry. **Protective services:** Law enforcement admin. **Psychology:** General. **Public administration:** Social work. **Social sciences:** Political science, sociology. **Theology:** Theology. **Visual/performing arts:** Art, dramatic, film/cinema, graphic design.

**Most popular majors.** Biology 6%, business/marketing 30%, education 10%, health sciences 15%, parks/recreation 8%, visual/performing arts 6%.

**Computing on campus.** 102 workstations in dormitories, library, computer center, student center. Dormitories wired for high-speed internet access and linked to campus network. Commuter students can connect to campus network. Online library, helpline, repair service, student web hosting, wireless network available.

**Student life. Freshman orientation:** Mandatory, $95 fee. Preregistration for classes offered. Orientation begins when students move onto campus, prior to beginning of classes. **Housing:** Guaranteed on-campus for freshmen. Coed dorms available. $150 fully refundable deposit. Pets allowed in dorm rooms. Quad suites available. **Activities:** Jazz band, campus ministries, choral groups, dance, drama, literary magazine, music ensembles, musical theater, opera, radio station, student government, student newspaper, Best Buddies, BCCares, Champions of Characters Council of Athletes, College Democrats, College Republicans, criminal justice club, departmental clubs, ethnic relations club, mentors in violence prevention.

**Athletics. NAIA. Intercollegiate:** Baseball M, basketball, cheerleading M, cross-country, football (tackle) M, golf, soccer, softball W, tennis, track and field, volleyball W, wrestling M. **Intramural:** Badminton, basketball, bowling, cross-country, football (non-tackle) M, golf, handball, racquetball, soccer, softball, table tennis, tennis, track and field, volleyball. **Team name:** Chargers.

**Student services.** Alcohol/substance abuse counseling, chaplain/spiritual director, career counseling, services for economically disadvantaged, student employment services, financial aid counseling, health services, personal counseling, placement for graduates. **Physically disabled:** Services for visually impaired.

**Contact.** E-mail: admissions@briarcliff.edu
Phone: (712) 279-5200 Toll-free number: (800) 662-3303 ext. 5200
Fax: (712) 279-1632
Sharisue Wilcoxon, Vice President for Enrollment Management, Briar Cliff University, 3303 Rebecca Street, Sioux City, IA 51104-0100

---

## Buena Vista University
**Storm Lake, Iowa**
**www.bvu.edu**                                     CB code: 6047

- Private 4-year liberal arts college affiliated with Presbyterian Church (USA)
- Residential campus in large town
- 939 degree-seeking undergraduates: 1% part-time, 51% women, 6% African American, 2% Asian American, 5% Hispanic American, 4% international

- 57 degree-seeking graduate students
- 72% of applicants admitted
- SAT or ACT (ACT writing optional) required
- 59% graduate within 6 years; 21% enter graduate study

**General.** Founded in 1891. Regionally accredited. 15 branch sites throughout Iowa and online programs provide educational opportunities for nontraditional students. **Degrees:** 597 bachelor's awarded; master's offered. **ROTC:** Army. **Location:** 150 miles from Des Moines, 80 miles from Sioux City. **Calendar:** 4-1-4, limited summer session. **Full-time faculty:** 83 total; 69% have terminal degrees, 5% minority, 45% women. **Part-time faculty:** 23 total; 9% minority, 52% women. **Class size:** 65% < 20, 34% 20-39, less than 1% 40-49, less than 1% 50-99. **Special facilities:** Multimedia production facilities, underground buildings, information technology center, digitally-controlled acoustic music practice rooms.

**Freshman class profile.** 1,433 applied, 1,027 admitted, 273 enrolled.

| Mid 50% test scores | | Rank in top quarter: | 38% |
|---|---|---|---|
| ACT composite: | 18-25 | Rank in top tenth: | 15% |
| GPA 3.75 or higher: | 22% | Return as sophomores: | 61% |
| GPA 3.50-3.74: | 18% | Out-of-state: | 26% |
| GPA 3.0-3.49: | 27% | Live on campus: | 96% |
| GPA 2.0-2.99: | 33% | International: | 4% |

**Basis for selection.** High school GPA and curriculum, rank in class, standardized test scores, interview, school and community activities important. Essay recommended.

**High school preparation.** College-preparatory program recommended. 15 units required. Required and recommended units include English 4, mathematics 4, social studies 2, history 2, science 2-4, foreign language 2 and computer science 1.

**2010-2011 Annual costs.** Tuition/fees: $26,306. Room/board: $7,582. Books/supplies: $1,000. Personal expenses: $1,500.

**2009-2010 Financial aid. Non-need-based:** Scholarships awarded for academics, art, minority status, music/drama, religious affiliation. **Additional information:** Portfolio required of art scholarship applicants, audition required of music and drama scholarship applicants.

**Application procedures. Admission:** No deadline. No application fee. Admission notification on a rolling basis. **Financial aid:** Priority date 6/1; no closing date. FAFSA required. Applicants notified on a rolling basis starting 2/15.

**Academics.** Students must earn credit by attending the Academic and Cultural Events Series, featuring lectures by national and international leaders and performances by world-famous classical performing groups and artists. **Special study options:** Combined bachelor's/graduate degree, distance learning, double major, dual enrollment of high school students, ESL, external degree, honors, independent study, internships, student-designed major, study abroad, teacher certification program, Washington semester. Rollins Fellows (competitive international internships). **Credit/placement by examination:** AP, CLEP, IB, ACT, institutional tests. 20 credit hours maximum toward bachelor's degree. **Support services:** Learning center, reduced course load, remedial instruction, study skills assistance, tutoring, writing center.

**Majors. Biology:** General. **Business:** Accounting, banking/financial services, entrepreneurial studies, human resources, international, management information systems, managerial economics, marketing. **Communications:** General, media studies, organizational. **Computer sciences:** Computer science. **Conservation:** Environmental science. **Education:** Art, biology, business, chemistry, computer, elementary, English, history, mathematics, music, physical, physics, psychology, reading, science, social science, Spanish, special, speech. **Foreign languages:** Spanish. **Health:** Athletic training. **History:** General. **Interdisciplinary:** Biological/physical sciences. **Math:** General. **Parks/recreation:** Exercise sciences, sports admin. **Philosophy/religion:** Philosophy. **Physical sciences:** Chemistry, physics. **Protective services:** Criminal justice. **Psychology:** General. **Public administration:** General, social work. **Social sciences:** General, political science, sociology. **Visual/performing arts:** Art, arts management, commercial/advertising art, music performance, theater history.

**Most popular majors.** Business/marketing 31%, education 17%, interdisciplinary studies 14%, psychology 13%, security/protective services 8%.

**Computing on campus.** 400 workstations in dormitories, library, computer center, student center. Dormitories wired for high-speed internet access and linked to campus network. Commuter students can connect to campus network. Online course registration, online library, helpline, repair service, wireless network available.

**Student life. Freshman orientation:** Mandatory. Preregistration for classes offered. Two-day orientation offered during summer. **Housing:** Guaranteed on-campus for all undergraduates. Coed dorms, single-sex dorms, wellness housing available. $200 nonrefundable deposit. **Activities:** Bands, campus ministries, choral groups, dance, drama, international student organizations, music ensembles, musical theater, radio station, student government, student newspaper, TV station, Circle-K, Students Concerned about Tomorrow's Environment, intervarsity multicultural club, Fellowship of Christian Athletes, College Democrats, College Republicans, Reshaping Our Campus Community.

**Athletics.** NCAA. **Intercollegiate:** Baseball M, basketball, cross-country, football (tackle) M, golf, soccer, softball W, tennis, track and field, volleyball W, wrestling M. **Intramural:** Basketball, football (non-tackle) M, racquetball, softball, table tennis, tennis, volleyball. **Team name:** Beavers.

**Student services.** Adult student services, alcohol/substance abuse counseling, chaplain/spiritual director, career counseling, student employment services, financial aid counseling, health services, minority student services, personal counseling, placement for graduates, veterans' counselor. **Physically disabled:** Services for visually, speech, hearing impaired.

**Contact.** E-mail: admissions@bvu.edu
Phone: (712) 749-2235 Toll-free number: (800) 383-9600
Fax: (712) 749-2037
Bridget Kurkowski, Director of Admissions, Buena Vista University, 610 West Fourth Street, Storm Lake, IA 50588

---

## Central College

**Pella, Iowa**                          **CB member**
**www.central.edu**                   **CB code: 6087**

- Private 4-year liberal arts college affiliated with Reformed Church in America
- Residential campus in large town
- 1,529 degree-seeking undergraduates: 1% part-time, 52% women, 2% African American, 2% Asian American, 2% Hispanic American, 1% international
- 74% of applicants admitted
- SAT or ACT (ACT writing optional) required
- 63% graduate within 6 years

**General.** Founded in 1853. Regionally accredited. **Degrees:** 266 bachelor's awarded. **Location:** 45 miles from Des Moines. **Calendar:** Semester, limited summer session. **Full-time faculty:** 88 total; 88% have terminal degrees, 7% minority, 43% women. **Part-time faculty:** 76 total; 29% have terminal degrees, 1% minority, 45% women. **Class size:** 51% < 20, 49% 20-39, less than 1% 40-49, less than 1% 50-99.

**Freshman class profile.** 2,451 applied, 1,823 admitted, 443 enrolled.

| Mid 50% test scores | | GPA 2.0-2.99: | 15% |
|---|---|---|---|
| SAT critical reading: | 470-670 | Rank in top quarter: | 54% |
| SAT math: | 480-650 | Rank in top tenth: | 28% |
| ACT composite: | 21-27 | Return as sophomores: | 80% |
| GPA 3.75 or higher: | 38% | Out-of-state: | 17% |
| GPA 3.50-3.74: | 22% | Live on campus: | 99% |
| GPA 3.0-3.49: | 25% | | |

**Basis for selection.** High school curriculum, GPA, class rank, test scores important. Recommendations, school and community activities, alumni affiliation also considered. Interview and essay recommended. Audition recommended for music and theater majors; required for scholarships. Portfolio recommended for art majors; required for scholarships. **Homeschooled:** Transcript of courses and grades required.

**High school preparation.** College-preparatory program recommended. 15 units recommended. Required and recommended units include English 4, mathematics 2-3, social studies 3, history 2, science 2-3 (laboratory 2) and foreign language 2.

**2010-2011 Annual costs.** Tuition/fees: $26,242. Room/board: $8,702.

**2009-2010 Financial aid. Need-based:** 443 full-time freshmen applied for aid; 394 were judged to have need; 394 of these received aid. Average need met was 87%. Average scholarship/grant was $17,824; average loan $3,928. 69% of total undergraduate aid awarded as scholarships/grants, 31% as loans/jobs. **Non-need-based:** Awarded to 438 full-time undergraduates, including 121 freshmen. Scholarships awarded for academics, alumni affiliation, art, minority status, music/drama, religious affiliation, state residency. **Additional information:** Institutional parent loan program and interest-earning, tuition prepayment savings account available.

**Application procedures. Admission:** No deadline. $25 fee, may be waived for applicants with need, free for online applicants. Admission notification on a rolling basis. **Financial aid:** Priority date 3/15; no closing date. FAFSA required. Applicants notified on a rolling basis starting 3/15; must reply by 5/1 or within 2 week(s) of notification.

**Academics. Special study options:** Combined bachelor's/graduate degree, cooperative education, double major, dual enrollment of high school students, honors, independent study, internships, student-designed major, study abroad, teacher certification program, urban semester, Washington semester. Study abroad in 9 countries (plus summer Ghana program) and programs in Washington, DC and Chicago. Dual degree programs in engineering, physical therapy/chiropractic and nursing. **Credit/placement by examination:** AP, CLEP, IB, SAT, ACT, institutional tests. **Support services:** Learning center, reduced course load, study skills assistance, tutoring, writing center.

**Majors. Biology:** General. **Business:** Accounting, actuarial science, business admin, international. **Communications:** General. **Computer sciences:** General, information systems. **Conservation:** Environmental studies. **Education:** Elementary, music. **Foreign languages:** French, German, linguistics, Spanish. **Health:** Athletic training. **History:** General. **Interdisciplinary:** Global studies, math/computer science, natural sciences. **Math:** General. **Parks/recreation:** Exercise sciences. **Philosophy/religion:** Philosophy, religion. **Physical sciences:** Chemistry, physics. **Psychology:** General. **Social sciences:** General, anthropology, economics, political science, sociology. **Visual/performing arts:** Art, dramatic.

**Most popular majors.** Biology 6%, business/marketing 15%, education 10%, foreign language 12%, parks/recreation 13%, social sciences 8%.

**Computing on campus.** 256 workstations in dormitories, library, computer center, student center. Dormitories wired for high-speed internet access and linked to campus network. Commuter students can connect to campus network. Online library, helpline, repair service, student web hosting, wireless network available.

**Student life. Freshman orientation:** Mandatory. Preregistration for classes offered. Held weekends in June. **Housing:** Guaranteed on-campus for all undergraduates. Coed dorms, single-sex dorms, special housing for disabled, apartments, fraternity/sorority housing, wellness housing available. $200 fully refundable deposit, deadline 5/1. Green housing available. **Activities:** Bands, campus ministries, choral groups, drama, international student organizations, literary magazine, music ensembles, radio station, student government, student newspaper, symphony orchestra, Young Democrats, Young Republicans, Fellowship of Christian Athletes, Inter-Varsity Christian Fellowship, alcohol awareness committee, multicultural campus association, Circle-K, Amnesty International, Students Against Apartheid, students concerned about the environment.

**Athletics.** NCAA. **Intercollegiate:** Baseball M, basketball, cross-country, football (tackle) M, golf, soccer, softball W, tennis, track and field, volleyball W, wrestling M. **Intramural:** Basketball, racquetball, rugby, softball, volleyball. **Team name:** Dutch.

**Student services.** Alcohol/substance abuse counseling, chaplain/spiritual director, career counseling, services for economically disadvantaged, student employment services, financial aid counseling, health services, minority student services, personal counseling, placement for graduates, veterans' counselor. **Physically disabled:** Services for visually, speech, hearing impaired. **Learning disabled:** Comprehensive services available.

**Contact.** E-mail: admissions@central.edu
Phone: (641) 628-5286 Toll-free number: (877) 462-3687
Fax: (641) 628-5316
Carol Williamson, Dean of Admission, Central College, 812 University Street, Pella, IA 50219-1999

---

## Clarke College

**Dubuque, Iowa**
**www.clarke.edu**                        **CB code: 6099**

- Private 4-year liberal arts college affiliated with Roman Catholic Church
- Residential campus in small city
- 938 degree-seeking undergraduates: 14% part-time, 68% women, 1% African American, 1% Asian American, 2% Hispanic American, 1% international
- 220 graduate students
- 77% of applicants admitted
- SAT or ACT (ACT writing optional) required
- 66% graduate within 6 years; 23% enter graduate study

**General.** Founded in 1843. Regionally accredited. **Degrees:** 226 bachelor's awarded; master's, professional offered. **ROTC:** Army. **Location:** 150 miles from Chicago. **Calendar:** Semester, limited summer session. **Full-time faculty:** 75 total; 68% have terminal degrees, 63% women. **Part-time faculty:** 60 total; 7% have terminal degrees, 57% women. **Class size:** 81% < 20, 19% 20-39, less than 1% 40-49. **Special facilities:** Planetarium, art and communications laboratory, writing center, art slide library, computerized mathematics laboratory, nursing laboratory, human gross anatomy laboratory with A.D.A.M. software.

**Freshman class profile.** 823 applied, 637 admitted, 148 enrolled.

| Mid 50% test scores | | GPA 2.0-2.99: | 28% |
|---|---|---|---|
| SAT critical reading: | 470-580 | Rank in top quarter: | 47% |
| SAT math: | 460-540 | Rank in top tenth: | 23% |
| SAT writing: | 510-560 | Return as sophomores: | 78% |
| ACT composite: | 20-26 | Out-of-state: | 58% |
| GPA 3.75 or higher: | 27% | Live on campus: | 88% |
| GPA 3.50-3.74: | 22% | International: | 1% |
| GPA 3.0-3.49: | 23% | | |

**Basis for selection.** High school record of primary importance. Particular attention paid to grades on college preparatory course work and test scores. Interview required of the academically weak. Auditions required of music and drama majors. Portfolio required of art majors.

**High school preparation.** 21 units required. Required and recommended units include English 4, mathematics 3-4, social studies 3, science 3-4 (laboratory 2), foreign language 2 and academic electives 4. 4 college preparatory math and science, including 3 lab, required for physical therapy program.

**2009-2010 Annual costs.** Tuition/fees: $23,520. Room/board: $6,840. Books/supplies: $700. Personal expenses: $700.

**2009-2010 Financial aid. Non-need-based:** Scholarships awarded for academics, alumni affiliation, art, athletics, leadership, music/drama, religious affiliation, state residency. **Additional information:** Reduced tuition for family members of BVMs.

**Application procedures. Admission:** No deadline. $25 fee, may be waived for applicants with need, free for online applicants. Admission notification on a rolling basis beginning on or about 1/15. Must reply by May 1 or within 3 week(s) if notified thereafter. **Financial aid:** Priority date 4/15; no closing date. Applicants notified on a rolling basis starting 3/11; must reply by 5/1 or within 2 week(s) of notification.

**Academics. Special study options:** Accelerated study, cooperative education, cross-registration, distance learning, double major, ESL, honors, independent study, internships, liberal arts/career combination, student-designed major, study abroad, teacher certification program. **Credit/placement by examination:** AP, CLEP, IB, SAT, ACT, institutional tests. 15 credit hours maximum toward associate degree, 30 toward bachelor's. Students applying for prior learning assessment (PLA) credit must be 24 years of age or older. Maximum of 30 credits granted for PLA, CLEP or DANTES within 5-year period. If more than 15 PLA credits are awarded based on portfolio evaluation, additional credit up to 30 hours must be matched by regular college credit. PLA does not count toward the 30 hour residency requirement and is awarded only after 5 hours in degree program are completed. Guidelines may vary by department. **Support services:** Learning center, reduced course load, study skills assistance, tutoring, writing center.

**Majors. Biology:** General, biochemistry. **Business:** Accounting, business admin. **Communications:** General. **Computer sciences:** General. **Education:** Elementary, music, physical. **Foreign languages:** Spanish. **Health:** Nursing (RN), predental, premedicine, prepharmacy, preveterinary. **History:** General. **Math:** General. **Parks/recreation:** Sports admin. **Philosophy/religion:** Philosophy, religion. **Physical sciences:** Chemistry. **Psychology:** General. **Public administration:** Social work. **Visual/performing arts:** Art, art history/conservation, dramatic, studio arts.

**Most popular majors.** Business/marketing 14%, communications/journalism 7%, education 15%, health sciences 24%, psychology 9%, visual/performing arts 7%.

**Computing on campus.** 237 workstations in dormitories, library, computer center, student center. Dormitories wired for high-speed internet access and linked to campus network. Commuter students can connect to campus network. Online course registration, online library, wireless network available.

**Student life. Freshman orientation:** Available. Preregistration for classes offered. **Housing:** Guaranteed on-campus for freshmen. Coed dorms, single-sex dorms, apartments, wellness housing available. $100 fully refundable deposit, deadline 7/15. **Activities:** Jazz band, campus ministries, choral groups, drama, literary magazine, music ensembles, musical theater, radio station,

student government, student newspaper, Amnesty International, peace and justice, peer ministry program, minority student organization, Walden Society.

**Athletics.** NAIA. **Intercollegiate:** Baseball M, basketball, bowling, cheerleading M, cross-country, golf, soccer, softball W, tennis, track and field, volleyball. **Intramural:** Basketball, bowling, football (non-tackle), softball, table tennis, tennis, volleyball. **Team name:** Crusaders.

**Student services.** Adult student services, alcohol/substance abuse counseling, chaplain/spiritual director, career counseling, student employment services, financial aid counseling, health services, minority student services, personal counseling. **Physically disabled:** Services for visually, hearing impaired.

**Contact.** E-mail: admissions@clarke.edu
Phone: (563) 588-6316 Toll-free number: (800) 383-2345
Fax: (563) 588-6789
Emily Kruse, Director of Admission, Clarke College, 1550 Clarke Drive, Dubuque, IA 52001-3198

---

**Coe College**
**Cedar Rapids, Iowa**                                    **CB member**
**www.coe.edu**                                          **CB code: 6101**

- Private 4-year nursing and liberal arts college affiliated with Presbyterian Church (USA)
- Residential campus in small city
- 1,278 degree-seeking undergraduates
- 65% of applicants admitted
- SAT or ACT (ACT writing optional), application essay required

**General.** Founded in 1851. Regionally accredited. **Degrees:** 277 bachelor's awarded; master's offered. **ROTC:** Army, Air Force. **Location:** 230 miles from Chicago, 300 miles from Minneapolis-St. Paul. **Calendar:** Semester, limited summer session. **Full-time faculty:** 90 total. **Part-time faculty:** 84 total. **Class size:** 68% < 20, 31% 20-39, less than 1% 40-49, less than 1% 50-99. **Special facilities:** Infrared spectrometer, analytical physiology units, music library, wilderness field station.

**Freshman class profile.** 2,063 applied, 1,336 admitted, 325 enrolled.

| Mid 50% test scores | | GPA 3.0-3.49: | 30% |
|---|---|---|---|
| SAT critical reading: | 540-640 | GPA 2.0-2.99: | 2% |
| SAT math: | 540-640 | Rank in top quarter: | 66% |
| SAT writing: | 530-610 | Rank in top tenth: | 30% |
| ACT composite: | 23-28 | Live on campus: | 97% |
| GPA 3.75 or higher: | 47% | Fraternities: | 17% |
| GPA 3.50-3.74: | 21% | | |

**Basis for selection.** School achievement record and test scores most important. Recommendations and school activities also important. Interview and community activities considered. **Homeschooled:** GED and portfolio required. **Learning Disabled:** Submission of disability assessment required.

**High school preparation.** College-preparatory program recommended. 18 units recommended. Recommended units include English 4, mathematics 3, social studies 3, science 3 (laboratory 1), foreign language 2 and academic electives 2.

**2009-2010 Annual costs.** Tuition/fees: $29,270. Cost per course for part-time students (fewer than 3 course credits) is $3,620. Room/board: $7,150. Books/supplies: $1,000. Personal expenses: $1,600.

**2009-2010 Financial aid. Non-need-based:** Scholarships awarded for academics, alumni affiliation, art, leadership, music/drama, ROTC.

**Application procedures. Admission:** Priority date 12/10; deadline 3/1 (postmark date). $30 fee, may be waived for applicants with need, free for online applicants. Admission notification on a rolling basis beginning on or about 10/1. Must reply by May 1 or within 2 week(s) if notified thereafter. **Financial aid:** Priority date 3/1; no closing date. FAFSA required. Applicants notified on a rolling basis starting 3/15; must reply by 5/1 or within 2 week(s) of notification.

**Academics.** Writing emphasis courses required. Semester practicum required for all students. **Special study options:** Accelerated study, combined bachelor's/graduate degree, cross-registration, double major, dual enrollment of high school students, ESL, exchange student, honors, independent study, internships, New York semester, student-designed major, study abroad, teacher certification program, urban semester, Washington semester. Oak Ridge science semester; research program at the Coe College wilderness field station- Minnesota Superior National Forest; tropical field research in

Costa Rica; travel abroad to England, Hong Kong, India, Italy, Japan, Russia, Latin America, Czech Republic, Tanzania, Germany, Sweden, Spain, France, Korea, Thailand, Ireland. **Credit/placement by examination:** AP, CLEP, IB, SAT, ACT, institutional tests. **Support services:** Pre-admission summer program, reduced course load, study skills assistance, tutoring, writing center.

**Majors.** **Area/ethnic studies:** African-American, American, Asian, French, German, Spanish/Iberian. **Biology:** General, biochemistry, molecular. **Business:** Accounting, business admin. **Communications:** General, public relations. **Computer sciences:** Computer science. **Conservation:** Environmental science. **Education:** General, art, elementary, middle, music, physical, science, secondary. **Foreign languages:** Classics, French, German, Spanish. **Health:** Athletic training, nursing (RN), predental, premedicine, preveterinary. **History:** General. **Interdisciplinary:** Accounting/computer science, biological/physical sciences, math/computer science. **Legal studies:** Prelaw. **Math:** General. **Parks/recreation:** Health/fitness. **Philosophy/religion:** Philosophy, religion. **Physical sciences:** General, chemistry, physics. **Psychology:** General. **Social sciences:** Economics, political science, sociology. **Visual/performing arts:** Acting, art, ceramics, directing/producing, dramatic, music performance, music theory/composition, painting, photography, studio arts, theater design.

**Most popular majors.** Biology 6%, business/marketing 23%, communications/journalism 6%, health sciences 8%, parks/recreation 6%, psychology 8%, social sciences 10%, visual/performing arts 10%.

**Computing on campus.** Dormitories wired for high-speed internet access and linked to campus network. Commuter students can connect to campus network. Online course registration, online library, helpline, student web hosting, wireless network available.

**Student life.** **Freshman orientation:** Mandatory, $150 fee. Four- or five-day program. **Policies:** Students must live on campus unless residing with relatives or granted off-campus permission by Department of Residence Life. **Housing:** Guaranteed on-campus for all undergraduates. Coed dorms, single-sex dorms, apartments, fraternity/sorority housing, wellness housing available. $200 nonrefundable deposit, deadline 5/1. **Activities:** Bands, campus ministries, choral groups, dance, drama, international student organizations, literary magazine, music ensembles, musical theater, radio station, student government, student newspaper, symphony orchestra, TV station, black self-education organization, Friends club, Egalitarians Supporting the Advancement of Women, Christian Fellowship, College Republicans, Habitat for Humanity, green club, College Democrats, Fellowship of Christian Athletes.

**Athletics.** NCAA. **Intercollegiate:** Baseball M, basketball, cheerleading M, cross-country, diving, football (tackle) M, golf, soccer, softball W, swimming, tennis, track and field, volleyball W, wrestling M. **Intramural:** Badminton, basketball, football (non-tackle) M, racquetball, soccer, softball, squash, table tennis, tennis, volleyball, wrestling M. **Team name:** Kohawks.

**Student services.** Adult student services, alcohol/substance abuse counseling, career counseling, student employment services, financial aid counseling, health services, minority student services, personal counseling, placement for graduates.

**Contact.** E-mail: admission@coe.edu
Phone: (319) 399-8500 Toll-free number: (877) 225-5263
Fax: (319) 399-8816
John Grundig, Dean of Admission, Coe College, 1220 First Avenue NE, Cedar Rapids, IA 52402

## Cornell College
**Mount Vernon, Iowa**
www.cornellcollege.edu

**CB member**
**CB code: 6119**

- Private 4-year liberal arts college affiliated with United Methodist Church
- Residential campus in small town
- 1,125 degree-seeking undergraduates: 52% women, 3% African American, 3% Asian American, 4% Hispanic American, 1% Native American, 5% international
- 44% of applicants admitted
- SAT or ACT (ACT writing optional), application essay required
- 64% graduate within 6 years; 51% enter graduate study

**General.** Founded in 1853. Regionally accredited. **Degrees:** 244 bachelor's awarded. **Location:** 15 miles from Cedar Rapids, 20 miles from Iowa City. **Calendar:** Nine terms of 3 and 1/2 weeks, one course per term. Extensive summer session. **Full-time faculty:** 87 total; 93% have terminal degrees, 7% minority, 48% women. **Part-time faculty:** 5 total; 80% have terminal degrees, 60% minority, 80% women. **Class size:** 67% < 20, 33% 20-39.

**Freshman class profile.** 3,208 applied, 1,411 admitted, 340 enrolled.

| Mid 50% test scores | | | |
|---|---|---|---|
| SAT critical reading: | 550-680 | GPA 2.0-2.99: | 16% |
| SAT math: | 550-680 | Rank in top quarter: | 57% |
| SAT writing: | 530-650 | Rank in top tenth: | 35% |
| ACT composite: | 24-29 | End year in good standing: | 99% |
| GPA 3.75 or higher: | 41% | Return as sophomores: | 79% |
| GPA 3.50-3.74: | 15% | Out-of-state: | 84% |
| GPA 3.0-3.49: | 28% | Live on campus: | 99% |

**Basis for selection.** Academic record, essay, co-curricular involvement, evidence of character, standardized test score, letters of reference, and recommended optional interview important. Primary consideration given to academic performance in college preparatory courses. **Homeschooled:** Transcript of courses and grades, interview, letter of recommendation (nonparent) required. Applicants asked to provide as many documents pertaining to their education as possible. **Learning Disabled:** Must have recent documentation of disability from official source if student requires special arrangements in academic setting.

**High school preparation.** College-preparatory program required. 15 units recommended. Recommended units include English 4, mathematics 3, social studies 3, science 3, foreign language 2 and academic electives 1. As many advanced, honors, and/or AP courses as possible recommended.

**2010-2011 Annual costs.** Tuition/fees (projected): $31,050. Room/board: $7,660. Books/supplies: $720. Personal expenses: $540.

**2009-2010 Financial aid. Need-based:** 277 full-time freshmen applied for aid; 242 were judged to have need; 242 of these received aid. Average need met was 95%. Average scholarship/grant was $22,730; average loan $3,517. 76% of total undergraduate aid awarded as scholarships/grants, 24% as loans/jobs. **Non-need-based:** Awarded to 877 full-time undergraduates, including 305 freshmen. Scholarships awarded for academics, art, leadership, minority status, music/drama, religious affiliation, state residency.

**Application procedures. Admission:** Priority date 12/1; deadline 2/1 (postmark date). $30 fee, may be waived for applicants with need, free for online applicants. Admission notification 3/20. Admission notification on a rolling basis. Must reply by May 1 or within 2 week(s) if notified thereafter. **Financial aid:** Closing date 3/1. FAFSA, institutional form required. Applicants notified on a rolling basis starting 3/1; must reply by 5/1 or within 2 week(s) of notification.

**Academics. Special study options:** Accelerated study, combined bachelor's/graduate degree, double major, ESL, exchange student, independent study, internships, liberal arts/career combination, semester at sea, student-designed major, study abroad, teacher certification program, urban semester, Washington semester. **Credit/placement by examination:** AP, CLEP, IB, institutional tests. **Support services:** Learning center, study skills assistance, tutoring, writing center.

**Majors. Area/ethnic studies:** Latin American, Russian/Slavic, women's. **Biology:** General, biochemistry, Biochemistry/biophysics and molecular biology, ecology, molecular, molecular biochemistry. **Computer sciences:** Computer science. **Conservation:** Environmental studies. **Education:** General, art, biology, chemistry, elementary, English, French, German, history, mathematics, middle, music, physical, physics, science, secondary, social science, social studies, Spanish. **Foreign languages:** General, classics, French, German, Russian, Spanish. **History:** General. **Math:** General. **Parks/recreation:** Exercise sciences, health/fitness. **Philosophy/religion:** Philosophy, religion. **Physical sciences:** Chemistry, geology, physics. **Psychology:** General. **Social sciences:** Anthropology, archaeology, economics, international relations, political science, sociology. **Visual/performing arts:** Art, art history/conservation, dramatic, music history, music performance, music theory/composition, stringed instruments, studio arts, theater design, voice/opera. **Other:** Ethnic studies, Medieval and early modern studies, sociology and anthropology.

**Most popular majors.** Biology 14%, education 8%, English 7%, foreign language 6%, history 10%, philosophy/religious studies 6%, psychology 11%, social sciences 19%, visual/performing arts 9%.

**Computing on campus.** 181 workstations in library, computer center, student center. Dormitories wired for high-speed internet access and linked to campus network. Commuter students can connect to campus network. Online course registration, online library, helpline, repair service, student web hosting, wireless network available.

**Student life. Freshman orientation:** Mandatory. Five-day orientation held before fall classes begin. **Housing:** Guaranteed on-campus for freshmen. Coed dorms, single-sex dorms, apartments, wellness housing available. $300 partly refundable deposit, deadline 5/1. First-year halls/floors available. **Activities:** Bands, campus ministries, choral groups, dance, drama, international student organizations, literary magazine, music ensembles, musical theater, opera, radio station, student government, student newspaper, symphony orchestra, Alpha Phi Omega, alumni student association, Fellowship of Christian Athletes, black awareness cultural organization, women's action group, Young Democrats, College Republicans, Habitat for Humanity, Organization for Latino Awareness, lunch buddies/youth mentoring.

**Athletics.** NCAA. **Intercollegiate:** Baseball M, basketball, cross-country, football (tackle) M, golf, soccer, softball W, tennis, track and field, volleyball W, wrestling M. **Intramural:** Badminton, basketball, bowling, football (non-tackle), racquetball, soccer, softball, table tennis, track and field, volleyball. **Team name:** Rams.

**Student services.** Adult student services, alcohol/substance abuse counseling, chaplain/spiritual director, career counseling, student employment services, financial aid counseling, health services, minority student services, personal counseling, women's services.

**Contact.** E-mail: admissions@cornellcollege.edu
Phone: (319) 895-4215 Toll-free number: (800) 747-1112
Fax: (319) 895-4451
Jonathan Stroud, Vice President for Enrollment/Dean of Admissions and Financial Aid, Cornell College, 600 First Street SW, Mount Vernon, IA 52314-1098

## Divine Word College
### Epworth, Iowa
### www.dwci.edu
### CB code: 6174

- Private 4-year liberal arts and seminary college for men affiliated with Roman Catholic Church
- Rural community
- 89 degree-seeking undergraduates
- Application essay, interview required

**General.** Founded in 1912. Regionally accredited. **Degrees:** 2 bachelor's, 1 associate awarded. **Location:** 15 miles from Dubuque. **Calendar:** Semester. **Full-time faculty:** 22 total. **Part-time faculty:** 3 total.

**Freshman class profile.**

| Mid 50% test scores | | |
|---|---|---|
| SAT critical reading: | 520-620 | SAT math: 520-570 |

**Basis for selection.** Interview and religious commitment most important. School achievement record, test scores, recommendations, and school and community activities also considered. Minnesota Multiphasic Personality Inventory (MMPI) used for admission and counseling. SAT or ACT writing component considered if submitted.

**High school preparation.** 16 units required. Required and recommended units include mathematics 3, social studies 3, science 3 and foreign language 2. 1 performing arts recommended.

**2009-2010 Annual costs.** Tuition/fees: $10,900. Room/board: $2,850. Books/supplies: $500.

**Application procedures.** **Admission:** Closing date 7/15. $25 fee, may be waived for applicants with need. Admission notification on a rolling basis beginning on or about 1/1. **Financial aid:** Priority date 8/31; no closing date. Applicants notified on a rolling basis starting 8/1.

**Academics.** **Special study options:** Double major, dual enrollment of high school students, independent study. **Credit/placement by examination:** AP, CLEP, institutional tests. **Support services:** Reduced course load, remedial instruction, tutoring.

**Majors.** **Interdisciplinary:** Intercultural. **Philosophy/religion:** Philosophy, religion.

**Computing on campus.** 26 workstations in computer center.

**Student life.** **Policies:** Religious observance required. **Housing:** All students live in dormitories on campus. **Activities:** Campus ministries, choral groups, student government, Vietnamese student organization, Sudanese student organization, social justice committee, Right to Life committee.

**Athletics.** **Intramural:** Basketball M, soccer M, swimming M, table tennis M, tennis M, volleyball M.

**Student services.** Career counseling, health services, personal counseling.

**Contact.** E-mail: svdvocations@dwci.edu
Phone: (563) 876-3332 Toll-free number: (800) 553-3321
Fax: (563) 876-5515
Len Uhal, Vice President for Recruitment and Admissions, Divine Word College, 102 Jacoby Drive SW, Epworth, IA 52045

## Dordt College
### Sioux Center, Iowa
### www.dordt.edu
### CB code: 6171

- Private 4-year liberal arts college affiliated with Christian Reformed Church
- Residential campus in small town
- 1,274 degree-seeking undergraduates: 1% part-time, 51% women, 1% Hispanic American, 15% international
- 84% of applicants admitted
- SAT or ACT (ACT writing optional) required
- 61% graduate within 6 years; 15% enter graduate study

**General.** Founded in 1955. Regionally accredited. **Degrees:** 277 bachelor's, 27 associate awarded; master's offered. **Location:** 45 miles from Sioux City; 55 miles from Sioux Falls, SD. **Calendar:** Semester. **Full-time faculty:** 79 total; 62% have terminal degrees, 4% minority, 23% women. **Part-time faculty:** 27 total; 11% have terminal degrees, 59% women. **Class size:** 61% < 20, 30% 20-39, 5% 40-49, 3% 50-99, less than 1% >100. **Special facilities:** Farm, biotechnology research facility, natural prairie plot.

**Freshman class profile.** 1,006 applied, 842 admitted, 364 enrolled.

| Mid 50% test scores | | | | |
|---|---|---|---|---|
| SAT critical reading: | 460-610 | GPA 2.0-2.99: | | 15% |
| SAT math: | 480-620 | Rank in top quarter: | | 57% |
| SAT writing: | 440-580 | Rank in top tenth: | | 35% |
| ACT composite: | 22-27 | Return as sophomores: | | 74% |
| GPA 3.75 or higher: | 40% | Out-of-state: | | 65% |
| GPA 3.50-3.74: | 17% | Live on campus: | | 90% |
| GPA 3.0-3.49: | 28% | International: | | 8% |

**Basis for selection.** School achievement record, high school GPA, test scores, religious affiliation or commitment important. Applicants with less than 2.25 GPA considered on individual basis, may be admitted provisionally. Interview recommended for academically borderline applicants. **Home-schooled:** Must submit certified GPA. **Learning Disabled:** Copies of prior testing and interview with learning disabilities advisor required.

**High school preparation.** College-preparatory program required. 19 units required; 25 recommended. Required and recommended units include English 3-4, mathematics 2-3, social studies 1, history 2, science 2-4, foreign language 2-3 and academic electives 6. 10 units must be in social science, English, foreign language, natural science, or math. Math must include algebra, geometry.

**2010-2011 Annual costs.** Tuition/fees: $23,180. Room/board: $6,320. Books/supplies: $780. Personal expenses: $2,000.

**2008-2009 Financial aid.** **Need-based:** 317 full-time freshmen applied for aid; 274 were judged to have need; 274 of these received aid. Average need met was 90%. Average scholarship/grant was $13,246; average loan $5,266. 56% of total undergraduate aid awarded as scholarships/grants, 44% as loans/jobs. **Non-need-based:** Awarded to 325 full-time undergraduates, including 94 freshmen. Scholarships awarded for academics, alumni affiliation, art, athletics, job skills, leadership, minority status, music/drama, religious affiliation, state residency.

**Application procedures.** **Admission:** Closing date 7/31. $25 fee, may be waived for applicants with need. Admission notification on a rolling basis beginning on or about 10/1. Must reply by May 1 or within 1 week(s) if notified thereafter. **Financial aid:** Priority date 4/1; no closing date. FAFSA, institutional form required. Applicants notified on a rolling basis starting 3/1; must reply within 3 week(s) of notification.

**Academics.** **Special study options:** Combined bachelor's/graduate degree, double major, ESL, honors, independent study, internships, liberal arts/career combination, student-designed major, study abroad, teacher certification program, urban semester, Washington semester. Iowa Legislative Intern program; China, England, Costa Rica, Russia, Latin America, Netherlands, and Germany semesters; Los Angeles-Film Institute semester, Chicago Metro semester, American Studies semester. **Credit/placement by examination:** AP, CLEP, IB, SAT, ACT, institutional tests. Registrar makes determination on case-by-case basis. Some credit may be given for work experience. **Support services:** Learning center, reduced course load, remedial instruction, study skills assistance, tutoring.

**Majors. Agriculture:** Agribusiness operations, animal sciences, business, plant sciences. **Biology:** General. **Business:** General, accounting, accounting/business management, information resources management, marketing. **Communications:** General, broadcast journalism, digital media, journalism, media studies, public relations. **Communications technology:** General, graphics. **Computer sciences:** General, computer science, information systems, LAN/WAN management, system admin. **Conservation:** General, environmental studies. **Education:** General, art, biology, business, chemistry, drama/dance, elementary, English, foreign languages, health, history, mathematics, middle, music, physical, physics, reading, science, secondary, social science, social studies, Spanish, special, speech. **Engineering:** General, agricultural, biomedical, civil, computer, electrical, mechanical. **Engineering technology:** General. **Foreign languages:** Dutch/Flemish, Spanish. **Health:** Athletic training, clinical lab science, clinical lab technology, health services, nursing (RN), predental, premedicine, prepharmacy, preveterinary. **History:** General. **Legal studies:** Prelaw. **Liberal arts:** Arts/sciences. **Math:** General. **Parks/recreation:** General, exercise sciences, health/fitness, sports admin. **Philosophy/religion:** Philosophy, religion. **Physical sciences:** General, chemistry, physics. **Protective services:** Police science. **Psychology:** General. **Public administration:** General, social work. **Social sciences:** General, political science. **Theology:** Missionary, sacred music, theology, youth ministry. **Visual/performing arts:** Art, commercial/advertising art, design, dramatic, piano/organ, stringed instruments, voice/opera.

**Most popular majors.** Business/marketing 19%, education 16%, engineering/engineering technologies 6%, parks/recreation 6%.

**Computing on campus.** 200 workstations in dormitories, library, computer center, student center. Dormitories wired for high-speed internet access and linked to campus network. Commuter students can connect to campus network. Online course registration, online library, helpline, wireless network available.

**Student life. Freshman orientation:** Mandatory. Preregistration for classes offered. Three-day program prior to beginning of classes. **Policies:** Non-smoking campus. Religious observance required. **Housing:** Guaranteed on-campus for all undergraduates. Single-sex dorms, special housing for disabled, apartments, wellness housing available. $100 deposit, deadline 6/1. **Activities:** Bands, campus ministries, choral groups, dance, drama, film society, international student organizations, literary magazine, music ensembles, musical theater, opera, radio station, student government, student newspaper, symphony orchestra, 50 clubs and student organizations.

**Athletics.** NAIA. **Intercollegiate:** Baseball M, basketball, cross-country, football (tackle) M, golf, ice hockey M, soccer, softball W, tennis, track and field, volleyball W. **Intramural:** Badminton, basketball, bowling, cross-country, field hockey, golf, racquetball, soccer, softball, swimming, tennis, volleyball, weight lifting. **Team name:** Defenders.

**Student services.** Adult student services, alcohol/substance abuse counseling, chaplain/spiritual director, career counseling, student employment services, financial aid counseling, health services, minority student services, personal counseling, placement for graduates, veterans' counselor, women's services. **Physically disabled:** Services for visually, speech, hearing impaired. **Learning disabled:** Comprehensive services available.

**Contact.** E-mail: admission@dordt.edu
Phone: (712) 722-6080 Toll-free number: (800) 343-6738
Fax: (712) 722-6035
Quentin Van Essen, Executive Director of Admissions, Dordt College, 498 Fourth Avenue, NE, Sioux Center, IA 51250

## Drake University
**Des Moines, Iowa** — CB member
www.drake.edu — CB code: 6168

- Private 4-year university
- Residential campus in large city
- 3,543 degree-seeking undergraduates: 6% part-time, 58% women, 3% African American, 3% Asian American, 3% Hispanic American, 7% international
- 2,002 degree-seeking graduate students
- 74% of applicants admitted
- SAT or ACT (ACT writing optional), application essay required
- 76% graduate within 6 years

**General.** Founded in 1881. Regionally accredited. **Degrees:** 846 bachelor's awarded; master's, doctoral, professional offered. **ROTC:** Army, Air Force. **Location:** 150 miles from Omaha, NE; 194 miles from Kansas City, MO. **Calendar:** Semester, extensive summer session. **Full-time faculty:** 275 total; 94% have terminal degrees, 12% minority, 46% women. **Part-time faculty:** 145 total. **Class size:** 29% < 20, 45% 20-39, 14% 40-49, 6% 50-99, 5% >100. **Special facilities:** Observatory, greenhouse.

**Freshman class profile.** 4,829 applied, 3,577 admitted, 863 enrolled.

| Mid 50% test scores | | | |
|---|---|---|---|
| SAT critical reading: | 510-640 | Rank in top quarter: | 70% |
| SAT math: | 530-660 | Rank in top tenth: | 38% |
| ACT composite: | 24-29 | Return as sophomores: | 88% |
| GPA 3.75 or higher: | 50% | Out-of-state: | 67% |
| GPA 3.50-3.74: | 19% | Live on campus: | 97% |
| GPA 3.0-3.49: | 24% | International: | 3% |
| GPA 2.0-2.99: | 7% | Fraternities: | 30% |
| | | Sororities: | 27% |

**Basis for selection.** High school academic record, test scores, extracurricular activities, counselor recommendation, and essay important. Comprehensive review completed and each item in student's file considered. Interview recommended for all, required for some. Audition required of music and theater majors. Portfolio recommended for art majors.

**High school preparation.** College-preparatory program recommended. 16 units recommended. Recommended units include English 4, mathematics 3, social studies 4, science 2 (laboratory 1) and foreign language 2.

**2010-2011 Annual costs.** Tuition/fees: $26,960. Room/board: $8,130. Books/supplies: $900. Personal expenses: $1,500.

**2009-2010 Financial aid. Need-based:** 726 full-time freshmen applied for aid; 546 were judged to have need; 546 of these received aid. Average need met was 84%. Average scholarship/grant was $14,496; average loan $4,499. 94% of total undergraduate aid awarded as scholarships/grants, 6% as loans/jobs. **Non-need-based:** Awarded to 1,653 full-time undergraduates, including 426 freshmen. Scholarships awarded for academics, alumni affiliation, art, athletics, music/drama, ROTC, state residency.

**Application procedures. Admission:** Priority date 3/1; no deadline. $25 fee, may be waived for applicants with need, free for online applicants. Admission notification on a rolling basis beginning on or about 10/15. **Financial aid:** Priority date 3/1; no closing date. FAFSA required. Applicants notified on a rolling basis starting 3/1; must reply by 5/1 or within 3 week(s) of notification.

**Academics.** Peer support through academic departments and residence halls offered. **Special study options:** Accelerated study, combined bachelor's/graduate degree, cooperative education, distance learning, double major, dual enrollment of high school students, ESL, honors, independent study, internships, liberal arts/career combination, semester at sea, student-designed major, study abroad, teacher certification program, Washington semester. **Credit/placement by examination:** AP, CLEP, IB, institutional tests. 66 credit hours maximum toward bachelor's degree. **Support services:** Study skills assistance, tutoring, writing center.

**Majors. Biology:** General, biochemistry, cellular/molecular, pharmacology. **Business:** General, accounting, actuarial science, finance, international, management information systems, management science, managerial economics, marketing. **Communications:** General, advertising, broadcast journalism, journalism, media studies, public relations, radio/tv. **Computer sciences:** General, computer science, information technology. **Conservation:** Environmental science, management/policy. **Education:** Curriculum, elementary, mathematics, music, secondary. **Health:** Health services, pharmaceutical sciences. **History:** General. **Interdisciplinary:** Neuroscience. **Legal studies:** General. **Math:** General. **Philosophy/religion:** Ethics, philosophy, religion. **Physical sciences:** Astronomy, chemistry, physics. **Psychology:** General. **Social sciences:** General, anthropology, economics, international relations, political science, sociology. **Visual/performing arts:** Acting, art history/conservation, commercial/advertising art, directing/producing, dramatic, drawing, music management, music performance, painting, printmaking, sculpture, theater design.

**Most popular majors.** Biology 8%, business/marketing 34%, communications/journalism 13%, education 8%, social sciences 8%, visual/performing arts 8%.

**Computing on campus.** 4,900 workstations in dormitories, library, computer center, student center. Dormitories wired for high-speed internet access and linked to campus network. Commuter students can connect to campus network. Online course registration, online library, helpline, repair service, student web hosting, wireless network available.

**Student life. Freshman orientation:** Available, $90 fee. Preregistration for classes offered. Four 1-1/2 day sessions held in June; includes parents. **Policies:** Student leaders must maintain 2.0 GPA. Students must live on-campus first 2 years following high school. **Housing:** Guaranteed on-campus for freshmen. Coed dorms, special housing for disabled, apartments, fraternity/sorority housing, wellness housing available. $250 nonrefundable deposit, deadline 5/1. **Activities:** Bands, campus ministries, choral groups, drama, international student organizations, literary magazine, music ensembles, Model UN, musical theater, radio station, student government, student newspaper, symphony orchestra, coalition of black students, Best Buddies, College Republicans, College Democrats, La Fuerza Latina,

Alpha Phi Omega, South Asian student association, Rainbow Union, Drake Hillel.

**Athletics.** NCAA. **Intercollegiate:** Basketball, cheerleading, cross-country, football (tackle) M, golf, rowing (crew) W, soccer, softball W, tennis, track and field, volleyball W. **Intramural:** Badminton, basketball, football (non-tackle), football (tackle) M, golf, racquetball, soccer, swimming, tennis, volleyball. **Team name:** Bulldogs.

**Student services.** Career counseling, student employment services, financial aid counseling, health services, legal services, personal counseling, placement for graduates. **Physically disabled:** Services for visually, speech, hearing impaired.

**Contact.** E-mail: admission@drake.edu
Phone: (515) 271-3181 Toll-free number: (800) 443-7253
Fax: (515) 271-2831
Laura Linn, Director of Admission, Drake University, 2507 University Avenue, Des Moines, IA 50311-4505

## Emmaus Bible College
### Dubuque, Iowa
### www.emmaus.edu
**CB code: 1215**

- Private 4-year Bible college affiliated with Brethren Church
- Residential campus in small city
- 245 degree-seeking undergraduates
- 64% of applicants admitted
- SAT or ACT (ACT writing optional), application essay required

**General.** Founded in 1942. Accredited by ABHE. **Degrees:** 40 bachelor's, 10 associate awarded. **Location:** 90 miles from Waterloo, 150 miles from Chicago. **Calendar:** Semester. **Full-time faculty:** 22 total. **Part-time faculty:** 14 total. **Class size:** 75% < 20, 14% 20-39, 4% 40-49, 7% 50-99.

**Freshman class profile.** 112 applied, 72 admitted, 45 enrolled.

| Mid 50% test scores | | | |
|---|---|---|---|
| SAT critical reading: | 480-650 | GPA 3.0-3.49: | 32% |
| SAT math: | 500-610 | GPA 2.0-2.99: | 27% |
| ACT composite: | 19-25 | Rank in top quarter: | 27% |
| GPA 3.75 or higher: | 17% | Rank in top tenth: | 2% |
| GPA 3.50-3.74: | 24% | Out-of-state: | 70% |
| | | Live on campus: | 99% |

**Basis for selection.** Recommendations and essay most important. GPA also important. Interview recommended. **Homeschooled:** Transcript of courses and grades, letter of recommendation (nonparent) required.

**2009-2010 Annual costs.** Tuition/fees: $11,578. Room/board: $5,396. Books/supplies: $600. Personal expenses: $1,600.

**Financial aid. Non-need-based:** Scholarships awarded for academics, music/drama.

**Application procedures. Admission:** Priority date 7/9; no deadline. $25 fee. Admission notification on a rolling basis. Must reply by May 1 or within 2 week(s) if notified thereafter. **Financial aid:** Priority date 5/15, closing date 7/1. FAFSA, institutional form required. Applicants notified on a rolling basis starting 3/1; must reply within 2 week(s) of notification.

**Academics. Special study options:** Combined bachelor's/graduate degree, double major, dual enrollment of high school students, ESL, internships, teacher certification program. **Credit/placement by examination:** AP, CLEP, IB, SAT, ACT, institutional tests. 9 credit hours maximum toward associate degree, 18 toward bachelor's. **Support services:** Reduced course load, remedial instruction, study skills assistance, tutoring.

**Majors. Computer sciences:** General. **Education:** Elementary, music. **Theology:** Bible, missionary, theology, youth ministry.

**Most popular majors.** Computer/information sciences 13%, education 25%, theological studies 25%.

**Computing on campus.** 60 workstations in library, computer center, student center. Dormitories wired for high-speed internet access and linked to campus network. Online library, wireless network available.

**Student life. Freshman orientation:** Mandatory. Held 4 days immediately preceding first day of class. **Policies:** No smoking, alcohol consumption, dancing. **Housing:** Guaranteed on-campus for all undergraduates. Single-sex dorms available. $170 nonrefundable deposit, deadline 7/9. **Activities:** Choral groups, drama, international student organizations, radio station, student government.

**Athletics.** NCCAA. **Intercollegiate:** Basketball. **Intramural:** Badminton, basketball, cross-country, football (non-tackle), golf, racquetball, soccer, softball, table tennis, tennis, volleyball. **Team name:** Eagles.

**Student services.** Chaplain/spiritual director, career counseling, student employment services, financial aid counseling, health services, personal counseling, veterans' counselor.

**Contact.** E-mail: info@emmaus.edu
Phone: (563) 588-8000 ext. 1310 Fax: (563) 588-1216
Israel Chavez, Director of Admissions, Emmaus Bible College, 2570 Asbury Road, Dubuque, IA 52001

## Faith Baptist Bible College and Theological Seminary
### Ankeny, Iowa
### www.faith.edu
**CB code: 6214**

- Private 4-year Bible and seminary college affiliated with General Association of Regular Baptist Churches
- Residential campus in large town
- 340 degree-seeking undergraduates: 10% part-time, 59% women, 1% African American, 1% Asian American, 2% Hispanic American, 1% Native American, 1% international
- 52 degree-seeking graduate students
- 57% of applicants admitted
- SAT or ACT (ACT writing optional), application essay required
- 47% graduate within 6 years

**General.** Founded in 1921. Regionally accredited; also accredited by ABHE. **Degrees:** 37 bachelor's, 14 associate awarded; master's offered. **Location:** 6 miles from Des Moines. **Calendar:** Semester, limited summer session. **Full-time faculty:** 21 total; 62% have terminal degrees, 10% minority, 14% women. **Part-time faculty:** 15 total; 27% have terminal degrees, 7% minority, 33% women. **Class size:** 65% < 20, 19% 20-39, 2% 40-49, 10% 50-99, 3% >100.

**Freshman class profile.** 179 applied, 102 admitted, 91 enrolled.

| Mid 50% test scores | | | |
|---|---|---|---|
| SAT critical reading: | 570-630 | GPA 3.0-3.49: | 25% |
| SAT math: | 540-570 | GPA 2.0-2.99: | 27% |
| SAT writing: | 580-620 | Rank in top quarter: | 42% |
| ACT composite: | 20-25 | Rank in top tenth: | 16% |
| GPA 3.75 or higher: | 31% | Return as sophomores: | 79% |
| GPA 3.50-3.74: | 17% | Out-of-state: | 53% |
| | | Live on campus: | 95% |

**Basis for selection.** Recommendations, church affiliation, character qualities important. Interview recommended for borderline applicants. **Homeschooled:** Transcript of courses and grades required. Validation by third-party testing recommended, such as SAT, ACT, GED. **Learning Disabled:** Request for accommodation must be submitted.

**High school preparation.** College-preparatory program required. Recommended units include English 4, mathematics 4, social studies 3, history 4, science 3 (laboratory 3), foreign language 2 and computer science 4.

**2009-2010 Annual costs.** Tuition/fees: $13,260. Room/board: $5,510.

**2008-2009 Financial aid. Non-need-based:** Scholarships awarded for academics, leadership, music/drama.

**Application procedures. Admission:** Priority date 6/1; deadline 8/1 (postmark date). $25 fee, may be waived for applicants with need. Application must be submitted on paper. Admission notification on a rolling basis. **Financial aid:** Priority date 4/1; no closing date. FAFSA required. Applicants notified on a rolling basis starting 3/15.

**Academics. Special study options:** Internships, liberal arts/career combination, study abroad, teacher certification program. **Credit/placement by examination:** AP, CLEP, institutional tests. 6 credit hours maximum toward associate degree, 12 toward bachelor's. **Support services:** Learning center, reduced course load, remedial instruction, study skills assistance, tutoring.

**Majors. Education:** Elementary, English, middle, music, secondary. **Theology:** Bible, missionary, religious ed, sacred music, theology.

**Most popular majors.** Education 35%, philosophy/religious studies 49%, theological studies 16%.

**Computing on campus.** 46 workstations in dormitories, library, computer center. Dormitories wired for high-speed internet access and linked to campus network. Repair service, wireless network available.

**Student life. Freshman orientation:** Mandatory. Preregistration for classes offered. Held weekend before classes start in fall. **Policies:** All single students under the age of 26 and not living at home must live in the residence halls. Religious observance required. **Housing:** Guaranteed on-campus for freshmen. Single-sex dorms, special housing for disabled, apartments available. $200 deposit, deadline 6/1. **Activities:** Bands, choral groups, drama, music ensembles, student government, student missionary fellowship, missionary kids fellowship, missions ambassadors, student association, Future Christian Teachers Association, ladies fellowship.

**Athletics.** NCCAA. **Intercollegiate:** Basketball, soccer, volleyball W. **Intramural:** Basketball, football (tackle). **Team name:** Eagles.

**Student services.** Career counseling, financial aid counseling, health services, personal counseling, placement for graduates, veterans' counselor.

**Contact.** E-mail: admissions@faith.edu
Phone: (515) 964-0601 ext. 233 Toll-free number: (888) 324-8448
Fax: (515) 964-1638
Patrick Odle, Vice President Enrollment/Constituency Services, Faith Baptist Bible College and Theological Seminary, 1900 NW Fourth Street, Ankeny, IA 50023

---

## Graceland University

Lamoni, Iowa
www.graceland.edu                              CB code: 6249

- Private 4-year university and liberal arts college affiliated with Community of Christ
- Residential campus in rural community
- 1,330 degree-seeking undergraduates: 12% part-time, 60% women, 10% African American, 2% Asian American, 3% Hispanic American, 1% Native American, 9% international
- 809 degree-seeking graduate students
- 88% of applicants admitted
- SAT or ACT (ACT writing optional) required
- 50% graduate within 6 years; 26% enter graduate study

**General.** Founded in 1895. Regionally accredited. Additional campus in Independence, MO. Evening and weekend programs offered at Indian Hills Community College and North Central Missouri College. **Degrees:** 425 bachelor's awarded; master's offered. **Location:** 75 miles from Des Moines, 110 miles from Kansas City. **Calendar:** 4-1-4, limited summer session. **Full-time faculty:** 85 total; 68% have terminal degrees, 16% minority, 56% women. **Part-time faculty:** 34 total; 24% have terminal degrees, 3% minority, 53% women. **Class size:** 64% < 20, 31% 20-39, 3% 40-49, 2% 50-99. **Special facilities:** International health center, Korean War study center, science center, nuclear magnetic resonance spectrometer, ultra-centrifuge, -80 degrees freezer.

**Freshman class profile.** 598 applied, 526 admitted, 222 enrolled.

| Mid 50% test scores | | | | |
|---|---|---|---|---|
| SAT critical reading: | 420-530 | Rank in top quarter: | 30% |
| SAT math: | 420-550 | Rank in top tenth: | 11% |
| ACT composite: | 16-23 | End year in good standing: | 69% |
| GPA 3.75 or higher: | 20% | Return as sophomores: | 68% |
| GPA 3.50-3.74: | 13% | Out-of-state: | 30% |
| GPA 3.0-3.49: | 23% | Live on campus: | 98% |
| GPA 2.0-2.99: | 42% | International: | 8% |

**Basis for selection.** Rank in upper 50% of class, 2.5 GPA, 21 ACT or 960 SAT (exclusive of Writing) important. Applicants who do not meet admissions criteria may be considered and will be required to take developmental courses if accepted. Some applicants must test for Chance Program prior to being considered. Interview required of applicants who do not meet admissions requirements, recommended for others. Portfolio recommended of art majors. **Homeschooled:** State certificate of completion of home study program required.

**High school preparation.** College-preparatory program recommended. 16 units recommended. Recommended units include English 4, mathematics 4, social studies 4 and science 4.

**2010-2011 Annual costs.** Tuition/fees: $20,980. Room/board: $7,040. Books/supplies: $1,000. Personal expenses: $1,760.

**2009-2010 Financial aid. Need-based:** 202 full-time freshmen applied for aid; 189 were judged to have need; 185 of these received aid. Average need met was 86%. Average scholarship/grant was $15,432; average loan $4,790. 53% of total undergraduate aid awarded as scholarships/grants, 47% as loans/jobs. **Non-need-based:** Awarded to 774 full-time undergraduates, including 176 freshmen. Scholarships awarded for academics, alumni affiliation, art, athletics, job skills, leadership, music/drama, religious affiliation. **Additional information:** Founders Scholarship will supplement other gift aid until percentage of calculated need has been met.

**Application procedures. Admission:** No deadline. $50 fee, may be waived for applicants with need, free for online applicants. Admission notification on a rolling basis. **Financial aid:** No deadline. FAFSA required. Applicants notified on a rolling basis starting 3/1; must reply within 2 week(s) of notification.

**Academics.** Distance Learning programs delivered to online cohorts and at multiple off-campus locations. Nursing program delivered through online study and on-campus residency sessions, and available only to individuals licensed as registered nurses in the U.S. **Special study options:** Accelerated study, combined bachelor's/graduate degree, distance learning, double major, dual enrollment of high school students, ESL, honors, independent study, internships, liberal arts/career combination, student-designed major, study abroad, teacher certification program. Accelerated nursing program available. **Credit/placement by examination:** AP, CLEP, IB, SAT, ACT, institutional tests. 30 credit hours maximum toward bachelor's degree. Credit by standardized examinations is awarded based on American Council on Education recommendations. **Support services:** Learning center, reduced course load, remedial instruction, study skills assistance, tutoring, writing center.

**Majors. Biology:** General. **Business:** Accounting, business admin. **Communications:** General. **Communications technology:** Desktop publishing. **Computer sciences:** General. **Education:** Elementary. **Family/consumer sciences:** Food/nutrition. **Foreign languages:** Spanish. **Health:** Athletic training, nursing (RN). **History:** General. **Interdisciplinary:** Global studies. **Liberal arts:** Arts/sciences. **Math:** General. **Parks/recreation:** General, health/fitness, sports admin. **Philosophy/religion:** Religion. **Physical sciences:** Chemistry. **Psychology:** General. **Social sciences:** Economics, sociology. **Visual/performing arts:** General, commercial/advertising art, dramatic, studio arts.

**Most popular majors.** Business/marketing 13%, education 30%, health sciences 28%, visual/performing arts 6%.

**Computing on campus.** 106 workstations in dormitories, library, computer center, student center. Dormitories wired for high-speed internet access and linked to campus network. Commuter students can connect to campus network. Online library, helpline, student web hosting, wireless network available.

**Student life. Freshman orientation:** Mandatory. Preregistration for classes offered. Early 1-day orientation sessions in spring and summer. Additional 2-3 day orientation at beginning of semester. **Policies:** No tobacco, alcohol, or drug use on campus. Students required to live on campus through sophomore year unless married or living with relatives. **Housing:** Guaranteed on-campus for all undergraduates. Single-sex dorms, special housing for disabled, apartments available. $200 fully refundable deposit, deadline 5/1. **Activities:** Bands, campus ministries, choral groups, dance, drama, film society, international student organizations, music ensembles, musical theater, radio station, student government, student newspaper, symphony orchestra, religious life program, social service projects, peace organization, Amnesty International, OASIS, Students for Free Enterprise, Habitat for Humanity, Young Republicans, Young Democrats.

**Athletics.** NAIA. **Intercollegiate:** Baseball M, basketball, cheerleading M, cross-country, football (tackle) M, golf, soccer, softball W, tennis, track and field, volleyball. **Intramural:** Badminton, baseball M, basketball, cross-country, football (non-tackle), golf, handball, racquetball, soccer, softball, swimming, table tennis, tennis, track and field, volleyball. **Team name:** Yellowjackets.

**Student services.** Adult student services, alcohol/substance abuse counseling, chaplain/spiritual director, career counseling, student employment services, financial aid counseling, health services, minority student services, personal counseling, placement for graduates, veterans' counselor. **Physically disabled:** Services for visually impaired.

**Contact.** E-mail: admissions@graceland.edu
Phone: (641) 784-5196 Toll-free number: (866) 472-2352
Fax: (641) 784-5480
Greg Sutherland, Vice President for Enrollment and Dean of Admissions, Graceland University, One University Place, Lamoni, IA 50140

---

## Grand View University

Des Moines, Iowa                                CB member
www.grandview.edu                               CB code: 6251

- Private 4-year liberal arts college affiliated with Evangelical Lutheran Church in America
- Commuter campus in large city

- 1,921 degree-seeking undergraduates: 17% part-time, 62% women, 7% African American, 3% Asian American, 3% Hispanic American, 1% international
- 21 degree-seeking graduate students
- 95% of applicants admitted
- SAT or ACT (ACT writing recommended) required
- 48% graduate within 6 years

**General.** Founded in 1896. Regionally accredited. **Degrees:** 409 bachelor's, 1 associate awarded; master's offered. **ROTC:** Army, Air Force. **Location:** 200 miles from Kansas City, Missouri; 250 miles from Minneapolis-St. Paul. **Calendar:** Semester, extensive summer session. **Full-time faculty:** 87 total; 58% have terminal degrees, 7% minority, 62% women. **Part-time faculty:** 116 total; 24% have terminal degrees, 3% minority, 56% women. **Class size:** 70% < 20, 30% 20-39, less than 1% 40-49.

**Freshman class profile.** 689 applied, 653 admitted, 233 enrolled.

| Mid 50% test scores | | | |
|---|---|---|---|
| SAT critical reading: | 410-500 | GPA 2.0-2.99: | 31% |
| SAT math: | 380-500 | Rank in top quarter: | 36% |
| SAT writing: | 410-480 | Rank in top tenth: | 16% |
| ACT composite: | 18-23 | Return as sophomores: | 70% |
| GPA 3.75 or higher: | 17% | Out-of-state: | 19% |
| GPA 3.50-3.74: | 14% | Live on campus: | 79% |
| GPA 3.0-3.49: | 38% | International: | 3% |

**Basis for selection.** Admissions based on individualized evaluation of applicant's secondary school record and SAT or ACT score. **Homeschooled:** Transcript of courses and grades required.

**High school preparation.** College-preparatory program recommended. 15 units recommended. Recommended units include English 4, mathematics 3, social studies 3, science 3 and foreign language 2.

**2009-2010 Annual costs.** Tuition/fees: $19,274. Room/board: $6,736. Books/supplies: $900. Personal expenses: $2,150.

**2009-2010 Financial aid.** **Need-based:** 219 full-time freshmen applied for aid; 191 were judged to have need; 191 of these received aid. Average need met was 86%. Average scholarship/grant was $14,884; average loan $3,772. 55% of total undergraduate aid awarded as scholarships/grants, 45% as loans/jobs. **Non-need-based:** Awarded to 484 full-time undergraduates, including 156 freshmen. Scholarships awarded for academics, alumni affiliation, art, athletics, leadership, music/drama, religious affiliation.

**Application procedures.** **Admission:** Closing date 8/15 (receipt date). $35 fee, may be waived for applicants with need. Admission notification on a rolling basis beginning on or about 9/15. **Financial aid:** Priority date 3/1; no closing date. FAFSA required. Applicants notified on a rolling basis starting 3/1; must reply by 5/1 or within 4 week(s) of notification.

**Academics.** University emphasizes integration of liberal arts core with career-related majors. Internships are primary focus in many majors. **Special study options:** Accelerated study, cooperative education, cross-registration, distance learning, double major, dual enrollment of high school students, honors, independent study, internships, liberal arts/career combination, student-designed major, study abroad, teacher certification program, Washington semester, weekend college. **Credit/placement by examination:** AP, CLEP, IB, SAT, ACT, institutional tests. 32 credit hours maximum toward bachelor's degree. ACT PEP credit accepted, DANTES accepted. **Support services:** Learning center, reduced course load, remedial instruction, study skills assistance, tutoring, writing center.

**Majors. Agriculture:** Business. **Biology:** General. **Business:** General, accounting, entrepreneurial studies, finance, hospitality admin, human resources, marketing, real estate. **Communications:** Broadcast journalism, journalism, media studies, public relations, radio/tv. **Communications technology:** Graphics. **Computer sciences:** General, information technology, programming. **Education:** Elementary, secondary. **Health:** Health services, nursing (RN), premedicine, prepharmacy. **History:** General. **Legal studies:** Paralegal, prelaw. **Liberal arts:** Arts/sciences. **Math:** Applied. **Parks/recreation:** Health/fitness, sports admin. **Philosophy/religion:** Religion. **Protective services:** Criminal justice. **Psychology:** General. **Public administration:** Human services. **Social sciences:** General, political science. **Visual/performing arts:** Dramatic, graphic design, studio arts.

**Most popular majors.** Business/marketing 21%, communications/journalism 6%, education 7%, health sciences 19%, liberal arts 7%, public administration/social services 6%, visual/performing arts 7%.

**Computing on campus.** Dormitories wired for high-speed internet access and linked to campus network. Commuter students can connect to campus network. Online course registration, online library, helpline, student web hosting, wireless network available.

**Student life. Freshman orientation:** Mandatory. Preregistration for classes offered. Three-day program just before start of fall semester, includes low ropes course at nearby camp. **Housing:** Coed dorms, apartments available. $200 deposit. University-owned on-campus houses available. **Activities:** Campus ministries, choral groups, dance, drama, international student organizations, literary magazine, music ensembles, radio station, student government, student newspaper, TV station, Campus Crusade, campus fellowship, campus ministries, criminal justice club, diversity alliance, international relations council, Viking Volunteers.

**Athletics.** NAIA. **Intercollegiate:** Baseball M, basketball, cross-country, football (tackle) M, golf, soccer, softball W, track and field, volleyball W, wrestling M. **Intramural:** Badminton, basketball, cheerleading W, football (non-tackle), soccer, softball, swimming, table tennis, tennis, track and field, volleyball. **Team name:** Vikings.

**Student services.** Adult student services, alcohol/substance abuse counseling, chaplain/spiritual director, career counseling, student employment services, financial aid counseling, health services, minority student services, personal counseling, placement for graduates, veterans' counselor. **Physically disabled:** Services for visually, speech, hearing impaired.

**Contact.** E-mail: admissions@GrandView.edu
Phone: (515) 263-2810 Toll-free number: (800) 444-6083
Fax: (515) 263-2974
Diane Johnson, Director of Admissions, Grand View University, 1200 Grandview Avenue, Des Moines, IA 50316-1599

## Grinnell College

**Grinnell, Iowa**        **CB member**
**www.grinnell.edu**        **CB code: 6252**

- Private 4-year liberal arts college
- Residential campus in small town
- 1,630 degree-seeking undergraduates: 53% women, 6% African American, 8% Asian American, 7% Hispanic American, 1% Native American, 11% international
- 34% of applicants admitted
- SAT or ACT (ACT writing optional), application essay required
- 84% graduate within 6 years

**General.** Founded in 1846. Regionally accredited. **Degrees:** 366 bachelor's awarded. **Location:** 55 miles from Des Moines. **Calendar:** Semester, limited summer session. **Full-time faculty:** 157 total; 98% have terminal degrees, 16% minority, 41% women. **Part-time faculty:** 46 total; 30% have terminal degrees, 11% minority, 56% women. **Class size:** 64% < 20, 36% 20-39. **Special facilities:** 365-acre environmental research area, observatory.

**Freshman class profile.** 3,291 applied, 1,108 admitted, 378 enrolled.

| Mid 50% test scores | | | |
|---|---|---|---|
| SAT critical reading: | 600-730 | Rank in top tenth: | 65% |
| SAT math: | 620-730 | Return as sophomores: | 95% |
| ACT composite: | 28-32 | Out-of-state: | 85% |
| Rank in top quarter: | 93% | Live on campus: | 100% |
| | | International: | 13% |

**Basis for selection.** Scholastic ability plus extracurricular pursuits, accomplishments most important. Curiosity, motivation, and persistence are stressed. Interview recommended. **Homeschooled:** Statement describing homeschool structure and mission, transcript of courses and grades, interview, letter of recommendation (nonparent) required. Copy of curriculum, writing sample required. SAT Subject Tests strongly recommended.

**High school preparation.** College-preparatory program recommended. 20 units recommended. Recommended units include English 4, mathematics 4, social studies 4, science 4 (laboratory 3) and foreign language 4.

**2010-2011 Annual costs.** Tuition/fees: $37,482. Room/board: $8,880. Books/supplies: $900. Personal expenses: $1,100.

**2009-2010 Financial aid.** **Need-based:** 321 full-time freshmen applied for aid; 270 were judged to have need; 269 of these received aid. Average need met was 100%. Average scholarship/grant was $28,905; average loan $2,854. 89% of total undergraduate aid awarded as scholarships/grants, 11% as loans/jobs. **Non-need-based:** Awarded to 435 full-time undergraduates, including 82 freshmen. Scholarships awarded for academics. **Additional information:** Need-blind admission policy, meets 100% of demonstrated institutional need for all domestic students, with loan cap programs. Students may apply financial aid to off-campus study programs.

**Application procedures. Admission:** Closing date 1/2 (postmark date). $30 fee, may be waived for applicants with need, free for online applicants. Admission notification 4/1. Must reply by 5/1. **Financial aid:** Closing date

2/1. FAFSA, institutional form required. Applicants notified by 4/1; must reply by 5/1.

**Academics.** Internships available in public agencies, private organizations, and corporations. **Special study options:** Accelerated study, double major, independent study, internships, liberal arts/career combination, student-designed major, study abroad, teacher certification program, urban semester, Washington semester. Study abroad available in more than 30 countries. Other programs include study in Washington, 3-2 engineering, architecture, and law. **Credit/placement by examination:** AP, CLEP, IB, institutional tests. **Support services:** Learning center, reduced course load, study skills assistance, tutoring, writing center.

**Majors.** **Biology:** General, biochemistry. **Computer sciences:** Computer science. **Foreign languages:** Classics, East Asian, French, German, Russian, Spanish. **History:** General. **Math:** General. **Philosophy/religion:** Philosophy, religion. **Physical sciences:** Chemistry, physics. **Psychology:** General. **Social sciences:** Anthropology, economics, political science, sociology. **Visual/performing arts:** Art, dramatic. **Other:** Gender, Women's and Sexuality Studies.

**Most popular majors.** Biology 10%, English 7%, foreign language 9%, history 6%, mathematics 6%, physical sciences 8%, psychology 8%, social sciences 26%, visual/performing arts 9%.

**Computing on campus.** 400 workstations in dormitories, library, computer center, student center. Dormitories wired for high-speed internet access and linked to campus network. Commuter students can connect to campus network. Online library, helpline, student web hosting, wireless network available.

**Student life. Freshman orientation:** Mandatory. Held immediately prior to start of classes. **Policies:** All residence halls and college-owned off-campus houses are self-governing: residents decide how their individual hall will operate and share responsibility for budget, quiet hours, social policy, regulations. **Housing:** Guaranteed on-campus for all undergraduates. Coed dorms, special housing for disabled, cooperative housing, wellness housing available. $200 nonrefundable deposit, deadline 5/1. Pets allowed in dorm rooms. **Activities:** Bands, campus ministries, choral groups, dance, drama, film society, international student organizations, literary magazine, music ensembles, Model UN, musical theater, radio station, student government, student newspaper, symphony orchestra, Muslim prayer group, Chalutzim, Investigating Religion and Spirituality, concerned black students, Asian student alliance, Latino student organization, Campus Democrats, College Republicans, Alternative Break, Native American student alliance.

**Athletics.** NCAA. **Intercollegiate:** Baseball M, basketball, cross-country, diving, football (tackle) M, golf, soccer, softball W, swimming, tennis, track and field, volleyball W. **Intramural:** Badminton, basketball, football (non-tackle), racquetball, rowing (crew), soccer, softball, table tennis, tennis, volleyball. **Team name:** Pioneers.

**Student services.** Alcohol/substance abuse counseling, chaplain/spiritual director, career counseling, financial aid counseling, health services, minority student services, personal counseling, placement for graduates, veterans' counselor. **Physically disabled:** Services for visually, speech, hearing impaired.

**Contact.** E-mail: askgrin@grinnell.edu
Phone: (641) 269-3600 Toll-free number: (800) 247-0113
Fax: (641) 269-4800
Seth Allen, Dean of Admission and Financial Aid, Grinnell College, 1103 Park Street, Grinnell, IA 50112-1690

## Hamilton Technical College
**Davenport, Iowa**
www.hamiltontechcollege.com      CB code: 1588

- For-profit 3-year technical college
- Commuter campus in small city
- 176 degree-seeking undergraduates
- Interview required

**General.** Founded in 1969. Accredited by ACCSC. **Degrees:** 33 bachelor's, 50 associate awarded. **Location:** 190 miles from Des Moines, 175 miles from Chicago. **Calendar:** Semester. **Full-time faculty:** 12 total.

**Basis for selection.** Open admission. Pseudoisochromatic Color Plates and Wonderlic required for placement.

**2009-2010 Annual costs.** Medical assistant and medical/insurance coding specialist programs tuition: $11,250; associate of science in electronic

engineering technology: $29,700; bachelor of science in electronic engineering technology: $39,600; includes all costs for entire degree program.

**Application procedures. Admission:** No deadline. No application fee. Admission notification on a rolling basis. **Financial aid:** No deadline. FAFSA, institutional form required. Applicants notified on a rolling basis.

**Academics. Credit/placement by examination:** CLEP. 35 credit hours maximum toward associate degree, 60 toward bachelor's. **Support services:** Tutoring.

**Majors.** BACHELOR'S. **Engineering technology:** Electrical. ASSOCIATE. **Engineering technology:** CAD/CADD, electrical.

**Computing on campus.** 125 workstations in library, computer center.

**Student services.** Career counseling, placement for graduates.

**Contact.** Phone: (563) 386-3570 Fax: (563) 386-6756
Scott Ervin, Admissions Director, Hamilton Technical College, 1011 East 53rd Street, Davenport, IA 52807

## Iowa State University
**Ames, Iowa**                               CB member
www.iastate.edu                           CB code: 6306

- Public 4-year university
- Residential campus in small city
- 21,959 degree-seeking undergraduates: 4% part-time, 43% women, 3% African American, 3% Asian American, 3% Hispanic American, 5% international
- 5,038 degree-seeking graduate students
- 85% of applicants admitted
- SAT or ACT (ACT writing optional) required
- 67% graduate within 6 years; 17% enter graduate study

**General.** Founded in 1858. Regionally accredited. State's land-grant research university. **Degrees:** 4,129 bachelor's awarded; master's, doctoral, professional offered. **ROTC:** Army, Naval, Air Force. **Location:** 30 miles from Des Moines. **Calendar:** Semester, extensive summer session. **Full-time faculty:** 1,435 total; 92% have terminal degrees, 20% minority, 32% women. **Part-time faculty:** 228 total; 73% have terminal degrees, 13% minority, 47% women. **Class size:** 33% < 20, 40% 20-39, 8% 40-49, 11% 50-99, 8% >100. **Special facilities:** Observatory, nature preserve, research park, molecular biology building, computation center, center for designing foods, Department of Energy laboratory, virtual reality applications center, crop utilization center, transportation research and education center, sustainable environmental technologies center, gardens, field-oriented lakeside research facility.

**Freshman class profile.** 12,536 applied, 10,662 admitted, 4,356 enrolled.

| Mid 50% test scores | | | |
|---|---|---|---|
| SAT critical reading: | 490-640 | Rank in top quarter: | 62% |
| SAT math: | 540-690 | Rank in top tenth: | 28% |
| ACT composite: | 22-28 | Return as sophomores: | 84% |
| GPA 3.75 or higher: | 36% | Out-of-state: | 31% |
| GPA 3.50-3.74: | 21% | Live on campus: | 90% |
| GPA 3.0-3.49: | 33% | International: | 5% |
| GPA 2.0-2.99: | 10% | Fraternities: | 13% |
| | | Sororities: | 17% |

**Basis for selection.** Rank in top half of graduating class and completion of prescribed set of college-preparatory high school courses important. Test scores considered as alternative criteria to class rank in some instances. Level of difficulty of courses also considered. **Homeschooled:** Emphasis placed on standardized examinations.

**High school preparation.** College-preparatory program required. 12 units required; 19 recommended. Required and recommended units include English 4, mathematics 3-4, social studies 2-4, science 3-4 (laboratory 2-3) and foreign language 2-3. 2 foreign language and 3 social studies required for College of Liberal Arts & Sciences.

**2009-2010 Annual costs.** Tuition/fees: $6,651; $17,871 out-of-state. Additional tuition for junior and senior engineering students of $1,808 for residents and $1,792 for non-residents; additional tuition for junior and senior business students of $500. Additional fees of $216 for engineering and computer science programs; $40 for business students. Room/board: $7,277. Books/supplies: $1,000. Personal expenses: $2,814.

**2009-2010 Financial aid. Need-based:** 3,623 full-time freshmen applied for aid; 2,358 were judged to have need; 2,328 of these received aid. Average need met was 83%. Average scholarship/grant was $6,560; average loan $3,780. 43% of total undergraduate aid awarded as scholarships/grants, 57% as loans/jobs. **Non-need-based:** Awarded to 11,976 full-time undergraduates, including 2,770 freshmen. Scholarships awarded for academics, art, athletics, leadership, minority status, music/drama, ROTC, state residency. **Additional information:** Short-term loan program available to meet unplanned needs. Financial counseling clinic provides budget and credit education assistance.

**Application procedures. Admission:** Closing date 7/1. $30 fee. Admission notification on a rolling basis. Must reply by May 1 or within 2 week(s) if notified thereafter. **Financial aid:** Priority date 3/1; no closing date. FAFSA required. Applicants notified on a rolling basis starting 4/1.

**Academics.** Classes offered over the Internet, by videotape, at distant locations through the state's fiber-optic communication network, and at off-campus locations taught face-to-face by the university's professors. **Special study options:** Accelerated study, combined bachelor's/graduate degree, co-operative education, cross-registration, distance learning, double major, dual enrollment of high school students, ESL, exchange student, external degree, honors, independent study, internships, liberal arts/career combination, student-designed major, study abroad, teacher certification program, Washington semester, weekend college. National Collegiate Honors Council Honors Semester. Combined bachelor's/graduate programs include: landscape architecture, agriculture and biosystems engineering, biochemistry and biophysics, electrical and computer engineering, civil and construction engineering, chemical engineering, food science and human nutrition, material science engineering, zoology and genetics. **Credit/placement by examination:** CLEP, IB, SAT, ACT, institutional tests. No limit on number of hours of credit by examination that may be counted toward degree. **Support services:** Learning center, pre-admission summer program, reduced course load, remedial instruction, study skills assistance, tutoring, writing center.

**Majors. Agriculture:** Agribusiness operations, agronomy, animal sciences, dairy, education services, farm/ranch, horticulture, international, mechanization, plant protection, plant sciences. **Architecture:** Architecture, landscape, urban/community planning. **Area/ethnic studies:** Women's. **Biology:** General, biochemistry, bioinformatics, biophysics, entomology, genetics, microbiology. **Business:** General, accounting, finance, hospitality admin, international, logistics, management information systems, managerial economics, marketing, operations, statistics. **Communications:** General, advertising, journalism. **Computer sciences:** General. **Conservation:** Environmental science, environmental studies, forestry. **Education:** General, agricultural, early childhood, elementary, family/consumer sciences, health, kindergarten/preschool, music, technology/industrial arts, trade/industrial. **Engineering:** General, aerospace, agricultural, chemical, civil, computer, construction, electrical, industrial, materials, materials science, mechanical, software. **Family/consumer sciences:** General, apparel marketing, clothing/textiles, family resources, family/community services, food/nutrition, housing, human nutrition, institutional food production, textile manufacture. **Foreign languages:** General, linguistics. **Health:** Dietetics, medical illustrating, premedicine, preveterinary. **History:** General. **Liberal arts:** Arts/sciences. **Math:** General, statistics. **Parks/recreation:** Exercise sciences. **Philosophy/religion:** Philosophy, religion. **Physical sciences:** Chemistry, geology, physics, planetary. **Psychology:** General. **Social sciences:** Anthropology, economics, international relations, political science, sociology. **Visual/performing arts:** General, art, commercial/advertising art, design, fashion design, graphic design, interior design. **Other:** Integrated studion arts.

**Most popular majors.** Agriculture 10%, business/marketing 21%, engineering/engineering technologies 17%, visual/performing arts 7%.

**Computing on campus.** 2,400 workstations in dormitories, library, computer center, student center. Dormitories wired for high-speed internet access and linked to campus network. Commuter students can connect to campus network. Online course registration, online library, helpline, repair service, wireless network available.

**Student life. Freshman orientation:** Available. Preregistration for classes offered. Two-day, overnight program. **Housing:** Guaranteed on-campus for all undergraduates. Coed dorms, single-sex dorms, special housing for disabled, apartments, cooperative housing, fraternity/sorority housing, wellness housing available. $135 partly refundable deposit, deadline 5/1. Learning communities, family, quiet, adult housing available. **Activities:** Bands, campus ministries, choral groups, dance, drama, film society, literary magazine, music ensembles, musical theater, opera, radio station, student government, student newspaper, symphony orchestra, TV station, more than 500 clubs and organizations.

**Athletics.** NCAA. **Intercollegiate:** Basketball, cross-country, football (tackle) M, golf, gymnastics W, soccer W, softball W, swimming W, tennis W, track and field, volleyball W, wrestling M. **Intramural:** Badminton, basketball, bowling, boxing M, cross-country, diving, golf, handball, ice hockey, racquetball, skiing, soccer, softball, squash, swimming, table tennis, tennis, volleyball, water polo, weight lifting, wrestling. **Team name:** Cyclones.

**Student services.** Adult student services, alcohol/substance abuse counseling, career counseling, student employment services, financial aid counseling, health services, legal services, minority student services, on-campus daycare, personal counseling, placement for graduates, veterans' counselor, women's services. **Physically disabled:** Services for visually, speech, hearing impaired. **Learning disabled:** Comprehensive services available.

**Contact.** E-mail: admissions@iastate.edu
Phone: (515) 294-5836 Toll-free number: (800) 262-3810
Fax: (515) 294-2592
Marc Harding, Director of Admissions, Iowa State University, 100 Enrollment Services Center, Ames, IA 50011-2011

## Iowa Wesleyan College
**Mount Pleasant, Iowa**     **CB member**
**www.iwc.edu**     **CB code: 6308**

- Private 4-year liberal arts college affiliated with United Methodist Church
- Residential campus in small town
- 858 degree-seeking undergraduates: 23% part-time, 60% women
- 68% of applicants admitted
- SAT or ACT (ACT writing optional) required

**General.** Founded in 1842. Regionally accredited. **Degrees:** 137 bachelor's awarded. **Location:** 47 miles from Iowa City, 25 miles from Burlington. **Calendar:** Semester, limited summer session. **Full-time faculty:** 49 total; 61% have terminal degrees, 8% minority, 43% women. **Part-time faculty:** 38 total; 8% have terminal degrees, 58% women. **Class size:** 86% < 20, 14% 20-39. **Special facilities:** Public interest institute, Harlan-Lincoln house museum.

**Freshman class profile.** 1,283 applied, 875 admitted, 154 enrolled.

| Mid 50% test scores | | | |
|---|---|---|---|
| SAT critical reading: | 390-490 | Out-of-state: | 67% |
| SAT math: | 380-480 | Live on campus: | 91% |
| ACT composite: | 17-22 | Fraternities: | 3% |
| Return as sophomores: | 49% | Sororities: | 8% |

**Basis for selection.** Upper 50% class rank preferred. Automatic acceptance with 2.5 GPA and 19 ACT. Audition recommended for music majors. Portfolio recommended for art, creative programs majors. Essay recommended for applicants who do not meet regular admission requirements. **Homeschooled:** Transcript of courses and grades required. GED or portfolio may be substituted for high school transcript requirement.

**High school preparation.** College-preparatory program recommended. 16 units recommended. Recommended units include English 4, mathematics 3, social studies 3, science 2 (laboratory 2) and academic electives 4.

**2009-2010 Annual costs.** Tuition/fees: $21,000. Room/board: $6,842. Books/supplies: $1,100. Personal expenses: $1,600.

**2009-2010 Financial aid. Need-based:** 142 full-time freshmen applied for aid; 142 were judged to have need; 142 of these received aid. 56% of total undergraduate aid awarded as scholarships/grants, 44% as loans/jobs. **Non-need-based:** Scholarships awarded for academics, art, athletics, music/drama.

**Application procedures. Admission:** Priority date 4/1; no deadline. $20 fee, may be waived for applicants with need, free for online applicants. Admission notification on a rolling basis beginning on or about 8/15. Must reply by May 1 or within 2 week(s) if notified thereafter. **Financial aid:** Priority date 4/1; no closing date. FAFSA required. Applicants notified on a rolling basis starting 1/1; must reply within 2 week(s) of notification.

**Academics. Special study options:** Combined bachelor's/graduate degree, cross-registration, distance learning, double major, dual enrollment of high school students, exchange student, independent study, internships, liberal arts/career combination, student-designed major, study abroad, teacher certification program, Washington semester. **Credit/placement by examination:** AP, CLEP, IB, institutional tests. 30 credit hours maximum toward bachelor's degree. **Support services:** Learning center, reduced course load, study skills assistance, tutoring, writing center.

**Majors. Biology:** General. **Business:** General, accounting, business admin, human resources. **Communications:** General. **Computer sciences:** General, computer science, web page design. **Conservation:** Forestry. **Education:** General, art, biology, chemistry, early childhood, elementary, English, health, history, mathematics, middle, music, physical, physics, secondary, social studies. **Engineering:** General. **Health:** Environmental health, nursing (RN), predental, premedicine, prepharmacy, preveterinary. **History:** General. **Legal studies:** Prelaw. **Math:** General. **Parks/recreation:** Exercise sciences, health/fitness, sports admin. **Philosophy/religion:** Christian, philosophy, religion. **Physical sciences:** Chemistry. **Protective services:** Criminal justice. **Psychology:** General. **Public administration:** Human services.

413

Social sciences: Sociology. **Visual/performing arts:** Design, studio arts. **Other:** Church leadership.

**Most popular majors.** Biology 6%, business/marketing 20%, education 12%, health sciences 12%, parks/recreation 13%, psychology 12%, social sciences 10%.

**Computing on campus.** 90 workstations in dormitories, library, computer center. Dormitories wired for high-speed internet access and linked to campus network. Commuter students can connect to campus network. Online library, repair service, wireless network available.

**Student life. Freshman orientation:** Mandatory. Preregistration for classes offered. Three-day program held weekend before classes begin. **Policies:** All full-time, unmarried students under the age of 22 who do not live with parents required to live in college residential facilities. Exemptions may be made for seniors, students with dependent children and veterans. **Housing:** Guaranteed on-campus for all undergraduates. Coed dorms, single-sex dorms, wellness housing available. $100 deposit, deadline 8/20. **Activities:** Bands, campus ministries, choral groups, international student organizations, literary magazine, music ensembles, radio station, student government, student newspaper, symphony orchestra, black awareness organization, Fellowship of Christian Athletics, Bacchus, Unidad.

**Athletics.** NAIA. **Intercollegiate:** Baseball M, basketball, cross-country, football (tackle) M, golf, soccer, softball W, track and field, volleyball W. **Intramural:** Badminton, basketball, bowling, football (non-tackle), softball, table tennis, volleyball. **Team name:** Tigers.

**Student services.** Adult student services, alcohol/substance abuse counseling, chaplain/spiritual director, career counseling, student employment services, financial aid counseling, health services, personal counseling, placement for graduates.

**Contact.** E-mail: admit@iwc.edu
Phone: (319) 385-6231 Toll-free number: (800) 582-2383 ext. 6231
Fax: (319) 385-6240
Mark Petty, Dean of Admissions, Iowa Wesleyan College, 601 North Main Street, Mount Pleasant, IA 52641-1398

## Kaplan University: Cedar Falls
Cedar Falls, Iowa
www.kucampus.edu

- For-profit 4-year university and branch campus college
- Commuter campus in small city
- 736 degree-seeking undergraduates
- Application essay, interview required

**General. Degrees:** 39 bachelor's, 115 associate awarded. **Location:** 120 miles from Des Moines. **Calendar:** Continuous, extensive summer session. **Full-time faculty:** 13 total. **Part-time faculty:** 41 total. **Class size:** 64% < 20, 33% 20-39, 3% 40-49.

**Basis for selection.** Open admission, but selective for some programs. Entrance test required for most programs.

**2009-2010 Annual costs.** Tuition/fees: $15,985. Tuition may vary by program; includes books.

**2008-2009 Financial aid.** All financial aid based on need.

**Application procedures. Admission:** No deadline. $25 fee. Application must be submitted on paper. Admission notification on a rolling basis. **Financial aid:** No deadline. FAFSA, institutional form required. Applicants notified on a rolling basis.

**Academics. Special study options:** Cooperative education, distance learning. **Credit/placement by examination:** AP, CLEP, institutional tests. 32 credit hours maximum toward associate degree. **Support services:** Learning center, tutoring.

**Majors. Business:** Business admin.

**Student life. Freshman orientation:** Available, $20 fee. **Activities:** Student government, student newspaper.

**Student services.** Student employment services, financial aid counseling, personal counseling, placement for graduates.

**Contact.** Phone: (319) 277-0220 Toll-free number: (800) 728-1220
Fax: (319) 243-2961
Jill Hansen, Director of Admissions, Kaplan University: Cedar Falls, 7009 Nordic Drive, Cedar Falls, IA 50613

## Kaplan University: Davenport
Davenport, Iowa
www.kucampus.edu                    CB code: 5848

- For-profit 4-year university
- Residential campus in large city
- 918 degree-seeking undergraduates
- Interview required

**General.** Founded in 1937. Regionally accredited. **Degrees:** 91 bachelor's, 95 associate awarded; master's offered. **Location:** 165 miles from Des Moines, 180 miles from Chicago. **Calendar:** Quarter, extensive summer session. **Full-time faculty:** 6 total. **Part-time faculty:** 31 total.

**Basis for selection.** Open admission, but selective for some programs.

**2009-2010 Annual costs.** Tuition/fees: $15,985. Tuition may vary by program; includes books.

**Financial aid. Non-need-based:** Scholarships awarded for academics.

**Application procedures. Admission:** No deadline. $25 fee, may be waived for applicants with need. Admission notification on a rolling basis. **Financial aid:** No deadline. FAFSA, institutional form required. Applicants notified on a rolling basis starting 3/4; must reply by 6/15 or within 2 week(s) of notification.

**Academics. Special study options:** Distance learning, double major, honors, internships, teacher certification program. **Credit/placement by examination:** CLEP, institutional tests. 22 credit hours maximum toward associate degree, 45 toward bachelor's. Up to 25% of all credit in a particular program can be earned through examination. **Support services:** Learning center, reduced course load, remedial instruction, study skills assistance, tutoring, writing center.

**Majors. Business:** Business admin. **Communications:** General. **Computer sciences:** Information technology, networking. **Health:** Nursing (RN). **Legal studies:** General, paralegal. **Protective services:** Criminal justice. **Psychology:** General.

**Most popular majors.** Business/marketing 35%, computer/information sciences 12%, health sciences 7%, legal studies 19%, security/protective services 28%.

**Computing on campus.** 121 workstations in library, student center. Online course registration, online library, helpline, student web hosting, wireless network available.

**Student life. Freshman orientation:** Mandatory, $20 fee. **Activities:** Student government, student newspaper.

**Student services.** Career counseling, student employment services, financial aid counseling, personal counseling, placement for graduates.

**Contact.** Phone: (563) 355-3500 Toll-free number: (800) 747-1035
Fax: (563) 355-1320
Jason Wilebski, Director of Admissions, Kaplan University: Davenport, 1801 East Kimberly Road, Suite 1, Davenport, IA 52807-2095

## Kaplan University: Des Moines
Urbandale, Iowa
www.kucampus.edu                    CB code: 3388

- For-profit 4-year university
- Commuter campus in large city
- 1,135 degree-seeking undergraduates
- Interview required

**General.** Regionally accredited. **Degrees:** 45 bachelor's, 211 associate awarded. **Location:** 4 miles from Des Moines. **Calendar:** Continuous, extensive summer session. **Full-time faculty:** 13 total. **Part-time faculty:** 67 total.

**Basis for selection.** Open admission, but selective for some programs.

**2009-2010 Annual costs.** Tuition/fees: $15,985. Tuition may vary by program; includes books. Personal expenses: $1,500.

**Financial aid.** All financial aid based on need.

**Application procedures. Admission:** No deadline. $25 fee, may be waived for applicants with need. Application must be submitted on paper.

Admission notification on a rolling basis. **Financial aid:** Priority date 6/30; no closing date. FAFSA, institutional form required.

**Academics. Special study options:** Accelerated study, distance learning, independent study, internships, liberal arts/career combination. **Credit/placement by examination:** AP, CLEP, institutional tests. 32 credit hours maximum toward associate degree, 32 toward bachelor's. **Support services:** Learning center, remedial instruction, study skills assistance, tutoring.

**Majors. Business:** Accounting, business admin. **Computer sciences:** Information technology. **Protective services:** Law enforcement admin.

**Computing on campus.** 195 workstations in library, computer center. Commuter students can connect to campus network. Online library, repair service available.

**Student life. Freshman orientation:** Mandatory, $20 fee. Preregistration for classes offered. **Activities:** Student government, student newspaper.

**Student services.** Adult student services, career counseling, student employment services, financial aid counseling, placement for graduates.

**Contact.** Phone: (515) 727-2100 Toll-free number: (800) 383-0253 Fax: (515) 727-2115
Mark Bandy, Director of Admissions, Kaplan University: Des Moines, 4655 121st Street, Urbandale, IA 50323

## Kaplan University: Mason City
**Mason City, Iowa**
**www.KU-Masoncity.edu**                                        CB code: 6289

- For-profit 4-year branch campus college
- Commuter campus in large town
- 428 degree-seeking undergraduates
- Interview required

**General.** Regionally accredited; also accredited by ACICS. **Degrees:** 32 bachelor's, 119 associate awarded. **Location:** 127 miles from Des Moines. **Calendar:** Continuous, extensive summer session. **Full-time faculty:** 12 total; 75% women. **Part-time faculty:** 19 total; 21% have terminal degrees, 5% minority, 74% women. **Class size:** 92% < 20, 8% 20-39.

**Basis for selection.** Open admission. **Homeschooled:** Transcript of courses and grades, state high school equivalency certificate required. GED required.

**2009-2010 Annual costs.** Tuition includes books and supplies; may vary by program. Personal expenses: $1,656.

**2008-2009 Financial aid. Non-need-based:** Scholarships awarded for academics.

**Application procedures. Admission:** No deadline. $20 fee. Application must be submitted on paper. Admission notification on a rolling basis. **Financial aid:** Closing date 6/1. FAFSA required. Applicants notified on a rolling basis.

**Academics. Special study options:** Accelerated study, combined bachelor's/graduate degree, distance learning, dual enrollment of high school students, independent study, internships, student-designed major, study abroad, teacher certification program. **Credit/placement by examination:** CLEP. **Support services:** Learning center, study skills assistance, tutoring.

**Majors. Business:** Accounting, business admin. **Computer sciences:** Information technology.

**Computing on campus.** 140 workstations in library, computer center. Commuter students can connect to campus network. Online library, helpline, repair service, wireless network available.

**Student life. Freshman orientation:** Mandatory. Preregistration for classes offered. **Activities:** Student government.

**Student services.** Adult student services, student employment services, financial aid counseling, placement for graduates. **Physically disabled:** Services for hearing impaired.

**Contact.** E-mail: mklacik@kaplan.edu
Phone: (641) 423-2530 Toll-free number: (800) 274-2530
Fax: (641) 423-7512
Michael Klacik, Director of Admissions, Kaplan University: Mason City, Plaza West 2570 Fourth Street, SW, Mason City, IA 50401

## Loras College
**Dubuque, Iowa**
**www.loras.edu**                                               CB code: 6370

- Private 4-year liberal arts college affiliated with Roman Catholic Church
- Residential campus in small city
- 1,481 degree-seeking undergraduates: 2% part-time, 49% women, 1% African American, 3% Hispanic American, 3% international
- 55 degree-seeking graduate students
- 61% of applicants admitted
- SAT or ACT (ACT writing optional) required
- 69% graduate within 6 years

**General.** Founded in 1839. Regionally accredited. **Degrees:** 299 bachelor's awarded; master's offered. **ROTC:** Army. **Location:** 180 miles from Chicago. **Calendar:** Semester, extensive summer session. **Full-time faculty:** 111 total; less than 1% have terminal degrees, 4% minority, 39% women. **Part-time faculty:** 48 total; 2% minority, 65% women. **Class size:** 57% < 20, 43% 20-39, less than 1% 50-99. **Special facilities:** Planetarium, observatory, residential arts complex.

**Freshman class profile.** 4,138 applied, 2,544 admitted, 414 enrolled.

| Mid 50% test scores | | Rank in top tenth: | 11% |
|---|---|---|---|
| ACT composite: | 19-26 | End year in good standing: | 95% |
| GPA 3.75 or higher: | 20% | Return as sophomores: | 73% |
| GPA 3.50-3.74: | 19% | Out-of-state: | 56% |
| GPA 3.0-3.49: | 36% | Live on campus: | 95% |
| GPA 2.0-2.99: | 25% | International: | 2% |
| Rank in top quarter: | 30% | | |

**Basis for selection.** High school academic record and test scores most important. Interview and essay recommended. **Learning Disabled:** All students applying for the enhanced learning disabilities program must have materials submitted by the required date. All files reviewed by learning disabilities program.

**High school preparation.** 16 units recommended. Recommended units include English 4, mathematics 3, social studies 3, history 3 and science 3.

**2010-2011 Annual costs.** Tuition/fees: $26,288. Room/board: $7,306. Books/supplies: $1,100.

**2008-2009 Financial aid. Need-based:** Average need met was 87%. Average scholarship/grant was $9,525; average loan $3,175. 75% of total undergraduate aid awarded as scholarships/grants, 25% as loans/jobs. **Non-need-based:** Scholarships awarded for academics, alumni affiliation, leadership, minority status, music/drama. **Additional information:** Audition or portfolio recommended for music and art financial aid applicants.

**Application procedures. Admission:** No deadline. $25 fee, may be waived for applicants with need. Admission notification on a rolling basis. Must reply by May 1 or within 2 week(s) if notified thereafter. **Financial aid:** Priority date 4/15; no closing date. FAFSA required. Applicants notified on a rolling basis starting 3/1; must reply within 3 week(s) of notification.

**Academics. Special study options:** Cooperative education, cross-registration, double major, dual enrollment of high school students, exchange student, honors, independent study, internships, student-designed major, study abroad, teacher certification program, urban semester, Washington semester. **Credit/placement by examination:** AP, CLEP, IB. **Support services:** Learning center, reduced course load, remedial instruction, study skills assistance, tutoring, writing center.

**Majors. Biology:** General, biochemistry. **Business:** General, accounting, business admin, finance, management information systems, marketing. **Communications:** Journalism, media studies, public relations. **Computer sciences:** Computer science. **Education:** General, art, early childhood, elementary, emotionally handicapped, mentally handicapped, multi-level teacher, physical, secondary, special. **Engineering:** Electrical, physics. **Foreign languages:** Spanish. **Health:** Athletic training. **History:** General. **Legal studies:** Prelaw. **Liberal arts:** Arts/sciences. **Math:** General. **Parks/recreation:** Exercise sciences. **Philosophy/religion:** Philosophy, religion. **Physical sciences:** General, chemistry. **Protective services:** Criminal justice. **Psychology:** General. **Public administration:** Social work. **Social sciences:** Economics, international relations, political science, sociology. **Visual/performing arts:** General.

**Most popular majors.** Biology 6%, business/marketing 8%, education 16%, English 9%, social sciences 7%.

**Computing on campus.** PC or laptop required. 20 workstations in library, computer center, student center. Dormitories wired for high-speed internet access and linked to campus network. Commuter students can connect to campus network. Online course registration, online library, helpline, repair service, student web hosting, wireless network available.

**Student life. Freshman orientation:** Mandatory. Preregistration for classes offered. Held from early June through the start of fall term. **Housing:** Guaranteed on-campus for freshmen. Coed dorms, apartments available. $100 fully refundable deposit. **Activities:** Bands, choral groups, dance, drama, film society, international student organizations, literary magazine, music ensembles, musical theater, radio station, student government, student newspaper, TV station, peace and justice club, African/Hispanic/Asian/Native American club, Amnesty International, environmental action forum, fellowship of Christian athletes.

**Athletics.** NCAA. **Intercollegiate:** Baseball M, basketball, cross-country, diving, football (tackle) M, golf, soccer, softball W, swimming, tennis W, track and field, volleyball W, wrestling M. **Intramural:** Badminton, baseball M, basketball, bowling, cheerleading, cross-country, diving, football (non-tackle), golf, handball, racquetball, soccer, softball, swimming, table tennis, tennis, track and field, volleyball, water polo, weight lifting, wrestling M. **Team name:** Duhawks.

**Student services.** Adult student services, alcohol/substance abuse counseling, chaplain/spiritual director, career counseling, student employment services, financial aid counseling, health services, minority student services, personal counseling, placement for graduates, veterans' counselor. **Physically disabled:** Services for visually, speech, hearing impaired. **Learning disabled:** Comprehensive services available.

**Contact.** E-mail: adms@loras.edu
Phone: (563) 588-7236 Toll-free number: (800) 245-6727
Fax: (563) 588-7119
Sharon Lyons, Director of Admissions, Loras College, 1450 Alta Vista Street, Dubuque, IA 52004-0178

---

## Luther College
Decorah, Iowa          **CB member**
www.luther.edu          **CB code: 6375**

◗ Private 4-year liberal arts college affiliated with Evangelical Lutheran Church in America

◗ Residential campus in small town

◗ 2,450 degree-seeking undergraduates: 1% part-time, 57% women, 2% African American, 2% Asian American, 2% Hispanic American, 5% international

◗ 70% of applicants admitted

◗ SAT or ACT (ACT writing optional), application essay required

◗ 75% graduate within 6 years; 19% enter graduate study

**General.** Founded in 1861. Regionally accredited. **Degrees:** 497 bachelor's awarded. **Location:** 70 miles from Rochester, MN; 50 miles from LaCrosse, WI. **Calendar:** 4-1-4, limited summer session. **Full-time faculty:** 177 total; 92% have terminal degrees, 3% minority, 39% women. **Part-time faculty:** 74 total; 38% have terminal degrees, 54% women. **Class size:** 53% < 20, 43% 20-39, 2% 40-49, 1% 50-99, less than 1% >100. **Special facilities:** Planetarium, Norwegian-American museum, extensive biology field study areas, cadaver laboratory.

**Freshman class profile.** 3,445 applied, 2,403 admitted, 657 enrolled.

| Mid 50% test scores | | | |
|---|---|---|---|
| SAT critical reading: | 500-640 | GPA 2.0-2.99: | 8% |
| SAT math: | 530-670 | Rank in top quarter: | 64% |
| SAT writing: | 490-640 | Rank in top tenth: | 35% |
| ACT composite: | 23-29 | End year in good standing: | 97% |
| GPA 3.75 or higher: | 48% | Return as sophomores: | 89% |
| GPA 3.50-3.74: | 21% | Out-of-state: | 69% |
| GPA 3.0-3.49: | 23% | Live on campus: | 100% |
| | | International: | 5% |

**Basis for selection.** Rigor of high school curriculum most important, followed by test scores and teacher recommendation(s). Applicants should rank in top half of high school class. Audition recommended for music scholarships. Portfolio recommended for art majors. Interview recommended for borderline students. **Homeschooled:** If graduate of non-diploma-granting organization, evidence of preparation for college required. Must provide at least 2 of the following: home school transcript listing all courses; detailed portfolio of high school work completed; bibliography of major books read, with brief essay on one of the selected works; additional reference letter completed by an educator assessing the applicant's academic preparation; scores from any AP exams and/or GED test results.

**High school preparation.** College-preparatory program recommended. 14 units recommended. Recommended units include English 4, mathematics 3, social studies 3, science 2 (laboratory 1) and foreign language 2.

**2010-2011 Annual costs.** Tuition/fees: $33,480. Room/board: $5,800. Books/supplies: $910. Personal expenses: $1,510.

**2009-2010 Financial aid. Need-based:** 569 full-time freshmen applied for aid; 478 were judged to have need; 478 of these received aid. Average need met was 91%. Average scholarship/grant was $18,292; average loan $5,956. 73% of total undergraduate aid awarded as scholarships/grants, 27% as loans/jobs. **Non-need-based:** Awarded to 481 full-time undergraduates, including 176 freshmen. Scholarships awarded for academics, alumni affiliation, art, minority status, music/drama.

**Application procedures. Admission:** No deadline. $25 fee, may be waived for applicants with need, free for online applicants. Admission notification on a rolling basis beginning on or about 9/1. Must reply by May 1 or within 4 week(s) if notified thereafter. **Financial aid:** Priority date 3/1; no closing date. FAFSA, institutional form required. Applicants notified on a rolling basis starting 3/15; must reply by 5/1 or within 4 week(s) of notification.

**Academics. Special study options:** Combined bachelor's/graduate degree, double major, dual enrollment of high school students, honors, independent study, internships, student-designed major, study abroad, teacher certification program, Washington semester. **Credit/placement by examination:** AP, CLEP, IB, institutional tests. No limit, but student must satisfy residency requirement. **Support services:** Learning center, reduced course load, remedial instruction, study skills assistance, tutoring, writing center.

**Majors. Area/ethnic studies:** African-American, Russian/Slavic, Scandinavian, women's. **Biology:** General. **Business:** Accounting, business admin, management information systems. **Communications:** Media studies. **Computer sciences:** Computer science. **Conservation:** Environmental studies. **Education:** Elementary, health, physical. **Foreign languages:** Ancient Greek, Biblical, classics, French, German, Latin, Spanish. **Health:** Nursing (RN). **History:** General. **Math:** General, statistics. **Parks/recreation:** Health/fitness, sports admin. **Philosophy/religion:** Philosophy, religion. **Physical sciences:** Chemistry, physics. **Psychology:** General. **Public administration:** Social work. **Social sciences:** Anthropology, economics, political science, sociology. **Visual/performing arts:** Art, dramatic.

**Most popular majors.** Biology 10%, business/marketing 13%, education 6%, foreign language 7%, psychology 6%, social sciences 8%, visual/performing arts 13%.

**Computing on campus.** 500 workstations in dormitories, library, computer center, student center. Dormitories wired for high-speed internet access and linked to campus network. Commuter students can connect to campus network. Online course registration, online library, helpline, student web hosting, wireless network available.

**Student life. Freshman orientation:** Mandatory. Preregistration for classes offered. Held prior to start of classes. **Housing:** Guaranteed on-campus for all undergraduates. Coed dorms, special housing for disabled, apartments, wellness housing available. Clusters, quiet floors, honors floor available. **Activities:** Bands, campus ministries, choral groups, dance, drama, international student organizations, literary magazine, music ensembles, Model UN, musical theater, radio station, student government, student newspaper, symphony orchestra, various religious and political clubs, black student union, Asian student association, Phi Beta Kappa, Amnesty International, Alpha Phi Omega.

**Athletics.** NCAA. **Intercollegiate:** Baseball M, basketball, cheerleading, cross-country, diving, football (tackle) M, golf, soccer, softball W, swimming, tennis, track and field, volleyball W, wrestling M. **Intramural:** Archery, badminton, basketball, football (non-tackle), handball, racquetball, soccer, softball, table tennis, tennis, track and field, volleyball. **Team name:** Norse.

**Student services.** Alcohol/substance abuse counseling, chaplain/spiritual director, career counseling, student employment services, financial aid counseling, health services, minority student services, personal counseling, placement for graduates. **Physically disabled:** Services for visually, hearing impaired.

**Contact.** E-mail: admissions@luther.edu
Phone: (563) 387-1287 Toll-free number: (800) 458-8437
Fax: (563) 387-2159
Scot Schaeffer, Vice President for Enrollment Management, Luther College, 700 College Drive, Decorah, IA 52101-1042

## Maharishi University of Management
**Fairfield, Iowa**
**www.mum.edu**                    CB code: 4497

- Private 4-year university and liberal arts college
- Residential campus in small town
- 271 degree-seeking undergraduates: 7% part-time, 43% women, 6% African American, 3% Asian American, 6% Hispanic American, 17% international
- 927 degree-seeking graduate students
- 38% of applicants admitted
- Application essay required
- 49% graduate within 6 years

**General.** Founded in 1971. Regionally accredited. **Degrees:** 39 bachelor's awarded; master's, doctoral offered. **Location:** 60 miles from Iowa City, 110 miles from Des Moines. **Calendar:** Semester. Modular block system: students study one subject per month, 10 subjects per year. Limited summer session. **Full-time faculty:** 52 total. **Special facilities:** Buildings for practice of transcendental meditation, organic greenhouses, college prep-school, indoor rock-climbing wall, basketball and tennis courts, weight training room, sustainable student center.

**Freshman class profile.** 126 applied, 48 admitted, 37 enrolled.

Live on campus:          78%      International:          23%

**Basis for selection.** Academics, grades, academic test scores, recommendations, high school and college transcripts, advanced placement tests, extracurricular activities, work experience, interview with admissions officer, and essay important. SAT or ACT recommended. Students encouraged to visit campus for 4-day weekend. **Homeschooled:** Must supply detailed record of courses and objectives. Home school certification required.

**High school preparation.** College-preparatory program recommended. 15 units recommended. Recommended units include English 4, mathematics 3, social studies 3, science 3 and foreign language 2.

**2009-2010 Annual costs.** Tuition/fees: $24,430. Room/board: $6,000. Books/supplies: $800. Personal expenses: $1,500.

**2008-2009 Financial aid. Additional information:** Students may earn scholarships through volunteer staff program.

**Application procedures. Admission:** No deadline. $30 fee. Application must be submitted online. Admission notification on a rolling basis. **Financial aid:** Priority date 7/15, closing date 7/30. FAFSA required. Applicants notified on a rolling basis starting 3/1; must reply within 4 week(s) of notification.

**Academics.** Offers consciousness-based education through Transcendental Meditation technique. **Special study options:** Double major, exchange student, honors, independent study, internships, liberal arts/career combination, study abroad, teacher certification program. **Credit/placement by examination:** CLEP, IB, institutional tests. 12 credit hours maximum toward bachelor's degree. **Support services:** Study skills assistance.

**Majors. Business:** Business admin. **Communications:** Media studies. **Computer sciences:** Computer science. **Education:** Elementary, secondary. **Health:** Premedicine. **Math:** General. **Visual/performing arts:** Studio arts. **Other:** Maharishi Vedic science, Sustainable living.

**Most popular majors.** Biology 6%, business/marketing 12%, computer/information sciences 6%, liberal arts 35%, mathematics 6%, natural resources/environmental science 18%, visual/performing arts 15%.

**Computing on campus.** 400 workstations in library, computer center, student center. Dormitories wired for high-speed internet access and linked to campus network. Commuter students can connect to campus network. Online library, helpline available.

**Student life. Freshman orientation:** Mandatory. 1-day program held the first day of class. **Policies:** Daily practice of Transcendental Meditation program by all students, faculty, and staff. Smoking, alcohol and drugs not permitted on campus. Organic, vegetarian food served in dining halls. **Housing:** Guaranteed on-campus for all undergraduates. Single-sex dorms, special housing for disabled, apartments, wellness housing available. $100 fully refundable deposit. Family housing, quiet dorms available. **Activities:** Choral groups, dance, drama, international student organizations, music ensembles, musical theater, radio station, student government, student newspaper, many clubs and activities available.

**Athletics. Team name:** Flyers.

**Student services.** Career counseling, financial aid counseling, health services, on-campus daycare, personal counseling, placement for graduates.

**Contact.** E-mail: admissions@mum.edu
Phone: (641) 472-1110 Toll-free number: (800) 369-6480
Fax: (641) 472-1179
Michelle Paton, U.S. Director of Admissions, Maharishi University of Management, Office of Admissions, Fairfield, IA 52557

## Mercy College of Health Sciences
**Des Moines, Iowa**
**www.mchs.edu**                    CB code: 2803

- Private 4-year health science college affiliated with Roman Catholic Church
- Commuter campus in large city
- 778 degree-seeking undergraduates
- SAT or ACT (ACT writing optional) required

**General.** Regionally accredited. Clinical education components at local medical facilities. **Degrees:** 59 bachelor's, 149 associate awarded. **Calendar:** Semester, limited summer session. **Full-time faculty:** 40 total; 18% have terminal degrees, 8% minority, 80% women. **Part-time faculty:** 8 total; 100% women. **Class size:** 85% < 20, 14% 20-39, 1% 40-49. **Special facilities:** Science and health care laboratory facilities.

**Basis for selection.** Admission decisions based primarily on secondary school record and standardized test scores. Recommendations and interview also important for some programs. **Homeschooled:** State high school equivalency certificate required.

**2009-2010 Annual costs.** Tuition/fees: $13,000. Books/supplies: $1,400. Personal expenses: $4,600.

**2008-2009 Financial aid. Need-based:** 30 full-time freshmen applied for aid; 25 were judged to have need; 24 of these received aid. Average need met was 40%. Average scholarship/grant was $5,772; average loan $3,284. 54% of total undergraduate aid awarded as scholarships/grants, 46% as loans/jobs. **Non-need-based:** Awarded to 155 full-time undergraduates, including 17 freshmen. Scholarships awarded for academics, minority status.

**Application procedures. Admission:** Priority date 7/20; no deadline. $25 fee, may be waived for applicants with need. Admission notification on a rolling basis. **Financial aid:** Closing date 7/1. FAFSA required. Applicants notified on a rolling basis starting 3/1; must reply by 8/1 or within 3 week(s) of notification.

**Academics. Special study options:** Accelerated study, distance learning, liberal arts/career combination. **Credit/placement by examination:** AP, CLEP, institutional tests. 24 hours total. **Support services:** Study skills assistance, tutoring, writing center.

**Majors. Health:** Health care admin, nursing (RN), premedicine. **Other:** Allied health education/leadership.

**Computing on campus.** 46 workstations in library, computer center. Commuter students can connect to campus network. Online library, wireless network available.

**Student life. Freshman orientation:** Mandatory. Preregistration for classes offered. One-day orientation and registration sessions held at various times before beginning of term. **Activities:** Campus ministries, student government, student newspaper.

**Student services.** Alcohol/substance abuse counseling, career counseling, student employment services, financial aid counseling, personal counseling.

**Contact.** E-mail: admissions@mchs.edu
Phone: (515) 643-6682 Toll-free number: (800) 637-2994 ext. 3-3180
Fax: (515) 643-6702
Kara Scholten, Admissions Manager, Mercy College of Health Sciences, 921 Sixth Avenue, Des Moines, IA 50309

## Morningside College
**Sioux City, Iowa**
**www.morningside.edu**                    CB code: 6415

- Private 4-year liberal arts college affiliated with United Methodist Church
- Residential campus in small city

- 1,199 degree-seeking undergraduates: 2% part-time, 54% women, 1% African American, 1% Asian American, 2% Hispanic American, 1% Native American, 2% international
- 463 degree-seeking graduate students
- 71% of applicants admitted
- SAT or ACT (ACT writing optional) required
- 47% graduate within 6 years; 14% enter graduate study

**General.** Founded in 1894. Regionally accredited. All full-time students receive notebook computers. **Degrees:** 256 bachelor's awarded; master's offered. **ROTC:** Army. **Location:** 90 miles from Omaha, NE; 90 miles from Sioux Falls, SD. **Calendar:** Semester, limited summer session. **Full-time faculty:** 70 total; 71% have terminal degrees, 4% minority, 49% women. **Part-time faculty:** 103 total; 2% minority, 72% women. **Class size:** 46% < 20, 51% 20-39, 2% 40-49, less than 1% 50-99. **Special facilities:** Biology research station.

**Freshman class profile.** 1,552 applied, 1,101 admitted, 325 enrolled.

| Mid 50% test scores | | End year in good standing: | 94% |
|---|---|---|---|
| ACT composite: | 20-25 | Return as sophomores: | 73% |
| GPA 3.75 or higher: | 25% | Out-of-state: | 36% |
| GPA 3.50-3.74: | 21% | Live on campus: | 94% |
| GPA 3.0-3.49: | 32% | International: | 2% |
| GPA 2.0-2.99: | 22% | Fraternities: | 3% |
| Rank in top quarter: | 41% | Sororities: | 3% |
| Rank in top tenth: | 16% | | |

**Basis for selection.** 20 ACT/1410 SAT and either rank in top half of class or 2.5 GPA required. Interview recommended. Audition or audition tape recommended for music majors and theater applicants. Portfolio recommended for art majors. **Homeschooled:** Transcript of courses and grades required. Home School Credit Evaluation form may be submitted in place of transcript.

**High school preparation.** College-preparatory program recommended. 10 units recommended. Recommended units include English 3, mathematics 2, social studies 3 and science 2. 4 units math and science required of math or science majors.

**2009-2010 Annual costs.** Tuition/fees: $22,020. Room/board: $6,740. Books/supplies: $940. Personal expenses: $1,765.

**2009-2010 Financial aid.** **Non-need-based:** Scholarships awarded for academics, alumni affiliation, art, athletics, job skills, leadership, music/drama, religious affiliation, ROTC, state residency.

**Application procedures.** **Admission:** Priority date 8/15; no deadline. No application fee. Admission notification on a rolling basis. **Financial aid:** Priority date 3/1; no closing date. FAFSA required. Applicants notified on a rolling basis starting 3/31.

**Academics.** **Special study options:** Distance learning, double major, dual enrollment of high school students, ESL, honors, independent study, internships, liberal arts/career combination, student-designed major, study abroad, teacher certification program, United Nations semester, Washington semester. **Credit/placement by examination:** AP, CLEP, IB, SAT, ACT, institutional tests. 32 credit hours maximum toward bachelor's degree. Maximum 12 hours may be used for general studies core requirements. **Support services:** Learning center, reduced course load, remedial instruction, study skills assistance, tutoring.

**Majors.** **Biology:** General. **Business:** Accounting, business admin, communications. **Communications:** Advertising, media studies. **Computer sciences:** Programming. **Education:** Art, biology, chemistry, elementary, English, history, mathematics, music, physics, science, Spanish, special. **Engineering:** Mechanics, physics. **Foreign languages:** Spanish. **Health:** Clinical lab science, nursing (RN). **History:** General, American. **Interdisciplinary:** Biopsychology. **Math:** General. **Philosophy/religion:** Philosophy, religion. **Physical sciences:** Chemistry, physics. **Psychology:** General, counseling, industrial. **Social sciences:** International relations, political science. **Visual/performing arts:** Dramatic, graphic design, music performance, photography, studio arts.

**Most popular majors.** Biology 8%, business/marketing 27%, communications/journalism 8%, education 20%, health sciences 9%, psychology 8%, visual/performing arts 8%.

**Computing on campus.** PC or laptop required. Dormitories wired for high-speed internet access and linked to campus network. Commuter students can connect to campus network. Online library, helpline, repair service, student web hosting, wireless network available.

**Student life.** **Freshman orientation:** Mandatory. Preregistration for classes offered. Held 4 days before school begins. **Housing:** Guaranteed on-campus for freshmen. Coed dorms, apartments, fraternity/sorority housing available. Apartments for adult non-traditional students available. **Activities:** Bands, campus ministries, choral groups, dance, drama, international student organizations, literary magazine, music ensembles, musical theater, radio station, student government, student newspaper, TV station, Civic Union, Project Hope, Fellowship of Christian Athletes, peace and justice club, mission trips, Cross by Color, Spanish club.

**Athletics.** NAIA. **Intercollegiate:** Baseball M, basketball, cross-country, football (tackle) M, golf, soccer, softball W, swimming, tennis, track and field, volleyball W. **Intramural:** Basketball, bowling, football (non-tackle), golf, soccer, softball, swimming, tennis, track and field, volleyball. **Team name:** Mustangs.

**Student services.** Alcohol/substance abuse counseling, career counseling, student employment services, financial aid counseling, health services, minority student services, personal counseling, placement for graduates, veterans' counselor. **Physically disabled:** Services for visually, speech, hearing impaired. **Learning disabled:** Comprehensive services available.

**Contact.** E-mail: mscadm@morningside.edu
Phone: (712) 274-5000 ext. 5511 Toll-free number: (800) 831-0806
Fax: (712) 274-5101
Amy Williams, Co-Director of Admissions, Morningside College, 1501 Morningside Avenue, Sioux City, IA 51106

## Mount Mercy College
### Cedar Rapids, Iowa
**www.mtmercy.edu**  CB code: 6417

- Private 4-year liberal arts college affiliated with Roman Catholic Church
- Commuter campus in small city
- 1,441 degree-seeking undergraduates: 35% part-time, 70% women, 2% African American, 2% Asian American, 3% Hispanic American, 2% international
- 168 degree-seeking graduate students
- 78% of applicants admitted
- SAT or ACT (ACT writing optional), application essay required
- 65% graduate within 6 years; 8% enter graduate study

**General.** Founded in 1928. Regionally accredited. **Degrees:** 381 bachelor's awarded; master's offered. **Location:** 220 miles from Chicago. **Calendar:** 4-1-4, limited summer session. **Full-time faculty:** 81 total; 60% have terminal degrees, 6% minority, 64% women. **Part-time faculty:** 71 total; 14% have terminal degrees, 6% minority, 55% women. **Class size:** 60% < 20, 37% 20-39, 2% 40-49. **Special facilities:** Campus buildings connected by tunnel system.

**Freshman class profile.** 366 applied, 284 admitted, 150 enrolled.

| Mid 50% test scores | | Rank in top tenth: | 15% |
|---|---|---|---|
| ACT composite: | 20-24 | End year in good standing: | 99% |
| GPA 3.75 or higher: | 28% | Return as sophomores: | 84% |
| GPA 3.50-3.74: | 28% | Out-of-state: | 5% |
| GPA 3.0-3.49: | 30% | Live on campus: | 94% |
| GPA 2.0-2.99: | 14% | International: | 5% |
| Rank in top quarter: | 38% | | |

**Basis for selection.** 2.5 GPA, rank in top half of class, 20 ACT required. **Homeschooled:** Transcript of courses and grades, letter of recommendation (nonparent) required. Submit records of studies or detailed account of subjects and materials.

**High school preparation.** College-preparatory program recommended. Recommended units include English 4, mathematics 3, social studies 3, history 3, science 3 (laboratory 1) and foreign language 2.

**2009-2010 Annual costs.** Tuition/fees: $22,100. Room/board: $6,980. Books/supplies: $1,000. Personal expenses: $2,010.

**2009-2010 Financial aid.** **Need-based:** Average need met was 71%. Average scholarship/grant was $11,381; average loan $4,225. 49% of total undergraduate aid awarded as scholarships/grants, 51% as loans/jobs. **Non-need-based:** Scholarships awarded for academics, alumni affiliation, art, athletics, leadership, music/drama, religious affiliation.

**Application procedures.** **Admission:** Closing date 8/15 (receipt date). $20 fee, may be waived for applicants with need, free for online applicants. Admission notification on a rolling basis. Must reply by May 1 or within 2 week(s) if notified thereafter. **Financial aid:** Priority date 3/1; no closing date. FAFSA required. Applicants notified on a rolling basis starting 3/15; must reply by 5/1 or within 3 week(s) of notification.

**Academics. Special study options:** Accelerated study, cross-registration, double major, dual enrollment of high school students, honors, independent study, internships, liberal arts/career combination, study abroad, teacher certification program. **Credit/placement by examination:** AP, CLEP, IB, ACT, institutional tests. 60 credit hours maximum toward bachelor's degree. **Support services:** Learning center, remedial instruction, study skills assistance, tutoring, writing center.

**Majors. Biology:** General. **Business:** General, accounting, business admin, finance, management information systems, marketing. **Communications:** General, digital media, journalism, public relations. **Computer sciences:** General, computer science. **Conservation:** General. **Education:** Elementary, secondary. **Health:** Clinical lab science, health care admin, nursing (RN). **History:** General. **Math:** General. **Philosophy/religion:** Philosophy, religion. **Protective services:** Law enforcement admin. **Psychology:** General. **Public administration:** Social work. **Social sciences:** International relations, political science, sociology. **Visual/performing arts:** Art, graphic design. **Other:** Applied management, Multi/interdisciplinary studies.

**Most popular majors.** Business/marketing 39%, education 10%, health sciences 23%, security/protective services 6%.

**Computing on campus.** 135 workstations in dormitories, library, computer center. Dormitories wired for high-speed internet access and linked to campus network. Commuter students can connect to campus network. Online library, helpline, wireless network available.

**Student life. Freshman orientation:** Available. Preregistration for classes offered. Four-day orientation held prior to start of fall term; 3 one-day orientation/registration sessions in the spring and summer. **Housing:** Guaranteed on-campus for freshmen. Coed dorms, apartments, wellness housing available. $200 nonrefundable deposit, deadline 8/15. **Activities:** Choral groups, drama, literary magazine, musical theater, student government, student newspaper, Best Buddies, biology club, Circle K International, criminal justice association, English club, green club, history club, honors student association.

**Athletics.** NAIA. **Intercollegiate:** Baseball M, basketball, cheerleading M, cross-country, golf, soccer, softball W, track and field, volleyball W. **Intramural:** Basketball, football (non-tackle) M, racquetball, soccer, softball, table tennis, tennis, volleyball. **Team name:** Mustangs.

**Student services.** Adult student services, alcohol/substance abuse counseling, chaplain/spiritual director, career counseling, student employment services, financial aid counseling, health services, personal counseling, placement for graduates, veterans' counselor. **Physically disabled:** Services for visually, speech, hearing impaired.

**Contact.** E-mail: admission@mtmercy.edu
Phone: (319) 368-6460 Toll-free number: (800) 248-4504
Fax: (319) 363-5270
Sue Oatey, Vice President for Enrollment and Student Services, Mount Mercy College, 1330 Elmhurst Drive NE, Cedar Rapids, IA 52402-4797

## Northwestern College
### Orange City, Iowa
**www.nwciowa.edu**                              **CB code: 6490**

❯ Private 4-year liberal arts college affiliated with Reformed Church in America
❯ Residential campus in small town
❯ 1,163 degree-seeking undergraduates: 1% part-time, 59% women, 1% African American, 1% Asian American, 2% Hispanic American, 3% international
❯ 75% of applicants admitted
❯ SAT or ACT (ACT writing optional) required
❯ 60% graduate within 6 years

**General.** Founded in 1882. Regionally accredited. **Degrees:** 278 bachelor's awarded. **Location:** 40 miles from Sioux City; 75 miles from Sioux Falls, SD. **Calendar:** Semester, limited summer session. **Full-time faculty:** 82 total; 77% have terminal degrees, 6% minority, 35% women. **Part-time faculty:** 46 total; 4% have terminal degrees, 61% women. **Class size:** 66% < 20, 32% 20-39, 2% 40-49, less than 1% 50-99. **Special facilities:** Natural prairie restoration project.

**Freshman class profile.** 1,356 applied, 1,018 admitted, 331 enrolled.

| Mid 50% test scores | | | |
|---|---|---|---|
| ACT composite: | 21-28 | Return as sophomores: | 78% |
| Rank in top quarter: | 54% | Out-of-state: | 48% |
| Rank in top tenth: | 29% | Live on campus: | 97% |
| | | International: | 2% |

**Basis for selection.** 2.0 GPA required. Rank in top half of class and test scores above 50th percentile most important. Recommendations also important. Interview and essay recommended. Audition recommended for theater, music majors. Portfolio recommended for art majors. **Homeschooled:** Transcript of courses and grades required. **Learning Disabled:** Students provide documentation to Director of Academic Support upon admittance.

**High school preparation.** College-preparatory program recommended. 16 units recommended. Recommended units include English 4, mathematics 3, social studies 3, science 3 and foreign language 3.

**2009-2010 Annual costs.** Tuition/fees: $22,240. 1-4 credits, $470 per credit hour; 5-8 credits, $700 per credit hour; 9-11 credits, $920 per credit hour. Room/board: $6,756. Books/supplies: $900. Personal expenses: $2,026.

**2008-2009 Financial aid. Need-based:** 243 full-time freshmen applied for aid; 243 were judged to have need; 243 of these received aid. Average need met was 90%. Average scholarship/grant was $7,506; average loan $3,808. 61% of total undergraduate aid awarded as scholarships/grants, 39% as loans/jobs. **Non-need-based:** Awarded to 1,438 full-time undergraduates, including 382 freshmen. Scholarships awarded for academics, alumni affiliation, art, athletics, music/drama, religious affiliation, state residency.

**Application procedures. Admission:** Priority date 6/2; no deadline. $25 fee, may be waived for applicants with need. Admission notification on a rolling basis beginning on or about 10/1. Must reply by May 1 or within 3 week(s) if notified thereafter. **Financial aid:** Priority date 4/1, closing date 6/30. FAFSA required. Applicants notified on a rolling basis starting 3/15; must reply within 3 week(s) of notification.

**Academics. Special study options:** Double major, ESL, honors, independent study, internships, liberal arts/career combination, student-designed major, study abroad, teacher certification program, Washington semester. American Studies Program (Washington, D.C.), AuSable Institute of Environmental Studies Program (Michigan), Los Angeles Film Studies Semester, Chicago Metropolitan Studies Program, China Studies Program (Xiaman), Middle East Studies Program (Cairo), Oxford Summer Program (Oxford), Russian Studies Program, Contemporary Music Center (Martha's Vineyard, MA), Latin American Studies Program (Costa Rica), Oxford Honours Programme (England), Trinity Christian College: Semester in Spain, Creation Care Study Program, Summer Institute of Journalism (Washington, D.C.), Semester in Romania, Semester in Oman. **Credit/placement by examination:** AP, CLEP, IB, SAT, ACT, institutional tests. 24 credit hours maximum toward bachelor's degree. **Support services:** Learning center, reduced course load, remedial instruction, study skills assistance, tutoring, writing center.

**Majors. Agriculture:** Business. **Biology:** General. **Business:** Accounting, actuarial science, business admin, finance, human resources, managerial economics, marketing. **Communications:** Digital media, journalism, public relations. **Computer sciences:** General, computer science. **Conservation:** General. **Education:** General, elementary. **Foreign languages:** Spanish. **Health:** Athletic training, clinical lab technology, nursing (RN). **History:** General. **Liberal arts:** Arts/sciences. **Math:** General. **Parks/recreation:** Exercise sciences, health/fitness. **Philosophy/religion:** Philosophy, religion. **Physical sciences:** Chemistry. **Psychology:** General. **Public administration:** Social work. **Social sciences:** Economics, political science, sociology. **Theology:** Religious ed. **Visual/performing arts:** Art, dramatic.

**Most popular majors.** Biology 6%, business/marketing 20%, education 22%, history 6%, social sciences 7%, visual/performing arts 9%.

**Computing on campus.** 250 workstations in dormitories, library, computer center, student center. Dormitories linked to campus network. Commuter students can connect to campus network. Online course registration, online library, helpline, repair service, wireless network available.

**Student life. Freshman orientation:** Available. Preregistration for classes offered. One-day orientation program in late May. **Policies:** Use of alcohol prohibited on campus. Resident living required for all students unless granted commuting status or living with parents. Religious observance required. **Housing:** Guaranteed on-campus for all undergraduates. Single-sex dorms, special housing for disabled, apartments available. $100 fully refundable deposit, deadline 8/1. **Activities:** Bands, campus ministries, choral groups, dance, drama, international student organizations, literary magazine, music ensembles, student government, student newspaper, symphony orchestra, TV station, student activities council, Fellowship of Christian Athletes, College Republicans, Campus Democrats, Phi Beta Lambda, Sigma Tau, Spanish club, education club.

**Athletics.** NAIA. **Intercollegiate:** Baseball M, basketball, cross-country, football (tackle) M, golf, soccer, softball W, tennis, track and field, volleyball W, wrestling M. **Intramural:** Badminton, basketball, bowling, football (non-tackle), golf, racquetball, soccer, softball, table tennis, tennis, volleyball. **Team name:** Red Raiders.

**Student services.** Alcohol/substance abuse counseling, career counseling, student employment services, financial aid counseling, health services, personal counseling, placement for graduates, veterans' counselor. **Physically disabled:** Services for visually, speech, hearing impaired.

**Contact.** E-mail: admissions@nwciowa.edu
Phone: (712) 707-7130 Toll-free number: (800) 747-4757
Fax: (712) 707-7164
Mark Bloemendaal, Director of Admissions, Northwestern College, 101 Seventh Street, SW, Orange City, IA 51041

## St. Ambrose University
Davenport, Iowa
www.sau.edu                                    CB code: 6617

- Private 4-year university and liberal arts college affiliated with Roman Catholic Church
- Residential campus in small city
- 2,821 degree-seeking undergraduates: 15% part-time, 61% women, 3% African American, 1% Asian American, 4% Hispanic American
- 811 degree-seeking graduate students
- 82% of applicants admitted
- SAT or ACT (ACT writing optional) required
- 65% graduate within 6 years

**General.** Founded in 1882. Regionally accredited. **Degrees:** 647 bachelor's awarded; master's, doctoral, professional offered. **Location:** 180 miles from Des Moines, 175 miles from Chicago. **Calendar:** Semester, extensive summer session. **Full-time faculty:** 185 total; 74% have terminal degrees, 8% minority, 46% women. **Part-time faculty:** 220 total; 6% have terminal degrees, 4% minority, 49% women. **Class size:** 61% < 20, 38% 20-39, less than 1% 40-49, less than 1% >100. **Special facilities:** Transmission electron microscope, cable television channel, observatory, national prairie garden, radio station.

**Freshman class profile.** 2,075 applied, 1,702 admitted, 577 enrolled.

| Mid 50% test scores | | Rank in top quarter: | 34% |
|---|---|---|---|
| ACT composite: | 20-25 | Rank in top tenth: | 14% |
| GPA 3.75 or higher: | 17% | End year in good standing: | 70% |
| GPA 3.50-3.74: | 13% | Return as sophomores: | 74% |
| GPA 3.0-3.49: | 29% | Out-of-state: | 71% |
| GPA 2.0-2.99: | 41% | Live on campus: | 91% |

**Basis for selection.** 2.5 GPA and 20 ACT/950 SAT (exclusive of Writing) or 18-19 ACT/870-950 SAT and rank in top half of class required. Interview recommended. Portfolio required for art majors. **Homeschooled:** Students without high school diploma required to score 50 on GED with 18 ACT or 860 SAT (exclusive of Writing).

**High school preparation.** College-preparatory program recommended. 18 units recommended. Recommended units include English 4, mathematics 3, social studies 1, history 1, science 2 (laboratory 2), foreign language 1 and academic electives 4.

**2010-2011 Annual costs.** Tuition/fees: $23,910. Room/board: $8,585. Books/supplies: $1,250. Personal expenses: $1,200.

**2009-2010 Financial aid. Need-based:** 576 full-time freshmen applied for aid; 433 were judged to have need; 430 of these received aid. Average need met was 24%. Average scholarship/grant was $11,544; average loan $3,896. 52% of total undergraduate aid awarded as scholarships/grants, 48% as loans/jobs. **Non-need-based:** Awarded to 1,479 full-time undergraduates, including 443 freshmen. Scholarships awarded for academics, alumni affiliation, art, athletics, job skills, music/drama. **Additional information:** Iowa applicants must apply for financial aid by July 1. Audition required for music, drama scholarship applicants.

**Application procedures. Admission:** No deadline. $25 fee, may be waived for applicants with need, free for online applicants. Admission notification on a rolling basis beginning on or about 10/1. Must reply by May 1 or within 2 week(s) if notified thereafter. **Financial aid:** Priority date 3/15; no closing date. FAFSA required. Applicants notified on a rolling basis starting 2/1; must reply within 2 week(s) of notification.

**Academics. Special study options:** Accelerated study, combined bachelor's/ graduate degree, cooperative education, distance learning, double major, independent study, internships, liberal arts/career combination, student-designed major, study abroad, teacher certification program. Service learning program in which students work as volunteers for community and earn 1-3 semester hours credit, license preparation for occupational therapy on campus, accounting majors volunteer to work on income tax forms for low income families on campus. **Credit/placement by examination:** AP, CLEP, IB, SAT, ACT, institutional tests. 60 credit hours maximum toward bachelor's degree. **Support services:** Learning center, pre-admission summer

program, reduced course load, remedial instruction, study skills assistance, tutoring, writing center.

**Majors. Biology:** General. **Business:** General, accounting, business admin, finance, international, management science, marketing, organizational behavior. **Communications:** General, advertising, broadcast journalism, journalism, media studies, public relations, radio/tv. **Computer sciences:** General, computer science, information systems, LAN/WAN management, security, systems analysis. **Education:** General, art, biology, business, chemistry, early childhood, elementary, English, foreign languages, French, German, health, history, mathematics, music, physical, physics, psychology, science, secondary, social science, Spanish. **Engineering:** Industrial, physics. **Foreign languages:** French, German, Spanish. **Health:** Nursing (RN). **History:** General. **Interdisciplinary:** Biological/physical sciences, natural sciences, neuroscience. **Math:** General. **Parks/recreation:** Exercise sciences, health/ fitness, sports admin. **Philosophy/religion:** Philosophy. **Physical sciences:** Chemistry, physics. **Protective services:** Criminal justice, criminalistics. **Psychology:** General, forensic. **Public administration:** General. **Social sciences:** Economics, political science, sociology. **Visual/performing arts:** Commercial/advertising art, dramatic, graphic design, multimedia, studio arts, theater arts management.

**Most popular majors.** Biology 8%, business/marketing 32%, education 10%, health sciences 9%, psychology 9%, social sciences 6%.

**Computing on campus.** 190 workstations in library, computer center, student center. Dormitories wired for high-speed internet access and linked to campus network. Commuter students can connect to campus network. Online course registration, online library, helpline, wireless network available.

**Student life. Freshman orientation:** Mandatory. Preregistration for classes offered. Held 2 days per month in April, June, August. **Policies:** All campus buildings smoke-free. **Housing:** Guaranteed on-campus for freshmen. Coed dorms, single-sex dorms, special housing for disabled, apartments, wellness housing available. $250 partly refundable deposit, deadline 5/1. Townhouses for seniors, houses for juniors and seniors available. **Activities:** Bands, campus ministries, choral groups, dance, drama, literary magazine, music ensembles, musical theater, opera, radio station, student government, student newspaper, symphony orchestra, TV station, Fellowship of Christian Athletes, black student union, philosophy club, Young Republicans, Young Democrats, veterans club, art club, music club, psychology club, multicultural club.

**Athletics.** NAIA. **Intercollegiate:** Baseball M, basketball, bowling, cheerleading, cross-country, football (tackle) M, golf, soccer, softball W, tennis, track and field, volleyball. **Intramural:** Badminton, basketball, bowling, football (non-tackle), golf, handball, racquetball, softball, tennis, triathlon, volleyball. **Team name:** Fighting Bees.

**Student services.** Adult student services, alcohol/substance abuse counseling, career counseling, student employment services, financial aid counseling, health services, minority student services, on-campus daycare, personal counseling, placement for graduates, veterans' counselor, women's services. **Physically disabled:** Services for visually, speech, hearing impaired.

**Contact.** E-mail: admit@sau.edu
Phone: (563) 333-6300 Toll-free number: (800) 383-2627
Fax: (563) 333-6243
Meg Halligan, Director of Admissions, St. Ambrose University, 518 West Locust Street, Davenport, IA 52803-2898

## Simpson College
Indianola, Iowa                                CB member
www.simpson.edu                                CB code: 6650

- Private 4-year liberal arts college affiliated with United Methodist Church
- Residential campus in large town
- 1,919 degree-seeking undergraduates: 23% part-time, 57% women, 2% African American, 2% Asian American, 2% Hispanic American, 1% international
- 35 degree-seeking graduate students
- 89% of applicants admitted
- SAT or ACT (ACT writing optional) required
- 65% graduate within 6 years; 18% enter graduate study

**General.** Founded in 1860. Regionally accredited. **Degrees:** 414 bachelor's awarded; master's offered. **Location:** 12 miles from Des Moines. **Calendar:** 4-4-1. Extensive summer session. **Full-time faculty:** 99 total; 88% have terminal degrees, 5% minority, 48% women. **Part-time faculty:** 96 total; 29% have terminal degrees, 5% minority, 32% women. **Class size:**

62% < 20, 36% 20-39, 1% 40-49, less than 1% 50-99. **Special facilities:** Antebellum-era literature collection, cadaver laboratory, art galleries, Iowa history center, urban studies institute, public policy center, vocation and integrative learning center, education lab.

**Freshman class profile.** 1,290 applied, 1,142 admitted, 390 enrolled.

| Mid 50% test scores | | Return as sophomores: | 85% |
|---|---|---|---|
| ACT composite: | 21-27 | Out-of-state: | 18% |
| Rank in top quarter: | 61% | Live on campus: | 90% |
| Rank in top tenth: | 31% | Fraternities: | 15% |
| End year in good standing: | 85% | Sororities: | 22% |

**Basis for selection.** High school record, class rank, GPA, and ACT/SAT most important. Recommendations also considered. Campus visit/interview recommended. Audition recommended for music, drama majors. Portfolio recommended for art majors. **Homeschooled:** Letter of recommendation (nonparent) required. Must submit GED or high school diploma and transcript(s) with course content descriptions. **Learning Disabled:** Students should submit documentation of disability to ensure adequate facilities and programming can be provided.

**High school preparation.** College-preparatory program recommended. 16 units recommended. Recommended units include English 4, mathematics 3, social studies 3, science 3 (laboratory 3) and foreign language 3. 2 algebra, 1 geometry required; 4 units for math or science majors recommended. Language units should be same language.

**2009-2010 Annual costs.** Tuition/fees: $25,733. Room/board: $7,261. Books/supplies: $900. Personal expenses: $1,300.

**2009-2010 Financial aid. Need-based:** 390 full-time freshmen applied for aid; 338 were judged to have need; 338 of these received aid. Average need met was 92%. Average scholarship/grant was $19,122; average loan $2,597. 71% of total undergraduate aid awarded as scholarships/grants, 29% as loans/jobs. **Non-need-based:** Awarded to 398 full-time undergraduates, including 114 freshmen. Scholarships awarded for academics, alumni affiliation, art, leadership, minority status, music/drama, religious affiliation, state residency. **Additional information:** Music and theater scholarships based on audition. Art scholarships based on portfolio.

**Application procedures. Admission:** Priority date 5/1; deadline 8/15. No application fee. Admission notification on a rolling basis beginning on or about 9/15. Must reply by May 1 or within 3 week(s) if notified thereafter. **Financial aid:** Priority date 4/1; no closing date. FAFSA required. Applicants notified on a rolling basis starting 3/12; must reply by 5/1 or within 3 week(s) of notification.

**Academics. Special study options:** Accelerated study, combined bachelor's/graduate degree, double major, honors, independent study, internships, liberal arts/career combination, New York semester, student-designed major, study abroad, teacher certification program, Washington semester. 3-2 and 4-2 engineering program with Washington University in St. Louis, Iowa State University, and Institute of Technology, University of Minnesota, Minneapolis. **Credit/placement by examination:** AP, CLEP, IB, ACT, institutional tests. 24 credit hours maximum toward bachelor's degree. **Support services:** Learning center, pre-admission summer program, reduced course load, study skills assistance, tutoring, writing center.

**Majors. Biology:** General, biochemistry. **Business:** Accounting, business admin, international, marketing. **Computer sciences:** Computer science, information systems. **Conservation:** Environmental science. **Education:** General, elementary, music, physical. **Foreign languages:** French, German, Spanish. **Health:** Athletic training, predental, premedicine, prepharmacy, preveterinary. **History:** General. **Legal studies:** Prelaw. **Liberal arts:** Arts/sciences. **Math:** General. **Parks/recreation:** Exercise sciences, sports admin. **Philosophy/religion:** Philosophy, religion. **Physical sciences:** Chemistry, physics. **Protective services:** Criminal justice, forensics. **Psychology:** General. **Public administration:** Social work. **Social sciences:** Economics, international relations, political science, sociology. **Theology:** Preministerial. **Visual/performing arts:** Art, dramatic, music performance. **Other:** Multimedia journalism, Pre-engineering, Pre-optometry.

**Most popular majors.** Biology 6%, business/marketing 25%, communications/journalism 6%, education 8%, liberal arts 6%, social sciences 8%, visual/performing arts 6%.

**Computing on campus.** 336 workstations in dormitories, library, computer center, student center. Dormitories wired for high-speed internet access and linked to campus network. Commuter students can connect to campus network. Online library, wireless network available.

**Student life. Freshman orientation:** Mandatory. Preregistration for classes offered. Four 1-day summer registration programs in June. Fall orientation held first week students are on campus. **Housing:** Guaranteed on-campus for all undergraduates. Coed dorms, apartments, fraternity/sorority housing, wellness housing available. $200 fully refundable deposit. Single sex rooms

and floors in co-ed dorms, medical single rooms available. **Activities:** Bands, campus ministries, choral groups, dance, drama, international student organizations, literary magazine, music ensembles, Model UN, musical theater, opera, radio station, student government, student newspaper, Religious Life Community, Interfaith Fellowship, Multicultural Student Alliance, Alpha Phi Omega Service Fraternity, College Democrats, College Republicans, Fellowship of Christian Athletes, Students Embracing Responsible Volunteer Experiences, Habitat for Humanity, Amnesty International.

**Athletics. NCAA. Intercollegiate:** Baseball M, basketball, cheerleading, cross-country, football (tackle) M, golf, soccer, softball W, swimming, tennis, track and field, volleyball W, wrestling M. **Intramural:** Badminton, basketball, football (non-tackle), golf, racquetball, soccer, softball, swimming, table tennis, tennis, volleyball, weight lifting. **Team name:** Storm.

**Student services.** Adult student services, alcohol/substance abuse counseling, chaplain/spiritual director, career counseling, services for economically disadvantaged, student employment services, financial aid counseling, health services, minority student services, personal counseling, women's services. **Physically disabled:** Services for visually, speech, hearing impaired.

**Contact.** E-mail: admiss@simpson.edu
Phone: (515) 961-1624 Toll-free number: (800) 362-2454 ext. 1624
Fax: (515) 961-1870
Deborah Tierney, Vice President for Enrollment, Simpson College, 701 North C Street, Indianola, IA 50125

---

| **University of Dubuque** | |
|---|---|
| Dubuque, Iowa | CB member |
| www.dbq.edu | CB code: 6869 |

- Private 4-year university and seminary college affiliated with Presbyterian Church (USA)
- Residential campus in small city
- 1,431 degree-seeking undergraduates: 6% part-time, 45% women, 12% African American, 2% Asian American, 4% Hispanic American, 1% Native American, 1% international
- 97 degree-seeking graduate students
- 75% of applicants admitted
- SAT or ACT (ACT writing optional), application essay required
- 43% graduate within 6 years; 35% enter graduate study

**General.** Founded in 1852. Regionally accredited. **Degrees:** 245 bachelor's, 2 associate awarded; master's, doctoral offered. **ROTC:** Army. **Location:** 180 miles from Chicago. **Calendar:** Semester, limited summer session. **Full-time faculty:** 83 total; 49% have terminal degrees, 7% minority, 36% women. **Part-time faculty:** 81 total; 51% women. **Class size:** 60% < 20, 39% 20-39, less than 1% 40-49, less than 1% 50-99. **Special facilities:** Floating laboratory on Mississippi River, curriculum laboratory for teachers, aviation operations center, studio laboratory for animation program, wetland area management, science center.

**Freshman class profile.** 1,181 applied, 882 admitted, 354 enrolled.

| Mid 50% test scores | | Rank in top quarter: | 22% |
|---|---|---|---|
| SAT critical reading: | 440-530 | Rank in top tenth: | 8% |
| SAT math: | 440-540 | End year in good standing: | 89% |
| ACT composite: | 18-23 | Return as sophomores: | 71% |
| GPA 3.75 or higher: | 10% | Out-of-state: | 72% |
| GPA 3.50-3.74: | 10% | Live on campus: | 90% |
| GPA 3.0-3.49: | 30% | Fraternities: | 4% |
| GPA 2.0-2.99: | 45% | Sororities: | 4% |

**Basis for selection.** 18 ACT, 860 SAT (exclusive of Writing), rank in top half of class most important. 2.0 GPA in college preparatory classes also considered. Rolling admission; must receive test scores before final enrollment. Recommendations required. **Learning Disabled:** Students must request assistance.

**High school preparation.** College-preparatory program recommended. 16 units required. Required and recommended units include English 4, mathematics 3, social studies 3, science 3, foreign language 2 and academic electives 3.

**2009-2010 Annual costs.** Tuition/fees: $20,770. Room/board: $6,990. Books/supplies: $950.

**2009-2010 Financial aid. Need-based:** 343 full-time freshmen applied for aid; 322 were judged to have need; 322 of these received aid. Average need met was 81%. Average scholarship/grant was $13,616; average loan $6,806. 60% of total undergraduate aid awarded as scholarships/grants, 40% as loans/jobs. **Non-need-based:** Awarded to 282 full-time undergraduates,

including 80 freshmen. Scholarships awarded for academics, alumni affiliation, leadership, music/drama, ROTC, state residency.

**Application procedures. Admission:** No deadline. $25 fee, may be waived for applicants with need. Admission notification on a rolling basis beginning on or about 9/1. Must reply by May 1 or within 4 week(s) if notified thereafter. **Financial aid:** Priority date 4/1; no closing date. FAFSA required. Applicants notified on a rolling basis starting 3/1; must reply within 3 week(s) of notification.

**Academics. Special study options:** Accelerated study, combined bachelor's/graduate degree, cooperative education, cross-registration, distance learning, double major, dual enrollment of high school students, independent study, internships, liberal arts/career combination, study abroad, teacher certification program, urban semester. Undergraduate students may take graduate courses. Off-campus study: semester-away programs. **Credit/placement by examination:** AP, CLEP, IB, SAT, ACT, institutional tests. 24 credit hours maximum toward associate degree, 24 toward bachelor's. **Support services:** Learning center, reduced course load, remedial instruction, study skills assistance, tutoring, writing center.

**Majors. Biology:** General, ecology. **Business:** Accounting, business admin. **Communications:** General. **Computer sciences:** General, computer graphics. **Conservation:** General, environmental studies. **Education:** General, elementary, physical. **Health:** Nursing (RN). **Parks/recreation:** General. **Philosophy/religion:** Philosophy, religion. **Physical sciences:** Planetary. **Protective services:** Criminal justice. **Psychology:** General. **Social sciences:** Sociology. **Transportation:** Aviation, aviation management, flight instructor. **Visual/performing arts:** Commercial/advertising art, graphic design.

**Most popular majors.** Biology 6%, business/marketing 20%, computer/information sciences 7%, education 11%, health sciences 12%, parks/recreation 6%, psychology 7%, social sciences 7%, trade and industry 15%.

**Computing on campus.** 200 workstations in dormitories, library, computer center, student center, student center. Dormitories wired for high-speed internet access and linked to campus network. Commuter students can connect to campus network. Online course registration, online library, helpline, student web hosting, wireless network available.

**Student life. Freshman orientation:** Mandatory, $100 fee. Preregistration for classes offered. Held 4 days prior to beginning of class. **Policies:** Students required to live on-campus through junior year, until they reach 21 years of age or unless living with parents within 50 miles of campus. **Housing:** Guaranteed on-campus for freshmen. Coed dorms, special housing for disabled, apartments, wellness housing available. $200 fully refundable deposit, deadline 6/1. Houses and townhouses available. **Activities:** Bands, campus ministries, choral groups, dance, drama, film society, international student organizations, literary magazine, music ensembles, student government, student newspaper, social service organizations, service fraternity, environmental group, student activities board, College Republicans, College Democrats.

**Athletics.** NCAA. **Intercollegiate:** Baseball M, basketball, cross-country, football (tackle) M, golf, soccer, softball W, tennis, track and field, volleyball W, wrestling M. **Intramural:** Archery, badminton, baseball M, basketball, bowling, cheerleading, football (non-tackle) M, golf, racquetball, soccer, softball, table tennis, tennis, volleyball. **Team name:** Spartans.

**Student services.** Alcohol/substance abuse counseling, chaplain/spiritual director, career counseling, student employment services, financial aid counseling, health services, minority student services, on-campus daycare, personal counseling, placement for graduates, veterans' counselor.

**Contact.** E-mail: admssns@dbq.edu
Phone: (563) 589-3200 Toll-free number: (800) 722-5583
Fax: (563) 589-3690
Jesse James, Dean of Admission, University of Dubuque, 2000 University Avenue, Dubuque, IA 52001-5099

## University of Iowa

**Iowa City, Iowa**                                    **CB member**
**www.uiowa.edu**                                  **CB code: 6681**

- Public 4-year university
- Residential campus in small city
- 19,899 degree-seeking undergraduates: 8% part-time, 51% women, 2% African American, 4% Asian American, 3% Hispanic American, 1% Native American, 4% international
- 8,413 graduate students
- 83% of applicants admitted
- SAT or ACT (ACT writing optional) required
- 66% graduate within 6 years

**General.** Founded in 1847. Regionally accredited. **Degrees:** 4,465 bachelor's awarded; master's, doctoral, professional offered. **ROTC:** Army, Air Force. **Location:** 20 miles from Cedar Rapids, 110 miles from Des Moines. **Calendar:** Semester, extensive summer session. **Full-time faculty:** 1,586 total; 97% have terminal degrees, 16% minority, 31% women. **Part-time faculty:** 93 total; 95% have terminal degrees, 10% minority, 26% women. **Class size:** 50% < 20, 37% 20-39, 4% 40-49, 6% 50-99, 4% >100. **Special facilities:** Field campus, accelerator, observatory, natural history museum, driving simulator.

**Freshman class profile.** 15,060 applied, 12,503 admitted, 4,063 enrolled.

| Mid 50% test scores | | GPA 2.0-2.99: | 6% |
|---|---|---|---|
| SAT critical reading: | 500-640 | Rank in top quarter: | 55% |
| SAT math: | 560-690 | Rank in top tenth: | 23% |
| ACT composite: | 23-28 | Return as sophomores: | 83% |
| GPA 3.75 or higher: | 35% | Out-of-state: | 49% |
| GPA 3.50-3.74: | 23% | Live on campus: | 94% |
| GPA 3.0-3.49: | 36% | International: | 6% |

**Basis for selection.** Regent Admission Index (RAI) computed based on ACT/SAT, class rank, GPA and number of high school core courses. Iowa residents must have 245 RAI; nonresidents must have 255 RAI. College of Engineering applicants must demonstrate success (A's or B's) in math and science courses; have 25 ACT with 25 ACT math or 1130 SAT (exclusive of Writing) with 620 SAT math; and have 265 RAI. Audition required of music, dance majors. **Homeschooled:** Personal essay describing homeschool experience strongly recommended and required in certain circumstances.

**High school preparation.** College-preparatory program required. 15 units required. Required and recommended units include English 4, mathematics 3-4, social studies 3, science 3 and foreign language 2-4. Math units must include 2 algebra, 1 geometry. Science units must include 2 of the following: biology, chemistry, and physics. Engineering majors require fourth unit of higher math, 1 chemistry and 1 physics, and only 2 units social studies.

**2010-2011 Annual costs.** Tuition/fees: $7,417; $23,713 out-of-state. Room/board: $8,331. Books/supplies: $1,090. Personal expenses: $2,625.

**2008-2009 Financial aid. Need-based:** 3,420 full-time freshmen applied for aid; 2,302 were judged to have need; 2,086 of these received aid. Average need met was 52%. Average scholarship/grant was $4,179; average loan $2,904. 41% of total undergraduate aid awarded as scholarships/grants, 59% as loans/jobs. **Non-need-based:** Awarded to 6,235 full-time undergraduates, including 2,100 freshmen. Scholarships awarded for academics, alumni affiliation, art, athletics, leadership, music/drama.

**Application procedures. Admission:** Closing date 4/1 (postmark date). $40 fee, may be waived for applicants with need. Admission notification on a rolling basis beginning on or about 9/15. Must reply by May 1 or within 2 week(s) if notified thereafter. **Financial aid:** Priority date 1/1; no closing date. FAFSA, institutional form required. Applicants notified on a rolling basis starting 3/15.

**Academics.** Bachelor of Liberal Studies and Bachelor of Applied Studies may be earned with distance education course work. **Special study options:** Accelerated study, combined bachelor's/graduate degree, cooperative education, distance learning, double major, dual enrollment of high school students, ESL, exchange student, external degree, honors, independent study, internships, New York semester, semester at sea, student-designed major, study abroad, teacher certification program, Washington semester. **Credit/placement by examination:** AP, CLEP, IB, SAT, ACT, institutional tests. 30 credit hours maximum toward bachelor's degree. **Support services:** Learning center, pre-admission summer program, reduced course load, remedial instruction, study skills assistance, tutoring, writing center.

**Majors. Area/ethnic studies:** African, African-American, American, Asian, Russian/Slavic, women's. **Biology:** General, biochemistry, microbiology. **Business:** Accounting, actuarial science, business admin, finance, human resources, labor relations, management information systems, management science, managerial economics, marketing. **Communications:** General, journalism, media studies. **Computer sciences:** General, computer science. **Conservation:** Environmental science, environmental studies. **Education:** Elementary. **Engineering:** General, biomedical, chemical, civil, electrical, industrial, mechanical. **Foreign languages:** Ancient Greek, Chinese, classics, comparative lit, French, German, Italian, Japanese, Latin, linguistics, Portuguese, Russian, Sanskrit, Spanish. **Health:** Athletic training, audiology/hearing, clinical lab science, music therapy, nuclear medical technology, nursing (RN), predental, premedicine, prenursing, prepharmacy, preveterinary, radiologic technology/medical imaging, recreational therapy. **History:** General. **Interdisciplinary:** Ancient studies, global studies. **Legal studies:** Prelaw. **Liberal arts:** Arts/sciences. **Math:** General, applied, statistics. **Parks/recreation:** General, exercise science, facilities management, sports admin. **Philosophy/religion:** Philosophy, religion. **Physical sciences:** Astronomy, chemistry, geology, physics. **Psychology:** General. **Public administration:** Social work. **Social sciences:** Anthropology, economics, geography, political science, sociology. **Visual/performing arts:** Art, art history/conservation, arts management, ceramics, cinematography, dance, dramatic, drawing, film/cinema, jazz, metal/jewelry, music management, music performance, music theory/composition, painting, photography, piano/organ, printmaking, sculpture, stringed instruments, studio arts, voice/opera. **Other:** Ethics and public policy.

**Most popular majors.** Business/marketing 19%, communications/journalism 10%, health sciences 8%, liberal arts 6%, psychology 8%, social sciences 9%, visual/performing arts 7%.

**Computing on campus.** 1,200 workstations in dormitories, library, computer center, student center. Dormitories wired for high-speed internet access and linked to campus network. Commuter students can connect to campus network. Online course registration, online library, helpline, repair service, student web hosting, wireless network available.

**Student life. Freshman orientation:** Mandatory, $250 fee. Preregistration for classes offered. 2-day summer program. Students meet academic advisers, learn about campus resources. Program for parents and guardians offered concurrently. **Policies:** Non-smoking campus. **Housing:** Coed dorms, special housing for disabled, apartments, fraternity/sorority housing, wellness housing available. $120 partly refundable deposit. Living-learning communities; international, freshman and transfer honors; career leadership and service; quiet houses; major-specific; Hispanic culture; sustainability; law housing. **Activities:** Bands, campus ministries, choral groups, dance, drama, film society, international student organizations, literary magazine, music ensembles, musical theater, opera, radio station, student government, student newspaper, symphony orchestra, TV station, College Republicans, University Democrats, American Indian student association, Hispanic Society, black student union, Amnesty International, gay/lesbian/bisexual/transgendered and allied union, honor societies, Habitat for Humanity, writer's club.

**Athletics.** NCAA. **Intercollegiate:** Baseball M, basketball, cheerleading, cross-country, diving, field hockey W, football (tackle) M, golf, gymnastics, rowing (crew) W, soccer W, softball W, swimming, tennis, track and field, volleyball W, wrestling M. **Intramural:** Badminton, basketball, bowling, football (non-tackle), golf, racquetball, soccer, softball, table tennis, tennis, volleyball, wrestling. **Team name:** Hawkeyes.

**Student services.** Adult student services, alcohol/substance abuse counseling, career counseling, services for economically disadvantaged, student employment services, financial aid counseling, health services, legal services, minority student services, on-campus daycare, personal counseling, placement for graduates, veterans' counselor, women's services. **Physically disabled:** Services for visually, speech, hearing impaired.

**Contact.** E-mail: admissions@uiowa.edu
Phone: (319) 335-3847 Toll-free number: (800) 553-4692
Fax: (319) 335-1535
Michael Barron, Assistant Provost for Enrollment Services, University of Iowa, 107 Calvin Hall, Iowa City, IA 52242-1396

---

## University of Northern Iowa
**Cedar Falls, Iowa**
www.uni.edu

CB member
CB code: 6307

- Public 4-year university
- Residential campus in small city
- 11,061 degree-seeking undergraduates: 8% part-time, 56% women, 3% African American, 1% Asian American, 3% Hispanic American, 2% international
- 1,459 degree-seeking graduate students
- 85% of applicants admitted
- SAT or ACT (ACT writing optional) required
- 67% graduate within 6 years

**General.** Founded in 1876. Regionally accredited. **Degrees:** 2,268 bachelor's awarded; master's, doctoral offered. **ROTC:** Army. **Location:** 63 miles from Cedar Rapids. **Calendar:** Semester, limited summer session. **Full-time faculty:** 632 total; 72% have terminal degrees, 13% minority, 45% women. **Part-time faculty:** 178 total; 28% have terminal degrees, 6% minority, 54% women. **Class size:** 36% <20, 47% 20-39, 8% 40-49, 6% 50-99, 3% >100. **Special facilities:** Performing arts center, center for energy and environmental education, NASA teacher resource center, observatory, natural preserve, museum, wellness and recreation center.

**Freshman class profile.** 4,133 applied, 3,505 admitted, 1,946 enrolled.

| Mid 50% test scores | | | |
|---|---|---|---|
| ACT composite: | 21-26 | Rank in top tenth: | 19% |
| GPA 3.75 or higher: | 30% | Return as sophomores: | 82% |
| GPA 3.50-3.74: | 22% | Out-of-state: | 5% |
| GPA 3.0-3.49: | 32% | Live on campus: | 90% |
| GPA 2.0-2.99: | 16% | International: | 1% |
| Rank in top quarter: | 49% | Fraternities: | 6% |
| | | Sororities: | 3% |

**Basis for selection.** Rank in top half of class, completion of high school curriculum requirements most important. In the absence of class rank, standardized test scores may carry greater weight. Audition required of music majors. Interview may be recommended for borderline applicants who do not meet admission requirements. **Homeschooled:** Statement describing homeschool structure and mission, transcript of courses and grades required.

**High school preparation.** 15 units required. Required and recommended units include English 4, mathematics 3, social studies 3, science 3 (laboratory 1), foreign language 2 and academic electives 2. English units must include 1 composition. Math units must include algebra, geometry and advanced algebra. 2 electives required in subjects listed above and/or fine arts.

**2009-2010 Annual costs.** Tuition/fees: $6,636; $14,900 out-of-state. Room/board: $6,960. Books/supplies: $1,035. Personal expenses: $2,777.

**2009-2010 Financial aid. Need-based:** 1,686 full-time freshmen applied for aid; 1,146 were judged to have need; 1,105 of these received aid. Average need met was 72%. Average scholarship/grant was $4,438; average loan $3,233. 42% of total undergraduate aid awarded as scholarships/grants, 58% as loans/jobs. **Non-need-based:** Awarded to 4,001 full-time undergraduates, including 1,291 freshmen. Scholarships awarded for academics, alumni affiliation, art, athletics, leadership, minority status, music/drama, ROTC, state residency.

**Application procedures. Admission:** Closing date 8/15 (postmark date). $40 fee. Admission notification on a rolling basis beginning on or about 9/1. **Financial aid:** No deadline. FAFSA required. Applicants notified on a rolling basis starting 3/1.

**Academics.** External undergraduate degree completion program available. **Special study options:** Accelerated study, combined bachelor's/graduate degree, cooperative education, distance learning, double major, dual enrollment of high school students, ESL, exchange student, external degree, honors, independent study, internships, liberal arts/career combination, student-designed major, study abroad, teacher certification program, Washington semester, weekend college. Combined bachelors/masters degree programs (BA/MA, BS/MS, BA/MS); undergraduate dual degree majors; Additional programs leading to combined bachelor's/graduate degree: biology, physics, and technology. **Credit/placement by examination:** AP, CLEP, IB, ACT, institutional tests. 32 credit hours maximum toward bachelor's degree. **Support services:** Learning center, pre-admission summer program, reduced course load, remedial instruction, study skills assistance, tutoring, writing center.

**Majors. Area/ethnic studies:** American, Latin American. **Biology:** General, biochemistry, bioinformatics, biomedical sciences, biotechnology, ecology, microbiology. **Business:** Accounting, actuarial science, business admin, construction management, finance, management information systems, marketing, real estate. **Communications:** General, digital media, organizational, public relations. **Communications technology:** Graphics. **Computer sciences:** General, computer science, networking. **Conservation:** Environmental science. **Education:** Business, elementary, ESL, foreign languages, health, kindergarten/preschool, middle, music, physical, reading, science, social science, speech, technology/industrial arts. **Engineering:** Physics. **Engineering technology:** Industrial, manufacturing. **Family/consumer sciences:** Clothing/textiles, family/community services. **Foreign languages:** General, French, German, Russian, Spanish. **Health:** Athletic training, speech pathology. **History:** General. **Interdisciplinary:** Biological/physical sciences, gerontology. **Liberal arts:** Arts/sciences, humanities. **Math:** General, applied. **Parks/recreation:** General, health/fitness. **Philosophy/religion:** Philosophy, religion. **Physical sciences:** Chemistry, geology, physics. **Psychology:** General. **Public administration:** General, social work. **Social sciences:** Anthropology, applied economics, criminology, econometrics, economics, geography, political science, sociology. **Visual/performing arts:** Acting, art, art history/conservation, dramatic, interior design, music performance, music theory/composition, studio arts, theater design. **Other:** Health promotion.

**Most popular majors.** Business/marketing 22%, communications/journalism 6%, education 15%, public administration/social services 6%, visual/performing arts 6%.

**Computing on campus.** 2,500 workstations in library, computer center, student center. Dormitories wired for high-speed internet access and linked to campus network. Online course registration, online library, helpline, student web hosting, wireless network available.

**Student life. Freshman orientation:** Available, $125 fee. Preregistration for classes offered. Nine 2-day sessions in summer and immediately preceding beginning of semesters. **Housing:** Coed dorms, single-sex dorms, special housing for disabled, apartments, fraternity/sorority housing available. $200 deposit. **Activities:** Bands, campus ministries, choral groups, dance, drama, international student organizations, literary magazine, music ensembles, Model UN, musical theater, opera, radio station, student government, student newspaper, symphony orchestra, Amnesty International, Asian American student union, black student union, Campus Crusade for Christ, Catholic student association, College Republicans, conservation club, Fellowship of Christian Athletes, Habitat for Humanity, Democrat club.

**Athletics.** NCAA. **Intercollegiate:** Basketball, cross-country, diving W, football (tackle) M, golf, soccer W, softball W, swimming W, tennis W, track and field, volleyball W, wrestling M. **Intramural:** Badminton, basketball, bowling, cheerleading, cross-country, football (non-tackle), football (tackle) M, golf, racquetball, soccer, softball, swimming, table tennis, tennis, track and field, volleyball, weight lifting, wrestling M. **Team name:** Panthers.

**Student services.** Adult student services, alcohol/substance abuse counseling, career counseling, student employment services, financial aid counseling, health services, minority student services, on-campus daycare, personal counseling, placement for graduates, veterans' counselor. **Physically disabled:** Services for visually, speech, hearing impaired.

**Contact.** E-mail: admissions@uni.edu
Phone: (319) 273-2281 Toll-free number: (800) 772-2037
Fax: (319) 273-2885
Christie Kangas, Director of Admissions, University of Northern Iowa, 1227 West 27th Street, Cedar Falls, IA 50614-0018

## Upper Iowa University
**Fayette, Iowa**
www.uiu.edu                                    CB code: 6885

- Private 4-year university
- Residential campus in rural community
- 5,811 degree-seeking undergraduates: 47% part-time, 61% women
- 447 graduate students
- 42% of applicants admitted
- 35% graduate within 6 years

**General.** Founded in 1857. Regionally accredited. **Degrees:** 1,097 bachelor's, 70 associate awarded; master's offered. **Location:** 50 miles from Waterloo, 70 miles from Cedar Rapids. **Calendar:** Semester, limited summer session. **Full-time faculty:** 60 total; 82% have terminal degrees, 7% minority, 43% women. **Part-time faculty:** 402 total; 15% minority, 46% women. **Special facilities:** Electron microscope lab, greenhouse, television and media lab with computer animation suite.

**Freshman class profile.** 1,293 applied, 544 admitted, 176 enrolled.

| Mid 50% test scores | | | |
|---|---|---|---|
| SAT critical reading: | 400-460 | GPA 3.0-3.49: | 35% |
| SAT math: | 410-530 | GPA 2.0-2.99: | 36% |
| ACT composite: | 17-22 | Return as sophomores: | 70% |
| GPA 3.75 or higher: | 11% | Out-of-state: | 50% |
| GPA 3.50-3.74: | 16% | Live on campus: | 17% |

**Basis for selection.** 2.0 GPA, 16 ACT, 760 SAT (exclusive of Writing) important. SAT or ACT recommended. Interview recommended for academically weak applicants. Portfolio recommended for art majors. **Homeschooled:** Letters of recommendation strongly encouraged. GED or proof of completed coursework required.

**High school preparation.** College-preparatory program recommended. 14 units recommended. Recommended units include English 4, mathematics 3, social studies 2, history 1, science 3 (laboratory 1).

**2009-2010 Annual costs.** Tuition/fees: $21,418. Room/board: $6,578. Books/supplies: $1,400. Personal expenses: $1,600.

**2008-2009 Financial aid. Need-based:** 816 full-time freshmen applied for aid; 628 were judged to have need; 610 of these received aid. Average need met was 64%. Average scholarship/grant was $9,828; average loan $3,218. 45% of total undergraduate aid awarded as scholarships/grants, 55% as loans/jobs. **Non-need-based:** Awarded to 985 full-time undergraduates, including 409 freshmen. Scholarships awarded for academics, alumni affiliation, athletics.

**Application procedures. Admission:** No deadline. $15 fee, may be waived for applicants with need. Admission notification on a rolling basis. **Financial aid:** Priority date 3/1; no closing date. FAFSA required. Applicants notified on a rolling basis starting 3/1; must reply within 9 week(s) of notification.

**Academics.** 2 consecutive 8-week terms equal one semester. **Special study options:** Accelerated study, combined bachelor's/graduate degree, distance learning, double major, dual enrollment of high school students, ESL, external degree, independent study, internships, liberal arts/career combination, student-designed major, study abroad, teacher certification program. **Credit/placement by examination:** AP, CLEP, IB, institutional tests. 30 credit hours maximum toward associate degree, 30 toward bachelor's. **Support services:** Learning center, tutoring.

**Majors. Area/ethnic studies:** American. **Biology:** General. **Business:** General, accounting, business admin, management information systems. **Communications:** General. **Conservation:** General, environmental science, forestry, management/policy. **Education:** General, biology, chemistry, early childhood, elementary, health, history, kindergarten/preschool, middle, physical, reading, science, secondary, social science, social studies, special. **Health:** Athletic training, facilities admin, health care admin, physical therapy assistant, predental, premedicine, prepharmacy, preveterinary. **Legal studies:** Prelaw. **Math:** General. **Parks/recreation:** Facilities management, health/fitness. **Personal/culinary services:** Mortuary science. **Physical sciences:** Chemistry. **Protective services:** Criminal justice. **Psychology:** General. **Public administration:** Human services. **Social sciences:** General, criminology, sociology. **Visual/performing arts:** Art, arts management, commercial/advertising art, studio arts.

**Most popular majors.** Business/marketing 41%, psychology 13%, public administration/social services 19%, security/protective services 7%.

**Computing on campus.** 4 workstations in dormitories, library, computer center, student center. Dormitories wired for high-speed internet access. Online course registration, online library, wireless network available.

**Student life. Freshman orientation:** Mandatory. Preregistration for classes offered. Held during summer, includes financial aid counseling. **Housing:** Guaranteed on-campus for all undergraduates. Coed dorms, single-sex dorms available. Suite-style housing available. **Activities:** Pep band, campus ministries, choral groups, international student organizations, student government, student newspaper, various organizations available.

**Athletics.** NCAA. **Intercollegiate:** Baseball M, basketball, cheerleading, football (tackle) M, golf, soccer, softball W, tennis, volleyball W, wrestling M. **Intramural:** Badminton, basketball, bowling, football (tackle), softball, table tennis, volleyball. **Team name:** Peacocks.

**Student services.** Career counseling, student employment services, financial aid counseling, health services, personal counseling, placement for graduates.

**Contact.** E-mail: admission@uiu.edu
Phone: (563) 425-5281 Toll-free number: (800) 553-4150 ext. 2
Fax: (563) 425-5323
Linc Morris, Vice President of Enrollment Management, Upper Iowa University, Parker Fox Hall, Fayette, IA 52142

## Waldorf College
**Forest City, Iowa**                          CB member
www.waldorf.edu                                CB code: 6925

- Private 4-year liberal arts college affiliated with Evangelical Lutheran Church in America
- Residential campus in small town
- 507 degree-seeking undergraduates: 3% part-time, 44% women
- 59% of applicants admitted
- SAT or ACT (ACT writing optional) required
- 35% graduate within 6 years; 9% enter graduate study

**General.** Founded in 1903. Regionally accredited. **Degrees:** 121 bachelor's, 1 associate awarded. **Location:** 125 miles from Des Moines. **Calendar:** Semester, limited summer session. **Full-time faculty:** 35 total; 57% have terminal degrees, 34% women. **Part-time faculty:** 22 total; 32% have terminal degrees, 46% women. **Class size:** 64% < 20, 36% 20-39. **Special facilities:** Digital multimedia lab, exercise physiology laboratory with hydrostatic metabolic chamber, GeoWall, FM radio station, cable access TV station.

**Freshman class profile.** 923 applied, 546 admitted, 95 enrolled.

| Mid 50% test scores | | | |
|---|---|---|---|
| ACT composite: | 18-23 | Rank in top quarter: | 16% |
| GPA 3.75 or higher: | 5% | Rank in top tenth: | 4% |
| GPA 3.50-3.74: | 16% | End year in good standing: | 79% |
| GPA 3.0-3.49: | 28% | Return as sophomores: | 47% |
| GPA 2.0-2.99: | 50% | Out-of-state: | 42% |
| | | Live on campus: | 90% |

**Basis for selection.** School record and test scores most important, recommendations important, class rank and interview (when administered) considered. Interview recommended. Audition and portfolio recommended for music, theater majors. **Learning Disabled:** Interview during campus visit required.

**High school preparation.** College-preparatory program recommended. 16 units recommended. Recommended units include English 4, mathematics 3, social studies 4, science 3 and foreign language 2.

**2009-2010 Annual costs.** Tuition/fees: $20,554. Room/board: $5,954. Books/supplies: $935. Personal expenses: $1,655.

**2008-2009 Financial aid. Need-based:** 113 full-time freshmen applied for aid; 96 were judged to have need; 96 of these received aid. Average need met was 77%. Average scholarship/grant was $12,191; average loan $4,129. 57% of total undergraduate aid awarded as scholarships/grants, 43% as loans/jobs. **Non-need-based:** Awarded to 164 full-time undergraduates, including 67 freshmen. Scholarships awarded for academics, alumni affiliation, athletics, job skills, leadership, music/drama, religious affiliation, state residency.

**Application procedures. Admission:** No deadline. No application fee. Admission notification on a rolling basis beginning on or about 9/9. **Financial aid:** Priority date 3/1; no closing date. FAFSA, institutional form required. Applicants notified on a rolling basis starting 3/1; must reply within 2 week(s) of notification.

**Academics.** Internships required in all baccalaureate programs. **Special study options:** Accelerated study, combined bachelor's/graduate degree, double major, dual enrollment of high school students, ESL, honors, independent study, internships, liberal arts/career combination, student-designed major, study abroad, teacher certification program. **Credit/placement by examination:** AP, CLEP, IB, SAT, ACT, institutional tests. 8 credit hours maximum toward associate degree, 8 toward bachelor's. **Support services:** Learning center, reduced course load, remedial instruction, study skills assistance, tutoring, writing center.

**Majors. Biology:** General. **Business:** General, business admin, finance, marketing. **Communications:** Broadcast journalism, journalism, media studies, radio/tv. **Communications technology:** General. **Computer sciences:** General, information systems. **Education:** Drama/dance, elementary, English, history, middle, multi-level teacher, music, science, secondary, social studies. **Family/consumer sciences:** Food/nutrition. **History:** General. **Legal studies:** Prelaw. **Liberal arts:** Arts/sciences, humanities. **Psychology:** General. **Social sciences:** General, political science. **Visual/performing arts:** General, arts management, dramatic, music management, music performance, piano/organ, theater arts management, voice/opera.

**Most popular majors.** Business/marketing 32%, communications/journalism 17%, education 15%, English 6%, health sciences 7%, history 6%, psychology 9%.

**Computing on campus.** PC or laptop required. Dormitories wired for high-speed internet access and linked to campus network. Online library, helpline, repair service, wireless network available.

**Student life. Freshman orientation:** Mandatory. Preregistration for classes offered. Held 2 days prior to start of school. **Policies:** No alcohol on campus. **Housing:** Guaranteed on-campus for all undergraduates. Coed dorms, single-sex dorms, special housing for disabled, apartments, wellness housing available. $100 fully refundable deposit, deadline 9/10. Pets allowed in dorm rooms. **Activities:** Bands, campus ministries, choral groups, dance, drama, film society, international student organizations, literary magazine, music ensembles, musical theater, radio station, student government, student newspaper, TV station, Fellowship of Christian athletes, science club, student senate, global culture club, Amnesty International, awareness ambassadors, praise and worship groups, history club, Gay Straight Alliance, Campus Democrats/Republicans.

**Athletics.** NAIA. **Intercollegiate:** Baseball M, basketball, cheerleading M, football (tackle) M, golf, soccer, softball W, volleyball W, wrestling M. **Intramural:** Badminton, basketball, bowling, football (non-tackle), racquetball, rugby W, skiing, soccer, softball, table tennis, tennis, volleyball, weight lifting. **Team name:** Warriors.

**Student services.** Alcohol/substance abuse counseling, chaplain/spiritual director, career counseling, student employment services, financial aid counseling, health services, personal counseling, placement for graduates. **Physically disabled:** Services for visually, hearing impaired. **Learning disabled:** Comprehensive services available.

**Contact.** E-mail: admissions@waldorf.edu
Phone: (641) 585-8112 Toll-free number: (800) 292-1903
Fax: (641) 585-8125
Carl Childs, Director of Admissions, Waldorf College, 106 South Sixth Street, Forest City, IA 50436-1713

## Wartburg College
**Waverly, Iowa**
**www.wartburg.edu**                                **CB code: 6926**

◗ Private 4-year liberal arts college affiliated with Evangelical Lutheran Church in America
◗ Residential campus in small town
◗ 1,755 degree-seeking undergraduates: 1% part-time, 52% women, 5% African American, 2% Asian American, 1% Hispanic American, 5% international
◗ 73% of applicants admitted
◗ SAT or ACT (ACT writing optional) required
◗ 64% graduate within 6 years; 20% enter graduate study

**General.** Founded in 1852. Regionally accredited. **Degrees:** 375 bachelor's awarded. **Location:** 15 miles from Waterloo-Cedar Falls. **Calendar:** 4-4-1. Limited summer session. **Full-time faculty:** 109 total; 84% have terminal degrees, 5% minority, 48% women. **Part-time faculty:** 72 total; 14% have terminal degrees, 8% minority, 50% women. **Class size:** 41% < 20, 51% 20-39, 5% 40-49, 3% 50-99. **Special facilities:** Planetarium/observatory, prairie preserve, math simulation laboratory, institute for leadership education, international museum, music laboratory, science center, center for community engagement.

**Freshman class profile.** 2,278 applied, 1,652 admitted, 480 enrolled.

| Mid 50% test scores | | | |
|---|---|---|---|
| SAT critical reading: | 420-600 | GPA 2.0-2.99: | 19% |
| SAT math: | 470-610 | Rank in top quarter: | 56% |
| SAT writing: | 410-570 | Rank in top tenth: | 28% |
| ACT composite: | 21-27 | End year in good standing: | 88% |
| GPA 3.75 or higher: | 39% | Return as sophomores: | 82% |
| GPA 3.50-3.74: | 20% | Out-of-state: | 26% |
| GPA 3.0-3.49: | 22% | Live on campus: | 98% |
| | | International: | 5% |

**Basis for selection.** Class rank, GPA, courses taken, test scores, recommendations important. Students with 18 ACT or below or who rank in lower half of high school class are reviewed by admission and scholarship committee for final decision. Interview recommended. Audition recommended for music majors. Portfolio recommended for art majors. **Learning Disabled:** Documentation of disability required.

**High school preparation.** College-preparatory program required. 15 units recommended. Recommended units include English 4, mathematics 3, social studies 2, science 3, foreign language 2 and computer science 1.

**2010-2011 Annual costs.** Tuition/fees: $29,020. Room/board: $7,975.

**2008-2009 Financial aid. Need-based:** 474 full-time freshmen applied for aid; 397 were judged to have need; 397 of these received aid. Average need met was 85%. Average scholarship/grant was $17,841; average loan $3,411. 73% of total undergraduate aid awarded as scholarships/grants, 27% as loans/jobs. **Non-need-based:** Awarded to 599 full-time undergraduates, including 191 freshmen. Scholarships awarded for academics, alumni affiliation, leadership, music/drama, religious affiliation.

**Application procedures. Admission:** Priority date 5/1; no deadline. No application fee. Admission notification on a rolling basis beginning on or about 9/1. **Financial aid:** Priority date 3/1; no closing date. FAFSA required. Applicants notified on a rolling basis starting 3/1; must reply within 2 week(s) of notification.

**Academics. Special study options:** Accelerated study, double major, dual enrollment of high school students, honors, independent study, internships, student-designed major, study abroad, teacher certification program, urban semester, Washington semester. Wartburg West urban academic internship experience in Denver, CO; Washington Center Academic Internship Program; cultural immersions in U.S. and around the world; Leadership Certificate Program; 3-2 engineering agreements; deferred admission program with the University of Iowa College of Dentistry, community-based learning courses and first-year seminars. **Credit/placement by examination:** AP, CLEP, SAT, ACT, institutional tests. **Support services:** Learning center, reduced course load, remedial instruction, study skills assistance, tutoring, writing center.

**Majors. Biology:** General, biochemistry. **Business:** Accounting, business admin, finance, international, marketing. **Communications:** General, broadcast journalism, journalism, public relations. **Computer sciences:** General, information systems. **Education:** Art, elementary, history, music, physical. **Engineering:** Science. **Foreign languages:** French, German, Spanish. **Health:** Clinical lab science, music therapy. **History:** General. **Math:** General. **Parks/recreation:** Sports admin. **Philosophy/religion:** Philosophy, religion. **Physical sciences:** Chemistry, physics. **Psychology:** General. **Public administration:** Social work. **Social sciences:** Economics, international relations, political science, sociology. **Theology:** Pastoral counseling, religious ed, sacred music. **Visual/performing arts:** Art, commercial/advertising art, dramatic, music performance, music theory/composition.

**Most popular majors.** Biology 13%, business/marketing 23%, communications/journalism 10%, education 13%.

**Computing on campus.** 275 workstations in dormitories, library, computer center, student center. Dormitories wired for high-speed internet access and linked to campus network. Commuter students can connect to campus network. Online course registration, online library, helpline, wireless network available.

**Student life. Freshman orientation:** Mandatory, $160 fee. Preregistration for classes offered. Two-day program in summer; continues in fall for 1 week. **Housing:** Guaranteed on-campus for freshmen. Coed dorms, single-sex dorms, apartments available. $100 deposit, deadline 5/1. Suite-style housing available. **Activities:** Bands, campus ministries, choral groups, dance, drama, film society, international student organizations, literary magazine, music ensembles, musical theater, opera, radio station, student government, student newspaper, symphony orchestra, TV station, campus ministry board, Democrat club, Republican club, Habitat for Humanity, Students for Peace and Justice, Fellowship of Christian Athletes, volunteer action center, EARTH, Mosaico Latino, Faith Alive.

**Athletics.** NCAA. **Intercollegiate:** Baseball M, basketball, cross-country, football (tackle) M, golf, soccer, softball W, tennis, track and field, volleyball W, wrestling M. **Intramural:** Basketball, bowling, football (nontackle), racquetball, softball, tennis, volleyball. **Team name:** Knights.

**Student services.** Alcohol/substance abuse counseling, chaplain/spiritual director, career counseling, student employment services, financial aid counseling, health services, minority student services, personal counseling.

**Contact.** E-mail: admissions@wartburg.edu
Phone: (319) 352-8264 Toll-free number: (800) 772-2085
Fax: (319) 352-8579
Todd Coleman, Assistant Vice President for Admissions and Alumni/Parent Programs, Wartburg College, 100 Wartburg Boulevard, PO Box 1003, Waverly, IA 50677-0903

## William Penn University
### Oskaloosa, Iowa
www.wmpenn.edu                                        CB code: 6943

- Private 4-year liberal arts college affiliated with Society of Friends (Quaker)
- Residential campus in small town
- 1,811 degree-seeking undergraduates
- 55% of applicants admitted
- SAT or ACT (ACT writing optional) required

**General.** Founded in 1873. Regionally accredited. Strong emphasis on leadership development. **Degrees:** 362 bachelor's, 73 associate awarded; master's offered. **Location:** 60 miles from Des Moines. **Calendar:** Differs by program, limited summer session. **Full-time faculty:** 53 total. **Part-time faculty:** 151 total. **Class size:** 62% < 20, 32% 20-39, 1% 40-49, 5% 50-99. **Special facilities:** Applied technology laboratories, multipurpose activity center, professional-level theater, Middle Eastern art collection, prairie wildlife preserve.

**Freshman class profile.** 759 applied, 418 admitted, 235 enrolled.

| Mid 50% test scores | | | |
|---|---|---|---|
| SAT critical reading: | 340-490 | SAT writing: | 380-480 |
| SAT math: | 400-500 | ACT composite: | 17-22 |

**Basis for selection.** Class rank, test scores, high school GPA important. Extracurricular activities, alumni relationship, recommendation, personal essay considered. Interview and essay recommended for academically marginal applicants. Audition recommended for music grants.

**High school preparation.** College-preparatory program recommended. 15 units required. Required and recommended units include English 4, mathematics 2, social studies 2, history 2, science 2 and academic electives 3.

**2009-2010 Annual costs.** Tuition/fees: $18,934. Room/board: $5,222. Books/supplies: $950. Personal expenses: $2,062.

**2008-2009 Financial aid. Non-need-based:** Scholarships awarded for academics, alumni affiliation, athletics, leadership, music/drama, religious affiliation.

**Application procedures. Admission:** No deadline. $20 fee, may be waived for applicants with need. Admission notification on a rolling basis beginning on or about 11/1. **Financial aid:** Priority date 4/15; no closing date. FAFSA required. Applicants notified on a rolling basis starting 1/1; must reply within 3 week(s) of notification.

**Academics.** College for Working Adults (CWA) degree program. Leadership core curriculum replaces general education requirements. **Special study options:** Accelerated study, distance learning, double major, dual enrollment of high school students, ESL, independent study, internships, liberal arts/career combination, study abroad, teacher certification program. 3-2 engineering program with Iowa State University. **Credit/placement by examination:** AP, CLEP, IB, SAT, ACT. 16 credit hours maximum toward associate degree, 32 toward bachelor's. **Support services:** Learning center, reduced course load, remedial instruction, study skills assistance, tutoring, writing center.

**Majors. Biology:** General. **Business:** Accounting, business admin. **Communications:** General. **Computer sciences:** General, information technology. **Education:** Elementary, secondary. **Engineering:** Mechanical. **Engineering technology:** Industrial. **History:** General. **Math:** General. **Parks/recreation:** Health/fitness. **Psychology:** General. **Public administration:** Human services. **Social sciences:** Sociology.

**Most popular majors.** Business/marketing 60%, education 10%, parks/recreation 12%.

**Computing on campus.** 125 workstations in dormitories, library, computer center, student center. Dormitories wired for high-speed internet access and linked to campus network. Commuter students can connect to campus network. Online library, helpline, repair service, wireless network available.

**Student life. Freshman orientation:** Mandatory. Preregistration for classes offered. Held the weekend prior to start of Fall classes; freshmen retreat hosted by faculty the weekend following first week of classes. **Policies:** Student Code of Conduct identifies academic conduct, conduct toward society, general conduct, and conduct toward others. **Housing:** Guaranteed on-campus for freshmen. Coed dorms, single-sex dorms, special housing for disabled, apartments, wellness housing available. $100 partly refundable deposit, deadline 8/1. **Activities:** Bands, campus ministries, choral groups, dance, drama, literary magazine, music ensembles, musical theater, radio station, student government, student newspaper, literary magazine, Students for Minority Interests, international student club, Presidents Diplomats, strength and conditioning club, Greek Council, honor societies, computer club.

**Athletics.** NAIA. **Intercollegiate:** Baseball M, basketball, cheerleading M, cross-country, football (tackle) M, golf M, soccer, softball W, track and field, volleyball W, wrestling M. **Intramural:** Basketball, bowling, football (non-tackle) M, softball, table tennis, tennis, volleyball. **Team name:** Lady Statesmen, Statesmen.

**Student services.** Adult student services, alcohol/substance abuse counseling, chaplain/spiritual director, career counseling, services for economically disadvantaged, student employment services, financial aid counseling, minority student services, personal counseling, placement for graduates, veterans' counselor. **Physically disabled:** Services for visually, hearing impaired.

**Contact.** E-mail: admissions@wmpenn.edu
Phone: (641) 673-1012 Toll-free number: (800) 779-7366
Fax: (641) 673-2113
Kerra Strong, Director of Admissions, William Penn University, 201 Trueblood Avenue, Oskaloosa, IA 52577

# Kansas

## Baker University

**Baldwin City, Kansas**
www.bakeru.edu

**CB member**
**CB code: 6031**

- Private 4-year liberal arts and teachers college affiliated with United Methodist Church
- Residential campus in small town
- 903 degree-seeking undergraduates: 1% part-time, 52% women, 8% African American, 1% Asian American, 1% Hispanic American, 1% Native American, 1% international
- 56% of applicants admitted
- SAT or ACT (ACT writing optional) required
- 54% graduate within 6 years; 30% enter graduate study

**General.** Founded in 1858. Regionally accredited. Additional campus locations include Overland Park, Topeka, Wichita, and Lee's Summit in Missouri. **Degrees:** 177 bachelor's awarded. **ROTC:** Army, Air Force. **Location:** 15 miles from Lawrence, 35 miles from Kansas City, Missouri. **Calendar:** 4-1-4, limited summer session. **Full-time faculty:** 65 total; 86% have terminal degrees, 5% minority, 42% women. **Part-time faculty:** 36 total; 22% have terminal degrees, 3% minority, 56% women. **Class size:** 74% < 20, 21% 20-39, 4% 40-49, less than 1% 50-99. **Special facilities:** Wetlands, museum, bible collections.

**Freshman class profile.** 1,266 applied, 706 admitted, 257 enrolled.

| Mid 50% test scores | | Rank in top quarter: | 54% |
|---|---|---|---|
| SAT critical reading: | 450-570 | Rank in top tenth: | 24% |
| SAT math: | 430-560 | Return as sophomores: | 75% |
| ACT composite: | 21-26 | Out-of-state: | 27% |
| GPA 3.75 or higher: | 30% | Live on campus: | 96% |
| GPA 3.50-3.74: | 24% | International: | 1% |
| GPA 3.0-3.49: | 34% | Fraternities: | 48% |
| GPA 2.0-2.99: | 12% | Sororities: | 43% |

**Basis for selection.** Strong core curriculum during high school very important. GPA, class rank, course selection, ACT or SAT, and recommendation from high school core teacher or guidance counselor important. Involvement in school, community and church activities considered. Interview and essay recommended. Audition recommended for music and theater majors. Portfolio recommended for art majors. **Homeschooled:** Letter of recommendation (nonparent) required.

**High school preparation.** College-preparatory program recommended. 17 units recommended. Recommended units include English 4, mathematics 3, social studies 3, science 3 (laboratory 1) and foreign language 2. One fine arts and one computing course recommended.

**2009-2010 Annual costs.** Tuition/fees: $21,130. Room/board: $6,800. Books/supplies: $1,200. Personal expenses: $1,550.

**2009-2010 Financial aid.** **Need-based:** 249 full-time freshmen applied for aid; 172 were judged to have need; 172 of these received aid. Average need met was 81%. Average scholarship/grant was $5,340; average loan $4,771. 52% of total undergraduate aid awarded as scholarships/grants, 48% as loans/jobs. **Non-need-based:** Awarded to 769 full-time undergraduates, including 235 freshmen. Scholarships awarded for academics, alumni affiliation, art, athletics, leadership, music/drama, religious affiliation.

**Application procedures. Admission:** No deadline. No application fee. Admission notification on a rolling basis. **Financial aid:** Priority date 3/1; no closing date. FAFSA, institutional form required. Applicants notified on a rolling basis starting 3/1; must reply by 5/1 or within 6 week(s) of notification.

**Academics.** Liberal arts core consisting of nine hours stressing critical thinking skills, strong writing ability, and application of these skills to various academic disciplines required. **Special study options:** Accelerated study, double major, honors, independent study, internships, liberal arts/career combination, student-designed major, study abroad, teacher certification program. **Credit/placement by examination:** AP, CLEP, IB, SAT, ACT. **Support services:** Learning center, reduced course load, study skills assistance, tutoring, writing center.

**Majors. Biology:** General, molecular, wildlife. **Business:** General, accounting, international. **Communications:** General, media studies. **Computer sciences:** Computer science, information systems, web page design. **Education:** Art, elementary, middle, music, secondary. **Foreign languages:** French, German, Spanish. **History:** General. **Interdisciplinary:** Global studies. **Math:** General. **Parks/recreation:** Exercise sciences, health/fitness, sports admin. **Philosophy/religion:** Philosophy, religion. **Physical sciences:** Chemistry, physics. **Psychology:** General. **Social sciences:** Economics, political science, sociology. **Visual/performing arts:** Art history/conservation, dramatic, studio arts.

**Most popular majors.** Biology 6%, business/marketing 25%, communications/journalism 6%, education 13%, parks/recreation 10%, social sciences 6%.

**Computing on campus.** 222 workstations in dormitories, library, computer center. Dormitories wired for high-speed internet access and linked to campus network. Online library, helpline, repair service, student web hosting, wireless network available.

**Student life. Freshman orientation:** Mandatory. Preregistration for classes offered. 4-day orientation program prior to start of fall term. **Policies:** Students required to live in campus or Greek housing unless granted permission to live off-campus. Freshmen not allowed to live in Greek housing. **Housing:** Guaranteed on-campus for freshmen. Coed dorms, single-sex dorms, special housing for disabled, apartments, fraternity/sorority housing available. $100 deposit. **Activities:** Bands, choral groups, dance, drama, international student organizations, literary magazine, music ensembles, radio station, student government, student newspaper, TV station, Fellowship of Christian Athletes, Parmentors, Baker Ambassadors, Earth We Are, College Republicans, Young Democrats, Baker Serves.

**Athletics.** NAIA. **Intercollegiate:** Baseball M, basketball, bowling W, cheerleading, cross-country, football (tackle) M, golf, soccer, softball W, tennis, track and field, volleyball W, wrestling M. **Intramural:** Basketball, football (non-tackle), softball, table tennis, volleyball. **Team name:** Wildcats.

**Student services.** Alcohol/substance abuse counseling, chaplain/spiritual director, career counseling, student employment services, financial aid counseling, health services, minority student services, personal counseling, placement for graduates, veterans' counselor, women's services. **Physically disabled:** Services for visually, hearing impaired.

**Contact.** E-mail: admission@bakeru.edu
Phone: (785) 594-8307 Toll-free number: (800) 873-4282
Fax: (785) 594-8372
Daniel McKinney, Director of Admissions, Baker University, 618 Eighth Street, Baldwin City, KS 66006-0065

## Barclay College

**Haviland, Kansas**
www.barclaycollege.edu

**CB code: 6228**

- Private 4-year Bible college affiliated with Evangelical Friends Alliance and Friends United Meeting
- Residential campus in rural community
- 194 degree-seeking undergraduates: 12% part-time, 49% women
- 77% of applicants admitted
- ACT (writing optional), application essay, interview required
- 31% graduate within 6 years; 15% enter graduate study

**General.** Founded in 1917. Accredited by ABHE. **Degrees:** 14 bachelor's, 4 associate awarded. **Location:** 100 miles from Wichita, 65 miles from Dodge City. **Calendar:** Semester, limited summer session. **Full-time faculty:** 7 total; 57% have terminal degrees, 14% minority, 14% women. **Part-time faculty:** 21 total; 14% have terminal degrees, 5% minority, 33% women. **Class size:** 81% < 20, 15% 20-39, 1% 40-49, 2% 50-99.

**Freshman class profile.** 70 applied, 54 admitted, 50 enrolled.

| Mid 50% test scores | | End year in good standing: | 74% |
|---|---|---|---|
| SAT critical reading: | 410-460 | Return as sophomores: | 71% |
| SAT math: | 410-440 | Out-of-state: | 69% |
| SAT writing: | 290-410 | International: | 2% |
| ACT composite: | 18-23 | | |

**Basis for selection.** Personal references and commitment to Christian vocation important. Committee reviews file and conducts phone interview. Audition recommended for music majors.

**2010-2011 Annual costs.** Tuition/fees (projected): $13,690. Room/board: $6,600. Books/supplies: $1,000. Personal expenses: $1,300.

**2009-2010 Financial aid. Need-based:** 67% of total undergraduate aid awarded as scholarships/grants, 33% as loans/jobs. **Non-need-based:** Scholarships awarded for academics, alumni affiliation, leadership, music/drama, state residency.

**Application procedures. Admission:** Closing date 9/1. $25 fee, may be waived for applicants with need, free for online applicants. Admission notification on a rolling basis. **Financial aid:** Priority date 5/31, closing date 7/15. FAFSA, institutional form required. Applicants notified on a rolling basis starting 1/1; must reply within 4 week(s) of notification.

**Academics.** Each student has Bible major in addition to individually chosen major. Emphasis on practicums and internships. **Special study options:** Cooperative education, distance learning, double major, dual enrollment of high school students, independent study, internships, liberal arts/career combination, teacher certification program. Cooperative classes with Pratt Community College. **Credit/placement by examination:** AP, CLEP, IB, SAT, ACT, institutional tests. 15 credit hours maximum toward associate degree, 30 toward bachelor's. **Support services:** Remedial instruction, study skills assistance, tutoring.

**Majors. Business:** General, business admin. **Education:** Elementary. **Philosophy/religion:** Religion. **Psychology:** General. **Theology:** Bible, missionary, pastoral counseling, sacred music, theology, youth ministry.

**Most popular majors.** Business/marketing 6%, psychology 17%, theological studies 78%.

**Computing on campus.** 18 workstations in library, computer center. Dormitories wired for high-speed internet access and linked to campus network. Commuter students can connect to campus network. Online course registration, online library, repair service, wireless network available.

**Student life. Freshman orientation:** Mandatory. Preregistration for classes offered. **Policies:** Christian and social work required. Religious observance required. **Housing:** Guaranteed on-campus for freshmen. Single-sex dorms, wellness housing available. $50 deposit. **Activities:** Jazz band, choral groups, drama, music ensembles, student government.

**Athletics. Intercollegiate:** Basketball, cheerleading M, golf, soccer M, tennis, volleyball W. **Intramural:** Baseball, basketball, bowling, softball, volleyball. **Team name:** Bears.

**Student services.** Chaplain/spiritual director, career counseling, student employment services, financial aid counseling, health services, personal counseling, placement for graduates.

**Contact.** E-mail: admissions@barclaycollege.edu
Phone: (620) 862-5252 ext. 21 Toll-free number: (800) 862-0226
Fax: (620) 862-5242
Justin Kendall, Director of Admissions, Barclay College, 607 North Kingman, Haviland, KS 67059

---

## Benedictine College
**Atchison, Kansas**

**CB member**

www.benedictine.edu

**CB code: 6056**

- Private 4-year liberal arts college affiliated with Roman Catholic Church
- Residential campus in large town
- 1,438 degree-seeking undergraduates: 1% part-time, 52% women, 4% African American, 5% Hispanic American, 1% international
- 59 degree-seeking graduate students
- SAT or ACT (ACT writing optional) required
- 59% graduate within 6 years; 24% enter graduate study

**General.** Founded in 1858. Regionally accredited. **Degrees:** 260 bachelor's awarded; master's offered. **ROTC:** Army. **Location:** 45 miles from Kansas City, Missouri. **Calendar:** Semester, limited summer session. **Full-time faculty:** 76 total; 84% have terminal degrees, 7% minority, 26% women. **Part-time faculty:** 38 total; 40% have terminal degrees, 3% minority, 60% women. **Class size:** 63% < 20, 35% 20-39, 1% 40-49, less than 1% 50-99. **Special facilities:** Biological research area, 2 performing arts theaters.

### Freshman class profile.

| Mid 50% test scores | | | |
|---|---|---|---|
| ACT composite: | 21-27 | Rank in top quarter: | 15% |
| GPA 3.75 or higher: | 30% | Rank in top tenth: | 5% |
| GPA 3.50-3.74: | 20% | Return as sophomores: | 72% |
| GPA 3.0-3.49: | 26% | Out-of-state: | 69% |
| GPA 2.0-2.99: | 24% | Live on campus: | 98% |
| | | International: | 1% |

**Basis for selection.** Applicant must satisfy 2 of following requirements: GPA above 2.0, rank in top half of class, requisite ACT or SAT scores. Recommendations and interview considered. Interview recommended for academically weak applicants.

**High school preparation.** Required and recommended units include English 4, mathematics 3-4, social studies 2, history 2, science 2-4 and foreign language 2-4.

**2009-2010 Annual costs. Tuition/fees:** $19,800. **Room/board:** $6,575. **Books/supplies:** $2,400. **Personal expenses:** $2,800.

**2009-2010 Financial aid. Need-based:** 368 full-time freshmen applied for aid; 299 were judged to have need; 299 of these received aid. Average need met was 76%. Average scholarship/grant was $13,106; average loan $2,412. 65% of total undergraduate aid awarded as scholarships/grants, 35% as loans/jobs. **Non-need-based:** Awarded to 409 full-time undergraduates, including 152 freshmen. Scholarships awarded for academics, alumni affiliation, art, athletics, job skills, leadership, minority status, music/drama, religious affiliation, ROTC.

**Application procedures. Admission:** No deadline. $25 fee, may be waived for applicants with need. Admission notification on a rolling basis. Must reply by May 1 or within 4 week(s) if notified thereafter. **Financial aid:** Priority date 3/15; no closing date. FAFSA required. Applicants notified on a rolling basis starting 2/1; must reply within 2 week(s) of notification.

**Academics. Special study options:** Combined bachelor's/graduate degree, cooperative education, double major, dual enrollment of high school students, ESL, exchange student, independent study, internships, liberal arts/career combination, student-designed major, study abroad, teacher certification program. **Credit/placement by examination:** AP, CLEP, IB, ACT, institutional tests. 30 credit hours maximum toward associate degree, 30 toward bachelor's. **Support services:** Learning center, reduced course load, remedial instruction, study skills assistance, tutoring.

**Majors. Biology:** General, biochemistry. **Business:** Accounting, business admin, finance, international. **Communications:** Media studies. **Computer sciences:** Computer science. **Education:** Elementary, music, physical, special. **Foreign languages:** French, Spanish. **Health:** Athletic training. **History:** General. **Interdisciplinary:** Natural sciences. **Liberal arts:** Arts/sciences. **Math:** General. **Philosophy/religion:** Philosophy, religion. **Physical sciences:** Astronomy, chemistry, physics. **Psychology:** General. **Social sciences:** General, economics, political science, sociology. **Theology:** Youth ministry. **Visual/performing arts:** Dramatic, music management, theater arts management.

**Most popular majors.** Business/marketing 24%, communications/journalism 7%, education 12%, parks/recreation 7%, theological studies 7%.

**Computing on campus.** 85 workstations in dormitories, library, computer center. Dormitories wired for high-speed internet access and linked to campus network. Commuter students can connect to campus network. Online course registration, online library, helpline, repair service, wireless network available.

**Student life. Freshman orientation:** Mandatory. Preregistration for classes offered. Weekend program before classes commence. **Housing:** Guaranteed on-campus for freshmen. Coed dorms, single-sex dorms, special housing for disabled available. $100 deposit. Off-campus college-owned housing available. **Activities:** Bands, campus ministries, choral groups, dance, drama, literary magazine, music ensembles, musical theater, student government, student newspaper, symphony orchestra, Ravens Respect Life, Young Democrats, Young Republicans, Knights of Columbus, hunger coalition, Fellowship of Catholic University Students, Students in Free Enterprise, Black Student Union, Amnesty International.

**Athletics. NAIA. Intercollegiate:** Baseball M, basketball, cheerleading, cross-country, football (tackle) M, golf, soccer, softball W, track and field, volleyball W. **Intramural:** Baseball M, basketball, handball, racquetball, soccer, softball, table tennis, volleyball. **Team name:** Ravens.

**Student services.** Alcohol/substance abuse counseling, chaplain/spiritual director, career counseling, student employment services, financial aid counseling, health services, personal counseling, placement for graduates, veterans' counselor. **Physically disabled:** Services for visually, speech, hearing impaired.

**Contact.** E-mail: bcadmiss@benedictine.edu
Phone: (913) 360-7476 Toll-free number: (800) 467-5340
Fax: (913) 367-5462
Pete Helgesen, Dean of Enrollment Management, Benedictine College, 1020 North Second Street, Atchison, KS 66002-1499

## Bethany College
**Lindsborg, Kansas**
**www.bethanylb.edu**                    CB code: 6034

- Private 4-year liberal arts college affiliated with Evangelical Lutheran Church in America
- Residential campus in small town
- 571 degree-seeking undergraduates
- 58% of applicants admitted
- SAT or ACT (ACT writing optional) required

**General.** Founded in 1881. Regionally accredited. **Degrees:** 101 bachelor's awarded. **Location:** 20 miles from Salina, 60 miles from Wichita. **Calendar:** 4-1-4, limited summer session. **Full-time faculty:** 43 total. **Part-time faculty:** 41 total. **Class size:** 84% < 20, 15% 20-39, less than 1% 40-49, less than 1% 50-99.

**Freshman class profile.** 831 applied, 485 admitted, 182 enrolled.

| Mid 50% test scores | | | |
|---|---|---|---|
| SAT critical reading: | 370-500 | GPA 2.0-2.99: | 20% |
| SAT math: | 420-560 | Rank in top quarter: | 42% |
| SAT writing: | 380-490 | Rank in top tenth: | 15% |
| ACT composite: | 19-24 | Out-of-state: | 63% |
| GPA 3.75 or higher: | 29% | Live on campus: | 95% |
| GPA 3.50-3.74: | 17% | Fraternities: | 2% |
| GPA 3.0-3.49: | 33% | Sororities: | 1% |

**Basis for selection.** High school GPA, course selection, trends in grades, class rank, and standardized test scores very important. Interview, letters of recommendation, leadership, curriculum, and involvement considered. Interview and essay recommended for some. Audition required of music and theater majors. Portfolio required of art majors.

**High school preparation.** College-preparatory program recommended. Recommended units include English 4, mathematics 3, social studies 3, science 3 (laboratory 2) and foreign language 2.

**2009-2010 Annual costs.** Tuition/fees: $19,065. Room/board: $5,876. Books/supplies: $1,000. Personal expenses: $1,900.

**2009-2010 Financial aid. Non-need-based:** Scholarships awarded for academics, alumni affiliation, art, athletics, leadership, music/drama, religious affiliation. **Additional information:** State financial aid deadline March 15.

**Application procedures. Admission:** Priority date 2/1; no deadline. No application fee. Admission notification on a rolling basis. **Financial aid:** Priority date 3/15; no closing date. FAFSA required. Applicants notified on a rolling basis starting 2/1; must reply within 3 week(s) of notification.

**Academics. Special study options:** Accelerated study, combined bachelor's/graduate degree, cross-registration, double major, dual enrollment of high school students, exchange student, honors, independent study, internships, liberal arts/career combination, student-designed major, study abroad, teacher certification program, urban semester, Washington semester. Special education program with Associated Colleges of Central Kansas. **Credit/placement by examination:** AP, CLEP, IB. 32 credit hours maximum toward bachelor's degree. **Support services:** Learning center, reduced course load, study skills assistance, tutoring, writing center.

**Majors. Biology:** General. **Business:** Accounting, business admin, finance, managerial economics, marketing. **Communications:** General. **Education:** General, art, biology, business, chemistry, elementary, English, health, history, mathematics, music, physical, secondary, social science. **Health:** Art therapy, athletic training. **History:** General. **Liberal arts:** Arts/sciences. **Math:** General. **Parks/recreation:** Facilities management, sports admin. **Philosophy/religion:** Christian. **Physical sciences:** Chemistry. **Protective services:** Criminal justice, police science. **Psychology:** General. **Public administration:** Social work. **Social sciences:** General, economics, sociology. **Visual/performing arts:** Art, music performance.

**Most popular majors.** Biology 15%, business/marketing 15%, education 24%, parks/recreation 7%, psychology 8%, security/protective services 6%, visual/performing arts 7%.

**Computing on campus.** 40 workstations in library, computer center. Dormitories wired for high-speed internet access and linked to campus network. Commuter students can connect to campus network. Online library available.

**Student life. Freshman orientation:** Mandatory. Preregistration for classes offered. One week of activities prior to first day of classes; planned and organized by returning students. **Policies:** No alcohol allowed on campus.

Full-time students required to live on campus until age 22 or special consideration given. **Housing:** Coed dorms, single-sex dorms, apartments, wellness housing available. $100 deposit, deadline 8/1. **Activities:** Bands, campus ministries, choral groups, dance, drama, international student organizations, music ensembles, musical theater, student government, student newspaper, symphony orchestra, SOAR, Blue Key, Gold Key, Alpha Omega, Bethany youth ministry program, Bread for the World, departmental organizations, honorary societies, Green Team.

**Athletics.** NAIA. **Intercollegiate:** Baseball M, basketball, cross-country, football (tackle) M, golf M, soccer, softball W, tennis, track and field, volleyball W. **Intramural:** Basketball, football (non-tackle), racquetball, soccer, softball, table tennis, volleyball, weight lifting. **Team name:** Swedes.

**Student services.** Alcohol/substance abuse counseling, chaplain/spiritual director, career counseling, student employment services, financial aid counseling, health services, minority student services, personal counseling, placement for graduates, veterans' counselor.

**Contact.** E-mail: admissions@bethanylb.edu
Phone: (785) 227-3380 ext. 8113 Toll-free number: (800) 826-2281
Fax: (785) 227-8993
Tricia Hawk, Dean of Admissions and Financial Aid, Bethany College, 335 East Swensson, Lindsborg, KS 67456-1897

## Bethel College
**North Newton, Kansas**
**www.bethelks.edu**                    CB code: 6037

- Private 4-year liberal arts college affiliated with Mennonite Church
- Residential campus in large town
- 437 degree-seeking undergraduates: 5% part-time, 49% women, 5% African American, 2% Asian American, 7% Hispanic American, 1% Native American, 3% international
- 75% of applicants admitted
- SAT or ACT (ACT writing optional) required
- 69% graduate within 6 years

**General.** Founded in 1887. Regionally accredited. **Degrees:** 119 bachelor's awarded. **Location:** 25 miles from Wichita. **Calendar:** 4-1-4, limited summer session. **Full-time faculty:** 40 total; 62% have terminal degrees, 5% minority, 42% women. **Part-time faculty:** 20 total; 25% have terminal degrees, 10% minority, 70% women. **Class size:** 75% < 20, 23% 20-39, less than 1% 40-49, less than 1% 50-99, less than 1% >100. **Special facilities:** Natural history museum, 80-acre natural history field laboratory, institute for peace and conflict resolution, Mennonite library and archives, observatory, conservatory.

**Freshman class profile.** 386 applied, 288 admitted, 92 enrolled.

| Mid 50% test scores | | | |
|---|---|---|---|
| SAT critical reading: | 420-700 | GPA 2.0-2.99: | 11% |
| SAT math: | 460-730 | Rank in top quarter: | 58% |
| SAT writing: | 430-690 | Rank in top tenth: | 36% |
| ACT composite: | 21-29 | End year in good standing: | 85% |
| GPA 3.75 or higher: | 51% | Return as sophomores: | 76% |
| GPA 3.50-3.74: | 18% | Out-of-state: | 31% |
| GPA 3.0-3.49: | 20% | Live on campus: | 97% |
| | | International: | 1% |

**Basis for selection.** Automatic admission generally given to students with high school GPA of 2.5 and ACT score of at least 19 or SAT of at least 890 (exclusive of Writing). Essay recommended for academically weak applicants. Audition recommended for drama and music majors. Portfolio recommended for art majors. **Homeschooled:** Evaluative transcript or GED score. ACT or SAT score is also required.

**High school preparation.** College-preparatory program recommended. 18 units recommended. Recommended units include English 4, mathematics 4, social studies 3, history 1, science 3, foreign language 2 and computer science 1.

**2009-2010 Annual costs.** Tuition/fees: $19,990. Room/board: $6,770. Books/supplies: $800. Personal expenses: $2,200.

**2008-2009 Financial aid. Need-based:** 108 full-time freshmen applied for aid; 95 were judged to have need; 95 of these received aid. Average need met was 96%. Average scholarship/grant was $4,793; average loan $5,079. 35% of total undergraduate aid awarded as scholarships/grants, 65% as loans/jobs. **Non-need-based:** Awarded to 632 full-time undergraduates, including 179 freshmen. Scholarships awarded for academics, alumni affiliation, art, athletics, minority status, music/drama, religious affiliation, state residency.

**Application procedures. Admission:** No deadline. $20 fee, may be waived for applicants with need. Admission notification on a rolling basis beginning on or about 9/1. **Financial aid:** Priority date 4/1; no closing date. FAFSA required. Applicants notified on a rolling basis starting 2/1; must reply within 2 week(s) of notification.

**Academics.** Curriculum founded on general education program in liberal arts and sciences. Distinctive elements include peace, justice and conflict studies, convocation, and cross-cultural learning requirements and senior capstone course focusing on basic issues of faith and life. **Special study options:** Cross-registration, double major, dual enrollment of high school students, independent study, internships, liberal arts/career combination, study abroad, teacher certification program, urban semester, Washington semester. **Credit/placement by examination:** AP, CLEP, IB, SAT, ACT, institutional tests. **Support services:** Learning center, study skills assistance, tutoring.

**Majors. Biology:** General. **Business:** General. **Communications:** Media studies. **Education:** Elementary. **Health:** Athletic training, nursing (RN). **History:** General. **Interdisciplinary:** Natural sciences. **Math:** General. **Parks/recreation:** Health/fitness. **Philosophy/religion:** Religion. **Physical sciences:** Chemistry. **Psychology:** General. **Public administration:** Social work. **Visual/performing arts:** Studio arts.

**Most popular majors.** Biology 7%, business/marketing 12%, health sciences 40%, public administration/social services 7%.

**Computing on campus.** 56 workstations in library, computer center. Dormitories wired for high-speed internet access and linked to campus network. Commuter students can connect to campus network. Helpline, repair service, student web hosting, wireless network available.

**Student life. Freshman orientation:** Mandatory. Preregistration for classes offered. Held the Wednesday through Monday before classes begin. **Policies:** Chapel services voluntary. 2 weekly convocations required and credited as part of general education. **Housing:** Guaranteed on-campus for all undergraduates. Coed dorms, special housing for disabled, apartments, wellness housing available. **Activities:** Bands, campus ministries, choral groups, dance, drama, international student organizations, literary magazine, music ensembles, musical theater, opera, radio station, student government, student newspaper, symphony orchestra, TV station, Student Community Action Network for voluntary services, peace club, Bethel Christian Fellowship, service corps-disaster response, Fellowship of Christian Athletes, environmental action club, Catholic student organization.

**Athletics.** NAIA. **Intercollegiate:** Basketball, cross-country, football (tackle) M, golf, soccer, tennis, track and field, volleyball W. **Intramural:** Badminton, basketball, football (non-tackle), golf, racquetball, softball, table tennis, tennis, volleyball. **Team name:** Threshers.

**Student services.** Alcohol/substance abuse counseling, chaplain/spiritual director, career counseling, student employment services, financial aid counseling, health services, minority student services, personal counseling. **Physically disabled:** Services for visually, hearing impaired.

**Contact.** E-mail: admissions@bethelks.edu
Phone: (316) 284-5230 Toll-free number: (800) 522-1887 ext. 230
Fax: (316) 284-5870
Todd Moore, Vice President for Admissions, Bethel College, 300 E 27th Street, North Newton, KS 67117-8061

---

## Central Christian College of Kansas
**McPherson, Kansas**
**www.centralchristian.edu**                     **CB code: 6088**

- Private 4-year liberal arts college affiliated with Free Methodist Church of North America
- Residential campus in large town
- 334 degree-seeking undergraduates: 2% part-time, 45% women, 15% African American, 1% Asian American, 4% Hispanic American, 2% Native American, 1% international
- 57% of applicants admitted
- 33% graduate within 6 years; 20% enter graduate study

**General.** Founded in 1884. Regionally accredited. **Degrees:** 46 bachelor's, 22 associate awarded. **Location:** 55 miles from Wichita. **Calendar:** 4-1-4, limited summer session. **Full-time faculty:** 18 total; 22% have terminal degrees, 33% women. **Part-time faculty:** 30 total; 47% women. **Class size:** 76% < 20, 19% 20-39, 2% 40-49, 3% 50-99, less than 1% >100.

**Freshman class profile.** 695 applied, 397 admitted, 110 enrolled.

| Mid 50% test scores | | | |
|---|---|---|---|
| SAT critical reading: | 370-540 | GPA 2.0-2.99: | 30% |
| SAT math: | 390-570 | Rank in top quarter: | 30% |
| SAT writing: | 390-510 | Rank in top tenth: | 8% |
| ACT composite: | 18-24 | End year in good standing: | 88% |
| GPA 3.75 or higher: | 22% | Return as sophomores: | 74% |
| GPA 3.50-3.74: | 13% | Out-of-state: | 66% |
| GPA 3.0-3.49: | 35% | Live on campus: | 99% |
| | | International: | 2% |

**Basis for selection.** Secondary school record, recommendations very important; test scores important. SAT or ACT recommended. Interview and essay recommended. **Homeschooled:** Transcript of courses and grades, letter of recommendation (nonparent) required. **Learning Disabled:** Provide Individualized Education Program (IEP).

**High school preparation.** College-preparatory program recommended. 22 units required. Required units include English 4, mathematics 2, social studies 2, history 1, science 2 (laboratory 1). One computer technology course recommended.

**2010-2011 Annual costs.** Tuition/fees (projected): $18,200. Room/board: $5,900. Books/supplies: $1,000. Personal expenses: $1,000.

**2008-2009 Financial aid. Non-need-based:** Scholarships awarded for academics, alumni affiliation, athletics, leadership, music/drama, religious affiliation.

**Application procedures. Admission:** Closing date 7/1 (receipt date). $20 fee, may be waived for applicants with need, free for online applicants. Admission notification on a rolling basis. **Financial aid:** Priority date 3/1; no closing date. FAFSA required. Applicants notified on a rolling basis starting 3/1; must reply within 4 week(s) of notification.

**Academics. Special study options:** Accelerated study, cooperative education, cross-registration, double major, dual enrollment of high school students, independent study, internships, liberal arts/career combination, student-designed major, teacher certification program, urban semester, Washington semester. **Credit/placement by examination:** AP, CLEP, IB, SAT, ACT. 30 credit hours maximum toward associate degree, 30 toward bachelor's. **Support services:** Learning center, reduced course load, remedial instruction, study skills assistance, tutoring.

**Majors. Biology:** General, exercise physiology. **Business:** General, accounting, accounting/business management, business admin, managerial economics, office management, small business admin. **Communications:** General, media studies. **Education:** Elementary, history, middle, physical, secondary. **Health:** Health services, preveterinary. **History:** General. **Interdisciplinary:** Accounting/computer science, natural sciences. **Legal studies:** Prelaw. **Liberal arts:** Arts/sciences. **Math:** General. **Parks/recreation:** Exercise sciences, facilities management, sports admin. **Philosophy/religion:** Religion. **Physical sciences:** Chemistry. **Protective services:** Law enforcement admin, police science, security management. **Psychology:** General. **Social sciences:** General. **Theology:** Bible, missionary, pastoral counseling, sacred music, theology, youth ministry. **Visual/performing arts:** General, dramatic, music performance, music theory/composition, piano/organ.

**Most popular majors.** Business/marketing 25%, English 6%, liberal arts 14%, natural resources/environmental science 10%, psychology 7%, theological studies 17%.

**Computing on campus.** 30 workstations in library, computer center, student center. Dormitories wired for high-speed internet access. Commuter students can connect to campus network. Online course registration, online library, helpline, repair service, wireless network available.

**Student life. Freshman orientation:** Mandatory. Preregistration for classes offered. Fall semester first seven weeks. Interterm and spring 1-2 days. **Policies:** Students must sign a life-style covenant. Alcohol, smoking, drugs not allowed on campus. **Housing:** Guaranteed on-campus for all undergraduates. Coed dorms, single-sex dorms, apartments, wellness housing available. $200 fully refundable deposit, deadline 8/1. Students 23 years of age or older can live off campus. **Activities:** Bands, campus ministries, choral groups, drama, literary magazine, music ensembles, musical theater, radio station, student government, student newspaper, symphony orchestra, Christian service organization, Flying Tigers, prison ministries, performing arts club, Share teams, C.O.L.O.R.S., PBL, student activities council.

**Athletics.** NAIA, NCCAA. **Intercollegiate:** Baseball M, basketball, cheerleading, cross-country, golf, soccer, softball W, tennis, volleyball W. **Intramural:** Badminton, basketball, bowling, football (non-tackle) M, golf, soccer, softball, table tennis, tennis, volleyball. **Team name:** Tigers.

**Student services.** Adult student services, chaplain/spiritual director, career counseling, student employment services, financial aid counseling, health services, personal counseling, placement for graduates. **Physically disabled:** Services for visually, speech impaired.

**Contact.** E-mail: admissions@centralchristian.edu
Phone: (620) 241-0723 ext. 337 Toll-free number: (800) 835-0078 ext. 337
Fax: (620) 241-6032
Rick Wyatt, Director of Admissions, Central Christian College of Kansas,
1200 South Main, McPherson, KS 67460-5740

---

## Emporia State University
Emporia, Kansas
www.emporia.edu                                      CB code: 6335

- Public 4-year university
- Commuter campus in large town
- 4,063 degree-seeking undergraduates: 10% part-time, 60% women, 6% African American, 1% Asian American, 5% Hispanic American, 1% Native American, 7% international
- 1,819 degree-seeking graduate students
- 88% of applicants admitted
- SAT or ACT (ACT writing optional) required
- 41% graduate within 6 years

**General.** Founded in 1863. Regionally accredited. **Degrees:** 830 bachelor's awarded; master's, doctoral offered. **Location:** 50 miles from Topeka, 77 miles from Wichita. **Calendar:** Semester, extensive summer session. **Full-time faculty:** 253 total; 81% have terminal degrees, 10% minority, 45% women. **Part-time faculty:** 25 total; 12% have terminal degrees, 76% women. **Class size:** 38% < 20, 44% 20-39, 12% 40-49, 5% 50-99, less than 1% >100. **Special facilities:** Planetarium, natural history reserve, natural history museum, National Teachers Hall of Fame, Great Plains study center.

**Freshman class profile.** 1,420 applied, 1,249 admitted, 677 enrolled.

| Mid 50% test scores | | End year in good standing: | 68% |
|---|---|---|---|
| ACT composite: | 19-25 | Return as sophomores: | 69% |
| GPA 3.75 or higher: | 21% | Out-of-state: | 9% |
| GPA 3.50-3.74: | 18% | Live on campus: | 72% |
| GPA 3.0-3.49: | 31% | International: | 3% |
| GPA 2.0-2.99: | 29% | Fraternities: | 6% |
| Rank in top quarter: | 33% | Sororities: | 6% |
| Rank in top tenth: | 14% | | |

**Basis for selection.** Applicants must have one of following: minimum ACT score of 21, rank in top third of high school class, minimum 2.0 GPA in Kansas Core Curriculum for in-state students, or 2.5 GPA for out-of-state students. Limited number of students who do not meet qualifications may be admitted through 10% exceptions window. ACT scores must be received by end of first semester of study. **Homeschooled:** State high school equivalency certificate required. GED must be submitted.

**High school preparation.** College-preparatory program recommended. Required units include English 4, mathematics 3, social studies 3, science 3 and academic electives 1. 1 computer technology recommended. These units required for students who do not have minimum ACT score of 21, or in top 1/3 of high school class.

**2009-2010 Annual costs.** Tuition/fees: $4,374; $13,578 out-of-state. Room/board: $6,146. Books/supplies: $900. Personal expenses: $2,896.

**2008-2009 Financial aid. Need-based:** 642 full-time freshmen applied for aid; 406 were judged to have need; 401 of these received aid. Average need met was 49%. Average scholarship/grant was $4,367; average loan $3,314. 41% of total undergraduate aid awarded as scholarships/grants, 59% as loans/jobs. **Non-need-based:** Awarded to 1,651 full-time undergraduates, including 375 freshmen. Scholarships awarded for academics, alumni affiliation, art, athletics, job skills, leadership, minority status, music/drama, religious affiliation, state residency. **Additional information:** Institution's own payment plan is available.

**Application procedures. Admission:** No deadline. $30 fee, may be waived for applicants with need. Admission notification on a rolling basis. Must reply by May 1 or within 2 week(s) if notified thereafter. **Financial aid:** Priority date 3/15; no closing date. FAFSA required. Applicants notified on a rolling basis starting 2/2; must reply within 2 week(s) of notification.

**Academics. Special study options:** Distance learning, double major, dual enrollment of high school students, ESL, honors, independent study, internships, student-designed major, study abroad, teacher certification program. Career development center and programs, continuing education courses, evening program, interdisciplinary or interdepartmental courses of study, learning

assistance programs, pass-fail grading option, service members' opportunity college, summer sessions, tutorial program, trio programs. **Credit/placement by examination:** AP, CLEP, IB, ACT, institutional tests. 30 credit hours maximum toward bachelor's degree. **Support services:** Remedial instruction, writing center.

**Majors. Biology:** General, Biochemistry/biophysics and molecular biology. **Business:** Accounting, business admin, human resources, marketing. **Communications:** General. **Computer sciences:** General, information systems, security. **Education:** Elementary, music, secondary. **Foreign languages:** General. **Health:** Athletic training, nursing (RN), public health ed, vocational rehab counseling. **History:** General. **Liberal arts:** Arts/sciences. **Math:** General. **Parks/recreation:** General. **Physical sciences:** General, chemistry, geology, physics. **Psychology:** General. **Social sciences:** General, economics, political science, sociology. **Visual/performing arts:** Art, dramatic. **Other:** Crime and delinquencies studies, Information resources studies.

**Most popular majors.** Business/marketing 18%, education 26%, health sciences 8%, social sciences 10%, visual/performing arts 6%.

**Computing on campus.** 410 workstations in dormitories, library, computer center, student center. Dormitories wired for high-speed internet access and linked to campus network. Commuter students can connect to campus network. Online course registration, online library, helpline, student web hosting, wireless network available.

**Student life. Freshman orientation:** Available, $35 fee. Preregistration for classes offered. One-day program for students and parents; held during summer and prior to start of classes. **Housing:** Guaranteed on-campus for freshmen. Coed dorms, single-sex dorms, special housing for disabled, apartments, cooperative housing, fraternity/sorority housing, wellness housing available. $145 partly refundable deposit, deadline 7/1. **Activities:** Bands, campus ministries, choral groups, dance, drama, film society, international student organizations, literary magazine, music ensembles, musical theater, opera, student government, student newspaper, symphony orchestra, Black Student Union, Hispanic American leadership organization, Catholic Campus Community, Christian student center, Black women's network, Muslim student association, Fellowship of Christian Athletes, Arabic language club, East Asian club, Campus Crusade for Christ.

**Athletics.** NCAA. **Intercollegiate:** Baseball M, basketball, cheerleading, cross-country, football (tackle) M, soccer W, softball W, tennis, track and field, volleyball W. **Intramural:** Badminton, basketball, football (non-tackle), soccer, softball, table tennis, volleyball. **Team name:** Hornets.

**Student services.** Adult student services, alcohol/substance abuse counseling, career counseling, services for economically disadvantaged, student employment services, financial aid counseling, health services, legal services, minority student services, on-campus daycare, personal counseling, placement for graduates, veterans' counselor, women's services. **Physically disabled:** Services for visually, speech, hearing impaired.

**Contact.** E-mail: go2esu@emporia.edu
Phone: (620) 341-5465 Toll-free number: (877) 468-6378
Fax: (620) 341-5599
Laura Eddy, Director of Admissions, Emporia State University, 1200 Commercial, Campus Box 4034, Emporia, KS 66801-5087

---

## Fort Hays State University
Hays, Kansas                                          CB member
www.fhsu.edu                                          CB code: 6218

- Public 4-year university
- Commuter campus in large town
- 8,455 degree-seeking undergraduates
- SAT or ACT with writing required

**General.** Founded in 1902. Regionally accredited. **Degrees:** 1,646 bachelor's, 59 associate awarded; master's offered. **Location:** 170 miles from Wichita, 270 miles from Kansas City. **Calendar:** Semester, extensive summer session. **Full-time faculty:** 268 total; 67% have terminal degrees, 6% minority, 40% women. **Part-time faculty:** 135 total; 22% have terminal degrees, 2% minority, 57% women. **Class size:** 50% < 20, 41% 20-39, 5% 40-49, 3% 50-99, less than 1% >100. **Special facilities:** Observatory, paleontology, natural history, archeology, history, geology, botanical-zoological museums.

**Contact.** E-mail: learn@friends.edu
Phone: (316) 295-5100 Toll-free number: (800) 577-2233
Fax: (316) 295-5101
Erin Haneberg, Director of Undergraduate Admissions, Friends University, 2100 University, Wichita, KS 67213

## Haskell Indian Nations University
### Lawrence, Kansas
www.haskell.edu                                    CB code: 0919

- Public 4-year university
- Residential campus in small city

**General.** Founded in 1884. Regionally accredited. **Location:** 38 miles from Kansas City, Missouri. **Calendar:** Semester.

**Annual costs/financial aid.** Haskell does not charge tuition. On-campus students pay $440 (includes room/board and required fees) for academic year; off-campus students pay $248 (required fees) for academic year. Books/supplies: $220. Need-based financial aid available to full-time and part-time students.

**Contact.** Phone: (785) 749-8454
Director of Admissions and Records, 155 Indian Avenue #5031, Lawrence, KS 66046-4800

## Kansas State University
### Manhattan, Kansas                          CB member
www.k-state.edu                                    CB code: 6334

- Public 4-year university
- Commuter campus in large town
- 18,230 degree-seeking undergraduates: 10% part-time, 48% women, 4% African American, 1% Asian American, 4% Hispanic American, 1% Native American, 5% international
- 3,627 degree-seeking graduate students
- 55% of applicants admitted
- 59% graduate within 6 years

**General.** Founded in 1863. Regionally accredited. Additional campus at Salina, Kansas. Off-campus site at Fort Riley army base. **Degrees:** 3,492 bachelor's, 63 associate awarded; master's, doctoral, professional offered. **ROTC:** Army, Air Force. **Location:** 120 miles from Kansas City, Missouri. **Calendar:** Semester, extensive summer session. **Full-time faculty:** 973 total; 81% have terminal degrees, 18% minority, 37% women. **Part-time faculty:** 138 total; 38% have terminal degrees, 6% minority, 51% women. **Class size:** 52% < 20, 31% 20-39, 7% 40-49, 6% 50-99, 4% >100. **Special facilities:** Prairie for biological research, laser laboratory, cancer research center, nuclear reactor, insect zoo.

**Freshman class profile.** 10,003 applied, 5,550 admitted, 4,016 enrolled.

| Mid 50% test scores | | | |
|---|---|---|---|
| ACT composite: | 21-27 | Rank in top tenth: | 22% |
| GPA 3.75 or higher: | 31% | Return as sophomores: | 79% |
| GPA 3.50-3.74: | 20% | Out-of-state: | 17% |
| GPA 3.0-3.49: | 30% | Live on campus: | 80% |
| GPA 2.0-2.99: | 18% | International: | 5% |
| Rank in top quarter: | 49% | Fraternities: | 21% |
| | | Sororities: | 26% |

**Basis for selection.** One of following required: minimum ACT score of 21, rank in top third of high school class, or minimum 2.0 GPA on Kansas pre-college curriculum (2.5 GPA for out-of-state students). SAT or ACT recommended. Audition recommended for music and theater majors. Portfolio recommended for art and architecture majors.

**High school preparation.** College-preparatory program recommended. 14 units recommended. Recommended units include English 4, mathematics 3, social studies 2, history 1.5 and science 3. One unit of technology recommended.

**2009-2010 Annual costs.** Tuition/fees: $6,870; $17,577 out-of-state. Room/board: $6,752. Books/supplies: $1,100. Personal expenses: $3,400.

**2008-2009 Financial aid. Need-based:** 2,563 full-time freshmen applied for aid; 1,706 were judged to have need; 1,663 of these received aid. Average need met was 82%. Average scholarship/grant was $3,822; average loan $3,309. 44% of total undergraduate aid awarded as scholarships/grants, 56% as loans/jobs. **Non-need-based:** Awarded to 3,575 full-time undergraduates, including 1,701 freshmen. Scholarships awarded for academics, alumni affiliation, art, athletics, leadership, music/drama, ROTC, state residency.

**Application procedures. Admission:** No deadline. $30 fee, may be waived for applicants with need. Admission notification on a rolling basis. **Financial aid:** Priority date 3/1; no closing date. FAFSA required. Applicants notified by 4/1; Applicants notified on a rolling basis starting 4/1; must reply within 2 week(s) of notification.

**Academics. Special study options:** Accelerated study, combined bachelor's/graduate degree, cooperative education, distance learning, double major, ESL, exchange student, honors, independent study, internships, study abroad, teacher certification program. **Credit/placement by examination:** AP, CLEP, IB, SAT, ACT. 10 credit hours maximum toward associate degree, 20 toward bachelor's. PEP, DANTES exams accepted for credit. **Support services:** Learning center, pre-admission summer program, reduced course load, remedial instruction, study skills assistance, tutoring, writing center.

**Majors. Agriculture:** Agronomy, animal sciences, business, communications, economics, food science, horticultural science, mechanization. **Area/ethnic studies:** Women's. **Biology:** General, biochemistry, microbiology, wildlife. **Business:** General, accounting, business admin, finance. **Communications:** General, journalism, media studies. **Computer sciences:** General, information systems, networking. **Education:** Agricultural, art, elementary, family/consumer sciences, music, secondary. **Engineering:** Agricultural, architectural, chemical, civil, computer, electrical, industrial, mechanical. **Engineering technology:** General, construction, electrical, industrial management. **Family/consumer sciences:** General, child development, clothing/textiles, family studies, human nutrition. **Foreign languages:** General. **Health:** Athletic training, communication disorders, dietetics, preveterinary. **History:** General. **Liberal arts:** Humanities. **Math:** General, statistics. **Mechanic/repair:** Aircraft. **Parks/recreation:** Exercise science, facilities management. **Philosophy/religion:** Philosophy. **Physical sciences:** General, chemistry, geology, physics. **Psychology:** General. **Public administration:** Social work. **Social sciences:** General, anthropology, economics, geography, political science, sociology. **Transportation:** Airline/commercial pilot. **Visual/performing arts:** Dramatic, interior design, music performance, studio arts. **Other:** Management of Animal health related organizations.

**Most popular majors.** Agriculture 11%, business/marketing 17%, education 10%, engineering/engineering technologies 13%, family/consumer sciences 6%, social sciences 12%.

**Computing on campus.** 547 workstations in dormitories, library, computer center, student center. Dormitories wired for high-speed internet access and linked to campus network. Commuter students can connect to campus network. Online course registration, online library, helpline, repair service, wireless network available.

**Student life. Freshman orientation:** Available, $25 fee. **Housing:** Coed dorms, single-sex dorms, apartments, cooperative housing, fraternity/sorority housing available. $25 deposit. **Activities:** Bands, campus ministries, choral groups, dance, drama, international student organizations, music ensembles, musical theater, radio station, student government, student newspaper, symphony orchestra, TV station, 340 religious, political, ethnic, and social service clubs and organizations available.

**Athletics.** NCAA. **Intercollegiate:** Baseball M, basketball, cross-country, equestrian W, football (tackle) M, golf, rowing (crew) W, tennis W, track and field, volleyball W. **Intramural:** Badminton, basketball, bowling, cross-country, golf, handball, soccer, softball, squash, swimming, table tennis, tennis, track and field, volleyball, water polo, wrestling M. **Team name:** Wildcats.

**Student services.** Adult student services, alcohol/substance abuse counseling, career counseling, student employment services, financial aid counseling, health services, legal services, minority student services, on-campus daycare, personal counseling, placement for graduates, veterans' counselor, women's services. **Physically disabled:** Services for visually, speech, hearing impaired.

**Contact.** E-mail: k-state@k-state.edu
Phone: (785) 532-6250 Toll-free number: (800) 432-8270
Fax: (785) 532-6393
Larry Moeder, Assistant Vice President for Student Financial Assistance and Admissions, Kansas State University, 119 Anderson Hall, Manhattan, KS 66506

## Kansas Wesleyan University
### Salina, Kansas
www.kwu.edu                                        CB code: 6337

- Private 4-year liberal arts college affiliated with United Methodist Church
- Residential campus in large town
- 783 degree-seeking undergraduates
- 47 graduate students

♦  55% of applicants admitted
♦  SAT or ACT (ACT writing optional) required

**General.** Founded in 1886. Regionally accredited. **Degrees:** 186 bachelor's awarded; master's offered. **Location:** 90 miles from Wichita, 180 miles from Kansas City. **Calendar:** Semester, limited summer session. **Full-time faculty:** 43 total. **Part-time faculty:** 25 total. **Class size:** 66% < 20, 26% 20-39, 6% 40-49, 1% 50-99, less than 1% >100. **Special facilities:** Observatory with 16-inch Cassegrain telescope.

**Freshman class profile.** 574 applied, 316 admitted, 139 enrolled.

| Mid 50% test scores | | | |
|---|---|---|---|
| | | ACT composite: | 19-25 |
| SAT critical reading: | 450-520 | Out-of-state: | 32% |
| SAT math: | 460-590 | Live on campus: | 67% |

**Basis for selection.** Applicant must have ACT composite score of 18 or SAT combined score of 850 (exclusive of Writing) and high school GPA of 2.5 or rank in top half of class. Interview recommended for academically weak applicants. Audition recommended for music majors. Portfolio recommended for art majors.

**2009-2010 Annual costs.** Tuition/fees: $19,200. $200 per-credit-hour charge for 1-5 credit hours; $1,800 per semester for 6-8 credit hours; $3,600 per semester for 9-11 credit hours. Room/board: $6,600. Books/supplies: $800. Personal expenses: $500.

**2009-2010 Financial aid. Non-need-based:** Scholarships awarded for academics, alumni affiliation, art, athletics, music/drama, state residency. **Additional information:** Awards available for residence hall students: minimum $7,000 for 3.0 GPA plus ACT score of 22 or SAT of 950 (exclusive of Writing); minimum $8,000 for 3.5 GPA plus ACT score of 22 or SAT score of 1030 (exclusive of Writing); minimum $9,000 for 3.75 GPA plus ACT score of 25 or SAT score of 1140 (exclusive of Writing). Application deadline March 15.

**Application procedures. Admission:** No deadline. $20 fee. Admission notification on a rolling basis. **Financial aid:** Closing date 3/15. FAFSA required. Applicants notified on a rolling basis starting 1/1; must reply by 8/1 or within 3 week(s) of notification.

**Academics. Special study options:** Accelerated study, cross-registration, double major, ESL, independent study, internships, liberal arts/career combination, student-designed major, teacher certification program. **Credit/placement by examination:** AP, CLEP, institutional tests. 30 credit hours maximum toward bachelor's degree. **Support services:** Learning center, reduced course load, remedial instruction, tutoring, writing center.

**Majors. Biology:** General. **Business:** General, accounting. **Communications:** General, public relations. **Computer sciences:** General, computer science. **Education:** Art, elementary, English, secondary. **Foreign languages:** General, German, Spanish. **Health:** Preop/surgical nursing. **History:** General. **Math:** General. **Parks/recreation:** Health/fitness. **Philosophy/religion:** Religion. **Physical sciences:** Chemistry, physics. **Protective services:** Criminal justice. **Psychology:** General. **Social sciences:** Sociology. **Theology:** Religious ed. **Visual/performing arts:** Arts management, dramatic, music performance, studio arts.

**Most popular majors.** Business/marketing 32%, education 9%, health sciences 9%, parks/recreation 7%, physical sciences 7%, social sciences 7%.

**Computing on campus.** 50 workstations in library, computer center. Dormitories wired for high-speed internet access and linked to campus network. Online library available.

**Student life. Freshman orientation:** Available. Preregistration for classes offered. **Housing:** Guaranteed on-campus for freshmen. Single-sex dorms, apartments available. $100 deposit. **Activities:** Jazz band, choral groups, dance, drama, literary magazine, music ensembles, musical theater, radio station, student government, student newspaper, Fellowship of Christian Athletes, Religious Life Committee.

**Athletics.** NAIA. **Intercollegiate:** Baseball M, basketball, cross-country, football (tackle) M, golf, soccer, softball W, tennis, track and field, volleyball W. **Intramural:** Basketball, softball, volleyball, weight lifting. **Team name:** Coyotes.

**Student services.** Adult student services, career counseling, student employment services, financial aid counseling, personal counseling, placement for graduates, veterans' counselor. **Physically disabled:** Services for visually impaired.

**Contact.**  E-mail: admissions@kwu.edu
Phone: (785) 827-5541 ext. 1285 Toll-free number: (800) 874-1154
Fax: (785) 827-0927
Jim Allen, Director of Admissions, Kansas Wesleyan University, 100 East Claflin Avenue, Salina, KS 67401-6196

---

## Manhattan Christian College
**Manhattan, Kansas**
www.mccks.edu                    CB code: 6392

♦  Private 4-year Bible college affiliated with Christian Church
♦  Residential campus in large town

**General.** Founded in 1927. Regionally accredited. **Location:** 130 miles west from Kansas City. **Calendar:** Semester.

**Annual costs/financial aid.** Tuition/fees (2009-2010): $11,478. Additional $6 required fee per-credit-hour, up to $72; $188 per-credit-hour charge for part-time, non-degree-seeking students. Part time non-degree and/or audit at $188 per-credit-hour. Room/board: $7,056. Books/supplies: $1,150. Personal expenses: $1,067. Need-based financial aid available to full-time and part-time students.

**Contact.**  Phone: (785) 539-3571
Director of Admissions, 1415 Anderson Avenue, Manhattan, KS 66502

---

## McPherson College
**McPherson, Kansas**
www.mcpherson.edu                    CB code: 6404

♦  Private 4-year liberal arts college affiliated with Church of the Brethren
♦  Residential campus in large town
♦  573 degree-seeking undergraduates: 5% part-time, 43% women
♦  87% of applicants admitted
♦  SAT or ACT (ACT writing optional) required

**General.** Founded in 1887. Regionally accredited. **Degrees:** 135 bachelor's awarded. **Location:** 60 miles from Wichita. **Calendar:** 4-1-4, limited summer session. **Full-time faculty:** 34 total; 82% have terminal degrees, 12% minority, 32% women. **Part-time faculty:** 20 total; 30% have terminal degrees, 10% minority, 45% women. **Class size:** 70% < 20, 29% 20-39, less than 1% 40-49.

**Freshman class profile.** 474 applied, 411 admitted, 137 enrolled.

| Mid 50% test scores | | | |
|---|---|---|---|
| | | GPA 3.0-3.49: | 30% |
| SAT critical reading: | 450-570 | GPA 2.0-2.99: | 25% |
| SAT math: | 420-560 | Rank in top quarter: | 38% |
| ACT composite: | 19-24 | Rank in top tenth: | 14% |
| GPA 3.75 or higher: | 21% | Out-of-state: | 10% |
| GPA 3.50-3.74: | 23% | | |

**Basis for selection.** Satisfactory high school performance or completion of GED, corresponding standardized test scores, and appropriate personal qualities. Portfolio required for auto restoration program.

**2009-2010 Annual costs.** Tuition/fees: $18,400. Room/board: $6,910. Books/supplies: $1,170. Personal expenses: $2,560.

**2009-2010 Financial aid. Need-based:** 52% of total undergraduate aid awarded as scholarships/grants, 48% as loans/jobs. **Non-need-based:** Scholarships awarded for academics, alumni affiliation, art, athletics, music/drama, religious affiliation, state residency.

**Application procedures. Admission:** Priority date 3/1; no deadline. $25 fee, may be waived for applicants with need. Admission notification on a rolling basis. Must reply by May 1 or within 4 week(s) if notified thereafter. **Financial aid:** Priority date 3/1; no closing date. FAFSA required. Applicants notified on a rolling basis starting 3/1; must reply within 3 week(s) of notification.

**Academics. Special study options:** Combined bachelor's/graduate degree, cross-registration, double major, dual enrollment of high school students, ESL, independent study, internships, liberal arts/career combination, student-designed major, study abroad, teacher certification program, urban semester. Only accreditied four year degree program in antique auto restoration in United States. **Credit/placement by examination:** AP, CLEP, IB, institutional tests. **Support services:** Learning center, reduced course load, remedial instruction, study skills assistance, tutoring, writing center.

**Majors. Biology:** General. **Business:** Accounting, business admin, finance, international. **Communications:** General. **Education:** General, art, biology, business, chemistry, computer, early childhood, elementary, English, foreign languages, history, mathematics, middle, music, physical, science, social studies, Spanish, special, speech, technology/industrial arts. **Foreign languages:** General, Spanish. **Health:** Predental, premedicine, prepharmacy, preveterinary. **History:** General. **Legal studies:** Prelaw. **Liberal arts:** Arts/sciences. **Math:** General. **Mechanic/repair:** Automotive. **Parks/**

**recreation:** Health/fitness. **Physical sciences:** Chemistry. **Psychology:** General. **Social sciences:** Sociology. **Visual/performing arts:** Art, dramatic, music performance.

**Most popular majors.** Biology 7%, business/marketing 27%, engineering/engineering technologies 21%, parks/recreation 8%, visual/performing arts 9%.

**Computing on campus.** 72 workstations in dormitories, library, computer center, student center. Dormitories wired for high-speed internet access and linked to campus network. Commuter students can connect to campus network. Online library, helpline, wireless network available.

**Student life. Freshman orientation:** Mandatory. Preregistration for classes offered. **Policies:** No alcohol permitted on campus. Unmarried students under 23 years old are required to live in residence halls. **Housing:** Guaranteed on-campus for all undergraduates. Coed dorms, single-sex dorms, special housing for disabled available. $150 nonrefundable deposit, deadline 5/1. **Activities:** Bands, choral groups, dance, drama, music ensembles, musical theater, student government, student newspaper, 28 clubs and organizations available.

**Athletics.** NAIA. **Intercollegiate:** Basketball, cheerleading, cross-country, football (tackle) M, softball W, track and field, volleyball W. **Intramural:** Badminton, basketball, football (non-tackle), football (tackle) M, handball, racquetball, soccer, softball, table tennis, volleyball. **Team name:** Bulldogs.

**Student services.** Adult student services, chaplain/spiritual director, career counseling, student employment services, financial aid counseling, health services, personal counseling, placement for graduates. **Physically disabled:** Services for hearing impaired.

**Contact.** E-mail: admiss@mcpherson.edu
Phone: (620) 241-0731 Toll-free number: (800) 695-7402
Fax: (620) 241-8443
David Barrett, Director of Admission, McPherson College, 1600 East Euclid Street, McPherson, KS 67460-1402

## MidAmerica Nazarene University
Olathe, Kansas
www.mnu.edu                                        CB code: 6437

▶ Private 4-year university and liberal arts college affiliated with Church of the Nazarene
▶ Residential campus in small city
▶ 1,335 degree-seeking undergraduates: 22% part-time, 58% women, 11% African American, 1% Asian American, 4% Hispanic American
▶ 363 degree-seeking graduate students
▶ 74% of applicants admitted
▶ SAT or ACT (ACT writing optional) required
▶ 60% graduate within 6 years

**General.** Founded in 1966. Regionally accredited. **Degrees:** 374 bachelor's, 12 associate awarded; master's offered. **ROTC:** Army, Air Force. **Location:** 19 miles from Kansas City. **Calendar:** Semester, limited summer session. **Full-time faculty:** 75 total; 45% have terminal degrees, 3% minority, 43% women. **Part-time faculty:** 123 total; 21% have terminal degrees, 48% women. **Class size:** 68% < 20, 24% 20-39, 4% 40-49, 4% 50-99.

**Freshman class profile.** 476 applied, 354 admitted, 196 enrolled.

| Mid 50% test scores | | | |
|---|---|---|---|
| SAT critical reading: | 440-590 | GPA 2.0-2.99: | 21% |
| SAT math: | 470-580 | Rank in top quarter: | 41% |
| ACT composite: | 20-25 | Rank in top tenth: | 23% |
| GPA 3.75 or higher: | 30% | Return as sophomores: | 76% |
| GPA 3.50-3.74: | 17% | Out-of-state: | 57% |
| GPA 3.0-3.49: | 31% | Live on campus: | 85% |

**Basis for selection.** Secondary school record, class rank, test scores, and moral principles important. Nursing, elementary education, and secondary education programs have higher standards for admission. Interview recommended for music, nursing, elementary and secondary education programs. Audition recommended for music majors. **Homeschooled:** Transcript of courses and grades, letter of recommendation (nonparent) required.

**High school preparation.** 15 units recommended. Recommended units include English 4, mathematics 3, social studies 3, science 3 and foreign language 1.

**2010-2011 Annual costs.** Tuition/fees (projected): $20,250. Room/board: $6,750. Books/supplies: $1,180. Personal expenses: $1,176.

**2009-2010 Financial aid. Need-based:** 182 full-time freshmen applied for aid; 156 were judged to have need; 156 of these received aid. Average need met was 75%. Average scholarship/grant was $12,739; average loan $3,587. 64% of total undergraduate aid awarded as scholarships/grants, 36% as loans/jobs. **Non-need-based:** Awarded to 524 full-time undergraduates, including 117 freshmen. Scholarships awarded for academics, athletics, leadership, music/drama, religious affiliation, ROTC.

**Application procedures. Admission:** Priority date 3/1; deadline 8/1 (postmark date). $25 fee. Admission notification on a rolling basis. **Financial aid:** Priority date 3/1; no closing date. FAFSA required. Applicants notified on a rolling basis starting 1/30; must reply within 2 week(s) of notification.

**Academics.** Adults 25 and older may earn bachelor's degree through evening division. **Special study options:** Accelerated study, cooperative education, cross-registration, distance learning, double major, dual enrollment of high school students, independent study, internships, student-designed major, study abroad, teacher certification program, Washington semester. Dual degree program in vocational agriculture with Kansas State University. **Credit/placement by examination:** AP, CLEP, IB, SAT, ACT, institutional tests. 34 credit hours maximum toward associate degree, 34 toward bachelor's. **Support services:** Learning center, reduced course load, remedial instruction, study skills assistance, tutoring.

**Majors. Biology:** General. **Business:** General, accounting, business admin, communications, human resources. **Communications:** General, media studies, public relations. **Computer sciences:** General, computer science, information systems. **Education:** Biology, business, elementary, English, foreign languages, health, mathematics, middle, music, physical, secondary, social studies, Spanish. **Foreign languages:** Spanish. **Health:** Athletic training, nursing (RN). **History:** General. **Math:** General. **Parks/recreation:** Exercise sciences, sports admin. **Philosophy/religion:** Religion. **Physical sciences:** Chemistry, physics. **Protective services:** Law enforcement admin. **Psychology:** General. **Social sciences:** General, sociology, urban studies. **Theology:** Missionary, religious ed, sacred music, youth ministry. **Visual/performing arts:** General, music performance, voice/opera.

**Most popular majors.** Business/marketing 53%, education 8%, health sciences 17%.

**Computing on campus.** 90 workstations in dormitories, library, computer center. Dormitories wired for high-speed internet access and linked to campus network. Commuter students can connect to campus network. Online course registration, online library, helpline, student web hosting, wireless network available.

**Student life. Freshman orientation:** Available, $44 fee. Preregistration for classes offered. Program concentrates on essential study skills, time management, value of liberal arts learning, career development aids, proficiency assessment. **Policies:** Religious observance required. **Housing:** Guaranteed on-campus for freshmen. Single-sex dorms, special housing for disabled, apartments, wellness housing available. $100 deposit, deadline 8/21. **Activities:** Bands, campus ministries, choral groups, drama, international student organizations, literary magazine, music ensembles, musical theater, radio station, student government, student newspaper, TV station, Circle K, College Republicans, gospel station, Fellowship of Christian Athletes, multicultural student asociation, BYTE, Psych Incorporated, medical careers club, covenant groups.

**Athletics.** NAIA. **Intercollegiate:** Baseball M, basketball, cheerleading, cross-country, football (tackle) M, soccer, softball W, track and field, volleyball W. **Intramural:** Basketball, bowling, football (non-tackle), football (tackle), golf, soccer, softball, table tennis, tennis, track and field, volleyball. **Team name:** Pioneers.

**Student services.** Adult student services, alcohol/substance abuse counseling, chaplain/spiritual director, career counseling, student employment services, financial aid counseling, health services, minority student services, personal counseling, placement for graduates, veterans' counselor. **Physically disabled:** Services for visually, speech, hearing impaired.

**Contact.** E-mail: admissions@mnu.edu
Phone: (913) 971-3380 Toll-free number: (800) 800-8887
Fax: (913) 971-3481
Brigit Mattox, Director of Admissions, MidAmerica Nazarene University, 2030 East College Way, Olathe, KS 66062-1899

## Newman University
Wichita, Kansas
www.newmanu.edu                                    CB code: 6615

▶ Private 4-year university and liberal arts college affiliated with Roman Catholic Church
▶ Commuter campus in large city

- 1,133 degree-seeking undergraduates: 14% part-time, 68% women, 6% African American, 4% Asian American, 11% Hispanic American, 2% Native American, 5% international
- 689 degree-seeking graduate students
- 42% of applicants admitted
- SAT and SAT Subject Tests or ACT (ACT writing optional) required
- 48% graduate within 6 years; 18% enter graduate study

**General.** Founded in 1933. Regionally accredited. The university is a sponsored ministry of the Adorers of the Blood of Christ. **Degrees:** 198 bachelor's, 59 associate awarded; master's offered. **Location:** 160 miles from Oklahoma City, 180 miles from Kansas City. **Calendar:** Semester, limited summer session. **Full-time faculty:** 77 total; 51% have terminal degrees, 3% minority, 53% women. **Part-time faculty:** 106 total; 8% minority, 71% women. **Class size:** 65% < 20, 30% 20-39, 4% 40-49, 1% 50-99. **Special facilities:** Photography laboratory, cadaver laboratory.

**Freshman class profile.** 2,193 applied, 913 admitted, 176 enrolled.

| Mid 50% test scores | | | |
|---|---|---|---|
| SAT critical reading: | 430-530 | GPA 2.0-2.99: | 19% |
| SAT math: | 420-570 | Rank in top quarter: | 52% |
| SAT writing: | 430-530 | Rank in top tenth: | 27% |
| ACT composite: | 19-27 | End year in good standing: | 82% |
| GPA 3.75 or higher: | 35% | Return as sophomores: | 72.2% |
| GPA 3.50-3.74: | 18% | Out-of-state: | 27% |
| GPA 3.0-3.49: | 28% | Live on campus: | 55% |
| | | International: | 6% |

**Basis for selection.** Minimum GPA 2.0, minimum ACT composite score of 18, or SAT score of 1290 (including Writing). Caliber of high school curriculum important. Portfolio recommended for art majors. **Learning Disabled:** Applicants should submit medical evaluation and recommendation.

**High school preparation.** College-preparatory program recommended. Recommended units include English 4, mathematics 3, social studies 3 and science 3.

**2009-2010 Annual costs.** Tuition/fees: $19,650. Room/board: $6,500. Books/supplies: $988.

**2009-2010 Financial aid. Need-based:** Average need met was 73%. Average scholarship/grant was $5,819; average loan $2,948. 32% of total undergraduate aid awarded as scholarships/grants, 68% as loans/jobs. **Non-need-based:** Scholarships awarded for academics, alumni affiliation, art, athletics, leadership, music/drama.

**Application procedures. Admission:** No deadline. $20 fee, may be waived for applicants with need, free for online applicants. Admission notification on a rolling basis. **Financial aid:** Priority date 3/1; no closing date. FAFSA required. Applicants notified on a rolling basis starting 2/1.

**Academics. Special study options:** Accelerated study, cooperative education, cross-registration, distance learning, double major, dual enrollment of high school students, honors, independent study, internships, liberal arts/career combination, student-designed major, study abroad, teacher certification program. **Credit/placement by examination:** AP, CLEP, IB, institutional tests. 30 credit hours maximum toward bachelor's degree. **Support services:** Learning center, remedial instruction, study skills assistance, tutoring, writing center.

**Majors. Biology:** General. **Business:** Accounting, business admin, management information systems. **Communications:** Media studies. **Computer sciences:** Information systems. **Education:** General, elementary, middle, secondary. **Health:** Nursing (RN), sonography. **History:** General. **Liberal arts:** Arts/sciences. **Math:** General. **Philosophy/religion:** Philosophy. **Physical sciences:** Chemistry. **Protective services:** Forensics, law enforcement admin. **Psychology:** General, counseling. **Social sciences:** Sociology. **Theology:** Pastoral counseling, theology. **Visual/performing arts:** Art. **Other:** Healthcare Science.

**Most popular majors.** Biology 11%, business/marketing 14%, education 24%, health sciences 29%, psychology 6%.

**Computing on campus.** 90 workstations in dormitories, library, computer center, student center. Dormitories wired for high-speed internet access and linked to campus network. Commuter students can connect to campus network. Online library, helpline, repair service, wireless network available.

**Student life. Freshman orientation:** Mandatory, $150 fee. Preregistration for classes offered. 4 days prior to first day of class. **Policies:** Freshmen required to live in college housing for first 2 years if not living with parents. **Housing:** Guaranteed on-campus for freshmen. Coed dorms, apartments, wellness housing available. $100 fully refundable deposit. **Activities:** Campus ministries, choral groups, international student organizations, literary

magazine, student government, student newspaper, Koinonia, Service Scholars, Newman Club, Peer Educators, Kansas Catholic College Student Convention, Peer Ministers.

**Athletics.** NCAA. **Intercollegiate:** Baseball M, basketball, cross-country, golf, soccer, softball W, tennis, volleyball W, wrestling M. **Intramural:** Baseball M, basketball, bowling, football (tackle), golf, soccer, softball W, table tennis, volleyball, weight lifting. **Team name:** Jets.

**Student services.** Adult student services, chaplain/spiritual director, career counseling, student employment services, financial aid counseling, personal counseling, placement for graduates. **Physically disabled:** Services for visually, speech, hearing impaired.

**Contact.** E-mail: admissions@newmanu.edu
Phone: (316) 942-4291 ext. 2144 Toll-free number: (877) 639-6268
Fax: (316) 942-4483
John Clayton, Dean of Admissions, Newman University, 3100 McCormick, Wichita, KS 67213-2097

## Ottawa University
**Ottawa, Kansas**
www.ottawa.edu

CB member
CB code: 6547

- Private 4-year university and liberal arts college affiliated with American Baptist Churches in the USA
- Residential campus in large town
- 526 degree-seeking undergraduates: 3% part-time, 48% women
- 70% of applicants admitted
- Application essay required
- 36% graduate within 6 years

**General.** Founded in 1865. Regionally accredited. Degree programs offered at additional campuses in Overland Park, KS; Phoenix, AZ; Milwaukee, WI; Jeffersonville, IN, and through Ottawa Online. **Degrees:** 78 bachelor's awarded. **Location:** 45 miles from Kansas City. **Calendar:** Semester, limited summer session. **Full-time faculty:** 25 total; 52% have terminal degrees, 16% minority, 48% women. **Part-time faculty:** 11 total; 46% have terminal degrees, 9% minority, 64% women. **Class size:** 76% < 20, 24% 20-39, less than 1% 40-49.

**Freshman class profile.** 1,421 applied, 993 admitted, 150 enrolled.

| Mid 50% test scores | | | |
|---|---|---|---|
| SAT critical reading: | 420-540 | GPA 2.0-2.99: | 25% |
| SAT math: | 440-510 | Rank in top quarter: | 36% |
| SAT writing: | 370-500 | Rank in top tenth: | 12% |
| ACT composite: | 19-23 | End year in good standing: | 40% |
| GPA 3.75 or higher: | 19% | Return as sophomores: | 50% |
| GPA 3.50-3.74: | 17% | Out-of-state: | 42% |
| GPA 3.0-3.49: | 37% | Live on campus: | 99% |

**Basis for selection.** Class ranking, cumulative GPA, standardized test scores, and personal essay are considered in the admissions decision. SAT or ACT recommended. Auditions recommended for music and drama majors. Portfolio recommended for art majors. **Homeschooled:** Transcript of courses and grades required. Must take ACT or SAT. Require a sample of most recent written work/portfolio.

**High school preparation.** College-preparatory program recommended. Recommended units include English 4, mathematics 3, social studies 1, history 2, science 3 (laboratory 2) and foreign language 1.

**2009-2010 Annual costs.** Tuition/fees: $19,360. Room/board: $6,084. Books/supplies: $1,100. Personal expenses: $1,800.

**2008-2009 Financial aid. Non-need-based:** Scholarships awarded for academics, alumni affiliation, athletics, music/drama, religious affiliation.

**Application procedures. Admission:** Priority date 6/1; no deadline. $25 fee, may be waived for applicants with need. Admission notification on a rolling basis. **Financial aid:** Priority date 3/15; no closing date. FAFSA required. Applicants notified on a rolling basis starting 2/1; must reply within 4 week(s) of notification.

**Academics. Special study options:** Distance learning, double major, dual enrollment of high school students, independent study, internships, liberal arts/career combination, student-designed major, study abroad, teacher certification program. **Credit/placement by examination:** CLEP, IB. **Support services:** Learning center, reduced course load, study skills assistance, tutoring.

**Majors. Biology:** General. **Business:** Accounting/business management, business admin. **Communications:** General. **Computer sciences:** Information technology. **Education:** Elementary. **History:** General. **Math:** General. **Parks/recreation:** Health/fitness. **Philosophy/religion:** Religion. **Psychology:** General. **Public administration:** Human services. **Social sciences:** Sociology. **Visual/performing arts:** Art, dramatic.

**Most popular majors.** Biology 6%, business/marketing 27%, communications/journalism 10%, education 11%, parks/recreation 22%.

**Computing on campus.** 59 workstations in library, computer center. Dormitories wired for high-speed internet access and linked to campus network. Commuter students can connect to campus network. Online course registration, online library, helpline, wireless network available.

**Student life. Freshman orientation:** Mandatory. Preregistration for classes offered. **Housing:** Guaranteed on-campus for freshmen. Coed dorms, single-sex dorms available. $150 fully refundable deposit. Pets allowed in dorm rooms. **Activities:** Jazz band, campus ministries, choral groups, dance, drama, music ensembles, radio station, student government, student newspaper, symphony orchestra, Christian Faith in Action, voluntary service organization, Whole Earth club, Fellowship of Christian Athletes, student activities force, Cognoscenti (literary group), Amnesty International.

**Athletics.** NAIA. **Intercollegiate:** Baseball M, basketball, cross-country, football (tackle) M, golf M, soccer, softball W, track and field, volleyball W. **Intramural:** Basketball, handball, racquetball, soccer, softball, track and field, volleyball. **Team name:** Braves.

**Student services.** Alcohol/substance abuse counseling, chaplain/spiritual director, career counseling, student employment services, financial aid counseling, health services, personal counseling, placement for graduates.

**Contact.** E-mail: admiss@ottawa.edu
Phone: (785) 242-5200 ext. 5421 Toll-free
number: (800) 755-5200 ext. 5421 Fax: (785) 229-1008
June Unrein, Dean of Enrollment Management, Ottawa University, 1001 South Cedar Street, #17, Ottawa, KS 66067-3399

## Pittsburg State University
**Pittsburg, Kansas**
www.pittstate.edu                    CB code: 6336

- Public 4-year university
- Residential campus in large town
- 5,462 degree-seeking undergraduates: 5% part-time, 46% women, 3% African American, 1% Asian American, 3% Hispanic American, 2% Native American, 4% international
- 1,268 degree-seeking graduate students
- 86% of applicants admitted
- ACT (writing optional) required
- 50% graduate within 6 years

**General.** Founded in 1903. Regionally accredited. Centers in Kansas City and Wichita. **Degrees:** 1,139 bachelor's, 17 associate awarded; master's offered. **ROTC:** Army. **Location:** 120 miles from Kansas City. **Calendar:** Semester, limited summer session. **Full-time faculty:** 308 total; 72% have terminal degrees, 10% minority, 39% women. **Part-time faculty:** 96 total; 15% have terminal degrees, 4% minority, 48% women. **Class size:** 46% < 20, 40% 20-39, 7% 40-49, 7% 50-99, less than 1% >100. **Special facilities:** Planetarium, observatory, field biology reserve, nature reach, herbarium, technology center, gorilla village, mammal collection, greenhouse, polymer research lab, broadcasting lab, cadaver lab.

**Freshman class profile.** 1,816 applied, 1,567 admitted, 864 enrolled.

| Mid 50% test scores | | | |
|---|---|---|---|
| ACT composite: | 19-24 | Rank in top tenth: | 18% |
| GPA 3.75 or higher: | 26% | Return as sophomores: | 75% |
| GPA 3.50-3.74: | 22% | Out-of-state: | 29% |
| GPA 3.0-3.49: | 28% | Live on campus: | 67% |
| GPA 2.0-2.99: | 23% | International: | 2% |
| Rank in top quarter: | 43% | Fraternities: | 7% |
| | | Sororities: | 8% |

**Basis for selection.** Academics, school record, class rank and test scores most important. **Homeschooled:** GED, record of course content and completion required.

**High school preparation.** College-preparatory program recommended. 13 units recommended. Recommended units include English 4, mathematics 3, social studies 3 and science 3.

**2009-2010 Annual costs.** Tuition/fees: $4,592; $13,116 out-of-state. Room/board: $5,744. Books/supplies: $1,000. Personal expenses: $2,150.

**2009-2010 Financial aid. Need-based:** Average need met was 94%. Average scholarship/grant was $5,375; average loan $3,314. 53% of total undergraduate aid awarded as scholarships/grants, 47% as loans/jobs. **Non-need-based:** Scholarships awarded for academics, alumni affiliation, art, athletics, leadership, music/drama, ROTC.

**Application procedures. Admission:** No deadline. $30 fee. Admission notification on a rolling basis. **Financial aid:** Priority date 3/1; no closing date. FAFSA, institutional form required. Applicants notified on a rolling basis; must reply within 2 week(s) of notification.

**Academics. Special study options:** Accelerated study, combined bachelor's/graduate degree, cooperative education, distance learning, double major, dual enrollment of high school students, ESL, exchange student, external degree, honors, independent study, internships, liberal arts/career combination, student-designed major, study abroad, teacher certification program. **Credit/placement by examination:** AP, CLEP, IB, ACT, institutional tests. 24 credit hours maximum toward bachelor's degree. **Support services:** Learning center, tutoring, writing center.

**Honors college/program.** Separate application required. Criteria for selection include minimum 28 ACT score, minimum 3.5 GPA, recommendations, record of participation in academic and other extracurricular activities. 36 incoming freshmen are accepted each year.

**Majors. Biology:** General, biochemistry, cellular/molecular, plant molecular, plant pathology, plant physiology. **Business:** Accounting, actuarial science, business admin, construction management, fashion, finance, human resources, international, managerial economics, marketing. **Communications:** General, advertising, journalism, photojournalism, public relations, radio/tv. **Computer sciences:** Information systems. **Education:** Art, biology, chemistry, early childhood, elementary, English, family/consumer sciences, French, mathematics, music, physical, physics, psychology, social studies, Spanish, technology/industrial arts, voc/tech. **Engineering technology:** Construction, electrical, manufacturing, mechanical, plastics. **Family/consumer sciences:** General, child development, family resources. **Foreign languages:** French, Spanish. **Health:** Clinical lab science, nursing (RN), predental, premedicine, prepharmacy, preveterinary, recreational therapy, substance abuse counseling. **History:** General. **Legal studies:** Prelaw. **Math:** General. **Mechanic/repair:** Auto body, automotive, diesel, motorcycle. **Parks/recreation:** General, facilities management. **Physical sciences:** Chemistry, physics, polymer chemistry. **Production:** Woodworking. **Psychology:** General, developmental. **Public administration:** Social work. **Social sciences:** Geography, international relations, political science, sociology. **Visual/performing arts:** Art, ceramics, commercial/advertising art, interior design, metal/jewelry, music performance, painting, theater arts management. **Other:** Communication education, Justice studies, Plant taxonomy, Pre-engineering (civil & mining), Pre-optometry.

**Most popular majors.** Business/marketing 14%, education 18%, health sciences 8%, trade and industry 10%.

**Computing on campus.** 425 workstations in library, computer center, student center. Dormitories wired for high-speed internet access and linked to campus network. Commuter students can connect to campus network. Online course registration, online library, repair service, student web hosting, wireless network available.

**Student life. Freshman orientation:** Mandatory, $20 fee. Eight individual sessions are offered and last approximately eight hours each. **Housing:** Guaranteed on-campus for freshmen. Coed dorms, special housing for disabled, apartments, wellness housing available. $145 partly refundable deposit. **Activities:** Bands, campus ministries, choral groups, dance, drama, film society, international student organizations, literary magazine, music ensembles, musical theater, opera, radio station, student government, student newspaper, symphony orchestra, TV station, Over 150 clubs and organizations available.

**Athletics.** NCAA. **Intercollegiate:** Baseball M, basketball, cheerleading, cross-country, football (tackle) M, golf M, softball W, track and field, volleyball W. **Intramural:** Badminton, basketball, football (non-tackle), racquetball, soccer, softball, table tennis, tennis, volleyball. **Team name:** Gorillas.

**Student services.** Alcohol/substance abuse counseling, chaplain/spiritual director, career counseling, student employment services, financial aid counseling, health services, legal services, minority student services, personal counseling, placement for graduates, veterans' counselor. **Physically disabled:** Services for visually, speech, hearing impaired.

**Contact.** E-mail: psuadmit@pittstate.edu
Phone: (620) 235-4251 Toll-free number: (800) 854-7488
Fax: (620) 235-6003
Melinda Roelfs, Director of Admission, Pittsburg State University, 1701 South Broadway, Pittsburg, KS 66762

## Southwestern College
### Winfield, Kansas
### www.sckans.edu
**CB code: 6670**

- Private 4-year liberal arts college affiliated with United Methodist Church
- Residential campus in large town
- 1,471 degree-seeking undergraduates: 61% part-time, 48% women, 8% African American, 2% Asian American, 6% Hispanic American, 2% Native American, 1% international
- 281 degree-seeking graduate students
- 90% of applicants admitted
- SAT or ACT (ACT writing optional), application essay required
- 45% graduate within 6 years

**General.** Founded in 1885. Regionally accredited. Laptop computers issued to all full-time students enrolled at main campus. **Degrees:** 520 bachelor's awarded; master's offered. **Location:** 40 miles from Wichita. **Calendar:** Semester, limited summer session. **Full-time faculty:** 47 total; 60% have terminal degrees, 6% minority, 38% women. **Part-time faculty:** 55 total; 7% have terminal degrees, 7% minority, 49% women. **Class size:** 83% < 20, 15% 20-39, less than 1% 40-49, 1% 50-99. **Special facilities:** Biological field station.

**Freshman class profile.** 293 applied, 264 admitted, 119 enrolled.

| Mid 50% test scores | | | |
|---|---|---|---|
| SAT critical reading: | 380-540 | Rank in top quarter: | 44% |
| SAT math: | 430-550 | Rank in top tenth: | 16% |
| SAT writing: | 390-560 | Return as sophomores: | 70% |
| ACT composite: | 19-24 | Out-of-state: | 50% |
| GPA 3.75 or higher: | 27% | Live on campus: | 98% |
| GPA 3.50-3.74: | 13% | International: | 3% |
| GPA 3.0-3.49: | 38% | | |
| GPA 2.0-2.99: | 22% | | |

**Basis for selection.** School achievement record, test scores and personal essay statement most important. Portfolio required. Interview recommended for nursing majors. Audition required for music and drama majors.

**High school preparation.** College-preparatory program recommended. 13.5 units required. Required units include English 4, mathematics 3, social studies 2.5, history 1, science 2 (laboratory 1). Computer or communication unit may be substituted for foreign language.

**2009-2010 Annual costs.** Tuition/fees: $19,680. Room/board: $5,750. Books/supplies: $600. Personal expenses: $3,748.

**2009-2010 Financial aid. Need-based:** 108 full-time freshmen applied for aid; 99 were judged to have need; 99 of these received aid. Average need met was 90%. Average scholarship/grant was $13,182; average loan $4,788. 47% of total undergraduate aid awarded as scholarships/grants, 53% as loans/jobs. **Non-need-based:** Awarded to 274 full-time undergraduates, including 57 freshmen. Scholarships awarded for academics, athletics, leadership, minority status, music/drama, religious affiliation.

**Application procedures. Admission:** Closing date 8/25 (receipt date). $25 fee, may be waived for applicants with need. Admission notification on a rolling basis beginning on or about 9/15. Must reply by May 1 or within 3 week(s) if notified thereafter. **Financial aid:** Priority date 4/1, closing date 8/15. FAFSA, institutional form required. Applicants notified on a rolling basis starting 2/1; must reply within 2 week(s) of notification.

**Academics. Special study options:** Accelerated study, distance learning, double major, honors, independent study, internships, student-designed major, teacher certification program, urban semester, Washington semester. **Credit/placement by examination:** AP, CLEP, ACT. 30 credit hours maximum toward bachelor's degree. **Support services:** Learning center, reduced course load, remedial instruction, study skills assistance, tutoring, writing center.

**Majors. Biology:** General, biochemistry, marine. **Business:** Accounting, business admin, communications, entrepreneurial studies, finance, management information systems, management science, marketing, nonprofit/public, operations, training/development. **Communications:** General, digital media, radio/tv. **Computer sciences:** General, computer science, programming, web page design. **Education:** General, business, drama/dance, early childhood, elementary, English, mathematics, music, physical, science, secondary, speech. **Engineering:** Physics. **Engineering technology:** Computer systems, manufacturing. **Health:** Athletic training, nursing (RN). **History:** General. **Liberal arts:** Arts/sciences. **Math:** General. **Parks/recreation:** Health/fitness, sports admin. **Philosophy/religion:** Philosophy, religion. **Physical sciences:** Chemistry, physics. **Protective services:** Criminal justice, security services. **Psychology:** General. **Theology:** Pastoral counseling. **Visual/performing arts:** Dramatic, film/cinema.

**Most popular majors.** Business/marketing 45%, computer/information sciences 13%, education 8%, security/protective services 12%.

**Computing on campus.** PC or laptop required. 10 workstations in dormitories, library, student center. Dormitories wired for high-speed internet access and linked to campus network. Commuter students can connect to campus network. Online library, helpline, repair service, student web hosting, wireless network available.

**Student life. Freshman orientation:** Mandatory. Preregistration for classes offered. 3-day orientation held before upperclassmen arrive on campus. **Policies:** Drug and alcohol-free campus. **Housing:** Guaranteed on-campus for freshmen. Coed dorms, single-sex dorms, apartments available. $150 deposit. **Activities:** Bands, campus ministries, choral groups, dance, drama, international student organizations, music ensembles, musical theater, radio station, student government, student newspaper, symphony orchestra, TV station, Black Student Union, Campus Council on Ministries, Sharp Ambassadors, Student Foundation, Business Students Association, Fellowship of Christian Athletes, Discipleship Southwestern, Leadership Southwestern, outreach teams, SC Association of Nursing Students.

**Athletics.** NAIA. **Intercollegiate:** Basketball, cheerleading, cross-country, football (tackle) M, golf, soccer, softball W, tennis, track and field, volleyball W. **Intramural:** Badminton, basketball, bowling, softball, swimming, tennis, volleyball. **Team name:** Moundbuilders.

**Student services.** Adult student services, alcohol/substance abuse counseling, chaplain/spiritual director, career counseling, student employment services, financial aid counseling, health services, minority student services, personal counseling, placement for graduates. **Physically disabled:** Services for visually, hearing impaired.

**Contact.** E-mail: scadmit@sckans.edu
Phone: (620) 229-6236 Toll-free number: (800) 846-1543 ext. 6236
Fax: (620) 229-6344
Marla Sexson, Director of Admission, Southwestern College, 100 College Street, Winfield, KS 67156

## Sterling College
### Sterling, Kansas
### www.sterling.edu
**CB code: 6684**

- Private 4-year liberal arts college affiliated with Presbyterian Church (USA)
- Residential campus in rural community
- 672 degree-seeking undergraduates: 11% part-time, 48% women, 7% African American, 1% Asian American, 7% Hispanic American, 2% Native American, 1% international
- 55% of applicants admitted
- SAT or ACT (ACT writing optional), application essay required
- 42% graduate within 6 years

**General.** Founded in 1887. Regionally accredited. **Degrees:** 96 bachelor's awarded. **Location:** 20 miles from Hutchinson, 70 miles from Wichita. **Calendar:** 4-1-4, limited summer session. **Full-time faculty:** 37 total; 49% have terminal degrees, 8% minority, 27% women. **Part-time faculty:** 20 total; 10% have terminal degrees, 5% minority, 35% women. **Class size:** 69% < 20, 25% 20-39, 2% 40-49, 4% 50-99.

**Freshman class profile.** 953 applied, 525 admitted, 187 enrolled.

| Mid 50% test scores | | | |
|---|---|---|---|
| SAT critical reading: | 410-530 | Rank in top quarter: | 25% |
| SAT math: | 450-540 | Rank in top tenth: | 8% |
| SAT writing: | 400-540 | End year in good standing: | 89% |
| ACT composite: | 19-24 | Return as sophomores: | 62% |
| GPA 3.75 or higher: | 14% | Out-of-state: | 53% |
| GPA 3.50-3.74: | 21% | Live on campus: | 95% |
| GPA 3.0-3.49: | 26% | International: | 1% |
| GPA 2.0-2.99: | 37% | | |

**Basis for selection.** High school record, test scores, recommendations from school counselor and pastor important; commitment to Christian values and service also important. Interview recommended. Audition required of performing arts majors. Portfolio recommended for art majors. **Homeschooled:** Transcript of courses and grades required. State certification strongly recommended for athletic eligibility. **Learning Disabled:** Must provide official documentation with recommended accommodations.

**High school preparation.** College-preparatory program recommended. 18 units recommended. Recommended units include English 4, mathematics 3, social studies 1, history 2, science 3 (laboratory 2), foreign language 2, computer science 1 and academic electives 1. Physical education recommended.

**2009-2010 Annual costs.** Tuition/fees: $18,100. Room/board: $6,430. Books/supplies: $600. Personal expenses: $700.

**2008-2009 Financial aid. Non-need-based:** Scholarships awarded for academics, athletics.

**Application procedures. Admission:** Priority date 3/1; no deadline. $25 fee, may be waived for applicants with need, free for online applicants. Admission notification on a rolling basis beginning on or about 9/15. **Financial aid:** Priority date 3/1; no closing date. FAFSA required. Applicants notified on a rolling basis starting 2/1; must reply within 3 week(s) of notification.

**Academics. Special study options:** Distance learning, double major, dual enrollment of high school students, honors, independent study, internships, liberal arts/career combination, student-designed major, study abroad, teacher certification program, urban semester, Washington semester. **Credit/placement by examination:** AP, CLEP, SAT, ACT, institutional tests. **Support services:** Learning center, reduced course load, remedial instruction, study skills assistance, tutoring, writing center.

**Majors. Biology:** General. **Business:** Business admin. **Communications:** General. **Education:** Elementary, mathematics, music. **Health:** Athletic training. **History:** General. **Math:** General. **Parks/recreation:** Health/fitness. **Physical sciences:** Chemistry. **Psychology:** General. **Theology:** Religious ed. **Visual/performing arts:** Art, dramatic.

**Most popular majors.** Biology 6%, business/marketing 27%, parks/recreation 20%, psychology 6%, theological studies 7%, visual/performing arts 6%.

**Computing on campus.** 120 workstations in dormitories, library, computer center, student center. Dormitories wired for high-speed internet access and linked to campus network. Commuter students can connect to campus network. Online course registration, online library, helpline, wireless network available.

**Student life. Freshman orientation:** Mandatory. Preregistration for classes offered. 3-day program prior to start of fall classes; includes service project. **Policies:** Prohibition of alcohol and tobacco products. All students under age 23 required to live in campus dormitories unless married or with dependents, living at home with parents, 5th-year senior, or by special circumstances. Religious observance required. **Housing:** Guaranteed on-campus for all undergraduates. Single-sex dorms, wellness housing available. $100 partly refundable deposit, deadline 8/1. **Activities:** Bands, campus ministries, choral groups, dance, drama, literary magazine, music ensembles, musical theater, radio station, student government, student newspaper, TV station, Future Science Professionals Association, Alpha Phi Omega, Fellowship of Christian Athletes, behavioral science club, Habitat for Humanity, Chi Beta Sigma, PEACE club, Pi Kappa Delta, Catholic student association.

**Athletics.** NAIA. **Intercollegiate:** Baseball M, basketball, cross-country, football (tackle) M, golf, soccer, softball W, tennis, track and field, volleyball W. **Intramural:** Basketball, bowling, football (non-tackle), softball, table tennis, volleyball. **Team name:** Warriors.

**Student services.** Chaplain/spiritual director, career counseling, student employment services, financial aid counseling, health services, personal counseling, veterans' counselor.

**Contact.** E-mail: admissions@sterling.edu
Phone: (620) 278-4275 Toll-free number: (800) 346-1017
Fax: (620) 278-4416
Dennis Dutton, Vice President for Enrollment Services, Sterling College, 125 West Cooper, Sterling, KS 67579

## Tabor College
### Hillsboro, Kansas
www.tabor.edu                                    CB code: 6815

- Private 4-year liberal arts college affiliated with Mennonite Brethren Church
- Residential campus in small town
- 617 degree-seeking undergraduates: 17% part-time, 49% women, 7% African American, 1% Asian American, 7% Hispanic American, 1% Native American, 1% international
- 22 degree-seeking graduate students
- 94% of applicants admitted
- SAT or ACT (ACT writing optional), application essay required
- 63% graduate within 6 years; 3% enter graduate study

**General.** Founded in 1908. Regionally accredited. Off-campus site in Wichita offers adult degree completion program and graduate studies. **Degrees:** 117

bachelor's, 1 associate awarded; master's offered. **Location:** 50 miles from Wichita. **Calendar:** 4-1-4, limited summer session. **Full-time faculty:** 30 total; 67% have terminal degrees, 3% minority, 40% women. **Part-time faculty:** 51 total; 14% have terminal degrees, 6% minority, 57% women. **Class size:** 63% < 20, 32% 20-39, 2% 40-49, 2% 50-99, less than 1% >100.

**Freshman class profile.** 343 applied, 321 admitted, 140 enrolled.

| Mid 50% test scores | | Rank in top tenth: | 14% |
|---|---|---|---|
| ACT composite: | 19-25 | End year in good standing: | 94.3% |
| GPA 3.75 or higher: | 24% | Return as sophomores: | 68% |
| GPA 3.50-3.74: | 15% | Out-of-state: | 46% |
| GPA 3.0-3.49: | 36% | Live on campus: | 99% |
| GPA 2.0-2.99: | 23% | International: | 1% |
| Rank in top quarter: | 19% | | |

**Basis for selection.** Life values and objectives, desire for Christian growth, and personal interviews important. Students must score a minimum of 18 on ACT and have ACT GPA (4.0 scale) product of 45 or above to be considered for admission. Audition recommended for music or drama. **Learning Disabled:** Must provide IEPs if special accommodations requested.

**High school preparation.** 17 units recommended. Recommended units include English 4, mathematics 3, social studies 2, history 2, science 3 and foreign language 1. 2 units of fine arts are also recommended.

**2010-2011 Annual costs.** Tuition/fees: $20,630. Room/board: $7,160. Books/supplies: $1,000. Personal expenses: $3,310.

**2009-2010 Financial aid. Need-based:** 140 full-time freshmen applied for aid; 124 were judged to have need; 124 of these received aid. Average need met was 85%. Average scholarship/grant was $5,330; average loan $6,810. 28% of total undergraduate aid awarded as scholarships/grants, 72% as loans/jobs. **Non-need-based:** Awarded to 779 full-time undergraduates, including 235 freshmen. Scholarships awarded for academics, alumni affiliation, athletics, music/drama, religious affiliation, state residency.

**Application procedures. Admission:** Priority date 4/1; no deadline. $30 fee, may be waived for applicants with need. Admission notification on a rolling basis beginning on or about 9/1. **Financial aid:** Priority date 3/1; no closing date. FAFSA required. Applicants notified by 3/15; Applicants notified on a rolling basis starting 3/1; must reply within 3 week(s) of notification.

**Academics. Special study options:** Accelerated study, combined bachelor's/graduate degree, cross registration, distance learning, double major, dual enrollment of high school students, exchange student, independent study, internships, liberal arts/career combination, student-designed major, study abroad, teacher certification program, Washington semester. **Credit/placement by examination:** AP, CLEP, IB, SAT, ACT. 30 credit hours maximum toward bachelor's degree. **Support services:** Learning center, reduced course load, remedial instruction, study skills assistance, tutoring, writing center.

**Majors. Biology:** General, biochemistry. **Business:** Accounting/business management, administrative services, business admin, marketing, office management. **Communications:** General, journalism, organizational, public relations. **Conservation:** Environmental studies. **Education:** General, biology, business, chemistry, developmentally delayed, elementary, emotionally handicapped, English, health, history, kindergarten/preschool, learning disabled, mathematics, mentally handicapped, middle, multi-level teacher, multiple handicapped, music, physical, science, secondary, social science, social studies, special. **Health:** Athletic training, clinical lab technology, predental, premedicine, preop/surgical nursing, prepharmacy, preveterinary. **History:** General. **Interdisciplinary:** Biological/physical sciences, math/computer science, natural sciences. **Legal studies:** Prelaw. **Liberal arts:** Humanities. **Math:** General. **Parks/recreation:** General, health/fitness, sports admin. **Philosophy/religion:** Philosophy, religion. **Physical sciences:** Chemistry. **Psychology:** General. **Social sciences:** General, sociology. **Theology:** Bible, theology, youth ministry. **Visual/performing arts:** Commercial/advertising art. **Other:** Social Welfare.

**Most popular majors.** Business/marketing 16%, education 12%, health sciences 17%, parks/recreation 6%, philosophy/religious studies 10%, visual/performing arts 8%.

**Computing on campus.** 58 workstations in library, computer center, student center. Dormitories wired for high-speed internet access and linked to campus network. Commuter students can connect to campus network. Online library, wireless network available.

**Student life. Freshman orientation:** Mandatory. Preregistration for classes offered. 3-day program prior to fall semester; includes service day. **Policies:** Students required to live on campus until age 23. Religious observance required. **Housing:** Guaranteed on-campus for freshmen. Single-sex dorms available. $175 fully refundable deposit, deadline 8/1. **Activities:** Bands, campus ministries, choral groups, drama, music ensembles, musical theater, student government, student newspaper, Science Club, Christian Ministries Council, Multicultural Student Union, Fellowship of Christian Athletes, CHUMS.

**Athletics.** NAIA. **Intercollegiate:** Baseball M, basketball, cheerleading, cross-country, football (tackle) M, soccer, softball W, tennis, track and field, volleyball W. **Intramural:** Basketball, football (non-tackle), racquetball, soccer, volleyball. **Team name:** Blue Jays.

**Student services.** Chaplain/spiritual director, career counseling, student employment services, financial aid counseling, minority student services, placement for graduates. **Physically disabled:** Services for visually, hearing impaired.

**Contact.** E-mail: admissions@tabor.edu
Phone: (620) 947-3121 ext. 1723 Toll-free number: (800) 822-6799
Fax: (620) 947-6276
Linda Cantwell, Vice President for Enrollment Management & Marketing, Tabor College, 400 South Jefferson, Hillsboro, KS 67063-1799

## University of Kansas

| Lawrence, Kansas | CB member |
|---|---|
| www.ku.edu | CB code: 6871 |

- Public 4-year university
- Commuter campus in small city
- 20,240 degree-seeking undergraduates: 9% part-time, 49% women, 4% African American, 4% Asian American, 4% Hispanic American, 1% Native American, 4% international
- 6,276 graduate students
- 91% of applicants admitted
- SAT or ACT (ACT writing optional) required
- 60% graduate within 6 years; 33% enter graduate study

**General.** Founded in 1866. Regionally accredited. **Degrees:** 3,867 bachelor's awarded; master's, doctoral, professional offered. **ROTC:** Army, Naval, Air Force. **Location:** 40 miles from Kansas City, 30 miles from Topeka. **Calendar:** Semester, extensive summer session. **Full-time faculty:** 1,021 total; 99% have terminal degrees, 18% minority, 32% women. **Part-time faculty:** 53 total; 94% have terminal degrees, 4% minority, 23% women. **Class size:** 39% < 20, 43% 20-39, 6% 40-49, 5% 50-99, 6% >100. **Special facilities:** 12 libraries including art and architecture, engineering, science, music, government documents and maps, rare books, manuscripts, and regional collections; art and natural history museums, space technology center, Institute for Life Span Studies, Performing Arts Center and Organ Recital Hall, Kansas Ecological Reserves, design lab, flight research lab, radar systems and remote sensing lab, film studio, Center for the Humanities, Multicultural Resource Center.

**Freshman class profile.** 10,653 applied, 9,740 admitted, 3,942 enrolled.

| Mid 50% test scores | | Rank in top quarter: | 57% |
|---|---|---|---|
| ACT composite: | 22-27 | Rank in top tenth: | 27% |
| GPA 3.75 or higher: | 29% | Return as sophomores: | 78% |
| GPA 3.50-3.74: | 19% | Out-of-state: | 27% |
| GPA 3.0-3.49: | 32% | Live on campus: | 57% |
| GPA 2.0-2.99: | 19% | International: | 5% |

**Basis for selection.** Admission to College of Liberal Arts and Sciences requires one of following for in-state students: minimum ACT score of 21 or SAT score of 980 (exclusive of Writing), rank in top third of high school class, or completion of required college preparatory curriculum with 2.0 GPA. For out-of-state students: minimum test scores are 24 on ACT or 1090 on SAT (exclusive of Writing); minimum GPA 2.5 on college preparatory curriculum; rank in top third of high school class. Admission policies for other colleges within university may vary. Audition required for music performance, music education, music therapy majors. **Homeschooled:** Admission based on test scores.

**High school preparation.** College-preparatory program required. 13 units required; 16 recommended. Required and recommended units include English 4, mathematics 3-4, social studies 3, science 3 and foreign language 2. 1 science unit must be chemistry or physics. 4 units mathematics recommended for mathematics, engineering and architecture majors. Social studies units include history.

**2009-2010 Annual costs.** Tuition/fees: $8,206; $20,174 out-of-state. Room/board: $6,802. Books/supplies: $800. Personal expenses: $2,324.

**2008-2009 Financial aid. Need-based:** 3,503 full-time freshmen applied for aid; 1,715 were judged to have need; 1,613 of these received aid. Average need met was 44%. Average scholarship/grant was $4,709; average

loan $2,873. 42% of total undergraduate aid awarded as scholarships/grants, 58% as loans/jobs. **Non-need-based:** Awarded to 4,844 full-time undergraduates, including 1,807 freshmen. Scholarships awarded for academics, alumni affiliation, art, athletics, leadership, minority status, music/drama, ROTC, state residency. **Additional information:** Students awarded federal work study are responsible for securing their own jobs on campus. There are positions on campus with a variety of schedules beyond 8-5.

**Application procedures. Admission:** Priority date 12/1; deadline 4/1 (receipt date). $30 fee. Admission notification on a rolling basis beginning on or about 9/1. Must reply by May 1 or within 2 week(s) if notified thereafter. **Financial aid:** Priority date 3/1; no closing date. FAFSA required. Applicants notified on a rolling basis starting 4/1; must reply within 2 week(s) of notification.

**Academics. Special study options:** Accelerated study, combined bachelor's/graduate degree, cooperative education, distance learning, double major, dual enrollment of high school students, ESL, honors, independent study, internships, liberal arts/career combination, study abroad, teacher certification program, Washington semester. **Credit/placement by examination:** AP, CLEP, IB, SAT, ACT, institutional tests. **Support services:** Learning center, remedial instruction, study skills assistance, tutoring, writing center.

**Honors college/program.** Students should have an ACT composite score of 30 or higher, a rigorous college preparatory curriculum, an un-weighted GPA of 3.75 or higher, participation in activities that supplement academic work and/or demonstrate community involvement and a sense of social responsibility, and an essay that reveals intellectual curiosity and academic rigor. Admission is competitive.

**Majors. Architecture:** History/criticism. **Area/ethnic studies:** African, American, European, Latin American, Russian/Slavic, women's. **Biology:** General, biochemistry, microbiology, molecular. **Business:** General, accounting, business admin, finance, logistics, management information systems, marketing. **Communications:** Journalism. **Computer sciences:** General. **Conservation:** Environmental studies. **Education:** Art, biology, chemistry, early childhood, elementary, English, foreign languages, history, mathematics, middle, music, physical, physics, science, secondary, social studies. **Engineering:** Aerospace, architectural, chemical, civil, computer, electrical, mechanical, petroleum, physics. **Foreign languages:** Classics, East Asian, French, Germanic, linguistics, Slavic, Spanish. **Health:** Athletic training, communication disorders, community health services, music therapy. **History:** General. **Interdisciplinary:** Ancient studies, behavioral sciences, global studies. **Liberal arts:** Arts/sciences, humanities. **Math:** General. **Parks/recreation:** Health/fitness. **Philosophy/religion:** Philosophy, religion. **Physical sciences:** Astronomy, atmospheric science, chemistry, geology, physics. **Psychology:** General, developmental. **Public administration:** General, social work. **Social sciences:** Anthropology, economics, geography, political science, sociology. **Visual/performing arts:** Art history/conservation, ceramics, commercial/advertising art, dance, design, dramatic, fiber arts, film/cinema, graphic design, illustration, industrial design, interior design, metal/jewelry, music performance, music theory/composition, musicology, painting, piano/organ, printmaking, sculpture, stringed instruments, studio arts, theater design, voice/opera.

**Most popular majors.** Biology 7%, business/marketing 14%, communications/journalism 7%, engineering/engineering technologies 6%, English 9%, psychology 7%, social sciences 12%, visual/performing arts 8%.

**Computing on campus.** 1,500 workstations in dormitories, library, computer center, student center. Dormitories wired for high-speed internet access and linked to campus network. Commuter students can connect to campus network. Online course registration, online library, helpline, student web hosting, wireless network available.

**Student life. Freshman orientation:** Available, $55 fee. Preregistration for classes offered. One-day program throughout summer; several 2 day programs available. Additional charges for parent participation and 2 day program. **Policies:** No alcohol permitted on campus, no smoking in any buildings. Parking by permit only. **Housing:** Coed dorms, single-sex dorms, apartments, cooperative housing, fraternity/sorority housing, wellness housing available. $335 partly refundable deposit. Scholarship halls available to students with high scholastic achievement and financial need. **Activities:** Bands, choral groups, dance, drama, international student organizations, literary magazine, music ensembles, musical theater, opera, radio station, student government, student newspaper, symphony orchestra, TV station, over 500 student organizations and activities.

**Athletics.** NCAA. **Intercollegiate:** Baseball M, basketball, cross-country, football (tackle) M, golf, rowing (crew) W, soccer W, softball W, swimming W, tennis W, track and field, volleyball W. **Intramural:** Basketball, bowling, football (non-tackle), golf, racquetball, soccer, softball, table tennis, tennis, volleyball. **Team name:** Jayhawks.

**Student services.** Adult student services, alcohol/substance abuse counseling, career counseling, services for economically disadvantaged, student employment services, financial aid counseling, health services, legal services, minority student services, on-campus daycare, personal counseling, placement for graduates, veterans' counselor, women's services. **Physically disabled:** Services for visually, speech, hearing impaired.

**Contact.** E-mail: adm@ku.edu
Phone: (785) 864-3911 Fax: (785) 864-5017
Lisa Pinamonti Kress, Director of Admissions and Scholarships, University of Kansas, 1502 Iowa Street, Lawrence, KS 66045-7576

## University of Kansas Medical Center
Kansas City, Kansas
www.kumc.edu                                    CB code: 0414

- Public two-year upper-division university and health science college
- Commuter campus in small city

**General.** Founded in 1905. Regionally accredited. **Degrees:** 230 bachelor's awarded; master's, doctoral, professional offered. **Location:** Downtown. **Calendar:** Semester, limited summer session. **Full-time faculty:** 267 total; 100% have terminal degrees, 21% minority, 55% women. **Part-time faculty:** 51 total; 100% have terminal degrees, 10% minority, 63% women. **Class size:** 83% < 20, 10% 20-39, 2% 50-99, 4% >100.

**Student profile.** 510 degree-seeking undergraduates, 2,505 degree-seeking graduate students. 135 applied as first time-transfer students.

| | | | |
|---|---|---|---|
| Women: | 84% | International: | 2% |
| African American: | 4% | Part-time: | 20% |
| Asian American: | 4% | Out-of-state: | 17% |
| Hispanic American: | 4% | 25 or older: | 40% |
| Native American: | 1% | | |

**Basis for selection.** College transcript required. Admissions regulations, policies and application closing dates vary by degree program. Transfer accepted as juniors, seniors.

**2009-2010 Annual costs.** Tuition/fees: $7,057; $17,740 out-of-state. Books/supplies: $1,440. Personal expenses: $3,790.

**Financial aid. Need-based:** 273 applied for aid; 245 were judged to have need; 245 of these received aid. Average need met was 62%. 32% of total undergraduate aid awarded as scholarships/grants, 68% as loans/jobs. **Non-need-based:** Awarded to 35 undergraduates. Scholarships awarded for academics, leadership, state residency.

**Application procedures. Admission:** $60 fee. Admissions deadlines vary by school and program. **Financial aid:** Priority date 2/14, no deadline. Applicants notified on a rolling basis starting 4/1.

**Academics.** Assessment and reading skills screened. Assistance offered in reviewing APA-style papers. **Special study options:** Combined bachelor's/graduate degree, distance learning, ESL, honors, independent study, internships, study abroad. **Credit/placement by examination:** CLEP.

**Majors. Health:** Clinical lab science, cytotechnology, medical records admin, nursing (RN), respiratory therapy technology. **Other:** Occupational therapy.

**Computing on campus.** 157 workstations in library, computer center, student center. Commuter students can connect to campus network. Online library, helpline, student web hosting, wireless network available.

**Student life. Activities:** International student organizations, literary magazine, student government, allied health student senate, graduate student council, medical student assembly, association of undergraduate nurses, Latino Midwest medical student association, American medical women's association, Students for Women's Wellness, Lifewatch Bible Study, Students Educating and Advocating for Diversity.

**Athletics. Intramural:** Basketball, racquetball, soccer, softball, swimming, volleyball.

**Student services.** Chaplain/spiritual director, career counseling, financial aid counseling, health services, legal services, personal counseling. **Physically disabled:** Services for visually, speech, hearing impaired.

**Contact.** E-mail: kumcregistrar@kumc.edu
Phone: (913) 588-7055 Fax: (913) 588-4697
University of Kansas Medical Center, 3901 Rainbow Boulevard, Kansas City, KS 66160-7116

## University of St. Mary
Leavenworth, Kansas
www.stmary.edu                                    CB code: 6630

- Private 4-year university affiliated with Roman Catholic Church
- Residential campus in large town
- 684 degree-seeking undergraduates: 25% part-time, 64% women, 12% African American, 1% Asian American, 8% Hispanic American, 1% Native American
- 286 degree-seeking graduate students
- 70% of applicants admitted
- SAT or ACT (ACT writing optional) required
- 37% graduate within 6 years

**General.** Founded in 1923. Regionally accredited. **Degrees:** 115 bachelor's awarded; master's offered. **ROTC:** Army, Air Force. **Location:** 26 miles from Kansas City. **Calendar:** Semester, limited summer session. **Full-time faculty:** 43 total; 60% have terminal degrees, 2% minority, 56% women. **Part-time faculty:** 67 total; 16% have terminal degrees, 55% women. **Class size:** 75% < 20, 24% 20-39, less than 1% 40-49, less than 1% 50-99, less than 1% >100. **Special facilities:** Sacred Scripture and History of the Catholic Church in Kansas collections in library.

**Freshman class profile.** 581 applied, 407 admitted, 129 enrolled.

| Mid 50% test scores | | GPA 2.0-2.99: | 35% |
|---|---|---|---|
| SAT critical reading: | 410-550 | Rank in top quarter: | 31% |
| SAT math: | 430-580 | Rank in top tenth: | 10% |
| ACT composite: | 18-24 | Return as sophomores: | 58% |
| GPA 3.75 or higher: | 15% | Out-of-state: | 34% |
| GPA 3.50-3.74: | 18% | Live on campus: | 81% |
| GPA 3.0-3.49: | 32% | | |

**Basis for selection.** 2.5 GPA, 18 ACT, 870 SAT (exclusive of Writing) required. Applicants below required GPA or ACT/SAT may be considered for admission. Portfolio recommended for fine and applied arts majors.

**High school preparation.** College-preparatory program recommended. 12 units required; 24 recommended. Required and recommended units include English 4, mathematics 2-4, social studies 2, history 2-4, science 2-4 (laboratory 2), foreign language 2 and academic electives 2. 1-2 computer programming recommended.

**2009-2010 Annual costs.** Tuition/fees: $18,950. Room/board: $5,900. Books/supplies: $1,200. Personal expenses: $1,910.

**2008-2009 Financial aid. Need-based:** 105 full-time freshmen applied for aid; 86 were judged to have need; 86 of these received aid. Average need met was 71%. Average scholarship/grant was $10,761; average loan $3,583. 53% of total undergraduate aid awarded as scholarships/grants, 47% as loans/jobs. **Non-need-based:** Awarded to 131 full-time undergraduates, including 44 freshmen. Scholarships awarded for academics, art, athletics, leadership, music/drama.

**Application procedures. Admission:** No deadline. $25 fee, may be waived for applicants with need. Admission notification on a rolling basis. Must reply by May 1 or within 4 week(s) if notified thereafter. **Financial aid:** Priority date 4/1; no closing date. FAFSA required. Applicants notified on a rolling basis starting 2/8; must reply within 2 week(s) of notification.

**Academics. Special study options:** Accelerated study, distance learning, double major, dual enrollment of high school students, exchange student, honors, independent study, internships, student-designed major, study abroad, teacher certification program. Degree completion programs. **Credit/placement by examination:** AP, CLEP, IB, SAT, ACT, institutional tests. 30 credit hours maximum toward bachelor's degree. **Support services:** Learning center, remedial instruction, study skills assistance, tutoring.

**Majors. Biology:** General. **Business:** General, accounting, business admin, international. **Communications:** General. **Computer sciences:** Information technology. **Education:** Elementary. **Family/consumer sciences:** Child development. **Health:** Nursing (RN). **History:** General. **Liberal arts:** Arts/sciences. **Math:** General. **Parks/recreation:** Sports admin. **Physical sciences:** Chemistry. **Psychology:** General. **Social sciences:** Criminology, political science. **Theology:** Pastoral counseling, theology. **Visual/performing arts:** Art, dramatic.

**Most popular majors.** Business/marketing 18%, education 8%, health sciences 24%, parks/recreation 8%, psychology 10%, social sciences 7%.

**Computing on campus.** 95 workstations in dormitories, library, computer center. Dormitories wired for high-speed internet access and linked to campus network. Helpline, student web hosting, wireless network available.

**Student life. Freshman orientation:** Mandatory. Preregistration for classes offered. Three-day program at beginning of fall semester. **Housing:** Guaranteed on-campus for freshmen. Coed dorms available. $100 nonrefundable deposit. **Activities:** Bands, campus ministries, choral groups, drama, international student organizations, literary magazine, music ensembles, musical theater, opera, student government, student newspaper, Bacchus, Aristotle Club, Amnesty International, Students in Free Enterprise, Young Democrats, Campus Republicans.

**Athletics.** NAIA. **Intercollegiate:** Baseball M, basketball, football (tackle) M, soccer, softball W, volleyball W. **Intramural:** Basketball, bowling, racquetball, softball, table tennis, volleyball. **Team name:** Spires.

**Student services.** Adult student services, alcohol/substance abuse counseling, chaplain/spiritual director, career counseling, student employment services, financial aid counseling, health services, on-campus daycare, personal counseling, placement for graduates, veterans' counselor.

**Contact.** E-mail: admiss@stmary.edu
Phone: (913) 758-6118 Toll-free number: (800) 752-7043
Fax: (913) 758-6140
Brandon Johnson, Director of Admissions, University of St. Mary, 4100 South Fourth Street Trafficway, Leavenworth, KS 66048

## Washburn University
### Topeka, Kansas
### www.washburn.edu
**CB code: 6928**

- Public 4-year university
- Commuter campus in small city
- 5,448 degree-seeking undergraduates: 30% part-time, 61% women
- 886 degree-seeking graduate students
- 42% graduate within 6 years

**General.** Founded in 1865. Regionally accredited. **Degrees:** 787 bachelor's, 143 associate awarded; master's, professional offered. **ROTC:** Army, Naval, Air Force. **Location:** 60 miles from Kansas City. **Calendar:** Semester, extensive summer session. **Full-time faculty:** 256 total; 86% have terminal degrees, 16% minority, 53% women. **Part-time faculty:** 243 total; 42% have terminal degrees, 9% minority, 53% women. **Class size:** 41% < 20, 50% 20-39, 6% 40-49, 3% 50-99. **Special facilities:** Concert hall, observatory, planetarium, 30-acre natural study and research area.

### Freshman class profile.

| | | | |
|---|---|---|---|
| GPA 3.75 or higher: | 23% | End year in good standing: | 62% |
| GPA 3.50-3.74: | 15% | Return as sophomores: | 66% |
| GPA 3.0-3.49: | 26% | Out-of-state: | 10% |
| GPA 2.0-2.99: | 31% | Live on campus: | 40% |
| Rank in top quarter: | 30% | Fraternities: | 10% |
| Rank in top tenth: | 12% | Sororities: | 10% |

**Basis for selection.** Open admission, but selective for some programs. Special requirements for health science programs, nursing, school of business, and education. ACT or ASSET required of all students for placement purposes.

**High school preparation.** College-preparatory program recommended. Recommended units include English 4, mathematics 3, social studies 3, history 1, science 3, foreign language 2 and computer science 1.

**2009-2010 Annual costs.** Tuition/fees: $6,116; $13,766 out-of-state. Room/board: $5,792. Books/supplies: $1,400. Personal expenses: $2,486.

**2009-2010 Financial aid. Need-based:** 655 full-time freshmen applied for aid; 454 were judged to have need; 451 of these received aid. Average need met was 35%. Average scholarship/grant was $4,693; average loan $3,331. 36% of total undergraduate aid awarded as scholarships/grants, 64% as loans/jobs. **Non-need-based:** Awarded to 1,739 full-time undergraduates, including 313 freshmen. Scholarships awarded for academics, alumni affiliation, art, athletics, job skills, leadership, minority status, music/drama, religious affiliation, ROTC, state residency.

**Application procedures. Admission:** Priority date 7/1; deadline 7/31. $20 fee. Admission notification on a rolling basis beginning on or about 9/1. **Financial aid:** Priority date 2/15; no closing date. FAFSA required. Applicants notified on a rolling basis starting 3/15; must reply within 4 week(s) of notification.

**Academics. Special study options:** Cooperative education, cross-registration, distance learning, double major, dual enrollment of high school students, ESL, honors, independent study, internships, liberal arts/career combination, student-designed major, study abroad, teacher certification program. Transformational Experience. **Credit/placement by examination:** AP,

CLEP, institutional tests. 40 credit hours maximum toward bachelor's degree. **Support services:** Learning center, remedial instruction, study skills assistance, tutoring, writing center.

**Majors. Biology:** General, biochemistry. **Business:** General, accounting, business admin, finance, managerial economics, marketing. **Communications:** General, media studies. **Computer sciences:** General, systems analysis. **Education:** General, art, biology, chemistry, early childhood, elementary, English, French, German, history, mathematics, music, physical, secondary, Spanish. **Foreign languages:** French, German, Spanish. **Health:** Athletic training, clinical lab technology, health services, nursing (RN), predental, premedicine, prepharmacy, preveterinary, sonography, substance abuse counseling. **History:** General. **Interdisciplinary:** Gerontology. **Legal studies:** Paralegal, prelaw. **Liberal arts:** Arts/sciences. **Math:** General. **Parks/recreation:** Exercise sciences, health/fitness, sports admin. **Philosophy/religion:** Philosophy, religion. **Physical sciences:** General, chemistry, physics. **Protective services:** Corrections, criminal justice, forensics, law enforcement admin, police science, security services. **Psychology:** General. **Public administration:** General, social work. **Social sciences:** Anthropology, economics, political science, sociology. **Visual/performing arts:** General, art, art history/conservation, dramatic, music performance, studio arts. **Other:** Design and applied arts.

**Most popular majors.** Business/marketing 19%, communications/journalism 6%, education 9%, health sciences 26%, security/protective services 8%.

**Computing on campus.** 1,200 workstations in dormitories, library, computer center, student center. Dormitories wired for high-speed internet access and linked to campus network. Commuter students can connect to campus network. Online course registration, online library, helpline, student web hosting, wireless network available.

**Student life. Freshman orientation:** Available. Preregistration for classes offered. Full day session in summer; 3-day session prior to start of classes. **Housing:** Coed dorms, apartments, fraternity/sorority housing, wellness housing available. $200 partly refundable deposit. **Activities:** Bands, campus ministries, choral groups, dance, drama, film society, international student organizations, literary magazine, music ensembles, Model UN, musical theater, student government, student newspaper, symphony orchestra, TV station, College Republicans, Learning in the Community, Campus Crusade for Christ, Circle K, Hispanic American Leadership Organization, Black Student Union, Student Educational Activists Coalition, Disaster Response Team, Student to Student, Literacy Education Action Project.

**Athletics.** NCAA. **Intercollegiate:** Baseball M, basketball, cheerleading, football (tackle) M, golf M, soccer W, softball W, tennis, volleyball W. **Intramural:** Badminton, basketball, football (non-tackle), golf, soccer, softball, swimming, table tennis, tennis, volleyball. **Team name:** Ichabods.

**Student services.** Adult student services, alcohol/substance abuse counseling, career counseling, services for economically disadvantaged, student employment services, financial aid counseling, health services, minority student services, personal counseling, placement for graduates, veterans' counselor. **Physically disabled:** Services for visually, hearing impaired.

**Contact.** E-mail: admissions@washburn.edu
Phone: (785) 670-1030 Toll-free number: (800) 332-0291 ext. 1030
Fax: (785) 670-1113
Richard Liedtke, Executive Director, Enrollment Management, Washburn University, 1700 SW College Avenue, Morgan 114, Topeka, KS 66621

## Wichita State University
### Wichita, Kansas
### www.wichita.edu
**CB code: 6884**

- Public 4-year university
- Commuter campus in large city
- 10,951 degree-seeking undergraduates: 27% part-time, 54% women, 6% African American, 6% Asian American, 5% Hispanic American, 1% Native American, 6% international
- 2,837 degree-seeking graduate students
- 89% of applicants admitted
- 41% graduate within 6 years

**General.** Founded in 1895. Regionally accredited. **Degrees:** 1,847 bachelor's, 76 associate awarded; master's, doctoral, professional offered. **Calendar:** Semester, extensive summer session. **Full-time faculty:** 448 total; 79% have terminal degrees, 17% minority, 42% women. **Part-time faculty:** 40 total; 50% have terminal degrees, 5% minority, 55% women. **Class size:** 41% < 20, 39% 20-39, 8% 40-49, 10% 50-99, 2% >100. **Special facilities:** Sculpture garden, wind tunnels, Marcusson pipe organ, flow-visualization water tunnel, National Aviation Research Institute, observatory, anthropology museum, rock climbing wall, bowling alley.

**Freshman class profile.** 2,963 applied, 2,625 admitted, 1,390 enrolled.

| Mid 50% test scores | | | |
|---|---|---|---|
| SAT critical reading: | 470-600 | **Rank in top tenth:** | 18% |
| SAT math: | 500-620 | **End year in good standing:** | 74% |
| ACT composite: | 21-26 | **Return as sophomores:** | 70% |
| GPA 3.75 or higher: | 24% | **Out-of-state:** | 6% |
| GPA 3.50-3.74: | 17% | **Live on campus:** | 34% |
| GPA 3.0-3.49: | 34% | **International:** | 2% |
| GPA 2.0-2.99: | 23% | **Fraternities:** | 15% |
| Rank in top quarter: | 45% | **Sororities:** | 11% |

**Basis for selection.** In-state criteria: 21 ACT or greater, rank in top 1/3 of high school class, or minimum 2.00 GPA in pre-college curriculum. Some academic colleges within WSU require a higher GPA for admission. Out-of-state criteria: varies by college. **Homeschooled:** State high school equivalency certificate required. ACT required.

**High school preparation.** College-preparatory program recommended. 14 units required. Required units include English 4, mathematics 3, social studies 3, science 3 and computer science 1.

**2009-2010 Annual costs.** Tuition/fees: $5,467; $13,501 out-of-state. Room/board: $6,060. Books/supplies: $945. Personal expenses: $1,661.

**2008-2009 Financial aid. Need-based:** 1,062 full-time freshmen applied for aid; 395 were judged to have need; 385 of these received aid. Average need met was 49%. Average scholarship/grant was $3,582; average loan $3,201. 38% of total undergraduate aid awarded as scholarships/grants, 62% as loans/jobs. **Non-need-based:** Awarded to 2,724 full-time undergraduates, including 742 freshmen. Scholarships awarded for academics, alumni affiliation, art, athletics, leadership, music/drama. **Additional information:** Top freshman applicants admitted by October 1 invited to university scholarship competition.

**Application procedures. Admission:** No deadline. $30 fee. Admission notification on a rolling basis. **Financial aid:** Priority date 3/1; no closing date. FAFSA required. Applicants notified on a rolling basis starting 3/1; must reply within 2 week(s) of notification.

**Academics.** 24-hour study room with Internet access. All library databases and other software maintained for student use. **Special study options:** Accelerated study, cooperative education, cross-registration, distance learning, double major, dual enrollment of high school students, ESL, exchange student, honors, independent study, internships, liberal arts/career combination, study abroad, teacher certification program, Washington semester. Peace Corps Returnee Program. **Credit/placement by examination:** AP, CLEP, IB, SAT, ACT, institutional tests. 30 credit hours maximum toward associate degree, 60 toward bachelor's. **Support services:** Learning center, pre-admission summer program, reduced course load, remedial instruction, study skills assistance, tutoring, writing center.

**Majors. Area/ethnic studies:** Women's. **Biology:** General, biochemistry. **Business:** Accounting, business admin, finance, human resources, international, management information systems, marketing. **Communications:** General. **Computer sciences:** General, computer science. **Education:** Art, early childhood, elementary, music, physical, secondary. **Engineering:** Aerospace, computer, electrical, industrial, manufacturing, mechanical. **Foreign languages:** French, Latin, Spanish. **Health:** Athletic training, communication disorders, dental hygiene, health care admin, physician assistant, staff services technology. **History:** General. **Interdisciplinary:** Classical/archaeology, gerontology, global studies. **Legal studies:** Prelaw. **Liberal arts:** Arts/sciences. **Math:** General. **Parks/recreation:** Exercise sciences, sports admin. **Philosophy/religion:** Philosophy, religion. **Physical sciences:** Chemistry, geology, physics. **Protective services:** Criminal justice. **Psychology:** General, school, social. **Public administration:** Social work. **Social sciences:** Anthropology, economics, geography, political science, sociology. **Visual/performing arts:** General, art, art history/conservation, commercial/advertising art, dramatic, music performance, music theory/composition, musical theater, studio arts, voice/opera.

**Most popular majors.** Business/marketing 24%, education 10%, engineering/engineering technologies 9%, health sciences 11%, psychology 6%, social sciences 6%.

**Computing on campus.** 1,500 workstations in dormitories, library, computer center, student center. Dormitories wired for high-speed internet access and linked to campus network. Commuter students can connect to campus network. Online course registration, online library, helpline, wireless network available.

**Student life. Freshman orientation:** Mandatory. Preregistration for classes offered. Held prior to fall semester and spring semester. **Policies:** Freshmen are required to live on campus, however, exceptions are made for freshmen who are 21 or older, married, living with a parent, legal gaurdian, grandparent, aunt or uncle in the greater Sedgwick County area, are taking fewer than 9 credit hours, or living in official Greek housing. **Housing:** Guaranteed on-campus for freshmen. Coed dorms, special housing for disabled, apartments, fraternity/sorority housing available. $200 nonrefundable deposit, deadline 8/19. Special floors available for Fine Arts, Emory Lindquist Honors Program, Shocker Sholars, Health Professions students. **Activities:** Bands, campus ministries, choral groups, dance, drama, film society, international student organizations, literary magazine, music ensembles, Model UN, musical theater, opera, radio station, student government, student newspaper, symphony orchestra, TV station, Campus Crusade for Christ, College Republicans, Chinese Student Friendship Association, Black Student Union, Hispanic American Leadership Association, Students in Free Enterprise, Association of Hindu Students, Muslim Student Association, That Gay Group, Emory Lindquist Honor Society.

**Athletics.** NCAA. **Intercollegiate:** Baseball M, basketball, cheerleading, cross-country, golf, softball W, tennis, track and field, volleyball W. **Intramural:** Badminton, basketball, football (non-tackle), golf, racquetball, rowing (crew), soccer, softball, swimming, table tennis, tennis, volleyball. **Team name:** Shockers.

**Student services.** Adult student services, alcohol/substance abuse counseling, chaplain/spiritual director, career counseling, services for economically disadvantaged, student employment services, financial aid counseling, health services, minority student services, on-campus daycare, personal counseling, placement for graduates, veterans' counselor, women's services. **Physically disabled:** Services for visually, speech, hearing impaired.

**Contact.** E-mail: admissions@wichita.edu
Phone: (316) 978-3085 Toll-free number: (800) 362-2594
Fax: (316) 978-3174
Bobby Gandu, Director of Admissions, Wichita State University, 1845 Fairmount Box 124, Wichita, KS 67260-0124

# Kentucky

## Alice Lloyd College
**Pippa Passes, Kentucky**
www.alc.edu                                         CB code: 1098

- Private 4-year liberal arts college
- Residential campus in rural community
- 650 degree-seeking undergraduates
- 9% of applicants admitted
- SAT or ACT (ACT writing optional) required

**General.** Founded in 1923. Regionally accredited. **Degrees:** 88 bachelor's awarded. **Location:** 150 miles from Lexington; 100 miles from Huntington, WV. **Calendar:** Semester. **Full-time faculty:** 30 total. **Part-time faculty:** 15 total. **Class size:** 41% < 20, 54% 20-39, 5% 40-49. **Special facilities:** Appalachian history collection, photographic archives.

**Freshman class profile.** 1,992 applied, 179 admitted, 179 enrolled.

| Mid 50% test scores | | | |
|---|---|---|---|
| SAT critical reading: | 440-590 | GPA 3.0-3.49: | 33% |
| SAT math: | 480-570 | GPA 2.0-2.99: | 23% |
| SAT writing: | 430-530 | Rank in top quarter: | 58% |
| ACT composite: | 17-23 | Rank in top tenth: | 21% |
| GPA 3.75 or higher: | 21% | Out-of-state: | 21% |
| GPA 3.50-3.74: | 21% | Live on campus: | 91% |

**Basis for selection.** High school record and test scores important. Essay and interview recommended. **Homeschooled:** Transcript of courses and grades, letter of recommendation (nonparent) required. Interview highly recommended.

**High school preparation.** 12 units required. Required units include English 4, mathematics 3, social studies 2 and science 3.

**2009-2010 Annual costs.** Tuition/fees: $7,600. Guaranteed tuition for students from 108-county central Appalachian service area in Kentucky, West Virginia, Virginia, Tennessee, and Ohio. Room/board: $5,850. Books/supplies: $850. Personal expenses: $1,300.

**2008-2009 Financial aid. Non-need-based:** Scholarships awarded for athletics, minority status, state residency. **Additional information:** All students receive financial aid through student work program. No student denied admission because of inability to pay. All full-time students required to work minimum of 10 hours per week.

**Application procedures. Admission:** Priority date 5/1; no deadline. No application fee. Admission notification on a rolling basis beginning on or about 9/1. **Financial aid:** Priority date 3/15; no closing date. FAFSA required. Applicants notified on a rolling basis starting 4/1; must reply within 6 week(s) of notification.

**Academics.** Scholarships for graduate work following graduation. **Special study options:** Double major, independent study, internships, liberal arts/career combination, student-designed major, study abroad, teacher certification program, Washington semester. **Credit/placement by examination:** AP, CLEP, IB, SAT, ACT, institutional tests. 30 credit hours maximum toward bachelor's degree. Limited number of hours of credit by examination may be counted toward degree, decided on individual basis. **Support services:** Reduced course load, remedial instruction, study skills assistance, tutoring, writing center.

**Majors. Biology:** General. **Business:** Business admin. **Education:** Biology, elementary, English, mathematics, middle, physical, science, secondary, social studies. **History:** General. **Interdisciplinary:** Biological/physical sciences. **Parks/recreation:** General. **Social sciences:** General.

**Most popular majors.** Biology 26%, business/marketing 18%, education 23%, English 6%, history 10%, social sciences 11%.

**Computing on campus.** 80 workstations in library, computer center. Dormitories wired for high-speed internet access and linked to campus network. Online library, helpline, repair service, wireless network available.

**Student life. Freshman orientation:** Mandatory. Preregistration for classes offered. Held 3 days before start of first semester. **Policies:** Zero tolerance of on-campus alcohol and/or drug usage or possession. **Housing:** Guaranteed on-campus for all undergraduates. Single-sex dorms available. $50 deposit, deadline 5/15. **Activities:** Choral groups, drama, radio station, student government, student newspaper, Students for Christ, Baptist student union, cultural diversity club, children's outreach club, community service volunteers, Circle K.

**Athletics.** NAIA. **Intercollegiate:** Baseball M, basketball, cheerleading M, cross-country, softball W. **Intramural:** Basketball, bowling, football (non-tackle), golf, racquetball, soccer, softball, swimming, table tennis, tennis, volleyball, weight lifting. **Team name:** Eagles.

**Student services.** Alcohol/substance abuse counseling, career counseling, student employment services, financial aid counseling, health services, on-campus daycare, personal counseling, placement for graduates, veterans' counselor.

**Contact.** E-mail: admissions@alc.edu
Phone: (606) 368-6036 Toll-free number: (888) 280-4252
Fax: (606) 368-6215
Ronnie Collins, Director of Admissions, Alice Lloyd College, 100 Purpose Road, Pippa Passes, KY 41844

## Asbury College
**Wilmore, Kentucky**                                CB member
www.asbury.edu                                       CB code: 1019

- Private 4-year university and liberal arts college affiliated with interdenominational tradition
- Residential campus in small town
- 1,371 degree-seeking undergraduates: 2% part-time, 62% women, 2% African American, 1% Asian American, 2% Hispanic American, 1% Native American, 1% international
- 137 degree-seeking graduate students
- 56% of applicants admitted
- SAT or ACT (ACT writing optional), application essay required
- 65% graduate within 6 years

**General.** Founded in 1890. Regionally accredited. **Degrees:** 293 bachelor's awarded; master's offered. **ROTC:** Army, Air Force. **Location:** 20 miles from Lexington. **Calendar:** Semester, limited summer session. **Full-time faculty:** 83 total; 71% have terminal degrees, 4% minority, 34% women. **Part-time faculty:** 84 total; 27% have terminal degrees, 7% minority, 45% women. **Class size:** 59% < 20, 33% 20-39, 7% 40-49, 1% 50-99. **Special facilities:** Indoor riding arena, horse stables.

**Freshman class profile.** 1,563 applied, 872 admitted, 315 enrolled.

| Mid 50% test scores | | | |
|---|---|---|---|
| SAT critical reading: | 510-650 | Rank in top quarter: | 63% |
| SAT math: | 490-630 | Rank in top tenth: | 32% |
| ACT composite: | 21-27 | End year in good standing: | 95% |
| GPA 3.75 or higher: | 45% | Return as sophomores: | 83% |
| GPA 3.50-3.74: | 18% | Out-of-state: | 48% |
| GPA 3.0-3.49: | 26% | Live on campus: | 96% |
| GPA 2.0-2.99: | 11% | International: | 1% |

**Basis for selection.** Careful consideration given to academic records, test scores, application essays, references, and ability to benefit. Probationary acceptance possible if GPA below 2.5. ACT required prior to admission to education department; both ACT and SAT required for presidential level scholarships. Interview recommended for music majors, academically weak applicants, scholarship applicants. Audition required for music majors. Portfolio recommended for art majors. **Homeschooled:** Transcript of courses and grades, state high school equivalency certificate required.

**High school preparation.** College-preparatory program recommended. 15 units recommended. Recommended units include English 4, mathematics 3, social studies 1, history 1, science 2 (laboratory 2) and foreign language 2.

**2010-2011 Annual costs.** Tuition/fees (projected): $23,303. Room/board: $5,566. Books/supplies: $815. Personal expenses: $1,240.

**2009-2010 Financial aid. Need-based:** 289 full-time freshmen applied for aid; 245 were judged to have need; 245 of these received aid. Average need met was 89%. Average scholarship/grant was $13,646; average loan $3,226. 62% of total undergraduate aid awarded as scholarships/grants, 38% as loans/jobs. **Non-need-based:** Awarded to 442 full-time undergraduates, including 153 freshmen. Scholarships awarded for academics, alumni affiliation, art, athletics, leadership, minority status, music/drama, religious affiliation, ROTC.

**Application procedures. Admission:** Priority date 5/1; no deadline. $30 fee, may be waived for applicants with need, free for online applicants. Admission notification on a rolling basis. Confirmation of intention to enroll requires $200 pre-tuition deposit within 30 days of admission notification. **Financial aid:** Priority date 3/1; no closing date. Institutional form required. Applicants notified on a rolling basis starting 1/31; must reply within 4 week(s) of notification.

**Academics. Special study options:** Double major, ESL, internships, study abroad, teacher certification program, urban semester, Washington semester. Exchange program with colleges in Christian College Consortium, 3-2 programs in engineering with the University of Kentucky. **Credit/placement by examination:** AP, CLEP, IB, SAT, ACT, institutional tests. **Support services:** Remedial instruction, study skills assistance, tutoring, writing center.

**Majors. Agriculture:** Equestrian studies. **Biology:** General, biochemistry. **Business:** General, accounting. **Communications:** Journalism. **Communications technology:** Radio/tv. **Education:** Art, elementary, middle, music, physical. **Foreign languages:** Biblical, classics, French, Spanish. **Health:** Health services. **History:** General. **Math:** General, computational. **Parks/recreation:** Facilities management, health/fitness, sports admin. **Philosophy/religion:** Philosophy. **Physical sciences:** General, chemistry. **Psychology:** General. **Public administration:** Social work. **Social sciences:** General, political science, sociology. **Theology:** Bible, missionary, religious ed, sacred music, youth ministry. **Visual/performing arts:** Dramatic, studio arts. **Other:** Mathematics, financial.

**Most popular majors.** Business/marketing 10%, communication technologies 14%, education 10%, English 11%, theological studies 10%, visual/performing arts 11%.

**Computing on campus.** 200 workstations in dormitories, library, computer center, student center. Dormitories wired for high-speed internet access and linked to campus network. Commuter students can connect to campus network. Online course registration, online library, helpline, repair service, wireless network available.

**Student life. Freshman orientation:** Mandatory. Preregistration for classes offered. Held weekend before fall semester begins. **Policies:** Christian values stressed. Religious observance required. **Housing:** Guaranteed on-campus for freshmen. Single-sex dorms, apartments available. **Activities:** Bands, campus ministries, choral groups, drama, literary magazine, music ensembles, musical theater, opera, radio station, student government, student newspaper, symphony orchestra, TV station, Christian service association, student fellowships, Impact, Asburians for Life, ministerial association, outdoors club.

**Athletics.** NAIA, NCCAA. **Intercollegiate:** Baseball M, basketball, cross-country, diving, soccer, softball W, swimming, tennis, volleyball W. **Intramural:** Basketball, football (non-tackle), golf, racquetball, soccer, softball, volleyball. **Team name:** Eagles.

**Student services.** Adult student services, chaplain/spiritual director, career counseling, student employment services, financial aid counseling, health services, minority student services, personal counseling.

**Contact.** E-mail: admissions@asbury.edu
Phone: (859) 858-3511 ext. 2142 Toll-free number: (800) 888-1818
Fax: (859) 858-3921
Lisa Harper, Director of Admissions, Asbury College, One Macklem Drive, Wilmore, KY 40390-1198

## Beckfield College
Florence, Kentucky
www.beckfield.edu                                    CB code: 3404

- For-profit 4-year business, health science and nursing college
- Commuter campus in large town
- 645 degree-seeking undergraduates
- Interview required

**General.** Accredited by ACICS. **Degrees:** 10 bachelor's, 143 associate awarded. **Location:** 10 miles from Cincinnati. **Calendar:** Quarter, extensive summer session. **Full-time faculty:** 20 total. **Part-time faculty:** 30 total. **Class size:** 100% < 20.

**Basis for selection.** Open admission, but selective for some programs. Nursing program requires qualifying ACT or SAT scores. **Homeschooled:** Transcript of courses and grades required. Accredited home study course will be considered for admission.

**2009-2010 Annual costs.** Tuition/fees: $13,353. Fees vary by program. Books/supplies: $1,500.

**2008-2009 Financial aid.** All financial aid based on need. **Additional information:** Deadline for filing of financial aid forms is end of first week of classes.

**Application procedures. Admission:** No deadline. $150 fee. Application must be submitted on paper. Admission notification on a rolling basis. **Financial aid:** FAFSA required. Applicants notified on a rolling basis.

**Academics. Special study options:** Combined bachelor's/graduate degree, independent study, internships. **Credit/placement by examination:** CLEP, IB, institutional tests. **Support services:** Reduced course load, remedial instruction, study skills assistance, tutoring.

**Majors. Business:** Business admin. **Health:** Nursing (RN). **Legal studies:** Paralegal. **Protective services:** Law enforcement admin.

**Computing on campus.** 90 workstations in library, computer center. Online library, wireless network available.

**Student life. Freshman orientation:** Mandatory. Preregistration for classes offered. Held for half day 3 days before beginning of quarter.

**Student services.** Alcohol/substance abuse counseling, career counseling, student employment services, financial aid counseling, personal counseling, placement for graduates, veterans' counselor.

**Contact.** Phone: (859) 371-9393 Fax: (859) 371-5096
Leah Boerger, Director of Admissions, Beckfield College, 16 Spiral Drive, Florence, KY 41042

## Bellarmine University
Louisville, Kentucky                                  CB member
www.bellarmine.edu                                   CB code: 1056

- Private 4-year university and liberal arts college affiliated with Roman Catholic Church
- Commuter campus in very large city
- 2,139 degree-seeking undergraduates: 5% part-time, 64% women, 3% African American, 3% Asian American, 2% Hispanic American, 1% international
- 653 degree-seeking graduate students
- 53% of applicants admitted
- SAT or ACT (ACT writing optional), application essay required
- 65% graduate within 6 years; 23% enter graduate study

**General.** Founded in 1950. Regionally accredited. **Degrees:** 466 bachelor's awarded; master's, professional offered. **ROTC:** Army, Air Force. **Location:** 7 miles from downtown, 100 miles from Cincinnati. **Calendar:** Semester, extensive summer session. **Full-time faculty:** 138 total; 80% have terminal degrees, 7% minority, 47% women. **Part-time faculty:** 162 total; 35% have terminal degrees, 8% minority, 49% women. **Class size:** 63% < 20, 32% 20-39, 2% 40-49, 2% 50-99.

**Freshman class profile.** 6,021 applied, 3,214 admitted, 603 enrolled.

| Mid 50% test scores | | | |
|---|---|---|---|
| SAT critical reading: | 480-600 | Rank in top quarter: | 51% |
| SAT math: | 510-600 | Rank in top tenth: | 23% |
| ACT composite: | 22-27 | End year in good standing: | 92% |
| GPA 3.75 or higher: | 31% | Return as sophomores: | 78% |
| GPA 3.50-3.74: | 25% | Out-of-state: | 36% |
| GPA 3.0-3.49: | 29% | Live on campus: | 79% |
| GPA 2.0-2.99: | 15% | Fraternities: | 1% |
| | | Sororities: | 1% |

**Basis for selection.** Admissions based on 2.5 GPA, college preparatory curriculum, 21 ACT or 1000 SAT (exclusive of Writing), strong high school recommendation, submission of acceptable essay (if requested). Applicants not meeting requirements may be admitted on strength of each criterion. School activities also considered. Interview recommended. Audition required of music majors. Portfolio recommended for art majors. **Homeschooled:** Transcript of courses and grades, letter of recommendation (nonparent) required.

**High school preparation.** College-preparatory program recommended. 20 units required; 26 recommended. Required and recommended units include English 4, mathematics 3-4, social studies 2-3, history 1-2, science 3-4 (laboratory 2), foreign language 2 and academic electives 5-7.

**2010-2011 Annual costs.** Tuition/fees: $30,310. Room/board: $8,550. Books/supplies: $764. Personal expenses: $3,693.

**2009-2010 Financial aid. Need-based:** 536 full-time freshmen applied for aid; 475 were judged to have need; 474 of these received aid. Average need met was 79%. Average scholarship/grant was $17,171; average loan

$3,303. 78% of total undergraduate aid awarded as scholarships/grants, 22% as loans/jobs. **Non-need-based:** Awarded to 1,153 full-time undergraduates, including 322 freshmen. Scholarships awarded for academics, alumni affiliation, art, athletics, leadership, minority status, music/drama, religious affiliation, ROTC, state residency.

**Application procedures. Admission:** Priority date 2/1; no deadline. $25 fee, may be waived for applicants with need, free for online applicants. Admission notification on a rolling basis beginning on or about 9/1. Must reply by May 1 or within 3 week(s) if notified thereafter. **Financial aid:** Priority date 3/1; no closing date. FAFSA required. Applicants notified on a rolling basis starting 3/15.

**Academics. Special study options:** Accelerated study, combined bachelor's/ graduate degree, cross-registration, double major, dual enrollment of high school students, honors, independent study, internships, liberal arts/career combination, semester at sea, student-designed major, study abroad, teacher certification program, Washington semester. **Credit/placement by examination:** AP, CLEP, IB, institutional tests. **Support services:** Learning center, reduced course load, study skills assistance, tutoring, writing center.

**Majors. Biology:** General, biochemistry. **Business:** Accounting, actuarial science, business admin, finance. **Communications:** General. **Computer sciences:** General, computer science, systems analysis. **Education:** Elementary, middle, special. **Engineering:** Computer. **Foreign languages:** Spanish. **Health:** Clinical lab science, nursing (RN), respiratory therapy technology. **History:** General. **Liberal arts:** Arts/sciences. **Math:** General. **Parks/ recreation:** Exercise sciences. **Philosophy/religion:** Philosophy. **Physical sciences:** Chemistry, physics. **Protective services:** Law enforcement admin. **Psychology:** General. **Social sciences:** Economics, political science, sociology. **Theology:** Theology. **Visual/performing arts:** Art, arts management. **Other:** Foreign languages and international studies.

**Most popular majors.** Business/marketing 17%, communications/ journalism 8%, health sciences 32%, psychology 10%.

**Computing on campus.** 600 workstations in dormitories, library, computer center, student center. Dormitories wired for high-speed internet access and linked to campus network. Commuter students can connect to campus network. Online course registration, helpline, repair service, wireless network available.

**Student life. Freshman orientation:** Mandatory, $300 fee. Preregistration for classes offered. Off-campus 3-day session held in August before classes begin. **Housing:** Guaranteed on-campus for freshmen. Coed dorms, single-sex dorms, special housing for disabled, apartments, wellness housing available. $200 fully refundable deposit, deadline 5/1. Pets allowed in dorm rooms. Suites available to upperclassmen. **Activities:** Bands, campus ministries, choral groups, dance, drama, literary magazine, music ensembles, musical theater, opera, radio station, student government, student newspaper, symphony orchestra, Catholic students association, Fellowship of Christian Athletes, Hillel, Highland community ministries, Habitat for Humanity.

**Athletics.** NCAA. **Intercollegiate:** Baseball M, basketball, bowling, cross-country, field hockey W, golf, lacrosse M, soccer, softball W, tennis, track and field, volleyball W. **Intramural:** Basketball, cheerleading, football (non-tackle) M, golf, soccer, softball, swimming, tennis, volleyball. **Team name:** Knights.

**Student services.** Adult student services, chaplain/spiritual director, career counseling, student employment services, financial aid counseling, health services, personal counseling, placement for graduates. **Physically disabled:** Services for visually, hearing impaired.

**Contact.** E-mail: admissions@bellarmine.edu
Phone: (502) 452-8131 Toll-free number: (800) 274-4723 ext. 8131
Fax: (502) 452-8002
Timothy Sturgeon, Dean of Admissions, Bellarmine University, 2001 Newburg Road, Louisville, KY 40205

## Berea College
**Berea, Kentucky**
**www.berea.edu**

**CB member**
**CB code: 1060**

- Private 4-year liberal arts college
- Residential campus in small town
- 1,496 degree-seeking undergraduates: 59% women, 18% African American, 1% Asian American, 3% Hispanic American, 1% Native American, 7% international
- 19% of applicants admitted
- SAT or ACT (ACT writing optional), application essay, interview required
- 65% graduate within 6 years

**General.** Founded in 1855. Regionally accredited. Each student is provided with a laptop computer. Departmental computer labs offer access to specialized functions such as video editing and graphical production. **Degrees:** 267 bachelor's awarded. **Location:** 40 miles from Lexington, 100 miles from Louisville. **Calendar:** 4-1-4, limited summer session. **Full-time faculty:** 130 total; 91% have terminal degrees, 12% minority, 43% women. **Part-time faculty:** 46 total; 35% have terminal degrees, 13% minority, 50% women. **Class size:** 62% < 20, 38% 20-39, less than 1% 40-49. **Special facilities:** Appalachian gallery, planetarium and observatory, geology museum, Ecovillage, child development laboratory, early technology lab, crafts program.

**Freshman class profile.** 2,745 applied, 516 admitted, 392 enrolled.

| Mid 50% test scores | | | |
|---|---|---|---|
| SAT critical reading: | 500-620 | GPA 2.0-2.99: | 18% |
| SAT math: | 470-590 | Rank in top quarter: | 69% |
| SAT writing: | 510-590 | Rank in top tenth: | 26% |
| ACT composite: | 21-26 | Return as sophomores: | 82% |
| GPA 3.75 or higher: | 28% | Out-of-state: | 54% |
| GPA 3.50-3.74: | 18% | Live on campus: | 97% |
| GPA 3.0-3.49: | 36% | International: | 6% |

**Basis for selection.** Admissions based on comprehensive review of application including academic credentials, recommendations, essay, financial eligibility, and interview. **Homeschooled:** List of courses and titles of textbooks required if transcript is not available.

**High school preparation.** College-preparatory program required. 13 units recommended. Recommended units include English 4, mathematics 3, social studies 1, history 1, science 2 (laboratory 2) and foreign language 2.

**2009-2010 Annual costs.** Only those with financial need admitted. All students awarded 4-year tuition scholarship. Amount of scholarship varies depending on financial need and presence of any additional outside scholarships. Resources cover entire cost of tuition, which totals $25,500. Financial aid and scholarships available for meeting additional costs of room/ board ($5,768) and fees ($876), depending on financial need. Books/ supplies: $750. Personal expenses: $1,376.

**2009-2010 Financial aid.** All financial aid based on need. 392 full-time freshmen applied for aid; 392 were judged to have need; 392 of these received aid. Average need met was 98%. Average scholarship/grant was $31,341; average loan $25. 93% of total undergraduate aid awarded as scholarships/ grants, 7% as loans/jobs.

**Application procedures. Admission:** Closing date 4/30. No application fee. Admission notification on a rolling basis beginning on or about 11/1. **Financial aid:** Priority date 3/15; no closing date. FAFSA required. Applicants notified on a rolling basis starting 4/1.

**Academics. Special study options:** Combined bachelor's/graduate degree, double major, ESL, exchange student, honors, independent study, internships, student-designed major, study abroad, teacher certification program. 3-2 engineering program with Washington University (MO) and University of Kentucky. **Credit/placement by examination:** AP, CLEP, SAT, ACT, institutional tests. Unlimited number of credit hours may be counted toward degree. **Support services:** Learning center, remedial instruction, study skills assistance, tutoring, writing center.

**Majors. Agriculture:** General. **Area/ethnic studies:** African-American, Asian, women's. **Biology:** General, neuroanatomy. **Business:** General, accounting, finance, marketing. **Communications:** Media studies. **Computer sciences:** General. **Education:** General, art, elementary, family/consumer sciences, kindergarten/preschool, middle, music, secondary, technology/industrial arts. **Engineering technology:** Manufacturing. **Family/consumer sciences:** General. **Foreign languages:** French, German, Latin, Spanish. **Health:** Nursing (RN). **History:** General. **Math:** General, applied. **Parks/recreation:** Exercise sciences, health/fitness. **Philosophy/religion:** Philosophy, religion. **Physical sciences:** Chemistry, physics. **Psychology:** General. **Social sciences:** Economics, political science, sociology. **Visual/performing arts:** Art, art history/conservation, dramatic, music performance, studio arts, voice/opera.

**Most popular majors.** Biology 7%, business/marketing 9%, engineering/ engineering technologies 8%, family/consumer sciences 7%, interdisciplinary studies 6%, social sciences 6%, visual/performing arts 11%.

**Computing on campus.** Dormitories wired for high-speed internet access and linked to campus network. Online course registration, online library, helpline, repair service, wireless network available.

**Student life. Freshman orientation:** Mandatory. Preregistration for classes offered. Choice of 3 long weekend sessions in summer; week-long session held before classes begin. **Housing:** Guaranteed on-campus for all undergraduates. Single-sex dorms, apartments, wellness housing available. Apartments for single parent students, Ecovillage. **Activities:** Bands, campus ministries, choral groups, dance, drama, international student organizations, literary magazine, music ensembles, student government, student newspaper, religious organizations, People Who Care, Students for Appalachia, Habitat for Humanity, Cosmopolitan Club.

**Athletics.** NAIA. **Intercollegiate:** Baseball M, basketball, cross-country, diving, golf M, soccer, softball W, swimming, tennis, track and field, volleyball W. **Intramural:** Basketball, football (non-tackle), soccer, softball, volleyball. **Team name:** Mountaineers.

**Student services.** Adult student services, alcohol/substance abuse counseling, chaplain/spiritual director, career counseling, services for economically disadvantaged, student employment services, financial aid counseling, health services, minority student services, on-campus daycare, personal counseling, placement for graduates, veterans' counselor, women's services. **Physically disabled:** Services for visually, speech, hearing impaired.

**Contact.** E-mail: admissions@berea.edu
Phone: (859) 985-3500 Toll-free number: (800) 326-5948
Fax: (859) 985-3512
Luke Hodson, Director of Admissions Operations, Berea College, CPO 2220, Berea, KY 40404

### Brescia University
**Owensboro, Kentucky**
**www.brescia.edu**                                    **CB code: 1071**

- Private 4-year university and liberal arts college affiliated with Roman Catholic Church
- Residential campus in small city
- 571 degree-seeking undergraduates: 16% part-time, 64% women
- 55 degree-seeking graduate students
- 67% of applicants admitted
- SAT or ACT (ACT writing optional), application essay required

**General.** Founded in 1950. Regionally accredited. Weekend college for nontraditional students. Lay ministry formation program nationally accredited. Online degree completion programs. **Degrees:** 69 bachelor's, 4 associate awarded; master's offered. **Location:** 120 miles from Louisville; 120 miles from Nashville, TN. **Calendar:** Semester, limited summer session. **Full-time faculty:** 41 total; 66% have terminal degrees, 12% minority, 54% women. **Part-time faculty:** 38 total; 5% have terminal degrees, 5% minority, 40% women. **Class size:** 78% < 20, 22% 20-39. **Special facilities:** Observatory, greenhouse.

**Freshman class profile.** 677 applied, 453 admitted, 122 enrolled.

| Mid 50% test scores | | | |
|---|---|---|---|
| | | GPA 3.0-3.49: | 31% |
| SAT math: | 440-510 | GPA 2.0-2.99: | 29% |
| ACT composite: | 18-24 | Out-of-state: | 11% |
| GPA 3.75 or higher: | 21% | Live on campus: | 83% |
| GPA 3.50-3.74: | 19% | International: | 1% |

**Basis for selection.** Students admitted based on high school grades and ACT/SAT scores. **Homeschooled:** Transcript of courses and grades required.

**High school preparation.** College-preparatory program required. 17 units recommended. Recommended units include English 4, mathematics 3, social studies 2, history 2, science 2, foreign language 2 and academic electives 2. 2 units in fine arts, 2 units in computer science also recommended.

**2009-2010 Annual costs.** Tuition/fees: $16,040. Room/board: $7,600. Books/supplies: $1,000. Personal expenses: $1,800.

**2009-2010 Financial aid. Non-need-based:** Scholarships awarded for academics, alumni affiliation, art, athletics, minority status, music/drama, religious affiliation, state residency.

**Application procedures. Admission:** No deadline. $25 fee, may be waived for applicants with need. Admission notification on a rolling basis beginning on or about 9/1. **Financial aid:** Priority date 8/1, closing date 8/23. FAFSA required. Applicants notified on a rolling basis starting 3/1; must reply within 3 week(s) of notification.

**Academics. Special study options:** Accelerated study, combined bachelor's/graduate degree, cross-registration, distance learning, double major, ESL, exchange student, honors, independent study, internships, liberal arts/career combination, student-designed major, teacher certification program, weekend college. **Credit/placement by examination:** AP, CLEP, IB, SAT, ACT, institutional tests. 18 credit hours maximum toward associate degree, 36 toward bachelor's. **Support services:** Pre-admission summer program, reduced course load, remedial instruction, study skills assistance, tutoring.

**Majors. Biology:** General. **Business:** General, accounting, business admin. **Computer sciences:** General. **Education:** Art, elementary, middle, secondary, social studies, Spanish, special. **Foreign languages:** Spanish. **Health:** Audiology/speech pathology, clinical lab science. **History:** General. **Interdisciplinary:** Biological/physical sciences, math/computer science. **Liberal arts:** Arts/sciences. **Math:** Applied. **Philosophy/religion:** Religion. **Physical sciences:** Chemistry. **Psychology:** General. **Public administration:** Social work. **Social sciences:** General, political science, sociology. **Theology:** Pastoral counseling, theology. **Visual/performing arts:** Art, commercial/advertising art.

**Most popular majors.** Business/marketing 22%, education 22%, liberal arts 8%, public administration/social services 16%, visual/performing arts 10%.

**Computing on campus.** 67 workstations in library, computer center, student center. Dormitories wired for high-speed internet access and linked to campus network. Commuter students can connect to campus network. Online library, wireless network available.

**Student life. Freshman orientation:** Available, $100 fee. Preregistration for classes offered. Sunday-Tuesday program held prior to start of classes. **Housing:** Guaranteed on-campus for freshmen. Coed dorms, single-sex dorms, special housing for disabled, apartments available. $100 fully refundable deposit, deadline 8/23. Shared apartment houses available. **Activities:** Pep band, campus ministries, choral groups, drama, international student organizations, literary magazine, student government, student newspaper, Fellowship of Christian Athletes, social work club, Council for Exceptional Children, Christian Life Experience, Grave Robbers, Alternative Spring Break, Right to Life.

**Athletics.** NAIA. **Intercollegiate:** Baseball M, basketball, cross-country, golf, soccer, softball W, tennis, track and field, volleyball W. **Intramural:** Basketball, racquetball, table tennis, volleyball. **Team name:** Bearcats.

**Student services.** Adult student services, alcohol/substance abuse counseling, chaplain/spiritual director, career counseling, services for economically disadvantaged, student employment services, financial aid counseling, personal counseling, placement for graduates, veterans' counselor, women's services. **Physically disabled:** Services for visually, speech, hearing impaired.

**Contact.** E-mail: admissions@brescia.edu
Phone: (270) 686-4241 Toll-free number: (877) 273-7242
Fax: (270) 686-4314
Chris Houk, Dean of Enrollment, Brescia University, 717 Frederica Street, Owensboro, KY 42301-3023

### Campbellsville University
**Campbellsville, Kentucky**                          **CB member**
**www.campbellsville.edu**                            **CB code: 1097**

- Private 4-year university affiliated with Baptist faith
- Residential campus in large town
- 1,888 degree-seeking undergraduates: 10% part-time, 54% women
- 442 degree-seeking graduate students
- 67% of applicants admitted
- SAT or ACT (ACT writing optional) required
- 39% graduate within 6 years

**General.** Founded in 1906. Regionally accredited. Affiliated with Kentucky Baptist Convention. **Degrees:** 251 bachelor's, 28 associate awarded; master's offered. **ROTC:** Army. **Location:** 80 miles from Louisville, 140 miles from Nashville, Tennessee. **Calendar:** Semester, extensive summer session. **Full-time faculty:** 115 total; 58% have terminal degrees, 6% minority, 51% women. **Part-time faculty:** 179 total; 10% minority, 59% women. **Class size:** 67% < 20, 31% 20-39, 1% 40-49, less than 1% 50-99. **Special facilities:** Educational and research woodland, American Civil War institute, fine arts center with computer-enhanced practice room with acoustical adjustment system.

**Freshman class profile.** 2,109 applied, 1,421 admitted, 518 enrolled.

| Mid 50% test scores | | | |
|---|---|---|---|
| | | GPA 2.0-2.99: | 35% |
| SAT critical reading: | 420-560 | Rank in top quarter: | 38% |
| SAT math: | 430-600 | Rank in top tenth: | 17% |
| ACT composite: | 18-23 | End year in good standing: | 89% |
| GPA 3.75 or higher: | 21% | Return as sophomores: | 65% |
| GPA 3.50-3.74: | 14% | Out-of-state: | 17% |
| GPA 3.0-3.49: | 27% | Live on campus: | 68% |

**Basis for selection.** Achievement in strong high school program and satisfactory ACT or SAT scores most important. Special consideration for entry to basic skills program may be given to other highly motivated and potentially successful applicants. Interview and essay recommended. **Home-schooled:** State high school equivalency certificate required.

**High school preparation.** College-preparatory program recommended. 21 units recommended. Recommended units include English 4, mathematics 3, social studies 2, history 2, science 3 (laboratory 1), foreign language 1 and academic electives 6. At least 2 units in the arts recommended for academic elective.

**2009-2010 Annual costs.** Tuition/fees: $18,810. Room/board: $6,540. Books/supplies: $1,000. Personal expenses: $1,900.

**2008-2009 Financial aid. Need-based:** 371 full-time freshmen applied for aid; 351 were judged to have need; 350 of these received aid. Average need met was 78%. Average scholarship/grant was $13,570; average loan $2,859. 67% of total undergraduate aid awarded as scholarships/grants, 33% as loans/jobs. **Non-need-based:** Awarded to 334 full-time undergraduates, including 89 freshmen. Scholarships awarded for academics, art, athletics, leadership, minority status, music/drama, religious affiliation, ROTC, state residency. **Additional information:** Matching scholarships available for students whose church contributes $200 annually. Performance grants available to members of marching band.

**Application procedures. Admission:** Priority date 4/15; no deadline. $20 fee, may be waived for applicants with need, free for online applicants. Admission notification on a rolling basis beginning on or about 1/2. **Financial aid:** Priority date 4/1; no closing date. FAFSA required. Applicants notified on a rolling basis starting 5/15.

**Academics. Special study options:** Cooperative education, distance learning, double major, dual enrollment of high school students, ESL, exchange student, honors, independent study, internships, study abroad, teacher certification program, Washington semester. London semester. **Credit/placement by examination:** AP, CLEP, institutional tests. 32 credit hours maximum toward bachelor's degree. Institutional/departmental examinations given in some areas. **Support services:** Learning center, preadmission summer program, reduced course load, remedial instruction, study skills assistance, tutoring, writing center.

**Majors. Biology:** General. **Business:** General, accounting, business admin, marketing, office management. **Communications:** General, broadcast journalism, journalism, public relations. **Computer sciences:** General. **Education:** General, art, biology, chemistry, early childhood, elementary, English, health, history, mathematics, middle, music, physical, physics, reading, science, secondary, social science, social studies. **Health:** Athletic training, predental, premedicine, prepharmacy, preveterinary. **History:** General. **Math:** General. **Parks/recreation:** General, exercise sciences, health/fitness. **Philosophy/religion:** Religion. **Physical sciences:** Chemistry, physics. **Protective services:** Law enforcement admin. **Psychology:** General. **Public administration:** Social work. **Social sciences:** General, economics, political science, sociology. **Theology:** Bible, religious ed, sacred music. **Visual/performing arts:** Art, conducting, dramatic, music performance, music theory/composition, piano/organ, studio arts, voice/opera.

**Most popular majors.** Business/marketing 23%, education 27%, theological studies 9%.

**Computing on campus.** 200 workstations in dormitories, library, computer center, student center. Dormitories wired for high-speed internet access and linked to campus network. Commuter students can connect to campus network. Online course registration, online library available.

**Student life. Freshman orientation:** Mandatory. Preregistration for classes offered. Held in June and July. **Policies:** Religious observance required. **Housing:** Guaranteed on-campus for all undergraduates. Single-sex dorms, apartments, wellness housing available. $100 deposit, deadline 7/1. **Activities:** Bands, campus ministries, choral groups, dance, drama, literary magazine, music ensembles, musical theater, opera, radio station, student government, student newspaper, symphony orchestra, TV station, Baptist student union, Young Republicans, Young Democrats, Student Foundation, Fellowship of Christian Athletes, student ambassadors, African American leadership league, world community club.

**Athletics.** NAIA. **Intercollegiate:** Baseball M, basketball, bowling, cheerleading, cross-country, football (tackle) M, golf, soccer, softball W, swimming W, tennis, track and field, volleyball W, wrestling M. **Intramural:** Basketball, racquetball, soccer, softball, swimming, table tennis, tennis, volleyball. **Team name:** Tigers.

**Student services.** Adult student services, alcohol/substance abuse counseling, chaplain/spiritual director, career counseling, student employment services, financial aid counseling, health services, personal counseling, placement for graduates, veterans' counselor.

**Contact.** E-mail: admissions@campbellsville.edu
Phone: (270) 789-5220 Toll-free number: (800) 264-6014
Fax: (270) 789-5071
David Walters, Vice President for Admissions, Campbellsville University, 1 University Drive, Campbellsville, KY 42718-2799

## Centre College
**Danville, Kentucky** — CB member
www.centre.edu — CB code: 1109

- Private 4-year liberal arts college affiliated with Presbyterian Church (USA)
- Residential campus in large town
- 1,214 degree-seeking undergraduates: 55% women, 4% African American, 3% Asian American, 2% Hispanic American, 2% international
- 69% of applicants admitted
- SAT or ACT (ACT writing optional), application essay required
- 81% graduate within 6 years

**General.** Founded in 1819. Regionally accredited. **Degrees:** 271 bachelor's awarded. **ROTC:** Army, Air Force. **Location:** 35 miles from Lexington, 85 miles from Louisville. **Calendar:** 4-1-4. **Full-time faculty:** 103 total; 92% have terminal degrees, 11% minority, 42% women. **Part-time faculty:** 17 total; 47% have terminal degrees, 6% minority, 41% women. **Class size:** 56% < 20, 44% 20-39. **Special facilities:** Regional performing arts center, hot glass studio.

**Freshman class profile.** 2,056 applied, 1,422 admitted, 333 enrolled.

| Mid 50% test scores | | | |
|---|---|---|---|
| SAT critical reading: | 550-670 | GPA 2.0-2.99: | 8% |
| SAT math: | 570-670 | Rank in top quarter: | 84% |
| SAT writing: | 530-670 | Rank in top tenth: | 59% |
| ACT composite: | 26-30 | Return as sophomores: | 91% |
| GPA 3.75 or higher: | 43% | Out-of-state: | 38% |
| GPA 3.50-3.74: | 22% | Live on campus: | 100% |
| GPA 3.0-3.49: | 27% | International: | 3% |

**Basis for selection.** Achievement and quality of high school program most important. Recommendations, test scores, academic and nonacademic interests, experiences considered. Interview recommended.

**High school preparation.** College-preparatory program required. 13 units required; 20 recommended. Required and recommended units include English 4, mathematics 3-4, social studies 1-2, history 1-2, science 2-4 (laboratory 2-3), foreign language 2-4 and visual/performing arts 1.

**2009-2010 Annual costs.** Comprehensive fee: $39,000. Reduced comprehensive fee may be available if student is approved to live off-campus by dean of students. Books/supplies: $1,000. Personal expenses: $1,300.

**2009-2010 Financial aid. Need-based:** 272 full-time freshmen applied for aid; 214 were judged to have need; 214 of these received aid. Average need met was 92%. Average scholarship/grant was $23,827; average loan $3,618. 85% of total undergraduate aid awarded as scholarships/grants, 15% as loans/jobs. **Non-need-based:** Awarded to 437 full-time undergraduates, including 110 freshmen. Scholarships awarded for academics, alumni affiliation, music/drama, ROTC.

**Application procedures. Admission:** Closing date 2/1 (postmark date). $40 fee, may be waived for applicants with need, free for online applicants. Admission notification 3/15. Must reply by May 1 or within 2 week(s) if notified thereafter. **Financial aid:** Closing date 3/1. FAFSA, institutional form required. Applicants notified by 3/25; must reply by 5/1 or within 2 week(s) of notification.

**Academics.** Unusual courses and off-campus study options offered during 3-week winter term. Long-term study abroad sites in England, France, Mexico, Japan, and Ireland. Winter-term international locations vary. **Special study options:** Double major, honors, independent study, internships, liberal arts/career combination, student-designed major, study abroad, teacher certification program, Washington semester. Science semester at Oak Ridge National Laboratories, Tennessee, and 5 other national science laboratories, 3-2 engineering program with Columbia University (NY), Washington University (MO), Vanderbilt University (TN), and University of Kentucky. **Credit/placement by examination:** AP, CLEP, IB, SAT, ACT, institutional tests. **Support services:** Study skills assistance, tutoring, writing center.

**Majors. Biology:** General, biochemistry, molecular. **Computer sciences:** Computer science. **Education:** Elementary. **Foreign languages:** Classics, French, German, Spanish. **History:** General. **Math:** General. **Philosophy/**

**religion:** Philosophy, religion. **Physical sciences:** Chemical physics, chemistry, physics. **Psychology:** General. **Social sciences:** Anthropology, economics, international relations, political science, sociology. **Visual/performing arts:** Art, dramatic.

**Most popular majors.** Biology 11%, English 11%, foreign language 10%, history 9%, philosophy/religious studies 6%, psychology 7%, social sciences 25%, visual/performing arts 7%.

**Computing on campus.** 170 workstations in dormitories, library, computer center, student center. Dormitories wired for high-speed internet access and linked to campus network. Commuter students can connect to campus network. Online course registration, helpline, repair service, student web hosting, wireless network available.

**Student life. Freshman orientation:** Mandatory. Preregistration for classes offered. Held at beginning of fall term. **Housing:** Guaranteed on-campus for all undergraduates. Coed dorms, single-sex dorms, special housing for disabled, apartments, fraternity/sorority housing, wellness housing available. **Activities:** Bands, campus ministries, choral groups, dance, drama, film society, international student organizations, literary magazine, music ensembles, student government, student newspaper, symphony orchestra, TV station, student activities council, volunteer services, diversity student union, Christian Fellowship, Campus Democrats and Republicans, ecumenical organization, peace organization, student environmental organization, Muslim student association.

**Athletics.** NCAA. **Intercollegiate:** Baseball M, basketball, cross-country, diving, field hockey W, football (tackle) M, golf, soccer, softball W, swimming, tennis, track and field, volleyball W. **Intramural:** Badminton, basketball, bowling, cross-country, fencing, field hockey W, football (tackle), golf, racquetball, rugby M, soccer, softball, swimming, table tennis, tennis, track and field, volleyball, wrestling M. **Team name:** Colonels.

**Student services.** Alcohol/substance abuse counseling, chaplain/spiritual director, career counseling, student employment services, financial aid counseling, health services, minority student services, personal counseling, placement for graduates. **Physically disabled:** Services for visually, hearing impaired.

**Contact.** E-mail: admission@centre.edu
Phone: (859) 238-5350 Toll-free number: (800) 423-6236
Fax: (859) 238-5373
Bob Nesmith, Director of Admission, Centre College, 600 West Walnut Street, Danville, KY 40422-1394

## Clear Creek Baptist Bible College
**Pineville, Kentucky**
**www.ccbbc.edu**                                    CB code: 5975

- Private 4-year Bible college affiliated with Southern Baptist Convention
- Residential campus in small town
- 168 degree-seeking undergraduates: 26% part-time, 21% women, 1% African American
- Application essay, interview required

**General.** Founded in 1926. Regionally accredited; also accredited by ABHE. Adult family Bible college affiliated with Kentucky Baptist Convention that trains individuals for ministry in local church. Prefer students to be at least 21 years of age. **Degrees:** 32 bachelor's, 6 associate awarded. **Location:** 110 miles from Lexington; 76 miles from Knoxville, TN. **Calendar:** Semester, limited summer session. **Full-time faculty:** 6 total; 83% have terminal degrees. **Part-time faculty:** 17 total; 35% have terminal degrees, 24% women. **Class size:** 80% < 20, 20% 20-39. **Special facilities:** Family life center, hiking/walking trails, campus thrift store.

**Freshman class profile.** 20 applied, 20 admitted, 20 enrolled.

**Basis for selection.** Open admission. Applicants must demonstrate a clear call to the gospel ministry. Recommendations by church required. **Homeschooled:** Transcript of courses and grades required.

**2009-2010 Annual costs.** Tuition/fees: $5,322. Room/board: $3,750. Books/supplies: $800. Personal expenses: $1,600.

**2008-2009 Financial aid. Non-need-based:** Scholarships awarded for academics.

**Application procedures. Admission:** Priority date 7/15; deadline 8/2 (receipt date). $40 fee. Admission notification on a rolling basis. **Financial aid:** Priority date 6/30; no closing date. FAFSA, institutional form required. Applicants notified on a rolling basis.

**Academics. Special study options:** Cross-registration, distance learning, double major, dual enrollment of high school students, independent study. **Credit/placement by examination:** CLEP, institutional tests. **Support services:** Reduced course load, remedial instruction, study skills assistance, tutoring.

**Majors. Theology:** Bible.

**Computing on campus.** 12 workstations in library, computer center. Dormitories wired for high-speed internet access and linked to campus network. Online course registration, online library, wireless network available.

**Student life. Freshman orientation:** Available. Preregistration for classes offered. Four-day program held week of registration. **Policies:** Dress code; no tobacco, alcohol, or drugs on campus. Religious observance required. **Housing:** Single-sex dorms, apartments, wellness housing available. $50 nonrefundable deposit, deadline 7/25. Cottages, family housing available. **Activities:** Campus ministries, choral groups, drama, music ensembles, radio station, student government, student newspaper, Women's Missionary Union, Brotherhood, Young Disciples, Acteens, Royal Ambassadors, Girls in Action, Mission Friends.

**Athletics. Intramural:** Basketball, football (non-tackle) M, softball, swimming, table tennis, tennis, volleyball.

**Student services.** Chaplain/spiritual director, career counseling, student employment services, financial aid counseling, health services, on-campus daycare, personal counseling, placement for graduates, veterans' counselor.

**Contact.** E-mail: ccbbc@ccbbc.edu
Phone: (606) 337-3196 Toll-free number: (866) 340-3196
Fax: (606) 337-2372
Billy Howell, Director of Admissions, Clear Creek Baptist Bible College, 300 Clear Creek Road, Pineville, KY 40977-9754

## Eastern Kentucky University
**Richmond, Kentucky**                              CB member
**www.eku.edu**                                     CB code: 1200

- Public 4-year university
- Residential campus in large town
- 13,151 degree-seeking undergraduates: 12% part-time, 57% women
- 2,277 graduate students
- 69% of applicants admitted
- SAT or ACT (ACT writing optional) required
- 38% graduate within 6 years

**General.** Founded in 1906. Regionally accredited. Courses offered at additional sites in Corbin, Danville, Manchester, Lancaster, London, Somerset and Barbourville. **Degrees:** 2,128 bachelor's, 195 associate awarded; master's offered. **ROTC:** Army. **Location:** 28 miles from Lexington, 110 miles from Cincinnati. **Calendar:** Semester, extensive summer session. **Full-time faculty:** 673 total. **Part-time faculty:** 451 total. **Class size:** 48% < 20, 44% 20-39, 4% 40-49, 3% 50-99, 1% >100. **Special facilities:** Planetarium, nature preserves, law enforcement facilities, music library.

**Freshman class profile.** 8,339 applied, 5,742 admitted, 2,564 enrolled.

| Mid 50% test scores | | | |
|---|---|---|---|
| SAT math: | 440-550 | Out-of-state: | 17% |
| ACT composite: | 18-24 | Live on campus: | 69% |
| Return as sophomores: | 68% | Fraternities: | 13% |
| | | Sororities: | 8% |

**Basis for selection.** Out-of-state applicants must rank in top half of graduating class or have 21 ACT or 890 SAT (exclusive of Writing). Resident applicants must have completed specified high school curriculum. Applicants without college preparatory courses subject to remediation. ACT only required for placement for in-state applicants. Interview recommended. Audition recommended for music majors. Portfolio recommended for art and graphic art majors. **Homeschooled:** Transcript of courses and grades required.

**High school preparation.** 25 units required. Required units include English 4, mathematics 3, social studies 3, science 3 (laboratory 1), foreign language 2 and academic electives 7. Art, drama, music, and computer science also recommended.

**2009-2010 Annual costs.** Tuition/fees: $6,312; $17,280 out-of-state. Room/board: $6,480. Books/supplies: $1,000. Personal expenses: $1,500.

**2009-2010 Financial aid. Non-need-based:** Scholarships awarded for academics, alumni affiliation, art, athletics, job skills, leadership, minority status, music/drama, ROTC.

**Application procedures. Admission:** Closing date 8/1. $30 fee, may be waived for applicants with need. Admission notification on a rolling basis beginning on or about 8/1. **Financial aid:** Priority date 3/15; no closing date. FAFSA required. Applicants notified on a rolling basis starting 4/1.

**Academics. Special study options:** Cooperative education, distance learning, double major, ESL, honors, independent study, internships, liberal arts/career combination, student-designed major, study abroad, teacher certification program. **Credit/placement by examination:** AP, CLEP, SAT, ACT, institutional tests. 30 credit hours maximum toward associate degree, 65 toward bachelor's. **Support services:** Learning center, pre-admission summer program, reduced course load, remedial instruction, study skills assistance, tutoring, writing center.

**Majors. Agriculture:** Ornamental horticulture, turf management. **Area/ethnic studies:** Canadian. **Biology:** General, bacteriology, ecology. **Business:** General, accounting, business admin, fashion, finance, insurance, management information systems, managerial economics, marketing, office management. **Communications:** General, broadcast journalism, journalism, public relations. **Computer sciences:** General, computer science. **Conservation:** Management/policy, wildlife. **Education:** Art, biology, business, Deaf/hearing impaired, elementary, family/consumer sciences, geography, mathematics, middle, music, physical, science, Spanish, special, speech impaired, technology/industrial arts, trade/industrial. **Engineering:** Science. **Engineering technology:** Architectural, manufacturing, water quality. **Family/consumer sciences:** Family studies, food/nutrition, housing. **Foreign languages:** General, French, German, sign language interpretation, Spanish. **Health:** Clinical lab assistant, clinical lab science, clinical lab technology, EMT paramedic, health care admin, medical assistant, medical records admin, medical records technology, nursing (RN), predental, premedicine, preop/surgical nursing, prepharmacy. **History:** General. **Legal studies:** Paralegal. **Liberal arts:** Arts/sciences. **Math:** General, statistics. **Parks/recreation:** General, facilities management. **Philosophy/religion:** Philosophy. **Physical sciences:** Chemistry, geology, physics. **Protective services:** Corrections, fire safety technology, forensics, police science, security services. **Psychology:** General. **Public administration:** Social work. **Social sciences:** Anthropology, economics, geography, political science, sociology. **Transportation:** Aviation. **Visual/performing arts:** Art, ceramics, dramatic, drawing, interior design, painting, printmaking, sculpture, studio arts.

**Most popular majors.** Business/marketing 11%, education 13%, health sciences 15%, security/protective services 15%.

**Computing on campus.** 250 workstations in dormitories, library, computer center, student center. Dormitories wired for high-speed internet access and linked to campus network. Commuter students can connect to campus network. Online course registration, online library, helpline, wireless network available.

**Student life. Freshman orientation:** Mandatory. Preregistration for classes offered. **Policies:** Students required to live on-campus until age 21 unless living with parent or guardian. **Housing:** Guaranteed on-campus for freshmen. Coed dorms, single-sex dorms, apartments, fraternity/sorority housing available. $100 fully refundable deposit. **Activities:** Bands, choral groups, dance, drama, literary magazine, music ensembles, musical theater, radio station, student government, student newspaper, symphony orchestra, 160 organizations available.

**Athletics.** NCAA. **Intercollegiate:** Baseball M, basketball, cheerleading, cross-country, football (tackle) M, golf, soccer W, softball W, swimming, tennis, track and field, volleyball W. **Intramural:** Basketball, football (tackle) M, golf, racquetball, softball, tennis, volleyball. **Team name:** Colonels.

**Student services.** Alcohol/substance abuse counseling, chaplain/spiritual director, career counseling, student employment services, financial aid counseling, health services, personal counseling, placement for graduates, veterans' counselor. **Physically disabled:** Services for visually, speech, hearing impaired.

**Contact.** E-mail: admissions@eku.edu
Phone: (859) 622-2106 Toll-free number: (800) 465-9191
Fax: (859) 622-8024
Steve Byrn, Director of Admissions, Eastern Kentucky University, SSB CPO 54, 521 Lancaster Avenue, Richmond, KY 40475-3102

## Georgetown College
### Georgetown, Kentucky
**www.georgetowncollege.edu**                    CB code: 1249

- Private 4-year liberal arts college affiliated with Southern Baptist Convention
- Residential campus in large town
- 1,297 degree-seeking undergraduates: 1% part-time, 56% women, 7% African American, 1% Hispanic American, 1% international

- 525 degree-seeking graduate students
- 79% of applicants admitted
- SAT or ACT (ACT writing optional) required
- 60% graduate within 6 years; 48% enter graduate study

**General.** Founded in 1829. Regionally accredited. **Degrees:** 273 bachelor's awarded; master's offered. **ROTC:** Army, Air Force. **Location:** 12 miles from Lexington, 60 miles from Louisville. **Calendar:** Semester, limited summer session. **Full-time faculty:** 110 total; 94% have terminal degrees, 6% minority, 42% women. **Part-time faculty:** 151 total; 2% minority, 17% women. **Class size:** 63% < 20, 37% 20-39, less than 1% 40-49. **Special facilities:** Planetarium, Foucault pendulum, arboretum, fine arts building.

**Freshman class profile.** 1,720 applied, 1,363 admitted, 378 enrolled.

| Mid 50% test scores | | | |
|---|---|---|---|
| SAT critical reading: | 430-570 | Rank in top quarter: | 60% |
| SAT math: | 480-560 | Rank in top tenth: | 31% |
| ACT composite: | 21-26 | Return as sophomores: | 79% |
| GPA 3.75 or higher: | 30% | Out-of-state: | 14% |
| GPA 3.50-3.74: | 27% | Live on campus: | 93% |
| GPA 3.0-3.49: | 32% | International: | 1% |
| GPA 2.0-2.99: | 11% | Fraternities: | 23% |
| | | Sororities: | 31% |

**Basis for selection.** School achievement record, test scores, and rank in top half of class most important. Interview recommended for academically weak or special needs applicants. Audition recommended for music and communication arts majors. Portfolio recommended for art majors. **Homeschooled:** Transcript of courses and grades required. Essay required.

**High school preparation.** College-preparatory program recommended. 20 units recommended. Recommended units include English 4, mathematics 3, social studies 2, science 3 and foreign language 2.

**2009-2010 Annual costs.** Tuition/fees: $26,080. Per-credit-hour charge for one course is $800; for more than one course or hours over 18 the per-credit-hour charge is $1,080. Room/board: $7,030.

**2009-2010 Financial aid. Need-based:** Average need met was 86.7%. Average scholarship/grant was $21,622; average loan $3,229. 83% of total undergraduate aid awarded as scholarships/grants, 17% as loans/jobs. **Non-need-based:** Scholarships awarded for academics, alumni affiliation, art, athletics, leadership, minority status, music/drama, religious affiliation, ROTC, state residency.

**Application procedures. Admission:** Priority date 5/1; deadline 8/1 (postmark date). $30 fee, may be waived for applicants with need. Admission notification on a rolling basis beginning on or about 10/1. Must reply by May 1 or within 4 week(s) if notified thereafter. **Financial aid:** Priority date 2/15, closing date 3/15. FAFSA, institutional form required. Must reply by 5/1.

**Academics. Special study options:** Accelerated study, cooperative education, double major, dual enrollment of high school students, honors, independent study, internships, liberal arts/career combination, student-designed major, study abroad, teacher certification program. 3-2 programs in Nursing and in Engineering with the University of Kentucky. **Credit/placement by examination:** AP, CLEP, IB, SAT, ACT, institutional tests. **Support services:** Study skills assistance, tutoring, writing center.

**Majors. Area/ethnic studies:** American, European. **Biology:** General, ecology. **Business:** General, accounting. **Communications:** Media studies. **Computer sciences:** General. **Education:** Elementary, middle, music, special. **Foreign languages:** French, German, Spanish. **Health:** Athletic training, predental, prenursing, prepharmacy, preveterinary. **History:** General. **Liberal arts:** Arts/sciences. **Math:** General. **Parks/recreation:** Exercise sciences, health/fitness. **Philosophy/religion:** Philosophy, religion. **Physical sciences:** Chemistry, physics. **Psychology:** General. **Social sciences:** Economics, political science, sociology. **Visual/performing arts:** Dramatic, studio arts. **Other:** Computational science, Environmental science, Security studies.

**Most popular majors.** Business/marketing 15%, communications/journalism 10%, education 8%, English 10%, parks/recreation 9%, psychology 11%, social sciences 11%.

**Computing on campus.** 115 workstations in library, computer center, student center. Dormitories wired for high-speed internet access and linked to campus network. Commuter students can connect to campus network. Online course registration, online library, helpline, repair service, wireless network available.

**Student life. Freshman orientation:** Mandatory, $100 fee. Preregistration for classes offered. Five-day orientation held prior to beginning of fall semester. **Policies:** Academic honor code enforced. **Housing:** Single-sex

dorms, fraternity/sorority housing available. $200 deposit, deadline 5/1. Mini-dorms of fewer than 80 students available; apartments available for seniors.
**Activities:** Bands, campus ministries, choral groups, dance, drama, literary magazine, music ensembles, Model UN, musical theater, radio station, student government, student newspaper, Baptist student union, Fellowship of Christian Athletes, union of black leaders.

**Athletics.** NAIA. **Intercollegiate:** Baseball M, basketball, cheerleading M, cross-country, football (tackle) M, golf, soccer, softball W, tennis, track and field, volleyball W. **Intramural:** Basketball, equestrian, football (non-tackle), golf, racquetball, soccer, softball, table tennis, tennis, volleyball. **Team name:** Tigers.

**Student services.** Alcohol/substance abuse counseling, chaplain/spiritual director, career counseling, student employment services, financial aid counseling, health services, minority student services, personal counseling, placement for graduates.

**Contact.** E-mail: admissions@georgetowncollege.edu
Phone: (502) 863-8009 Toll-free number: (800) 788-9985
Fax: (502) 868-7733
Georgetown College, 400 East College Street, Georgetown, KY 40324

## ITT Technical Institute: Louisville
**Louisville, Kentucky**
www.itt-tech.edu                          CB code: 2728

- For-profit 4-year technical college
- Large city

**General.** Accredited by ACICS. **Calendar:** Quarter.

**Contact.** Phone: (502) 327-7424
Director of Recruitment, 10509 Timberwood Circle, Louisville, KY 40223

## Kentucky Christian University
**Grayson, Kentucky**
www.kcu.edu                               CB code: 1377

- Private 4-year Bible and liberal arts college affiliated with Independent Christian Church/Church of Christ
- Residential campus in small town
- 675 degree-seeking undergraduates
- 70% of applicants admitted
- SAT or ACT (ACT writing optional), application essay required

**General.** Founded in 1919. Regionally accredited. **Degrees:** 98 bachelor's awarded; master's offered. **ROTC:** Army. **Location:** 25 miles from Ashland, 100 miles from Lexington. **Calendar:** Semester, limited summer session. **Full-time faculty:** 34 total; 71% have terminal degrees, 26% women. **Part-time faculty:** 25 total; 8% have terminal degrees, 40% women. **Class size:** 78% < 20, 15% 20-39, 4% 40-49, 3% 50-99.

**Freshman class profile.** 381 applied, 267 admitted, 144 enrolled.

| Mid 50% test scores | | ACT composite: | 15-24 |
|---|---|---|---|
| SAT critical reading: | 370-520 | Out-of-state: | 44% |
| SAT math: | 390-510 | Live on campus: | 91% |

**Basis for selection.** High school grades, rank in class, ACT or SAT test scores, personal references, and religious commitment given equal weight. Interview recommended for academically weak. **Learning Disabled:** Students with special needs should contact Director of Campus Counseling to make arrangements for special accommodations.

**2009-2010 Annual costs.** Tuition/fees: $13,220. Room/board: $5,800.

**2008-2009 Financial aid. Non-need-based:** Scholarships awarded for academics, alumni affiliation, leadership, minority status, music/drama, religious affiliation.

**Application procedures. Admission:** No deadline. $30 fee. Admission notification on a rolling basis. **Financial aid:** Priority date 3/1; no closing date. FAFSA required. Applicants notified on a rolling basis starting 3/15; must reply within 2 week(s) of notification.

**Academics.** All students required to major in Bible as a second degree. **Special study options:** Distance learning, double major, dual enrollment of high school students, independent study, internships, liberal arts/career combination, study abroad, teacher certification program. **Credit/placement by examination:** AP, CLEP, IB, ACT. **Support services:** Learning center, reduced course load, remedial instruction, study skills assistance, tutoring, writing center.

**Majors. Business:** Business admin. **Education:** Elementary, English, middle, music, secondary, social studies. **Health:** Nursing (RN). **History:** General. **Liberal arts:** Humanities. **Psychology:** Counseling. **Public administration:** Social work. **Theology:** Bible, pastoral counseling, sacred music. **Visual/performing arts:** Music management, music performance. **Other:** University studies.

**Most popular majors.** Business/marketing 12%, education 24%, health sciences 14%, interdisciplinary studies 8%, liberal arts 6%, social sciences 10%, theological studies 23%.

**Computing on campus.** 50 workstations in library, computer center, student center. Dormitories wired for high-speed internet access and linked to campus network. Commuter students can connect to campus network. Online library, helpline, repair service, wireless network available.

**Student life. Freshman orientation:** Mandatory. Preregistration for classes offered. **Policies:** All students under 26 not living with parents must live in on-campus housing. Religious observance required. **Housing:** Guaranteed on-campus for all undergraduates. Single-sex dorms, special housing for disabled, apartments available. $100 nonrefundable deposit. **Activities:** Bands, campus ministries, choral groups, drama, international student organizations, music ensembles, student government, Global Mission Awareness, Pi Chi Delta, Collegiate Music Educators National Conference, Herodotus Society, Laos Protos, American Association of Christian Counselors, Students in Free Enterprise.

**Athletics.** NAIA, NCCAA. **Intercollegiate:** Basketball, cheerleading M, cross-country, football (tackle) M, soccer, volleyball W. **Intramural:** Basketball, football (non-tackle) M, soccer, softball, table tennis, volleyball. **Team name:** Knights.

**Student services.** Chaplain/spiritual director, career counseling, financial aid counseling, health services, minority student services, personal counseling, women's services. **Physically disabled:** Services for visually, hearing impaired.

**Contact.** E-mail: knights@kcu.edu
Phone: (606) 474-3266 Toll-free number: (800) 522-3181
Fax: (606) 474-3155
Sandra Deakins, Vice President of Enrollment Management, Kentucky Christian University, 100 Academic Parkway, Grayson, KY 41143-2205

## Kentucky Mountain Bible College
**Vancleve, Kentucky**
www.kmbc.edu                              CB code: 1384

- Private 4-year Bible college affiliated with Kentucky Mountain Holiness Association
- Residential campus in rural community
- 60 degree-seeking undergraduates
- ACT (writing optional), application essay required

**General.** Founded in 1931. Accredited by ABHE. **Degrees:** 8 bachelor's, 1 associate awarded. **Location:** 75 miles from Lexington. **Calendar:** Semester. **Part-time faculty:** 16 total; 12% have terminal degrees, 19% women. **Class size:** 84% < 20, 16% 20-39.

**Freshman class profile.**

| Mid 50% test scores | | GPA 2.0-2.99: | 50% |
|---|---|---|---|
| ACT composite: | 15-21 | Rank in top quarter: | 11% |
| GPA 3.75 or higher: | 7% | Rank in top tenth: | 11% |
| GPA 3.50-3.74: | 29% | Out-of-state: | 30% |
| GPA 3.0-3.49: | 14% | Live on campus: | 100% |

**Basis for selection.** Open admission, but selective for some programs and for out-of-state students. All students must have C average or above and provide 2 recommendations. 15 ACT required. Provisional admission granted. Interview recommended.

**High school preparation.** 18 units required. Required and recommended units include English 4, mathematics 2, history 2 and science 2. A total of 10 units in English, math, science or language required out of 18 units.

**2009-2010 Annual costs.** Tuition/fees: $6,330. Room/board: $3,900. Books/supplies: $400. Personal expenses: $250.

**2009-2010 Financial aid. Need-based:** 55% of total undergraduate aid awarded as scholarships/grants, 45% as loans/jobs. **Non-need-based:** Scholarships awarded for academics, job skills, leadership, music/drama.

**Application procedures. Admission:** Priority date 6/1; no deadline. $25 fee, may be waived for applicants with need. Admission notification on a rolling basis. **Financial aid:** Priority date 4/1, closing date 6/30. FAFSA, institutional form required. Applicants notified on a rolling basis starting 3/15.

**Academics.** **Special study options:** Combined bachelor's/graduate degree, distance learning, independent study, internships, teacher certification program. **Credit/placement by examination:** AP, CLEP, ACT. 20 credit hours maximum toward associate degree, 20 toward bachelor's. **Support services:** Reduced course load, remedial instruction, study skills assistance, tutoring.

**Majors.** **Communications:** General. **Education:** Elementary. **Theology:** Missionary, religious ed, sacred music, theology.

**Computing on campus.** 12 workstations in library, computer center. Dormitories wired for high-speed internet access and linked to campus network. Commuter students can connect to campus network. Wireless network available.

**Student life.** **Freshman orientation:** Mandatory. Preregistration for classes offered. 2-day program held immediately before semester; includes Bible-knowledge testing. **Policies:** Religious observance required. **Housing:** Guaranteed on-campus for all undergraduates. Single-sex dorms, apartments, wellness housing available. Pets allowed in dorm rooms. **Activities:** Campus ministries, choral groups, drama, radio station, student government, student newspaper, missionary student involvement group, student council, class organizations.

**Athletics.** **Intramural:** Basketball M, volleyball W.

**Student services.** Chaplain/spiritual director, financial aid counseling, health services, personal counseling.

**Contact.**  E-mail: kmbc@kmbc.edu
Phone: (606) 693-5000 ext. 130 Toll-free number: (800) 879-5622 ext. 130
Fax: (606) 693-4884
David Lorimer, Chief Admissions Counselor, Kentucky Mountain Bible College, Box 10, Vancleve, KY 41385-0010

## Kentucky State University
**Frankfort, Kentucky**                      **CB member**
www.kysu.edu                                 **CB code: 1368**

- Public 4-year university and liberal arts college
- Residential campus in large town
- 2,326 degree-seeking undergraduates: 12% part-time, 58% women, 64% African American, 1% Hispanic American, 1% international
- 181 degree-seeking graduate students
- SAT or ACT (ACT writing optional) required

**General.** Founded in 1886. Regionally accredited. **Degrees:** 184 bachelor's, 39 associate awarded; master's offered. **ROTC:** Army, Air Force. **Location:** 50 miles from Louisville, 25 miles from Lexington. **Calendar:** Semester, limited summer session. **Full-time faculty:** 130 total; 68% have terminal degrees, 35% minority, 43% women. **Part-time faculty:** 52 total; 2% have terminal degrees, 35% minority, 65% women. **Class size:** 58% < 20, 40% 20-39, 1% 40-49, less than 1% >100. **Special facilities:** Center of excellence for the study of Kentucky African Americans, land grant institution.

### Freshman class profile.

| Mid 50% test scores | | | |
|---|---|---|---|
| SAT critical reading: | 360-460 | GPA 3.50-3.74: | 6% |
| SAT math: | 340-460 | GPA 3.0-3.49: | 16% |
| SAT writing: | 350-440 | GPA 2.0-2.99: | 62% |
| ACT composite: | 15-19 | Return as sophomores: | 51% |
| GPA 3.75 or higher: | 2% | Out-of-state: | 58% |
| | | Live on campus: | 71% |

**Basis for selection.** Unconditional admission for graduates of accredited high schools who meet Pre-College Curriculum requirements and have 430 admission index. Interview recommended for nursing majors. Audition recommended for music majors. Portfolio recommended for art majors. Interview recommended and essay required of applicants to College of Leadership Studies. **Homeschooled:** Transcript of courses and grades required. Notarized statement from the homeschool teacher detailing the content and duration of the student's homeschool curriculum required.

**High school preparation.** College-preparatory program recommended. 17 units required. Required units include English 4, mathematics 3, social studies 3, science 3, foreign language 2 and visual/performing arts 1.

**2009-2010 Annual costs.** Tuition/fees: $5,920; $14,208 out-of-state. Room/board: $6,480. Books/supplies: $1,300. Personal expenses: $3,000.

**2009-2010 Financial aid.** **Need-based:** 457 full-time freshmen applied for aid; 455 were judged to have need; 414 of these received aid. Average need met was 18%. Average scholarship/grant was $5,739; average loan $3,441. 50% of total undergraduate aid awarded as scholarships/grants, 50% as loans/jobs. **Non-need-based:** Awarded to 1,035 full-time undergraduates, including 263 freshmen. Scholarships awarded for academics, alumni affiliation, art, athletics, minority status, music/drama.

**Application procedures.** **Admission:** No deadline. $30 fee, may be waived for applicants with need. Admission notification on a rolling basis. **Financial aid:** Priority date 4/15; no closing date. FAFSA required. Applicants notified by 4/1; must reply within 2 week(s) of notification.

**Academics.** **Special study options:** Combined bachelor's/graduate degree, cooperative education, distance learning, double major, dual enrollment of high school students, ESL, honors, independent study, internships, liberal arts/career combination, student-designed major, study abroad, teacher certification program. **Credit/placement by examination:** AP, CLEP, IB, SAT, ACT. **Support services:** Learning center, pre-admission summer program, reduced course load, remedial instruction, study skills assistance, tutoring, writing center.

**Majors.** **Biology:** General. **Business:** General. **Communications:** Journalism. **Computer sciences:** General, information technology. **Education:** Elementary, physical. **Family/consumer sciences:** Family studies. **Health:** Nursing (RN). **Liberal arts:** Arts/sciences. **Math:** General. **Physical sciences:** Chemistry. **Protective services:** Criminal justice. **Psychology:** General. **Public administration:** General, social work. **Social sciences:** General, political science. **Visual/performing arts:** Studio arts.

**Most popular majors.** Biology 10%, business/marketing 15%, computer/information sciences 6%, education 7%, liberal arts 17%, public administration/social services 7%, security/protective services 8%, social sciences 6%.

**Computing on campus.** 306 workstations in dormitories, library, student center. Dormitories wired for high-speed internet access and linked to campus network. Commuter students can connect to campus network. Online library, helpline, repair service, wireless network available.

**Student life.** **Freshman orientation:** Mandatory. Preregistration for classes offered. **Housing:** Guaranteed on-campus for freshmen. Coed dorms, single-sex dorms available. $300 nonrefundable deposit. **Activities:** Bands, campus ministries, choral groups, dance, drama, international student organizations, music ensembles, musical theater, opera, student government, student newspaper, Young Democrats, Baptist campus ministries, NAACP, criminal justice club, Wesley Foundation, Apostolic Lighthouse, Students in Free Enterprise, National Society for Black Engineers, Minorities in Agriculture.

**Athletics.** NCAA. **Intercollegiate:** Baseball M, basketball, cheerleading M, cross-country, football (tackle) M, golf M, softball W, track and field, volleyball W. **Team name:** Thorobreds.

**Student services.** Adult student services, alcohol/substance abuse counseling, career counseling, services for economically disadvantaged, student employment services, financial aid counseling, health services, minority student services, personal counseling, placement for graduates, veterans' counselor. **Physically disabled:** Services for visually, hearing impaired.

**Contact.**  E-mail: admissions@kysu.edu
Phone: (502) 597-6813 Toll-free number: (877) 367-5978
Fax: (502) 597-5814
James Burrell, Director of Admissions, Kentucky State University, 400 East Main Street, ASB 312, Frankfort, KY 40601

## Kentucky Wesleyan College
**Owensboro, Kentucky**                      **CB member**
www.kwc.edu                                  **CB code: 1369**

- Private 4-year liberal arts college affiliated with United Methodist Church
- Residential campus in small city
- 862 degree-seeking undergraduates: 3% part-time, 47% women, 9% African American, 1% Hispanic American, 1% international
- 67% of applicants admitted
- SAT or ACT (ACT writing optional) required
- 52% graduate within 6 years; 21% enter graduate study

**General.** Founded in 1858. Regionally accredited. **Degrees:** 138 bachelor's awarded. **ROTC:** Army. **Location:** 116 miles from Louisville; 120 miles from Nashville, TN. **Calendar:** Semester, extensive summer session. **Full-time faculty:** 43 total; 84% have terminal degrees, 9% minority, 40% women. **Part-time faculty:** 44 total; 23% have terminal degrees, 2% minority, 54% women. **Class size:** 70% < 20, 29% 20-39, 1% 40-49. **Special**

**facilities:** Center for the sciences, center for the arts, fully computerized writing workshop, center for business studies.

**Freshman class profile.** 1,240 applied, 828 admitted, 227 enrolled.

| Mid 50% test scores | | | |
|---|---|---|---|
| SAT critical reading: | 450-550 | Rank in top quarter: | 36% |
| SAT math: | 430-520 | Rank in top tenth: | 18% |
| SAT writing: | 390-490 | End year in good standing: | 86% |
| ACT composite: | 19-24 | Return as sophomores: | 63% |
| GPA 3.75 or higher: | 20% | Out-of-state: | 25% |
| GPA 3.50-3.74: | 15% | Live on campus: | 70% |
| GPA 3.0-3.49: | 31% | International: | 1% |
| GPA 2.0-2.99: | 31% | Fraternities: | 10% |
| | | Sororities: | 12% |

**Basis for selection.** Secondary school record very important. Test scores, GPA, class rank, and school activities important. **Homeschooled:** Transcript of courses and grades required.

**High school preparation.** College-preparatory program recommended. 13 units required. Required and recommended units include English 4, mathematics 3, social studies 3, science 3 and foreign language 2.

**2009-2010 Annual costs.** Tuition/fees: $16,870. Room/board: $6,440. Books/supplies: $1,250. Personal expenses: $1,000.

**2009-2010 Financial aid. Need-based:** 210 full-time freshmen applied for aid; 200 were judged to have need; 197 of these received aid. Average need met was 80%. Average scholarship/grant was $14,085; average loan $3,347. 75% of total undergraduate aid awarded as scholarships/grants, 25% as loans/jobs. **Non-need-based:** Awarded to 239 full-time undergraduates, including 46 freshmen. Scholarships awarded for academics, alumni affiliation, art, athletics, leadership, music/drama, religious affiliation, state residency.

**Application procedures. Admission:** No deadline. No application fee. Admission notification on a rolling basis beginning on or about 9/1. **Financial aid:** Closing date 3/15. FAFSA required. Applicants notified on a rolling basis starting 2/15; must reply within 2 week(s) of notification.

**Academics.** Co-curricular leadership program available. **Special study options:** Double major, independent study, internships, liberal arts/career combination, student-designed major, study abroad, teacher certification program, Washington semester. **Credit/placement by examination:** AP, CLEP, IB, SAT, ACT, institutional tests. 42 credit hours maximum toward bachelor's degree. International Baccalaureate Diploma credit will be awarded for advanced course scores of 6 or 7, with up to 10 hours of credit awarded. **Support services:** Learning center, reduced course load, remedial instruction, study skills assistance, tutoring, writing center.

**Majors. Biology:** General, zoology. **Business:** General, accounting, business admin, communications. **Communications:** General. **Computer sciences:** General. **Education:** Art, biology, chemistry, elementary, English, mathematics, middle, physical, social studies, Spanish. **Foreign languages:** Spanish. **History:** General. **Math:** General. **Parks/recreation:** Sports admin. **Philosophy/religion:** Religion. **Physical sciences:** Chemistry, physics. **Protective services:** Criminal justice. **Psychology:** General. **Public administration:** Human services. **Social sciences:** Political science, sociology. **Visual/performing arts:** Art, music management, music performance, studio arts. **Other:** Interdisciplinary studies.

**Most popular majors.** Biology 10%, business/marketing 20%, communications/journalism 6%, education 13%, history 6%, parks/recreation 9%, psychology 9%, security/protective services 9%.

**Computing on campus.** 125 workstations in dormitories, library, computer center, student center. Dormitories wired for high-speed internet access and linked to campus network. Commuter students can connect to campus network. Online course registration, online library, helpline, repair service, wireless network available.

**Student life. Freshman orientation:** Mandatory, $125 fee. Preregistration for classes offered. **Housing:** Guaranteed on-campus for freshmen. Coed dorms, single-sex dorms, special housing for disabled, apartments, fraternity/sorority housing, wellness housing available. $100 fully refundable deposit, deadline 5/1. **Activities:** Bands, campus ministries, choral groups, dance, drama, literary magazine, music ensembles, radio station, student government, student newspaper, student activities programming board, Baptist student union, United Methodist student fellowship, Brothers and Sisters in Christ, criminal justice association, singing club, College Republicans, Young Democrats, Fellowship of Christian Athletes, psychology club.

**Athletics.** NCAA. **Intercollegiate:** Baseball M, basketball, cheerleading, cross-country, football (tackle) M, golf, soccer, softball W, tennis W, volleyball W. **Intramural:** Basketball, bowling, football (non-tackle), soccer, softball, table tennis, tennis, volleyball. **Team name:** Panthers.

**Student services.** Alcohol/substance abuse counseling, chaplain/spiritual director, career counseling, student employment services, financial aid counseling, health services, personal counseling, placement for graduates. **Physically disabled:** Services for visually impaired. **Learning disabled:** Comprehensive services available.

**Contact.** E-mail: admitme@kwc.edu
Phone: (270) 852-3120 Toll-free number: (800) 999-0592
Fax: (270) 852-3133
Lauren Werner, Director of Admissions, Kentucky Wesleyan College, 3000 Frederica Street, Owensboro, KY 42301

## Lindsey Wilson College
**Columbia, Kentucky**
**www.lindsey.edu**                    CB code: 1409

- Private 4-year liberal arts college affiliated with United Methodist Church
- Residential campus in small town
- 1,700 degree-seeking undergraduates

**General.** Founded in 1903. Regionally accredited. **Degrees:** 311 bachelor's, 18 associate awarded; master's offered. **Location:** 100 miles from Louisville. **Calendar:** Semester, limited summer session. **Full-time faculty:** 70 total. **Part-time faculty:** 45 total.

**Freshman class profile.**

| | | | |
|---|---|---|---|
| GPA 3.75 or higher: | 15% | GPA 2.0-2.99: | 42% |
| GPA 3.50-3.74: | 13% | Out-of-state: | 5% |
| GPA 3.0-3.49: | 25% | Live on campus: | 69% |

**Basis for selection.** Open admission, but selective for some programs. Special requirements for education and human services programs. ACCUPLACER or ACT required for placement. Interview recommended.

**2009-2010 Annual costs.** Tuition/fees: $17,870. Room/board: $7,280. Books/supplies: $900. Personal expenses: $1,200.

**2008-2009 Financial aid.** All financial aid based on need.

**Application procedures. Admission:** Priority date 6/1; no deadline. No application fee. Admission notification on a rolling basis beginning on or about 1/1. **Financial aid:** Priority date 4/15; no closing date. FAFSA, institutional form required. Applicants notified on a rolling basis starting 5/1; must reply within 2 week(s) of notification.

**Academics. Special study options:** Dual enrollment of high school students, independent study, internships, student-designed major, study abroad, teacher certification program, weekend college. On-campus and extension evening program for associate degree in business management and computer science, weekend extension program in human services. **Credit/placement by examination:** AP, CLEP. 16 credit hours maximum toward associate degree, 32 toward bachelor's. **Support services:** Learning center, reduced course load, remedial instruction, study skills assistance, tutoring, writing center.

**Majors. Area/ethnic studies:** American. **Biology:** General. **Business:** Business admin. **Communications:** General, journalism. **Education:** Art, biology, elementary, English, mathematics, middle, physical, secondary, social science. **History:** General. **Legal studies:** Prelaw. **Liberal arts:** Humanities. **Math:** General. **Parks/recreation:** Health/fitness. **Philosophy/religion:** Christian. **Protective services:** Criminal justice. **Psychology:** General. **Social sciences:** General. **Visual/performing arts:** Studio arts.

**Most popular majors.** Biology 6%, business/marketing 13%, communications/journalism 7%, education 7%, public administration/social services 47%.

**Computing on campus.** 100 workstations in library, computer center. Dormitories wired for high-speed internet access and linked to campus network. Commuter students can connect to campus network. Online course registration, online library, wireless network available.

**Student life. Freshman orientation:** Available. Preregistration for classes offered. **Policies:** All students not living with family must live in campus housing. **Housing:** Single-sex dorms, apartments, wellness housing available. $40 deposit. **Activities:** Pep band, choral groups, drama, literary magazine, music ensembles, student government, student newspaper, Christian student organizations, Student Ambassadors, black student union, Students in Free Enterprise, Raider Republicans, international student association.

**Athletics.** NAIA. **Intercollegiate:** Baseball M, basketball, bowling, cross-country, golf, soccer, softball W, tennis, track and field, volleyball W. **Intramural:** Basketball, football (tackle), softball, table tennis, tennis, volleyball. **Team name:** Blue Raiders.

**Student services.** Alcohol/substance abuse counseling, chaplain/spiritual director, career counseling, student employment services, financial aid counseling, health services, personal counseling, placement for graduates. **Physically disabled:** Services for visually impaired.

**Contact.** E-mail: admissions@lindsey.edu
Phone: (270) 384-8100 Toll-free number: (800) 264-0138
Fax: (270) 384-8591
Traci Pooler, Dean of Admissions, Lindsey Wilson College, 210 Lindsey Wilson Street, Columbia, KY 42728

## Mid-Continent University
**Mayfield, Kentucky**
**www.midcontinent.edu**       **CB code: 0254**

- Private 4-year Bible and liberal arts college affiliated with Southern Baptist Convention
- Commuter campus in large town
- 1,822 degree-seeking undergraduates: 13% part-time, 64% women, 13% African American, 1% Hispanic American, 2% international
- 57% of applicants admitted
- SAT or ACT (ACT writing optional), application essay required

**General.** Founded in 1949. Regionally accredited. **Degrees:** 321 bachelor's, 178 associate awarded; master's offered. **Location:** 20 miles from Paducah; 125 miles from Nashville, TN. **Calendar:** Semester, limited summer session. **Full-time faculty:** 33 total; 39% have terminal degrees, 18% minority, 15% women. **Part-time faculty:** 113 total; 12% have terminal degrees, 6% minority, 37% women. **Class size:** 82% < 20, 17% 20-39, less than 1% 40-49, less than 1% 50-99.

**Freshman class profile.** 508 applied, 289 admitted, 190 enrolled.

| Mid 50% test scores | | GPA 2.0-2.99: | 48% |
|---|---|---|---|
| SAT critical reading: | 420-450 | Rank in top quarter: | 15% |
| SAT math: | 390-450 | Rank in top tenth: | 2% |
| SAT writing: | 440-440 | End year in good standing: | 93% |
| ACT composite: | 17-21 | Return as sophomores: | 69% |
| GPA 3.75 or higher: | 6% | Out-of-state: | 9% |
| GPA 3.50-3.74: | 4% | Live on campus: | 14% |
| GPA 3.0-3.49: | 38% | International: | 2% |

**Basis for selection.** Secondary school record and standardized test scores most important. Entering students tested in mathematics and English. **Homeschooled:** Statement describing homeschool structure and mission, transcript of courses and grades, letter of recommendation (nonparent) required.

**High school preparation.** College-preparatory program recommended. Required units include English 4, mathematics 2, social studies 2, science 2 and foreign language 1.

**2009-2010 Annual costs.** Tuition/fees: $13,700. Room/board: $6,500. Books/supplies: $1,200. Personal expenses: $1,500.

**2009-2010 Financial aid.** **Need-based:** Average need met was 33%. Average scholarship/grant was $5,479; average loan $2,338. 46% of total undergraduate aid awarded as scholarships/grants, 54% as loans/jobs. **Non-need-based:** Scholarships awarded for academics.

**Application procedures.** **Admission:** Priority date 8/1; no deadline. $20 fee ($20 out-of-state), may be waived for applicants with need. Admission notification on a rolling basis. **Financial aid:** Priority date 3/15, closing date 5/30. FAFSA, institutional form required. Applicants notified on a rolling basis starting 4/1; must reply within 2 week(s) of notification.

**Academics.** Bachelor of Ministry degree awarded after 36 hours above earned baccalaureate degree from regionally accredited institution. Accelerated programs in Business Management for adult learners available. **Special study options:** Accelerated study, combined bachelor's/graduate degree, double major, dual enrollment of high school students, independent study, study abroad, teacher certification program. **Credit/placement by examination:** AP, CLEP, SAT, ACT, institutional tests. 30 credit hours maximum toward bachelor's degree. **Support services:** Remedial instruction, tutoring.

**Majors.** **Business:** Business admin, organizational behavior. **Education:** Elementary. **Math:** General. **Philosophy/religion:** Christian. **Psychology:** General, counseling. **Social sciences:** General. **Theology:** Bible, missionary, religious ed.

**Most popular majors.** Business/marketing 90%.

**Computing on campus.** 43 workstations in library, computer center, student center. Dormitories wired for high-speed internet access. Online library, wireless network available.

---

**Student life. Freshman orientation:** Mandatory. Preregistration for classes offered. 2-3 day orientation process at beginning of academic year. **Policies:** Religious observance required. **Housing:** Single-sex dorms available. $200 fully refundable deposit, deadline 8/1. **Activities:** Student government, student newspaper, Baptist Student Union, Fellowship of Christian Athletes, psychology club, international student association.

**Athletics.** NAIA, NCCAA. **Intercollegiate:** Baseball M, basketball, soccer M, softball W, volleyball W. **Team name:** Cougars, Lady Cougars.

**Student services.** Chaplain/spiritual director, career counseling, financial aid counseling, personal counseling, veterans' counselor. **Physically disabled:** Services for visually, hearing impaired.

**Contact.** E-mail: admissions@midcontinent.edu
Phone: (270) 247-8521 ext. 238 Toll-free number: (866) 894-8878
Fax: (270) 247-3115
Debbie Smith, Director of Admissions, Mid-Continent University, 99 Powell Road East, Mayfield, KY 42066-0357

## Midway College
**Midway, Kentucky**       **CB member**
**www.midway.edu**       **CB code: 1467**

- Private 4-year liberal arts college for women affiliated with Christian Church (Disciples of Christ)
- Commuter campus in small town
- 1,316 degree-seeking undergraduates
- 62 graduate students
- 47% of applicants admitted
- SAT or ACT required

**General.** Founded in 1847. Regionally accredited. Men admitted to evening, weekend and online programs. **Degrees:** 271 bachelor's, 69 associate awarded; master's offered. **ROTC:** Army. **Location:** 12 miles from Lexington, 60 miles from Louisville. **Calendar:** Semester, limited summer session. **Full-time faculty:** 52 total. **Part-time faculty:** 61 total. **Class size:** 80% < 20, 19% 20-39, 1% 40-49. **Special facilities:** Equine science center, riding arena, campus farm.

**Freshman class profile.** 648 applied, 303 admitted, 193 enrolled.

| Mid 50% test scores | | GPA 3.0-3.49: | 36% |
|---|---|---|---|
| SAT critical reading: | 440-480 | GPA 2.0-2.99: | 24% |
| SAT math: | 470-540 | Rank in top quarter: | 42% |
| SAT writing: | 440-500 | Rank in top tenth: | 16% |
| ACT composite: | 18-22 | Out-of-state: | 9% |
| GPA 3.75 or higher: | 15% | Live on campus: | 45% |
| GPA 3.50-3.74: | 23% | | |

**Basis for selection.** High school record and test scores important. Essay and letters of recommendation encouraged. More competitive requirements established for certain programs such as biology, education, nursing. Interview required for majors in nursing; also required of academically weak. Essay recommended for students who are conditionally admitted.

**High school preparation.** 15 units required. Required and recommended units include English 4, mathematics 3, social studies 1, history 1 and science 2. Specific college-preparatory program required for some majors.

**2009-2010 Annual costs.** Tuition/fees: $18,000. Room/board: $6,800. Books/supplies: $1,200. Personal expenses: $1,000.

**Financial aid.** **Non-need-based:** Scholarships awarded for academics, alumni affiliation, art, athletics, leadership, minority status, religious affiliation. **Additional information:** Audition required of applicants for music scholarships. Portfolio required for art scholarships.

**Application procedures.** **Admission:** Priority date 4/1; no deadline. $25 fee, may be waived for applicants with need, free for online applicants. Admission notification on a rolling basis. Must reply by May 1 or within 4 week(s) if notified thereafter. **Financial aid:** Priority date 4/1, closing date 8/1. FAFSA, institutional form required. Applicants notified on a rolling basis; must reply within 4 week(s) of notification.

**Academics.** **Special study options:** Accelerated study, cooperative education, distance learning, double major, dual enrollment of high school students, independent study, internships, liberal arts/career combination, study abroad, teacher certification program. Evening programs in business, nursing and teacher certification. **Credit/placement by examination:** AP, CLEP, IB, institutional tests. 12 credit hours maximum toward associate degree, 12 toward bachelor's. **Support services:** Learning center, reduced course load, remedial instruction, tutoring, writing center.

**Majors. Agriculture:** Equestrian studies. **Biology:** General. **Business:** General, human resources, organizational behavior. **Computer sciences:** General. **Conservation:** Environmental science. **Education:** Elementary, middle, multi-level teacher, secondary, special. **Health:** Health care admin, nursing (RN). **Interdisciplinary:** Intercultural. **Liberal arts:** Arts/sciences. **Math:** General. **Parks/recreation:** Sports admin. **Protective services:** Emergency management/homeland security. **Psychology:** General.

**Most popular majors.** Agriculture 8%, business/marketing 31%, education 48%.

**Computing on campus.** 60 workstations in dormitories, library, computer center, student center. Dormitories wired for high-speed internet access and linked to campus network. Commuter students can connect to campus network. Online course registration, online library, helpline available.

**Student life. Freshman orientation:** Mandatory. Preregistration for classes offered. 2-3 day orientation prior to start of term. **Policies:** All students under 21, unmarried, and not living at home required to live in campus housing. **Housing:** Guaranteed on-campus for all undergraduates. Special housing for disabled, wellness housing available. $100 nonrefundable deposit, deadline 5/1. **Activities:** Campus ministries, choral groups, international student organizations, student government, commuters committee, Fellowship of Christian Athletes, Disciples on Campus, Ruth Slack Roach Scholars.

**Athletics.** NAIA. **Intercollegiate:** Basketball W, cross-country W, equestrian W, soccer W, softball W, tennis W, track and field W, volleyball W. **Team name:** Eagles.

**Student services.** Adult student services, chaplain/spiritual director, career counseling, student employment services, financial aid counseling, health services, personal counseling, placement for graduates.

**Contact.** E-mail: admissions@midway.edu
Phone: (859) 846-5347 Toll-free number: (800) 755-0031
Fax: (859) 846-5787
Jim Wombles, Chief Enrollment Officer, Midway College, 512 East Stephens Street, Midway, KY 40347-1120

## Morehead State University
**Morehead, Kentucky**
**www.moreheadstate.edu**                         CB code: 1487

- Public 4-year university
- Residential campus in large town
- 6,725 degree-seeking undergraduates: 17% part-time, 60% women, 3% African American, 1% Hispanic American
- 1,232 degree-seeking graduate students
- 80% of applicants admitted
- SAT or ACT (ACT writing optional) required
- 39% graduate within 6 years

**General.** Founded in 1922. Regionally accredited. **Degrees:** 952 bachelor's, 150 associate awarded; master's offered. **ROTC:** Army. **Location:** 65 miles from Lexington; 70 miles from Huntington, West Virginia. **Calendar:** Semester, extensive summer session. **Full-time faculty:** 371 total; 67% have terminal degrees, 11% minority, 48% women. **Part-time faculty:** 96 total; 9% minority, 57% women. **Class size:** 52% < 20, 38% 20-39, 7% 40-49, 3% 50-99, less than 1% >100. **Special facilities:** Planetarium, agriculture complex, outdoor learning center at Cave Run, Kentucky folk art center, space science center, space tracking radio telescope, Center for Traditional Music.

**Freshman class profile.** 2,772 applied, 2,217 admitted, 1,260 enrolled.

| Mid 50% test scores | | Rank in top quarter: | 46% |
|---|---|---|---|
| SAT critical reading: | 440-560 | Rank in top tenth: | 21% |
| SAT math: | 460-570 | Return as sophomores: | 71% |
| ACT composite: | 19-24 | Out-of-state: | 15% |
| GPA 3.75 or higher: | 27% | Live on campus: | 71% |
| GPA 3.50-3.74: | 16% | Fraternities: | 12% |
| GPA 3.0-3.49: | 29% | Sororities: | 11% |
| GPA 2.0-2.99: | 26% | | |

**Basis for selection.** Test scores and GPA used to calculate index to determine admission. Status and review of pre-college curriculum important. Interview recommended for applicants to specialized allied health programs. Audition recommended for music majors. Students not meeting academic requirements may request an interview and submit additional documentation in order to be admitted with conditions. **Homeschooled:**

Statement describing homeschool structure and mission, transcript of courses and grades required.

**High school preparation.** College-preparatory program required. 22 units required. Required units include English 4, mathematics 3, social studies 3, history 1, science 3 (laboratory 1), foreign language 2, computer science 1, visual/performing arts 1 and academic electives 7. 1 unit history and appreciation of fine arts required.

**2009-2010 Annual costs.** Tuition/fees: $6,036; $15,096 out-of-state. Tuition is based on enrollment of 15 credit hours. Room/board: $6,192. Books/supplies: $912. Personal expenses: $1,200.

**2008-2009 Financial aid. Need-based:** 1,146 full-time freshmen applied for aid; 891 were judged to have need; 881 of these received aid. Average need met was 76%. Average scholarship/grant was $5,126; average loan $2,954. 87% of total undergraduate aid awarded as scholarships/grants, 13% as loans/jobs. **Non-need-based:** Awarded to 3,301 full-time undergraduates, including 1,064 freshmen. Scholarships awarded for academics, alumni affiliation, art, athletics, leadership, minority status, music/drama, ROTC, state residency.

**Application procedures. Admission:** No deadline. $30 fee. Admission notification on a rolling basis. **Financial aid:** Priority date 3/15; no closing date. FAFSA, institutional form required. Applicants notified on a rolling basis.

**Academics.** 2-year transfer programs in prechiropractic, predentistry, preengineering, preforestry, prelaw, premedicine, preoptometry, prepharmacy, prephysical therapy, preveterinary medicine, and others offered. **Special study options:** Accelerated study, cooperative education, cross-registration, distance learning, double major, dual enrollment of high school students, exchange student, honors, independent study, internships, student-designed major, study abroad, teacher certification program, Washington semester, weekend college. **Credit/placement by examination:** AP, CLEP, IB, SAT, ACT, institutional tests. 16 credit hours maximum toward associate degree, 32 toward bachelor's. **Support services:** Learning center, pre-admission summer program, remedial instruction, study skills assistance, tutoring, writing center.

**Majors. Agriculture:** General. **Biology:** General. **Business:** Accounting, business admin, finance, management information systems, managerial economics, marketing, real estate. **Communications:** General. **Computer sciences:** General. **Education:** Business, early childhood, elementary, health, middle, physical, special. **Engineering technology:** Manufacturing. **Foreign languages:** French, Spanish. **Health:** Medical radiologic technology/radiation therapy, nursing (RN). **History:** General. **Legal studies:** Paralegal. **Math:** General. **Parks/recreation:** Exercise sciences. **Philosophy/religion:** Philosophy. **Physical sciences:** Chemistry, geology, physics. **Psychology:** General. **Public administration:** Social work. **Social sciences:** General, geography, political science, sociology. **Visual/performing arts:** Dramatic, studio arts.

**Most popular majors.** Business/marketing 10%, education 17%, health sciences 7%, liberal arts 15%, parks/recreation 6%, public administration/social services 7%, social sciences 7%.

**Computing on campus.** 2,100 workstations in dormitories, library, computer center, student center. Dormitories wired for high-speed internet access and linked to campus network. Commuter students can connect to campus network. Online course registration, online library, helpline, repair service, student web hosting, wireless network available.

**Student life. Freshman orientation:** Mandatory. Preregistration for classes offered. Offered several times in June and July. **Housing:** Coed dorms, special housing for disabled, apartments, fraternity/sorority housing available. $100 fully refundable deposit. Limited housing available at agriculture complex for agriculture science students. Housing for handicapped students and private rooms available. **Activities:** Bands, choral groups, dance, drama, literary magazine, music ensembles, musical theater, opera, radio station, student government, student newspaper, symphony orchestra, TV station, six religious organizations, Young Democrats, Young Republicans, several service organizations.

**Athletics.** NCAA. **Intercollegiate:** Baseball M, basketball, cheerleading, cross-country, football (tackle) M, golf M, rifle, soccer W, softball W, tennis, track and field, volleyball W. **Intramural:** Archery, badminton, basketball, bowling, football (non-tackle) M, golf, racquetball, soccer M, softball, swimming, table tennis, tennis, track and field, volleyball. **Team name:** Eagles.

**Student services.** Adult student services, alcohol/substance abuse counseling, career counseling, services for economically disadvantaged, student employment services, financial aid counseling, health services, minority student services, personal counseling, veterans' counselor. **Physically disabled:** Services for visually, hearing impaired.

**Contact.** E-mail: admissions@moreheadstate.edu
Phone: (606) 783-2000 Toll-free number: (800) 585-6781
Fax: (606) 783-5038
Jeffrey Liles, Assistant Vice President of Enrollment Services, Morehead State University, 100 Admissions Center, Morehead, KY 40351

---

## Murray State University
**Murray, Kentucky**
**www.murraystate.edu**

**CB member**
**CB code: 1494**

- Public 4-year university
- Residential campus in large town
- 7,571 degree-seeking undergraduates: 11% part-time, 59% women, 6% African American, 1% Asian American, 1% Hispanic American, 2% international
- 1,638 degree-seeking graduate students
- ACT (writing recommended) required
- 49% graduate within 6 years

**General.** Founded in 1922. Regionally accredited. **Degrees:** 1,542 bachelor's, 10 associate awarded; master's offered. **ROTC:** Army. **Location:** 115 miles from Nashville, TN. **Calendar:** Semester, limited summer session. **Full-time faculty:** 406 total; 77% have terminal degrees, 13% minority, 41% women. **Part-time faculty:** 161 total; 35% have terminal degrees, 4% minority, 56% women. **Class size:** 54% < 20, 37% 20-39, 5% 40-49, 3% 50-99, less than 1% >100. **Special facilities:** Biological research station, aquatic wildlife area, veterinary diagnostic research center, center of excellence for reservoir research, NASA-related technology transfer station, 2 farms, archaeological research and excavation site, West Kentucky regional museum, state center of excellence for telecommunication systems management.

**Freshman class profile.** 1,391 enrolled.

| Mid 50% test scores | | | |
|---|---|---|---|
| ACT composite: | 21-25 | Rank in top tenth: | 27% |
| GPA 3.75 or higher: | 26% | Return as sophomores: | 72% |
| GPA 3.50-3.74: | 15% | Out-of-state: | 31% |
| GPA 3.0-3.49: | 32% | Live on campus: | 82% |
| GPA 2.0-2.99: | 26% | International: | 2% |
| Rank in top quarter: | 64% | Fraternities: | 12% |
| | | Sororities: | 10% |

**Basis for selection.** Selective admission to nursing, business and social work programs. Students must rank in top half of class or have 3.0 GPA, 18 ACT and complete precollege curriculum. Interview recommended for art, music, nursing majors. Auditions recommended for music majors. Portfolio recommended for art majors. **Homeschooled:** Transcript of courses and grades required. Students may be asked to verify lab experience and provide GED if ACT score is less than average. **Learning Disabled:** Students should contact Office for Students with Learning Disabilities.

**High school preparation.** College-preparatory program required. 22 units required. Required and recommended units include English 4, mathematics 3-4, social studies 3, science 3-4 (laboratory 1), foreign language 2 and academic electives 5. 1 art appreciation required. Social sciences must include U.S. history and world civilization. 1 arts and 1 computer science recommended. Math must include 3 algebra I and above. Sciences must include biology and chemistry or physics.

**2009-2010 Annual costs.** Tuition/fees: $5,976; $8,852 out-of-district; $16,236 out-of-state. Room/board: $6,562. Books/supplies: $990. Personal expenses: $1,500.

**2009-2010 Financial aid. Need-based:** Average scholarship/grant was $2,912; average loan $2,044. 58% of total undergraduate aid awarded as scholarships/grants, 42% as loans/jobs. **Non-need-based:** Awarded to 3,842 full-time undergraduates, including 684 freshmen. Scholarships awarded for academics, alumni affiliation, art, athletics, job skills, leadership, minority status, music/drama, ROTC, state residency. **Additional information:** Tuition discount for children and grandchildren of out-of-state alumni. Regional tuition for students from certain counties in Illinois, Tennessee, Missouri, and Indiana.

**Application procedures. Admission:** Closing date 8/1 (postmark date). $30 fee, may be waived for applicants with need. Admission notification on a rolling basis. **Financial aid:** Priority date 4/1; no closing date. FAFSA, institutional form required. Applicants notified on a rolling basis starting 4/15.

**Academics. Special study options:** Combined bachelor's/graduate degree, cooperative education, cross-registration, distance learning, double major, dual enrollment of high school students, ESL, exchange student, external degree, honors, independent study, internships, liberal arts/career combination, semester at sea, study abroad, teacher certification program,

weekend college. Cooperative center for study in Britain, Kentucky Institute for International Studies, national and international student exchange. **Credit/placement by examination:** AP, CLEP, ACT, institutional tests. 96 credit hours maximum toward bachelor's degree. **Support services:** Learning center, pre-admission summer program, reduced course load, remedial instruction, study skills assistance, tutoring, writing center.

**Honors college/program.** Based on standardized test scores, GPA, evidence of creative and leadership abilities as displayed in extracurricular interests and activities, and faculty recommendation.

**Majors. Agriculture:** General. **Biology:** General. **Business:** General, accounting, business admin, finance, international, management information systems, marketing. **Communications:** Advertising, journalism, organizational, public relations, radio/tv. **Communications technology:** Desktop publishing, printing management. **Computer sciences:** General, information systems. **Conservation:** Wildlife. **Education:** Art, early childhood, elementary, health, middle, music, special. **Engineering:** Electrical, physics. **Engineering technology:** Civil, drafting, electromechanical, manufacturing, occupational safety, water quality. **Family/consumer sciences:** Food/nutrition. **Foreign languages:** French, German, Spanish. **Health:** Audiology/speech pathology, nursing (RN), veterinary technology/assistant. **History:** General. **Liberal arts:** Arts/sciences. **Math:** General. **Parks/recreation:** Exercise sciences, facilities management, health/fitness. **Philosophy/religion:** Philosophy. **Physical sciences:** Chemistry, geology, physics. **Protective services:** Criminal justice. **Psychology:** General. **Public administration:** Social work. **Social sciences:** Economics, international relations, political science, sociology. **Visual/performing arts:** Dramatic, music management, studio arts.

**Most popular majors.** Business/marketing 13%, communications/journalism 8%, education 15%, engineering/engineering technologies 8%, health sciences 11%, liberal arts 9%.

**Computing on campus.** 1,800 workstations in dormitories, library, computer center, student center. Dormitories wired for high-speed internet access and linked to campus network. Commuter students can connect to campus network. Online course registration, online library, helpline, repair service, student web hosting, wireless network available.

**Student life. Freshman orientation:** Available, $100 fee. Preregistration for classes offered. **Housing:** Guaranteed on-campus for freshmen. Coed dorms, single-sex dorms, special housing for disabled, apartments, fraternity/sorority housing, wellness housing available. $75 deposit, deadline 3/1. **Activities:** Bands, campus ministries, choral groups, dance, drama, film society, international student organizations, literary magazine, music ensembles, musical theater, opera, radio station, student government, student newspaper, symphony orchestra, TV station, Rotaract, Young Democrats, Young Republicans, black student council, Newman center, Baptist student center, Chi Alpha, Christian fellowship, Wesley Foundation.

**Athletics.** NCAA. **Intercollegiate:** Baseball M, basketball, bowling M, cheerleading, cross-country, equestrian, football (tackle) M, golf, rifle, rodeo, soccer W, softball W, tennis, track and field W, volleyball W. **Intramural:** Basketball, football (non-tackle), golf, racquetball, soccer, softball, tennis, volleyball. **Team name:** Racers.

**Student services.** Adult student services, alcohol/substance abuse counseling, chaplain/spiritual director, career counseling, services for economically disadvantaged, student employment services, financial aid counseling, health services, legal services, minority student services, on-campus daycare, personal counseling, placement for graduates, veterans' counselor, women's services. **Physically disabled:** Services for visually, hearing impaired. **Learning disabled:** Comprehensive services available.

**Contact.** E-mail: admissions@murraystate.edu
Phone: (270) 809-2896 Toll-free number: (800) 272-4678
Fax: (270) 809-3780
Shawn Smee, Director Office of Recruitment, Murray State University, 102 Curris Center Murray State University, Murray, KY 42071

---

## Northern Kentucky University
**Highland Heights, Kentucky**
**www.nku.edu**

**CB member**
**CB code: 1574**

- Public 4-year university
- Commuter campus in small town
- 12,461 degree-seeking undergraduates: 20% part-time, 56% women, 6% African American, 1% Asian American, 1% Hispanic American, 1% international
- 2,028 degree-seeking graduate students
- 69% of applicants admitted
- SAT or ACT required

**General.** Founded in 1968. Regionally accredited. **Degrees:** 1,836 bachelor's, 124 associate awarded; master's, doctoral, professional offered. **ROTC:** Army, Air Force. **Location:** 7 miles from Cincinnati. **Calendar:** Semester, extensive summer session. **Full-time faculty:** 536 total; 14% minority, 49% women. **Part-time faculty:** 617 total; 8% minority, 57% women. **Special facilities:** Planetarium, anthropology museum, biology museum, cadaver lab.

**Freshman class profile.** 6,887 applied, 4,767 admitted, 2,239 enrolled.

| Mid 50% test scores | | GPA 2.0-2.99: | 37% |
|---|---|---|---|
| SAT critical reading: | 420-540 | Return as sophomores: | 65% |
| SAT math: | 430-540 | Out-of-state: | 30% |
| ACT composite: | 19-24 | Live on campus: | 34% |
| GPA 3.75 or higher: | 17% | International: | 1% |
| GPA 3.50-3.74: | 13% | Fraternities: | 5% |
| GPA 3.0-3.49: | 29% | Sororities: | 5% |

**Basis for selection.** Requirements vary by program. Students with 2 or more deficiencies may be required to submit essay, letters of recommendation, and activities portfoloio. **Homeschooled:** Transcript of courses and grades required.

**High school preparation.** College-preparatory program required. 22 units required. Required units include English 4, mathematics 3, social studies 3, history 1, science 3 (laboratory 1), foreign language 2, computer science 1, visual/performing arts 1 and academic electives 5.

**2009-2010 Annual costs.** Tuition/fees: $6,792; $12,792 out-of-state. Room/board: $7,210.

**2008-2009 Financial aid. Need-based:** 1,609 full-time freshmen applied for aid; 1,178 were judged to have need; 1,167 of these received aid. Average need met was 58%. Average scholarship/grant was $5,379; average loan $2,971. 32% of total undergraduate aid awarded as scholarships/grants, 68% as loans/jobs. **Non-need-based:** Awarded to 3,100 full-time undergraduates, including 1,017 freshmen. Scholarships awarded for academics, alumni affiliation, art, athletics, leadership, music/drama, state residency.

**Application procedures. Admission:** Priority date 5/1; deadline 8/1 (postmark date). $40 fee, may be waived for applicants with need. Admission notification on a rolling basis beginning on or about 9/15. Must reply by May 1 or within 2 week(s) if notified thereafter. **Financial aid:** Priority date 3/1; no closing date. FAFSA required. Applicants notified on a rolling basis starting 4/1.

**Academics. Special study options:** Accelerated study, cooperative education, cross-registration, distance learning, double major, dual enrollment of high school students, ESL, exchange student, honors, independent study, internships, liberal arts/career combination, student-designed major, study abroad, teacher certification program, weekend college. Introductory-level courses and some graduate-level courses and business seminars available at University College Campus in Covington; Summer NKU Academy gives remediation for denied students. **Credit/placement by examination:** CLEP, IB, institutional tests. 24 credit hours maximum toward associate degree, 45 toward bachelor's. Credit awarded for CLEP, military, vocational, and National Occupational Competency Testing Institute exams. **Support services:** Learning center, pre-admission summer program, reduced course load, remedial instruction, study skills assistance, tutoring, writing center.

**Honors college/program.** 26 ACT or 1760 SAT, 3.5 GPA, and rank in top 10% of high school class required. Students can take courses towards honors minor. Courses vary in topic on a semester basis and most classes have 15 students or less. 550 total students currently enrolled.

**Majors. Biology:** General. **Business:** General, accounting, business admin, entrepreneurial studies, finance, management information systems, managerial economics, marketing, organizational behavior. **Communications:** Broadcast journalism, journalism, public relations. **Computer sciences:** General, information systems, information technology. **Conservation:** Environmental science. **Education:** Business, elementary, kindergarten/preschool, middle, physical, trade/industrial. **Engineering technology:** Architectural, electrical, industrial. **Foreign languages:** French, German, Spanish. **Health:** Athletic training, health services, mental health services, nursing (RN). **Liberal arts:** Arts/sciences. **Math:** General. **Parks/recreation:** Sports admin. **Philosophy/religion:** Philosophy. **Physical sciences:** Chemistry, geology, physics. **Protective services:** Criminal justice. **Psychology:** General. **Public administration:** Social work. **Social sciences:** General, anthropology, geography, international relations, political science, sociology. **Visual/performing arts:** Commercial/advertising art, dramatic, studio arts.

**Most popular majors.** Business/marketing 24%, communications/journalism 6%, education 11%, health sciences 12%, social sciences 7%, visual/performing arts 8%.

**Computing on campus.** 1,500 workstations in dormitories, library, computer center, student center. Dormitories wired for high-speed internet access and linked to campus network. Commuter students can connect to campus network. Online course registration, online library, helpline, repair service, student web hosting, wireless network available.

**Student life. Freshman orientation:** Mandatory, $45 fee. Preregistration for classes offered. 2-day summer program. **Policies:** Student organizations required to register annually and attend student organization orientation session annually. **Housing:** Coed dorms, single-sex dorms, special housing for disabled, apartments, fraternity/sorority housing, wellness housing available. $200 nonrefundable deposit, deadline 5/1. **Activities:** Bands, campus ministries, choral groups, dance, drama, international student organizations, literary magazine, music ensembles, Model UN, musical theater, radio station, student government, student newspaper, symphony orchestra, TV station, Baptist student union, Newman Center, Schools for Schools, Up til Dawn, black united students, Common Ground, College Republicans, Campus Democrats, Latino student union.

**Athletics.** NCAA. **Intercollegiate:** Baseball M, basketball, cheerleading, cross-country, golf, soccer, softball W, tennis, volleyball W. **Intramural:** Basketball, bowling, football (non-tackle), racquetball, soccer, softball, tennis, volleyball, water polo, weight lifting. **Team name:** Norse.

**Student services.** Adult student services, alcohol/substance abuse counseling, career counseling, services for economically disadvantaged, student employment services, financial aid counseling, health services, minority student services, on-campus daycare, personal counseling, placement for graduates. **Physically disabled:** Services for visually, speech, hearing impaired.

**Contact.** E-mail: admitnku@nku.edu
Phone: (859) 572-5220 Toll-free number: (800) 637-9948
Fax: (859) 572-6665
Melissa Gorbandt, Director of Admissions - Outreach, Northern Kentucky University, Administrative Center 401, Northern Kentucky University, Highland Heights, KY 41099

## Pikeville College

**Pikeville, Kentucky** — CB member
**www.pc.edu** — CB code: 1625

- Private 4-year liberal arts college affiliated with Presbyterian Church (USA)
- Residential campus in small town
- 673 degree-seeking undergraduates: 7% part-time, 51% women, 10% African American, 1% Asian American, 1% Hispanic American
- 300 degree-seeking graduate students
- 34% graduate within 6 years; 40% enter graduate study

**General.** Founded in 1889. Regionally accredited. **Degrees:** 131 bachelor's, 21 associate awarded; professional offered. **ROTC:** Army. **Location:** 150 miles from Lexington; 140 miles from Charleston, WV. **Calendar:** Semester, limited summer session. **Full-time faculty:** 53 total; 53% have terminal degrees, 55% women. **Part-time faculty:** 17 total; 24% have terminal degrees, 59% women. **Class size:** 69% < 20, 31% 20-39, less than 1% 40-49.

**Freshman class profile.** 770 applied, 770 admitted, 186 enrolled.

| Mid 50% test scores | | GPA 2.0-2.99: | 28% |
|---|---|---|---|
| ACT composite: | 17-23 | End year in good standing: | 66% |
| GPA 3.75 or higher: | 25% | Return as sophomores: | 53% |
| GPA 3.50-3.74: | 17% | Out-of-state: | 37% |
| GPA 3.0-3.49: | 26% | Live on campus: | 73% |

**Basis for selection.** Open admission, but selective for some programs. 19 ACT required for nursing, 21 ACT required for education majors.

**High school preparation.** College-preparatory program recommended. 13 units recommended. Recommended units include English 4, mathematics 3, social studies 2, history 1 and science 3.

**2009-2010 Annual costs.** Tuition/fees: $14,535. Room/board: $6,000. Books/supplies: $2,000. Personal expenses: $2,000.

**2009-2010 Financial aid.** All financial aid based on need. 185 full-time freshmen applied for aid; 184 were judged to have need; 184 of these received aid. Average need met was 93%. Average scholarship/grant was $12,894; average loan $3,457. 63% of total undergraduate aid awarded as scholarships/grants, 37% as loans/jobs.

**Application procedures. Admission:** Priority date 3/15; deadline 8/15 (receipt date). No application fee. Admission notification on a rolling basis beginning on or about 9/15. **Financial aid:** Priority date 3/15; no closing date. FAFSA, institutional form required. Applicants notified on a rolling basis starting 2/1; must reply by 5/1 or within 2 week(s) of notification.

**Academics. Special study options:** Combined bachelor's/graduate degree, double major, dual enrollment of high school students, independent study, internships, liberal arts/career combination, student-designed major, study abroad, teacher certification program, Washington semester. **Credit/placement by examination:** AP, CLEP. 15 credit hours maximum toward associate degree, 15 toward bachelor's. **Support services:** Reduced course load, remedial instruction, study skills assistance, tutoring, writing center.

**Majors. Biology:** General. **Business:** Business admin. **Communications:** General. **Computer sciences:** General. **Education:** Elementary, middle. **History:** General. **Math:** General. **Philosophy/religion:** Religion. **Physical sciences:** Chemistry. **Protective services:** Criminal justice. **Psychology:** General. **Public administration:** Social work. **Social sciences:** Sociology. **Visual/performing arts:** Art.

**Most popular majors.** Biology 11%, business/marketing 30%, communications/journalism 7%, education 7%, history 10%, psychology 11%, security/protective services 7%.

**Computing on campus.** 162 workstations in library, computer center. Dormitories wired for high-speed internet access and linked to campus network. Commuter students can connect to campus network. Online library, student web hosting, wireless network available.

**Student life. Freshman orientation:** Mandatory. Preregistration for classes offered. Held first 3 days before start of classes. **Policies:** No alcohol allowed on campus. **Housing:** Guaranteed on-campus for freshmen. Coed dorms, single-sex dorms available. $50 nonrefundable deposit, deadline 5/30. **Activities:** Pep band, choral groups, dance, literary magazine, student government, student newspaper, academic team, Appalachian Association for Justice, Baptist student union, Blessed Unity of God, Fellowship of Christian Athletes, Lambda Sigma society, Phi Beta Lambda, Psi Chi, Sigma Tau Delta, Young Republicans.

**Athletics.** NAIA. **Intercollegiate:** Baseball M, basketball, bowling, cheerleading, cross-country, football (tackle) M, golf, soccer, softball W, tennis, volleyball W. **Intramural:** Basketball, football (non-tackle), softball. **Team name:** Bears.

**Student services.** Financial aid counseling, health services, personal counseling, veterans' counselor.

**Contact.** E-mail: wewantyou@pc.edu
Phone: (606) 218-5251 Toll-free number: (866) 232-7700
Fax: (606) 218-5255
Amanda Slone, Assistant Dean, Admissions, Pikeville College, 147 Sycamore Street, Pikeville, KY 41501-1194

## St. Catharine College
### St. Catharine, Kentucky
**www.sccky.edu**      **CB code: 1690**

♦ Private 4-year health science and liberal arts college affiliated with Roman Catholic Church
♦ Commuter campus in small town
♦ 600 full-time, degree-seeking undergraduates

**General.** Founded in 1931. Regionally accredited. **Degrees:** 11 bachelor's, 84 associate awarded. **Location:** 50 miles from Louisville and Lexington. **Calendar:** Semester, limited summer session. **Full-time faculty:** 48 total; 25% have terminal degrees, 19% minority, 56% women. **Part-time faculty:** 40 total; 15% have terminal degrees, 2% minority, 65% women.

**Freshman class profile.** 620 applied, 620 admitted, 171 enrolled.

**Basis for selection.** Open admission. Assessment tests in mathematics, English and reading administered upon admission for course placement or remediation.

**2009-2010 Annual costs.** Tuition/fees: $14,740. Higher tuition applies for health science program. Room/board: $7,210. Books/supplies: $700. Personal expenses: $1,200.

**Financial aid.** All financial aid based on need.

**Application procedures. Admission:** No deadline. $15 fee, may be waived for applicants with need. Application must be submitted on paper. Admission notification on a rolling basis. **Financial aid:** Priority date 3/15; no closing date. FAFSA, institutional form required. Applicants notified on a rolling basis.

**Academics. Special study options:** Distance learning, dual enrollment of high school students, independent study, internships, liberal arts/career combination, student-designed major, study abroad, teacher certification program, weekend college. **Credit/placement by examination:** AP, CLEP, institutional tests. 35 credit hours maximum toward associate degree, 35 toward

bachelor's. **Support services:** Learning center, reduced course load, remedial instruction, study skills assistance, tutoring.

**Majors. Business:** Business admin. **Education:** Elementary, middle. **Health:** Health services, sonography. **Liberal arts:** Arts/sciences. **Psychology:** General. **Other:** Criminal Justic/Law Enforcement Administration.

**Most popular majors.** Business/marketing 31%, education 22%, liberal arts 22%, psychology 18%, social sciences 7%.

**Computing on campus.** 35 workstations in library, computer center. Dormitories wired for high-speed internet access. Online library, wireless network available.

**Student life. Freshman orientation:** Mandatory, $40 fee. Preregistration for classes offered. 3-day program held before start of classes. **Housing:** Single-sex dorms, special housing for disabled, wellness housing available. $25 nonrefundable deposit, deadline 8/15. **Activities:** Campus ministries, choral groups, drama, literary magazine, student government, student newspaper, Phi Theta Kappa, Students Above Traditional Age, student ambassadors, health occupations student association.

**Athletics.** NAIA. **Intercollegiate:** Baseball M, basketball, bowling, cross-country, golf, soccer, softball W, track and field, volleyball W. **Team name:** Patriots.

**Student services.** Chaplain/spiritual director, career counseling, student employment services, financial aid counseling, legal services, on-campus daycare, personal counseling, veterans' counselor.

**Contact.** E-mail: twiley@sccky.edu
Phone: (859) 336-5082 ext. 1259 Toll-free
number: (800) 599-2000 ext. 1259 Fax: (859) 336-9381
Toni Wiley, Director of Admissions, St. Catharine College, 2735 Bardstown Road, St. Catharine, KY 40061

## Spalding University
### Louisville, Kentucky      CB member
**www.spalding.edu**      **CB code: 1552**

♦ Private 4-year university affiliated with Roman Catholic Church
♦ Commuter campus in large city
♦ 1,180 degree-seeking undergraduates: 27% part-time, 74% women, 31% African American, 1% Asian American, 2% Hispanic American
♦ 894 degree-seeking graduate students
♦ 49% of applicants admitted
♦ SAT or ACT (ACT writing optional) required
♦ 35% graduate within 6 years

**General.** Founded in 1814. Regionally accredited. **Degrees:** 171 bachelor's, 4 associate awarded; master's, doctoral offered. **ROTC:** Army, Air Force. **Location:** One mile from downtown. **Calendar:** Continuous, extensive summer session. **Full-time faculty:** 87 total; 68% have terminal degrees, 13% minority, 67% women. **Part-time faculty:** 138 total; 46% have terminal degrees, 16% minority, 56% women. **Class size:** 61% < 20, 37% 20-39, 2% 40-49. **Special facilities:** Historical collection of Edith Stein works, Huff Gallery.

**Freshman class profile.** 406 applied, 197 admitted, 109 enrolled.

| Mid 50% test scores | | | |
|---|---|---|---|
| SAT critical reading: | 440-570 | GPA 3.50-3.74: | 5% |
| SAT math: | 470-520 | GPA 3.0-3.49: | 27% |
| SAT writing: | 430-470 | GPA 2.0-2.99: | 57% |
| ACT composite: | 16-20 | Return as sophomores: | 73% |
| GPA 3.75 or higher: | 5% | Out-of-state: | 1% |
| | | Live on campus: | 3% |

**Basis for selection.** Automatic admission for students with 2.5 GPA and 20 ACT or 950 SAT (exclusive of Writing). Applicants who do not meet the stated automatic admission criteria must submit personal statement. **Home-schooled:** Transcript of courses and grades, state high school equivalency certificate required.

**High school preparation.** College-preparatory program recommended. 13 units recommended. Recommended units include English 4, mathematics 3, social studies 2, science 2 and foreign language 2.

**2009-2010 Annual costs.** Tuition/fees: $18,000. Room only: $2,000. Books/supplies: $1,260. Personal expenses: $2,700.

**2008-2009 Financial aid. Non-need-based:** Scholarships awarded for academics, religious affiliation.

**Application procedures. Admission:** No deadline. $20 fee, may be waived for applicants with need, free for online applicants. Admission notification on a rolling basis. **Financial aid:** Priority date 3/1; no closing date. FAFSA required. Applicants notified on a rolling basis starting 3/31; must reply within 2 week(s) of notification.

**Academics. Special study options:** Accelerated study, cross-registration, distance learning, double major, dual enrollment of high school students, independent study, internships, study abroad, teacher certification program, weekend college. **Credit/placement by examination:** AP, CLEP, SAT, ACT, institutional tests. 32 credit hours maximum toward associate degree, 32 toward bachelor's. **Support services:** Learning center, reduced course load, remedial instruction, study skills assistance, tutoring, writing center.

**Majors. Business:** General, accounting. **Communications:** General. **Education:** General, elementary, middle, special. **Health:** Nursing (RN), occupational therapy assistant. **Interdisciplinary:** Natural sciences. **Liberal arts:** Humanities. **Psychology:** General. **Public administration:** Social work. **Social sciences:** General.

**Most popular majors.** Business/marketing 24%, education 6%, health sciences 45%, psychology 12%.

**Computing on campus.** 250 workstations in dormitories, library, student center. Dormitories wired for high-speed internet access and linked to campus network. Commuter students can connect to campus network. Online course registration, online library, helpline, wireless network available.

**Student life. Freshman orientation:** Mandatory, $55 fee. Preregistration for classes offered. **Housing:** Guaranteed on-campus for freshmen. Coed dorms available. $100 fully refundable deposit. **Activities:** Campus ministries, international student organizations, student government, international club, Campus Crusade for Christ, Fellowship of Christian Athletes, black student association, Advocates for Campus Accessibility.

**Athletics.** NCAA. **Intercollegiate:** Baseball M, basketball, bowling W, cross-country, golf, soccer, softball W, tennis W, volleyball W. **Team name:** Golden Eagles.

**Student services.** Adult student services, alcohol/substance abuse counseling, chaplain/spiritual director, career counseling, services for economically disadvantaged, student employment services, financial aid counseling, minority student services, personal counseling. **Physically disabled:** Services for visually, speech, hearing impaired. **Learning disabled:** Comprehensive services available.

**Contact.** E-mail: admissions@spalding.edu
Phone: (502) 585-9911 ext. 2111 Toll-free
number: (800) 896-8941 ext. 2111 Fax: (502) 992-2418
Christopher Hart, Dean of Enrollment Management, Spalding University, 845 So 3rd St, Louisville, KY 40203

## Sullivan University
**Louisville, Kentucky**
www.sullivan.edu                                       CB code: 0811

- For-profit 4-year university
- Commuter campus in large city
- 5,122 undergraduates
- 397 graduate students
- Interview required

**General.** Founded in 1962. Regionally accredited. **Degrees:** 450 bachelor's, 603 associate awarded; master's, doctoral, professional offered. **Location:** 110 miles from Indianapolis, 110 miles from Cincinnati. **Calendar:** Quarter, extensive summer session. **Full-time faculty:** 104 total; 26% have terminal degrees. **Part-time faculty:** 191 total; 28% have terminal degrees. **Special facilities:** University-operated fine dining restaurant.

**Freshman class profile.**

| | | | |
|---|---|---|---|
| Out-of-state: | 17% | **Live on campus:** | 19% |

**Basis for selection.** Test scores, interview, high school record important. CPAT required for placement if no ACT or SAT scores are available.

**2009-2010 Annual costs.** Tuition, fees and per-credit-hour charges vary by program. Tuition costs range from $15,600 to $16,860 per academic year. Room only: $4,950. Books/supplies: $1,800. Personal expenses: $1,200.

**Financial aid.** All financial aid based on need.

**Application procedures. Admission:** No deadline. $100 fee. Admission notification on a rolling basis. **Financial aid:** No deadline. FAFSA required. Applicants notified on a rolling basis starting 1/2.

**Academics.** Day classes meet Monday-Thursday; special program on Friday for additional help. Night/Weekend classes meet Monday-Sunday. **Special study options:** Accelerated study, distance learning, double major, independent study, weekend college. **Credit/placement by examination:** CLEP, IB, SAT, ACT, institutional tests. **Support services:** Reduced course load, remedial instruction, study skills assistance, tutoring.

**Majors. Business:** Accounting, business admin, tourism promotion. **Computer sciences:** General, applications programming. **Legal studies:** Paralegal. **Personal/culinary services:** Culinary arts.

**Computing on campus.** 252 workstations in dormitories, library, computer center. Commuter students can connect to campus network. Online course registration, online library, helpline, wireless network available.

**Student life. Freshman orientation:** Mandatory. 1- and 2-day sessions held at beginning of quarter. **Housing:** Apartments, wellness housing available. $95 nonrefundable deposit, deadline 9/30. Housing available for freshmen under 21 who live outside a 75-mile radius from Louisville. **Activities:** Student newspaper, student activities committee, travel club, culinary competition team, student paralegal association, International Association of Administrative Professionals, Rotarac.

**Athletics. Intramural:** Basketball, bowling, softball, volleyball.

**Student services.** Career counseling, student employment services, financial aid counseling, personal counseling, placement for graduates, veterans' counselor.

**Contact.** E-mail: admissions@sullivan.edu
Phone: (502) 456-6505 Toll-free number: (800) 844-1354
Fax: (502) 456-0040
Terri Thomas, Director of Admissions, Sullivan University, 3101 Bardstown Road, Louisville, KY 40205

## Thomas More College
**Crestview Hills, Kentucky**                          CB member
www.thomasmore.edu                                     CB code: 1876

- Private 4-year liberal arts college affiliated with Roman Catholic Church
- Commuter campus in small town
- 1,415 degree-seeking undergraduates: 7% part-time, 53% women, 5% African American, 1% Asian American, 1% Hispanic American, 1% Native American
- 147 degree-seeking graduate students
- 93% of applicants admitted
- SAT or ACT (ACT writing optional) required
- 50% graduate within 6 years

**General.** Founded in 1921. Regionally accredited. **Degrees:** 256 bachelor's, 69 associate awarded; master's offered. **ROTC:** Army, Air Force. **Location:** 8 miles from Cincinnati. **Calendar:** Semester, limited summer session. **Full-time faculty:** 75 total; 68% have terminal degrees, 5% minority, 47% women. **Part-time faculty:** 58 total; 3% minority, 52% women. **Class size:** 73% < 20, 27% 20-39. **Special facilities:** Biology field station, observatory.

**Freshman class profile.** 1,047 applied, 974 admitted, 312 enrolled.

| Mid 50% test scores | | | |
|---|---|---|---|
| SAT critical reading: | 440-560 | Rank in top quarter: | 36% |
| SAT math: | 430-550 | Rank in top tenth: | 13% |
| ACT composite: | 20-25 | Return as sophomores: | 67% |
| GPA 3.75 or higher: | 21% | Out-of-state: | 49% |
| GPA 3.50-3.74: | 14% | Live on campus: | 52% |
| GPA 3.0-3.49: | 36% | Fraternities: | 1% |
| GPA 2.0-2.99: | 28% | Sororities: | 4% |

**Basis for selection.** Students must have C+ average or 2.5 GPA; 20 ACT English/480 SAT verbal; and 20 ACT or 1010 SAT. Students not meeting these requirements may be conditionally admitted.

**High school preparation.** College-preparatory program required. 17 units required. Required units include English 4, mathematics 3, social studies 3, science 3, foreign language 2, computer science 1 and visual/performing arts 1.

**2009-2010 Annual costs.** Tuition/fees: $23,220. Tiered tuition with a guaranteed 3% increase pre year which allows planning the cost of a degree. Each level has different tuition and figures given are for incoming Freshmen only, with other classes lower. Room/board: $6,560. Books/supplies: $1,000. Personal expenses: $2,300.

**2009-2010 Financial aid. Need-based:** 278 full-time freshmen applied for aid; 241 were judged to have need; 240 of these received aid. Average need met was 78%. Average scholarship/grant was $11,950; average loan $3,538. 76% of total undergraduate aid awarded as scholarships/grants, 24% as loans/jobs. **Non-need-based:** Awarded to 548 full-time undergraduates, including 145 freshmen. Scholarships awarded for academics, alumni affiliation, art, job skills, leadership, minority status, music/drama, religious affiliation, ROTC, state residency.

**Application procedures. Admission:** Closing date 8/1 (postmark date). $25 fee, may be waived for applicants with need, free for online applicants. Admission notification on a rolling basis beginning on or about 10/1. **Financial aid:** Priority date 3/15; no closing date. FAFSA required. Applicants notified on a rolling basis starting 10/1.

**Academics. Special study options:** Accelerated study, cooperative education, cross-registration, double major, dual enrollment of high school students, honors, independent study, internships, student-designed major, study abroad, teacher certification program. **Credit/placement by examination:** AP, CLEP, IB, SAT, ACT, institutional tests. 30 credit hours maximum toward associate degree, 60 toward bachelor's. **Support services:** Learning center, pre-admission summer program, reduced course load, remedial instruction, study skills assistance, tutoring, writing center.

**Majors. Biology:** General. **Business:** General, accounting. **Communications:** General. **Computer sciences:** General. **Conservation:** Environmental science. **Education:** Art, business, elementary, middle, secondary, social studies. **Foreign languages:** Spanish. **Health:** Clinical lab science, nursing (RN). **History:** General. **Liberal arts:** Arts/sciences, humanities. **Math:** General. **Parks/recreation:** Sports admin. **Philosophy/religion:** Philosophy, religion. **Physical sciences:** Chemistry, physics. **Protective services:** Forensics, law enforcement admin. **Psychology:** General. **Social sciences:** Economics, international relations, political science, sociology. **Visual/performing arts:** Dramatic, studio arts.

**Most popular majors.** Biology 6%, business/marketing 51%, health sciences 8%, liberal arts 7%.

**Computing on campus.** 95 workstations in library, computer center, student center. Dormitories wired for high-speed internet access and linked to campus network. Commuter students can connect to campus network. Online library, helpline, student web hosting, wireless network available.

**Student life. Freshman orientation:** Mandatory, $125 fee. Preregistration for classes offered. Two-day program held at beginning of fall semester in August. **Housing:** Coed dorms, single-sex dorms, special housing for disabled available. $100 nonrefundable deposit, deadline 5/1. **Activities:** Campus ministries, choral groups, drama, international student organizations, literary magazine, student government, student activities board, residence hall government association, African American Society, Habitat for Humanity, business society, social issues commune, student government association, campus ministry, international student organization.

**Athletics.** NCAA. **Intercollegiate:** Baseball M, basketball, cross-country, football (tackle) M, golf, soccer, softball W, tennis, volleyball W. **Intramural:** Basketball, football (non-tackle), soccer, softball, volleyball. **Team name:** Saints.

**Student services.** Adult student services, alcohol/substance abuse counseling, chaplain/spiritual director, career counseling, student employment services, financial aid counseling, health services, minority student services, personal counseling, placement for graduates, veterans' counselor. **Physically disabled:** Services for visually, speech, hearing impaired.

**Contact.** E-mail: admissions@thomasmore.edu
Phone: (859) 344-3332 Toll-free number: (800) 825-4557
Fax: (859) 344-3444
Billy Sarge, Assistant Director of Admissions, Thomas More College, 333 Thomas More Parkway, Crestview Hills, KY 41017-3495

---

## Transylvania University
**Lexington, Kentucky**
www.transy.edu

CB member
CB code: 1808

- Private 4-year liberal arts college affiliated with Christian Church (Disciples of Christ)
- Residential campus in large city
- 1,088 degree-seeking undergraduates: 59% women
- 81% of applicants admitted
- SAT or ACT (ACT writing optional), application essay required

**General.** Founded in 1780. Regionally accredited. **Degrees:** 290 bachelor's awarded. **ROTC:** Army, Air Force. **Location:** 80 miles from Louisville, 80 miles from Cincinnati. **Calendar:** 4-1-4, limited summer session.

---

**Full-time faculty:** 90 total; 93% have terminal degrees, 4% minority, 39% women. **Part-time faculty:** 10 total; 10% have terminal degrees, 40% women. **Class size:** 61% < 20, 39% 20-39. **Special facilities:** Museum of early scientific apparatus, special library collections of early medical and scientific works and Kentucky books.

**Freshman class profile.** 1,374 applied, 1,118 admitted, 283 enrolled.

| Mid 50% test scores | | GPA 2.0-2.99: | 7% |
|---|---|---|---|
| SAT critical reading: | 530-640 | Rank in top quarter: | 66% |
| SAT math: | 530-640 | Rank in top tenth: | 40% |
| SAT writing: | 510-640 | Out-of-state: | 11% |
| ACT composite: | 24-29 | Live on campus: | 95% |
| GPA 3.75 or higher: | 54% | Fraternities: | 55% |
| GPA 3.50-3.74: | 19% | Sororities: | 60% |
| GPA 3.0-3.49: | 20% | | |

**Basis for selection.** Rigor of curriculum, GPA, and test scores most important. Recommendations, essay, extracurricular activities, excellence of character and high personal goals important. Interview recommended. Audition required for music scholarship applicants. Portfolio required for art scholarship applicants. **Learning Disabled:** Students should meet with coordinator of disability services.

**High school preparation.** 12 units required; 16 recommended. Required and recommended units include English 4, mathematics 3-4, social studies 2, history 1, science 3-4 (laboratory 2), foreign language 2 and academic electives 1. Broad high school curriculum important to allow full participation in required liberal arts course work. Solid background in English highly recommended.

**2009-2010 Annual costs.** Tuition/fees: $25,280. Room/board: $7,770. Books/supplies: $750. Personal expenses: $1,250.

**2009-2010 Financial aid. Need-based:** 73% of total undergraduate aid awarded as scholarships/grants, 27% as loans/jobs. **Non-need-based:** Scholarships awarded for academics, art, leadership, minority status, music/drama, religious affiliation, ROTC, state residency. **Additional information:** Auditions and portfolios required for music and art scholarships respectively. Essays required for other scholarship programs. Applications for William T. Young scholarships must be received by December 1.

**Application procedures. Admission:** Priority date 12/1; deadline 2/1 (postmark date). $30 fee, may be waived for applicants with need, free for online applicants. Admission notification 3/1. Must reply by 5/1. **Financial aid:** Priority date 3/1; no closing date. FAFSA required. Applicants notified on a rolling basis starting 3/15; must reply by 5/1 or within 2 week(s) of notification.

**Academics. Special study options:** Combined bachelor's/graduate degree, double major, independent study, internships, liberal arts/career combination, student-designed major, study abroad, teacher certification program, Washington semester. **Credit/placement by examination:** AP, CLEP, IB, ACT, institutional tests. No limit to credit for AP or IB. **Support services:** Learning center, study skills assistance, tutoring, writing center.

**Majors. Biology:** General. **Business:** General, accounting. **Computer sciences:** General. **Education:** Elementary, middle, music, physical. **Foreign languages:** Classics, French, Spanish. **History:** General. **Liberal arts:** Arts/sciences. **Math:** General. **Parks/recreation:** Exercise sciences. **Philosophy/religion:** Philosophy, religion. **Physical sciences:** Chemistry, physics. **Psychology:** General. **Social sciences:** Anthropology, economics, political science, sociology. **Visual/performing arts:** Dramatic, music performance, studio arts.

**Most popular majors.** Biology 9%, business/marketing 20%, English 6%, foreign language 11%, interdisciplinary studies 7%, psychology 10%, social sciences 17%.

**Computing on campus.** 250 workstations in dormitories, library, computer center, student center. Dormitories wired for high-speed internet access and linked to campus network. Commuter students can connect to campus network. Online library, helpline, student web hosting, wireless network available.

**Student life. Freshman orientation:** Mandatory. Preregistration for classes offered. One-day summer event; 4-day program before classes begin. **Housing:** Guaranteed on-campus for freshmen. Coed dorms, single-sex dorms, special housing for disabled, apartments, wellness housing available. $200 nonrefundable deposit, deadline 5/1. Efficiency apartment option for upperclassmen; two units with facilities for disabled students available. **Activities:** Bands, choral groups, dance, drama, literary magazine, music ensembles, musical theater, opera, radio station, student government, student newspaper, Diversity Action Council, College Democrats, College Republicans, Alternative Spring Break, Campus Crusade, student government association, student activities board, student alumni association, Transylvania Environmental Rights and Responsibilities Alliance.

**Athletics.** NCAA. **Intercollegiate:** Baseball M, basketball, cross-country, diving, field hockey W, golf, soccer, softball W, swimming, tennis, track and field, volleyball W. **Intramural:** Badminton, basketball, bowling, cross-country, football (non-tackle), football (tackle), golf, handball, racquetball, soccer, softball, swimming, table tennis, tennis, volleyball. **Team name:** Pioneers.

**Student services.** Alcohol/substance abuse counseling, chaplain/spiritual director, career counseling, student employment services, financial aid counseling, health services, minority student services, personal counseling, veterans' counselor. **Physically disabled:** Services for visually, hearing impaired.

**Contact.** E-mail: admissions@transy.edu
Phone: (859) 233-8242 Toll-free number: (800) 872-6798
Fax: (859) 281-3649
Brad Goan, Director of Admissions, Transylvania University, 300 North Broadway, Lexington, KY 40508-1797

## Union College
### Barbourville, Kentucky
www.unionky.edu                                    CB code: 1825

- Private 4-year liberal arts and teachers college affiliated with United Methodist Church
- Residential campus in small town
- 811 degree-seeking undergraduates: 6% part-time, 46% women
- 541 degree-seeking graduate students
- 28% of applicants admitted
- SAT or ACT (ACT writing recommended) required

**General.** Founded in 1879. Regionally accredited. **Degrees:** 106 bachelor's awarded; master's offered. **ROTC:** Army. **Location:** 107 miles from Lexington; 107 miles from Knoxville, TN. **Calendar:** Semester, limited summer session. **Full-time faculty:** 61 total; 72% have terminal degrees, 10% minority, 44% women. **Part-time faculty:** 43 total; 30% have terminal degrees, 51% women. **Class size:** 78% < 20, 22% 20-39, less than 1% 40-49.

**Freshman class profile.** 1,226 applied, 348 admitted, 191 enrolled.

| Mid 50% test scores | | | |
|---|---|---|---|
| SAT critical reading: | 420-460 | GPA 3.50-3.74: | 11% |
| SAT math: | 440-510 | GPA 3.0-3.49: | 27% |
| ACT composite: | 17-21 | GPA 2.0-2.99: | 52% |
| GPA 3.75 or higher: | 8% | End year in good standing: | 54% |
| | | Return as sophomores: | 55% |

**Basis for selection.** School achievement record, course work, class rank, SAT or ACT scores important. ACT preferred for all, required for teacher education program. Interview recommended. **Homeschooled:** Statement describing homeschool structure and mission, transcript of courses and grades, letter of recommendation (nonparent) required. Academic calender with attendance required. Submission of writing sample, summary of travel-related exerience or work history may be requested. **Learning Disabled:** Students must provide documentation to coordinator of special program to receive necessary accommodations.

**High school preparation.** College-preparatory program recommended. Recommended units include English 4, mathematics 3, social studies 2, science 2 (laboratory 2) and foreign language 1.

**2010-2011 Annual costs.** Tuition/fees (projected): $18,849. Room/board: $5,950. Books/supplies: $1,400. Personal expenses: $1,600.

**2009-2010 Financial aid. Need-based:** 183 full-time freshmen applied for aid; 183 were judged to have need; 170 of these received aid. Average need met was 75%. Average scholarship/grant was $12,644; average loan $6,280. 60% of total undergraduate aid awarded as scholarships/grants, 40% as loans/jobs. **Non-need-based:** Awarded to 155 full-time undergraduates, including 36 freshmen. Scholarships awarded for academics, athletics, leadership, music/drama, religious affiliation, state residency.

**Application procedures. Admission:** No deadline. $10 fee, may be waived for applicants with need. Admission notification on a rolling basis. **Financial aid:** Priority date 3/15; no closing date. FAFSA required. Applicants notified on a rolling basis starting 3/1; must reply within 2 week(s) of notification.

**Academics. Special study options:** Combined bachelor's/graduate degree, distance learning, double major, honors, independent study, internships, liberal arts/career combination, student-designed major, study abroad, teacher certification program. **Credit/placement by examination:** AP, CLEP, ACT, institutional tests. 30 credit hours maximum toward bachelor's degree. **Support services:** Learning center, remedial instruction, study skills assistance, tutoring, writing center.

**Majors. Biology:** General. **Business:** Accounting, business admin. **Communications:** General. **Education:** Elementary, health, middle, physical, science, secondary, social studies, special. **History:** General. **Math:** General. **Parks/recreation:** Facilities management, sports admin. **Philosophy/religion:** Religion. **Physical sciences:** Chemistry. **Protective services:** Law enforcement admin. **Psychology:** General. **Social sciences:** Sociology. **Theology:** Religious ed.

**Most popular majors.** Business/marketing 38%, education 25%, psychology 9%.

**Computing on campus.** 230 workstations in dormitories, library, computer center, student center. Dormitories wired for high-speed internet access and linked to campus network. Commuter students can connect to campus network. Online course registration, online library, wireless network available.

**Student life. Freshman orientation:** Mandatory. Preregistration for classes offered. One day sessions offered in May, June, and July. **Housing:** Guaranteed on-campus for freshmen. Single-sex dorms, apartments available. $50 fully refundable deposit. Private rooms occasionally available to upperclassmen. **Activities:** Pep band, choral groups, drama, literary magazine, student government, student newspaper, TV station, Fellowship of Christian Athletes, Appalachian wilderness club, Baptist student union, Methodist student organizations, Newman club, student ambassadors, science society, philosophy society.

**Athletics.** NAIA. **Intercollegiate:** Baseball M, basketball, bowling, cross-country, football (tackle) M, golf, soccer, softball W, swimming, tennis, track and field, volleyball W. **Intramural:** Basketball, football (non-tackle), soccer, softball, table tennis, tennis, volleyball. **Team name:** Bulldogs.

**Student services.** Alcohol/substance abuse counseling, chaplain/spiritual director, career counseling, services for economically disadvantaged, student employment services, financial aid counseling, health services, personal counseling, placement for graduates. **Physically disabled:** Services for visually, hearing impaired.

**Contact.** E-mail: enrollme@unionky.edu
Phone: (606) 546-1229 Toll-free number: (800) 489-8646
Fax: (606) 546-1667
Jerry Jackson, Dean of Enrollment Management, Union College, 310 College Street, Box 005, Barbourville, KY 40906

## University of Kentucky
### Lexington, Kentucky
www.uky.edu
CB member
CB code: 1837

- Public 4-year university
- Commuter campus in large city
- 18,806 degree-seeking undergraduates: 7% part-time, 50% women, 7% African American, 2% Asian American, 2% Hispanic American, 1% international
- 6,775 degree-seeking graduate students
- 74% of applicants admitted
- SAT or ACT (ACT writing optional) required

**General.** Founded in 1865. Regionally accredited. **Degrees:** 3,650 bachelor's awarded; master's, doctoral, professional offered. **ROTC:** Army, Air Force. **Location:** 80 miles from Louisville, 90 miles from Cincinnati. **Calendar:** Semester, limited summer session. **Full-time faculty:** 1,301 total; 91% have terminal degrees, 17% minority, 34% women. **Part-time faculty:** 382 total; 49% have terminal degrees, 6% minority, 48% women. **Class size:** 23% < 20, 53% 20-39, 6% 40-49, 11% 50-99, 7% >100. **Special facilities:** Center for the arts, Van de Graaff accelerator, equine research center, center for the humanities.

**Freshman class profile.** 12,195 applied, 8,966 admitted, 4,153 enrolled.

| Mid 50% test scores | | | |
|---|---|---|---|
| SAT critical reading: | 500-620 | GPA 3.0-3.49: | 24% |
| SAT math: | 500-630 | GPA 2.0-2.99: | 14% |
| ACT composite: | 22-27 | Rank in top quarter: | 50% |
| GPA 3.75 or higher: | 46% | Rank in top tenth: | 23% |
| GPA 3.50-3.74: | 16% | Out-of-state: | 21% |
| | | International: | 1% |

**Basis for selection.** Test scores and GPA should indicate potential for academic success. Required course work and extracurricular activities also considered. Students out of high school 2 years or more with no college credit admitted on probationary basis. Audition required of music majors. **Homeschooled:** List of textbooks, attendance record and 2 letters of recommendation from persons outside family required.

**High school preparation.** 22 units required. Required and recommended units include English 4, mathematics 3-4, social studies 3, science 3-4, foreign language 2 and academic electives 5. 1 fine or performing arts, .5 health, .5 physical education required.

**2009-2010 Annual costs.** Tuition/fees: $8,123; $16,678 out-of-state. Room/board: $9,125. Books/supplies: $800. Personal expenses: $1,460.

**2009-2010 Financial aid. Non-need-based:** Scholarships awarded for academics, alumni affiliation, art, athletics, job skills, leadership, minority status, music/drama, ROTC, state residency.

**Application procedures. Admission:** Closing date 2/15 (postmark date). $40 fee, may be waived for applicants with need. Admission notification on a rolling basis beginning on or about 10/1. Reply by 05/01 preferred. **Financial aid:** Closing date 2/15. FAFSA required. Applicants notified on a rolling basis starting 4/1; must reply within 3 week(s) of notification.

**Academics. Special study options:** Accelerated study, combined bachelor's/graduate degree, cooperative education, distance learning, double major, ESL, exchange student, honors, independent study, internships, study abroad, teacher certification program, weekend college. **Credit/placement by examination:** AP, CLEP, IB, SAT, ACT, institutional tests. Students who receive Advanced Placement credit for a course may apply this credit the same way credit earned by passing a course is applied. **Support services:** Learning center, reduced course load, remedial instruction, tutoring, writing center.

**Majors. Agriculture:** Agronomy, animal sciences, economics, food science. **Architecture:** Architecture, landscape. **Area/ethnic studies:** Latin American. **Biology:** General. **Business:** General, accounting, finance, hospitality admin, management science, managerial economics, marketing. **Communications:** General, advertising, journalism, radio/tv. **Computer sciences:** General. **Conservation:** General, forest sciences. **Education:** Art, early childhood, elementary, health, mathematics, middle, music, physical, science, special. **Engineering:** Agricultural, chemical, civil, electrical, materials, mechanical, mining. **Family/consumer sciences:** General, food/nutrition. **Foreign languages:** Classics, French, German, linguistics, Russian, Spanish. **Health:** Audiology/speech pathology, clinical lab science, health care admin. **History:** General. **Math:** General. **Philosophy/religion:** Philosophy. **Physical sciences:** Chemistry, geology, physics. **Psychology:** General. **Public administration:** Social work. **Social sciences:** General, anthropology, economics, geography, political science, sociology. **Visual/performing arts:** Art history/conservation, arts management, dramatic, interior design, music history, music performance.

**Most popular majors.** Biology 6%, business/marketing 18%, communications/journalism 10%, education 8%, engineering/engineering technologies 7%, psychology 6%, social sciences 9%.

**Computing on campus.** 810 workstations in dormitories, library, computer center, student center. Dormitories wired for high-speed internet access and linked to campus network. Commuter students can connect to campus network. Online course registration, online library, helpline, wireless network available.

**Student life. Freshman orientation:** Mandatory, $40 fee. Preregistration for classes offered. $20 additional charge per guest. **Housing:** Coed dorms, single-sex dorms, special housing for disabled, apartments, fraternity/sorority housing available. $300 deposit, deadline 6/1. **Activities:** Bands, choral groups, dance, drama, literary magazine, music ensembles, musical theater, opera, radio station, student government, student newspaper, symphony orchestra, more than 300 organizations available.

**Athletics.** NCAA. **Intercollegiate:** Baseball M, basketball, cross-country, diving, football (tackle) M, golf, gymnastics W, rifle, soccer, softball W, swimming, tennis, track and field, volleyball W. **Intramural:** Archery, badminton, basketball, bowling, cross-country, fencing, field hockey W, football (non-tackle), golf, handball, ice hockey M, lacrosse, racquetball, rugby M, skiing, soccer, softball, squash, swimming, table tennis, tennis, track and field, volleyball, wrestling M. **Team name:** Wildcats.

**Student services.** Adult student services, career counseling, student employment services, health services, on-campus daycare, personal counseling, placement for graduates, veterans' counselor. **Physically disabled:** Services for visually, speech, hearing impaired.

**Contact.** E-mail: admisso@uky.edu
Phone: (859) 257-2000 Toll-free number: (800) 432-0967
Fax: (859) 257-3823
Don Witt, Assistant Provost for Enrollment Management, University of Kentucky, 100 W.D. Funkhouser Building, Lexington, KY 40506-0054

---

### University of Louisville
Louisville, Kentucky
www.louisville.edu

CB member
CB code: 1838

- Public 4-year university
- Commuter campus in very large city

---

- 14,591 degree-seeking undergraduates: 19% part-time, 51% women, 13% African American, 3% Asian American, 2% Hispanic American, 1% international
- 5,539 graduate students
- 73% of applicants admitted
- SAT or ACT (ACT writing optional) required

**General.** Founded in 1798. Regionally accredited. **Degrees:** 2,482 bachelor's, 20 associate awarded; master's, doctoral offered. **ROTC:** Army, Air Force. **Location:** 3 miles from downtown, 92 miles from Cincinnati. **Calendar:** Semester, extensive summer session. **Full-time faculty:** 862 total; 90% have terminal degrees, 20% minority, 40% women. **Part-time faculty:** 492 total; 43% have terminal degrees, 11% minority, 52% women. **Class size:** 26% < 20, 54% 20-39, 8% 40-49, 9% 50-99, 4% >100. **Special facilities:** Planetarium, computer-aided engineering building with robotics laboratory, rapid prototype facility with Sinterstation 2000 system.

**Freshman class profile.** 7,755 applied, 5,625 admitted, 2,478 enrolled.

| Mid 50% test scores | | Rank in top quarter: | 52% |
|---|---|---|---|
| SAT critical reading: | 500-640 | Rank in top tenth: | 25% |
| SAT math: | 510-650 | Out-of-state: | 15% |
| ACT composite: | 21-27 | Live on campus: | 62% |
| GPA 3.75 or higher: | 34% | International: | 1% |
| GPA 3.50-3.74: | 18% | Fraternities: | 24% |
| GPA 3.0-3.49: | 32% | Sororities: | 13% |
| GPA 2.0-2.99: | 16% | | |

**Basis for selection.** High school grades, curriculum, rank in top half of class and test scores very important. Diagnostic testing/interview option for students lacking requirements. Partnership with local community college for those lacking required academic units. SAT/ACT score reports must be received by registration before the first day of class. **Homeschooled:** Transcript of courses and grades required.

**High school preparation.** College-preparatory program required. 22 units required. Required and recommended units include English 4, mathematics 3-4, social studies 3, science 3-4 (laboratory 1), foreign language 2-3, visual/performing arts 1 and academic electives 5. History requirement included in social studies, 5 electives must be rigorous.

**2009-2010 Annual costs.** Tuition/fees: $7,944; $19,272 out-of-state. All full-time students not living on campus are required to purchase a $175 meal plan per semester. Room/board: $5,437. Books/supplies: $1,000. Personal expenses: $4,086.

**2009-2010 Financial aid. Non-need-based:** Scholarships awarded for academics, art, athletics, leadership, minority status, music/drama, ROTC.

**Application procedures. Admission:** Priority date 2/15; deadline 8/25 (receipt date). $40 fee, may be waived for applicants with need. Admission notification on a rolling basis. **Financial aid:** Priority date 3/15; no closing date. FAFSA required. Applicants notified on a rolling basis starting 4/1.

**Academics. Special study options:** Accelerated study, combined bachelor's/graduate degree, cooperative education, cross-registration, distance learning, double major, dual enrollment of high school students, ESL, honors, independent study, internships, student-designed major, study abroad, teacher certification program. **Credit/placement by examination:** AP, CLEP, IB, SAT, ACT, institutional tests. 24 credit hours maximum toward bachelor's degree. Candidates for the nursing program may apply no more than 37 semester hours of CLEP credit toward the bachelor's degree. **Support services:** Learning center, pre-admission summer program, reduced course load, remedial instruction, tutoring.

**Majors. Area/ethnic studies:** African-American, women's. **Biology:** General. **Business:** Accounting, business admin, finance, management information systems, managerial economics, marketing. **Communications:** General. **Education:** Elementary, music, trade/industrial. **Engineering:** General, biomedical, chemical, civil, computer, electrical, industrial, mechanical. **Foreign languages:** French, Spanish. **Health:** Dental hygiene, music therapy, nursing (RN). **History:** General. **Liberal arts:** Arts/sciences, humanities. **Math:** General. **Parks/recreation:** Health/fitness, sports admin. **Philosophy/religion:** Philosophy. **Physical sciences:** Chemistry, physics. **Protective services:** Law enforcement admin. **Psychology:** General. **Social sciences:** Anthropology, economics, geography, political science, sociology. **Visual/performing arts:** Art history/conservation, dramatic, studio arts. **Other:** Equine business, Science - medical and dental.

**Most popular majors.** Business/marketing 22%, communications/journalism 7%, engineering/engineering technologies 8%, health sciences 8%, parks/recreation 7%, psychology 8%, social sciences 10%.

**Computing on campus.** 327 workstations in dormitories, library, computer center, student center. Dormitories wired for high-speed internet access and linked to campus network. Commuter students can connect to campus network. Online course registration, online library, helpline, repair service, student web hosting, wireless network available.

**Student life. Freshman orientation:** Mandatory, $125 fee. Preregistration for classes offered. **Housing:** Coed dorms, special housing for disabled, apartments, fraternity/sorority housing available. $200 fully refundable deposit. Special residence hall floors with in-house computer facilities for honors students, coed suites available. **Activities:** Bands, campus ministries, choral groups, dance, drama, international student organizations, literary magazine, music ensembles, musical theater, opera, radio station, student government, student newspaper, symphony orchestra, Alpha Phi Omega, College Democrats, College Republicans, UNICEF, Common Ground, L-Raisers, Baptist Student Union, Debate Society, Rho Lambda Honor Society, The Redshirt Company.

**Athletics.** NCAA. **Intercollegiate:** Baseball M, basketball, cross-country, diving, field hockey W, football (tackle) M, golf, soccer, softball W, swimming, tennis, track and field, volleyball W. **Intramural:** Badminton, basketball, bowling, cheerleading, football (non-tackle) M, golf, racquetball, soccer, swimming, table tennis, tennis, track and field, volleyball. **Team name:** Cardinals.

**Student services.** Alcohol/substance abuse counseling, chaplain/spiritual director, career counseling, student employment services, financial aid counseling, health services, legal services, minority student services, personal counseling, placement for graduates, women's services. **Physically disabled:** Services for visually, speech, hearing impaired.

**Contact.** E-mail: admitme@gwise.louisville.edu
Phone: (502) 852-6531 Toll-free number: (800) 334-8635 ext. 6531
Fax: (502) 852-4776
Jenny Sawyer, Director of Admissions, University of Louisville, 2211 South Brook Street, Louisville, KY 40292

## University of the Cumberlands
**Williamsburg, Kentucky**                    **CB member**
**www.ucumberlands.edu**                      **CB code: 1145**

▶ Private 4-year university and liberal arts college affiliated with Baptist faith

▶ Residential campus in small town

▶ 1,461 degree-seeking undergraduates: 3% part-time, 50% women, 9% African American, 1% Asian American, 3% Hispanic American, 3% international

▶ 1,000 degree-seeking graduate students

▶ 73% of applicants admitted

▶ SAT or ACT (ACT writing optional) required

▶ 40% graduate within 6 years; 30% enter graduate study

**General.** Founded in 1889. Regionally accredited. **Degrees:** 264 bachelor's awarded; master's, doctoral offered. **ROTC:** Army. **Location:** 100 miles from Lexington; 65 miles from Knoxville, TN. **Calendar:** Semester, limited summer session. **Full-time faculty:** 96 total; 72% have terminal degrees, 7% minority, 40% women. **Part-time faculty:** 58 total; 53% have terminal degrees, 52% women. **Class size:** 58% < 20, 36% 20-39, 4% 40-49, 2% 50-99, less than 1% >100. **Special facilities:** Life science museum, greenhouse, conference center and inn.

**Freshman class profile.** 1,633 applied, 1,193 admitted, 454 enrolled.

| Mid 50% test scores | | GPA 2.0-2.99: | 25% |
|---|---|---|---|
| SAT critical reading: | 420-550 | Rank in top quarter: | 45% |
| SAT math: | 460-560 | Rank in top tenth: | 21% |
| ACT composite: | 19-24 | End year in good standing: | 76% |
| GPA 3.75 or higher: | 30% | Return as sophomores: | 63% |
| GPA 3.50-3.74: | 13% | Out-of-state: | 39% |
| GPA 3.0-3.49: | 31% | Live on campus: | 75% |

**Basis for selection.** School achievement and activities, test scores important. **Homeschooled:** Must have GED or high school transcript.

**High school preparation.** College-preparatory program recommended. Required and recommended units include English 4, mathematics 3, social studies 1-2 and science 2-3.

**2010-2011 Annual costs.** Tuition/fees: $17,000. Room/board: $6,826. Books/supplies: $1,000. Personal expenses: $2,950.

**2009-2010 Financial aid. Need-based:** 438 full-time freshmen applied for aid; 403 were judged to have need; 403 of these received aid. Average need met was 81%. Average scholarship/grant was $13,211; average loan $3,239. 68% of total undergraduate aid awarded as scholarships/grants, 32% as loans/jobs. **Non-need-based:** Awarded to 468 full-time undergraduates, including 144 freshmen. Scholarships awarded for academics, athletics.

**Application procedures. Admission:** Priority date 3/1; deadline 8/15 (receipt date). $30 fee, may be waived for applicants with need. Admission

notification on a rolling basis beginning on or about 9/1. Must reply by May 1 or within 2 week(s) if notified thereafter. **Financial aid:** Priority date 3/1; no closing date. FAFSA required. Applicants notified on a rolling basis starting 4/1; must reply within 2 week(s) of notification.

**Academics.** All students encouraged to take advantage of individualized or computerized tutoring assistance. **Special study options:** Accelerated study, distance learning, double major, honors, independent study, internships, liberal arts/career combination, student-designed major, study abroad, teacher certification program. **Credit/placement by examination:** AP, CLEP, IB, SAT, ACT, institutional tests. 30 credit hours maximum toward bachelor's degree. **Support services:** Learning center, reduced course load, remedial instruction, study skills assistance, tutoring, writing center.

**Majors. Biology:** General. **Business:** General, accounting, management information systems, organizational behavior. **Communications:** General. **Education:** Art, computer, elementary, health, middle, music, physical, social studies, Spanish, special. **Foreign languages:** Spanish. **Health:** Community health services. **History:** General. **Math:** General. **Parks/recreation:** Health/fitness, sports admin. **Physical sciences:** Chemistry, physics. **Protective services:** Criminal justice. **Psychology:** General. **Public administration:** Human services, social work. **Social sciences:** Political science. **Theology:** Religious ed. **Visual/performing arts:** Dramatic, studio arts. **Other:** Applied science - engineering transfer, History & government, Philosophy & religion.

**Most popular majors.** Biology 12%, business/marketing 25%, education 14%, health sciences 8%, parks/recreation 8%, psychology 6%.

**Computing on campus.** 300 workstations in dormitories, library, computer center, student center. Dormitories wired for high-speed internet access and linked to campus network. Commuter students can connect to campus network. Online library, helpline, wireless network available.

**Student life. Freshman orientation:** Mandatory. Preregistration for classes offered. One-day session in summer. **Policies:** All students required to complete 40-hour community service project. Religious observance required. **Housing:** Guaranteed on-campus for all undergraduates. Single-sex dorms available. $125 partly refundable deposit, deadline 8/15. **Activities:** Bands, campus ministries, choral groups, dance, drama, international student organizations, music ensembles, musical theater, radio station, student government, student newspaper, TV station, Baptist student union, Fellowship of Christian Athletes, Appalachian ministries, Mountain Outreach.

**Athletics.** NAIA. **Intercollegiate:** Baseball M, basketball, cheerleading, cross-country, football (non-tackle) M, football (tackle) M, golf, soccer, softball W, swimming, tennis, track and field, volleyball W, wrestling. **Intramural:** Archery, badminton, basketball, football (non-tackle), golf, soccer, softball, table tennis, volleyball. **Team name:** Patriots.

**Student services.** Alcohol/substance abuse counseling, chaplain/spiritual director, career counseling, services for economically disadvantaged, student employment services, financial aid counseling, health services, personal counseling, placement for graduates, veterans' counselor, women's services. **Physically disabled:** Services for visually, speech, hearing impaired.

**Contact.** E-mail: admiss@ucumberlands.edu
Phone: (606) 539-4241 Toll-free number: (800) 343-1609
Fax: (606) 539-4303
Erica Harris, Director of Admissions, University of the Cumberlands, 6178 College Station Drive, Williamsburg, KY 40769

## Western Kentucky University
**Bowling Green, Kentucky**
**www.wku.edu**                              **CB code: 1901**

▶ Public 4-year university

▶ Commuter campus in small city

▶ 16,436 degree-seeking undergraduates: 16% part-time, 57% women, 11% African American, 1% Asian American, 1% Hispanic American, 2% international

▶ 2,563 degree-seeking graduate students

▶ 50% graduate within 6 years

**General.** Founded in 1906. Regionally accredited. Branch campus located in Glasgow offering general education, nursing, and elementary education programs. Upper division and graduate courses also offered at branch campuses in Owensboro and Fort Knox/Elizabethtown area. **Degrees:** 2,382 bachelor's, 217 associate awarded; master's, doctoral offered. **ROTC:** Army, Air Force. **Location:** 110 miles from Louisville; 65 miles from Nashville, TN. **Calendar:** Semester, limited summer session. **Full-time faculty:** 735 total; 72% have terminal degrees, 14% minority, 48% women. **Part-time faculty:** 415 total; 17% have terminal degrees, 4% minority, 51% women.

**Class size:** 41% < 20, 46% 20-39, 8% 40-49, 5% 50-99, less than 1% >100.
**Special facilities:** University farm, planetarium, observatory,.

**Freshman class profile.** 7,757 applied, 7,331 admitted, 3,387 enrolled.

| Mid 50% test scores | | | | |
|---|---|---|---|---|
| SAT critical reading: | 430-540 | Rank in top quarter: | 38% |
| SAT math: | 430-550 | Rank in top tenth: | 17% |
| ACT composite: | 18-24 | Return as sophomores: | 74% |
| GPA 3.75 or higher: | 20% | Out-of-state: | 17% |
| GPA 3.50-3.74: | 15% | Live on campus: | 71% |
| GPA 3.0-3.49: | 28% | International: | 1% |
| GPA 2.0-2.99: | 33% | Fraternities: | 7% |
| | | Sororities: | 10% |

**Basis for selection.** Open admission, but selective for some programs.

**High school preparation.** College-preparatory program required. 22 units required. Required units include English 4, mathematics 3, social studies 3, science 3 (laboratory 1), foreign language 2, visual/performing arts .5. 0.5 credits required in health, physical education, history, performing arts.

**2009-2010 Annual costs.** Tuition/fees: $7,200; $17,784 out-of-state. Room/board: $6,138. Books/supplies: $1,000. Personal expenses: $1,679.

**2008-2009 Financial aid. Need-based:** 2,654 full-time freshmen applied for aid; 1,943 were judged to have need; 1,924 of these received aid. Average need met was 32%. Average scholarship/grant was $5,247; average loan $3,018. 52% of total undergraduate aid awarded as scholarships/grants, 48% as loans/jobs. **Non-need-based:** Awarded to 5,924 full-time undergraduates, including 2,036 freshmen. Scholarships awarded for academics, alumni affiliation, art, athletics, job skills, leadership, minority status, music/drama, religious affiliation, ROTC, state residency.

**Application procedures. Admission:** Closing date 8/1 (postmark date). $40 fee, may be waived for applicants with need. Admission notification on a rolling basis. **Financial aid:** Priority date 4/1; no closing date. FAFSA required. Applicants notified on a rolling basis starting 3/1.

**Academics. Special study options:** Cooperative education, distance learning, double major, dual enrollment of high school students, ESL, exchange student, external degree, honors, independent study, internships, New York semester, student-designed major, study abroad, teacher certification program, Washington semester. **Credit/placement by examination:** CLEP, IB, institutional tests. Unlimited number of hours of credit by examination may be counted toward degree. **Support services:** Learning center, pre-admission summer program, reduced course load, remedial instruction, study skills assistance, tutoring, writing center.

**Honors college/program.** Students must have 27 ACT or 1210 SAT (exclusive of Writing), 3.8 unweighted GPA and be in top 15% of class.

**Majors. Agriculture:** General. **Architecture:** Technology. **Biology:** General, biochemistry. **Business:** Accounting, business admin, entrepreneurial studies, finance, hospitality admin, management information systems, managerial economics, marketing. **Communications:** General, advertising, journalism, organizational, photojournalism, public relations, radio/tv. **Computer sciences:** General, information technology. **Education:** Business, early childhood, elementary, family/consumer sciences, middle, physical, special, trade/industrial. **Engineering:** Civil, electrical, mechanical. **Engineering technology:** Construction, industrial, manufacturing. **Family/consumer sciences:** Clothing/textiles. **Foreign languages:** French, German, Spanish. **Health:** Clinical lab science, communication disorders, community health, dental hygiene, environmental health, health care admin, health services, nursing (RN). **History:** General. **Math:** General. **Parks/recreation:** Exercise sciences, facilities management, sports admin. **Philosophy/religion:** Philosophy, religion. **Physical sciences:** Chemistry, geology, meteorology, physics. **Psychology:** General. **Public administration:** Social work. **Social sciences:** General, anthropology, cartography, economics, geography, political science, sociology. **Visual/performing arts:** General, dance, dramatic, studio arts.

**Most popular majors.** Business/marketing 16%, communications/journalism 10%, education 14%, health sciences 8%, liberal arts 8%, social sciences 9%.

**Computing on campus.** 1,350 workstations in dormitories, library, computer center, student center. Dormitories wired for high-speed internet access and linked to campus network. Commuter students can connect to campus network. Online course registration, online library, helpline, repair service, student web hosting, wireless network available.

**Student life. Freshman orientation:** Mandatory, $45 fee. Preregistration for classes offered. **Housing:** Guaranteed on-campus for freshmen. Coed dorms, single-sex dorms, special housing for disabled, fraternity/sorority housing, wellness housing available. $150 partly refundable deposit, deadline 3/31. Learning communities, diversity housing, honors community available. **Activities:** Bands, campus ministries, choral groups, dance, drama,

film society, international student organizations, literary magazine, music ensembles, Model UN, musical theater, opera, radio station, student government, student newspaper, symphony orchestra, TV station, American Democracy Project, Amnesty International, Habitat for Humanity, College Republicans, College Democrats, Campus Crusade, Women in Transition, NAACP, black student alliance, Green Party, mock trial club, ONE Campaign Challenge.

**Athletics.** NCAA. **Intercollegiate:** Baseball M, basketball, cross-country, diving, football (tackle) M, golf, rifle, soccer, softball W, swimming, tennis, track and field, volleyball W. **Intramural:** Archery, badminton, basketball, bowling, equestrian, football (non-tackle), golf, handball, racquetball, soccer, softball, swimming, table tennis, triathlon, volleyball, water polo, wrestling M. **Team name:** Hilltoppers.

**Student services.** Adult student services, alcohol/substance abuse counseling, chaplain/spiritual director, career counseling, services for economically disadvantaged, student employment services, financial aid counseling, health services, minority student services, on-campus daycare, personal counseling, placement for graduates, veterans' counselor, women's services. **Physically disabled:** Services for visually, speech, hearing impaired.

**Contact.** E-mail: admission@wku.edu
Phone: (270) 745-2551 Toll-free number: (800) 495-8463
Fax: (270) 745-6133
Scott Gordon, Director of Admission and Academic Services, Western Kentucky University, 1906 College Heights Boulevard, Bowling Green, KY 42101

# Louisiana

## Centenary College of Louisiana

| Shreveport, Louisiana | CB member |
| --- | --- |
| www.centenary.edu | CB code: 6082 |

- Private 4-year liberal arts college affiliated with United Methodist Church
- Residential campus in small city
- 879 degree-seeking undergraduates: 1% part-time, 56% women, 10% African American, 3% Asian American, 3% Hispanic American, 1% international
- 86 degree-seeking graduate students
- SAT or ACT (ACT writing optional) required
- 61% graduate within 6 years

**General.** Founded in 1825. Regionally accredited. **Degrees:** 164 bachelor's awarded; master's offered. **Location:** 325 miles from New Orleans, 189 miles from Dallas. **Calendar:** Semester, extensive summer session. **Full-time faculty:** 71 total; 96% have terminal degrees, 4% minority, 35% women. **Part-time faculty:** 39 total; 28% have terminal degrees, 5% minority, 46% women. **Class size:** 72% < 20, 27% 20-39, less than 1% 40-49. **Special facilities:** Amphitheater, playhouse, music library, archives, Jack London collection.

### Freshman class profile.

| Mid 50% test scores | | Rank in top quarter: | 67% |
| --- | --- | --- | --- |
| SAT critical reading: | 510-620 | Rank in top tenth: | 37% |
| SAT math: | 500-610 | Return as sophomores: | 75% |
| SAT writing: | 480-610 | Out-of-state: | 45% |
| ACT composite: | 22-27 | International: | 1% |

**Basis for selection.** Academic achievement record, high school GPA, test scores, essay, letters of recommendation, interview recommended. Extracurricular activities and leadership ability considered. Audition required of music, theater, dance majors. Portfolio recommended for art majors. **Homeschooled:** Transcript of courses and grades required.

**High school preparation.** 15 units recommended. Recommended units include English 4, mathematics 3, social studies 3, science 3 (laboratory 2) and foreign language 2.

**2009-2010 Annual costs.** Tuition/fees: $22,900. Room/board: $7,940. Books/supplies: $1,200. Personal expenses: $1,820.

**2009-2010 Financial aid. Non-need-based:** Scholarships awarded for academics, art, athletics, leadership, music/drama, religious affiliation, state residency.

**Application procedures. Admission:** Priority date 2/15; deadline 8/1 (postmark date). $30 fee, may be waived for applicants with need. Admission notification on a rolling basis beginning on or about 11/15. Must reply by May 1 or within 3 week(s) if notified thereafter. **Financial aid:** Priority date 2/15; no closing date. FAFSA, institutional form required. Applicants notified on a rolling basis starting 2/15.

**Academics. Special study options:** Combined bachelor's/graduate degree, double major, dual enrollment of high school students, independent study, internships, liberal arts/career combination, student-designed major, study abroad, teacher certification program, Washington semester. Oak Ridge National Laboratory semester, 3-2 engineering program, 3-2 communication disorders program. **Credit/placement by examination:** AP, CLEP, IB, institutional tests. 40 credit hours maximum toward bachelor's degree. Credit awarded only when the student has not already attempted to earn credit in a college classroom at or below the level of the subject covered by the exam. **Support services:** Learning center, reduced course load, study skills assistance, tutoring, writing center.

**Majors. Biology:** General, biochemistry, biophysics. **Business:** Accounting, accounting/business management, accounting/finance, business admin, finance, managerial economics. **Communications:** General, digital media, media studies. **Conservation:** Environmental science. **Education:** Art, biology, chemistry, drama/dance, elementary, English, foreign languages, French, German, health, history, mathematics, middle, multi-level teacher, music, physical, psychology, science, secondary, social studies, Spanish. **Foreign languages:** General, classics, French, German, Latin, Spanish. **Health:** Predental, premedicine, prepharmacy, preveterinary, speech pathology. **History:** General. **Interdisciplinary:** Neuroscience. **Legal studies:** Prelaw. **Liberal arts:** Arts/sciences. **Math:** General. **Parks/recreation:** Exercise sciences, health/fitness. **Philosophy/religion:** Philosophy, religion. **Physical sciences:** Chemistry, geology, physics. **Psychology:** General. **Social sciences:** Applied economics, economics, political science, sociology. **Theology:** Sacred music. **Visual/performing arts:** General, art, cinematography, dance, dramatic, music performance, music theory/composition, painting, piano/organ, sculpture, studio arts, theater design, voice/opera.

**Most popular majors.** Biology 18%, business/marketing 16%, communication technologies 6%, parks/recreation 7%, psychology 7%, visual/performing arts 7%.

**Computing on campus.** 250 workstations in dormitories, library, computer center. Dormitories linked to campus network. Commuter students can connect to campus network. Online course registration, student web hosting, wireless network available.

**Student life. Freshman orientation:** Mandatory, $100 fee. Held 4 days prior to beginning of fall classes. **Policies:** Students participate on enrollment management committee, academic affairs committee, student/faculty discipline and other college-wide committees. All students 21 years of age or younger who are not local residents required to live in college housing. **Housing:** Guaranteed on-campus for all undergraduates. Coed dorms, single-sex dorms, fraternity/sorority housing available. $200 partly refundable deposit, deadline 7/1. **Activities:** Bands, choral groups, dance, drama, film society, music ensembles, musical theater, opera, radio station, student government, student newspaper, symphony orchestra, church careers institute, United Methodist student movement, Baptist collegiate ministry, Canterbury House, Fellowship of Christian Athletes, student government association, Young Democrats, Young Republicans, Students for Diversity, tutoring service.

**Athletics.** NCAA. **Intercollegiate:** Baseball M, basketball, cross-country, golf, gymnastics W, soccer, softball W, swimming, tennis, volleyball W. **Intramural:** Archery, badminton, basketball, bowling, football (nontackle), golf, lacrosse M, racquetball, rowing (crew), soccer, softball, table tennis, tennis, volleyball. **Team name:** Gents/Ladies.

**Student services.** Alcohol/substance abuse counseling, chaplain/spiritual director, career counseling, financial aid counseling, health services, personal counseling, veterans' counselor. **Physically disabled:** Services for visually impaired.

**Contact.** E-mail: tcrowley@centenary.edu
Phone: (318) 869-5131 Toll-free number: (800) 234-4448
Fax: (318) 869-5005
Tim Crowley, Director of Admissions, Centenary College of Louisiana, Box 41188, Shreveport, LA 71134-1188

## Dillard University

| New Orleans, Louisiana | CB member |
| --- | --- |
| www.dillard.edu | CB code: 6164 |

- Private 4-year university and liberal arts college affiliated with United Church of Christ and United Methodist Church
- Residential campus in large city
- 1,011 degree-seeking undergraduates: 6% part-time, 73% women, 96% African American, 1% Hispanic American
- 48% of applicants admitted
- SAT or ACT (ACT writing optional), application essay required

**General.** Founded in 1869. Regionally accredited. **Degrees:** 171 bachelor's awarded. **ROTC:** Army, Naval, Air Force. **Calendar:** Semester, limited summer session. **Full-time faculty:** 92 total; 70% have terminal degrees, 91% minority, 53% women. **Part-time faculty:** 23 total; 70% minority, 61% women. **Class size:** 60% < 20, 34% 20-39, 5% 40-49, 1% 50-99, less than 1% >100.

**Freshman class profile.** 3,993 applied, 1,900 admitted, 326 enrolled.

| Mid 50% test scores | | ACT composite: | 16-20 |
| --- | --- | --- | --- |
| SAT critical reading: | 370-470 | Rank in top quarter: | 33% |
| SAT math: | 340-440 | Rank in top tenth: | 11% |
| SAT writing: | 360-480 | Out-of-state: | 46% |

**Basis for selection.** Preference to applicants in top 25% of class with 2.5 GPA. Test scores, class rank, participation in extracurricular activities and community projects considered. Interview recommended. **Homeschooled:** Recommended that student apply for state diploma.

**High school preparation.** 19 units required. Required and recommended units include English 4, mathematics 3, social studies 3, science 3, foreign language 2 and academic electives 6.

**2009-2010 Annual costs.** Tuition/fees: $13,540. Room/board: $8,210. Books/supplies: $1,000. Personal expenses: $1,533.

**Financial aid.** All financial aid based on need.

**Application procedures. Admission:** Priority date 12/1; deadline 7/1 (postmark date). $30 fee, may be waived for applicants with need. Admission notification on a rolling basis. Must reply by May 1 or within 2 week(s) if notified thereafter. **Financial aid:** Priority date 12/1, closing date 5/1. FAFSA, institutional form required. Applicants notified on a rolling basis starting 3/1; must reply by 5/1 or within 2 week(s) of notification.

**Academics. Special study options:** Combined bachelor's/graduate degree, double major, dual enrollment of high school students, exchange student, honors, independent study, internships, liberal arts/career combination, study abroad, teacher certification program. **Credit/placement by examination:** AP, CLEP, IB, SAT, ACT, institutional tests. 20 credit hours maximum toward bachelor's degree. **Support services:** Learning center, pre-admission summer program, reduced course load, remedial instruction, tutoring, writing center.

**Majors. Area/ethnic studies:** African. **Biology:** General. **Business:** Accounting, business admin, finance. **Communications:** General. **Computer sciences:** Computer science. **Education:** Brain injured, early childhood, early childhood special, elementary, physical, secondary, special. **Foreign languages:** General, French, German, Spanish. **Health:** Nursing (RN), premedicine, public health ed. **History:** General. **Math:** General. **Philosophy/religion:** Philosophy, religion. **Physical sciences:** Chemistry, physics. **Psychology:** General. **Public administration:** Social work. **Social sciences:** Criminology, economics, political science, sociology, urban studies. **Visual/performing arts:** Art, arts management, dramatic, music management.

**Most popular majors.** Biology 9%, business/marketing 13%, communications/journalism 12%, health sciences 21%, psychology 8%, social sciences 20%.

**Computing on campus.** 400 workstations in dormitories, library, computer center. Dormitories wired for high-speed internet access and linked to campus network. Commuter students can connect to campus network. Online library, helpline, repair service available.

**Student life. Freshman orientation:** Mandatory, $200 fee. Preregistration for classes offered. One-week program held the week before classes begin; includes advising and registration. **Housing:** Guaranteed on-campus for freshmen. Coed dorms, single-sex dorms, special housing for disabled, apartments, wellness housing available. $300 nonrefundable deposit, deadline 5/1. **Activities:** Jazz band, choral groups, dance, drama, music ensembles, musical theater, radio station, student government, student newspaper, service sororities and fraternities, honor societies, religious groups, NAACP, Santa Filomena, Young Republicans, Baptist student union.

**Athletics.** NAIA. **Intercollegiate:** Basketball, cross-country, softball W, track and field, volleyball W. **Intramural:** Basketball, football (non-tackle), football (tackle) M, softball, tennis, volleyball. **Team name:** Blue Devils.

**Student services.** Chaplain/spiritual director, career counseling, student employment services, financial aid counseling, health services, personal counseling, placement for graduates.

**Contact.** E-mail: admission@dillard.edu
Phone: (504) 816-4670 Toll-free number: (800) 216-6637
Fax: (504) 816-4895
Meredith Reed, Director of Admissions, Dillard University, 2601 Gentilly Boulevard, New Orleans, LA 70122-3097

## Grambling State University
**Grambling, Louisiana**
www.gram.edu                              CB code: 6250

- Public 4-year university
- Residential campus in small town
- 4,534 degree-seeking undergraduates: 7% part-time, 61% women, 88% African American, 10% international
- 446 degree-seeking graduate students
- SAT or ACT (ACT writing optional) required
- 31% graduate within 6 years

**General.** Founded in 1901. Regionally accredited. **Degrees:** 554 bachelor's, 33 associate awarded; master's, doctoral offered. **ROTC:** Army, Air

Force. **Location:** 35 miles from Monroe, 65 miles from Shreveport. **Calendar:** Semester, limited summer session. **Full-time faculty:** 242 total; 58% have terminal degrees, 65% minority, 44% women. **Part-time faculty:** 17 total; 47% minority. **Class size:** 44% < 20, 44% 20-39, 8% 40-49, 4% 50-99.

**Freshman class profile.**

| Mid 50% test scores | | |
|---|---|---|
| SAT critical reading: | 370-470 | |
| SAT math: | 380-480 | |
| ACT composite: | 16-19 | |
| GPA 3.75 or higher: | 2% | |
| GPA 3.50-3.74: | 5% | |
| GPA 3.0-3.49: | 25% | |

| | |
|---|---|
| GPA 2.0-2.99: | 64% |
| Rank in top quarter: | 33% |
| Rank in top tenth: | 4% |
| End year in good standing: | 58% |
| Return as sophomores: | 57% |
| Out-of-state: | 46% |
| International: | 3% |

**Basis for selection.** GED not accepted. 2.0 GPA or 20 ACT and completion of 17.5 high school core units required for in-state applicants. Graduates of non-Louisiana high schools must complete the required units plus have either a 2.0 GPA and 20 ACT or have a 23 ACT. Neither group can require more than 1 developmental course. **Homeschooled:** State high school equivalency certificate required.

**High school preparation.** College-preparatory program recommended. 16.5 units required. Required units include English 4, mathematics 3, history 3, science 3, foreign language 2, computer science .5 and visual/performing arts 1. One additional unit of advanced math (geometry or above) or advanced science required (biology II, chemistry II, physics, or above). Foreign language units must be of the same language.

**2009-2010 Annual costs.** Tuition/fees: $4,016; $9,902 out-of-state. Room/board: $5,468. Books/supplies: $1,200. Personal expenses: $3,638.

**2009-2010 Financial aid. Need-based:** Average scholarship/grant was $1,729; average loan $1,734. 48% of total undergraduate aid awarded as scholarships/grants, 52% as loans/jobs. **Non-need-based:** Awarded to 947 full-time undergraduates, including 52 freshmen. Scholarships awarded for academics, alumni affiliation, art, athletics, job skills, leadership, minority status, music/drama, religious affiliation, ROTC, state residency.

**Application procedures. Admission:** Priority date 4/1; deadline 6/1 (receipt date). $20 fee. Admission notification on a rolling basis. **Financial aid:** Priority date 4/1, closing date 6/1. FAFSA required. Applicants notified on a rolling basis starting 3/1; must reply within 2 week(s) of notification.

**Academics. Special study options:** Cooperative education, cross-registration, distance learning, double major, exchange student, honors, independent study, internships, study abroad, teacher certification program. **Credit/placement by examination:** AP, CLEP, SAT, ACT, institutional tests. 30 credit hours maximum toward associate degree, 30 toward bachelor's. **Support services:** Learning center, reduced course load, remedial instruction, study skills assistance, tutoring, writing center.

**Honors college/program.** 25 ACT/SAT equivalent and 3.5 GPA required.

**Majors. Biology:** General. **Business:** Accounting, business admin, hotel/motel admin, managerial economics, marketing. **Communications:** Media studies. **Computer sciences:** Computer science, information systems. **Education:** Art, biology, early childhood, elementary, English, French, mathematics, middle, music, physical, physics, social studies, special. **Engineering technology:** Drafting, electrical. **Foreign languages:** French, Spanish. **Health:** Nursing (RN). **History:** General. **Legal studies:** Paralegal, prelaw. **Math:** General. **Parks/recreation:** General. **Physical sciences:** Chemistry, physics. **Protective services:** Criminal justice. **Psychology:** General. **Public administration:** Social work. **Social sciences:** Political science, sociology. **Visual/performing arts:** Art, dramatic, music performance.

**Most popular majors.** Business/marketing 19%, computer/information sciences 7%, education 7%, health sciences 19%, security/protective services 13%.

**Computing on campus.** 300 workstations in dormitories, library, computer center, student center. Dormitories wired for high-speed internet access and linked to campus network. Commuter students can connect to campus network. Online course registration, online library, helpline, wireless network available.

**Student life. Freshman orientation:** Mandatory. Preregistration for classes offered. **Housing:** Single-sex dorms, special housing for disabled, apartments, wellness housing available. $50 fully refundable deposit, deadline 7/15. **Activities:** Bands, campus ministries, choral groups, dance, drama, international student organizations, music ensembles, Model UN, opera, radio station, student government, student newspaper, symphony orchestra, TV station, Bayou Boyz social organization, Favrot student union, College Democrats, Ladies of Essence, NAACP, Bayou Girlz.

**Athletics.** NCAA. **Intercollegiate:** Baseball M, basketball, bowling W, cross-country, football (tackle) M, golf, soccer W, softball W, tennis, track and field, volleyball W. **Intramural:** Badminton, baseball M, basketball, bowling, cross-country, golf, gymnastics M, softball W, swimming, tennis, track and field, volleyball. **Team name:** Tigers.

**Student services.** Career counseling, student employment services, financial aid counseling, health services, personal counseling, placement for graduates, veterans' counselor. **Physically disabled:** Services for visually, speech, hearing impaired.

**Contact.** E-mail: admissions@gram.edu
Phone: (318) 274-6183 Toll-free number: (888) 863-3655
Fax: (318) 274-3292
Annie Moss, Director of Admissions and Recruitment, Grambling State University, 403 Main Street, GSU Box 4200, Grambling, LA 71245

## Herzing University
Kenner, Louisiana
www.herzing.edu                         CB code: 3430

- For-profit 4-year branch campus and technical college
- Commuter campus in very large city
- 356 degree-seeking undergraduates
- 100% of applicants admitted
- Interview required

**General.** Regionally accredited. **Degrees:** 12 bachelor's, 50 associate awarded. **Location:** 10 miles from downtown New Orleans. **Calendar:** Semester, extensive summer session. **Full-time faculty:** 4 total. **Part-time faculty:** 20 total. **Class size:** 16% < 20, 84% 20-39.

**Basis for selection.** Wonderlic entrance test required.

**2009-2010 Annual costs.** Tuition costs vary by program, $360-$390 per credit hour.

**Application procedures. Admission:** No deadline. No application fee.

**Academics. Special study options:** Combined bachelor's/graduate degree, distance learning, liberal arts/career combination, weekend college. **Credit/placement by examination:** CLEP, IB, institutional tests. **Support services:** Learning center, reduced course load, study skills assistance, tutoring.

**Majors. Business:** Accounting, business admin, management information systems. **Computer sciences:** Information technology, LAN/WAN management, programming.

**Computing on campus.** 115 workstations in library, computer center, student center. Online library, helpline, repair service available.

**Student life. Freshman orientation:** Mandatory. **Activities:** Student government.

**Student services.** Career counseling, student employment services, financial aid counseling, placement for graduates. **Physically disabled:** Services for visually, hearing impaired.

**Contact.** E-mail: info@nor.herzing.edu
Phone: (504) 733-0074 Fax: (504) 733-0020
Chrissy Kalivitis, Adult Leaner Admissions Advisor, Herzing University, 2400 Veterans Boulevard, Suite 410, Kenner, LA 70062

## ITT Technical Institute: St. Rose
St. Rose, Louisiana
www.itt-tech.edu                         CB code: 2766

- For-profit 4-year technical college
- Commuter campus in small town

**General.** Accredited by ACICS. **Calendar:** Quarter.

**Contact.** Phone: (504) 463-0338
Director of Recruitment, 140 James Drive East, St. Rose, LA 70087

## Louisiana College
Pineville, Louisiana
www.lacollege.edu                         CB code: 6371

- Private 4-year liberal arts college affiliated with Southern Baptist Convention
- Residential campus in small city
- 1,037 degree-seeking undergraduates: 7% part-time, 49% women
- 424 degree-seeking graduate students
- 51% of applicants admitted
- SAT or ACT (ACT writing optional) required
- 43% graduate within 6 years

**General.** Founded in 1906. Regionally accredited. **Degrees:** 152 bachelor's awarded; master's offered. **ROTC:** Army. **Location:** 110 miles from Shreveport, 140 miles from Baton Rouge. **Calendar:** Semester, limited summer session. **Full-time faculty:** 67 total; 61% have terminal degrees, 3% minority, 46% women. **Part-time faculty:** 34 total; 12% have terminal degrees, 44% women. **Class size:** 70% < 20, 26% 20-39, 3% 40-49, less than 1% 50-99.

**Freshman class profile.** 1,091 applied, 560 admitted, 255 enrolled.

| Mid 50% test scores | | SAT writing: | 400-600 |
|---|---|---|---|
| SAT critical reading: | 430-600 | ACT composite: | 17-24 |
| SAT math: | 420-600 | Return as sophomores: | 64% |

**Basis for selection.** 20 ACT (930 SAT) and 2.0 GPA or 17 ACT (810 SAT) and 2.0 GPA and rank in the upper 50% of graduating class required. Interview required of nursing, respiratory care majors. Portfolio recommended for art majors.

**High school preparation.** 17 units required. Required units include English 4, mathematics 3, social studies 3, science 3 (laboratory 2) and academic electives 4.

**2009-2010 Annual costs.** Tuition/fees: $12,530. Room/board: $4,450. Books/supplies: $535. Personal expenses: $1,040.

**Financial aid. Non-need-based:** Scholarships awarded for academics, art, leadership, music/drama, ROTC.

**Application procedures. Admission:** Closing date 8/15. $25 fee, may be waived for applicants with need. Admission notification on a rolling basis. Must reply by May 1 or within 2 week(s) if notified thereafter. **Financial aid:** Priority date 3/31; no closing date. FAFSA, institutional form required. Applicants notified on a rolling basis starting 3/1; must reply by 5/1 or within 2 week(s) of notification.

**Academics. Special study options:** Double major, dual enrollment of high school students, independent study, internships, liberal arts/career combination, student-designed major, study abroad, teacher certification program. **Credit/placement by examination:** AP, CLEP, institutional tests. 30 credit hours maximum toward bachelor's degree. **Support services:** Preadmission summer program, reduced course load, remedial instruction, tutoring.

**Majors. Biology:** General. **Business:** General, accounting, business admin, finance, marketing. **Communications:** General, journalism, media studies. **Computer sciences:** Webmaster. **Education:** General, art, business, elementary, English, foreign languages, French, health, mathematics, middle, music, physical, physically handicapped, science, secondary, social studies, Spanish. **Foreign languages:** General, French. **Health:** Athletic training, clinical lab technology, nursing (RN), physical therapy assistant, predental, premedicine, prepharmacy, preveterinary. **History:** General. **Interdisciplinary:** Biological/physical sciences. **Legal studies:** Prelaw. **Math:** General. **Parks/recreation:** Health/fitness. **Philosophy/religion:** Religion. **Physical sciences:** Chemistry. **Protective services:** Law enforcement admin. **Psychology:** General. **Public administration:** General, social work. **Social sciences:** General, economics, political science, sociology. **Theology:** Religious ed, sacred music. **Visual/performing arts:** Commercial/advertising art, dramatic, music pedagogy, music performance, piano/organ, studio arts, voice/opera.

**Most popular majors.** Biology 10%, business/marketing 7%, communications/journalism 6%, education 11%, health sciences 15%, history 8%, public administration/social services 7%, social sciences 9%, visual/performing arts 7%.

**Computing on campus.** 242 workstations in library, computer center, student center. Dormitories linked to campus network.

**Student life. Freshman orientation:** Mandatory. Preregistration for classes offered. **Policies:** Religious observance required. **Housing:** Guaranteed on-campus for all undergraduates. Single-sex dorms, apartments, wellness housing available. $75 deposit, deadline 8/1. **Activities:** Bands, campus ministries, choral groups, drama, international student organizations, literary magazine, music ensembles, musical theater, opera, radio station, student government, student newspaper, Lamda Chi Beta, Delta Xi Omega, Sigma Theta, Kappa Tau Beta, Union Board, church vocation fellowship, Fellowship of Christian Athletes, Jacob's Society.

**Athletics.** NCAA, NCCAA. **Intercollegiate:** Baseball M, basketball, cheerleading, cross-country, football (tackle) M, golf M, soccer, softball W, tennis W. **Intramural:** Badminton, basketball, bowling, golf, softball, swimming, table tennis, tennis, volleyball. **Team name:** Wildcats.

**Student services.** Chaplain/spiritual director, career counseling, student employment services, financial aid counseling, health services, personal counseling, placement for graduates. **Physically disabled:** Services for visually impaired.

**Contact.** E-mail: admissions@lacollege.edu
Phone: (318) 487-7259 Toll-free number: (800) 487-1906
Fax: (318) 487-7550
Byron McGee, Director of Enrollment Management and Admissions, Louisiana College, LC Box 566, Pineville, LA 71359

## Louisiana State University and Agricultural and Mechanical College

| Baton Rouge, Louisiana | CB member |
| --- | --- |
| www.lsu.edu | CB code: 6373 |

- Public 4-year university and agricultural college
- Commuter campus in large city
- 22,625 degree-seeking undergraduates: 6% part-time, 51% women, 9% African American, 3% Asian American, 3% Hispanic American, 2% international
- 5,397 degree-seeking graduate students
- 69% of applicants admitted
- SAT or ACT (ACT writing recommended) required
- 61% graduate within 6 years

**General.** Founded in 1860. Regionally accredited. **Degrees:** 4,734 bachelor's awarded; master's, doctoral, professional offered. **ROTC:** Army, Naval, Air Force. **Location:** 80 miles from New Orleans. **Calendar:** Semester, extensive summer session. **Full-time faculty:** 1,309 total; 88% have terminal degrees, 15% minority, 35% women. **Part-time faculty:** 146 total; 62% have terminal degrees, 8% minority, 38% women. **Class size:** 35% < 20, 38% 20-39, 7% 40-49, 11% 50-99, 8% >100. **Special facilities:** Mycological herbarium, lichenological herbarium, natural science museum, geoscience museum, rural life museum, Anglo-American art museum, Civil War center, biomedical research center, coastal ecology center, center for advanced microstructures and devices.

**Freshman class profile.** 15,917 applied, 11,012 admitted, 4,789 enrolled.

| Mid 50% test scores | | GPA 2.0-2.99: | 8% |
| --- | --- | --- | --- |
| SAT critical reading: | 510-630 | Rank in top quarter: | 53% |
| SAT math: | 540-650 | Rank in top tenth: | 25% |
| SAT writing: | 490-600 | End year in good standing: | 86% |
| ACT composite: | 23-28 | Return as sophomores: | 84% |
| GPA 3.75 or higher: | 28% | Out-of-state: | 24% |
| GPA 3.50-3.74: | 25% | Live on campus: | 67% |
| GPA 3.0-3.49: | 39% | International: | 2% |

**Basis for selection.** Criteria include number of academic units earned, GPA, ACT or SAT scores. Students must also meet minimum Board of Regents Master Plan requirements. Applicants not meeting course units and/or grades or test score requirements may be considered by admissions committee. Audition required for MDA majors. Portfolio required for Art and Landscape Architecture majors. **Homeschooled:** Statement describing homeschool structure and mission, transcript of courses and grades required. Students with ACT score below 26 will be reviewed by admission committee. **Learning Disabled:** Students with learning disabilities who do not meet regular admission requirements may appeal to admission committee and submit documentation explaining positions.

**High school preparation.** College-preparatory program required. 18 units required. Required and recommended units include English 4, mathematics 3-4, social studies 1, history 2, science 3, foreign language 2, academic electives 2.5. Computer literacy (.5 units) also required. Specific courses required in some subject areas.

**2009-2010 Annual costs.** Tuition/fees: $5,233; $14,383 out-of-state. Room/board: $7,738. Books/supplies: $1,500. Personal expenses: $1,820.

**2008-2009 Financial aid.** **Need-based:** 3,117 full-time freshmen applied for aid; 1,750 were judged to have need; 1,750 of these received aid.

Average need met was 74%. Average scholarship/grant was $8,549; average loan $3,157. 55% of total undergraduate aid awarded as scholarships/grants, 45% as loans/jobs. **Non-need-based:** Awarded to 4,239 full-time undergraduates, including 1,657 freshmen. Scholarships awarded for academics, alumni affiliation, athletics, leadership, music/drama, ROTC, state residency.

**Application procedures. Admission:** Priority date 11/15; deadline 4/15 (receipt date). $40 fee, may be waived for applicants with need. Application must be submitted online. Admission notification on a rolling basis. **Financial aid:** Priority date 7/1; no closing date. FAFSA required. Applicants notified on a rolling basis starting 4/1; must reply by 5/1 or within 3 week(s) of notification.

**Academics. Special study options:** Accelerated study, cooperative education, cross-registration, distance learning, double major, dual enrollment of high school students, ESL, exchange student, honors, independent study, internships, student-designed major, study abroad, teacher certification program. **Credit/placement by examination:** AP, CLEP, IB, SAT, ACT, institutional tests. 30 credit hours maximum toward bachelor's degree. **Support services:** Learning center, study skills assistance, tutoring, writing center.

**Honors college/program.** 30 ACT with 30 English, or 29 ACT with 31 English, or 1320 SAT (exclusive of Writing) with 660 Verbal. 3.5 GPA and essay required. ACT/SAT writing component required.

**Majors. Agriculture:** Animal sciences, business, food science, plant sciences. **Architecture:** Architecture, interior, landscape. **Area/ethnic studies:** Women's. **Biology:** General, biochemistry, microbiology. **Business:** Accounting, business admin, construction management, fashion, finance, international, management science, managerial economics, marketing. **Communications:** Media studies. **Computer sciences:** Computer science. **Conservation:** Environmental science, forest management, management/policy. **Education:** Adult/continuing, agricultural, business, early childhood, elementary, family/consumer sciences, music, physical, sales/marketing, secondary. **Engineering:** Biomedical, chemical, civil, computer, electrical, environmental, industrial, mechanical, petroleum. **Family/consumer sciences:** General. **Foreign languages:** French, German, Latin, Spanish. **Health:** Audiology/speech pathology, dietetics. **History:** General. **Interdisciplinary:** Global studies. **Liberal arts:** Arts/sciences. **Math:** General. **Parks/recreation:** Sports admin. **Philosophy/religion:** Philosophy. **Physical sciences:** Chemistry, geology, oceanography, physics. **Psychology:** General. **Social sciences:** Anthropology, economics, geography, political science, sociology. **Visual/performing arts:** Dramatic, music performance, studio arts.

**Most popular majors.** Biology 9%, business/marketing 18%, education 8%, engineering/engineering technologies 8%, English 6%, liberal arts 9%, social sciences 9%.

**Computing on campus.** 1,500 workstations in dormitories, library, student center. Dormitories wired for high-speed internet access and linked to campus network. Commuter students can connect to campus network. Online course registration, online library, helpline, student web hosting, wireless network available.

**Student life. Freshman orientation:** Mandatory, $116 fee. Preregistration for classes offered. Held in June, July, and August; Spring Invitational held in April. **Housing:** Coed dorms, single-sex dorms, special housing for disabled, apartments, fraternity/sorority housing available. $150 partly refundable deposit. **Activities:** Bands, campus ministries, choral groups, dance, drama, film society, international student organizations, literary magazine, music ensembles, musical theater, opera, radio station, student government, student newspaper, symphony orchestra, TV station, various religious, professional, honorary, political, service, and special interest organizations.

**Athletics.** NCAA. **Intercollegiate:** Baseball M, basketball, cross-country, football (tackle) M, golf, gymnastics W, soccer W, softball W, swimming, tennis, track and field, volleyball W. **Intramural:** Badminton, basketball, football (non-tackle), golf, racquetball, soccer, softball, table tennis, tennis, volleyball. **Team name:** Tigers.

**Student services.** Adult student services, alcohol/substance abuse counseling, career counseling, student employment services, financial aid counseling, health services, minority student services, on-campus daycare, personal counseling, placement for graduates, veterans' counselor, women's services. **Physically disabled:** Services for visually, speech, hearing impaired.

**Contact.** E-mail: admissions@lsu.edu
Phone: (225) 578-1175 Fax: (225) 578-4433
Mary Parker, Executive Director of Undergraduate Admissions & Student Aid, Louisiana State University and Agricultural and Mechanical College, 1146 Pleasant Halll, Baton Rouge, LA 70803-2750

## Louisiana State University at Alexandria
**Alexandria, Louisiana**
www.lsua.edu                               CB code: 1632

♦ Public 4-year university
♦ Commuter campus in small city
♦ 1,287 full-time, degree-seeking undergraduates
♦ 75% of applicants admitted
♦ ACT required

**General.** Founded in 1959. Regionally accredited. **Degrees:** 166 bachelor's, 151 associate awarded. **ROTC:** Army. **Location:** 10 miles from downtown. **Calendar:** Semester, extensive summer session. **Full-time faculty:** 111 total. **Part-time faculty:** 65 total. **Class size:** 42% < 20, 50% 20-39, 4% 40-49, 3% 50-99.

**Freshman class profile.** 646 applied, 485 admitted, 378 enrolled.

Mid 50% test scores                Out-of-state:            1%
  ACT composite:        18-23

**Basis for selection.** Admissibility based on high school curriculum, GPA, class rank, ACT, and the need, if any, for developmental course work. Completion of Regents high school core curriculum required, along with one of the following: 2.0 GPA or rank in top 50% of class or 20 ACT. Students must also need no more than one developmental course by having one of the following: 18 ACT English or 19 ACT math. **Homeschooled:** Applicants must submit transcript of high school level work with graduation date.

**High school preparation.** 17.5 units required. Required units include English 4, mathematics 3, social studies 3, science 3 and foreign language 2. 1 additional unit in math or science, .5 units in computer studies and 1 unit in fine arts survey required. Foreign language units must be in same language.

**2009-2010 Annual costs.** Tuition/fees: $3,576; $6,284 out-of-state. Room/board: $6,234. Books/supplies: $1,200. Personal expenses: $1,726.

**Financial aid.** Non-need-based: Scholarships awarded for academics, state residency.

**Application procedures. Admission:** Priority date 8/1; no deadline. $20 fee. Admission notification on a rolling basis. **Financial aid:** Priority date 4/1; no closing date. FAFSA, institutional form required. Applicants notified on a rolling basis starting 4/20; must reply within 3 week(s) of notification.

**Academics. Special study options:** Distance learning, dual enrollment of high school students. **Credit/placement by examination:** AP, CLEP, institutional tests. Credit by examination limited to one-fourth number of hours required for degree. **Support services:** Learning center, pre-admission summer program, remedial instruction, study skills assistance, tutoring, writing center.

**Majors. Biology:** General. **Business:** Business admin. **Education:** General, elementary. **Health:** Nursing (RN). **History:** General. **Liberal arts:** Arts/sciences. **Math:** General. **Protective services:** Criminal justice. **Psychology:** General.

**Most popular majors.** Education 24%, liberal arts 74%.

**Computing on campus.** 163 workstations in library, computer center, student center. Commuter students can connect to campus network.

**Student life. Freshman orientation:** Mandatory. Preregistration for classes offered. **Housing:** Apartments available. **Activities:** Choral groups, drama, literary magazine, student government, student newspaper, Baptist ministry, Catholic student organization, Apostolic student fellowship, Canterbury club, College Republicans, College Democrats, international student organization, nontraditional student organization, Identity, Circle K.

**Athletics. Intramural:** Basketball, cross-country, football (non-tackle) M, soccer, softball, tennis, volleyball. **Team name:** Generals.

**Student services.** Adult student services, chaplain/spiritual director, career counseling, student employment services, financial aid counseling, minority student services, on-campus daycare, personal counseling, placement for graduates, veterans' counselor.

**Contact.** E-mail: generalinfo@lsua.edu
Phone: (318) 473-6417 Toll-free number: (888) 473-6417
Fax: (318) 473-6418
Teresa Seymour, Registrar, Louisiana State University at Alexandria, 8100 Highway 71 South, Alexandria, LA 71302-9121

## Louisiana State University Health Sciences Center
**New Orleans, Louisiana**
www.lsuhsc.edu                             CB code: 1192

♦ Public two-year upper-division health science and nursing college
♦ Commuter campus in large city
♦ Interview required

**General.** Founded in 1931. Regionally accredited. **Degrees:** 255 bachelor's, 6 associate awarded; master's, doctoral, professional offered. **Articulation:** Agreement with University of New Orleans. **Calendar:** Differs by program, limited summer session. **Part-time faculty:** 9 total.

**Student profile.** 836 undergraduates, 1,808 graduate students.

Out-of-state:          1%     25 or older:        28%
Live on campus:       20%

**Basis for selection.** College transcript, interview required. Application closing, notification, and response dates vary by program. Transfer accepted as sophomores, juniors, seniors.

**2009-2010 Annual costs.** Allied Health Professions: $5,548 residents, $8,992 non-residents. Dental Hygiene: $3,314 residents, $4,856 non-residents. Dental Laboratory Technology: $3,039 residents, $4,581 non-residents. School of Nursing: $3,360 residents, $5,234 non-residents. Books/supplies: $3,262.

**Financial aid.** Non-need-based: Scholarships awarded for academics.

**Application procedures. Admission:** $50 fee. **Financial aid:** FAFSA, institutional form required.

**Academics. Special study options:** Cross-registration, double major, honors, independent study, internships. **Credit/placement by examination:** CLEP.

**Majors. Health:** Cardiovascular technology, clinical lab science, dental hygiene, dental lab technology, nursing (RN), vocational rehab counseling.

**Computing on campus.** 227 workstations in dormitories, library, computer center, student center. Dormitories wired for high-speed internet access and linked to campus network. Commuter students can connect to campus network. Online library, helpline, repair service, wireless network available.

**Student life. Housing:** Coed dorms, apartments, wellness housing available. **Activities:** Choral groups, student government.

**Student services.** Alcohol/substance abuse counseling, career counseling, financial aid counseling, health services, personal counseling. **Physically disabled:** Services for visually, speech, hearing impaired.

**Contact.** Phone: (504) 568-4808
Louisiana State University Health Sciences Center, 433 Bolivar Street, New Orleans, LA 70112-2223

## Louisiana State University in Shreveport
**Shreveport, Louisiana**
www.lsus.edu                               CB code: 6355

♦ Public 4-year university and liberal arts college
♦ Commuter campus in large city
♦ 3,260 degree-seeking undergraduates
♦ 447 graduate students
♦ 80% of applicants admitted
♦ ACT (writing optional), application essay required

**General.** Founded in 1965. Regionally accredited. **Degrees:** 533 bachelor's awarded; master's offered. **ROTC:** Army. **Location:** 180 miles from Dallas. **Calendar:** Semester, extensive summer session. **Full-time faculty:** 150 total. **Part-time faculty:** 53 total. **Class size:** 42% < 20, 40% 20-39, 9% 40-49, 8% 50-99, less than 1% >100. **Special facilities:** Life science museum, pioneer heritage center.

**Freshman class profile.** 750 applied, 600 admitted, 402 enrolled.

| Mid 50% test scores | | | |
|---|---|---|---|
| SAT critical reading: | 530-550 | GPA 3.0-3.49: | 35% |
| SAT math: | 490-560 | GPA 2.0-2.99: | 34% |
| ACT composite: | 20-24 | End year in good standing: | 96% |
| GPA 3.75 or higher: | 17% | Return as sophomores: | 41% |
| GPA 3.50-3.74: | 14% | Out-of-state: | 9% |

**Basis for selection.** Completion of Regents high school core curriculum of 16.5 course units and one of the following required: 2.0 GPA, high school rank in top 50% of class, or 20 ACT. For early admission, principal's recommendation, 29 ACT, 15 specific high school units, 3.0 GPA required. Regardless of age, students who have accumulated at least 12 term hours of non-developmental college credit may transfer if all transfer requirements met. **Homeschooled:** GED required.

**High school preparation.** Recommended units include English 4, mathematics 3, social studies 3, science 3, foreign language 2, computer science 1 and visual/performing arts 1.

**2009-2010 Annual costs.** Tuition/fees: $3,925; $8,695 out-of-state. Books/supplies: $1,200. Personal expenses: $1,819.

**Application procedures. Admission:** Closing date 7/15 (receipt date). $10 fee. Application must be submitted on paper. Admission notification on a rolling basis. **Financial aid:** No deadline. Applicants notified on a rolling basis.

**Academics. Special study options:** Combined bachelor's/graduate degree, cooperative education, distance learning, double major, dual enrollment of high school students, independent study, internships, student-designed major, study abroad, teacher certification program, Washington semester. Cooperative education program with Southern University at Shreveport. **Credit/placement by examination:** AP, CLEP, ACT, institutional tests. 62 credit hours maximum toward bachelor's degree. **Support services:** Learning center, remedial instruction, study skills assistance, tutoring, writing center.

**Majors. Biology:** General, biochemistry. **Business:** Accounting, banking/financial services, business admin, financial planning, managerial economics, marketing. **Communications:** General, media studies. **Computer sciences:** Computer science, information systems. **Conservation:** Environmental science. **Education:** Art, biology, chemistry, early childhood, elementary, English, mathematics, physical, physics, science, social studies. **Foreign languages:** French, Spanish. **History:** General. **Liberal arts:** Arts/sciences. **Math:** General. **Parks/recreation:** Health/fitness. **Physical sciences:** Chemistry, physics. **Protective services:** Criminal justice. **Psychology:** General. **Social sciences:** Geography, political science, sociology. **Visual/performing arts:** Art.

**Most popular majors.** Biology 12%, business/marketing 25%, education 13%, liberal arts 17%, psychology 9%.

**Computing on campus.** 250 workstations in library, computer center, student center. Commuter students can connect to campus network. Online course registration, online library, helpline, student web hosting, wireless network available.

**Student life. Freshman orientation:** Mandatory. Preregistration for classes offered. **Housing:** Guaranteed on-campus for all undergraduates. Apartments available. Pets allowed in dorm rooms. **Activities:** Jazz band, dance, literary magazine, radio station, student government, student newspaper, Baptist student union, College Republicans, government and law society, Catholic student union, Rotaract, foreign language club, psychology club, black student association.

**Athletics.** NAIA. **Intercollegiate:** Baseball M. **Intramural:** Badminton, basketball, football (non-tackle), golf, racquetball, soccer, softball, swimming, table tennis, tennis, track and field, volleyball. **Team name:** Pilots.

**Student services.** Career counseling, student employment services, financial aid counseling, minority student services, personal counseling, placement for graduates, veterans' counselor. **Physically disabled:** Services for visually, speech, hearing impaired.

**Contact.** E-mail: admissions@pilot.lsus.edu
Phone: (318) 797-5061 Toll-free number: (800) 229-5957
Fax: (318) 797-5286
Mickey Diez, Dean of Enrollment Services & Registrar, Louisiana State University in Shreveport, One University Place, Shreveport, LA 71115-2399

## Louisiana Tech University

**Ruston, Louisiana**
www.latech.edu

CB member
CB code: 6372

- Public 4-year university
- Commuter campus in large town
- 7,101 degree-seeking undergraduates
- 63% of applicants admitted
- SAT or ACT (ACT writing optional) required

**General.** Founded in 1894. Regionally accredited. **Degrees:** 1,322 bachelor's, 94 associate awarded; master's, doctoral offered. **ROTC:** Army, Naval. **Location:** 70 miles from Shreveport, 30 miles from Monroe. **Calendar:** Quarter, extensive summer session. **Full-time faculty:** 378 total. **Part-time faculty:** 98 total. **Class size:** 37% < 20, 42% 20-39, 11% 40-49, 8% 50-99, 2% >100. **Special facilities:** Natural history museum, on-campus lab school, arboretum, planetarium, rehabilitation science and biomedical engineering center, micromanufacturing institute, water resource center.

**Freshman class profile.** 4,734 applied, 2,973 admitted, 1,507 enrolled.

| Mid 50% test scores | | | |
|---|---|---|---|
| SAT critical reading: | 440-550 | Out-of-state: | 14% |
| SAT math: | 460-590 | Fraternities: | 9% |
| ACT composite: | 20-26 | Sororities: | 17% |

**Basis for selection.** High school record, test scores most important. Special talents, school and community activities, recommendations considered. To be admitted, applicant must need no more than one remedial course. Admission deadline for scholarship consideration is January 2 for the following fall term. **Homeschooled:** Applicants must have 2.5 GPA, 23 ACT/1060 SAT (exclusive of Writing).

**High school preparation.** Required units include English 4, mathematics 3, social studies 3, science 3, academic electives 4.5. 2 algebra required. Social studies must include 1 U.S. history. 4.5 units of electives from foreign language, sciences, math, social studies, speech, advanced fine arts, or computer literacy required. Prefer English courses that emphasize grammar, composition, and literature.

**2009-2010 Annual costs.** Tuition/fees: $5,079; $12,000 out-of-state. Room/board: $5,055. Books/supplies: $1,800. Personal expenses: $1,500.

**2009-2010 Financial aid. Non-need-based:** Scholarships awarded for academics, art, athletics, leadership, music/drama, ROTC.

**Application procedures. Admission:** Priority date 8/1; no deadline. $20 fee, may be waived for applicants with need. Admission notification on a rolling basis beginning on or about 6/1. **Financial aid:** Priority date 4/15; no closing date. FAFSA, institutional form required. Applicants notified on a rolling basis starting 3/18; must reply within 4 week(s) of notification.

**Academics. Special study options:** Combined bachelor's/graduate degree, cooperative education, cross-registration, distance learning, double major, dual enrollment of high school students, ESL, honors, independent study, internships, liberal arts/career combination, study abroad, teacher certification program. Cooperative programs with Grambling State University. **Credit/placement by examination:** AP, CLEP, institutional tests. 30 credit hours maximum toward associate degree, 30 toward bachelor's. **Support services:** Remedial instruction, study skills assistance, tutoring.

**Majors. Agriculture:** Animal sciences, business. **Architecture:** Architecture, interior. **Biology:** General. **Business:** Accounting, business admin, finance, human resources, management information systems, management science, managerial economics, marketing. **Communications:** Journalism. **Computer sciences:** Computer science. **Conservation:** General, forest resources, forestry. **Education:** Art, early childhood, elementary, French, music, physical, secondary, special, speech impaired. **Engineering:** Biomedical, chemical, civil, electrical, mechanical. **Engineering technology:** Civil, electrical. **Family/consumer sciences:** Family studies. **Foreign languages:** French, Spanish. **Health:** Audiology/speech pathology, clinical lab science, medical records admin. **History:** General. **Liberal arts:** Arts/sciences. **Math:** General. **Parks/recreation:** Health/fitness. **Physical sciences:** Chemistry, geology, physics. **Psychology:** General. **Social sciences:** Geography, political science, sociology. **Transportation:** Aviation, aviation management. **Visual/performing arts:** Art, commercial/advertising art, music performance, photography. **Other:** Nanosystems engineering.

**Computing on campus.** 1,800 workstations in dormitories, library, computer center. Dormitories linked to campus network.

**Student life. Freshman orientation:** Available, $55 fee. Preregistration for classes offered. Four sessions offered during summer. **Housing:** Guaranteed on-campus for freshmen. Single-sex dorms, special housing for disabled, apartments available. $50 deposit, deadline 7/15. **Activities:** Bands, choral groups, dance, drama, music ensembles, musical theater, radio station, student government, student newspaper, Wesley Foundation, Baptist student union, Union Board, College Republicans, Campus Crusade for Christ, international student association, NAACP, Circle K, Angel Flight.

**Athletics.** NCAA. **Intercollegiate:** Baseball M, basketball, bowling W, cross-country, football (tackle) M, golf M, soccer W, softball W, tennis W, track and field, volleyball W. **Intramural:** Badminton, basketball, bowling, golf M, racquetball, soccer, softball, tennis, volleyball. **Team name:** Bulldogs (M), Lady Techsters (W).

**Student services.** Chaplain/spiritual director, career counseling, student employment services, financial aid counseling, health services, legal services, minority student services, personal counseling, placement for graduates, veterans' counselor, women's services. **Physically disabled:** Services for speech impaired.

**Contact.** E-mail: bulldog@latech.edu
Phone: (318) 257-3036 Toll-free number: (800) 528-3241
Fax: (318) 257-2499
Jan Albritton, Director of Admissions, College of Basic and Career Studies, Louisiana Tech University, Box 3178, Ruston, LA 71272

---

## Loyola University New Orleans

**New Orleans, Louisiana**      **CB member**
www.loyno.edu/      **CB code: 6374**

- Private 4-year university and liberal arts college affiliated with Roman Catholic Church
- Residential campus in large city
- 2,721 degree-seeking undergraduates: 10% part-time, 57% women, 14% African American, 5% Asian American, 11% Hispanic American, 1% Native American, 3% international
- 1,881 degree-seeking graduate students
- 58% of applicants admitted
- SAT or ACT (ACT writing optional), application essay required
- 63% graduate within 6 years; 61% enter graduate study

**General.** Founded in 1912. Regionally accredited. **Degrees:** 599 bachelor's awarded; master's, doctoral, professional offered. **ROTC:** Army, Naval, Air Force. **Location:** Uptown. **Calendar:** Semester, limited summer session. **Full-time faculty:** 283 total; 88% have terminal degrees, 13% minority, 44% women. **Part-time faculty:** 158 total; 37% have terminal degrees, 11% minority, 46% women. **Class size:** 59% < 20, 39% 20-39, 2% 40-49, less than 1% 50-99. **Special facilities:** Humanities lab, 24-hour microcomputer labs, computer science lab, graphics lab, visual arts lab, ad club/communications lab, RATHE business computer lab, multi-media training center, non-profit communications center, television broadcast studio, multimedia studio, audio recording studio, editing studio, multimedia exhibit room, international education center, suspended pool, career development center, Jesuit social research institute.

**Freshman class profile.** 4,345 applied, 2,538 admitted, 809 enrolled.

| Mid 50% test scores | | | |
|---|---|---|---|
| SAT critical reading: | 570-670 | Rank in top quarter: | 60% |
| SAT math: | 550-660 | Rank in top tenth: | 29% |
| SAT writing: | 550-660 | End year in good standing: | 91% |
| ACT composite: | 24-29 | Return as sophomores: | 80% |
| GPA 3.75 or higher: | 46% | Out-of-state: | 53% |
| GPA 3.50-3.74: | 19% | Live on campus: | 63% |
| GPA 3.0-3.49: | 32% | International: | 3% |
| GPA 2.0-2.99: | 3% | Fraternities: | 15% |
| | | Sororities: | 21% |

**Basis for selection.** High school performance, test scores, counselor/teacher evaluation, personal essay, extracurricular activity, community involvement and work experience considered. Interview recommended. Audition required for music, theater arts and dance majors. Portfolio required for visual arts program applicants. **Homeschooled:** Require proof of high school graduation or its equivalent.

**High school preparation.** College-preparatory program recommended. 17 units required; 22 recommended. Required and recommended units include English 4, mathematics 2-3, social studies 2, science 2-3 (laboratory 1) and foreign language 2.

**2010-2011 Annual costs.** Tuition/fees (projected): $31,504. Room/board: $10,388. Books/supplies: $1,000. Personal expenses: $1,500.

**2009-2010 Financial aid. Need-based:** 627 full-time freshmen applied for aid; 510 were judged to have need; 510 of these received aid. Average need met was 88%. Average scholarship/grant was $18,146; average loan $3,562. 81% of total undergraduate aid awarded as scholarships/grants, 19%

as loans/jobs. **Non-need-based:** Awarded to 1,953 full-time undergraduates, including 733 freshmen. Scholarships awarded for academics, alumni affiliation, art, leadership, ROTC.

**Application procedures. Admission:** Priority date 12/1; no deadline. $20 fee, may be waived for applicants with need, free for online applicants. Admission notification on a rolling basis beginning on or about 10/20. Must reply by May 1 or within 2 week(s) if notified thereafter. Students recommended by high school principals and considered ready for college work by the Committee on Admissions may be admitted immediately following completion of junior year of high school. Program intended to serve applicants of unusual promise who will benefit from beginning college careers a year early. **Financial aid:** Priority date 2/15, closing date 6/1. FAFSA required. Applicants notified on a rolling basis starting 3/1; must reply by 5/1 or within 2 week(s) of notification.

**Academics.** Jesuit tradition of contributing to the liberal education of the whole person emphasized. **Special study options:** Accelerated study, combined bachelor's/graduate degree, cross-registration, distance learning, double major, dual enrollment of high school students, ESL, exchange student, honors, independent study, internships, liberal arts/career combination, student-designed major, study abroad, teacher certification program, Washington semester. Evening courses, internet-based program in nursing. **Credit/placement by examination:** AP, CLEP, IB, SAT, ACT, institutional tests. 30 credit hours maximum toward bachelor's degree. **Support services:** Learning center, pre-admission summer program, reduced course load, remedial instruction, study skills assistance, tutoring, writing center.

**Majors. Biology:** General. **Business:** Accounting, business admin, finance, international, managerial economics, marketing. **Communications:** General. **Education:** Music. **Foreign languages:** General, ancient Greek, French, German, Spanish. **Health:** Music therapy, nursing (RN), predental, premedicine, preveterinary. **History:** General. **Math:** General. **Philosophy/religion:** Christian, philosophy, religion. **Physical sciences:** Chemistry, physics. **Protective services:** Criminal justice, forensics. **Psychology:** General. **Social sciences:** General, criminology, economics, political science, sociology. **Visual/performing arts:** General, art, commercial/advertising art, dramatic, jazz, music management, music performance, music theory/composition, studio arts. **Other:** Jazz, music business.

**Most popular majors.** Business/marketing 20%, communications/journalism 9%, health sciences 7%, psychology 10%, social sciences 15%, visual/performing arts 15%.

**Computing on campus.** 525 workstations in dormitories, library, computer center, student center. Dormitories wired for high-speed internet access and linked to campus network. Commuter students can connect to campus network. Online course registration, online library, helpline, repair service, student web hosting, wireless network available.

**Student life. Freshman orientation:** Mandatory, $150 fee. Preregistration for classes offered. Required session held in summer; optional session held the weekend before classes begin. **Housing:** Guaranteed on-campus for freshmen. Coed dorms, special housing for disabled, wellness housing available. $100 nonrefundable deposit, deadline 5/1. Honors floors available. **Activities:** Bands, campus ministries, choral groups, dance, drama, film society, international student organizations, literary magazine, music ensembles, musical theater, opera, radio station, student government, student newspaper, symphony orchestra, black student union, community action program, international student association, Muslim student association, Asian student organization, gay/lesbian outreach, university programming board, Big Brothers/Big Sisters, civic engagement society.

**Athletics.** NAIA. **Intercollegiate:** Baseball M, basketball, cross-country, track and field, volleyball W. **Intramural:** Basketball, racquetball, soccer, softball, swimming, volleyball, weight lifting. **Team name:** Wolfpack.

**Student services.** Adult student services, alcohol/substance abuse counseling, chaplain/spiritual director, career counseling, student employment services, financial aid counseling, health services, on-campus daycare, personal counseling, placement for graduates, women's services. **Physically disabled:** Services for visually, speech, hearing impaired.

**Contact.** E-mail: admit@loyno.edu
Phone: (504) 865-3240 Toll-free number: (800) 456-9652
Fax: (504) 865-3383
Salvadore Liberto, Vice President for Enrollment Management, Loyola University New Orleans, 6363 St. Charles Avenue, New Orleans, LA 70118-6195

---

## McNeese State University

**Lake Charles, Louisiana**
www.mcneese.edu      **CB code: 6403**

- Public 4-year university
- Commuter campus in small city

◆ 7,018 degree-seeking undergraduates: 15% part-time, 61% women, 19% African American, 1% Asian American, 1% Hispanic American, 1% Native American, 4% international

◆ 854 degree-seeking graduate students

◆ 67% of applicants admitted

◆ SAT or ACT (ACT writing optional) required

◆ 37% graduate within 6 years

**General.** Founded in 1939. Regionally accredited. **Degrees:** 1,049 bachelor's, 122 associate awarded; master's offered. **ROTC:** Army. **Location:** 193 miles from New Orleans, 124 miles from Houston. **Calendar:** Semester, extensive summer session. **Full-time faculty:** 308 total; 66% have terminal degrees, 15% minority, 45% women. **Part-time faculty:** 109 total; 19% have terminal degrees, 7% minority, 63% women. **Class size:** 40% < 20, 41% 20-39, 12% 40-49, 6% 50-99, less than 1% >100. **Special facilities:** Environmental research center, vertebrate museum, farm, community health care clinic.

**Freshman class profile.** 2,904 applied, 1,946 admitted, 1,334 enrolled.

| Mid 50% test scores | | Rank in top quarter: | 40% |
|---|---|---|---|
| ACT composite: | 18-23 | Rank in top tenth: | 19% |
| GPA 3.75 or higher: | 19% | Return as sophomores: | 67% |
| GPA 3.50-3.74: | 15% | Out-of-state: | 8% |
| GPA 3.0-3.49: | 33% | International: | 2% |
| GPA 2.0-2.99: | 32% | | |

**Basis for selection.** Applicants must complete Louisiana Board of Regents high school core curriculum and have 18 ACT English or 19 math score (450 SAT Verbal or 460 Math). Either 2.0 GPA, 20 ACT, or rank in top 50% of graduating class also required. Audition required of music majors. **Homeschooled:** Transcript of courses and grades required. Applicant must not be in need of any developmental courses. **Learning Disabled:** Applicants should register with Office of Services for Students with Disabilities.

**High school preparation.** College-preparatory program required. 17.5 units required. Required units include English 4, mathematics 3, social studies 1, history 2, science 3, foreign language 2, computer science .5 and visual/performing arts 1. 1 additional math or science recommended.

**2009-2010 Annual costs.** Tuition/fees: $3,588; $10,260 out-of-state. Room/board: $5,770. Books/supplies: $1,200. Personal expenses: $1,820.

**2008-2009 Financial aid. Non-need-based:** Scholarships awarded for academics, alumni affiliation, art, athletics, leadership, minority status, music/drama, state residency. **Additional information:** Books may be charged and paid in 2 installments during semester.

**Application procedures. Admission:** Priority date 7/15; no deadline. $20 fee. Admission notification on a rolling basis beginning on or about 3/15. **Financial aid:** Priority date 5/1; no closing date. FAFSA, institutional form required. Applicants notified on a rolling basis starting 4/15; must reply within 2 week(s) of notification.

**Academics. Special study options:** Accelerated study, cooperative education, distance learning, double major, dual enrollment of high school students, ESL, honors, independent study, internships, study abroad, teacher certification program. **Credit/placement by examination:** CLEP, ACT, institutional tests. 24 credit hours maximum toward associate degree, 45 toward bachelor's. **Support services:** Learning center, remedial instruction, tutoring, writing center.

**Honors college/program.** Requirements include 27 ACT, 3.4 GPA, essay, interview, and 3 recommendations.

**Majors. Agriculture:** General. **Biology:** General. **Business:** Accounting, business admin, finance, marketing. **Communications:** Media studies. **Computer sciences:** Computer science. **Conservation:** Wildlife. **Education:** Agricultural, art, biology, business, chemistry, early childhood, elementary, English, family/consumer sciences, foreign languages, mathematics, music, physical, social studies, special, speech. **Engineering:** General. **Engineering technology:** General. **Family/consumer sciences:** General. **Foreign languages:** French, Spanish. **Health:** Athletic training, clinical lab science, nursing (RN), radiologic technology/medical imaging. **History:** General. **Liberal arts:** Arts/sciences. **Math:** General. **Parks/recreation:** Exercise sciences. **Physical sciences:** Chemistry, physics. **Protective services:** Criminal justice. **Psychology:** General. **Social sciences:** Political science, sociology. **Visual/performing arts:** Art, dramatic, music performance. **Other:** Environmental science education.

**Most popular majors.** Business/marketing 18%, education 10%, engineering/engineering technologies 6%, health sciences 18%, liberal arts 18%.

**Computing on campus.** 450 workstations in dormitories, library, computer center, student center. Dormitories wired for high-speed internet access and linked to campus network. Commuter students can connect to campus network. Online course registration, online library, helpline, student web hosting, wireless network available.

**Student life. Freshman orientation:** Mandatory, $50 fee. Preregistration for classes offered. 5 conferences offered in summer. **Housing:** Coed dorms, apartments, fraternity/sorority housing available. $325 partly refundable deposit. **Activities:** Bands, campus ministries, choral groups, dance, drama, international student organizations, literary magazine, music ensembles, musical theater, opera, student government, student newspaper, symphony orchestra, 93 organizations available.

**Athletics.** NCAA. **Intercollegiate:** Baseball M, basketball, cheerleading, cross-country, football (tackle) M, golf, rodeo, soccer W, softball W, tennis W, track and field, volleyball W. **Intramural:** Badminton, basketball, bowling, football (non-tackle), golf, handball, racquetball, softball, swimming, table tennis, tennis, volleyball, water polo. **Team name:** Cowboys.

**Student services.** Adult student services, alcohol/substance abuse counseling, chaplain/spiritual director, career counseling, student employment services, financial aid counseling, health services, minority student services, personal counseling, placement for graduates, veterans' counselor. **Physically disabled:** Services for visually, speech, hearing impaired.

**Contact.** E-mail: info@mcneese.edu
Phone: (337) 475-5356 Toll-free number: (800) 622-3352 ext. 5356
Fax: (337) 475-5151
Kara Smith, Director of Admissions and Recruiting, McNeese State University, Box 91740 MSU, Lake Charles, LA 70609-1740

---

## New Orleans Baptist Theological Seminary: Leavell College

**New Orleans, Louisiana**
**www.nobts.edu**     **CB code: 5034**

◆ Private 4-year Bible and seminary college affiliated with Southern Baptist Convention

◆ Very large city

**General.** Regionally accredited. **Calendar:** Semester.

**Annual costs/financial aid.** Tuition/fees (2009-2010): $4,940. Tuition reported for Southern Baptist students. Other Baptist and non-Baptist students pay tuition at a slightly higher rate. Room: $2,400. Books/supplies: $500.

**Contact.** Phone: (504) 282-4455
Registrar and Dean of Admissions, 3939 Gentilly Boulevard, New Orleans, LA 70126-4858

---

## Nicholls State University

**Thibodaux, Louisiana**
**www.nicholls.edu**     **CB code: 6221**

◆ Public 4-year university

◆ Commuter campus in large town

◆ 6,443 degree-seeking undergraduates: 20% part-time, 62% women, 18% African American, 1% Asian American, 2% Hispanic American, 2% Native American, 2% international

◆ 266 degree-seeking graduate students

◆ 78% of applicants admitted

◆ SAT or ACT (ACT writing optional) required

◆ 34% graduate within 6 years

**General.** Founded in 1948. Regionally accredited. **Degrees:** 861 bachelor's, 175 associate awarded; master's offered. **Location:** 60 miles from New Orleans, 75 miles from Baton Rouge. **Calendar:** Semester, extensive summer session. **Full-time faculty:** 265 total; 57% have terminal degrees, 11% minority, 51% women. **Part-time faculty:** 6 total; 33% have terminal degrees, 17% minority, 67% women. **Class size:** 40% < 20, 45% 20-39, 13% 40-49, 1% 50-99, 1% >100. **Special facilities:** Marine research facility, culinary institute, center for women and government, marine biology laboratory, center for study of dyslexia, center for economic education, small business development center, center for traditional boat building, economic council.

**Freshman class profile.** 1,887 applied, 1,478 admitted, 1,247 enrolled.

| Mid 50% test scores | | End year in good standing: | 78% |
|---|---|---|---|
| ACT composite: | 19-23 | Return as sophomores: | 67% |
| GPA 3.75 or higher: | 14% | Out-of-state: | 4% |
| GPA 3.50-3.74: | 15% | Live on campus: | 42% |
| GPA 3.0-3.49: | 35% | International: | 1% |
| GPA 2.0-2.99: | 35% | Fraternities: | 13% |
| Rank in top quarter: | 40% | Sororities: | 9% |
| Rank in top tenth: | 16% | | |

**Basis for selection.** Must meet the Board of Regents Core (TOPS Core) requirement, have a 2.0 GPA, and meet at least one of the following: 20 ACT or rank in the top half of graduating class.

**High school preparation.** College-preparatory program recommended. 16.5 units required. Required units include English 4, mathematics 3, social studies 1, history 2, science 3, foreign language 2, academic electives 1.5.

**2009-2010 Annual costs.** Tuition/fees: $3,965; $11,795 out-of-state. Room/board: $7,310. Books/supplies: $1,200. Personal expenses: $1,692.

**2008-2009 Financial aid.** Need-based: 1,108 full-time freshmen applied for aid; 579 were judged to have need; 577 of these received aid. Average need met was 95%. Average scholarship/grant was $5,070; average loan $2,743. 68% of total undergraduate aid awarded as scholarships/grants, 32% as loans/jobs. **Non-need-based:** Awarded to 1,179 full-time undergraduates, including 512 freshmen. Scholarships awarded for academics, athletics, state residency.

**Application procedures.** Admission: Priority date 8/15; no deadline. $20 fee ($30 out-of-state). Admission notification on a rolling basis beginning on or about 9/1. **Financial aid:** Priority date 4/15, closing date 6/30. FAFSA, institutional form required. Applicants notified on a rolling basis; must reply within 2 week(s) of notification.

**Academics.** Special study options: Cooperative education, cross-registration, distance learning, dual enrollment of high school students, exchange student, honors, independent study, internships, study abroad, teacher certification program. **Credit/placement by examination:** AP, CLEP, SAT, ACT, institutional tests. 15 credit hours maximum toward associate degree, 30 toward bachelor's. **Support services:** Learning center, pre-admission summer program, reduced course load, remedial instruction, study skills assistance, tutoring, writing center.

**Majors.** Biology: General. **Business:** Accounting, business admin, finance, management information systems, marketing. **Communications:** Media studies. **Computer sciences:** Computer science. **Education:** Art, business, early childhood, elementary, English, French, mathematics, middle, music, physical, science, social studies. **Engineering technology:** Petroleum, surveying. **Family/consumer sciences:** General. **Health:** Audiology/speech pathology, dietetics, health services, nursing (RN). **History:** General. **Math:** General. **Personal/culinary services:** Chef training. **Physical sciences:** Chemistry. **Protective services:** Police science. **Psychology:** General. **Social sciences:** Political science, sociology. **Visual/performing arts:** Art.

**Most popular majors.** Business/marketing 25%, education 8%, health sciences 23%, liberal arts 12%.

**Computing on campus.** 285 workstations in dormitories, library, computer center. Dormitories wired for high-speed internet access and linked to campus network. Commuter students can connect to campus network. Online course registration, online library, wireless network available.

**Student life.** Freshman orientation: Mandatory, $50 fee. Preregistration for classes offered. **Housing:** Guaranteed on-campus for all undergraduates. Coed dorms, single-sex dorms, special housing for disabled, apartments, wellness housing available. $200 partly refundable deposit, deadline 8/15. **Activities:** Bands, choral groups, dance, drama, film society, international student organizations, literary magazine, music ensembles, musical theater, radio station, student government, student newspaper, TV station, Baptist student union, Circle K, Young Democrats, Support for Older and Returning Students, Order of Athena, Young Republicans, UNITE, Newman club, Muslim student association.

**Athletics.** NCAA. **Intercollegiate:** Baseball M, basketball, cross-country, football (tackle) M, golf, soccer W, softball W, tennis, track and field W, volleyball W. **Intramural:** Basketball, football (non-tackle), softball, volleyball. **Team name:** Colonels.

**Student services.** Adult student services, alcohol/substance abuse counseling, chaplain/spiritual director, career counseling, services for economically disadvantaged, student employment services, financial aid counseling, health services, legal services, minority student services, personal counseling, placement for graduates, veterans' counselor, women's services. **Physically disabled:** Services for visually, speech, hearing impaired. **Learning disabled:** Comprehensive services available.

**Contact.** E-mail: nicholls@nicholls.edu
Phone: (985) 448-4507 Toll-free number: (877) 642-4655
Fax: (985) 448-4929
Becky Durocher, Director of Admissions, Nicholls State University, PO Box 2004-NSU, Thibodaux, LA 70310

## Northwestern State University
**Natchitoches, Louisiana**
www.nsula.edu — CB code: 6492

- Public 4-year university
- Commuter campus in large town
- 7,443 degree-seeking undergraduates: 28% part-time, 67% women, 30% African American, 1% Asian American, 2% Hispanic American, 2% Native American, 1% international
- 972 degree-seeking graduate students
- 81% of applicants admitted
- SAT or ACT (ACT writing optional) required
- 36% graduate within 6 years

**General.** Founded in 1884. Regionally accredited. Additional campuses in Shreveport, Leesville, Alexandria, and off-campus sites. **Degrees:** 1,075 bachelor's, 289 associate awarded; master's offered. **ROTC:** Army, Air Force. **Location:** 75 miles from Shreveport, 57 miles from Alexandria. **Calendar:** Semester, extensive summer session. **Full-time faculty:** 318 total; 57% have terminal degrees, 11% minority, 55% women. **Part-time faculty:** 213 total; 27% have terminal degrees, 15% minority, 61% women. **Class size:** 53% < 20, 32% 20-39, 6% 40-49, 9% 50-99, less than 1% >100. **Special facilities:** Regional folklife center, Creole heritage center, southern studies institute, heritage resources laboratory, preservation technology and training center, aquaculture center.

**Freshman class profile.** 2,781 applied, 2,249 admitted, 1,340 enrolled.

| Mid 50% test scores | | GPA 2.0-2.99: | 38% |
|---|---|---|---|
| SAT critical reading: | 420-530 | Rank in top quarter: | 36% |
| SAT math: | 430-560 | Rank in top tenth: | 12% |
| ACT composite: | 18-23 | End year in good standing: | 87% |
| GPA 3.75 or higher: | 11% | Return as sophomores: | 69% |
| GPA 3.50-3.74: | 14% | Out-of-state: | 10% |
| GPA 3.0-3.49: | 36% | Live on campus: | 51% |

**Basis for selection.** Applicants must have completed the 17.5 unit college preparatory program, need no more than one developmental class, and must have one of the following: 20 ACT (or SAT equivalent), 2.0 GPA, or be in top 50% of graduating class. Out-of-state and homeschooled students admitted based on ACT/SAT scores.

**High school preparation.** College-preparatory program required. 17.5 units required. Required units include English 4, mathematics 3, social studies 1, history 2, science 3 (laboratory 3), foreign language 2, computer science .5 and visual/performing arts 1. Additional unit of math or science.

**2009-2010 Annual costs.** Tuition/fees: $3,786; $10,472 out-of-state. Room/board: $6,680. Books/supplies: $1,200. Personal expenses: $1,819.

**2008-2009 Financial aid.** Need-based: 986 full-time freshmen applied for aid; 816 were judged to have need; 792 of these received aid. Average need met was 61%. Average scholarship/grant was $4,372; average loan $5,064. 47% of total undergraduate aid awarded as scholarships/grants, 53% as loans/jobs. **Non-need-based:** Awarded to 3,039 full-time undergraduates, including 855 freshmen. Scholarships awarded for academics, alumni affiliation, art, athletics, job skills, leadership, minority status, music/drama, religious affiliation, ROTC, state residency.

**Application procedures.** Admission: Closing date 7/6 (receipt date). $20 fee. Admission notification on a rolling basis. Applications may be submitted after fall deadline but consideration is not guaranteed. **Financial aid:** Priority date 5/1; no closing date. FAFSA, institutional form required. Applicants notified on a rolling basis starting 5/1; must reply within 4 week(s) of notification.

**Academics.** Special study options: Cooperative education, distance learning, double major, dual enrollment of high school students, honors, independent study, internships, study abroad, teacher certification program. **Credit/placement by examination:** AP, CLEP, SAT, ACT, institutional tests. 30 credit hours maximum toward associate degree, 62 toward bachelor's. Maximum semester hours of credit by examination may not exceed half the number of credits required for degree. **Support services:** Learning center, pre-admission summer program, reduced course load, remedial instruction, study skills assistance, tutoring, writing center.

**Honors college/program.** Student must have 25 ACT/1130 SAT (exclusive of Writing), score 20 on each ACT subscore or 480 on SAT verbal and math, and have 3.0 high school GPA in the Louisiana core curriculum or 3.0 college GPA.

**Majors. Biology:** General. **Business:** Accounting, business admin, hospitality admin. **Communications:** Journalism. **Computer sciences:** Information systems. **Education:** Biology, business, chemistry, early childhood, elementary, English, family/consumer sciences, mathematics, middle, music, physical, physics, social studies, speech. **Engineering technology:** Electrical, industrial. **Family/consumer sciences:** General. **Health:** Nursing (RN), radiologic technology/medical imaging, substance abuse counseling. **History:** General. **Interdisciplinary:** Cultural resource management. **Liberal arts:** Arts/sciences. **Math:** General. **Parks/recreation:** Health/fitness. **Physical sciences:** Chemistry, physics. **Protective services:** Criminal justice. **Psychology:** General. **Public administration:** Social work. **Social sciences:** Political science, sociology. **Visual/performing arts:** Dramatic, music performance, studio arts. **Other:** Unified public safety administration.

**Most popular majors.** Business/marketing 14%, education 8%, health sciences 18%, liberal arts 17%, psychology 11%.

**Computing on campus.** Dormitories linked to campus network. Commuter students can connect to campus network. Online course registration, online library, helpline, student web hosting, wireless network available.

**Student life. Freshman orientation:** Available, $80 fee. Preregistration for classes offered. One- to 2-day program held 5 times during the summer; includes program for parents. **Housing:** Coed dorms, special housing for disabled, apartments, fraternity/sorority housing available. $175 nonrefundable deposit, deadline 3/5. **Activities:** Bands, campus ministries, choral groups, dance, drama, international student organizations, literary magazine, music ensembles, musical theater, opera, radio station, student government, student newspaper, symphony orchestra, TV station, Catholic student organization, Fellowship of Christian Athletes, Wesley Westminster Ministry, Latterday Saints institute, honor society, Purple Jackets, College Republicans, College Democrats, African-American caucus.

**Athletics.** NCAA. **Intercollegiate:** Baseball M, basketball, cross-country, football (tackle) M, soccer W, softball W, tennis W, track and field, volleyball W. **Intramural:** Badminton, baseball, basketball, bowling, football (nontackle), golf, racquetball, soccer, softball, table tennis, tennis, volleyball, water polo. **Team name:** Demons.

**Student services.** Adult student services, alcohol/substance abuse counseling, chaplain/spiritual director, career counseling, services for economically disadvantaged, student employment services, financial aid counseling, health services, minority student services, personal counseling, placement for graduates, veterans' counselor. **Physically disabled:** Services for visually, speech, hearing impaired. **Learning disabled:** Comprehensive services available.

**Contact.** E-mail: applications@nsula.edu
Phone: (318) 357-4078 Toll-free number: (800) 767-8115
Fax: (318) 357-4660
Andrea Maley, Director of Admissions, Northwestern State University, Roy Hall, Room 209, Natchitoches, LA 71497

## Our Lady of Holy Cross College
### New Orleans, Louisiana
### www.olhcc.edu                      CB code: 6002

- Private 4-year liberal arts college affiliated with Roman Catholic Church
- Commuter campus in very large city
- 535 full-time, degree-seeking undergraduates
- 200 graduate students
- ACT required

**General.** Founded in 1916. Regionally accredited. Campus offerings available for senior citizens. **Degrees:** 148 bachelor's, 1 associate awarded; master's offered. **ROTC:** Army, Naval, Air Force. **Location:** 3 miles from downtown. **Calendar:** Semester, limited summer session. **Full-time faculty:** 45 total. **Part-time faculty:** 85 total. **Class size:** 51% < 20, 43% 20-39, 3% 40-49, 2% 50-99. **Special facilities:** Training and counseling center.

**Freshman class profile.**

| Mid 50% test scores | | Out-of-state: | 1% |
|---|---|---|---|
| ACT composite: | 17-21 | | |

**Basis for selection.** Those with 2.0 GPA and 20 ACT unconditionally accepted. Students with less than 2.0 GPA and 17 ACT will be denied. Students entering directly from high school required to submit ACT, while others must take institutional test. English and math proficiency tests required.

**High school preparation.** 17.5 units recommended. Recommended units include English 4, mathematics 2, social studies 3, science 4 and foreign language 2. .5 unit of computer literacy recommended.

**2009-2010 Annual costs.** Tuition/fees: $10,320. Books/supplies: $1,200. Personal expenses: $1,819.

**2009-2010 Financial aid. Non-need-based:** Scholarships awarded for academics, state residency.

**Application procedures. Admission:** Priority date 12/1; no deadline. $25 fee. Admission notification on a rolling basis. **Financial aid:** Priority date 7/1; no closing date. FAFSA required. Applicants notified on a rolling basis starting 5/15; must reply within 4 week(s) of notification.

**Academics. Special study options:** Cross-registration, distance learning, dual enrollment of high school students, exchange student, independent study, internships, study abroad, teacher certification program. **Credit/placement by examination:** AP, CLEP, institutional tests. 60 credit hours maximum toward bachelor's degree. **Support services:** Learning center, preadmission summer program, reduced course load, remedial instruction, tutoring.

**Majors. Biology:** General. **Business:** Accounting, business admin. **Education:** Business, elementary, English, mathematics, secondary, social studies, special. **Health:** Medical radiologic technology/radiation therapy, respiratory therapy technology. **History:** General. **Interdisciplinary:** Biological/physical sciences. **Liberal arts:** Arts/sciences. **Social sciences:** General.

**Computing on campus.** 68 workstations in library, computer center. Commuter students can connect to campus network. Online library, wireless network available.

**Student life. Freshman orientation:** Mandatory. Preregistration for classes offered. **Activities:** Campus ministries, choral groups, drama, international student organizations, literary magazine, student government, student newspaper, Rotaract Club, various honor societies.

**Athletics. Intramural:** Bowling, soccer M, softball, volleyball. **Team name:** Hurricanes.

**Student services.** Adult student services, chaplain/spiritual director, career counseling, student employment services, financial aid counseling, health services, personal counseling, placement for graduates, veterans' counselor.

**Contact.** E-mail: admissions@olhcc.edu
Phone: (504) 394-7744 ext. 175 Toll-free number: (800) 259-7744
Fax: (504) 394-1182
Kristine Hatfield, Vice President for Enrollment Services, Our Lady of Holy Cross College, 4123 Woodland Drive, New Orleans, LA 70131-7399

## Our Lady of the Lake College
### Baton Rouge, Louisiana
### www.ololcollege.edu                 CB code: 3928

- Private 4-year health science and nursing college affiliated with Roman Catholic Church
- Commuter campus in large city
- 1,692 degree-seeking undergraduates: 33% part-time, 85% women, 23% African American, 3% Asian American, 2% Hispanic American
- 149 degree-seeking graduate students
- 88% of applicants admitted
- SAT or ACT (ACT writing optional) required

**General.** Regionally accredited. **Degrees:** 81 bachelor's, 386 associate awarded; master's offered. **ROTC:** Army, Air Force. **Calendar:** Semester, extensive summer session. **Full-time faculty:** 84 total; 25% have terminal degrees, 80% women. **Part-time faculty:** 61 total; 36% have terminal degrees, 43% women. **Class size:** 52% < 20, 43% 20-39, 3% 40-49, 2% 50-99.

**Freshman class profile.** 237 applied, 209 admitted, 91 enrolled.

| Mid 50% test scores | | GPA 3.0-3.49: | 50% |
|---|---|---|---|
| ACT composite: | 19-22 | GPA 2.0-2.99: | 30% |
| GPA 3.75 or higher: | 5% | Return as sophomores: | 74% |
| GPA 3.50-3.74: | 15% | Out-of-state: | 4% |

**Basis for selection.** High school record and test scores important. **Homeschooled:** State high school equivalency certificate required.

**High school preparation.** Required units include English 4, mathematics 3, social studies 3, science 3, foreign language 2, computer science .5 and academic electives 2.

**2009-2010 Annual costs.** Tuition/fees: $9,864. Books/supplies: $1,512. Personal expenses: $1,820.

**2008-2009 Financial aid. Need-based:** 90 full-time freshmen applied for aid; 69 were judged to have need; 68 of these received aid. Average scholarship/grant was $4,910; average loan $9,918. 22% of total undergraduate aid awarded as scholarships/grants, 78% as loans/jobs. **Non-need-based:** Awarded to 137 full-time undergraduates, including 40 freshmen.

**Application procedures. Admission:** Priority date 7/15; deadline 8/15 (receipt date). $35 fee, may be waived for applicants with need. Admission notification on a rolling basis. **Financial aid:** Closing date 3/1. FAFSA required.

**Academics. Special study options:** Accelerated study, combined bachelor's/graduate degree. **Credit/placement by examination:** CLEP, ACT, institutional tests. 15 credit hours maximum toward associate degree, 30 toward bachelor's. **Support services:** Learning center, reduced course load, study skills assistance, tutoring.

**Majors. Biology:** General, biomedical sciences. **Health:** Clinical lab science, facilities admin, health care admin, health services, health services admin, nursing (RN), premedicine. **Liberal arts:** Humanities. **Psychology:** General.

**Most popular majors.** Biology 7%, health sciences 86%.

**Computing on campus.** 150 workstations in library. Commuter students can connect to campus network. Online library, helpline, wireless network available.

**Student life. Freshman orientation:** Mandatory. Preregistration for classes offered. One-day program held the week before classes begin. **Policies:** Smoke-free campus. **Activities:** Campus ministries, student government, American College of Healthcare Executives, Beta Epsilon Fraternity of Radiologic Technology Students, Beta Sigma Mu, Christian student fellowship, clinical laboratory scientist association, cultural arts association, Epsilon Mu Theta, math and science association, Phi Theta Alpha.

**Student services.** Adult student services, chaplain/spiritual director, career counseling, financial aid counseling.

**Contact.** E-mail: admission@ololcollege.edu
Phone: (225) 768-1700 Toll-free number: (877) 242-3509
Fax: (225) 768-1726
Rebecca Cannon, Director of Admissions, Our Lady of the Lake College, 7434 Perkins Road, Baton Rouge, LA 70808

## St. Joseph Seminary College
**St. Benedict, Louisiana**
**www.sjasc.edu**     **CB code: 6689**

- Private 4-year liberal arts and seminary college for men affiliated with Roman Catholic Church
- Residential campus in rural community
- 83 degree-seeking undergraduates: 4% African American, 4% Asian American, 27% Hispanic American, 1% Native American
- ACT (writing optional) required

**General.** Founded in 1891. Regionally accredited. Non-seminarian, non-degree-seeking students may attend part-time. **Degrees:** 14 bachelor's awarded. **Location:** 40 miles from New Orleans. **Calendar:** Semester. **Full-time faculty:** 9 total; 33% have terminal degrees, 67% women. **Part-time faculty:** 16 total; 44% have terminal degrees, 25% women. **Class size:** 69% < 20, 31% 20-39. **Special facilities:** 1,200 acres of forest, Romanesque abbey church.

### Freshman class profile.

| | | | |
|---|---|---|---|
| End year in good standing: | 6% | Out-of-state: | 50% |
| Return as sophomores: | 12% | Live on campus: | 100% |

**Basis for selection.** Recommendation by diocesan bishop, academic standing, and test scores required. Interview, essay required by dioceses prior to application to college. **Homeschooled:** State high school equivalency certificate required.

**High school preparation.** 10 units recommended. Recommended units include English 3, mathematics 2, history 1, science 2 and foreign language 2. Additional units in English, second foreign language, social science and math recommended.

**2009-2010 Annual costs.** Tuition/fees: $13,082. Room/board: $11,168. Books/supplies: $1,200. Personal expenses: $1,387.

**2009-2010 Financial aid. Need-based:** 10 full-time freshmen applied for aid; 5 were judged to have need; 5 of these received aid. Average scholarship/grant was $6,200. **Non-need-based:** Scholarships awarded for academics, leadership.

**Application procedures. Admission:** No deadline. No application fee. Application must be submitted on paper. **Financial aid:** Priority date 3/15; no closing date. FAFSA required. Applicants notified on a rolling basis starting 7/1; must reply within 4 week(s) of notification.

**Academics. Special study options:** ESL. **Credit/placement by examination:** AP, CLEP, IB, institutional tests. 24 credit hours maximum toward bachelor's degree. **Support services:** Remedial instruction, tutoring, writing center.

**Majors. Liberal arts:** Arts/sciences.

**Computing on campus.** 14 workstations in dormitories, library, computer center. Dormitories wired for high-speed internet access. Online library, repair service, wireless network available.

**Student life. Freshman orientation:** Mandatory. Preregistration for classes offered. **Policies:** Closed formation weekends. Religious observance required. **Housing:** Guaranteed on-campus for all undergraduates. All students live on campus. **Activities:** Campus ministries, choral groups, student government.

**Athletics. Intramural:** Basketball M, football (non-tackle) M, softball M, volleyball M. **Team name:** Ravens.

**Student services.** Chaplain/spiritual director, financial aid counseling, health services, personal counseling, veterans' counselor. **Physically disabled:** Services for visually, speech, hearing impaired.

**Contact.** E-mail: acdean@sjasc.edu
Phone: (985) 867-2273 Fax: (985) 327-1085
Registrar, St. Joseph Seminary College, 75376 River Road, St. Benedict, LA 70457-9990

## Southeastern Louisiana University
**Hammond, Louisiana**
**www.selu.edu**     **CB code: 6656**

- Public 4-year university
- Commuter campus in large town
- 13,086 degree-seeking undergraduates: 15% part-time, 62% women, 18% African American, 1% Asian American, 2% Hispanic American, 1% international
- 1,071 degree-seeking graduate students
- 92% of applicants admitted
- ACT (writing optional) required
- 31% graduate within 6 years

**General.** Founded in 1925. Regionally accredited. **Degrees:** 1,880 bachelor's, 67 associate awarded; master's, doctoral offered. **ROTC:** Army. **Location:** 55 miles from New Orleans, 40 miles from Baton Rouge. **Calendar:** Semester, extensive summer session. **Full-time faculty:** 522 total; 63% have terminal degrees, 13% minority, 56% women. **Part-time faculty:** 117 total; 35% have terminal degrees, 9% minority, 62% women. **Class size:** 19% < 20, 59% 20-39, 12% 40-49, 9% 50-99, 2% >100. **Special facilities:** Environmental research station, social science research center, maritime museum, contemporary art gallery, performing arts theatre.

**Freshman class profile.** 3,609 applied, 3,329 admitted, 2,487 enrolled.

| Mid 50% test scores | | Rank in top tenth: | 11% |
|---|---|---|---|
| ACT composite: | 19-23 | End year in good standing: | 69% |
| GPA 3.75 or higher: | 11% | Return as sophomores: | 67% |
| GPA 3.50-3.74: | 11% | Out-of-state: | 3% |
| GPA 3.0-3.49: | 31% | Live on campus: | 44% |
| GPA 2.0-2.99: | 46% | International: | 3% |
| Rank in top quarter: | 28% | | |

**Basis for selection.** In-state students must have completion of Regents high school core curriculum; 20 ACT, or rank in upper 50% of high school graduating class, or 2.0 GPA, and have no more than 1 developmental course requirement. Out-of-state students must meet same criteria as in-state students, or score 23 ACT composite and have no more than 1 development course requirement, or meet all of following criteria: 20 ACT composite, rank in upper 50% of high school graduating class, 2.0 cumulative high school GPA. Audition recommended for music majors. **Homeschooled:** Program must be state-approved, applicant must have 23 ACT, and have no more than one developmental course requirement. **Learning Disabled:** No special requirements or procedures.

**High school preparation.** College-preparatory program required. 17.5 units required. Required units include English 4, mathematics 3, social studies 3, science 3, foreign language 2, computer science .5 and visual/performing arts 1. 1 additional math or science unit required.

**2009-2010 Annual costs.** Tuition/fees: $3,655; $10,910 out-of-state. Room/board: $6,110. Books/supplies: $1,200. Personal expenses: $1,818.

**2008-2009 Financial aid. Need-based:** 2,276 full-time freshmen applied for aid; 1,420 were judged to have need; 1,345 of these received aid. Average scholarship/grant was $5,876; average loan $2,844. 47% of total undergraduate aid awarded as scholarships/grants, 53% as loans/jobs. **Non-need-based:** Awarded to 3,333 full-time undergraduates, including 1,012 freshmen. Scholarships awarded for academics, athletics, job skills, leadership, music/drama, state residency.

**Application procedures. Admission:** Priority date 7/15; deadline 8/1 (postmark date). $20 fee. Admission notification on a rolling basis. High school students who have completed six semesters of high school and meet the following criteria will qualify for early admission: 3.0 GPA, 25 ACT, and recommendation from the high school principal. **Financial aid:** Priority date 5/1; no closing date. FAFSA required. Applicants notified on a rolling basis starting 3/1; must reply within 2 week(s) of notification.

**Academics. Special study options:** Accelerated study, cross-registration, distance learning, double major, dual enrollment of high school students, ESL, honors, independent study, internships, liberal arts/career combination, study abroad, teacher certification program. **Credit/placement by examination:** AP, CLEP, SAT, ACT, institutional tests. 30 credit hours maximum toward bachelor's degree. Maximum of 60 hours through all types of nontraditional educational experiences, i.e., advanced placement credit, correspondence courses, and military service credits. **Support services:** Learning center, remedial instruction, study skills assistance, tutoring, writing center.

**Majors. Biology:** General. **Business:** Accounting, business admin, finance, logistics, marketing. **Communications:** General. **Computer sciences:** Computer science. **Education:** Art, computer, early childhood, elementary, English, family/consumer sciences, French, health, mathematics, middle, music, physical, science, social studies, Spanish, special, speech. **Engineering technology:** General, industrial, occupational safety. **Family/consumer sciences:** General. **Foreign languages:** French, Spanish. **Health:** Athletic training, audiology/speech pathology, nursing (RN), public health ed, radiologic technology/medical imaging. **History:** General. **Liberal arts:** Arts/sciences. **Math:** General. **Parks/recreation:** Sports admin. **Physical sciences:** Chemistry, physics. **Protective services:** Criminal justice. **Psychology:** General. **Public administration:** Social work. **Social sciences:** Political science, sociology. **Visual/performing arts:** Art, arts management, music performance.

**Most popular majors.** Business/marketing 30%, education 12%, health sciences 12%, liberal arts 17%.

**Computing on campus.** 833 workstations in library, computer center, student center. Dormitories wired for high-speed internet access and linked to campus network. Commuter students can connect to campus network. Online course registration, online library, helpline, repair service, student web hosting, wireless network available.

**Student life. Freshman orientation:** Mandatory, $75 fee. Preregistration for classes offered. Students may take orientation either during summer or at beginning of first semester. Must pay room and board for summer session. **Policies:** Freshmen and sophomores must live on campus. **Housing:** Coed dorms, single-sex dorms, apartments, fraternity/sorority housing available. $150 nonrefundable deposit, deadline 6/15. **Activities:** Bands, campus ministries, choral groups, dance, drama, film society, international student organizations, literary magazine, music ensembles, musical theater, opera, radio station, student government, student newspaper, symphony orchestra, TV station, gospel choir, Baptist collegiate ministries, student government association, international student organization, Wesley Foundation, campus activities board, black student union, campus outreach, Circle K International, Best Buddies.

**Athletics.** NCAA. **Intercollegiate:** Baseball M, basketball, cross-country, football (tackle) M, golf M, soccer W, softball W, tennis W, track and field, volleyball W. **Intramural:** Basketball, football (non-tackle), soccer, softball, volleyball. **Team name:** Lions, Lady Lions.

**Student services.** Adult student services, alcohol/substance abuse counseling, career counseling, services for economically disadvantaged, student employment services, financial aid counseling, health services, minority student services, personal counseling, placement for graduates, veterans' counselor. **Physically disabled:** Services for visually, speech, hearing impaired.

**Contact.** E-mail: admissions@selu.edu
Phone: (985) 549-5637 Toll-free number: (800) 222-7358
Fax: (985) 549-5882
Jeff Rhodes, Dean of Enrollment Management, Southeastern Louisiana University, SLU 10752, Hammond, LA 70402

## Southern University and Agricultural and Mechanical College
### Baton Rouge, Louisiana
www.subr.edu    CB code: 6663

- Public 4-year university
- Commuter campus in large city
- 6,280 degree-seeking undergraduates: 8% part-time, 60% women
- 1,071 degree-seeking graduate students
- 39% of applicants admitted
- SAT or ACT (ACT writing optional) required
- 30% graduate within 6 years; 10% enter graduate study

**General.** Founded in 1880. Regionally accredited. **Degrees:** 896 bachelor's, 2 associate awarded; master's, doctoral offered. **ROTC:** Army, Naval, Air Force. **Location:** 80 miles from New Orleans. **Calendar:** Semester, extensive summer session. **Full-time faculty:** 405 total; 66% have terminal degrees, 85% minority, 47% women. **Part-time faculty:** 141 total; 43% have terminal degrees, 86% minority, 57% women. **Class size:** 37% < 20, 46% 20-39, 10% 40-49, 5% 50-99, 2% >100. **Special facilities:** Experimental (laboratory) farm, outdoor learning resource center (nature trail), meat processing plant, Black heritage museum.

**Freshman class profile.** 4,627 applied, 1,783 admitted, 1,008 enrolled.

| Mid 50% test scores | | Rank in top quarter: | 10% |
|---|---|---|---|
| ACT composite: | 17-20 | Rank in top tenth: | 3% |
| GPA 3.75 or higher: | 21% | End year in good standing: | 56% |
| GPA 3.50-3.74: | 14% | Return as sophomores: | 72% |
| GPA 3.0-3.49: | 23% | Out-of-state: | 21% |
| GPA 2.0-2.99: | 29% | Live on campus: | 70% |

**Basis for selection.** 20 ACT (940 SAT) or 2.0 GPA or rank in top 50% of class and require no more than 1 remedial course by having 18 ACT English and Math (450 SAT Verbal or 430 Math) as well as 16.5-unit core class requirements. Auditions required for music program. **Homeschooled:** Transcript of courses and grades required. 20 ACT or 940 SAT (exclusive of writing) required.

**High school preparation.** College-preparatory program required. 16.5 units required. Required units include English 4, mathematics 3, social studies 2, history 1, science 3 and foreign language 2. .5 computer literacy, 1 fine arts required.

**2009-2010 Annual costs.** Tuition/fees: $4,100; $9,892 out-of-state. Cable and internet, key deposit, and mail box rental $166. Room/board: $5,666. Books/supplies: $1,200. Personal expenses: $1,726.

**2008-2009 Financial aid. Non-need-based:** Scholarships awarded for academics, athletics, ROTC, state residency.

**Application procedures. Admission:** Closing date 7/1 (postmark date). $20 fee. Admission notification on a rolling basis. Admission can be deferred for 2 semesters. High school students admitted early must be in good academic standing and have approval from their high school. **Financial aid:** Priority date 1/31, closing date 3/30. FAFSA required. Applicants notified on a rolling basis starting 5/1; must reply within 3 week(s) of notification.

**Academics. Special study options:** Combined bachelor's/graduate degree, cooperative education, cross-registration, distance learning, double major, dual enrollment of high school students, exchange student, honors, independent study, internships, study abroad, teacher certification program, weekend college. **Credit/placement by examination:** AP, CLEP, SAT, ACT, institutional tests. 30 credit hours maximum toward bachelor's degree. **Support services:** Learning center, pre-admission summer program, reduced course load, remedial instruction, study skills assistance, tutoring, writing center.

**Honors college/program.** Must have 23 ACT (1070 SAT, exclusive of Writing) and 3.0 GPA.

**Majors. Agriculture:** Animal sciences, economics. **Architecture:** Architecture. **Biology:** General. **Business:** Accounting, business admin, e-commerce, finance, managerial economics, marketing. **Communications:** Media studies. **Computer sciences:** Computer science. **Conservation:** Urban forestry.

**Education:** Agricultural, art, biology, chemistry, computer, early childhood, elementary, English, French, mathematics, middle, music, physical, physics, science, secondary, social studies, Spanish, special. **Engineering:** Civil, electrical, mechanical. **Engineering technology:** Electrical. **Family/ consumer sciences:** General. **Foreign languages:** French, Spanish. **Health:** Audiology/speech pathology, nursing (RN), recreational therapy, vocational rehab counseling. **History:** General. **Math:** General. **Physical sciences:** Chemistry, physics. **Protective services:** Criminal justice. **Psychology:** General. **Public administration:** Social work. **Social sciences:** Political science, sociology. **Visual/performing arts:** Dramatic, music performance, studio arts.

**Most popular majors.** Business/marketing 17%, engineering/ engineering technologies 9%, family/consumer sciences 7%, health sciences 17%, psychology 9%, security/protective services 6%, social sciences 6%.

**Computing on campus.** 1,500 workstations in library, computer center. Dormitories wired for high-speed internet access and linked to campus network. Commuter students can connect to campus network. Online course registration, online library, helpline, wireless network available.

**Student life. Freshman orientation:** Mandatory. Preregistration for classes offered. Two-day program held during registration. **Housing:** Guaranteed on-campus for freshmen. Single-sex dorms, special housing for disabled, apartments, wellness housing available. $50 fully refundable deposit, deadline 12/20. **Activities:** Bands, campus ministries, choral groups, dance, drama, international student organizations, literary magazine, music ensembles, musical theater, radio station, student government, student newspaper, TV station, Catholic student club, Committed to Christ student organization, Love Alive Christian Fellowship, Muslim student organization, Nation of Islam student organization, Sigma Omega Delta social service organization, College Democrats, College Republicans, Collegiate 100 Black Men.

**Athletics.** NCAA. **Intercollegiate:** Baseball M, basketball, bowling W, cross-country, football (tackle) M, golf M, soccer W, softball W, tennis W, track and field, volleyball W. **Intramural:** Football (non-tackle). **Team name:** Jaguars.

**Student services.** Career counseling, student employment services, financial aid counseling, health services, personal counseling, placement for graduates, veterans' counselor. **Physically disabled:** Services for visually, speech, hearing impaired.

**Contact.** E-mail: admit@subr.edu
Phone: (225) 771-2430 Toll-free number: (800) 256-1531
Fax: (225) 771-2500
Velva Thomas, Director of Admissions, Southern University and Agricultural and Mechanical College, T.H. Harris Hall, Baton Rouge, LA 70813

## Southern University at New Orleans
### New Orleans, Louisiana
**www.suno.edu**          CB code: 1647

- Public 4-year university
- Commuter campus in large city
- 2,603 degree-seeking undergraduates

**General.** Founded in 1959. Regionally accredited. Part of Southern University System. **Degrees:** 228 bachelor's, 11 associate awarded; master's offered. **ROTC:** Army, Naval, Air Force. **Location:** Downtown. **Calendar:** Semester, limited summer session. **Full-time faculty:** 99 total. **Part-time faculty:** 2 total. **Class size:** 49% < 20, 47% 20-39, 3% 40-49, less than 1% 50-99, less than 1% >100.

**Basis for selection.** Open admission. ACT required by state law for placement.

**High school preparation.** 16 units recommended. Recommended units include English 4, mathematics 3, social studies 3, science 3 (laboratory 2) and foreign language 1.

**2009-2010 Annual costs.** Tuition/fees: $3,161; $6,899 out-of-state. Books/ supplies: $1,000. Personal expenses: $6,000.

**Financial aid.** All financial aid based on need.

**Application procedures. Admission:** Closing date 7/1. $5 fee ($15 out-of-state). Admission notification on a rolling basis. **Financial aid:** Closing date 4/1. FAFSA required. Applicants notified by 5/15; must reply within 1 week(s) of notification.

**Academics. Special study options:** Combined bachelor's/graduate degree, cooperative education, cross-registration, distance learning, double major, dual enrollment of high school students, internships, teacher certification program, weekend college. **Credit/placement by examination:** CLEP. 30 credit hours maximum toward bachelor's degree. **Support services:** Reduced course load, remedial instruction, study skills assistance, tutoring, writing center.

**Majors. Biology:** General. **Business:** Entrepreneurial studies, management information systems. **Education:** Early childhood, elementary. **Family/ consumer sciences:** Family studies. **Health:** Medical records admin, substance abuse counseling. **Physical sciences:** Physics. **Protective services:** Criminal justice. **Psychology:** General. **Public administration:** General, social work. **Social sciences:** Sociology.

**Most popular majors.** Biology 6%, business/marketing 18%, computer/ information sciences 9%, liberal arts 15%, psychology 13%, public administration/social services 9%, security/protective services 13%.

**Computing on campus.** 60 workstations in library, computer center. Online library, helpline, wireless network available.

**Student life. Freshman orientation:** Available. Preregistration for classes offered. **Housing:** Wellness housing available. **Activities:** Student government.

**Athletics.** NAIA. **Intercollegiate:** Basketball, cross-country. **Team name:** Knights.

**Student services.** Chaplain/spiritual director, career counseling, student employment services, financial aid counseling, health services, personal counseling, placement for graduates. **Physically disabled:** Services for visually, speech, hearing impaired.

**Contact.** Phone: (504) 286-5000 ext. 5314 Fax: (504) 284-5481
Rene Gill Pratt, Director of Recruitment, Admissions, & Retention, Southern University at New Orleans, 6801 Press Drive, New Orleans, LA 70126

## Southwest University
### Kenner, Louisiana
**www.southwest.edu**

- For-profit 4-year virtual university
- Very large city
- 562 degree-seeking undergraduates

**General.** Accredited by DETC. **Degrees:** 36 bachelor's awarded; master's offered. **Calendar:** Continuous. **Full-time faculty:** 6 total. **Part-time faculty:** 41 total.

**Basis for selection.** Open admission.

**2009-2010 Annual costs.** Tuition/fees: $5,500. Graduate tuition $250 per credit hour.

**Application procedures. Admission:** No deadline. $50 fee. Admission notification on a rolling basis.

**Academics. Special study options:** Accelerated study, distance learning, double major, independent study. **Credit/placement by examination:** CLEP.

**Majors. Business:** Business admin, management science. **Protective services:** Law enforcement admin.

**Computing on campus.** Online library available.

**Student services.** Adult student services, veterans' counselor.

**Contact.** E-mail: admissions@southwest.edu
Phone: (504) 468-2900 Toll-free number: (800) 433-5923
Fax: (504) 468-3213
Lydia Ocmand, Director of Admissions, Southwest University, 2200 Veterans Memorial Boulevard, Kenner, LA 70062-4005

## Tulane University
### New Orleans, Louisiana          CB member
**www.tulane.edu**          CB code: 6832

- Private 4-year university
- Residential campus in very large city

◗ 7,160 degree-seeking undergraduates: 24% part-time, 55% women, 10% African American, 4% Asian American, 4% Hispanic American, 2% Native American, 3% international

◗ 4,701 degree-seeking graduate students

◗ 26% of applicants admitted

◗ SAT or ACT with writing, application essay required

◗ 73% graduate within 6 years

**General.** Founded in 1834. Regionally accredited. **Degrees:** 1,405 bachelor's, 32 associate awarded; master's, doctoral, professional offered. **ROTC:** Army, Naval, Air Force. **Location:** 4 miles from downtown. **Calendar:** Semester, limited summer session. **Full-time faculty:** 572 total; 94% have terminal degrees, 18% minority, 36% women. **Part-time faculty:** 612 total; 50% have terminal degrees, 14% minority, 42% women. **Class size:** 65% < 20, 24% 20-39, 4% 40-49, 6% 50-99, 1% >100. **Special facilities:** Jazz archive, Louisiana collection of historical materials, Southeastern architecture archive, center for research on women, political economy institute, center for Latin American studies, middle American research institute, center for bioenvironmental research, performing arts center, Amistad research center.

**Freshman class profile.** 39,887 applied, 10,563 admitted, 1,502 enrolled.

| Mid 50% test scores | | | |
|---|---|---|---|
| SAT critical reading: | 630-700 | GPA 2.0-2.99: | 9% |
| SAT math: | 620-700 | Rank in top quarter: | 88% |
| SAT writing: | 630-710 | Rank in top tenth: | 60% |
| ACT composite: | 29-32 | Return as sophomores: | 91% |
| GPA 3.75 or higher: | 30% | Out-of-state: | 84% |
| GPA 3.50-3.74: | 24% | Live on campus: | 97% |
| GPA 3.0-3.49: | 37% | International: | 2% |

**Basis for selection.** High school achievement record most important, followed by test scores, recommendation, personal qualities; special consideration for children of alumni and minority applicants. Candidates should be in top third of graduating class with 3.5 GPA. Audition recommended for music majors. Portfolio recommended for architecture, art majors. **Home-schooled:** State high school equivalency certificate, letter of recommendation (nonparent) required. SAT Subject Tests required.

**High school preparation.** Recommended units include English 4, mathematics 4, social studies 3, science 4 (laboratory 4), foreign language 3 and academic electives 3. Chemistry and physics recommended for science or engineering majors.

**2009-2010 Annual costs.** Tuition/fees: $40,584. Room/board: $9,606. Books/supplies: $1,200. Personal expenses: $936.

**2008-2009 Financial aid. Need-based:** 925 full-time freshmen applied for aid; 598 were judged to have need; 598 of these received aid. Average need met was 96%. Average scholarship/grant was $22,910; average loan $5,320. 76% of total undergraduate aid awarded as scholarships/grants, 24% as loans/jobs. **Non-need-based:** Awarded to 2,701 full-time undergraduates, including 1,024 freshmen. Scholarships awarded for academics, athletics, leadership, music/drama, state residency. **Additional information:** Application deadline for merit scholarships December 1.

**Application procedures. Admission:** Closing date 1/15 (postmark date). No application fee. Admission notification 4/1. Admission notification on a rolling basis. Must reply by May 1 or within 2 week(s) if notified thereafter. **Financial aid:** Closing date 2/15. FAFSA, CSS PROFILE required. Applicants notified on a rolling basis starting 3/15; must reply within 2 week(s) of notification.

**Academics. Special study options:** Accelerated study, combined bachelor's/graduate degree, cross-registration, distance learning, double major, ESL, exchange student, honors, independent study, internships, liberal arts/career combination, student-designed major, study abroad, teacher certification program, Washington semester. **Credit/placement by examination:** AP, CLEP, IB, institutional tests. **Support services:** Learning center, study skills assistance, tutoring, writing center.

**Majors. Architecture:** Architecture. **Area/ethnic studies:** African, American, Asian, German, Latin American, Russian/Slavic, women's. **Biology:** General, biochemistry, cell/histology, ecology, evolutionary, molecular. **Business:** General, accounting, business admin, finance, management information systems, marketing. **Communications:** Media studies. **Conservation:** Environmental science, environmental studies. **Engineering:** Biomedical, chemical, physics. **Foreign languages:** Classics, French, German, Italian, linguistics, modern Greek, Portuguese, Russian, Spanish. **History:** General. **Interdisciplinary:** Medieval/Renaissance, neuroscience. **Legal studies:** General, paralegal. **Math:** General. **Philosophy/religion:** Judaic, philosophy. **Physical sciences:** Chemistry, geology, physics. **Psychology:** General. **Social sciences:** Anthropology, economics, international economics, political

science, sociology, urban studies. **Visual/performing arts:** Art, art history/conservation, dance, dramatic, multimedia, music performance, music theory/composition, musical theater, studio arts, theater history. **Other:** Earth sciences, Legal studies in business, Mathematical economics, Social policy and practice.

**Most popular majors.** Architecture 8%, biology 7%, business/marketing 20%, psychology 6%, social sciences 15%.

**Computing on campus.** 556 workstations in dormitories, library, computer center, student center. Dormitories wired for high-speed internet access and linked to campus network. Commuter students can connect to campus network. Online course registration, online library, helpline, repair service, student web hosting, wireless network available.

**Student life. Freshman orientation:** Mandatory, $400 fee. Preregistration for classes offered. **Policies:** Alcohol, substance abuse and sexual harrassment policies in place. **Housing:** Guaranteed on-campus for freshmen. Coed dorms, single-sex dorms, special housing for disabled, apartments, wellness housing available. $300 nonrefundable deposit, deadline 5/1. Honors program residence hall, language floors, women in science, healthy lifestyle, engineering and technology, performing and creative arts, pre-med and pre-law special living floors, quiet-study floors, and international living floors available. **Activities:** Bands, choral groups, dance, drama, film society, international student organizations, literary magazine, music ensembles, musical theater, radio station, student government, student newspaper, symphony orchestra, TV station, Hillel, Episcopal center, Inter-Varsity Christian Fellowship, Catholic center, Baptist student union, African-American Congress, Latin American students association, Amnesty International.

**Athletics.** NCAA. **Intercollegiate:** Baseball M, basketball, cross-country, diving W, football (tackle) M, golf W, swimming W, tennis, track and field, volleyball W. **Intramural:** Badminton, basketball, football (tackle) M, racquetball, softball, squash, swimming, tennis, triathlon, volleyball, wrestling M. **Team name:** Green Wave.

**Student services.** Alcohol/substance abuse counseling, chaplain/spiritual director, career counseling, student employment services, financial aid counseling, health services, legal services, minority student services, personal counseling, women's services. **Physically disabled:** Services for visually, speech, hearing impaired.

**Contact.** E-mail: undergrad.admission@tulane.edu
Phone: (504) 865-5731 Toll-free number: (800) 873-9283
Fax: (504) 862-8715
Earl Retif, Vice President for Enrollment Management and University Registrar, Tulane University, 6823 St. Charles Avenue, New Orleans, LA 70118-5680

---

## University of Louisiana at Lafayette

| Lafayette, Louisiana | CB member |
|---|---|
| www.louisiana.edu | CB code: 6672 |

◗ Public 4-year university

◗ Commuter campus in small city

◗ 14,349 degree-seeking undergraduates: 13% part-time, 57% women, 19% African American, 2% Asian American, 2% Hispanic American, 2% international

◗ 1,397 degree-seeking graduate students

◗ SAT or ACT (ACT writing optional) required

**General.** Founded in 1898. Regionally accredited. **Degrees:** 2,142 bachelor's, 2 associate awarded; master's, doctoral offered. **ROTC:** Army. **Location:** 130 miles from New Orleans, 200 miles from Houston. **Calendar:** Semester, extensive summer session. **Full-time faculty:** 591 total; 74% have terminal degrees, 15% minority, 42% women. **Part-time faculty:** 156 total; 20% have terminal degrees, 8% minority, 53% women. **Class size:** 30% < 20, 50% 20-39, 13% 40-49, 5% 50-99, 2% >100. **Special facilities:** 2 nuclear accelerators, 2 electron microscopes, CAD/CAM laboratory, Acadiana folklore archives, confocal microscope, atomic force microscope, Louisiana Emersive Technology Center, on campus restaurant and hotel (which include instructional facilities), nursery school laboratory, 600-acre sustainable farm, television production studio, marine research facility.

**Freshman class profile.**

| Mid 50% test scores | | | |
|---|---|---|---|
| ACT composite: | 20-24 | Rank in top quarter: | 39% |
| GPA 3.75 or higher: | 16% | Rank in top tenth: | 15% |
| GPA 3.50-3.74: | 16% | Out-of-state: | 4% |
| GPA 3.0-3.49: | 37% | International: | 1% |
| GPA 2.0-2.99: | 31% | Fraternities: | 6% |
| | | Sororities: | 8% |

**Basis for selection.** Guaranteed admissions for students who complete Louisiana Board of Regents' high school core curriculum with 19 ACT math (460 SAT math) or 18 ACT English (450 SAT verbal) and one of the following: 2.5 unweighted GPA or 23 ACT (1050 SAT math and verbal) with 2.0 GPA or rank in top 25% of class with 2.0 GPA. Audition required of music majors. Portfolio required of art, architecture majors. Essays required for some applicants.

**High school preparation.** College-preparatory program required. Required units include English 4, mathematics 4, social studies 1, history 2, science 3, foreign language 2 and visual/performing arts 1. Suggested electives: .5 unit computer science, 1 unit fine arts, 1 unit speech.

**2009-2010 Annual costs.** Tuition/fees: $4,046; $12,618 out-of-state. Room/board: $4,682. Books/supplies: $1,200. Personal expenses: $1,819.

**2008-2009 Financial aid.** All financial aid based on need.

**Application procedures. Admission:** Priority date 7/20; no deadline. $25 fee. Admission notification on a rolling basis. **Financial aid:** Priority date 5/1; no closing date. FAFSA required. Applicants notified on a rolling basis starting 4/1; must reply within 2 week(s) of notification.

**Academics. Special study options:** Accelerated study, cooperative education, cross-registration, distance learning, double major, dual enrollment of high school students, exchange student, honors, independent study, internships, student-designed major, study abroad, teacher certification program, Washington semester. **Credit/placement by examination:** AP, CLEP, SAT, ACT, institutional tests. 30 credit hours maximum toward bachelor's degree. **Support services:** Learning center, reduced course load, remedial instruction, study skills assistance, tutoring, writing center.

**Majors. Agriculture:** General. **Architecture:** Architecture, interior. **Biology:** General, conservation, microbiology. **Business:** Accounting, business admin, fashion, finance, hospitality admin, insurance, management information systems, managerial economics, marketing. **Communications:** General, media studies, public relations. **Computer sciences:** Computer science. **Conservation:** Land use planning, management/policy. **Education:** Agricultural, art, biology, business, chemistry, early childhood, early childhood special, elementary, English, family/consumer sciences, French, German, mathematics, middle, music, physical, physics, science, secondary, social studies, Spanish, special, speech, technology/industrial arts. **Engineering:** Chemical, civil, computer, electrical, mechanical, petroleum. **Engineering technology:** Industrial. **Family/consumer sciences:** Family studies. **Foreign languages:** General. **Health:** Athletic training, audiology/speech pathology, dental hygiene, dietetics, medical records admin, nursing (RN). **History:** General. **Math:** General. **Philosophy/religion:** Philosophy. **Physical sciences:** Chemistry, geology, physics. **Protective services:** Criminal justice. **Psychology:** General. **Social sciences:** Anthropology, political science, sociology. **Visual/performing arts:** General, art, industrial design, music performance. **Other:** Earth science education grades 6-12.

**Most popular majors.** Business/marketing 23%, education 13%, engineering/engineering technologies 7%, health sciences 9%, liberal arts 16%.

**Computing on campus.** 2,000 workstations in dormitories, library, computer center, student center. Commuter students can connect to campus network. Online course registration, online library, helpline, wireless network available.

**Student life. Freshman orientation:** Mandatory, $75 fee. Preregistration for classes offered. **Housing:** Single-sex dorms, apartments, fraternity/sorority housing available. $50 deposit, deadline 6/15. **Activities:** Bands, campus ministries, choral groups, dance, drama, international student organizations, literary magazine, music ensembles, musical theater, opera, radio station, student government, student newspaper, symphony orchestra, Young Republicans, Young Democrats, Omega Phi Alpha, Afro-American student groups.

**Athletics.** NCAA. **Intercollegiate:** Baseball M, basketball, cheerleading, cross-country, football (tackle) M, golf M, soccer W, softball W, tennis, track and field, volleyball W. **Intramural:** Basketball, football (non-tackle), racquetball, soccer, softball, tennis, volleyball, water polo. **Team name:** Ragin' Cajuns.

**Student services.** Adult student services, career counseling, student employment services, financial aid counseling, health services, minority student services, on-campus daycare, personal counseling, placement for graduates, veterans' counselor. **Physically disabled:** Services for visually, speech, hearing impaired.

**Contact.** E-mail: enroll@louisiana.edu
Phone: (337) 482-6553 Toll-free number: (800) 752-6553
Fax: (337) 482-1112
Leroy Broussard, Director of Admissions, University of Louisiana at Lafayette, Box 41210, Lafayette, LA 70504-1210

## University of Louisiana at Monroe
### Monroe, Louisiana
### www.ulm.edu            CB code: 6482

▶ Public 4-year university
▶ Commuter campus in small city
▶ 7,793 degree-seeking undergraduates: 23% part-time, 63% women, 28% African American, 2% Asian American, 1% Hispanic American, 1% international
▶ 1,092 degree-seeking graduate students
▶ 74% of applicants admitted
▶ SAT or ACT (ACT writing optional) required
▶ 31% graduate within 6 years; 6% enter graduate study

**General.** Founded in 1931. Regionally accredited. **Degrees:** 890 bachelor's, 33 associate awarded; master's, doctoral, professional offered. **ROTC:** Army. **Location:** 90 miles from Shreveport, 120 miles from Jackson, Mississippi. **Calendar:** Semester, extensive summer session. **Full-time faculty:** 370 total; 12% minority, 50% women. **Part-time faculty:** 73 total; 11% minority, 60% women. **Class size:** 35% < 20, 45% 20-39, 8% 40-49, 10% 50-99, 2% >100. **Special facilities:** National Public Radio station, Louisiana state cancer tumor registry archives, regional small business development center, weather research center, museum of natural history, flight simulator.

**Freshman class profile.** 2,585 applied, 1,924 admitted, 1,345 enrolled.

| Mid 50% test scores | | | |
|---|---|---|---|
| SAT critical reading: | 420-520 | Rank in top quarter: | 45% |
| SAT math: | 410-530 | Rank in top tenth: | 20% |
| ACT composite: | 19-23 | End year in good standing: | 64% |
| GPA 3.75 or higher: | 17% | Return as sophomores: | 69% |
| GPA 3.50-3.74: | 16% | Out-of-state: | 8% |
| GPA 3.0-3.49: | 33% | Live on campus: | 54% |
| GPA 2.0-2.99: | 30% | International: | 1% |

**Basis for selection.** Students who do not meet defined criteria evaluated on other evidence of academic promise for admittance by exception. Only limited number of students will be granted admittance by exception. **Homeschooled:** Transcript of courses and grades required. Must submit official transcript of grades and official proof of graduation or original diploma to admissions office.

**High school preparation.** College-preparatory program required. 17.5 units required. Required units include English 4, mathematics 4, social studies 1, history 2, science 3, foreign language 2, computer science .5. 1 fine arts, 0.5 free enterprise, 0.5 civics required.

**2009-2010 Annual costs.** Tuition/fees: $4,024; $12,206 out-of-state. Room/board: $5,790. Books/supplies: $1,200.

**Financial aid. Non-need-based:** Scholarships awarded for academics, alumni affiliation, art, athletics, job skills, leadership, minority status, music/drama, religious affiliation, ROTC, state residency.

**Application procedures. Admission:** Priority date 4/1; no deadline. $20 fee, may be waived for applicants with need. Admission notification on a rolling basis. **Financial aid:** Priority date 4/1; no closing date. FAFSA required. Applicants notified on a rolling basis starting 6/1; must reply within 2 week(s) of notification.

**Academics.** Credit hours toward graduation may be earned through examination, military service, correspondence and extension courses taken through accredited extension divisions of other colleges and universities. **Special study options:** Accelerated study, combined bachelor's/graduate degree, cooperative education, distance learning, double major, dual enrollment of high school students, ESL, honors, independent study, internships, study abroad, teacher certification program. Evening college. **Credit/placement by examination:** AP, CLEP, SAT, ACT, institutional tests. 22 credit hours maximum toward associate degree, 43 toward bachelor's. Maximum of one-third of credits required for degree may be earned through examination, military experience, and correspondence courses. **Support services:** Learning center, reduced course load, remedial instruction, study skills assistance, tutoring, writing center.

**Majors. Agriculture:** Business. **Biology:** General, toxicology. **Business:** Accounting, business admin, finance, insurance, management information systems, marketing. **Communications:** Media studies. **Computer sciences:** Computer science. **Education:** Art, biology, chemistry, elementary, English, family/consumer sciences, French, mathematics, music, physical, social studies, Spanish, speech. **Engineering technology:** Construction. **Foreign languages:** French, Spanish. **Health:** Audiology/speech pathology, clinical lab science, dental hygiene, health care admin, health services, nursing (RN), radiologic technology/medical imaging. **History:** General. **Math:** General. **Parks/recreation:** Exercise sciences. **Physical sciences:** Atmospheric science, chemistry. **Protective services:** Criminal justice. **Psychology:** General, educational. **Public administration:** Social work. **Social sciences:** Political science, sociology. **Transportation:** Airline/commercial pilot. **Visual/performing arts:** Music performance, studio arts. **Other:** Earth science education, grades 6-12.

**Most popular majors.** Business/marketing 19%, education 6%, health sciences 21%, liberal arts 11%, parks/recreation 6%.

**Computing on campus.** Dormitories wired for high-speed internet access and linked to campus network. Commuter students can connect to campus network. Online course registration, online library, helpline, repair service, student web hosting, wireless network available.

**Student life. Freshman orientation:** Mandatory. Preregistration for classes offered. Five regular sessions plus one computer PREP session available. **Housing:** Coed dorms, single-sex dorms, apartments, fraternity/sorority housing, wellness housing available. $50 partly refundable deposit, deadline 7/1. **Activities:** Bands, campus ministries, choral groups, dance, drama, international student organizations, literary magazine, music ensembles, musical theater, opera, radio station, student government, student newspaper, symphony orchestra.

**Athletics.** NCAA. **Intercollegiate:** Baseball M, basketball, cheerleading, cross-country, football (tackle) M, golf, soccer W, softball W, swimming, track and field, volleyball W. **Intramural:** Basketball, cross-country, football (non-tackle), golf, racquetball, soccer, softball, swimming, tennis, track and field, volleyball, weight lifting. **Team name:** Warhawks.

**Student services.** Adult student services, alcohol/substance abuse counseling, chaplain/spiritual director, career counseling, student employment services, financial aid counseling, health services, on-campus daycare, personal counseling, placement for graduates, veterans' counselor. **Physically disabled:** Services for visually, speech, hearing impaired.

**Contact.** E-mail: self@ulm.edu
Phone: (318) 342-5430 Toll-free number: (800) 372-5127
Fax: (318) 342-1915
Susan Duggins, Executive Director of Recruitment and Admissions, University of Louisiana at Monroe, 700 University Avenue, Monroe, LA 71209-1160

## University of New Orleans
**New Orleans, Louisiana**                          CB member
**www.uno.edu**                                     CB code: 6379

◆ Public 4-year university
◆ Commuter campus in very large city
◆ 8,515 degree-seeking undergraduates: 22% part-time, 51% women, 18% African American, 6% Asian American, 7% Hispanic American, 1% Native American, 4% international
◆ 2,619 degree-seeking graduate students
◆ 57% of applicants admitted
◆ SAT or ACT (ACT writing optional) required

**General.** Founded in 1956. Regionally accredited. **Degrees:** 1,356 bachelor's awarded; master's, doctoral offered. **ROTC:** Army, Naval, Air Force. **Calendar:** Semester, extensive summer session. **Full-time faculty:** 442 total; 69% have terminal degrees, 15% minority, 41% women. **Part-time faculty:** 188 total; 31% have terminal degrees, 17% minority, 47% women. **Class size:** 35% < 20, 43% 20-39, 9% 40-49, 9% 50-99, 4% >100.

**Freshman class profile.** 3,764 applied, 2,130 admitted, 1,259 enrolled.

| Mid 50% test scores | | GPA 2.0-2.99: | 44% |
|---|---|---|---|
| SAT critical reading: | 470-600 | Rank in top quarter: | 33% |
| SAT math: | 480-630 | Rank in top tenth: | 13% |
| SAT writing: | 460-570 | Return as sophomores: | 69% |
| ACT composite: | 20-24 | Out-of-state: | 6% |
| GPA 3.75 or higher: | 8% | Live on campus: | 8% |
| GPA 3.50-3.74: | 13% | International: | 6% |
| GPA 3.0-3.49: | 35% | | |

**Basis for selection.** Students who graduate from state-approved high schools must complete Louisiana Board of Regents core curriculum, require no more than one developmental/remedial course and satisfy one of the following (students who do not meet core curriculum must satisfy all of the following): 23 ACT (or SAT equivalent), 2.5 GPA and non-remedial in English and Math subscores, and/or rank in top 25% of class. If these are not met, student must have 26 ACT (SAT equivalent) and require no more than one remedial/developmental course. Audition required of music majors. Fine

Arts studio majors may apply for bypass credit for 1000 level studio courses by submitting a portfolio.

**High school preparation.** College-preparatory program required. 17.5 units required. Required units include English 4, mathematics 3, social studies 1, history 2, science 3, foreign language 2, computer science .5 and visual/performing arts 1. 1 additional math or science required.

**2009-2010 Annual costs.** Tuition/fees: $4,372; $12,528 out-of-state. Room/board: $6,700. Books/supplies: $1,200. Personal expenses: $2,143.

**2009-2010 Financial aid. Need-based:** 1,110 full-time freshmen applied for aid; 833 were judged to have need; 799 of these received aid. Average need met was 68%. Average scholarship/grant was $6,780; average loan $3,048. 63% of total undergraduate aid awarded as scholarships/grants, 37% as loans/jobs. **Non-need-based:** Awarded to 1,852 full-time undergraduates, including 606 freshmen. Scholarships awarded for academics, athletics. **Additional information:** Students in good academic and financial standing eligible to participate in Extended Payment Plan option.

**Application procedures. Admission:** Priority date 7/1; deadline 8/20 (receipt date). $40 fee. Application must be submitted online. Admission notification on a rolling basis beginning on or about 10/1. **Financial aid:** Priority date 5/15; no closing date. FAFSA required. Applicants notified on a rolling basis starting 4/20; must reply within 4 week(s) of notification.

**Academics. Special study options:** Cooperative education, cross-registration, distance learning, double major, dual enrollment of high school students, ESL, exchange student, honors, independent study, internships, student-designed major, study abroad, teacher certification program, Washington semester, weekend college. **Credit/placement by examination:** AP, CLEP, IB, SAT, ACT, institutional tests. 30 credit hours maximum toward bachelor's degree. **Support services:** Learning center, remedial instruction, tutoring, writing center.

**Majors. Area/ethnic studies:** Women's. **Biology:** General. **Business:** Accounting, business admin, entrepreneurial studies, finance, hospitality admin, management information systems, managerial economics, marketing. **Communications:** General. **Computer sciences:** Computer science. **Conservation:** Environmental studies. **Education:** Biology, chemistry, early childhood, elementary, English, mathematics, music, secondary, social studies. **Engineering:** Civil, electrical, marine, mechanical. **Foreign languages:** French, Spanish. **History:** General. **Interdisciplinary:** Global studies. **Math:** General. **Philosophy/religion:** Philosophy. **Physical sciences:** Chemistry, geology, physics. **Psychology:** General. **Social sciences:** Anthropology, geography, political science, sociology, urban studies. **Visual/performing arts:** Art history/conservation, studio arts. **Other:** Earth science education.

**Most popular majors.** Business/marketing 40%, communications/journalism 7%, liberal arts 11%, psychology 8%, social sciences 6%.

**Computing on campus.** Dormitories wired for high-speed internet access and linked to campus network. Commuter students can connect to campus network. Online course registration, online library, helpline, wireless network available.

**Student life. Freshman orientation:** Mandatory, $100 fee. Preregistration for classes offered. **Housing:** Coed dorms, special housing for disabled, apartments available. **Activities:** Bands, campus ministries, choral groups, dance, drama, film society, international student organizations, literary magazine, music ensembles, musical theater, opera, radio station, student government, student newspaper, African students organization, Chinese students and scholars association, international student organization, InterVarsity Christian Fellowship, Latin American student association, Muslim student association, Pakistan students association, College Republicans, Taiwanese students association, Vietnamese American student association.

**Athletics.** NCAA. **Intercollegiate:** Baseball M, basketball, diving, golf M, swimming, tennis, volleyball W. **Intramural:** Basketball, football (non-tackle), racquetball, soccer, softball, swimming, table tennis, tennis, volleyball. **Team name:** Privateers.

**Student services.** Adult student services, alcohol/substance abuse counseling, career counseling, student employment services, financial aid counseling, health services, legal services, minority student services, on-campus daycare, personal counseling, placement for graduates, veterans' counselor, women's services. **Physically disabled:** Services for visually, speech, hearing impaired.

**Contact.** E-mail: admissions@uno.edu
Phone: (504) 280-6595 Toll-free number: (800) 256-5866
Fax: (504) 280-5522
Andy Benoit, Director of Admissions Office, University of New Orleans, Administration Building Room 103, New Orleans, LA 70148

## Xavier University of Louisiana
**New Orleans, Louisiana**

www.xula.edu

CB member

CB code: 6975

- Private 4-year university affiliated with Roman Catholic Church
- Commuter campus in very large city
- 2,644 degree-seeking undergraduates: 3% part-time, 72% women, 74% African American, 10% Asian American, 1% Hispanic American, 2% international
- 672 degree-seeking graduate students
- 67% of applicants admitted
- SAT or ACT (ACT writing optional) required
- 41% graduate within 6 years

**General.** Founded in 1915. Regionally accredited. **Degrees:** 353 bachelor's awarded; master's, professional offered. **ROTC:** Army, Naval, Air Force. **Location:** One mile from downtown. **Calendar:** Semester, limited summer session. **Full-time faculty:** 228 total; 87% have terminal degrees, 52% minority, 49% women. **Part-time faculty:** 29 total; 52% have terminal degrees, 48% minority, 48% women. **Class size:** 45% < 20, 44% 20-39, 4% 40-49, 4% 50-99, 3% >100.

**Freshman class profile.** 3,278 applied, 2,193 admitted, 765 enrolled.

| Mid 50% test scores | | | |
|---|---|---|---|
| SAT critical reading: | 420-530 | GPA 2.0-2.99: | 36% |
| SAT math: | 410-530 | Rank in top quarter: | 34% |
| SAT writing: | 420-540 | Rank in top tenth: | 20% |
| ACT composite: | 18-24 | Return as sophomores: | 70% |
| GPA 3.75 or higher: | 24% | Out-of-state: | 44% |
| GPA 3.50-3.74: | 13% | Live on campus: | 56% |
| GPA 3.0-3.49: | 24% | International: | 1% |

**Basis for selection.** High school record or GED scores, standardized test results, and recommendation from counselor important. Interview recommended for academically weak. Audition required for music majors. Portfolio required for art majors.

**High school preparation.** College-preparatory program recommended. 16 units required. Required and recommended units include English 4, mathematics 2-4, social studies 1, history 1, science 1-3, foreign language 1 and academic electives 8. Math must include 1 algebra.

**2009-2010 Annual costs.** Tuition/fees: $15,825. Required fees for academic year cover information technology ($400), student government ($80), identification card ($20), and yearbook ($25). Room/board: $7,000. Books/supplies: $1,200.

**2008-2009 Financial aid. Need-based:** Average need met was 11%. Average scholarship/grant was $5,137; average loan $3,373. 34% of total undergraduate aid awarded as scholarships/grants, 66% as loans/jobs. **Non-need-based:** Awarded to 152 full-time undergraduates, including 70 freshmen. Scholarships awarded for music/drama.

**Application procedures. Admission:** Priority date 3/1; deadline 7/1 (postmark date). $25 fee, may be waived for applicants with need. Admission notification on a rolling basis. Must reply by May 1 or within 2 week(s) if notified thereafter. **Financial aid:** Priority date 1/1; no closing date. FAFSA required. Applicants notified on a rolling basis starting 4/1; must reply within 2 week(s) of notification.

**Academics. Special study options:** Accelerated study, combined bachelor's/graduate degree, cooperative education, cross-registration, double major, dual enrollment of high school students, exchange student, honors, independent study, internships, study abroad. **Credit/placement by examination:** AP, CLEP, SAT, ACT, institutional tests. 30 credit hours maximum toward bachelor's degree. **Support services:** Learning center, pre-admission summer program, reduced course load, remedial instruction, study skills assistance, tutoring, writing center.

**Majors. Biology:** General, biochemistry, microbiology. **Business:** Accounting, business admin, finance, management science, marketing. **Communications:** Media studies. **Computer sciences:** General, computer science. **Education:** General, art, biology, chemistry, early childhood, elementary, English, foreign languages, French, history, mathematics, multi-level teacher, music, physical, science, social studies, Spanish, special. **Engineering:** Computer. **Foreign languages:** French, Spanish. **Health:** Predental, premedicine, prepharmacy, preveterinary, speech pathology. **History:** General. **Legal studies:** Prelaw. **Math:** General, statistics. **Parks/recreation:** Health/fitness. **Philosophy/religion:** Philosophy. **Physical sciences:** Chemistry, physics. **Psychology:** General. **Social sciences:** Political science, sociology. **Theology:** Theology. **Visual/performing arts:** Art, music performance, piano/organ, stringed instruments, voice/opera.

**Most popular majors.** Biology 39%, business/marketing 10%, physical sciences 16%, psychology 15%, social sciences 6%.

**Computing on campus.** 350 workstations in dormitories, library, computer center. Dormitories wired for high-speed internet access and linked to campus network. Commuter students can connect to campus network. Online course registration, online library, helpline available.

**Student life. Freshman orientation:** Mandatory, $150 fee. Preregistration for classes offered. One-week program. **Policies:** All recognized student organizations must perform 2 community service activities per semester. **Housing:** Coed dorms, single-sex dorms, special housing for disabled available. $100 partly refundable deposit, deadline 4/9. **Activities:** Bands, campus ministries, choral groups, dance, drama, international student organizations, literary magazine, music ensembles, opera, student government, student newspaper, symphony orchestra, TV station, over 30 organizations.

**Athletics.** NAIA. **Intercollegiate:** Basketball, cross-country, tennis, volleyball W. **Intramural:** Basketball, cheerleading, football (non-tackle), softball, swimming, table tennis, tennis, track and field, volleyball. **Team name:** Gold Rush.

**Student services.** Adult student services, alcohol/substance abuse counseling, chaplain/spiritual director, career counseling, student employment services, financial aid counseling, health services, personal counseling, placement for graduates, veterans' counselor, women's services. **Physically disabled:** Services for visually, speech, hearing impaired.

**Contact.** E-mail: apply@xula.edu
Phone: (504) 520-7388 Toll-free number: (877) 928-4378
Fax: (504) 520-7941
Winston Brown, Dean of Admissions, Xavier University of Louisiana, 1 Drexel Drive, New Orleans, LA 70125-1098

# Maine

Four-Year Colleges

## Bates College

| | |
|---|---|
| Lewiston, Maine | CB member |
| www.bates.edu | CB code: 3076 |

- Private 4-year liberal arts college
- Residential campus in large town
- 1,738 degree-seeking undergraduates: 53% women, 5% African American, 7% Asian American, 4% Hispanic American, 1% Native American, 6% international
- 27% of applicants admitted
- Application essay required
- 91% graduate within 6 years

**General.** Founded in 1855. Regionally accredited. **Degrees:** 472 bachelor's awarded. **Location:** 35 miles from Portland. **Calendar:** 4-4-1 semester system. **Full-time faculty:** 163 total; 91% have terminal degrees, 15% minority, 49% women. **Part-time faculty:** 31 total; 64% have terminal degrees, 13% minority, 58% women. **Class size:** 64% < 20, 28% 20-39, 5% 40-49, 3% 50-99. **Special facilities:** Mountain seacoast conservation area, Edmund S. Muskie Archives, art museum, observatory.

**Freshman class profile.** 4,767 applied, 1,284 admitted, 469 enrolled.

| Mid 50% test scores | | | | |
|---|---|---|---|---|
| SAT critical reading: | 620-700 | End year in good standing: | 99% |
| SAT math: | 640-710 | Return as sophomores: | 94% |
| SAT writing: | 620-710 | Out-of-state: | 92% |
| Rank in top quarter: | 91% | Live on campus: | 100% |
| Rank in top tenth: | 63% | International: | 5% |

**Basis for selection.** GED not accepted. School achievement record, recommendations, special talents, leadership, essay, interview all important. Submission of standardized test scores is optional for admission. Interviews are strongly recommended.

**High school preparation.** College-preparatory program required. 17 units required; 23 recommended. Required and recommended units include English 4, mathematics 3-4, social studies 3-4, science 3-4 (laboratory 2-3) and foreign language 2-4. History included in social studies requirement.

**2009-2010 Annual costs.** Comprehensive fee: $51,300. Books/supplies: $1,150.

**2009-2010 Financial aid.** All financial aid based on need. 229 full-time freshmen applied for aid; 198 were judged to have need; 189 of these received aid. Average need met was 100%. Average scholarship/grant was $32,732; average loan $3,555. 88% of total undergraduate aid awarded as scholarships/grants, 12% as loans/jobs. **Additional information:** Priority date for filing required financial aid forms for early decision students is 11/15.

**Application procedures. Admission:** Closing date 1/1 (postmark date). $60 fee, may be waived for applicants with need. Admission notification 3/31. Must reply by 5/1. **Financial aid:** Closing date 2/1. FAFSA, CSS PROFILE required. Applicants notified by 4/1; must reply by 5/1.

**Academics. Special study options:** Accelerated study, combined bachelor's/graduate degree, cooperative education, double major, honors, independent study, internships, liberal arts/career combination, semester at sea, student-designed major, study abroad, teacher certification program, urban semester, Washington semester. Marine studies program at Mystic Seaport, liberal arts-engineering dual degree program with 5 universities. **Credit/placement by examination:** AP, CLEP, IB, institutional tests. **Support services:** Reduced course load, study skills assistance, tutoring, writing center.

**Majors. Area/ethnic studies:** African-American, American, East Asian, women's. **Biology:** General, biochemistry. **Conservation:** Environmental studies. **Engineering:** General. **Foreign languages:** Chinese, French, German, Japanese, Russian, Spanish. **History:** General. **Interdisciplinary:** Ancient studies, neuroscience. **Math:** General. **Philosophy/religion:** Philosophy, religion. **Physical sciences:** Chemistry, geology, physics. **Psychology:** General. **Social sciences:** Anthropology, economics, political science, sociology. **Visual/performing arts:** Art, dramatic.

**Most popular majors.** Biology 6%, English 7%, foreign language 9%, history 10%, psychology 11%, social sciences 28%, visual/performing arts 7%.

**Computing on campus.** 415 workstations in dormitories, library, computer center. Dormitories wired for high-speed internet access and linked to campus network. Commuter students can connect to campus network. Online course registration, helpline, repair service, student web hosting, wireless network available.

**Student life. Freshman orientation:** Mandatory. Preregistration for classes offered. Held 5 days prior to start of classes. **Housing:** Guaranteed on-campus for all undergraduates. Coed dorms, single-sex dorms, wellness housing available. $300 nonrefundable deposit, deadline 5/1. **Activities:** Bands, campus ministries, choral groups, dance, drama, film society, international student organizations, literary magazine, music ensembles, Model UN, radio station, student government, student newspaper, symphony orchestra, Amandla!, Bates Christian Fellowship, Bates Democrats, Bates Hindu Awareness Group, College Republicans, Feminist Action Coalition, Hillel, Latinos Unidos, Mushahada Club, OUTFront.

**Athletics.** NCAA. **Intercollegiate:** Baseball M, basketball, cross-country, diving, field hockey W, football (tackle) M, golf, lacrosse, rowing (crew), skiing, soccer, softball W, squash, swimming, tennis, track and field, volleyball W. **Intramural:** Badminton, baseball M, basketball, football (tackle), golf, handball, ice hockey, lacrosse, racquetball, rugby, sailing, soccer, softball, squash, table tennis, tennis, volleyball. **Team name:** Bobcats.

**Student services.** Alcohol/substance abuse counseling, chaplain/spiritual director, career counseling, student employment services, financial aid counseling, health services, minority student services, personal counseling, placement for graduates, women's services. **Physically disabled:** Services for visually, hearing impaired.

**Contact.** E-mail: admissions@bates.edu
Phone: (207) 786-6000 Fax: (207) 786-6025
Wylie Mitchell, Dean of Admissions, Bates College, 23 Campus Avenue, Lindholm House, Lewiston, ME 04240-9917

## Bowdoin College

| | |
|---|---|
| Brunswick, Maine | CB member |
| www.bowdoin.edu | CB code: 3089 |

- Private 4-year liberal arts college
- Residential campus in large town
- 1,772 degree-seeking undergraduates: 51% women, 6% African American, 12% Asian American, 10% Hispanic American, 1% Native American, 3% international
- 19% of applicants admitted
- Application essay required
- 94% graduate within 6 years; 15% enter graduate study

**General.** Founded in 1794. Regionally accredited. **Degrees:** 452 bachelor's awarded. **Location:** 25 miles from Portland, 120 miles from Boston. **Calendar:** Semester. **Full-time faculty:** 177 total; 98% have terminal degrees, 18% minority, 48% women. **Part-time faculty:** 40 total; 95% have terminal degrees, 25% minority, 58% women. **Class size:** 64% < 20, 27% 20-39, 7% 40-49, 3% 50-99. **Special facilities:** Arctic museum, arctic studies center, coastal marine biology and ornithology research facility, scientific station, farm, center for learning and teaching, 2 theaters, visual arts center, hall of music, environmental studies center, outdoor leadership center, community service resource center, African-American center, women's resource center, educational research and development program, career planning center, boathouse, electronic classroom, recital hall, nature trails, language media center, recording studio, crafts center, ceramic studio and photography darkroom.

**Freshman class profile.** 5,940 applied, 1,153 admitted, 494 enrolled.

| Mid 50% test scores | | | | |
|---|---|---|---|---|
| SAT critical reading: | 660-750 | Rank in top tenth: | 81% |
| SAT math: | 660-750 | Return as sophomores: | 96% |
| SAT writing: | 660-750 | Out-of-state: | 87% |
| ACT composite: | 30-33 | Live on campus: | 100% |
| Rank in top quarter: | 96% | International: | 4% |

**Basis for selection.** GED not accepted. Academic record, level of challenge represented in the candidate's course work, counselor/teacher recommendations, interview, quality of application and essay, character and personal qualities, extracurricular activities, talents and abilities, and overall academic potential most important. Test scores considered, but not required.

Motivation of candidate also considered. Interview recommended. Candidates with unusual talent in music, theater or visual arts encouraged to complete Arts Supplement when applying for admission. Audition recommended for music majors. Portfolio recommended for art majors. **Homeschooled:** Applicants applying from systems providing written evaluations rather than grades are required to submit either SAT or ACT-plus-SAT-Subject Test results. SAT Subject Tests should include Math Level 1 or Math Level 2 and one science. Personal interview strongly recommended.

**High school preparation.** College-preparatory program required. 20 units recommended. Recommended units include English 4, mathematics 4, social studies 4, science 4 (laboratory 3) and foreign language 4. Arts, music and computer science or computer literacy recommended.

**2009-2010 Annual costs.** Tuition/fees: $40,020. Room/board: $10,880. Books/supplies: $800. Personal expenses: $1,200.

**2008-2009 Financial aid. Need-based:** 273 full-time freshmen applied for aid; 201 were judged to have need; 201 of these received aid. Average need met was 100%. Average scholarship/grant was $34,289. 96% of total undergraduate aid awarded as scholarships/grants, 4% as loans/jobs. **Non-need-based:** Awarded to 65 full-time undergraduates, including 19 freshmen. Scholarships awarded for academics, leadership. **Additional information:** Regardless of financial circumstances, students admitted will receive money they need to attend. International students for regular admission must submit their financial aid applications by January 1st.

**Application procedures. Admission:** Closing date 1/1 (receipt date). $60 fee, may be waived for applicants with need. Admission notification on a rolling basis beginning on or about 4/5. Must reply by May 1 or within 1 week(s) if notified thereafter. **Financial aid:** Closing date 2/15. FAFSA, CSS PROFILE required. Applicants notified by 4/5; must reply by 5/1 or within 1 week(s) of notification.

**Academics.** Most students pursue independent scholarly research, working closely with a faculty advisor, through an independent study or honors project. About half of the student body studies abroad for one or 2 semesters, usually during the junior year. First-year seminars are limited to 16 first-year students and emphasize college-level reading and writing. Interdisciplinary and self-designed majors are available. **Special study options:** Accelerated study, combined bachelor's/graduate degree, double major, exchange student, independent study, liberal arts/career combination, semester at sea, student-designed major, study abroad, teacher certification program, Washington semester. 3-2 or 4-2 engineering degree programs with California Institute of Technology, Dartmouth College, Columbia University or University of Maine, Orono, 3-3 legal studies program with Columbia University Law School, first-year seminars, summer research fellowships, service-learning courses, The Writing Project, Quantitative Skills Program, Legal Studies Advisory Group, Health Professions Advising, ESL Writing Tutor. **Credit/placement by examination:** AP, CLEP, IB, institutional tests. **Support services:** Learning center, reduced course load, study skills assistance, tutoring, writing center.

**Majors. Area/ethnic studies:** African, Asian, Central/Eastern European, Latin American, women's. **Biology:** General, biochemistry. **Computer sciences:** Computer science. **Conservation:** Environmental studies. **Foreign languages:** Classics, French, German, Romance, Russian, Spanish. **History:** General. **Interdisciplinary:** Ancient studies, classical/archaeology, math/computer science, neuroscience. **Math:** General. **Philosophy/religion:** Philosophy, religion. **Physical sciences:** Chemical physics, chemistry, geochemistry, geology, geophysics, physics. **Psychology:** General. **Social sciences:** Anthropology, archaeology, econometrics, economics, political science, sociology. **Visual/performing arts:** Art history/conservation, studio arts, theater history.

**Most popular majors.** Biology 8%, English 6%, foreign language 10%, history 8%, psychology 6%, social sciences 29%, visual/performing arts 6%.

**Computing on campus.** 450 workstations in dormitories, library, computer center, student center. Dormitories wired for high-speed internet access and linked to campus network. Commuter students can connect to campus network. Online library, helpline, repair service, student web hosting, wireless network available.

**Student life. Freshman orientation:** Mandatory. 4-5 day program at the end of August, just before the start of classes. Pre-orientation outing trips offered over 4 nights prior to formal orientation; separate charge depending on the trip. **Policies:** Honor code, social code, judicial authority, drug and alcohol policies, policies on sexual misconduct, smoking, illegal drugs, discrimination, information technology use, residential life. **Housing:** Guaranteed on-campus for freshmen. Coed dorms, special housing for disabled, apartments, wellness housing available. Three small college houses and 8 college system houses available. **Activities:** Bands, choral groups, dance, drama, film society, international student organizations, literary magazine,

music ensembles, musical theater, radio station, student government, student newspaper, symphony orchestra, TV station, African-American society, Asian student organization, Latin American student organization, Hillel, Catholic student union, Christian fellowship, community service council, Evergreens, Democrats, Republicans.

**Athletics.** NCAA. **Intercollegiate:** Baseball M, basketball, cross-country, diving, field hockey W, football (tackle) M, golf, ice hockey, lacrosse, rugby W, sailing, skiing, soccer, softball W, squash, swimming, tennis, track and field, volleyball W. **Intramural:** Badminton, basketball M, cricket, cross-country, field hockey, football (non-tackle), ice hockey, rugby, soccer, softball, squash, tennis, volleyball, water polo. **Team name:** Polar Bears.

**Student services.** Alcohol/substance abuse counseling, career counseling, student employment services, health services, minority student services, on-campus daycare, personal counseling, placement for graduates, women's services. **Physically disabled:** Services for visually, speech, hearing impaired.

**Contact.** E-mail: admissions@bowdoin.edu
Phone: (207) 725-3100 Fax: (207) 725-3101
Scott Meiklejohn, Dean of Admissions and Student Aid, Bowdoin College, 5000 College Station, Brunswick, ME 04011-8441

---

## Colby College
**Waterville, Maine**
**www.colby.edu**

**CB member**
**CB code: 3280**

- Private 4-year liberal arts college
- Residential campus in large town
- 1,838 degree-seeking undergraduates: 54% women, 3% African American, 8% Asian American, 3% Hispanic American, 1% Native American, 5% international
- 34% of applicants admitted
- Application essay required
- 88% graduate within 6 years; 27% enter graduate study

**General.** Founded in 1813. Regionally accredited. Off-campus facilities available for teaching and research in biology, ecology, geology. **Degrees:** 508 bachelor's awarded. **ROTC:** Army. **Location:** 180 miles from Boston, 75 miles from Portland. **Calendar:** 4-1-4. **Full-time faculty:** 165 total; 96% have terminal degrees, 13% minority, 44% women. **Part-time faculty:** 57 total; 44% have terminal degrees, 4% minority, 58% women. **Class size:** 66% < 20, 28% 20-39, 4% 40-49, 2% 50-99. **Special facilities:** Astronomical observatory, arboretum, research greenhouses, kettlehole research bog, professional blacksmith's forge, woodworking shop, crew rowing center, technical climbing wall, Nordic ski trails, two synthetic turf fields, community radio station, scanning and transmission electron microscopes, laser flash photolysis, 400 MHz NMR, x-ray diffractometer, spectrophotometers, chromatographs, GIS lab, microcalorimeters, piezometers (groundwater monitoring wells).

**Freshman class profile.** 4,520 applied, 1,544 admitted, 480 enrolled.

| Mid 50% test scores | | | |
|---|---|---|---|
| SAT critical reading: | 630-720 | Rank in top tenth: | 59% |
| SAT math: | 640-720 | End year in good standing: | 96% |
| SAT writing: | 630-710 | Return as sophomores: | 94% |
| ACT composite: | 28-31 | Out-of-state: | 86% |
| Rank in top quarter: | 89% | Live on campus: | 100% |
| | | International: | 7% |

**Basis for selection.** School record and personal qualities very important. Test scores, recommendations, potential contribution to college life, and essay important. Interview, social, economic, racial, and geographic diversity considered. SAT/ACT or three Subject Tests of the student's choice are required.

**High school preparation.** 16 units recommended. Recommended units include English 4, mathematics 3, social studies 2, science 2 (laboratory 2), foreign language 3 and academic electives 2. Social studies units recommended could include history courses.

**2009-2010 Annual costs.** Comprehensive fee: $50,320. Books/supplies: $700. Personal expenses: $900.

**2009-2010 Financial aid.** All financial aid based on need. **Additional information:** Institutional loans have been replaced with institutional grants.

**Application procedures. Admission:** Closing date 1/1 (postmark date). $65 fee, may be waived for applicants with need, free for online applicants. Admission notification 4/1. Must reply by 5/1. **Financial aid:** Closing date 2/1. FAFSA, CSS PROFILE required. Applicants notified by 4/1; must reply by 5/1.

**Academics. Special study options:** Combined bachelor's/graduate degree, cross-registration, double major, exchange student, honors, independent study, internships, semester at sea, student-designed major, study abroad, teacher certification program, Washington semester. Numerous research, service learning, and internship opportunities through the Goldfarb Center for Public Affairs and Civic Engagement; summer research assistantships; course exchange programs with Bowdoin College, Bates College, Thomas College; stipends to enable student internships; coordinated 3-2 engineering program with Dartmouth; Idea Network of Biomedical Research Excellence (partnerships with Jackson Labs, Mt. Desert Island Biological Labs, and other colleges), exchange programs with Howard University and Pomona College, January Program term for focused studies, extensive study-abroad opportunities, Colby in Washington program. **Credit/placement by examination:** AP, CLEP, IB, institutional tests. 12 credit hours maximum toward bachelor's degree. When appropriate, distribution requirements, as well as certain requirements for the major, may be absolved by examination without course enrollment at the discretion of the department concerned. Matriculated students may earn credit by examination in 100- or 200-level courses to a maximum of 12 hours. Departmental examinations or external examinations approved by the department may be used, with credit given for the equivalent of at least C-level work. The cost of each examination is paid by the student. The college will exempt students from the language requirement for attaining before entrance a score of 64 in a SAT Subject Test in a foreign language or for attaining a score of 64 in Colby's placement test during first-year orientation; in either case, no academic credit will be granted. **Support services:** Tutoring, writing center.

**Majors. Area/ethnic studies:** African-American, American, East Asian, Latin American, Russian/Slavic, women's. **Biology:** General, biochemistry, cell/histology, environmental, molecular, molecular biochemistry, neurobiology/physiology. **Computer sciences:** Computer science. **Conservation:** Environmental science, environmental studies. **Foreign languages:** Classics, French, German, Spanish. **History:** General. **Interdisciplinary:** Classical/archaeology, global studies, neuroscience, science/society. **Math:** General. **Philosophy/religion:** Philosophy, religion. **Physical sciences:** Chemistry, geology, physics. **Psychology:** General. **Social sciences:** Anthropology, econometrics, economics, international relations, political science, sociology. **Visual/performing arts:** Art, art history/conservation, dramatic, studio arts. **Other:** Classical civilization: English, Human Development.

**Most popular majors.** Biology 12%, English 8%, foreign language 7%, history 8%, interdisciplinary studies 9%, mathematics 6%, physical sciences 8%, social sciences 24%.

**Computing on campus.** 350 workstations in library, computer center, student center. Dormitories wired for high-speed internet access and linked to campus network. Commuter students can connect to campus network. Online course registration, online library, helpline, repair service, student web hosting, wireless network available.

**Student life. Freshman orientation:** Mandatory. Preregistration for classes offered. 4-day optional outdoor component ($175); 3-day on-campus component follows, both held the week before classes begin. **Policies:** Students participate in forming policies and governing social and community activities through student government and serving on official college committees up to and including the Board of Trustees. **Housing:** Guaranteed on-campus for all undergraduates. Coed dorms, wellness housing available. Senior apartments. **Activities:** Bands, choral groups, dance, drama, film society, international student organizations, literary magazine, music ensembles, musical theater, radio station, student government, student newspaper, symphony orchestra, Approximately 100 student clubs and organizations.

**Athletics.** NCAA. **Intercollegiate:** Baseball M, basketball, cross-country, diving, field hockey W, football (tackle) M, golf, ice hockey, lacrosse, rowing (crew), skiing, soccer, softball W, squash, swimming, tennis, track and field, volleyball W. **Intramural:** Basketball, field hockey, football (non-tackle), soccer, softball. **Team name:** White Mules.

**Student services.** Alcohol/substance abuse counseling, chaplain/spiritual director, career counseling, student employment services, financial aid counseling, health services, minority student services, personal counseling, placement for graduates, women's services. **Physically disabled:** Services for visually, hearing impaired.

**Contact.** E-mail: admissions@colby.edu
Phone: (800) 723-3032 Toll-free number: (800) 723-3032
Fax: (207) 859-4828
Parker Beverage, Dean of Admissions and Financial Aid, Colby College, 4800 Mayflower Hill, Waterville, ME 04901-8848

## College of the Atlantic
**Bar Harbor, Maine**
**www.coa.edu**
CB code: 3305

- Private 4-year liberal arts college
- Residential campus in small town

- 321 degree-seeking undergraduates: 5% part-time, 69% women, 1% African American, 2% Asian American, 1% Hispanic American, 1% Native American, 15% international
- 5 degree-seeking graduate students
- 75% of applicants admitted
- Application essay required
- 61% graduate within 6 years; 15% enter graduate study

**General.** Founded in 1969. Regionally accredited. **Degrees:** 74 bachelor's awarded; master's offered. **Location:** 300 miles from Boston, 50 miles from Bangor. **Calendar:** Trimester, limited summer session. **Full-time faculty:** 24 total; 88% have terminal degrees, 4% minority, 29% women. **Part-time faculty:** 14 total; 29% have terminal degrees, 7% minority, 50% women. **Class size:** 89% < 20, 11% 20-39. **Special facilities:** Natural history museum, whale museum, herbarium, greenhouse, pier, research boat, organic farm, island research stations.

**Freshman class profile.** 322 applied, 241 admitted, 76 enrolled.

| Mid 50% test scores | | | |
|---|---|---|---|
| SAT critical reading: | 620-690 | GPA 2.0-2.99: | 11% |
| SAT math: | 510-620 | Rank in top quarter: | 63% |
| SAT writing: | 570-670 | Rank in top tenth: | 26% |
| ACT composite: | 21-27 | Return as sophomores: | 80% |
| GPA 3.75 or higher: | 29% | Out-of-state: | 79% |
| GPA 3.50-3.74: | 33% | Live on campus: | 99% |
| GPA 3.0-3.49: | 27% | International: | 18% |

**Basis for selection.** Academic ability, motivation, intellectual enthusiasm, independence, creativity, and commitment to ecological concerns and to goals and philosophies of college as demonstrated by high school record, recommendations, and interview important. **Homeschooled:** Thorough outline of topics covered, books read, homework completed, the evaluation process used in assessing work and the progress made over the years required. Standardized test scores recommended. **Learning Disabled:** Meeting with dean of academic services recommended.

**High school preparation.** College-preparatory program recommended. 15 units required; 19 recommended. Required and recommended units include English 4, mathematics 3-4, social studies 2, history 2, science 2-3 (laboratory 2), foreign language 2 and academic electives 1.

**2009-2010 Annual costs.** Tuition/fees: $33,060. Room/board: $8,490. Books/supplies: $600. Personal expenses: $630.

**2009-2010 Financial aid.** All financial aid based on need. 69 full-time freshmen applied for aid; 67 were judged to have need; 67 of these received aid. Average need met was 96%. Average scholarship/grant was $30,576; average loan $4,132. 83% of total undergraduate aid awarded as scholarships/grants, 17% as loans/jobs.

**Application procedures. Admission:** Closing date 2/15 (postmark date). $45 fee, may be waived for applicants with need. Admission notification 4/1. Must reply by May 1 or within 2 week(s) if notified thereafter. **Financial aid:** Closing date 2/15. FAFSA, institutional form required. Applicants notified by 4/1; must reply by 5/1.

**Academics.** Interdisciplinary curriculum consists of problem-solving course work, strong mentorships, seminars, independent study, tutorials, specialized skill courses, supervised internships away from college. **Special study options:** Independent study, internships, semester at sea, student-designed major, study abroad, teacher certification program. Winter Term program in Yucatan, Mexico. Consortium agreement (Eco-League) with four other colleges for student exchanges (Alaska Pacific University, Green Mountain College, Northland College, Prescott College); as well as academic partnerships with Olin College of Engineering, SALT Institute for Documentary Studies, National Outdoor Leadership School, and Sea Education Association. **Credit/placement by examination:** AP, CLEP, IB. 30 credit hours maximum toward bachelor's degree. **Support services:** Reduced course load, remedial instruction, study skills assistance, tutoring, writing center.

**Majors. Biology:** Ecology.

**Computing on campus.** 50 workstations in library, computer center. Dormitories wired for high-speed internet access and linked to campus network. Online course registration, online library, helpline, student web hosting, wireless network available.

**Student life. Freshman orientation:** Mandatory, $120 fee. Preregistration for classes offered. 4 days on campus with optional 6-day outdoor adventure trips available. **Policies:** Students participate in developing college policy and operate student activities fund. **Housing:** Guaranteed on-campus for freshmen. Coed dorms, special housing for disabled, wellness housing available. $150 nonrefundable deposit, deadline 5/1. **Activities:** Bands, choral groups, dance, drama, international student organizations, literary magazine, music ensembles, student government, student newspaper, SustainUs, outdoor experience program, life-drawing club, Student Democrats, international culture and issue group, GLBTQ group, sustainability committee.

**Athletics. Intramural:** Badminton, cricket, ice hockey, sailing, soccer, softball, table tennis, volleyball, water polo. **Team name:** Black Flies.

**Student services.** Alcohol/substance abuse counseling, career counseling, student employment services, financial aid counseling, health services, minority student services, personal counseling, placement for graduates. **Physically disabled:** Services for visually, hearing impaired.

**Contact.** E-mail: inquiry@coa.edu
Phone: (207) 801-5641 Toll-free number: (800) 528-0025
Fax: (207) 288-4126
Sarah Baker, Dean of Admission, College of the Atlantic, 105 Eden Street, Bar Harbor, ME 04609

---

## Husson University
**Bangor, Maine**
www.husson.edu
CB member
CB code: 3440

- Private 4-year business and health science college
- Residential campus in large town
- 2,383 degree-seeking undergraduates: 20% part-time, 58% women
- 376 degree-seeking graduate students
- 64% of applicants admitted
- SAT or ACT with writing, application essay required

**General.** Founded in 1898. Regionally accredited. **Degrees:** 381 bachelor's, 42 associate awarded; master's, professional offered. **ROTC:** Army, Naval. **Location:** 125 miles from Portland. **Calendar:** Semester, extensive summer session. **Full-time faculty:** 101 total; 67% have terminal degrees, 5% minority, 44% women. **Part-time faculty:** 8 total; 88% women. **Class size:** 49% < 20, 43% 20-39, 6% 40-49, less than 1% 50-99, less than 1% >100. **Special facilities:** Center for family business.

**Freshman class profile.** 1,280 applied, 813 admitted, 532 enrolled.

| Mid 50% test scores | | | |
|---|---|---|---|
| SAT critical reading: | 410-510 | GPA 3.0-3.49: | 35% |
| SAT math: | 420-510 | GPA 2.0-2.99: | 32% |
| SAT writing: | 390-500 | Rank in top quarter: | 30% |
| ACT composite: | 16-22 | Rank in top tenth: | 11% |
| GPA 3.75 or higher: | 10% | End year in good standing: | 67% |
| GPA 3.50-3.74: | 18% | Out-of-state: | 18% |
| | | Live on campus: | 63% |

**Basis for selection.** Class rank and school achievement record most important. Counselor recommendations considered. Test scores important for nursing applicants and occupational and physical therapy applicants. Test scores are used only for placement purposes for business and humanities school applicants. SAT recommended but not required for 2-year program and undeclared majors. Interview recommended. **Homeschooled:** Transcript of courses and grades, state high school equivalency certificate, letter of recommendation (nonparent) required. GED required for financial aid to be awarded. **Learning Disabled:** School must be apprised of special accommodation needs at time of payment of tuition deposit.

**High school preparation.** College-preparatory program recommended. Recommended units include English 4, mathematics 3, social studies 1, history 1, science 3 (laboratory 2).

**2009-2010 Annual costs.** Tuition/fees: $12,990. Room/board: $6,994. Books/supplies: $970. Personal expenses: $1,070.

**2009-2010 Financial aid. Need-based:** Average need met was 75%. Average scholarship/grant was $8,979; average loan $3,079. 50% of total undergraduate aid awarded as scholarships/grants, 50% as loans/jobs. **Non-need-based:** Scholarships awarded for academics, leadership.

**Application procedures. Admission:** Priority date 3/1; deadline 9/1 (postmark date). $25 fee, may be waived for applicants with need. Admission notification on a rolling basis beginning on or about 12/1. Must reply by May 1 or within 2 week(s) if notified thereafter. **Financial aid:** Priority date 4/15; no closing date. FAFSA required. Applicants notified on a rolling basis starting 4/1; must reply by 5/1 or within 2 week(s) of notification.

**Academics.** Strong liberal arts core within business programs. **Special study options:** Combined bachelor's/graduate degree, cooperative education, double major, independent study, internships, liberal arts/career combination, student-designed major, teacher certification program, weekend college. **Credit/placement by examination:** AP, CLEP, IB, SAT, institutional

tests. 30 credit hours maximum toward bachelor's degree. **Support services:** Learning center, pre-admission summer program, reduced course load, remedial instruction, study skills assistance, tutoring, writing center.

**Majors. Biology:** General. **Business:** General, accounting, accounting/business management, banking/financial services, business admin, entrepreneurial studies, finance, hospitality admin, hospitality/recreation, hotel/motel admin, international, international marketing, management information systems, managerial economics, market research, marketing, public finance, sales/distribution, small business admin. **Computer sciences:** Applications programming, programming, systems analysis. **Education:** Biology, elementary, English, physical, secondary. **Health:** Nursing (RN), prepharmacy. **Legal studies:** Paralegal. **Liberal arts:** Arts/sciences. **Parks/recreation:** Facilities management, health/fitness, sports admin. **Physical sciences:** Chemistry. **Protective services:** Criminal justice, law enforcement admin. **Psychology:** General, clinical. **Social sciences:** Criminology.

**Most popular majors.** Business/marketing 40%, education 6%, health sciences 30%, legal studies 10%, psychology 10%.

**Computing on campus.** 115 workstations in library, computer center, student center. Dormitories wired for high-speed internet access and linked to campus network. Commuter students can connect to campus network. Online course registration, online library, helpline, student web hosting, wireless network available.

**Student life. Freshman orientation:** Mandatory, $75 fee. Preregistration for classes offered. **Housing:** Guaranteed on-campus for all undergraduates. Coed dorms, fraternity/sorority housing, wellness housing available. **Activities:** Bands, campus ministries, drama, international student organizations, literary magazine, radio station, student government, student newspaper, campus crusade for Christ, Chi Alpha, political clubs.

**Athletics.** NCAA. **Intercollegiate:** Baseball M, basketball, field hockey W, football (tackle) M, golf M, lacrosse, soccer, softball W, swimming W, volleyball W. **Intramural:** Basketball, football (non-tackle) M, ice hockey, lacrosse, soccer, swimming W, tennis, volleyball. **Team name:** Eagles.

**Student services.** Adult student services, alcohol/substance abuse counseling, chaplain/spiritual director, career counseling, student employment services, financial aid counseling, health services, personal counseling, placement for graduates, veterans' counselor.

**Contact.** E-mail: admit@husson.edu
Phone: (207) 941-7100 Toll-free number: (800) 448-7766
Fax: (207) 941-7935
Carlena Bean, Director of Admissions, Husson University, One College Circle, Bangor, ME 04401-2999

---

## Maine College of Art
**Portland, Maine**
www.meca.edu
CB member
CB code: 3701

- Private 4-year visual arts college
- Commuter campus in small city
- 304 degree-seeking undergraduates: 3% part-time, 69% women
- 21 degree-seeking graduate students
- 77% of applicants admitted
- Application essay required
- 44% graduate within 6 years

**General.** Founded in 1882. Regionally accredited. Personal studio space for all juniors and seniors. **Degrees:** 71 bachelor's awarded; master's offered. **Location:** 100 miles from Boston. **Calendar:** Semester. **Full-time faculty:** 5 total; 100% have terminal degrees, 40% minority, 20% women. **Part-time faculty:** 40 total; 72% have terminal degrees, 2% minority, 58% women. **Class size:** 71% < 20, 29% 20-39. **Special facilities:** 2 art galleries, visual arts library.

**Freshman class profile.** 359 applied, 278 admitted, 69 enrolled.

| Mid 50% test scores | | | |
|---|---|---|---|
| SAT critical reading: | 460-600 | GPA 3.50-3.74: | 12% |
| SAT math: | 420-550 | GPA 3.0-3.49: | 37% |
| SAT writing: | 440-580 | GPA 2.0-2.99: | 41% |
| ACT composite: | 17-27 | Rank in top quarter: | 31% |
| GPA 3.75 or higher: | 10% | Rank in top tenth: | 10% |
| | | Out-of-state: | 64% |

**Basis for selection.** Decision based on interview and portfolio in conjunction with high school achievement record; essay, recommendations important, test scores considered. Interview recommended. Portfolio required. **Homeschooled:** Transcript of courses and grades required. Show evidence through the State Certification of Completion of high school program or

GED. **Learning Disabled:** Submit proper documentation to Director of Student Affairs (once admitted) and request specific accommodations.

**High school preparation.** 27 units recommended. Recommended units include English 4, mathematics 3, social studies 4, history 4, science 3, foreign language 2 and academic electives 3. 4 units of art strongly recommended.

**2009-2010 Annual costs.** Tuition/fees: $28,090. Studio fees vary per class. Room/board: $9,875. Books/supplies: $2,150. Personal expenses: $1,220.

**2009-2010 Financial aid. Non-need-based:** Scholarships awarded for academics, art.

**Application procedures. Admission:** Priority date 2/1; no deadline. $40 fee, may be waived for applicants with need. Admission notification on a rolling basis beginning on or about 1/2. Students strongly encouraged to reply by May 1 or within 3 weeks if notified thereafter. **Financial aid:** Priority date 3/1; no closing date. FAFSA required. Applicants notified on a rolling basis starting 2/15; must reply within 2 week(s) of notification.

**Academics.** 1 to 2 year foundation program in drawing, color, digital imaging, and 2 and 3 dimensional design, followed by transitional year, and final 2 years in major. **Special study options:** Combined bachelor's/ graduate degree, cross-registration, double major, exchange student, independent study, internships, liberal arts/career combination, study abroad, teacher certification program. Mobility program with 36 AICAD (Associated Independent Colleges of Art and Design) across the country and in Canada, cross-registration program with 4 other colleges and universities in the greater Portland area; special exchange program with Hanoi Fine Arts College, Vietnam; BFA credit available through Provincetown, MA Fine Arts Work Center. **Credit/placement by examination:** AP, CLEP. **Support services:** Learning center, study skills assistance, tutoring, writing center.

**Majors. Visual/performing arts:** Art, ceramics, graphic design, illustration, metal/jewelry, painting, photography, printmaking, sculpture, studio arts.

**Computing on campus.** 86 workstations in library, computer center, student center. Dormitories wired for high-speed internet access and linked to campus network. Commuter students can connect to campus network. Online library, helpline, student web hosting, wireless network available.

**Student life. Freshman orientation:** Mandatory. Preregistration for classes offered. Held the week before the start of classes. **Housing:** Coed dorms, wellness housing available. $500 partly refundable deposit. **Activities:** Film society, student government, student senate, community action group, green group, movie club, peer mentor scholarships.

**Student services.** Adult student services, alcohol/substance abuse counseling, career counseling, student employment services, financial aid counseling, minority student services, personal counseling.

**Contact.** E-mail: admissions@meca.edu
Phone: (207) 699-5026 Toll-free number: (800) 699-1509
Fax: (207) 699-5080
Grace Hopkins-Lisle, Director of Admissions, Maine College of Art, 522 Congress Street, Portland, ME 04101

---

### Maine Maritime Academy
Castine, Maine
www.mainemaritime.edu                    CB code: 3505

- Public 4-year maritime college
- Residential campus in rural community
- 921 degree-seeking undergraduates: 1% part-time, 17% women
- 18 degree-seeking graduate students
- SAT or ACT with writing required
- 64% graduate within 6 years

**General.** Founded in 1941. Regionally accredited. **Degrees:** 141 bachelor's, 4 associate awarded; master's offered. **ROTC:** Army, Naval. **Location:** 38 miles from Bangor. **Calendar:** Semester. **Full-time faculty:** 69 total; 33% have terminal degrees, 4% minority, 26% women. **Part-time faculty:** 21 total; 52% women. **Special facilities:** 500-foot training ship, 40-foot marine research vessel, 80-foot ocean going tugboat and barge, two-masted arctic schooner, steam and diesel engine laboratories, power plant simulators, bridge simulator, planetarium, ocean classrooms.

**Freshman class profile.**

| Mid 50% test scores | | ACT composite: | 18-25 |
|---|---|---|---|
| SAT critical reading: | 450-560 | Out-of-state: | 31% |
| SAT math: | 480-570 | Live on campus: | 95% |
| SAT writing: | 430-550 | | |

**Basis for selection.** High school academic record followed by SAT/ ACT test scores the most important. Interview, school and community activities, work ethic, and recommendations also considered. Interview and personal statement are highly recommended. **Homeschooled:** Transcript of courses and grades, letter of recommendation (nonparent) required. ACT/ SAT scores and possibly have transcripts/course records evaluated by Maine Department of Education.

**High school preparation.** College-preparatory program required. Required and recommended units include English 4, mathematics 4, science 2-3 (laboratory 2) and foreign language 2. 1 unit computer literacy recommended.

**2009-2010 Annual costs.** Tuition/fees: $10,105; $14,055 out-of-district; $17,805 out-of-state. Fee of $3,000 for U.S. Coast Guard licensing programs. Room/board: $8,450. Books/supplies: $1,000. Personal expenses: $800.

**2008-2009 Financial aid. Need-based:** 174 full-time freshmen applied for aid; 130 were judged to have need; 129 of these received aid. Average need met was 51%. Average scholarship/grant was $5,606; average loan $4,227. 36% of total undergraduate aid awarded as scholarships/grants, 64% as loans/jobs. **Non-need-based:** Awarded to 61 full-time undergraduates, including 27 freshmen. Scholarships awarded for academics, leadership, state residency.

**Application procedures. Admission:** Priority date 5/31; deadline 7/1 (receipt date). $15 fee, may be waived for applicants with need, free for online applicants. Admission notification on a rolling basis beginning on or about 1/1. Must reply by 5/1. **Financial aid:** Priority date 4/15; no closing date. FAFSA required. Applicants notified on a rolling basis starting 4/1; must reply within 4 week(s) of notification.

**Academics. Special study options:** Cooperative education, double major, internships, liberal arts/career combination, semester at sea, student-designed major, study abroad, teacher certification program. 2-month training cruise for USCG unlimited license majors. **Credit/placement by examination:** AP, CLEP, institutional tests. **Support services:** Study skills assistance, tutoring, writing center.

**Majors. Biology:** Marine. **Business:** General, business admin, entrepreneurial studies, international, logistics. **Engineering:** Marine, systems. **Engineering technology:** General. **Physical sciences:** Oceanography. **Transportation:** Maritime/Merchant Marine.

**Most popular majors.** Biology 8%, business/marketing 8%, engineering/ engineering technologies 64%, trade and industry 20%.

**Computing on campus.** PC or laptop required. 40 workstations in dormitories, library. Dormitories wired for high-speed internet access and linked to campus network. Commuter students can connect to campus network. Online library, helpline, repair service, wireless network available.

**Student life. Freshman orientation:** Mandatory. Preregistration for classes offered. 2.5 days available through 4 different sessions in August. **Policies:** Regimental lifestyle optional for the 2-year program and those majoring in power engineering, ocean studies, international business, and small vessel operations. Regiment is mandatory for United States Coast Guard unlimited license programs (marine transportation and marine engineering). No military obligation. Students required to live on-campus unless married, over age 23, or have completed 2 or more years of active military service or 6 semesters of study. **Housing:** Guaranteed on-campus for all undergraduates. Coed dorms, apartments, wellness housing available. $200 nonrefundable deposit, deadline 8/15. **Activities:** Bands, choral groups, drama, music ensembles, student government, student newspaper, Alpha Phi Omega, other service organizations.

**Athletics.** NCAA. **Intercollegiate:** Basketball, cross-country, football (tackle) M, golf M, lacrosse M, sailing, soccer, softball W, volleyball W. **Intramural:** Basketball, golf, handball, ice hockey M, racquetball, rifle, rugby M, sailing, skiing, soccer, softball, squash, tennis, volleyball, water polo. **Team name:** Mariners.

**Student services.** Alcohol/substance abuse counseling, career counseling, student employment services, financial aid counseling, health services, personal counseling, placement for graduates, veterans' counselor, women's services.

Contact. E-mail: admissions@mma.edu
Phone: (207) 326-2206 Toll-free number: (800) 227-8465
Fax: (207) 326-2515
Jeffrey Wright, Director of Admissions, Maine Maritime Academy, Pleasant Street, Castine, ME 04420

## New England School of Communications
### Bangor, Maine
**www.nescom.edu**                                **CB code: 3101**

- Private 4-year college of communications
- Residential campus in small city
- 496 degree-seeking undergraduates: 5% part-time, 26% women, 2% African American, 1% Asian American, 2% Hispanic American
- 64% of applicants admitted
- Application essay, interview required

**General.** Accredited by ACCSC. **Degrees:** 27 bachelor's, 17 associate awarded. **ROTC:** Army. **Location:** 250 miles from Boston. **Calendar:** Semester, limited summer session. **Full-time faculty:** 20 total; 15% have terminal degrees, 10% women. **Part-time faculty:** 49 total; 10% have terminal degrees, 2% minority, 31% women. **Class size:** 56% < 20, 42% 20-39, less than 1% 40-49, less than 1% 50-99. **Special facilities:** Sound recording studio, digital photography lab, mobile production studio.

**Freshman class profile.** 354 applied, 228 admitted, 132 enrolled.

| | | | |
|---|---|---|---|
| Out-of-state: | 23% | Sororities: | 2% |
| Live on campus: | 69% | | |

**Basis for selection.** Interview and Placement Test most important. High school record and essay also important. SAT or ACT recommended. Timed scholastic placement exam, audio reading required for on-air candidates. **Homeschooled:** Transcript of courses and grades, state high school equivalency certificate, interview, letter of recommendation (nonparent) required. Require GED score if homeschooling is not through an accredited curriculum-based program. **Learning Disabled:** Students requiring additional placement test time must provide professional evaluation documentation requesting extra time prior to interview date.

**High school preparation.** College-preparatory program recommended. Recommended units include English 4, mathematics 2, social studies 1, history 2, science 2, foreign language 2, computer science 1 and visual/performing arts 1. Recommend additional computer, public speaking, creative arts coursework.

**2009-2010 Annual costs.** Tuition/fees: $11,200. Additional cost of $160 for FireWire hard drive. Room/board: $6,994. Books/supplies: $1,500. Personal expenses: $1,000.

**2008-2009 Financial aid. Need-based:** Average need met was 16%. Average scholarship/grant was $4,559; average loan $3,430. 43% of total undergraduate aid awarded as scholarships/grants, 57% as loans/jobs. **Non-need-based:** Scholarships awarded for academics, leadership.

**Application procedures. Admission:** Priority date 4/1; no deadline. $25 fee, may be waived for applicants with need. Admission notification on a rolling basis. **Financial aid:** Priority date 4/15; no closing date. FAFSA, institutional form required. Applicants notified on a rolling basis starting 2/1; must reply by 8/15.

**Academics. Special study options:** Cross-registration, double major, internships, liberal arts/career combination, student-designed major. **Credit/placement by examination:** AP, CLEP, institutional tests. 6 credit hours maximum toward associate degree, 15 toward bachelor's. **Support services:** Reduced course load, study skills assistance, tutoring, writing center.

**Majors. Business:** Marketing. **Communications:** Advertising, broadcast journalism, digital media, photojournalism, public relations, radio/tv. **Communications technology:** General, photo/film/video, radio/tv, recording arts. **Computer sciences:** Web page design.

**Computing on campus.** 195 workstations in dormitories, library, computer center, student center. Dormitories wired for high-speed internet access and linked to campus network. Commuter students can connect to campus network. Online library, helpline, wireless network available.

**Student life. Freshman orientation:** Mandatory. Preregistration for classes offered. 3 days before start of fall session. Spring orientation held the Monday before classes start. **Housing:** Guaranteed on-campus for freshmen. Coed dorms, fraternity/sorority housing, wellness housing available. **Activities:** Pep band, campus ministries, choral groups, drama, international student organizations, literary magazine, music ensembles, musical theater, radio

station, student government, student newspaper, TV station, Crusade for Christ, Diversity Club, Habitat for Humanity.

**Athletics. Intramural:** Baseball, basketball, cheerleading, diving, field hockey, football (non-tackle), skiing, soccer, softball, swimming, table tennis, tennis, volleyball, water polo.

**Student services.** Adult student services, alcohol/substance abuse counseling, chaplain/spiritual director, career counseling, student employment services, financial aid counseling, health services, personal counseling, placement for graduates, veterans' counselor.

**Contact.** E-mail: info@nescom.edu
Phone: (207) 941-7176 Toll-free number: (888) 877-1876 ext. 1093
Fax: (207) 947-3987
Louise Grant, Director of Admissions, New England School of Communications, One College Circle, Bangor, ME 04401

## Saint Joseph's College of Maine
### Standish, Maine                              CB member
**www.sjcme.edu**                                **CB code: 3755**

- Private 4-year liberal arts college affiliated with Roman Catholic Church
- Residential campus in small town
- 1,039 degree-seeking undergraduates
- 87% of applicants admitted
- SAT or ACT (ACT writing recommended), application essay required

**General.** Founded in 1912. Regionally accredited. **Degrees:** 282 bachelor's awarded; master's offered. **ROTC:** Army. **Location:** 18 miles from Portland, 120 miles from Boston. **Calendar:** Semester, limited summer session. **Full-time faculty:** 66 total. **Part-time faculty:** 74 total. **Class size:** 60% < 20, 36% 20-39, 2% 40-49, 1% 50-99. **Special facilities:** Telescope, observatory.

**Freshman class profile.** 1,200 applied, 1,043 admitted, 267 enrolled.

| Mid 50% test scores | | | |
|---|---|---|---|
| SAT critical reading: | 430-530 | SAT writing: | 440-530 |
| SAT math: | 440-540 | Out-of-state: | 44% |
| | | Live on campus: | 93% |

**Basis for selection.** School record, class rank, test scores, recommendations, essays, extracurricular activities all considered. Interview optional, but recommended.

**High school preparation.** 16 units recommended. Recommended units include English 4, mathematics 3, social studies 2, history 2, science 2 (laboratory 2) and foreign language 2. Laboratory biology and laboratory chemistry required for nursing and science applicants. For any intended major, transcripts from candidates for admission should include 16 or more college-preparatory courses.

**2009-2010 Annual costs.** Tuition/fees: $26,050. Room/board: $10,350. Books/supplies: $1,100. Personal expenses: $1,200.

**2009-2010 Financial aid. Non-need-based:** Scholarships awarded for academics, leadership.

**Application procedures. Admission:** Priority date 3/1; no deadline. No application fee. Admission notification on a rolling basis beginning on or about 12/15. Must reply by May 1 or within 3 week(s) if notified thereafter. **Financial aid:** Priority date 3/1; no closing date. FAFSA, institutional form required. Applicants notified on a rolling basis starting 3/1; must reply within 3 week(s) of notification.

**Academics.** College belongs to Greater Portland Alliance, a 5-college consortium with cross registration. **Special study options:** Combined bachelor's/graduate degree, cooperative education, cross-registration, distance learning, double major, honors, independent study, internships, liberal arts/career combination, semester at sea, student-designed major, study abroad, teacher certification program, Washington semester. **Credit/placement by examination:** AP, CLEP, SAT, ACT, institutional tests. 30 credit hours maximum toward bachelor's degree. **Support services:** Study skills assistance, tutoring, writing center.

**Majors. Biology:** General. **Business:** Accounting, business admin, finance, human resources, international, marketing. **Communications:** Digital media, journalism, public relations. **Conservation:** Environmental science, environmental studies. **Education:** Biology, elementary, English, history, mathematics, physical. **Health:** Medical radiologic technology/radiation therapy, nursing (RN). **History:** General. **Interdisciplinary:** Marine science. **Math:** General. **Parks/recreation:** Exercise sciences, sports admin. **Philosophy/religion:** Philosophy. **Physical sciences:** Chemistry. **Protective services:**

Criminal justice. **Psychology:** General. **Social sciences:** General, political science, sociology. **Theology:** Theology.

**Most popular majors.** Biology 6%, business/marketing 20%, communications/journalism 8%, education 13%, health sciences 21%, parks/recreation 6%, social sciences 6%.

**Computing on campus.** 102 workstations in library, computer center, student center. Dormitories wired for high-speed internet access and linked to campus network. Commuter students can connect to campus network. Helpline, repair service, wireless network available.

**Student life. Freshman orientation:** Available, $50 fee. Preregistration for classes offered. Two-day session in June or July. **Policies:** Mass available daily on campus. **Housing:** Guaranteed on-campus for all undergraduates. Coed dorms, single-sex dorms, wellness housing available. $100 deposit, deadline 5/1. **Activities:** Choral groups, dance, drama, literary magazine, radio station, student government, student newspaper, Habitat for Humanity, High Adventure, Superkids, business club, campus ministry, culture and heritage club, interhall council, student nurses association.

**Athletics.** NCAA. **Intercollegiate:** Baseball M, basketball, cross-country, field hockey W, golf M, lacrosse, soccer, softball W, swimming, volleyball W. **Intramural:** Basketball, football (non-tackle), soccer, softball, swimming, volleyball. **Team name:** Monks.

**Student services.** Alcohol/substance abuse counseling, chaplain/spiritual director, career counseling, student employment services, financial aid counseling, health services, personal counseling, placement for graduates, veterans' counselor. **Physically disabled:** Services for visually, speech, hearing impaired. **Learning disabled:** Comprehensive services available.

**Contact.** E-mail: admission@sjcme.edu
Phone: (207) 893-7746 Toll-free number: (800) 338-7057
Fax: (207) 893-7862
Jennifer Gronros, Dean of Admission, Saint Joseph's College of Maine, 278 Whites Bridge Road, Standish, ME 04084-5263

## Thomas College
**Waterville, Maine**
www.thomas.edu
**CB member**
**CB code: 3903**

- Private 4-year business and liberal arts college
- Residential campus in large town
- 740 degree-seeking undergraduates: 12% part-time, 50% women, 3% African American, 2% Asian American, 1% Hispanic American, 1% Native American
- 129 degree-seeking graduate students
- 94% of applicants admitted
- SAT or ACT (ACT writing optional), application essay required
- 41% graduate within 6 years

**General.** Founded in 1894. Regionally accredited. Evening division (undergraduate and graduate) on trimester system. **Degrees:** 104 bachelor's, 11 associate awarded; master's offered. **Location:** 75 miles from Portland. **Calendar:** Semester, limited summer session. **Full-time faculty:** 25 total; 52% have terminal degrees, 40% women. **Part-time faculty:** 53 total; 19% have terminal degrees, 51% women. **Class size:** 41% < 20, 59% 20-39.

**Freshman class profile.** 606 applied, 571 admitted, 218 enrolled.

| Mid 50% test scores | | GPA 2.0-2.99: | 33% |
|---|---|---|---|
| SAT critical reading: | 400-500 | Rank in top quarter: | 30% |
| SAT math: | 450-510 | Rank in top tenth: | 13% |
| SAT writing: | 420-480 | End year in good standing: | 91% |
| GPA 3.75 or higher: | 3% | Return as sophomores: | 66% |
| GPA 3.50-3.74: | 7% | Out-of-state: | 21% |
| GPA 3.0-3.49: | 51% | Live on campus: | 82% |

**Basis for selection.** Academic transcripts most important. Letters of recommendation, SAT, ACT and/or TOEFL Exam scores also important. Recommend minimum 2.0 overall GPA, rank in top half of class. Test scores required of bachelor's degree candidates, not required for associate degree candidates. Interview recommended. **Homeschooled:** Transcript of courses and grades, state high school equivalency certificate, letter of recommendation (nonparent) required.

**High school preparation.** College-preparatory program recommended. 16 units recommended. Recommended units include English 4, mathematics 3, social studies 2, history 2, science 3 and foreign language 2.

**2009-2010 Annual costs.** Tuition/fees: $20,440. Room/board: $8,410. Books/supplies: $800. Personal expenses: $1,000.

**2009-2010 Financial aid. Need-based:** 210 full-time freshmen applied for aid; 206 were judged to have need; 206 of these received aid. Average need met was 85%. Average scholarship/grant was $13,611; average loan $4,005. 71% of total undergraduate aid awarded as scholarships/grants, 29% as loans/jobs. **Non-need-based:** Awarded to 369 full-time undergraduates, including 158 freshmen. Scholarships awarded for academics, leadership, state residency.

**Application procedures. Admission:** No deadline. $50 fee, may be waived for applicants with need. Admission notification on a rolling basis beginning on or about 12/1. Must reply by May 1 or within 4 week(s) if notified thereafter. **Financial aid:** Priority date 2/15; no closing date. FAFSA required. Applicants notified on a rolling basis starting 3/15; must reply within 2 week(s) of notification.

**Academics. Special study options:** Combined bachelor's/graduate degree, cross-registration, double major, dual enrollment of high school students, independent study, internships, study abroad, teacher certification program, Washington semester. **Credit/placement by examination:** AP, CLEP. 15 credit hours maximum toward associate degree, 15 toward bachelor's. **Support services:** Learning center, reduced course load, study skills assistance, tutoring.

**Majors. Business:** Accounting, business admin, finance, hospitality admin, human resources, international, marketing. **Communications:** General. **Computer sciences:** Computer science, information technology. **Education:** Early childhood, elementary. **Parks/recreation:** Sports admin. **Protective services:** Criminal justice, law enforcement admin. **Psychology:** General, forensic. **Social sciences:** Political science.

**Most popular majors.** Business/marketing 43%, education 10%, parks/recreation 9%, psychology 10%, security/protective services 19%.

**Computing on campus.** 120 workstations in dormitories, library, computer center, student center. Dormitories wired for high-speed internet access and linked to campus network. Commuter students can connect to campus network. Online course registration, online library, helpline, repair service, student web hosting, wireless network available.

**Student life. Freshman orientation:** Mandatory. Preregistration for classes offered. 3-day program held at the end of August; extended programs during fall semester. **Housing:** Guaranteed on-campus for freshmen. Coed dorms, wellness housing available. $200 nonrefundable deposit, deadline 5/1. **Activities:** Dance, drama, student government, student newspaper, Fellowship Group, Habitat for Humanity, Environmental Awareness Club, ASSIST (A Society of Students in Service Together), Student Veterans Organization.

**Athletics.** NCAA. **Intercollegiate:** Baseball M, basketball, cross-country, field hockey W, golf M, lacrosse, soccer, softball W, tennis, volleyball W. **Intramural:** Badminton, basketball, bowling, football (non-tackle), soccer, softball, table tennis, tennis, volleyball, weight lifting. **Team name:** Terriers.

**Student services.** Alcohol/substance abuse counseling, chaplain/spiritual director, career counseling, student employment services, financial aid counseling, health services, personal counseling, placement for graduates.

**Contact.** E-mail: admiss@thomas.edu
Phone: (207) 859-1101 Toll-free number: (800) 339-7001
Fax: (207) 859-1114
Wendy Martin, Associate Dean for Undergraduate Admissions, Thomas College, 180 West River Road, Waterville, ME 04901

## Unity College
**Unity, Maine**
www.unity.edu
**CB code: 3925**

- Private 4-year liberal arts college
- Residential campus in rural community
- 558 degree-seeking undergraduates: 1% part-time, 49% women
- 77% of applicants admitted
- 52% graduate within 6 years; 12% enter graduate study

**General.** Founded in 1965. Regionally accredited. **Degrees:** 90 bachelor's, 4 associate awarded. **ROTC:** Army. **Location:** 20 miles from Waterville. **Calendar:** Semester, limited summer session. **Full-time faculty:** 36 total; 92% have terminal degrees, 42% women. **Part-time faculty:** 23 total; 83% have terminal degrees. **Class size:** 59% < 20, 39% 20-39, 1% 40-49, less than 1% 50-99. **Special facilities:** Wetlands research area.

**Freshman class profile.** 677 applied, 521 admitted, 169 enrolled.

| Mid 50% test scores | | | |
|---|---|---|---|
| SAT critical reading: | 460-590 | GPA 3.0-3.49: | 27% |
| SAT math: | 450-570 | GPA 2.0-2.99: | 37% |
| SAT writing: | 440-560 | End year in good standing: | 91% |
| GPA 3.75 or higher: | 15% | Return as sophomores: | 74% |
| GPA 3.50-3.74: | 20% | Out-of-state: | 78% |
| | | Live on campus: | 94% |

**Basis for selection.** High school transcripts, interviews, recommendations and essay most important. Test scores not required but highly recommended. SAT or ACT recommended. Interview is optional but recommended. **Homeschooled:** Informative portfolio.

**High school preparation.** College-preparatory program recommended. 18 units recommended. Required and recommended units include English 4, mathematics 4, social studies 3, history 3, science 3 (laboratory 3) and foreign language 2.

**2009-2010 Annual costs.** Tuition/fees: $21,640. Room/board: $8,060. Books/supplies: $450. Personal expenses: $800.

**2009-2010 Financial aid. Need-based:** 161 full-time freshmen applied for aid; 150 were judged to have need; 150 of these received aid. Average need met was 73%. Average scholarship/grant was $12,395; average loan $4,720. 79% of total undergraduate aid awarded as scholarships/grants, 21% as loans/jobs. **Non-need-based:** Awarded to 87 full-time undergraduates, including 15 freshmen. Scholarships awarded for academics, leadership, minority status.

**Application procedures. Admission:** Priority date 7/1; no deadline. $25 fee, may be waived for applicants with need, free for online applicants. Admission notification on a rolling basis. **Financial aid:** Priority date 3/1; no closing date. FAFSA required. Applicants notified on a rolling basis starting 3/10; must reply within 2 week(s) of notification.

**Academics. Special study options:** Accelerated study, combined bachelor's/graduate degree, cooperative education, double major, independent study, internships, semester at sea, student-designed major, study abroad, teacher certification program, Washington semester. **Credit/placement by examination:** AP, CLEP, IB, SAT, ACT, institutional tests. 15 credit hours maximum toward associate degree, 15 toward bachelor's. **Support services:** Learning center, reduced course load, remedial instruction, study skills assistance, tutoring, writing center.

**Majors. Agriculture:** Aquaculture, ornamental horticulture. **Biology:** Ecology, environmental, marine, wildlife. **Conservation:** Environmental science, environmental studies, forestry, management/policy, wildlife. **Education:** General. **Health:** Recreational therapy. **Liberal arts:** Arts/sciences. **Parks/recreation:** General, facilities management.

**Most popular majors.** Agriculture 7%, biology 30%, natural resources/environmental science 33%, parks/recreation 18%.

**Computing on campus.** 80 workstations in dormitories, library, computer center, student center. Dormitories wired for high-speed internet access and linked to campus network. Commuter students can connect to campus network. Online course registration, online library, helpline, wireless network available.

**Student life. Freshman orientation:** Mandatory, $100 fee. A 5-day outdoor wilderness-based program. **Housing:** Guaranteed on-campus for all undergraduates. Coed dorms, single-sex dorms, cooperative housing, wellness housing available. $100 nonrefundable deposit. **Activities:** Drama, literary magazine, student government, student newspaper, search and rescue crew, photography club, Environmental Awareness, recycling, community service.

**Student services.** Alcohol/substance abuse counseling, chaplain/spiritual director, career counseling, student employment services, financial aid counseling, health services, personal counseling, placement for graduates, veterans' counselor. **Physically disabled:** Services for hearing impaired.

**Contact.** E-mail: admissions@unity.edu
Phone: (207) 948-3131 ext. 231 Toll-free number: (800) 624-1024
Fax: (207) 948-2928
Kay Fiedler, Director of Admission, Unity College, P.O. 532, Unity, ME 04988-0532

---

## University of Maine
**Orono, Maine**
www.umaine.edu

CB member
CB code: 3916

- Public 4-year university
- Residential campus in large town
- 8,759 degree-seeking undergraduates: 9% part-time, 48% women, 1% African American, 1% Asian American, 1% Hispanic American, 2% Native American, 2% international
- 1,731 degree-seeking graduate students
- 80% of applicants admitted
- SAT or ACT (ACT writing recommended), application essay required
- 59% graduate within 6 years

**General.** Founded in 1865. Regionally accredited. **Degrees:** 1,614 bachelor's awarded; master's, doctoral offered. **ROTC:** Army, Naval. **Location:** 12 miles from Bangor. **Calendar:** Semester, extensive summer session. **Full-time faculty:** 567 total; 76% have terminal degrees, 6% minority, 34% women. **Part-time faculty:** 231 total; 33% have terminal degrees, 4% minority, 59% women. **Class size:** 49% < 20, 31% 20-39, 7% 40-49, 10% 50-99, 4% >100. **Special facilities:** Advanced manufacturing center, machine tool lab, laboratory for surface science and technology, planetarium, anthropology museum, woodland preserve, botanical garden, art museum, observatory, environmental research facility, performing arts hall, Canadian-American center, Franco-American center, digital media lab, farm museum, marine lab, aquatic production facility, climbing wall, center for undergraduate research, student innovation center.

**Freshman class profile.** 6,786 applied, 5,435 admitted, 1,731 enrolled.

| Mid 50% test scores | | | |
|---|---|---|---|
| SAT critical reading: | 470-580 | GPA 2.0-2.99: | 21% |
| SAT math: | 480-590 | Rank in top quarter: | 52% |
| SAT writing: | 460-560 | Rank in top tenth: | 20% |
| ACT composite: | 20-26 | Return as sophomores: | 79% |
| GPA 3.75 or higher: | 21% | Out-of-state: | 18% |
| GPA 3.50-3.74: | 8% | Live on campus: | 87% |
| GPA 3.0-3.49: | 50% | International: | 2% |

**Basis for selection.** Strong emphasis on grades earned, GPA, class rank (if available) and standardized test scores. Academic requirements for admission may vary by program. Interviews available. Audition required of music majors. Portfolio recommended for art majors. **Homeschooled:** Statement describing homeschool structure and mission, transcript of courses and grades, state high school equivalency certificate, letter of recommendation (nonparent) required. GED requirement may be waived if thorough records submitted.

**High school preparation.** College-preparatory program required. 17 units required. Required and recommended units include English 4, mathematics 3-4, social studies 2-3, history 1, science 2-4 (laboratory 2), foreign language 2, computer science 1, visual/performing arts 1 and academic electives 2-3. 1 unit physical education required of all College of Education candidates.

**2009-2010 Annual costs.** Tuition/fees: $9,626; $23,876 out-of-state. New England Regional Student Program tuition is $11,400. Room/board: $8,348. Books/supplies: $700. Personal expenses: $1,100.

**2008-2009 Financial aid. Need-based:** Average need met was 76%. Average scholarship/grant was $6,608; average loan $4,312. 45% of total undergraduate aid awarded as scholarships/grants, 55% as loans/jobs. **Non-need-based:** Scholarships awarded for academics, alumni affiliation, art, athletics, job skills, leadership, minority status, music/drama, religious affiliation, ROTC, state residency. **Additional information:** Financial aid is available for students entering in the spring.

**Application procedures. Admission:** Priority date 3/1; no deadline. $40 fee, may be waived for applicants with need. Admission notification on a rolling basis beginning on or about 2/1. Must reply by May 1 or within 2 week(s) if notified thereafter. **Financial aid:** Priority date 3/1; no closing date. FAFSA required. Applicants notified on a rolling basis starting 3/15; must reply by 5/1 or within 2 week(s) of notification.

**Academics. Special study options:** Accelerated study, combined bachelor's/graduate degree, cooperative education, distance learning, double major, dual enrollment of high school students, ESL, honors, independent study, internships, liberal arts/career combination, semester at sea, study abroad, teacher certification program. **Credit/placement by examination:** AP, CLEP, IB, institutional tests. Duplicate credit may not be granted. Each department may develop or adopt examinations other than CLEP examinations for the purpose of granting credit for specific courses. **Support services:** Reduced course load, remedial instruction, study skills assistance, tutoring, writing center.

**Honors college/program.** Admission for first-time and transfer students based on test scores and high school record.

**Majors. Agriculture:** Animal sciences, business, economics, food science, greenhouse operations, horticultural science, landscaping, nursery operations, ornamental horticulture, plant sciences, soil science, turf management. **Area/ethnic studies:** Women's. **Biology:** General, bacteriology, biochemistry, biomedical sciences, botany, cell/histology, ecology, entomology, marine, molecular, pathology, zoology. **Business:** General, accounting, business admin, finance, labor relations, management information systems, managerial economics. **Communications:** General, journalism. **Computer sciences:** General. **Conservation:** General, environmental studies, forest management, forest resources, forestry, management/policy, wildlife, wood science. **Education:** General, art, biology, chemistry, elementary, English, foreign languages, French, history, mathematics, music, physical, science, secondary, social studies, Spanish. **Engineering:** General, agricultural, chemical, civil, computer, electrical, forest, mechanical, physics, systems. **Engineering technology:** Civil, electrical, surveying. **Family/consumer sciences:** Family/community services, food/nutrition. **Foreign languages:** General, French, German, Latin, Spanish. **Health:** Audiology/speech pathology, clinical lab science, communication disorders, nursing (RN). **History:** General. **Interdisciplinary:** Biological/physical sciences, natural sciences. **Liberal arts:** Arts/sciences. **Math:** General. **Parks/recreation:** Facilities management. **Philosophy/religion:** Philosophy. **Physical sciences:** Chemistry, geology, oceanography, physics. **Psychology:** General. **Public administration:** General, social work. **Social sciences:** Anthropology, economics, international relations, political science, sociology. **Visual/performing arts:** Art history/conservation, dramatic, music performance, studio arts.

**Most popular majors.** Business/marketing 14%, communications/journalism 6%, education 11%, engineering/engineering technologies 16%, health sciences 8%, psychology 6%, social sciences 7%.

**Computing on campus.** 500 workstations in library, computer center, student center. Dormitories wired for high-speed internet access and linked to campus network. Commuter students can connect to campus network. Online course registration, online library, helpline, repair service, student web hosting, wireless network available.

**Student life. Freshman orientation:** Available. Preregistration for classes offered. 2-day events in June, parents invited; 4-day welcome program in fall; additional adventure orientations available. **Housing:** Guaranteed on-campus for freshmen. Coed dorms, special housing for disabled, apartments, fraternity/sorority housing, wellness housing available. Academic grouping wings, men-only sections, women-only sections available. **Activities:** Bands, campus ministries, choral groups, dance, drama, film society, international student organizations, literary magazine, music ensembles, Model UN, musical theater, opera, radio station, student government, student newspaper, symphony orchestra, TV station, InterVarsity Christian Fellowship, Campus Crusade for Christ, Catholic Student Association, Hillel, Maine Christian Association, Muslim student organization, Newman Center.

**Athletics.** NCAA. **Intercollegiate:** Baseball M, basketball, cheerleading, cross-country, diving, field hockey W, football (tackle) M, ice hockey, soccer, softball, swimming, track and field, volleyball W. **Intramural:** Badminton, basketball, cross-country, diving, field hockey W, football (non-tackle) M, golf, racquetball, skiing, soccer, softball, squash, swimming, table tennis, tennis, track and field, triathlon, volleyball, water polo. **Team name:** Black Bears.

**Student services.** Adult student services, alcohol/substance abuse counseling, chaplain/spiritual director, career counseling, services for economically disadvantaged, student employment services, financial aid counseling, health services, legal services, minority student services, on-campus daycare, personal counseling, placement for graduates, veterans' counselor, women's services. **Physically disabled:** Services for visually, speech, hearing impaired.

**Contact.** E-mail: um-admit@maine.edu
Phone: (207) 581-1561 Toll-free number: (877) 486-2364
Fax: (207) 581-1213
Sharon Oliver, Director of Admissions, University of Maine, 5713 Chadbourne Hall, Orono, ME 04469-5713

## University of Maine at Augusta
**Augusta, Maine**      **CB member**
**www.uma.edu**      **CB code: 3929**

- Public 4-year university
- Commuter campus in large town
- 4,370 degree-seeking undergraduates: 62% part-time, 74% women, 1% African American, 1% Asian American, 1% Hispanic American, 3% Native American

**General.** Founded in 1965. Regionally accredited. Additional centers in Rockland, Brunswick, Rumford, Saco, Ellsworth, East Millinocket; additional campus in Bangor. **Degrees:** 244 bachelor's, 279 associate awarded. **ROTC:** Army, Naval, Air Force. **Location:** 2 miles from downtown, 65 miles from Portland. **Calendar:** Semester, extensive summer session. **Full-time faculty:** 104 total; 54% have terminal degrees, 57% women. **Part-time faculty:** 180 total; 53% women. **Class size:** 64% < 20, 33% 20-39, 1% 40-49, 2% 50-99. **Special facilities:** Holocaust center, human rights center.

**Basis for selection.** Open admission, but selective for some programs. High school achievement record and test scores considered for admission to allied health and bachelor's degree programs. Talent/ability assessed for admission to music programs. TOEFL is requested of non-native English speakers. Interviews required of dental hygiene and medical laboratory technology majors. Audition required of music majors. **Homeschooled:** Transcript of courses and grades required. Documentation of high school completion required.

**High school preparation.** College-preparatory program recommended. Recommended units include English 4, mathematics 2, social studies 2, history 2, science 2 (laboratory 2). Applicants to health science programs must have biology, chemistry, and Algebra II. Business administration and public administration applicants must have Algebra II and geometry.

**2009-2010 Annual costs.** Tuition/fees: $6,855; $15,375 out-of-state. New England Regional Student Program tuition is $9,000. Books/supplies: $1,040. Personal expenses: $1,800.

**2009-2010 Financial aid. Need-based:** Average need met was 63%. Average scholarship/grant was $4,628; average loan $3,087. 53% of total undergraduate aid awarded as scholarships/grants, 47% as loans/jobs. **Non-need-based:** Scholarships awarded for academics, athletics, leadership, music/drama, state residency.

**Application procedures. Admission:** Priority date 6/15; deadline 8/30 (receipt date). $40 fee, may be waived for applicants with need. Admission notification on a rolling basis. Must reply by May 1 or within 2 week(s) if notified thereafter. **Financial aid:** Priority date 3/1; no closing date. FAFSA required. Applicants notified on a rolling basis starting 3/15; must reply within 2 week(s) of notification.

**Academics. Special study options:** Combined bachelor's/graduate degree, cross-registration, distance learning, double major, dual enrollment of high school students, honors, independent study, internships, liberal arts/career combination, student-designed major, study abroad. **Credit/placement by examination:** AP, CLEP, institutional tests. 45 credit hours maximum toward associate degree, 90 toward bachelor's. **Support services:** Reduced course load, remedial instruction, study skills assistance, tutoring.

**Majors. Architecture:** Technology. **Biology:** General. **Business:** Accounting, business admin, financial planning. **Computer sciences:** General. **Health:** Dental hygiene, nursing (RN). **Liberal arts:** Library science. **Protective services:** Law enforcement admin. **Public administration:** General. **Social sciences:** General. **Visual/performing arts:** Studio arts.

**Most popular majors.** Business/marketing 19%, health sciences 32%, liberal arts 14%, library sciences 8%.

**Computing on campus.** 191 workstations in library, computer center. Commuter students can connect to campus network. Online course registration, online library, wireless network available.

**Student life. Freshman orientation:** Available. Preregistration for classes offered. One-day program held 1 week prior to start of each semester and mid-summer. **Activities:** Bands, drama, international student organizations, music ensembles, student government, student newspaper, art and architectural student association, Gay Lesbian Bisexual Transgender friends and associates, honors English program, English society, student nursing association, Pi Alpha Alpha, College Republicans, mental health and human services club, campus crusade.

**Athletics.** USCAA. **Intercollegiate:** Basketball, golf, soccer W. **Intramural:** Basketball, racquetball, soccer. **Team name:** Moose.

**Student services.** Adult student services, alcohol/substance abuse counseling, career counseling, services for economically disadvantaged, financial aid counseling, personal counseling, veterans' counselor. **Physically disabled:** Services for visually, hearing impaired.

**Contact.** E-mail: umaadm@maine.edu
Phone: (207) 621-3465 Toll-free number: (877) 862-1234
Fax: (207) 621-3333
Jonathan Henry, Dean of Enrollment and Director of Admissions, University of Maine at Augusta, 46 University Drive, Augusta, ME 04330

# University of Maine at Farmington

**Farmington, Maine**  **CB member**
**www.farmington.edu**  **CB code: 3506**

- Public 4-year liberal arts and teachers college
- Residential campus in small town
- 2,046 degree-seeking undergraduates: 4% part-time, 65% women, 1% African American, 1% Asian American, 1% Hispanic American, 1% Native American
- 47 graduate students
- 80% of applicants admitted
- Application essay required
- 62% graduate within 6 years

**General.** Founded in 1863. Regionally accredited. **Degrees:** 467 bachelor's awarded; master's offered. **Location:** 38 miles from Augusta, 80 miles from Portland. **Calendar:** Semester, extensive summer session. **Full-time faculty:** 125 total; 87% have terminal degrees, 4% minority, 54% women. **Part-time faculty:** 39 total; 38% have terminal degrees, 59% women. **Class size:** 65% < 20, 33% 20-39, less than 1% 40-49, 1% 50-99, less than 1% >100. **Special facilities:** Archaeology research center, campus-wide wireless laptop network, 24/7 computer center, on-site nursery school, day care center teaching labs, multi-media graphics lab, observatory.

**Freshman class profile.** 1,534 applied, 1,232 admitted, 519 enrolled.

| Mid 50% test scores | | | |
|---|---|---|---|
| SAT critical reading: | 440-560 | GPA 2.0-2.99: | 15% |
| SAT math: | 450-550 | Rank in top quarter: | 42% |
| SAT writing: | 460-570 | Rank in top tenth: | 13% |
| GPA 3.75 or higher: | 1% | Return as sophomores: | 70% |
| GPA 3.50-3.74: | 3% | Out-of-state: | 19% |
| GPA 3.0-3.49: | 81% | Live on campus: | 90% |

**Basis for selection.** School achievement record and recommendation most important. School and community activities, interviews and personal essay also important. On campus placement tests required for those below SAT 490 Verbal, 450 Math. Interview recommended. 13-15 page writing sample required for Creative Writing BFA. **Homeschooled:** Transcript of courses and grades, state high school equivalency certificate required. **Learning Disabled:** Students may submit disclosure of learning disability to learning center after admission.

**High school preparation.** 19 units recommended. Required and recommended units include English 4, mathematics 3-4, social studies 2-3, science 2-3 (laboratory 2-3), foreign language 2-3 and academic electives 3. Algebra I and II and geometry required. Two years of same foreign language required. General college preparatory program required for all except those admitted to Liberal Studies Bridge.

**2009-2010 Annual costs.** Tuition/fees: $8,446; $16,862 out-of-state. New England Regional Student Program tuition and fees: $11,616. Room/board: $7,552. Books/supplies: $720. Personal expenses: $1,992.

**2008-2009 Financial aid. Non-need-based:** Scholarships awarded for academics, leadership, minority status, state residency. **Additional information:** FAFSA must arrive at Federal processor by 3/1.

**Application procedures. Admission:** No deadline. $40 fee, may be waived for applicants with need. Admission notification on a rolling basis beginning on or about 12/15. Must reply by May 1 or within 3 week(s) if notified thereafter. **Financial aid:** Priority date 3/1; no closing date. FAFSA required. Applicants notified on a rolling basis starting 3/15; must reply within 2 week(s) of notification.

**Academics.** Interdisciplinary first year seminar. **Special study options:** Accelerated study, cross-registration, distance learning, double major, dual enrollment of high school students, exchange student, honors, independent study, internships, liberal arts/career combination, semester at sea, student-designed major, study abroad, teacher certification program. **Credit/placement by examination:** AP, CLEP, IB, SAT, institutional tests. 16 credit hours maximum toward bachelor's degree. CLEP tests must have been taken prior to matriculation. **Support services:** Learning center, pre-admission summer program, reduced course load, remedial instruction, study skills assistance, tutoring, writing center.

**Majors. Area/ethnic studies:** Women's. **Biology:** General. **Business:** Managerial economics. **Computer sciences:** Computer science. **Conservation:** Environmental science, land use planning. **Education:** Biology, early childhood, early childhood special, elementary, English, health, kindergarten/preschool, mathematics, science, secondary, social science, special. **Health:** Community health, public health ed. **History:** General. **Interdisciplinary:** Global studies. **Math:** General. **Physical sciences:** Geochemistry, geology.

**Psychology:** General. **Social sciences:** Anthropology, geography, political science. **Visual/performing arts:** Art, arts management, dramatic, music management, theater arts management. **Other:** Interdisciplinary studies, Philosophy and religious studies, Rehabilitation administration and rehabilitation services.

**Most popular majors.** Business/marketing 6%, education 37%, English 6%, health sciences 16%, interdisciplinary studies 9%, psychology 10%.

**Computing on campus.** 180 workstations in library, computer center, student center. Dormitories wired for high-speed internet access and linked to campus network. Commuter students can connect to campus network. Online course registration, online library, helpline, wireless network available.

**Student life. Freshman orientation:** Available, $175 fee. Preregistration for classes offered. Held immediately before classes; includes outdoor activities and community service. **Housing:** Guaranteed on-campus for freshmen. Coed dorms, single-sex dorms, special housing for disabled, wellness housing available. Housing for students maintaining certain GPA, medical single rooms, quiet floors, wellness community, independent living environment housing available. **Activities:** Concert band, choral groups, dance, drama, literary magazine, music ensembles, radio station, student government, student newspaper, symphony orchestra, Justice Uniting Students Together, student environmental and political awareness club, Amnesty International, InterVarsity Christian Fellowship, student alcohol educators, student admissions club, Alpha Phi Omega, literary guild, Newman Club, student-run entertainment board.

**Athletics.** NCAA. **Intercollegiate:** Baseball M, basketball, cross-country, field hockey W, golf, soccer, softball W, volleyball W. **Intramural:** Basketball, football (non-tackle), soccer, softball, swimming, tennis, volleyball. **Team name:** Beavers.

**Student services.** Alcohol/substance abuse counseling, career counseling, services for economically disadvantaged, student employment services, financial aid counseling, health services, on-campus daycare, personal counseling, placement for graduates, veterans' counselor, women's services. **Physically disabled:** Services for visually, hearing impaired.

**Contact.** E-mail: umfadmit@maine.edu
Phone: (207) 778-7050 Fax: (207) 778-8182
Elaine Vincent, Director of Admission, University of Maine at Farmington, 246 Main Street, Farmington, ME 04938

# University of Maine at Fort Kent

**Fort Kent, Maine**  **CB member**
**www.umfk.maine.edu**  **CB code: 3393**

- Public 4-year university and branch campus college
- Commuter campus in small town
- 1,063 degree-seeking undergraduates: 46% part-time, 66% women
- 78% of applicants admitted
- Application essay required
- 34% graduate within 6 years; 3% enter graduate study

**General.** Founded in 1878. Regionally accredited. Bilingual Franco-American region. **Degrees:** 212 bachelor's, 28 associate awarded. **Location:** 200 miles from Bangor, 21 miles from Edmundston, Canada. **Calendar:** Semester, extensive summer session. **Full-time faculty:** 41 total; 78% have terminal degrees, 2% minority, 42% women. **Part-time faculty:** 29 total; 7% have terminal degrees, 66% women. **Class size:** 65% < 20, 32% 20-39, 2% 40-49, 2% 50-99. **Special facilities:** 16-acre biological park, Acadian Archives, interactive television site, Northern Maine Center for Rural Health Science, Center for Sustainable Rural Development.

**Freshman class profile.** 280 applied, 217 admitted, 125 enrolled.

| Mid 50% test scores | | | |
|---|---|---|---|
| SAT critical reading: | 350-480 | GPA 3.0-3.49: | 41% |
| SAT math: | 350-470 | GPA 2.0-2.99: | 41% |
| SAT writing: | 320-470 | Rank in top quarter: | 19% |
| ACT composite: | 18-22 | Rank in top tenth: | 2% |
| GPA 3.75 or higher: | 9% | End year in good standing: | 85% |
| GPA 3.50-3.74: | 1% | Return as sophomores: | 76% |
|  |  | International: | 6% |

**Basis for selection.** High school courses and achievement record most important. Recommendations considered. SAT, ACT scores, or on-campus placement exams required. Interview recommended.

**High school preparation.** 16 units required. Required and recommended units include English 4, mathematics 2, social studies 2, science 2 and foreign language 2. Biology and chemistry required for nursing and environmental studies.

**2009-2010 Annual costs.** Tuition/fees: $6,803; $15,953 out-of-state. New England Regional Student Program tuition is $9,060. Room/board: $7,080. Books/supplies: $1,000. Personal expenses: $1,000.

**2009-2010 Financial aid.** **Non-need-based:** Scholarships awarded for academics, leadership, state residency.

**Application procedures.** **Admission:** No deadline. $40 fee, may be waived for applicants with need. Admission notification on a rolling basis. Must reply by May 1 or within 4 week(s) if notified thereafter. **Financial aid:** Priority date 3/1, closing date 2/1. FAFSA, institutional form required. Applicants notified on a rolling basis starting 3/15; must reply within 2 week(s) of notification.

**Academics.** **Special study options:** Accelerated study, cross-registration, distance learning, double major, dual enrollment of high school students, honors, independent study, internships, liberal arts/career combination, student-designed major, study abroad, teacher certification program. **Credit/ placement by examination:** AP, CLEP, IB, SAT, ACT, institutional tests. 30 credit hours maximum toward associate degree, 90 toward bachelor's. **Support services:** Learning center, pre-admission summer program, reduced course load, remedial instruction, tutoring, writing center.

**Majors.** **Biology:** General. **Business:** General, business admin, e-commerce, management information systems. **Computer sciences:** General, information technology. **Conservation:** Environmental science, management/ policy. **Education:** General, business, elementary, English, multi-level teacher, music, science, secondary, social studies. **Foreign languages:** General, comparative lit, French. **Health:** Nursing (RN). **Interdisciplinary:** Math/ computer science. **Liberal arts:** Arts/sciences. **Psychology:** General. **Public administration:** Social work. **Social sciences:** General. **Other:** Public Safety Administration.

**Most popular majors.** Biology 6%, education 61%, health sciences 20%.

**Computing on campus.** 100 workstations in dormitories, library, computer center, student center. Dormitories wired for high-speed internet access and linked to campus network. Commuter students can connect to campus network. Online course registration, helpline, repair service, student web hosting, wireless network available.

**Student life.** **Freshman orientation:** Mandatory. Preregistration for classes offered. 3-day social and educational orientation; includes workshops. **Housing:** Coed dorms available. $100 partly refundable deposit, deadline 8/15. **Activities:** Choral groups, dance, drama, musical theater, student government, Christian Fellowship, Newman Club.

**Athletics.** NAIA. **Intercollegiate:** Basketball, skiing, soccer, volleyball W. **Intramural:** Baseball, basketball, golf, ice hockey M, racquetball, skiing, soccer, softball, table tennis, tennis, volleyball, weight lifting. **Team name:** Bengals.

**Student services.** Adult student services, alcohol/substance abuse counseling, career counseling, services for economically disadvantaged, financial aid counseling, health services, personal counseling, placement for graduates, veterans' counselor. **Physically disabled:** Services for visually, speech, hearing impaired.

**Contact.** E-mail: umfkadm@maine.edu
Phone: (207) 834-7600 Toll-free number: (888) 879-8635
Fax: (207) 834-7609
Jill Cairns, Director of Admissions, University of Maine at Fort Kent, 23 University Drive, Fort Kent, ME 04743

---

## University of Maine at Machias
**Machias, Maine**

**www.umm.maine.edu**

**CB member**

**CB code: 3956**

- Public 4-year university and liberal arts college
- Commuter campus in rural community
- 573 degree-seeking undergraduates: 21% part-time, 65% women, 3% African American, 1% Asian American, 2% Hispanic American, 4% Native American, 3% international
- 74% of applicants admitted
- SAT or ACT (ACT writing optional), application essay required

**General.** Founded in 1909. Regionally accredited. **Degrees:** 78 bachelor's, 4 associate awarded. **Location:** 85 miles from Bangor, 65 miles from Bar Harbor. **Calendar:** Semester, limited summer session. **Full-time faculty:** 30 total; 77% have terminal degrees, 3% minority, 33% women. **Part-time faculty:** 40 total; 35% have terminal degrees, 2% minority, 50% women. **Class size:** 72% < 20, 28% 20-39. **Special facilities:** Institute for applied

marine research and education, mariculture student research facility, greenhouse, GIS lab, early childhood center, field station, international park, sail loft.

**Freshman class profile.** 374 applied, 276 admitted, 105 enrolled.

| Mid 50% test scores | | | |
|---|---|---|---|
| SAT critical reading: | 420-520 | GPA 2.0-2.99: | 36% |
| SAT math: | 390-490 | Rank in top quarter: | 24% |
| SAT writing: | 410-520 | Rank in top tenth: | 13% |
| ACT composite: | 17-22 | Return as sophomores: | 71% |
| GPA 3.75 or higher: | 9% | Out-of-state: | 29% |
| GPA 3.50-3.74: | 7% | Live on campus: | 76% |
| GPA 3.0-3.49: | 48% | International: | 1% |

**Basis for selection.** Applicants should rank in top half of class and have a B average. Recommendations and test scores important. Essay and outstanding nonacademic achievement (extracurricular, community, military, life, or work) considered. SAT/ACT not required of applicants for associate of science degree. Test score for fall-term admission must be received before first day of classes. Interview recommended. **Homeschooled:** Statement describing homeschool structure and mission, transcript of courses and grades required. Records of all completed coursework plus documentation verifying proficiency in coursework (such as examples of writing, math skills). Portfolio beneficial for some coursework. Standardized test scores required; campus visit with interview important. **Learning Disabled:** Students evaluated on results of required college preparatory work. Documentation of disability important if seeking assistance from Student Resource Center.

**High school preparation.** 11 units required. Required and recommended units include English 4, mathematics 3, social studies 2, science 2 (laboratory 2), foreign language 2, computer science 1 and academic electives 3. Social studies may include history. Computer applications, fine arts also recommended.

**2009-2010 Annual costs.** Tuition/fees: $6,775; $17,515 out-of-state. New England Regional Student Program tuition is $9,060. Room/board: $6,936. Books/supplies: $800. Personal expenses: $1,600.

**Financial aid.** **Non-need-based:** Scholarships awarded for academics, alumni affiliation, art, job skills, leadership, minority status, music/drama, state residency.

**Application procedures.** **Admission:** Closing date 8/15 (receipt date). $40 fee, may be waived for applicants with need. Admission notification on a rolling basis. Must reply by May 1 or within 2 week(s) if notified thereafter. **Financial aid:** Priority date 3/1; no closing date. FAFSA required. Applicants notified on a rolling basis starting 2/15; must reply within 2 week(s) of notification.

**Academics.** Internships and/or cooperative education program available in business studies, recreation management, biology, environmental studies, and behavioral science. **Special study options:** Cooperative education, distance learning, double major, dual enrollment of high school students, independent study, internships, student-designed major, study abroad, teacher certification program. **Credit/placement by examination:** AP, CLEP, SAT, ACT, institutional tests. **Support services:** Learning center, reduced course load, remedial instruction, study skills assistance, tutoring, writing center.

**Majors.** **Biology:** General, ecology, marine. **Business:** General, accounting, business admin, hospitality admin, hospitality/recreation, marketing, office management, office/clerical, tourism promotion, tourism/travel. **Conservation:** General, environmental studies. **Education:** Business, elementary, middle, secondary. **Health:** Mental health services. **History:** General. **Interdisciplinary:** Behavioral sciences. **Liberal arts:** Arts/sciences. **Parks/ recreation:** General, facilities management. **Psychology:** General. **Public administration:** Human services. **Visual/performing arts:** General.

**Most popular majors.** Biology 22%, business/marketing 10%, education 8%, interdisciplinary studies 22%, natural resources/environmental science 7%, parks/recreation 12%.

**Computing on campus.** 117 workstations in dormitories, library, computer center. Dormitories wired for high-speed internet access and linked to campus network. Commuter students can connect to campus network. Online course registration, online library, helpline, repair service, wireless network available.

**Student life.** **Freshman orientation:** Available. Preregistration for classes offered. Orientation in June, August, and January. **Policies:** Students over 21 may drink in their rooms. Firearms must be stored in safe in Resident Director's office. **Housing:** Guaranteed on-campus for all undergraduates. Coed dorms, wellness housing available. $100 deposit. Pets allowed in dorm rooms. **Activities:** Concert band, choral groups, dance, drama, literary magazine, music ensembles, musical theater, radio station, student government, Newman Club, Students of Service.

**Athletics.** NAIA. **Intercollegiate:** Basketball, cross-country, soccer, volleyball W. **Intramural:** Basketball, cheerleading W, fencing, football (non-tackle), soccer, softball W, water polo. **Team name:** Clippers.

**Student services.** Career counseling, student employment services, financial aid counseling, health services, on-campus daycare, personal counseling, placement for graduates, veterans' counselor.

**Contact.** E-mail: ummadmissions@maine.edu
Phone: (207) 255-1318 Toll-free number: (888) 468-6866
Fax: (207) 255-1363
Stewart Bennett, Director of Admissions, University of Maine at Machias, 9 O'Brien Avenue, Machias, ME 04654

## University of Maine at Presque Isle
Presque Isle, Maine — CB member
www.umpi.edu — CB code: 3008

- Public 4-year university
- Commuter campus in small town
- 1,243 degree-seeking undergraduates: 26% part-time, 65% women
- Application essay required

**General.** Founded in 1903. Regionally accredited. **Degrees:** 286 bachelor's, 8 associate awarded. **Location:** 165 miles from Bangor. **Calendar:** Semester, limited summer session. **Full-time faculty:** 55 total. **Part-time faculty:** 65 total. **Class size:** 63% < 20, 37% 20-39. **Special facilities:** Small business institute, kinesiology laboratory, local history center, human services laboratory, museum of natural science.

**Freshman class profile.**

| Mid 50% test scores | | | |
|---|---|---|---|
| SAT critical reading: | 390-530 | Rank in top quarter: | 23% |
| SAT math: | 390-500 | Rank in top tenth: | 8% |
| GPA 3.75 or higher: | 12% | Return as sophomores: | 70% |
| GPA 3.50-3.74: | 9% | Out-of-state: | 4% |
| GPA 3.0-3.49: | 38% | Live on campus: | 38% |
| GPA 2.0-2.99: | 40% | International: | 4% |

**Basis for selection.** Admissions based on secondary school record, class rank, recommendations, and essay. Interview also important. Interview recommended for academically borderline. Portfolio required of bachelor of fine arts applicants.

**High school preparation.** 16 units required. Required units include English 4, mathematics 3, social studies 3, science 2 (laboratory 2), foreign language 2 and academic electives 2. Medical laboratory technology and nursing programs: 4 English, 1 biology w/lab, 1 chemistry w/lab, 2 math, 1 social studies, 6 electives, totaling 15.

**2009-2010 Annual costs.** Tuition/fees: $6,670; $15,820 out-of-state. Room/board: $6,192. Books/supplies: $800. Personal expenses: $1,100.

**2009-2010 Financial aid. Non-need-based:** Scholarships awarded for academics, alumni affiliation, art, job skills, leadership, minority status, music/drama, state residency.

**Application procedures. Admission:** No deadline. $40 fee, may be waived for applicants with need. Admission notification on a rolling basis. **Financial aid:** Priority date 4/1; no closing date. FAFSA required. Applicants notified on a rolling basis starting 3/1; must reply within 2 week(s) of notification.

**Academics. Special study options:** Accelerated study, combined bachelor's/graduate degree, cooperative education, cross-registration, distance learning, double major, exchange student, honors, independent study, internships, student-designed major, study abroad, teacher certification program. **Credit/placement by examination:** AP, CLEP, IB, SAT, ACT, institutional tests. 30 credit hours maximum toward associate degree, 60 toward bachelor's. Scores of 3, 4, and 5 acceptable on AP tests; hours awarded decided on case-by-case basis. **Support services:** Learning center, reduced course load, remedial instruction, study skills assistance, tutoring, writing center.

**Majors. Biology:** General. **Business:** Accounting, business admin, communications. **Conservation:** Environmental studies. **Education:** General, art, elementary, health, physical, secondary. **Health:** Athletic training. **Interdisciplinary:** Behavioral sciences. **Liberal arts:** Arts/sciences. **Parks/recreation:** General. **Physical sciences:** Geology. **Protective services:** Law enforcement admin. **Psychology:** General. **Public administration:** Social work. **Social sciences:** International relations, political science, sociology. **Visual/performing arts:** Art, studio arts.

**Most popular majors.** Business/marketing 9%, education 17%, liberal arts 46%.

**Computing on campus.** 120 workstations in library, computer center. Dormitories wired for high-speed internet access and linked to campus network. Commuter students can connect to campus network. Helpline available.

**Student life. Freshman orientation:** Mandatory, $35 fee. Preregistration for classes offered. Held during the spring, summer, and in January. **Housing:** Guaranteed on-campus for freshmen. Coed dorms, apartments available. $100 deposit, deadline 8/1. **Activities:** Drama, radio station, student government, student newspaper, Geo-ecology club, honors club, Campus Crusade for Christ, outdoor adventure program, physical education majors club, games club, Big Brothers and Big Sisters, accounting/business/MIS club.

**Athletics. Intercollegiate:** Baseball M, basketball, cross-country, golf M, skiing, soccer, softball W, volleyball W. **Team name:** Owls.

**Student services.** Adult student services, chaplain/spiritual director, career counseling, student employment services, financial aid counseling, health services, on-campus daycare, personal counseling, placement for graduates, veterans' counselor. **Physically disabled:** Services for visually, hearing impaired.

**Contact.** E-mail: erin.benson@umpi.edu
Phone: (207) 768-9532 Fax: (207) 768-9777
Erin Benson, Director of Admissions, University of Maine at Presque Isle, 181 Main Street, Presque Isle, ME 04769

## University of New England
Biddeford, Maine — CB member
www.une.edu — CB code: 3751

- Private 4-year university
- Residential campus in small city
- 2,149 degree-seeking undergraduates: 5% part-time, 70% women, 1% African American, 2% Asian American, 1% Hispanic American, 1% international
- 2,001 degree-seeking graduate students
- 80% of applicants admitted
- SAT or ACT (ACT writing optional) required
- 49% graduate within 6 years

**General.** Founded in 1831. Regionally accredited. **Degrees:** 362 bachelor's, 86 associate awarded; master's, professional offered. **ROTC:** Army. **Location:** 15 miles from Portland. **Calendar:** Semester, limited summer session. **Full-time faculty:** 180 total; 72% have terminal degrees, 6% minority, 49% women. **Part-time faculty:** 140 total; 32% have terminal degrees, 4% minority, 54% women. **Class size:** 45% < 20, 47% 20-39, 4% 40-49, 4% 50-99, less than 1% >100. **Special facilities:** Maine Women Writers collection, osteopathic center, performance enhancement and evaluation center, marine science education and research center.

**Freshman class profile.** 3,315 applied, 2,661 admitted, 607 enrolled.

| Mid 50% test scores | | | |
|---|---|---|---|
| SAT critical reading: | 480-570 | Rank in top quarter: | 59% |
| SAT math: | 490-590 | Rank in top tenth: | 25% |
| GPA 3.75 or higher: | 13% | Return as sophomores: | 77% |
| GPA 3.50-3.74: | 15% | Out-of-state: | 65% |
| GPA 3.0-3.49: | 39% | Live on campus: | 90% |
| GPA 2.0-2.99: | 32% | International: | 1% |

**Basis for selection.** School achievement record most important. Test scores, school, community activities considered. Exposure to health careers recommended if seeking admission to health science majors. Rigor of curriculum considered. Essay recommended. Interview required for nursing program, recommended for all, strongly recommended for academically weaker students. **Homeschooled:** Statement describing homeschool structure and mission, transcript of courses and grades required.

**High school preparation.** College-preparatory program recommended. 16 units required; 20 recommended. Required and recommended units include English 4, mathematics 3-4, social studies 1-2, history 1-2, science 2-3 (laboratory 2-3), foreign language 2 and academic electives 2-4.

**2009-2010 Annual costs.** Tuition/fees: $27,920. Room/board: $10,870. Books/supplies: $1,350. Personal expenses: $1,400.

**2008-2009 Financial aid. Non-need-based:** Scholarships awarded for academics, alumni affiliation, leadership.

**Application procedures. Admission:** Priority date 12/1; deadline 2/15 (postmark date). $40 fee, may be waived for applicants with need. Admission notification on a rolling basis beginning on or about 12/15. Must reply by May 1 or within 4 week(s) if notified thereafter. **Financial aid:** Priority date 5/1; no closing date. FAFSA required. Applicants notified on a rolling basis starting 2/1.

**Academics. Special study options:** Combined bachelor's/graduate degree, cooperative education, cross-registration, distance learning, double major, dual enrollment of high school students, honors, independent study, internships, liberal arts/career combination, student-designed major, study abroad, teacher certification program. **Credit/placement by examination:** AP, CLEP, IB, SAT, ACT, institutional tests. **Support services:** Learning center, reduced course load, remedial instruction, study skills assistance, tutoring, writing center.

**Majors. Agriculture:** Aquaculture. **Biology:** General, biochemistry, marine. **Business:** Business admin. **Conservation:** Environmental science, environmental studies. **Education:** General, art, elementary. **Health:** Athletic training, clinical lab technology, dental hygiene, health services admin, nursing (RN). **History:** General. **Liberal arts:** Arts/sciences. **Math:** General. **Parks/recreation:** Exercise sciences, sports admin. **Physical sciences:** Chemistry. **Psychology:** General, psychobiology, social. **Social sciences:** Political science, sociology.

**Most popular majors.** Biology 29%, health sciences 28%, parks/recreation 11%, psychology 14%.

**Computing on campus.** 170 workstations in dormitories, library, computer center, student center. Dormitories wired for high-speed internet access and linked to campus network. Commuter students can connect to campus network. Online course registration, online library, helpline, student web hosting, wireless network available.

**Student life. Freshman orientation:** Mandatory. Preregistration for classes offered. **Housing:** Guaranteed on-campus for freshmen. Coed dorms, single-sex dorms, wellness housing available. $200 partly refundable deposit, deadline 5/1. **Activities:** Literary magazine, student government, Earth's ECO, Rotoract, Marine Animal Stranding Helpline, Make A Wish, EMS, campus diversity club, Intervarsity Christian Fellowship, Cross Seekers, Habitat for Humanity, College Democrats.

**Athletics.** NCAA. **Intercollegiate:** Basketball, cross-country, field hockey W, golf M, lacrosse, soccer, softball W, swimming W, volleyball W. **Intramural:** Basketball, gymnastics, racquetball, soccer, softball, table tennis, volleyball W, water polo. **Team name:** Nor-easters.

**Student services.** Adult student services, alcohol/substance abuse counseling, chaplain/spiritual director, career counseling, student employment services, financial aid counseling, health services, minority student services, personal counseling, veterans' counselor.

**Contact.** E-mail: admissions@une.edu
Phone: (207) 283-0170 ext. 2297 Toll-free number: (800) 477-4863
Fax: (207) 602-5900
Robert Pecchia, Associate Dean of Admissions, University of New England, Hills Beach Road, Biddeford, ME 04005

---

## University of Southern Maine

**Portland, Maine**   **CB member**
**www.usm.maine.edu**   **CB code: 3691**

- Public 4-year university and liberal arts college
- Commuter campus in small city
- 6,548 degree-seeking undergraduates: 27% part-time, 57% women, 2% African American, 2% Asian American, 1% Hispanic American, 2% Native American, 2% international
- 1,582 degree-seeking graduate students
- 84% of applicants admitted
- SAT or ACT with writing, application essay required

**General.** Founded in 1878. Regionally accredited. **Degrees:** 1,101 bachelor's, 8 associate awarded; master's, doctoral, professional offered. **ROTC:** Army, Air Force. **Location:** 110 miles from Boston. **Calendar:** Semester, extensive summer session. **Full-time faculty:** 335 total. **Part-time faculty:** 292 total. **Special facilities:** Planetarium, cartographic collection, Olympic-sized ice arena.

**Freshman class profile.** 4,141 applied, 3,458 admitted, 924 enrolled.

| Mid 50% test scores | | | |
|---|---|---|---|
| SAT critical reading: | 450-560 | GPA 3.0-3.49: | 33% |
| SAT math: | 450-560 | GPA 2.0-2.99: | 44% |
| SAT writing: | 440-550 | Rank in top quarter: | 29% |
| ACT composite: | 18-23 | Rank in top tenth: | 8% |
| GPA 3.75 or higher: | 14% | Out-of-state: | 19% |
| GPA 3.50-3.74: | 7% | International: | 1% |

**Basis for selection.** Level and content of academic program with performance or achievement record, class rank, and standardized test scores most important. Counselor recommendation, essay, and experience outside classroom also important. Interview recommended for all. Audition required of music majors. **Homeschooled:** Transcript of courses and grades, letter of recommendation (nonparent) required. SAT or ACT, annual assessment of courses, and GED required for financial aid purposes. **Learning Disabled:** Must be otherwise qualified to be admitted, may be asked to provide documentation.

**High school preparation.** 16 units required. Required and recommended units include English 4, mathematics 3-4, social studies 2-3, history 2-3, science 2-3 (laboratory 2-3) and foreign language 2-3. 3 lab sciences for science majors. Math, business and electrical engineering majors require 4 years of math.

**2009-2010 Annual costs.** Tuition/fees: $7,814; $20,024 out-of-state. New England Regional Student Program tuition is $10,410. Room/board: $8,762. Books/supplies: $1,000. Personal expenses: $2,000.

**2009-2010 Financial aid. Non-need-based:** Scholarships awarded for academics, music/drama.

**Application procedures. Admission:** Priority date 2/15; no deadline. $40 fee, may be waived for applicants with need. Admission notification on a rolling basis beginning on or about 1/1. Must reply by May 1 or within 2 week(s) if notified thereafter. **Financial aid:** Priority date 2/15; no closing date. FAFSA required. Applicants notified on a rolling basis starting 3/15; must reply by 5/1 or within 2 week(s) of notification.

**Academics. Special study options:** Accelerated study, combined bachelor's/graduate degree, cooperative education, cross-registration, distance learning, double major, ESL, exchange student, honors, independent study, internships, liberal arts/career combination, semester at sea, student-designed major, study abroad, teacher certification program, Washington semester, weekend college. Preengineering program with University of Maine at Orono, living/learning scholars program, Greater Portland Alliance - cross registration with University of New England, St. Joseph's (Maine), Southern Maine Technical College, and Maine College of Art. **Credit/placement by examination:** AP, CLEP, IB, institutional tests. No numerical limit. Students must meet all course requirements and 30 credit residency for BA/BS and 15 credit residency for AA/AS degrees. **Support services:** Learning center, reduced course load, remedial instruction, study skills assistance, tutoring, writing center.

**Honors college/program.** Honors application required. Several course options available. Interdisciplinary curriculum with small seminar classes.

**Majors. Area/ethnic studies:** Chicano/Hispanic-American/Latino, French, Russian/Slavic, women's. **Biology:** General, biotechnology. **Business:** General, accounting, accounting/finance, business admin, finance, management information systems, marketing, organizational behavior. **Communications:** General, media studies. **Computer sciences:** General, applications programming, computer science, programming. **Conservation:** Environmental science, environmental studies. **Construction:** Site management. **Education:** Art, elementary, mathematics, music, technology/industrial arts, voc/tech. **Engineering:** Electrical, mechanical. **Engineering technology:** Electrical, manufacturing. **Foreign languages:** General, classics, French, linguistics. **Health:** Athletic training, environmental health, medical radiologic technology/radiation therapy, nursing (RN), pediatric nursing, predental, premedicine, preop/surgical nursing, preveterinary, psychiatric nursing, recreational therapy. **History:** General. **Interdisciplinary:** Behavioral sciences, global studies, math/computer science, natural sciences. **Legal studies:** Prelaw. **Liberal arts:** Arts/sciences, humanities. **Math:** General. **Parks/recreation:** General, exercise sciences. **Philosophy/religion:** Philosophy. **Physical sciences:** Chemistry, geology, physics. **Psychology:** General. **Public administration:** Social work. **Social sciences:** General, anthropology, criminology, economics, geography, international relations, political science, sociology. **Visual/performing arts:** General, acting, art, art history/conservation, arts management, directing/producing, dramatic, drawing, jazz, music performance, painting, piano/organ, sculpture, stringed instruments, studio arts, theater arts management, voice/opera.

**Most popular majors.** Business/marketing 13%, communications/journalism 10%, health sciences 20%, psychology 6%, social sciences 19%.

**Computing on campus.** 410 workstations in dormitories, library, computer center, student center. Dormitories wired for high-speed internet access and linked to campus network. Commuter students can connect to campus network. Online course registration, helpline, repair service, wireless network available.

**Student life. Freshman orientation:** Mandatory, $150 fee. Preregistration for classes offered. Sessions in summer and autumn. **Policies:** Smoking is not allowed within 50 feet of any dormitory. **Housing:** Coed dorms, special housing for disabled, apartments, fraternity/sorority housing, wellness housing available. $75 deposit, deadline 5/1. **Activities:** Bands, choral groups, dance, drama, international student organizations, literary magazine, music ensembles, musical theater, opera, radio station, student government, student newspaper, symphony orchestra, TV station, American Indian student association, Environmental Coalition, College Republicans, Alliance of Sexual Diversity, Women's Forum, Bahai Association, ethnic student association.

**Athletics.** NCAA. **Intercollegiate:** Baseball M, basketball, cheerleading, cross-country, field hockey W, golf, ice hockey, lacrosse, soccer, softball W, tennis, track and field, volleyball W, wrestling M. **Intramural:** Basketball, cheerleading W, football (non-tackle), football (tackle) M, ice hockey, lacrosse, racquetball, rugby, sailing, skiing, soccer, softball, squash, table tennis, tennis, volleyball, weight lifting. **Team name:** Huskies.

**Student services.** Adult student services, alcohol/substance abuse counseling, chaplain/spiritual director, career counseling, services for economically disadvantaged, student employment services, financial aid counseling, health services, legal services, minority student services, on-campus daycare, personal counseling, placement for graduates, veterans' counselor, women's services. **Physically disabled:** Services for visually, speech, hearing impaired.

**Contact.** E-mail: usmadm@usm.maine.edu
Phone: (207) 780-5670 Toll-free number: (800) 800-4876 ext. 5670
Fax: (207) 780-5640
Scott Steinberg, Dean of Undergraduate Admission, University of Southern Maine, PO Box 9300, Portland, ME 04104

# Maryland

## Baltimore International College
**Baltimore, Maryland**
www.bic.edu                    CB code: 5086

- Private 4-year culinary school and business college
- Commuter campus in very large city
- 482 degree-seeking undergraduates

**General.** Founded in 1972. Regionally accredited. **Degrees:** 26 bachelor's, 106 associate awarded; master's offered. **Location:** Downtown. **Calendar:** Semester, limited summer session. **Full-time faculty:** 15 total. **Part-time faculty:** 20 total. **Class size:** 46% < 20, 52% 20-39, 2% 40-49.

**Freshman class profile.**

| | | | |
|---|---|---|---|
| Out-of-state: | 18% | Live on campus: | 23% |

**Basis for selection.** Institutional placement evaluation most important. School achievement record, interview, test scores, and recommendations also important. Interview recommended. **Homeschooled:** Must be an accredited home school program or approved by the local school district.

**2009-2010 Annual costs.** Tuition/fees: $27,390. Fees shown are for culinary school and include use of computer, culinary supplies, upgrading and maintenance of kitchen equipment and facilities. Day students provided one full meal daily. Business program students pay lower fees. ($1406). Room/board: $10,320. Books/supplies: $1,500.

**2008-2009 Financial aid. Non-need-based:** Scholarships awarded for academics, alumni affiliation, job skills, leadership, state residency.

**Application procedures. Admission:** $50 fee. Admission notification on a rolling basis. **Financial aid:** FAFSA, institutional form required. Applicants notified on a rolling basis; must reply within 2 week(s) of notification.

**Academics. Special study options:** Accelerated study, cooperative education, double major, honors, internships, liberal arts/career combination, study abroad. Honors program available at the Virginia Park campus in Ireland. **Credit/placement by examination:** AP, CLEP, institutional tests. **Support services:** Remedial instruction, study skills assistance, tutoring.

**Majors. Personal/culinary services:** Restaurant/catering.

**Computing on campus.** 45 workstations in dormitories, library, computer center.

**Student life. Freshman orientation:** Mandatory. One-day program held approximately a week before first day of classes. **Policies:** Freshmen under 21, single, with permanent residence more than 50 miles from campus required to live on campus. **Housing:** Guaranteed on-campus for all undergraduates. Coed dorms available. $100 nonrefundable deposit. **Activities:** Student government, student newspaper, American Culinary Foundation-Greater Baltimore Chapter, Residence Hall Programming Board, Sigma Kappa Epsilon Sorority, Tau Eta Omega Fraternity, Students In Free Enterprise.

**Student services.** Alcohol/substance abuse counseling, career counseling, services for economically disadvantaged, student employment services, financial aid counseling, health services, minority student services, personal counseling, placement for graduates, veterans' counselor, women's services.

**Contact.** E-mail: admissions@bic.edu
Phone: (410) 752-4710 ext. 120 Toll-free number: (800) 624-9926 ext. 120
Fax: (410) 752-3730
Elaine Novotny, Director of Admissions, Baltimore International College, 17 Commerce Street, Baltimore, MD 21202-3230

## Bowie State University
**Bowie, Maryland**                    CB member
www.bowiestate.edu                    CB code: 5401

- Public 4-year university
- Commuter campus in small city

- 4,244 degree-seeking undergraduates: 16% part-time, 64% women, 90% African American, 2% Asian American, 2% Hispanic American, 1% international
- 1,172 degree-seeking graduate students
- 48% of applicants admitted
- SAT or ACT (ACT writing optional) required
- 39% graduate within 6 years

**General.** Founded in 1865. Regionally accredited. Limited courses offered at off-site locations. **Degrees:** 613 bachelor's awarded; master's, doctoral offered. **ROTC:** Army, Air Force. **Location:** 25 miles from Baltimore, 20 miles from Washington, DC. **Calendar:** Semester, limited summer session. **Full-time faculty:** 230 total; 92% have terminal degrees, 79% minority, 49% women. **Part-time faculty:** 176 total; 50% have terminal degrees, 83% minority, 44% women. **Class size:** 41% < 20, 53% 20-39, 4% 40-49, 2% 50-99. **Special facilities:** NASA operations and control center, art gallery, green house, super computer center(limited access).

**Freshman class profile.** 3,526 applied, 1,704 admitted, 642 enrolled.

| Mid 50% test scores | | SAT math: | 470-800 |
|---|---|---|---|
| SAT critical reading: | 450-800 | SAT writing: | 420-800 |

**Basis for selection.** School achievement record in college-preparatory curriculum, test scores, minimum GPA of 2.0, counselor/school recommendation important. Audition required for music program. Portfolio required for art program. Praxis I required for education program. **Homeschooled:** Statement describing homeschool structure and mission required.

**High school preparation.** Required units include English 4, mathematics 3, social studies 1, history 2, science 3 and foreign language 2.

**2009-2010 Annual costs.** Tuition/fees: $6,040; $16,479 out-of-state. Room/board: $7,536. Books/supplies: $1,338. Personal expenses: $1,804.

**2009-2010 Financial aid. Need-based:** 496 full-time freshmen applied for aid; 494 were judged to have need; 494 of these received aid. Average need met was 47%. Average scholarship/grant was $6,730; average loan $3,413. 51% of total undergraduate aid awarded as scholarships/grants, 49% as loans/jobs. **Non-need-based:** Scholarships awarded for academics, alumni affiliation, art, athletics, leadership, music/drama, ROTC, state residency.

**Application procedures. Admission:** No deadline. $40 fee, may be waived for applicants with need. Admission notification on a rolling basis. **Financial aid:** Closing date 3/1. FAFSA required. Applicants notified on a rolling basis starting 4/1; must reply within 2 week(s) of notification.

**Academics.** For more information please contact Monica Turner at (301) 860-3296. **Special study options:** Combined bachelor's/graduate degree, cooperative education, cross-registration, distance learning, double major, dual enrollment of high school students, exchange student, honors, independent study, internships, liberal arts/career combination, study abroad, teacher certification program. Dual degree programs in engineering and dentistry with cooperating universities. **Credit/placement by examination:** AP, CLEP, institutional tests. 60 credit hours maximum toward bachelor's degree. **Support services:** Learning center, pre-admission summer program, reduced course load, remedial instruction, tutoring, writing center.

**Majors. Biology:** General. **Business:** Business admin. **Communications technology:** Radio/tv. **Computer sciences:** Computer science. **Education:** Elementary, kindergarten/preschool, science. **Family/consumer sciences:** Child development. **Health:** Nursing (RN). **History:** General. **Math:** General. **Psychology:** General. **Public administration:** Social work. **Social sciences:** Sociology. **Visual/performing arts:** Art, dramatic. **Other:** Technology.

**Most popular majors.** Business/marketing 24%, communication technologies 14%, education 8%, psychology 9%, social sciences 15%.

**Computing on campus.** 150 workstations in dormitories, library, computer center. Dormitories wired for high-speed internet access and linked to campus network. Commuter students can connect to campus network. Online course registration, online library, helpline, repair service, wireless network available.

**Student life. Freshman orientation:** Mandatory, $75 fee. Preregistration for classes offered. One-day session in the 2nd or 3rd week of August. **Policies:** Zero tolerance policy for illegal substance use and violence. **Housing:** Coed dorms, single-sex dorms, apartments, wellness housing available. $150 fully refundable deposit. **Activities:** Bands, campus ministries, choral groups, dance, drama, international student organizations, music ensembles, musical theater, radio station, student government, student newspaper, TV station, NAACP, greater Washington urban league chapter, commuter senate.

**Athletics.** NCAA. **Intercollegiate:** Basketball, bowling W, cross-country, football (tackle) M, softball W, tennis W, track and field, volleyball W.

**Intramural:** Basketball, football (non-tackle), golf, gymnastics, racquetball, soccer, softball, swimming, table tennis, tennis, volleyball, weight lifting. **Team name:** Bulldogs.

**Student services.** Adult student services, alcohol/substance abuse counseling, chaplain/spiritual director, career counseling, student employment services, financial aid counseling, health services, personal counseling, placement for graduates, veterans' counselor. **Physically disabled:** Services for visually, hearing impaired.

**Contact.** E-mail: dkiah@bowiestate.edu
Phone: (301) 860-3415 Fax: (301) 860-3438
Don Kiah, Assistant Vice President, Enrollment Management, Bowie State University, 14000 Jericho Park Road, Bowie, MD 20715

## Capitol College
Laurel, Maryland
www.capitol-college.edu                    CB code: 5101

♦ Private 4-year business and engineering college
♦ Commuter campus in large town
♦ 307 degree-seeking undergraduates
♦ SAT or ACT (ACT writing optional), application essay required

**General.** Founded in 1964. Regionally accredited. **Degrees:** 50 bachelor's awarded; master's offered. **ROTC:** Army. **Location:** 19 miles from Washington, DC, 22 miles from Baltimore. **Calendar:** Semester, limited summer session. **Full-time faculty:** 20 total. **Part-time faculty:** 60 total. **Special facilities:** Video lab, interactive computer classrooms, two engineering labs, telecommunications lab.

### Freshman class profile.

| Mid 50% test scores | | | |
|---|---|---|---|
| | | ACT composite: | 12-20 |
| SAT critical reading: | 380-510 | Live on campus: | 20% |
| SAT math: | 430-540 | | |

**Basis for selection.** Academic preparation, school record and test scores most important. Mathematics foundation necessary for successful completion of programs. Interview and essay recommended.

**High school preparation.** 20 units required. Required and recommended units include English 4, mathematics 3-4, social studies 2, history 2, science 1-3 (laboratory 1-2) and academic electives 2-3. Mathematic units include algebra I, geometry, algebra II/trigonometry. Calculus recommended for advanced standing.

**2009-2010 Annual costs.** Tuition/fees: $20,030. Room only: $4,676. Books/supplies: $800. Personal expenses: $1,900.

**2009-2010 Financial aid. Non-need-based:** Scholarships awarded for academics, alumni affiliation, leadership, minority status.

**Application procedures. Admission:** Priority date 5/1; no deadline. $25 fee, may be waived for applicants with need, free for online applicants. Admission notification on a rolling basis beginning on or about 3/1. Must reply by May 1 or within 3 week(s) if notified thereafter. **Financial aid:** Priority date 2/1; no closing date. FAFSA, institutional form required. Applicants notified on a rolling basis starting 6/3; must reply by 5/1 or within 3 week(s) of notification.

**Academics. Special study options:** Combined bachelor's/graduate degree, cooperative education, distance learning, double major, independent study, liberal arts/career combination, weekend college. **Credit/placement by examination:** AP, CLEP, institutional tests. **Support services:** Learning center, pre-admission summer program, reduced course load, remedial instruction, tutoring.

**Majors. Business:** Business admin. **Computer sciences:** Computer science. **Engineering:** Computer, electrical, software. **Engineering technology:** Aerospace, electrical, telecommunications. **Other:** Information assurance.

**Most popular majors.** Business/marketing 12%, computer/information sciences 29%, engineering/engineering technologies 59%.

**Computing on campus.** 60 workstations in library, computer center. Dormitories wired for high-speed internet access and linked to campus network. Helpline, wireless network available.

**Student life. Freshman orientation:** Mandatory. **Housing:** Coed dorms available. $200 deposit, deadline 5/1. **Activities:** Drama, literary magazine, radio station, student government, student newspaper, computer club, chess club, robotics club, music club, Society of Black Engineers, Society of Women Engineers.

**Athletics. Intramural:** Basketball M, boxing M, fencing M, golf M, soccer M, softball M, table tennis, tennis, track and field, volleyball, water polo.

**Student services.** Adult student services, career counseling, student employment services, personal counseling, placement for graduates, veterans' counselor.

**Contact.** E-mail: admissions@capitol-college.edu
Phone: (301) 369-2800 Toll-free number: (800) 950-1992
Fax: (301) 953-1442
Tony Miller, Director of Admissions, Capitol College, 11301 Springfield Road, Laurel, MD 20708

## College of Notre Dame of Maryland
Baltimore, Maryland                         CB member
www.ndm.edu                                 CB code: 5114

♦ Private 4-year liberal arts college for women affiliated with Roman Catholic Church
♦ Residential campus in very large city
♦ 1,254 degree-seeking undergraduates
♦ 1,717 graduate students
♦ 86% of applicants admitted
♦ SAT or ACT (ACT writing recommended), application essay required

**General.** Founded in 1873. Regionally accredited. Men admitted only to undergraduate and graduate weekend college programs. **Degrees:** 376 bachelor's awarded; master's, professional offered. **ROTC:** Army. **Location:** 5 miles from Baltimore, 37 miles from Washington, DC. **Calendar:** Semester, limited summer session. **Full-time faculty:** 102 total. **Part-time faculty:** 11 total. **Class size:** 78% < 20, 22% 20-39. **Special facilities:** Planetarium, photography laboratories.

### Freshman class profile. 460 applied, 397 admitted, 103 enrolled.

| Mid 50% test scores | | | |
|---|---|---|---|
| | | Rank in top quarter: | 46% |
| SAT critical reading: | 450-590 | Rank in top tenth: | 15% |
| SAT math: | 450-570 | Out-of-state: | 14% |
| ACT composite: | 19-26 | Live on campus: | 66% |

**Basis for selection.** Careful evaluation of academic record, high school curriculum, test scores, recommendations, personal abilities/talents and goals, intellectual potential and eagerness to learn and be challenged. Students should take SAT by December of senior year. Interview and campus visit highly recommended; visits required for scholarship consideration. Audition recommended for music majors. Portfolio recommended for art, writing majors. **Homeschooled:** Transcript or GED required. **Learning Disabled:** Students with learning disabilities should self-report during admissions process.

**High school preparation.** College-preparatory program required. 18 units required. Required units include English 4, mathematics 3, social studies 2, science 2 (laboratory 2), foreign language 3 and academic electives 4.

**2009-2010 Annual costs.** Tuition/fees: $27,250. Room/board: $9,100. Books/supplies: $1,200. Personal expenses: $1,000.

**2009-2010 Financial aid. Non-need-based:** Scholarships awarded for academics, alumni affiliation, art, leadership, music/drama, ROTC. **Additional information:** Maximum consideration for financial aid if application received by February 15. Auditions and portfolios in areas of art, music and writing considered for scholarships.

**Application procedures. Admission:** Priority date 2/15; no deadline. $45 fee, may be waived for applicants with need. Admission notification on a rolling basis beginning on or about 10/1. Must reply by May 1 or within 2 week(s) if notified thereafter. **Financial aid:** Priority date 2/15; no closing date. FAFSA required. Applicants notified on a rolling basis starting 3/15; must reply by 5/1 or within 2 week(s) of notification.

**Academics. Special study options:** Accelerated study, combined bachelor's/graduate degree, cross-registration, double major, dual enrollment of high school students, ESL, honors, independent study, internships, liberal arts/career combination, student-designed major, study abroad, teacher certification program, weekend college. 3-2 programs in engineering and nursing with Johns Hopkins University; academic consortium with seven local colleges and universities. **Credit/placement by examination:** AP, CLEP, IB, institutional tests. 30 credit hours maximum toward bachelor's degree. AP, CLEP and IB credits are posted upon admissions to college. Students should send testing information with their admissions application or prior to start of their first semester. **Support services:** Learning center, reduced course load, study skills assistance, tutoring, writing center.

**Majors. Biology:** General. **Business:** General, finance, international, nonprofit/public. **Communications:** General. **Computer sciences:** General, computer science. **Education:** Early childhood, elementary, secondary, special. **Engineering:** General. **Foreign languages:** General, classics, French, Spanish. **Health:** Medical radiologic technology/radiation therapy. **History:** General. **Interdisciplinary:** Biopsychology. **Legal studies:** Prelaw. **Liberal arts:** Arts/sciences. **Math:** General. **Philosophy/religion:** Philosophy, religion. **Physical sciences:** Chemistry, physics. **Psychology:** General. **Public administration:** Community org/advocacy. **Social sciences:** Criminology, economics, international relations, political science. **Visual/performing arts:** Art, art history/conservation, photography, studio arts.

**Most popular majors.** Biology 7%, business/marketing 21%, communications/journalism 8%, education 14%, health sciences 7%, interdisciplinary studies 6%, liberal arts 11%.

**Computing on campus.** 80 workstations in dormitories, library, computer center, student center. Dormitories wired for high-speed internet access and linked to campus network. Commuter students can connect to campus network. Online course registration, online library, helpline, repair service, wireless network available.

**Student life. Freshman orientation:** Mandatory. Preregistration for classes offered. 2-day program in June; 4-day program prior to start of school in late August/early September. **Policies:** Must abide by honor code. **Housing:** Guaranteed on-campus for all undergraduates. Wellness housing available. $200 nonrefundable deposit, deadline 5/1. **Activities:** Campus ministries, choral groups, dance, drama, film society, international student organizations, literary magazine, music ensembles, musical theater, radio station, student government, student newspaper, TV station, community service organization, Hispanic society, black student organization, interorganizational council.

**Athletics.** NCAA. **Intercollegiate:** Basketball W, field hockey W, lacrosse W, soccer W, softball W, swimming W, tennis W, volleyball W. **Intramural:** Basketball W, cross-country W, lacrosse W, soccer W, softball W. **Team name:** Gators.

**Student services.** Adult student services, alcohol/substance abuse counseling, chaplain/spiritual director, career counseling, student employment services, financial aid counseling, health services, personal counseling, placement for graduates, veterans' counselor.

**Contact.** E-mail: admiss@ndm.edu
Phone: (410) 532-5330 Toll-free number: (800) 435-0200
Fax: (410) 532-6287
Lucas Sifuentes, Director of Admissions, College of Notre Dame of Maryland, 4701 North Charles Street, Baltimore, MD 21210

---

## Coppin State University
**Baltimore, Maryland**          CB member
**www.coppin.edu**               CB code: 5122

- Public 4-year liberal arts college
- Commuter campus in very large city
- 3,227 degree-seeking undergraduates: 21% part-time, 77% women, 88% African American, 4% international
- 324 degree-seeking graduate students
- 50% of applicants admitted
- SAT or ACT (ACT writing optional) required

**General.** Founded in 1900. Regionally accredited. Manages Rosemont Elementary School; educational corridor between Coppin and selected elementary, middle, and high schools; mentorship program with elementary students. **Degrees:** 358 bachelor's awarded; master's offered. **ROTC:** Army. **Location:** 50 miles from Washington, DC. **Calendar:** Semester, extensive summer session. **Full-time faculty:** 162 total; 59% have terminal degrees, 56% women. **Part-time faculty:** 139 total; 20% have terminal degrees, 56% women.

**Freshman class profile.** 4,503 applied, 2,261 admitted, 574 enrolled.

| Mid 50% test scores | | GPA 3.0-3.49: | 24% |
|---|---|---|---|
| SAT critical reading: | 400-480 | GPA 2.0-2.99: | 62% |
| SAT math: | 390-470 | Return as sophomores: | 62% |
| GPA 3.75 or higher: | 3% | Out-of-state: | 16% |
| GPA 3.50-3.74: | 5% | International: | 3% |

**Basis for selection.** Minimum GPA of 2.5 and predictive index based on test scores and school achievement record. Essay recommended. Interview recommended for nursing majors. Portfolio recommended for art majors.

**Homeschooled:** Location must be certified by Maryland Department of Education.

**High school preparation.** 16 units required. Required units include English 4, mathematics 3, social studies 3, science 2 (laboratory 2) and foreign language 2. 2 years of advanced tech program courses can be substituted for foreign language requirement.

**2009-2010 Annual costs.** Tuition/fees: $5,276; $13,971 out-of-state. Room/board: $7,496. Books/supplies: $700. Personal expenses: $3,085.

**2009-2010 Financial aid. Non-need-based:** Scholarships awarded for academics, alumni affiliation, athletics, ROTC, state residency. **Additional information:** Funds allocated by State of Maryland for minority students enrolled for at least 6 credits who are Maryland residents and U.S. citizens (Other Race Grant).

**Application procedures. Admission:** Closing date 7/15. $35 fee, may be waived for applicants with need. Admission notification on a rolling basis beginning on or about 3/15. **Financial aid:** Priority date 3/1; no closing date. FAFSA required. Applicants notified on a rolling basis starting 4/15; must reply within 2 week(s) of notification.

**Academics. Special study options:** Accelerated study, combined bachelor's/graduate degree, cooperative education, distance learning, double major, dual enrollment of high school students, external degree, honors, independent study, internships, liberal arts/career combination, study abroad, teacher certification program, weekend college. 3-2 programs in engineering, pharmacy, dentistry, physical therapy. **Credit/placement by examination:** AP, CLEP, IB, SAT, institutional tests. 30 credit hours maximum toward bachelor's degree. **Support services:** Learning center, pre-admission summer program, remedial instruction, study skills assistance, tutoring, writing center.

**Majors. Biology:** General. **Business:** Management science. **Computer sciences:** Computer science. **Education:** Biology, chemistry, early childhood, elementary, mathematics, secondary, special. **Health:** Medical records admin, nursing (RN). **History:** General. **Liberal arts:** Arts/sciences. **Math:** General. **Parks/recreation:** Sports admin. **Physical sciences:** Chemistry. **Protective services:** Criminal justice. **Psychology:** General. **Public administration:** Social work. **Social sciences:** General, political science, sociology. **Visual/performing arts:** Art. **Other:** Rehabilitation and Therapeutic Professions.

**Computing on campus.** 371 workstations in dormitories, library, computer center, student center. Dormitories wired for high-speed internet access and linked to campus network. Commuter students can connect to campus network. Online course registration, online library, helpline, repair service, student web hosting, wireless network available.

**Student life. Freshman orientation:** Mandatory. Preregistration for classes offered. **Housing:** Coed dorms, special housing for disabled, wellness housing available. $150 deposit. **Activities:** Campus ministries, choral groups, dance, drama, film society, international student organizations, music ensembles, radio station, student government, student newspaper, TV station, criminal justice club, gospel choir, history club, psychology club, Thurgood Marshall Club, social work association.

**Athletics.** NCAA. **Intercollegiate:** Baseball M, basketball, bowling W, cheerleading M, cross-country, golf W, softball W, tennis, track and field, volleyball W. **Intramural:** Basketball, football (non-tackle), softball, tennis, volleyball. **Team name:** Eagles.

**Student services.** Adult student services, alcohol/substance abuse counseling, career counseling, services for economically disadvantaged, student employment services, financial aid counseling, health services, minority student services, personal counseling, placement for graduates, veterans' counselor, women's services. **Physically disabled:** Services for visually, hearing impaired.

**Contact.** E-mail: admissions@coppin.edu
Phone: (410) 951-3600 Toll-free number: (800) 635-3674
Fax: (410) 523-7351
Michelle Gross, Director of Admissions, Coppin State University, 2500 West North Avenue, Baltimore, MD 21216

---

## DeVry University: Bethesda
**Bethesda, Maryland**
**www.devry.edu**

- For-profit 4-year university
- Commuter campus in small city
- 68 degree-seeking undergraduates: 57% part-time, 51% women, 47% African American, 3% Asian American, 21% Hispanic American
- 74 degree-seeking graduate students

**General. Degrees:** 3 bachelor's awarded; master's offered. **Calendar:** Semester. **Part-time faculty:** 21 total; 48% minority, 33% women.

**Basis for selection.** Interview important.

**2009-2010 Annual costs.** Tuition/fees: $14,240. Books/supplies: $1,300. Personal expenses: $5,082.

**2008-2009 Financial aid. Non-need-based:** Scholarships awarded for academics.

**Application procedures. Admission:** No deadline. $50 fee. Admission notification on a rolling basis. **Financial aid:** No deadline. FAFSA required. Applicants notified on a rolling basis.

**Academics. Special study options:** Accelerated study, distance learning. **Credit/placement by examination:** CLEP.

**Majors. Business:** Business admin. **Computer sciences:** General. **Other:** Technical management.

**Contact.** Phone: (301) 652-8477 Fax: (301) 652-8577
DeVry University: Bethesda, 4550 Montgomery Avenue, Suite 100 N, Bethesda, MD 20814

## Frostburg State University
**Frostburg, Maryland**
**www.frostburg.edu**

**CB member**
**CB code: 5402**

- Public 4-year university and teachers college
- Residential campus in small town
- 4,634 degree-seeking undergraduates: 5% part-time, 49% women, 24% African American, 2% Asian American, 3% Hispanic American
- 593 degree-seeking graduate students
- 59% of applicants admitted
- SAT or ACT (ACT writing optional) required
- 49% graduate within 6 years

**General.** Founded in 1898. Regionally accredited. Center in Hagerstown offers upper-division undergraduate and graduate courses. **Degrees:** 752 bachelor's awarded; master's offered. **Location:** 150 miles from Baltimore. **Calendar:** Semester, limited summer session. **Full-time faculty:** 242 total; 85% have terminal degrees, 13% minority, 39% women. **Part-time faculty:** 118 total; 17% have terminal degrees, 5% minority, 56% women. **Class size:** 42% < 20, 51% 20-39, 3% 40-49, 3% 50-99, less than 1% >100. **Special facilities:** Planetarium, arboretum, electron microscope, exploratorium.

**Freshman class profile.** 4,476 applied, 2,624 admitted, 1,041 enrolled.

| Mid 50% test scores | | | | |
|---|---|---|---|---|
| SAT critical reading: | 430-530 | GPA 3.50-3.74: | | 11% |
| SAT math: | 430-530 | GPA 3.0-3.49: | | 37% |
| SAT writing: | 420-520 | GPA 2.0-2.99: | | 42% |
| ACT composite: | 17-22 | Return as sophomores: | | 72% |
| GPA 3.75 or higher: | 10% | Out-of-state: | | 7% |
| | | Live on campus: | | 73% |

**Basis for selection.** High school record and SAT scores most important. Interview recommended. Audition required of music majors. Portfolio required of art majors.

**High school preparation.** 15 units required. Required units include English 4, mathematics 3, social studies 3, science 3 (laboratory 2) and foreign language 2.

**2009-2010 Annual costs.** Tuition/fees: $6,684; $16,880 out-of-state. Room/board: $7,304. Books/supplies: $750. Personal expenses: $900.

**2009-2010 Financial aid. Non-need-based:** Scholarships awarded for academics, leadership, minority status.

**Application procedures. Admission:** No deadline. $30 fee, may be waived for applicants with need. Admission notification on a rolling basis beginning on or about 11/1. Must reply by May 1 or within 4 week(s) if notified thereafter. **Financial aid:** Priority date 3/1; no closing date. FAFSA required. Applicants notified on a rolling basis starting 3/15; must reply within 3 week(s) of notification.

**Academics. Special study options:** Combined bachelor's/graduate degree, distance learning, double major, dual enrollment of high school students, honors, independent study, internships, study abroad, teacher certification program. International student exchange program, dual degree program, combined bachelor's program. **Credit/placement by examination:** AP, CLEP, IB, institutional tests. 30 credit hours maximum toward bachelor's degree.

**Support services:** Learning center, reduced course load, remedial instruction, tutoring, writing center.

**Majors. Architecture:** Urban/community planning. **Biology:** General. **Business:** Accounting, business admin. **Communications:** General. **Computer sciences:** General, information technology. **Conservation:** General, environmental studies, fisheries, wildlife. **Education:** Early childhood, elementary, English, mathematics, music, physical, social science. **Engineering:** General. **Foreign languages:** General. **Health:** Nursing (RN), predental, premedicine, prenursing, prepharmacy, preveterinary. **History:** General. **Liberal arts:** Arts/sciences. **Math:** General. **Parks/recreation:** General, exercise sciences, health/fitness, sports admin. **Philosophy/religion:** Philosophy. **Physical sciences:** Chemistry, physics. **Protective services:** Law enforcement admin, police science. **Psychology:** General. **Public administration:** Social work. **Social sciences:** General, economics, geography, international relations, political science, sociology. **Visual/performing arts:** General, commercial/advertising art, dramatic, studio arts. **Other:** Ethnobotany.

**Most popular majors.** Business/marketing 16%, education 12%, liberal arts 8%, parks/recreation 7%, psychology 6%, security/protective services 6%, social sciences 11%, visual/performing arts 7%.

**Computing on campus.** 668 workstations in dormitories, library, computer center, student center. Dormitories wired for high-speed internet access and linked to campus network. Commuter students can connect to campus network. Online course registration, online library, helpline, wireless network available.

**Student life. Freshman orientation:** Mandatory. **Housing:** Coed dorms, single-sex dorms, special housing for disabled, wellness housing available. $100 deposit. **Activities:** Bands, campus ministries, choral groups, dance, drama, literary magazine, music ensembles, Model UN, radio station, student government, student newspaper, TV station, social, religious, political, and ethnic organizations.

**Athletics.** NCAA. **Intercollegiate:** Baseball M, basketball, cross-country, diving, field hockey W, football (tackle) M, lacrosse W, soccer, softball W, swimming, tennis, track and field, volleyball W. **Intramural:** Basketball, field hockey, football (tackle), golf, lacrosse, racquetball, rugby M, soccer, softball, table tennis, tennis, volleyball, weight lifting, wrestling M. **Team name:** Bobcats.

**Student services.** Chaplain/spiritual director, career counseling, student employment services, health services, minority student services, on-campus daycare, personal counseling, placement for graduates, veterans' counselor. **Physically disabled:** Services for visually, speech, hearing impaired.

**Contact.** E-mail: fsuadmissions@frostburg.edu
Phone: (301) 687-4201 Fax: (301) 687-7074
Trish Gregory, Director of Admissions, Frostburg State University, 101 Braddock Road, Frostburg, MD 21532-1099

## Goucher College
**Baltimore, Maryland**
**www.goucher.edu**

**CB member**
**CB code: 5257**

- Private 4-year liberal arts college
- Residential campus in small city
- 1,464 degree-seeking undergraduates: 2% part-time, 69% women, 8% African American, 3% Asian American, 5% Hispanic American, 1% Native American, 1% international
- 513 degree-seeking graduate students
- 46% of applicants admitted
- Application essay required
- 68% graduate within 6 years

**General.** Founded in 1885. Regionally accredited. Students are required to study abroad and are given a voucher of at least $1,200 to help offset travel expenses. **Degrees:** 309 bachelor's awarded; master's offered. **ROTC:** Army. **Location:** 8 miles from Baltimore. **Calendar:** Semester. **Full-time faculty:** 130 total; 89% have terminal degrees, 15% minority, 62% women. **Part-time faculty:** 79 total; 46% have terminal degrees, 10% minority, 60% women. **Class size:** 74% < 20, 23% 20-39, 1% 40-49, less than 1% 50-99, less than 1% >100.

**Freshman class profile.** 3,651 applied, 1,664 admitted, 400 enrolled.

| Mid 50% test scores | | | |
|---|---|---|---|
| SAT critical reading: | 550-670 | GPA 2.0-2.99: | 37% |
| SAT math: | 510-630 | Rank in top quarter: | 52% |
| SAT writing: | 540-650 | Rank in top tenth: | 26% |
| ACT composite: | 23-29 | Return as sophomores: | 75% |
| GPA 3.75 or higher: | 14% | Out-of-state: | 76% |
| GPA 3.50-3.74: | 12% | Live on campus: | 96% |
| GPA 3.0-3.49: | 37% | International: | 1% |

**Basis for selection.** Record in traditional college-preparatory program, secondary school record, and recommendations most important. Interview recommended. **Homeschooled:** Statement describing homeschool structure and mission, transcript of courses and grades, state high school equivalency certificate, letter of recommendation (nonparent) required.

**High school preparation.** College-preparatory program required. 16 units required; 20 recommended. Required and recommended units include English 4-4, mathematics 3-4, social studies 3-3, science 2-3, foreign language 2-4 and academic electives 2-2.

**2010-2011 Annual costs.** Tuition/fees: $35,142. Room/board: $10,283. Books/supplies: $800. Personal expenses: $800.

**2008-2009 Financial aid. Need-based:** 242 full-time freshmen applied for aid; 192 were judged to have need; 190 of these received aid. Average need met was 81%. Average scholarship/grant was $22,609; average loan $3,394. 80% of total undergraduate aid awarded as scholarships/grants, 20% as loans/jobs. **Non-need-based:** Awarded to 388 full-time undergraduates, including 83 freshmen. Scholarships awarded for academics, art, leadership, music/drama.

**Application procedures. Admission:** Closing date 2/1 (postmark date). $55 fee, may be waived for applicants with need. Admission notification 4/1. Must reply by 5/1. **Financial aid:** Closing date 2/1. FAFSA, CSS PRO-FILE required. Applicants notified on a rolling basis starting 4/1; must reply by 5/1 or within 2 week(s) of notification.

**Academics. Special study options:** Combined bachelor's/graduate degree, cross-registration, distance learning, double major, dual enrollment of high school students, independent study, internships, student-designed major, study abroad, teacher certification program, Washington semester. Community service, service learning. **Credit/placement by examination:** AP, CLEP, IB, SAT, ACT, institutional tests. 30 credit hours maximum toward bachelor's degree. **Support services:** Learning center, reduced course load, study skills assistance, tutoring, writing center.

**Majors. Area/ethnic studies:** American, women's. **Biology:** General. **Business:** Business admin. **Communications:** Media studies. **Computer sciences:** Computer science. **Education:** Elementary, special. **Foreign languages:** French, Russian, Spanish. **History:** General. **Interdisciplinary:** Peace/conflict. **Math:** General. **Philosophy/religion:** Philosophy, religion. **Physical sciences:** Chemistry, physics. **Psychology:** General. **Social sciences:** Economics, international relations, political science, sociology. **Visual/performing arts:** Art, dance, dramatic. **Other:** Multi-interdisciplinary studies.

**Most popular majors.** Biology 7%, communications/journalism 10%, English 10%, history 6%, psychology 13%, social sciences 12%, visual/performing arts 18%.

**Computing on campus.** 190 workstations in library, computer center, student center. Dormitories wired for high-speed internet access and linked to campus network. Commuter students can connect to campus network. Online course registration, online library, helpline, repair service, student web hosting, wireless network available.

**Student life. Freshman orientation:** Mandatory. Preregistration for classes offered. **Housing:** Guaranteed on-campus for freshmen. Coed dorms, single-sex dorms, special housing for disabled, apartments, wellness housing available. $100 fully refundable deposit, deadline 5/1. **Activities:** Jazz band, campus ministries, choral groups, dance, drama, film society, international student organizations, literary magazine, music ensembles, Model UN, musical theater, opera, radio station, student government, student newspaper, symphony orchestra, TV station, African alliance, community action program, Prism, Hillel, Christian fellowship, Amnesty International, environmental organization, Jubilate Deo, Concern for International Children.

**Athletics.** NCAA. **Intercollegiate:** Basketball, cross-country, equestrian M, field hockey W, lacrosse, soccer, swimming, tennis, track and field, volleyball W. **Intramural:** Basketball, football (tackle). **Team name:** Gophers.

**Student services.** Adult student services, alcohol/substance abuse counseling, chaplain/spiritual director, career counseling, services for economically disadvantaged, student employment services, financial aid counseling, health services, minority student services, personal counseling, placement for graduates, veterans' counselor, women's services. **Physically disabled:** Services for visually, hearing impaired.

**Contact.** E-mail: admissions@goucher.edu
Phone: (410) 337-6100 Toll-free number: (800) 468-2437
Fax: (410) 337-6354
Carlton Surbeck, Director of Admissions, Goucher College, 1021 Dulaney Valley Road, Baltimore, MD 21204-2753

## Griggs University
### Silver Spring, Maryland
### www.griggs.edu

- Private 4-year virtual Bible college affiliated with Seventh-day Adventists
- Small city
- 750 degree-seeking undergraduates
- Application essay required

**General.** Accredited by DETC. **Degrees:** 25 bachelor's, 13 associate awarded; master's offered. **Location:** 30 miles from Washington, DC. **Calendar:** Semester. **Part-time faculty:** 60 total.

**Basis for selection.** Minimum secondary school grade average of 2.00 required. SAT or ACT recommended. **Homeschooled:** Statement describing homeschool structure and mission required.

**High school preparation.** 21 units required; 24 recommended. Required and recommended units include English 4, mathematics 3-4, social studies 1-2, history 2, science 3-4 (laboratory 2-3), foreign language 2, computer science 1, visual/performing arts 1 and academic electives 2-3.

**2009-2010 Annual costs.** Tuition/fees: $9,380.

**Application procedures. Admission:** No deadline. $50 fee, may be waived for applicants with need. Admission notification on a rolling basis. **Financial aid:** No deadline. Institutional form required.

**Academics. Special study options:** Cross-registration, distance learning, dual enrollment of high school students, independent study, student-designed major, study abroad. **Credit/placement by examination:** AP, CLEP, IB, SAT, ACT, institutional tests. 12 credit hours maximum toward associate degree, 24 toward bachelor's. **Support services:** Reduced course load, remedial instruction, tutoring.

**Majors. Business:** Business admin. **Philosophy/religion:** Religion. **Theology:** Bible, religious ed.

**Computing on campus.** PC or laptop required.

**Contact.** Phone: (301) 680-6570
Marietta Fowler, Registrar Assistant, Griggs University, 12501 Old Columbia Pike, Silver Spring, MD 20904-6600

## Hood College
### Frederick, Maryland                              CB member
### www.hood.edu                                      CB code: 5296

- Private 4-year liberal arts college
- Residential campus in small city
- 1,363 degree-seeking undergraduates: 9% part-time, 68% women, 11% African American, 2% Asian American, 4% Hispanic American, 2% international
- 924 degree-seeking graduate students
- 72% of applicants admitted
- SAT or ACT (ACT writing optional) required
- 70% graduate within 6 years; 68% enter graduate study

**General.** Founded in 1893. Regionally accredited. **Degrees:** 349 bachelor's awarded; master's offered. **ROTC:** Army. **Location:** 52 miles from Baltimore, 52 miles from Washington, DC. **Calendar:** Semester, limited summer session. **Full-time faculty:** 81 total; 98% have terminal degrees, 12% minority, 58% women. **Part-time faculty:** 175 total; 42% have terminal degrees, 8% minority, 50% women. **Class size:** 62% < 20, 37% 20-39, less than 1% 40-49, less than 1% 50-99. **Special facilities:** Psychology and preschool laboratories, observatory.

**Freshman class profile.** 1,622 applied, 1,166 admitted, 251 enrolled.

| Mid 50% test scores | | | |
|---|---|---|---|
| SAT critical reading: | 490-600 | GPA 2.0-2.99: | 18% |
| SAT math: | 470-590 | Rank in top quarter: | 51% |
| SAT writing: | 480-600 | Rank in top tenth: | 20% |
| ACT composite: | 20-25 | Return as sophomores: | 85% |
| GPA 3.75 or higher: | 37% | Out-of-state: | 23% |
| GPA 3.50-3.74: | 14% | Live on campus: | 80% |
| GPA 3.0-3.49: | 31% | International: | 3% |

**Basis for selection.** High school record, class rank, test scores important. Recommendations, contributions to school, family and community, essay considered. Interview recommended; essay required of some. **Homeschooled:** Interview, letter of recommendation (nonparent) required. Must interview and present bibliography of all reading materials used; two recommendations; partial portfolio of work.

**High school preparation.** College-preparatory program required. 18 units required. Required and recommended units include English 4, mathematics 3-4, social studies 2, history 1, science 3 (laboratory 2), foreign language 2 and academic electives 1.

**2009-2010 Annual costs.** Tuition/fees: $28,170. Room/board: $9,440. Books/supplies: $1,000. Personal expenses: $1,100.

**2009-2010 Financial aid. Need-based:** 231 full-time freshmen applied for aid; 202 were judged to have need; 194 of these received aid. Average need met was 80%. Average scholarship/grant was $20,993; average loan $3,153. 76% of total undergraduate aid awarded as scholarships/grants, 24% as loans/jobs. **Non-need-based:** Awarded to 404 full-time undergraduates, including 89 freshmen. Scholarships awarded for academics, alumni affiliation, music/drama, ROTC.

**Application procedures. Admission:** Priority date 2/15; no deadline. $35 fee, may be waived for applicants with need, free for online applicants. Admission notification on a rolling basis beginning on or about 12/1. Must reply by May 1 or within 2 week(s) if notified thereafter. Early Action closing dates of 10/1, 11/1 and 12/1. Applications received after February 1 considered on a space available basis. **Financial aid:** Priority date 2/15; no closing date. FAFSA required. Applicants notified on a rolling basis starting 3/1; must reply by 5/1 or within 3 week(s) of notification.

**Academics.** Students in all fields may earn academic credits for internships. Opportunities available for students to earn degree in 3 years, 2 degrees in 4 years, or bachelor's and master's in 5 years. **Special study options:** Combined bachelor's/graduate degree, double major, dual enrollment of high school students, honors, independent study, internships, liberal arts/career combination, student-designed major, study abroad, teacher certification program, Washington semester. **Credit/placement by examination:** AP, CLEP, IB, SAT, ACT, institutional tests. 30 credit hours maximum toward bachelor's degree. **Support services:** Learning center, reduced course load, remedial instruction, study skills assistance, tutoring.

**Majors. Area/ethnic studies:** Latin American. **Biology:** General, biochemistry. **Business:** Business admin. **Communications:** General. **Computer sciences:** Computer science. **Conservation:** Environmental science. **Education:** Early childhood, special. **Foreign languages:** French, German, Spanish. **History:** General. **Legal studies:** General. **Math:** General. **Philosophy/religion:** Philosophy, religion. **Physical sciences:** Chemistry. **Psychology:** General. **Public administration:** Social work. **Social sciences:** Economics, political science, sociology. **Visual/performing arts:** Art. **Other:** Art and archaeology, French/German.

**Most popular majors.** Biology 9%, business/marketing 10%, communications/journalism 8%, education 13%, history 8%, psychology 14%, social sciences 9%, visual/performing arts 6%.

**Computing on campus.** 252 workstations in dormitories, library, computer center, student center. Dormitories wired for high-speed internet access and linked to campus network. Commuter students can connect to campus network. Online course registration, online library, helpline, wireless network available.

**Student life. Freshman orientation:** Mandatory. Preregistration for classes offered. Choice of 3 programs held on weekends in June for preregistration with the final program 4 days prior to start of classes. **Policies:** Students responsible for governing themselves through honor code. **Housing:** Guaranteed on-campus for all undergraduates. Coed dorms, single-sex dorms available. $300 nonrefundable deposit, deadline 5/1. **Activities:** Jazz band, campus ministries, choral groups, dance, drama, film society, international student organizations, literary magazine, music ensembles, Model UN, musical theater, radio station, student government, student newspaper, Black student union, Circle K, La Union Latina, Best Buddies, intervarsity christian fellowship, College Democrats, Jewish student union, College Republicans, For Goodness Sake.

**Athletics.** NCAA. **Intercollegiate:** Basketball, cross-country, field hockey W, golf, lacrosse, soccer, softball W, swimming, tennis, track and field, volleyball W. **Intramural:** Basketball, football (tackle) M, soccer, table tennis, volleyball W. **Team name:** Blazers.

**Student services.** Adult student services, alcohol/substance abuse counseling, chaplain/spiritual director, career counseling, student employment services, financial aid counseling, health services, minority student services, personal counseling, placement for graduates, veterans' counselor, women's services. **Physically disabled:** Services for speech, hearing impaired.

**Contact.** E-mail: admissions@hood.edu
Phone: (301) 696-3400 Toll-free number: (800) 922-1599
Fax: (301) 696-3819
David Adams, Director of Admissions, Hood College, 401 Rosemont Avenue, Frederick, MD 21701-8575

## ITT Technical Institute: Owings Mills
### Owings Mills, Maryland

▶ For-profit 4-year business and technical college
▶ Large town

**General.** Accredited by ACICS. **Calendar:** Quarter.

**Contact.** 11301 Red Run Boulevard, Owings Mills, MD 21117

## Johns Hopkins University
### Baltimore, Maryland
### www.jhu.edu

**CB member**
**CB code: 5332**

▶ Private 4-year university
▶ Residential campus in very large city
▶ 4,970 degree-seeking undergraduates: 47% women, 7% African American, 23% Asian American, 7% Hispanic American, 7% international
▶ 1,729 degree-seeking graduate students
▶ 27% of applicants admitted
▶ SAT or ACT with writing, application essay required
▶ 93% graduate within 6 years; 41% enter graduate study

**General.** Founded in 1876. Regionally accredited. Centers in Bologna and Florence, Italy, and Nanjing, China. **Degrees:** 1,487 bachelor's awarded; master's, doctoral, professional offered. **ROTC:** Army, Air Force. **Location:** 4 miles from downtown. **Calendar:** 4-1-4, limited summer session. **Full-time faculty:** 451 total; 94% have terminal degrees, 12% minority, 25% women. **Part-time faculty:** 74 total; 8% minority, 31% women. **Class size:** 65% < 20, 22% 20-39, 3% 40-49, 6% 50-99, 5% >100. **Special facilities:** Space telescope science institute.

**Freshman class profile.** 16,122 applied, 4,308 admitted, 1,349 enrolled.

| Mid 50% test scores | | | |
|---|---|---|---|
| SAT critical reading: | 630-730 | Rank in top quarter: | 95% |
| SAT math: | 670-770 | Rank in top tenth: | 80% |
| SAT writing: | 650-730 | End year in good standing: | 96% |
| ACT composite: | 29-33 | Return as sophomores: | 97% |
| GPA 3.75 or higher: | 47% | Out-of-state: | 89% |
| GPA 3.50-3.74: | 30% | Live on campus: | 99% |
| GPA 3.0-3.49: | 22% | International: | 11% |
| GPA 2.0-2.99: | 1% | Fraternities: | 24% |
| | | Sororities: | 27% |

**Basis for selection.** School achievement record most important, with emphasis on course grades related to applicant's major field of academic interest. Intellectual interests and accomplishments, recommendations, personal character, extracurricular activities significant. Test scores also important. Students wishing to enroll in the biomedical engineering major (BME) must indicate BME as their first-choice major. Students are admitted specifically into the BME major based on evaluation of credentials and space availability. SAT Subject Tests recommended. Early Decision applicants should have test scores in by November 1. Recommend 3 SAT Subject Tests. SAT Math Level 2 recommended for students applying to the school of engineering. Interview recommended. Audition required of applicants to dual-degree program with Peabody Institute. **Homeschooled:** Statement describing homeschool structure and mission, transcript of courses and grades, letter of recommendation (nonparent) required. Secondary school report must include summary of program, complete transcript with course descriptions, bibliography of textbooks, description of evaluation methods, and actual grades or evaluations.

**High school preparation.** College-preparatory program recommended. Recommended units include English 4, mathematics 4, social studies 2, history 2, science 4 and foreign language 4. 4 combined units recommended for social studies and history.

**2010-2011 Annual costs.** Tuition/fees: $41,180. Room/board: $12,510. Books/supplies: $1,200. Personal expenses: $1,000.

**2009-2010 Financial aid. Need-based:** 801 full-time freshmen applied for aid; 577 were judged to have need; 570 of these received aid. Average need met was 94%. Average scholarship/grant was $27,523; average loan $3,395. 79% of total undergraduate aid awarded as scholarships/grants, 21% as loans/jobs. **Non-need-based:** Scholarships awarded for academics, athletics, leadership, ROTC, state residency. **Additional information:** Selected students receive aid packages without loan expectation, grants to full need. Private merit aid does not reduce Hopkins grant.

**Application procedures. Admission:** Closing date 1/1 (postmark date). $70 fee, may be waived for applicants with need. Admission notification 4/1. Must reply by May 1 or within 2 week(s) if notified thereafter. **Financial aid:** Closing date 3/1. FAFSA, CSS PROFILE required. Applicants notified by 4/1; must reply by 5/1 or within 2 week(s) of notification.

**Academics. Special study options:** Combined bachelor's/graduate degree, cross-registration, double major, dual enrollment of high school students, independent study, internships, student-designed major, study abroad, Washington semester. Combined bachelor's/master's programs. **Credit/placement by examination:** AP, CLEP, IB, institutional tests. **Support services:** Pre-admission summer program, reduced course load, study skills assistance, tutoring, writing center.

**Majors. Area/ethnic studies:** African-American, East Asian, Latin American, Near/Middle Eastern. **Biology:** General, biophysics, cell/histology, molecular. **Computer sciences:** General. **Conservation:** Environmental studies. **Engineering:** General, biomedical, chemical, civil, computer, electrical, environmental, materials, materials science, mechanical, mechanics. **Foreign languages:** Classics, French, German, Italian, Spanish. **History:** General, science/technology. **Interdisciplinary:** Behavioral sciences, cognitive science, neuroscience. **Liberal arts:** Arts/sciences. **Math:** General, statistics. **Philosophy/religion:** Philosophy. **Physical sciences:** Astronomy, chemistry, geology, physics. **Psychology:** General. **Public administration:** Policy analysis. **Social sciences:** General, anthropology, archaeology, economics, geography, international relations, political science, sociology. **Visual/performing arts:** Art history/conservation, film/cinema. **Other:** Film and media studies.

**Most popular majors.** Biology 14%, engineering/engineering technologies 17%, health sciences 22%, liberal arts 8%, social sciences 8%, visual/performing arts 6%.

**Computing on campus.** 140 workstations in dormitories, library, computer center. Dormitories wired for high-speed internet access and linked to campus network. Commuter students can connect to campus network. Online course registration, online library, helpline, repair service, student web hosting, wireless network available.

**Student life. Freshman orientation:** Mandatory. Preregistration for classes offered. 5-day extensive program held 1 week prior to start of fall semester. **Policies:** Freshmen and sophomores required to live on campus unless they live with a parent or legal guardian within commuting distance. **Housing:** Guaranteed on-campus for freshmen. Coed dorms, single-sex dorms, special housing for disabled, apartments, fraternity/sorority housing, wellness housing available. $200 nonrefundable deposit, deadline 5/30. Substance-free and vacation housing floors available. Specific spaces accessible or modified for disabled students. **Activities:** Bands, campus ministries, choral groups, dance, drama, film society, international student organizations, literary magazine, music ensembles, Model UN, musical theater, radio station, student government, student newspaper, symphony orchestra, Jewish Student Association, Catholic Community, Christian Fellowship, Black Student Union, Organizacion Latina Estudiantil, Chinese Student Association, emergency response organization, senior citizens community outreach program, College Democrats, College Republicans.

**Athletics.** NCAA. **Intercollegiate:** Baseball M, basketball, cross-country, diving, fencing, field hockey W, football (tackle) M, lacrosse, soccer, swimming, tennis, track and field, volleyball W, water polo M, wrestling M. **Intramural:** Basketball, football (non-tackle), soccer, volleyball. **Team name:** Blue Jays.

**Student services.** Alcohol/substance abuse counseling, chaplain/spiritual director, career counseling, student employment services, financial aid counseling, health services, minority student services, personal counseling, placement for graduates. **Physically disabled:** Services for visually, speech, hearing impaired.

**Contact.** E-mail: gotojhu@jhu.edu
Phone: (410) 516-8171 Fax: (410) 516-6025
John Latting, Dean of Undergraduate Admissions, Johns Hopkins University, 3400 North Charles Street, Mason Hall, Baltimore, MD 21218

## Johns Hopkins University: Peabody Conservatory of Music
**Baltimore, Maryland**
**www.peabody.jhu.edu**                                   CB code: 5532

- Private 4-year music college
- Residential campus in very large city
- 340 degree-seeking undergraduates: 2% part-time, 46% women, 3% African American, 14% Asian American, 6% Hispanic American, 17% international
- 328 degree-seeking graduate students
- 39% of applicants admitted
- SAT or ACT required
- 79% graduate within 6 years

**General.** Founded in 1857. Regionally accredited. **Degrees:** 74 bachelor's awarded; master's, doctoral offered. **Location:** 36 miles from Washington, DC. **Calendar:** Semester. **Full-time faculty:** 74 total; 30% women. **Part-time faculty:** 82 total; 34% women. **Special facilities:** Concert halls.

**Freshman class profile.** 801 applied, 312 admitted, 93 enrolled.

| | | | |
|---|---|---|---|
| End year in good standing: | 90% | Live on campus: | 100% |
| Return as sophomores: | 92% | International: | 15% |

**Basis for selection.** Audition most important; secondary school record, test scores also important. Interview recommended. Audition required. **Homeschooled:** Statement describing homeschool structure and mission, state high school equivalency certificate required.

**2009-2010 Annual costs.** Tuition/fees: $35,375. Room/board: $11,100. Books/supplies: $750. Personal expenses: $1,400.

**2008-2009 Financial aid. Need-based:** 73 full-time freshmen applied for aid; 64 were judged to have need; 64 of these received aid. Average need met was 73%. Average scholarship/grant was $14,130; average loan $3,027. 51% of total undergraduate aid awarded as scholarships/grants, 49% as loans/jobs. **Non-need-based:** Awarded to 175 full-time undergraduates, including 29 freshmen. Scholarships awarded for academics, music/drama.

**Application procedures. Admission:** Priority date 12/1; deadline 4/1 (postmark date). $100 fee, may be waived for applicants with need. Admission notification 4/1. Must reply by 5/1. Must apply by December 15 for guarantee of scholarship consideration. **Financial aid:** Priority date 2/1, closing date 2/1. FAFSA, institutional form required. Applicants notified by 4/1; must reply by 5/1.

**Academics. Special study options:** Cross-registration, double major, internships, study abroad, teacher certification program. **Credit/placement by examination:** AP, CLEP, IB, institutional tests. 8 credit hours maximum toward bachelor's degree. **Support services:** Remedial instruction, tutoring.

**Majors. Communications technology:** Recording arts. **Education:** Music. **Visual/performing arts:** Music performance, music theory/composition, piano/organ, voice/opera.

**Most popular majors.** Visual/performing arts 97%.

**Computing on campus.** 28 workstations in dormitories, library, computer center. Dormitories linked to campus network. Commuter students can connect to campus network. Online library, helpline, repair service, wireless network available.

**Student life. Freshman orientation:** Available. **Housing:** Guaranteed on-campus for freshmen. Coed dorms, single-sex dorms available. $250 partly refundable deposit, deadline 1/7. **Activities:** Bands, choral groups, music ensembles, opera, student government, symphony orchestra.

**Student services.** Alcohol/substance abuse counseling, career counseling, student employment services, financial aid counseling, health services, personal counseling, placement for graduates. **Physically disabled:** Services for visually, speech, hearing impaired.

**Contact.** Phone: (410) 234-4848 Toll-free number: (800) 368-2521 Fax: (410) 659-8102
David Lane, Director of Admissions, Johns Hopkins University: Peabody Conservatory of Music, One East Mount Vernon Place, Baltimore, MD 21202

## Loyola University Maryland

**Baltimore, Maryland**    CB member
www.loyola.edu    CB code: 5370

- Private 4-year business and liberal arts college affiliated with Roman Catholic Church
- Residential campus in very large city
- 3,757 degree-seeking undergraduates: 1% part-time, 59% women, 4% African American, 3% Asian American, 4% Hispanic American, 1% international
- 2,310 degree-seeking graduate students
- 66% of applicants admitted
- 83% graduate within 6 years

**General.** Founded in 1852. Regionally accredited. A Catholic, Jesuit comprehensive university in Baltimore. **Degrees:** 808 bachelor's awarded; master's, doctoral, professional offered. **ROTC:** Army, Air Force. **Location:** 38 miles from Washington, DC, 103 miles from Philadelphia. **Calendar:** Semester, extensive summer session. **Full-time faculty:** 333 total; 79% have terminal degrees, 12% minority, 46% women. **Part-time faculty:** 230 total; 8% have terminal degrees, 10% minority, 45% women. **Class size:** 48% < 20, 51% 20-39, less than 1% 40-49, less than 1% 50-99.

**Freshman class profile.** 9,117 applied, 6,008 admitted, 968 enrolled.

| Mid 50% test scores | | | |
|---|---|---|---|
| SAT critical reading: | 530-630 | GPA 3.0-3.49: | 40% |
| SAT math: | 540-640 | GPA 2.0-2.99: | 11% |
| SAT writing: | 550-640 | Rank in top quarter: | 65% |
| ACT composite: | 24-28 | Rank in top tenth: | 31% |
| GPA 3.75 or higher: | 20% | Return as sophomores: | 89% |
| GPA 3.50-3.74: | 29% | Out-of-state: | 84% |
| | | Live on campus: | 98% |

**Basis for selection.** School record, academic qualifications most important. Extracurricular activities, recommendations, personal background, class rank also considered. Mid-year senior grades and additional requirements for borderline applicants.

**High school preparation.** College-preparatory program required. 15 units required; 19 recommended. Required and recommended units include English 4, mathematics 3, social studies 2-3, history 2-3, science 3-4, foreign language 3-4, computer science 1 and visual/performing arts 1.

**2009-2010 Annual costs.** Tuition/fees: $37,610. Room/board: $10,200. Books/supplies: $1,050. Personal expenses: $1,095.

**2009-2010 Financial aid. Need-based:** 705 full-time freshmen applied for aid; 548 were judged to have need; 548 of these received aid. Average need met was 100%. Average scholarship/grant was $18,750; average loan $5,445. 81% of total undergraduate aid awarded as scholarships/grants, 19% as loans/jobs. **Non-need-based:** Awarded to 904 full-time undergraduates, including 196 freshmen. Scholarships awarded for academics, athletics, ROTC.

**Application procedures. Admission:** Priority date 11/1; deadline 6/1. $50 fee, may be waived for applicants with need. Admission notification 5/1. Must reply by May 1 or within 3 week(s) if notified thereafter. **Financial aid:** Priority date 2/15, closing date 2/15. FAFSA, CSS PROFILE required. Applicants notified by 4/1; must reply by 5/1.

**Academics.** Service learning courses available. **Special study options:** Cross-registration, double major, dual enrollment of high school students, honors, independent study, internships, liberal arts/career combination, study abroad, teacher certification program. **Credit/placement by examination:** AP, CLEP, IB, institutional tests. 30 credit hours maximum toward bachelor's degree. **Support services:** Learning center, remedial instruction, study skills assistance, tutoring.

**Majors. Biology:** General. **Business:** General, accounting. **Communications:** General. **Computer sciences:** General. **Education:** Elementary. **Engineering:** General, electrical. **Foreign languages:** Classics, French, German, Latin, Spanish. **Health:** Speech pathology. **History:** General. **Math:** Applied. **Philosophy/religion:** Philosophy, religion. **Physical sciences:** Chemistry, physics. **Psychology:** General. **Social sciences:** Economics, political science, sociology. **Visual/performing arts:** Art.

**Most popular majors.** Biology 7%, business/marketing 37%, communications/journalism 11%, English 6%, psychology 7%, social sciences 7%.

**Computing on campus.** 775 workstations in dormitories, library, computer center, student center. Dormitories wired for high-speed internet access and linked to campus network. Commuter students can connect to campus network. Online course registration, helpline, student web hosting, wireless network available.

**Student life. Freshman orientation:** Mandatory, $165 fee. Preregistration for classes offered. Must attend 1 of 4 programs offered in summer; parents invited to attend. **Housing:** Guaranteed on-campus for freshmen. Coed dorms, cooperative housing, wellness housing available. $500 nonrefundable deposit; deadline 5/1. **Activities:** Campus ministries, choral groups, dance, drama, literary magazine, music ensembles, musical theater, radio station, student government, student newspaper, TV station, black student association, College Republicans, Korean students association, Circle K, Amnesty International, Jewish students association, College Democrats, Evergreens for Life.

**Athletics.** NCAA. **Intercollegiate:** Basketball, cross-country, diving, golf M, lacrosse, rowing (crew), soccer, swimming, tennis, track and field W, volleyball W. **Intramural:** Baseball M, basketball, racquetball, soccer, softball, squash, tennis, track and field M, volleyball. **Team name:** Greyhounds.

**Student services.** Alcohol/substance abuse counseling, chaplain/spiritual director, career counseling, student employment services, financial aid counseling, health services, minority student services, personal counseling, placement for graduates, women's services. **Physically disabled:** Services for visually, speech, hearing impaired.

**Contact.** E-mail: admissions@loyola.edu
Phone: (410) 617-5012 Toll-free number: (800) 221-9107
Fax: (410) 617-2176
Elena Hicks, Director of Undergraduate Admission, Loyola University Maryland, 4501 North Charles Street, Baltimore, MD 21210-2699

## Maryland Institute College of Art

**Baltimore, Maryland**    CB member
www.mica.edu    CB code: 5399

- Private 4-year visual arts college
- Residential campus in very large city
- 1,699 degree-seeking undergraduates: 1% part-time, 71% women, 4% African American, 11% Asian American, 4% Hispanic American, 4% international
- 217 degree-seeking graduate students
- 47% of applicants admitted
- SAT or ACT (ACT writing optional), application essay required
- 68% graduate within 6 years; 23% enter graduate study

**General.** Founded in 1826. Regionally accredited. **Degrees:** 336 bachelor's awarded; master's offered. **ROTC:** Army. **Location:** 180 miles from New York City, 50 miles from Washington, DC. **Calendar:** Semester, extensive summer session. **Full-time faculty:** 129 total; 83% have terminal degrees, 12% minority, 54% women. **Part-time faculty:** 168 total; 83% have terminal degrees, 12% minority, 54% women. **Class size:** 75% < 20, 25% 20-39, less than 1% 40-49. **Special facilities:** Nature library, slide library with over 250,000 slides, graphics laboratory, independent studios, digital print studio.

**Freshman class profile.** 2,892 applied, 1,348 admitted, 459 enrolled.

| Mid 50% test scores | | | |
|---|---|---|---|
| SAT critical reading: | 530-660 | Return as sophomores: | 83% |
| SAT math: | 510-620 | Out-of-state: | 83% |
| SAT writing: | 530-650 | Live on campus: | 88% |
| End year in good standing: | 98% | International: | 4% |

**Basis for selection.** Emphasis placed on artistic ability as demonstrated in portfolio, academic achievement, test scores, GPA, and level of coursework. Essays, recommendations, interview, and extra-curricular activities also considered. Interview recommended. Portfolio of 15-20 pieces of artwork required. **Learning Disabled:** Students with documented learning disabilities not required to submit SAT or ACT test scores.

**High school preparation.** College-preparatory program required. 24 units required. Required and recommended units include English 4, mathematics 2-3, social studies 4, history 3-4, science 2-3 (laboratory 1) and academic electives 6. 2 studio art required, 4 studio art recommended, 1 art history recommended.

**2010-2011 Annual costs.** Tuition/fees: $35,690. Room/board: $9,850. Books/supplies: $1,450. Personal expenses: $675.

**Financial aid. Non-need-based:** Scholarships awarded for academics, art.

**Application procedures. Admission:** Closing date 2/13 (receipt date). $60 fee, may be waived for applicants with need. Application must be submitted on paper. Admission notification 3/13. Must reply by 5/1. **Financial**

**aid:** Closing date 3/1. FAFSA, institutional form required. Applicants notified by 4/10; must reply by 5/1.

**Academics.** One-third of course work in liberal arts and two-thirds in studio art required for graduation. Minors available in academic subjects. Independent studio and study requirement sometimes met by job internships. Foundation program required in the first year. **Special study options:** Accelerated study, combined bachelor's/graduate degree, cross-registration, distance learning, double major, dual enrollment of high school students, exchange student, independent study, internships, New York semester, student-designed major, study abroad, teacher certification program. Cooperative exchange programs with Johns Hopkins University, Goucher College, Peabody Conservatory of Music, University of Baltimore, Loyola College, Notre Dame College, University of Maryland Baltimore County, Morgan State University, Baltimore Hebrew Institute and Towson University; 5-year BFA/MAT. **Credit/placement by examination:** CLEP, IB, institutional tests. 27 credit hours maximum toward bachelor's degree. **Support services:** Learning center, reduced course load, remedial instruction, study skills assistance, tutoring, writing center.

**Majors. Education:** Art. **Visual/performing arts:** Art history/conservation, ceramics, drawing, fiber arts, graphic design, illustration, interior design, multimedia, painting, photography, printmaking, sculpture. **Other:** Interaction design and art.

**Most popular majors.** Education 6%, visual/performing arts 94%.

**Computing on campus.** 440 workstations in dormitories, library, computer center, student center. Dormitories wired for high-speed internet access and linked to campus network. Commuter students can connect to campus network. Helpline, student web hosting, wireless network available.

**Student life. Freshman orientation:** Mandatory, $140 fee. Preregistration for classes offered. **Housing:** Guaranteed on-campus for freshmen. Coed dorms, special housing for disabled, apartments available. $650 partly refundable deposit, deadline 5/1. **Activities:** Choral groups, dance, drama, film society, international student organizations, literary magazine, student government, Amnesty International, Prisoner Writing, Asian Student Alliance, Black Student Union, Disciples on Campus, Koinonia Christian Fellowship, Korean Student Association, Mission in Christian Artists, Student Voice Association, Students for a Sustainable Campus.

**Student services.** Alcohol/substance abuse counseling, career counseling, student employment services, financial aid counseling, health services, minority student services, personal counseling, placement for graduates.

**Contact.** E-mail: admissions@mica.edu
Phone: (410) 225-2222 Fax: (410) 225-2337
Theresa Bedoya, Vice President and Dean of Admission and Financial Aid, Maryland Institute College of Art, 1300 Mount Royal Avenue, Baltimore, MD 21217-4134

---

## McDaniel College
**Westminster, Maryland**
**www.mcdaniel.edu**
**CB member**
**CB code: 5898**

- Private 4-year liberal arts college
- Residential campus in large town
- 1,666 degree-seeking undergraduates: 1% part-time, 54% women, 6% African American, 4% Asian American, 3% Hispanic American
- 1,553 degree-seeking graduate students
- 79% of applicants admitted
- SAT or ACT (ACT writing optional), application essay required
- 70% graduate within 6 years; 97% enter graduate study

**General.** Founded in 1867. Regionally accredited. **Degrees:** 469 bachelor's awarded; master's offered. **ROTC:** Army. **Location:** 30 miles from Baltimore, 60 miles from Washington, DC. **Calendar:** 4-1-4, limited summer session. **Full-time faculty:** 103 total; 98% have terminal degrees, 12% minority, 50% women. **Part-time faculty:** 266 total; 28% have terminal degrees, 8% minority, 56% women. **Class size:** 67% < 20, 33% 20-39, less than 1% 50-99. **Special facilities:** 9-hole golf course, film/video production laboratory, photography studio, audiology laboratory, human performance laboratory, graphics laboratory, physics observatory.

**Freshman class profile.** 2,532 applied, 2,006 admitted, 425 enrolled.

| Mid 50% test scores | | | |
|---|---|---|---|
| SAT critical reading: | 500-620 | Rank in top quarter: | 52% |
| SAT math: | 500-620 | Rank in top tenth: | 27% |
| ACT composite: | 22-29 | End year in good standing: | 88% |
| GPA 3.75 or higher: | 30% | Return as sophomores: | 81% |
| GPA 3.50-3.74: | 16% | Out-of-state: | 40% |
| GPA 3.0-3.49: | 34% | Live on campus: | 96% |
| GPA 2.0-2.99: | 20% | International: | 1% |

**Basis for selection.** Rigor of course work completed and academic performance test scores, writing skills, personal and academic accomplishments, recommendations by counselors and teachers, leadership and participation in non-academic activities. Academic recommendations required. Interview recommended. **Homeschooled:** Statement describing home-school structure and mission, transcript of courses and grades, letter of recommendation (nonparent) required. Must submit documentation used to satisfy your state graduation requirement.

**High school preparation.** College-preparatory program required. 16 units required; 19 recommended. Required and recommended units include English 4, mathematics 3-4, social studies 3, science 3-4 (laboratory 3) and foreign language 3-4.

**2010-2011 Annual costs.** Tuition/fees: $33,280. Room/board: $7,020. Books/supplies: $1,200. Personal expenses: $1,000.

**2009-2010 Financial aid. Need-based:** 354 full-time freshmen applied for aid; 301 were judged to have need; 301 of these received aid. Average need met was 95%. Average scholarship/grant was $21,937; average loan $4,393. 83% of total undergraduate aid awarded as scholarships/grants, 17% as loans/jobs. **Non-need-based:** Awarded to 372 full-time undergraduates, including 86 freshmen. Scholarships awarded for academics, ROTC, state residency.

**Application procedures. Admission:** Priority date 2/15; deadline 2/15 (postmark date). $50 fee, may be waived for applicants with need. Admission notification 1/1. Must reply by May 1 or within 2 week(s) if notified thereafter. **Financial aid:** Priority date 3/1; no closing date. FAFSA, institutional form required. Applicants notified on a rolling basis starting 2/15; must reply by 5/1 or within 2 week(s) of notification.

**Academics.** January term offered as a two-credit period of concentrated study. May include travel, classroom study or independent study. **Special study options:** Double major, dual enrollment of high school students, honors, independent study, internships, New York semester, semester at sea, student-designed major, study abroad, teacher certification program, United Nations semester, Washington semester. 3-2 program in engineering with University of Maryland. **Credit/placement by examination:** AP, CLEP, IB, SAT, ACT, institutional tests. 32 credit hours maximum toward bachelor's degree. **Support services:** Learning center, reduced course load, remedial instruction, study skills assistance, tutoring, writing center.

**Majors. Biology:** General, biochemistry, environmental. **Business:** Business admin. **Communications:** General. **Computer sciences:** General. **Conservation:** Environmental science. **Foreign languages:** French, German, Spanish. **History:** General. **Math:** General. **Parks/recreation:** Exercise sciences. **Philosophy/religion:** Philosophy, religion. **Physical sciences:** Chemistry, physics. **Psychology:** General. **Public administration:** Social work. **Social sciences:** Economics, political science, sociology. **Visual/performing arts:** Art, art history/conservation, dramatic.

**Most popular majors.** Biology 6%, business/marketing 14%, communications/journalism 9%, English 7%, psychology 12%, social sciences 23%, visual/performing arts 6%.

**Computing on campus.** 175 workstations in library, computer center. Dormitories wired for high-speed internet access and linked to campus network. Commuter students can connect to campus network. Online course registration, helpline, wireless network available.

**Student life. Freshman orientation:** Mandatory. Preregistration for classes offered. 5-day program. **Housing:** Guaranteed on-campus for freshmen. Coed dorms, single-sex dorms, apartments, fraternity/sorority housing, wellness housing available. Single-family homes available. **Activities:** Bands, campus ministries, choral groups, dance, drama, literary magazine, music ensembles, musical theater, radio station, student government, student newspaper, symphony orchestra, TV station, Jewish student union, Christian fellowship, Circle K, ecology club, Black student union, multicultural student association, German club, French club, Spanish club.

**Athletics.** NCAA. **Intercollegiate:** Baseball M, basketball, cross-country, field hockey W, football (tackle) M, golf, lacrosse, soccer, softball W, swimming, tennis, track and field, volleyball W, wrestling M. **Intramural:** Badminton, basketball, football (non-tackle) M, golf, soccer, softball, swimming, tennis, volleyball. **Team name:** The Green Terror.

**Student services.** Career counseling, student employment services, financial aid counseling, health services, minority student services, personal counseling. **Physically disabled:** Services for visually, hearing impaired. **Learning disabled:** Comprehensive services available.

**Contact.** E-mail: admissions@mcdaniel.edu
Phone: (410) 857-2230 Toll-free number: (800) 638-5005
Fax: (410) 857-2757
Florence Hines, Vice President for Enrollment Management and Dean of Admissions, McDaniel College, Two College Hill, Westminster, MD 21157-4390

---

## Morgan State University

**Baltimore, Maryland**
**www.morgan.edu**

**CB member**
**CB code: 5416**

- Public 4-year university and liberal arts college
- Commuter campus in large city
- 6,171 degree-seeking undergraduates: 10% part-time, 56% women, 93% African American, 1% Asian American, 1% Hispanic American, 4% international
- 983 degree-seeking graduate students
- 32% of applicants admitted
- 32% graduate within 6 years

**General.** Founded in 1867. Regionally accredited. **Degrees:** 843 bachelor's awarded; master's, doctoral offered. **ROTC:** Army. **Location:** 45 miles from Washington, DC, 100 miles from Philadelphia. **Calendar:** Semester, limited summer session. **Full-time faculty:** 440 total; 74% have terminal degrees, 75% minority, 40% women. **Part-time faculty:** 109 total; 44% have terminal degrees, 90% minority, 49% women. **Special facilities:** Historical and government documents collections, special collections of African American history, super computer, engineering complex.

**Freshman class profile.** 12,154 applied, 3,864 admitted, 1,283 enrolled.

| Mid 50% test scores | | Return as sophomores: | 71% |
|---|---|---|---|
| SAT critical reading: | 400-490 | Out-of-state: | 7% |
| SAT math: | 400-500 | International: | 2% |

**Basis for selection.** School achievement record and test scores most important. 820 SAT (exclusive of Writing) with 2.5 high school GPA or 900 SAT (exclusive of Writing) with 2.0 high school GPA, principal's recommendation, and parents' consent form (for minors) required. Interview and essay recommended. Audition recommended for music majors. **Homeschooled:** State high school equivalency certificate required. State-recognized diploma. **Learning Disabled:** Students with learning disability must provide documentation and take untimed SAT with assistance from counseling center.

**High school preparation.** College-preparatory program recommended. 13 units recommended. Recommended units include English 4, mathematics 3, social studies 2, history 3, science 3 and foreign language 1. History can be substituted for social studies; computer science can be used in place of foreign language.

**2010-2011 Annual costs.** Tuition/fees (projected): $6,548; $15,418 out-of-state. Room/board: $8,340. Books/supplies: $721. Personal expenses: $2,369.

**Application procedures. Admission:** Priority date 2/15; deadline 4/15. $35 fee, may be waived for applicants with need. Admission notification on a rolling basis beginning on or about 11/15. Must reply by May 1 or within 2 week(s) if notified thereafter. **Financial aid:** Priority date 4/1; no closing date. FAFSA required. Applicants notified on a rolling basis starting 6/1; must reply within 2 week(s) of notification.

**Academics. Special study options:** Cooperative education, cross-registration, distance learning, double major, dual enrollment of high school students, honors, independent study, internships, liberal arts/career combination, teacher certification program, weekend college. Fulbright Program. **Credit/placement by examination:** CLEP, institutional tests. 46 credit hours maximum toward bachelor's degree. Proficiency tests in general education requirements. **Support services:** Learning center, pre-admission summer program, reduced course load, remedial instruction, study skills assistance, tutoring, writing center.

**Majors. Architecture:** Architecture, environmental design. **Area/ethnic studies:** African-American. **Biology:** General. **Business:** Accounting, business admin, finance, hospitality admin, marketing. **Computer sciences:** Computer science, information systems, networking. **Education:** Elementary, health, physical, science. **Engineering:** General, civil, electrical, industrial, physics. **Family/consumer sciences:** Food/nutrition. **Health:** Staff services technology. **History:** General. **Math:** General. **Physical sciences:** Chemistry,

physics. **Psychology:** General. **Social sciences:** Economics, political science, sociology. **Visual/performing arts:** Dramatic, studio arts.

**Most popular majors.** Biology 8%, business/marketing 26%, communications/journalism 11%, education 8%, engineering/engineering technologies 9%, psychology 6%, social sciences 6%.

**Computing on campus.** Dormitories wired for high-speed internet access and linked to campus network. Commuter students can connect to campus network. Online course registration, online library, helpline, repair service, student web hosting, wireless network available.

**Student life. Freshman orientation:** Mandatory. Preregistration for classes offered. Held twice during summer for 5 days. **Housing:** Coed dorms, single-sex dorms, special housing for disabled, apartments, wellness housing available. $200 nonrefundable deposit, deadline 5/1. **Activities:** Bands, choral groups, dance, drama, film society, international student organizations, music ensembles, musical theater, radio station, student government, student newspaper, TV station, Council on Religious Life.

**Athletics.** NCAA. **Intercollegiate:** Basketball, bowling W, cheerleading M, cross-country, football (tackle) M, softball W, tennis, track and field, volleyball W. **Intramural:** Basketball, cross-country, handball, racquetball, rifle, soccer, softball, swimming, table tennis, tennis, track and field, volleyball. **Team name:** Bears.

**Student services.** Alcohol/substance abuse counseling, career counseling, student employment services, health services, on-campus daycare, personal counseling, placement for graduates, veterans' counselor. **Physically disabled:** Services for visually, speech, hearing impaired.

**Contact.** E-mail: admissions@morgan.edu
Phone: (443) 885-3000 Toll-free number: (800) 332-6674
Fax: (443) 885-8260
Shonda Gray, Director of Admissions/ Recruitment, Morgan State University, 1700 East Cold Spring Lane, Baltimore, MD 21251

---

## Mount St. Mary's University

**Emmitsburg, Maryland**
**www.msmary.edu**

**CB member**
**CB code: 5421**

- Private 4-year university and liberal arts college affiliated with Roman Catholic Church
- Residential campus in rural community
- 1,609 degree-seeking undergraduates: 7% part-time, 57% women, 8% African American, 3% Asian American, 6% Hispanic American, 1% Native American, 1% international
- 443 degree-seeking graduate students
- 84% of applicants admitted
- SAT or ACT (ACT writing optional) required
- 73% graduate within 6 years; 30% enter graduate study

**General.** Founded in 1808. Regionally accredited. **Degrees:** 403 bachelor's awarded; master's offered. **ROTC:** Army. **Location:** 65 miles from Washington, DC, 50 miles from Baltimore. **Calendar:** Semester, limited summer session. **Full-time faculty:** 112 total; 86% have terminal degrees, 4% minority, 44% women. **Part-time faculty:** 75 total; 28% have terminal degrees, 7% minority, 45% women. **Class size:** 48% < 20, 50% 20-39, 1% 40-49, less than 1% 50-99. **Special facilities:** 300 acre recreation area.

**Freshman class profile.** 2,963 applied, 2,497 admitted, 465 enrolled.

| Mid 50% test scores | | GPA 2.0-2.99: | 39% |
|---|---|---|---|
| SAT critical reading: | 470-580 | Rank in top quarter: | 45% |
| SAT math: | 460-590 | Rank in top tenth: | 21% |
| SAT writing: | 470-580 | End year in good standing: | 90% |
| ACT composite: | 20-25 | Return as sophomores: | 78% |
| GPA 3.75 or higher: | 13% | Out-of-state: | 45% |
| GPA 3.50-3.74: | 15% | Live on campus: | 94% |
| GPA 3.0-3.49: | 32% | International: | 1% |

**Basis for selection.** High school record most important followed by standardized test scores, character, extracurricular activities. Interview and essay recommended. Auditions and/or portfolios are recommended for VPA majors, but not required. **Homeschooled:** Statement describing homeschool structure and mission, letter of recommendation (nonparent) required. **Learning Disabled:** Current and valid documentation of disability, including functional limitations and the impact of disability on academic performance, is required.

**High school preparation.** College-preparatory program required. 16 units required. Required units include English 4, mathematics 3, social studies 3, science 3 (laboratory 2), foreign language 2 and academic electives 1.

**2010-2011 Annual costs.** Tuition/fees: $30,350. Room/board: $10,308. Books/supplies: $1,000. Personal expenses: $500.

**2009-2010 Financial aid. Need-based:** 400 full-time freshmen applied for aid; 343 were judged to have need; 343 of these received aid. Average need met was 76%. Average scholarship/grant was $16,102; average loan $4,150. 67% of total undergraduate aid awarded as scholarships/grants, 33% as loans/jobs. **Non-need-based:** Awarded to 813 full-time undergraduates, including 220 freshmen. Scholarships awarded for academics, art, athletics, leadership, minority status, music/drama, ROTC.

**Application procedures. Admission:** No deadline. $35 fee, may be waived for applicants with need. Admission notification on a rolling basis beginning on or about 12/1. Must reply by May 1 or within 2 week(s) if notified thereafter. **Financial aid:** Closing date 3/1. FAFSA, institutional form required. Applicants notified on a rolling basis starting 2/15; must reply by 5/1.

**Academics.** Liberal arts core curriculum integrated over 4 years includes: western civilization (clustered with literature and art courses), American experience, philosophy, theology, ethics, non-western cultures, mathematical science, foreign language, social science, written and oral communication. Undergraduate professional studies programs in business and criminal justice in an accelerated format offered off-campus; open to adult students only. **Special study options:** Accelerated study, combined bachelor's/graduate degree, cross-registration, double major, dual enrollment of high school students, honors, independent study, internships, liberal arts/career combination, student-designed major, study abroad, teacher certification program, Washington semester, weekend college. 3-2 with Johns Hopkins University (BS Biology, BS Nursing), 3-3 with Sacred Heart University (BS in Biology, Ph.D in Physical Therapy), 4-2 with Sacred Heart University (BS in Biology, MS in Occupational Therapy). **Credit/placement by examination:** AP, CLEP, IB, SAT, ACT, institutional tests. 30 credit hours maximum toward bachelor's degree. **Support services:** Learning center, reduced course load, remedial instruction, study skills assistance, tutoring, writing center.

**Majors. Biology:** General, biochemistry. **Business:** General, accounting, information resources management. **Communications:** General. **Computer sciences:** General. **Conservation:** Environmental studies. **Education:** Elementary. **Foreign languages:** French, German, Spanish. **History:** General. **Math:** General. **Parks/recreation:** Sports admin. **Philosophy/religion:** Philosophy. **Physical sciences:** Chemistry. **Protective services:** Criminal justice. **Psychology:** General. **Social sciences:** General, economics, international relations, political science, sociology. **Theology:** Theology. **Visual/performing arts:** General.

**Most popular majors.** Biology 9%, business/marketing 28%, communications/journalism 8%, education 10%, history 6%, psychology 6%, social sciences 11%.

**Computing on campus.** 100 workstations in library, computer center, student center. Dormitories wired for high-speed internet access and linked to campus network. Commuter students can connect to campus network. Online course registration, helpline, repair service, student web hosting, wireless network available.

**Student life. Freshman orientation:** Mandatory. Preregistration for classes offered. 3-day weekend in August and choice of 1 of 2 weekends in June for pre-registration. **Housing:** Guaranteed on-campus for all undergraduates. Coed dorms, special housing for disabled, apartments, wellness housing available. **Activities:** Bands, campus ministries, choral groups, dance, drama, international student organizations, literary magazine, music ensembles, musical theater, radio station, student government, student newspaper, TV station, College Democrats, College Republicans, Amnesty International, Circle K, Heritage, Commuter Student Association, Habitat for Humanity, Students for Life.

**Athletics.** NCAA. **Intercollegiate:** Baseball M, basketball, cross-country, golf, lacrosse, soccer, softball W, swimming W, tennis, track and field. **Intramural:** Basketball, field hockey W, football (non-tackle) M, racquetball, skiing, soccer, softball, swimming, tennis, volleyball. **Team name:** Mountaineers.

**Student services.** Adult student services, alcohol/substance abuse counseling, chaplain/spiritual director, career counseling, student employment services, financial aid counseling, health services, minority student services, personal counseling, placement for graduates. **Physically disabled:** Services for visually, hearing impaired.

**Contact.** E-mail: admissions@msmary.edu
Phone: (301) 447-5214 Toll-free number: (800) 448-4347
Fax: (301) 447-5860
Michael Post, Dean of Admissions and Enrollment Management, Mount St. Mary's University, 16300 Old Emmitsburg Road, Emmitsburg, MD 21727

## National Labor College
**Silver Spring, Maryland**
www.nlc.edu — CB code: 3930

- Private 4-year liberal arts and career college
- Commuter campus in small city
- 222 undergraduates
- Application essay required

**General.** Regionally accredited. **Degrees:** 9 bachelor's awarded. **Calendar:** Semester, limited summer session. **Full-time faculty:** 12 total. **Part-time faculty:** 6 total.

**Basis for selection.** Open admission. **Homeschooled:** Transcript of courses and grades required.

**2009-2010 Annual costs.** $158 per-credit-hour for union members affiliated with the AFL-CIO. $210 per-credit-hour for union members not affiliated with the AFL-CIO. $1031 per-credit-hour for non-union members.

**Application procedures. Admission:** No deadline. $60 fee. Admission notification on a rolling basis.

**Academics. Credit/placement by examination:** CLEP. **Support services:** Reduced course load, study skills assistance, tutoring, writing center.

**Majors. Business:** Labor studies. **Health:** Occupational health. **Other:** Labor Safety and Health.

**Computing on campus.** 30 workstations in computer center. Dormitories wired for high-speed internet access. Commuter students can connect to campus network. Online course registration, online library, wireless network available.

**Student life. Freshman orientation:** Mandatory.

**Student services.** Personal counseling.

**Contact.** E-mail: registration@nlc.edu
Phone: (301) 431-6400 Toll-free number: (800) 462-4237
Fax: (301) 628-0160
Karen Banks, Director of Admissions, National Labor College, 10000 New Hampshire Avenue, Silver Spring, MD 20903

## Ner Israel Rabbinical College
**Baltimore, Maryland**
CB code: 0839

- Private 4-year rabbinical college for men affiliated with Jewish faith
- Very large city

**General.** Accredited by AARTS. **Calendar:** Semester.

**Contact.** Phone: (410) 484-7200
Admissions Director, 400 Mount Wilson Lane, Baltimore, MD 21208

## St. John's College
**Annapolis, Maryland** — CB member
www.stjohnscollege.edu — CB code: 5598

- Private 4-year liberal arts college
- Residential campus in large town
- 464 degree-seeking undergraduates: 50% women, 1% Asian American, 4% Hispanic American, 1% Native American, 4% international
- 77 degree-seeking graduate students
- 81% of applicants admitted
- Application essay required
- 66% graduate within 6 years

**General.** Founded in 1784. Regionally accredited. Second campus in Santa Fe, New Mexico. Students may transfer between campuses. **Degrees:** 109 bachelor's awarded; master's offered. **Location:** 35 miles from Washington, DC, 30 miles from Baltimore. **Calendar:** Semester. **Full-time faculty:** 67 total; 78% have terminal degrees, 4% minority, 24% women. **Part-time faculty:** 3 total; 67% have terminal degrees, 33% women. **Class size:** 94% < 20, 5% 20-39, less than 1% >100. **Special facilities:** Planetarium, boathouse, observatory.

**Freshman class profile.** 390 applied, 314 admitted, 137 enrolled.

| Mid 50% test scores | | | |
|---|---|---|---|
| SAT critical reading: | 630-730 | End year in good standing: | 88% |
| SAT math: | 570-670 | Return as sophomores: | 82% |
| Rank in top quarter: | 56% | Out-of-state: | 88% |
| Rank in top tenth: | 29% | Live on campus: | 100% |
| | | International: | 9% |

**Basis for selection.** One optional and 3 required essays most important. School achievement record and teacher recommendations important. 2-day campus visit and interview recommended. Standardized tests required for homeschooled and international students. **Homeschooled:** Statement describing homeschool structure and mission, letter of recommendation (nonparent) required. Must submit results of PSAT, SAT, or ACT if high school diploma will not be earned.

**High school preparation.** College-preparatory program recommended. 5 units required. Required and recommended units include English 4, mathematics 3-4, social studies 2, history 2, science 3 (laboratory 3) and foreign language 2-4.

**2010-2011 Annual costs.** Tuition/fees: $42,192. Room/board: $9,984. Books/supplies: $280. Personal expenses: $750.

**2009-2010 Financial aid.** All financial aid based on need. 70% of total undergraduate aid awarded as scholarships/grants, 30% as loans/jobs.

**Application procedures. Admission:** Priority date 3/1; no deadline. No application fee. Admission notification on a rolling basis. Must reply by May 1 or within 2 week(s) if notified thereafter. Early application encouraged as class generally fills by first week in May. **Financial aid:** Priority date 2/15; no closing date. FAFSA, CSS PROFILE required. Applicants notified on a rolling basis starting 1/15; must reply by 5/1.

**Academics. Special study options:** Internships. **Credit/placement by examination:** CLEP. **Support services:** Tutoring, writing center.

**Majors. Area/ethnic studies:** Western European. **Liberal arts:** Arts/sciences, humanities.

**Computing on campus.** 20 workstations in library, computer center. Dormitories wired for high-speed internet access and linked to campus network. Commuter students can connect to campus network.

**Student life. Freshman orientation:** Mandatory. 2-day program, after registration and prior to start of classes. **Policies:** Freshmen required to live in dormitories. **Housing:** Guaranteed on-campus for freshmen. Coed dorms, wellness housing available. **Activities:** Choral groups, dance, drama, film society, international student organizations, literary magazine, music ensembles, musical theater, student government, student newspaper, Political Forum, Project Politae, Pink Triangle Society, Christian Fellowship, Jewish Students Society, Student Committee on Instruction, Environmental Club, Amnesty International, Delegate Council.

**Athletics. Intramural:** Badminton, basketball, boxing M, fencing, football (non-tackle) M, handball, rowing (crew), sailing, soccer, softball, table tennis, tennis, track and field, volleyball.

**Student services.** Alcohol/substance abuse counseling, career counseling, student employment services, financial aid counseling, health services, personal counseling, placement for graduates, women's services.

**Contact.** E-mail: admissions@sjca.edu
Phone: (410) 626-2522 Toll-free number: (800) 727-9238
Fax: (410) 269-7916
John Christensen, Director of Admissions, St. John's College, PO Box 2800, Annapolis, MD 21404

---

## St. Mary's College of Maryland

St. Mary's City, Maryland
www.smcm.edu

**CB member**
**CB code: 5601**

- Public 4-year liberal arts college
- Residential campus in large town
- 1,978 degree-seeking undergraduates: 2% part-time, 57% women, 8% African American, 4% Asian American, 4% Hispanic American, 1% Native American, 2% international
- 43 degree-seeking graduate students
- 57% of applicants admitted
- SAT or ACT (ACT writing optional), application essay required
- 79% graduate within 6 years; 46% enter graduate study

**General.** Founded in 1840. Regionally accredited. **Degrees:** 448 bachelor's awarded; master's offered. **Location:** 70 miles from Washington, DC.

**Calendar:** Semester, limited summer session. **Full-time faculty:** 142 total; 98% have terminal degrees, 16% minority, 46% women. **Part-time faculty:** 83 total; 39% have terminal degrees, 11% minority, 49% women. **Class size:** 65% < 20, 32% 20-39, 1% 40-49, 1% 50-99. **Special facilities:** Archaeological site of Historic St. Mary's City, electron microscope, marine research vessel, fresh and salt water research facilities.

**Freshman class profile.** 2,411 applied, 1,381 admitted, 488 enrolled.

| Mid 50% test scores | | | |
|---|---|---|---|
| SAT critical reading: | 580-690 | GPA 2.0-2.99: | 7% |
| SAT math: | 550-650 | Rank in top quarter: | 78% |
| SAT writing: | 560-670 | Rank in top tenth: | 47% |
| ACT composite: | 24-29 | Return as sophomores: | 91% |
| GPA 3.75 or higher: | 39% | Out-of-state: | 17% |
| GPA 3.50-3.74: | 27% | Live on campus: | 96% |
| GPA 3.0-3.49: | 27% | International: | 2% |

**Basis for selection.** High school record, SAT or ACT scores, recommendations by counselors/teachers, co-curricular resume, and essay most important. Interview recommended for admissions. **Homeschooled:** Transcript of courses and grades, state high school equivalency certificate required.

**High school preparation.** College-preparatory program recommended. 20 units required; 24 recommended. Required and recommended units include English 4, mathematics 3-4, social studies 2, history 1-2, science 3 (laboratory 2), foreign language 2-4 and academic electives 3.

**2010-2011 Annual costs.** Tuition/fees: $13,630; $25,023 out-of-state. Room/board: $10,235. Books/supplies: $1,000. Personal expenses: $1,800.

**2008-2009 Financial aid. Need-based:** 320 full-time freshmen applied for aid; 205 were judged to have need; 205 of these received aid. Average need met was 59%. Average scholarship/grant was $3,000; average loan $3,500. 62% of total undergraduate aid awarded as scholarships/grants, 38% as loans/jobs. **Non-need-based:** Awarded to 833 full-time undergraduates, including 223 freshmen. Scholarships awarded for academics, alumni affiliation.

**Application procedures. Admission:** Closing date 1/1 (postmark date). $50 fee, may be waived for applicants with need. Admission notification 4/1. Must reply by May 1 or within 2 week(s) if notified thereafter. **Financial aid:** Priority date 2/15, closing date 3/1. FAFSA required. Applicants notified by 4/1; must reply by 5/1.

**Academics. Special study options:** Double major, dual enrollment of high school students, exchange student, honors, independent study, internships, student-designed major, study abroad, teacher certification program, Washington semester. International study programs in Argentina, Australia, Belize, China, Costa Rica, England, France, the Gambia, Germany, Japan, India, Italy, New Zealand, Slovenia, Thailand, other countries by special arrangements; pre-engineering 3-2 program with University of Maryland School of Engineering. Opportunities for participating in colonial and archaeological research. **Credit/placement by examination:** AP, CLEP, IB, SAT, institutional tests. 45 credit hours maximum toward bachelor's degree. **Support services:** Reduced course load, study skills assistance, tutoring, writing center.

**Majors. Area/ethnic studies:** Asian. **Biology:** General, biochemistry. **Computer sciences:** General. **Foreign languages:** General. **History:** General. **Interdisciplinary:** Biological/physical sciences. **Liberal arts:** Humanities. **Math:** General. **Philosophy/religion:** Philosophy, religion. **Physical sciences:** Chemistry, physics. **Psychology:** General. **Public administration:** Policy analysis. **Social sciences:** Anthropology, economics, political science, sociology. **Visual/performing arts:** Art, dramatic.

**Most popular majors.** Biology 13%, English 14%, history 9%, psychology 17%, social sciences 24%, visual/performing arts 6%.

**Computing on campus.** 400 workstations in library, computer center, student center. Dormitories wired for high-speed internet access and linked to campus network. Commuter students can connect to campus network. Online course registration, online library, helpline, student web hosting, wireless network available.

**Student life. Freshman orientation:** Mandatory, $100 fee. Preregistration for classes offered. Offered in July; additional program in August. **Housing:** Guaranteed on-campus for all undergraduates. Coed dorms, single-sex dorms, special housing for disabled, apartments, wellness housing available. $500 nonrefundable deposit, deadline 5/1. Pets allowed in dorm rooms. Townhouses and suites available for upper-class students. **Activities:** Jazz band, choral groups, dance, drama, film society, international student organizations, literary magazine, music ensembles, musical theater, radio station, student government, student newspaper, symphony orchestra, Black student union, College Republicans, College Democrats, Amnesty International, For Goodness Sake, Hillel, Habitat for Humanity, Student Environmental Action Coalition, Intervarsity Christian Fellowship, St. Mary's Triangle.

**Athletics.** NCAA. **Intercollegiate:** Baseball M, basketball, cross-country, field hockey W, lacrosse, sailing, soccer, swimming, tennis, volleyball W. **Intramural:** Basketball, cross-country, football (non-tackle), handball, soccer, softball, water polo. **Team name:** Seahawks.

**Student services.** Alcohol/substance abuse counseling, career counseling, student employment services, financial aid counseling, health services, minority student services, personal counseling, veterans' counselor, women's services. **Physically disabled:** Services for visually, hearing impaired.

**Contact.** E-mail: admissions@smcm.edu
Phone: (240) 895-5000 Toll-free number: (800) 492-7181
Fax: (240) 895-5001
Richard Edgar, Director of Admissions, St. Mary's College of Maryland, 18952 East Fisher Road, St. Mary's City, MD 20686-3001

## Salisbury University
**Salisbury, Maryland**
www.salisbury.edu
**CB member**
**CB code: 5403**

- Public 4-year university and liberal arts college
- Residential campus in large town
- 7,285 degree-seeking undergraduates: 5% part-time, 55% women, 11% African American, 3% Asian American, 3% Hispanic American, 1% Native American, 1% international
- 543 degree-seeking graduate students
- 54% of applicants admitted
- 69% graduate within 6 years; 23% enter graduate study

**General.** Founded in 1925. Regionally accredited. **Degrees:** 1,608 bachelor's awarded; master's offered. **ROTC:** Army, Air Force. **Location:** 110 miles from Baltimore and Washington, DC. **Calendar:** 4-1-4, extensive summer session. **Full-time faculty:** 380 total; 85% have terminal degrees, 12% minority, 46% women. **Part-time faculty:** 191 total; 15% have terminal degrees, 4% minority, 62% women. **Class size:** 32% < 20, 61% 20-39, 3% 40-49, 3% 50-99, 1% >100. **Special facilities:** Arboretum, galleries, history and culture research center, center for conflict resolution, small business development center, museum of wildfowl art.

**Freshman class profile.** 7,525 applied, 4,026 admitted, 1,276 enrolled.

| Mid 50% test scores | | | | |
|---|---|---|---|---|
| SAT critical reading: | 520-600 | GPA 2.0-2.99: | 9% |
| SAT math: | 520-620 | Rank in top quarter: | 58% |
| SAT writing: | 530-600 | Rank in top tenth: | 23% |
| ACT composite: | 21-26 | End year in good standing: | 82% |
| GPA 3.75 or higher: | 35% | Return as sophomores: | 80% |
| GPA 3.50-3.74: | 31% | Out-of-state: | 16% |
| GPA 3.0-3.49: | 25% | Live on campus: | 86% |
| | | International: | 1% |

**Basis for selection.** Rigor of secondary school record, including level of courses, depth of subjects, GPA, most important. Activities, leadership roles, artistic or athletic talents, ability to contribute to a culturally diverse community also important. SAT/ACT scores optional for applicants with high school GPA of 3.5 or higher. Auditions required for music and fine art programs. Essays recommended.

**High school preparation.** College-preparatory program recommended. 15 units required; 21 recommended. Required and recommended units include English 4, mathematics 3-4, social studies 3, science 3-4 (laboratory 2-3), foreign language 2-3 and academic electives 3.

**2009-2010 Annual costs.** Tuition/fees: $6,618; $15,114 out-of-state. Room/board: $7,810. Books/supplies: $1,300. Personal expenses: $1,500.

**2008-2009 Financial aid. Need-based:** 961 full-time freshmen applied for aid; 490 were judged to have need; 478 of these received aid. Average need met was 63%. Average scholarship/grant was $5,398; average loan $3,002. 37% of total undergraduate aid awarded as scholarships/grants, 63% as loans/jobs. **Non-need-based:** Awarded to 565 full-time undergraduates, including 270 freshmen. Scholarships awarded for academics, alumni affiliation, art, leadership, music/drama, state residency.

**Application procedures. Admission:** Closing date 1/15. $45 fee, may be waived for applicants with need. Application must be submitted online. Admission notification 3/15. Must reply by 5/1. **Financial aid:** Closing date 3/1. FAFSA required. Applicants notified by 3/15; Applicants notified on a rolling basis starting 3/15; must reply by 5/1 or within 2 week(s) of notification.

**Academics. Special study options:** Accelerated study, combined bachelor's/graduate degree, cooperative education, cross-registration, distance learning, double major, dual enrollment of high school students, ESL, exchange student, external degree, honors, independent study, internships, liberal arts/career combination, student-designed major, study abroad, teacher certification program, Washington semester. **Credit/placement by examination:** AP, CLEP, IB, institutional tests. 60 credit hours maximum toward bachelor's degree. **Support services:** Learning center, study skills assistance, tutoring, writing center.

**Majors. Biology:** General. **Business:** Accounting, business admin, finance, marketing. **Communications:** General. **Computer sciences:** General, information systems. **Conservation:** Environmental science. **Education:** Early childhood, elementary, ESL, health, physical. **Foreign languages:** French, Spanish. **Health:** Athletic training, clinical lab science, environmental health, nursing (RN), respiratory therapy technology. **History:** General. **Interdisciplinary:** Global studies, peace/conflict. **Math:** General. **Parks/recreation:** Exercise sciences. **Philosophy/religion:** Philosophy. **Physical sciences:** Chemistry, physics. **Psychology:** General. **Public administration:** Social work. **Social sciences:** Economics, geography, political science, sociology. **Visual/performing arts:** Art, dramatic, studio arts. **Other:** Interdisciplinary studies.

**Most popular majors.** Biology 6%, business/marketing 23%, communications/journalism 10%, education 11%, health sciences 8%, psychology 6%, social sciences 6%.

**Computing on campus.** 423 workstations in library, computer center, student center. Dormitories wired for high-speed internet access and linked to campus network. Commuter students can connect to campus network. Online course registration, online library, helpline, repair service, student web hosting, wireless network available.

**Student life. Freshman orientation:** Mandatory. Preregistration for classes offered. Orientation fee varies per program. **Policies:** Class attendance policies vary by instructor. Hazing and smoking is prohibited. **Housing:** Coed dorms, single-sex dorms, apartments, wellness housing available. $300 non-refundable deposit. Affiliated off-campus apartments. **Activities:** Bands, campus ministries, choral groups, dance, drama, film society, international student organizations, literary magazine, music ensembles, musical theater, radio station, student government, student newspaper, symphony orchestra, TV station, Campus Crusade for Christ, Christian fellowship, reformed university fellowship, Muslim student organization, junior gospel choir, Union of African-Americans, NAACP, African American historical & philosophical society.

**Athletics.** NCAA. **Intercollegiate:** Baseball M, basketball, cross-country, field hockey W, football (tackle) M, lacrosse, soccer, softball W, swimming, tennis, track and field, volleyball W. **Intramural:** Basketball, cross-country, fencing, football (non-tackle), golf, racquetball, soccer, softball W, swimming, tennis, track and field, volleyball, water polo. **Team name:** Seagulls.

**Student services.** Alcohol/substance abuse counseling, career counseling, student employment services, financial aid counseling, health services, minority student services, personal counseling, veterans' counselor. **Physically disabled:** Services for visually, speech, hearing impaired.

**Contact.** E-mail: admissions@salisbury.edu
Phone: (410) 543-6161 Toll-free number: (888) 543-0148
Fax: (410) 546-6016
Aaron Basko, Director of Admissions, Salisbury University, 1200 Camden Avenue, Salisbury, MD 21801-6862

## Sojourner-Douglass College
**Baltimore, Maryland**
www.sdc.edu
**CB code: 0504**

- Private 4-year liberal arts college
- Very large city
- 1,250 degree-seeking undergraduates
- Interview required

**General.** Founded in 1980. Regionally accredited. Campus in the Bahamas. **Degrees:** 153 bachelor's awarded; master's offered. **Location:** Downtown. **Calendar:** Semester. **Full-time faculty:** 60 total. **Part-time faculty:** 150 total. **Special facilities:** Learning resource center, writing lab.

**Basis for selection.** Open admission.

**2009-2010 Annual costs.** Tuition/fees: $8,360. Books/supplies: $800. Personal expenses: $2,800.

**Application procedures. Admission:** No deadline. $25 fee, may be waived for applicants with need. Admission notification on a rolling basis.

**Financial aid:** Priority date 3/1; no closing date. FAFSA, institutional form required. Applicants notified on a rolling basis; must reply within 2 week(s) of notification.

**Academics. Special study options:** Accelerated study, cooperative education, honors, independent study, internships. **Credit/placement by examination:** CLEP. **Support services:** Learning center, remedial instruction, tutoring.

**Majors. Business:** Business admin, hospitality admin, management information systems. **Health:** Health care admin. **Interdisciplinary:** Gerontology. **Public administration:** Social work. **Social sciences:** General.

**Most popular majors.** Business/marketing 26%, education 11%, psychology 19%, public administration/social services 45%.

**Computing on campus.** 100 workstations in computer center.

**Student life. Freshman orientation:** Available. Held the Saturday before classes start in the fall. **Activities:** Student government, student newspaper, Phi Beta Sigma, Zeta Phi Beta, Sigma Beta Delta honor society, student government association, Association for the Study of African American Life and History.

**Student services.** Career counseling, on-campus daycare, personal counseling.

**Contact.** Phone: (410) 276-0306 ext. 248 Fax: (410) 675-1811
Diana Samuels, Coordinator of Admissions, Sojourner-Douglass College, 500 North Caroline Street, Baltimore, MD 21205

---

## Stevenson University

**Stevenson, Maryland**          **CB member**
**www.stevenson.edu**            **CB code: 5856**

- Private 4-year university and career college
- Residential campus in very large city
- 3,133 degree-seeking undergraduates: 16% part-time, 70% women, 17% African American, 3% Asian American, 2% Hispanic American, 1% Native American
- 255 degree-seeking graduate students
- 57% of applicants admitted
- SAT or ACT (ACT writing optional), application essay required
- 58% graduate within 6 years

**General.** Founded in 1947. Regionally accredited. **Degrees:** 663 bachelor's, 1 associate awarded; master's offered. **ROTC:** Army. **Location:** 8 miles from Baltimore. **Calendar:** Semester, extensive summer session. **Full-time faculty:** 110 total; 66% have terminal degrees, 11% minority, 57% women. **Part-time faculty:** 239 total; 9% minority, 50% women. **Class size:** 67% < 20, 33% 20-39. **Special facilities:** Theater.

**Freshman class profile.** 4,107 applied, 2,345 admitted, 527 enrolled.

| Mid 50% test scores | | GPA 3.0-3.49: | 33% |
|---|---|---|---|
| SAT critical reading: | 450-560 | GPA 2.0-2.99: | 22% |
| SAT math: | 450-560 | Rank in top quarter: | 38% |
| SAT writing: | 450-560 | Rank in top tenth: | 16% |
| ACT composite: | 18-22 | Return as sophomores: | 79% |
| GPA 3.75 or higher: | 30% | Out-of-state: | 14% |
| GPA 3.50-3.74: | 15% | Live on campus: | 73% |

**Basis for selection.** High school record and test scores most important. Optional interview, recommendations, essay, extracurricular activities also important. Interviews are recommended but not required.

**High school preparation.** College-preparatory program recommended. 17 units required. Required and recommended units include English 4, mathematics 3, social studies 2, history 1, science 3 (laboratory 2), foreign language 2 and academic electives 4.

**2009-2010 Annual costs.** Tuition/fees: $20,644. Room and board fees includes laundry. Room/board: $10,296.

**2008-2009 Financial aid.** **Need-based:** 545 full-time freshmen applied for aid; 437 were judged to have need; 436 of these received aid. Average need met was 59%. Average scholarship/grant was $11,823; average loan $4,616. 69% of total undergraduate aid awarded as scholarships/grants, 31% as loans/jobs. **Non-need-based:** Awarded to 811 full-time undergraduates, including 193 freshmen. Scholarships awarded for academics, art, leadership, music/drama, ROTC. **Additional information:** Cooperative Education Program allows students to work in their field of study with area corporations.

**Application procedures. Admission:** Priority date 3/1; no deadline. $40 fee, may be waived for applicants with need, free for online applicants. Admission notification on a rolling basis beginning on or about 12/1. Must reply by May 1 or within 2 week(s) if notified thereafter. **Financial aid:** Priority date 2/15; no closing date. FAFSA required. Applicants notified on a rolling basis starting 3/15; must reply by 5/1 or within 2 week(s) of notification.

**Academics.** Advanced technology programs, forensic science program and forensic studies programs offered. Cooperative education program available to third- and fourth-year students. Career Architecture, a program for personal and professional development, is integrated into all programs. **Special study options:** Accelerated study, cooperative education, cross-registration, distance learning, double major, dual enrollment of high school students, honors, independent study, internships, liberal arts/career combination, student-designed major, study abroad, teacher certification program, Washington semester. **Credit/placement by examination:** AP, CLEP, IB, SAT, ACT, institutional tests. 15 credit hours maximum toward associate degree, 30 toward bachelor's. **Support services:** Learning center, pre-admission summer program, reduced course load, remedial instruction, study skills assistance, tutoring, writing center.

**Majors. Biology:** General, biotechnology. **Business:** Accounting, business admin, communications, management information systems. **Computer sciences:** Programming. **Education:** Elementary, kindergarten/preschool, middle. **Family/consumer sciences:** Family/community services. **Health:** Clinical lab science, nursing (RN). **History:** Public archives. **Legal studies:** Paralegal. **Math:** Applied. **Physical sciences:** Chemistry. **Protective services:** Law enforcement admin. **Psychology:** General. **Visual/performing arts:** Design, film/cinema.

**Most popular majors.** Business/marketing 24%, computer/information sciences 8%, education 8%, health sciences 19%, interdisciplinary studies 6%, legal studies 7%, visual/performing arts 9%.

**Computing on campus.** 600 workstations in library, computer center, student center. Dormitories wired for high-speed internet access and linked to campus network. Commuter students can connect to campus network. Online course registration, online library, helpline, repair service, wireless network available.

**Student life. Freshman orientation:** Mandatory. Preregistration for classes offered. Full-day program, conducted by major, normally held during June. Freshmen also attend second orientation in August, prior to start of fall semester. **Housing:** Apartments available. Suite style housing (2 bedrooms, share bath). **Activities:** Bands, campus ministries, choral groups, dance, drama, international student organizations, literary magazine, music ensembles, student government, student newspaper, symphony orchestra, Black Student Union, Service Corps, Campus Crusade for Christ, Extreme Acts, Reformed University Fellowship, Angus Dei.

**Athletics.** NCAA. **Intercollegiate:** Baseball M, basketball, cross-country, field hockey W, golf, lacrosse, soccer, softball W, tennis, track and field, volleyball. **Intramural:** Badminton, basketball, fencing, football (non-tackle) M, sailing, skiing, soccer, table tennis, tennis, track and field, volleyball. **Team name:** Mustangs.

**Student services.** Adult student services, alcohol/substance abuse counseling, career counseling, student employment services, financial aid counseling, health services, personal counseling, placement for graduates, veterans' counselor.

**Contact.** E-mail: admissions@stevenson.edu
Phone: (410) 486-7001 Toll-free number: (877) 468-6852
Fax: (443) 352-4440
Mark Hergan, Vice President for Enrollment Management, Stevenson University, 1525 Greenspring Valley Road, Stevenson, MD 21153-0641

---

## Towson University

**Towson, Maryland**          **CB member**
**www.towson.edu**           **CB code: 5404**

- Public 4-year university
- Commuter campus in large city
- 16,598 degree-seeking undergraduates: 9% part-time, 60% women, 12% African American, 4% Asian American, 3% Hispanic American, 3% international
- 3,346 degree-seeking graduate students
- 63% of applicants admitted
- SAT or ACT with writing required
- 73% graduate within 6 years

**General.** Founded in 1866. Regionally accredited. **Degrees:** 3,380 bachelor's awarded; master's, doctoral, professional offered. **ROTC:** Army, Air Force. **Location:** 1.5 miles from Baltimore. **Calendar:** Semester, extensive summer session. **Full-time faculty:** 822 total; 74% have terminal degrees, 14% minority, 53% women. **Part-time faculty:** 723 total; 27% have terminal degrees, 10% minority, 53% women. **Class size:** 36% < 20, 59% 20-39, 3% 40-49, 1% 50-99. **Special facilities:** Planetarium, Asian art collection, concert hall, greenhouse, herbarium, observatory, animal museum.

**Freshman class profile.** 15,423 applied, 9,696 admitted, 2,405 enrolled.

| Mid 50% test scores | | Rank in top quarter: | 23% |
|---|---|---|---|
| SAT critical reading: | 490-580 | Rank in top tenth: | 9% |
| SAT math: | 490-590 | Return as sophomores: | 84% |
| SAT writing: | 500-580 | Out-of-state: | 27% |
| ACT composite: | 21-24 | Live on campus: | 85% |
| GPA 3.75 or higher: | 27% | International: | 1% |
| GPA 3.50-3.74: | 28% | Fraternities: | 9% |
| GPA 3.0-3.49: | 43% | Sororities: | 10% |
| GPA 2.0-2.99: | 2% | | |

**Basis for selection.** High school record, test scores important; class rank, recommendations, essay considered. Interview and essay recommended. Audition required of music, dance majors. **Homeschooled:** Writing samples, 3 letters of recommendation, course-work summary required.

**High school preparation.** 21 units required. Required units include English 4, mathematics 3, social studies 3, science 3 (laboratory 2), foreign language 2 and academic electives 6.

**2009-2010 Annual costs.** Tuition/fees: $7,418; $18,232 out-of-state. Room/board: $8,670. Books/supplies: $1,080. Personal expenses: $2,050.

**2009-2010 Financial aid. Need-based:** 1,941 full-time freshmen applied for aid; 1,275 were judged to have need; 1,202 of these received aid. Average need met was 67%. Average scholarship/grant was $8,753; average loan $3,237. 58% of total undergraduate aid awarded as scholarships/grants, 42% as loans/jobs. **Non-need-based:** Awarded to 3,344 full-time undergraduates, including 768 freshmen. Scholarships awarded for academics, art, athletics, music/drama, ROTC.

**Application procedures. Admission:** Priority date 12/1; deadline 2/15 (postmark date). $45 fee, may be waived for applicants with need. Admission notification on a rolling basis beginning on or about 10/15. Must reply by May 1 or within 2 week(s) if notified thereafter. **Financial aid:** Closing date 2/10. FAFSA required. Applicants notified on a rolling basis starting 3/21; must reply by 5/1 or within 2 week(s) of notification.

**Academics. Special study options:** Combined bachelor's/graduate degree, cooperative education, cross-registration, distance learning, double major, dual enrollment of high school students, ESL, exchange student, honors, independent study, internships, liberal arts/career combination, student-designed major, study abroad, teacher certification program. 3-2 engineering with University of Maryland, College Park. **Credit/placement by examination:** AP, CLEP, IB, SAT, ACT, institutional tests. 45 credit hours maximum toward bachelor's degree. Portfolio reviews, oral exams, demonstrations or written reports/papers considered for credit. **Support services:** Learning center, remedial instruction, study skills assistance, tutoring, writing center.

**Honors college/program.** Guaranteed admission with unweighted GPA of 3.60 on 4.00 scale and score of 1800 on SAT. If either criterion lacking, admission based on comprehensive review of course selection, HS curriculum, and skills.

**Majors. Area/ethnic studies:** American, women's. **Biology:** General, Biochemistry/biophysics and molecular biology, ecology. **Business:** Accounting, business admin. **Communications:** General, journalism, media studies. **Communications technology:** Radio/tv. **Computer sciences:** General, computer science, information technology. **Conservation:** Environmental studies. **Education:** Art, early childhood, elementary, music, physical, special. **Family/consumer sciences:** Family systems. **Foreign languages:** General. **Health:** Athletic training, audiology/speech pathology, health care admin, health services, nursing (RN), substance abuse counseling. **History:** General. **Interdisciplinary:** Biological/physical sciences, gerontology. **Legal studies:** General. **Math:** General. **Parks/recreation:** Exercise sciences, sports admin. **Philosophy/religion:** Judaic, philosophy, religion. **Physical sciences:** Chemistry, geology, physics, planetary. **Protective services:** Forensics. **Psychology:** General. **Social sciences:** General, economics, geography, international relations, political science, sociology, urban studies. **Visual/performing arts:** Art, dance, dramatic, studio arts.

**Most popular majors.** Business/marketing 18%, communications/journalism 10%, education 11%, health sciences 10%, psychology 8%, social sciences 11%, visual/performing arts 6%.

**Computing on campus.** 1,200 workstations in dormitories, library, computer center, student center. Dormitories wired for high-speed internet access and linked to campus network. Commuter students can connect to campus network. Online course registration, online library, helpline, student web hosting, wireless network available.

**Student life. Freshman orientation:** Mandatory. Preregistration for classes offered. **Policies:** Students play active role in university governance. **Housing:** Guaranteed on-campus for freshmen. Coed dorms, special housing for disabled, apartments, wellness housing available. $350 nonrefundable deposit, deadline 5/1. Honors hall, alcohol free floors, academic emphasis floors, non-traditional age area, non-smoking floors, leadership floor, special quiet floors available. **Activities:** Bands, campus ministries, choral groups, dance, drama, international student organizations, literary magazine, music ensembles, musical theater, radio station, student government, student newspaper, symphony orchestra, TV station, Black student union, Jewish student association, Circle K, student ambassadors, Newman Club, Campus Crusades, Hillel, sisterhood.

**Athletics.** NCAA. **Intercollegiate:** Baseball M, basketball, cheerleading, cross-country, diving, field hockey W, football (tackle) M, golf M, gymnastics W, lacrosse, soccer, softball W, swimming, tennis, track and field, volleyball W. **Intramural:** Basketball, cross-country, football (non-tackle), lacrosse, racquetball, soccer, softball, tennis, triathlon, volleyball. **Team name:** Tigers.

**Student services.** Adult student services, alcohol/substance abuse counseling, chaplain/spiritual director, career counseling, student employment services, financial aid counseling, health services, minority student services, on-campus daycare, personal counseling, placement for graduates, veterans' counselor, women's services. **Physically disabled:** Services for visually, speech, hearing impaired.

**Contact.** E-mail: admissions@towson.edu
Phone: (410) 704-2113 Toll-free number: (888) 486-9766
Fax: (410) 704-3030
Louise Shulack, Director of Undergraduate Admissions, Towson University, 8000 York Road, Towson, MD 21252-0001

---

## United States Naval Academy
**Annapolis, Maryland**  **CB member**
**www.usna.edu**  **CB code: 5809**

- Public 4-year military college
- Residential campus in large town
- 4,552 degree-seeking undergraduates: 20% women, 5% African American, 4% Asian American, 12% Hispanic American, 1% international
- 10% of applicants admitted
- SAT or ACT (ACT writing optional), application essay, interview required
- 85% graduate within 6 years; 2% enter graduate study

**General.** Founded in 1845. Regionally accredited. **Degrees:** 1,055 bachelor's awarded. **Location:** 30 miles from Baltimore, 35 miles from Washington, DC. **Calendar:** Semester, limited summer session. **Full-time faculty:** 525 total; 64% have terminal degrees, 9% minority, 22% women. **Class size:** 59% < 20, 41% 20-39, less than 1% 50-99. **Special facilities:** Observatory, planetarium, satellite EarthStation, oceanographic research vessel, weather station, tow tanks, propulsion laboratory, transsonic and hypersonic wind tunnels, museum.

**Freshman class profile.** 15,342 applied, 1,464 admitted, 1,251 enrolled.

| Mid 50% test scores | | End year in good standing: | 98% |
|---|---|---|---|
| SAT critical reading: | 570-700 | Return as sophomores: | 98% |
| SAT math: | 600-700 | Out-of-state: | 95% |
| Rank in top quarter: | 81% | Live on campus: | 100% |
| Rank in top tenth: | 56% | International: | 1% |

**Basis for selection.** Test scores, school achievement record, interview, recommendations of school officials, participation in sports, school, and community activities important. Rank in top 40% of class usually required. Successful candidate must be qualified medically, pass a candidate physical fitness assessment, and be nominated by an official source.

**High school preparation.** College-preparatory program recommended. Recommended units include English 4, mathematics 4, history 2, science 2 (laboratory 2) and foreign language 2. Familiarity with the use of personal computers, including the Windows operating system, word processing, spreadsheets, and the Internet required.

**2010-2011 Annual costs.** Tuition, room and board, and medical and dental care provided by United States government. Each midshipman receives monthly salary of about $929 to cover costs of books, supplies, uniforms, laundry, and equipment, including microcomputer.

**Application procedures. Admission:** Closing date 1/31 (receipt date). No application fee. Application must be submitted online. Admission notification on a rolling basis beginning on or about 9/1. Must reply by May 1 or within 2 week(s) if notified thereafter. Nomination essential prior to consideration for appointment. Nominating authorities include President, Vice President, Secretary of Navy, members of Congress, delegates to Congress, governors of United States Territories, and resident commissioner of Puerto Rico. Applicants for presidential appointments limited by law to sons and daughters of career military personnel, active or retired. Applicants encouraged to apply to the Academy and nominating authority by May one year prior to desired admission.

**Academics.** Military environment and organization under student leadership with military officer supervision. Professional training at US bases and with units of the United States Navy and United States Marine Corps during summer months. Graduates receive B.S. degree with a major in one of 23 disciplines, plus commission as Ensign in US Navy or Second Lieutenant in US Marine Corps. **Special study options:** Double major, exchange student, honors, independent study, study abroad. Qualified students have opportunities to begin work in senior year towards a Master's degree at local graduate schools. Selected midshipmen can also engage in research with thesis, or work towards honors in their majors. **Credit/placement by examination:** CLEP, IB, SAT, ACT, institutional tests. Midshipmen take local examinations after admission for placement. AP Exam scores also used for validation of some courses. **Support services:** Learning center, remedial instruction, study skills assistance, tutoring, writing center.

**Majors. Computer sciences:** General, information technology. **Engineering:** General, aerospace, computer hardware, electrical, marine, mechanical, ocean, systems. **Foreign languages:** Arabic, Chinese. **History:** General. **Math:** General, applied. **Physical sciences:** General, chemistry, oceanography, physics. **Social sciences:** Econometrics, economics, political science.

**Most popular majors.** Engineering/engineering technologies 34%, English 6%, history 9%, physical sciences 13%, social sciences 31%.

**Computing on campus.** PC or laptop required. Dormitories wired for high-speed internet access and linked to campus network. Online course registration, helpline, repair service available.

**Student life. Freshman orientation:** Mandatory. All freshmen (plebes) report in late June/early July for approximately 6 weeks of military indoctrination. **Policies:** The Naval Academy has an Honor Concept administered by the Brigade of Midshipmen. **Housing:** Guaranteed on-campus for all undergraduates. Coed dorms, wellness housing available. Midshipmen must live in the dormitory on campus all four years. **Activities:** Bands, choral groups, drama, film society, literary magazine, music ensembles, musical theater, radio station, student newspaper, Fellowship of Christian Athletes, Black Studies Club, Midshipmen Action Group, Officers' Christian Fellowship, Foreign Affairs Conference, Women's Professional Association.

**Athletics.** NCAA. **Intercollegiate:** Baseball M, basketball, cross-country, diving, football (tackle) M, golf M, gymnastics M, lacrosse, rifle, rowing (crew), sailing, soccer, squash M, swimming, tennis, track and field, volleyball W, water polo M, wrestling M. **Intramural:** Basketball, boxing, cross-country, football (non-tackle), golf, handball, judo, racquetball, sailing, soccer, softball, swimming, volleyball, weight lifting, wrestling. **Team name:** Midshipmen.

**Student services.** Alcohol/substance abuse counseling, chaplain/spiritual director, career counseling, health services, legal services, minority student services, personal counseling, placement for graduates, women's services.

**Contact.** E-mail: webmail@usna.edu
Phone: (410) 293-4361 Toll-free number: (888) 249-7707
Fax: (410) 293-1815
Dean of Admissions, United States Naval Academy, 117 Decatur Road, Annapolis, MD 21402-5018

---

## University of Baltimore
**Baltimore, Maryland**  CB member
**www.ubalt.edu**  CB code: 5810

- Public 4-year business and liberal arts college
- Commuter campus in very large city
- 2,967 degree-seeking undergraduates: 41% part-time, 58% women, 38% African American, 4% Asian American, 2% Hispanic American, 1% Native American, 1% international

---

- 3,084 degree-seeking graduate students
- 65% of applicants admitted
- SAT or ACT (ACT writing optional), application essay required

**General.** Founded in 1925. Regionally accredited. Active career center, off-campus housing support. **Degrees:** 528 bachelor's awarded; master's, doctoral, professional offered. **ROTC:** Army. **Location:** Midtown Baltimore. **Calendar:** Semester, limited summer session. **Full-time faculty:** 178 total; 84% have terminal degrees, 23% minority, 43% women. **Part-time faculty:** 195 total; 53% have terminal degrees, 18% minority, 38% women. **Class size:** 30% < 20, 63% 20-39, 3% 40-49, 4% 50-99. **Special facilities:** Graphics laboratory, business center, interactive video network.

**Freshman class profile.** 748 applied, 488 admitted, 203 enrolled.

| Mid 50% test scores | | SAT writing: | 470-550 |
|---|---|---|---|
| SAT critical reading: | 480-570 | Out-of-state: | 2% |
| SAT math: | 460-570 | International: | 1% |

**Basis for selection.** Application, high school transcript, standardized test scores (ACT/SAT) and personal essay.

**High school preparation.** 22 units required; 24 recommended. Required and recommended units include English 4, mathematics 3, social studies 3, history 3, science 3, foreign language 1-2, computer science 1-2 and academic electives 4.

**2009-2010 Annual costs.** Tuition/fees: $7,171; $20,678 out-of-state. Books/supplies: $730.

**Application procedures. Admission:** No deadline. $30 fee, may be waived for applicants with need. Admission notification on a rolling basis beginning on or about 9/15. Must reply by 5/1. **Financial aid:** No deadline. FAFSA, institutional form required. Applicants notified on a rolling basis.

**Academics.** All undergraduate students take 9 hours in an upper-level core curriculum in a general humanities-based general education. **Special study options:** Accelerated study, combined bachelor's/graduate degree, cooperative education, cross-registration, distance learning, dual enrollment of high school students, exchange student, honors, independent study, internships, student-designed major, study abroad, weekend college. **Credit/placement by examination:** AP, CLEP, IB, institutional tests. 30 credit hours maximum toward bachelor's degree. **Support services:** Learning center, reduced course load, remedial instruction, study skills assistance, tutoring, writing center.

**Majors. Business:** General, accounting, business admin, communications, entrepreneurial studies, finance, human resources, international, management information systems, managerial economics, marketing, real estate. **Communications:** Public relations. **Computer sciences:** General, game design. **Health:** Health care admin. **History:** General. **Legal studies:** Prelaw. **Liberal arts:** Arts/sciences. **Protective services:** Criminal justice, forensics. **Psychology:** General. **Public administration:** Human services. **Social sciences:** Political science.

**Most popular majors.** Business/marketing 46%, communications/journalism 6%, computer/information sciences 10%, security/protective services 11%.

**Computing on campus.** 155 workstations in library, computer center, student center. Commuter students can connect to campus network. Online library, helpline, wireless network available.

**Student life. Freshman orientation:** Available. **Activities:** International student organizations, literary magazine, student government, student newspaper, 60 student organizations.

**Athletics. Intramural:** Badminton, basketball, golf, judo, racquetball, rowing (crew), skiing, soccer W, table tennis, tennis, volleyball.

**Student services.** Career counseling, student employment services, health services, personal counseling, placement for graduates, veterans' counselor. **Physically disabled:** Services for visually, speech, hearing impaired.

**Contact.** E-mail: admissions@ubalt.edu
Phone: (410) 837-4777 Toll-free number: (877) 277-5982
Fax: (410) 837-4793
Valarie Trimarchi, Director of Freshman Admission, University of Baltimore, 1420 North Charles Street, Baltimore, MD 21201-5779

---

## University of Maryland: Baltimore
**Baltimore, Maryland**
**www.umaryland.edu**  CB code: 0527

- Public two-year upper-division university and health science college
- Commuter campus in very large city
- 48% of applicants admitted

rfffffffffrrfffr

fff

ffffffffffffffffffffffffff

---

**General.** Founded in 1807. Regionally accredited. **Degrees:** 349 bachelor's awarded; master's, doctoral, professional offered. **Articulation:** Agreements with all Maryland community colleges. **Location:** Downtown. **Calendar:** 4-1-4, limited summer session. **Full-time faculty:** 399 total; 76% have terminal degrees, 22% minority, 61% women. **Part-time faculty:** 609 total; 54% have terminal degrees, 19% minority, 60% women. **Special facilities:** Dental, medical, pharmacy and nursing museums; law library, health sciences library, center for health policy and health services research, center for research on aging, center for vaccine development, biotechnology institute, center for health and homeland security.

**Student profile.** 840 degree-seeking undergraduates, 5,377 degree-seeking graduate students. 690 applied as first time-transfer students, 330 admitted, 247 enrolled. 45% transferred from two-year, 55% transferred from four-year institutions.

| | | | |
|---|---|---|---|
| Women: | 85% | International: | 5% |
| African American: | 25% | Part-time: | 35% |
| Asian American: | 13% | Out-of-state: | 6% |
| Hispanic American: | 4% | 25 or older: | 64% |
| Native American: | 1% | | |

**Basis for selection.** College transcript required. Undergraduate deadlines range from February 1 to August 15 (nursing, dental hygiene, medical technology). Transfer accepted as juniors, seniors.

**2009-2010 Annual costs.** Tuition/fees: $7,941; $23,650 out-of-state. Books/supplies: $1,955. Personal expenses: $425.

**Financial aid.** **Additional information:** Maryland state deadline 3/1.

**Application procedures.** Admission: $50 fee. Admission process, fees, and dates differ among undergraduate programs (nursing, dental hygiene, medical technology). **Financial aid:** FAFSA required.

**Academics.** **Special study options:** Distance learning, double major. **Credit/placement by examination:** CLEP, institutional tests. 30 credit hours maximum toward bachelor's degree.

**Majors.** **Health:** Clinical lab science, dental hygiene, nursing (RN).

**Computing on campus.** 100 workstations in library, computer center, student center. Dormitories wired for high-speed internet access and linked to campus network. Commuter students can connect to campus network. Online library, helpline, wireless network available.

**Student life.** **Housing:** Apartments available. **Activities:** International student organizations, student government, Newman Center, African-American student association, Community Volunteer Program.

**Athletics.** **Intramural:** Badminton, basketball, football (non-tackle), golf, racquetball, soccer, softball, squash, tennis, volleyball.

**Student services.** Alcohol/substance abuse counseling, career counseling, services for economically disadvantaged, student employment services, financial aid counseling, health services, minority student services, on-campus daycare, personal counseling, placement for graduates, women's services. **Physically disabled:** Services for visually, speech, hearing impaired.

**Contact.**  E-mail: gradinfo@umaryland.edu
Phone: (410) 706-7480 Fax: (410) 706-4053
Thomas Day, Director of Records and Registration, University of Maryland: Baltimore, 620 West Lexington Street, Baltimore, MD 21201

---

## University of Maryland: Baltimore County

**Baltimore, Maryland**     CB member
**www.umbc.edu**     CB code: 5835

- Public 4-year university
- Residential campus in large city
- 9,815 degree-seeking undergraduates: 12% part-time, 46% women, 17% African American, 21% Asian American, 4% Hispanic American, 1% Native American, 4% international
- 2,644 degree-seeking graduate students
- 69% of applicants admitted
- SAT or ACT (ACT writing optional), application essay required
- 60% graduate within 6 years

**General.** Founded in 1963. Regionally accredited. **Degrees:** 1,798 bachelor's awarded; master's, doctoral offered. **ROTC:** Army, Air Force. **Location:** 5 miles from Baltimore, 35 miles from Washington, DC. **Calendar:** 4-1-4, extensive summer session. **Full-time faculty:** 480 total; 87% have terminal degrees, 18% minority, 42% women. **Part-time faculty:** 250 total; 33% have terminal degrees, 20% minority, 42% women. **Class size:** 41% < 20, 39% 20-39, 8% 40-49, 9% 50-99, 4% >100. **Special facilities:** Research telescope, greenhouse, research spectrometers, nuclear magnetic resonance machines, electron microscope facility, imaging/digital art laboratory, healthcare informatics laboratory, two galleries - contemporary art and photography, conservation and environmental research area.

**Freshman class profile.** 6,047 applied, 4,168 admitted, 1,532 enrolled.

| Mid 50% test scores | | | |
|---|---|---|---|
| SAT critical reading: | 530-630 | GPA 2.0-2.99: | 13% |
| SAT math: | 550-660 | Rank in top quarter: | 52% |
| SAT writing: | 530-630 | Rank in top tenth: | 24% |
| ACT composite: | 22-29 | Return as sophomores: | 85% |
| GPA 3.75 or higher: | 42% | Out-of-state: | 9% |
| GPA 3.50-3.74: | 18% | Live on campus: | 72% |
| GPA 3.0-3.49: | 27% | International: | 5% |

**Basis for selection.** High school record, test scores important. Audition required for music, dance, theater majors. Portfolio required for visual arts majors.

**High school preparation.** College-preparatory program recommended. Required and recommended units include English 4, mathematics 3, social studies 3, science 3-4 and foreign language 2. Algebra I and II, and geometry required. History combined with Social Studies.

**2009-2010 Annual costs.** Tuition/fees: $8,872; $18,213 out-of-state. Room/board: $9,303. Books/supplies: $1,200. Personal expenses: $1,450.

**2008-2009 Financial aid.** **Need-based:** 1,102 full-time freshmen applied for aid; 675 were judged to have need; 675 of these received aid. Average need met was 88%. Average scholarship/grant was $9,612; average loan $3,574. 61% of total undergraduate aid awarded as scholarships/grants, 39% as loans/jobs. **Non-need-based:** Awarded to 1,742 full-time undergraduates, including 710 freshmen. Scholarships awarded for academics, alumni affiliation, art, athletics, music/drama.

**Application procedures.** Admission: Priority date 11/1; deadline 2/1 (postmark date). $50 fee, may be waived for applicants with need. Admission notification on a rolling basis beginning on or about 12/15. Must reply by May 1 or within 2 week(s) if notified thereafter. **Financial aid:** Priority date 2/14; no closing date. FAFSA required. Applicants notified by 3/15; Applicants notified on a rolling basis starting 3/15; must reply within 2 week(s) of notification.

**Academics.** **Special study options:** Accelerated study, combined bachelor's/graduate degree, cooperative education, cross-registration, double major, dual enrollment of high school students, ESL, exchange student, honors, independent study, internships, semester at sea, student-designed major, study abroad, teacher certification program. **Credit/placement by examination:** AP, CLEP, IB, institutional tests. 60 credit hours maximum toward bachelor's degree. **Support services:** Learning center, remedial instruction, study skills assistance, tutoring, writing center.

**Honors college/program.** Minimum 1300 SAT (exclusive of Writing) and 3.5 GPA required. Approximately 140 students accepted each year, with average SAT of 1300 (exclusive of Writing) and 3.81 GPA. Each semester 40-50 courses offered along with non-curricular activities.

**Majors.** **Area/ethnic studies:** African-American, American. **Biology:** General, Biochemistry/biophysics and molecular biology, bioinformatics. **Communications:** Media studies. **Computer sciences:** General, information systems. **Conservation:** Environmental science, environmental studies. **Education:** Physics. **Engineering:** General, chemical, computer, mechanical. **Foreign languages:** General, linguistics. **Health:** EMT paramedic, health services. **History:** General. **Interdisciplinary:** Ancient studies. **Math:** General, statistics. **Philosophy/religion:** Philosophy. **Physical sciences:** Chemistry, physics. **Psychology:** General. **Public administration:** Social work. **Social sciences:** Anthropology, economics, geography, political science, sociology. **Visual/performing arts:** General, acting, dance, dramatic. **Other:** Gender Studies, Physics Education.

**Most popular majors.** Biology 13%, computer/information sciences 12%, engineering/engineering technologies 9%, psychology 14%, social sciences 17%, visual/performing arts 9%.

**Computing on campus.** 1,100 workstations in dormitories, library, computer center, student center. Dormitories wired for high-speed internet access and linked to campus network. Commuter students can connect to campus network. Online course registration, online library, helpline, repair service, student web hosting, wireless network available.

**Student life.** **Freshman orientation:** Mandatory, $125 fee. Preregistration for classes offered. Held June and July. Separate program for honors college students. **Housing:** Guaranteed on-campus for freshmen. Coed dorms, special housing for disabled, apartments available. $200 nonrefundable deposit, deadline 5/1. **Activities:** Bands, campus ministries, choral groups, dance, drama, film society, international student organizations, literary magazine, music ensembles, Model UN, musical theater, radio station, student government, student newspaper, symphony orchestra, Black student union, Chinese student association, Jewish student association, Korean club, gay and lesbian organization, progressive action committee, Christian Fellowship, women's union.

**Athletics.** NCAA. **Intercollegiate:** Baseball M, basketball, cheerleading, cross-country, diving, lacrosse, soccer, softball W, swimming, tennis, track and field, volleyball W. **Intramural:** Basketball, football (non-tackle), handball, lacrosse, soccer, softball, tennis, volleyball, weight lifting. **Team name:** Retrievers.

**Student services.** Adult student services, alcohol/substance abuse counseling, chaplain/spiritual director, career counseling, services for economically disadvantaged, student employment services, financial aid counseling, health services, minority student services, on-campus daycare, personal counseling, placement for graduates, veterans' counselor, women's services. **Physically disabled:** Services for visually, hearing impaired.

**Contact.** E-mail: admissions@umbc.edu
Phone: (410) 455-2291 Toll-free number: (800) 862-2482
Fax: (410) 455-1094
Dale Bittinger, Director of Admissions, University of Maryland: Baltimore County, 1000 Hilltop Circle, Baltimore, MD 21250

---

## University of Maryland: College Park

College Park, Maryland  **CB member**
www.maryland.edu  **CB code: 5814**

- Public 4-year university
- Commuter campus in large town
- 25,898 degree-seeking undergraduates: 5% part-time, 47% women, 12% African American, 15% Asian American, 6% Hispanic American, 2% international
- 9,965 degree-seeking graduate students
- 42% of applicants admitted
- SAT or ACT with writing, application essay required
- 82% graduate within 6 years

**General.** Founded in 1856. Regionally accredited. Research and internship opportunities at Smithsonian Institution, National Institutes for Health, NASA, US Capitol, White House, FBI, Department of Agriculture, other federal agencies. **Degrees:** 6,704 bachelor's awarded; master's, doctoral, professional offered. **ROTC:** Army, Naval, Air Force. **Location:** 30 miles from Baltimore, 3 miles from Washington, DC. **Calendar:** Semester, extensive summer session. **Full-time faculty:** 1,644 total; 92% have terminal degrees, 20% minority, 34% women. **Part-time faculty:** 629 total; 50% have terminal degrees, 12% minority, 44% women. **Class size:** 34% < 20, 44% 20-39, 7% 40-49, 8% 50-99, 7% >100. **Special facilities:** National Archives II, astronomy observatory, engineering wind tunnel, space systems lab, nuclear reactor, performing arts center, center for young children, agricultural biotechnology, superconductivity research, institute for systems research, fire and rescue institute.

**Freshman class profile.** 28,331 applied, 11,870 admitted, 4,202 enrolled.

| Mid 50% test scores | | | |
|---|---|---|---|
| SAT critical reading: | 580-680 | Return as sophomores: | 93% |
| SAT math: | 620-710 | Out-of-state: | 33% |
| GPA 3.75 or higher: | 68% | Live on campus: | 93% |
| GPA 3.50-3.74: | 17% | International: | 2% |
| GPA 3.0-3.49: | 13% | Fraternities: | 16% |
| GPA 2.0-2.99: | 2% | Sororities: | 21% |

**Basis for selection.** Academic record, rigor of the high school academic program, standardized admission test scores, class rank (if available), essay, extracurricular activities, counselor recommendation, and other letters of recommendation reviewed. For priority deadline, we will do our best to consider scores from November testing date and for the final January application deadline, we will do our best to consider December scores. Audition required of music majors. Portfolio recommended for architecture majors. **Homeschooled:** Statement describing homeschool structure and mission, transcript of courses and grades required. Transcript should include description of course work, books used, method of evaluation and actual grades or evaluation. Letter of recommendation required and must be from academic professional.

**High school preparation.** College-preparatory program recommended. 15 units required; 16 recommended. Required and recommended units include English 4, mathematics 3-4, social studies 3, science 3 (laboratory 2) and foreign language 2. Algebra I and II, plane geometry required. Social studies units should include history.

**2009-2010 Annual costs.** Tuition/fees: $8,053; $23,990 out-of-state. Room/board: $9,377. Books/supplies: $1,025. Personal expenses: $2,268.

**2008-2009 Financial aid. Non-need-based:** Scholarships awarded for academics, art, athletics, music/drama. **Additional information:** Prepaid tuition plans available through state.

**Application procedures. Admission:** Priority date 11/1; deadline 1/20 (receipt date). $55 fee, may be waived for applicants with need. Admission notification 4/1. Must reply by May 1 or within 4 week(s) if notified thereafter. **Financial aid:** Priority date 2/15; no closing date. FAFSA required. Applicants notified on a rolling basis starting 4/1.

**Academics. Special study options:** Accelerated study, combined bachelor's/graduate degree, cooperative education, cross-registration, distance learning, double major, dual enrollment of high school students, ESL, exchange student, external degree, honors, independent study, internships, liberal arts/career combination, semester at sea, student-designed major, study abroad, teacher certification program. Living/learning programs. **Credit/placement by examination:** AP, CLEP, IB, SAT, ACT, institutional tests. 60 credit hours maximum toward bachelor's degree. **Support services:** Learning center, pre-admission summer program, reduced course load, remedial instruction, study skills assistance, tutoring, writing center.

**Majors. Agriculture:** General, animal sciences, economics, food science. **Architecture:** Architecture, landscape. **Area/ethnic studies:** African-American, American, Russian/Slavic, women's. **Biology:** General, biochemistry, ecology, microbiology. **Business:** General, accounting, finance, international, logistics, management science, marketing. **Communications:** General, journalism. **Computer sciences:** General, information systems. **Conservation:** General, environmental science. **Education:** Art, elementary, English, foreign languages, health, kindergarten/preschool, mathematics, music, physical, science, social studies, special. **Engineering:** General, aerospace, agricultural, chemical, civil, computer, electrical, materials, mechanical. **Family/consumer sciences:** Family/community services, food/nutrition. **Foreign languages:** Arabic, Chinese, classics, French, German, Italian, Japanese, linguistics, Persian, Romance, Russian, Spanish. **Health:** Communication disorders, dietetics, nursing (RN), predental, preveterinary. **History:** General. **Legal studies:** Prelaw. **Math:** General. **Parks/recreation:** Exercise sciences. **Philosophy/religion:** Judaic, philosophy. **Physical sciences:** General, astronomy, chemistry, geology, physics. **Psychology:** General. **Social sciences:** Anthropology, criminology, economics, geography, political science, sociology. **Visual/performing arts:** Art history/conservation, dance, dramatic, music performance, studio arts. **Other:** Public health science.

**Most popular majors.** Biology 8%, business/marketing 16%, communications/journalism 6%, engineering/engineering technologies 9%, social sciences 21%.

**Computing on campus.** 11,637 workstations in dormitories, library, computer center, student center. Dormitories wired for high-speed internet access and linked to campus network. Commuter students can connect to campus network. Online course registration, online library, helpline, student web hosting, wireless network available.

**Student life. Freshman orientation:** Mandatory, $160 fee. Preregistration for classes offered. 2-day program. **Housing:** Guaranteed on-campus for freshmen. Coed dorms, single-sex dorms, special housing for disabled, apartments, cooperative housing, fraternity/sorority housing, wellness housing available. **Activities:** Bands, campus ministries, choral groups, dance, drama, film society, international student organizations, literary magazine, music ensembles, Model UN, musical theater, opera, radio station, student government, student newspaper, symphony orchestra, TV station, Black student union, Asian American student union, Latino student union, Native American student union, Alpha Phi Omega, Habitat for Humanity.

**Athletics.** NCAA. **Intercollegiate:** Baseball M, basketball, cheerleading M, cross-country, equestrian, field hockey W, football (tackle) M, golf, gymnastics W, lacrosse, soccer, softball W, swimming, tennis, track and field, volleyball W, water polo W, wrestling M. **Intramural:** Badminton, basketball, football (non-tackle), golf, ice hockey W, racquetball, soccer, softball, table tennis, tennis, track and field, volleyball, wrestling M. **Team name:** Terrapins.

**Student services.** Adult student services, alcohol/substance abuse counseling, chaplain/spiritual director, career counseling, services for economically disadvantaged, student employment services, financial aid counseling, health services, legal services, minority student services, on-campus daycare, personal counseling, placement for graduates, veterans' counselor, women's services. **Physically disabled:** Services for visually, speech, hearing impaired.

**Contact.** E-mail: um-admit@uga.umd.edu
Phone: (301) 314-8385 Toll-free number: (800) 422-5867
Fax: (301) 314-9693
Barbara Gill, Director of Undergraduate Admissions, University of
Maryland: College Park, Mitchell Building, College Park, MD 20742-5235

## University of Maryland: Eastern Shore
**Princess Anne, Maryland**                          CB member
**www.umes.edu**                                     CB code: 5400

- Public 4-year university
- Residential campus in rural community
- 3,827 degree-seeking undergraduates: 6% part-time, 59% women, 83%
  African American, 1% Asian American, 1% Hispanic American, 3%
  international
- 490 degree-seeking graduate students
- 56% of applicants admitted
- SAT or ACT (ACT writing optional), application essay required
- 38% graduate within 6 years

**General.** Founded in 1886. Regionally accredited. **Degrees:** 429 bachelor's awarded; master's, doctoral, professional offered. **Location:** 12 miles
from Salisbury. **Calendar:** Semester, extensive summer session. **Full-time
faculty:** 178 total; 70% have terminal degrees, 56% minority, 44% women.
**Part-time faculty:** 121 total; 15% have terminal degrees, 37% minority,
51% women. **Class size:** 41% < 20, 33% 20-39, 24% 40-49, 3% 50-99, less
than 1% >100. **Special facilities:** Arts and technology center, performing
arts center, hydroponic greenhouse, education center.

**Freshman class profile.** 4,317 applied, 2,409 admitted, 881 enrolled.

| Mid 50% test scores | | | |
|---|---|---|---|
| SAT critical reading: | 380-470 | GPA 3.0-3.49: | 23% |
| SAT math: | 370-460 | GPA 2.0-2.99: | 68% |
| SAT writing: | 380-460 | Return as sophomores: | 70% |
| ACT composite: | 15-18 | Out-of-state: | 28% |
| GPA 3.75 or higher: | 4% | Live on campus: | 93% |
| GPA 3.50-3.74: | 4% | International: | 2% |

**Basis for selection.** School record, class rank, and test scores most important. Interview recommended for honors program and physical therapy
applicants. Audition required for music majors. **Homeschooled:** Transcript
of courses and grades required. Must demonstrate compliance with state
and local education regulations.

**High school preparation.** 20 units required. Required units include English 4, mathematics 3, social studies 3, science 2, foreign language 2 and
academic electives 6.

**2009-2010 Annual costs.** Tuition/fees: $6,082; $13,306 out-of-state. Room/
board: $7,230. Books/supplies: $1,800. Personal expenses: $1,800.

**2008-2009 Financial aid. Need-based:** 789 full-time freshmen applied
for aid; 710 were judged to have need; 710 of these received aid. Average
scholarship/grant was $6,110; average loan $2,950. 62% of total undergraduate aid awarded as scholarships/grants, 38% as loans/jobs. **Non-need-
based:** Awarded to 1,004 full-time undergraduates, including 146 freshmen.
Scholarships awarded for academics, alumni affiliation, art, athletics, leadership, music/drama, ROTC, state residency.

**Application procedures. Admission:** Priority date 3/1; deadline 7/15.
$25 fee, may be waived for applicants with need. Admission notification
9/14. Admission notification on a rolling basis. **Financial aid:** Priority date
3/1, closing date 4/1. FAFSA required. Applicants notified on a rolling basis
starting 4/15.

**Academics.** The doctoral program in organizational leadership is a weekend program to meet scheduling needs of its students who are mostly full-
time employees. The Library opens in the evenings. **Special study options:**
Accelerated study, cooperative education, cross-registration, distance learning, double major, dual enrollment of high school students, exchange student, honors, independent study, internships, liberal arts/career combination, New York semester, study abroad, teacher certification program. **Credit/
placement by examination:** AP, CLEP, IB, institutional tests. 60 credit
hours maximum toward bachelor's degree. **Support services:** Learning center, pre-admission summer program, reduced course load, remedial instruction, study skills assistance, tutoring, writing center.

**Majors. Agriculture:** General, business. **Area/ethnic studies:** African-
American. **Biology:** General, ecology. **Business:** Accounting, business admin, golf management, hospitality admin, hotel/motel admin. **Computer
sciences:** General. **Education:** Agricultural, art, biology, business, chemistry, English, mathematics, music, physical, social studies, special, technology/

industrial arts. **Engineering:** General. **Engineering technology:** General,
civil. **Family/consumer sciences:** General. **Health:** Physician assistant. **History:** General. **Liberal arts:** Arts/sciences. **Math:** General. **Parks/
recreation:** Exercise sciences. **Physical sciences:** Chemistry. **Protective services:** Police science. **Social sciences:** Sociology. **Transportation:** Aviation.
**Visual/performing arts:** Commercial/advertising art. **Other:** General studies, Rehabilitation services.

**Most popular majors.** Biology 7%, business/marketing 20%, engineering/
engineering technologies 6%, English 6%, family/consumer sciences 6%,
health sciences 8%, security/protective services 17%, social sciences 11%.

**Computing on campus.** 739 workstations in dormitories, library, computer center. Dormitories wired for high-speed internet access and linked to
campus network. Commuter students can connect to campus network. Online library, helpline, wireless network available.

**Student life. Freshman orientation:** Mandatory, $100 fee. Preregistra-
tion for classes offered. 2 day program in the Fall. **Housing:** Coed dorms,
single-sex dorms, apartments, wellness housing available. $300 partly re-
fundable deposit, deadline 5/1. **Activities:** Bands, campus ministries, choral
groups, dance, drama, international student organizations, music ensembles,
radio station, student government, student newspaper, NAACP, Students for
Progressive Action, Phenomenal Women, Rotaract club, College Democrats
of America, Students in Free Enterprise, For Sisters Only, National Student
Business League.

**Athletics.** NCAA. **Intercollegiate:** Baseball M, basketball, bowling W,
cheerleading M, cross-country, golf M, softball W, tennis, track and field,
volleyball W. **Intramural:** Basketball, bowling, football (non-tackle) M,
soccer, softball W, swimming, table tennis, volleyball. **Team name:** Hawks.

**Student services.** Adult student services, career counseling, student employment services, financial aid counseling, health services, on-campus daycare, personal counseling, placement for graduates, veterans' counselor. **Physically disabled:** Services for speech, hearing impaired.

**Contact.** E-mail: umesadmissions@umes.edu
Phone: (410) 651-6410 Fax: (410) 651-7922
Tyrone Young, Director of Admissions and Recruitment, University of
Maryland: Eastern Shore, Student Development Center, Suite 1140,
Princess Anne, MD 21853

## University of Maryland: University College
**Adelphi, Maryland**
**www.umuc.edu**                                     CB code: 0551

- Public 4-year university
- Commuter campus in large town
- 23,168 degree-seeking undergraduates: 85% part-time, 56% women,
  32% African American, 4% Asian American, 6% Hispanic American,
  1% Native American, 2% international
- 12,565 degree-seeking graduate students

**General.** Founded in 1947. Regionally accredited. Courses held at over 20
locations throughout Maryland, Virginia and Washington, DC. Associate
degree programs available only to active military personnel. Courses offered at more than 100 locations in Europe and Asia. **Degrees:** 2,698 bachelor's, 248 associate awarded; master's, professional offered. **Location:** 9
miles from Washington, DC. **Calendar:** Semester, extensive summer session. **Full-time faculty:** 228 total; 83% have terminal degrees, 13% minority, 48% women. **Part-time faculty:** 1,730 total; 69% have terminal degrees, 14% minority, 40% women. **Class size:** 53% < 20, 44% 20-39, 2%
40-49.

**Freshman class profile.**

| Out-of-state: | 36% | International: | 2% |
|---|---|---|---|

**Basis for selection.** Open admission.

**2009-2010 Annual costs.** Tuition/fees: $5,820; $12,276 out-of-state. Books/
supplies: $2,000. Personal expenses: $5,500.

**2008-2009 Financial aid. Need-based:** 81 full-time freshmen applied
for aid; 74 were judged to have need; 68 of these received aid. Average
need met was 17%. Average scholarship/grant was $3,447; average loan
$2,594. 17% of total undergraduate aid awarded as scholarships/grants, 83%
as loans/jobs. **Non-need-based:** Awarded to 290 full-time undergraduates,
including 6 freshmen. Scholarships awarded for academics, leadership.

**Application procedures. Admission:** No deadline. $50 fee. Admission
notification on a rolling basis. **Financial aid:** Priority date 6/1; no closing
date. FAFSA required. Applicants notified on a rolling basis starting 5/1;
must reply within 2 week(s) of notification.

**Academics.** Degree programs offered primarily for adults attending part-time. No traditional freshman class. **Special study options:** Accelerated study, cooperative education, cross-registration, distance learning, double major, dual enrollment of high school students, external degree, independent study, internships, teacher certification program, weekend college. **Credit/placement by examination:** AP, CLEP, IB, institutional tests. 30 credit hours maximum toward associate degree, 60 toward bachelor's. **Support services:** Tutoring, writing center.

**Majors. Area/ethnic studies:** Asian. **Biology:** Biomedical sciences. **Business:** General, accounting, business admin, finance, human resources, management science, marketing. **Communications:** General. **Computer sciences:** General, information systems, security. **Conservation:** General. **History:** General. **Interdisciplinary:** Gerontology. **Legal studies:** General. **Liberal arts:** Arts/sciences, humanities. **Protective services:** Criminal justice, fire services admin, firefighting, forensics. **Psychology:** General. **Public administration:** General. **Social sciences:** General, political science.

**Most popular majors.** Business/marketing 38%, computer/information sciences 21%, interdisciplinary studies 8%, psychology 7%.

**Computing on campus.** Commuter students can connect to campus network. Online course registration, online library, helpline, student web hosting, wireless network available.

**Student life. Freshman orientation:** Available.

**Student services.** Adult student services, career counseling, financial aid counseling, veterans' counselor. **Physically disabled:** Services for visually, speech, hearing impaired.

**Contact.** E-mail: enroll@umuc.edu
Phone: (301) 985-7000 Toll-free number: (800) 888-8682
Fax: (240) 684-2151
Jessica Sadaka, Director of Admissions, University of Maryland: University College, 3501 University Boulevard East, Adelphi, MD 20783

## Washington Adventist University
**Takoma Park, Maryland**
www.cuc.edu                                   CB code: 5890

- Private 4-year liberal arts college affiliated with Seventh-day Adventists
- Residential campus in large town
- 986 degree-seeking undergraduates: 22% part-time, 65% women, 52% African American, 6% Asian American, 11% Hispanic American
- 100 degree-seeking graduate students
- 41% of applicants admitted
- SAT or ACT (ACT writing optional) required

**General.** Founded in 1904. Regionally accredited. **Degrees:** 190 bachelor's, 12 associate awarded; master's offered. **Location:** 1 mile from Washington, DC. **Calendar:** Semester, limited summer session. **Full-time faculty:** 41 total; 51% have terminal degrees, 51% women. **Part-time faculty:** 68 total; 4% have terminal degrees, 48% women.

**Freshman class profile.** 1,293 applied, 531 admitted, 144 enrolled.

**Basis for selection.** High school GPA of 2.5, school achievement record, test scores very important; recommendations considered. Audition required of music majors. **Homeschooled:** Transcript of courses and grades required. Recognized high school diploma or GED required. **Learning Disabled:** Students must provide written documentation of disabilities and submit written request for all needed services for review by the Disabilities Coordinator three months before registration. All forms may be obtained from Center for Learning Resources.

**High school preparation.** 18 units required; 29 recommended. Required and recommended units include English 4, mathematics 2-4, social studies 2, history 4, science 2-4 (laboratory 2), foreign language 2, computer science 1 and academic electives 4. One unit of computer science also recommended.

**2010-2011 Annual costs.** Tuition/fees (projected): $19,480. Room/board: $7,200. Books/supplies: $1,200. Personal expenses: $1,250.

**2008-2009 Financial aid. Non-need-based:** Scholarships awarded for academics, athletics, leadership, music/drama, state residency.

**Application procedures. Admission:** Closing date 8/1 (postmark date). $25 fee, may be waived for applicants with need, free for online applicants. Admission notification on a rolling basis. Must reply by 8/15. **Financial aid:** Closing date 3/31. FAFSA required. Applicants notified on a rolling basis starting 5/31; must reply within 4 week(s) of notification.

**Academics. Special study options:** Accelerated study, combined bachelor's/graduate degree, cooperative education, cross-registration, distance learning, double major, dual enrollment of high school students, ESL, external degree, honors, independent study, internships, liberal arts/career combination, student-designed major, study abroad, teacher certification program, Washington semester. Co-Op Programs: Business,Biochemistry, Communications/Journalism, Computer Science, English. **Credit/placement by examination:** AP, CLEP, SAT, ACT, institutional tests. 12 credit hours maximum toward associate degree, 24 toward bachelor's. CLEP business exams not accepted for traditional business majors. **Support services:** Learning center, reduced course load, remedial instruction, study skills assistance, tutoring, writing center.

**Majors. Biology:** General, biochemistry. **Business:** Accounting, business admin, marketing, organizational behavior. **Communications:** General, broadcast journalism, journalism. **Computer sciences:** General, computer science, information systems. **Education:** General, elementary, English, mathematics, music, physical, science, secondary. **Health:** Health care admin, nursing (RN), predental, premedicine, prepharmacy, preveterinary. **History:** General. **Legal studies:** Prelaw. **Liberal arts:** Arts/sciences. **Math:** General. **Parks/recreation:** Health/fitness, sports admin. **Philosophy/religion:** Religion. **Physical sciences:** Chemistry. **Psychology:** General, counseling. **Social sciences:** Political science. **Theology:** Religious ed, theology. **Visual/performing arts:** Music performance. **Other:** Health/fitness management, Philosophy and religion.

**Most popular majors.** Business/marketing 15%, education 7%, health sciences 31%, liberal arts 7%, psychology 18%.

**Computing on campus.** Dormitories wired for high-speed internet access and linked to campus network. Commuter students can connect to campus network. Online library, wireless network available.

**Student life. Freshman orientation:** Mandatory, $150 fee. Preregistration for classes offered. **Policies:** Attendance required at weekly chapel service. Resident students required to attend dormitory worships. Religious observance required. **Housing:** Guaranteed on-campus for freshmen. Single-sex dorms, apartments available. $200 fully refundable deposit, deadline 8/15. **Activities:** Bands, campus ministries, choral groups, international student organizations, literary magazine, music ensembles, musical theater, radio station, student government, student newspaper, symphony orchestra, Humanitas, Loaves and Fishes, Shepherd's Hands (puppet ministry), Teach-a-Kid, Youth-to-Youth (drug prevention), student mission club.

**Athletics.** NCAA. **Intercollegiate:** Baseball M, basketball, cross-country, soccer, softball W, track and field. **Intramural:** Basketball M, soccer M, volleyball. **Team name:** Pioneers.

**Student services.** Adult student services, chaplain/spiritual director, career counseling, student employment services, financial aid counseling, health services, personal counseling, placement for graduates, veterans' counselor.

**Contact.** E-mail: admissions@cuc.edu
Phone: (301) 891-4080 Toll-free number: (800) 835-4212
Fax: (301) 891-4230
Elaine Oliver, Vice President of Enrollment Management, Washington Adventist University, 7600 Flower Avenue, Takoma Park, MD 20912

## Washington Bible College
**Lanham, Maryland**
www.bible.edu                                 CB code: 5884

- Private 4-year Bible and seminary college affiliated with nondenominational tradition
- Commuter campus in large town
- 300 degree-seeking undergraduates
- SAT or ACT (ACT writing optional), application essay required

**General.** Founded in 1938. Regionally accredited; also accredited by ABHE. Main Campus in Lanham, MD. Branch sites in Annapolis, MD and in Springfield, VA. **Degrees:** 25 bachelor's, 1 associate awarded; master's offered. **Location:** 10 miles from Washington, DC. **Calendar:** Semester, limited summer session. **Full-time faculty:** 9 total. **Part-time faculty:** 16 total.

**Freshman class profile.**

| Mid 50% test scores | | Out-of-state: | 31% |
|---|---|---|---|
| SAT critical reading: | 420-580 | Live on campus: | 68% |
| SAT math: | 410-550 | | |

**Basis for selection.** Student's spiritual qualifications most important, followed by academic achievement, test scores, essay, recommendations. 2 references required. Interview recommended. Audition required of music majors.

**High school preparation.** 15 units recommended. Recommended units include English 4, mathematics 2, social studies 2, science 2 and academic electives 5. Typing recommended.

**2009-2010 Annual costs.** Tuition/fees: $13,230. Room/board: $6,770. Books/supplies: $500. Personal expenses: $1,300.

**2008-2009 Financial aid. Non-need-based:** Scholarships awarded for academics, leadership, music/drama, state residency.

**Application procedures. Admission:** Closing date 8/1 (receipt date). $35 fee, may be waived for applicants with need, free for online applicants. Admission notification on a rolling basis. Campus visit suggested. Deadline for housing deposit 30 days after acceptance. **Financial aid:** Closing date 3/1. FAFSA, institutional form required. Applicants notified on a rolling basis starting 7/1; must reply within 2 week(s) of notification.

**Academics.** All students major in Bible; other areas may be studied for concentrations. **Special study options:** Accelerated study, double major, ESL, independent study, internships, study abroad, teacher certification program. **Credit/placement by examination:** AP, CLEP, SAT, ACT, institutional tests. 15 credit hours maximum toward bachelor's degree. **Support services:** Reduced course load, tutoring, writing center.

**Majors. Education:** General, early childhood, elementary, multi-level teacher, music, physical, school counseling. **Family/consumer sciences:** Work/family studies. **Psychology:** Counseling. **Theology:** Bible, missionary, pastoral counseling, preministerial, religious ed, sacred music, theology, youth ministry. **Visual/performing arts:** Music performance, piano/organ, voice/opera.

**Computing on campus.** 10 workstations in library, student center. Dormitories wired for high-speed internet access and linked to campus network. Commuter students can connect to campus network. Online library, helpline, wireless network available.

**Student life. Freshman orientation:** Mandatory. 2-day spring and summer programs. **Policies:** Religious observance required. **Housing:** Guaranteed on-campus for freshmen. Single-sex dorms, apartments, wellness housing available. $100 nonrefundable deposit, deadline 6/1. **Activities:** Choral groups, drama, music ensembles, student government, student newspaper, Student Missions Fellowship, Fellowship of Christian Athletes.

**Athletics.** NCCAA. **Intercollegiate:** Basketball M, volleyball W. **Intramural:** Basketball, cheerleading, football (tackle) M, racquetball, soccer, table tennis, volleyball, weight lifting. **Team name:** Cougars.

**Student services.** Chaplain/spiritual director, career counseling, student employment services, financial aid counseling, health services, personal counseling, placement for graduates, veterans' counselor. **Physically disabled:** Services for visually, hearing impaired.

**Contact.** E-mail: iadmissions@bible.edu
Phone: (301) 552-1400 ext. 1212 Toll-free
number: (877) 793-7227 ext. 1212 Fax: (301) 552-2775
Bernt King, Director of Admission, Washington Bible College, 6511 Princess Garden Parkway, Lanham, MD 20706-3599

## Washington College
**Chestertown, Maryland**
www.washcoll.edu

CB member
CB code: 5888

- Private 4-year liberal arts college
- Residential campus in small town
- 1,268 degree-seeking undergraduates: 59% women, 5% African American, 2% Asian American, 1% Hispanic American, 2% international
- 58 degree-seeking graduate students
- 72% of applicants admitted
- SAT or ACT (ACT writing optional), application essay required
- 79% graduate within 6 years; 30% enter graduate study

**General.** Founded in 1782. Regionally accredited. **Degrees:** 293 bachelor's awarded; master's offered. **Location:** 70 miles from Baltimore, 75 miles from Washington, DC. **Calendar:** Semester, limited summer session. **Full-time faculty:** 87 total; 93% have terminal degrees, 13% minority, 37% women. **Part-time faculty:** 66 total; 44% have terminal degrees, 12% minority, 50% women. **Class size:** 67% < 20, 31% 20-39, 1% 40-49, less than 1% 50-99. **Special facilities:** Center for the Study of the American Experience, Center for the Environment and Society.

**Freshman class profile.** 4,498 applied, 3,240 admitted, 378 enrolled.

| Mid 50% test scores | | | |
|---|---|---|---|
| SAT critical reading: | 520-620 | Rank in top quarter: | 71% |
| SAT math: | 510-610 | Rank in top tenth: | 30% |
| SAT writing: | 520-620 | Return as sophomores: | 84% |
| ACT composite: | 22-29 | Out-of-state: | 50% |
| GPA 3.75 or higher: | 30% | Live on campus: | 98% |
| GPA 3.50-3.74: | 22% | International: | 2% |
| GPA 3.0-3.49: | 28% | Fraternities: | 6% |
| GPA 2.0-2.99: | 20% | Sororities: | 12% |

**Basis for selection.** High school program and grades, class rank, test scores, recommendations important, extracurricular activities considered. Interview recommended. **Homeschooled:** Interview required.

**High school preparation.** College-preparatory program required. 16 units required; 20 recommended. Required and recommended units include English 4, mathematics 3-4, social studies 2-4, history 2, science 3-4 (laboratory 2-3) and foreign language 2-4.

**2009-2010 Annual costs.** Tuition/fees: $35,350. Room/board: $7,460. Books/supplies: $1,250. Personal expenses: $1,500.

**2009-2010 Financial aid. Need-based:** 300 full-time freshmen applied for aid; 219 were judged to have need; 219 of these received aid. Average need met was 81%. Average scholarship/grant was $21,904; average loan $4,087. 77% of total undergraduate aid awarded as scholarships/grants, 23% as loans/jobs. **Non-need-based:** Awarded to 426 full-time undergraduates, including 140 freshmen. Scholarships awarded for academics.

**Application procedures. Admission:** Priority date 2/15; deadline 3/1 (postmark date). $55 fee, may be waived for applicants with need. Admission notification on a rolling basis beginning on or about 10/15. Must reply by May 1 or within 2 week(s) if notified thereafter. Applicants applying after February 15 may be wait-listed. **Financial aid:** Priority date 2/15; no closing date. FAFSA, institutional form required. Applicants notified on a rolling basis starting 2/1; must reply by 5/1.

**Academics. Special study options:** Combined bachelor's/graduate degree, cross-registration, double major, dual enrollment of high school students, exchange student, honors, independent study, internships, liberal arts/career combination, student-designed major, study abroad, teacher certification program, Washington semester. **Credit/placement by examination:** AP, CLEP, IB, institutional tests. **Support services:** Learning center, reduced course load, study skills assistance, tutoring, writing center.

**Majors. Area/ethnic studies:** American. **Biology:** General. **Business:** General. **Computer sciences:** Computer science. **Conservation:** Environmental studies. **Education:** General. **Foreign languages:** French, German, Spanish. **History:** General. **Interdisciplinary:** Math/computer science, neuroscience. **Liberal arts:** Arts/sciences, humanities. **Philosophy/religion:** Philosophy. **Physical sciences:** Chemistry, physics. **Psychology:** General. **Social sciences:** Anthropology, economics, international relations, political science, sociology. **Visual/performing arts:** Art, dramatic. **Other:** Interdisciplinary studies.

**Most popular majors.** Biology 9%, business/marketing 14%, English 13%, history 7%, liberal arts 6%, psychology 12%, social sciences 19%.

**Computing on campus.** 200 workstations in dormitories, library, computer center, student center. Dormitories wired for high-speed internet access and linked to campus network. Commuter students can connect to campus network. Online course registration, online library, helpline, repair service, student web hosting, wireless network available.

**Student life. Freshman orientation:** Mandatory. Preregistration for classes offered. Thursday - Sunday before classes begin. **Housing:** Guaranteed on-campus for freshmen. Coed dorms, single-sex dorms, special housing for disabled, fraternity/sorority housing, wellness housing available. $200 nonrefundable deposit, deadline 6/1. **Activities:** Bands, campus ministries, choral groups, dance, drama, international student organizations, literary magazine, music ensembles, Model UN, radio station, student government, student newspaper, College Republicans, Christian Fellowship, Amnesty International, Hillel, Black Student Alliance, Cleopatra's Daughters, College Democrats, Best Buddies, EROS, Newman Club.

**Athletics.** NCAA. **Intercollegiate:** Baseball M, basketball, field hockey W, lacrosse, rowing (crew), sailing, soccer, softball W, swimming, tennis, volleyball W. **Intramural:** Basketball, fencing, golf M, ice hockey M, racquetball, rugby, sailing, soccer, softball, squash, tennis, volleyball. **Team name:** Shoremen/Shorewomen.

**Student services.** Adult student services, alcohol/substance abuse counseling, career counseling, student employment services, financial aid counseling, health services, minority student services, personal counseling, placement for graduates, veterans' counselor. **Physically disabled:** Services for hearing impaired.

**Contact.** E-mail: adm.off@washcoll.edu
Phone: (410) 778-7700 Toll-free number: (800) 442-1782
Fax: (410) 778-7287
Kevin Coveney, Vice President for Admissions, Washington College, 300
Washington Avenue, Chestertown, MD 21620-1197

## Yeshiva College of the Nations Capital
### Silver Spring, Maryland

- Private 4-year rabbinical college for men affiliated with Jewish faith
- Residential campus in small city

**General.** Accredited by AARTS. **Calendar:** Continuous.

**Contact.** Phone: (301) 593-2534
Academic Dean, 1216 Arcola Avenue, Silver Spring, MD 20902

# Massachusetts

## American International College
**Springfield, Massachusetts**  CB member
www.aic.edu  CB code: 3002

- Private 4-year liberal arts college
- Residential campus in small city
- 1,729 degree-seeking undergraduates: 9% part-time, 58% women, 27% African American, 3% Asian American, 9% Hispanic American, 1% Native American, 2% international
- 1,672 graduate students
- 79% of applicants admitted
- SAT or ACT (ACT writing recommended) required

**General.** Founded in 1885. Regionally accredited. **Degrees:** 288 bachelor's, 3 associate awarded; master's, doctoral, professional offered. **ROTC:** Army, Air Force. **Location:** 90 miles from Boston; 27 miles from Hartford, Connecticut. **Calendar:** Semester, extensive summer session. **Full-time faculty:** 89 total; 47% have terminal degrees, 7% minority, 60% women. **Part-time faculty:** 234 total; 19% have terminal degrees, 5% minority, 55% women. **Class size:** 53% < 20, 42% 20-39, 1% 40-49, 2% 50-99, less than 1% >100. **Special facilities:** Cultural arts center, performing arts center, anatomical laboratory, communications media laboratory.

**Freshman class profile.** 1,469 applied, 1,162 admitted, 350 enrolled.

| Mid 50% test scores | | | |
|---|---|---|---|
| SAT critical reading: | 420-510 | Rank in top quarter: | 28% |
| SAT math: | 420-520 | Rank in top tenth: | 22% |
| SAT writing: | 420-500 | End year in good standing: | 87% |
| ACT composite: | 17-23 | Return as sophomores: | 63% |
| GPA 3.75 or higher: | 4% | Out-of-state: | 51% |
| GPA 3.50-3.74: | 8% | Live on campus: | 79% |
| GPA 3.0-3.49: | 38% | | |
| GPA 2.0-2.99: | 46% | | |

**Basis for selection.** Must have satisfied school's graduation requirements except for one course in English and one course in Social Studies. Must have unqualified approval of school counselor or principal and must possess strong academic skills and maturity necessary for success in college. Essay or personal statement recommended. **Homeschooled:** Statement describing homeschool structure and mission, transcript of courses and grades, interview, letter of recommendation (nonparent) required. **Learning Disabled:** Wechsler Adult Intelligence Scale, interview, diagnostic documentation recommended.

**High school preparation.** College-preparatory program recommended. 16 units required. Required and recommended units include English 4, mathematics 3-4, social studies 1-2, history 2, science 2-3 (laboratory 2), foreign language 1-2 and academic electives 4.

**2009-2010 Annual costs.** Tuition/fees: $25,500. Room/board: $10,560. Books/supplies: $1,500. Personal expenses: $1,000.

**2008-2009 Financial aid. Need-based:** 339 full-time freshmen applied for aid; 320 were judged to have need; 320 of these received aid. Average need met was 70%. Average scholarship/grant was $16,590; average loan $3,100. 60% of total undergraduate aid awarded as scholarships/grants, 40% as loans/jobs. **Non-need-based:** Awarded to 399 full-time undergraduates, including 144 freshmen. Scholarships awarded for academics, alumni affiliation, athletics, leadership.

**Application procedures. Admission:** Priority date 7/1; no deadline. $25 fee, may be waived for applicants with need. Admission notification on a rolling basis beginning on or about 12/1. Must reply by May 1 or within 2 week(s) if notified thereafter. **Financial aid:** Priority date 5/1; no closing date. FAFSA required. Applicants notified on a rolling basis starting 3/15; must reply by 5/1 or within 2 week(s) of notification.

**Academics. Special study options:** Accelerated study, combined bachelor's/graduate degree, cross-registration, distance learning, double major, dual enrollment of high school students, ESL, honors, independent study, internships, liberal arts/career combination, study abroad, teacher certification program, Washington semester, weekend college. **Credit/placement by examination:** AP, CLEP, IB, institutional tests. 30 credit hours maximum toward

bachelor's degree. **Support services:** Learning center, reduced course load, remedial instruction, study skills assistance, tutoring, writing center.

**Majors. Area/ethnic studies:** American. **Biology:** General, biochemistry. **Business:** General, accounting, business admin, finance, international, management science, managerial economics, marketing. **Communications:** Advertising, broadcast journalism, journalism, media studies, public relations, radio/tv. **Computer sciences:** Computer science, information systems. **Education:** Early childhood, elementary, middle, secondary, special. **Health:** Nursing (RN), predental, premedicine, preveterinary. **History:** General. **Interdisciplinary:** Accounting/computer science, biological/physical sciences. **Legal studies:** Prelaw. **Liberal arts:** Arts/sciences. **Parks/recreation:** General, sports admin. **Physical sciences:** Chemistry. **Protective services:** Criminal justice, law enforcement admin, police science. **Psychology:** General. **Social sciences:** Criminology, economics, international relations, political science, sociology.

**Most popular majors.** Business/marketing 24%, health sciences 26%, interdisciplinary studies 6%, psychology 7%, security/protective services 12%, social sciences 8%.

**Computing on campus.** 100 workstations in dormitories, library, computer center, student center. Dormitories wired for high-speed internet access and linked to campus network. Commuter students can connect to campus network. Online course registration, online library, helpline, wireless network available.

**Student life. Freshman orientation:** Available. Preregistration for classes offered. Three-day program in early September prior to start of Fall term. **Housing:** Guaranteed on-campus for all undergraduates. Coed dorms, single-sex dorms, apartments, wellness housing available. $100 fully refundable deposit, deadline 8/1. **Activities:** Pep band, campus ministries, choral groups, dance, drama, international student organizations, literary magazine, musical theater, radio station, student government, student newspaper, Model Congress, minority student organizations, Partners, Best Buddies, Intervarsity Christian Fellowship, Young Professionals for International Cooperation.

**Athletics.** NCAA. **Intercollegiate:** Baseball M, basketball, cheerleading, cross-country, field hockey W, football (tackle) M, golf M, ice hockey M, lacrosse, soccer, softball W, tennis, track and field, volleyball W, wrestling M. **Intramural:** Basketball, football (non-tackle) M, skiing, soccer, softball, swimming, volleyball. **Team name:** Yellow Jackets.

**Student services.** Adult student services, alcohol/substance abuse counseling, chaplain/spiritual director, career counseling, services for economically disadvantaged, student employment services, financial aid counseling, health services, minority student services, personal counseling, placement for graduates, veterans' counselor, women's services. **Physically disabled:** Services for visually impaired. **Learning disabled:** Comprehensive services available.

**Contact.** E-mail: inquiry@aic.edu
Phone: (413) 205-3201 Toll-free number: (800) 242-3142
Fax: (413) 205-3051
Peter Miller, Vice President for Admission Services, American International College, 1000 State Street, Springfield, MA 01109

## Amherst College
**Amherst, Massachusetts**  CB member
www.amherst.edu  CB code: 3003

- Private 4-year liberal arts college
- Residential campus in large town
- 1,744 degree-seeking undergraduates: 50% women, 11% African American, 10% Asian American, 11% Hispanic American, 8% international
- 15% of applicants admitted
- SAT and SAT Subject Tests or ACT (ACT writing recommended), application essay required
- 95% graduate within 6 years

**General.** Founded in 1821. Regionally accredited. **Degrees:** 419 bachelor's awarded. **ROTC:** Air Force. **Location:** 90 miles from Boston, 150 miles from New York City. **Calendar:** Semester. **Full-time faculty:** 203 total; 19% minority, 42% women. **Part-time faculty:** 21 total; 14% minority, 43% women. **Class size:** 70% < 20, 23% 20-39, 4% 40-49, 2% 50-99, less than 1% >100. **Special facilities:** Recital hall, observatory, planetarium, center for Russian culture, Dickinson homestead, natural history museum, fine arts museum, center for community engagement.

**Freshman class profile.** 7,745 applied, 1,144 admitted, 438 enrolled.

| Mid 50% test scores | | | |
|---|---|---|---|
| SAT critical reading: | 660-760 | Rank in top quarter: | 95% |
| SAT math: | 660-760 | Rank in top tenth: | 79% |
| SAT writing: | 670-760 | Out-of-state: | 90% |
| ACT composite: | 28-33 | Live on campus: | 100% |
| | | International: | 10% |

**Basis for selection.** Grades, test scores, essays, recommendations, independent work, quality of individual's secondary school program, achievements outside of classroom most important.

**High school preparation.** College-preparatory program recommended. Recommended units include English 4, mathematics 4, social studies 2, history 2, science 3 (laboratory 1) and foreign language 4.

**2009-2010 Annual costs.** Tuition/fees: $38,928. Health Insurance (waivable): $950. Room/board: $10,150. Books/supplies: $1,000. Personal expenses: $1,700.

**2008-2009 Financial aid.** All financial aid based on need. 249 full-time freshmen applied for aid; 224 were judged to have need; 224 of these received aid. Average need met was 100%. Average scholarship/grant was $36,075; average loan $2,375. 95% of total undergraduate aid awarded as scholarships/grants, 5% as loans/jobs.

**Application procedures.** Admission: Closing date 1/1 (postmark date). $60 fee, may be waived for applicants with need. Admission notification 4/1. Must reply by 5/1. Financial aid: Priority date 2/15; no closing date. FAFSA, CSS PROFILE required. Applicants notified by 4/1; must reply by 5/1.

**Academics.** First-year students must choose 1 seminar from range of 20 special topics, often interdisciplinary. No core curriculum, no distribution requirements. Students select major at end of sophomore year. **Special study options:** Cross-registration, double major, exchange student, honors, independent study, internships, student-designed major, study abroad, teacher certification program. Member of 5-college consortium. **Credit/placement by examination:** AP, CLEP, IB, institutional tests. **Support services:** Study skills assistance, tutoring, writing center.

**Majors. Area/ethnic studies:** African, African-American, American, Asian, Central/Eastern European, European, Western European, women's. **Biology:** General. **Computer sciences:** Computer science. **Foreign languages:** Ancient Greek, classics, French, German, Latin, Russian, Spanish. **History:** General. **Interdisciplinary:** Math/computer science, neuroscience. **Legal studies:** General. **Math:** General. **Philosophy/religion:** Philosophy, religion. **Physical sciences:** Astronomy, chemistry, geology, physics. **Psychology:** General. **Social sciences:** Anthropology, economics, political science, sociology. **Visual/performing arts:** Dance, dramatic, studio arts.

**Most popular majors.** Biology 7%, English 9%, foreign language 9%, history 6%, physical sciences 8%, psychology 7%, social sciences 28%, visual/performing arts 7%.

**Computing on campus.** 230 workstations in library, computer center, student center. Dormitories wired for high-speed internet access and linked to campus network. Commuter students can connect to campus network. Helpline, repair service, wireless network available.

**Student life. Freshman orientation:** Mandatory. Eight-day orientation with events planned by student groups and cultural organizations. **Housing:** Guaranteed on-campus for all undergraduates. Coed dorms, cooperative housing, wellness housing available. Language and other theme houses available including French/Spanish, Russian/German, Latino, African American, health and wellness house, and arts house. Men's and women's floors available to all students. **Activities:** Jazz band, choral groups, dance, drama, film society, international student organizations, literary magazine, music ensembles, Model UN, musical theater, opera, radio station, student government, student newspaper, symphony orchestra, Hillel, service organization, Christian association, Newman club, black student union, Asian student association, Cambodian family tutoring, LaCausa, Christian Fellowship, Korean American students association.

**Athletics.** NCAA. **Intercollegiate:** Baseball M, basketball, cross-country, diving, field hockey W, football (tackle) M, golf, ice hockey, lacrosse, soccer, softball W, squash, swimming, tennis, track and field, volleyball W. **Intramural:** Badminton, basketball, football (non-tackle), golf, ice hockey, soccer, softball, squash, table tennis, tennis, volleyball. **Team name:** Lord Jeffs.

**Student services.** Alcohol/substance abuse counseling, chaplain/spiritual director, career counseling, services for economically disadvantaged, student employment services, financial aid counseling, health services, minority student services, personal counseling, placement for graduates, women's services. **Physically disabled:** Services for visually, speech, hearing impaired.

**Contact.** E-mail: admission@amherst.edu
Phone: (413) 542-2328 Fax: (413) 542-2040
Katharine Fretwell, Director of Admission & Senior Associate Dean of Admission, Amherst College, PO Box 5000, Amherst, MA 01002-5000

## Anna Maria College
**Paxton, Massachusetts** — CB member
www.annamaria.edu — CB code: 3005

- Private 4-year liberal arts college affiliated with Roman Catholic Church
- Residential campus in small town
- 1,168 degree-seeking undergraduates: 18% part-time, 51% women, 8% African American, 1% Asian American, 6% Hispanic American, 1% Native American
- 371 degree-seeking graduate students
- 71% of applicants admitted
- SAT or ACT (ACT writing optional) required
- 55% graduate within 6 years

**General.** Founded in 1946. Regionally accredited. **Degrees:** 162 bachelor's, 14 associate awarded; master's offered. **ROTC:** Air Force. **Location:** 8 miles from Worcester, 40 miles from Boston. **Calendar:** Semester, limited summer session. **Full-time faculty:** 52 total; 60% have terminal degrees, 64% women. **Part-time faculty:** 147 total; 22% have terminal degrees, 43% women. **Class size:** 65% < 20, 35% 20-39. **Special facilities:** Nature trails, arts building.

**Freshman class profile.** 2,042 applied, 1,441 admitted, 373 enrolled.

| Mid 50% test scores | | | |
|---|---|---|---|
| SAT critical reading: | 400-500 | GPA 3.50-3.74: | 6% |
| SAT math: | 390-500 | GPA 3.0-3.49: | 18% |
| SAT writing: | 380-490 | GPA 2.0-2.99: | 72% |
| ACT composite: | 18-21 | Return as sophomores: | 62% |
| GPA 3.75 or higher: | 2% | Out-of-state: | 25% |
| | | Live on campus: | 84% |

**Basis for selection.** High school record most important, followed by test scores, recommendations, school and community activities, interview. Audition required of music majors; portfolio required of art majors, essays required of nursing and transfer students.

**High school preparation.** College-preparatory program recommended. 21 units required. Required units include English 4, mathematics 3, social studies 2, history 2, science 3 (laboratory 1), foreign language 2 and academic electives 4.

**2009-2010 Annual costs.** Tuition/fees: $26,620. Annual tuition for music program: $27,588. Room/board: $9,730. Books/supplies: $800. Personal expenses: $1,200.

**2009-2010 Financial aid. Non-need-based:** Scholarships awarded for academics, alumni affiliation, music/drama, religious affiliation, state residency.

**Application procedures. Admission:** Priority date 3/1; no deadline. $40 fee, may be waived for applicants with need, free for online applicants. Admission notification on a rolling basis. **Financial aid:** Priority date 3/1; no closing date. FAFSA required. Applicants notified on a rolling basis starting 4/1; must reply within 4 week(s) of notification.

**Academics. Special study options:** Accelerated study, combined bachelor's/graduate degree, cooperative education, cross-registration, double major, honors, independent study, internships, liberal arts/career combination, student-designed major, study abroad, teacher certification program, Washington semester. Member of 13-college Worcester Consortium. **Credit/placement by examination:** AP, CLEP, institutional tests. 30 credit hours maximum toward bachelor's degree. **Support services:** Learning center, reduced course load, remedial instruction, study skills assistance, tutoring, writing center.

**Majors. Business:** Business admin, management information systems. **Communications:** Media studies. **Computer sciences:** General. **Conservation:** Environmental science. **Education:** Art, elementary, English, history, kindergarten/preschool, music. **Foreign languages:** Spanish. **Health:** Art therapy, health services, music therapy, nursing (RN). **History:** General. **Legal studies:** Paralegal. **Liberal arts:** Arts/sciences. **Parks/recreation:** Sports admin. **Protective services:** Criminal justice, firefighting. **Psychology:** General. **Public administration:** Human services, policy analysis, social work. **Social sciences:** Political science, sociology. **Theology:** Theology. **Visual/performing arts:** Art, graphic design, music performance. **Other:** Related humanities.

**Most popular majors.** Business/marketing 13%, health sciences 12%, public administration/social services 19%, security/protective services 28%.

**Computing on campus.** 94 workstations in dormitories, library, computer center, student center. Dormitories wired for high-speed internet access and linked to campus network. Online course registration, online library, wireless network available.

**Student life. Freshman orientation:** Mandatory. Preregistration for classes offered. **Housing:** Guaranteed on-campus for freshmen. Coed dorms, special housing for disabled, wellness housing available. $300 fully refundable deposit, deadline 5/1. **Activities:** Bands, campus ministries, choral groups, dance, drama, music ensembles, musical theater, student government, student newspaper.

**Athletics.** NCAA. **Intercollegiate:** Baseball M, basketball, cross-country, field hockey W, football (tackle) M, golf, lacrosse, soccer, softball W, tennis, volleyball W. **Intramural:** Baseball, basketball, football (non-tackle), volleyball. **Team name:** Amcats.

**Student services.** Alcohol/substance abuse counseling, chaplain/spiritual director, career counseling, student employment services, financial aid counseling, health services, minority student services, personal counseling, placement for graduates. **Physically disabled:** Services for visually, speech, hearing impaired.

**Contact.** E-mail: admission@annamaria.edu
Phone: (508) 849-3360 Toll-free number: (800) 344-4586 ext. 360
Fax: (508) 849-3362
Meghan McDonough, Director of Admissions, Anna Maria College, 50 Sunset Lane, Box O, Paxton, MA 01612-1198

---

## Art Institute of Boston at Lesley University
**Boston, Massachusetts**
www.aiboston.edu                          CB code: 3777

- Private 4-year visual arts college
- Residential campus in very large city
- 517 degree-seeking undergraduates
- 33 graduate students
- SAT or ACT (ACT writing optional), application essay, interview required
- 62% graduate within 6 years

**General.** Regionally accredited. One of two undergraduate institutions within Lesley University. **Degrees:** 125 bachelor's awarded; master's offered. **Location:** Downtown. **Calendar:** Semester, limited summer session. **Full-time faculty:** 73 total; 84% have terminal degrees, 15% minority, 58% women. **Part-time faculty:** 185 total; 24% have terminal degrees, 58% women. **Class size:** 77% < 20, 22% 20-39, less than 1% 40-49, less than 1% 50-99. **Special facilities:** Animation lab, clay studio, wood-working studio, print-making studio, photo lab, digital-printing lab.

### Freshman class profile.

| Mid 50% test scores | | | |
|---|---|---|---|
| SAT critical reading: | 470-600 | GPA 3.0-3.49: | 34% |
| SAT math: | 450-580 | GPA 2.0-2.99: | 46% |
| SAT writing: | 470-600 | Rank in top quarter: | 43% |
| ACT composite: | 20-26 | Rank in top tenth: | 14% |
| GPA 3.75 or higher: | 3% | Out-of-state: | 48% |
| GPA 3.50-3.74: | 13% | Live on campus: | 85% |

**Basis for selection.** Admission based on art portfolio, academic record, test scores, personal interview, essay, extracurricular activities, and letters of recommendation. Portfolios required.

**High school preparation.** College-preparatory program required. 4 units required; 14 recommended. Required and recommended units include English 4, mathematics 1, social studies 2, history 2, science 1, foreign language 1, computer science 2 and visual/performing arts 2.

**2010-2011 Annual costs.** Tuition/fees: $27,600. Room/board: $12,800. Books/supplies: $1,575. Personal expenses: $1,580.

**2009-2010 Financial aid. Need-based:** Average need met was 74%. Average scholarship/grant was $15,193; average loan $3,715. 64% of total undergraduate aid awarded as scholarships/grants, 36% as loans/jobs. **Non-need-based:** Scholarships awarded for academics, art, leadership, minority status.

**Application procedures. Admission:** Priority date 2/15; no deadline. $40 fee, may be waived for applicants with need, free for online applicants. Admission notification on a rolling basis beginning on or about 12/15. Must reply by May 1 or within 2 week(s) if notified thereafter. **Financial aid:** Priority date 2/15; no closing date. FAFSA required. Applicants notified on a rolling basis starting 2/15.

**Academics. Special study options:** Accelerated study, combined bachelor's/graduate degree, cross-registration, distance learning, double major, dual enrollment of high school students, exchange student, honors, independent study, internships, liberal arts/career combination, New York semester, student-designed major, study abroad, teacher certification program. Studio courses. **Credit/placement by examination:** AP, CLEP, SAT, ACT, institutional tests. **Support services:** Learning center, pre-admission summer program, reduced course load, study skills assistance, tutoring, writing center.

**Majors. Education:** Art. **Visual/performing arts:** General, art, art history/conservation, commercial photography, commercial/advertising art, drawing, graphic design, illustration, painting, photography, printmaking, studio arts.

**Most popular majors.** Business/marketing 7%, education 9%, liberal arts 37%, psychology 14%, visual/performing arts 27%.

**Computing on campus.** 80 workstations in dormitories, library, computer center, student center. Dormitories wired for high-speed internet access and linked to campus network. Commuter students can connect to campus network. Online course registration, online library, helpline, repair service, student web hosting, wireless network available.

**Student life. Freshman orientation:** Mandatory. Preregistration for classes offered. **Housing:** Coed dorms, single-sex dorms available. $300 nonrefundable deposit, deadline 5/1. Victorian houses and suite-style residence available. **Activities:** Campus ministries, choral groups, dance, drama, international student organizations, literary magazine, musical theater, student government, student newspaper, peer advisors, ski club, international student association, student gallery committee, literary journal, Prism, women for social justice.

**Athletics.** NCAA. **Intercollegiate:** Baseball M, basketball, cross-country, soccer, softball W, tennis, volleyball. **Team name:** Lesley Lynx.

**Student services.** Adult student services, alcohol/substance abuse counseling, chaplain/spiritual director, career counseling, student employment services, financial aid counseling, health services, minority student services, personal counseling, placement for graduates, women's services. **Physically disabled:** Services for visually, speech, hearing impaired.

**Contact.** E-mail: admissions@aiboston.edu
Phone: (617) 585-6710 Toll-free number: (800) 773-0494 ext. 6710
Fax: (617) 585-6720
Bob Gielow, Director of Operations, Art Institute of Boston at Lesley University, 700 Beacon Street, Boston, MA 02215-2598

---

## Assumption College
**Worcester, Massachusetts**                  CB member
www.assumption.edu                            CB code: 3009

- Private 4-year liberal arts college affiliated with Roman Catholic Church
- Residential campus in small city
- 2,114 degree-seeking undergraduates: 58% women, 2% African American, 1% Asian American, 3% Hispanic American, 1% international
- 436 degree-seeking graduate students
- 79% of applicants admitted
- Application essay required
- 66% graduate within 6 years; 23% enter graduate study

**General.** Founded in 1904. Regionally accredited. Students may register for courses at 11 area colleges. Volunteer programs available: comprehensive 2-week programs in Mexico and Puerto Rico, 1-week spring break programs in various locations. **Degrees:** 443 bachelor's awarded; master's offered. **ROTC:** Army, Air Force. **Location:** 45 miles from Boston. **Calendar:** Semester, limited summer session. **Full-time faculty:** 154 total; 93% have terminal degrees, 6% minority, 42% women. **Part-time faculty:** 70 total; 60% have terminal degrees, 11% minority, 49% women. **Class size:** 47% < 20, 52% 20-39, less than 1% 40-49. **Special facilities:** French institute (academic research center for study of Francophone questions).

**Freshman class profile.** 3,719 applied, 2,947 admitted, 515 enrolled.

| Mid 50% test scores | | GPA 2.0-2.99: | 1% |
|---|---|---|---|
| SAT critical reading: | 480-580 | Rank in top quarter: | 44% |
| SAT math: | 490-590 | Rank in top tenth: | 14% |
| ACT composite: | 20-25 | End year in good standing: | 96% |
| GPA 3.75 or higher: | 4% | Return as sophomores: | 81% |
| GPA 3.50-3.74: | 28% | Out-of-state: | 38% |
| GPA 3.0-3.49: | 67% | Live on campus: | 95% |

**Basis for selection.** School achievement most important, followed by class rank in top 40%, extracurricular activities, interview, recommendations. **Homeschooled:** Statement describing homeschool structure and mission, letter of recommendation (nonparent) required.

**High school preparation.** College-preparatory program required. 18 units required. Required units include English 4, mathematics 3, history 2, science 2, foreign language 2 and academic electives 5.

**2009-2010 Annual costs.** Tuition/fees: $30,171. Room/board: $10,070. Books/supplies: $1,000. Personal expenses: $1,000.

**2009-2010 Financial aid. Need-based:** 468 full-time freshmen applied for aid; 400 were judged to have need; 400 of these received aid. Average need met was 70%. Average scholarship/grant was $16,000; average loan $3,430. 68% of total undergraduate aid awarded as scholarships/grants, 32% as loans/jobs. **Non-need-based:** Awarded to 572 full-time undergraduates, including 146 freshmen. Scholarships awarded for academics, athletics.

**Application procedures. Admission:** Closing date 2/15 (postmark date). $50 fee, may be waived for applicants with need. Admission notification 5/1. Admission notification on a rolling basis. Must reply by May 1 or within 2 week(s) if notified thereafter. **Financial aid:** Closing date 2/15. FAFSA required. Applicants notified on a rolling basis starting 2/16; must reply by 5/1.

**Academics. Special study options:** Combined bachelor's/graduate degree, cross-registration, double major, honors, independent study, internships, semester at sea, student-designed major, study abroad, teacher certification program, Washington semester. Worcester Consortium gerontology studies program; 3-2 engineering program (BA/BS) with Worcester Polytechnic Institute. **Credit/placement by examination:** AP, CLEP, IB, institutional tests. **Support services:** Learning center, study skills assistance, tutoring, writing center.

**Majors. Area/ethnic studies:** Latin American. **Biology:** General, biotechnology. **Business:** Accounting, business admin, international, marketing. **Communications:** Organizational. **Computer sciences:** General. **Conservation:** Environmental science. **Foreign languages:** General, classics, French, Italian, Spanish. **History:** General. **Interdisciplinary:** Global studies. **Math:** General. **Philosophy/religion:** Philosophy. **Physical sciences:** Chemistry. **Psychology:** General. **Social sciences:** Economics, political science, sociology. **Theology:** Theology. **Visual/performing arts:** General. **Other:** Human services and rehabilitation studies.

**Most popular majors.** Biology 8%, business/marketing 24%, communications/journalism 10%, English 7%, history 6%, psychology 11%, social sciences 10%.

**Computing on campus.** 315 workstations in dormitories, library, computer center, student center. Dormitories wired for high-speed internet access and linked to campus network. Commuter students can connect to campus network. Online course registration, online library, helpline, repair service, student web hosting, wireless network available.

**Student life. Freshman orientation:** Mandatory, $265 fee. Preregistration for classes offered. Two-day program in June includes choosing rooms, testing, scheduling fall courses, meeting faculty, workshops. **Housing:** Guaranteed on-campus for all undergraduates. Coed dorms, single-sex dorms, special housing for disabled, wellness housing available. Freshman dorms, substance-free dorms, living/learning center available. **Activities:** Bands, campus ministries, choral groups, drama, film society, literary magazine, musical theater, student government, student newspaper, TV station, ALANA network, College Democrats, College Republicans, student volunteer organization, students advocating change, student health network, service program, Omicron Delta Kappa leadership circle, retreat programs.

**Athletics.** NCAA. **Intercollegiate:** Baseball M, basketball, cross-country, field hockey W, football (tackle) M, golf M, ice hockey M, lacrosse, rowing (crew) W, soccer, softball W, swimming W, tennis, track and field, volleyball W. **Intramural:** Basketball, football (non-tackle) M, golf, ice hockey, racquetball, soccer, softball, volleyball. **Team name:** Greyhounds.

**Student services.** Alcohol/substance abuse counseling, chaplain/spiritual director, career counseling, student employment services, financial aid counseling, health services, minority student services, personal counseling, placement for graduates. **Physically disabled:** Services for visually, speech, hearing impaired.

**Contact.** E-mail: admiss@assumption.edu
Phone: (508) 767-7285 Toll-free number: (866) 477-7776
Fax: (508) 799-4412
Evan Lipp, Vice President for Enrollment Management, Assumption College, 500 Salisbury Street, Worcester, MA 01609-1296

## Atlantic Union College
### South Lancaster, Massachusetts
www.auc.edu                                      CB code: 3010

- Private 4-year professional school affiliated with Seventh-day Adventists
- Residential campus in small town
- 431 degree-seeking undergraduates: 16% part-time, 68% women, 54% African American, 4% Asian American, 19% Hispanic American
- 59% of applicants admitted

**General.** Founded in 1882. Regionally accredited. **Degrees:** 68 bachelor's, 27 associate awarded; master's offered. **Location:** 45 miles from Boston. **Calendar:** Semester, limited summer session. **Full-time faculty:** 26 total; 62% have terminal degrees, 54% women. **Part-time faculty:** 46 total; 41% women. **Class size:** 81% < 20, 17% 20-39, 2% 40-49, less than 1% 50-99. **Special facilities:** Music conservatory.

**Freshman class profile.** 224 applied, 133 admitted, 89 enrolled.

| GPA 3.75 or higher: | 8% | GPA 2.0-2.99: | 45% |
|---|---|---|---|
| GPA 3.50-3.74: | 13% | Return as sophomores: | 58% |
| GPA 3.0-3.49: | 33% | | |

**Basis for selection.** School achievement record, interview, recommendations, test scores important. SAT or ACT recommended. Interview recommended for non-Seventh-day Adventists. Audition required of music majors. Portfolio recommended for art majors. **Homeschooled:** Transcript of courses and grades required. GED test score accepted in lieu of transcript.

**High school preparation.** 14 units required. Required and recommended units include English 4, mathematics 3, social studies 2, science 2 (laboratory 1), foreign language 2 and computer science 1.

**2010-2011 Annual costs.** Tuition/fees (projected): $17,066. Room/board: $5,150. Books/supplies: $1,000. Personal expenses: $2,300.

**2009-2010 Financial aid. Need-based:** Average need met was 67%. Average scholarship/grant was $6,325; average loan $3,695. 39% of total undergraduate aid awarded as scholarships/grants, 61% as loans/jobs. **Non-need-based:** Scholarships awarded for academics, art, leadership, music/drama.

**Application procedures. Admission:** Closing date 8/1. $25 fee, may be waived for applicants with need. Admission notification on a rolling basis. **Financial aid:** Priority date 3/1, closing date 9/16. FAFSA, institutional form required. Applicants notified on a rolling basis starting 3/1; must reply by 9/12 or within 2 week(s) of notification.

**Academics.** External degree program of directed independent study for those 25 and over. Master of education program available summer session only. **Special study options:** Accelerated study, combined bachelor's/graduate degree, cooperative education, cross-registration, distance learning, double major, dual enrollment of high school students, ESL, external degree, honors, independent study, internships, liberal arts/career combination, study abroad, teacher certification program. **Credit/placement by examination:** AP, CLEP, IB, institutional tests. 32 credit hours maximum toward bachelor's degree. **Support services:** Learning center, reduced course load, remedial instruction, study skills assistance, tutoring, writing center.

**Majors. Biology:** General. **Business:** Accounting, business admin. **Education:** Early childhood, elementary, secondary. **Health:** Nursing (RN). **Liberal arts:** Arts/sciences. **Philosophy/religion:** Religion. **Psychology:** General. **Theology:** Theology. **Visual/performing arts:** Studio arts.

**Computing on campus.** 84 workstations in dormitories, library, computer center. Dormitories linked to campus network. Commuter students can connect to campus network. Wireless network available.

**Student life. Freshman orientation:** Mandatory, $150 fee. Preregistration for classes offered. Program held one week before official registration. **Policies:** Religious observance required. **Housing:** Single-sex dorms, apartments available. $350 deposit, deadline 8/1. **Activities:** Concert band, campus ministries, choral groups, drama, music ensembles, student government, student newspaper, symphony orchestra, campus community outreach, Black Christian Union, Council of Hispanic students for Progressive Action, ministerial student association.

**Athletics. Intramural:** Cross-country, golf, gymnastics, racquetball, sailing, skiing, skin diving, softball, swimming, tennis, track and field, volleyball.

**Student services.** Chaplain/spiritual director, career counseling, student employment services, financial aid counseling, health services, personal counseling, placement for graduates.

**Contact.** E-mail: bordes.henry-saturne@auc.edu
Phone: (978) 368-2235 Toll-free number: (800) 282-2030
Fax: (978) 368-2015
Bordes Henry-Saturne, Director of Admissions, Atlantic Union College, Main Street, South Lancaster, MA 01561

## Babson College
**Babson Park, Massachusetts**                          **CB member**
**www.babson.edu**                                        **CB code: 3075**

- Private 4-year business college
- Residential campus in large town
- 1,898 degree-seeking undergraduates: 43% women, 5% African American, 13% Asian American, 8% Hispanic American, 22% international
- 1,517 degree-seeking graduate students
- 40% of applicants admitted
- SAT or ACT with writing, application essay required
- 91% graduate within 6 years

**General.** Founded in 1919. Regionally accredited. **Degrees:** 429 bachelor's awarded; master's offered. **ROTC:** Army, Naval, Air Force. **Location:** 14 miles from Boston. **Calendar:** Semester, limited summer session. **Full-time faculty:** 174 total; 88% have terminal degrees, 16% minority, 31% women. **Part-time faculty:** 94 total; 40% have terminal degrees, 5% minority, 32% women. **Class size:** 19% < 20, 67% 20-39, 11% 40-49, 3% 50-99. **Special facilities:** Entrepreneurship center, woman's leadership center, social entrepreneurship institute.

**Freshman class profile.** 4,150 applied, 1,675 admitted, 471 enrolled.

| Mid 50% test scores | | | |
|---|---|---|---|
| SAT critical reading: | 560-650 | Rank in top quarter: | 86% |
| SAT math: | 610-700 | Rank in top tenth: | 50% |
| SAT writing: | 560-670 | Return as sophomores: | 92% |
| ACT composite: | 25-29 | Out-of-state: | 79% |
| GPA 3.75 or higher: | 31% | Live on campus: | 99% |
| GPA 3.50-3.74: | 27% | International: | 26% |
| GPA 3.0-3.49: | 36% | Fraternities: | 15% |
| GPA 2.0-2.99: | 6% | Sororities: | 21% |

**Basis for selection.** Academic performance and level of course work (college preparation, honors, Advanced Placement) most important; followed by academic motivation, including interest in learning and willingness to challenge oneself; test scores; writing ability; involvement in cocurricular activities and/or work experience; leadership, creativity, enthusiasm. SAT Subject Tests recommended. **Homeschooled:** Statement describing homeschool structure and mission, transcript of courses and grades, state high school equivalency certificate, letter of recommendation (nonparent) required. Provide information about completed courses, schooling, testing, and diploma requirements.

**High school preparation.** College-preparatory program required. 20 units required. Required and recommended units include English 4, mathematics 4, social studies 2, history 2, science 4 (laboratory 3) and foreign language 4. Pre-calculus strongly recommended.

**2009-2010 Annual costs.** Tuition/fees: $37,824. Room/board: $12,500. Books/supplies: $1,000. Personal expenses: $900.

**2009-2010 Financial aid.** All financial aid based on need. 265 full-time freshmen applied for aid; 213 were judged to have need; 213 of these received aid. Average need met was 92%. Average scholarship/grant was $24,739; average loan $2,862. 82% of total undergraduate aid awarded as scholarships/grants, 18% as loans/jobs.

**Application procedures. Admission:** Priority date 11/1; deadline 1/15 (postmark date). $65 fee, may be waived for applicants with need. Admission notification 4/1. Must reply by 5/1. **Financial aid:** Closing date 2/15. FAFSA, CSS PROFILE required. Applicants notified by 4/1; must reply by 5/1.

**Academics. Special study options:** Accelerated study, combined bachelor's/graduate degree, cross-registration, exchange student, honors, independent study, internships, liberal arts/career combination, semester at sea, student-designed major, study abroad. **Credit/placement by examination:** AP, CLEP, IB, institutional tests. 63 credit hours maximum toward bachelor's degree. **Support services:** Reduced course load, study skills assistance, tutoring, writing center.

**Majors. Business:** General, accounting, accounting/business management, accounting/finance, auditing, business admin, communications, entrepreneurial studies, finance, international, international finance, international marketing, investments/securities, management information systems, management science, managerial economics, marketing, office management, operations, sales/distribution, small business admin, statistics. **Communications:** Advertising. **Computer sciences:** General, information systems. **Legal studies:** Prelaw.

**Computing on campus.** PC or laptop required. 290 workstations in dormitories, library, computer center, student center. Dormitories wired for high-speed internet access and linked to campus network. Commuter students can connect to campus network. Online course registration, online library, helpline, repair service, wireless network available.

**Student life. Freshman orientation:** Mandatory. Preregistration for classes offered. Three-day program preceding start of classes. **Policies:** First-year students required to live on campus unless commuting from home (must live within 25-mile radius of campus). **Housing:** Guaranteed on-campus for all undergraduates. Coed dorms, single-sex dorms, special housing for disabled, fraternity/sorority housing, wellness housing available. $500 partly refundable deposit, deadline 5/1. Cultural, nontraditional, suite style, single-sex floors, wings for women available. **Activities:** Jazz band, campus ministries, choral groups, dance, drama, film society, international student organizations, literary magazine, music ensembles, musical theater, radio station, student government, student newspaper, symphony orchestra, 68 student-run organizations available.

**Athletics. NCAA. Intercollegiate:** Baseball M, basketball, cross-country, diving, field hockey W, golf M, ice hockey M, lacrosse, skiing, soccer, softball W, swimming, tennis, track and field, volleyball W. **Intramural:** Basketball, football (non-tackle), ice hockey, racquetball, soccer, softball, squash, tennis, volleyball, water polo. **Team name:** Beavers.

**Student services.** Alcohol/substance abuse counseling, chaplain/spiritual director, career counseling, student employment services, financial aid counseling, health services, minority student services, personal counseling; placement for graduates, women's services. **Physically disabled:** Services for visually, speech, hearing impaired.

**Contact.** E-mail: ugradadmission@babson.edu
Phone: (781) 239-5522 Toll-free number: (800) 488-3696
Fax: (781) 239-4135
Grant Gosselin, Dean of Undergraduate Admission, Babson College, 231 Forest Street, Babson Park, MA 02457-0310

## Bard College at Simon's Rock
**Great Barrington, Massachusetts**
**www.simons-rock.edu**                                   **CB code: 3795**

- Private 4-year liberal arts college
- Residential campus in small town
- 421 degree-seeking undergraduates: 60% women
- 84% of applicants admitted
- Application essay, interview required

**General.** Founded in 1964. Regionally accredited. Provides students with the opportunity to begin college in a residential environment after completing the 10th or 11th grade. **Degrees:** 60 bachelor's, 125 associate awarded. **Location:** 135 miles from Boston, 132 miles from New York. **Calendar:** Semester. **Full-time faculty:** 43 total; 91% have terminal degrees, 7% minority, 42% women. **Part-time faculty:** 42 total; 40% have terminal degrees, 5% minority, 45% women. **Class size:** 94% < 20, 6% 20-39. **Special facilities:** Visual and performing arts center, environmental research center.

**Freshman class profile.** 332 applied, 280 admitted, 179 enrolled.

| Mid 50% test scores | | | |
|---|---|---|---|
| SAT critical reading: | 560-690 | GPA 2.0-2.99: | 27% |
| SAT math: | 530-680 | Rank in top quarter: | 82% |
| ACT composite: | 25-30 | Rank in top tenth: | 60% |
| GPA 3.75 or higher: | 31% | Return as sophomores: | 74% |
| GPA 3.50-3.74: | 24% | Out-of-state: | 90% |
| GPA 3.0-3.49: | 18% | Live on campus: | 93% |

**Basis for selection.** School achievement record, essays, recommendations (counselor and teacher), interview most important. Institutional testing used for math and foreign language placement. **Homeschooled:** Statement describing homeschool structure and mission, transcript of courses and grades, interview required.

**High school preparation.** 15 units recommended. Recommended units include English 2, mathematics 2, social studies 2, history 2, science 2 (laboratory 1), foreign language 2 and academic electives 2. Applicants who have completed 10th or 11th grade should have 2 or 3 years college-preparatory curriculum respectively.

**2009-2010 Annual costs.** Tuition/fees: $39,380. Annual health services fee of $640. Student activity fee $150. Room/board: $10,960. Books/supplies: $1,000. Personal expenses: $640.

**2009-2010 Financial aid. Need-based:** 139 full-time freshmen applied for aid; 118 were judged to have need; 112 of these received aid. Average need met was 77%. Average scholarship/grant was $19,325. 69% of total undergraduate aid awarded as scholarships/grants, 31% as loans/jobs. **Non-need-based:** Awarded to 291 full-time undergraduates, including 122 freshmen. Scholarships awarded for academics, alumni affiliation, minority status, state residency.

**Application procedures. Admission:** Priority date 5/1; no deadline. $50 fee, may be waived for applicants with need. Application must be submitted on paper. Admission notification on a rolling basis beginning on or about 4/15. **Financial aid:** Priority date 4/15; no closing date. FAFSA, CSS PROFILE required. Applicants notified on a rolling basis starting 4/15; must reply within 2 week(s) of notification.

**Academics.** Upper-class students may take courses at Bard College. **Special study options:** External degree, independent study, internships, student-designed major, study abroad. Globalization and International Affairs, undergraduate summer research fellows program with Rockefeller University, International Human Rights Exchange, 3/2 engineering program with Columbia University. **Credit/placement by examination:** AP, CLEP, institutional tests. 10 credit hours maximum toward associate degree, 10 toward bachelor's. Credit for Advanced Placement determined by individual divisions. **Support services:** Learning center, reduced course load, study skills assistance, tutoring, writing center.

**Majors. Area/ethnic studies:** African, African-American, American, Asian, Central/Eastern European, Chinese, East Asian, European, French, gay/lesbian, German, Latin American, regional, Russian/Slavic, South Asian, Southeast Asian, Spanish/Iberian, Western European, women's. **Biology:** General, ecology. **Communications technology:** Photo/film/video. **Computer sciences:** Computer science. **Conservation:** Environmental science, environmental studies. **Engineering:** General. **Foreign languages:** General, Arabic, Chinese, comparative lit, French, German, Germanic, Latin, linguistics, Spanish. **History:** American. **Interdisciplinary:** Math/computer science. **Liberal arts:** Arts/sciences. **Math:** General. **Philosophy/religion:** Philosophy. **Physical sciences:** Chemistry, physics. **Psychology:** General. **Social sciences:** General, anthropology, political science, sociology. **Visual/performing arts:** General, acting, art history/conservation, ceramics, cinematography, dance, dramatic, drawing, music history, music performance, music theory/composition, painting, photography, play/screenwriting, printmaking, sculpture, studio arts, theater history.

**Most popular majors.** Area/ethnic studies 11%, biology 16%, engineering/engineering technologies 7%, foreign language 11%, psychology 7%, social sciences 10%, visual/performing arts 12%.

**Computing on campus.** 72 workstations in dormitories, library, student center. Dormitories wired for high-speed internet access and linked to campus network. Commuter students can connect to campus network. Online library, helpline, repair service, student web hosting, wireless network available.

**Student life. Freshman orientation:** Mandatory, $500 fee. Preregistration for classes offered. One-week writing and thinking workshop held prior to start of semester. **Policies:** No alcohol, illegal drugs or weapons allowed on campus. **Housing:** Guaranteed on-campus for freshmen. Coed dorms, single-sex dorms available. **Activities:** Concert band, choral groups, dance, drama, international student organizations, literary magazine, music ensembles, Model UN, student government, student newspaper, black student union, Latino student union, international students club, Amnesty International, Bible study group, QueerSA, women's center.

**Athletics. Intercollegiate:** Basketball, cricket, cross-country, fencing, field hockey W, racquetball, soccer, softball, swimming. **Intramural:** Archery, basketball, cricket, cross-country, diving, fencing, field hockey W, handball, racquetball, skiing, soccer, softball, squash, swimming. **Team name:** Llamas.

**Student services.** Alcohol/substance abuse counseling, chaplain/spiritual director, career counseling, student employment services, financial aid counseling, health services, minority student services, personal counseling, placement for graduates, women's services.

**Contact.** E-mail: admit@simons-rock.edu
Phone: (413) 528-7312 Toll-free number: (800) 235-7186
Fax: (413) 541-0081
Mary Davidson, Dean of Admission and Student Affairs, Bard College at Simon's Rock, Office of Admission, Great Barrington, MA 01230-1990

## Bay Path College
**Longmeadow, Massachusetts**
www.baypath.edu                    CB code: 3078

- Private 4-year liberal arts college for women
- Residential campus in large town
- 1,481 degree-seeking undergraduates: 19% part-time, 100% women, 11% African American, 2% Asian American, 11% Hispanic American
- 553 degree-seeking graduate students
- 67% of applicants admitted
- SAT or ACT (ACT writing recommended) required
- 54% graduate within 6 years

**General.** Founded in 1897. Regionally accredited. Member of 8-college consortium. **Degrees:** 282 bachelor's, 48 associate awarded; master's offered. **ROTC:** Army, Air Force. **Location:** 5 miles from Springfield; 23 miles from Hartford, Connecticut. **Calendar:** Semester, limited summer session. **Full-time faculty:** 45 total. **Part-time faculty:** 180 total. **Class size:** 63% < 20, 37% 20-39, less than 1% 50-99. **Special facilities:** Academic development center, occupational therapy laboratory, business hall, career development center.

**Freshman class profile.** 853 applied, 575 admitted, 147 enrolled.

| Mid 50% test scores | | | |
|---|---|---|---|
| SAT critical reading: | 420-550 | GPA 3.0-3.49: | 29% |
| SAT math: | 410-530 | GPA 2.0-2.99: | 38% |
| SAT writing: | 420-540 | Rank in top quarter: | 43% |
| ACT composite: | 19-24 | Rank in top tenth: | 21% |
| GPA 3.75 or higher: | 22% | Return as sophomores: | 75% |
| GPA 3.50-3.74: | 11% | Out-of-state: | 57% |
| | | Live on campus: | 83% |

**Basis for selection.** High school transcript and performance, class rank, GPA, SAT or ACT, letters of recommendation, and essay. Interview and essay or personal statement recommended. **Homeschooled:** Statement describing homeschool structure and mission, transcript of courses and grades, state high school equivalency certificate, letter of recommendation (nonparent) required.

**High school preparation.** College-preparatory program recommended. 15 units required; 20 recommended. Required and recommended units include English 4, mathematics 3-4, social studies 2, history 1-2, science 2-3 (laboratory 2) and foreign language 2.

**2009-2010 Annual costs.** Tuition/fees: $24,530. Room/board: $10,035. Books/supplies: $1,000. Personal expenses: $900.

**2009-2010 Financial aid. Need-based:** 187 full-time freshmen applied for aid; 177 were judged to have need; 168 of these received aid. Average need met was 76%. Average scholarship/grant was $15,286; average loan $4,821. 69% of total undergraduate aid awarded as scholarships/grants, 31% as loans/jobs. **Non-need-based:** Awarded to 175 full-time undergraduates, including 27 freshmen. Scholarships awarded for academics, music/drama. **Additional information:** Opportunity Grant program for students whose family may be facing financial difficulties paying tuition resulting from economic conditions. Additional funding available in an endowment program to assist students who qualify.

**Application procedures. Admission:** Priority date 12/15; no deadline. $25 fee, may be waived for applicants with need, free for online applicants. Admission notification on a rolling basis beginning on or about 9/15. Must reply by May 1 or within 2 week(s) if notified thereafter. **Financial aid:** Priority date 3/1; no closing date. FAFSA required. Applicants notified on a rolling basis starting 3/1; must reply within 2 week(s) of notification.

**Academics. Special study options:** Accelerated study, combined bachelor's/graduate degree, cooperative education, cross-registration, distance learning, double major, ESL, exchange student, honors, independent study, internships, student-designed major, study abroad, teacher certification program, Washington semester, weekend college. **Credit/placement by examination:** AP, CLEP, IB, institutional tests. **Support services:** Learning center, study skills assistance, tutoring, writing center.

**Majors. Biology:** General, biotechnology. **Business:** General, business admin, marketing. **Education:** Early childhood, elementary. **Legal studies:** General, prelaw. **Liberal arts:** Arts/sciences. **Protective services:** Criminal justice. **Psychology:** General, child, forensic. **Visual/performing arts:** Interior design.

**Most popular majors.** Business/marketing 23%, legal studies 11%, liberal arts 33%, psychology 17%, security/protective services 14%.

**Computing on campus.** 214 workstations in dormitories, library, computer center, student center. Dormitories wired for high-speed internet access and linked to campus network. Commuter students can connect to campus network. Online course registration, online library, helpline, wireless network available.

**Student life. Freshman orientation:** Mandatory. Preregistration for classes offered. **Policies:** No smoking or alcohol in dormitories. **Housing:** Guaranteed on-campus for all undergraduates. $300 nonrefundable deposit, deadline 5/1. **Activities:** Choral groups, dance, drama, international student organizations, literary magazine, Model UN, musical theater, student government, student newspaper, interfaith council, Habitat for Humanity, women of culture, Alliance, Phi Beta Lambda.

**Athletics.** NCAA. **Intercollegiate:** Basketball W, cross-country W, field hockey W, soccer W, softball W, tennis W, volleyball W. **Intramural:** Lacrosse W, track and field W. **Team name:** Wildcats.

**Student services.** Adult student services, career counseling, student employment services, financial aid counseling, health services, minority student services, personal counseling, placement for graduates, women's services.

**Contact.** E-mail: admiss@baypath.edu
Phone: (413) 565-1000 ext. 1331 Toll-free
number: (800) 782-7284 ext. 1331 Fax: (413) 565-1105
Dawn Bryden, Director of Admissions, Bay Path College, 588
Longmeadow Street, Longmeadow, MA 01106

## Becker College
**Worcester, Massachusetts**
www.becker.edu

**CB member**
**CB code: 3079**

- Private 4-year liberal arts college
- Residential campus in small city
- 1,742 degree-seeking undergraduates: 18% part-time, 67% women
- 82% of applicants admitted
- SAT or ACT with writing required

**General.** Founded in 1887. Regionally accredited. Additional campus in Leicester. Member of Colleges of the Worcester Consortium. **Degrees:** 152 bachelor's, 112 associate awarded. **ROTC:** Army, Naval, Air Force. **Location:** 49 miles from Boston; 39 miles from Providence, Rhode Island. **Calendar:** Semester, limited summer session. **Full-time faculty:** 49 total; 69% women. **Part-time faculty:** 82 total; 62% women. **Class size:** 68% < 20, 31% 20-39, less than 1% 40-49, less than 1% 50-99. **Special facilities:** Veterinary clinic, on-site preschool and day-care facility, 96-acre off-campus stable for equine programs.

**Freshman class profile.** 1,902 applied, 1,555 admitted, 365 enrolled.

| Mid 50% test scores | | Rank in top quarter: | 40% |
|---|---|---|---|
| SAT critical reading: | 450-540 | Rank in top tenth: | 8% |
| SAT math: | 370-420 | Out-of-state: | 34% |
| ACT composite: | 12-20 | | |

**Basis for selection.** High school record, GPA, extracurricular activities important. Recommendations, interview considered. Additional prerequisites for nursing, veterinary technology, and veterinary science programs. Essay recommended. **Homeschooled:** Statement describing homeschool structure and mission, letter of recommendation (nonparent) required. Official transcript required from high school with which student is affiliated.

**High school preparation.** College-preparatory program required. Required and recommended units include English 4, mathematics 3, social studies 1, history 2 and science 2. 2 math including 1 algebra, 1 chemistry with lab, 1 biology with lab required for nursing, veterinary technician, veterinary science, pre-vet programs.

**2009-2010 Annual costs.** Tuition/fees: $24,780. Additional one-time charge of $285 for nursing program. Room/board: $9,760. Books/supplies: $1,000. Personal expenses: $1,170.

**2009-2010 Financial aid. Non-need-based:** Scholarships awarded for academics.

**Application procedures. Admission:** No deadline. $30 fee, may be waived for applicants with need. Admission notification on a rolling basis. Must reply by May 1 or within 4 week(s) if notified thereafter. **Financial aid:** Priority date 3/1; no closing date. FAFSA required. Applicants notified on a rolling basis starting 2/1; must reply within 2 week(s) of notification.

**Academics. Special study options:** Accelerated study, cross-registration, distance learning, dual enrollment of high school students, independent study, internships, liberal arts/career combination, study abroad, teacher certification program. **Credit/placement by examination:** AP, CLEP, IB, institutional tests. 30 credit hours maximum toward associate degree, 60 toward bachelor's. **Support services:** Learning center, reduced course load, remedial instruction, study skills assistance, tutoring, writing center.

**Majors. Biology:** General. **Business:** Accounting, business admin, hospitality admin, human resources, marketing, tourism/travel. **Communications technology:** General. **Computer sciences:** Networking. **Education:** Early childhood, elementary. **Health:** Nursing (RN), preveterinary, veterinary technology/assistant. **Legal studies:** General, prelaw. **Liberal arts:** Arts/sciences. **Parks/recreation:** Health/fitness, sports admin. **Protective services:** Criminal justice. **Psychology:** General. **Public administration:** Human services. **Visual/performing arts:** Commercial/advertising art, interior design.

**Most popular majors.** Business/marketing 58%, health sciences 7%, psychology 6%, visual/performing arts 18%.

**Computing on campus.** 155 workstations in dormitories, library, computer center. Dormitories wired for high-speed internet access and linked to campus network. Commuter students can connect to campus network. Online course registration, online library, helpline, wireless network available.

**Student life. Freshman orientation:** Mandatory. Preregistration for classes offered. **Housing:** Guaranteed on-campus for freshmen. Coed dorms, single-sex dorms, apartments, wellness housing available. $100 nonrefundable deposit. Substance-free dormitory and over-21 housing available. **Activities:** Choral groups, dance, drama, student government, student newspaper, campus community service club, international club, animal health club, business club, commuter club, early childhood education club, outdoors club, travel club, nursing club.

**Athletics.** NCAA. **Intercollegiate:** Baseball M, basketball, equestrian, field hockey W, football (tackle) M, golf M, ice hockey M, lacrosse, soccer, softball W, tennis, volleyball W. **Intramural:** Badminton, basketball, soccer, table tennis, volleyball. **Team name:** Hawks.

**Student services.** Adult student services, alcohol/substance abuse counseling, career counseling, student employment services, financial aid counseling, health services, on-campus daycare, personal counseling, placement for graduates. **Physically disabled:** Services for visually, speech, hearing impaired.

**Contact.** E-mail: admissions@beckercollege.edu
Phone: (508) 373-9400 Toll-free number: (877) 523-2537
Fax: (508) 890-1500
Michael Perron, Director of Admissions, Becker College, 61 Sever Street, Worcester, MA 01609

## Bentley University
**Waltham, Massachusetts**
www.bentley.edu

**CB member**
**CB code: 3096**

- Private 4-year business college
- Residential campus in small city
- 4,179 degree-seeking undergraduates: 5% part-time, 40% women, 3% African American, 7% Asian American, 5% Hispanic American, 9% international
- 1,378 degree-seeking graduate students
- 43% of applicants admitted
- SAT or ACT with writing, application essay required
- 88% graduate within 6 years; 24% enter graduate study

**General.** Founded in 1917. Regionally accredited. **Degrees:** 1,073 bachelor's, 2 associate awarded; master's, doctoral offered. **ROTC:** Army, Air Force. **Location:** 10 miles from Boston. **Calendar:** Semester, extensive summer session. **Full-time faculty:** 279 total; 82% have terminal degrees, 13% minority, 39% women. **Part-time faculty:** 178 total; 36% have terminal degrees, 8% minority, 41% women. **Class size:** 31% < 20, 69% 20-39, less than 1% 40-49. **Special facilities:** Academic technology center; alliance for ethics and social responsibility; business ethics center; international students and scholars center; languages and international collaboration center; marketing technology center; quantitative analysis center; international center; cyber law center; design and usability center; financial services center; library, media and culture labs and studio; service-learning center; trading room; arts and sciences center; accounting center; women's leadership institute.

**Freshman class profile.** 6,675 applied, 2,842 admitted, 949 enrolled.

| Mid 50% test scores | | | |
|---|---|---|---|
| SAT critical reading: | 540-630 | Return as sophomores: | 93% |
| SAT math: | 600-680 | Out-of-state: | 56% |
| SAT writing: | 550-640 | Live on campus: | 98% |
| ACT composite: | 25-28 | International: | 10% |
| Rank in top quarter: | 79% | Fraternities: | 10% |
| Rank in top tenth: | 38% | Sororities: | 10% |

**Basis for selection.** Decisions based on application with essay, secondary school transcript(s), standardized test scores, recommendations. Any supplemental information submitted by applicant will also be considered. Interviews recommended. **Homeschooled:** Statement describing homeschool structure and mission, transcript of courses and grades, letter of recommendation (nonparent) required. Interview strongly recommended.

**High school preparation.** College-preparatory program required. 19 units recommended. Recommended units include English 4, mathematics 4, social studies 3, science 3 (laboratory 3) and foreign language 3. 2 additional units English, math, social or lab science, or foreign language recommended.

**2009-2010 Annual costs.** Tuition/fees: $35,828. Room/board: $11,740. Books/supplies: $1,050. Personal expenses: $1,135.

**2008-2009 Financial aid. Need-based:** 752 full-time freshmen applied for aid; 479 were judged to have need; 477 of these received aid. Average need met was 94%. Average scholarship/grant was $20,801; average loan $4,498. 74% of total undergraduate aid awarded as scholarships/grants, 26% as loans/jobs. **Non-need-based:** Awarded to 1,264 full-time undergraduates, including 366 freshmen. Scholarships awarded for academics, athletics, leadership, minority status. **Additional information:** Deadlines for receipt of CSS PROFILE: early decision 12/1, early action and regular decision 2/1.

**Application procedures. Admission:** Closing date 1/15 (postmark date). $50 fee, may be waived for applicants with need. Admission notification 4/1. Must reply by 5/1. **Financial aid:** Closing date 2/1. FAFSA required. CSS PROFILE required if student is applying for institutional grants. Applicants notified on a rolling basis starting 3/25.

**Academics. Special study options:** Accelerated study, combined bachelor's/graduate degree, cross-registration, double major, honors, independent study, internships, liberal arts/career combination, semester at sea, student-designed major, study abroad. 5-year bachelor's/master's programs in business administration, accountancy, finance, marketing analytics, information technology, financial planning, taxation. **Credit/placement by examination:** AP, CLEP, IB, SAT, ACT, institutional tests. 30 credit hours maximum toward bachelor's degree. CLEP credit for French, German, Spanish not available to native speakers. Language exams require oral test with department. **Support services:** Learning center, reduced course load, study skills assistance, tutoring, writing center.

**Majors. Business:** General, accounting, business admin, communications, finance, managerial economics, marketing. **Computer sciences:** General. **History:** General. **Liberal arts:** Arts/sciences. **Math:** General. **Philosophy/religion:** Philosophy.

**Most popular majors.** Business/marketing 94%.

**Computing on campus.** PC or laptop required. 4,665 workstations in dormitories, library, computer center, student center. Dormitories wired for high-speed internet access and linked to campus network. Commuter students can connect to campus network. Online course registration, online library, helpline, repair service, student web hosting, wireless network available.

**Student life. Freshman orientation:** Available. Preregistration for classes offered. Three-day program, usually held in June; family members invited on last day. **Policies:** Academic honesty system, minimum GPA for student leaders. **Housing:** Guaranteed on-campus for all undergraduates. Coed dorms, special housing for disabled, apartments, wellness housing available. Global living floors available. **Activities:** Bands, campus ministries, choral groups, dance, drama, film society, international student organizations, literary magazine, music ensembles, Model UN, radio station, student government, student newspaper, TV station, black united body, South Asian student association, La Cultura Latina, People Respecting Individuality and Diversity Through Education, green society, Muslim students' association, Circle K, Habitat For Humanity, Hillel, Christian Fellowship.

**Athletics.** NCAA. **Intercollegiate:** Baseball M, basketball, cross-country, diving, field hockey W, football (tackle) M, golf M, ice hockey M, lacrosse, soccer, softball W, swimming, tennis, track and field, volleyball W. **Intramural:** Basketball, football (non-tackle) M, soccer, softball, volleyball. **Team name:** Falcons.

**Student services.** Adult student services, alcohol/substance abuse counseling, chaplain/spiritual director, career counseling, student employment services, financial aid counseling, health services, minority student services, personal counseling, placement for graduates, veterans' counselor, women's services. **Physically disabled:** Services for visually, speech, hearing impaired. **Learning disabled:** Comprehensive services available.

**Contact.** E-mail: ugadmission@bentley.edu
Phone: (781) 891-2244 Toll-free number: (800) 523-2354
Fax: (781) 891-3414
Erika Vardaro, Director of Admissions, Bentley University, 175 Forest Street, Waltham, MA 02452-4705

## Berklee College of Music
**Boston, Massachusetts**  CB member
**www.berklee.edu**  CB code: 3107

- Private 4-year music college
- Commuter campus in very large city
- 3,531 degree-seeking undergraduates: 8% part-time, 29% women, 8% African American, 4% Asian American, 8% Hispanic American, 20% international
- 42% of applicants admitted
- Application essay, interview required
- 47% graduate within 6 years

**General.** Founded in 1945. Regionally accredited. **Degrees:** 654 bachelor's awarded. **Calendar:** Semester, extensive summer session. **Full-time faculty:** 234 total; 17% minority, 21% women. **Part-time faculty:** 296 total; 20% minority, 30% women. **Class size:** 94% < 20, 6% 20-39, less than 1% 40-49, less than 1% 50-99. **Special facilities:** Performance center, student-run music venue and coffee house, music technology facilities and practice spaces, synthesizer laboratories, recording studios, film scoring laboratories, technology labs, media center.

**Freshman class profile.** 3,636 applied, 1,545 admitted, 863 enrolled.

| | | | |
|---|---|---|---|
| GPA 3.75 or higher: | 32% | Return as sophomores: | 79% |
| GPA 3.50-3.74: | 23% | Out-of-state: | 85% |
| GPA 3.0-3.49: | 33% | Live on campus: | 58% |
| GPA 2.0-2.99: | 11% | International: | 13% |

**Basis for selection.** Musical training and experience, recommendations, academic record, test scores, extracurricular music activities, interview important. Auditions required. **Homeschooled:** Statement describing homeschool structure and mission, state high school equivalency certificate required. **Learning Disabled:** Students with disabilities should contact Special Services Coordinator.

**High school preparation.** Recommended units include English 4, mathematics 1, history 1, science 1 (laboratory 1) and academic electives 6. Minimum 2 years recent formal musical study on principal instrument covering standard methods/materials and/or significant practical performance experience plus knowledge of written-music fundamentals normally required of all applicants.

**2009-2010 Annual costs.** Tuition/fees: $33,653. Required fees include one-time charge $2,950 for purchase of laptop, which all freshmen must purchase. Room/board: $15,080. Books/supplies: $470. Personal expenses: $2,378.

**2009-2010 Financial aid. Need-based:** Average need met was 31%. Average scholarship/grant was $5,979; average loan $4,647. 42% of total undergraduate aid awarded as scholarships/grants, 58% as loans/jobs.

**Application procedures. Admission:** Closing date 1/15 (postmark date). $150 fee, may be waived for applicants with need. Application must be submitted online. Admission notification 3/31. Must reply by May 1 or within 4 week(s) if notified thereafter. Applicants should submit completed application materials well in advance of deadline to ensure placement in desired entry class. **Financial aid:** Closing date 5/1. Applicants notified on a rolling basis starting 3/7; must reply within 2 week(s) of notification.

**Academics.** Bachelor's degree program includes 30 credits general education courses. Four-year professional diploma available (not including general education). **Special study options:** Cooperative education, cross-registration, distance learning, double major, dual enrollment of high school students, ESL, independent study, internships, student-designed major, study abroad, teacher certification program. ProArts Consortium with Boston Architectural Center, Boston Conservatory, Emerson College, Massachusetts College of Art, School of the Museum of Fine Arts. **Credit/placement by examination:** CLEP, institutional tests. 60 credit hours maximum toward bachelor's degree. **Support services:** Learning center, pre-admission summer program, tutoring, writing center.

**Majors. Health:** Music therapy. **Visual/performing arts:** Jazz, music management, music performance, music theory/composition, piano/organ, voice/opera. **Other:** Music business/management, Music synthesis.

**Most popular majors.** Business/marketing 17%, engineering/engineering technologies 17%, visual/performing arts 61%.

**Computing on campus.** PC or laptop required. 50 workstations in dormitories, library, computer center. Dormitories wired for high-speed internet access and linked to campus network. Online library, helpline, repair service, student web hosting, wireless network available.

**Student life. Freshman orientation:** Available. Series of events before and during registration week. **Housing:** Coed dorms available. $300 nonrefundable deposit. Residence space limited. **Activities:** Bands, choral groups, dance, film society, international student organizations, literary magazine, music ensembles, musical theater, radio station, student government, student newspaper, black student union, Christian Fellowship, Berklee Cares, women musicians' network, Latinos association, GLBT Allies at Berklee, Korean student association, Amnesty International.

**Athletics. Intramural:** Basketball, football (non-tackle), ice hockey, soccer. **Team name:** IceCats.

**Student services.** Career counseling, student employment services, minority student services, personal counseling, veterans' counselor. **Physically disabled:** Services for visually impaired.

**Contact.** E-mail: admissions@berklee.edu
Phone: (617) 747-2221 Toll-free number: (800) 237-5533
Fax: (617) 747-2047
Damien Bracken, Director of Admissions/OSSE, Berklee College of Music, 1140 Boylston Street, Boston, MA 02215

---

### Boston Architectural College
**Boston, Massachusetts**
www.the-bac.edu                                    CB code: 1168

- Private 6-year architecture and design college
- Commuter campus in very large city
- 636 degree-seeking undergraduates: 3% part-time, 32% women
- 511 degree-seeking graduate students

**General.** Founded in 1889. Regionally accredited. Program offers practice-based learning with simultaneous employment in field and academic study. **Degrees:** 39 bachelor's awarded; master's offered. **Location:** Downtown. **Calendar:** Semester, limited summer session. **Full-time faculty:** 1 total; 100% have terminal degrees, 100% women. **Part-time faculty:** 364 total; 100% have terminal degrees, 16% minority, 50% women. **Class size:** 96% < 20, less than 1% 20-39, 2% 40-49, less than 1% 50-99, less than 1% >100. **Special facilities:** On-campus gallery featuring exhibits of architectural and interior design interest, CAD lab, photography studio.

**Freshman class profile.**

| | | | |
|---|---|---|---|
| GPA 3.75 or higher: | 3% | Rank in top quarter: | 34% |
| GPA 3.50-3.74: | 14% | Rank in top tenth: | 11% |
| GPA 3.0-3.49: | 28% | Out-of-state: | 63% |
| GPA 2.0-2.99: | 46% | | |

**Basis for selection.** Open admission. Portfolio required for transfer credits for design courses.

**2009-2010 Annual costs.** Tuition/fees: $11,468. Academic Only program tuition is $15,340 plus $20 required fees. Books/supplies: $1,516. Personal expenses: $3,006.

**2009-2010 Financial aid. Need-based:** Average need met was 32%. Average scholarship/grant was $5,765; average loan $4,941. 15% of total undergraduate aid awarded as scholarships/grants, 85% as loans/jobs. **Non-need-based:** Scholarships awarded for academics, art, leadership.

**Application procedures. Admission:** Priority date 5/15; deadline 8/31 (receipt date). $50 fee, may be waived for applicants with need. Admission notification on a rolling basis beginning on or about 1/26. Must reply by May 1 or within 2 week(s) if notified thereafter. **Financial aid:** Priority date 4/15; no closing date. FAFSA required. Applicants notified on a rolling basis starting 3/30; must reply within 2 week(s) of notification.

**Academics.** Bachelor of architecture or interior design awarded after 6-year program of concurrent work and academic curriculum. Students usually transfer into program during second or third years. **Special study options:** Cross-registration, distance learning, independent study, internships, liberal arts/career combination. Member Professional Arts Consortium. **Credit/**

**placement by examination:** AP, CLEP, institutional tests. **Support services:** Learning center, tutoring, writing center.

**Majors. Architecture:** Architecture, environmental design, interior, landscape.

**Computing on campus.** 63 workstations in library, computer center. Commuter students can connect to campus network. Online library, helpline, wireless network available.

**Student life. Freshman orientation:** Mandatory. Preregistration for classes offered. Several dates; includes writing test. **Policies:** Campus code of conduct. **Housing:** Dormitory space, when available, at ProArts Consortium schools. **Activities:** Student government.

**Student services.** Adult student services, career counseling, student employment services, financial aid counseling, minority student services, veterans' counselor. **Physically disabled:** Services for visually, speech, hearing impaired.

**Contact.** E-mail: admissions@the-bac.edu
Phone: (617) 585-0123 Toll-free number: (877) 585-0100
Fax: (617) 585-0121
Richard Moyer, Director of Admissions, Boston Architectural College, 320 Newbury Street, Boston, MA 02115-2795

---

### Boston Baptist College
**Boston, Massachusetts**
www.boston.edu/

- Private 4-year Bible college affiliated with Baptist
- Very large city
- 121 degree-seeking undergraduates
- SAT or ACT required

**General.** Regionally accredited; also accredited by TRACS. **Degrees:** 23 bachelor's awarded. **Calendar:** Semester. **Full-time faculty:** 8 total. **Part-time faculty:** 29 total.

**Basis for selection.** Test scores, recommendation very important. **Homeschooled:** Letter of recommendation (nonparent) required.

**High school preparation.** College-preparatory program recommended.

**Application procedures. Admission:** No deadline. $40 fee, may be waived for applicants with need.

**Academics. Credit/placement by examination:** CLEP.

**Majors. Theology:** Bible.

**Contact.** E-mail: admissions@boston.edu
Phone: (617) 364-3510 ext. 217
Karen Fox, Director of Admissions, Boston Baptist College, 950 Metropolitan Avenue, Boston, MA 02136

---

### Boston College
**Chestnut Hill, Massachusetts**                    CB member
www.bc.edu                                          CB code: 3083

- Private 4-year university affiliated with Roman Catholic Church
- Residential campus in small city
- 9,171 degree-seeking undergraduates: 52% women, 5% African American, 10% Asian American, 8% Hispanic American, 3% international
- 4,960 graduate students
- 30% of applicants admitted
- SAT and SAT Subject Tests or ACT with writing, application essay required
- 91% graduate within 6 years; 27% enter graduate study

**General.** Founded in 1863. Regionally accredited. **Degrees:** 2,300 bachelor's awarded; master's, doctoral, professional offered. **ROTC:** Army, Naval, Air Force. **Location:** 6 miles from downtown Boston. **Calendar:** Semester, extensive summer session. **Full-time faculty:** 708 total; 98% have terminal degrees, 13% minority, 38% women. **Part-time faculty:** 615 total. **Class size:** 47% < 20, 37% 20-39, 8% 40-49, 5% 50-99, 2% >100. **Special facilities:** Observatory, theater, arts center, chemistry center.

**Freshman class profile.** 29,289 applied, 8,804 admitted, 2,171 enrolled.

| Mid 50% test scores | | Rank in top tenth: | 80% |
|---|---|---|---|
| SAT critical reading: | 610-700 | Return as sophomores: | 95% |
| SAT math: | 640-730 | Out-of-state: | 76% |
| SAT writing: | 630-720 | Live on campus: | 99% |
| ACT composite: | 29-32 | International: | 4% |
| Rank in top quarter: | 96% | | |

**Basis for selection.** Evidence of academic ability, intellectual curiosity, strength of character, motivation, creativity, energy, and promise for personal growth and development very important. Recommendations by counselors and teachers, required personal statement and extracurricular activities important. 2 SAT Subject Tests of student's choice required if SAT is submitted. Portfolio recommended for studio art majors. Students interested in music, theater, or dance encouraged to send examples of work via DVD or CD. **Learning Disabled:** May provide documentation of disability at option of applicant.

**High school preparation.** College-preparatory program recommended. 20 units recommended. Recommended units include English 4, mathematics 4, social studies 4, science 4 (laboratory 4) and foreign language 4. 4 combined social studies and history recommended. 2 laboratory science (including 1 chemistry) required of nursing applicants.

**2009-2010 Annual costs.** Tuition/fees: $39,130. Room/board: $11,840. Books/supplies: $900. Personal expenses: $1,000.

**2009-2010 Financial aid. Need-based:** 1,198 full-time freshmen applied for aid; 957 were judged to have need; 957 of these received aid. Average need met was 100%. Average scholarship/grant was $27,618; average loan $3,521. 78% of total undergraduate aid awarded as scholarships/grants, 22% as loans/jobs. **Non-need-based:** Awarded to 494 full-time undergraduates, including 134 freshmen. Scholarships awarded for academics, athletics, leadership, ROTC.

**Application procedures. Admission:** Closing date 1/1 (postmark date). $70 fee, may be waived for applicants with need. Admission notification 4/15. Must reply by 5/1. **Financial aid:** Priority date 2/1; no closing date. FAFSA, CSS PROFILE required. Applicants notified on a rolling basis starting 4/1.

**Academics. Special study options:** Accelerated study, combined bachelor's/graduate degree, cross-registration, distance learning, double major, ESL, exchange student, honors, independent study, internships, liberal arts/career combination, student-designed major, study abroad, teacher certification program, Washington semester. 3-2 program in engineering with Boston University; Tufts Medical School Early Acceptance Program. **Credit/placement by examination:** AP, CLEP, IB. 24 credit hours maximum toward bachelor's degree. **Support services:** Learning center, pre-admission summer program, reduced course load, study skills assistance, tutoring, writing center.

**Majors. Area/ethnic studies:** Chicano/Hispanic-American/Latino. **Biology:** General, biochemistry. **Business:** Accounting, business admin, finance, human resources, management information systems, managerial economics, operations. **Communications:** General. **Computer sciences:** General, computer science, information systems. **Education:** Early childhood, elementary, secondary. **Foreign languages:** Ancient Greek, classics, French, German, Italian, Latin, linguistics, Russian, Spanish. **Health:** Nursing (RN). **History:** General. **Math:** General. **Philosophy/religion:** Philosophy. **Physical sciences:** Chemistry, geology, geophysics, physics. **Psychology:** General. **Social sciences:** Economics, political science, sociology. **Visual/performing arts:** Art history/conservation, dramatic, film/cinema, studio arts.

**Most popular majors.** Biology 6%, business/marketing 23%, communications/journalism 10%, English 7%, history 7%, psychology 10%, social sciences 15%.

**Computing on campus.** 1,000 workstations in library, computer center, student center. Dormitories wired for high-speed internet access and linked to campus network. Commuter students can connect to campus network. Online course registration, online library, helpline, repair service, student web hosting, wireless network available.

**Student life. Freshman orientation:** Mandatory, $408 fee. Preregistration for classes offered. Three-day, 2-night program; 4-6 scheduled options offered during summer. **Policies:** Alcohol prohibited for students under 21, smoking prohibited in all residence halls. Halogen lights, space heaters, egg crate style foam mattress pads, and candles prohibited in dorm rooms. **Housing:** Guaranteed on-campus for freshmen. Coed dorms, single-sex dorms, special housing for disabled, wellness housing available. $250 partly refundable deposit, deadline 5/1. Honors house, multicultural floor, 24-hour quiet living floor, social justice floor available. Apartment-style housing and townhouse-style housing available for upperclassmen. **Activities:** Bands, campus ministries, choral groups, dance, drama, film society, international student organizations, literary magazine, music ensembles, musical theater, radio station, student government, student newspaper, symphony orchestra, TV station, 4Boston, Amnesty International, Appalachia Volunteers, Asian Caucus, Black Student Forum, Buddhist club, Hillel, Ignatian Society, Puerto Rican association, Muslim students association.

**Athletics.** NCAA. **Intercollegiate:** Baseball M, basketball, cross-country, diving, fencing, field hockey W, football (tackle) M, golf, ice hockey, lacrosse W, rowing (crew) W, sailing, skiing, soccer, softball W, swimming, tennis, track and field, volleyball W. **Intramural:** Basketball, football (non-tackle), golf, ice hockey, racquetball, soccer, softball, squash, tennis, volleyball. **Team name:** Eagles.

**Student services.** Alcohol/substance abuse counseling, chaplain/spiritual director, career counseling, services for economically disadvantaged, student employment services, financial aid counseling, health services, minority student services, on-campus daycare, personal counseling, placement for graduates, women's services. **Physically disabled:** Services for visually, speech, hearing impaired.

**Contact.** Phone: (617) 552-3100 Toll-free number: (800) 360-2522 Fax: (617) 552-0798
John Mahoney, Director of Undergraduate Admission, Boston College, 140 Commonwealth Avenue, Devlin Hall 208, Chestnut Hill, MA 02467-3809

---

## Boston Conservatory
**Boston, Massachusetts**     CB member
**www.bostonconservatory.edu**     CB code: 3084

- Private 4-year music and performing arts college
- Residential campus in very large city
- 489 degree-seeking undergraduates: 58% women, 2% Asian American, 9% international
- 187 degree-seeking graduate students
- 34% of applicants admitted
- SAT or ACT (ACT writing optional), application essay required
- 66% graduate within 6 years

**General.** Founded in 1867. Regionally accredited. **Degrees:** 83 bachelor's awarded; master's offered. **Location:** Downtown. **Calendar:** Semester, limited summer session. **Full-time faculty:** 74 total. **Part-time faculty:** 115 total. **Class size:** 89% < 20, 9% 20-39, less than 1% 40-49, less than 1% 50-99. **Special facilities:** College operated theater.

**Freshman class profile.** 1,191 applied, 407 admitted, 130 enrolled.

| Return as sophomores: | 76% | International: | 11% |
|---|---|---|---|
| Out-of-state: | 75% | Sororities: | 5% |
| Live on campus: | 98% | | |

**Basis for selection.** Audition carries most weight. Academic record and artistic background strongly considered. Test scores, recommendations, personal essay, school and community activities, interview important. Audition required. Interview required of music education, composition majors. **Homeschooled:** Statement describing homeschool structure and mission, transcript of courses and grades, state high school equivalency certificate required.

**High school preparation.** College-preparatory program required.

**2009-2010 Annual costs.** Tuition/fees: $33,976. Room/board: $15,880. Books/supplies: $750. Personal expenses: $2,580.

**2009-2010 Financial aid. Need-based:** Average need met was 40%. Average scholarship/grant was $15,215; average loan $3,546. 57% of total undergraduate aid awarded as scholarships/grants, 43% as loans/jobs. **Non-need-based:** Scholarships awarded for music/drama.

**Application procedures. Admission:** Closing date 12/1 (postmark date). $110 fee, may be waived for applicants with need. Application must be submitted online. Admission notification 4/1. Must reply by 5/1. **Financial aid:** Priority date 3/1; no closing date. FAFSA required. Applicants notified on a rolling basis.

**Academics. Special study options:** Cross-registration, double major, ESL, independent study, teacher certification program. **Credit/placement by examination:** AP, CLEP, institutional tests. 75 credit hours maximum toward bachelor's degree. **Support services:** Pre-admission summer program, study skills assistance, tutoring, writing center.

**Majors. Visual/performing arts:** Dance, music performance, music theory/composition, piano/organ, voice/opera.

**Computing on campus.** 20 workstations in dormitories, library, student center. Dormitories linked to campus network. Online library available.

**Student life. Freshman orientation:** Mandatory, $366 fee. Held the week prior to registration includes college life seminar, advising, parent luncheon, school tours, city-wide tours, placements, auditions. Fee for music education students is $95. **Housing:** Coed dorms, single-sex dorms available. $250 deposit, deadline 5/1. **Activities:** International student organizations, literary magazine, student government, student newspaper, African American artists' association, community services association, Christian Fellowship, environmental awareness group, peer support aides, Taiwan Chinese student association, gay and lesbian artists' association, Organizacion De Artistas Hispanos, Korean society.

**Student services.** Career counseling, health services, personal counseling.

**Contact.** E-mail: admissions@bostonconservatory.edu
Phone: (617) 912-9153 Fax: (617) 536-3176
Kristy Errera-Solomon, Dean of Enrollment Services, Boston Conservatory, 8 The Fenway, Boston, MA 02215

## Boston University
**Boston, Massachusetts**
www.bu.edu
CB member
CB code: 3087

- Private 4-year university
- Residential campus in very large city
- 16,295 degree-seeking undergraduates: 3% part-time, 60% women, 3% African American, 14% Asian American, 7% Hispanic American, 9% international
- 13,136 degree-seeking graduate students
- 58% of applicants admitted
- SAT or ACT with writing, SAT Subject Tests, application essay required
- 82% graduate within 6 years

**General.** Founded in 1839. Regionally accredited. **Degrees:** 4,233 bachelor's awarded; master's, doctoral, professional offered. **ROTC:** Army, Naval, Air Force. **Location:** Downtown. **Calendar:** Semester, extensive summer session. **Full-time faculty:** 1,549 total; 78% have terminal degrees, 12% minority, 36% women. **Part-time faculty:** 1,079 total; 6% minority, 43% women. **Class size:** 55% < 20, 31% 20-39, 5% 40-49, 6% 50-99, 4% >100. **Special facilities:** Biodiversity station in Ecuador, dedicated management library, planetarium, National Public Radio station, 20th century archives, professional theater/theater company, center for remote sensing, speech, language and hearing clinic, culinary center, communication multimedia lab.

**Freshman class profile.** 37,795 applied, 22,101 admitted, 4,130 enrolled.

| Mid 50% test scores | | | |
|---|---|---|---|
| SAT critical reading: | 570-660 | Rank in top quarter: | 86% |
| SAT math: | 600-690 | Rank in top tenth: | 51% |
| SAT writing: | 590-680 | Return as sophomores: | 90% |
| ACT composite: | 26-30 | Out-of-state: | 80% |
| GPA 3.75 or higher: | 23% | Live on campus: | 99% |
| GPA 3.50-3.74: | 33% | International: | 11% |
| GPA 3.0-3.49: | 39% | Fraternities: | 5% |
| GPA 2.0-2.99: | 5% | Sororities: | 15% |

**Basis for selection.** Evidence of strong academic performance in challenging college-prep curriculum most important. SAT Subject Tests in Chemistry and Math (level 2) required for accelerated medical and dental programs. Others required to submit 2 subject tests in subject areas of their choice. Subject Tests recommended for College of Fine Arts, College of General Studies and the Science and Engineering Program in Metropolitan College. Interview required for accelerated medical/dental programs, all nonperformance theater arts majors. Audition required for music, theater performance programs. Portfolio required of visual arts, stage management, theatrical design majors. Portfolio or audition required for College of Fine Arts. **Homeschooled:** Students should contact Office of Admissions prior to application.

**High school preparation.** College-preparatory program required. 15 units required; 20 recommended. Required and recommended units include English 4, mathematics 3-4, social studies 3-4, science 3-4 (laboratory 3-4) and foreign language 2-4. Pre-calculus required. Social studies should include history.

**2009-2010 Annual costs.** Tuition/fees: $38,440. Room/board: $11,848. Books/supplies: $940. Personal expenses: $1,226.

**2009-2010 Financial aid. Need-based:** 2,497 full-time freshmen applied for aid; 2,065 were judged to have need; 2,063 of these received aid. Average need met was 91%. Average scholarship/grant was $24,183; average loan $6,331. 72% of total undergraduate aid awarded as scholarships/grants, 28% as loans/jobs. **Non-need-based:** Awarded to 3,471 full-time undergraduates, including 1,142 freshmen. Scholarships awarded for academics, alumni affiliation, art, athletics, leadership, music/drama, religious affiliation, ROTC, state residency. **Additional information:** Financial aid deadline for early decision applicants: 11/01; notification date: 2/15. Graduates of Boston's public high schools who complete their financial aid application and demonstrate need will be awarded financial aid packages which contain no loans and meet their full demonstrated need.

**Application procedures. Admission:** Closing date 1/1 (receipt date). $75 fee, may be waived for applicants with need. Admission notification 4/15. Must reply by 5/1. Application deadline December 1 for accelerated medical and dental combined degree and trustee, Boston high school, Cardinal Medeiros Scholar programs. **Financial aid:** Closing date 2/15. FAFSA, CSS PROFILE required. Applicants notified on a rolling basis starting 3/15; must reply by 5/1 or within 2 week(s) of notification.

**Academics. Special study options:** Accelerated study, combined bachelor's/graduate degree, cooperative education, cross-registration, distance learning, double major, dual enrollment of high school students, ESL, honors, independent study, internships, liberal arts/career combination, semester at sea, student-designed major, study abroad, teacher certification program, Washington semester, weekend college. Extensive opportunities for study abroad as well as internships available in South and Central America, Europe, Africa, China, Pacific Rim, Russia. Field study in marine science at Woods Hole Institute, in environmental/ecological science in Ecuador, and at Photonics Center, combined bachelor's/master's degrees, 6-year physical therapy (BS/DPT) program, 5-year occupational therapy (BS/MS) program; 7-year accelerated MD, DMD programs. **Credit/placement by examination:** AP, CLEP, IB, SAT, ACT, institutional tests. 32 credit hours maximum toward bachelor's degree. Credits assigned vary by school and college. Scores higher than minimums may result in additional credit depending on department. **Support services:** Learning center, study skills assistance, tutoring, writing center.

**Majors. Area/ethnic studies:** American, East Asian, Italian, Latin American, Russian/Slavic. **Biology:** General, biochemistry, ecology, marine, molecular. **Business:** Accounting, business admin, entrepreneurial studies, finance, hospitality admin, international, international finance, management information systems, market research, marketing, operations, organizational behavior. **Communications:** General, advertising, broadcast journalism, journalism, public relations. **Computer sciences:** General. **Conservation:** General, environmental science, environmental studies, management/policy. **Education:** General, art, bilingual, chemistry, Deaf/hearing impaired, drama/dance, early childhood, elementary, English, mathematics, music, physical, science, social studies, special. **Engineering:** General, aerospace, biomedical, computer, electrical, mechanical. **Foreign languages:** General, ancient Greek, classics, French, German, Italian, Latin, linguistics, modern Greek, Russian, Spanish. **Health:** Athletic training, communication disorders, dental lab technology. **History:** General. **Interdisciplinary:** Math/computer science, neuroscience, nutrition sciences. **Legal studies:** Legal secretary, paralegal. **Math:** General. **Parks/recreation:** Exercise sciences. **Philosophy/religion:** Philosophy, religion. **Physical sciences:** Astronomy, astrophysics, chemistry, geology, geophysics, physics, planetary. **Psychology:** General. **Social sciences:** Anthropology, archaeology, economics, geography, international relations, political science, sociology, urban studies. **Visual/performing arts:** General, acting, art history/conservation, cinematography, commercial/advertising art, directing/producing, drawing, music history, music performance, music theory/composition, painting, piano/organ, sculpture, theater design, theater history, voice/opera.

**Most popular majors.** Biology 6%, business/marketing 17%, communications/journalism 16%, engineering/engineering technologies 6%, health sciences 7%, psychology 7%, social sciences 17%, visual/performing arts 6%.

**Computing on campus.** 750 workstations in dormitories, library, computer center, student center. Dormitories wired for high-speed internet access and linked to campus network. Commuter students can connect to campus network. Online course registration, online library, helpline, repair service, student web hosting, wireless network available.

**Student life. Freshman orientation:** Mandatory, $135 fee. Preregistration for classes offered. Summer program. **Policies:** Campus residents must abide by guest/visitor policy. **Housing:** Guaranteed on-campus for all undergraduates. Coed dorms, single-sex dorms, special housing for disabled, apartments, cooperative housing, wellness housing available. $650 nonrefundable deposit, deadline 5/1. Specialty halls/floors available for groups of students with common interest or academic major. **Activities:** Bands, campus ministries, choral groups, dance, drama, film society, international student organizations, literary magazine, music ensembles, Model UN, musical theater, opera, radio station, student government, student newspaper, symphony orchestra, TV station, 525 student organizations available.

**Athletics.** NCAA. **Intercollegiate:** Basketball, cross-country, diving, field hockey W, golf, ice hockey, lacrosse W, rowing (crew), soccer, softball W, swimming, tennis, track and field, wrestling M. **Intramural:** Basketball, football (non-tackle), ice hockey W, soccer, softball, swimming, tennis, volleyball, water polo. **Team name:** Terriers.

**Student services.** Adult student services, chaplain/spiritual director, career counseling, student employment services, financial aid counseling, health services, minority student services, personal counseling, placement for graduates, veterans' counselor. **Physically disabled:** Services for visually, speech, hearing impaired. **Learning disabled:** Comprehensive services available.

**Contact.**  E-mail: admissions@bu.edu
Phone: (617) 353-2300 Fax: (617) 353-9695
Kelly Walter, Director, Office of Undergraduate Admissions, Boston University, 121 Bay State Road, Boston, MA 02215

---

## Brandeis University
**Waltham, Massachusetts**  CB member
**www.brandeis.edu**  CB code: 3092

- Private 4-year university
- Residential campus in small city
- 3,299 degree-seeking undergraduates: 56% women, 5% African American, 11% Asian American, 5% Hispanic American, 10% international
- 2,061 degree-seeking graduate students
- 40% of applicants admitted
- SAT or ACT with writing, application essay required
- 87% graduate within 6 years

**General.** Founded in 1948. Regionally accredited. **Degrees:** 783 bachelor's awarded; master's, doctoral offered. **ROTC:** Army, Air Force. **Location:** 10 miles from Boston. **Calendar:** Semester, limited summer session. **Full-time faculty:** 358 total; 96% have terminal degrees, 12% minority, 38% women. **Part-time faculty:** 130 total; 66% have terminal degrees, 6% minority, 55% women. **Class size:** 61% < 20, 27% 20-39, 3% 40-49, 6% 50-99, 2% >100. **Special facilities:** Basic medical sciences research center, spatial orientation laboratory, center for complex systems, astronomical observatory.

**Freshman class profile.** 6,815 applied, 2,756 admitted, 781 enrolled.

| Mid 50% test scores | | GPA 2.0-2.99: | 2% |
|---|---|---|---|
| SAT critical reading: | 620-730 | Rank in top quarter: | 97% |
| SAT math: | 640-730 | Rank in top tenth: | 79% |
| SAT writing: | 620-720 | Return as sophomores: | 94% |
| ACT composite: | 27-31 | Out-of-state: | 71% |
| GPA 3.75 or higher: | 51% | Live on campus: | 99% |
| GPA 3.50-3.74: | 29% | International: | 12% |
| GPA 3.0-3.49: | 18% | | |

**Basis for selection.** Evidence of accomplishment and development most important. School and teacher statements, test scores also important. Interview recommended.

**High school preparation.** College-preparatory program required. 20 units recommended. Recommended units include English 4, mathematics 4, social studies 4, science 4 (laboratory 2) and foreign language 4.

**2009-2010 Annual costs.** Tuition/fees: $38,762. Room/board: $10,800. Books/supplies: $1,000. Personal expenses: $1,500.

**2009-2010 Financial aid. Need-based:** 546 full-time freshmen applied for aid; 451 were judged to have need; 446 of these received aid. Average need met was 82%. Average scholarship/grant was $27,392; average loan $3,696. 42% of total undergraduate aid awarded as scholarships/grants, 58% as loans/jobs. **Non-need-based:** Awarded to 528 full-time undergraduates, including 69 freshmen. Scholarships awarded for academics.

**Application procedures. Admission:** Closing date 1/15 (receipt date). $55 fee, may be waived for applicants with need. Admission notification 4/1. Must reply by May 1 or within 2 week(s) if notified thereafter. **Financial aid:** Priority date 2/1; no closing date. FAFSA, CSS PROFILE required. Applicants notified on a rolling basis starting 4/1.

**Academics. Special study options:** Cross-registration, double major, independent study, internships, student-designed major, study abroad. 5-year BA/MA programs in international economics and finance, computer science, computational linguistics, and Near Eastern and Judaic studies; early admission to Mt. Sinai Medical School and Tufts Medical School. **Credit/**

**placement by examination:** AP, CLEP, IB, institutional tests. **Support services:** Reduced course load, remedial instruction, study skills assistance, tutoring, writing center.

**Majors. Area/ethnic studies:** African-American, American, East Asian, European, Italian, Latin American, Near/Middle Eastern, women's. **Biology:** General, biochemistry, biophysics. **Business:** General. **Computer sciences:** Computer science. **Conservation:** Environmental studies. **Education:** General. **Foreign languages:** Classics, comparative lit, French, German, Hebrew, linguistics, Russian, Spanish. **Health:** Health care admin. **History:** General. **Interdisciplinary:** Global studies, neuroscience. **Math:** General. **Philosophy/religion:** Judaic, philosophy. **Physical sciences:** Chemistry, physics. **Psychology:** General. **Social sciences:** Anthropology, economics, political science, sociology, U.S. government. **Visual/performing arts:** Art history/conservation, dramatic, film/cinema, studio arts.

**Most popular majors.** Area/ethnic studies 10%, biology 10%, history 7%, interdisciplinary studies 9%, psychology 8%, social sciences 28%, visual/performing arts 6%.

**Computing on campus.** 104 workstations in library, computer center, student center. Dormitories wired for high-speed internet access and linked to campus network. Commuter students can connect to campus network. Online course registration, online library, helpline, repair service, student web hosting, wireless network available.

**Student life. Freshman orientation:** Mandatory, $185 fee. Preregistration for classes offered. Five-day program begins weekend before Labor Day weekend. **Housing:** Guaranteed on-campus for freshmen. Coed dorms, single-sex dorms, special housing for disabled, apartments available. Thematic learning communities available. **Activities:** Bands, campus ministries, choral groups, dance, drama, film society, international student organizations, literary magazine, music ensembles, musical theater, radio station, student government, student newspaper, symphony orchestra, TV station, 246 recognized clubs and organizations.

**Athletics.** NCAA. **Intercollegiate:** Baseball M, basketball, cross-country, diving, fencing, golf M, soccer, softball W, swimming, tennis, track and field, volleyball W. **Intramural:** Basketball, equestrian, football (non-tackle), soccer, softball, squash, tennis, volleyball, water polo. **Team name:** Judges.

**Student services.** Alcohol/substance abuse counseling, chaplain/spiritual director, career counseling, student employment services, financial aid counseling, health services, minority student services, on-campus daycare, personal counseling, placement for graduates, veterans' counselor, women's services. **Physically disabled:** Services for visually, speech, hearing impaired.

**Contact.**  E-mail: admissions@brandeis.edu
Phone: (781) 736-3500 Toll-free number: (800) 622-0622
Fax: (781) 736-3536
Jean Eddy, Senior Vice-President for Students and Enrollment, Brandeis University, Box 549110, Waltham, MA 02454-9110

---

## Bridgewater State College
**Bridgewater, Massachusetts**  CB member
**www.bridgew.edu**  CB code: 3517

- Public 4-year liberal arts and teachers college
- Commuter campus in large town
- 8,725 degree-seeking undergraduates: 14% part-time, 60% women, 6% African American, 2% Asian American, 3% Hispanic American, 1% international
- 1,265 degree-seeking graduate students
- 61% of applicants admitted
- SAT or ACT (ACT writing optional) required
- 54% graduate within 6 years

**General.** Founded in 1840. Regionally accredited. **Degrees:** 1,492 bachelor's awarded; master's offered. **ROTC:** Army, Air Force. **Location:** 30 miles from Boston; 35 miles from Providence, Rhode Island. **Calendar:** Semester, extensive summer session. **Full-time faculty:** 304 total; 93% have terminal degrees, 12% minority, 49% women. **Part-time faculty:** 260 total; 6% minority, 46% women. **Class size:** 40% < 20, 58% 20-39, 2% 40-49, less than 1% 50-99.

**Freshman class profile.** 7,448 applied, 4,559 admitted, 1,479 enrolled.

| Mid 50% test scores | | | |
|---|---|---|---|
| SAT critical reading: | 460-560 | GPA 2.0-2.99: | 43% |
| SAT math: | 470-560 | Rank in top quarter: | 32% |
| ACT composite: | 20-24 | Rank in top tenth: | 8% |
| GPA 3.75 or higher: | 9% | Return as sophomores: | 82% |
| GPA 3.50-3.74: | 9% | Out-of-state: | 4% |
| GPA 3.0-3.49: | 39% | Live on campus: | 63% |

**Basis for selection.** High school achievement most important, including weighted high school GPA and completion of 16 college preparatory courses. Test scores, essay, extracurricular activities also important. Class rank, recommendations considered. Essay recommended. **Learning Disabled:** Exemption from admissions standardized testing upon documentation of diagnostic test results. Must complete 16 required academic courses with 3.0 GPA or present evidence of potential for academic success.

**High school preparation.** 16 units required. Required units include English 4, mathematics 3, social studies 1, history 1, science 3 (laboratory 2), foreign language 2 and academic electives 2.

**2009-2010 Annual costs.** Tuition/fees: $6,473; $12,613 out-of-state. Room/board: $8,116. Books/supplies: $1,000. Personal expenses: $2,000.

**2008-2009 Financial aid. Need-based:** 1,251 full-time freshmen applied for aid; 871 were judged to have need; 866 of these received aid. Average scholarship/grant was $4,184; average loan $3,442. 40% of total undergraduate aid awarded as scholarships/grants, 60% as loans/jobs. **Non-need-based:** Awarded to 550 full-time undergraduates, including 247 freshmen. Scholarships awarded for academics, leadership, minority status, state residency.

**Application procedures. Admission:** No deadline. $25 fee, may be waived for applicants with need. Admission notification on a rolling basis beginning on or about 12/15. **Financial aid:** Priority date 3/1; no closing date. FAFSA required.

**Academics. Special study options:** Accelerated study, combined bachelor's/graduate degree, cross-registration, distance learning, double major, dual enrollment of high school students, ESL, exchange student, honors, independent study, internships, study abroad, teacher certification program, Washington semester. **Credit/placement by examination:** CLEP, IB, institutional tests. **Support services:** Learning center, pre-admission summer program, reduced course load, remedial instruction, study skills assistance, tutoring, writing center.

**Majors. Architecture:** Urban/community planning. **Biology:** General, biochemistry, biomedical sciences, cellular/molecular, environmental. **Business:** Accounting, business admin, finance, international, management information systems, marketing, transportation. **Communications:** General. **Computer sciences:** Computer science. **Education:** Art, biology, drama/dance, early childhood, elementary, English, health, health occupations, kindergarten/preschool, music, physical, special. **Foreign languages:** Spanish. **Health:** Athletic training, communication disorders, kinesiotherapy. **History:** General. **Legal studies:** General. **Math:** General. **Parks/recreation:** General, exercise sciences, sports admin. **Philosophy/religion:** Ethics, philosophy. **Physical sciences:** Chemistry, geochemistry, geology, physics. **Protective services:** Criminal justice. **Psychology:** General. **Public administration:** Social work. **Social sciences:** Anthropology, archaeology, economics, geography, international relations, political science, sociology, U.S. government, urban studies. **Transportation:** Airline/commercial pilot, aviation management. **Visual/performing arts:** Art history/conservation, crafts, dramatic, graphic design, photography, studio arts.

**Most popular majors.** Business/marketing 18%, communications/journalism 8%, education 14%, psychology 11%, security/protective services 9%, social sciences 6%.

**Computing on campus.** PC or laptop required. 780 workstations in library, computer center, student center. Dormitories wired for high-speed internet access and linked to campus network. Commuter students can connect to campus network. Online course registration, online library, helpline, repair service, wireless network available.

**Student life. Freshman orientation:** Mandatory, $160 fee. Preregistration for classes offered. **Housing:** Coed dorms, single-sex dorms, apartments, wellness housing available. Quiet floor, nonsmoking floor available in residence hall. Housing available over breaks for athletes, student teachers, international students. **Activities:** Bands, campus ministries, choral groups, dance, drama, literary magazine, music ensembles, musical theater, radio station, student government, student newspaper, Christian Fellowship, College Democrats, Afro-American society, international club, La Sociedad Latina, Amnesty International, Big Brothers/Big Sisters, Habitat for Humanity.

**Athletics.** NCAA. **Intercollegiate:** Baseball M, basketball, cross-country, diving, field hockey W, football (tackle) M, lacrosse W, soccer, softball W, swimming, tennis, track and field, volleyball W, wrestling M. **Intramural:** Basketball, football (tackle) M, lacrosse M, soccer, softball, tennis, volleyball, water polo. **Team name:** Bears.

**Student services.** Adult student services, chaplain/spiritual director, career counseling, student employment services, financial aid counseling, health services, minority student services, on-campus daycare, personal counseling, placement for graduates, veterans' counselor, women's services. **Physically disabled:** Services for visually, speech, hearing impaired.

**Contact.** E-mail: admission@bridgew.edu
Phone: (508) 531-1237 Fax: (508) 531-1746
Gregg Meyer, Director of Admissions, Bridgewater State College, Gates House, Bridgewater, MA 02325

## Cambridge College
**Cambridge, Massachusetts**
**www.cambridgecollege.edu**　　　　**CB code: 3612**

- Private 4-year liberal arts and teachers college
- Commuter campus in small city
- 1,287 degree-seeking undergraduates: 29% African American, 3% Asian American, 19% Hispanic American, 1% international
- 3,663 graduate students
- Application essay required

**General.** Regionally accredited. **Degrees:** 202 bachelor's awarded; master's, doctoral offered. **Calendar:** Continuous, extensive summer session. **Full-time faculty:** 26 total; 69% have terminal degrees, 38% minority, 54% women. **Part-time faculty:** 545 total; 60% have terminal degrees, 36% minority, 60% women. **Class size:** 81% < 20, 19% 20-39.

**Basis for selection.** Open admission.

**2009-2010 Annual costs.** Tuition/fees: $10,950. Books/supplies: $750. Personal expenses: $900.

**2009-2010 Financial aid.** All financial aid based on need. Average need met was 26%. Average scholarship/grant was $5,092; average loan $3,478. 22% of total undergraduate aid awarded as scholarships/grants, 78% as loans/jobs.

**Application procedures. Admission:** No deadline. $30 fee, may be waived for applicants with need. Admission notification on a rolling basis beginning on or about 8/1. **Financial aid:** Priority date 9/1; no closing date. FAFSA, institutional form required. Applicants notified on a rolling basis starting 6/1.

**Academics. Special study options:** Accelerated study, distance learning, double major, independent study, internships, weekend college. **Credit/placement by examination:** CLEP. **Support services:** Learning center, reduced course load, remedial instruction, tutoring, writing center.

**Majors. Business:** General. **Liberal arts:** Arts/sciences. **Psychology:** General, community.

**Most popular majors.** Business/marketing 31%, liberal arts 46%, psychology 23%.

**Computing on campus.** Commuter students can connect to campus network. Online course registration, online library, wireless network available.

**Student life. Freshman orientation:** Available. Preregistration for classes offered. **Activities:** Student government.

**Student services.** Adult student services, services for economically disadvantaged, financial aid counseling. **Physically disabled:** Services for visually, speech, hearing impaired. **Learning disabled:** Comprehensive services available.

**Contact.** E-mail: admit@cambridgecollege.edu
Phone: (888) 800-4723 Toll-free number: (800) 877-4723
Stephen Lyons, Director of Undergraduate and Graduate Admissions, Cambridge College, 1000 Massachusetts Avenue, Cambridge, MA 02138-5304

## Clark University
**Worcester, Massachusetts**　　　　**CB member**
**www.clarku.edu**　　　　**CB code: 3279**

- Private 4-year university and liberal arts college
- Residential campus in small city

- 2,243 degree-seeking undergraduates: 2% part-time, 61% women, 2% African American, 4% Asian American, 2% Hispanic American, 8% international
- 1,055 degree-seeking graduate students
- 64% of applicants admitted
- SAT or ACT (ACT writing optional), application essay required
- 78% graduate within 6 years; 38% enter graduate study

**General.** Founded in 1887. Regionally accredited. **Degrees:** 537 bachelor's awarded; master's, doctoral offered. **ROTC:** Army, Naval, Air Force. **Location:** 50 miles from Boston. **Calendar:** Semester, limited summer session. **Full-time faculty:** 187 total; 96% have terminal degrees, 19% minority, 42% women. **Part-time faculty:** 105 total; 42% women. **Class size:** 57% < 20, 34% 20-39, 4% 40-49, 4% 50-99, less than 1% >100. **Special facilities:** Robert Goddard exhibition, map library, rare book room, NMR research facility, observatory, electronic music facility, arboretum, crafts studio, 2 theaters, environmental education laboratory, student-run recycling center, pulsed magnetic field laboratory, Holocaust studies center.

**Freshman class profile.** 4,271 applied, 2,741 admitted, 550 enrolled.

| Mid 50% test scores | | | |
|---|---|---|---|
| SAT critical reading: | 550-650 | GPA 2.0-2.99: | 13% |
| SAT math: | 530-640 | Rank in top quarter: | 71% |
| SAT writing: | 550-650 | Rank in top tenth: | 34% |
| ACT composite: | 24-29 | End year in good standing: | 92% |
| GPA 3.75 or higher: | 27% | Return as sophomores: | 88% |
| GPA 3.50-3.74: | 25% | Out-of-state: | 60% |
| GPA 3.0-3.49: | 35% | Live on campus: | 98% |
| | | International: | 8% |

**Basis for selection.** School achievement record and courses, recommendations, test scores most important. Special talents, accomplishments, motivation, and individual circumstances, including outside activities and jobs, also important. Interview recommended. Portfolio recommended for art majors. **Learning Disabled:** Students should self-identify as soon as possible.

**High school preparation.** College-preparatory program required. 16 units recommended. Recommended units include English 4, mathematics 3, social studies 2, history 2, science 3 (laboratory 2) and foreign language 2.

**2009-2010 Annual costs.** Tuition/fees: $35,220. New student contingency fee: $50. Fifth-year tuition waived for eligible undergraduates admitted to accelerated bachelor's/master's programs. Room/board: $6,750. Books/supplies: $800. Personal expenses: $700.

**2009-2010 Financial aid. Need-based:** 404 full-time freshmen applied for aid; 306 were judged to have need; 303 of these received aid. Average need met was 94%. Average scholarship/grant was $20,705; average loan $3,288. 77% of total undergraduate aid awarded as scholarships/grants, 23% as loans/jobs. **Non-need-based:** Awarded to 1,271 full-time undergraduates, including 317 freshmen. Scholarships awarded for academics, leadership.

**Application procedures. Admission:** Closing date 1/15 (postmark date). $55 fee, may be waived for applicants with need. Admission notification 4/1. Must reply by May 1 or within 2 week(s) if notified thereafter. **Financial aid:** Closing date 2/1. FAFSA, CSS PROFILE required. Applicants notified by 3/31; must reply by 5/1.

**Academics.** Interdisciplinary majors, special programs, and accelerated bachelor's/master's program with fifth-year tuition-free available. **Special study options:** Combined bachelor's/graduate degree, cross-registration, double major, ESL, independent study, internships, liberal arts/career combination, student-designed major, study abroad, teacher certification program, Washington semester. Courses at Bermuda Biological Station, May term at Clark European Center in Luxembourg, semester-long environmental science program at marine biological laboratory at Woods Hole Oceanographic Institute. 3-2 engineering programs with Columbia University, Worcester Polytechnic Institute, Washington University. **Credit/placement by examination:** AP, CLEP, IB, SAT, institutional tests. 16 credit hours maximum toward bachelor's degree. **Support services:** Reduced course load, study skills assistance, writing center.

**Majors. Area/ethnic studies:** Women's. **Biology:** General, biochemistry, bioinformatics, molecular. **Business:** General, business admin. **Communications:** General. **Computer sciences:** General, computer science. **Conservation:** Environmental science, environmental studies. **Foreign languages:** General, classics, comparative lit, French, Spanish. **History:** General. **Interdisciplinary:** Global studies, math/computer science, science/society. **Liberal arts:** Arts/sciences. **Math:** General. **Philosophy/religion:** Philosophy. **Physical sciences:** Chemistry, physics. **Psychology:** General. **Public administration:** General. **Social sciences:** Economics, geography, international relations, political science, sociology. **Visual/performing arts:** General, art, art history/conservation, dramatic, film/cinema, studio arts.

**Most popular majors.** Biology 8%, business/marketing 7%, communications/journalism 6%, English 6%, psychology 14%, social sciences 31%, visual/performing arts 8%.

**Computing on campus.** 110 workstations in dormitories, library, computer center, student center. Dormitories wired for high-speed internet access and linked to campus network. Commuter students can connect to campus network. Online course registration, online library, helpline, student web hosting, wireless network available.

**Student life. Freshman orientation:** Mandatory, $200 fee. Preregistration for classes offered. Program held during week prior to fall semester; includes course selection and registration. **Housing:** Guaranteed on-campus for freshmen. Coed dorms, single-sex dorms, special housing for disabled, apartments, wellness housing available. $100 nonrefundable deposit, deadline 5/1. Some university-owned off-campus housing available. Year-round house, quiet house, other special interest houses available. All residence halls nonsmoking. **Activities:** Bands, campus ministries, choral groups, dance, drama, film society, international student organizations, literary magazine, music ensembles, Model UN, musical theater, radio station, student government, student newspaper, symphony orchestra, TV station, 115 student clubs and organizations.

**Athletics.** NCAA. **Intercollegiate:** Baseball M, basketball, cross-country, diving, field hockey W, lacrosse M, rowing (crew), soccer, softball W, swimming, tennis, volleyball W. **Intramural:** Basketball, racquetball, soccer, softball, water polo. **Team name:** Cougars.

**Student services.** Adult student services, alcohol/substance abuse counseling, chaplain/spiritual director, career counseling, services for economically disadvantaged, student employment services, financial aid counseling, health services, minority student services, personal counseling, placement for graduates, women's services. **Physically disabled:** Services for visually, speech, hearing impaired.

**Contact.** E-mail: admissions@clarku.edu
Phone: (508) 793-7431 Toll-free number: (800) 462-5275
Fax: (508) 793-8821
Donald Honeman, Dean of Admissions, Clark University, 950 Main Street, Worcester, MA 01610-1477

## College of the Holy Cross
**Worcester, Massachusetts**
www.holycross.edu
CB member
CB code: 3282

- Private 4-year liberal arts college affiliated with Roman Catholic Church
- Residential campus in small city
- 2,897 degree-seeking undergraduates: 55% women, 4% African American, 6% Asian American, 8% Hispanic American, 1% international
- 36% of applicants admitted
- Application essay required
- 89% graduate within 6 years; 24% enter graduate study

**General.** Founded in 1843. Regionally accredited. Campus is a registered arboretum. **Degrees:** 678 bachelor's awarded. **ROTC:** Army, Naval, Air Force. **Location:** 45 miles from Boston. **Calendar:** Semester. **Full-time faculty:** 244 total; 98% have terminal degrees, 45% women. **Part-time faculty:** 62 total; 48% women. **Class size:** 53% < 20, 44% 20-39, 2% 40-49, 1% 50-99. **Special facilities:** Greenhouse, facilities for aquatic research, research-level scientific equipment.

**Freshman class profile.** 6,652 applied, 2,426 admitted, 747 enrolled.

| Mid 50% test scores | | | |
|---|---|---|---|
| SAT critical reading: | 600-680 | GPA 2.0-2.99: | 2% |
| SAT math: | 610-690 | Rank in top quarter: | 93% |
| SAT writing: | 600-690 | Rank in top tenth: | 66% |
| ACT composite: | 26-30 | Return as sophomores: | 96% |
| GPA 3.75 or higher: | 58% | Out-of-state: | 66% |
| GPA 3.50-3.74: | 21% | Live on campus: | 100% |
| GPA 3.0-3.49: | 19% | International: | 2% |

**Basis for selection.** Candidates urged to complete the most challenging college-preparatory program available at their school. Evidence of superior achievement in analytical reading and writing are of particular importance. Advanced placement and honors courses recommended. Standardized test scores are optional. Students may submit scores if they believe the results present a fuller picture of their achievements and potential. Students who do not submit scores will not be at any disadvantage in admissions decisions. Personal interview optional but highly recommended. **Homeschooled:** On-campus interview highly encouraged. Applicants should submit course work samples, personal statement, and college transcripts if applicable. If home-schooling associated with particular organization or program, submit description.

**High school preparation.** College-preparatory program required. 20 units recommended. Recommended units include English 4, mathematics 4, social studies 2, history 2, science 4 (laboratory 2) and foreign language 4.

**2010-2011 Annual costs.** Tuition/fees: $39,892. Room/board: $10,940. Books/supplies: $700. Personal expenses: $900.

**2009-2010 Financial aid. Need-based:** 522 full-time freshmen applied for aid; 438 were judged to have need; 411 of these received aid. Average need met was 100%. Average scholarship/grant was $26,977; average loan $5,262. 72% of total undergraduate aid awarded as scholarships/grants, 28% as loans/jobs. **Non-need-based:** Awarded to 104 full-time undergraduates, including 44 freshmen. Scholarships awarded for academics, athletics, ROTC. **Additional information:** Cost of tuition waived above the amount of the Pell Grant award for Worcester residents whose families earn less than $50,000.

**Application procedures. Admission:** Closing date 1/15 (receipt date). $60 fee, may be waived for applicants with need. Admission notification 4/1. Must reply by 5/1. **Financial aid:** Closing date 2/1. FAFSA required. CSS PROFILE required of all students applying for institutional aid. Applicants notified by 3/30; must reply by 5/1.

**Academics.** Students encouraged to participate in Oxford-style tutorials. 32 courses of 1 or more units required for graduation. 10 to 14 courses of 1 or more units required in major. **Special study options:** Accelerated study, cross-registration, double major, dual enrollment of high school students, exchange student, honors, independent study, internships, liberal arts/career combination, semester at sea, student-designed major, study abroad, teacher certification program, Washington semester. First-year living and learning academic enrichment program. **Credit/placement by examination:** AP, CLEP, IB, institutional tests. Language placement determined by departmental testing. **Support services:** Learning center, study skills assistance, tutoring, writing center.

**Majors. Architecture:** Architecture. **Area/ethnic studies:** Asian, German, Italian, Russian/Slavic. **Biology:** General. **Business:** Accounting. **Computer sciences:** General. **Conservation:** Environmental studies. **Foreign languages:** Classics, comparative lit, French, German, Italian, Russian, Spanish. **History:** General. **Interdisciplinary:** Medieval/Renaissance. **Math:** General. **Philosophy/religion:** Philosophy, religion. **Physical sciences:** Chemistry, physics. **Psychology:** General. **Social sciences:** Anthropology, economics, political science, sociology. **Visual/performing arts:** Art history/conservation, dramatic, studio arts. **Other:** Catholic studies.

**Most popular majors.** Biology 7%, English 12%, foreign language 9%, history 8%, psychology 12%, social sciences 35%.

**Computing on campus.** 485 workstations in dormitories, library, computer center, student center. Dormitories wired for high-speed internet access and linked to campus network. Commuter students can connect to campus network. Online library, helpline, repair service, student web hosting, wireless network available.

**Student life. Freshman orientation:** Available, $220 fee. Two-day programs available in mid-June; 3-day orientation prior to fall registration. **Policies:** Responsible drinking policy for students 21 and older. Initiation hazing prohibited. **Housing:** Guaranteed on-campus for all undergraduates. Coed dorms, special housing for disabled, apartments, wellness housing available. $500 nonrefundable deposit, deadline 5/1. **Activities:** Bands, campus ministries, choral groups, dance, drama, international student organizations, literary magazine, music ensembles, musical theater, radio station, student government, student newspaper, black student union, Purple Key society, student program for urban development, women's forum, Latin American student organization, Asian student society, Muslim student association, Appalachia service project, Habitat for Humanity, association of bisexuals/gays/lesbians.

**Athletics.** NCAA. **Intercollegiate:** Baseball M, basketball, cross-country, diving, field hockey W, football (tackle) M, golf, ice hockey, lacrosse, rowing (crew), soccer, softball W, swimming, tennis, track and field, volleyball W. **Intramural:** Basketball, football (non-tackle), soccer, softball, volleyball. **Team name:** Crusaders.

**Student services.** Alcohol/substance abuse counseling, chaplain/spiritual director, career counseling, student employment services, financial aid counseling, health services, minority student services, personal counseling, placement for graduates, women's services. **Physically disabled:** Services for visually, hearing impaired.

**Contact.** E-mail: admissions@holycross.edu
Phone: (508) 793-2443 Toll-free number: (800) 442-2421
Fax: (508) 793-3888
Ann McDermott, Director of Admissions, College of the Holy Cross, One College Street, Worcester, MA 01610-2395

---

## Curry College
**Milton, Massachusetts**
www.curry.edu
CB member
CB code: 3285

- Private 4-year nursing and liberal arts college
- Residential campus in large town
- 2,703 degree-seeking undergraduates: 27% part-time, 56% women, 8% African American, 1% Asian American, 3% Hispanic American, 1% international
- 282 degree-seeking graduate students
- 75% of applicants admitted
- Application essay required
- 48% graduate within 6 years

**General.** Founded in 1879. Regionally accredited. **Degrees:** 716 bachelor's awarded; master's offered. **ROTC:** Army, Air Force. **Location:** Seven miles from downtown Boston. **Calendar:** Semester, limited summer session. **Full-time faculty:** 119 total; 63% have terminal degrees, 6% minority, 65% women. **Part-time faculty:** 302 total; 18% have terminal degrees, 8% minority, 58% women. **Class size:** 51% < 20, 49% 20-39, less than 1% 40-49. **Special facilities:** Communication center, television studio with full TV production services.

**Freshman class profile.** 4,355 applied, 3,268 admitted, 623 enrolled.

| Mid 50% test scores | | | |
|---|---|---|---|
| SAT critical reading: | 420-510 | GPA 3.0-3.49: | 22% |
| SAT math: | 420-520 | GPA 2.0-2.99: | 61% |
| SAT writing: | 420-510 | Rank in top quarter: | 16% |
| ACT composite: | 18-22 | Rank in top tenth: | 2% |
| GPA 3.75 or higher: | 2% | Return as sophomores: | 61% |
| GPA 3.50-3.74: | 4% | Out-of-state: | 34% |
| | | Live on campus: | 85% |

**Basis for selection.** High school record, recommendations, extracurricular activities most important. Test scores also important. Interviews strongly recommended. **Homeschooled:** Statement describing homeschool structure and mission, transcript of courses and grades, state high school equivalency certificate required. **Learning Disabled:** Wechsler Adult Intelligence Scale required of learning disabled applicants and replaces SAT requirement. SAT or ACT still recommended.

**High school preparation.** College-preparatory program required. 16 units required. Required and recommended units include English 4, mathematics 3, social studies 2, history 2, science 2-3 (laboratory 2) and foreign language 2. 3 math through algebra II, 1 chemistry, and 1 biology required for nursing applicants.

**2009-2010 Annual costs.** Tuition/fees: $29,370. PAL (Program for Advancement of Learning) students pay additional program participation fee of up to $6,250. Room/board: $11,110. Books/supplies: $800. Personal expenses: $1,000.

**2008-2009 Financial aid. Need-based:** 382 full-time freshmen applied for aid; 382 were judged to have need; 382 of these received aid. Average need met was 61%. Average scholarship/grant was $11,768; average loan $3,422. 72% of total undergraduate aid awarded as scholarships/grants, 28% as loans/jobs. **Non-need-based:** Awarded to 89 full-time undergraduates, including 35 freshmen. Scholarships awarded for academics, leadership.

**Application procedures. Admission:** Closing date 4/1 (postmark date). $50 fee, may be waived for applicants with need. Admission notification on a rolling basis beginning on or about 12/1. Must reply by May 1 or within 2 week(s) if notified thereafter. **Financial aid:** Priority date 3/1; no closing date. FAFSA required. Applicants notified on a rolling basis starting 3/1; must reply by 5/1 or within 2 week(s) of notification.

**Academics. Special study options:** Accelerated study, cross-registration, double major, honors, independent study, internships, New York semester, semester at sea, student-designed major, study abroad, teacher certification program. **Credit/placement by examination:** AP, CLEP, IB, SAT, institutional tests. 60 credit hours maximum toward bachelor's degree. **Support services:** Learning center, pre-admission summer program, reduced course load, remedial instruction, study skills assistance, tutoring, writing center.

**Majors. Biology:** General. **Business:** Business admin. **Communications:** General. **Computer sciences:** General. **Conservation:** Environmental science. **Education:** General, early childhood, elementary, special. **Health:** Health services, nursing (RN). **Liberal arts:** Arts/sciences. **Philosophy/religion:** Philosophy. **Protective services:** Criminal justice. **Psychology:** General. **Social sciences:** Sociology. **Visual/performing arts:** Graphic design, studio arts. **Other:** Politics and history.

**Most popular majors.** Business/marketing 16%, communications/journalism 17%, health sciences 25%, psychology 7%, security/protective services 21%.

**Computing on campus.** 100 workstations in dormitories, library, computer center. Dormitories wired for high-speed internet access and linked to campus network. Commuter students can connect to campus network. Helpline, student web hosting, wireless network available.

**Student life. Freshman orientation:** Available, $150 fee. Preregistration for classes offered. Three summer 2-day programs and 2-day August program available. **Housing:** Guaranteed on-campus for all undergraduates. Coed dorms, single-sex dorms, special housing for disabled available. $300 nonrefundable deposit, deadline 5/1. Honors housing available. **Activities:** Campus ministries, choral groups, dance, drama, film society, international student organizations, literary magazine, music ensembles, musical theater, radio station, student government, student newspaper, TV station, nursing association, student activities board, community service organization, Hillel, One Curry, Newman club, Curry Cares.

**Athletics.** NCAA. **Intercollegiate:** Baseball M, basketball, cross-country W, football (tackle) M, ice hockey M, lacrosse, soccer, softball W, tennis. **Intramural:** Basketball, cheerleading W, field hockey W, football (non-tackle), golf, rugby M, skiing, softball, tennis, volleyball. **Team name:** Colonels.

**Student services.** Adult student services, alcohol/substance abuse counseling, chaplain/spiritual director, career counseling, student employment services, financial aid counseling, health services, minority student services, on-campus daycare, personal counseling, placement for graduates, veterans' counselor, women's services. **Learning disabled:** Comprehensive services available.

**Contact.** E-mail: curryadm@curry.edu
Phone: (617) 333-2210 Toll-free number: (800) 669-0686
Fax: (617) 333-2114
Jane Fidler, Dean of Admission, Curry College, 1071 Blue Hill Avenue, Milton, MA 02186-9984

---

## Eastern Nazarene College
**Quincy, Massachusetts**     **CB member**
**www.enc.edu**     **CB code: 3365**

- Private 4-year liberal arts college affiliated with Church of the Nazarene
- Residential campus in small city
- 833 degree-seeking undergraduates: 2% part-time, 59% women
- 221 graduate students
- 60% of applicants admitted
- SAT or ACT with writing, application essay, interview required
- 54% graduate within 6 years

**General.** Founded in 1900. Regionally accredited. **Degrees:** 206 bachelor's, 25 associate awarded; master's offered. **ROTC:** Army, Air Force. **Location:** 2 miles from Boston. **Calendar:** Semester, limited summer session. **Full-time faculty:** 45 total; 82% have terminal degrees, 9% minority, 29% women. **Part-time faculty:** 103 total. **Class size:** 74% < 20, 21% 20-39, 4% 40-49, 1% 50-99. **Special facilities:** Arboretum; early childhood education center; center for history, law, and government; business center.

**Freshman class profile.** 834 applied, 503 admitted, 206 enrolled.

| Mid 50% test scores | | | |
|---|---|---|---|
| SAT critical reading: | 440-580 | GPA 3.0-3.49: | 29% |
| SAT math: | 430-570 | GPA 2.0-2.99: | 45% |
| SAT writing: | 440-570 | Rank in top quarter: | 31% |
| ACT composite: | 20-27 | Rank in top tenth: | 14% |
| GPA 3.75 or higher: | 15% | Return as sophomores: | 66% |
| GPA 3.50-3.74: | 9% | Out-of-state: | 62% |
| | | Live on campus: | 85% |

**Basis for selection.** Applicants should demonstrate academic achievement, extracurricular involvement, and community engagement. SAT Subject Tests recommended. Accuplacer test may also be required. Interviews may be conducted over the phone. Audition required of students intending to major in music. **Homeschooled:** Statement describing homeschool structure and mission, transcript of courses and grades, interview, letter of recommendation (nonparent) required.

**High school preparation.** College-preparatory program required. 15 units required. Required and recommended units include English 4, mathematics 2-4, social studies 1-2, history 1-2, science 2-4 (laboratory 2-4), foreign language 2-4, visual/performing arts 1-2 and academic electives 5.

**2010-2011 Annual costs.** Tuition/fees (projected): $23,772. Room/board: $7,250. Books/supplies: $1,100.

**2008-2009 Financial aid. Need-based:** 164 full-time freshmen applied for aid; 147 were judged to have need; 147 of these received aid. Average need met was 71%. Average scholarship/grant was $9,499; average loan $8,298. 45% of total undergraduate aid awarded as scholarships/grants, 55% as loans/jobs. **Non-need-based:** Awarded to 121 full-time undergraduates, including 41 freshmen. Scholarships awarded for academics, alumni affiliation, leadership, religious affiliation, ROTC. **Additional information:** Participant in Massachusetts University pre-payment plan.

**Application procedures. Admission:** Priority date 1/1; no deadline. $25 fee, may be waived for applicants with need. Application must be submitted online. Admission notification on a rolling basis. **Financial aid:** Priority date 3/1, closing date 8/1. FAFSA, institutional form required. Applicants notified on a rolling basis starting 3/14; must reply by 8/1 or within 2 week(s) of notification.

**Academics. Special study options:** Accelerated study, combined bachelor's/graduate degree, cross-registration, double major, dual enrollment of high school students, exchange student, honors, independent study, internships, liberal arts/career combination, semester at sea, study abroad, teacher certification program, urban semester, Washington semester. **Credit/placement by examination:** AP, CLEP, IB, SAT, ACT, institutional tests. **Support services:** Learning center, pre-admission summer program, remedial instruction, study skills assistance, tutoring, writing center.

**Majors. Biology:** General, biochemistry. **Business:** General, accounting, accounting/business management, accounting/finance, business admin, marketing. **Communications:** Journalism. **Conservation:** Environmental science, environmental studies. **Education:** General, biology, business, chemistry, early childhood, elementary, English, history, kindergarten/preschool, mathematics, middle, music, physical, physics, science, social studies, special. **Engineering:** General, computer, electrical, physics. **Health:** Movement therapy, predental, premedicine, prenursing, prepharmacy, preveterinary. **History:** General. **Interdisciplinary:** Biological/physical sciences. **Legal studies:** Prelaw. **Liberal arts:** Arts/sciences. **Math:** General. **Parks/recreation:** Health/fitness, sports admin. **Philosophy/religion:** Religion. **Physical sciences:** Chemistry, physics. **Protective services:** Criminal justice, forensics, law enforcement admin, police science. **Psychology:** General, clinical, counseling, developmental, social. **Public administration:** Social work. **Theology:** Pastoral counseling, preministerial, sacred music, theology, youth ministry. **Visual/performing arts:** Dramatic, music history, music management, music pedagogy, music performance, music theory/composition, piano/organ, stringed instruments, theater arts management, voice/opera.

**Most popular majors.** Business/marketing 14%, communications/journalism 6%, education 9%, English 6%, liberal arts 11%, philosophy/religious studies 6%, psychology 16%, social sciences 6%.

**Computing on campus.** 98 workstations in library, computer center, student center. Dormitories wired for high-speed internet access and linked to campus network. Commuter students can connect to campus network. Online library, helpline, repair service, wireless network available.

**Student life. Freshman orientation:** Mandatory. Preregistration for classes offered. **Policies:** Students must abstain from use of illegal drugs, alcohol and tobacco, and are to avoid attendance at bars, clubs, or other activities or places of entertainment that promote themes of inappropriate sexuality, violence, profanity, pornography or activities demeaning to human life. Religious observance required. **Housing:** Guaranteed on-campus for all undergraduates. Coed dorms, single-sex dorms, special housing for disabled, apartments available. $300 nonrefundable deposit, deadline 8/25. **Activities:** Bands, campus ministries, choral groups, dance, drama, film society, literary magazine, music ensembles, musical theater, student government, student newspaper, symphony orchestra, ACTS/JUMP, Barnabas, Big Brother Big Sister, Causeway, Fellowship of Christian Athletes, Germantown Tutoring, Open Hand Open Heart, Refiner's Fire, Students for Social Justice, Women of Grace.

**Athletics.** NCAA. **Intercollegiate:** Baseball M, basketball, cross-country, soccer, softball W, tennis, volleyball W. **Intramural:** Basketball, field hockey W, football (non-tackle), lacrosse, skiing, soccer, volleyball. **Team name:** Lions.

**Student services.** Adult student services, alcohol/substance abuse counseling, chaplain/spiritual director, career counseling, services for economically disadvantaged, student employment services, financial aid counseling, health services, minority student services, personal counseling, placement for graduates, veterans' counselor, women's services. **Physically disabled:** Services for visually impaired.

**Contact.** E-mail: admissions@enc.edu
Phone: (617) 745-3711 Toll-free number: (800) 883-6288
Fax: (617) 745-3992
Andrew Wright, Director of Admissions, Eastern Nazarene College, 23 East Elm Avenue, Quincy, MA 02170

## Elms College
**Chicopee, Massachusetts**
www.elms.edu

**CB member**
**CB code: 3283**

- Private 4-year liberal arts college affiliated with Roman Catholic Church
- Residential campus in small city
- 1,010 degree-seeking undergraduates
- 299 graduate students
- 85% of applicants admitted
- SAT or ACT with writing, application essay required

**General.** Founded in 1928. Regionally accredited. **Degrees:** 230 bachelor's, 7 associate awarded; master's offered. **ROTC:** Army, Air Force. **Location:** 2 miles from Springfield; 30 miles from Hartford, Connecticut. **Calendar:** Semester, limited summer session. **Full-time faculty:** 58 total; 66% have terminal degrees, 3% minority, 69% women. **Part-time faculty:** 57 total; 12% have terminal degrees, 12% minority, 61% women. **Special facilities:** Rare book collection, Federal Depository, Irish cultural center, Polish center for discovery and learning.

**Freshman class profile.** 557 applied, 474 admitted, 151 enrolled.

| Mid 50% test scores | | GPA 3.0-3.49: | 36% |
|---|---|---|---|
| SAT critical reading: | 420-530 | GPA 2.0-2.99: | 40% |
| SAT math: | 420-530 | Rank in top quarter: | 35% |
| SAT writing: | 440-540 | Rank in top tenth: | 10% |
| ACT composite: | 18-23 | Out-of-state: | 22% |
| GPA 3.75 or higher: | 10% | Live on campus: | 54% |
| GPA 3.50-3.74: | 13% | | |

**Basis for selection.** Students should rank in top half of high school class; 2.8 GPA, 1000 SAT (exclusive of Writing) recommended. Interview recommended. **Homeschooled:** Transcript of courses and grades, letter of recommendation (nonparent) required.

**High school preparation.** College-preparatory program recommended. 15 units required; 22 recommended. Required and recommended units include English 4, mathematics 2-4, social studies 1-2, history 2, science 2-4 (laboratory 2) and foreign language 2-4. Algebra II, biology, chemistry required for nursing applicants.

**2010-2011 Annual costs.** Tuition/fees (projected): $27,045. Room/board: $9,810. Books/supplies: $1,000. Personal expenses: $1,000.

**2009-2010 Financial aid. Non-need-based:** Scholarships awarded for academics, alumni affiliation, leadership, religious affiliation, state residency.

**Application procedures. Admission:** No deadline. $30 fee, may be waived for applicants with need. Admission notification on a rolling basis beginning on or about 12/15. Must reply by May 1 or within 2 week(s) if notified thereafter. **Financial aid:** Priority date 3/1; no closing date. FAFSA required. Applicants notified on a rolling basis starting 3/10; must reply by 5/1 or within 2 week(s) of notification.

**Academics.** Tutor training certified by College Reading and Learning Association. **Special study options:** Cross-registration, distance learning, double major, dual enrollment of high school students, ESL, exchange student, honors, independent study, internships, liberal arts/career combination, study abroad, teacher certification program, Washington semester, weekend college. **Credit/placement by examination:** AP, CLEP, IB, SAT, ACT, institutional tests. 12 credit hours maximum toward bachelor's degree. **Support services:** Learning center, reduced course load, study skills assistance, tutoring, writing center.

**Majors. Area/ethnic studies:** American, Spanish/Iberian. **Biology:** General. **Business:** Accounting, accounting/business management, business admin, international, marketing. **Communications:** General. **Computer sciences:** General. **Education:** General, bilingual, Deaf/hearing impaired, early childhood, elementary, English, ESL, secondary, special. **Foreign languages:** Spanish. **Health:** Audiology/hearing, audiology/speech pathology, communication disorders, facilities admin, health care admin, health services admin, nursing (RN), pediatric nursing, predental, premedicine, preop/surgical nursing, preveterinary, public health nursing, speech pathology, speech-language pathology assistant. **History:** General, American, European. **Interdisciplinary:** Biological/physical sciences, natural sciences. **Legal studies:** General, paralegal, prelaw. **Liberal arts:** Arts/sciences. **Math:** General. **Parks/recreation:** Sports admin. **Philosophy/religion:** Religion. **Physical sciences:** Chemistry. **Psychology:** General. **Public administration:** Social work. **Social sciences:** International relations, sociology. **Visual/performing arts:** Studio arts.

**Most popular majors.** Business/marketing 14%, health sciences 43%, legal studies 6%, social sciences 12%.

**Computing on campus.** 70 workstations in dormitories, library, computer center, student center. Dormitories wired for high-speed internet access and linked to campus network. Commuter students can connect to campus network. Helpline, wireless network available.

**Student life. Freshman orientation:** Mandatory. Preregistration for classes offered. One-day programs held in June and August. **Housing:** Guaranteed on-campus for all undergraduates. Coed dorms, wellness housing available. **Activities:** Campus ministries, choral groups, dance, drama, international student organizations, literary magazine, music ensembles, radio station, student government, student newspaper, student government association, social work club, foreign language club, speech pathology and audiology club, Student Ambassadors organization, affirmative action committee, student nurse association.

**Athletics.** NCAA. **Intercollegiate:** Baseball M, basketball, cross-country, field hockey W, golf M, lacrosse W, soccer, softball W, swimming, volleyball. **Intramural:** Baseball M, basketball, cross-country, field hockey W, football (non-tackle), golf M, lacrosse W, soccer, softball W, swimming, volleyball. **Team name:** Blazers.

**Student services.** Adult student services, alcohol/substance abuse counseling, chaplain/spiritual director, career counseling, student employment services, financial aid counseling, health services, minority student services, personal counseling, placement for graduates. **Physically disabled:** Services for visually, speech, hearing impaired.

**Contact.** E-mail: admissions@elms.edu
Phone: (413) 592-3189 Toll-free number: (800) 255-3567
Fax: (413) 594-2781
Joseph Wagner, Director of Admission, Elms College, 291 Springfield Street, Chicopee, MA 01013-2839

## Emerson College
**Boston, Massachusetts**
www.emerson.edu

**CB member**
**CB code: 3367**

- Private 4-year college of communication and the arts
- Residential campus in very large city
- 3,454 degree-seeking undergraduates: 1% part-time, 59% women, 3% African American, 5% Asian American, 8% Hispanic American, 3% international
- 839 degree-seeking graduate students
- 42% of applicants admitted
- SAT or ACT with writing, application essay required
- 78% graduate within 6 years; 9% enter graduate study

**General.** Founded in 1880. Regionally accredited. **Degrees:** 863 bachelor's awarded; master's, doctoral offered. **Calendar:** Semester, limited summer session. **Full-time faculty:** 177 total; 71% have terminal degrees, 18% minority, 44% women. **Part-time faculty:** 254 total; 33% have terminal degrees, 7% minority, 43% women. **Class size:** 63% < 20, 30% 20-39, 6% 40-49, 2% 50-99. **Special facilities:** 2 historic theaters, performance and production center, sound treated television studios, integrated digital newsroom, film production facilities and film screening room, clinics/programs to observe speech and hearing therapy, marketing research suite.

**Freshman class profile.** 6,943 applied, 2,926 admitted, 766 enrolled.

| Mid 50% test scores | | GPA 2.0-2.99: | 5% |
|---|---|---|---|
| SAT critical reading: | 570-670 | Rank in top quarter: | 77% |
| SAT math: | 540-640 | Rank in top tenth: | 42% |
| SAT writing: | 580-670 | Return as sophomores: | 88% |
| ACT composite: | 24-29 | Out-of-state: | 80% |
| GPA 3.75 or higher: | 36% | Live on campus: | 99% |
| GPA 3.50-3.74: | 29% | International: | 4% |
| GPA 3.0-3.49: | 30% | | |

**Basis for selection.** Secondary school record, recommendations, writing competency, and personal qualities as seen in extracurricular activities, community involvement, demonstrated leadership important. Performing arts applicants must submit theatrical resume and, depending upon the major, either audition/interview or submit portfolio/essay. Candidates for film program must submit either a 5-8 minute video (20MB) accompanied by statement describing their role in its production or 5-10 page script. **Homeschooled:** State high school equivalency certificate required. Common Application Home School Supplement required.

**High school preparation.** College-preparatory program required. 16 units required; 20 recommended. Required and recommended units include English 4, mathematics 3, social studies 3, (laboratory 3), foreign language 3 and academic electives 4.

**2009-2010 Annual costs.** Tuition/fees: $29,928. Room/board: $12,280. Books/supplies: $720. Personal expenses: $1,431.

**2008-2009 Financial aid. Need-based:** 644 full-time freshmen applied for aid; 486 were judged to have need; 486 of these received aid. Average need met was 89%. Average scholarship/grant was $14,243; average loan $3,865. 56% of total undergraduate aid awarded as scholarships/grants, 44% as loans/jobs. **Non-need-based:** Awarded to 151 full-time undergraduates, including 61 freshmen. Scholarships awarded for academics, leadership, music/drama, state residency. **Additional information:** Massachusetts Loan Plan available for parents of dependent undergraduates.

**Application procedures. Admission:** Closing date 1/5 (postmark date). $65 fee, may be waived for applicants with need. Admission notification 4/1. Must reply by May 1 or within 2 week(s) if notified thereafter. **Financial aid:** Priority date 3/1; no closing date. FAFSA, CSS PROFILE required. Applicants notified by 4/1; must reply by 5/1 or within 3 week(s) of notification.

**Academics. Special study options:** Cross-registration, double major, honors, independent study, internships, liberal arts/career combination, student-designed major, study abroad, teacher certification program, Washington semester. Study and internship programs in Los Angeles and Washington, DC. Course cross-registration through the six-member Boston ProArts Consortium (Berklee College of Music, Boston Architectural Center, Boston Conservatory, Emerson, Massachusetts College of Art, School of the Museum of Fine Arts). **Credit/placement by examination:** AP, CLEP, IB, SAT, ACT, institutional tests. 32 credit hours maximum toward bachelor's degree. Math requirement waived with 550 SAT math or 24 ACT math. **Support services:** Learning center, reduced course load, study skills assistance, tutoring, writing center.

**Majors. Business:** Communications, marketing. **Communications:** General, advertising, broadcast journalism, journalism, media studies, political, public relations, publishing. **Education:** Autistic, Deaf/hearing impaired, drama/dance, speech, speech impaired. **Health:** Audiology/hearing, audiology/speech pathology, communication disorders, speech pathology. **Visual/performing arts:** General, acting, cinematography, directing/producing, dramatic, film/cinema, play/screenwriting, theater arts management, theater design.

**Most popular majors.** Business/marketing 14%, communications/journalism 33%, English 19%, visual/performing arts 31%.

**Computing on campus.** 480 workstations in dormitories, library, computer center, student center. Dormitories wired for high-speed internet access and linked to campus network. Commuter students can connect to campus network. Online course registration, online library, helpline, repair service, wireless network available.

**Student life. Freshman orientation:** Mandatory, $145 fee. Preregistration for classes offered. Multi-day event preceding first day of classes that includes computer workshops, library tours, advising, social activities, and field trips around Boston. **Housing:** Coed dorms, wellness housing available. $500 nonrefundable deposit, deadline 5/1. **Activities:** Campus ministries, choral groups, dance, drama, film society, international student organizations, literary magazine, music ensembles, Model UN, musical theater, radio station, student government, student newspaper, TV station, Hillel, Newman Club, Goodnews Fellowship, Islamic community, Alliance of Gays and Lesbians and Everyone, Latino student organization, international club, Earth Emerson, Asian Students for Intercultural Awareness, Amnesty International.

**Athletics.** NCAA. **Intercollegiate:** Baseball M, basketball, cross-country, golf, lacrosse, soccer, softball W, tennis, track and field, volleyball W. **Team name:** Lions.

**Student services.** Adult student services, chaplain/spiritual director, career counseling, student employment services, financial aid counseling, health services, minority student services, personal counseling, placement for graduates. **Physically disabled:** Services for visually, speech, hearing impaired.

**Contact.** E-mail: admission@emerson.edu
Phone: (617) 824-8600 Fax: (617) 824-8609
Sara Ramirez, Director of Undergraduate Admission, Emerson College, 120 Boylston Street, Boston, MA 02116-4624

---

## Emmanuel College

**Boston, Massachusetts**
**www.emmanuel.edu**

**CB member**
**CB code: 3368**

- Private 4-year liberal arts college affiliated with Roman Catholic Church
- Residential campus in very large city

---

- 1,997 degree-seeking undergraduates: 18% part-time, 74% women, 7% African American, 3% Asian American, 5% Hispanic American, 1% international
- 277 degree-seeking graduate students
- 56% of applicants admitted
- SAT or ACT (ACT writing optional), application essay required
- 63% graduate within 6 years

**General.** Founded in 1919. Regionally accredited. Through the Colleges of the Fenway consortium, students can cross-register at Simmons College, Wentworth Institute of Technology, Wheelock College, Massachusetts College of Art, and Massachusetts College of Pharmacy and Health Sciences. **Degrees:** 459 bachelor's awarded; master's offered. **ROTC:** Army. **Calendar:** Semester, limited summer session. **Full-time faculty:** 82 total; 84% have terminal degrees, 15% minority, 62% women. **Part-time faculty:** 109 total; 35% have terminal degrees, 6% minority, 52% women. **Class size:** 71% < 20, 29% 20-39. **Special facilities:** Science center with 14 laboratories, community leadership center, mission and spirituality center.

**Freshman class profile.** 5,518 applied, 3,100 admitted, 424 enrolled.

| Mid 50% test scores | | | | |
|---|---|---|---|---|
| SAT critical reading: | 510-590 | GPA 2.0-2.99: | 23% |
| SAT math: | 480-570 | Rank in top quarter: | 41% |
| SAT writing: | 500-590 | Rank in top tenth: | 12% |
| ACT composite: | 20-24 | Return as sophomores: | 79% |
| GPA 3.75 or higher: | 26% | Out-of-state: | 44% |
| GPA 3.50-3.74: | 20% | Live on campus: | 92% |
| GPA 3.0-3.49: | 31% | International: | 3% |

**Basis for selection.** High school curriculum and record most important, followed by recommendations, test scores, essay, creativity, initiative. Interviews encouraged. **Homeschooled:** Portfolio, on-campus interview recommended.

**High school preparation.** College-preparatory program required. 16 units required. Required units include English 4, mathematics 3, social studies 2, science 2 (laboratory 2) and foreign language 2.

**2009-2010 Annual costs.** Tuition/fees: $29,490. Room/board: $11,950. Books/supplies: $880. Personal expenses: $1,935.

**2009-2010 Financial aid. Need-based:** 385 full-time freshmen applied for aid; 344 were judged to have need; 344 of these received aid. Average need met was 75%. Average scholarship/grant was $20,527; average loan $3,688. 59% of total undergraduate aid awarded as scholarships/grants, 41% as loans/jobs. **Non-need-based:** Awarded to 844 full-time undergraduates, including 351 freshmen. Scholarships awarded for academics, alumni affiliation, leadership.

**Application procedures. Admission:** Priority date 12/1; deadline 3/1 (postmark date). $40 fee, may be waived for applicants with need, free for online applicants. Admission notification on a rolling basis beginning on or about 12/1. Must reply by May 1 or within 2 week(s) if notified thereafter. **Financial aid:** Priority date 4/1; no closing date. FAFSA, institutional form required. Applicants notified on a rolling basis starting 3/15.

**Academics.** Each student required to complete 1-semester Capstone Experience designed to provide an opportunity to integrate and present content and methodology acquired in the major. This course may take the form of a seminar, internship, research project or creative project. **Special study options:** Accelerated study, cross-registration, distance learning, double major, exchange student, honors, independent study, internships, liberal arts/career combination, semester at sea, student-designed major, study abroad, teacher certification program, Washington semester. **Credit/placement by examination:** AP, CLEP, IB, SAT, ACT, institutional tests. **Support services:** Learning center, pre-admission summer program, reduced course load, remedial instruction, study skills assistance, tutoring, writing center.

**Majors. Area/ethnic studies:** American. **Biology:** General, biochemistry, biostatistics. **Business:** Business admin. **Communications:** General. **Conservation:** Environmental studies. **Education:** Elementary, secondary. **Foreign languages:** Spanish. **Health:** Art therapy. **History:** General. **Interdisciplinary:** Global studies, neuroscience. **Liberal arts:** Arts/sciences. **Math:** General. **Physical sciences:** Chemistry, forensic chemistry. **Psychology:** General, counseling, developmental. **Social sciences:** Political science, sociology. **Visual/performing arts:** Graphic design, studio arts.

**Most popular majors.** Business/marketing 16%, communications/journalism 9%, education 9%, English 8%, liberal arts 7%, psychology 13%, social sciences 8%, visual/performing arts 6%.

**Computing on campus.** 196 workstations in dormitories, library, computer center, student center. Dormitories wired for high-speed internet access and linked to campus network. Commuter students can connect to campus network. Online course registration, online library, helpline, student web hosting, wireless network available.

**Student life. Freshman orientation:** Mandatory, $100 fee. Preregistration for classes offered. Three 2-day sessions during the summer; includes assessment of foundation skills, course selection, placement exams, academic advising and educational sessions. **Policies:** No alcohol permitted on campus. **Housing:** Guaranteed on-campus for all undergraduates. Coed dorms, special housing for disabled available. $200 nonrefundable deposit, deadline 5/1. **Activities:** Bands, campus ministries, choral groups, dance, drama, film society, international student organizations, literary magazine, music ensembles, Model UN, musical theater, radio station, student government, student newspaper, symphony orchestra, Association of Countries Cultures Events Nations and Traditions, Asian student association, black student union, Helping Unite Latinos to Lead and Achieve Success, College Democrats, College Republicans, social awareness club, students for environmental action, Core Ministry team.

**Athletics.** NCAA. **Intercollegiate:** Basketball, cross-country, golf M, lacrosse W, soccer, softball W, tennis W, track and field, volleyball. **Intramural:** Badminton, basketball, bowling, football (non-tackle), racquetball, soccer, softball, tennis, volleyball. **Team name:** Saints.

**Student services.** Adult student services, alcohol/substance abuse counseling, chaplain/spiritual director, career counseling, student employment services, financial aid counseling, health services, minority student services, personal counseling, placement for graduates, veterans' counselor. **Physically disabled:** Services for visually, speech, hearing impaired.

**Contact.** E-mail: enroll@emmanuel.edu
Phone: (617) 735-9715 Fax: (617) 735-9801
Sandra Robbins, Dean of Enrollment, Emmanuel College, 400 The Fenway, Boston, MA 02115

## Endicott College
**Beverly, Massachusetts**  **CB member**
**www.endicott.edu**  **CB code: 3369**

- Private 4-year liberal arts college
- Residential campus in large town
- 2,273 degree-seeking undergraduates: 7% part-time, 58% women, 1% African American, 1% Asian American, 2% Hispanic American, 2% international
- 567 degree-seeking graduate students
- 53% of applicants admitted
- SAT or ACT with writing, application essay required
- 72% graduate within 6 years; 26% enter graduate study

**General.** Founded in 1939. Regionally accredited. **Degrees:** 463 bachelor's, 1 associate awarded; master's offered. **ROTC:** Army, Air Force. **Location:** 24 miles from Boston. **Calendar:** 4-1-4, limited summer session. **Full-time faculty:** 77 total; 66% have terminal degrees, 6% minority, 53% women. **Part-time faculty:** 111 total; 30% have terminal degrees, 5% minority, 58% women. **Class size:** 52% < 20, 48% 20-39. **Special facilities:** Art galleries, student-run restaurant/classroom, archives museum, nature trails, private beaches.

**Freshman class profile.** 3,885 applied, 2,072 admitted, 561 enrolled.

| Mid 50% test scores | | Rank in top tenth: | 10% |
|---|---|---|---|
| SAT critical reading: | 490-580 | Return as sophomores: | 83% |
| SAT math: | 500-590 | Out-of-state: | 58% |
| SAT writing: | 480-580 | Live on campus: | 97% |
| ACT composite: | 20-25 | International: | 2% |
| Rank in top quarter: | 41% | | |

**Basis for selection.** School achievement record and SAT/ACT scores most important. Class rank, essay, volunteer work, extracurricular activities, leadership also important. Teacher, counselor recommendations considered. Interview recommended. **Homeschooled:** Verification that curriculum has been certified by local school system or state, or GED.

**High school preparation.** College-preparatory program recommended. 16 units recommended. Recommended units include English 4, mathematics 3, social studies 2, history 1, science 2 and academic electives 4. One chemistry with laboratory and algebra required for nursing and athletic training programs.

**2009-2010 Annual costs.** Tuition/fees: $25,376. Room/board: $11,836. Books/supplies: $1,000. Personal expenses: $1,000.

**2009-2010 Financial aid. Need-based:** 503 full-time freshmen applied for aid; 371 were judged to have need; 367 of these received aid. Average need met was 60%. Average scholarship/grant was $9,439; average loan $3,803. 67% of total undergraduate aid awarded as scholarships/grants, 33%

as loans/jobs. **Non-need-based:** Awarded to 1,095 full-time undergraduates, including 337 freshmen. Scholarships awarded for academics, alumni affiliation, art, job skills, leadership, music/drama, religious affiliation, ROTC, state residency.

**Application procedures. Admission:** Closing date 2/15. $40 fee, may be waived for applicants with need. Admission notification on a rolling basis beginning on or about 11/1. Must reply by May 1 or within 1 week(s) if notified thereafter. **Financial aid:** Priority date 3/15; no closing date. FAFSA, institutional form required. Applicants notified on a rolling basis starting 3/15; must reply within 2 week(s) of notification.

**Academics.** Three Internships required of all traditional undergraduates. **Special study options:** Accelerated study, combined bachelor's/graduate degree, cross-registration, distance learning, dual enrollment of high school students, exchange student, honors, independent study, internships, liberal arts/career combination, student-designed major, study abroad, teacher certification program, Washington semester. **Credit/placement by examination:** AP, CLEP, IB, SAT, institutional tests. 32 credit hours maximum toward associate degree, 85 toward bachelor's. **Support services:** Learning center, study skills assistance, tutoring, writing center.

**Majors. Biology:** Biotechnology. **Business:** Accounting, business admin, hospitality admin. **Communications:** Media studies. **Computer sciences:** Computer science. **Conservation:** Environmental studies. **Education:** Early childhood, elementary, physical. **Health:** Athletic training, nursing (RN). **History:** General. **Interdisciplinary:** Global studies. **Liberal arts:** Arts/sciences. **Parks/recreation:** Sports admin. **Protective services:** Criminal justice. **Psychology:** General. **Public administration:** Human services. **Visual/performing arts:** Design, interior design, studio arts.

**Most popular majors.** Business/marketing 32%, communications/journalism 10%, education 6%, health sciences 8%, parks/recreation 12%, security/protective services 6%, visual/performing arts 9%.

**Computing on campus.** 232 workstations in library, computer center. Dormitories wired for high-speed internet access and linked to campus network. Commuter students can connect to campus network. Online course registration, online library, helpline, repair service, wireless network available.

**Student life. Freshman orientation:** Available. Preregistration for classes offered. Sessions held in July and September; includes preparation for fall course assignment. **Housing:** Guaranteed on-campus for freshmen. Coed dorms, single-sex dorms, special housing for disabled, apartments, wellness housing available. $500 deposit, deadline 5/1. Single-parent housing, suite-type, modular housing available. **Activities:** Bands, campus ministries, choral groups, dance, drama, film society, international student organizations, literary magazine, music ensembles, Model UN, musical theater, student government, student newspaper, TV station, intercultural club, Phi Theta Kappa, ALANA, friendship club, political debate society, Rotaract service club.

**Athletics.** NCAA. **Intercollegiate:** Baseball M, basketball, cross-country, equestrian, field hockey W, football (tackle) M, golf M, lacrosse, rowing (crew), sailing, soccer, softball W, tennis, volleyball. **Intramural:** Basketball, football (non-tackle), lacrosse, racquetball, soccer, softball, volleyball. **Team name:** Gulls.

**Student services.** Alcohol/substance abuse counseling, chaplain/spiritual director, career counseling, financial aid counseling, health services, personal counseling, women's services. **Physically disabled:** Services for visually, hearing impaired.

**Contact.** E-mail: admission@endicott.edu
Phone: (978) 921-1000 Toll-free number: (800) 325-1114
Fax: (978) 232-2520
Thomas Redman, Vice President for Admissions and Financial Aid, Endicott College, 376 Hale Street, Beverly, MA 01915-9985

## Fitchburg State College
**Fitchburg, Massachusetts**  **CB member**
**www.fsc.edu**  **CB code: 3518**

- Public 4-year liberal arts and teachers college
- Residential campus in small city
- 3,987 degree-seeking undergraduates: 13% part-time, 53% women, 4% African American, 2% Asian American, 4% Hispanic American
- 1,066 degree-seeking graduate students
- 64% of applicants admitted
- SAT or ACT (ACT writing optional), application essay required
- 52% graduate within 6 years

**General.** Founded in 1894. Regionally accredited. **Degrees:** 640 bachelor's awarded; master's offered. **ROTC:** Army. **Location:** 50 miles from Boston, 25 miles from Worcester. **Calendar:** Semester, limited summer session. **Full-time faculty:** 179 total; 91% have terminal degrees, 13% minority, 46% women. **Part-time faculty:** 86 total; 28% have terminal degrees, 6% minority, 57% women. **Class size:** 43% < 20, 57% 20-39, less than 1% 40-49. **Special facilities:** Teacher education laboratory school, 120-acre conservation area.

**Freshman class profile.** 3,809 applied, 2,456 admitted, 783 enrolled.

| Mid 50% test scores | | | |
|---|---|---|---|
| SAT critical reading: | 460-560 | GPA 3.0-3.49: | 30% |
| SAT math: | 460-560 | GPA 2.0-2.99: | 50% |
| SAT writing: | 450-550 | Return as sophomores: | 77% |
| ACT composite: | 19-23 | Out-of-state: | 11% |
| GPA 3.75 or higher: | 11% | Live on campus: | 71% |
| GPA 3.50-3.74: | 9% | Fraternities: | 3% |
| | | Sororities: | 8% |

**Basis for selection.** Secondary school record, test scores, essay important. Recommendations considered. Interview recommended for nursing, undeclared major, computer science, business administration, communications/media majors. **Learning Disabled:** Students with professionally diagnosed learning disabilities exempt from standardized test requirements.

**High school preparation.** College-preparatory program required. 16 units required. Required units include English 4, mathematics 3, social studies 1, history 1, science 3 (laboratory 2), foreign language 2 and academic electives 2. Additional units of math and science preferred for nursing, medical technology, computer science, business applicants.

**2009-2010 Annual costs.** Tuition/fees: $6,900; $12,980 out-of-state. Room/board: $7,632. Books/supplies: $800. Personal expenses: $1,500.

**2008-2009 Financial aid. Need-based:** 727 full-time freshmen applied for aid; 443 were judged to have need; 432 of these received aid. Average need met was 93%. Average scholarship/grant was $4,391; average loan $2,463. 50% of total undergraduate aid awarded as scholarships/grants, 50% as loans/jobs. **Non-need-based:** Awarded to 211 full-time undergraduates, including 139 freshmen. Scholarships awarded for academics, alumni affiliation, leadership, ROTC, state residency.

**Application procedures. Admission:** Priority date 1/1; no deadline. $25 fee ($40 out-of-state), may be waived for applicants with need. Admission notification on a rolling basis beginning on or about 12/1. Must reply by May 1 or within 2 week(s) if notified thereafter. **Financial aid:** Priority date 3/1; no closing date. FAFSA required. Applicants notified on a rolling basis starting 3/15.

**Academics.** Many major programs include internship, practicum, or clinical experience. All degree programs require completion of 48 credits in liberal arts and sciences. **Special study options:** Cross-registration, distance learning, double major, dual enrollment of high school students, honors, independent study, internships, liberal arts/career combination, student-designed major, study abroad, teacher certification program. **Credit/placement by examination:** AP, CLEP, institutional tests. 60 credit hours maximum toward bachelor's degree. **Support services:** Learning center, pre-admission summer program, reduced course load, remedial instruction, study skills assistance, tutoring, writing center.

**Honors college/program.** Selected freshmen students invited to join Leadership Academy based on high school preparation, test scores, and leadership potential. Students complete integrated sequence of courses over 4-year period. Students expected to demonstrate leadership through extracurricular activities, volunteer positions, and service learning placements. A 3.3 GPA is required to continue in the program.

**Majors. Architecture:** Technology. **Biology:** General, biotechnology, environmental, exercise physiology. **Business:** Accounting, business admin, finance, international, management science, marketing. **Communications:** General, digital media. **Computer sciences:** General, computer science. **Education:** General, biology, early childhood, elementary, English, geography, history, mathematics, middle, secondary, special, technology/industrial arts, trade/industrial. **Engineering technology:** Architectural, construction, electrical, industrial, manufacturing. **Health:** Nursing (RN). **History:** General. **Liberal arts:** Arts/sciences. **Math:** General. **Parks/recreation:** Exercise sciences, sports admin. **Protective services:** Criminal justice. **Psychology:** General, developmental, industrial. **Public administration:** Human services. **Social sciences:** Economics, geography, international economics, political science, sociology. **Visual/performing arts:** Cinematography, dramatic, graphic design, photography, theater design.

**Most popular majors.** Business/marketing 15%, education 10%, health sciences 6%, liberal arts 11%, security/protective services 6%, visual/performing arts 15%.

**Computing on campus.** PC or laptop required. 150 workstations in dormitories, library, computer center, student center. Dormitories wired for high-speed internet access and linked to campus network. Commuter students can connect to campus network. Online course registration, online library, helpline, wireless network available.

**Student life. Freshman orientation:** Mandatory. Preregistration for classes offered. Testing, academic advising, registration for classes are key components of the program. **Housing:** Coed dorms, special housing for disabled, apartments, wellness housing available. $150 nonrefundable deposit, deadline 5/1. Quiet halls available. **Activities:** Bands, choral groups, dance, drama, film society, literary magazine, Model UN, radio station, student government, student newspaper, student government association, Christian Fellowship, black student union, Habitat for Humanity, Latin American student organization, MASSPIRG, peer educators, First Responders, Chavarium.

**Athletics.** NCAA. **Intercollegiate:** Baseball M, basketball, cross-country, field hockey W, football (tackle) M, ice hockey M, lacrosse W, soccer, softball W, track and field. **Intramural:** Basketball, bowling, football (non-tackle), racquetball, soccer, softball, volleyball. **Team name:** Falcons.

**Student services.** Alcohol/substance abuse counseling, career counseling, services for economically disadvantaged, student employment services, financial aid counseling, health services, minority student services, personal counseling. **Physically disabled:** Services for visually, speech, hearing impaired. **Learning disabled:** Comprehensive services available.

**Contact.** E-mail: admissions@fsc.edu
Phone: (978) 665-3144 Toll-free number: (800) 705-9692
Fax: (978) 665-4540
Pamela McCafferty, Dean of Enrollment Management, Fitchburg State College, 160 Pearl Street, Fitchburg, MA 01420-2697

---

## Framingham State College
**Framingham, Massachusetts**
**www.framingham.edu**
CB member
CB code: 3519

- Public 4-year liberal arts and teachers college
- Residential campus in small city
- 3,485 degree-seeking undergraduates: 12% part-time, 66% women, 5% African American, 2% Asian American, 4% Hispanic American, 1% international
- 804 degree-seeking graduate students
- 63% of applicants admitted
- SAT or ACT with writing, application essay required
- 52% graduate within 6 years

**General.** Founded in 1839. Regionally accredited. **Degrees:** 664 bachelor's awarded; master's offered. **Location:** 20 miles from Boston. **Calendar:** Semester, extensive summer session. **Full-time faculty:** 164 total; 77% have terminal degrees, 5% minority, 57% women. **Part-time faculty:** 86 total; 48% women. **Class size:** 36% < 20, 62% 20-39, less than 1% 40-49, 1% 50-99. **Special facilities:** Global education center, social research center, learning center, economic research center, STEM pipeline center, food and nutrition institute, greenhouse, early childhood demonstration lab, education curriculum library.

**Freshman class profile.** 3,384 applied, 2,141 admitted, 724 enrolled.

| Mid 50% test scores | | | |
|---|---|---|---|
| SAT critical reading: | 460-560 | GPA 2.0-2.99: | 36% |
| SAT math: | 480-560 | Rank in top quarter: | 32% |
| SAT writing: | 470-560 | Rank in top tenth: | 9% |
| ACT composite: | 20-21 | Return as sophomores: | 73% |
| GPA 3.75 or higher: | 13% | Out-of-state: | 5% |
| GPA 3.50-3.74: | 10% | Live on campus: | 82% |
| GPA 3.0-3.49: | 41% | International: | 1% |

**Basis for selection.** Strength of high school curriculum, weighted high school GPA, class rank, test scores most important. Some attention given to organized and volunteer activities, recommendations and special talents. Consideration given to students whose educational opportunities have been limited due to economic disadvantage. Admission standards policy of Massachusetts Department of Higher Education requires 16 college-preparatory courses with 3.0 weighted GPA. Students with lower GPA may qualify based on sliding scale combining SAT scores with GPA. Portfolio required of studio art majors. **Homeschooled:** Students may be required to submit results of additional nationally normed tests, such as SAT Subject Tests. **Learning Disabled:** Students with diagnosed learning disability must submit individualized educational plan/504 plan along with all psychoeducational testing current within last 3 years.

**High school preparation.** College-preparatory program required. 16 units required; 21 recommended. Required and recommended units include English 4, mathematics 3-4, social studies 1, history 1-2, science 3-4 (laboratory 2-3), foreign language 2-4 and academic electives 2. Math must include algebra I, algebra II, and geometry. Additional unit of math strongly recommended for computer science, math, pre-engineering, and science majors. Additional units of biology, chemistry, physics recommended for science majors. Foreign language must be 2 units of same language. All units must be college-preparatory level.

**2009-2010 Annual costs.** Tuition/fees: $6,540; $12,620 out-of-state. Fees include mandatory laptop purchase by new students. New England Regional tuition rate $1,455. Room/board: $8,148. Books/supplies: $900. Personal expenses: $1,200.

**2008-2009 Financial aid. Need-based:** 526 full-time freshmen applied for aid; 367 were judged to have need; 367 of these received aid. Average need met was 76%. Average scholarship/grant was $4,060; average loan $4,525. 35% of total undergraduate aid awarded as scholarships/grants, 65% as loans/jobs. **Non-need-based:** Awarded to 310 full-time undergraduates, including 98 freshmen. Scholarships awarded for academics.

**Application procedures. Admission:** Priority date 2/15; no deadline. $50 fee, may be waived for applicants with need. Admission notification on a rolling basis beginning on or about 1/15. Must reply by May 1 or within 2 week(s) if notified thereafter. Students should contact admissions office after priority date of 2/15 to determine if applications are still being accepted. Some majors and on-campus housing may be filled by priority date. Application fee waiver available to students who submit College Board fee waiver. **Financial aid:** Priority date 3/1; no closing date. FAFSA required. Applicants notified on a rolling basis starting 3/15; must reply by 5/1 or within 2 week(s) of notification.

**Academics.** E-tutoring available on-line. **Special study options:** Cross-registration, distance learning, double major, honors, independent study, internships, liberal arts/career combination, study abroad, teacher certification program, Washington semester. Pre-engineering program in conjunction with University of Massachusetts at Amherst, University of Massachusetts at Dartmouth, University of Massachusetts at Lowell. **Credit/placement by examination:** AP, CLEP, IB, institutional tests. 64 credit hours maximum toward bachelor's degree. **Support services:** Learning center, reduced course load, remedial instruction, study skills assistance, tutoring, writing center.

**Majors. Agriculture:** Food science. **Biology:** General. **Business:** General, knowledge management. **Computer sciences:** General. **Conservation:** Environmental studies. **Education:** Early childhood, elementary. **Family/consumer sciences:** General, clothing/textiles, food/nutrition. **Foreign languages:** General. **Health:** Nursing (RN). **History:** General. **Liberal arts:** Arts/sciences. **Math:** General. **Physical sciences:** Chemistry. **Psychology:** General. **Social sciences:** Economics, geography, political science, sociology. **Visual/performing arts:** Art.

**Most popular majors.** Business/marketing 18%, communication technologies 8%, education 7%, family/consumer sciences 12%, history 7%, psychology 11%, social sciences 11%.

**Computing on campus.** PC or laptop required. 232 workstations in dormitories, library, computer center, student center. Dormitories wired for high-speed internet access and linked to campus network. Commuter students can connect to campus network. Online course registration, online library, helpline, wireless network available.

**Student life. Freshman orientation:** Mandatory. Preregistration for classes offered. Weekend session held during the summer; additional 1-day session in late August or early September. **Housing:** Coed dorms, single-sex dorms, wellness housing available. $150 nonrefundable deposit, deadline 5/1. **Activities:** Campus ministries, choral groups, dance, drama, international student organizations, literary magazine, musical theater, radio station, student government, student newspaper, active sociologists, black student union, Christian fellowship, Newman Association, student union activities board, international student union, 10% Alliance and Allies, Amnesty International, animal rights, global change initiative.

**Athletics.** NCAA. **Intercollegiate:** Baseball M, basketball, cross-country, field hockey W, football (tackle) M, ice hockey M, lacrosse W, soccer, softball W, volleyball W. **Intramural:** Basketball, football (non-tackle), golf, soccer, tennis, volleyball, weight lifting. **Team name:** Rams.

**Student services.** Adult student services, alcohol/substance abuse counseling, chaplain/spiritual director, career counseling, services for economically disadvantaged, student employment services, financial aid counseling, health services, minority student services, on-campus daycare, personal counseling, placement for graduates, veterans' counselor. **Physically disabled:** Services for visually, hearing impaired.

**Contact.** E-mail: admissions@framingham.edu
Phone: (508) 626-4500 Fax: (508) 626-4017
Nick Figueroa, Dean of Undergraduate Admissions, Framingham State College, PO Box 9101, Framingham, MA 01701-9101

## Franklin W. Olin College of Engineering
**Needham, Massachusetts**     CB member
www.olin.edu     CB code: 2824

- Private 4-year engineering college
- Residential campus in large town
- 330 degree-seeking undergraduates: 45% women
- 16% of applicants admitted
- SAT or ACT (ACT writing optional), SAT Subject Tests, application essay required
- 95% graduate within 6 years; 28% enter graduate study

**General.** Regionally accredited. All students receive Olin Scholarship, currently valued at one-half tuition. Additional need-based aid available to cover other costs. **Degrees:** 62 bachelor's awarded. **Location:** 14 miles from Boston. **Calendar:** Semester. **Full-time faculty:** 35 total; 100% have terminal degrees, 17% minority, 34% women. **Part-time faculty:** 7 total; 86% have terminal degrees, 14% minority, 14% women. **Class size:** 53% < 20, 45% 20-39, 3% 40-49.

**Freshman class profile.** 874 applied, 143 admitted, 85 enrolled.

| Mid 50% test scores | | | |
|---|---|---|---|
| | | ACT composite: | 32-35 |
| SAT critical reading: | 700-790 | Out-of-state: | 91% |
| SAT math: | 740-800 | Live on campus: | 100% |
| SAT writing: | 670-770 | International: | 9% |

**Basis for selection.** Secondary school achievement, course rigor, test scores, personal character most important; creativity and entrepreneurial spirit also very important. Cultural, economic, geographic diversity encouraged. Candidates for admission selected from all applicants. Candidates required to attend 1 of 2 weekends on campus to participate in design project, individual interviews, and team exercises. Incoming class selected from this group. 2 SAT Subject Tests required: Math (Level 2 preferred, Level 1 accepted) and any science subject. **Homeschooled:** Statement describing homeschool structure and mission, transcript of courses and grades, letter of recommendation (nonparent) required.

**High school preparation.** College-preparatory program recommended. Recommended units include English 4, mathematics 4, social studies 2, history 2, science 3 (laboratory 3) and foreign language 2. 1 calculus unit and 1 physics unit required.

**2009-2010 Annual costs.** Tuition/fees: $36,795. All incoming students will receive Olin Scholarship, currently valued at one-half tuition. Additional need-based aid available to cover other costs. Room/board: $13,230. Books/supplies: $750.

**2009-2010 Financial aid. Need-based:** 89% of total undergraduate aid awarded as scholarships/grants, 11% as loans/jobs. **Non-need-based:** Scholarships awarded for academics, leadership. **Additional information:** Financial aid forms not needed for one-half tuition scholarship which all students receive; FAFSA forms required for need-based aid considerations.

**Application procedures. Admission:** Closing date 1/1 (postmark date). $80 fee, may be waived for applicants with need. Application must be submitted online. Admission notification 3/22. Must reply by 5/1. **Financial aid:** Priority date 2/15; no closing date. FAFSA required. Applicants notified on a rolling basis starting 3/31; must reply by 5/1.

**Academics. Special study options:** Combined bachelor's/graduate degree, cross-registration, exchange student, independent study, internships, liberal arts/career combination, semester at sea, student-designed major, study abroad. **Credit/placement by examination:** CLEP. **Support services:** Study skills assistance, tutoring, writing center.

**Majors. Engineering:** General, electrical, mechanical.

**Computing on campus.** PC or laptop required. Dormitories wired for high-speed internet access and linked to campus network. Commuter students can connect to campus network. Online course registration, online library, helpline, repair service, student web hosting, wireless network available.

**Student life. Freshman orientation:** Mandatory. **Policies:** All students sign honor code that addresses personal and academic integrity. **Housing:** Guaranteed on-campus for all undergraduates. Coed dorms, special housing for disabled available. **Activities:** Jazz band, choral groups, dance, drama, film society, music ensembles, musical theater, student government, symphony orchestra, Christian fellowship, Support, Encourage and Recognize Volunteerism, Korean club, political caucus, martial arts club, Chinese club, Catholic association, Japanese club, Judaism at Olin.

**Athletics. Intramural:** Basketball, football (non-tackle), ice hockey, racquetball, soccer, softball, squash, tennis, volleyball.

**Student services.** Alcohol/substance abuse counseling, chaplain/spiritual director, career counseling, student employment services, financial aid counseling, health services, minority student services, personal counseling, placement for graduates, veterans' counselor, women's services. **Physically disabled:** Services for hearing impaired.

**Contact.** E-mail: info@olin.edu
Phone: (781) 292-2222 Fax: (781) 292-2210
Charles Nolan, Dean of Admission, Franklin W. Olin College of Engineering, Olin Way, Needham, MA 02492-1245

---

## Gordon College

| Wenham, Massachusetts | CB member |
| www.gordon.edu | CB code: 3417 |

- Private 4-year liberal arts college affiliated with nondenominational tradition
- Residential campus in small town
- 1,572 degree-seeking undergraduates: 2% part-time, 62% women, 2% African American, 2% Asian American, 3% Hispanic American, 4% international
- 87 degree-seeking graduate students
- 66% of applicants admitted
- SAT or ACT with writing, application essay, interview required
- 72% graduate within 6 years

**General.** Founded in 1889. Regionally accredited. Full ropes course. **Degrees:** 374 bachelor's awarded; master's offered. **ROTC:** Army, Air Force. **Location:** 25 miles from Boston. **Calendar:** Semester, limited summer session. **Full-time faculty:** 93 total; 81% have terminal degrees, 11% minority, 30% women. **Part-time faculty:** 52 total; 2% minority, 56% women. **Class size:** 67% < 20, 27% 20-39, 3% 40-49, 2% 50-99, 1% >100. **Special facilities:** Christian studies center, international office for Christians in the visual arts, electron microscope, gene sequencing machine, Shakespearean folios, center for balance and mobility.

**Freshman class profile.** 1,664 applied, 1,106 admitted, 382 enrolled.

| Mid 50% test scores | | Rank in top tenth: | 32% |
|---|---|---|---|
| SAT critical reading: | 520-650 | Return as sophomores: | 90% |
| SAT math: | 500-640 | Out-of-state: | 77% |
| SAT writing: | 560-640 | Live on campus: | 99% |
| ACT composite: | 24-28 | International: | 3% |
| Rank in top quarter: | 58% | | |

**Basis for selection.** High school course selection and grades, rank in class, essay of Christian commitment, test scores, references, interview important. School and community activities considered. SAT Subject Tests not required but may be used for placement. Audition required of music majors. Portfolio required of visual art majors. **Homeschooled:** Statement describing homeschool structure and mission, transcript of courses and grades, letter of recommendation (nonparent) required. Information regarding course of study, including description of curriculum and reading list required. **Learning Disabled:** Students with diagnosed learning disability may submit documentation with application, as well as any learning plans used through high school.

**High school preparation.** College-preparatory program required. 20 units required; 25 recommended. Required and recommended units include English 4, mathematics 2-3, social studies 2-3, science 2-3 (laboratory 1-3), foreign language 2-4 and academic electives 5. Academic profile should include AP, honors, or accelerated courses.

**2010-2011 Annual costs.** Tuition/fees: $29,458. Room/board: $8,100. Books/supplies: $800. Personal expenses: $1,000.

**2009-2010 Financial aid. Need-based:** Average need met was 73%. Average scholarship/grant was $12,753; average loan $4,995. 58% of total undergraduate aid awarded as scholarships/grants, 42% as loans/jobs. **Non-need-based:** Scholarships awarded for academics, alumni affiliation, art, leadership, minority status, music/drama, religious affiliation.

**Application procedures. Admission:** Priority date 3/1; no deadline. $50 fee, may be waived for applicants with need. Admission notification on a rolling basis beginning on or about 12/15. Must reply by May 1 or within 2

week(s) if notified thereafter. **Financial aid:** Closing date 3/1. FAFSA required. Applicants notified on a rolling basis starting 4/15; must reply by 5/1 or within 2 week(s) of notification.

**Academics.** Study abroad in England, France, Israel, Italy, Egypt, Russia, China, Canada, Belize, Latin America, Uganda. Extensive domestic programs include marine biology, film studies in Hollywood. Great Books Honors Program in Jerusalem and Athens. Outdoor education immersion semester in urban Boston, South Africa. **Special study options:** Combined bachelor's/graduate degree, cooperative education, cross-registration, double major, honors, independent study, internships, liberal arts/career combination, student-designed major, study abroad, teacher certification program, urban semester, Washington semester. Programs in Boston; Aix-en-Provence, France; Orvieto, Italy. Outdoor Education Immersion Semester; Kinesiology Semester; Public History Semester; Oregon Extension; co-op programs in arts, business, computer science, education, engineering, health professions, humanities, natural science, social/behavioral science. **Credit/placement by examination:** AP, CLEP, IB, SAT, institutional tests. **Support services:** Learning center, reduced course load, remedial instruction, study skills assistance, tutoring, writing center.

**Majors. Biology:** General, exercise physiology. **Business:** Accounting, business admin, finance. **Communications:** General. **Computer sciences:** Computer science. **Education:** Early childhood, elementary, middle, music, secondary, special. **Engineering:** Physics. **Foreign languages:** General, French, German, Spanish. **History:** General. **Math:** General. **Parks/recreation:** General. **Philosophy/religion:** Christian, philosophy. **Physical sciences:** Chemistry, physics. **Psychology:** General. **Public administration:** Social work. **Social sciences:** Economics, international relations, political science, sociology. **Theology:** Youth ministry. **Visual/performing arts:** Art, dramatic, music performance.

**Most popular majors.** Biology 6%, business/marketing 13%, communications/journalism 7%, education 9%, English 7%, history 6%, psychology 8%, public administration/social services 6%, social sciences 12%, theological studies 8%.

**Computing on campus.** 125 workstations in dormitories, library, computer center, student center. Dormitories wired for high-speed internet access and linked to campus network. Commuter students can connect to campus network. Online library, helpline, repair service, wireless network available.

**Student life. Freshman orientation:** Mandatory. Preregistration for classes offered. Five-day program held in the days prior to start of semester; includes program for parents on days 1 and 2. **Policies:** No alcohol or smoking allowed on campus or at college-sponsored events. Religious observance required. **Housing:** Guaranteed on-campus for all undergraduates. Coed dorms, single-sex dorms, special housing for disabled, apartments, wellness housing available. $250 nonrefundable deposit. Mentoring hall. **Activities:** Bands, campus ministries, choral groups, drama, film society, international student organizations, literary magazine, music ensembles, Model UN, musical theater, student government, student newspaper, symphony orchestra, society for new politics, advocates for cultural diversity, Christians for social action, fellowship group for children of missionaries, ministry to deaf persons, outreach service, short-term mission trips, Amnesty International, ALANA.

**Athletics.** NCAA. **Intercollegiate:** Baseball M, basketball, cross-country, field hockey W, golf, lacrosse, soccer, softball W, swimming, tennis, track and field, volleyball W. **Intramural:** Basketball, football (non-tackle), racquetball, soccer, softball, table tennis. **Team name:** Fighting Scots.

**Student services.** Alcohol/substance abuse counseling, chaplain/spiritual director, career counseling, student employment services, financial aid counseling, health services, minority student services, personal counseling, placement for graduates. **Physically disabled:** Services for visually, speech, hearing impaired.

**Contact.** E-mail: admissions@gordon.edu
Phone: (978) 867-4218 Toll-free number: (866) 464-6736
Fax: (978) 867-4682
Brook Berry, Vice President of Enrollment, Gordon College, 255 Grapevine Road, Wenham, MA 01984

---

## Hampshire College

| Amherst, Massachusetts | CB member |
| www.hampshire.edu | CB code: 3447 |

- Private 4-year liberal arts college
- Residential campus in large town
- 1,438 degree-seeking undergraduates: 60% women
- 63% of applicants admitted
- Application essay required
- 64% graduate within 6 years; 10% enter graduate study

**General.** Founded in 1965. Regionally accredited. All students work closely with faculty advisors to design individual academic programs and complete capstone project. **Degrees:** 300 bachelor's awarded. **ROTC:** Army. **Location:** 90 miles from Boston, 20 miles from Springfield. **Calendar:** 4-1-4. **Full-time faculty:** 99 total; 83% have terminal degrees, 20% minority, 54% women. **Part-time faculty:** 60 total; 73% have terminal degrees, 13% minority, 42% women. **Class size:** 68% < 20, 31% 20-39, less than 1% 40-49. **Special facilities:** Bioshelter (integrated greenhouse/aquaculture facility), farm center, electronic music production studio, extensive film and photography facilities, fabrication center, national Yiddish book center, picture-book art museum.

**Freshman class profile.** 2,515 applied, 1,578 admitted, 373 enrolled.

| Mid 50% test scores | | GPA 2.0-2.99: | 14% |
|---|---|---|---|
| SAT critical reading: | 600-710 | Rank in top quarter: | 69% |
| SAT math: | 530-660 | Rank in top tenth: | 27% |
| SAT writing: | 590-700 | Return as sophomores: | 87% |
| ACT composite: | 25-29 | Out-of-state: | 81% |
| GPA 3.75 or higher: | 33% | Live on campus: | 100% |
| GPA 3.50-3.74: | 19% | International: | 3% |
| GPA 3.0-3.49: | 34% | | |

**Basis for selection.** Criteria include desire to do rigorous independent work, school record, academic writing samples, recommendations, school and community activities. Interview recommended.

**High school preparation.** College-preparatory program required. 16 units required; 20 recommended. Required and recommended units include English 4, mathematics 3-4, history 3-4, science 3-4 (laboratory 2) and foreign language 3-4.

**2010-2011 Annual costs.** Tuition/fees: $41,404. Room/board: $10,798. Books/supplies: $700. Personal expenses: $700.

**2009-2010 Financial aid. Need-based:** Average need met was 98%. Average scholarship/grant was $30,240; average loan $3,500. 82% of total undergraduate aid awarded as scholarships/grants, 18% as loans/jobs. **Non-need-based:** Scholarships awarded for academics, leadership.

**Application procedures. Admission:** Priority date 11/15; deadline 1/1 (receipt date). $60 fee, may be waived for applicants with need, free for online applicants. Admission notification 4/1. Must reply by May 1 or within 2 week(s) if notified thereafter. **Financial aid:** Closing date 2/1. FAFSA, CSS PROFILE required. Applicants notified by 4/1; must reply by 5/1.

**Academics.** All students pursue individualized program of study. Requirements for graduation not based on credit, but on completion of division one courses in all 5 schools, an independent concentration consisting of combination of courses, independent project work, year-long thesis. **Special study options:** Exchange student, independent study, internships, student-designed major, study abroad, teacher certification program. Member 5-college consortium; may take classes at other member institutions. **Credit/placement by examination:** AP, CLEP. **Support services:** Study skills assistance, writing center.

**Majors. Agriculture:** General. **Architecture:** Architecture. **Area/ethnic studies:** African, African-American, American, Asian, Asian-American, Chicano/Hispanic-American/Latino, East Asian, European, gay/lesbian, Latin American, Native American, Near/Middle Eastern, South Asian, women's. **Biology:** General, animal behavior, neurobiology/physiology. **Communications:** General. **Communications technology:** Animation/special effects. **Computer sciences:** Computer graphics, computer science. **Conservation:** Environmental studies. **Education:** General. **Foreign languages:** Linguistics. **Health:** Premedicine. **History:** General. **Interdisciplinary:** Cognitive science, peace/conflict. **Legal studies:** General, prelaw. **Liberal arts:** Arts/sciences, humanities. **Math:** General. **Philosophy/religion:** Philosophy, religion. **Physical sciences:** Astronomy, chemistry, geology, physics. **Psychology:** General. **Public administration:** Policy analysis. **Social sciences:** Anthropology, economics, international economics, international relations, political science, sociology, urban studies. **Visual/performing arts:** General, art history/conservation, dance, design, dramatic, film/cinema, photography, studio arts.

**Most popular majors.** Area/ethnic studies 9%, English 11%, social sciences 10%, visual/performing arts 31%.

**Computing on campus.** 215 workstations in library, computer center, student center. Dormitories wired for high-speed internet access and linked to campus network. Commuter students can connect to campus network. Online course registration, online library, helpline, repair service, student web hosting, wireless network available.

**Student life. Freshman orientation:** Mandatory, $175 fee. Preregistration for classes offered. Program held during week immediately before matriculation. **Policies:** Students design individual concentrations of study, test

theory with off-campus study and community service, and complete original research and projects. **Housing:** Guaranteed on-campus for freshmen. Coed dorms, special housing for disabled, apartments, wellness housing available. $200 nonrefundable deposit, deadline 5/1. **Activities:** Jazz band, choral groups, dance, drama, film society, international student organizations, music ensembles, radio station, student government, student newspaper, Jewish student union, Amnesty International, Pan Asian student association, Counselor Advocates, Blacksmiths Collective, outing club.

**Student services.** Alcohol/substance abuse counseling, chaplain/spiritual director, career counseling, financial aid counseling, health services, minority student services, on-campus daycare, personal counseling, women's services. **Physically disabled:** Services for visually, speech, hearing impaired. **Learning disabled:** Comprehensive services available.

**Contact.** E-mail: admissions@hampshire.edu
Phone: (413) 559-5471 Toll-free number: (877) 937-4267
Fax: (413) 559-5631
Karen Parker, Director of Admissions, Hampshire College, 893 West Street, Amherst, MA 01002-9988

---

## Harvard College
**Cambridge, Massachusetts**
**www.college.harvard.edu**

**CB member**
**CB code: 3434**

- Private 4-year university and liberal arts college
- Residential campus in large city
- 6,655 degree-seeking undergraduates: 51% women, 8% African American, 17% Asian American, 7% Hispanic American, 1% Native American, 11% international
- 3,738 degree-seeking graduate students
- 7% of applicants admitted
- SAT or ACT with writing, SAT Subject Tests, application essay, interview required
- 97% graduate within 6 years

**General.** Founded in 1636. Regionally accredited. Harvard College is the undergraduate program within Harvard University, part of the faculty of arts and sciences, and offers programs in liberal arts. **Degrees:** 1,664 bachelor's awarded; master's, doctoral offered. **ROTC:** Army, Naval, Air Force. **Location:** 3 miles from Boston. **Calendar:** Semester, extensive summer session. **Full-time faculty:** 1,712 total; 99% have terminal degrees, 14% minority, 32% women. **Part-time faculty:** 410 total; 99% have terminal degrees, 13% minority, 33% women. **Class size:** 80% < 20, 10% 20-39, 2% 40-49, 5% 50-99, 3% >100. **Special facilities:** Museum of Scandinavian and Germanic art; experimental forest in New York state; center for study of Italian Renaissance in Florence, Italy; center for Byzantine studies in Washington, DC; Smithsonian astrophysical observatory.

**Freshman class profile.** 29,114 applied, 2,175 admitted, 1,663 enrolled.

| Mid 50% test scores | | Rank in top quarter: | 100% |
|---|---|---|---|
| SAT critical reading: | 690-780 | Rank in top tenth: | 95% |
| SAT math: | 690-790 | Return as sophomores: | 98% |
| SAT writing: | 690-780 | Out-of-state: | 85% |
| ACT composite: | 31-34 | International: | 10% |

**Basis for selection.** Secondary school record most important; character, creative ability in some discipline or activity, leadership, liveliness of mind, demonstrated stamina and ability to carry out demanding college program, and strong sense of social responsibility important. Any 3 SAT Subject Tests required. Interview with alumnus/alumna required of all applicants if possible; documentation of special talents encouraged.

**High school preparation.** College-preparatory program recommended. Recommended units include English 4, mathematics 4, social studies 3, history 2, science 4 and foreign language 4. Applicants encouraged to take rigorous courses and make the most of any opportunities for enrichment.

**2009-2010 Annual costs.** Tuition/fees: $36,828. Room/board: $11,856. Books/supplies: $1,000. Personal expenses: $2,132.

**2009-2010 Financial aid.** All financial aid based on need. 1,202 full-time freshmen applied for aid; 1,060 were judged to have need; 1,060 of these received aid. Average need met was 100%. Average scholarship/grant was $39,803; average loan $2,948. 93% of total undergraduate aid awarded as scholarships/grants, 7% as loans/jobs. **Additional information:** Institution meets full need of all admitted students. Aid includes no loans; home equity and retirement excluded from need analysis; families with incomes below $60,000 have zero parent contribution; $60,000 to $180,000 and standard assets have parent contributions from 0-10% of income.

**Application procedures. Admission:** Closing date 1/1 (postmark date). $75 fee, may be waived for applicants with need. Admission notification 4/1. Must reply by 5/1. **Financial aid:** Closing date 2/1. FAFSA, CSS PROFILE required. Applicants notified by 4/1; must reply by 5/1 or within 2 week(s) of notification.

**Academics.** Require 12 one-term courses for completion of major and 32 one-term courses for graduation. **Special study options:** Accelerated study, cross-registration, double major, exchange student, honors, independent study, internships, student-designed major, study abroad, teacher certification program. **Credit/placement by examination:** AP, CLEP, IB, institutional tests. SAT Subject Test policy varies depending on subject matter and score. Sophomore standing available on basis of 4 AP exams with qualifying scores, or on basis of IB scores. Students with fewer than 4 AP qualifying scores eligible for placement in more challenging courses. **Support services:** Learning center, study skills assistance, tutoring, writing center.

**Majors. Area/ethnic studies:** African-American, East Asian, Near/Middle Eastern, women's. **Biology:** General, biochemistry, evolutionary, neurobiology/physiology. **Computer sciences:** Computer science. **Conservation:** Environmental studies. **Engineering:** Science. **Foreign languages:** Ancient Greek, classics, comparative lit, German, Latin, linguistics, Romance, Sanskrit, Slavic. **History:** General, science/technology. **Interdisciplinary:** Classical/archaeology. **Liberal arts:** Arts/sciences. **Math:** General, applied, statistics. **Philosophy/religion:** Philosophy, religion. **Physical sciences:** Chemistry, geology, molecular physics, physics. **Psychology:** General. **Social sciences:** General, anthropology, economics, political science, sociology. **Visual/performing arts:** General, art history/conservation.

**Most popular majors.** Biology 14%, history 8%, mathematics 6%, physical sciences 7%, psychology 6%, social sciences 36%.

**Computing on campus.** 605 workstations in dormitories, library, computer center. Dormitories wired for high-speed internet access and linked to campus network. Commuter students can connect to campus network. Online course registration, online library, helpline, repair service, student web hosting, wireless network available.

**Student life. Freshman orientation:** Mandatory. Week-long program in early September. **Housing:** Guaranteed on-campus for all undergraduates. Coed dorms, special housing for disabled, apartments, cooperative housing available. All freshmen live together. Other students and some faculty members reside in 13 on-campus houses, self-contained communities offering seminars and tutorials. **Activities:** Bands, campus ministries, choral groups, dance, drama, film society, international student organizations, literary magazine, music ensembles, Model UN, musical theater, opera, radio station, student government, student newspaper, symphony orchestra, TV station, over 320 official clubs available.

**Athletics.** NCAA. **Intercollegiate:** Baseball M, basketball, cross-country, diving, fencing, field hockey W, football (tackle) M, golf, ice hockey, lacrosse, rowing (crew), sailing, skiing, soccer, softball W, squash, swimming, tennis, track and field, volleyball, water polo, wrestling M. **Intramural:** Basketball, cross-country, fencing, football (non-tackle), ice hockey, rowing (crew), soccer, softball, squash, swimming, table tennis, tennis, volleyball. **Team name:** Crimson.

**Student services.** Alcohol/substance abuse counseling, chaplain/spiritual director, career counseling, services for economically disadvantaged, student employment services, financial aid counseling, health services, on-campus daycare, personal counseling, placement for graduates, women's services. **Physically disabled:** Services for visually, speech, hearing impaired.

**Contact.** E-mail: college@fas.harvard.edu
Phone: (617) 495-1551 Fax: (617) 495-8821
William Fitzsimmons, Dean of Admissions, Harvard College, 86 Brattle Street, Cambridge, MA 02138

---

## Hellenic College/Holy Cross
**Brookline, Massachusetts**
www.hchc.edu
**CB member**
**CB code: 3449**

- Private 4-year liberal arts and seminary college affiliated with Eastern Orthodox Church
- Residential campus in large town
- 69 degree-seeking undergraduates
- 121 graduate students
- SAT or ACT (ACT writing optional), application essay, interview required

**General.** Founded in 1937. Regionally accredited. **Degrees:** 22 bachelor's awarded; master's offered. **Location:** 5 miles from downtown Boston. **Calendar:** Semester, limited summer session. **Full-time faculty:** 14 total; 79%

have terminal degrees, 50% women. **Part-time faculty:** 19 total; 47% have terminal degrees, 21% women. **Class size:** 49% < 20, 51% 20-39.

**Freshman class profile.**

| Mid 50% test scores | | | |
|---|---|---|---|
| SAT critical reading: | 480-620 | GPA 3.75 or higher: | 10% |
| SAT math: | 460-520 | GPA 3.0-3.49: | 60% |
| SAT writing: | 430-610 | GPA 2.0-2.99: | 30% |
| ACT composite: | 21-27 | Out-of-state: | 90% |
| | | Live on campus: | 95% |

**Basis for selection.** High school achievement, GPA, 2 recommendations from instructors, test scores very important, school and community activities also important. For religious studies majors, 2 letters from clergy important if members of Orthodox Christian Church. **Homeschooled:** Transcript of courses and grades, state high school equivalency certificate required.

**High school preparation.** 15 units required. Required units include English 4, mathematics 2, social studies 2, history 2, science 3 and foreign language 2.

**2009-2010 Annual costs.** Tuition/fees: $18,850. Room/board: $11,780. Books/supplies: $1,000. Personal expenses: $1,500.

**2008-2009 Financial aid.** All financial aid based on need.

**Application procedures. Admission:** Priority date 5/1; deadline 8/15 (receipt date). $50 fee, may be waived for applicants with need. Admission notification on a rolling basis. Students who apply by December 1 eligible to have application fee waived and receive priority consideration for scholarships; early applications encouraged. **Financial aid:** Closing date 4/1. FAFSA, institutional form required. Applicants notified on a rolling basis starting 10/1; must reply within 2 week(s) of notification.

**Academics. Special study options:** Cross-registration, exchange student, honors, independent study, internships, liberal arts/career combination, study abroad. **Credit/placement by examination:** AP, CLEP, IB, institutional tests. Credit granted varies by degree program. **Support services:** Tutoring.

**Majors. Education:** Elementary. **Family/consumer sciences:** Family studies. **Foreign languages:** Classics. **Liberal arts:** Arts/sciences. **Psychology:** General. **Theology:** Theology.

**Computing on campus.** Online library, wireless network available.

**Student life. Freshman orientation:** Available. **Policies:** Religious observance required for some students. **Housing:** Guaranteed on-campus for freshmen. Single sex dorms, apartments available. $300 nonrefundable deposit. **Activities:** Campus ministries, choral groups, dance, drama, music ensembles, student government, several Orthodox groups, prison ministry, missions group.

**Athletics. Intramural:** Basketball, soccer M, table tennis, tennis, volleyball.

**Student services.** Chaplain/spiritual director, career counseling, student employment services, financial aid counseling, health services, personal counseling, placement for graduates.

**Contact.** E-mail: admissions@hchc.edu
Phone: (617) 850-1260 Toll-free number: (866) 424-2338
Fax: (617) 850-1460
Gregory Floor, Director of Admissions and Records, Hellenic College/Holy Cross, 50 Goddard Avenue, Brookline, MA 02445

---

## Lasell College
**Newton, Massachusetts**
www.lasell.edu
**CB member**
**CB code: 3481**

- Private 4-year liberal arts college
- Residential campus in small city
- 1,520 degree-seeking undergraduates: 1% part-time, 67% women, 6% African American, 3% Asian American, 4% Hispanic American, 2% international
- 129 degree-seeking graduate students
- 64% of applicants admitted
- SAT or ACT (ACT writing optional), application essay required
- 45% graduate within 6 years; 26% enter graduate study

**General.** Founded in 1851. Regionally accredited. **Degrees:** 222 bachelor's awarded; master's offered. **Location:** 8 miles from Boston. **Calendar:** Semester. **Full-time faculty:** 68 total; 87% have terminal degrees,

10% minority, 66% women. **Part-time faculty:** 117 total; 14% have terminal degrees, 3% minority, 60% women. **Class size:** 65% < 20, 35% 20-39. **Special facilities:** Community-based learning center, art and cultural center with antique clothing collection, center for research on aging and intergenerational studies, institute for values and public life, technology for learning center, 2 child study centers.

**Freshman class profile.** 3,378 applied, 2,156 admitted, 522 enrolled.

| Mid 50% test scores | | GPA 2.0-2.99: | 60% |
|---|---|---|---|
| SAT critical reading: | 450-530 | Rank in top quarter: | 15% |
| SAT math: | 460-540 | Rank in top tenth: | 3% |
| SAT writing: | 450-540 | End year in good standing: | 69% |
| ACT composite: | 19-23 | Return as sophomores: | 73% |
| GPA 3.75 or higher: | 4% | Out-of-state: | 53% |
| GPA 3.50-3.74: | 9% | Live on campus: | 93% |
| GPA 3.0-3.49: | 26% | International: | 1% |

**Basis for selection.** GPA, curriculum, class rank, interview, recommendations, extracurricular activities, personal essay, and standardized test scores considered. Interview recommended.

**High school preparation.** College-preparatory program required. 15 units required; 21 recommended. Required and recommended units include English 4, mathematics 3-4, social studies 2-3, history 2-3, science 2-3 (laboratory 2) and foreign language 2.

**2009-2010 Annual costs.** Tuition/fees: $25,300. Room/board: $10,500. Books/supplies: $1,000. Personal expenses: $2,000.

**2009-2010 Financial aid. Need-based:** 480 full-time freshmen applied for aid; 431 were judged to have need; 431 of these received aid. Average need met was 89%. Average scholarship/grant was $16,546; average loan $2,075. 65% of total undergraduate aid awarded as scholarships/grants, 35% as loans/jobs. **Non-need-based:** Awarded to 200 full-time undergraduates, including 89 freshmen. Scholarships awarded for academics, alumni affiliation.

**Application procedures. Admission:** Priority date 3/15; no deadline. $40 fee, may be waived for applicants with need, free for online applicants. Admission notification on a rolling basis beginning on or about 12/15. Must reply by May 1 or within 2 week(s) if notified thereafter. **Financial aid:** Priority date 3/1; no closing date. FAFSA, institutional form required. Applicants notified on a rolling basis starting 2/15; must reply by 5/1 or within 2 week(s) of notification.

**Academics.** Free tutoring available in many academic subjects. **Special study options:** Double major, honors, independent study, internships, liberal arts/career combination, student-designed major, study abroad, teacher certification program. **Credit/placement by examination:** AP, CLEP, IB, SAT, ACT, institutional tests. **Support services:** Learning center, reduced course load, study skills assistance, tutoring.

**Majors. Business:** Accounting, accounting/business management, accounting/finance, business admin, entrepreneurial studies, fashion, finance, hospitality admin, hotel/motel admin, international, marketing, tourism/travel. **Communications:** General, advertising, digital media, journalism, media studies, public relations, radio/tv. **Conservation:** Environmental studies. **Education:** Early childhood, elementary, English, history, mathematics, secondary. **Family/consumer sciences:** Fashion consultant. **Health:** Athletic training. **History:** General. **Legal studies:** General, prelaw. **Liberal arts:** Humanities. **Parks/recreation:** Exercise sciences, sports admin. **Protective services:** Law enforcement admin. **Psychology:** General. **Public administration:** Human services. **Social sciences:** General, sociology. **Visual/performing arts:** Fashion design, graphic design.

**Most popular majors.** Business/marketing 47%, parks/recreation 13%, visual/performing arts 14%.

**Computing on campus.** 175 workstations in dormitories, library, computer center, student center. Dormitories wired for high-speed internet access and linked to campus network. Commuter students can connect to campus network. Online course registration, online library, helpline, wireless network available.

**Student life. Freshman orientation:** Mandatory, $40 fee. Preregistration for classes offered. **Housing:** Guaranteed on-campus for all undergraduates. Coed dorms, single-sex dorms, wellness housing available. $200 nonrefundable deposit, deadline 5/1. Community service, special interest housing available. **Activities:** Jazz band, campus ministries, choral groups, dance, drama, international student organizations, literary magazine, music ensembles, musical theater, radio station, student government, student newspaper, Amnesty International, Ninos de Veracruz, multicultural student union, students advocating for equality, fashion and service society, environment club, religious club.

**Athletics.** NCAA. **Intercollegiate:** Baseball M, basketball, cross-country, field hockey W, lacrosse, soccer, softball W, track and field, volleyball. **Intramural:** Basketball, football (non-tackle), soccer, softball, volleyball. **Team name:** Lasers.

**Student services.** Alcohol/substance abuse counseling, chaplain/spiritual director, career counseling, student employment services, financial aid counseling, health services, personal counseling, placement for graduates.

**Contact.** E-mail: info@lasell.edu
Phone: (617) 243-2225 Toll-free number: (888) 527-3554
Fax: (617) 243-2380
James Tweed, Dean of Undergraduate Admission, Lasell College, 1844 Commonwealth Avenue, Newton, MA 02466-2709

## Lesley University
**Cambridge, Massachusetts** — CB member
www.lesley.edu — CB code: 3483

- Private 4-year liberal arts and teachers college
- Residential campus in very large city
- 1,369 degree-seeking undergraduates: 3% part-time, 75% women, 4% African American, 3% Asian American, 5% Hispanic American, 1% Native American, 1% international
- 3,732 degree-seeking graduate students
- 67% of applicants admitted
- SAT or ACT with writing, application essay, interview required
- 62% graduate within 6 years

**General.** Founded in 1909. Regionally accredited. Lesley University includes 2 undergraduate colleges, Lesley College and The Art Institute of Boston. Main campus in Cambridge. **Degrees:** 381 bachelor's awarded; master's, doctoral offered. **Calendar:** Semester, limited summer session. **Full-time faculty:** 73 total; 84% have terminal degrees, 15% minority, 58% women. **Part-time faculty:** 185 total; 24% have terminal degrees, 58% women. **Class size:** 77% < 20, 22% 20-39, less than 1% 40-49, less than 1% 50-99. **Special facilities:** Center for teaching resources, media production facility, fine arts studios.

**Freshman class profile.** 2,611 applied, 1,754 admitted, 385 enrolled.

| Mid 50% test scores | | GPA 3.0-3.49: | 34% |
|---|---|---|---|
| SAT critical reading: | 470-600 | GPA 2.0-2.99: | 46% |
| SAT math: | 450-580 | Rank in top quarter: | 43% |
| SAT writing: | 470-600 | Rank in top tenth: | 14% |
| ACT composite: | 20-26 | Return as sophomores: | 75% |
| GPA 3.75 or higher: | 3% | Out-of-state: | 48% |
| GPA 3.50-3.74: | 13% | Live on campus: | 85% |

**Basis for selection.** Primary focus given to academic record, both grades and challenging courses. Test scores, recommendations, interview, community service, leadership experience also considered.

**High school preparation.** College-preparatory program required. 18 units required; 20 recommended. Required and recommended units include English 4, mathematics 3-4, social studies 1-2, history 1-2, science 3-4 (laboratory 2), foreign language 2 and academic electives 4. 2 units visual/performing arts recommended for some programs in art or expressive therapies.

**2010-2011 Annual costs.** Tuition/fees: $29,400. Room/board: $12,800. Books/supplies: $700. Personal expenses: $1,580.

**2009-2010 Financial aid. Need-based:** 326 full-time freshmen applied for aid; 294 were judged to have need; 294 of these received aid. Average need met was 74%. Average scholarship/grant was $15,193; average loan $3,715. 64% of total undergraduate aid awarded as scholarships/grants, 36% as loans/jobs. **Non-need-based:** Awarded to 466 full-time undergraduates, including 47 freshmen. Scholarships awarded for academics, art, leadership, minority status, state residency.

**Application procedures. Admission:** Priority date 2/15; no deadline. $50 fee, may be waived for applicants with need, free for online applicants. Admission notification on a rolling basis beginning on or about 1/15. Must reply by May 1 or within 2 week(s) if notified thereafter. **Financial aid:** Priority date 2/15; no closing date. FAFSA required. Applicants notified on a rolling basis starting 2/15.

**Academics.** Students complete between 450 and 650 hours of significant internship experience that begins freshman year. **Special study options:** Accelerated study, combined bachelor's/graduate degree, cross-registration, distance learning, double major, dual enrollment of high school students, exchange student, honors, independent study, internships, liberal arts/career combination, New York semester, student-designed major, study abroad, teacher certification program, Washington semester. Studio courses. **Credit/ placement by examination:** AP, CLEP, IB, SAT, ACT, institutional tests. 16 credit hours maximum toward bachelor's degree. **Support services:** Learning center, pre-admission summer program, reduced course load, study skills assistance, tutoring, writing center.

**Majors. Area/ethnic studies:** American. **Biology:** General. **Business:** Business admin. **Communications technology:** General. **Conservation:** Environmental studies. **Education:** General, art, early childhood, early childhood special, elementary, English, kindergarten/preschool, mathematics, middle, science, secondary, social studies, special. **Family/consumer sciences:** Child development, family studies. **Health:** Art therapy, health services. **Interdisciplinary:** Global studies, natural sciences. **Liberal arts:** Arts/sciences. **Math:** General. **Social sciences:** General. **Visual/performing arts:** Art, studio arts.

**Most popular majors.** Business/marketing 6%, education 7%, liberal arts 31%, psychology 12%, public administration/social services 18%, visual/ performing arts 22%.

**Computing on campus.** 195 workstations in dormitories, library, computer center, student center. Dormitories wired for high-speed internet access and linked to campus network. Commuter students can connect to campus network. Online course registration, online library, helpline, wireless network available.

**Student life. Freshman orientation:** Mandatory. Begins 1 week prior to start of classes. **Housing:** Guaranteed on-campus for all undergraduates. Coed dorms, single-sex dorms, wellness housing available. $300 nonrefundable deposit, deadline 5/1. Victorian houses and suite-style residences available. **Activities:** Campus ministries, choral groups, dance, drama, film society, international student organizations, literary magazine, musical theater, student government, student newspaper, women for social justice, Hillel, Third Wave women's group, Prism, students for a free Tibet, ALANA, Christian fellowship.

**Athletics.** NCAA. **Intercollegiate:** Baseball M, basketball, cross-country, soccer, softball W, tennis, volleyball. **Team name:** Lynx.

**Student services.** Adult student services, alcohol/substance abuse counseling, chaplain/spiritual director, career counseling, student employment services, financial aid counseling, health services, minority student services, personal counseling, placement for graduates. **Physically disabled:** Services for visually, speech, hearing impaired. **Learning disabled:** Comprehensive services available.

**Contact.** E-mail: lcadmissions@lesley.edu
Phone: (617) 349-8800 Toll-free number: (800) 999-1959 ext. 8800
Fax: (617) 349-8810
Deb Kocar, Director of Admissions, Lesley University, 29 Everett Street, Cambridge, MA 02140-2790

---

## Massachusetts College of Art and Design

**Boston, Massachusetts**  CB member
**www.massart.edu**  CB code: 3516

- Public 4-year visual arts college
- Residential campus in very large city
- 1,772 degree-seeking undergraduates: 10% part-time, 67% women, 3% African American, 6% Asian American, 5% Hispanic American, 1% Native American, 2% international
- 160 degree-seeking graduate students
- 51% of applicants admitted
- SAT or ACT with writing, application essay required
- 64% graduate within 6 years

**General.** Founded in 1873. Regionally accredited. **Degrees:** 290 bachelor's awarded; master's offered. **Calendar:** Semester, extensive summer session. **Full-time faculty:** 101 total; 78% have terminal degrees, 13% minority, 54% women. **Part-time faculty:** 143 total. **Class size:** 85% < 20, 15% 20-39. **Special facilities:** 7 art galleries, foundry, glass furnaces, ceramic kilns, video and film studios, performance and studio spaces, Polaroid 20X24 camera.

**Freshman class profile.** 1,631 applied, 837 admitted, 315 enrolled.

| Mid 50% test scores | | | |
|---|---|---|---|
| SAT critical reading: | 510-610 | GPA 2.0-2.99: | 22% |
| SAT math: | 490-590 | Rank in top quarter: | 51% |
| SAT writing: | 500-600 | Rank in top tenth: | 18% |
| GPA 3.75 or higher: | 17% | Return as sophomores: | 88% |
| GPA 3.50-3.74: | 17% | Out-of-state: | 34% |
| GPA 3.0-3.49: | 44% | Live on campus: | 87% |
| | | International: | 1% |

**Basis for selection.** Emphasis on portfolio, academic record, essay, test scores, recommendations. 3.0 GPA recommended. For GPA between 2.0 and 2.9, SAT/ACT scores considered in combination with GPA on sliding scale. Applicants must meet Massachusetts public college admission standards. Portfolio of at least 15 pieces of artwork required, presented as 35 mm 2x2 slides. Work may also be submitted on VHS videotape or digital media. **Homeschooled:** Students who earn high school diploma must provide course curriculum that includes evaluations/grades as well as SAT or ACT scores. Students who do not earn high school diploma must submit official GED exam scores. **Learning Disabled:** Testing may be waived for applicants with professionally certified learning disabilities.

**High school preparation.** 17 units required. Required units include English 4, mathematics 3, social studies 2, science 3 (laboratory 2), foreign language 2 and academic electives 2. At least 2 additional academic units of computer science, humanities, or visual and performing arts required. Social Studies requirement must include 1 U.S. history course. Foreign language units must be in same language.

**2009-2010 Annual costs.** Tuition/fees: $8,400; $24,400 out-of-state. Tuition for New England resident students $14,900. Room/board: $11,288. Books/supplies: $200. Personal expenses: $1,312.

**2008-2009 Financial aid. Need-based:** 227 full-time freshmen applied for aid; 176 were judged to have need; 176 of these received aid. Average scholarship/grant was $7,271; average loan $3,611. 46% of total undergraduate aid awarded as scholarships/grants, 54% as loans/jobs. **Non-need-based:** Awarded to 129 full-time undergraduates, including 47 freshmen. Scholarships awarded for academics, art, leadership, state residency. **Additional information:** Tuition waiver available to Vietnam veterans.

**Application procedures. Admission:** Closing date 2/1. $30 fee ($65 out-of-state), may be waived for applicants with need. Admission notification on a rolling basis. Must reply by May 1 or within 3 week(s) if notified thereafter. **Financial aid:** Priority date 3/1; no closing date. FAFSA required. Applicants notified on a rolling basis starting 3/15; must reply within 3 week(s) of notification.

**Academics.** Three-year certificates available. **Special study options:** Cross-registration, double major, exchange student, independent study, internships, liberal arts/career combination, student-designed major, study abroad. Member of American Independent Colleges of Art and Design (AICAD), College Academic Program Sharing (CAPS), Colleges of the Fenway, and Pro Arts Consortium. Exchange programs available in Holland, England, Germany, Ireland, Italy, France. Study abroad available in Spain, Greece, China, Mexico. **Credit/placement by examination:** CLEP, IB, institutional tests. **Support services:** Pre-admission summer program, reduced course load, remedial instruction, study skills assistance, tutoring.

**Majors. Education:** Art. **Visual/performing arts:** Art history/ conservation, ceramics, cinematography, design, fashion design, fiber arts, film/cinema, graphic design, industrial design, metal/jewelry, multimedia, painting, photography, printmaking, sculpture, studio arts.

**Most popular majors.** Education 9%, visual/performing arts 91%.

**Computing on campus.** 370 workstations in library, computer center. Dormitories wired for high-speed internet access and linked to campus network. Commuter students can connect to campus network. Online course registration, online library, helpline, wireless network available.

**Student life. Freshman orientation:** Mandatory. **Policies:** Intercollegiate sports program available through Emerson College. **Housing:** Coed dorms available. $240 nonrefundable deposit, deadline 5/1. Additional housing available in Simmons College dorm. **Activities:** Dance, drama, film society, music ensembles, radio station, student government, student newspaper, TV station, minority student organization, gay/lesbian organization, student-run design firm, international student organization, nontraditional student organization.

**Athletics. Intramural:** Basketball, cross-country, field hockey, football (non-tackle), ice hockey, soccer, softball W, table tennis, tennis, volleyball.

**Student services.** Adult student services, career counseling, student employment services, health services, personal counseling, placement for graduates, veterans' counselor. **Physically disabled:** Services for visually, hearing impaired.

**Contact.** E-mail: admissions@massart.edu
Phone: (617) 879-7222 Fax: (617) 879-7250
Karen Townsend, Dean of Admissions, Massachusetts College of Art and Design, 621 Huntington Avenue, Boston, MA 02115-5882

## Massachusetts College of Liberal Arts
### North Adams, Massachusetts　　CB member
### www.mcla.edu　　CB code: 3521

- Public 4-year liberal arts college
- Residential campus in large town
- 1,625 degree-seeking undergraduates: 10% part-time, 60% women, 6% African American, 1% Asian American, 5% Hispanic American
- 242 degree-seeking graduate students
- 70% of applicants admitted
- SAT or ACT (ACT writing optional), application essay required
- 50% graduate within 6 years

**General.** Founded in 1894. Regionally accredited. **Degrees:** 293 bachelor's awarded; master's offered. **Location:** 60 miles from Springfield, 120 miles from Boston. **Calendar:** Semester, limited summer session. **Full-time faculty:** 87 total; 82% have terminal degrees, 6% minority, 45% women. **Part-time faculty:** 86 total; 2% minority, 46% women. **Class size:** 65% < 20, 35% 20-39, less than 1% 50-99.

**Freshman class profile.** 1,685 applied, 1,187 admitted, 351 enrolled.

| Mid 50% test scores | | | |
|---|---|---|---|
| SAT critical reading: | 470-590 | GPA 2.0-2.99: | 51% |
| SAT math: | 440-560 | Rank in top quarter: | 42% |
| ACT composite: | 20-24 | Rank in top tenth: | 16% |
| GPA 3.75 or higher: | 12% | Return as sophomores: | 75% |
| GPA 3.50-3.74: | 8% | Out-of-state: | 26% |
| GPA 3.0-3.49: | 29% | Live on campus: | 91% |

**Basis for selection.** Secondary school record most important; test scores, essay also important; recommendations, extracurricular activities considered. Interview recommended. **Homeschooled:** State high school equivalency certificate required. **Learning Disabled:** Massachusetts law prohibits requiring standardized test scores from students with documented learning disabilities.

**High school preparation.** College-preparatory program required. 16 units required. Required units include English 4, mathematics 3, science 3 (laboratory 2), foreign language 2 and academic electives 2.

**2009-2010 Annual costs.** Tuition/fees: $7,015; $15,960 out-of-state. Room/board: $7,868.

**2009-2010 Financial aid. Need-based:** 332 full-time freshmen applied for aid; 259 were judged to have need; 258 of these received aid. Average scholarship/grant was $5,728; average loan $3,270. 41% of total undergraduate aid awarded as scholarships/grants, 59% as loans/jobs. **Non-need-based:** Awarded to 457 full-time undergraduates, including 147 freshmen. Scholarships awarded for academics, alumni affiliation, art, leadership, minority status, music/drama.

**Application procedures. Admission:** Priority date 3/1; no deadline. $35 fee, may be waived for applicants with need. Admission notification on a rolling basis beginning on or about 12/15. Must reply by May 1 or within 2 week(s) if notified thereafter. **Financial aid:** Priority date 3/1; no closing date. FAFSA, institutional form required. Applicants notified on a rolling basis starting 3/1; must reply by 5/1 or within 2 week(s) of notification.

**Academics. Special study options:** Accelerated study, combined bachelor's/graduate degree, cross-registration, distance learning, double major, dual enrollment of high school students, exchange student, honors, independent study, internships, liberal arts/career combination, semester at sea, student-designed major, study abroad, teacher certification program, Washington semester. **Credit/placement by examination:** AP, CLEP, IB, institutional tests. **Support services:** Learning center, pre-admission summer program, reduced course load, remedial instruction, tutoring, writing center.

**Majors. Biology:** General. **Business:** Business admin. **Communications:** General. **Computer sciences:** General. **Conservation:** Environmental studies. **Education:** General. **Health:** Athletic training. **History:** General. **Liberal arts:** Arts/sciences. **Math:** General. **Philosophy/religion:** Philosophy. **Physical sciences:** Physics. **Psychology:** General. **Public administration:** Policy analysis. **Social sciences:** Political science, sociology. **Visual/performing arts:** General, art, arts management. **Other:** Interdisciplinary studies.

**Most popular majors.** Business/marketing 19%, English 21%, history 7%, interdisciplinary studies 6%, psychology 9%, social sciences 15%, visual/performing arts 8%.

**Computing on campus.** PC or laptop required. 125 workstations in dormitories, library, computer center, student center. Dormitories wired for high-speed internet access and linked to campus network. Commuter students can connect to campus network. Online course registration, helpline, wireless network available.

**Student life. Freshman orientation:** Mandatory, $75 fee. **Housing:** Guaranteed on-campus for all undergraduates. Coed dorms, special housing for disabled available. $100 nonrefundable deposit. **Activities:** Bands, choral groups, dance, drama, international student organizations, literary magazine, music ensembles, radio station, student government, student newspaper, TV station, interfaith association, Campus Christian Fellowship, Jewish student organization, Newman club, gay and lesbian student society, multicultural society.

**Athletics.** NCAA. **Intercollegiate:** Baseball M, basketball, cross-country, golf M, soccer, softball W, tennis W, volleyball W. **Intramural:** Basketball, bowling, equestrian, football (non-tackle), soccer, softball, swimming, tennis, volleyball, water polo M. **Team name:** Trailblazers.

**Student services.** Adult student services, career counseling, student employment services, financial aid counseling, health services, minority student services, personal counseling, placement for graduates, veterans' counselor, women's services. **Physically disabled:** Services for visually, hearing impaired.

**Contact.** E-mail: admissions@mcla.edu
Phone: (413) 662-5410 Toll-free number: (800) 969-6252
Fax: (413) 662-5179
Steve King, Assistant Dean, Director of Admission and Student Records, Massachusetts College of Liberal Arts, 375 Church Street, North Adams, MA 01247

## Massachusetts College of Pharmacy and Health Sciences
### Boston, Massachusetts　　CB member
### www.mcphs.edu　　CB code: 3512

- Private 4-year health science and pharmacy college
- Commuter campus in very large city
- 2,883 degree-seeking undergraduates: 4% part-time, 68% women, 5% African American, 28% Asian American, 3% Hispanic American, 3% international
- 1,369 degree-seeking graduate students
- 55% of applicants admitted
- SAT or ACT (ACT writing optional), application essay required
- 69% graduate within 6 years

**General.** Founded in 1823. Regionally accredited. Member of Fenway College Consortium, 14-college library consortium, Worcester Consortium, and Manchester Area College Consortium. Students have access to Harvard Medical School library. Accelerated PharmD program available at Worcester campus and Manchester campus; Physician Assistant program and Nursing also offered at Boston, Manchester, and Worcester campuses. **Degrees:** 279 bachelor's awarded; master's, doctoral, professional offered. **ROTC:** Army, Naval, Air Force. **Calendar:** Semester, limited summer session. **Full-time faculty:** 206 total; 85% have terminal degrees, 65% women. **Part-time faculty:** 4 total; 100% have terminal degrees, 75% women. **Class size:** 24% < 20, 47% 20-39, 9% 40-49, 9% 50-99, 11% >100. **Special facilities:** Pharmacy practice lab, dental hygiene clinic, patient assessment lab, nursing skills and technology lab.

**Freshman class profile.** 3,011 applied, 1,643 admitted, 685 enrolled.

| Mid 50% test scores | | | |
|---|---|---|---|
| SAT critical reading: | 480-570 | GPA 3.0-3.49: | 37% |
| SAT math: | 520-620 | GPA 2.0-2.99: | 15% |
| SAT writing: | 490-590 | Return as sophomores: | 83% |
| ACT composite: | 21-26 | Out-of-state: | 43% |
| GPA 3.75 or higher: | 27% | Live on campus: | 78% |
| GPA 3.50-3.74: | 21% | International: | 3% |

**Basis for selection.** School academic record most important, with emphasis on math and science courses. Student's interest, aptitude for pharmacy and allied health fields considered. **Homeschooled:** Require documentation of curriculum and program of study; equivalency exam. **Learning Disabled:** Must submit documents to Academic Support Services.

**High school preparation.** College-preparatory program required. 16 units required. Required units include English 4, mathematics 3, social studies 1, history 1, science 2 (laboratory 2) and academic electives 5.

**2009-2010 Annual costs.** Tuition/fees: $24,550. Room/board: $11,900. Books/supplies: $850. Personal expenses: $2,140.

**2009-2010 Financial aid. Need-based:** Average need met was 48%. Average scholarship/grant was $10,934; average loan $5,165. 59% of total undergraduate aid awarded as scholarships/grants, 41% as loans/jobs. **Non-need-based:** Scholarships awarded for academics.

**Application procedures. Admission:** Priority date 2/15; no deadline. $70 fee, may be waived for applicants with need. Admission notification on a rolling basis beginning on or about 2/15. Must reply by May 1 or within 2 week(s) if notified thereafter. **Financial aid:** Priority date 3/15; no closing date. FAFSA required. Applicants notified on a rolling basis.

**Academics. Special study options:** Accelerated study, combined bachelor's/graduate degree, cross-registration, distance learning, double major, independent study, internships, study abroad. **Credit/placement by examination:** AP, CLEP, IB, SAT, ACT, institutional tests. 6 credit hours maximum toward bachelor's degree. CLEP exams must be taken before student's first semester of enrollment in order for credit to be granted. **Support services:** Learning center, reduced course load, study skills assistance, tutoring, writing center.

**Majors. Biology:** Pharmacology/toxicology. **Health:** Dental hygiene, health services, medical radiologic technology/radiation therapy, nuclear medical technology, nursing (RN), pharmaceutical sciences, premedicine, preveterinary, radiologic technology/medical imaging. **Physical sciences:** Chemistry. **Psychology:** Medical. **Other:** Pharmaceutical marketing and management.

**Most popular majors.** Health sciences 97%.

**Computing on campus.** 752 workstations in dormitories, library, computer center, student center. Dormitories wired for high-speed internet access and linked to campus network. Commuter students can connect to campus network. Online library, helpline, wireless network available.

**Student life. Freshman orientation:** Mandatory, $100 fee. Preregistration for classes offered. Two-day overnight program in summer; 1-day freshman parent orientation. **Policies:** Identification must be worn and displayed while on campus. Academic honesty policy, alcohol and drug abuse policies; electronic communications policy; good neighbor policy; hazing policy; smoke-free policy; sexual harassment policy. **Housing:** Guaranteed on-campus for freshmen. Coed dorms, single-sex dorms, wellness housing available. $250 fully refundable deposit, deadline 5/1. **Activities:** Concert band, choral groups, dance, drama, international student organizations, literary magazine, music ensembles, student government, student newspaper, symphony orchestra, Academy of Student Pharmacists, Kappa Psi fraternity, Vietnamese student association, black student union, physician assistant student society, campus activities board, student government association, Indian student organization, Asian student association.

**Athletics. Intramural:** Badminton, basketball, bowling, field hockey, football (non-tackle), racquetball, soccer, softball, table tennis, tennis, volleyball. **Team name:** Cardinals.

**Student services.** Adult student services, alcohol/substance abuse counseling, career counseling, student employment services, financial aid counseling, health services, minority student services, personal counseling, placement for graduates, veterans' counselor, women's services. **Physically disabled:** Services for visually, speech, hearing impaired.

**Contact.** E-mail: admissions@mcphs.edu
Phone: (617) 732-2850 Toll-free number: (800) 225-5506
Fax: (617) 732-2118
Kathleen Ryan, Executive Director of Admission, Massachusetts College of Pharmacy and Health Sciences, 179 Longwood Avenue, Boston, MA 02115-5896

## Massachusetts Institute of Technology

**Cambridge, Massachusetts**  CB member
**web.mit.edu**  CB code: 3514

- Private 4-year university
- Residential campus in small city
- 4,218 degree-seeking undergraduates: 1% part-time, 45% women, 8% African American, 26% Asian American, 13% Hispanic American, 1% Native American, 9% international
- 6,032 degree-seeking graduate students
- 11% of applicants admitted
- SAT or ACT with writing, SAT Subject Tests, application essay required
- 91% graduate within 6 years; 48% enter graduate study

**General.** Founded in 1861. Regionally accredited. **Degrees:** 1,146 bachelor's awarded; master's, doctoral offered. **ROTC:** Army, Naval, Air Force.

**Location:** One mile from Boston. **Calendar:** 4-1-4, limited summer session. **Full-time faculty:** 1,326 total; 90% have terminal degrees, 15% minority, 22% women. **Part-time faculty:** 452 total; 70% have terminal degrees, 8% minority, 23% women. **Class size:** 65% < 20, 18% 20-39, 5% 40-49, 9% 50-99, 4% >100. **Special facilities:** Museum, visual arts center, computer science and artificial intelligence laboratory, institute for soldier nanotechnologies, institute for learning and memory.

**Freshman class profile.** 15,663 applied, 1,676 admitted, 1,072 enrolled.

| Mid 50% test scores | | End year in good standing: | 97% |
|---|---|---|---|
| SAT critical reading: | 650-760 | Return as sophomores: | 97% |
| SAT math: | 720-800 | Out-of-state: | 90% |
| SAT writing: | 660-760 | Live on campus: | 100% |
| ACT composite: | 32-35 | International: | 8% |
| Rank in top quarter: | 100% | Fraternities: | 52% |
| Rank in top tenth: | 95% | Sororities: | 40% |

**Basis for selection.** Holistic review of application. Important factors include character, creativity, grades, leadership, love of learning, personal accomplishments, quality of academic program, recommendations, resiliency, test scores. Applicant's context considered. 1 math and 1 science SAT Subject Test required. Interviews strongly recommended.

**High school preparation.** College-preparatory program recommended. Recommended units include English 4, mathematics 4, social studies 2, science 4 and foreign language 2.

**2009-2010 Annual costs.** Tuition/fees: $37,782. Room/board: $11,360. Books/supplies: $1,150. Personal expenses: $1,708.

**2008-2009 Financial aid.** All financial aid based on need. 834 full-time freshmen applied for aid; 673 were judged to have need; 673 of these received aid. Average need met was 100%. Average scholarship/grant was $34,136; average loan $2,127. 92% of total undergraduate aid awarded as scholarships/grants, 8% as loans/jobs. **Additional information:** Filing deadline 2/15 for CSS PROFILE.

**Application procedures. Admission:** Closing date 1/1 (postmark date). $75 fee, may be waived for applicants with need. Admission notification 3/20. Must reply by May 1 or within 2 week(s) if notified thereafter. **Financial aid:** Closing date 2/15. FAFSA, CSS PROFILE required. Applicants notified by 4/1; must reply by 5/1.

**Academics. Special study options:** Combined bachelor's/graduate degree, cooperative education, cross-registration, double major, internships, semester at sea, study abroad, teacher certification program, Washington semester. Undergraduate research opportunities program, independent activities period, freshman learning communities. **Credit/placement by examination:** AP, CLEP, IB, institutional tests. **Support services:** Learning center, pre-admission summer program, study skills assistance, tutoring, writing center.

**Majors. Architecture:** Architecture, urban/community planning. **Biology:** General. **Business:** General. **Communications:** Media studies. **Computer sciences:** Computer science. **Engineering:** Aerospace, biomedical, chemical, civil, electrical, environmental, materials, mechanical, nuclear. **Foreign languages:** General, linguistics. **History:** General. **Interdisciplinary:** Cognitive science, math/computer science, neuroscience, science/society. **Liberal arts:** Arts/sciences. **Math:** General. **Philosophy/religion:** Philosophy. **Physical sciences:** Chemistry, geology, physics. **Social sciences:** Anthropology, economics, political science.

**Most popular majors.** Biology 6%, business/marketing 6%, computer/information sciences 15%, engineering/engineering technologies 40%, interdisciplinary studies 6%, mathematics 8%, physical sciences 10%.

**Computing on campus.** 1,100 workstations in dormitories, library, computer center, student center. Dormitories wired for high-speed internet access and linked to campus network. Commuter students can connect to campus network. Online course registration, online library, helpline, repair service, student web hosting, wireless network available.

**Student life. Freshman orientation:** Mandatory. Held last 2 weeks of August. Includes programs for parents and international students. Additional 20 optional pre-orientation programs held week prior to orientation. **Policies:** Many undergraduate buildings designated smoke-free. **Housing:** Guaranteed on-campus for freshmen. Coed dorms, single-sex dorms, special housing for disabled, apartments, cooperative housing, fraternity/sorority housing, wellness housing available. Independent living group housing, housing for students with children, cultural theme housing, living learning communities available. **Activities:** Bands, campus ministries, choral groups, dance, drama, film society, international student organizations, literary magazine, music ensembles, Model UN, musical theater, radio station, student government, student newspaper, symphony orchestra, TV station, numerous recognized organizations available.

**Athletics.** NCAA. **Intercollegiate:** Baseball M, basketball, cross-country, diving, fencing, field hockey W, football (tackle) M, lacrosse, rifle, rowing (crew), sailing, soccer, softball W, squash M, swimming, tennis, track and field, volleyball, water polo M. **Intramural:** Badminton, basketball, bowling, football (non-tackle), ice hockey, soccer, softball, table tennis, tennis, volleyball, water polo. **Team name:** Engineers.

**Student services.** Alcohol/substance abuse counseling, chaplain/spiritual director, career counseling, student employment services, financial aid counseling, health services, on-campus daycare, personal counseling, placement for graduates. **Physically disabled:** Services for visually, speech, hearing impaired.

**Contact.** E-mail: admissions@mit.edu
Phone: (617) 253-3400 Fax: (617) 258-8304
Stuart Schmill, Dean of Admissions, Massachusetts Institute of Technology, 77 Massachusetts Avenue, Room 3-108, Cambridge, MA 02139-4307

---

## Massachusetts Maritime Academy
**Buzzards Bay, Massachusetts** — CB member
**www.maritime.edu** — CB code: 3515

- Public 4-year maritime college
- Residential campus in large town
- 1,097 degree-seeking undergraduates: 3% part-time, 8% women
- 87 degree-seeking graduate students
- SAT or ACT (ACT writing optional), application essay required

**General.** Founded in 1891. Regionally accredited. **Degrees:** 203 bachelor's awarded; master's offered. **ROTC:** Army, Naval, Air Force. **Location:** 55 miles from Boston; 50 miles from Providence, Rhode Island. **Calendar:** 4-1-4, limited summer session. **Full-time faculty:** 60 total. **Part-time faculty:** 20 total. **Class size:** 43% < 20, 57% 20-39, less than 1% 40-49. **Special facilities:** 540-foot training ship with classrooms, labs, marine engineering, and environmental protection; diesel simulator; video full-function bridge navigation simulator; commercial fishing simulator; spill management simulator; cargo handling simulator; hands-on aquaculture center; emergency management simulator; 248-foot tall 660-kilowatt wind turbine; bio-diesel re-generator; 81kW of solar power.

**Freshman class profile.**

| Mid 50% test scores | | ACT composite: | 17-23 |
|---|---|---|---|
| SAT critical reading: | 440-560 | Live on campus: | 100% |
| SAT math: | 480-580 | | |

**Basis for selection.** School achievement record, test scores, extracurricular accomplishments most important. Character and personality emphasized, leadership potential desirable. Interview recommended.

**High school preparation.** 18 units required. Required units include English 4, mathematics 3, social studies 2, history 2, science 3 (laboratory 2) and foreign language 2. Math units must include 2 algebra, 1 plane geometry. Science units must include 1 chemistry, or two courses with a lab. Physics recommended.

**2009-2010 Annual costs.** Tuition/fees: $6,119; $18,758 out-of-state. Semester at Sea cost: $3,499. Room/board: $8,917. Books/supplies: $800. Personal expenses: $1,200.

**2008-2009 Financial aid.** Non-need-based: Scholarships awarded for academics, leadership, music/drama.

**Application procedures.** Admission: No deadline. $50 fee, may be waived for applicants with need, free for online applicants. Admission notification on a rolling basis beginning on or about 11/15. Must reply by May 1 or within 1 week(s) if notified thereafter. **Financial aid:** Priority date 4/30; no closing date. FAFSA, institutional form required. Applicants notified on a rolling basis starting 3/1.

**Academics.** Technical and practical training for third assistant engineer and third mate licenses. Graduates may apply for commissions in U.S. Navy, Coast Guard, Marine Reserve, Army, or Air Force. **Special study options:** Combined bachelor's/graduate degree, cooperative education, double major, internships, liberal arts/career combination, semester at sea. **Credit/placement by examination:** AP, CLEP, IB, institutional tests. 6 credit hours maximum toward bachelor's degree. **Support services:** Learning center, pre-admission summer program, reduced course load, study skills assistance, tutoring.

**Majors. Business:** Transportation. **Engineering:** General. **Engineering technology:** Industrial management. **Protective services:** Security management. **Transportation:** Maritime/Merchant Marine.

**Most popular majors.** Engineering/engineering technologies 50%, natural resources/environmental science 15%, security/protective services 15%, trade and industry 20%.

**Computing on campus.** PC or laptop required. 70 workstations in dormitories, library, computer center. Dormitories wired for high-speed internet access and linked to campus network. Commuter students can connect to campus network. Helpline, wireless network available.

**Student life. Freshman orientation:** Mandatory, $400 fee. Preregistration for classes offered. Held last 2 weeks of August, paramilitary style orientation. **Policies:** No mandatory military obligation. **Housing:** Guaranteed on-campus for all undergraduates. Coed dorms, wellness housing available. All majors required to live on campus. **Activities:** Bands, drama, literary magazine, music ensembles, student government, student newspaper, Newman Club, marine careers group, Association of Industrial Plant Engineers.

**Athletics.** NCAA. **Intercollegiate:** Baseball M, cross-country, football (tackle) M, lacrosse M, rifle, rowing (crew), sailing, soccer M, softball W, track and field W, volleyball W. **Intramural:** Basketball, boxing M, football (tackle) M, ice hockey, racquetball, rifle, sailing, soccer, softball, swimming, table tennis, tennis, track and field W, volleyball, water polo, wrestling M. **Team name:** Buccaneers.

**Student services.** Adult student services, alcohol/substance abuse counseling, chaplain/spiritual director, career counseling, student employment services, financial aid counseling, health services, personal counseling, placement for graduates, veterans' counselor, women's services. **Learning disabled:** Comprehensive services available.

**Contact.** E-mail: admissions@maritime.edu
Phone: (508) 830-5000 ext. 1102 Toll-free number: (800) 544-3411
Fax: (508) 830-5077
Roy Fulgueras, Director of Admissions, Massachusetts Maritime Academy, 101 Academy Drive, Buzzards Bay, MA 02532-1803

---

## Merrimack College
**North Andover, Massachusetts** — CB member
**www.merrimack.edu** — CB code: 3525

- Private 4-year business and liberal arts college affiliated with Roman Catholic Church
- Residential campus in large town
- 1,927 degree-seeking undergraduates
- 79% of applicants admitted
- Application essay required

**General.** Founded in 1947. Regionally accredited. Associated with Augustinian Friars. **Degrees:** 488 bachelor's awarded; master's offered. **ROTC:** Air Force. **Location:** 25 miles from Boston. **Calendar:** Semester, limited summer session. **Full-time faculty:** 132 total. **Part-time faculty:** 110 total. **Class size:** 64% < 20, 35% 20-39, less than 1% 40-49, less than 1% 50-99, less than 1% >100. **Special facilities:** Astronomy dome and telescope, arts center.

**Freshman class profile.** 3,890 applied, 3,075 admitted, 550 enrolled.

**Basis for selection.** School achievement record, course selection, class rank, essay, recommendations important. Interview recommended. **Home-schooled:** State certificate of completion, list of coursework, interview required.

**High school preparation.** 17 units required; 22 recommended. Required and recommended units include English 4, mathematics 3-4, social studies 1-2, history 1-2, science 3-4 (laboratory 3-4), foreign language 2-3 and academic electives 3. Math must include algebra I and II and plane geometry. 1 additional math and 3 science, including physics, required of math, science, engineering, and computer science applicants.

**2009-2010 Annual costs.** Tuition/fees: $29,810. Room/board: $10,190. Books/supplies: $800. Personal expenses: $2,750.

**2008-2009 Financial aid.** Non-need-based: Scholarships awarded for academics, athletics, leadership, minority status, religious affiliation. **Additional information:** Accept the Challenge program provides tuition for students from Lawrence who meet program criteria.

**Application procedures.** Admission: Closing date 2/1 (postmark date). $60 fee, may be waived for applicants with need. Admission notification 4/1. Admission notification on a rolling basis. Must reply by May 1 or within 2 week(s) if notified thereafter. **Financial aid:** Closing date 2/1. FAFSA required. Applicants notified by 3/15; must reply by 5/1 or within 2 week(s) of notification.

**Academics.** Writing intensive courses available in all areas. Associate degree and M.Ed programs offered through continuing education division only. **Special study options:** Accelerated study, combined bachelor's/graduate degree, cooperative education, cross-registration, double major, dual enrollment of high school students, ESL, independent study, internships, liberal arts/career combination, student-designed major, study abroad, teacher certification program, Washington semester. 5-year combined BA/BS program. **Credit/placement by examination:** AP, CLEP, IB, institutional tests. **Support services:** Learning center, reduced course load, remedial instruction, study skills assistance, tutoring, writing center.

**Majors. Biology:** General, biochemistry. **Business:** Business admin. **Communications:** General. **Computer sciences:** Computer science. **Engineering:** General, civil, computer, electrical. **Foreign languages:** French, Romance, Spanish. **Health:** Athletic training, health services. **History:** General. **Liberal arts:** Arts/sciences. **Math:** General. **Philosophy/religion:** Philosophy, religion. **Physical sciences:** Chemistry, physics. **Psychology:** General. **Public administration:** Human services. **Social sciences:** Economics, political science, sociology. **Visual/performing arts:** Studio arts.

**Most popular majors.** Biology 6%, business/marketing 32%, engineering/engineering technologies 7%, health sciences 6%, psychology 9%, social sciences 10%.

**Computing on campus.** Dormitories wired for high-speed internet access and linked to campus network. Commuter students can connect to campus network. Online course registration, online library, helpline, repair service, wireless network available.

**Student life. Freshman orientation:** Mandatory, $150 fee. Preregistration for classes offered. Two-day June sessions and 3-day August pre-class orientation. **Policies:** All residence halls are drug-free. **Housing:** Guaranteed on-campus for freshmen. Coed dorms, special housing for disabled, apartments, cooperative housing, wellness housing available. $300 fully refundable deposit, deadline 5/1. Townhouses for upperclassmen. Applications accepted from groups of students for theme housing in townhouses. Austin Scholars residential program available to selected students. **Activities:** Bands, campus ministries, choral groups, dance, drama, film society, international student organizations, music ensembles, Model UN, musical theater, student government, student newspaper, TV station, student tutoring group, community service organizations, College Democrats, College Republicans, Society Organized Against Racism, Latinos Organization.

**Athletics.** NCAA. **Intercollegiate:** Baseball M, basketball, cross-country, field hockey W, football (tackle) M, ice hockey M, lacrosse, soccer, softball W, tennis, volleyball W. **Intramural:** Basketball, ice hockey M, soccer, softball, volleyball. **Team name:** Warriors.

**Student services.** Adult student services, alcohol/substance abuse counseling, chaplain/spiritual director, career counseling, student employment services, financial aid counseling, health services, minority student services, personal counseling, placement for graduates.

**Contact.** E-mail: admission@merrimack.edu
Phone: (978) 837-5000 ext. 5100 Fax: (978) 837-5133
Jorge Hernandez, Director of Freshman Admission, Merrimack College, 315 Turnpike Street, North Andover, MA 01845

## Montserrat College of Art
**Beverly, Massachusetts**  CB member
www.montserrat.edu  CB code: 9101

- Private 4-year visual arts college
- Residential campus in large town
- 339 degree-seeking undergraduates: 1% part-time, 73% women, 2% African American, 2% Asian American, 3% Hispanic American, 1% international
- 77% of applicants admitted
- Application essay required
- 48% graduate within 6 years

**General.** Founded in 1970. Regionally accredited. **Degrees:** 42 bachelor's awarded. **Location:** 18 miles from Boston. **Calendar:** Semester, limited summer session. **Full-time faculty:** 19 total; 74% have terminal degrees, 5% minority, 58% women. **Part-time faculty:** 45 total; 84% have terminal degrees, 7% minority, 51% women. **Class size:** 87% < 20, 13% 20-39. **Special facilities:** Computer design laboratories, various art facilities, college-operated galleries; student-operated gallery.

**Freshman class profile.** 435 applied, 335 admitted, 128 enrolled.

| Mid 50% test scores | | | |
|---|---|---|---|
| SAT critical reading: | 440-600 | GPA 3.0-3.49: | 18% |
| SAT math: | 420-570 | GPA 2.0-2.99: | 58% |
| SAT writing: | 420-590 | End year in good standing: | 88% |
| ACT composite: | 19-27 | Return as sophomores: | 75% |
| GPA 3.75 or higher: | 6% | Out-of-state: | 60% |
| GPA 3.50-3.74: | 2% | Live on campus: | 90% |

**Basis for selection.** Visual art portfolio most important. High school record, interview, artist statement, and letters of recommendation required of BFA applicants. If personal visit is impractical, portfolio in digital or slide form may be sent; follow-up telephone interview will be conducted. SAT or ACT scores required for applicants with GED. Interview recommended; portfolio required. **Homeschooled:** Transcript of courses and grades, state high school equivalency certificate, letter of recommendation (nonparent) required. Must take SAT/ACT and successfully pass GED. **Learning Disabled:** Official documentation of disability and any previous accommodation plans required if accommodation requested.

**High school preparation.** College-preparatory program recommended. Recommended units include English 4, social studies 2, history 2 and visual/performing arts 2. Visual arts courses including drawing recommended.

**2010-2011 Annual costs.** Tuition/fees (projected): $24,790. Room/board: $6,370. Books/supplies: $1,200. Personal expenses: $1,300.

**2009-2010 Financial aid. Need-based:** 122 full-time freshmen applied for aid; 105 were judged to have need; 104 of these received aid. Average need met was 58%. Average scholarship/grant was $12,132; average loan $4,017. 54% of total undergraduate aid awarded as scholarships/grants, 46% as loans/jobs. **Non-need-based:** Awarded to 56 full-time undergraduates, including 29 freshmen. Scholarships awarded for academics, art.

**Application procedures. Admission:** Priority date 2/15; no deadline. $50 fee, may be waived for applicants with need. Admission notification on a rolling basis beginning on or about 12/20. Must reply by May 1 or within 3 week(s) if notified thereafter. If completed admissions application and financial aid application is received by 1/2, admissions decision and estimated financial aid package will be sent by 1/15. **Financial aid:** Priority date 3/1; no closing date. FAFSA, institutional form required. Applicants notified on a rolling basis starting 12/20; must reply within 2 week(s) of notification.

**Academics.** In addition to frequent class critiques, students' work is reviewed by faculty panel in semester-end evaluations. **Special study options:** Cross-registration, double major, dual enrollment of high school students, exchange student, independent study, internships, New York semester, student-designed major, study abroad, teacher certification program. Summer study abroad opportunities in Italy and Japan; winter study abroad opportunities in Africa and Puerto Rico; on-campus summer and winter session classes available. **Credit/placement by examination:** AP, CLEP, IB. **Support services:** Learning center, pre-admission summer program, reduced course load, remedial instruction, study skills assistance, tutoring, writing center.

**Majors. Visual/performing arts:** Art, design, drawing, graphic design, illustration, painting, photography, printmaking, sculpture, studio arts.

**Computing on campus.** 158 workstations in dormitories, library, computer center, student center. Dormitories wired for high-speed internet access. Online library, helpline, wireless network available.

**Student life. Freshman orientation:** Mandatory, $100 fee. Preregistration for classes offered. **Housing:** Coed dorms, single-sex dorms, wellness housing available. $275 nonrefundable deposit, deadline 5/1. **Activities:** Literary magazine, music ensembles, student government, student newspaper, Cooking Outside the Lines.

**Athletics. Intramural:** Basketball, football (tackle).

**Student services.** Adult student services, alcohol/substance abuse counseling, career counseling, student employment services, financial aid counseling, personal counseling, placement for graduates. **Physically disabled:** Services for visually, speech, hearing impaired.

**Contact.** E-mail: admiss@montserrat.edu
Phone: (978) 921-4242 ext. 1153 Toll-free number: (800) 836-0487 ext. 1153 Fax: (978) 921-4241
Rick Longo, Dean of Admissions and Enrollment Management, Montserrat College of Art, 23 Essex Street, Beverly, MA 01915

## Mount Holyoke College

**South Hadley, Massachusetts**  **CB member**
www.mtholyoke.edu  **CB code: 3529**

◆ Private 4-year liberal arts college for women
◆ Residential campus in large town
◆ 2,247 degree-seeking undergraduates: 2% part-time, 100% women, 7% African American, 10% Asian American, 6% Hispanic American, 20% international
◆ 15 degree-seeking graduate students
◆ 58% of applicants admitted
◆ Application essay required
◆ 83% graduate within 6 years; 22% enter graduate study

**General.** Founded in 1837. Regionally accredited. Member of 5-college consortium with Amherst College, Hampshire College, Smith College, and University of Massachusetts at Amherst. Member of 12 College Exchange with Amherst College, Bowdoin, Connecticut College, Dartmouth College, O'Neill National Theatre Institute, Smith College, Trinity College, Vassar, Wellesley College, Wesleyan University, Wheaton College, Williams/ Mystic Seaport Program in Maritime Studies. **Degrees:** 565 bachelor's awarded; master's offered. **ROTC:** Army, Air Force. **Location:** 10 miles from Springfield; 40 miles from Hartford, CT. **Calendar:** Semester. **Full-time faculty:** 224 total; 95% have terminal degrees, 25% minority, 55% women. **Part-time faculty:** 63 total; 57% have terminal degrees, 14% minority, 59% women. **Class size:** 62% < 20, 30% 20-39, 4% 40-49, 4% 50-99, less than 1% >100. **Special facilities:** Nuclear accelerator, nuclear magnetic resonance equipment, electron microscope, bronze-casting foundry, solar greenhouse, Japanese meditation garden and tea house, equestrian center, language learning center with satellite communication and interactive video, child study center, global initiatives center, greenhouse and botanical garden, leadership and liberal arts center, art museum, center for the environment, observatory.

**Freshman class profile.** 3,061 applied, 1,771 admitted, 574 enrolled.

| Mid 50% test scores | | GPA 2.0-2.99: | 5% |
|---|---|---|---|
| SAT critical reading: | 610-730 | Rank in top quarter: | 87% |
| SAT math: | 600-720 | Rank in top tenth: | 62% |
| SAT writing: | 620-710 | Return as sophomores: | 90% |
| ACT composite: | 27-31 | Out-of-state: | 77% |
| GPA 3.75 or higher: | 41% | Live on campus: | 100% |
| GPA 3.50-3.74: | 26% | International: | 23% |
| GPA 3.0-3.49: | 28% | | |

**Basis for selection.** School record most important, followed by special talents, particular goals, evidence of determination. Personal interview on campus recommended if candidate lives within 200 miles of college, or with alumna admissions representative if applicant resides outside of area. **Homeschooled:** Detailed outline of study and 5 SAT Subject Tests recommended.

**High school preparation.** College-preparatory program recommended. Recommended units include English 4, mathematics 3, history 3, science 3 (laboratory 3), foreign language 3 and academic electives 1. History requirement includes U.S. and world history. Either 4 units of one foreign language, or 2 units of one and 3 units of a second foreign language recommended.

**2009-2010 Annual costs.** Tuition/fees: $39,126. Room/board: $11,450. Books/supplies: $1,900.

**2009-2010 Financial aid. Need-based:** 469 full-time freshmen applied for aid; 401 were judged to have need; 401 of these received aid. Average need met was 100%. Average scholarship/grant was $31,435; average loan $3,250. 80% of total undergraduate aid awarded as scholarships/grants, 20% as loans/jobs. **Non-need-based:** Scholarships awarded for academics, leadership.

**Application procedures. Admission:** Closing date 1/15 (postmark date). $60 fee, may be waived for applicants with need, free for online applicants. Admission notification 4/1. Must reply by 5/1. **Financial aid:** Priority date 2/15, closing date 3/1. FAFSA, CSS PROFILE required. Applicants notified by 4/1; must reply by 5/1.

**Academics.** Honor system and self-scheduled examinations practiced. All students must complete minor. **Special study options:** Combined bachelor's/ graduate degree, cooperative education, cross-registration, double major, exchange student, independent study, internships, liberal arts/career combination, semester at sea, student-designed major, study abroad, teacher certification program, Washington semester. Community-based learning courses, first-year seminars. **Credit/placement by examination:** AP, CLEP, IB, institutional tests. 32 credit hours maximum toward bachelor's degree. Credit will

not satisfy any distribution or language requirement, but may satisfy some prerequisites. **Support services:** Reduced course load, study skills assistance, tutoring, writing center.

**Majors. Architecture:** Architecture. **Area/ethnic studies:** African-American, American, Asian, European, German, Latin American, Russian/ Slavic. **Biology:** General, biochemistry. **Business:** Organizational behavior. **Computer sciences:** Computer science. **Conservation:** Environmental studies. **Education:** General. **Foreign languages:** Ancient Greek, classics, French, Italian, Latin, Romance, Spanish. **History:** General. **Interdisciplinary:** Ancient studies, medieval/Renaissance, neuroscience. **Math:** General, statistics. **Philosophy/religion:** Philosophy, religion. **Physical sciences:** Astronomy, chemistry, geology, physics. **Psychology:** General. **Social sciences:** Anthropology, economics, geography, international relations, political science, sociology. **Visual/performing arts:** Art history/conservation, dance, dramatic, film/cinema, studio arts. **Other:** Critical social thought, Gender studies.

**Most popular majors.** Area/ethnic studies 6%, biology 9%, English 8%, foreign language 6%, interdisciplinary studies 7%, psychology 7%, social sciences 27%, visual/performing arts 9%.

**Computing on campus.** 586 workstations in dormitories, library, computer center, student center. Dormitories wired for high-speed internet access and linked to campus network. Commuter students can connect to campus network. Online course registration, online library, helpline, repair service, student web hosting, wireless network available.

**Student life. Freshman orientation:** Available. Preregistration for classes offered. Program held week before start of classes. **Policies:** Smoke-free campus. **Housing:** Guaranteed on-campus for all undergraduates. Special housing for disabled, apartments available. $200 nonrefundable deposit, deadline 5/15. Kosher/halal kitchen available; special accommodations by need. **Activities:** Jazz band, campus ministries, choral groups, dance, drama, film society, international student organizations, literary magazine, music ensembles, Model UN, musical theater, radio station, student government, student newspaper, symphony orchestra, community service organizations, religious organizations, cultural/ethnic organizations, political/activist organizations.

**Athletics.** NCAA. **Intercollegiate:** Basketball W, cross-country W, diving W, equestrian W, field hockey W, golf W, lacrosse W, rowing (crew) W, soccer W, squash W, swimming W, tennis W, track and field W, volleyball W. **Team name:** Lyons.

**Student services.** Adult student services, alcohol/substance abuse counseling, chaplain/spiritual director, career counseling, student employment services, financial aid counseling, health services, minority student services, personal counseling, placement for graduates, women's services. **Physically disabled:** Services for visually, speech, hearing impaired.

**Contact.** E-mail: admission@mtholyoke.edu
Phone: (413) 538-2023 Fax: (413) 538-2409
Diane Anci, Dean of Admission, Mount Holyoke College, Newhall Center, South Hadley, MA 01075-1488

## Mount Ida College

**Newton, Massachusetts**  **CB member**
www.mountida.edu  **CB code: 3530**

◆ Private 4-year business and liberal arts college
◆ Residential campus in small city
◆ 1,479 degree-seeking undergraduates: 5% part-time, 65% women, 12% African American, 2% Asian American, 6% Hispanic American, 5% international
◆ 10 degree-seeking graduate students
◆ 74% of applicants admitted
◆ SAT or ACT (ACT writing recommended) required

**General.** Founded in 1899. Regionally accredited. **Degrees:** 192 bachelor's, 32 associate awarded; master's offered. **Location:** 8 miles from downtown Boston. **Calendar:** Semester, limited summer session. **Full-time faculty:** 65 total; 57% have terminal degrees, 9% minority, 58% women. **Part-time faculty:** 135 total; 23% have terminal degrees, 7% minority, 62% women. **Class size:** 68% < 20, 31% 20-39, less than 1% 40-49, less than 1% 50-99. **Special facilities:** Darkroom, blueprint making facility, veterinary kennel and operating facility, dental laboratory, design labs.

**Freshman class profile.** 2,004 applied, 1,477 admitted, 434 enrolled.

| Mid 50% test scores | | | |
| --- | --- | --- | --- |
| SAT critical reading: | 400-490 | **GPA 3.0-3.49:** | 20% |
| SAT math: | 390-490 | **GPA 2.0-2.99:** | 60% |
| SAT writing: | 390-490 | **End year in good standing:** | 74% |
| ACT composite: | 16-20 | **Return as sophomores:** | 63% |
| **GPA 3.75 or higher:** | 3% | **Out-of-state:** | 44% |
| **GPA 3.50-3.74:** | 6% | **Live on campus:** | 88% |
| | | **International:** | 3% |

**Basis for selection.** School record, GPA, recommendations, test scores, and essay most important. Essay or personal statement, campus visit strongly recommended. Interviews may be required.

**High school preparation.** College-preparatory program recommended. 14 units recommended. Recommended units include English 4, mathematics 3, social studies 2, science 3 (laboratory 3) and foreign language 2. 4 math and 2 physical science strongly recommended for science majors.

**2009-2010 Annual costs.** Tuition/fees: $23,100. Room/board: $11,450. Books/supplies: $1,000. Personal expenses: $1,200.

**Application procedures. Admission:** No deadline. $45 fee, may be waived for applicants with need, free for online applicants. Admission notification on a rolling basis beginning on or about 10/1. **Financial aid:** Priority date 4/15; no closing date. FAFSA, institutional form required. Applicants notified on a rolling basis starting 3/1; must reply within 3 week(s) of notification.

**Academics.** Professionally intensive courses of study coupled with liberal arts requirements. **Special study options:** Distance learning, double major, ESL, honors, independent study, internships, semester at sea, study abroad, teacher certification program. **Credit/placement by examination:** AP, CLEP, IB, institutional tests. **Support services:** Learning center, reduced course load, remedial instruction, study skills assistance, tutoring, writing center.

**Majors. Agriculture:** Equestrian studies. **Biology:** General. **Business:** Business admin, fashion, hospitality admin. **Communications technology:** Animation/special effects. **Education:** Early childhood. **Health:** Veterinary technology/assistant. **History:** American. **Liberal arts:** Arts/sciences. **Parks/recreation:** Sports admin. **Personal/culinary services:** Mortuary science. **Protective services:** Criminal justice, forensics. **Psychology:** General. **Public administration:** Human services. **Visual/performing arts:** Fashion design, graphic design, interior design.

**Most popular majors.** Business/marketing 33%, health sciences 12%, psychology 7%, security/protective services 8%, visual/performing arts 21%.

**Computing on campus.** 122 workstations in library, computer center. Dormitories wired for high-speed internet access and linked to campus network. Online library, wireless network available.

**Student life. Freshman orientation:** Mandatory. Preregistration for classes offered. Held in July; students able to choose roommate. Activities also held prior to first day of class in late August. **Housing:** Guaranteed on-campus for freshmen. Coed dorms, single-sex dorms, special housing for disabled, wellness housing available. $300 partly refundable deposit. **Activities:** Choral groups, dance, drama, international student organizations, literary magazine, radio station, student government, student newspaper, black student achievement coalition, gay/lesbian and everyone else, Jewish student society, student association for Latino and Spanish Americans.

**Athletics.** NCAA. **Intercollegiate:** Basketball, cheerleading, cross-country W, equestrian W, football (tackle) M, lacrosse, soccer, softball W, tennis W, volleyball. **Intramural:** Basketball, football (non-tackle), rugby, soccer. **Team name:** Mustangs.

**Student services.** Adult student services, alcohol/substance abuse counseling, chaplain/spiritual director, career counseling, services for economically disadvantaged, student employment services, financial aid counseling, health services, minority student services, personal counseling, placement for graduates.

**Contact.** E-mail: admissions@mountida.edu
Phone: (617) 928-4553 Fax: (617) 928-4507
Jay Titus, Dean of Admissions, Mount Ida College, 777 Dedham Street, Newton, MA 02459

---

## New England Conservatory of Music
**Boston, Massachusetts**      CB member
**www.necmusic.edu**      CB code: 3659

- Private 4-year music college
- Commuter campus in very large city

---

- 405 degree-seeking undergraduates: 8% part-time, 46% women, 4% African American, 9% Asian American, 6% Hispanic American, 24% international
- 333 degree-seeking graduate students
- 33% of applicants admitted
- Application essay required
- 72% graduate within 6 years

**General.** Founded in 1867. Regionally accredited. In close proximity to Symphony Hall. Faculty includes members of Boston Symphony Orchestra. **Degrees:** 71 bachelor's awarded; master's, doctoral offered. **Location:** 2 miles from downtown. **Calendar:** Semester, limited summer session. **Full-time faculty:** 90 total; 26% have terminal degrees, 6% minority, 33% women. **Part-time faculty:** 124 total; 7% have terminal degrees, 7% minority, 27% women. **Class size:** 79% < 20, 20% 20-39, 2% 40-49. **Special facilities:** Listening library.

**Freshman class profile.** 1,153 applied, 379 admitted, 113 enrolled.

| | | | |
| --- | --- | --- | --- |
| **End year in good standing:** | 100% | **Out-of-state:** | 91% |
| **Return as sophomores:** | 94% | **Live on campus:** | 96% |

**Basis for selection.** Audition most important, followed by recommendations, high school record, essay. Accepted students permitted to postpone admission one-half year. Live or taped auditions required. **Homeschooled:** Must provide curriculum overview.

**2009-2010 Annual costs.** Tuition/fees: $33,325. On-campus residents and all incoming students pay $440 health center fee. Room/board: $11,600. Books/supplies: $700. Personal expenses: $2,386.

**2009-2010 Financial aid. Need-based:** 65 full-time freshmen applied for aid; 58 were judged to have need; 58 of these received aid. Average need met was 59%. Average scholarship/grant was $16,675; average loan $2,938. 64% of total undergraduate aid awarded as scholarships/grants, 36% as loans/jobs. **Non-need-based:** Awarded to 159 full-time undergraduates, including 37 freshmen. Scholarships awarded for academics, music/drama.

**Application procedures. Admission:** Priority date 12/1; no deadline. $100 fee. Admission notification on a rolling basis beginning on or about 4/1. Must reply by May 1 or within 4 week(s) if notified thereafter. **Financial aid:** Closing date 12/1. FAFSA, institutional form required. Applicants notified by 4/1; must reply by 5/1 or within 2 week(s) of notification.

**Academics.** Undergraduate diploma available in lieu of bachelor's degree (performance-oriented, with fewer academic requirements). Artist's diploma (professional degree) available for particularly gifted performers. Graduate diploma also available. **Special study options:** Cross-registration, dual enrollment of high school students, ESL, independent study, internships, study abroad. 5-year double degree program with Tufts University; 5-year AB/MM program with Harvard University. **Credit/placement by examination:** AP, CLEP, IB, institutional tests. 12 credit hours maximum toward bachelor's degree. **Support services:** Tutoring, writing center.

**Majors. Visual/performing arts:** Jazz, music history, music performance, music theory/composition, musicology, piano/organ, stringed instruments, voice/opera.

**Computing on campus.** 48 workstations in dormitories, library, computer center, student center. Online library, wireless network available.

**Student life. Freshman orientation:** Mandatory. Preregistration for classes offered. Held 5 days before start of classes. **Housing:** Guaranteed on-campus for freshmen. Coed dorms available. $500 fully refundable deposit, deadline 5/1. **Activities:** Bands, choral groups, music ensembles, opera, student government, student newspaper, symphony orchestra, Christian Fellowship, feminist and minority student organizations.

**Athletics. Team name:** Penguins.

**Student services.** Career counseling, student employment services, financial aid counseling, health services, personal counseling, placement for graduates. **Physically disabled:** Services for visually impaired.

**Contact.** E-mail: ADMStaff@necmusic.edu
Phone: (617) 585-1101 Fax: (617) 585-1115
Christina Daly, Director of Admissions, New England Conservatory of Music, 290 Huntington Avenue, Boston, MA 02115

---

## New England Institute of Art
**Brookline, Massachusetts**
**www.artinstitutes.edu/boston**      CB code: 3636

- For-profit 4-year visual arts and technical college
- Commuter campus in very large city

- 1,700 degree-seeking undergraduates
- 41% of applicants admitted
- Application essay, interview required

**General.** Regionally accredited. **Degrees:** 293 bachelor's, 24 associate awarded. **Calendar:** Semester, extensive summer session. **Full-time faculty:** 30 total. **Part-time faculty:** 50 total. **Class size:** 79% < 20, 19% 20-39, 2% 40-49. **Special facilities:** Audio production studios, drafting rooms, animation studio.

**Freshman class profile.** 1,362 applied, 563 admitted, 563 enrolled.

**Basis for selection.** Essay and interview most important, followed by secondary school record. Class rank, recommendations, test scores considered. Second interview required for audio programs. Portfolio required for Media Arts and Animation program.

**Financial aid.** **Non-need-based:** Scholarships awarded for academics.

**Application procedures.** **Admission:** No deadline. $150 fee. Admission notification on a rolling basis. **Financial aid:** Priority date 5/1; no closing date. FAFSA, institutional form required. Applicants notified on a rolling basis starting 3/1.

**Academics.** Bachelor's degrees offered in graphic design and web design & interactive media. Non-collegiate certificates offered in web site development and digital graphic design. **Special study options:** Internships. **Credit/placement by examination:** AP, CLEP, institutional tests. **Support services:** Learning center, remedial instruction, study skills assistance, tutoring.

**Majors. Business:** Fashion. **Communications:** Digital media. **Communications technology:** Graphics, photo/film/video, recording arts. **Computer sciences:** Web page design. **Visual/performing arts:** Commercial/advertising art, fashion design, graphic design, illustration, multimedia.

**Computing on campus.** Dormitories wired for high-speed internet access. Student web hosting available.

**Student life. Freshman orientation:** Mandatory. Half-day program held prior to start of semester. **Policies:** Student code of conduct. **Housing:** Coed dorms, apartments available. $400 nonrefundable deposit. **Activities:** Film society, literary magazine, radio station, student government.

**Student services.** Adult student services, alcohol/substance abuse counseling, career counseling, student employment services, financial aid counseling, personal counseling, placement for graduates.

**Contact.** E-mail: neiaadm@aii.edu
Phone: (617) 739-1700 Toll-free number: (800) 903-4425
Fax: (617) 582-4500
Dr. Susan Lane, President, New England Institute of Art, 10 Brookline Place West, Brookline, MA 02445-7295

## Newbury College
**Brookline, Massachusetts**
www.newbury.edu

CB member
CB code: 3639

- Private 4-year business and liberal arts college
- Commuter campus in large city
- 887 degree-seeking undergraduates: 3% part-time, 58% women
- 66% of applicants admitted
- Application essay required

**General.** Founded in 1962. Regionally accredited. **Degrees:** 207 bachelor's, 32 associate awarded. **Location:** 3 miles from Boston. **Calendar:** Semester, limited summer session. **Full-time faculty:** 31 total. **Part-time faculty:** 78 total. **Class size:** 33% < 20, 67% 20-39. **Special facilities:** 7 culinary arts production kitchens, on-campus restaurant open to the public.

**Freshman class profile.** 3,166 applied, 2,099 admitted, 333 enrolled.

| | | | |
|---|---|---|---|
| GPA 3.75 or higher: | 1% | Out-of-state: | 35% |
| GPA 3.50-3.74: | 3% | Live on campus: | 59% |
| GPA 3.0-3.49: | 22% | International: | 4% |
| GPA 2.0-2.99: | 63% | | |

**Basis for selection.** Holistic approach includes application, essay, high school transcript, extra-curricular activities and 2 letters of recommendation. Interviews recommended.

**High school preparation.** College-preparatory program recommended. Recommended units include English 3, mathematics 3, social studies 3, history 3, science 2, foreign language 2 and computer science 1.

**2009-2010 Annual costs.** Tuition/fees: $23,650. Room/board: $11,230. Books/supplies: $750. Personal expenses: $1,000.

**Financial aid.** All financial aid based on need.

**Application procedures. Admission:** Priority date 3/1; no deadline. $25 fee, may be waived for applicants with need, free for online applicants. Admission notification on a rolling basis beginning on or about 11/1. Must reply by May 1 or within 4 week(s) if notified thereafter. **Financial aid:** Closing date 5/1. FAFSA required. Applicants notified on a rolling basis starting 3/1; must reply by 5/1 or within 2 week(s) of notification.

**Academics.** Academic enrichment program available for students entering who demonstrate need for academic support. **Special study options:** Combined bachelor's/graduate degree, cross-registration, double major, honors, independent study, internships, liberal arts/career combination, study abroad, weekend college. **Credit/placement by examination:** AP, CLEP, IB, institutional tests. 30 credit hours maximum toward associate degree, 60 toward bachelor's. **Support services:** Learning center, remedial instruction, study skills assistance, tutoring.

**Majors. Architecture:** Interior. **Business:** Accounting, business admin, fashion, finance, hospitality admin, international, marketing. **Communications:** General, journalism, media studies. **Computer sciences:** General, computer graphics, computer science. **Engineering technology:** Computer systems. **Health:** Health care admin. **Legal studies:** General, paralegal, prelaw. **Personal/culinary services:** Chef training, culinary arts, food service, restaurant/catering. **Protective services:** Law enforcement admin. **Psychology:** General. **Visual/performing arts:** Graphic design, interior design.

**Most popular majors.** Business/marketing 66%, computer/information sciences 10%, legal studies 15%.

**Computing on campus.** 65 workstations in dormitories, library, computer center, student center. Dormitories wired for high-speed internet access and linked to campus network. Online course registration, online library, helpline, wireless network available.

**Student life. Freshman orientation:** Mandatory, $150 fee. Preregistration for classes offered. Information sessions and activities held a few days before each semester. **Housing:** Guaranteed on-campus for freshmen. Coed dorms, single-sex dorms available. $250 nonrefundable deposit, deadline 5/1. Summer housing available. **Activities:** Jazz band, choral groups, dance, drama, radio station, student government, TV station, international student organization, black student union, Latino student association, Habitat for Humanity, innkeepers club, business club, radio club, student programming board.

**Athletics.** NCAA. **Intercollegiate:** Basketball, cross-country, golf, soccer, softball W, tennis, volleyball. **Intramural:** Lacrosse. **Team name:** Nighthawks.

**Student services.** Alcohol/substance abuse counseling, career counseling, student employment services, financial aid counseling, personal counseling, placement for graduates.

**Contact.** E-mail: admissions@newbury.edu
Phone: (617) 730-7007 Toll-free number: (800) 639-2879
Fax: (617) 731-9618
Joseph Chillo, Vice President for Enrollment Management, Newbury College, 129 Fisher Avenue, Brookline, MA 02445

## Nichols College
**Dudley, Massachusetts**
www.nichols.edu

CB member
CB code: 3666

- Private 4-year business and liberal arts college
- Residential campus in small town
- 1,319 degree-seeking undergraduates: 12% part-time, 40% women, 5% African American, 2% Asian American, 4% Hispanic American, 1% international
- 194 degree-seeking graduate students
- 74% of applicants admitted
- SAT or ACT (ACT writing recommended), application essay required
- 52% graduate within 6 years

**General.** Founded in 1815. Regionally accredited. One-credit Professional Development Seminar program required each year; coursework helps with resume writing, building a work portfolio and successful interviewing skills. **Degrees:** 175 bachelor's, 17 associate awarded; master's offered. **ROTC:** Army. **Location:** 20 miles from Worcester, 50 miles from Boston. **Calendar:** Semester, limited summer session. **Full-time faculty:** 36 total; 61% have terminal degrees, 6% minority, 33% women. **Part-time faculty:** 44

total; 20% have terminal degrees, 2% minority, 39% women. **Class size:** 41% < 20, 58% 20-39, less than 1% 40-49. **Special facilities:** Policy and cultural institute, observatory.

**Freshman class profile.** 1,983 applied, 1,463 admitted, 352 enrolled.

| Mid 50% test scores | | GPA 3.50-3.74: | 4% |
|---|---|---|---|
| SAT critical reading: | 410-500 | GPA 3.0-3.49: | 18% |
| SAT math: | 420-520 | GPA 2.0-2.99: | 72% |
| SAT writing: | 400-500 | Return as sophomores: | 67% |
| ACT composite: | 17-22 | Out-of-state: | 46% |
| GPA 3.75 or higher: | 1% | Live on campus: | 90% |

**Basis for selection.** Secondary school record most important; test scores important, followed by recommendations, essay and interview. Interview recommended. **Homeschooled:** Statement describing homeschool structure and mission, state high school equivalency certificate, interview, letter of recommendation (nonparent) required.

**High school preparation.** College-preparatory program recommended. 16 units required. Required and recommended units include English 4, mathematics 3-4, social studies 2, science 2-3 (laboratory 2-3), foreign language 2 and academic electives 5. 2 foreign language recommended for liberal arts majors.

**2009-2010 Annual costs.** Tuition/fees: $28,040. Room/board: $9,200. Books/supplies: $1,050. Personal expenses: $1,200.

**2009-2010 Financial aid. Need-based:** Average need met was 77%. Average scholarship/grant was $18,579; average loan $3,028. 60% of total undergraduate aid awarded as scholarships/grants, 40% as loans/jobs. **Non-need-based:** Scholarships awarded for academics, alumni affiliation, ROTC.

**Application procedures. Admission:** Priority date 3/1; no deadline. $25 fee, may be waived for applicants with need, free for online applicants. Admission notification on a rolling basis beginning on or about 10/1. Must reply by May 1 or within 2 week(s) if notified thereafter. **Financial aid:** Priority date 3/1, closing date 6/1. FAFSA required. Applicants notified on a rolling basis starting 2/26; must reply within 4 week(s) of notification.

**Academics. Special study options:** Combined bachelor's/graduate degree, cooperative education, distance learning, double major, honors, independent study, internships, liberal arts/career combination, semester at sea, study abroad, teacher certification program, Washington semester. **Credit/placement by examination:** AP, CLEP. 30 credit hours maximum toward bachelor's degree. **Support services:** Learning center, reduced course load, remedial instruction, study skills assistance, tutoring, writing center.

**Majors. Business:** Accounting, business admin, communications, finance, human resources, international, management information systems, managerial economics, marketing, training/development. **Education:** Secondary. **History:** General. **Legal studies:** General. **Math:** General. **Parks/recreation:** Sports admin. **Protective services:** Criminal justice. **Psychology:** General. **Social sciences:** Economics. **Other:** Arts and entertainment management.

**Most popular majors.** Business/marketing 94%.

**Computing on campus.** 111 workstations in library, computer center, student center. Dormitories wired for high-speed internet access and linked to campus network. Commuter students can connect to campus network. Online course registration, online library, helpline, wireless network available.

**Student life. Freshman orientation:** Mandatory. Preregistration for classes offered. Overnight pre-college summer programs for students and parents. **Housing:** Guaranteed on-campus for all undergraduates. Coed dorms, single-sex dorms, special housing for disabled, apartments, wellness housing available. $250 deposit, deadline 5/1. **Activities:** Campus ministries, drama, literary magazine, radio station, student government, student newspaper, TV station, Institute for American Values, Republican club, Young Democrats, Umoja.

**Athletics.** NCAA. **Intercollegiate:** Baseball M, basketball, field hockey W, football (tackle) M, golf M, ice hockey, lacrosse, soccer, softball W, tennis. **Intramural:** Basketball, football (non-tackle), racquetball, rugby, softball M, volleyball. **Team name:** Bison.

**Student services.** Alcohol/substance abuse counseling, chaplain/spiritual director, career counseling, student employment services, financial aid counseling, health services, personal counseling, placement for graduates.

**Contact.** E-mail: admissions@nichols.edu
Phone: (508) 213-2203 Toll-free number: (800) 470-3379
Fax: (508) 943-9885
Tom Cafaro, Vice President of Enrollment and Marketing, Nichols College, PO Box 5000, Dudley, MA 01571-5000

---

## Northeastern University
**Boston, Massachusetts**      **CB member**
www.northeastern.edu      **CB code: 3667**

- Private 4-year university
- Residential campus in very large city
- 15,699 degree-seeking undergraduates: 51% women, 4% African American, 9% Asian American, 5% Hispanic American, 8% international
- 6,392 graduate students
- 41% of applicants admitted
- SAT or ACT with writing, application essay required
- 75% graduate within 6 years

**General.** Founded in 1898. Regionally accredited. **Degrees:** 2,808 bachelor's awarded; master's, doctoral, professional offered. **ROTC:** Army, Naval, Air Force. **Location:** Downtown. **Calendar:** Semester, extensive summer session. **Full-time faculty:** 984 total; 88% have terminal degrees, 17% minority, 39% women. **Part-time faculty:** 439 total; 52% women. **Class size:** 61% < 20, 21% 20-39, 11% 40-49, 5% 50-99, 2% >100. **Special facilities:** Complex network research center, drug discovery center, chemical and biological analysis institute, high rate nanomanufacturing center, subsurface sensing and imaging systems center, information assurance institute, urban health research institute, urban and regional policy center, African-American institute, race and justice institute, global innovation management institute.

**Freshman class profile.** 34,005 applied, 13,948 admitted, 2,833 enrolled.

| Mid 50% test scores | | Rank in top tenth: | 50% |
|---|---|---|---|
| SAT critical reading: | 580-670 | Return as sophomores: | 91% |
| SAT math: | 620-700 | Out-of-state: | 68% |
| SAT writing: | 580-670 | Live on campus: | 97% |
| ACT composite: | 27-31 | International: | 9% |
| Rank in top quarter: | 81% | | |

**Basis for selection.** Academic achievement as measured by grades, quality of classes, test scores most important. Recommendations, personal statement, school and community activities also important. Portfolios/auditions required for art and design, music technology programs. **Homeschooled:** Transcript of courses and grades required. Students should submit comprehensive outline of academic curriculum, list of textbooks, special projects and activities.

**High school preparation.** College-preparatory program required. 17 units required. Required and recommended units include English 4, mathematics 3-4, social studies 3, history 2, science 3-4 (laboratory 2-3) and foreign language 2-3. Each department and college of university may have more specific recommendations for additional preparation.

**2009-2010 Annual costs.** Tuition/fees: $35,362. Room/board: $12,350. Books/supplies: $1,000. Personal expenses: $900.

**2009-2010 Financial aid. Non-need-based:** Scholarships awarded for academics, athletics, minority status.

**Application procedures. Admission:** Closing date 1/15 (postmark date). $70 fee, may be waived for applicants with need. Admission notification 4/1. Must reply by May 1 or within 4 week(s) if notified thereafter. **Financial aid:** Closing date 2/15. FAFSA, CSS PROFILE required. Applicants notified on a rolling basis starting 3/15; must reply by 5/1.

**Academics. Special study options:** Accelerated study, combined bachelor's/graduate degree, cooperative education, cross-registration, distance learning, double major, ESL, exchange student, honors, independent study, internships, liberal arts/career combination, semester at sea, student-designed major, study abroad, teacher certification program, Washington semester. ROTC. **Credit/placement by examination:** AP, CLEP, IB, institutional tests. **Support services:** Learning center, pre-admission summer program, reduced course load, remedial instruction, study skills assistance, tutoring, writing center.

**Majors. Architecture:** Architecture. **Area/ethnic studies:** African-American, Asian, Near/Middle Eastern. **Biology:** General, biochemistry, biophysics, toxicology. **Business:** General, accounting, business admin, entrepreneurial studies, finance, human resources, international, logistics, management information systems, marketing. **Communications:** General, journalism. **Communications technology:** Animation/special effects. **Computer sciences:** General, computer science, information systems. **Conservation:** Environmental studies. **Engineering:** General, architectural, chemical, civil, computer, electrical, industrial, mechanical. **Foreign languages:** American Sign Language, East Asian, French, linguistics, Spanish. **Health:** Athletic training, audiology/speech pathology, cardiopulmonary technology, clinical lab science, health services, nursing (RN). **History:** General. **Interdisciplinary:** Neuroscience. **Liberal arts:** Arts/sciences. **Math:** General. **Philosophy/religion:** Judaic, philosophy, religion. **Physical sciences:** Chemistry, geology, physics. **Protective services:** Criminal justice. **Psychology:** General. **Public administration:** Human services. **Social sciences:** Economics, international economic development, international relations, political science, sociology. **Visual/performing arts:** Art, dramatic, film/cinema, graphic design, illustration, multimedia, studio arts.

**Most popular majors.** Business/marketing 21%, communications/journalism 7%, engineering/engineering technologies 15%, health sciences 11%, security/protective services 7%, social sciences 10%, visual/performing arts 7%.

**Computing on campus.** 1,993 workstations in dormitories, library, computer center, student center. Dormitories wired for high-speed internet access and linked to campus network. Commuter students can connect to campus network. Online course registration, online library, helpline, repair service, student web hosting, wireless network available.

**Student life. Freshman orientation:** Mandatory, $350 fee. Preregistration for classes offered. **Housing:** Guaranteed on-campus for freshmen. Coed dorms, special housing for disabled, apartments, wellness housing available. $400 deposit, deadline 5/1. **Activities:** Bands, campus ministries, choral groups, dance, drama, international student organizations, literary magazine, music ensembles, Model UN, musical theater, radio station, student government, student newspaper, symphony orchestra, TV station, Over 250 student organizations available.

**Athletics.** NCAA. **Intercollegiate:** Baseball M, basketball, cross-country, diving W, field hockey W, ice hockey, rowing (crew), soccer, swimming W, track and field, volleyball W. **Intramural:** Basketball, ice hockey, racquetball, soccer, softball, squash, tennis, volleyball, water polo. **Team name:** Huskies.

**Student services.** Alcohol/substance abuse counseling, chaplain/spiritual director, career counseling, services for economically disadvantaged, student employment services, financial aid counseling, health services, legal services, minority student services, personal counseling, placement for graduates, women's services. **Physically disabled:** Services for visually, speech, hearing impaired. **Learning disabled:** Comprehensive services available.

**Contact.** E-mail: admissions@neu.edu
Phone: (617) 373-2200 Fax: (617) 373-8780
Ronne Turner, Dean of Undergraduate Admissions, Northeastern University, 360 Huntington Avenue, 150 Richards Hall, Boston, MA 02115-9959

## Pine Manor College
**Chestnut Hill, Massachusetts**　　**CB member**
**www.pmc.edu**　　**CB code: 3689**

- Private 4-year liberal arts college for women
- Residential campus in very large city
- 161 degree-seeking undergraduates: 1% part-time, 100% women, 43% African American, 2% Asian American, 22% Hispanic American, 3% international
- 63% of applicants admitted
- SAT or ACT, application essay required
- 36% graduate within 6 years

**General.** Founded in 1911. Regionally accredited. **Degrees:** 67 bachelor's awarded; master's offered. **ROTC:** Army, Air Force. **Location:** 5 miles from Boston. **Calendar:** Semester, limited summer session. **Full-time faculty:** 32 total; 75% have terminal degrees, 12% minority, 75% women. **Part-time faculty:** 44 total; 57% have terminal degrees, 14% minority, 75% women. **Class size:** 83% < 20, 17% 20-39. **Special facilities:** Center for inclusive leadership and social responsibility, child study center.

**Freshman class profile.** 611 applied, 385 admitted, 161 enrolled.

| Mid 50% test scores | | Return as sophomores: | 77% |
|---|---|---|---|
| SAT critical reading: | 340-450 | Out-of-state: | 26% |
| SAT math: | 340-460 | Live on campus: | 93% |
| ACT composite: | 15-17 | | |

**Basis for selection.** School achievement record, test scores, GPA, and recommendations important. Rolling deadline for SAT/ACT score submission. Interview recommended. **Learning Disabled:** Students may be required to submit learning disability documentation.

**High school preparation.** Required units include English 4, mathematics 3, social studies 2, science 3 and foreign language 2.

**2009-2010 Annual costs.** Tuition/fees: $20,189. Room/board: $11,670. Books/supplies: $800. Personal expenses: $1,000.

**2008-2009 Financial aid. Non-need-based:** Scholarships awarded for academics, alumni affiliation, leadership.

**Application procedures. Admission:** No deadline. $25 fee, may be waived for applicants with need, free for online applicants. Admission notification on a rolling basis. Must reply by May 1 or within 2 week(s) if notified thereafter. **Financial aid:** Priority date 5/1; no closing date. FAFSA required. Applicants notified on a rolling basis starting 3/1; must reply by 5/1 or within 2 week(s) of notification.

**Academics.** All students required to participate in internship program. All students receive comprehensive advising. **Special study options:** Cross-registration, double major, honors, independent study, internships, liberal arts/career combination, semester at sea, student-designed major, study abroad, teacher certification program, Washington semester. Students with sophomore status or higher eligible to take courses offered by Marine Studies Consortium. **Credit/placement by examination:** AP, CLEP, IB, institutional tests. 24 credit hours maximum toward bachelor's degree. **Support services:** Learning center, reduced course load, study skills assistance, tutoring, writing center.

**Majors. Biology:** General. **Business:** Business admin. **Communications:** Media studies. **History:** General. **Liberal arts:** Arts/sciences. **Psychology:** General. **Social sciences:** Political science. **Visual/performing arts:** General.

**Most popular majors.** Biology 18%, business/marketing 19%, psychology 26%, visual/performing arts 11%.

**Computing on campus.** 108 workstations in dormitories, library, computer center, student center. Dormitories wired for high-speed internet access and linked to campus network. Commuter students can connect to campus network. Online course registration, helpline, repair service available.

**Student life. Freshman orientation:** Mandatory, $150 fee. Preregistration for classes offered. Held in June and September. **Housing:** Guaranteed on-campus for freshmen. Wellness housing available. $250 nonrefundable deposit. Quiet residence halls available. **Activities:** Choral groups, dance, drama, literary magazine, radio station, student government, Ladies of Various Ebony Shades, African American/Latina/Asian/Native American and All club, Alianza Latina, bisexuals/gays/lesbians and allies in diversity club, Cape Verdean student alliance, dance ensemble, student government association, student health advisory board, Imani Christian club, Camerata singers.

**Athletics.** NCAA. **Intercollegiate:** Basketball W, cross-country W, lacrosse W, soccer W, softball W, tennis W, volleyball W. **Team name:** Gators.

**Student services.** Alcohol/substance abuse counseling, career counseling, services for economically disadvantaged, student employment services, financial aid counseling, health services, minority student services, personal counseling, placement for graduates, women's services.

**Contact.** E-mail: admission@pmc.edu
Phone: (617) 731-7104 Toll-free number: (800) 762-1357
Fax: (617) 731-7102
William Boffi, Dean for Student Recruitment and Retention, Pine Manor College, 400 Heath Street, Chestnut Hill, MA 02467

## Regis College
**Weston, Massachusetts**　　**CB member**
**www.regiscollege.edu**　　**CB code: 3723**

- Private 4-year nursing and liberal arts college affiliated with Roman Catholic Church
- Residential campus in large town
- 972 degree-seeking undergraduates: 23% part-time, 82% women, 22% African American, 5% Asian American, 9% Hispanic American, 1% Native American, 1% international
- 614 degree-seeking graduate students
- 73% of applicants admitted
- SAT or ACT (ACT writing optional), application essay required
- 63% graduate within 6 years; 31% enter graduate study

**General.** Founded in 1927. Regionally accredited. College founded by Sisters of St. Joseph. **Degrees:** 227 bachelor's, 136 associate awarded; master's, professional offered. **ROTC:** Army. **Location:** 12 miles from Boston. **Calendar:** Semester, limited summer session. **Full-time faculty:** 69 total; 71% have terminal degrees, 4% minority, 77% women. **Part-time faculty:** 69 total; 44% have terminal degrees, 12% minority, 88% women. **Class size:** 64% < 20, 35% 20-39, less than 1% 40-49. **Special facilities:** Philatelic museum, fine arts center, 2 digital imaging studios, music laboratory with electronic keyboards and computers.

**Freshman class profile.** 1,735 applied, 1,270 admitted, 241 enrolled.

| Mid 50% test scores | | GPA 2.0-2.99: | 61% |
|---|---|---|---|
| SAT critical reading: | 420-520 | Rank in top quarter: | 37% |
| SAT math: | 420-520 | Rank in top tenth: | 10% |
| SAT writing: | 420-520 | End year in good standing: | 83% |
| ACT composite: | 17-21 | Return as sophomores: | 68% |
| GPA 3.75 or higher: | 3% | Out-of-state: | 11% |
| GPA 3.50-3.74: | 8% | Live on campus: | 78% |
| GPA 3.0-3.49: | 27% | International: | 1% |

**Basis for selection.** All credentials within student's file reviewed. At times, interview or additional grades requested or guidance counselors called. Interview highly recommended. Portfolio recommended for art majors. **Homeschooled:** Statement describing homeschool structure and mission, transcript of courses and grades, letter of recommendation (nonparent) required. **Learning Disabled:** Should apprise Director of Student Disabilities of disability status and document condition to receive appropriate accommodations.

**High school preparation.** 16 units required. Required units include English 4, mathematics 3, social studies 2, science 2 (laboratory 1), foreign language 2 and academic electives 3.

**2009-2010 Annual costs.** Tuition/fees: $28,900. Room/board: $12,190. Books/supplies: $1,000. Personal expenses: $1,520.

**2009-2010 Financial aid.** **Non-need-based:** Scholarships awarded for academics, alumni affiliation, leadership, ROTC. **Additional information:** Family tuition discount scholarship; offered during any semester in which 2 or more unmarried, dependent siblings attend full-time.

**Application procedures.** **Admission:** No deadline. $50 fee, may be waived for applicants with need. Admission notification on a rolling basis beginning on or about 12/1. Must reply by May 1 or within 2 week(s) if notified thereafter. Students encouraged to apply by January 1. **Financial aid:** Priority date 2/15; no closing date. FAFSA, institutional form required. Applicants notified on a rolling basis starting 3/15; must reply by 5/1 or within 2 week(s) of notification.

**Academics.** Online tutoring assistance, professional math and writing tutor, and academic skills workshops available. **Special study options:** Accelerated study, combined bachelor's/graduate degree, cross-registration, double major, ESL, exchange student, honors, independent study, internships, student-designed major, study abroad, teacher certification program, Washington semester. **Credit/placement by examination:** AP, CLEP, IB, SAT, ACT, institutional tests. 24 credit hours maximum toward bachelor's degree. **Support services:** Learning center, reduced course load, remedial instruction, study skills assistance, tutoring, writing center.

**Majors.** **Biology:** General, biochemistry. **Business:** General. **Communications:** General, public relations. **Computer sciences:** General, computer science. **Education:** Mathematics. **Foreign languages:** Spanish. **Health:** Nursing (RN). **History:** General. **Interdisciplinary:** Museum. **Liberal arts:** Arts/sciences. **Physical sciences:** Chemistry. **Psychology:** General. **Public administration:** Social work. **Social sciences:** International relations, political science, sociology. **Visual/performing arts:** Dramatic, graphic design. **Other:** Health and fitness, Human computer interaction, Law and government.

**Most popular majors.** Biology 7%, business/marketing 7%, communications/journalism 8%, health sciences 55%, social sciences 10%.

**Computing on campus.** 199 workstations in library, computer center, student center. Dormitories wired for high-speed internet access and linked to campus network. Commuter students can connect to campus network. Online course registration, online library, helpline, wireless network available.

**Student life.** **Freshman orientation:** Mandatory, $195 fee. Preregistration for classes offered. Two-day summer session and 2-day fall session during opening weekend. **Policies:** Must complete series of effective decision-making courses in order to obtain guest privileges. All residences smoke-free. **Housing:** Guaranteed on-campus for all undergraduates. Coed dorms, single-sex dorms, special housing for disabled, wellness housing available. $450 nonrefundable deposit, deadline 5/1. Quiet floors available. **Activities:** Campus ministries, choral groups, dance, drama, international student

organizations, literary magazine, music ensembles, Model UN, musical theater, radio station, student government, Asian American, African American, Hispanic, Asian, and Native American organizations; student organization for Latino culture; campus activities board; student government association; student athletic advisory committee.

**Athletics.** NCAA. **Intercollegiate:** Basketball, cheerleading, diving, field hockey W, lacrosse, soccer, softball W, swimming, tennis, track and field, volleyball. **Intramural:** Basketball, soccer, softball. **Team name:** Regis Pride.

**Student services.** Adult student services, alcohol/substance abuse counseling, chaplain/spiritual director, career counseling, services for economically disadvantaged, student employment services, financial aid counseling, health services, minority student services, on-campus daycare, personal counseling, placement for graduates, veterans' counselor. **Physically disabled:** Services for visually, hearing impaired.

**Contact.** E-mail: admission@regiscollege.edu
Phone: (781) 768-7100 Toll-free number: (866) 438-7344
Fax: (781) 768-7071
Wanda Suriel, Director of Admission, Regis College, 235 Wellesley Street, Weston, MA 02493-1571

---

## Salem State College
**Salem, Massachusetts**
**www.salemstate.edu/**

CB member
CB code: 3522

- Public 4-year university
- Commuter campus in large town
- 7,086 degree-seeking undergraduates: 18% part-time, 62% women, 9% African American, 3% Asian American, 7% Hispanic American, 3% international
- 1,367 degree-seeking graduate students
- 60% of applicants admitted
- SAT or ACT (ACT writing optional) required
- 43% graduate within 6 years

**General.** Founded in 1854. Regionally accredited. **Degrees:** 1,203 bachelor's awarded; master's offered. **ROTC:** Army, Air Force. **Location:** 15 miles from Boston. **Calendar:** Semester, extensive summer session. **Full-time faculty:** 331 total; 9% minority, 53% women. **Part-time faculty:** 428 total; 4% minority, 60% women. **Class size:** 53% < 20, 43% 20-39, 3% 40-49, less than 1% 50-99. **Special facilities:** Media facility, center for creative and performing arts, observatories, glass blowing studio.

**Freshman class profile.** 5,835 applied, 3,514 admitted, 994 enrolled.

| Mid 50% test scores | | GPA 2.0-2.99: | 59% |
|---|---|---|---|
| SAT critical reading: | 440-540 | Return as sophomores: | 75% |
| SAT math: | 440-540 | Out-of-state: | 3% |
| GPA 3.75 or higher: | 8% | Live on campus: | 63% |
| GPA 3.50-3.74: | 6% | International: | 1% |
| GPA 3.0-3.49: | 27% | | |

**Basis for selection.** Students with 3.0 GPA and college prep curriculum admitted. Students with less than 3.0 GPA admitted with balancing SAT/ACT scores. Special consideration possible. Some majors require higher GPA. Recommendations considered. Interview recommended. Portfolio required for art applicants. Audition required for music applicants. **Homeschooled:** Transcript of courses and grades, state high school equivalency certificate required.

**High school preparation.** College-preparatory program required. Required and recommended units include English 4, mathematics 3, social studies 2-3, history 2, science 3 (laboratory 2), foreign language 2, computer science 1 and visual/performing arts 1. Additional requirements for some programs.

**2009-2010 Annual costs.** Tuition/fees: $6,790; $12,930 out-of-state. Room/board: $9,330.

**Application procedures.** **Admission:** No deadline. $50 fee, may be waived for applicants with need. Admission notification on a rolling basis beginning on or about 12/1. Must reply within 30 days. **Financial aid:** Priority date 4/1; no closing date. FAFSA required. Applicants notified on a rolling basis starting 4/1; must reply within 2 week(s) of notification.

**Academics.** Reading lab available. **Special study options:** Cooperative education, distance learning, double major, dual enrollment of high school students, ESL, honors, independent study, internships, study abroad, teacher certification program. **Credit/placement by examination:** AP, CLEP, institutional tests. **Support services:** Pre-admission summer program, remedial instruction, tutoring, writing center.

**Majors. Biology:** General, biochemistry, ecology, marine. **Business:** Accounting, accounting/finance, business admin, entrepreneurial studies, finance, hospitality admin, human resources, international, management information systems, managerial economics, marketing, tourism/travel. **Communications:** General, advertising, journalism, media studies, public relations. **Computer sciences:** General. **Education:** General, early childhood, elementary, middle, physical, secondary, Spanish. **Foreign languages:** Comparative lit, Spanish, translation. **Health:** Athletic training, clinical lab science, nuclear medical technology, nursing (RN). **History:** General, American, European, public archives. **Interdisciplinary:** Math/computer science. **Liberal arts:** Arts/sciences. **Math:** General. **Parks/recreation:** General, exercise sciences, health/fitness, sports admin. **Physical sciences:** Chemistry, geology. **Protective services:** Fire services admin, law enforcement admin. **Psychology:** General. **Public administration:** Social work. **Social sciences:** Cartography, economics, geography, political science, sociology. **Visual/performing arts:** Acting, art, art history/conservation, commercial/advertising art, dramatic, drawing, painting, photography, printmaking, sculpture, theater design, theater history.

**Most popular majors.** Business/marketing 19%, communications/journalism 8%, education 9%, health sciences 15%, psychology 9%, security/protective services 8%, social sciences 7%, visual/performing arts 6%.

**Computing on campus.** PC or laptop required. 84 workstations in library, computer center, student center. Dormitories wired for high-speed internet access and linked to campus network. Commuter students can connect to campus network. Online course registration, online library, helpline, repair service, student web hosting, wireless network available.

**Student life. Freshman orientation:** Mandatory, $175 fee. Preregistration for classes offered. Sessions held prior to start of semester. **Housing:** Coed dorms, wellness housing available. $225 nonrefundable deposit, deadline 6/1. **Activities:** Bands, choral groups, dance, drama, literary magazine, music ensembles, musical theater, radio station, student government, student newspaper, Hispanic-American society, multicultural student association, international student association, Asian student association, community service group, campus educators on sexual asault, political science academy, student action resource team.

**Athletics.** NCAA. **Intercollegiate:** Baseball M, basketball, cross-country, field hockey W, golf M, ice hockey M, lacrosse M, soccer, softball W, tennis, track and field, volleyball W. **Intramural:** Baseball M, basketball, cheerleading W, football (non-tackle), ice hockey, softball W, volleyball. **Team name:** Vikings.

**Student services.** Adult student services, alcohol/substance abuse counseling, chaplain/spiritual director, career counseling, services for economically disadvantaged, student employment services, financial aid counseling, health services, legal services, minority student services, on-campus daycare, personal counseling, placement for graduates, veterans' counselor, women's services. **Physically disabled:** Services for visually, speech, hearing impaired. **Learning disabled:** Comprehensive services available.

**Contact.** E-mail: admissions@salemstate.edu
Phone: (978) 542-6200 Fax: (978) 542-6893
Mary Dunn, Assistant Dean of Admissions, Salem State College, 352 Lafayette Street, Salem, MA 01970-5353

## School of the Museum of Fine Arts
**Boston, Massachusetts**
www.smfa.edu                                    CB code: 3794

- Private 4-year visual arts college
- Commuter campus in very large city
- 564 degree-seeking undergraduates: 5% part-time, 66% women, 1% African American, 4% Asian American, 6% Hispanic American, 8% international
- 109 degree-seeking graduate students
- 81% of applicants admitted
- Application essay required
- 50% graduate within 6 years

**General.** Founded in 1876. Part of the Museum of Fine Arts,. **Degrees:** 119 bachelor's awarded; master's offered. **Location:** One mile from downtown. **Calendar:** Semester, limited summer session. **Full-time faculty:** 46 total; 70% have terminal degrees, 6% minority, 48% women. **Part-time faculty:** 50 total; 40% have terminal degrees, 6% minority, 60% women. **Class size:** 89% < 20, 10% 20-39, less than 1% 50-99.

**Freshman class profile.** 743 applied, 599 admitted, 102 enrolled.

| Mid 50% test scores | | | |
|---|---|---|---|
| SAT critical reading: | 510-640 | End year in good standing: | 79% |
| SAT math: | 450-590 | Return as sophomores: | 81% |
| SAT writing: | 490-630 | Out-of-state: | 71% |
| ACT composite: | 21-26 | Live on campus: | 59% |
| | | International: | 8% |

**Basis for selection.** Portfolio, previous schooling, and quality and content of essays important; grades and test scores important for BFA applicants, considered for Studio Diploma applicants. Combined Degree program applicants must apply to the Museum School and Tufts University simultaneously. Scores accepted on a rolling basis after February 1. Portfolio required. Interview available by appointment. **Homeschooled:** Transcript of courses and grades required. Must have graduation date indicating successful completion of program; must be signed and dated by recognized record keeper, which may include outside testing agency, homeschool representative, or parent.

**2009-2010 Annual costs.** Tuition/fees: $30,660. Room only: $13,046. Books/supplies: $1,500. Personal expenses: $1,091.

**2009-2010 Financial aid. Need-based:** 81 full-time freshmen applied for aid; 70 were judged to have need; 70 of these received aid. Average need met was 58%. Average scholarship/grant was $14,944; average loan $3,441. 63% of total undergraduate aid awarded as scholarships/grants, 37% as loans/jobs. **Non-need-based:** Awarded to 60 full-time undergraduates, including 38 freshmen. Scholarships awarded for art.

**Application procedures. Admission:** Priority date 2/1; no deadline. $65 fee, may be waived for applicants with need. Admission notification on a rolling basis beginning on or about 3/15. Must reply by May 1 or within 2 week(s) if notified thereafter. Students may apply early and request early notification of admission. **Financial aid:** Closing date 3/15. FAFSA, institutional form required. Applicants notified by 4/15; must reply by 5/1 or within 2 week(s) of notification.

**Academics.** Credit for studio work awarded through a Review Board, which consists of 2 faculty members and 2 student reviewers who evaluate the work. **Special study options:** Combined bachelor's/graduate degree, cross-registration, double major, ESL, exchange student, independent study, internships, liberal arts/career combination, New York semester, student-designed major, study abroad, teacher certification program. 5-year BFA/BA with Tufts University, Studio art elective Diploma program, optional fifth-year certificate program for Studio Diploma recipients. Additional BFA also offered through Northeastern University, Boston. Degree affiliations with Tufts and Northeastern Universities; extensive exchange and cross-registration opportunities within Boston, the United States, and around the world. Studio programs are interdisciplinary and self-directed. **Credit/placement by examination:** CLEP. **Support services:** Pre-admission summer program, study skills assistance, writing center.

**Majors. Communications technology:** Animation/special effects. **Visual/performing arts:** Art, ceramics, cinematography, drawing, illustration, metal/jewelry, multimedia, painting, photography, printmaking, sculpture, studio arts. **Other:** Video.

**Most popular majors.** Visual/performing arts 95%.

**Computing on campus.** 170 workstations in library, computer center, student center. Dormitories wired for high-speed internet access. Online course registration, wireless network available.

**Student life. Freshman orientation:** Mandatory, $125 fee. Preregistration for classes offered. Typically held during last week in August, right before beginning of semester. **Housing:** Coed dorms available. $450 nonrefundable deposit, deadline 5/1. Professional off-campus housing assistance available. **Activities:** Film society, student government, Open Forum (GLBT), SMFA in New Orleans, environmental club.

**Student services.** Adult student services, career counseling, student employment services, financial aid counseling, personal counseling, placement for graduates. **Physically disabled:** Services for hearing impaired.

**Contact.** E-mail: admissions@smfa.edu
Phone: (617) 369-3626 Toll-free number: (800) 643-6078
Fax: (617) 369-4264
Susan Clain, Dean of Admissions, School of the Museum of Fine Arts, 230 The Fenway, Boston, MA 02115

## Simmons College
**Boston, Massachusetts**                       CB member
www.simmons.edu                                 CB code: 3761

- Private 4-year health science and liberal arts college for women
- Residential campus in very large city

◆ 1,933 degree-seeking undergraduates: 10% part-time, 100% women, 6% African American, 7% Asian American, 4% Hispanic American, 3% international
◆ 2,889 degree-seeking graduate students
◆ 57% of applicants admitted
◆ SAT or ACT (ACT writing optional), application essay required
◆ 70% graduate within 6 years

**General.** Founded in 1899. Regionally accredited. **Degrees:** 477 bachelor's awarded; master's, professional offered. **ROTC:** Army. **Location:** 2 miles from downtown. **Calendar:** Semester, extensive summer session. **Full-time faculty:** 230 total; 81% have terminal degrees. **Part-time faculty:** 325 total. **Class size:** 68% < 20, 25% 20-39, 2% 40-49, 6% 50-99. **Special facilities:** Art gallery, technology resource center.

**Freshman class profile.** 3,522 applied, 2,013 admitted, 354 enrolled.

| Mid 50% test scores | | | |
|---|---|---|---|
| SAT critical reading: | 500-590 | GPA 2.0-2.99: | 35% |
| SAT math: | 490-600 | Rank in top quarter: | 55% |
| SAT writing: | 510-610 | Rank in top tenth: | 19% |
| ACT composite: | 22-26 | Return as sophomores: | 75% |
| GPA 3.75 or higher: | 7% | Out-of-state: | 44% |
| GPA 3.50-3.74: | 16% | Live on campus: | 85% |
| GPA 3.0-3.49: | 42% | International: | 6% |

**Basis for selection.** School achievement record most important. Test scores, 2 recommendations, essay, interview (if available), personal qualities also important. Interests, accomplishments considered. **Homeschooled:** Statement describing homeschool structure and mission, transcript of courses and grades, letter of recommendation (nonparent) required.

**High school preparation.** College-preparatory program required. 19 units required; 22 recommended. Required and recommended units include English 4, mathematics 3-4, social studies 3-4, history 3, science 3 and foreign language 3-4.

**2009-2010 Annual costs.** Tuition/fees: $31,220. Room/board: $12,050. Books/supplies: $800. Personal expenses: $1,250.

**2009-2010 Financial aid. Need-based:** 344 full-time freshmen applied for aid; 276 were judged to have need; 276 of these received aid. Average need met was 65%. Average scholarship/grant was $15,937; average loan $4,126. 67% of total undergraduate aid awarded as scholarships/grants, 33% as loans/jobs. **Non-need-based:** Awarded to 374 full-time undergraduates, including 71 freshmen. Scholarships awarded for academics, alumni affiliation, leadership, minority status.

**Application procedures. Admission:** Closing date 2/1 (postmark date). $55 fee, may be waived for applicants with need, free for online applicants. Admission notification 4/15. Must reply by May 1 or within 2 week(s) if notified thereafter. **Financial aid:** Priority date 2/15, closing date 3/1. FAFSA, institutional form required. Applicants notified on a rolling basis starting 3/15; must reply by 5/1 or within 4 week(s) of notification.

**Academics. Special study options:** Accelerated study, combined bachelor's/graduate degree, cross-registration, double major, dual enrollment of high school students, ESL, exchange student, honors, independent study, internships, liberal arts/career combination, semester at sea, student-designed major, study abroad, teacher certification program, Washington semester. Exchange programs with Mills College, Spelman College, Fisk University, American University, Colleges of the Fenway; double degree programs with Massachusetts College of Pharmacy and Health Sciences and Hebrew College. **Credit/placement by examination:** AP, CLEP, IB, institutional tests. 32 credit hours maximum toward bachelor's degree. **Support services:** Learning center, reduced course load, study skills assistance, tutoring, writing center.

**Majors. Area/ethnic studies:** African-American, East Asian, women's. **Biology:** General, biochemistry. **Business:** Business admin, finance, management information systems, sales/distribution. **Communications:** General, public relations. **Computer sciences:** General. **Conservation:** General, environmental science. **Education:** General, early childhood, elementary, ESL, middle, secondary, social studies, special. **Foreign languages:** Comparative lit, French, Spanish. **Health:** Nursing (RN), predental, premedicine, prepharmacy. **History:** General. **Interdisciplinary:** Nutrition sciences. **Math:** General. **Philosophy/religion:** Philosophy. **Physical sciences:** Chemistry, physics. **Psychology:** General, psychobiology. **Public administration:** Policy analysis. **Social sciences:** Economics, international relations, political science, sociology. **Visual/performing arts:** Art history/conservation, arts management, commercial/advertising art, graphic design, music history, music performance.

**Most popular majors.** Biology 7%, business/marketing 8%, communications/journalism 9%, health sciences 35%, psychology 11%, social sciences 11%.

**Computing on campus.** 630 workstations in dormitories, library, computer center, student center. Dormitories wired for high-speed internet access and linked to campus network. Commuter students can connect to campus network. Online course registration, online library, helpline, wireless network available.

**Student life. Freshman orientation:** Mandatory. Preregistration for classes offered. **Housing:** Special housing for disabled, wellness housing available. $250 fully refundable deposit, deadline 5/1. Special interest housing available. **Activities:** Choral groups, dance, drama, film society, literary magazine, radio station, student government, student newspaper, symphony orchestra, Asian student association, black students organization, Organizacion Latino Americana, Hillel, Amnesty International, women's center, The Alliance, chemistry-physics liaison, dance company, ALANA nursing liaison.

**Athletics.** NCAA. **Intercollegiate:** Basketball W, diving W, field hockey W, lacrosse W, rowing (crew) W, soccer W, softball W, swimming W, tennis W, volleyball W. **Team name:** Sharks.

**Student services.** Adult student services, alcohol/substance abuse counseling, chaplain/spiritual director, career counseling, student employment services, financial aid counseling, health services, personal counseling, placement for graduates, veterans' counselor, women's services. **Physically disabled:** Services for visually, speech, hearing impaired.

**Contact.** E-mail: ugadm@simmons.edu
Phone: (617) 521-2051 Toll-free number: (800) 345-8468
Fax: (617) 521-3190
Catherine Capolupo, Director of Undergraduate Admissions, Simmons College, 300 The Fenway, Boston, MA 02115-5898

---

**Smith College**
**Northampton, Massachusetts**     **CB member**
www.smith.edu     **CB code: 3762**

◆ Private 4-year liberal arts college for women
◆ Residential campus in large town
◆ 2,614 degree-seeking undergraduates: 1% part-time, 100% women, 7% African American, 13% Asian American, 7% Hispanic American, 1% Native American, 8% international
◆ 506 degree-seeking graduate students
◆ 47% of applicants admitted
◆ Application essay required
◆ 84% graduate within 6 years

**General.** Founded in 1871. Regionally accredited. **Degrees:** 679 bachelor's awarded; master's, doctoral offered. **ROTC:** Army, Air Force. **Location:** 35 miles from Hartford, Connecticut; 90 miles from Boston. **Calendar:** Semester. **Full-time faculty:** 281 total; 98% have terminal degrees, 17% minority, 54% women. **Part-time faculty:** 25 total; 88% have terminal degrees, 4% minority, 44% women. **Class size:** 67% < 20, 25% 20-39, 3% 40-49, 4% 50-99, less than 1% >100. **Special facilities:** Physiology and horticultural laboratories, printmaking studio, darkroom and sculpture (including bronze casting studio) facilities, dance, theater and television studios, electronic music studio, recital hall, digital design studio, animal care facilities, electron microscopes, on-campus elementary school, multimedia language lab, greenhouses, astronomy observatories.

**Freshman class profile.** 4,011 applied, 1,904 admitted, 665 enrolled.

| Mid 50% test scores | | | |
|---|---|---|---|
| SAT critical reading: | 610-710 | GPA 2.0-2.99: | 1% |
| SAT math: | 580-690 | Rank in top quarter: | 94% |
| SAT writing: | 610-710 | Rank in top tenth: | 66% |
| ACT composite: | 27-30 | End year in good standing: | 96% |
| GPA 3.75 or higher: | 48% | Return as sophomores: | 91% |
| GPA 3.50-3.74: | 35% | Out-of-state: | 83% |
| GPA 3.0-3.49: | 16% | Live on campus: | 100% |
| | | International: | 12% |

**Basis for selection.** Secondary school record, including GPA and difficulty of courses, recommendations most important. Class rank, essay, school and community activities and test scores also important. Interview strongly recommended, may be conducted off-campus by alumna. **Homeschooled:** Statement describing homeschool structure and mission, transcript of courses and grades, letter of recommendation (nonparent) required. Submit portfolio and evaluation of coursework and sample of short research or analytical paper with evaluator's remarks.

**High school preparation.** College-preparatory program recommended. 15 units recommended. Recommended units include English 4, mathematics 3, history 2, science 3 (laboratory 3) and foreign language 3. 3 units of 1 foreign language or 2 each of 2 languages recommended.

**2009-2010 Annual costs.** Tuition/fees: $37,758. Room/board: $12,622. Books/supplies: $800. Personal expenses: $1,550.

**2008-2009 Financial aid. Need-based:** 526 full-time freshmen applied for aid; 406 were judged to have need; 406 of these received aid. Average need met was 100%. Average scholarship/grant was $31,980; average loan $3,198. 83% of total undergraduate aid awarded as scholarships/grants, 17% as loans/jobs. **Non-need-based:** Awarded to 144 full-time undergraduates, including 35 freshmen. Scholarships awarded for academics, state residency. **Additional information:** Financial aid policy guarantees to meet full financial need, as calculated by college, of all admitted students who have met application deadlines.

**Application procedures. Admission:** Closing date 1/15 (postmark date). $60 fee, may be waived for applicants with need, free for online applicants. Notification by early April. Must reply by May 1 or within 2 week(s) if notified thereafter. **Financial aid:** Closing date 2/15. FAFSA, CSS PROFILE required. Applicants notified by 4/1; must reply by 5/1.

**Academics.** Academic honor code; writing course required in first year. **Special study options:** Accelerated study, cross-registration, double major, exchange student, honors, independent study, internships, semester at sea, student-designed major, study abroad, teacher certification program, Washington semester. Member of Five College Consortium, program in engineering and technology, engineering science program within liberal arts curriculum leading to BS degree, post-baccalaureate certificate in American studies (available to international students). **Credit/placement by examination:** AP, CLEP, IB, institutional tests. 32 credit hours maximum toward bachelor's degree. **Support services:** Learning center, study skills assistance, tutoring, writing center.

**Majors. Area/ethnic studies:** African-American, American, Asian, Latin American, women's. **Biology:** General, biochemistry. **Computer sciences:** Computer science. **Education:** General. **Engineering:** General, biomedical, chemical, civil, computer, electrical, environmental, mechanical, mechanics, science. **Foreign languages:** Ancient Greek, classics, comparative lit, East Asian, French, German, Italian, Latin, Portuguese, Russian, Spanish. **History:** General. **Interdisciplinary:** Ancient studies, medieval/Renaissance, neuroscience. **Math:** General. **Philosophy/religion:** Philosophy, religion. **Physical sciences:** Astronomy, astrophysics, chemistry, geology, physics. **Psychology:** General. **Social sciences:** Anthropology, economics, political science, sociology. **Visual/performing arts:** Art, art history/conservation, dance, dramatic, film/cinema, studio arts.

**Most popular majors.** Area/ethnic studies 10%, biology 6%, English 7%, foreign language 9%, psychology 10%, social sciences 24%, visual/performing arts 10%.

**Computing on campus.** 582 workstations in dormitories, library, computer center, student center. Dormitories wired for high-speed internet access and linked to campus network. Commuter students can connect to campus network. Online course registration, online library, helpline, repair service, student web hosting, wireless network available.

**Student life. Freshman orientation:** Mandatory. Program held 4-5 days prior to beginning of classes; includes parent day. **Policies:** Each residence self-governed within framework of college regulations. Residents determine house responsibilities. **Housing:** Guaranteed on-campus for all undergraduates. Cooperative housing available. $200 nonrefundable deposit, deadline 5/1. French-speaking house, senior house, nontraditional age house, apartment complexes for juniors and seniors available. **Activities:** Bands, campus ministries, choral groups, dance, drama, international student organizations, literary magazine, music ensembles, Model UN, musical theater, radio station, student government, student newspaper, TV station, service organizations, women's resource center, black student alliance, Asian student association, Hillel, Newman Club, Christian council, international relations club, Latina organization, Native American organization.

**Athletics.** NCAA. **Intercollegiate:** Basketball W, cross-country W, diving W, equestrian W, field hockey W, lacrosse W, rowing (crew) W, skiing W, soccer W, softball W, squash W, swimming W, tennis W, track and field W, volleyball W. **Intramural:** Basketball W, soccer W. **Team name:** Pioneers.

**Student services.** Adult student services, alcohol/substance abuse counseling, chaplain/spiritual director, career counseling, services for economically disadvantaged, student employment services, financial aid counseling, health services, minority student services, on-campus daycare, personal counseling, placement for graduates, women's services. **Physically disabled:** Services for visually, speech, hearing impaired.

**Contact.** E-mail: admission@smith.edu
Phone: (413) 585-2500 Fax: (413) 585-2527
Debra Shaver, Director of Admission, Smith College, 7 College Lane, Northampton, MA 01063

## Springfield College
**Springfield, Massachusetts**
www.springfieldcollege.edu
**CB member**
**CB code: 3763**

- Private 4-year health science and liberal arts college
- Residential campus in small city
- 2,292 degree-seeking undergraduates
- 69% of applicants admitted
- SAT or ACT with writing, application essay required

**General.** Founded in 1885. Regionally accredited. Adult weekend programs at 11 sites across the country. **Degrees:** 962 bachelor's awarded; master's, doctoral offered. **ROTC:** Army, Air Force. **Location:** 90 miles from Boston; 26 miles from Hartford, Connecticut. **Calendar:** Semester, limited summer session. **Full-time faculty:** 210 total. **Part-time faculty:** 155 total. **Class size:** 46% < 20, 52% 20-39, less than 1% 40-49, less than 1% 50-99, less than 1% >100. **Special facilities:** 57-acre campground and outdoor adventure area.

**Freshman class profile.** 2,392 applied, 1,650 admitted, 579 enrolled.

| Mid 50% test scores | | Rank in top tenth: | 13% |
|---|---|---|---|
| SAT critical reading: | 450-550 | Out-of-state: | 72% |
| SAT math: | 470-580 | Live on campus: | 98% |
| Rank in top quarter: | 38% | | |

**Basis for selection.** School achievement record, essay, extracurricular activities, personal references, and test scores important. Portfolio required of art majors. **Homeschooled:** Statement describing homeschool structure and mission, transcript of courses and grades, letter of recommendation (nonparent) required.

**High school preparation.** College-preparatory program required. 16 units required. Required and recommended units include English 4, mathematics 3, social studies 2, history 1, science 3 (laboratory 2) and foreign language 3. Emphasis on science for majors in allied health fields.

**2009-2010 Annual costs.** Tuition/fees: $26,480. Room/board: $11,050. Books/supplies: $900. Personal expenses: $1,200.

**2008-2009 Financial aid. Additional information:** Co-operative education program available to students after freshman year.

**Application procedures. Admission:** Priority date 3/1; deadline 4/1 (postmark date). $50 fee, may be waived for applicants with need. Admission notification on a rolling basis beginning on or about 12/1. Must reply by May 1 or within 2 week(s) if notified thereafter. Application closing date for athletic training, physical therapy majors 12/1; closing date for physician assistant and occupational therapy majors 1/15. **Financial aid:** Priority date 3/15; no closing date. FAFSA, institutional form, CSS PROFILE required. Applicants notified on a rolling basis starting 3/15; must reply by 5/1 or within 2 week(s) of notification.

**Academics.** Emphasis on practical fieldwork experiences to supplement classroom learning. **Special study options:** Combined bachelor's/graduate degree, cooperative education, cross-registration, double major, ESL, independent study, internships, liberal arts/career combination, study abroad, teacher certification program, weekend college. **Credit/placement by examination:** AP, CLEP, IB, SAT, ACT, institutional tests. 30 credit hours maximum toward bachelor's degree. **Support services:** Learning center, reduced course load, study skills assistance, tutoring, writing center.

**Majors. Biology:** General. **Business:** Business admin. **Computer sciences:** General, computer graphics, information systems. **Conservation:** General, environmental studies. **Education:** Art, early childhood, elementary, health, physical, secondary, special. **Health:** Art therapy, athletic training, clinical lab science, clinical lab technology, EMT paramedic, health care admin, medical records admin, physician assistant, predental, recreational therapy. **History:** General. **Interdisciplinary:** Biological/physical sciences. **Legal studies:** Prelaw. **Liberal arts:** Arts/sciences. **Math:** General. **Parks/recreation:** Exercise sciences, facilities management, health/fitness, sports admin. **Protective services:** Law enforcement admin. **Psychology:** General. **Public administration:** Community org/advocacy, human services. **Social sciences:** Political science, sociology. **Visual/performing arts:** Art, dance.

**Computing on campus.** 235 workstations in dormitories, library, computer center, student center. Dormitories wired for high-speed internet access and linked to campus network. Commuter students can connect to campus network. Online course registration, helpline, wireless network available.

**Student life. Freshman orientation:** Mandatory, $125 fee. Four-day program immediately preceding fall semester. **Housing:** Guaranteed on-campus for all undergraduates. Coed dorms, single-sex dorms, special housing for disabled, apartments, wellness housing available. **Activities:** Jazz band, campus ministries, choral groups, dance, drama, international student organizations, literary magazine, music ensembles, musical theater, radio station, student government, student newspaper, environmental club, Fellowship of Christian Athletes, Habitat for Humanity, Hillel, Newman community, outreach committee, student society for cultural diversity, students against violence everywhere, international student organization.

**Athletics.** NCAA. **Intercollegiate:** Baseball M, basketball, cross-country, diving, field hockey W, football (tackle) M, golf, gymnastics, lacrosse, soccer, softball W, swimming, tennis, track and field, volleyball, wrestling M. **Intramural:** Basketball, bowling, field hockey, football (non-tackle), golf, handball, lacrosse, racquetball, soccer, softball, swimming, tennis, track and field, volleyball, wrestling M. **Team name:** Pride.

**Student services.** Adult student services, alcohol/substance abuse counseling, chaplain/spiritual director, career counseling, student employment services, financial aid counseling, health services, minority student services, on-campus daycare, personal counseling, placement for graduates, veterans' counselor, women's services. **Physically disabled:** Services for visually, speech, hearing impaired.

**Contact.** E-mail: admissions@spfldcol.edu
Phone: (413) 748-3136 Toll-free number: (800) 343-1257
Fax: (413) 748-3694
Richard Veres, Director of Admissions, Springfield College, 263 Alden Street, Springfield, MA 01109

---

## Stonehill College
### Easton, Massachusetts
**CB member**
### www.stonehill.edu
**CB code: 3770**

- Private 4-year liberal arts college affiliated with Roman Catholic Church
- Residential campus in large town
- 2,448 degree-seeking undergraduates: 1% part-time, 60% women, 3% African American, 1% Asian American, 4% Hispanic American
- 56% of applicants admitted
- Application essay required
- 82% graduate within 6 years; 32% enter graduate study

**General.** Founded in 1948. Regionally accredited. **Degrees:** 569 bachelor's awarded. **ROTC:** Army. **Location:** 19 miles from Boston, 25 miles from Providence. **Calendar:** Semester, limited summer session. **Full-time faculty:** 151 total; 82% have terminal degrees, 9% minority, 39% women. **Part-time faculty:** 103 total; 39% have terminal degrees, 7% minority, 37% women. **Class size:** 42% < 20, 56% 20-39, less than 1% 40-49, less than 1% 50-99. **Special facilities:** Observatory, shovel museum.

**Freshman class profile.** 5,871 applied, 3,313 admitted, 684 enrolled.

| Mid 50% test scores | | | |
|---|---|---|---|
| SAT critical reading: | 550-630 | GPA 2.0-2.99: | 8% |
| SAT math: | 570-650 | Rank in top quarter: | 87% |
| ACT composite: | 24-28 | Rank in top tenth: | 50% |
| GPA 3.75 or higher: | 26% | Return as sophomores: | 89% |
| GPA 3.50-3.74: | 29% | Out-of-state: | 48% |
| GPA 3.0-3.49: | 37% | Live on campus: | 97% |

**Basis for selection.** Competitive high school course profile, grades, weighted GPA, class rank, high school profile, counselor recommendation important. **Homeschooled:** Statement describing homeschool structure and mission, transcript of courses and grades required. Common Application Home Schooled Supplement form required.

**High school preparation.** College-preparatory program required. 16 units required; 20 recommended. Required and recommended units include English 4, mathematics 3-4, history 3, science 1-3 (laboratory 1-2), foreign language 2-3 and academic electives 3. Foreign language units should be in same language. 3 combined units in history, political science, social science required. Math units should consist of algegra I, algebra II, and geometry. Additional units in science and math recommended for science applicants. Additional math units recommended for business applicants.

**2009-2010 Annual costs.** Tuition/fees: $31,210. Room/board: $12,240. Books/supplies: $1,200. Personal expenses: $836.

**2009-2010 Financial aid. Need-based:** 617 full-time freshmen applied for aid; 485 were judged to have need; 485 of these received aid. Average need met was 76%. Average scholarship/grant was $18,707; average loan $3,430. 67% of total undergraduate aid awarded as scholarships/grants, 33% as loans/jobs. **Non-need-based:** Awarded to 706 full-time undergraduates, including 248 freshmen. Scholarships awarded for academics, art, athletics, leadership, minority status, music/drama, ROTC.

**Application procedures. Admission:** Closing date 1/15 (postmark date). $60 fee, may be waived for applicants with need. Admission notification 3/15. Admission notification on a rolling basis. Must reply by 5/1. **Financial aid:** Priority date 2/1; no closing date. FAFSA, CSS PROFILE required. Applicants notified by 4/1; must reply by 5/1.

**Academics. Special study options:** Cross-registration, double major, dual enrollment of high school students, honors, independent study, internships, liberal arts/career combination, New York semester, student-designed major, study abroad, teacher certification program, Washington semester. Full-semester international internship sites in Dublin, Geneva, London, Madrid, and Paris; 3-2 computer engineering BA/BS program with University of Notre Dame, Indiana; Stonehill Undergraduate Research Experience (SURE) program. **Credit/placement by examination:** AP, CLEP, IB, SAT, ACT, institutional tests. **Support services:** Learning center, reduced course load, study skills assistance, tutoring, writing center.

**Majors. Area/ethnic studies:** American. **Biology:** General, biochemistry. **Business:** Accounting, business admin, finance, international, marketing. **Communications:** General. **Computer sciences:** Computer science. **Conservation:** Environmental studies. **Education:** Early childhood, elementary. **Foreign languages:** General, French, Spanish. **Health:** Health care admin. **History:** General. **Interdisciplinary:** Neuroscience. **Math:** General. **Philosophy/religion:** Christian, philosophy, religion. **Physical sciences:** Chemistry, physics. **Psychology:** General. **Public administration:** General. **Social sciences:** Criminology, economics, international relations, political science, sociology. **Visual/performing arts:** General, art history/conservation, graphic design, studio arts.

**Most popular majors.** Biology 6%, business/marketing 24%, communications/journalism 8%, education 7%, English 6%, psychology 11%, social sciences 15%.

**Computing on campus.** 370 workstations in library, computer center, student center. Dormitories wired for high-speed internet access and linked to campus network. Commuter students can connect to campus network. Online course registration, online library, helpline, repair service, student web hosting, wireless network available.

**Student life. Freshman orientation:** Mandatory. Preregistration for classes offered. Two-day program in June. **Housing:** Guaranteed on-campus for all undergraduates. Coed dorms, single-sex dorms, special housing for disabled, wellness housing available. $300 nonrefundable deposit, deadline 5/1. Special interest housing proposals considered for groups. **Activities:** Pep band, campus ministries, choral groups, dance, drama, film society, literary magazine, music ensembles, musical theater, radio station, student government, student newspaper, College Republicans, College Democrats, PRIDE, BACCHUS, Asian American Society, Habitat for Humanity, Circle K, Diversity on Campus, Fear No People.

**Athletics.** NCAA. **Intercollegiate:** Baseball M, basketball, cross-country, equestrian W, field hockey W, football (tackle) M, ice hockey M, lacrosse W, soccer, softball W, tennis, track and field, volleyball W. **Intramural:** Basketball, field hockey, football (non-tackle), handball, soccer, softball, tennis, volleyball. **Team name:** Skyhawks.

**Student services.** Adult student services, alcohol/substance abuse counseling, chaplain/spiritual director, career counseling, services for economically disadvantaged, student employment services, financial aid counseling, health services, minority student services, on-campus daycare, personal counseling, placement for graduates, women's services. **Physically disabled:** Services for visually, speech, hearing impaired.

**Contact.** E-mail: admissions@stonehill.edu
Phone: (508) 565-1373 Fax: (508) 565-1545
Brian Murphy, Dean of Admissions and Enrollment, Stonehill College, 320 Washington Street, Easton, MA 02357-0100

---

## Suffolk University
### Boston, Massachusetts
**CB member**
### www.suffolk.edu
**CB code: 3771**

- Private 4-year university
- Commuter campus in very large city
- 5,617 degree-seeking undergraduates: 6% part-time, 56% women, 4% African American, 7% Asian American, 7% Hispanic American, 10% international
- 1,882 degree-seeking graduate students
- 85% of applicants admitted
- SAT or ACT with writing required
- 54% graduate within 6 years; 27% enter graduate study

**General.** Founded in 1906. Regionally accredited. Campuses in Spain and Senegal. Branch campuses in Cape Cod, Merrimack, and Franklin. **Degrees:** 1,105 bachelor's awarded; master's, doctoral, professional offered. **ROTC:** Army. **Location:** Downtown. **Calendar:** Semester, extensive summer session. **Full-time faculty:** 425 total; 91% have terminal degrees, 12% minority, 39% women. **Part-time faculty:** 564 total; 12% have terminal degrees, 11% minority, 43% women. **Class size:** 54% < 20, 44% 20-39, 1% 40-49, less than 1% 50-99, less than 1% >100. **Special facilities:** Marine biology station, poetry center, energy research lab, political research center, television studio.

**Freshman class profile.** 9,036 applied, 7,661 admitted, 1,254 enrolled.

| Mid 50% test scores | | GPA 2.0-2.99: | 47% |
|---|---|---|---|
| SAT critical reading: | 450-560 | Rank in top quarter: | 38% |
| SAT math: | 450-560 | Rank in top tenth: | 12% |
| SAT writing: | 450-560 | End year in good standing: | 84% |
| ACT composite: | 19-24 | Return as sophomores: | 72% |
| GPA 3.75 or higher: | 7% | Out-of-state: | 36% |
| GPA 3.50-3.74: | 10% | Live on campus: | 68% |
| GPA 3.0-3.49: | 36% | International: | 7% |

**Basis for selection.** High school record including courses taken, level of study, class rank, test scores, essay important. Counselor recommendation considered. Interview recommended. Portfolio required for BFA program applicants. **Homeschooled:** Transcript of courses and grades, state high school equivalency certificate, letter of recommendation (nonparent) required. Admission interview highly recommended. Transcript/Record of courses and grades or written evaluation of work required.

**High school preparation.** College-preparatory program recommended. 17 units required; 22 recommended. Required and recommended units include English 4, mathematics 3-4, history 1-4, science 2-4 (laboratory 1), foreign language 2-3 and academic electives 4.

**2009-2010 Annual costs.** Tuition/fees: $27,208. Room/board: $14,544. Books/supplies: $1,000. Personal expenses: $2,400.

**2009-2010 Financial aid. Need-based:** 1,016 full-time freshmen applied for aid; 873 were judged to have need; 868 of these received aid. Average need met was 72%. Average scholarship/grant was $13,201; average loan $3,466. 36% of total undergraduate aid awarded as scholarships/grants, 64% as loans/jobs. **Non-need-based:** Awarded to 1,523 full-time undergraduates, including 307 freshmen. Scholarships awarded for academics, alumni affiliation. **Additional information:** Foreign students may apply for institutional employment awards.

**Application procedures. Admission:** Closing date 3/1. $50 fee, may be waived for applicants with need. Admission notification on a rolling basis beginning on or about 2/5. Must reply by May 1 or within 2 week(s) if notified thereafter. Strongly suggest housing deposit before March 15. Housing awarded on first-come first-served basis by date of the admission deposit. **Financial aid:** Closing date 3/1. FAFSA, institutional form required. Applicants notified on a rolling basis starting 2/5.

**Academics. Special study options:** Accelerated study, combined bachelor's/graduate degree, cooperative education, cross-registration, distance learning, double major, ESL, exchange student, honors, independent study, internships, liberal arts/career combination, study abroad, Washington semester. **Credit/placement by examination:** AP, CLEP, IB, SAT, ACT, institutional tests. 30 credit hours maximum toward associate degree, 30 toward bachelor's. **Support services:** Learning center, pre-admission summer program, reduced course load, remedial instruction, study skills assistance, tutoring, writing center.

**Honors college/program.** Separate application required. Class rank, GPA, personal essay, interview, and quality of secondary school curriculum, including advanced placement, honors, and other types of accelerated courses, and any other relevant information considered. Applicants from the College of Arts and Sciences and Sawyer Business School will normally meet at least 2 of the following criteria: 3.7 GPA, class rank within upper 10% (if class rank is available), 1300 SAT (exclusive of Writing), or 29 ACT.

**Majors. Area/ethnic studies:** African-American, French, German, women's. **Biology:** General, biochemistry, biomedical sciences, biophysics, environmental, marine, radiobiology. **Business:** General, accounting, business admin, entrepreneurial studies, finance, international, management information systems, marketing, office technology. **Communications:** General, advertising, broadcast journalism, journalism, media studies, organizational, political, public relations. **Communications technology:** General, radio/tv. **Computer sciences:** General, computer science, information systems. **Conservation:** Environmental science. **Education:** General. **Engineering:** Computer, electrical, environmental. **Engineering technology:** Biomedical. **Foreign languages:** General, French, German, Spanish. **History:** General, American, European. **Legal studies:** Paralegal, prelaw. **Liberal arts:** Arts/sciences, humanities. **Math:** General. **Philosophy/religion:** Philosophy. **Physical sciences:** General, chemistry, physics. **Protective services:** Law enforcement admin. **Psychology:** General. **Public administration:** General, policy

analysis. **Social sciences:** General, criminology, economics, international economics, international relations, political science, sociology, U.S. government. **Visual/performing arts:** General, acting, art, art history/conservation, arts management, commercial/advertising art, dramatic, film/cinema, interior design, studio arts, theater history.

**Most popular majors.** Business/marketing 39%, communications/journalism 15%, social sciences 16%, visual/performing arts 6%.

**Computing on campus.** 539 workstations in dormitories, library, computer center, student center. Dormitories wired for high-speed internet access and linked to campus network. Commuter students can connect to campus network. Online course registration, online library, helpline, wireless network available.

**Student life. Freshman orientation:** Mandatory, $85 fee. Preregistration for classes offered. Three-day orientation held in June and August. **Housing:** Coed dorms, apartments, wellness housing available. $600 fully refundable deposit, deadline 5/1. **Activities:** Jazz band, campus ministries, choral groups, dance, drama, literary magazine, music ensembles, musical theater, radio station, student government, student newspaper, TV station, Islamic cultural society, Newman club, Jewish society, finance committee, student government association, student judiciary review board, Jumpstart Inc., S.O.U.L.S., Best Buddies, Up 'Til Dawn.

**Athletics.** NCAA. **Intercollegiate:** Baseball M, basketball, cross-country, golf M, ice hockey M, soccer M, softball W, tennis, volleyball W. **Intramural:** Basketball, football (non-tackle), soccer W, table tennis, volleyball. **Team name:** Rams.

**Student services.** Adult student services, alcohol/substance abuse counseling, chaplain/spiritual director, career counseling, student employment services, financial aid counseling, health services, minority student services, personal counseling, placement for graduates, veterans' counselor, women's services. **Physically disabled:** Services for visually, speech, hearing impaired.

**Contact.** E-mail: admission@suffolk.edu
Phone: (617) 573-8460 Toll-free number: (800) 678-3365
Fax: (617) 557-1574
John Hamel, Director of Admissions, Suffolk University, 8 Ashburton Place, Boston, MA 02108

---

## Tufts University
**Medford, Massachusetts** — CB member
**www.tufts.edu** — CB code: 3901

- Private 4-year university
- Residential campus in small city
- 5,146 degree-seeking undergraduates: 1% part-time, 51% women, 5% African American, 13% Asian American, 6% Hispanic American, 6% international
- 4,724 degree-seeking graduate students
- 27% of applicants admitted
- SAT and SAT Subject Tests or ACT with writing, application essay required
- 91% graduate within 6 years

**General.** Founded in 1852. Regionally accredited. **Degrees:** 1,371 bachelor's awarded; master's, doctoral, professional offered. **ROTC:** Army, Naval, Air Force. **Location:** 5 miles from Boston. **Calendar:** Semester, limited summer session. **Full-time faculty:** 675 total; 95% have terminal degrees, 21% minority, 40% women. **Part-time faculty:** 422 total; 65% have terminal degrees, 13% minority, 50% women. **Class size:** 71% < 20, 22% 20-39, 3% 40-49, 3% 50-99, 2% >100. **Special facilities:** Computer-aided design laboratory, arts center, theater in the round, engineering project design center.

**Freshman class profile.** 15,042 applied, 3,995 admitted, 1,314 enrolled.

| Mid 50% test scores | | Rank in top tenth: | 85% |
|---|---|---|---|
| SAT critical reading: | 680-750 | Return as sophomores: | 96% |
| SAT math: | 680-750 | Out-of-state: | 77% |
| SAT writing: | 680-760 | Live on campus: | 100% |
| ACT composite: | 30-33 | International: | 7% |
| Rank in top quarter: | 98% | | |

**Basis for selection.** School achievement record most important. School recommendations, test scores, character, personality, extracurricular participation, special talents also important. Geographical distribution, alumni relationship, minority status, socioeconomic status all considered. For applicants who submit SAT scores: 2 SAT Subject Tests required of liberal arts applicants; Math 1 or 2 and either physics or chemistry required of engineering applicants. Interview optional but recommended. **Homeschooled:** Transcript of courses and grades required.

**High school preparation.** College-preparatory program required. Recommended units include English 4, mathematics 4, history 4, science 4 and foreign language 4. 4 math, 2 laboratory science recommended for engineering, math, and science majors.

**2009-2010 Annual costs.** Tuition/fees: $40,342. Room/board: $10,746.

**2009-2010 Financial aid.** All financial aid based on need.

**Application procedures. Admission:** Closing date 1/1 (postmark date). $70 fee, may be waived for applicants with need. Admission notification 4/1. Must reply by 5/1. **Financial aid:** Closing date 2/15. FAFSA, CSS PROFILE required. Applicants notified by 4/1; must reply by 5/1.

**Academics. Special study options:** Combined bachelor's/graduate degree, cross-registration, double major, exchange student, independent study, internships, liberal arts/career combination, semester at sea, student-designed major, study abroad, teacher certification program, Washington semester. Experimental college, semester exchange with Lincoln University and Swarthmore College, 3-2 programs with New England Conservatory of Music (BA/BM), School of the Museum of Fine Arts (BA/BFA) European Center in Talloires, France. **Credit/placement by examination:** AP, CLEP, IB, SAT, institutional tests. Limit 1 year of credit by acceleration. **Support services:** Learning center, study skills assistance, tutoring.

**Majors. Area/ethnic studies:** African, African-American, American, Asian, Central/Eastern European, East Asian, European, Latin American, Near/Middle Eastern, Russian/Slavic, Western European, women's. **Biology:** General, ecology. **Computer sciences:** General, computer science, information systems, programming. **Education:** Early childhood. **Engineering:** General, architectural, biomedical, chemical, civil, computer, electrical, environmental, mechanical, physics, science. **Foreign languages:** General, ancient Greek, Chinese, classics, comparative lit, French, German, Italian, Japanese, Latin, Russian, Spanish. **History:** General. **Interdisciplinary:** Math/computer science, peace/conflict. **Liberal arts:** Arts/sciences. **Math:** General, applied. **Philosophy/religion:** Philosophy, religion. **Physical sciences:** Astronomy, chemistry, geology, physics. **Psychology:** General. **Social sciences:** Anthropology, archaeology, economics, international relations, political science, sociology. **Visual/performing arts:** Art history/conservation, music history, music theory/composition, musicology, studio arts, theater history.

**Most popular majors.** Engineering/engineering technologies 11%, foreign language 7%, psychology 7%, social sciences 30%, visual/performing arts 9%.

**Computing on campus.** 500 workstations in library, computer center. Dormitories wired for high-speed internet access and linked to campus network. Commuter students can connect to campus network. Online course registration, online library, helpline, repair service, student web hosting, wireless network available.

**Student life. Freshman orientation:** Mandatory. Preregistration for classes offered. Three-day program prior to beginning of fall semester. **Housing:** Guaranteed on-campus for freshmen. Coed dorms, single-sex dorms, special housing for disabled, apartments, cooperative housing, fraternity/sorority housing, wellness housing available. Culture, special interest, language houses available. **Activities:** Bands, campus ministries, choral groups, dance, drama, film society, international student organizations, literary magazine, music ensembles, Model UN, musical theater, opera, radio station, student government, student newspaper, symphony orchestra, TV station, over 200 student organizations.

**Athletics.** NCAA. **Intercollegiate:** Baseball M, basketball, cross-country, diving, fencing W, field hockey W, football (tackle) M, golf M, ice hockey M, lacrosse, rowing (crew), rugby, sailing, soccer, softball W, squash, swimming, tennis, track and field, volleyball W. **Intramural:** Basketball, fencing M, handball, racquetball, softball, squash, tennis, volleyball. **Team name:** Jumbos.

**Student services.** Adult student services, alcohol/substance abuse counseling, chaplain/spiritual director, career counseling, services for economically disadvantaged, student employment services, financial aid counseling, health services, legal services, minority student services, on-campus daycare, personal counseling, placement for graduates, women's services. **Physically disabled:** Services for visually, speech, hearing impaired.

**Contact.** E-mail: admissions.inquiry@ase.tufts.edu
Phone: (617) 627-3170 Fax: (617) 627-3860
Lee Coffin, Dean of Undergraduate Admissions and Enrollment Management, Tufts University, Bendetson Hall, Medford, MA 02155

## University of Massachusetts Amherst

**Amherst, Massachusetts** — CB member
**www.umass.edu** — CB code: 3917

- Public 4-year university
- Residential campus in large town
- 20,287 degree-seeking undergraduates: 5% part-time, 50% women, 5% African American, 8% Asian American, 4% Hispanic American, 1% international
- 5,546 degree-seeking graduate students
- 67% of applicants admitted
- SAT or ACT (ACT writing recommended), application essay required
- 66% graduate within 6 years

**General.** Founded in 1863. Regionally accredited. **Degrees:** 4,573 bachelor's, 74 associate awarded; master's, doctoral offered. **ROTC:** Army, Air Force. **Location:** 90 miles from Boston, 30 miles from Springfield. **Calendar:** Semester, limited summer session. **Full-time faculty:** 1,170 total; 93% have terminal degrees, 19% minority, 38% women. **Part-time faculty:** 145 total; 61% have terminal degrees, 6% minority, 56% women. **Class size:** 35% < 20, 41% 20-39, 6% 40-49, 9% 50-99, 9% >100. **Special facilities:** Observatory, botanical gardens, sports arena with ice rink.

**Freshman class profile.** 29,452 applied, 19,703 admitted, 4,124 enrolled.

| Mid 50% test scores | | | |
|---|---|---|---|
| SAT critical reading: | 520-630 | Rank in top quarter: | 67% |
| SAT math: | 540-650 | Rank in top tenth: | 27% |
| ACT composite: | 23-28 | Return as sophomores: | 87% |
| GPA 3.75 or higher: | 33% | Out-of-state: | 23% |
| GPA 3.50-3.74: | 28% | Live on campus: | 97% |
| GPA 3.0-3.49: | 37% | International: | 2% |
| GPA 2.0-2.99: | 2% | Fraternities: | 2% |
| | | Sororities: | 3% |

**Basis for selection.** High school grades most important, followed by test scores, extracurricular activities, essay and recommendations. Audition required of music and dance majors. Portfolio required of art and design majors. **Homeschooled:** Detailed transcript required. **Learning Disabled:** Applicants must submit diagnostic data and/or individualized educational plan. Massachusetts residents with documented learning disabilities not required to submit standardized test scores for admissions consideration.

**High school preparation.** College-preparatory program required. 16 units required. Required units include English 4, mathematics 3, social studies 2, science 3 (laboratory 2), foreign language 2 and academic electives 2.

**2009-2010 Annual costs.** Tuition/fees: $11,917; $23,414 out-of-state. Room/board: $8,276. Books/supplies: $1,000. Personal expenses: $1,000.

**2008-2009 Financial aid. Need-based:** 3,646 full-time freshmen applied for aid; 2,203 were judged to have need; 2,136 of these received aid. Average need met was 84%. Average scholarship/grant was $7,952; average loan $3,463. 49% of total undergraduate aid awarded as scholarships/grants, 51% as loans/jobs. **Non-need-based:** Awarded to 1,896 full-time undergraduates, including 421 freshmen. Scholarships awarded for academics, art, athletics, music/drama, ROTC, state residency.

**Application procedures. Admission:** Closing date 1/15 (postmark date). $40 fee ($50 out-of-state), may be waived for applicants with need. Admission notification on a rolling basis beginning on or about 3/7. Must reply by 5/1. **Financial aid:** Priority date 2/14; no closing date. FAFSA required. Applicants notified on a rolling basis starting 3/1.

**Academics.** Students may take courses at Amherst, Hampshire, Mt. Holyoke and Smith Colleges at no extra charge. **Special study options:** Cooperative education, cross-registration, distance learning, double major, dual enrollment of high school students, ESL, exchange student, honors, independent study, internships, liberal arts/career combination, student-designed major, study abroad, teacher certification program, Washington semester. University Without Walls program offers individualized degrees to working adults; residential academic programs allow first-year students to live and take classes together. **Credit/placement by examination:** AP, CLEP, IB, institutional tests. 30 credit hours maximum toward bachelor's degree. Credit awarded for International Baccalaureate scores of 4-7. **Support services:** Learning center, study skills assistance, tutoring, writing center.

**Honors college/program.** First-year students admitted by invitation, approximately 600 freshmen admitted. Interdisciplinary seminars, enriched honors courses, colloquia, independent study, service learning offered; honors thesis, project, or activity required.

**Majors. Agriculture:** Animal sciences, economics, food science, plant sciences. **Architecture:** Environmental design, interior, landscape. **Area/**

**ethnic studies:** African-American, Near/Middle Eastern, Russian/Slavic, women's. **Biology:** General, Biochemistry/biophysics and molecular biology, exercise physiology, microbiology. **Business:** Accounting, apparel, business admin, finance, hospitality admin, marketing. **Communications:** General, journalism. **Computer sciences:** Computer science. **Conservation:** General, environmental science, wood science. **Engineering:** Chemical, civil, computer, electrical, industrial, mechanical. **Family/consumer sciences:** Family resources, human nutrition. **Foreign languages:** Chinese, classics, comparative lit, French, German, Italian, Japanese, linguistics, Portuguese, Spanish. **Health:** Communication disorders, nursing (RN), predental, premedicine, preveterinary. **History:** General. **Interdisciplinary:** Biological/physical sciences. **Legal studies:** General. **Math:** General. **Parks/recreation:** Sports admin. **Philosophy/religion:** Judaic, philosophy. **Physical sciences:** Astronomy, chemistry, geology, physics. **Psychology:** General. **Social sciences:** Anthropology, economics, geography, political science, sociology. **Visual/performing arts:** Art history/conservation, dance, dramatic, music performance, studio arts. **Other:** Social thought and political economy.

**Most popular majors.** Biology 8%, business/marketing 18%, communications/journalism 8%, health sciences 6%, psychology 9%, social sciences 12%.

**Computing on campus.** 450 workstations in dormitories, library, computer center, student center. Dormitories wired for high-speed internet access and linked to campus network. Commuter students can connect to campus network. Online course registration, online library, helpline, repair service, student web hosting, wireless network available.

**Student life. Freshman orientation:** Mandatory. Preregistration for classes offered. Two-and-a-half-day sessions in June or July, with a make-up orientation at end of August. **Policies:** Students required to live on-campus through freshman year unless eligible for housing exemption (parents of dependent children, veterans, commuting students). **Housing:** Guaranteed on-campus for freshmen. Coed dorms, single-sex dorms, special housing for disabled, apartments, fraternity/sorority housing, wellness housing available. Special interest housing; residential academic programs for first-year students. Gradual penalty for cancellation of housing up to $300. **Activities:** Bands, campus ministries, choral groups, dance, drama, film society, international student organizations, literary magazine, music ensembles, Model UN, musical theater, opera, radio station, student government, student newspaper, symphony orchestra, TV station, Over 300 student organizations.

**Athletics.** NCAA. **Intercollegiate:** Baseball M, basketball, cross-country, diving, field hockey W, football (tackle) M, ice hockey M, lacrosse, rowing (crew) W, soccer, softball W, swimming, tennis W, track and field. **Intramural:** Basketball, field hockey W, football (non-tackle), ice hockey, soccer, softball, tennis, volleyball. **Team name:** Minutemen, Minutewomen.

**Student services.** Adult student services, alcohol/substance abuse counseling, chaplain/spiritual director, career counseling, student employment services, financial aid counseling, health services, legal services, minority student services, on-campus daycare, personal counseling, placement for graduates, veterans' counselor, women's services. **Physically disabled:** Services for visually, speech, hearing impaired. **Learning disabled:** Comprehensive services available.

**Contact.** E-mail: mail@admissions.umass.edu
Phone: (413) 545-0222 Fax: (413) 545-4312
Kevin Kelly, Director of Admissions, University of Massachusetts Amherst, University Admissions Center, Amherst, MA 01003-9291

## University of Massachusetts Boston

**Boston, Massachusetts**     **CB member**
www.umb.edu     **CB code: 3924**

- Public 4-year university
- Commuter campus in very large city
- 10,130 degree-seeking undergraduates: 26% part-time, 58% women, 16% African American, 13% Asian American, 9% Hispanic American, 4% international
- 3,122 degree-seeking graduate students
- 61% of applicants admitted
- SAT or ACT (ACT writing recommended), application essay required
- 39% graduate within 6 years

**General.** Founded in 1964. Regionally accredited. One of 5 campuses of the University of Massachusetts. **Degrees:** 1,608 bachelor's awarded; master's, doctoral, professional offered. **ROTC:** Army, Naval, Air Force. **Location:** 3 miles from downtown. **Calendar:** Semester, extensive summer session. **Full-time faculty:** 499 total; 93% have terminal degrees, 21% minority, 48% women. **Part-time faculty:** 465 total; 30% have terminal degrees, 11% minority, 62% women. **Class size:** 32% < 20, 60% 20-39, 3% 40-49,

3% 50-99, 2% >100. **Special facilities:** Tropical greenhouse, observatory, adaptive computer laboratory.

**Freshman class profile.** 6,050 applied, 3,718 admitted, 987 enrolled.

| Mid 50% test scores | | | |
|---|---|---|---|
| SAT critical reading: | 460-570 | GPA 3.0-3.49: | 33% |
| SAT math: | 480-580 | GPA 2.0-2.99: | 46% |
| GPA 3.75 or higher: | 11% | Return as sophomores: | 77% |
| GPA 3.50-3.74: | 10% | Out-of-state: | 6% |
| | | International: | 4% |

**Basis for selection.** School achievement record, range of test scores, GPA most important. Recommendations, essay also important. Extracurricular activities considered. Grades for college preparatory background should be B- or better. Interview recommended for nontraditional students.

**High school preparation.** College-preparatory program required. 16 units required. Required units include English 4, mathematics 3, social studies 1, history 1, science 3 (laboratory 2), foreign language 2 and academic electives 2.

**2009-2010 Annual costs.** Tuition/fees: $10,611; $22,797 out-of-state. Books/supplies: $800. Personal expenses: $1,170.

**2008-2009 Financial aid. Need-based:** 737 full-time freshmen applied for aid; 616 were judged to have need; 616 of these received aid. Average need met was 90%. Average scholarship/grant was $6,757; average loan $3,730. 47% of total undergraduate aid awarded as scholarships/grants, 53% as loans/jobs. **Non-need-based:** Awarded to 268 full-time undergraduates, including 109 freshmen. Scholarships awarded for academics, leadership, state residency. **Additional information:** Some Massachusetts state employees and Massachusetts Vietnam veterans eligible for tuition waiver. Some waivers available based on talent and academic excellence.

**Application procedures. Admission:** Priority date 3/1; deadline 6/1. $40 fee ($60 out-of-state), may be waived for applicants with need. Admission notification on a rolling basis. Must reply by May 1 or within 3 week(s) if notified thereafter. **Financial aid:** Priority date 3/1; no closing date. FAFSA required. Applicants notified on a rolling basis starting 3/21.

**Academics. Special study options:** Combined bachelor's/graduate degree, cooperative education, cross-registration, distance learning, double major, dual enrollment of high school students, ESL, exchange student, honors, independent study, internships, liberal arts/career combination, student-designed major, study abroad, teacher certification program. 2-2 programs in engineering with area institutions. **Credit/placement by examination:** AP, CLEP, SAT, ACT, institutional tests. 90 credit hours maximum toward bachelor's degree. **Support services:** Learning center, pre-admission summer program, reduced course load, remedial instruction, study skills assistance, tutoring, writing center.

**Majors. Area/ethnic studies:** African-American, American, women's. **Biology:** General, biochemistry, biotechnology. **Business:** Business admin. **Computer sciences:** General, information technology. **Engineering:** Physics. **Foreign languages:** Classics, French, Italian, Spanish. **Health:** Nursing (RN). **History:** General. **Interdisciplinary:** Gerontology. **Legal studies:** General. **Math:** General. **Parks/recreation:** Health/fitness. **Philosophy/religion:** Philosophy. **Physical sciences:** Chemistry, geology, physics. **Protective services:** Criminal justice. **Psychology:** General. **Public administration:** General, community org/advocacy, human services. **Social sciences:** General, anthropology, economics, political science, sociology. **Visual/performing arts:** Art, dramatic. **Other:** Individual major.

**Most popular majors.** Biology 7%, business/marketing 19%, English 6%, health sciences 14%, psychology 13%, security/protective services 6%, social sciences 14%.

**Computing on campus.** 350 workstations in library, computer center, student center. Commuter students can connect to campus network. Online course registration, online library, helpline, repair service, wireless network available.

**Student life. Freshman orientation:** Mandatory, $25 fee. Preregistration for classes offered. **Housing:** Housing referral services available. **Activities:** Bands, campus ministries, choral groups, dance, drama, film society, international student organizations, literary magazine, music ensembles, Model UN, radio station, student government, student newspaper, symphony orchestra.

**Athletics.** NCAA. **Intercollegiate:** Baseball M, basketball, cross-country, ice hockey M, lacrosse M, soccer, softball W, tennis, track and field, volleyball W. **Intramural:** Basketball, ice hockey M, racquetball, sailing, soccer, softball, squash, tennis, volleyball. **Team name:** Beacons.

**Student services.** Adult student services, alcohol/substance abuse counseling, chaplain/spiritual director, career counseling, student employment services, health services, legal services, minority student services, on-campus daycare, personal counseling, placement for graduates, veterans' counselor, women's services. **Physically disabled:** Services for visually, speech, hearing impaired.

**Contact.** E-mail: enrollment.info@umb.edu
Phone: (617) 287-6000 Fax: (617) 287-5999
Liliana Mickle, Director of Admissions, University of Massachusetts Boston, 100 Morrissey Boulevard, Boston, MA 02125-3393

---

## University of Massachusetts Dartmouth
### North Dartmouth, Massachusetts — CB member
### www.umassd.edu — CB code: 3786

- Public 4-year university
- Residential campus in large town
- 7,775 degree-seeking undergraduates: 9% part-time, 48% women, 8% African American, 3% Asian American, 3% Hispanic American, 1% Native American
- 1,115 degree-seeking graduate students
- 68% of applicants admitted
- SAT or ACT (ACT writing optional), application essay required
- 46% graduate within 6 years

**General.** Founded in 1895. Regionally accredited. **Degrees:** 1,245 bachelor's awarded; master's, doctoral offered. **ROTC:** Army. **Location:** 60 miles from Boston; 30 miles from Providence, Rhode Island. **Calendar:** Semester, extensive summer session. **Full-time faculty:** 369 total; 86% have terminal degrees, 23% minority, 40% women. **Part-time faculty:** 219 total; 11% minority, 49% women. **Class size:** 36% < 20, 41% 20-39, 10% 40-49, 11% 50-99, 2% >100. **Special facilities:** Observatory, marine research vessel, coastal marine laboratory, full art studios, Jewish culture and Portuguese studies centers, Robert F. Kennedy assassination archive.

**Freshman class profile.** 7,149 applied, 4,876 admitted, 1,511 enrolled.

| Mid 50% test scores | | | |
|---|---|---|---|
| SAT critical reading: | 470-570 | GPA 3.0-3.49: | 32% |
| SAT math: | 490-590 | GPA 2.0-2.99: | 45% |
| ACT composite: | 20-25 | Rank in top quarter: | 36% |
| GPA 3.75 or higher: | 13% | Rank in top tenth: | 14% |
| GPA 3.50-3.74: | 10% | Out-of-state: | 5% |
| | | Live on campus: | 77% |

**Basis for selection.** High school record, test scores most important; class rank, essay, recommendations considered. Minimum 2.0 GPA required. 3.0 GPA recommended. Audition required for music majors; portfolio required for design majors. **Homeschooled:** State high school equivalency certificate required. Must get certification or equivalency from local high school. **Learning Disabled:** SAT scores may be waived for Massachusetts students with documented disability.

**High school preparation.** College-preparatory program required. 16 units required. Required units include English 4, mathematics 3, social studies 1, history 1, science 3 (laboratory 2), foreign language 2 and academic electives 2. 1 U.S. history required. Programs in science, engineering and business require additional math. Science and engineering require physical science. 2 foreign language must be same language.

**2009-2010 Annual costs.** Tuition/fees: $10,358; $20,061 out-of-state. Room/board: $9,699. Books/supplies: $1,200. Personal expenses: $1,320.

**2008-2009 Financial aid.** **Need-based:** 1,454 full-time freshmen applied for aid; 1,101 were judged to have need; 1,101 of these received aid. Average need met was 91%. Average scholarship/grant was $6,186; average loan $5,631. 38% of total undergraduate aid awarded as scholarships/grants, 62% as loans/jobs. **Non-need-based:** Awarded to 584 full-time undergraduates, including 220 freshmen. Scholarships awarded for academics, minority status, ROTC, state residency.

**Application procedures.** **Admission:** No deadline. $40 fee ($60 out-of-state), may be waived for applicants with need. Admission notification on a rolling basis beginning on or about 1/1. Must reply by May 1 or within 2 week(s) if notified thereafter. Competitive programs may be filled by March 1. Nursing closes by late January. Freshman applicants advised to apply before end of December and not later than March. **Financial aid:** Priority date 3/1; no closing date. FAFSA required. Applicants notified on a rolling basis starting 3/25; must reply within 3 week(s) of notification.

**Academics.** Alternative admissions program for academically disadvantaged Massachusetts residents; program offers special freshman curriculum and counseling support. **Special study options:** Combined bachelor's/graduate degree, cooperative education, cross-registration, distance learning, double major, dual enrollment of high school students, exchange student, honors, independent study, internships, semester at sea, student-designed major, study abroad, teacher certification program, Washington semester. **Credit/placement by examination:** AP, CLEP, IB, SAT, ACT, institutional tests. 30 credit hours maximum toward bachelor's degree. **Support services:** Learning center, reduced course load, remedial instruction, study skills assistance, tutoring, writing center.

**Majors.** **Area/ethnic studies:** Women's. **Biology:** General. **Business:** Accounting, business admin, finance, management information systems, marketing. **Computer sciences:** General. **Education:** Art. **Engineering:** Civil, computer, electrical, mechanical, textile. **Foreign languages:** French, Portuguese, Spanish. **Health:** Clinical lab science, nursing (RN). **History:** General. **Liberal arts:** Arts/sciences. **Math:** General. **Philosophy/religion:** Philosophy. **Physical sciences:** Chemistry, physics. **Psychology:** General. **Social sciences:** Criminology, economics, political science, sociology. **Visual/performing arts:** General, art history/conservation, ceramics, commercial/advertising art, design, fiber arts, metal/jewelry, multimedia, painting, photography, sculpture, studio arts.

**Most popular majors.** Business/marketing 34%, engineering/engineering technologies 8%, health sciences 10%, psychology 7%, social sciences 10%, visual/performing arts 8%.

**Computing on campus.** 650 workstations in dormitories, library, computer center, student center. Dormitories wired for high-speed internet access and linked to campus network. Commuter students can connect to campus network. Helpline, repair service, wireless network available.

**Student life. Freshman orientation:** Mandatory, $200 fee. Preregistration for classes offered. Three-day, 2-night program in June and July. **Housing:** Coed dorms, special housing for disabled, apartments, wellness housing available. $200 nonrefundable deposit, deadline 5/1. Quiet, substance-free, smoke-free housing, program-dedicated suites available. **Activities:** Bands, choral groups, dance, drama, international student organizations, literary magazine, music ensembles, musical theater, radio station, student government, student newspaper, symphony orchestra, women's center, Portuguese center, Unity House, Indian student organization, Arab student organization, Luso-American student organization, Taiwanese student organization, MASSPIRG.

**Athletics.** NCAA. **Intercollegiate:** Baseball M, basketball, cheerleading M, cross-country, diving, equestrian W, field hockey W, football (tackle) M, golf M, ice hockey M, lacrosse, soccer, softball W, swimming, tennis, track and field, volleyball W. **Intramural:** Badminton, basketball, cross-country, football (non-tackle), sailing, soccer, softball, swimming, table tennis, tennis, volleyball. **Team name:** Corsairs.

**Student services.** Adult student services, alcohol/substance abuse counseling, chaplain/spiritual director, career counseling, student employment services, financial aid counseling, health services, minority student services, on-campus daycare, personal counseling, placement for graduates, veterans' counselor, women's services. **Physically disabled:** Services for visually, speech, hearing impaired.

**Contact.** E-mail: admissions@umassd.edu
Phone: (508) 999-8605 Fax: (508) 999-8755
Director of Admissions, University of Massachusetts Dartmouth, 285 Old Westport Road, North Dartmouth, MA 02747-2300

---

## University of Massachusetts Lowell
### Lowell, Massachusetts — CB member
### www.uml.edu — CB code: 3911

- Public 4-year university
- Commuter campus in small city
- 9,615 degree-seeking undergraduates: 22% part-time, 40% women
- 3,054 degree-seeking graduate students
- 73% of applicants admitted
- SAT or ACT (ACT writing optional), application essay required
- 46% graduate within 6 years; 81% enter graduate study

**General.** Founded in 1894. Regionally accredited. **Degrees:** 1,337 bachelor's, 29 associate awarded; master's, doctoral, professional offered. **ROTC:** Air Force. **Location:** 40 miles from Boston, 45 miles from Worcester. **Calendar:** Semester, extensive summer session. **Full-time faculty:** 402 total; 86% have terminal degrees, 17% minority, 35% women. **Part-time faculty:** 312 total; 6% minority, 44% women. **Class size:** 49% < 20, 36% 20-39, 10% 40-49, 3% 50-99, 2% >100. **Special facilities:** Tsongas Industrial History center, teaching and research laboratories in sound recording technology, digital imaging, wellness resource room.

**Freshman class profile.** 5,913 applied, 4,287 admitted, 1,522 enrolled.

| Mid 50% test scores | | | |
|---|---|---|---|
| SAT critical reading: | 480-570 | GPA 2.0-2.99: | 37% |
| SAT math: | 500-610 | Rank in top quarter: | 43% |
| GPA 3.75 or higher: | 13% | Rank in top tenth: | 15% |
| GPA 3.50-3.74: | 11% | Out-of-state: | 11% |
| GPA 3.0-3.49: | 39% | Live on campus: | 54% |

**Basis for selection.** School record, test scores, recommendations most important. Interview recommended. Audition required of music majors. **Homeschooled:** Statement describing homeschool structure and mission, transcript of courses and grades, state high school equivalency certificate, letter of recommendation (nonparent) required. **Learning Disabled:** Students with documented learning differences do not have to submit SAT or ACT.

**High school preparation.** College-preparatory program recommended. 16 units required. Required and recommended units include English 4, mathematics 3-4, social studies 2, science 3-4 (laboratory 2), foreign language 2 and academic electives 2.

**2009-2010 Annual costs.** Tuition/fees: $10,422; $22,843 out-of-state. Room/board: $8,635. Books/supplies: $800. Personal expenses: $850.

**2009-2010 Financial aid. Need-based:** 1,362 full-time freshmen applied for aid; 926 were judged to have need; 926 of these received aid. Average need met was 94%. Average scholarship/grant was $6,805; average loan $5,359. 39% of total undergraduate aid awarded as scholarships/grants, 61% as loans/jobs. **Non-need-based:** Awarded to 1,871 full-time undergraduates, including 498 freshmen. Scholarships awarded for academics, alumni affiliation, art, athletics, job skills, leadership, minority status, music/drama, ROTC, state residency.

**Application procedures. Admission:** Priority date 7/1; no deadline. $40 fee, may be waived for applicants with need. Admission notification on a rolling basis beginning on or about 4/1. Must reply within 2 weeks of notification of acceptance. **Financial aid:** Priority date 3/1; no closing date. FAFSA required. Applicants notified on a rolling basis starting 3/20.

**Academics.** Special focus on applied science and technology; coursework emphasizes context and implications of each discipline. Funded research initiatives available in nanotechnology, bioinformatics, advanced materials, photonics. **Special study options:** Accelerated study, combined bachelor's/graduate degree, cooperative education, cross-registration, distance learning, double major, dual enrollment of high school students, honors, internships, liberal arts/career combination, study abroad, teacher certification program. **Credit/placement by examination:** AP, CLEP, SAT, ACT, institutional tests. 30 credit hours maximum toward bachelor's degree. **Support services:** Learning center, pre-admission summer program, reduced course load, study skills assistance, tutoring, writing center.

**Majors. Area/ethnic studies:** American. **Biology:** General. **Business:** Business admin, entrepreneurial studies. **Computer sciences:** Computer science, information systems. **Education:** Health, music. **Engineering:** Chemical, civil, electrical, mechanical, polymer. **Engineering technology:** Civil, electrical, industrial. **Foreign languages:** General. **Health:** Clinical lab science, nursing (RN). **History:** General. **Liberal arts:** Arts/sciences. **Math:** General, applied. **Philosophy/religion:** Philosophy. **Physical sciences:** Chemistry, physics. **Protective services:** Law enforcement admin. **Psychology:** General. **Social sciences:** Economics, political science, sociology. **Visual/performing arts:** General, graphic design, music performance, studio arts.

**Most popular majors.** Business/marketing 19%, computer/information sciences 9%, engineering/engineering technologies 14%, health sciences 11%, liberal arts 6%, psychology 7%, security/protective services 12%, visual/performing arts 6%.

**Computing on campus.** 4,000 workstations in dormitories, library, computer center, student center. Dormitories wired for high-speed internet access and linked to campus network. Commuter students can connect to campus network. Online course registration, online library, helpline available.

**Student life. Freshman orientation:** Mandatory. Preregistration for classes offered. **Housing:** Guaranteed on-campus for freshmen. Coed dorms, single-sex dorms, special housing for disabled, apartments, cooperative housing available. $200 nonrefundable deposit, deadline 4/15. **Activities:** Bands, choral groups, dance, drama, film society, literary magazine, music ensembles, radio station, student government, student newspaper, symphony orchestra, Abundant Life Christian Fellowship, Chi Alpha, Latter-day Saints student association, association of students of African origin, Cambodian student association, Latin American student association, community service organization, College Democrats, College Republicans.

**Athletics.** NCAA. **Intercollegiate:** Baseball M, basketball, cross-country, field hockey W, golf M, ice hockey M, rowing (crew), soccer, softball W, track and field, volleyball W. **Intramural:** Badminton, basketball, bowling, diving, equestrian W, ice hockey, racquetball, rowing (crew), soccer, softball, squash, swimming, table tennis, tennis M, volleyball. **Team name:** River Hawks.

**Student services.** Adult student services, alcohol/substance abuse counseling, chaplain/spiritual director, career counseling, financial aid counseling, health services, personal counseling, placement for graduates, veterans' counselor. **Physically disabled:** Services for visually, speech, hearing impaired.

**Contact.** E-mail: admissions@uml.edu
Phone: (978) 934-3931 Toll-free number: (800) 410-4607
Fax: (978) 934-3086
Kerri Johnston, Director Undergraduate Admissions, University of Massachusetts Lowell, 883 Broadway Street, Room 110, Lowell, MA 01854-5104

---

## Wellesley College
**Wellesley, Massachusetts**
www.wellesley.edu

CB member
CB code: 3957

- Private 4-year liberal arts college for women
- Residential campus in large town
- 2,193 degree-seeking undergraduates: 1% part-time, 100% women, 7% African American, 26% Asian American, 8% Hispanic American, 1% Native American, 10% international
- 35% of applicants admitted
- SAT and SAT Subject Tests or ACT with writing, application essay required
- 90% graduate within 6 years

**General.** Founded in 1870. Regionally accredited. **Degrees:** 594 bachelor's awarded. **ROTC:** Army, Air Force. **Location:** 12 miles from Boston. **Calendar:** Semester, limited summer session. **Full-time faculty:** 259 total; 96% have terminal degrees, 24% minority, 56% women. **Part-time faculty:** 55 total; 80% have terminal degrees, 16% minority, 74% women. **Class size:** 68% < 20, 31% 20-39, less than 1% 40-49, less than 1% 50-99. **Special facilities:** Science center with X-ray diffractometer, nuclear magnetic resonance, spectrometers (NMR and microMRI), electron microscopes, argon and dye lasers, observatory with three telescopes (6-, 12-, and 24-inch), cultural center, greenhouses, botanic gardens, arboretum, media and technology center with linear editing room for video, digital-based video editing suite, plotter, film recorder, slide scanner.

**Freshman class profile.** 4,156 applied, 1,463 admitted, 589 enrolled.

| Mid 50% test scores | | | |
|---|---|---|---|
| SAT critical reading: | 640-740 | Rank in top tenth: | 78% |
| SAT math: | 640-730 | Return as sophomores: | 94% |
| SAT writing: | 650-740 | Out-of-state: | 86% |
| ACT composite: | 29-32 | Live on campus: | 100% |
| Rank in top quarter: | 96% | International: | 15% |

**Basis for selection.** Evidence in student's record, both in and out of the classroom, of ability to meet rigorous academic standards and willingness to engage in the community is important. Candidates should have taken full advantage of the opportunities available in high school. 2 SAT Subject Tests required if SAT is submitted; at least one quantitative Subject Test recommended. Interviews recommended; on- and off-campus interviews available. **Homeschooled:** Statement describing homeschool structure and mission, transcript of courses and grades, letter of recommendation (nonparent) required. Applicants must meet homeschooling requirements of their state.

**High school preparation.** College-preparatory program recommended. Recommended units include English 4, mathematics 4, social studies 4, history 4, science 3 (laboratory 2) and foreign language 4.

**2009-2010 Annual costs.** Tuition/fees: $38,062. Room/board: $11,786. Books/supplies: $800. Personal expenses: $1,200.

**2009-2010 Financial aid.** All financial aid based on need. 413 full-time freshmen applied for aid; 341 were judged to have need; 341 of these received aid. Average need met was 100%. Average scholarship/grant was $34,246; average loan $2,601. 91% of total undergraduate aid awarded as scholarships/grants, 9% as loans/jobs. **Additional information:** No student will graduate with more than $12,825 in packaged student loans. Students from families with a calculated income between $60,000 and $100,000 will graduate with no more than $8,600 in packaged student loans. Students from families with the greatest need ($60,000 income or less) will graduate with $0 in packaged student loans; their packages will consist of scholarship and work-study money.

**Application procedures. Admission:** Closing date 1/15 (postmark date). $50 fee, may be waived for applicants with need, free for online applicants.

Admission notification 4/1. Must reply by 5/1. **Financial aid:** Closing date 1/15. FAFSA, CSS PROFILE required. Applicants notified by 4/1; must reply by 5/1.

**Academics. Special study options:** Cross-registration, double major, dual enrollment of high school students, exchange student, honors, independent study, internships, semester at sea, student-designed major, study abroad, teacher certification program, Washington semester. **Credit/placement by examination:** AP, CLEP, IB, institutional tests. 16 credit hours maximum toward bachelor's degree. Students may receive credit for score of 5 on most AP exams or a 5, 6, or 7 on most IB exams. **Support services:** Learning center, reduced course load, study skills assistance, tutoring, writing center.

**Majors. Architecture:** Architecture. **Area/ethnic studies:** African, African-American, American, Asian, Central/Eastern European, East Asian, European, French, German, Latin American, Near/Middle Eastern, Russian/Slavic, South Asian, women's. **Biology:** General, biochemistry. **Computer sciences:** General, computer science. **Conservation:** Environmental studies. **Engineering:** General. **Foreign languages:** General, African, ancient Greek, Arabic, Chinese, classics, comparative lit, French, German, Italian, Japanese, Latin, linguistics, Russian, Spanish. **History:** General. **Interdisciplinary:** Biological/physical sciences, classical/archaeology, medieval/Renaissance, neuroscience, peace/conflict, science/society. **Math:** General. **Philosophy/religion:** Judaic, philosophy, religion. **Physical sciences:** Astronomy, astrophysics, chemistry, geology, physics. **Psychology:** General. **Social sciences:** Anthropology, archaeology, economics, international relations, political science, sociology. **Visual/performing arts:** Art history/conservation, dramatic, music history, studio arts.

**Most popular majors.** Area/ethnic studies 8%, English 7%, foreign language 10%, interdisciplinary studies 8%, psychology 7%, social sciences 27%, visual/performing arts 9%.

**Computing on campus.** 481 workstations in dormitories, library, computer center, student center. Dormitories wired for high-speed internet access and linked to campus network. Commuter students can connect to campus network. Online course registration, online library, helpline, repair service, student web hosting, wireless network available.

**Student life. Freshman orientation:** Mandatory. Preregistration for classes offered. Held the week before classes begin. **Policies:** Honor Code in effect. **Housing:** Guaranteed on-campus for all undergraduates. Apartments, cooperative housing, wellness housing available. Pets allowed in dorm rooms. French and Spanish language houses available. **Activities:** Jazz band, campus ministries, choral groups, dance, drama, film society, international student organizations, literary magazine, music ensembles, Model UN, musical theater, opera, radio station, student government, student newspaper, symphony orchestra, black student club, Latina student club, Asian student union, Hillel, Al-Muslimat, Intervarsity Christian Fellowship, political and legislative action organization, Best Buddies, Habitat for Humanity.

**Athletics.** NCAA. **Intercollegiate:** Basketball W, cross-country W, diving W, fencing W, field hockey W, golf W, lacrosse W, rowing (crew) W, soccer W, softball W, squash W, swimming W, tennis W, track and field W, volleyball W. **Intramural:** Basketball W, ice hockey W, racquetball W, rowing (crew) W, rugby W, sailing W, soccer W, table tennis W. **Team name:** Wellesley Blue.

**Student services.** Adult student services, alcohol/substance abuse counseling, chaplain/spiritual director, career counseling, services for economically disadvantaged, student employment services, financial aid counseling, health services, minority student services, on-campus daycare, personal counseling, placement for graduates, women's services. **Physically disabled:** Services for visually, hearing impaired.

**Contact.** E-mail: admission@wellesley.edu
Phone: (781) 283-2270 Fax: (781) 283-3678
Jennifer Desjarlais, Dean of Admission and Financial Aid, Wellesley College, 106 Central Street, Wellesley, MA 02481

## Wentworth Institute of Technology
**Boston, Massachusetts**      **CB member**
**www.wit.edu**      **CB code: 3958**

- Private 4-year engineering and technical college
- Residential campus in very large city
- 3,781 degree-seeking undergraduates: 11% part-time, 19% women, 4% African American, 5% Asian American, 4% Hispanic American, 3% international
- 84 degree-seeking graduate students
- 67% of applicants admitted
- SAT or ACT (ACT writing optional), application essay required
- 55% graduate within 6 years; 3% enter graduate study

**General.** Founded in 1904. Regionally accredited. Mandatory cooperative education program. Member of Colleges of the Fenway. **Degrees:** 721 bachelor's, 37 associate awarded; master's offered. **ROTC:** Army, Air Force. **Location:** 2 miles from downtown. **Calendar:** Semester, limited summer session. **Full-time faculty:** 139 total; 56% have terminal degrees, 11% minority, 23% women. **Part-time faculty:** 168 total; 11% minority, 28% women. **Class size:** 37% < 20, 59% 20-39, 2% 40-49, 2% 50-99, less than 1% >100.

**Freshman class profile.** 4,845 applied, 3,251 admitted, 852 enrolled.

| Mid 50% test scores | | | |
|---|---|---|---|
| SAT critical reading: | 460-560 | GPA 3.0-3.49: | 35% |
| SAT math: | 500-610 | GPA 2.0-2.99: | 50% |
| SAT writing: | 450-550 | End year in good standing: | 92% |
| ACT composite: | 20-25 | Return as sophomores: | 79% |
| GPA 3.75 or higher: | 3% | Out-of-state: | 42% |
| GPA 3.50-3.74: | 9% | Live on campus: | 82% |
| | | International: | 3% |

**Basis for selection.** School achievement record most important, followed by test scores. Teacher recommendations, personal statement, extracurricular activities also considered. **Homeschooled:** Transcript of courses and grades, letter of recommendation (nonparent) required. Course content description may be requested.

**High school preparation.** College-preparatory program recommended. Required and recommended units include English 4, mathematics 3-4, social studies 1, science 2 (laboratory 1). 3 college-preparatory math, 1 physics recommended for many programs. 4 years of mathematics required for some programs.

**2009-2010 Annual costs.** Tuition/fees: $21,800. Tuition includes cost of laptop computer; students in architecture and design programs pay $2,000 in required fees for academic year. Room/board: $10,500. Books/supplies: $1,500. Personal expenses: $1,000.

**2009-2010 Financial aid. Need-based:** 751 full-time freshmen applied for aid; 660 were judged to have need; 660 of these received aid. Average need met was 52%. Average scholarship/grant was $6,402; average loan $3,460. 54% of total undergraduate aid awarded as scholarships/grants, 46% as loans/jobs. **Non-need-based:** Awarded to 2,702 full-time undergraduates, including 746 freshmen. Scholarships awarded for academics, leadership, ROTC, state residency.

**Application procedures. Admission:** Priority date 5/1; no deadline. $50 fee, may be waived for applicants with need. Admission notification on a rolling basis beginning on or about 10/30. Must reply by May 1 or within 2 week(s) if notified thereafter. **Financial aid:** Priority date 3/1; no closing date. FAFSA required. Applicants notified on a rolling basis starting 3/15; must reply within 2 week(s) of notification.

**Academics.** Some bachelor's programs require 5 years. All bachelor's candidates required to complete 2 semesters full-time co-op. **Special study options:** Cooperative education, cross-registration, distance learning, study abroad. Cross-registration with Simmons College, Emmanuel College, Wheelock College, Massachusetts College of Pharmacy and Health Sciences, Massachusetts College of Art (Colleges of the Fenway). **Credit/placement by examination:** AP, CLEP, IB, institutional tests. 32 credit hours maximum toward associate degree, 64 toward bachelor's. Students may only receive maximum of one half of total credit requirement from credit by examination. **Support services:** Learning center, reduced course load, study skills assistance, tutoring, writing center.

**Majors. Architecture:** Architecture. **Business:** Business admin, construction management, operations. **Computer sciences:** General, computer science. **Engineering technology:** General, civil, computer, electrical, mechanical. **Visual/performing arts:** Industrial design, interior design. **Other:** Electromechanical Engineering.

**Most popular majors.** Architecture 23%, computer/information sciences 11%, engineering/engineering technologies 39%, visual/performing arts 22%.

**Computing on campus.** PC or laptop required. 300 workstations in dormitories, library, computer center. Dormitories wired for high-speed internet access and linked to campus network. Commuter students can connect to campus network. Online course registration, online library, helpline, repair service, wireless network available.

**Student life. Freshman orientation:** Mandatory. Preregistration for classes offered. Week-long session held week before classes begin. **Policies:** Alcohol permitted in certain residential halls if every resident of the room is 21 or older. Smoke-free campus. **Housing:** Coed dorms available. $500 fully refundable deposit, deadline 5/1. Apartments available for upperclassmen. **Activities:** Dance, film society, international student organizations, radio station, student government, honor society, Society of Women Engineers, Student Association of Interior Design, National Society of Black Engineers, Asian student association, architecture club, American Society of Civil

Engineers, anime club, competitive video gaming club, Institute of Electrical & Electronic Engineers.

**Athletics.** NCAA. **Intercollegiate:** Baseball M, basketball, golf M, ice hockey M, lacrosse M, rifle, soccer, softball W, tennis, volleyball. **Intramural:** Basketball, football (non-tackle), sailing, softball, volleyball. **Team name:** Leopards.

**Student services.** Alcohol/substance abuse counseling, career counseling, student employment services, financial aid counseling, health services, minority student services, personal counseling, placement for graduates, veterans' counselor, women's services. **Physically disabled:** Services for hearing impaired.

**Contact.** E-mail: admissions@wit.edu
Phone: (617) 989-4000 Toll-free number: (800) 556-0610
Fax: (617) 989-4010
Maureen Dischino, Director of Admissions, Wentworth Institute of Technology, 550 Huntington Avenue, Boston, MA 02115

---

## Western New England College
**Springfield, Massachusetts** — CB member
www.wnec.edu — CB code: 3962

- Private 4-year university
- Residential campus in small city
- 2,716 degree-seeking undergraduates: 9% part-time, 40% women, 4% African American, 2% Asian American, 4% Hispanic American
- 959 degree-seeking graduate students
- 81% of applicants admitted
- SAT or ACT (ACT writing optional) required
- 55% graduate within 6 years

**General.** Founded in 1919. Regionally accredited. **Degrees:** 584 bachelor's, 4 associate awarded; master's, doctoral, professional offered. **ROTC:** Army, Air Force. **Location:** 95 miles from Boston, 20 miles from Hartford. **Calendar:** Semester, limited summer session. **Full-time faculty:** 188 total; 89% have terminal degrees, 7% minority, 37% women. **Part-time faculty:** 113 total. **Class size:** 45% < 20, 54% 20-39, less than 1% 40-49, less than 1% 50-99.

**Freshman class profile.** 4,769 applied, 3,861 admitted, 689 enrolled.

| Mid 50% test scores | | | |
|---|---|---|---|
| SAT critical reading: | 470-560 | GPA 2.0-2.99: | 43% |
| SAT math: | 490-600 | Rank in top quarter: | 42% |
| ACT composite: | 21-25 | Rank in top tenth: | 14% |
| GPA 3.75 or higher: | 23% | Return as sophomores: | 74% |
| GPA 3.50-3.74: | 11% | Out-of-state: | 61% |
| GPA 3.0-3.49: | 23% | Live on campus: | 88% |

**Basis for selection.** School achievement record, test scores, recommendation most important. Interview, class rank, extracurricular activities also considered. Interview and essay recommended.

**High school preparation.** College-preparatory program required. 10 units required; 18 recommended. Required and recommended units include English 4, mathematics 2-4, social studies 1-2, history 1-2, science 1-2 (laboratory 1-2) and foreign language 2. 1 American history required. Additional science and math required for certain programs.

**2009-2010 Annual costs.** Tuition/fees: $28,816. Room/board: $10,980. Books/supplies: $1,100. Personal expenses: $1,400.

**2009-2010 Financial aid. Need-based:** 612 full-time freshmen applied for aid; 535 were judged to have need; 535 of these received aid. Average need met was 70%. Average scholarship/grant was $15,024; average loan $4,122. 70% of total undergraduate aid awarded as scholarships/grants, 30% as loans/jobs. **Non-need-based:** Awarded to 396 full-time undergraduates, including 139 freshmen. Scholarships awarded for academics, music/drama, ROTC.

**Application procedures. Admission:** Priority date 2/15; no deadline. $50 fee, may be waived for applicants with need. Admission notification on a rolling basis beginning on or about 12/1. Must reply by May 1 or within 2 week(s) if notified thereafter. **Financial aid:** Priority date 4/15, closing date 5/1. FAFSA required. Applicants notified on a rolling basis starting 3/15; must reply by 5/1 or within 2 week(s) of notification.

**Academics. Special study options:** Accelerated study, combined bachelor's/graduate degree, cross-registration, distance learning, double major, dual enrollment of high school students, honors, independent study, internships, liberal arts/career combination, student-designed major, study abroad, teacher

certification program, Washington semester. 3+3 law program. Accelerated part-time degree completion. 3+2 programs for completion of MBA or MSA for a variety of majors. **Credit/placement by examination:** AP, CLEP, IB, SAT, ACT, institutional tests. **Support services:** Pre-admission summer program, reduced course load, study skills assistance, tutoring, writing center.

**Majors. Biology:** General, molecular. **Business:** General, accounting, business admin, finance, management information systems, marketing. **Communications:** General, advertising, journalism, media studies, public relations. **Computer sciences:** Computer science, information systems. **Education:** Elementary, secondary. **Engineering:** Biomedical, electrical, industrial, mechanical. **Health:** Prepharmacy. **History:** General. **Interdisciplinary:** Global studies. **Legal studies:** General. **Liberal arts:** Arts/sciences. **Math:** General. **Parks/recreation:** Sports admin. **Philosophy/religion:** Philosophy. **Physical sciences:** Chemistry. **Protective services:** Criminal justice. **Psychology:** General. **Public administration:** Social work. **Social sciences:** Economics, political science, sociology.

**Most popular majors.** Business/marketing 37%, engineering/engineering technologies 8%, parks/recreation 8%, psychology 12%, security/protective services 11%.

**Computing on campus.** 400 workstations in dormitories, library, computer center, student center. Dormitories wired for high-speed internet access and linked to campus network. Commuter students can connect to campus network. Online library, helpline, repair service, wireless network available.

**Student life. Freshman orientation:** Available. Preregistration for classes offered. Two-day program held over summer for students and parents. Parents assessed meals and materials fee. **Housing:** Guaranteed on-campus for freshmen. Coed dorms, special housing for disabled, apartments available. $300 nonrefundable deposit, deadline 5/1. **Activities:** Bands, campus ministries, choral groups, dance, drama, international student organizations, literary magazine, music ensembles, radio station, student government, student newspaper, United and Mutually Equal, Helping Hands Society.

**Athletics.** NCAA. **Intercollegiate:** Baseball M, basketball, bowling, cross-country, field hockey W, football (tackle) M, golf M, ice hockey M, lacrosse, soccer, softball W, swimming W, tennis, volleyball W, wrestling M. **Intramural:** Badminton, basketball, football (non-tackle), handball, soccer, softball, table tennis, volleyball, water polo. **Team name:** Golden Bears.

**Student services.** Adult student services, alcohol/substance abuse counseling, chaplain/spiritual director, career counseling, student employment services, financial aid counseling, health services, minority student services, personal counseling, veterans' counselor. **Physically disabled:** Services for visually, hearing impaired.

**Contact.** E-mail: ugradmis@wnec.edu
Phone: (413) 782-1321 Toll-free number: (800) 325-1122 ext. 1321
Fax: (413) 782-1777
Charles Pollock, Vice President for Enrollment Management, Western New England College, 1215 Wilbraham Road, Springfield, MA 01119-2684

---

## Westfield State College
**Westfield, Massachusetts** — CB member
www.wsc.ma.edu — CB code: 3523

- Public 4-year liberal arts and teachers college
- Residential campus in large town
- 4,925 degree-seeking undergraduates: 8% part-time, 52% women, 4% African American, 1% Asian American, 4% Hispanic American
- 420 degree-seeking graduate students
- 58% of applicants admitted
- SAT or ACT (ACT writing optional) required
- 57% graduate within 6 years

**General.** Founded in 1838. Regionally accredited. **Degrees:** 1,026 bachelor's awarded; master's offered. **ROTC:** Army, Air Force. **Location:** 10 miles from Springfield, 100 miles from Boston. **Calendar:** Semester, limited summer session. **Full-time faculty:** 208 total; 80% have terminal degrees, 14% minority, 48% women. **Part-time faculty:** 240 total; 20% have terminal degrees, 45% women. **Class size:** 41% < 20, 57% 20-39, 1% 40-49, 1% 50-99, less than 1% >100. **Special facilities:** Television production studio, natural history museum/collections, art gallery, GIS lab.

**Freshman class profile.** 5,391 applied, 3,124 admitted, 1,140 enrolled.

| Mid 50% test scores | | | |
|---|---|---|---|
| SAT critical reading: | 460-550 | GPA 2.0-2.99: | 46% |
| SAT math: | 470-560 | Rank in top quarter: | 27% |
| ACT composite: | 19-23 | Rank in top tenth: | 8% |
| GPA 3.75 or higher: | 8% | End year in good standing: | 86% |
| GPA 3.50-3.74: | 9% | Return as sophomores: | 78% |
| GPA 3.0-3.49: | 37% | Out-of-state: | 6% |
| | | Live on campus: | 84% |

**Basis for selection.** Rigor of secondary school record, academic grade point average, and standardized testing are the most important factors. Personal essay and recommendations may be considered if submitted. Extracurricular activities, community involvement, and family educational background may also be considered. Essay recommended. Audition required of music majors. Portfolio required of art majors. **Homeschooled:** Requirements based on AACROA standards. **Learning Disabled:** SAT/ACT test score requirement waived for students with documented learning disability. Interview required for learning disabled applicants at the request of the Director of Disability Services.

**High school preparation.** College-preparatory program required. 16 units required. Required units include English 4, mathematics 3, social studies 1, history 1, science 3 (laboratory 2), foreign language 2 and academic electives 2.

**2009-2010 Annual costs.** Tuition/fees: $7,016; $13,096 out-of-state. Room/board: $7,728. Books/supplies: $950. Personal expenses: $1,200.

**2008-2009 Financial aid. Need-based:** 948 full-time freshmen applied for aid; 572 were judged to have need; 556 of these received aid. Average need met was 70%. Average scholarship/grant was $4,634; average loan $3,151. 40% of total undergraduate aid awarded as scholarships/grants, 60% as loans/jobs. **Non-need-based:** Awarded to 401 full-time undergraduates, including 152 freshmen.

**Application procedures. Admission:** Closing date 3/1 (postmark date). $50 fee, may be waived for applicants with need. Admission notification 4/15. Admission notification on a rolling basis. Must reply by May 1 or within 2 week(s) if notified thereafter. **Financial aid:** Priority date 3/1; no closing date. FAFSA required. Applicants notified on a rolling basis starting 4/1.

**Academics. Special study options:** Cooperative education, cross-registration, distance learning, double major, dual enrollment of high school students, exchange student, honors, independent study, internships, semester at sea, student-designed major, study abroad, teacher certification program, Washington semester. **Credit/placement by examination:** AP, CLEP, institutional tests. 60 credit hours maximum toward bachelor's degree. Maximum of 3 credits awarded for AP tests in English. Students taking CLEP tests in English Composition with Essay or Freshman Composition must also submit writing portfolio; portfolio evaluated before credit can be awarded. Maximum of 3 credits awarded for composition. **Support services:** Learning center, pre-admission summer program, reduced course load, study skills assistance, tutoring, writing center.

**Majors. Architecture:** Urban/community planning. **Biology:** General. **Business:** General. **Communications:** General. **Computer sciences:** Computer science, information systems. **Conservation:** Environmental science. **Education:** Art, biology, business, elementary, English, history, kindergarten/preschool, mathematics, music, physical, science, special, technology/industrial arts. **History:** General. **Liberal arts:** Arts/sciences. **Math:** General. **Parks/recreation:** Health/fitness. **Physical sciences:** General, chemistry. **Protective services:** Criminal justice. **Psychology:** General. **Public administration:** Social work. **Social sciences:** Economics, political science, sociology. **Visual/performing arts:** Art, dramatic.

**Most popular majors.** Business/marketing 13%, communications/journalism 8%, education 11%, liberal arts 14%, psychology 9%, security/protective services 17%.

**Computing on campus.** 275 workstations in dormitories, library, student center. Dormitories wired for high-speed internet access and linked to campus network. Commuter students can connect to campus network. Online course registration, online library, helpline, student web hosting, wireless network available.

**Student life. Freshman orientation:** Available. Several 2-day sessions held in June and August; includes mandatory testing, course selection. **Housing:** Coed dorms, special housing for disabled, apartments available. $100 nonrefundable deposit, deadline 5/1. Living/learning (academic intensive), quiet living, honors housing. **Activities:** Bands, campus ministries, choral groups, dance, drama, international student organizations, literary magazine, music ensembles, musical theater, opera, radio station, student government, student newspaper, symphony orchestra, TV station, third world group,

public interest research group, Campus Crusade, Circle K, Habitat for Humanity, international relations club, Latino association for empowerment, gay straight alliance, peace and justice club, Republican club.

**Athletics.** NCAA. **Intercollegiate:** Baseball M, basketball, cheerleading, cross-country, diving W, field hockey W, football (tackle) M, golf, ice hockey M, lacrosse W, soccer, softball W, swimming W, track and field, volleyball W. **Intramural:** Badminton, basketball, football (non-tackle), racquetball, soccer, softball, table tennis, volleyball, water polo. **Team name:** Owls.

**Student services.** Adult student services, alcohol/substance abuse counseling, career counseling, services for economically disadvantaged, student employment services, financial aid counseling, health services, minority student services, personal counseling, placement for graduates, veterans' counselor. **Physically disabled:** Services for visually, speech, hearing impaired. **Learning disabled:** Comprehensive services available.

**Contact.** E-mail: admission@wsc.ma.edu
Phone: (413) 572-5218 Toll-free number: (800) 322-8401
Fax: (413) 572-0520
Michael Cole, Director of Admission, Westfield State College, 577 Western Avenue, Westfield, MA 01086-1630

## Wheaton College
**Norton, Massachusetts**
www.wheatoncollege.edu/
**CB member**
**CB code: 3963**

- Private 4-year liberal arts college
- Residential campus in large town
- 1,632 degree-seeking undergraduates: 62% women, 5% African American, 2% Asian American, 4% Hispanic American, 5% international
- 59% of applicants admitted
- Application essay required
- 75% graduate within 6 years; 38% enter graduate study

**General.** Founded in 1834. Regionally accredited. **Degrees:** 460 bachelor's awarded. **ROTC:** Army. **Location:** 35 miles from Boston; 15 miles from Providence, Rhode Island. **Calendar:** Semester. **Full-time faculty:** 139 total; 88% have terminal degrees, 19% minority, 51% women. **Part-time faculty:** 30 total; 27% have terminal degrees, 27% minority, 70% women. **Class size:** 68% < 20, 25% 20-39, 3% 40-49, 4% 50-99. **Special facilities:** Observatory, language laboratory, early childhood lab school.

**Freshman class profile.** 3,304 applied, 1,947 admitted, 424 enrolled.

| Mid 50% test scores | | | |
|---|---|---|---|
| SAT critical reading: | 570-680 | GPA 2.0-2.99: | 17% |
| SAT math: | 560-670 | End year in good standing: | 95% |
| ACT composite: | 27-30 | Return as sophomores: | 88% |
| GPA 3.75 or higher: | 28% | Out-of-state: | 64% |
| GPA 3.50-3.74: | 21% | Live on campus: | 99% |
| GPA 3.0-3.49: | 34% | International: | 8% |

**Basis for selection.** School record, essay/writing sample, personal academic portfolio, extracurricular activities, recommendations, interview important. Standardized testing optional. Interviews strongly recommended. **Homeschooled:** Statement describing homeschool structure and mission, transcript of courses and grades required. **Learning Disabled:** Students who have diagnosed learning difference encouraged to submit supporting testing for review.

**High school preparation.** College-preparatory program recommended. 20 units recommended. Recommended units include English 4, mathematics 4, social studies 3, history 2, science 3 (laboratory 2) and foreign language 4. English should emphasize composition skills.

**2010-2011 Annual costs.** Tuition/fees: $41,084. Freshmen pay one-time $50 general fee (non-refundable). Room/board: $10,180. Books/supplies: $940. Personal expenses: $760.

**2009-2010 Financial aid. Need-based:** 289 full-time freshmen applied for aid; 257 were judged to have need; 257 of these received aid. Average need met was 96%. Average scholarship/grant was $25,818; average loan $3,897. 80% of total undergraduate aid awarded as scholarships/grants, 20% as loans/jobs. **Non-need-based:** Awarded to 221 full-time undergraduates, including 72 freshmen. Scholarships awarded for academics.

**Application procedures. Admission:** Closing date 1/15 (postmark date). $55 fee, may be waived for applicants with need, free for online applicants. Admission notification 4/1. Must reply by 5/1. **Financial aid:** Closing date 2/1. FAFSA, CSS PROFILE required. Applicants notified by 4/1; must reply by 5/1.

**Academics. Special study options:** Accelerated study, combined bachelor's/graduate degree, cross-registration, double major, dual enrollment of high school students, exchange student, honors, independent study, internships, liberal arts/career combination, student-designed major, study abroad, teacher certification program, Washington semester. BS in engineering with George Washington University and Dartmouth College; MA in Intergrated Marketing Communications with Emerson College; MBA in management with University of Rochester; BFA in studio art with School of the Museum of Fine Arts; MA in religion with Andover Newton Theological School; Doctor of Optometry with New England School of Optometry. **Credit/placement by examination:** AP, CLEP, IB, institutional tests. 8 credit hours maximum toward bachelor's degree. **Support services:** Learning center, pre-admission summer program, reduced course load, tutoring, writing center.

**Majors. Area/ethnic studies:** American, Asian, French, German, Italian, Latin American, Russian/Slavic, women's. **Biology:** General, biochemistry, bioinformatics. **Computer sciences:** General, computer science. **Conservation:** Environmental science. **Foreign languages:** Classics, French, German, Italian, Latin, modern Greek, Russian, Spanish. **History:** General. **Interdisciplinary:** Biological/physical sciences, math/computer science. **Liberal arts:** Arts/sciences. **Math:** General. **Philosophy/religion:** Philosophy, religion. **Physical sciences:** Astronomy, chemistry, physics. **Psychology:** General, psychobiology. **Social sciences:** Anthropology, economics, international relations, political science, sociology. **Visual/performing arts:** Art history/conservation, studio arts. **Other:** Ancient studies, Classical civilization, Mathematics and economics, Religion and history, Theatre and English dramatic literature.

**Most popular majors.** Area/ethnic studies 10%, biology 6%, English 10%, psychology 20%, social sciences 26%, visual/performing arts 12%.

**Computing on campus.** 375 workstations in library, computer center, student center. Dormitories wired for high-speed internet access and linked to campus network. Commuter students can connect to campus network. Online course registration, online library, helpline, repair service, student web hosting, wireless network available.

**Student life. Freshman orientation:** Mandatory. Preregistration for classes offered. Held 2-3 days prior to start of classes. **Housing:** Guaranteed on-campus for all undergraduates. Coed dorms, single-sex dorms, special housing for disabled, wellness housing available. Quiet housing available. **Activities:** Bands, choral groups, dance, drama, film society, international student organizations, literary magazine, music ensembles, Model UN, musical theater, radio station, student government, student newspaper, symphony orchestra, Amnesty International, student art league, black students association, Latino students association, Asian American coalition.

**Athletics.** NCAA. **Intercollegiate:** Baseball M, basketball, cross-country, diving, field hockey W, lacrosse, soccer, softball W, swimming, synchronized swimming W, tennis, track and field, volleyball W. **Intramural:** Badminton, basketball, football (non-tackle), soccer, softball, tennis, volleyball. **Team name:** Lyons.

**Student services.** Career counseling, student employment services, financial aid counseling, health services, minority student services, personal counseling, placement for graduates, women's services. **Physically disabled:** Services for visually, hearing impaired.

**Contact.** E-mail: admission@wheatoncollege.edu
Phone: (508) 286-8251 Toll-free number: (800) 394-6003
Fax: (508) 286-8271
Gail Berson, Vice President for Enrollment and Dean of Admission and Student Aid, Wheaton College, 26 East Main Street, Norton, MA 02766

---

## Wheelock College

| Boston, Massachusetts | CB member |
|---|---|
| www.wheelock.edu | CB code: 3964 |

- Private 4-year liberal arts and teachers college
- Residential campus in very large city
- 746 degree-seeking undergraduates: 3% part-time, 90% women, 9% African American, 2% Asian American, 8% Hispanic American, 1% Native American, 1% international
- 287 degree-seeking graduate students
- 75% of applicants admitted
- SAT or ACT (ACT writing optional), application essay required

**General.** Founded in 1888. Regionally accredited. Member of the Colleges of the Fenway. **Degrees:** 152 bachelor's awarded; master's offered. **Calendar:** Semester, limited summer session. **Full-time faculty:** 63 total; 87% have terminal degrees, 24% minority, 78% women. **Part-time faculty:** 80 total; 26% have terminal degrees, 25% minority, 78% women. **Class size:** 71% < 20, 29% 20-39, less than 1% 40-49.

**Freshman class profile.** 1,092 applied, 819 admitted, 191 enrolled.

| Mid 50% test scores | | | |
|---|---|---|---|
| SAT critical reading: | 440-550 | GPA 3.0-3.49: | 28% |
| SAT math: | 430-540 | GPA 2.0-2.99: | 49% |
| SAT writing: | 440-550 | Rank in top quarter: | 35% |
| ACT composite: | 18-24 | Rank in top tenth: | 10% |
| GPA 3.75 or higher: | 15% | Out-of-state: | 56% |
| GPA 3.50-3.74: | 8% | Live on campus: | 91% |

**Basis for selection.** School achievement record most important. Test scores, school and community activities considered. Interview recommended.

**High school preparation.** College-preparatory program recommended. 16 units required. Required units include English 4, mathematics 3, social studies 2, science 2 (laboratory 1). Child development course recommended.

**2009-2010 Annual costs.** Tuition/fees: $28,160. Room/board: $11,200. Books/supplies: $880. Personal expenses: $1,400.

**2009-2010 Financial aid. Need-based:** 177 full-time freshmen applied for aid; 170 were judged to have need; 170 of these received aid. Average need met was 74%. Average scholarship/grant was $18,775; average loan $3,815. 63% of total undergraduate aid awarded as scholarships/grants, 37% as loans/jobs. **Non-need-based:** Awarded to 147 full-time undergraduates, including 32 freshmen. Scholarships awarded for academics, job skills, leadership.

**Application procedures. Admission:** Priority date 3/1; no deadline. $15 fee, may be waived for applicants with need, free for online applicants. Admission notification on a rolling basis beginning on or about 1/4. Must reply by May 1 or within 2 week(s) if notified thereafter. **Financial aid:** Closing date 2/15. FAFSA required. Applicants notified on a rolling basis starting 3/1; must reply by 5/1.

**Academics.** Fieldwork throughout all 4 years supplements classwork in day care, infant and toddler behavior, museum teaching, children in health care settings, elementary education, special education, social work programs. Students choose major and professional studies concentration in early childhood care and education, elementary school education, juvenile justice, social work, or child life. **Special study options:** Combined bachelor's/graduate degree, cross-registration, double major, exchange student, honors, independent study, internships, liberal arts/career combination, study abroad, teacher certification program. **Credit/placement by examination:** AP, CLEP, institutional tests. 32 credit hours maximum toward bachelor's degree. **Support services:** Learning center, pre-admission summer program, reduced course load, remedial instruction, study skills assistance, tutoring, writing center.

**Majors. Area/ethnic studies:** American. **Communications:** Media studies. **Education:** Early childhood, elementary, special. **Family/consumer sciences:** Child care, child development, family studies. **Liberal arts:** Arts/sciences, humanities. **Math:** General. **Public administration:** Social work, youth services. **Visual/performing arts:** General.

**Most popular majors.** Education 27%, family/consumer sciences 43%, public administration/social services 8%, visual/performing arts 8%.

**Computing on campus.** 120 workstations in dormitories, library, computer center, student center. Dormitories wired for high-speed internet access and linked to campus network. Commuter students can connect to campus network. Online course registration, online library, helpline, repair service, wireless network available.

**Student life. Freshman orientation:** Mandatory, $200 fee. Preregistration for classes offered. Two-day program held in summer; students have choice of 2 sessions. **Housing:** Guaranteed on-campus for freshmen. Coed dorms, single-sex dorms, special housing for disabled, cooperative housing, wellness housing available. $100 nonrefundable deposit, deadline 5/1. Smoke-free areas, wellness floor available. **Activities:** Choral groups, dance, drama, musical theater, student government, social work club, women's center, Boston Association for the Education of Young Children, child life council, sign language club, Bible study, juvenile justice and youth advocacy council.

**Athletics.** NCAA. **Intercollegiate:** Basketball, field hockey W, lacrosse, soccer W, softball, tennis. **Intramural:** Basketball, racquetball, soccer, softball, squash, volleyball. **Team name:** Wildcats.

**Student services.** Alcohol/substance abuse counseling, career counseling, student employment services, financial aid counseling, health services, personal counseling, placement for graduates, women's services. **Physically disabled:** Services for visually, speech, hearing impaired.

**Contact.** E-mail: undergrad@wheelock.edu
Phone: (617) 879-2206 Toll-free number: (800) 734-5212
Fax: (617) 879-2449
Lisa Slavin, Dean of Enrollment and Financial Aid, Wheelock College, 200
The Riverway, Boston, MA 02215-4176

## Williams College
**Williamstown, Massachusetts**     **CB member**
**www.williams.edu**     **CB code: 3965**

- Private 4-year liberal arts college affiliated with United Church of Christ
- Residential campus in small town
- 2,032 degree-seeking undergraduates: 52% women, 10% African American, 12% Asian American, 10% Hispanic American, 7% international
- 56 degree-seeking graduate students
- 20% of applicants admitted
- SAT and SAT Subject Tests or ACT with writing, application essay required
- 96% graduate within 6 years

**General.** Founded in 1793. Regionally accredited. **Degrees:** 512 bachelor's awarded; master's offered. **ROTC:** Air Force. **Location:** 35 miles from Albany, New York; 150 miles from Boston. **Calendar:** 4-1-4. **Full-time faculty:** 267 total; 96% have terminal degrees, 19% minority, 40% women. **Part-time faculty:** 48 total; 56% have terminal degrees, 12% minority, 46% women. **Class size:** 74% < 20, 20% 20-39, 2% 40-49, 3% 50-99, less than 1% >100. **Special facilities:** Performing arts center, experimental forest, environmental studies center, observatory, electron-scanning microscope, transmission microscopes, studio art center, nuclear magnetic resonance imager, college museum.

**Freshman class profile.** 6,017 applied, 1,229 admitted, 546 enrolled.

| Mid 50% test scores | | | |
|---|---|---|---|
| SAT critical reading: | 660-770 | Rank in top tenth: | 88% |
| SAT math: | 650-760 | Return as sophomores: | 98% |
| ACT composite: | 30-34 | Out-of-state: | 87% |
| Rank in top quarter: | 99% | Live on campus: | 100% |
| | | International: | 6% |

**Basis for selection.** School achievement record, character and personal promise, test scores, essay important. College seeks diversity of social, economic, and geographic backgrounds. Leadership and accomplishment in extracurricular activities also considered.

**High school preparation.** College-preparatory program required. Recommended units include English 4, mathematics 4, social studies 3, science 3 (laboratory 3) and foreign language 4. Writing skills stressed. Course work should be at highest level available.

**2009-2010 Annual costs.** Tuition/fees: $39,490. Room/board: $10,390. Books/supplies: $800. Personal expenses: $1,200.

**2009-2010 Financial aid.** All financial aid based on need. 346 full-time freshmen applied for aid; 289 were judged to have need; 289 of these received aid. Average need met was 100%. Average scholarship/grant was $37,175. 96% of total undergraduate aid awarded as scholarships/grants, 4% as loans/jobs.

**Application procedures. Admission:** Closing date 1/1 (postmark date). $60 fee, may be waived for applicants with need. Admission notification 4/1. Must reply by May 1 or within 2 week(s) if notified thereafter. **Financial aid:** Closing date 2/1. FAFSA, CSS PROFILE required. Applicants notified by 4/1; must reply by 5/1.

**Academics. Special study options:** Combined bachelor's/graduate degree, cross-registration, double major, independent study, internships, student-designed major, study abroad. Summer science research program, Williams in Oxford, Mystic maritime studies program, tutorials, 3-2 engineering program with Columbia University and Washington University. **Credit/placement by examination:** AP, CLEP, IB, institutional tests. **Support services:** Pre-admission summer program, study skills assistance, tutoring, writing center.

**Majors. Area/ethnic studies:** American, Asian. **Biology:** General. **Computer sciences:** Computer science. **Foreign languages:** Chinese, classics, comparative lit, French, German, Japanese, Russian, Spanish. **History:** General. **Math:** General. **Philosophy/religion:** Philosophy, religion. **Physical sciences:** Astronomy, astrophysics, chemistry, geology, physics. **Psychology:** General. **Social sciences:** Anthropology, economics, political science, sociology. **Visual/performing arts:** Art history/conservation, dramatic, studio arts.

**Most popular majors.** Biology 8%, English 9%, foreign language 8%, history 8%, mathematics 8%, physical sciences 8%, psychology 8%, social sciences 22%, visual/performing arts 10%.

**Computing on campus.** 247 workstations in library, computer center, student center. Dormitories wired for high-speed internet access and linked to campus network. Commuter students can connect to campus network. Online course registration, helpline, repair service, student web hosting, wireless network available.

**Student life. Freshman orientation:** Mandatory. Preregistration for classes offered. **Housing:** Guaranteed on-campus for all undergraduates. Coed dorms, cooperative housing available. $200 nonrefundable deposit, deadline 5/1. **Activities:** Pep band, choral groups, dance, drama, film society, international student organizations, literary magazine, music ensembles, radio station, student government, student newspaper, symphony orchestra, black student union, Purple Key, Asian Link, Hispanic students club, Korean club, minority coalition, nonviolent alternatives committee, women's club, Hillel, LGBTQ Student organization.

**Athletics.** NCAA. **Intercollegiate:** Baseball M, basketball, cross-country, diving, field hockey W, football (tackle) M, golf, ice hockey, lacrosse, rowing (crew), skiing, soccer, softball W, squash, swimming, tennis, track and field, volleyball W, wrestling M. **Intramural:** Badminton, basketball, ice hockey M, skiing, soccer, softball, volleyball. **Team name:** Ephs.

**Student services.** Alcohol/substance abuse counseling, chaplain/spiritual director, career counseling, services for economically disadvantaged, student employment services, financial aid counseling, health services, minority student services, personal counseling, placement for graduates. **Physically disabled:** Services for visually, hearing impaired.

**Contact.** E-mail: admission@williams.edu
Phone: (413) 597-2211 Fax: (413) 597-4052
Richard Nesbitt, Director of Admissions, Williams College, 33 Stetson Court, Williamstown, MA 01267

## Worcester Polytechnic Institute
**Worcester, Massachusetts**     **CB member**
**www.wpi.edu**     **CB code: 3969**

- Private 4-year university
- Residential campus in small city
- 3,391 degree-seeking undergraduates: 3% part-time, 28% women, 3% African American, 6% Asian American, 6% Hispanic American, 1% Native American, 9% international
- 1,153 degree-seeking graduate students
- 63% of applicants admitted
- Application essay required
- 80% graduate within 6 years; 26% enter graduate study

**General.** Founded in 1865. Regionally accredited. Participation by most students in overseas or off-campus projects; over 20 project centers located throughout North America, Central America, Africa, Australia, Asia and Europe. **Degrees:** 620 bachelor's awarded; master's, doctoral offered. **ROTC:** Army, Naval, Air Force. **Location:** 35 miles from Boston. **Calendar:** Quarter, limited summer session. **Full-time faculty:** 263 total; 94% have terminal degrees, 16% minority, 22% women. **Part-time faculty:** 102 total; 50% have terminal degrees, 7% minority, 28% women. **Class size:** 67% < 20, 21% 20-39, 4% 40-49, 7% 50-99, 2% >100. **Special facilities:** Centers for life sciences and bioengineering, biomaterials, bioprocessing, comparative neuroimaging, molecular sensors, nanoscience and technology, untethered healthcare, water research, computer-controlled machining, holographic studies and laser technology, wireless information network studies, fuel cell, industrial math and statistics, fire science laboratory, pavement research laboratory, atomic force microscopy laboratory.

**Freshman class profile.** 6,284 applied, 3,989 admitted, 925 enrolled.

| Mid 50% test scores | | | |
|---|---|---|---|
| SAT critical reading: | 560-660 | Rank in top quarter: | 88% |
| SAT math: | 630-720 | Rank in top tenth: | 55% |
| SAT writing: | 560-660 | End year in good standing: | 92% |
| ACT composite: | 26-31 | Return as sophomores: | 95% |
| GPA 3.75 or higher: | 61% | Out-of-state: | 54% |
| GPA 3.50-3.74: | 23% | Live on campus: | 90% |
| GPA 3.0-3.49: | 15% | International: | 10% |
| GPA 2.0-2.99: | 1% | Fraternities: | 30% |
| | | Sororities: | 32% |

**Basis for selection.** High school record including academic rigor most important. Extracurricular activities, recommendations, motivation, creativity, initiative important. In lieu of test scores, students may submit alternative documentation of potential for academic success. SAT/ACT scores or alternative materials that will better reflect the applicant's potential for success (Flex Path) required. Students who choose the Flex Path encouraged to submit examples of academic work or extracurricular projects that reflect a high level of organization, motivation, creativity and problem-solving ability. Interviews offered, but not required. **Homeschooled:** Statement describing homeschool structure and mission, transcript of courses and grades, interview, letter of recommendation (nonparent) required. Submit as much relevant support material as possible and outside recommendations. Detailed course descriptions recommended.

**High school preparation.** College-preparatory program required. 10 units required. Required and recommended units include English 4, mathematics 4, social studies 2, history 1, science 2-4 (laboratory 2), foreign language 2 and computer science 1. Math requirement includes algebra, geometry, trigonometry and pre-calculus. Science should include physics, chemistry, or biology.

**2010-2011 Annual costs.** Tuition/fees (projected): $38,920. Room/board: $11,610. Books/supplies: $1,000. Personal expenses: $1,000.

**2008-2009 Financial aid. Non-need-based:** Scholarships awarded for academics, leadership, minority status, ROTC.

**Application procedures. Admission:** Closing date 2/1 (postmark date). $60 fee, may be waived for applicants with need. Admission notification 4/1. Must reply by May 1 or within 2 week(s) if notified thereafter. Second early action closing date January 1; notification date February 10. **Financial aid:** Closing date 2/1. FAFSA, CSS PROFILE required. Applicants notified by 4/1; must reply by 5/1.

**Academics. Special study options:** Accelerated study, combined bachelor's/graduate degree, cooperative education, cross-registration, distance learning, double major, dual enrollment of high school students, ESL, honors, independent study, liberal arts/career combination, New York semester, student-designed major, study abroad, teacher certification program, Washington semester. Completion of degree-required projects at off-campus locations (international and domestic) supervised by institution's faculty. **Credit/placement by examination:** AP, CLEP, IB, institutional tests. **Support services:** Reduced course load, study skills assistance, tutoring, writing center.

**Majors. Biology:** General, biochemistry, biotechnology. **Business:** Actuarial science, business admin, management information systems, management science, operations. **Computer sciences:** A.i./robotics, computer science, game design, web page design. **Conservation:** Environmental studies. **Engineering:** Aerospace, biomedical, chemical, civil, electrical, environmental, industrial, mechanical, physics, systems. **Engineering technology:** Industrial management. **Health:** Predental, premedicine, preveterinary. **Interdisciplinary:** Biological/physical sciences, global studies, science/society. **Legal studies:** Prelaw. **Liberal arts:** Humanities. **Math:** General, applied. **Physical sciences:** Chemistry, physics. **Social sciences:** General, economics. **Other:** Robotics engineering.

**Most popular majors.** Biology 12%, computer/information sciences 9%, engineering/engineering technologies 62%.

**Computing on campus.** 300 workstations in dormitories, library, computer center, student center. Dormitories wired for high-speed internet access and linked to campus network. Commuter students can connect to campus network. Online course registration, online library, helpline, repair service, student web hosting, wireless network available.

**Student life. Freshman orientation:** Available, $200 fee. Preregistration for classes offered. Program held in late August. **Housing:** Guaranteed on-campus for freshmen. Coed dorms, special housing for disabled, apartments, fraternity/sorority housing, wellness housing available. Special interest housing available. **Activities:** Bands, campus ministries, choral groups, dance, drama, film society, international student organizations, literary magazine, music ensembles, musical theater, radio station, student government, student newspaper, symphony orchestra, African American cultural society, volunteer tutoring group, Big Brother/Big Sister, World House, European student association, Asian society, Hispanic student association, women's awareness group, students for social awareness, Amnesty International.

**Athletics.** NCAA. **Intercollegiate:** Baseball M, basketball, cross-country, field hockey W, football (tackle) M, rowing (crew), soccer, softball W, swimming, track and field, volleyball W, wrestling M. **Intramural:** Basketball, bowling, cross-country, fencing, football (non-tackle) M, racquetball, soccer, softball, swimming, table tennis, volleyball, water polo M, wrestling M. **Team name:** Engineers.

**Student services.** Adult student services, alcohol/substance abuse counseling, chaplain/spiritual director, career counseling, student employment services, financial aid counseling, health services, minority student services, personal counseling, placement for graduates, veterans' counselor, women's services. **Physically disabled:** Services for visually, speech, hearing impaired.

**Contact.** E-mail: admissions@wpi.edu
Phone: (508) 831-5286 Fax: (508) 831-5875
Edward Connor, Director of Admissions, Worcester Polytechnic Institute, 100 Institute Road, Worcester, MA 01609-2280

## Worcester State College
**Worcester, Massachusetts**    CB member
**www.worcester.edu**    CB code: 3524

- Public 4-year liberal arts and teachers college
- Commuter campus in small city
- 4,211 degree-seeking undergraduates: 17% part-time, 59% women, 6% African American, 3% Asian American, 6% Hispanic American, 1% Native American, 1% international
- 487 degree-seeking graduate students
- 59% of applicants admitted
- SAT or ACT with writing required
- 44% graduate within 6 years

**General.** Founded in 1874. Regionally accredited. **Degrees:** 810 bachelor's awarded; master's offered. **ROTC:** Army, Naval, Air Force. **Location:** 45 miles from Boston; 65 miles from Hartford, Connecticut. **Calendar:** Semester, extensive summer session. **Full-time faculty:** 179 total; 74% have terminal degrees, 20% minority, 52% women. **Part-time faculty:** 199 total; 8% minority, 51% women. **Class size:** 49% < 20, 51% 20-39. **Special facilities:** Photographic labs, multimedia classrooms with satellite connectivity, speech/language/hearing clinic.

**Freshman class profile.** 3,559 applied, 2,101 admitted, 695 enrolled.

| Mid 50% test scores | | | |
|---|---|---|---|
| SAT critical reading: | 460-550 | GPA 3.50-3.74: | 9% |
| SAT math: | 470-560 | GPA 3.0-3.49: | 33% |
| SAT writing: | 450-550 | GPA 2.0-2.99: | 47% |
| ACT composite: | 19-24 | Return as sophomores: | 77% |
| GPA 3.75 or higher: | 11% | Out-of-state: | 4% |
| | | Live on campus: | 56% |

**Basis for selection.** Secondary school record most important; test scores important; extracurricular activities considered. Interview and personal essay recommended for academically weak. **Homeschooled:** Student must submit documentation that home school plan meets district curriculum standards. **Learning Disabled:** SAT waiver available for students with learning disabilities with IEP plan.

**High school preparation.** College-preparatory program required. 16 units required. Required units include English 4, mathematics 3, social studies 1, history 1, science 3 (laboratory 1), foreign language 2 and academic electives 2. History unit must be US history.

**2009-2010 Annual costs.** Tuition/fees: $6,605; $12,685 out-of-state. Room/board: $9,067.

**2008-2009 Financial aid. Need-based:** 598 full-time freshmen applied for aid; 378 were judged to have need; 372 of these received aid. Average need met was 82%. Average scholarship/grant was $4,643; average loan $1,876. 58% of total undergraduate aid awarded as scholarships/grants, 42% as loans/jobs. **Non-need-based:** Awarded to 616 full-time undergraduates, including 201 freshmen. Scholarships awarded for academics, ROTC. **Additional information:** Veterans, Native Americans and those certified by Massachusetts Rehabilitation Commission and Massachusetts Commission for the Blind considered for tuition waivers while funds available. Tuition also waived for needy Massachusetts residents and in-state National Guard members.

**Application procedures. Admission:** Priority date 2/1; deadline 5/1 (receipt date). $40 fee, may be waived for applicants with need. Admission notification on a rolling basis beginning on or about 12/1. Must reply by May 1 or within 4 week(s) if notified thereafter. **Financial aid:** Priority date 3/1, closing date 5/1. FAFSA required. Applicants notified on a rolling basis starting 3/1; must reply within 2 week(s) of notification.

**Academics. Special study options:** Combined bachelor's/graduate degree, cross-registration, distance learning, double major, ESL, exchange student, honors, independent study, internships, liberal arts/career combination, study abroad, teacher certification program, Washington semester. Foreign exchange student program. **Credit/placement by examination:** AP, CLEP, IB, institutional tests. 30 credit hours maximum toward bachelor's degree. **Support services:** Learning center, pre-admission summer program, reduced course load, remedial instruction, study skills assistance, tutoring, writing center.

**Majors. Biology:** General, biotechnology. **Business:** Business admin. **Communications:** General, media studies. **Communications technology:** Radio/tv. **Computer sciences:** General. **Education:** Early childhood, elementary.

**Foreign languages:** Spanish. **Health:** Adult health nursing, communication disorders, community health services, health services, nursing (RN). **History:** General. **Math:** General. **Physical sciences:** General, chemistry. **Protective services:** Criminal justice. **Psychology:** General. **Social sciences:** Economics, geography, sociology, urban studies. **Visual/performing arts:** General.

**Most popular majors.** Biology 8%, business/marketing 22%, communications/journalism 9%, education 7%, health sciences 15%, psychology 12%, security/protective services 7%.

**Computing on campus.** PC or laptop required. 300 workstations in dormitories, library, computer center, student center. Dormitories wired for high-speed internet access and linked to campus network. Commuter students can connect to campus network. Online course registration, online library, helpline, repair service, student web hosting, wireless network available.

**Student life. Freshman orientation:** Mandatory, $75 fee. Preregistration for classes offered. Four-hour parent orientation in Spring; 4-1/2 day session for students last week in August. **Housing:** Coed dorms, single-sex dorms, special housing for disabled available. $150 nonrefundable deposit, deadline 2/15. **Activities:** Bands, campus ministries, choral groups, dance, drama, international student organizations, music ensembles, radio station, student government, student newspaper, TV station, student events committee, Third World alliance, campus ambassadors, gay-straight alliance, surreal games and sci-fi, ski/snow board club.

**Athletics.** NCAA. **Intercollegiate:** Baseball M, basketball, cheerleading, cross-country, field hockey W, football (tackle) M, golf M, ice hockey M, lacrosse W, soccer, softball W, tennis W, track and field, volleyball. **Intramural:** Baseball M, basketball, cheerleading, cross-country, field hockey W, football (tackle) M, golf M, ice hockey M, lacrosse W, rowing (crew), soccer, softball W, tennis W, track and field, volleyball. **Team name:** Lancers.

**Student services.** Adult student services, alcohol/substance abuse counseling, chaplain/spiritual director, career counseling, services for economically disadvantaged, student employment services, financial aid counseling, health services, minority student services, personal counseling, placement for graduates, veterans' counselor, women's services. **Physically disabled:** Services for visually, speech, hearing impaired.

**Contact.** E-mail: admissions@worcester.edu
Phone: (508) 929-8040 Fax: (508) 929-8183
Beth Axelson, Admissions Director, Worcester State College, Office of Undergraduate Admission, Worcester, MA 01602-2597

## Zion Bible College
**Haverhill, Massachusetts**
www.zbc.edu                         CB code: 3942

▸ Private 4-year Bible college affiliated with Assemblies of God
▸ Residential campus in small city
▸ 258 degree-seeking undergraduates: 14% part-time, 46% women, 11% African American, 4% Asian American, 14% Hispanic American, 2% international
▸ Application essay required
▸ 64% graduate within 6 years; 10% enter graduate study

**General.** Accredited by ABHE. **Degrees:** 40 bachelor's awarded. **Location:** 40 miles from Boston. **Calendar:** Semester, limited summer session. **Full-time faculty:** 10 total; 20% have terminal degrees, 10% women. **Part-time faculty:** 14 total; 14% have terminal degrees, 7% minority, 36% women. **Class size:** 68% < 20, 27% 20-39, 4% 40-49, 1% 50-99.

**Freshman class profile.**

| | | | |
|---|---|---|---|
| End year in good standing: | 66% | Live on campus: | 95% |
| Return as sophomores: | 53% | International: | 2% |
| Out-of-state: | 67% | | |

**Basis for selection.** Open admission. Three references required, including pastoral recommendation; high school transcript, immunizations, health certificate, and test scores also required. **Homeschooled:** Transcript of courses and grades required. Applicants must produce diploma and transcript that verify graduation by the state department of education, local school district or accrediting association. Students who cannot produce this must submit a GED.

**2009-2010 Annual costs.** Tuition/fees: $8,470. Room/board: $6,200. Books/supplies: $600.

**2009-2010 Financial aid. Non-need-based:** Scholarships awarded for academics, leadership, minority status, state residency.

**Application procedures. Admission:** No deadline. $35 fee. Admission notification on a rolling basis. Letter of Intent with deposit (tuition and board) required one month after notification. **Financial aid:** Priority date 6/1; no closing date. FAFSA required. Applicants notified on a rolling basis; must reply within 4 week(s) of notification.

**Academics. Special study options:** Independent study, internships, weekend college. **Credit/placement by examination:** AP, CLEP. **Support services:** Learning center, reduced course load, study skills assistance.

**Majors. Theology:** Bible.

**Computing on campus.** 15 workstations in library, computer center. Dormitories wired for high-speed internet access. Online library, wireless network available.

**Student life. Freshman orientation:** Mandatory. **Policies:** Nightly curfew of 10:30, except for Fridays (11:00 or midnight for seniors). Chapel attendance required Tuesday through Friday. No alcohol, drugs, or smoking permitted on or off-campus. Full-time students assigned to assist in an area church. Religious observance required. **Housing:** Guaranteed on-campus for all undergraduates. Single-sex dorms available. $100 fully refundable deposit. **Activities:** Campus ministries, choral groups, music ensembles, student government.

**Student services.** Chaplain/spiritual director, financial aid counseling.

**Contact.** E-mail: admissions@zbc.edu
Phone: (978) 478-3400 ext. 3431 Toll-free number: (800) 356-4014
Fax: (978) 478-3406
David Hodge, Director of Admissions and Records, Zion Bible College, 320 South Main Street, Haverhill, MA 01835

# Michigan

## Adrian College
Adrian, Michigan
www.adrian.edu

**CB member**
**CB code: 1001**

- Private 4-year liberal arts college affiliated with United Methodist Church
- Residential campus in large town
- 1,500 degree-seeking undergraduates
- 58% of applicants admitted
- SAT or ACT (ACT writing optional) required

**General.** Founded in 1859. Regionally accredited. **Degrees:** 146 bachelor's awarded. **Location:** 75 miles from Detroit, 30 miles from Toledo, Ohio. **Calendar:** Semester, limited summer session. **Full-time faculty:** 85 total. **Class size:** 66% < 20, 33% 20-39, less than 1% 40-49, 1% 50-99. **Special facilities:** Observatory, planetarium, arboretum, solar greenhouse, human anatomy laboratory, writing laboratory, educational curriculum center.

**Freshman class profile.** 3,944 applied, 2,288 admitted, 503 enrolled.

| Mid 50% test scores | | | |
|---|---|---|---|
| ACT composite: | 20-25 | Rank in top quarter: | 51% |
| GPA 3.75 or higher: | 25% | Rank in top tenth: | 24% |
| GPA 3.50-3.74: | 16% | Out-of-state: | 23% |
| GPA 3.0-3.49: | 57% | Live on campus: | 93% |
| | | GPA 2.0-2.99: | 2% |

**Basis for selection.** School achievement most important, followed by test scores. Applicants should rank in top half of high school class. School recommendations and extracurricular activities considered. ACT preferred. **Homeschooled:** Must have transcript approved by school district.

**High school preparation.** College-preparatory program recommended. 15 units recommended. Recommended units include English 4, mathematics 3, social studies 1, history 1, science 2 (laboratory 1), foreign language 2 and academic electives 2.

**2009-2010 Annual costs.** Tuition/fees: $24,440. Room/board: $7,660. Books/supplies: $400. Personal expenses: $928.

**2008-2009 Financial aid. Non-need-based:** Scholarships awarded for academics, alumni affiliation, art, leadership, music/drama, religious affiliation, state residency.

**Application procedures. Admission:** No deadline. No application fee. Admission notification on a rolling basis beginning on or about 9/1. **Financial aid:** Priority date 3/1; no closing date. FAFSA required. Applicants notified on a rolling basis starting 3/15; must reply by 5/1 or within 2 week(s) of notification.

**Academics. Special study options:** Combined bachelor's/graduate degree, double major, dual enrollment of high school students, honors, independent study, internships, student-designed major, study abroad, teacher certification program, Washington semester. **Credit/placement by examination:** AP, CLEP, IB, institutional tests. 15 credit hours maximum toward associate degree, 30 toward bachelor's. **Support services:** Learning center, pre-admission summer program, reduced course load, remedial instruction, study skills assistance, tutoring, writing center.

**Majors. Area/ethnic studies:** Japanese. **Biology:** General. **Business:** Accounting, business admin, international, international marketing, management science, marketing. **Communications:** General, journalism, media studies. **Conservation:** Environmental science, environmental studies. **Education:** General, art, elementary, health, multi-level teacher, music, physical, secondary, social science. **Foreign languages:** French, German, Spanish. **Health:** Athletic training, predental, premedicine, prepharmacy, preveterinary. **History:** General. **Interdisciplinary:** Global studies. **Legal studies:** Prelaw. **Math:** General. **Parks/recreation:** Exercise sciences, health/fitness. **Philosophy/religion:** Philosophy, religion. **Physical sciences:** Chemistry, geology, physics. **Protective services:** Criminal justice. **Psychology:** General. **Public administration:** Social work. **Social sciences:** Economics, political science, sociology. **Theology:** Preministerial. **Visual/performing arts:** Art, arts management, dramatic, interior design, musical theater.

**Most popular majors.** Business/marketing 10%, education 8%, parks/recreation 9%, visual/performing arts 17%.

**Computing on campus.** 170 workstations in library, computer center, student center. Dormitories wired for high-speed internet access and linked to campus network. Commuter students can connect to campus network. Online course registration, online library, helpline, student web hosting, wireless network available.

**Student life. Freshman orientation:** Mandatory. Preregistration for classes offered. Week-long program in August. Students take placement exams and take a first-year trip. **Policies:** Freshmen, sophomores, and juniors required to live on campus unless living with family. **Housing:** Guaranteed on-campus for all undergraduates. Coed dorms, single-sex dorms, apartments, fraternity/sorority housing available. $100 deposit, deadline 7/1. **Activities:** Bands, campus ministries, choral groups, dance, drama, international student organizations, literary magazine, music ensembles, Model UN, musical theater, radio station, student government, student newspaper, symphony orchestra, Wesley Fellowship, Circle K, Religious Life Council, Habitat for Humanity, African-American Leaders Promoting Higher Achievement, Leaders in College Service, Catholic student organization.

**Athletics.** NCAA. **Intercollegiate:** Baseball M, basketball, cross-country, football (tackle) M, golf, ice hockey, lacrosse, soccer, softball W, tennis, track and field, volleyball W. **Intramural:** Basketball, bowling, football (non-tackle), lacrosse, racquetball, soccer, softball, tennis, volleyball. **Team name:** Bulldogs.

**Student services.** Adult student services, alcohol/substance abuse counseling, chaplain/spiritual director, career counseling, student employment services, financial aid counseling, health services, minority student services, personal counseling, placement for graduates. **Physically disabled:** Services for visually, speech, hearing impaired.

**Contact.** E-mail: admissions@adrian.edu
Phone: (517) 265-5161 ext. 4326 Toll-free number: (800) 877-2246
Fax: (517) 264-3878
Carolyn Quinlan, Director of Admissions, Adrian College, 110 South Madison Street, Adrian, MI 49221-2575

## Albion College
Albion, Michigan
www.albion.edu

**CB member**
**CB code: 1007**

- Private 4-year liberal arts college affiliated with United Methodist Church
- Residential campus in small town
- 1,722 degree-seeking undergraduates: 1% part-time, 52% women, 3% African American, 3% Asian American, 1% Hispanic American, 2% international
- 79% of applicants admitted
- SAT or ACT (ACT writing optional), application essay required
- 74% graduate within 6 years

**General.** Founded in 1835. Regionally accredited. **Degrees:** 450 bachelor's awarded. **Location:** 55 miles from Lansing, 55 miles from Ann Arbor. **Calendar:** Semester, limited summer session. **Full-time faculty:** 124 total; 94% have terminal degrees, 14% minority, 39% women. **Part-time faculty:** 38 total; 45% have terminal degrees, 3% minority, 40% women. **Class size:** 57% < 20, 40% 20-39, 2% 40-49, less than 1% 50-99. **Special facilities:** Science complex, 144-acre nature center, observatory, equestrian center.

**Freshman class profile.** 1,780 applied, 1,413 admitted, 434 enrolled.

| Mid 50% test scores | | | |
|---|---|---|---|
| SAT critical reading: | 530-660 | Rank in top quarter: | 56% |
| SAT math: | 560-670 | Rank in top tenth: | 27% |
| ACT composite: | 22-28 | Return as sophomores: | 85% |
| GPA 3.75 or higher: | 35% | Out-of-state: | 7% |
| GPA 3.50-3.74: | 23% | Live on campus: | 98% |
| GPA 3.0-3.49: | 29% | International: | 6% |
| GPA 2.0-2.99: | 13% | Fraternities: | 52% |
| | | Sororities: | 46% |

**Basis for selection.** Admission based on school achievement record, ACT/SAT test scores, recommendations from counselor or principal. Interview recommended. Audition recommended for music and theater majors.

**High school preparation.** College-preparatory program required. 15 units required; 19 recommended. Required and recommended units include English 4, mathematics 3-4, social studies 3-4, science 3-4 (laboratory 2) and foreign language 2-3.

**2009-2010 Annual costs.** Tuition/fees: $30,272. Room/board: $8,510. Books/supplies: $650. Personal expenses: $350.

**2009-2010 Financial aid. Need-based:** 362 full-time freshmen applied for aid; 312 were judged to have need; 312 of these received aid. Average need met was 89%. Average scholarship/grant was $21,528; average loan $4,429. 81% of total undergraduate aid awarded as scholarships/grants, 19% as loans/jobs. **Non-need-based:** Awarded to 1,644 full-time undergraduates, including 428 freshmen. Scholarships awarded for academics, alumni affiliation, art, music/drama, state residency.

**Application procedures. Admission:** No deadline. $40 fee, may be waived for applicants with need, free for online applicants. Admission notification on a rolling basis beginning on or about 11/1. **Financial aid:** Priority date 3/1; no closing date. FAFSA required. Applicants notified on a rolling basis starting 3/15; must reply by 5/1 or within 2 week(s) of notification.

**Academics. Special study options:** Combined bachelor's/graduate degree, double major, dual enrollment of high school students, honors, independent study, internships, liberal arts/career combination, New York semester, semester at sea, student-designed major, study abroad, teacher certification program, urban semester, Washington semester. Environmental institute, public service institute, liberal arts program in professional management. **Credit/placement by examination:** AP, CLEP, IB, institutional tests. **Support services:** Learning center, reduced course load, study skills assistance, tutoring, writing center.

**Majors. Area/ethnic studies:** American. **Biology:** General, biochemistry. **Business:** Business admin. **Communications:** General. **Computer sciences:** General, computer science. **Conservation:** Environmental science, environmental studies. **Education:** Art, biology, chemistry, English, foreign languages, French, German, history, mathematics, music, physical, physics, science, social studies, Spanish. **Foreign languages:** French, German, Spanish. **History:** General. **Interdisciplinary:** Behavioral sciences, biological/physical sciences, math/computer science, natural sciences, neuroscience. **Math:** General. **Philosophy/religion:** Philosophy, religion. **Physical sciences:** Chemistry, geology, physics. **Psychology:** General. **Public administration:** Policy analysis. **Social sciences:** Anthropology, economics, international relations, political science, sociology. **Visual/performing arts:** General, art, art history/conservation, dramatic, music performance, studio arts.

**Most popular majors.** Biology 10%, business/marketing 18%, communications/journalism 7%, English 8%, history 6%, philosophy/religious studies 6%, physical sciences 7%, psychology 10%, social sciences 10%.

**Computing on campus.** 435 workstations in dormitories, library, computer center, student center. Dormitories wired for high-speed internet access and linked to campus network. Commuter students can connect to campus network. Online course registration, online library, helpline, repair service, wireless network available.

**Student life. Freshman orientation:** Mandatory. Preregistration for classes offered. **Housing:** Guaranteed on-campus for all undergraduates. Coed dorms, single-sex dorms, special housing for disabled, apartments, cooperative housing, fraternity/sorority housing available. $300 partly refundable deposit, deadline 5/1. Special interest annexes available. **Activities:** Bands, campus ministries, choral groups, dance, drama, international student organizations, literary magazine, music ensembles, Model UN, musical theater, radio station, student government, student newspaper, symphony orchestra, 110 campus organizations.

**Athletics.** NCAA. **Intercollegiate:** Baseball M, basketball, cheerleading, cross-country, diving, equestrian, football (tackle) M, golf, soccer, softball W, swimming, tennis, track and field, volleyball W. **Intramural:** Badminton, basketball, diving, football (non-tackle), football (tackle) M, racquetball, rugby, soccer, softball, swimming, tennis, volleyball. **Team name:** Britons.

**Student services.** Alcohol/substance abuse counseling, chaplain/spiritual director, career counseling, services for economically disadvantaged, student employment services, financial aid counseling, health services, minority student services, personal counseling, placement for graduates, women's services. **Physically disabled:** Services for visually, hearing impaired.

**Contact.** E-mail: admissions@albion.edu
Phone: (517) 629-0321 Toll-free number: (800) 858-6770
Fax: (517) 629-0569
Kevin Kropf, Director of Admission, Albion College, 611 East Porter Street, Albion, MI 49224-1831

## Alma College
**Alma, Michigan**  **CB member**
**www.alma.edu**  **CB code: 1010**

- Private 4-year liberal arts college affiliated with Presbyterian Church (USA)
- Residential campus in small town

- 1,394 degree-seeking undergraduates: 2% part-time, 55% women
- 75% of applicants admitted
- SAT or ACT (ACT writing optional) required
- 63% graduate within 6 years

**General.** Founded in 1886. Regionally accredited. Scottish heritage honored through marching band clad in kilts, Scottish dance troupe, student pipers, tartan, Alma Highland Festival and Games. **Degrees:** 261 bachelor's awarded. **ROTC:** Army. **Location:** 50 miles from Lansing, 45 miles from Saginaw. **Calendar:** 4-4-1 semester system. Limited summer session. **Full-time faculty:** 85 total; 89% have terminal degrees, 8% minority, 38% women. **Part-time faculty:** 49 total; 26% have terminal degrees, 6% minority, 45% women. **Class size:** 55% < 20, 38% 20-39, 4% 40-49, 3% 50-99. **Special facilities:** Planetarium, performing arts center, climbing wall, ecological station.

**Freshman class profile.** 1,778 applied, 1,334 admitted, 396 enrolled.

| Mid 50% test scores | | Rank in top quarter: | 57% |
|---|---|---|---|
| SAT critical reading: | 470-710 | Rank in top tenth: | 30% |
| SAT math: | 480-670 | End year in good standing: | 96% |
| SAT writing: | 500-710 | Return as sophomores: | 80% |
| ACT composite: | 21-27 | Out-of-state: | 7% |
| GPA 3.75 or higher: | 30% | Live on campus: | 96% |
| GPA 3.50-3.74: | 21% | International: | 1% |
| GPA 3.0-3.49: | 33% | Fraternities: | 22% |
| GPA 2.0-2.99: | 16% | Sororities: | 23% |

**Basis for selection.** Applicant should be in top half of class, have 3.0 high school GPA or 22 ACT or 1030 SAT (exclusive of Writing). Co-curricular activities considered. Portfolio recommended for art majors. Interview recommended for all, strongly recommended for academically weak and those whose grades and test scores show discrepancies.

**High school preparation.** College-preparatory program required. 16 units required. Required and recommended units include English 4, mathematics 3, social studies 3, science 3 and foreign language 2.

**2009-2010 Annual costs.** Tuition/fees: $26,068. Room/board: $8,518. Books/supplies: $800. Personal expenses: $710.

**2009-2010 Financial aid. Need-based:** 386 full-time freshmen applied for aid; 338 were judged to have need; 338 of these received aid. Average need met was 87%. Average scholarship/grant was $19,894; average loan $4,156. 75% of total undergraduate aid awarded as scholarships/grants, 25% as loans/jobs. **Non-need-based:** Awarded to 442 full-time undergraduates, including 127 freshmen. Scholarships awarded for academics, alumni affiliation, art, minority status, music/drama. **Additional information:** Auditions required for music, drama, dance scholarship candidates. Portfolios required for art scholarship candidates.

**Application procedures. Admission:** No deadline. $25 fee, may be waived for applicants with need, free for online applicants. Admission notification on a rolling basis beginning on or about 9/1. Must reply by May 1 or within 3 week(s) if notified thereafter. **Financial aid:** Priority date 3/1; no closing date. FAFSA required. Applicants notified on a rolling basis starting 3/1; must reply within 3 week(s) of notification.

**Academics.** One-month spring term provides special opportunities for study in United States or overseas. Students required to complete 2 spring terms. **Special study options:** Combined bachelor's/graduate degree, double major, dual enrollment of high school students, exchange student, honors, independent study, internships, New York semester, student-designed major, study abroad, teacher certification program, urban semester, Washington semester. Pre-engineering 3-2 programs with University of Michigan, Michigan Technological University; pre-occupational therapy 3-2 program with Washington University (MO). **Credit/placement by examination:** AP, CLEP, IB, SAT, ACT, institutional tests. 32 credit hours maximum toward bachelor's degree. **Support services:** Pre-admission summer program, reduced course load, remedial instruction, study skills assistance, tutoring, writing center.

**Majors. Biology:** General, biochemistry. **Business:** Accounting, business admin, finance, international, marketing. **Communications:** Media studies. **Computer sciences:** Computer science. **Education:** General, elementary, secondary. **Foreign languages:** French, German, Spanish. **Health:** Medical illustrating, predental, premedicine, preveterinary. **History:** General. **Interdisciplinary:** Biological/physical sciences, gerontology. **Legal studies:** Prelaw. **Liberal arts:** Arts/sciences, humanities. **Math:** General. **Parks/recreation:** Exercise sciences. **Philosophy/religion:** Philosophy, religion. **Physical sciences:** Chemistry, physics. **Psychology:** General. **Social sciences:** Anthropology, economics, political science, sociology. **Theology:** Preministerial. **Visual/performing arts:** General, art, art history/conservation, dance, design, dramatic, graphic design, music performance, studio arts.

**Most popular majors.** Biology 12%, business/marketing 17%, education 7%, health sciences 10%, history 8%, psychology 6%, social sciences 10%, visual/performing arts 10%.

**Computing on campus.** 357 workstations in dormitories, library, computer center, student center. Dormitories wired for high-speed internet access and linked to campus network. Commuter students can connect to campus network. Online course registration, online library, helpline, student web hosting, wireless network available.

**Student life. Freshman orientation:** Mandatory, $330 fee. Preregistration for classes offered. Last weekend of August prior to the start of the fall term. **Housing:** Guaranteed on-campus for all undergraduates. Coed dorms, fraternity/sorority housing available. $200 nonrefundable deposit, deadline 5/1. **Activities:** Bands, campus ministries, choral groups, dance, drama, international student organizations, music ensembles, Model UN, radio station, student government, student newspaper, symphony orchestra, College Republicans/College Democrats, Amnesty International, Big Brothers/Big Sisters, Catholic student organization, Habitat for Humanity, Multicultural Black Student Union, Students Offering Service, New Life Campus Ministries.

**Athletics.** NCAA. **Intercollegiate:** Baseball M, basketball, cross-country, diving, football (tackle) M, golf, soccer, softball W, swimming, tennis, track and field, volleyball W. **Intramural:** Basketball, soccer W, softball, volleyball. **Team name:** Scots.

**Student services.** Alcohol/substance abuse counseling, chaplain/spiritual director, career counseling, student employment services, financial aid counseling, health services, personal counseling. **Physically disabled:** Services for visually, hearing impaired.

**Contact.** E-mail: admissions@alma.edu
Phone: (989) 463-7139 Toll-free number: (800) 321-2562
Fax: (989) 463-7057
Karen Jezewski, Senior Associate Director of Admissions, Alma College, 614 West Superior Street, Alma, MI 48801-1599

## Andrews University
**Berrien Springs, Michigan**
**www.andrews.edu**                           **CB code: 1030**

- Private 4-year university affiliated with Seventh-day Adventists
- Residential campus in small town
- 1,817 degree-seeking undergraduates: 7% part-time, 54% women, 26% African American, 11% Asian American, 12% Hispanic American, 12% international
- 1,587 degree-seeking graduate students
- 49% of applicants admitted
- SAT or ACT (ACT writing optional), application essay required
- 58% graduate within 6 years

**General.** Founded in 1874. Regionally accredited. **Degrees:** 341 bachelor's, 2 associate awarded; master's, doctoral offered. **Location:** 10 miles from St. Joseph-Benton Harbor, 25 miles from South Bend, Indiana. **Calendar:** Semester, limited summer session. **Full-time faculty:** 216 total; 74% have terminal degrees, 26% minority, 34% women. **Part-time faculty:** 82 total; 38% have terminal degrees, 18% minority, 55% women. **Class size:** 59% < 20, 29% 20-39, 4% 40-49, 7% 50-99, 1% >100. **Special facilities:** Natural history museum, archaeology museum, performing arts center, arboretum.

**Freshman class profile.** 1,809 applied, 879 admitted, 377 enrolled.

| Mid 50% test scores | | GPA 2.0-2.99: | 24% |
|---|---|---|---|
| SAT critical reading: | 450-580 | Rank in top quarter: | 21% |
| SAT math: | 430-580 | Rank in top tenth: | 15% |
| SAT writing: | 440-580 | Return as sophomores: | 79% |
| ACT composite: | 19-25 | Out-of-state: | 69% |
| GPA 3.75 or higher: | 30% | Live on campus: | 87% |
| GPA 3.50-3.74: | 17% | International: | 9% |
| GPA 3.0-3.49: | 28% | | |

**Basis for selection.** School achievement record, test scores, recommendations important. Interview recommended. Audition recommended for music majors. Portfolios recommended for architecture, art majors. **Home-schooled:** Portfolio required. **Learning Disabled:** Must advise student services of learning disability prior to admission interview and testing.

**High school preparation.** College-preparatory program recommended. 13 units required; 15 recommended. Required and recommended units include English 3-4, mathematics 2-3, social studies 1, history 2, science 2

and academic electives 3. Additional 1 unit chemistry, 1 unit physics, 1 unit computer recommended.

**2009-2010 Annual costs.** Tuition/fees: $21,170. Room/board: $6,860. Books/supplies: $1,050. Personal expenses: $800.

**2008-2009 Financial aid. Non-need-based:** Scholarships awarded for academics, alumni affiliation, leadership, music/drama, religious affiliation.

**Application procedures. Admission:** No deadline. $30 fee. Admission notification on a rolling basis beginning on or about 1/1. **Financial aid:** Priority date 3/31; no closing date. FAFSA, institutional form required. Applicants notified on a rolling basis starting 3/15.

**Academics. Special study options:** Accelerated study, combined bachelor's/graduate degree, cooperative education, distance learning, double major, dual enrollment of high school students, ESL, honors, internships, student-designed major, study abroad, teacher certification program. **Credit/placement by examination:** AP, CLEP, IB, institutional tests. 32 credit hours maximum toward associate degree, 32 toward bachelor's. DANTES (for nontraditional students). **Support services:** Learning center, pre-admission summer program, reduced course load, remedial instruction, study skills assistance, tutoring, writing center.

**Majors. Agriculture:** Animal sciences, business, horticulture. **Architecture:** Architecture. **Biology:** General, biochemistry, biophysics, botany, molecular, zoology. **Business:** Accounting, business admin, entrepreneurial studies, finance, managerial economics, nonprofit/public, training/development. **Communications:** General, journalism, public relations. **Communications technology:** General. **Computer sciences:** General, information systems. **Conservation:** Environmental science. **Education:** Elementary, mathematics, secondary, social science, social studies. **Engineering:** General, electrical, industrial, mechanical. **Family/consumer sciences:** Family studies, food/nutrition. **Foreign languages:** French, Spanish. **Health:** Audiology/speech pathology, clinical lab science, dietetics, nursing (RN). **History:** General. **Interdisciplinary:** Biological/physical sciences, neuroscience. **Math:** General. **Mechanic/repair:** Aircraft. **Philosophy/religion:** Religion. **Physical sciences:** Chemistry, physics. **Psychology:** General. **Public administration:** Social work. **Social sciences:** General, anthropology, economics, international economic development, political science, sociology. **Theology:** Religious ed, sacred music, theology, youth ministry. **Transportation:** Aviation. **Visual/performing arts:** General, art, art history/conservation, ceramics, commercial/advertising art, design, graphic design, multimedia, music performance, painting, photography, printmaking, studio arts.

**Most popular majors.** Biology 8%, business/marketing 10%, foreign language 8%, health sciences 20%, visual/performing arts 6%.

**Computing on campus.** 130 workstations in dormitories, library, computer center. Dormitories wired for high-speed internet access and linked to campus network. Commuter students can connect to campus network. Online course registration, online library, helpline, repair service, student web hosting, wireless network available.

**Student life. Freshman orientation:** Mandatory. Preregistration for classes offered. Held week before fall registration. **Policies:** Students expected to abide by ethical and moral standards of the university, which are mission-driven as published in official documents. Resident students required to stay in dorm until age 22. Religious observance required. **Housing:** Guaranteed on-campus for all undergraduates. Single-sex dorms, apartments, wellness housing available. $200 deposit. **Activities:** Concert band, choral groups, drama, international student organizations, music ensembles, musical theater, radio station, student government, student newspaper, symphony orchestra, Christian Youth Action.

**Athletics. Intramural:** Badminton, basketball, field hockey, football (nontackle), soccer, softball, triathlon, volleyball.

**Student services.** Chaplain/spiritual director, career counseling, student employment services, financial aid counseling, health services, on-campus daycare, personal counseling, placement for graduates, veterans' counselor. **Physically disabled:** Services for visually, speech, hearing impaired.

**Contact.** E-mail: enroll@andrews.edu
Phone: (800) 253-2874 Toll-free number: (800) 253-2874
Fax: (269) 471-3228
Stephen Payne, Vice President for Enrollment Management, Andrews University, 100 US Highway 31, Berrien Springs, MI 49104

## Aquinas College
**Grand Rapids, Michigan**
**www.aquinas.edu**                           **CB code: 1018**

- Private 4-year liberal arts college affiliated with Roman Catholic Church
- Residential campus in small city

- 1,879 degree-seeking undergraduates: 13% part-time, 64% women, 4% African American, 2% Asian American, 4% Hispanic American
- 237 degree-seeking graduate students
- 80% of applicants admitted
- SAT or ACT (ACT writing optional) required
- 56% graduate within 6 years; 21% enter graduate study

**General.** Founded in 1886. Regionally accredited. **Degrees:** 320 bachelor's, 3 associate awarded; master's offered. **Location:** 140 miles from Detroit, 180 miles from Chicago. **Calendar:** Semester, extensive summer session. **Full-time faculty:** 94 total; 87% have terminal degrees, 8% minority, 49% women. **Part-time faculty:** 150 total; 23% have terminal degrees, 4% minority, 47% women. **Class size:** 57% < 20, 40% 20-39, 1% 40-49, 1% 50-99. **Special facilities:** Greenhouse, astronomy tower, nature trails, community theater, center for sustainability.

**Freshman class profile.** 2,192 applied, 1,761 admitted, 402 enrolled.

| Mid 50% test scores | | Rank in top quarter: | 48% |
|---|---|---|---|
| ACT composite: | 20-26 | Rank in top tenth: | 19% |
| GPA 3.75 or higher: | 26% | Return as sophomores: | 72% |
| GPA 3.50-3.74: | 21% | Out-of-state: | 3% |
| GPA 3.0-3.49: | 33% | Live on campus: | 85% |
| GPA 2.0-2.99: | 20% | | |

**Basis for selection.** GED not accepted. 2.5 high school GPA in academic subjects. Test scores important. Interview required for applicants with above average test scores but less than 2.5 high school GPA in academic subjects, recommended for others. Audition recommended for music majors. Portfolio recommended for art majors. **Homeschooled:** Transcript of courses and grades required. Greater emphasis placed upon results of ACT or SAT. Students may be required to complete Ability to Benefit test. **Learning Disabled:** Make appointment with Academic Achievement Center to express needed accommodations prior to enrollment.

**High school preparation.** College-preparatory program recommended. 15 units required. Required units include English 4, mathematics 4, social studies 4 and science 3.

**2009-2010 Annual costs.** Tuition/fees: $22,314. Room/board: $7,014. Books/supplies: $798. Personal expenses: $788.

**2009-2010 Financial aid. Need-based:** 381 full-time freshmen applied for aid; 347 were judged to have need; 347 of these received aid. Average need met was 90%. Average scholarship/grant was $18,803; average loan $2,750. 81% of total undergraduate aid awarded as scholarships/grants, 19% as loans/jobs. **Non-need-based:** Awarded to 1,513 full-time undergraduates, including 466 freshmen. Scholarships awarded for academics, alumni affiliation, art, athletics, leadership, music/drama.

**Application procedures. Admission:** No deadline. No application fee. Admission notification on a rolling basis beginning on or about 8/1. **Financial aid:** Priority date 3/1; no closing date. FAFSA required. Applicants notified on a rolling basis starting 2/15; must reply within 2 week(s) of notification.

**Academics. Special study options:** Accelerated study, cooperative education, cross-registration, distance learning, double major, dual enrollment of high school students, exchange student, honors, independent study, internships, liberal arts/career combination, student-designed major, study abroad, teacher certification program, urban semester. **Credit/placement by examination:** AP, CLEP, institutional tests. 30 credit hours maximum toward bachelor's degree. **Support services:** Learning center, remedial instruction, study skills assistance, tutoring, writing center.

**Majors. Biology:** General. **Business:** Accounting, accounting/finance, business admin, communications, international, management information systems. **Communications:** General. **Computer sciences:** General. **Conservation:** Environmental science, environmental studies. **Education:** General, English, learning disabled, music, physical, science, social science, social studies, special. **Foreign languages:** French, German, Japanese, Spanish. **Health:** Athletic training. **History:** General. **Liberal arts:** Arts/sciences, humanities. **Math:** General. **Parks/recreation:** General, health/fitness, sports admin. **Philosophy/religion:** Philosophy, religion. **Physical sciences:** Chemistry. **Psychology:** General. **Public administration:** Community org/advocacy. **Social sciences:** General, economics, geography, international relations, political science, sociology. **Theology:** Sacred music. **Visual/performing arts:** Art, art history/conservation, arts management, theater arts management. **Other:** Sustainable business.

**Most popular majors.** Biology 6%, business/marketing 31%, communications/journalism 6%, education 11%, social sciences 9%.

**Computing on campus.** 162 workstations in dormitories, library, computer center, student center. Dormitories wired for high-speed internet access and linked to campus network. Commuter students can connect to campus network. Online library, helpline, wireless network available.

**Student life. Freshman orientation:** Mandatory, $100 fee. Preregistration for classes offered. 3 days during week before fall classes begin. Includes start of common freshman class. **Policies:** Students serve on administrative and faculty committees. **Housing:** Guaranteed on-campus for freshmen. Coed dorms, single-sex dorms, apartments, wellness housing available. $100 deposit, deadline 8/15. **Activities:** Jazz band, campus ministries, choral groups, dance, drama, international student organizations, literary magazine, music ensembles, radio station, student government, student newspaper, community action volunteers, social action commission, community senate, Bible Study, College Democrats, College Republicans, Catholic studies club, Habitat for Humanity.

**Athletics.** NAIA. **Intercollegiate:** Baseball M, basketball, cross-country, golf, soccer, softball W, tennis, track and field, volleyball W. **Intramural:** Basketball, bowling, fencing M, golf, ice hockey M, lacrosse, skiing, soccer, softball, tennis, volleyball. **Team name:** Saints.

**Student services.** Adult student services, alcohol/substance abuse counseling, chaplain/spiritual director, career counseling, services for economically disadvantaged, student employment services, financial aid counseling, health services, minority student services, personal counseling, placement for graduates, veterans' counselor, women's services. **Physically disabled:** Services for visually, speech, hearing impaired.

**Contact.** E-mail: admissions@aquinas.edu
Phone: (616) 632-2900 Toll-free number: (800) 678-9593
Fax: (616) 732-4469
Angela Schlosser-Bacon, Director of Admissions, Aquinas College, 1607 Robinson Road Southeast, Grand Rapids, MI 49506-1799

## Art Institute of Michigan
**Novi, Michigan**
**www.artinstitutes.edu/detroit**

- For-profit 4-year branch campus and visual arts college
- Large city
- 300 degree-seeking undergraduates
- Application essay, interview required

**General.** Regionally accredited; also accredited by ACCSC. **Calendar:** Quarter. **Full-time faculty:** 3 total. **Part-time faculty:** 27 total.

**Basis for selection.** Academic record and interview very important. SAT or ACT recommended. **Homeschooled:** Transcript of courses and grades, state high school equivalency certificate required.

**2009-2010 Annual costs.** Tuition/fees: $21,105. Required fees vary by program.

**Application procedures. Admission:** Closing date 10/12 (receipt date). $50 fee, may be waived for applicants with need. Admission notification on a rolling basis. **Financial aid:** Closing date 10/12.

**Academics. Credit/placement by examination:** CLEP, SAT, ACT.

**Majors. Business:** Fashion. **Communications:** Advertising. **Personal/culinary services:** Restaurant/catering. **Visual/performing arts:** Interior design. **Other:** Interactive media design, Visual communications.

**Contact.** Phone: (248) 675-3800
Senior Director of Admissions, Art Institute of Michigan, 28125 Cabot Drive, Suite 120, Novi, MI 48377

## Baker College of Allen Park
**Allen Park, Michigan**
**www.baker.edu**

- Private 4-year business and health science college
- Commuter campus in large city
- 3,384 degree-seeking undergraduates

**General.** Regionally accredited. **Degrees:** 48 bachelor's, 210 associate awarded. **Location:** 10 miles from Detroit. **Calendar:** Quarter, limited summer session. **Full-time faculty:** 5 total. **Part-time faculty:** 100 total.

**Basis for selection.** Open admission, but selective for some programs. **Homeschooled:** Transcript of courses and grades required.

**2009-2010 Annual costs.** Tuition/fees: $8,775.

**Application procedures. Admission:** No deadline. $20 fee, may be waived for applicants with need. Admission notification on a rolling basis.

**Academics. Special study options:** Combined bachelor's/graduate degree, cooperative education, distance learning, double major, dual enrollment of high school students, independent study, internships, teacher certification program. **Credit/placement by examination:** CLEP. **Support services:** Learning center, remedial instruction, study skills assistance, tutoring.

**Majors. Business:** Human resources. **Computer sciences:** Information technology. **Education:** Elementary, middle, secondary. **Health:** Health services. **Public administration:** Human services.

**Computing on campus.** 208 workstations in library, computer center, student center. Online library, helpline, wireless network available.

**Student life. Freshman orientation:** Mandatory.

**Contact.** Phone: (313) 425-3700
Steve Peterson, Vice President for Admissions, Baker College of Allen Park, 4500 Enterprise Drive, Allen Park, MI 48101

## Baker College of Auburn Hills
### Auburn Hills, Michigan
www.baker.edu                    CB code: 1457

- Private 4-year business and technical college
- Commuter campus in small city
- 4,285 degree-seeking undergraduates

**General.** Founded in 1990. Regionally accredited. Part of multi-campus system specializing in career education. **Degrees:** 169 bachelor's, 351 associate awarded. **Location:** 30 miles from Detroit. **Calendar:** Quarter, limited summer session. **Full-time faculty:** 10 total. **Part-time faculty:** 150 total. **Class size:** 45% < 20, 55% 20-39.

**Basis for selection.** Open admission. Specific entrance requirements for allied health programs and bachelor of business leadership degree program. Interview recommended.

**2009-2010 Annual costs.** Tuition/fees: $8,775. Books/supplies: $1,000.

**Financial aid. Non-need-based:** Scholarships awarded for academics, alumni affiliation.

**Application procedures. Admission:** No deadline. $20 fee, may be waived for applicants with need. Admission notification on a rolling basis. **Financial aid:** Priority date 2/21, closing date 9/1. FAFSA, institutional form required. Applicants notified on a rolling basis starting 4/1.

**Academics.** 2+2 system allows students to begin required courses in major while completing associate degree. **Special study options:** Accelerated study, combined bachelor's/graduate degree, distance learning, double major, dual enrollment of high school students, independent study, internships, liberal arts/career combination, teacher certification program. **Credit/placement by examination:** AP, CLEP, IB, institutional tests. 48 credit hours maximum toward associate degree, 96 toward bachelor's. **Support services:** Learning center, reduced course load, remedial instruction, study skills assistance, tutoring, writing center.

**Majors. Business:** General, accounting, business admin, management science. **Education:** General, elementary, middle, multi-level teacher, secondary.

**Computing on campus.** 131 workstations in library, computer center, student center. Commuter students can connect to campus network. Helpline available.

**Student life. Freshman orientation:** Mandatory. **Activities:** Accounting club, management club, interior design society, society of automotive engineers, marketing club.

**Student services.** Career counseling, student employment services, financial aid counseling, personal counseling, placement for graduates, veterans' counselor. **Physically disabled:** Services for visually, hearing impaired.

**Contact.** Phone: (248) 340-0600 Toll-free number: (888) 429-0410
Fax: (248) 340-0600
Jan Bohlen, Vice President for Admissions, Baker College of Auburn Hills, 1500 University Drive, Auburn Hills, MI 48326

## Baker College of Cadillac
### Cadillac, Michigan
www.baker.edu                    CB code: 1381

- Private 4-year business and health science college
- Commuter campus in large town
- 2,070 degree-seeking undergraduates

**General.** Founded in 1911. Regionally accredited. Part of multicampus system specializing in career education. **Degrees:** 39 bachelor's, 132 associate awarded. **Location:** 90 miles from Grand Rapids, 45 miles from Traverse City. **Calendar:** Quarter, limited summer session. **Full-time faculty:** 5 total. **Part-time faculty:** 100 total. **Class size:** 68% < 20, 31% 20-39, 1% 40-49. **Special facilities:** Mock operating room, massage therapy room.

**Basis for selection.** Open admission. Some allied health programs require health appraisal. Interview recommended.

**2009-2010 Annual costs.** Tuition/fees: $8,775. Books/supplies: $1,000.

**Financial aid. Non-need-based:** Scholarships awarded for academics.

**Application procedures. Admission:** No deadline. $20 fee, may be waived for applicants with need. Admission notification on a rolling basis beginning on or about 10/1. **Financial aid:** Priority date 2/21; no closing date. FAFSA, institutional form required. Applicants notified on a rolling basis starting 5/1.

**Academics. Special study options:** Accelerated study, combined bachelor's/graduate degree, cooperative education, distance learning, double major, dual enrollment of high school students, external degree, independent study, internships, liberal arts/career combination, weekend college. 2+2 bachelor's degree and bachelor of business leadership degree. **Credit/placement by examination:** AP, CLEP, IB, institutional tests. 48 credit hours maximum toward associate degree, 96 toward bachelor's. **Support services:** Learning center, reduced course load, remedial instruction, study skills assistance, tutoring, writing center.

**Majors. Business:** Accounting, business admin, human resources, office management. **Computer sciences:** Computer science. **Public administration:** Human services.

**Computing on campus.** 154 workstations in library, computer center. Commuter students can connect to campus network. Online library, helpline, repair service available.

**Student life. Freshman orientation:** Mandatory. Preregistration for classes offered. **Activities:** Student activities group, professional student organizations.

**Student services.** Career counseling, student employment services, financial aid counseling, personal counseling, placement for graduates, veterans' counselor. **Physically disabled:** Services for visually, hearing impaired.

**Contact.** E-mail: mike.tisdale@baker.edu
Phone: (231) 876-3100 Toll-free number: (888) 313-3463
Fax: (231) 775-8505
Mike Tisdale, Director of Admissions, Baker College of Cadillac, 9600 East 13th Street, Cadillac, MI 49601

## Baker College of Clinton Township
### Clinton Township, Michigan
www.baker.edu                    CB code: 1386

- Private 4-year business and technical college
- Commuter campus in very large city
- 6,455 degree-seeking undergraduates

**General.** Founded in 1911. Regionally accredited. Part of multicampus system specializing in career education. **Degrees:** 212 bachelor's, 396 associate awarded. **Location:** 15 miles from Detroit. **Calendar:** Quarter, limited summer session. **Full-time faculty:** 20 total. **Part-time faculty:** 195 total. **Class size:** 25% < 20, 74% 20-39, less than 1% 40-49.

**Basis for selection.** Open admission, but selective for some programs. Physical exam may be required for some programs. Interview recommended. **Learning Disabled:** Students must complete special needs intake form signed by professional.

**High school preparation.** Recommended units include English 4, mathematics 4, social studies 2, science 3 and foreign language 4.

**2009-2010 Annual costs.** Tuition/fees: $8,775. Books/supplies: $1,000. Personal expenses: $2,000.

**Financial aid. Non-need-based:** Scholarships awarded for academics, minority status.

**Application procedures. Admission:** Priority date 9/1; no deadline. $20 fee, may be waived for applicants with need. Admission notification on a rolling basis. **Financial aid:** Priority date 2/21, closing date 9/1. FAFSA, institutional form required. Applicants notified on a rolling basis starting 4/1.

**Academics.** 2+2 system allows students to begin required courses in major while completing associate degree. **Special study options:** Accelerated study, combined bachelor's/graduate degree, cooperative education, distance learning, double major, dual enrollment of high school students, external degree, independent study, internships, teacher certification program. **Credit/placement by examination:** AP, CLEP, IB, institutional tests. 48 credit hours maximum toward associate degree, 96 toward bachelor's. **Support services:** Learning center, reduced course load, remedial instruction, study skills assistance, tutoring, writing center.

**Majors. Business:** Accounting, administrative services, business admin, human resources, management science, office management. **Computer sciences:** General, computer science. **Education:** Elementary, middle, multi-level teacher, secondary. **Health:** Health care admin, nursing (RN), office admin. **Public administration:** Human services.

**Computing on campus.** 120 workstations in library, computer center. Commuter students can connect to campus network. Helpline available.

**Student life. Freshman orientation:** Mandatory. Preregistration for classes offered.

**Student services.** Adult student services, career counseling, student employment services, financial aid counseling, personal counseling, placement for graduates, veterans' counselor. **Physically disabled:** Services for visually, hearing impaired.

**Contact.** E-mail: adm_mc@baker.edu
Phone: (586) 791-3000 Toll-free number: (888) 272-2842
Fax: (586) 791-6610
Annette Looser, Director of Admissions, Baker College of Clinton Township, 34950 Little Mack Avenue, Clinton Township, MI 48035

## Baker College of Flint
Flint, Michigan
www.baker.edu                                        CB code: 0806

- Private 4-year business and technical college
- Commuter campus in large city
- 7,305 degree-seeking undergraduates

**General.** Founded in 1911. Regionally accredited. Corporate services division offers degree-granting programs on campus and/or at work site, coordinated with corporate training and professional development programs. Part of multicampus system specializing in career education. **Degrees:** 203 bachelor's, 557 associate awarded; master's offered. **Location:** 10 miles from downtown, 60 miles from Detroit. **Calendar:** Quarter, limited summer session. **Full-time faculty:** 40 total. **Part-time faculty:** 300 total. **Special facilities:** Polysommnography sleep lab, orthotic/prosthetic lab.

**Freshman class profile.**

Out-of-state:               2%       Live on campus:              5%

**Basis for selection.** Open admission, but selective for some programs. Health applicants must have health appraisal. Occupational therapy applicants must present minimum of 1 year biology, 1 year chemistry/physics, 2 years math including algebra or equivalent. All health programs require 2.0 GPA for entrance to professional classes. Class size may be limited. Trucking programs require drug screening prior to enrollment acceptance. Interview recommended.

**2009-2010 Annual costs.** Tuition/fees: $8,775. Additional fees vary with program. Room only: $2,700. Books/supplies: $900.

**Financial aid. Non-need-based:** Scholarships awarded for academics, minority status.

**Application procedures. Admission:** Priority date 9/1; no deadline. $20 fee, may be waived for applicants with need. Admission notification on a rolling basis. **Financial aid:** Priority date 2/21, closing date 9/1. FAFSA, institutional form required. Applicants notified on a rolling basis starting 4/1.

**Academics.** 2+2 system allows students to begin required courses in major while completing associate degree. Calendar based on 10-week quarters. **Special study options:** Accelerated study, combined bachelor's/graduate degree, cooperative education, distance learning, double major, dual enrollment of high school students, external degree, independent study, internships. **Credit/placement by examination:** AP, CLEP, IB, institutional tests. 48 credit hours maximum toward associate degree, 96 toward bachelor's.

**Support services:** Learning center, reduced course load, remedial instruction, study skills assistance, tutoring, writing center.

**Majors. Business:** Accounting, business admin, management information systems, office management, operations. **Computer sciences:** General. **Education:** Elementary, middle, multi-level teacher, secondary. **Engineering:** Mechanical. **Engineering technology:** Electrical. **Health:** Health care admin, medical records admin, nursing (RN). **Transportation:** Aviation management. **Visual/performing arts:** Commercial/advertising art, interior design.

**Most popular majors.** Business/marketing 65%, health sciences 25%.

**Computing on campus.** 300 workstations in library, computer center. Commuter students can connect to campus network. Helpline available.

**Student life. Freshman orientation:** Mandatory. Preregistration for classes offered. **Housing:** Guaranteed on-campus for freshmen. Coed dorms, wellness housing available. $50 deposit, deadline 9/20. **Activities:** Literary magazine, National Association of Accountants, American Marketing Association, Interior Design Society, travel club, environmental club, physical therapy assistant club, medical assistants student organization, Health Information Management Association, graphic communications club, Society of Manufacturing Engineers student chapter.

**Athletics. Intramural:** Basketball, volleyball.

**Student services.** Career counseling, student employment services, on-campus daycare, personal counseling, placement for graduates, veterans' counselor. **Physically disabled:** Services for visually, hearing impaired.

**Contact.** E-mail: adm-fl@baker.edu
Phone: (810) 766-4000 Toll-free number: (800) 964-4299
Fax: (810) 766-4293
Jodi Cuneaz, Director of Admissions, Baker College of Flint, 1050 West Bristol Road, Flint, MI 48507

## Baker College of Jackson
Jackson, Michigan
www.baker.edu                                        CB code: 1887

- Private 4-year business and technical college
- Commuter campus in small city
- 2,432 degree-seeking undergraduates

**General.** Founded in 1994. Regionally accredited. Part of multicampus system specializing in career education. **Degrees:** 91 bachelor's, 173 associate awarded. **Location:** 40 miles from Lansing, 40 miles from Ann Arbor. **Calendar:** Quarter, limited summer session. **Full-time faculty:** 5 total. **Part-time faculty:** 95 total.

**Basis for selection.** Open admission, but selective for some programs. Physical exam may be required for allied health programs. All health programs require specific GPA. Interview recommended.

**2009-2010 Annual costs.** Tuition/fees: $8,775. Books/supplies: $975.

**Financial aid. Non-need-based:** Scholarships awarded for academics, minority status.

**Application procedures. Admission:** No deadline. $20 fee, may be waived for applicants with need. Admission notification on a rolling basis. **Financial aid:** Priority date 2/21, closing date 9/1. FAFSA, institutional form required. Applicants notified on a rolling basis starting 4/1.

**Academics.** 2+2 system allows students to begin required courses in major while completing associate degree. **Special study options:** Accelerated study, combined bachelor's/graduate degree, cooperative education, distance learning, double major, dual enrollment of high school students, external degree, independent study, internships. **Credit/placement by examination:** AP, CLEP, IB, institutional tests. 48 credit hours maximum toward associate degree, 96 toward bachelor's. **Support services:** Learning center, reduced course load, remedial instruction, study skills assistance, tutoring, writing center.

**Majors. Business:** General, accounting. **Education:** Elementary, middle, multi-level teacher, secondary.

**Computing on campus.** 114 workstations in library, computer center. Commuter students can connect to campus network. Helpline available.

**Student life. Freshman orientation:** Mandatory. Preregistration for classes offered. **Activities:** Student government.

**Student services.** Career counseling, student employment services, personal counseling, placement for graduates, veterans' counselor. **Physically disabled:** Services for visually, hearing impaired.

**Contact.** E-mail: adm-jk@baker.edu
Phone: (517) 788-7800 Toll-free number: (888) 343-3683
Fax: (517) 789-7331
Kevin Pnacek, Vice President for Admissions, Baker College of Jackson, 2800 Springport Road, Jackson, MI 49202

## Baker College of Muskegon
**Muskegon, Michigan**
www.baker.edu                                    CB code: 1527

- Private 4-year business and technical college
- Commuter campus in small city
- 6,132 degree-seeking undergraduates

**General.** Founded in 1888. Regionally accredited. Part of multicampus system specializing in career education. All associate degree programs include internship, co-op or clinical affiliation experience. **Degrees:** 161 bachelor's, 520 associate awarded. **Location:** 40 miles from Grand Rapids. **Calendar:** Quarter, limited summer session. **Full-time faculty:** 20 total. **Part-time faculty:** 170 total. **Class size:** 38% < 20, 57% 20-39, 3% 40-49, 2% 50-99. **Special facilities:** Restaurant run by culinary and food and beverage management students.

**Basis for selection.** Open admission, but selective for some programs. 2.75 GPA required for admission to occupational therapy assisting, physical therapist assisting, veterinary technician, surgical technology, teacher preparation. Class size may be limited in some programs. Physical examination, background check required for some programs. Interview recommended. **Homeschooled:** Basic skills placement assessments in math, language arts, and reading part of orientation/registration process. **Learning Disabled:** Learning disability must be documented and presented to counseling staff before registering for classes.

**2009-2010 Annual costs.** Tuition/fees: $8,775. Room only: $2,965. Books/supplies: $975. Personal expenses: $2,000.

**Financial aid. Non-need-based:** Scholarships awarded for academics, minority status.

**Application procedures. Admission:** Priority date 9/1; no deadline. $20 fee, may be waived for applicants with need. Admission notification on a rolling basis. **Financial aid:** Priority date 2/21; no closing date. FAFSA, institutional form required. Applicants notified on a rolling basis starting 4/1.

**Academics.** 2+2 system allows students to begin required courses in major while completing associate degree. Maximum number of credits awarded for prior work and/or life experiences, 48 for associate and 144 for bachelor. **Special study options:** Accelerated study, combined bachelor's/graduate degree, cooperative education, distance learning, double major, dual enrollment of high school students, external degree, independent study, internships, liberal arts/career combination, teacher certification program. Accelerated bachelor of business administration offered in weekend delivery format. **Credit/placement by examination:** AP, CLEP, IB, institutional tests. 48 credit hours maximum toward associate degree, 144 toward bachelor's. **Support services:** Learning center, reduced course load, remedial instruction, study skills assistance, tutoring.

**Majors. Business:** Accounting, accounting/business management, administrative services, business admin, human resources, management science, marketing, office management, restaurant/food services. **Computer sciences:** General, computer science, information systems, systems analysis. **Education:** Elementary, kindergarten/preschool, middle, multi-level teacher, secondary. **Engineering technology:** Industrial management. **Health:** Health care admin. **Personal/culinary services:** General, culinary arts, restaurant/catering. **Public administration:** Human services. **Transportation:** Aviation management.

**Computing on campus.** 180 workstations in dormitories, library, computer center. Dormitories wired for high-speed internet access and linked to campus network. Commuter students can connect to campus network. Online course registration, online library, helpline, wireless network available.

**Student life. Freshman orientation:** Mandatory. Preregistration for classes offered. 3-4 hour session prior to start of quarter; includes COMPASS testing, registration, academic advising. **Policies:** No drug or alcohol use permitted anywhere on campus or in residence halls. **Housing:** Coed dorms, special housing for disabled, apartments, wellness housing available. $50 deposit, deadline 9/1. **Activities:** Student government, travel club, rehab club, residence hall association, culinary arts club, human resource management club.

**Athletics. Intramural:** Bowling.

**Student services.** Adult student services, career counseling, student employment services, financial aid counseling, personal counseling, placement for graduates, veterans' counselor. **Physically disabled:** Services for visually, hearing impaired.

**Contact.** E-mail: kathy.jacobson@baker.edu
Phone: (231) 777-5200 Toll-free number: (800) 937-0337
Fax: (231) 777-5201
Kathy Jacobson, Vice President and Director of Admissions, Baker College of Muskegon, 1903 Marquette Avenue, Muskegon, MI 49442

## Baker College of Owosso
**Owosso, Michigan**
www.baker.edu                                    CB code: 5270

- Private 4-year business and technical college
- Commuter campus in large town
- 3,637 degree-seeking undergraduates

**General.** Founded in 1911. Regionally accredited. Part of multicampus system, with affiliated graduate school, specializing in career education. Master's degree available at Flint campus. **Degrees:** 65 bachelor's, 280 associate awarded. **Location:** 30 miles from Lansing, 300 miles from Flint. **Calendar:** Quarter, limited summer session. **Full-time faculty:** 10 total. **Part-time faculty:** 150 total. **Special facilities:** Diesel technology center.

**Freshman class profile.**

| | | | |
|---|---|---|---|
| Out-of-state: | 3% | Live on campus: | 30% |

**Basis for selection.** Open admission. Limited enrollment for medical programs.

**2009-2010 Annual costs.** Tuition/fees: $8,775. Room only: $2,700. Books/supplies: $1,000.

**Financial aid. Non-need-based:** Scholarships awarded for academics, minority status.

**Application procedures. Admission:** Priority date 9/1; no deadline. $20 fee, may be waived for applicants with need. Admission notification on a rolling basis. **Financial aid:** Priority date 2/21, closing date 9/1. FAFSA, institutional form required. Applicants notified on a rolling basis starting 4/1.

**Academics.** 2+2 system allows students to begin required courses in major while completing associate degree. **Special study options:** Accelerated study, combined bachelor's/graduate degree, cooperative education, distance learning, double major, dual enrollment of high school students, external degree, independent study, internships. **Credit/placement by examination:** AP, CLEP, IB, institutional tests. 48 credit hours maximum toward associate degree, 96 toward bachelor's. **Support services:** Learning center, reduced course load, remedial instruction, study skills assistance, tutoring, writing center.

**Majors. Business:** Accounting, administrative services, business admin, human resources, management information systems, marketing, office management. **Communications technology:** Graphics. **Computer sciences:** General, computer graphics, computer science. **Education:** Elementary, middle, multi-level teacher, secondary. **Health:** Health care admin. **Public administration:** Human services.

**Computing on campus.** 226 workstations in dormitories, library, computer center. Dormitories wired for high-speed internet access. Commuter students can connect to campus network. Online library, helpline available.

**Student life. Freshman orientation:** Mandatory. Preregistration for classes offered. **Housing:** Guaranteed on-campus for freshmen. Coed dorms, wellness housing available. $50 deposit. **Activities:** Student newspaper, accounting club, MLT club, interior design club, radiology club, graphics club.

**Athletics. Intramural:** Basketball, volleyball.

**Student services.** Adult student services, career counseling, services for economically disadvantaged, student employment services, financial aid counseling, on-campus daycare, personal counseling, placement for graduates, veterans' counselor. **Physically disabled:** Services for visually, speech, hearing impaired.

**Contact.** E-mail: michael.konopacke@baker.edu
Phone: (989) 729-3350 Toll-free number: (800) 879-3797
Fax: (989) 729-3359
Michael Konopacke, Vice President of Admissions, Baker College of Owosso, 1020 South Washington Street, Owosso, MI 48867

## Baker College of Port Huron
**Port Huron, Michigan**
www.baker.edu                    CB code: 1413

- Private 4-year business and technical college
- Commuter campus in large town
- 1,984 degree-seeking undergraduates

**General.** Founded in 1911. Regionally accredited. Part of multicampus system specializing in career education. **Degrees:** 62 bachelor's, 178 associate awarded; master's offered. **Location:** 60 miles from Detroit. **Calendar:** Quarter, limited summer session. **Full-time faculty:** 10 total. **Part-time faculty:** 115 total. **Class size:** 58% < 20, 37% 20-39, 1% 40-49, 4% 50-99. **Special facilities:** Dental hygiene clinic.

**Basis for selection.** Open admission, but selective for some programs. Specific entrance requirements for health and human services programs. Waiting list for Dental Hygiene. Interview recommended.

**2009-2010 Annual costs.** Tuition/fees: $8,775. Books/supplies: $1,000. Personal expenses: $2,000.

**Financial aid.** All financial aid based on need.

**Application procedures. Admission:** Priority date 9/1; no deadline. $20 fee, may be waived for applicants with need. Admission notification on a rolling basis. **Financial aid:** Priority date 2/21; no closing date. FAFSA, institutional form required. Applicants notified on a rolling basis starting 4/1.

**Academics.** 2+2 system allows students to begin required courses in major while completing associate degree. Accelerated BBA available. **Special study options:** Accelerated study, combined bachelor's/graduate degree, cooperative education, distance learning, double major, dual enrollment of high school students, external degree, independent study, internships, liberal arts/career combination. **Credit/placement by examination:** AP, CLEP, IB, institutional tests. 48 credit hours maximum toward associate degree, 96 toward bachelor's. **Support services:** Learning center, reduced course load, remedial instruction, study skills assistance, tutoring, writing center.

**Majors. Business:** General, accounting, administrative services, business admin, human resources, international, management information systems, marketing, office management. **Computer sciences:** General, computer science, information systems. **Health:** Health care admin.

**Computing on campus.** 229 workstations in library, computer center. Commuter students can connect to campus network. Online course registration, helpline available.

**Student life. Freshman orientation:** Mandatory. Preregistration for classes offered. **Activities:** Dental hygiene society.

**Student services.** Adult student services, career counseling, student employment services, personal counseling, placement for graduates, veterans' counselor. **Physically disabled:** Services for visually, hearing impaired.

**Contact.** E-mail: daniel.kenny@baker.edu
Phone: (810) 985-7000 Toll-free number: (888) 262-2442
Fax: (810) 985-7066
Dan Kenny, Vice President of Admissions, Baker College of Port Huron, 3403 Lapeer Road, Port Huron, MI 48060-2597

## Calvin College
**Grand Rapids, Michigan**          CB member
www.calvin.edu                      CB code: 1095

- Private 4-year liberal arts college affiliated with Christian Reformed Church
- Residential campus in large city
- 3,939 degree-seeking undergraduates: 2% part-time, 54% women, 2% African American, 3% Asian American, 2% Hispanic American, 8% international
- 43 degree-seeking graduate students
- 93% of applicants admitted
- SAT or ACT (ACT writing optional), application essay required
- 75% graduate within 6 years; 41% enter graduate study

**General.** Founded in 1876. Regionally accredited. **Degrees:** 882 bachelor's awarded; master's offered. **ROTC:** Army. **Location:** 150 miles from Detroit and Chicago. **Calendar:** 4-1-4, limited summer session. **Full-time faculty:** 326 total; 82% have terminal degrees, 10% minority, 34% women.

**Part-time faculty:** 69 total; 17% have terminal degrees, 3% minority, 52% women. **Class size:** 39% < 20, 58% 20-39, 1% 40-49, 1% 50-99. **Special facilities:** Ecosystem preserve and interpretive center, electron microscope, rhetoric center, observatory.

**Freshman class profile.** 2,529 applied, 2,346 admitted, 945 enrolled.

| Mid 50% test scores | | | |
|---|---|---|---|
| SAT critical reading: | 520-670 | Rank in top quarter: | 57% |
| SAT math: | 550-660 | Rank in top tenth: | 29% |
| ACT composite: | 23-29 | End year in good standing: | 91% |
| GPA 3.75 or higher: | 44% | Return as sophomores: | 86% |
| GPA 3.50-3.74: | 22% | Out-of-state: | 48% |
| GPA 3.0-3.49: | 23% | Live on campus: | 96% |
| GPA 2.0-2.99: | 11% | International: | 8% |

**Basis for selection.** Genuine interest in Christian goals of college and 2.5 GPA required. Recommendation, personal statement important. Minimum 20 ACT or 470 SAT Verbal and 470 SAT Math recommended. GED accepted only for those age 19 years or over. SAT Subject Tests recommended. **Homeschooled:** Must provide some form of transcript with grades.

**High school preparation.** College-preparatory program recommended. 12 units required; 17 recommended. Required and recommended units include English 3-4, mathematics 3, social studies 2-3, science 2 (laboratory 1), foreign language 2 and academic electives 3. Math must include algebra and geometry.

**2009-2010 Annual costs.** Tuition/fees: $24,035. Room/board: $8,275. Books/supplies: $980. Personal expenses: $1,150.

**2008-2009 Financial aid. Need-based:** 778 full-time freshmen applied for aid; 599 were judged to have need; 598 of these received aid. Average need met was 84%. Average scholarship/grant was $10,791; average loan $4,625. 58% of total undergraduate aid awarded as scholarships/grants, 42% as loans/jobs. **Non-need-based:** Awarded to 1,831 full-time undergraduates, including 479 freshmen. Scholarships awarded for academics, alumni affiliation, art, leadership, minority status, music/drama, religious affiliation, state residency.

**Application procedures. Admission:** Closing date 8/15 (postmark date). $35 fee, may be waived for applicants with need. Admission notification on a rolling basis beginning on or about 11/1. Must reply by May 1 or within 4 week(s) if notified thereafter. **Financial aid:** Priority date 2/15; no closing date. FAFSA required. Applicants notified on a rolling basis starting 3/15.

**Academics.** Importance of faith perspective in all disciplines and co-curricular activities emphasized. **Special study options:** Accelerated study, combined bachelor's/graduate degree, double major, dual enrollment of high school students, honors, independent study, internships, student-designed major, study abroad, teacher certification program, urban semester, Washington semester. Overseas programs with Central College, January interim exchange with other colleges, academically-based service-learning. **Credit/placement by examination:** AP, CLEP, IB, institutional tests. **Support services:** Learning center, reduced course load, remedial instruction, study skills assistance, tutoring, writing center.

**Majors. Area/ethnic studies:** Asian. **Biology:** General, biochemistry, biotechnology. **Business:** General, accounting, business admin, communications, management information systems. **Communications:** General, digital media, media studies. **Computer sciences:** General, computer science, information systems, networking, programming. **Conservation:** Environmental science. **Education:** General, art, bilingual, biology, chemistry, Deaf/hearing impaired, early childhood, elementary, English, French, German, history, mathematics, mentally handicapped, middle, music, physical, physics, reading, science, secondary, social science, social studies, Spanish, special, speech impaired. **Engineering:** General, chemical, civil, electrical, mechanical. **Foreign languages:** Ancient Greek, Biblical, Chinese, classics, Dutch/Flemish, French, German, Japanese, Latin, modern Greek, Spanish. **Health:** Athletic training, audiology/speech pathology, communication disorders, nursing (RN), predental, premedicine, prepharmacy, preveterinary, recreational therapy, speech pathology. **History:** General, American, European. **Interdisciplinary:** Biological/physical sciences, classical/archaeology, natural sciences. **Legal studies:** Prelaw. **Liberal arts:** Arts/sciences. **Math:** General. **Parks/recreation:** General, exercise sciences, health/fitness. **Philosophy/religion:** Philosophy, religion. **Physical sciences:** Chemistry, geology, physics. **Psychology:** General. **Public administration:** General, social work. **Social sciences:** General, economics, geography, international economic development, international relations, political science, sociology. **Theology:** Bible, sacred music. **Visual/performing arts:** General, art, art history/conservation, cinematography, conducting, dramatic, film/cinema, music history, music performance, music theory/composition, piano/organ, studio arts, voice/opera.

**Most popular majors.** Business/marketing 13%, education 8%, engineering/engineering technologies 6%, foreign language 8%, health sciences 8%, social sciences 9%, visual/performing arts 9%.

**Computing on campus.** 900 workstations in dormitories, library, computer center. Dormitories wired for high-speed internet access and linked to campus network. Commuter students can connect to campus network. Online course registration, online library, helpline, student web hosting, wireless network available.

**Student life. Freshman orientation:** Mandatory, $225 fee. 2-day program held in summer. **Policies:** Strong emphasis on student leadership and service. Religious observance strongly expected and encouraged. First- and second-year students (under 21) not living at home required to live in residence halls. **Housing:** Guaranteed on-campus for freshmen. Single-sex dorms, apartments available. $50 deposit, deadline 5/1. Project Neighborhood houses available. **Activities:** Bands, campus ministries, choral groups, dance, drama, film society, international student organizations, literary magazine, music ensembles, Model UN, musical theater, student government, student newspaper, symphony orchestra, Amnesty International, Asia Club, Calvin College Democrats, Calvin College Conservatives, Democracy Matters, Engineers Without Borders, Environmental Stewardship, Global Business Brigades, International Health and Development.

**Athletics.** NCAA. **Intercollegiate:** Baseball M, basketball, cross-country, diving, golf, soccer, softball W, swimming, tennis, track and field, volleyball W. **Intramural:** Badminton, basketball, football (non-tackle), golf, racquetball, soccer, softball, swimming, table tennis, tennis, track and field, volleyball, water polo. **Team name:** Knights.

**Student services.** Adult student services, alcohol/substance abuse counseling, chaplain/spiritual director, career counseling, student employment services, financial aid counseling, health services, minority student services, personal counseling, placement for graduates. **Physically disabled:** Services for visually, speech, hearing impaired.

**Contact.** E-mail: admissions@calvin.edu
Phone: (616) 526-6106 Toll-free number: (800) 688-0122
Fax: (616) 526-6777
Dale Kuiper, Director of Admissions and Financial Aid, Calvin College, 3201 Burton Street Southeast, Grand Rapids, MI 49546

## Central Michigan University
**Mount Pleasant, Michigan**

www.cmich.edu

CB member

CB code: 1106

- Public 4-year university
- Residential campus in large town
- 20,141 degree-seeking undergraduates: 10% part-time, 55% women, 6% African American, 1% Asian American, 2% Hispanic American, 1% Native American, 1% international
- 6,254 degree-seeking graduate students
- 73% of applicants admitted
- ACT (writing recommended) required
- 57% graduate within 6 years

**General.** Founded in 1892. Regionally accredited. 60 off-campus locations in the United States and surrounding countries. **Degrees:** 3,571 bachelor's awarded; master's, doctoral, professional offered. **ROTC:** Army. **Location:** 70 miles from Lansing. **Calendar:** Semester, limited summer session. **Full-time faculty:** 752 total; 81% have terminal degrees, 17% minority, 40% women. **Part-time faculty:** 438 total; 26% have terminal degrees, 11% minority, 51% women. **Class size:** 33% < 20, 44% 20-39, 12% 40-49, 8% 50-99, 3% >100. **Special facilities:** Center for clinical care and education, English language institute, center for applied research and rural studies, Michigan services for children and young adults who are deaf-blind, psychological training and consultation center, language learning center, biological station, conservation genetics lab, water research center, museum of cultural and natural history, historical library, 255-acre natural woodland.

**Freshman class profile.** 16,887 applied, 12,273 admitted, 3,691 enrolled.

| Mid 50% test scores | | | |
|---|---|---|---|
| SAT critical reading: | 440-560 | Rank in top tenth: | 16% |
| SAT math: | 450-570 | End year in good standing: | 77% |
| ACT composite: | 20-25 | Return as sophomores: | 76% |
| GPA 3.75 or higher: | 19% | Out-of-state: | 3% |
| GPA 3.50-3.74: | 19% | Live on campus: | 96% |
| GPA 3.0-3.49: | 39% | International: | 1% |
| GPA 2.0-2.99: | 23% | Fraternities: | 4% |
| Rank in top quarter: | 41% | Sororities: | 6% |

**Basis for selection.** School achievement record, test scores, and recommendations are important. Transfer students with over 30 credits are not required to take the ACT. Interview and essay are recommended of some. Auditions may be required for music majors. **Learning Disabled:** Students

are prompted to register with Student Disability Services following admission.

**High school preparation.** College-preparatory program recommended. 20 units recommended. Recommended units include English 4, mathematics 4, social studies 2, history 2, science 4 (laboratory 1), foreign language 2, computer science 1 and visual/performing arts 1.

**2009-2010 Annual costs.** Tuition/fees: $10,170; $23,670 out-of-state. Room/board: $7,896. Books/supplies: $1,000. Personal expenses: $1,050.

**2008-2009 Financial aid. Need-based:** 3,139 full-time freshmen applied for aid; 2,198 were judged to have need; 2,150 of these received aid. Average need met was 83%. Average scholarship/grant was $5,822; average loan $5,410. 36% of total undergraduate aid awarded as scholarships/grants, 64% as loans/jobs. **Non-need-based:** Awarded to 2,320 full-time undergraduates, including 734 freshmen. Scholarships awarded for academics, alumni affiliation, art, athletics, leadership, minority status, music/drama, ROTC, state residency. **Additional information:** Tuition waiver for Native American students qualifying under state program criteria.

**Application procedures. Admission:** Priority date 10/1; deadline 7/1 (receipt date). $35 fee, may be waived for applicants with need. Admission notification on a rolling basis beginning on or about 9/1. Must reply by May 1 or within 2 week(s) if notified thereafter. **Financial aid:** Priority date 3/1; no closing date. FAFSA required. Applicants notified on a rolling basis starting 4/1.

**Academics. Special study options:** Accelerated study, combined bachelor's/graduate degree, distance learning, double major, dual enrollment of high school students, ESL, honors, independent study, internships, semester at sea, student-designed major, study abroad, teacher certification program, Washington semester. Leadership Institute, Pre-professional studies. **Credit/placement by examination:** AP, CLEP, IB, ACT, institutional tests. 40 credit hours maximum toward bachelor's degree. Credit by examination may not be used to repeat any course previously taken. **Support services:** Learning center, pre-admission summer program, reduced course load, remedial instruction, study skills assistance, tutoring, writing center.

**Honors college/program.** Applicants must have 3.75 GPA or 3.6 GPA and 25 ACT.

**Majors. Architecture:** Interior. **Area/ethnic studies:** European, women's. **Biology:** General, biochemistry, biomedical sciences. **Business:** Accounting, actuarial science, business admin, entrepreneurial studies, fashion, finance, financial planning, hospitality admin, hotel/motel admin, human resources, international, logistics, management information systems, marketing, operations, purchasing, real estate, retailing. **Communications:** General, advertising, journalism, organizational, photojournalism, public relations. **Computer sciences:** Computer science, information technology. **Conservation:** General, environmental science, environmental studies. **Education:** Art, biology, business, chemistry, early childhood, elementary, emotionally handicapped, English, family/consumer sciences, French, geography, German, health, history, mathematics, mentally handicapped, music, physical, physics, science, social studies, Spanish, speech, technology/industrial arts. **Engineering:** Electrical, manufacturing, mechanical. **Engineering technology:** Automotive, computer systems, construction, electrical, manufacturing, mechanical. **Family/consumer sciences:** Child development, family systems, institutional food production. **Foreign languages:** French, German, Spanish. **Health:** Athletic training, clinical lab science, communication disorders, dietetics, health care admin, public health ed, recreational therapy. **History:** General. **Interdisciplinary:** Cognitive science, math/computer science, neuroscience. **Legal studies:** General. **Liberal arts:** Arts/sciences. **Math:** General, statistics. **Parks/recreation:** General, exercise sciences, facilities management, health/fitness, sports admin. **Philosophy/religion:** Philosophy, religion. **Physical sciences:** Astronomy, chemistry, geology, meteorology, oceanography, physics. **Psychology:** General. **Public administration:** Community org/advocacy, social work. **Social sciences:** General, anthropology, economics, geography, international relations, political science, sociology. **Visual/performing arts:** Acting, art, dramatic, graphic design, music theory/composition, studio arts, theater design.

**Most popular majors.** Business/marketing 27%, communications/journalism 8%, education 17%, parks/recreation 8%, social sciences 6%.

**Computing on campus.** 3,000 workstations in dormitories, library, computer center, student center. Dormitories wired for high-speed internet access and linked to campus network. Commuter students can connect to campus network. Online course registration, online library, helpline, repair service, student web hosting, wireless network available.

**Student life. Freshman orientation:** Mandatory, $175 fee. Preregistration for classes offered. One-day sessions; morning refreshments and lunch provided. **Housing:** Guaranteed on-campus for freshmen. Coed dorms, single-sex dorms, special housing for disabled, apartments, fraternity/sorority housing, wellness housing available. $800 partly refundable deposit, deadline

5/1. **Activities:** Bands, choral groups, dance, drama, film society, international student organizations, literary magazine, music ensembles, musical theater, radio station, student government, student newspaper, TV station, Asian cultural organization, Hispanic student organization, North American Indian student organization, organization for black unity, gay/lesbian/bisexual club, College Republicans, University Democrats, Baha'i club, Campus Crusade for Christ, Fellowship of Christian Athletes.

**Athletics.** NCAA. **Intercollegiate:** Baseball M, basketball, cross-country, field hockey W, football (tackle) M, gymnastics W, soccer W, softball W, track and field, volleyball W, wrestling M. **Intramural:** Basketball, football (non-tackle), golf, racquetball, soccer, softball, table tennis, tennis, volleyball, wrestling M. **Team name:** Chippewas.

**Student services.** Alcohol/substance abuse counseling, career counseling, services for economically disadvantaged, student employment services, financial aid counseling, health services, minority student services, personal counseling, placement for graduates, veterans' counselor. **Physically disabled:** Services for visually, speech, hearing impaired.

**Contact.** E-mail: cmuadmit@cmich.edu
Phone: (989) 774-3076 Toll-free number: (888) 292-5366
Fax: (989) 774-7267
Betty Wagner, Director of Admissions, Central Michigan University, Admissions Office, Mount Pleasant, MI 48859

## Cleary University
### Howell, Michigan
### www.cleary.edu
### CB code: 1123

- Private 4-year university and business college
- Commuter campus in small city
- 626 degree-seeking undergraduates: 34% part-time, 60% women, 8% African American, 1% Asian American, 2% Hispanic American, 1% international
- 121 graduate students

**General.** Founded in 1883. Regionally accredited. Campuses in Howell and Ann Arbor; extension sites throughout Southeastern Michigan. **Degrees:** 172 bachelor's, 62 associate awarded; master's offered. **Location:** 55 miles from Detroit, 27 miles from Ann Arbor. **Calendar:** Quarter, limited summer session. **Full-time faculty:** 4 total; 25% have terminal degrees, 25% minority, 50% women. **Part-time faculty:** 146 total; 9% have terminal degrees, 10% minority, 40% women. **Special facilities:** Nature trails.

**Freshman class profile.** 78 applied, 66 admitted, 37 enrolled.

**Basis for selection.** Open admission, but selective for some programs. 2.0 GPA, high school record or GED most important. 20 ACT or 1000 SAT (exclusive of Writing) recommended. Regular, special, guest, dual, provisional, transfer, and international admissions available. Applicants with below 2.0 GPA may be accepted if probable success in chosen program indicated.

**High school preparation.** 24 units recommended. Recommended units include English 4, mathematics 2, social studies 2, history 2, science 2 and academic electives 12.

**2009-2010 Annual costs.** Tuition/fees: $15,600. Tuition prices guaranteed if student enrolled continuously. Tuition includes all books and fees.

**2009-2010 Financial aid. Need-based:** Average need met was 14%. Average scholarship/grant was $1,322; average loan $1,323. 55% of total undergraduate aid awarded as scholarships/grants, 45% as loans/jobs. **Non-need-based:** Scholarships awarded for academics. **Additional information:** Filing electronically preferred; paper applications available. Tuition guarantee based on continuous enrollment. Essay and recommendations required for scholarship consideration.

**Application procedures. Admission:** Closing date 8/15. $25 fee, may be waived for applicants with need. Admission notification on a rolling basis. **Financial aid:** Priority date 3/15, closing date 8/15. FAFSA required. Applicants notified on a rolling basis; must reply within 2 week(s) of notification.

**Academics.** Compressed academic calendar reduces time to degree completion. First-time college students can complete bachelor's degree in 3.5 years and adults with previous college experience can complete degree in just over 1 year. **Special study options:** Accelerated study, combined bachelor's/graduate degree, cooperative education, distance learning, double major, dual enrollment of high school students, independent study, internships. **Credit/placement by examination:** CLEP, institutional tests. 36 credit hours maximum toward bachelor's degree. **Support services:** Pre-admission summer program, reduced course load, remedial instruction, study skills assistance, tutoring.

**Majors. Business:** Accounting, business admin, e-commerce, entrepreneurial studies, financial planning, human resources, management information systems, marketing, nonprofit/public, public finance. **Computer sciences:** Security.

**Computing on campus.** 60 workstations in computer center, student center. Commuter students can connect to campus network. Online library, helpline, wireless network available.

**Student life. Freshman orientation:** Mandatory. Preregistration for classes offered. **Activities:** DECA, Rotaract, Automation Alley, Michigan Quality Council, Livingston Economic Club, Washtenaw Economic Club.

**Athletics. Intramural:** Basketball. **Team name:** Cougars.

**Student services.** Adult student services, career counseling, student employment services, financial aid counseling, placement for graduates.

**Contact.** E-mail: admissions@cleary.edu
Phone: (517) 338-3330 Toll-free number: (888) 525-3279
Fax: (517) 338-3336
Carrie Bonofiglio, Director of Admissions, Cleary University, 3750 Cleary Drive, Howell, MI 48843

## College for Creative Studies
### Detroit, Michigan
### CB member
### www.collegeforcreativestudies.edu
### CB code: 1035

- Private 4-year visual arts college
- Commuter campus in very large city
- 1,382 degree-seeking undergraduates: 14% part-time, 45% women, 7% African American, 4% Asian American, 5% Hispanic American, 1% Native American, 6% international
- 18 degree-seeking graduate students
- 39% of applicants admitted
- SAT or ACT (ACT writing optional) required

**General.** Founded in 1926. Regionally accredited. **Degrees:** 243 bachelor's awarded. **Location:** 4 miles from downtown. **Calendar:** Semester, limited summer session. **Full-time faculty:** 58 total; 60% have terminal degrees, 16% minority, 31% women. **Part-time faculty:** 190 total; 42% women. **Special facilities:** Extensive studio space, art gallery for student exhibitions, foundry, computer studios, wood shop, metals shop, glassblowing studio, ceramic studio, fiber studio.

**Freshman class profile.** 1,434 applied, 556 admitted, 235 enrolled.

| Mid 50% test scores | | GPA 2.0-2.99: | 40% |
|---|---|---|---|
| ACT composite: | 18-23 | Out-of-state: | 18% |
| GPA 3.75 or higher: | 10% | Live on campus: | 64% |
| GPA 3.50-3.74: | 11% | International: | 5% |
| GPA 3.0-3.49: | 39% | | |

**Basis for selection.** Art portfolio, test scores, and high school record important. Minimum 2.5 high school GPA for applicants. ACT/SAT scores required. Portfolio required. **Homeschooled:** Transcript of courses and grades required.

**High school preparation.** 13 units recommended. Recommended units include English 4, mathematics 3, social studies 2, science 2 and foreign language 2. College-preparatory program recommended, art courses highly recommended.

**2010-2011 Annual costs.** Tuition/fees (projected): $31,275. Room/board: $8,500. Books/supplies: $2,500. Personal expenses: $1,500.

**2008-2009 Financial aid. Need-based:** 52% of total undergraduate aid awarded as scholarships/grants, 48% as loans/jobs. **Non-need-based:** Scholarships awarded for academics, art.

**Application procedures. Admission:** Priority date 3/1; deadline 8/1 (postmark date). $35 fee, may be waived for applicants with need, free for online applicants. Admission notification on a rolling basis beginning on or about 9/15. Must reply by May 1 or within 3 week(s) if notified thereafter. **Financial aid:** Priority date 7/1; no closing date. FAFSA required. Applicants notified on a rolling basis starting 3/15; must reply within 3 week(s) of notification.

**Academics. Special study options:** Cooperative education, cross-registration, double major, dual enrollment of high school students, exchange student, independent study, internships, New York semester, study abroad, teacher certification program. Advanced students may petition for 1 semester in New York studio space. **Credit/placement by examination:** AP, CLEP, IB, institutional tests. 6 credit hours maximum toward bachelor's degree. **Support services:** Learning center, pre-admission summer program, reduced course load, remedial instruction, study skills assistance, tutoring, writing center.

**Majors. Business:** Transportation. **Communications:** Digital media. **Communications technology:** Animation/special effects. **Production:** Furniture. **Visual/performing arts:** Ceramics, cinematography, commercial photography, commercial/advertising art, crafts, design, drawing, fiber arts, graphic design, illustration, industrial design, interior design, metal/jewelry, multimedia, painting, photography, printmaking, sculpture, studio arts.

**Computing on campus.** 400 workstations in dormitories, library, computer center. Dormitories wired for high-speed internet access and linked to campus network. Commuter students can connect to campus network. Online library, student web hosting, wireless network available.

**Student life. Freshman orientation:** Mandatory. Preregistration for classes offered. **Housing:** Apartments available. $200 fully refundable deposit, deadline 5/1. Furnished, college-owned apartments available. **Activities:** Student government, black student club, women artists club, industrial design students club.

**Student services.** Alcohol/substance abuse counseling, career counseling, student employment services, financial aid counseling, minority student services, personal counseling, placement for graduates. **Physically disabled:** Services for hearing impaired.

**Contact.** E-mail: admissions@collegeforcreativestudies.edu
Phone: (313) 664-7425 Toll-free number: (800) 952-2787
Fax: (313) 872-2739
Lori Watson, Director of Admissions, College for Creative Studies, 201 East Kirby, Detroit, MI 48202-4034

---

## Concordia University
### Ann Arbor, Michigan
### www.cuaa.edu
**CB code: 1094**

◗ Private 4-year liberal arts and teachers college affiliated with Lutheran Church - Missouri Synod
◗ Residential campus in small city

**General.** Founded in 1962. Regionally accredited. **Location:** 40 miles from Detroit. **Calendar:** Semester.

**Annual costs/financial aid.** Tuition/fees (2009-2010): $20,460. Additional one-time fees for all undergraduates include: $125 pre-enrollment deposit, $100 matriculation fee. Room/board: $7,606. Books/supplies: $1,000. Personal expenses: $1,175. Need-based financial aid available to full-time and part-time students.

**Contact.** Phone: (734) 995-7322
Executive Director of Enrollment Services, 4090 Geddes Road, Ann Arbor, MI 48105

---

## Cornerstone University
### Grand Rapids, Michigan
### www.cornerstone.edu
**CB code: 1253**

◗ Private 4-year university and liberal arts college affiliated with interdenominational tradition
◗ Residential campus in small city
◗ 1,833 degree-seeking undergraduates: 22% part-time, 59% women, 10% African American, 1% Asian American, 3% Hispanic American, 1% international
◗ 714 graduate students
◗ 79% of applicants admitted
◗ SAT or ACT (ACT writing recommended), application essay required
◗ 53% graduate within 6 years; 10% enter graduate study

**General.** Founded in 1941. Regionally accredited. **Degrees:** 362 bachelor's, 36 associate awarded; master's offered. **Location:** 4 miles from downtown. **Calendar:** Semester, limited summer session. **Full-time faculty:** 58 total; 47% have terminal degrees, 3% minority, 33% women. **Part-time faculty:** 70 total; 6% have terminal degrees, 3% minority, 23% women. **Class size:** 61% < 20, 34% 20-39, 3% 40-49, 2% 50-99.

**Freshman class profile.** 1,024 applied, 808 admitted, 331 enrolled.

| Mid 50% test scores | | | |
|---|---|---|---|
| SAT critical reading: | 490-570 | GPA 3.0-3.49: | 26% |
| SAT math: | 480-560 | GPA 2.0-2.99: | 18% |
| SAT writing: | 460-560 | End year in good standing: | 90% |
| ACT composite: | 20-26 | Return as sophomores: | 64% |
| GPA 3.75 or higher: | 32% | Out-of-state: | 21% |
| GPA 3.50-3.74: | 24% | Live on campus: | 87% |
| | | International: | 1% |

**Basis for selection.** Statement of Christian commitment, pastoral reference, 2.5 high school GPA, and ACT score of 19. Students with lower scores and GPA may be admitted conditionally. Interview recommended. Audition required for music majors. **Homeschooled:** Statement describing homeschool structure and mission, transcript of courses and grades, letter of recommendation (nonparent) required.

**High school preparation.** College-preparatory program recommended. 18 units recommended. Recommended units include English 4, mathematics 3, social studies 2, history 1, science 2 (laboratory 1), foreign language 2 and academic electives 4.

**2009-2010 Annual costs.** Tuition/fees: $20,520. Tuition includes laptop computer. Room/board: $6,510. Books/supplies: $1,000. Personal expenses: $1,234.

**2009-2010 Financial aid. Need-based:** Average need met was 89%. Average scholarship/grant was $15,398; average loan $3,394. 58% of total undergraduate aid awarded as scholarships/grants, 42% as loans/jobs. **Non-need-based:** Scholarships awarded for academics, athletics, leadership, music/drama, state residency. **Additional information:** Audition required for music scholarship applicants.

**Application procedures. Admission:** No deadline. $25 fee, may be waived for applicants with need, free for online applicants. Admission notification on a rolling basis. **Financial aid:** Priority date 3/1; no closing date. FAFSA required. Applicants notified on a rolling basis starting 3/15; must reply within 2 week(s) of notification.

**Academics.** All students must complete internship in major field. Core curriculum. **Special study options:** Accelerated study, cross-registration, distance learning, double major, dual enrollment of high school students, ESL, honors, independent study, internships, liberal arts/career combination, study abroad, teacher certification program, urban semester, Washington semester, weekend college. **Credit/placement by examination:** AP, CLEP, IB, ACT, institutional tests. 15 credit hours maximum toward associate degree, 30 toward bachelor's. **Support services:** Learning center, reduced course load, remedial instruction, study skills assistance, tutoring, writing center.

**Honors college/program.** Requires 28 ACT; 12-15 admitted annually.

**Majors. Biology:** General, environmental. **Business:** Accounting, business admin, financial planning, international, management information systems, management science, marketing. **Communications:** General, digital media, media studies. **Education:** Biology, early childhood, elementary, English, history, mathematics, music, physical, science, secondary, social science, social studies, voc/tech. **Family/consumer sciences:** Family systems, work/family studies. **Foreign languages:** Spanish. **Health:** Health services, predental, premedicine, preveterinary. **History:** General. **Math:** General. **Parks/recreation:** Exercise sciences, sports admin. **Psychology:** General, family. **Public administration:** Social work. **Social sciences:** General. **Theology:** Bible, youth ministry. **Visual/performing arts:** Music performance, music theory/composition.

**Most popular majors.** Business/marketing 50%, education 17%, theological studies 11%.

**Computing on campus.** PC or laptop required. 117 workstations in dormitories, library, computer center, student center. Dormitories wired for high-speed internet access and linked to campus network. Commuter students can connect to campus network. Online course registration, online library, helpline, repair service, wireless network available.

**Student life. Freshman orientation:** Mandatory. Preregistration for classes offered. 4-day program held prior to start of Fall classes. **Policies:** Dry campus; chapel attendance required. Students under 21 with fewer than 63 credit hours must live on campus unless living with immediate family. Religious observance required. **Housing:** Guaranteed on-campus for all undergraduates. Single-sex dorms, special housing for disabled, apartments available. $150 fully refundable deposit, deadline 5/29. All housing is alcohol, drug, and smoke-free. **Activities:** Bands, campus ministries, choral groups, dance, drama, film society, international student organizations, literary magazine, music ensembles, musical theater, opera, radio station, student government, student newspaper, student outreach committee, Young Republicans, cross-cultural ministries, social committee, fine arts committee, literature club, diversity club, right-to-life campus organization.

**Athletics.** NAIA. **Intercollegiate:** Basketball, cross-country, golf, soccer, softball W, track and field, volleyball W. **Intramural:** Basketball, football (non-tackle), ice hockey M, racquetball, soccer, softball, volleyball. **Team name:** Golden Eagles.

**Student services.** Adult student services, alcohol/substance abuse counseling, chaplain/spiritual director, career counseling, student employment services, financial aid counseling, health services, personal counseling, placement for graduates, veterans' counselor. **Physically disabled:** Services for visually, hearing impaired.

**Contact.** E-mail: admissions@cornerstone.edu
Phone: (616) 222-1426 Toll-free number: (800) 787-9778
Fax: (616) 222-1418
Lisa Link, Director of Admissions, Cornerstone University, 1001 East Beltline NE, Grand Rapids, MI 49525-5897

## Davenport University
### Grand Rapids, Michigan
www.davenport.edu                                    CB code: 1183

▶ Private 4-year university and business college
▶ Commuter campus in small city
▶ 9,951 degree-seeking undergraduates: 66% part-time, 67% women
▶ 1,476 graduate students

**General.** Founded in 1866. Regionally accredited. Locations in Alma, Battle Creek, Caro, Flint, Gaylord, Holland, Kalamazoo, Lansing, Livonia, Midland, Saginaw, Traverse City, and Warren. **Degrees:** 988 bachelor's, 643 associate awarded; master's offered. **Location:** 10 miles from Grand Rapids. **Calendar:** Semester, extensive summer session. **Full-time faculty:** 150 total; 23% have terminal degrees, 8% minority, 60% women. **Part-time faculty:** 793 total; 21% minority, 50% women. **Class size:** 58% < 20, 41% 20-39, less than 1% 40-49, less than 1% 50-99.

**Freshman class profile.**

| | | | |
|---|---|---|---|
| Out-of-state: | 3% | Live on campus: | 5% |

**Basis for selection.** GPA and test scores important; prospective students without ACT or SAT scores may take standard COMPASS assessment as arranged by a Davenport representative. SAT or ACT recommended. Interview recommended.

**High school preparation.** Recommended units include English 6.

**2009-2010 Annual costs.** Tuition/fees: $13,970. Books/supplies: $1,600. Personal expenses: $1,300.

**2008-2009 Financial aid. Non-need-based:** Scholarships awarded for academics, alumni affiliation, athletics, leadership.

**Application procedures. Admission:** No deadline. $25 fee. Admission notification on a rolling basis beginning on or about 9/1. **Financial aid:** Priority date 3/1; no closing date. FAFSA required. Applicants notified on a rolling basis starting 3/1; must reply within 2 week(s) of notification.

**Academics. Special study options:** Accelerated study, distance learning, dual enrollment of high school students, ESL, honors, independent study, internships, study abroad. **Credit/placement by examination:** AP, CLEP, IB, ACT, institutional tests. 40 credit hours maximum toward associate degree, 40 toward bachelor's. **Support services:** Learning center, remedial instruction, tutoring, writing center.

**Majors. Biology:** Bioinformatics. **Business:** General, accounting, business admin, finance, human resources, international, marketing. **Communications technology:** Animation/special effects. **Computer sciences:** Networking, security. **Health:** Health care admin, management/clinical assistant, medical records admin, nursing (RN). **Legal studies:** Paralegal. **Parks/recreation:** Sports admin. **Protective services:** Security management. **Other:** Service management and marketing.

**Most popular majors.** Business/marketing 78%, computer/information sciences 15%, health sciences 7%.

**Computing on campus.** 3,224 workstations in dormitories, library, computer center, student center. Dormitories wired for high-speed internet access and linked to campus network. Commuter students can connect to campus network. Online course registration, online library, helpline, wireless network available.

**Student life. Freshman orientation:** Mandatory. Preregistration for classes offered. **Housing:** Coed dorms, wellness housing available. $300 fully refundable deposit. **Activities:** Minority student association, Alternative Spring

Break, Business Professionals of America, Delta Epsilon Chi, global student organization, health information management student association, legal assistants club, residence hall community council, Society of Human Resource Management, student activities committee.

**Athletics.** NAIA. **Intercollegiate:** Baseball M, basketball, bowling, cheerleading M, cross-country, golf, ice hockey M, lacrosse, rugby M, soccer, softball, tennis, track and field, volleyball. **Team name:** Panthers.

**Student services.** Career counseling, student employment services, financial aid counseling, personal counseling.

**Contact.** E-mail: gradmiss@davenport.edu
Phone: (616) 698-7111 Toll-free number: (866) 925-3884
Daryl Kingrey, Executive Director of Admissions, Davenport University, 6191 Kraft Avenue SE, Grand Rapids, MI 49512-5926

## Eastern Michigan University
### Ypsilanti, Michigan                               CB member
www.emich.edu                                        CB code: 1201

▶ Public 4-year university
▶ Residential campus in small city
▶ 17,399 degree-seeking undergraduates: 27% part-time, 57% women, 21% African American, 2% Asian American, 3% Hispanic American, 1% Native American, 2% international
▶ 4,087 degree-seeking graduate students
▶ 71% of applicants admitted
▶ SAT or ACT (ACT writing optional) required
▶ 40% graduate within 6 years

**General.** Founded in 1849. Regionally accredited. **Degrees:** 2,944 bachelor's awarded; master's offered. **ROTC:** Army, Naval, Air Force. **Location:** 7 miles from Ann Arbor, 35 miles from Detroit. **Calendar:** Semester, limited summer session. **Full-time faculty:** 780 total; 79% have terminal degrees, 17% minority, 49% women. **Part-time faculty:** 535 total; 10% have terminal degrees, 14% minority, 60% women. **Class size:** 36% < 20, 53% 20-39, 6% 40-49, 5% 50-99, less than 1% >100. **Special facilities:** Corporate education center, observatory, laser laboratory, textiles research and training institute.

**Freshman class profile.** 10,341 applied, 7,337 admitted, 2,277 enrolled.

| Mid 50% test scores | | | |
|---|---|---|---|
| SAT critical reading: | 440-580 | GPA 2.0-2.99: | 43% |
| SAT math: | 450-580 | Rank in top quarter: | 36% |
| SAT writing: | 430-560 | Rank in top tenth: | 11% |
| ACT composite: | 18-24 | End year in good standing: | 86% |
| GPA 3.75 or higher: | 10% | Return as sophomores: | 71% |
| GPA 3.50-3.74: | 12% | Out-of-state: | 13% |
| GPA 3.0-3.49: | 35% | Live on campus: | 69% |
| | | International: | 2% |

**Basis for selection.** School achievement record and test scores important. Grades and test results combined to predict academic success. Michigan English Language Assessment Battery accepted in place of TOEFL with minimum score 72 for unconditional acceptance. Essay recommended. Audition required of music majors. Portfolio required of art majors.

**High school preparation.** College-preparatory program recommended. 21 units recommended. Recommended units include English 4, mathematics 4, social studies 2, history 1, science 4 (laboratory 1), foreign language 2 and academic electives 4. 2 units fine arts and 1 computer literacy also recommended.

**2009-2010 Annual costs.** Tuition/fees: $8,378; $22,283 out-of-state. Room/board: $7,785. Books/supplies: $900. Personal expenses: $1,150.

**2008-2009 Financial aid. Need-based:** 1,839 full-time freshmen applied for aid; 1,485 were judged to have need; 1,453 of these received aid. Average need met was 62%. Average scholarship/grant was $4,231; average loan $3,700. 31% of total undergraduate aid awarded as scholarships/grants, 69% as loans/jobs. **Non-need-based:** Awarded to 3,565 full-time undergraduates, including 1,376 freshmen. Scholarships awarded for academics, alumni affiliation, art, athletics, leadership, minority status, music/drama, ROTC, state residency.

**Application procedures. Admission:** Priority date 2/15; no deadline. $30 fee, may be waived for applicants with need. Admission notification on a rolling basis beginning on or about 10/1. **Financial aid:** Priority date 3/15; no closing date. FAFSA required. Applicants notified on a rolling basis starting 3/1.

**Academics. Special study options:** Accelerated study, combined bachelor's/ graduate degree, cooperative education, distance learning, double major, dual enrollment of high school students, ESL, external degree, honors, independent study, internships, student-designed major, study abroad, teacher certification program, Washington semester, weekend college. Dual enrollment program requires students to apply for admission to EMU. **Credit/ placement by examination:** AP, CLEP, IB, SAT, ACT, institutional tests. 30 credit hours maximum toward bachelor's degree. **Support services:** Learning center, reduced course load, remedial instruction, tutoring, writing center.

**Honors college/program.** Admission based on high school GPA, test scores, letters of recommendation. Approximately 250 freshmen per year admitted; reduced class size emphasizing student-professor interaction.

**Majors. Architecture:** Architecture, urban/community planning. **Area/ ethnic studies:** African-American, women's. **Biology:** General, biochemistry, toxicology. **Business:** General, accounting, actuarial science, business admin, construction management, entrepreneurial studies, fashion, finance, hospitality admin, international, labor studies, logistics, management information systems, managerial economics, marketing, office management. **Communications:** General, journalism, public relations. **Communications technology:** General, radio/tv. **Computer sciences:** General, computer science. **Education:** Art, biology, business, chemistry, computer, Deaf/hearing impaired, elementary, emotionally handicapped, English, foreign languages, French, German, history, mathematics, mentally handicapped, music, physical, physically handicapped, physics, reading, sales/marketing, science, secondary, social science, social studies, Spanish, special, speech impaired, technology/industrial arts, visually handicapped. **Engineering:** Physics. **Engineering technology:** CAD/CADD, computer, electrical, industrial, industrial management, manufacturing, mechanical, mechanical drafting, plastics. **Family/consumer sciences:** Facilities/event planning. **Foreign languages:** French, German, Germanic, Japanese, linguistics, Spanish. **Health:** Athletic training, clinical lab science, dietetics, health care admin, music therapy, nursing (RN), predental, premedicine, prepharmacy, preveterinary, recreational therapy, speech pathology. **History:** General. **Interdisciplinary:** Biological/physical sciences, science/society. **Legal studies:** Paralegal, prelaw. **Math:** General, statistics. **Parks/recreation:** Facilities management, health/ fitness. **Personal/culinary services:** Mortuary science. **Philosophy/ religion:** Philosophy. **Physical sciences:** Chemistry, geology, geophysics, physics. **Psychology:** General. **Public administration:** General, social work. **Social sciences:** General, anthropology, criminology, economics, geography, political science, sociology. **Transportation:** Airline/commercial pilot, aviation management. **Visual/performing arts:** Art, art history/ conservation, arts management, dance, dramatic, film/cinema, interior design, music performance.

**Most popular majors.** Business/marketing 22%, communications/ journalism 6%, education 20%, health sciences 10%, social sciences 8%, visual/performing arts 7%.

**Computing on campus.** 1,500 workstations in dormitories, library, computer center, student center. Dormitories wired for high-speed internet access and linked to campus network. Commuter students can connect to campus network. Online course registration, online library, helpline, student web hosting, wireless network available.

**Student life. Freshman orientation:** Mandatory, $300 fee. Preregistration for classes offered. 4-day orientation held Saturday through Tuesday. **Housing:** Coed dorms, special housing for disabled, apartments, fraternity/ sorority housing, wellness housing available. $200 partly refundable deposit, deadline 5/1. **Activities:** Bands, campus ministries, choral groups, dance, drama, film society, international student organizations, literary magazine, music ensembles, musical theater, opera, radio station, student government, student newspaper, symphony orchestra, TV station, Over 140 student organizations.

**Athletics.** NCAA. **Intercollegiate:** Baseball M, basketball, cross-country, diving, football (tackle), golf, gymnastics W, rowing (crew) W, soccer W, softball W, swimming, tennis W, track and field, volleyball W, wrestling M. **Intramural:** Badminton, basketball, bowling, cross-country, football (non-tackle), golf, racquetball, soccer, softball, swimming, table tennis, tennis, track and field, volleyball, weight lifting. **Team name:** Eagles.

**Student services.** Adult student services, alcohol/substance abuse counseling, chaplain/spiritual director, career counseling, student employment services, health services, minority student services, on-campus daycare, personal counseling, placement for graduates, veterans' counselor, women's services. **Physically disabled:** Services for visually, speech, hearing impaired.

**Contact.** E-mail: admissions@emich.edu
Phone: (734) 487-3060 Toll-free number: (800) 468-6368
Fax: (734) 487-6559
Kathryn Orscheln, Director, Admissions, Eastern Michigan University, 400 Pierce Hall, Ypsilanti, MI 48197

---

## Ferris State University
**Big Rapids, Michigan**
www.ferris.edu

**CB member**
**CB code: 1222**

- Public 4-year university
- Residential campus in large town
- 12,208 degree-seeking undergraduates: 25% part-time, 49% women, 7% African American, 1% Asian American, 2% Hispanic American, 1% Native American, 1% international
- 1,250 degree-seeking graduate students
- 55% of applicants admitted
- SAT or ACT (ACT writing optional) required
- 49% graduate within 6 years

**General.** Founded in 1884. Regionally accredited. **Degrees:** 1,976 bachelor's, 805 associate awarded; master's, professional offered. **ROTC:** Army. **Location:** 55 miles from Grand Rapids. **Calendar:** Semester, limited summer session. **Full-time faculty:** 613 total; 27% have terminal degrees, 8% minority, 41% women. **Part-time faculty:** 290 total; 11% have terminal degrees, 3% minority, 48% women. **Class size:** 33% < 20, 55% 20-39, 8% 40-49, 3% 50-99, 1% >100. **Special facilities:** Observatory, wildlife museum, Jim Crow museum, art walk, greenhouse.

**Freshman class profile.** 10,743 applied, 5,942 admitted, 2,242 enrolled.

| Mid 50% test scores | | | |
|---|---|---|---|
| ACT composite: | 18-24 | Return as sophomores: | 71% |
| GPA 3.75 or higher: | 15% | Out-of-state: | 6% |
| GPA 3.50-3.74: | 13% | Live on campus: | 74% |
| GPA 3.0-3.49: | 32% | | |

GPA 2.0-2.99: 40%

**Basis for selection.** School achievement record most important. General admission requirements: 2.5 GPA (509 GED) or 17 ACT/1210 SAT. Specific program requirements vary. ACT and SAT scores used for admissions purposes for marginal applicants. Interview recommended. Portfolio recommended of visual communication majors. **Learning Disabled:** Students with learning disabilities should submit documentation from professional psychologist or social worker to Disabilities Services Office in the Educational and Career Services Counseling Center.

**High school preparation.** College-preparatory program recommended. 24 units recommended. Recommended units include English 4, mathematics 4, social studies 2, history 2, science 4 (laboratory 2), foreign language 3 and academic electives 3. 2 units in fine arts and 1 unit in computer literacy recommended.

**2009-2010 Annual costs.** Tuition/fees: $9,480; $16,770 out-of-state. Midwest Compact states of Illinois, Indiana, Kansas, Minnesota, Missouri, Nebraska, Ohio, and Wisconsin tuition is $14,220. Room/board: $8,940. Books/ supplies: $1,100. Personal expenses: $797.

**2009-2010 Financial aid. Need-based:** Average need met was 88%. Average scholarship/grant was $5,154; average loan $3,313. 44% of total undergraduate aid awarded as scholarships/grants, 56% as loans/jobs. **Non-need-based:** Scholarships awarded for academics, alumni affiliation, art, athletics, leadership, minority status, music/drama, religious affiliation, ROTC.

**Application procedures. Admission:** Closing date 8/1 (postmark date). $30 fee, may be waived for applicants with need, free for online applicants. Admission notification on a rolling basis beginning on or about 7/1. **Financial aid:** Priority date 3/1; no closing date. FAFSA required. Applicants notified on a rolling basis starting 3/1; must reply within 3 week(s) of notification.

**Academics. Special study options:** Accelerated study, cooperative education, cross-registration, distance learning, double major, dual enrollment of high school students, exchange student, external degree, honors, independent study, internships, liberal arts/career combination, student-designed major, study abroad, teacher certification program. **Credit/placement by examination:** AP, CLEP, SAT, ACT, institutional tests. **Support services:** Learning center, remedial instruction, study skills assistance, tutoring, writing center.

**Majors. Architecture:** Interior. **Biology:** General, biochemistry, biotechnology, environmental. **Business:** Accounting, accounting technology, accounting/finance, business admin, construction management, e-commerce, entrepreneurial studies, finance, golf management, hospitality admin, hospitality/ recreation, hotel/motel admin, human resources, international, marketing, operations. **Communications:** General, advertising, public relations. **Communications technology:** Animation/special effects, graphic/printing, printing management, radio/tv. **Computer sciences:** Information technology. **Education:** Art, biology, business, chemistry, elementary, English, family/ consumer sciences, history, mathematics, social science, social studies, voc/

tech. **Engineering technology:** Automotive, electrical, energy systems, environmental, industrial, manufacturing, mechanical, plastics, quality control, surveying, telecommunications. **Family/consumer sciences:** Child care. **Health:** Clinical lab science, dental hygiene, health care admin, medical records admin, nuclear medical technology, nursing (RN). **History:** General. **Math:** General, applied, statistics. **Mechanic/repair:** Heavy equipment. **Parks/recreation:** Facilities management. **Physical sciences:** Chemistry. **Protective services:** Police science. **Psychology:** General. **Public administration:** General, social work. **Social sciences:** Political science, sociology. **Visual/performing arts:** Art history/conservation, commercial/advertising art, design, graphic design, illustration, industrial design, interior design, metal/jewelry, music management, painting, photography, sculpture, studio arts. **Other:** Business administration/leadership-organizational development, Furniture design, Rubber technology.

**Most popular majors.** Business/marketing 25%, education 8%, engineering/engineering technologies 14%, health sciences 11%, security/protective services 11%, visual/performing arts 11%.

**Computing on campus.** 2,373 workstations in dormitories, library, computer center, student center. Dormitories wired for high-speed internet access and linked to campus network. Commuter students can connect to campus network. Online course registration, online library, helpline, repair service, wireless network available.

**Student life. Freshman orientation:** Mandatory, $75 fee. Preregistration for classes offered. **Policies:** All students sign ethics statement during orientation. **Housing:** Guaranteed on-campus for all undergraduates. Coed dorms, special housing for disabled, apartments, wellness housing available. $200 nonrefundable deposit, deadline 5/31. **Activities:** Bands, choral groups, dance, drama, international student organizations, music ensembles, radio station, student government, student newspaper, symphony orchestra, TV station, Alpha Omega Co-ed Christian Fraternity, Circle K, Diverse Sexuality and Gender Alliance, Lyrical Praise Gospel Choir, Habitat for Humanity, Indian students association, international student organization, National Organization for Women, Red Cross Student Chapter, Young Americans for Liberty.

**Athletics. NCAA. Intercollegiate:** Basketball, cheerleading, cross-country, football (tackle) M, golf, ice hockey M, soccer W, softball W, tennis, track and field, volleyball W. **Intramural:** Badminton, basketball, football (non-tackle), golf, handball, ice hockey M, racquetball, softball, swimming, table tennis, tennis, volleyball, water polo M. **Team name:** Bulldogs.

**Student services.** Adult student services, alcohol/substance abuse counseling, chaplain/spiritual director, career counseling, services for economically disadvantaged, student employment services, financial aid counseling, health services, legal services, minority student services, on-campus daycare, personal counseling, placement for graduates, veterans' counselor. **Physically disabled:** Services for visually, speech, hearing impaired.

**Contact.** E-mail: admissions@ferris.edu
Phone: (231) 591-2100 Toll-free number: (800) 433-7747
Fax: (231) 591-3944
Kristen Salomonson, Dean of Enrollment Services, Ferris State University, 1201 South State Street, CSS 201, Big Rapids, MI 49307-2714

## Finlandia University
**Hancock, Michigan**
**www.finlandia.edu**                          **CB code: 1743**

▸ Private 4-year university and liberal arts college affiliated with Evangelical Lutheran Church in America
▸ Commuter campus in small town
▸ 559 degree-seeking undergraduates: 10% part-time, 63% women, 4% African American, 1% Asian American, 2% Hispanic American, 1% Native American, 1% international
▸ 90% of applicants admitted
▸ Application essay required
▸ 52% graduate within 6 years

**General.** Founded in 1896. Regionally accredited. **Degrees:** 76 bachelor's, 32 associate awarded. **ROTC:** Army, Naval, Air Force. **Location:** 100 miles from Marquette, 220 miles from Green Bay, Wisconsin. **Calendar:** Semester, limited summer session. **Full-time faculty:** 32 total; 22% have terminal degrees, 72% women. **Part-time faculty:** 36 total; 14% have terminal degrees, 67% women. **Class size:** 69% < 20, 27% 20-39, 4% 40-49. **Special facilities:** Finnish-American historical archive.

**Freshman class profile.** 634 applied, 568 admitted, 136 enrolled.

| | | | |
|---|---|---|---|
| GPA 3.75 or higher: | 4% | Return as sophomores: | 67% |
| GPA 3.50-3.74: | 3% | Out-of-state: | 19% |
| GPA 3.0-3.49: | 33% | Live on campus: | 28% |
| GPA 2.0-2.99: | 59% | International: | 2% |
| End year in good standing: | 77% | | |

**Basis for selection.** One unit of algebra and chemistry with grade of 3.0 and 2.5 cumulative GPA required for nursing. 1 unit of algebra and biology with grade of 3.0 and 3.0 cumulative GPA required for physical therapist assistant. GPA of 2.0 required of all other programs. If GPA below 2.0, special consideration given in determining admission. Student may obtain admission into academic warning program based on placement test results. Nursing applicants should apply by March 15, physical therapy assistant applicants by April 15. SAT or ACT recommended. **Homeschooled:** Transcript of courses and grades required. Placement tests required. **Learning Disabled:** Evaluation results and/or IEP that specifically states the disability is required for eligibility for accommodations, but not for admission to the university.

**High school preparation.** College-preparatory program recommended. Recommended units include English 4, mathematics 2, science 2 (laboratory 2).

**2009-2010 Annual costs.** Tuition/fees: $18,436. Room/board: $5,974. Books/supplies: $1,300. Personal expenses: $100.

**2009-2010 Financial aid. Non-need-based:** Scholarships awarded for academics, leadership, religious affiliation, state residency. **Additional information:** Work/study program; up to $2,800 per year.

**Application procedures. Admission:** Priority date 8/1; deadline 8/25 (postmark date). $30 fee, may be waived for applicants with need, free for online applicants. Admission notification on a rolling basis. **Financial aid:** Priority date 3/1; no closing date. FAFSA, institutional form required. Applicants notified on a rolling basis starting 3/1; must reply within 2 week(s) of notification.

**Academics. Special study options:** Double major, dual enrollment of high school students, ESL, exchange student, honors, independent study, internships, liberal arts/career combination, student-designed major, study abroad, teacher certification program. **Credit/placement by examination:** AP, CLEP, IB, SAT, ACT, institutional tests. 18 credit hours maximum toward associate degree, 30 toward bachelor's. **Support services:** Learning center, remedial instruction, study skills assistance, tutoring, writing center.

**Majors. Business:** Accounting, business admin, international, marketing. **Education:** Elementary. **Health:** Nursing (RN). **Liberal arts:** Arts/sciences. **Psychology:** General. **Public administration:** Human services. **Social sciences:** General. **Visual/performing arts:** Art, ceramics, commercial/advertising art, design, drawing, fashion design, fiber arts, graphic design, illustration, interior design, painting, studio arts.

**Most popular majors.** Business/marketing 19%, education 8%, health sciences 38%, liberal arts 8%, public administration/social services 8%, visual/performing arts 19%.

**Computing on campus.** 80 workstations in dormitories, library, computer center. Dormitories wired for high-speed internet access and linked to campus network. Online library, helpline, wireless network available.

**Student life. Freshman orientation:** Mandatory. Preregistration for classes offered. 3-day program includes testing, workshops, and special speakers. **Housing:** Guaranteed on-campus for all undergraduates. Coed dorms available. $100 nonrefundable deposit, deadline 8/25. **Activities:** Pep band, campus ministries, choral groups, dance, drama, music ensembles, musical theater, student government, student newspaper, servant leadership program, local agency volunteer programs.

**Athletics. NCAA. Intercollegiate:** Baseball M, basketball, cross-country, golf, ice hockey, soccer, softball W, tennis W, volleyball W. **Intramural:** Bowling, football (non-tackle), softball, swimming, table tennis, volleyball. **Team name:** Lions.

**Student services.** Chaplain/spiritual director, career counseling, services for economically disadvantaged, student employment services, financial aid counseling, personal counseling, placement for graduates, veterans' counselor. **Learning disabled:** Comprehensive services available.

**Contact.** E-mail: admissions@finlandia.edu
Phone: (906) 487-7274 Toll-free number: (877) 202-5491
Fax: (906) 487-7383
Martin Kinard, Director of Admissions, Finlandia University, 601 Quincy Street, Hancock, MI 49930-1882

## Grace Bible College
### Grand Rapids, Michigan
www.gbcol.edu                                    CB code: 0809

- Private 4-year Bible and liberal arts college affiliated with Grace Gospel Fellowship
- Residential campus in small city
- 192 degree-seeking undergraduates: 6% part-time, 44% women, 3% African American, 1% Asian American, 1% Hispanic American
- 61% of applicants admitted
- SAT or ACT (ACT writing optional) required
- 75% graduate within 6 years

**General.** Founded in 1945. Regionally accredited; also accredited by ABHE. **Degrees:** 31 bachelor's, 8 associate awarded. **ROTC:** Army. **Location:** 50 miles from Kalamazoo. **Calendar:** Semester. **Full-time faculty:** 7 total; 43% have terminal degrees, 29% women. **Part-time faculty:** 9 total; 33% have terminal degrees, 22% women. **Class size:** 66% < 20, 30% 20-39, 4% 50-99.

**Freshman class profile.** 138 applied, 84 admitted, 48 enrolled.

| Mid 50% test scores | | | |
|---|---|---|---|
| SAT critical reading: | 460-560 | GPA 3.0-3.49: | 24% |
| SAT math: | 470-550 | GPA 2.0-2.99: | 29% |
| SAT writing: | 410-600 | Rank in top quarter: | 41% |
| ACT composite: | 18-24 | Rank in top tenth: | 19% |
| GPA 3.75 or higher: | 29% | Return as sophomores: | 79% |
| GPA 3.50-3.74: | 16% | Out-of-state: | 35% |
| | | Live on campus: | 65% |

**Basis for selection.** Evidence of personal salvation through Jesus Christ important. 2.5 GPA, 20 ACT, and rank in top half of class for regular admission. Probationary admission for those in third quarter of class. Interview may be recommended.

**High school preparation.** Recommended units include English 4, mathematics 3, social studies 3, science 3 and foreign language 1.

**2009-2010 Annual costs.** Tuition/fees: $13,920. Room/board: $6,850. Books/supplies: $548. Personal expenses: $976.

**2008-2009 Financial aid. Non-need-based:** Scholarships awarded for academics, music/drama, religious affiliation.

**Application procedures. Admission:** Closing date 6/1 (receipt date). No application fee. Admission notification on a rolling basis. Must reply by May 1 or within 4 week(s) if notified thereafter. **Financial aid:** Priority date 3/1; no closing date. FAFSA required. Applicants notified on a rolling basis starting 5/15; must reply within 2 week(s) of notification.

**Academics.** All students major in Bible and theology in addition to degree major. **Special study options:** Combined bachelor's/graduate degree, cross-registration, double major, dual enrollment of high school students, independent study, internships, liberal arts/career combination. **Credit/placement by examination:** AP, CLEP, institutional tests. **Support services:** Reduced course load, remedial instruction, tutoring.

**Majors. Business:** General, accounting, business admin, international, management science, marketing. **Communications technology:** Photo/film/video, recording arts. **Computer sciences:** General, information technology, web page design. **Education:** Early childhood, elementary, music, secondary. **Liberal arts:** Arts/sciences. **Public administration:** Human services. **Theology:** Bible, missionary, pastoral counseling, religious ed, sacred music, theology, youth ministry.

**Most popular majors.** Business/marketing 7%, education 35%, interdisciplinary studies 13%, public administration/social services 13%, theological studies 16%, visual/performing arts 13%.

**Computing on campus.** 25 workstations in library, computer center. Dormitories wired for high-speed internet access and linked to campus network. Helpline, wireless network available.

**Student life. Freshman orientation:** Mandatory. Preregistration for classes offered. Freshmen meet for 5 days prior to start of fall semester. **Policies:** Religious observance required. **Housing:** Guaranteed on-campus for freshmen. Single-sex dorms, apartments, wellness housing available. $100 deposit, deadline 5/1. **Activities:** Jazz band, campus ministries, choral groups, drama, music ensembles, student government.

**Athletics.** NCCAA. **Intercollegiate:** Basketball, soccer M, volleyball W. **Intramural:** Basketball M, bowling, racquetball, soccer, tennis, volleyball. **Team name:** Tigers.

---

**Student services.** Chaplain/spiritual director, career counseling, student employment services, financial aid counseling, health services, personal counseling, placement for graduates.

**Contact.**  E-mail: gbc@gbcol.edu
Phone: (616) 538-2330 Toll-free number: (800) 968-1887
Fax: (616) 538-0599
Kevin Gilliam, Enrollment Director, Grace Bible College, 1011 Aldon Street SW, PO Box 910, Grand Rapids, MI 49509

## Grand Valley State University
### Allendale, Michigan                          CB member
www.gvsu.edu                                     CB code: 1258

- Public 4-year university
- Residential campus in large town
- 20,731 degree-seeking undergraduates: 11% part-time, 59% women, 5% African American, 3% Asian American, 3% Hispanic American, 1% Native American, 1% international
- 3,140 degree-seeking graduate students
- 81% of applicants admitted
- SAT or ACT (ACT writing recommended) required
- 56% graduate within 6 years; 21% enter graduate study

**General.** Founded in 1960. Regionally accredited. **Degrees:** 3,710 bachelor's awarded; master's, professional offered. **Location:** 12 miles from Grand Rapids. **Calendar:** Semester, extensive summer session. **Full-time faculty:** 1,051 total; 54% have terminal degrees, 16% minority, 46% women. **Part-time faculty:** 536 total; 8% have terminal degrees, 7% minority, 54% women. **Class size:** 24% < 20, 58% 20-39, 12% 40-49, 5% 50-99, 2% >100. **Special facilities:** Cross-country fitness trail, recital hall, two Great Lakes research vessels, water resources research institute, center for presidential studies.

**Freshman class profile.** 13,051 applied, 10,520 admitted, 3,727 enrolled.

| Mid 50% test scores | | | |
|---|---|---|---|
| SAT critical reading: | 480-610 | GPA 2.0-2.99: | 4% |
| SAT math: | 520-640 | Rank in top quarter: | 55% |
| SAT writing: | 470-580 | Rank in top tenth: | 21% |
| ACT composite: | 22-26 | End year in good standing: | 96% |
| GPA 3.75 or higher: | 30% | Return as sophomores: | 83% |
| GPA 3.50-3.74: | 26% | Out-of-state: | 5% |
| GPA 3.0-3.49: | 40% | Live on campus: | 84% |
| | | International: | 1% |

**Basis for selection.** Admission based on secondary school grades, courses, personal and academic data, ACT/SAT results.

**High school preparation.** College-preparatory program recommended. Required units include English 4, mathematics 3, social studies 3, science 3 (laboratory 1) and foreign language 2.

**2009-2010 Annual costs.** Tuition/fees: $8,630; $12,944 out-of-state. Room/board: $7,448. Books/supplies: $1,000. Personal expenses: $2,330.

**2008-2009 Financial aid. Need-based:** 3,279 full-time freshmen applied for aid; 2,097 were judged to have need; 2,087 of these received aid. Average need met was 83%. Average scholarship/grant was $5,721; average loan $4,169. 47% of total undergraduate aid awarded as scholarships/grants, 53% as loans/jobs. **Non-need-based:** Awarded to 2,460 full-time undergraduates, including 681 freshmen. Scholarships awarded for academics, alumni affiliation, art, athletics, music/drama, state residency.

**Application procedures. Admission:** Closing date 5/1. $30 fee, may be waived for applicants with need. Admission notification on a rolling basis. Application closing date December 31 for scholarships. **Financial aid:** Priority date 3/1; no closing date. FAFSA required. Applicants notified on a rolling basis starting 4/1; must reply by 5/1 or within 4 week(s) of notification.

**Academics. Special study options:** Combined bachelor's/graduate degree, distance learning, double major, dual enrollment of high school students, ESL, honors, independent study, internships, student-designed major, study abroad, teacher certification program, Washington semester. Undergraduates may take graduate level classes as seniors; co-op programs in education, engineering, health professions. **Credit/placement by examination:** AP, CLEP, IB, SAT, ACT, institutional tests. 32 credit hours maximum toward bachelor's degree. **Support services:** Learning center, preadmission summer program, remedial instruction, study skills assistance, tutoring, writing center.

**Honors college/program.** 3.5 GPA and 28 ACT required.

**Majors. Architecture:** Urban/community planning. **Area/ethnic studies:** Chinese, Russian/Slavic. **Biology:** General, biochemistry, cellular/molecular. **Business:** Accounting, business admin, finance, human resources, international, management science, managerial economics, marketing, tourism promotion, tourism/travel. **Communications:** General, advertising, broadcast journalism, journalism, public relations. **Computer sciences:** General, computer science, information systems, programming. **Conservation:** Management/policy. **Education:** Music, physical, science, special. **Engineering:** Electrical, manufacturing, mechanical. **Engineering technology:** Occupational safety. **Foreign languages:** Ancient Greek, classics, French, German, Latin, Spanish. **Health:** Athletic training, clinical lab science, medical radiologic technology/radiation therapy, nursing (RN), occupational health, predental, premedicine, prepharmacy, preveterinary. **History:** General. **Interdisciplinary:** Behavioral sciences, biological/physical sciences, biopsychology. **Legal studies:** General, paralegal. **Liberal arts:** Arts/sciences. **Math:** General, statistics. **Parks/recreation:** General, health/fitness. **Philosophy/religion:** Philosophy. **Physical sciences:** Chemistry, geochemistry, geology, physics. **Protective services:** Law enforcement admin, security services. **Psychology:** General, social. **Public administration:** General, social work. **Social sciences:** General, anthropology, economics, geography, international relations, political science, sociology. **Visual/performing arts:** Art, art history/conservation, ceramics, commercial/advertising art, dance, dramatic, film/cinema, metal/jewelry, painting, photography, printmaking, sculpture, studio arts.

**Most popular majors.** Biology 9%, business/marketing 20%, communications/journalism 7%, English 6%, health sciences 10%, psychology 8%, social sciences 9%.

**Computing on campus.** 1,270 workstations in dormitories, library, computer center, student center. Dormitories wired for high-speed internet access and linked to campus network. Commuter students can connect to campus network. Online course registration, helpline, repair service, student web hosting, wireless network available.

**Student life. Freshman orientation:** Mandatory, $75 fee. Preregistration for classes offered. One day long and held for small groups on 50 possible dates through May, June, July, and August. Students register for classes for full year. **Housing:** Guaranteed on-campus for freshmen. Coed dorms, apartments, fraternity/sorority housing available. $150 deposit, deadline 3/1. **Activities:** Bands, campus ministries, choral groups, dance, drama, international student organizations, literary magazine, music ensembles, musical theater, radio station, student government, student newspaper, symphony orchestra, TV station, 143 registered organizations.

**Athletics. NCAA. Intercollegiate:** Baseball M, basketball, cheerleading, cross-country, diving, football (tackle) M, golf, soccer W, softball W, swimming, tennis, track and field, volleyball W. **Intramural:** Archery, badminton, basketball, bowling, cross-country, diving, fencing, field hockey, football (tackle) M, golf, gymnastics, racquetball, rowing (crew), skiing, skin diving, soccer, softball, squash, swimming, table tennis, tennis, volleyball, wrestling M. **Team name:** Lakers.

**Student services.** Adult student services, alcohol/substance abuse counseling, chaplain/spiritual director, career counseling, services for economically disadvantaged, student employment services, financial aid counseling, health services, minority student services, on-campus daycare, personal counseling, placement for graduates, women's services. **Physically disabled:** Services for visually, speech, hearing impaired.

**Contact.** E-mail: go2gvsu@gvsu.edu
Phone: (616) 331-2025 Toll-free number: (800) 748-0246
Fax: (616) 331-2000
Jodi Chycinski, Director of Admissions, Grand Valley State University, 1 Campus Drive, Allendale, MI 49401-9403

## Great Lakes Christian College
**Lansing, Michigan**
**www.glcc.edu**                          **CB code: 7320**

- Private 4-year Bible college affiliated with Church of Christ / Christian Church
- Residential campus in small city
- 232 degree-seeking undergraduates
- SAT or ACT (ACT writing optional) required
- 36% graduate within 6 years

**General.** Founded in 1949. Accredited by ABHE. **Degrees:** 17 bachelor's, 7 associate awarded. **Location:** 90 miles from Detroit, 65 miles from Grand Rapids. **Calendar:** Semester, limited summer session. **Full-time faculty:** 10 total. **Part-time faculty:** 11 total.

**Basis for selection.** Recommendations of character from applicant's minister and church leaders required. Students with GPA below 2.25 or ACT

below 16 or SAT below 820 (exclusive of Writing) admitted on probation. **Homeschooled:** Transcript of courses and grades, letter of recommendation (nonparent) required.

**2009-2010 Annual costs.** Tuition/fees: $11,980. Room/board: $7,000. Books/supplies: $950. Personal expenses: $1,800.

**2009-2010 Financial aid. Non-need-based:** Scholarships awarded for academics, alumni affiliation, music/drama.

**Application procedures. Admission:** Closing date 8/1 (receipt date). $30 fee, may be waived for applicants with need. Admission notification on a rolling basis. **Financial aid:** Priority date 8/1; no closing date. FAFSA, institutional form required. Applicants notified on a rolling basis starting 5/1; must reply within 3 week(s) of notification.

**Academics. Special study options:** Combined bachelor's/graduate degree, cooperative education, double major, dual enrollment of high school students, internships. **Credit/placement by examination:** CLEP. **Support services:** Remedial instruction, study skills assistance, tutoring.

**Majors. History:** General. **Theology:** Bible, religious ed, sacred music.

**Computing on campus.** 23 workstations in library, computer center, student center. Dormitories wired for high-speed internet access and linked to campus network. Commuter students can connect to campus network. Online library, helpline, repair service, wireless network available.

**Student life. Freshman orientation:** Mandatory. Preregistration for classes offered. **Policies:** Regular Christian service participation required of all graduates. Religious observance required. **Housing:** Single-sex dorms, apartments, wellness housing available. $200 fully refundable deposit, deadline 6/1. **Activities:** Campus ministries, choral groups, drama, music ensembles, musical theater, student government, student newspaper.

**Athletics. NCCAA. Intercollegiate:** Basketball M, soccer M. **Intramural:** Volleyball M. **Team name:** Crusaders.

**Student services.** Chaplain/spiritual director, financial aid counseling, personal counseling. **Physically disabled:** Services for visually, hearing impaired.

**Contact.** E-mail: admissions@glcc.edu
Phone: (517) 321-0242 ext. 221 Toll-free number: (800) 937-4522
Fax: (517) 321-5902
Lloyd Scharer, Director of Admissions and College Relations, Great Lakes Christian College, 6211 West Willow Highway, Lansing, MI 48917-1231

## Hillsdale College
**Hillsdale, Michigan**                          **CB member**
**www.hillsdale.edu**                          **CB code: 1295**

- Private 4-year liberal arts college
- Residential campus in large town
- 1,378 degree-seeking undergraduates
- 61% of applicants admitted
- SAT or ACT (ACT writing optional), application essay required
- 75% graduate within 6 years; 41% enter graduate study

**General.** Founded in 1844. Regionally accredited. **Degrees:** 270 bachelor's awarded. **Location:** 120 miles from Detroit, 75 miles from Ann Arbor. **Calendar:** Semester, limited summer session. **Full-time faculty:** 117 total. **Part-time faculty:** 37 total. **Class size:** 77% < 20, 22% 20-39, less than 1% 40-49, less than 1% 50-99. **Special facilities:** Arboretum, preschool, K-12 private academy, economics library, special collections library for first editions, 685-acre lake biological station, Kirby Center for Constitutional Studies and Citizenship.

**Freshman class profile.** 1,632 applied, 1,000 admitted, 362 enrolled.

| Mid 50% test scores | | | |
|---|---|---|---|
| SAT critical reading: | 640-720 | Rank in top quarter: | 75% |
| SAT math: | 570-660 | Rank in top tenth: | 47% |
| SAT writing: | 610-690 | End year in good standing: | 92% |
| ACT composite: | 25-30 | Return as sophomores: | 96% |
| GPA 3.75 or higher: | 60% | Out-of-state: | 63% |
| GPA 3.50-3.74: | 22% | Live on campus: | 99% |
| GPA 3.0-3.49: | 15% | Fraternities: | 30% |
| GPA 2.0-2.99: | 3% | Sororities: | 40% |

**Basis for selection.** Minimum 3.3 GPA, class rank in top third preferred. Test scores, recommendations, interview, personal essay important. SAT Subject Tests recommended. Portfolio recommended for art majors.

Audition required for music scholarship applicants. **Homeschooled:** Transcript of courses and grades required.

**High school preparation.** College-preparatory program recommended. 16 units recommended. Recommended units include English 4, mathematics 4, social studies 1, history 2, science 3 (laboratory 1) and foreign language 2.

**2009-2010 Annual costs.** Tuition/fees: $19,920. Room/board: $7,750. Books/supplies: $900. Personal expenses: $500.

**2009-2010 Financial aid. Need-based:** 50% of total undergraduate aid awarded as scholarships/grants, 50% as loans/jobs. **Non-need-based:** Scholarships awarded for academics, alumni affiliation, art, athletics, leadership, music/drama, state residency. **Additional information:** Campus employment available.

**Application procedures. Admission:** Priority date 11/15; deadline 2/15 (postmark date). $35 fee. Admission notification on a rolling basis beginning on or about 12/1. Must reply by 5/1. **Financial aid:** Priority date 3/1, closing date 3/15. Institutional form required. CSS PROFILE required for returning students only. Applicants notified on a rolling basis starting 2/1; must reply by 5/1 or within 4 week(s) of notification.

**Academics.** Highly qualified students may study at Oxford University, England for semester or summer. Summer business program at Regents College, London, England as well as study abroad programs in France, Germany and Spain. **Special study options:** Accelerated study, double major, dual enrollment of high school students, honors, independent study, internships, study abroad, teacher certification program, Washington semester. **Credit/placement by examination:** AP, CLEP, IB, SAT, ACT, institutional tests. **Support services:** Reduced course load, study skills assistance, tutoring, writing center.

**Majors. Area/ethnic studies:** American, European. **Biology:** General. **Business:** General, accounting, business admin, finance, international marketing, marketing. **Communications:** General, journalism. **Computer sciences:** Computer science. **Education:** General, early childhood, elementary, multi-level teacher, physical, secondary. **Foreign languages:** Classics, comparative lit, French, German, Spanish. **Health:** Predental, premedicine, prenursing, prepharmacy, preveterinary. **History:** General. **Interdisciplinary:** Math/computer science. **Legal studies:** Prelaw. **Liberal arts:** Arts/sciences. **Math:** General, computational. **Philosophy/religion:** Christian, philosophy, religion. **Physical sciences:** Chemistry, physics. **Psychology:** General. **Social sciences:** Economics, political science, sociology. **Theology:** Preministerial. **Visual/performing arts:** Art, dramatic.

**Most popular majors.** Biology 7%, business/marketing 15%, education 12%, English 11%, history 14%, social sciences 13%, visual/performing arts 7%.

**Computing on campus.** 220 workstations in library, computer center, student center. Dormitories wired for high-speed internet access and linked to campus network. Commuter students can connect to campus network. Online library, helpline, repair service, wireless network available.

**Student life. Freshman orientation:** Mandatory. Preregistration for classes offered. 3-day program in the fall. **Housing:** Guaranteed on-campus for all undergraduates. Single-sex dorms, apartments, fraternity/sorority housing, wellness housing available. $300 nonrefundable deposit, deadline 5/1. **Activities:** Bands, campus ministries, choral groups, dance, drama, international student organizations, literary magazine, music ensembles, musical theater, student government, student newspaper, symphony orchestra, Catholic student council, Varsity H-Club, student federation, enterprising leaders, Intervarsity Christian Fellowship, Fellowship of Christian Athletes, College Republicans, Young Life, Praxis, Charis.

**Athletics.** NCAA. **Intercollegiate:** Baseball M, basketball, cross-country, diving W, equestrian W, football (tackle) M, softball W, swimming W, track and field, volleyball W. **Intramural:** Basketball, football (non-tackle), handball, racquetball, soccer, softball, swimming, table tennis, tennis, track and field, volleyball. **Team name:** Chargers.

**Student services.** Chaplain/spiritual director, career counseling, student employment services, financial aid counseling, health services, personal counseling, placement for graduates. **Physically disabled:** Services for visually impaired.

**Contact.** E-mail: admissions@hillsdale.edu
Phone: (517) 607-2327 Fax: (517) 607-2223
Jeffrey Lantis, Director of Admissions, Hillsdale College, 33 East College Street, Hillsdale, MI 49242

## Hope College
Holland, Michigan
www.hope.edu
CB member
CB code: 1301

- Private 4-year liberal arts college affiliated with Reformed Church in America
- Residential campus in small city
- 3,153 degree-seeking undergraduates: 2% part-time, 60% women, 2% African American, 2% Asian American, 4% Hispanic American, 1% international
- 84% of applicants admitted
- SAT or ACT (ACT writing optional), application essay required
- 79% graduate within 6 years; 30% enter graduate study

**General.** Founded in 1862. Regionally accredited. **Degrees:** 735 bachelor's awarded. **ROTC:** Army. **Location:** 30 miles from Grand Rapids, 160 miles from Chicago. **Calendar:** Semester, limited summer session. **Full-time faculty:** 230 total; 78% have terminal degrees, 10% minority, 45% women. **Part-time faculty:** 73 total; 23% have terminal degrees, 4% minority, 58% women. **Class size:** 53% < 20, 44% 20-39, less than 1% 40-49, 2% 50-99. **Special facilities:** Museum, Pelletron particle accelerator, biological field station, electron microscopes, laser research, cadaver lab.

**Freshman class profile.** 2,941 applied, 2,483 admitted, 803 enrolled.

| Mid 50% test scores | | | |
|---|---|---|---|
| SAT critical reading: | 520-660 | Rank in top quarter: | 63% |
| SAT math: | 540-670 | Rank in top tenth: | 34% |
| ACT composite: | 23-29 | End year in good standing: | 98% |
| GPA 3.75 or higher: | 50% | Return as sophomores: | 88% |
| GPA 3.50-3.74: | 19% | Out-of-state: | 30% |
| GPA 3.0-3.49: | 23% | Live on campus: | 99% |
| GPA 2.0-2.99: | 8% | International: | 1% |

**Basis for selection.** Strength of curriculum, achievement, test scores, perceived ability to succeed important. Interviews recommended. **Homeschooled:** Transcript of courses and grades, letter of recommendation (nonparent) required. Paper of at least 3 pages from final 2 years of homeschooling, list of non-textbooks read in last 2 years of homeschooling required. **Learning Disabled:** Students should consult the director of the academic support program to ensure available resources and personnel to accommodate the disability.

**High school preparation.** College-preparatory program recommended. 18 units recommended. Recommended units include English 4, mathematics 3, science 2 (laboratory 2), foreign language 2 and academic electives 5.

**2009-2010 Annual costs.** Tuition/fees: $25,660. Room/board: $7,870.

**2009-2010 Financial aid. Need-based:** 673 full-time freshmen applied for aid; 533 were judged to have need; 533 of these received aid. Average need met was 84%. Average scholarship/grant was $18,368; average loan $3,733. 74% of total undergraduate aid awarded as scholarships/grants, 26% as loans/jobs. **Non-need-based:** Awarded to 2,112 full-time undergraduates, including 600 freshmen. Scholarships awarded for academics, art, minority status, music/drama, religious affiliation.

**Application procedures. Admission:** Priority date 3/1; no deadline. $50 fee, may be waived for applicants with need. Admission notification on a rolling basis beginning on or about 12/15. Must reply by May 1 or within 2 week(s) if notified thereafter. **Financial aid:** Priority date 3/1; no closing date. FAFSA, institutional form required. Applicants notified on a rolling basis starting 3/15.

**Academics.** Extensive undergraduate scientific research opportunities available. All fine arts divisions nationally accredited. **Special study options:** Distance learning, double major, ESL, independent study, internships, New York semester, student-designed major, study abroad, teacher certification program, urban semester, Washington semester. Internships in Chicago, New York City, Washington DC, Philadelphia. **Credit/placement by examination:** AP, CLEP, IB, institutional tests. 32 credit hours maximum toward bachelor's degree. **Support services:** Reduced course load, study skills assistance, tutoring, writing center.

**Majors. Area/ethnic studies:** Japanese, women's. **Biology:** General. **Business:** Accounting, business admin, managerial economics. **Communications:** General, journalism. **Computer sciences:** General. **Conservation:** Environmental science. **Education:** Art, biology, chemistry, drama/dance, emotionally handicapped, English, French, German, history, learning disabled, mathematics, music, physical, physics, science, social studies, Spanish. **Engineering:** General. **Foreign languages:** Classics, French, German, Spanish. **Health:** Athletic training, nursing (RN). **History:** General. **Interdisciplinary:** Global studies. **Math:** General. **Parks/recreation:** Exercise sciences. **Philosophy/religion:** Philosophy, religion. **Physical sciences:** Chemistry, physics. **Psychology:** General. **Public administration:** Social work. **Social sciences:** Economics, political science, sociology. **Visual/ performing arts:** Art history/conservation, dance, dramatic, jazz, music performance, music theory/composition, piano/organ, stringed instruments, studio arts, voice/opera.

**Most popular majors.** Business/marketing 11%, communications/ journalism 7%, education 10%, foreign language 7%, physical sciences 7%, psychology 8%, social sciences 7%, visual/performing arts 7%.

**Computing on campus.** 350 workstations in dormitories, library, computer center, student center. Dormitories wired for high-speed internet access and linked to campus network. Commuter students can connect to campus network. Online library, helpline, repair service, student web hosting, wireless network available.

**Student life. Freshman orientation:** Mandatory. Preregistration for classes offered. 3-day orientation for students and parents begins Friday before school starts. **Policies:** Visitors of opposite gender not allowed after 12 a.m. on weekdays and 2 a.m. on weekends. No alcohol allowed on campus. **Housing:** Guaranteed on-campus for all undergraduates. Coed dorms, single-sex dorms, special housing for disabled, apartments, fraternity/sorority housing, wellness housing available. $300 nonrefundable deposit, deadline 5/1. Cottages (houses on or near campus). **Activities:** Bands, campus ministries, choral groups, dance, drama, international student organizations, literary magazine, music ensembles, Model UN, musical theater, radio station, student government, student newspaper, symphony orchestra, TV station, Fellowship of Christian Athletes, Inter-Varsity Christian Fellowship, Fellowship of Christian Students, College Republicans and Democrats, Higher Horizons, black student union, Hispanic students organization, Catholic student union.

**Athletics.** NCAA. **Intercollegiate:** Baseball M, basketball, cheerleading, cross-country, diving, football (tackle) M, golf, soccer, softball W, swimming, tennis, track and field, volleyball W. **Intramural:** Basketball, bowling, football (non-tackle), racquetball, soccer, softball, tennis, volleyball, water polo. **Team name:** Flying Dutchmen, Flying Dutch.

**Student services.** Adult student services, alcohol/substance abuse counseling, chaplain/spiritual director, career counseling, student employment services, financial aid counseling, health services, minority student services, personal counseling, placement for graduates, women's services. **Physically disabled:** Services for visually, hearing impaired.

**Contact.** E-mail: admissions@hope.edu
Phone: (616) 395-7850 Toll-free number: (800) 968-7850
Fax: (616) 395-7130
William Vanderbilt, Vice President for Admissions, Hope College, 69 East 10th Street, Holland, MI 49422-9000

## International Academy of Design and Technology: Detroit
**Troy, Michigan**
**www.iadtdetroit.com/**

▸ For-profit 4-year visual arts and technical college
▸ Small city
▸ 987 degree-seeking undergraduates

**General.** Accredited by ACICS. **Degrees:** 82 bachelor's, 21 associate awarded. **Calendar:** Semester. **Full-time faculty:** 14 total. **Part-time faculty:** 70 total.

**Freshman class profile.** 147 enrolled.

**Basis for selection.** Open admission.

**Application procedures. Admission:** No deadline. $50 fee. Admission notification on a rolling basis. **Financial aid:** No deadline.

**Academics. Special study options:** Distance learning. **Credit/placement by examination:** CLEP.

**Majors. Communications technology:** Desktop publishing, graphics. **Computer sciences:** Game design. **Visual/performing arts:** Fashion design, graphic design, interior design.

**Contact.** Phone: (248) 457-2700
Richard Reed, Senior Director of Admissions, International Academy of Design and Technology: Detroit, 1850 Research Drive, Troy, MI 48083

## Kalamazoo College
**Kalamazoo, Michigan**
**www.kzoo.edu**
CB member
CB code: 1365

▸ Private 4-year liberal arts college
▸ Residential campus in small city
▸ 1,356 degree-seeking undergraduates: 57% women, 4% African American, 5% Asian American, 4% Hispanic American, 3% international
▸ 48% of applicants admitted
▸ SAT or ACT with writing, application essay required
▸ 75% graduate within 6 years

**General.** Founded in 1833. Regionally accredited. Study abroad centers in Kenya, Senegal, Egypt, India, Thailand, Chile, Japan, Australia, UK, Ecuador, Spain, France, Germany, Mexico, and China. **Degrees:** 316 bachelor's awarded. **ROTC:** Army. **Location:** 140 miles from Detroit, 140 miles from Chicago. **Calendar:** Trimester. **Full-time faculty:** 93 total; 86% have terminal degrees, 18% minority, 48% women. **Part-time faculty:** 18 total; 50% have terminal degrees, 22% minority, 61% women. **Class size:** 61% < 20, 36% 20-39, 3% 40-49, less than 1% 50-99. **Special facilities:** 3 theaters, rare books collection, science center, 100 acre arboretum.

**Freshman class profile.** 1,979 applied, 949 admitted, 391 enrolled.

| Mid 50% test scores | | | |
|---|---|---|---|
| SAT critical reading: | 570-690 | GPA 2.0-2.99: | 4% |
| SAT math: | 560-680 | Rank in top quarter: | 84% |
| SAT writing: | 550-680 | Rank in top tenth: | 46% |
| ACT composite: | 26-30 | Return as sophomores: | 89% |
| GPA 3.75 or higher: | 37% | Out-of-state: | 35% |
| GPA 3.50-3.74: | 31% | Live on campus: | 100% |
| GPA 3.0-3.49: | 28% | International: | 5% |

**Basis for selection.** Curriculum, grades, essay, recommendations, and special accomplishments influence decision. Interview recommended. **Homeschooled:** Statement describing homeschool structure and mission, transcript of courses and grades, interview, letter of recommendation (nonparent) required.

**High school preparation.** College-preparatory program required. 18 units required. Required and recommended units include English 4, mathematics 3-4, social studies 2, history 2, science 3-4 and foreign language 3-4.

**2009-2010 Annual costs.** Tuition/fees: $32,643. Room/board: $7,776. Books/supplies: $750. Personal expenses: $828.

**2008-2009 Financial aid. Non-need-based:** Scholarships awarded for academics, alumni affiliation, art, leadership, minority status, music/drama. **Additional information:** Paid career development internship and senior project experiences available on campus.

**Application procedures. Admission:** Priority date 11/20; deadline 2/1 (postmark date). $40 fee, may be waived for applicants with need. Application must be submitted online. Admission notification 4/1. Must reply by 5/1. **Financial aid:** Priority date 2/15; no closing date. FAFSA, institutional form required. CSS PROFILE required for Early Decision applicants requesting need-based financial aid. Applicants notified on a rolling basis starting 3/21; must reply by 5/1.

**Academics.** Most students participate in career internships and study abroad. College subsidizes most study abroad expenses. Students complete a senior individualized project as part of graduation requirements. **Special study options:** Combined bachelor's/graduate degree, cross-registration, double major, dual enrollment of high school students, exchange student, independent study, internships, New York semester, student-designed major, study abroad, urban semester. **Credit/placement by examination:** AP, CLEP, IB, institutional tests. 18 credit hours maximum toward bachelor's degree. **Support services:** Learning center, reduced course load, study skills assistance, tutoring, writing center.

**Majors. Biology:** General. **Business:** General. **Computer sciences:** General. **Family/consumer sciences:** Family studies. **Foreign languages:** Classics, French, German, Spanish. **Health:** Predental, premedicine, preveterinary. **History:** General. **Legal studies:** Prelaw. **Math:** General. **Philosophy/ religion:** Philosophy, religion. **Physical sciences:** Chemistry, physics. **Psychology:** General. **Social sciences:** Anthropology, economics, political science, sociology. **Visual/performing arts:** Art, art history/conservation, dramatic.

**Most popular majors.** Biology 12%, English 7%, foreign language 9%, history 7%, physical sciences 7%, psychology 10%, social sciences 24%, visual/performing arts 8%.

**Computing on campus.** 130 workstations in library, computer center, student center. Dormitories wired for high-speed internet access and linked to campus network. Commuter students can connect to campus network. Online course registration, online library, helpline, student web hosting, wireless network available.

**Student life. Freshman orientation:** Mandatory. Preregistration for classes offered. Held on campus the week before fall classes begin. **Housing:** Guaranteed on-campus for all undergraduates. Coed dorms, wellness housing available. **Activities:** Bands, campus ministries, choral groups, dance, drama, international student organizations, literary magazine, music ensembles, Model UN, musical theater, radio station, student government, student newspaper, symphony orchestra, TV station, African American student organization, women's equity coalition, volunteer bureau, environmental organization, film society, Habitat for Humanity, Amnesty International, coalition on racial diversity.

**Athletics.** NCAA. **Intercollegiate:** Baseball M, basketball, cross-country, diving, football (tackle) M, golf, soccer, softball W, swimming, tennis, volleyball W. **Intramural:** Basketball, cheerleading W, golf, gymnastics W, racquetball, rugby, skiing, soccer, softball, squash, table tennis, tennis, volleyball, water polo. **Team name:** Hornets.

**Student services.** Alcohol/substance abuse counseling, chaplain/spiritual director, career counseling, student employment services, financial aid counseling, health services, minority student services, personal counseling, placement for graduates, women's services. **Physically disabled:** Services for visually, hearing impaired.

**Contact.** E-mail: admission@kzoo.edu
Phone: (269) 337-7166 Toll-free number: (800) 253-3602
Fax: (269) 337-7390
Eric Staab, Dean of Admission, Kalamazoo College, 1200 Academy Street, Kalamazoo, MI 49006

## Kendall College of Art and Design of Ferris State University
**Grand Rapids, Michigan**
www.kcad.edu                                          CB code: 1376

- Public 4-year visual arts college
- Commuter campus in large city
- 1,149 degree-seeking undergraduates
- 53 graduate students
- SAT or ACT (ACT writing optional), application essay required

**General.** Founded in 1928. Regionally accredited. **Degrees:** 155 bachelor's awarded; master's offered. **Location:** 175 miles from Detroit, 160 miles from Chicago. **Calendar:** Semester, extensive summer session. **Full-time faculty:** 54 total. **Part-time faculty:** 97 total.

**Basis for selection.** High school GPA, statement of purpose/essay, ACT or SAT test scores, and portfolio considered in admission process. Portfolio not required for the following 3 programs: Art History, Furniture Design, Interior Design. Applicants for Interior Design are required to complete an Observation Exercise. **Homeschooled:** Transcript of courses and grades required. **Learning Disabled:** Highly recommended that students with learning disabilities meet college counselor to discuss education needs/assistance to help achieve learning success.

**2009-2010 Annual costs.** Tuition/fees: $15,642; $23,322 out-of-state. Studio art courses: $613 per credit hour in-state and $920 out-of-state. General education courses: $316 per credit hour in-state and $474 out-of-state. Books/supplies: $3,554. Personal expenses: $732.

**2009-2010 Financial aid.** All financial aid based on need.

**Application procedures. Admission:** Priority date 6/1; no deadline. $30 fee, may be waived for applicants with need, free for online applicants. Admission notification on a rolling basis. **Financial aid:** Priority date 2/15; no closing date. FAFSA required. Applicants notified on a rolling basis starting 4/15.

**Academics.** For bachelor's degree, 42-54 credits in major required, depending on specified major. **Special study options:** Combined bachelor's/graduate degree, double major, dual enrollment of high school students, independent study, internships, liberal arts/career combination, New York semester, study abroad, teacher certification program. **Credit/placement by examination:** AP, CLEP, institutional tests. **Support services:** Reduced course load, study skills assistance, tutoring, writing center.

**Majors. Education:** Art. **Production:** Furniture. **Visual/performing arts:** Art history/conservation, commercial/advertising art, design, digital art, drawing, graphic design, illustration, industrial design, interior design, metal/

jewelry, multimedia, painting, photography, printmaking, sculpture, studio arts.

**Most popular majors.** Visual/performing arts 99%.

**Computing on campus.** PC or laptop required. Commuter students can connect to campus network. Online course registration, online library, wireless network available.

**Student life. Freshman orientation:** Available. Preregistration for classes offered. **Housing:** Apartments available.

**Student services.** Adult student services, career counseling, student employment services, financial aid counseling, personal counseling, placement for graduates, veterans' counselor. **Physically disabled:** Services for hearing impaired.

**Contact.** E-mail: kcadadmissions@ferris.edu
Phone: (616) 451-2787 Toll-free number: (800) 676-2787
Fax: (616) 831-9689
Sandra Britton, Director of Enrollment Management, Kendall College of Art and Design of Ferris State University, 17 Fountain Street NW, Grand Rapids, MI 49503-3002

## Kettering University
**Flint, Michigan**                                    CB member
www.kettering.edu                                      CB code: 1246

- Private 4-year university and engineering college
- Residential campus in small city
- 2,009 degree-seeking undergraduates: 1% part-time, 17% women
- 324 degree-seeking graduate students
- 64% of applicants admitted
- SAT or ACT (ACT writing optional) required
- 56% graduate within 6 years

**General.** Founded in 1919. Regionally accredited. Formerly GMI Engineering and Management Institute. **Degrees:** 442 bachelor's awarded; master's offered. **Location:** 70 miles from Detroit. **Calendar:** Semester, extensive summer session. **Full-time faculty:** 116 total; 90% have terminal degrees, 22% minority, 20% women. **Part-time faculty:** 35 total; 14% have terminal degrees, 11% minority, 31% women. **Class size:** 47% < 20, 46% 20-39, 6% 40-49, 1% 50-99. **Special facilities:** Computer-integrated manufacturing laboratory, GM-PACE e-design and e-manufacturing studio, acoustics laboratory, polymer optimization center, engine test center, SAE vehicle development laboratory, mechatronics laboratory, biomedical laboratories on campus and at nearby medical center, Ford design simulation studio, crash study lab, fuel cell research center.

**Freshman class profile.** 3,465 applied, 2,227 admitted, 444 enrolled.

| Mid 50% test scores | | | |
|---|---|---|---|
| SAT critical reading: | 530-650 | Rank in top quarter: | 67% |
| SAT math: | 600-690 | Rank in top tenth: | 27% |
| ACT composite: | 24-29 | End year in good standing: | 79% |
| GPA 3.75 or higher: | 34% | Return as sophomores: | 86% |
| GPA 3.50-3.74: | 30% | Out-of-state: | 32% |
| GPA 3.0-3.49: | 32% | Live on campus: | 100% |
| GPA 2.0-2.99: | 4% | International: | 2% |

**Basis for selection.** GED not accepted. Strength of preparation, performance in school, test scores, nonscholastic activities and achievements most important. Accepted students encouraged to confirm enrollment plans early so co-op employment search process can begin. SAT Subject Tests (especially math level II, chemistry, and physics), while not required, helpful when presented. Interview recommended. **Homeschooled:** Laboratory science experience very important and may need to be documented.

**High school preparation.** College-preparatory program required. 10.5 units required; 21 recommended. Required and recommended units include English 3-4, mathematics 3.5-4, social studies 2, history 2, science 2-3 (laboratory 2-3), foreign language 2 and computer science 1. At least 1 unit of either chemistry or physics with laboratory required. Both chemistry and physics strongly recommended. Algebra I and II, geometry and trigonometry required. Drafting or CAD recommended, especially for those considering engineering.

**2010-2011 Annual costs.** Tuition/fees: $29,270. Room/board: $6,390. Books/supplies: $1,111. Personal expenses: $2,955.

**2009-2010 Financial aid. Need-based:** 406 full-time freshmen applied for aid; 363 were judged to have need; 363 of these received aid. Average need met was 91%. Average scholarship/grant was $17,135; average loan

$3,402. 56% of total undergraduate aid awarded as scholarships/grants, 44% as loans/jobs. **Non-need-based:** Awarded to 538 full-time undergraduates, including 118 freshmen. Scholarships awarded for academics, leadership, minority status, state residency.

**Application procedures. Admission:** No deadline. $35 fee, may be waived for applicants with need, free for online applicants. Admission notification on a rolling basis beginning on or about 10/15. Must reply by May 1 or within 3 week(s) if notified thereafter. Enrollment may be postponed 1 year after admission. **Financial aid:** Priority date 2/14; no closing date. FAFSA required. Applicants notified on a rolling basis starting 1/31.

**Academics. Special study options:** Accelerated study, combined bachelor's/graduate degree, cooperative education, distance learning, double major, dual enrollment of high school students, independent study, study abroad. Paid professional co-op experience in industry required of all undergraduates. Co-op typically begins in first year. Each 24-week semester divided into 11 weeks of classes and 12 weeks of co-op. **Credit/placement by examination:** AP, CLEP, IB, institutional tests. **Support services:** Learning center, study skills assistance, tutoring, writing center.

**Majors. Biology:** Biochemistry. **Business:** Business admin. **Computer sciences:** Computer science. **Engineering:** Computer, electrical, industrial, mechanical. **Math:** Applied. **Physical sciences:** Applied physics, chemistry. **Other:** Engineering physics, Manufacturing management.

**Most popular majors.** Engineering/engineering technologies 90%.

**Computing on campus.** 450 workstations in dormitories, library, computer center, student center. Dormitories wired for high-speed internet access and linked to campus network. Commuter students can connect to campus network. Online library, helpline, wireless network available.

**Student life. Freshman orientation:** Mandatory, $150 fee. Four-day program; begins Thursday before start of classes. **Policies:** Grade requirement to be eligible to join or maintain active membership in Greek letter organizations. **Housing:** Guaranteed on-campus for freshmen. Coed dorms, apartments, fraternity/sorority housing, wellness housing available. $100 fully refundable deposit, deadline 6/1. **Activities:** Jazz band, campus ministries, dance, drama, international student organizations, literary magazine, music ensembles, Model UN, radio station, student government, student newspaper, Christians in Action, Real Service, Engineers Without Borders, National Society of Black Engineers, National Society of Hispanic Engineers, Asian American Association, Black Unity Congress, Kettering Crusade for Christ, India Student Organization.

**Athletics. Intramural:** Basketball, bowling, football (non-tackle), handball, racquetball, soccer, softball, squash, tennis, volleyball, water polo. **Team name:** Bulldogs.

**Student services.** Alcohol/substance abuse counseling, career counseling, student employment services, financial aid counseling, health services, minority student services, personal counseling, placement for graduates, women's services. **Physically disabled:** Services for visually, speech, hearing impaired.

**Contact.** E-mail: admissions@kettering.edu
Phone: (810) 762-7865 Toll-free number: (800) 955-4464 ext. 7865
Fax: (810) 762-9837
Shari Luck, Director of Admissions, Kettering University, 1700 University Avenue, Flint, MI 48504-6214

---

## Kuyper College
**Grand Rapids, Michigan**
www.kuyper.edu
CB code: 1672

- Private 4-year Bible college affiliated with Reformed
- Residential campus in large city
- 341 degree-seeking undergraduates: 11% part-time, 50% women, 4% African American, 2% Asian American, 2% Hispanic American, 8% international
- 1 degree-seeking graduate students
- SAT or ACT (ACT writing optional), application essay required
- 41% graduate within 6 years

**General.** Founded in 1939. Regionally accredited; also accredited by ABHE. **Degrees:** 48 bachelor's awarded. **ROTC:** Army. **Location:** 7 miles from downtown, 180 miles from Chicago. **Calendar:** Semester. **Full-time faculty:** 14 total; 43% have terminal degrees, 14% minority, 50% women. **Part-time faculty:** 23 total; 26% have terminal degrees, 30% women. **Class size:** 65% < 20, 34% 20-39, 1% 40-49.

**Freshman class profile.** 76 enrolled.

| Mid 50% test scores | | |
|---|---|---|
| SAT critical reading: | 550-620 | |
| SAT math: | 530-580 | |
| SAT writing: | 560-590 | |
| ACT composite: | 18-25 | |
| GPA 3.75 or higher: | 19% | |
| GPA 3.50-3.74: | 19% | |
| GPA 3.0-3.49: | 26% | |
| GPA 2.0-2.99: | 36% | |
| Rank in top quarter: | 19% | |
| Rank in top tenth: | 8% | |
| Return as sophomores: | 72% | |
| Out-of-state: | 21% | |
| Live on campus: | 75% | |
| International: | 3% | |

**Basis for selection.** Secondary school record, test scores important. Applicants with 2.0-2.5 GPA evaluated individually and possibly admitted on conditional acceptance. Interview required for borderline applicants. **Homeschooled:** Transcript of courses and grades required.

**High school preparation.** Recommended units include English 4, mathematics 3, social studies 3, science 3, foreign language 1 and academic electives 3.

**2009-2010 Annual costs.** Tuition/fees: $15,218. Room/board: $6,200. Books/supplies: $676. Personal expenses: $848.

**2009-2010 Financial aid. Need-based:** 73 full-time freshmen applied for aid; 67 were judged to have need; 67 of these received aid. Average need met was 67%. Average scholarship/grant was $7,565; average loan $4,336. 54% of total undergraduate aid awarded as scholarships/grants, 46% as loans/jobs. **Non-need-based:** Awarded to 130 full-time undergraduates, including 34 freshmen. Scholarships awarded for academics, leadership, minority status.

**Application procedures. Admission:** Priority date 8/15; no deadline. $25 fee, may be waived for applicants with need, free for online applicants. Admission notification on a rolling basis. **Financial aid:** Priority date 3/1; no closing date. FAFSA required. Applicants notified on a rolling basis starting 3/15; must reply within 2 week(s) of notification.

**Academics. Special study options:** Combined bachelor's/graduate degree, cooperative education, double major, dual enrollment of high school students, ESL, independent study, internships, study abroad, teacher certification program. **Credit/placement by examination:** AP, CLEP, SAT, ACT, institutional tests. **Support services:** Learning center, pre-admission summer program, reduced course load, remedial instruction, study skills assistance, tutoring, writing center.

**Majors. Business:** Accounting, business admin, international. **Communications:** General, journalism, media studies, public relations. **Education:** Elementary, kindergarten/preschool, secondary. **Health:** Prenursing. **Parks/recreation:** Exercise sciences. **Public administration:** Social work. **Theology:** Bible, missionary, preministerial, religious ed, sacred music, youth ministry. **Visual/performing arts:** Dramatic.

**Most popular majors.** Education 6%, liberal arts 19%, public administration/social services 16%, theological studies 54%.

**Computing on campus.** 54 workstations in dormitories, library, computer center. Dormitories linked to campus network. Commuter students can connect to campus network. Online library, helpline, student web hosting, wireless network available.

**Student life. Freshman orientation:** Available. Preregistration for classes offered. Held first week of fall semester. **Policies:** Smoke-free campus, alcohol and drug-free campus, standards of conduct and housing policies in accordance with school's moral values. **Housing:** Guaranteed on-campus for freshmen. Coed dorms, special housing for disabled, apartments, wellness housing available. $100 nonrefundable deposit. **Activities:** Choral groups, drama, international student organizations, music ensembles, student government, Bible studies, Student Activities Committee, Spiritual Life Committee, Social Work organization, Intramurals Committee, Street Team.

**Athletics.** NCCAA. **Intercollegiate:** Basketball. **Intramural:** Baseball, basketball, field hockey, football (non-tackle), soccer, softball, table tennis, volleyball. **Team name:** Cougars.

**Student services.** Alcohol/substance abuse counseling, chaplain/spiritual director, career counseling, student employment services, financial aid counseling, health services, minority student services, personal counseling, placement for graduates, veterans' counselor. **Physically disabled:** Services for visually impaired. **Learning disabled:** Comprehensive services available.

**Contact.** E-mail: admissions@kuyper.edu
Phone: (616) 988-3621 Toll-free number: (800) 511-3749
Fax: (616) 988-3608
Ryan Struck-VanderHaak, Vice President for Enrollment, Kuyper College, 3333 East Beltline Avenue Northeast, Grand Rapids, MI 49525-9749

## Lake Superior State University
### Sault Ste. Marie, Michigan
### www.lssu.edu

**CB member**
**CB code: 1421**

◗ Public 4-year university and engineering college
◗ Residential campus in large town
◗ 2,528 degree-seeking undergraduates: 14% part-time, 52% women, 1% African American, 1% Hispanic American, 8% Native American, 11% international
◗ 17 degree-seeking graduate students
◗ 88% of applicants admitted
◗ SAT or ACT (ACT writing recommended) required

**General.** Founded in 1946. Regionally accredited. **Degrees:** 457 bachelor's, 109 associate awarded; master's offered. **Calendar:** Semester, limited summer session. **Full-time faculty:** 104 total; 7% minority, 39% women. **Part-time faculty:** 80 total; 1% minority, 55% women. **Class size:** 55% < 20, 33% 20-39, 6% 40-49, 5% 50-99, less than 1% >100. **Special facilities:** Aquatic research laboratory with fish hatchery and toxicology lab, planetarium, natural science museum, 200-acre biology station, robotics laboratory, indoor rifle range, indoor ice arena.

**Freshman class profile.** 677 applied, 597 admitted, 512 enrolled.

| Mid 50% test scores | | Return as sophomores: | 68% |
|---|---|---|---|
| ACT composite: | 19-24 | Out-of-state: | 1% |
| Rank in top quarter: | 28% | Live on campus: | 63% |
| Rank in top tenth: | 12% | International: | 6% |

**Basis for selection.** Cumulative GPA, high school course curriculum, and ACT or SAT most important. **Learning Disabled:** Students with learning disabilities referred to coordinator for Resource Center for Students with Disabilities.

**High school preparation.** College-preparatory program recommended. 18 units recommended. Recommended units include English 4, mathematics 3, social studies 2, history 1, science 3 (laboratory 3) and foreign language 2. Specific academic units required vary by college program.

**2009-2010 Annual costs.** Tuition/fees: $8,284; $16,468 out-of-state. Residents of Ontario pay in-state tuition. Residents of Kansas, Minnesota, Missouri, Nebraska, and North Dakota eligible for Midwest Consortium agreement rate of $512 per credit. Room/board: $7,923. Books/supplies: $900. Personal expenses: $1,397.

**2008-2009 Financial aid. Need-based:** 27% of total undergraduate aid awarded as scholarships/grants, 73% as loans/jobs. **Non-need-based:** Scholarships awarded for academics, alumni affiliation, athletics, state residency.

**Application procedures. Admission:** No deadline. $35 fee, may be waived for applicants with need. Admission notification on a rolling basis beginning on or about 9/15. **Financial aid:** Priority date 3/1; no closing date. FAFSA required. Applicants notified on a rolling basis starting 11/1; must reply within 3 week(s) of notification.

**Academics. Special study options:** Combined bachelor's/graduate degree, cooperative education, cross-registration, distance learning, double major, dual enrollment of high school students, honors, independent study, internships, student-designed major, study abroad, teacher certification program, weekend college. **Credit/placement by examination:** AP, CLEP, IB, SAT, ACT, institutional tests. **Support services:** Learning center, reduced course load, remedial instruction, study skills assistance, tutoring, writing center.

**Majors. Biology:** General. **Business:** General, accounting, business admin, managerial economics. **Communications:** General. **Computer sciences:** General. **Conservation:** General, environmental science, fisheries, management/policy, wildlife. **Education:** Early childhood, elementary, multi-level teacher, secondary. **Engineering:** Computer, electrical, mechanical. **Engineering technology:** Electrical, industrial management, manufacturing. **Foreign languages:** French, Spanish. **Health:** Clinical lab science, nursing (RN), recreational therapy. **History:** General. **Interdisciplinary:** Math/computer science. **Legal studies:** Paralegal. **Liberal arts:** Arts/sciences. **Math:** General. **Parks/recreation:** Exercise sciences, facilities management. **Physical sciences:** Chemistry, forensic chemistry, geology. **Protective services:** Fire safety technology, law enforcement admin. **Psychology:** General. **Social sciences:** General, political science, sociology. **Visual/performing arts:** Studio arts.

**Most popular majors.** Business/marketing 17%, education 12%, health sciences 11%, security/protective services 20%.

**Computing on campus.** 450 workstations in library, computer center, student center. Dormitories wired for high-speed internet access and linked to campus network. Commuter students can connect to campus network.

Online course registration, online library, helpline, wireless network available.

**Student life. Freshman orientation:** Mandatory, $125 fee. Preregistration for classes offered. One-day program held during the summer; 5 dates available. **Housing:** Guaranteed on-campus for freshmen. Coed dorms, single-sex dorms, apartments, fraternity/sorority housing, wellness housing available. $300 partly refundable deposit, deadline 6/1. **Activities:** Bands, campus ministries, choral groups, dance, drama, literary magazine, music ensembles, musical theater, radio station, student government, student newspaper, symphony orchestra, Campus Crusade for Christ, Christian fellowship, Newman Center, Native American students' council, political science club, environmental awareness club, professional organizations.

**Athletics.** NCAA. **Intercollegiate:** Basketball, cross-country, golf, ice hockey M, softball W, tennis, track and field, volleyball W. **Intramural:** Badminton, basketball, football (non-tackle) M, handball, ice hockey, racquetball, soccer, softball, tennis, track and field, volleyball, water polo, wrestling M. **Team name:** Lakers.

**Student services.** Adult student services, alcohol/substance abuse counseling, chaplain/spiritual director, career counseling, services for economically disadvantaged, student employment services, financial aid counseling, health services, minority student services, on-campus daycare, personal counseling, placement for graduates, veterans' counselor. **Physically disabled:** Services for visually, speech, hearing impaired.

**Contact.** E-mail: admissions@lssu.edu
Phone: (906) 635-2231 Toll-free number: (888) 800-5778
Fax: (906) 635-6696
Susan Camp, Director of Admissions, Lake Superior State University, 650 West Easterday Avenue, Sault Ste. Marie, MI 49783-1699

## Lawrence Technological University
### Southfield, Michigan
### www.ltu.edu

**CB member**
**CB code: 1399**

◗ Private 4-year university
◗ Commuter campus in small city
◗ 2,257 degree-seeking undergraduates: 28% part-time, 26% women, 13% African American, 4% Asian American, 2% Hispanic American, 7% international
◗ 1,327 degree-seeking graduate students
◗ 50% of applicants admitted
◗ SAT or ACT (ACT writing optional), application essay required
◗ 45% graduate within 6 years

**General.** Founded in 1932. Regionally accredited. **Degrees:** 451 bachelor's, 21 associate awarded; master's, doctoral offered. **ROTC:** Air Force. **Location:** 20 miles from Detroit. **Calendar:** Semester, extensive summer session. **Full-time faculty:** 129 total; 72% have terminal degrees, 10% minority, 26% women. **Part-time faculty:** 301 total; 36% have terminal degrees, 11% minority, 22% women. **Class size:** 75% < 20, 23% 20-39, less than 1% 40-49, less than 1% 50-99. **Special facilities:** Frank Lloyd Wright-designed residence for academic study.

**Freshman class profile.** 1,698 applied, 845 admitted, 344 enrolled.

| Mid 50% test scores | | End year in good standing: | 82% |
|---|---|---|---|
| ACT composite: | 21-27 | Return as sophomores: | 72% |
| GPA 3.75 or higher: | 24% | Out-of-state: | 1% |
| GPA 3.50-3.74: | 19% | Live on campus: | 44% |
| GPA 3.0-3.49: | 30% | International: | 2% |
| GPA 2.0-2.99: | 27% | Fraternities: | 18% |
| Rank in top quarter: | 56% | Sororities: | 13% |
| Rank in top tenth: | 26% | | |

**Basis for selection.** Minimum 2.50 GPA required; Architecture/Transportation Design program requires 2.75. **Homeschooled:** Transcript of courses and grades, letter of recommendation (nonparent) required.

**High school preparation.** College-preparatory program recommended. 12 units required. Required and recommended units include English 4, mathematics 3-4, social studies 3, history 2, science 2-4 (laboratory 2).

**2009-2010 Annual costs.** Tuition/fees: $22,958. Room/board: $9,253. Books/supplies: $1,270. Personal expenses: $2,000.

**2008-2009 Financial aid. Need-based:** 262 full-time freshmen applied for aid; 210 were judged to have need; 208 of these received aid. Average need met was 69%. Average scholarship/grant was $11,703; average loan $6,079. 48% of total undergraduate aid awarded as scholarships/grants, 52% as loans/jobs. **Non-need-based:** Awarded to 902 full-time undergraduates,

including 197 freshmen. Scholarships awarded for academics, alumni affiliation, art, job skills, leadership, minority status, ROTC, state residency. **Additional information:** March 1 state deadline for Michigan Competitive Scholarship and Michigan Tuition Grant.

**Application procedures. Admission:** No deadline. $30 fee, may be waived for applicants with need. Admission notification on a rolling basis. **Financial aid:** Priority date 4/1; no closing date. FAFSA required. Applicants notified on a rolling basis starting 3/1; must reply within 2 week(s) of notification.

**Academics. Special study options:** Cooperative education, cross-registration, distance learning, double major, dual enrollment of high school students, ESL, honors, independent study, internships, liberal arts/career combination, study abroad, weekend college. **Credit/placement by examination:** AP, CLEP, IB, institutional tests. **Support services:** Learning center, pre-admission summer program, reduced course load, remedial instruction, study skills assistance, tutoring, writing center.

**Majors. Architecture:** Architecture, environmental design, interior. **Biology:** Biochemistry, molecular. **Business:** Business admin, construction management, international. **Communications:** General. **Communications technology:** General. **Computer sciences:** Computer science, information technology. **Engineering:** Architectural, biomedical, civil, computer, electrical, industrial, mechanical. **Engineering technology:** General, industrial, industrial management. **Interdisciplinary:** Math/computer science. **Liberal arts:** Humanities. **Math:** General. **Physical sciences:** Chemistry, physics. **Psychology:** General. **Visual/performing arts:** Design, illustration.

**Most popular majors.** Architecture 35%, computer/information sciences 6%, engineering/engineering technologies 47%.

**Computing on campus.** PC or laptop required. 100 workstations in dormitories, library, computer center, student center. Dormitories wired for high-speed internet access and linked to campus network. Commuter students can connect to campus network. Online course registration, online library, helpline, repair service, student web hosting, wireless network available.

**Student life. Freshman orientation:** Mandatory. **Housing:** Special housing for disabled, apartments, wellness housing available. $200 nonrefundable deposit, deadline 6/30. **Activities:** Literary magazine, music ensembles, student government, student newspaper, Campus Crusade for Christ, Alpha Kappa Alpha Sorority, Phi Beta Sigma Fraternity, National Society of Black Engineers, Young Republicans, Alpha Phi Omega.

**Athletics. Intramural:** Badminton, basketball, bowling, cricket M, football (non-tackle), golf, racquetball, skiing, soccer, softball, table tennis, tennis, volleyball. **Team name:** Blue Devils.

**Student services.** Alcohol/substance abuse counseling, career counseling, services for economically disadvantaged, student employment services, financial aid counseling, minority student services, personal counseling, placement for graduates, veterans' counselor. **Physically disabled:** Services for visually, speech, hearing impaired.

**Contact.** E-mail: admissions@ltu.edu
Phone: (248) 204-3160 Toll-free number: (800) 225-5588
Fax: (248) 204-2228
Jane Rohrback, Director of Admissions, Lawrence Technological University, 21000 West Ten Mile Road, Southfield, MI 48075-1058

## Madonna University
**Livonia, Michigan**
**www.madonna.edu**      **CB code: 1437**

◗ Private 4-year university and liberal arts college affiliated with Roman Catholic Church
◗ Commuter campus in small city
◗ 2,854 degree-seeking undergraduates: 42% part-time, 75% women, 14% African American, 2% Asian American, 3% Hispanic American, 5% international
◗ 1,334 graduate students
◗ 74% of applicants admitted
◗ SAT or ACT (ACT writing recommended), application essay required
◗ 53% graduate within 6 years

**General.** Founded in 1947. Regionally accredited. **Degrees:** 608 bachelor's, 20 associate awarded; master's, professional offered. **Location:** 18 miles from Detroit, 20 miles from Ann Arbor. **Calendar:** Semester, limited summer session. **Full-time faculty:** 120 total; 100% have terminal degrees, 7% minority, 58% women. **Part-time faculty:** 210 total; 98% have terminal

degrees, 9% minority, 60% women. **Class size:** 70% < 20, 26% 20-39, less than 1% 40-49, 3% 50-99.

**Freshman class profile.** 702 applied, 516 admitted, 189 enrolled.

| Mid 50% test scores | | | |
|---|---|---|---|
| SAT critical reading: | 480-670 | GPA 2.0-2.99: | 26% |
| SAT math: | 470-630 | Rank in top quarter: | 40% |
| SAT writing: | 500-770 | Rank in top tenth: | 16% |
| ACT composite: | 19-23 | End year in good standing: | 94% |
| GPA 3.75 or higher: | 21% | Return as sophomores: | 93% |
| GPA 3.50-3.74: | 15% | Out-of-state: | 2% |
| GPA 3.0-3.49: | 34% | Live on campus: | 25% |
| | | International: | 2% |

**Basis for selection.** GPA and curriculum most important. Majors in sciences, allied health and nursing, and math require specific high school subjects. ACT test results important. Some majors require letters of recommendation. ACT preferred. Interview recommended.

**High school preparation.** College-preparatory program recommended. 19 units required. Required and recommended units include English 3-4, mathematics 2-4, social studies 3-4, history 4, science 3-4 (laboratory 1) and foreign language 2. 1 biology, 1 chemistry, 1 algebra required for nursing applicants; biology, 1 chemistry, 2 algebra recommended for medical and radiologic technology program applicants.

**2009-2010 Annual costs.** Tuition/fees: $13,150. Nursing students pay $466 per credit hour. Nonresident aliens pay $2,500 deposit. Room/board: $6,808. Books/supplies: $992. Personal expenses: $1,076.

**2008-2009 Financial aid. Need-based:** 126 full-time freshmen applied for aid; 93 were judged to have need; 93 of these received aid. Average need met was 49%. Average scholarship/grant was $5,825; average loan $2,970. 36% of total undergraduate aid awarded as scholarships/grants, 64% as loans/jobs. **Non-need-based:** Awarded to 259 full-time undergraduates, including 114 freshmen. Scholarships awarded for academics, alumni affiliation, art, athletics, leadership, minority status, music/drama, religious affiliation, state residency.

**Application procedures. Admission:** Priority date 9/1; no deadline. $25 fee, may be waived for applicants with need. Admission notification on a rolling basis. **Financial aid:** Priority date 2/21; no closing date. FAFSA required. Applicants notified on a rolling basis starting 3/15; must reply by 9/1 or within 2 week(s) of notification.

**Academics. Special study options:** Accelerated study, combined bachelor's/graduate degree, cooperative education, cross-registration, distance learning, double major, dual enrollment of high school students, ESL, independent study, internships, liberal arts/career combination, student-designed major, study abroad, teacher certification program. **Credit/placement by examination:** AP, CLEP, IB, ACT, institutional tests. 30 credit hours maximum toward associate degree, 60 toward bachelor's. **Support services:** Learning center, pre-admission summer program, reduced course load, remedial instruction, study skills assistance, tutoring, writing center.

**Majors. Biology:** General, biochemistry. **Business:** Accounting, business admin, hospitality admin, human resources, international, management information systems, marketing. **Communications:** General, journalism. **Computer sciences:** Computer science. **Conservation:** Environmental science. **Education:** Early childhood, mathematics, physical, science, social studies. **Engineering technology:** Occupational safety. **Family/consumer sciences:** General, aging, child development, food/nutrition, merchandising. **Foreign languages:** American Sign Language, Spanish. **Health:** Clinical lab science, clinical lab technology, health care admin, nursing (RN), predental, premedicine, prenursing, prepharmacy, preveterinary. **History:** General. **Interdisciplinary:** Gerontology, natural sciences. **Legal studies:** Paralegal, prelaw. **Liberal arts:** Humanities. **Math:** General. **Parks/recreation:** Sports admin. **Philosophy/religion:** Philosophy, religion. **Physical sciences:** Chemistry, physics. **Protective services:** Criminal justice, firefighting, forensics. **Psychology:** General, industrial. **Public administration:** Social work. **Social sciences:** Political science, sociology. **Theology:** Sacred music, theology. **Visual/performing arts:** Art history/conservation, design, graphic design, music performance, studio arts. **Other:** Applied science, Engineering, pre-engineering, Health/medical preparatory programs, Occupational safety and health/fire science, Pastoral counseling and specialized ministries, Psychological trauma research, Security and protective services, Television and video communications.

**Most popular majors.** Business/marketing 14%, family/consumer sciences 6%, health sciences 21%, security/protective services 13%.

**Computing on campus.** 157 workstations in dormitories, library, computer center. Dormitories wired for high-speed internet access and linked to campus network. Commuter students can connect to campus network. Online course registration, online library, helpline, wireless network available.

**Student life. Freshman orientation:** Mandatory. Preregistration for classes offered. All day orientation held in May, June, and July; evening orientation for adult and transfer students in January, June, and July; Saturday orientation held in August and December. **Policies:** Use of alcohol or drugs prohibited on campus; all buildings smoke-free; sexual assault, harassment policies in place. **Housing:** Single-sex dorms, wellness housing available. $75 nonrefundable deposit, deadline 9/1. **Activities:** Campus ministries, choral groups, international student organizations, music ensembles, musical theater, radio station, student government, student newspaper, TV station, social work student association, gerontology association, student-faculty academic clubs, athletic club, nursing student association, business professional association, student teacher association.

**Athletics.** NAIA. **Intercollegiate:** Baseball M, basketball, cross-country, golf, soccer, softball W, volleyball W. **Team name:** Crusaders.

**Student services.** Adult student services, alcohol/substance abuse counseling, chaplain/spiritual director, career counseling, services for economically disadvantaged, student employment services, financial aid counseling, health services, minority student services, personal counseling, placement for graduates, women's services. **Physically disabled:** Services for visually, speech, hearing impaired.

**Contact.** E-mail: muinfo@madonna.edu
Phone: (734) 432-5339 Toll-free number: (800) 852-4951
Fax: (734) 432-5424
Michael Quattro, Director of Undergraduate Admission, Madonna University, 36600 Schoolcraft Road, Livonia, MI 48150-1176

## Marygrove College
### Detroit, Michigan
### www.marygrove.edu
### CB code: 1452

- Private 4-year liberal arts college affiliated with Roman Catholic Church
- Commuter campus in very large city
- 911 degree-seeking undergraduates
- 31% of applicants admitted
- Application essay required

**General.** Founded in 1905. Regionally accredited. **Degrees:** 81 bachelor's, 9 associate awarded; master's offered. **Location:** 6 miles from downtown. **Calendar:** Semester, limited summer session. **Full-time faculty:** 56 total. **Part-time faculty:** 8 total.

**Freshman class profile.** 1,364 applied, 419 admitted, 156 enrolled.

| Mid 50% test scores | ACT composite: | 15-19 |
|---|---|---|

**Basis for selection.** School achievement record and test scores most important. ACT recommended. Audition required of music, theater, dance majors. Portfolio required of art majors. Interview required of older applicants and academically weak applicants.

**High school preparation.** College-preparatory program recommended. 17 units recommended. Recommended units include English 4, mathematics 2, social studies 2, history 2, science 3 (laboratory 1), foreign language 2 and computer science 1.

**2009-2010 Annual costs.** Tuition/fees: $16,280. Room/board: $7,000. Books/supplies: $1,040. Personal expenses: $2,200.

**2009-2010 Financial aid.** All financial aid based on need.

**Application procedures. Admission:** Priority date 12/1; deadline 3/15 (postmark date). $25 fee, may be waived for applicants with need. Admission notification on a rolling basis. Must reply by 5/1. **Financial aid:** Priority date 3/15; no closing date. FAFSA, institutional form required. Applicants notified on a rolling basis starting 5/15; must reply within 2 week(s) of notification.

**Academics. Special study options:** Cooperative education, cross-registration, distance learning, double major, dual enrollment of high school students, honors, independent study, internships, student-designed major, study abroad, teacher certification program. **Credit/placement by examination:** AP, CLEP, ACT, institutional tests. 16 credit hours maximum toward associate degree, 32 toward bachelor's. Credit awarded for score of 3 or higher on AP exam. Credit hours awarded determined by faculty. **Support services:** Learning center, pre-admission summer program, reduced course load, remedial instruction, study skills assistance, tutoring, writing center.

**Majors. Biology:** General. **Business:** General, accounting, business admin, international. **Computer sciences:** General. **Conservation:** Environmental science. **Education:** General, early childhood, special. **Health:** Art therapy.

**History:** General. **Interdisciplinary:** Natural sciences. **Math:** General. **Philosophy/religion:** Religion. **Physical sciences:** Chemistry. **Psychology:** General. **Public administration:** Social work. **Social sciences:** General, political science. **Visual/performing arts:** Art, dance, music performance, music theory/composition, studio arts.

**Computing on campus.** 50 workstations in dormitories, library, computer center, student center. Dormitories wired for high-speed internet access and linked to campus network. Commuter students can connect to campus network. Online course registration, online library, helpline, wireless network available.

**Student life. Freshman orientation:** Mandatory. Preregistration for classes offered. 2-day weekday program; students spend night in dorms. **Housing:** Coed dorms available. $250 deposit, deadline 8/1. **Activities:** Campus ministries, choral groups, dance, international student organizations, music ensembles, student government, student newspaper, debate teams (political & philosophical), Black social worker club, Ensemble gospel choir, art club, diversity club, optimist club, criminal justice, math & science club, English Honors Society, Hype Squad.

**Athletics.** NAIA. **Intercollegiate:** Basketball, cross-country, soccer, volleyball W. **Intramural:** Badminton, basketball, bowling, football (non-tackle), golf, soccer, softball, table tennis, track and field, volleyball. **Team name:** Mustangs.

**Student services.** Alcohol/substance abuse counseling, chaplain/spiritual director, career counseling, services for economically disadvantaged, student employment services, financial aid counseling, health services, on-campus daycare, personal counseling, placement for graduates, women's services.

**Contact.** E-mail: info@marygrove.edu
Phone: (313) 927-1240 Toll-free number: (866) 313-1927
Fax: (313) 927-1345
Edwina Tansil, Marygrove College, 8425 West McNichols Road, Detroit, MI 48221

## Michigan Jewish Institute
### West Bloomfield, Michigan
### www.mji.edu
### CB code: 1505

- Private 4-year business and liberal arts college affiliated with Jewish faith
- Commuter campus in very large city
- 75 degree-seeking undergraduates

**General.** Accredited by ACICS. **Degrees:** 5 bachelor's awarded. **Calendar:** Semester, limited summer session. **Full-time faculty:** 3 total. **Part-time faculty:** 15 total. **Special facilities:** Synagogue available on West Bloomfield campus.

**Basis for selection.** Open admission, but selective for some programs. 2.0 GPA required; applicants with less than 2.0 GPA or with GED may be accepted under provisional status. **Homeschooled:** Statement describing homeschool structure and mission, transcript of courses and grades, interview, letter of recommendation (nonparent) required.

**High school preparation.** Recommended units include English 3, mathematics 3, social studies 1, history 2, science 3 (laboratory 1), foreign language 2 and computer science 1.

**2009-2010 Annual costs.** Tuition/fees: $10,500. Books/supplies: $1,215. Personal expenses: $1,060.

**Financial aid. Non-need-based:** Scholarships awarded for academics.

**Application procedures. Admission:** No deadline. $50 fee. Admission notification on a rolling basis. High school students may enroll in dual studies program to earn high school and college credits for the same courses. Students may also be admitted into the college for up to 6 months before high school graduation. Should an admitted student not complete high school within the 6 months, they will not be able to continue until proof of high school graduation or GED is provided.

**Academics. Special study options:** Accelerated study, cooperative education, distance learning, double major, dual enrollment of high school students, ESL, independent study, internships, liberal arts/career combination, study abroad, weekend college. **Credit/placement by examination:** AP, CLEP, IB, institutional tests. **Support services:** Learning center, reduced course load, remedial instruction, study skills assistance, tutoring.

**Majors. Business:** Business admin. **Computer sciences:** General. **Philosophy/religion:** Judaic. **Other:** Judaic education, Judaic organizational leadership.

**Most popular majors.** Area/ethnic studies 10%, business/marketing 30%, computer/information sciences 20%, education 10%, philosophy/religious studies 20%, theological studies 10%.

**Computing on campus.** PC or laptop required. 16 workstations in library, computer center, student center. Online library, helpline, wireless network available.

**Student life. Freshman orientation:** Available. Preregistration for classes offered. Scheduled onsite sessions and online tutorials available.

**Student services.** Adult student services, alcohol/substance abuse counseling, chaplain/spiritual director, career counseling, student employment services, financial aid counseling, personal counseling.

**Contact.**  E-mail: info@mji.edu
Phone: (248) 414-6900 ext. 105 Fax: (248) 414-6907
Fran Herman, Registrar, Michigan Jewish Institute, 6890 West Maple Road, West Bloomfield, MI 48322

---

### Michigan State University
**East Lansing, Michigan**  CB member
**www.msu.edu**  CB code: 1465

- Public 4-year university
- Residential campus in small city
- 36,224 degree-seeking undergraduates: 8% part-time, 52% women, 8% African American, 5% Asian American, 3% Hispanic American, 1% Native American, 7% international
- 9,455 degree-seeking graduate students
- 73% of applicants admitted
- SAT or ACT with writing, application essay required
- 75% graduate within 6 years; 25% enter graduate study

**General.** Founded in 1855. Regionally accredited. **Degrees:** 7,814 bachelor's awarded; master's, doctoral, professional offered. **ROTC:** Army, Air Force. **Location:** 3 miles from Lansing, 80 miles from Detroit. **Calendar:** Semester, extensive summer session. **Full-time faculty:** 2,620 total; 93% have terminal degrees, 23% minority, 36% women. **Part-time faculty:** 352 total; 60% have terminal degrees, 14% minority, 54% women. **Class size:** 24% < 20, 47% 20-39, 7% 40-49, 9% 50-99, 12% >100. **Special facilities:** Planetarium, observatory, botanical garden, center for environmental toxicology, superconducting cyclotron laboratory, pesticide research center, experimental farms, 2 museums, center for performing arts, 2 golf courses, agricultural and livestock pavilion, children's garden.

**Freshman class profile.** 25,349 applied, 18,383 admitted, 7,416 enrolled.

| Mid 50% test scores | | GPA 2.0-2.99: | 6% |
|---|---|---|---|
| SAT critical reading: | 470-610 | Rank in top quarter: | 70% |
| SAT math: | 540-660 | Rank in top tenth: | 31% |
| SAT writing: | 480-610 | Return as sophomores: | 91% |
| ACT composite: | 23-27 | Out-of-state: | 13% |
| GPA 3.75 or higher: | 37% | Live on campus: | 94% |
| GPA 3.50-3.74: | 29% | International: | 9% |
| GPA 3.0-3.49: | 28% | | |

**Basis for selection.** Freshman admission based upon academic performance in high school, strength and quality of curriculum, recent trends in academic performance, class rank, test scores, leadership, talents, conduct and diversity of experience. Recommended that test scores be received no later than April. Audition required of music majors. **Homeschooled:** Submit grades, even if from parent. List or provide information on curriculum and be prepared to answer questions. Test scores have stronger emphasis; transcript required.

**High school preparation.** College-preparatory program recommended. Required and recommended units include English 4, mathematics 3, social studies 2, history 1-2, science 2 (laboratory 2) and foreign language 2.

**2009-2010 Annual costs.** Tuition/fees: $10,880; $27,343 out-of-state. Room/board: $7,394. Books/supplies: $962. Personal expenses: $1,246.

**2009-2010 Financial aid.** All financial aid based on need. 5,427 full-time freshmen applied for aid; 3,700 were judged to have need; 3,675 of these received aid. Average need met was 70%. Average scholarship/grant was $9,119; average loan $3,464. 55% of total undergraduate aid awarded as scholarships/grants, 45% as loans/jobs.

**Application procedures. Admission:** No deadline. $35 fee, may be waived for applicants with need. Admission notification on a rolling basis. Must reply by May 1 or within 4 week(s) if notified thereafter. Common

Application accepted, use of internal application preferred. Early Action by invitation only. Test scores should be submitted by April. **Financial aid:** No deadline. FAFSA required. Applicants notified on a rolling basis starting 3/15; must reply within 4 week(s) of notification.

**Academics. Special study options:** Accelerated study, combined bachelor's/graduate degree, cooperative education, distance learning, double major, dual enrollment of high school students, ESL, exchange student, honors, independent study, internships, liberal arts/career combination, student-designed major, study abroad, teacher certification program, weekend college. **Credit/placement by examination:** AP, CLEP, IB, SAT, ACT, institutional tests. 60 credit hours maximum toward bachelor's degree. **Support services:** Learning center, pre-admission summer program, reduced course load, remedial instruction, study skills assistance, tutoring, writing center.

**Honors college/program.** Selection criteria include test scores and class rank. Number admitted varies.

**Majors. Agriculture:** Animal sciences, business, economics, food science, horticultural science, soil science. **Architecture:** Landscape, urban/community planning. **Area/ethnic studies:** African-American, American, Asian, Central/Eastern European, Native American, Russian/Slavic, women's. **Biology:** General, biochemistry, Biochemistry/biophysics and molecular biology, botany, entomology, environmental, microbiology, molecular, molecular genetics, physiology, plant pathology, zoology. **Business:** Accounting, apparel, business admin, construction management, fashion, finance, hospitality admin, human resources, information resources management, logistics, management information systems, marketing. **Communications:** General, advertising, journalism, public relations, radio/tv. **Communications technology:** General. **Computer sciences:** General, information systems. **Conservation:** Economics, environmental science, environmental studies, fisheries, forestry, wildlife. **Education:** General, art, biology, chemistry, computer, Deaf/hearing impaired, early childhood, elementary, family/consumer sciences, French, geography, German, health, history, kindergarten/preschool, learning disabled, mathematics, middle, music, physical, physics, reading, science, secondary, social science, social studies, Spanish, special. **Engineering:** General, agricultural, biomedical, chemical, civil, computer, electrical, materials, materials science, mechanical. **Engineering technology:** Construction. **Family/consumer sciences:** General, apparel marketing, child development, clothing/textiles, family/community services, textile manufacture, textile science. **Foreign languages:** Arabic, Chinese, East Asian, French, German, Japanese, linguistics, Russian, Spanish. **Health:** Athletic training, audiology/speech pathology, clinical lab science, communication disorders, community health services, dietetics, marriage/family therapy, nurse practitioner, nursing (RN), premedicine, veterinary technology/assistant. **History:** General. **Interdisciplinary:** Biological/physical sciences, classical/archaeology, global studies, nutrition sciences, science/society. **Legal studies:** Prelaw. **Liberal arts:** Humanities. **Math:** General, computational, statistics. **Parks/recreation:** General, exercise sciences. **Philosophy/religion:** Philosophy, religion. **Physical sciences:** General, astrophysics, chemical physics, chemistry, geology, geophysics, physics. **Protective services:** Criminal justice, law enforcement admin. **Psychology:** General. **Public administration:** General, policy analysis, social work. **Social sciences:** General, anthropology, economics, geography, international relations, political science, sociology. **Visual/performing arts:** Acting, art, art history/conservation, design, dramatic, fashion design, interior design, jazz, music pedagogy, music performance, music theory/composition, theater arts management. **Other:** Packaging.

**Most popular majors.** Biology 9%, business/marketing 19%, communications/journalism 13%, engineering/engineering technologies 8%, health sciences 6%, social sciences 11%.

**Computing on campus.** PC or laptop required. 2,000 workstations in dormitories, library, computer center, student center. Dormitories wired for high-speed internet access and linked to campus network. Commuter students can connect to campus network. Online course registration, online library, helpline, repair service, student web hosting, wireless network available.

**Student life. Freshman orientation:** Mandatory, $175 fee. Preregistration for classes offered. One-and-a-half day session in summer; includes placement tests. **Housing:** Guaranteed on-campus for freshmen. Coed dorms, single-sex dorms, special housing for disabled, apartments, cooperative housing, fraternity/sorority housing, wellness housing available. $250 fully refundable deposit, deadline 5/1. **Activities:** Bands, campus ministries, choral groups, dance, drama, film society, international student organizations, literary magazine, music ensembles, Model UN, musical theater, opera, radio station, student government, student newspaper, symphony orchestra, TV station, over 500 organizations.

**Athletics.** NCAA. **Intercollegiate:** Baseball M, basketball, cheerleading, cross-country, diving, field hockey W, football (tackle) M, golf, gymnastics W, ice hockey M, rowing (crew) W, soccer, softball W, swimming, tennis, track and field, volleyball W, wrestling M. **Intramural:** Archery, baseball M, basketball, cross-country, fencing, football (non-tackle) M, golf, gymnastics, ice hockey, lacrosse M, racquetball, rowing (crew) M, rugby, sailing, skiing, soccer, softball, squash, swimming, tennis, track and field, volleyball, water polo, wrestling M. **Team name:** Spartans.

**Student services.** Adult student services, alcohol/substance abuse counseling, career counseling, services for economically disadvantaged, student employment services, financial aid counseling, health services, legal services, minority student services, on-campus daycare, personal counseling, placement for graduates, veterans' counselor, women's services. **Physically disabled:** Services for visually, speech, hearing impaired. **Learning disabled:** Comprehensive services available.

**Contact.**   E-mail: admis@msu.edu
Phone: (517) 355-8332 Fax: (517) 353-1647
James Cotter, Director of Admissions, Michigan State University, 250
Administration Building, East Lansing, MI 48824

## Michigan Technological University
**Houghton, Michigan**                                    CB member
**www.mtu.edu**                                          CB code: 1464

- Public 4-year university
- Residential campus in small town
- 5,835 degree-seeking undergraduates: 5% part-time, 24% women, 2% African American, 1% Asian American, 2% Hispanic American, 1% Native American, 7% international
- 1,050 degree-seeking graduate students
- 73% of applicants admitted
- SAT or ACT (ACT writing optional) required
- 66% graduate within 6 years

**General.** Founded in 1885. Regionally accredited. **Degrees:** 1,073 bachelor's, 23 associate awarded; master's, doctoral offered. **ROTC:** Army, Air Force. **Location:** 210 miles from Green Bay, Wisconsin, 325 miles from Milwaukee. **Calendar:** Semester, limited summer session. **Full-time faculty:** 379 total; 86% have terminal degrees, 14% minority, 29% women. **Part-time faculty:** 66 total; 56% have terminal degrees, 14% minority, 44% women. **Class size:** 47% < 20, 32% 20-39, 10% 40-49, 9% 50-99, 3% >100. **Special facilities:** Anechoic chamber, mineral museum, performing arts center, forestry center and research forest, cosmic ray observatory, X-ray fluorescence spectrometer, process simulation and control center, remote sensing institute, computer-aided engineering lab, microfabrication lab, subsurface visualization lab.

**Freshman class profile.** 4,719 applied, 3,456 admitted, 1,160 enrolled.

| Mid 50% test scores | | | | |
|---|---|---|---|---|
| SAT critical reading: | 530-650 | Rank in top quarter: | 57% |
| SAT math: | 570-700 | Rank in top tenth: | 28% |
| SAT writing: | 490-620 | Return as sophomores: | 83% |
| ACT composite: | 23-28 | Out-of-state: | 25% |
| GPA 3.75 or higher: | 35% | Live on campus: | 89% |
| GPA 3.50-3.74: | 22% | International: | 4% |
| GPA 3.0-3.49: | 30% | Fraternities: | 3% |
| GPA 2.0-2.99: | 13% | Sororities: | 4% |

**Basis for selection.** Academic record, ACT or SAT scores, and class rank (if available) are very important. SAT or ACT scores should be received as soon as possible to process the application and to be considered for merit-based scholarships. Students applying for programs within the visual and performing arts department are required to submit additional admission materials including essay response and a portfolio of creative work or performance audition. **Homeschooled:** Transcript of courses and grades required. ACT or SAT required.

**High school preparation.** College-preparatory program recommended. 8 units required; 20 recommended. Required and recommended units include English 3-4, mathematics 3-4, social studies 3, history 1, science 2-3, foreign language 2, computer science 1 and academic electives 2.

**2009-2010 Annual costs.** Tuition/fees: $11,348; $23,618 out-of-state. Room/board: $8,121.

**2009-2010 Financial aid.** **Need-based:** Average need met was 74%. Average scholarship/grant was $6,037; average loan $3,366. 44% of total undergraduate aid awarded as scholarships/grants, 56% as loans/jobs. **Non-need-based:** Scholarships awarded for academics, alumni affiliation, art, athletics, job skills, leadership, music/drama, ROTC, state residency.

**Application procedures.** **Admission:** Priority date 1/15; no deadline. No application fee. Admission notification on a rolling basis beginning on or about 9/15. Must reply by May 1 or within 2 week(s) if notified thereafter. Students applying by 1/15 for fall term admission receive priority consideration for admission and scholarships. **Financial aid:** No deadline. FAFSA required. Applicants notified on a rolling basis.

**Academics.** **Special study options:** Cooperative education, distance learning, double major, dual enrollment of high school students, ESL, exchange student, honors, independent study, internships, semester at sea, study abroad, teacher certification program. **Credit/placement by examination:** AP, CLEP, IB, SAT, ACT, institutional tests. **Support services:** Learning center, reduced course load, study skills assistance, tutoring, writing center.

**Majors.** **Biology:** General, Biochemistry/biophysics and molecular biology, bioinformatics. **Business:** Business admin, construction management. **Communications:** General. **Communications technology:** Recording arts. **Computer sciences:** General, networking, system admin. **Conservation:** Environmental science, forest management, forestry, wildlife. **Engineering:** General, biomedical, chemical, civil, computer, electrical, environmental, geological, materials, mechanical, software, surveying. **Engineering technology:** Electrical, industrial, mechanical. **Health:** Clinical lab science. **History:** General. **Liberal arts:** Arts/sciences. **Math:** General. **Parks/recreation:** Exercise sciences, health/fitness. **Physical sciences:** Chemistry, geology, geophysics, physics. **Psychology:** General. **Social sciences:** General, anthropology, economics. **Visual/performing arts:** General, theater design. **Other:** Chemistry, Communication, journalism, and related programs.

**Most popular majors.** Business/marketing 11%, computer/information sciences 7%, engineering/engineering technologies 61%.

**Computing on campus.** Dormitories wired for high-speed internet access and linked to campus network. Commuter students can connect to campus network. Online course registration, online library, helpline, student web hosting, wireless network available.

**Student life.** **Freshman orientation:** Mandatory, $250 fee. Preregistration for classes offered. Week-long program before start of classes. **Housing:** Guaranteed on-campus for freshmen. Coed dorms, special housing for disabled, apartments, fraternity/sorority housing, wellness housing available. **Activities:** Bands, campus ministries, choral groups, dance, drama, film society, international student organizations, literary magazine, music ensembles, musical theater, opera, radio station, student government, student newspaper, symphony orchestra.

**Athletics.** NCAA. **Intercollegiate:** Basketball, cross-country, football (tackle) M, ice hockey M, skiing, tennis, track and field, volleyball W. **Intramural:** Archery, badminton, basketball, bowling, cross-country, football (non-tackle), golf, ice hockey, racquetball, rifle, soccer, softball, squash, swimming, table tennis, tennis, volleyball, water polo, wrestling. **Team name:** Huskies.

**Student services.** Adult student services, alcohol/substance abuse counseling, chaplain/spiritual director, career counseling, services for economically disadvantaged, student employment services, financial aid counseling, health services, minority student services, on-campus daycare, personal counseling, placement for graduates, veterans' counselor, women's services. **Physically disabled:** Services for visually, speech, hearing impaired.

**Contact.**   E-mail: mtu4u@mtu.edu
Phone: (906) 487-2335 Toll-free number: (888) 688-1885
Fax: (906) 487-2125
Allison Carter, Director of Admissions, Michigan Technological University, 1400 Townsend Drive, Houghton, MI 49931-1295

## Michigan Theological Seminary
**Plymouth, Michigan**
**www.mts.edu**

- Private 4-year seminary college
- Small town

**General.** Regionally accredited. **Calendar:** Semester.

**Annual costs/financial aid.** Tuition/fees (2009-2010): $11,960.

**Contact.**   Phone: (734) 207-9581
Registrar, 41550 East Ann Arbor Trail, Plymouth, MI 48170-1622

## Northern Michigan University
**Marquette, Michigan**                                   CB member
**www.nmu.edu**                                          CB code: 1560

- Public 4-year university
- Residential campus in large town

- 8,386 degree-seeking undergraduates: 7% part-time, 53% women, 2% African American, 1% Asian American, 1% Hispanic American, 3% Native American, 1% international
- 465 degree-seeking graduate students
- 73% of applicants admitted
- SAT or ACT (ACT writing optional) required
- 49% graduate within 6 years; 13% enter graduate study

**General.** Founded in 1899. Regionally accredited. Every full-time student receives a ThinkPad or MacBook Pro notebook computer as part of tuition and fees, which are replaced every 2 years. **Degrees:** 1,223 bachelor's, 126 associate awarded; master's offered. **ROTC:** Army. **Location:** 300 miles from Milwaukee, 380 miles from Chicago. **Calendar:** Semester, limited summer session. **Full-time faculty:** 317 total; 80% have terminal degrees, 7% minority, 41% women. **Part-time faculty:** 145 total; 1% have terminal degrees, 8% minority, 46% women. **Class size:** 23% < 20, 61% 20-39, 4% 40-49, 9% 50-99, 2% >100. **Special facilities:** Education center, center for teaching and learning science and math, art and design studios, observatory with 12.5 F:6 Newtonian telescope, 120-acre nature preserve.

**Freshman class profile.** 5,955 applied, 4,338 admitted, 1,772 enrolled.

| Mid 50% test scores | | End year in good standing: | 82% |
|---|---|---|---|
| ACT composite: | 19-24 | Return as sophomores: | 73% |
| GPA 3.75 or higher: | 15% | Out-of-state: | 26% |
| GPA 3.50-3.74: | 9% | Live on campus: | 76% |
| GPA 3.0-3.49: | 23% | International: | 1% |
| GPA 2.0-2.99: | 41% | | |

**Basis for selection.** High school record, test scores most important. Recommendations considered. Students who do not fulfill normal requirements for admission may be conditionally admitted for freshman probation and college transition programs. Applicants may re-take exams and submit new scores any time prior to the first day of fall classes. Some certificate, diploma and associate degree programs do not require test scores. Audition recommended for music, drama majors. Portfolio recommended for art majors. Interview, extracurricular activities, talent/ability considered for borderline students. **Homeschooled:** Transcript of courses and grades required.

**High school preparation.** College-preparatory program recommended. 19 units recommended. Recommended units include English 4, mathematics 4, social studies 4, science 4 and foreign language 3.

**2009-2010 Annual costs.** Tuition/fees: $7,454; $11,828 out-of-state. Excludes one-time $200 athletic fee for first time freshmen. All full-time students provided with ThinkPad or MacBook computer as part of tuition and fees. Room/board: $7,646. Books/supplies: $830. Personal expenses: $1,110.

**2008-2009 Financial aid. Need-based:** 1,681 full-time freshmen applied for aid; 1,144 were judged to have need; 1,112 of these received aid. Average need met was 60%. Average scholarship/grant was $4,544; average loan $2,921. 41% of total undergraduate aid awarded as scholarships/grants, 59% as loans/jobs. **Non-need-based:** Awarded to 2,092 full-time undergraduates, including 669 freshmen. Scholarships awarded for academics, art, athletics, leadership, minority status, music/drama, religious affiliation, ROTC, state residency. **Additional information:** Audition or portfolio required for music, drama, and art scholarship applicants. Alumni Dependent Tuition Program gives resident tuition rates to nonresident dependents of NMU alumni who received master's, baccalaureate, or associate degree; renewable.

**Application procedures. Admission:** No deadline. $30 fee, may be waived for applicants with need. Admission notification on a rolling basis. Students may defer enrollment for one year. After one year, they must re-apply. **Financial aid:** Priority date 3/1; no closing date. FAFSA required. Applicants notified on a rolling basis starting 4/1; must reply within 2 week(s) of notification.

**Academics. Special study options:** Combined bachelor's/graduate degree, distance learning, double major, dual enrollment of high school students, ESL, honors, independent study, internships, liberal arts/career combination, student-designed major, study abroad, teacher certification program, Washington semester, weekend college. **Credit/placement by examination:** AP, CLEP, IB, SAT, ACT, institutional tests. 11 credit hours maximum toward associate degree, 32 toward bachelor's. 8 credits may be counted toward certificate. **Support services:** Learning center, pre-admission summer program, reduced course load, remedial instruction, study skills assistance, tutoring, writing center.

**Honors college/program.** Limited to 50 students; requires 3.5 GPA and 27 ACT or equivalent.

**Majors. Biology:** General, biochemistry, botany, ecology, microbiology, physiology, zoology. **Business:** General, accounting, accounting/finance, business admin, entrepreneurial studies, finance, financial planning, hospitality admin, management information systems, marketing, small business admin. **Communications:** General, digital media, public relations. **Computer sciences:** General, LAN/WAN management, networking, webmaster. **Conservation:** General, environmental science. **Education:** Art, biology, chemistry, elementary, emotionally handicapped, English, French, geography, health, history, mathematics, mentally handicapped, music, physical, physics, science, secondary, social science, social studies, Spanish, special, technology/industrial arts. **Engineering technology:** Construction, electrical, industrial, manufacturing, mechanical. **Foreign languages:** French, Spanish. **Health:** Athletic training, clinical lab science, community health services, cytogenetics, nursing (RN), predental, premedicine, prepharmacy, preveterinary, radiologic technology/medical imaging, respiratory therapy technology, speech pathology, surgical technology. **History:** General. **Interdisciplinary:** Behavioral sciences. **Legal studies:** Prelaw. **Liberal arts:** Arts/sciences. **Math:** General. **Parks/recreation:** General, exercise sciences, health/fitness, sports admin. **Philosophy/religion:** Philosophy. **Physical sciences:** Chemistry, forensic chemistry, geology, physics. **Protective services:** Criminal justice, security services. **Psychology:** General, developmental, experimental. **Public administration:** General, social work. **Social sciences:** Cartography, economics, geography, international relations, political science, sociology. **Visual/performing arts:** Art, art history/conservation, ceramics, cinematography, digital art, dramatic, drawing, graphic design, illustration, metal/jewelry, painting, photography, printmaking, sculpture. **Other:** Digital cinema, Earth science teacher education, Entertainment/sports promotion, Forensic biochemistry, human geography, Pre-architecture, Pre-engineering, Pre-optometry.

**Most popular majors.** Biology 7%, business/marketing 14%, education 12%, health sciences 11%, social sciences 7%, visual/performing arts 8%.

**Computing on campus.** PC or laptop required. 9,500 workstations in library. Dormitories wired for high-speed internet access and linked to campus network. Commuter students can connect to campus network. Online course registration, online library, helpline, repair service, student web hosting, wireless network available.

**Student life. Freshman orientation:** Mandatory, $75 fee. Preregistration for classes offered. 3-day sessions held throughout the summer prior to start of classes. **Housing:** Guaranteed on-campus for all undergraduates. Coed dorms, special housing for disabled, apartments, wellness housing available. $125 partly refundable deposit. **Activities:** Bands, campus ministries, choral groups, dance, drama, film society, international student organizations, literary magazine, music ensembles, Model UN, musical theater, opera, radio station, student government, student newspaper, symphony orchestra, TV station, Room at the Inn Student Chapter, Catholic Campus Ministry, Presque Isle Zen Community, Amnesty International, Political Review, Native American Student Association, All Nations Club, International Dancers, Superior Edge citizen-leader program, Student Leader Fellowship Program.

**Athletics.** NCAA. **Intercollegiate:** Basketball, cheerleading, cross-country W, diving W, football (tackle) M, golf M, ice hockey M, lacrosse M, rowing (crew), sailing, skiing, soccer, swimming W, track and field, volleyball W. **Intramural:** Badminton, basketball, football (non-tackle), ice hockey, racquetball, soccer, softball, table tennis, volleyball. **Team name:** Wildcats.

**Student services.** Adult student services, chaplain/spiritual director, career counseling, student employment services, financial aid counseling, health services, minority student services, personal counseling, placement for graduates, veterans' counselor. **Physically disabled:** Services for visually, speech, hearing impaired.

**Contact.** E-mail: admiss@nmu.edu
Phone: (906) 227-2650 Toll-free number: (800) 682-9797
Fax: (906) 227-1747
Gerri Daniels, Director of Admissions, Northern Michigan University, 1401 Presque Isle Avenue, Marquette, MI 49855

---

## Northwood University: Michigan
**Midland, Michigan**
**www.northwood.edu**                    CB code: 1568

- Private 4-year university and business college
- Residential campus in large town
- 1,814 degree-seeking undergraduates: 3% part-time, 39% women, 12% African American, 1% Asian American, 2% Hispanic American, 1% Native American, 9% international
- 422 degree-seeking graduate students
- 73% of applicants admitted
- SAT or ACT (ACT writing optional), application essay required
- 54% graduate within 6 years; 10% enter graduate study

**General.** Founded in 1959. Regionally accredited. Specialty university offering only business degrees in professional management; 3 residential campuses in Michigan, Florida, and Texas; 40 program centers; library center in Maine. **Degrees:** 511 bachelor's, 260 associate awarded; master's offered. **Location:** 125 miles from Detroit, 25 miles from Saginaw. **Calendar:** Semester, extensive summer session. **Full-time faculty:** 50 total; 32% have terminal degrees, 14% minority, 30% women. **Part-time faculty:** 51 total; 18% have terminal degrees, 2% minority, 41% women. **Class size:** 35% < 20, 52% 20-39, 12% 40-49, less than 1% 50-99, less than 1% >100. **Special facilities:** Creativity center, university-operated hotel.

**Freshman class profile.** 1,527 applied, 1,122 admitted, 343 enrolled.

| Mid 50% test scores | | | |
|---|---|---|---|
| SAT critical reading: | 410-480 | Rank in top quarter: | 28% |
| SAT math: | 430-570 | Rank in top tenth: | 9% |
| ACT composite: | 18-23 | End year in good standing: | 84% |
| GPA 3.75 or higher: | 11% | Return as sophomores: | 77% |
| GPA 3.50-3.74: | 14% | Out-of-state: | 11% |
| GPA 3.0-3.49: | 33% | Live on campus: | 88% |
| GPA 2.0-2.99: | 39% | International: | 3% |

**Basis for selection.** Minimum 2.0 GPA and strong interest in business or related field important. Test scores considered. Students with lower GPA possibly admitted on probation. Interview recommended. **Homeschooled:** State high school equivalency certificate required.

**High school preparation.** College-preparatory program recommended. 17 units recommended. Recommended units include English 4, mathematics 3, social studies 3, science 3 (laboratory 2), foreign language 1 and computer science 1.

**2009-2010 Annual costs.** Tuition/fees: $18,408. Room/board: $7,923. Books/supplies: $1,581. Personal expenses: $120.

**2009-2010 Financial aid. Need-based:** 283 full-time freshmen applied for aid; 256 were judged to have need; 256 of these received aid. Average need met was 58%. Average scholarship/grant was $5,766; average loan $3,307. 58% of total undergraduate aid awarded as scholarships/grants, 42% as loans/jobs. **Non-need-based:** Awarded to 799 full-time undergraduates, including 169 freshmen. Scholarships awarded for academics, athletics, leadership, minority status, ROTC.

**Application procedures. Admission:** No deadline. $25 fee, may be waived for applicants with need, free for online applicants. Admission notification on a rolling basis beginning on or about 9/1. **Financial aid:** No deadline. FAFSA required. Applicants notified on a rolling basis starting 3/1.

**Academics. Special study options:** Accelerated study, combined bachelor's/graduate degree, double major, dual enrollment of high school students, ESL, external degree, honors, independent study, internships, study abroad. **Credit/placement by examination:** AP, CLEP, IB, SAT, ACT, institutional tests. 12 credit hours maximum toward bachelor's degree. **Support services:** Learning center, pre-admission summer program, reduced course load, remedial instruction, study skills assistance, tutoring.

**Majors. Business:** Accounting, business admin, entrepreneurial studies, fashion, finance, hotel/motel admin, international, management information systems, managerial economics, marketing, vehicle parts marketing. **Communications:** Advertising. **Computer sciences:** General. **Parks/recreation:** Sports admin.

**Most popular majors.** Business/marketing 93%.

**Computing on campus.** 215 workstations in dormitories, library, computer center. Dormitories wired for high-speed internet access and linked to campus network. Commuter students can connect to campus network. Online course registration, online library, helpline, student web hosting, wireless network available.

**Student life. Freshman orientation:** Mandatory. Preregistration for classes offered. **Housing:** Guaranteed on-campus for freshmen. Single-sex dorms, apartments, wellness housing available. $100 fully refundable deposit, deadline 8/1. **Activities:** Choral groups, drama, international student organizations, student government, student newspaper, Business Professionals of America, American Marketing Association, ambassador club, Rotaract, law club, International Business Association, Minority Business Women, American Advertising Federation, The Church Reloaded, diversity club.

**Athletics.** NCAA. **Intercollegiate:** Baseball M, basketball, cheerleading, cross-country, football (tackle) M, golf, soccer, softball W, tennis, track and field, volleyball W. **Intramural:** Badminton, basketball, field hockey, football (non-tackle) M, soccer, tennis, volleyball. **Team name:** Timberwolves.

**Student services.** Adult student services, alcohol/substance abuse counseling, career counseling, student employment services, financial aid counseling, health services, minority student services, personal counseling, placement for graduates, veterans' counselor. **Physically disabled:** Services for visually, speech, hearing impaired.

**Contact.** E-mail: miadmit@northwood.edu
Phone: (989) 837-4273 Toll-free number: (800) 457-7878
Fax: (989) 837-4490
Daniel Toland, Dean of Admissions, Northwood University: Michigan, 4000 Whiting Drive, Midland, MI 48640

---

## Oakland University
### Rochester, Michigan
**www.oakland.edu**

**CB member**
**CB code: 1497**

- Public 4-year university
- Commuter campus in small city
- 14,728 degree-seeking undergraduates: 24% part-time, 61% women, 9% African American, 4% Asian American, 2% Hispanic American, 1% international
- 3,492 degree-seeking graduate students
- 69% of applicants admitted
- 41% graduate within 6 years; 20% enter graduate study

**General.** Founded in 1957. Regionally accredited. **Degrees:** 2,226 bachelor's awarded; master's, doctoral, professional offered. **ROTC:** Air Force. **Location:** 30 miles from Detroit. **Calendar:** Semester, limited summer session. **Full-time faculty:** 509 total; 90% have terminal degrees, 21% minority, 45% women. **Class size:** 39% < 20, 41% 20-39, 8% 40-49, 9% 50-99, 2% >100. **Special facilities:** Music pavilion, engineering and science research laboratories, robotics laboratory, product development and manufacturing center.

**Freshman class profile.** 10,070 applied, 6,912 admitted, 2,466 enrolled.

| Mid 50% test scores | | | |
|---|---|---|---|
| ACT composite: | 19-25 | End year in good standing: | 83% |
| GPA 3.75 or higher: | 16% | Return as sophomores: | 74% |
| GPA 3.50-3.74: | 17% | Out-of-state: | 2% |
| GPA 3.0-3.49: | 39% | Live on campus: | 37% |
| GPA 2.0-2.99: | 28% | International: | 1% |
| Rank in top quarter: | 42% | Fraternities: | 5% |
| | | Sororities: | 4% |

**Basis for selection.** Admission based on 2.5 GPA in academic subjects, school and community activities, recommendations. Applicants with minimum 2.0 GPA may be admitted to summer program. Engineering, business, education, nursing, and physical therapy programs require higher GPA. TOEFL required of all non-native speakers of English. SAT or ACT recommended. Except for home schooled students, ACT scores used only for placement and scholarship purposes. Audition required of music, theatre, dance majors. **Homeschooled:** ACT composite score of 20 or above.

**High school preparation.** College-preparatory program recommended. Required and recommended units include English 4, mathematics 3, social studies 3, science 3 and foreign language 2.

**2009-2010 Annual costs.** Tuition/fees: $8,783; $20,498 out-of-state. Room/board: $7,350. Books/supplies: $1,107. Personal expenses: $2,022.

**2009-2010 Financial aid. Non-need-based:** Scholarships awarded for academics, art, athletics, leadership, music/drama, state residency.

**Application procedures. Admission:** No deadline. No application fee. Admission notification on a rolling basis. **Financial aid:** Priority date 2/15; no closing date. FAFSA required. Applicants notified on a rolling basis starting 3/15.

**Academics. Special study options:** Accelerated study, cooperative education, distance learning, double major, ESL, honors, independent study, internships, student-designed major, study abroad, teacher certification program. **Credit/placement by examination:** AP, CLEP, IB, ACT, institutional tests. 60 credit hours maximum toward bachelor's degree. **Support services:** Learning center, pre-admission summer program, reduced course load, remedial instruction, study skills assistance, tutoring, writing center.

**Majors. Area/ethnic studies:** African, East Asian, Latin American, Slavic, South Asian, women's. **Biology:** General, biochemistry, biophysics. **Business:** General, accounting, finance, human resources, management information systems, managerial economics, marketing, operations, training/development. **Communications:** General, journalism. **Computer sciences:**

General, information technology. **Education:** Elementary, music. **Engineering:** Computer, electrical, industrial, mechanical, physics. **Foreign languages:** General, French, German, Japanese, linguistics, Spanish. **Health:** Clinical lab science, cytotechnology, environmental health, health services, histologic technology, medical radiologic technology/radiation therapy, nuclear medical technology, nursing (RN), occupational health, radiologic technology/medical imaging. **History:** General. **Liberal arts:** Arts/sciences. **Math:** General, statistics. **Philosophy/religion:** Philosophy. **Physical sciences:** Chemistry, physics. **Psychology:** General. **Public administration:** General, social work. **Social sciences:** Anthropology, economics, international relations, political science, sociology. **Visual/performing arts:** Acting, art history/conservation, dance, dramatic, drawing, film/cinema, multimedia, music performance, musical theater, painting, photography, piano/organ, studio arts, theater design, voice/opera. **Other:** Engineering chemistry, engineering biology, Wellness health promotion/ injury prevention, writing and rhetoric.

**Most popular majors.** Business/marketing 20%, communications/journalism 10%, education 10%, health sciences 18%, psychology 6%, social sciences 7%.

**Computing on campus.** Dormitories linked to campus network. Commuter students can connect to campus network. Online course registration, online library, helpline, student web hosting, wireless network available.

**Student life. Freshman orientation:** Mandatory. Preregistration for classes offered. Held on weekdays from end of June through mid-July. 1.5-day program requires overnight stay in residence halls. Condensed 1-day orientation available. **Housing:** Guaranteed on-campus for freshmen. Coed dorms, special housing for disabled, apartments, cooperative housing, fraternity/sorority housing, wellness housing available. $100 nonrefundable deposit, deadline 9/1. Residence halls easily accessible to handicapped persons. **Activities:** Bands, campus ministries, choral groups, dance, drama, film society, international student organizations, literary magazine, music ensembles, musical theater, radio station, student government, student newspaper, symphony orchestra, TV station, association of black students, Indian students association, Arab American association, College Democrats, College Republicans, Inter varsity Christian Fellowship, Hillel, Muslim student association, Chinese friendship association, gay/straight alliance.

**Athletics.** NCAA. **Intercollegiate:** Baseball M, basketball, cross-country, diving, golf, soccer, softball W, swimming, tennis W, track and field, volleyball W. **Intramural:** Badminton, basketball, bowling, football (non-tackle), racquetball, soccer, softball, table tennis, volleyball. **Team name:** Golden Grizzlies.

**Student services.** Alcohol/substance abuse counseling, chaplain/spiritual director, career counseling, student employment services, financial aid counseling, health services, minority student services, on-campus daycare, personal counseling, placement for graduates. **Physically disabled:** Services for visually, speech, hearing impaired.

**Contact.** E-mail: ouinfo@oakland.edu
Phone: (248) 370-3360 Toll-free number: (800) 625-8648
Fax: (248) 370-4462
Eleanor Reynolds, Assistant Vice President Student Affairs Admissions, Oakland University, 101 North Foundation Hall, Rochester, MI 48309-4401

## Olivet College
**Olivet, Michigan**          **CB member**
**www.olivetcollege.edu**     **CB code: 1595**

- Private 4-year liberal arts college affiliated with Congregational Christian Churches and United Church of Christ
- Residential campus in rural community

**General.** Founded in 1844. Regionally accredited. **Location:** 30 miles from Lansing, 120 miles from Detroit. **Calendar:** Semester.

**Annual costs/financial aid.** Books/supplies: $900. Personal expenses: $1,000. Need-based financial aid available to full-time and part-time students.

**Contact.** Phone: (269) 749-7635
Vice President for Enrollment Management, Admissions Office, Olivet, MI 49076

## Rochester College
**Rochester Hills, Michigan**
**www.rc.edu**          **CB code: 1516**

- Private 4-year liberal arts college affiliated with Church of Christ
- Residential campus in small city

- 950 degree-seeking undergraduates
- ACT (writing optional), application essay required

**General.** Founded in 1959. Regionally accredited. **Degrees:** 278 bachelor's, 14 associate awarded; master's offered. **Location:** 25 miles from Detroit. **Calendar:** Semester, limited summer session. **Full-time faculty:** 50 total. **Part-time faculty:** 115 total. **Class size:** 86% < 20, 14% 20-39, less than 1% 40-49.

**Freshman class profile.**

| Mid 50% test scores | | | |
|---|---|---|---|
| SAT critical reading: | 420-520 | GPA 3.50-3.74: | 15% |
| SAT math: | 390-480 | GPA 3.0-3.49: | 26% |
| ACT composite: | 19-24 | GPA 2.0-2.99: | 38% |
| GPA 3.75 or higher: | 18% | Rank in top quarter: | 28% |
| | | Rank in top tenth: | 14% |

**Basis for selection.** ACT score and high school GPA most important. Recommendations and interview considered. **Homeschooled:** Transcript of courses and grades required.

**2009-2010 Annual costs.** Tuition/fees: $17,362. Room/board: $5,496. Books/supplies: $600. Personal expenses: $750.

**Financial aid. Non-need-based:** Scholarships awarded for academics, alumni affiliation, athletics, leadership, music/drama, state residency.

**Application procedures. Admission:** No deadline. $35 fee. Admission notification on a rolling basis. **Financial aid:** Priority date 8/1; no closing date. FAFSA required. Applicants notified on a rolling basis starting 6/1; must reply within 2 week(s) of notification.

**Academics. Special study options:** Accelerated study, combined bachelor's/graduate degree, cross-registration, double major, dual enrollment of high school students, honors, independent study, internships, liberal arts/career combination, study abroad, teacher certification program, weekend college. **Credit/placement by examination:** AP, CLEP, IB, institutional tests. 32 credit hours maximum toward associate degree, 64 toward bachelor's. Credit awarded for successful completion of selected DANTES Subject Standardized Testing Program. **Support services:** Learning center, reduced course load, remedial instruction, study skills assistance, tutoring, writing center.

**Majors. Business:** Accounting, business admin, management information systems, marketing. **Communications:** General. **Computer sciences:** General. **Education:** General, early childhood, elementary, English, history, mathematics, middle, music, science, secondary. **History:** General. **Philosophy/religion:** Religion. **Psychology:** General. **Public administration:** Social work. **Theology:** Bible, theology. **Visual/performing arts:** Music performance.

**Most popular majors.** Business/marketing 35%, communications/journalism 6%, education 22%, psychology 20%.

**Computing on campus.** 34 workstations in dormitories, library, computer center. Dormitories wired for high-speed internet access and linked to campus network. Online library, helpline, student web hosting, wireless network available.

**Student life. Freshman orientation:** Mandatory, $100 fee. Preregistration for classes offered. **Housing:** Guaranteed on-campus for freshmen. Single-sex dorms, apartments available. $180 deposit, deadline 5/1. **Activities:** Bands, choral groups, drama, music ensembles, musical theater, opera, student government, student newspaper, service and mission organizations, social clubs, departmental organizations, honor societies.

**Athletics.** NCCAA. **Intercollegiate:** Baseball M, basketball, soccer, softball W, volleyball W. **Intramural:** Basketball, football (non-tackle), softball, volleyball. **Team name:** Warriors.

**Student services.** Adult student services, alcohol/substance abuse counseling, chaplain/spiritual director, career counseling, student employment services, financial aid counseling, minority student services, personal counseling, placement for graduates, veterans' counselor. **Physically disabled:** Services for visually, speech, hearing impaired.

**Contact.** E-mail: admissions@rc.edu
Phone: (248) 218-2031 Toll-free number: (800) 521-6010
Fax: (248) 218-2035
Klint Pleasant, Rochester College, 800 West Avon Road, Rochester Hills, MI 48307

## Sacred Heart Major Seminary
**Detroit, Michigan**
**www.shms.org**          **CB code: 1686**

- Private 4-year seminary college affiliated with Roman Catholic Church
- Commuter campus in very large city

- 88 degree-seeking undergraduates: 43% part-time, 31% women, 2% African American, 5% Hispanic American, 2% international
- 168 degree-seeking graduate students
- 100% of applicants admitted
- SAT or ACT (ACT writing optional), application essay, interview required
- 50% graduate within 6 years

**General.** Founded in 1919. Regionally accredited. **Degrees:** 14 bachelor's, 1 associate awarded; master's offered. **Calendar:** Semester, limited summer session. **Full-time faculty:** 30 total; 80% have terminal degrees, 7% minority, 17% women. **Part-time faculty:** 39 total; 26% have terminal degrees, 8% minority, 33% women. **Class size:** 81% < 20, 19% 20-39.

**Freshman class profile.** 6 applied, 6 admitted, 6 enrolled.

| Mid 50% test scores | | | |
|---|---|---|---|
| ACT composite: | 22-29 | Live on campus: | 83% |
| GPA 3.75 or higher: | 80% | | |
| GPA 2.0-2.99: | 20% | | |

**Basis for selection.** Recommendations of parish pastor, high school principal, and college counselor vital. School, community, and church-related activities viewed as important formative experiences. Religious commitment very important. Interview required for priesthood candidates. **Home-schooled:** Transcript of courses and grades, interview, letter of recommendation (nonparent) required. **Learning Disabled:** Once admitted, students should contact the Office of the Dean of Studies for accommodations.

**High school preparation.** College-preparatory program recommended. 13 units required. Required and recommended units include English 4, mathematics 3, social studies 3, science 1 (laboratory 1) and foreign language 2.

**2009-2010 Annual costs.** Tuition/fees: $14,390. Room/board: $7,800. Books/supplies: $1,366. Personal expenses: $3,150.

**2008-2009 Financial aid. Need-based:** 92% of total undergraduate aid awarded as scholarships/grants, 8% as loans/jobs. **Non-need-based:** Scholarships awarded for academics, religious affiliation.

**Application procedures. Admission:** Closing date 8/15 (postmark date). $30 fee. Application must be submitted online. Admission notification 8/22. **Financial aid:** No deadline. FAFSA, institutional form required. Applicants notified on a rolling basis; must reply within 2 week(s) of notification.

**Academics.** 30 to 40% of undergraduate course work taken at other consortium colleges. **Special study options:** Double major, dual enrollment of high school students, ESL, independent study. **Credit/placement by examination:** AP, CLEP, institutional tests. 6 credit hours maximum toward associate degree, 12 toward bachelor's. Must accumulate 15 hours at SHMS before credit is recorded. **Support services:** Learning center, reduced course load, study skills assistance, tutoring.

**Majors. Liberal arts:** Arts/sciences. **Philosophy/religion:** Philosophy.

**Most popular majors.** Liberal arts 50%, philosophy/religious studies 50%.

**Computing on campus.** 12 workstations in library, computer center. Online library available.

**Student life. Freshman orientation:** Mandatory. 3 days for seminarians, 1 day for commuters at beginning of fall term. **Policies:** On-campus housing available and guaranteed to seminarians only. Religious observance required. **Housing:** On-campus housing available and guaranteed to seminarians only. **Activities:** Campus ministries, choral groups, music ensembles, student government, student newspaper.

**Student services.** Chaplain/spiritual director, financial aid counseling.

**Contact.** E-mail: IFM@shms.edu
Phone: (313) 883-8520 Fax: (313) 883-8530
Janet Diaz, Director of Admissions and Enrollment Management, Sacred Heart Major Seminary, 2701 Chicago Boulevard, Detroit, MI 48206-1799

## Saginaw Valley State University
**University Center, Michigan**
www.svsu.edu
CB code: 1766

- Public 4-year university
- Commuter campus in small city
- 8,609 degree-seeking undergraduates: 15% part-time, 58% women, 9% African American, 1% Asian American, 3% Hispanic American, 3% international
- 1,698 degree-seeking graduate students

- 86% of applicants admitted
- ACT (writing optional) required
- 38% graduate within 6 years

**General.** Founded in 1963. Regionally accredited. **Degrees:** 1,097 bachelor's awarded; master's offered. **Location:** 10 miles from Bay City and Saginaw. **Calendar:** Semester, limited summer session. **Full-time faculty:** 297 total; 73% have terminal degrees. **Part-time faculty:** 300 total. **Class size:** 30% < 20, 62% 20-39, 3% 40-49, 4% 50-99. **Special facilities:** Fine arts center, sculpture museum, observatory.

**Freshman class profile.** 6,103 applied, 5,244 admitted, 1,740 enrolled.

| Mid 50% test scores | | | |
|---|---|---|---|
| ACT composite: | 18-24 | Rank in top tenth: | 18% |
| GPA 3.75 or higher: | 20% | End year in good standing: | 71% |
| GPA 3.50-3.74: | 15% | Return as sophomores: | 71% |
| GPA 3.0-3.49: | 28% | Out-of-state: | 1% |
| GPA 2.0-2.99: | 37% | Live on campus: | 72% |
| Rank in top quarter: | 40% | International: | 1% |

**Basis for selection.** Minimum high school GPA of 2.5 preferred. **Home-schooled:** Interview required.

**High school preparation.** Required and recommended units include English 4, mathematics 3-4, social studies 3-4, science 2-4 and foreign language 2. One unit of communications recommended.

**2009-2010 Annual costs.** Tuition/fees: $6,900; $16,200 out-of-state. Room/board: $7,270. Books/supplies: $900. Personal expenses: $1,000.

**2008-2009 Financial aid. Need-based:** 1,596 full-time freshmen applied for aid; 1,141 were judged to have need; 1,120 of these received aid. Average need met was 65%. Average scholarship/grant was $3,542; average loan $2,986. 38% of total undergraduate aid awarded as scholarships/grants, 62% as loans/jobs. **Non-need-based:** Awarded to 3,030 full-time undergraduates, including 1,103 freshmen. Scholarships awarded for academics, art, athletics, leadership, minority status, music/drama.

**Application procedures. Admission:** No deadline. $25 fee, may be waived for applicants with need. Admission notification on a rolling basis. **Financial aid:** Priority date 2/14; no closing date. FAFSA required. Applicants notified on a rolling basis starting 3/20; must reply within 10 week(s) of notification.

**Academics. Special study options:** Accelerated study, cooperative education, distance learning, double major, dual enrollment of high school students, ESL, honors, independent study, internships, student-designed major, study abroad, teacher certification program. **Credit/placement by examination:** AP, CLEP, IB, ACT, institutional tests. 62 credit hours maximum toward bachelor's degree. **Support services:** Learning center, reduced course load, remedial instruction, study skills assistance, tutoring, writing center.

**Majors. Biology:** General, biochemistry. **Business:** General, accounting, business admin, finance, international, managerial economics, marketing, operations. **Communications:** General. **Computer sciences:** General, systems analysis. **Education:** Elementary, physical, special. **Engineering:** Electrical, mechanical. **Engineering technology:** General. **Foreign languages:** French, Spanish. **Health:** Athletic training, clinical lab science, health services, nursing (RN). **History:** General. **Interdisciplinary:** Global studies. **Math:** General, applied. **Parks/recreation:** Exercise sciences. **Physical sciences:** Chemical physics, chemistry, optics, physics. **Protective services:** Criminal justice. **Psychology:** General. **Public administration:** General, social work. **Social sciences:** Economics, political science, sociology. **Visual/performing arts:** Art, dramatic, graphic design, studio arts. **Other:** Applied studies, Business chemistry.

**Most popular majors.** Business/marketing 10%, communications/journalism 36%, education 12%, health sciences 9%.

**Computing on campus.** 1,100 workstations in library, computer center, student center. Dormitories linked to campus network. Commuter students can connect to campus network. Online course registration, online library, helpline, student web hosting, wireless network available.

**Student life. Freshman orientation:** Mandatory, $55 fee. Preregistration for classes offered. Day-long sessions before each semester include university placement testing, advising, and registration. **Housing:** Coed dorms, special housing for disabled, apartments, wellness housing available. $200 partly refundable deposit. **Activities:** Bands, campus ministries, choral groups, dance, drama, film society, international student organizations, literary magazine, music ensembles, Model UN, musical theater, student government, student newspaper, over 110 student clubs and organizations.

**Athletics.** NCAA. **Intercollegiate:** Baseball M, basketball, bowling M, cheerleading, cross-country, football (tackle) M, golf M, soccer, softball W, tennis W, track and field, volleyball W. **Intramural:** Badminton, basketball, football (non-tackle), golf, lacrosse, racquetball, soccer, softball, squash, table tennis, tennis, volleyball. **Team name:** Cardinals.

**Student services.** Adult student services, alcohol/substance abuse counseling, career counseling, services for economically disadvantaged, student employment services, financial aid counseling, health services, legal services, minority student services, personal counseling, placement for graduates, veterans' counselor, women's services. **Physically disabled:** Services for visually, hearing impaired.

**Contact.** E-mail: admissions@svsu.edu
Phone: (989) 964-4200 Toll-free number: (800) 968-9500
Fax: (989) 790-0180
Jennifer Pahl, Director of Admissions, Saginaw Valley State University, 7400 Bay Road, University Center, MI 48710

---

## Siena Heights University
**Adrian, Michigan**  **CB member**
www.sienaheights.edu  **CB code: 1719**

- Private 4-year university and liberal arts college affiliated with Roman Catholic Church
- Residential campus in large town
- 1,938 degree-seeking undergraduates: 49% part-time, 59% women
- 323 graduate students
- 69% of applicants admitted
- SAT or ACT (ACT writing recommended) required
- 56% graduate within 6 years; 57% enter graduate study

**General.** Founded in 1919. Regionally accredited. Degree completion programs offered in Ann Arbor, Battle Creek, Benton Harbor, Jackson, Lansing, Monroe, Port Huron and Southfield. **Degrees:** 627 bachelor's, 17 associate awarded; master's offered. **Location:** 30 miles from Toledo, Ohio; 60 miles from Detroit. **Calendar:** Semester, limited summer session. **Full-time faculty:** 66 total. **Part-time faculty:** 152 total.

**Freshman class profile.** 957 applied, 659 admitted, 208 enrolled.

| | | | |
|---|---|---|---|
| **GPA 3.75 or higher:** | 15% | **End year in good standing:** | 70% |
| **GPA 3.50-3.74:** | 13% | **Return as sophomores:** | 75% |
| **GPA 3.0-3.49:** | 33% | **Out-of-state:** | 10% |
| **GPA 2.0-2.99:** | 39% | **Live on campus:** | 70% |

**Basis for selection.** Admission for a first time freshmen is determined by high school grades and standardized test scores. Admission for a student transferring from another university is determined by post high school grades. **Homeschooled:** Transcript of courses and grades required. Must complete GED for state or federal assistance.

**High school preparation.** College-preparatory program recommended. Recommended units include English 4, mathematics 3, social studies 3, history 3, science 3, foreign language 2, computer science 1 and visual/performing arts 1.

**2009-2010 Annual costs.** Tuition/fees: $19,210. Room/board: $7,070. Books/supplies: $750. Personal expenses: $788.

**2008-2009 Financial aid. Non-need-based:** Scholarships awarded for academics, alumni affiliation, art, athletics, music/drama, religious affiliation.

**Application procedures. Admission:** No deadline. $25 fee, may be waived for applicants with need. Application must be submitted online. Admission notification on a rolling basis. **Financial aid:** Priority date 3/15, closing date 8/15. FAFSA, institutional form, CSS PROFILE required. Applicants notified on a rolling basis starting 2/15.

**Academics. Special study options:** Combined bachelor's/graduate degree, cooperative education, distance learning, double major, dual enrollment of high school students, ESL, exchange student, external degree, internships, liberal arts/career combination, student-designed major, study abroad, teacher certification program, weekend college. **Credit/placement by examination:** AP, CLEP, ACT, institutional tests. 18 credit hours maximum toward associate degree, 36 toward bachelor's. **Support services:** Learning center, pre-admission summer program, reduced course load, remedial instruction, study skills assistance, tutoring, writing center.

**Majors. Area/ethnic studies:** American. **Biology:** General. **Business:** General, accounting, hospitality/recreation. **Communications:** General. **Computer sciences:** General. **Education:** Business, elementary, secondary. **Foreign languages:** Spanish. **Health:** Predental, premedicine, prepharmacy. **History:** General. **Interdisciplinary:** Natural sciences. **Legal studies:** Prelaw. **Liberal arts:** Arts/sciences. **Math:** General. **Parks/recreation:** Sports

admin. **Philosophy/religion:** Philosophy, religion. **Physical sciences:** Chemistry. **Protective services:** Criminal justice. **Psychology:** General. **Public administration:** Social work. **Social sciences:** General. **Visual/performing arts:** Art, ceramics, commercial/advertising art, dramatic, drawing, metal/jewelry, painting, photography, sculpture, studio arts.

**Computing on campus.** 80 workstations in dormitories, library, computer center. Dormitories linked to campus network. Commuter students can connect to campus network. Online course registration, online library, helpline, repair service, wireless network available.

**Student life. Freshman orientation:** Mandatory. Preregistration for classes offered. One-day Registration program offered in May, June, July, and August. Students arrive on campus early for a five day Welcome Week program immediately before the semester begins. **Housing:** Guaranteed on-campus for all undergraduates. Coed dorms, single-sex dorms, apartments available. $100 nonrefundable deposit. **Activities:** Jazz band, campus ministries, choral groups, dance, drama, film society, international student organizations, literary magazine, music ensembles, musical theater, student government, student newspaper, Siena Heights African American Knowledge Association, Student Programming Association, Greek Council, Residence Hall Council.

**Athletics.** NAIA. **Intercollegiate:** Baseball M, basketball, cross-country, golf, lacrosse, soccer, softball W, track and field, volleyball. **Intramural:** Basketball, softball, volleyball. **Team name:** Saints.

**Student services.** Adult student services, alcohol/substance abuse counseling, chaplain/spiritual director, career counseling, student employment services, financial aid counseling, health services, personal counseling, placement for graduates, veterans' counselor. **Physically disabled:** Services for visually, hearing impaired.

**Contact.** E-mail: admissions@sienaheights.edu
Phone: (517) 264-7180 Toll-free number: (800) 521-0009 ext. 7180
Fax: (517) 264-7745
Sara Johnson, Director of Admissions, Siena Heights University, 1247 East Siena Heights Drive, Adrian, MI 49221-1796

---

## Spring Arbor University
**Spring Arbor, Michigan**
www.arbor.edu  **CB code: 1732**

- Private 4-year university and liberal arts college affiliated with Free Methodist Church of North America
- Residential campus in rural community
- 2,710 degree-seeking undergraduates: 27% part-time, 69% women
- 1,163 degree-seeking graduate students
- 78% of applicants admitted
- SAT or ACT (ACT writing optional) required
- 58% graduate within 6 years; 29% enter graduate study

**General.** Founded in 1873. Regionally accredited. School of Professional Studies offers nine degree completion programs available at 14 regional sites. **Degrees:** 752 bachelor's awarded; master's offered. **ROTC:** Army, Air Force. **Location:** 8 miles from Jackson, 40 miles from Lansing. **Calendar:** Semester, limited summer session. **Full-time faculty:** 83 total; 60% have terminal degrees, 6% minority, 31% women. **Part-time faculty:** 57 total; 19% have terminal degrees, 5% minority, 63% women. **Class size:** 60% < 20, 34% 20-39, 4% 40-49, 2% 50-99. **Special facilities:** Trading center.

**Freshman class profile.** 2,022 applied, 1,583 admitted, 381 enrolled.

| Mid 50% test scores | | | |
|---|---|---|---|
| **SAT critical reading:** | 480-600 | **GPA 2.0-2.99:** | 20% |
| **SAT math:** | 470-600 | **Rank in top quarter:** | 49% |
| **SAT writing:** | 460-570 | **Rank in top tenth:** | 25% |
| **ACT composite:** | 20-26 | **Return as sophomores:** | 72% |
| **GPA 3.75 or higher:** | 30% | **Out-of-state:** | 16% |
| **GPA 3.50-3.74:** | 21% | **Live on campus:** | 90% |
| **GPA 3.0-3.49:** | 28% | **International:** | 1% |

**Basis for selection.** An ACT composite score of 20 or an SAT of 930 and a High School GPA of 2.60 GPA are recommended. Applicants whose scores are below these recommendations may be admitted conditionally. Interview recommended for borderline applicants. **Homeschooled:** Letter of recommendation from the parent/teacher and a 2-3 page paper regarding applicant's homeschool experience.

**High school preparation.** College-preparatory program required. 14 units required. Required and recommended units include English 4, mathematics

3, history 3, science 3 (laboratory 3), foreign language 2 and computer science 1.

**2009-2010 Annual costs.** Tuition/fees: $19,790. Room/board: $6,950. Books/supplies: $800. Personal expenses: $880.

**2009-2010 Financial aid. Need-based:** 371 full-time freshmen applied for aid; 333 were judged to have need; 333 of these received aid. Average need met was 92%. Average scholarship/grant was $12,493; average loan $3,674. 65% of total undergraduate aid awarded as scholarships/grants, 35% as loans/jobs. **Non-need-based:** Scholarships awarded for academics, art, athletics, minority status, music/drama, religious affiliation.

**Application procedures. Admission:** Priority date 2/15; deadline 8/1 (receipt date). $30 fee, may be waived for applicants with need, free for online applicants. Admission notification on a rolling basis beginning on or about 9/1. **Financial aid:** Priority date 3/1; no closing date. FAFSA required. Applicants notified on a rolling basis starting 3/1; must reply within 2 week(s) of notification.

**Academics. Special study options:** Accelerated study, combined bachelor's/graduate degree, cross-registration, distance learning, double major, dual enrollment of high school students, ESL, honors, independent study, internships, student-designed major, study abroad, teacher certification program, Washington semester, weekend college. Environmental study semester offered at AuSable Trails Institute in northern Michigan; cross-cultural program with several destinations. **Credit/placement by examination:** AP, CLEP, IB, SAT, ACT, institutional tests. 10 credit hours maximum toward associate degree, 60 toward bachelor's. No more than 1/3 of credits for a major can be earned through credit by examination. **Support services:** Learning center, pre-admission summer program, reduced course load, remedial instruction, study skills assistance, tutoring.

**Majors. Biology:** General, biochemistry. **Business:** Accounting, actuarial science, business admin, finance, management information systems, managerial economics, operations. **Communications:** General, advertising, broadcast journalism, public relations. **Computer sciences:** Computer science. **Education:** Art, elementary, secondary, special. **Engineering technology:** General. **Family/consumer sciences:** Family studies. **Foreign languages:** Spanish. **Health:** Health care admin, nursing (RN). **History:** General. **Interdisciplinary:** Global studies. **Math:** General. **Parks/recreation:** General, health/fitness. **Philosophy/religion:** Christian, philosophy, religion. **Physical sciences:** Chemistry, theoretical physics. **Psychology:** General. **Public administration:** Social work. **Social sciences:** General, political science, sociology, urban studies. **Theology:** Bible, missionary, pastoral counseling, sacred music, theology, youth ministry. **Visual/performing arts:** Art, design, film/cinema, graphic design. **Other:** Biology health careers.

**Most popular majors.** Business/marketing 31%, education 11%, family/consumer sciences 18%, health sciences 11%, public administration/social services 8%.

**Computing on campus.** 362 workstations in dormitories, library, computer center, student center. Dormitories wired for high-speed internet access and linked to campus network. Commuter students can connect to campus network. Online course registration, helpline, repair service, student web hosting, wireless network available.

**Student life. Freshman orientation:** Mandatory. Preregistration for classes offered. 3-day session held at the beginning of September each year; parents are encouraged to attend the first day. **Policies:** Emphasis placed on an active commitment to Jesus Christ and his teachings. Chapel attendance is required twice a week. Religious observance required. **Housing:** Guaranteed on-campus for freshmen. Single-sex dorms, special housing for disabled, apartments, wellness housing available. $200 fully refundable deposit, deadline 5/1. Community homes on campus. **Activities:** Bands, campus ministries, choral groups, drama, film society, international student organizations, literary magazine, music ensembles, musical theater, student government, student newspaper, symphony orchestra, Inter-faith Shelter Ministries, Habitat for Humanity.

**Athletics.** NAIA, NCCAA. **Intercollegiate:** Baseball M, basketball, cross-country, golf M, soccer, softball W, tennis, track and field, volleyball W. **Intramural:** Basketball, field hockey M, football (non-tackle) M, golf M, soccer, softball, table tennis, tennis, volleyball. **Team name:** Cougars.

**Student services.** Adult student services, chaplain/spiritual director, career counseling, student employment services, financial aid counseling, health services, minority student services, personal counseling, placement for graduates, veterans' counselor. **Physically disabled:** Services for visually, speech, hearing impaired.

**Contact.** E-mail: admissions@arbor.edu
Phone: (517) 750-6468 Toll-free number: (800) 968-0011
Fax: (517) 750-6620
Randy Comfort, Executive Director of Admissions, Spring Arbor University, 106 East Main Street, Spring Arbor, MI 49283-9799

## University of Detroit Mercy
Detroit, Michigan — CB member
www.udmercy.edu — CB code: 1835

- Private 4-year university affiliated with Roman Catholic Church
- Commuter campus in very large city
- 3,149 undergraduates
- 2,436 graduate students
- 64% of applicants admitted
- SAT or ACT (ACT writing optional) required

**General.** Founded in 1991. Regionally accredited. **Degrees:** 634 bachelor's awarded; master's, doctoral, professional offered. **Calendar:** Semester, extensive summer session. **Full-time faculty:** 250 total. **Part-time faculty:** 321 total. **Class size:** 61% < 20, 35% 20-39, 3% 40-49, 2% 50-99.

**Freshman class profile.** 3,173 applied, 2,020 admitted, 608 enrolled.

| Mid 50% test scores | | |
| --- | --- | --- |
| ACT composite: | 21-26 | |
| Rank in top quarter: | 63% | |
| Rank in top tenth: | 31% | |
| Return as sophomores: | | 77% |
| Out-of-state: | | 4% |
| Live on campus: | | 45% |

**Basis for selection.** High school GPA in college-preparatory work, test scores, counselor's recommendation considered. Interview required for University College applicants, recommended for all others.

**High school preparation.** College-preparatory program required. 16 units required. Required and recommended units include English 4, mathematics 3-4, social studies 2, history 2, science 2-3 (laboratory 1) and academic electives 4. Units in speech, foreign language, music, art recommended.

**2010-2011 Annual costs.** Tuition/fees (projected): $30,660. Room/board: $8,930. Books/supplies: $1,568. Personal expenses: $3,167.

**Financial aid. Non-need-based:** Scholarships awarded for academics, alumni affiliation, athletics, leadership, minority status, music/drama, religious affiliation.

**Application procedures. Admission:** Closing date 7/1. $25 fee, may be waived for applicants with need, free for online applicants. Admission notification on a rolling basis beginning on or about 9/1. Must reply by May 1 or within 3 week(s) if notified thereafter. **Financial aid:** Priority date 3/1; no closing date. FAFSA required. Applicants notified on a rolling basis starting 3/1; must reply within 3 week(s) of notification.

**Academics. Special study options:** Combined bachelor's/graduate degree, cooperative education, distance learning, double major, dual enrollment of high school students, ESL, honors, independent study, internships, liberal arts/career combination, study abroad, teacher certification program, Washington semester, weekend college. Bachelor's degree completion program for registered nurses, 5-year program leading to master's degree in architecture. **Credit/placement by examination:** AP, CLEP, institutional tests. 30 credit hours maximum toward bachelor's degree. **Support services:** Learning center, reduced course load, remedial instruction, study skills assistance, tutoring, writing center.

**Majors. Architecture:** Architecture. **Biology:** General, biochemistry. **Business:** General, accounting, business admin, marketing. **Communications:** General, broadcast journalism, journalism, public relations. **Computer sciences:** General, computer science, systems analysis. **Education:** General, biology, chemistry, elementary, emotionally handicapped, history, mathematics, mentally handicapped, middle, reading, science, secondary, social science, social studies, special. **Engineering:** General, civil, computer, electrical, manufacturing, mechanical. **Health:** Dental hygiene, health care admin, nursing (RN), predental, premedicine, substance abuse counseling. **History:** General. **Legal studies:** Paralegal, prelaw. **Liberal arts:** Arts/sciences. **Math:** General, applied. **Philosophy/religion:** Philosophy, religion. **Physical sciences:** Chemistry. **Protective services:** Criminal justice, law enforcement admin, police science. **Psychology:** General, developmental. **Public administration:** Social work. **Social sciences:** Economics, political science, sociology. **Visual/performing arts:** Dramatic.

**Most popular majors.** Biology 8%, business/marketing 12%, engineering/engineering technologies 13%, health sciences 36%.

**Computing on campus.** 250 workstations in dormitories, library, computer center, student center. Dormitories wired for high-speed internet access and linked to campus network. Commuter students can connect to campus network. Online library, helpline, repair service, student web hosting, wireless network available.

**Student life. Freshman orientation:** Available, $200 fee. Preregistration for classes offered. **Housing:** Coed dorms available. $100 deposit. **Activities:** Pep band, campus ministries, dance, drama, international student organizations, literary magazine, radio station, student government, student newspaper, American Institute of Architecture students, College Democrats, College Republicans, minority student association, NAACP, philosophy club, chemistry club, engineering societies, poet and writers forum, student environmental club.

**Athletics.** NCAA. **Intercollegiate:** Basketball, cheerleading, cross-country, fencing, golf, lacrosse, soccer, softball W, tennis W, track and field. **Intramural:** Baseball M, basketball, racquetball, soccer M, softball, table tennis, tennis, volleyball. **Team name:** Detroit Titans.

**Student services.** Adult student services, alcohol/substance abuse counseling, chaplain/spiritual director, career counseling, student employment services, financial aid counseling, health services, personal counseling, placement for graduates.

**Contact.** E-mail: admissions@udmercy.edu
Phone: (313) 993-1245 Toll-free number: (800) 635-5020
Fax: (313) 993-3326
Denise Williams, Vice President for Enrollment Management and Student Life, University of Detroit Mercy, 4001 West McNichols Road, Detroit, MI 48221-3038

## University of Michigan
### Ann Arbor, Michigan — CB member
### www.umich.edu — CB code: 1839

- Public 4-year university
- Residential campus in small city
- 26,033 degree-seeking undergraduates: 3% part-time, 49% women
- 13,840 degree-seeking graduate students
- 50% of applicants admitted
- SAT or ACT (ACT writing optional), application essay required
- 88% graduate within 6 years; 14% enter graduate study

**General.** Founded in 1817. Regionally accredited. Over 150 first-year seminars and several thousand undergraduate research opportunities. **Degrees:** 6,473 bachelor's awarded; master's, doctoral, professional offered. **ROTC:** Army, Naval, Air Force. **Location:** 40 miles from Detroit. **Calendar:** Trimester, limited summer session. **Full-time faculty:** 2,479 total; 91% have terminal degrees, 24% minority, 37% women. **Part-time faculty:** 595 total; 74% have terminal degrees, 14% minority, 52% women. **Class size:** 45% < 20, 34% 20-39, 4% 40-49, 11% 50-99, 7% >100. **Special facilities:** Botanical garden, biological station in northern Michigan, arboretum, planetarium, laboratories, observatory, field station in the greater Yellowstone ecosystem, exhibit museum, art museum, herbarium, galleries.

**Freshman class profile.** 29,965 applied, 14,970 admitted, 6,079 enrolled.

| Mid 50% test scores | | | |
|---|---|---|---|
| SAT critical reading: | 590-690 | Rank in top quarter: | 99% |
| SAT math: | 640-740 | Rank in top tenth: | 92% |
| SAT writing: | 600-700 | Return as sophomores: | 96% |
| ACT composite: | 27-31 | Out-of-state: | 32% |
| GPA 3.75 or higher: | 62% | Live on campus: | 97% |
| GPA 3.50-3.74: | 27% | International: | 4% |
| GPA 3.0-3.49: | 10% | Fraternities: | 19% |
| GPA 2.0-2.99: | 1% | Sororities: | 23% |

**Basis for selection.** Admissions based on school achievement record, including quality of school and courses elected, and test scores. Talents and extracurricular activities considered. Audition required for music majors; portfolio required for art majors. **Homeschooled:** Students must submit 3-4 SAT Subject Tests or other proficiency results depending on school/college of application.

**High school preparation.** College-preparatory program recommended. 16 units required; 20 recommended. Required and recommended units include English 4, mathematics 3-4, social studies 3, history 3, science 3-4 (laboratory 1), foreign language 2-4, computer science 1, visual/performing arts 2 and academic electives 1. Recommend AP, IB, honors, enriched, accelerated courses.

**2009-2010 Annual costs.** Tuition/fees: $11,659; $34,937 out-of-state. Room/board: $8,924. Books/supplies: $1,048. Personal expenses: $2,090.

**2008-2009 Financial aid.** **Need-based:** 3,788 full-time freshmen applied for aid; 2,622 were judged to have need; 2,622 of these received aid. Average need met was 90%. Average scholarship/grant was $8,375; average loan $4,340. 49% of total undergraduate aid awarded as scholarships/grants, 51% as loans/jobs. **Non-need-based:** Awarded to 16,718 full-time undergraduates, including 4,944 freshmen. Scholarships awarded for academics, alumni affiliation, art, athletics, leadership, music/drama, religious affiliation, ROTC, state residency.

**Application procedures. Admission:** Priority date 11/1; deadline 2/1 (postmark date). $40 fee, may be waived for applicants with need. Admission notification on a rolling basis beginning on or about 11/1. Must reply by May 1 or within 2 week(s) if notified thereafter. Students should apply early in the fall of senior year. Applications may be considered after 2/1 for School of Art and Design, School of Music, Theatre and Dance, School of Natural Resources and Environment, and School of Nursing programs on space availability basis. **Financial aid:** Priority date 4/29, closing date 5/29. FAFSA, CSS PROFILE required. Applicants notified on a rolling basis starting 3/15.

**Academics.** Small-scale, interdisciplinary instruction programs in residence halls; freshman and sophomore seminars, undergraduate research, study abroad opportunities. Numerous interdisciplinary undergraduate programs between Engineering, LSA, Business, and other schools/colleges. For School of Public Health's On Job/On Campus program, students attend classes one four-day weekend per month for 18-25 months for a master's degree. The Community Health Nursing Program involves staying on-campus from Friday through Sunday once a month for 47-credit master's degree. **Special study options:** Accelerated study, combined bachelor's/graduate degree, co-operative education, cross-registration, distance learning, double major, dual enrollment of high school students, ESL, exchange student, external degree, honors, independent study, internships, liberal arts/career combination, semester at sea, student-designed major, study abroad, teacher certification program, Washington semester, weekend college. Numerous graduate/professional programs in Engineering and Business (some offered on-line or through blended coursework); customized programs for Engineering professionals; dual and combined baccalaureate degree options in the College of Engineering; dual degree options in the Ross School of Business, College of Literature, Science and Arts, School of Kinesiology, and School of Music, Theatre and Dance. **Credit/placement by examination:** CLEP, IB, institutional tests. 60 credit hours maximum toward bachelor's degree. Policies on credit by examination varies by exam. **Support services:** Learning center, reduced course load, study skills assistance, tutoring, writing center.

**Honors college/program.** Roughly 500 members of each incoming freshman class admitted; grades, test scores, recommendations, essay used in decision process.

**Majors. Architecture:** Architecture. **Area/ethnic studies:** African-American, American, Asian, Chicano/Hispanic-American/Latino, East Asian, Latin American, Near/Middle Eastern, Russian/Slavic, women's. **Biology:** General, biochemistry, biophysics, botany, cellular/molecular, ecology, microbiology. **Business:** Business admin, organizational behavior. **Communications:** General. **Computer sciences:** General. **Conservation:** Environmental studies. **Education:** Elementary, music, physical. **Engineering:** General, aerospace, biomedical, chemical, civil, computer, electrical, geological, industrial, marine, materials science, mechanical, nuclear, physics, science. **Foreign languages:** Ancient Greek, Arabic, classics, comparative lit, French, German, Hebrew, Italian, Latin, linguistics, modern Greek, Russian, Spanish, Turkish. **Health:** Athletic training, dental hygiene, nursing (RN), pharmaceutical sciences. **History:** General. **Interdisciplinary:** Ancient studies, classical/archaeology, global studies, medieval/Renaissance, neuroscience. **Liberal arts:** Humanities. **Math:** General, statistics. **Parks/recreation:** Exercise sciences, sports admin. **Philosophy/religion:** Judaic, philosophy, religion. **Physical sciences:** Astronomy, atmospheric science, chemistry, geology, oceanography, physics. **Psychology:** General, cognitive. **Public administration:** Policy analysis. **Social sciences:** General, anthropology, economics, political science, sociology. **Visual/performing arts:** General, art, art history/conservation, ceramics, dance, dramatic, drawing, fiber arts, film/cinema, graphic design, illustration, industrial design, jazz, metal/jewelry, music history, music performance, music theory/composition, photography, printmaking, sculpture, theater design. **Other:** Anthropology-zoology, Environmental geosciences, Sound engineering.

**Most popular majors.** Biology 6%, business/marketing 6%, engineering/engineering technologies 15%, psychology 11%, social sciences 18%.

**Computing on campus.** 2,072 workstations in dormitories, library, computer center, student center. Dormitories wired for high-speed internet access and linked to campus network. Commuter students can connect to campus network. Online course registration, online library, helpline, repair service, student web hosting, wireless network available.

**Student life. Freshman orientation:** Mandatory, $270 fee. Preregistration for classes offered. Students must attend 1 of several 3-day summer programs. **Housing:** Guaranteed on-campus for freshmen. Coed dorms, single-sex dorms, special housing for disabled, apartments, cooperative housing, fraternity/sorority housing, wellness housing available. Living-learning communities. **Activities:** Bands, campus ministries, choral groups, dance, drama, film society, international student organizations, literary magazine, music ensembles, Model UN, musical theater, opera, radio station, student government, student newspaper, symphony orchestra, TV station, over 1,000 student organizations.

**Athletics.** NCAA. **Intercollegiate:** Baseball M, basketball, cheerleading, cross-country, diving, field hockey W, football (tackle) M, golf, gymnastics, ice hockey M, rowing (crew), soccer, softball W, swimming, tennis, track and field, volleyball W, water polo, wrestling M. **Intramural:** Badminton, basketball, cross-country, diving, football (non-tackle), golf, racquetball, soccer, softball, swimming, table tennis, tennis, track and field, volleyball, water polo, wrestling. **Team name:** Wolverines.

**Student services.** Adult student services, alcohol/substance abuse counseling, chaplain/spiritual director, career counseling, student employment services, financial aid counseling, health services, legal services, minority student services, on-campus daycare, personal counseling, placement for graduates, veterans' counselor, women's services. **Physically disabled:** Services for visually, speech, hearing impaired.

**Contact.** Phone: (734) 764-7433 Fax: (734) 936-0740
Theodore Spencer, Associate Vice Provost and Executive Director, Undergraduate Admissions, University of Michigan, 1220 Student Activities Building, Ann Arbor, MI 48109-1316

---

### University of Michigan: Dearborn

| Dearborn, Michigan | CB member |
|---|---|
| www.umd.umich.edu | CB code: 1861 |

- Public 4-year university
- Commuter campus in small city
- 6,509 degree-seeking undergraduates: 28% part-time, 52% women, 11% African American, 6% Asian American, 3% Hispanic American, 1% international
- 1,504 degree-seeking graduate students
- 67% of applicants admitted
- SAT or ACT (ACT writing optional) required
- 54% graduate within 6 years

**General.** Founded in 1959. Regionally accredited. **Degrees:** 1,139 bachelor's awarded; master's, doctoral offered. **ROTC:** Army, Naval, Air Force. **Location:** 10 miles from Detroit. **Calendar:** Semester, limited summer session. **Full-time faculty:** 306 total; 85% have terminal degrees, 29% minority, 37% women. **Part-time faculty:** 201 total; 35% have terminal degrees, 10% minority, 39% women. **Class size:** 23% < 20, 56% 20-39, 14% 40-49, 6% 50-99, less than 1% >100. **Special facilities:** Henry Ford's Fairlane estate, environmental study area, extensive rotating art collection, engineering CAD-CAM robotics laboratory, Armenian research center.

**Freshman class profile.** 3,711 applied, 2,492 admitted, 922 enrolled.

| Mid 50% test scores | | GPA 2.0-2.99: | 16% |
|---|---|---|---|
| SAT critical reading: | 500-630 | Rank in top quarter: | 60% |
| SAT math: | 530-680 | Rank in top tenth: | 26% |
| SAT writing: | 600-720 | Return as sophomores: | 78% |
| ACT composite: | 21-27 | Out-of-state: | .6% |
| GPA 3.75 or higher: | 34% | International: | 1% |
| GPA 3.50-3.74: | 18% | Fraternities: | 2% |
| GPA 3.0-3.49: | 32% | Sororities: | 2% |

**Basis for selection.** Minimum 3.0 GPA with 500 SAT verbal and math or 22 ACT preferred; class rank considered. Interview recommended for applicants with less than 3.0 GPA or 20 ACT or 1000 SAT (exclusive of Writing). Essay recommended for all.

**High school preparation.** 15 units required; 20 recommended. Required and recommended units include English 4, mathematics 4, social studies 4, history 4, science 2 (laboratory 1) and foreign language 2. 1 unit information technology and 1 unit fine and performing arts recommended.

**2009-2010 Annual costs.** Tuition/fees: $9,100; $19,883 out-of-state.

**2008-2009 Financial aid. Non-need-based:** Scholarships awarded for academics, alumni affiliation, athletics, job skills, leadership, minority status, ROTC.

**Application procedures. Admission:** Priority date 5/1; no deadline. $30 fee, may be waived for applicants with need. Admission notification on a rolling basis beginning on or about 9/1. Must reply by May 1 or within 4 week(s) if notified thereafter. **Financial aid:** Priority date 2/15; no closing date. FAFSA required. Applicants notified on a rolling basis starting 3/10; must reply within 3 week(s) of notification.

**Academics. Special study options:** Cooperative education, cross-registration, distance learning, double major, dual enrollment of high school

students, honors, independent study, internships, liberal arts/career combination, student-designed major, study abroad, teacher certification program, Washington semester. Professional development courses in education, engineering, liberal arts, and management. **Credit/placement by examination:** AP, CLEP, institutional tests. 30 credit hours maximum toward bachelor's degree. **Support services:** Learning center, pre-admission summer program, tutoring, writing center.

**Majors. Area/ethnic studies:** American. **Biology:** General, bacteriology, biochemistry, ecology. **Business:** Business admin, management science. **Communications:** General. **Computer sciences:** General, programming. **Conservation:** General, environmental studies. **Education:** General, art, business, chemistry, early childhood, foreign languages, mathematics, science, secondary, social studies. **Engineering:** General, computer, electrical, manufacturing, mechanical. **Foreign languages:** French, Spanish. **Health:** Health care admin. **History:** General. **Interdisciplinary:** Behavioral sciences. **Liberal arts:** Arts/sciences. **Math:** General. **Philosophy/religion:** Philosophy. **Physical sciences:** Chemistry, physics. **Psychology:** General. **Public administration:** General. **Social sciences:** Anthropology, economics, political science, sociology. **Visual/performing arts:** Painting.

**Most popular majors.** Biology 6%, business/marketing 21%, education 16%, engineering/engineering technologies 16%, psychology 10%, social sciences 6%.

**Computing on campus.** 140 workstations in library, computer center, student center. Commuter students can connect to campus network. Online course registration, helpline, wireless network available.

**Student life. Freshman orientation:** Mandatory, $50 fee. Preregistration for classes offered. **Activities:** Campus ministries, choral groups, drama, film society, literary magazine, radio station, student government, student newspaper, TV station, Arab student union, African American association, campus engineers, Asian American association, student activities board, professional accounting society, Muslim student association.

**Athletics.** NAIA. **Intercollegiate:** Basketball, softball W, volleyball W. **Intramural:** Basketball, volleyball. **Team name:** Wolves.

**Student services.** Adult student services, alcohol/substance abuse counseling, career counseling, services for economically disadvantaged, student employment services, financial aid counseling, health services, on-campus daycare, personal counseling, placement for graduates, veterans' counselor, women's services. **Physically disabled:** Services for visually, speech, hearing impaired.

**Contact.** E-mail: admissions@umd.umich.edu
Phone: (313) 593-5100 Fax: (313) 436-9167
Christopher Tremblay, Director of Admissions and Orientation, University of Michigan: Dearborn, 4901 Evergreen Road, 1145 UC, Dearborn, MI 48128-1491

---

### University of Michigan: Flint

| Flint, Michigan | CB member |
|---|---|
| www.umflint.edu | CB code: 1853 |

- Public 4-year university and branch campus college
- Commuter campus in small city
- 6,280 degree-seeking undergraduates: 31% part-time, 61% women, 14% African American, 2% Asian American, 3% Hispanic American, 1% Native American, 1% international
- 1,158 degree-seeking graduate students
- 82% of applicants admitted
- SAT or ACT (ACT writing optional) required
- 43% graduate within 6 years

**General.** Founded in 1956. Regionally accredited. Institution shares many resources of entire University of Michigan system. **Degrees:** 903 bachelor's awarded; master's, professional offered. **Location:** 60 miles from Detroit. **Calendar:** Semester, limited summer session. **Full-time faculty:** 257 total; 70% have terminal degrees, 17% minority, 52% women. **Part-time faculty:** 237 total; 26% have terminal degrees, 9% minority, 57% women. **Class size:** 40% < 20, 48% 20-39, 7% 40-49, 5% 50-99, less than 1% >100. **Special facilities:** Green Arts Project House.

**Freshman class profile.** 2,693 applied, 2,213 admitted, 768 enrolled.

| Mid 50% test scores | | | |
|---|---|---|---|
| SAT critical reading: | 390-570 | Rank in top quarter: | 43% |
| SAT math: | 430-550 | Rank in top tenth: | 19% |
| SAT writing: | 400-540 | End year in good standing: | 74% |
| ACT composite: | 18-24 | Return as sophomores: | 73% |
| GPA 3.75 or higher: | 17% | Out-of-state: | 1% |
| GPA 3.50-3.74: | 16% | Live on campus: | 17% |
| GPA 3.0-3.49: | 33% | International: | 1% |
| GPA 2.0-2.99: | 34% | Fraternities: | 2% |
| | | Sororities: | 3% |

**Basis for selection.** GPA of 2.7 or higher and test scores equaling national average automatically admitted. Essay and interview recommended. Audition required for art and music majors. **Homeschooled:** Transcript of courses and grades required.

**High school preparation.** College-preparatory program recommended. 9 units required; 22 recommended. Required and recommended units include English 4, mathematics 3-4, social studies 3, history 3, science 2-4 (laboratory 2) and foreign language 2. Fine arts and computer science courses recommended.

**2009-2010 Annual costs.** Tuition/fees: $8,279; $15,793 out-of-state. Room/board: $6,874. Books/supplies: $1,000. Personal expenses: $1,380.

**2008-2009 Financial aid.** **Need-based:** 721 full-time freshmen applied for aid; 558 were judged to have need; 552 of these received aid. Average need met was 78%. Average scholarship/grant was $6,159; average loan $3,346. 31% of total undergraduate aid awarded as scholarships/grants, 69% as loans/jobs. **Non-need-based:** Awarded to 2,237 full-time undergraduates, including 538 freshmen. Scholarships awarded for academics, art, leadership, minority status, music/drama. **Additional information:** SAT/ACT scores must be submitted for scholarship consideration.

**Application procedures.** **Admission:** No deadline. $30 fee, may be waived for applicants with need. Admission notification on a rolling basis beginning on or about 12/1. Must reply by May 1 or within 2 week(s) if notified thereafter. **Financial aid:** Priority date 3/1; no closing date. FAFSA required. Applicants notified on a rolling basis starting 3/15.

**Academics.** **Special study options:** Combined bachelor's/graduate degree, cooperative education, distance learning, double major, dual enrollment of high school students, ESL, honors, independent study, internships, student-designed major, study abroad, teacher certification program. **Credit/placement by examination:** AP, CLEP, SAT, ACT, institutional tests. 9 credit hours maximum toward bachelor's degree. Maximum of 3 courses may be passed by examination in Arts & Sciences, School of Management and Nursing. **Support services:** Learning center, reduced course load, remedial instruction, study skills assistance, tutoring, writing center.

**Majors.** **Area/ethnic studies:** African-American. **Biology:** General, Biochemistry/biophysics and molecular biology, biomedical sciences, ecology, molecular, wildlife. **Business:** Accounting, actuarial science, business admin, finance, international, marketing, operations, organizational behavior. **Communications:** General, journalism, media studies, organizational. **Computer sciences:** General, computer science, information systems. **Conservation:** Environmental science. **Education:** General, art, biology, chemistry, elementary, English, foreign languages, French, history, mathematics, music, physics, science, secondary, social studies, Spanish. **Engineering:** Mechanical, science. **Foreign languages:** French, Spanish. **Health:** Clinical lab science, health care admin, health services, medical radiologic technology/radiation therapy, nursing (RN), public health ed. **History:** General. **Liberal arts:** Arts/sciences. **Math:** General. **Philosophy/religion:** Ethics, philosophy. **Physical sciences:** Chemistry, physics. **Protective services:** Law enforcement admin. **Psychology:** General, clinical. **Public administration:** General, social work. **Social sciences:** General, anthropology, economics, political science, sociology. **Visual/performing arts:** Acting, ceramics, dramatic, graphic design, music performance, painting, photography, printmaking, sculpture, studio arts, theater design, theater history.

**Most popular majors.** Biology 6%, business/marketing 18%, education 13%, health sciences 20%, public administration/social services 6%.

**Computing on campus.** 205 workstations in library, computer center, student center. Dormitories wired for high-speed internet access and linked to campus network. Commuter students can connect to campus network. Online course registration, online library, helpline, repair service, student web hosting, wireless network available.

**Student life.** **Freshman orientation:** Mandatory, $80 fee. Preregistration for classes offered. One-day program for students and parents before start of fall semester. **Housing:** Coed dorms available. **Activities:** Bands, choral groups, dance, drama, literary magazine, music ensembles, musical theater, student government, student newspaper, TV station, College Democrats, College Republicans, College Libertarians, Intervarsity Christian Fellowship,

Muslim student association, Students Moving the UCEN Forward, Voices for Women on Campus, chess club, Michigan Poetry Society.

**Athletics.** **Intramural:** Basketball, football (non-tackle), golf, racquetball, soccer, table tennis, volleyball.

**Student services.** Adult student services, alcohol/substance abuse counseling, career counseling, student employment services, financial aid counseling, health services, minority student services, on-campus daycare, personal counseling, veterans' counselor, women's services. **Physically disabled:** Services for visually, speech, hearing impaired.

**Contact.** E-mail: admissions@umflint.edu
Phone: (810) 762-3300 Fax: (810) 762-3272
Kimberley Buster-Williams, Director of Admissions, University of Michigan: Flint, 303 East Kearsley Street, Flint, MI 48502-1950

---

## Walsh College of Accountancy and Business Administration
**Troy, Michigan**
**www.walshcollege.edu**                    **CB code: 0372**

▶ Private two-year upper-division business college
▶ Commuter campus in large city
▶ 74% of applicants admitted

**General.** Founded in 1922. Regionally accredited. **Degrees:** 374 bachelor's awarded; master's, professional offered. **Articulation:** Agreements with Henry Ford CC, Oakland CC, Macomb CC, Mott CC, Schoolcraft College, Washtenaw CC, St. Clair County CC, Wayne County CC, Kellogg CC, Jackson CC, Lansing CC. **Location:** 17 miles from Detroit. **Calendar:** Semester, extensive summer session. **Full-time faculty:** 18 total; 50% have terminal degrees, 6% minority, 44% women. **Part-time faculty:** 114 total; 30% have terminal degrees, 9% minority, 29% women. **Class size:** 25% < 20, 64% 20-39, 11% 40-49.

**Student profile.** 1,076 degree-seeking undergraduates, 1,980 degree-seeking graduate students. 454 applied as first time-transfer students, 337 admitted, 293 enrolled. 100% entered as juniors.

| Women: | 53% | International: | 3% |
|---|---|---|---|
| African American: | 5% | Part-time: | 86% |
| Asian American: | 3% | Out-of-state: | 2% |
| Hispanic American: | 1% | 25 or older: | 64% |

**Basis for selection.** Open admission. College transcript required. 30 transferred credits must be in liberal arts, including course in English composition or written communication. Transfer accepted as juniors.

**2010-2011 Annual costs.** Tuition/fees (projected): $11,355.

**Financial aid.** **Need-based:** 150 applied for aid; 130 were judged to have need; 128 of these received aid. Average need met was 58%. 17% of total undergraduate aid awarded as scholarships/grants, 83% as loans/jobs. **Non-need-based:** Awarded to 45 undergraduates. Scholarships awarded for academics.

**Application procedures.** **Admission:** Rolling admission. $25 fee, may be waived for applicants with need. **Financial aid:** Priority date 3/1, no deadline. Applicants notified on a rolling basis. FAFSA required.

**Academics.** **Special study options:** Accelerated study, combined bachelor's/graduate degree, distance learning, double major, internships. Joint partnerships with area community colleges to offer 150-hour honors program in which students complete associate, bachelor and MBA degrees in 5 years. **Credit/placement by examination:** CLEP, IB.

**Majors.** **Business:** General, accounting, business admin, finance. **Computer sciences:** General, information technology.

**Most popular majors.** Business/marketing 98%.

**Computing on campus.** 200 workstations in library, computer center. Commuter students can connect to campus network. Online course registration, online library, helpline, wireless network available.

**Student life.** **Activities:** International student organizations, student government, American Marketing Association, finance/economics club, National Association of Black Accountants, accounting club, Association of Information Technology Professionals, international club.

**Student services.** Career counseling, student employment services, financial aid counseling, placement for graduates. **Physically disabled:** Services for visually, hearing impaired.

**Contact.** E-mail: admissions@walshcollege.edu
Phone: (248) 823-1610 Toll-free number: (800) 925-7401
Fax: (248) 823-1662
Jeremy Guc, Director of Admissions and Academic Advising, Walsh
College of Accountancy and Business Administration, PO Box 7006, Troy,
MI 48007-7006

## Wayne State University
### Detroit, Michigan
**CB member**
www.wayne.edu
**CB code: 1898**

- Public 4-year university
- Commuter campus in very large city
- 19,650 degree-seeking undergraduates: 34% part-time, 58% women, 32% African American, 7% Asian American, 3% Hispanic American, 1% Native American, 3% international
- 10,650 degree-seeking graduate students
- 75% of applicants admitted
- SAT or ACT (ACT writing optional) required
- 32% graduate within 6 years

**General.** Founded in 1868. Regionally accredited. 4 extension center locations, 2 university centers and an advanced technology center at Southeastern Michigan community colleges. **Degrees:** 2,635 bachelor's awarded; master's, doctoral, professional offered. **ROTC:** Army, Air Force. **Location:** 3 miles from downtown. **Calendar:** Semester, extensive summer session. **Full-time faculty:** 1,055 total; 76% have terminal degrees, 27% minority, 42% women. **Part-time faculty:** 988 total; 22% have terminal degrees, 27% minority, 55% women. **Class size:** 44% < 20, 39% 20-39, 7% 40-49, 7% 50-99, 3% >100. **Special facilities:** 3 theaters, planetarium.

**Freshman class profile.** 10,689 applied, 8,063 admitted, 3,046 enrolled.

| Mid 50% test scores | | | |
|---|---|---|---|
| ACT composite: | 17-24 | Return as sophomores: | 76% |
| GPA 3.75 or higher: | 16% | Out-of-state: | 1% |
| GPA 3.50-3.74: | 14% | Live on campus: | 32% |
| GPA 3.0-3.49: | 29% | International: | 2% |
| GPA 2.0-2.99: | 40% | Fraternities: | 1% |
| End year in good standing: | 75% | Sororities: | 1% |

**Basis for selection.** High school record and test scores are important. Minimum 2.75 GPA or 2.0 GPA combined with 21 ACT is acceptable for admission although all applications are considered on an individual basis. Audition required for music or dance applicants.

**High school preparation.** College-preparatory program recommended. 18 units recommended. Recommended units include English 4, mathematics 4, social studies 3, science 3, foreign language 2 and visual/performing arts 2. Computer literacy.

**2009-2010 Annual costs.** Tuition/fees: $8,599; $18,412 out-of-state. Room/board: $7,210. Books/supplies: $972. Personal expenses: $1,841.

**2008-2009 Financial aid. Need-based:** 2,241 full-time freshmen applied for aid; 1,800 were judged to have need; 1,764 of these received aid. Average need met was 72%. Average scholarship/grant was $5,546; average loan $3,549. 32% of total undergraduate aid awarded as scholarships/grants, 68% as loans/jobs. **Non-need-based:** Awarded to 4,211 full-time undergraduates, including 1,255 freshmen. Scholarships awarded for academics, art, athletics, leadership, music/drama. **Additional information:** Need-based institutional grants cover tuition and fees with grants and EFC (no loans).

**Application procedures. Admission:** No deadline. $30 fee, may be waived for applicants with need. Admission notification on a rolling basis. **Financial aid:** Priority date 2/15, closing date 4/30. FAFSA required. Applicants notified on a rolling basis starting 3/1; must reply within 2 week(s) of notification.

**Academics. Special study options:** Accelerated study, combined bachelor's/graduate degree, cooperative education, cross-registration, distance learning, double major, dual enrollment of high school students, ESL, honors, independent study, internships, liberal arts/career combination, study abroad, teacher certification program. Off-campus courses for credit, city-wide adult education program, international exchange student programs. **Credit/placement by examination:** AP, CLEP, IB, institutional tests. 32 credit hours maximum toward bachelor's degree. **Support services:** Learning center, pre-admission summer program, reduced course load, remedial instruction, study skills assistance, tutoring, writing center.

**Honors college/program.** Selected incoming freshmen are invited into the program each year through Scholars Day and are awarded at least $2,000 in a tuition scholarship for four years.

**Majors. Area/ethnic studies:** African-American, American, East Asian. **Biology:** General. **Business:** Accounting, finance, international, labor studies, management information systems, marketing, organizational behavior. **Communications:** General, journalism, public relations, radio/tv. **Computer sciences:** General, information systems. **Conservation:** Environmental science. **Education:** Art, elementary, English, health, mathematics, physical, science, social studies, special, speech impaired, voc/tech. **Engineering:** Chemical, civil, electrical, industrial, mechanical. **Engineering technology:** Computer systems, construction, electrical, electromechanical, industrial, manufacturing, mechanical. **Family/consumer sciences:** Apparel marketing, food/nutrition. **Foreign languages:** General, classics, German, linguistics, Slavic. **Health:** Clinical lab science, communication disorders, dietetics, health services, medical radiologic technology/radiation therapy, pathology assistant. **History:** General. **Math:** General. **Personal/culinary services:** Funeral direction. **Philosophy/religion:** Philosophy. **Physical sciences:** Chemistry, geology, physics. **Protective services:** Criminal justice. **Psychology:** General. **Public administration:** General, social work. **Social sciences:** Anthropology, economics, political science, sociology, urban studies. **Visual/performing arts:** Art, art history/conservation, cinematography, dance, dramatic, film/cinema. **Other:** Biomedical physics, Elementary language arts, Near eastern languages, Near eastern studies, Product design engineering technology, Technical and interdisciplinary studies.

**Most popular majors.** Biology 8%, business/marketing 17%, education 10%, engineering/engineering technologies 8%, health sciences 10%, psychology 8%, social sciences 6%, visual/performing arts 7%.

**Computing on campus.** 1,020 workstations in library. Dormitories wired for high-speed internet access and linked to campus network. Commuter students can connect to campus network. Online course registration, online library, helpline, repair service, wireless network available.

**Student life. Freshman orientation:** Mandatory, $75 fee. Preregistration for classes offered. Held at the Welcome Center several times a year. **Housing:** Coed dorms, special housing for disabled, apartments, fraternity/sorority housing, wellness housing available. $150 nonrefundable deposit. **Activities:** Bands, campus ministries, choral groups, dance, drama, international student organizations, literary magazine, music ensembles, Model UN, musical theater, radio station, student government, student newspaper, symphony orchestra, TV station, Indian student association, Albanian American student association, cultural diversity council, Slavic club, Campus Crusade for Christ, College Democrats, cancer awareness association, Habitat for Humanity, UNICEF, university mentors.

**Athletics.** NCAA. **Intercollegiate:** Baseball M, basketball, cross-country, diving, fencing, football (tackle) M, golf M, ice hockey W, softball W, swimming, tennis, volleyball W. **Intramural:** Badminton, basketball, bowling, cheerleading, football (non-tackle), racquetball, soccer, softball, tennis, volleyball. **Team name:** Warriors.

**Student services.** Adult student services, alcohol/substance abuse counseling, chaplain/spiritual director, career counseling, services for economically disadvantaged, student employment services, financial aid counseling, health services, legal services, minority student services, on-campus daycare, personal counseling, placement for graduates, veterans' counselor, women's services. **Physically disabled:** Services for visually, speech, hearing impaired. **Learning disabled:** Comprehensive services available.

**Contact.** E-mail: admissions@wayne.edu
Phone: (313) 577-3577 Toll-free number: (877) 978-4636
Fax: (313) 577-7536
Judy Tatum, Senior Director of Undergraduate Admissions, Wayne State University, 42 West Warren, Detroit, MI 48201

## Western Michigan University
### Kalamazoo, Michigan
**CB member**
www.wmich.edu
**CB code: 1902**

- Public 4-year university
- Residential campus in small city
- 19,302 degree-seeking undergraduates: 12% part-time, 49% women, 8% African American, 2% Asian American, 3% Hispanic American, 1% Native American, 3% international
- 4,476 degree-seeking graduate students
- 83% of applicants admitted
- SAT or ACT (ACT writing recommended) required
- 55% graduate within 6 years

**General.** Founded in 1903. Regionally accredited. **Degrees:** 3,969 bachelor's awarded; master's, doctoral, professional offered. **ROTC:** Army. **Location:** 140 miles from Detroit, 140 miles from Chicago. **Calendar:** Semester, extensive summer session. **Full-time faculty:** 908 total; 80% have terminal degrees, 14% minority, 40% women. **Part-time faculty:** 527 total; 54% women. **Class size:** 37% < 20, 43% 20-39, 9% 40-49, 7% 50-99, 4% >100. **Special facilities:** Van de Graaff particle accelerator, pilot plant for manufacturing and printing of paper and fiber recovery, aviation flight simulators, business technology park.

**Freshman class profile.** 12,379 applied, 10,253 admitted, 3,193 enrolled.

| Mid 50% test scores | | Rank in top quarter: | 32% |
|---|---|---|---|
| ACT composite: | 20-25 | Rank in top tenth: | 12% |
| GPA 3.75 or higher: | 18% | Return as sophomores: | 72% |
| GPA 3.50-3.74: | 13% | Out-of-state: | 10% |
| GPA 3.0-3.49: | 38% | Live on campus: | 87% |
| GPA 2.0-2.99: | 31% | International: | 1% |

**Basis for selection.** School achievement record, test scores most important. Trend of grades and number of solid high school academic subjects completed considered; students not meeting college-preparatory program requirements may be admitted conditionally if they meet other admission requirements. Interview recommended. Audition required for dance, music, and theater applicants. Portfolio required for some art applicants. **Homeschooled:** State high school equivalency certificate, letter of recommendation (nonparent) required.

**High school preparation.** College-preparatory program required. 15 units required; 17 recommended. Required and recommended units include English 4, mathematics 3, social studies 2, history 1, science 2 (laboratory 1), foreign language 1, computer science 1, visual/performing arts 1 and academic electives 2.

**2009-2010 Annual costs.** Tuition/fees: $8,382; $19,502 out-of-state. Room/board: $7,784. Books/supplies: $1,000.

**2008-2009 Financial aid. Need-based:** 3,800 full-time freshmen applied for aid; 3,468 were judged to have need; 3,468 of these received aid. Average need met was 85%. Average scholarship/grant was $4,566; average loan $3,422. 38% of total undergraduate aid awarded as scholarships/grants, 62% as loans/jobs. **Non-need-based:** Awarded to 8,369 full-time undergraduates, including 1,672 freshmen. Scholarships awarded for academics, alumni affiliation, art, athletics, minority status, music/drama, ROTC, state residency.

**Application procedures. Admission:** Priority date 2/1; deadline 8/1. $35 fee, may be waived for applicants with need. Admission notification on a rolling basis beginning on or about 7/1. Must reply by 5/1. **Financial aid:** Priority date 3/15; no closing date. FAFSA required. Applicants notified on a rolling basis starting 3/15.

**Academics. Special study options:** Accelerated study, combined bachelor's/graduate degree, cross-registration, distance learning, double major, dual enrollment of high school students, ESL, exchange student, honors, independent study, internships, student-designed major, study abroad, teacher certification program, Washington semester. **Credit/placement by examination:** AP, CLEP, IB, SAT, ACT, institutional tests. Maximum semester hours of credit by examination which may be counted toward degree varies by department. Credit by examination may not be used to satisfy minimum residency requirement of 30 semester hours. **Support services:** Learning center, pre-admission summer program, reduced course load, remedial instruction, study skills assistance, tutoring, writing center.

**Honors college/program.** ACT composite score of at least 26 and a GPA of 3.6 or can demonstrate a rank within the top 10% of their high school class; must provide two letters of reference from teachers, instructors, professors, and/or counselors who can describe their academic ability along with application.

**Majors. Architecture:** Urban/community planning. **Area/ethnic studies:** African-American, women's. **Biology:** General, biochemistry, biomedical sciences. **Business:** General, accounting, e-commerce, finance, financial planning, information resources management, management science, marketing, travel services. **Communications:** General, advertising, journalism, organizational, public relations. **Computer sciences:** General, computer science. **Conservation:** Environmental studies. **Education:** Art, biology, business, chemistry, early childhood, elementary, emotionally handicapped, English, family/consumer sciences, French, geography, German, health, history, Latin, mathematics, mentally handicapped, physical, physics, sales/marketing, science, social science, social studies, Spanish, technology/industrial arts, trade/industrial. **Engineering:** Aerospace, chemical, civil, computer, electrical, industrial, manufacturing, mechanical, structural. **Engineering technology:** Industrial management. **Family/consumer sciences:** Child development, clothing/textiles, family systems, institutional food production. **Foreign languages:** French, German, Latin, Spanish. **Health:** Athletic training, audiology/speech pathology, dietetics, music therapy, nursing (RN). **History:** General, public archives. **Interdisciplinary:** Global studies. **Math:** General, statistics. **Mechanic/repair:** Avionics. **Parks/recreation:** General, exercise sciences. **Philosophy/religion:** Philosophy, religion. **Physical sciences:** Chemistry, geochemistry, geology, geophysics, hydrology, physics. **Protective services:** Criminal justice. **Psychology:** General. **Public administration:** Social work. **Social sciences:** Anthropology, economics, geography, political science, sociology. **Transportation:** Airline/commercial pilot, aviation management. **Visual/performing arts:** Art history/conservation, dance, graphic design, interior design, jazz, music performance, music theory/composition, studio arts, theater history. **Other:** Business-oriented chemistry, Career and tech education, Economics: business, Engineering graphics and design technology, Food and consumer package goods marketing, Interdisciplinary health services, Musical theater performance, Paper Engineering: Process, Student-planned major.

**Most popular majors.** Business/marketing 25%, communications/journalism 7%, education 15%, engineering/engineering technologies 6%, health sciences 8%, visual/performing arts 6%.

**Computing on campus.** 2,000 workstations in dormitories, library, computer center, student center. Dormitories wired for high-speed internet access and linked to campus network. Commuter students can connect to campus network. Online course registration, helpline, repair service, student web hosting, wireless network available.

**Student life. Freshman orientation:** Mandatory, $195 fee. Preregistration for classes offered. 2-day program in June; includes session for parents. **Housing:** Guaranteed on-campus for freshmen. Coed dorms, single-sex dorms, special housing for disabled, apartments, fraternity/sorority housing, wellness housing available. $100 fully refundable deposit, deadline 6/1. Aviation, business, engineering and applied sciences houses, fine arts house, health and human services house, honors community, second year experience, transfer student communities, Magellan house, Umma scholars house. **Activities:** Bands, campus ministries, choral groups, dance, drama, film society, international student organizations, literary magazine, music ensembles, musical theater, opera, radio station, student government, student newspaper, symphony orchestra, nearly 300 organizations available.

**Athletics.** NCAA. **Intercollegiate:** Baseball M, basketball, cross-country W, football (tackle) M, golf W, gymnastics W, ice hockey M, soccer, softball W, tennis, track and field W, volleyball W. **Intramural:** Badminton, basketball, bowling, equestrian, fencing, football (tackle), golf M, ice hockey, lacrosse, racquetball, rugby, sailing, skiing, soccer, softball, swimming, table tennis, tennis, volleyball. **Team name:** Broncos.

**Student services.** Adult student services, alcohol/substance abuse counseling, chaplain/spiritual director, career counseling, student employment services, financial aid counseling, health services, minority student services, on-campus daycare, personal counseling, placement for graduates, veterans' counselor, women's services. **Physically disabled:** Services for visually, speech, hearing impaired.

**Contact.** E-mail: ask-wmu@wmich.edu
Phone: (269) 387-2000 Fax: (269) 387-2096
Penny Bundy, Director of Admissions, Western Michigan University, 1903 West Michigan Avenue, Kalamazoo, MI 49008-5211

## Yeshiva Beth Yehuda-Yeshiva Gedolah of Greater Detroit
### Oak Park, Michigan
**CB code: 7010**

- Private 5-year rabbinical college for men affiliated with Jewish faith
- Residential campus in large town

**General.** Accredited by AARTS. **Calendar:** Semester.

**Annual costs/financial aid.** Books/supplies: $500. Personal expenses: $200.

**Contact.** Phone: (248) 968-3360
24600 Greenfield Road, Oak Park, MI 48237

# Minnesota

## Argosy University: Twin Cities
**Eagan, Minnesota**
**www.argosy.edu/twincities**

- For-profit 4-year university
- Very large city
- 1,536 degree-seeking undergraduates

**General. Degrees:** 26 bachelor's, 304 associate awarded; master's, doctoral, professional offered. **Calendar:** Continuous. **Full-time faculty:** 71 total. **Part-time faculty:** 185 total.

**Freshman class profile.** 305 enrolled.

**Basis for selection.** Open admission.

**Academics. Credit/placement by examination:** CLEP.

**Majors. Business:** Business admin. **Health:** Clinical lab science. **Liberal arts:** Arts/sciences. **Protective services:** Police science. **Psychology:** General.

**Contact.** E-mail: autcadmissions@argosy.edu
Phone: (651) 846-3300
Argosy University: Twin Cities, 1515 Central Parkway, Eagan, MN 55121

## Art Institutes International Minnesota
**Minneapolis, Minnesota**
**www.artinstitutes.edu/minneapolis**          CB code: 2332

- For-profit 4-year culinary school and visual arts college
- Commuter campus in large city
- 1,974 degree-seeking undergraduates
- Application essay, interview required
- 43% graduate within 6 years

**General.** Accredited by ACICS. **Degrees:** 261 bachelor's, 113 associate awarded. **Calendar:** Quarter, extensive summer session. **Full-time faculty:** 56 total; 36% women. **Part-time faculty:** 63 total; 44% women. **Special facilities:** Student-run dining lab, wireless internet.

**Basis for selection.** Open admission. School tour required prior to admission. **Homeschooled:** Transcript of courses and grades, interview required. **Learning Disabled:** Notify Dean of Student Affairs.

**2009-2010 Annual costs.** Tuition/fees: $22,416. Typical full-time credit load 16 credits/quarter. Starter kits for most programs $350 to $1,300. Books/supplies: $1,649. Personal expenses: $2,880.

**Application procedures. Admission:** No deadline. $50 fee. Admission notification on a rolling basis. **Financial aid:** FAFSA required.

**Academics. Special study options:** Cooperative education, distance learning, honors, independent study, internships, study abroad, weekend college. **Credit/placement by examination:** AP, CLEP, institutional tests. **Support services:** Learning center, remedial instruction, study skills assistance, tutoring.

**Majors. Business:** Customer service, fashion, hospitality admin, hospitality/recreation, hotel/motel admin, marketing, merchandising, resort management, restaurant/food services, retailing, selling. **Communications:** Advertising, digital media, photojournalism. **Communications technology:** Animation/special effects, graphics. **Computer sciences:** Computer graphics, web page design, webmaster. **Personal/culinary services:** Restaurant/catering. **Visual/performing arts:** Arts management, cinematography, commercial photography, commercial/advertising art, design, film/cinema, graphic design, interior design, multimedia, photography. **Other:** Culinary management, Digital film and video production.

**Computing on campus.** 320 workstations in library, computer center, student center. Dormitories wired for high-speed internet access. Online library, student web hosting, wireless network available.

**Student life. Freshman orientation:** Mandatory. Preregistration for classes offered. **Housing:** Apartments, wellness housing available. $250 deposit. **Activities:** Campus ministries, film society, student government, student newspaper.

**Student services.** Alcohol/substance abuse counseling, career counseling, student employment services, financial aid counseling, personal counseling, placement for graduates, veterans' counselor. **Physically disabled:** Services for hearing impaired.

**Contact.** E-mail: aimadm@aii.edu
Phone: (612) 332-3361 Toll-free number: (800) 777-3643
Fax: (612) 332-3934
Mary Strand, Senior Director of Admissions, Art Institutes International Minnesota, 15 South Ninth Street, Minneapolis, MN 55402

## Augsburg College
**Minneapolis, Minnesota**          **CB member**
**www.augsburg.edu**          **CB code: 6014**

- Private 4-year liberal arts college affiliated with Evangelical Lutheran Church in America
- Residential campus in large city
- 2,979 degree-seeking undergraduates: 16% part-time, 54% women, 8% African American, 6% Asian American, 3% Hispanic American, 2% Native American, 1% international
- 892 degree-seeking graduate students
- 52% of applicants admitted
- Application essay required
- 62% graduate within 6 years; 24% enter graduate study

**General.** Founded in 1869. Regionally accredited. **Degrees:** 577 bachelor's awarded; master's offered. **ROTC:** Army, Naval, Air Force. **Location:** 5 miles from downtown. **Calendar:** Differs by program, extensive summer session. **Full-time faculty:** 200 total; 36% have terminal degrees, 9% minority, 48% women. **Part-time faculty:** 209 total; 35% have terminal degrees, 11% minority, 50% women. **Class size:** 62% < 20, 36% 20-39, less than 1% 40-49, less than 1% 50-99. **Special facilities:** Center for atmospheric research.

**Freshman class profile.** 2,330 applied, 1,211 admitted, 449 enrolled.

| Mid 50% test scores | | GPA 2.0-2.99: | 33% |
|---|---|---|---|
| SAT critical reading: | 510-640 | Rank in top quarter: | 37% |
| SAT math: | 500-640 | Rank in top tenth: | 11% |
| SAT writing: | 480-600 | End year in good standing: | 90% |
| ACT composite: | 20-25 | Return as sophomores: | 81% |
| GPA 3.75 or higher: | 21% | Out-of-state: | 13% |
| GPA 3.50-3.74: | 11% | Live on campus: | 90% |
| GPA 3.0-3.49: | 34% | International: | 3% |

**Basis for selection.** School achievement record, class rank in top half, test scores, essays and recommendations very important; extracurricular activities important. SAT or ACT recommended. Interview recommended.

**High school preparation.** College-preparatory program recommended. 15 units required. Required and recommended units include English 4, mathematics 3, social studies 2-4, history 2, science 3 and foreign language 2.

**2009-2010 Annual costs.** Tuition/fees: $27,628. Room/board: $7,514. Books/supplies: $1,000. Personal expenses: $1,670.

**2008-2009 Financial aid. Non-need-based:** Scholarships awarded for academics, alumni affiliation, leadership, minority status, music/drama, religious affiliation.

**Application procedures. Admission:** Priority date 5/1; deadline 8/1 (receipt date). $25 fee, may be waived for applicants with need, free for online applicants. Admission notification on a rolling basis beginning on or about 11/1. Must reply by May 1 or within 2 week(s) if notified thereafter. **Financial aid:** Priority date 4/15, closing date 8/1. FAFSA required. Applicants notified on a rolling basis starting 3/1; must reply within 3 week(s) of notification.

**Academics. Special study options:** Combined bachelor's/graduate degree, cooperative education, cross-registration, double major, dual enrollment of high school students, ESL, honors, independent study, internships, liberal arts/career combination, student-designed major, study abroad, teacher certification program, urban semester, weekend college. Metro-urban studies internship program; global education program in Central America, Mexico, Namibia and Norway. **Credit/placement by examination:** AP, CLEP, IB, institutional tests. 1 credit hours maximum toward bachelor's degree. **Support services:** Learning center, pre-admission summer program, reduced course load, remedial instruction, study skills assistance, tutoring, writing center.

**Majors. Area/ethnic studies:** Central/Eastern European, East Asian, Native American, Scandinavian, women's. **Biology:** General. **Business:** Accounting, accounting/business management, business admin, finance, international, management information systems, marketing. **Communications:** General, media studies, organizational. **Computer sciences:** Computer science. **Education:** General, biology, early childhood, elementary, emotionally handicapped, health, music, physical, secondary. **Engineering:** General. **Foreign languages:** French, German, Scandinavian, Spanish. **Health:** Clinical lab science, music therapy, nursing (RN), public health nursing. **History:** General. **Interdisciplinary:** Medieval/Renaissance. **Liberal arts:** Arts/sciences. **Math:** General. **Philosophy/religion:** Philosophy, religion. **Physical sciences:** Chemistry, physics. **Psychology:** General. **Public administration:** Social work. **Social sciences:** General, applied economics, economics, international relations, political science, sociology, urban studies. **Theology:** Youth ministry. **Visual/performing arts:** Art history/conservation, dramatic, film/cinema, music management, music performance, studio arts, theater history. **Other:** Media writing.

**Most popular majors.** Business/marketing 31%, communications/journalism 9%, education 9%, health sciences 10%, social sciences 6%, visual/performing arts 6%.

**Computing on campus.** 260 workstations in dormitories, library, computer center, student center. Dormitories wired for high-speed internet access and linked to campus network. Commuter students can connect to campus network. Online course registration, online library, helpline, student web hosting, wireless network available.

**Student life. Freshman orientation:** Available, $100 fee. Preregistration for classes offered. Students attend in June or July; lasts Friday through Saturday morning. **Housing:** Guaranteed on-campus for freshmen. Coed dorms, special housing for disabled, apartments, wellness housing available. $350 partly refundable deposit, deadline 6/1. **Activities:** Bands, campus ministries, choral groups, drama, international student organizations, literary magazine, music ensembles, radio station, student government, student newspaper, symphony orchestra, Auggie Ultimate Frisbee, art club, chemistry society, Spanish club, Muslim student association, Fellowship of Christian Athletes, Tri-Beta Biology honor society, cycling club, KAUG radio.

**Athletics.** NCAA. **Intercollegiate:** Baseball M, basketball, cross-country, football (tackle) M, golf, ice hockey, soccer, softball W, swimming W, tennis, track and field, volleyball W, wrestling M. **Intramural:** Basketball, softball, tennis, volleyball. **Team name:** Auggies.

**Student services.** Adult student services, alcohol/substance abuse counseling, chaplain/spiritual director, career counseling, student employment services, financial aid counseling, health services, minority student services, personal counseling, placement for graduates. **Physically disabled:** Services for visually, speech, hearing impaired.

**Contact.** E-mail: admissions@augsburg.edu
Phone: (612) 330-1001 Toll-free number: (800) 788-5678
Fax: (612) 330-1590
Carrie Carroll, Director of Admissions, Augsburg College, 2211 Riverside Avenue, Minneapolis, MN 55454

---

## Bemidji State University
**Bemidji, Minnesota**
**www.bemidjistate.edu**                          CB code: 6676

- Public 4-year university
- Residential campus in large town
- 4,235 degree-seeking undergraduates: 16% part-time, 52% women, 1% African American, 1% Asian American, 1% Hispanic American, 4% Native American, 3% international
- 245 degree-seeking graduate students
- 81% of applicants admitted
- ACT (writing optional) required
- 46% graduate within 6 years; 12% enter graduate study

**General.** Founded in 1919. Regionally accredited. Arrowhead University Center located on Minnesota's Mesabi Iron Range offers several degree programs. **Degrees:** 838 bachelor's, 34 associate awarded; master's offered. **Location:** 150 miles from Duluth, 230 miles from Minneapolis-St. Paul. **Calendar:** Semester, extensive summer session. **Full-time faculty:** 182 total; 69% have terminal degrees, 7% minority, 43% women. **Part-time faculty:** 94 total; 8% have terminal degrees, 2% minority, 51% women. **Class**

**size:** 45% < 20, 44% 20-39, 6% 40-49, 3% 50-99, 2% >100. **Special facilities:** Freshwater aquatics laboratory, research center, forest and nature preserve.

**Freshman class profile.** 2,167 applied, 1,747 admitted, 810 enrolled.

| Mid 50% test scores | | | |
|---|---|---|---|
| ACT composite: | 19-24 | Rank in top tenth: | 7% |
| GPA 3.75 or higher: | 13% | End year in good standing: | 82% |
| GPA 3.50-3.74: | 14% | Return as sophomores: | 72% |
| GPA 3.0-3.49: | 35% | Out-of-state: | 6% |
| GPA 2.0-2.99: | 37% | Live on campus: | 83% |
| Rank in top quarter: | 25% | International: | 3% |

**Basis for selection.** Rank in top half of class or test scores above 50th percentile preferred. ACT scores considered for applicants in bottom half of class. Composite score of 21 or higher preferred. Interview recommended. Audition recommended for music applicants; portfolio recommended for art applicants. **Learning Disabled:** Students encouraged to identify themselves to Office of Disabilities to be apprised of services available.

**High school preparation.** 16 units required. Required units include English 4, mathematics 3, social studies 3, science 3, foreign language 2 and academic electives 1. 1 unit of art, music, world culture required.

**2010-2011 Annual costs.** Tuition/fees (projected): $7,510; $7,510 out-of-state. Room/board: $6,425. Books/supplies: $840. Personal expenses: $1,350.

**2009-2010 Financial aid. Need-based:** 662 full-time freshmen applied for aid; 471 were judged to have need; 470 of these received aid. Average need met was 76%. Average scholarship/grant was $5,877; average loan $336. 52% of total undergraduate aid awarded as scholarships/grants, 48% as loans/jobs. **Non-need-based:** Awarded to 2,418 full-time undergraduates, including 610 freshmen. Scholarships awarded for academics, alumni affiliation, art, athletics, music/drama.

**Application procedures. Admission:** Priority date 8/13; no deadline. $20 fee, may be waived for applicants with need. Admission notification on a rolling basis. **Financial aid:** Priority date 5/15; no closing date. FAFSA, institutional form required. Applicants notified on a rolling basis starting 5/15.

**Academics. Special study options:** Accelerated study, combined bachelor's/graduate degree, cooperative education, distance learning, double major, dual enrollment of high school students, ESL, external degree, honors, independent study, internships, liberal arts/career combination, study abroad, teacher certification program. Exchange program with other Minnesota state universities, Euro-spring semester, Sino-summer semester. **Credit/placement by examination:** AP, CLEP, IB, ACT, institutional tests. Department defined number of hours of credit by examination may be counted towards degree. **Support services:** Learning center, reduced course load, remedial instruction, study skills assistance, tutoring, writing center.

**Majors. Area/ethnic studies:** Native American. **Biology:** General, marine. **Business:** Accounting, business admin. **Communications:** Journalism. **Computer sciences:** General, computer science. **Conservation:** General. **Construction:** General. **Education:** General, elementary, voc/tech. **Engineering:** Physics. **Foreign languages:** German, Spanish. **Health:** Clinical lab science, preop/surgical nursing. **History:** General. **Liberal arts:** Arts/sciences. **Math:** General. **Parks/recreation:** Health/fitness. **Philosophy/religion:** Philosophy. **Physical sciences:** Chemistry, geology, physics. **Protective services:** Criminal justice. **Psychology:** General. **Public administration:** Community org/advocacy, social work. **Social sciences:** General, economics, geography, political science, sociology. **Visual/performing arts:** Art, commercial/advertising art, dramatic.

**Most popular majors.** Business/marketing 15%, education 24%, engineering/engineering technologies 9%, psychology 8%, security/protective services 6%, visual/performing arts 6%.

**Computing on campus.** 1,600 workstations in dormitories, library, computer center, student center. Dormitories wired for high-speed internet access and linked to campus network. Commuter students can connect to campus network. Online course registration, online library, helpline, repair service, student web hosting, wireless network available.

**Student life. Freshman orientation:** Available, $25 fee. Preregistration for classes offered. One-day orientation for students and parents. Student orientation program is also scheduled the weekend prior to first day of class. **Policies:** Zero tolerance for discrimination, racism, sexual violence, illegal activities including drug use. **Housing:** Coed dorms, single-sex dorms, apartments, wellness housing available. $100 partly refundable deposit. Single parents hall (includes child care facilities), quiet floors, hall/dorm for students older than average age. **Activities:** Bands, campus ministries, choral groups, dance, drama, film society, international student organizations, literary magazine, music ensembles, Model UN, musical theater, opera, radio station, student government, student newspaper, symphony orchestra, TV station, Newman Center, Lutheran center, Young Republicans, Young Democrats, social service organization, veterans club, Council of Indian Students, Black Student Coalition.

**Athletics.** NCAA. **Intercollegiate:** Baseball M, basketball, cross-country, football (tackle) M, golf, ice hockey, soccer W, softball W, tennis W, track and field, volleyball W. **Intramural:** Badminton, baseball, basketball, field hockey, football (non-tackle), golf, ice hockey, racquetball, skiing, soccer, softball, table tennis, tennis, triathlon, volleyball, weight lifting M, wrestling M. **Team name:** Beavers.

**Student services.** Adult student services, alcohol/substance abuse counseling, chaplain/spiritual director, career counseling, services for economically disadvantaged, student employment services, financial aid counseling, health services, minority student services, on-campus daycare, personal counseling, placement for graduates, veterans' counselor, women's services. **Physically disabled:** Services for visually, speech, hearing impaired.

**Contact.** E-mail: admissions@bemidjistate.edu
Phone: (218) 755-2040 Toll-free number: (800) 475-2001
Fax: (218) 755-2390
Russ Kreager, Director of Admissions, Bemidji State University, 1500 Birchmont Drive NE, #13, Bemidji, MN 56601

## Bethany Lutheran College
**Mankato, Minnesota**
www.blc.edu                                                   **CB code: 6035**

- Private 4-year liberal arts college affiliated with Evangelical Lutheran Synod
- Residential campus in large town
- 615 degree-seeking undergraduates
- 83% of applicants admitted
- SAT or ACT (ACT writing optional), application essay required

**General.** Founded in 1927. Regionally accredited. **Degrees:** 85 bachelor's awarded. **ROTC:** Army. **Location:** 80 miles from Minneapolis-St. Paul. **Calendar:** Semester. **Full-time faculty:** 42 total; 43% have terminal degrees, 21% women. **Part-time faculty:** 24 total; 42% women. **Class size:** 70% < 20, 28% 20-39, less than 1% 40-49, less than 1% 50-99.

**Freshman class profile.** 437 applied, 361 admitted, 168 enrolled.

| Mid 50% test scores | | GPA 2.0-2.99: | 32% |
|---|---|---|---|
| ACT composite: | 19-26 | Rank in top quarter: | 35% |
| GPA 3.75 or higher: | 21% | Rank in top tenth: | 15% |
| GPA 3.50-3.74: | 21% | Out-of-state: | 26% |
| GPA 3.0-3.49: | 26% | Live on campus: | 97% |

**Basis for selection.** College-prep GPA, overall GPA, test scores most important. **Learning Disabled:** Students with learning disabilities must meet with head of tutorial program.

**High school preparation.** College-preparatory program recommended. Recommended units include English 4, mathematics 3, social studies 3, history 3, science 3 (laboratory 1) and foreign language 2.

**2009-2010 Annual costs.** Tuition/fees: $19,650. Room/board: $6,200. Books/supplies: $800. Personal expenses: $1,500.

**2008-2009 Financial aid.** **Need-based:** 167 full-time freshmen applied for aid; 152 were judged to have need; 151 of these received aid. Average need met was 86%. Average scholarship/grant was $11,909; average loan $3,952. 65% of total undergraduate aid awarded as scholarships/grants, 35% as loans/jobs. **Non-need-based:** Awarded to 138 full-time undergraduates, including 38 freshmen. Scholarships awarded for academics, art, music/drama.

**Application procedures.** **Admission:** Closing date 7/1 (postmark date). No application fee. Admission notification on a rolling basis beginning on or about 9/15. **Financial aid:** Priority date 4/15; no closing date. FAFSA, institutional form required. Applicants notified on a rolling basis starting 3/1; must reply within 2 week(s) of notification.

**Academics.** **Special study options:** Combined bachelor's/graduate degree, cross-registration, double major, dual enrollment of high school students, independent study, internships, student-designed major, study abroad, teacher certification program. **Credit/placement by examination:** AP, CLEP, IB, SAT, ACT, institutional tests. 15 credit hours maximum toward associate degree, 15 toward bachelor's. **Support services:** Learning center, reduced course load, remedial instruction, tutoring.

**Majors. Biology:** Biomedical sciences. **Business:** Business admin. **Communications:** General. **Education:** Elementary. **History:** General. **Liberal**

**arts:** Arts/sciences. **Physical sciences:** General, chemistry. **Psychology:** General. **Social sciences:** General, sociology. **Theology:** Sacred music. **Visual/performing arts:** Dramatic, studio arts.

**Most popular majors.** Biology 10%, business/marketing 14%, communications/journalism 16%, education 11%, English 6%, liberal arts 9%, psychology 12%, social sciences 7%, visual/performing arts 9%.

**Computing on campus.** 100 workstations in dormitories, library, computer center, student center. Dormitories wired for high-speed internet access and linked to campus network. Commuter students can connect to campus network. Helpline, repair service, student web hosting, wireless network available.

**Student life. Freshman orientation:** Mandatory. Preregistration for classes offered. **Policies:** Freshmen and sophomores not living with family required to live on campus. **Housing:** Guaranteed on-campus for all undergraduates. Single-sex dorms, apartments, wellness housing available. **Activities:** Bands, choral groups, dance, drama, literary magazine, music ensembles, musical theater, student government, student newspaper, TV station, spiritual life committee, Lutherans for Life, student senate, Lambda Pi Eta, scholastic leadership society.

**Athletics.** NCAA, NCCAA. **Intercollegiate:** Baseball M, basketball, cross-country, golf, soccer, softball W, tennis, volleyball W. **Intramural:** Baseball M, basketball, football (non-tackle), soccer, softball, table tennis, tennis, volleyball. **Team name:** Vikings.

**Student services.** Chaplain/spiritual director, career counseling, financial aid counseling, health services, minority student services, personal counseling.

**Contact.** E-mail: admissions@blc.edu
Phone: (507) 344-7331 Toll-free number: (800) 944-3066
Fax: (507) 344-7376
Don Westphal, Dean of Admissions, Bethany Lutheran College, 700 Luther Drive, Mankato, MN 56001-4490

## Bethel University
**Saint Paul, Minnesota**                                      **CB member**
www.bethel.edu                                                 **CB code: 6038**

- Private 4-year university and liberal arts college affiliated with Baptist General Conference
- Residential campus in large city
- 3,335 degree-seeking undergraduates: 19% part-time, 61% women, 4% African American, 2% Asian American, 1% Hispanic American
- 1,991 degree-seeking graduate students
- 80% of applicants admitted
- SAT or ACT (ACT writing optional), application essay required
- 75% graduate within 6 years; 21% enter graduate study

**General.** Founded in 1871. Regionally accredited. **Degrees:** 899 bachelor's, 6 associate awarded; master's, doctoral, professional offered. **ROTC:** Army, Air Force. **Location:** 10 miles from Minneapolis-St. Paul. **Calendar:** Differs by program, limited summer session. **Full-time faculty:** 188 total; 78% have terminal degrees, 11% minority, 42% women. **Part-time faculty:** 105 total; 26% have terminal degrees, 6% minority, 61% women. **Class size:** 52% < 20, 40% 20-39, 6% 40-49, 2% 50-99, 1% >100.

**Freshman class profile.** 2,179 applied, 1,734 admitted, 727 enrolled.

| Mid 50% test scores | | GPA 2.0-2.99: | 14% |
|---|---|---|---|
| SAT critical reading: | 510-680 | Rank in top quarter: | 55% |
| SAT math: | 510-670 | Rank in top tenth: | 31% |
| ACT composite: | 21-28 | End year in good standing: | 90% |
| GPA 3.75 or higher: | 39% | Return as sophomores: | 85% |
| GPA 3.50-3.74: | 20% | Out-of-state: | 22% |
| GPA 3.0-3.49: | 26% | Live on campus: | 89% |

**Basis for selection.** Rank in top half of class, 92 PSAT, 21 ACT, or 920 SAT (exclusive of Writing). Applicant must make personal statement regarding Christian commitment and agree to live in accordance with college's lifestyle. Interview recommended for art, drama, and music applicants; audition recommended for music applicants; portfolio recommended for art applicants.

**High school preparation.** College-preparatory program required. 14 units required. Required and recommended units include English 4, mathematics 3, social studies 4, history 1, science 3 (laboratory 3), foreign language 2, computer science 1 and visual/performing arts 1.

**2009-2010 Annual costs.** Tuition/fees: $27,020. Rate frozen as long as student continues to reside in campus housing. Room/board: $7,920. Books/supplies: $980. Personal expenses: $1,640.

**2008-2009 Financial aid. Need-based:** 517 full-time freshmen applied for aid; 442 were judged to have need; 442 of these received aid. Average need met was 78%. Average scholarship/grant was $15,158; average loan $4,132. 61% of total undergraduate aid awarded as scholarships/grants, 39% as loans/jobs. **Non-need-based:** Awarded to 762 full-time undergraduates, including 177 freshmen. Scholarships awarded for academics, alumni affiliation, art, leadership, music/drama, state residency.

**Application procedures. Admission:** Priority date 3/1; no deadline. No application fee. Admission notification on a rolling basis beginning on or about 10/1. Must reply by May 1 or within 3 week(s) if notified thereafter. **Financial aid:** Priority date 4/15; no closing date. FAFSA, institutional form required. Applicants notified on a rolling basis starting 3/1.

**Academics. Special study options:** Combined bachelor's/graduate degree, double major, exchange student, honors, independent study, internships, New York semester, semester at sea, student-designed major, study abroad, teacher certification program, urban semester, Washington semester. Dual degree program for engineering science with the University of Minnesota or other schools on individual basis. Terms in South Africa, Guatemala, Spain, Australia, England, Thailand; New York Center for Art and Media Studies (NYCAMS). **Credit/placement by examination:** AP, CLEP, IB, institutional tests. 30 credit hours maximum toward associate degree, 30 toward bachelor's. **Support services:** Learning center, study skills assistance, tutoring, writing center.

**Majors. Biology:** General. **Business:** Accounting/finance, business admin, human resources, organizational behavior. **Communications:** General, journalism, media studies. **Computer sciences:** General. **Conservation:** Environmental science, environmental studies. **Education:** General, art, biology, business, chemistry, early childhood, elementary, English, ESL, French, health, kindergarten/preschool, mathematics, middle, music, physical, physics, secondary, social studies, Spanish. **Engineering:** Science. **Foreign languages:** French, Spanish. **Health:** Athletic training, community health services, nursing (RN). **History:** General. **Interdisciplinary:** Peace/conflict. **Math:** General. **Parks/recreation:** Exercise sciences, health/fitness. **Philosophy/religion:** Philosophy. **Physical sciences:** Chemistry, physics. **Psychology:** General. **Public administration:** Social work. **Social sciences:** General, economics, international relations, political science. **Theology:** Bible, sacred music, youth ministry. **Visual/performing arts:** Art, dramatic, music performance. **Other:** Biochemistry and molecular biology, Business and political science, Third World studies.

**Most popular majors.** Business/marketing 14%, communications/journalism 9%, education 16%, health sciences 11%, interdisciplinary studies 6%, psychology 6%, social sciences 6%.

**Computing on campus.** 420 workstations in dormitories, library, computer center. Dormitories wired for high-speed internet access and linked to campus network. Commuter students can connect to campus network. Online course registration, online library, helpline, student web hosting, wireless network available.

**Student life. Freshman orientation:** Mandatory. Preregistration for classes offered. 2 days prior to the start of classes. **Policies:** High moral standards stressed. Use of tobacco and alcohol prohibited. **Housing:** Guaranteed on-campus for freshmen. Coed dorms, special housing for disabled, apartments available. $150 fully refundable deposit. **Activities:** Bands, campus ministries, choral groups, dance, drama, film society, international student organizations, literary magazine, music ensembles, musical theater, radio station, student government, student newspaper, symphony orchestra, United Cultures of Bethel, College Republicans, College Democrats, Habitat for Humanity, dormitory discipleship programs, Mu Kappa (for students from missionary homes), Twin Cities Outreach.

**Athletics.** NCAA. **Intercollegiate:** Baseball M, basketball, cross-country, football (tackle) M, golf, ice hockey, soccer, softball W, tennis, track and field, volleyball W. **Intramural:** Badminton, basketball, football (non-tackle) M, ice hockey, softball, volleyball. **Team name:** Royals.

**Student services.** Adult student services, alcohol/substance abuse counseling, chaplain/spiritual director, career counseling, student employment services, financial aid counseling, health services, minority student services, on-campus daycare, personal counseling, placement for graduates, women's services. **Physically disabled:** Services for visually, speech, hearing impaired.

**Contact.** E-mail: buadmissions-cas@bethel.edu
Phone: (651) 638-6242 Toll-free number: (800) 255-8706 ext. 6242
Fax: (651) 635-1490
Jay Fedje, Director of Admissions, Bethel University, 3900 Bethel Drive, Saint Paul, MN 55112

## Brown College
**Mendota Heights, Minnesota**
**www.browncollege.edu**                      CB code: 1210

- For-profit 4-year business and liberal arts college
- Commuter campus in small city
- 1,195 degree-seeking undergraduates
- Interview required

**General.** Founded in 1946. Accredited by ACCSC. **Degrees:** 236 bachelor's, 190 associate awarded. **Location:** 14 miles from Minneapolis-St. Paul. **Calendar:** Quarter, extensive summer session. **Full-time faculty:** 56 total. **Part-time faculty:** 77 total.

**Freshman class profile.** 1,430 applied, 1,000 admitted, 676 enrolled.

**Basis for selection.** Open admission, but selective for some programs. ACCUPLACER Test required in lieu of other tests. **Learning Disabled:** IEP's and/or other requests for ADA-level accommodations accepted. Eligible students must complete brief Application for Auxiliary Aid and return with any supporting documentation available well in advance of enrollment.

**High school preparation.** Recommended units include English 4, mathematics 2 and science 1.

**2009-2010 Annual costs.** Tuition/fees: $16,956. Books/supplies: $3,000. Personal expenses: $1,600.

**Financial aid. Non-need-based:** Scholarships awarded for academics.

**Application procedures. Admission:** No deadline. $25 fee. Admission notification on a rolling basis beginning on or about 1/1. **Financial aid:** Priority date 7/1; no closing date. FAFSA, institutional form required. Applicants notified on a rolling basis starting 1/1; must reply within 2 week(s) of notification.

**Academics. Special study options:** Cooperative education, internships, liberal arts/career combination. **Credit/placement by examination:** AP, CLEP, institutional tests. **Support services:** Learning center, reduced course load, remedial instruction, study skills assistance, tutoring, writing center.

**Majors. Business:** General. **Communications:** General. **Communications technology:** Graphics. **Computer sciences:** Information systems, information technology. **Protective services:** Criminal justice. **Visual/performing arts:** Design.

**Computing on campus.** PC or laptop required. 231 workstations in library, computer center. Commuter students can connect to campus network. Online course registration, online library, helpline, repair service, wireless network available.

**Student life. Freshman orientation:** Mandatory. **Housing:** Apartments available. **Activities:** Radio station, student government, student senate, Campus Crusade for Christ, minority students club.

**Athletics. Intramural:** Football (non-tackle) M.

**Student services.** Adult student services, career counseling, student employment services, financial aid counseling, placement for graduates.

**Contact.** E-mail: info@browncollege.edu
Phone: (651) 905-3400 Toll-free number: (800) 627-6966 ext. 240
Fax: (651) 905-3540
Rick Hubbard, Vice President Admissions and Marketing, Brown College, 1440 Northland Drive, Mendota Heights, MN 55120

## Capella University
**Minneapolis, Minnesota**
**www.capella.edu**                      CB code: 3829

- For-profit 4-year virtual university
- Very large city
- 5,619 degree-seeking undergraduates
- 26,379 graduate students

**General.** Regionally accredited. **Degrees:** 573 bachelor's awarded; master's, doctoral offered. **Calendar:** Quarter, extensive summer session.

**Basis for selection.** Open admission, but selective for some programs. Applicants must be at least 24 years of age unless in military or unless they enter with 90 college level credits from previous institution. Bachelor's programs are completion programs for students who have associate's degree or at least 90 quarter credits of undergraduate coursework completed.

**2009-2010 Annual costs.** Tuition/fees: $13,275.

**Application procedures. Admission:** No deadline. $75 fee. Admission notification on a rolling basis.

**Academics. Special study options:** Accelerated study, combined bachelor's/graduate degree, distance learning, internships. **Credit/placement by examination:** CLEP, IB. **Support services:** Learning center, tutoring, writing center.

**Majors. Business:** Accounting, finance, human resources, marketing. **Computer sciences:** Computer graphics, information technology, LAN/WAN management, security, web page design.

**Most popular majors.** Business/marketing 39%, computer/information sciences 61%.

**Computing on campus.** PC or laptop required.

**Student life. Freshman orientation:** Available. Preregistration for classes offered. Online seminar that provides students with knowledge, skills, and advice needed to be successful in Capella's online environment.

**Student services.** Adult student services, career counseling, financial aid counseling. **Physically disabled:** Services for visually, hearing impaired.

**Contact.** E-mail: info@capella.edu
Phone: (888) 227-2736
Rebecca Miller, Enrollment Services Director, Capella University, 225 South Sixth Street, 9th Floor, Minneapolis, MN 55402

## Carleton College
**Northfield, Minnesota**　　　　　　　**CB member**
**www.carleton.edu**　　　　　　　　**CB code: 6081**

- Private 4-year liberal arts college
- Residential campus in large town
- 1,986 degree-seeking undergraduates: 52% women, 5% African American, 10% Asian American, 6% Hispanic American, 1% Native American, 7% international
- 30% of applicants admitted
- SAT or ACT with writing, application essay required
- 92% graduate within 6 years; 23% enter graduate study

**General.** Founded in 1866. Regionally accredited. Sustainability initiatives include green roofs, eco-building class, eco house built by students, 1.65 megawatt wind turbine. **Degrees:** 507 bachelor's awarded. **Location:** 35 miles from Minneapolis-St. Paul. **Calendar:** Trimester. **Full-time faculty:** 217 total; 95% have terminal degrees, 22% minority, 45% women. **Part-time faculty:** 21 total; 48% have terminal degrees, 10% minority, 29% women. **Class size:** 60% < 20, 37% 20-39, 2% 40-49, 1% 50-99. **Special facilities:** 955 acre arboretum, 35 acre virgin prairie, greenhouse, observatory, scanning and transmission electron microscope, refractor and reflector telescopes, nuclear magnet resonance spectrometer.

**Freshman class profile.** 4,784 applied, 1,459 admitted, 529 enrolled.

| Mid 50% test scores | | | |
|---|---|---|---|
| SAT critical reading: | 660-760 | Rank in top tenth: | 78% |
| SAT math: | 660-740 | Return as sophomores: | 97% |
| SAT writing: | 670-750 | Out-of-state: | 77% |
| ACT composite: | 29-33 | Live on campus: | 100% |
| Rank in top quarter: | 96% | International: | 9% |

**Basis for selection.** School achievement record and recommendations most important. Test scores, extracurricular school and community activities also important. SAT Subject Tests recommended. Interview recommended. **Learning Disabled:** Untimed standardized tests and GED accepted.

**High school preparation.** College-preparatory program recommended. Recommended units include English 4, mathematics 3, social studies 3, science 3 (laboratory 1) and foreign language 3. 3 units distributed between history and social sciences recommended.

**2009-2010 Annual costs.** Tuition/fees: $39,777. Room/board: $10,428. Books/supplies: $700. Personal expenses: $631.

**2008-2009 Financial aid. Need-based:** 406 full-time freshmen applied for aid; 311 were judged to have need; 311 of these received aid. Average need met was 100%. Average scholarship/grant was $28,868; average loan $3,979. 78% of total undergraduate aid awarded as scholarships/grants, 22% as loans/jobs. **Non-need-based:** Awarded to 360 full-time undergraduates, including 79 freshmen. Scholarships awarded for academics. **Additional information:** Full financial need of all admitted applicants met through combination of work, loans, grants. Carleton Access Scholarship reduces loans for entering students whose family income is below $75,000.

**Application procedures. Admission:** Closing date 1/15 (postmark date). $30 fee, may be waived for applicants with need, free for online applicants. Admission notification 4/15. Must reply by May 1 or within 2 week(s) if notified thereafter. **Financial aid:** Closing date 2/15. FAFSA, CSS PROFILE required. Applicants notified by 4/1; must reply by 5/1 or within 2 week(s) of notification.

**Academics.** 15-20 freshman seminars offered, enrollment limited to 15 students each. **Special study options:** Accelerated study, cross-registration, double major, dual enrollment of high school students, independent study, internships, student-designed major, study abroad, teacher certification program, urban semester. **Credit/placement by examination:** AP, CLEP, IB, institutional tests. 36 credit hours maximum toward bachelor's degree. **Support services:** Learning center, tutoring, writing center.

**Majors. Area/ethnic studies:** African, African-American, American, Asian, Latin American, Russian/Slavic, women's. **Biology:** General. **Computer sciences:** Computer science. **Foreign languages:** Ancient Greek, classics, French, German, Hebrew, Latin, Romance, Russian, Spanish. **History:** General. **Interdisciplinary:** Math/computer science. **Math:** General. **Philosophy/religion:** Philosophy, religion. **Physical sciences:** Chemistry, geology, physics. **Psychology:** General. **Social sciences:** Anthropology, economics, international relations, political science, sociology. **Visual/performing arts:** Art history/conservation, studio arts.

**Most popular majors.** Biology 12%, English 7%, history 8%, philosophy/religious studies 6%, physical sciences 13%, psychology 8%, social sciences 22%, visual/performing arts 7%.

**Computing on campus.** 300 workstations in library, computer center, student center. Dormitories wired for high-speed internet access and linked to campus network. Online course registration, online library, helpline, repair service, student web hosting, wireless network available.

**Student life. Freshman orientation:** Mandatory. Preregistration for classes offered. 4 days prior to start of fall classes. **Housing:** Guaranteed on-campus for all undergraduates. Coed dorms, special housing for disabled, apartments, wellness housing available. 25 college-owned houses within 2 blocks of campus, some coeducational, with varying board options. Several for special interest groups. **Activities:** Bands, campus ministries, choral groups, dance, drama, film society, international student organizations, literary magazine, music ensembles, Model UN, musical theater, radio station, student government, student newspaper, symphony orchestra, 132 registered student organizations.

**Athletics.** NCAA. **Intercollegiate:** Baseball M, basketball, cross-country, diving, football (tackle) M, golf, soccer, softball W, swimming, synchronized swimming W, tennis, track and field, volleyball W, wrestling M. **Intramural:** Basketball, ice hockey, racquetball, soccer, softball, table tennis, tennis, triathlon, volleyball. **Team name:** Knights.

**Student services.** Alcohol/substance abuse counseling, chaplain/spiritual director, career counseling, student employment services, financial aid counseling, health services, minority student services, personal counseling, placement for graduates, women's services. **Physically disabled:** Services for visually, hearing impaired.

**Contact.** E-mail: admissions@carleton.edu
Phone: (507) 222-4190 Toll-free number: (800) 995-2275
Fax: (507) 222-4526
Paul Thiboutot, Vice President and Dean of Admissions and Financial Aid, Carleton College, 100 South College Street, Northfield, MN 55057

## College of St. Benedict
**St. Joseph, Minnesota**　　　　　　　**CB member**
**www.csbsju.edu**　　　　　　　　　**CB code: 6104**

- Private 4-year liberal arts college for women affiliated with Roman Catholic Church
- Residential campus in small town
- 2,106 degree-seeking undergraduates: 2% part-time, 100% women, 1% African American, 4% Asian American, 2% Hispanic American, 6% international
- 85% of applicants admitted

♦ SAT or ACT (ACT writing optional), application essay required

♦ 78% graduate within 6 years; 25% enter graduate study

**General.** Founded in 1887. Regionally accredited. CSB located six miles from St. John's University; students enrolled on both campuses have access to classes, activities held by the two institutions. **Degrees:** 488 bachelor's awarded. **ROTC:** Army. **Location:** 10 miles from St. Cloud, 70 miles from Minneapolis-St. Paul. **Calendar:** Semester, limited summer session. **Full-time faculty:** 159 total; 84% have terminal degrees, 8% minority, 48% women. **Part-time faculty:** 34 total; 35% have terminal degrees, 6% minority, 41% women. **Class size:** 53% < 20, 46% 20-39, less than 1% 40-49, less than 1% 50-99, less than 1% >100. **Special facilities:** Observatory, ecumenical center, museum and manuscript library, liturgical press, nature preserve, arboretum, natural history museum, pottery kiln.

**Freshman class profile.** 1,604 applied, 1,369 admitted, 551 enrolled.

| Mid 50% test scores | | GPA 2.0-2.99: | 1% |
|---|---|---|---|
| SAT critical reading: | 510-660 | Rank in top quarter: | 76% |
| SAT math: | 510-670 | Rank in top tenth: | 40% |
| SAT writing: | 510-670 | End year in good standing: | 94% |
| ACT composite: | 23-28 | Return as sophomores: | 88% |
| GPA 3.75 or higher: | 57% | Out-of-state: | 19% |
| GPA 3.50-3.74: | 22% | Live on campus: | 100% |
| GPA 3.0-3.49: | 20% | International: | 6% |

**Basis for selection.** Course selection, scholastic achievement, GPA, test scores and essay are most important. Extracurricular involvement and recommendations are also important. Interview recommended for conditionally accepted/academically weak applicants. **Homeschooled:** Applicants are not required to have a high school diploma but are required to provide appropriate documentation of college preparatory curriculum.

**High school preparation.** College-preparatory program required. 15 units required. Required and recommended units include English 4, mathematics 3, social studies 2, science 2 (laboratory 2), foreign language 2 and academic electives 4.

**2009-2010 Annual costs.** Tuition/fees: $30,136. Room/board: $8,358. Books/supplies: $900. Personal expenses: $800.

**2009-2010 Financial aid. Need-based:** 447 full-time freshmen applied for aid; 375 were judged to have need; 375 of these received aid. Average need met was 94%. Average scholarship/grant was $20,316; average loan $3,422. 61% of total undergraduate aid awarded as scholarships/grants, 39% as loans/jobs. **Non-need-based:** Awarded to 1,874 full-time undergraduates, including 513 freshmen. Scholarships awarded for academics, art, leadership, music/drama, ROTC. **Additional information:** Scholarship letters will be mailed on a rolling basis approximately two weeks from the time the admission acceptance letter is sent.

**Application procedures. Admission:** Priority date 11/15; no deadline. No application fee. A non-refundable enrollment deposit of $300 is due May 1. **Financial aid:** Priority date 3/15; no closing date. FAFSA, institutional form required. Applicants notified on a rolling basis starting 3/15; must reply by 5/1.

**Academics. Special study options:** Combined bachelor's/graduate degree, cross-registration, double major, dual enrollment of high school students, ESL, honors, independent study, internships, student-designed major, study abroad, teacher certification program. 3-2 program in engineering with University of Minnesota, 3-1 program in dentistry with University of Minnesota, cross registration with St. Cloud State University. **Credit/placement by examination:** AP, CLEP, IB, SAT, ACT, institutional tests. **Support services:** Reduced course load, study skills assistance, tutoring, writing center.

**Majors. Area/ethnic studies:** Women's. **Biology:** General, biochemistry. **Business:** Accounting, business admin. **Computer sciences:** Computer science. **Conservation:** Environmental studies. **Education:** General, elementary. **Foreign languages:** Classics, French, German, Spanish. **Health:** Dietetics, nursing (RN), predental, premedicine, prepharmacy, preveterinary. **History:** General. **Interdisciplinary:** Biological/physical sciences, math/computer science, natural sciences, nutrition sciences, peace/conflict. **Legal studies:** Prelaw. **Liberal arts:** Arts/sciences, humanities. **Math:** General. **Philosophy/religion:** Philosophy. **Physical sciences:** Chemistry, physics. **Psychology:** General. **Social sciences:** General, economics, political science, sociology. **Theology:** Theology. **Visual/performing arts:** Art, dramatic.

**Most popular majors.** Biology 11%, business/marketing 12%, education 7%, English 15%, foreign language 9%, health sciences 7%, interdisciplinary studies 6%, psychology 10%, social sciences 10%.

**Computing on campus.** 860 workstations in dormitories, library, computer center, student center. Dormitories wired for high-speed internet access and linked to campus network. Commuter students can connect to campus network. Online course registration, online library, helpline, repair service, student web hosting, wireless network available.

**Student life. Freshman orientation:** Mandatory. Preregistration for classes offered. Fall orientation begins the evening of move-in day and concludes with convocation the first day of classes. **Policies:** There is a 4 year residency requirement. **Housing:** Guaranteed on-campus for freshmen. Special housing for disabled, apartments, wellness housing available. **Activities:** Bands, campus ministries, choral groups, dance, drama, international student organizations, literary magazine, music ensembles, Model UN, musical theater, opera, radio station, student government, student newspaper, symphony orchestra, Volunteers in Service to Others, College Republicans, College Democrats, Joints Events Council, Asia Club, Student Coalition for Global Solidarity, Students in Free Enterprise, Magis, Cultural Fusion Club, Outdoor Leadership Center.

**Athletics.** NCAA. **Intercollegiate:** Basketball W, cross-country W, diving W, golf W, ice hockey W, skiing W, soccer W, softball W, swimming W, tennis W, track and field W, volleyball W. **Intramural:** Badminton W, basketball W, racquetball W, soccer W, softball W, table tennis W, tennis W, volleyball W. **Team name:** Blazers.

**Student services.** Alcohol/substance abuse counseling, chaplain/spiritual director, career counseling, financial aid counseling, health services, minority student services, personal counseling, placement for graduates, women's services. **Physically disabled:** Services for hearing impaired.

**Contact.** E-mail: admissions@csbsju.edu
Phone: (320) 363-2196 Toll-free number: (800) 544-1489
Fax: (320) 363-2750
Cal Mosley, Vice President for Admission and Financial Aid, College of St. Benedict, College of St Benedict/St John's University, Collegeville, MN 56321-7155

## College of St. Scholastica
**Duluth, Minnesota**                          **CB member**
**www.css.edu**                                **CB code: 6107**

♦ Private 4-year liberal arts college affiliated with Roman Catholic Church

♦ Residential campus in small city

♦ 2,144 degree-seeking undergraduates: 2% part-time, 68% women, 2% African American, 1% Asian American, 1% Hispanic American, 3% Native American, 4% international

♦ 917 degree-seeking graduate students

♦ 85% of applicants admitted

♦ SAT or ACT (ACT writing optional) required

♦ 66% graduate within 6 years; 27% enter graduate study

**General.** Founded in 1912. Regionally accredited. **Degrees:** 670 bachelor's awarded; master's, professional offered. **ROTC:** Air Force. **Location:** 2 miles from downtown, 150 miles from Minneapolis-St. Paul. **Calendar:** Semester, limited summer session. **Full-time faculty:** 166 total; 58% have terminal degrees, 8% minority, 60% women. **Part-time faculty:** 145 total. **Class size:** 50% < 20, 43% 20-39, 3% 40-49, 3% 50-99, 1% >100. **Special facilities:** Wellness center with climbing wall.

**Freshman class profile.** 1,864 applied, 1,581 admitted, 530 enrolled.

| Mid 50% test scores | | GPA 2.0-2.99: | 14% |
|---|---|---|---|
| SAT critical reading: | 460-610 | Rank in top quarter: | 54% |
| SAT math: | 490-670 | Rank in top tenth: | 23% |
| SAT writing: | 450-640 | End year in good standing: | 93% |
| ACT composite: | 21-26 | Return as sophomores: | 77% |
| GPA 3.75 or higher: | 34% | Out-of-state: | 14% |
| GPA 3.50-3.74: | 23% | Live on campus: | 87% |
| GPA 3.0-3.49: | 29% | International: | 4% |

**Basis for selection.** School achievement record and test scores most important. Interview recommended.

**High school preparation.** College-preparatory program recommended. Recommended units include English 4, mathematics 2, social studies 3, history 3, science 3 and foreign language 3.

**2009-2010 Annual costs.** Tuition/fees: $27,284. Room/board: $7,278. Books/supplies: $1,000. Personal expenses: $1,074.

**2009-2010 Financial aid. Need-based:** Average need met was 82%. Average scholarship/grant was $8,043; average loan $3,434. 60% of total undergraduate aid awarded as scholarships/grants, 40% as loans/jobs. **Non-need-based:** Scholarships awarded for academics, alumni affiliation, music/drama, religious affiliation, ROTC, state residency.

**Application procedures. Admission:** No deadline. $25 fee, may be waived for applicants with need, free for online applicants. Admission notification on a rolling basis beginning on or about 9/1. Must reply by May 1

or within 2 week(s) if notified thereafter. **Financial aid:** Priority date 3/1; no closing date. FAFSA required. Applicants notified on a rolling basis starting 3/1; must reply by 5/1 or within 2 week(s) of notification.

**Academics. Special study options:** Accelerated study, combined bachelor's/graduate degree, cross-registration, distance learning, double major, dual enrollment of high school students, external degree, honors, independent study, internships, liberal arts/career combination, student-designed major, study abroad, teacher certification program, Washington semester. **Credit/placement by examination:** AP, CLEP, IB, ACT, institutional tests. 96 credit hours maximum toward bachelor's degree. All external credit meeting score expectations will be accepted; last 32 semester hours must be completed in residence. **Support services:** Pre-admission summer program, reduced course load, study skills assistance, tutoring, writing center.

**Honors college/program.** Should meet 2 of the following: top 15% of high school class, 26 ACT or 1100 (exclusive of Writing) SAT, GPA of 3.5; others may apply by contacting the honors director. Students must complete 20 honors credits, at least 8 of which are upper-level credits.

**Majors. Biology:** General, biochemistry, exercise physiology. **Business:** Accounting, business admin, finance, marketing, organizational behavior. **Communications:** General, advertising, journalism. **Computer sciences:** General. **Education:** Elementary, multi-level teacher, Native American, school librarian, social science. **Foreign languages:** Spanish. **Health:** Health services, medical records admin, nursing (RN). **History:** General. **Interdisciplinary:** Global studies. **Liberal arts:** Humanities. **Math:** General. **Philosophy/religion:** Christian, religion. **Physical sciences:** Chemistry. **Psychology:** General. **Public administration:** Social work. **Social sciences:** General, applied economics. **Visual/performing arts:** Art, music performance.

**Most popular majors.** Biology 9%, business/marketing 25%, health sciences 38%, public administration/social services 6%.

**Computing on campus.** 407 workstations in dormitories, library, computer center, student center. Dormitories wired for high-speed internet access and linked to campus network. Commuter students can connect to campus network. Online course registration, online library, helpline, student web hosting, wireless network available.

**Student life. Freshman orientation:** Mandatory. Preregistration for classes offered. **Housing:** Guaranteed on-campus for freshmen. Coed dorms, special housing for disabled, apartments, wellness housing available. $150 fully refundable deposit, deadline 2/1. Quiet or study wing; apartments for students with dependent children. **Activities:** Bands, campus ministries, choral groups, dance, drama, international student organizations, literary magazine, music ensembles, student government, student newspaper, TV station, Circle-K, InterVarsity Christian Fellowship, Indigenous Students' Association, Benedictine Friends, Volunteers Involved Through Action, Amnesty International, Kaleidoscope Multicultural Club, Habitat for Humanity, United for Africa, Earth Action.

**Athletics.** NCAA. **Intercollegiate:** Baseball M, basketball, cross-country, football (tackle) M, ice hockey, skiing, soccer, softball W, tennis, track and field, volleyball W. **Intramural:** Badminton, basketball, bowling, football (non-tackle), tennis, volleyball. **Team name:** Saints.

**Student services.** Adult student services, alcohol/substance abuse counseling, chaplain/spiritual director, career counseling, student employment services, financial aid counseling, health services, minority student services, personal counseling, placement for graduates, veterans' counselor, women's services. **Physically disabled:** Services for visually, hearing impaired.

**Contact.** E-mail: admissions@css.edu
Phone: (218) 723-6046 Toll-free number: (800) 249-6412
Fax: (218) 723-5991
Eric Berg, Vice President for Enrollment Management, College of St. Scholastica, 1200 Kenwood Avenue, Duluth, MN 55811-4199

## College of Visual Arts
**Saint Paul, Minnesota**
**www.cva.edu**                                      **CB code: 6147**

- Private 4-year visual arts college
- Commuter campus in large city
- 180 degree-seeking undergraduates: 2% part-time, 66% women
- 67% of applicants admitted
- SAT or ACT (ACT writing optional), application essay required
- 32% graduate within 6 years

**General.** Founded in 1924. Regionally accredited. **Degrees:** 37 bachelor's awarded. **Calendar:** Semester, limited summer session. **Full-time faculty:** 7 total; 29% have terminal degrees, 71% women. **Part-time faculty:** 43 total; 12% have terminal degrees, 2% minority, 44% women. **Class size:**

92% < 20, 8% 20-39. **Special facilities:** Exhibition gallery, photography facilities, sculpture studio, printmaking studio, drawing studio, painting studio.

**Freshman class profile.** 139 applied, 93 admitted, 51 enrolled.

| | | | |
|---|---|---|---|
| End year in good standing: | 79% | Out-of-state: | 19% |
| Return as sophomores: | 73% | | |

**Basis for selection.** Statement of interest, test scores, transcript and portfolio very important. Students with 30+ college credits are not required to submit ACT/SAT scores. Review of portfolio required. **Homeschooled:** Transcript of courses and grades required. List of classes, textbooks used. **Learning Disabled:** Documentation of disabilities required.

**High school preparation.** Recommended units include English 4, mathematics 4, social studies 4, science 4 and foreign language 2. Progression of classes in art preferred.

**2009-2010 Annual costs.** Tuition/fees: $23,194. Books/supplies: $2,424.

**2009-2010 Financial aid. Need-based:** 36 full-time freshmen applied for aid; 34 were judged to have need; 34 of these received aid. Average need met was 58%. Average scholarship/grant was $12,407; average loan $3,328. 12% of total undergraduate aid awarded as scholarships/grants, 88% as loans/jobs. **Non-need-based:** Awarded to 42 full-time undergraduates, including 5 freshmen. Scholarships awarded for academics, art.

**Application procedures. Admission:** Priority date 3/9; no deadline. $40 fee, may be waived for applicants with need. Admission notification on a rolling basis. Must reply by May 1 or within 2 week(s) if notified thereafter. **Financial aid:** Priority date 3/1; no closing date. FAFSA, institutional form required. Applicants notified on a rolling basis starting 2/15; must reply within 2 week(s) of notification.

**Academics. Special study options:** Honors, independent study, internships, study abroad. **Credit/placement by examination:** AP, CLEP, SAT, ACT. **Support services:** Learning center, study skills assistance, tutoring, writing center.

**Majors. Visual/performing arts:** Commercial/advertising art, design, drawing, illustration, painting, photography, printmaking, sculpture, studio arts.

**Computing on campus.** 50 workstations in library, computer center. Online library, helpline available.

**Student life. Freshman orientation:** Mandatory. Preregistration for classes offered. **Housing:** Housing coordinator and roommate matching services. **Activities:** Film society, student government.

**Student services.** Alcohol/substance abuse counseling, career counseling, services for economically disadvantaged, student employment services, financial aid counseling, minority student services, personal counseling, placement for graduates.

**Contact.** E-mail: admissions@cva.edu
Phone: (651) 757-4040 Toll-free number: (800) 224-1536
Fax: (651) 757-4010
Elyan Paz, Senior Associate Director of Admission, College of Visual Arts, 344 Summit Avenue, Saint Paul, MN 55102-2199

## Concordia College: Moorhead
**Moorhead, Minnesota**                                **CB member**
**www.concordiacollege.edu**                            **CB code: 6113**

- Private 4-year liberal arts college affiliated with Evangelical Lutheran Church in America
- Residential campus in small city
- 2,744 degree-seeking undergraduates: 1% part-time, 61% women, 1% African American, 1% Asian American, 1% Hispanic American, 3% international
- 23 degree-seeking graduate students
- 79% of applicants admitted
- SAT or ACT (ACT writing optional) required
- 67% graduate within 6 years; 25% enter graduate study

**General.** Founded in 1891. Regionally accredited. **Degrees:** 559 bachelor's awarded; master's offered. **ROTC:** Army, Air Force. **Location:** 234 miles from Minneapolis-St. Paul, 1 mile from Fargo, North Dakota. **Calendar:** Semester, limited summer session. **Full-time faculty:** 194 total; 81% have terminal degrees, 8% minority, 45% women. **Part-time faculty:** 54 total; 20% have terminal degrees, 57% women. **Class size:** 48% < 20, 47% 20-39, 3% 40-49, 2% 50-99. **Special facilities:** Observatory, microparticle accelerator, language villages, television production studio, biology research facility, nursing lab, eco-friendly classroom/lab building located 40 miles from campus.

**Freshman class profile.** 2,851 applied, 2,254 admitted, 726 enrolled.

| Mid 50% test scores | | | |
|---|---|---|---|
| SAT critical reading: | 510-680 | **GPA 2.0-2.99:** | 7% |
| SAT math: | 520-660 | **Rank in top quarter:** | 66% |
| ACT composite: | 22-28 | **Rank in top tenth:** | 32% |
| GPA 3.75 or higher: | 45% | **Return as sophomores:** | 84% |
| GPA 3.50-3.74: | 23% | **Out-of-state:** | 34% |
| GPA 3.0-3.49: | 25% | **Live on campus:** | 97% |
| | | **International:** | 2% |

**Basis for selection.** Academic record (types of courses and grades) most important, followed by test scores and recommendations. Interview recommended. **Homeschooled:** Transcript of courses and grades, letter of recommendation (nonparent) required.

**High school preparation.** College-preparatory program recommended. Recommended units include English 4, mathematics 3, social studies 3, science 3, foreign language 2, computer science 1 and visual/performing arts 1.

**2010-2011 Annual costs.** Tuition/fees: $27,160. Room/board: $6,510. Books/supplies: $740. Personal expenses: $1,170.

**2008-2009 Financial aid.** **Need-based:** 674 full-time freshmen applied for aid; 558 were judged to have need; 558 of these received aid. Average need met was 88%. Average scholarship/grant was $14,140; average loan $3,791. 63% of total undergraduate aid awarded as scholarships/grants, 37% as loans/jobs. **Non-need-based:** Awarded to 1,020 full-time undergraduates, including 295 freshmen. Scholarships awarded for academics, art, leadership, minority status, music/drama.

**Application procedures.** **Admission:** No deadline. $20 fee, may be waived for applicants with need, free for online applicants. Admission notification on a rolling basis beginning on or about 6/15. **Financial aid:** No deadline. FAFSA required. Applicants notified on a rolling basis starting 3/15.

**Academics.** **Special study options:** Cooperative education, double major, exchange student, honors, independent study, internships, liberal arts/career combination, semester at sea, study abroad, teacher certification program, urban semester, Washington semester. Urban studies program in Chicago; Lutheran Consortium with Dar es Salaam University in East Africa; a wide variety of global education opportunities including exploration seminars, summer field studies, long term programs, May seminars, and summer school abroad. **Credit/placement by examination:** AP, CLEP, IB, institutional tests. 20 credit hours maximum toward bachelor's degree. **Support services:** Learning center, reduced course load, study skills assistance, tutoring, writing center.

**Majors.** **Area/ethnic studies:** French, German, Russian/Slavic, Scandinavian, Spanish/Iberian. **Biology:** General. **Business:** General, accounting, business admin, international, marketing. **Communications:** General. **Computer sciences:** Computer science. **Conservation:** Environmental studies. **Education:** Art, biology, business, chemistry, elementary, English, French, German, health, history, Latin, mathematics, music, physical, physics, secondary, social science, social studies, Spanish, speech. **Foreign languages:** Chinese, classics, French, German, Latin, Russian, Scandinavian, Spanish. **Health:** Health care admin, nursing (RN). **History:** General. **Interdisciplinary:** Global studies, math/computer science, nutrition sciences. **Liberal arts:** Arts/sciences. **Math:** General. **Parks/recreation:** Exercise sciences, health/fitness. **Philosophy/religion:** Philosophy, religion. **Physical sciences:** Chemistry, physics. **Psychology:** General. **Public administration:** Social work. **Social sciences:** Economics, political science, sociology. **Visual/performing arts:** Art, dramatic, music performance, music theory/composition. **Other:** Clinical laboratory science.

**Most popular majors.** Biology 8%, business/marketing 14%, communications/journalism 9%, education 11%, foreign language 8%, health sciences 6%, social sciences 8%, visual/performing arts 6%.

**Computing on campus.** 570 workstations in dormitories, library, computer center, student center. Dormitories wired for high-speed internet access and linked to campus network. Commuter students can connect to campus network. Online course registration, online library, helpline, repair service, student web hosting, wireless network available.

**Student life.** **Freshman orientation:** Mandatory. Preregistration for classes offered. 4-day program prior to the beginning of fall semester classes. **Housing:** Guaranteed on-campus for freshmen. Coed dorms, single-sex dorms, apartments, wellness housing available. $200 fully refundable deposit, deadline 8/1. Students studying Spanish, French, or German have opportunity to live with native speakers in campus apartments. **Activities:** Bands, campus ministries, choral groups, dance, drama, international student organizations, literary magazine, music ensembles, musical theater, radio station, student government, student newspaper, symphony orchestra, TV station, over 100 clubs and organizations.

**Athletics.** NCAA. **Intercollegiate:** Baseball M, basketball, cheerleading M, cross-country, diving W, football (tackle) M, golf, ice hockey, soccer, softball W, swimming W, tennis, track and field, volleyball W, wrestling M. **Intramural:** Badminton, basketball, football (non-tackle), rugby, softball, swimming, table tennis, tennis, volleyball. **Team name:** Cobbers.

**Student services.** Alcohol/substance abuse counseling, chaplain/spiritual director, career counseling, student employment services, financial aid counseling, health services, minority student services, on-campus daycare, personal counseling, placement for graduates. **Physically disabled:** Services for visually, speech, hearing impaired.

**Contact.** E-mail: admissions@cord.edu
Phone: (218) 299-3004 Toll-free number: (800) 699-9897
Fax: (218) 299-4720
Scott Ellingson, Admissions Director, Concordia College: Moorhead, 901 Eighth Street South, Moorhead, MN 56562

## Concordia University: St. Paul

**St. Paul, Minnesota** — CB member
**www.csp.edu** — CB code: 6114

▶ Private 4-year university affiliated with Lutheran Church - Missouri Synod
▶ Residential campus in large city
▶ 1,471 degree-seeking undergraduates: 9% part-time, 57% women, 10% African American, 7% Asian American, 2% Hispanic American, 1% Native American
▶ 1,026 degree-seeking graduate students
▶ 56% of applicants admitted
▶ SAT or ACT (ACT writing optional) required
▶ 50% graduate within 6 years

**General.** Founded in 1893. Regionally accredited. **Degrees:** 424 bachelor's, 4 associate awarded; master's offered. **ROTC:** Army, Naval, Air Force. **Calendar:** Semester, limited summer session. **Full-time faculty:** 74 total; 66% have terminal degrees, 5% minority, 53% women. **Part-time faculty:** 211 total; 26% have terminal degrees, 6% minority, 51% women. **Class size:** 73% < 20, 26% 20-39, less than 1% 40-49.

**Freshman class profile.** 1,106 applied, 621 admitted, 184 enrolled.

| Mid 50% test scores | | | |
|---|---|---|---|
| ACT composite: | 18-24 | **Rank in top tenth:** | 6% |
| GPA 3.75 or higher: | 10% | **End year in good standing:** | 76% |
| GPA 3.50-3.74: | 16% | **Return as sophomores:** | 72% |
| GPA 3.0-3.49: | 24% | **Out-of-state:** | 21% |
| GPA 2.0-2.99: | 47% | **Live on campus:** | 76% |
| Rank in top quarter: | 24% | **International:** | 1% |

**Basis for selection.** School record, test scores, recommendations important. ACT preferred. Interview recommended.

**High school preparation.** College-preparatory program recommended. 15 units required; 16 recommended. Required and recommended units include English 4, mathematics 2, social studies 1, history 1, science 2 (laboratory 2) and foreign language 1. 2 units of fine arts, 1 unit of health/physical education.

**2010-2011 Annual costs.** Tuition/fees: $27,400. Room/board: $7,500. Books/supplies: $740. Personal expenses: $1,095.

**2009-2010 Financial aid.** **Need-based:** 183 full-time freshmen applied for aid; 162 were judged to have need; 162 of these received aid. Average need met was 80%. Average scholarship/grant was $16,705; average loan $4,320. 52% of total undergraduate aid awarded as scholarships/grants, 48% as loans/jobs. **Non-need-based:** Awarded to 160 full-time undergraduates, including 26 freshmen. Scholarships awarded for academics, art, athletics, minority status, music/drama, religious affiliation. **Additional information:** Church districts and local congregations are major sources of aid for church-vocation students.

**Application procedures.** **Admission:** Priority date 5/1; deadline 8/1 (receipt date). $30 fee, may be waived for applicants with need. Admission notification on a rolling basis. **Financial aid:** Priority date 5/1; no closing date. FAFSA, institutional form required. Applicants notified on a rolling basis starting 3/1.

**Academics.** Offers a variety of non-traditional undergraduate degree completion programs designed for working adults in both face-to-face and distance education formats. Approximately 35% of the undergraduates fall into this non-traditional category. **Special study options:** Accelerated study, cross-registration, distance learning, double major, dual enrollment of high school students, exchange student, honors, independent study, internships, student-designed major, study abroad, teacher certification program. **Credit/placement by examination:** AP, CLEP, IB, ACT, institutional tests. **Support services:** Learning center, reduced course load, remedial instruction, study skills assistance, tutoring, writing center.

**Majors. Biology:** General. **Business:** Accounting, business admin, finance, marketing, sales/distribution. **Communications:** Media studies. **Education:** Art, bilingual, biology, chemistry, early childhood, elementary, English, ESL, health, history, kindergarten/preschool, mathematics, middle, music, physical, science, secondary, social studies. **Family/consumer sciences:** Child development, family studies. **History:** General. **Math:** General. **Parks/recreation:** Exercise sciences, health/fitness. **Protective services:** Criminal justice, law enforcement admin. **Psychology:** General. **Social sciences:** Sociology. **Theology:** Missionary, religious ed, sacred music, theology. **Visual/performing arts:** Art, dramatic, graphic design, studio arts.

**Most popular majors.** Business/marketing 43%, computer/information sciences 8%, family/consumer sciences 12%, security/protective services 7%.

**Computing on campus.** Dormitories wired for high-speed internet access and linked to campus network. Commuter students can connect to campus network. Helpline, repair service, wireless network available.

**Student life. Freshman orientation:** Mandatory. Preregistration for classes offered. 3-day program prior to start of fall semester provides information about student life, support services, social programs, employment opportunities, and technology training. **Housing:** Guaranteed on-campus for freshmen. Coed dorms, single-sex dorms, special housing for disabled, apartments, wellness housing available. $125 deposit. **Activities:** Bands, campus ministries, choral groups, dance, drama, music ensembles, musical theater, student government, student newspaper, TV station, Fellowship of Christian Athletes, Southeast Asian student association, United Minds of Joint Action, student senate, mission society.

**Athletics.** NCAA. **Intercollegiate:** Baseball M, basketball, cross-country, football (tackle) M, golf, soccer W, softball W, track and field, volleyball W. **Intramural:** Basketball, cheerleading, football (non-tackle), racquetball, softball, volleyball. **Team name:** Golden Bears.

**Student services.** Adult student services, alcohol/substance abuse counseling, chaplain/spiritual director, career counseling, services for economically disadvantaged, student employment services, financial aid counseling, health services, minority student services, on-campus daycare, personal counseling, placement for graduates. **Physically disabled:** Services for visually, speech, hearing impaired.

**Contact.**  E-mail: admission@csp.edu
Phone: (651) 641-8230 Toll-free number: (800) 333-4705
Fax: (651) 603-6320
Kristin Schoon, Director of Undergraduate Admission, Concordia University: St. Paul, 275 Syndicate Street North, St. Paul, MN 55104-5494

## Crossroads College
**Rochester, Minnesota**
**www.crossroadscollege.edu**          CB code: 6412

▸ Private 4-year Bible college affiliated with Christian Church
▸ Residential campus in small city
▸ 170 degree-seeking undergraduates
▸ SAT or ACT (ACT writing recommended), application essay required

**General.** Founded in 1913. Accredited by ABHE. **Degrees:** 30 bachelor's, 7 associate awarded. **Location:** 85 miles from Minneapolis-St. Paul. **Calendar:** Semester, limited summer session. **Full-time faculty:** 10 total. **Part-time faculty:** 20 total. **Class size:** 79% < 20, 16% 20-39, 2% 40-49, 4% 50-99. **Special facilities:** 38-acre wooded area with nature trails, pond.

**Freshman class profile.** 33 enrolled.

| Mid 50% test scores | | Rank in top quarter: | 58% |
|---|---|---|---|
| SAT critical reading: | 470-540 | Out-of-state: | 28% |
| SAT math: | 640-660 | Live on campus: | 86% |
| ACT composite: | 17-23 | | |

**Basis for selection.** High school rank, experience, aptitude for Christian ministry, character references, and personal statement of goals considered. High school GPA, rank and ACT/SAT scores determine number of credit hours a student may take during first semester if accepted. Interview recommended. **Learning Disabled:** Provide Vice President of Student Development with verification of learning disability.

**2009-2010 Annual costs.** Tuition/fees: $14,290. Room only: $3,950. Books/supplies: $700. Personal expenses: $1,500.

**2009-2010 Financial aid. Non-need-based:** Scholarships awarded for academics, leadership, music/drama, religious affiliation.

**Application procedures. Admission:** Closing date 8/15 (receipt date). $30 fee. Admission notification on a rolling basis. **Financial aid:** Priority date 4/1; no closing date. FAFSA, institutional form required. Applicants notified on a rolling basis starting 2/1; must reply within 4 week(s) of notification.

**Academics.** Minors in religious music, counseling psychology, biblical and classical languages, missions, youth ministries. **Special study options:** Double major, independent study, internships, liberal arts/career combination, student-designed major. **Credit/placement by examination:** AP, CLEP, SAT, ACT, institutional tests. 30 credit hours maximum toward bachelor's degree. **Support services:** Reduced course load, remedial instruction, study skills assistance, tutoring, writing center.

**Majors. Business:** Business admin, nonprofit/public. **Psychology:** Counseling. **Theology:** Missionary, religious ed, sacred music, theology, youth ministry.

**Computing on campus.** 17 workstations in library, computer center. Dormitories wired for high-speed internet access. Wireless network available.

**Student life. Freshman orientation:** Mandatory. Preregistration for classes offered. 2-day session with some placement testing in August; one-day session in January. **Policies:** Attendance required at weekly Chapel and Spiritual Formation Group meetings; Field Service participation required. Religious observance required. **Housing:** Guaranteed on-campus for freshmen. Single-sex dorms, special housing for disabled, apartments, wellness housing available. **Activities:** Choral groups, drama, music ensembles, student government, student newspaper, Christians outdoors, ambassadors group, international students fellowship.

**Athletics. Intercollegiate:** Baseball M, basketball, golf M, soccer M, softball W, tennis, volleyball W. **Intramural:** Bowling, golf, ice hockey, racquetball, skiing, soccer W, swimming, table tennis, tennis, volleyball. **Team name:** Knights.

**Student services.** Adult student services, chaplain/spiritual director, career counseling, student employment services, financial aid counseling, personal counseling, placement for graduates, veterans' counselor.

**Contact.**  E-mail: admissions@crossroads.edu
Phone: (507) 288-4563 ext. 313 Toll-free number: (800) 456-7651
Fax: (507) 288-9046
Scott Klaehn, Director of Admissions, Crossroads College, 920 Mayowood Road, SW, Rochester, MN 55902

## Crown College
**St. Bonifacius, Minnesota**
**www.crown.edu**          CB code: 6639

▸ Private 4-year liberal arts college affiliated with Christian and Missionary Alliance
▸ Residential campus in small town
▸ 936 degree-seeking undergraduates: 17% part-time, 56% women
▸ 160 degree-seeking graduate students
▸ 66% of applicants admitted
▸ SAT or ACT (ACT writing optional), application essay required
▸ 68% graduate within 6 years

**General.** Founded in 1916. Regionally accredited. **Degrees:** 211 bachelor's, 13 associate awarded; master's offered. **ROTC:** Army. **Location:** 25 miles from Minneapolis-St. Paul. **Calendar:** Semester, limited summer session. **Full-time faculty:** 35 total. **Class size:** 68% < 20, 25% 20-39, 5% 40-49, 3% 50-99. **Special facilities:** Nursing lab.

**Freshman class profile.** 457 applied, 303 admitted, 149 enrolled.

| Mid 50% test scores | | | |
|---|---|---|---|
| SAT critical reading: | 500-660 | GPA 2.0-2.99: | 24% |
| SAT math: | 470-640 | Rank in top quarter: | 44% |
| ACT composite: | 20-24 | Rank in top tenth: | 11% |
| GPA 3.75 or higher: | 29% | Return as sophomores: | 74% |
| GPA 3.50-3.74: | 24% | Out-of-state: | 37% |
| GPA 3.0-3.49: | 22% | Live on campus: | 93% |

**Basis for selection.** Applicants must profess personal faith in Jesus Christ. Pastor's and general recommendations very important, academic records and test scores important. **Learning Disabled:** Applicant should meet with director of academic support.

**High school preparation.** College-preparatory program recommended. Recommended units include English 4, mathematics 3, social studies 3, science 3 and foreign language 2.

**2009-2010 Annual costs.** Tuition/fees: $19,870. Room/board: $7,366. Books/supplies: $1,600. Personal expenses: $2,340.

**2009-2010 Financial aid. Need-based:** Average need met was 66%. Average scholarship/grant was $6,547; average loan $3,693. 53% of total undergraduate aid awarded as scholarships/grants, 47% as loans/jobs. **Non-need-based:** Scholarships awarded for academics, alumni affiliation, leadership, minority status, music/drama, religious affiliation.

**Application procedures. Admission:** Closing date 8/18 (postmark date). $35 fee, may be waived for applicants with need. Admission notification on a rolling basis. Within 30 days of their acceptance notification. **Financial aid:** Priority date 4/1, closing date 8/1. FAFSA, institutional form required. Applicants notified on a rolling basis starting 4/1; must reply within 3 week(s) of notification.

**Academics. Special study options:** Accelerated study, combined bachelor's/graduate degree, distance learning, double major, dual enrollment of high school students, ESL, exchange student, honors, independent study, internships, liberal arts/career combination, study abroad, teacher certification program, urban semester, weekend college. 2-2 with non-accredited Bible colleges. **Credit/placement by examination:** AP, CLEP, IB, ACT, institutional tests. 30 credit hours maximum toward associate degree, 30 toward bachelor's. **Support services:** Learning center, reduced course load, remedial instruction, study skills assistance, tutoring, writing center.

**Majors. Biology:** General. **Business:** General, business admin, operations. **Computer sciences:** System admin. **Education:** Early childhood, elementary, English, ESL, history, music, physical, science, secondary, social studies. **Foreign languages:** Linguistics. **Health:** Nursing (RN), public health nursing. **History:** General. **Legal studies:** General. **Liberal arts:** Arts/sciences. **Parks/recreation:** Sports admin. **Physical sciences:** General. **Psychology:** General. **Social sciences:** Urban studies. **Theology:** Bible, missionary, pastoral counseling, religious ed, sacred music, theology, youth ministry. **Visual/performing arts:** Dramatic, music performance. **Other:** Counseling psychology, Intercultural studies, Music education, Relational communication, Social entrepreneurship, TESOL (Teaching English to Speakers of Other Languages), Urban studies.

**Computing on campus.** 105 workstations in library, computer center. Dormitories wired for high-speed internet access and linked to campus network. Commuter students can connect to campus network. Online library, helpline, wireless network available.

**Student life. Freshman orientation:** Available. Preregistration for classes offered. 2-day orientation program at the beginning of the spring semester, 4 days prior to fall semester. **Policies:** Must abide by Crown College Covenant. Religious observance required. **Housing:** Guaranteed on-campus for all undergraduates. Single-sex dorms, special housing for disabled, apartments, wellness housing available. $100 fully refundable deposit. **Activities:** Bands, campus ministries, choral groups, dance, drama, film society, international student organizations, literary magazine, music ensembles, musical theater, radio station, student government, student newspaper, symphony orchestra, Christian service groups, mission support groups, Student Missionary Society, ethnic clubs, activity planning group, student family association, Intercultural Experiences, College Conservatives, Missionary Cabinet, Hmong Student Fellowship.

**Athletics.** NCAA. **Intercollegiate:** Baseball M, basketball, cross-country, football (tackle) M, golf, soccer, softball W, volleyball W. **Intramural:** Basketball, soccer, volleyball. **Team name:** The Storm.

**Student services.** Adult student services, chaplain/spiritual director, career counseling, student employment services, financial aid counseling, health services, personal counseling. **Physically disabled:** Services for visually, hearing impaired.

**Contact.** E-mail: info@crown.edu
Phone: (952) 446-4100 ext. 4142 Toll-free number: (800) 682-7696
Fax: (952) 446-4149
Jill Pautz, Director of Admissions, Crown College, 8700 College View Drive, St. Bonifacius, MN 55375-9001

## DeVry University: Edina
### Edina, Minnesota
www.devry.edu

▶ For-profit 4-year university
▶ Commuter campus in large town
▶ 309 degree-seeking undergraduates: 67% part-time, 41% women
▶ 79 degree-seeking graduate students

**General. Degrees:** 32 bachelor's, 1 associate awarded; master's offered. **Calendar:** Semester. **Part-time faculty:** 12 total; 33% women.

**Freshman class profile.** 26 enrolled.

**Basis for selection.** Interview and GPA important, test scores and class rank considered.

**2009-2010 Annual costs.** Tuition/fees: $14,160. Books/supplies: $1,310. Personal expenses: $3,270.

**2008-2009 Financial aid. Non-need-based:** Scholarships awarded for academics.

**Application procedures. Admission:** No deadline. $50 fee. Admission notification on a rolling basis. **Financial aid:** No deadline. FAFSA required. Applicants notified on a rolling basis.

**Academics. Special study options:** Accelerated study, distance learning. **Credit/placement by examination:** CLEP.

**Majors. Business:** Business admin. **Computer sciences:** Game design, networking, security, systems analysis, web page design. **Engineering:** Software.

**Most popular majors.** Business/marketing 81%, computer/information sciences 19%.

**Student life. Housing:** Private apartments, student-plan housing, private rooms available.

**Contact.** Phone: (877) 733-3879
DeVry University: Edina, 7700 France Avenue South, Suite 575, Edina, MN 55435

## Globe University
### Woodbury, Minnesota
www.globeuniversity.edu                    CB code: 2296

▶ For-profit 4-year business and health science college
▶ Commuter campus in small city
▶ 890 degree-seeking undergraduates: 12% part-time, 71% women, 7% African American, 9% Asian American, 4% Hispanic American, 1% Native American
▶ 45 degree-seeking graduate students
▶ Interview required

**General.** Accredited by ACICS. **Degrees:** 34 bachelor's, 113 associate awarded; master's offered. **Location:** 8 miles from Minneapolis-St. Paul. **Calendar:** Quarter, extensive summer session. **Full-time faculty:** 16 total. **Part-time faculty:** 56 total. **Class size:** 87% < 20, 13% 20-39. **Special facilities:** Music business labs, health fitness labs, research vet tech facility with full AVMA accreditation.

**Basis for selection.** Open admission. **Learning Disabled:** Interview with Dean of Students.

**2009-2010 Annual costs.** Tuition/fees: $18,675. Books/supplies: $900. Personal expenses: $2,502.

**Application procedures. Admission:** No deadline. $50 fee. Admission notification on a rolling basis. **Financial aid:** No deadline. FAFSA, institutional form required. Applicants notified on a rolling basis starting 5/1.

**Academics. Special study options:** Distance learning, honors, independent study, internships, liberal arts/career combination. **Credit/placement**

**by examination:** AP, CLEP, institutional tests. **Support services:** Learning center, reduced course load, remedial instruction, study skills assistance, tutoring, writing center.

**Majors. Agriculture:** Animal sciences. **Business:** Accounting, business admin. **Computer sciences:** General, information technology, LAN/WAN management, security, system admin, web page design. **Engineering:** Software. **Engineering technology:** Computer, computer hardware, computer systems, software. **Health:** Office admin. **Legal studies:** Paralegal. **Parks/recreation:** Exercise sciences.

**Computing on campus.** 173 workstations in library, computer center, student center. Commuter students can connect to campus network. Online course registration, online library, helpline, repair service, wireless network available.

**Student life. Freshman orientation:** Mandatory. Preregistration for classes offered. Day and evening sessions available and run 12-1:30 or 5:30-7:00 pm the week prior to classes starting. **Activities:** Student government, student newspaper, Vet Tech club, Medical Assisting club, paralegal club, accounting club, business/professional club.

**Student services.** Career counseling, services for economically disadvantaged, student employment services, financial aid counseling, placement for graduates. **Physically disabled:** Services for visually, speech, hearing impaired.

**Contact.** E-mail: admissions@globeuniversity.edu
Phone: (651) 730-5100 Toll-free number: (800) 231-0660
Fax: (651) 730-5151
Stacy Severson, Director of Admissions, Globe University, 8089 Globe Drive, Woodbury, MN 55125

## Gustavus Adolphus College
**St. Peter, Minnesota** — CB member
www.gustavus.edu — CB code: 6253

- Private 4-year liberal arts college affiliated with Evangelical Lutheran Church in America
- Residential campus in small town
- 2,462 degree-seeking undergraduates: 1% part-time, 58% women, 3% African American, 6% Asian American, 2% Hispanic American, 2% international
- 74% of applicants admitted
- Application essay required
- 81% graduate within 6 years; 23% enter graduate study

**General.** Founded in 1862. Regionally accredited. **Degrees:** 608 bachelor's awarded. **ROTC:** Army. **Location:** 65 miles from Minneapolis-St. Paul. **Calendar:** 4-1-4, limited summer session. **Full-time faculty:** 194 total; 86% have terminal degrees, 14% minority, 46% women. **Part-time faculty:** 43 total; 46% have terminal degrees, 7% minority, 49% women. **Class size:** 51% < 20, 40% 20-39, 6% 40-49, 2% 50-99. **Special facilities:** Arboretum with walking and skiing paths, theme gardens, native woods and prairies, art museum, interpretive center.

**Freshman class profile.** 2,929 applied, 2,154 admitted, 620 enrolled.

| Mid 50% test scores | | Rank in top tenth: | 32% |
|---|---|---|---|
| ACT composite: | 24-29 | End year in good standing: | 96% |
| GPA 3.75 or higher: | 46% | Return as sophomores: | 96% |
| GPA 3.50-3.74: | 24% | Out-of-state: | 19% |
| GPA 3.0-3.49: | 24% | Live on campus: | 99% |
| GPA 2.0-2.99: | 6% | International: | 2% |
| Rank in top quarter: | 82% | | |

**Basis for selection.** School achievement record, test scores, recommendations, interview, essay or personal statement, school and community activities most important. Special consideration given to children of alumni and minority applicants. SAT or ACT recommended. **Homeschooled:** Statement describing homeschool structure and mission, interview, letter of recommendation (nonparent) required.

**High school preparation.** College-preparatory program recommended. 17 units required; 22 recommended. Required and recommended units include English 4, mathematics 3-4, social studies 2, history 2, science 2-3 (laboratory 2-3), foreign language 2-3 and academic electives 2.

**2009-2010 Annual costs.** Tuition/fees: $32,110. Room/board: $7,900. Books/supplies: $900. Personal expenses: $610.

**2009-2010 Financial aid. Non-need-based:** Scholarships awarded for academics, alumni affiliation, art, music/drama, religious affiliation, ROTC.

**Application procedures. Admission:** Closing date 4/1. No application fee. Admission notification 4/15. Admission notification on a rolling basis beginning on or about 11/20. Must reply by May 1 or within 2 week(s) if notified thereafter. **Financial aid:** Priority date 2/15, closing date 4/15. FAFSA required. CSS PROFILE required of students applying for need-based assistance. Applicants notified on a rolling basis starting 12/20; must reply by 5/1 or within 2 week(s) of notification.

**Academics. Special study options:** Cooperative education, cross-registration, double major, dual enrollment of high school students, exchange student, honors, independent study, internships, liberal arts/career combination, student-designed major, study abroad, teacher certification program, Washington semester. **Credit/placement by examination:** AP, CLEP, IB, institutional tests. **Support services:** Reduced course load, study skills assistance, tutoring, writing center.

**Majors. Area/ethnic studies:** Japanese, Russian/Slavic, Scandinavian, women's. **Biology:** General, biochemistry. **Business:** General, accounting, international. **Communications:** General. **Computer sciences:** General, computer science. **Conservation:** General, environmental studies. **Education:** General, elementary, secondary. **Foreign languages:** Classics, French, German, Japanese, Russian, Scandinavian, Spanish. **Health:** Athletic training, nursing (RN), predental, premedicine, preveterinary. **History:** General. **Legal studies:** Prelaw. **Math:** General. **Parks/recreation:** Health/fitness. **Philosophy/religion:** Philosophy, religion. **Physical sciences:** Chemistry, geology, physics. **Protective services:** Criminal justice. **Psychology:** General. **Social sciences:** Anthropology, economics, geography, political science, sociology. **Theology:** Sacred music. **Visual/performing arts:** Art, art history/conservation, dance, dramatic, music performance.

**Most popular majors.** Biology 11%, business/marketing 16%, communications/journalism 8%, education 8%, physical sciences 6%, psychology 10%, social sciences 15%.

**Computing on campus.** 440 workstations in dormitories, library, computer center, student center. Dormitories wired for high-speed internet access and linked to campus network. Commuter students can connect to campus network. Online course registration, online library, helpline, repair service, student web hosting, wireless network available.

**Student life. Freshman orientation:** Mandatory, $100 fee. Preregistration for classes offered. On-campus registration and pre-orientation sessions take place in June for students and families. Orientation program begins for first-year students four days prior to the beginning of classes. **Housing:** Guaranteed on-campus for all undergraduates. Coed dorms, special housing for disabled, apartments, wellness housing available. $300 nonrefundable deposit, deadline 5/1. **Activities:** Bands, campus ministries, choral groups, dance, drama, international student organizations, literary magazine, music ensembles, musical theater, radio station, student government, student newspaper, symphony orchestra, TV station, over 100 religious, political, ethnic, and social service organizations.

**Athletics.** NCAA. **Intercollegiate:** Baseball M, basketball, cross-country, diving, football (tackle) M, golf, gymnastics W, ice hockey, skiing, soccer, softball W, swimming, tennis, track and field, volleyball W. **Intramural:** Badminton, basketball, football (non-tackle) M, golf, handball, ice hockey, lacrosse M, racquetball, rugby, skiing, soccer, softball, swimming, table tennis, tennis, volleyball. **Team name:** Gusties.

**Student services.** Alcohol/substance abuse counseling, chaplain/spiritual director, career counseling, student employment services, financial aid counseling, health services, minority student services, personal counseling, placement for graduates, women's services. **Physically disabled:** Services for visually, hearing impaired.

**Contact.** E-mail: admission@gustavus.edu
Phone: (507) 933-7676 Toll-free number: (800) 487-8288
Fax: (507) 933-7474
Mark Anderson, Vice-President for Enrollment Management, Gustavus Adolphus College, 800 West College Avenue, St. Peter, MN 56082

## Hamline University
**St. Paul, Minnesota** — CB member
www.hamline.edu — CB code: 6265

- Private 4-year university and liberal arts college affiliated with United Methodist Church
- Residential campus in very large city
- 1,826 degree-seeking undergraduates: 3% part-time, 55% women, 7% African American, 5% Asian American, 3% Hispanic American, 1% Native American, 3% international
- 2,547 degree-seeking graduate students
- 75% of applicants admitted

- SAT or ACT (ACT writing optional), application essay required
- 66% graduate within 6 years; 26% enter graduate study

**General.** Founded in 1854. Regionally accredited. **Degrees:** 590 bachelor's awarded; master's, doctoral, professional offered. **ROTC:** Army, Air Force. **Location:** 5 miles from downtown. **Calendar:** 4-1-4, extensive summer session. **Full-time faculty:** 192 total; 90% have terminal degrees, 16% minority, 50% women. **Part-time faculty:** 339 total; 33% have terminal degrees, 6% minority, 59% women. **Class size:** 56% < 20, 38% 20-39, 3% 40-49, 4% 50-99.

**Freshman class profile.** 2,176 applied, 1,637 admitted, 400 enrolled.

| Mid 50% test scores | | GPA 2.0-2.99: | 20% |
|---|---|---|---|
| SAT critical reading: | 510-630 | Rank in top quarter: | 50% |
| SAT math: | 480-590 | Rank in top tenth: | 21% |
| SAT writing: | 480-600 | End year in good standing: | 88% |
| ACT composite: | 21-27 | Return as sophomores: | 79% |
| GPA 3.75 or higher: | 28% | Out-of-state: | 23% |
| GPA 3.50-3.74: | 21% | Live on campus: | 89% |
| GPA 3.0-3.49: | 31% | International: | 2% |

**Basis for selection.** Class rank, high school GPA, and selection of college-preparatory courses of primary importance. Test scores, extracurricular activities, recommendations of teacher and guidance counselor also emphasized. ACT writing exam preferred but not required. Interview recommended.

**High school preparation.** College-preparatory program recommended. 20 units recommended. Recommended units include English 4, mathematics 3, social studies 4, science 3 (laboratory 3), foreign language 2 and academic electives 4.

**2010-2011 Annual costs.** Tuition/fees (projected): $30,763. Room/board: $8,396. Books/supplies: $1,200.

**2008-2009 Financial aid. Need-based:** 410 full-time freshmen applied for aid; 358 were judged to have need; 358 of these received aid. Average need met was 85%. Average scholarship/grant was $15,448; average loan $4,856. 70% of total undergraduate aid awarded as scholarships/grants, 30% as loans/jobs. **Non-need-based:** Awarded to 476 full-time undergraduates, including 107 freshmen. Scholarships awarded for academics, alumni affiliation, art, leadership, minority status, music/drama, religious affiliation.

**Application procedures. Admission:** Priority date 4/20; no deadline. No application fee. Admission notification on a rolling basis beginning on or about 10/1. Must reply by May 1 or within 2 week(s) if notified thereafter. **Financial aid:** Priority date 3/1; no closing date. FAFSA required. Applicants notified on a rolling basis starting 3/1; must reply within 2 week(s) of notification.

**Academics.** Intensive fall semester course for conditionally-admitted students. **Special study options:** Combined bachelor's/graduate degree, cross-registration, double major, dual enrollment of high school students, ESL, exchange student, honors, independent study, internships, student-designed major, study abroad, teacher certification program, urban semester, Washington semester. **Credit/placement by examination:** AP, CLEP, IB. **Support services:** Learning center, study skills assistance, tutoring, writing center.

**Majors. Area/ethnic studies:** East Asian, Latin American, women's. **Biology:** General, biochemistry. **Business:** General, accounting, business admin, finance, international, marketing. **Communications:** General. **Conservation:** Environmental studies. **Education:** General, art, elementary, ESL, health, music, physical, science, secondary. **Foreign languages:** French, German, Spanish. **Health:** Predental, premedicine, preveterinary. **History:** General. **Interdisciplinary:** Peace/conflict. **Legal studies:** General, paralegal. **Math:** General. **Parks/recreation:** Exercise sciences, health/fitness. **Philosophy/religion:** Philosophy, religion. **Physical sciences:** Chemistry, physics. **Protective services:** Criminal justice. **Psychology:** General. **Social sciences:** General, anthropology, economics, international relations, political science, sociology, urban studies. **Visual/performing arts:** General, art history/conservation, dramatic, music performance, music theory/composition, studio arts. **Other:** International journalism, Multi-/interdisciplinary studies.

**Most popular majors.** Biology 6%, business/marketing 12%, legal studies 8%, psychology 12%, security/protective services 8%, social sciences 20%.

**Computing on campus.** 150 workstations in dormitories, library, computer center. Dormitories wired for high-speed internet access and linked to campus network. Commuter students can connect to campus network. Online course registration, online library, helpline, repair service, student web hosting, wireless network available.

**Student life. Freshman orientation:** Mandatory, $220 fee. Preregistration for classes offered. Fall orientation begins in September, three days before classes start, and lasts one week. A preview of orientation is held in July, with make-up times available in September. **Housing:** Guaranteed on-campus for freshmen. Coed dorms, special housing for disabled, apartments, fraternity/sorority housing, wellness housing available. $50 deposit, deadline 5/1. PRIDE Black Student Alliance House, Spanish Language House, Spectrum Gay Lesbian Bisexual Transgender and Allies House, and Graduate International Student House. **Activities:** Bands, choral groups, dance, drama, international student organizations, literary magazine, music ensembles, Model UN, musical theater, radio station, student government, student newspaper, symphony orchestra, TV station, Asian Pacific American Coalition, College Democrats, College Republicans, Habitat for Humanity, Hamline African Student Association, Hmong Student Association, InterVarsity Christian Fellowship, Minnesota Public Interest Research Group, PRIDE Black Student Alliance, Spectrum (awareness of LGBT issues).

**Athletics.** NCAA. **Intercollegiate:** Baseball M, basketball, cross-country, diving, football (tackle) M, gymnastics W, ice hockey, soccer, softball W, swimming, tennis, track and field, volleyball W. **Intramural:** Basketball, football (non-tackle), volleyball. **Team name:** Pipers.

**Student services.** Alcohol/substance abuse counseling, chaplain/spiritual director, career counseling, student employment services, financial aid counseling, health services, minority student services, personal counseling, placement for graduates, women's services. **Physically disabled:** Services for visually, speech, hearing impaired.

**Contact.** E-mail: admission@hamline.edu
Phone: (651) 523-2207 Toll-free number: (800) 753-9753
Fax: (651) 523-2458
Brian Peterson, Associate Dean of Admission, Hamline University, 1536 Hewitt Avenue, St. Paul, MN 55104-1284

## Macalester College

**St. Paul, Minnesota**
**www.macalester.edu/admissions**
**CB member**
**CB code: 6390**

- Private 4-year liberal arts college affiliated with Presbyterian Church (USA)
- Residential campus in very large city
- 1,965 degree-seeking undergraduates: 58% women, 4% African American, 9% Asian American, 4% Hispanic American, 1% Native American, 12% international
- 46% of applicants admitted
- SAT or ACT (ACT writing optional), application essay required
- 86% graduate within 6 years; 16% enter graduate study

**General.** Founded in 1874. Regionally accredited. **Degrees:** 439 bachelor's awarded. **ROTC:** Army, Naval, Air Force. **Location:** 5 miles from Minneapolis-St. Paul. **Calendar:** Semester. **Full-time faculty:** 163 total; 96% have terminal degrees, 20% minority, 47% women. **Part-time faculty:** 73 total; 58% have terminal degrees, 18% minority, 52% women. **Class size:** 67% < 20, 31% 20-39, 1% 40-49, less than 1% 50-99. **Special facilities:** Observatory with DT-M 16 inch F/8 cassegrain telescope, 250-acre nature preserve, nuclear accelerator, computer modeling facilities, laser spectroscopy laboratory, x-ray diffractometer and a nuclear magnetic spectrometer, fully equipped animal operant chamber, international research center, econometrics lab, ethnographic lab, geographic information systems (GIS) lab.

**Freshman class profile.** 4,565 applied, 2,109 admitted, 565 enrolled.

| Mid 50% test scores | | Rank in top tenth: | 67% |
|---|---|---|---|
| SAT critical reading: | 660-740 | End year in good standing: | 98% |
| SAT math: | 630-710 | Return as sophomores: | 94% |
| SAT writing: | 640-730 | Out-of-state: | 80% |
| ACT composite: | 29-32 | Live on campus: | 100% |
| Rank in top quarter: | 92% | International: | 13% |

**Basis for selection.** Test scores and curriculum most important. Leadership potential and extracurricular involvements also important, with special attention given to service to others. Students whose native language is not English must also submit the results of English as a Foreign Language (TOEFL) or the English Language Proficiency Test (ELPT). SAT Reading is not required of these students. Interview recommended. **Homeschooled:** Transcript of courses and grades, letter of recommendation (nonparent) required.

**High school preparation.** College-preparatory program recommended. Recommended units include English 4, mathematics 3, social studies 3, science 3 (laboratory 3) and foreign language 3. Honors, AP, or IB level courses recommended.

**2009-2010 Annual costs.** Tuition/fees: $38,174. Room/board: $8,768. Books/supplies: $950. Personal expenses: $850.

**2009-2010 Financial aid. Need-based:** 454 full-time freshmen applied for aid; 400 were judged to have need; 400 of these received aid. Average need met was 100%. Average scholarship/grant was $28,280; average loan $2,909. 80% of total undergraduate aid awarded as scholarships/grants, 20% as loans/jobs. **Non-need-based:** Awarded to 149 full-time undergraduates, including 66 freshmen. Scholarships awarded for academics, minority status. **Additional information:** College meets full need for all admitted students. Minnesota Self Loan available to qualified students.

**Application procedures. Admission:** Closing date 1/15 (postmark date). $40 fee, may be waived for applicants with need. Admission notification 3/30. Must reply by May 1 or within 2 week(s) if notified thereafter. **Financial aid:** Priority date 2/8, closing date 3/1. FAFSA, CSS PROFILE required. Applicants notified by 4/1; must reply by 5/1 or within 1 week(s) of notification.

**Academics. Special study options:** Cross-registration, double major, honors, independent study, internships, New York semester, student-designed major, study abroad, urban semester, Washington semester. BA/masters in architecture with Washington University of St. Louis, BA/BS in engineering with Washington University of St. Louis and with the University of Minnesota. **Credit/placement by examination:** AP, CLEP, IB, institutional tests. **Support services:** Learning center, remedial instruction, study skills assistance, tutoring, writing center.

**Majors. Area/ethnic studies:** Asian, Latin American, women's. **Biology:** General. **Computer sciences:** General. **Conservation:** Environmental studies. **Education:** General. **Foreign languages:** Classics, French, German, Japanese, linguistics, Russian, Spanish. **History:** General. **Interdisciplinary:** Global studies, intercultural, neuroscience. **Liberal arts:** Humanities. **Math:** General. **Philosophy/religion:** Philosophy, religion. **Physical sciences:** Chemistry, geology, physics. **Psychology:** General. **Social sciences:** Anthropology, economics, geography, political science, sociology. **Visual/performing arts:** Dramatic.

**Most popular majors.** Biology 6%, English 7%, foreign language 10%, interdisciplinary studies 8%, psychology 7%, social sciences 29%, visual/performing arts 6%.

**Computing on campus.** 400 workstations in dormitories, library, computer center, student center. Dormitories wired for high-speed internet access and linked to campus network. Commuter students can connect to campus network. Online library, helpline, repair service, student web hosting, wireless network available.

**Student life. Freshman orientation:** Mandatory. Preregistration for classes offered. 5 days prior to classes in September. **Housing:** Guaranteed on-campus for freshmen. Coed dorms, apartments available. $300 nonrefundable deposit, deadline 5/1. 6 language houses (French, German, Russian, Spanish, Japanese, Chinese), Jewish cultural house, vegetarian co-op housing available. 2-year residency requirement for first-year students, single-sex floors within coed dorms. **Activities:** Bands, campus ministries, choral groups, dance, drama, international student organizations, literary magazine, music ensembles, Model UN, radio station, student government, student newspaper, symphony orchestra, Conservation & Renewable Energy Society, Voices of Tamani, Asian Student Alliance, Habitat for Humanity, Model United Nations, Amnesty International, Council for Religious Understanding, Macalester Multifaith Council, Mac Christian Fellowship, Afrika.

**Athletics.** NCAA. **Intercollegiate:** Baseball M, basketball, cross-country, diving, football (tackle) M, golf, soccer, softball W, swimming, tennis, track and field, volleyball W, water polo W. **Intramural:** Badminton, basketball, bowling, football (non-tackle), racquetball, soccer, softball, table tennis, tennis, volleyball, water polo. **Team name:** Fighting Scots.

**Student services.** Alcohol/substance abuse counseling, chaplain/spiritual director, career counseling, student employment services, financial aid counseling, health services, minority student services, personal counseling, placement for graduates. **Physically disabled:** Services for visually, speech, hearing impaired.

**Contact.** E-mail: admissions@macalester.edu
Phone: (651) 696-6357 Toll-free number: (800) 231-7974
Fax: (651) 696-6724
Lorne Robinson, Dean of Admissions and Financial Aid, Macalester College, 1600 Grand Avenue, St. Paul, MN 55105-1899

## Martin Luther College
**New Ulm, Minnesota**
**www.mlc-wels.edu**   CB code: 6435

- Private 4-year college of theology and education affiliated with Wisconsin Evangelical Lutheran Synod
- Residential campus in large town

- 722 degree-seeking undergraduates: 3% part-time, 51% women, 1% African American, 1% Asian American, 2% international
- 70 degree-seeking graduate students
- 98% of applicants admitted
- ACT (writing optional) required
- 71% graduate within 6 years

**General.** Founded in 1995. Regionally accredited. Offers programs of study in early childhood education and staff ministry. **Degrees:** 145 bachelor's awarded; master's offered. **Location:** 90 miles from Minneapolis-St. Paul. **Calendar:** Semester, limited summer session. **Full-time faculty:** 49 total; 53% have terminal degrees, 14% women. **Part-time faculty:** 26 total; 27% have terminal degrees, 38% women. **Class size:** 40% < 20, 57% 20-39, 2% 40-49, less than 1% 50-99, less than 1% >100.

**Freshman class profile.** 213 applied, 208 admitted, 158 enrolled.

| Mid 50% test scores | | Rank in top quarter: | 35% |
|---|---|---|---|
| ACT composite: | 22-27 | Rank in top tenth: | 9% |
| GPA 3.75 or higher: | 33% | Return as sophomores: | 85% |
| GPA 3.50-3.74: | 18% | Out-of-state: | 90% |
| GPA 3.0-3.49: | 31% | Live on campus: | 100% |
| GPA 2.0-2.99: | 18% | International: | 2% |

**Basis for selection.** Primarily pastor's letter of recommendation, high school transcript, and test scores required. Rating provided by student's high school considered.

**High school preparation.** College-preparatory program required. 14 units required. Required units include English 4, mathematics 3, social studies 2, science 3 (laboratory 2), foreign language 2 and academic electives 2. 5 units in foreign language required for pastoral program.

**2009-2010 Annual costs.** Tuition/fees: $10,660. Room/board: $4,140. Books/supplies: $800. Personal expenses: $2,000.

**2008-2009 Financial aid. Need-based:** 165 full-time freshmen applied for aid; 130 were judged to have need; 130 of these received aid. Average need met was 60%. Average scholarship/grant was $4,150; average loan $3,847. 67% of total undergraduate aid awarded as scholarships/grants, 33% as loans/jobs. **Non-need-based:** Awarded to 398 full-time undergraduates, including 108 freshmen. Scholarships awarded for academics, music/drama.

**Application procedures. Admission:** Closing date 4/15 (postmark date). $25 fee, may be waived for applicants with need. Admission notification on a rolling basis beginning on or about 9/15. Must reply by May 1 or within 2 week(s) if notified thereafter. **Financial aid:** Priority date 4/15, closing date 9/30. FAFSA, institutional form required. Applicants notified on a rolling basis starting 3/15.

**Academics. Special study options:** Distance learning, double major, teacher certification program. **Credit/placement by examination:** AP, CLEP, ACT, institutional tests. **Support services:** Learning center, reduced course load, remedial instruction, study skills assistance, tutoring.

**Majors. Education:** Early childhood, elementary, multi-level teacher. **Theology:** Theology.

**Computing on campus.** 129 workstations in dormitories, library, computer center. Dormitories linked to campus network. Helpline, repair service available.

**Student life. Freshman orientation:** Mandatory, $20 fee. **Policies:** Religious observance required. **Housing:** Guaranteed on-campus for freshmen. Single-sex dorms available. $100 nonrefundable deposit, deadline 5/1. **Activities:** Bands, campus ministries, choral groups, dance, drama, literary magazine, music ensembles, musical theater, student government, symphony orchestra.

**Athletics.** NAIA, NCAA. **Intercollegiate:** Baseball M, basketball, cross-country, football (tackle) M, golf M, soccer, softball W, tennis, track and field, volleyball W. **Intramural:** Badminton, basketball, bowling, football (tackle) M, soccer, softball, tennis, volleyball. **Team name:** Knights.

**Student services.** Chaplain/spiritual director, student employment services, financial aid counseling, health services, personal counseling.

**Contact.** E-mail: mlcadmit@mlc-wels.edu
Phone: (507) 354-8221 Fax: (507) 354-8225
Ronald Brutlag, Director of Admissions, Martin Luther College, 1995 Luther Court, New Ulm, MN 56073-3965

## Metropolitan State University
St. Paul, Minnesota
www.metrostate.edu                                    CB code: 1245

- Public 4-year university
- Commuter campus in very large city
- 6,178 degree-seeking undergraduates: 62% part-time, 58% women
- 595 degree-seeking graduate students
- 100% of applicants admitted

**General.** Founded in 1971. Regionally accredited. **Degrees:** 1,348 bachelor's awarded; master's, doctoral offered. **Calendar:** Semester, extensive summer session. **Full-time faculty:** 126 total; 79% have terminal degrees, 21% minority, 55% women. **Part-time faculty:** 375 total; 23% have terminal degrees, 14% minority, 47% women. **Class size:** 34% < 20, 64% 20-39, less than 1% 40-49, less than 1% 50-99.

**Freshman class profile.** 288 applied, 288 admitted, 92 enrolled.

| Mid 50% test scores | | Rank in top tenth: | 8% |
|---|---|---|---|
| ACT composite: | 16-24 | Out-of-state: | 2% |
| Rank in top quarter: | 24% | International: | 3% |

**Basis for selection.** School achievement record and test scores most important. ACT or SAT at or above national median or high school rank in upper half of class. Interview and essays only used as part of the appeals process if admission was denied.

**High school preparation.** 16 units required. Required units include English 4, mathematics 3, social studies 3, science 3 (laboratory 1) and academic electives 3. 3 years of electives from language, world culture, or arts.

**2009-2010 Annual costs.** Tuition/fees: $5,627; $11,173 out-of-state. Books/supplies: $1,500. Personal expenses: $1,976.

**2009-2010 Financial aid. Non-need-based:** Scholarships awarded for academics, leadership, minority status, state residency.

**Application procedures. Admission:** Closing date 6/15. $20 fee, may be waived for applicants with need. Admission notification on a rolling basis. **Financial aid:** Priority date 5/1; no closing date. FAFSA required. Applicants notified on a rolling basis starting 5/1; must reply within 2 week(s) of notification.

**Academics. Special study options:** Cross-registration, distance learning, double major, dual enrollment of high school students, external degree, independent study, internships, liberal arts/career combination, student-designed major, teacher certification program, weekend college. **Credit/placement by examination:** AP, CLEP, IB, institutional tests. 90 credit hours maximum toward bachelor's degree. **Support services:** Learning center, reduced course load, study skills assistance, tutoring, writing center.

**Majors. Area/ethnic studies:** Women's. **Biology:** General. **Business:** Accounting, business admin, finance, hospitality admin, human resources, information resources management, international, management information systems, marketing, operations, sales/distribution. **Communications:** General, advertising. **Computer sciences:** Computer science, information systems, security. **Education:** Biology, elementary, English, kindergarten/preschool, mathematics, social studies. **Health:** Dental hygiene, nursing (RN), substance abuse counseling. **History:** General. **Liberal arts:** Arts/sciences. **Math:** Applied. **Philosophy/religion:** Philosophy. **Protective services:** Criminal justice, police science. **Psychology:** General, developmental. **Public administration:** Human services, social work. **Social sciences:** General, economics. **Visual/performing arts:** Dramatic, play/screenwriting.

**Most popular majors.** Business/marketing 38%, health sciences 9%, liberal arts 18%, psychology 7%, public administration/social services 6%.

**Computing on campus.** 550 workstations in library, computer center. Commuter students can connect to campus network. Online course registration, helpline, wireless network available.

**Student life. Freshman orientation:** Mandatory, $10 fee. Preregistration for classes offered. Orientation sessions of 3-1/2 hours are held several times each semester. **Policies:** Annual registration required of all student organizations. **Activities:** Drama, international student organizations, literary magazine, student government, student newspaper, Asian student organization, Lavender Bridge, African-American student association, graduate student advisory committee, Voice of Indian Council for Educational Success, social work student association, psychology club, Muslim student association, Urban Teachers Student Program Organization.

**Student services.** Adult student services, career counseling, minority student services, personal counseling, veterans' counselor, women's services. **Physically disabled:** Services for visually, speech, hearing impaired.

**Contact.** E-mail: admission.metro@metrostate.edu
Phone: (651) 793-1300 Fax: (651) 793-1310
Monir Johnson, Admissions Director, Metropolitan State University, 700 East Seventh Street, St. Paul, MN 55106-5000

## Minneapolis College of Art and Design
Minneapolis, Minnesota                                CB member
www.mcad.edu                                          CB code: 6411

- Private 4-year visual arts college
- Residential campus in very large city
- 655 degree-seeking undergraduates: 4% part-time, 58% women
- 30 degree-seeking graduate students
- 67% of applicants admitted
- SAT or ACT (ACT writing optional), application essay required
- 59% graduate within 6 years

**General.** Founded in 1886. Regionally accredited. **Degrees:** 148 bachelor's awarded; master's offered. **Calendar:** Semester, limited summer session. **Full-time faculty:** 43 total; 100% have terminal degrees, 35% women. **Part-time faculty:** 85 total; 85% have terminal degrees, 47% women. **Class size:** 84% < 20, 16% 20-39. **Special facilities:** Art and design galleries, personal on-campus studio space, 3-D furniture/sculpture studios, animation studios, drawing studios, film studios, print/paper/book studios, painting studios, photo studios, on-campus professional design studio.

**Freshman class profile.** 424 applied, 285 admitted, 111 enrolled.

| Mid 50% test scores | | GPA 3.50-3.74: | 19% |
|---|---|---|---|
| SAT critical reading: | 540-670 | GPA 3.0-3.49: | 43% |
| SAT math: | 470-590 | GPA 2.0-2.99: | 10% |
| SAT writing: | 480-600 | Return as sophomores: | 78% |
| ACT composite: | 21-27 | Out-of-state: | 58% |
| GPA 3.75 or higher: | 28% | Live on campus: | 81% |

**Basis for selection.** Bachelor of Fine Arts applicants required to submit a portfolio of creative work. For all students (BFA & BS), academic record and test scores reviewed. Level of interest and motivation determined through personal statement of interest, letter of recommendation and essay requirement. Tests not required for transfer applicants who have completed 12 or more satisfactory credits (C or better) at the college level. Interview recommended. Personal statement required on specific topic. Visual arts portfolio required for all BFA applications; essay on specific topic required for all BS applications.

**High school preparation.** College-preparatory program recommended. Recommended units include English 4, social studies 4, history 4 and visual/performing arts 6.

**2009-2010 Annual costs.** Tuition/fees: $31,500. Housing costs vary; figure quoted is for double-occupancy (furnished) one-bedroom apartment. Required fees include $1800 laptop computer that freshmen must purchase. Room only: $4,340. Books/supplies: $2,200. Personal expenses: $1,000.

**2009-2010 Financial aid. Non-need-based:** Scholarships awarded for academics, alumni affiliation, art.

**Application procedures. Admission:** Priority date 2/15; deadline 5/1 (receipt date). $50 fee, may be waived for applicants with need. Admission notification on a rolling basis. Must reply by 5/1. **Financial aid:** Priority date 3/15, closing date 3/15. FAFSA required. Applicants notified by 4/1; Applicants notified on a rolling basis starting 4/1; must reply by 5/1 or within 2 week(s) of notification.

**Academics. Special study options:** Combined bachelor's/graduate degree, cooperative education, cross-registration, distance learning, exchange student, independent study, internships, New York semester, study abroad. **Credit/placement by examination:** AP, CLEP, IB. **Support services:** Learning center, reduced course load, study skills assistance, tutoring, writing center.

**Majors. Communications:** Advertising, public relations. **Communications technology:** Animation/special effects. **Production:** Furniture. **Visual/performing arts:** Drawing, graphic design, illustration, painting, photography, printmaking, sculpture, studio arts. **Other:** Comic art, Print and web communications, Project management.

**Computing on campus.** PC or laptop required. 160 workstations in library, computer center, student center. Dormitories wired for high-speed internet access and linked to campus network. Commuter students can connect to campus network. Online library, helpline, repair service, student web hosting, wireless network available.

**Student life. Freshman orientation:** Mandatory. Preregistration for classes offered. 3 days prior to first day of fall semester classes; includes 1 day for parent/guardian orientation. **Housing:** Guaranteed on-campus for freshmen. Coed dorms, apartments available. $175 fully refundable deposit, deadline 5/1. **Activities:** Film society, international student organizations, student government, animation club, anime club, bike club, Comic Heads, film club, musicians club, design club, green club, OH NO HOMO, recess club.

**Student services.** Alcohol/substance abuse counseling, career counseling, student employment services, financial aid counseling, personal counseling, placement for graduates.

**Contact.** E-mail: admissions@mcad.edu
Phone: (612) 874-3760 Toll-free number: (800) 874-6223 ext. 1
Fax: (612) 874-3701
William Mullen, Vice President, Enrollment Management, Minneapolis College of Art and Design, 2501 Stevens Avenue, Minneapolis, MN 55404

## Minnesota School of Business
### Minneapolis, Minnesota
www.msbcollege.edu                          CB code: 3313

- For-profit 4-year business and technical college
- Commuter campus in very large city
- 402 full-time, degree-seeking undergraduates
- Interview required

**General.** Accredited by ACICS. **Degrees:** 71 bachelor's, 129 associate awarded; master's offered. **Calendar:** Quarter, extensive summer session. **Full-time faculty:** 12 total; 33% have terminal degrees, 33% women. **Part-time faculty:** 63 total; 8% have terminal degrees, 8% minority, 44% women. **Class size:** 97% < 20, 3% 20-39.

**Basis for selection.** Standardized test scores most important. Interview also important. Scores are used to exempt applicants from entrance exam. **Learning Disabled:** Students with learning disabilities are allowed 90 minutes for exams while all other students are allowed 60 minutes.

**2009-2010 Annual costs.** Tuition/fees: $18,675. Books/supplies: $1,500. Personal expenses: $2,178.

**Application procedures. Admission:** No deadline. $50 fee. Application must be submitted online. Admission notification on a rolling basis. **Financial aid:** No deadline. FAFSA, institutional form required. Applicants notified on a rolling basis starting 7/1; must reply within 2 week(s) of notification.

**Academics. Special study options:** Combined bachelor's/graduate degree, distance learning, liberal arts/career combination. **Credit/placement by examination:** CLEP. **Support services:** Study skills assistance, tutoring, writing center.

**Majors. Business:** Accounting, business admin. **Computer sciences:** Information technology. **Health:** Nursing (RN). **Legal studies:** Paralegal.

**Computing on campus.** 12 workstations in library, computer center. Online library, helpline, wireless network available.

**Student life. Freshman orientation:** Mandatory.

**Student services.** Student employment services, financial aid counseling, placement for graduates.

**Contact.** E-mail: pmurray@msbcollege.edu
Phone: (612) 861-2000 Toll-free number: (800) 752-4223
Fax: (612) 861-5548
Patricia Murray, Director of Admissions, Minnesota School of Business, 1401 West 76 Street, Suite 500, Richfield, MN 55423

## Minnesota School of Business: Blaine
### Blaine, Minnesota
www.msbcollege.edu

- For-profit 4-year branch campus and business college
- Very large city
- 946 degree-seeking undergraduates

**General.** Regionally accredited; also accredited by ACICS. **Degrees:** 4 bachelor's, 56 associate awarded. **Calendar:** Quarter, extensive summer session. **Full-time faculty:** 8 total. **Part-time faculty:** 30 total.

**Freshman class profile.** 103 applied, 103 admitted, 103 enrolled.

**Basis for selection.** Open admission, but selective for some programs.

**2009-2010 Annual costs.** Tuition/fees: $18,675.

**Application procedures. Admission:** No deadline. $50 fee.

**Academics. Credit/placement by examination:** CLEP.

**Majors. Business:** Accounting, business admin. **Computer sciences:** Information technology.

**Student life. Activities:** Student newspaper.

**Contact.** E-mail: kswanson@msbcollege.edu
Kristen Swanson, Director of Admissions, Minnesota School of Business: Blaine, 3680 Pheasant Ridge Dr. NE, Blaine, MN 55449

## Minnesota School of Business: Plymouth
### Plymouth, Minnesota
www.msbcollege.edu

- For-profit 4-year business and technical college
- Small city

**General.** Accredited by ACICS. **Calendar:** Quarter.

**Annual costs/financial aid.** Tuition/fees (2009-2010): $18,675.

**Contact.** Phone: (866) 476-2121
Director of Admissions, 1455 County Road 101 North, Plymouth, MN 55447

## Minnesota School of Business: Rochester
### Rochester, Minnesota
www.msbcollege.edu

- For-profit 4-year career college
- Small city
- 427 full-time, degree-seeking undergraduates

**General.** Accredited by ACICS. **Degrees:** 11 bachelor's, 77 associate awarded. **Calendar:** Quarter. **Full-time faculty:** 11 total. **Part-time faculty:** 42 total.

**Basis for selection.** Admissions based on results of Accuplacer entrance exam.

**2009-2010 Annual costs.** Tuition/fees: $18,675. Books/supplies: $1,200.

**Application procedures. Admission:** Closing date 10/1. $50 fee. Application must be submitted online. Admission notification on a rolling basis.

**Academics. Special study options:** Distance learning. **Credit/placement by examination:** CLEP. **Support services:** Learning center, remedial instruction, study skills assistance, tutoring, writing center.

**Majors. Business:** Accounting, business admin.

**Computing on campus.** 14 workstations in library, student center. Online library, helpline, wireless network available.

**Contact.** Phone: (507) 536-9500
Angie Helm, Director of Admissions, Minnesota School of Business: Rochester, 2521 Pennington Drive NW, Rochester, MN 55901

## Minnesota School of Business: St. Cloud
### Waite Park, Minnesota
www.msbcollege.edu

- For-profit 4-year virtual university
- Small city
- 1,003 degree-seeking undergraduates
- 100% of applicants admitted

**General.** Accredited by ACICS. **Degrees:** 20 bachelor's, 187 associate awarded; master's offered. **Calendar:** Quarter, extensive summer session. **Full-time faculty:** 13 total. **Part-time faculty:** 41 total.

**Freshman class profile.** 168 applied, 168 admitted, 168 enrolled.

**Basis for selection.** Applicants to all diploma, associate, and bachelor degree programs must achieve minimum scores on the Accuplacer test administered at the college: 35 (reading comprehension), 35 (sentence skills), 21 (arithmetic). **Homeschooled:** State high school equivalency certificate required.

**2009-2010 Annual costs.** Tuition/fees: $18,675.

**Application procedures. Admission:** No deadline. $50 fee. Application must be submitted online. Admission notification on a rolling basis.

**Academics. Special study options:** Combined bachelor's/graduate degree, distance learning, internships. **Credit/placement by examination:** CLEP. **Support services:** Remedial instruction, study skills assistance, tutoring, writing center.

**Majors. Business:** Accounting, business admin. **Computer sciences:** Information technology. **Health:** Health care admin. **Other:** Health fitness specialist, Paralegal.

**Computing on campus.** Online course registration, helpline, wireless network available.

**Contact.** E-mail: info@msbcollege.edu
Phone: (866) 403-3333
Candi Janssen, Director of Admissions, Minnesota School of Business: St. Cloud, 1201 Second Street South, Waite Park, MN 55387

## Minnesota School of Business: Shakopee
### Shakopee, Minnesota
### www.msbcollege.edu

- For-profit 4-year business and technical college
- Commuter campus in large town
- 460 degree-seeking undergraduates
- 54% of applicants admitted
- Interview required

**General.** Accredited by ACICS. **Degrees:** 19 bachelor's, 74 associate awarded; master's offered. **Calendar:** Quarter. **Full-time faculty:** 10 total; 30% have terminal degrees, 60% women. **Part-time faculty:** 31 total; 13% have terminal degrees, 3% minority, 45% women. **Class size:** 97% < 20, 3% 20-39.

**Basis for selection.** Interview with admissions and SAT, ACT, or entrance exam (Accuplacer) important.

**2009-2010 Annual costs.** Tuition/fees: $18,675.

**2009-2010 Financial aid. Non-need-based:** Scholarships awarded for academics.

**Application procedures. Admission:** No deadline. $50 fee. Admission notification on a rolling basis. **Financial aid:** No deadline. FAFSA, institutional form required. Applicants notified on a rolling basis.

**Academics. Special study options:** Combined bachelor's/graduate degree, distance learning, liberal arts/career combination. **Credit/placement by examination:** CLEP, SAT, ACT, institutional tests. 75 credit hours maximum toward associate degree, 75 toward bachelor's. **Support services:** Learning center, remedial instruction, study skills assistance, tutoring, writing center.

**Majors. Business:** Business admin.

**Computing on campus.** 50 workstations in computer center. Online course registration, online library, helpline, wireless network available.

**Student life. Freshman orientation:** Mandatory.

**Contact.** Phone: (866) 776-1200
Gretchen Seifert, Director of Admissions, Minnesota School of Business: Shakopee, 1200 Shakopee Town Square, Shakopee, MN 55379

## Minnesota State University Mankato
### Mankato, Minnesota
### www.mnsu.edu
**CB member**
**CB code: 6677**

- Public 4-year university
- Residential campus in large town
- 12,825 degree-seeking undergraduates
- 1,910 graduate students
- 88% of applicants admitted

- SAT or ACT (ACT writing optional) required
- 52% graduate within 6 years

**General.** Founded in 1867. Regionally accredited. **Degrees:** 2,129 bachelor's, 46 associate awarded; master's offered. **ROTC:** Army. **Location:** 85 miles from Minneapolis-St. Paul. **Calendar:** Semester, extensive summer session. **Full-time faculty:** 499 total; 82% have terminal degrees, 9% minority, 45% women. **Part-time faculty:** 262 total; 8% have terminal degrees, 2% minority, 60% women. **Class size:** 33% < 20, 49% 20-39, 7% 40-49, 8% 50-99, 3% >100. **Special facilities:** 2 observatories, ropes course.

**Freshman class profile.** 6,417 applied, 5,640 admitted, 2,383 enrolled.

| Mid 50% test scores | | | |
|---|---|---|---|
| ACT composite: | 20-24 | Return as sophomores: | 77% |
| Rank in top quarter: | 27% | Out-of-state: | 14% |
| Rank in top tenth: | 7% | Live on campus: | 85% |

**Basis for selection.** Students must rank in top 50 percent of high school class or score 21 or better on the ACT. College preparatory courses also reviewed. ACT used only when admission cannot be achieved using high school rank and college preparatory courses. Essays and/or recommendations used only for contract/admission review by faculty committees. **Homeschooled:** Must submit standardized test results in lieu of rank/record.

**High school preparation.** 16 units required. Required units include English 4, mathematics 3, social studies 2, history 1, science 3 (laboratory 3) and foreign language 2. One year world culture course or arts course.

**2009-2010 Annual costs.** Tuition/fees: $6,429; $12,861 out-of-state. Room/board: $6,019. Books/supplies: $820. Personal expenses: $2,600.

**2008-2009 Financial aid. Need-based:** 1,968 full-time freshmen applied for aid; 1,206 were judged to have need; 1,206 of these received aid. Average need met was 80%. Average scholarship/grant was $4,528; average loan $2,963. 45% of total undergraduate aid awarded as scholarships/grants, 55% as loans/jobs. **Non-need-based:** Awarded to 1,644 full-time undergraduates, including 578 freshmen. Scholarships awarded for academics, art, athletics, leadership, minority status, music/drama.

**Application procedures. Admission:** Closing date 8/15. $20 fee, may be waived for applicants with need. Admission notification on a rolling basis. **Financial aid:** Priority date 3/15; no closing date. FAFSA required. Applicants notified on a rolling basis starting 3/30; must reply within 2 week(s) of notification.

**Academics. Special study options:** Combined bachelor's/graduate degree, cross-registration, distance learning, double major, dual enrollment of high school students, ESL, exchange student, external degree, honors, independent study, internships, semester at sea, student-designed major, study abroad, teacher certification program. **Credit/placement by examination:** AP, CLEP, IB, institutional tests. **Support services:** Learning center, reduced course load, remedial instruction, study skills assistance, tutoring, writing center.

**Majors. Agriculture:** Food science, plant sciences. **Architecture:** Urban/community planning. **Area/ethnic studies:** French, German, Scandinavian, women's. **Biology:** General, anatomy, bacteriology, biochemistry, biotechnology, botany, ecology, genetics, toxicology, zoology. **Business:** General, accounting, banking/financial services, business admin, finance, financial planning, human resources, international, management information systems, management science, operations. **Communications:** General, journalism, media studies, public relations. **Computer sciences:** General, computer science. **Conservation:** General, environmental studies. **Construction:** Maintenance. **Education:** General, art, biology, business, chemistry, computer, curriculum, drama/dance, early childhood, elementary, English, family/consumer sciences, foreign languages, French, German, health, health occupations, history, mathematics, middle, music, physical, physics, science, secondary, social science, social studies, Spanish, speech, technology/industrial arts, voc/tech. **Engineering:** General, civil, computer, electrical, mechanical. **Engineering technology:** Automotive, computer, electrical, manufacturing, mechanical. **Family/consumer sciences:** General, clothing/textiles, family studies, family/community services, food/nutrition, housing. **Foreign languages:** French, German, Spanish. **Health:** Athletic training, communication disorders, cytotechnology, dental hygiene, health care admin, nursing (RN), predental, premedicine, preop/surgical nursing, prepharmacy, preveterinary, public health ed, recreational therapy. **History:** General. **Interdisciplinary:** Biological/physical sciences, gerontology, math/computer science. **Legal studies:** Prelaw. **Math:** General. **Mechanic/repair:** Automotive. **Parks/recreation:** General, exercise sciences, facilities management, health/fitness, sports admin. **Philosophy/religion:** Philosophy. **Physical sciences:** Astronomy, chemistry, physics. **Protective services:** Corrections, law enforcement admin, police science. **Psychology:** General. **Public administration:** General, human services, social work. **Social**

**sciences:** Anthropology, economics, geography, international relations, political science, sociology, urban studies. **Transportation:** Aviation management. **Visual/performing arts:** General, art, art history/conservation, ceramics, commercial/advertising art, dramatic, drawing, fiber arts, music management, music performance, painting, sculpture, studio arts, theater design.

**Most popular majors.** Business/marketing 23%, education 12%, engineering/engineering technologies 6%, health sciences 11%, parks/recreation 6%, social sciences 6%.

**Computing on campus.** 900 workstations in dormitories, library, computer center, student center. Dormitories wired for high-speed internet access and linked to campus network. Commuter students can connect to campus network. Online course registration, online library, helpline, repair service, student web hosting, wireless network available.

**Student life. Freshman orientation:** Mandatory, $65 fee. Preregistration for classes offered. Includes overnight stay. **Housing:** Coed dorms, special housing for disabled available. $250 partly refundable deposit. **Activities:** Bands, campus ministries, choral groups, dance, drama, international student organizations, music ensembles, musical theater, radio station, student government, student newspaper, symphony orchestra, Hmong student association, American Indian student association, Chicano Latino AM student association, Fellowship of Christian Athletes, InterVarsity, MSU Pagan Organization.

**Athletics.** NCAA. **Intercollegiate:** Baseball M, basketball, bowling W, cheerleading, cross-country, diving, football (tackle) M, golf, ice hockey, soccer W, softball W, swimming, tennis, track and field, volleyball W, wrestling M. **Intramural:** Archery, basketball, bowling, football (non-tackle), golf, ice hockey, racquetball, rugby, soccer, softball, swimming, tennis, track and field, triathlon, volleyball, wrestling M. **Team name:** Mavericks.

**Student services.** Adult student services, alcohol/substance abuse counseling, chaplain/spiritual director, career counseling, services for economically disadvantaged, student employment services, financial aid counseling, health services, legal services, minority student services, on-campus daycare, personal counseling, placement for graduates, veterans' counselor, women's services. **Physically disabled:** Services for visually, speech, hearing impaired.

**Contact.** E-mail: admissions@mnsu.edu
Phone: (507) 389-1822 Toll-free number: (800) 722-0544
Fax: (507) 389-1511
Brian Jones, Director of Admissions, Minnesota State University Mankato, 122 Taylor Center, Mankato, MN 56001

## Minnesota State University Moorhead
**Moorhead, Minnesota**
www.mnstate.edu                                    CB code: 6678

- Public 4-year university
- Residential campus in small city
- 6,567 degree-seeking undergraduates: 13% part-time, 56% women, 3% African American, 1% Asian American, 1% Hispanic American, 1% Native American, 5% international
- 364 degree-seeking graduate students
- 77% of applicants admitted
- SAT or ACT (ACT writing optional) required
- 40% graduate within 6 years

**General.** Founded in 1885. Regionally accredited. **Degrees:** 1,328 bachelor's, 25 associate awarded; master's, doctoral offered. **ROTC:** Army, Air Force. **Location:** 240 miles from Minneapolis-St. Paul. **Calendar:** Semester, limited summer session. **Full-time faculty:** 307 total. **Part-time faculty:** 185 total. **Special facilities:** Planetarium, biology museum.

**Freshman class profile.** 2,900 applied, 2,241 admitted, 1,055 enrolled.

| Mid 50% test scores | | | |
|---|---|---|---|
| ACT composite: | 19-24 | Return as sophomores: | 67% |
| Rank in top quarter: | 27% | Out-of-state: | 37% |
| Rank in top tenth: | 9% | Live on campus: | 82% |
| | | International: | 3% |

**Basis for selection.** Applicants must rank in top half of class or have minimum ACT composite score of 21 or equivalent scores on SAT or PSAT/NMSQT. Some applicants not meeting requirements will be admitted to transitional college program. Applicants must also fulfill minimum requirements of secondary course work. Students not meeting automatic admission standards may apply through alternative admissions program, Corrick Center. **Learning Disabled:** Contact Office of Disability Services to make sure appropriate accommodations can be provided.

**High school preparation.** College-preparatory program required. 16 units required. Required units include English 4, mathematics 3, social studies 3, science 3 (laboratory 1) and foreign language 2. One unit fine arts, .5 computer science recommended.

**2009-2010 Annual costs.** Tuition/fees: $6,598. Out-of-state students pay same rate as in-state. Room/board: $6,242. Books/supplies: $800. Personal expenses: $2,206.

**2009-2010 Financial aid. Non-need-based:** Scholarships awarded for academics, art, athletics, leadership, minority status, music/drama, state residency.

**Application procedures. Admission:** Closing date 8/1 (postmark date). $20 fee. Admission notification on a rolling basis beginning on or about 10/1. **Financial aid:** Priority date 2/15; no closing date. FAFSA required. Applicants notified on a rolling basis starting 6/1; must reply within 2 week(s) of notification.

**Academics. Special study options:** Cross-registration, distance learning, double major, dual enrollment of high school students, exchange student, external degree, honors, independent study, internships, student-designed major, study abroad, teacher certification program. Reciprocal bachelor's degree programs with North Dakota State University. **Credit/placement by examination:** AP, CLEP, ACT, institutional tests. 12 credit hours maximum toward bachelor's degree. **Support services:** Pre-admission summer program, reduced course load, remedial instruction, study skills assistance, tutoring, writing center.

**Majors. Area/ethnic studies:** American, East Asian. **Biology:** General. **Business:** Accounting, business admin, finance, international, management information systems, marketing. **Communications:** Media studies. **Computer sciences:** General, computer science. **Education:** Art, biology, chemistry, elementary, English, health, kindergarten/preschool, mathematics, music, physical, physics, science, social studies, Spanish, special, speech. **Engineering technology:** Construction, industrial. **Foreign languages:** Spanish. **Health:** Athletic training, audiology/speech pathology, clinical lab science, community health services, health care admin, nurse practitioner, predental, premedicine, prepharmacy, preveterinary. **History:** General. **Interdisciplinary:** Gerontology. **Legal studies:** General, paralegal. **Math:** General. **Parks/recreation:** Exercise sciences, health/fitness. **Philosophy/religion:** Philosophy. **Physical sciences:** Chemistry, physics. **Protective services:** Criminal justice. **Psychology:** General. **Public administration:** Social work. **Social sciences:** Anthropology, economics, political science, sociology. **Visual/performing arts:** Art, commercial/advertising art, dramatic, music management, music performance.

**Most popular majors.** Business/marketing 18%, communications/journalism 6%, education 19%, health sciences 10%, public administration/social services 6%, visual/performing arts 9%.

**Computing on campus.** 791 workstations in dormitories, library, computer center. Dormitories linked to campus network. Commuter students can connect to campus network. Online course registration, online library, helpline, repair service, student web hosting, wireless network available.

**Student life. Freshman orientation:** Available. Preregistration for classes offered. **Housing:** Coed dorms, single-sex dorms, special housing for disabled, apartments, fraternity/sorority housing available. $250 partly refundable deposit, deadline 3/15. Students participating in our Learning Communities program take at least three of their fall semester classes together as well as live together on the same residence hall floor. **Activities:** Bands, campus ministries, choral groups, dance, drama, film society, international student organizations, literary magazine, music ensembles, Model UN, musical theater, radio station, student government, student newspaper, symphony orchestra, TV station, 125 student clubs, including Spanish club, Habitat for Humanity, volunteer visions, sci-fi club, Dragons 4 Wellness, Chinese club, Dragon baseball club, Colleges Against Cancer.

**Athletics.** NCAA. **Intercollegiate:** Basketball, cross-country, diving W, football (tackle) M, golf W, soccer W, softball W, swimming W, tennis W, track and field, volleyball W, wrestling M. **Intramural:** Basketball, football (tackle) M, golf, ice hockey M, lacrosse M, racquetball, rugby, soccer, softball, swimming, tennis, track and field, volleyball, water polo. **Team name:** Dragons.

**Student services.** Adult student services, alcohol/substance abuse counseling, career counseling, student employment services, financial aid counseling, health services, minority student services, on-campus daycare, personal counseling, placement for graduates, veterans' counselor, women's services. **Physically disabled:** Services for visually, speech, hearing impaired.

**Contact.** E-mail: dragon@mnstate.edu
Phone: (218) 477-2161 Toll-free number: (800) 593-7246
Fax: (218) 477-4374
Jeremy Johnson, Director of Admissions, Minnesota State University Moorhead, Owens Hall, Moorhead, MN 56563

## National American University: Bloomington
**Bloomington, Minnesota**
**www.national.edu**                    **CB code: 5358**

- For-profit 4-year branch campus and business college
- Commuter campus in very large city
- 400 degree-seeking undergraduates

**General.** Founded in 1974. Regionally accredited. Campuses in Bloomington/ Mall of America, Brooklyn Center and Roseville. **Degrees:** 20 bachelor's, 13 associate awarded; master's offered. **Calendar:** Quarter, extensive summer session. **Full-time faculty:** 5 total. **Part-time faculty:** 65 total. **Class size:** 95% < 20, 5% 20-39.

**Basis for selection.** Open admission.

**2009-2010 Annual costs.** Tuition/fees: $14,975. Required fees include a one-time matriculation fee ($50) and one-time assessment fee ($75). Books/ supplies: $1,000.

**Financial aid. Non-need-based:** Scholarships awarded for academics.

**Application procedures. Admission:** No deadline. $25 fee. Admission notification on a rolling basis. **Financial aid:** Priority date 8/21; no closing date. FAFSA required. Applicants notified on a rolling basis.

**Academics. Special study options:** Accelerated study, distance learning, double major, independent study, internships. **Credit/placement by examination:** AP, CLEP, IB, institutional tests. **Support services:** Reduced course load, tutoring.

**Majors. Business:** General, accounting, business admin, hospitality admin, international, management information systems, marketing. **Computer sciences:** General, programming.

**Computing on campus.** 112 workstations in library, computer center. Online library available.

**Student life. Freshman orientation:** Mandatory. Preregistration for classes offered. **Activities:** Student government, student business club, Southeast Asian student organization, student government, international student organizations.

**Athletics. Team name:** Mavericks.

**Student services.** Career counseling, student employment services, placement for graduates.

**Contact.** E-mail: mmottl@national.edu
Phone: (952) 883-0439 Toll-free number: (866) 628-6387
Fax: (952) 883-0439
Michael Curtis, Director of Admissions, National American University: Bloomington, Mall of America West 112 West Market, Bloomington, MN 55425

## National American University: Roseville
**Roseville, Minnesota**
**www.national.edu**

- For-profit 4-year university and branch campus college
- Very large city
- 322 degree-seeking undergraduates

**General.** Regionally accredited. **Degrees:** 45 bachelor's, 34 associate awarded. **Calendar:** Quarter. **Part-time faculty:** 39 total.

**Basis for selection.** Open admission.

**2009-2010 Annual costs.** Tuition/fees: $14,975. Required fees include a one-time matriculation fee ($50) and a one-time disk assessment fee ($75).

**Application procedures. Admission:** $25 fee. **Financial aid:** Closing date 8/25.

**Academics. Credit/placement by examination:** CLEP.

**Majors. Business:** Business admin. **Computer sciences:** General.

**Contact.** Nicole Ryan, Director of Admissions, National American University: Roseville, 1550 West Highway 36, Roseville, MN 55431

## North Central University
**Minneapolis, Minnesota**
**www.northcentral.edu**                    **CB code: 0051**

- Private 4-year university and Bible college affiliated with Assemblies of God
- Residential campus in large city
- 1,050 degree-seeking undergraduates: 16% part-time, 57% women
- 100% of applicants admitted
- SAT or ACT (ACT writing optional), application essay required

**General.** Founded in 1930. Regionally accredited. **Degrees:** 204 bachelor's, 10 associate awarded. **ROTC:** Army, Air Force. **Calendar:** Semester, limited summer session. **Full-time faculty:** 42 total; 55% have terminal degrees, 17% minority, 40% women. **Part-time faculty:** 80 total; 15% minority. **Class size:** 49% < 20, 37% 20-39, 10% 40-49, 2% 50-99, 1% >100. **Special facilities:** Private recording studio on-campus, center for youth and leadership, children's literature library.

**Freshman class profile.** 577 applied, 575 admitted, 273 enrolled.

| Mid 50% test scores | | | |
|---|---|---|---|
| SAT critical reading: | 480-580 | GPA 3.0-3.49: | 34% |
| SAT math: | 450-570 | GPA 2.0-2.99: | 34% |
| ACT composite: | 18-24 | Rank in top quarter: | 31% |
| GPA 3.75 or higher: | 14% | Rank in top tenth: | 14% |
| GPA 3.50-3.74: | 17% | Out-of-state: | 61% |
| | | Live on campus: | 93% |

**Basis for selection.** School achievement record, essay character recommendation, and pastor's recommendation are most important. Conditional admission available for students not in good standing at previous institution. Applicants with GPA below 2.2 or ACT scores below 18 may be provisionally admitted. The writing portions of the ACT and SAT are not required and not taken into consideration for admission or scholarship. **Homeschooled:** Statement describing homeschool structure and mission, transcript of courses and grades required. Must meet their state's requirements for graduation.

**High school preparation.** 9 units recommended. Recommended units include English 3, mathematics 1, social studies 2, history 1, science 1 and foreign language 1.

**2010-2011 Annual costs.** Tuition/fees (projected): $16,671. Room/ board: $5,610. Books/supplies: $900.

**2008-2009 Financial aid. Non-need-based:** Scholarships awarded for academics, leadership, music/drama.

**Application procedures. Admission:** Priority date 1/15; deadline 6/1 (postmark date). $25 fee, may be waived for applicants with need. Admission notification on a rolling basis. **Financial aid:** No deadline. FAFSA required. Applicants notified on a rolling basis starting 3/1; must reply within 2 week(s) of notification.

**Academics. Special study options:** Combined bachelor's/graduate degree, double major, dual enrollment of high school students, exchange student, independent study, internships, liberal arts/career combination, student-designed major, study abroad, teacher certification program, weekend college. **Credit/placement by examination:** CLEP, SAT, ACT. **Support services:** Learning center, pre-admission summer program, reduced course load, remedial instruction, study skills assistance, tutoring, writing center.

**Majors. Business:** Business admin. **Communications:** Journalism, media studies. **Education:** Elementary, ESL, secondary. **Foreign languages:** American Sign Language, sign language interpretation. **Health:** Substance abuse counseling. **Interdisciplinary:** Intercultural. **Parks/recreation:** Sports admin. **Philosophy/religion:** Christian, religion. **Psychology:** General. **Public administration:** Social work. **Social sciences:** Urban studies. **Theology:** Bible, missionary, pastoral counseling, religious ed, sacred music, theology, youth ministry. **Visual/performing arts:** Dramatic, music management, music performance. **Other:** Children and family mInistries, deaf culture, worship arts.

**Most popular majors.** Business/marketing 9%, education 9%, family/ consumer sciences 6%, interdisciplinary studies 25%, psychology 10%, theological studies 23%, visual/performing arts 9%.

**Computing on campus.** 120 workstations in dormitories, library, computer center, student center. Dormitories wired for high-speed internet access and linked to campus network. Commuter students can connect to campus network. Online course registration, online library, helpline, wireless network available.

**Student life. Freshman orientation:** Mandatory, $115 fee. Preregistration for classes offered. 4-5 optional dates in the summer months. **Policies:**

North Central requires all members of the community to refrain from any form of sexual immorality. Students must refrain from the possession, use or distribution of non-medical drugs, alcoholic beverages, and tobacco in any form. Religious observance required. **Housing:** Guaranteed on-campus for freshmen. Single-sex dorms, special housing for disabled, apartments, wellness housing available. $200 partly refundable deposit, deadline 6/1. **Activities:** Bands, campus ministries, choral groups, dance, drama, literary magazine, music ensembles, musical theater, student government, student newspaper, leadership development committee, student committee, the Northern Light, SIFE, Alpha Kai, deaf culture fellowship, student senate, student missions fellowship, student activities committee.

**Athletics.** NCAA, NCCAA. **Intercollegiate:** Baseball M, basketball, cross-country, golf M, soccer, softball W, track and field, volleyball W. **Intramural:** Basketball M, football (non-tackle). **Team name:** Rams.

**Student services.** Chaplain/spiritual director, career counseling, student employment services, financial aid counseling, health services, personal counseling, placement for graduates, women's services. **Physically disabled:** Services for visually, speech, hearing impaired.

**Contact.** E-mail: admissions@northcentral.edu
Phone: (612) 343-4460 Toll-free number: (800) 289-6222
Fax: (612) 343-4146
Troy Pearson, Director of Admissions, North Central University, 910 Elliot Avenue, Minneapolis, MN 55404

## Northwestern College
### Saint Paul, Minnesota
www.nwc.edu                              CB code: 6489

- Private 4-year liberal arts college affiliated with nondenominational tradition
- Residential campus in very large city
- 1,852 degree-seeking undergraduates: 3% part-time, 57% women, 2% African American, 4% Asian American, 2% Hispanic American
- 89 degree-seeking graduate students
- 98% of applicants admitted
- SAT or ACT (ACT writing optional), application essay required
- 61% graduate within 6 years; 6% enter graduate study

**General.** Founded in 1902. Regionally accredited. **Degrees:** 376 bachelor's, 6 associate awarded; master's offered. **ROTC:** Army, Air Force. **Location:** 9 miles from Minneapolis-St. Paul. **Calendar:** Semester, limited summer session. **Full-time faculty:** 101 total; 61% have terminal degrees, 10% minority, 35% women. **Part-time faculty:** 81 total; 35% have terminal degrees, 5% minority, 56% women. **Class size:** 52% < 20, 39% 20-39, 5% 40-49, 4% 50-99, less than 1% >100.

**Freshman class profile.** 1,053 applied, 1,032 admitted, 439 enrolled.

| Mid 50% test scores | | | |
|---|---|---|---|
| SAT critical reading: | 520-650 | Rank in top quarter: | 47% |
| SAT math: | 460-610 | Rank in top tenth: | 21% |
| ACT composite: | 21-27 | End year in good standing: | 94% |
| GPA 3.75 or higher: | 34% | Return as sophomores: | 79% |
| GPA 3.50-3.74: | 23% | Out-of-state: | 29% |
| GPA 3.0-3.49: | 27% | Live on campus: | 92% |
| GPA 2.0-2.99: | 15% | International: | 1% |

**Basis for selection.** Evidence that student will benefit from the education and contribute to the community important. School record, recommendations, test scores, essay, character, and religious affiliation very important. ACT recommended. Audition required for music students. Portfolio recommended for art students. Interview recommended for borderline students.

**High school preparation.** College-preparatory program recommended. 16 units recommended. Recommended units include English 4, mathematics 3, social studies 3, science 3, foreign language 2 and academic electives 1.

**2010-2011 Annual costs.** Tuition/fees: $24,570. Room/board: $7,720. Books/supplies: $610. Personal expenses: $1,600.

**2008-2009 Financial aid. Need-based:** 408 full-time freshmen applied for aid; 348 were judged to have need; 348 of these received aid. Average need met was 70%. Average scholarship/grant was $11,949; average loan $3,830. 62% of total undergraduate aid awarded as scholarships/grants, 38% as loans/jobs. **Non-need-based:** Awarded to 392 full-time undergraduates, including 94 freshmen. Scholarships awarded for academics, alumni affiliation, leadership, music/drama. **Additional information:** Students enrolled at least half-time in the FOCUS or Distance Education degree programs may apply for financial aid from the same Federal and state sources as

traditional undergraduates. However, their expense budgets and aid are less due to lower tuition: FOCUS, $345/credit; Center for Distance Education, $260/credit.

**Application procedures. Admission:** Priority date 5/1; deadline 8/1 (receipt date). $30 fee, may be waived for applicants with need. Admission notification on a rolling basis beginning on or about 10/1. **Financial aid:** Priority date 3/1, closing date 8/1. FAFSA, institutional form required. Applicants notified on a rolling basis starting 3/1; must reply within 2 week(s) of notification.

**Academics.** Core curriculum built around a biblical worldview theme thoroughly integrates general education and biblical studies (64-68 credits). Transfer students meet core curriculum requirements on a proportional basis. **Special study options:** Combined bachelor's/graduate degree, distance learning, double major, exchange student, honors, independent study, internships, liberal arts/career combination, student-designed major, study abroad, teacher certification program, Washington semester. **Credit/placement by examination:** AP, CLEP, IB, SAT, ACT, institutional tests. 32 credit hours maximum toward associate degree, 32 toward bachelor's. **Support services:** Learning center, reduced course load, remedial instruction, study skills assistance, tutoring.

**Majors. Biology:** General, biochemistry. **Business:** Accounting, business admin, finance, international, management information systems, marketing. **Communications:** General, journalism, public relations, radio/tv. **Communications technology:** Animation/special effects. **Education:** Art, early childhood, elementary, English, ESL, mathematics, music, physical, social studies. **Foreign languages:** Spanish. **History:** General. **Math:** General. **Parks/recreation:** Exercise sciences, health/fitness. **Protective services:** Criminal justice. **Psychology:** General. **Social sciences:** Urban studies. **Theology:** Bible, missionary, preministerial, youth ministry. **Visual/performing arts:** Dramatic, graphic design, music performance, music theory/composition, piano/organ, stringed instruments, studio arts, voice/opera. **Other:** Children and family ministry.

**Most popular majors.** Business/marketing 16%, communications/journalism 10%, education 19%, psychology 10%, theological studies 17%, visual/performing arts 8%.

**Computing on campus.** PC or laptop required. 100 workstations in dormitories, library, computer center, student center. Dormitories wired for high-speed internet access and linked to campus network. Commuter students can connect to campus network. Online course registration, online library, helpline, student web hosting, wireless network available.

**Student life. Freshman orientation:** Mandatory. Preregistration for classes offered. 6 one-day events during summer. General orientation: 4 days prior to start of classes. Multicultural orientation: 4 days prior to general orientation. **Policies:** Religious observance required. **Housing:** Guaranteed on-campus for freshmen. Single-sex dorms, special housing for disabled, apartments, wellness housing available. **Activities:** Bands, campus ministries, choral groups, drama, literary magazine, music ensembles, musical theater, opera, radio station, student government, student newspaper, symphony orchestra, TV station, Student Missions Fellowship, The Gathering, Transfer Student Organization, Guardian Angels, Mu Kappa, Inter-cultural Unity Organization, Young Republicans.

**Athletics.** NCAA, NCCAA. **Intercollegiate:** Baseball M, basketball, cross-country, football (tackle) M, golf M, soccer, softball W, tennis, track and field, volleyball W. **Intramural:** Basketball, football (non-tackle), softball, table tennis, tennis, volleyball. **Team name:** Eagles.

**Student services.** Adult student services, chaplain/spiritual director, career counseling, student employment services, financial aid counseling, health services, minority student services, personal counseling, placement for graduates.

**Contact.** E-mail: admissions@nwc.edu
Phone: (651) 631-5111 Toll-free number: (800) 827-6827
Fax: (651) 631-5680
Kenneth Faffler, Director of Admissions, Northwestern College, 3003 Snelling Avenue North, Saint Paul, MN 55113-1598

## Northwestern Health Sciences University
### Bloomington, Minnesota
www.nwhealth.edu

- Private two-year upper-division university and health science college
- Very large city

**General.** Regionally accredited. **Degrees:** 44 bachelor's awarded; master's, professional offered. **Calendar:** Trimester, limited summer session. **Full-time faculty:** 80 total. **Part-time faculty:** 38 total.

**Student profile.** 64 degree-seeking undergraduates, 764 graduate students.

**2009-2010 Annual costs.** Massage therapy certificate program: $318 per-credit-hour charge (tuition), $190 per-trimester (required fees); undergraduate studies program: $348 per-credit-hour charge (tuition), $85 per-trimester (required fees). Books/supplies: $972. Personal expenses: $2,400.

**Application procedures.** Admission: $50 fee.

**Academics.** Credit/placement by examination: CLEP.

**Majors.** Other: Human biology.

**Computing on campus.** Wireless network available.

**Contact.** E-mail: admit@nwhealth.edu
Phone: (952) 888-4777 ext. 409
Bill Kuehl, Director of Admissions, Northwestern Health Sciences University, 2501 West 84th Street, Bloomington, MN 55431

## Oak Hills Christian College
### Bemidji, Minnesota
### www.oakhills.edu
CB code: 7247

- Private 4-year Bible college affiliated with interdenominational tradition
- Residential campus in large town
- 149 degree-seeking undergraduates: 17% part-time, 52% women
- 67% of applicants admitted
- Application essay required

**General.** Founded in 1946. Accredited by ABHE. **Degrees:** 27 bachelor's, 3 associate awarded. **Location:** 4 miles from Bemidji, 230 miles from Minneapolis-St. Paul. **Calendar:** Semester. **Full-time faculty:** 6 total; 67% have terminal degrees, 33% women. **Part-time faculty:** 11 total; 27% have terminal degrees, 36% women. **Class size:** 67% < 20, 22% 20-39, 9% 40-49, 2% 50-99. **Special facilities:** Center for Indian ministries resource center.

**Freshman class profile.** 58 applied, 39 admitted, 38 enrolled.

| Mid 50% test scores | | | |
|---|---|---|---|
| ACT composite: | 17-23 | GPA 2.0-2.99: | 55% |
| GPA 3.75 or higher: | 7% | Rank in top quarter: | 17% |
| GPA 3.50-3.74: | 18% | Return as sophomores: | 78% |
| GPA 3.0-3.49: | 15% | Out-of-state: | 30% |
| | | Live on campus: | 96% |

**Basis for selection.** Applicants must have high school GPA of 2.0 or above and/or ACT score of 18 or above to be eligible for consideration. Applicants not meeting minimum requirements considered on individual basis. SAT/ACT scores must be received at latest 4 weeks after first day of classes. Not required if student has 1 year of college credit or if 2 years out of high school. An essay or personal statement may generate an interview. **Homeschooled:** Transcript of courses and grades, letter of recommendation (nonparent) required. Proof of graduation from high school. **Learning Disabled:** All special education or diagnostic (IEP) records required. Interview may be requested.

**2010-2011 Annual costs.** Tuition/fees (projected): $13,730. Room/board: $4,840. Books/supplies: $730. Personal expenses: $2,975.

**2008-2009 Financial aid.** Non-need-based: Scholarships awarded for academics, alumni affiliation.

**Application procedures.** Admission: No deadline. $25 fee, may be waived for applicants with need. Admission notification on a rolling basis beginning on or about 9/1. Early Admission of high school students is allowed if they are PSEO students. **Financial aid:** No deadline. FAFSA, institutional form required. Applicants notified on a rolling basis starting 3/1.

**Academics.** Special study options: Combined bachelor's/graduate degree, cooperative education, double major, independent study, internships. **Credit/placement by examination:** AP, CLEP, ACT, institutional tests. **Support services:** Learning center, reduced course load, remedial instruction, study skills assistance, tutoring, writing center.

**Majors.** Liberal arts: Arts/sciences. Psychology: General. Theology: Bible, missionary, sacred music, youth ministry. Other: Children's Ministry, Small Business Administration.

**Most popular majors.** Liberal arts 17%, theological studies 83%.

**Computing on campus.** 12 workstations in library. Dormitories wired for high-speed internet access and linked to campus network. Online course registration, online library, wireless network available.

**Student life.** Freshman orientation: Mandatory. Preregistration for classes offered. Held first weekend prior to start of fall classes. **Policies:** Mandatory chapel, no alcohol, illegal drugs, gambling, or smoking on campus. Religious observance required. **Housing:** Guaranteed on-campus for freshmen. Single-sex dorms, special housing for disabled, apartments, wellness housing available. $100 nonrefundable deposit, deadline 8/31. Apartments for students with dependent children. **Activities:** Campus ministries, choral groups, music ensembles, student government, married students group, students older than average group, women's group, engaged couples group, many outreach programs, single student cell groups.

**Athletics.** Intercollegiate: Basketball M, volleyball W. **Intramural:** Basketball, football (non-tackle), golf, racquetball, soccer, softball, table tennis, volleyball. **Team name:** Wolfpack.

**Student services.** Adult student services, chaplain/spiritual director, career counseling, student employment services, financial aid counseling, health services, placement for graduates. **Physically disabled:** Services for visually, speech, hearing impaired. **Learning disabled:** Comprehensive services available.

**Contact.** E-mail: admissions@oakhills.edu
Phone: (218) 751-8671 ext. 1285 Toll-free number: (888) 751-8670 ext. 1285 Fax: (218) 751-8825
Karen Stish, Director of Admissions, Oak Hills Christian College, 1600 Oak Hills Road SW, Bemidji, MN 56601-8826

## Rasmussen College: Lake Elmo/Woodbury
### Lake Elmo, Minnesota
### www.rasmussen.edu

- For-profit 4-year technical college
- Small city
- 749 degree-seeking undergraduates

**General.** Regionally accredited. **Degrees:** 2 bachelor's, 50 associate awarded. **Calendar:** Quarter. **Full-time faculty:** 11 total. **Part-time faculty:** 20 total.

**Basis for selection.** Open admission, but selective for some programs.

**2009-2010 Annual costs.** Regular courses are $420 per credit hour; networking classes: $535/credit; child care classes: $295/credit. Personal expenses: $2,214.

**Application procedures.** Admission: $60 fee.

**Academics.** Credit/placement by examination: CLEP.

**Majors.** Business: Business admin.

**Contact.** E-mail: patrick.green@rasmussen.edu
Phone: (651) 259-6600
Patrick Green, Director of Admissions, Rasmussen College: Lake Elmo/Woodbury, 8565 Eagle Point Circle, Lake Elmo, MN 55042-8637

## St. Catherine University
### Saint Paul, Minnesota
CB member
### www.stkate.edu
CB code: 6105

- Private 4-year health science and liberal arts college for women affiliated with Roman Catholic Church
- Commuter campus in large city
- 3,689 degree-seeking undergraduates: 33% part-time, 97% women, 11% African American, 10% Asian American, 3% Hispanic American, 1% Native American, 1% international
- 1,480 degree-seeking graduate students
- 67% of applicants admitted
- SAT or ACT (ACT writing optional) required
- 63% graduate within 6 years

**General.** Founded in 1905. Regionally accredited. Men may attend classes through cross-registration. Traditional day, weekend and graduate programs offered on St. Paul campus. 2-year associate's program in various health professions at Minneapolis campus. **Degrees:** 557 bachelor's, 181 associate awarded; master's, professional offered. **ROTC:** Army, Air Force. **Location:** 6 miles from downtown. **Calendar:** 4-1-4, extensive summer session. **Full-time faculty:** 286 total; 76% have terminal degrees, 8% minority, 81%

women. **Part-time faculty:** 161 total; 52% have terminal degrees, 8% minority, 79% women. **Class size:** 55% < 20, 41% 20-39, 2% 40-49, 2% 50-99, less than 1% >100. **Special facilities:** Center for women's research, observatory.

**Freshman class profile.** 2,151 applied, 1,445 admitted, 414 enrolled.

| Mid 50% test scores | | | |
|---|---|---|---|
| ACT composite: | 21-26 | Rank in top quarter: | 60% |
| GPA 3.75 or higher: | 32% | Rank in top tenth: | 26% |
| GPA 3.50-3.74: | 27% | Return as sophomores: | 78% |
| GPA 3.0-3.49: | 34% | Out-of-state: | 11% |
| GPA 2.0-2.99: | 7% | Live on campus: | 79% |
| | | International: | 1% |

**Basis for selection.** School achievement record with rank in top half of class and test scores important. Extracurricular and community involvement also considered. Recommendations important. Interview recommended for all applicants, required for marginal students. Audition recommended for music students; portfolio recommended for art students. Essay recommended for marginal students.

**High school preparation.** College-preparatory program recommended. 15 units recommended. Recommended units include English 4, mathematics 3, social studies 2, science 2 and foreign language 4.

**2009-2010 Annual costs.** Tuition/fees: $27,078. Room/board: $7,330. Books/supplies: $625. Personal expenses: $400.

**2008-2009 Financial aid. Need-based:** 340 full-time freshmen applied for aid; 305 were judged to have need; 305 of these received aid. Average need met was 86%. Average scholarship/grant was $11,400; average loan $6,250. 38% of total undergraduate aid awarded as scholarships/grants, 62% as loans/jobs. **Non-need-based:** Awarded to 1,156 full-time undergraduates, including 293 freshmen. Scholarships awarded for academics, alumni affiliation, leadership, state residency. **Additional information:** Audition required for music scholarships.

**Application procedures. Admission:** No deadline. No application fee. Admission notification on a rolling basis. Must reply by May 1 or within 2 week(s) if notified thereafter. Students must be accepted by 2/1 to be eligible to compete in merit scholarship competition. **Financial aid:** Priority date 4/15; no closing date. FAFSA, institutional form required. Applicants notified on a rolling basis starting 3/30; must reply within 2 week(s) of notification.

**Academics. Special study options:** Combined bachelor's/graduate degree, cross-registration, double major, dual enrollment of high school students, exchange student, honors, independent study, internships, student-designed major, study abroad, teacher certification program, urban semester, Washington semester, weekend college. Cooperative program in fashion merchandising with Fashion Institute of Technology in New York City and Fashion Institute of Design in Los Angeles, academic year of study in New York City, exchange program with other Carondolet Colleges, internship program includes over 500 sites in Twin Cities area. **Credit/placement by examination:** AP, CLEP, IB, institutional tests. 32 credit hours maximum toward bachelor's degree. **Support services:** Learning center, reduced course load, study skills assistance, tutoring, writing center.

**Majors. Area/ethnic studies:** Women's. **Biology:** General, biochemistry. **Business:** Accounting, business admin, fashion, international, management information systems, sales/distribution. **Communications:** General. **Computer sciences:** General, information systems. **Education:** General, art, business, early childhood, elementary, English, family/consumer sciences, foreign languages, mathematics, middle, music, physical, secondary. **Family/consumer sciences:** General, food/nutrition. **Foreign languages:** American Sign Language, French, sign language interpretation, Spanish. **Health:** Dietetics, medical records admin, nursing (RN), predental, premedicine, prepharmacy, preveterinary, respiratory therapy technology. **History:** General. **Interdisciplinary:** Intercultural. **Legal studies:** Prelaw. **Math:** General. **Parks/recreation:** Exercise sciences. **Philosophy/religion:** Philosophy. **Physical sciences:** Chemistry, physics. **Psychology:** General. **Public administration:** Social work. **Social sciences:** General, economics, international relations, political science, sociology. **Theology:** Theology. **Visual/performing arts:** Art history/conservation, dramatic, fashion design, music performance, studio arts.

**Most popular majors.** Business/marketing 15%, English 7%, foreign language 6%, health sciences 23%, social sciences 6%.

**Computing on campus.** 350 workstations in dormitories, library, computer center, student center. Dormitories wired for high-speed internet access and linked to campus network. Commuter students can connect to campus network. Online course registration, online library, helpline available.

**Student life. Freshman orientation:** Mandatory. **Housing:** Guaranteed on-campus for freshmen. Apartments available. $100 deposit. Apartments for student-parents available. **Activities:** Concert band, campus ministries,

choral groups, dance, drama, international student organizations, literary magazine, music ensembles, musical theater, student government, student newspaper, Volunteers in Action, League of Women Voters, Minnesota Public Interest Research Group, Women of Color, clubs for majors, women's issues groups.

**Athletics.** NCAA. **Intercollegiate:** Basketball W, cross-country W, diving W, ice hockey W, soccer W, softball W, swimming W, tennis W, track and field W, volleyball W. **Intramural:** Basketball W, cheerleading W, football (non-tackle) W, golf W, lacrosse W, racquetball W, soccer W, softball W, tennis W, volleyball W. **Team name:** Wildcats.

**Student services.** Adult student services, chaplain/spiritual director, career counseling, student employment services, financial aid counseling, health services, minority student services, on-campus daycare, personal counseling, placement for graduates, women's services. **Physically disabled:** Services for visually, speech, hearing impaired.

**Contact.** E-mail: admissions@stkate.edu
Phone: (651) 690-8850 Toll-free number: (800) 945-4599
Fax: (651) 690-8824
Brian Bruess, Vice President of Enrollment Management and Dean of Students, St. Catherine University, 2004 Randolph Avenue #4-02, St. Paul, MN 55105

## Saint Cloud State University
St. Cloud, Minnesota
www.stcloudstate.edu — CB code: 6679

- Public 4-year university
- Commuter campus in small city
- 13,718 degree-seeking undergraduates: 12% part-time, 50% women, 4% African American, 3% Asian American, 1% Hispanic American, 1% Native American, 6% international
- 1,732 degree-seeking graduate students
- 87% of applicants admitted
- SAT or ACT (ACT writing optional) required
- 48% graduate within 6 years

**General.** Founded in 1869. Regionally accredited. **Degrees:** 2,581 bachelor's, 120 associate awarded; master's, doctoral offered. **ROTC:** Army. **Location:** 80 miles from Minneapolis-St. Paul. **Calendar:** Semester, limited summer session. **Full-time faculty:** 668 total; 82% have terminal degrees. **Part-time faculty:** 271 total; 22% have terminal degrees. **Class size:** 32% < 20, 55% 20-39, 7% 40-49, 4% 50-99, 2% >100. **Special facilities:** Planetarium, greenhouse, nature preserve, observatory, GIS cartographic center, aviation facilities, weather labs, National Hockey Center, AVID editing equipment.

**Freshman class profile.** 6,025 applied, 5,241 admitted, 2,390 enrolled.

| Mid 50% test scores | | | |
|---|---|---|---|
| ACT composite: | 19-24 | Return as sophomores: | 71% |
| Rank in top quarter: | 22% | Out-of-state: | 10% |
| Rank in top tenth: | 5% | Live on campus: | 71% |
| | | International: | 2% |

**Basis for selection.** Each application individually reviewed and evaluated using a combination of high school rank, GPA, curriculum, test scores, and other indicators of academic performance and potential.

**High school preparation.** College-preparatory program required. 16 units required. Required units include English 4, mathematics 3, social studies 2, history 1, science 3 (laboratory 1), foreign language 2 and visual/performing arts 1.

**2009-2010 Annual costs.** Tuition/fees: $6,330; $13,844 out-of-state. Room/board: $6,016. Books/supplies: $1,200. Personal expenses: $2,884.

**2009-2010 Financial aid. Non-need-based:** Scholarships awarded for academics, art, athletics, leadership, music/drama.

**Application procedures. Admission:** Priority date 5/1; deadline 6/1 (receipt date). $20 fee, may be waived for applicants with need. Admission notification on a rolling basis beginning on or about 9/15. Early application recommended for those who want to live on-campus. **Financial aid:** No deadline. FAFSA, institutional form required. Applicants notified on a rolling basis starting 6/15.

**Academics. Special study options:** Accelerated study, cooperative education, cross-registration, distance learning, double major, dual enrollment of high school students, ESL, honors, independent study, internships, student-designed major, study abroad, teacher certification program, weekend college. **Credit/placement by examination:** AP, CLEP, IB, institutional tests.

32 credit hours maximum toward bachelor's degree. **Support services:** Learning center, pre-admission summer program, remedial instruction, study skills assistance, tutoring, writing center.

**Majors. Area/ethnic studies:** Latin American, women's. **Biology:** General, aquatic, biochemistry, biotechnology, cellular/anatomical, ecology, marine. **Business:** General, accounting, business admin, entrepreneurial studies, finance, human resources, insurance, international, management information systems, marketing, real estate, tourism/travel. **Communications:** General, advertising, broadcast journalism, journalism, media studies, public relations, radio/tv. **Computer sciences:** General, computer science, networking, security. **Conservation:** Environmental science, environmental studies. **Education:** Art, biology, chemistry, drama/dance, driver/safety, early childhood, elementary, English, foreign languages, French, German, health, history, instructional media, kindergarten/preschool, mathematics, multi-level teacher, music, physical, physics, psychology, reading, science, secondary, social science, social studies, Spanish, special, speech, technology/industrial arts, voc/tech. **Engineering:** Computer, electrical, manufacturing, mechanical. **Engineering technology:** Surveying. **Foreign languages:** French, German, linguistics, Spanish. **Health:** Audiology/speech pathology, clinical lab science, communication disorders, community health services, medical radiologic technology/radiation therapy, nuclear medical technology, nursing (RN), predental, premedicine, prepharmacy, preveterinary, public health ed, recreational therapy, substance abuse counseling. **History:** General. **Interdisciplinary:** Gerontology, global studies, natural sciences. **Legal studies:** Prelaw. **Liberal arts:** Arts/sciences, library science. **Math:** General, statistics. **Parks/recreation:** General, health/fitness. **Philosophy/religion:** Philosophy. **Physical sciences:** General, atmospheric science, chemistry, geology, hydrology, meteorology, physics, planetary. **Protective services:** Criminal justice. **Psychology:** General, community. **Public administration:** General, social work. **Social sciences:** General, anthropology, econometrics, economics, geography, international relations, political science, sociology, urban studies. **Transportation:** Air traffic control, airline/commercial pilot, aviation management, flight instructor. **Visual/performing arts:** Acting, art, art history/conservation, ceramics, dramatic, drawing, film/cinema, jazz, music history, music performance, painting, piano/organ, printmaking, sculpture, stringed instruments, studio arts, voice/opera. **Other:** Business economics, Earth science.

**Most popular majors.** Business/marketing 27%, communications/journalism 9%, education 12%, psychology 9%, social sciences 7%.

**Computing on campus.** 1,489 workstations in dormitories, library, computer center, student center. Dormitories wired for high-speed internet access and linked to campus network. Commuter students can connect to campus network. Online course registration, online library, helpline, repair service, student web hosting, wireless network available.

**Student life. Freshman orientation:** Mandatory. Preregistration for classes offered. Includes assistance with fall term registration. **Housing:** Coed dorms, single-sex dorms, special housing for disabled, apartments available. $100 fully refundable deposit, deadline 3/31. **Activities:** Bands, campus ministries, choral groups, dance, drama, film society, international student organizations, literary magazine, music ensembles, Model UN, musical theater, opera, radio station, student government, student newspaper, symphony orchestra, TV station, more than 240 clubs and departmental organizations.

**Athletics.** NCAA. **Intercollegiate:** Baseball M, basketball, cross-country, diving, football (tackle) M, golf, ice hockey, skiing W, soccer W, softball W, swimming, tennis, track and field, volleyball W, wrestling M. **Intramural:** Badminton, basketball, football (non-tackle), golf, ice hockey, racquetball, soccer, softball, tennis, volleyball, water polo. **Team name:** Huskies.

**Student services.** Adult student services, alcohol/substance abuse counseling, career counseling, student employment services, financial aid counseling, health services, legal services, minority student services, on-campus daycare, personal counseling, placement for graduates, veterans' counselor, women's services. **Physically disabled:** Services for visually, speech, hearing impaired.

**Contact.** E-mail: scsu4u@stcloudstate.edu
Phone: (320) 308-2244 Toll-free number: (877) 654-7278
Fax: (320) 308-2243
Richard Shearer, Director of Admissions, Saint Cloud State University, 720 Fourth Avenue South, St. Cloud, MN 56301

---

## St. John's University

**Collegeville, Minnesota**

www.csbsju.edu

CB member
CB code: 6624

- Private 4-year university and liberal arts college for men affiliated with Roman Catholic Church
- Residential campus in rural community

---

- 1,915 degree-seeking undergraduates: 3% part-time, 2% African American, 3% Asian American, 2% Hispanic American, 7% international
- 105 graduate students
- 84% of applicants admitted
- SAT or ACT (ACT writing optional), application essay required
- 80% graduate within 6 years; 15% enter graduate study

**General.** Founded in 1857. Regionally accredited. SJU located six miles from the College of Saint Benedict; students enrolled on both campuses have access to classes, activities held by the two institutions. **Degrees:** 408 bachelor's awarded; master's offered. **ROTC:** Army. **Location:** 70 miles from Minneapolis-St. Paul, 15 miles from St. Cloud. **Calendar:** Semester, limited summer session. **Full-time faculty:** 147 total; 84% have terminal degrees, 9% minority, 49% women. **Part-time faculty:** 30 total; 37% have terminal degrees, 3% minority, 40% women. **Class size:** 53% < 20, 46% 20-39, less than 1% 40-49, less than 1% 50-99, less than 1% >100. **Special facilities:** Observatory, ecumenical center, Hill Museum and Manuscript library, arboretum, natural history museum, pottery studio, greenhouse and herbarium.

**Freshman class profile.** 1,344 applied, 1,125 admitted, 461 enrolled.

| Mid 50% test scores | | | |
|---|---|---|---|
| SAT critical reading: | 490-650 | GPA 2.0-2.99: | 8% |
| SAT math: | 520-680 | Rank in top quarter: | 58% |
| SAT writing: | 480-590 | Rank in top tenth: | 23% |
| ACT composite: | 23-29 | End year in good standing: | 92% |
| GPA 3.75 or higher: | 32% | Return as sophomores: | 90% |
| GPA 3.50-3.74: | 28% | Out-of-state: | 18% |
| GPA 3.0-3.49: | 32% | Live on campus: | 100% |
| | | International: | 8% |

**Basis for selection.** Course selection, scholastic achievement, GPA, test scores and essay are most important. Extracurricular involvement and recommendations are also important. Scholarship letters will be mailed on a rolling basis approximately two weeks from the time the admission acceptance letter is sent. Interview recommended for conditionally accepted/academically weak students. **Homeschooled:** Applicants are not required to have a high school diploma, but are required to provide appropriate documentation of college preparatory curriculum.

**High school preparation.** College-preparatory program required. 15 units required. Required and recommended units include English 4, mathematics 3, social studies 2, science 2 (laboratory 2), foreign language 2 and academic electives 4.

**2009-2010 Annual costs.** Tuition/fees: $29,886. Room/board: $7,714. Books/supplies: $900. Personal expenses: $800.

**2009-2010 Financial aid. Need-based:** 361 full-time freshmen applied for aid; 275 were judged to have need; 275 of these received aid. Average need met was 96%. Average scholarship/grant was $20,744; average loan $4,234. 62% of total undergraduate aid awarded as scholarships/grants, 38% as loans/jobs. **Non-need-based:** Awarded to 1,652 full-time undergraduates, including 410 freshmen. Scholarships awarded for academics, art, leadership, music/drama, ROTC.

**Application procedures. Admission:** Priority date 11/15; no deadline. No application fee. A non-refundable enrollment deposit of $300 is due by May 1. **Financial aid:** Priority date 3/15; no closing date. FAFSA, institutional form required. Applicants notified on a rolling basis starting 3/15; must reply by 5/1.

**Academics. Special study options:** Combined bachelor's/graduate degree, cross-registration, double major, dual enrollment of high school students, ESL, exchange student, honors, independent study, internships, student-designed major, study abroad, teacher certification program. 3-2 program in engineering with University of Minnesota, 3-1 program in dentistry with University of Minnesota, cross registration with St. Cloud State University. **Credit/placement by examination:** AP, CLEP, IB, SAT, ACT, institutional tests. **Support services:** Reduced course load, study skills assistance, tutoring, writing center.

**Majors. Area/ethnic studies:** Women's. **Biology:** General, biochemistry. **Business:** Accounting, business admin. **Computer sciences:** Computer science. **Conservation:** Environmental science. **Education:** General, elementary. **Foreign languages:** Classics, French, German, Spanish. **Health:** Dietetics, nursing (RN), predental, premedicine, prepharmacy, preveterinary. **History:** General. **Interdisciplinary:** Biological/physical sciences, math/computer science, natural sciences, nutrition sciences, peace/conflict. **Legal studies:** Prelaw. **Liberal arts:** Arts/sciences, humanities. **Math:** General. **Philosophy/religion:** Philosophy. **Physical sciences:** Chemistry, physics. **Psychology:** General. **Social sciences:** General, economics, political science, sociology. **Theology:** Preministerial, theology. **Visual/performing arts:** Art, dramatic.

**Most popular majors.** Biology 8%, business/marketing 31%, English 9%, social sciences 14%.

**Computing on campus.** 860 workstations in dormitories, library, computer center, student center. Dormitories wired for high-speed internet access and linked to campus network. Commuter students can connect to campus network. Online course registration, online library, helpline, repair service, student web hosting, wireless network available.

**Student life. Freshman orientation:** Mandatory. Preregistration for classes offered. Fall orientation begins the evening of move-in day and concludes with convocation the first day of classes. **Policies:** Four year residency requirement. **Housing:** Guaranteed on-campus for freshmen. Special housing for disabled, apartments available. **Activities:** Bands, campus ministries, choral groups, dance, drama, international student organizations, literary magazine, music ensembles, Model UN, musical theater, opera, radio station, student government, student newspaper, symphony orchestra, Volunteers in Service to Others, College Republicans, College Democrats, Joints Events Council, Asia club, Student Coalition for Global Solidarity, Students in Free Enterprise, Magis, Cultural Fusion Club, Outdoor Leadership center.

**Athletics.** NCAA. **Intercollegiate:** Baseball M, basketball M, cross-country M, diving M, football (tackle) M, golf M, ice hockey M, skiing M, soccer M, swimming M, tennis M, track and field M, wrestling M. **Intramural:** Basketball M, football (tackle) M, ice hockey M, racquetball M, soccer M, softball M, table tennis M, tennis M, volleyball M, water polo M. **Team name:** Johnnies.

**Student services.** Alcohol/substance abuse counseling, chaplain/spiritual director, career counseling, financial aid counseling, health services, minority student services, personal counseling, placement for graduates. **Physically disabled:** Services for hearing impaired.

**Contact.** E-mail: admissions@csbsju.edu
Phone: (320) 363-2196 Toll-free number: (800) 544-1489
Fax: (320) 363-2750
Cal Mosley, Vice President for Admission and Financial Aid, St. John's University, College of St Benedict/St John's University, Collegeville, MN 56321-7155

## St. Mary's University of Minnesota

| Winona, Minnesota | CB member |
| www.smumn.edu | CB code: 6632 |

- Private 4-year university affiliated with Roman Catholic Church
- Residential campus in large town
- 2,046 degree-seeking undergraduates: 30% part-time, 52% women, 3% African American, 2% Asian American, 3% Hispanic American, 3% international
- 3,217 degree-seeking graduate students
- 72% of applicants admitted
- SAT or ACT (ACT writing optional), application essay required
- 55% graduate within 6 years

**General.** Founded in 1912. Regionally accredited. **Degrees:** 437 bachelor's awarded; master's, doctoral, professional offered. **ROTC:** Army. **Location:** 110 miles from Minneapolis-St. Paul, 45 miles from Rochester. **Calendar:** Semester, limited summer session. **Full-time faculty:** 103 total; 84% have terminal degrees, 3% minority, 38% women. **Part-time faculty:** 482 total; 38% have terminal degrees, 7% minority, 53% women. **Class size:** 51% < 20, 48% 20-39, less than 1% 40-49. **Special facilities:** Woodland and stream, nature preserve, observatory.

**Freshman class profile.** 1,408 applied, 1,020 admitted, 330 enrolled.

| Mid 50% test scores | | GPA 2.0-2.99: | 35% |
| --- | --- | --- | --- |
| SAT critical reading: | 500-560 | Rank in top quarter: | 41% |
| SAT math: | 460-610 | Rank in top tenth: | 18% |
| ACT composite: | 19-26 | Return as sophomores: | 75% |
| GPA 3.75 or higher: | 22% | Out-of-state: | 35% |
| GPA 3.50-3.74: | 13% | Live on campus: | 97% |
| GPA 3.0-3.49: | 27% | International: | 3% |

**Basis for selection.** Minimum 2.5 GPA, upper half of class, 50th percentile on standardized tests, essay, college prep coursework required. Recommendations, interview, school and community activities considered. Interview recommended for academically marginal students. **Homeschooled:** Statement describing homeschool structure and mission, transcript of courses and grades required.

**High school preparation.** College-preparatory program required. 18 units required. Required and recommended units include English 4, mathematics 3, social studies 2, science 3 (laboratory 2), foreign language 2 and academic electives 6.

**2009-2010 Annual costs.** Tuition/fees: $25,100. Room/board: $6,700. Books/supplies: $1,220. Personal expenses: $850.

**2009-2010 Financial aid. Need-based:** 300 full-time freshmen applied for aid; 269 were judged to have need; 269 of these received aid. Average need met was 82%. Average scholarship/grant was $16,374; average loan $4,091. 62% of total undergraduate aid awarded as scholarships/grants, 38% as loans/jobs. **Non-need-based:** Awarded to 345 full-time undergraduates, including 58 freshmen. Scholarships awarded for academics, alumni affiliation, art, leadership, minority status, music/drama.

**Application procedures. Admission:** Priority date 4/1; deadline 5/1 (postmark date). $25 fee, may be waived for applicants with need, free for online applicants. Admission notification 5/1. Admission notification on a rolling basis. Must reply by May 1 or within 2 week(s) if notified thereafter. **Financial aid:** Priority date 3/15; no closing date. FAFSA required. Applicants notified on a rolling basis starting 2/1; must reply within 3 week(s) of notification.

**Academics. Special study options:** Cooperative education, cross-registration, double major, dual enrollment of high school students, ESL, honors, independent study, internships, student-designed major, study abroad, teacher certification program, urban semester, Washington semester. **Credit/placement by examination:** AP, CLEP, IB, SAT, ACT, institutional tests. 15 credit hours maximum toward bachelor's degree. **Support services:** Learning center, reduced course load, remedial instruction, study skills assistance, tutoring, writing center.

**Majors. Biology:** General, biochemistry, biophysics, environmental. **Business:** General, accounting, business admin, entrepreneurial studies, human resources, international, marketing, sales/distribution. **Communications:** Journalism, public relations. **Communications technology:** General. **Computer sciences:** General, computer science, information systems. **Education:** Biology, chemistry, elementary, English, foreign languages, French, mathematics, music, physics, social science, Spanish. **Engineering:** Computer, physics. **Engineering technology:** Industrial. **Foreign languages:** French, Spanish. **Health:** Clinical lab science, cytogenetics, cytotechnology, nuclear medical technology, nursing (RN). **History:** General. **Interdisciplinary:** Global studies, math/computer science. **Math:** General. **Parks/recreation:** Sports admin. **Philosophy/religion:** Philosophy. **Physical sciences:** Chemistry. **Protective services:** Corrections, criminal justice, law enforcement admin, police science, security management. **Psychology:** General. **Public administration:** Human services. **Social sciences:** General, political science, sociology. **Theology:** Preministerial, religious ed, sacred music, theology, youth ministry. **Visual/performing arts:** Dramatic, graphic design, music management, music performance, studio arts. **Other:** Allied healthcare, E-business technology, Electronic publishing.

**Most popular majors.** Business/marketing 46%, security/protective services 9%, visual/performing arts 6%.

**Computing on campus.** 365 workstations in dormitories, library, computer center, student center. Dormitories wired for high-speed internet access and linked to campus network. Commuter students can connect to campus network. Online course registration, online library, helpline, student web hosting, wireless network available.

**Student life. Freshman orientation:** Mandatory. Preregistration for classes offered. Held during summer prior to fall enrollment. **Housing:** Guaranteed on-campus for all undergraduates. Coed dorms, single-sex dorms, special housing for disabled, apartments available. **Activities:** Bands, campus ministries, choral groups, dance, drama, international student organizations, literary magazine, music ensembles, musical theater, radio station, student government, student newspaper, Big and Little Pals, College Democrats, College Republicans, Serving Others United in Love, Intercultural Awareness Association, liturgical ministers, BUDDIES, Habitat for Humanity, Colleges Against Cancer.

**Athletics.** NCAA. **Intercollegiate:** Baseball M, basketball, cross-country, diving, golf, ice hockey, soccer, softball W, swimming, tennis, track and field, volleyball W. **Intramural:** Basketball, football (non-tackle), ice hockey M, racquetball, soccer, softball, tennis, volleyball. **Team name:** Cardinals.

**Student services.** Alcohol/substance abuse counseling, chaplain/spiritual director, career counseling, financial aid counseling, health services, personal counseling. **Physically disabled:** Services for visually, hearing impaired.

**Contact.** E-mail: admission@smumn.edu
Phone: (507) 457-1700 Toll-free number: (800) 635-5987
Fax: (507) 457-1722
Anthony Piscitiello, Vice President for Admission, St. Mary's University of Minnesota, 700 Terrace Heights #2, Winona, MN 55987-1399

## St. Olaf College
**Northfield, Minnesota**
www.stolaf.edu

CB member
CB code: 6638

- Private 4-year liberal arts college affiliated with Evangelical Lutheran Church in America
- Residential campus in large town
- 3,033 degree-seeking undergraduates: 55% women, 2% African American, 5% Asian American, 2% Hispanic American, 2% international
- 57% of applicants admitted
- SAT or ACT (ACT writing optional), application essay required
- 87% graduate within 6 years; 29% enter graduate study

**General.** Founded in 1874. Regionally accredited. **Degrees:** 690 bachelor's awarded. **Location:** 35 miles from Minneapolis-St. Paul. **Calendar:** 4-1-4, limited summer session. **Full-time faculty:** 207 total; 90% have terminal degrees, 11% minority, 44% women. **Part-time faculty:** 120 total; 63% have terminal degrees, 3% minority, 46% women. **Class size:** 60% < 20, 34% 20-39, 2% 40-49, 4% 50-99. **Special facilities:** 325 acres of restored native tallgrass prairie, wetlands, and woodlands, a student-run organic farm adjacent to the campus.

**Freshman class profile.** 3,882 applied, 2,230 admitted, 778 enrolled.

| Mid 50% test scores | | | |
|---|---|---|---|
| SAT critical reading: | 590-710 | GPA 2.0-2.99: | 8% |
| SAT math: | 590-690 | Rank in top quarter: | 82% |
| ACT composite: | 26-31 | Rank in top tenth: | 53% |
| GPA 3.75 or higher: | 52% | Return as sophomores: | 93% |
| GPA 3.50-3.74: | 17% | Out-of-state: | 51% |
| GPA 3.0-3.49: | 23% | Live on campus: | 100% |
| | | International: | 4% |

**Basis for selection.** Academic achievement most important, with academic aptitude and personal qualifications, as well as leadership and significant involvement in school and community, strongly considered. Interview recommended. Audition required for music students. **Learning Disabled:** Personal interview recommended. Untimed standardized tests accepted.

**High school preparation.** College-preparatory program recommended. 24 units recommended. Recommended units include English 4, mathematics 4, social studies 4, science 4 (laboratory 2) and foreign language 4.

**2009-2010 Annual costs.** Tuition/fees: $35,500. Room/board: $8,200. Books/supplies: $1,000. Personal expenses: $900.

**2009-2010 Financial aid. Non-need-based:** Scholarships awarded for academics, leadership, music/drama. **Additional information:** Limited number of music lesson fee waivers available for music majors, awarded on audition basis only.

**Application procedures. Admission:** Closing date 1/15 (postmark date). $40 fee, may be waived for applicants with need, free for online applicants. Admission notification 3/20. Must reply by May 1 or within 2 week(s) if notified thereafter. **Financial aid:** Priority date 1/15, closing date 2/1. FAFSA, CSS PROFILE required. Applicants notified on a rolling basis starting 3/1; must reply by 5/1 or within 2 week(s) of notification.

**Academics.** Students may propose self-designed integrative majors. **Special study options:** Combined bachelor's/graduate degree, cross-registration, double major, dual enrollment of high school students, independent study, internships, student-designed major, study abroad, teacher certification program, urban semester, Washington semester. Great Conversation: 5-semester program emphasizing reading, writing, and outside-of-the-classroom discussion available to 70 incoming students each year; BA/BS in engineering with Washington University (MO), University of Minnesota, Minneapolis; Center for Experiential Learning; undergraduate research in humanities and the sciences, Center for Integrative Studies; study-travel programs in 38 different countries; includes Global semester, Term in Asia, Environmental Studies in Australia, ACM and HECUA program, 30-40 different interims, both domestic and abroad, all with a St. Olaf College faculty member as leader/instructor. **Credit/placement by examination:** AP, CLEP, IB, SAT, ACT, institutional tests. 5 credit hours maximum toward bachelor's degree. **Support services:** Learning center, pre-admission summer program, reduced course load, study skills assistance, tutoring, writing center.

**Majors. Area/ethnic studies:** American, Asian, Latin American, Russian/Slavic, women's. **Biology:** General. **Computer sciences:** Computer science. **Conservation:** Environmental studies. **Education:** Music, social studies. **Foreign languages:** Ancient Greek, classics, French, German, Latin, Norwegian, Russian, Spanish. **Health:** Nursing (RN). **History:** General. **Interdisciplinary:** Ancient studies, medieval/Renaissance. **Liberal arts:** Arts/sciences. **Math:** General. **Parks/recreation:** Exercise sciences. **Philosophy/**

**religion:** Philosophy, religion. **Physical sciences:** Chemistry, physics. **Psychology:** General. **Public administration:** Social work. **Social sciences:** Economics, political science, sociology. **Theology:** Sacred music. **Visual/performing arts:** Art, art history/conservation, dance, dramatic, music performance, music theory/composition. **Other:** American racial and multicultural studies.

**Most popular majors.** Area/ethnic studies 6%, biology 12%, English 6%, foreign language 7%, mathematics 6%, physical sciences 6%, psychology 6%, social sciences 17%, visual/performing arts 12%.

**Computing on campus.** 855 workstations in dormitories, library, computer center, student center. Dormitories wired for high-speed internet access and linked to campus network. Commuter students can connect to campus network. Helpline, wireless network available.

**Student life. Freshman orientation:** Mandatory. Preregistration for classes offered. Held 5 days before start of fall classes. **Policies:** Alcohol not permitted on campus. **Housing:** Guaranteed on-campus for all undergraduates. Coed dorms, special housing for disabled, wellness housing available. Honor houses, language houses, quiet halls, first-year only dorms. **Activities:** Bands, campus ministries, choral groups, dance, drama, film society, international student organizations, literary magazine, music ensembles, Model UN, musical theater, opera, radio station, student government, student newspaper, symphony orchestra, TV station, 193 registered student organizations.

**Athletics.** NCAA. **Intercollegiate:** Baseball M, basketball, cross-country, diving, football (tackle) M, golf, ice hockey, skiing, soccer, softball W, swimming, tennis, track and field, volleyball W, wrestling M. **Intramural:** Basketball, football (non-tackle), golf, racquetball, soccer, softball, swimming, table tennis, tennis, triathlon, volleyball, wrestling. **Team name:** Oles.

**Student services.** Alcohol/substance abuse counseling, chaplain/spiritual director, career counseling, services for economically disadvantaged, student employment services, financial aid counseling, health services, minority student services, personal counseling. **Physically disabled:** Services for visually, hearing impaired.

**Contact.** E-mail: admissions@stolaf.edu
Phone: (507) 786-3025 Toll-free number: (800) 800-3025
Fax: (507) 786-3832
Derek Gueldenzoph, Dean of Admissions, St. Olaf College, 1520 St. Olaf Avenue, Northfield, MN 55057

## Southwest Minnesota State University
**Marshall, Minnesota**
www.smsu.edu

CB code: 6703

- Public 4-year university and liberal arts college
- Residential campus in large town
- 2,584 degree-seeking undergraduates: 13% part-time, 55% women, 3% African American, 3% Asian American, 2% Hispanic American, 8% international
- 509 degree-seeking graduate students
- 65% of applicants admitted
- SAT or ACT (ACT writing optional) required
- 40% graduate within 6 years

**General.** Founded in 1963. Regionally accredited. **Degrees:** 539 bachelor's, 5 associate awarded; master's offered. **Location:** 150 miles from Minneapolis-St. Paul. **Calendar:** Semester, limited summer session. **Full-time faculty:** 122 total; 83% have terminal degrees, 13% minority, 44% women. **Part-time faculty:** 63 total; 33% have terminal degrees, 8% minority, 59% women. **Class size:** 41% < 20, 49% 20-39, 7% 40-49, 3% 50-99, less than 1% >100. **Special facilities:** Natural history museum, anthropology museum, planetarium, wildlife area.

**Freshman class profile.** 2,054 applied, 1,336 admitted, 461 enrolled.

| Mid 50% test scores | | | |
|---|---|---|---|
| ACT composite: | 19-24 | Rank in top tenth: | 13% |
| GPA 3.75 or higher: | 17% | End year in good standing: | 80% |
| GPA 3.50-3.74: | 14% | Return as sophomores: | 69% |
| GPA 3.0-3.49: | 32% | Out-of-state: | 22% |
| GPA 2.0-2.99: | 34% | Live on campus: | 88% |
| Rank in top quarter: | 20% | International: | 4% |

**Basis for selection.** Class rank in top half of class or SAT combined score of 970 (exclusive of Writing) or ACT composite score of 21. Provisional admission may be granted to students who rank in top two-thirds of class or have ACT composite score of 19 or SAT combined score of 890. GED students must submit ACT. ACT recommended. PSAT/NMSQT may be submitted in place of SAT or ACT. Interview recommended for academically weak students; audition recommended for music students. **Home-schooled:** Transcript of courses and grades required.

**High school preparation.** College-preparatory program required. 16 units required. Required units include English 4, mathematics 3, social studies 3, history 1, science 3 and foreign language 2. Social studies units must include American history and geography.

**2009-2010 Annual costs.** Tuition/fees: $6,932. Out-of-state students pay same rate as in-state. Room/board: $6,520. Books/supplies: $1,000. Personal expenses: $1,578.

**2009-2010 Financial aid. Need-based:** 394 full-time freshmen applied for aid; 295 were judged to have need; 291 of these received aid. Average need met was 61%. Average scholarship/grant was $5,598; average loan $3,438. 45% of total undergraduate aid awarded as scholarships/grants, 55% as loans/jobs. **Non-need-based:** Awarded to 1,165 full-time undergraduates, including 300 freshmen. Scholarships awarded for academics, alumni affiliation, art, athletics, leadership, minority status, music/drama, state residency.

**Application procedures. Admission:** Priority date 8/15; deadline 9/1 (receipt date). $20 fee. Admission notification on a rolling basis. **Financial aid:** Priority date 3/1; no closing date. FAFSA, institutional form required. Applicants notified on a rolling basis starting 6/1.

**Academics. Special study options:** Accelerated study, combined bachelor's/graduate degree, cooperative education, cross-registration, distance learning, double major, dual enrollment of high school students, ESL, external degree, honors, independent study, internships, student-designed major, study abroad, teacher certification program. 2+2 bachelor's programs with Ridgewater College, St. Cloud Technical College, Minnesota West, South Central (Mankato) and Riverland College. Visiting Exchange Student Program. **Credit/placement by examination:** CLEP, ACT, institutional tests. 36 credit hours maximum toward associate degree, 36 toward bachelor's. **Support services:** Learning center, reduced course load, remedial instruction, study skills assistance, tutoring, writing center.

**Majors. Agriculture:** Agribusiness operations, food science, soil science. **Biology:** General, cell/histology, ecology. **Business:** Accounting, business admin, finance, hospitality admin, marketing, nonprofit/public, restaurant/food services. **Communications:** General, broadcast journalism, public relations, radio/tv. **Computer sciences:** General, information technology. **Conservation:** Environmental science. **Education:** Art, biology, chemistry, drama/dance, early childhood, elementary, health, mathematics, music, physical, science, speech. **Foreign languages:** Spanish. **History:** General. **Liberal arts:** Arts/sciences. **Math:** General. **Parks/recreation:** Health/fitness. **Philosophy/religion:** Philosophy. **Physical sciences:** Chemistry. **Protective services:** Criminal justice, fire services admin, law enforcement admin. **Psychology:** General. **Public administration:** General, social work. **Social sciences:** Political science, sociology. **Visual/performing arts:** Art, dramatic, music management.

**Most popular majors.** Business/marketing 41%, education 20%, parks/recreation 6%.

**Computing on campus.** 300 workstations in dormitories, library, computer center, student center. Dormitories wired for high-speed internet access and linked to campus network. Commuter students can connect to campus network. Online course registration, online library, helpline, repair service, student web hosting, wireless network available.

**Student life. Freshman orientation:** Available, $125 fee. Preregistration for classes offered. **Housing:** Coed dorms, single-sex dorms, special housing for disabled, apartments available. $100 fully refundable deposit. **Activities:** Bands, campus ministries, choral groups, dance, drama, film society, international student organizations, literary magazine, music ensembles, musical theater, radio station, student government, student newspaper, symphony orchestra, TV station, Black Student Union, Inter-Varsity Christian Fellowship, Lutheran Student Commission, student activities committee, Republican Speakers Club, Young DFL, non-traditional students organization.

**Athletics.** NAIA. **Intercollegiate:** Baseball M, basketball, football (tackle) M, golf W, soccer W, softball W, tennis W, volleyball W, wrestling M. **Intramural:** Basketball, ice hockey M, racquetball, skiing, softball, tennis, track and field, volleyball, wrestling M. **Team name:** Mustangs.

**Student services.** Adult student services, alcohol/substance abuse counseling, chaplain/spiritual director, career counseling, student employment services, financial aid counseling, health services, minority student services, on-campus daycare, personal counseling, placement for graduates, veterans' counselor, women's services. **Physically disabled:** Services for visually, speech, hearing impaired.

**Contact.** E-mail: LeAnn.Thooft@smsu.edu
Phone: (507) 537-6286 Toll-free number: (800) 642-0684
Fax: (507) 537-7154
LeAnn Thooft, Director of Admissions, Southwest Minnesota State University; 1501 State Street, Marshall, MN 56258-1598

## University of Minnesota: Crookston
**Crookston, Minnesota**
www.UMCrookston.edu                              CB code: 6893

- Public 4-year branch campus college
- Commuter campus in small town
- 1,310 degree-seeking undergraduates: 18% part-time, 42% women, 5% African American, 2% Asian American, 3% Hispanic American, 1% Native American, 8% international
- 83% of applicants admitted
- SAT or ACT (ACT writing optional) required
- 33% graduate within 6 years

**General.** Founded in 1965. Regionally accredited. **Degrees:** 239 bachelor's, 14 associate awarded. **ROTC:** Air Force. **Location:** 25 miles from Grand Forks, North Dakota, 170 miles from Winnipeg, Canada. **Calendar:** Semester, limited summer session. **Class size:** 54% < 20, 35% 20-39, 8% 40-49, 3% 50-99. **Special facilities:** 85-acre Red River Valley natural history area with prairie, marshes and forests.

**Freshman class profile.** 769 applied, 635 admitted, 285 enrolled.

| Mid 50% test scores | | | |
|---|---|---|---|
| SAT critical reading: | 410-560 | Rank in top quarter: | 27% |
| SAT math: | 420-590 | Rank in top tenth: | 10% |
| SAT writing: | 380-590 | Out-of-state: | 38% |
| ACT composite: | 19-24 | Live on campus: | 77% |
| GPA 3.75 or higher: | 15% | International: | 6% |
| GPA 3.50-3.74: | 12% | Fraternities: | 4% |
| GPA 3.0-3.49: | 29% | Sororities: | 1% |
| GPA 2.0-2.99: | 43% | | |

**Basis for selection.** High school class rank and ACT test scores most important. ACT recommended. **Learning Disabled:** Students encouraged to contact Disability Services early in the admissions process to insure availability of appropriate services.

**High school preparation.** College-preparatory program recommended. 13 units required. Required and recommended units include English 4, mathematics 3, social studies 3, science 3 (laboratory 2) and foreign language 2.

**2009-2010 Annual costs.** Tuition/fees: $9,988. In-state and out-of-state tuition rates are the same. Room/board: $6,254. Books/supplies: $800. Personal expenses: $1,000.

**2009-2010 Financial aid. Non-need-based:** Scholarships awarded for academics, alumni affiliation, athletics, leadership, minority status, music/drama, ROTC, state residency.

**Application procedures. Admission:** Priority date 2/1; no deadline. $30 fee, may be waived for applicants with need. Admission notification on a rolling basis beginning on or about 9/1. **Financial aid:** Priority date 2/15; no closing date. FAFSA required. Applicants notified on a rolling basis starting 3/15.

**Academics. Special study options:** Cross-registration, distance learning, double major, dual enrollment of high school students, ESL, honors, independent study, internships, student-designed major, study abroad, teacher certification program. **Credit/placement by examination:** AP, CLEP, IB, ACT. Proficiency examinations are administered by appropriate academic department, require no fee, and yield no credit or grade but may fulfill prerequisites for advanced courses or satisfy requirements. Special Examinations for Credit have fee of $50 per credit. Credits earned by examination do not count as residence credits. Exams given at discretion of appropriate academic department. **Support services:** Learning center, pre-admission summer program, reduced course load, remedial instruction, study skills assistance, tutoring, writing center.

**Majors. Agriculture:** Agribusiness operations, agronomy, animal sciences, business, business technology, crop production, equestrian studies, equine science, greenhouse operations, horticultural science, landscaping, power machinery, turf management. **Biology:** General. **Business:** Accounting, business admin, entrepreneurial studies, hospitality admin, hotel/motel admin, management information systems, marketing, resort management, restaurant/food services. **Communications:** General. **Conservation:** General, management/policy, urban forestry, wildlife. **Education:** Agricultural, kindergarten/preschool, science, technology/industrial arts. **Engineering:** Industrial, software, water resource. **Engineering technology:** Quality control. **Health:** Health care admin, health services, respiratory therapy assistant. **Parks/recreation:** Facilities management, sports admin. **Protective services:** Corrections, law enforcement admin, police science. **Psychology:** Community, industrial. **Transportation:** Airline/commercial pilot, aviation. **Other:** Applied Studies, Respiratory Care.

**Most popular majors.** Agriculture 25%, business/marketing 24%, engineering/engineering technologies 9%, interdisciplinary studies 6%, natural resources/environmental science 20%.

**Computing on campus.** PC or laptop required. 1,350 workstations in dormitories, library, computer center, student center. Dormitories wired for high-speed internet access and linked to campus network. Commuter students can connect to campus network. Online course registration, online library, helpline, repair service, student web hosting, wireless network available.

**Student life. Freshman orientation:** Mandatory, $75 fee. Preregistration for classes offered. The new student orientation program for the fall term begins three days before the first day of class. **Housing:** Coed dorms, special housing for disabled, apartments available. $100 partly refundable deposit, deadline 9/1. **Activities:** Bands, campus ministries, choral groups, drama, international student organizations, student government, multicultural club, UMC Ambassadors, Students in Free Enterprise, Wildlife Society Chapter, Collegiate FFA, flying club, Habitat for Humanity, Rodeo Association, Student Athletic Advisory Committee.

**Athletics.** NCAA. **Intercollegiate:** Baseball M, basketball, equestrian W, football (tackle) M, golf, soccer W, softball W, tennis W, volleyball W. **Intramural:** Basketball, football (non-tackle), golf, racquetball, soccer, softball, table tennis, tennis, volleyball. **Team name:** Golden Eagles.

**Student services.** Adult student services, alcohol/substance abuse counseling, chaplain/spiritual director, career counseling, services for economically disadvantaged, student employment services, financial aid counseling, health services, minority student services, on-campus daycare, personal counseling, placement for graduates, veterans' counselor, women's services. **Physically disabled:** Services for visually, hearing impaired.

**Contact.** E-mail: info@umn.edu
Phone: (218) 281-8569 Toll-free number: (800) 862-6466
Fax: (218) 281-8575 ext. 369
Amber Evans-Dailey, Director of Admissions, University of Minnesota: Crookston, 2900 University Avenue, Crookston, MN 56716-5001

## University of Minnesota: Duluth
Duluth, Minnesota
www.d.umn.edu                              CB code: 6873

▶ Public 4-year university
▶ Residential campus in small city
▶ 9,422 degree-seeking undergraduates: 4% part-time, 47% women, 1% African American, 3% Asian American, 1% Hispanic American, 1% Native American, 1% international
▶ 1,112 degree-seeking graduate students
▶ 71% of applicants admitted
▶ SAT or ACT with writing required
▶ 50% graduate within 6 years; 7% enter graduate study

**General.** Founded in 1947. Regionally accredited. All buildings at UMD are connected by a unique skyway and concourse system. **Degrees:** 1,783 bachelor's awarded; master's, professional offered. **ROTC:** Air Force. **Location:** 160 miles from Minneapolis-St. Paul. **Calendar:** Semester, extensive summer session. **Full-time faculty:** 463 total; 75% have terminal degrees, 19% minority, 43% women. **Part-time faculty:** 88 total; 33% have terminal degrees, 6% minority, 54% women. **Class size:** 29% < 20, 50% 20-39, 5% 40-49, 9% 50-99, 6% >100. **Special facilities:** Planetarium, visual imaging laboratory, Tweed Museum of Art, Glensheen Historic Congdon Estate, nature center, multi-cultural center.

**Freshman class profile.** 7,936 applied, 5,669 admitted, 2,118 enrolled.

| Mid 50% test scores | | Return as sophomores: | 81% |
|---|---|---|---|
| ACT composite: | 20-26 | Out-of-state: | 12% |
| Rank in top quarter: | 42% | Live on campus: | 92% |
| Rank in top tenth: | 17% | International: | 1% |
| End year in good standing: | 81% | | |

**Basis for selection.** 65th percentile of high school class or above typically admitted. Test scores are required. Students ranking between the 40th

and 64th percentile are selectively admitted based on test scores and academic preparation. Essays or personal statements considered in an admissions decision appeals process. Audition required for music students. **Learning Disabled:** Students must meet our general admission policy.

**High school preparation.** College-preparatory program required. 15 units required. Required units include English 4, mathematics 3, social studies 1, history 1, science 3, foreign language 2, computer science 1 and visual/performing arts 1. One year of physical and biological science required; mathematics sequence includes algebra, geometry, and higher algebra. Visual and performing arts courses and computer skills courses strongly recommended.

**2009-2010 Annual costs.** Tuition/fees: $11,004; $13,004 out-of-state. Room/board: $6,176. Books/supplies: $1,100. Personal expenses: $1,600.

**2008-2009 Financial aid. Need-based:** 1,782 full-time freshmen applied for aid; 1,229 were judged to have need; 1,228 of these received aid. Average need met was 81%. Average scholarship/grant was $7,967; average loan $4,220. 47% of total undergraduate aid awarded as scholarships/grants, 53% as loans/jobs. **Non-need-based:** Awarded to 2,287 full-time undergraduates, including 694 freshmen. Scholarships awarded for academics, athletics, ROTC.

**Application procedures. Admission:** Priority date 12/15; deadline 8/1 (receipt date). $35 fee. Admission notification on a rolling basis beginning on or about 9/17. Must reply by May 1 or within 4 week(s) if notified thereafter. Applications are accepted on a space available basis after 2/01. **Financial aid:** Priority date 3/1; no closing date. FAFSA required. Applicants notified on a rolling basis starting 3/1; must reply within 2 week(s) of notification.

**Academics. Special study options:** Accelerated study, cross-registration, distance learning, double major, dual enrollment of high school students, exchange student, honors, independent study, internships, liberal arts/career combination, study abroad, teacher certification program, weekend college. **Credit/placement by examination:** AP, CLEP, IB, ACT, institutional tests. **Support services:** Learning center, reduced course load, remedial instruction, study skills assistance, tutoring.

**Majors. Area/ethnic studies:** German, Native American, women's. **Biology:** General, biochemistry, cell/histology, molecular. **Business:** Accounting, actuarial science, business admin, finance, human resources, management information systems, marketing. **Communications:** General. **Computer sciences:** General, computer science, information systems. **Conservation:** Environmental science, environmental studies. **Education:** Art, biology, chemistry, early childhood, elementary, English, French, German, health, mathematics, middle, music, physical, physics, science, secondary, social studies, Spanish. **Engineering:** Chemical, civil, computer, electrical, industrial, mechanical. **Family/consumer sciences:** Child development. **Foreign languages:** German, Spanish. **Health:** Athletic training, communication disorders, health care admin. **History:** General. **Interdisciplinary:** Global studies. **Math:** General, statistics. **Parks/recreation:** General, exercise sciences. **Philosophy/religion:** Philosophy. **Physical sciences:** Applied physics, chemistry, geology, physics. **Psychology:** General. **Social sciences:** Anthropology, criminology, economics, geography, political science, sociology, urban studies. **Visual/performing arts:** Acting, art, art history/conservation, digital art, dramatic, graphic design, jazz, music pedagogy, music performance, musical theater, studio arts, theater design.

**Most popular majors.** Biology 10%, business/marketing 20%, communications/journalism 6%, education 11%, engineering/engineering technologies 6%, psychology 8%, social sciences 13%, visual/performing arts 7%.

**Computing on campus.** 465 workstations in library, computer center. Dormitories wired for high-speed internet access and linked to campus network. Commuter students can connect to campus network. Online course registration, online library, helpline, repair service, student web hosting, wireless network available.

**Student life. Freshman orientation:** Mandatory, $40 fee. Preregistration for classes offered. Academic advisement and registration (orientation) is held from March 1st to August 30. **Policies:** Smoke and alcohol free campus. **Housing:** Single-sex dorms, special housing for disabled, wellness housing available. $200 partly refundable deposit, deadline 5/1. Housing facilities are fully accessible to persons with physical disabilities. All facilities are smoke free. **Activities:** Bands, campus ministries, choral groups, dance, drama, film society, international student organizations, literary magazine, music ensembles, Model UN, musical theater, opera, radio station, student government, student newspaper, symphony orchestra, Intervarsity Christian Fellowship, Minnesota Public Interest Research Group, Anishinabe club, Black student association, Queer and Allied Students Union, Hispanic organization, Southeast Asian association, Students Engaged in Rewarding Volunteer Experiences.

**Athletics.** NCAA. **Intercollegiate:** Baseball M, basketball, cross-country, football (tackle) M, ice hockey, soccer W, softball W, tennis W, track and field, volleyball W. **Intramural:** Badminton, basketball, bowling, football (non-tackle), golf, ice hockey, sailing, skiing, soccer, softball, table tennis, tennis, track and field, volleyball, water polo. **Team name:** Bulldogs.

**Student services.** Adult student services, chaplain/spiritual director, career counseling, student employment services, financial aid counseling, health services, minority student services, on-campus daycare, personal counseling, placement for graduates, veterans' counselor, women's services. **Physically disabled:** Services for visually, speech, hearing impaired.

**Contact.** E-mail: umdadmis@d.umn.edu
Phone: (218) 726-7171 Toll-free number: (800) 232-1339
Fax: (218) 726-7040
Beth Esselstrom, Director of Admissions, University of Minnesota: Duluth, 25 Solon Campus Center, Duluth, MN 55812-3000

## University of Minnesota: Morris
**Morris, Minnesota**
www.morris.umn.edu                    CB code: 6890

- Public 4-year university and liberal arts college
- Residential campus in small town
- 1,599 degree-seeking undergraduates
- 73% of applicants admitted
- SAT or ACT with writing required

**General.** Founded in 1959. Regionally accredited. **Degrees:** 308 bachelor's awarded. **Location:** 150 miles from Minneapolis-St. Paul; 100 miles from Fargo, North Dakota. **Calendar:** Semester, limited summer session. **Full-time faculty:** 106 total. **Part-time faculty:** 62 total. **Class size:** 69% < 20, 25% 20-39, 3% 40-49, 3% 50-99. **Special facilities:** Tropical conservatory, prairie gate press, historical center, experiment station, USDA soil laboratory, center for small towns, observatory.

**Freshman class profile.** 1,467 applied, 1,077 admitted, 405 enrolled.

| Mid 50% test scores | | Rank in top quarter: | 60% |
|---|---|---|---|
| SAT critical reading: | 520-710 | Rank in top tenth: | 32% |
| SAT math: | 520-710 | Out-of-state: | 13% |
| SAT writing: | 500-660 | Live on campus: | 98% |
| ACT composite: | 22-28 | | |

**Basis for selection.** Admission based on four primary factors: high school performance, ACT/SAT scores, extra-curricular involvement/leadership experience/honors. Interview recommended. Audition required for music students receiving scholarships. **Homeschooled:** Submit portfolio of works studied.

**High school preparation.** 17 units recommended. Recommended units include English 4, mathematics 3, social studies 4, history 4, science 3 (laboratory 2) and foreign language 2. Science units must include 1 biological science and 1 physical science.

**2009-2010 Annual costs.** Tuition/fees: $10,716. In-state and out-of-state tuition rates are the same. Room/board: $7,056. Books/supplies: $600. Personal expenses: $1,200.

**2009-2010 Financial aid. Non-need-based:** Scholarships awarded for academics, alumni affiliation, leadership, minority status, music/drama. **Additional information:** Land-grant program waiving tuition for Native Americans.

**Application procedures. Admission:** Priority date 12/15; deadline 3/15 (postmark date). $35 fee, may be waived for applicants with need. Admission notification on a rolling basis beginning on or about 9/1. Must reply by May 1 or within 2 week(s) if notified thereafter. **Financial aid:** Priority date 3/1; no closing date. FAFSA required. Applicants notified on a rolling basis starting 3/1; must reply within 3 week(s) of notification.

**Academics.** Academic opportunities that allow students to assist faculty in research or teaching endeavors and receive a stipend or expense allowances include: The Undergraduate Research Opportunities Program, The Morris Academic Partnership, The Minority Mentorship Program, The Morris Administrative Internship, and The Student Internship Program. **Special study options:** Combined bachelor's/graduate degree, cooperative education, cross-registration, distance learning, double major, exchange student, honors, independent study, internships, liberal arts/career combination, New York semester, semester at sea, student-designed major, study abroad, teacher certification program, United Nations semester, urban semester, Washington semester. **Credit/placement by examination:** AP, CLEP, IB, ACT, institutional tests. No limit for credit by exam, but the credit awarded does not count as resident credit; must have 30 resident credits. **Support services:** Learning center, pre-admission summer program, reduced course load, study skills assistance, tutoring, writing center.

**Majors. Area/ethnic studies:** European, Latin American, Native American, women's. **Biology:** General. **Business:** Management science. **Communications:** General. **Computer sciences:** Computer science. **Conservation:** Environmental studies. **Education:** Elementary. **Foreign languages:** French, German, Spanish. **History:** General. **Liberal arts:** Humanities. **Math:** General, statistics. **Philosophy/religion:** Philosophy. **Physical sciences:** Chemistry, geology, physics. **Psychology:** General. **Public administration:** Social work. **Social sciences:** Anthropology, economics, political science, sociology. **Visual/performing arts:** Art history/conservation, dramatic, music performance, studio arts.

**Computing on campus.** 220 workstations in dormitories, library, computer center, student center. Dormitories wired for high-speed internet access and linked to campus network. Commuter students can connect to campus network. Online course registration, online library, helpline, repair service, wireless network available.

**Student life. Freshman orientation:** Mandatory. Preregistration for classes offered. Held 4 days prior to fall semester. **Housing:** Guaranteed on-campus for all undergraduates. Coed dorms, special housing for disabled, wellness housing available. $200 deposit, deadline 8/1. **Activities:** Bands, choral groups, dance, drama, film society, literary magazine, music ensembles, musical theater, radio station, student government, student newspaper, symphony orchestra, TV station, Amnesty International, Big Friend/Little Friend, Campus Aglow Outreach, E-Quality, Habitat for Humanity, Intervarsity Christian Fellowship, Minnesota Public Interest Research Group (MPIRG), Morris Campus Student Association (MCSA), Positive Spirituality, Women of Color Association.

**Athletics.** NCAA. **Intercollegiate:** Baseball M, basketball, cross-country, diving W, football (tackle) M, golf, soccer, softball W, swimming W, tennis, track and field, volleyball W. **Intramural:** Baseball, basketball, bowling, field hockey, football (non-tackle), ice hockey, softball, triathlon, volleyball. **Team name:** Cougars.

**Student services.** Alcohol/substance abuse counseling, career counseling, student employment services, financial aid counseling, health services, minority student services, personal counseling, placement for graduates, veterans' counselor, women's services. **Physically disabled:** Services for visually, speech, hearing impaired. **Learning disabled:** Comprehensive services available.

**Contact.** E-mail: admissions@morris.umn.edu
Phone: (320) 589-6035 Toll-free number: (888) 866-3382
Fax: (320) 589-1673
Bryan Herrmann, Director of Admission, University of Minnesota: Morris, 600 East 4th Street, Morris, MN 56267

## University of Minnesota: Rochester
**Rochester, Minnesota**
www.r.umn.edu                    CB code: 5877

- Public 4-year university and health science college
- Small city
- 200 degree-seeking undergraduates

**General.** Regionally accredited. **Calendar:** Semester. **Full-time faculty:** 9 total.

**Freshman class profile.** 50 enrolled.

**Academics. Credit/placement by examination:** CLEP.

**Majors. Health:** Health services.

**Contact.** E-mail: applyumr@umn.edu
Phone: (507) 258-8687 Toll-free number: (877) 280-4699
Jade Bakke, Director of Admissions, University of Minnesota: Rochester, 111 South Broadway, Rochester, MN 55904

## University of Minnesota: Twin Cities
**Minneapolis, Minnesota**                    CB member
www.umn.edu/tc                    CB code: 6874

- Public 4-year university
- Residential campus in very large city
- 29,921 degree-seeking undergraduates: 8% part-time, 52% women, 5% African American, 10% Asian American, 2% Hispanic American, 1% Native American, 5% international
- 17,795 degree-seeking graduate students
- 50% of applicants admitted

♦ SAT or ACT with writing required
♦ 66% graduate within 6 years

**General.** Founded in 1851. Regionally accredited. Campuses in Minneapolis and St. Paul. **Degrees:** 6,686 bachelor's awarded; master's, doctoral, professional offered. **ROTC:** Army, Naval, Air Force. **Calendar:** Semester, extensive summer session. **Full-time faculty:** 1,834 total; 81% have terminal degrees, 15% minority, 39% women. **Part-time faculty:** 937 total; 47% have terminal degrees, 8% minority, 42% women. **Class size:** 40% < 20, 37% 20-39, 6% 40-49, 10% 50-99, 7% >100. **Special facilities:** West bank arts quarter, natural history museum, showboat, rehabilitation museum, arboretum, concert hall.

**Freshman class profile.** 33,910 applied, 16,960 admitted, 5,400 enrolled.

| Mid 50% test scores | | | |
|---|---|---|---|
| SAT critical reading: | 520-670 | Rank in top tenth: | 43% |
| SAT math: | 600-710 | Return as sophomores: | 90% |
| SAT writing: | 530-650 | Out-of-state: | 29% |
| ACT composite: | 24-29 | Live on campus: | 83% |
| Rank in top quarter: | 83% | International: | 6% |

**Basis for selection.** Successful completion of a college preparatory curriculum, high school rank percentile, grade point average, ACT or SAT scores, and strength of curriculum very important. Writing tests required. Results considered as secondary admission factor.

**High school preparation.** College-preparatory program required. 16 units required. Required units include English 4, mathematics 3, social studies 3, history 1, science 3 and foreign language 2. 1 year of visual and/or performing arts also required. Management, biological sciences, and technology applicants require a fourth year of mathematics and 3 years of science including 1 year each of biological science, chemistry, and physics.

**2009-2010 Annual costs.** Tuition/fees: $11,287; $15,287 out-of-state. Room/board: $7,392.

**2009-2010 Financial aid.** All financial aid based on need. 4,292 full-time freshmen applied for aid; 2,786 were judged to have need; 2,783 of these received aid. Average need met was 87%. Average scholarship/grant was $8,703; average loan $4,532. 48% of total undergraduate aid awarded as scholarships/grants, 52% as loans/jobs.

**Application procedures. Admission:** Priority date 12/15; no deadline. $45 fee, may be waived for applicants with need. Admission notification on a rolling basis. Must reply by May 1 or within 2 week(s) if notified thereafter. **Financial aid:** Priority date 3/1; no closing date. FAFSA, institutional form required. Applicants notified on a rolling basis starting 2/15.

**Academics.** Four year graduation guarantee offered. **Special study options:** Accelerated study, combined bachelor's/graduate degree, cooperative education, cross-registration, distance learning, double major, dual enrollment of high school students, ESL, exchange student, external degree, honors, independent study, internships, liberal arts/career combination, student-designed major, study abroad, teacher certification program. Qualified undergraduates may take graduate-level classes. **Credit/placement by examination:** AP, CLEP, IB, SAT, ACT, institutional tests. **Support services:** Learning center, pre-admission summer program, reduced course load, remedial instruction, study skills assistance, tutoring, writing center.

**Majors. Agriculture:** Animal sciences, business, economics, food science. **Architecture:** Architecture, environmental design, landscape. **Area/ethnic studies:** African, African-American, American, Chicano/Hispanic-American/Latino, East Asian, European, Latin American, Native American, Near/Middle Eastern, Russian/Slavic, women's. **Biology:** General, bacteriology, biochemistry, biostatistics, cell/histology, ecology. **Business:** Accounting, actuarial science, business admin, human resources, insurance, international, labor relations, logistics, management information systems, marketing, sales/distribution. **Communications:** Journalism. **Computer sciences:** Computer science, networking. **Conservation:** General, fisheries, forest resources, forestry, wildlife. **Construction:** Maintenance. **Education:** Agricultural, art, business, early childhood, elementary, foundations, mathematics, music, physical, sales/marketing, technology/industrial arts. **Engineering:** Aerospace, agricultural, chemical, civil, computer, electrical, geological, materials, materials science, mechanical. **Family/consumer sciences:** General, clothing/textiles, family studies, food/nutrition, housing. **Foreign languages:** General, ancient Greek, Chinese, classics, comparative lit, French, German, Hebrew, Italian, Japanese, Latin, linguistics, Portuguese, Russian, Scandinavian, Spanish. **Health:** Audiology/speech pathology, dental hygiene, music therapy, nurse anesthetist, nursing (RN), predental, premedicine, prepharmacy, preveterinary. **History:** General. **Interdisciplinary:** Biological/physical sciences, nutrition sciences. **Legal studies:** Prelaw. **Liberal arts:** Arts/sciences. **Math:** General, statistics. **Parks/recreation:** General.

**Personal/culinary services:** Mortuary science. **Philosophy/religion:** Judaic, philosophy, religion. **Physical sciences:** Astronomy, astrophysics, chemistry, geology, geophysics, physics. **Psychology:** General. **Social sciences:** Anthropology, applied economics, criminology, econometrics, economics, geography, international relations, political science, sociology, urban studies. **Visual/performing arts:** Art history/conservation, commercial/advertising art, dance, design, dramatic, fashion design, film/cinema, interior design, music performance. **Other:** Bio-based products engineering.

**Most popular majors.** Biology 8%, business/marketing 8%, engineering/engineering technologies 10%, English 7%, psychology 7%, social sciences 12%, visual/performing arts 6%.

**Computing on campus.** Dormitories wired for high-speed internet access and linked to campus network. Commuter students can connect to campus network. Online course registration, online library, helpline, repair service, student web hosting, wireless network available.

**Student life. Freshman orientation:** Mandatory. **Housing:** Guaranteed on-campus for freshmen. Coed dorms, special housing for disabled, apartments, cooperative housing, fraternity/sorority housing, wellness housing available. $100 fully refundable deposit, deadline 5/1. Honors housing available. 24 living and learning communities. **Activities:** Bands, choral groups, dance, drama, film society, international student organizations, literary magazine, music ensembles, musical theater, opera, radio station, student government, student newspaper, symphony orchestra, TV station, 600 student-run organizations.

**Athletics.** NCAA. **Intercollegiate:** Baseball, basketball, cheerleading, cross-country, diving, football (tackle), golf, gymnastics, ice hockey, rowing (crew) W, soccer W, softball W, swimming, tennis, track and field, volleyball W, wrestling M. **Intramural:** Badminton, baseball, basketball, bowling, fencing, football (tackle) M, golf, gymnastics, handball, ice hockey, judo, lacrosse, racquetball, rugby, sailing, skiing, soccer, softball, squash, swimming, synchronized swimming, tennis, volleyball, water polo, wrestling M. **Team name:** Golden Gophers.

**Student services.** Adult student services, alcohol/substance abuse counseling, chaplain/spiritual director, career counseling, services for economically disadvantaged, student employment services, financial aid counseling, health services, legal services, minority student services, on-campus daycare, personal counseling, placement for graduates, veterans' counselor, women's services. **Physically disabled:** Services for visually, speech, hearing impaired.

**Contact.** Phone: (612) 625-2008 Toll-free number: (800) 752-1000 Fax: (612) 626-1693
Wayne Sigler, Director of Admissions, University of Minnesota: Twin Cities, 240 Williamson Hall, 231 Pillsbury Drive SE, Minneapolis, MN 55455-0115

---

**University of St. Thomas**
St. Paul, Minnesota
www.stthomas.edu

CB member
CB code: 6110

♦ Private 4-year university and liberal arts college affiliated with Roman Catholic Church
♦ Commuter campus in very large city
♦ 5,992 degree-seeking undergraduates: 4% part-time, 45% women, 3% African American, 5% Asian American, 4% Hispanic American, 1% international
♦ 4,376 degree-seeking graduate students
♦ 87% of applicants admitted
♦ SAT or ACT (ACT writing optional), application essay required
♦ 72% graduate within 6 years

**General.** Founded in 1885. Regionally accredited. **Degrees:** 1,322 bachelor's awarded; master's, doctoral, professional offered. **ROTC:** Army, Naval, Air Force. **Location:** St. Paul campus is 5 miles from the downtowns of St. Paul and Minneapolis; Minneapolis campus is in the heart of the city. **Calendar:** 4-1-4, limited summer session. **Class size:** 42% < 20, 55% 20-39, 1% 40-49, 2% 50-99, less than 1% >100. **Special facilities:** American Museum of Asmat Art, O'Shaughnessy-Frey Library Department of Special Collections.

**Freshman class profile.** 5,065 applied, 4,389 admitted, 1,352 enrolled.

| Mid 50% test scores | | GPA 2.0-2.99: | 9% |
|---|---|---|---|
| SAT critical reading: | 520-630 | Rank in top quarter: | 50% |
| SAT math: | 540-650 | Rank in top tenth: | 21% |
| ACT composite: | 23-28 | Return as sophomores: | 86% |
| GPA 3.75 or higher: | 33% | Out-of-state: | 20% |
| GPA 3.50-3.74: | 24% | Live on campus: | 92% |
| GPA 3.0-3.49: | 34% | International: | 1% |

**Basis for selection.** Admissions decision by formula using combination of high school rank and standardized test scores, including consideration of the contributions the student has made to their school, community or church. Interview recommended. **Homeschooled:** Submit course descriptions.

**High school preparation.** College-preparatory program recommended. Required and recommended units include English 4, mathematics 3-4, social studies 2, science 2 and foreign language 4. Some departments may require 3 units social studies (includes 1 geography), 1 US history, 1 unit visual or performing arts.

**2009-2010 Annual costs.** Tuition/fees: $29,467. Room/board: $8,042. Books/supplies: $1,491. Personal expenses: $2,100.

**2009-2010 Financial aid. Need-based:** 1,109 full-time freshmen applied for aid; 841 were judged to have need; 841 of these received aid. Average need met was 94%. Average scholarship/grant was $19,162; average loan $5,981. 67% of total undergraduate aid awarded as scholarships/grants, 33% as loans/jobs. **Non-need-based:** Awarded to 966 full-time undergraduates, including 375 freshmen. Scholarships awarded for academics, music/drama, ROTC.

**Application procedures. Admission:** No deadline. No application fee. Admission notification on a rolling basis beginning on or about 10/1. Applications accepted until class is full; reviewed starting 10/1. **Financial aid:** Priority date 4/1; no closing date. FAFSA required. Applicants notified on a rolling basis starting 3/1; must reply within 3 week(s) of notification.

**Academics. Special study options:** Cross-registration, double major, exchange student, honors, independent study, internships, semester at sea, student-designed major, study abroad, teacher certification program, urban semester, Washington semester. Renaissance Program in which students major in a liberal arts area, take career-oriented classes as a minor, and after graduation can take additional undergraduate business courses free of charge. **Credit/placement by examination:** AP, CLEP, IB, institutional tests. Typically credit by exam can be used for only 1/8 of a student's courses. CLEP credit awarded if student scores at 50th percentile or above for those examinations that have been approved by the department in which the subject is usually taught. **Support services:** Learning center, reduced course load, study skills assistance, tutoring, writing center.

**Majors. Area/ethnic studies:** Women's. **Biology:** General, biochemistry. **Business:** Accounting, actuarial science, business admin, entrepreneurial studies, finance, human resources, international, marketing, operations, real estate. **Communications:** General, journalism. **Computer sciences:** Computer science, information systems, information technology, security. **Conservation:** Environmental science, environmental studies. **Education:** Chemistry, elementary, English, French, German, health, mathematics, middle, multi-level teacher, music, physical, physics, science, social studies, Spanish. **Engineering:** General, electrical, mechanical. **Foreign languages:** Classics, comparative lit, French, German, Latin, Spanish. **Health:** Predental, preveterinary, public health ed. **History:** General. **Interdisciplinary:** Classical/archaeology, neuroscience, peace/conflict. **Legal studies:** Prelaw. **Liberal arts:** Arts/sciences. **Math:** General, statistics. **Philosophy/religion:** Philosophy, religion. **Physical sciences:** Chemistry, geology, physics. **Psychology:** General. **Public administration:** Social work. **Social sciences:** General, criminology, econometrics, economics, geography, international economics, international relations, political science, sociology. **Theology:** Preministerial. **Visual/performing arts:** Art history/conservation, music performance. **Other:** Business communication leadership, Lay ministry, Pre-engineering.

**Most popular majors.** Biology 6%, business/marketing 44%, communications/journalism 10%, philosophy/religious studies 6%, social sciences 8%.

**Computing on campus.** 4,280 workstations in dormitories, library, computer center, student center. Dormitories wired for high-speed internet access and linked to campus network. Commuter students can connect to campus network. Online course registration, online library, helpline, student web hosting, wireless network available.

**Student life. Freshman orientation:** Mandatory. Preregistration for classes offered. One day orientation for students and parents during the summer; students and parents can stay overnight in the dorms. Separate programs for students and parents. **Housing:** Single-sex dorms, apartments available. $200 fully refundable deposit, deadline 5/1. Chemical-free lifestyle, women in science house, first year experience houses, Catholic women's and Catholic men's communities. **Activities:** Bands, campus ministries, choral groups,

dance, drama, literary magazine, music ensembles, Model UN, radio station, student government, student newspaper, Globally Minded Student Association, Volunteers in Action, Student Coalition for Social Justice, African Nations Students Association, Fellowship of Christian Athletes, St. Paul's Outreach student organization, theology club, Black Empowerment Student Alliance.

**Athletics.** NCAA. **Intercollegiate:** Baseball M, basketball, cross-country, football (tackle) M, golf, ice hockey, soccer, softball W, swimming, tennis, track and field, volleyball W. **Intramural:** Basketball, football (non-tackle), racquetball, soccer, softball, tennis, volleyball. **Team name:** Tommies.

**Student services.** Adult student services, alcohol/substance abuse counseling, chaplain/spiritual director, career counseling, student employment services, financial aid counseling, health services, minority student services, on-campus daycare, personal counseling, veterans' counselor, women's services. **Physically disabled:** Services for visually, speech, hearing impaired. **Learning disabled:** Comprehensive services available.

**Contact.** E-mail: admissions@stthomas.edu
Phone: (651) 962-6150 Toll-free number: (800) 328-6819 ext. 26150
Fax: (651) 962-6160
Marla Friederichs, Associate Vice President for Enrollment Management, University of St. Thomas, 2115 Summit Avenue, 32F, St. Paul, MN 55105-1096

## Walden University
**Minneapolis, Minnesota**
**www.waldenu.edu**

- For-profit 4-year virtual university
- Large city
- 5,227 degree-seeking undergraduates: 88% part-time, 73% women, 35% African American, 1% Asian American, 11% Hispanic American, 1% Native American, 1% international
- 35,313 degree-seeking graduate students
- Application essay required

**General.** Walden University is a fully online institution accredited by the Higher Learning Commission's North Central Association offering programs in a variety of disciplines and degree levels, from undergraduate to doctorate. **Degrees:** 272 bachelor's awarded; master's, doctoral offered. **Calendar:** Differs by program, extensive summer session. **Full-time faculty:** 146 total; 96% have terminal degrees. **Part-time faculty:** 1,708 total; 84% have terminal degrees.

**Basis for selection.** Open admission, but selective for some programs. In addition to high school diploma or equivalent, applicants must also meet one of the following criteria: be at least 24 years old, be active in the military or a veteran, have already earned minimum 90 college-level quarter credit hours. Additional exceptions and requirements may apply. Admission decisions based on transcript and years of work experience in profession.

**2009-2010 Annual costs.** Tuition/fees: $11,790. Books/supplies: $2,100.

**2008-2009 Financial aid.** All financial aid based on need. 15% of total undergraduate aid awarded as scholarships/grants, 85% as loans/jobs.

**Application procedures. Admission:** No deadline. $50 fee, may be waived for applicants with need. Application must be submitted online. Admission notification on a rolling basis. Offer remains in effect for 12 months. **Financial aid:** No deadline. FAFSA required. Applicants notified on a rolling basis.

**Academics. Special study options:** Distance learning, internships, student-designed major, teacher certification program. **Credit/placement by examination:** AP, CLEP, IB. 30 credit hours maximum toward bachelor's degree. **Support services:** Remedial instruction, tutoring, writing center.

**Majors. Business:** Accounting, business admin, finance, human resources, international, knowledge management, management information systems, marketing, training/development. **Communications:** General, media studies. **Computer sciences:** General, information technology, security. **Education:** Instructional media. **Family/consumer sciences:** Child care, child development. **Health:** Health care admin, medical informatics, medical records technology, nursing (RN). **Protective services:** Criminal justice, law enforcement admin, police science. **Psychology:** General. **Public administration:** Policy analysis. **Social sciences:** Criminology. **Other:** Human computer interaction, New media.

**Computing on campus.** PC or laptop required. Commuter students can connect to campus network. Online course registration, online library, helpline available.

**Student life. Freshman orientation:** Available.

**Student services.** Career counseling, financial aid counseling, personal counseling, veterans' counselor. **Physically disabled:** Services for visually, speech, hearing impaired. **Learning disabled:** Comprehensive services available.

**Contact.** E-mail: admissions@waldenu.edu
Phone: (800) 925-3368 Toll-free number: (800) 925-3368
Reginald White, Enrollment Manager, Walden University, 650 South Exeter Street, 8th Floor, Baltimore, MD 21202

---

## Winona State University
### Winona, Minnesota
### www.winona.edu
### CB code: 6680

♦ Public 4-year university
♦ Residential campus in large town
♦ 7,872 degree-seeking undergraduates: 6% part-time, 60% women, 1% African American, 2% Asian American, 1% Hispanic American, 3% international
♦ 358 degree-seeking graduate students
♦ 71% of applicants admitted
♦ SAT and SAT Subject Tests or ACT (ACT writing optional) required
♦ 52% graduate within 6 years

**General.** Founded in 1858. Regionally accredited. **Degrees:** 1,426 bachelor's, 29 associate awarded; master's, doctoral offered. **ROTC:** Army. **Location:** 90 miles from Minneapolis-St. Paul. **Calendar:** Semester, extensive summer session. **Full-time faculty:** 340 total; 15% minority, 44% women. **Part-time faculty:** 136 total; 2% minority, 67% women. **Class size:** 27% < 20, 59% 20-39, 7% 40-49, 6% 50-99, 2% >100.

**Freshman class profile.** 6,500 applied, 4,607 admitted, 1,813 enrolled.

| Mid 50% test scores | | GPA 2.0-2.99: | 25% |
|---|---|---|---|
| SAT critical reading: | 440-600 | Rank in top quarter: | 33% |
| SAT math: | 510-640 | Rank in top tenth: | 10% |
| ACT composite: | 21-25 | Return as sophomores: | 75% |
| GPA 3.75 or higher: | 15% | Out-of-state: | 37% |
| GPA 3.50-3.74: | 21% | Live on campus: | 92% |
| GPA 3.0-3.49: | 38% | | |

**Basis for selection.** 16 units of college prep high school courses and rank in top 2/3 of class and SAT combined score of 1000 (exclusive of Writing) or ACT composite score of 21 required or top half of class with and ACT 18 or higher for regular admission. Interview required for academically marginal students.

**High school preparation.** College-preparatory program required. 16 units required. Required units include English 4, mathematics 3, social studies 2, history 1, science 3 (laboratory 3), foreign language 2 and academic electives 1. One English unit may be speech.

**2009-2010 Annual costs.** Tuition/fees: $7,809; $12,639 out-of-state. Fees include mandatory laptop lease for full-time students. Room/board: $6,680. Books/supplies: $1,160. Personal expenses: $2,050.

**2008-2009 Financial aid. Non-need-based:** Scholarships awarded for academics, alumni affiliation, art, athletics, leadership, minority status, music/drama, ROTC, state residency.

**Application procedures. Admission:** Priority date 3/1; deadline 7/30 (postmark date). $20 fee, may be waived for applicants with need. Admission notification on a rolling basis beginning on or about 8/15. **Financial aid:** No deadline. FAFSA required. Applicants notified on a rolling basis starting 5/1; must reply within 3 week(s) of notification.

**Academics. Special study options:** Accelerated study, cross-registration, distance learning, double major, dual enrollment of high school students, ESL, external degree, independent study, internships, student-designed major, study abroad, teacher certification program. **Credit/placement by examination:** AP, CLEP, IB, institutional tests. **Support services:** Learning center, reduced course load, study skills assistance, tutoring, writing center.

**Majors. Biology:** General, cell/histology, molecular. **Business:** General, accounting, administrative services, business admin, finance, human resources, management information systems, management science, managerial economics, market research, office/clerical, operations. **Communications:** General, advertising, broadcast journalism, journalism, media studies, photojournalism, public relations. **Communications technology:** General. **Computer sciences:** General, applications programming, computer science,

information technology, programming. **Conservation:** General, environmental studies. **Education:** General, art, bilingual, biology, business, chemistry, curriculum, drama/dance, early childhood, elementary, emotionally handicapped, English, foreign languages, French, German, health, health occupations, history, learning disabled, mathematics, mentally handicapped, middle, multi-level teacher, multiple handicapped, music, physical, physically handicapped, physics, reading, science, secondary, social science, social studies, Spanish, special, speech. **Engineering:** Materials, materials science, polymer. **Foreign languages:** General, French, German, Spanish. **Health:** Athletic training, clinical lab technology, cytotechnology, health care admin, nursing (RN), predental, premedicine, preop/surgical nursing, prepharmacy, preveterinary, public health ed, recreational therapy. **History:** General. **Interdisciplinary:** Biological/physical sciences. **Legal studies:** Paralegal, prelaw. **Liberal arts:** Arts/sciences. **Math:** General, applied, statistics. **Parks/recreation:** General, exercise sciences, facilities management, health/fitness, sports admin. **Physical sciences:** Chemistry, geology, physics, planetary, polymer chemistry. **Protective services:** Corrections, criminal justice, law enforcement admin, police science, security services. **Psychology:** General. **Public administration:** General, social work. **Social sciences:** General, economics, political science, sociology, urban studies. **Visual/performing arts:** General, art, commercial/advertising art, design, dramatic, music management, music performance, studio arts.

**Most popular majors.** Biology 6%, business/marketing 21%, communications/journalism 7%, education 18%, health sciences 11%.

**Computing on campus.** PC or laptop required. 125 workstations in dormitories, library, computer center, student center. Dormitories wired for high-speed internet access and linked to campus network. Commuter students can connect to campus network. Online course registration, helpline, repair service, student web hosting, wireless network available.

**Student life. Freshman orientation:** Available, $25 fee. Preregistration for classes offered. **Housing:** Guaranteed on-campus for freshmen. Coed dorms, single-sex dorms, special housing for disabled, apartments available. $175 partly refundable deposit, deadline 3/1. Residence hall with classrooms and faculty offices. **Activities:** Bands, choral groups, dance, drama, film society, international student organizations, literary magazine, music ensembles, musical theater, radio station, student government, student newspaper, symphony orchestra, TV station, over 130 organizations.

**Athletics.** NCAA. **Intercollegiate:** Baseball M, basketball, cross-country, football (tackle) M, golf, gymnastics W, soccer W, softball W, tennis W, track and field W, volleyball W. **Intramural:** Archery, badminton, baseball M, basketball, bowling, cross-country, diving, equestrian, fencing, field hockey, golf, gymnastics W, handball, ice hockey, racquetball, rifle, rugby, skiing, soccer, softball, swimming, table tennis, tennis, track and field, volleyball, wrestling M. **Team name:** Warriors.

**Student services.** Adult student services, alcohol/substance abuse counseling, chaplain/spiritual director, career counseling, services for economically disadvantaged, student employment services, financial aid counseling, health services, legal services, minority student services, on-campus daycare, personal counseling, placement for graduates, veterans' counselor, women's services. **Physically disabled:** Services for visually, speech, hearing impaired.

**Contact.** E-mail: admissions@winona.edu
Phone: (507) 457-5100 Toll-free number: (800) 342-5978
Fax: (507) 457-5620
Carl Stange, Director of Admissions, Winona State University, Office of Admissions, Winona, MN 55987

# Mississippi

## Alcorn State University
### Alcorn State, Mississippi
www.alcorn.edu

CB member
CB code: 1008

- Public 4-year university and agricultural college
- Residential campus in rural community
- 2,700 degree-seeking undergraduates: 10% part-time, 67% women, 93% African American, 1% Hispanic American, 1% international
- 634 degree-seeking graduate students
- 40% of applicants admitted
- SAT or ACT (ACT writing optional), application essay, interview required
- 39% graduate within 6 years; 34% enter graduate study

**General.** Founded in 1871. Regionally accredited. School of Nursing is located in Natchez. **Degrees:** 439 bachelor's, 27 associate awarded; master's offered. **ROTC:** Army. **Location:** 40 miles from Natchez, 45 miles from Vicksburg. **Calendar:** Semester, limited summer session. **Full-time faculty:** 184 total; 64% have terminal degrees, 76% minority, 49% women. **Part-time faculty:** 38 total; 53% have terminal degrees, 87% minority, 58% women. **Special facilities:** Nature trails, lakes.

**Freshman class profile.** 3,195 applied, 1,291 admitted, 464 enrolled.

| Mid 50% test scores | | | |
|---|---|---|---|
| SAT critical reading: | 390-470 | GPA 3.0-3.49: | 26% |
| SAT math: | 400-460 | GPA 2.0-2.99: | 50% |
| ACT composite: | 16-19 | Return as sophomores: | 70% |
| GPA 3.75 or higher: | 5% | Out-of-state: | 21% |
| GPA 3.50-3.74: | 8% | Live on campus: | 91% |

**Basis for selection.** Test scores, school achievement record important; specific academic units considered. Test score requirements depend upon high school GPA. Audition required for music majors. **Homeschooled:** Transcript of courses and grades, state high school equivalency certificate required.

**High school preparation.** College-preparatory program required. 15.5 units required. Required and recommended units include English 4, mathematics 3, social studies 3, science 3 (laboratory 2), foreign language 1, computer science .5 and academic electives 2. One advanced elective must be in foreign language or world geography.

**2009-2010 Annual costs.** Tuition/fees: $4,498; $11,064 out-of-state. Room/board: $5,384. Books/supplies: $1,452. Personal expenses: $2,419.

**2009-2010 Financial aid.** **Need-based:** 462 full-time freshmen applied for aid; 431 were judged to have need; 431 of these received aid. Average need met was 77%. Average scholarship/grant was $5,400; average loan $3,370. 57% of total undergraduate aid awarded as scholarships/grants, 43% as loans/jobs. **Non-need-based:** Awarded to 1,266 full-time undergraduates, including 330 freshmen. Scholarships awarded for academics, athletics, ROTC.

**Application procedures.** **Admission:** No deadline. No application fee. Application must be submitted on paper. Admission notification on a rolling basis. **Financial aid:** Priority date 4/1; no closing date. FAFSA, institutional form required. Applicants notified on a rolling basis starting 4/1; must reply within 4 week(s) of notification.

**Academics.** **Special study options:** Accelerated study, cooperative education, distance learning, double major, dual enrollment of high school students, honors, independent study, internships, liberal arts/career combination, study abroad, teacher certification program. **Credit/placement by examination:** AP, CLEP, SAT, ACT, institutional tests. 15 credit hours maximum toward associate degree, 30 toward bachelor's. Student must earn 12 hours at Alcorn State University before credit by examination may be recorded on the student's transcript. **Support services:** Learning center, preadmission summer program, reduced course load, remedial instruction, tutoring.

**Majors.** **Agriculture:** General, business, economics. **Biology:** General. **Business:** Accounting, business admin. **Communications:** Media studies. **Computer sciences:** General, LAN/WAN management. **Education:** Elementary,

special. **Engineering technology:** Robotics. **Family/consumer sciences:** Child development, food/nutrition. **Health:** Athletic training, nursing (RN). **History:** General. **Liberal arts:** Arts/sciences. **Math:** General. **Parks/recreation:** General. **Physical sciences:** Chemistry. **Protective services:** Criminal justice. **Psychology:** General, educational. **Social sciences:** Economics, political science, sociology. **Visual/performing arts:** Music performance.

**Most popular majors.** Biology 13%, business/marketing 9%, health sciences 13%, liberal arts 20%, social sciences 6%.

**Computing on campus.** 500 workstations in library, computer center, student center. Dormitories wired for high-speed internet access and linked to campus network. Commuter students can connect to campus network. Online course registration, online library, helpline, repair service available.

**Student life.** **Freshman orientation:** Mandatory. Preregistration for classes offered. Entrance and placement exams given. **Housing:** Guaranteed on-campus for all undergraduates. Single-sex dorms available. $75 fully refundable deposit. **Activities:** Bands, choral groups, dance, drama, music ensembles, radio station, student government, student newspaper, TV station, Wesley Foundation, NAACP, YWCA, PHA Masonic Order, ASU Heritage Committee.

**Athletics.** NCAA. **Intercollegiate:** Baseball M, basketball, cross-country, football (tackle) M, golf, soccer W, softball W, tennis, track and field, volleyball W. **Intramural:** Basketball. **Team name:** Braves.

**Student services.** Career counseling, student employment services, health services, on-campus daycare, personal counseling, placement for graduates, veterans' counselor.

**Contact.** E-mail: jbmcdonald@alcorn.edu
Phone: (601) 877-6147 Toll-free number: (800) 222-6790
Fax: (601) 877-6347
Johnny McDonald, Director of Admissions and Recruiting, Alcorn State University, 1000 ASU Drive #300, Alcorn State, MS 39096-7500

## Belhaven University
### Jackson, Mississippi
www.belhaven.edu

CB code: 1055

- Private 4-year liberal arts college affiliated with Presbyterian Church (USA)
- Commuter campus in large city
- 2,298 degree-seeking undergraduates: 5% part-time, 65% women
- 451 degree-seeking graduate students
- 52% of applicants admitted
- SAT or ACT (ACT writing optional), application essay required
- 49% graduate within 6 years; 24% enter graduate study

**General.** Founded in 1883. Regionally accredited. Christian liberal arts college. **Degrees:** 230 bachelor's awarded; master's offered. **ROTC:** Army, Air Force. **Location:** 188 miles from New Orleans, 200 miles from Memphis, Tennessee. **Calendar:** Semester, extensive summer session. **Full-time faculty:** 63 total; 73% have terminal degrees, 35% women. **Part-time faculty:** 84 total; 32% have terminal degrees, 56% women. **Class size:** 71% < 20, 21% 20-39, 8% 40-49, less than 1% 50-99. **Special facilities:** Museum, heritage room.

**Freshman class profile.** 1,380 applied, 712 admitted, 191 enrolled.

| Mid 50% test scores | | | |
|---|---|---|---|
| SAT critical reading: | 490-610 | GPA 2.0-2.99: | 27% |
| SAT math: | 460-570 | Rank in top quarter: | 55% |
| ACT composite: | 19-24 | Rank in top tenth: | 35% |
| GPA 3.75 or higher: | 26% | End year in good standing: | 82% |
| GPA 3.50-3.74: | 23% | Return as sophomores: | 67% |
| GPA 3.0-3.49: | 24% | Out-of-state: | 62% |
| | | Live on campus: | 86% |

**Basis for selection.** Test scores, school record, recommendations, and character important. Interview recommended for art, dance, music, and theater majors; portfolio recommended for art majors. Audition required for dance, music, and theater majors.

**High school preparation.** 16 units required. Required units include English 4, mathematics 2, social studies 1, science 1, computer science 1 and academic electives 8.

**2010-2011 Annual costs.** Tuition/fees: $17,700. Room/board: $6,500. Books/supplies: $1,400.

**2009-2010 Financial aid.** **Need-based:** 165 full-time freshmen applied for aid; 139 were judged to have need; 138 of these received aid. Average need met was 62%. Average scholarship/grant was $11,499; average loan

$3,260. 46% of total undergraduate aid awarded as scholarships/grants, 54% as loans/jobs. **Non-need-based:** Awarded to 227 full-time undergraduates, including 66 freshmen. Scholarships awarded for academics, alumni affiliation, art, athletics, job skills, leadership, music/drama.

**Application procedures. Admission:** No deadline. $25 fee, may be waived for applicants with need. Admission notification on a rolling basis. Accepted applicants must reply within 30 days. **Financial aid:** Priority date 1/31; no closing date. FAFSA required. Applicants notified on a rolling basis starting 2/1.

**Academics. Special study options:** Accelerated study, combined bachelor's/graduate degree, distance learning, double major, dual enrollment of high school students, ESL, honors, independent study, internships, student-designed major, study abroad, teacher certification program, weekend college. **Credit/placement by examination:** AP, CLEP, IB, SAT, ACT, institutional tests. 30 credit hours maximum toward bachelor's degree. **Support services:** Learning center, reduced course load, remedial instruction, study skills assistance, tutoring, writing center.

**Majors. Biology:** General. **Business:** Accounting, business admin. **Communications:** General. **Computer sciences:** General, computer science. **Education:** Elementary. **Health:** Health care admin. **History:** General. **Interdisciplinary:** Global studies. **Liberal arts:** Humanities. **Math:** General. **Parks/recreation:** Exercise sciences, sports admin. **Philosophy/religion:** Philosophy. **Physical sciences:** Chemistry. **Psychology:** General. **Social sciences:** General, political science. **Theology:** Bible. **Visual/performing arts:** Art, arts management, dance, dramatic. **Other:** Sports ministry.

**Most popular majors.** Business/marketing 17%, education 9%, parks/recreation 11%, psychology 8%, social sciences 6%, visual/performing arts 22%.

**Computing on campus.** 40 workstations in library, computer center. Dormitories wired for high-speed internet access and linked to campus network. Commuter students can connect to campus network. Online course registration, online library, wireless network available.

**Student life. Freshman orientation:** Mandatory. Preregistration for classes offered. Held 5 days before fall classes begin. **Policies:** Religious observance required. **Housing:** Guaranteed on-campus for all undergraduates. Single-sex dorms, wellness housing available. $100 fully refundable deposit, deadline 6/1. **Activities:** Bands, campus ministries, choral groups, dance, drama, international student organizations, literary magazine, music ensembles, student government, student newspaper, Baptist Student Union, College Republicans, Fellowship of Christian Athletes, Praise & Worship Fellowship, Reformed University Fellowship, Student Missions Fellowship.

**Athletics.** NAIA. **Intercollegiate:** Baseball M, basketball, cross-country, football (tackle) M, golf, soccer, softball W, tennis, volleyball W. **Intramural:** Basketball, football (non-tackle), soccer W, softball, volleyball, weight lifting W. **Team name:** Blazers.

**Student services.** Adult student services, chaplain/spiritual director, career counseling, student employment services, financial aid counseling, health services, personal counseling.

**Contact.** E-mail: admission@belhaven.edu
Phone: (601) 968-5940 Toll-free number: (800) 960-5940
Fax: (601) 968-8946
Suzanne Sullivan, Director of Admission, Belhaven University, 1500 Peachtree Street, Jackson, MS 39202

## Blue Mountain College
**Blue Mountain, Mississippi**
www.bmc.edu    CB code: 1066

- Private 4-year liberal arts college affiliated with Southern Baptist Convention
- Commuter campus in rural community
- 479 degree-seeking undergraduates: 12% part-time, 67% women, 15% African American, 1% Hispanic American
- 11 degree-seeking graduate students
- 44% of applicants admitted
- SAT or ACT (ACT writing optional) required
- 50% graduate within 6 years

**General.** Founded in 1873. Regionally accredited. **Degrees:** 95 bachelor's awarded; master's offered. **Location:** 69 miles from Memphis, Tennessee. **Calendar:** Semester, limited summer session. **Full-time faculty:** 27 total; 70% have terminal degrees, 4% minority, 52% women. **Part-time faculty:** 17 total; 29% have terminal degrees, 76% women. **Class size:** 67% < 20, 27% 20-39, 4% 40-49, 2% 50-99.

**Freshman class profile.** 272 applied, 119 admitted, 75 enrolled.

| Mid 50% test scores | | | |
|---|---|---|---|
| ACT composite: | 18-24 | Rank in top quarter: | 52% |
| GPA 3.75 or higher: | 39% | Rank in top tenth: | 21% |
| GPA 3.50-3.74: | 16% | End year in good standing: | 90% |
| GPA 3.0-3.49: | 21% | Return as sophomores: | 67% |
| GPA 2.0-2.99: | 20% | Out-of-state: | 29% |
| | | Live on campus: | 84% |

**Basis for selection.** High school record, test scores, and individual motivation considered.

**High school preparation.** College-preparatory program recommended. 15 units recommended. Recommended units include English 4, mathematics 3, social studies 1, history 2, science 3 (laboratory 2) and foreign language 2.

**2009-2010 Annual costs.** Tuition/fees: $8,790. Room/board: $3,800. Books/supplies: $750. Personal expenses: $500.

**2008-2009 Financial aid. Non-need-based:** Scholarships awarded for academics, alumni affiliation, art, athletics, leadership, music/drama, religious affiliation, state residency.

**Application procedures. Admission:** No deadline. $10 fee, may be waived for applicants with need, free for online applicants. Admission notification on a rolling basis beginning on or about 10/1. **Financial aid:** Priority date 3/1, closing date 7/31. FAFSA, institutional form required. Applicants notified on a rolling basis starting 4/1; must reply within 2 week(s) of notification.

**Academics. Special study options:** Accelerated study, combined bachelor's/graduate degree, double major, dual enrollment of high school students, honors, internships, teacher certification program. **Credit/placement by examination:** AP, CLEP, IB, SAT, ACT, institutional tests. 30 credit hours maximum toward bachelor's degree. **Support services:** Learning center, reduced course load, remedial instruction.

**Majors. Biology:** General. **Business:** Business admin. **Education:** Biology, elementary, English, mathematics, music, physical, science, social science, Spanish. **Foreign languages:** Spanish. **Health:** Clinical lab science. **History:** General. **Interdisciplinary:** Natural sciences. **Math:** General. **Parks/recreation:** Health/fitness. **Psychology:** General. **Social sciences:** General. **Theology:** Bible, sacred music. **Visual/performing arts:** General.

**Most popular majors.** Business/marketing 7%, education 51%, psychology 14%, theological studies 16%.

**Computing on campus.** 41 workstations in dormitories, library. Online library, wireless network available.

**Student life. Freshman orientation:** Mandatory, $50 fee. Preregistration for classes offered. Held the week prior to the opening of the fall semester; designed to provide opportunities for learning methods that support college success. **Policies:** Smoking and alcoholic beverages forbidden. Chapel attendance is required of all full-time students. Unmarried full-time students under the age of 21 are required to live on campus unless they are independent students, are living at home with parents or immediate family and commuting to school. **Housing:** Single-sex dorms, wellness housing available. $50 fully refundable deposit. **Activities:** Choral groups, drama, literary magazine, music ensembles, musical theater, student government, Alpha Psi Omega, Baptist Student Union, Cap and Gown Honor Society, Mississippi Association of Educators student chapter, psychology club, Society of Mathematicians and Scientists, Vivace club, Ministerial Association, Koinonia, social societies.

**Athletics.** NAIA. **Intercollegiate:** Basketball, cross-country. **Intramural:** Basketball, cross-country, football (non-tackle) M, golf M, softball, swimming, table tennis, tennis W, volleyball W. **Team name:** Toppers.

**Student services.** Health services, placement for graduates. **Physically disabled:** Services for visually, hearing impaired.

**Contact.** E-mail: admissions@bmc.edu
Phone: (662) 685-4771 ext. 166 Toll-free number: (800) 235-0136
Fax: (662) 685-4776
Maria Teel, Director of Admissions, Blue Mountain College, 201 West Main Street, PO Box 160, Blue Mountain, MS 38610-0160

## Delta State University
**Cleveland, Mississippi**    CB member
www.deltastate.edu    CB code: 1163

- Public 4-year university
- Commuter campus in large town

- 3,115 degree-seeking undergraduates: 20% part-time, 61% women, 39% African American, 1% Asian American, 1% Hispanic American, 2% international
- 916 degree-seeking graduate students
- 24% of applicants admitted
- ACT (writing optional) required
- 45% graduate within 6 years

**General.** Founded in 1924. Regionally accredited. **Degrees:** 599 bachelor's awarded; master's, doctoral offered. **ROTC:** Army. **Location:** 40 miles from Greenville, 110 miles from Memphis, Tennessee. **Calendar:** Semester, extensive summer session. **Full-time faculty:** 192 total; 70% have terminal degrees, 14% minority, 50% women. **Part-time faculty:** 67 total; 48% have terminal degrees, 9% minority, 57% women. **Class size:** 66% < 20, 31% 20-39, 2% 40-49, less than 1% 50-99. **Special facilities:** Planetarium, airport, archives & museum.

**Freshman class profile.** 1,919 applied, 469 admitted, 373 enrolled.

| Mid 50% test scores | | | |
|---|---|---|---|
| ACT composite: | 18-22 | GPA 2.0-2.99: | 36% |
| GPA 3.75 or higher: | 14% | Return as sophomores: | 63% |
| GPA 3.50-3.74: | 15% | Out-of-state: | 16% |
| GPA 3.0-3.49: | 33% | Live on campus: | 78% |
| | | International: | 3% |

**Basis for selection.** Combination of college preparatory curriculum, test scores, class rank. Mississippi residents must take ACT for admission. Interview required for art, music majors. Audition recommended for music majors; portfolio recommended for art majors.

**High school preparation.** College-preparatory program required. 15.5 units required. Required units include English 4, mathematics 3, social studies 3, science 3 (laboratory 2), computer science .5 and academic electives 2.

**2009-2010 Annual costs.** Tuition/fees: $4,449; $11,519 out-of-state. Room/board: $5,705. Books/supplies: $800.

**2008-2009 Financial aid.** **Need-based:** 295 full-time freshmen applied for aid; 249 were judged to have need; 249 of these received aid. Average scholarship/grant was $3,574. 33% of total undergraduate aid awarded as scholarships/grants, 67% as loans/jobs. **Non-need-based:** Awarded to 272 full-time undergraduates, including 45 freshmen. Scholarships awarded for academics, alumni affiliation, art, athletics, leadership, music/drama, state residency.

**Application procedures. Admission:** Priority date 8/1; no deadline. $25 fee. Admission notification on a rolling basis. **Financial aid:** Priority date 3/1; no closing date. FAFSA required. Applicants notified on a rolling basis starting 5/1.

**Academics. Special study options:** Distance learning, double major, dual enrollment of high school students, honors, independent study, internships, study abroad, teacher certification program. **Credit/placement by examination:** AP, CLEP, SAT, ACT, institutional tests. 30 credit hours maximum toward bachelor's degree. **Support services:** Learning center, preadmission summer program, remedial instruction, study skills assistance, tutoring, writing center.

**Majors. Biology:** General. **Business:** General, accounting, business admin, finance, hospitality admin, insurance, management information systems, marketing. **Communications:** Journalism. **Education:** Elementary, English, mathematics, music, physical, social science. **Family/consumer sciences:** General. **Foreign languages:** General. **Health:** Athletic training, audiology/speech pathology, nursing (RN). **History:** General. **Interdisciplinary:** Biological/physical sciences. **Math:** General. **Physical sciences:** Chemistry. **Protective services:** Criminal justice. **Psychology:** General. **Public administration:** Social work. **Social sciences:** General, political science. **Transportation:** Airline/commercial pilot, aviation. **Visual/performing arts:** General.

**Most popular majors.** Business/marketing 23%, education 18%, family/consumer sciences 8%, health sciences 14%, visual/performing arts 6%.

**Computing on campus.** 293 workstations in dormitories, library, computer center, student center. Dormitories wired for high-speed internet access and linked to campus network. Commuter students can connect to campus network. Online course registration, online library, helpline, repair service, student web hosting, wireless network available.

**Student life. Freshman orientation:** Available, $35 fee. Preregistration for classes offered. Provides opportunity for academic advisement. **Housing:** Guaranteed on-campus for all undergraduates. Single-sex dorms, apartments, fraternity/sorority housing available. $50 fully refundable deposit, deadline 8/1. **Activities:** Bands, campus ministries, choral groups, dance,

drama, international student organizations, literary magazine, music ensembles, musical theater, opera, student government, student newspaper, several religious, ethnic, social, political organizations available on campus.

**Athletics.** NCAA. **Intercollegiate:** Baseball M, basketball, cross-country W, diving, football (tackle) M, golf M, soccer, softball W, swimming, tennis. **Intramural:** Badminton, basketball, bowling, cross-country, diving, football (non-tackle), golf, racquetball, rifle, soccer, softball, swimming, table tennis, tennis, triathlon, volleyball. **Team name:** Statesmen; Lady Statesmen.

**Student services.** Alcohol/substance abuse counseling, career counseling, student employment services, financial aid counseling, health services, on-campus daycare, personal counseling, placement for graduates. **Physically disabled:** Services for speech, hearing impaired.

**Contact.** E-mail: admissions@deltastate.edu
Phone: (662) 846-4655 Toll-free number: (800) 468-6378
Fax: (662) 846-4684
Debbie Heslep, Dean of Enrollment Management, Delta State University, 117 Kent Wyatt Hall, Cleveland, MS 38733

---

## Jackson State University
**Jackson, Mississippi**  CB member
www.jsums.edu  CB code: 1341

- Public 4-year university
- Commuter campus in small city
- 6,810 degree-seeking undergraduates: 19% part-time, 62% women, 95% African American
- 1,978 degree-seeking graduate students
- 54% of applicants admitted
- SAT or ACT required
- 36% graduate within 6 years

**General.** Founded in 1877. Regionally accredited. **Degrees:** 905 bachelor's awarded; master's, doctoral offered. **ROTC:** Army, Air Force. **Location:** 210 miles from Memphis, Tennessee, 190 miles from New Orleans. **Calendar:** Semester, extensive summer session. **Full-time faculty:** 411 total; 79% have terminal degrees, 82% minority, 46% women. **Part-time faculty:** 114 total; 51% have terminal degrees, 85% minority, 52% women. **Special facilities:** National research center, science observatory, academic research and computing center.

**Freshman class profile.** 8,002 applied, 4,290 admitted, 853 enrolled.

| Mid 50% test scores | | | |
|---|---|---|---|
| ACT composite: | 17-20 | Rank in top quarter: | 33% |
| GPA 3.75 or higher: | 8% | End year in good standing: | 66% |
| GPA 3.50-3.74: | 9% | Return as sophomores: | 76% |
| GPA 3.0-3.49: | 25% | Out-of-state: | 38% |
| GPA 2.0-2.99: | 51% | Live on campus: | 75% |

**Basis for selection.** Test scores and high school transcript important. Audition recommended for music majors.

**High school preparation.** 15 units required. Required units include English 4, mathematics 3, social studies 3, science 3, foreign language 2 and academic electives 2.

**2009-2010 Annual costs.** Tuition/fees: $4,634; $11,359 out-of-state. Room/board: $6,254. Books/supplies: $800. Personal expenses: $2,250.

**2008-2009 Financial aid.** All financial aid based on need.

**Application procedures. Admission:** Priority date 8/1; no deadline. No application fee. Admission notification on a rolling basis beginning on or about 1/1. **Financial aid:** Priority date 4/1, closing date 5/1. FAFSA required. Applicants notified on a rolling basis starting 5/1.

**Academics. Special study options:** Distance learning, double major, dual enrollment of high school students, ESL, honors, independent study, internships, study abroad, teacher certification program, weekend college. **Credit/placement by examination:** AP, CLEP, SAT, ACT. 30 credit hours maximum toward bachelor's degree. **Support services:** Learning center, preadmission summer program, reduced course load, remedial instruction, study skills assistance, tutoring, writing center.

**Majors. Biology:** General. **Business:** Accounting, business admin, finance, marketing. **Communications:** Media studies. **Computer sciences:** General. **Education:** Elementary, instructional media, music, physical, social science, special. **Engineering:** Civil, computer, electrical. **Engineering technology:** Industrial. **Foreign languages:** General. **Health:** Communication disorders, health care admin, predental. **History:** General. **Math:** General. **Physical sciences:** Atmospheric science, chemistry, geology, physics. **Protective services:** Criminal justice. **Psychology:** General. **Public administration:** Social work. **Social sciences:** General, political science, sociology, urban studies. **Visual/performing arts:** General, music performance. **Other:** Professional interdiscplinary studies.

**Most popular majors.** Biology 10%, business/marketing 21%, education 14%, interdisciplinary studies 11%, social sciences 6%.

**Computing on campus.** Dormitories wired for high-speed internet access and linked to campus network. Commuter students can connect to campus network. Online course registration, helpline, wireless network available.

**Student life. Freshman orientation:** Mandatory. Preregistration for classes offered. **Housing:** Single-sex dorms available. $50 nonrefundable deposit. **Activities:** Bands, choral groups, dance, drama, film society, literary magazine, music ensembles, opera, radio station, student government, student newspaper, symphony orchestra, TV station, Pierre Toussaint Catholic Student Union, Baptist Student Union, Church of God in Christ club, NAACP, Alpha Phi Omega,.

**Athletics.** NCAA. **Intercollegiate:** Baseball M, basketball, bowling, cross-country, football (tackle) M, golf, rifle, soccer W, softball W, tennis, track and field, volleyball W. **Intramural:** Basketball, rifle, swimming, tennis, volleyball. **Team name:** JSU Tigers.

**Student services.** Adult student services, career counseling, student employment services, financial aid counseling, health services, on-campus daycare, personal counseling, placement for graduates, veterans' counselor. **Physically disabled:** Services for visually, speech, hearing impaired.

**Contact.** E-mail: admappl@jsums.edu
Phone: (601) 979-2100 Toll-free number: (800) 848-6917
Fax: (601) 979-2237
Stephanie Chatman, Director of Admissions and Financial Aid, Jackson State University, 1400 JR Lynch Street, Jackson, MS 39217

---

## Millsaps College
### Jackson, Mississippi
www.millsaps.edu                                      CB code: 1471

▶ Private 4-year business and liberal arts college affiliated with United Methodist Church
▶ Residential campus in large city
▶ 1,002 degree-seeking undergraduates: 1% part-time, 50% women, 11% African American, 4% Asian American, 2% Hispanic American, 2% international
▶ 97 degree-seeking graduate students
▶ 74% of applicants admitted
▶ SAT or ACT (ACT writing optional), application essay required
▶ 66% graduate within 6 years; 49% enter graduate study

**General.** Founded in 1890. Regionally accredited. 4,000-acre biocultural reserve and learning center in the state of Yucatan, Mexico Yucatan program also includes teaching and living facility for international business studies, in the city of Merida. **Degrees:** 238 bachelor's awarded; master's offered. **ROTC:** Army. **Location:** 190 miles from New Orleans, 210 miles from Memphis, Tennessee. **Calendar:** Semester, limited summer session. **Full-time faculty:** 96 total; 94% have terminal degrees, 12% minority, 44% women. **Part-time faculty:** 20 total; 30% have terminal degrees, 5% minority, 60% women. **Class size:** 66% < 20, 33% 20-39, less than 1% >100. **Special facilities:** Molecular biology/functional genomics research laboratory, fluorescence microscopy suite and imaging facility, GIS workstation, microsurgical lab for animal surgeries, hydrogeologic monitoring station, computational modeling laboratory, sorbent and environmental laboratory.

**Freshman class profile.** 1,348 applied, 992 admitted, 283 enrolled.

| Mid 50% test scores | | Rank in top quarter: | 50% |
|---|---|---|---|
| SAT critical reading: | 510-640 | Rank in top tenth: | 33% |
| SAT math: | 520-640 | Return as sophomores: | 78% |
| ACT composite: | 23-29 | Out-of-state: | 56% |
| GPA 3.75 or higher: | 38% | Live on campus: | 96% |
| GPA 3.50-3.74: | 21% | International: | 2% |
| GPA 3.0-3.49: | 25% | Fraternities: | 48% |
| GPA 2.0-2.99: | 16% | Sororities: | 52% |

**Basis for selection.** Test scores, GPA in academic courses, recommendations, essays, and school and community activities are important. Advanced credit is awarded for A-Levels, International Baccalaureate, and some other systems. Students interested in fine and performing arts scholarships

are required to submit a portfolio and/or audition for scholarships. **Homeschooled:** Statement describing homeschool structure and mission, transcript of courses and grades, letter of recommendation (nonparent) required. **Learning Disabled:** Students requiring accommodations should submit appropriate documentation from their physician.

**High school preparation.** 14 units required; 20 recommended. Required and recommended units include English 4, mathematics 3-4, social studies 2, history 2, science 3-4 (laboratory 1), foreign language 2 and academic electives 2.

**2010-2011 Annual costs.** Tuition/fees: $27,812. Room/board: $9,728. Books/supplies: $1,050. Personal expenses: $1,110.

**2009-2010 Financial aid. Need-based:** 245 full-time freshmen applied for aid; 186 were judged to have need; 186 of these received aid. Average need met was 92%. Average scholarship/grant was $22,158; average loan $3,071. 79% of total undergraduate aid awarded as scholarships/grants, 21% as loans/jobs. **Non-need-based:** Awarded to 530 full-time undergraduates, including 147 freshmen. Scholarships awarded for academics, art, leadership, music/drama, religious affiliation.

**Application procedures. Admission:** No deadline. No application fee. Admission notification on a rolling basis beginning on or about 10/1. Must reply by May 1 or within 2 week(s) if notified thereafter. Early action priority deadline is January 12, with notification 2 weeks after applying. **Financial aid:** Priority date 3/1; no closing date. FAFSA required. Applicants notified on a rolling basis starting 3/15; must reply by 5/1 or within 2 week(s) of notification.

**Academics. Special study options:** Accelerated study, combined bachelor's/graduate degree, double major, honors, independent study, internships, liberal arts/career combination, New York semester, semester at sea, student-designed major, study abroad, teacher certification program, United Nations semester, urban semester, Washington semester. Faith & Work Initiative; pre-health, pre-law, pre-social work, pre-ministerial programs; direct exchange programs with Akita International University in Japan, Hochschule Liechtenstein in Liechtenstein, and Queens University, the University of Ulster, and Belfast Metropolitan College in Northern Ireland; dual degrees in engineering, applied science and nursing through Auburn University, Columbia University, Vanderbilt University, Washington University, and University of Mississippi Medical Center; Study Abroad programs in Albania, Belgium, Cambodia, China, Costa Rica, Ecuador, England, France, Germany, Ghana, Greece, Israel, Italy, Japan, Jordan, Mexico (Yucatan), Tanzania and Viet Nam. **Credit/placement by examination:** AP, CLEP, IB, SAT, ACT, institutional tests. 28 credit hours maximum toward bachelor's degree. Limited to two courses in any discipline and seven courses overall. **Support services:** Pre-admission summer program, reduced course load, study skills assistance, tutoring, writing center.

**Majors. Area/ethnic studies:** European, Latin American. **Biology:** General, biochemistry. **Business:** Accounting, business admin. **Communications:** General. **Computer sciences:** General, computer science. **Education:** Elementary. **Foreign languages:** Classics, French, Spanish. **History:** General. **Math:** General, applied. **Philosophy/religion:** Philosophy, religion. **Physical sciences:** Chemistry, geology, physics. **Psychology:** General. **Public administration:** General. **Social sciences:** Anthropology, economics, political science, sociology. **Visual/performing arts:** Art history/conservation, dramatic, studio arts.

**Most popular majors.** Biology 11%, business/marketing 24%, English 6%, foreign language 6%, psychology 12%, social sciences 13%.

**Computing on campus.** 150 workstations in dormitories, library, computer center, student center. Dormitories wired for high-speed internet access and linked to campus network. Commuter students can connect to campus network. Online course registration, online library, helpline, student web hosting, wireless network available.

**Student life. Freshman orientation:** Mandatory. Preregistration for classes offered. 3 days before classes start. 8 days of educational and social activities and 8-week Foundations program held once weekly to explore student issues and involvement in campus activities. **Policies:** Students required to live on campus through sophomore year. Students with family in the area may be exempted. **Housing:** Guaranteed on-campus for freshmen. Coed dorms, single-sex dorms, special housing for disabled, fraternity/sorority housing available. Community service theme housing available. **Activities:** Pep band, campus ministries, choral groups, dance, drama, international student organizations, literary magazine, music ensembles, Model UN, musical theater, student government, student newspaper, Circle K, Christian Fellowship, Black student association, Habitat for Humanity, Catholic student association, Fellowship of Christian Athletes, College Republicans, Young Democrats, Multicultural Affairs Diversity Group, E.A.R.T.H. (environmental service club), Jewish cultural organization.

**Athletics.** NCAA. **Intercollegiate:** Baseball M, basketball, cross-country, football (tackle) M, golf, lacrosse, soccer, softball W, tennis, track and field, volleyball W. **Intramural:** Basketball, football (non-tackle), racquetball, soccer, softball, table tennis, volleyball. **Team name:** Millsaps Majors, Lady Majors.

**Student services.** Adult student services, alcohol/substance abuse counseling, chaplain/spiritual director, career counseling, student employment services, financial aid counseling, health services, minority student services, personal counseling, placement for graduates, women's services.

**Contact.** E-mail: admissions@millsaps.edu
Phone: (601) 974-1050 Toll-free number: (800) 352-1050
Fax: (601) 974-1059
Michael Thorp, Dean of Enrollment Management, Millsaps College, 1701 North State Street, Jackson, MS 39210-0001

---

## Mississippi College
### Clinton, Mississippi
www.mc.edu                                           CB code: 1477

- Private 4-year university affiliated with Southern Baptist Convention
- Residential campus in large city
- 3,084 degree-seeking undergraduates: 13% part-time, 60% women, 25% African American, 1% Asian American, 1% Hispanic American, 2% international
- 1,636 degree-seeking graduate students
- 61% of applicants admitted
- SAT or ACT (ACT writing optional) required
- 52% graduate within 6 years; 37% enter graduate study

**General.** Founded in 1826. Regionally accredited. **Degrees:** 522 bachelor's awarded; master's, doctoral, professional offered. **ROTC:** Army, Air Force. **Location:** 10 miles from Jackson. **Calendar:** Semester, limited summer session. **Full-time faculty:** 180 total; 77% have terminal degrees, 5% minority, 48% women. **Part-time faculty:** 244 total; 53% have terminal degrees, 12% minority, 48% women. **Class size:** 50% < 20, 37% 20-39, 10% 40-49, 2% 50-99. **Special facilities:** Baptist healthplex, Choctaw trails.

**Freshman class profile.** 1,763 applied, 1,080 admitted, 466 enrolled.

| Mid 50% test scores | | | |
|---|---|---|---|
| SAT critical reading: | 450-600 | GPA 2.0-2.99: | 27% |
| SAT math: | 470-600 | Rank in top quarter: | 50% |
| ACT composite: | 20-27 | Rank in top tenth: | 24% |
| GPA 3.75 or higher: | 34% | End year in good standing: | 82% |
| GPA 3.50-3.74: | 15% | Return as sophomores: | 67% |
| GPA 3.0-3.49: | 22% | Out-of-state: | 35% |
| | | Live on campus: | 94% |

**Basis for selection.** ACT/SAT scores most important, followed by high school record. Recommendations considered in marginal cases. For placement purposes, provisional admission if ACT score is less than 18. Admission and advising affects course load and course selection. Audition recommended for music majors; portfolio recommended for art majors. **Homeschooled:** Transcript of courses and grades required.

**High school preparation.** College-preparatory program recommended. 22 units recommended. Recommended units include English 4, mathematics 4, social studies 2, history 2, science 4 (laboratory 2), foreign language 1, computer science .5, visual/performing arts 1, academic electives 3.5. 2 units of advanced electives recommended.

**2010-2011 Annual costs.** Tuition/fees: $13,550. Room/board: $6,150. Books/supplies: $1,000. Personal expenses: $1,775.

**2009-2010 Financial aid. Need-based:** 452 full-time freshmen applied for aid; 284 were judged to have need; 283 of these received aid. Average need met was 80%. Average scholarship/grant was $10,549; average loan $5,685. 50% of total undergraduate aid awarded as scholarships/grants, 50% as loans/jobs. **Non-need-based:** Awarded to 1,198 full-time undergraduates, including 245 freshmen. Scholarships awarded for academics, alumni affiliation, art, leadership, music/drama, religious affiliation. **Additional information:** Student reply date for institutional scholarships: May 1.

**Application procedures. Admission:** No deadline. No application fee. Admission notification on a rolling basis. Either SAT or ACT may be substituted for TOEFL scores for foreign students. **Financial aid:** Priority date 3/1; no closing date. FAFSA required. Applicants notified on a rolling basis starting 3/1; must reply by 5/1.

**Academics. Special study options:** Accelerated study, combined bachelor's/graduate degree, distance learning, double major, dual enrollment of high school students, ESL, honors, independent study, internships, study abroad, teacher certification program. **Credit/placement by examination:** AP, CLEP, IB, ACT, institutional tests. 30 credit hours maximum toward bachelor's

degree. **Support services:** Reduced course load, remedial instruction, study skills assistance, tutoring, writing center.

**Majors. Biology:** General, biochemistry, biomedical sciences. **Business:** Accounting, business admin, marketing. **Communications:** General, journalism, media studies, public relations. **Computer sciences:** General, computer science. **Education:** Art, biology, business, chemistry, elementary, English, French, mathematics, music, physical, secondary, social studies, Spanish, special. **Engineering:** Physics. **Foreign languages:** French, Spanish, translation. **Health:** Nursing (RN). **History:** General. **Interdisciplinary:** Global studies. **Legal studies:** Paralegal, prelaw. **Math:** General. **Parks/recreation:** Exercise sciences, sports admin. **Philosophy/religion:** Christian. **Physical sciences:** Chemistry, physics. **Protective services:** Law enforcement admin. **Psychology:** General. **Public administration:** Social work. **Social sciences:** Political science, sociology. **Theology:** Sacred music. **Visual/performing arts:** Art, graphic design, interior design, music performance, music theory/composition, piano/organ, studio arts, voice/opera. **Other:** French and German.

**Most popular majors.** Biology 10%, business/marketing 26%, communications/journalism 7%, education 12%, health sciences 11%.

**Computing on campus.** 340 workstations in dormitories, library, computer center. Dormitories wired for high-speed internet access and linked to campus network. Commuter students can connect to campus network. Online course registration, helpline, student web hosting, wireless network available.

**Student life. Freshman orientation:** Available, $65 fee. Preregistration for classes offered. Held on a Thursday, Friday, and Saturday in July. **Policies:** No alcohol allowed, no smoking in front of buildings. **Housing:** Single-sex dorms, special housing for disabled, apartments, wellness housing available. $100 nonrefundable deposit, deadline 7/15. **Activities:** Bands, campus ministries, choral groups, dance, drama, international student organizations, literary magazine, music ensembles, musical theater, opera, radio station, student government, student newspaper, Baptist Student Union, Civitan, Circle-K, Rotoract, Young Democrats, Young Republicans, Black Student Association, 5 women's social/service clubs, Reformed University Fellowship, Habitat for Humanity.

**Athletics.** NCAA. **Intercollegiate:** Baseball M, basketball, cheerleading, cross-country, equestrian, football (tackle) M, golf, soccer, softball W, table tennis, tennis, track and field, volleyball W. **Intramural:** Badminton, basketball, field hockey, football (non-tackle), soccer, softball, table tennis, tennis, volleyball. **Team name:** Choctaws.

**Student services.** Adult student services, chaplain/spiritual director, career counseling, student employment services, financial aid counseling, health services, personal counseling, placement for graduates. **Physically disabled:** Services for visually, speech, hearing impaired.

**Contact.** E-mail: enrollment-services@mc.edu
Phone: (601) 925-3800 Toll-free number: (800) 738-1236
Fax: (601) 925-3950
Chad Phillips, Director of Admissions, Mississippi College, PO Box 4026, Clinton, MS 39058

---

## Mississippi State University
### Mississippi State, Mississippi                    CB member
www.msstate.edu                                      CB code: 1480

- Public 4-year university and agricultural college
- Residential campus in large town
- 13,730 degree-seeking undergraduates: 9% part-time, 48% women, 20% African American, 1% Asian American, 1% Hispanic American, 1% Native American, 2% international
- 3,615 degree-seeking graduate students
- 65% of applicants admitted
- SAT or ACT (ACT writing optional) required
- 60% graduate within 6 years

**General.** Founded in 1878. Regionally accredited. Branch campus located in Meridian; extension offices in all 82 counties; branch experiment stations and research units in 15 locations. **Degrees:** 2,656 bachelor's awarded; master's, doctoral, professional offered. **ROTC:** Army, Air Force. **Location:** 112 miles from Jackson, 116 miles from Birmingham, AL. **Calendar:** Semester, extensive summer session. **Full-time faculty:** 844 total; 80% have terminal degrees, 14% minority, 34% women. **Part-time faculty:** 168 total; 49% have terminal degrees, 8% minority, 56% women. **Class size:** 40% < 20, 41% 20-39, 7% 40-49, 10% 50-99, 3% >100. **Special facilities:** Clock museum, historic costume and textiles collection, archaeology museum, Mississippi entomological museum, arboretum, music museum, observatory, advanced vehicular systems center, computational sciences center, computer security research center, DoD user productivity enhancement and technology transfer, computational simulation and design center, geosystems research institute, high performance computing collaboratory, high voltage laboratory, industrial assessment center, industrial outreach service, clean energy technology institute, digital biology institute, neurocognitive science and technology institute, microsystems prototyping laboratory, Mississippi transportation research center, flight research laboratory, forensics training center, sustainable energy research center.

**Freshman class profile.** 7,839 applied, 5,109 admitted, 2,450 enrolled.

| Mid 50% test scores | | | |
|---|---|---|---|
| SAT critical reading: | 470-610 | Rank in top quarter: | 27% |
| SAT math: | 490-640 | Rank in top tenth: | 27% |
| ACT composite: | 20-27 | Return as sophomores: | 82% |
| GPA 3.75 or higher: | 22% | Out-of-state: | 29% |
| GPA 3.50-3.74: | 14% | Live on campus: | 91% |
| GPA 3.0-3.49: | 28% | International: | 2% |
| GPA 2.0-2.99: | 34% | Fraternities: | 24% |
| | | Sororities: | 35% |

**Basis for selection.** Admission based on standardized test scores, GPA, class rank. Students with academic deficiencies may be admitted after additional review. Requirements may vary by department; student should contact department to ensure that requirements are met. Successful completion of summer developmental program results in admission for fall term with mandatory participation in academic support program freshmen year. Audition, portfolio required. Interview recommended for architecture, professional golf management, and veterinary medicine students. **Homeschooled:** Transcript of courses and grades required.

**High school preparation.** College-preparatory program recommended. 15.5 units required; 20.5 recommended. Required and recommended units include English 4, mathematics 3-4, social studies 1-2, history 2, science 3-4 (laboratory 2), foreign language 1, computer science .5 and academic electives 2. One of the two academic electives must be a foreign language or world geography. Additional unit recommended.

**2009-2010 Annual costs.** Tuition/fees: $5,151; $13,021 out-of-state. Room/board: $7,520. Books/supplies: $1,200. Personal expenses: $2,250.

**2008-2009 Financial aid. Need-based:** 1,714 full-time freshmen applied for aid; 1,402 were judged to have need; 1,385 of these received aid. Average need met was 68%. Average scholarship/grant was $5,170; average loan $3,246. 36% of total undergraduate aid awarded as scholarships/grants, 64% as loans/jobs. **Non-need-based:** Awarded to 3,533 full-time undergraduates, including 1,047 freshmen. Scholarships awarded for academics, alumni affiliation, art, athletics, job skills, leadership, minority status, music/drama, ROTC, state residency. **Additional information:** No institutional closing date for FAFSA.

**Application procedures. Admission:** No deadline. $35 fee, may be waived for applicants with need. Admission notification on a rolling basis beginning on or about 9/1. **Financial aid:** Priority date 4/1; no closing date. FAFSA required. Applicants notified on a rolling basis starting 12/1; must reply by 5/1.

**Academics. Special study options:** Combined bachelor's/graduate degree, cooperative education, distance learning, double major, dual enrollment of high school students, ESL, exchange student, external degree, honors, independent study, internships, liberal arts/career combination, student-designed major, study abroad, teacher certification program, weekend college. **Credit/placement by examination:** AP, CLEP, IB, SAT, ACT, institutional tests. Maximum of 25 percent of any curriculum may be earned by examination which includes AP Credit, CLEP, correspondence, and military. **Support services:** Learning center, pre-admission summer program, reduced course load, remedial instruction, study skills assistance, tutoring, writing center.

**Honors college/program.** ACT composite score of 30 or above (SAT 1230) and a 3.8 high school core GPA.

**Majors. Agriculture:** General, agribusiness operations, agronomy, animal sciences, economics, food science, horticultural science, landscaping, plant protection, poultry. **Architecture:** Architecture, interior, landscape. **Biology:** General, bacteriology, biochemistry. **Business:** Accounting, business admin, construction management, finance, insurance, management information systems, managerial economics, marketing, real estate. **Communications:** General. **Computer sciences:** General. **Conservation:** Forestry, wildlife. **Education:** Agricultural, business, elementary, music, physical, secondary, special, voc/tech. **Engineering:** Aerospace, biomedical, chemical, civil, computer, electrical, industrial, mechanical. **Engineering technology:** Industrial. **Family/consumer sciences:** General. **Foreign languages:** General. **Health:** Clinical lab science. **History:** General. **Interdisciplinary:** Biological/physical sciences. **Liberal arts:** Arts/sciences. **Math:** General. **Philosophy/religion:** Philosophy. **Physical sciences:** Chemistry, geology, physics. **Psychology:** General, educational. **Public administration:** Social work. **Social sciences:** Anthropology, economics, political science, sociology. **Visual/**

**performing arts:** General. **Other:** Agricultural engineering technology and business, Computational engineering, Instructional technology, Veterinary medical science.

**Most popular majors.** Agriculture 6%, business/marketing 22%, education 20%, engineering/engineering technologies 14%, interdisciplinary studies 6%.

**Computing on campus.** 1,000 workstations in dormitories, library, computer center, student center. Dormitories wired for high-speed internet access and linked to campus network. Commuter students can connect to campus network. Online course registration, online library, helpline, repair service, student web hosting, wireless network available.

**Student life. Freshman orientation:** Available, $30 fee. Preregistration for classes offered. 2-day program for freshmen; 1-day program for transfer students. Held three times during the summer and prior to the beginning of each semester. Orientation fees and parents' fees vary for freshman and transfer students. **Policies:** Freshmen are required to live in residence hall and purchase a meal plan. **Housing:** Guaranteed on-campus for freshmen. Single-sex dorms, apartments, fraternity/sorority housing available. $50 nonrefundable deposit. Co-residential housing available. Residence halls are ADA accessible. **Activities:** Bands, campus ministries, choral groups, dance, drama, international student organizations, music ensembles, Model UN, musical theater, radio station, student government, student newspaper, TV station, more than 300 organizations on campus.

**Athletics.** NCAA. **Intercollegiate:** Baseball M, basketball, cross-country, football (tackle) M, golf, soccer W, softball W, tennis, track and field, volleyball W. **Intramural:** Badminton, basketball, bowling, football (non-tackle), golf, racquetball, soccer, softball, table tennis, tennis, volleyball, water polo, weight lifting. **Team name:** Bulldogs.

**Student services.** Adult student services, alcohol/substance abuse counseling, chaplain/spiritual director, career counseling, services for economically disadvantaged, student employment services, financial aid counseling, health services, minority student services, on-campus daycare, personal counseling, veterans' counselor. **Physically disabled:** Services for visually, speech, hearing impaired.

**Contact.** E-mail: admit@msstate.edu
Phone: (662) 325-2224 Fax: (662) 325-1678
Phil Bonfanti, Director of Admissions and Scholarships, Mississippi State University, Box 6334, Mississippi State, MS 39762

## Mississippi University for Women
Columbus, Mississippi                    CB member
www.muw.edu                              CB code: 1481

- Public 4-year university and liberal arts college
- Commuter campus in large town
- 2,069 degree-seeking undergraduates: 15% part-time, 84% women, 40% African American, 1% Asian American, 1% Hispanic American, 1% international
- 204 graduate students
- 42% of applicants admitted
- 41% graduate within 6 years

**General.** Founded in 1884. Regionally accredited. **Degrees:** 406 bachelor's, 33 associate awarded; master's offered. **ROTC:** Army, Air Force. **Location:** 120 miles from Birmingham, Alabama, 160 miles from Memphis, Tennessee. **Calendar:** Semester, limited summer session. **Full-time faculty:** 134 total; 55% have terminal degrees, 8% minority, 62% women. **Part-time faculty:** 51 total; 29% have terminal degrees, 8% minority, 63% women. **Class size:** 60% < 20, 33% 20-39, 4% 40-49, 2% 50-99, 2% >100. **Special facilities:** Environmental education center.

**Freshman class profile.** 1,376 applied, 580 admitted, 222 enrolled.

| Mid 50% test scores | | | |
|---|---|---|---|
| SAT critical reading: | 410-640 | Rank in top quarter: | 61% |
| SAT math: | 390-530 | Rank in top tenth: | 30% |
| ACT composite: | 18-24 | Return as sophomores: | 68% |
| GPA 3.75 or higher: | 23% | Out-of-state: | 10% |
| GPA 3.50-3.74: | 18% | Live on campus: | 66% |
| GPA 3.0-3.49: | 29% | International: | 3% |
| GPA 2.0-2.99: | 30% | Fraternities: | 42% |
| | | Sororities: | 43% |

**Basis for selection.** Test scores, high school GPA, academic achievement considered in that order. SAT or ACT recommended. Students with a 3.2 GPA or higher not required to provide test scores. Interview required for students who are taking a placement test. **Homeschooled:** Portfolio of work and/or transcript is required. Placement test may be required.

**High school preparation.** College-preparatory program recommended. 16 units required; 20 recommended. Required and recommended units include English 4, mathematics 3-4, social studies 3, science 3-4 (laboratory 2), foreign language 1, computer science .5 and academic electives 2. One elective of foreign language or world geography required; other elective must be in foreign language, world geography, 4th year mathematics, or 4th year laboratory science.

**2009-2010 Annual costs.** Tuition/fees: $4,423; $12,051 out-of-state. Room/board: $5,249. Books/supplies: $800. Personal expenses: $1,200.

**2009-2010 Financial aid. Non-need-based:** Scholarships awarded for academics, alumni affiliation, leadership, minority status, music/drama, ROTC, state residency.

**Application procedures. Admission:** No deadline. No application fee. Admission notification on a rolling basis. **Financial aid:** Priority date 3/1; no closing date. FAFSA required. Applicants notified on a rolling basis starting 3/15; must reply within 2 week(s) of notification.

**Academics. Special study options:** Cross-registration, distance learning, double major, dual enrollment of high school students, honors, independent study, internships, study abroad, teacher certification program, weekend college. **Credit/placement by examination:** AP, CLEP, SAT, ACT, institutional tests. 60 credit hours maximum toward bachelor's degree. **Support services:** Learning center, pre-admission summer program, remedial instruction, tutoring.

**Majors. Biology:** General, bacteriology. **Business:** Accounting, business admin. **Communications:** General. **Education:** Art, elementary, music. **Family/consumer sciences:** Family systems. **Foreign languages:** Spanish. **Health:** Music therapy, nursing (RN), speech pathology. **History:** General. **Legal studies:** Paralegal. **Liberal arts:** Arts/sciences. **Math:** General. **Parks/recreation:** Health/fitness. **Personal/culinary services:** Culinary arts. **Physical sciences:** General, chemistry. **Psychology:** General. **Social sciences:** General, political science. **Visual/performing arts:** General.

**Most popular majors.** Business/marketing 9%, education 15%, health sciences 33%.

**Computing on campus.** 500 workstations in dormitories, library, computer center. Dormitories wired for high-speed internet access and linked to campus network. Commuter students can connect to campus network. Online course registration, online library, helpline, student web hosting available.

**Student life. Freshman orientation:** Available, $50 fee. Preregistration for classes offered. **Housing:** Guaranteed on-campus for all undergraduates. Single-sex dorms, apartments, wellness housing available. $100 partly refundable deposit. **Activities:** Jazz band, choral groups, drama, international student organizations, literary magazine, music ensembles, radio station, student government, student newspaper, Methodist, Presbyterian, Episcopal, Baptist, Catholic, Student Interfaith Association, Black student organizations, College Republicans, Young Democrats.

**Athletics. Intramural:** Badminton, basketball, football (non-tackle), golf, racquetball, soccer, softball, table tennis, tennis, volleyball.

**Student services.** Adult student services, alcohol/substance abuse counseling, career counseling, student employment services, financial aid counseling, health services, on-campus daycare, personal counseling, placement for graduates, veterans' counselor. **Physically disabled:** Services for visually, speech, hearing impaired.

**Contact.**  E-mail: admissions@muw.edu
Phone: (662) 329-7106 Toll-free number: (877) 462-8439
Fax: (662) 241-7481
Cassie Derden, Director of Admissions, Mississippi University for Women, 1100 College St. MUW-1613, Columbus, MS 39701

---

## Mississippi Valley State University
**Itta Bena, Mississippi**                                   CB member
**www.mvsu.edu**                                             CB code: 1482

- Public 4-year university and liberal arts college
- Commuter campus in small town
- 2,357 degree-seeking undergraduates: 7% part-time, 62% women, 93% African American, 1% Hispanic American
- 416 degree-seeking graduate students
- 30% of applicants admitted
- SAT or ACT (ACT writing optional) required
- 51% graduate within 6 years

**General.** Founded in 1946. Regionally accredited. **Degrees:** 308 bachelor's awarded; master's offered. **ROTC:** Army. **Location:** 100 miles from Jackson, 130 miles from Memphis, Tennessee. **Calendar:** Semester, extensive summer session. **Full-time faculty:** 133 total; 58% have terminal degrees, 30% minority, 46% women. **Part-time faculty:** 46 total; 24% have terminal degrees, 15% minority, 65% women. **Class size:** 58% < 20, 36% 20-39, 4% 40-49, 2% 50-99.

**Freshman class profile.** 6,086 applied, 1,796 admitted, 415 enrolled.

| Mid 50% test scores | | | |
|---|---|---|---|
| ACT composite: | 15-19 | GPA 2.0-2.99: | 57% |
| GPA 3.75 or higher: | 3% | Return as sophomores: | 39% |
| GPA 3.50-3.74: | 3% | Out-of-state: | 24% |
| GPA 3.0-3.49: | 24% | Live on campus: | 81% |

**Basis for selection.** High school curriculum and test scores very important. Audition required for music education majors. Interview required of some students, but recommended for all students.

**High school preparation.** 16 units required; 18 recommended. Required and recommended units include English 4, mathematics 3, social studies 3, science 3 (laboratory 2), foreign language 1 and academic electives 2. Mathematics requirement includes algebra I and II and geometry. Social sciences must include US government and US history. Sciences must be chosen from introductory and advanced biology, physics, and chemistry. Advanced science or mathematics may be substituted for a foreign language.

**2009-2010 Annual costs.** Tuition/fees: $4,575; $11,410 out-of-state. Room/board: $5,081.

**Financial aid. Non-need-based:** Scholarships awarded for academics, athletics, minority status, ROTC.

**Application procedures. Admission:** Priority date 8/1; deadline 8/17 (receipt date). No application fee. Admission notification on a rolling basis. **Financial aid:** Priority date 3/1, closing date 5/1. FAFSA, institutional form required. Applicants notified on a rolling basis starting 4/1; must reply within 2 week(s) of notification.

**Academics. Special study options:** Cooperative education, double major, dual enrollment of high school students, honors, independent study, internships, teacher certification program. **Credit/placement by examination:** AP, CLEP, ACT. 30 credit hours maximum toward bachelor's degree. **Support services:** Learning center, pre-admission summer program, reduced course load, remedial instruction, study skills assistance, tutoring, writing center.

**Majors. Biology:** General. **Business:** Accounting, business admin, office management. **Communications:** General. **Computer sciences:** General. **Education:** Biology, early childhood, elementary, English, mathematics, music, physical, social science. **Engineering technology:** Industrial. **Health:** Environmental health. **History:** General. **Math:** General. **Physical sciences:** Chemistry. **Protective services:** Criminal justice. **Public administration:** General, social work. **Social sciences:** Political science, sociology. **Visual/performing arts:** Music management, studio arts.

**Most popular majors.** Biology 6%, business/marketing 18%, education 29%, public administration/social services 21%, security/protective services 10%.

**Computing on campus.** 600 workstations in dormitories, library, computer center. Dormitories wired for high-speed internet access and linked to campus network. Commuter students can connect to campus network. Online course registration, online library, wireless network available.

**Student life. Freshman orientation:** Mandatory, $75 fee. Preregistration for classes offered. **Housing:** Single-sex dorms, apartments available. $50 deposit, deadline 7/31. **Activities:** Bands, choral groups, dance, drama, music ensembles, radio station, student government, student newspaper, TV station, numerous honor societies, political, social, religious organizations, prelaw club.

**Athletics. NCAA. Intercollegiate:** Baseball M, basketball, bowling, cross-country, football (tackle) M, golf, soccer W, softball W, tennis, track and field, volleyball W. **Intramural:** Baseball M, basketball, bowling, cross-country, softball W, swimming, tennis, volleyball. **Team name:** Delta Devils (M), Devilettes (W).

**Student services.** Adult student services, career counseling, student employment services, financial aid counseling, health services, on-campus daycare, personal counseling, placement for graduates, veterans' counselor.

**Contact.** E-mail: nbtaylor@mvsu.edu
Phone: (662) 254-3347 Fax: (662) 254-3759
Nora Taylor, Director of Admissions and Recruitment, Mississippi Valley State University, 14000 Highway 82 West, Itta Bena, MS 38941-1400

## Rust College
### Holly Springs, Mississippi
### www.rustcollege.edu
**CB code: 1669**

- Private 4-year liberal arts college affiliated with United Methodist Church
- Residential campus in small town
- 1,200 degree-seeking undergraduates
- 55% of applicants admitted
- ACT (writing optional) required
- 59% graduate within 6 years; 35% enter graduate study

**General.** Founded in 1866. Regionally accredited. **Degrees:** 118 bachelor's, 5 associate awarded. **Location:** 35 miles from Memphis, Tennessee. **Calendar:** Semester, limited summer session. **Full-time faculty:** 46 total. **Part-time faculty:** 4 total. **Class size:** 59% < 20, 19% 20-39, 4% 40-49, 12% 50-99, 5% >100. **Special facilities:** Library for ministers and ministerial students, Inuit and African art collections, international artifacts collection.

**Freshman class profile.** 571 applied, 313 admitted, 313 enrolled.

| Mid 50% test scores | | GPA 3.0-3.49: | 17% |
|---|---|---|---|
| ACT composite: | 14-17 | GPA 2.0-2.99: | 71% |
| GPA 3.75 or higher: | 6% | End year in good standing: | 80% |
| GPA 3.50-3.74: | 6% | Out-of-state: | 52% |

**Basis for selection.** School achievement record and recommendations most important. Test scores also important. **Homeschooled:** State high school equivalency certificate, letter of recommendation (nonparent) required.

**High school preparation.** 19 units required. Required units include English 4, mathematics 3, social studies 3, science 3 and academic electives 6.

**2009-2010 Annual costs.** Tuition/fees: $7,410. Room/board: $3,220. Books/supplies: $500. Personal expenses: $1,450.

**2008-2009 Financial aid. Need-based:** Average need met was 92%. Average scholarship/grant was $4,314; average loan $2,945. 48% of total undergraduate aid awarded as scholarships/grants, 52% as loans/jobs. **Non-need-based:** Scholarships awarded for academics, leadership, music/drama, religious affiliation, state residency.

**Application procedures. Admission:** Priority date 5/5; no deadline. $10 fee, may be waived for applicants with need. Admission notification on a rolling basis. Must reply by May 1 or within 2 week(s) if notified thereafter. **Financial aid:** Closing date 5/1. FAFSA, institutional form required. Applicants notified on a rolling basis starting 5/1; must reply within 2 week(s) of notification.

**Academics. Special study options:** Double major, honors, independent study, internships, liberal arts/career combination, study abroad, teacher certification program. Nursing and medical technology cooperative program with other institutions. **Credit/placement by examination:** AP, CLEP, ACT, institutional tests. 12 credit hours maximum toward associate degree, 12 toward bachelor's. **Support services:** Learning center, pre-admission summer program, reduced course load, remedial instruction, study skills assistance, tutoring, writing center.

**Majors. Biology:** General. **Business:** Business admin. **Communications:** Broadcast journalism, journalism. **Computer sciences:** Computer science. **Education:** Biology, business, elementary, English, mathematics, social science. **Family/consumer sciences:** Child care. **Math:** General. **Physical sciences:** Chemistry. **Public administration:** Social work. **Social sciences:** General, political science, sociology.

**Most popular majors.** Biology 27%, business/marketing 14%, computer/information sciences 12%, English 7%, family/consumer sciences 12%, public administration/social services 8%, social sciences 9%.

**Computing on campus.** 220 workstations in dormitories, library, computer center. Dormitories wired for high-speed internet access and linked to campus network. Commuter students can connect to campus network. Online library, helpline, wireless network available.

**Student life. Freshman orientation:** Mandatory. Orientation and assessment program begins 1 week prior to registration. **Housing:** Guaranteed on-campus for all undergraduates. Single-sex dorms, apartments available.

$50 deposit. **Activities:** Bands, choral groups, dance, drama, music ensembles, radio station, student government, student newspaper, TV station, Methodist Student Movement, Baptist Student Union, Catholic Student Association, pre-law club, NAACP, social work club, Sunday School Association, international student association, All Saints Student Movement.

**Athletics.** NCAA. **Intercollegiate:** Baseball M, basketball, cheerleading, cross-country, soccer M, softball W, tennis, track and field, volleyball. **Intramural:** Badminton, baseball, basketball, bowling, cheerleading, cross-country, football (non-tackle), soccer, softball, swimming, table tennis, tennis, track and field, volleyball, weight lifting. **Team name:** Bearcats.

**Student services.** Adult student services, career counseling, student employment services, health services, minority student services, on-campus daycare, personal counseling, placement for graduates, veterans' counselor.

**Contact.** E-mail: jascott@rustcollege.edu
Phone: (662) 252-8000 ext. 4059 Toll-free number: (888) 886-8492 ext. 4059 Fax: (662) 252-8895
JoAnn Scott, Director of Enrollment Services, Rust College, 150 Rust Avenue, Holly Springs, MS 38635-2328

## Southeastern Baptist College
### Laurel, Mississippi
### www.southeasternbaptist.edu
**CB code: 1781**

- Private 4-year Bible college affiliated with Baptist faith
- Commuter campus in large town

**General.** Founded in 1949. Accredited by ABHE. **Location:** 90 miles from Jackson. **Calendar:** Semester.

**Annual costs/financial aid.** Tuition/fees (2009-2010): $5,650. Room: $800. Books/supplies: $300. Personal expenses: $350.

**Contact.** Phone: (601) 426-6346
Academic Dean, 4229 Highway 15 North, Laurel, MS 39440

## Tougaloo College
### Tougaloo, Mississippi
### www.tougaloo.edu
**CB member**
**CB code: 1807**

- Private 4-year liberal arts college affiliated with United Christian Mission Society and United Church of Christ
- Residential campus in large city
- 930 degree-seeking undergraduates: 3% part-time, 67% women, 98% African American
- 100% of applicants admitted
- SAT or ACT (ACT writing optional) required
- 38% graduate within 6 years

**General.** Founded in 1869. Regionally accredited. Cooperative program with Brown University provides exchange of financial resources and students. Exchange opportunities available between New York and Boston universities in pre-med and other areas. **Degrees:** 148 bachelor's, 1 associate awarded. **ROTC:** Army, Naval. **Calendar:** Semester, limited summer session. **Full-time faculty:** 74 total; 35% minority, 55% women. **Part-time faculty:** 22 total; 4% minority, 82% women. **Class size:** 68% < 20, 30% 20-39, 2% 40-49, less than 1% 50-99. **Special facilities:** Civil rights documents and prints, East and West African art and artifacts.

**Freshman class profile.** 1,141 applied, 1,138 admitted, 235 enrolled.

| Mid 50% test scores | | End year in good standing: | 97% |
|---|---|---|---|
| SAT critical reading: | 480-550 | Return as sophomores: | 74% |
| SAT math: | 500-510 | Out-of-state: | 26% |
| ACT composite: | 24-28 | Live on campus: | 90% |

**Basis for selection.** Transcript, test scores important. Minimum 3.0 GPA and ACT composite score of 18 required of applicants in junior year of high school. Audition required for music majors. Portfolio recommended for art majors.

**High school preparation.** College-preparatory program recommended. 16 units required. Required and recommended units include English 3, mathematics 2, social studies 2, science 2, foreign language 2 and academic electives 9.

**2010-2011 Annual costs.** Tuition/fees (projected): $9,718. Room/board: $6,330. Books/supplies: $500. Personal expenses: $800.

**2009-2010 Financial aid. Need-based:** 210 full-time freshmen applied for aid; 200 were judged to have need; 195 of these received aid. Average need met was 60%. Average scholarship/grant was $7,350; average loan $3,500. 31% of total undergraduate aid awarded as scholarships/grants, 69% as loans/jobs. **Non-need-based:** Awarded to 317 full-time undergraduates, including 72 freshmen. Scholarships awarded for academics, athletics, ROTC.

**Application procedures. Admission:** Priority date 4/15; no deadline. $25 fee, may be waived for applicants with need. Admission notification on a rolling basis. **Financial aid:** Priority date 4/15; no closing date. FAFSA, institutional form required. Applicants notified on a rolling basis starting 5/1; must reply within 2 week(s) of notification.

**Academics. Special study options:** Accelerated study, cooperative education, cross-registration, double major, dual enrollment of high school students, exchange student, honors, independent study, internships, liberal arts/career combination, New York semester, student-designed major, study abroad, teacher certification program, Washington semester. 3-2 program in pre-engineering and physical sciences with Brown University, Georgia Institute of Technology, University of Mississippi, University of Wisconsin Madison, Tuskegee Institute, Washington University St. Louis, Howard University, University of Memphis, Florida A&M. **Credit/placement by examination:** AP, CLEP, IB, SAT, ACT, institutional tests. 12 credit hours maximum toward bachelor's degree. **Support services:** Learning center, pre-admission summer program, reduced course load, remedial instruction, study skills assistance, tutoring, writing center.

**Majors. Biology:** General. **Communications:** Media studies. **Education:** Elementary, health, kindergarten/preschool, secondary, special. **History:** General. **Interdisciplinary:** Math/computer science. **Liberal arts:** Arts/sciences. **Math:** General. **Physical sciences:** Chemistry, physics. **Psychology:** General. **Social sciences:** Economics, political science, sociology. **Visual/performing arts:** Art.

**Most popular majors.** Biology 8%, education 7%, English 12%, history 8%, psychology 20%, social sciences 25%.

**Computing on campus.** 4 workstations in dormitories, library, computer center, student center. Dormitories linked to campus network. Commuter students can connect to campus network. Helpline, repair service available.

**Student life. Freshman orientation:** Mandatory. Preregistration for classes offered. **Housing:** Single-sex dorms, wellness housing available. $50 non-refundable deposit. **Activities:** Jazz band, choral groups, dance, drama, music ensembles, radio station, student government, student newspaper, Baptist student union, biology club, Afro-American studies group, College Republicans, foreign students club, French club, pre-health club, prelaw club, honor societies, human services clubs.

**Athletics.** NAIA. **Intercollegiate:** Baseball M, basketball, cross-country, golf, tennis. **Intramural:** Badminton, baseball M, basketball, cheerleading, cross-country M, football (non-tackle) M, golf, soccer M, softball, tennis, volleyball. **Team name:** Bulldogs.

**Student services.** Adult student services, chaplain/spiritual director, career counseling, student employment services, financial aid counseling, health services, personal counseling, placement for graduates, veterans' counselor.

**Contact.** E-mail: info@tougaloo.edu
Phone: (601) 977-7765 Toll-free number: (888) 424-2566
Fax: (601) 977-4501
Junoesque Jacobs, Director of Admissions, Tougaloo College, 500 West County Line Road, Tougaloo, MS 39174

---

## University of Mississippi
### University, Mississippi
www.olemiss.edu

**CB member**
**CB code: 1840**

♦ Public 4-year university
♦ Residential campus in large town
♦ 13,024 degree-seeking undergraduates: 8% part-time, 53% women, 15% African American, 2% Asian American, 1% Hispanic American, 1% international
♦ 2,523 degree-seeking graduate students
♦ 79% of applicants admitted
♦ 61% graduate within 6 years

**General.** Founded in 1844. Regionally accredited. **Degrees:** 2,506 bachelor's awarded; master's, doctoral, professional offered. **ROTC:** Army, Naval, Air Force. **Location:** 75 miles from Memphis, Tennessee. **Calendar:** Semester, extensive summer session. **Full-time faculty:** 729 total; 84% have terminal degrees, 20% minority, 39% women. **Part-time faculty:** 148 total; 56% have terminal degrees, 10% minority, 53% women. **Class size:** 49%

< 20, 32% 20-39, 5% 40-49, 11% 50-99, 3% >100. **Special facilities:** Accredited teaching museum, William Faulkner home and grounds, Southern culture center, National Center for Physical Acoustics, 2 super computers, National Center for the Development of Natural Products, National School Food Service Management Institute, water and wetland resources center.

**Freshman class profile.** 8,595 applied, 6,833 admitted, 2,576 enrolled.

| Mid 50% test scores | | | |
|---|---|---|---|
| SAT critical reading: | 460-580 | GPA 3.0-3.49: | 30% |
| SAT math: | 460-600 | GPA 2.0-2.99: | 28% |
| ACT composite: | 20-26 | Rank in top quarter: | 48% |
| GPA 3.75 or higher: | 25% | Rank in top tenth: | 26% |
| GPA 3.50-3.74: | 16% | International: | 1% |

**Basis for selection.** School achievement record and test scores important. SAT or ACT may be required for students with core GPA of under 3.2. Essay required for Croft Institute for International Studies, honors college; audition required for music, theater majors. Portfolio recommended for art majors. **Homeschooled:** Transcript of courses and grades required. **Learning Disabled:** Report and document disabilities to student disabilities office.

**High school preparation.** College-preparatory program required. 15 units required. Required and recommended units include English 4, mathematics 3-4, social studies 1-2, history 2, science 3-4 (laboratory 2), foreign language 1-2, computer science .5 and academic electives 1. Mathematics units must include algebra and 2 higher courses. Social sciences units must include U.S. history and U.S. government. Academic electives must include 1 year world geography and fourth year math or science.

**2009-2010 Annual costs.** Tuition/fees: $5,106; $13,046 out-of-state. Room/board: $6,190.

**2008-2009 Financial aid. Need-based:** 1,507 full-time freshmen applied for aid; 976 were judged to have need; 949 of these received aid. Average need met was 77%. Average scholarship/grant was $7,169; average loan $3,513. 44% of total undergraduate aid awarded as scholarships/grants, 56% as loans/jobs. **Non-need-based:** Awarded to 3,042 full-time undergraduates, including 835 freshmen. Scholarships awarded for academics, alumni affiliation, art, athletics, leadership, minority status, music/drama, ROTC, state residency.

**Application procedures. Admission:** Priority date 4/1; deadline 7/20 (postmark date). $30 fee ($50 out-of-state), may be waived for applicants with need. Admission notification on a rolling basis beginning on or about 9/15. Online out-of-state application fee: $50. **Financial aid:** Priority date 3/15; no closing date. FAFSA required. Applicants notified on a rolling basis starting 4/1; must reply within 3 week(s) of notification.

**Academics. Special study options:** Accelerated study, combined bachelor's/graduate degree, cooperative education, distance learning, double major, ESL, exchange student, honors, independent study, internships, study abroad, teacher certification program. **Credit/placement by examination:** AP, CLEP, IB, institutional tests. 63 credit hours maximum toward bachelor's degree. Student must earn 12 hours in residence before any credit-by-examination hours are recorded on transcript. **Support services:** Learning center, pre-admission summer program, reduced course load, remedial instruction, study skills assistance, tutoring, writing center.

**Honors college/program.** Requires test scores, transcript, essays, and recommendations. 120 students admitted each fall. Unique courses which meet general education requirements taught by senior/master faculty. Senior thesis required.

**Majors. Area/ethnic studies:** African-American. **Biology:** General. **Business:** Accounting, business admin, finance, hospitality admin, insurance, management information systems, managerial economics, marketing, real estate. **Communications:** Journalism. **Computer sciences:** General. **Education:** Elementary, English, foreign languages, mathematics, science, social studies, special. **Engineering:** General, chemical, civil, electrical, geological, mechanical. **Foreign languages:** Chinese, classics, French, German, linguistics, Spanish. **Health:** Audiology/speech pathology, clinical lab science, dietetics, pharmaceutical sciences. **History:** General. **Legal studies:** Paralegal. **Liberal arts:** Arts/sciences. **Math:** General. **Parks/recreation:** Exercise sciences, facilities management. **Philosophy/religion:** Philosophy. **Physical sciences:** Chemistry, geology, physics. **Protective services:** Forensics, law enforcement admin. **Psychology:** General. **Public administration:** Policy analysis, social work. **Social sciences:** Anthropology, economics, international relations, political science, sociology. **Visual/performing arts:** General, art history/conservation, dramatic. **Other:** Marketing communications, Southern studies.

**Most popular majors.** Business/marketing 31%, communications/journalism 6%, education 12%, psychology 6%.

**Computing on campus.** 638 workstations in dormitories, library, computer center. Dormitories wired for high-speed internet access and linked to campus network. Commuter students can connect to campus network. Online course registration, online library, helpline, repair service, student web hosting, wireless network available.

**Student life. Freshman orientation:** Mandatory. Preregistration for classes offered. 2 days in June, additional session immediately before beginning of term. **Housing:** Guaranteed on-campus for freshmen. Single-sex dorms, apartments, fraternity/sorority housing, wellness housing available. $75 nonrefundable deposit. Intensive study floors available to honors and other students. Special interest, graduate/older students, substance-free, environmental interest housing available. **Activities:** Bands, campus ministries, choral groups, dance, drama, international student organizations, music ensembles, musical theater, opera, radio station, student government, student newspaper, symphony orchestra, TV station, Wesley Foundation, Baptist student union, Black student union, Students for Environmental Awareness, Mortar Board, Habitat for Humanity, Students Envisioning Equality through Diversity.

**Athletics.** NCAA. **Intercollegiate:** Baseball M, basketball, cheerleading, cross-country, fencing, football (tackle) M, golf, lacrosse M, racquetball M, rifle W, rugby M, skiing M, soccer, softball W, tennis, track and field, volleyball W. **Intramural:** Badminton, basketball, bowling, football (tackle), golf, handball, rifle, soccer, softball, swimming, table tennis, tennis, track and field, volleyball, water polo. **Team name:** Rebels.

**Student services.** Adult student services, alcohol/substance abuse counseling, chaplain/spiritual director, career counseling, student employment services, financial aid counseling, health services, legal services, minority student services, personal counseling, placement for graduates, veterans' counselor, women's services. **Physically disabled:** Services for visually, speech, hearing impaired.

**Contact.** E-mail: admissions@olemiss.edu
Phone: (662) 915-7226 Toll-free number: (800) 653-6477
Fax: (662) 915-5869
Charlotte Fant, Director of Admissions and Registrar, University of Mississippi, 145 Martindale, University, MS 38677-1848

## University of Mississippi Medical Center
### Jackson, Mississippi
www.umc.edu                              CB code: 0358

▶ Public two-year upper-division health science college
▶ Commuter campus in large city

**General.** Founded in 1955. Regionally accredited. **Location:** 200 miles from Memphis, Tennessee. **Calendar:** Quarter.

**Annual costs/financial aid.** Tuition/fees (2009-2010): $5,106; $13,046 out-of-state. Tuition and fees quoted are for nursing and other health-related undergraduate programs. Books/supplies: $1,596. Need-based financial aid available to full-time and part-time students.

**Contact.** Phone: (601) 984-1080
Registrar, 2500 North State Street, Jackson, MS 39216

## University of Southern Mississippi
### Hattiesburg, Mississippi                CB member
www.usm.edu                              CB code: 1479

▶ Public 4-year university
▶ Residential campus in small city
▶ 12,383 degree-seeking undergraduates: 14% part-time, 61% women, 30% African American, 1% Asian American, 2% Hispanic American, 1% international
▶ 2,910 degree-seeking graduate students
▶ 56% of applicants admitted
▶ SAT or ACT (ACT writing optional) required
▶ 45% graduate within 6 years

**General.** Founded in 1910. Regionally accredited. Dual campus with main campus in Hattiesburg and nonresidential, nontraditional campus in Long Beach; other sites along Mississippi Gulf Coast. **Degrees:** 2,374 bachelor's awarded; master's, doctoral offered. **ROTC:** Army, Air Force. **Location:** 85 miles from Jackson, 110 miles from New Orleans. **Calendar:** Semester, extensive summer session. **Full-time faculty:** 758 total; 74% have terminal degrees, 15% minority, 47% women. **Part-time faculty:** 185 total; 38% have terminal degrees, 6% minority, 55% women. **Class size:** 46% < 20, 38% 20-39, 6% 40-49, 7% 50-99, 3% >100. **Special facilities:** Marine education center, aquarium.

**Freshman class profile.** 5,081 applied, 2,860 admitted, 1,602 enrolled.

| Mid 50% test scores | | | |
|---|---|---|---|
| SAT critical reading: | 460-560 | Rank in top quarter: | 41% |
| SAT math: | 450-570 | Rank in top tenth: | 15% |
| ACT composite: | 18-24 | Return as sophomores: | 74% |
| GPA 3.75 or higher: | 14% | Out-of-state: | 22% |
| GPA 3.50-3.74: | 12% | Live on campus: | 91% |
| GPA 3.0-3.49: | 29% | International: | 1% |
| GPA 2.0-2.99: | 44% | Fraternities: | 17% |
| | | Sororities: | 20% |

**Basis for selection.** Test scores, GPA, class rank important. Applicants who don't meet criteria may be required to participate in screening process that includes testing. Test not required of some students.

**High school preparation.** College-preparatory program required. 15.5 units required; 17.5 recommended. Required and recommended units include English 4, mathematics 3, social studies 3, science 3, foreign language 2, computer science .5 and academic electives 2. Mathematics must include algebra I and II, geometry or higher mathematics. Social sciences must include US government, US history, world history, and economics or geography. Sciences must be chosen from introductory and advanced biology, physics, and chemistry. 2 units world geography, or additional science or mathematics may be substituted for 1 foreign language.

**2009-2010 Annual costs.** Tuition/fees: $5,096; $13,051 out-of-state. Room/board: $5,972. Books/supplies: $1,400. Personal expenses: $3,314.

**2008-2009 Financial aid. Need-based:** 1,433 full-time freshmen applied for aid; 1,172 were judged to have need; 1,143 of these received aid. Average need met was 84%. Average scholarship/grant was $4,771; average loan $4,057. 44% of total undergraduate aid awarded as scholarships/grants, 56% as loans/jobs. **Non-need-based:** Awarded to 4,255 full-time undergraduates, including 964 freshmen.

**Application procedures. Admission:** No deadline. $35 fee, may be waived for applicants with need. Admission notification on a rolling basis beginning on or about 9/1. **Financial aid:** Priority date 3/15; no closing date. FAFSA, institutional form required.

**Academics. Special study options:** Combined bachelor's/graduate degree, distance learning, double major, dual enrollment of high school students, honors, independent study, internships, study abroad, teacher certification program. **Credit/placement by examination:** AP, CLEP, SAT, ACT, institutional tests. 30 credit hours maximum toward bachelor's degree. **Support services:** Learning center, pre-admission summer program, reduced course load, remedial instruction, study skills assistance, tutoring, writing center.

**Honors college/program.** Requires an ACT score of 26 or equivalent GPA requirement, and essay.

**Majors. Architecture:** Interior. **Area/ethnic studies:** American. **Biology:** General, marine. **Business:** Accounting, business admin, finance, hotel/motel admin, human resources, international, management information systems, managerial economics, marketing, tourism/travel. **Communications:** General, advertising, journalism, radio/tv. **Computer sciences:** General, data processing. **Education:** Business, Deaf/hearing impaired, elementary, music, physical, special, technology/industrial arts. **Engineering technology:** Architectural, computer, electrical, industrial. **Family/consumer sciences:** Clothing/textiles, family studies, family systems. **Foreign languages:** General. **Health:** Athletic training, audiology/speech pathology, clinical lab science, dietetics, health services, nursing (RN). **History:** General. **Interdisciplinary:** Biological/physical sciences. **Legal studies:** Paralegal. **Liberal arts:** Library science. **Math:** General. **Parks/recreation:** General, sports admin. **Personal/culinary services:** Mortuary science. **Philosophy/religion:** Philosophy, religion. **Physical sciences:** Chemistry, geology, oceanography, physics. **Protective services:** Criminal justice, forensics. **Psychology:** General. **Public administration:** Social work. **Social sciences:** Anthropology, geography, international relations, political science, sociology. **Visual/performing arts:** General, dance, dramatic, music management. **Other:** Applied technology.

**Most popular majors.** Business/marketing 23%, education 10%, health sciences 13%, psychology 8%.

**Computing on campus.** 202 workstations in dormitories, library, computer center. Dormitories wired for high-speed internet access and linked to campus network. Commuter students can connect to campus network. Online course registration, online library, helpline, student web hosting, wireless network available.

**Student life. Freshman orientation:** Available. Preregistration for classes offered. **Policies:** Freshmen who reside in area may live at home. All freshmen who request campus housing required to live in freshman dormitories. **Housing:** Single-sex dorms, special housing for disabled, apartments, fraternity/

sorority housing available. $75 nonrefundable deposit, deadline 2/1. **Activities:** Bands, campus ministries, choral groups, dance, drama, film society, international student organizations, literary magazine, music ensembles, musical theater, opera, radio station, student government, student newspaper, symphony orchestra, Honor societies, service and religious Organizations, Young Republicans, Young Democrats.

**Athletics.** NCAA. **Intercollegiate:** Baseball M, basketball, cross-country, football (tackle) M, golf, rugby M, soccer W, softball W, tennis, track and field, volleyball W. **Intramural:** Badminton, basketball, bowling, golf, racquetball, soccer, softball, squash, swimming, table tennis, tennis, track and field, volleyball. **Team name:** Golden Eagles.

**Student services.** Adult student services, career counseling, student employment services, health services, minority student services, on-campus daycare, personal counseling, placement for graduates, veterans' counselor, women's services. **Physically disabled:** Services for visually, speech, hearing impaired. **Learning disabled:** Comprehensive services available.

**Contact.**   E-mail: admissions@usm.edu
Phone: (601) 266-5000 Fax: (601) 266-5148
Amanda Belsom, Admissions Operations, University of Southern Mississippi, 118 College Drive #5166, Hattiesburg, MS 39406-0001

---

## Wesley College
### Florence, Mississippi
www.wesleycollege.edu                 CB code: 1923

▶ Private 4-year Bible college affiliated with Congregational Methodist Church
▶ Residential campus in small town
▶ 143 degree-seeking undergraduates
▶ 100% of applicants admitted
▶ SAT or ACT (ACT writing optional), application essay required

**General.** Founded in 1972. Accredited by ABHE. **Degrees:** 9 bachelor's awarded. **Location:** 12 miles from Jackson. **Calendar:** Semester, limited summer session. **Full-time faculty:** 5 total. **Part-time faculty:** 13 total. **Class size:** 82% < 20, 18% 20-39.

**Freshman class profile.** 17 applied, 17 admitted, 17 enrolled.

| Mid 50% test scores | | | |
|---|---|---|---|
| SAT critical reading: | 430-580 | Rank in top quarter: | 12% |
| SAT math: | 440-600 | Rank in top tenth: | 2% |
| ACT composite: | 14-21 | Out-of-state: | 46% |
| | | Live on campus: | 92% |

**Basis for selection.** Test scores, school achievement record, essay important. **Homeschooled:** Must have certified diploma, GED, or meet minimum ACT/SAT scores as specified in current college catalog. **Learning Disabled:** Copies of previous diagnostic records requested.

**High school preparation.** 15 units recommended. Recommended units include English 4, mathematics 2, social studies 4, science 3 and academic electives 2.

**2009-2010 Annual costs.** Tuition/fees: $9,084. Room/board: $4,800. Books/supplies: $700. Personal expenses: $650.

**2008-2009 Financial aid.** **Non-need-based:** Scholarships awarded for academics, alumni affiliation, leadership, religious affiliation.

**Application procedures. Admission:** Priority date 7/1; deadline 8/15 (receipt date). $25 fee. Admission notification on a rolling basis. Must reply by May 1 or within 4 week(s) if notified thereafter. **Financial aid:** Closing date 5/14. FAFSA required. Applicants notified on a rolling basis starting 7/1; must reply within 2 week(s) of notification.

**Academics. Special study options:** Distance learning, double major, dual enrollment of high school students, independent study, internships. **Credit/placement by examination:** AP, CLEP, institutional tests. 15 credit hours maximum toward associate degree, 15 toward bachelor's. **Support services:** Learning center, reduced course load, remedial instruction, study skills assistance, tutoring.

**Majors. Philosophy/religion:** Religion. **Theology:** Bible, missionary, pastoral counseling, religious ed, theology, youth ministry.

**Most popular majors.** Theological studies 99%.

**Computing on campus.** 4 workstations in library, student center. Dormitories wired for high-speed internet access. Wireless network available.

**Student life. Freshman orientation:** Mandatory. Preregistration for classes offered. **Policies:** Religious observance required. **Housing:** Single-sex dorms,

apartments, wellness housing available. $50 deposit, deadline 8/15. **Activities:** Choral groups, drama, music ensembles, student government, missionary prayer band, ministerial partnership, Christian service program.

**Athletics.** NCCAA. **Intercollegiate:** Basketball M. **Intramural:** Basketball, table tennis, volleyball. **Team name:** Warriors.

**Student services.** Chaplain/spiritual director, career counseling, student employment services, financial aid counseling, personal counseling.

**Contact.**   E-mail: admissions@wesleycollege.edu
Phone: (601) 845-5747 Toll-free number: (800) 748-9972
Fax: (601) 845-2266
Robin Moffitt, Director of Enrollment, Wesley College, PO Box 1070, Florence, MS 39073-0070

---

## William Carey University
### Hattiesburg, Mississippi
www.wmcarey.edu                 CB code: 1907

▶ Private 4-year university and liberal arts college affiliated with Baptist faith
▶ Commuter campus in small city

**General.** Founded in 1906. Regionally accredited. **Location:** 110 miles from New Orleans. **Calendar:** Trimester.

**Annual costs/financial aid.** Tuition/fees (2009-2010): $9,750. Room/board: $3,915. Books/supplies: $2,850. Personal expenses: $1,350. Need-based financial aid available to full-time and part-time students.

**Contact.**   Phone: (601) 318-6103
Dean of Enrollment Management & Records, 498 Tuscan Avenue, Hattiesburg, MS 39401

# Missouri

## Avila University
**Kansas City, Missouri**
www.avila.edu                                      CB code: 6109

- Private 4-year university and liberal arts college affiliated with Roman Catholic Church
- Commuter campus in very large city
- 1,120 degree-seeking undergraduates: 18% part-time, 67% women, 15% African American, 1% Asian American, 5% Hispanic American, 1% Native American, 4% international
- 726 degree-seeking graduate students
- 43% of applicants admitted
- SAT or ACT (ACT writing optional) required
- 44% graduate within 6 years

**General.** Founded in 1916. Regionally accredited. **Degrees:** 246 bachelor's awarded; master's offered. **ROTC:** Army. **Calendar:** Semester, extensive summer session. **Full-time faculty:** 65 total; 74% have terminal degrees, 8% minority, 57% women. **Part-time faculty:** 149 total; 26% have terminal degrees, 5% minority, 56% women. **Class size:** 74% < 20, 24% 20-39, 2% 40-49, less than 1% 50-99. **Special facilities:** Theater, radiological laboratory, 30 off-campus medical-clinical learning sites, campus media production facilities, nursing learning resource center, photography lab.

**Freshman class profile.** 1,036 applied, 446 admitted, 119 enrolled.

| Mid 50% test scores | | GPA 2.0-2.99: | 26% |
|---|---|---|---|
| SAT critical reading: | 540-560 | Rank in top quarter: | 56% |
| SAT math: | 460-540 | Rank in top tenth: | 23% |
| ACT composite: | 20-25 | Return as sophomores: | 71% |
| GPA 3.75 or higher: | 30% | Out-of-state: | 21% |
| GPA 3.50-3.74: | 19% | Live on campus: | 79% |
| GPA 3.0-3.49: | 25% | International: | 1% |

**Basis for selection.** Unconditional acceptance for applicants with minimum GPA of 2.5 and ACT composite of 20 or higher. Others may be considered. Use ACT subscores for placement in math and English. Audition recommended for drama, music students. **Homeschooled:** SAT or ACT and home school transcripts required. GED may be requested.

**High school preparation.** 17 units required. Required units include English 4, mathematics 3, social studies 3, science 3 (laboratory 1), foreign language 3 and visual/performing arts 1.

**2009-2010 Annual costs.** Tuition/fees: $20,900. Room/board: $6,100. Books/supplies: $1,000. Personal expenses: $3,000.

**2008-2009 Financial aid. Need-based:** 114 full-time freshmen applied for aid; 114 were judged to have need; 114 of these received aid. Average need met was 65%. Average scholarship/grant was $6,600; average loan $2,970. 70% of total undergraduate aid awarded as scholarships/grants, 30% as loans/jobs. **Non-need-based:** Awarded to 1,334 full-time undergraduates, including 285 freshmen. Scholarships awarded for academics, alumni affiliation, art, athletics, music/drama, religious affiliation. **Additional information:** Financial aid adjusted for increases in tuition based on need.

**Application procedures. Admission:** No deadline. $25 fee, may be waived for applicants with need, free for online applicants. Admission notification on a rolling basis. **Financial aid:** Priority date 3/1, closing date 4/1. FAFSA, institutional form required. Applicants notified on a rolling basis starting 2/1; must reply within 2 week(s) of notification.

**Academics.** Outcome-based core curriculum; interdisciplinary course work at junior level required; unique senior experience bridges transition from college to community. **Special study options:** Accelerated study, combined bachelor's/graduate degree, cooperative education, cross-registration, distance learning, double major, dual enrollment of high school students, ESL, exchange student, independent study, internships, liberal arts/career combination, study abroad, teacher certification program, Washington semester, weekend college. **Credit/placement by examination:** AP, CLEP, IB, SAT, ACT, institutional tests. 32 credit hours maximum toward bachelor's degree. **Support services:** Learning center, reduced course load, remedial instruction, study skills assistance, tutoring, writing center.

**Majors. Biology:** General. **Business:** General, accounting, business admin, entrepreneurial studies, finance, human resources, international, marketing. **Communications:** General, public relations. **Computer sciences:** General. **Education:** Elementary, middle, secondary, special. **Health:** Facilities admin, nursing (RN). **History:** General. **Interdisciplinary:** Biological/physical sciences. **Legal studies:** Paralegal. **Philosophy/religion:** Religion. **Physical sciences:** Chemistry. **Psychology:** General. **Public administration:** Social work. **Social sciences:** Political science, sociology. **Visual/performing arts:** Dramatic, music performance, studio arts.

**Most popular majors.** Business/marketing 24%, education 7%, health sciences 31%, psychology 7%, visual/performing arts 11%.

**Computing on campus.** 156 workstations in dormitories, library, computer center, student center. Dormitories wired for high-speed internet access and linked to campus network. Commuter students can connect to campus network. Online course registration, online library, helpline, wireless network available.

**Student life. Freshman orientation:** Mandatory. Preregistration for classes offered. Held 3 days prior to first day of classes; programs available for freshmen-adult transfer students and friends/family of new students. **Policies:** First-time, first-year students not living at home with parents/guardians required to live on campus through sophomore year. **Housing:** Guaranteed on-campus for freshmen. Coed dorms, apartments, wellness housing available. Single-sex floors available. **Activities:** Campus ministries, choral groups, dance, drama, international student organizations, literary magazine, musical theater, student government, student newspaper, student nurses association, psychology club, Black Student Union, premedical club, English club, education club, Association of Radiological Science, social work association, National Association of Masters in Psychology, Society of Life Scientists.

**Athletics.** NAIA. **Intercollegiate:** Baseball M, basketball, cheerleading M, football (tackle) M, golf W, soccer, softball W, volleyball W. **Intramural:** Basketball, table tennis, volleyball. **Team name:** Eagles.

**Student services.** Adult student services, alcohol/substance abuse counseling, chaplain/spiritual director, career counseling, student employment services, financial aid counseling, health services, on-campus daycare, personal counseling, placement for graduates, veterans' counselor, women's services. **Physically disabled:** Services for visually, speech, hearing impaired.

**Contact.** E-mail: admission@avila.edu
Phone: (816) 501-2400 Toll-free number: (800) 462-8452
Fax: (816) 501-2453
Patricia Harper, Director of Admission, Avila University, 11901 Wornall Road, Kansas City, MO 64145-1007

## Baptist Bible College
**Springfield, Missouri**
www.gobbc.edu                                      CB code: 0991

- Private 4-year Bible and seminary college affiliated with Baptist faith
- Residential campus in small city
- 481 degree-seeking undergraduates

**General.** Founded in 1950. Candidate for regional accreditation.; also accredited by ABHE. **Degrees:** 89 bachelor's, 9 associate awarded; master's offered. **Location:** 180 miles from Kansas City, 225 miles from St. Louis. **Calendar:** Semester. **Full-time faculty:** 25 total. **Part-time faculty:** 10 total.

**Basis for selection.** Open admission. Baptist pastor's recommendation required. **Homeschooled:** Ability To Benefit test required.

**2009-2010 Annual costs.** Tuition/fees: $13,610. Room/board: $5,400. Books/supplies: $840.

**2008-2009 Financial aid. Non-need-based:** Scholarships awarded for academics.

**Application procedures. Admission:** Priority date 8/1; no deadline. $40 fee. Admission notification on a rolling basis. **Financial aid:** Closing date 5/1. FAFSA, institutional form required. Applicants notified on a rolling basis; must reply within 2 week(s) of notification.

**Academics. Special study options:** Distance learning. **Credit/placement by examination:** AP, CLEP. **Support services:** Learning center, reduced course load, study skills assistance, tutoring.

**Majors. Business:** Administrative services. **Education:** Elementary, music. **Philosophy/religion:** Religion. **Theology:** Missionary, pastoral counseling, religious ed, sacred music, theology.

**Computing on campus.** 70 workstations in library, computer center, student center. Dormitories wired for high-speed internet access and linked to campus network. Online library, helpline, repair service available.

**Student life. Freshman orientation:** Mandatory. Preregistration for classes offered. **Policies:** Religious observance required. **Housing:** Guaranteed on-campus for freshmen. Single-sex dorms, apartments available. **Activities:** Concert band, choral groups, music ensembles, radio station, student government.

**Athletics.** NCCAA. **Intercollegiate:** Basketball, soccer M, volleyball W. **Intramural:** Basketball. **Team name:** Patriots.

**Student services.** Chaplain/spiritual director, financial aid counseling, health services, on-campus daycare, personal counseling, veterans' counselor.

**Contact.** E-mail: cmcgee@gobbc.edu
Phone: (417) 268-6013 Toll-free number: (800) 228-5754 ext. 6021
Fax: (417) 268-6694
Jon Slayden, Director of Enrollment Services, Baptist Bible College, 628 East Kearney Street, Springfield, MO 65803

---

## Calvary Bible College and Theological Seminary
### Kansas City, Missouri
### www.calvary.edu
**CB code: 6331**

- Private 4-year Bible and seminary college affiliated with nondenominational tradition
- Residential campus in large city
- 214 degree-seeking undergraduates: 33% part-time, 46% women, 8% African American, 1% Asian American, 2% Hispanic American, 2% Native American
- 57 degree-seeking graduate students
- 30% graduate within 6 years

**General.** Founded in 1932. Regionally accredited; also accredited by ABHE. **Degrees:** 56 bachelor's, 4 associate awarded; master's offered. **ROTC:** Army. **Location:** 20 miles from Kansas City. **Calendar:** Semester, limited summer session. **Full-time faculty:** 12 total; 50% have terminal degrees, 8% minority, 33% women. **Part-time faculty:** 14 total; 21% have terminal degrees, 29% women. **Class size:** 89% < 20, 9% 20-39, 2% 40-49.

**Freshman class profile.** 46 applied, 37 admitted, 32 enrolled.

| Mid 50% test scores | | Return as sophomores: | 52% |
|---|---|---|---|
| ACT composite: | 19-24 | Out-of-state: | 72% |

**Basis for selection.** Open admission, but selective for some programs. Christian character stressed along with academic preparation. Pastor's and personal reference forms required. School achievement record and test scores considered. Applicants are required to submit a written Personal Testimony/Confirmation and Statement of Faith. Audition required for music students. **Homeschooled:** Transcripts are required in compliance with state's homeschool policies. **Learning Disabled:** Students should contact the Director of Admissions.

**2009-2010 Annual costs.** Tuition/fees: $8,772. Room/board: $4,400. Books/supplies: $500. Personal expenses: $150.

**2009-2010 Financial aid. Non-need-based:** Scholarships awarded for academics, alumni affiliation, job skills, music/drama, religious affiliation, ROTC.

**Application procedures. Admission:** Closing date 7/15 (receipt date). $25 fee. Admission notification on a rolling basis. **Financial aid:** Priority date 3/1, closing date 4/1. FAFSA, institutional form required. Applicants notified on a rolling basis starting 5/1.

**Academics.** Each student carries major in Bible and theology and second major in a professional area. These majors prepare students for vocational and/or volunteer involvement in Christian ministry. **Special study options:** Cooperative education, double major, dual enrollment of high school students, independent study, internships, student-designed major, teacher certification program. **Credit/placement by examination:** CLEP, IB, institutional tests. **Support services:** Learning center, reduced course load, remedial instruction, study skills assistance, tutoring.

**Majors. Business:** Organizational behavior. **Communications:** Broadcast journalism, media studies. **Education:** Elementary, music, secondary. **Social sciences:** Urban studies. **Theology:** Bible, missionary, pastoral counseling, preministerial, religious ed, sacred music, theology, youth ministry. **Visual/**

**performing arts:** Music performance, piano/organ, voice/opera. **Other:** Christian broadcasting, Christian ministry, Organizational leadership.

**Most popular majors.** Business/marketing 11%, education 9%, theological studies 73%.

**Computing on campus.** 21 workstations in library, student center. Dormitories wired for high-speed internet access. Online course registration, repair service, wireless network available.

**Student life. Freshman orientation:** Mandatory, $50 fee. **Policies:** Weekly Christian ministry, chapel and church attendance required. Single students required to live in college housing unless living with parents or at least 23 years of age. Religious observance required. **Housing:** Guaranteed on-campus for all undergraduates. Single-sex dorms, apartments available. $50 fully refundable deposit, deadline 8/15. Duplexes for married students available. **Activities:** Pep band, campus ministries, choral groups, drama, music ensembles, musical theater, radio station, student government, Missionary Prayer Fellowship, short-term missions.

**Athletics.** NCCAA. **Intercollegiate:** Basketball, soccer M, volleyball W. **Team name:** Warriors.

**Student services.** Alcohol/substance abuse counseling, chaplain/spiritual director, student employment services, financial aid counseling, health services, personal counseling, veterans' counselor, women's services.

**Contact.** E-mail: admissions@calvary.edu
Phone: (816) 326-3960 Toll-free number: (800) 326-3960
Fax: (816) 331-4474
Robert Crank, Director of Admissions, Calvary Bible College and Theological Seminary, 15800 Calvary Road, Kansas City, MO 64147-1341

---

## Central Bible College
### Springfield, Missouri
### www.cbcag.edu
**CB code: 6085**

- Private 4-year Bible college affiliated with Assemblies of God
- Residential campus in small city
- 625 degree-seeking undergraduates
- 89% of applicants admitted
- Application essay required

**General.** Founded in 1922. Accredited by ABHE. **Degrees:** 128 bachelor's, 20 associate awarded. **ROTC:** Army, Air Force. **Location:** 210 miles from St. Louis, 174 miles from Kansas City. **Calendar:** Semester, extensive summer session. **Full-time faculty:** 34 total. **Part-time faculty:** 30 total.

**Freshman class profile.** 255 applied, 228 admitted, 210 enrolled.

| Mid 50% test scores | | SAT writing: | 400-620 |
|---|---|---|---|
| SAT critical reading: | 400-620 | ACT composite: | 18-24 |
| SAT math: | 410-600 | | |

**Basis for selection.** Special consideration given to members of Assemblies of God and others committed to Christian principles, and applicants who rank in top half of graduating class who meet entrance requirements. Interview recommended for all students; audition recommended for music students. **Homeschooled:** Transcript of courses and grades required.

**High school preparation.** Strong background in English, math, and science recommended. Computer literacy course recommended.

**2009-2010 Annual costs.** Tuition/fees: $11,466. Room/board: $5,132. Books/supplies: $550.

**Application procedures. Admission:** Priority date 8/15; no deadline. $25 fee, may be waived for applicants with need. Admission notification on a rolling basis. **Financial aid:** Priority date 5/1; no closing date. FAFSA required. Applicants notified on a rolling basis starting 5/15; must reply within 3 week(s) of notification.

**Academics. Special study options:** Accelerated study, cooperative education, cross-registration, double major, independent study, internships. **Credit/placement by examination:** CLEP, SAT, ACT, institutional tests. 24 credit hours maximum toward bachelor's degree. **Support services:** Reduced course load, remedial instruction, tutoring.

**Majors. Theology:** Bible, missionary, pastoral counseling, religious ed, sacred music, theology, youth ministry. **Other:** Ministry in arts.

**Computing on campus.** 20 workstations in library, computer center.

**Student life. Freshman orientation:** Mandatory. Preregistration for classes offered. Held within week prior to start of both fall and spring classes; orientation sessions for all new students. **Policies:** Practices which are known to be morally wrong by Biblical teaching are not acceptable for members of the college community. Religious observance required. **Housing:** Guaranteed on-campus for freshmen. Single-sex dorms, apartments, wellness housing available. **Activities:** Jazz band, choral groups, drama, music ensembles, radio station, student government, student newspaper, Campus Missions Fellowship, Delta Chi, FOCAL, student government association, student ministries, multicultural club.

**Athletics.** NCCAA. **Intercollegiate:** Basketball, soccer M, volleyball W. **Intramural:** Basketball, softball. **Team name:** Spartans.

**Student services.** Student employment services, financial aid counseling, health services, personal counseling, placement for graduates, veterans' counselor. **Physically disabled:** Services for hearing impaired.

**Contact.** E-mail: info@cbcag.edu
Phone: (417) 833-2551 ext. 1290 Toll-free number: (800) 831-4222
Fax: (417) 833-5141
Bill Davis, Registrar, Central Bible College, 3000 North Grant Avenue, Springfield, MO 65803-1069

## Central Christian College of the Bible
**Moberly, Missouri**
**www.cccb.edu**                                    **CB code: 6145**

- Private 4-year Bible college affiliated with Christian Church
- Residential campus in large town
- 391 degree-seeking undergraduates
- 65% of applicants admitted
- ACT (writing recommended), application essay required

**General.** Founded in 1957. Accredited by ABHE. Every full-time student receives a full-tuition scholarship. **Degrees:** 60 bachelor's, 35 associate awarded. **Location:** 35 miles from Columbia. **Calendar:** Semester, limited summer session. **Full-time faculty:** 14 total. **Part-time faculty:** 12 total. **Special facilities:** 71,000 volume library with computer lab and foreign language lab.

**Freshman class profile.** 354 applied, 230 admitted, 76 enrolled.

| Mid 50% test scores | | | |
|---|---|---|---|
| SAT critical reading: | 490-550 | SAT writing: | 500-590 |
| SAT math: | 470-580 | ACT composite: | 18-23 |
| | | Live on campus: | 100% |

**Basis for selection.** High school transcript, ACT/SAT scores and references very important. Students with GPA below 2.0 assigned reduced course load.

**High school preparation.** 15 units recommended. Recommended units include English 2, mathematics 2, social studies 1 and science 2.

**2009-2010 Annual costs.** Full-time students receive full scholarship for tuition only, $8,800. Room and board $5,790 for two semesters. Required fees $1,540 per semester.Off-campus students pay a $650 facilities usage fee per semester. Books/supplies: $947. Personal expenses: $4,635.

**Application procedures. Admission:** No deadline. No application fee. Admission notification on a rolling basis beginning on or about 12/1. Admitted applicants must reply within 6 weeks of notification. **Financial aid:** Priority date 3/15, closing date 4/1. FAFSA required. Applicants notified by 5/15; must reply within 2 week(s) of notification.

**Academics. Special study options:** Cooperative education, distance learning, dual enrollment of high school students, internships. **Credit/placement by examination:** CLEP. 6 credit hours maximum toward bachelor's degree. **Support services:** Reduced course load, study skills assistance, tutoring.

**Majors. Philosophy/religion:** Religion. **Theology:** Pastoral counseling, religious ed, sacred music, theology.

**Computing on campus.** 30 workstations in library, student center. Dormitories wired for high-speed internet access and linked to campus network. Commuter students can connect to campus network. Wireless network available.

**Student life. Freshman orientation:** Mandatory, $250 fee. Preregistration for classes offered. **Policies:** Religious observance required. **Housing:** Guaranteed on-campus for all undergraduates. Single-sex dorms, wellness housing available. **Activities:** Choral groups, international student organizations, music ensembles, student government, Harvesters missions group, Gospel choir.

**Athletics.** NCCAA. **Intercollegiate:** Basketball, soccer M, volleyball W. **Intramural:** Basketball, bowling, softball, table tennis, tennis, volleyball. **Team name:** Heralds.

**Student services.** Chaplain/spiritual director, career counseling, financial aid counseling, personal counseling, placement for graduates, veterans' counselor.

**Contact.** E-mail: admissions2@cccb.edu
Phone: (888) 263-3900 Toll-free number: (888) 263-3900
Fax: (888) 263-3936
Aaron Merritt, Director of Admission, Central Christian College of the Bible, 911 East Urbandale Drive, Moberly, MO 65270-1997

## Central Methodist University
**Fayette, Missouri**
**www.centralmethodist.edu**                        **CB code: 6089**

- Private 4-year university and liberal arts college affiliated with United Methodist Church
- Residential campus in small town
- 1,022 degree-seeking undergraduates: 2% part-time, 51% women, 7% African American, 2% Hispanic American, 1% Native American, 3% international
- 67% of applicants admitted
- SAT or ACT (ACT writing optional) required
- 40% graduate within 6 years

**General.** Founded in 1854. Regionally accredited. **Degrees:** 191 bachelor's, 2 associate awarded; master's offered. **ROTC:** Army, Air Force. **Location:** 25 miles from Columbia, 150 miles from St. Louis. **Calendar:** Semester, limited summer session. **Full-time faculty:** 59 total; 56% have terminal degrees, 3% minority, 41% women. **Part-time faculty:** 29 total; 21% have terminal degrees, 48% women. **Class size:** 63% < 20, 29% 20-39, 5% 40-49, 3% 50-99. **Special facilities:** Observatory and laboratory, natural history museum, music conservatory.

**Freshman class profile.** 1,146 applied, 764 admitted, 260 enrolled.

| Mid 50% test scores | | | |
|---|---|---|---|
| ACT composite: | 19-24 | Rank in top tenth: | 12% |
| GPA 3.75 or higher: | 22% | End year in good standing: | 90% |
| GPA 3.50-3.74: | 22% | Return as sophomores: | 65% |
| GPA 3.0-3.49: | 35% | Out-of-state: | 7% |
| GPA 2.0-2.99: | 21% | Live on campus: | 96% |
| Rank in top quarter: | 33% | International: | 2% |

**Basis for selection.** Full acceptance requires 2.5 GPA and 21 ACT or equivalent SAT. Interview required for nursing applicants; audition recommended for drama, music students.

**High school preparation.** College-preparatory program recommended. 24 units recommended. Recommended units include English 4, mathematics 3, social studies 3, science 3 and foreign language 2. 2 humanities recommended.

**2009-2010 Annual costs.** Tuition/fees: $18,670. Room/board: $6,240. Books/supplies: $900. Personal expenses: $2,250.

**2009-2010 Financial aid. Non-need-based:** Scholarships awarded for academics, alumni affiliation, athletics, leadership, music/drama, religious affiliation, ROTC.

**Application procedures. Admission:** No deadline. $20 fee, may be waived for applicants with need, free for online applicants. Admission notification on a rolling basis beginning on or about 10/1. Must reply by May 1 or within 4 week(s) if notified thereafter. **Financial aid:** Priority date 3/15; no closing date. FAFSA required. Applicants notified on a rolling basis starting 1/30; must reply within 2 week(s) of notification.

**Academics. Special study options:** Accelerated study, combined bachelor's/graduate degree, distance learning, double major, dual enrollment of high school students, honors, independent study, internships, liberal arts/career combination, student-designed major, study abroad, teacher certification program. 3-year bachelor's degree, 2-week January travel program. **Credit/placement by examination:** AP, CLEP, IB, ACT, institutional tests. 32 credit hours maximum toward associate degree, 32 toward bachelor's. **Support services:** Learning center, reduced course load, study skills assistance, tutoring.

**Majors. Biology:** General, marine. **Business:** General, accounting, banking/financial services, business admin, entrepreneurial studies, international, management science, marketing. **Communications:** General. **Computer sciences:** Computer science. **Conservation:** Environmental science. **Education:**

Biology, chemistry, early childhood, elementary, foreign languages, middle, music, physical, physics, science, secondary, social science, special. **Family/consumer sciences:** Child development. **Foreign languages:** Spanish. **Health:** Athletic training, nursing (RN). **History:** General. **Math:** General. **Parks/recreation:** Facilities management. **Philosophy/religion:** Philosophy, religion. **Physical sciences:** Chemistry, physics. **Protective services:** Law enforcement admin. **Psychology:** General. **Social sciences:** Political science, sociology. **Visual/performing arts:** Dramatic, music performance.

**Most popular majors.** Business/marketing 28%, education 21%, health sciences 15%.

**Computing on campus.** 300 workstations in dormitories, library, computer center, student center. Dormitories wired for high-speed internet access and linked to campus network. Commuter students can connect to campus network. Online library, helpline, repair service, wireless network available.

**Student life. Freshman orientation:** Mandatory. Preregistration for classes offered. **Housing:** Guaranteed on-campus for all undergraduates. Coed dorms, single-sex dorms, apartments, fraternity/sorority housing available. $100 fully refundable deposit. **Activities:** Bands, campus ministries, choral groups, dance, drama, international student organizations, literary magazine, music ensembles, musical theater, radio station, student government, student newspaper, Alpha Phi Omega, prelaw club, religious, service, business, music organizations, Students in Free Enterprise.

**Athletics. NAIA. Intercollegiate:** Baseball M, basketball, cheerleading M, cross-country, football (tackle) M, golf, soccer, softball W, track and field, volleyball W. **Intramural:** Basketball, football (non-tackle), racquetball, soccer, softball, tennis, track and field, volleyball. **Team name:** Eagles.

**Student services.** Alcohol/substance abuse counseling, chaplain/spiritual director, career counseling, student employment services, financial aid counseling, health services, personal counseling, placement for graduates.

**Contact.** E-mail: admissions@centralmethodist.edu
Phone: (660) 248-6251 Toll-free number: (877) 268-1854
Fax: (660) 248-1872
Lawrence Anderson, Director of Admissions, Central Methodist University, 411 Central Methodist Square, Fayette, MO 65248-1198

## Chamberlain College of Nursing
**St. Louis, Missouri**
www.chamberlain.edu                    **CB code: 3139**

- For-profit 4-year nursing college affiliated with United Church of Christ
- Commuter campus in very large city

**General.** Founded in 1889. Regionally accredited. **Calendar:** Semester.

**Annual costs/financial aid.** Books/supplies: $1,100. Personal expenses: $550. Need-based financial aid available to full-time and part-time students.

**Contact.** Phone: (314) 768-7528
6150 Oakland Avenue, St. Louis, MO 63139

## College of the Ozarks
**Point Lookout, Missouri**
www.cofo.edu                    **CB code: 6713**

- Private 4-year liberal arts college affiliated with interdenominational tradition
- Residential campus in small town
- 1,350 degree-seeking undergraduates: 1% part-time, 57% women, 1% African American, 1% Asian American, 1% Hispanic American, 1% Native American, 1% international
- 9% of applicants admitted
- SAT or ACT (ACT writing optional), interview required
- 62% graduate within 6 years; 14% enter graduate study

**General.** Founded in 1906. Regionally accredited. No tuition; students work at a campus job rather than pay tuition. **Degrees:** 245 bachelor's awarded. **ROTC:** Army. **Location:** 2 miles from Branson, 45 miles from Springfield. **Calendar:** Semester. **Full-time faculty:** 95 total; 57% have terminal degrees, 2% minority, 35% women. **Part-time faculty:** 35 total; 14% have terminal degrees, 49% women. **Class size:** 62% < 20, 34% 20-39, 1% 40-49, 2% 50-99. **Special facilities:** Greenhouses, college-operated hotel, observatory, nature preserve, museum with extensive collection of regional history.

**Freshman class profile.** 3,025 applied, 263 admitted, 245 enrolled.

| Mid 50% test scores | | | |
|---|---|---|---|
| ACT composite: | 20-25 | Rank in top tenth: | 22% |
| GPA 3.75 or higher: | 41% | End year in good standing: | 75% |
| GPA 3.50-3.74: | 21% | Return as sophomores: | 82% |
| GPA 3.0-3.49: | 30% | Out-of-state: | 16% |
| GPA 2.0-2.99: | 8% | Live on campus: | 99% |
| Rank in top quarter: | 59% | International: | 2% |

**Basis for selection.** High school record, financial need, test scores, class rank, recommendations, activities and interview important. Academic interest and growth, development of intellectual skills considered. ACT preferred. Audition recommended for music students; portfolio recommended for art students. **Homeschooled:** Pass grades are not acceptable. Candidates must present a transcript with a letter or percentage grade.

**High school preparation.** College-preparatory program recommended. 24 units recommended. Recommended units include English 4, mathematics 3, social studies 3, science 2 (laboratory 1) and foreign language 2. Public speaking, visual and performing arts recommended.

**2010-2011 Annual costs.** Cost of full-time tuition met through combination of institutional work program and federal, state, and institutional funding. Full-time students participating in work program work 15 hours per week for 16 weeks and one 40-hour work week per semester. Part-time students (commuters only) pay $295 per credit hour for tuition. Required fees for academic year, $410. Room/board: $5,300. Books/supplies: $800. Personal expenses: $410.

**2009-2010 Financial aid. Need-based:** Average need met was 80%. Average scholarship/grant was $11,067. 79% of total undergraduate aid awarded as scholarships/grants, 21% as loans/jobs. **Non-need-based:** Scholarships awarded for academics, art, athletics, leadership, music/drama, ROTC, state residency.

**Application procedures. Admission:** Closing date 2/15 (receipt date). No application fee. Admission notification on a rolling basis beginning on or about 3/1. Must reply by May 1 or within 2 week(s) if notified thereafter. Housing deposit due within two weeks of admission offer. **Financial aid:** Priority date 2/15; no closing date. FAFSA required. Applicants notified by 7/1.

**Academics.** Curriculum offers liberal arts foundation with intensive concentration in special areas. **Special study options:** Combined bachelor's/graduate degree, double major, dual enrollment of high school students, independent study, internships, student-designed major, teacher certification program. 3-2 engineering program, interdisciplinary programs, paraprofessional counseling certificate, pre-professional programs, dietetics program. **Credit/placement by examination:** AP, CLEP, IB, ACT, institutional tests. Five "credits by exam" classes unless specific approval by academic dean. **Support services:** Learning center, reduced course load, remedial instruction, study skills assistance, tutoring, writing center.

**Majors. Agriculture:** Agronomy, animal sciences, business, horticultural science, horticulture, mechanization. **Biology:** General. **Business:** Accounting, business admin, hospitality admin, international, managerial economics, marketing, restaurant/food services. **Communications:** General, broadcast journalism, journalism, public relations. **Computer sciences:** General, computer science. **Conservation:** Wildlife. **Education:** Agricultural, art, biology, business, chemistry, early childhood, elementary, English, family/consumer sciences, history, mathematics, music, physical, science, secondary, social studies, technology/industrial arts. **Family/consumer sciences:** General, child development, food/nutrition. **Foreign languages:** Spanish. **Health:** Dietetics, health services, nursing (RN). **History:** General. **Math:** General. **Parks/recreation:** Facilities management; health/fitness. **Personal/culinary services:** Chef training, restaurant/catering. **Philosophy/religion:** Philosophy, religion. **Physical sciences:** Chemistry. **Protective services:** Corrections, police science. **Psychology:** General. **Public administration:** Social work. **Social sciences:** Sociology. **Theology:** Sacred music. **Visual/performing arts:** Art, dramatic, studio arts, theater design.

**Most popular majors.** Business/marketing 19%, education 19%, English 6%, visual/performing arts 7%.

**Computing on campus.** 160 workstations in dormitories, library. Dormitories wired for high-speed internet access and linked to campus network. Commuter students can connect to campus network. Online course registration, online library, helpline, wireless network available.

**Student life. Freshman orientation:** Mandatory. Preregistration for classes offered. 10-day program held the week before classes begin. **Policies:** Convocations and chapel attendance required for some students. All full-time students must live in residence halls unless they meet one of the following criteria: 21 years of age or older, married, living with parents, or veteran of armed services. Religious observance required. **Housing:** Guaranteed on-campus for all undergraduates. Single-sex dorms, wellness housing available. $100 fully refundable deposit. **Activities:** Bands, campus ministries, choral groups, drama, film society, literary magazine, music ensembles, musical theater, radio station, student government, student newspaper, Baptist Student Union, fire department, InterVarsity Christian Fellowship, Wilderness Activities Club, Aggie club, Business Undergraduate Society, Bonner Organization, College Republicans, College Democrats.

**Athletics.** NAIA. **Intercollegiate:** Baseball M, basketball, volleyball W. **Intramural:** Baseball M, basketball, football (non-tackle) M, racquetball, softball, tennis, volleyball. **Team name:** Bobcats.

**Student services.** Chaplain/spiritual director, career counseling, student employment services, financial aid counseling, health services, on-campus daycare, personal counseling, placement for graduates, veterans' counselor.

**Contact.** E-mail: admiss4@cofo.edu
Phone: (417) 690-2636 Toll-free number: (800) 222-0525
Fax: (417) 690-2635
Marci Linson, Dean of Admissions, College of the Ozarks, PO Box 17, Point Lookout, MO 65726-0017

## Columbia College
### Columbia, Missouri
**www.ccis.edu**                                    CB code: 6095

- Private 4-year liberal arts college affiliated with Christian Church (Disciples of Christ)
- Commuter campus in small city
- 1,038 degree-seeking undergraduates: 18% part-time, 59% women, 6% African American, 1% Asian American, 2% Hispanic American, 1% Native American, 9% international
- 260 degree-seeking graduate students
- 47% of applicants admitted
- SAT or ACT (ACT writing optional) required
- 42% graduate within 6 years; 8% enter graduate study

**General.** Founded in 1851. Regionally accredited. Programs for adult students offered on campus and at 34 teaching locations in United States and Cuba. **Degrees:** 213 bachelor's, 5 associate awarded; master's offered. **ROTC:** Army, Naval, Air Force. **Location:** 120 miles from Kansas City, 120 miles from St. Louis. **Calendar:** Semester, extensive summer session. **Full-time faculty:** 66 total; 79% have terminal degrees, 6% minority, 46% women. **Part-time faculty:** 45 total; 18% have terminal degrees, 53% women. **Class size:** 76% < 20, 24% 20-39, less than 1% 40-49.

**Freshman class profile.** 1,137 applied, 536 admitted, 174 enrolled.

| Mid 50% test scores | | | |
|---|---|---|---|
| SAT critical reading: | 430-570 | **GPA 2.0-2.99:** | 22% |
| SAT math: | 550-680 | **Rank in top quarter:** | 50% |
| ACT composite: | 20-26 | **Rank in top tenth:** | 24% |
| GPA 3.75 or higher: | 32% | **End year in good standing:** | 83% |
| GPA 3.50-3.74: | 18% | **Return as sophomores:** | 60% |
| GPA 3.0-3.49: | 27% | **Out-of-state:** | 11% |
| | | **Live on campus:** | 72% |

**Basis for selection.** School achievement, class rank, test scores most important. Also use IB (International Baccalaureate) for placement. **Home-schooled:** Statement describing homeschool structure and mission, transcript of courses and grades required. ACT/SAT required; no GED requirement.

**High school preparation.** College-preparatory program recommended. 14 units recommended. Recommended units include English 4, mathematics 3, social studies 2, science 3 and foreign language 2.

**2010-2011 Annual costs.** Tuition/fees (projected): $15,596. Room/board: $6,074. Books/supplies: $800. Personal expenses: $4,908.

**2008-2009 Financial aid.** **Need-based:** 51% of total undergraduate aid awarded as scholarships/grants, 49% as loans/jobs. **Non-need-based:** Scholarships awarded for academics, alumni affiliation, art, athletics, job skills, leadership, music/drama, religious affiliation, ROTC, state residency.

**Application procedures.** **Admission:** Closing date 8/9 (postmark date). $35 fee, may be waived for applicants with need. Admission notification on a rolling basis beginning on or about 9/15. **Financial aid:** No deadline. FAFSA required. Applicants notified on a rolling basis starting 3/1.

**Academics.** Evening degree program available based on 8-week ongoing terms. **Special study options:** Combined bachelor's/graduate degree, cooperative education, cross-registration, distance learning, double major, dual

enrollment of high school students, ESL, honors, independent study, internships, student-designed major, study abroad, teacher certification program. **Credit/placement by examination:** AP, CLEP, IB, SAT, ACT, institutional tests. 45 credit hours maximum toward associate degree, 60 toward bachelor's. **Support services:** Tutoring, writing center.

**Honors college/program.** High school GPA of 3.5 or greater, ACT in 78th percentile or higher required for admission.

**Majors.** **Area/ethnic studies:** American. **Biology:** General. **Business:** General, accounting, business admin, finance, human resources, international, marketing. **Communications:** General. **Computer sciences:** General, computer science. **Conservation:** Environmental science. **History:** General. **Math:** General. **Physical sciences:** Chemistry. **Protective services:** Forensics, law enforcement admin. **Psychology:** General. **Public administration:** Human services. **Social sciences:** Political science, sociology. **Visual/performing arts:** Art, ceramics, graphic design, painting, photography, printmaking. **Other:** Philosophy and religious studies.

**Most popular majors.** Biology 11%, business/marketing 36%, English 6%, psychology 9%, security/protective services 9%.

**Computing on campus.** 83 workstations in dormitories, library, computer center, student center. Dormitories wired for high-speed internet access and linked to campus network. Commuter students can connect to campus network. Online course registration, online library, helpline, repair service, wireless network available.

**Student life.** **Freshman orientation:** Available. Preregistration for classes offered. Held weekend before classes start. **Policies:** Alcohol and illegal drugs forbidden on campus. Students with less than 52 credit hours must live on campus. **Housing:** Guaranteed on-campus for freshmen. Coed dorms, single-sex dorms, special housing for disabled, apartments, wellness housing available. **Activities:** Campus ministries, choral groups, dance, drama, international student organizations, literary magazine, music ensembles, Model UN, student government, student newspaper, International Student Association, Mock Trial Association, Student Leaders Advocating Teaching Excellence, Partners in Education, Criminal Justice Association, Elysium Players, Fellowship of Christian Athletes, Delta Epsilon Chi.

**Athletics.** NAIA. **Intercollegiate:** Basketball, soccer M, softball W, volleyball W. **Intramural:** Basketball, bowling, football (non-tackle), golf, soccer, softball, volleyball. **Team name:** Cougars.

**Student services.** Alcohol/substance abuse counseling, career counseling, services for economically disadvantaged, student employment services, financial aid counseling, health services, personal counseling, placement for graduates, veterans' counselor. **Physically disabled:** Services for visually, speech, hearing impaired.

**Contact.** E-mail: admissions@ccis.edu
Phone: (573) 875-7352 Toll-free number: (800) 231-2391 ext. 7352
Fax: (573) 875-7506
Samantha White, Director, Admissions, Columbia College, 1001 Rogers Street, Columbia, MO 65216

## Conception Seminary College
### Conception, Missouri
**www.conception.edu**                              CB code: 6112

- Private 4-year seminary college for men affiliated with Roman Catholic Church
- Residential campus in rural community
- 112 degree-seeking undergraduates
- ACT (writing optional), application essay required

**General.** Founded in 1883. Regionally accredited. Operated by Benedictine Monks of Conception Abbey, for both independent seminary students and candidates affiliated with sponsoring diocese. Women may enroll on part-time basis. **Degrees:** 13 bachelor's awarded. **Location:** 100 miles from Kansas City, 45 miles from St. Joseph. **Calendar:** Semester. **Full-time faculty:** 10 total. **Part-time faculty:** 18 total. **Special facilities:** Abbey Basilica of the Immaculate Conception.

**Freshman class profile.**

| Mid 50% test scores | | | |
|---|---|---|---|
| ACT composite: | 19-26 | **Live on campus:** | 100% |

**Basis for selection.** ACT composite scores tend to count more heavily than high school grades. Class rank considered. Applicants must be sponsored. Interview recommended.

**High school preparation.** 16 units required. Required units include English 4, social studies 4 and science 4.

**2009-2010 Annual costs.** Tuition/fees: $15,786. Room/board: $9,362. Books/supplies: $650. Personal expenses: $850.

**Financial aid. Non-need-based:** Scholarships awarded for academics.

**Application procedures. Admission:** Priority date 6/1; deadline 7/31 (receipt date). No application fee. Admission notification on a rolling basis beginning on or about 2/1. Must reply by 8/10. Foreign applications require written certification of financial, ecclesiastical sponsorship. **Financial aid:** No deadline. FAFSA required. Applicants notified on a rolling basis starting 8/1; must reply by 8/20.

**Academics.** Curriculum combines liberal arts and pre-theology training to accommodate varying degrees of vocational commitment. **Special study options:** ESL, independent study. **Credit/placement by examination:** AP, CLEP, ACT, institutional tests. 12 credit hours maximum toward bachelor's degree. **Support services:** Learning center, reduced course load, remedial instruction, study skills assistance, tutoring.

**Majors. Philosophy/religion:** Philosophy.

**Computing on campus.** 15 workstations in dormitories, library, computer center. Dormitories wired for high-speed internet access and linked to campus network. Online library, helpline, repair service, wireless network available.

**Student life. Freshman orientation:** Mandatory. Preregistration for classes offered. **Policies:** Religious observance required. **Housing:** Guaranteed on-campus for all undergraduates. Wellness housing available. $50 deposit. **Activities:** Choral groups, drama, music ensembles, musical theater, student government, student newspaper, apostolic work, mission club, social concerns, community council, Inner-Life.

**Athletics. Intercollegiate:** Basketball M, soccer M, volleyball M. **Intramural:** Basketball M, football (non-tackle) M, racquetball M, soccer M, softball M, swimming M, table tennis M, tennis M, track and field M, volleyball M, weight lifting M. **Team name:** Blue Knights.

**Student services.** Adult student services, alcohol/substance abuse counseling, chaplain/spiritual director, career counseling, financial aid counseling, health services, personal counseling.

**Contact.** E-mail: vocations@conception.edu
Phone: (660) 944-2886 Fax: (660) 944-2829
Fr. Pachomius Meade, Director of Admissions, Conception Seminary College, Box 502, Conception, MO 64433-0502

---

## Cox College
**Springfield, Missouri**
www.coxcollege.edu                          CB code: 3932

- Private 4-year health science and nursing college
- Commuter campus in small city
- 509 degree-seeking undergraduates

**General.** Regionally accredited. **Degrees:** 74 bachelor's, 61 associate awarded. **Calendar:** Semester, limited summer session. **Full-time faculty:** 31 total. **Part-time faculty:** 12 total. **Special facilities:** Nursing resource center.

**Basis for selection.** Minimum GPA and ACT composite score required. TOEFL required of non-native English speakers and all international applicants. ACT or SAT scores required for early decision candidates. If ACT or SAT scores are less than 5 years old, student may be exempt from pre-entrance placement testing. **Homeschooled:** Applicants must submit official transcript from a state accredited institution or official GED or high school equivalency score report.

**High school preparation.** Recommended units include English 4, mathematics 2 and science 2. Early Decision candidates must achieve grade of C or better in biology, chemistry, 4 units English, 2 units math, including algebra.

**2009-2010 Annual costs.** Tuition/fees: $9,720. Educational fee of $40 per credit hour. Books/supplies: $1,200.

**Application procedures. Admission:** Closing date 8/1 (receipt date). $45 fee, may be waived for applicants with need. Application must be submitted on paper. Admission notification on a rolling basis. **Financial aid:** Priority date 3/1; no closing date.

**Academics. Special study options:** Accelerated study. **Credit/placement by examination:** CLEP, SAT, ACT, institutional tests. 6 credit

hours maximum toward associate degree, 6 toward bachelor's. **Support services:** Remedial instruction, study skills assistance, tutoring, writing center.

**Majors. Health:** Nursing (RN).

**Computing on campus.** 34 workstations in dormitories, library, computer center.

**Student life. Freshman orientation:** Available. **Housing:** Coed dorms available. $100 deposit. **Activities:** Student government, National Student Nurses Association, student council, residence hall council, Christian Fellowship.

**Student services.** Financial aid counseling.

**Contact.** E-mail: admissions@coxcollege.edu
Phone: (417) 269-3068 Toll-free number: (866) 898-5355
Fax: (417) 269-3586
Lindy Biglieni, Director of Admission, Cox College, 1423 North Jefferson Avenue, Springfield, MO 65802

---

## Culver-Stockton College
**Canton, Missouri**                          CB member
www.culver.edu                          CB code: 6123

- Private 4-year liberal arts college affiliated with Christian Church (Disciples of Christ)
- Residential campus in small town
- 723 degree-seeking undergraduates: 3% part-time, 55% women, 9% African American, 1% Asian American, 2% Hispanic American, 1% Native American, 3% international
- 60% of applicants admitted
- SAT or ACT (ACT writing optional) required
- 49% graduate within 6 years; 19% enter graduate study

**General.** Founded in 1853. Regionally accredited. **Degrees:** 129 bachelor's awarded. **Location:** 130 miles from St. Louis, 20 miles from Quincy, IL. **Calendar:** Semester, limited summer session. **Full-time faculty:** 45 total; 76% have terminal degrees, 9% minority, 36% women. **Part-time faculty:** 39 total; 15% have terminal degrees, 10% minority, 44% women. **Class size:** 71% < 20, 27% 20-39, less than 1% 40-49, less than 1% 50-99.

**Freshman class profile.** 1,263 applied, 762 admitted, 148 enrolled.

| Mid 50% test scores | | | |
|---|---|---|---|
| SAT critical reading: | 410-750 | Rank in top quarter: | 36% |
| SAT math: | 460-700 | Rank in top tenth: | 14% |
| ACT composite: | 19-24 | Return as sophomores: | 59% |
| GPA 3.75 or higher: | 27% | Out-of-state: | 44% |
| GPA 3.50-3.74: | 14% | Live on campus: | 93% |
| GPA 3.0-3.49: | 28% | International: | 5% |
| GPA 2.0-2.99: | 30% | Fraternities: | 47% |
| | | Sororities: | 45% |

**Basis for selection.** Secondary school record and test scores most important; recommendations, application essay and alumni relation considered. ACT recommended. **Learning Disabled:** Must request accommodations and submit appropriate documentation.

**High school preparation.** College-preparatory program recommended. 15 units required. Required and recommended units include English 4, mathematics 2, social studies 3 and science 4.

**2010-2011 Annual costs.** Tuition/fees: $22,550. Room/board: $7,400. Books/supplies: $1,000. Personal expenses: $340.

**2009-2010 Financial aid. Need-based:** 141 full-time freshmen applied for aid; 132 were judged to have need; 132 of these received aid. Average need met was 78%. Average scholarship/grant was $17,385; average loan $3,916. 66% of total undergraduate aid awarded as scholarships/grants, 34% as loans/jobs. **Non-need-based:** Awarded to 85 full-time undergraduates, including 49 freshmen. Scholarships awarded for academics, alumni affiliation, art, athletics, job skills, leadership, music/drama, religious affiliation, state residency.

**Application procedures. Admission:** Priority date 5/1; no deadline. No application fee. Admission notification on a rolling basis beginning on or about 10/15. **Financial aid:** Priority date 3/1, closing date 6/1. FAFSA required. Applicants notified on a rolling basis starting 2/15; must reply within 2 week(s) of notification.

**Academics. Special study options:** Combined bachelor's/graduate degree, distance learning, double major, dual enrollment of high school students, honors, independent study, internships, liberal arts/career combination, semester at sea, student-designed major, study abroad, teacher certification program, Washington semester. **Credit/placement by examination:** AP, CLEP, IB, ACT, institutional tests. 90 credit hours maximum toward bachelor's degree. **Support services:** Learning center, reduced course load, remedial instruction, study skills assistance, tutoring, writing center.

**Majors. Biology:** General, biochemistry. **Business:** Accounting, business admin, finance. **Communications:** General. **Education:** General, art, elementary, music, physical, speech. **Health:** Athletic training, nursing (RN). **History:** General. **Liberal arts:** Arts/sciences. **Math:** General. **Parks/recreation:** Sports admin. **Philosophy/religion:** Religion. **Protective services:** Law enforcement admin. **Psychology:** General. **Social sciences:** Political science. **Visual/performing arts:** Art, arts management, dramatic, musical theater.

**Most popular majors.** Business/marketing 20%, education 15%, health sciences 23%, parks/recreation 7%, psychology 8%, security/protective services 9%, visual/performing arts 7%.

**Computing on campus.** 75 workstations in dormitories, library, computer center, student center. Dormitories wired for high-speed internet access and linked to campus network. Commuter students can connect to campus network. Online course registration, online library, helpline, repair service, student web hosting, wireless network available.

**Student life. Freshman orientation:** Mandatory, $150 fee. Preregistration for classes offered. Held for 3 days prior to the beginning of fall semester. **Policies:** All students under age 21 are required to live on campus unless living with parents. Students have voting representation on faculty committees. **Housing:** Guaranteed on-campus for all undergraduates. Coed dorms, fraternity/sorority housing, wellness housing available. $200 deposit, deadline 8/15. **Activities:** Bands, campus ministries, choral groups, dance, drama, international student organizations, literary magazine, music ensembles, Model UN, musical theater, radio station, student government, student newspaper, Disciples on Campus, Christians in Action, Fellowship of Christian Athletes, Black Student Union, International Students Club, Psychology Club, HOPE, Student Nurses Organization, Circle K International, Up 'Til Dawn.

**Athletics.** NAIA. **Intercollegiate:** Baseball M, basketball, cheerleading, cross-country, football (tackle) M, golf, soccer, softball W, track and field, volleyball W. **Intramural:** Basketball, football (non-tackle), golf, racquetball, soccer, softball, volleyball. **Team name:** Wildcats.

**Student services.** Adult student services, alcohol/substance abuse counseling, chaplain/spiritual director, career counseling, student employment services, financial aid counseling, personal counseling, placement for graduates, veterans' counselor.

**Contact.** E-mail: enrollment@culver.edu
Phone: (573) 288-6331 Toll-free number: (800) 537-1883
Fax: (573) 288-6618
Jim Lynes, Director of Admissions, Culver-Stockton College, One College Hill, Canton, MO 63435-1299

## DeVry University: Kansas City
Kansas City, Missouri
www.devry.edu                                    CB code: 6092

- For-profit 4-year university
- Commuter campus in large city
- 1,052 degree-seeking undergraduates: 46% part-time, 32% women, 18% African American, 3% Asian American, 4% Hispanic American, 1% Native American
- 216 degree-seeking graduate students
- Interview required
- 36% graduate within 6 years

**General.** Founded in 1931. Regionally accredited. **Degrees:** 167 bachelor's, 47 associate awarded; master's offered. **Location:** 15 miles from downtown. **Calendar:** Semester, extensive summer session. **Full-time faculty:** 28 total; 7% minority, 25% women. **Part-time faculty:** 53 total; 4% minority, 42% women.

**Freshman class profile.** 186 enrolled.

**Basis for selection.** Applicants must have high school diploma or equivalent degree from accredited postsecondary institution and be at least 17 years of age on the first day of classes. New students may enter at beginning of any semester. CPT also accepted.

**High school preparation.** Required units include mathematics 1. Math unit must be algebra or higher.

**2009-2010 Annual costs.** Tuition/fees: $14,160. Books/supplies: $1,310. Personal expenses: $3,574.

**2008-2009 Financial aid.** All financial aid based on need.

**Application procedures. Admission:** No deadline. $50 fee, may be waived for applicants with need. Admission notification on a rolling basis. **Financial aid:** No deadline. FAFSA required. Applicants notified on a rolling basis.

**Academics. Special study options:** Accelerated study, distance learning, weekend college. **Credit/placement by examination:** CLEP, institutional tests. **Support services:** Learning center, remedial instruction, tutoring.

**Majors. Business:** Business admin. **Computer sciences:** Networking, systems analysis, web page design. **Engineering technology:** Biomedical, computer, electrical. **Other:** Technical management.

**Most popular majors.** Business/marketing 41%, computer/information sciences 47%, engineering/engineering technologies 11%.

**Computing on campus.** 1,300 workstations in library, computer center. Online course registration, online library, helpline available.

**Student life. Freshman orientation:** Mandatory. **Activities:** Association of Information Technology Professionals, Campus Crusade for Christ, Institute for Electrical & Electronics Engineers, Phi Beta Lambda, Tau Alpha Pi, professional certification club, drama club, Gamma Beta Phi.

**Athletics. Intramural:** Volleyball.

**Student services.** Career counseling, student employment services, financial aid counseling, placement for graduates, veterans' counselor. **Physically disabled:** Services for visually, hearing impaired.

**Contact.** E-mail: ssmeed@kc.devry.edu
Phone: (816) 941-2810 Toll-free number: (800) 821-3766
Fax: (816) 941-0896
Shane Smeed, Director of Admissions, DeVry University: Kansas City, 11224 Holmes Street, Kansas City, MO 64131-3626

## Drury University
Springfield, Missouri
www.drury.edu                                    CB code: 6169

- Private 4-year university and liberal arts college affiliated with United Church of Christ and Christian Church (Disciples of Christ)
- Residential campus in large city
- 1,538 degree-seeking undergraduates: 2% part-time, 53% women
- 526 degree-seeking graduate students
- 70% of applicants admitted
- SAT or ACT (ACT writing optional) required
- 64% graduate within 6 years

**General.** Founded in 1873. Regionally accredited. **Degrees:** 331 bachelor's awarded; master's offered. **ROTC:** Army. **Location:** 220 miles from St. Louis, 170 miles from Kansas City. **Calendar:** Semester, limited summer session. **Full-time faculty:** 131 total; 92% have terminal degrees, 8% minority. **Part-time faculty:** 48 total; 12% have terminal degrees, 6% minority. **Class size:** 65% < 20, 34% 20-39, less than 1% 40-49, less than 1% 50-99. **Special facilities:** Science center, greenhouse, astronomical observation station, electronic music lab.

**Freshman class profile.** 1,184 applied, 832 admitted, 338 enrolled.

| Mid 50% test scores | | Rank in top tenth: | 35% |
|---|---|---|---|
| ACT composite: | 23-29 | Return as sophomores: | 83% |
| GPA 3.75 or higher: | 60% | Out-of-state: | 28% |
| GPA 3.50-3.74: | 15% | Live on campus: | 62% |
| GPA 3.0-3.49: | 15% | International: | 6% |
| GPA 2.0-2.99: | 10% | Fraternities: | 33% |
| Rank in top quarter: | 67% | Sororities: | 36% |

**Basis for selection.** School achievement record, test scores, reference from high school counselor, essay important. Interview recommended for all students. Audition recommended for music, theater students; portfolio recommended for architecture, art students.

**High school preparation.** College-preparatory program recommended. 12 units required. Required and recommended units include English 4, mathematics 3-4, social studies 3, science 3 and foreign language 2.

**2010-2011 Annual costs.** Tuition/fees: $19,944. Room/board: $6,971. Books/supplies: $1,500. Personal expenses: $1,500.

**2009-2010 Financial aid. Need-based:** 338 full-time freshmen applied for aid; 309 were judged to have need; 309 of these received aid. Average need met was 84%. Average scholarship/grant was $5,680; average loan $4,500. 28% of total undergraduate aid awarded as scholarships/grants, 72% as loans/jobs. **Non-need-based:** Awarded to 1,777 full-time undergraduates, including 353 freshmen. Scholarships awarded for academics, alumni affiliation, art, athletics, job skills, leadership, minority status, music/drama, religious affiliation.

**Application procedures. Admission:** Priority date 1/15; deadline 8/1 (postmark date). $25 fee, may be waived for applicants with need. Admission notification on a rolling basis beginning on or about 10/1. Must reply by May 1 or within 3 week(s) if notified thereafter. Application fee waived if applicant visits campus. **Financial aid:** Closing date 3/1. FAFSA, institutional form required. Applicants notified on a rolling basis starting 3/30; must reply within 2 week(s) of notification.

**Academics.** General education curriculum leads to minor in global studies for each student. **Special study options:** Accelerated study, combined bachelor's/graduate degree, cooperative education, distance learning, double major, dual enrollment of high school students, ESL, honors, independent study, internships, liberal arts/career combination, student-designed major, study abroad, teacher certification program, Washington semester. Living-learning communities, leadership/community service communities, Drury Center in Volos, Greece. **Credit/placement by examination:** AP, CLEP, IB, institutional tests. **Support services:** Pre-admission summer program, reduced course load, remedial instruction, study skills assistance, tutoring, writing center.

**Majors. Architecture:** Architecture. **Biology:** General, exercise physiology. **Business:** Accounting, business admin, finance. **Communications:** General, advertising, public relations. **Computer sciences:** General, computer science. **Conservation:** Environmental science, environmental studies. **Education:** General, elementary, music, physical. **Engineering technology:** General. **Foreign languages:** French, German, Spanish. **Health:** Environmental health, music therapy, nursing (RN), physician assistant, predental, premedicine, prenursing, prepharmacy, preveterinary. **History:** General. **Liberal arts:** Arts/sciences. **Math:** General. **Parks/recreation:** Exercise sciences. **Philosophy/religion:** Philosophy, religion. **Physical sciences:** Applied physics, chemistry. **Psychology:** General. **Social sciences:** Criminology, economics, international relations, political science, sociology, U.S. government. **Visual/performing arts:** General, art, art history/conservation, arts management, design, dramatic, music theory/composition, piano/organ, studio arts, voice/opera. **Other:** Integrated media, Pre-occupational therapy.

**Most popular majors.** Biology 9%, business/marketing 13%, communications/journalism 8%, education 8%, English 6%, psychology 16%, security/protective services 10%, social sciences 6%.

**Computing on campus.** 389 workstations in dormitories, library, computer center, student center. Dormitories wired for high-speed internet access and linked to campus network. Commuter students can connect to campus network. Online course registration, online library, helpline, repair service, student web hosting, wireless network available.

**Student life. Freshman orientation:** Mandatory, $145 fee. Preregistration for classes offered. 4-day program; includes parent session. **Housing:** Guaranteed on-campus for freshmen. Coed dorms, special housing for disabled, apartments, fraternity/sorority housing available. $200 fully refundable deposit, deadline 6/1. Living-learning, leadership/service communities available. **Activities:** Bands, campus ministries, choral groups, dance, drama, film society, international student organizations, literary magazine, music ensembles, musical theater, opera, radio station, student government, student newspaper, symphony orchestra, TV station, Think Green, Student Union Board, Mortar Board, Habitat for Humanity, Students in Free Enterprise, Ad Team, student teacher association, Bacchus, Fellowship of Christian Athletes, outdoor club.

**Athletics.** NCAA. **Intercollegiate:** Baseball M, basketball, cheerleading M, cross-country, diving, golf, soccer, softball W, swimming, tennis, track and field, volleyball W. **Intramural:** Basketball, football (non-tackle), racquetball, rugby M, soccer, softball W, volleyball. **Team name:** Panthers.

**Student services.** Adult student services, alcohol/substance abuse counseling, chaplain/spiritual director, career counseling, services for economically disadvantaged, student employment services, financial aid counseling, health services, minority student services, personal counseling, placement for graduates, veterans' counselor, women's services. **Physically disabled:** Services for visually, speech, hearing impaired.

**Contact.** E-mail: druryad@drury.edu
Phone: (417) 873-7205 Toll-free number: (800) 922-2274
Fax: (417) 866-3873
Dawn Hiles, Dean of Admission, Drury University, 900 North Benton Avenue, Springfield, MO 65802-3712

## Evangel University
### Springfield, Missouri
www.evangel.edu                           CB code: 6198

- Private 4-year liberal arts college affiliated with Assemblies of God
- Residential campus in small city
- 1,735 degree-seeking undergraduates
- 74% of applicants admitted
- SAT or ACT with writing required

**General.** Founded in 1955. Regionally accredited. **Degrees:** 322 bachelor's, 2 associate awarded; master's offered. **ROTC:** Army. **Location:** 170 miles from Kansas City, 212 miles from St. Louis. **Calendar:** Semester, limited summer session. **Full-time faculty:** 93 total. **Part-time faculty:** 32 total. **Class size:** 64% < 20, 29% 20-39, 4% 40-49, 3% 50-99.

**Freshman class profile.** 1,163 applied, 857 admitted, 432 enrolled.

| Mid 50% test scores | | Out-of-state: | 60% |
|---|---|---|---|
| ACT composite: | 20-25 | Live on campus: | 90% |

**Basis for selection.** Minimum 2.0 high school GPA, acceptance of college's moral and religious standards, acceptable ACT or SAT scores, rank in top half of graduating class. Statement of Christian faith required. Audition required for music, sport students. Essay and portfolio recommended. **Homeschooled:** Letter of recommendation (nonparent) required. Admissions based upon ACT/SAT scores and letters of recommendation.

**High school preparation.** Recommended units include English 3, mathematics 2, social studies 2 and science 1.

**2009-2010 Annual costs.** Tuition/fees: $16,000. Room/board: $5,730.

**2008-2009 Financial aid.** All financial aid based on need.

**Application procedures. Admission:** Closing date 8/1 (receipt date). $25 fee, may be waived for applicants with need. Admission notification on a rolling basis. **Financial aid:** Priority date 4/1, closing date 6/30. FAFSA required. Applicants notified on a rolling basis starting 4/1; must reply within 3 week(s) of notification.

**Academics. Special study options:** Cross-registration, double major, dual enrollment of high school students, internships, liberal arts/career combination, study abroad, teacher certification program, Washington semester. **Credit/placement by examination:** AP, CLEP, IB, ACT, institutional tests. 30 credit hours maximum toward associate degree, 30 toward bachelor's. **Support services:** Learning center, reduced course load, remedial instruction, study skills assistance, tutoring, writing center.

**Majors. Biology:** General. **Business:** General, accounting, business admin, marketing. **Communications:** General, broadcast journalism, journalism. **Communications technology:** General. **Computer sciences:** General. **Education:** Art, business, early childhood, elementary, English, foreign languages, mathematics, middle, music, physical, science, secondary, social studies, special. **Foreign languages:** Spanish. **Health:** Clinical lab technology, predental, premedicine, preveterinary. **History:** General. **Interdisciplinary:** Math/computer science. **Legal studies:** Prelaw. **Math:** General. **Parks/recreation:** General. **Physical sciences:** Chemistry. **Protective services:** Criminal justice. **Psychology:** General. **Public administration:** Social work. **Social sciences:** General, criminology, political science, sociology. **Theology:** Bible, missionary, sacred music. **Visual/performing arts:** Dramatic, music performance, studio arts.

**Most popular majors.** Business/marketing 15%, communications/journalism 9%, education 21%, philosophy/religious studies 12%, psychology 10%, social sciences 7%.

**Computing on campus.** 407 workstations in dormitories, library, computer center, student center. Dormitories wired for high-speed internet access and linked to campus network. Online library, helpline, wireless network available.

**Student life. Freshman orientation:** Mandatory, $50 fee. Preregistration for classes offered. **Policies:** Religious observance required. **Housing:** Guaranteed on-campus for freshmen. Coed dorms, single-sex dorms, apartments, wellness housing available. $200 deposit, deadline 8/1. **Activities:** Bands, campus ministries, choral groups, drama, literary magazine, music ensembles, radio station, student government, student newspaper, symphony orchestra, TV station, international students club, honor fraternities, student ministries.

**Athletics.** NAIA. **Intercollegiate:** Baseball M, basketball, cross-country, football (tackle) M, golf, softball W, tennis, track and field, volleyball W. **Intramural:** Basketball, football (non-tackle), soccer, softball, volleyball W. **Team name:** Crusaders.

**Student services.** Chaplain/spiritual director, career counseling, student employment services, financial aid counseling, health services, personal counseling, placement for graduates, veterans' counselor. **Physically disabled:** Services for visually, hearing impaired.

**Contact.** E-mail: admission@evangel.edu
Phone: (417) 865-2811 ext. 7205 Toll-free number: (800) 382-6435
Fax: (417) 865-9599
Jeff Burnett, Director of Admissions, Evangel University, 1111 North Glenstone, Springfield, MO 65802

---

## Everest College: Springfield
### Springfield, Missouri
**www.springfield-college.com**      **CB code: 1478**

▶ For-profit 4-year technical college
▶ Commuter campus in small city

**General.** Founded in 1979. Accredited by ACICS. **Location:** 250 miles from St. Louis, 190 miles from Kansas City. **Calendar:** Quarter.

**Contact.** Phone: (417) 864-7220
Director of Admissions, 1010 West Sunshine, Springfield, MO 65807

---

## Fontbonne University
### St. Louis, Missouri      CB member
**www.fontbonne.edu**      **CB code: 6216**

▶ Private 4-year university and liberal arts college affiliated with Roman Catholic Church
▶ Commuter campus in large city
▶ 1,972 degree-seeking undergraduates: 26% part-time, 71% women, 33% African American, 1% Asian American, 2% Hispanic American, 2% international
▶ 896 degree-seeking graduate students
▶ 85% of applicants admitted
▶ SAT or ACT (ACT writing recommended) required
▶ 52% graduate within 6 years; 40% enter graduate study

**General.** Founded in 1923. Regionally accredited. **Degrees:** 468 bachelor's awarded; master's offered. **ROTC:** Army, Air Force. **Location:** 6 miles from downtown. **Calendar:** Semester, limited summer session. **Full-time faculty:** 82 total; 76% have terminal degrees, 10% minority, 70% women. **Part-time faculty:** 165 total. **Class size:** 62% < 20, 38% 20-39. **Special facilities:** Theater, speech, language, and hearing clinic, academic resource and ADA accommodations center.

**Freshman class profile.** 517 applied, 442 admitted, 180 enrolled.

| Mid 50% test scores | | | |
|---|---|---|---|
| ACT composite: | 20-25 | End year in good standing: | 56% |
| GPA 3.75 or higher: | 16% | Return as sophomores: | 67% |
| GPA 3.50-3.74: | 22% | Out-of-state: | 17% |
| GPA 3.0-3.49: | 27% | Live on campus: | 40% |
| GPA 2.0-2.99: | 35% | International: | 5% |
| Rank in top quarter: | 38% | | |
| Rank in top tenth: | 18% | | |

**Basis for selection.** High school GPA, class rank, test scores considered. Recommendations may be requested. Essay and interview recommended. Audition required for theater students; portfolio required for art students.

**High school preparation.** College-preparatory program required. 16 units required. Required units include English 4, mathematics 3, social studies 3, science 3 (laboratory 1), visual/performing arts 1 and academic electives 2. Core electives 3 units. Must include foreign language and 1 unit visual or performing arts.

**2010-2011 Annual costs.** Tuition/fees: $20,380. Room/board: $7,600. Books/supplies: $650. Personal expenses: $640.

**2008-2009 Financial aid.** **Need-based:** 141 full-time freshmen applied for aid; 117 were judged to have need; 117 of these received aid. 46% of total undergraduate aid awarded as scholarships/grants, 54% as loans/jobs. **Non-need-based:** Awarded to 840 full-time undergraduates, including 118 freshmen. Scholarships awarded for academics, alumni affiliation, art, leadership, minority status, music/drama, religious affiliation, state residency.

**Application procedures.** **Admission:** Priority date 12/15; no deadline. $25 fee, may be waived for applicants with need. Admission notification on

a rolling basis. Must reply by May 1 or within 3 week(s) if notified thereafter. **Financial aid:** Closing date 4/1. FAFSA, institutional form required. Applicants notified on a rolling basis starting 2/1; must reply within 2 week(s) of notification.

**Academics.** **Special study options:** Accelerated study, combined bachelor's/graduate degree, cooperative education, cross-registration, distance learning, double major, dual enrollment of high school students, ESL, exchange student, honors, independent study, internships, liberal arts/career combination, semester at sea, student-designed major, study abroad, teacher certification program, weekend college. 3-2 program in social work or engineering with Washington University. **Credit/placement by examination:** CLEP, IB, institutional tests. 30 credit hours maximum toward bachelor's degree. Fontbonne will accept undergraduate credit by exam for non-standardized examinations given by accredited institutions. Course number, title, and credit hours must appear on official transcript. Determination as to fulfillment of certain course requirements will be reviewed and considered by department chairperson. **Support services:** Learning center, reduced course load, remedial instruction, study skills assistance, tutoring, writing center.

**Majors.** **Biology:** General. **Business:** Business admin, organizational behavior. **Communications:** General, advertising. **Computer sciences:** General. **Education:** Deaf/hearing impaired, early childhood, elementary, family/consumer sciences, middle, special. **Family/consumer sciences:** Clothing/textiles. **Health:** Dietetics, speech pathology. **History:** General. **Legal studies:** Prelaw. **Liberal arts:** Arts/sciences. **Math:** General. **Parks/recreation:** Sports admin. **Psychology:** General. **Public administration:** Human services, social work. **Social sciences:** Sociology. **Visual/performing arts:** Art, dramatic, studio arts. **Other:** Global studies.

**Most popular majors.** Business/marketing 49%, education 14%.

**Computing on campus.** 285 workstations in dormitories, library, computer center. Dormitories wired for high-speed internet access and linked to campus network. Commuter students can connect to campus network. Online course registration, online library, helpline, repair service, wireless network available.

**Student life.** **Freshman orientation:** Mandatory, $75 fee. Preregistration for classes offered. Held during week prior to classes, includes community service. **Housing:** Coed dorms, special housing for disabled, apartments, wellness housing available. $150 fully refundable deposit. Apartment style residence halls available. **Activities:** Campus ministries, choral groups, dance, drama, international student organizations, literary magazine, music ensembles, musical theater, radio station, student government, student newspaper, College Republicans, College Democrats, Fontbonne in Service and Humility, Straights and Gays for Equality, Students for the Enhancement of Black Awareness.

**Athletics.** NCAA. **Intercollegiate:** Baseball M, basketball, bowling, cross-country, golf, lacrosse, soccer, softball W, tennis, track and field, volleyball. **Intramural:** Badminton, basketball, bowling, football (non-tackle), soccer, softball, table tennis, tennis, volleyball. **Team name:** Griffins.

**Student services.** Adult student services, alcohol/substance abuse counseling, chaplain/spiritual director, career counseling, student employment services, financial aid counseling, health services, minority student services, personal counseling, placement for graduates. **Physically disabled:** Services for speech, hearing impaired.

**Contact.** Phone: (314) 889-1400 Toll-free number: (800) 205-5862
Fax: (314) 889-1451
Peggy Musen, Vice President for Enrollment Management, Fontbonne University, 6800 Wydown Boulevard, St. Louis, MO 63105

---

## Global University
### Springfield, Missouri
**www.globaluniversity.edu**      **CB code: 4916**

▶ Private 4-year Bible and seminary college affiliated with Assemblies of God
▶ Commuter campus in small city
▶ 4,551 degree-seeking undergraduates

**General.** Founded in 1948. Accredited by DETC. All course work completed via distance education. **Degrees:** 250 bachelor's, 6 associate awarded; master's offered. **Location:** 200 miles from St. Louis, 170 miles from Kansas City. **Calendar:** Continuous, extensive summer session. **Full-time faculty:** 55 total. **Part-time faculty:** 450 total.

**Freshman class profile.** 536 applied, 536 admitted, 536 enrolled.

**Basis for selection.** Open admission.

**2009-2010 Annual costs.** Tuition/fees: $3,300. Quoted tuition is for U.S. students. Tuition for international students varies by country. Books/supplies: $650.

**Application procedures. Admission:** No deadline. $40 fee. Admission notification on a rolling basis. Global University allows for rolling applications year round.

**Academics. Special study options:** Distance learning, external degree, independent study. **Credit/placement by examination:** CLEP. 16 credit hours maximum toward associate degree, 32 toward bachelor's. **Support services:** Study skills assistance.

**Majors. Theology:** Bible, missionary, religious ed, theology.

**Computing on campus.** Online library available.

**Student services.** Chaplain/spiritual director.

**Contact.** E-mail: info@globaluniversity.edu
Phone: (417) 862-9533 Toll-free number: (800) 443-1083
Fax: (417) 865-7167
C. Kroh, Registrar and Associate Dean of Student Services, Global University, 1211 South Glenstone Avenue, Springfield, MO 65804

## Goldfarb School of Nursing at Barnes-Jewish College
**St. Louis, Missouri**
www.barnesjewishcollege.edu          CB code: 6329

- Private two-year upper-division nursing college
- Commuter campus in very large city
- 84% of applicants admitted

**General.** Regionally accredited. Affiliated with Barnes-Jewish Hospital and Washington University Medical Center. **Degrees:** 262 bachelor's, 60 associate awarded; master's, doctoral offered. **Location:** Downtown. **Calendar:** Trimester, extensive summer session. **Full-time faculty:** 24 total; 79% have terminal degrees, 12% minority, 92% women. **Class size:** 31% < 20, 30% 20-39, 7% 40-49, 31% 50-99.

**Student profile.** 517 degree-seeking undergraduates, 121 degree-seeking graduate students. 266 applied as first time-transfer students, 223 admitted, 157 enrolled. 80% transferred from two-year, 20% transferred from four-year institutions.

| | | | |
|---|---|---|---|
| Women: | 88% | Out-of-state: | 5% |
| Part-time: | 29% | 25 or older: | 85% |

**Basis for selection.** Open admission. College transcript required. Transfer accepted as juniors, seniors.

**2010-2011 Annual costs.** Tuition/fees: $14,953. Books/supplies: $1,260.

**Financial aid. Non-need-based:** Scholarships awarded for academics, leadership.

**Application procedures. Admission:** Rolling admission. $50 fee. Application must be submitted on paper. **Financial aid:** No deadline. Applicants notified on a rolling basis. FAFSA required.

**Academics. Special study options:** Accelerated study, combined bachelor's/graduate degree. **Credit/placement by examination:** AP, CLEP, IB, institutional tests. **Support services:** Tutoring, writing center.

**Majors. Health:** Nursing (RN).

**Computing on campus.** 60 workstations in library, computer center. Commuter students can connect to campus network. Online library, helpline, wireless network available.

**Student life. Activities:** Student newspaper.

**Student services.** Career counseling, financial aid counseling, personal counseling.

**Contact.** E-mail: bjcon-admissions@bjc.org
Phone: (314) 454-7057 Toll-free number: (800) 832-9009
Fax: (314) 362-9250
Michael Ward, Associate Dean for Student Programs, Goldfarb School of Nursing at Barnes-Jewish College, 4483 Duncan Avenue, St. Louis, MO 63110-1091

## Grantham University
**Kansas City, Missouri**
www.grantham.edu          CB code: 2244

- For-profit 4-year virtual university
- Large city
- 5,542 degree-seeking undergraduates
- 609 graduate students

**General.** Founded in 1951. Accredited by DETC. Degree programs are 100 percent online. **Degrees:** 274 bachelor's, 385 associate awarded; master's offered. **Calendar:** Continuous, extensive summer session. **Full-time faculty:** 17 total; 71% women. **Part-time faculty:** 166 total; 52% women.

**Basis for selection.** Open admission. High school diploma, GED, or equivalent required. Basic computer skills and use of computer with Windows, Internet access, e-mail account, printer also required. **Home-schooled:** Requirements for home schooled student high school graduation vary by state, or state institution granting high school accreditation. Will accept any documentation certifying high school graduation if it is approved by issuing state or the military.

**High school preparation.** College-preparatory program recommended.

**2009-2010 Annual costs.** Tuition/fees: $7,980. Grantham's tuition includes required textbooks, software and shipping (within U.S.).

**2009-2010 Financial aid. Additional information:** DANTES and some employer reimbursement programs available.

**Application procedures. Admission:** No deadline. No application fee. Admission notification on a rolling basis. **Financial aid:** No deadline.

**Academics. Special study options:** Accelerated study, distance learning, independent study. **Credit/placement by examination:** CLEP, IB. 45 credit hours maximum toward associate degree, 90 toward bachelor's. **Support services:** Learning center, tutoring.

**Majors. Business:** Business admin. **Computer sciences:** Computer science, information systems. **Engineering technology:** Electrical, software. **Protective services:** Law enforcement admin.

**Most popular majors.** Business/marketing 47%, computer/information sciences 31%, engineering/engineering technologies 15%.

**Computing on campus.** PC or laptop required. Online library available.

**Student life. Freshman orientation:** Mandatory.

**Student services.** Adult student services, financial aid counseling, veterans' counselor.

**Contact.** E-mail: admissions@grantham.edu
Phone: (800) 955-2527 Toll-free number: (800) 955-2527
Fax: (816) 595-5757
Richard Lee, Associate Director of Addmissions, Grantham University, 7200 NW 86th Street, Kansas City, MO 64153

## Hannibal-LaGrange College
**Hannibal, Missouri**
www.hlg.edu          CB code: 6266

- Private 4-year liberal arts college affiliated with Southern Baptist Convention
- Residential campus in large town
- 902 degree-seeking undergraduates: 6% part-time, 63% women, 3% African American, 1% Asian American, 2% Hispanic American, 9% international
- 23 degree-seeking graduate students
- 94% of applicants admitted
- SAT or ACT (ACT writing optional), interview required

**General.** Founded in 1858. Regionally accredited. Christian environment. **Degrees:** 244 bachelor's, 48 associate awarded; master's offered. **Location:** 100 miles from St. Louis. **Calendar:** Semester, limited summer session. **Full-time faculty:** 63 total; 27% have terminal degrees, 2% minority, 52% women. **Part-time faculty:** 83 total; 5% have terminal degrees, 4% minority, 55% women. **Class size:** 75% < 20, 24% 20-39, 1% 40-49. **Special facilities:** Nature trail, fine arts theater, mission center.

**Freshman class profile.** 646 applied, 607 admitted, 189 enrolled.

| Mid 50% test scores | | | |
|---|---|---|---|
| ACT composite: | 18-26 | Return as sophomores: | 56% |
| Rank in top quarter: | 37% | Out-of-state: | 27% |
| Rank in top tenth: | 21% | Live on campus: | 86% |
| | | International: | 14% |

**Basis for selection.** Most applicants admitted. Test scores important. 20 or above ACT composite required. Applicants with 16-19 ACT composite admitted provisionally. ACT administered on campus on registration day. Applications without English Composition 1 and college algebra must submit ACT scores and take mathematics placement exam. Interviews required for performance and honor students. **Homeschooled:** Transcript of courses and grades required. ACT score required. **Learning Disabled:** Must provide appropriate ADA documentation.

**High school preparation.** College-preparatory program recommended. Recommended units include English 4, mathematics 3, history 3, science 2 (laboratory 1).

**2009-2010 Annual costs.** Tuition/fees: $15,480. Room/board: $6,000. Books/supplies: $800. Personal expenses: $2,061.

**2009-2010 Financial aid. Need-based:** Average loan was $14,241. 36% of total undergraduate aid awarded as scholarships/grants, 64% as loans/jobs. **Non-need-based:** Awarded to 250 full-time undergraduates, including 89 freshmen. Scholarships awarded for academics, art, athletics, music/drama, religious affiliation. **Additional information:** Work-study opportunities vary according to on- and off-campus needs.

**Application procedures. Admission:** Closing date 8/26. $25 fee. Admission notification on a rolling basis beginning on or about 9/1. **Financial aid:** Closing date 7/1. FAFSA, institutional form required. Applicants notified on a rolling basis; must reply by 8/31.

**Academics. Special study options:** Accelerated study, distance learning, double major, dual enrollment of high school students, ESL, honors, independent study, internships, student-designed major, study abroad, teacher certification program, weekend college. **Credit/placement by examination:** AP, CLEP, SAT, ACT, institutional tests. 16 credit hours maximum toward associate degree, 30 toward bachelor's. No more than 8 credit hours in one discipline. **Support services:** Remedial instruction, study skills assistance, tutoring.

**Honors college/program.** Minimum ACT-27, essay. Additional 21 hours plus research project required, must maintain requirements for eligibility each semester.

**Majors. Biology:** General. **Business:** General, accounting, business admin, finance, marketing, organizational behavior. **Communications:** General. **Computer sciences:** General. **Education:** General, art, business, early childhood, elementary, English, mathematics, music, physical, science, secondary, social studies. **Health:** Nursing (RN). **History:** General. **Liberal arts:** Arts/sciences. **Math:** General. **Parks/recreation:** Facilities management. **Protective services:** Law enforcement admin. **Psychology:** General. **Public administration:** Human services. **Social sciences:** Sociology. **Theology:** Bible, religious ed, sacred music. **Visual/performing arts:** Art, dramatic, music performance. **Other:** Intercultural missions.

**Computing on campus.** 91 workstations in library, computer center, student center. Dormitories linked to campus network. Commuter students can connect to campus network. Online library, repair service, wireless network available.

**Student life. Freshman orientation:** Mandatory, $50 fee. Preregistration for classes offered. Conducted 4 days before classes begin. **Policies:** Students under 21 years of age at beginning of enrollment required to live in residence housing unless living with approved relative. Religious observance required. **Housing:** Single-sex dorms, special housing for disabled, apartments, wellness housing available. $100 fully refundable deposit, deadline 8/26. **Activities:** Jazz band, campus ministries, choral groups, drama, international student organizations, music ensembles, student government, student newspaper, Democratic club, Fellowship of Christian Athletes, Phi Beta Delta (men's service), Phi Beta Lambda, Gatekeepers (mentoring), Students for Life, Natures Investigation Circulus, Missouri State Teachers Association, Republican club, art club, science club.

**Athletics.** NAIA, NCCAA. **Intercollegiate:** Baseball M, basketball, cross-country, golf, soccer, softball W, swimming, track and field, volleyball, wrestling M. **Intramural:** Badminton, basketball, racquetball, table tennis, volleyball. **Team name:** Trojans.

**Student services.** Career counseling, student employment services. **Physically disabled:** Services for visually, hearing impaired.

---

**Contact.** E-mail: admissio@hlg.edu
Phone: (573) 629-3264 Toll-free number: (800) 454-1119
Fax: (573) 221-6594
Ray Carty, Vice President of Enrollment Management, Hannibal-LaGrange College, 2800 Palmyra Road, Hannibal, MO 63401

## Harris-Stowe State University
### St. Louis, Missouri
**www.hssu.edu**   CB code: 6269

- Public 4-year university
- Commuter campus in large city
- 1,844 degree-seeking undergraduates: 24% part-time, 67% women, 92% African American, 1% Hispanic American, 1% international
- 94% of applicants admitted

**General.** Founded in 1857. Regionally accredited. **Degrees:** 132 bachelor's awarded. **ROTC:** Army, Air Force. **Location:** Midtown. **Calendar:** Semester, limited summer session. **Full-time faculty:** 56 total. **Part-time faculty:** 134 total. **Class size:** 70% < 20, 30% 20-39. **Special facilities:** Jazz institute.

**Freshman class profile.** 1,534 applied, 1,449 admitted, 391 enrolled.

| Mid 50% test scores | | | |
|---|---|---|---|
| ACT composite: | 14-18 | Rank in top tenth: | 3% |
| GPA 3.75 or higher: | 1% | End year in good standing: | 10% |
| GPA 3.50-3.74: | 2% | Return as sophomores: | 47% |
| GPA 3.0-3.49: | 9% | Out-of-state: | 11% |
| GPA 2.0-2.99: | 54% | Live on campus: | 31% |
| Rank in top quarter: | 12% | Fraternities: | 1% |
| | | Sororities: | 1% |

**Basis for selection.** ACT composite score of 21, or combined ACT composite percentile rank and high school class percentile rank greater than or equal to 100. Full-time, first-year freshmen are encouraged to meet the Missouri High School Core Curriculum requirements. SAT or ACT recommended. Applicants with scores below 18 on any section of the ACT or below 440 on any section of the SAT must take institutional placement test. **Learning Disabled:** Submit documentation of disability for review by Director of Academic Support Services.

**High school preparation.** College-preparatory program recommended. Required and recommended units include English 4, mathematics 3, social studies 3, science 3 (laboratory 1), foreign language 2 and academic electives 7. 1 visual/performing arts required. Social studies must include American government. Electives must be from above list.

**2009-2010 Annual costs.** Tuition/fees: $5,340; $10,092 out-of-state. Books/supplies: $500. Personal expenses: $2,000.

**2009-2010 Financial aid. Need-based:** 414 full-time freshmen applied for aid; 400 were judged to have need; 400 of these received aid. Average need met was 98%. Average scholarship/grant was $1,375; average loan $3,500. 59% of total undergraduate aid awarded as scholarships/grants, 41% as loans/jobs. **Non-need-based:** Awarded to 1,346 full-time undergraduates, including 202 freshmen. Scholarships awarded for academics, athletics, music/drama, state residency.

**Application procedures. Admission:** No deadline. $15 fee. Application must be submitted on paper. Admission notification on a rolling basis. **Financial aid:** Priority date 4/1; no closing date. FAFSA, institutional form required. Applicants notified on a rolling basis starting 4/1; must reply within 3 week(s) of notification.

**Academics. Special study options:** Accelerated study, cooperative education, ESL, internships, student-designed major, teacher certification program. **Credit/placement by examination:** AP, CLEP, SAT, ACT, institutional tests. **Support services:** Learning center, pre-admission summer program, reduced course load, remedial instruction, study skills assistance, tutoring, writing center.

**Majors. Business:** General, accounting, business admin, entrepreneurial studies, hospitality admin, marketing. **Computer sciences:** General, information systems, networking. **Education:** Early childhood, elementary, middle, multi-level teacher, secondary. **Health:** Health services admin. **Protective services:** Juvenile corrections, law enforcement admin. **Public administration:** General. **Social sciences:** Urban studies.

**Most popular majors.** Business/marketing 39%, education 43%, security/protective services 10%.

**Computing on campus.** 205 workstations in dormitories, library, computer center. Dormitories wired for high-speed internet access. Commuter students can connect to campus network. Wireless network available.

**Student life. Freshman orientation:** Mandatory. Program directed by counseling staff during semester. **Housing:** Coed dorms available. $500 nonrefundable deposit. **Activities:** Choral groups, drama, international student organizations, literary magazine, music ensembles, student government, student newspaper, African American Studies Society, multicultural council, 100 Strong, Organization for Cultrual Progress, Student Ambassadors.

**Athletics.** NAIA. **Intercollegiate:** Baseball M, basketball, cheerleading, soccer, softball W, volleyball W. **Intramural:** Basketball, volleyball. **Team name:** Hornets.

**Student services.** Career counseling, student employment services, financial aid counseling, health services, personal counseling, placement for graduates, veterans' counselor.

**Contact.** E-mail: admissions@hssu.edu
Phone: (314) 340-3300 Fax: (314) 340-3555
Lashanda Boone, Executive Director of Enrollment Management, Harris-Stowe State University, 3026 Laclede Avenue, St. Louis, MO 63103-2199

## Hickey College
### St. Louis, Missouri
www.hickeycollege.edu          CB code: 2308

◗ For-profit 4-year business and technical college
◗ Commuter campus in very large city
◗ 444 degree-seeking undergraduates

**General.** Founded in 1933. Accredited by ACICS. **Degrees:** 30 bachelor's, 167 associate awarded. **Location:** 15 miles from downtown. **Calendar:** Semester. **Full-time faculty:** 18 total. **Part-time faculty:** 24 total.

**Basis for selection.** Open admission, but selective for some programs. Selective enrollment for paralegal and veterinary technician programs.

**2009-2010 Annual costs.** Books/supplies: $1,000.

**Application procedures. Admission:** No deadline. $50 fee. Admission notification on a rolling basis. **Financial aid:** No deadline. FAFSA required. Applicants notified on a rolling basis.

**Academics. Credit/placement by examination:** CLEP.

**Majors. Business:** Management science.

**Computing on campus.** 134 workstations in library, computer center.

**Student life. Housing:** Apartments available.

**Student services.** Placement for graduates.

**Contact.** E-mail: admin@hickeycollege.edu
Phone: (314) 434-2212 Toll-free number: (800) 777-1544
Fax: (314) 434-1974
James Rowe, Director of Admissions, Hickey College, 940 West Port Plaza, St. Louis, MO 63146

## ITT Technical Institute: Arnold
### Arnold, Missouri
www.itt-tech.edu          CB code: 2691

◗ For-profit 4-year technical college
◗ Commuter campus in large town

**General.** Accredited by ACICS. **Calendar:** Quarter.

**Annual costs/financial aid.** Books/supplies: $3,100.

**Contact.** Phone: (636) 464-6600
Director of Recruitment, 1930 Meyer Drury Drive, Arnold, MO 63010

## ITT Technical Institute: Earth City
### Earth City, Missouri
www.itt-tech.edu          CB code: 1216

◗ For-profit 4-year technical college
◗ Commuter campus in large city

**General.** Founded in 1936. Accredited by ACICS. **Location:** 15 miles from St. Louis. **Calendar:** Quarter.

**Contact.** Phone: (314) 298-7800
Director of Recruitment, 13505 Lakefront Drive, Earth City, MO 63045

## Kansas City Art Institute
### Kansas City, Missouri
www.kcai.edu          CB code: 6330

◗ Private 4-year visual arts college
◗ Residential campus in large city
◗ 679 degree-seeking undergraduates: 2% part-time, 59% women
◗ 69% of applicants admitted
◗ SAT or ACT (ACT writing optional), application essay required
◗ 59% graduate within 6 years; 10% enter graduate study

**General.** Founded in 1885. Regionally accredited. **Degrees:** 125 bachelor's awarded. **Location:** 250 miles from St. Louis, 500 miles from Denver. **Calendar:** Semester, limited summer session. **Full-time faculty:** 46 total; 91% have terminal degrees, 4% minority, 39% women. **Part-time faculty:** 55 total; 38% have terminal degrees, 2% minority, 46% women. **Class size:** 83% < 20, 17% 20-39.

**Freshman class profile.** 527 applied, 365 admitted, 185 enrolled.

| Mid 50% test scores | | | |
|---|---|---|---|
| SAT critical reading: | 450-590 | Rank in top quarter: | 10% |
| SAT math: | 450-530 | Rank in top tenth: | 1% |
| SAT writing: | 430-550 | End year in good standing: | 91% |
| ACT composite: | 20-25 | Return as sophomores: | 74% |
| GPA 3.75 or higher: | 14% | Out-of-state: | 69% |
| GPA 3.50-3.74: | 13% | Live on campus: | 90% |
| GPA 3.0-3.49: | 37% | | |
| GPA 2.0-2.99: | 35% | | |

**Basis for selection.** High school or GED academic record, 2 letters of recommendation, ACT, SAT or TOEFL scores and a statement of purpose are all used to determine admissions decisions. Portfolio of minimum of 15 pieces of artwork is required/evaluated for admission decisions. **Home-schooled:** State high school equivalency certificate required. **Learning Disabled:** Disclosure of special needs recommended but not required.

**High school preparation.** College-preparatory program recommended. 20 units recommended. Recommended units include English 4, mathematics 3, social studies 3, science 3, visual/performing arts 4 and academic electives 3.

**2009-2010 Annual costs.** Tuition/fees: $28,580. Room/board: $8,710. Books/supplies: $1,500. Personal expenses: $2,000.

**2009-2010 Financial aid. Need-based:** 166 full-time freshmen applied for aid; 152 were judged to have need; 152 of these received aid. Average need met was 70%. Average scholarship/grant was $18,537; average loan $4,459. 71% of total undergraduate aid awarded as scholarships/grants, 29% as loans/jobs. **Non-need-based:** Awarded to 44 full-time undergraduates, including 37 freshmen. Scholarships awarded for academics, art.

**Application procedures. Admission:** Priority date 2/1; deadline 8/1 (postmark date). $35 fee, may be waived for applicants with need. Admission notification on a rolling basis beginning on or about 9/1. Must reply by May 1 or within 2 week(s) if notified thereafter. **Financial aid:** Priority date 3/15, closing date 4/1. FAFSA required. Applicants notified on a rolling basis starting 4/1; must reply within 2 week(s) of notification.

**Academics. Special study options:** Double major, ESL, exchange student, independent study, internships, New York semester, study abroad. **Credit/placement by examination:** CLEP, IB. 15 credit hours maximum toward bachelor's degree. **Support services:** Learning center, reduced course load, remedial instruction, study skills assistance, tutoring, writing center.

**Majors. Visual/performing arts:** Art history/conservation, ceramics, cinematography, fiber arts, graphic design, painting, photography, printmaking, sculpture. **Other:** Digital media.

**Computing on campus.** 50 workstations in dormitories, library, computer center. Dormitories wired for high-speed internet access and linked to campus network. Commuter students can connect to campus network. Online course registration, online library, helpline, wireless network available.

**Student life. Freshman orientation:** Mandatory. Preregistration for classes offered. 3-day program held prior to start of academic year. **Housing:** Guaranteed on-campus for freshmen. Coed dorms, apartments, wellness housing available. $225 nonrefundable deposit, deadline 6/1. **Activities:** Film society, international student organizations, literary magazine, student government, student newspaper, Xenos Society.

**Student services.** Adult student services, alcohol/substance abuse counseling, career counseling, student employment services, financial aid counseling, minority student services, personal counseling, veterans' counselor. **Physically disabled:** Services for visually, hearing impaired. **Learning disabled:** Comprehensive services available.

**Contact.** E-mail: admiss@kcai.edu
Phone: (816) 474-5224 Toll-free number: (800) 522-5224
Fax: (816) 802-3309
Kansas City Art Institute, 4415 Warwick Boulevard, Kansas City, MO 64111

## Lincoln University
### Jefferson City, Missouri
### www.lincolnu.edu
### CB code: 6366

- Public 4-year university and liberal arts college
- Commuter campus in large town
- 2,650 degree-seeking undergraduates: 21% part-time, 59% women, 46% African American, 1% Asian American, 2% Hispanic American, 2% international
- 147 degree-seeking graduate students

**General.** Founded in 1866. Regionally accredited. 1890 land-grant institution. **Degrees:** 297 bachelor's, 69 associate awarded; master's offered. **ROTC:** Army, Naval, Air Force. **Location:** 132 miles from St. Louis, 157 miles from Kansas City. **Calendar:** Semester, limited summer session. **Full-time faculty:** 139 total; 29% minority, 50% women. **Part-time faculty:** 109 total. **Class size:** 55% < 20, 41% 20-39, 3% 40-49, less than 1% 50-99. **Special facilities:** Ethnic studies center and archives, 3 research farms, agriculture and extension information center.

### Freshman class profile.

| Mid 50% test scores | | | |
|---|---|---|---|
| SAT critical reading: | 380-450 | GPA 2.0-2.99: | 52% |
| SAT math: | 380-460 | Rank in top quarter: | 16% |
| ACT composite: | 14-20 | Rank in top tenth: | 3% |
| GPA 3.75 or higher: | 5% | Return as sophomores: | 52% |
| GPA 3.50-3.74: | 6% | Out-of-state: | 23% |
| GPA 3.0-3.49: | 17% | Live on campus: | 61% |

**Basis for selection.** Open admission, but selective for some programs and for out-of-state students. Special requirements for nursing and education programs. ACT or SAT scores required but used for placement purposes only. Audition required for sacred music and music education students. **Homeschooled:** Must submit a transcript with the parent's notarized signature, demonstrating completion of the Missouri Minimum Core Curriculum or its equivalency, as determined by the University. **Learning Disabled:** Comprehensive documentation of disability by qualified professional must be on file to request accommodations.

**High school preparation.** College-preparatory program recommended. 16 units recommended. Recommended units include English 4, mathematics 3, social studies 3, science 2 (laboratory 1), foreign language 2, visual/performing arts 1 and academic electives 1. Social studies courses should include 1 unit of U.S. history and at least 1 semester of government.

**2010-2011 Annual costs.** Tuition/fees (projected): $6,175; $10,885 out-of-state. Students enrolled full-time must pay $233 per fall/spring semester or $96 per summer semester for health insurance if they do not provide proof of other coverage. Enrollment in the student health insurance program is required for international students. Room/board: $4,660. Books/supplies: $950. Personal expenses: $166.

**2009-2010 Financial aid. Non-need-based:** Scholarships awarded for academics, art, athletics, job skills, leadership, minority status, music/drama, ROTC, state residency.

**Application procedures. Admission:** Closing date 7/15 (postmark date). $20 fee. Admission notification on a rolling basis. **Financial aid:** Priority date 3/1; no closing date. FAFSA, institutional form required. Applicants notified by 3/15; Applicants notified on a rolling basis starting 3/15; must reply within 2 week(s) of notification.

**Academics. Special study options:** Accelerated study, distance learning, double major, dual enrollment of high school students, exchange student, honors, independent study, internships, study abroad, teacher certification program. Senior citizen program. **Credit/placement by examination:** AP, CLEP, institutional tests. 15 credit hours maximum toward associate degree, 20 toward bachelor's. Total number of alternative credit hours cannot exceed 30. Students may receive credit only for courses numbered 100-299. Each examination may be taken only once. Students must be currently enrolled during the semester in which he/she elects to take the exam. **Support**

services: Learning center, pre-admission summer program, reduced course load, remedial instruction, study skills assistance, tutoring, writing center.

**Majors. Agriculture:** General, business. **Biology:** General. **Business:** Accounting, business admin, managerial economics, marketing. **Communications:** Journalism. **Computer sciences:** Information systems. **Conservation:** Environmental science. **Education:** Art, biology, business, chemistry, elementary, English, mathematics, music, physical, physics, social science, special. **Engineering technology:** Civil, mechanical. **Foreign languages:** Spanish. **Health:** Clinical lab science, nursing (RN). **History:** General. **Liberal arts:** Arts/sciences. **Math:** General. **Physical sciences:** Chemistry, physics. **Protective services:** Law enforcement admin. **Psychology:** General. **Public administration:** General, social work. **Social sciences:** Political science, sociology. **Theology:** Sacred music. **Visual/performing arts:** Studio arts. **Other:** Wellness.

**Most popular majors.** Business/marketing 25%, communications/journalism 6%, education 14%, health sciences 6%, liberal arts 7%, psychology 6%, security/protective services 8%.

**Computing on campus.** 315 workstations in dormitories, library, computer center, student center. Dormitories wired for high-speed internet access and linked to campus network. Online library, helpline, wireless network available.

**Student life. Freshman orientation:** Mandatory, $50 fee. Preregistration for classes offered. Summer orientations are one and a half day programs. Other sessions throughout the year. **Policies:** Unmarried freshmen and sophomores under 21 years of age, whose primary domicile is beyond a 60-mile radius of the University, are required to live in residence halls for four consecutive semesters. Armed Forces veterans and any student who has established a primary domicile one year prior to entering the University are exempted from this policy. **Housing:** Guaranteed on-campus for freshmen. Coed dorms, single-sex dorms, wellness housing available. $125 fully refundable deposit, deadline 7/1. Honors housing available. **Activities:** Bands, campus ministries, choral groups, dance, drama, international student organizations, literary magazine, music ensembles, radio station, student government, student newspaper, TV station, Baptist Student Center, College Republicans, College Democrats, Barrier Breakers, Wesley Foundation, Kathleen McGuire Newman Center.

**Athletics.** NCAA. **Intercollegiate:** Baseball M, basketball, cheerleading M, cross-country W, football (tackle) M, golf, softball W, tennis W, track and field. **Intramural:** Basketball, bowling. **Team name:** Blue Tigers.

**Student services.** Career counseling, services for economically disadvantaged, financial aid counseling, health services, personal counseling, veterans' counselor. **Physically disabled:** Services for visually, speech, hearing impaired.

**Contact.** E-mail: enroll@lincolnu.edu
Phone: (573) 681-5599 Toll-free number: (800) 521-5052
Fax: (573) 681-5889
Mike Kosher, Director of Admissions, Lincoln University, 820 Chestnut Stree, B7 Young Hall, Jefferson City, MO 65102-0029

## Lindenwood University
### Saint Charles, Missouri
### www.lindenwood.edu/
### CB code: 6367

- Private 4-year university and liberal arts college affiliated with Presbyterian Church (USA)
- Residential campus in very large city
- 6,384 degree-seeking undergraduates: 4% part-time, 56% women, 10% African American, 1% Asian American, 3% Hispanic American, 10% international
- 3,624 degree-seeking graduate students
- 57% of applicants admitted
- SAT or ACT (ACT writing optional) required
- 46% graduate within 6 years

**General.** Founded in 1827. Regionally accredited. **Degrees:** 1,243 bachelor's awarded; master's, doctoral offered. **ROTC:** Army. **Location:** 20 miles from St. Louis. **Calendar:** 4-1-4, limited summer session. **Full-time faculty:** 210 total; 70% have terminal degrees, 8% minority, 38% women. **Part-time faculty:** 310 total; 29% have terminal degrees, 12% minority, 45% women. **Class size:** 64% < 20, 35% 20-39, less than 1% 40-49. **Special facilities:** Greenhouse, wetland program facility, success center, natural history.

**Freshman class profile.** 3,261 applied, 1,852 admitted, 1,105 enrolled.

| Mid 50% test scores | | | |
|---|---|---|---|
| SAT critical reading: | 450-570 | Rank in top quarter: | 26% |
| SAT math: | 480-590 | Rank in top tenth: | 8% |
| SAT writing: | 390-470 | Return as sophomores: | 72% |
| ACT composite: | 20-24 | Out-of-state: | 27% |
| GPA 3.75 or higher: | 11% | Live on campus: | 87% |
| GPA 3.50-3.74: | 14% | International: | 14% |
| GPA 3.0-3.49: | 34% | Fraternities: | 1% |
| GPA 2.0-2.99: | 38% | Sororities: | 1% |

**Basis for selection.** Class rank, school record, high school GPA very important. **Homeschooled:** Transcript of courses and grades required.

**High school preparation.** College-preparatory program recommended. 19 units recommended. Recommended units include English 4, mathematics 3, social studies 3, history 3, science 3 (laboratory 1), foreign language 2 and visual/performing arts 1.

**2010-2011 Annual costs.** Tuition/fees: $13,600. Room/board: $7,120.

**2009-2010 Financial aid. Need-based:** 744 full-time freshmen applied for aid; 637 were judged to have need; 637 of these received aid. Average need met was 90%. Average scholarship/grant was $3,274; average loan $2,472. 55% of total undergraduate aid awarded as scholarships/grants, 45% as loans/jobs. **Non-need-based:** Awarded to 2,393 full-time undergraduates, including 597 freshmen. Scholarships awarded for academics, alumni affiliation, art, job skills, leadership, music/drama, ROTC.

**Application procedures. Admission:** No deadline. $30 fee, may be waived for applicants with need. Admission notification on a rolling basis. **Financial aid:** Priority date 4/1; no closing date. FAFSA required. Applicants notified on a rolling basis.

**Academics. Special study options:** Accelerated study, combined bachelor's/graduate degree, cooperative education, distance learning, double major, dual enrollment of high school students, ESL, external degree, honors, independent study, internships, student-designed major, study abroad, teacher certification program. **Credit/placement by examination:** CLEP, IB, institutional tests. **Support services:** Learning center, reduced course load, study skills assistance, tutoring, writing center.

**Majors. Area/ethnic studies:** American. **Biology:** General, environmental. **Business:** General, accounting, business admin, communications, entrepreneurial studies, finance, hospitality admin, human resources, international, management information systems, marketing, nonprofit/public, retailing. **Communications:** General, advertising, digital media, journalism, media studies, organizational. **Computer sciences:** General, computer science, information technology. **Conservation:** Environmental science. **Education:** Art, biology, business, chemistry, early childhood, early childhood special, elementary, French, history, middle, physical, science, social studies, Spanish, technology/industrial arts, trade/industrial. **Foreign languages:** French, Spanish. **Health:** Athletic training, health care admin. **History:** General. **Interdisciplinary:** Gerontology. **Math:** General. **Parks/recreation:** Exercise sciences, sports admin. **Personal/culinary services:** Funeral direction, mortuary science. **Philosophy/religion:** Christian, philosophy, religion. **Physical sciences:** Chemistry. **Protective services:** Criminal justice, fire services admin. **Psychology:** General. **Public administration:** General, human services, social work. **Social sciences:** Criminology, international relations, political science, sociology. **Theology:** Pastoral counseling, youth ministry. **Visual/performing arts:** General, acting, art, art history/conservation, arts management, dance, directing/producing, dramatic, fashion design, multimedia, music management, music performance, music theory/composition, musical theater, studio arts, theater arts management, theater design.

**Most popular majors.** Business/marketing 47%, communications/journalism 6%, education 12%, social sciences 9%, visual/performing arts 6%.

**Computing on campus.** 153 workstations in library, computer center, student center. Dormitories wired for high-speed internet access and linked to campus network. Commuter students can connect to campus network. Online course registration, online library, helpline, wireless network available.

**Student life. Freshman orientation:** Mandatory. Preregistration for classes offered. Held 5 days before the beginning of fall semester. **Policies:** Zero tolerance of illegal substances. **Housing:** Guaranteed on-campus for all undergraduates. Single-sex dorms, apartments, fraternity/sorority housing available. $300 nonrefundable deposit. Housing for single parents with children available. **Activities:** Bands, campus ministries, choral groups, dance, drama, international student organizations, literary magazine, music ensembles, musical theater, radio station, student government, student newspaper, TV station, Campus Crusade for Christ, intercultural club, American Humanics, Circle K, Reform Campus Fellowship, Lewis & Clark Historical Society,

Eastern Debating Society, Christian Life Group, Fellowship of Christian Athletes.

**Athletics.** NAIA. **Intercollegiate:** Baseball M, basketball, bowling, cheerleading, cross-country, diving, field hockey W, football (tackle) M, golf, ice hockey, rifle, soccer, softball W, swimming, synchronized swimming, tennis W, track and field, volleyball, water polo, wrestling. **Intramural:** Basketball, bowling, football (non-tackle), soccer, softball, swimming, table tennis, tennis, volleyball, water polo. **Team name:** Lions.

**Student services.** Adult student services, chaplain/spiritual director, career counseling, student employment services, financial aid counseling, health services, personal counseling, placement for graduates, veterans' counselor. **Physically disabled:** Services for visually, hearing impaired.

**Contact.** E-mail: admissions@lindenwood.edu
Phone: (636) 949-4949 Fax: (636) 949-4989
Joe Parisi, Dean of Undergraduate Day Admissions, Lindenwood University, 209 South Kingshighway, St. Charles, MO 63301

## Maryville University of Saint Louis
St. Louis, Missouri — CB member
www.maryville.edu — CB code: 6399

- Private 4-year university
- Commuter campus in very large city
- 2,826 degree-seeking undergraduates: 41% part-time, 76% women, 7% African American, 2% Asian American, 2% Hispanic American, 1% international
- 600 degree-seeking graduate students
- 66% of applicants admitted
- SAT or ACT (ACT writing optional) required
- 61% graduate within 6 years; 9% enter graduate study

**General.** Founded in 1872. Regionally accredited. **Degrees:** 653 bachelor's awarded; master's, doctoral offered. **ROTC:** Army. **Location:** 20 miles from downtown. **Calendar:** Semester, limited summer session. **Full-time faculty:** 111 total; 86% have terminal degrees, 13% minority, 59% women. **Part-time faculty:** 282 total; 49% have terminal degrees, 9% minority, 63% women. **Class size:** 67% < 20, 32% 20-39, 1% 40-49, less than 1% 50-99. **Special facilities:** Observatory, auditorium, outdoor walking trails, coffeehouse, teaching laboratory, clinical laboratories, communications laboratory, multi-media classrooms,.

**Freshman class profile.** 1,154 applied, 764 admitted, 374 enrolled.

| Mid 50% test scores | | | |
|---|---|---|---|
| ACT composite: | 22-27 | Rank in top tenth: | 26% |
| GPA 3.75 or higher: | 37% | End year in good standing: | 94% |
| GPA 3.50-3.74: | 22% | Return as sophomores: | 82% |
| GPA 3.0-3.49: | 24% | Out-of-state: | 20% |
| GPA 2.0-2.99: | 17% | Live on campus: | 64% |
| Rank in top quarter: | 56% | International: | 1% |

**Basis for selection.** School record most important. Recommendations and extracurricular activities considered. ACT or SAT very important. Interview and 20 hours observation in clinical setting required for physical therapy students. Audition required for music therapy students; portfolio required for art education, graphic design, interior design, and studio art majors. **Homeschooled:** Increased weight placed on ACT or SAT scores.

**High school preparation.** College-preparatory program recommended. 22 units required. Required and recommended units include English 4, mathematics 3, social studies 2, science 2, foreign language 3 and academic electives 8. Applicants for actuarial science, art, education, interior design, clinical laboratory science, nursing, occupational therapy, and physical therapy must meet other specific requirements.

**2010-2011 Annual costs.** Tuition/fees: $21,910. Room/board: $8,500. Books/supplies: $1,600. Personal expenses: $2,100.

**2009-2010 Financial aid. Need-based:** 292 full-time freshmen applied for aid; 254 were judged to have need; 254 of these received aid. Average need met was 79%. Average scholarship/grant was $13,040; average loan $3,010. 50% of total undergraduate aid awarded as scholarships/grants, 50% as loans/jobs. **Non-need-based:** Awarded to 423 full-time undergraduates, including 114 freshmen. Scholarships awarded for academics, alumni affiliation, art, athletics, leadership, minority status, ROTC.

**Application procedures. Admission:** Closing date 8/15. $30 fee, may be waived for applicants with need, free for online applicants. Admission notification on a rolling basis. Must reply by May 1 or within 4 week(s) if notified thereafter. **Financial aid:** Priority date 3/1; no closing date. FAFSA required. Applicants notified on a rolling basis starting 3/1; must reply by 5/1 or within 2 week(s) of notification.

**Academics. Special study options:** Accelerated study, combined bachelor's/graduate degree, cooperative education, cross-registration, distance learning, double major, dual enrollment of high school students, honors, independent study, internships, liberal arts/career combination, semester at sea, student-designed major, study abroad, teacher certification program, Washington semester, weekend college. **Credit/placement by examination:** AP, CLEP, IB, SAT, ACT, institutional tests. 30 credit hours maximum toward bachelor's degree. **Support services:** Learning center, reduced course load, study skills assistance, tutoring, writing center.

**Majors. Biology:** General, biochemistry, biomedical sciences. **Business:** General, accounting, actuarial science, business admin, e-commerce, management information systems, marketing. **Communications:** Media studies. **Computer sciences:** Computer science. **Conservation:** Environmental science, environmental studies. **Education:** Art, early childhood, elementary, middle. **Health:** Clinical lab science, music therapy, nursing (RN), predental, vocational rehab counseling. **History:** General. **Interdisciplinary:** Biological/physical sciences. **Legal studies:** Paralegal. **Liberal arts:** Arts/sciences. **Math:** General, applied. **Parks/recreation:** Sports admin. **Physical sciences:** Chemistry. **Psychology:** General, industrial, social. **Social sciences:** Criminology, sociology. **Visual/performing arts:** Graphic design, interior design, studio arts.

**Most popular majors.** Business/marketing 29%, education 6%, health sciences 35%, psychology 8%, visual/performing arts 6%.

**Computing on campus.** 494 workstations in dormitories, library, computer center, student center, student center. Dormitories wired for high-speed internet access and linked to campus network. Commuter students can connect to campus network. Online course registration, online library, helpline, student web hosting, wireless network available.

**Student life. Freshman orientation:** Available. Preregistration for classes offered. 3-day program prior to start of classes. **Housing:** Guaranteed on-campus for all undergraduates. Coed dorms, apartments, wellness housing available. $150 partly refundable deposit, deadline 5/1. **Activities:** Bands, campus ministries, choral groups, dance, drama, literary magazine, music ensembles, student government, student newspaper, symphony orchestra, student academic majors clubs, Baptist student union, Campus Crusade for Christ, Roman Catholic student community, Reformed Campus Fellowship, Fellowship of Christian Athletes, Association of Black Collegians, multicultural club, community service club.

**Athletics.** NCAA. **Intercollegiate:** Baseball M, basketball, cross-country, golf, soccer, softball W, tennis, track and field, volleyball W. **Intramural:** Basketball, bowling, cheerleading, football (non-tackle), soccer, softball, table tennis, volleyball. **Team name:** Saints.

**Student services.** Adult student services, alcohol/substance abuse counseling, chaplain/spiritual director, career counseling, student employment services, financial aid counseling, health services, minority student services, personal counseling, placement for graduates, veterans' counselor. **Physically disabled:** Services for visually, speech, hearing impaired.

**Contact.** E-mail: admissions@maryville.edu
Phone: (314) 529-9350 Toll-free number: (800) 627-9855 ext. 9350
Fax: (314) 529-9927
Shani Lenore-Jenkins, Assistant Vice President of Enrollment, Maryville University of Saint Louis, 650 Maryville University Drive, St. Louis, MO 63141-7299

## Midwest University
**Wentzville, Missouri**
**www.midwest.edu**

▶ Private two-year upper-division university and seminary college
▶ Large town

**General.** Regionally accredited; also accredited by TRACS. **Degrees:** 9 bachelor's awarded; master's, doctoral offered. **Calendar:** Semester. **Full-time faculty:** 5 total. **Part-time faculty:** 4 total.

**Student profile.** 90 degree-seeking undergraduates.

**2009-2010 Annual costs.** Tuition/fees: $6,100. Room/board: $5,100.

**Application procedures. Admission:** $100 fee.

**Academics. Credit/placement by examination:** CLEP.

**Majors. Philosophy/religion:** Religion.

**Contact.** E-mail: usa@midwest.edu
Phone: (636) 327-4645
Jeoung Ham, Registrar and Director of Admissions, Midwest University, 851 Parr Road, Wentzville, MO 63385

## Missouri Baptist University
**St. Louis, Missouri**
**www.mobap.edu**                          **CB code: 2258**

▶ Private 4-year university and liberal arts college affiliated with Baptist faith
▶ Commuter campus in very large city
▶ 1,541 degree-seeking undergraduates: 18% part-time, 60% women, 11% African American, 1% Asian American, 3% Hispanic American, 1% Native American, 3% international
▶ 1,372 degree-seeking graduate students
▶ 59% of applicants admitted
▶ 45% graduate within 6 years

**General.** Founded in 1963. Regionally accredited. **Degrees:** 325 bachelor's awarded; master's, professional offered. **ROTC:** Army. **Location:** 10 miles from downtown. **Calendar:** Semester, limited summer session. **Full-time faculty:** 70 total; 54% have terminal degrees, 44% women. **Part-time faculty:** 176 total; 17% have terminal degrees, 47% women.

**Freshman class profile.** 821 applied, 482 admitted, 223 enrolled.

| Mid 50% test scores | | ACT composite: | 19-24 |
|---|---|---|---|
| SAT critical reading: | 450-500 | Return as sophomores: | 70% |
| SAT math: | 400-550 | International: | 3% |

**Basis for selection.** Minimum 2.0 high school GPA. Minimum score of 20 is required for ACT and/or a minimum score of 950 (exclusive of Writing) on SAT. Final class rank must be in the upper 50 percent of the graduating class. Applicants with high school GPA below 2.0 may be admitted on a probational status. Interview and/or essay required for academically weak students; audition required for music majors. **Learning Disabled:** Students must self-identify to the Special Needs Access Office, provide current written documentation of disability from qualified professional or agency, and request accommodations. Documentation must meet institutional documentation criteria, indicate a substantial limitation in the education environment, and be completed at least six weeks prior to the start of the semester or class.

**High school preparation.** 22 units required. Required and recommended units include English 4, mathematics 3, social studies 2, history 1, science 2 (laboratory 1), foreign language 2 and academic electives 3. One visual and performing arts required.

**2009-2010 Annual costs.** Tuition/fees: $17,860. Room/board: $7,090.

**2008-2009 Financial aid. Non-need-based:** Scholarships awarded for academics, alumni affiliation, athletics, leadership, music/drama, religious affiliation.

**Application procedures. Admission:** No deadline. $30 fee, may be waived for applicants with need, free for online applicants. Admission notification on a rolling basis. **Financial aid:** Priority date 4/1; no closing date. FAFSA, institutional form required. Applicants notified on a rolling basis starting 4/15; must reply within 2 week(s) of notification.

**Academics. Special study options:** Accelerated study, combined bachelor's/graduate degree, cooperative education, cross-registration, distance learning, double major, dual enrollment of high school students, independent study, internships, liberal arts/career combination, student-designed major, study abroad, teacher certification program, urban semester, Washington semester. **Credit/placement by examination:** AP, CLEP, institutional tests. 45 credit hours maximum toward bachelor's degree. No single source may account for more than 30 of the 45 credit-hour maximum. **Support services:** Learning center, reduced course load, remedial instruction, study skills assistance, tutoring, writing center.

**Majors. Biology:** General, biotechnology. **Business:** Accounting, business admin, marketing, operations. **Communications:** General. **Computer sciences:** General. **Education:** Business, early childhood, elementary, health, middle, music, physical, science. **Family/consumer sciences:** Family studies. **Health:** Athletic training. **History:** General. **Liberal arts:** Arts/sciences. **Math:** General. **Parks/recreation:** Sports admin. **Philosophy/religion:** Christian. **Physical sciences:** Chemistry. **Protective services:** Criminal justice. **Psychology:** General. **Public administration:** Human services. **Social sciences:** General. **Theology:** Religious ed, sacred music, theology. **Visual/performing arts:** Music performance. **Other:** Worship arts.

**Computing on campus.** 60 workstations in dormitories, library, computer center, student center. Dormitories wired for high-speed internet access and linked to campus network. Commuter students can connect to campus network. Online library, helpline, wireless network available.

**Student life. Freshman orientation:** Mandatory. **Policies:** Religious observance required. **Housing:** Single-sex dorms, apartments, wellness housing available. $250 deposit, deadline 7/1. **Activities:** Bands, campus ministries, choral groups, drama, international student organizations, literary magazine, music ensembles, musical theater, opera, radio station, student government, student newspaper, Baptist Student Union, Fellowship of Christian Athletes, Student Mission, state teachers association, Ministerial Alliance, international club, science club, computer club, College Music Educators National Conference, Students in Free Enterprise.

**Athletics.** NAIA. **Intercollegiate:** Baseball M, basketball, bowling, cheerleading, cross-country, golf, lacrosse W, soccer, softball W, tennis W, track and field, volleyball, wrestling M. **Intramural:** Basketball, softball, volleyball. **Team name:** Spartans.

**Student services.** Adult student services, chaplain/spiritual director, career counseling, student employment services, financial aid counseling, personal counseling, placement for graduates, veterans' counselor. **Physically disabled:** Services for visually, hearing impaired.

**Contact.** E-mail: admissions@mobap.edu
Phone: (314) 392-2290 Toll-free number: (877) 434-1115
Fax: (314) 392-2292
Terry Cruse, Dean of Enrollment Services, Missouri Baptist University, One College Park Drive, St. Louis, MO 63141-8698

## Missouri Southern State University
### Joplin, Missouri
**www.mssu.edu**   CB code: 6322

- Public 4-year university and liberal arts college
- Commuter campus in large town
- 5,195 degree-seeking undergraduates: 21% part-time, 58% women
- 62 degree-seeking graduate students
- 95% of applicants admitted
- SAT or ACT (ACT writing optional), SAT Subject Tests required
- 31% graduate within 6 years

**General.** Founded in 1937. Regionally accredited. Extension courses offered in Lamar, Monett, Nevada (evening only), limited weekend courses. Television and online courses offered. **Degrees:** 732 bachelor's, 134 associate awarded; master's offered. **Location:** 138 miles from Kansas City, 126 miles from Tulsa, Oklahoma. **Calendar:** Semester, extensive summer session. **Full-time faculty:** 208 total; 58% have terminal degrees, 8% minority, 39% women. **Part-time faculty:** 87 total; 16% have terminal degrees, 5% minority, 51% women. **Class size:** 46% < 20, 52% 20-39, 2% 40-49, less than 1% 50-99. **Special facilities:** Biology pond, crime lab, child development center, small business development center, indoor "livefire" firearms range, performing arts center, greenhouse, law library, cyber coffee shop.

**Freshman class profile.** 1,568 applied, 1,483 admitted, 858 enrolled.

| Mid 50% test scores | | |
|---|---|---|
| ACT composite: | 18-24 | |
| GPA 3.75 or higher: | 21% | |
| GPA 3.50-3.74: | 15% | |
| GPA 3.0-3.49: | 26% | |
| GPA 2.0-2.99: | 35% | |
| Rank in top quarter: | | 22% |
| Rank in top tenth: | | 11% |
| Out-of-state: | | 1.9% |
| Live on campus: | | 70% |
| Fraternities: | | 1% |
| Sororities: | | 1% |

**Basis for selection.** Minimum 18 ACT or rank in upper 50% of class. ACT recommended. International students must score in 75th percentile on Michigan Test for English as foreign language. **Homeschooled:** Transcript of courses and grades required. Transccript with GPA; final transcript with date of graduation needed prior to enrollment; ACT composite score of 21 or GPA of 2.25. Must meet high school core requirements. **Learning Disabled:** Submission of documentation is not the same as the request for services. Request for services and/or accommodations must be initiated by the student after admission.

**High school preparation.** 16 units required. Required and recommended units include English 4, mathematics 3, social studies 3, science 2 (laboratory 1), foreign language 2 and academic electives 3. 1 unit from visual arts, music, dance or theater required.

**2009-2010 Annual costs.** Tuition/fees: $4,816; $9,106 out-of-state. Room/board: $5,382. Books/supplies: $800. Personal expenses: $1,500.

**2008-2009 Financial aid. Need-based:** 671 full-time freshmen applied for aid; 468 were judged to have need; 463 of these received aid. Average

need met was 65%. Average scholarship/grant was $3,607; average loan $2,671. 50% of total undergraduate aid awarded as scholarships/grants, 50% as loans/jobs. **Non-need-based:** Awarded to 1,445 full-time undergraduates, including 579 freshmen. Scholarships awarded for academics, alumni affiliation, art, minority status, music/drama.

**Application procedures. Admission:** Priority date 8/1; no deadline. $15 fee, may be waived for applicants with need. Admission notification on a rolling basis beginning on or about 9/1. **Financial aid:** Priority date 5/1; no closing date. FAFSA, institutional form required. Applicants notified by 3/1; Applicants notified on a rolling basis.

**Academics. Special study options:** Accelerated study, combined bachelor's/graduate degree, cooperative education, distance learning, double major, dual enrollment of high school students, ESL, exchange student, honors, independent study, internships, liberal arts/career combination, study abroad, teacher certification program, weekend college. **Credit/placement by examination:** AP, CLEP, IB, SAT, ACT, institutional tests. **Support services:** Learning center, reduced course load, remedial instruction, study skills assistance, tutoring, writing center.

**Honors college/program.** Entrance by invitation. Approximately 30 students admitted each year. Application closing date March 1. Require 28 ACT or 3.5 GPA.

**Majors. Biology:** General, bacteriology, biochemistry, biotechnology, conservation, ecology, genetics, marine. **Business:** General, accounting, finance, financial planning, international, management science, marketing, operations. **Communications:** General, media studies. **Computer sciences:** General, computer science, information systems, programming. **Conservation:** General, management/policy. **Education:** General, art, biology, business, chemistry, early childhood, elementary, English, ESL, foreign languages, French, German, health, history, mathematics, middle, multi-level teacher, music, physical, physics, reading, science, secondary, social science, Spanish, special, speech, technology/industrial arts. **Engineering:** Industrial. **Foreign languages:** French, German, Spanish. **Health:** Environmental health, nursing (RN), predental, premedicine, prepharmacy, preveterinary. **History:** General. **Math:** General, computational. **Parks/recreation:** Health/fitness. **Physical sciences:** Chemistry, physics. **Protective services:** Forensics, law enforcement admin. **Psychology:** General. **Social sciences:** General, international relations, political science, sociology. **Visual/performing arts:** Dramatic, studio arts.

**Most popular majors.** Biology 6%, business/marketing 25%, engineering/engineering technologies 14%, health sciences 10%, liberal arts 7%, security/protective services 12%.

**Computing on campus.** 522 workstations in library, computer center, student center. Dormitories wired for high-speed internet access and linked to campus network. Commuter students can connect to campus network. Online library, helpline, repair service, student web hosting, wireless network available.

**Student life. Freshman orientation:** Mandatory, $30 fee. Preregistration for classes offered. One-day introduction to campus and enrollment process during summer, plus 8-week course. **Policies:** Freshmen must live in residence halls if space is available, unless married, residing with relatives, or excused by the Coordinator of Student Housing. **Housing:** Guaranteed on-campus for freshmen. Coed dorms, single-sex dorms, special housing for disabled, apartments, wellness housing available. $150 fully refundable deposit, deadline 5/1. **Activities:** Bands, campus ministries, choral groups, dance, drama, film society, international student organizations, literary magazine, music ensembles, Model UN, musical theater, radio station, student government, student newspaper, symphony orchestra, TV station, over 90 clubs and organizations available.

**Athletics.** NCAA. **Intercollegiate:** Baseball M, basketball, cheerleading, cross-country, football (tackle) M, golf M, soccer, softball W, tennis W, track and field, volleyball W. **Intramural:** Basketball, football (non-tackle), golf, racquetball, soccer, softball, table tennis, tennis, volleyball. **Team name:** Lions, Lady Lions.

**Student services.** Adult student services, alcohol/substance abuse counseling, career counseling, services for economically disadvantaged, student employment services, financial aid counseling, health services, on-campus daycare, personal counseling, placement for graduates, veterans' counselor. **Physically disabled:** Services for visually, speech, hearing impaired. **Learning disabled:** Comprehensive services available.

**Contact.** E-mail: admissions@mssu.edu
Phone: (417) 625-9378 Toll-free number: (866) 818-6778
Fax: (417) 659-4429
Derek Skaggs, Director of Enrollment Services, Missouri Southern State University, 3950 East Newman Road, Joplin, MO 64801-1595

# Missouri State University
## Springfield, Missouri
www.missouristate.edu    CB code: 6665

- Public 4-year university
- Commuter campus in small city
- 14,974 degree-seeking undergraduates: 11% part-time, 55% women, 4% African American, 2% Asian American, 2% Hispanic American, 1% Native American, 3% international
- 2,888 degree-seeking graduate students
- 52% of applicants admitted
- SAT or ACT (ACT writing optional) required
- 54% graduate within 6 years

**General.** Founded in 1906. Regionally accredited. **Degrees:** 3,015 bachelor's awarded; master's, professional offered. **ROTC:** Army. **Location:** 180 miles from Kansas City. **Calendar:** Semester, extensive summer session. **Full-time faculty:** 737 total; 80% have terminal degrees, 8% minority, 43% women. **Part-time faculty:** 356 total; 26% have terminal degrees, 3% minority, 49% women. **Class size:** 28% < 20, 50% 20-39, 11% 40-49, 10% 50-99, 2% >100. **Special facilities:** Observatory, 125-acre agriculture research and demonstration center, summer tent theater, archaeological research center, social research center, agriculture research center.

**Freshman class profile.** 8,946 applied, 4,672 admitted, 2,659 enrolled.

| Mid 50% test scores | | Rank in top tenth: | 23% |
|---|---|---|---|
| ACT composite: | 21-27 | Return as sophomores: | 76% |
| GPA 3.75 or higher: | 37% | Out-of-state: | 11% |
| GPA 3.50-3.74: | 16% | Live on campus: | 83% |
| GPA 3.0-3.49: | 30% | International: | 1% |
| GPA 2.0-2.99: | 16% | Fraternities: | 15% |
| Rank in top quarter: | 51% | Sororities: | 19% |

**Basis for selection.** Applicant must have 108 or higher on selection index (sum of high school class rank percentile and test score percentile).

**High school preparation.** College-preparatory program required. 24 units required. Required and recommended units include English 4, mathematics 3, social studies 2, history 1, science 3 (laboratory 1), foreign language 2, visual/performing arts 1 and academic electives 3. 7 additional electives required.

**2009-2010 Annual costs.** Tuition/fees: $6,276; $11,556 out-of-state. Room/board: $5,836. Books/supplies: $900. Personal expenses: $3,500.

**2008-2009 Financial aid. Need-based:** 1,945 full-time freshmen applied for aid; 1,311 were judged to have need; 1,289 of these received aid. Average need met was 71%. Average scholarship/grant was $5,897; average loan $3,122. 43% of total undergraduate aid awarded as scholarships/grants, 57% as loans/jobs. **Non-need-based:** Awarded to 629 full-time undergraduates, including 211 freshmen. Scholarships awarded for academics, alumni affiliation, art, athletics, job skills, leadership, minority status, music/drama, ROTC, state residency. **Additional information:** Extensive scholarship program offered to freshmen and transfer students. Out-of-state fee stipends available. Student employment service available to assist students in securing employment on campus and in community.

**Application procedures. Admission:** Priority date 3/1; deadline 7/20 (postmark date). $35 fee, may be waived for applicants with need. Admission notification on a rolling basis beginning on or about 7/1. **Financial aid:** Priority date 3/31; no closing date. FAFSA required. Applicants notified on a rolling basis starting 4/30; must reply within 4 week(s) of notification.

**Academics. Special study options:** Accelerated study, combined bachelor's/graduate degree, cooperative education, distance learning, double major, dual enrollment of high school students, ESL, exchange student, honors, independent study, internships, liberal arts/career combination, student-designed major, study abroad, teacher certification program. London semester. **Credit/placement by examination:** AP, CLEP, IB, SAT, ACT, institutional tests. **Support services:** Learning center, pre-admission summer program, study skills assistance, tutoring, writing center.

**Honors college/program.** Minimum 27 ACT or 1220 (exclusive of Writing) SAT and rank in top 10th percentile of class required. Approximately 250 to 300 freshmen enroll each year. Program includes freshman honors seminar, honors general education courses, departmental honors courses, senior project, senior honors seminar.

**Majors. Agriculture:** General, agribusiness operations, agronomy, animal sciences, business, horticultural science. **Architecture:** Urban/community planning. **Biology:** General, cellular/molecular. **Business:** General, accounting, business admin, construction management, entrepreneurial studies, finance, hospitality admin, insurance, logistics, management information systems, marketing. **Communications:** General, journalism, media studies, political, public relations. **Computer sciences:** Computer science. **Conservation:** Wildlife. **Education:** Agricultural, art, biology, business, chemistry, drama/dance, early childhood, elementary, English, family/consumer sciences, French, geography, German, history, Latin, mathematics, middle, music, physical, physics, school counseling, science, Spanish, special, speech, technology/industrial arts. **Engineering technology:** Industrial management. **Family/consumer sciences:** General, clothing/textiles, family studies, housing. **Foreign languages:** French, German, Latin, Spanish. **Health:** Athletic training, audiology/speech pathology, clinical lab science, dietetics, nursing (RN), preop/surgical nursing, radiologic technology/medical imaging, respiratory therapy technology. **History:** General. **Interdisciplinary:** Gerontology. **Liberal arts:** Humanities. **Math:** General. **Parks/recreation:** General, exercise sciences. **Philosophy/religion:** Philosophy, religion. **Physical sciences:** Chemistry, geology, physics. **Psychology:** General. **Public administration:** General, social work. **Social sciences:** Anthropology, cartography, criminology, economics, geography, political science, sociology. **Visual/performing arts:** General, art, art history/conservation, dance, design, dramatic, multimedia, music performance, studio arts. **Other:** Electronic arts, Entertainment management, Physical science technologies.

**Most popular majors.** Business/marketing 35%, communications/journalism 6%, education 14%, health sciences 6%, social sciences 7%.

**Computing on campus.** 1,800 workstations in dormitories, library, computer center, student center. Dormitories wired for high-speed internet access and linked to campus network. Commuter students can connect to campus network. Online library, helpline, student web hosting, wireless network available.

**Student life. Freshman orientation:** Mandatory, $40 fee. Preregistration for classes offered. 2-day program held during summer. **Housing:** Guaranteed on-campus for freshmen. Coed dorms, special housing for disabled, apartments, fraternity/sorority housing available. $100 fully refundable deposit, deadline 7/1. Nontraditional, upper-class, honor, transfer student housing available. **Activities:** Bands, campus ministries, choral groups, dance, drama, film society, international student organizations, literary magazine, music ensembles, Model UN, musical theater, opera, radio station, student government, student newspaper, symphony orchestra, TV station, nearly 300 student organizations available.

**Athletics.** NCAA. **Intercollegiate:** Baseball M, basketball, cross-country, field hockey W, football (tackle) M, golf, soccer, softball W, swimming, track and field, volleyball W. **Intramural:** Basketball, bowling, football (non-tackle), golf, racquetball, soccer, softball, table tennis, tennis, track and field, volleyball, weight lifting, wrestling. **Team name:** Bears.

**Student services.** Adult student services, alcohol/substance abuse counseling, chaplain/spiritual director, career counseling, services for economically disadvantaged, student employment services, financial aid counseling, health services, legal services, minority student services, on-campus daycare, personal counseling, placement for graduates, veterans' counselor. **Physically disabled:** Services for visually, speech, hearing impaired. **Learning disabled:** Comprehensive services available.

**Contact.** E-mail: info@missouristate.edu
Phone: (417) 836-5517 Toll-free number: (800) 492-7900
Fax: (417) 836-6334
Donald Simpson, Director of Admissions, Missouri State University, 901 South National Avenue, Springfield, MO 65897

# Missouri Technical School
## St. Charles, Missouri
www.motech.edu    CB code: 2383

- For-profit 4-year engineering and technical college
- Commuter campus in very large city
- 130 degree-seeking undergraduates
- Interview required

**General.** Founded in 1932. Accredited by ACCSC. **Degrees:** 16 bachelor's, 30 associate awarded. **Location:** 20 miles from downtown. **Calendar:** Semester, extensive summer session. **Full-time faculty:** 6 total; 83% have terminal degrees. **Part-time faculty:** 9 total.

**Basis for selection.** Test scores and interview most important.

**High school preparation.** Math and science courses recommended.

**2009-2010 Annual costs.** Tuition is $500 per credit hour. Fees are $95 per 2-month term. Books/supplies: $800.

**Financial aid.** All financial aid based on need.

**Application procedures. Admission:** No deadline. $125 fee. Admission notification on a rolling basis. **Financial aid:** No deadline. FAFSA, institutional form required. Applicants notified on a rolling basis.

**Academics.** Classes held 4 days per week; academic year is three 17 week semesters of 2 segments each. **Special study options:** Accelerated study, double major, independent study, internships. **Credit/placement by examination:** CLEP, IB, institutional tests. **Support services:** Reduced course load, remedial instruction, study skills assistance, tutoring.

**Majors. Computer sciences:** Computer graphics, computer science, information systems, LAN/WAN management, programming, systems analysis. **Engineering:** Computer, electrical, software. **Engineering technology:** Electrical. **Health:** Substance abuse counseling.

**Computing on campus.** 120 workstations in library, computer center, student center. Commuter students can connect to campus network. Helpline, repair service available.

**Student life. Freshman orientation:** Mandatory. Preregistration for classes offered. Held for 2 hours on Saturday before the term starts. **Housing:** Single-sex dorms, wellness housing available. $175 deposit. Apartment housing available. **Activities:** Student government, student newspaper.

**Student services.** Adult student services, alcohol/substance abuse counseling, career counseling, student employment services, financial aid counseling, placement for graduates. **Physically disabled:** Services for visually, hearing impaired.

**Contact.** Toll-free number: (800) 960-8324
Director of Admissions, Missouri Technical School, 1690 Country Club Plaza Drive, St. Charles, MO 63303

## Missouri University of Science and Technology
**Rolla, Missouri**
**www.mst.edu**

**CB member**
**CB code: 6876**

- Public 4-year university
- Residential campus in large town
- 5,145 degree-seeking undergraduates: 5% part-time, 22% women, 5% African American, 2% Asian American, 2% Hispanic American, 1% Native American, 3% international
- 1,593 degree-seeking graduate students
- 93% of applicants admitted
- SAT or ACT (ACT writing optional) required
- 63% graduate within 6 years

**General.** Founded in 1870. Regionally accredited. **Degrees:** 920 bachelor's awarded; master's, doctoral offered. **ROTC:** Army, Air Force. **Location:** 100 miles from St. Louis, 100 miles from Springfield. **Calendar:** Semester, extensive summer session. **Full-time faculty:** 360 total; 89% have terminal degrees, 28% minority, 19% women. **Part-time faculty:** 96 total; 43% have terminal degrees, 24% minority, 28% women. **Class size:** 32% < 20, 39% 20-39, 12% 40-49, 11% 50-99, 6% >100. **Special facilities:** Computerized manufacturing system, nuclear reactor, observatory, experimental mine, rocks, minerals, and gemstones museum, centers for environmental research, virtual reality laboratory; student design team center, wind tunnel.

**Freshman class profile.** 2,620 applied, 2,430 admitted, 1,108 enrolled.

| Mid 50% test scores | | | |
|---|---|---|---|
| SAT critical reading: | 550-670 | Rank in top quarter: | 71% |
| SAT math: | 610-700 | Rank in top tenth: | 43% |
| ACT composite: | 25-31 | Return as sophomores: | 88% |
| GPA 3.75 or higher: | 46% | Out-of-state: | 19% |
| GPA 3.50-3.74: | 21% | Live on campus: | 94% |
| GPA 3.0-3.49: | 23% | International: | 2% |
| GPA 2.0-2.99: | 10% | Fraternities: | 23% |
| | | Sororities: | 28% |

**Basis for selection.** Admission based on secondary school record, class rank, and standardized test scores. Recommendations considered. ACT or SAT score percentage, plus high school class rank percentile should equal 120 (minimum). Exceptions may be made on an individual basis. ACT recommended. Campus visit and personal statement encouraged. **Home-schooled:** Transcript of courses and grades required. Must submit a standardized test score. **Learning Disabled:** Should submit voluntary declaration of disability to receive accommodation.

**High school preparation.** College-preparatory program required. 17 units required. Required units include English 4, mathematics 4, social studies 3, science 3 (laboratory 1), foreign language 2 and visual/performing arts 1. Foreign language units must be in same language.

**2009-2010 Annual costs.** Tuition/fees: $8,488; $19,579 out-of-state. Room/board: $7,545. Books/supplies: $960. Personal expenses: $3,366.

**2008-2009 Financial aid. Need-based:** 905 full-time freshmen applied for aid; 587 were judged to have need; 587 of these received aid. Average need met was 46%. Average scholarship/grant was $8,616; average loan $4,088. 57% of total undergraduate aid awarded as scholarships/grants, 43% as loans/jobs. **Non-need-based:** Awarded to 2,501 full-time undergraduates, including 719 freshmen. Scholarships awarded for academics, alumni affiliation, athletics, job skills, leadership, minority status, music/drama, religious affiliation, ROTC, state residency.

**Application procedures. Admission:** Priority date 12/1; deadline 7/1 (postmark date). $45 fee, may be waived for applicants with need. Admission notification on a rolling basis beginning on or about 10/1. Must reply by May 1 or within 3 week(s) if notified thereafter. **Financial aid:** Priority date 3/1; no closing date. FAFSA required. Applicants notified on a rolling basis; must reply within 3 week(s) of notification.

**Academics. Special study options:** Accelerated study, combined bachelor's/graduate degree, cooperative education, distance learning, double major, dual enrollment of high school students, ESL, honors, independent study, internships, liberal arts/career combination, student-designed major, study abroad, teacher certification program. **Credit/placement by examination:** AP, CLEP, IB, institutional tests. **Support services:** Learning center, pre-admission summer program, reduced course load, study skills assistance, tutoring, writing center.

**Majors. Biology:** General, biochemistry, biophysics. **Business:** General, business admin, management information systems. **Computer sciences:** General, computer science, information systems, information technology. **Engineering:** Aerospace, architectural, ceramic, chemical, civil, computer, electrical, environmental, geological, mechanical, mechanics, metallurgical, mining, nuclear, petroleum, polymer. **Engineering technology:** Industrial management. **Health:** Predental, premedicine. **History:** General. **Legal studies:** Prelaw. **Math:** Applied. **Philosophy/religion:** Philosophy. **Physical sciences:** Chemistry, geochemistry, geology, geophysics, physics. **Psychology:** General. **Social sciences:** Economics.

**Most popular majors.** Computer/information sciences 6%, engineering/engineering technologies 75%.

**Computing on campus.** PC or laptop required. 812 workstations in dormitories, library, computer center. Dormitories wired for high-speed internet access and linked to campus network. Commuter students can connect to campus network. Online course registration, online library, helpline, repair service, student web hosting, wireless network available.

**Student life. Freshman orientation:** Mandatory, $135 fee. Preregistration for classes offered. **Housing:** Guaranteed on-campus for freshmen. Coed dorms, special housing for disabled, apartments, cooperative housing, fraternity/sorority housing, wellness housing available. $160 partly refundable deposit, deadline 6/1. Residential college available. **Activities:** Bands, campus ministries, choral groups, dance, drama, international student organizations, literary magazine, music ensembles, musical theater, radio station, student government, student newspaper, symphony orchestra, over 200 student groups avaliable.

**Athletics.** NCAA. **Intercollegiate:** Baseball M, basketball, cheerleading, cross-country, football (tackle) M, soccer, softball W, swimming M, track and field, volleyball W. **Intramural:** Badminton, basketball, bowling, cross-country, football (non-tackle), golf, racquetball, soccer, softball, swimming, table tennis, tennis, track and field, volleyball, weight lifting. **Team name:** Miners.

**Student services.** Adult student services, alcohol/substance abuse counseling, career counseling, student employment services, financial aid counseling, health services, legal services, minority student services, personal counseling, placement for graduates, women's services. **Physically disabled:** Services for visually, speech, hearing impaired. **Learning disabled:** Comprehensive services available.

**Contact.** E-mail: admissions@mst.edu
Phone: (573) 341-4164 Toll-free number: (800) 522-0938
Fax: (573) 341-4082
Rance Larsen, Director of Admissions, Missouri University of Science and Technology, 106 Parker Hall, Rolla, MO 65409-1060

## Missouri Valley College
**Marshall, Missouri**
**www.moval.edu**

**CB code: 6413**

- Private 4-year liberal arts college affiliated with Presbyterian Church (USA)
- Residential campus in large town

◗ 1,450 degree-seeking undergraduates
◗ SAT or ACT (ACT writing optional) required

**General.** Founded in 1889. Regionally accredited. **Degrees:** 195 bachelor's, 1 associate awarded. **ROTC:** Army. **Location:** 75 miles from Kansas City, 65 miles from Columbia. **Calendar:** Semester, limited summer session. **Full-time faculty:** 70 total. **Part-time faculty:** 50 total. **Class size:** 45% < 20, 54% 20-39, less than 1% 40-49, less than 1% 50-99.

**Freshman class profile.**

| Mid 50% test scores | | Rank in top tenth: | 6% |
|---|---|---|---|
| SAT critical reading: | 410-490 | Out-of-state: | 25% |
| SAT math: | 440-550 | Live on campus: | 90% |
| ACT composite: | 17-20 | Fraternities: | 25% |
| Rank in top quarter: | 19% | Sororities: | 25% |

**Basis for selection.** Interview, recommendations, high school record, test scores important; extracurricular activities, personal attributes also important; class rank considered. Essay recommended for academically weak students. Audition recommended for drama majors; portfolio recommended for art majors. **Homeschooled:** Transcript of courses and grades required. GED in addition to acceptable ACT/SAT score is sufficient.

**High school preparation.** Recommended units include English 4, mathematics 3, social studies 1, history 3, science 3 and foreign language 1.

**2010-2011 Annual costs.** Tuition/fees: $17,170. Room/board: $6,450. Books/supplies: $1,300. Personal expenses: $2,900.

**Financial aid.** **Non-need-based:** Scholarships awarded for academics, state residency.

**Application procedures.** **Admission:** Priority date 3/1; no deadline. $15 fee, may be waived for applicants with need, free for online applicants. Admission notification on a rolling basis. Must reply by May 1 or within 4 week(s) if notified thereafter. **Financial aid:** Priority date 3/1; no closing date. FAFSA required. Applicants notified on a rolling basis starting 2/1; must reply within 6 week(s) of notification.

**Academics.** **Special study options:** Combined bachelor's/graduate degree, double major, dual enrollment of high school students, ESL, external degree, independent study, internships, liberal arts/career combination, student-designed major, study abroad, teacher certification program. **Credit/placement by examination:** AP, CLEP, SAT, ACT, institutional tests. 30 credit hours maximum toward bachelor's degree. **Support services:** Learning center, reduced course load, remedial instruction, study skills assistance, tutoring, writing center.

**Majors.** **Biology:** General. **Business:** Accounting, business admin. **Communications:** Media studies. **Computer sciences:** General. **Education:** Elementary, multiple handicapped, physical, secondary, social studies, special. **Health:** Athletic training, nursing (RN), substance abuse counseling. **History:** General. **Interdisciplinary:** Biological/physical sciences. **Liberal arts:** Arts/sciences. **Math:** General. **Parks/recreation:** Exercise sciences, facilities management. **Philosophy/religion:** Philosophy, religion. **Protective services:** Law enforcement admin. **Psychology:** General. **Public administration:** General. **Social sciences:** Economics, political science, sociology. **Visual/performing arts:** Art, dance, dramatic. **Other:** Hospitality and tourism management.

**Computing on campus.** 172 workstations in library, computer center, student center. Dormitories wired for high-speed internet access and linked to campus network. Commuter students can connect to campus network. Online library, helpline, repair service, wireless network available.

**Student life.** **Freshman orientation:** Available. Preregistration for classes offered. **Housing:** Guaranteed on-campus for all undergraduates. Single-sex dorms, apartments, fraternity/sorority housing available. **Activities:** Bands, campus ministries, choral groups, dance, drama, film society, international student organizations, literary magazine, music ensembles, musical theater, radio station, student government, student newspaper, symphony orchestra, TV station, American Humanics, minority student union, Fellowship of Christian Athletes, student council for exceptional children.

**Athletics.** NAIA. **Intercollegiate:** Baseball M, basketball, cheerleading, cross-country, football (tackle) M, golf, rodeo, soccer, softball W, tennis, track and field, volleyball, wrestling. **Intramural:** Badminton, baseball M, basketball, bowling, cross-country, football (non-tackle), soccer, softball, table tennis, track and field, volleyball, weight lifting. **Team name:** Vikings.

**Student services.** Alcohol/substance abuse counseling, chaplain/spiritual director, career counseling, student employment services, financial aid counseling, health services, personal counseling, placement for graduates, veterans' counselor.

**Contact.** E-mail: admissions@moval.edu
Phone: (660) 831-4114 Fax: (660) 831-4233
Tennille Langdon, Director of Admissions, Missouri Valley College, 500 East College Street, Marshall, MO 65340

## Missouri Western State University
**St. Joseph, Missouri**
**www.missouriwestern.edu**                    CB code: 6625

◗ Public 4-year business and liberal arts college
◗ Commuter campus in small city
◗ 5,071 degree-seeking undergraduates: 20% part-time, 58% women, 11% African American, 1% Asian American, 2% Hispanic American, 1% Native American
◗ 69 graduate students

**General.** Founded in 1915. Regionally accredited. **Degrees:** 662 bachelor's, 66 associate awarded; master's offered. **ROTC:** Army. **Location:** 48 miles from Kansas City. **Calendar:** Semester, extensive summer session. **Full-time faculty:** 187 total. **Part-time faculty:** 140 total. **Class size:** 40% < 20, 53% 20-39, 3% 40-49, 4% 50-99, less than 1% >100. **Special facilities:** Biology nature study area, planetarium.

**Freshman class profile.** 4,467 applied, 2,783 admitted, 1,464 enrolled.

| Mid 50% test scores | | Out-of-state: | 6% |
|---|---|---|---|
| ACT composite: | 16-22 | Live on campus: | 46% |

**Basis for selection.** Open admission, but selective for some programs. School record, test scores, interview, recommendations important for education, nursing, mathematics, computer science, social work applicants. Special talents important for music, art applicants. High school units mandated by state law may vary by program. Interview required for education, nursing, social work programs. Portfolio recommended for art majors, audition recommended for music majors.

**High school preparation.** College-preparatory program required. 16 units required. Required and recommended units include English 4, mathematics 3, social studies 3, science 2 (laboratory 1), foreign language 2, visual/performing arts 1 and academic electives 3.

**2010-2011 Annual costs.** Tuition/fees (projected): $5,460; $9,818 out-of-state. Room/board: $6,500. Books/supplies: $800. Personal expenses: $3,200.

**2008-2009 Financial aid.** **Non-need-based:** Scholarships awarded for academics, alumni affiliation, art, athletics, job skills, leadership, minority status, music/drama, state residency.

**Application procedures.** **Admission:** Priority date 3/1; deadline 6/1. $15 fee, may be waived for applicants with need. Admission notification on a rolling basis. **Financial aid:** Closing date 3/1. FAFSA, institutional form required. Applicants notified on a rolling basis starting 4/5; must reply within 3 week(s) of notification.

**Academics.** **Special study options:** Combined bachelor's/graduate degree, distance learning, double major, dual enrollment of high school students, honors, internships, liberal arts/career combination, teacher certification program, weekend college. **Credit/placement by examination:** AP, CLEP, institutional tests. 30 credit hours maximum toward associate degree, 30 toward bachelor's. **Support services:** Learning center, pre-admission summer program, reduced course load, remedial instruction, study skills assistance, tutoring, writing center.

**Majors.** **Biology:** General, biochemistry. **Business:** Accounting, business admin, finance, marketing. **Communications:** General. **Computer sciences:** General, information systems. **Education:** Art, elementary, English, French, middle, music, Spanish. **Engineering technology:** Computer, construction, electrical. **Foreign languages:** French, Spanish. **Health:** Clinical lab technology, nursing (RN). **History:** General. **Interdisciplinary:** Natural sciences. **Liberal arts:** Arts/sciences. **Math:** General. **Parks/recreation:** Facilities management, health/fitness. **Physical sciences:** Chemistry. **Protective services:** Criminal justice. **Psychology:** General. **Public administration:** Social work. **Social sciences:** Economics, political science. **Visual/performing arts:** Art, graphic design.

**Computing on campus.** 300 workstations in dormitories, library, computer center, student center. Dormitories linked to campus network. Commuter students can connect to campus network. Online course registration available.

**Student life.** **Freshman orientation:** Available, $60 fee. Preregistration for classes offered. **Housing:** Coed dorms, apartments, fraternity/sorority housing available. $100 deposit. **Activities:** Bands, choral groups, dance, drama, music ensembles, musical theater, student government, student newspaper, symphony orchestra, over 70 organizations.

**Athletics.** NCAA. **Intercollegiate:** Baseball M, basketball, football (tackle) M, golf, soccer W, softball W, tennis W, volleyball W, wrestling M. **Intramural:** Archery, badminton, baseball M, basketball, bowling, golf, handball, racquetball, rugby M, soccer M, softball, table tennis, tennis, volleyball. **Team name:** Griffons.

**Student services.** Adult student services, alcohol/substance abuse counseling, career counseling, student employment services, financial aid counseling, health services, minority student services, on-campus daycare, personal counseling, placement for graduates, veterans' counselor.

**Contact.**   E-mail: admissions@missouriwestern.edu
Phone: (816) 271-4200 Toll-free number: (800) 662-7041
Fax: (816) 271-5833
Howard McCauley, Director of Admissions, Missouri Western State University, 4525 Downs Drive, St. Joseph, MO 64507

---

## National American University: Kansas City
### Independence, Missouri
www.national.edu                                    CB code: 5357

▶   For-profit 4-year university
▶   Commuter campus in large city

**General.** Founded in 1941. Regionally accredited. **Location:** 8 miles from downtown. **Calendar:** Quarter.

**Annual costs/financial aid.** Tuition/fees (2009-2010): $13,055. Need-based financial aid available to full-time and part-time students.

**Contact.**   Phone: (866) 628-1288
Director of Admissions, 3620 Arrowhead Avenue, Independence, MO 64057

---

## Northwest Missouri State University
### Maryville, Missouri
www.nwmissouri.edu                                  CB code: 6488

▶   Public 4-year university
▶   Residential campus in large town
▶   5,740 degree-seeking undergraduates: 5% part-time, 55% women, 5% African American, 1% Asian American, 2% Hispanic American, 2% international
▶   876 degree-seeking graduate students
▶   70% of applicants admitted
▶   SAT or ACT (ACT writing optional) required
▶   52% graduate within 6 years; 27% enter graduate study

**General.** Founded in 1905. Regionally accredited. **Degrees:** 1,020 bachelor's, 63 associate awarded; master's offered. **ROTC:** Army. **Location:** 100 miles from Kansas City. **Calendar:** Trimester, extensive summer session. **Full-time faculty:** 261 total; 69% have terminal degrees, 44% women. **Part-time faculty:** 64 total. **Class size:** 42% < 20, 46% 20-39, 4% 40-49, 7% 50-99, less than 1% >100. **Special facilities:** Arboretum, lake-front outdoor education recreation area, laboratory school, dairy operation, swine herd, horticulture complex, experimental farmland, center for innovation and entrepreneurship (incubator), studio/black box experimental theater, alternative energy learning center, observatory, online museum, science museum, agriculture museum, computing museum, museum of broadcasting.

**Freshman class profile.** 5,420 applied, 3,784 admitted, 1,561 enrolled.

| Mid 50% test scores | | | |
|---|---|---|---|
| SAT critical reading: | 410-540 | **Rank in top tenth:** | 14% |
| SAT math: | 480-560 | **End year in good standing:** | 65% |
| ACT composite: | 20-25 | **Return as sophomores:** | 73% |
| GPA 3.75 or higher: | 21% | **Out-of-state:** | 24% |
| GPA 3.50-3.74: | 20% | **Live on campus:** | 91% |
| GPA 3.0-3.49: | 32% | **International:** | 2% |
| GPA 2.0-2.99: | 27% | **Fraternities:** | 18% |
| Rank in top quarter: | 40% | **Sororities:** | 14% |

**Basis for selection.** School achievement record and test scores most important. Index based on class rank and national test. Audition recommended for dramatic arts and music students; portfolio recommended for art students. **Homeschooled:** Transcript of courses and grades, state high school equivalency certificate required.

**High school preparation.** College-preparatory program recommended. 16 units required. Required and recommended units include English 4, mathematics 3-4, social studies 3, science 2-3 (laboratory 1), foreign language 2, visual/performing arts 1 and academic electives 3. One fine arts required. Foreign language and additional math and science highly recommended.

**2009-2010 Annual costs.** Tuition/fees: $7,032; $11,753 out-of-state. Tuition/fees includes free laptop for full-time students and textbook rental for primary textbooks. Room/board: $6,790. Books/supplies: $500. Personal expenses: $1,400.

**2008-2009 Financial aid. Need-based:** 1,348 full-time freshmen applied for aid; 966 were judged to have need; 966 of these received aid. Average need met was 65%. Average scholarship/grant was $4,678; average loan $3,243. 45% of total undergraduate aid awarded as scholarships/grants, 55% as loans/jobs. **Non-need-based:** Awarded to 2,818 full-time undergraduates, including 1,253 freshmen. Scholarships awarded for academics, alumni affiliation, art, athletics, job skills, leadership, minority status, music/drama, ROTC, state residency.

**Application procedures. Admission:** No deadline. $25 fee, may be waived for applicants with need, free for online applicants. Admission notification on a rolling basis beginning on or about 9/1. **Financial aid:** Priority date 4/1; no closing date. FAFSA required. Applicants notified on a rolling basis starting 3/15; must reply within 4 week(s) of notification.

**Academics. Special study options:** Cross-registration, distance learning, double major, dual enrollment of high school students, ESL, exchange student, honors, independent study, internships, liberal arts/career combination, study abroad, teacher certification program, Washington semester. **Credit/placement by examination:** AP, CLEP, IB, SAT, ACT, institutional tests. **Support services:** Learning center, reduced course load, remedial instruction, study skills assistance, tutoring, writing center.

**Majors. Agriculture:** General, agribusiness operations, agronomy, animal sciences, economics, horticultural science. **Biology:** General, marine. **Business:** Accounting, administrative services, business admin, finance, international, management information systems, managerial economics, marketing. **Communications:** Advertising, journalism, organizational, public relations, radio/tv. **Computer sciences:** General, web page design. **Conservation:** Wildlife. **Education:** Agricultural, art, biology, business, chemistry, curriculum, elementary, English, family/consumer sciences, mathematics, middle, multiple handicapped, music, physical, physics, science, social science, Spanish. **Engineering technology:** GIS. **Family/consumer sciences:** Apparel marketing, family studies, institutional food production. **Foreign languages:** Spanish. **Health:** Clinical lab science, dietetics, nursing (RN), preveterinary. **History:** General. **Interdisciplinary:** Biological/physical sciences, biopsychology. **Liberal arts:** Humanities. **Math:** General, statistics. **Parks/recreation:** Facilities management. **Philosophy/religion:** Philosophy. **Physical sciences:** Chemistry, geology, physics. **Psychology:** General, industrial, psychobiology, social. **Public administration:** General. **Social sciences:** Economics, geography, political science, sociology. **Visual/performing arts:** Acting, dramatic, studio arts, theater design. **Other:** Alternative energy, Geographic information science, Speech/theatre education.

**Most popular majors.** Agriculture 7%, business/marketing 28%, education 17%, psychology 10%.

**Computing on campus.** 6,450 workstations in dormitories, library, computer center, student center. Dormitories wired for high-speed internet access and linked to campus network. Commuter students can connect to campus network. Online course registration, online library, helpline, repair service, student web hosting, wireless network available.

**Student life. Freshman orientation:** Mandatory, $100 fee. Preregistration for classes offered. One-day program in June plus 4-day program held before classes begin in August. **Policies:** Alcohol- and smoke-free campus. **Housing:** Guaranteed on-campus for freshmen. Coed dorms, special housing for disabled, apartments, fraternity/sorority housing available. $150 nonrefundable deposit. **Activities:** Bands, choral groups, dance, drama, film society, international student organizations, literary magazine, music ensembles, musical theater, radio station, student government, student newspaper, symphony orchestra, TV station, more than 180 student organizations available.

**Athletics.** NCAA. **Intercollegiate:** Baseball M, basketball, cheerleading, cross-country, football (tackle) M, golf W, soccer W, softball W, tennis, track and field, volleyball W. **Intramural:** Badminton, basketball, cross-country, football (non-tackle), golf, racquetball, skiing, softball W, swimming, table tennis, tennis, track and field, volleyball. **Team name:** Bearcats.

**Student services.** Alcohol/substance abuse counseling, chaplain/spiritual director, career counseling, services for economically disadvantaged, student employment services, financial aid counseling, health services, minority student services, personal counseling, placement for graduates. **Physically disabled:** Services for visually, speech, hearing impaired.

**Contact.** E-mail: admissions@nwmissouri.edu
Phone: (660) 562-1562 Toll-free number: (800) 633-1175
Fax: (660) 562-1121
Beverly Schenkel, Dean of Enrollment Management, Northwest Missouri State University, 800 University Drive, Maryville, MO 64468-6001

## Ozark Christian College
### Joplin, Missouri
www.occ.edu                          CB code: 6542

- Private 4-year Bible college affiliated with nondenominational tradition
- Residential campus in large town
- 616 degree-seeking undergraduates: 14% part-time, 45% women, 1% African American, 1% Asian American, 1% Hispanic American, 3% Native American, 3% international
- 63% of applicants admitted
- SAT or ACT (ACT writing optional), application essay required
- 42% graduate within 6 years

**General.** Founded in 1942. Accredited by ABHE. **Degrees:** 106 bachelor's, 26 associate awarded. **Location:** 70 miles from Springfield, 100 miles from Tulsa, Oklahoma. **Calendar:** Semester, limited summer session. **Full-time faculty:** 27 total; 26% have terminal degrees, 7% women. **Part-time faculty:** 33 total; 12% have terminal degrees, 27% women. **Class size:** 64% < 20, 26% 20-39, 5% 40-49, 6% 50-99.

**Freshman class profile.** 283 applied, 179 admitted, 143 enrolled.

| | | | |
|---|---|---|---|
| Return as sophomores: | 68% | International: | 1% |
| Live on campus: | 90% | | |

**Basis for selection.** Secondary school record, test scores, essay important. 2 references required. Audition required for music ministry students. **Homeschooled:** Transcript of courses and grades required. Provide notarized transcript of grades signed by student and parents.

**High school preparation.** 15 units recommended. Recommended units include English 3, mathematics 2, history 1, science 2 and academic electives 7.

**2009-2010 Annual costs.** Tuition/fees: $8,450. Room/board: $4,170. Books/supplies: $600. Personal expenses: $1,560.

**2008-2009 Financial aid. Need-based:** 44% of total undergraduate aid awarded as scholarships/grants, 56% as loans/jobs. **Non-need-based:** Scholarships awarded for academics, leadership.

**Application procedures. Admission:** Closing date 8/5 (receipt date). $30 fee, may be waived for applicants with need. Admission notification on a rolling basis. Applicant must submit high school transcript through first half of senior year. **Financial aid:** Priority date 4/1; no closing date. FAFSA required. Applicants notified on a rolling basis starting 4/15; must reply within 4 week(s) of notification.

**Academics. Special study options:** Combined bachelor's/graduate degree, cooperative education, distance learning, double major, independent study, internships. 5-year bachelor's degree program in theology. **Credit/placement by examination:** CLEP, ACT, institutional tests. **Support services:** Learning center, study skills assistance, tutoring.

**Majors. Theology:** Bible, missionary, religious ed, sacred music, theology.

**Computing on campus.** 23 workstations in library, computer center, student center. Dormitories wired for high-speed internet access and linked to campus network. Commuter students can connect to campus network. Online library, helpline, repair service, wireless network available.

**Student life. Freshman orientation:** Mandatory. Preregistration for classes offered. **Policies:** Religious observance required. **Housing:** Guaranteed on-campus for all undergraduates. Single-sex dorms, wellness housing available. $90 deposit, deadline 8/5. **Activities:** Choral groups, drama, music ensembles, musical theater, student government.

**Athletics.** NCCAA. **Intercollegiate:** Baseball M, basketball, volleyball W. **Intramural:** Basketball, racquetball, volleyball. **Team name:** Ambassadors.

**Student services.** Adult student services, chaplain/spiritual director, career counseling, student employment services, financial aid counseling, health services, personal counseling, placement for graduates, veterans' counselor. **Physically disabled:** Services for hearing impaired.

**Contact.** E-mail: admissions@occ.edu
Phone: (417) 624-2518 Toll-free number: (800) 299-4622
Fax: (417) 624-0090
Troy Nelson, Director of Admissions, Ozark Christian College, 1111 North Main Street, Joplin, MO 64801

## Park University
### Parkville, Missouri
www.park.edu                          CB code: 6574

- Private 4-year university
- Commuter campus in small town
- 11,135 degree-seeking undergraduates: 88% part-time, 52% women
- 743 degree-seeking graduate students
- 70% of applicants admitted

**General.** Founded in 1875. Regionally accredited. MetroPark School for adult education in Kansas City offers bachelor's degree. School for Extended Learning (SEL) offers degree programs in 21 states. **Degrees:** 2,483 bachelor's, 55 associate awarded; master's offered. **ROTC:** Army. **Location:** 12 miles from downtown Kansas City. **Calendar:** Semester, extensive summer session. **Full-time faculty:** 119 total. **Part-time faculty:** 881 total. **Special facilities:** 700 acres of woodland.

**Freshman class profile.** 554 applied, 389 admitted, 205 enrolled.

| Mid 50% test scores | | Rank in top tenth: | 24% |
|---|---|---|---|
| ACT composite: | 18-25 | Out-of-state: | 14% |
| Rank in top quarter: | 49% | Live on campus: | 58% |

**Basis for selection.** GPA (minimum 2.0), followed by test scores and rank in top half of class important. Exceptions considered on individual merit. Students with 3.0 GPA not required to submit SAT/ACT for admission; however, institutional placement test must be substituted. Entering freshmen with GPA of 2.0 to 3.0 must either be in top half of graduating class or submit satisfactory SAT/ACT scores. Interview recommended for academically weak students; audition recommended for music and theater students; portfolio recommended for art students.

**High school preparation.** 19 units recommended. Recommended units include English 3, mathematics 2, social studies 3, history 1, science 2 (laboratory 1), foreign language 2 and academic electives 6.

**2009-2010 Annual costs.** Tuition/fees: $8,820. Tuition varies by program. Room/board: $5,850. Books/supplies: $1,200. Personal expenses: $2,745.

**2008-2009 Financial aid. Non-need-based;** Scholarships awarded for academics, alumni affiliation, art, athletics, job skills, leadership, minority status, music/drama, religious affiliation, ROTC.

**Application procedures. Admission:** Priority date 4/15; deadline 8/1. $25 fee, may be waived for applicants with need. Admission notification on a rolling basis. **Financial aid:** Priority date 4/1, closing date 8/1. FAFSA, institutional form required. Applicants notified on a rolling basis starting 4/1.

**Academics. Special study options:** Accelerated study, cross-registration, distance learning, double major, dual enrollment of high school students, ESL, honors, independent study, internships, student-designed major, study abroad, teacher certification program, Washington semester, weekend college. **Credit/placement by examination:** AP, CLEP, ACT, institutional tests. **Support services:** Learning center, reduced course load, remedial instruction, study skills assistance, tutoring, writing center.

**Majors. Biology:** General. **Business:** Accounting, accounting/business management, business admin, logistics, management information systems, managerial economics, marketing. **Communications:** General. **Computer sciences:** General, computer science. **Education:** Early childhood, elementary. **Family/consumer sciences:** Child development. **Foreign languages:** Spanish. **Health:** Athletic training. **History:** General. **Interdisciplinary:** Math/computer science, natural sciences. **Legal studies:** General. **Liberal arts:** Arts/sciences. **Math:** General. **Physical sciences:** Chemistry. **Protective services:** Fire services admin, law enforcement admin. **Psychology:** General. **Public administration:** General, social work. **Social sciences:** Economics, geography, political science, sociology. **Transportation:** Aviation management. **Visual/performing arts:** Dramatic, graphic design, interior design, studio arts.

**Most popular majors.** Business/marketing 66%, psychology 16%, security/protective services 9%.

**Computing on campus.** 570 workstations in dormitories, library, computer center, student center. Dormitories linked to campus network. Commuter students can connect to campus network. Online course registration available.

**Student life. Freshman orientation:** Mandatory. Preregistration for classes offered. **Housing:** Guaranteed on-campus for freshmen. Coed dorms, apartments available. $100 deposit. **Activities:** Choral groups, drama, literary magazine, radio station, student government, student newspaper, symphony orchestra, service organizations, Christian Fellowship, World Student Union, Brothers and Sisters United, accounting society, Latin American student organization, marketing club, honors club, non-traditional student organization.

**Athletics. NAIA. Intercollegiate:** Baseball M, basketball, cross-country, golf W, soccer, softball W, track and field, volleyball. **Intramural:** Basketball, soccer, softball, volleyball. **Team name:** Pirates.

**Student services.** Career counseling, student employment services, financial aid counseling, health services, on-campus daycare, personal counseling, placement for graduates, veterans' counselor. **Physically disabled:** Services for visually, speech, hearing impaired.

**Contact.** E-mail: admissions@park.edu
Phone: (816) 584-6215 Toll-free number: (800) 745-7275
Fax: (816) 741-4462
Cathy Colapietro, Director of Admissions and Student Financial Services, Park University, 8700 NW River Park Drive, Parkville, MO 64152

---

## Research College of Nursing
### Kansas City, Missouri
www.researchcollege.edu                     CB code: 6612

- For-profit 4-year nursing college
- Residential campus in very large city
- 328 degree-seeking undergraduates
- 80 graduate students
- 68% of applicants admitted
- SAT or ACT (ACT writing optional) required

**General.** Founded in 1905. Regionally accredited. Natural science, social science, and liberal arts courses taken at Rockhurst University. Students have access to facilities, organizations, sports and activities on both campuses. Bachelor of Science in Nursing is awarded jointly by Research College of Nursing and Rockhurst University. **Degrees:** 120 bachelor's awarded; master's offered. **ROTC:** Army. **Location:** 5 miles from downtown. **Calendar:** Semester, limited summer session. **Full-time faculty:** 35 total; 26% have terminal degrees, 6% minority, 97% women. **Part-time faculty:** 2 total; 100% women. **Class size:** 100% 50-99. **Special facilities:** Medical library, 532-bed research medical center.

**Freshman class profile.** 244 applied, 165 admitted, 55 enrolled.

| Mid 50% test scores | | Out-of-state: | 25% |
|---|---|---|---|
| ACT composite: | 22-26 | Live on campus: | 77% |

**Basis for selection.** Academic record, high school GPA, rank in top half of class, counselor's recommendation, test scores very important. ACT score of 20 required. Interview, high school activities considered. Interview recommended for all; strongly recommended for applicants with ACT scores below 20.

**High school preparation.** College-preparatory program recommended. 18 units recommended. Recommended units include English 4, mathematics 3, social studies 3, science 4 and foreign language 2. Visual or performing arts also recommended. Mathematics should include algebra II, science should include chemistry.

**2009-2010 Annual costs.** Tuition/fees: $25,690. Room/board: $7,480. Books/supplies: $720. Personal expenses: $915.

**2009-2010 Financial aid. Non-need-based:** Scholarships awarded for academics, alumni affiliation, leadership. **Additional information:** Financial aid handled by Rockhurst University for freshmen and sophomores.

**Application procedures. Admission:** Priority date 3/1; no deadline. $20 fee, may be waived for applicants with need, free for online applicants. Admission notification on a rolling basis beginning on or about 10/1. Must reply by May 1 or within 4 week(s) if notified thereafter. **Financial aid:** Priority date 3/15; no closing date. FAFSA, institutional form required. Applicants notified on a rolling basis starting 3/15.

**Academics.** Students admitted into nursing program in freshman year guaranteed place in upper-division nursing courses if academic requirements maintained. **Special study options:** Accelerated study, cross-registration, double major, dual enrollment of high school students, exchange student, honors, independent study, study abroad. **Credit/placement by examination:** AP, CLEP, IB, ACT, institutional tests. 32 credit hours

---

maximum toward bachelor's degree. **Support services:** Learning center, reduced course load, tutoring.

**Majors. Health:** Nursing (RN).

**Computing on campus.** 300 workstations in dormitories, library, computer center. Dormitories wired for high-speed internet access and linked to campus network. Commuter students can connect to campus network. Online course registration, helpline, wireless network available.

**Student life. Freshman orientation:** Mandatory, $50 fee. Preregistration for classes offered. **Housing:** Guaranteed on-campus for freshmen. Coed dorms, single-sex dorms, apartments, fraternity/sorority housing available. $200 fully refundable deposit. Freshman nursing students not living at home must live on Rockhurst College campus. All other undergraduates may choose to live on Research College campus or at Rockhurst College. **Activities:** Campus ministries, choral groups, drama, music ensembles, musical theater, radio station, student government, student newspaper, Alpha Phi Omega, Black Student Union, Young Republicans, Young Democrats, Missouri Student Nurses Association, National Student Nurses Association, Rockhurst Organization of Collegiate Women.

**Athletics. NCAA. Intercollegiate:** Baseball M, basketball, cross-country, golf, soccer, softball W, tennis, volleyball W. **Intramural:** Basketball, lacrosse, racquetball, rugby, table tennis, volleyball.

**Student services.** Chaplain/spiritual director, career counseling, student employment services, financial aid counseling, health services, on-campus daycare, personal counseling, placement for graduates, veterans' counselor.

**Contact.** Phone: (816) 995-2812 Toll-free number: (866) 855-0296
Fax: (816) 995-2813
Lane Ramey, Director of Freshmen Admission, Research College of Nursing, 2525 East Meyer Boulevard, Kansas City, MO 64132-1199

---

## Rockhurst University
### Kansas City, Missouri
www.rockhurst.edu                   CB member
                                     CB code: 6611

- Private 4-year business and liberal arts college affiliated with Roman Catholic Church
- Residential campus in very large city
- 1,541 degree-seeking undergraduates: 9% part-time, 63% women, 6% African American, 3% Asian American, 6% Hispanic American, 1% international
- 901 degree-seeking graduate students
- 76% of applicants admitted
- SAT or ACT (ACT writing optional) required
- 67% graduate within 6 years

**General.** Founded in 1910. Regionally accredited. Students graduate with community service transcript in addition to academic transcript. **Degrees:** 476 bachelor's awarded; master's, professional offered. **ROTC:** Army. **Location:** 5 miles from downtown. **Calendar:** Semester, limited summer session. **Full-time faculty:** 127 total; 81% have terminal degrees, 9% minority, 52% women. **Part-time faculty:** 101 total; 28% have terminal degrees, 7% minority, 58% women. **Class size:** 36% < 20, 57% 20-39, 2% 40-49, 4% 50-99, less than 1% >100.

**Freshman class profile.** 2,107 applied, 1,611 admitted, 419 enrolled.

| Mid 50% test scores | | GPA 2.0-2.99: | 14% |
|---|---|---|---|
| SAT critical reading: | 530-650 | End year in good standing: | 99% |
| SAT math: | 530-640 | Return as sophomores: | 84% |
| ACT composite: | 22-28 | Out-of-state: | 67% |
| GPA 3.75 or higher: | 37% | Live on campus: | 89% |
| GPA 3.50-3.74: | 17% | International: | 1% |
| GPA 3.0-3.49: | 32% | | |

**Basis for selection.** High school GPA, class rank, test scores, recommendations most important; school and community activities considered. Interviews recommended for all students. Essay or personal statement may be required or requested. **Homeschooled:** Transcript of courses and grades, state high school equivalency certificate required. GED requested dependent on quality of grades presented on transcript.

**High school preparation.** College-preparatory program recommended. 16 units recommended. Recommended units include English 4, mathematics 3, social studies 3, history 2, science 3 (laboratory 3), foreign language 2 and academic electives 4.

**2010-2011 Annual costs.** Tuition/fees: $27,390. Room/board: $7,490. Books/supplies: $1,400. Personal expenses: $1,029.

**2009-2010 Financial aid. Need-based:** 417 full-time freshmen applied for aid; 380 were judged to have need; 379 of these received aid. Average need met was 100%. Average scholarship/grant was $7,413; average loan $2,988. 75% of total undergraduate aid awarded as scholarships/grants, 25% as loans/jobs. **Non-need-based:** Awarded to 300 full-time undergraduates, including 445 freshmen. Scholarships awarded for academics, alumni affiliation, athletics, leadership, music/drama. **Additional information:** Auditions, portfolios required for some scholarships.

**Application procedures. Admission:** No deadline. $25 fee, may be waived for applicants with need, free for online applicants. Admission notification on a rolling basis beginning on or about 9/1. Must reply by May 1 or within 2 week(s) if notified thereafter. **Financial aid:** Priority date 3/1; no closing date. FAFSA required. Applicants notified on a rolling basis starting 3/1; must reply within 4 week(s) of notification.

**Academics.** Core curriculum based on 7 "modes of inquiry," different ways people approach reality to seek truth including artistic, literary, historical, scientific-causal, scientific-relational, philosophical, and theological. **Special study options:** Accelerated study, combined bachelor's/graduate degree, cooperative education, cross-registration, double major, dual enrollment of high school students, exchange student, honors, independent study, internships, liberal arts/career combination, New York semester, semester at sea, study abroad, teacher certification program, Washington semester. **Credit/placement by examination:** AP, CLEP, IB, SAT, ACT, institutional tests. 32 credit hours maximum toward bachelor's degree. **Support services:** Learning center, study skills assistance, tutoring, writing center.

**Majors. Biology:** General, biochemistry. **Business:** Business admin, communications, nonprofit/public. **Communications:** General. **Education:** Elementary, secondary. **Foreign languages:** French, Spanish. **Health:** Clinical lab science, nursing (RN), speech pathology. **History:** General. **Interdisciplinary:** Global studies. **Math:** General. **Parks/recreation:** Exercise sciences. **Philosophy/religion:** Philosophy, religion. **Physical sciences:** Chemistry, physics. **Psychology:** General. **Public administration:** Community org/advocacy. **Social sciences:** General, economics, political science.

**Computing on campus.** 227 workstations in dormitories, library, computer center, student center. Dormitories wired for high-speed internet access and linked to campus network. Commuter students can connect to campus network. Online course registration, online library, helpline, student web hosting, wireless network available.

**Student life. Freshman orientation:** Mandatory, $150 fee. Preregistration for classes offered. Programs held 4 days before fall semester begins. Includes participation in community service projects. **Policies:** Full-time unmarried freshmen and sophomores must live on campus if not living with family. **Housing:** Coed dorms, single-sex dorms, special housing for disabled, apartments, fraternity/sorority housing, wellness housing available. $200 nonrefundable deposit. **Activities:** Campus ministries, choral groups, dance, drama, international student organizations, literary magazine, student government, student newspaper, Alpha Phi Omega, Black Student Union, Multicultural Affairs Office, American Humanics, Student Senate, Delta Sigma Pi Business Fraternity, Student Activities Board, Student Organization of Latinos, theatre troupe.

**Athletics.** NCAA. **Intercollegiate:** Baseball M, basketball, golf, soccer, softball W, tennis, volleyball W. **Intramural:** Badminton, basketball, cross-country, field hockey, football (tackle), golf, handball M, racquetball, soccer, softball, tennis, volleyball, weight lifting M, wrestling M. **Team name:** Hawks.

**Student services.** Alcohol/substance abuse counseling, chaplain/spiritual director, career counseling, student employment services, financial aid counseling, health services, personal counseling, placement for graduates, veterans' counselor. **Physically disabled:** Services for visually, speech, hearing impaired.

**Contact.** E-mail: admission@rockhurst.edu
Phone: (816) 501-4100 Toll-free number: (800) 842-6776
Fax: (816) 501-4241
Lane Ramey, Director of Freshman Admissions, Rockhurst University, 1100 Rockhurst Road, Kansas City, MO 64110-2561

## St. Louis Christian College
**Florissant, Missouri**
www.slcconline.edu  CB code: 0334

- Private 4-year Bible college affiliated with Church of Christ
- Residential campus in small city
- 333 degree-seeking undergraduates: 12% part-time, 42% women, 23% African American, 1% Asian American, 3% Hispanic American, 4% international

- 43% of applicants admitted
- ACT (writing optional), application essay required
- 30% graduate within 6 years

**General.** Founded in 1956. Candidate for regional accreditation.; also accredited by ABHE. Students highly involved in service and field education. **Degrees:** 54 bachelor's, 21 associate awarded. **Location:** 15 miles from downtown St. Louis. **Calendar:** Semester, limited summer session. **Full-time faculty:** 12 total; 17% have terminal degrees, 17% women. **Part-time faculty:** 24 total; 25% have terminal degrees, 38% women.

**Freshman class profile.** 150 applied, 64 admitted, 56 enrolled.

| Mid 50% test scores | | | |
| --- | --- | --- | --- |
| ACT composite: | 17-25 | Out-of-state: | 46% |
| | | Live on campus: | 94% |

**Basis for selection.** ACT score, high school class rank, and GPA very important. English and Math placement based on ACT subscores or ACCUPLACER tests. Interview recommended for all. Audition required for religious music students. **Homeschooled:** ACT required, GED recommended.

**High school preparation.** Recommended units include English 4, mathematics 3, social studies 3, science 3, foreign language 2 and academic electives 4.

**2009-2010 Annual costs.** Full-time residential students maintaining an acceptable GPA receive full scholarships for tuition; required fees are $1300 annually. Full-time commuter students pay $173 per-credit-hour; required fees, $1300. Room/board: $6,600. Books/supplies: $800. Personal expenses: $600.

**2009-2010 Financial aid. Non-need-based:** Scholarships awarded for academics, alumni affiliation, leadership, music/drama, religious affiliation.

**Application procedures. Admission:** Priority date 1/15; deadline 8/7 (receipt date). $25 fee, may be waived for applicants with need. Admission notification on a rolling basis beginning on or about 10/1. **Financial aid:** Closing date 8/1. FAFSA, institutional form required. Applicants notified on a rolling basis starting 7/20; must reply within 2 week(s) of notification.

**Academics.** Preparation for ministries in preaching, education, youth work, mission fields, music, worship and pre-seminary education. **Special study options:** Cross-registration, internships. **Credit/placement by examination:** CLEP, ACT, institutional tests. 30 credit hours maximum toward associate degree, 30 toward bachelor's. **Support services:** Learning center, remedial instruction, study skills assistance, tutoring, writing center.

**Majors. Education:** General. **Theology:** Bible, missionary, religious ed, sacred music, theology.

**Computing on campus.** 13 workstations in library, computer center. Dormitories wired for high-speed internet access and linked to campus network.

**Student life. Freshman orientation:** Mandatory, $250 fee. Preregistration for classes offered. Held weekend before first day of class. **Policies:** Students involved in evangelistic activities of area churches. Religious observance required. **Housing:** Guaranteed on-campus for all undergraduates. Single-sex dorms, apartments available. **Activities:** Choral groups, drama, music ensembles, student government, missions interest group, ministry teams.

**Athletics.** NCCAA. **Intercollegiate:** Baseball M, basketball M, cross-country W, volleyball W. **Intramural:** Baseball M, basketball, cross-country, softball, tennis, volleyball. **Team name:** Soldiers.

**Student services.** Adult student services, chaplain/spiritual director, career counseling, student employment services, personal counseling. **Physically disabled:** Services for visually, hearing impaired.

**Contact.** E-mail: admissions@slcconline.edu
Phone: (314) 837-6777 ext. 8110 Toll-free number: (800) 877-7522
Fax: (314) 837-8291
Carrie Chapman, Director of Admissions, St. Louis Christian College, 1360 Grandview Drive, Florissant, MO 63033

## Saint Louis University
**Saint Louis, Missouri**
www.slu.edu  CB member  CB code: 6629

- Private 4-year university affiliated with Roman Catholic Church
- Residential campus in very large city
- 7,945 degree-seeking undergraduates: 10% part-time, 59% women, 8% African American, 6% Asian American, 3% Hispanic American, 7% international

- 5,092 degree-seeking graduate students
- 71% of applicants admitted
- SAT or ACT (ACT writing optional), application essay required
- 73% graduate within 6 years; 35% enter graduate study

**General.** Founded in 1818. Regionally accredited. Institution maintains campus in Madrid, Spain. **Degrees:** 1,617 bachelor's awarded; master's, doctoral, professional offered. **ROTC:** Army, Air Force. **Location:** Midtown. **Calendar:** Semester, extensive summer session. **Full-time faculty:** 639 total; 90% have terminal degrees, 10% minority, 44% women. **Part-time faculty:** 437 total; 14% have terminal degrees, 8% minority, 55% women. **Class size:** 55% < 20, 36% 20-39, 4% 40-49, 4% 50-99, 2% >100. **Special facilities:** Vatican manuscripts microfilm library, art museums, biological station, entrepreneurial studies center, earthquake research center, supersonic wind tunnel, water tunnel, shock tube, flight simulators, airport, fabrication labs, sculpture/ceramics studio, performing arts center, physiology and gait research labs, student media broadcasting (TV, radio), demonstration clinics in counseling and family therapy, child development, speech and hearing, psychology, dental, occupational and physical therapy, organic gardening and food service.

**Freshman class profile.** 10,707 applied, 7,616 admitted, 1,597 enrolled.

| Mid 50% test scores | | | |
|---|---|---|---|
| SAT critical reading: | 540-650 | Rank in top tenth: | 39% |
| SAT math: | 540-670 | End year in good standing: | 91% |
| ACT composite: | 24-30 | Return as sophomores: | 85% |
| GPA 3.75 or higher: | 53% | Out-of-state: | 65% |
| GPA 3.50-3.74: | 17% | Live on campus: | 91% |
| GPA 3.0-3.49: | 21% | International: | 4% |
| GPA 2.0-2.99: | 9% | Fraternities: | 11% |
| Rank in top quarter: | 71% | Sororities: | 15% |

**Basis for selection.** Secondary school record, standardized test scores important; recommendations, essay, extracurricular activities, character/personal qualities, volunteer work considered. Academic performance is most important for international applicants. Audition recommended for music majors; portfolio recommended for art majors. **Homeschooled:** Appplicants strongly recommended to present 5 academic courses each semester for all four years. Should include 4 years of English, 4 years of mathematics (algebra I & II, and geometry), 3 years each of foreign language, natural science, social science and academic electives. **Learning Disabled:** Students with learning disabilities are responsible for contacting Disabilities Services.

**High school preparation.** College-preparatory program recommended. 20 units required. Required units include English 4, mathematics 4, social studies 3, science 3, foreign language 3 and academic electives 3.

**2010-2011 Annual costs.** Tuition/fees: $32,656. Room/board: $9,170. Books/supplies: $1,660. Personal expenses: $3,692.

**2008-2009 Financial aid. Need-based:** 1,260 full-time freshmen applied for aid; 1,043 were judged to have need; 1,043 of these received aid. Average need met was 73%. Average scholarship/grant was $19,795; average loan $3,973. 78% of total undergraduate aid awarded as scholarships/grants, 22% as loans/jobs. **Non-need-based:** Awarded to 2,550 full-time undergraduates, including 620 freshmen. Scholarships awarded for academics, art, athletics, leadership, music/drama, religious affiliation, ROTC. **Additional information:** Presidential scholarship applications are due by December 1. Martin Luther King Jr. (MLK) scholarship applications have a priority date of February 1.

**Application procedures. Admission:** Closing date 12/1 (receipt date). $25 fee. Admission notification 8/1. Admission notification on a rolling basis. Must reply by May 1 or within 2 week(s) if notified thereafter. **Financial aid:** Priority date 3/1; no closing date. FAFSA required. Applicants notified on a rolling basis starting 3/1; must reply by 5/1 or within 4 week(s) of notification.

**Academics. Special study options:** Accelerated study, combined bachelor's/graduate degree, cooperative education, cross-registration, distance learning, double major, dual enrollment of high school students, ESL, honors, independent study, internships, liberal arts/career combination, student-designed major, study abroad, teacher certification program. **Credit/placement by examination:** AP, CLEP, IB, SAT, ACT, institutional tests. 30 credit hours maximum toward bachelor's degree. **Support services:** Pre-admission summer program, reduced course load, study skills assistance, tutoring, writing center.

**Honors college/program.** 30 ACT/1320 SAT (exclusive of Writing), 3.8 GPA required. Approximately 225 freshman admitted each year. Academic offerings include honors core classes, honors opportunities in major, senior honors thesis.

**Majors. Area/ethnic studies:** American, Latin American, women's. **Biology:** General, biochemistry. **Business:** Business admin, human resources, management information systems, management science, marketing, organizational behavior, purchasing. **Communications:** General. **Computer sciences:** General. **Conservation:** Environmental science. **Education:** Multilevel teacher. **Engineering:** Aerospace, biomedical, civil, computer, electrical, mechanical, physics. **Engineering technology:** Aerospace, electrical, industrial management. **Family/consumer sciences:** Food/nutrition. **Foreign languages:** General, classics, French, German, Italian, modern Greek, Russian, Spanish. **Health:** Athletic training, audiology/speech pathology, clinical lab science, cytotechnology, medical radiologic technology/radiation therapy, medical records admin, nuclear medical technology, nursing (RN). **History:** General. **Legal studies:** General. **Liberal arts:** Humanities. **Math:** General. **Parks/recreation:** Exercise sciences. **Philosophy/religion:** Philosophy. **Physical sciences:** Atmospheric science, chemistry, geology, geophysics, physics. **Protective services:** Corrections, criminal justice, law enforcement admin. **Psychology:** General. **Public administration:** Social work. **Social sciences:** Economics, international relations, political science, sociology, urban studies. **Theology:** Theology. **Transportation:** Airline/commercial pilot, aviation management. **Visual/performing arts:** Art history/conservation, dramatic, studio arts.

**Most popular majors.** Biology 7%, business/marketing 26%, health sciences 16%, social sciences 7%.

**Computing on campus.** 300 workstations in dormitories, library, computer center, student center. Dormitories wired for high-speed internet access and linked to campus network. Commuter students can connect to campus network. Online course registration, online library, helpline, student web hosting, wireless network available.

**Student life. Freshman orientation:** Mandatory. Preregistration for classes offered. 2-day program scheduled 7 times in summer before fall enrollment. **Housing:** Coed dorms, single-sex dorms, special housing for disabled, apartments, fraternity/sorority housing available. $250 fully refundable deposit, deadline 5/1. Foreign language housing available. **Activities:** Bands, campus ministries, choral groups, dance, drama, film society, international student organizations, literary magazine, music ensembles, Model UN, musical theater, radio station, student government, student newspaper, TV station, Black Student Alliance, College Democrats, College Republicans, student activities board, Muslim students' Association, Relay for Life, Amnesty International, International Student Federation, Interfaith Ministries.

**Athletics.** NCAA. **Intercollegiate:** Baseball M, basketball, cross-country, diving, field hockey W, soccer, softball W, swimming, tennis, track and field, volleyball W. **Intramural:** Badminton, basketball, bowling, football (non-tackle), golf, handball, racquetball, soccer, softball, squash, swimming, table tennis, tennis, volleyball. **Team name:** Billikens.

**Student services.** Adult student services, alcohol/substance abuse counseling, chaplain/spiritual director, career counseling, services for economically disadvantaged, student employment services, financial aid counseling, health services, minority student services, personal counseling, veterans' counselor, women's services. **Physically disabled:** Services for visually, speech, hearing impaired.

**Contact.** E-mail: admitme@slu.edu
Phone: (314) 977-2500 Toll-free number: (800) 758-3678
Fax: (314) 977-7136
Jean Gilman, Dean of Undergraduate Admission, Saint Louis University, 221 North Grand Boulevard, St. Louis, MO 63103

## St. Luke's College
### Kansas City, Missouri
www.saintlukescollege.edu

CB code: 7127

- Private two-year upper-division nursing college affiliated with Episcopal Church
- Commuter campus in large city
- 20% of applicants admitted
- Application essay, interview required

**General.** Founded in 1903. Regionally accredited. **Degrees:** 56 bachelor's awarded. **Calendar:** Semester, limited summer session. **Full-time faculty:** 18 total; 44% have terminal degrees, 6% minority, 94% women. **Class size:** 33% < 20, 44% 20-39, 6% 40-49, 17% 50-99. **Special facilities:** Simulated clinical settings for nursing students.

**Student profile.** 123 degree-seeking undergraduates. 302 applied as first time-transfer students, 61 admitted, 61 enrolled. 100% entered as juniors.

| | | | |
|---|---|---|---|
| Women: | 88% | Hispanic American: | 3% |
| African American: | 3% | Part-time: | 2% |
| Asian American: | 2% | 25 or older: | 46% |

**Basis for selection.** High school transcript, college transcript, application essay, interview required. Recommendations required. Health care-related work and community service considered. Transfer accepted as juniors.

**2010-2011 Annual costs.** Tuition/fees (projected): $12,373. Books/supplies: $1,000.

**Financial aid. Need-based:** 103 applied for aid; 93 were judged to have need; 93 of these received aid. Average need met was 75%. 30% of total undergraduate aid awarded as scholarships/grants, 70% as loans/jobs. **Non-need-based:** Awarded to 20 undergraduates.

**Application procedures. Admission:** Deadline 12/31. $35 fee. Application must be submitted on paper. Admission notification 3/1.

**Academics. Special study options:** Combined bachelor's/graduate degree, study abroad. **Credit/placement by examination:** AP, CLEP. 15 credit hours maximum toward bachelor's degree. Exams must not be older than 10 years Only CLEP and AP exams accepted.

**Majors. Health:** Nursing (RN).

**Computing on campus.** 30 workstations in library, computer center. Helpline available.

**Student life. Activities:** Student government.

**Student services.** Career counseling, financial aid counseling, health services, personal counseling.

**Contact.** E-mail: slc-admissions@saint-lukes.org
Phone: (816) 932-2367 Fax: (816) 932-9064
St. Luke's College, 8320 Ward Parkway, Suite 300, Kansas City, MO 64114

---

## Southeast Missouri State University

**Cape Girardeau, Missouri**  **CB member**
**www.semo.edu**  **CB code: 6655**

- Public 4-year university
- Commuter campus in large town
- 8,882 degree-seeking undergraduates: 19% part-time, 58% women, 9% African American, 1% Asian American, 1% Hispanic American, 2% international
- 805 degree-seeking graduate students
- 92% of applicants admitted
- SAT or ACT (ACT writing optional) required
- 51% graduate within 6 years

**General.** Founded in 1873. Regionally accredited. **Degrees:** 1,510 bachelor's, 15 associate awarded; master's offered. **ROTC:** Air Force. **Location:** 120 miles from St. Louis. **Calendar:** Semester, extensive summer session. **Full-time faculty:** 420 total; 76% have terminal degrees, 13% minority, 46% women. **Part-time faculty:** 172 total; 18% have terminal degrees, 7% minority, 55% women. **Class size:** 40% < 20, 56% 20-39, 2% 40-49, 1% 50-99, less than 1% >100. **Special facilities:** Demonstration farm, NASA educator resource center, mobile teaching and learning center, mobile health center, museum of archeology, history, and fine art.

**Freshman class profile.** 4,164 applied, 3,835 admitted, 1,805 enrolled.

| Mid 50% test scores | | | |
|---|---|---|---|
| SAT critical reading: | 440-570 | Rank in top quarter: | 41% |
| SAT math: | 460-580 | Rank in top tenth: | 16% |
| ACT composite: | 20-25 | End year in good standing: | 73% |
| GPA 3.75 or higher: | 25% | Return as sophomores: | 72% |
| GPA 3.50-3.74: | 15% | Out-of-state: | 15% |
| GPA 3.0-3.49: | 29% | Live on campus: | 60% |
| GPA 2.0-2.99: | 29% | Fraternities: | 16% |
| | | Sororities: | 10% |

**Basis for selection.** Standard test scores, academic GPA, rigor of secondary school records very important. Non-traditional students may take the ASSET exam, but ACT preferred; SAT accepted. Audition required for music and theater majors.

**High school preparation.** College-preparatory program recommended. 17 units required. Required units include English 4, mathematics 3, social studies 2, history 1, science 3 (laboratory 1), visual/performing arts 1 and academic electives 3. Of social studies requirements, .5 units must be in U.S. government.

**2009-2010 Annual costs.** Tuition/fees: $6,255; $10,890 out-of-state. Room/board: $6,358. Books/supplies: $447. Personal expenses: $2,230.

**2008-2009 Financial aid. Need-based:** 1,318 full-time freshmen applied for aid; 901 were judged to have need; 900 of these received aid. Average need met was 77%. Average scholarship/grant was $5,718; average loan $3,054. 42% of total undergraduate aid awarded as scholarships/grants, 58% as loans/jobs. **Non-need-based:** Awarded to 1,567 full-time undergraduates, including 659 freshmen. Scholarships awarded for academics, alumni affiliation, art, athletics, job skills, leadership, minority status, music/drama, ROTC, state residency.

**Application procedures. Admission:** Priority date 12/15; deadline 5/1 (postmark date). $25 fee, may be waived for applicants with need. Admission notification on a rolling basis beginning on or about 9/1. Must reply by 5/1. **Financial aid:** Priority date 3/1; no closing date. FAFSA required. Applicants notified on a rolling basis starting 4/1; must reply within 3 week(s) of notification.

**Academics. Special study options:** Accelerated study, distance learning, double major, dual enrollment of high school students, ESL, honors, independent study, internships, liberal arts/career combination, student-designed major, study abroad, teacher certification program. **Credit/placement by examination:** AP, CLEP, SAT, ACT, institutional tests. 30 credit hours maximum toward associate degree, 30 toward bachelor's. Departmental exams offered. **Support services:** Learning center, pre-admission summer program, reduced course load, remedial instruction, study skills assistance, tutoring, writing center.

**Majors. Agriculture:** General, agribusiness operations, animal sciences, horticultural science, plant sciences. **Biology:** General. **Business:** Accounting, business admin, finance, marketing, office management. **Communications:** General. **Computer sciences:** General, programming. **Conservation:** Environmental studies. **Education:** Art, business, elementary, English, family/consumer sciences, foreign languages, kindergarten/preschool, mathematics, middle, music, physical, science, social studies, special, speech, technology/industrial arts. **Engineering:** Physics. **Engineering technology:** General, industrial. **Family/consumer sciences:** General. **Foreign languages:** French, German, Spanish. **Health:** Clinical lab science, communication disorders, nursing (RN). **History:** General. **Interdisciplinary:** Global studies. **Liberal arts:** Humanities. **Math:** General. **Parks/recreation:** General, health/fitness, sports admin. **Philosophy/religion:** Philosophy. **Physical sciences:** Chemistry, physics. **Protective services:** Corrections. **Psychology:** General. **Public administration:** Social work. **Social sciences:** Anthropology, economics, political science. **Visual/performing arts:** General, art, dramatic.

**Most popular majors.** Business/marketing 14%, communications/journalism 8%, education 17%, family/consumer sciences 6%, health sciences 6%, liberal arts 12%, parks/recreation 6%.

**Computing on campus.** 1,311 workstations in dormitories, library, computer center, student center. Dormitories wired for high-speed internet access and linked to campus network. Online course registration, online library, helpline, student web hosting, wireless network available.

**Student life. Freshman orientation:** Mandatory, $50 fee. Preregistration for classes offered. One-day program offered many times throughout the semester. **Housing:** Coed dorms, fraternity/sorority housing, wellness housing available. $150 partly refundable deposit. Apartments for students with dependents available. **Activities:** Bands, campus ministries, choral groups, dance, drama, international student organizations, literary magazine, music ensembles, Model UN, musical theater, opera, radio station, student government, student newspaper, symphony orchestra, Baptist Student Union, Lutheran Student Fellowship, Association of Black Collegians, College Republicans, College Democrats, Friends Without Borders, Indian Subcontinent Student Association, Catholic Campus Ministries, Chinese Students & Scholars Association.

**Athletics.** NCAA. **Intercollegiate:** Baseball M, basketball, cheerleading, cross-country, football (tackle) M, gymnastics W, soccer W, softball W, tennis W, track and field, volleyball W. **Intramural:** Badminton, basketball, bowling, football (non-tackle), golf, racquetball, soccer, softball, swimming, table tennis, tennis, volleyball, wrestling. **Team name:** Redhawks.

**Student services.** Adult student services, alcohol/substance abuse counseling, chaplain/spiritual director, career counseling, services for economically disadvantaged, student employment services, financial aid counseling, health services, minority student services, on-campus daycare, personal counseling, placement for graduates, veterans' counselor. **Physically disabled:** Services for visually, speech, hearing impaired. **Learning disabled:** Comprehensive services available.

**Contact.**  E-mail: admissions@semo.edu
Phone: (573) 651-2590 Fax: (573) 651-5936
Deborah Below, Director, Southeast Missouri State University, One
University Plaza, Cape Girardeau, MO 63701

## Southwest Baptist University
### Bolivar, Missouri
www.sbuniv.edu                                    CB code: 6664

- Private 4-year university affiliated with Southern Baptist Convention
- Residential campus in small town
- 2,646 degree-seeking undergraduates: 24% part-time, 66% women, 4% African American, 1% Asian American, 1% Hispanic American, 1% Native American, 1% international
- 545 degree-seeking graduate students
- 92% of applicants admitted
- SAT or ACT (ACT writing optional) required
- 49% graduate within 6 years

**General.** Founded in 1878. Regionally accredited. **Degrees:** 312 bachelor's, 179 associate awarded; master's, professional offered. **ROTC:** Army. **Location:** 25 miles from Springfield, 120 miles from Kansas City. **Calendar:** Semester, extensive summer session. **Full-time faculty:** 116 total; 60% have terminal degrees, 2% minority, 41% women. **Part-time faculty:** 144 total; 24% have terminal degrees, less than 1% minority, 56% women. **Class size:** 66% < 20, 27% 20-39, 5% 40-49, 2% 50-99.

**Freshman class profile.** 1,617 applied, 1,493 admitted, 458 enrolled.

| Mid 50% test scores | | | |
|---|---|---|---|
| SAT critical reading: | 410-560 | Rank in top quarter: | 41% |
| SAT math: | 450-600 | Rank in top tenth: | 22% |
| ACT composite: | 20-26 | End year in good standing: | 82% |
| GPA 3.75 or higher: | 41% | Return as sophomores: | 70% |
| GPA 3.50-3.74: | 18% | Out-of-state: | 30% |
| GPA 3.0-3.49: | 22% | Live on campus: | 95% |
| GPA 2.0-2.99: | 18% | International: | 1% |

**Basis for selection.** Must meet 2 of 3 qualifiers: 2.50 GPA, 21 ACT or 990 SAT score (exclusive of Writing), top 50% high school class rank. Interview required for conditionally admitted applicants, recommended for all. Audition recommended for music, speech, and theater students.

**High school preparation.** College-preparatory program recommended. 13 units recommended. Recommended units include English 4, mathematics 3, social studies 2, science 2 and academic electives 2. 2 additional units of foreign language or computer science or 2 units of English, math, social studies or natural sciences recommended.

**2010-2011 Annual costs.** Tuition/fees: $17,280. Room/board: $5,720. Books/supplies: $1,000. Personal expenses: $1,000.

**2009-2010 Financial aid. Need-based:** 437 full-time freshmen applied for aid; 381 were judged to have need; 380 of these received aid. Average need met was 84%. Average scholarship/grant was $4,023; average loan $3,092. 35% of total undergraduate aid awarded as scholarships/grants, 65% as loans/jobs. **Non-need-based:** Awarded to 1,837 full-time undergraduates, including 507 freshmen. Scholarships awarded for academics, art, athletics, minority status, music/drama, state residency.

**Application procedures. Admission:** No deadline. $30 fee, may be waived for applicants with need. Admission notification on a rolling basis beginning on or about 9/1. **Financial aid:** Priority date 3/15; no closing date. FAFSA, institutional form required. Applicants notified on a rolling basis starting 3/1; must reply within 2 week(s) of notification.

**Academics. Special study options:** Cooperative education, distance learning, double major, dual enrollment of high school students, honors, independent study, internships, student-designed major, study abroad, teacher certification program, Washington semester. **Credit/placement by examination:** AP, CLEP, IB, SAT, ACT, institutional tests. 16 credit hours maximum toward associate degree, 32 toward bachelor's. **Support services:** Learning center, reduced course load, remedial instruction, study skills assistance, tutoring, writing center.

**Majors. Biology:** General. **Business:** Accounting, business admin, customer service, finance, international, marketing, office management. **Communications:** General. **Computer sciences:** General, computer science. **Education:** Art, biology, chemistry, elementary, English, health, middle, music, physical, science, social science. **Foreign languages:** Spanish. **Health:** Athletic training, clinical lab science, nursing (RN). **History:** General. **Math:** General. **Parks/recreation:** General, health/fitness, sports admin. **Philosophy/religion:** Religion. **Physical sciences:** Chemistry. **Protective services:** Law

enforcement admin. **Psychology:** General. **Public administration:** Human services. **Social sciences:** Political science, sociology. **Theology:** Bible, missionary, religious ed, sacred music, theology. **Visual/performing arts:** Art, commercial/advertising art, dramatic. **Other:** Science and Christian faith.

**Most popular majors.** Business/marketing 15%, education 21%, health sciences 12%, psychology 10%, theological studies 11%.

**Computing on campus.** 242 workstations in dormitories, library, computer center, student center. Dormitories linked to campus network. Commuter students can connect to campus network. Online library, helpline, wireless network available.

**Student life. Freshman orientation:** Available. Preregistration for classes offered. 5-days prior to start of the fall semester. **Policies:** Religious observance required. **Housing:** Guaranteed on-campus for freshmen. Single-sex dorms, apartments, wellness housing available. $100 deposit. **Activities:** Bands, campus ministries, choral groups, drama, international student organizations, music ensembles, musical theater, opera, student government, student newspaper, symphony orchestra, University Missions, Habitat for Humanity, Christian Service Organization, Theatrical Evangelism and Mission, Students in Free Enterprise, Discipleship-Now teams.

**Athletics.** NCAA. **Intercollegiate:** Baseball M, basketball, cheerleading, cross-country, football (tackle) M, golf M, soccer W, softball W, tennis, track and field, volleyball W. **Intramural:** Basketball, football (non-tackle), racquetball, soccer, softball, volleyball. **Team name:** Bearcats.

**Student services.** Chaplain/spiritual director, career counseling, student employment services, financial aid counseling, health services, personal counseling, placement for graduates.

**Contact.** E-mail: dcrowder@sbuniv.edu
Phone: (417) 328-1810 Toll-free number: (800) 526-5859
Fax: (417) 328-1808
Darren Crowder, Director of Admissions, Southwest Baptist University, 1600 University Avenue, Bolivar, MO 65613-2597

## Stephens College
### Columbia, Missouri
www.stephens.edu                  CB member          CB code: 6683

- Private 4-year liberal arts college
- Residential campus in small city
- 948 degree-seeking undergraduates: 17% part-time, 97% women, 13% African American, 1% Asian American, 3% Hispanic American, 1% Native American
- 248 degree-seeking graduate students
- 72% of applicants admitted
- SAT or ACT (ACT writing optional), application essay required
- 57% graduate within 6 years; 18% enter graduate study

**General.** Founded in 1833. Regionally accredited. **Degrees:** 193 bachelor's, 1 associate awarded; master's offered. **ROTC:** Army, Naval, Air Force. **Location:** 125 miles from St. Louis and Kansas City. **Calendar:** Semester, limited summer session. **Full-time faculty:** 60 total; 38% have terminal degrees, 2% minority, 78% women. **Part-time faculty:** 53 total; 11% minority, 66% women. **Class size:** 75% < 20, 23% 20-39, 1% 40-49, less than 1% 50-99. **Special facilities:** Professional-level theater, private elementary school and child study center, 60-horse stables, historical costume collection.

**Freshman class profile.** 676 applied, 487 admitted, 231 enrolled.

| Mid 50% test scores | | | |
|---|---|---|---|
| | | GPA 2.0-2.99: | 25% |
| SAT critical reading: | 510-600 | Rank in top quarter: | 36% |
| SAT math: | 460-550 | Rank in top tenth: | 11% |
| SAT writing: | 500-580 | End year in good standing: | 90% |
| ACT composite: | 19-25 | Return as sophomores: | 65% |
| GPA 3.75 or higher: | 19% | Out-of-state: | 44% |
| GPA 3.50-3.74: | 20% | Live on campus: | 100% |
| GPA 3.0-3.49: | 36% | Sororities: | 9% |

**Basis for selection.** School achievement record most important, followed by test scores. Interview recommended for all students; audition mandatory for dance, recommended for theater, musical theater students. **Homeschooled:** Statement describing homeschool structure and mission, transcript of courses and grades, letter of recommendation (nonparent) required. Require short narrative by primary instructor describing secondary-level education. Examples of student's work may be provided as supplemental information. Visit to campus for individual meeting with admissions counselor encouraged.

**High school preparation.** College-preparatory program recommended. 12 units recommended. Recommended units include English 4, mathematics 3, social studies 1, science 2 and foreign language 2.

**2010-2011 Annual costs.** Tuition/fees: $25,400. Room/board: $8,070. Books/supplies: $1,400. Personal expenses: $2,150.

**2009-2010 Financial aid. Non-need-based:** Scholarships awarded for academics, alumni affiliation, athletics, leadership, music/drama, state residency.

**Application procedures. Admission:** Priority date 1/1; no deadline. $25 fee, may be waived for applicants with need, free for online applicants. Admission notification on a rolling basis beginning on or about 9/15. **Financial aid:** Priority date 3/15; no closing date. FAFSA required. Applicants notified on a rolling basis starting 3/1.

**Academics. Special study options:** Combined bachelor's/graduate degree, cross-registration, distance learning, double major, dual enrollment of high school students, external degree, independent study, internships, liberal arts/career combination, semester at sea, student-designed major, study abroad, teacher certification program. **Credit/placement by examination:** AP, CLEP, IB, SAT, ACT. 15 credit hours maximum toward associate degree, 30 toward bachelor's. **Support services:** Learning center, pre-admission summer program, study skills assistance, tutoring, writing center.

**Majors. Agriculture:** Equine science. **Biology:** General. **Business:** General, accounting, business admin, fashion, marketing. **Communications:** General, advertising, broadcast journalism, journalism, media studies, public relations. **Education:** General, early childhood, elementary. **Family/consumer sciences:** Clothing/textiles, family studies. **Health:** Medical records admin. **Legal studies:** Prelaw. **Liberal arts:** Arts/sciences. **Psychology:** General. **Visual/performing arts:** General, commercial/advertising art, dance, dramatic, fashion design, film/cinema, graphic design, interior design.

**Computing on campus.** 107 workstations in dormitories, library, computer center. Dormitories linked to campus network. Commuter students can connect to campus network. Online library, helpline, repair service, student web hosting, wireless network available.

**Student life. Freshman orientation:** Mandatory. Preregistration for classes offered. Typically held third week of August, one week prior to start of classes. Registration held mid-June on campus with academic advisor. **Housing:** Guaranteed on-campus for all undergraduates. Single-sex dorms, apartments available. $100 deposit. Pets allowed in dorm rooms. Freshman academic residence hall available. **Activities:** Choral groups, dance, drama, film society, literary magazine, music ensembles, musical theater, radio station, student government, student newspaper, TV station, more than 45 clubs and organizations.

**Athletics.** NAIA. **Intercollegiate:** Basketball W, cross-country W, softball W, swimming W, tennis W, volleyball W. **Intramural:** Equestrian W. **Team name:** Stars.

**Student services.** Adult student services, career counseling, student employment services, financial aid counseling, health services, personal counseling, placement for graduates, women's services.

**Contact.** E-mail: apply@stephens.edu
Phone: (573) 876-7207 Toll-free number: (800) 876-7207
Fax: (573) 876-7237
David Adams, Dean of Enrollment Management, Stephens College, 1200 East Broadway, Columbia, MO 65215

## Truman State University

**Kirksville, Missouri**   CB member
**www.truman.edu**   CB code: 6483

- Public 4-year university and liberal arts college
- Residential campus in large town
- 5,381 degree-seeking undergraduates: 2% part-time, 58% women, 4% African American, 2% Asian American, 2% Hispanic American, 1% Native American, 5% international
- 247 degree-seeking graduate students
- 72% of applicants admitted
- SAT or ACT (ACT writing optional), application essay required
- 71% graduate within 6 years

**General.** Founded in 1867. Regionally accredited. State's only public liberal arts and sciences university. **Degrees:** 1,217 bachelor's awarded; master's offered. **ROTC:** Army. **Location:** 195 miles from St. Louis, 170 miles from Kansas City. **Calendar:** Semester, extensive summer session. **Full-time faculty:** 345 total; 82% have terminal degrees, 11% minority, 38% women. **Part-time faculty:** 27 total; 48% have terminal degrees, 7% minority, 56% women. **Class size:** 37% < 20, 59% 20-39, 2% 40-49, 2% 50-99, less than 1% >100. **Special facilities:** Observatory, greenhouse, local history museum, 400-acre farm, human performance laboratory, speech and hearing clinic, biofeedback laboratory, IR and NMR instrumentation, independent learning center for nursing, art gallery, radio station, television studio.

**Freshman class profile.** 4,608 applied, 3,333 admitted, 1,342 enrolled.

| Mid 50% test scores | | | |
|---|---|---|---|
| SAT critical reading: | 540-660 | Rank in top tenth: | 46% |
| SAT math: | 560-660 | End year in good standing: | 85% |
| ACT composite: | 25-30 | Return as sophomores: | 84% |
| GPA 3.75 or higher: | 60% | Out-of-state: | 20% |
| GPA 3.50-3.74: | 20% | Live on campus: | 98% |
| GPA 3.0-3.49: | 17% | International: | 2% |
| GPA 2.0-2.99: | 3% | Fraternities: | 19% |
| Rank in top quarter: | 95% | Sororities: | 15% |

**Basis for selection.** High school performance (class rank, GPA, college preparatory curriculum), test scores, and essay are most important; special ability, talent and achievement are considered. Portfolio recommended for fine arts students. Audition required for music students. **Homeschooled:** Transcript of courses and grades required. **Learning Disabled:** Students are welcome to provide additional documentation of their learning disability.

**High school preparation.** College-preparatory program required. 16 units required; 17 recommended. Required and recommended units include English 4, mathematics 3-4, social studies 2, history 1, science 3 (laboratory 1-2), foreign language 2 and visual/performing arts 1.

**2009-2010 Annual costs.** Tuition/fees: $6,692; $11,543 out-of-state. Room/board: $6,854. Books/supplies: $1,000. Personal expenses: $2,500.

**2008-2009 Financial aid. Need-based:** 1,064 full-time freshmen applied for aid; 634 were judged to have need; 634 of these received aid. Average need met was 85%. Average scholarship/grant was $3,821; average loan $3,556. 47% of total undergraduate aid awarded as scholarships/grants, 53% as loans/jobs. **Non-need-based:** Awarded to 4,411 full-time undergraduates, including 1,438 freshmen. Scholarships awarded for academics, alumni affiliation, art, athletics, leadership, minority status, music/drama, ROTC, state residency. **Additional information:** Out-of-state students whose parents work in Missouri may deduct $1 for every dollar paid in Missouri income taxes from out-of-state tuition.

**Application procedures. Admission:** Priority date 12/15; no deadline. No application fee. Admission notification on a rolling basis. Must reply by May 1 or within 3 week(s) if notified thereafter. **Financial aid:** Priority date 4/1; no closing date. FAFSA, institutional form required. Applicants notified on a rolling basis starting 3/1; must reply within 4 week(s) of notification.

**Academics. Special study options:** Combined bachelor's/graduate degree, double major, dual enrollment of high school students, honors, independent study, internships, semester at sea, student-designed major, study abroad, teacher certification program, Washington semester. **Credit/placement by examination:** AP, CLEP, IB, institutional tests. **Support services:** Learning center, pre-admission summer program, remedial instruction, study skills assistance, tutoring, writing center.

**Majors. Agriculture:** General. **Biology:** General. **Business:** Accounting, business admin. **Communications:** General. **Computer sciences:** Computer science. **Foreign languages:** Classics, French, German, linguistics, Romance, Russian, Spanish. **Health:** Communication disorders, nursing (RN). **History:** General. **Math:** General. **Parks/recreation:** Exercise sciences, health/fitness. **Physical sciences:** Chemistry, physics. **Protective services:** Criminal justice. **Psychology:** General. **Social sciences:** Economics, political science, sociology. **Visual/performing arts:** Art, art history/conservation, dramatic, music performance. **Other:** Philosophy and religious studies.

**Most popular majors.** Biology 9%, business/marketing 16%, communications/journalism 6%, English 9%, parks/recreation 8%, psychology 9%, social sciences 7%, visual/performing arts 8%.

**Computing on campus.** 271 workstations in dormitories, library, computer center, student center. Dormitories wired for high-speed internet access and linked to campus network. Commuter students can connect to campus network. Online course registration, online library, helpline, repair service, student web hosting, wireless network available.

**Student life. Freshman orientation:** Mandatory, $305 fee. Preregistration for classes offered. Sessions held during June and August, with additional "Truman Week" program a few days before fall semester begins. **Housing:** Guaranteed on-campus for freshmen. Coed dorms, special housing for disabled, apartments, wellness housing available. $150 partly refundable deposit, deadline 5/1. Sorority housing, Spanish and French language housing, International roommate options available. **Activities:** Bands, campus ministries, choral groups, dance, drama, film society, international student organizations, literary magazine, music ensembles, Model UN, musical theater, opera, radio station, student government, student newspaper, symphony orchestra, TV station, Alpha Phi Omega, Association of Black Collegians, College Republicans, Campus Christian Fellowship, Amnesty International, Blue Key, Cardinal Key, Circle-K, College Democrats, Baptist Student Union.

**Athletics.** NCAA. **Intercollegiate:** Baseball M, basketball, cross-country, football (tackle) M, golf, soccer, softball W, swimming, tennis, track and field, volleyball W, wrestling M. **Intramural:** Badminton, basketball, bowling, football (non-tackle), racquetball, soccer, softball, swimming, table tennis, tennis, track and field, volleyball, weight lifting. **Team name:** Bulldogs.

**Student services.** Career counseling, services for economically disadvantaged, student employment services, financial aid counseling, health services, minority student services, personal counseling, placement for graduates, veterans' counselor, women's services. **Physically disabled:** Services for visually, speech, hearing impaired.

**Contact.**  E-mail: admissions@truman.edu
Phone: (660) 785-4114 Toll-free number: (800) 892-7792
Fax: (660) 785-7456
Melody Chambers, Director of Admission, Truman State University, 100 East Normal Street, Kirksville, MO 63501-9980

## University of Central Missouri
**Warrensburg, Missouri**

www.ucmo.edu                                    CB code: 6090

- Public 4-year university
- Commuter campus in large town
- 8,401 degree-seeking undergraduates: 11% part-time, 55% women, 8% African American, 1% Asian American, 2% Hispanic American, 1% Native American, 2% international
- 1,957 degree-seeking graduate students
- 85% of applicants admitted
- SAT or ACT (ACT writing optional) required
- 48% graduate within 6 years

**General.** Founded in 1871. Regionally accredited. **Degrees:** 1,673 bachelor's, 2 associate awarded; master's offered. **ROTC:** Army, Air Force. **Location:** 50 miles from Kansas City. **Calendar:** Semester, extensive summer session. **Full-time faculty:** 445 total; 69% have terminal degrees, 13% minority, 42% women. **Class size:** 49% < 20, 43% 20-39, 5% 40-49, 3% 50-99, less than 1% >100. **Special facilities:** Airport, 260-acre farm, children's literature collection, musical instruments collection, child development lab, advanced technology library.

**Freshman class profile.** 3,653 applied, 3,091 admitted, 1,504 enrolled.

| Mid 50% test scores | | Rank in top quarter: | 38% |
|---|---|---|---|
| SAT critical reading: | 450-580 | Rank in top tenth: | 14% |
| SAT math: | 450-510 | Return as sophomores: | 71% |
| SAT writing: | 420-560 | Out-of-state: | 9% |
| ACT composite: | 20-24 | Live on campus: | 92% |
| GPA 3.75 or higher: | 23% | International: | 2% |
| GPA 3.50-3.74: | 17% | Fraternities: | 9% |
| GPA 3.0-3.49: | 29% | Sororities: | 9% |
| GPA 2.0-2.99: | 30% | | |

**Basis for selection.** Applicant must be in top two-thirds of high school class, complete 16-unit core curriculum and have minimum ACT score of 20. Essay required for some programs; audition recommended for music students. **Homeschooled:** Recommend ACT, GED, or equivalent.

**High school preparation.** College-preparatory program required. 16 units required. Required and recommended units include English 4, mathematics 3, social studies 3, science 2 (laboratory 1), foreign language 2 and academic electives 3. 1 fine/performing arts required.

**2009-2010 Annual costs.** Tuition/fees: $6,885; $12,444 out-of-state. Room/board: $6,320. Books/supplies: $600. Personal expenses: $1,000.

**2008-2009 Financial aid.** **Need-based:** 1,193 full-time freshmen applied for aid; 499 were judged to have need; 499 of these received aid. Average need met was 88%. Average scholarship/grant was $3,406; average loan $4,084. 43% of total undergraduate aid awarded as scholarships/grants, 57% as loans/jobs. **Non-need-based:** Awarded to 2,702 full-time undergraduates, including 762 freshmen. Scholarships awarded for academics, alumni

affiliation, art, athletics, leadership, minority status, music/drama, ROTC, state residency.

**Application procedures. Admission:** Priority date 6/1; no deadline. $30 fee, may be waived for applicants with need. Admission notification on a rolling basis beginning on or about 8/18. Deferred admission is allowed for one semester. **Financial aid:** Priority date 3/1; no closing date. FAFSA required. Applicants notified on a rolling basis starting 3/1; must reply within 2 week(s) of notification.

**Academics.** Online services and resources include library, technical support, writing center and bookstore. Extensive international exchange program. **Special study options:** Combined bachelor's/graduate degree, cooperative education, cross-registration, distance learning, double major, dual enrollment of high school students, ESL, honors, internships, liberal arts/career combination, student-designed major, study abroad, teacher certification program, weekend college. Engineering program with University of Missouri (Columbia, Rolla) and University of Indiana, MIssouri University of Science & Technology at Rolla. **Credit/placement by examination:** AP, CLEP, IB, SAT, ACT, institutional tests. 15 credit hours maximum toward associate degree, 30 toward bachelor's. **Support services:** Learning center, remedial instruction, study skills assistance, tutoring, writing center.

**Honors college/program.** Minimum ACT score of 25; 319 freshmen admitted; requires 48 credit hours.

**Majors. Agriculture:** General, business, economics. **Biology:** General. **Business:** Accounting, actuarial science, business admin, finance, hotel/motel admin, human resources, management information systems, marketing, office management, tourism promotion. **Communications:** General, broadcast journalism, journalism, public relations. **Communications technology:** Graphic/printing. **Computer sciences:** General, data processing. **Education:** Agricultural, art, biology, business, chemistry, elementary, English, family/consumer sciences, foreign languages, French, German, mathematics, middle, music, physical, physics, science, secondary, social studies, Spanish, special, speech, technology/industrial arts. **Engineering technology:** Architectural, construction, drafting, electrical, industrial. **Family/consumer sciences:** General, child development, clothing/textiles, family studies. **Foreign languages:** French, German, Spanish. **Health:** Nursing (RN), speech pathology. **History:** General. **Math:** General. **Parks/recreation:** General, facilities management. **Physical sciences:** Chemistry, geology, physics, planetary. **Protective services:** Law enforcement admin. **Psychology:** General. **Public administration:** Social work. **Social sciences:** Economics, geography, political science, sociology. **Visual/performing arts:** Art, commercial/advertising art, dramatic, interior design, photography, studio arts.

**Most popular majors.** Business/marketing 18%, education 20%, engineering/engineering technologies 10%, health sciences 7%, security/protective services 9%, visual/performing arts 7%.

**Computing on campus.** 2,785 workstations in dormitories, library, computer center, student center. Dormitories wired for high-speed internet access and linked to campus network. Commuter students can connect to campus network. Online course registration, online library, helpline, student web hosting, wireless network available.

**Student life. Freshman orientation:** Mandatory. Preregistration for classes offered. 8 one-day sessions in early summer. **Housing:** Guaranteed on-campus for all undergraduates. Coed dorms, single-sex dorms, special housing for disabled, apartments, fraternity/sorority housing, wellness housing available. $100 nonrefundable deposit, deadline 6/1. Honors hall, economy suites available. **Activities:** Bands, campus ministries, choral groups, dance, drama, film society, international student organizations, literary magazine, music ensembles, musical theater, opera, radio station, student government, student newspaper, symphony orchestra, TV station, Association of Black Collegians, nontraditional student association, student ambassadors, College Republicans, College Democrats, United Students for Equal Access, Student Government Association.

**Athletics.** NCAA. **Intercollegiate:** Baseball M, basketball, bowling W, cross-country, football (tackle) M, golf M, soccer W, softball W, track and field, volleyball W, wrestling M. **Intramural:** Archery M, badminton M, basketball, bowling, cross-country, diving, football (tackle), golf, racquetball, rifle, rugby M, soccer, softball, swimming, table tennis, tennis, track and field, volleyball, water polo, weight lifting M, wrestling M. **Team name:** Mules (M), Jennies (W).

**Student services.** Adult student services, alcohol/substance abuse counseling, chaplain/spiritual director, career counseling, student employment services, financial aid counseling, health services, minority student services, on-campus daycare, personal counseling, placement for graduates, veterans' counselor, women's services. **Physically disabled:** Services for visually, speech, hearing impaired.

**Contact.** E-mail: admit@ucmovmb.ucmo.edu
Phone: (660) 543-4290 Toll-free number: (877) 729-8266
Fax: (660) 543-8517
Ann Nordyke, Chief Admissions Officer, University of Central Missouri,
WDE 1400, Warrensburg, MO 64093

## University of Missouri: Columbia
**Columbia, Missouri**                          **CB member**
**www.missouri.edu**                            **CB code: 6875**

- Public 4-year university
- Residential campus in small city
- 23,529 degree-seeking undergraduates: 5% part-time, 52% women, 7% African American, 2% Asian American, 2% Hispanic American, 1% Native American, 2% international
- 6,892 degree-seeking graduate students
- 83% of applicants admitted
- SAT or ACT (ACT writing optional) required
- 68% graduate within 6 years

**General.** Founded in 1839. Regionally accredited. Students with common academic interest housed in same residence hall and enrolled in 3 classes together. **Degrees:** 4,855 bachelor's awarded; master's, doctoral, professional offered. **ROTC:** Army, Naval, Air Force. **Location:** 125 miles from Kansas City, 125 miles from St. Louis. **Calendar:** Semester, limited summer session. **Full-time faculty:** 1,266 total; 91% have terminal degrees, 18% minority, 35% women. **Part-time faculty:** 75 total; 93% have terminal degrees, 9% minority, 44% women. **Special facilities:** Observatory, research nuclear reactor, freedom of information center, Food for 21st Century program, engineering experiment station, center for research in social behavior, equine center, university research farms, child development laboratory, daily city newspaper production, nightly newscasts, black culture center.

**Freshman class profile.** 16,436 applied, 13,659 admitted, 5,593 enrolled.

| Mid 50% test scores | | Return as sophomores: | 85% |
|---|---|---|---|
| SAT critical reading: | 530-650 | Out-of-state: | 28% |
| SAT math: | 530-650 | Live on campus: | 86% |
| ACT composite: | 23-28 | International: | 1% |
| Rank in top quarter: | 55% | Fraternities: | 19% |
| Rank in top tenth: ' | 25% | Sororities: | 26% |

**Basis for selection.** Admission based on required core courses and combination of high school rank and test scores. Individual programs may have additional requirements. Trial summer admission open to Missouri residents. Students must complete math and English with C or better to continue enrollment on probation in fall. ACT preferred.

**High school preparation.** College-preparatory program required. 17 units required. Required units include English 4, mathematics 4, social studies 3, science 3 (laboratory 1) and foreign language 2. 1 fine arts required. Math must include algebra I and higher.

**2009-2010 Annual costs.** Tuition/fees: $8,501; $19,682 out-of-state. Room/board: $8,285. Books/supplies: $1,020. Personal expenses: $1,490.

**2008-2009 Financial aid.** **Need-based:** 4,201 full-time freshmen applied for aid; 2,722 were judged to have need; 2,654 of these received aid. Average need met was 87%. Average scholarship/grant was $7,660; average loan $3,515. 51% of total undergraduate aid awarded as scholarships/grants, 49% as loans/jobs. **Non-need-based:** Awarded to 5,372 full-time undergraduates, including 1,694 freshmen. Scholarships awarded for academics, alumni affiliation, art, athletics, leadership, minority status, music/drama, ROTC, state residency. **Additional information:** Scholarship available for international students based on success during 1st semester.

**Application procedures.** **Admission:** Priority date 5/1; no deadline. $45 fee, may be waived for applicants with need. Admission notification on a rolling basis beginning on or about 1/15. Must reply by May 1 or within 4 week(s) if notified thereafter. **Financial aid:** No deadline. FAFSA required. Applicants notified on a rolling basis.

**Academics.** Guaranteed admission to School of Law with 30 ACT, and maintenance of 3.3 GPA. Early admission to School of Medicine with 30 ACT, maintenance of 3.4 GPA, and required interview. Early admission to School of Nursing with 29 ACT and rank in top 10% of high school class. Project for Excellence in Teaching offered. **Special study options:** Accelerated study, combined bachelor's/graduate degree, cooperative education, cross-registration, distance learning, double major, dual enrollment of high school students, ESL, exchange student, external degree, honors, independent study, internships, New York semester, student-designed major, study abroad, teacher

certification program, Washington semester. **Credit/placement by examination:** AP, CLEP, IB, ACT, institutional tests. Credit by examination policy varies by school/college. **Support services:** Learning center, pre-admission summer program, reduced course load, study skills assistance, tutoring, writing center.

**Honors college/program.** 29 ACT or 1280 SAT and top 10% of high school graduating class required. If school does not rank, core GPA of 3.71 necessary. Core GPA includes all English courses, all math courses Algebra I and higher, and all science, social studies, and foreign language courses.

**Majors. Agriculture:** General, animal sciences, business, communications, economics, food science, plant sciences, soil science. **Area/ethnic studies:** African-American, East Asian, European, Latin American, South Asian, women's. **Biology:** General, biochemistry, conservation, microbiology. **Business:** General, accounting, banking/financial services, business admin, hotel/motel admin, international, marketing, real estate, restaurant/food services, travel services. **Communications:** General, advertising, broadcast journalism, journalism, photojournalism, radio/tv. **Computer sciences:** General, computer science, information technology. **Conservation:** Fisheries, forestry, wildlife. **Education:** General, agricultural, art, biology, business, chemistry, early childhood, elementary, English, foreign languages, mathematics, middle, multiple handicapped, music, physics, science, secondary, social studies, Spanish, voc/tech. **Engineering:** Agricultural, biomedical, chemical, civil, computer, electrical, industrial, mechanical. **Family/consumer sciences:** Clothing/textiles, family resources, family studies, food/nutrition, housing, human nutrition. **Foreign languages:** Classics, East Asian, French, German, linguistics, Russian, South Asian, Spanish. **Health:** Audiology/speech pathology, dietetics, health services admin, medical radiologic technology/radiation therapy, nuclear medical technology, nursing (RN), premedicine, prepharmacy, preveterinary, radiologic technology/medical imaging, respiratory therapy technology, sonography. **History:** General. **Interdisciplinary:** Behavioral sciences, nutrition sciences, peace/conflict. **Math:** General, statistics. **Military:** General. **Parks/recreation:** General, exercise sciences. **Philosophy/religion:** Philosophy, religion. **Physical sciences:** Atmospheric science, chemistry, geology, physics. **Psychology:** General. **Public administration:** Social work. **Social sciences:** Anthropology, archaeology, economics, geography, political science, sociology. **Visual/performing arts:** Art, dramatic.

**Most popular majors.** Business/marketing 19%, communications/journalism 13%, engineering/engineering technologies 7%, family/consumer sciences 6%, health sciences 7%, social sciences 6%.

**Computing on campus.** 1,200 workstations in dormitories, library, computer center, student center. Dormitories wired for high-speed internet access and linked to campus network. Commuter students can connect to campus network. Online course registration, online library, helpline, repair service, student web hosting, wireless network available.

**Student life. Freshman orientation:** Available. Preregistration for classes offered. Nineteen 2-day sessions during summer. **Policies:** Alcohol-free and smoke-free campus buildings, residence halls, and Greek housing available. **Housing:** Guaranteed on-campus for freshmen. Coed dorms, single-sex dorms, apartments, fraternity/sorority housing, wellness housing available. $300 fully refundable deposit, deadline 4/1. Specialized living/learning communities and freshman interest groups in residence halls available. **Activities:** Bands, campus ministries, choral groups, dance, drama, film society, international student organizations, literary magazine, music ensembles, Model UN, musical theater, opera, radio station, student government, student newspaper, symphony orchestra, TV station, Over 40 clubs available.

**Athletics.** NCAA. **Intercollegiate:** Baseball M, basketball, cross-country, diving, football (tackle) M, golf, gymnastics W, soccer W, softball W, swimming, tennis W, track and field, volleyball W, wrestling M. **Intramural:** Basketball, football (non-tackle), golf, soccer, softball, volleyball. **Team name:** Tigers.

**Student services.** Alcohol/substance abuse counseling, chaplain/spiritual director, career counseling, services for economically disadvantaged, student employment services, financial aid counseling, health services, legal services, minority student services, on-campus daycare, personal counseling, placement for graduates, veterans' counselor, women's services. **Physically disabled:** Services for visually, speech, hearing impaired.

**Contact.** E-mail: mu4u@missouri.edu
Phone: (573) 882-7786 Toll-free number: (800) 225-6075
Fax: (573) 882-7887
Barbara Rupp, Director of Admissions, University of Missouri: Columbia, 230 Jesse Hall, Columbia, MO 65211

## University of Missouri: Kansas City
**Kansas City, Missouri**                        **CB member**
**www.umkc.edu**                                 **CB code: 6872**

- Public 4-year university
- Residential campus in large city

◗ 7,721 degree-seeking undergraduates: 20% part-time, 58% women

◗ 5,102 degree-seeking graduate students

◗ 62% of applicants admitted

◗ SAT or ACT (ACT writing optional) required

◗ 45% graduate within 6 years

**General.** Founded in 1929. Regionally accredited. **Degrees:** 1,496 bachelor's awarded; master's, doctoral, professional offered. **ROTC:** Army. **Location:** 500 miles from Chicago, 250 miles from St. Louis. **Calendar:** Semester, extensive summer session. **Full-time faculty:** 713 total; 75% have terminal degrees, 22% minority, 44% women. **Part-time faculty:** 422 total; 33% have terminal degrees, 10% minority, 48% women. **Class size:** 56% < 20, 32% 20-39, 5% 40-49, 6% 50-99, 2% >100. **Special facilities:** Observatory, science and technology library, music conservatory, miniature toy museum.

**Freshman class profile.** 4,117 applied, 2,564 admitted, 1,004 enrolled.

| Mid 50% test scores | | Rank in top tenth: | 31% |
|---|---|---|---|
| SAT critical reading: | 520-650 | End year in good standing: | 76% |
| SAT math: | 550-690 | Return as sophomores: | 74% |
| ACT composite: | 21-28 | Out-of-state: | 23% |
| GPA 3.75 or higher: | 28% | Live on campus: | 64% |
| GPA 3.50-3.74: | 16% | International: | 3% |
| GPA 3.0-3.49: | 30% | Fraternities: | 18% |
| GPA 2.0-2.99: | 26% | Sororities: | 18% |
| Rank in top quarter: | 58% | | |

**Basis for selection.** Admission based on class rank, test scores, and high school course requirements. Admission is very selective to combined arts and sciences/medical; highly selective to pharmacy program; and selective to Conservatory of Music. Interview required for six-year medicine applicants; audition required for Conservatory of Music and Dance applicants. **Homeschooled:** Transcript of courses and grades required. ACT or SAT score required.

**High school preparation.** College-preparatory program required. 17 units required. Required units include English 4, mathematics 4, social studies 3, science 3 (laboratory 1), foreign language 2 and visual/performing arts 1.

**2009-2010 Annual costs.** Tuition/fees: $8,272; $19,363 out-of-state. Room/board: $8,773. Books/supplies: $1,180. Personal expenses: $4,900.

**2009-2010 Financial aid. Need-based:** 814 full-time freshmen applied for aid; 659 were judged to have need; 643 of these received aid. Average need met was 56%. Average scholarship/grant was $7,882; average loan $6,358. 39% of total undergraduate aid awarded as scholarships/grants, 61% as loans/jobs. **Non-need-based:** Awarded to 994 full-time undergraduates, including 261 freshmen. Scholarships awarded for academics, alumni affiliation, art, athletics, leadership, minority status, music/drama, state residency.

**Application procedures. Admission:** Priority date 4/1; no deadline. $45 fee, may be waived for applicants with need. Admission notification on a rolling basis. Architecture, six-year medicine, conservatory and pharmacy programs have separate application deadlines and specific admissions requirements. **Financial aid:** Priority date 3/1; no closing date. FAFSA required. Applicants notified on a rolling basis starting 4/15; must reply within 2 week(s) of notification.

**Academics. Special study options:** Accelerated study, combined bachelor's/graduate degree, cooperative education, distance learning, double major, dual enrollment of high school students, ESL, honors, independent study, internships, liberal arts/career combination, student-designed major, study abroad, teacher certification program. **Credit/placement by examination:** AP, CLEP, IB, ACT, institutional tests. 30 credit hours maximum toward bachelor's degree. **Support services:** Learning center, reduced course load, study skills assistance, tutoring, writing center.

**Majors. Architecture:** Architecture, urban/community planning. **Area/ethnic studies:** American. **Biology:** General. **Business:** General, accounting, accounting/business management, accounting/finance, business admin, entrepreneurial studies, finance, market research. **Communications:** General. **Computer sciences:** Computer science, information technology. **Conservation:** Environmental science, environmental studies. **Education:** General, art, bilingual, biology, chemistry, early childhood, elementary, English, foreign languages, French, geography, German, history, kindergarten/preschool, middle, music, physics, science, secondary, social science, social studies, Spanish. **Engineering:** Civil, electrical, mechanical. **Foreign languages:** French, German, Spanish. **Health:** Clinical lab science, dental hygiene, music therapy, nursing (RN), pharmaceutical sciences, predental, premedicine, prenursing, prepharmacy. **History:** General. **Legal studies:** Prelaw. **Liberal arts:** Arts/sciences. **Math:** General, statistics. **Philosophy/religion:** Philosophy. **Physical sciences:** Chemistry, geology, physics. **Protective services:** Criminal justice, law enforcement admin, police science.

**Psychology:** General. **Social sciences:** Criminology, economics, geography, political science, sociology, urban studies. **Visual/performing arts:** Art, art history/conservation, dance, dramatic, music performance, music theory/composition, piano/organ, stringed instruments, studio arts, voice/opera. **Other:** History and Judaic studies, Pre-Health sciences.

**Most popular majors.** Business/marketing 13%, communications/journalism 7%, education 9%, health sciences 9%, liberal arts 17%, psychology 6%, visual/performing arts 7%.

**Computing on campus.** 680 workstations in dormitories, library, computer center, student center. Dormitories wired for high-speed internet access and linked to campus network. Commuter students can connect to campus network. Online course registration, online library, helpline, wireless network available.

**Student life. Freshman orientation:** Mandatory, $40 fee. Preregistration for classes offered. Several day-long orientations offered in spring and summer. **Housing:** Coed dorms, apartments, fraternity/sorority housing, wellness housing available. $300 partly refundable deposit. University owned houses available. **Activities:** Bands, campus ministries, choral groups, dance, drama, international student organizations, literary magazine, music ensembles, musical theater, opera, radio station, student government, student newspaper, symphony orchestra, over 300 religious, political, ethnic, and social service organizations.

**Athletics.** NCAA. **Intercollegiate:** Basketball, cheerleading, cross-country, golf, soccer M, softball W, tennis, track and field, volleyball W. **Intramural:** Basketball, football (tackle), golf, racquetball, softball, table tennis, volleyball. **Team name:** Kangaroos.

**Student services.** Adult student services, alcohol/substance abuse counseling, career counseling, student employment services, financial aid counseling, health services, minority student services, on-campus daycare, personal counseling, placement for graduates, veterans' counselor, women's services. **Physically disabled:** Services for visually, speech, hearing impaired.

**Contact.** E-mail: admit@umkc.edu
Phone: (816) 235-1111 Toll-free number: (800) 775-8652
Fax: (816) 235-5544
W.C. Vance, Director of Admissions, University of Missouri: Kansas City, 5100 Rockhill Road, AC120, Kansas City, MO 64110-2499

---

## University of Missouri: St. Louis
**St. Louis, Missouri**    **CB member**
**www.umsl.edu**    **CB code: 6889**

◗ Public 4-year university

◗ Commuter campus in very large city

◗ 8,933 degree-seeking undergraduates: 34% part-time, 58% women, 21% African American, 3% Asian American, 2% Hispanic American, 3% international

◗ 3,395 degree-seeking graduate students

◗ 79% of applicants admitted

◗ SAT or ACT (ACT writing optional) required

◗ 46% graduate within 6 years

**General.** Founded in 1963. Regionally accredited. **Degrees:** 2,018 bachelor's awarded; master's, doctoral, professional offered. **ROTC:** Army, Air Force. **Location:** 7 miles from downtown. **Calendar:** Semester, extensive summer session. **Full-time faculty:** 480 total; 76% have terminal degrees, 18% minority, 48% women. **Part-time faculty:** 378 total; 25% have terminal degrees, 14% minority, 62% women. **Class size:** 44% < 20, 40% 20-39, 7% 40-49, 8% 50-99, 1% >100. **Special facilities:** Mercantile library, observatory, 3 art galleries, performing arts center.

**Freshman class profile.** 1,619 applied, 1,278 admitted, 525 enrolled.

| Mid 50% test scores | | Return as sophomores: | 69% |
|---|---|---|---|
| ACT composite: | 20-26 | Out-of-state: | 15% |
| Rank in top quarter: | 48% | Live on campus: | 38% |
| Rank in top tenth: | 22% | International: | 6% |
| End year in good standing: | 74% | | |

**Basis for selection.** Class rank, test scores and high school course requirements most important. Audition required for music majors; not required for admission but for the purpose of placement with instrument. **Homeschooled:** ACT scores are key factor in determining admission. Students should strive for score of 24 or higher.

**High school preparation.** College-preparatory program required. 17 units required. Required units include English 4, mathematics 4, social studies 3, science 3 (laboratory 1) and foreign language 2. 1 fine art required.

**2009-2010 Annual costs.** Tuition/fees: $8,595; $19,686 out-of-state. Room/board: $8,164. Books/supplies: $950. Personal expenses: $6,140.

**2009-2010 Financial aid. Need-based:** 410 full-time freshmen applied for aid; 355 were judged to have need; 348 of these received aid. Average need met was 54%. Average scholarship/grant was $6,842; average loan $3,368. 35% of total undergraduate aid awarded as scholarships/grants, 65% as loans/jobs. **Non-need-based:** Awarded to 662 full-time undergraduates, including 110 freshmen. Scholarships awarded for academics, alumni affiliation, art, athletics, music/drama, ROTC, state residency.

**Application procedures. Admission:** Closing date 8/23. $35 fee, may be waived for applicants with need. Admission notification on a rolling basis beginning on or about 10/1. **Financial aid:** Priority date 4/1; no closing date. FAFSA required. Applicants notified on a rolling basis starting 4/1; must reply within 2 week(s) of notification.

**Academics. Special study options:** Accelerated study, combined bachelor's/graduate degree, cooperative education, cross-registration, distance learning, double major, dual enrollment of high school students, ESL, exchange student, honors, independent study, internships, liberal arts/career combination, semester at sea, student-designed major, study abroad, teacher certification program. **Credit/placement by examination:** AP, CLEP, IB, SAT, ACT, institutional tests. 30 credit hours maximum toward bachelor's degree. **Support services:** Learning center, pre-admission summer program, study skills assistance, tutoring, writing center.

**Honors college/program.** Selection based on scores, class rank, extracurricular activities, test scores, 2 recommendations, essay, interview with Dean. Approximately 50 freshmen admitted each fall. Academic program includes honors classes.

**Majors. Biology:** General, biochemistry. **Business:** General, accounting, business admin, finance, international, logistics, management information systems, marketing, operations, organizational behavior. **Communications:** General, media studies. **Computer sciences:** General. **Education:** General, early childhood, elementary, music, physical, secondary, special. **Engineering:** Civil, electrical, mechanical. **Foreign languages:** French, German, Spanish. **Health:** Nursing (RN). **History:** General. **Liberal arts:** Arts/sciences. **Math:** General, applied. **Philosophy/religion:** Philosophy. **Physical sciences:** Chemistry, physics. **Psychology:** General. **Public administration:** General, social work. **Social sciences:** Anthropology, criminology, economics, political science, sociology. **Visual/performing arts:** Art, art history/conservation, dramatic, music history.

**Most popular majors.** Business/marketing 28%, communications/journalism 6%, education 14%, health sciences 9%, psychology 6%, social sciences 9%.

**Computing on campus.** 1,200 workstations in dormitories, library, computer center, student center. Dormitories wired for high-speed internet access and linked to campus network. Commuter students can connect to campus network. Online course registration, online library, helpline, student web hosting, wireless network available.

**Student life. Freshman orientation:** Available. Preregistration for classes offered. One day program held several times throughout summer. Spring orientation session offered in January. **Housing:** Guaranteed on-campus for all undergraduates. Coed dorms, special housing for disabled, apartments, fraternity/sorority housing, wellness housing available. $200 partly refundable deposit, deadline 7/1. Optometry housing available. **Activities:** Bands, campus ministries, choral groups, dance, drama, film society, international student organizations, literary magazine, music ensembles, Model UN, musical theater, opera, radio station, student government, student newspaper, Associated Black Collegians, Spanish club, Alpha Phi Omega, Amnesty International, Pan-Hellenic Council, College Republicans, Catholic Students at Newman Center, Campus Crusade for Christ, Sigma Gamma Rho.

**Athletics.** NCAA. **Intercollegiate:** Baseball M, basketball, golf, soccer, softball W, tennis, volleyball W. **Intramural:** Football (tackle). **Team name:** Tritons.

**Student services.** Adult student services, alcohol/substance abuse counseling, chaplain/spiritual director, career counseling, services for economically disadvantaged, student employment services, financial aid counseling, health services, minority student services, on-campus daycare, personal counseling, placement for graduates, veterans' counselor, women's services. **Physically disabled:** Services for visually, speech, hearing impaired.

**Contact.** E-mail: admissions@umsl.edu
Phone: (314) 516-5451 Toll-free number: (888) 462-8675
Fax: (314) 516-5310
J. McCalley, Associate Vice Provost, University of Missouri: St. Louis, One University Boulevard, St. Louis, MO 63121-4400

## Washington University in St. Louis
St. Louis, Missouri
www.wustl.edu

CB member
CB code: 6929

- Private 4-year university
- Residential campus in large city
- 6,436 degree-seeking undergraduates: 5% part-time, 50% women, 9% African American, 14% Asian American, 3% Hispanic American, 6% international
- 6,315 degree-seeking graduate students
- 22% of applicants admitted
- SAT or ACT (ACT writing optional), application essay required
- 93% graduate within 6 years

**General.** Founded in 1853. Regionally accredited. **Degrees:** 1,637 bachelor's awarded; master's, doctoral, professional offered. **ROTC:** Army, Air Force. **Location:** 7 miles from downtown St. Louis. **Calendar:** Semester, extensive summer session. **Full-time faculty:** 916 total; 98% have terminal degrees, 35% women. **Part-time faculty:** 176 total; 42% women. **Class size:** 72% < 20, 15% 20-39, 4% 40-49, 6% 50-99, 3% >100. **Special facilities:** Research center, 59-acre medical campus, observatory, plant growth facility, international writer's center, planetarium, business/economics experimental laboratory, laboratory science building, outdoor research center, theater.

**Freshman class profile.** 23,105 applied, 5,128 admitted, 1,510 enrolled.

| Mid 50% test scores | | Out-of-state: | 92% |
|---|---|---|---|
| SAT critical reading: | 680-750 | Live on campus: | 99% |
| SAT math: | 710-780 | International: | 8% |
| ACT composite: | 32-34 | Fraternities: | 25% |
| Return as sophomores: | 97% | Sororities: | 25% |

**Basis for selection.** Rigor of high school curriculum and academic performance, GPA, test scores, extracurricular activities, essay, recommendations very important. Counselor and teacher recommendations required of all applicants. Portfolio optional for students applying to the College of Art and the College of Architecture. **Homeschooled:** Letter of recommendation (nonparent) required.

**High school preparation.** College-preparatory program recommended. 20 units recommended. Recommended units include English 4, mathematics 4, social studies 4, history 4, science 4 (laboratory 4) and foreign language 2.

**2010-2011 Annual costs.** Tuition/fees: $40,374. Room/board: $12,941. Books/supplies: $1,300. Personal expenses: $2,290.

**2009-2010 Financial aid. Need-based:** 996 full-time freshmen applied for aid; 566 were judged to have need; 556 of these received aid. Average need met was 100%. Average scholarship/grant was $27,699; average loan $5,275. 85% of total undergraduate aid awarded as scholarships/grants, 15% as loans/jobs. **Non-need-based:** Awarded to 1,089 full-time undergraduates, including 329 freshmen. Scholarships awarded for academics, ROTC.

**Application procedures. Admission:** Closing date 1/15. $55 fee, may be waived for applicants with need. Admission notification 4/1. Must reply by 5/1. **Financial aid:** Closing date 2/15. FAFSA, CSS PROFILE required. Applicants notified by 4/1; must reply by 5/1.

**Academics. Special study options:** Accelerated study, combined bachelor's/graduate degree, cooperative education, cross-registration, double major, dual enrollment of high school students, ESL, exchange student, independent study, internships, liberal arts/career combination, student-designed major, study abroad, teacher certification program, Washington semester. University Scholars Program. **Credit/placement by examination:** AP, CLEP, IB, institutional tests. **Support services:** Learning center, pre-admission summer program, reduced course load, study skills assistance, tutoring, writing center.

**Majors. Architecture:** Architecture, technology. **Area/ethnic studies:** African-American, American, Asian, East Asian, European, German, Latin American, Near/Middle Eastern, women's. **Biology:** General, biochemistry, biophysics, ecology. **Business:** General, accounting, business admin, entrepreneurial studies, finance, human resources, international, international finance, managerial economics, marketing, operations. **Communications:** Advertising, journalism. **Computer sciences:** General, computer science, data processing, information systems. **Conservation:** Environmental studies. **Education:** General, art, biology, chemistry, drama/dance, elementary, English, French, German, history, mathematics, middle, physics, science, secondary, social science, social studies, Spanish. **Engineering:** Biomedical, chemical, computer, electrical, mechanical, systems. **Foreign languages:** General, ancient Greek,

Arabic, Chinese, classics, comparative lit, French, German, Germanic, Hebrew, Italian, Japanese, Latin, linguistics, Romance, Spanish. **Health:** Health care admin, predental, premedicine, prepharmacy, preveterinary. **History:** General. **Interdisciplinary:** Ancient studies, biological/physical sciences, biopsychology, math/computer science, neuroscience, science/society, systems science. **Liberal arts:** Arts/sciences, humanities. **Math:** General, applied, statistics. **Philosophy/religion:** Islamic, Judaic, philosophy, religion. **Physical sciences:** Chemistry, geology, physics, planetary. **Psychology:** General, industrial. **Social sciences:** General, anthropology, archaeology, economics, international relations, political science, urban studies. **Visual/performing arts:** General, art, art history/conservation, ceramics, commercial/advertising art, dance, design, dramatic, drawing, fashion design, film/cinema, graphic design, illustration, music history, music theory/composition, painting, photography, printmaking, sculpture, studio arts, theater history, voice/opera.

**Most popular majors.** Biology 6%, business/marketing 13%, engineering/engineering technologies 14%, psychology 9%, social sciences 17%, visual/performing arts 9%.

**Computing on campus.** 2,500 workstations in dormitories, library, computer center, student center. Dormitories wired for high-speed internet access and linked to campus network. Commuter students can connect to campus network. Online course registration, online library, helpline, repair service, student web hosting, wireless network available.

**Student life. Freshman orientation:** Mandatory. Preregistration for classes offered. **Housing:** Guaranteed on-campus for freshmen. Coed dorms, apartments, cooperative housing, fraternity/sorority housing, wellness housing available. $250 deposit, deadline 5/1. Special interest suites, upper-class housing, single-sex floors in coed buildings, on-campus housing for transfer students, small-group housing available. **Activities:** Bands, campus ministries, choral groups, dance, drama, film society, international student organizations, literary magazine, music ensembles, Model UN, musical theater, opera, radio station, student government, student newspaper, symphony orchestra, TV station, Approximately 200 social clubs and organizations including religious, political, community service, ethnic, and many other organizations are available.

**Athletics.** NCAA. **Intercollegiate:** Baseball M, basketball, cross-country, diving, football (tackle) M, golf W, soccer, softball W, swimming, tennis, track and field, volleyball W. **Intramural:** Badminton, basketball, bowling, cross-country, football (non-tackle), golf, racquetball, soccer, softball, swimming, table tennis, tennis, track and field, volleyball, water polo. **Team name:** Bears.

**Student services.** Adult student services, alcohol/substance abuse counseling, chaplain/spiritual director, career counseling, services for economically disadvantaged, student employment services, financial aid counseling, health services, minority student services, on-campus daycare, personal counseling, placement for graduates, veterans' counselor, women's services. **Physically disabled:** Services for visually, speech, hearing impaired.

**Contact.** E-mail: admissions@wustl.edu
Phone: (314) 935-6000 Toll-free number: (800) 638-0700
Fax: (314) 935-4290
Julie Shimabukuro, Director of Admissions, Washington University in St. Louis, Campus Box 1089, One Brookings Drive, St. Louis, MO 63130-4899

---

## Webster University
**St. Louis, Missouri**
**www.webster.edu**

**CB member**
**CB code: 6933**

- Private 4-year university
- Commuter campus in large city
- 3,411 degree-seeking undergraduates: 23% part-time, 58% women, 12% African American, 2% Asian American, 3% Hispanic American, 1% Native American, 1% international
- 4,565 degree-seeking graduate students
- 52% of applicants admitted
- SAT or ACT (ACT writing recommended), application essay required
- 65% graduate within 6 years; 16% enter graduate study

**General.** Founded in 1915. Regionally accredited. Additional programs offered at five St. Louis area campuses. Undergraduate degrees offered at extended campus locations in California, South Carolina, Florida, and international campuses in Vienna; Leiden, The Netherlands; Geneva, Switzerland; Cha-am, Thailand; London. **Degrees:** 826 bachelor's awarded; master's, doctoral offered. **ROTC:** Army, Air Force. **Location:** 12 miles from St. Louis. **Calendar:** Semester, limited summer session. **Full-time faculty:** 187 total; 73% have terminal degrees, 9% minority, 46% women. **Part-time faculty:** 718 total; 8% minority, 40% women. **Class size:** 86% < 20, 14%

---

20-39, less than 1% 40-49. **Special facilities:** Repertory theater, opera theater, community music school.

**Freshman class profile.** 1,584 applied, 828 admitted, 494 enrolled.

| Mid 50% test scores | | | |
|---|---|---|---|
| SAT critical reading: | 520-650 | GPA 2.0-2.99: | 19% |
| SAT math: | 460-630 | Rank in top quarter: | 55% |
| ACT composite: | 21-28 | Rank in top tenth: | 24% |
| GPA 3.75 or higher: | 34% | Return as sophomores: | 80% |
| GPA 3.50-3.74: | 15% | Out-of-state: | 30% |
| GPA 3.0-3.49: | 32% | Live on campus: | 65% |

**Basis for selection.** School achievement record, test scores important. Rank in top half of class recommended. Recommendation, essay, resume of activities considered. Interview recommended for all students. Audition required for dance, music, music theater, and theater students; portfolio required for art and film students. **Homeschooled:** Transcripts, ACT or SAT scores, recommendations from community leader or employer must be submitted.

**High school preparation.** College-preparatory program recommended. 21 units recommended. Recommended units include English 4, mathematics 3, social studies 3, science 3 (laboratory 2), foreign language 2, visual/performing arts 1 and academic electives 3.

**2009-2010 Annual costs.** Tuition/fees: $21,056. Tuition $24,556for theater conservatory students. Room/board: $9,070. Books/supplies: $800. Personal expenses: $1,500.

**2008-2009 Financial aid. Non-need-based:** Scholarships awarded for academics, art, music/drama, state residency.

**Application procedures. Admission:** Priority date 3/1; deadline 6/1. $35 fee, may be waived for applicants with need. Admission notification on a rolling basis beginning on or about 9/1. Must reply by May 1 or within 4 week(s) if notified thereafter. **Financial aid:** Priority date 4/1; no closing date. FAFSA, institutional form required. Applicants notified on a rolling basis starting 2/9; must reply within 2 week(s) of notification.

**Academics.** Professional Actors Equity theater company in residence for theater program. Internships and practicums available in most areas. **Special study options:** Accelerated study, combined bachelor's/graduate degree, cooperative education, cross-registration, distance learning, double major, dual enrollment of high school students, ESL, exchange student, honors, independent study, internships, liberal arts/career combination, student-designed major, study abroad, teacher certification program. Certificate programs and combination bachelor's/master's degree in many subject areas, student leadership development program, individualized majors. **Credit/placement by examination:** AP, CLEP, IB. 64 credit hours maximum toward bachelor's degree. **Support services:** Learning center, reduced course load, remedial instruction, study skills assistance, tutoring, writing center.

**Majors. Area/ethnic studies:** American. **Biology:** General. **Business:** General, accounting, accounting/finance, business admin, finance, international, marketing. **Communications:** General, advertising, broadcast journalism, digital media, journalism, public relations. **Communications technology:** Recording arts. **Computer sciences:** Computer science. **Education:** General, music. **Foreign languages:** General, French, German, Spanish. **Health:** Nursing (RN). **History:** General. **Interdisciplinary:** Global studies. **Legal studies:** General, paralegal. **Liberal arts:** Arts/sciences, humanities. **Math:** General. **Philosophy/religion:** Ethics, philosophy, religion. **Psychology:** General. **Social sciences:** General, anthropology, economics, international relations, political science, sociology. **Visual/performing arts:** Acting, art, cinematography, dance, directing/producing, dramatic, film/cinema, musical theater, photography, studio arts. **Other:** Media literacy.

**Most popular majors.** Business/marketing 36%, communications/journalism 15%, psychology 7%, social sciences 8%, visual/performing arts 11%.

**Computing on campus.** 450 workstations in dormitories, library, computer center, student center. Dormitories wired for high-speed internet access and linked to campus network. Online course registration, online library, helpline, student web hosting, wireless network available.

**Student life. Freshman orientation:** Available. **Housing:** Guaranteed on-campus for freshmen. Coed dorms, apartments available. $150 fully refundable deposit, deadline 4/1. Pets allowed in dorm rooms. **Activities:** Jazz band, campus ministries, choral groups, dance, drama, film society, international student organizations, literary magazine, music ensembles, musical theater, opera, radio station, student government, student newspaper, symphony orchestra, TV station, Africa student association, Amnesty International, Campus Crusade for Christ, Chinese student association, College Republicans, Habitat for Humanity, Japanese student association, Latin American student association, Sustainability Initiative, Webster LGBTQ Alliance.

**Athletics.** NCAA. **Intercollegiate:** Baseball M, basketball, cross-country, golf M, soccer, softball W, tennis, track and field, volleyball W. **Intramural:** Bowling, soccer, table tennis, volleyball M. **Team name:** Gorloks.

**Student services.** Alcohol/substance abuse counseling, chaplain/spiritual director, career counseling, student employment services, financial aid counseling, health services, minority student services, personal counseling, placement for graduates, veterans' counselor, women's services. **Physically disabled:** Services for visually, speech, hearing impaired.

**Contact.** E-mail: admit@webster.edu
Phone: (314) 968-6991 Toll-free number: (800) 753-6765
Fax: (314) 968-7115
Matt Nolan, Dean of Admissions, Webster University, 470 East Lockwood Avenue, St. Louis, MO 63119-3194

---

### Westminster College
**Fulton, Missouri**
www.westminster-mo.edu

**CB member**
**CB code: 6937**

- Private 4-year liberal arts college affiliated with Presbyterian Church (USA)
- Residential campus in large town
- 1,067 degree-seeking undergraduates: 1% part-time, 44% women
- 78% of applicants admitted
- SAT or ACT (ACT writing optional) required
- 58% graduate within 6 years; 28% enter graduate study

**General.** Founded in 1851. Regionally accredited. **Degrees:** 203 bachelor's awarded. **ROTC:** Army, Air Force. **Location:** 100 miles from St. Louis, 24 miles from Jefferson City. **Calendar:** Semester, limited summer session. **Full-time faculty:** 61 total; 77% have terminal degrees, 41% women. **Part-time faculty:** 30 total; 27% have terminal degrees, 40% women. **Class size:** 61% < 20, 39% 20-39. **Special facilities:** Winston Churchill memorial and library, 12th century church from London re-built on campus.

**Freshman class profile.** 1,356 applied, 1,057 admitted, 311 enrolled.

| Mid 50% test scores | | | |
|---|---|---|---|
| SAT critical reading: | 440-620 | Rank in top quarter: | 45% |
| SAT math: | 490-630 | Rank in top tenth: | 16% |
| SAT writing: | 450-580 | Return as sophomores: | 83% |
| ACT composite: | 21-28 | Out-of-state: | 29% |
| GPA 3.75 or higher: | 29% | Live on campus: | 96% |
| GPA 3.50-3.74: | 23% | International: | 14% |
| GPA 3.0-3.49: | 28% | Fraternities: | 55% |
| GPA 2.0-2.99: | 19% | Sororities: | 44% |

**Basis for selection.** High school achievement (including class rank, involvement, ACT scores, curriculum, GPA) and recommendations most important. Interview recommended for borderline students, required for students with learning disabilities. **Learning Disabled:** Learning Disabilities Program applicants must have completed applications credentials and personal interview prior to April 1, including untimed SAT/ACT results.

**High school preparation.** College-preparatory program recommended. 16 units recommended. Required and recommended units include English 4, mathematics 3, social studies 2, science 2 (laboratory 2), foreign language 2 and academic electives 2. Pre-med and pre-dental students should have at least 3 lab science, 1 advanced math.

**2009-2010 Annual costs.** Tuition/fees: $18,700. Room/board: $7,120. Books/supplies: $800. Personal expenses: $2,480.

**2009-2010 Financial aid. Need-based:** 249 full-time freshmen applied for aid; 186 were judged to have need; 186 of these received aid. Average need met was 82%. Average scholarship/grant was $14,707; average loan $3,403. 87% of total undergraduate aid awarded as scholarships/grants, 13% as loans/jobs. **Non-need-based:** Awarded to 430 full-time undergraduates, including 122 freshmen. Scholarships awarded for academics, alumni affiliation, leadership, minority status, music/drama, religious affiliation, ROTC, state residency.

**Application procedures. Admission:** Priority date 2/1; no deadline. No application fee. Admission notification on a rolling basis beginning on or about 10/1. Must reply by May 1 or within 3 week(s) if notified thereafter. **Financial aid:** Priority date 2/15; no closing date. FAFSA required. Applicants notified on a rolling basis starting 3/1; must reply within 3 week(s) of notification.

**Academics.** First-year seminar fosters communication, critical thinking and study skills. **Special study options:** Combined bachelor's/graduate degree, cooperative education, cross-registration, double major, dual enrollment of high school students, exchange student, honors, independent study,

internships, liberal arts/career combination, New York semester, student-designed major, study abroad, teacher certification program, urban semester, Washington semester. **Credit/placement by examination:** AP, CLEP, IB, institutional tests. 30 credit hours maximum toward bachelor's degree. **Support services:** Learning center, reduced course load, remedial instruction, study skills assistance, tutoring, writing center.

**Majors. Biology:** General, biochemistry. **Business:** Accounting, business admin, management information systems. **Communications:** Advertising, journalism, media studies. **Computer sciences:** General. **Conservation:** Environmental science, environmental studies. **Education:** Elementary, middle, physical, secondary. **Foreign languages:** French, Spanish. **History:** General. **Math:** General. **Philosophy/religion:** Philosophy, religion. **Physical sciences:** Chemistry, physics. **Psychology:** General. **Social sciences:** Anthropology, economics, international relations, political science, sociology.

**Most popular majors.** Biology 13%, business/marketing 28%, education 12%, English 8%, social sciences 9%.

**Computing on campus.** 200 workstations in library, computer center. Dormitories wired for high-speed internet access and linked to campus network. Commuter students can connect to campus network. Online course registration, online library, helpline, student web hosting, wireless network available.

**Student life. Freshman orientation:** Mandatory. Preregistration for classes offered. Held three days before classes start. **Housing:** Guaranteed on-campus for freshmen. Coed dorms, single-sex dorms, apartments, fraternity/sorority housing available. **Activities:** Pep band, campus ministries, choral groups, dance, drama, international student organizations, literary magazine, music ensembles, Model UN, student government, student newspaper, Young Democrats, Young Republicans, Big Brother-Big Sister program, Environmentally Concerned Students, Chapel Leadership Council, Habitat For Humanity, Fellowship of Christian Athletes.

**Athletics.** NCAA. **Intercollegiate:** Baseball M, basketball, cheerleading M, cross-country, football (tackle) M, golf, soccer, softball W, tennis, track and field, volleyball W. **Intramural:** Basketball, football (non-tackle), soccer, softball, volleyball. **Team name:** Blue Jays.

**Student services.** Alcohol/substance abuse counseling, chaplain/spiritual director, career counseling, student employment services, financial aid counseling, health services, minority student services, personal counseling, placement for graduates, women's services. **Physically disabled:** Services for visually, speech, hearing impaired. **Learning disabled:** Comprehensive services available.

**Contact.** E-mail: admissions@westminster-mo.edu
Phone: (573) 592-5251 Toll-free number: (800) 475-3361
Fax: (573) 592-5255
George Wolf, Vice President and Dean of Enrollment Services, Westminster College, 501 Westminster Avenue, Fulton, MO 65251-1299

---

### William Jewell College
**Liberty, Missouri**
www.jewell.edu

**CB member**
**CB code: 6941**

- Private 4-year liberal arts college
- Residential campus in large town
- 1,083 degree-seeking undergraduates: 5% part-time, 60% women, 4% African American, 2% Asian American, 3% Hispanic American, 1% Native American, 2% international
- 55% of applicants admitted
- SAT or ACT (ACT writing recommended), application essay required
- 63% graduate within 6 years; 30% enter graduate study

**General.** Founded in 1849. Regionally accredited. Campus in Harlaxton, England. **Degrees:** 267 bachelor's awarded. **ROTC:** Army. **Location:** 14 miles from downtown Kansas City. **Calendar:** Semester, limited summer session. **Full-time faculty:** 70 total; 86% have terminal degrees, 3% minority, 49% women. **Part-time faculty:** 77 total; 4% have terminal degrees, 6% minority, 60% women. **Class size:** 67% < 20, 32% 20-39, less than 1% 40-49. **Special facilities:** Observatory, flow cytometer, high and low-ropes course, outdoor environmental learning lab, Quimby pipe organ.

**Freshman class profile.** 2,497 applied, 1,374 admitted, 282 enrolled.

| Mid 50% test scores | | | |
|---|---|---|---|
| SAT critical reading: | 490-640 | Rank in top tenth: | 34% |
| SAT math: | 510-650 | End year in good standing: | 83% |
| ACT composite: | 23-29 | Return as sophomores: | 78% |
| GPA 3.75 or higher: | 54% | Out-of-state: | 36% |
| GPA 3.50-3.74: | 17% | Live on campus: | 96% |
| GPA 3.0-3.49: | 21% | International: | 3% |
| GPA 2.0-2.99: | 8% | Fraternities: | 27% |
| Rank in top quarter: | 68% | Sororities: | 42% |

**Basis for selection.** Admissions based on secondary school record. Class rank, standardized test scores, and essay also important. Audition or portfolio required for scholarship seeking music, theater, or art students.

**High school preparation.** College-preparatory program required. 15 units required; 19 recommended. Required and recommended units include English 4, mathematics 3-4, social studies 3, science 3 (laboratory 1), foreign language 2-3 and academic electives 2.

**2010-2011 Annual costs.** Tuition/fees: $28,450. Room/board: $7,200. Books/supplies: $1,100. Personal expenses: $2,520.

**2009-2010 Financial aid.** **Need-based:** 258 full-time freshmen applied for aid; 217 were judged to have need; 217 of these received aid. Average need met was 89%. Average loan was $5,205. 71% of total undergraduate aid awarded as scholarships/grants, 29% as loans/jobs. **Non-need-based:** Awarded to 111 full-time undergraduates, including 27 freshmen. Scholarships awarded for academics, alumni affiliation, art, athletics, music/drama, ROTC.

**Application procedures.** **Admission:** Priority date 12/1; deadline 8/15 (postmark date). $25 fee, may be waived for applicants with need, free for online applicants. Admission notification on a rolling basis beginning on or about 9/15. Must reply by May 1 or within 2 week(s) if notified thereafter. **Financial aid:** Priority date 3/1; no closing date. FAFSA required. Applicants notified on a rolling basis starting 2/15; must reply within 1.5 week(s) of notification.

**Academics.** Interdisciplinary core curriculum required. **Special study options:** Accelerated study, combined bachelor's/graduate degree, double major, dual enrollment of high school students, honors, independent study, internships, liberal arts/career combination, semester at sea, student-designed major, study abroad, teacher certification program, Washington semester. Pryor Leadership Studies. **Credit/placement by examination:** AP, CLEP, IB, SAT, ACT, institutional tests. No limit to credit by examination, but student must complete a minimum of 30 hours in residence. **Support services:** Study skills assistance, tutoring, writing center.

**Honors college/program.** Oxbridge Honors Program allows students to study their major subject using tutorial mode of instruction used at Oxford University and Cambridge University (England). Minimum 3.8 GPA, ACT score of 28 required for admission.

**Majors.** **Biology:** General, biochemistry, biomedical sciences, molecular. **Business:** Accounting, business admin, international, managerial economics, nonprofit/public. **Communications:** General, organizational. **Education:** Art, biology, chemistry, drama/dance, elementary, English, foreign languages, French, mathematics, music, physical, physics, secondary, social studies, Spanish, speech. **Foreign languages:** French, Spanish. **Health:** Clinical lab science, nursing (RN). **History:** General. **Liberal arts:** Arts/sciences. **Math:** General. **Parks/recreation:** General. **Philosophy/religion:** Philosophy, religion. **Physical sciences:** Chemistry, physics. **Psychology:** General. **Social sciences:** International relations, political science. **Theology:** Sacred music. **Visual/performing arts:** Art, dramatic, music history, music performance, music theory/composition. **Other:** Oxbridge history of ideas, Oxbridge institutions and policy, Oxbridge science.

**Most popular majors.** Biology 6%, business/marketing 22%, education 8%, health sciences 17%, psychology 11%.

**Computing on campus.** 240 workstations in library, computer center, student center. Dormitories wired for high-speed internet access and linked to campus network. Commuter students can connect to campus network. Online course registration, online library, helpline, student web hosting, wireless network available.

**Student life.** **Freshman orientation:** Mandatory. Preregistration for classes offered. 3-day program prior to the first day of classes. **Housing:** Guaranteed on-campus for all undergraduates. Coed dorms, single-sex dorms, special housing for disabled, fraternity/sorority housing, wellness housing available. $300 fully refundable deposit, deadline 5/1. **Activities:** Bands, campus ministries, choral groups, dance, drama, music ensembles, musical theater, opera, radio station, student government, student newspaper, symphony orchestra, Young Democrats, College Republicans, Progressive Students for

America, Amnesty International, Student Senate, UNITY, Rotaract, Fellowship of Christian Athletes, Black Student Association.

**Athletics.** NAIA. **Intercollegiate:** Baseball M, basketball, cheerleading, cross-country, football (tackle) M, golf, soccer, softball W, tennis, track and field, volleyball W. **Intramural:** Basketball, football (non-tackle), golf, racquetball, soccer, softball, tennis, volleyball. **Team name:** Cardinals.

**Student services.** Alcohol/substance abuse counseling, chaplain/spiritual director, career counseling, student employment services, financial aid counseling, health services, minority student services, personal counseling, placement for graduates. **Physically disabled:** Services for visually, speech, hearing impaired.

**Contact.** E-mail: admission@william.jewell.edu
Phone: (816) 415-7511 Toll-free number: (888) 253-9355
Fax: (816) 415-5040
Bridget Gramling, Dean of Admission, William Jewell College, 500 College Hill, Liberty, MO 64068

---

## William Woods University

**Fulton, Missouri**    **CB member**
**www.williamwoods.edu**    **CB code: 6944**

- Private 4-year university and liberal arts college affiliated with Christian Church (Disciples of Christ)
- Residential campus in large town
- 1,068 degree-seeking undergraduates: 19% part-time, 76% women, 5% African American, 1% Asian American, 1% Hispanic American, 1% Native American, 1% international
- 1,296 degree-seeking graduate students
- 77% of applicants admitted
- SAT or ACT (ACT writing recommended) required
- 48% graduate within 6 years

**General.** Founded in 1870. Regionally accredited. Students may enroll in courses offered at 4 other mid-Missouri colleges and universities. **Degrees:** 215 bachelor's, 20 associate awarded; master's offered. **ROTC:** Army, Naval, Air Force. **Location:** 100 miles from St. Louis, 30 miles from Columbia. **Calendar:** Semester, limited summer session. **Full-time faculty:** 62 total. **Part-time faculty:** 266 total. **Class size:** 76% < 20, 23% 20-39, less than 1% 40-49. **Special facilities:** Equestrian studies facilities, observatory, broadcasting laboratory, computer laboratories, model courtroom, ASL interpreting laboratories.

**Freshman class profile.** 877 applied, 672 admitted, 243 enrolled.

| Mid 50% test scores | | | |
|---|---|---|---|
| SAT critical reading: | 490-610 | GPA 2.0-2.99: | 23% |
| SAT math: | 480-580 | Rank in top quarter: | 39% |
| SAT writing: | 460-580 | Rank in top tenth: | 18% |
| ACT composite: | 19-26 | Return as sophomores: | 78% |
| GPA 3.75 or higher: | 27% | Out-of-state: | 36% |
| GPA 3.50-3.74: | 15% | Live on campus: | 92% |
| GPA 3.0-3.49: | 35% | Fraternities: | 38% |
| | | Sororities: | 46% |

**Basis for selection.** Secondary school record, class rank, test scores most important; extracurricular activities, 2 academic references also important; interview considered. Interview recommended for all students. Audition required for performing arts students; portfolio required for visual arts students. **Homeschooled:** Letter of recommendation (nonparent) required. GED required; ACT/SAT must be submitted. Minimum ACT of 19/minimum SAT of 860. Must submit two letters of recommendation.

**High school preparation.** College-preparatory program recommended. 16 units required; 20 recommended. Required and recommended units include English 4, mathematics 3, social studies 2, history 3, science 3 (laboratory 3) and foreign language 2.

**2009-2010 Annual costs.** Tuition/fees: $17,310. Commuter students pay additional $50 fee per year. Room/board: $6,950. Books/supplies: $1,200. Personal expenses: $3,000.

**2009-2010 Financial aid.** **Need-based:** 236 full-time freshmen applied for aid; 176 were judged to have need; 169 of these received aid. Average need met was 73%. Average scholarship/grant was $12,823; average loan $3,219. 62% of total undergraduate aid awarded as scholarships/grants, 38% as loans/jobs. **Non-need-based:** Awarded to 389 full-time undergraduates, including 118 freshmen. Scholarships awarded for academics, alumni affiliation, art, athletics, leadership, music/drama, religious affiliation.

**Application procedures.** **Admission:** Priority date 3/1; no deadline. $25 fee, may be waived for applicants with need, free for online applicants. Admission notification on a rolling basis. Must reply by May 1 or within 2 week(s) if notified thereafter. **Financial aid:** Priority date 3/1; no closing date. FAFSA, institutional form required. Applicants notified on a rolling basis starting 3/15; must reply within 2 week(s) of notification.

**Academics.** ASL interpreting available. **Special study options:** Accelerated study, cross-registration, double major, dual enrollment of high school students, ESL, honors, independent study, internships, liberal arts/career combination, New York semester, student-designed major, study abroad, teacher certification program, Washington semester, Hollywood semester, qualified students may complete bachelor's degree in 3 years through Century Scholars program. **Credit/placement by examination:** AP, CLEP, IB, SAT, ACT, institutional tests. 30 credit hours maximum toward bachelor's degree. **Support services:** Pre-admission summer program, reduced course load, remedial instruction, study skills assistance, tutoring, writing center.

**Majors. Agriculture:** Equestrian studies. **Biology:** General. **Business:** Accounting, business admin, international, management information systems, managerial economics. **Communications:** General, advertising, broadcast journalism, journalism, public relations. **Computer sciences:** General. **Education:** General, art, elementary, English, mathematics, middle, physical, science, secondary, social science, special. **Foreign languages:** American Sign Language, Spanish. **Health:** Athletic training. **History:** General. **Legal studies:** General, paralegal. **Math:** General. **Parks/recreation:** Sports admin. **Physical sciences:** General. **Psychology:** General. **Public administration:** Social work. **Social sciences:** Political science. **Visual/performing arts:** Art, design, dramatic, graphic design, studio arts.

**Most popular majors.** Agriculture 16%, business/marketing 29%, education 16%, foreign language 6%.

**Computing on campus.** 75 workstations in dormitories, library, computer center, student center. Dormitories wired for high-speed internet access and linked to campus network. Online course registration, online library, helpline, repair service, wireless network available.

**Student life. Freshman orientation:** Mandatory. Preregistration for classes offered. 7 days prior to start of fall term. **Policies:** All residence halls nonsmoking. Students under 23 must reside on campus unless married or living with parent or guardian; lottery offered to students who wish to move off campus in spring for following fall semester. **Housing:** Guaranteed on-campus for all undergraduates. Coed dorms, single-sex dorms, special housing for disabled, apartments, fraternity/sorority housing, wellness housing available. $250 partly refundable deposit, deadline 8/15. Senior housing, single rooms, independent housing, learning communities, upper-class halls and apartments available. **Activities:** Campus ministries, choral groups, dance, drama, international student organizations, literary magazine, musical theater, radio station, student government, student newspaper, Big Brothers/Big Sisters, campus activities board, Association of Christian Ecumenical Students, community action network, Jesters, Students for Social Work, departmental clubs.

**Athletics.** NAIA. **Intercollegiate:** Baseball M, basketball, cross-country, golf, soccer, softball W, track and field, volleyball. **Intramural:** Badminton, baseball M, basketball, equestrian, football (non-tackle), softball, table tennis, tennis, volleyball, weight lifting. **Team name:** Owls.

**Student services.** Adult student services, alcohol/substance abuse counseling, chaplain/spiritual director, career counseling, financial aid counseling, health services, personal counseling. **Physically disabled:** Services for visually, speech, hearing impaired.

**Contact.** E-mail: admissions@williamwoods.edu
Phone: (573) 592-4221 Toll-free number: (800) 995-3159
Fax: (573) 592-1146
Sarah Munns, Dean of Admissions, William Woods University, One University Avenue, Fulton, MO 65251-2388

# Montana

## Carroll College

| Helena, Montana | CB member |
| --- | --- |
| www.carroll.edu | CB code: 4041 |

- Private 4-year liberal arts college affiliated with Roman Catholic Church
- Residential campus in large town

**General.** Founded in 1909. Regionally accredited. **Location:** 90 miles from Great Falls, 240 miles from Billings. **Calendar:** Semester.

**Annual costs/financial aid.** Tuition/fees (2009-2010): $22,424. Room/board: $7,188. Books/supplies: $800. Personal expenses: $1,600. Need-based financial aid available to full-time and part-time students.

**Contact.** Phone: (406) 447-4384
Director of Admissions and Enrollment, 1601 North Benton Avenue, Helena, MT 59625

## Montana State University: Billings

| Billings, Montana | CB member |
| --- | --- |
| www.msubillings.edu | CB code: 4298 |

- Public 4-year university and technical college
- Commuter campus in small city
- 4,425 degree-seeking undergraduates: 28% part-time, 62% women, 1% African American, 1% Asian American, 4% Hispanic American, 6% Native American
- 355 degree-seeking graduate students
- 100% of applicants admitted
- SAT or ACT (ACT writing recommended) required

**General.** Founded in 1927. Regionally accredited. College of Professional Studies and Lifelong Learning located in downtown Billings. **Degrees:** 540 bachelor's, 222 associate awarded; master's offered. **ROTC:** Army. **Location:** 224 miles from Helena, 560 miles from Denver. **Calendar:** Semester, limited summer session. **Full-time faculty:** 154 total; 65% have terminal degrees, 4% minority, 40% women. **Part-time faculty:** 136 total; 4% minority, 63% women. **Class size:** 44% < 20, 48% 20-39, 4% 40-49, 4% 50-99, less than 1% >100. **Special facilities:** Biological station, center for business enterprise, Montana Center for Disabilities, special education learning center, center for gerontological studies, small business institute, urban institute, public radio, center for applied economic research.

**Freshman class profile.** 1,384 applied, 1,382 admitted, 900 enrolled.

| Mid 50% test scores | | GPA 2.0-2.99: | 40% |
| --- | --- | --- | --- |
| SAT critical reading: | 460-580 | Rank in top quarter: | 25% |
| SAT math: | 460-590 | Rank in top tenth: | 11% |
| ACT composite: | 18-24 | End year in good standing: | 65% |
| GPA 3.75 or higher: | 13% | Return as sophomores: | 59% |
| GPA 3.50-3.74: | 13% | Out-of-state: | 8% |
| GPA 3.0-3.49: | 30% | Live on campus: | 32% |

**Basis for selection.** Applicants must meet one of the following: 2.5 GPA, 22 ACT/1030 SAT (exclusive of Writing), or rank in upper half of graduating class. **Homeschooled:** Applicants may be admitted based on GED, ACT, or COMPASS scores.

**High school preparation.** College-preparatory program required. 14 units required. Required units include English 4, mathematics 3, social studies 3, science 2 (laboratory 2). 2 years foreign language, computer science, visual and performing arts, or vocational education also recommended.

**2009-2010 Annual costs.** Tuition/fees: $5,207; $14,543 out-of-state. Room/board: $5,460. Books/supplies: $1,000. Personal expenses: $3,400.

**2008-2009 Financial aid. Need-based:** 533 full-time freshmen applied for aid; 419 were judged to have need; 403 of these received aid. Average need met was 67%. Average scholarship/grant was $4,044; average loan $2,850. 41% of total undergraduate aid awarded as scholarships/grants, 59% as loans/jobs. **Non-need-based:** Awarded to 201 full-time undergraduates, including 46 freshmen. Scholarships awarded for academics, alumni affiliation, art, athletics, job skills, leadership, minority status, music/drama, state residency. **Additional information:** Veterans and honors fee waivers offered.

**Application procedures. Admission:** Priority date 7/1; no deadline. $30 fee. Admission notification on a rolling basis. **Financial aid:** Priority date 3/1; no closing date. FAFSA required. Applicants notified on a rolling basis starting 4/1; must reply within 3 week(s) of notification.

**Academics.** Full degree programs and many courses designed for working professionals. **Special study options:** Accelerated study, cooperative education, cross-registration, distance learning, double major, dual enrollment of high school students, ESL, external degree, honors, independent study, internships, liberal arts/career combination, study abroad, teacher certification program, weekend college. Evening College, with extensive online programs and courses. College of Technology offers training and retraining for employment by combining academics and vocational opportunities. **Credit/placement by examination:** AP, CLEP, SAT, ACT, institutional tests. **Support services:** Learning center, reduced course load, remedial instruction, study skills assistance, tutoring, writing center.

**Majors. Biology:** General. **Business:** General. **Communications:** General, media studies, public relations. **Conservation:** Environmental studies. **Education:** General, art, biology, chemistry, curriculum, elementary, English, foreign languages, health, history, mathematics, music, physical, physics, science, secondary, social science, social studies, Spanish, special. **Foreign languages:** Spanish. **Health:** Athletic training, health care admin, vocational rehab counseling. **History:** General. **Liberal arts:** Arts/sciences. **Math:** General. **Parks/recreation:** Health/fitness, sports admin. **Physical sciences:** Chemistry. **Protective services:** Criminal justice. **Psychology:** General. **Public administration:** Human services. **Social sciences:** Political science, sociology. **Visual/performing arts:** Art, dramatic, music performance.

**Most popular majors.** Business/marketing 26%, education 24%, liberal arts 9%, psychology 9%.

**Computing on campus.** 1,250 workstations in dormitories, library, computer center, student center. Dormitories wired for high-speed internet access and linked to campus network. Commuter students can connect to campus network. Online course registration, online library, helpline, student web hosting, wireless network available.

**Student life. Freshman orientation:** Mandatory, $75 fee. Preregistration for classes offered. One-day orientations held throughout summer. **Housing:** Coed dorms, single-sex dorms, special housing for disabled, apartments, wellness housing available. $75 fully refundable deposit. **Activities:** Bands, campus ministries, choral groups, drama, international student organizations, literary magazine, music ensembles, musical theater, radio station, student government, student newspaper, more than 50 student groups available.

**Athletics.** NCAA. **Intercollegiate:** Baseball M, basketball, cheerleading, cross-country, golf, soccer, softball W, tennis, track and field, volleyball W. **Intramural:** Archery, basketball, cross-country, golf, racquetball, skiing, softball, swimming, table tennis, tennis, volleyball. **Team name:** Yellowjackets.

**Student services.** Adult student services, alcohol/substance abuse counseling, chaplain/spiritual director, career counseling, services for economically disadvantaged, student employment services, financial aid counseling, health services, legal services, minority student services, on-campus daycare, personal counseling, placement for graduates, veterans' counselor. **Physically disabled:** Services for visually, speech, hearing impaired.

**Contact.** E-mail: cjohannes@msubillings.edu
Phone: (406) 657-2158 Toll-free number: (800) 656-6782
Fax: (406) 657-2051
Shelly Andersen, Director of Admissions, Montana State University: Billings, 1500 University Drive, Billings, MT 59101-0298

## Montana State University: Bozeman

| Bozeman, Montana | CB member |
| --- | --- |
| www.montana.edu | CB code: 4488 |

- Public 4-year university
- Residential campus in large town
- 10,754 degree-seeking undergraduates: 17% part-time, 45% women
- 1,581 degree-seeking graduate students
- 64% of applicants admitted
- SAT or ACT with writing required
- 48% graduate within 6 years

**General.** Founded in 1893. Regionally accredited. **Degrees:** 1,889 bachelor's awarded; master's, doctoral offered. **ROTC:** Army, Air Force. **Location:** 139 miles from Billings. **Calendar:** Semester, limited summer session. **Full-time faculty:** 569 total; 78% have terminal degrees, 3% minority, 36% women. **Part-time faculty:** 239 total; 36% have terminal degrees, 2% minority, 58% women. **Class size:** 43% < 20, 34% 20-39, 9% 40-49, 8% 50-99, 6% >100. **Special facilities:** Museum of the Rockies, agricultural bioscience center, wind tunnel, electron microscope, center for biofilm engineering, planetarium, telecommunication center, geographic information and analysis center, thermal biology institute, rural dwellers center.

**Freshman class profile.** 8,033 applied, 5,106 admitted, 2,316 enrolled.

Mid 50% test scores
| | | | |
|---|---|---|---|
| SAT critical reading: | 500-620 | Rank in top quarter: | 41% |
| SAT math: | 500-640 | Rank in top tenth: | 17% |
| ACT composite: | 21-27 | Return as sophomores: | 72% |
| GPA 3.75 or higher: | 25% | Out-of-state: | 38% |
| GPA 3.50-3.74: | 16% | Live on campus: | 73% |
| GPA 3.0-3.49: | 29% | Fraternities: | 3% |
| GPA 2.0-2.99: | 29% | Sororities: | 3% |

**Basis for selection.** Minimum 2.5 GPA or 22 ACT/SAT equivalent, or rank in top half of graduating class. Completion of state college-preparatory requirements important. Students may use SAT/ACT math scores for placement or take departmental exam. Students with 27 ACT English or 640 SAT verbal can waive freshman composition. Varies by program. **Home-schooled:** GED required.

**High school preparation.** College-preparatory program required. 14 units required. Required units include English 4, mathematics 3, social studies 3, science 2 (laboratory 2). 4 math recommended for science majors. Substitutions for foreign language requirement possible. 2 foreign language, preferably 2 computer science, visual and performing arts, or approved vocational education units.

**2009-2010 Annual costs.** Tuition/fees: $5,988; $17,651 out-of-state. Non-resident alien fees: $1,379 in required fees, in addition to $150 administrative fee. Room/board: $7,578. Books/supplies: $1,100. Personal expenses: $1,830.

**2008-2009 Financial aid. Need-based:** 35% of total undergraduate aid awarded as scholarships/grants, 65% as loans/jobs. **Non-need-based:** Scholarships awarded for academics, alumni affiliation, art, athletics, job skills, leadership, minority status, music/drama, ROTC, state residency.

**Application procedures. Admission:** No deadline. $30 fee. Admission notification on a rolling basis. **Financial aid:** Priority date 3/1; no closing date. FAFSA required. Applicants notified on a rolling basis starting 4/1; must reply within 3 week(s) of notification.

**Academics. Special study options:** Combined bachelor's/graduate degree, cooperative education, cross-registration, distance learning, double major, ESL, exchange student, honors, independent study, internships, student-designed major, study abroad, teacher certification program. Combined bachelor's/master's programs in environmental design/architecture and construction engineering technology/construction engineering management. **Credit/placement by examination:** AP, CLEP, IB, SAT, ACT, institutional tests. No more than 30 semester credits earned by correspondence, extension, or continuing education counted toward bachelor's degree. **Support services:** Learning center, remedial instruction, study skills assistance, tutoring, writing center.

**Majors. Agriculture:** Business, horticultural science, plant sciences, range science. **Architecture:** Environmental design. **Biology:** General, bacteriology, biotechnology. **Business:** General. **Computer sciences:** Computer science. **Conservation:** General, management/policy. **Education:** Agricultural, elementary, music, secondary, technology/industrial arts. **Engineering:** Chemical, civil, computer, electrical, mechanical. **Engineering technology:** Construction. **Family/consumer sciences:** General. **Foreign languages:** General. **Health:** Nursing (RN). **History:** General. **Math:** General. **Parks/recreation:** Sports admin. **Philosophy/religion:** Philosophy. **Physical sciences:** Chemistry, physics, planetary. **Psychology:** General. **Social sciences:** Anthropology, economics, political science, sociology. **Visual/performing arts:** Art, cinematography.

**Most popular majors.** Biology 8%, business/marketing 12%, education 9%, engineering/engineering technologies 15%, family/consumer sciences 6%, health sciences 10%, visual/performing arts 8%.

**Computing on campus.** 850 workstations in dormitories, library, computer center. Dormitories wired for high-speed internet access and linked to campus network. Commuter students can connect to campus network. Online course registration, helpline, wireless network available.

**Student life. Freshman orientation:** Mandatory, $65 fee. Preregistration for classes offered. **Housing:** Guaranteed on-campus for freshmen. Coed dorms, single-sex dorms, apartments, fraternity/sorority housing, wellness housing available. $200 nonrefundable deposit. Older student floors available. **Activities:** Bands, campus ministries, choral groups, dance, drama, film society, international student organizations, literary magazine, music ensembles, musical theater, radio station, student newspaper, TV station, campus service organizations, Circle-K, Native American club, international coordinating council, black student union, Campus Crusade for Christ, Intervarsity Christian Fellowship.

**Athletics.** NCAA. **Intercollegiate:** Basketball, cheerleading, cross-country, football (tackle) M, golf W, rodeo, skiing, tennis, track and field, volleyball W. **Intramural:** Archery, badminton, basketball, bowling, cross-country, golf, gymnastics, handball, racquetball, rodeo, skiing, soccer, softball, swimming, table tennis, tennis, track and field, volleyball, water polo, weight lifting, wrestling M. **Team name:** Bobcats.

**Student services.** Adult student services, alcohol/substance abuse counseling, chaplain/spiritual director, career counseling, student employment services, financial aid counseling, health services, legal services, minority student services, on-campus daycare, personal counseling, placement for graduates, veterans' counselor, women's services. **Physically disabled:** Services for visually, speech, hearing impaired.

**Contact.** E-mail: admissions@montana.edu
Phone: (406) 994-2452 Toll-free number: (888) 678-2287
Fax: (406) 994-1923
Ronda Russell, Director, Admissions and Enrollment Services, Montana State University: Bozeman, PO Box 172190, Bozeman, MT 59717-2190

## Montana State University: Northern
**Havre, Montana**
www.msun.edu
**CB code: 4538**

- Public 4-year university and liberal arts college
- Commuter campus in large town

**General.** Founded in 1929. Regionally accredited. **Location:** 115 miles from Great Falls. **Calendar:** Semester.

**Annual costs/financial aid.** Tuition/fees (2009-2010): $4,440; $15,085 out-of-state. Room/board: $6,157. Books/supplies: $800. Personal expenses: $558. Need-based financial aid available to full-time and part-time students.

**Contact.** Phone: (406) 265-3704
Director of Admissions, Box 7751, Havre, MT 59501

## Montana Tech of the University of Montana
**Butte, Montana**
www.mtech.edu
**CB code: 4487**

- Public 4-year engineering and technical college
- Commuter campus in large town
- 2,345 degree-seeking undergraduates: 8% part-time, 38% women, 1% African American, 1% Asian American, 2% Hispanic American, 2% Native American, 9% international
- 130 degree-seeking graduate students
- 91% of applicants admitted
- SAT or ACT (ACT writing recommended) required
- 38% graduate within 6 years; 17% enter graduate study

**General.** Founded in 1893. Regionally accredited. **Degrees:** 256 bachelor's, 87 associate awarded; master's offered. **Location:** 82 miles from Bozeman, 65 miles from Helena. **Calendar:** Semester, extensive summer session. **Full-time faculty:** 127 total; 57% have terminal degrees, 9% minority, 35% women. **Part-time faculty:** 74 total; 5% minority, 43% women. **Class size:** 59% < 20, 25% 20-39, 5% 40-49, 10% 50-99, less than 1% >100. **Special facilities:** Mineral museum, earthquake studies office.

**Freshman class profile.** 821 applied, 746 admitted, 490 enrolled.

Mid 50% test scores
| | | | |
|---|---|---|---|
| SAT critical reading: | 450-580 | GPA 3.0-3.49: | 33% |
| SAT math: | 490-620 | GPA 2.0-2.99: | 21% |
| SAT writing: | 430-540 | Rank in top quarter: | 47% |
| ACT composite: | 21-26 | Rank in top tenth: | 14% |
| GPA 3.75 or higher: | 28% | Out-of-state: | 11% |
| GPA 3.50-3.74: | 17% | Live on campus: | 43% |
| | | International: | 2% |

**Basis for selection.** Rank in top half of graduating class, or graduate with minimum cumulative GPA of 2.5, or achieve minimum composite score on ACT of 22, or minimum total score on SAT of 1530; meet math and English standards, and complete preparatory requirements.

**High school preparation.** College-preparatory program required. Required and recommended units include English 4, mathematics 3-4, social studies 3, history 3, science 2 (laboratory 2). Combined 3 years of foreign language, visual and performing arts, computer science, or vocational education required.

**2009-2010 Annual costs.** Tuition/fees: $5,872; $16,149 out-of-state. Room/board: $6,602. Books/supplies: $1,000. Personal expenses: $1,600.

**2008-2009 Financial aid.** Non-need-based: Scholarships awarded for academics, alumni affiliation, athletics, minority status, state residency.

**Application procedures.** Admission: No deadline. $30 fee. Admission notification on a rolling basis. **Financial aid:** Priority date 3/1; no closing date. FAFSA, institutional form required. Applicants notified on a rolling basis starting 4/1; must reply within 2 week(s) of notification.

**Academics.** Special study options: Combined bachelor's/graduate degree, cooperative education, cross-registration, distance learning, double major, dual enrollment of high school students, external degree, honors, independent study, internships, teacher certification program. 3-2 liberal arts-engineering program with Carroll College, dual enrollment agreement with Flathead Valley Community College, collaborative programs with UM Helena (BAS Business, BS BIT, BAS General Studies), UM Western (Elementary Education Certification and Secondary Education Certification in Biological Sciences, General Sciences, and Mathematical Sciences), and UM-COT (AAS Surgical Technology). **Credit/placement by examination:** AP, CLEP, IB, SAT, ACT, institutional tests. 10 credit hours maximum toward associate degree, 30 toward bachelor's. **Support services:** Learning center, pre-admission summer program, reduced course load, study skills assistance, tutoring.

**Majors.** Biology: General. **Business:** General. **Computer sciences:** Computer science, networking. **Engineering:** General, electrical, environmental, geological, metallurgical, mining, petroleum, software. **Health:** Medical informatics, nursing (RN), occupational health. **Liberal arts:** Arts/sciences. **Math:** General. **Physical sciences:** General, chemistry. **Other:** Business information technology.

**Most popular majors.** Business/marketing 13%, engineering/engineering technologies 59%, health sciences 10%.

**Computing on campus.** 491 workstations in dormitories, library, computer center, student center. Dormitories wired for high-speed internet access and linked to campus network. Commuter students can connect to campus network. Online course registration, online library, helpline, repair service, student web hosting, wireless network available.

**Student life. Freshman orientation:** Mandatory. Preregistration for classes offered. Held several days before semester start. **Housing:** Guaranteed on-campus for freshmen. Coed dorms, special housing for disabled, apartments available. $100 fully refundable deposit. **Activities:** Pep band, campus ministries, international student organizations, radio station, student government, student newspaper, Baptist student union, Circle-K, Baha'i club, Prospectors, American Indian Science and Engineering Society, Students in Engineering Programs, Newman Club.

**Athletics.** NAIA. **Intercollegiate:** Basketball, football (tackle) M, golf, volleyball W. **Intramural:** Basketball, football (non-tackle), racquetball, softball, volleyball. **Team name:** Orediggers.

**Student services.** Adult student services, alcohol/substance abuse counseling, chaplain/spiritual director, career counseling, student employment services, financial aid counseling, health services, minority student services, personal counseling, placement for graduates, veterans' counselor, women's services. **Physically disabled:** Services for visually, hearing impaired.

**Contact.** E-mail: enrollment@mtech.edu
Phone: (406) 496-4256 Toll-free number: (800) 445-8324
Fax: (406) 496-4710
Tony Campeau, Director of Enrollment Management, Montana Tech of the University of Montana, 1300 West Park Street, Butte, MT 59701-8997

## Rocky Mountain College
**Billings, Montana**
www.rocky.edu
CB code: 4660

- Private 4-year liberal arts college affiliated with United Church of Christ, United Methodist Church, United Presbyterian Church
- Commuter campus in small city

---

- 811 degree-seeking undergraduates: 4% part-time, 50% women, 2% African American, 1% Asian American, 3% Hispanic American, 4% Native American, 5% international
- 66 degree-seeking graduate students
- 63% of applicants admitted
- SAT or ACT (ACT writing optional) required
- 47% graduate within 6 years; 22% enter graduate study

**General.** Founded in 1878. Regionally accredited. **Degrees:** 180 bachelor's awarded; master's offered. **ROTC:** Army. **Calendar:** Semester, limited summer session. **Full-time faculty:** 65 total; 69% have terminal degrees, 2% minority, 43% women. **Part-time faculty:** 37 total; 11% have terminal degrees, 40% women. **Class size:** 71% < 20, 20% 20-39, 3% 40-49, 3% 50-99, 2% >100. **Special facilities:** Outdoor recreation center, flight school, equestrian facilities, geology library, rock climbing wall.

**Freshman class profile.** 927 applied, 587 admitted, 234 enrolled.

| Mid 50% test scores | | | |
|---|---|---|---|
| SAT critical reading: | 440-450 | GPA 3.0-3.49: | 33% |
| SAT math: | 450-550 | GPA 2.0-2.99: | 25% |
| SAT writing: | 410-550 | End year in good standing: | 85% |
| ACT composite: | 20-26 | Return as sophomores: | 60% |
| GPA 3.75 or higher: | 22% | Out-of-state: | 39% |
| GPA 3.50-3.74: | 20% | Live on campus: | 80% |
| | | International: | 7% |

**Basis for selection.** 2.5 GPA, ACT 21 or combined critical reading/math SAT of 1000 meets requirement for regular admission. Essay recommended for all students. Interview recommended for students not meeting regular admission requirements. Audition recommended for music, theater students. Portfolio recommended for art students. **Homeschooled:** Applicants must either have GED or pass ACT based on college entrance standards.

**High school preparation.** College-preparatory program recommended. 19 units required. Required units include English 4, mathematics 4, social studies 3, history 2, science 3 and academic electives 3.

**2010-2011 Annual costs.** Tuition/fees (projected): $21,100. Room/board: $6,580. Books/supplies: $1,200. Personal expenses: $1,400.

**2008-2009 Financial aid.** Non-need-based: Scholarships awarded for academics, alumni affiliation, art, athletics, leadership, minority status, music/drama, religious affiliation, state residency.

**Application procedures.** Admission: No deadline. $35 fee, may be waived for applicants with need, free for online applicants. Admission notification on a rolling basis. **Financial aid:** Priority date 3/1; no closing date. FAFSA, institutional form required. Applicants notified on a rolling basis starting 2/1; must reply within 4 week(s) of notification.

**Academics.** Special study options: Accelerated study, combined bachelor's/graduate degree, distance learning, double major, dual enrollment of high school students, ESL, honors, independent study, internships, student-designed major, study abroad, teacher certification program. **Credit/placement by examination:** AP, CLEP, IB, SAT, ACT, institutional tests. 15 credit hours maximum toward associate degree, 31 toward bachelor's. **Support services:** Learning center, reduced course load, remedial instruction, study skills assistance, tutoring.

**Majors.** Agriculture: Business, equestrian studies. **Biology:** General. **Business:** Accounting, accounting/business management, business admin, management information systems, management science. **Communications:** General. **Computer sciences:** Computer science. **Conservation:** Environmental science, environmental studies. **Education:** General, art, biology, drama/dance, elementary, English, history, mathematics, middle, multi-level teacher, music, physical, secondary, social studies. **Health:** Athletic training. **History:** General. **Math:** General. **Parks/recreation:** Exercise sciences, health/fitness, sports admin. **Physical sciences:** Chemistry, geology. **Psychology:** General. **Social sciences:** Economics, political science, sociology. **Transportation:** Airline/commercial pilot, aviation management. **Visual/performing arts:** Art, dramatic, music performance, theater design. **Other:** Philosophy and religious thought.

**Most popular majors.** Biology 7%, business/marketing 35%, education 15%, parks/recreation 7%, trade and industry 10%.

**Computing on campus.** 129 workstations in dormitories, library, computer center, student center. Dormitories wired for high-speed internet access and linked to campus network. Commuter students can connect to campus network. Online course registration, online library, helpline, student web hosting, wireless network available.

**Student life. Freshman orientation:** Mandatory. Preregistration for classes offered. Held during the 4 days before classes start; includes mountain getaway trip. **Housing:** Guaranteed on-campus for freshmen. Coed dorms, special housing for disabled, apartments available. $250 fully refundable deposit. Suites available. **Activities:** Bands, choral groups, drama, international student organizations, musical theater, student government, student newspaper, symphony orchestra, Pi Kappa Delta-National Honorary Forensics Fraternity, Alpha Eta Rho National Aviation Fraternity Ambassador's club, American Indian cultural association, American Indian science and engineering society, investing club, Intervarsity Christian Fellowship, geology club, equestrian club, ski club, Newman club.

**Athletics.** NAIA. **Intercollegiate:** Basketball, cheerleading M, cross-country, equestrian, football (tackle) M, golf, skiing, soccer, volleyball W. **Intramural:** Basketball, football (tackle) M, golf, handball, racquetball, skiing, soccer, softball, swimming, table tennis, tennis, volleyball. **Team name:** Battlin' Bears.

**Student services.** Adult student services, alcohol/substance abuse counseling, chaplain/spiritual director, career counseling, student employment services, financial aid counseling, health services, on-campus daycare, personal counseling, placement for graduates. **Physically disabled:** Services for visually, speech, hearing impaired.

**Contact.** E-mail: admissions@rocky.edu
Phone: (406) 657-1026 Toll-free number: (800) 877-6259
Fax: (406) 657-1189
Kelly Edwards, Director of Admissions, Rocky Mountain College, 1511 Poly Drive, Billings, MT 59102-1796

## Salish Kootenai College
### Pablo, Montana
### www.skc.edu
### CB code: 0898

- Private 4-year liberal arts college
- Commuter campus in rural community
- 1,090 degree-seeking undergraduates

**General.** Founded in 1977. Regionally accredited. Native American cultural heritage. **Degrees:** 35 bachelor's, 61 associate awarded. **Location:** 55 miles from Missoula, 65 miles from Kalispell. **Calendar:** Quarter, limited summer session. **Full-time faculty:** 74 total. **Part-time faculty:** 38 total.

**Freshman class profile.** 370 applied, 370 admitted, 135 enrolled.

**Basis for selection.** Open admission, but selective for some programs. Special requirements for highway construction worker training, social work, dental assisting technology and nursing. Highway construction worker training program has special application which includes drug testing. Third-year applicants to social work program must complete special application which includes background check. Dental assisting technology and nursing also require special applications.

**2009-2010 Annual costs.** Full-time tuition for Native American students, $2,844 ($79 per credit hour); full-time tuition for students of Native American descent, $3,492 ($97 per credit hour). Academic year required fees, $1,071. Books/supplies: $1,050. Personal expenses: $2,000.

**Application procedures. Admission:** Priority date 7/1; no deadline. No application fee. Application must be submitted on paper. Admission notification on a rolling basis. **Financial aid:** Priority date 3/31; no closing date. FAFSA required. Applicants notified on a rolling basis starting 7/15; must reply within 6 week(s) of notification.

**Academics. Special study options:** Combined bachelor's/graduate degree, cooperative education, distance learning, double major, dual enrollment of high school students, independent study, internships. **Credit/placement by examination:** CLEP, institutional tests. **Support services:** Learning center, remedial instruction, study skills assistance, tutoring, writing center.

**Majors. Business:** Administrative services. **Computer sciences:** General. **Conservation:** General. **Health:** Nursing (RN). **Public administration:** Social work.

**Most popular majors.** Business/marketing 16%, computer/information sciences 8%, health sciences 20%, natural resources/environmental science 12%, public administration/social services 44%.

**Computing on campus.** 42 workstations in library, computer center, student center. Dormitories wired for high-speed internet access. Online course registration, online library, helpline, wireless network available.

**Student life. Freshman orientation:** Mandatory. Preregistration for classes offered. Held prior to registration day; one-half to one-day session. **Housing:** Special housing for disabled, apartments available. Housing costs based on income. **Activities:** Student government, student newspaper, TV station.

**Athletics. Intercollegiate:** Basketball. **Intramural:** Basketball, skiing, softball, volleyball. **Team name:** Bison.

**Student services.** Career counseling, student employment services, on-campus daycare, personal counseling, placement for graduates, veterans' counselor. **Physically disabled:** Services for visually, speech, hearing impaired.

**Contact.** E-mail: jackie_moran@skc.edu
Phone: (406) 275-4866 Fax: (406) 275-4810
Jackie Moran, Admissions, Salish Kootenai College, PO Box 70, Pablo, MT 59855

## University of Great Falls
### Great Falls, Montana
### www.ugf.edu
### CB code: 4058

- Private 4-year university and liberal arts college affiliated with Roman Catholic Church
- Residential campus in small city
- 775 degree-seeking undergraduates: 24% part-time, 63% women, 4% African American, 1% Asian American, 5% Hispanic American, 4% Native American, 2% international
- 75 degree-seeking graduate students
- 31% of applicants admitted
- Application essay required

**General.** Founded in 1932. Regionally accredited. **Degrees:** 171 bachelor's, 8 associate awarded; master's offered. **Location:** 600 miles from Seattle, 370 miles from Spokane, Washington. **Calendar:** Semester, limited summer session. **Full-time faculty:** 41 total; 80% have terminal degrees, 2% minority, 56% women. **Part-time faculty:** 72 total; 15% have terminal degrees, 4% minority, 56% women. **Class size:** 79% < 20, 21% 20-39. **Special facilities:** Herbarium.

**Freshman class profile.** 516 applied, 160 admitted, 146 enrolled.

| Mid 50% test scores | | | |
|---|---|---|---|
| SAT critical reading: | 440-520 | GPA 3.0-3.49: | 27% |
| SAT math: | 440-520 | GPA 2.0-2.99: | 34% |
| ACT composite: | 18-22 | Return as sophomores: | 57% |
| GPA 3.75 or higher: | 18% | Out-of-state: | 42% |
| GPA 3.50-3.74: | 20% | Live on campus: | 90% |
| | | International: | 2% |

**Basis for selection.** High school record and character most important. ACT/SAT scores may be considered when making scholarship decisions. SAT or ACT, SAT Subject Tests recommended. Interview recommended. **Homeschooled:** Transcript of courses and grades required. Applicants should submit SAT/ACT test scores, bibliography of school literature and essay describing and evaluating preparation for university-level work.

**High school preparation.** 20 units required; 22 recommended. Required and recommended units include English 4, mathematics 3, social studies 1-2, history 3, science 3 (laboratory 1) and academic electives 5.

**2009-2010 Annual costs.** Tuition/fees: $18,212. Room/board: $6,610. Books/supplies: $800. Personal expenses: $750.

**2009-2010 Financial aid. Need-based:** Average need met was 64%. Average scholarship/grant was $4,919; average loan $3,405. 62% of total undergraduate aid awarded as scholarships/grants, 38% as loans/jobs. **Non-need-based:** Scholarships awarded for academics, art, athletics, religious affiliation.

**Application procedures. Admission:** Priority date 5/1; deadline 9/1 (postmark date). $35 fee, may be waived for applicants with need. Admission notification on a rolling basis beginning on or about 10/1. Must reply by May 1 or within 2 week(s) if notified thereafter. Admission granted with 6th semester transcripts. **Financial aid:** Priority date 5/1; no closing date. FAFSA required. Applicants notified on a rolling basis starting 3/1; must reply within 2 week(s) of notification.

**Academics.** Trio Title IV Student Support Services program available to eligible students. **Special study options:** Combined bachelor's/graduate degree, cooperative education, distance learning, double major, dual enrollment of high school students, exchange student, honors, independent study, internships, liberal arts/career combination, study abroad, teacher certification program, weekend college. **Credit/placement by examination:** AP, CLEP, IB, SAT, ACT, institutional tests. 30 credit hours maximum toward associate degree, 30 toward bachelor's. **Support services:** Learning center, pre-admission summer program, reduced course load, remedial instruction, study skills assistance, tutoring, writing center.

**Majors. Biology:** General, botany. **Business:** Accounting, accounting/business management, business admin. **Computer sciences:** General, applications programming, computer graphics, computer science, data processing, LAN/WAN management, networking, programming, security, system

Four-Year Colleges

admin, systems analysis. **Education:** Art, biology, chemistry, early childhood, elementary, English, gifted/talented, health, history, kindergarten/preschool, mathematics, middle, physical, psychology, reading, science, secondary, social science, social studies, special. **Health:** Predental, premedicine, preveterinary, substance abuse counseling. **History:** General. **Legal studies:** Paralegal. **Math:** General. **Parks/recreation:** Health/fitness. **Philosophy/religion:** Religion. **Physical sciences:** Chemistry. **Protective services:** Corrections, criminal justice, forensics, juvenile corrections, police science. **Psychology:** General. **Social sciences:** General, political science, sociology. **Visual/performing arts:** Art. **Other:** Health and human performance.

**Most popular majors.** Business/marketing 16%, education 31%, psychology 16%, security/protective services 10%.

**Computing on campus.** 120 workstations in dormitories, library, computer center, student center. Dormitories wired for high-speed internet access and linked to campus network. Commuter students can connect to campus network. Online course registration, online library, helpline, repair service, student web hosting, wireless network available.

**Student life. Freshman orientation:** Mandatory, $75 fee. Preregistration for classes offered. Programs held 3 days prior to fall and spring semesters; includes float trip down Missouri River. **Policies:** No drugs, alcohol, firearms or weapons allowed on campus. **Housing:** Guaranteed on-campus for freshmen. Coed dorms, apartments, wellness housing available. $150 fully refundable deposit, deadline 8/15. **Activities:** Bands, campus ministries, choral groups, dance, drama, film society, music ensembles, musical theater, student government, student newspaper, symphony orchestra, United Tribes Club, Americorps, drama club, art club, Students In Free Enterprise, international law and justice club, medical science club, student Montana education association, paralegal club.

**Athletics.** NAIA. **Intercollegiate:** Basketball, cross-country, golf, soccer W, softball W, volleyball W, wrestling M. **Intramural:** Baseball, basketball, bowling, cheerleading, football (non-tackle), softball, tennis, volleyball. **Team name:** Argonauts.

**Student services.** Adult student services, alcohol/substance abuse counseling, chaplain/spiritual director, career counseling, services for economically disadvantaged, student employment services, financial aid counseling, health services, minority student services, on-campus daycare, personal counseling, placement for graduates, veterans' counselor, women's services. **Physically disabled:** Services for visually, hearing impaired.

**Contact.** E-mail: enroll@ugf.edu
Phone: (406) 791-5200 Toll-free number: (800) 856-9544
Fax: (406) 791-5209
April Clutter, Assistant Director of Admissions, University of Great Falls, 1301 20th Street South, Great Falls, MT 59405

---

## University of Montana
**Missoula, Montana**                      **CB member**
**www.umt.edu**                            **CB code: 4489**

♦ Public 4-year university and liberal arts college
♦ Residential campus in small city
♦ 12,673 degree-seeking undergraduates
♦ 83% of applicants admitted
♦ SAT or ACT (ACT writing recommended) required

**General.** Founded in 1893. Regionally accredited. Two-year technical college provides technical training, education and postsecondary academic preparation through general associate programs. **Degrees:** 1,759 bachelor's, 247 associate awarded; master's, doctoral, professional offered. **ROTC:** Army. **Location:** 210 miles from Spokane, Washington. **Calendar:** Semester, extensive summer session. **Full-time faculty:** 564 total. **Part-time faculty:** 236 total. **Class size:** 45% <20, 36% 20-39, 6% 40-49, 8% 50-99, 5% >100. **Special facilities:** Broadcast media center (public radio and TV) and performing arts building; 3 art galleries; wildlife biology museum; 29,000-acre experimental forest; biological research station; geology field camp; biological, biomedical, kinesiology, physiology, and forestry-related research centers and labs; environmental studies laboratory; primate colony; forensics lab; clinical psychology center; practical ethics center; Fort Missoula field research center.

**Freshman class profile.** 4,670 applied, 3,884 admitted, 1,886 enrolled.

| Mid 50% test scores | | Out-of-state: | 27% |
|---|---|---|---|
| SAT critical reading: | 480-580 | Live on campus: | 69% |
| SAT math: | 480-590 | Fraternities: | 6% |
| SAT writing: | 450-580 | Sororities: | 5% |
| ACT composite: | 20-26 | | |

**Basis for selection.** Must meet one of the following: 2.5 GPA, 22 ACT, 1540 SAT, or rank in top half of graduating class. TOEFL or Michigan Test and statement of intent and personal contribution required for international students. SAT/ACT not required for nontraditional students or international students.

**High school preparation.** Required and recommended units include English 4, mathematics 3, social studies 3, history 1-2, science 2 (laboratory 2), foreign language 2 and academic electives 2. Computer science, visual and performing arts, and/or vocational education.

**2009-2010 Annual costs.** Tuition/fees: $5,330; $17,763 out-of-state. Room/board: $6,611. Books/supplies: $850. Personal expenses: $3,700.

**2009-2010 Financial aid. Non-need-based:** Scholarships awarded for academics, art, athletics, leadership, music/drama, ROTC, state residency.

**Application procedures. Admission:** Priority date 3/1; no deadline. $30 fee. Admission notification on a rolling basis beginning on or about 9/15. **Financial aid:** Priority date 2/15; no closing date. FAFSA, institutional form, CSS PROFILE required. Applicants notified on a rolling basis starting 4/1; must reply by 8/1 or within 4 week(s) of notification.

**Academics. Special study options:** Combined bachelor's/graduate degree, cooperative education, cross-registration, distance learning, double major, ESL, exchange student, honors, independent study, internships, study abroad, teacher certification program. English language institute, combined programs with other institutions for bachelor in nursing and master in public administration with Montana State University-Bozeman. **Credit/placement by examination:** CLEP, institutional tests. 10 credit hours maximum toward associate degree. Credit hours awarded determined by academic department. **Support services:** Learning center, pre-admission summer program, reduced course load, remedial instruction, study skills assistance, tutoring, writing center.

**Majors. Architecture:** Urban/community planning. **Area/ethnic studies:** Asian, Native American, women's. **Biology:** General, bacteriology, botany, cellular/molecular, zoology. **Business:** General, business admin, finance, international, management information systems, marketing. **Communications:** General, broadcast journalism, journalism. **Computer sciences:** Computer science. **Conservation:** General, forestry, wildlife. **Education:** General, art, biology, business, elementary, English, mathematics, music, physical, secondary. **Foreign languages:** Classics, French, German, Japanese, Latin, Russian, Spanish. **Health:** Athletic training, clinical lab science. **History:** General. **Interdisciplinary:** Math/computer science. **Liberal arts:** Arts/sciences. **Math:** General. **Parks/recreation:** Exercise sciences, facilities management, health/fitness. **Philosophy/religion:** Philosophy. **Physical sciences:** Chemistry, geology, physics. **Psychology:** General. **Public administration:** Social work. **Social sciences:** Anthropology, cartography, criminology, economics, geography, international relations, political science, sociology. **Visual/performing arts:** General, art, art history/conservation, dance, dramatic, music performance, music theory/composition.

**Computing on campus.** 1,800 workstations in dormitories, library, computer center, student center. Dormitories wired for high-speed internet access and linked to campus network. Commuter students can connect to campus network. Online course registration, online library, helpline, repair service, wireless network available.

**Student life. Freshman orientation:** Mandatory, $45 fee. Preregistration for classes offered. Three-day summer session which includes parent track. **Housing:** Guaranteed on-campus for freshmen. Coed dorms, single-sex dorms, special housing for disabled, apartments, fraternity/sorority housing available. $120 deposit, deadline 3/1. Honors floors, international floors, quiet floors, activity dorms, personal development housing available. **Activities:** Bands, choral groups, dance, drama, literary magazine, music ensembles, musical theater, opera, radio station, student government, student newspaper, symphony orchestra, TV station, Associated Students of University of Montana, University of Montana Advocates, Mortar Board, Spurs, Circle-K, forestry student association, honors student association, Kyi-Yo (Native American organization), environmental action club, American Indian Business Leaders.

**Athletics.** NCAA. **Intercollegiate:** Basketball, cheerleading, cross-country, football (tackle) M, golf W, rodeo, soccer W, tennis, track and field, volleyball W. **Intramural:** Badminton, baseball M, basketball, football (tackle), golf, handball, racquetball, soccer, softball, swimming, table tennis, tennis, track and field, triathlon, volleyball. **Team name:** Grizzlies.

**Student services.** Adult student services, alcohol/substance abuse counseling, chaplain/spiritual director, career counseling, services for economically disadvantaged, student employment services, financial aid counseling, health services, legal services, minority student services, on-campus daycare, personal counseling, placement for graduates, veterans' counselor, women's services. **Physically disabled:** Services for visually, speech, hearing impaired.

**Contact.** E-mail: admiss@umontana.edu
Phone: (406) 243-6266 Toll-free number: (800) 462-8636
Fax: (406) 243-5711
Jed Liston, Assistant Vice President for Enrollment Services, University of Montana, Lommasson Center 103, Missoula, MT 59812

## University of Montana: Western
**Dillon, Montana**     CB member
www.umwestern.edu     CB code: 4945

- Public 4-year liberal arts and teachers college
- Residential campus in small town
- 1,207 degree-seeking undergraduates: 15% part-time, 55% women
- 38% graduate within 6 years; 15% enter graduate study

**General.** Founded in 1893. Regionally accredited. **Degrees:** 128 bachelor's, 30 associate awarded. **Location:** 65 miles from Butte, 145 miles from Idaho Falls. **Calendar:** Semester, extensive summer session. **Full-time faculty:** 61 total; 75% have terminal degrees, 48% women. **Part-time faculty:** 28 total; 25% have terminal degrees, 46% women. **Special facilities:** Outdoor education center, wildlife exhibit, office simulation center, public gallery, affiliation with La Cense, Montana Ranch.

**Freshman class profile.** 477 applied, 334 admitted, 240 enrolled.

| Mid 50% test scores | | | |
|---|---|---|---|
| SAT critical reading: | 400-540 | GPA 2.0-2.99: | 49% |
| SAT math: | 400-550 | Rank in top quarter: | 19% |
| ACT composite: | 17-22 | Rank in top tenth: | 6% |
| GPA 3.75 or higher: | 8% | End year in good standing: | 93% |
| GPA 3.50-3.74: | 11% | Return as sophomores: | 74% |
| GPA 3.0-3.49: | 28% | Out-of-state: | 27% |
| | | Live on campus: | 99% |

**Basis for selection.** Open admission, but selective for some programs. **Homeschooled:** State high school equivalency certificate required.

**High school preparation.** College-preparatory program required. 16 units recommended. Recommended units include English 4, mathematics 3, social studies 3, science 3 (laboratory 3) and academic electives 2. Vocational education, computer education, foreign language, visual or performing arts recommended.

**2009-2010 Annual costs.** Tuition/fees: $3,689; $12,745 out-of-state. Room/board: $5,510. Books/supplies: $750. Personal expenses: $2,000.

**2008-2009 Financial aid. Need-based:** Average need met was 16%. Average scholarship/grant was $2,494; average loan $3,589. 43% of total undergraduate aid awarded as scholarships/grants, 57% as loans/jobs. **Non-need-based:** Awarded to 526 full-time undergraduates, including 201 freshmen. Scholarships awarded for academics, alumni affiliation, art, athletics, leadership, minority status, state residency. **Additional information:** Tuition and/or fee waivers for veterans, American Indian, senior citizens, and dependents of Montana University System employees.

**Application procedures. Admission:** Priority date 7/1; no deadline. $30 fee. Admission notification on a rolling basis. **Financial aid:** Priority date 3/1; no closing date. FAFSA, institutional form required. Applicants notified on a rolling basis starting 4/1; must reply within 4 week(s) of notification.

**Academics.** Montana Western offers classes in a block scheduling system. All students take 1 course at a time in 3-1/2 week blocks (18 days). Blocks end with final exam and are followed by 4 day break prior to next block. 4 blocks per semester; most classes are 4 credits. **Special study options:** Cooperative education, distance learning, double major, dual enrollment of high school students, honors, independent study, internships, liberal arts/career combination, teacher certification program. **Credit/placement by examination:** AP, CLEP, institutional tests. 30 credit hours maximum toward associate degree, 30 toward bachelor's. **Support services:** Learning center, reduced course load, remedial instruction, study skills assistance, tutoring.

**Majors. Agriculture:** Equestrian studies. **Area/ethnic studies:** Women's. **Biology:** General, cellular/molecular, wildlife. **Business:** General, business admin, office management, small business admin, tourism/travel. **Communications:** General. **Computer sciences:** Networking. **Conservation:** General, environmental science, wildlife. **Education:** General, art, biology, business, chemistry, early childhood, elementary, English, health, history, mathematics, multi-level teacher, music, physical, school librarian, science, secondary, social studies, technology/industrial arts. **History:** General. **Legal studies:** Prelaw. **Liberal arts:** Arts/sciences. **Math:** General, applied. **Physical sciences:** Chemistry, geology. **Psychology:** General. **Social sciences:** General, anthropology, political science, sociology. **Visual/performing arts:** General, art, dramatic, illustration, studio arts. **Other:**

Biological mathematics, Environmental interpretation, Health and human performance, Industrial technology, Natural horsemanship, Restorative justice.

**Most popular majors.** Business/marketing 21%, education 44%, liberal arts 38%.

**Computing on campus.** 140 workstations in dormitories, library, computer center. Dormitories linked to campus network. Commuter students can connect to campus network. Online course registration, wireless network available.

**Student life. Freshman orientation:** Mandatory, $60 fee. Preregistration for classes offered. **Housing:** Guaranteed on-campus for freshmen. Coed dorms, single-sex dorms, special housing for disabled, apartments, wellness housing available. $100 fully refundable deposit. Students with fewer than 30 credits not living with family required to live in dormitory. Transfer students under 21 with fewer than 30 credits not living with parents required to live on campus. **Activities:** Campus ministries, choral groups, drama, literary magazine, music ensembles, radio station, student government, student newspaper, admissions ambassadors, Chi Alpha-Christian fellowship, outdoor club, Polynesian club, rodeo club, IT club, academic clubs.

**Athletics.** NAIA. **Intercollegiate:** Basketball, equestrian, football (tackle) M, golf, rodeo, volleyball W. **Intramural:** Basketball, golf, racquetball, skiing, soccer, softball, volleyball. **Team name:** Bulldogs, Lady Bulldogs.

**Student services.** Alcohol/substance abuse counseling, career counseling, student employment services, financial aid counseling, legal services, on-campus daycare, personal counseling, placement for graduates, veterans' counselor. **Physically disabled:** Services for visually, speech, hearing impaired.

**Contact.** E-mail: admissions@umwestern.edu
Phone: (406) 683-7331 Toll-free number: (877) 683-7331
Fax: (406) 683-7493
Catherine Redhead, Director of Admissions, University of Montana: Western, 710 South Atlantic Street, Dillon, MT 59725

# Nebraska

## Bellevue University
**Bellevue, Nebraska**
**www.bellevue.edu**

CB code: 6053

- Private 4-year university and business college
- Commuter campus in large city
- 6,194 degree-seeking undergraduates: 42% part-time, 48% women, 12% African American, 2% Asian American, 8% Hispanic American, 1% Native American, 5% international
- 2,638 degree-seeking graduate students

**General.** Founded in 1965. Regionally accredited. Satellite operations throughout a five-state area in the Midwest. Focus on adult learners, non-traditional students and customized programs for organizations and corporations. **Degrees:** 1,840 bachelor's awarded; master's, doctoral offered. **ROTC:** Army, Air Force. **Calendar:** Continuous, extensive summer session. **Full-time faculty:** 87 total; 59% have terminal degrees, 12% minority, 45% women. **Part-time faculty:** 176 total; 44% have terminal degrees, 7% minority, 42% women.

**Basis for selection.** Open admission, but selective for some programs. Students dismissed from another institution for academic or disciplinary reasons will be accepted for admission after 1 year has lapsed since dismissal from that institution. Admission to Professional Studies program requires roughly 60 transfer credit hours from accredited institution. Michigan English Language Assessment Battery used for placement after arrival. IELT also accepted. **Homeschooled:** Students should submit official verification of completion.

**High school preparation.** Recommended units include English 3, mathematics 3, social studies 3, history 3, science 3 (laboratory 1), foreign language 3 and academic electives 3.

**2010-2011 Annual costs.** Tuition/fees (projected): $7,050. Books/supplies: $1,500. Personal expenses: $1,845.

**2008-2009 Financial aid. Need-based:** Average scholarship/grant was $2,459; average loan $3,010. 10% of total undergraduate aid awarded as scholarships/grants, 90% as loans/jobs. **Non-need-based:** Scholarships awarded for academics, athletics, leadership.

**Application procedures. Admission:** No deadline. $50 fee, may be waived for applicants with need. Admission notification on a rolling basis. **Financial aid:** Priority date 4/15; no closing date. FAFSA, institutional form required. Applicants notified on a rolling basis starting 4/15; must reply within 2 week(s) of notification.

**Academics. Special study options:** Accelerated study, cross-registration, distance learning, double major, dual enrollment of high school students, ESL, independent study, internships, liberal arts/career combination, weekend college. **Credit/placement by examination:** AP, CLEP, IB, institutional tests. Offer 12 computer proficiency exams, each worth 1 credit. Maximum of 12 credits allowed. **Support services:** Learning center, remedial instruction, study skills assistance, tutoring, writing center.

**Majors. Biology:** General. **Business:** General, accounting, business admin, e-commerce, human resources, management information systems, marketing. **Communications:** General. **Computer sciences:** General, information systems, information technology, web page design. **Education:** Physical. **Health:** Health care admin, premedicine, substance abuse counseling. **History:** General. **Legal studies:** Prelaw. **Liberal arts:** Arts/sciences. **Parks/recreation:** Sports admin. **Protective services:** Law enforcement admin. **Psychology:** General. **Public administration:** General, human services. **Social sciences:** General, sociology. **Visual/performing arts:** Art, art history/conservation, arts management, commercial/advertising art, studio arts.

**Most popular majors.** Business/marketing 37%, computer/information sciences 9%, security/protective services 8%, social sciences 12%, visual/performing arts 6%.

**Computing on campus.** 600 workstations in library, computer center. Commuter students can connect to campus network. Online course registration, online library, helpline, wireless network available.

**Student life. Freshman orientation:** Available. Preregistration for classes offered. 2-day programs held the beginning week of fall, winter and spring

semesters. **Policies:** No alcohol at any student events. Any event must be coordinated through the Student Activities Office. **Activities:** Student government, Alpha Chi, Campus Crusade for Christ, computer graphic design club, Delta Epsilon Chi, economics club, institute of management accountants, multicultural student organization, student advisory council, toastmasters, chapter of Student Veterans Association.

**Athletics.** NAIA. **Intercollegiate:** Baseball M, basketball M, soccer, softball W, volleyball W. **Team name:** Bruins.

**Student services.** Career counseling, student employment services, financial aid counseling, personal counseling, placement for graduates, veterans' counselor. **Physically disabled:** Services for visually, speech, hearing impaired.

**Contact.** E-mail: info@bellevue.edu
Phone: (402) 293-2000 Toll-free number: (800) 756-7920
Fax: (402) 557-7230
Nick Baker, Director, Undergraduate Admissions, Bellevue University, 1000 Galvin Road South, Bellevue, NE 68005-3098

## BryanLGH College of Health Sciences
**Lincoln, Nebraska**
**www.bryanlghcollege.edu**

- Private 4-year health science college
- Commuter campus in large city
- 449 degree-seeking undergraduates: 43% part-time, 92% women
- 33 degree-seeking graduate students
- 85% of applicants admitted
- SAT or ACT (ACT writing optional), application essay, interview required

**General.** Regionally accredited. **Degrees:** 57 bachelor's, 15 associate awarded; master's offered. **ROTC:** Army, Naval. **Calendar:** Semester, limited summer session. **Full-time faculty:** 32 total; 9% have terminal degrees, 3% minority, 97% women. **Part-time faculty:** 31 total; 16% have terminal degrees, 13% minority, 77% women. **Class size:** 65% < 20, 26% 20-39, 3% 40-49, 6% 50-99. **Special facilities:** William Jennings Bryan home and museum, health system facilities, patient simulators, plastinates.

**Freshman class profile.** 39 applied, 33 admitted, 27 enrolled.

| Mid 50% test scores | | | |
|---|---|---|---|
| ACT composite: | 21-24 | GPA 3.0-3.49: | 26% |
| GPA 3.75 or higher: | 44% | End year in good standing: | 96% |
| GPA 3.50-3.74: | 30% | Return as sophomores: | 96% |
| | | Out-of-state: | 3% |

**Basis for selection.** Applicants are reviewed by a faculty admissions committee. Students scoring above a certain rubric level are admitted. **Homeschooled:** Transcript of courses and grades required.

**High school preparation.** College-preparatory program recommended. 23 units recommended. Recommended units include English 4, mathematics 4, social studies 4, science 4 (laboratory 2), foreign language 4 and computer science 1.

**2009-2010 Annual costs.** Tuition/fees: $11,400. Clinical Fees Nursing: $175/course; Clinical Fees Allied Health: $250/semester; Board Registry Fee estimated: $90/semester (Allied Health); ATI Testing Fee (Nursing): $60/semester. Books/supplies: $1,000. Personal expenses: $3,120.

**2008-2009 Financial aid. Need-based:** 28 full-time freshmen applied for aid; 28 were judged to have need; 28 of these received aid. Average need met was 17%. Average scholarship/grant was $2,160; average loan $3,500. 15% of total undergraduate aid awarded as scholarships/grants, 85% as loans/jobs. **Non-need-based:** Awarded to 112 full-time undergraduates, including 11 freshmen. Scholarships awarded for academics, leadership.

**Application procedures. Admission:** Closing date 2/1 (postmark date). $40 fee, may be waived for applicants with need. Application must be submitted on paper. Admission notification on a rolling basis beginning on or about 3/1. Must reply by May 1 or within 4 week(s) if notified thereafter. **Financial aid:** Closing date 5/1. FAFSA, institutional form required. Applicants notified on a rolling basis starting 5/1; must reply within 3 week(s) of notification.

**Academics. Special study options:** Independent study. **Credit/placement by examination:** AP, CLEP, institutional tests. 1 credit hours maximum toward associate degree, 2 toward bachelor's. **Support services:** Learning center, pre-admission summer program, remedial instruction, study skills assistance, tutoring.

**Majors. Health:** Nursing (RN).

**Computing on campus.** 30 workstations in library, student center. Commuter students can connect to campus network. Online library, helpline, wireless network available.

**Student life. Freshman orientation:** Mandatory. Preregistration for classes offered. Held on-campus the Thursday and Friday before classes begin each term. **Activities:** Student government, Red Cross, Caring with Christ, Action for Students, student nurses association, health promotion organization.

**Student services.** Alcohol/substance abuse counseling, financial aid counseling, health services, personal counseling.

**Contact.** E-mail: admissions@bryanlghcollege.edu
Phone: (402) 481-8697 Toll-free number: (800) 742-7844 ext. 18697
Fax: (402) 481-8697
Sara Malsbury, Director of Enrollment Management, BryanLGH College of Health Sciences, 5035 Everett Street, Lincoln, NE 68506

## Chadron State College
### Chadron, Nebraska
**www.csc.edu**      **CB code: 6466**

- Public 4-year business, liberal arts and teachers college
- Residential campus in small town
- 2,100 degree-seeking undergraduates

**General.** Founded in 1911. Regionally accredited. Limited distance education classes and programs offered online and at Scottsbluff, Alliance, Sidney, and throughout western Nebraska and eastern Wyoming. **Degrees:** 350 bachelor's awarded; master's offered. **ROTC:** Army. **Location:** 100 miles from Scottsbluff. **Calendar:** Semester, limited summer session. **Full-time faculty:** 100 total. **Part-time faculty:** 40 total. **Class size:** 65% < 20, 30% 20-39, 4% 40-49, less than 1% 50-99. **Special facilities:** Planetarium, herbarium, geological museum, high plains heritage center.

### Freshman class profile.

| Mid 50% test scores | | | |
|---|---|---|---|
| ACT composite: | 17-24 | GPA 2.0-2.99: | 28% |
| GPA 3.75 or higher: | 20% | Rank in top quarter: | 26% |
| GPA 3.50-3.74: | 11% | Rank in top tenth: | 11% |
| GPA 3.0-3.49: | 22% | Out-of-state: | 29% |
| | | Live on campus: | 90% |

**Basis for selection.** Open admission, but selective for some programs. Test scores must be submitted for placement, but no minimum score required. Audition recommended for music program.

**High school preparation.** 12 units recommended. Recommended units include English 4, mathematics 3, social studies 3, science 2 (laboratory 2). Units in visual or performing arts, computer literacy, or foreign language recommended.

**2009-2010 Annual costs.** Tuition/fees: $4,831; $8,506 out-of-state. Room/board: $4,888. Books/supplies: $600. Personal expenses: $972.

**Financial aid. Non-need-based:** Scholarships awarded for academics, alumni affiliation, art, athletics, leadership, minority status, music/drama, state residency.

**Application procedures. Admission:** No deadline. $15 fee. Admission notification on a rolling basis. **Financial aid:** Priority date 6/1; no closing date. FAFSA, institutional form required. Applicants notified on a rolling basis starting 4/1; must reply within 2 week(s) of notification.

**Academics. Special study options:** Accelerated study, combined bachelor's/graduate degree, cooperative education, distance learning, double major, dual enrollment of high school students, honors, independent study, internships, student-designed major, study abroad, teacher certification program. **Credit/placement by examination:** AP, CLEP, SAT, ACT, institutional tests. 65 credit hours maximum toward bachelor's degree. **Support services:** Learning center, pre-admission summer program, reduced course load, remedial instruction, study skills assistance, tutoring, writing center.

**Majors. Agriculture:** Range science. **Biology:** General. **Business:** Accounting, business admin, finance, management information systems, management science, office management. **Computer sciences:** Information systems. **Education:** Art, biology, business, chemistry, drama/dance, elementary, English, family/consumer sciences, history, mathematics, middle, music, physical, physics, science, secondary, social science, Spanish, technology/industrial arts, trade/industrial. **Family/consumer sciences:** General. **Foreign languages:** Spanish. **History:** General. **Legal studies:** General, prelaw. **Liberal arts:** Arts/sciences, library science. **Math:** General. **Parks/recreation:** General. **Physical sciences:** Chemistry. **Psychology:** General. **Public administration:** Social work. **Social sciences:** General, sociology. **Visual/performing arts:** Art, dramatic.

**Most popular majors.** Biology 11%, business/marketing 20%, education 27%.

**Computing on campus.** 120 workstations in dormitories, library, computer center, student center. Dormitories wired for high-speed internet access and linked to campus network. Commuter students can connect to campus network. Online course registration, online library, helpline, wireless network available.

**Student life. Freshman orientation:** Available, $50 fee. Preregistration for classes offered. Four or five 2-day weekend orientations held prior to start of fall term. **Housing:** Guaranteed on-campus for freshmen. Coed dorms, single-sex dorms, special housing for disabled, apartments, wellness housing available. $100 deposit, deadline 6/1. **Activities:** Bands, choral groups, dance, drama, international student organizations, music ensembles, musical theater, student government, student newspaper, Circle K, student education association, multicultural club, Intervarsity Christian Fellowship, White Buffalo Club.

**Athletics.** NCAA. **Intercollegiate:** Basketball, football (tackle) M, golf W, track and field, volleyball W, wrestling M. **Intramural:** Archery, badminton, basketball, bowling, golf, racquetball, rugby M, softball, track and field, volleyball, wrestling M. **Team name:** Eagles.

**Student services.** Adult student services, alcohol/substance abuse counseling, career counseling, services for economically disadvantaged, student employment services, financial aid counseling, health services, on-campus daycare, personal counseling, placement for graduates, veterans' counselor. **Physically disabled:** Services for visually, speech, hearing impaired.

**Contact.** E-mail: inquire@csc.edu
Phone: (308) 432-6263 Toll-free number: (800) 242-3766
Fax: (308) 432-6229
Tena Cook, Director of Admissions, Chadron State College, 1000 Main Street, Chadron, NE 69337

## Clarkson College
### Omaha, Nebraska
**www.clarksoncollege.edu**      **CB code: 2250**

- Private 4-year health science college affiliated with Episcopal Church
- Commuter campus in large city
- 750 degree-seeking undergraduates
- Application essay required

**General.** Founded in 1888. Regionally accredited. **Degrees:** 118 bachelor's, 46 associate awarded; master's offered. **ROTC:** Army, Air Force. **Location:** 50 miles from Lincoln. **Calendar:** Semester, extensive summer session. **Full-time faculty:** 45 total. **Part-time faculty:** 55 total. **Class size:** 66% < 20, 30% 20-39, less than 1% 40-49, 3% 50-99. **Special facilities:** Health care clinical facilities for professional education (more than 180 clinical sites), fully energized radiologic technology lab.

**Freshman class profile.** 725 applied, 435 admitted, 244 enrolled.

| Mid 50% test scores | | | |
|---|---|---|---|
| ACT composite: | 19-24 | Out-of-state: | 79% |

**Basis for selection.** Open admission, but selective for some programs. GPA, class rank, test scores, essay important. ACT recommended. **Home-schooled:** Must take GED and submit ACT scores. Essay required. Transcript or portfolio recommended.

**High school preparation.** 9 units required. Required and recommended units include English 3-4, mathematics 2-4, social studies 2-3, history 2, science 2-4 (laboratory 1-2) and foreign language 2.

**2009-2010 Annual costs.** Tuition/fees: $13,530. Room/board: $6,400. Books/supplies: $1,380. Personal expenses: $2,600.

**2008-2009 Financial aid. Non-need-based:** Scholarships awarded for academics, alumni affiliation, minority status, religious affiliation.

**Application procedures. Admission:** No deadline. $35 fee. Application must be submitted on paper. Admission notification on a rolling basis. Must reply by May 1 or within 4 week(s) if notified thereafter. Application deadlines may vary by program. Students should check with admissions office for program deadlines. **Financial aid:** Priority date 4/1; no closing date. FAFSA, institutional form required. Applicants notified on a rolling basis starting 4/13; must reply within 3 week(s) of notification.

**Academics. Special study options:** Accelerated study, combined bachelor's/graduate degree, cooperative education, cross-registration, distance learning, double major, dual enrollment of high school students, external degree, independent study, internships, study abroad. **Credit/placement by examination:** CLEP, institutional tests. 40 credit hours maximum toward associate degree, 88 toward bachelor's. Unlimited number of hours of credit by examination may be counted toward degree if residency requirement of 40 hours is met. **Support services:** Learning center, reduced course load, study skills assistance, tutoring, writing center.

**Majors. Business:** General, business admin. **Health:** Health care admin, medical radiologic technology/radiation therapy, nursing (RN), preop/surgical nursing, radiologic technology/medical imaging.

**Computing on campus.** 60 workstations in dormitories, library, computer center. Dormitories wired for high-speed internet access. Commuter students can connect to campus network. Online library, helpline, repair service available.

**Student life. Freshman orientation:** Mandatory. Preregistration for classes offered. One-day program held on Friday before classes begin. **Housing:** Guaranteed on-campus for freshmen. Coed dorms, apartments available. $250 deposit, deadline 6/30. Board plan not available, kitchens located in each apartment. **Activities:** Student government, student newspaper, Christian Fellowship, Red Cross, National Student Nurses Association, Fellows club, Ambassador club, student leadership council.

**Athletics. Intercollegiate:** Skiing M.

**Student services.** Adult student services, alcohol/substance abuse counseling, career counseling, student employment services, financial aid counseling, health services, minority student services, on-campus daycare, personal counseling, placement for graduates. **Physically disabled:** Services for visually, hearing impaired.

**Contact.** E-mail: admiss@clarksoncollege.edu
Phone: (402) 552-3041 Toll-free number: (800) 647-5500
Fax: (402) 552-6057
Denise Work, Director of Admission, Clarkson College, 101 South 42nd Street, Omaha, NE 68131-2739

## College of Saint Mary
**Omaha, Nebraska**
**www.csm.edu**                          CB code: 6106

- Private 4-year nursing, liberal arts and teachers college for women affiliated with Roman Catholic Church
- Commuter campus in large city
- 816 degree-seeking undergraduates: 16% part-time, 100% women, 12% African American, 1% Asian American, 9% Hispanic American, 1% Native American, 1% international
- 265 degree-seeking graduate students
- 42% of applicants admitted
- SAT or ACT (ACT writing optional) required
- 45% graduate within 6 years

**General.** Founded in 1923. Regionally accredited. Weekend accelerated master's in teaching program, extensive integrated service learning. **Degrees:** 112 bachelor's, 88 associate awarded; master's, doctoral offered. **ROTC:** Army, Air Force. **Location:** 10 miles from downtown. **Calendar:** Semester, limited summer session. **Full-time faculty:** 57 total; 58% have terminal degrees, 16% minority, 81% women. **Part-time faculty:** 112 total; 23% have terminal degrees, 5% minority, 78% women. **Class size:** 73% < 20, 23% 20-39, 2% 40-49, 2% 50-99. **Special facilities:** Nursing labs, on-site child development center.

**Freshman class profile.** 510 applied, 216 admitted, 108 enrolled.

| Mid 50% test scores | | | |
|---|---|---|---|
| ACT composite: | 18-23 | Rank in top quarter: | 42% |
| GPA 3.75 or higher: | 30% | Rank in top tenth: | 14% |
| GPA 3.50-3.74: | 21% | End year in good standing: | 79% |
| GPA 3.0-3.49: | 24% | Return as sophomores: | 64% |
| GPA 2.0-2.99: | 25% | Out-of-state: | 7% |
| | | Live on campus: | 67% |

**Basis for selection.** Test scores, secondary school record, class rank important factors. Recommendations also considered. Nursing program requires a specific minimum score on the TEAS test. **Homeschooled:** Must take ACT exam and submit scores.

**High school preparation.** Required and recommended units include English 4, mathematics 2-3, social studies 2 and science 2-3. Chemistry and biology required of nursing, occupational therapy and pre-professional studies students.

**2009-2010 Annual costs.** Tuition/fees: $22,260. Room/board: $6,400. Books/supplies: $1,200. Personal expenses: $1,670.

**2009-2010 Financial aid. Need-based:** Average need met was 76%. Average scholarship/grant was $17,861; average loan $3,730. 50% of total undergraduate aid awarded as scholarships/grants, 50% as loans/jobs. **Non-need-based:** Scholarships awarded for academics, athletics, music/drama.

**Application procedures. Admission:** No deadline. $30 fee, may be waived for applicants with need. Admission notification on a rolling basis. **Financial aid:** Priority date 3/1; no closing date. FAFSA required. Applicants notified on a rolling basis starting 3/1; must reply within 2 week(s) of notification.

**Academics. Special study options:** Accelerated study, combined bachelor's/graduate degree, cooperative education, distance learning, double major, dual enrollment of high school students, exchange student, honors, independent study, internships, liberal arts/career combination, student-designed major, study abroad, teacher certification program, weekend college. **Credit/placement by examination:** AP, CLEP, IB, ACT, institutional tests. 15 credit hours maximum toward associate degree, 15 toward bachelor's. 10 percent of program may be earned through credit by examination. **Support services:** Learning center, reduced course load, remedial instruction, study skills assistance, tutoring, writing center.

**Majors. Biology:** General. **Business:** Business admin. **Computer sciences:** General. **Education:** Biology, chemistry, early childhood, elementary, English, mathematics, middle, science, secondary, social science, special. **Foreign languages:** Spanish. **Health:** Clinical lab technology, nursing (RN), predental, premedicine, prepharmacy, preveterinary. **Legal studies:** Paralegal. **Liberal arts:** Arts/sciences. **Math:** General. **Physical sciences:** General, chemistry. **Psychology:** General. **Theology:** Theology. **Visual/performing arts:** Studio arts.

**Most popular majors.** Business/marketing 17%, education 8%, health sciences 41%, legal studies 6%, liberal arts 8%, psychology 14%.

**Computing on campus.** 90 workstations in dormitories, library, computer center, student center. Dormitories wired for high-speed internet access and linked to campus network. Commuter students can connect to campus network. Online course registration, online library, helpline, wireless network available.

**Student life. Freshman orientation:** Mandatory. Preregistration for classes offered. One-day program offered several times during late spring and summer. **Policies:** Student Senate and Multicultural Association of Students members must have an overall 2.5 GPA to be eligible. **Housing:** Guaranteed on-campus for freshmen. $125 nonrefundable deposit, deadline 8/1. Residence hall for single mothers with children available. **Activities:** Campus ministries, choral groups, student government, Do Unto Others Board, residence hall council, Golden S (service club), campus activities board, Student Education Association of Nebraska, business student association, College Democrats, Multicultural Association of Students, student nurse association, green team, math/science club.

**Athletics.** NAIA. **Intercollegiate:** Basketball W, cross-country W, soccer W, softball W, swimming W, volleyball W. **Intramural:** Volleyball W. **Team name:** Flames.

**Student services.** Adult student services, alcohol/substance abuse counseling, chaplain/spiritual director, career counseling, services for economically disadvantaged, student employment services, financial aid counseling, health services, minority student services, on-campus daycare, personal counseling, placement for graduates, veterans' counselor, women's services. **Physically disabled:** Services for visually, speech, hearing impaired.

**Contact.** E-mail: enroll@csm.edu
Phone: (402) 399-2355 Toll-free number: (800) 926-5534
Fax: (402) 399-2412
Joe Szejk, Vice President for Enrollment Services and Marketing, College of Saint Mary, 7000 Mercy Road, Omaha, NE 68106

## Concordia University
**Seward, Nebraska**
**www.cune.edu**                          CB code: 6116

- Private 4-year university affiliated with Lutheran Church - Missouri Synod
- Residential campus in small town
- 1,129 degree-seeking undergraduates: 6% part-time, 51% women, 4% African American, 1% Asian American, 2% Hispanic American, 1% international
- 460 degree-seeking graduate students
- 75% of applicants admitted
- SAT or ACT (ACT writing optional) required
- 61% graduate within 6 years; 30% enter graduate study

**General.** Founded in 1894. Regionally accredited. **Degrees:** 234 bachelor's awarded; master's offered. **ROTC:** Army, Air Force. **Location:** 25 miles from Lincoln, 75 miles from Omaha. **Calendar:** Semester, limited summer session. **Full-time faculty:** 55 total; 66% have terminal degrees, 2% minority, 27% women. **Part-time faculty:** 88 total; 30% have terminal degrees, 3% minority, 58% women. **Class size:** 50% < 20, 45% 20-39, 5% 40-49, less than 1% 50-99. **Special facilities:** Rock museum, observatory, arboretum.

**Freshman class profile.** 1,281 applied, 962 admitted, 288 enrolled.

| Mid 50% test scores | | | |
|---|---|---|---|
| SAT critical reading: | 440-590 | GPA 2.0-2.99: | 18% |
| SAT math: | 430-640 | Rank in top quarter: | 51% |
| ACT composite: | 21-28 | Rank in top tenth: | 25% |
| GPA 3.75 or higher: | 43% | Return as sophomores: | 76% |
| GPA 3.50-3.74: | 19% | Out-of-state: | 57% |
| GPA 3.0-3.49: | 20% | Live on campus: | 99% |
| | | International: | 1% |

**Basis for selection.** High school GPA and SAT/ACT scores important in admissions decisions. Audition required for drama, music, and speech programs; portfolio required for art program. **Homeschooled:** Statement describing homeschool structure and mission, transcript of courses and grades, state high school equivalency certificate required.

**High school preparation.** College-preparatory program recommended. 16 units recommended. Recommended units include English 4, mathematics 3, social studies 3, science 2, foreign language 1 and academic electives 3. One unit each in music, art, and physical education recommended.

**2009-2010 Annual costs.** Tuition/fees: $21,250. Room/board: $5,520. Books/supplies: $750. Personal expenses: $1,200.

**2009-2010 Financial aid. Non-need-based:** Scholarships awarded for academics, alumni affiliation, art, athletics, leadership, music/drama, religious affiliation.

**Application procedures. Admission:** Priority date 7/1; deadline 8/1 (receipt date). No application fee. Admission notification on a rolling basis beginning on or about 9/1. Must reply within 30 days of receipt of acceptance letter or request extension. **Financial aid:** Priority date 3/1; no closing date. FAFSA required. Applicants notified on a rolling basis starting 3/1; must reply within 4 week(s) of notification.

**Academics.** Curriculum for degree completion program for bachelor of arts in organizational management contains 16 modules taken sequentially one night a week for 18 months. Summer term offering hybrid online and face to face instruction. **Special study options:** Accelerated study, distance learning, double major, dual enrollment of high school students, ESL, exchange student, independent study, internships, study abroad, teacher certification program. Undergraduate students may take graduate level classes. **Credit/placement by examination:** AP, CLEP, IB, SAT, ACT. **Support services:** Learning center, reduced course load, study skills assistance, tutoring, writing center.

**Majors. Agriculture:** Business. **Biology:** General, environmental. **Business:** General, accounting, business admin, communications, management information systems. **Communications:** General, journalism. **Computer sciences:** Computer science. **Education:** General, art, biology, business, chemistry, computer, elementary, English, ESL, family/consumer sciences, geography, health, history, mathematics, middle, multi-level teacher, music, physical, physics, science, secondary, social studies, Spanish, speech, technology/industrial arts. **Foreign languages:** Spanish. **Health:** Predental, premedicine, prenursing, prepharmacy, preveterinary. **History:** General. **Interdisciplinary:** Behavioral sciences. **Legal studies:** Prelaw. **Math:** General. **Parks/recreation:** Exercise sciences, health/fitness, sports admin. **Physical sciences:** General, chemistry, forensic chemistry. **Psychology:** General. **Social sciences:** Geography. **Theology:** Preministerial, religious ed, sacred music, theology, youth ministry. **Visual/performing arts:** General, art, arts management, dramatic, graphic design, piano/organ, studio arts, voice/opera.

**Most popular majors.** Biology 6%, business/marketing 12%, education 38%, psychology 9%, theological studies 10%, visual/performing arts 7%.

**Computing on campus.** 199 workstations in dormitories, library, computer center, student center. Dormitories wired for high-speed internet access and linked to campus network. Commuter students can connect to campus network. Online course registration, online library, helpline, student web hosting, wireless network available.

**Student life. Freshman orientation:** Mandatory. Preregistration for classes offered. 3 days before classes start. Includes community service events and community building. **Policies:** University responsibly maintains Christian standards of conduct among its students, faculty and staff. **Housing:** Guaranteed on-campus for all undergraduates. Single-sex dorms, special housing for disabled, apartments, wellness housing available. $200 fully refundable deposit, deadline 8/24. **Activities:** Bands, campus ministries, choral groups, dance, drama, literary magazine, music ensembles, musical theater, student government, student newspaper, symphony orchestra, Circle K, Ongoing Ambassadors for Christ, multicultural awareness club, Peers and Leaders Serving, Habitat for Humanity, Leaders in Physical Health Education, Mission Minded Students, Students in Free Enterprise, Students with Families Association.

**Athletics.** NAIA. **Intercollegiate:** Baseball M, basketball, cross-country, football (tackle) M, golf, soccer, softball W, tennis, track and field, volleyball W, wrestling M. **Intramural:** Basketball, bowling, football (nontackle), racquetball, soccer, softball, table tennis, tennis, track and field, volleyball. **Team name:** Bulldogs.

**Student services.** Adult student services, alcohol/substance abuse counseling, chaplain/spiritual director, career counseling, student employment services, financial aid counseling, health services, personal counseling, placement for graduates. **Physically disabled:** Services for visually, speech, hearing impaired.

**Contact.** E-mail: admiss@cune.edu
Phone: (800) 535-5494 Toll-free number: (800) 535-5494
Fax: (402) 643-4073
Aaron Roberts, Director of Undergraduate Recruitment, Concordia University, 800 North Columbia Avenue, Seward, NE 68434-1556

## Creative Center
**Omaha, Nebraska**
**www.creativecenter.edu**

- For-profit 4-year visual arts and career college
- Commuter campus in large city
- 125 degree-seeking undergraduates: 2% part-time, 60% women
- Application essay, interview required

**General.** Accredited by ACCSC. **Degrees:** 13 bachelor's, 40 associate awarded. **Calendar:** Semester, limited summer session. **Full-time faculty:** 4 total; 50% women. **Part-time faculty:** 15 total; 47% women. **Class size:** 29% 20-39, 36% 40-49, 36% 50-99.

**Basis for selection.** Students must provide a letter of recommendation, letter of intent, high school transcript and portfolio to be reviewed and approved. Portfolio required.

**2010-2011 Annual costs.** Tuition/fees: $21,600. Tuition/fees may vary by program.

**Financial aid. Non-need-based:** Scholarships awarded for academics, art.

**Application procedures. Admission:** No deadline. $100 fee. Application must be submitted on paper. Admission notification on a rolling basis. **Financial aid:** No deadline. FAFSA required. Applicants notified on a rolling basis starting 1/1.

**Academics. Credit/placement by examination:** CLEP. **Support services:** Reduced course load, study skills assistance, tutoring.

**Majors. Visual/performing arts:** Graphic design.

**Computing on campus.** PC or laptop required. 8 workstations in library. Online library, helpline, student web hosting, wireless network available.

**Student life. Freshman orientation:** Mandatory. Orientation held throughout first week of class.

**Student services.** Career counseling, financial aid counseling, placement for graduates.

**Contact.** E-mail: admissions@creativecenter.edu
Phone: (402) 898-1000 Toll-free number: (888) 898-1789
Fax: (402) 898-1301
Beth Connor, Admissions and Placement Coordinator, Creative Center, 10850 Emmet Street, Omaha, NE 68164

## Creighton University
**Omaha, Nebraska**
**www.creighton.edu**
**CB member**
**CB code: 6121**

- Private 4-year university affiliated with Roman Catholic Church
- Residential campus in very large city

- 4,133 degree-seeking undergraduates: 6% part-time, 59% women, 3% African American, 10% Asian American, 4% Hispanic American, 1% Native American, 2% international
- 3,252 degree-seeking graduate students
- 82% of applicants admitted
- SAT or ACT (ACT writing optional), application essay required
- 75% graduate within 6 years; 45% enter graduate study

**General.** Founded in 1878. Regionally accredited. **Degrees:** 944 bachelor's, 4 associate awarded; master's, doctoral, professional offered. **ROTC:** Army, Air Force. **Location:** 167 miles from Kansas City, 290 miles from Minneapolis. **Calendar:** Semester, extensive summer session. **Full-time faculty:** 532 total; 83% have terminal degrees, 12% minority, 42% women. **Part-time faculty:** 203 total; 21% have terminal degrees, 10% minority, 49% women. **Class size:** 45% < 20, 46% 20-39, 4% 40-49, 4% 50-99, less than 1% >100.

**Freshman class profile.** 4,752 applied, 3,888 admitted, 1,054 enrolled.

| Mid 50% test scores | | | |
|---|---|---|---|
| SAT critical reading: | 520-640 | Rank in top tenth: | 41% |
| SAT math: | 540-650 | End year in good standing: | 93% |
| ACT composite: | 24-29 | Return as sophomores: | 89% |
| GPA 3.75 or higher: | 58% | Out-of-state: | 72% |
| GPA 3.50-3.74: | 17% | Live on campus: | 93% |
| GPA 3.0-3.49: | 20% | International: | 2% |
| GPA 2.0-2.99: | 5% | Fraternities: | 26% |
| Rank in top quarter: | 73% | Sororities: | 28% |

**Basis for selection.** School record, high school GPA, test scores, and application essay important. Class rank considered. **Homeschooled:** GED required.

**High school preparation.** College-preparatory program recommended. 16 units required; 21 recommended. Required and recommended units include English 4, mathematics 3-4, social studies 2-3, history 1, science 2-3, foreign language 2-3 and academic electives 3.

**2009-2010 Annual costs.** Tuition/fees: $29,544. Room/board: $8,814. Books/supplies: $1,000. Personal expenses: $1,400.

**2009-2010 Financial aid. Need-based:** 840 full-time freshmen applied for aid; 651 were judged to have need; 651 of these received aid. Average need met was 93%. Average scholarship/grant was $20,675; average loan $5,755. 72% of total undergraduate aid awarded as scholarships/grants, 28% as loans/jobs. **Non-need-based:** Scholarships awarded for academics, alumni affiliation, art, athletics, leadership, minority status, music/drama, ROTC.

**Application procedures. Admission:** Priority date 12/1; deadline 2/15. $40 fee, may be waived for applicants with need, free for online applicants. Admission notification on a rolling basis beginning on or about 12/15. Must reply by May 1 or within 2 week(s) if notified thereafter. **Financial aid:** Priority date 3/1; no closing date. FAFSA, institutional form required. Applicants notified on a rolling basis starting 3/15; must reply by 5/1 or within 4 week(s) of notification.

**Academics.** Institution's students given admissions preference into all of university's professional schools. Core curriculum required (61 semester hours from 5 areas: cultures, ideas and civilizations; theology, philosophy and ethics; natural science; social and behavioral sciences; skills). **Special study options:** Accelerated study, combined bachelor's/graduate degree, cross-registration, distance learning, double major, dual enrollment of high school students, ESL, exchange student, honors, independent study, internships, liberal arts/career combination, study abroad, teacher certification program, Washington semester. 2-3 program in engineering with Marquette and University of Detroit Mercy, 3-3 Law Program within Creighton University, study abroad opportunities at 110 partner institutions in 40 countries. **Credit/placement by examination:** AP, CLEP, IB, SAT, ACT, institutional tests. CLEP Subject Examinations must be taken with essay where applicable. **Support services:** Learning center, pre-admission summer program, reduced course load, remedial instruction, study skills assistance, tutoring, writing center.

**Honors college/program.** The College of Arts and Sciences offers an Honors Program with a special curricula. Admission is by invitation only. In fall 2009, 54 freshmen began the honors program, 7% of those admitted to the College of Arts and Sciences.

**Majors. Area/ethnic studies:** American, Native American. **Biology:** General. **Business:** Accounting, business admin, communications, e-commerce, entrepreneurial studies, finance, international, management information systems, marketing. **Communications:** General, journalism, organizational. **Computer sciences:** Computer science. **Education:** Chemistry, elementary, Latin, secondary. **Foreign languages:** Ancient Greek, classics, French, German, Latin, Spanish. **Health:** Athletic training, EMT paramedic, health care admin, nursing (RN). **History:** General. **Interdisciplinary:** Peace/conflict. **Math:** General, applied. **Parks/recreation:** Exercise sciences. **Philosophy/religion:** Philosophy, religion. **Physical sciences:** Atmospheric science, chemistry, physics. **Psychology:** General. **Public administration:** Social work. **Social sciences:** Anthropology, economics, international relations, political science, sociology. **Visual/performing arts:** Art, dramatic, graphic design, music performance, studio arts.

**Most popular majors.** Biology 12%, business/marketing 21%, communications/journalism 7%, health sciences 20%, psychology 8%.

**Computing on campus.** 550 workstations in dormitories, library, computer center, student center. Dormitories wired for high-speed internet access and linked to campus network. Commuter students can connect to campus network. Online course registration, online library, helpline, repair service, student web hosting, wireless network available.

**Student life. Freshman orientation:** Mandatory, $60 fee. Preregistration for classes offered. Held first week of fall semester. **Housing:** Guaranteed on-campus for freshmen. Coed dorms, single-sex dorms, special housing for disabled, apartments, wellness housing available. $100 fully refundable deposit, deadline 5/1. **Activities:** Bands, campus ministries, choral groups, dance, drama, international student organizations, literary magazine, music ensembles, Model UN, musical theater, student government, student newspaper, symphony orchestra, TV station, world hunger awareness group, Afro-American students association, international relations club, women's resource center, community service center, Christian life community, Young Democrats, Young Republicans.

**Athletics.** NCAA. **Intercollegiate:** Baseball M, basketball, cross-country, golf, rowing (crew) W, soccer, softball W, tennis, volleyball W. **Intramural:** Badminton, basketball, bowling, football (non-tackle), golf, racquetball, soccer, softball, tennis, volleyball. **Team name:** Bluejays.

**Student services.** Adult student services, alcohol/substance abuse counseling, chaplain/spiritual director, career counseling, services for economically disadvantaged, student employment services, financial aid counseling, health services, minority student services, on-campus daycare, personal counseling, placement for graduates, veterans' counselor, women's services. **Physically disabled:** Services for visually, speech, hearing impaired. **Learning disabled:** Comprehensive services available.

**Contact.** E-mail: admissions@creighton.edu
Phone: (402) 280-2703 Toll-free number: (800) 282-5835
Fax: (402) 280-2685
Joe Bezousek, Director of Admissions, Creighton University, 2500 California Plaza, Omaha, NE 68178-0001

---

## Dana College
**Blair, Nebraska**
www.dana.edu

**CB member**
**CB code: 6157**

- Private 4-year liberal arts college affiliated with Evangelical Lutheran Church in America
- Residential campus in small town
- 590 degree-seeking undergraduates: 2% part-time, 46% women, 6% African American, 2% Asian American, 5% Hispanic American, 1% Native American
- 66% of applicants admitted
- SAT or ACT (ACT writing optional) required
- 49% graduate within 6 years

**General.** Founded in 1884. Regionally accredited. **Degrees:** 114 bachelor's awarded. **ROTC:** Army, Air Force. **Location:** 20 miles from Omaha. **Calendar:** 4-1-4, limited summer session. **Full-time faculty:** 32 total; 69% have terminal degrees, 3% minority, 47% women. **Part-time faculty:** 26 total; 19% have terminal degrees, 8% minority, 38% women. **Class size:** 62% < 20, 32% 20-39, 5% 40-49, 1% 50-99. **Special facilities:** Fine arts center, Danish heritage room, Danish immigrant archives.

**Freshman class profile.** 1,087 applied, 721 admitted, 174 enrolled.

| Mid 50% test scores | | | |
|---|---|---|---|
| | | GPA 2.0-2.99: | 32% |
| SAT critical reading: | 390-480 | Rank in top quarter: | 31% |
| SAT math: | 410-520 | Rank in top tenth: | 8% |
| ACT composite: | 20-25 | Return as sophomores: | 57% |
| GPA 3.75 or higher: | 21% | Out-of-state: | 42% |
| GPA 3.50-3.74: | 16% | Live on campus: | 97% |
| GPA 3.0-3.49: | 31% | International: | 1% |

**Basis for selection.** 2.0 cumulative GPA in college preparatory courses, standardized test scores important. Recommendations by school officials considered. **Homeschooled:** Transcript of courses and grades required. ACT composite of 18 or above or combined SAT score of 860 or above (exclusive of Writing), plus one of the following: transcript from high school or college where courses were taken, GED score of 500 or above, portfolio of representative work.

**High school preparation.** College-preparatory program recommended. 16 units recommended. Recommended units include English 4, mathematics 3, social studies 4, science 3 (laboratory 2) and foreign language 2.

**2009-2010 Annual costs.** Tuition/fees: $21,100. Room/board: $6,690. Books/supplies: $1,280. Personal expenses: $1,900.

**2009-2010 Financial aid. Need-based:** 172 full-time freshmen applied for aid; 151 were judged to have need; 151 of these received aid. Average need met was 86%. Average scholarship/grant was $5,604; average loan $3,398. 53% of total undergraduate aid awarded as scholarships/grants, 47% as loans/jobs. **Non-need-based:** Awarded to 756 full-time undergraduates, including 259 freshmen. Scholarships awarded for academics, alumni affiliation, art, athletics, music/drama, religious affiliation, ROTC, state residency. **Additional information:** Auditions recommended for music and drama scholarship applicants. Portfolios recommended for art, graphic design, and cheerleading/dance scholarship applicants.

**Application procedures. Admission:** No deadline. No application fee. Admission notification on a rolling basis. **Financial aid:** Priority date 4/9; no closing date. FAFSA, institutional form required. Applicants notified on a rolling basis starting 3/9; must reply within 3 week(s) of notification.

**Academics. Special study options:** Accelerated study, cross-registration, double major, dual enrollment of high school students, honors, independent study, internships, liberal arts/career combination, New York semester, semester at sea, student-designed major, study abroad, teacher certification program, United Nations semester, urban semester. **Credit/placement by examination:** AP, CLEP, IB, ACT, institutional tests. 30 credit hours maximum toward bachelor's degree. **Support services:** Learning center, reduced course load, remedial instruction, study skills assistance, tutoring.

**Majors. Biology:** General. **Business:** Accounting, business admin, communications, management information systems. **Communications:** Journalism. **Conservation:** Environmental studies. **Education:** General, art, biology, business, chemistry, elementary, English, history, kindergarten/ preschool, mathematics, music, social science, Spanish, special. **Foreign languages:** Spanish. **History:** General. **Interdisciplinary:** Global studies. **Liberal arts:** Arts/sciences. **Math:** General. **Parks/recreation:** Sports admin. **Philosophy/religion:** Religion. **Physical sciences:** Chemistry. **Protective services:** Criminal justice. **Psychology:** General. **Public administration:** Social work. **Social sciences:** General. **Visual/performing arts:** Art, graphic design, musical theater. **Other:** Integrated studies, Public accounting.

**Most popular majors.** Business/marketing 28%, communications/ journalism 6%, education 21%, parks/recreation 9%, security/protective services 6%.

**Computing on campus.** 110 workstations in dormitories, library, computer center, student center. Dormitories wired for high-speed internet access and linked to campus network. Commuter students can connect to campus network. Online library, student web hosting, wireless network available.

**Student life. Freshman orientation:** Mandatory. Preregistration for classes offered. **Housing:** Guaranteed on-campus for all undergraduates. Coed dorms, single-sex dorms, wellness housing available. $100 fully refundable deposit. Suite style housing - 4 students per apartment. **Activities:** Bands, campus ministries, choral groups, dance, drama, literary magazine, music ensembles, musical theater, radio station, student government, student newspaper, TV station, Fellowship of Christian Athletes, social awareness organization, student activities board, German club, Help Our People Expand, communication club.

**Athletics.** NAIA. **Intercollegiate:** Baseball M, basketball, cross-country, football (tackle) M, golf W, soccer, softball W, track and field, volleyball W, wrestling M. **Intramural:** Basketball, bowling, handball, soccer, softball, swimming, table tennis, tennis, volleyball. **Team name:** Vikings.

**Student services.** Adult student services, alcohol/substance abuse counseling, chaplain/spiritual director, career counseling, student employment services, financial aid counseling, health services, personal counseling, placement for graduates, veterans' counselor. **Physically disabled:** Services for visually, hearing impaired.

**Contact.** E-mail: admissions@acad2.dana.edu
Phone: (402) 426-7222 Toll-free number: (800) 444-3262
Fax: (402) 426-7386
Tina Blair, Director of Admission, Dana College, 2848 College Drive, Blair, NE 68008-1099

## Doane College
Crete, Nebraska
www.doane.edu

**CB member**
**CB code: 6165**

- Private 4-year liberal arts college affiliated with United Church of Christ
- Residential campus in small town
- 966 degree-seeking undergraduates: 49% women, 3% African American, 1% Asian American, 4% Hispanic American, 1% Native American, 1% international
- 76% of applicants admitted
- SAT or ACT (ACT writing optional) required
- 64% graduate within 6 years

**General.** Founded in 1872. Regionally accredited. Campuses also in Lincoln and Grand Island. **Degrees:** 198 bachelor's awarded; master's offered. **ROTC:** Army, Air Force. **Location:** 25 miles from Lincoln, 75 miles from Omaha. **Calendar:** 4-1-4, limited summer session. **Full-time faculty:** 70 total; 79% have terminal degrees, 6% minority, 49% women. **Part-time faculty:** 49 total. **Class size:** 75% < 20, 21% 20-39, 3% 40-49, less than 1% 50-99. **Special facilities:** Arboretum, open-air theater, observatory, all-American rose test garden, ropes challenge course, fitness trail.

**Freshman class profile.** 1,379 applied, 1,048 admitted, 312 enrolled.

| Mid 50% test scores | | | |
|---|---|---|---|
| SAT critical reading: | 440-550 | GPA 2.0-2.99: | 19% |
| SAT math: | 460-580 | Rank in top quarter: | 42% |
| SAT writing: | 420-600 | Rank in top tenth: | 15% |
| ACT composite: | 20-26 | End year in good standing: | 92% |
| GPA 3.75 or higher: | 34% | Return as sophomores: | 77% |
| GPA 3.50-3.74: | 18% | Out-of-state: | 21% |
| GPA 3.0-3.49: | 29% | Live on campus: | 99% |

**Basis for selection.** Academic and personal record, recommendations, test scores important. Class rank considered. Interview required for academically marginal students; audition required for drama, music programs and forensics; portfolio required for art program.

**High school preparation.** College-preparatory program recommended. 13 units recommended. Recommended units include English 4, mathematics 3, social studies 3 and science 3.

**2009-2010 Annual costs.** Tuition/fees: $21,040. Room/board: $5,970. Books/supplies: $800. Personal expenses: $1,100.

**2009-2010 Financial aid. Need-based:** 305 full-time freshmen applied for aid; 265 were judged to have need; 265 of these received aid. Average need met was 96%. Average scholarship/grant was $14,148; average loan $3,920. 66% of total undergraduate aid awarded as scholarships/grants, 34% as loans/jobs. **Non-need-based:** Awarded to 198 full-time undergraduates, including 48 freshmen. Scholarships awarded for academics, art, athletics, music/drama.

**Application procedures. Admission:** No deadline. No application fee. Admission notification on a rolling basis beginning on or about 9/15. Must reply by May 1 or within 4 week(s) if notified thereafter. **Financial aid:** Priority date 3/1; no closing date. FAFSA required. Applicants notified on a rolling basis starting 3/1; must reply within 2 week(s) of notification.

**Academics.** Midwest Institute for International Students prepares students to meet English language requirement for admission to Doane and other American colleges. **Special study options:** Combined bachelor's/ graduate degree, double major, ESL, honors, independent study, internships, student-designed major, study abroad, teacher certification program. 3-2 programs in engineering with Washington University, Columbia University, 3-2 program in environmental and forestry studies with Duke University. **Credit/ placement by examination:** AP, CLEP, IB, SAT, ACT, institutional tests. 36 credit hours maximum toward bachelor's degree. International students who successfully complete Midwest Institute ESL program may be admitted without TOEFL scores. **Support services:** Learning center, reduced course load, remedial instruction, study skills assistance, tutoring, writing center.

**Majors. Biology:** General, biochemistry. **Business:** Accounting, business admin, human resources. **Communications:** Journalism, organizational. **Computer sciences:** General, computer science, information systems. **Conservation:** Environmental studies. **Education:** Elementary, ESL, physical, special. **Foreign languages:** French, German, Spanish. **History:** General. **Interdisciplinary:** Global studies, natural sciences. **Legal studies:** Paralegal. **Liberal arts:** Arts/sciences. **Math:** General. **Philosophy/religion:** Philosophy, religion. **Physical sciences:** Chemistry, physics. **Psychology:** General. **Public administration:** General. **Social sciences:** General, economics, international relations, political science, sociology. **Visual/performing arts:** Art, dramatic, graphic design.

**Most popular majors.** Biology 9%, business/marketing 16%, education 25%, social sciences 11%, visual/performing arts 9%.

**Computing on campus.** 400 workstations in dormitories, library, computer center, student center. Dormitories wired for high-speed internet access and linked to campus network. Commuter students can connect to campus network. Online course registration, online library, helpline, student web hosting, wireless network available.

**Student life. Freshman orientation:** Available. Preregistration for classes offered. **Policies:** Unmarried students under 22 not living with parents expected to live on campus. **Housing:** Guaranteed on-campus for freshmen. Coed dorms, single-sex dorms available. $200 fully refundable deposit. **Activities:** Bands, campus ministries, choral groups, dance, drama, film society, literary magazine, music ensembles, musical theater, radio station, student government, student newspaper, TV station, student education association, Doane speakers, Club Internationale, Fellowship of Christian Athletes, American Minority Student Alliance, College Republicans, Young Democrats.

**Athletics.** NAIA. **Intercollegiate:** Baseball M, basketball, bowling, cheerleading M, cross-country, football (tackle) M, golf, soccer, softball W, tennis, track and field, volleyball W. **Intramural:** Basketball, cheerleading W, football (tackle) M, golf, softball, swimming, tennis, volleyball. **Team name:** Tigers.

**Student services.** Adult student services, chaplain/spiritual director, career counseling, student employment services, financial aid counseling, health services, personal counseling, placement for graduates, veterans' counselor.

**Contact.** E-mail: admissions@doane.edu
Phone: (402) 826-8222 Toll-free number: (800) 333-6263
Fax: (402) 826-8600
Joal Weyand, vicwe President for Admission, Doane College, 1014 Boswell Avenue, Crete, NE 68333

## Grace University
**Omaha, Nebraska**
**www.graceuniversity.edu**                    CB code: 6248

- Private 4-year university and Bible college affiliated with interdenominational tradition
- Residential campus in very large city
- 399 degree-seeking undergraduates
- 87 graduate students
- 65% of applicants admitted
- ACT (writing optional), application essay required

**General.** Founded in 1943. Regionally accredited; also accredited by ABHE. **Degrees:** 68 bachelor's, 4 associate awarded; master's offered. **ROTC:** Air Force. **Calendar:** Semester, limited summer session. **Full-time faculty:** 27 total. **Part-time faculty:** 39 total. **Class size:** 81% < 20, 13% 20-39, 3% 40-49, 2% 50-99, less than 1% >100.

**Freshman class profile.** 184 applied, 119 admitted, 62 enrolled.

Mid 50% test scores              **ACT composite:**              20-25

**Basis for selection.** School achievement record, religious affiliation/commitment, test scores, and student profile important. Conditional admission for students who have not taken SAT/ACT. Audition required for music programs. **Homeschooled:** Transcript of courses and grades required. ACT score of 20 or GED required.

**High school preparation.** College-preparatory program recommended. Teacher education program requires 4 language arts, 2 mathematics, 2 sciences, 2 social sciences.

**2010-2011 Annual costs.** Tuition/fees (projected): $15,390. Room/board: $5,900. Books/supplies: $800.

**2009-2010 Financial aid. Need-based:** 55% of total undergraduate aid awarded as scholarships/grants, 45% as loans/jobs. **Non-need-based:** Scholarships awarded for academics, alumni affiliation, leadership, minority status, music/drama.

**Application procedures. Admission:** Priority date 2/1; deadline 8/15 (receipt date). $35 fee, may be waived for applicants with need. Admission notification on a rolling basis. High school students can take up to 12 credits prior to their high school graduation at a reduced cost. **Financial aid:** Priority date 3/1, closing date 4/1. FAFSA, institutional form required. Applicants notified on a rolling basis starting 3/1; must reply within 2 week(s) of notification.

**Academics. Special study options:** Accelerated study, combined bachelor's/graduate degree, cooperative education, distance learning, double major, dual

enrollment of high school students, independent study, internships, liberal arts/career combination, student-designed major, study abroad, teacher certification program, urban semester. **Credit/placement by examination:** AP, CLEP, ACT. 15 credit hours maximum toward bachelor's degree. **Support services:** Learning center, reduced course load, study skills assistance, tutoring, writing center.

**Majors. Business:** Management science. **Communications technology:** General. **Computer sciences:** General. **Education:** Business, elementary, English, ESL, history, mathematics, middle, music, secondary, social science. **Health:** Nursing (RN). **Liberal arts:** Arts/sciences. **Psychology:** General. **Theology:** Bible, missionary, religious ed, sacred music, theology. **Visual/performing arts:** Music performance, music theory/composition, piano/organ, voice/opera.

**Computing on campus.** 43 workstations in dormitories, library, computer center. Dormitories wired for high-speed internet access and linked to campus network. Commuter students can connect to campus network. Online library, helpline, wireless network available.

**Student life. Freshman orientation:** Mandatory. Preregistration for classes offered. **Policies:** All on campus housing is alcohol/drug/smoke-free. Religious observance required. **Housing:** Guaranteed on-campus for freshmen. Single-sex dorms, apartments, wellness housing available. $150 partly refundable deposit. **Activities:** Concert band, campus ministries, choral groups, drama, music ensembles, radio station, student government.

**Athletics.** NCCAA. **Intercollegiate:** Basketball, soccer M, volleyball W. **Intramural:** Basketball M, football (tackle), volleyball W. **Team name:** Royals.

**Student services.** Adult student services, chaplain/spiritual director, career counseling, student employment services, financial aid counseling, health services, personal counseling, placement for graduates.

**Contact.** E-mail: admissions@graceuniversity.edu
Phone: (402) 449-2831 Toll-free number: (800) 383-1422
Fax: (402) 449-2999
Chris Pruitt, Dean of Enrollment Managment, Grace University, 1311 South Ninth Street, Omaha, NE 68108-3629

## Hastings College
**Hastings, Nebraska**
**www.hastings.edu**                    CB code: 6270

- Private 4-year liberal arts college affiliated with Presbyterian Church (USA)
- Residential campus in large town

**General.** Founded in 1882. Regionally accredited. **Location:** 90 miles from Lincoln, 150 miles from Omaha. **Calendar:** 4-1-4.

**Annual costs/financial aid.** Tuition/fees (2009-2010): $21,782. Room/board: $6,000. Books/supplies: $750. Personal expenses: $1,800. Need-based financial aid available to full-time and part-time students.

**Contact.** Phone: (402) 461-7403
Director of Admissions, 710 North Turner Avenue, Hastings, NE 68901-7621

## ITT Technical Institute: Omaha
**Omaha, Nebraska**
**www.itt-tech.edu**                    CB code: 2740

- For-profit 4-year technical college
- Commuter campus in large city

**General.** Accredited by ACICS. **Calendar:** Quarter.

**Contact.** Phone: (402) 331-2900
Director of Recruitment, 9814 M Street, Omaha, NE 68127

## Midland Lutheran College
**Fremont, Nebraska**
**www.mlc.edu**                    CB code: 6406

- Private 4-year liberal arts college affiliated with Evangelical Lutheran Church in America
- Residential campus in large town

**General.** Founded in 1883. Regionally accredited. **Location:** 35 miles from Omaha, 52 miles from Lincoln. **Calendar:** 4-1-4.

**Annual costs/financial aid.** Tuition/fees (2009-2010): $22,984. Room/board: $5,612. Books/supplies: $1,000. Personal expenses: $1,200. Need-based financial aid available to full-time and part-time students.

**Contact.** Phone: (402) 941-6501
Director of Admissions, 900 North Clarkson, Fremont, NE 68025

## Nebraska Christian College
### Papillion, Nebraska
www.nechristian.edu
CB code: 1332

▶ Private 4-year Bible college affiliated with Christian Church/Churches of Christ
▶ Residential campus in large town
▶ 142 degree-seeking undergraduates
▶ SAT or ACT (ACT writing optional), application essay required
▶ 59% graduate within 6 years; 35% enter graduate study

**General.** Founded in 1944. Accredited by ABHE. **Degrees:** 27 bachelor's, 12 associate awarded. **Location:** 10 miles from Omaha. **Calendar:** Semester, limited summer session. **Full-time faculty:** 11 total; 64% have terminal degrees. **Part-time faculty:** 7 total.

**Freshman class profile.**

| | | | |
|---|---|---|---|
| End year in good standing: | 89% | Out-of-state: | 45% |
| Return as sophomores: | 81% | | |

**Basis for selection.** Christian commitment and references very important; high school transcript or GED required. Standardized test scores required. Transcript of any previous college work required.

**2009-2010 Annual costs.** Tuition/fees: $10,500. Room/board: $4,800. Books/supplies: $600. Personal expenses: $1,900.

**2008-2009 Financial aid. Non-need-based:** Scholarships awarded for academics, leadership.

**Application procedures. Admission:** Closing date 8/1 (postmark date). $25 fee, may be waived for applicants with need, free for online applicants. Admission notification on a rolling basis. **Financial aid:** Priority date 6/1; no closing date. FAFSA, institutional form required. Applicants notified on a rolling basis starting 5/5.

**Academics. Special study options:** Combined bachelor's/graduate degree, cooperative education, double major, dual enrollment of high school students, independent study, internships, teacher certification program. **Credit/placement by examination:** AP, CLEP. **Support services:** Learning center, reduced course load, study skills assistance, tutoring, writing center.

**Majors. Theology:** Bible, missionary, religious ed, sacred music, theology.

**Computing on campus.** 10 workstations in library, computer center. Dormitories wired for high-speed internet access. Wireless network available.

**Student life. Freshman orientation:** Mandatory. Preregistration for classes offered. **Policies:** Religious observance required. **Housing:** Single-sex dorms, special housing for disabled, apartments, wellness housing available. $200 nonrefundable deposit, deadline 6/30. **Activities:** Pep band, campus ministries, choral groups, drama, literary magazine, music ensembles, student government.

**Athletics.** NCCAA. **Intercollegiate:** Basketball M, volleyball W. **Intramural:** Basketball, football (non-tackle), soccer, volleyball. **Team name:** Parsons.

**Student services.** Adult student services, alcohol/substance abuse counseling, chaplain/spiritual director, career counseling, student employment services, financial aid counseling, health services, personal counseling, placement for graduates.

**Contact.** E-mail: admissions@nechristian.edu
Phone: (402) 935-9400 Fax: (402) 935-9500
David Huskey, Chief Student Officer, Nebraska Christian College, 12550 South 114th Street, Papillion, NE 68046

## Nebraska Methodist College of Nursing and Allied Health
### Omaha, Nebraska
www.methodistcollege.edu
CB code: 6510

▶ Private 4-year health science and nursing college affiliated with United Methodist Church
▶ Commuter campus in large city
▶ 568 degree-seeking undergraduates: 28% part-time, 90% women, 3% African American, 3% Asian American, 1% Hispanic American, 1% Native American
▶ 81 degree-seeking graduate students
▶ 38% of applicants admitted
▶ SAT or ACT (ACT writing optional) required
▶ 69% graduate within 6 years

**General.** Founded in 1891. Regionally accredited. **Degrees:** 124 bachelor's, 46 associate awarded; master's offered. **ROTC:** Army. **Location:** 120 miles from Des Moines, Iowa, 180 miles from Kansas City, Missouri. **Calendar:** Semester, limited summer session. **Full-time faculty:** 47 total; 28% have terminal degrees, 2% minority, 89% women. **Part-time faculty:** 11 total; 36% have terminal degrees, 100% women. **Class size:** 48% < 20, 46% 20-39, 3% 40-49, 3% 50-99. **Special facilities:** Human cadaver lab, human simulation labs, center for health partnerships.

**Freshman class profile.** 248 applied, 94 admitted, 60 enrolled.

| Mid 50% test scores | | | |
|---|---|---|---|
| ACT composite: | 19-25 | GPA 2.0-2.99: | 23% |
| GPA 3.75 or higher: | 27% | Rank in top quarter: | 35% |
| GPA 3.50-3.74: | 14% | Out-of-state: | 15% |
| GPA 3.0-3.49: | 36% | Live on campus: | 40% |

**Basis for selection.** School achievement, test scores most important. Personal statement, interview important. Recommendations, school and community activities considered. Deadlines vary by program. ACT or SAT is required of all current high school graduates and of students making application within two years of high school graduation. Departmental interview for specific programs. Written statement is required for all applicants. **Homeschooled:** Submit GED equivalent. The State of NE does not issue high school diplomas to exempt students.

**High school preparation.** 10 units required. Required units include English 4, mathematics 2, social studies 2, science 2 (laboratory 2). Chemistry, biology, algebra, anatomy and physiology recommended. A background in physics is strongly recommended for applicants for radiologic technology, sonography, and physical therapist assistant.

**2009-2010 Annual costs.** Tuition/fees: $14,130. Room/board: $6,510. Books/supplies: $962. Personal expenses: $1,395.

**2009-2010 Financial aid. Need-based:** Average need met was 77%. Average scholarship/grant was $7,211; average loan $2,852. 28% of total undergraduate aid awarded as scholarships/grants, 72% as loans/jobs. **Non-need-based:** Scholarships awarded for academics, leadership, religious affiliation, ROTC.

**Application procedures. Admission:** No deadline. $25 fee, may be waived for applicants with need. Admission notification on a rolling basis. Required within two weeks of acceptance. Application deadlines vary by program. **Financial aid:** Priority date 5/1; no closing date. FAFSA, institutional form required. Applicants notified on a rolling basis starting 3/1; must reply within 3 week(s) of notification.

**Academics.** Peer tutoring available for most courses; study seminars available for science and professional courses. **Special study options:** Accelerated study, combined bachelor's/graduate degree, distance learning, independent study, internships. **Credit/placement by examination:** AP, CLEP, institutional tests. 9 credit hours maximum toward associate degree, 9 toward bachelor's. Credit by examination considered on an individual basis. **Support services:** Learning center, reduced course load, remedial instruction, study skills assistance, tutoring, writing center.

**Majors. Health:** Cardiovascular technology, nursing (RN), radiologic technology/medical imaging, respiratory therapy technology, sonography.

**Computing on campus.** 47 workstations in library, computer center, student center. Dormitories linked to campus network. Online course registration, online library, helpline available.

**Student life. Freshman orientation:** Mandatory. Preregistration for classes offered. 2-days held in August, one-day transfer orientation for allied health students held in May. **Housing:** Guaranteed on-campus for all undergraduates. Coed dorms, apartments, wellness housing available. $150 nonrefundable deposit. **Activities:** Campus ministries, student government, student nurse association (state and national), allied health student association, College Ambassadors, minority student organization, Pathfinders, residence hall council.

**Student services.** Adult student services, alcohol/substance abuse counseling, chaplain/spiritual director, career counseling, student employment services, financial aid counseling, health services, minority student services, personal counseling, placement for graduates, veterans' counselor.

**Contact.** E-mail: admissions@methodistcollege.edu
Phone: (402) 354-7200 Toll-free number: (800) 335-5510
Fax: (402) 354-7020
Sara Bonney, Director of Enrollment Services, Nebraska Methodist College of Nursing and Allied Health, 720 North 87th Street, Omaha, NE 68114

## Nebraska Wesleyan University
### Lincoln, Nebraska
www.nebrwesleyan.edu                    CB code: 6470

- Private 4-year liberal arts college affiliated with United Methodist Church
- Residential campus in small city
- 1,790 degree-seeking undergraduates: 11% part-time, 58% women, 2% African American, 2% Asian American, 1% Hispanic American
- 241 degree-seeking graduate students
- 82% of applicants admitted
- SAT or ACT (ACT writing optional) required
- 66% graduate within 6 years

**General.** Founded in 1887. Regionally accredited. Non-traditional programs on accelerated semesters. **Degrees:** 404 bachelor's awarded; master's offered. **ROTC:** Army, Air Force. **Location:** 55 miles from Omaha, 200 miles from Kansas City, Missouri. **Calendar:** Semester, limited summer session. **Full-time faculty:** 103 total; 88% have terminal degrees, 2% minority, 52% women. **Part-time faculty:** 65 total; 29% have terminal degrees, 3% minority, 51% women. **Class size:** 57% <20, 39% 20-39, 2% 40-49, 2% 50-99. **Special facilities:** Planetarium, laboratory theater, greenhouse, herbarium, nuclear magnetic resonance laboratory, sleep laboratory, art gallery.

**Freshman class profile.** 1,428 applied, 1,178 admitted, 393 enrolled.

| Mid 50% test scores | | Out-of-state: | 12% |
|---|---|---|---|
| ACT composite: | 23-27 | Live on campus: | 92% |
| Rank in top quarter: | 60% | International: | 1% |
| Rank in top tenth: | 25% | Fraternities: | 28% |
| End year in good standing: | 95% | Sororities: | 32% |
| Return as sophomores: | 79% | | |

**Basis for selection.** Students who rank in the top half of their graduating class or achieve an ACT composite score of 20 or an SAT combined score of 950 (exclusive of Writing) are invited to apply for admission. Campus visit recommended for all students; audition required for drama, music scholarships; portfolio required for art scholarships. **Homeschooled:** Transcript of courses and grades required. GED scores.

**High school preparation.** College-preparatory program recommended. Recommended units include English 4, mathematics 3, social studies 3, science 3 and foreign language 2.

**2009-2010 Annual costs.** Tuition/fees: $22,312. Room/board: $6,230.

**2009-2010 Financial aid. Need-based:** 345 full-time freshmen applied for aid; 298 were judged to have need; 297 of these received aid. Average need met was 74%. Average scholarship/grant was $12,819; average loan $4,335. 66% of total undergraduate aid awarded as scholarships/grants, 34% as loans/jobs. **Non-need-based:** Awarded to 552 full-time undergraduates, including 130 freshmen. Scholarships awarded for academics, alumni affiliation, art, minority status, music/drama.

**Application procedures. Admission:** Closing date 8/15 (postmark date). $20 fee, may be waived for applicants with need, free for online applicants. Admission notification on a rolling basis beginning on or about 1/15. Must reply by May 1 or within 4 week(s) if notified thereafter. **Financial aid:** No deadline. FAFSA required. Applicants notified on a rolling basis starting 3/1; must reply within 4 week(s) of notification.

**Academics. Special study options:** Combined bachelor's/graduate degree, double major, dual enrollment of high school students, exchange student, independent study, internships, liberal arts/career combination, semester at sea, study abroad, teacher certification program, United Nations semester, urban semester, Washington semester. 3-2 engineering with Washington University or Columbia University; Capitol Hill Internship Program; Chicago Center for Urban Life and Culture; summer research fellowships in the natural sciences; faculty led international study tours. **Credit/placement by examination:** AP, CLEP, IB, institutional tests. Unlimited number of hours of credit by examination may be counted toward degree. **Support services:** Reduced course load, study skills assistance, tutoring, writing center.

**Majors. Biology:** General, biochemistry, Biochemistry/biophysics and molecular biology. **Business:** Accounting, business admin, international. **Communications:** General, political. **Computer sciences:** Computer science, information technology. **Education:** Elementary, English, middle, music, physical, science, social science, special. **Foreign languages:** French, German, Spanish. **Health:** Athletic training, nursing (RN). **History:** General. **Interdisciplinary:** Biopsychology, global studies. **Math:** General. **Parks/recreation:** Exercise sciences, health/fitness, sports admin. **Philosophy/religion:** Philosophy, religion. **Physical sciences:** Chemistry, physics. **Psychology:** General, industrial. **Public administration:** Social work. **Social sciences:** Economics, political science, sociology. **Visual/performing arts:** Art, dramatic, music performance, studio arts. **Other:** Business-sociology, Gender studies.

**Most popular majors.** Biology 10%, business/marketing 23%, education 7%, English 8%, health sciences 9%, parks/recreation 8%, psychology 8%, visual/performing arts 7%.

**Computing on campus.** 360 workstations in dormitories, library, computer center, student center. Dormitories wired for high-speed internet access and linked to campus network. Commuter students can connect to campus network. Online course registration, online library, helpline, repair service, student web hosting, wireless network available.

**Student life. Freshman orientation:** Mandatory. Preregistration for classes offered. Summer 1-day registration sessions in June; 4-day orientation program before fall classes begin. **Housing:** Guaranteed on-campus for all undergraduates. Coed dorms, single-sex dorms, special housing for disabled, apartments, fraternity/sorority housing available. $100 nonrefundable deposit, deadline 7/1. Residence hall suites and townhomes. **Activities:** Bands, campus ministries, choral groups, drama, international student organizations, literary magazine, music ensembles, musical theater, opera, student government, student newspaper, Student Fellowship, Fellowship of Christian Athletes, Meeting of Students Addressing Intercultural Concerns, College Republicans, Young Democrats, Nebraskans for Peace, International Relations Organization, Circle K, Environmental Action, Global Service Learning.

**Athletics.** NAIA, NCAA. **Intercollegiate:** Baseball M, basketball, cross-country, football (tackle) M, golf, soccer, softball W, tennis, track and field, volleyball W. **Intramural:** Basketball, bowling, football (non-tackle), racquetball, soccer, softball, tennis, volleyball, water polo. **Team name:** Prairie Wolves.

**Student services.** Adult student services, chaplain/spiritual director, career counseling, student employment services, financial aid counseling, health services, minority student services, personal counseling, placement for graduates, women's services. **Physically disabled:** Services for visually, speech, hearing impaired.

**Contact.** E-mail: admissions@nebrwesleyan.edu
Phone: (402) 465-2218 Toll-free number: (800) 541-3818
Fax: (402) 465-2177
David Duzik, Director of Admissions, Nebraska Wesleyan University, 5000 St. Paul Avenue, Lincoln, NE 68504

## Peru State College
### Peru, Nebraska
www.peru.edu                    CB code: 6468

- Public 4-year liberal arts and teachers college
- Residential campus in rural community
- 1,997 degree-seeking undergraduates

**General.** Founded in 1867. Regionally accredited. Elementary school teacher certification courses offered at Offutt Air Force Base. Online graduate degrees in education and organizational management offered. **Degrees:** 316 bachelor's awarded; master's offered. **Location:** 64 miles from Omaha, 67 miles from Lincoln. **Calendar:** Semester, limited summer session. **Full-time faculty:** 46 total; 85% have terminal degrees, 4% minority, 37% women. **Part-time faculty:** 67 total; 51% women.

## Freshman class profile.

| | | | |
|---|---|---|---|
| Out-of-state: | 7% | Live on campus: | 75% |

**Basis for selection.** Open admission, but selective for out-of-state students. SAT/ACT scores required of all, however scores are only used in admissions decisions for out-of-state applicants. Out-of-state applicants must rank in top half of graduating class or have ACT score of 14 or SAT score of 560 (exclusive of Writing), and 2.0 GPA. **Homeschooled:** Transcript of courses and grades required. **Learning Disabled:** There are no special admissions requirements for students with learning disabilities, but depending upon their test scores, they may qualify for various tutoring opportunities, or other assistance through our Center for Achievement and Transition Services department.

**High school preparation.** 16 units recommended. Recommended units include English 4, mathematics 2, social studies 3, science 2 and foreign language 1.

**2009-2010 Annual costs.** Tuition/fees: $4,581; $4,581 out-of-state. Peru State College has eliminated out-of-state (non-resident) tuition beginning in 2009 fall as part of a three-year pilot program. That means that every student, regardless of your residency status, has the opportunity to pay the in-state tuition rate. Since we already offer a single tuition rate for online courses, the program applies only to those students pursuing their degrees on-site. Room/board: $4,962. Books/supplies: $600. Personal expenses: $1,000.

**2008-2009 Financial aid.** All financial aid based on need.

**Application procedures. Admission:** Priority date 12/1; no deadline. No application fee. Admission notification on a rolling basis beginning on or about 9/1. **Financial aid:** Priority date 3/1; no closing date. FAFSA, institutional form required. Applicants notified on a rolling basis starting 3/1; must reply within 2 week(s) of notification.

**Academics. Special study options:** Cooperative education, cross-registration, distance learning, double major, dual enrollment of high school students, honors, independent study, internships, liberal arts/career combination, study abroad, teacher certification program. **Credit/placement by examination:** CLEP, IB. 16 credit hours maximum toward bachelor's degree. **Support services:** Learning center, reduced course load, remedial instruction, study skills assistance, tutoring.

**Majors. Biology:** Plant physiology. **Business:** Business admin, office technology. **Computer sciences:** General, computer science, programming. **Education:** General, art, biology, computer, early childhood, elementary, English, history, mathematics, middle, music, physical, physics, science, secondary, social science, special, speech, voc/tech. **Interdisciplinary:** Natural sciences. **Math:** General. **Protective services:** Law enforcement admin. **Psychology:** General. **Social sciences:** General, sociology. **Visual/performing arts:** Art.

**Most popular majors.** Business/marketing 38%, education 47%, psychology 6%.

**Computing on campus.** 140 workstations in dormitories, library, computer center, student center. Dormitories linked to campus network.

**Student life. Freshman orientation:** Mandatory. Preregistration for classes offered. 5 different 1-day sessions in June, July, August. **Housing:** Guaranteed on-campus for freshmen. Coed dorms, single-sex dorms, apartments, wellness housing available. $100 deposit. **Activities:** Bands, choral groups, drama, literary magazine, music ensembles, musical theater, student government, student newspaper, TV station, Fellowship of Christian Athletes, multicultural committee, Phi Beta Lambda, Peru Players, Women's Athletic Association, Ambassadors.

**Athletics.** NAIA. **Intercollegiate:** Baseball M, basketball, football (tackle) M, golf W, softball W, volleyball W. **Intramural:** Basketball, soccer, softball, swimming, table tennis, tennis, volleyball, water polo M. **Team name:** Bobcats.

**Student services.** Adult student services, alcohol/substance abuse counseling, chaplain/spiritual director, career counseling, student employment services, financial aid counseling, health services, on-campus daycare, personal counseling, placement for graduates, veterans' counselor. **Physically disabled:** Services for visually, hearing impaired.

**Contact.** E-mail: admissions@oakmail.peru.edu
Phone: (402) 872-2221 Toll-free number: (800) 742-4412
Fax: (402) 872-2296
Micki Willis, Vice President for Enrollment Management and Student Affairs, Peru State College, Box 10, Peru, NE 68421-0010

---

## Union College
**Lincoln, Nebraska**
www.ucollege.edu

**CB code: 6865**

- Private 4-year liberal arts college affiliated with Seventh-day Adventists
- Residential campus in small city
- 736 degree-seeking undergraduates: 10% part-time, 58% women, 3% African American, 3% Asian American, 8% Hispanic American, 1% Native American, 7% international
- 70 graduate students
- 41% of applicants admitted
- SAT or ACT (ACT writing optional), application essay required
- 57% graduate within 6 years

**General.** Founded in 1889. Regionally accredited. **Degrees:** 178 bachelor's, 22 associate awarded; master's offered. **Location:** 50 miles from Omaha. **Calendar:** Semester, limited summer session. **Full-time faculty:** 57 total; 42% have terminal degrees, 9% minority, 35% women. **Part-time faculty:** 35 total; 14% have terminal degrees, 11% minority, 60% women. **Class size:** 74% < 20, 23% 20-39, 2% 40-49, 2% 50-99. **Special facilities:** Arboretum.

**Freshman class profile.** 392 applied, 162 admitted, 117 enrolled.

| Mid 50% test scores | | | |
|---|---|---|---|
| ACT composite: | 20-25 | Rank in top quarter: | 19% |
| GPA 3.75 or higher: | 34% | Rank in top tenth: | 13% |
| GPA 3.50-3.74: | 22% | Return as sophomores: | 65% |
| GPA 3.0-3.49: | 26% | Out-of-state: | 79% |
| GPA 2.0-2.99: | 17% | Live on campus: | 96% |

**Basis for selection.** School achievement record and 3 references (including 1 from pastor) very important. Interview recommended for all students; audition recommended for music program; portfolio recommended for art program.

**High school preparation.** College-preparatory program recommended. 20 units required. Required and recommended units include English 3-4, mathematics 2-3, social studies 1, history 1, science 2-3 (laboratory 1), foreign language 1 and academic electives 3. 2 algebra, 1 geometry, trigonometry recommended for mathematics and science-related programs. Physics and chemistry recommended for nursing, biology, chemistry, physics, engineering, medical technology, premedicine, and predental programs.

**2010-2011 Annual costs.** Tuition/fees (projected): $18,150. Room/board: $5,900. Books/supplies: $1,000. Personal expenses: $1,200.

**2008-2009 Financial aid. Non-need-based:** Scholarships awarded for academics. **Additional information:** Special institutional grants offered to all freshmen and sophomores demonstrating exceptional financial need.

**Application procedures. Admission:** No deadline. No application fee. Admission notification on a rolling basis. **Financial aid:** Priority date 5/1; no closing date. FAFSA required. Applicants notified on a rolling basis starting 4/15; must reply by 5/1 or within 3 week(s) of notification.

**Academics. Special study options:** Cross-registration, double major, dual enrollment of high school students, ESL, honors, independent study, internships, student-designed major, study abroad, teacher certification program. **Credit/placement by examination:** AP, CLEP, IB, ACT, institutional tests. **Support services:** Learning center, reduced course load, remedial instruction, study skills assistance, tutoring, writing center.

**Majors. Biology:** General, biochemistry. **Business:** Accounting, business admin, finance, international finance, management science. **Communications:** Journalism, public relations. **Computer sciences:** Computer science, information systems, systems analysis. **Education:** General, elementary, secondary. **Foreign languages:** French, German, Spanish. **History:** General. **Math:** General. **Parks/recreation:** Health/fitness, sports admin. **Philosophy/religion:** Religion. **Physical sciences:** Chemistry, physics. **Psychology:** General. **Public administration:** Social work. **Social sciences:** General. **Theology:** Pastoral counseling, religious ed, theology. **Visual/performing arts:** Commercial/advertising art, music performance, studio arts. **Other:** International relief and rescue.

**Most popular majors.** Business/marketing 15%, communications/journalism 6%, education 12%, health sciences 29%, theological studies 7%.

**Computing on campus.** 80 workstations in dormitories, library, computer center, student center. Dormitories wired for high-speed internet access and linked to campus network. Commuter students can connect to campus network. Online library, helpline, student web hosting, wireless network available.

**Student life. Freshman orientation:** Mandatory. Preregistration for classes offered. **Policies:** Religious observance required. **Housing:** Guaranteed on-campus for all undergraduates. Single-sex dorms, apartments available. **Activities:** Concert band, choral groups, drama, literary magazine, music ensembles, student government, student newspaper, Collegiate Adventists for Better Living, Union for Christ, Union for Kids.

**Athletics. Intercollegiate:** Basketball, soccer. **Intramural:** Badminton, basketball, bowling, football (non-tackle), golf, gymnastics, racquetball, soccer, softball, tennis, volleyball. **Team name:** Warriors and Lady Warriors.

**Student services.** Chaplain/spiritual director, career counseling, student employment services, financial aid counseling, health services, minority student services, personal counseling, placement for graduates. **Physically disabled:** Services for visually, speech, hearing impaired.

**Contact.** E-mail: ucenroll@ucollege.edu
Phone: (402) 486-2504 Toll-free number: (800) 228-4600
Fax: (402) 486-2895
Huda McClelland, Director of Admission, Union College, 3800 South 48th Street, Lincoln, NE 68506-4300

---

## University of Nebraska - Kearney
### Kearney, Nebraska
### www.unk.edu
**CB code: 6467**

- Public 4-year university
- Residential campus in large town
- 4,904 degree-seeking undergraduates: 8% part-time, 52% women, 1% African American, 1% Asian American, 5% Hispanic American, 8% international
- 1,619 degree-seeking graduate students
- 77% of applicants admitted
- SAT or ACT (ACT writing optional) required
- 59% graduate within 6 years

**General.** Founded in 1903. Regionally accredited. **Degrees:** 966 bachelor's awarded; master's offered. **ROTC:** Army. **Location:** 180 miles from Omaha. **Calendar:** Semester, extensive summer session. **Full-time faculty:** 305 total; 78% have terminal degrees, 7% minority, 47% women. **Part-time faculty:** 101 total; 22% have terminal degrees, 5% minority, 57% women. **Class size:** 44% < 20, 45% 20-39, 6% 40-49, 4% 50-99, less than 1% >100. **Special facilities:** Nebraska state art collection, state arboretum, planetarium.

**Freshman class profile.** 2,895 applied, 2,215 admitted, 983 enrolled.

| Mid 50% test scores | | | |
|---|---|---|---|
| SAT critical reading: | 400-660 | GPA 3.0-3.49: | 25% |
| SAT math: | 370-700 | GPA 2.0-2.99: | 25% |
| SAT writing: | 380-670 | Rank in top quarter: | 42% |
| ACT composite: | 20-25 | Rank in top tenth: | 17% |
| GPA 3.75 or higher: | 31% | Out-of-state: | 7% |
| GPA 3.50-3.74: | 18% | Live on campus: | 88% |
| | | International: | 5% |

**Basis for selection.** Test scores, school achievement record most important. Applicants who show promise of academic success, but do not meet admission requirements, may be admitted on conditional basis.

**High school preparation.** 16 units required. Required units include English 4, mathematics 3, social studies 3, science 3 (laboratory 1), foreign language 2 and academic electives 1.

**2009-2010 Annual costs.** Tuition/fees: $5,635; $10,397 out-of-state. Room/board: $6,830. Books/supplies: $952. Personal expenses: $2,556.

**2009-2010 Financial aid. Need-based:** 820 full-time freshmen applied for aid; 657 were judged to have need; 649 of these received aid. Average need met was 83%. Average scholarship/grant was $6,283; average loan $2,573. 49% of total undergraduate aid awarded as scholarships/grants, 51% as loans/jobs. **Non-need-based:** Awarded to 1,819 full-time undergraduates, including 397 freshmen. Scholarships awarded for academics, alumni affiliation, art, athletics, leadership, minority status, music/drama, ROTC, state residency.

**Application procedures. Admission:** Priority date 8/1; no deadline. $45 fee, may be waived for applicants with need. Admission notification on a rolling basis beginning on or about 10/1. **Financial aid:** Priority date 4/1; no closing date. FAFSA, institutional form required. Applicants notified on a rolling basis starting 3/15; must reply within 2 week(s) of notification.

**Academics. Special study options:** Cooperative education, distance learning, double major, dual enrollment of high school students, ESL, exchange student, honors, independent study, internships, study abroad, teacher certification program. International student exchange program with Sapporo University and Kansai Gaidai, Japan; Nebraska semester abroad. **Credit/placement by examination:** CLEP, SAT, ACT, institutional tests. 45 credit hours maximum toward bachelor's degree. **Support services:** Learning center, study skills assistance, tutoring, writing center.

**Majors. Agriculture:** Business. **Biology:** General. **Business:** Business admin, office management, office/clerical, operations, tourism/travel. **Communications:** General, advertising, broadcast journalism, journalism. **Computer sciences:** General, information systems. **Education:** General, art, biology, business, chemistry, early childhood, elementary, English, ESL, family/consumer sciences, foreign languages, French, German, health, history, learning disabled, mathematics, mentally handicapped, middle, multiple handicapped, music, physical, physically handicapped, physics, science, secondary, social science, Spanish, special, speech, speech impaired, technology/industrial arts, trade/industrial. **Family/consumer sciences:** General, business, clothing/textiles, family studies, housing. **Foreign languages:** French, German, Spanish, translation. **Health:** Medical radiologic technology/radiation therapy, respiratory therapy technology, speech pathology. **History:** General. **Liberal arts:** Arts/sciences. **Math:** General. **Parks/recreation:** Facilities management, sports admin. **Philosophy/religion:** Philosophy. **Physical sciences:** Chemistry, physics. **Protective services:** Criminal justice, police science. **Psychology:** General. **Public administration:** Social work. **Social sciences:** General, economics, geography, international relations, political science, sociology. **Visual/performing arts:** General, art, art history/conservation, commercial/advertising art, dramatic, music performance, studio arts.

**Most popular majors.** Business/marketing 25%, education 17%, parks/recreation 8%.

**Computing on campus.** 411 workstations in dormitories, library, computer center, student center. Dormitories wired for high-speed internet access and linked to campus network. Commuter students can connect to campus network. Online course registration, helpline, repair service, wireless network available.

**Student life. Freshman orientation:** Available. Preregistration for classes offered. **Housing:** Guaranteed on-campus for freshmen. Coed dorms, single-sex dorms, apartments, fraternity/sorority housing available. $50 nonrefundable deposit. **Activities:** Bands, campus ministries, choral groups, dance, drama, international student organizations, music ensembles, Model UN, musical theater, radio station, student government, student newspaper, symphony orchestra, TV station, Young Republicans, Young Democrats, Alpha Phi Omega, Fellowship of Christian Athletes, People of Color.

**Athletics. NCAA. Intercollegiate:** Baseball M, basketball, cross-country, diving W, football (tackle) M, golf, softball W, swimming W, tennis, track and field, volleyball W, wrestling M. **Intramural:** Archery, badminton, basketball, bowling, cross-country, diving, football (non-tackle), golf, racquetball, soccer, softball, swimming, table tennis, tennis, track and field, volleyball, water polo, wrestling M. **Team name:** Lopers.

**Student services.** Alcohol/substance abuse counseling, career counseling, student employment services, financial aid counseling, health services, minority student services, on-campus daycare, personal counseling, placement for graduates, veterans' counselor, women's services. **Physically disabled:** Services for visually, hearing impaired.

**Contact.** E-mail: admissionsug@unk.edu
Phone: (308) 865-8526 Toll-free number: (800) 532-7639
Fax: (308) 865-8987
Dusty Newton, Director of Admissions, University of Nebraska - Kearney, 905 West 25th, Kearney, NE 68849

---

## University of Nebraska - Lincoln
### Lincoln, Nebraska
### www.unl.edu
**CB member**
**CB code: 6877**

- Public 4-year university
- Residential campus in small city
- 18,955 degree-seeking undergraduates: 6% part-time, 46% women, 3% African American, 3% Asian American, 4% Hispanic American, 1% Native American, 3% international
- 4,444 degree-seeking graduate students
- 63% of applicants admitted
- SAT or ACT (ACT writing optional) required
- 63% graduate within 6 years

**General.** Founded in 1869. Regionally accredited. Nebraska's only land-grant university. Research opportunities impacting state's economic development available to students. **Degrees:** 3,219 bachelor's, 8 associate awarded;

master's, doctoral, professional offered. **ROTC:** Army, Naval, Air Force. **Location:** 50 miles from Omaha. **Calendar:** Semester, extensive summer session. **Full-time faculty:** 1,102 total; 96% have terminal degrees, 18% minority, 29% women. **Part-time faculty:** 9 total; 100% have terminal degrees, 11% minority, 33% women. **Class size:** 38% < 20, 42% 20-39, 6% 40-49, 7% 50-99, 7% >100. **Special facilities:** State museum, planetarium, center for performing arts, arboretum, center for Asian culture, center for Great Plains studies, center for biomaterials and genetic research.

### Freshman class profile. 9,455 applied, 5,943 admitted, 3,986 enrolled.

| Mid 50% test scores | | | |
|---|---|---|---|
| SAT critical reading: | 510-670 | Return as sophomores: | 84% |
| SAT math: | 530-680 | Out-of-state: | 19% |
| ACT composite: | 22-29 | Live on campus: | 91% |
| Rank in top quarter: | 54% | International: | 2% |
| Rank in top tenth: | 27% | Fraternities: | 21% |
| | | Sororities: | 25% |

**Basis for selection.** Students must meet minimum requirements of 20 ACT composite score, SAT combined score of 950 (exclusive of Writing) or rank in top half of class. Audition required for music program. **Home-schooled:** Statement describing homeschool structure and mission, transcript of courses and grades required.

**High school preparation.** College-preparatory program required. 16 units required. Required and recommended units include English 4, mathematics 4, social studies 3, history 1, science 3 (laboratory 1) and foreign language 2. Mathematics must include algebra I and II, geometry, and 1 higher level math. 2 units of foreign language must be in same language. At least 1 social studies should be U.S. and/or world history and 1 additional unit should be history, American government, and/or geography. College of Engineering & Technology requires 1 pre-calculus/trigonometry, 1 physics and 1 chemistry. Architecture requires 0.5 trigonometry or pre-calculus for pre-architecture.

**2009-2010 Annual costs.** Tuition/fees: $6,857; $17,897 out-of-state. Room/board: $7,260. Books/supplies: $990. Personal expenses: $2,091.

**2008-2009 Financial aid.** **Need-based:** 2,956 full-time freshmen applied for aid; 1,917 were judged to have need; 1,884 of these received aid. Average need met was 89%. Average scholarship/grant was $7,585; average loan $3,198. 49% of total undergraduate aid awarded as scholarships/grants, 51% as loans/jobs. **Non-need-based:** Awarded to 2,695 full-time undergraduates, including 1,044 freshmen. Scholarships awarded for academics, alumni affiliation, art, athletics, leadership, minority status, music/drama, state residency.

**Application procedures. Admission:** Priority date 1/15; deadline 5/1 (receipt date). $45 fee, may be waived for applicants with need. Admission notification on a rolling basis beginning on or about 9/1. Must reply by 5/1. **Financial aid:** Priority date 4/15; no closing date. FAFSA required. Applicants notified on a rolling basis starting 4/1.

**Academics.** Comprehensive Education Program (CEP) is required of all entering students. Master of architecture professional degree available. **Special study options:** Accelerated study, combined bachelor's/graduate degree, cooperative education, cross-registration, distance learning, double major, dual enrollment of high school students, ESL, exchange student, honors, independent study, internships, liberal arts/career combination, student-designed major, study abroad, teacher certification program. **Credit/placement by examination:** AP, CLEP, IB, SAT, ACT, institutional tests. Individual colleges have different policies. **Support services:** Learning center, pre-admission summer program, reduced course load, remedial instruction, study skills assistance, tutoring, writing center.

**Honors college/program.** Formal application required. Acceptance based on evaluation of the student's potential by the faculty committee.

**Majors. Agriculture:** General, agronomy, animal sciences, business, communications, economics, food science, horticultural science, landscaping, mechanization, plant protection, products processing, range science, soil science. **Architecture:** Architecture, interior, landscape. **Area/ethnic studies:** Latin American, regional, Western European, women's. **Biology:** General, biochemistry, botany. **Business:** Accounting, actuarial science, business admin, finance, hospitality admin, international, management science, managerial economics, marketing. **Communications:** General, advertising, broadcast journalism, journalism. **Computer sciences:** General. **Conservation:** General, environmental studies, management/policy. **Education:** Agricultural, art, biology, business, chemistry, computer, Deaf/hearing impaired, elementary, English, ESL, foreign languages, French, German, health, history, mathematics, middle, multi-level teacher, music, physical, physics, reading, sales/marketing, science, social science, Spanish, technology/industrial arts, trade/industrial. **Engineering:** Agricultural, architectural, biomedical, chemical, civil, computer, electrical, industrial, mechanical. **Engineering technology:** Construction, electrical, industrial. **Family/consumer sciences:** General, clothing/textiles, food/nutrition, housing. **Foreign languages:** Ancient Greek, classics, French, German, Latin, Russian, Spanish.

**Health:** Athletic training, community health services, predental, premedicine, prepharmacy, preveterinary, speech pathology, veterinary technology/assistant. **History:** General. **Interdisciplinary:** Ancient studies, medieval/Renaissance. **Liberal arts:** Arts/sciences, humanities. **Math:** General. **Parks/recreation:** Exercise sciences. **Philosophy/religion:** Philosophy. **Physical sciences:** Atmospheric science, chemistry, geology, hydrology, physics. **Protective services:** Forensics. **Psychology:** General. **Social sciences:** Anthropology, economics, geography, international relations, political science, sociology. **Visual/performing arts:** Art history/conservation, dance, dramatic, film/cinema, studio arts. **Other:** Child, youth and family studies, Technical education.

**Most popular majors.** Agriculture 6%, business/marketing 22%, communications/journalism 6%, education 10%, engineering/engineering technologies 12%, family/consumer sciences 8%, social sciences 6%.

**Computing on campus.** 650 workstations in dormitories, library, computer center, student center. Dormitories wired for high-speed internet access and linked to campus network. Commuter students can connect to campus network. Online course registration, online library, helpline, student web hosting, wireless network available.

**Student life. Freshman orientation:** Available. Preregistration for classes offered. Day-long program conducted from mid-June to mid-July. **Policies:** No smoking allowed in University buildings. No alcohol or firearms on campus. Freshmen required to live on campus if not living with parents or close relatives. **Housing:** Guaranteed on-campus for freshmen. Coed dorms, single-sex dorms, special housing for disabled, apartments, cooperative housing, fraternity/sorority housing available. $250 partly refundable deposit, deadline 5/1. Pets allowed in dorm rooms. Special interest floors available. **Activities:** Bands, campus ministries, choral groups, dance, drama, film society, international student organizations, literary magazine, music ensembles, musical theater, opera, radio station, student government, student newspaper, symphony orchestra, TV station, Afrikaan People's Union, University of Nebraska Inter-Tribal Exchange, Mexican-American student association, adult student network, Ecology Now, student foundation, student-alumni association, UNL Entrepreneurial Society.

**Athletics.** NCAA. **Intercollegiate:** Baseball M, basketball, bowling W, cross-country, diving W, football (tackle) M, golf, gymnastics, rifle W, rodeo, rowing (crew), soccer W, softball W, swimming W, tennis, track and field, volleyball W, wrestling M. **Intramural:** Football (non-tackle), soccer, softball, tennis, track and field, volleyball, water polo, wrestling M. **Team name:** Cornhuskers.

**Student services.** Adult student services, alcohol/substance abuse counseling, chaplain/spiritual director, career counseling, services for economically disadvantaged, student employment services, financial aid counseling, health services, legal services, minority student services, on-campus daycare, personal counseling, placement for graduates, veterans' counselor, women's services. **Physically disabled:** Services for visually, speech, hearing impaired.

**Contact.** E-mail: admissions@unl.edu
Phone: (402) 472-2023 Toll-free number: (800) 742-8800
Fax: (402) 472-0670
Alan Cerveny, Dean of Admissions, University of Nebraska - Lincoln, 1410 Q Street, Lincoln, NE 68588-0417

---

## University of Nebraska - Omaha
**Omaha, Nebraska**
**www.unomaha.edu**

**CB member**
**CB code: 6420**

- Public 4-year university
- Commuter campus in large city
- 11,323 degree-seeking undergraduates: 20% part-time, 52% women, 6% African American, 3% Asian American, 4% Hispanic American, 1% Native American, 2% international
- 2,785 degree-seeking graduate students
- 80% of applicants admitted
- SAT or ACT (ACT writing optional) required
- 45% graduate within 6 years

**General.** Founded in 1908. Regionally accredited. Cooperative classes at Offutt Air Force Base. Cooperative programs with UNMC medical center. **Degrees:** 1,969 bachelor's awarded; master's, doctoral offered. **ROTC:** Army, Air Force. **Location:** 160 miles from Kansas City, Missouri. **Calendar:** Semester, limited summer session. **Full-time faculty:** 500 total; 82% have terminal degrees, 19% minority, 42% women. **Part-time faculty:** 398 total; 24% have terminal degrees, 12% minority, 47% women. **Class size:** 32% < 20, 46% 20-39, 10% 40-49, 11% 50-99, 2% >100. **Special facilities:** Outdoor venture center, climbing wall, nature preserve, planetarium, Nebraska Book Arts Center.

**Freshman class profile.** 4,845 applied, 3,896 admitted, 1,816 enrolled.

| Mid 50% test scores | | Rank in top tenth: | 11% |
|---|---|---|---|
| ACT composite: | 20-26 | Return as sophomores: | 72% |
| GPA 3.75 or higher: | 26% | Out-of-state: | 8% |
| GPA 3.50-3.74: | 16% | Live on campus: | 39% |
| GPA 3.0-3.49: | 29% | International: | 2% |
| GPA 2.0-2.99: | 28% | Fraternities: | 5% |
| Rank in top quarter: | 35% | Sororities: | 4% |

**Basis for selection.** School achievement record, test scores important. Must have ACT score of 20, comparable SAT score or class rank in upper half of graduating class. Admitted for special talent consideration on case by case basis. Open admission for non-degree applicants and non-traditional adult freshman applicants. Audition required for music program. **Homeschooled:** Applicants must submit official GED scores verifying successful completion of the GED. An ACT composite score of 25+ may be substituted in lieu of the GED score.

**High school preparation.** College-preparatory program required. 16 units required. Required units include English 4, mathematics 3, social studies 1, history 2, science 3 (laboratory 1), foreign language 2 and academic electives 1. Specific course requirements for programs in business administration, human resources and family services for College of Engineering and Technology.

**2009-2010 Annual costs.** Tuition/fees: $6,229; $16,189 out-of-state. Room/board: $7,230. Books/supplies: $900. Personal expenses: $2,110.

**2008-2009 Financial aid. Need-based:** 1,304 full-time freshmen applied for aid; 869 were judged to have need; 841 of these received aid. Average scholarship/grant was $1,888; average loan $2,643. 47% of total undergraduate aid awarded as scholarships/grants, 53% as loans/jobs. **Non-need-based:** Awarded to 2,365 full-time undergraduates, including 803 freshmen. Scholarships awarded for academics, alumni affiliation, art, athletics, leadership, minority status, music/drama, ROTC, state residency.

**Application procedures. Admission:** Closing date 8/1 (postmark date). $45 fee. Admission notification on a rolling basis. **Financial aid:** Priority date 3/1; no closing date. FAFSA required. Applicants notified on a rolling basis starting 4/15; must reply within 2 week(s) of notification.

**Academics.** Associate degree program available on Omaha campus through University of Nebraska-Lincoln in construction, drafting and design technology, electronic technology, fire control and safety technology, fire protection, manufacturing technology. On-line courses in aviation studies also available. **Special study options:** Combined bachelor's/graduate degree, cooperative education, cross-registration, distance learning, double major, dual enrollment of high school students, ESL, exchange student, honors, independent study, internships, student-designed major, study abroad, teacher certification program. **Credit/placement by examination:** AP, CLEP, ACT, institutional tests. 30 credit hours maximum toward bachelor's degree. CLEP exams in American History and Western Civilization must be accompanied by essay. **Support services:** Reduced course load, study skills assistance, tutoring, writing center.

**Majors. Area/ethnic studies:** African-American, Latin American, women's. **Biology:** General, bioinformatics, biotechnology. **Business:** General, accounting, banking/financial services, business admin, finance, investments/securities, management information systems, managerial economics, marketing, real estate, small business admin. **Communications:** General, broadcast journalism, journalism. **Computer sciences:** Computer science. **Conservation:** Environmental studies. **Education:** Elementary, music, physical, secondary, special, speech impaired. **Engineering:** Architectural, chemical, civil, computer, electrical, physics. **Engineering technology:** Construction, industrial, manufacturing. **Family/consumer sciences:** General, communication, family resources. **Foreign languages:** French, German, Spanish. **Health:** Community health services, health care admin, premedicine. **History:** General. **Interdisciplinary:** Gerontology, global studies, natural sciences. **Liberal arts:** Library science. **Math:** General. **Parks/recreation:** General, exercise sciences. **Philosophy/religion:** Philosophy, religion. **Physical sciences:** Chemistry, geology, physics. **Protective services:** Criminal justice. **Psychology:** General. **Public administration:** General, social work. **Social sciences:** Geography, political science, sociology, urban studies. **Transportation:** Aviation, aviation management. **Visual/performing arts:** Art, art history/conservation, dramatic, music performance, music theory/composition, piano/organ, stringed instruments, studio arts, voice/opera.

**Most popular majors.** Business/marketing 25%, communications/journalism 6%, education 12%, psychology 6%, security/protective services 7%.

**Computing on campus.** 2,415 workstations in dormitories, library, computer center, student center. Dormitories wired for high-speed internet access and linked to campus network. Commuter students can connect to campus network. Online course registration, online library, helpline, student web hosting, wireless network available.

**Student life. Freshman orientation:** Mandatory. Preregistration for classes offered. Held every week April 15 thru August 1st. **Housing:** Coed dorms available. $260 partly refundable deposit. **Activities:** Bands, campus ministries, choral groups, dance, drama, film society, international student organizations, literary magazine, music ensembles, musical theater, opera, radio station, student government, student newspaper, symphony orchestra, TV station, American multi-cultural students, chapter summary Bible study, student government legislative & public relations, Campus Crusade for Christ, honor societies, Greek letter organizations.

**Athletics.** NCAA. **Intercollegiate:** Baseball M, basketball, cross-country W, football (tackle) M, golf W, ice hockey M, soccer W, softball W, swimming W, tennis, track and field W, volleyball W, wrestling M. **Intramural:** Badminton, basketball, bowling, football (non-tackle), golf, gymnastics, handball, racquetball, soccer, softball, squash, swimming, tennis, track and field, volleyball, wrestling. **Team name:** Mavericks.

**Student services.** Adult student services, alcohol/substance abuse counseling, chaplain/spiritual director, career counseling, services for economically disadvantaged, student employment services, financial aid counseling, health services, minority student services, on-campus daycare, personal counseling, placement for graduates, veterans' counselor, women's services. **Physically disabled:** Services for visually, speech, hearing impaired.

**Contact.** E-mail: unoadm@mail.unomaha.edu
Phone: (402) 554-2393 Toll-free number: (800) 858-8648
Fax: (402) 554-3472
Jolene Adams, Director of Admissions, University of Nebraska - Omaha, 6001 Dodge Street, Omaha, NE 68182-0005

## University of Nebraska Medical Center
**Omaha, Nebraska**
**www.unmc.edu**　　　　　　　　　　　　　**CB code: 6896**

▶ Public two-year upper-division health science college
▶ Commuter campus in very large city

**General.** Founded in 1869. Regionally accredited. Students must have 30 plus transfer hours to be admitted to UNMC. **Degrees:** 343 bachelor's awarded; master's, doctoral, professional offered. **ROTC:** Army, Air Force. **Calendar:** Semester, limited summer session. **Full-time faculty:** 989 total; 87% have terminal degrees, 19% minority, 40% women. **Part-time faculty:** 201 total; 87% have terminal degrees, 8% minority, 46% women.

**Student profile.** 790 degree-seeking undergraduates, 2,426 degree-seeking graduate students. 16% entered as juniors, 12% entered as seniors. 5% transferred from two-year, 95% transferred from four-year institutions.

| | | | |
|---|---|---|---|
| Women: | 91% | International: | 1% |
| African American: | 2% | Part-time: | 9% |
| Asian American: | 2% | Out-of-state: | 10% |
| Hispanic American: | 4% | 25 or older: | 31% |
| Native American: | 1% | | |

**Basis for selection.** College transcript required. Admissions requirements, application procedures, and closing dates vary by program. Health professions program applicants must have completed prerequisite courses at another institution. Transfer accepted as sophomores, juniors, seniors.

**2009-2010 Annual costs.** Tuition/fees: $5,990; $17,030 out-of-state. Tuition varies by program. Books/supplies: $900. Personal expenses: $1,500.

**Financial aid. Need-based:** 835 applied for aid; 710 were judged to have need; 686 of these received aid. Average need met was 54%. 38% of total undergraduate aid awarded as scholarships/grants, 62% as loans/jobs. **Non-need-based:** Awarded to 144 undergraduates.

**Application procedures. Admission:** $45 fee, may be waived for applicants with need. Application must be submitted online. **Financial aid:** No deadline. Applicants notified on a rolling basis starting 5/1; must reply within 2 weeks of notification. FAFSA, institutional form required.

**Academics. Special study options:** Accelerated study, combined bachelor's/graduate degree, distance learning, honors. **Credit/placement by examination:** CLEP, IB, institutional tests. 24 credit hours maximum toward bachelor's degree.

**Majors. Health:** Clinical lab science, dental hygiene, medical radiologic technology/radiation therapy, nuclear medical technology, nursing (RN), radiologic technology/medical imaging, sonography.

**Computing on campus.** 108 workstations in library, computer center, student center. Commuter students can connect to campus network. Online library, helpline, repair service, wireless network available.

**Student life. Housing:** Apartments available. **Activities:** Student government, committee on minority concerns, American Academy of Physician Assistants, Religious Life Council, Christian Fellowship, student association for rural health, student services council, student professional organizations.

**Athletics. Intramural:** Basketball, softball, volleyball.

**Student services.** Alcohol/substance abuse counseling, career counseling, services for economically disadvantaged, financial aid counseling, health services, minority student services, on-campus daycare, personal counseling, veterans' counselor. **Physically disabled:** Services for hearing impaired.

**Contact.** E-mail: ttonjes@unmc.edu
Phone: (402) 559-6468 Toll-free number: (800) 626-8431 ext. 96468
Fax: (402) 559-6796
University of Nebraska Medical Center, 984230 Nebraska Medical Center, Omaha, NE 68198-4230

## Wayne State College
Wayne, Nebraska
www.wsc.edu

**CB member**
**CB code: 6469**

♦ Public 4-year liberal arts and teachers college
♦ Residential campus in small town
♦ 2,924 degree-seeking undergraduates: 8% part-time, 54% women, 3% African American, 1% Asian American, 2% Hispanic American, 1% Native American, 1% international
♦ 570 degree-seeking graduate students
♦ 48% graduate within 6 years

**General.** Founded in 1909. Regionally accredited. Campus is state arboretum. **Degrees:** 491 bachelor's awarded; master's offered. **ROTC:** Army. **Location:** 45 miles from Sioux City, Iowa. **Calendar:** Semester, extensive summer session. **Full-time faculty:** 122 total; 76% have terminal degrees, 6% minority, 48% women. **Part-time faculty:** 98 total; 11% have terminal degrees, 7% minority, 70% women. **Class size:** 42% < 20, 51% 20-39, 6% 40-49, 1% 50-99. **Special facilities:** Planetarium, outdoor amphitheater.

**Freshman class profile.**

| | | | |
|---|---|---|---|
| GPA 3.75 or higher: | 24% | Rank in top tenth: | 11% |
| GPA 3.50-3.74: | 18% | Return as sophomores: | 67% |
| GPA 3.0-3.49: | 26% | Out-of-state: | 14% |
| GPA 2.0-2.99: | 27% | Live on campus: | 95% |
| Rank in top quarter: | 30% | International: | 1% |

**Basis for selection.** Open admission.

**High school preparation.** College-preparatory program recommended. 18 units recommended. Recommended units include English 4, mathematics 3, social studies 3, science 2, foreign language 2, computer science 2 and visual/performing arts 2.

**2009-2010 Annual costs.** Tuition/fees: $4,805; $8,480 out-of-state. Room/board: $5,280. Books/supplies: $1,000. Personal expenses: $900.

**2009-2010 Financial aid. Need-based:** 596 full-time freshmen applied for aid; 476 were judged to have need; 461 of these received aid. Average need met was 60%. Average scholarship/grant was $3,916; average loan $3,329. 49% of total undergraduate aid awarded as scholarships/grants, 51% as loans/jobs. **Non-need-based:** Awarded to 1,054 full-time undergraduates, including 235 freshmen. Scholarships awarded for academics, art, athletics, leadership, minority status, music/drama, religious affiliation, state residency.

**Application procedures. Admission:** Priority date 12/1; deadline 8/20. $30 fee. Admission notification on a rolling basis beginning on or about 9/15. **Financial aid:** Priority date 4/1; no closing date. FAFSA required. Applicants notified on a rolling basis starting 3/1; must reply within 4 week(s) of notification.

**Academics. Special study options:** Cooperative education, distance learning, double major, dual enrollment of high school students, honors, independent study, internships, student-designed major, study abroad, teacher certification program. Learning Communities, First-Year Experience. **Credit/placement by examination:** AP, CLEP, institutional tests. **Support services:** Learning center, reduced course load, study skills assistance, tutoring, writing center.

**Majors. Biology:** General. **Business:** Business admin. **Communications:** General, journalism, media studies. **Computer sciences:** General, information systems. **Education:** Art, biology, business, chemistry, drama/dance,

early childhood, elementary, English, family/consumer sciences, foreign languages, geography, history, mathematics, middle, music, physical, psychology, social science, special, speech, technology/industrial arts. **Engineering technology:** General. **Family/consumer sciences:** General, food/nutrition. **Foreign languages:** General, Spanish. **Health:** Athletic training. **History:** General. **Math:** General. **Parks/recreation:** Exercise sciences, health/fitness, sports admin. **Physical sciences:** Chemistry. **Protective services:** Criminal justice. **Psychology:** General. **Social sciences:** General, geography, political science, sociology. **Visual/performing arts:** Art, dramatic, graphic design.

**Most popular majors.** Business/marketing 22%, education 22%, parks/recreation 8%, psychology 7%, security/protective services 6%.

**Computing on campus.** 365 workstations in library, computer center, student center. Dormitories wired for high-speed internet access and linked to campus network. Commuter students can connect to campus network. Online course registration, helpline, wireless network available.

**Student life. Freshman orientation:** Available, $75 fee. Preregistration for classes offered. **Housing:** Guaranteed on-campus for freshmen. Coed dorms, wellness housing available. $100 fully refundable deposit. **Activities:** Bands, campus ministries, choral groups, dance, drama, international student organizations, literary magazine, music ensembles, musical theater, radio station, student government, student newspaper, TV station.

**Athletics. NCAA. Intercollegiate:** Baseball M, basketball, cross-country, football (tackle) M, golf, soccer W, softball W, track and field, volleyball W. **Intramural:** Archery, badminton, basketball, bowling, football (non-tackle), golf, handball, racquetball, softball, swimming, table tennis, tennis, track and field, volleyball, weight lifting M, wrestling M. **Team name:** Wildcats.

**Student services.** Alcohol/substance abuse counseling, chaplain/spiritual director, career counseling, services for economically disadvantaged, student employment services, financial aid counseling, health services, minority student services, personal counseling, placement for graduates, veterans' counselor. **Physically disabled:** Services for visually, speech, hearing impaired.

**Contact.** E-mail: admit1@wsc.edu
Phone: (402) 375-7234 Toll-free number: (800) 228-9972
Fax: (402) 375-7204
Kevin Halle, Director of Admissions, Wayne State College, 1111 Main Street, Wayne, NE 68787

## York College
York, Nebraska
www.york.edu

**CB code: 6984**

♦ Private 4-year liberal arts and teachers college affiliated with Church of Christ
♦ Residential campus in small town
♦ 410 degree-seeking undergraduates
♦ 60% of applicants admitted
♦ SAT or ACT (ACT writing optional) required

**General.** Founded in 1956. Regionally accredited. **Degrees:** 53 bachelor's, 6 associate awarded. **ROTC:** Army, Naval, Air Force. **Location:** 50 miles from Lincoln. **Calendar:** Semester, limited summer session. **Full-time faculty:** 24 total; 42% have terminal degrees, 4% minority, 38% women. **Part-time faculty:** 24 total; 21% have terminal degrees, 38% women. **Class size:** 85% < 20, 13% 20-39, 2% 40-49, less than 1% 50-99. **Special facilities:** 35,000 sq. ft. indoor sports practice facility, historic prayer chapel.

**Freshman class profile.** 484 applied, 290 admitted, 116 enrolled.

| Mid 50% test scores | | | |
|---|---|---|---|
| | | GPA 2.0-2.99: | 36% |
| SAT critical reading: | 330-470 | Rank in top quarter: | 24% |
| SAT math: | 330-460 | Rank in top tenth: | 11% |
| ACT composite: | 18-24 | Out-of-state: | 66% |
| GPA 3.75 or higher: | 21% | Live on campus: | 95% |
| GPA 3.50-3.74: | 10% | Fraternities: | 66% |
| GPA 3.0-3.49: | 30% | Sororities: | 76% |

**Basis for selection.** ACT/SAT test scores, high school GPA, class rank very important. Essay recommended but not required. **Homeschooled:** Transcript of courses and grades required. **Learning Disabled:** Submission of high school IEP is recommended for students who self-identify learning disabilities.

**High school preparation.** College-preparatory program recommended. 15 units required; 21 recommended. Required and recommended units include English 3-4, mathematics 2-4, social studies 1-4, history 1-4, science 2-4 and foreign language 3.

**2009-2010 Annual costs.** Tuition/fees: $14,000. Room/board: $4,500. Books/supplies: $1,500. Personal expenses: $2,400.

**2008-2009 Financial aid. Non-need-based:** Scholarships awarded for academics, alumni affiliation, athletics, leadership, music/drama.

**Application procedures. Admission:** Priority date 3/31; deadline 8/31 (receipt date). $20 fee, may be waived for applicants with need. Admission notification on a rolling basis. Must reply by 9/1. **Financial aid:** Priority date 4/1; no closing date. FAFSA required. Applicants notified on a rolling basis starting 3/1; must reply within 4 week(s) of notification.

**Academics. Special study options:** Accelerated study, double major, dual enrollment of high school students, independent study, internships, student-designed major, teacher certification program. **Credit/placement by examination:** AP, CLEP, IB, SAT, ACT, institutional tests. 12 credit hours maximum toward associate degree, 32 toward bachelor's. **Support services:** Reduced course load, remedial instruction, study skills assistance, tutoring.

**Majors. Biology:** General. **Business:** Accounting, business admin, finance, human resources. **Communications:** General. **Education:** General, art, biology, business, drama/dance, elementary, English, history, mathematics, middle, multi-level teacher, music, physical, reading, secondary, social science, special, speech. **History:** General. **Math:** General. **Philosophy/religion:** Religion. **Psychology:** General. **Social sciences:** Criminology. **Theology:** Bible, religious ed. **Visual/performing arts:** Voice/opera. **Other:** Sports management.

**Most popular majors.** Biology 7%, business/marketing 26%, education 30%, liberal arts 11%, psychology 9%.

**Computing on campus.** 57 workstations in dormitories, library, computer center. Dormitories wired for high-speed internet access and linked to campus network. Online library, helpline, wireless network available.

**Student life. Freshman orientation:** Mandatory. Preregistration for classes offered. **Policies:** Students expected to conform to Christian norms. Alcohol and tobacco prohibited. Unmarried, full-time students under 21 required to live on campus or with relatives or staff off campus. **Housing:** Guaranteed on-campus for all undergraduates. Single-sex dorms, apartments, wellness housing available. $100 fully refundable deposit, deadline 8/31. **Activities:** Campus ministries, choral groups, drama, music ensembles, musical theater, student government, student newspaper, service clubs, Chi Rho, spiritual life committee.

**Athletics.** NAIA. **Intercollegiate:** Baseball M, basketball, soccer, softball W, volleyball W, wrestling M. **Intramural:** Basketball, football (non-tackle), soccer, softball, table tennis, volleyball. **Team name:** Panthers.

**Student services.** Adult student services, chaplain/spiritual director, career counseling, student employment services, financial aid counseling, personal counseling, placement for graduates, veterans' counselor.

**Contact.** E-mail: enroll@york.edu
Phone: (402) 363-5627 Toll-free number: (800) 950-9675
Fax: (402) 363-5623
Willie Sanchez, Director of Admissions, York College, 1125 East 8th Street, York, NE 68467

# Nevada

## Art Institute of Las Vegas
Henderson, Nevada
www.artinstitutes.edu/lasvegas/     CB code: 3141

- For-profit 3-year culinary school and visual arts college
- Commuter campus in very large city
- 1,182 degree-seeking undergraduates
- Application essay, interview required

**General.** Accredited by ACCSC. The Art Institute of Las Vegas occupies approximately space at 2350 Corporate Circle and 2340 Corporate Circle. **Degrees:** 127 bachelor's, 57 associate awarded. **Location:** 10 miles from Las Vegas. **Calendar:** Quarter, extensive summer session. **Full-time faculty:** 26 total; 8% have terminal degrees. **Part-time faculty:** 41 total; 7% have terminal degrees. **Class size:** 77% < 20, 19% 20-39, 2% 40-49, 2% 50-99. **Special facilities:** Sound-mixing studio, control room, isolation chamber, student-run restaurant, print and service bureaus, photography lab, supply store, learning resource center.

**Freshman class profile.** 356 applied, 351 admitted, 224 enrolled.

| | | | |
|---|---|---|---|
| GPA 3.75 or higher: | 2% | GPA 2.0-2.99: | 60% |
| GPA 3.50-3.74: | 4% | Out-of-state: | 7% |
| GPA 3.0-3.49: | 17% | Live on campus: | 12% |

**Basis for selection.** Open admission, but selective for some programs. Minimum GPA of 2.5 required for game art & design and 2.0 for audio production applicants. Face-to-face or phone interview, an original essay of at least 150 words required. Personal portfolio may be required, depending upon the desired academic curriculum. Official transcripts for high school, GED, and/or college, ACCUPLACER test or satisfactory SAT or ACT scores required of all applicants. **Homeschooled:** Institution must be recognized by state or national department of education. **Learning Disabled:** Accommodations to qualified students with disabilities available through the Student Affairs office.

**2009-2010 Annual costs.** Tuition/fees: $22,002.

**2009-2010 Financial aid.** **Non-need-based:** Scholarships awarded for academics, state residency.

**Application procedures.** **Admission:** No deadline. $150 fee. Application must be submitted on paper. Admission notification on a rolling basis. **Financial aid:** No deadline. Applicants notified on a rolling basis.

**Academics.** **Special study options:** Distance learning, honors, independent study, internships, liberal arts/career combination, study abroad. **Credit/placement by examination:** CLEP, IB, institutional tests. 28 credit hours maximum toward associate degree, 48 toward bachelor's. **Support services:** Learning center, pre-admission summer program, reduced course load, remedial instruction, study skills assistance, tutoring, writing center.

**Majors.** **BACHELOR'S. Communications technology:** Animation/special effects, recording arts. **Computer sciences:** Computer graphics, game design. **Personal/culinary services:** Restaurant/catering. **Visual/performing arts:** General, cinematography, design, fashion design, graphic design, interior design, multimedia, photography. **ASSOCIATE. Personal/culinary services:** Baking, chef training.

**Most popular majors.** Visual/performing arts 30%.

**Computing on campus.** 221 workstations in library, computer center. Commuter students can connect to campus network. Online course registration, online library, student web hosting, wireless network available.

**Student life.** **Freshman orientation:** Mandatory. Preregistration for classes offered. **Policies:** Resident Advisor (RA) available to on-campus students, apartment information and roommate referrals available to off-campus students. **Housing:** Apartments, wellness housing available. $150 partly refundable deposit. **Activities:** Film society.

**Student services.** Adult student services, alcohol/substance abuse counseling, career counseling, services for economically disadvantaged, student employment services, financial aid counseling, personal counseling, placement for graduates. **Physically disabled:** Services for visually, speech, hearing impaired. **Learning disabled:** Comprehensive services available.

**Contact.** Phone: (702) 369-9944
Laurie Perdue, Director of Admissions, Art Institute of Las Vegas, 2350 Corporate Circle, Henderson, NV 89074-7737

## DeVry University: Henderson
Henderson, Nevada
www.devry.edu

- For-profit 4-year university
- Commuter campus in large city
- 279 degree-seeking undergraduates: 50% part-time, 42% women, 20% African American, 11% Asian American, 19% Hispanic American
- 90 degree-seeking graduate students

**General.** **Degrees:** 19 bachelor's, 9 associate awarded; master's offered. **Calendar:** Semester. **Full-time faculty:** 2 total. **Part-time faculty:** 27 total; 22% minority, 41% women.

**Freshman class profile.** 37 enrolled.

**Basis for selection.** Academic record and interview most important.

**High school preparation.** College-preparatory program recommended.

**2009-2010 Annual costs.** Tuition/fees: $14,160. Books/supplies: $1,310. Personal expenses: $3,574.

**2008-2009 Financial aid.** **Non-need-based:** Scholarships awarded for academics.

**Application procedures.** **Admission:** No deadline. $50 fee. Admission notification on a rolling basis. **Financial aid:** No deadline. FAFSA required. Applicants notified on a rolling basis.

**Academics.** **Special study options:** Accelerated study, distance learning. **Credit/placement by examination:** CLEP.

**Majors.** **Business:** Business admin. **Other:** Technology management.

**Contact.** Phone: (702) 933-9700
DeVry University: Henderson, 2490 Paseo Verde Parkway, Suite 150, Henderson, NV 89074-7120

## Great Basin College
Elko, Nevada
www.gbcnv.edu     CB code: 4293

- Public 4-year community and teachers college
- Commuter campus in large town
- 2,389 degree-seeking undergraduates
- Application essay, interview required

**General.** Founded in 1967. Regionally accredited. **Degrees:** 46 bachelor's, 228 associate awarded. **Location:** 280 miles from Reno, 220 miles from Salt Lake City. **Calendar:** Semester, limited summer session. **Full-time faculty:** 104 total. **Part-time faculty:** 178 total.

**Freshman class profile.**

| | | | |
|---|---|---|---|
| Out-of-state: | 5% | Live on campus: | 3% |

**Basis for selection.** Open admission, but selective for some programs. Placement test required for some English and math courses. Nursing applicants selected on basis of point system. Points given for courses completed, grades, current work experience in health field, certifications, letters of recommendation, and scores obtained on required entrance exam which measures math and reading comprehension skills.

**2009-2010 Annual costs.** Tuition/fees: $2,130; $8,318 out-of-state. Discounted tuition (Good Neighbor rates) available for nonresident students residing in certain counties bordering Nevada. On-campus room only $2,090-$3,300 (extended semester has additional costs). Room only: $3,300. Books/supplies: $1,400.

**Application procedures.** **Admission:** No deadline. $10 fee. Admission notification on a rolling basis. **Financial aid:** Priority date 6/1; no closing date. FAFSA required. Applicants notified on a rolling basis starting 7/1.

**Academics.** **Special study options:** Cooperative education, distance learning, dual enrollment of high school students, ESL, independent study, liberal arts/career combination, teacher certification program. **Credit/placement by examination:** AP, CLEP, institutional tests. 15 credit hours

**Four-Year Colleges**

maximum toward associate degree, 30 toward bachelor's. **Support services:** Learning center, reduced course load, remedial instruction, study skills assistance, tutoring, writing center.

**Majors. Agriculture:** Business. **Business:** Business admin. **Education:** Agricultural, biology, elementary, history, mathematics, science, secondary, social science, trade/industrial. **Engineering:** Surveying. **Health:** Nursing (RN). **Interdisciplinary:** Cultural resource management. **Liberal arts:** Arts/sciences. **Social sciences:** General.

**Computing on campus.** 200 workstations in dormitories, library, computer center. Dormitories linked to campus network. Commuter students can connect to campus network. Online course registration, online library, helpline, wireless network available.

**Student life. Freshman orientation:** Mandatory, $26 fee. Preregistration for classes offered. **Housing:** Coed dorms, apartments, wellness housing available. **Activities:** Choral groups, drama, musical theater, student government, vocational clubs, nursing club, rodeo, intramural sports, student ambassadors.

**Athletics. Intramural:** Rodeo, table tennis, volleyball.

**Student services.** Adult student services, career counseling, services for economically disadvantaged, student employment services, financial aid counseling, minority student services, on-campus daycare, personal counseling, placement for graduates, veterans' counselor. **Physically disabled:** Services for visually, speech, hearing impaired.

**Contact.** E-mail: admissions@gbcnv.edu
Phone: (775) 753-2311 Fax: (775) 738-8771
Julie Byrnes, Director of Enrollment Management, Great Basin College, 1500 College Parkway, Elko, NV 89801

## International Academy of Design and Technology: Henderson
Henderson, Nevada
www.iadtvegas.com

‣ For-profit 3-year visual arts and technical college
‣ Very large city
‣ 514 degree-seeking undergraduates

**General.** Accredited by ACICS. **Degrees:** 38 bachelor's, 25 associate awarded. **Location:** 10 miles from Las Vegas. **Calendar:** Quarter. **Full-time faculty:** 6 total. **Part-time faculty:** 36 total. **Class size:** 84% < 20, 16% 20-39.

**Basis for selection.** Open admission. **Homeschooled:** ACT or SAT scores.

**2009-2010 Annual costs.** Tuition/fees: $17,525. Costs of books and supplies vary from $4,200 to $9,600 for entire program depending on course of study. Additional fees may apply.

**Application procedures. Admission:** No deadline. $50 fee. **Financial aid:** No deadline.

**Academics. Special study options:** Distance learning, independent study, internships, study abroad. **Credit/placement by examination:** AP, CLEP. **Support services:** Tutoring.

**Majors. BACHELOR'S. Computer sciences:** Game design. **Visual/performing arts:** Fashion design, graphic design, interior design. **ASSOCIATE. Visual/performing arts:** Fashion design, graphic design, interior design.

**Computing on campus.** Online course registration, online library, wireless network available.

**Student life. Freshman orientation:** Mandatory.

**Contact.** E-mail: vegas_web@iadtvegas.com
Phone: (702) 990-0150 Toll-free number: (866) 400-4238
Maggie Balderas, Director of Admissions, International Academy of Design and Technology: Henderson, 2495 Village View Drive, Henderson, NV 89074

## ITT Technical Institute: Henderson
Henderson, Nevada
www.itt-tech.edu     CB code: 2710

‣ For-profit 4-year technical college
‣ Commuter campus in small city

**General.** Accredited by ACICS. **Calendar:** Quarter.

**Contact.** Phone: (702) 558-5404
Director of Recruitment, 168 North Gibson Road, Henderson, NV 89014

## Morrison University
Reno, Nevada
www.morrisonuniversity.com     CB code: 2114

‣ For-profit 4-year university and business college
‣ Commuter campus in small city
‣ 164 degree-seeking undergraduates
‣ 32 graduate students
‣ Interview required

**General.** Founded in 1902. Accredited by ACICS. **Degrees:** 13 bachelor's, 10 associate awarded; master's offered. **Location:** Half of mile from downtown. **Calendar:** Quarter, extensive summer session. **Full-time faculty:** 1 total; 100% minority, 100% women. **Part-time faculty:** 22 total; 18% have terminal degrees, 4% minority, 32% women. **Class size:** 71% < 20, 29% 20-39.

**Basis for selection.** Open admission.

**2009-2010 Annual costs.** Tuition/fees: $9,025. Books/supplies: $800.

**Application procedures. Admission:** No deadline. $50 fee, may be waived for applicants with need. Application must be submitted on paper. Admission notification on a rolling basis. **Financial aid:** No deadline. FAFSA required. Applicants notified on a rolling basis starting 7/1.

**Academics. Special study options:** Accelerated study, combined bachelor's/graduate degree, weekend college. **Credit/placement by examination:** CLEP, IB. 8 credit hours maximum toward associate degree, 20 toward bachelor's. A student enrolled in and attending a course may earn credit in that course by advanced standing examination up to the end of the add/drop period. **Support services:** Learning center, reduced course load, remedial instruction, study skills assistance, tutoring, writing center.

**Majors. Business:** Accounting, business admin.

**Computing on campus.** 62 workstations in library, computer center. Online library, wireless network available.

**Student life. Freshman orientation:** Available. Preregistration for classes offered. **Policies:** Dress code, appropriate conduct policy, zero tolerance for alcohol and drug use while in school. **Activities:** Student government, student newspaper.

**Student services.** Adult student services, alcohol/substance abuse counseling, career counseling, student employment services, financial aid counseling, personal counseling, placement for graduates, veterans' counselor.

**Contact.** E-mail: jdecker@morrison.anthem.edu
Phone: (775) 335-3900 Toll-free number: (866) 502-2627
Fax: (775) 850-0711
Joyce Decker, Director of Admissions, Morrison University, 10315 Professional Circle, #201, Reno, NV 89521

## Nevada State College
Henderson, Nevada
www.nsc.nevada.edu

‣ Public 4-year nursing, liberal arts and teachers college
‣ Commuter campus in large city
‣ 1,990 degree-seeking undergraduates: 49% part-time, 76% women, 9% African American, 13% Asian American, 15% Hispanic American, 1% Native American
‣ 72% of applicants admitted

**General.** Regionally accredited. Satellite campus in downtown Henderson and off-site locations throughout the state of Nevada. **Degrees:** 211 bachelor's awarded. **Location:** Downtown. **Calendar:** Semester, limited summer session. **Full-time faculty:** 48 total; 27% have terminal degrees, 27% minority, 56% women. **Part-time faculty:** 97 total; 22% minority, 63% women. **Class size:** 40% < 20, 55% 20-39, 5% 40-49. **Special facilities:** 42,000-square-foot liberal arts & sciences building ("smart" classrooms, seismograph for detecting earthquake activity, weather center), anatomy and physiology cadaver laboratories.

**Freshman class profile.** 796 applied, 574 admitted, 282 enrolled.

| Mid 50% test scores | | | |
|---|---|---|---|
| SAT critical reading: | 400-470 | GPA 3.0-3.49: | 27% |
| SAT math: | 390-490 | GPA 2.0-2.99: | 60% |
| SAT writing: | 380-470 | Rank in top quarter: | 24% |
| ACT composite: | 16-23 | Rank in top tenth: | 9% |
| GPA 3.75 or higher: | 3% | Return as sophomores: | 67% |
| GPA 3.50-3.74: | 9% | Out-of-state: | 3% |

**Basis for selection.** Admission based on academic record. National college entrance tests, ACT/SAT, will be used as benchmarks for placement in English and mathematics courses. **Homeschooled:** SAT/ACT required.

**High school preparation.** College-preparatory program required. 12 units required. Required units include English 4, mathematics 3, social studies 3, science 2 (laboratory 1).

**2009-2010 Annual costs.** Tuition/fees: $3,260; $12,524 out-of-state. Books/supplies: $1,300. Personal expenses: $2,220.

**2008-2009 Financial aid. Need-based:** 68 full-time freshmen applied for aid; 62 were judged to have need; 61 of these received aid. Average need met was 62%. Average scholarship/grant was $4,300; average loan $3,200. 37% of total undergraduate aid awarded as scholarships/grants, 63% as loans/jobs. **Non-need-based:** Awarded to 230 full-time undergraduates, including 38 freshmen.

**Application procedures. Admission:** Closing date 8/29. $30 fee, may be waived for applicants with need. Admission notification on a rolling basis. **Financial aid:** Priority date 3/1, closing date 6/1. FAFSA, institutional form required. Applicants notified on a rolling basis starting 5/1.

**Academics. Special study options:** Accelerated study, combined bachelor's/graduate degree, distance learning, double major, dual enrollment of high school students, independent study, internships, liberal arts/career combination, student-designed major, teacher certification program. **Credit/placement by examination:** AP, CLEP, SAT, ACT, institutional tests. 30 credit hours maximum toward bachelor's degree. **Support services:** Learning center, remedial instruction, study skills assistance, tutoring, writing center.

**Majors. Biology:** General. **Business:** Business admin, management science. **Communications:** General. **Computer sciences:** General, computer science. **Conservation:** Environmental science. **Education:** General, bilingual, biology, elementary, English, history, mathematics, secondary, special. **Health:** Nursing (RN), speech pathology. **History:** General. **Interdisciplinary:** Gerontology. **Math:** General. **Protective services:** Law enforcement admin. **Psychology:** General. **Social sciences:** Economics, sociology.

**Most popular majors.** Business/marketing 17%, education 13%, health sciences 44%, psychology 7%, security/protective services 7%.

**Computing on campus.** 136 workstations in library, computer center, student center. Commuter students can connect to campus network. Online course registration, online library, helpline, student web hosting, wireless network available.

**Student life. Freshman orientation:** Available. Preregistration for classes offered. One-day program held prior to start of Spring and Fall terms for freshman and transfer students. A separate program for parents and family members offered concurrently to student orientation. **Activities:** Choral groups, international student organizations, student government, student newspaper, Alpha Phi Omega/Venture Crew, Young Democrats, Asian Pacific Islander Coalition, Black Student Organization, American Sign Language Club.

**Athletics. Team name:** Scorpions.

**Student services.** Financial aid counseling, minority student services. **Physically disabled:** Services for visually, speech, hearing impaired.

**Contact.** E-mail: admissions@nsc.nevada.edu
Phone: (702) 992-2130
Patricia Ring, Admissions/Registrar, Director, Nevada State College, 1125 Nevada State Drive, Henderson, NV 89002

## Sierra Nevada College
**Incline Village, Nevada**
www.sierranevada.edu
CB code: 4757

▶ Private 4-year liberal arts college
▶ Residential campus in small town
▶ 379 degree-seeking undergraduates
▶ SAT or ACT with writing, application essay required

**General.** Founded in 1969. Regionally accredited. **Degrees:** 52 bachelor's awarded; master's offered. **ROTC:** Army. **Location:** 35 miles from Reno. **Calendar:** Semester, limited summer session. **Full-time faculty:** 29 total. **Part-time faculty:** 100 total. **Class size:** 84% < 20, 16% 20-39. **Special facilities:** Entertainment technology lab, center for environmental sciences.

**Freshman class profile.**

| Mid 50% test scores | | | |
|---|---|---|---|
| SAT critical reading: | 400-560 | Rank in top quarter: | 35% |
| SAT math: | 440-580 | Rank in top tenth: | 10% |
| ACT composite: | 19-23 | Out-of-state: | 71% |
| | | Live on campus: | 90% |

**Basis for selection.** Motivation as evidenced in personal interview and/or autobiographical statement very important. Applicants with GPA below 2.0 may be admitted provisionally, upon review by faculty admission committee. Interview recommended. **Homeschooled:** Submit any course plans or transcripts along with any home schooling plans that are available.

**High school preparation.** Recommended units include English 4, mathematics 3, social studies 2, history 2, science 2 and foreign language 2.

**2009-2010 Annual costs.** Tuition/fees: $22,978. Room/board: $8,824. Books/supplies: $1,454. Personal expenses: $3,147.

**2009-2010 Financial aid. Non-need-based:** Scholarships awarded for academics, art, athletics.

**Application procedures. Admission:** Priority date 2/15; deadline 4/1. No application fee. Admission notification on a rolling basis beginning on or about 11/1. Must reply by May 1 or within 3 week(s) if notified thereafter. **Financial aid:** Priority date 4/1; no closing date. FAFSA, institutional form required. Applicants notified on a rolling basis; must reply by 5/1 or within 4 week(s) of notification.

**Academics.** Interdisciplinary studies in business, environmental science, fine arts, and the humanities. **Special study options:** Combined bachelor's/graduate degree, double major, honors, independent study, internships, liberal arts/career combination, study abroad, teacher certification program. Tuition exchange. **Credit/placement by examination:** AP, CLEP, IB, SAT, ACT, institutional tests. 30 credit hours maximum toward bachelor's degree. **Support services:** Remedial instruction, study skills assistance, tutoring, writing center.

**Majors. Biology:** General, ecology. **Business:** Business admin, hospitality admin, resort management. **Computer sciences:** General, computer science. **Conservation:** Environmental science, management/policy. **Health:** Premedicine, prenursing, prepharmacy. **Interdisciplinary:** Global studies. **Liberal arts:** Arts/sciences. **Psychology:** General. **Visual/performing arts:** General, ceramics, drawing, painting, printmaking, sculpture, studio arts.

**Most popular majors.** Business/marketing 31%, English 9%, liberal arts 12%, psychology 7%, visual/performing arts 24%.

**Computing on campus.** PC or laptop required. 30 workstations in dormitories, library, computer center, student center. Dormitories wired for high-speed internet access and linked to campus network. Commuter students can connect to campus network. Online library, helpline, repair service, wireless network available.

**Student life. Freshman orientation:** Mandatory. Preregistration for classes offered. Week-long program held the week prior to first day of classes. **Housing:** Guaranteed on-campus for all undergraduates. Coed dorms, wellness housing available. $200 nonrefundable deposit, deadline 5/1. **Activities:** Jazz band, choral groups, drama, literary magazine, music ensembles, musical theater, student government, student newspaper, recycling club, Christian club, Amnesty International.

**Athletics.** NCAA. **Intercollegiate:** Skiing. **Intramural:** Basketball, bowling, skiing, soccer, softball, volleyball. **Team name:** Eagles.

**Student services.** Alcohol/substance abuse counseling, career counseling, student employment services, financial aid counseling, health services, personal counseling, placement for graduates, veterans' counselor.

**Contact.** E-mail: admissions@sierranevada.edu
Phone: (775) 831-1314 Toll-free number: (866) 412-4636
Fax: (775) 831-6223
Bernie McConnell, Director of Admission, Sierra Nevada College, 999 Tahoe Boulevard, Incline Village, NV 89451-4269

## University of Nevada: Las Vegas
**Las Vegas, Nevada**
www.unlv.edu
CB member
CB code: 4861

▶ Public 4-year university
▶ Commuter campus in very large city

- 22,708 degree-seeking undergraduates
- 5,556 graduate students
- 39% graduate within 6 years

**General.** Founded in 1957. Regionally accredited. Credit courses available at Nellis Air Force Base. Unique majors: gaming management, entertainment engineering and design. International campus in Singapore. **Degrees:** 3,747 bachelor's awarded; master's, doctoral, professional offered. **ROTC:** Army, Air Force. **Location:** 268 miles from Los Angeles, 290 miles from Phoenix. **Calendar:** Semester, extensive summer session. **Full-time faculty:** 950 total; 88% have terminal degrees, 19% minority, 35% women. **Part-time faculty:** 727 total. **Class size:** 37% < 20, 41% 20-39, 9% 40-49, 10% 50-99, 2% >100. **Special facilities:** National supercomputing center for energy and environment, natural history museum, arboretum, theaters, concert hall, international gaming institute, professional practice school for teachers, student recreation and wellness center.

**Freshman class profile.**

| Mid 50% test scores | | GPA 2.0-2.99: | 21% |
|---|---|---|---|
| SAT critical reading: | 450-560 | Rank in top quarter: | 50% |
| SAT math: | 460-580 | Rank in top tenth: | 18% |
| ACT composite: | 19-24 | Out-of-state: | 20% |
| GPA 3.75 or higher: | 13% | Live on campus: | 30% |
| GPA 3.50-3.74: | 18% | Fraternities: | 8% |
| GPA 3.0-3.49: | 47% | Sororities: | 6% |

**Basis for selection.** GED not accepted. High school record must show minimum 3.0 minimum GPA in core courses. ACT/SAT can waive GPA requirements, but all students must have the core. Recommendations, personal essay and test scores considered for students applying through Alternate Criteria program. ACT/SAT required for English and math course placement. SAT or ACT recommended. SAT/ACT required for students appealing admission through alternate criteria and for placement into English/math courses. Audition recommended for music, theater arts programs; portfolio recommended for art program. **Homeschooled:** Transcript of courses and grades, letter of recommendation (nonparent) required. Personal statement, two letters of recommendation, ACT/SAT test scores required.

**High school preparation.** 13 units required. Required units include English 4, mathematics 3, social studies 3, science 3 (laboratory 2). Algebra or higher level math required.

**2009-2010 Annual costs.** Tuition/fees: $4,527; $16,867 out-of-state. Discounted tuition (Good Neighbor rates) available for nonresident students residing in certain counties bordering Nevada. Room/board: $10,456. Books/supplies: $1,000. Personal expenses: $1,800.

**2008-2009 Financial aid. Non-need-based:** Scholarships awarded for academics, alumni affiliation, art, athletics, job skills, leadership, minority status, music/drama, ROTC, state residency. **Additional information:** Tuition reduction for state residents through consortium programs and for out-of-state students graduating from high schools in designated counties bordering Nevada, for military dependents residing in-state, and for dependents of children of alumni not residing in-state.

**Application procedures. Admission:** Priority date 2/1; no deadline. $60 fee. Admission notification on a rolling basis beginning on or about 2/28. **Financial aid:** Priority date 2/1; no closing date. FAFSA, institutional form required. Applicants notified on a rolling basis starting 3/20; must reply within 2 week(s) of notification.

**Academics. Special study options:** Accelerated study, combined bachelor's/graduate degree, cooperative education, cross-registration, distance learning, double major, dual enrollment of high school students, ESL, exchange student, honors, independent study, internships, student-designed major, study abroad, teacher certification program. 2+2 culinary arts program with College of Southern Nevada. **Credit/placement by examination:** AP, CLEP, IB, SAT, ACT, institutional tests. 30 credit hours maximum toward bachelor's degree. **Support services:** Learning center, pre-admission summer program, remedial instruction, study skills assistance, tutoring, writing center.

**Honors college/program.** Honors College applicants must complete the honors application, letters of recommendation, test scores, personal statements, and essay response.

**Majors. Architecture:** Architecture, interior, landscape, urban/community planning. **Area/ethnic studies:** Asian, Latin American, women's. **Biology:** General. **Business:** Accounting, finance, hospitality admin, human resources, international marketing, management information systems, managerial economics, marketing, real estate. **Communications:** General. **Computer sciences:** Computer science. **Conservation:** General, environmental studies, management/policy. **Education:** Adult/continuing, computer, early childhood, elementary, health, physical, secondary, special. **Engineering:** Civil, computer, electrical, mechanical, software. **Engineering technology:** Construction. **Foreign languages:** French, German, Spanish. **Health:** Athletic training, clinical lab science, health care admin, medical radiologic technology/radiation therapy, nuclear medical technology, nursing (RN), physics/radiologic health. **History:** General. **Interdisciplinary:** Nutrition sciences. **Liberal arts:** Arts/sciences. **Math:** General, applied. **Parks/recreation:** General, exercise sciences, health/fitness. **Personal/culinary services:** Culinary arts. **Philosophy/religion:** Philosophy. **Physical sciences:** Chemistry, geology, physics. **Psychology:** General. **Public administration:** Social work. **Social sciences:** Anthropology, political science, sociology. **Visual/performing arts:** Art, dance, dramatic, film/cinema, jazz, studio arts.

**Most popular majors.** Business/marketing 29%, communications/journalism 6%, education 9%, psychology 7%, social sciences 6%, visual/performing arts 6%.

**Computing on campus.** 1,550 workstations in dormitories, library, computer center, student center. Dormitories wired for high-speed internet access and linked to campus network. Commuter students can connect to campus network. Online course registration, online library, helpline, wireless network available.

**Student life. Freshman orientation:** Mandatory, $120 fee. Preregistration for classes offered. **Housing:** Guaranteed on-campus for freshmen. Coed dorms, special housing for disabled, wellness housing available. $125 partly refundable deposit. All-female, study intensive floors and special interest floors available; handicapped accessible suites in all complexes. **Activities:** Bands, campus ministries, choral groups, dance, drama, film society, international student organizations, literary magazine, music ensembles, musical theater, opera, radio station, student government, student newspaper, symphony orchestra, TV station, Young Democrats/Republicans, Rebel Christian Fellowship, Hillel, ethnic student council, student organization of Latinos, black student association, Latter-day Saints student organization, Hawaii club, Circle K.

**Athletics.** NCAA. **Intercollegiate:** Baseball M, basketball, cheerleading, cross-country W, diving, football (tackle) M, golf, soccer, softball W, swimming, tennis, track and field W, volleyball W. **Intramural:** Badminton, basketball, bowling, cross-country, football (non-tackle), golf, racquetball, soccer, softball, swimming, table tennis, tennis, track and field, volleyball. **Team name:** Rebels.

**Student services.** Adult student services, alcohol/substance abuse counseling, career counseling, services for economically disadvantaged, student employment services, financial aid counseling, health services, legal services, minority student services, on-campus daycare, personal counseling, placement for graduates, veterans' counselor, women's services. **Physically disabled:** Services for visually, speech, hearing impaired. **Learning disabled:** Comprehensive services available.

**Contact.** E-mail: admissions@unlv.edu
Phone: (702) 774-8658 Fax: (702) 774-8008
Luke Schultheis, Executive Director of Admissions & Recruitment, University of Nevada: Las Vegas, 4505 Maryland Parkway Box 451021, Las Vegas, NV 89154-1021

---

## University of Nevada: Reno
Reno, Nevada
www.unr.edu

CB member
CB code: 4844

- Public 4-year university
- Commuter campus in small city
- 12,878 degree-seeking undergraduates: 17% part-time, 54% women, 3% African American, 7% Asian American, 10% Hispanic American, 1% Native American, 2% international
- 2,538 degree-seeking graduate students
- 88% of applicants admitted
- 48% graduate within 6 years

**General.** Founded in 1874. Regionally accredited. **Degrees:** 2,218 bachelor's awarded; master's, doctoral, professional offered. **ROTC:** Army. **Location:** 225 miles from San Francisco, 35 miles from Lake Tahoe. **Calendar:** Semester, extensive summer session. **Full-time faculty:** 585 total; 94% have terminal degrees, 17% minority, 38% women. **Part-time faculty:** 19 total; 79% have terminal degrees, 10% minority, 42% women. **Class size:** 38% < 20, 40% 20-39, 7% 40-49, 9% 50-99, 6% >100. **Special facilities:** Mineral museum, planetarium, arboretum, disability resource center, ethnic student resource center, internship center.

**Freshman class profile.** 5,045 applied, 4,457 admitted, 2,172 enrolled.

| Mid 50% test scores | | | |
|---|---|---|---|
| SAT critical reading: | 470-580 | GPA 2.0-2.99: | 17% |
| SAT math: | 470-600 | End year in good standing: | 76% |
| SAT writing: | 450-570 | Return as sophomores: | 80% |
| ACT composite: | 20-26 | Out-of-state: | 15% |
| GPA 3.75 or higher: | 20% | Live on campus: | 54% |
| GPA 3.50-3.74: | 19% | International: | 1% |
| GPA 3.0-3.49: | 44% | Fraternities: | 11% |
| | | Sororities: | 14% |

**Basis for selection.** GED not accepted. Secondary school record most important, with 3.0 GPA in academic core of English, math, social sciences and natural sciences. Students who do not meet Board of Regents admission requirements may appeal for special admission. If student does not meet GPA requirement, 1040 SAT or 22 ACT may be used in place of GPA requirement. All students applying for scholarships must submit test scores. Interview recommended for nursing program; audition recommended for music program; portfolio recommended for fine arts program. **Home-schooled:** Home schooled students who do not meet Board of Regents admission requirements may appeal for special admission.

**High school preparation.** College-preparatory program required. 13 units required. Required units include English 4, mathematics 3, social studies 3, science 3 (laboratory 2).

**2009-2010 Annual costs.** Tuition/fees: $4,901; $17,241 out-of-state. Discounted tuition (Good Neighbor rates) available for nonresident students residing in certain counties bordering Nevada. Discounted tuition also available for Western Undergraduate Exchange students. Room/board: $10,595. Books/supplies: $1,300. Personal expenses: $2,578.

**2008-2009 Financial aid. Need-based:** 1,363 full-time freshmen applied for aid; 855 were judged to have need; 831 of these received aid. Average need met was 55%. Average scholarship/grant was $5,605; average loan $3,182. 88% of total undergraduate aid awarded as scholarships/grants, 12% as loans/jobs. **Non-need-based:** Awarded to 7,460 full-time undergraduates, including 1,956 freshmen. Scholarships awarded for academics, alumni affiliation, art, athletics, music/drama. **Additional information:** Reduced out-of-state tuition available for children of alumni and for non-residents from some neighboring counties in California and participants in WUE program.

**Application procedures. Admission:** Priority date 3/1; no deadline. $60 fee, may be waived for applicants with need. Admission notification on a rolling basis. **Financial aid:** Priority date 3/1; no closing date. FAFSA required. Applicants notified on a rolling basis starting 4/1; must reply within 2 week(s) of notification.

**Academics. Special study options:** Distance learning, double major, dual enrollment of high school students, ESL, honors, independent study, internships, study abroad, teacher certification program. **Credit/placement by examination:** AP, CLEP, IB, SAT, ACT, institutional tests. 60 credit hours maximum toward bachelor's degree. **Support services:** Learning center, pre-admission summer program, reduced course load, remedial instruction, study skills assistance, tutoring, writing center.

**Majors. Agriculture:** Animal breeding, animal sciences, economics. **Area/ethnic studies:** Women's. **Biology:** General, biochemistry, biotechnology. **Business:** General, accounting, entrepreneurial studies, finance, hospitality admin, human resources, international, logistics, managerial economics, marketing. **Communications:** General, journalism. **Computer sciences:** General, computer science. **Conservation:** General, environmental science, forestry, management/policy, wildlife. **Education:** Agricultural, art, business, elementary, English, family/consumer sciences, foreign languages, health, mathematics, music, physical, science, secondary, social science, social studies, special, technology/industrial arts, trade/industrial. **Engineering:** Chemical, civil, computer, electrical, environmental, geological, mechanical, metallurgical, mining, physics, water resource. **Engineering technology:** Construction. **Family/consumer sciences:** Child development, family studies, food/nutrition. **Foreign languages:** French, German, Spanish. **Health:** Nursing (RN), preveterinary, speech pathology. **History:** General. **Interdisciplinary:** Neuroscience, nutrition sciences, science/society. **Math:** General. **Philosophy/religion:** Philosophy. **Physical sciences:** Atmospheric science, chemistry, geology, geophysics, physics. **Psychology:** General, social. **Public administration:** Social work. **Social sciences:** Anthropology, criminology, geography, international relations, political science, sociology. **Visual/performing arts:** Art, art history/conservation, dramatic, music performance. **Other:** English language and linguistics, Health ecology, Speech communication teacher education.

**Most popular majors.** Biology 8%, business/marketing 17%, communications/journalism 6%, education 6%, engineering/engineering technologies 8%, health sciences 10%, liberal arts 6%, social sciences 11%.

**Computing on campus.** Dormitories wired for high-speed internet access and linked to campus network. Commuter students can connect to campus network. Online course registration, online library, helpline, repair service, student web hosting, wireless network available.

**Student life. Freshman orientation:** Mandatory, $99 fee. Preregistration for classes offered. Sessions held before each semester. Family members welcome. **Housing:** Coed dorms, single-sex dorms, special housing for disabled, apartments, wellness housing available. $325 partly refundable deposit. Special interest floors (fitness, arts and culture, stereo limitation, alcohol prohibition, honors) available. **Activities:** Bands, choral groups, dance, drama, film society, international student organizations, literary magazine, music ensembles, Model UN, musical theater, opera, radio station, student government, student newspaper, symphony orchestra, Intervarsity Christian Fellowship, black student union, American Indian organization, Asian American Alliance, Chinese students association, Young Republicans, Young Democrats, Hillel, MEXA.

**Athletics.** NCAA. **Intercollegiate:** Baseball M, basketball, cross-country W, diving W, football (tackle) M, golf, rifle, soccer W, softball W, swimming W, tennis, track and field W, volleyball W. **Intramural:** Badminton, basketball, bowling, football (non-tackle), golf, racquetball, soccer, softball, swimming, table tennis, tennis, track and field, volleyball, water polo, weight lifting. **Team name:** Wolf Pack.

**Student services.** Adult student services, alcohol/substance abuse counseling, career counseling, services for economically disadvantaged, student employment services, financial aid counseling, health services, legal services, minority student services, on-campus daycare, personal counseling, placement for graduates, veterans' counselor, women's services. **Physically disabled:** Services for visually, speech, hearing impaired.

**Contact.** E-mail: asknevada@unr.edu
Phone: (775) 784-1110 Toll-free number: (866) 263-8232
Fax: (775) 784-4283
Steve Maples, Director of Admissions, University of Nevada: Reno, Mail Stop 120, Reno, NV 89557

## University of Southern Nevada
**Henderson, Nevada**
**www.usn.edu**

- Private two-year upper-division university
- Commuter campus in very large city
- 69% of applicants admitted
- Test scores, application essay, interview required

**General.** Candidate for regional accreditation. **Degrees:** 50 bachelor's awarded; master's, professional offered. **Articulation:** Agreement with Lake Tahoe Community College. **Location:** 9 miles from Las Vegas. **Calendar:** Differs by program. **Full-time faculty:** 56 total; 68% have terminal degrees, 36% minority, 61% women. **Part-time faculty:** 21 total; 67% have terminal degrees, 24% minority, 19% women. **Class size:** 8% 20-39, 92% 50-99.

**Student profile.** 142 degree-seeking undergraduates, 681 degree-seeking graduate students. 128 applied as first time-transfer students, 88 admitted, 63 enrolled. 59% transferred from two-year, 41% transferred from four-year institutions.

| | | | |
|---|---|---|---|
| Women: | 79% | International: | 5% |
| African American: | 23% | Out-of-state: | 67% |
| Asian American: | 47% | 25 or older: | 68% |
| Hispanic American: | 4% | | |

**Basis for selection.** College transcript, application essay, interview, standardized test scores required. Must complete specified courses. Transfer accepted as juniors.

**2009-2010 Annual costs.** Tuition/fees: $27,625. Books/supplies: $1,000. Personal expenses: $2,500.

**Financial aid. Need-based:** 102 applied for aid; 102 were judged to have need; 102 of these received aid. Average need met was 75%. 40% of total undergraduate aid awarded as scholarships/grants, 60% as loans/jobs. **Non-need-based:** Awarded to 101 undergraduates.

**Application procedures. Admission:** Rolling admission. $100 fee. Application must be submitted on paper. **Financial aid:** Priority date 1/1, closing date 4/1. Applicants notified on a rolling basis starting 7/1; must reply within 2 weeks of notification.

**Academics. Special study options:** Accelerated study. **Credit/placement by examination:** CLEP.

**Majors. Health:** Nursing (RN).

**Computing on campus.** PC or laptop required. 28 workstations in library. Commuter students can connect to campus network. Online library, helpline, repair service, wireless network available.

**Student services.** Financial aid counseling, placement for graduates. **Physically disabled:** Services for visually, hearing impaired.

**Contact.**   E-mail: bsnadmission@usn.edu
Phone: (702) 968-2075 Fax: (702) 968-2097
University of Southern Nevada, 11 Sunset Way, Henderson, NV
89014-2333

student government, Student Senate, Campus Activities Board, Team Chester (service organization), Gay-Straight Alliance.

**Student services.** Alcohol/substance abuse counseling, career counseling, financial aid counseling, personal counseling.

**Contact.** E-mail: admissions@chestercollege.edu
Phone: (603) 887-7400 Toll-free number: (800) 974-6372
Fax: (603) 887-1777
Sarah Vogell, Director of Admission, Chester College of New England, 40 Chester Street, Chester, NH 03036

# New Hampshire

---

## Chester College of New England
**Chester, New Hampshire**
www.chestercollege.edu
**CB member**
**CB code: 3977**

- Private 4-year visual arts and liberal arts college
- Residential campus in rural community
- 187 degree-seeking undergraduates: 9% part-time, 66% women, 1% African American, 2% Asian American, 3% Hispanic American, 1% Native American
- 53% of applicants admitted
- Application essay, interview required

**General.** Founded in 1965. Regionally accredited. **Degrees:** 33 bachelor's awarded. **Location:** 10 miles from Manchester, 50 miles from Boston. **Calendar:** Semester, limited summer session. **Full-time faculty:** 12 total; 100% have terminal degrees, 8% minority, 67% women. **Part-time faculty:** 28 total; 54% have terminal degrees, 4% minority, 43% women. **Class size:** 98% < 20, 2% 20-39.

**Freshman class profile.** 182 applied, 97 admitted, 51 enrolled.

| | | | |
|---|---|---|---|
| GPA 3.75 or higher: | 2% | GPA 2.0-2.99: | 60% |
| GPA 3.50-3.74: | 7% | Out-of-state: | 32% |
| GPA 3.0-3.49: | 22% | Live on campus: | 67% |

**Basis for selection.** High school achievement record, recommendations important; SAT/ACT scores considered. Interview and portfolio review required. **Homeschooled:** Statement describing homeschool structure and mission, interview, letter of recommendation (nonparent) required. Students may be required to complete an essay under examination conditions. SAT scores required.

**High school preparation.** Recommended units include English 4, mathematics 3, social studies 2, history 2, science 3 and foreign language 1.

**2009-2010 Annual costs.** Tuition/fees: $17,680. Lab fees vary per student; average cost $600. Room/board: $8,210. Books/supplies: $700. Personal expenses: $1,320.

**2008-2009 Financial aid. Need-based:** 56 full-time freshmen applied for aid; 51 were judged to have need; 51 of these received aid. Average need met was 20%. Average scholarship/grant was $2,800; average loan $3,500. 25% of total undergraduate aid awarded as scholarships/grants, 75% as loans/jobs. **Non-need-based:** Awarded to 165 full-time undergraduates, including 55 freshmen. Scholarships awarded for academics, art, state residency.

**Application procedures. Admission:** No deadline. $35 fee, may be waived for applicants with need. Admission notification on a rolling basis beginning on or about 1/15. Must reply by May 1 or within 2 week(s) if notified thereafter. **Financial aid:** Priority date 3/15; no closing date. FAFSA required. Applicants notified on a rolling basis starting 12/1; must reply within 2 week(s) of notification.

**Academics. Special study options:** Cross-registration, double major, independent study, internships, liberal arts/career combination, student-designed major, study abroad. **Credit/placement by examination:** AP, CLEP. 60 credit hours maximum toward bachelor's degree. **Support services:** Reduced course load, remedial instruction, study skills assistance, tutoring.

**Majors. Communications:** Digital media, media studies. **Computer sciences:** Web page design. **Visual/performing arts:** Art, graphic design, photography, studio arts.

**Most popular majors.** English 31%, interdisciplinary studies 7%, visual/performing arts 62%.

**Computing on campus.** 60 workstations in library, computer center, student center. Dormitories wired for high-speed internet access. Online library, wireless network available.

**Student life. Freshman orientation:** Mandatory. Preregistration for classes offered. Three-day orientation. **Housing:** Guaranteed on-campus for all undergraduates. Coed dorms available. $300 nonrefundable deposit, deadline 8/15. Pets allowed in dorm rooms. **Activities:** Drama, literary magazine,

---

## Colby-Sawyer College
**New London, New Hampshire**
www.colby-sawyer.edu
**CB member**
**CB code: 3281**

- Private 4-year liberal arts college
- Residential campus in small town
- 1,100 degree-seeking undergraduates
- 80% of applicants admitted
- Application essay required

**General.** Founded in 1837. Regionally accredited. **Degrees:** 190 bachelor's, 6 associate awarded. **ROTC:** Army, Air Force. **Location:** 30 miles from Hanover, 35 miles from Concord. **Calendar:** Semester. **Full-time faculty:** 60 total. **Part-time faculty:** 67 total. **Class size:** 65% < 20, 35% 20-39, less than 1% 40-49. **Special facilities:** Fine arts center, laboratory school (preschool, K-3), library learning center, conservatory and greenhouse, science center, weather station.

**Freshman class profile.** 3,224 applied, 2,579 admitted, 464 enrolled.

| | | | |
|---|---|---|---|
| GPA 3.75 or higher: | 5% | GPA 2.0-2.99: | 42% |
| GPA 3.50-3.74: | 12% | Out-of-state: | 67% |
| GPA 3.0-3.49: | 40% | Live on campus: | 98% |

**Basis for selection.** High school transcript most important. Recommendations, school and community activities, essay also considered. Interviews highly recommended, but not required. Test scores considered if submitted. Portfolio recommended for art program.

**High school preparation.** 15 units required. Required units include English 4, mathematics 3, social studies 3, science 3 (laboratory 3) and foreign language 2. Nursing applicants strongly encouraged to have 3 years of college-preparatory lab sciences, including biology and chemistry.

**2009-2010 Annual costs.** Tuition/fees: $31,090. Room/board: $10,860. Books/supplies: $750. Personal expenses: $1,000.

**2009-2010 Financial aid. Non-need-based:** Scholarships awarded for academics, alumni affiliation, art, leadership, minority status, music/drama.

**Application procedures. Admission:** No deadline. $45 fee, may be waived for applicants with need, free for online applicants. Admission notification on a rolling basis beginning on or about 12/15. Must reply by May 1 or within 2 week(s) if notified thereafter. **Financial aid:** Priority date 2/15, closing date 3/1. FAFSA required. Applicants notified on a rolling basis starting 1/1; must reply by 5/1 or within 2 week(s) of notification.

**Academics.** Liberal arts and experiential education integrated. Internships or senior research projects required in all major programs. **Special study options:** Accelerated study, cross-registration, double major, dual enrollment of high school students, ESL, exchange student, honors, independent study, internships, semester at sea, student-designed major, study abroad, teacher certification program, Washington semester. **Credit/placement by examination:** AP, CLEP, IB, institutional tests. 30 credit hours maximum toward associate degree, 60 toward bachelor's. **Support services:** Learning center, reduced course load, study skills assistance, tutoring.

**Majors. Biology:** General. **Business:** Business admin. **Communications:** Media studies. **Conservation:** Environmental studies. **Education:** Art, early childhood, English, social studies. **Health:** Athletic training, health services, nursing (RN). **Parks/recreation:** Exercise sciences, sports admin. **Psychology:** General, developmental. **Social sciences:** Sociology. **Visual/performing arts:** Art, graphic design, studio arts.

**Most popular majors.** Business/marketing 12%, communications/journalism 7%, education 12%, health sciences 16%, parks/recreation 11%, psychology 17%, visual/performing arts 12%.

**Computing on campus.** 150 workstations in library, computer center, student center. Dormitories wired for high-speed internet access and linked to campus network. Commuter students can connect to campus network. Online library, helpline, wireless network available.

**Student life. Freshman orientation:** Mandatory. Preregistration for classes offered. Two days immediately preceding beginning of fall semester. **Housing:** Guaranteed on-campus for all undergraduates. Coed dorms, single-sex dorms, special housing for disabled, wellness housing available. **Activities:** Choral groups, dance, drama, literary magazine, musical theater, radio station, student government, student newspaper, community service club, Safe Zones, cross cultural club, Christian Fellowship, Coalition for Peace and Justice, Student Democrats.

**Athletics. NCAA. Intercollegiate:** Baseball M, basketball, cross-country, diving, equestrian, field hockey W, lacrosse W, skiing, soccer, swimming, tennis, track and field, volleyball W. **Intramural:** Basketball, football (non-tackle), golf, soccer, volleyball. **Team name:** Chargers.

**Student services.** Alcohol/substance abuse counseling, career counseling, student employment services, financial aid counseling, health services, personal counseling. **Physically disabled:** Services for visually, hearing impaired.

**Contact.** E-mail: admissions@colby-sawyer.edu
Phone: (603) 526-3700 Toll-free number: (800) 272-1015
Fax: (603) 526-3452
Tracey Perkins, Director of Admission Counseling, Colby-Sawyer College, 541 Main Street, New London, NH 03257-7835

---

## Daniel Webster College
### Nashua, New Hampshire
**www.dwc.edu**
**CB member**
**CB code: 3648**

- Private 4-year business, engineering and liberal arts college
- Residential campus in small city
- 730 degree-seeking undergraduates
- SAT or ACT (ACT writing optional), application essay required

**General.** Founded in 1965. Regionally accredited. STEM institution: (Science, Technology, Engineering & Management), AT-CTI (Air Traffic Collegiate Training Initiative), FAA 141 Flight School. **Degrees:** 142 bachelor's, 23 associate awarded; master's offered. **ROTC:** Army, Air Force. **Location:** 18 miles from Manchester, 47 miles from Boston. **Calendar:** Semester, limited summer session. **Full-time faculty:** 40 total. **Part-time faculty:** 45 total. **Special facilities:** On-campus flight center, aircraft, four flight simulators, air-traffic-control simulation system, wind tunnel, robotic arm.

**Basis for selection.** High school transcript, recommendations, test scores and essay most important. Extracurricular activities considered. Interviews highly recommended. **Homeschooled:** Statement describing homeschool structure and mission, transcript of courses and grades, state high school equivalency certificate, interview, letter of recommendation (nonparent) required. Must submit portfolio outline of high school work.

**High school preparation.** College-preparatory program recommended. 16 units required. Required and recommended units include English 4, mathematics 3-4, social studies 2, history 2, science 3 (laboratory 2), foreign language 2 and computer science 1.

**2009-2010 Annual costs.** Tuition/fees: $28,614. Room/board: $9,698.

**2008-2009 Financial aid. Non-need-based:** Scholarships awarded for academics, alumni affiliation, leadership.

**Application procedures. Admission:** No deadline. $35 fee, may be waived for applicants with need. Application must be submitted online. Admission notification on a rolling basis. Must reply by May 1 or within 2 week(s) if notified thereafter. **Financial aid:** Priority date 3/1; no closing date. FAFSA, institutional form required. Applicants notified on a rolling basis starting 3/15; must reply within 2 week(s) of notification.

**Academics.** Credit granted for pilot licenses. Flight students must have FAA Class II medical examination. Flight operations majors must pass FAA written examinations and flight tests to earn pilot ratings. **Special study options:** Accelerated study, combined bachelor's/graduate degree, cooperative education, cross-registration, distance learning, double major, dual enrollment of high school students, independent study, internships, liberal arts/career combination, semester at sea, study abroad, Washington semester. **Credit/placement by examination:** AP, CLEP, IB, SAT, ACT, institutional tests. 30 credit hours maximum toward associate degree, 30 toward bachelor's. **Support services:** Learning center, study skills assistance, tutoring, writing center.

**Majors. Business:** General, business admin, management information systems, marketing. **Computer sciences:** General, a.i./robotics, computer science, game design, information systems, LAN/WAN management. **Engineering:** Aerospace, mechanical. **Parks/recreation:** Sports admin. **Protective

---

**services:** Emergency management/homeland security. **Psychology:** General. **Social sciences:** General. **Transportation:** Air traffic control, aviation, aviation management.

**Computing on campus.** 182 workstations in library, computer center, student center. Dormitories wired for high-speed internet access and linked to campus network. Helpline, repair service, wireless network available.

**Student life. Freshman orientation:** Mandatory, $250 fee. 4-day program. **Housing:** Guaranteed on-campus for freshmen. Coed dorms, single-sex dorms available. Townhouses and suites for 4 to 7 students available. **Activities:** Jazz band, campus ministries, music ensembles, student government, Campus Crusade for Christ, Gay-Straight Alliance, Intercultural Club.

**Athletics. NCAA. Intercollegiate:** Baseball M, basketball, cross-country, field hockey W, golf, lacrosse, soccer, softball W, volleyball. **Intramural:** Basketball, football (non-tackle), ice hockey M, soccer, volleyball. **Team name:** Eagles.

**Student services.** Adult student services, alcohol/substance abuse counseling, career counseling, student employment services, financial aid counseling, health services, personal counseling, placement for graduates, veterans' counselor.

**Contact.** E-mail: admissions@dwc.edu
Phone: (603) 577-6600 Toll-free number: (800) 325-6876 ext. 3
Fax: (603) 577-6001
Daniel Monahan, Dean of Admissions and Financial Assistance, Daniel Webster College, 20 University Drive, Nashua, NH 03063

---

## Dartmouth College
### Hanover, New Hampshire
**www.dartmouth.edu**
**CB member**
**CB code: 3351**

- Private 4-year university and liberal arts college
- Residential campus in large town
- 4,090 degree-seeking undergraduates: 50% women, 8% African American, 15% Asian American, 7% Hispanic American, 4% Native American, 7% international
- 1,739 degree-seeking graduate students
- 13% of applicants admitted
- SAT or ACT with writing, SAT Subject Tests, application essay required
- 94% graduate within 6 years

**General.** Founded in 1769. Regionally accredited. **Degrees:** 1,054 bachelor's awarded; master's, doctoral, professional offered. **ROTC:** Army. **Location:** 130 miles from Boston. **Calendar:** Quarter, extensive summer session. **Full-time faculty:** 492 total. **Part-time faculty:** 155 total. **Special facilities:** Observatory, centers for humanities, social sciences, physical science, performing arts, ethics, life science, computation.

**Freshman class profile.** 18,132 applied, 2,279 admitted, 1,094 enrolled.

| Mid 50% test scores | | | |
|---|---|---|---|
| SAT critical reading: | 660-770 | Rank in top tenth: | 91% |
| SAT math: | 680-780 | Return as sophomores: | 98% |
| SAT writing: | 670-780 | Out-of-state: | 98% |
| ACT composite: | 30-34 | Live on campus: | 100% |
| Rank in top quarter: | 99% | International: | 6% |

**Basis for selection.** Evidence of intellectual capability, motivation, and personal integrity of primary importance. Talent, accomplishment, and involvement in nonacademic areas also evaluated. 2 SAT Subject Tests of student's choice required. Interview optional.

**High school preparation.** College-preparatory program recommended. Recommended units include English 4, mathematics 4, social studies 3, history 3 and science 3. Strongest academic program available to applicant recommended.

**2009-2010 Annual costs.** Tuition/fees: $38,789. Room/board: $11,295. Books/supplies: $1,618. Personal expenses: $1,381.

**2008-2009 Financial aid.** All financial aid based on need. 678 full-time freshmen applied for aid; 535 were judged to have need; 535 of these received aid. Average need met was 100%. Average scholarship/grant was $34,939; average loan $2,401. 90% of total undergraduate aid awarded as scholarships/grants, 10% as loans/jobs.

**Application procedures. Admission:** Closing date 1/1 (postmark date). $70 fee, may be waived for applicants with need. Admission notification

4/10. Must reply by 5/1. **Financial aid:** Closing date 2/1. FAFSA, CSS PROFILE required. Applicants notified by 4/10; must reply by 5/1.

**Academics.** Undergraduate research encouraged. **Special study options:** Combined bachelor's/graduate degree, double major, exchange student, honors, independent study, internships, semester at sea, student-designed major, study abroad, teacher certification program, Washington semester. Williams Mystic Seaport Maritime Studies program, study at Eugene O'Neill National Theater Institute, Twelve College Exchange, University of California-San Diego exchange program, McGill University exchange program, exchange programs with over 50 foreign universities, special academic programs in Washington, DC and Tucson, AZ. **Credit/placement by examination:** AP, CLEP, IB, SAT, ACT, institutional tests. **Support services:** Learning center, study skills assistance, tutoring, writing center.

**Majors. Area/ethnic studies:** African, African-American, Asian, Caribbean, Chicano/Hispanic-American/Latino, German, Latin American, Native American, Near/Middle Eastern, Russian/Slavic, Spanish/Iberian, women's. **Biology:** General, biochemistry, Biochemistry/biophysics and molecular biology, cell/histology, ecology, evolutionary, genetics, molecular. **Computer sciences:** Computer science. **Conservation:** General, environmental studies. **Engineering:** Biomedical, physics, science. **Foreign languages:** Arabic, Chinese, classics, comparative lit, French, German, Hebrew, Italian, Japanese, linguistics, Russian, South Asian, Spanish. **History:** General. **Interdisciplinary:** Ancient studies, classical/archaeology, neuroscience. **Math:** General. **Philosophy/religion:** Philosophy, religion. **Physical sciences:** Astronomy, chemistry, physics, planetary. **Psychology:** General. **Social sciences:** Anthropology, economics, geography, political science, sociology. **Visual/performing arts:** Art history/conservation, dramatic, film/cinema, studio arts.

**Most popular majors.** Area/ethnic studies 7%, biology 7%, English 6%, foreign language 6%, history 7%, psychology 6%, social sciences 31%.

**Computing on campus.** PC or laptop required. Dormitories wired for high-speed internet access and linked to campus network. Commuter students can connect to campus network. Online course registration, online library, helpline, repair service, student web hosting, wireless network available.

**Student life. Freshman orientation:** Mandatory. Held week before fall classes begin; freshmen trips led by Dartmouth outing club. **Housing:** Guaranteed on-campus for freshmen. Coed dorms, apartments, cooperative housing, fraternity/sorority housing, wellness housing available. Academic affinity housing, faculty-in-residence programs, special interest housing available. **Activities:** Bands, campus ministries, choral groups, dance, drama, film society, international student organizations, literary magazine, music ensembles, Model UN, musical theater, opera, radio station, student government, student newspaper, symphony orchestra, TV station, community and service programs, religious groups, and political and ethnic organizations available.

**Athletics.** NCAA. **Intercollegiate:** Baseball M, basketball, cross-country, diving, equestrian, field hockey W, football (tackle) M, golf, ice hockey, lacrosse, rowing (crew), sailing, skiing, soccer, softball W, squash, swimming, tennis, track and field, volleyball W. **Intramural:** Baseball M, basketball, bowling, cross-country, football (non-tackle), golf, handball, ice hockey, lacrosse, racquetball, skiing, soccer, softball, squash, swimming, table tennis, tennis, track and field, volleyball, water polo, wrestling M. **Team name:** Big Green.

**Student services.** Alcohol/substance abuse counseling, chaplain/spiritual director, career counseling, student employment services, financial aid counseling, health services, minority student services, on-campus daycare, personal counseling, placement for graduates, women's services. **Physically disabled:** Services for visually, speech, hearing impaired.

**Contact.** E-mail: admissions.office@dartmouth.edu
Phone: (603) 646-2875 Fax: (603) 646-1216
Maria Laskaris, Dean of Admissions and Financial Aid, Dartmouth College, 6016 McNutt Hall, Hanover, NH 03755

## Franklin Pierce University
**Rindge, New Hampshire**
www.franklinpierce.edu

**CB member**
**CB code: 3395**

- Private 4-year university and liberal arts college
- Residential campus in small town
- 1,846 degree-seeking undergraduates: 14% part-time, 54% women, 3% African American, 1% Asian American, 3% Hispanic American, 2% international
- 524 degree-seeking graduate students
- 81% of applicants admitted
- SAT or ACT with writing, application essay required
- 45% graduate within 6 years

**General.** Founded in 1962. Regionally accredited. 4 satellite campuses offer continuing education sequence of 8-week undergraduate and 12-week graduate sessions on-campus and online. Associate, bachelor's, MBA, DPT, MEd, DA and PA offered through graduate and professional studies division campuses in Concord, Lebanon, Manchester and Portsmouth, NH as well as online. **Degrees:** 442 bachelor's, 48 associate awarded; master's, doctoral, professional offered. **ROTC:** Army, Air Force. **Location:** 20 miles from Keene, 60 miles from Boston. **Calendar:** Semester, limited summer session. **Full-time faculty:** 110 total; 68% have terminal degrees, 8% minority, 50% women. **Part-time faculty:** 141 total; 23% have terminal degrees, 4% minority, 48% women. **Class size:** 75% < 20, 25% 20-39, less than 1% 40-49. **Special facilities:** Glass blowing studio, ceramic studio and firing kiln, graphic design workshop, archaeological dig site, physical therapy labs, television studio, media production studios.

**Freshman class profile.** 2,562 applied, 2,079 admitted, 389 enrolled.

| | | | |
|---|---|---|---|
| GPA 3.75 or higher: | 1% | Return as sophomores: | 59% |
| GPA 3.50-3.74: | 5% | Out-of-state: | 80% |
| GPA 3.0-3.49: | 19% | Live on campus: | 100% |
| GPA 2.0-2.99: | 46% | International: | 1% |

**Basis for selection.** School achievement record, difficulty of course work, recommendations and school involvement primary considerations. Test scores also important. Test of English as a Foreign Language (TOEFL) is required for English speakers of other languages. Interview and campus visit recommended for all. **Homeschooled:** Letter of recommendation (nonparent) required.

**High school preparation.** College-preparatory program recommended. 16 units recommended. Recommended units include English 4, mathematics 3, social studies 2, history 1, science 3 (laboratory 2) and foreign language 1.

**2009-2010 Annual costs.** Tuition/fees: $29,000. Room/board: $9,800.

**2008-2009 Financial aid. Need-based:** 406 full-time freshmen applied for aid; 357 were judged to have need; 353 of these received aid. Average need met was 71%. Average scholarship/grant was $15,681. 59% of total undergraduate aid awarded as scholarships/grants, 41% as loans/jobs. **Non-need-based:** Awarded to 464 full-time undergraduates, including 150 freshmen. Scholarships awarded for academics, alumni affiliation, art, athletics, leadership.

**Application procedures. Admission:** No deadline. $40 fee. Admission notification on a rolling basis beginning on or about 10/1. Must reply by May 1 or within 2 week(s) if notified thereafter. **Financial aid:** Closing date 3/1. FAFSA required. Applicants notified on a rolling basis starting 3/1; must reply within 2 week(s) of notification.

**Academics. Special study options:** Accelerated study, combined bachelor's/graduate degree, distance learning, double major, dual enrollment of high school students, ESL, exchange student, honors, independent study, internships, liberal arts/career combination, student-designed major, study abroad, teacher certification program, Washington semester. Semester abroad touring Costa Rica, Vienna, Athens or Lyons. **Credit/placement by examination:** AP, CLEP, IB, SAT, ACT, institutional tests. 12 credit hours maximum toward associate degree, 30 toward bachelor's. **Support services:** Learning center, reduced course load, remedial instruction, study skills assistance, tutoring, writing center.

**Majors. Area/ethnic studies:** American. **Biology:** General. **Business:** Accounting/finance, management information systems, management science, marketing. **Communications:** Media studies. **Computer sciences:** Information technology. **Conservation:** Environmental science. **Education:** General. **History:** General. **Liberal arts:** Arts/sciences. **Math:** General. **Parks/recreation:** Facilities management. **Protective services:** Criminal justice. **Psychology:** General. **Public administration:** Social work. **Social sciences:** Anthropology, political science. **Visual/performing arts:** Arts management, commercial/advertising art, dance, dramatic, music performance, studio arts.

**Most popular majors.** Business/marketing 28%, communications/journalism 7%, liberal arts 6%, security/protective services 11%, visual/performing arts 8%.

**Computing on campus.** 109 workstations in dormitories, library, computer center. Dormitories wired for high-speed internet access and linked to campus network. Commuter students can connect to campus network. Online library, helpline, repair service, wireless network available.

**Student life. Freshman orientation:** Mandatory. Preregistration for classes offered. Held immediately prior to start of semester. **Housing:** Guaranteed on-campus for all undergraduates. Coed dorms, apartments, wellness housing available. $250 nonrefundable deposit, deadline 7/15. **Activities:** Bands, campus ministries, choral groups, dance, drama, international student organizations, literary magazine, music ensembles, musical theater, radio station, student government, student newspaper, TV station, student senate, law club, business club, black student alliance, Pierce Pals, community service, environmental awareness club, emergency medical services club, education club.

**Athletics.** NCAA. **Intercollegiate:** Baseball M, basketball, cross-country W, field hockey W, golf M, ice hockey M, lacrosse, rowing (crew), soccer, softball W, tennis, volleyball W. **Intramural:** Baseball M, basketball, cross-country W, field hockey W, sailing, skiing, soccer, softball, table tennis, tennis, volleyball. **Team name:** Ravens.

**Student services.** Alcohol/substance abuse counseling, chaplain/spiritual director, career counseling, student employment services, financial aid counseling, health services, minority student services, personal counseling, placement for graduates, women's services.

**Contact.** E-mail: admissions@franklinpierce.edu
Phone: (603) 899-4050 Toll-free number: (800) 437-0048
Fax: (603) 899-4394
Linda Quimby, Director, Admissions, Franklin Pierce University, 40 University Drive, Rindge, NH 03461-0060

## Granite State College
### Concord, New Hampshire
### www.granite.edu
**CB code: 0458**

- Public 4-year liberal arts college
- Commuter campus in large town
- 1,338 degree-seeking undergraduates: 50% part-time, 72% women
- 216 graduate students
- Application essay required
- 52% graduate within 6 years

**General.** Founded in 1972. Regionally accredited. **Degrees:** 221 bachelor's, 89 associate awarded. **ROTC:** Army. **Calendar:** Trimester, limited summer session. **Part-time faculty:** 166 total; 25% have terminal degrees, less than 1% minority, 67% women. **Class size:** 98% < 20, 2% 20-39.

**Freshman class profile.** 95 applied, 95 admitted, 52 enrolled.

**Basis for selection.** Open admission. Accuplacer tests used for placement. **Homeschooled:** State high school equivalency certificate required.

**2009-2010 Annual costs.** Tuition/fees: $7,695; $8,145 out-of-state. Books/supplies: $900. Personal expenses: $2,475.

**2008-2009 Financial aid.** All financial aid based on need. 97% of total undergraduate aid awarded as scholarships/grants, 3% as loans/jobs.

**Application procedures. Admission:** No deadline. $45 fee. Admission notification on a rolling basis. **Financial aid:** No deadline. FAFSA, institutional form required. Applicants notified on a rolling basis starting 4/15.

**Academics. Special study options:** Accelerated study, cross-registration, distance learning, double major, independent study, internships, liberal arts/career combination, student-designed major, teacher certification program. **Credit/placement by examination:** AP, CLEP, institutional tests. 32 credit hours maximum toward associate degree, 64 toward bachelor's. Exams must support degree program. **Support services:** Learning center, remedial instruction, study skills assistance, tutoring.

**Majors. Business:** Management science. **Education:** Early childhood. **Interdisciplinary:** Behavioral sciences. **Liberal arts:** Arts/sciences. **Protective services:** Criminal justice, law enforcement admin. **Other:** Applied Studies.

**Most popular majors.** Business/marketing 27%, interdisciplinary studies 30%, liberal arts 31%.

**Computing on campus.** 139 workstations in computer center, student center. Commuter students can connect to campus network. Online course registration, online library, helpline, wireless network available.

**Student life. Freshman orientation:** Available. Faculty, academic resource coordinators and advisors meet with new students twice a year for approximately three hours. This includes a Blackboard orientation. **Activities:** Alumni Learner Association, Green Team.

**Student services.** Adult student services, career counseling, financial aid counseling, veterans' counselor.

**Contact.** E-mail: ruth.nawn@granite.edu
Phone: (603) 228-3000 ext. 339 Toll-free number: (888) 228-3000 ext. 339
Fax: (603) 513-1386
Ruth Nawn, Associate Director of Admissions, Granite State College, 8 Old Suncook Road, Concord, NH 03301-7317

## Hesser College
### Manchester, New Hampshire
### www.hesser.edu
**CB code: 3452**

- For-profit 4-year business and junior college
- Residential campus in small city

**General.** Founded in 1900. Regionally accredited. **Location:** 50 miles from Boston. **Calendar:** Semester.

**Annual costs/financial aid.** Books/supplies: $1,200. Personal expenses: $450. Need-based financial aid available to full-time and part-time students.

**Contact.** Phone: (603) 668-6660 ext. 2110
Director of Admissions, 3 Sundial Avenue, Manchester, NH 03103

## Keene State College
### Keene, New Hampshire
### www.keene.edu
**CB member**
**CB code: 3472**

- Public 4-year liberal arts and teachers college
- Residential campus in large town
- 4,990 degree-seeking undergraduates: 3% part-time, 57% women, 1% Hispanic American
- 88 degree-seeking graduate students
- 71% of applicants admitted
- SAT or ACT (ACT writing recommended), application essay required
- 57% graduate within 6 years; 28% enter graduate study

**General.** Founded in 1909. Regionally accredited. **Degrees:** 945 bachelor's, 32 associate awarded; master's offered. **ROTC:** Air Force. **Location:** 52 miles from Concord, 85 miles from Boston. **Calendar:** Semester, extensive summer session. **Full-time faculty:** 195 total; 84% have terminal degrees, 4% minority, 47% women. **Part-time faculty:** 265 total; 56% women. **Class size:** 53% < 20, 43% 20-39, 3% 40-49, 1% 50-99. **Special facilities:** Arboretum and gardens, center for Holocaust studies, child development center, community research center, curriculum materials library, small business institute, college-owned camp, 400-acre preserve, theater complex.

**Freshman class profile.** 4,997 applied, 3,537 admitted, 1,188 enrolled.

| Mid 50% test scores | | GPA 2.0-2.99: | 43% |
|---|---|---|---|
| SAT critical reading: | 440-550 | Rank in top quarter: | 22% |
| SAT math: | 440-550 | Rank in top tenth: | 5% |
| SAT writing: | 450-540 | End year in good standing: | 95% |
| GPA 3.75 or higher: | 5% | Return as sophomores: | 79% |
| GPA 3.50-3.74: | 10% | Out-of-state: | 55% |
| GPA 3.0-3.49: | 41% | Live on campus: | 94% |

**Basis for selection.** High school record, including challenging courses, most important. SAT or ACT scores do not hold nearly as much weight as high school performance. Audition required for music education and music performance programs; portfolio required for art program. **Homeschooled:** Statement describing homeschool structure and mission required. **Learning Disabled:** Documented proof of disability required for some services.

**High school preparation.** College-preparatory program recommended. 14 units required. Required units include English 4, mathematics 3, social studies 2, science 3 and academic electives 2.

**2009-2010 Annual costs.** Tuition/fees: $9,334; $17,504 out-of-state. New England Regional tuition is 175% of in-state public institution tuition. Room/board: $8,444. Books/supplies: $800. Personal expenses: $750.

**2008-2009 Financial aid. Need-based:** 1,103 full-time freshmen applied for aid; 746 were judged to have need; 728 of these received aid. Average need met was 65%. Average scholarship/grant was $5,512; average loan $3,386. 41% of total undergraduate aid awarded as scholarships/grants, 59% as loans/jobs. **Non-need-based:** Awarded to 565 full-time undergraduates, including 167 freshmen. Scholarships awarded for academics, alumni affiliation, art, music/drama.

**Application procedures. Admission:** Closing date 4/1 (receipt date). $40 fee, may be waived for applicants with need. Admission notification on a rolling basis. Must reply by 5/1. **Financial aid:** Closing date 3/1. FAFSA required. Applicants notified on a rolling basis; must reply within 4 week(s) of notification.

**Academics. Special study options:** Cooperative education, double major, ESL, exchange student, honors, independent study, internships, liberal arts/career combination, student-designed major, study abroad, teacher certification program. **Credit/placement by examination:** AP, CLEP. 30 credit hours maximum toward associate degree, 60 toward bachelor's. **Support services:** Learning center, pre-admission summer program, reduced course load, study skills assistance, tutoring, writing center.

**Majors. Architecture:** Architecture. **Area/ethnic studies:** American. **Biology:** General. **Business:** Business admin. **Communications:** General, journalism. **Computer sciences:** General. **Conservation:** Environmental studies. **Education:** Biology, chemistry, computer, early childhood, elementary, English, French, health, history, mathematics, music, physical, science, secondary, social studies, Spanish, technology/industrial arts. **Engineering technology:** Architectural, occupational safety. **Foreign languages:** French, Spanish. **Health:** Athletic training, dietetics, substance abuse counseling. **History:** General, American, European. **Interdisciplinary:** Biological/physical sciences. **Math:** General. **Parks/recreation:** Health/fitness. **Physical sciences:** General, chemistry, geology. **Psychology:** General, clinical, developmental, experimental, social. **Social sciences:** General, economics, geography, political science, sociology. **Visual/performing arts:** Acting, cinematography, commercial/advertising art, dance, directing/producing, film/cinema, music history, music performance, music theory/composition, studio arts, theater design, theater history. **Other:** Chemistry physics, Computer mathematics, Individualized, Math physics, Music technology, Technology studies.

**Most popular majors.** Business/marketing 9%, communications/journalism 7%, education 17%, engineering/engineering technologies 9%, psychology 15%, social sciences 12%, visual/performing arts 9%.

**Computing on campus.** 500 workstations in dormitories, library, computer center, student center. Dormitories wired for high-speed internet access and linked to campus network. Commuter students can connect to campus network. Online course registration, online library, helpline, repair service, student web hosting, wireless network available.

**Student life. Freshman orientation:** Mandatory. Preregistration for classes offered. **Housing:** Coed dorms, single-sex dorms, apartments, fraternity/sorority housing, wellness housing available. $100 nonrefundable deposit, deadline 5/1. Language/Culture, leadership, quiet study available. **Activities:** Bands, campus ministries, choral groups, dance, drama, film society, international student organizations, literary magazine, music ensembles, musical theater, radio station, student government, student newspaper, TV station, Habitat for Humanity, Amnesty International, student government, campus ecology, civil liberties union, student volunteer organization, environmental outing club, KSC Pride, Circle K.

**Athletics. NCAA. Intercollegiate:** Baseball M, basketball, cheerleading, cross-country, diving, field hockey W, lacrosse, soccer, softball W, swimming, track and field, volleyball W. **Intramural:** Badminton, basketball, cross-country, football (non-tackle), racquetball, soccer, softball, tennis, track and field, volleyball, water polo. **Team name:** Owls.

**Student services.** Adult student services, alcohol/substance abuse counseling, chaplain/spiritual director, career counseling, student employment services, financial aid counseling, health services, minority student services, on-campus daycare, personal counseling, placement for graduates, veterans' counselor. **Physically disabled:** Services for visually, speech, hearing impaired.

**Contact.** E-mail: admissions@keene.edu
Phone: (603) 358-2276 Toll-free number: (800) 572-1909
Fax: (603) 358-2767
Margaret Richmond, Director of Admissions, Keene State College, 229 Main Street, Keene, NH 03435-2604

## Magdalen College
Warner, New Hampshire
www.magdalen.edu                          CB code: 3562

- Private 4-year liberal arts college affiliated with Roman Catholic Church
- Residential campus in small town
- 68 degree-seeking undergraduates
- 66% of applicants admitted
- SAT or ACT (ACT writing recommended), application essay, interview required

**General.** Regionally accredited. **Degrees:** 10 bachelor's, 1 associate awarded. **Location:** 20 miles from Concord. **Calendar:** Semester. **Full-time faculty:** 6 total. **Part-time faculty:** 1 total. **Special facilities:** Observatory.

**Freshman class profile.** 50 applied, 33 admitted, 21 enrolled.

Mid 50% test scores
SAT critical reading: 510-670        ACT composite: 21-24
SAT math: 390-570                    Out-of-state: 78%
                                     Live on campus: 100%

**Basis for selection.** Campus visit required (may be waived due to hardship). Academic GPA and high school transcript important.

**High school preparation.** 24 units recommended. Recommended units include English 4, mathematics 4, social studies 3, history 2, science 3, foreign language 2 and academic electives 6.

**2009-2010 Annual costs.** Tuition/fees: $14,200. Room/board: $6,750. Books/supplies: $400. Personal expenses: $200.

**2008-2009 Financial aid.** All financial aid based on need.

**Application procedures. Admission:** No deadline. $35 fee. Application must be submitted on paper. Admission notification on a rolling basis. Must reply by May 1 or within 4 week(s) if notified thereafter. **Financial aid:** Closing date 6/30. Institutional form required. Applicants notified by 7/1; must reply by 7/1 or within 4 week(s) of notification.

**Academics. Special study options:** Study abroad. **Credit/placement by examination:** CLEP. **Support services:** Learning center, pre-admission summer program, remedial instruction, study skills assistance, tutoring.

**Majors. Liberal arts:** Arts/sciences.

**Computing on campus.** 20 workstations in dormitories, library. Online library available.

**Student life. Freshman orientation:** Mandatory. 2-day program in early September. **Policies:** Dress code for class. Required attendance at meals. Curfews in dormitories. No-cut policy for class. Campus service required. Sunday mass required for Catholic students. Religious observance required. **Housing:** Guaranteed on-campus for all undergraduates. Single-sex dorms, wellness housing available. $500 deposit, deadline 6/15. **Activities:** Choral groups, drama, music ensembles, musical theater, campus service organization, college choir.

**Athletics. Intramural:** Basketball, football (non-tackle) M, soccer, volleyball.

**Student services.** Chaplain/spiritual director, career counseling, student employment services, financial aid counseling, personal counseling.

**Contact.** E-mail: admissions@magdalen.edu
Phone: (603) 456-2656 ext. 14 Toll-free number: (877) 498-1723
Fax: (603) 456-2660
Bobbie Anne Abson, Director of Admissions and Financial Aid, Magdalen College, 511 Kearsarge Mountain Road, Warner, NH 03278

## New England College
Henniker, New Hampshire
www.nec.edu                               CB code: 3657

- Private 4-year business, liberal arts and teachers college
- Residential campus in small town
- 997 degree-seeking undergraduates: 6% part-time, 50% women, 6% African American, 1% Asian American, 3% Hispanic American, 5% international
- 852 degree-seeking graduate students
- 81% of applicants admitted
- Application essay required
- 42% graduate within 6 years; 23% enter graduate study

**General.** Founded in 1946. Regionally accredited. Cross-registration with other 4-year institutions available through New Hampshire College and University Council. **Degrees:** 182 bachelor's awarded; master's offered. **ROTC:** Army, Air Force. **Location:** 18 miles from Concord. **Calendar:** Semester, limited summer session. **Full-time faculty:** 65 total; 69% have terminal degrees, 3% minority, 46% women. **Part-time faculty:** 115 total; 26% have terminal degrees, less than 1% minority, 56% women. **Class size:** 78% < 20, 22% 20-39. **Special facilities:** Center for Educational Innovation.

## New England College

**Freshman class profile.** 1,767 applied, 1,428 admitted, 258 enrolled.

| Mid 50% test scores | | | |
|---|---|---|---|
| SAT critical reading: | 390-500 | Rank in top quarter: | 6% |
| SAT math: | 390-500 | Rank in top tenth: | 2% |
| SAT writing: | 380-480 | End year in good standing: | 74% |
| ACT composite: | 17-23 | Return as sophomores: | 58% |
| GPA 3.75 or higher: | 2% | Out-of-state: | 70% |
| GPA 3.50-3.74: | 5% | Live on campus: | 94% |
| GPA 3.0-3.49: | 31% | International: | 2% |
| GPA 2.0-2.99: | 52% | Fraternities: | 4% |
| | | Sororities: | 4% |

**Basis for selection.** School achievement record most important, followed by recommendations, essay or personal statement, evidence of leadership and extracurricular activities. Interview recommended for all; portfolio recommended for art program. **Homeschooled:** Transcript of courses and grades, state high school equivalency certificate, letter of recommendation (nonparent) required.

**High school preparation.** College-preparatory program recommended. 12 units required. Required and recommended units include English 4, mathematics 2-3, social studies 2-3, science 2-3 (laboratory 1-2) and foreign language 2.

**2009-2010 Annual costs.** Tuition/fees: $27,450. Room/board: $9,626. Books/supplies: $850. Personal expenses: $1,300.

**2009-2010 Financial aid. Need-based:** 223 full-time freshmen applied for aid; 209 were judged to have need; 209 of these received aid. Average need met was 81%. Average scholarship/grant was $16,469; average loan $8,098. 60% of total undergraduate aid awarded as scholarships/grants, 40% as loans/jobs. **Non-need-based:** Awarded to 271 full-time undergraduates, including 60 freshmen. Scholarships awarded for academics, alumni affiliation, art, job skills, leadership, music/drama, state residency.

**Application procedures. Admission:** No deadline. $30 fee, may be waived for applicants with need. Admission notification on a rolling basis beginning on or about 11/1. **Financial aid:** Priority date 4/1; no closing date. FAFSA, institutional form required. Applicants notified on a rolling basis starting 1/12; must reply within 2 week(s) of notification.

**Academics. Special study options:** Accelerated study, combined bachelor's/graduate degree, cross-registration, distance learning, double major, dual enrollment of high school students, ESL, exchange student, external degree, honors, independent study, internships, liberal arts/career combination, semester at sea, student-designed major, study abroad, teacher certification program, Washington semester. Exchange programs with Regent's College, London; American University of Paris; 18 colleges in Quebec, Canada; University of the Sunshine Coast, Australia. Students keep all financial aid when abroad. **Credit/placement by examination:** AP, CLEP, IB, institutional tests. 21 credit hours maximum toward associate degree, 21 toward bachelor's. **Support services:** Learning center, reduced course load, remedial instruction, study skills assistance, tutoring, writing center.

**Majors. Biology:** General. **Business:** Accounting, business admin, entrepreneurial studies, finance, human resources, management information systems, marketing. **Communications:** General, advertising, public relations. **Computer sciences:** General. **Conservation:** Environmental science. **Education:** Art, biology, elementary, English, learning disabled, mathematics, physical, science, secondary, social science, social studies, special. **Engineering:** Civil. **Foreign languages:** Comparative lit. **Health:** Health care admin, premedicine. **History:** General. **Legal studies:** Prelaw. **Liberal arts:** Arts/sciences. **Math:** General. **Parks/recreation:** General, exercise sciences, facilities management, sports admin. **Philosophy/religion:** Philosophy. **Protective services:** Criminal justice. **Psychology:** General. **Social sciences:** Political science, sociology. **Visual/performing arts:** Art, art history/conservation, dramatic, photography.

**Most popular majors.** Business/marketing 20%, education 11%, health sciences 8%, parks/recreation 15%, psychology 11%, security/protective services 7%, visual/performing arts 11%.

**Computing on campus.** 200 workstations in library, computer center, student center. Dormitories wired for high-speed internet access and linked to campus network. Commuter students can connect to campus network. Online course registration, online library, helpline, wireless network available.

**Student life. Freshman orientation:** Available. Preregistration for classes offered. Held 3 days prior to first day of classes and 3 mid-summer options. **Housing:** Guaranteed on-campus for all undergraduates. Coed dorms, apartments, fraternity/sorority housing, wellness housing available. $100 nonrefundable deposit. Quiet study options, special interest housing available. **Activities:** Choral groups, dance, drama, international student organizations, literary magazine, radio station, student government, student newspaper, international student association, Hillel, Servcorps, environmental action committee, Womyn's Network, international diplomacy council, Adventure Bound.

**Athletics. NCAA. Intercollegiate:** Baseball M, basketball, cross-country, field hockey W, ice hockey, lacrosse, soccer, softball W. **Intramural:** Baseball M, basketball, ice hockey, soccer, softball, table tennis, tennis, volleyball. **Team name:** Pilgrims.

**Student services.** Adult student services, alcohol/substance abuse counseling, career counseling, student employment services, financial aid counseling, health services, personal counseling, placement for graduates, veterans' counselor.

**Contact.** E-mail: admission@nec.edu
Phone: (603) 428-2223 Toll-free number: (800) 521-7642
Fax: (603) 428-3155
Diane Raymond, Director of Admissions, New England College, 102 Bridge Street, Henniker, NH 03242

## Plymouth State University
**Plymouth, New Hampshire**
www.plymouth.edu

CB member
CB code: 3690

- Public 4-year university and teachers college
- Residential campus in small town
- 4,155 degree-seeking undergraduates: 3% part-time, 46% women
- 842 degree-seeking graduate students
- 70% of applicants admitted
- SAT or ACT with writing, application essay required
- 55% graduate within 6 years

**General.** Founded in 1871. Regionally accredited. **Degrees:** 877 bachelor's awarded; master's, doctoral offered. **ROTC:** Army, Air Force. **Location:** 60 miles from Manchester, 115 miles from Boston. **Calendar:** Semester, limited summer session. **Full-time faculty:** 189 total; 82% have terminal degrees, 7% minority, 41% women. **Part-time faculty:** 236 total; 30% have terminal degrees, 2% minority, 68% women. **Class size:** 48% < 20, 48% 20-39, 3% 40-49, 1% 50-99, less than 1% >100. **Special facilities:** Planetarium, cultural arts center, child development and family center, geographic information systems lab, meteorology institute, center for the environment, climbing wall, ropes course.

**Freshman class profile.** 4,239 applied, 2,957 admitted, 969 enrolled.

| Mid 50% test scores | | | |
|---|---|---|---|
| SAT critical reading: | 430-530 | GPA 2.0-2.99: | 67% |
| SAT math: | 440-530 | Rank in top quarter: | 17% |
| ACT composite: | 18-23 | Rank in top tenth: | 4% |
| GPA 3.75 or higher: | 4% | Return as sophomores: | 78% |
| GPA 3.50-3.74: | 7% | Out-of-state: | 45% |
| GPA 3.0-3.49: | 22% | Live on campus: | 94% |

**Basis for selection.** Decision made by committee, based on school achievement record (most important) followed by test scores, recommendations, essay and extracurricular activities. SAT/ACT not required for resident or non-resident aliens. Audition required for music and theater programs. Portfolio required for art program. **Homeschooled:** Transcript of any work attempted in secondary school, SAT or ACT, GED or homeschool diploma, outline of homeschool curriculum required.

**High school preparation.** College-preparatory program required. 13 units required; 18 recommended. Required and recommended units include English 4, mathematics 3, social studies 2-3, history 1-2, science 2-3 (laboratory 1) and foreign language 2.

**2009-2010 Annual costs.** Tuition/fees: $8,944; $17,114 out-of-state. New England Regional tuition: 175% of in-state tuition. Room/board: $9,134.

**2008-2009 Financial aid. Non-need-based:** Scholarships awarded for academics, minority status, music/drama.

**Application procedures. Admission:** Closing date 4/1 (postmark date). $45 fee, may be waived for applicants with need. Admission notification on a rolling basis beginning on or about 11/1. Must reply by 5/1. **Financial aid:** Priority date 3/1; no closing date. FAFSA required. Applicants notified on a rolling basis starting 2/15; must reply by 5/1.

**Academics. Special study options:** Cross-registration, distance learning, double major, dual enrollment of high school students, ESL, exchange student, external degree, honors, independent study, internships, student-designed major, study abroad, teacher certification program. **Credit/placement by examination:** AP, CLEP, institutional tests. 30 credit hours maximum toward bachelor's degree. **Support services:** Study skills assistance, tutoring, writing center.

**Majors. Architecture:** Urban/community planning. **Biology:** General, biotechnology, environmental. **Business:** General, accounting, business admin, marketing. **Communications:** General. **Computer sciences:** Computer science, information technology. **Conservation:** Environmental studies. **Education:** Art, early childhood, elementary, mathematics, music. **Foreign languages:** French, Spanish. **Health:** Athletic training, public health ed. **History:** General. **Liberal arts:** Humanities. **Math:** General. **Parks/recreation:** Health/fitness. **Philosophy/religion:** Philosophy. **Physical sciences:** Atmospheric science, chemistry. **Protective services:** Criminal justice. **Psychology:** General. **Public administration:** General, social work. **Social sciences:** General, applied economics, geography, political science. **Visual/performing arts:** Art, commercial/advertising art, dramatic, studio arts. **Other:** Adventure education.

**Most popular majors.** Business/marketing 27%, education 15%, parks/recreation 7%, security/protective services 6%, visual/performing arts 8%.

**Computing on campus.** 500 workstations in dormitories, library, computer center, student center. Dormitories wired for high-speed internet access and linked to campus network. Commuter students can connect to campus network. Online course registration, online library, helpline, repair service, student web hosting, wireless network available.

**Student life. Freshman orientation:** Mandatory, $188 fee. Preregistration for classes offered. 5 sessions in June, one session in September. **Housing:** Guaranteed on-campus for all undergraduates. Coed dorms, apartments, wellness housing available. $90 partly refundable deposit, deadline 5/1. Music/theater/dance housing, honors housing, special interest housing, community service, non-traditional, and quiet study/academic housing available. **Activities:** Bands, campus ministries, choral groups, dance, drama, film society, international student organizations, music ensembles, Model UN, musical theater, radio station, student government, student newspaper, Chi Alpha Christian Fellowship, multicultural student organization, Nicaragua club, volunteer club, social work club, health and wellness club, peer educators, Alternative Spring Break.

**Athletics.** NCAA. **Intercollegiate:** Baseball M, basketball, cheerleading M, diving W, field hockey W, football (tackle) M, ice hockey, lacrosse, skiing, soccer, softball W, swimming W, tennis W, volleyball W, wrestling M. **Intramural:** Basketball, bowling, cross-country, football (non-tackle), golf, racquetball, soccer, softball, table tennis, tennis, triathlon, volleyball. **Team name:** Panthers.

**Student services.** Alcohol/substance abuse counseling, chaplain/spiritual director, career counseling, student employment services, financial aid counseling, health services, on-campus daycare, personal counseling, placement for graduates, veterans' counselor, women's services. **Physically disabled:** Services for visually, hearing impaired.

**Contact.** E-mail: plymouthadmit@plymouth.edu
Phone: (603) 535-2237 Toll-free number: (800) 842-6900
Fax: (603) 535-2714
Eugene Fahey, Senior Associate Director of Admission, Plymouth State University, 17 High Street MSC 52, Plymouth, NH 03264-1595

## Rivier College

| Nashua, New Hampshire | |
|---|---|
| www.rivier.edu | CB member |
| | CB code: 3728 |

- Private 4-year liberal arts and teachers college affiliated with Roman Catholic Church
- Commuter campus in small city
- 1,406 degree-seeking undergraduates: 31% part-time, 82% women, 2% African American, 2% Asian American, 4% Hispanic American, 1% Native American
- 564 degree-seeking graduate students
- SAT or ACT with writing, application essay required
- 50% graduate within 6 years

**General.** Founded in 1933. Regionally accredited. Founded in 1933 by the Sisters of the Presentation of Mary Convent. **Degrees:** 276 bachelor's, 132 associate awarded; master's offered. **ROTC:** Army, Naval, Air Force. **Location:** 19 miles from Manchester, 45 miles from Boston. **Calendar:** Semester, limited summer session. **Full-time faculty:** 71 total; 76% have terminal degrees, 62% women. **Part-time faculty:** 122 total; 18% have terminal degrees, 70% women. **Class size:** 49% < 20, 47% 20-39, 2% 40-49, 2% 50-99. **Special facilities:** Center for finance and economics, early childhood center/laboratory school, biology research lab.

**Freshman class profile.** 878 applied, 713 admitted, 236 enrolled.

| Mid 50% test scores | | | |
|---|---|---|---|
| | | **ACT composite:** | 17-22 |
| **SAT critical reading:** | 430-510 | **Return as sophomores:** | 77% |
| **SAT math:** | 420-530 | **Out-of-state:** | 60% |
| **SAT writing:** | 440-530 | **Live on campus:** | 72% |

**Basis for selection.** Open admission, but selective for some programs. High school academic record (course selection, course level, grades), test scores, extracurricular activities, application essay, and letters of recommendation considered. Interview recommended for all; portfolio required for art programs. **Homeschooled:** Transcript of courses and grades, interview required. Portfolio.

**High school preparation.** College-preparatory program recommended. 16 units recommended. Recommended units include English 4, mathematics 3, social studies 2, history 1, science 1 (laboratory 1), foreign language 2 and academic electives 3. Nursing program applicants must have completed chemistry and algebra.

**2010-2011 Annual costs.** Tuition/fees (projected): $25,050. Room/board: $9,428. Books/supplies: $1,200. Personal expenses: $1,500.

**2009-2010 Financial aid. Need-based:** 229 full-time freshmen applied for aid; 203 were judged to have need; 202 of these received aid. Average need met was 64%. Average scholarship/grant was $13,076; average loan $3,457. **Non-need-based:** Awarded to 169 full-time undergraduates, including 43 freshmen. Scholarships awarded for academics, alumni affiliation.

**Application procedures. Admission:** Priority date 3/1; no deadline. $25 fee, may be waived for applicants with need. Admission notification on a rolling basis beginning on or about 11/1. Must reply by May 1 or within 4 week(s) if notified thereafter. **Financial aid:** Priority date 3/1; no closing date. FAFSA required. Applicants notified on a rolling basis starting 3/1; must reply by 5/1 or within 2 week(s) of notification.

**Academics.** Formal programs for learning disabled students not offered, but Office of Special Needs Services has part-time learning disabilities specialist available. **Special study options:** Combined bachelor's/graduate degree, cross-registration, double major, ESL, honors, independent study, internships, liberal arts/career combination, study abroad, teacher certification program. **Credit/placement by examination:** AP, CLEP, IB, institutional tests. 12 credit hours maximum toward associate degree, 12 toward bachelor's. **Support services:** Learning center, reduced course load, study skills assistance, tutoring, writing center.

**Honors college/program.** Honors program limited to 15 students per class. Special application and interview required. Scholarship available to all participants. SAT 1200 plus (exclusive of Writing), top 20% of high school class. Honors classes will fulfill some core requirements.

**Majors. Biology:** General. **Business:** Business admin, management information systems, management science. **Communications:** General, broadcast journalism, journalism, public relations. **Computer sciences:** Computer science. **Education:** General, biology, early childhood, elementary, English, foreign languages, history, mathematics, science, secondary, social science, social studies, Spanish. **Foreign languages:** Spanish. **Health:** Nursing (RN), predental, premedicine, preop/surgical nursing, preveterinary. **History:** General. **Legal studies:** Prelaw. **Liberal arts:** Arts/sciences. **Math:** General. **Psychology:** General. **Social sciences:** General, political science, sociology. **Visual/performing arts:** Design, photography, studio arts.

**Most popular majors.** Business/marketing 20%, education 13%, health sciences 28%, psychology 8%.

**Computing on campus.** 150 workstations in dormitories, library, computer center, student center. Dormitories linked to campus network. Commuter students can connect to campus network. Online course registration, online library, helpline, repair service, wireless network available.

**Student life. Freshman orientation:** Mandatory, $100 fee. Preregistration for classes offered. 2-day on-campus program in June. Parallel program for parents. **Housing:** Guaranteed on-campus for all undergraduates. Coed dorms, special housing for disabled, wellness housing available. $100 fully refundable deposit, deadline 5/1. **Activities:** Campus ministries, choral groups, dance, drama, international student organizations, literary magazine, Model UN, student government, student newspaper, symphony orchestra, TV station, REACT (Rivier Environmental Activists), Amnesty International, Chinese student association, America Reads, Americorps, Habitat for Humanity.

**Athletics.** NCAA. **Intercollegiate:** Baseball M, basketball, cross-country, soccer, softball W, track and field, volleyball. **Intramural:** Basketball, soccer, softball, table tennis, volleyball, weight lifting. **Team name:** Raiders.

**Student services.** Adult student services, alcohol/substance abuse counseling, chaplain/spiritual director, career counseling, student employment services, financial aid counseling, health services, minority student services, on-campus daycare, personal counseling, placement for graduates.

**Contact.** E-mail: rivadmit@rivier.edu
Phone: (603) 897-8507 Toll-free number: (800) 447-4843
Fax: (603) 891-1799
David Boisvert, Vice President for Enrollment Management, Rivier College, 420 South Main Street, Nashua, NH 03060-5086

## Saint Anselm College
**Manchester, New Hampshire**
www.anselm.edu

CB member
CB code: 3748

- Private 4-year nursing and liberal arts college affiliated with Roman Catholic Church
- Residential campus in small city
- 1,889 degree-seeking undergraduates: 1% part-time, 57% women, 1% African American, 1% Asian American, 2% Hispanic American, 1% Native American
- 77% of applicants admitted
- SAT or ACT (ACT writing optional), application essay required
- 73% graduate within 6 years

**General.** Founded in 1889. Regionally accredited. Administered by Order of St. Benedict. **Degrees:** 404 bachelor's awarded. **ROTC:** Army, Air Force. **Location:** 50 miles from Boston. **Calendar:** Semester, limited summer session. **Full-time faculty:** 144 total; 92% have terminal degrees, 8% minority, 51% women. **Part-time faculty:** 64 total; 44% have terminal degrees, 5% minority, 50% women. **Class size:** 56% < 20, 40% 20-39, less than 1% 40-49, 3% 50-99, less than 1% >100. **Special facilities:** Observatory, institute of politics, ice arena, humanities and performing arts center, art center, Abbey Church.

**Freshman class profile.** 3,664 applied, 2,830 admitted, 531 enrolled.

| Mid 50% test scores | | | |
|---|---|---|---|
| SAT critical reading: | 500-590 | GPA 3.50-3.74: | 11% |
| SAT math: | 510-580 | GPA 3.0-3.49: | 49% |
| SAT writing: | 490-590 | GPA 2.0-2.99: | 34% |
| ACT composite: | 20-26 | Return as sophomores: | 85% |
| GPA 3.75 or higher: | 6% | Out-of-state: | 80% |
| | | Live on campus: | 96% |

**Basis for selection.** School achievement record and character most important, followed by test scores, 2 recommendations, essay. Interview recommended. **Homeschooled:** Statement describing homeschool structure and mission, interview, letter of recommendation (nonparent) required.

**High school preparation.** College-preparatory program required. 16 units required. Required and recommended units include English 4, mathematics 3-4, social studies 2, science 3-4 (laboratory 2) and foreign language 2.

**2009-2010 Annual costs.** Tuition/fees: $30,470. Room/board: $11,240. Books/supplies: $800.

**2009-2010 Financial aid. Need-based:** 475 full-time freshmen applied for aid; 390 were judged to have need; 390 of these received aid. Average need met was 83%. Average scholarship/grant was $19,133; average loan $4,584. 68% of total undergraduate aid awarded as scholarships/grants, 32% as loans/jobs. **Non-need-based:** Awarded to 448 full-time undergraduates, including 152 freshmen. Scholarships awarded for academics, alumni affiliation, athletics, state residency.

**Application procedures. Admission:** Closing date 3/1 (postmark date). $55 fee, may be waived for applicants with need. Admission notification on a rolling basis beginning on or about 1/15. Must reply by May 1 or within 2 week(s) if notified thereafter. **Financial aid:** Closing date 3/15. FAFSA, CSS PROFILE required. Applicants notified on a rolling basis starting 3/1; must reply by 5/1 or within 2 week(s) of notification.

**Academics.** 4-semester humanities program required of all students. Special studies certificates in addition to major concentrations available in fine arts (visual arts, theater, music), international studies, communications, computational physical science, human relations and work, French, Spanish, German, Latin, Greek, Russian area studies, Latin American studies, Asian studies, Catholic studies, medieval studies, neuroscience, public policy studies, web design. **Special study options:** Cross-registration, honors, independent study, internships, liberal arts/career combination, New York semester, semester at sea, study abroad, teacher certification program, Washington semester. **Credit/placement by examination:** AP, CLEP, IB, institutional tests. 30 credit hours maximum toward bachelor's degree. **Support services:** Learning center, reduced course load, study skills assistance, tutoring, writing center.

**Majors. Biology:** General, biochemistry. **Business:** General, accounting, finance, managerial economics. **Communications:** Media studies. **Computer sciences:** Computer science. **Conservation:** Environmental science. **Engineering:** General, physics. **Foreign languages:** Classics, French, Spanish. **Health:** Nursing (RN), predental, premedicine. **History:** General. **Interdisciplinary:** Biological/physical sciences, math/computer science. **Legal studies:** Prelaw. **Liberal arts:** Arts/sciences. **Math:** General. **Philosophy/religion:** Philosophy. **Physical sciences:** Chemistry, physics. **Protective services:** Criminal justice. **Psychology:** General. **Social sciences:** Economics, international relations, political science, sociology. **Theology:** Theology. **Visual/performing arts:** Art.

**Most popular majors.** Biology 7%, business/marketing 19%, English 8%, health sciences 15%, history 7%, psychology 7%, social sciences 26%.

**Computing on campus.** 400 workstations in dormitories, library, computer center, student center. Dormitories wired for high-speed internet access and linked to campus network. Commuter students can connect to campus network. Online course registration, online library, helpline, repair service, wireless network available.

**Student life. Freshman orientation:** Available, $25 fee. Preregistration for classes offered. Held 3 days prior to fall semester. **Housing:** Guaranteed on-campus for all undergraduates. Coed dorms, single-sex dorms, special housing for disabled, apartments, wellness housing available. $200 nonrefundable deposit. **Activities:** Bands, campus ministries, choral groups, dance, drama, film society, international student organizations, literary magazine, Model UN, musical theater, radio station, student government, student newspaper, TV station, Muslim student associations, black student alliance, Knights of Columbus, College Republicans, College Democrats, rugby club, Oxford Companions, volunteers center, music society, Radio Flyers.

**Athletics.** NCAA. **Intercollegiate:** Baseball M, basketball, cross-country, field hockey W, football (tackle) M, golf, ice hockey, lacrosse, skiing, soccer, softball W, tennis, volleyball W. **Intramural:** Basketball, football (non-tackle), handball, ice hockey, racquetball, skiing, soccer, softball, table tennis, tennis, volleyball. **Team name:** Hawks.

**Student services.** Alcohol/substance abuse counseling, chaplain/spiritual director, career counseling, student employment services, financial aid counseling, health services, minority student services, personal counseling, placement for graduates, veterans' counselor.

**Contact.** E-mail: admission@anselm.edu
Phone: (603) 641-7500 Toll-free number: (888) 426-7356
Fax: (603) 641-7550
Nancy Griffin, Dean of Admission, Saint Anselm College, 100 Saint Anselm Drive, Manchester, NH 03102-1310

## Southern New Hampshire University
**Manchester, New Hampshire**
www.snhu.edu

CB member
CB code: 3649

- Private 4-year university
- Residential campus in small city
- 1,929 degree-seeking undergraduates: 2% part-time, 52% women, 1% African American, 1% Asian American, 2% Hispanic American, 5% international
- 2,314 degree-seeking graduate students
- 87% of applicants admitted
- Application essay required

**General.** Founded in 1932. Regionally accredited. Continuing Education Centers in Manchester, Nashua, Salem, Seacoast, Brunswick (ME) and online. Graduate programs in Manchester, Nashua, Seacoast, Salem, Brunswick (ME), and online. **Degrees:** 1,091 bachelor's, 157 associate awarded; master's, doctoral offered. **ROTC:** Army, Air Force. **Location:** 55 miles from Boston. **Calendar:** Differs by program, extensive summer session. **Full-time faculty:** 120 total; 76% have terminal degrees, 12% minority, 38% women. **Part-time faculty:** 303 total; 5% minority, 45% women. **Class size:** 58% < 20, 42% 20-39. **Special facilities:** Culinary institute, financial studies center, advertising agency, audiovisual studio, psychology observation lab, career development center, iMAC graphics lab.

**Freshman class profile.** 3,036 applied, 2,631 admitted, 471 enrolled.

| Mid 50% test scores | | | |
|---|---|---|---|
| | | GPA 2.0-2.99: | 51% |
| SAT critical reading: | 440-520 | Rank in top quarter: | 25% |
| SAT math: | 440-540 | Rank in top tenth: | 8% |
| SAT writing: | 430-530 | Out-of-state: | 60% |
| ACT composite: | 18-21 | Live on campus: | 85% |
| GPA 3.75 or higher: | 4% | International: | 5% |
| GPA 3.50-3.74: | 12% | Fraternities: | 4% |
| GPA 3.0-3.49: | 33% | Sororities: | 3% |

**Basis for selection.** High school academic record weighed most heavily, including courses and course levels, grades, and class rank (if applicable). SAT/ACT scores, extracurricular activities, work experience, recommendations, and essay also considered. Interview required for 3-year bachelor's program. Creative writing majors must submit samples of their original writing. Culinary arts and baking and pastry arts applicants not required to submit SAT or ACT scores. SAT or ACT recommended. Interview recommended.

**High school preparation.** College-preparatory program required. 12 units required. Required units include English 4, mathematics 3, social studies 2, history 2, science 3 (laboratory 2) and foreign language 2.

**2009-2010 Annual costs.** Tuition/fees: $26,442. Room/board: $10,176. Books/supplies: $1,000. Personal expenses: $1,000.

**2009-2010 Financial aid. Non-need-based:** Scholarships awarded for academics, alumni affiliation, athletics, leadership, state residency.

**Application procedures. Admission:** Priority date 3/15; no deadline. $40 fee, may be waived for applicants with need. Admission notification on a rolling basis. Must reply by May 1 or within 4 week(s) if notified thereafter. **Financial aid:** Priority date 3/15; no closing date. FAFSA required. Applicants notified on a rolling basis starting 3/1; must reply within 3 week(s) of notification.

**Academics.** All undergraduate day students required to have laptop computer. **Special study options:** Accelerated study, combined bachelor's/graduate degree, cooperative education, distance learning, double major, dual enrollment of high school students, ESL, honors, independent study, internships, semester at sea, student-designed major, study abroad, teacher certification program, United Nations semester, Washington semester, weekend college. Three-year honors program in business administration. **Credit/placement by examination:** AP, CLEP, IB, institutional tests. 15 credit hours maximum toward associate degree, 15 toward bachelor's. **Support services:** Learning center, pre-admission summer program, reduced course load, remedial instruction, study skills assistance, tutoring.

**Majors. Business:** Accounting, business admin, hospitality admin, international, marketing, retailing, tourism/travel. **Communications:** General, advertising, digital media, public relations. **Computer sciences:** General. **Conservation:** Environmental studies. **Education:** General, business, early childhood, elementary, English, social studies. **Family/consumer sciences:** Child development. **History:** General. **Interdisciplinary:** Accounting/computer science. **Parks/recreation:** Sports admin. **Psychology:** General. **Public administration:** General. **Social sciences:** General, economics, political science. **Visual/performing arts:** Graphic design. **Other:** Justice Studies, Technical Management.

**Most popular majors.** Business/marketing 61%, education 6%, personal/culinary services 7%, psychology 7%.

**Computing on campus.** PC or laptop required. 674 workstations in library, computer center. Dormitories wired for high-speed internet access and linked to campus network. Commuter students can connect to campus network. Online course registration, online library, helpline, repair service, wireless network available.

**Student life. Freshman orientation:** Mandatory, $150 fee. Preregistration for classes offered. Five 1-day sessions held in June; 3-day program held at the opening of the fall term. **Housing:** Guaranteed on-campus for all undergraduates. Coed dorms, special housing for disabled, apartments, wellness housing available. $200 fully refundable deposit, deadline 5/1. Women's floor and wellness housing available. **Activities:** Campus ministries, choral groups, dance, drama, international student organizations, literary magazine, Model UN, musical theater, radio station, student government, student newspaper, TV station.

**Athletics.** NCAA. **Intercollegiate:** Baseball M, basketball, cheerleading, cross-country, golf M, ice hockey M, lacrosse, soccer, softball W, tennis, volleyball W. **Intramural:** Badminton, basketball, football (tackle), racquetball, skiing, soccer, softball, table tennis, tennis, volleyball W. **Team name:** Penmen.

**Student services.** Adult student services, alcohol/substance abuse counseling, chaplain/spiritual director, career counseling, student employment services, financial aid counseling, health services, personal counseling, placement for graduates, veterans' counselor. **Physically disabled:** Services for visually, speech, hearing impaired.

**Contact.** E-mail: admission@snhu.edu
Phone: (603) 645-9611 Toll-free number: (800) 642-4968
Fax: (603) 645-9693
Steve Soba, Director of Admission, Southern New Hampshire University, 2500 North River Road, Manchester, NH 03106-1045

## Thomas More College of Liberal Arts
**Merrimack, New Hampshire**
**www.thomasmorecollege.edu**  CB code: 3892

- Private 4-year liberal arts college affiliated with Roman Catholic Church
- Residential campus in large town
- 80 degree-seeking undergraduates
- SAT or ACT (ACT writing optional), application essay required

**General.** Founded in 1978. Regionally accredited. **Degrees:** 25 bachelor's awarded. **Location:** 45 miles from Boston. **Calendar:** Semester. **Full-time faculty:** 7 total. **Part-time faculty:** 2 total. **Class size:** 80% < 20, 10% 20-39, 10% 50-99.

**Basis for selection.** Evidence of student's desire to learn important. Complete application includes essay, 2 academic letters of recommendation, high school transcript, and SAT or ACT scores. Interviews and/or visits are strongly recommended.

**High school preparation.** 17 units required. Required units include English 4, mathematics 3, social studies 2, history 2, science 2 (laboratory 2) and foreign language 2. Recommended languages: Latin, French, German, Greek. Recommended electives: music, art.

**2009-2010 Annual costs.** Tuition/fees: $14,500. Room/board: $9,100. Books/supplies: $350. Personal expenses: $150.

**2009-2010 Financial aid. Non-need-based:** Scholarships awarded for academics.

**Application procedures. Admission:** No deadline. No application fee. **Financial aid:** Priority date 5/1; no closing date. FAFSA required. Applicants notified on a rolling basis starting 5/15; must reply within 2 week(s) of notification.

**Academics.** Each student, regardless of major, takes 6-hour humanities course every semester throughout 4 years: philosophy, literature, politics, history, theology taught by faculty from various disciplines. **Special study options:** Independent study, internships, liberal arts/career combination, study abroad. Sophomore semester in Rome, Italy. **Credit/placement by examination:** CLEP. **Support services:** Tutoring, writing center.

**Majors. Biology:** General. **Liberal arts:** Arts/sciences. **Philosophy/religion:** Philosophy. **Social sciences:** Political science.

**Computing on campus.** 7 workstations in library.

**Student life. Freshman orientation:** Mandatory. **Housing:** Guaranteed on-campus for all undergraduates. Single-sex dorms available. Pets allowed in dorm rooms. **Activities:** Campus ministries, choral groups, dance, drama, literary magazine, music ensembles, student government.

**Athletics. Intramural:** Basketball, football (non-tackle), racquetball, skiing, soccer, swimming, table tennis, tennis, volleyball M, weight lifting.

**Student services.** Chaplain/spiritual director, career counseling, financial aid counseling, personal counseling.

**Contact.** E-mail: admissions@thomasmorecollege.edu
Phone: (800) 880-8308 ext. 14 Toll-free number: (800) 880-8308 ext. 14
Fax: (603) 880-9280
Mark Schwerdt, Director of Admissions, Thomas More College of Liberal Arts, Six Manchester Street, Merrimack, NH 03054-4818

## University of New Hampshire
**Durham, New Hampshire**  CB member
**www.unh.edu**  CB code: 3918

- Public 4-year university
- Residential campus in small town
- 12,226 degree-seeking undergraduates: 2% part-time, 56% women, 2% African American, 2% Asian American, 2% Hispanic American, 1% international
- 2,266 degree-seeking graduate students
- 72% of applicants admitted
- SAT or ACT with writing, application essay required
- 73% graduate within 6 years; 36% enter graduate study

**General.** Founded in 1866. Regionally accredited. **Degrees:** 2,682 bachelor's, 151 associate awarded; master's, doctoral offered. **ROTC:** Army, Air Force. **Location:** 50 miles from Boston, 50 miles from Portland, ME. **Calendar:** Semester, extensive summer session. **Full-time faculty:** 618 total; 84% have terminal degrees, 9% minority, 38% women. **Part-time faculty:** 358 total; 16% have terminal degrees, 1% minority, 59% women. **Class size:** 41% < 20, 35% 20-39, 7% 40-49, 10% 50-99, 7% >100. **Special facilities:** Journalism laboratory, optical observatory, marine research laboratory, experiential learning center, child development center, agricultural and equine facilities, electron microscope, sawmill, nature preserve, radio station, research centers, survey center, TV station.

**Freshman class profile.** 16,132 applied, 11,583 admitted, 3,004 enrolled.

| Mid 50% test scores | | | |
|---|---|---|---|
| SAT critical reading: | 510-610 | Return as sophomores: | 87% |
| SAT math: | 520-630 | Out-of-state: | 46% |
| Rank in top quarter: | 71% | Live on campus: | 92% |
| Rank in top tenth: | 25% | International: | 1% |
| End year in good standing: | 93% | Fraternities: | 8% |
| | | Sororities: | 6% |

**Basis for selection.** School achievement record most important, followed by course selection, class rank, recommendations, test scores. Cocurricular activities, character/leadership considered. SAT Subject Tests can satisfy a foreign language requirement for students in a BA program. Audition required for music programs. **Homeschooled:** Supporting documents include GED scores, transcripts, education plans, syllabi, SAT or ACT scores, homeschool association information.

**High school preparation.** College-preparatory program required. 17 units required; 22 recommended. Required and recommended units include English 4, mathematics 3-4, social studies 3, science 3-4 (laboratory 2-3), foreign language 2-3 and visual/performing arts 1. Additional requirements determined by intended major.

**2009-2010 Annual costs.** Tuition/fees: $12,743; $26,713 out-of-state. New England Regional Student Program tuition 175% of in-state tuition. College of Earth and Physical Science charges additional $793 per year. Whittemore School of Business charges additional $777 per year. Music majors pay additional $800 per year. Room/board: $9,674. Books/supplies: $1,200. Personal expenses: $2,231.

**2008-2009 Financial aid. Need-based:** 2,101 full-time freshmen applied for aid; 1,542 were judged to have need; 1,519 of these received aid. Average need met was 84%. Average scholarship/grant was $4,283; average loan $2,658. 46% of total undergraduate aid awarded as scholarships/grants, 54% as loans/jobs. **Non-need-based:** Awarded to 2,981 full-time undergraduates, including 708 freshmen. Scholarships awarded for academics, art, athletics, leadership, music/drama, religious affiliation, ROTC.

**Application procedures. Admission:** Closing date 2/1 (postmark date). $50 fee ($65 out-of-state), may be waived for applicants with need. Admission notification 4/15. Admission notification on a rolling basis. Must reply by 5/1. **Financial aid:** Closing date 3/1. FAFSA required. Applicants notified on a rolling basis starting 3/1; must reply by 5/1.

**Academics.** All students must complete a set of writing intensive courses, including Freshman Composition and three additional courses, one of which must be in the student's major and one of which must be an upper-level course. **Special study options:** Accelerated study, combined bachelor's/graduate degree, cooperative education, cross-registration, distance learning, double major, ESL, exchange student, honors, independent study, internships, semester at sea, student-designed major, study abroad, teacher certification program, United Nations semester, Washington semester. Undergraduate research opportunities, International Undergraduate Research Opportunities Program, Service Learning, Capstone experiences, Experiential learning. **Credit/placement by examination:** AP, CLEP, IB, institutional tests. 32 credit hours maximum toward associate degree, 64 toward bachelor's. **Support services:** Learning center, reduced course load, study skills assistance, tutoring, writing center.

**Majors. Agriculture:** Animal sciences, dairy, equestrian studies, horticultural science. **Architecture:** Urban/community planning. **Area/ethnic studies:** European, French, women's. **Biology:** General, bacteriology, Biochemistry/biophysics and molecular biology, biomedical sciences, botany, genetics, microbiology, zoology. **Business:** General, business admin, hospitality admin. **Communications:** General, digital media. **Computer sciences:** General, information technology. **Conservation:** General, economics, environmental science, environmental studies, forestry, wildlife. **Education:** Art, mathematics. **Engineering:** General, chemical, civil, computer, electrical, environmental, materials science, mechanical, ocean, systems. **Engineering technology:** Electrical, mechanical. **Family/consumer sciences:** Child development, family studies, family/community services. **Foreign languages:** Ancient Greek, classics, French, German, Latin, linguistics, Russian, Spanish. **Health:** Athletic training, clinical lab science, health care admin, nursing (RN), recreational therapy. **History:** General. **Interdisciplinary:** Nutrition sciences. **Liberal arts:** Humanities. **Math:** General. **Parks/recreation:** Exercise sciences, facilities management. **Philosophy/religion:** Philosophy. **Physical sciences:** Chemistry, geology, hydrology, physics. **Psychology:** General. **Public administration:** Social work. **Social sciences:** Anthropology, criminology, economics, geography, political science, sociology. **Visual/performing arts:** Art, dramatic, studio arts. **Other:** Adult and occupational education, Ecogastronomy, Horticulture and agronomy, Interdisciplinary mathematics, Resource economics.

**Most popular majors.** Biology 6%, business/marketing 16%, communications/journalism 6%, engineering/engineering technologies 8%, English 6%, health sciences 10%, psychology 8%, social sciences 10%.

**Computing on campus.** 345 workstations in library, computer center, student center. Dormitories wired for high-speed internet access and linked to campus network. Commuter students can connect to campus network. Online course registration, online library, helpline, repair service, student web hosting, wireless network available.

**Student life. Freshman orientation:** Mandatory. Preregistration for classes offered. Two-day program held in June with additional session in fall. A minority student orientation is also offered. **Housing:** Guaranteed on-campus for freshmen. Coed dorms, apartments, fraternity/sorority housing, wellness housing available. $200 partly refundable deposit, deadline 5/1. **Activities:** Bands, campus ministries, choral groups, dance, drama, film society, international student organizations, literary magazine, music ensembles, Model UN, musical theater, radio station, student government, student newspaper, symphony orchestra, TV station, Diversity Support Coalition, Black student union, Indian student association, United Asian Coalition, Chinese Students and Scholars Association, Intervarsity Christian Fellowship, Young Life, Catholic student organization, College Democrats, College Republicans.

**Athletics.** NCAA. **Intercollegiate:** Basketball, cross-country, diving W, field hockey W, football (tackle) M, gymnastics W, ice hockey, lacrosse W, skiing, soccer, swimming W, track and field, volleyball W. **Intramural:** Basketball, field hockey W, football (non-tackle), ice hockey, racquetball, soccer, softball, swimming, table tennis, tennis, volleyball, water polo. **Team name:** Wildcats.

**Student services.** Adult student services, alcohol/substance abuse counseling, chaplain/spiritual director, career counseling, services for economically disadvantaged, student employment services, financial aid counseling, health services, legal services, minority student services, on-campus daycare, personal counseling, placement for graduates, veterans' counselor, women's services. **Physically disabled:** Services for visually, speech, hearing impaired.

**Contact.** E-mail: admissions@unh.edu
Phone: (603) 862-1360 Fax: (603) 862-0077
Robert McGann, Director of Admissions, University of New Hampshire, Grant House, Durham, NH 03824

---

## University of New Hampshire at Manchester
**Manchester, New Hampshire**   CB member
www.unhm.unh.edu   CB code: 2094

- Public 4-year university and liberal arts college
- Commuter campus in small city
- 844 degree-seeking undergraduates: 20% part-time, 54% women
- 80% of applicants admitted
- SAT or ACT (ACT writing optional), application essay required

**General.** Founded in 1985. Regionally accredited. **Degrees:** 166 bachelor's, 28 associate awarded; master's offered. **ROTC:** Army, Air Force. **Location:** 35 miles from Concord, 55 miles from Boston. **Calendar:** Semester, limited summer session. **Full-time faculty:** 36 total. **Part-time faculty:** 104 total.

**Freshman class profile.** 307 applied, 247 admitted, 159 enrolled.

| Mid 50% test scores | | | |
|---|---|---|---|
| | | SAT writing: | 440-550 |
| SAT critical reading: | 450-560 | Out-of-state: | 1% |
| SAT math: | 430-570 | | |

**Basis for selection.** Achievement in high school college preparatory program most important. SAT scores should be consistent with achievement. Recommendation, essay, interview very helpful for students of moderate achievement or in nontraditional cases. Non-native speakers of English must submit TOEFL scores. Interview necessary for college transition program. **Homeschooled:** Transcript of courses and grades, state high school equivalency certificate, letter of recommendation (nonparent) required. Encourage GED, SAT, syllabus of curriculum; diploma from homeschool association if available. **Learning Disabled:** To be eligible for services, students must provide documentation of their disability as determined by a licensed physician and/or certified psychologist who is skilled in the diagnosis of such disability. This documentation must be current (generally within three years).

**High school preparation.** College-preparatory program recommended. Required and recommended units include English 4, mathematics 3-4, social studies 2, science 3-4 (laboratory 1) and foreign language 2-3.

**2009-2010 Annual costs.** Tuition/fees: $10,136; $24,406 out-of-state. New England Regional Student tuition 175% of in-state public institution tuition. Books/supplies: $700. Personal expenses: $2,020.

**2009-2010 Financial aid.** **Non-need-based:** Scholarships awarded for academics, state residency.

**Application procedures.** **Admission:** Priority date 4/1; deadline 6/15 (postmark date). $45 fee ($60 out-of-state), may be waived for applicants with need. Admission notification on a rolling basis. Must reply by May 1 or within 3 week(s) if notified thereafter. **Financial aid:** Closing date 3/1. FAFSA required. Applicants notified on a rolling basis starting 4/1; must reply within 2 week(s) of notification.

**Academics.** **Special study options:** Combined bachelor's/graduate degree, cross-registration, double major, ESL, exchange student, external degree, independent study, internships, semester at sea, student-designed major, study abroad, teacher certification program, Washington semester. **Credit/placement by examination:** AP, CLEP, IB, institutional tests. 48 credit hours maximum toward associate degree, 64 toward bachelor's. **Support services:** Learning center, pre-admission summer program, reduced course load, remedial instruction, study skills assistance, tutoring, writing center.

**Majors.** **Biology:** General. **Business:** Business admin. **Communications:** General. **Computer sciences:** General. **Engineering technology:** Electrical. **Foreign languages:** Sign language interpretation. **History:** General. **Liberal arts:** Arts/sciences, humanities. **Psychology:** General. **Social sciences:** Political science.

**Computing on campus.** 64 workstations in library, computer center. Commuter students can connect to campus network. Online library, helpline, wireless network available.

**Student life.** **Freshman orientation:** Mandatory, $30 fee. Preregistration for classes offered. 3-day (or evening) program held in June, August, and January. June attendees able to preregister for fall courses. **Housing:** Students may reside in dormitories at New Hampshire Institute of Art. **Activities:** Choral groups, dance, student government.

**Athletics.** **Team name:** Wildcats.

**Student services.** Career counseling, financial aid counseling, veterans' counselor. **Physically disabled:** Services for visually, speech, hearing impaired.

**Contact.** E-mail: unhm.admissions@unh.edu
Phone: (603) 641-4150 Fax: (603) 641-4342
Miho Bean, Associate Director of Admissions, University of New Hampshire at Manchester, 400 Commercial Street, Manchester, NH 03101-1113

# New Jersey

## Berkeley College

**Woodland Park, New Jersey**

www.berkeleycollege.edu

**CB member**

**CB code: 2061**

- For-profit 4-year business and career college
- Commuter campus in large town
- 3,688 degree-seeking undergraduates: 15% part-time, 71% women

**General.** Founded in 1931. Regionally accredited. Branch campuses in Paramus, Newark, and Woodbridge. **Degrees:** 331 bachelor's, 262 associate awarded. **Location:** 20 miles from New York City. **Calendar:** Quarter, extensive summer session. **Full-time faculty:** 73 total. **Part-time faculty:** 156 total. **Class size:** 36% < 20, 64% 20-39, less than 1% 40-49.

**Basis for selection.** Class rank, high school record, interview most important. Passing grade on school entrance/placement exam required. Interviews strongly recommended.

**2010-2011 Annual costs.** Tuition/fees (projected): $20,700. Room/board: $10,812. Books/supplies: $1,360. Personal expenses: $3,000.

**Financial aid. Non-need-based:** Scholarships awarded for academics, alumni affiliation. **Additional information:** Alumni scholarship examination given in November and December. Full and partial scholarships awarded.

**Application procedures. Admission:** No deadline. $50 fee. Admission notification on a rolling basis. Admitted applicants must reply within 2 weeks of notification. **Financial aid:** No deadline. FAFSA required. Applicants notified on a rolling basis starting 3/1; must reply within 6 week(s) of notification.

**Academics. Special study options:** Accelerated study, distance learning, internships, New York semester, study abroad. **Credit/placement by examination:** AP, CLEP, SAT, ACT, institutional tests. **Support services:** Learning center, pre-admission summer program, remedial instruction, study skills assistance, tutoring, writing center.

**Majors. Business:** Accounting, business admin, entrepreneurial studies, fashion, financial planning, human resources, international, marketing, nonprofit/public. **Health:** Health care admin. **Protective services:** Law enforcement admin. **Other:** Interior design management.

**Computing on campus.** 358 workstations in library, computer center, student center. Dormitories linked to campus network. Commuter students can connect to campus network. Online library, helpline, wireless network available.

**Student life. Freshman orientation:** Mandatory. **Housing:** Coed dorms available. $400 deposit. **Activities:** Choral groups, drama, literary magazine, student government, Phi Beta Lambda, paralegal club, interior design club, athletic club, fashion and marketing club, Phi Theta Kappa.

**Athletics. Team name:** Bulldogs.

**Student services.** Adult student services, career counseling, student employment services, financial aid counseling, personal counseling, placement for graduates, veterans' counselor.

**Contact.** E-mail: info@berkeleycollege.edu
Phone: (973) 278-5400 ext. 1210 Toll-free number: (800) 446-5400
Fax: (973) 278-9141
David Bertone, Director for High School Admissions, Berkeley College, 44 Rifle Camp Road, Woodland Park, NJ 07424-0440

## Beth Medrash Govoha

**Lakewood, New Jersey**

**CB code: 2166**

- Private 4-year rabbinical college for men affiliated with Jewish faith
- Residential campus in small city
- 2,711 degree-seeking undergraduates
- Interview required

**General.** Founded in 1943. Accredited by AARTS. **Degrees:** 420 bachelor's awarded; master's offered. **Calendar:** Semester. **Full-time faculty:** 130 total. **Part-time faculty:** 20 total.

**Basis for selection.** Interviews required.

**2009-2010 Annual costs.** Books/supplies: $450.

**Application procedures. Admission:** Closing date 8/15. $125 fee, may be waived for applicants with need. **Financial aid:** No deadline.

**Academics. Credit/placement by examination:** CLEP.

**Majors. Theology:** Talmudic.

**Student life. Housing:** Apartments available.

**Student services.** Financial aid counseling, placement for graduates.

**Contact.** Phone: (732) 367-1060 Fax: (732) 370-6559
Rabbi. Abraham Feuer, Director of Admissions, Beth Medrash Govoha, 617 Sixth Street, Lakewood, NJ 08701

## Bloomfield College

**Bloomfield, New Jersey**

www.bloomfield.edu

**CB member**

**CB code: 2044**

- Private 4-year liberal arts and teachers college affiliated with Presbyterian Church (USA)
- Commuter campus in large town
- 2,131 degree-seeking undergraduates: 19% part-time, 65% women, 50% African American, 3% Asian American, 20% Hispanic American, 1% international
- 52% of applicants admitted
- SAT or ACT (ACT writing optional), application essay required
- 33% graduate within 6 years; 7% enter graduate study

**General.** Founded in 1868. Regionally accredited. **Degrees:** 281 bachelor's awarded. **ROTC:** Army. **Location:** 7 miles from Newark, 15 miles from New York City. **Calendar:** Semester, limited summer session. **Full-time faculty:** 68 total; 74% have terminal degrees, 21% minority, 57% women. **Part-time faculty:** 170 total; 12% have terminal degrees, 35% minority, 49% women. **Class size:** 74% < 20, 25% 20-39, less than 1% 40-49, less than 1% 50-99, less than 1% >100. **Special facilities:** Technology and multimedia center, performing arts center, art gallery.

**Freshman class profile.** 3,242 applied, 1,680 admitted, 483 enrolled.

| Mid 50% test scores | | | |
|---|---|---|---|
| SAT critical reading: | 370-450 | Rank in top tenth: | 8% |
| SAT math: | 360-460 | End year in good standing: | 67% |
| GPA 3.75 or higher: | 1% | Return as sophomores: | 71% |
| GPA 3.50-3.74: | 2% | Out-of-state: | 4% |
| GPA 3.0-3.49: | 18% | Live on campus: | 36% |
| GPA 2.0-2.99: | 72% | Fraternities: | 20% |
| Rank in top quarter: | 24% | Sororities: | 30% |

**Basis for selection.** Acceptance for regular admission requires 900 SAT (exclusive of Writing) and 2.8 GPA. Interviews not required but strongly recommended. Essays must be self-recommendations or reflections on previous educational experiences. Recent graded term paper can be substituted for essay. **Homeschooled:** Statement describing homeschool structure and mission, transcript of courses and grades, state high school equivalency certificate, interview, letter of recommendation (nonparent) required. Applicants must submit SAT scores and official transcript with information about organization that performed accreditation/conversion. **Learning Disabled:** Students must meet regular admission requirements, and should ask for special accommodations for SAT testing.

**High school preparation.** College-preparatory program required. 14 units required.

**2010-2011 Annual costs.** Tuition/fees (projected): $22,000. Room/board: $10,600. Books/supplies: $1,000. Personal expenses: $1,800.

**2009-2010 Financial aid. Need-based:** 451 full-time freshmen applied for aid; 437 were judged to have need; 435 of these received aid. Average need met was 62%. Average scholarship/grant was $16,016; average loan $7,409. 76% of total undergraduate aid awarded as scholarships/grants, 24% as loans/jobs. **Non-need-based:** Awarded to 772 full-time undergraduates, including 253 freshmen. Scholarships awarded for academics, alumni affiliation, athletics, music/drama, religious affiliation.

**Application procedures. Admission:** Priority date 3/14; deadline 8/1 (receipt date). $40 fee, may be waived for applicants with need. Admission notification on a rolling basis beginning on or about 10/1. Must reply by May 1 or within 2 week(s) if notified thereafter. **Financial aid:** Priority date 3/15, closing date 6/1. FAFSA required. Applicants notified on a rolling basis starting 3/15; must reply within 2 week(s) of notification.

**Academics.** Organized into 7 divisions: Business and Computer Information Systems, Creative Arts and Technology, Humanities, Natural Science and Mathematics, Nursing, and Social and Behavioral Sciences, and Education. **Special study options:** Accelerated study, distance learning, double major, dual enrollment of high school students, ESL, honors, independent study, internships, liberal arts/career combination, student-designed major, study abroad, teacher certification program. Four-year clinical laboratory science program and allied health technologies major offered in conjunction with University of Medicine and Dentistry of New Jersey; joint BS/MS in computer information systems program offered with NJIT; special programs offered by the Institute for Technology and Professional Studies. **Credit/placement by examination:** AP, CLEP, institutional tests. 16 credit hours maximum toward bachelor's degree. Maximum of 16 course units may be earned through combination of CLEP examinations, portfolio assessment, and nursing assessment. **Support services:** Learning center, pre-admission summer program, remedial instruction, study skills assistance, tutoring, writing center.

**Majors. Biology:** General. **Business:** Accounting, business admin, e-commerce. **Computer sciences:** General, networking. **Education:** General. **Health:** Nursing (RN). **History:** General. **Math:** General, applied. **Philosophy/religion:** Philosophy, religion. **Physical sciences:** Chemistry. **Psychology:** General. **Social sciences:** Political science, sociology. **Visual/performing arts:** General. **Other:** Allied health technologies.

**Most popular majors.** Biology 7%, business/marketing 17%, education 8%, health sciences 12%, psychology 15%, social sciences 17%, visual/performing arts 10%.

**Computing on campus.** 100 workstations in dormitories, library, computer center, student center. Dormitories wired for high-speed internet access and linked to campus network. Commuter students can connect to campus network. Online library, helpline, student web hosting, wireless network available.

**Student life. Freshman orientation:** Available. Preregistration for classes offered. Multi-day sessions offered prior to beginning of fall semester. **Policies:** Statement of Shared Values adopted, addressing student conduct and standards for behavior. **Housing:** Coed dorms available. $100 fully refundable deposit, deadline 5/1. **Activities:** Campus ministries, dance, drama, international student organizations, radio station, student government, African student association, association of Latin American students, Team Infinite, Christian Fellowship, First Ladies, Modern Era Japanese club, gentlemen's club, gay/non gay alliance.

**Athletics.** NCAA. **Intercollegiate:** Baseball M, basketball, cross-country, soccer, softball W, tennis M, volleyball W. **Intramural:** Basketball, volleyball M. **Team name:** Deacons.

**Student services.** Adult student services, alcohol/substance abuse counseling, chaplain/spiritual director, career counseling, student employment services, financial aid counseling, health services, personal counseling, placement for graduates. **Physically disabled:** Services for visually, speech, hearing impaired. **Learning disabled:** Comprehensive services available.

**Contact.** E-mail: admission@bloomfield.edu
Phone: (973) 748-9000 ext. 230 Toll-free number: (800) 848-4555
Fax: (973) 748-0916
Adam Castro, Director of Admissions, Bloomfield College, One Park Place, Bloomfield, NJ 07003

## Caldwell College
**Caldwell, New Jersey**
**www.caldwell.edu**

**CB member**
**CB code: 2072**

- Private 4-year liberal arts college affiliated with Roman Catholic Church
- Commuter campus in large town
- 1,548 degree-seeking undergraduates
- 57% of applicants admitted
- SAT or ACT with writing, application essay required

**General.** Founded in 1939. Regionally accredited. **Degrees:** 315 bachelor's awarded; master's offered. **ROTC:** Army. **Location:** 20 miles from New York City. **Calendar:** Semester, limited summer session. **Full-time faculty:** 82 total. **Part-time faculty:** 129 total. **Class size:** 79% < 20, 21% 20-39.

**Freshman class profile.** 1,740 applied, 995 admitted, 274 enrolled.

| Mid 50% test scores | | | |
|---|---|---|---|
| SAT critical reading: | 450-560 | Rank in top tenth: | 10% |
| SAT math: | 440-570 | Out-of-state: | 7% |
| Rank in top quarter: | 23% | Live on campus: | 56% |

**Basis for selection.** Class rank in top half, school achievement record, test scores, interview, extracurricular activities very important. Counselor's recommendation, volunteer work important. Essay, interview recommended for all, audition required for music programs, portfolio required for art programs.

**High school preparation.** 16 units required. Required units include English 4, mathematics 2, history 1, science 2 (laboratory 1), foreign language 2 and academic electives 5.

**2009-2010 Annual costs.** Tuition/fees: $24,600. Room/board: $10,000. Books/supplies: $1,200. Personal expenses: $1,000.

**2009-2010 Financial aid. Non-need-based:** Scholarships awarded for academics, alumni affiliation, art, athletics, leadership, music/drama, religious affiliation.

**Application procedures. Admission:** Priority date 12/1; no deadline. $40 fee, may be waived for applicants with need. Admission notification on a rolling basis beginning on or about 12/31. Must reply by May 1 or within 2 week(s) if notified thereafter. **Financial aid:** Priority date 4/1; no closing date. FAFSA, institutional form required. Applicants notified on a rolling basis starting 3/1; must reply within 4 week(s) of notification.

**Academics. Special study options:** Accelerated study, combined bachelor's/graduate degree, cooperative education, distance learning, double major, ESL, external degree, honors, independent study, internships, liberal arts/career combination, student-designed major, study abroad, teacher certification program, Washington semester, weekend college. Offers affiliation programs with institutions such as New York University, Columbia University, Temple University, UMDNJ and others where students earn bachelor's degree, typically in biology, and professional degree from the affiliated school. **Credit/placement by examination:** AP, CLEP, IB, institutional tests. 30 credit hours maximum toward bachelor's degree. Credit by exam only available during first year (30 credits) of matriculation. Credit toward major dependent on departmental approval. Prior Learning Assessment (PLA) for adult students who must attend PLA workshop. **Support services:** Learning center, pre-admission summer program, remedial instruction, study skills assistance, tutoring, writing center.

**Majors. Biology:** General. **Business:** Accounting, business admin, international, management science, marketing. **Communications:** General. **Computer sciences:** General, computer science. **Education:** Elementary. **Foreign languages:** French, Spanish. **Health:** Clinical lab technology. **History:** General. **Math:** General. **Physical sciences:** Chemistry. **Protective services:** Criminal justice. **Psychology:** General. **Social sciences:** General, political science, sociology. **Theology:** Theology. **Visual/performing arts:** Art, studio arts.

**Most popular majors.** Business/marketing 20%, communications/journalism 8%, education 12%, psychology 13%, security/protective services 9%.

**Computing on campus.** 210 workstations in dormitories, library, computer center, student center. Dormitories wired for high-speed internet access and linked to campus network. Commuter students can connect to campus network. Online course registration, online library, helpline, student web hosting, wireless network available.

**Student life. Freshman orientation:** Mandatory, $200 fee. Preregistration for classes offered. Held Sunday and Monday prior to beginning of classes in August. **Housing:** Guaranteed on-campus for all undergraduates. Coed dorms, wellness housing available. $200 nonrefundable deposit, deadline 5/1. **Activities:** Jazz band, campus ministries, choral groups, drama, international student organizations, literary magazine, music ensembles, musical theater, student government, student newspaper, Circle K, black students cooperative union, Latin American student association, Portuguese club, Irish club.

**Athletics.** NCAA. **Intercollegiate:** Baseball M, basketball, cross-country W, golf M, soccer, softball W, tennis. **Intramural:** Basketball, football (non-tackle), soccer, softball, volleyball. **Team name:** Cougars.

**Student services.** Adult student services, alcohol/substance abuse counseling, chaplain/spiritual director, career counseling, services for economically disadvantaged, student employment services, financial aid counseling, health services, minority student services, personal counseling, placement for graduates, women's services. **Physically disabled:** Services for visually, hearing impaired.

**Contact.** E-mail: admissions@caldwell.edu
Phone: (973) 618-3500 Toll-free number: (888) 864-9516
Fax: (973) 618-3600
Kathryn Reilly, Executive Director of Admissions and Financial Aid,
Caldwell College, 9 Ryerson Avenue, Caldwell, NJ 07006-6195

## Centenary College
**Hackettstown, New Jersey**
www.centenarycollege.edu

**CB member**
**CB code: 2080**

- Private 4-year liberal arts college affiliated with United Methodist Church
- Residential campus in large town
- 2,140 degree-seeking undergraduates: 8% part-time, 63% women
- 799 graduate students
- 89% of applicants admitted
- SAT or ACT, application essay required

**General.** Founded in 1867. Regionally accredited. **Degrees:** 481 bachelor's, 77 associate awarded; master's offered. **Location:** 55 miles from New York City. **Calendar:** Semester, limited summer session. **Full-time faculty:** 69 total; 56% have terminal degrees, 7% minority, 56% women. **Part-time faculty:** 270 total; 52% women. **Class size:** 60% < 20, 39% 20-39, 1% 40-49. **Special facilities:** Textile laboratory, equestrian center.

**Freshman class profile.** 754 applied, 673 admitted, 271 enrolled.

| Mid 50% test scores | | | |
|---|---|---|---|
| SAT critical reading: | 410-510 | GPA 2.0-2.99: | 67% |
| SAT math: | 420-510 | Rank in top quarter: | 30% |
| SAT writing: | 410-510 | Rank in top tenth: | 14% |
| ACT composite: | 16-20 | Return as sophomores: | 76% |
| GPA 3.75 or higher: | 3% | Out-of-state: | 24% |
| GPA 3.50-3.74: | 8% | Live on campus: | 79% |
| GPA 3.0-3.49: | 20% | Fraternities: | 5% |
| | | Sororities: | 5% |

**Basis for selection.** School achievement record, standardized test scores most important. Interview, recommendations, community activities also strongly considered. Interviews required for academically marginal students with special needs; recommended for others. Portfolio required for art and design, graphic arts majors. **Homeschooled:** State high school equivalency certificate required. **Learning Disabled:** Interview with Director of Services, documentation of psycho-education evaluation and IEP required for supportive services programs.

**High school preparation.** College-preparatory program required. 16 units required; 20 recommended. Required and recommended units include English 4, mathematics 3-4, social studies 2, science 2-4 (laboratory 1-2) and foreign language 2. Major-related courses on high school level recommended.

**2009-2010 Annual costs.** Tuition/fees: $26,534. Additional fees required for equine majors and for comprehensive learning support program. Room/board: $9,434. Books/supplies: $1,200. Personal expenses: $850.

**2008-2009 Financial aid. Need-based:** 265 full-time freshmen applied for aid; 224 were judged to have need; 224 of these received aid. Average need met was 75%. Average scholarship/grant was $14,806; average loan $5,143. 60% of total undergraduate aid awarded as scholarships/grants, 40% as loans/jobs. **Non-need-based:** Awarded to 472 full-time undergraduates, including 68 freshmen. Scholarships awarded for academics, alumni affiliation, art, leadership, minority status, music/drama, religious affiliation, state residency.

**Application procedures. Admission:** Priority date 3/1; no deadline. $30 fee, may be waived for applicants with need, free for online applicants. Admission notification on a rolling basis beginning on or about 12/15. Must reply by May 1 or within 4 week(s) if notified thereafter. **Financial aid:** Priority date 4/1, closing date 6/1. FAFSA required. Applicants notified on a rolling basis starting 3/1.

**Academics.** Core curriculum required. Educational program balances career and liberal arts. **Special study options:** Accelerated study, combined bachelor's/graduate degree, cross-registration, distance learning, double major, dual enrollment of high school students, ESL, exchange student, honors, independent study, internships, liberal arts/career combination, student-designed major, study abroad, teacher certification program, weekend college. **Credit/placement by examination:** AP, CLEP, IB. 15 credit hours maximum toward associate degree, 30 toward bachelor's. **Support services:** Learning center, pre-admission summer program, reduced course load, remedial instruction, study skills assistance, tutoring, writing center.

**Majors. Agriculture:** Equestrian studies. **Biology:** General. **Business:** Accounting, business admin. **Communications:** General. **Computer sciences:**

General. **Education:** General. **History:** General. **Math:** General. **Protective services:** Criminal justice. **Psychology:** General. **Social sciences:** Political science, sociology. **Visual/performing arts:** Commercial/advertising art, dramatic, fashion design.

**Most popular majors.** Business/marketing 49%, history 6%, psychology 10%, security/protective services 7%, social sciences 10%, visual/performing arts 7%.

**Computing on campus.** PC or laptop required. 750 workstations in dormitories, library, computer center. Dormitories wired for high-speed internet access and linked to campus network. Commuter students can connect to campus network. Online course registration, online library, helpline, repair service, wireless network available.

**Student life. Freshman orientation:** Mandatory. Preregistration for classes offered. Three-day orientation prior to start of classes. **Housing:** Coed dorms available. $150 deposit, deadline 5/1. **Activities:** Campus ministries, choral groups, dance, drama, film society, international student organizations, literary magazine, music ensembles, Model UN, musical theater, radio station, student government, student newspaper, TV station, art guild, student activities committee, service groups, fashion group, academic clubs, professional and honor societies, special interest clubs, Students in Free Enterprise.

**Athletics.** NCAA. **Intercollegiate:** Baseball M, basketball, cross-country, equestrian, golf, lacrosse, soccer, softball W, volleyball W, wrestling M. **Intramural:** Basketball M, equestrian M. **Team name:** Cyclones.

**Student services.** Adult student services, alcohol/substance abuse counseling, chaplain/spiritual director, career counseling, services for economically disadvantaged, student employment services, financial aid counseling, health services, minority student services, personal counseling, placement for graduates, women's services. **Learning disabled:** Comprehensive services available.

**Contact.** E-mail: admissions@centenarycollege.edu
Phone: (908) 852-1400 ext. 2217 Toll-free number: (800) 236-8679
Fax: (908) 852-3454
Dianne Finnan, Vice President for Enrollment Management and Strategic Branding, Centenary College, 400 Jefferson Street, Hackettstown, NJ 07840-9989

## The College of New Jersey
**Ewing, New Jersey**
www.tcnj.edu

**CB code: 2519**

- Public 4-year liberal arts college
- Residential campus in large town
- 6,197 degree-seeking undergraduates: 2% part-time, 59% women, 6% African American, 6% Asian American, 9% Hispanic American, 1% international
- 598 degree-seeking graduate students
- 46% of applicants admitted
- SAT or ACT (ACT writing optional), application essay required
- 86% graduate within 6 years; 32% enter graduate study

**General.** Founded in 1855. Regionally accredited. **Degrees:** 1,487 bachelor's awarded; master's offered. **ROTC:** Army, Air Force. **Location:** 35 miles from Philadelphia. **Calendar:** Semester, limited summer session. **Full-time faculty:** 348 total; 88% have terminal degrees, 22% minority, 50% women. **Part-time faculty:** 402 total; 24% have terminal degrees, 9% minority, 54% women. **Class size:** 42% < 20, 54% 20-39, 3% 40-49, less than 1% 50-99. **Special facilities:** Concert hall, electron microscopy lab, nuclear magnetic resonance lab, optical spectroscopy lab, observatory, planetarium, greenhouse.

**Freshman class profile.** 9,283 applied, 4,267 admitted, 1,284 enrolled.

| Mid 50% test scores | | | |
|---|---|---|---|
| SAT critical reading: | 560-660 | Rank in top tenth: | 61% |
| SAT math: | 590-690 | Return as sophomores: | 95% |
| SAT writing: | 570-670 | Out-of-state: | 6% |
| Rank in top quarter: | 92% | Live on campus: | 95% |

**Basis for selection.** Standardized test scores, high school rank and choice of curriculum very important. Extracurricular service, activities and community involvement considered. Audition required for music; portfolio required for art. **Homeschooled:** Statement describing homeschool structure and mission, transcript of courses and grades, state high school equivalency certificate, letter of recommendation (nonparent) required.

**High school preparation.** College-preparatory program recommended. 18 units required; 20 recommended. Required and recommended units include English 4, mathematics 3, social studies 2-3, science 3 (laboratory 2-3) and foreign language 2-3.

**2009-2010 Annual costs.** Tuition/fees: $12,722; $21,408 out-of-state. Room/board: $9,996. Books/supplies: $1,000. Personal expenses: $1,500.

**2008-2009 Financial aid. Need-based:** 1,124 full-time freshmen applied for aid; 633 were judged to have need; 596 of these received aid. Average need met was 47%. Average scholarship/grant was $14,125; average loan $3,285. 43% of total undergraduate aid awarded as scholarships/grants, 57% as loans/jobs. **Non-need-based:** Awarded to 2,068 full-time undergraduates, including 535 freshmen. Scholarships awarded for academics. **Additional information:** Merit scholarships available to New Jersey high school graduates based on academic distinction. Limited number of scholarships available to out-of-state students who demonstrate exceptional academic achievement in high school and on SAT. The EOF Promise Award meets the direct cost of attendance freshman and sophomore years, with merit scholarship awards available in junior and senior years.

**Application procedures. Admission:** Priority date 11/15; deadline 1/15 (postmark date). $70 fee, may be waived for applicants with need. Admission notification on a rolling basis beginning on or about 1/15. Must reply by 4/1. **Financial aid:** Priority date 3/1, closing date 10/1. FAFSA required. Applicants notified on a rolling basis starting 6/1; must reply within 2 week(s) of notification.

**Academics. Special study options:** Accelerated study, combined bachelor's/graduate degree, double major, dual enrollment of high school students, exchange student, honors, independent study, internships, liberal arts/career combination, semester at sea, student-designed major, study abroad, teacher certification program, Washington semester. Mentored Undergraduate Summer Experience (MUSE). **Credit/placement by examination:** AP, CLEP, IB, SAT, institutional tests. 30 credit hours maximum toward bachelor's degree. **Support services:** Learning center, pre-admission summer program, reduced course load, remedial instruction, study skills assistance, tutoring, writing center.

**Majors. Area/ethnic studies:** Women's. **Biology:** General. **Business:** Accounting, business admin. **Computer sciences:** General. **Education:** Art, biology, chemistry, Deaf/hearing impaired, early childhood, elementary, English, foreign languages, health, history, mathematics, middle, music, physical, physics, social studies, special, technology/industrial arts. **Engineering:** Biomedical, civil, computer, electrical, mechanical, science. **Foreign languages:** Spanish. **Health:** Nursing (RN). **History:** General. **Math:** General. **Philosophy/religion:** Philosophy. **Physical sciences:** Chemistry, physics. **Protective services:** Law enforcement admin. **Psychology:** General. **Social sciences:** Economics, international relations, political science, sociology. **Visual/performing arts:** General, art, commercial/advertising art, multimedia, studio arts.

**Most popular majors.** Biology 6%, business/marketing 16%, education 22%, English 10%, psychology 10%, social sciences 6%.

**Computing on campus.** 631 workstations in dormitories, library, computer center, student center. Dormitories wired for high-speed internet access and linked to campus network. Commuter students can connect to campus network. Online course registration, online library, helpline, repair service, student web hosting, wireless network available.

**Student life. Freshman orientation:** Mandatory, $165 fee. Preregistration for classes offered. Four-part program including June advisement week, summer readings, welcome week, college seminar. **Housing:** Guaranteed on-campus for freshmen. Coed dorms, single-sex dorms, special housing for disabled, apartments, wellness housing available. $150 nonrefundable deposit, deadline 5/1. Pets allowed in dorm rooms. Housing for transfer students available. **Activities:** Bands, campus ministries, choral groups, dance, drama, international student organizations, literary magazine, music ensembles, Model UN, musical theater, opera, radio station, student government, student newspaper, symphony orchestra, TV station, black student union, Amnesty International, Circle K, EOF Alliance, PRISM, Islamic society, outreach association, students acting for the environment, Jewish student union, ACTION: activist coalition.

**Athletics.** NCAA. **Intercollegiate:** Baseball M, basketball, cross-country, diving, field hockey W, football (tackle) M, lacrosse W, soccer, softball W, swimming, tennis, track and field, wrestling M. **Intramural:** Basketball, bowling, fencing, field hockey, football (non-tackle), ice hockey M, lacrosse M, racquetball, rugby, skiing, soccer, softball, swimming, tennis, volleyball, water polo. **Team name:** Lions.

**Student services.** Adult student services, alcohol/substance abuse counseling, chaplain/spiritual director, career counseling, services for economically disadvantaged, student employment services, financial aid counseling, health services, minority student services, personal counseling, placement for graduates, veterans' counselor, women's services. **Physically disabled:** Services for visually, speech, hearing impaired.

**Contact.** E-mail: tcnjinfo@tcnj.edu
Phone: (609) 771-2131 Fax: (609) 637-5174
Lisa Angeloni, Dean of Admissions, The College of New Jersey, Box 7718, Ewing, NJ 08628

## College of St. Elizabeth
**Morristown, New Jersey**
**www.cse.edu**

CB member
CB code: 2090

- Private 4-year liberal arts college for women affiliated with Roman Catholic Church
- Residential campus in large town
- 1,216 degree-seeking undergraduates: 45% part-time, 89% women
- 872 degree-seeking graduate students
- 83% of applicants admitted
- SAT or ACT (ACT writing optional), application essay required
- 62% graduate within 6 years

**General.** Founded in 1899. Regionally accredited. Men admitted to adult undergraduate programs and master's programs. **Degrees:** 253 bachelor's awarded; master's, doctoral offered. **Location:** 40 miles from New York City. **Calendar:** Semester, limited summer session. **Full-time faculty:** 72 total; 86% have terminal degrees, 4% minority, 67% women. **Part-time faculty:** 139 total; 18% have terminal degrees, 6% minority, 68% women. **Class size:** 82% < 20, 17% 20-39, less than 1% 40-49, less than 1% >100. **Special facilities:** Library of rare books and manuscripts, Greek theater, Shakespeare garden, Holocaust education resource center, center for Catholic women's history, center for theological and spiritual development.

**Freshman class profile.** 509 applied, 424 admitted, 179 enrolled.

| Mid 50% test scores | | | |
|---|---|---|---|
| SAT critical reading: | 390-500 | Rank in top tenth: | 15% |
| SAT math: | 370-490 | Return as sophomores: | 72% |
| SAT writing: | 380-510 | Out-of-state: | 5% |
| Rank in top quarter: | 34% | Live on campus: | 83% |

**Basis for selection.** School achievement record and recommendations most important, followed by test scores, class rank; interview recommended. **Homeschooled:** Letter of recommendation (nonparent) required. Applicants processed on individual basis. Must provide approved curriculum guide.

**High school preparation.** College-preparatory program required. 16 units required; 23 recommended. Required and recommended units include English 3-4, mathematics 2-3, history 1-3, science 1-2 (laboratory 1-2), foreign language 2 and academic electives 7.

**2009-2010 Annual costs.** Tuition/fees: $25,058. Room/board: $10,904. Books/supplies: $1,200. Personal expenses: $1,312.

**2008-2009 Financial aid. Non-need-based:** Scholarships awarded for academics, alumni affiliation, art, leadership, state residency.

**Application procedures. Admission:** Priority date 3/1; deadline 8/15 (receipt date). $35 fee, may be waived for applicants with need. Admission notification on a rolling basis beginning on or about 11/15. Must reply by May 1 or within 2 week(s) if notified thereafter. **Financial aid:** Priority date 3/1; no closing date. FAFSA required. Applicants notified on a rolling basis starting 11/15; must reply by 5/1 or within 2 week(s) of notification.

**Academics.** Students with 60 undergraduate credits may take accelerated program in business or communication on Saturdays and complete bachelor's degree in 2 years. **Special study options:** Accelerated study, combined bachelor's/graduate degree, cross-registration, distance learning, double major, dual enrollment of high school students, ESL, exchange student, honors, independent study, internships, liberal arts/career combination, student-designed major, study abroad, teacher certification program, United Nations semester, weekend college. Accelerated co-ed baccalaureate program with majors in business, communication, nursing and psychology for adults over age 23 with classes evenings and on Saturdays. **Credit/placement by examination:** AP, CLEP, IB, institutional tests. 30 credit hours maximum toward bachelor's degree. Credit for prior work and/or life experience offered via portfolio. **Support services:** Learning center, pre-admission summer program, reduced course load, remedial instruction, study skills assistance, tutoring.

**Majors. Area/ethnic studies:** American, women's. **Biology:** General, biochemistry. **Business:** Business admin. **Communications:** General. **Computer sciences:** Computer science. **Education:** Elementary, special. **Foreign languages:** Spanish. **Health:** Dietetics, nursing (RN). **History:** General.

**Interdisciplinary:** Global studies. **Math:** General. **Philosophy/religion:** Philosophy. **Physical sciences:** Chemistry. **Psychology:** General. **Social sciences:** Economics, sociology. **Theology:** Theology. **Visual/performing arts:** Art. **Other:** Alllied health studies, Justice studies, applied science.

**Most popular majors.** Biology 6%, business/marketing 17%, communications/journalism 11%, education 9%, health sciences 25%, interdisciplinary studies 11%, psychology 7%.

**Computing on campus.** 127 workstations in dormitories, library, computer center. Dormitories wired for high-speed internet access and linked to campus network. Commuter students can connect to campus network. Helpline, wireless network available.

**Student life. Freshman orientation:** Mandatory, $200 fee. Preregistration for classes offered. Comprehensive program held before start of classes for Women's College students. **Housing:** Guaranteed on-campus for all undergraduates. Wellness housing available. $200 deposit. **Activities:** Campus ministries, choral groups, drama, literary magazine, music ensembles, student government, student newspaper, volunteer services center, international/intercultural club, Latin Roots, Students Take Action Committee, foreign language club, American Chemical Society Affiliates, psychology club, sociology club.

**Athletics.** NCAA. **Intercollegiate:** Basketball W, equestrian W, soccer W, softball W, swimming W, tennis W, volleyball W. **Intramural:** Volleyball W. **Team name:** Eagles.

**Student services.** Adult student services, alcohol/substance abuse counseling, chaplain/spiritual director, career counseling, services for economically disadvantaged, student employment services, financial aid counseling, health services, minority student services, personal counseling, placement for graduates, women's services. **Physically disabled:** Services for visually, speech, hearing impaired.

**Contact.** E-mail: apply@cse.edu
Phone: (973) 290-4700 Toll-free number: (800) 210-7900
Fax: (973) 290-4710
Donna Tatarka, Dean of Admission, College of St. Elizabeth, 2 Convent Road, Morristown, NJ 07960-6989

## DeVry University: North Brunswick
**North Brunswick, New Jersey**
www.devry.edu                     **CB code: 2203**

- For-profit 4-year university
- Commuter campus in small city
- 1,432 degree-seeking undergraduates: 42% part-time, 28% women, 24% African American, 8% Asian American, 21% Hispanic American, 1% Native American, 1% international
- Interview required

**General.** Founded in 1996. Regionally accredited. **Degrees:** 176 bachelor's, 178 associate awarded. **Location:** 30 miles from New York City. **Calendar:** Semester, extensive summer session. **Full-time faculty:** 37 total; 24% minority, 30% women. **Part-time faculty:** 118 total; 25% minority, 48% women.

**Basis for selection.** Applicants must have high school diploma or equivalent, degree from an accredited postsecondary institution, or submit acceptable test scores and be at least 17 years of age on the first day of classes. New students may enter at beginning of any semester. SAT or ACT recommended. CPT also accepted.

**High school preparation.** Required units include mathematics 1. Math unit must be algebra or higher.

**2009-2010 Annual costs.** Tuition/fees: $14,800. Books/supplies: $1,300. Personal expenses: $3,152.

**2008-2009 Financial aid.** All financial aid based on need.

**Application procedures. Admission:** No deadline. $50 fee. Admission notification on a rolling basis. **Financial aid:** No deadline. FAFSA required. Applicants notified on a rolling basis.

**Academics. Special study options:** Accelerated study, cooperative education, distance learning, weekend college. **Credit/placement by examination:** CLEP, institutional tests. **Support services:** Learning center, remedial instruction, tutoring.

**Majors. Business:** Business admin. **Computer sciences:** Networking, systems analysis. **Engineering technology:** Biomedical, electrical. **Other:** Technical management.

**Most popular majors.** Business/marketing 37%, computer/information sciences 46%, engineering/engineering technologies 16%.

**Computing on campus.** 575 workstations in library, computer center. Online course registration, online library, helpline available.

**Student life. Freshman orientation:** Mandatory. **Activities:** Student government, Phi Theta Kappa, Golden Key, Institution of Electrical and Electronics Engineers, cultural exchange club, chess club, art club, Crusade for Christ.

**Student services.** Career counseling, student employment services, financial aid counseling, on-campus daycare, placement for graduates, veterans' counselor. **Physically disabled:** Services for visually, hearing impaired.

**Contact.** E-mail: admissions@devry.edu
Phone: (732) 435-4850 Toll-free number: (800) 333-3879
Fax: (732) 435-4850
Gerald Wargo, Director of Admissions, DeVry University: North Brunswick, 630 US Highway One, North Brunswick, NJ 08902-3362

## Drew University
**Madison, New Jersey**                     **CB member**
www.drew.edu                                 **CB code: 2193**

- Private 4-year university and liberal arts college affiliated with United Methodist Church
- Residential campus in large town
- 1,684 degree-seeking undergraduates: 1% part-time, 61% women, 8% African American, 6% Asian American, 10% Hispanic American, 2% international
- 893 degree-seeking graduate students
- 74% of applicants admitted
- 77% graduate within 6 years

**General.** Founded in 1867. Regionally accredited. **Degrees:** 335 bachelor's awarded; master's, doctoral, professional offered. **Location:** 30 miles from New York City. **Calendar:** Semester, limited summer session. **Full-time faculty:** 159 total; 96% have terminal degrees, 20% minority, 50% women. **Part-time faculty:** 99 total. **Class size:** 71% < 20, 24% 20-39, 3% 40-49, 2% 50-99. **Special facilities:** 80-acre forest preserve, arboretum, photography gallery, observatory, research greenhouse, laser holography laboratory, center for the arts, music hall.

**Freshman class profile.** 5,392 applied, 3,991 admitted, 506 enrolled.

| Mid 50% test scores | | GPA 2.0-2.99: | 26% |
|---|---|---|---|
| SAT critical reading: | 510-630 | Rank in top quarter: | 67% |
| SAT math: | 500-620 | Rank in top tenth: | 38% |
| SAT writing: | 510-630 | Return as sophomores: | 79% |
| ACT composite: | 21-27 | Out-of-state: | 44% |
| GPA 3.75 or higher: | 18% | Live on campus: | 90% |
| GPA 3.50-3.74: | 16% | International: | 1% |
| GPA 3.0-3.49: | 40% | | |

**Basis for selection.** School achievement record most important; test scores also important. Graded analytical writing sample required if test scores not submitted. Interview recommended. **Homeschooled:** Statement describing homeschool structure and mission, transcript of courses and grades required.

**High school preparation.** College-preparatory program recommended. Recommended units include English 4, mathematics 3, social studies 2, history 2, science 2 (laboratory 2), foreign language 2 and academic electives 3.

**2009-2010 Annual costs.** Tuition/fees: $38,017. Room/board: $10,368. Books/supplies: $1,228.

**2008-2009 Financial aid. Need-based:** 83% of total undergraduate aid awarded as scholarships/grants, 17% as loans/jobs. **Non-need-based:** Scholarships awarded for academics, art, minority status, music/drama.

**Application procedures. Admission:** Closing date 2/15. $50 fee, may be waived for applicants with need. Applicants notified by third week in March. Must reply by 5/1. **Financial aid:** Closing date 2/15. FAFSA, CSS PROFILE required. Must reply by 5/1.

**Academics.** RISE program enables students to conduct scientific research with retired scientists. **Special study options:** Accelerated study, combined bachelor's/graduate degree, cross-registration, double major, exchange student, honors, independent study, internships, New York semester, student-designed major, study abroad, teacher certification program, United Nations semester, Washington semester. Seven year dual degree (BA/MD) program with UMDNJ - New Jersey Medical School. Five year dual degree (BA/BS or B Eng) programs in engineering and technologies with Columbia University, Stevens Institute of Technology, and Washington University. Five year dual degree (BA/Master of Forestry or Master of Environmental Management) program with Duke University. **Credit/placement by examination:** AP, CLEP, IB, institutional tests. 32 credit hours maximum toward bachelor's degree. **Support services:** Learning center, pre-admission summer program, reduced course load, study skills assistance, tutoring, writing center.

**Majors. Area/ethnic studies:** African, women's. **Biology:** General, Biochemistry/biophysics and molecular biology. **Business:** Business admin, managerial economics. **Computer sciences:** Computer science. **Conservation:** Environmental studies. **Foreign languages:** Chinese, classics, French, German, Spanish. **History:** General. **Interdisciplinary:** Behavioral sciences, neuroscience. **Math:** General. **Philosophy/religion:** Philosophy, religion. **Physical sciences:** Chemistry, physics. **Psychology:** General. **Social sciences:** Anthropology, economics, political science, sociology. **Visual/performing arts:** Art, art history/conservation, dramatic. **Other:** Biological anthropology.

**Most popular majors.** Biology 7%, English 6%, foreign language 9%, history 7%, interdisciplinary studies 6%, psychology 11%, social sciences 31%, visual/performing arts 13%.

**Computing on campus.** PC or laptop required. Dormitories wired for high-speed internet access and linked to campus network. Commuter students can connect to campus network. Online course registration, online library, helpline, repair service, wireless network available.

**Student life. Freshman orientation:** Mandatory, $250 fee. Preregistration for classes offered. Held the week before start of fall semester. **Housing:** Guaranteed on-campus for all undergraduates. Coed dorms, special housing for disabled, wellness housing available. **Activities:** Campus ministries, choral groups, dance, drama, film society, literary magazine, music ensembles, radio station, student government, student newspaper, symphony orchestra, TV station, Amnesty International, Hispanic student organization, College Democrats, College Republicans, Pan-African student organization, Inter-Varsity Christian Fellowship, Jewish student organization/Hillel, environmental action league, Students Against Violence Everywhere, The Alliance.

**Athletics. NCAA. Intercollegiate:** Baseball M, basketball, cross-country, equestrian, fencing, field hockey W, lacrosse, soccer, softball W, swimming, tennis. **Intramural:** Basketball, football (non-tackle), racquetball, soccer, softball, squash, table tennis, volleyball. **Team name:** Rangers.

**Student services.** Adult student services, alcohol/substance abuse counseling, chaplain/spiritual director, career counseling, services for economically disadvantaged, student employment services, financial aid counseling, health services, minority student services, on-campus daycare, personal counseling, placement for graduates, women's services. **Physically disabled:** Services for visually, hearing impaired.

**Contact.** E-mail: cadm@drew.edu
Phone: (973) 408-3739 Fax: (973) 408-3068
Alyssa McCloud, Vice President for Enrollment Management, Drew University, 36 Madison Avenue, Madison, NJ 07940-4063

## Fairleigh Dickinson University: College at Florham

**Madison, New Jersey**
www.fdu.edu
**CB code: 2262**

- Private 4-year university
- Residential campus in large town
- 2,419 degree-seeking undergraduates: 6% part-time, 53% women, 8% African American, 3% Asian American, 8% Hispanic American, 1% international
- 1,000 degree-seeking graduate students
- 67% of applicants admitted
- SAT or ACT (ACT writing optional) required
- 52% graduate within 6 years

**General.** Regionally accredited. Additional campus locations: Wroxton College, England and Vancouver, Canada. **Degrees:** 522 bachelor's awarded; master's offered. **ROTC:** Army, Air Force. **Location:** 27 miles from New York City. **Calendar:** Semester, extensive summer session. **Full-time faculty:** 120 total. **Part-time faculty:** 200 total. **Special facilities:** ITV multimedia classrooms, web-iab, regional center for students with learning disabilities, cyber crime lab.

**Freshman class profile.** 3,907 applied, 2,601 admitted, 645 enrolled.

| Mid 50% test scores | | | |
|---|---|---|---|
| SAT critical reading: | 460-550 | GPA 2.0-2.99: | 37% |
| SAT math: | 470-570 | Rank in top quarter: | 43% |
| SAT writing: | 450-560 | Rank in top tenth: | 16% |
| GPA 3.75 or higher: | 16% | Return as sophomores: | 75% |
| GPA 3.50-3.74: | 15% | Out-of-state: | 18% |
| GPA 3.0-3.49: | 32% | Live on campus: | 86% |

**Basis for selection.** GPA, test scores, difficulty of high school curriculum most important. FDU placement tests required for all. **Learning Disabled:** Separate application along with admissions application.

**High school preparation.** 16 units required. Required and recommended units include English 4, mathematics 3, social studies 2, history 2, science 2-3 (laboratory 2-3), foreign language 2 and academic electives 3.

**2009-2010 Annual costs.** Tuition/fees: $31,264. Room/board: $11,058.

**Application procedures. Admission:** Priority date 3/15; no deadline. $40 fee, may be waived for applicants with need, free for online applicants. Admission notification on a rolling basis beginning on or about 11/1. Must reply by May 1 or within 2 week(s) if notified thereafter. **Financial aid:** Priority date 2/15; no closing date. FAFSA required. Applicants notified on a rolling basis starting 2/1; must reply by 5/1 or within 4 week(s) of notification.

**Academics. Special study options:** Accelerated study, combined bachelor's/graduate degree, cooperative education, cross-registration, distance learning, double major, external degree, honors, independent study, internships, liberal arts/career combination, teacher certification program, Washington semester, weekend college. **Credit/placement by examination:** CLEP, institutional tests. 30 credit hours maximum toward bachelor's degree. **Support services:** Learning center, pre-admission summer program, reduced course load, remedial instruction, study skills assistance, tutoring, writing center.

**Majors. Biology:** General, biochemistry, marine. **Business:** Accounting, business admin, entrepreneurial studies, hospitality admin, managerial economics, marketing. **Communications:** General. **Computer sciences:** General. **Foreign languages:** French, Spanish. **Health:** Clinical lab science, health services, medical radiologic technology/radiation therapy, nursing (RN), respiratory therapy technology. **History:** General. **Liberal arts:** Humanities. **Math:** General. **Philosophy/religion:** Philosophy. **Physical sciences:** Chemistry. **Psychology:** General. **Social sciences:** Economics, political science, sociology. **Visual/performing arts:** General, cinematography, dramatic. **Other:** Allied health technology.

**Most popular majors.** Business/marketing 33%, communications/journalism 8%, English 8%, liberal arts 7%, psychology 15%, social sciences 6%, visual/performing arts 9%.

**Computing on campus.** 140 workstations in library, computer center. Dormitories wired for high-speed internet access and linked to campus network. Commuter students can connect to campus network. Online library, helpline, student web hosting, wireless network available.

**Student life. Freshman orientation:** Mandatory. Preregistration for classes offered. **Housing:** Guaranteed on-campus for freshmen. Coed dorms, special housing for disabled available. $350 partly refundable deposit, deadline 5/1. **Activities:** Campus ministries, choral groups, dance, drama, film society, international student organizations, literary magazine, musical theater, opera, radio station, student government, student newspaper, Green Club, Greek organizations, Florham Programming Committee, Association of Black Collegians.

**Athletics. NCAA. Intercollegiate:** Baseball M, basketball, cross-country, field hockey W, football (tackle) M, golf M, lacrosse, soccer, softball W, swimming, tennis, volleyball W. **Intramural:** Basketball, football (non-tackle) M, ice hockey M, soccer, softball, volleyball. **Team name:** Devils.

**Student services.** Adult student services, alcohol/substance abuse counseling, chaplain/spiritual director, career counseling, services for economically disadvantaged, student employment services, financial aid counseling, health services, minority student services, personal counseling, placement for graduates, veterans' counselor, women's services. **Physically disabled:** Services for visually, speech, hearing impaired. **Learning disabled:** Comprehensive services available.

**Contact.** E-mail: globaleducation@fdu.edu
Phone: (800) 338-8803 Toll-free number: (800) 338-8803
Fax: (973) 443-8088
Jonathan Wexler, Associate Vice President for Admissions and Financial Aid, Fairleigh Dickinson University: College at Florham, 285 Madison Avenue, Madison, NJ 07940

## Fairleigh Dickinson University: Metropolitan Campus
**Teaneck, New Jersey**
www.fdu.edu                    CB code: 2263

- Private 4-year university
- Commuter campus in large town
- 3,672 degree-seeking undergraduates: 34% part-time, 57% women, 14% African American, 6% Asian American, 26% Hispanic American, 7% international
- 2,629 degree-seeking graduate students
- 57% of applicants admitted
- SAT or ACT (ACT writing optional) required
- 40% graduate within 6 years

**General.** Founded in 1942. Regionally accredited. Additional campus at Wroxton College, England and Vancouver, Canada. **Degrees:** 784 bachelor's, 41 associate awarded; master's, professional offered. **ROTC:** Army, Air Force. **Location:** 13 miles from New York City. **Calendar:** Semester, extensive summer session. **Full-time faculty:** 185 total. **Part-time faculty:** 440 total. **Special facilities:** ITV multimedia classrooms, photonics lab, regional center for students with learning disabilities, psychological services center, marine biology lab, cyber crime lab.

**Freshman class profile.** 5,108 applied, 2,916 admitted, 711 enrolled.

| Mid 50% test scores | | | |
|---|---|---|---|
| SAT critical reading: | 440-530 | GPA 2.0-2.99: | 37% |
| SAT math: | 450-560 | Rank in top quarter: | 39% |
| SAT writing: | 430-530 | Rank in top tenth: | 17% |
| GPA 3.75 or higher: | 17% | Return as sophomores: | 73% |
| GPA 3.50-3.74: | 16% | Out-of-state: | 13% |
| GPA 3.0-3.49: | 30% | Live on campus: | 44% |
| | | International: | 9% |

**Basis for selection.** Rigor of secondary school record and GPA most important. Recommendations, standardized test scores, extracurricular activities important. Placement tests required for all students. **Learning Disabled:** Regional Center for College Students with Learning Disabilities requires additional application.

**High school preparation.** College-preparatory program required. 16 units required. Required and recommended units include English 4, mathematics 3, social studies 2, history 2, science 2-3 (laboratory 2-3), foreign language 2 and academic electives 3.

**2009-2010 Annual costs.** Tuition/fees: $29,066. Room/board: $11,398.

**Application procedures. Admission:** Priority date 3/15; no deadline. $40 fee, may be waived for applicants with need, free for online applicants. Admission notification on a rolling basis beginning on or about 11/1. Must reply by May 1 or within 2 week(s) if notified thereafter. **Financial aid:** Priority date 2/15; no closing date. Applicants notified on a rolling basis starting 3/1; must reply by 5/1 or within 2 week(s) of notification.

**Academics.** Core curriculum consists of 4 interdisciplinary courses. **Special study options:** Accelerated study, combined bachelor's/graduate degree, cooperative education, cross-registration, distance learning, ESL, honors, independent study, internships, student-designed major, study abroad, teacher certification program, Washington semester, weekend college. **Credit/placement by examination:** CLEP, institutional tests. 30 credit hours maximum toward bachelor's degree. **Support services:** Learning center, preadmission summer program, reduced course load, remedial instruction, study skills assistance, tutoring, writing center.

**Majors. Biology:** General, biochemistry, marine. **Business:** Accounting, business admin, entrepreneurial studies, hospitality admin, managerial economics, marketing. **Computer sciences:** Computer science, information technology. **Conservation:** Environmental science. **Engineering:** Electrical. **Engineering technology:** Civil, construction, electrical, mechanical. **Foreign languages:** French, Spanish. **Health:** Clinical lab science, nursing (RN), radiologic technology/medical imaging. **History:** General. **Interdisciplinary:** Biological/physical sciences. **Liberal arts:** Humanities. **Math:** General. **Parks/recreation:** Sports admin. **Philosophy/religion:** Philosophy. **Physical sciences:** Chemistry, physics. **Protective services:** Law enforcement admin. **Psychology:** General. **Social sciences:** Economics, international relations, political science, sociology. **Visual/performing arts:** General. **Other:** Allied health, Communication studies, Interdisciplinary studies.

**Most popular majors.** Business/marketing 11%, health sciences 12%, liberal arts 49%, psychology 7%, security/protective services 6%.

**Computing on campus.** 245 workstations in library, computer center. Dormitories wired for high-speed internet access and linked to campus network. Commuter students can connect to campus network. Online course registration, online library, helpline, wireless network available.

**Student life. Freshman orientation:** Mandatory. Preregistration for classes offered. **Housing:** Coed dorms, special housing for disabled available. $350 partly refundable deposit, deadline 5/1. L.I.F.E. house, honor's house, global scholar's hall. **Activities:** Pep band, campus ministries, choral groups, dance, drama, film society, international student organizations, literary magazine, Model UN, radio station, student government, student newspaper, student program board, multicultural council, Indian cultural experience, nubian ladies.

**Athletics.** NCAA. **Intercollegiate:** Baseball M, basketball, bowling W, cross-country, fencing W, golf, soccer, softball W, tennis, track and field, volleyball W. **Intramural:** Badminton, baseball, basketball, football (nontackle), soccer, tennis, volleyball. **Team name:** Knights.

**Student services.** Adult student services, alcohol/substance abuse counseling, chaplain/spiritual director, career counseling, services for economically disadvantaged, student employment services, financial aid counseling, health services, personal counseling, placement for graduates, veterans' counselor, women's services. **Physically disabled:** Services for visually, speech, hearing impaired. **Learning disabled:** Comprehensive services available.

**Contact.** E-mail: globaleducation@fdu.edu
Phone: (201) 692-2553 Toll-free number: (800) 338-8803
Fax: (201) 692-7319
Jonathan Wexler, Associate Vice President for Admissions and Financial Aid, Fairleigh Dickinson University: Metropolitan Campus, 1000 River Road, H-DH3-10, Teaneck, NJ 07666-1996

## Felician College
**Lodi, New Jersey**
www.felician.edu                    CB code: 2321

- Private 4-year liberal arts college affiliated with Roman Catholic Church
- Commuter campus in large town
- 1,675 degree-seeking undergraduates: 20% part-time, 77% women, 13% African American, 9% Asian American, 19% Hispanic American
- 353 degree-seeking graduate students
- 84% of applicants admitted
- SAT or ACT (ACT writing optional) required

**General.** Founded in 1942. Regionally accredited. Additional campus in Rutherford. All programs spread through both campuses. **Degrees:** 317 bachelor's, 19 associate awarded; master's offered. **ROTC:** Army, Air Force. **Location:** 12 miles from New York City. **Calendar:** Semester, limited summer session. **Full-time faculty:** 102 total; 60% women. **Part-time faculty:** 89 total; 44% women. **Class size:** 76% < 20, 23% 20-39, less than 1% 40-49, less than 1% 50-99, less than 1% >100. **Special facilities:** Nursing skills laboratory, performance and theater facilities.

**Freshman class profile.** 1,618 applied, 1,358 admitted, 254 enrolled.

| Mid 50% test scores | | | |
|---|---|---|---|
| SAT critical reading: | 400-500 | Return as sophomores: | 68% |
| SAT math: | 390-490 | Out-of-state: | 6% |

**Basis for selection.** School achievement record, test scores most important. Interview, school and community activities, recommendations of high school counselor considered. Interview recommended for all; portfolio recommended for art programs.

**High school preparation.** College-preparatory program recommended. 19 units recommended. Recommended units include English 4, mathematics 3, social studies 3, science 3 and academic electives 6. Biology, chemistry, algebra required for nursing and medical laboratory technology applicants.

**2009-2010 Annual costs.** Tuition/fees: $25,050. Room/board: $9,700. Books/supplies: $1,200. Personal expenses: $1,890.

**2008-2009 Financial aid. Non-need-based:** Scholarships awarded for academics, alumni affiliation, athletics, religious affiliation.

**Application procedures. Admission:** No deadline. $30 fee, may be waived for applicants with need. Admission notification on a rolling basis beginning on or about 11/15. Must reply by May 1 or within 2 week(s) if notified thereafter. **Financial aid:** Priority date 6/1; no closing date. FAFSA required. Applicants notified on a rolling basis starting 4/1; must reply within 2 week(s) of notification.

**Academics.** Post-baccalaureate certification available in elementary and secondary education. **Special study options:** Accelerated study, combined bachelor's/graduate degree, cooperative education, cross-registration, distance learning, double major, dual enrollment of high school students, ESL, honors, independent study, internships, liberal arts/career combination, student-designed major, study abroad, teacher certification program. **Credit/placement by examination:** AP, CLEP, IB, institutional tests. 15 credit hours maximum toward associate degree, 30 toward bachelor's. **Support services:** Learning center, tutoring, writing center.

**Majors. Biology:** General, toxicology. **Business:** Accounting, business admin, international, marketing. **Communications:** General, broadcast journalism, digital media, journalism. **Computer sciences:** General, computer science. **Education:** Early childhood, early childhood special, elementary, mathematics, multi-level teacher, secondary. **Health:** Cytotechnology, health services, nuclear medical technology, nursing (RN), nursing admin, respiratory therapy technology. **History:** General. **Interdisciplinary:** Natural sciences. **Liberal arts:** Humanities. **Math:** General. **Philosophy/religion:** Philosophy, religion. **Protective services:** Law enforcement admin. **Psychology:** General. **Social sciences:** General, political science, sociology. **Visual/performing arts:** Art, studio arts.

**Most popular majors.** Business/marketing 31%, education 17%, health sciences 27%.

**Computing on campus.** 140 workstations in dormitories, library, computer center. Dormitories wired for high-speed internet access and linked to campus network. Commuter students can connect to campus network. Online library, repair service, wireless network available.

**Student life. Freshman orientation:** Mandatory. 3 summer programs available. **Policies:** No drugs or alcohol on campus. **Housing:** Guaranteed on-campus for freshmen. Coed dorms, single-sex dorms, special housing for disabled available. $200 nonrefundable deposit. **Activities:** Campus ministries, choral groups, international student organizations, literary magazine, radio station, student government, Angelicum club, history club, RCIA, Kappa Sigma Xi, aspiring authors, Students in Free Enterprise, Kappa Gamma Pi.

**Athletics.** NAIA, NCAA. **Intercollegiate:** Baseball M, basketball, cross-country, golf M, soccer, softball W, track and field, volleyball W. **Intramural:** Basketball M, bowling. **Team name:** Golden Falcons.

**Student services.** Chaplain/spiritual director, career counseling, financial aid counseling, health services. **Learning disabled:** Comprehensive services available.

**Contact.** E-mail: admissions@inet.felician.edu
Phone: (201) 559-6131 Fax: (201) 559-6188
Alexander Scott, Dean of Undergraduate Admissions, Felician College, 262 South Main Street, Lodi, NJ 07644-2198

## Georgian Court University
**Lakewood, New Jersey**
www.georgian.edu

CB member
CB code: 2274

- Private 4-year university and liberal arts college for women affiliated with Roman Catholic Church
- Residential campus in large town
- 1,736 degree-seeking undergraduates: 13% part-time, 94% women, 11% African American, 2% Asian American, 8% Hispanic American
- 801 degree-seeking graduate students
- 62% of applicants admitted
- 55% graduate within 6 years

**General.** Founded in 1908. Regionally accredited. Evening and graduate divisions coeducational. **Degrees:** 438 bachelor's awarded; master's offered. **Location:** 60 miles from New York City and Philadelphia. **Calendar:** Semester, limited summer session. **Full-time faculty:** 103 total; 84% have terminal degrees, 13% minority, 64% women. **Part-time faculty:** 186 total; 30% have terminal degrees, 8% minority. **Class size:** 75% < 20, 25% 20-39, less than 1% 40-49. **Special facilities:** Arboretum, Gould estate and gardens, NASA Education Resource Center.

**Freshman class profile.** 1,008 applied, 624 admitted, 253 enrolled.

| | | | |
|---|---|---|---|
| GPA 3.75 or higher: | 13% | Rank in top tenth: | 16% |
| GPA 3.50-3.74: | 15% | Return as sophomores: | 78% |
| GPA 3.0-3.49: | 34% | Out-of-state: | 8% |
| GPA 2.0-2.99: | 37% | Live on campus: | 61% |
| Rank in top quarter: | 41% | International: | 1% |

**Basis for selection.** Completed high school program reviewed for rigor of courses and grades received. Students should be completing program of 16 academic units with grades of 2.5 or higher. Students not meeting criteria referred to faculty committee for review. SAT or ACT recommended.

**Homeschooled:** Statement describing homeschool structure and mission required.

**High school preparation.** College-preparatory program required. 16 units required. Required units include English 4, mathematics 2, history 1, (laboratory 1), foreign language 2 and academic electives 6.

**2010-2011 Annual costs.** Tuition/fees: $26,176. Room/board: $9,856. Books/supplies: $1,350. Personal expenses: $2,100.

**2009-2010 Financial aid. Need-based:** 250 full-time freshmen applied for aid; 224 were judged to have need; 224 of these received aid. Average need met was 73%. Average scholarship/grant was $18,731; average loan $3,656. 66% of total undergraduate aid awarded as scholarships/grants, 34% as loans/jobs. **Non-need-based:** Awarded to 239 full-time undergraduates, including 52 freshmen. Scholarships awarded for academics, alumni affiliation, art, athletics, leadership, minority status, music/drama, religious affiliation.

**Application procedures. Admission:** Closing date 8/1 (receipt date). $40 fee, may be waived for applicants with need. Admission notification on a rolling basis beginning on or about 10/1. Must reply by May 1 or within 2 week(s) if notified thereafter. **Financial aid:** Priority date 3/1; no closing date. FAFSA, institutional form required. Applicants notified on a rolling basis starting 2/1; must reply within 2 week(s) of notification.

**Academics. Special study options:** Accelerated study, combined bachelor's/graduate degree, distance learning, double major, dual enrollment of high school students, ESL, honors, independent study, internships, liberal arts/career combination, study abroad, teacher certification program. **Credit/placement by examination:** AP, CLEP, institutional tests. 30 credit hours maximum toward bachelor's degree. **Support services:** Learning center, reduced course load, remedial instruction, study skills assistance, tutoring.

**Majors. Biology:** General, biochemistry. **Business:** Accounting, business admin, hospitality admin. **Communications:** General. **Education:** Elementary. **Foreign languages:** Spanish. **Health:** Clinical lab science, nursing (RN). **History:** General. **Interdisciplinary:** Natural sciences. **Liberal arts:** Humanities. **Math:** General. **Parks/recreation:** Exercise sciences. **Philosophy/religion:** Religion. **Physical sciences:** Chemistry. **Protective services:** Criminal justice. **Psychology:** General. **Public administration:** Social work. **Social sciences:** Sociology. **Visual/performing arts:** Art, dance. **Other:** Allied health technologies, Applied arts and sciences.

**Most popular majors.** Business/marketing 12%, education 25%, English 9%, history 7%, psychology 23%.

**Computing on campus.** 197 workstations in dormitories, library, computer center. Dormitories wired for high-speed internet access and linked to campus network. Commuter students can connect to campus network. Online course registration, online library, helpline, wireless network available.

**Student life. Freshman orientation:** Mandatory, $155 fee. Held during the week before classes begin. **Housing:** Guaranteed on-campus for all undergraduates. Wellness housing available. $250 deposit, deadline 5/1. **Activities:** Bands, campus ministries, choral groups, dance, international student organizations, literary magazine, music ensembles, Model UN, student government, student newspaper, council for exceptional children, Sisters United, Re-Entry women's club, Alliance Francaise, Amnesty International, black student union, LASO, living/learning communities.

**Athletics.** NCAA. **Intercollegiate:** Basketball W, cross-country W, lacrosse W, soccer W, softball W, tennis W, track and field W, volleyball W. **Team name:** Lions.

**Student services.** Chaplain/spiritual director, career counseling, financial aid counseling, health services, personal counseling. **Physically disabled:** Services for visually, speech, hearing impaired.

**Contact.** E-mail: admissions@georgian.edu
Phone: (732) 987-2200 ext. 2700 Toll-free number: (800) 458-8422 ext. 2760 Fax: (732) 987-2000
Kathie Gallant, Director of Admissions, Georgian Court University, 900 Lakewood Avenue, Lakewood, NJ 08701-2697

## Kean University
**Union, New Jersey**
www.kean.edu

CB member
CB code: 2517

- Public 4-year university and liberal arts college
- Commuter campus in small city
- 11,730 degree-seeking undergraduates: 21% part-time, 62% women, 19% African American, 7% Asian American, 21% Hispanic American, 2% international

- 1,913 degree-seeking graduate students
- 62% of applicants admitted
- SAT or ACT (ACT writing optional), application essay required
- 45% graduate within 6 years

**General.** Founded in 1855. Regionally accredited. **Degrees:** 2,082 bachelor's awarded; master's, doctoral offered. **ROTC:** Army, Air Force. **Location:** 12 miles from New York City. **Calendar:** Semester, limited summer session. **Full-time faculty:** 352 total; 91% have terminal degrees, 28% minority, 46% women. **Part-time faculty:** 977 total; 22% minority, 52% women. **Class size:** 41% < 20, 58% 20-39, less than 1% 40-49, less than 1% 50-99. **Special facilities:** Holocaust resource center, ethnic studies center, Center for New Jersey Science, Technology and Mathematics Education, institute for foreign service and diplomacy.

**Freshman class profile.** 5,955 applied, 3,693 admitted, 1,548 enrolled.

| Mid 50% test scores | | | |
|---|---|---|---|
| SAT critical reading: | 410-500 | Rank in top quarter: | 26% |
| SAT math: | 420-510 | Rank in top tenth: | 8% |
| GPA 3.75 or higher: | 7% | Return as sophomores: | 81% |
| GPA 3.50-3.74: | 9% | Out-of-state: | 3% |
| GPA 3.0-3.49: | 36% | Live on campus: | 44% |
| GPA 2.0-2.99: | 47% | International: | 1% |

**Basis for selection.** High school GPA at or above 2.9, test scores, counselor recommendations important. Consideration given to class rank, military service, work, personal life experiences. Non-US-educated applicants evaluated based on academic record in home country. If needed, applicants advised of specific additional requirements.

**High school preparation.** College-preparatory program required. 16 units required. Required and recommended units include English 4, mathematics 3, social studies 2, history 2, science 2 (laboratory 2), foreign language 2 and academic electives 5.

**2009-2010 Annual costs.** Tuition/fees: $9,446; $14,081 out-of-state. Room/board: $12,264.

**2009-2010 Financial aid. Need-based:** 1,331 full-time freshmen applied for aid; 1,095 were judged to have need; 1,009 of these received aid. Average need met was 58%. Average scholarship/grant was $8,414; average loan $3,550. 57% of total undergraduate aid awarded as scholarships/grants, 43% as loans/jobs. **Non-need-based:** Awarded to 840 full-time undergraduates, including 153 freshmen. Scholarships awarded for academics, alumni affiliation, art, leadership, music/drama.

**Application procedures. Admission:** Priority date 5/1; deadline 5/31 (postmark date). $50 fee, may be waived for applicants with need. Admission notification on a rolling basis beginning on or about 11/1. Must reply by May 1 or within 2 week(s) if notified thereafter. **Financial aid:** Priority date 3/15; no closing date. FAFSA required. Applicants notified on a rolling basis starting 3/15; must reply by 5/1.

**Academics. Special study options:** Accelerated study, combined bachelor's/graduate degree, cooperative education, distance learning, double major, dual enrollment of high school students, ESL, honors, independent study, internships, liberal arts/career combination, semester at sea, study abroad, teacher certification program, Washington semester, weekend college. 2-year bachelor's degree program for RNs, Foreign Transfer Programs, TraveLearn. **Credit/placement by examination:** AP, CLEP, IB, SAT, institutional tests. **Support services:** Learning center, pre-admission summer program, reduced course load, remedial instruction, study skills assistance, tutoring, writing center.

**Majors. Biology:** General. **Business:** Accounting, business admin, finance, marketing. **Communications:** General. **Communications technology:** Printing management. **Computer sciences:** General, networking. **Conservation:** Environmental science. **Education:** Elementary, kindergarten/preschool, music, physical, special, speech. **Engineering technology:** Electrical. **Foreign languages:** Spanish. **Health:** Athletic training, clinical lab science, medical records admin. **History:** General. **Liberal arts:** Arts/sciences. **Math:** General. **Parks/recreation:** Facilities management. **Physical sciences:** Chemistry, geology. **Protective services:** Law enforcement admin. **Psychology:** General. **Public administration:** General, social work. **Social sciences:** Economics, political science, sociology. **Visual/performing arts:** Acting, art, art history/conservation, design, dramatic, film/cinema, industrial design, interior design, studio arts, theater design. **Other:** Philosophy and religion, Psychology rehabilitation, Science and technology, Speech, language & hearing science.

**Most popular majors.** Business/marketing 22%, education 18%, psychology 10%, security/protective services 6%, social sciences 6%, visual/performing arts 6%.

**Computing on campus.** 1,700 workstations in dormitories, library, computer center, student center. Dormitories wired for high-speed internet access and linked to campus network. Commuter students can connect to campus network. Online course registration, student web hosting, wireless network available.

**Student life. Freshman orientation:** Mandatory, $50 fee. Preregistration for classes offered. **Housing:** Coed dorms, special housing for disabled, apartments available. $100 nonrefundable deposit, deadline 5/1. Freshmen housing, floor for women-only housing. **Activities:** Bands, campus ministries, choral groups, dance, drama, film society, international student organizations, literary magazine, music ensembles, musical theater, radio station, student government, student newspaper, symphony orchestra, TV station, Asian Culture Club, Association of Indian Students, Association of Latin American Students, Pan African Student Association, Intervarsity Christian Fellowship, Haitian Student Association, Hamor's Head Club for Democrats, Jewish Culture Club, Muslim Student Association.

**Athletics.** NCAA. **Intercollegiate:** Baseball M, basketball, field hockey W, football (tackle) M, lacrosse, soccer, softball W, tennis W, track and field, volleyball W. **Intramural:** Basketball, football (non-tackle), soccer, softball, tennis, volleyball, weight lifting. **Team name:** Cougars.

**Student services.** Adult student services, alcohol/substance abuse counseling, chaplain/spiritual director, career counseling, services for economically disadvantaged, student employment services, financial aid counseling, health services, minority student services, on-campus daycare, personal counseling, placement for graduates, veterans' counselor, women's services. **Physically disabled:** Services for visually, speech, hearing impaired. **Learning disabled:** Comprehensive services available.

**Contact.** E-mail: admitme@kean.edu
Phone: (908) 737-7100 Fax: (908) 737-7105
Valerie Winslow, Director of Admissions, Kean University, 1000 Morris Avenue, Union, NJ 07083-0411

---

## Monmouth University
**West Long Branch, New Jersey**
www.monmouth.edu

**CB member**
**CB code: 2416**

- Private 4-year university
- Residential campus in small town
- 4,633 degree-seeking undergraduates: 7% part-time, 58% women, 4% African American, 2% Asian American, 6% Hispanic American, 1% international
- 1,633 degree-seeking graduate students
- 62% of applicants admitted
- SAT or ACT with writing required
- 61% graduate within 6 years

**General.** Founded in 1933. Regionally accredited. **Degrees:** 1,061 bachelor's, 4 associate awarded; master's offered. **ROTC:** Air Force. **Location:** 50 miles from New York City, 75 miles from Philadelphia. **Calendar:** Semester, limited summer session. **Full-time faculty:** 247 total; 84% have terminal degrees, 16% minority, 53% women. **Part-time faculty:** 313 total; 23% have terminal degrees, 6% minority, 50% women. **Class size:** 44% < 20, 56% 20-39, less than 1% 40-49. **Special facilities:** Multimedia communications center with TV and radio station, sculpture garden, ice house-gallery, multipurpose activity center with 4100 seat arena, fitness center, 6 lane indoor track.

**Freshman class profile.** 6,738 applied, 4,160 admitted, 998 enrolled.

| Mid 50% test scores | | | |
|---|---|---|---|
| SAT critical reading: | 490-570 | GPA 2.0-2.99: | 23% |
| SAT math: | 510-600 | Rank in top quarter: | 46% |
| SAT writing: | 490-570 | Rank in top tenth: | 18% |
| ACT composite: | 22-26 | End year in good standing: | 97% |
| GPA 3.75 or higher: | 16% | Return as sophomores: | 78% |
| GPA 3.50-3.74: | 20% | Out-of-state: | 19% |
| GPA 3.0-3.49: | 41% | Live on campus: | 80% |
| | | International: | 1% |

**Basis for selection.** School record, GPA, test scores important followed by recommendations and essay. Resume of activities including community involvement and leadership positions encouraged. Audition recommended for music programs; portfolio recommended for art programs. Interview recommended for Music and Theatre Arts Department. **Homeschooled:** State high school equivalency certificate required. All students who submit portfolio of coursework in lieu of transcript must also complete institution's curriculum chart for homeschooled students.

**High school preparation.** College-preparatory program recommended. 16 units required; 20 recommended. Required and recommended units include English 4, mathematics 3, social studies 2, history 2, science 2 (laboratory 1), foreign language 2 and academic electives 5.

**2010-2011 Annual costs.** Tuition/fees: $26,356. Room/board: $9,936. Books/supplies: $1,000. Personal expenses: $1,996.

**2009-2010 Financial aid. Need-based:** 878 full-time freshmen applied for aid; 706 were judged to have need; 706 of these received aid. Average need met was 74%. Average scholarship/grant was $12,972; average loan $3,444. 56% of total undergraduate aid awarded as scholarships/grants, 44% as loans/jobs. **Non-need-based:** Awarded to 4,058 full-time undergraduates, including 990 freshmen. Scholarships awarded for academics, alumni affiliation, art, athletics, leadership.

**Application procedures. Admission:** Priority date 12/1; deadline 3/1 (receipt date). $50 fee, may be waived for applicants with need. Admission notification 4/1. Must reply by 5/1. All deposits non-refundable after May 1. **Financial aid:** Priority date 2/15; no closing date. FAFSA required. Applicants notified on a rolling basis starting 2/15; must reply within 2 week(s) of notification.

**Academics. Special study options:** Accelerated study, combined bachelor's/graduate degree, cooperative education, cross-registration, double major, dual enrollment of high school students, honors, independent study, internships, liberal arts/career combination, student-designed major, study abroad, teacher certification program, Washington semester. **Credit/placement by examination:** AP, CLEP, IB, SAT, ACT, institutional tests. 30 credit hours maximum toward bachelor's degree. AP credit awarded only for institutional course equivalents. **Support services:** Learning center, reduced course load, remedial instruction, study skills assistance, tutoring, writing center.

**Honors college/program.** Students admitted to honors school with 1750 SAT (with no section score less than 520) and 3.3 GPA.

**Majors. Biology:** General, environmental. **Business:** Business admin, international. **Communications:** General. **Computer sciences:** General. **Education:** General, special. **Engineering:** Software. **Foreign languages:** General. **Health:** Clinical lab science, health services, nursing (RN). **History:** General. **Math:** General. **Parks/recreation:** Health/fitness. **Physical sciences:** Chemistry. **Protective services:** Criminal justice. **Psychology:** General. **Public administration:** Social work. **Social sciences:** Anthropology, political science, sociology. **Visual/performing arts:** Art, dramatic, studio arts. **Other:** History and political science, Interdisciplinary studies.

**Most popular majors.** Business/marketing 32%, communications/journalism 13%, education 15%, security/protective services 6%, visual/performing arts 6%.

**Computing on campus.** 453 workstations in dormitories, library, computer center, student center. Dormitories wired for high-speed internet access and linked to campus network. Commuter students can connect to campus network. Online library, helpline, student web hosting, wireless network available.

**Student life. Freshman orientation:** Mandatory, $200 fee. Preregistration for classes offered. Two-day orientation held in July. **Policies:** Must complete at least 12 credit hours to associate with a fraternity or sorority. Students must have 2.2 GPA and be registered full-time. Transfer students taking 12 or more credits may also associate. **Housing:** Guaranteed on-campus for freshmen. Coed dorms, apartments, wellness housing available. $150 deposit, deadline 5/1. Honors, 24-hour quiet floors, leadership floors available. **Activities:** Bands, choral groups, dance, drama, international student organizations, literary magazine, music ensembles, musical theater, radio station, student government, student newspaper, TV station, Hillel, Christian Ambassadors, Catholic center, African-American student union, Latin American club, Circle K, Rotaract Club, alternative lifestyles clubs.

**Athletics.** NCAA. **Intercollegiate:** Baseball M, basketball, cross-country, field hockey W, football (tackle) M, golf, lacrosse W, sailing, soccer, softball W, tennis, track and field. **Intramural:** Badminton, basketball, football (non-tackle), soccer, softball, tennis, volleyball, water polo. **Team name:** Hawks.

**Student services.** Adult student services, alcohol/substance abuse counseling, chaplain/spiritual director, career counseling, services for economically disadvantaged, student employment services, financial aid counseling, health services, legal services, personal counseling, placement for graduates, veterans' counselor, women's services. **Physically disabled:** Services for visually, speech, hearing impaired.

**Contact.** E-mail: admission@monmouth.edu
Phone: (732) 571-3456 Toll-free number: (800) 543-9671
Fax: (732) 263-5166
Lauren Cifelli, Director of Undergraduate Admission, Monmouth University, 400 Cedar Avenue, West Long Branch, NJ 07764-1898

---

## Montclair State University
**Upper Montclair, New Jersey**
www.montclair.edu
CB member
CB code: 2520

- Public 4-year university
- Residential campus in large town
- 13,542 degree-seeking undergraduates: 14% part-time, 61% women, 9% African American, 6% Asian American, 20% Hispanic American, 2% international
- 2,949 degree-seeking graduate students
- 47% of applicants admitted
- SAT or ACT (ACT writing recommended) required
- 62% graduate within 6 years; 26% enter graduate study

**General.** Founded in 1908. Regionally accredited. Includes Institute for the Humanities, Institute for the Advancement of Philosophy for Children, Institute for Critical Thinking, New Jersey School of Conservation in Stokes State Forest, Branchville, and Center for Continuing Education. **Degrees:** 2,675 bachelor's awarded; master's, doctoral offered. **ROTC:** Army, Naval, Air Force. **Location:** 14 miles from New York City. **Calendar:** Semester, limited summer session. **Full-time faculty:** 553 total; 92% have terminal degrees, 25% minority, 48% women. **Part-time faculty:** 936 total; 6% have terminal degrees, 11% minority, 56% women. **Class size:** 34% < 20, 62% 20-39, 1% 40-49, 2% 50-99, 1% >100.

**Freshman class profile.** 13,469 applied, 6,332 admitted, 2,117 enrolled.

| Mid 50% test scores | | | |
|---|---|---|---|
| SAT critical reading: | 440-540 | GPA 2.0-2.99: | 33% |
| SAT math: | 450-550 | Rank in top quarter: | 40% |
| SAT writing: | 450-550 | Rank in top tenth: | 10% |
| GPA 3.75 or higher: | 8% | Out-of-state: | 3% |
| GPA 3.50-3.74: | 14% | Live on campus: | 51% |
| GPA 3.0-3.49: | 45% | International: | 1% |

**Basis for selection.** School achievement record most important. Extracurricular activities, test scores, community activities also important. Consideration given to disadvantaged applicants. Interview required for art, music, music therapy, speech, theater, and dance programs; audition required for dance, music, speech, theater programs; portfolio required for art programs. **Homeschooled:** Statement describing homeschool structure and mission, transcript of courses and grades required.

**High school preparation.** College-preparatory program required. 16 units required. Required units include English 4, mathematics 3, social studies 2, science 2 (laboratory 2), foreign language 2 and academic electives 3. 4 math (including trigonometry) required of computer science majors. Algebra II required for business administration majors. 3 additional units in English, social studies, science, math, or foreign language required.

**2009-2010 Annual costs.** Tuition/fees: $9,771; $17,783 out-of-state. Room/board: $10,208. Books/supplies: $1,200. Personal expenses: $4,062.

**2009-2010 Financial aid. Need-based:** 1,440 full-time freshmen applied for aid; 1,156 were judged to have need; 1,114 of these received aid. Average need met was 63%. Average scholarship/grant was $8,932; average loan $3,444. 53% of total undergraduate aid awarded as scholarships/grants, 47% as loans/jobs. **Non-need-based:** Awarded to 1,181 full-time undergraduates, including 270 freshmen. Scholarships awarded for academics, alumni affiliation, art, leadership, minority status, music/drama, ROTC, state residency.

**Application procedures. Admission:** Closing date 3/1 (postmark date). $60 fee, may be waived for applicants with need. Admission notification on a rolling basis beginning on or about 10/1. Must reply by 5/1. Immediate decision process available to seniors at some local high schools. **Financial aid:** Priority date 3/1; no closing date. FAFSA required. Applicants notified on a rolling basis starting 4/1; must reply within 2 week(s) of notification.

**Academics. Special study options:** Combined bachelor's/graduate degree, cooperative education, double major, ESL, honors, independent study, internships, study abroad, teacher certification program, Washington semester. Joint admission with UMDNJ. **Credit/placement by examination:** AP, CLEP, IB, institutional tests. 24 credit hours maximum toward bachelor's degree. **Support services:** Learning center, pre-admission summer program, reduced course load, remedial instruction, tutoring, writing center.

**Honors college/program.** Two of the following required: rank in top 10% of high school class; 600 SAT verbal or math; 1200 SAT (exclusive of Writing); unusual ability in creative arts or exceptional leadership or other extraordinary accomplishment.

**Majors. Area/ethnic studies:** Women's. **Biology:** General, biochemistry, molecular. **Business:** Business admin. **Communications:** Broadcast journalism, organizational, radio/tv. **Communications technology:** Animation/special effects. **Computer sciences:** General, computer science, information technology. **Education:** Business, drama/dance, health, physical, technology/industrial arts. **Family/consumer sciences:** General, food/nutrition. **Foreign languages:** Classics, French, Italian, Latin, linguistics, Spanish. **Health:** Athletic training, health services, music therapy. **History:** General. **Interdisciplinary:** Peace/conflict. **Liberal arts:** Arts/sciences, humanities. **Math:** General. **Philosophy/religion:** Philosophy, religion. **Physical sciences:** Chemistry, geology, physics. **Psychology:** General. **Social sciences:** Anthropology, economics, geography, political science, sociology. **Visual/performing arts:** Art, cinematography, dance, dramatic, fashion design, graphic design, illustration, industrial design, music performance. **Other:** Justice studies.

**Computing on campus.** 700 workstations in dormitories, library, computer center, student center. Dormitories wired for high-speed internet access and linked to campus network. Commuter students can connect to campus network. Online course registration, online library, helpline, repair service, wireless network available.

**Student life. Freshman orientation:** Mandatory, $175 fee. Preregistration for classes offered. **Housing:** Coed dorms, single-sex dorms, special housing for disabled, apartments available. $125 nonrefundable deposit, deadline 5/1. Pets allowed in dorm rooms. **Activities:** Bands, campus ministries, choral groups, dance, drama, international student organizations, literary magazine, music ensembles, musical theater, opera, radio station, student government, student newspaper, symphony orchestra, TV station, Newman center, college life union board, recreation board, organization for students of African unity, Latin American student organization, LEAD.

**Athletics.** NCAA. **Intercollegiate:** Baseball M, basketball, diving, field hockey W, football (tackle) M, lacrosse, soccer, softball W, swimming, track and field, volleyball W. **Intramural:** Badminton, basketball, bowling, football (tackle) M, golf, racquetball, softball, tennis, volleyball, water polo. **Team name:** Red Hawks.

**Student services.** Adult student services, alcohol/substance abuse counseling, chaplain/spiritual director, career counseling, services for economically disadvantaged, student employment services, financial aid counseling, health services, on-campus daycare, personal counseling, placement for graduates, veterans' counselor, women's services. **Physically disabled:** Services for visually, speech, hearing impaired. **Learning disabled:** Comprehensive services available.

**Contact.** E-mail: undergraduate.admissions@mail.montclair.edu
Phone: (973) 655-4444 Toll-free number: (800) 331-9205
Fax: (973) 655-7700
Jason Langdon, Director of Admissions, Montclair State University, One Normal Avenue, Upper Montclair, NJ 07043-1624

---

## New Jersey City University

**Jersey City, New Jersey**    **CB member**
**www.njcu.edu**    **CB code: 2516**

◗ Public 4-year university

◗ Commuter campus in small city

◗ 6,325 degree-seeking undergraduates: 26% part-time, 61% women, 20% African American, 7% Asian American, 35% Hispanic American, 1% international

◗ 1,026 degree-seeking graduate students

◗ 35% of applicants admitted

◗ SAT or ACT, application essay required

◗ 34% graduate within 6 years

**General.** Founded in 1927. Regionally accredited. **Degrees:** 1,002 bachelor's awarded; master's offered. **Location:** 5 miles from New York City. **Calendar:** Semester, extensive summer session. **Full-time faculty:** 246 total; 89% have terminal degrees, 25% minority, 50% women. **Part-time faculty:** 461 total; 18% minority, 42% women. **Class size:** 47% < 20, 49% 20-39, 2% 40-49, 3% 50-99. **Special facilities:** Laboratory school for multihandicapped children, computer technology center, cooperative education, media studies center.

**Freshman class profile.** 4,339 applied, 1,509 admitted, 754 enrolled.

| Mid 50% test scores | | | |
|---|---|---|---|
| SAT critical reading: | 420-500 | Out-of-state: | 1% |
| SAT math: | 430-520 | Live on campus: | 4% |
| SAT writing: | 420-500 | International: | 1% |
| Rank in top quarter: | 33% | Fraternities: | 2% |
| Rank in top tenth: | 9% | Sororities: | 2% |

**Basis for selection.** High school courses, grades, class rank, and test scores most important, followed by essay or personal statement. Special program for educationally disadvantaged applicants available with above criteria. Interview recommended for all; audition required for music programs; portfolio recommended for art programs.

**High school preparation.** College-preparatory program recommended. 16 units required; 21 recommended. Required and recommended units include English 4, mathematics 4, social studies 4, science 4 (laboratory 2-3) and foreign language 2.

**2009-2010 Annual costs.** Tuition/fees: $8,990; $16,268 out-of-state. Room/board: $9,043. Books/supplies: $1,988. Personal expenses: $2,425.

**2008-2009 Financial aid.** Need-based: 572 full-time freshmen applied for aid; 517 were judged to have need; 480 of these received aid. Average need met was 58%. Average scholarship/grant was $7,661; average loan $3,417. 66% of total undergraduate aid awarded as scholarships/grants, 34% as loans/jobs. **Non-need-based:** Awarded to 346 full-time undergraduates, including 84 freshmen.

**Application procedures. Admission:** Closing date 4/1. $35 fee, may be waived for applicants with need, free for online applicants. Admission notification on a rolling basis beginning on or about 1/1. Must reply by May 1 or within 3 week(s) if notified thereafter. **Financial aid:** Priority date 4/15; no closing date. FAFSA required. Applicants notified by 5/5.

**Academics.** Cooperative education placement offered in all majors. Professional diploma in school psychology offered. **Special study options:** Cooperative education, cross-registration, distance learning, double major, dual enrollment of high school students, ESL, honors, independent study, internships, liberal arts/career combination, study abroad, teacher certification program, Washington semester, weekend college. **Credit/placement by examination:** AP, CLEP, IB, institutional tests. 30 credit hours maximum toward bachelor's degree. **Support services:** Learning center, pre-admission summer program, reduced course load, remedial instruction, tutoring, writing center.

**Majors. Biology:** General. **Business:** Business admin. **Communications:** General. **Computer sciences:** General. **Education:** Early childhood, elementary, reading, special. **Foreign languages:** Spanish. **Health:** Clinical lab science, health services, nursing (RN). **History:** General. **Math:** General. **Philosophy/religion:** Philosophy. **Physical sciences:** Chemistry, geology, physics. **Protective services:** Firefighting, security services. **Psychology:** General. **Social sciences:** Economics, political science, sociology. **Visual/performing arts:** Art, studio arts.

**Most popular majors.** Business/marketing 23%, English 7%, health sciences 10%, history 6%, psychology 10%, security/protective services 12%, social sciences 9%.

**Computing on campus.** 704 workstations in dormitories, library, computer center, student center. Dormitories wired for high-speed internet access and linked to campus network. Commuter students can connect to campus network. Online course registration, online library, helpline, wireless network available.

**Student life. Freshman orientation:** Mandatory. **Housing:** Coed dorms, apartments available. $150 deposit, deadline 8/13. **Activities:** Bands, campus ministries, choral groups, dance, drama, film society, international student organizations, literary magazine, music ensembles, musical theater, opera, radio station, student government, student newspaper, symphony orchestra, Campus Christian fellowship, black freedom society, Latin power association, Africana journal.

**Athletics.** NCAA. **Intercollegiate:** Baseball M, basketball, bowling W, cross-country, soccer, softball W, track and field, volleyball. **Intramural:** Basketball, bowling, racquetball, soccer, softball, swimming, table tennis, volleyball, weight lifting. **Team name:** Gothic Knights.

**Student services.** Chaplain/spiritual director, career counseling, student employment services, financial aid counseling, health services, on-campus daycare, personal counseling, placement for graduates, veterans' counselor, women's services. **Physically disabled:** Services for visually, speech, hearing impaired.

**Contact.** E-mail: admissions@njcu.edu
Phone: (201) 200-3234 Toll-free number: (888) 441-6528
Jose Balda, Director of Admissions, New Jersey City University, 2039
Kennedy Boulevard, Jersey City, NJ 07305-1597

## New Jersey Institute of Technology
### Newark, New Jersey
### www.njit.edu
**CB member**
**CB code: 2513**

- Public 4-year university
- Residential campus in large city
- 5,528 degree-seeking undergraduates: 14% part-time, 20% women, 10% African American, 21% Asian American, 20% Hispanic American, 1% Native American, 4% international
- 2,759 degree-seeking graduate students
- 67% of applicants admitted
- SAT or ACT with writing required
- 55% graduate within 6 years; 75% enter graduate study

**General.** Founded in 1881. Regionally accredited. **Degrees:** 857 bachelor's awarded; master's, doctoral offered. **ROTC:** Army, Air Force. **Location:** 10 miles from New York City. **Calendar:** Semester, extensive summer session. **Full-time faculty:** 403 total; 100% have terminal degrees, 24% minority, 19% women. **Part-time faculty:** 237 total; 4% minority, 21% women. **Class size:** 39% < 20, 53% 20-39, 4% 40-49, 4% 50-99, less than 1% >100. **Special facilities:** Computer chip manufacturing laboratory, multi-lifecycle engineering center, numerous government and industry-sponsored research laboratories, hazardous waste management research center, factory floor manufacturing center, observatory.

**Freshman class profile.** 4,315 applied, 2,874 admitted, 973 enrolled.

| Mid 50% test scores | | | |
|---|---|---|---|
| SAT critical reading: | 490-590 | Return as sophomores: | 84% |
| SAT math: | 550-660 | Out-of-state: | 6% |
| SAT writing: | 480-580 | Live on campus: | 50% |
| Rank in top quarter: | 55% | International: | 4% |
| Rank in top tenth: | 26% | Fraternities: | 8% |
| | | Sororities: | 5% |

**Basis for selection.** Class rank, test scores, secondary school record including grades and curriculum most important. Grades in math and science very important, especially for engineering, engineering science and computer science applicants. Essay and interview required for honors college; interview and portfolio required for architecture programs. Interview required for conditional admission, educational opportunity program.

**High school preparation.** College-preparatory program required. 16 units required. Required and recommended units include English 4, mathematics 4, social studies 1, history 1, science 2 (laboratory 2), foreign language 2 and academic electives 2. 3 math required of management majors and science, technology and society majors. One lab science required for management majors.

**2009-2010 Annual costs.** Tuition/fees: $12,860; $22,604 out-of-state. Room/board: $9,504. Books/supplies: $1,200. Personal expenses: $1,100.

**2009-2010 Financial aid. Need-based:** 809 full-time freshmen applied for aid; 691 were judged to have need; 691 of these received aid. Average need met was 63%. Average scholarship/grant was $15,000; average loan $3,100. 78% of total undergraduate aid awarded as scholarships/grants, 22% as loans/jobs. **Non-need-based:** Awarded to 2,260 full-time undergraduates, including 655 freshmen. Scholarships awarded for academics, athletics, job skills, leadership, minority status, ROTC, state residency. **Additional information:** Extensive co-op program for all majors.

**Application procedures. Admission:** Closing date 4/1. $50 fee, may be waived for applicants with need. Admission notification on a rolling basis beginning on or about 11/15. Must reply by May 1 or within 2 week(s) if notified thereafter. **Financial aid:** Priority date 3/15, closing date 5/15. FAFSA required. Applicants notified on a rolling basis starting 3/1; must reply within 2 week(s) of notification.

**Academics.** Numerous research opportunities available. **Special study options:** Accelerated study, combined bachelor's/graduate degree, cooperative education, cross-registration, distance learning, double major, ESL, honors, independent study, internships, study abroad. Environmental Scholars Program, Career Advancement Plan, University Research Experience. **Credit/placement by examination:** AP, CLEP, SAT, institutional tests. **Support services:** Learning center, pre-admission summer program, reduced course load, remedial instruction, study skills assistance, tutoring.

**Majors. Architecture:** Architecture. **Biology:** General. **Business:** Business admin. **Computer sciences:** General, information systems, information technology. **Conservation:** Environmental science. **Engineering:** Biomedical, chemical, civil, computer, electrical, environmental, geological, industrial, manufacturing, mechanical, science. **Engineering technology:** General. **History:** General. **Interdisciplinary:** Science/society. **Math:** Applied. **Physical sciences:** Chemistry, physics.

**Most popular majors.** Architecture 13%, business/marketing 12%, computer/information sciences 16%, engineering/engineering technologies 51%.

**Computing on campus.** PC or laptop required. 1,500 workstations in dormitories, library, computer center, student center. Dormitories wired for high-speed internet access and linked to campus network. Commuter students can connect to campus network. Online course registration, online library, helpline, repair service, student web hosting, wireless network available.

**Student life. Freshman orientation:** Mandatory. **Housing:** Guaranteed on-campus for freshmen. Coed dorms available. $100 nonrefundable deposit, deadline 6/2. **Activities:** Bands, dance, drama, international student organizations, literary magazine, musical theater, radio station, student government, student newspaper, Arab student association, black student engineers association, Caribbean student association, Chinese student association, Hispanic students in technology association, Intervarsity Christian Federation, Polish student association, Islamic student association, women engineers club.

**Athletics.** NCAA. **Intercollegiate:** Baseball M, basketball, cheerleading, cross-country, fencing, soccer, swimming, tennis, volleyball. **Intramural:** Badminton, basketball, bowling, cricket, fencing, racquetball, soccer, swimming, table tennis, tennis, track and field, volleyball, weight lifting. **Team name:** Highlanders.

**Student services.** Adult student services, alcohol/substance abuse counseling, career counseling, services for economically disadvantaged, student employment services, financial aid counseling, health services, minority student services, on-campus daycare, personal counseling, placement for graduates, veterans' counselor, women's services. **Physically disabled:** Services for visually, speech, hearing impaired.

**Contact.** E-mail: admissions@njit.edu
Phone: (973) 596-3300 Toll-free number: (800) 925-6548
Fax: (973) 596-3461
Stephen Eck, Director of Admissions, New Jersey Institute of Technology, University Heights, Newark, NJ 07102

## Princeton University
### Princeton, New Jersey
### www.princeton.edu
**CB member**
**CB code: 2672**

- Private 4-year university
- Residential campus in large town
- 5,029 degree-seeking undergraduates: 49% women, 8% African American, 16% Asian American, 8% Hispanic American, 10% international
- 2,450 degree-seeking graduate students
- 10% of applicants admitted
- SAT or ACT with writing, SAT Subject Tests, application essay required
- 96% graduate within 6 years

**General.** Founded in 1746. Regionally accredited. **Degrees:** 1,136 bachelor's awarded; master's, doctoral offered. **ROTC:** Army, Air Force. **Location:** 50 miles from New York City, 45 miles from Philadelphia. **Calendar:** Semester. **Full-time faculty:** 846 total; 93% have terminal degrees, 17% minority, 28% women. **Part-time faculty:** 212 total; 60% have terminal degrees, 19% minority, 43% women. **Class size:** 73% < 20, 14% 20-39, 2% 40-49, 7% 50-99, 4% >100. **Special facilities:** Institute for integrative genomics, center for theoretical physics, institute in neuroscience, center for creative and performing arts, center for human values, plasma physics laboratory, council of the humanities, institute for international and regional studies, observatory, center for energy and the environment.

**Freshman class profile.** 21,963 applied, 2,209 admitted, 1,320 enrolled.

| Mid 50% test scores | | | |
|---|---|---|---|
| SAT critical reading: | 690-790 | GPA 3.0-3.49: | 6% |
| SAT math: | 700-790 | Rank in top quarter: | 100% |
| SAT writing: | 700-780 | Rank in top tenth: | 95% |
| ACT composite: | 31-35 | Return as sophomores: | 98% |
| GPA 3.75 or higher: | 83% | Live on campus: | 100% |
| GPA 3.50-3.74: | 11% | International: | 10% |

**Basis for selection.** School achievement record and recommendations of guidance counselor and 2 teachers very important. SAT or ACT with Writing required along with 2 SAT Subject Test scores. Prospective students in engineering should take SAT Subject Tests in either math 1 or 2 and either physics or chemistry. Interview recommended when possible. Submission of supplementary materials for the visual and performing arts considered. **Homeschooled:** Statement describing homeschool structure and mission required.

**High school preparation.** College-preparatory program recommended. Recommended units include English 4, mathematics 4, social studies 2, history 2, science 4 (laboratory 2) and foreign language 4. 1 physics or chemistry (preferably both) and 4 math encouraged for prospective engineering majors.

**2010-2011 Annual costs.** Tuition/fees: $36,640. Room/board: $11,940. Books/supplies: $1,200. Personal expenses: $2,295.

**2008-2009 Financial aid.** All financial aid based on need. 816 full-time freshmen applied for aid; 697 were judged to have need; 697 of these received aid. Average need met was 100%. Average scholarship/grant was $33,671. 97% of total undergraduate aid awarded as scholarships/grants, 3% as loans/jobs. **Additional information:** All aid need-based; all aid grant money (no loans); institution meets full demonstrated need.

**Application procedures. Admission:** Closing date 1/1 (postmark date). $65 fee, may be waived for applicants with need. Admission notification 4/1. Must reply by May 1 or within 1 week(s) if notified thereafter. **Financial aid:** Priority date 2/1; no closing date. FAFSA, institutional form required. Applicants notified by 4/1; must reply by 5/1.

**Academics.** Independent project in junior year and senior thesis required for graduation. **Special study options:** Cross-registration, exchange student, independent study, student-designed major, study abroad, teacher certification program. **Credit/placement by examination:** AP, CLEP, IB, institutional tests. **Support services:** Learning center, pre-admission summer program, study skills assistance, tutoring, writing center.

**Majors. Architecture:** Architecture. **Area/ethnic studies:** East Asian, Near/Middle Eastern. **Biology:** Ecology, molecular. **Engineering:** Chemical, civil, computer, electrical, mechanical, operations research. **Foreign languages:** Classics, comparative lit, German, Italian, Slavic, Spanish. **History:** General. **Math:** General. **Philosophy/religion:** Philosophy, religion. **Physical sciences:** Astrophysics, chemistry, geology, physics. **Psychology:** General. **Public administration:** General. **Social sciences:** Anthropology, economics, political science, sociology. **Visual/performing arts:** Art history/conservation.

**Most popular majors.** Biology 8%, engineering/engineering technologies 15%, English 8%, history 8%, public administration/social services 7%, social sciences 27%.

**Computing on campus.** 500 workstations in dormitories, library, computer center, student center. Dormitories wired for high-speed internet access and linked to campus network. Commuter students can connect to campus network. Online course registration, online library, helpline, repair service, student web hosting, wireless network available.

**Student life. Freshman orientation:** Mandatory. Three-day orientation. Optional 1-week trip with Outdoor Action or Student Volunteer Council. **Housing:** Guaranteed on-campus for all undergraduates. Coed dorms, special housing for disabled, apartments available. Residential colleges for freshmen and sophomores. Kosher dining facilities available. **Activities:** Bands, campus ministries, choral groups, dance, drama, film society, international student organizations, literary magazine, music ensembles, Model UN, musical theater, opera, radio station, student government, student newspaper, symphony orchestra, over 200 student organizations available.

**Athletics.** NCAA. **Intercollegiate:** Baseball M, basketball, cross-country, diving, fencing, field hockey W, football (tackle) M, golf, ice hockey, lacrosse, rowing (crew), soccer, softball W, squash, swimming, tennis, track and field, volleyball, water polo, wrestling M. **Intramural:** Badminton, basketball, bowling, football (non-tackle), golf, ice hockey, judo, racquetball, soccer, softball, tennis, water polo. **Team name:** Tigers.

**Student services.** Alcohol/substance abuse counseling, chaplain/spiritual director, career counseling, student employment services, financial aid counseling, health services, minority student services, personal counseling, placement for graduates, women's services. **Physically disabled:** Services for visually, speech, hearing impaired.

**Contact.** E-mail: uaoffice@princeton.edu
Phone: (609) 258-3060 Fax: (609) 258-6743
Janet Rapelye, Dean of Admission, Princeton University, Box 430, Princeton, NJ 08542-0430

## Rabbi Jacob Joseph School
### Edison, New Jersey

- Private 4-year rabbinical college
- Large town

**General.** Accredited by AARTS. **Calendar:** Semester.

**Contact.** Phone: (732) 985-6533
One Plainfield Avenue, Edison, NJ 08817

## Rabbinical College of America
### Morristown, New Jersey
**CB code: 1546**

- Private 4-year rabbinical college for men affiliated with Jewish faith
- Residential campus in large town

**General.** Founded in 1956. Accredited by AARTS. **Location:** One mile from downtown, 35 miles from New York City. **Calendar:** Semester.

**Contact.** Phone: (973) 267-9404
Registrar, 226 Sussex Avenue, CN 1996, Morristown, NJ 07962-1996

## Ramapo College of New Jersey
### Mahwah, New Jersey
**CB member**
www.ramapo.edu
**CB code: 2884**

- Public 4-year liberal arts college
- Residential campus in large town
- 5,529 degree-seeking undergraduates: 7% part-time, 58% women, 5% African American, 5% Asian American, 9% Hispanic American, 2% international
- 213 degree-seeking graduate students
- 51% of applicants admitted
- SAT, application essay required
- 70% graduate within 6 years

**General.** Founded in 1969. Regionally accredited. **Degrees:** 1,142 bachelor's awarded; master's offered. **ROTC:** Air Force. **Location:** 35 miles from New York City. **Calendar:** Semester, extensive summer session. **Full-time faculty:** 213 total; 94% have terminal degrees, 22% minority, 45% women. **Part-time faculty:** 195 total. **Class size:** 24% < 20, 73% 20-39, 3% 40-49. **Special facilities:** International telecommunications center, electron microscope, Holocaust center, performing arts center, international and intercultural education office, environmental studies/sustainability education center, greenhouse center, astronomical observatory, global financial markets trading laboratory.

**Freshman class profile.** 5,114 applied, 2,627 admitted, 937 enrolled.

| Mid 50% test scores | | | |
|---|---|---|---|
| SAT critical reading: | 520-600 | GPA 2.0-2.99: | 16% |
| SAT math: | 550-630 | Rank in top quarter: | 62% |
| SAT writing: | 530-610 | Rank in top tenth: | 24% |
| GPA 3.75 or higher: | 21% | Out-of-state: | 3% |
| GPA 3.50-3.74: | 21% | Live on campus: | 85% |
| GPA 3.0-3.49: | 42% | International: | 1% |

**Basis for selection.** School achievement record, test scores most important. Applicants should rank in top 25% of high school class. SAT Reading and ACT Reading/English may be used for academic advising. Certain majors have additional entrance requirements.

**High school preparation.** College-preparatory program required. 18 units required. Required units include English 4, mathematics 3, social studies 3, science 3 (laboratory 2), foreign language 2 and academic electives 3. Math must consist of algebra I, geometry, and algebra II.

**2009-2010 Annual costs.** Tuition/fees: $11,416; $19,099 out-of-state. Room/board: $11,290. Books/supplies: $1,200. Personal expenses: $2,250.

**2008-2009 Financial aid. Need-based:** 697 full-time freshmen applied for aid; 479 were judged to have need; 448 of these received aid. Average need met was 69%. Average scholarship/grant was $11,114; average loan $3,349. 48% of total undergraduate aid awarded as scholarships/grants, 52% as loans/jobs. **Non-need-based:** Awarded to 1,102 full-time undergraduates, including 205 freshmen. Scholarships awarded for academics, state residency.

**Application procedures. Admission:** Closing date 3/1. $60 fee, may be waived for applicants with need. Admission notification on a rolling basis beginning on or about 11/15. Must reply by 5/1. **Financial aid:** Priority date 3/1; no closing date. FAFSA required. Applicants notified on a rolling basis starting 4/1; must reply by 5/1 or within 2 week(s) of notification.

**Academics.** Thematic learning communities. **Special study options:** Accelerated study, combined bachelor's/graduate degree, cooperative education, cross-registration, distance learning, double major, dual enrollment of high school students, exchange student, external degree, honors, independent study, internships, liberal arts/career combination, student-designed major, study abroad, teacher certification program. **Credit/placement by examination:** AP, CLEP, IB, SAT. 65 credit hours maximum toward bachelor's degree. **Support services:** Learning center, pre-admission summer program, reduced course load, remedial instruction, study skills assistance, tutoring, writing center.

**Majors. Area/ethnic studies:** American. **Biology:** General, biochemistry, bioinformatics. **Business:** Accounting, business admin, international. **Communications:** General. **Computer sciences:** General, information systems. **Conservation:** Environmental science, environmental studies. **Foreign languages:** Comparative lit, Spanish. **Health:** Clinical lab science, health services. **History:** General. **Interdisciplinary:** Biological/physical sciences, global studies. **Legal studies:** General. **Liberal arts:** Arts/sciences, humanities. **Math:** General. **Physical sciences:** Chemistry, physics. **Psychology:** General. **Public administration:** Social work. **Social sciences:** Economics, political science, sociology. **Visual/performing arts:** General, art, dramatic, multimedia.

**Most popular majors.** Business/marketing 20%, communications/journalism 10%, education 6%, health sciences 8%, psychology 13%, visual/performing arts 9%.

**Computing on campus.** 1,058 workstations in dormitories, library, computer center, student center. Dormitories wired for high-speed internet access and linked to campus network. Commuter students can connect to campus network. Online course registration, online library, helpline, repair service, student web hosting, wireless network available.

**Student life. Freshman orientation:** Mandatory, $130 fee. Preregistration for classes offered. Several sessions held throughout summer. **Policies:** Smoking prohibited in all physical buildings on campus. Smokers must stand 25 feet away from buildings. **Housing:** Guaranteed on-campus for freshmen. Coed dorms, special housing for disabled, apartments, cooperative housing available. $200 partly refundable deposit, deadline 5/1. **Activities:** Campus ministries, choral groups, dance, drama, international student organizations, literary magazine, music ensembles, Model UN, musical theater, radio station, student government, student newspaper, TV station, United Asian Americans, College Democrats, College Republicans, Hillel, Intervarsity Christian Fellowship, Muslim student association, Community Builders Coalition, culture club, Organization for African Unity.

**Athletics.** NCAA. **Intercollegiate:** Baseball M, basketball, cheerleading M, cross-country, field hockey W, lacrosse W, soccer, softball W, swimming, tennis, track and field, volleyball. **Intramural:** Basketball, bowling, football (non-tackle) M, soccer, softball, volleyball. **Team name:** Roadrunners.

**Student services.** Adult student services, alcohol/substance abuse counseling, chaplain/spiritual director, career counseling, services for economically disadvantaged, student employment services, financial aid counseling, health services, minority student services, personal counseling, placement for graduates, veterans' counselor, women's services. **Physically disabled:** Services for visually, speech, hearing impaired. **Learning disabled:** Comprehensive services available.

**Contact.** E-mail: admissions@ramapo.edu
Phone: (201) 684-7300 Toll-free number: (800) 972-6276
Fax: (201) 684-7964
Peter Rice, Director of Admissions, Ramapo College of New Jersey, 505 Ramapo Valley Road, Mahwah, NJ 07430-1680

## Richard Stockton College of New Jersey

Pomona, New Jersey — CB member
www.stockton.edu — CB code: 2889

- Public 4-year liberal arts college
- Residential campus in large town
- 6,717 degree-seeking undergraduates: 10% part-time, 57% women, 8% African American, 6% Asian American, 7% Hispanic American
- 664 degree-seeking graduate students
- 61% of applicants admitted
- SAT or ACT (ACT writing optional), application essay required
- 66% graduate within 6 years; 28% enter graduate study

**General.** Founded in 1969. Regionally accredited. 7-acre marine science field station located off-campus. **Degrees:** 1,757 bachelor's awarded; master's, professional offered. **Location:** 12 miles from Atlantic City, 50 miles from Philadelphia. **Calendar:** Semester, extensive summer session. **Full-time faculty:** 264 total; 95% have terminal degrees, 22% minority, 50% women. **Part-time faculty:** 255 total; 38% have terminal degrees, 10% minority, 46% women. **Class size:** 22% < 20, 74% 20-39, 2% 40-49, 1% 50-99, less than 1% >100. **Special facilities:** Arboretum, forestry nursery, ecologic succession plots and study preserve, child care center, interdisciplinary natural sciences laboratory, observatory, Holocaust center, geothermal plant, ITV classroom, performing arts theater, hospital located on college grounds.

**Freshman class profile.** 4,547 applied, 2,783 admitted, 870 enrolled.

| Mid 50% test scores | | | |
|---|---|---|---|
| SAT critical reading: | 490-590 | Rank in top tenth: | 26% |
| SAT math: | 510-610 | End year in good standing: | 90% |
| SAT writing: | 480-580 | Return as sophomores: | 81% |
| ACT composite: | 19-23 | Out-of-state: | 1% |
| Rank in top quarter: | 60% | Live on campus: | 86% |

**Basis for selection.** Secondary school record, class rank, test scores most important; essay, recommendations, extracurricular activities also important; interview, work experience considered. **Homeschooled:** Statement describing homeschool structure and mission, transcript of courses and grades required.

**High school preparation.** College-preparatory program recommended. 16 units required; 18 recommended. Required and recommended units include English 4, mathematics 3, social studies 2, science 2 (laboratory 2), foreign language 2 and academic electives 5.

**2009-2010 Annual costs.** Tuition/fees: $10,940; $16,624 out-of-state. Room/board: $10,286. Books/supplies: $1,400. Personal expenses: $1,614.

**2009-2010 Financial aid. Non-need-based:** Scholarships awarded for academics, art, leadership, minority status, music/drama, state residency. **Additional information:** Institutional grants provided for majority of neediest incoming students.

**Application procedures. Admission:** Priority date 2/1; deadline 6/1 (postmark date). $50 fee, may be waived for applicants with need. Admission notification on a rolling basis beginning on or about 10/1. Must reply by May 1 or within 2 week(s) if notified thereafter. **Financial aid:** Priority date 3/1; no closing date. FAFSA required. Applicants notified on a rolling basis starting 4/1; must reply within 2 week(s) of notification.

**Academics. Special study options:** Accelerated study, combined bachelor's/graduate degree, cross-registration, distance learning, double major, dual enrollment of high school students, honors, independent study, internships, liberal arts/career combination, semester at sea, study abroad, teacher certification program, Washington semester. Dual degree bachelor's program in engineering with Rutgers University and New Jersey Institute of Technology, preceptorial advising, opportunities for specialized research, extensive Washington internship available. Accelerated Health Professions Program. **Credit/placement by examination:** AP, CLEP, IB, SAT, ACT, institutional tests. 32 credit hours maximum toward bachelor's degree. **Support services:** Learning center, pre-admission summer program, reduced course load, remedial instruction, study skills assistance, tutoring, writing center.

**Majors. Biology:** General, biochemistry, marine. **Business:** Business admin, hospitality admin. **Communications:** General. **Computer sciences:** Information systems. **Conservation:** Environmental studies. **Education:** Multilevel teacher. **Foreign languages:** General. **Health:** Audiology/speech pathology, nursing (RN). **History:** General. **Liberal arts:** Arts/sciences. **Math:** General. **Physical sciences:** Chemistry, geology, physics. **Psychology:** General. **Public administration:** Social work. **Social sciences:** Criminology, economics, political science, sociology. **Visual/performing arts:** General. **Other:** Computational science, Philosophy and religion.

**Most popular majors.** Biology 11%, business/marketing 20%, education 11%, psychology 11%, social sciences 13%.

**Computing on campus.** 810 workstations in dormitories, library, computer center, student center. Dormitories wired for high-speed internet access and linked to campus network. Commuter students can connect to campus network. Online course registration, online library, helpline, student web hosting, wireless network available.

**Student life. Freshman orientation:** Mandatory, $90 fee. Preregistration for classes offered. Program includes parents' sessions. **Housing:** Guaranteed on-campus for freshmen. Coed dorms, special housing for disabled, apartments, wellness housing available. $150 partly refundable deposit, deadline 5/1. **Activities:** Concert band, campus ministries, choral groups, dance, drama, international student organizations, literary magazine, music ensembles, radio station, student government, student newspaper, TV station, Books Without Borders, unified black students society, Christian Fellowship, Jewish student union, Circle K International, Amnesty International, action volunteers for the environment, Water Watch, CHANGE, campus religious council.

**Athletics.** NCAA. **Intercollegiate:** Baseball M, basketball, cheerleading; cross-country, field hockey W, lacrosse M, rowing (crew) W, soccer, softball W, tennis W, track and field, volleyball W. **Intramural:** Basketball, football (non-tackle), soccer, softball, table tennis, volleyball. **Team name:** Ospreys.

**Student services.** Adult student services, alcohol/substance abuse counseling, chaplain/spiritual director, career counseling, services for economically disadvantaged, student employment services, financial aid counseling, health services, on-campus daycare, personal counseling, placement for graduates, veterans' counselor, women's services. **Physically disabled:** Services for visually, speech, hearing impaired. **Learning disabled:** Comprehensive services available.

**Contact.** E-mail: admissions@stockton.edu
Phone: (609) 652-4261 Toll-free number: (866) 772-2885
Fax: (609) 748-5541
John Iacovelli, Dean of Enrollment Management, Richard Stockton College of New Jersey, Jim Leeds Road, Pomona, NJ 08240-0195

---

## Rider University
### Lawrenceville, New Jersey
### www.rider.edu

CB member
CB code: 2758

- Private 4-year university
- Residential campus in small town
- 4,712 degree-seeking undergraduates: 14% part-time, 61% women, 10% African American, 3% Asian American, 6% Hispanic American, 3% international
- 930 degree-seeking graduate students
- 75% of applicants admitted
- SAT or ACT with writing, application essay required
- 60% graduate within 6 years; 16% enter graduate study

**General.** Founded in 1865. Regionally accredited. Westminster College of the Arts, located in Lawrenceville and Princeton campuses. **Degrees:** 982 bachelor's, 4 associate awarded; master's offered. **ROTC:** Army. **Location:** 5 miles from Princeton, 3 miles from Trenton. **Calendar:** Semester, extensive summer session. **Full-time faculty:** 243 total; 97% have terminal degrees, 14% minority, 42% women. **Part-time faculty:** 383 total; 47% have terminal degrees, 19% minority, 50% women. **Class size:** 50% < 20, 45% 20-39, 4% 40-49, less than 1% 50-99, less than 1% >100. **Special facilities:** Holocaust/genocide center, teaching and learning center, art gallery.

**Freshman class profile.** 7,372 applied, 5,534 admitted, 1,026 enrolled.

| Mid 50% test scores | | | |
|---|---|---|---|
| SAT critical reading: | 460-560 | GPA 2.0-2.99: | 26% |
| SAT math: | 470-580 | Rank in top quarter: | 45% |
| SAT writing: | 470-580 | Rank in top tenth: | 16% |
| ACT composite: | 19-24 | Return as sophomores: | 80% |
| GPA 3.75 or higher: | 16% | Out-of-state: | 28% |
| GPA 3.50-3.74: | 21% | Live on campus: | 88% |
| GPA 3.0-3.49: | 37% | International: | 2% |

**Basis for selection.** High school curriculum most important, followed by GPA, test scores, essay, and recommendations. Extracurricular activities, interview considered. Interview recommended for all; audition required for music program with Westminster College of the Arts. **Homeschooled:** Information about syllabi, reading lists, and/or course descriptions recommended.

**High school preparation.** College-preparatory program required. 16 units required. Required and recommended units include English 4, mathematics 3-4, social studies 2, history 2, science 4 (laboratory 4) and foreign language 2. Algebra I and II and geometry required for business administration, science, math majors.

**2009-2010 Annual costs.** Tuition/fees: $29,060. Room/board: $10,720. Books/supplies: $1,500. Personal expenses: $590.

**2009-2010 Financial aid. Need-based:** 938 full-time freshmen applied for aid; 789 were judged to have need; 789 of these received aid. Average need met was 75%. Average scholarship/grant was $17,170; average loan $3,590. 57% of total undergraduate aid awarded as scholarships/grants, 43% as loans/jobs. **Non-need-based:** Awarded to 1,505 full-time undergraduates, including 402 freshmen. Scholarships awarded for academics, alumni affiliation, athletics, leadership, minority status, music/drama.

**Application procedures. Admission:** Priority date 1/15; no deadline. $50 fee, may be waived for applicants with need. Admission notification on a rolling basis beginning on or about 12/15. Must reply by May 1 or within 4 week(s) if notified thereafter. Notification of admission decision sent within 3-4 weeks of receiving application. **Financial aid:** Priority date 3/1; no closing date. FAFSA required. Applicants notified on a rolling basis starting 2/20.

**Academics. Special study options:** Cooperative education, cross-registration, distance learning, double major, honors, independent study, internships, liberal arts/career combination, study abroad, teacher certification program, weekend college. **Credit/placement by examination:** AP, CLEP, SAT, ACT, institutional tests. Policy varies by major. 30 hours of credit by general examination may be counted toward degree. No limit for subject examinations. Not acceptable for last 30 credits of degree program. 4-8 AP courses (24 credits) required for sophomore standing. **Support services:** Learning center, reduced course load, remedial instruction, study skills assistance, tutoring, writing center.

**Majors. Area/ethnic studies:** American. **Biology:** General, biochemistry. **Business:** Accounting, actuarial science, administrative services, business admin, entrepreneurial studies, finance, human resources, international, management science, managerial economics, marketing, office management, organizational behavior. **Communications:** Advertising, journalism. **Computer sciences:** General. **Conservation:** Environmental science. **Education:** Business, elementary, music, sales/marketing, science, secondary. **Foreign languages:** French, German, Russian, Spanish. **History:** General. **Interdisciplinary:** Biopsychology. **Liberal arts:** Arts/sciences. **Math:** General. **Philosophy/religion:** Philosophy. **Physical sciences:** Chemistry, geology, oceanography, physics. **Psychology:** General. **Social sciences:** Economics, international relations, political science, sociology. **Theology:** Sacred music. **Visual/performing arts:** Art, arts management, music theory/composition, musical theater, piano/organ, studio arts, voice/opera. **Other:** Global supply chain management.

**Most popular majors.** Business/marketing 31%, education 16%, English 14%, liberal arts 9%, psychology 6%, visual/performing arts 7%.

**Computing on campus.** 300 workstations in library, computer center, student center. Dormitories wired for high-speed internet access and linked to campus network. Commuter students can connect to campus network. Online course registration, online library, helpline, student web hosting, wireless network available.

**Student life. Freshman orientation:** Mandatory, $250 fee. Preregistration for classes offered. Two-day program for new students and family members. **Housing:** Guaranteed on-campus for freshmen. Coed dorms, single-sex dorms, special housing for disabled, apartments, fraternity/sorority housing, wellness housing available. $300 nonrefundable deposit, deadline 5/1. Faculty-in-residence options, suites available. **Activities:** Bands, campus ministries, choral groups, dance, drama, film society, international student organizations, literary magazine, music ensembles, Model UN, musical theater, opera, radio station, student government, student newspaper, TV station, student entertainment council, residence hall association, finance board, Asian student organization, interfraternity council, hunger and homelessness awareness, College Republicans, Latin American student organization.

**Athletics.** NCAA. **Intercollegiate:** Baseball M, basketball, cheerleading, cross-country, diving, field hockey W, golf M, soccer, softball W, swimming, tennis, track and field, volleyball W, wrestling M. **Intramural:** Basketball, football (non-tackle), ice hockey M, lacrosse, soccer, softball, track and field, volleyball. **Team name:** Broncs.

**Student services.** Adult student services, alcohol/substance abuse counseling, chaplain/spiritual director, career counseling, services for economically disadvantaged, student employment services, financial aid counseling, health services, minority student services, personal counseling, placement for graduates, veterans' counselor, women's services. **Physically disabled:** Services for visually, speech, hearing impaired.

**Contact.** E-mail: admissions@rider.edu
Phone: (609) 896-5042 Toll-free number: (800) 257-9026
Fax: (609) 895-6645
William Larrousse, Director of Undergraduate Admissions, Rider University, 2083 Lawrenceville Road, Lawrenceville, NJ 08648-3099

## Rowan University
**Glassboro, New Jersey**
**www.rowan.edu**
**CB member**
**CB code: 2515**

- Public 4-year university
- Residential campus in large town
- 9,292 degree-seeking undergraduates: 11% part-time, 52% women, 9% African American, 4% Asian American, 7% Hispanic American
- 997 degree-seeking graduate students
- 68% of applicants admitted
- SAT or ACT (ACT writing optional) required
- 62% graduate within 6 years; 4% enter graduate study

**General.** Founded in 1923. Regionally accredited. **Degrees:** 2,096 bachelor's awarded; master's, professional offered. **ROTC:** Army. **Location:** 20 miles from Philadelphia. **Calendar:** Semester, extensive summer session. **Full-time faculty:** 407 total; 84% have terminal degrees, 22% minority, 42% women. **Part-time faculty:** 530 total; 26% have terminal degrees, 10% minority, 46% women. **Class size:** 39% < 20, 60% 20-39, less than 1% 40-49, less than 1% 50-99, less than 1% >100. **Special facilities:** Observatory, glass-blowing museum, on-campus early childhood demonstration center, animal penthouse, greenhouse for biological studies, concert hall.

**Freshman class profile.** 7,486 applied, 5,073 admitted, 1,602 enrolled.

| Mid 50% test scores | | | |
|---|---|---|---|
| SAT critical reading: | 480-580 | GPA 2.0-2.99: | 13% |
| SAT math: | 500-600 | Rank in top quarter: | 48% |
| SAT writing: | 480-580 | Rank in top tenth: | 24% |
| GPA 3.75 or higher: | 28% | Return as sophomores: | 82% |
| GPA 3.50-3.74: | 21% | Out-of-state: | 3% |
| GPA 3.0-3.49: | 38% | Live on campus: | 80% |

**Basis for selection.** School achievement record and test scores most important, followed by recommendations. Audition required for music, theater programs; portfolio interview required for art program. **Home-schooled:** Transcript of courses and grades required.

**High school preparation.** College-preparatory program required. 16 units required. Required and recommended units include English 4, mathematics 3, science 2 and foreign language 2. Engineering applicants should have 3 units of laboratory science including physics and chemistry, and 4 units of college preparatory math including precalculus. Calculus strongly recommended.

**2009-2010 Annual costs.** Tuition/fees: $11,234; $18,308 out-of-state. Room/board: $9,958. Books/supplies: $1,500. Personal expenses: $1,000.

**2008-2009 Financial aid. Need-based:** 979 full-time freshmen applied for aid; 620 were judged to have need; 573 of these received aid. Average need met was 81%. Average scholarship/grant was $7,589; average loan $3,128. 32% of total undergraduate aid awarded as scholarships/grants, 68% as loans/jobs. **Non-need-based:** Awarded to 1,252 full-time undergraduates, including 127 freshmen. Scholarships awarded for academics, art, music/drama.

**Application procedures. Admission:** Closing date 3/1 (receipt date). $50 fee, may be waived for applicants with need. Admission notification on a rolling basis beginning on or about 10/15. Must reply by 5/1. **Financial aid:** Priority date 3/15; no closing date. FAFSA required. Applicants notified on a rolling basis starting 3/15.

**Academics.** Camden campus offers general education courses and major programs in elementary education, business administration, law/justice, and sociology. **Special study options:** Accelerated study, combined bachelor's/graduate degree, distance learning, double major, dual enrollment of high school students, ESL, honors, independent study, internships, study abroad, teacher certification program, weekend college. **Credit/placement by examination:** AP, CLEP, IB, SAT, ACT. 30 credit hours maximum toward bachelor's degree. **Support services:** Pre-admission summer program, remedial instruction, study skills assistance, tutoring, writing center.

**Majors. Biology:** General, biochemistry. **Business:** Accounting, business admin, finance, human resources, management information systems, management science, marketing. **Communications:** Advertising, journalism, public relations. **Computer sciences:** Computer science. **Education:** General, art, early childhood, elementary, music, secondary, special. **Engineering:** Chemical, civil, electrical, mechanical. **Foreign languages:** Spanish. **Health:** Athletic training. **History:** General. **Liberal arts:** Arts/sciences. **Math:** General. **Parks/recreation:** Health/fitness, sports admin. **Physical sciences:** Chemistry, physics. **Protective services:** Criminal justice. **Psychology:** General, developmental. **Social sciences:** Economics, geography, political science, sociology. **Visual/performing arts:** Art, dance, dramatic, film/cinema, jazz, music performance, music theory/composition, studio arts.

**Most popular majors.** Business/marketing 16%, communications/journalism 11%, communication technologies 6%, education 18%, security/protective services 7%, social sciences 6%.

**Computing on campus.** 1,200 workstations in dormitories, library, computer center. Commuter students can connect to campus network. Online course registration, online library, helpline, repair service, wireless network available.

**Student life. Freshman orientation:** Available. Preregistration for classes offered. Overnight program for freshmen and their families during summer. **Housing:** Guaranteed on-campus for freshmen. Coed dorms, special housing for disabled, apartments, wellness housing available. $200 nonrefundable deposit, deadline 5/1. Townhouses. **Activities:** Bands, choral groups, dance, drama, film society, music ensembles, radio station, student government, student newspaper, symphony orchestra, TV station, Over 100 clubs and student organizations available.

**Athletics.** NCAA. **Intercollegiate:** Baseball M, basketball, cross-country, diving, field hockey W, football (tackle) M, lacrosse W, soccer, softball W, swimming, track and field, volleyball W. **Intramural:** Basketball, bowling, golf, handball, racquetball, soccer, softball, table tennis, tennis, volleyball. **Team name:** Profs.

**Student services.** Adult student services, alcohol/substance abuse counseling, chaplain/spiritual director, career counseling, student employment services, financial aid counseling, health services, legal services, minority student services, on-campus daycare, personal counseling, placement for graduates, veterans' counselor, women's services. **Physically disabled:** Services for visually, speech, hearing impaired.

**Contact.** E-mail: admissions@rowan.edu
Phone: (856) 256-4200 Toll-free number: (877) 787-6926
Fax: (856) 256-4430
Albert Betts, Director of Admissions, Rowan University, Savitz Hall, 201 Mullica Hill Road, Glassboro, NJ 08028

## Rutgers, The State University of New Jersey: Camden Regional Campus
**Camden, New Jersey**
**www.rutgers.edu**
**CB member**
**CB code: 2742**

- Public 4-year university
- Commuter campus in small city
- 4,067 degree-seeking undergraduates: 18% part-time, 55% women, 16% African American, 8% Asian American, 9% Hispanic American, 1% international
- 1,598 degree-seeking graduate students
- 49% of applicants admitted
- SAT or ACT with writing required
- 59% graduate within 6 years

**General.** Founded in 1927. Regionally accredited. Undergraduate schools: Camden College of Arts and Sciences, University College-Camden, School of Business-Camden. Graduate degrees available at School of Business. Graduate schools: Graduate School-Camden, School of Law-Camden. **Degrees:** 862 bachelor's awarded; master's, professional offered. **ROTC:** Army, Air Force. **Location:** One mile from Philadelphia. **Calendar:** Semester, extensive summer session. **Full-time faculty:** 252 total; 99% have terminal degrees, 16% minority, 38% women. **Part-time faculty:** 182 total; 99% have terminal degrees, 12% minority, 41% women. **Class size:** 42% < 20, 42% 20-39, 7% 40-49, 6% 50-99, 3% >100. **Special facilities:** Fine arts center.

**Freshman class profile.** 5,529 applied, 2,683 admitted, 352 enrolled.

| Mid 50% test scores | | | |
|---|---|---|---|
| SAT critical reading: | 490-600 | Rank in top tenth: | 17% |
| SAT math: | 510-600 | Return as sophomores: | 81% |
| SAT writing: | 480-580 | Out-of-state: | 6% |
| Rank in top quarter: | 23% | Live on campus: | 59% |

**Basis for selection.** School achievement record (including grades, rank, strength of program, honors) and test scores most important. Extracurricular activities, talent, disadvantaged status considered. SAT Subject Tests required for applicants who will not have diploma from accredited high school by entrance date. May also be required of GED holders. SAT/ACT scores should be submitted by December of senior year. **Homeschooled:** SAT Subject Tests required for applicants who will not have diploma from accredited high school by entrance date.

**High school preparation.** College-preparatory program required. 16 units required. Required and recommended units include English 4, mathematics 3-4, science 2, foreign language 2 and academic electives 5. Math requirement includes algebra I and II and geometry. 4 math, 1 chemistry, 1 physics required for engineering applicants.

**2009-2010 Annual costs.** Tuition/fees: $11,698; $22,330 out-of-state. Room/board: $9,788. Books/supplies: $1,431. Personal expenses: $1,631.

**2009-2010 Financial aid. Non-need-based:** Scholarships awarded for academics, alumni affiliation, art, athletics, leadership, minority status, music/drama, state residency.

**Application procedures. Admission:** Closing date 12/1. $65 fee, may be waived for applicants with need. Application must be submitted online. Admission notification on a rolling basis beginning on or about 2/28. Must reply by May 1 or within 2 week(s) if notified thereafter. May apply to up to 3 Rutgers colleges with 1 application. Students applying by December 1 notified by February 28. **Financial aid:** Priority date 3/15; no closing date. FAFSA required. Applicants notified on a rolling basis starting 2/1; must reply within 2 week(s) of notification.

**Academics. Special study options:** Accelerated study, combined bachelor's/graduate degree, cooperative education, cross-registration, distance learning, double major, dual enrollment of high school students, ESL, exchange student, honors, independent study, internships, liberal arts/career combination, student-designed major, study abroad, teacher certification program, weekend college. Cooperative baccalaureate program in Engineering with School of Engineering (New Brunswick Campus); Interdisciplinary program in African-American studies, general science. Cooperative baccalaureate in medical technology with approved hospital. BA/MA in Childhood Studies; English, History, Liberal Studies or Psychology; BA/MS in Biology, Chemistry or Mathematics (with the Graduate School-Camden). BA in Economics or Political Science/Master of Public Administration (with the Graduate School-Camden); BS/Master of Business and Science (MBS). **Credit/placement by examination:** AP, CLEP, IB, institutional tests. No more than 8 credits given for elementary or intermediate levels of any foreign language. Graduating seniors may take no more than one examination in their final term. **Support services:** Learning center, pre-admission summer program, reduced course load, remedial instruction, study skills assistance, tutoring, writing center.

**Majors. Area/ethnic studies:** African-American. **Biology:** General, biomedical sciences. **Business:** Accounting, business admin, finance, hospitality admin, marketing. **Computer sciences:** Computer science. **Engineering:** Biomedical, ceramic, chemical, civil, electrical, mechanical, science. **Foreign languages:** French, German, Spanish. **Health:** Nursing (RN), predental, premedicine. **History:** General. **Interdisciplinary:** Biological/physical sciences. **Legal studies:** Prelaw. **Liberal arts:** Arts/sciences. **Math:** General. **Philosophy/religion:** Philosophy. **Physical sciences:** Chemistry, physics. **Protective services:** Criminal justice. **Psychology:** General. **Public administration:** Social work. **Social sciences:** Economics, political science, sociology, urban studies. **Visual/performing arts:** Art, dramatic.

**Most popular majors.** Business/marketing 25%, English 8%, history 6%, psychology 13%, security/protective services 6%, social sciences 11%.

**Computing on campus.** 187 workstations in dormitories, library, computer center, student center. Dormitories linked to campus network. Commuter students can connect to campus network. Online course registration, helpline, repair service, wireless network available.

**Student life. Freshman orientation:** Available. **Housing:** Coed dorms, special housing for disabled, apartments available. $200 nonrefundable deposit. **Activities:** Drama, international student organizations, literary magazine, radio station, student government, student newspaper, accounting society, forensics society, political science association, black student union, Latin American students organization, physics society, Jewish student union, marketing association, psychology club.

**Athletics.** NCAA. **Intercollegiate:** Baseball M, basketball, cross-country, golf M, rowing (crew) W, soccer, softball W, track and field, volleyball W. **Intramural:** Badminton, basketball, football (tackle) M, handball, racquetball, soccer, softball, squash, volleyball. **Team name:** Scarlet Raptors.

**Student services.** Career counseling, student employment services, health services, on-campus daycare, personal counseling, placement for graduates, veterans' counselor. **Physically disabled:** Services for visually, speech, hearing impaired.

**Contact.** E-mail: admissions@ugadm.rutgers.edu
Phone: (856) 225-6104 Fax: (856) 225-6498
Deborah Bowles, Director of Admissions, Rutgers, The State University of New Jersey: Camden Regional Campus, 406 Penn Street, Camden, NJ 08102

## Rutgers, The State University of New Jersey: New Brunswick/Piscataway Campus

**Piscataway, New Jersey**  CB member
**www.rutgers.edu**  CB code: 2765

- Public 4-year university
- Residential campus in large town
- 28,817 degree-seeking undergraduates: 4% part-time, 48% women, 8% African American, 25% Asian American, 10% Hispanic American, 2% international
- 7,336 degree-seeking graduate students
- 61% of applicants admitted
- SAT or ACT with writing required
- 75% graduate within 6 years

**General.** Founded in 1969. Regionally accredited. Undergraduate schools include: School of Environmental and Biological Sciences, School of Arts and Sciences, School of Engineering, School of the Arts, School of Planning and Public Policy, College of Nursing, School of Pharmacy, School of Business-New Brunswick, School of Communication and Information. **Degrees:** 5,752 bachelor's awarded; master's, doctoral, professional offered. **ROTC:** Army, Air Force. **Location:** 33 miles from New York City. **Calendar:** Semester, extensive summer session. **Full-time faculty:** 1,678 total; 99% have terminal degrees, 18% minority, 37% women. **Part-time faculty:** 867 total; 99% have terminal degrees, 16% minority, 51% women. **Class size:** 41% < 20, 30% 20-39, 7% 40-49, 11% 50-99, 10% >100. **Special facilities:** Geology museum, ecological preserve, 2 theaters, center for urban policy research, institute for health, health care policy and aging research, journalism resources institute, laboratory for computer science research, center for math, science and computer education.

**Freshman class profile.** 28,624 applied, 17,598 admitted, 5,835 enrolled.

| Mid 50% test scores | | | |
|---|---|---|---|
| SAT critical reading: | 530-630 | Return as sophomores: | 92% |
| SAT math: | 560-680 | Out-of-state: | 8% |
| SAT writing: | 540-640 | Live on campus: | 85% |
| | | International: | 2% |

**Basis for selection.** School achievement record (including grades, rank, strength of program, honors, AP) and test scores most important. Extracurricular activities, leadership talent, minority, disadvantaged status considered. State residents with educationally and economically disadvantaged backgrounds given consideration through state Educational Opportunity Fund program. SAT Subject Tests required of applicants who, by expected date of entrance, will not have diploma from accredited high school. May also be required of GED holders. Recommended that SAT/ACT be submitted by December of senior year. Interview, audition, portfolio review required for School of the Arts. **Homeschooled:** SAT Subject Tests required of graduates from non-accredited high schools.

**High school preparation.** College-preparatory program required. 16 units required. Required and recommended units include English 4, mathematics 3-4, science 2, foreign language 2 and academic electives 5. Math requirement includes algebra I and II and geometry. 4 math, 1 chemistry, 1 physics required for engineering program. One biology, 1 chemistry required for nursing program. 5-9 academic electives required, depending on college.

**2009-2010 Annual costs.** Tuition/fees: $11,886; $22,518 out-of-state. Tuition and fees may vary by program. Room/board: $10,676. Books/supplies: $1,431. Personal expenses: $1,631.

**2009-2010 Financial aid. Non-need-based:** Scholarships awarded for academics, alumni affiliation, art, athletics, leadership, minority status, music/drama, state residency.

**Application procedures. Admission:** Closing date 12/1. $65 fee, may be waived for applicants with need. Application must be submitted online. Admission notification on a rolling basis. Must reply by May 1 or within 2 week(s) if notified thereafter. May apply to up to 3 Rutgers colleges with 1 application. Applications received by December 1 will be answered by February 28. **Financial aid:** Priority date 3/15; no closing date. FAFSA required. Applicants notified on a rolling basis starting 2/1; must reply within 2 week(s) of notification.

**Academics. Special study options:** Accelerated study, combined bachelor's/ graduate degree, cooperative education, cross-registration, distance learning, double major, dual enrollment of high school students, ESL, exchange student, honors, independent study, internships, liberal arts/career combination, student-designed major, study abroad, teacher certification program, Washington semester, weekend college. 5-year BA or BS/MPA program in Rutgers Business School; BS in Business Discipline/MBA; BA or BS in Science Discipline/MBA; 8-year Bachelor/Medical Dual Degree program with UMDNJ-Robert Wood Johnson Medical School; 5-year BS/BS in Bioenvironmental Engineering with the School of Engineering; 5-year accelerated baccalaureate-MBA with RU Business School; Bureau of Engineering Research, supported by the University, industry, state and federal government, provides research opportunities for students and faculty; continuing professional education; Exchange program between School of Engineering and the City University of London for qualified students majoring in civil, electrical, or mechanical engineering; 5-year BA/BS degree program in liberal arts and engineering; 5-year BA or BS/M.Ed. with the Graduate School of Education; interdepartmental programs and certificate programs are available; BA/Master of Communication and Information Studies (with SCI); BA/MLER with School of Management and Labor Relations; Baccalaureate/ MCRP, MPH or MPP with EJB School of Planning and Public Policy; Baccalaureate in Business major/Master of Human Resources Management with School of Management and Labor Relations (SMLR); BS/Master of Business and Science (MBS). **Credit/placement by examination:** AP, CLEP, IB, institutional tests. 30 credit hours maximum toward bachelor's degree. **Support services:** Learning center, pre-admission summer program, reduced course load, remedial instruction, study skills assistance, tutoring, writing center.

**Majors. Agriculture:** Animal sciences, food science, plant sciences. **Architecture:** Environmental design, urban/community planning. **Area/ethnic studies:** African, African-American, American, Caribbean, Central/Eastern European, Chicano/Hispanic-American/Latino, East Asian, Latin American, Near/Middle Eastern, Russian/Slavic, women's. **Biology:** General, bacteriology, biochemistry, biometrics, biotechnology, cell/histology, genetics, marine, molecular. **Business:** Accounting, business admin, finance, labor relations, management information systems, management science, marketing. **Communications:** General, journalism. **Computer sciences:** Computer science. **Conservation:** General, environmental studies, management/policy. **Engineering:** Biomedical, ceramic, chemical, civil, electrical, environmental, mechanical, science. **Foreign languages:** Chinese, classics, comparative lit, French, German, Italian, linguistics, Portuguese, Russian, Spanish. **Health:** Clinical lab technology, nursing (RN), physician assistant, predental, premedicine. **History:** General. **Interdisciplinary:** Medieval/ Renaissance, nutrition sciences. **Legal studies:** Prelaw. **Math:** General, statistics. **Parks/recreation:** Exercise sciences. **Philosophy/religion:** Judaic, philosophy, religion. **Physical sciences:** Atmospheric science, chemistry, geology, physics. **Protective services:** Law enforcement admin. **Psychology:** General. **Public administration:** Social work. **Social sciences:** Anthropology, economics, geography, political science, sociology, urban studies. **Visual/performing arts:** Art, art history/conservation, dance, dramatic.

**Most popular majors.** Biology 10%, business/marketing 7%, communications/journalism 10%, engineering/engineering technologies 8%, psychology 11%, social sciences 17%.

**Computing on campus.** 1,450 workstations in dormitories, library, computer center, student center. Dormitories linked to campus network. Commuter students can connect to campus network. Helpline, repair service available.

**Student life. Freshman orientation:** Available. **Housing:** Guaranteed on-campus for freshmen. Coed dorms, single-sex dorms, special housing for disabled, apartments, cooperative housing, fraternity/sorority housing available. $100 deposit, deadline 6/15. **Activities:** Bands, campus ministries, choral groups, dance, drama, film society, international student organizations, literary magazine, music ensembles, musical theater, opera, radio station, student government, student newspaper, symphony orchestra, TV station, 400 organizations available.

**Athletics.** NCAA. **Intercollegiate:** Baseball M, basketball, cross-country, diving W, fencing M, field hockey W, football (tackle) M, golf, gymnastics W, lacrosse, rowing (crew), soccer, softball W, swimming W, tennis W, track and field, volleyball W, wrestling M. **Intramural:** Badminton, basketball, bowling, cross-country, golf, racquetball, soccer, softball, squash, swimming W, table tennis, tennis, track and field, volleyball, water polo, wrestling M. **Team name:** Scarlet Knights.

**Student services.** Adult student services, career counseling, student employment services, health services, on-campus daycare, personal counseling, placement for graduates, veterans' counselor. **Physically disabled:** Services for visually, speech, hearing impaired.

**Contact.** E-mail: admissions@ugadm.rutgers.edu
Phone: (732) 932-4636 Fax: (732) 445-0237
Diane Harris, Director of Undergraduate Admissions, Rutgers, The State University of New Jersey: New Brunswick/Piscataway Campus, 65 Davidson Road, Room 202, Piscataway, NJ 08854-8097

---

## Rutgers, The State University of New Jersey: Newark Regional Campus
### Newark, New Jersey
www.rutgers.edu      CB code: 2753

- Public 4-year university
- Commuter campus in large city
- 6,677 degree-seeking undergraduates: 14% part-time, 54% women, 19% African American, 24% Asian American, 21% Hispanic American, 2% international
- 3,924 degree-seeking graduate students
- 60% of applicants admitted
- SAT or ACT with writing required
- 59% graduate within 6 years

**General.** Founded in 1930. Regionally accredited. **Degrees:** 1,357 bachelor's awarded; master's, doctoral, professional offered. **ROTC:** Army, Air Force. **Location:** 10 miles from New York City. **Calendar:** Semester, extensive summer session. **Full-time faculty:** 447 total; 99% have terminal degrees, 21% minority, 38% women. **Part-time faculty:** 257 total; 99% have terminal degrees, 22% minority, 52% women. **Class size:** 26% < 20, 34% 20-39, 18% 40-49, 18% 50-99, 4% >100. **Special facilities:** Biology learning center, jazz institute, animal behavior institute, center for molecular and behavioral neuroscience, center for negotiation and conflict resolution.

**Freshman class profile.** 12,462 applied, 7,430 admitted, 872 enrolled.

| Mid 50% test scores | | | |
|---|---|---|---|
| SAT critical reading: | 470-570 | Rank in top tenth: | 29% |
| SAT math: | 510-620 | Return as sophomores: | 86% |
| SAT writing: | 480-580 | Out-of-state: | 4% |
| Rank in top quarter: | 30% | Live on campus: | 45% |
| | | International: | 1% |

**Basis for selection.** School achievement record and test scores most important. Extracurricular activities, leadership talent, minority, disadvantaged status considered. State residents with educational and economically disadvantaged backgrounds given consideration through state Educational Opportunity Fund program. SAT Subject Tests required of applicants who, by expected date of entrance, will not have diploma from accredited high school. May also be required of GED holders. SAT/ACT scores should be submitted by December of senior year.

**High school preparation.** College-preparatory program required. 16 units required. Required and recommended units include English 4, mathematics 3-4, science 2, foreign language 2 and academic electives 5. Math requirement includes algebra I, II and geometry. 4 math, 1 chemistry, 1 physics required for engineering program. One biology, 1 chemistry required for nursing program. Foreign language recommended.

**2009-2010 Annual costs.** Tuition/fees: $11,414; $22,046 out-of-state. Tuition and fees may vary by program. Room/board: $11,155. Books/ supplies: $1,431. Personal expenses: $1,631.

**2009-2010 Financial aid. Non-need-based:** Scholarships awarded for academics, alumni affiliation, art, athletics, leadership, minority status, music/ drama, religious affiliation, state residency.

**Application procedures. Admission:** Priority date 12/1; no deadline. $65 fee, may be waived for applicants with need. Application must be submitted online. Admission notification on a rolling basis beginning on or about 2/28. Must reply by May 1 or within 2 week(s) if notified thereafter. May apply to up to 3 Rutgers colleges with 1 application. Applications completed by December 1 will be answered by February 28. **Financial aid:** Priority date 3/15; no closing date. FAFSA required. Applicants notified on a rolling basis starting 2/1; must reply within 2 week(s) of notification.

**Academics. Special study options:** Accelerated study, combined bachelor's/ graduate degree, cooperative education, cross-registration, distance learning, double major, dual enrollment of high school students, ESL, exchange student, honors, independent study, internships, liberal arts/career combination, student-designed major, study abroad, teacher certification program, Washington semester, weekend college. 5-year baccalaureate-MBA with RU Business School; BS in Business Discipline/MBA; BA or BS in Science Discipline/MBA; Baccalaureate/MA in Criminal Justice with the School of Criminal Justice; Baccalaureate/MPA with the School of Public Affairs and Administration; Cooperative baccalaureate program with the School of Engineering (New Brunswick campus); Cooperative baccalaureate in medical technology with affiliated hospitals; interdisciplinary program in archaeology, international affairs, legal studies, women's studies; continuing professional education; Baccalaureate in Business Major/Master of Human Resource Management (with School of Management and Labor Relations in New Brunswick); Baccalaureate-Master's dual degree programs with the

School of Criminal Justice and Rutgers Business School; BA or BS in Biology/MS in Biology; BA in Chemistry/MS in Chemistry; BA in Economics/MA in Economics; BS in Environmental Sciences/MS in Environmental Geology; BS in Environmental Sciences/MS in Environmental Sciences; BA in Political Science, Sociology or Anthropology/MS in Global Affairs; BA in History/MA in History, Sociology or Anthropology/MA in Jazz History and Research; BA in Political Science/MA in Political Science; BS in Computer Science or Information Science/Master of Information Technology; BS in Accounting/Master of Accountancy (Governmental Accounting or Financial Accounting); BS in Accounting/MBA in Professional Accounting; BS in Finance/Master of Quantitative Finance; The College of Nursing offers a program on the New Brunswick Campus. Students are admitted in the fall semester only; BS in Nursing/MS in Nursing. **Credit/placement by examination:** AP, CLEP, IB, institutional tests. 24 credit hours maximum toward bachelor's degree. **Support services:** Learning center, pre-admission summer program, reduced course load, remedial instruction, study skills assistance, tutoring, writing center.

**Honors college/program.** By invitation.

**Majors. Area/ethnic studies:** African, African-American, American, Caribbean, Chicano/Hispanic-American/Latino, women's. **Biology:** General, botany, zoology. **Business:** Accounting, business admin, finance, marketing. **Communications:** Journalism. **Computer sciences:** Computer science, information systems. **Conservation:** General. **Engineering:** Biomedical, ceramic, chemical, civil, electrical, mechanical. **Foreign languages:** French, Spanish. **Health:** Clinical lab science, clinical lab technology, nursing (RN), predental, premedicine. **History:** General. **Interdisciplinary:** Science/society. **Legal studies:** Prelaw. **Math:** General, applied. **Philosophy/religion:** Philosophy. **Physical sciences:** Chemistry, geology, physics. **Protective services:** Criminal justice. **Psychology:** General. **Public administration:** Social work. **Social sciences:** Anthropology, economics, political science, sociology. **Visual/performing arts:** Art, dramatic.

**Most popular majors.** Biology 11%, business/marketing 32%, health sciences 16%, psychology 9%, security/protective services 9%, social sciences 7%.

**Computing on campus.** 450 workstations in dormitories, library, computer center. Dormitories linked to campus network. Commuter students can connect to campus network. Helpline, repair service available.

**Student life. Freshman orientation:** Available. **Housing:** Coed dorms, special housing for disabled, apartments, fraternity/sorority housing available. $100 deposit. **Activities:** Choral groups, drama, international student organizations, radio station, student government, student newspaper, black organization of students, Puerto Rican and Latin American student organizations, political organizations, religious organizations, service organizations.

**Athletics.** NCAA. **Intercollegiate:** Baseball M, basketball, soccer, softball W, tennis, volleyball. **Intramural:** Basketball, racquetball, soccer, tennis, volleyball. **Team name:** Scarlet Raiders.

**Student services.** Career counseling, student employment services, health services, personal counseling, placement for graduates, veterans' counselor. **Physically disabled:** Services for visually, speech, hearing impaired.

**Contact.** Phone: (973) 353-5205 Fax: (973) 353-1440
Bruce Neimeyer, Director of Admissions at Newark, Rutgers, The State University of New Jersey: Newark Regional Campus, 249 University Avenue, Newark, NJ 07102-1896

## Saint Peter's College
**Jersey City, New Jersey** — **CB member**
www.spc.edu — **CB code: 2806**

- Private 4-year liberal arts college affiliated with Roman Catholic Church
- Commuter campus in small city
- 2,322 degree-seeking undergraduates: 10% part-time, 57% women, 25% African American, 11% Asian American, 28% Hispanic American, 3% international
- 586 degree-seeking graduate students
- 49% of applicants admitted
- SAT or ACT (ACT writing optional), application essay required
- 52% graduate within 6 years

**General.** Founded in 1872. Regionally accredited. Extensive evening program on main campus, at branch locations at Englewood Cliffs and South Amboy for adult learners, and other locations throughout metropolitan area. **Degrees:** 419 bachelor's, 20 associate awarded; master's offered. **ROTC:**

Army, Air Force. **Location:** 3 miles from New York City. **Calendar:** Semester, extensive summer session. **Full-time faculty:** 115 total; 80% have terminal degrees, 10% minority, 46% women. **Part-time faculty:** 171 total; 26% have terminal degrees, 19% minority, 34% women. **Class size:** 61% < 20, 39% 20-39, less than 1% 40-49.

**Freshman class profile.** 6,547 applied, 3,181 admitted, 539 enrolled.

| Mid 50% test scores | | | |
|---|---|---|---|
| SAT critical reading: | 420-510 | GPA 2.0-2.99: | 34% |
| SAT math: | 420-530 | Rank in top quarter: | 41% |
| SAT writing: | 420-510 | Rank in top tenth: | 14% |
| ACT composite: | 17-24 | End year in good standing: | 74% |
| GPA 3.75 or higher: | 19% | Return as sophomores: | 76% |
| GPA 3.50-3.74: | 16% | Out-of-state: | 22% |
| GPA 3.0-3.49: | 30% | Live on campus: | 56% |
| | | International: | 2% |

**Basis for selection.** Admissions decision based on (in rank order) school achievement record, test scores, essay, letters of recommendation, class activities. Interview recommended.

**High school preparation.** 16 units required; 19 recommended. Required and recommended units include English 4, mathematics 3-4, history 2-3, science 2-3 (laboratory 1), foreign language 2 and academic electives 3.

**2009-2010 Annual costs.** Tuition/fees: $26,870. Room/board: $10,854. Books/supplies: $800. Personal expenses: $600.

**2008-2009 Financial aid. Need-based:** 575 full-time freshmen applied for aid; 480 were judged to have need; 480 of these received aid. Average need met was 80%. Average scholarship/grant was $18,601; average loan $3,251. 76% of total undergraduate aid awarded as scholarships/grants, 24% as loans/jobs. **Non-need-based:** Awarded to 440 full-time undergraduates, including 141 freshmen. Scholarships awarded for academics, athletics. **Additional information:** Cooperative education internships available in all majors, with average salaries exceeding $5,200.

**Application procedures. Admission:** Priority date 4/1; no deadline. No application fee. Admission notification on a rolling basis beginning on or about 11/1. **Financial aid:** Priority date 3/15; no closing date. FAFSA required. Applicants notified on a rolling basis starting 2/15; must reply by 5/1 or within 2 week(s) of notification.

**Academics.** Joint Pre-Med/MD program with UMDNJ, joint Pre-Law/Law and Occupational Therapy program with Seton Hall University, joint Pharmacy and Physical Therapy program with Rutgers University, joint Engineering Program with New Jersey Institute of Technology. **Special study options:** Accelerated study, combined bachelor's/graduate degree, cooperative education, double major, dual enrollment of high school students, exchange student, honors, independent study, internships, liberal arts/career combination, student-designed major, study abroad, teacher certification program, Washington semester. Joint degree in clinical laboratory sciences with University of Medicine and Dentistry of New Jersey. **Credit/placement by examination:** AP, CLEP, IB, institutional tests. 30 credit hours maximum toward bachelor's degree. **Support services:** Learning center, pre-admission summer program, reduced course load, remedial instruction, study skills assistance, tutoring, writing center.

**Majors. Area/ethnic studies:** American. **Biology:** General, biochemistry, toxicology. **Business:** Accounting, actuarial science, banking/financial services, business admin, international, management information systems, managerial economics. **Communications:** General. **Computer sciences:** General, computer science, information systems, programming. **Education:** Elementary. **Foreign languages:** General, classics, Spanish. **Health:** Clinical lab science, cytotechnology, nursing (RN). **History:** General. **Interdisciplinary:** Biological/physical sciences. **Math:** General. **Philosophy/religion:** Philosophy, religion. **Physical sciences:** Chemistry, physics. **Psychology:** General. **Public administration:** Policy analysis. **Social sciences:** General, economics, political science, sociology, urban studies. **Visual/performing arts:** Studio arts.

**Most popular majors.** Biology 7%, business/marketing 34%, education 8%, health sciences 8%, security/protective services 11%, social sciences 6%.

**Computing on campus.** 225 workstations in dormitories, library, computer center, student center. Dormitories wired for high-speed internet access and linked to campus network. Commuter students can connect to campus network. Online library, helpline, student web hosting, wireless network available.

**Student life. Freshman orientation:** Mandatory, $200 fee. Preregistration for classes offered. Three-day sessions held throughout July. Program features academic advising, social activities, and introduction to community service. **Housing:** Guaranteed on-campus for all undergraduates. Coed dorms, special housing for disabled, apartments available. $200 partly refundable deposit, deadline 5/1. **Activities:** Choral groups, drama, international student organizations, literary magazine, radio station, student government, student newspaper, Alpha Phi Omega, Emmaus Spiritual Retreats, Circle K, Young Republicans, Hispanic culture club, Irish American club, Asian American student union, Black Action Committee, Indo-Pak culture club.

**Athletics.** NCAA. **Intercollegiate:** Baseball M, basketball, bowling, cheerleading, cross-country, diving, golf M, soccer, softball W, swimming, tennis, track and field, volleyball W. **Intramural:** Baseball M, basketball, bowling, racquetball, soccer, softball, swimming, table tennis, tennis, volleyball, water polo. **Team name:** Peacocks/Peahens.

**Student services.** Adult student services, alcohol/substance abuse counseling, chaplain/spiritual director, career counseling, services for economically disadvantaged, student employment services, financial aid counseling, health services, minority student services, personal counseling, placement for graduates, veterans' counselor. **Physically disabled:** Services for visually, speech, hearing impaired.

**Contact.** E-mail: admissions@spc.edu
Phone: (201) 761-7100 Toll-free number: (888) 772-9933
Fax: (201) 761-7105
Joe Giglio, Executive Director of Admission and Enrollment Marketing, Saint Peter's College, 2641 Kennedy Boulevard, Jersey City, NJ 07306

## Seton Hall University
**South Orange, New Jersey**      **CB member**
**www.shu.edu**      **CB code: 2811**

- Private 4-year university affiliated with Roman Catholic Church
- Residential campus in large town
- 4,972 degree-seeking undergraduates: 6% part-time, 58% women, 14% African American, 7% Asian American, 12% Hispanic American, 2% international
- 4,079 degree-seeking graduate students
- 79% of applicants admitted
- SAT or ACT with writing, application essay required
- 61% graduate within 6 years

**General.** Founded in 1856. Regionally accredited. Immaculate Conception Seminary and School of Theology located on campus. Off-campus sites for nursing and education. **Degrees:** 1,017 bachelor's awarded; master's, doctoral, professional offered. **ROTC:** Army. **Location:** 14 miles from New York City. **Calendar:** Semester, extensive summer session. **Full-time faculty:** 460 total; 88% have terminal degrees, 48% women. **Part-time faculty:** 419 total; 48% women. **Class size:** 45% < 20, 49% 20-39, 3% 40-49, 2% 50-99, less than 1% >100. **Special facilities:** Computer graphics and communications laboratories, educational media center, nursing demonstration room, art center, music laboratories, special collections center.

**Freshman class profile.** 10,851 applied, 8,602 admitted, 1,139 enrolled.

| Mid 50% test scores | | GPA 2.0-2.99: | 38% |
|---|---|---|---|
| SAT critical reading: | 470-570 | Rank in top quarter: | 50% |
| SAT math: | 470-580 | Rank in top tenth: | 22% |
| SAT writing: | 480-580 | Return as sophomores: | 82% |
| ACT composite: | 20-25 | Out-of-state: | 29% |
| GPA 3.75 or higher: | 13% | Live on campus: | 72% |
| GPA 3.50-3.74: | 15% | International: | 1% |
| GPA 3.0-3.49: | 33% | | |

**Basis for selection.** School achievement record, test scores, recommendations, essay most important. Extracurricular activities, volunteer work, work experience important. Class rank, interview, talent/ability, character/personal qualities considered. Interview strongly recommended. Audition required for music majors. **Homeschooled:** Statement describing homeschool structure and mission required. Must submit GED (total score of at least 225 with no individual score below 45) and copy of homeschool curriculum with list of textbooks used for each of the major unit requirements.

**High school preparation.** College-preparatory program required. 16 units required. Required units include English 4, mathematics 3, social studies 2, science 1 (laboratory 1), foreign language 2 and academic electives 4. Nursing majors must have additional 2 units in science (biology and chemistry).

**2010-2011 Annual costs.** Tuition/fees: $31,890. Room/board: $12,050.

**2008-2009 Financial aid. Non-need-based:** Scholarships awarded for academics, alumni affiliation, athletics, minority status, ROTC, state residency.

**Application procedures. Admission:** Priority date 3/1; no deadline. $55 fee, may be waived for applicants with need. Admission notification on a rolling basis beginning on or about 12/1. Must reply by May 1 or within 4 week(s) if notified thereafter. **Financial aid:** Priority date 2/15; no closing date. FAFSA required. Applicants notified on a rolling basis starting 3/1; must reply by 5/1 or within 4 week(s) of notification.

**Academics. Special study options:** Accelerated study, combined bachelor's/graduate degree, cooperative education, cross-registration, distance learning, double major, dual enrollment of high school students, ESL, honors, independent study, internships, liberal arts/career combination, study abroad, teacher certification program, Washington semester. **Credit/placement by examination:** AP, CLEP, IB, SAT, institutional tests. 30 credit hours maximum toward bachelor's degree. **Support services:** Pre-admission summer program, reduced course load, remedial instruction, study skills assistance, tutoring, writing center.

**Majors. Area/ethnic studies:** African-American, Asian, Latin American. **Biology:** General, biochemistry. **Business:** Accounting, business admin, finance, information resources management, labor relations, management information systems, managerial economics, marketing. **Communications:** General, journalism, public relations, radio/tv. **Computer sciences:** General. **Conservation:** Environmental studies. **Education:** Art, early childhood, elementary, secondary, special. **Foreign languages:** General, classics, French, Italian, Spanish. **Health:** Nursing (RN). **History:** General. **Liberal arts:** Arts/sciences, humanities. **Math:** General. **Parks/recreation:** Sports admin. **Philosophy/religion:** Christian, philosophy, religion. **Physical sciences:** Chemistry, physics. **Protective services:** Criminal justice. **Psychology:** General. **Public administration:** Social work. **Social sciences:** Anthropology, economics, international relations, political science, sociology. **Theology:** Religious ed, theology. **Visual/performing arts:** General, art history/conservation, commercial/advertising art, dramatic, music history, music performance, theater arts management.

**Most popular majors.** Biology 6%, business/marketing 19%, communications/journalism 6%, education 8%, health sciences 12%, liberal arts 8%, social sciences 11%.

**Computing on campus.** PC or laptop required. 350 workstations in dormitories, library, computer center, student center. Dormitories wired for high-speed internet access and linked to campus network. Online course registration, online library, helpline, repair service, student web hosting, wireless network available.

**Student life. Freshman orientation:** Mandatory, $300 fee. Preregistration for classes offered. 2-day program held at various times from June through July. **Policies:** 1.8 GPA housing requirement. **Housing:** Coed dorms, special housing for disabled, apartments, wellness housing available. $250 deposit, deadline 5/1. **Activities:** Pep band, campus ministries, choral groups, drama, international student organizations, radio station, student government, student newspaper, TV station, Adelante, black students union, community service organizations, Puerto Rican Institute, Amnesty International, student ambassadors.

**Athletics.** NCAA. **Intercollegiate:** Baseball M, basketball, cross-country, golf, soccer, softball W, swimming, tennis W, volleyball W. **Intramural:** Basketball, football (non-tackle), racquetball, soccer, softball, tennis, volleyball. **Team name:** Pirates.

**Student services.** Alcohol/substance abuse counseling, chaplain/spiritual director, career counseling, services for economically disadvantaged, student employment services, financial aid counseling, health services, minority student services, personal counseling, placement for graduates. **Physically disabled:** Services for visually, speech, hearing impaired.

**Contact.** E-mail: thehall@shu.edu
Phone: (973) 313-6146 Toll-free number: (800) 843-4255
Fax: (973) 275-2040
Peter Nacy, Assistant Vice President for Admissions, Seton Hall University, 400 South Orange Avenue, South Orange, NJ 07079-2680

## Somerset Christian College
**Zarephath, New Jersey**
**www.somerset.edu**      **CB code: 3933**

- Private 4-year Bible and liberal arts college affiliated with Pillar of Fire International
- Commuter campus in small town
- 242 degree-seeking undergraduates
- SAT or ACT with writing, application essay required

**General.** Candidate for regional accreditation.; also accredited by ABHE. **Degrees:** 10 bachelor's, 8 associate awarded. **Location:** 45 miles from New York City and Philadelphia. **Calendar:** Semester, limited summer session.

**Full-time faculty:** 5 total. **Part-time faculty:** 4 total. **Class size:** 48% < 20, 52% 20-39.

**Basis for selection.** Recommendations most important. High school record, standardized test scores, essay also important. **Homeschooled:** Interview, letter of recommendation (nonparent) required. Transcript of study including subjects, grades and GPA required. Students must send proof of graduation date or GED scores. **Learning Disabled:** Students must have documented diagnosis and portfolio of prior school collaboration in accommodating students' learning disabilities.

**High school preparation.** 15 units required. Required units include English 4, mathematics 1, social studies 3, science 2, foreign language 2 and academic electives 3.

**2009-2010 Annual costs.** Tuition/fees: $11,294. Personal expenses: $1,120.

**Financial aid.** All financial aid based on need.

**Application procedures. Admission:** Closing date 8/30 (postmark date). $35 fee, may be waived for applicants with need. Application must be submitted online. Admission notification on a rolling basis. **Financial aid:** No deadline. FAFSA required. Applicants notified on a rolling basis starting 1/31.

**Academics. Special study options:** Distance learning, dual enrollment of high school students, independent study, internships. **Credit/placement by examination:** AP, CLEP, IB, institutional tests. **Support services:** Learning center, reduced course load, remedial instruction, study skills assistance, tutoring, writing center.

**Majors. Philosophy/religion:** Christian. **Theology:** Bible.

**Computing on campus.** 30 workstations in library, computer center. Online course registration, online library, wireless network available.

**Student life. Freshman orientation:** Mandatory. Preregistration for classes offered. **Policies:** Religious observance required. **Activities:** Student government, student newspaper.

**Student services.** Chaplain/spiritual director, career counseling, financial aid counseling.

**Contact.** E-mail: info@somerset.edu
Phone: (732) 356-1595 Toll-free number: (800) 234-9305
Fax: (732) 356-4846
Rich Valdes, Director of Admissions, Somerset Christian College, 10 College Way, Zarephath, NJ 08890

---

## Stevens Institute of Technology
**Hoboken, New Jersey**  **CB member**
**www.stevens.edu**  **CB code: 2819**

- Private 4-year university and engineering college
- Residential campus in small city
- 2,234 degree-seeking undergraduates: 26% women
- 3,623 degree-seeking graduate students
- 51% of applicants admitted
- SAT or ACT (ACT writing optional), application essay, interview required
- 76% graduate within 6 years; 24% enter graduate study

**General.** Founded in 1870. Regionally accredited. **Degrees:** 419 bachelor's awarded; master's, doctoral offered. **ROTC:** Army, Air Force. **Location:** One mile from New York City. **Calendar:** Semester, extensive summer session. **Full-time faculty:** 251 total; 90% have terminal degrees, 13% minority, 18% women. **Part-time faculty:** 187 total. **Class size:** 43% < 20, 47% 20-39, 4% 40-49, 4% 50-99, 2% >100. **Special facilities:** Laboratory for coastal, ocean and naval engineering, environmental laboratory, design and manufacturing institute, advanced telecommunications institute, geoenvironmental laboratory, optical communications lab, quantum cascade laser, center for mass spectrometry, center for microchemical systems, computer visualization laboratory.

**Freshman class profile.** 2,972 applied, 1,514 admitted, 561 enrolled.

| Mid 50% test scores | | | |
|---|---|---|---|
| SAT critical reading: | 550-650 | Rank in top quarter: | 85% |
| SAT math: | 620-710 | Rank in top tenth: | 58% |
| SAT writing: | 540-650 | Return as sophomores: | 90% |
| ACT composite: | 24-29 | Out-of-state: | 38% |
| GPA 3.75 or higher: | 57% | Live on campus: | 91% |
| GPA 3.50-3.74: | 23% | International: | 2% |
| GPA 3.0-3.49: | 18% | Fraternities: | 27% |
| GPA 2.0-2.99: | 2% | Sororities: | 26% |

**Basis for selection.** GED not accepted. Admissions committee meets to review applicant's file once official transcript and standardized test scores received and interview requirement completed. Other information submitted considered as well. SAT Subject Tests required for accelerated premed, predentistry, or prelaw programs and recommended for all others. Students who live outside 250-mile radius and are unable to visit campus may schedule phone interview. Additional interview with departmental committee required of applicants to accelerated premed, predentistry, and prelaw programs. **Homeschooled:** Letter of recommendation (nonparent) required.

**High school preparation.** College-preparatory program required. 16 units required. Required and recommended units include English 4, mathematics 4, social studies 2, history 2, science 3-4 (laboratory 3-4), foreign language 2 and academic electives 4. Business, engineering, computer science, and applied science programs require 2 algebra, 1 geometry, 1 pre-calculus or calculus, 1 chemistry, 1 physics, 1 biology.

**2009-2010 Annual costs.** Tuition/fees: $38,600. Room/board: $12,150. Books/supplies: $900. Personal expenses: $750.

**2009-2010 Financial aid. Non-need-based:** Scholarships awarded for academics, leadership, music/drama, ROTC.

**Application procedures. Admission:** Priority date 11/15; deadline 2/1 (postmark date). $55 fee, may be waived for applicants with need, free for online applicants. Admission notification 4/1. Must reply by May 1 or within 2 week(s) if notified thereafter. **Financial aid:** Priority date 2/15; no closing date. FAFSA required. Applicants notified on a rolling basis starting 3/30; must reply by 5/1 or within 2 week(s) of notification.

**Academics. Special study options:** Accelerated study, combined bachelor's/graduate degree, cooperative education, cross-registration, distance learning, double major, dual enrollment of high school students, honors, independent study, internships, study abroad. 4-year bachelor's/master's programs in all engineering and science disciplines; dual enrollment program with New York University. **Credit/placement by examination:** AP, CLEP, IB. **Support services:** Pre-admission summer program, reduced course load, remedial instruction, study skills assistance, tutoring, writing center.

**Majors. Biology:** Biochemistry, bioinformatics. **Business:** Business admin, management information systems. **Computer sciences:** General, networking, security. **Engineering:** General, biomedical, chemical, civil, computer, electrical, environmental, materials science, mechanical, physics. **Engineering technology:** Industrial management. **History:** General. **Interdisciplinary:** Math/computer science. **Liberal arts:** Arts/sciences. **Math:** Applied. **Philosophy/religion:** Philosophy. **Physical sciences:** Chemistry, physics. **Other:** Music and technology, Quantitative finance.

**Most popular majors.** Biology 8%, business/marketing 13%, engineering/engineering technologies 68%.

**Computing on campus.** PC or laptop required. 500 workstations in dormitories, library, computer center, student center. Dormitories wired for high-speed internet access and linked to campus network. Commuter students can connect to campus network. Online course registration, online library, helpline, repair service, student web hosting, wireless network available.

**Student life. Freshman orientation:** Mandatory, $500 fee. Preregistration for classes offered. 3-day program. **Policies:** Honor system observed. Freshmen not living at home must live on campus. **Housing:** Guaranteed on-campus for all undergraduates. Coed dorms, single-sex dorms, apartments, fraternity/sorority housing, wellness housing available. $350 nonrefundable deposit, deadline 6/15. **Activities:** Bands, campus ministries, choral groups, dance, drama, international student organizations, literary magazine, music ensembles, musical theater, radio station, student government, student newspaper, TV station, over 70 organizations.

**Athletics.** NCAA. **Intercollegiate:** Baseball M, basketball, cross-country, equestrian W, fencing, field hockey W, golf M, lacrosse, soccer, softball W, swimming, tennis, track and field, volleyball, wrestling M. **Intramural:** Archery, badminton, basketball, cricket, football (non-tackle), lacrosse M, racquetball, soccer, softball, squash, tennis, volleyball. **Team name:** Ducks.

**Student services.** Alcohol/substance abuse counseling, chaplain/spiritual director, career counseling, services for economically disadvantaged, student employment services, financial aid counseling, health services, minority student services, personal counseling, placement for graduates, veterans' counselor, women's services. **Physically disabled:** Services for visually, speech, hearing impaired.

**Contact.** E-mail: admissions@stevens.edu
Phone: (201) 216-5194 Toll-free number: (800) 458-5323
Fax: (201) 216-8348
Daniel Gallagher, Dean of University Admissions, Stevens Institute of Technology, 1 Castle Point on Hudson, Hoboken, NJ 07030

## Talmudical Academy of New Jersey
### Adelphia, New Jersey
CB code: 0686

▶ Private 4-year rabbinical college for men affiliated with Jewish faith
▶ Large town

**General.** Founded in 1967. Accredited by AARTS. **Calendar:** Semester.

**Contact.** Phone: (732) 431-1600
Registrar and Admissions Director, Route 524, PO Box 7, Adelphia, NJ 07710

## Thomas Edison State College
### Trenton, New Jersey
CB member
www.tesc.edu
CB code: 0682

▶ Public 4-year liberal arts college
▶ Small city
▶ 17,320 degree-seeking undergraduates: 100% part-time, 38% women
▶ 886 degree-seeking graduate students

**General.** Founded in 1972. Regionally accredited. **Degrees:** 1,970 bachelor's, 454 associate awarded; master's offered. **Location:** 45 miles from Philadelphia, 76 miles from New York City. **Calendar:** Continuous.

**Basis for selection.** Open admission, but selective for some programs. Applicants should be at least 21 years old. Certain programs in health professions limited to persons holding appropriate certification. Admission to bachelor's degree nursing program limited to registered nurses (RNs) currently licensed in the USA. Admission to Master of Arts in Educational Leadership degree limited to person with valid Teacher's Certificate. Applicants under the age of 21 may be accepted on case-by-case basis, or if they are member of a special population such as a corporate partner or member of U.S. military.

**2009-2010 Annual costs.** Tuition/fees: $4,695; $6,720 out-of-state. Two tuition plans available. Comprehensive Tuition Plan: covers up to 36 credits per year for all credit-earning options, at $4,695 per year for in-state students and military personnel, $6,720 for out-of-state students; Enrolled Options Plan: $1,390 per year (state residents and military personnel), $2,520 (out-of-state), and $3,440 (international) for annual enrollment tuition and a technology services fee ($103); tests, portfolios, courses and other fees at additional cost.

**2008-2009 Financial aid. Need-based:** 20% of total undergraduate aid awarded as scholarships/grants, 80% as loans/jobs. **Additional information:** Financial aid applications should be received two months before each new term begins.

**Application procedures. Admission:** No deadline. $75 fee. Admission notification on a rolling basis. **Financial aid:** No deadline. FAFSA, institutional form required. Applicants notified on a rolling basis; must reply within 4 week(s) of notification.

**Academics.** Provides flexibility to complete degree, including credit by examination, assessment of experiential learning, guided study, online courses, e-pack courses and credit for licenses and certificates, corporate and military training. Contracts with subject matter experts to act as mentors to academic units of college. **Special study options:** Combined bachelor's/graduate degree, distance learning, dual enrollment of high school students, external degree, independent study, student-designed major. Bachelor of Science in Health Sciences program offered in partnership with University of Medicine and Dentistry of New Jersey School of Health-Related Professions. The 121-credit program is designed for those employed in the allied health field and requires students to possess professional certifications and licensures. **Credit/placement by examination:** CLEP. 60 credit hours maximum toward associate degree, 120 toward bachelor's.

**Majors. Agriculture:** Horticulture. **Biology:** General. **Business:** Accounting, business admin, entrepreneurial studies, finance, hospitality admin, human resources, international, labor relations, marketing, operations, real estate. **Communications:** General, journalism. **Computer sciences:** Computer science. **Conservation:** Environmental science, environmental studies, forestry. **Engineering technology:** Architectural drafting, biomedical, civil, construction, electrical, manufacturing, mechanical, nuclear, surveying. **Family/consumer sciences:** Child care. **Foreign languages:** General. **Health:** Clinical lab science, cytotechnology, dental hygiene, facilities admin, health services, medical radiologic technology/radiation therapy, nuclear medical technology, nursing (RN), perfusion technology, public health ed, radiation protection, respiratory therapy technology, veterinary technology/assistant. **History:** General. **Interdisciplinary:** Gerontology, natural sciences. **Legal studies:** Paralegal. **Liberal arts:** Arts/sciences, humanities. **Math:** General. **Mechanic/repair:** Aircraft. **Parks/recreation:** General. **Philosophy/religion:** Philosophy, religion. **Protective services:** Criminal justice, fire safety technology, law enforcement admin. **Psychology:** General. **Public administration:** General, community org/advocacy, human services. **Social sciences:** General, anthropology, economics, political science, sociology. **Transportation:** Air traffic control. **Visual/performing arts:** Art, dramatic, photography. **Other:** Aviation flight technology, Computer information systems, Emergency disaster services/Homeland Security, Engineering graphics, Imaging science, Kitchen and bath design.

**Most popular majors.** Business/marketing 14%, engineering/engineering technologies 15%, health sciences 9%, liberal arts 25%, psychology 6%, social sciences 7%.

**Computing on campus.** Commuter students can connect to campus network. Online course registration, online library, wireless network available.

**Student life. Activities:** Student newspaper.

**Student services.** Adult student services, financial aid counseling, veterans' counselor. **Physically disabled:** Services for visually, hearing impaired.

**Contact.** E-mail: admissions@tesc.edu
Phone: (888) 442-8372 Toll-free number: (888) 442-8372
Fax: (609) 984-8447
David Hoftiezer, Director, Admissions, Thomas Edison State College, 101 West State Street, Trenton, NJ 08608-1176

## University of Medicine and Dentistry of New Jersey: School of Health Related Professions
### Newark, New Jersey
www.shrp.umdnj.edu
CB code: 0598

▶ Public two-year upper-division health science college
▶ Commuter campus in large city
▶ Application essay, interview required

**General.** Founded in 1976. Regionally accredited. Courses offered through videoconferencing in Newark, Scotch Plains, and Stratford. Possible opppurtunity to cross-enroll in courses offered by other schools within UMDNJ. **Degrees:** 100 bachelor's, 80 associate awarded; master's offered. **Location:** 15 miles from New York City. **Calendar:** Semester, limited summer session. **Full-time faculty:** 110 total. **Part-time faculty:** 20 total.

**Student profile.** 525 degree-seeking undergraduates.

**Basis for selection.** Open admission. College transcript, application essay, interview required. Admission requirements vary per program; transfer applicants evaluated by faculty and associate dean. Minimum GPA and interview most important; health-related experience and letters of recommendation also important. Qualified minority, disabled and disadvantaged students encouraged to apply. Application procedures and closing dates vary per program. Transfer accepted as sophomores, juniors, seniors.

**2009-2010 Annual costs.** Books/supplies: $1,000.

**Application procedures. Admission:** Rolling admission. $75 fee. **Financial aid:** FAFSA, institutional form required.

**Academics. Special study options:** Accelerated study, combined bachelor's/graduate degree, cross-registration, distance learning, double major, dual enrollment of high school students, independent study, internships, liberal arts/career combination, student-designed major. **Credit/placement by examination:** CLEP, IB, institutional tests. Maximum of half of graduation requirement credits for professional component may be earned by examination.

**Majors. Health:** Clinical lab science, cytotechnology, dental hygiene, health services, medical radiologic technology/radiation therapy, nuclear medical technology, respiratory therapy technology, sonography.

**Computing on campus.** Commuter students can connect to campus network. Online course registration, online library, helpline, repair service available.

**Student life. Housing:** Coed dorms available. **Activities:** Student professional organizations.

**Student services.** Career counseling, services for economically disadvantaged, health services, personal counseling.

**Contact.** E-mail: shrpadm@umdnj.edu
Phone: (973) 972-5454 Fax: (973) 972-7463
Brian Lewis, Assistant Dean for Enrollment Services, University of Medicine and Dentistry of New Jersey: School of Health Related Professions, 65 Bergen Street, Newark, NJ 07101-1709

---

## University of Medicine and Dentistry of New Jersey: School of Nursing
**Newark, New Jersey**
www.sn.umdnj.edu                     CB code: 0769

- Public 4-year nursing college
- Commuter campus in large city
- 390 degree-seeking undergraduates

**General.** Founded in 1992. Regionally accredited. **Degrees:** 200 bachelor's awarded; master's offered. **Location:** 10 miles from New York City. **Calendar:** Semester, extensive summer session.

**Basis for selection.** Each program has established criteria for admissions. Minimum GPA and interview most important. Nursing and health related experiences and letters of recommendation also important. Qualified minority, handicapped, and disadvantaged students encouraged to apply. Essay, interview recommended.

**High school preparation.** Specific high school course requirements vary by program.

**2009-2010 Annual costs.** Tuition/fees: $13,302; $17,652 out-of-state. Costs vary by program; costs cited are for BSN program. Additional insurance fee ($2,065) for students not covered by equivalent plan.

**Application procedures. Admission:** No deadline. $50 fee. Admission notification on a rolling basis. Closing date varies for each program. **Financial aid:** Priority date 3/1; no closing date. Applicants notified on a rolling basis.

**Academics. Special study options:** Accelerated study, combined bachelor's/graduate degree, double major, independent study. 3 joint degree programs: AS in nursing with Middlesex County College and BSN with Ramapo College of NJ and New Jersey Institute of Technology, MS in nursing transition option for registered nurses. **Credit/placement by examination:** CLEP. **Support services:** Reduced course load, tutoring.

**Computing on campus.** Commuter students can connect to campus network. Online library, helpline, repair service, wireless network available.

**Student life. Housing:** Coed dorms available. **Activities:** Student government, student newspaper, Student professional organizations by nursing specialty.

**Student services.** Health services, personal counseling. **Physically disabled:** Services for visually, hearing impaired.

**Contact.** E-mail: snadmissions@umdnj.edu
Phone: (973) 972-5336 Fax: (973) 972-7453
Brian Lewis, Assistant Dean of Enrollment Services, University of Medicine and Dentistry of New Jersey: School of Nursing, 65 Bergen Street Room 149, Newark, NJ 07101-1709

---

## William Paterson University of New Jersey
**Wayne, New Jersey**                     CB member
www.wpunj.edu                     CB code: 2518

- Public 4-year university and liberal arts college
- Commuter campus in large town

---

- 9,055 degree-seeking undergraduates: 15% part-time, 55% women, 14% African American, 6% Asian American, 19% Hispanic American, 1% international
- 858 degree-seeking graduate students
- 65% of applicants admitted
- SAT or ACT (ACT writing optional) required
- 51% graduate within 6 years

**General.** Founded in 1855. Regionally accredited. **Degrees:** 1,534 bachelor's awarded; master's offered. **ROTC:** Air Force. **Location:** 20 miles from New York City. **Calendar:** Semester, limited summer session. **Full-time faculty:** 371 total; 93% have terminal degrees, 34% minority, 47% women. **Part-time faculty:** 571 total. **Class size:** 48% < 20, 49% 20-39, 2% 40-49, less than 1% 50-99, less than 1% >100. **Special facilities:** 5 Silicon Graphics Iris workstations, satellite uplink and downlink capabilities, 2 theaters.

**Freshman class profile.** 6,969 applied, 4,552 admitted, 1,453 enrolled.

| Mid 50% test scores | | Rank in top tenth: | 9% |
|---|---|---|---|
| SAT critical reading: | 440-530 | Return as sophomores: | 78% |
| SAT math: | 450-550 | Out-of-state: | 3% |
| Rank in top quarter: | 29% | Live on campus: | 48% |

**Basis for selection.** School record and test score most important; recommendations also important; class rank and essay considered. Audition required for music programs; portfolio required for art programs. Essays recommended. **Homeschooled:** Transcript of courses and grades, state high school equivalency certificate required.

**High school preparation.** College-preparatory program required. 16 units required. Required units include English 4, mathematics 3, social studies 2, science 2 (laboratory 2) and academic electives 5. Five additional college preparatory courses (advanced math, literature, foreign language, social science) also required.

**2009-2010 Annual costs.** Tuition/fees: $10,838; $17,592 out-of-state. Room/board: $9,480. Books/supplies: $1,300. Personal expenses: $2,300.

**2009-2010 Financial aid. Non-need-based:** Scholarships awarded for academics, alumni affiliation, music/drama.

**Application procedures. Admission:** Priority date 4/1; deadline 5/1 (postmark date). $50 fee, may be waived for applicants with need. Admission notification on a rolling basis beginning on or about 10/1. Must reply by May 1 or within 2 week(s) if notified thereafter. **Financial aid:** Priority date 4/1; no closing date. FAFSA required. Applicants notified on a rolling basis starting 3/15.

**Academics.** Honors programs available in biopsychology, humanities, cognitive science, life science and environmental ethics, music, nursing, performing and literary arts. **Special study options:** Accelerated study, combined bachelor's/graduate degree, cross-registration, distance learning, double major, dual enrollment of high school students, ESL, exchange student, honors, independent study, internships, study abroad, teacher certification program, Washington semester. Cluster courses (program that provides opportunities for students and faculty to study and learn together in courses grouped in interdisciplinary clusters of three). **Credit/placement by examination:** AP, CLEP, SAT, ACT, institutional tests. 90 credit hours maximum toward bachelor's degree. **Support services:** Learning center, pre-admission summer program, reduced course load, remedial instruction, study skills assistance, tutoring, writing center.

**Honors college/program.** Generally, students accepted with 1200 SAT (math and reading) and solid B+ or above high school average. About 100 first-year students admitted to each year.

**Majors. Area/ethnic studies:** African, African-American, Caribbean, French, Latin American, women's. **Biology:** General, biotechnology. **Business:** Accounting, business admin, finance, international finance, managerial economics. **Communications:** General. **Computer sciences:** General, computer science. **Conservation:** General, environmental science. **Education:** General, art, early childhood, elementary, health, kindergarten/preschool, mathematics, music, physical, special. **Foreign languages:** French, Spanish. **Health:** Nursing (RN), public health nursing, speech pathology. **History:** General. **Math:** General. **Parks/recreation:** Exercise sciences. **Philosophy/religion:** Philosophy. **Physical sciences:** Chemistry. **Psychology:** General. **Social sciences:** Anthropology, economics, geography, political science, sociology. **Visual/performing arts:** Art, jazz, music management, music performance.

**Most popular majors.** Business/marketing 21%, communications/journalism 11%, education 15%, English 7%, health sciences 6%, psychology 11%, social sciences 10%, visual/performing arts 6%.

**Computing on campus.** 700 workstations in dormitories, library, computer center. Dormitories wired for high-speed internet access and linked to campus network. Commuter students can connect to campus network. On-line course registration, online library, helpline, student web hosting, wireless network available.

**Student life. Freshman orientation:** Mandatory, $75 fee. Two-day program held twice in early summer. Freshmen and parents invited to stay overnight for nominal fee. **Housing:** Guaranteed on-campus for all undergraduates. Coed dorms, special housing for disabled, apartments, wellness housing available. $150 nonrefundable deposit, deadline 4/1. Hall reserved for students 21-and-older, apartment-style housing, women's floor, academic interest housing available. **Activities:** Bands, campus ministries, choral groups, dance, drama, film society, international student organizations, literary magazine, music ensembles, Model UN, radio station, student government, student newspaper, TV station, black student association, Christian Fellowship club, Jewish student association, Feminist Collective, organization of Latin American students, United Asian Americans, coalition of lesbians/gays/friends.

**Athletics.** NCAA. **Intercollegiate:** Baseball M, basketball, field hockey W, football (tackle) M, soccer, softball W, swimming, volleyball W. **Intramural:** Basketball, field hockey W, soccer W, softball, volleyball. **Team name:** Pioneers.

**Student services.** Adult student services, alcohol/substance abuse counseling, chaplain/spiritual director, career counseling, services for economically disadvantaged, student employment services, financial aid counseling, health services, legal services, minority student services, on-campus daycare, personal counseling, placement for graduates, veterans' counselor, women's services. **Physically disabled:** Services for visually, speech, hearing impaired.

**Contact.** E-mail: admissions@wpunj.edu
Phone: (973) 720-2125 Toll-free number: (877) 978-3923
Fax: (973) 720-2910
Colleen O'Connor, Director of Admissions, William Paterson University of New Jersey, 300 Pompton Road, Wayne, NJ 07470

# New Mexico

## Art Center Design College
**Albuquerque, New Mexico**
www.theartcenter.edu

CB code: 3039

- For-profit 4-year visual arts college
- Commuter campus in very large city
- 274 degree-seeking undergraduates: 53% part-time, 60% women
- SAT or ACT (ACT writing optional), application essay, interview required

**General. Degrees:** 23 bachelor's awarded. **Calendar:** Semester, extensive summer session. **Full-time faculty:** 8 total. **Part-time faculty:** 25 total.

**Freshman class profile.**

| Mid 50% test scores | | | |
|---|---|---|---|
| SAT critical reading: | 450-520 | SAT math: | 370-450 |
| | | ACT composite: | 17-23 |

**Basis for selection.** High school transcripts (GED accepted), ACT or SAT scores, essay, interview, personal statement form, and art work for illustration, animation, fine arts and graphic design programs. Applications accepted based on an evaluation of strengths, academic preparedness and communication skills. **Homeschooled:** Transcript of courses and grades required.

**High school preparation.** College-preparatory program recommended.

**2009-2010 Annual costs.** Tuition/fees: $16,680. Books/supplies: $1,250. Personal expenses: $3,204.

**2009-2010 Financial aid. Non-need-based:** Scholarships awarded for academics.

**Application procedures. Admission:** No deadline. $25 fee. Admission notification on a rolling basis. **Financial aid:** FAFSA required.

**Academics. Special study options:** Double major, independent study, internships, liberal arts/career combination. **Credit/placement by examination:** AP, CLEP, IB, SAT, ACT, institutional tests. **Support services:** Learning center, reduced course load, remedial instruction, study skills assistance, tutoring, writing center.

**Majors. Business:** Marketing. **Communications:** Advertising. **Communications technology:** Animation/special effects. **Visual/performing arts:** Graphic design, illustration, interior design, photography, studio arts.

**Computing on campus.** Online course registration, online library, student web hosting, wireless network available.

**Student life. Freshman orientation:** Mandatory. Preregistration for classes offered.

**Student services.** Adult student services, career counseling, student employment services, financial aid counseling, personal counseling, placement for graduates, veterans' counselor.

**Contact.** E-mail: inquire@theartcenter.edu
Phone: (505) 254-7575 Toll-free number: (800) 825-8753
Fax: (505) 254-4754
Cindy Whitaker, Director of Admissions, Art Center Design College, 5000 Marble Avenue NE, Albuquerque, NM 87119

## College of Santa Fe
**Santa Fe, New Mexico**
www.csf.edu

CB member
CB code: 4676

- Private 4-year visual arts college
- Residential campus in small city
- 650 undergraduates
- 99% of applicants admitted
- SAT or ACT with writing, application essay, interview required

**General.** Founded in 1947. Regionally accredited. **Degrees:** 194 bachelor's awarded; master's offered. **Location:** 60 miles from Albuquerque. **Calendar:** Semester, limited summer session. **Full-time faculty:** 75 total. **Part-time faculty:** 105 total. **Class size:** 89% < 20, 10% 20-39, less than 1% 40-49, less than 1% 50-99. **Special facilities:** Sound stages for film and video, visual arts center, theater center with two stages, digital arts laboratory, recording studios.

**Freshman class profile.** 557 applied, 551 admitted, 165 enrolled.

| Mid 50% test scores | | | |
|---|---|---|---|
| SAT critical reading: | 510-650 | GPA 3.0-3.49: | 36% |
| SAT math: | 460-580 | GPA 2.0-2.99: | 32% |
| SAT writing: | 500-640 | Rank in top quarter: | 40% |
| ACT composite: | 21-27 | Rank in top tenth: | 12% |
| GPA 3.75 or higher: | 14% | Out-of-state: | 87% |
| GPA 3.50-3.74: | 17% | Live on campus: | 95% |

**Basis for selection.** Admissions based on secondary school record, interview, talent, ability, character, and personal qualities. Class rank, recommendations, standardized test scores, essay, and volunteer work also important. **Homeschooled:** Statement describing homeschool structure and mission, transcript of courses and grades, interview required.

**High school preparation.** 16 units required. Required and recommended units include English 4, mathematics 2-3, social studies 2, history 2, science 2-3 (laboratory 2-3), foreign language 2 and academic electives 6.

**2009-2010 Annual costs.** Books/supplies: $1,180. Personal expenses: $1,380.

**2008-2009 Financial aid. Non-need-based:** Scholarships awarded for academics, alumni affiliation, art, athletics, leadership, minority status, music/drama.

**Application procedures. Admission:** Priority date 3/15; no deadline. $35 fee, may be waived for applicants with need. Admission notification on a rolling basis beginning on or about 1/15. Must reply by May 1 or within 2 week(s) if notified thereafter. **Financial aid:** Priority date 3/15; no closing date. FAFSA required. Applicants notified on a rolling basis starting 3/1; must reply by 5/1 or within 2 week(s) of notification.

**Academics. Special study options:** Cooperative education, double major, dual enrollment of high school students, exchange student, independent study, internships, New York semester, student-designed major, study abroad. London semester, Lasallian Consortium for Study Abroad. **Credit/placement by examination:** AP, CLEP, institutional tests. 48 credit hours maximum toward bachelor's degree. **Support services:** Learning center, reduced course load, remedial instruction, study skills assistance, tutoring, writing center.

**Majors. Visual/performing arts:** Acting, art history/conservation, dramatic, film/cinema, graphic design, multimedia, music performance, music theory/composition, musical theater, painting, photography, sculpture, studio arts, theater arts management, theater design.

**Most popular majors.** Business/marketing 10%, education 7%, English 6%, psychology 9%, visual/performing arts 48%.

**Computing on campus.** 84 workstations in library, computer center. Dormitories wired for high-speed internet access and linked to campus network. Online course registration, online library, helpline, student web hosting, wireless network available.

**Student life. Freshman orientation:** Mandatory. Preregistration for classes offered. Four-day program involves meetings with faculty advisors, social activities, club sign-ups, off-campus trips to learn more about the community. **Housing:** Guaranteed on-campus for freshmen. Coed dorms, single-sex dorms, special housing for disabled, apartments, wellness housing available. $200 fully refundable deposit. Separate quiet floors available. **Activities:** Dance, drama, literary magazine, musical theater, student government, student newspaper, TV station.

**Student services.** Alcohol/substance abuse counseling, chaplain/spiritual director, career counseling, financial aid counseling, health services, personal counseling. **Physically disabled:** Services for visually, speech, hearing impaired. **Learning disabled:** Comprehensive services available.

**Contact.** E-mail: admissions@csf.edu
Phone: (505) 473-6133 Toll-free number: (800) 456-2673
Fax: (505) 473-6129
Jackie Donohoe, Executive Director of Admissions, College of Santa Fe, 1600 Saint Michael's Drive, Santa Fe, NM 87505-7634

## Eastern New Mexico University
Portales, New Mexico
www.enmu.edu
CB code: 4299

▶ Public 4-year university
▶ Residential campus in large town
▶ 3,442 degree-seeking undergraduates: 27% part-time, 56% women, 7% African American, 1% Asian American, 29% Hispanic American, 3% Native American, 3% international
▶ 624 degree-seeking graduate students
▶ 65% of applicants admitted
▶ SAT or ACT (ACT writing optional) required

**General.** Founded in 1927. Regionally accredited. **Degrees:** 458 bachelor's, 11 associate awarded; master's offered. **Location:** 225 miles from Albuquerque, 120 miles from Lubbock, Texas. **Calendar:** Semester, extensive summer session. **Full-time faculty:** 149 total; 76% have terminal degrees, 13% minority, 47% women. **Part-time faculty:** 169 total; 17% have terminal degrees, 18% minority, 49% women. **Class size:** 55% < 20, 38% 20-39, 5% 40-49, 2% 50-99. **Special facilities:** Natural history museum, mineral museum, scanning and transmission electron microscopes.

**Freshman class profile.** 1,176 applied, 762 admitted, 634 enrolled.

| Mid 50% test scores | | | |
|---|---|---|---|
| SAT critical reading: | 420-530 | GPA 2.0-2.99: | 32% |
| SAT math: | 410-540 | Rank in top quarter: | 34% |
| ACT composite: | 17-22 | Rank in top tenth: | 11% |
| GPA 3.75 or higher: | 16% | Return as sophomores: | 61% |
| GPA 3.50-3.74: | 15% | Out-of-state: | 21% |
| GPA 3.0-3.49: | 36% | Live on campus: | 75% |
| | | International: | 2% |

**Basis for selection.** Test scores, school record, recommendations important. Students not meeting regular admission standards may be admitted on probation. **Homeschooled:** Transcript of courses and grades required.

**High school preparation.** College-preparatory program recommended. 14 units recommended. Recommended units include English 4, mathematics 4, social studies 2 and science 2.

**2009-2010 Annual costs.** Tuition/fees: $3,552; $9,102 out-of-state. Room/board: $5,374. Books/supplies: $1,200. Personal expenses: $3,000.

**2009-2010 Financial aid. Need-based:** 390 full-time freshmen applied for aid; 390 were judged to have need; 390 of these received aid. Average need met was 40%. Average scholarship/grant was $4,191; average loan $3,243. 48% of total undergraduate aid awarded as scholarships/grants, 52% as loans/jobs. **Non-need-based:** Scholarships awarded for academics, alumni affiliation, art, athletics, leadership, music/drama, state residency.

**Application procedures. Admission:** Priority date 8/15; no deadline. No application fee. Admission notification on a rolling basis. **Financial aid:** Priority date 3/1; no closing date. FAFSA required. Applicants notified by 4/1.

**Academics. Special study options:** Accelerated study, combined bachelor's/graduate degree, distance learning, double major, dual enrollment of high school students, ESL, exchange student, independent study, internships, student-designed major, teacher certification program. **Credit/placement by examination:** AP, CLEP, ACT, institutional tests. 32 credit hours maximum toward associate degree, 50 toward bachelor's. **Support services:** Learning center, pre-admission summer program, remedial instruction, tutoring.

**Majors. Agriculture:** Agribusiness operations, dairy. **Biology:** General. **Business:** Accounting, business admin, finance, human resources, management information systems, managerial economics, marketing. **Communications:** General, broadcast journalism, journalism. **Computer sciences:** General, computer science. **Conservation:** Environmental science, wildlife. **Education:** Agricultural, business, early childhood, elementary, music, physical, sales/marketing, special. **Engineering technology:** General. **Family/consumer sciences:** General. **Foreign languages:** Spanish. **Health:** Audiology/speech pathology, clinical lab science, nursing (RN). **History:** General. **Liberal arts:** Arts/sciences. **Math:** General. **Parks/recreation:** Health/fitness. **Philosophy/religion:** Religion. **Physical sciences:** Chemistry, geology. **Protective services:** Criminal justice, forensics. **Psychology:** General. **Public administration:** Social work. **Social sciences:** General, anthropology, political science, sociology. **Transportation:** Aviation management. **Visual/performing arts:** Art, dramatic.

**Most popular majors.** Business/marketing 15%, education 25%, health sciences 6%, liberal arts 14%.

**Computing on campus.** 370 workstations in dormitories, library, computer center. Dormitories linked to campus network. Commuter students can connect to campus network. Helpline, repair service, wireless network available.

**Student life. Freshman orientation:** Mandatory, $60 fee. Preregistration for classes offered. **Housing:** Guaranteed on-campus for freshmen. Coed dorms, single-sex dorms, special housing for disabled, apartments, fraternity/sorority housing available. $150 fully refundable deposit. **Activities:** Bands, campus ministries, choral groups, dance, drama, film society, international student organizations, literary magazine, music ensembles, radio station, student government, student newspaper, symphony orchestra, TV station, several religious, political, honorary, and service organizations.

**Athletics.** NCAA. **Intercollegiate:** Baseball M, basketball, cross-country, football (tackle) M, rodeo, soccer, softball W, track and field, volleyball W. **Intramural:** Badminton, basketball, cross-country, football (non-tackle) M, golf, racquetball, soccer, softball, tennis, volleyball. **Team name:** Greyhounds.

**Student services.** Adult student services, career counseling, student employment services, financial aid counseling, health services, minority student services, on-campus daycare, personal counseling, placement for graduates, veterans' counselor. **Physically disabled:** Services for visually, speech, hearing impaired.

**Contact.** Phone: (575) 562-2178 Toll-free number: (800) 367-3668 Fax: (575) 562-2566
Donna Kittrell, Director of Enrollment Services, Eastern New Mexico University, Station Seven, Portales, NM 88130

## Institute of American Indian Arts
Santa Fe, New Mexico
www.iaia.edu
CB code: 0180

▶ Public 4-year visual arts and liberal arts college
▶ Residential campus in small city
▶ 250 undergraduates
▶ Application essay required

**General.** Founded in 1962. Regionally accredited. Dedicated to providing education in fine arts and cultural studies to American Indians and Alaska Natives. **Degrees:** 22 bachelor's, 7 associate awarded. **Location:** 60 miles from Albuquerque. **Calendar:** Semester, limited summer session. **Full-time faculty:** 19 total. **Part-time faculty:** 15 total. **Special facilities:** Native American contemporary arts museum.

**Freshman class profile.**

| Mid 50% test scores | | | |
|---|---|---|---|
| SAT critical reading: | 400-500 | ACT composite: | 15-21 |
| SAT math: | 200-300 | Live on campus: | 90% |

**Basis for selection.** Admissions decisions based on GPA, high school record, recommendations, SAT or ACT or Accuplacer test scores. SAT or ACT recommended. Personal statement of educational intention required.

**2009-2010 Annual costs.** Tuition/fees: $3,156. Room/board: $4,900. Books/supplies: $2,500. Personal expenses: $2,400.

**2008-2009 Financial aid. Non-need-based:** Scholarships awarded for academics, art. **Additional information:** For American Indian and Alaskan natives, financial aid available through Tribe or Native Corporation in which student is enrolled.

**Application procedures. Admission:** Closing date 8/4. $5 fee. Admission notification on a rolling basis beginning on or about 5/1. Must reply by May 1 or within 1 week(s) if notified thereafter. **Financial aid:** Priority date 3/15; no closing date. FAFSA, institutional form required. Applicants notified on a rolling basis starting 5/1.

**Academics.** Most courses emphasize American Indian perspective. **Special study options:** Cross-registration, double major, exchange student, independent study, internships. **Credit/placement by examination:** AP, CLEP, SAT, ACT, institutional tests. **Support services:** Learning center, remedial instruction, study skills assistance, tutoring.

**Majors. Interdisciplinary:** Museum. **Visual/performing arts:** Studio arts. **Other:** Indigenous liberal studies, New media arts.

**Computing on campus.** 3 workstations in dormitories, library, computer center. Dormitories linked to campus network.

**Student life. Freshman orientation:** Mandatory. Preregistration for classes offered. Conducted each semester one week before registration. **Housing:** Guaranteed on-campus for freshmen. Coed dorms available. $150 deposit.

**Activities:** Literary magazine, student government, student newspaper, TV station, student senate, Pow-Wow club, traditional dance club, museum club, photography club, theater club, campus cleanup club.

**Athletics. Intramural:** Basketball M, skiing, softball, swimming, table tennis, tennis, volleyball.

**Student services.** Alcohol/substance abuse counseling, career counseling, student employment services, financial aid counseling, personal counseling, placement for graduates.

**Contact.** E-mail: admissions@iaia.edu
Phone: (505) 424-2332 Toll-free number: (800) 804-6422
Fax: (505) 424-4500
Nena Anaya, Director of Admissions, Records & Enrollment, Institute of American Indian Arts, 83 Avan Nu Po Road, Santa Fe, NM 87508-1300

---

## ITT Technical Institute: Albuquerque
**Albuquerque, New Mexico**
www.itt-tech.edu                              CB code: 2690

- For-profit 4-year technical college
- Commuter campus in large city

**General.** Accredited by ACICS. **Calendar:** Quarter.

**Contact.** Phone: (505) 828-1114
Director of Recruitment, 5100 Masthead Street NE, Albuquerque, NM 87109

---

## National American University: Rio Rancho
**Rio Rancho, New Mexico**
www.national.edu                              CB code: 5360

- For-profit 4-year business college
- Large city

**General.** Founded in 1941. Regionally accredited. **Calendar:** Quarter.

**Annual costs/financial aid.** Annual tuition of year-round program is $15,120; required fees: $500. Books/supplies: $1,200.

**Contact.** Phone: (505) 348-3750
Director of Admissions, 4775 Indian School Road NE, Suite 200, Albuquerque, NM 87110

---

## New Mexico Highlands University
**Las Vegas, New Mexico**                     CB member
www.nmhu.edu                                  CB code: 4532

- Public 4-year university
- Commuter campus in large town
- 2,107 degree-seeking undergraduates: 23% part-time, 59% women
- 1,175 degree-seeking graduate students
- 56% of applicants admitted

**General.** Founded in 1893. Regionally accredited. **Degrees:** 302 bachelor's awarded; master's offered. **Location:** 68 miles from Santa Fe, 120 miles from Albuquerque. **Calendar:** Semester, limited summer session. **Full-time faculty:** 149 total.

**Freshman class profile.** 3,228 applied, 1,803 admitted, 398 enrolled.

| Mid 50% test scores | | | |
|---|---|---|---|
| ACT composite: | 16-20 | GPA 2.0-2.99: | 46% |
| GPA 3.75 or higher: | 12% | Rank in top quarter: | 28% |
| GPA 3.50-3.74: | 8% | Rank in top tenth: | 6% |
| GPA 3.0-3.49: | 30% | Return as sophomores: | 45% |

**Basis for selection.** Minimum 2.0 GPA required. All tests used for placement purposes. COMPASS may be submitted in place of ACT. **Home-schooled:** Transcript of courses and grades, state high school equivalency certificate required.

**2009-2010 Annual costs.** Tuition/fees: $2,755; $4,323 out-of-state. Room/board: $5,650. Books/supplies: $850. Personal expenses: $1,870.

**2008-2009 Financial aid. Non-need-based:** Scholarships awarded for academics, athletics, leadership, minority status, music/drama, state residency. **Additional information:** Work study funds available on no-need basis to state residents.

**Application procedures. Admission:** No deadline. $15 fee, may be waived for applicants with need. Admission notification on a rolling basis. **Financial aid:** Priority date 3/1, closing date 5/1. FAFSA, institutional form required. Applicants notified on a rolling basis starting 5/15; must reply within 2 week(s) of notification.

**Academics. Special study options:** Combined bachelor's/graduate degree, cooperative education, distance learning, double major, dual enrollment of high school students, ESL, honors, independent study, internships, liberal arts/career combination, teacher certification program. **Credit/placement by examination:** AP, CLEP, SAT, ACT, institutional tests. As approved by appropriate department. **Support services:** Learning center, remedial instruction, study skills assistance, tutoring, writing center.

**Majors. Biology:** General. **Business:** Accounting, business admin, finance, international, management information systems, marketing. **Communications:** Media studies. **Computer sciences:** Computer science. **Conservation:** Forest management. **Education:** Art, biology, early childhood, elementary, mathematics, music, science, secondary, special. **Foreign languages:** Spanish. **Health:** Nursing (RN). **History:** General. **Math:** General. **Parks/recreation:** Health/fitness, sports admin. **Physical sciences:** Chemistry, forensic chemistry, geology. **Protective services:** Criminal justice, forensics. **Psychology:** General. **Public administration:** Social work. **Social sciences:** Anthropology, criminology, political science, sociology. **Visual/performing arts:** Art, music performance, studio arts.

**Most popular majors.** Business/marketing 15%, education 33%, social sciences 8%.

**Computing on campus.** 250 workstations in dormitories, library, computer center, student center. Dormitories wired for high-speed internet access and linked to campus network. Commuter students can connect to campus network. Online library, helpline, repair service, wireless network available.

**Student life. Freshman orientation:** Mandatory, $50 fee. Preregistration for classes offered. **Housing:** Guaranteed on-campus for freshmen. Coed dorms, single-sex dorms, apartments available. $100 partly refundable deposit. **Activities:** Bands, choral groups, dance, drama, film society, international student organizations, music ensembles, musical theater, radio station, student government, student newspaper, TV station, social work club, several ethnic and religious groups.

**Athletics.** NAIA, NCAA. **Intercollegiate:** Baseball M, basketball, cross-country, football (tackle) M, rodeo, soccer W, softball W, track and field W, volleyball W, wrestling M. **Intramural:** Baseball M, basketball, golf, handball, racquetball, rifle, rugby, skiing, softball, swimming, table tennis, tennis, track and field. **Team name:** Cowboys, Cowgirls.

**Student services.** Adult student services, career counseling, services for economically disadvantaged, student employment services, financial aid counseling, health services, minority student services, on-campus daycare, personal counseling, placement for graduates, veterans' counselor. **Physically disabled:** Services for visually, speech, hearing impaired.

**Contact.** E-mail: mdbassett@nmhu.edu
Phone: (505) 454-3434 Toll-free number: (877) 850-9064
Fax: (505) 454-3552
John Coca, Director of Admissions, New Mexico Highlands University, Box 9000, Las Vegas, NM 87701

---

## New Mexico Institute of Mining and Technology
**Socorro, New Mexico**                       CB member
www.nmt.edu                                   CB code: 4533

- Public 4-year engineering and liberal arts college
- Residential campus in small town
- 1,151 degree-seeking undergraduates: 5% part-time, 27% women, 1% African American, 3% Asian American, 25% Hispanic American, 3% Native American, 2% international
- 436 degree-seeking graduate students
- 79% of applicants admitted
- SAT or ACT (ACT writing optional) required
- 46% graduate within 6 years

**General.** Founded in 1889. Regionally accredited. Student employment opportunities in research facilities and in faculty research. **Degrees:** 194 bachelor's, 5 associate awarded; master's, doctoral offered. **Location:** 75

miles from Albuquerque. **Calendar:** Semester, limited summer session. **Full-time faculty:** 124 total; 97% have terminal degrees, 13% minority, 20% women. **Part-time faculty:** 29 total; 31% have terminal degrees, 21% minority, 17% women. **Class size:** 63% < 20, 30% 20-39, 4% 40-49, 4% 50-99. **Special facilities:** Experimental mine, mineral museum, laboratory for atmospheric physics and chemistry, energetic materials research, seismic research network, scanning electron microscope, scanning transmission electron microscope, transmission electron microscope, New Mexico Bureau of Geology, observatory.

**Freshman class profile.** 445 applied, 353 admitted, 255 enrolled.

| Mid 50% test scores | | | |
|---|---|---|---|
| SAT critical reading: | 530-650 | GPA 3.0-3.49: | 25% |
| SAT math: | 570-680 | GPA 2.0-2.99: | 15% |
| ACT composite: | 23-28 | Rank in top quarter: | 66% |
| GPA 3.75 or higher: | 38% | Rank in top tenth: | 36% |
| GPA 3.50-3.74: | 22% | Return as sophomores: | 71% |
| | | Out-of-state: | 16% |

**Basis for selection.** Test scores and high school GPA most important. Minimum 2.5 GPA required. Minimum 21 ACT or 970 SAT (exclusive of Writing) required. ACT recommended. Interview and recommendations considered if GPA and test scores are borderline or if other issues need to be addressed. **Homeschooled:** Transcript of courses and grades required. Must supply documentation of courses completed.

**High school preparation.** College-preparatory program recommended. 15 units required; 18 recommended. Required and recommended units include English 4, mathematics 3-4, social studies 2-3, history 1, science 2-4 (laboratory 2-3), foreign language 2 and academic electives 3.

**2009-2010 Annual costs.** Tuition/fees: $4,607; $13,568 out-of-state. Room/board: $5,702. Books/supplies: $1,050. Personal expenses: $1,592.

**2008-2009 Financial aid. Need-based:** 280 full-time freshmen applied for aid; 124 were judged to have need; 122 of these received aid. Average need met was 94%. Average scholarship/grant was $4,567; average loan $3,819. 44% of total undergraduate aid awarded as scholarships/grants, 56% as loans/jobs. **Non-need-based:** Awarded to 705 full-time undergraduates, including 235 freshmen. Scholarships awarded for academics, alumni affiliation, minority status, state residency. **Additional information:** Campus research projects offer student employment based on merit.

**Application procedures. Admission:** Priority date 3/1; deadline 8/1. $15 fee, may be waived for applicants with need. Admission notification on a rolling basis beginning on or about 3/1. Must reply by May 1 or within 2 week(s) if notified thereafter. **Financial aid:** Priority date 6/1; no closing date. FAFSA, institutional form required. Applicants notified on a rolling basis starting 4/1; must reply within 2 week(s) of notification.

**Academics. Special study options:** Accelerated study, cooperative education, distance learning, double major, dual enrollment of high school students, exchange student, independent study, internships, student-designed major, teacher certification program. **Credit/placement by examination:** AP, CLEP, SAT, ACT, institutional tests. No limit to number of credits. Must have permission of instructor. **Support services:** Pre-admission summer program, reduced course load, study skills assistance, tutoring, writing center.

**Majors. Biology:** General, biochemistry. **Business:** Business admin. **Computer sciences:** General, computer science, information technology. **Conservation:** General, environmental studies. **Engineering:** General, chemical, civil, electrical, environmental, materials, mechanical, metallurgical, mining, petroleum. **Math:** General, applied. **Physical sciences:** Astrophysics, atmospheric physics, chemistry, geology, geophysics, physics. **Psychology:** General.

**Most popular majors.** Biology 10%, computer/information sciences 14%, engineering/engineering technologies 43%, liberal arts 7%, physical sciences 11%.

**Computing on campus.** 225 workstations in dormitories, library, computer center, student center. Dormitories wired for high-speed internet access and linked to campus network. Commuter students can connect to campus network. Helpline, student web hosting, wireless network available.

**Student life. Freshman orientation:** Available, $40 fee. Preregistration for classes offered. 2-day event held weekend before classes start. **Policies:** Students living on-campus must purchase meal plan. **Housing:** Coed dorms, single-sex dorms, apartments, wellness housing available. $100 partly refundable deposit, deadline 6/1. **Activities:** Bands, choral groups, dance, drama, film society, international student organizations, music ensembles, musical theater, radio station, student government, student newspaper, many organizations available.

**Athletics. Intramural:** Badminton, basketball, fencing, golf, racquetball, rifle, rugby, soccer, softball, table tennis, tennis, volleyball.

**Student services.** Adult student services, career counseling, student employment services, health services, on-campus daycare, personal counseling, placement for graduates. **Physically disabled:** Services for visually, hearing impaired.

**Contact.** E-mail: admission@admin.nmt.edu
Phone: (575) 835-5424 Toll-free number: (800) 428-8324
Fax: (575) 835-5989
Mike Kloeppel, Director of Admission, New Mexico Institute of Mining and Technology, 801 Leroy Place, Socorro, NM 87801

## New Mexico State University

| Las Cruces, New Mexico | CB member |
|---|---|
| www.nmsu.edu | CB code: 4531 |

- Public 4-year university
- Commuter campus in small city
- 14,536 degree-seeking undergraduates: 14% part-time, 55% women, 3% African American, 1% Asian American, 44% Hispanic American, 4% Native American, 5% international
- 3,701 degree-seeking graduate students
- 96% of applicants admitted
- SAT or ACT with writing required
- 44% graduate within 6 years

**General.** Founded in 1888. Regionally accredited. **Degrees:** 2,204 bachelor's, 30 associate awarded; master's, doctoral offered. **ROTC:** Army, Air Force. **Location:** 42 miles from El Paso, Texas. **Calendar:** Semester, extensive summer session. **Full-time faculty:** 699 total; 75% have terminal degrees, 20% minority, 40% women. **Part-time faculty:** 324 total; 25% have terminal degrees, 14% minority, 57% women. **Class size:** 45% < 20, 36% 20-39, 8% 40-49, 7% 50-99, 3% >100. **Special facilities:** Observatory, horse farm, rodeo grounds, electron microscope, CRAY supercomputer, sports medicine training clinic.

**Freshman class profile.** 6,650 applied, 6,404 admitted, 2,878 enrolled.

| Mid 50% test scores | | | |
|---|---|---|---|
| SAT critical reading: | 420-540 | GPA 2.0-2.99: | 26% |
| SAT math: | 430-550 | Rank in top quarter: | 42% |
| SAT writing: | 410-530 | Rank in top tenth: | 15% |
| ACT composite: | 18-23 | End year in good standing: | 73.9% |
| GPA 3.75 or higher: | 23% | Return as sophomores: | 76% |
| GPA 3.50-3.74: | 17% | Out-of-state: | 23% |
| GPA 3.0-3.49: | 33% | International: | 4% |

**Basis for selection.** School achievement record, test scores most important.

**High school preparation.** 10 units required. Required units include English 4, mathematics 3, science 2 (laboratory 2) and foreign language 1. English must include at least 2 composition, 1 of which must be at junior or senior level. Math must be algebra I, algebra II, geometry, trigonometry or advanced math. Will accept 1 foreign language or 1 fine arts.

**2009-2010 Annual costs.** Tuition/fees: $4,998; $15,150 out-of-state. Room/board: $6,338. Books/supplies: $1,032. Personal expenses: $2,212.

**2008-2009 Financial aid. Need-based:** 1,470 full-time freshmen applied for aid; 1,142 were judged to have need; 929 of these received aid. Average need met was 52%. Average scholarship/grant was $5,455; average loan $3,261. 46% of total undergraduate aid awarded as scholarships/grants, 54% as loans/jobs. **Non-need-based:** Awarded to 193 full-time undergraduates, including 43 freshmen. Scholarships awarded for academics, alumni affiliation, athletics, leadership, minority status, state residency.

**Application procedures. Admission:** No deadline. $20 fee. Admission notification on a rolling basis. **Financial aid:** Priority date 3/1; no closing date. FAFSA, institutional form required. Applicants notified on a rolling basis starting 3/1.

**Academics. Special study options:** Accelerated study, cooperative education, cross-registration, distance learning, double major, exchange student, honors, independent study, internships, student-designed major, study abroad, teacher certification program, weekend college. **Credit/placement by examination:** CLEP, institutional tests. **Support services:** Learning center, reduced course load, study skills assistance, tutoring, writing center.

**Majors. Agriculture:** General, agribusiness operations, agronomy, animal sciences, horticultural science, range science, soil science, turf management. **Architecture:** Urban/community planning. **Area/ethnic studies:** Women's. **Biology:** General, bacteriology, biochemistry, ecology, plant pathology. **Business:** General, accounting, business admin, finance, hospitality admin, international, marketing, real estate. **Communications:** Journalism. **Computer sciences:** General, information systems, information technology. **Conservation:** Environmental science, wildlife. **Education:** General, agricultural, early childhood, elementary, family/consumer sciences, music, physical, secondary. **Engineering:** Aerospace, agricultural, chemical, civil, electrical, industrial, mechanical, physics. **Engineering technology:** Surveying. **Family/consumer sciences:** Clothing/textiles, family studies, food/nutrition. **Foreign languages:** General. **Health:** Athletic training, clinical lab science, environmental health, nursing (RN), public health ed. **History:** General. **Math:** General. **Parks/recreation:** Facilities management. **Philosophy/religion:** Philosophy. **Physical sciences:** Chemistry, geology, physics. **Protective services:** Criminal justice. **Psychology:** General. **Public administration:** Community org/advocacy, social work. **Social sciences:** Anthropology, economics, geography, political science, sociology. **Visual/performing arts:** General, cinematography, dance, dramatic, music performance, studio arts.

**Most popular majors.** Business/marketing 19%, education 12%, engineering/engineering technologies 8%, health sciences 7%, security/protective services 6%.

**Computing on campus.** 743 workstations in dormitories, library, computer center, student center. Dormitories wired for high-speed internet access and linked to campus network. Commuter students can connect to campus network. Online course registration, online library, helpline, repair service, student web hosting, wireless network available.

**Student life. Freshman orientation:** Available. Preregistration for classes offered. **Housing:** Coed dorms, single-sex dorms, special housing for disabled, apartments, fraternity/sorority housing, wellness housing available. $100 deposit, deadline 7/1. Upper division dorms available. **Activities:** Bands, campus ministries, choral groups, dance, drama, literary magazine, music ensembles, musical theater, opera, radio station, student government, student newspaper, symphony orchestra, TV station, Baptist student union, Catholic center, Young Democrats, College Republicans, Black Allied Student Association, Movimiento Estudiantil Chicano de Azatlan, Native American organization.

**Athletics.** NCAA. **Intercollegiate:** Baseball M, basketball, cross-country, equestrian, football (tackle) M, golf, softball W, swimming W, tennis, track and field W, volleyball W. **Intramural:** Archery, badminton, basketball, cheerleading, football (non-tackle), football (tackle), golf, racquetball, soccer, softball, tennis, volleyball, water polo, weight lifting, wrestling M. **Team name:** Aggies.

**Student services.** Adult student services, alcohol/substance abuse counseling, career counseling, student employment services, health services, personal counseling, placement for graduates, veterans' counselor. **Physically disabled:** Services for visually, speech, hearing impaired.

**Contact.** E-mail: admissions@nmsu.edu
Phone: (575) 646-3121 Toll-free number: (800) 662-6678
Fax: (575) 646-6330
Valerie Pickett, Director of Admissions, New Mexico State University, Box 30001, MSC 3A, Las Cruces, NM 88003-8001

---

## St. John's College

| Santa Fe, New Mexico | CB member |
|---|---|
| www.sjcsf.edu | CB code: 4737 |

◗  Private 4-year liberal arts college

◗  Residential campus in small city

◗  414 degree-seeking undergraduates: 39% women, 4% Asian American, 7% Hispanic American, 1% Native American, 5% international

◗  85 degree-seeking graduate students

◗  85% of applicants admitted

◗  Application essay required

◗  60% graduate within 6 years; 10% enter graduate study

**General.** Founded in 1964. Regionally accredited. Second campus in Annapolis, MD, where students may transfer during their 4 years. **Degrees:** 86 bachelor's awarded; master's offered. **Location:** 60 miles from Albuquerque. **Calendar:** Semester, limited summer session. **Full-time faculty:** 68 total; 81% have terminal degrees, 6% minority, 26% women. **Class size:** 96% < 20, 4% 20-39. **Special facilities:** Search and rescue center, Ptolemy stone, forest with hiking trails.

**Freshman class profile.** 297 applied, 253 admitted, 123 enrolled.

| Mid 50% test scores | | | |
|---|---|---|---|
| SAT critical reading: | 610-720 | End year in good standing: | 92% |
| SAT math: | 570-690 | Return as sophomores: | 74% |
| ACT composite: | 26-30 | Out-of-state: | 90% |
| Rank in top quarter: | 50% | Live on campus: | 98% |
| Rank in top tenth: | 22% | International: | 6% |

**Basis for selection.** Three essays describing educational and personal background and goals are most important along with 2 letters of reference from teachers; secondary school reference from guidance counselor or other school official is requested. High school achievement record considered. SAT or ACT required of early admission, homeschooled, and international applicants; optional for others. Interview and over-night campus visit are strongly encouraged, as are interviews off-campus when offered by admissions officers. **Homeschooled:** Statement describing homeschool structure and mission, transcript of courses and grades, letter of recommendation (nonparent) required.

**High school preparation.** College-preparatory program recommended. 5 units required; 22 recommended. Required and recommended units include English 4, mathematics 3-4, history 2, science 3 (laboratory 3) and foreign language 2-4. Math includes 2 algebra, 1 geometry; precalculus or trigonometry recommended.

**2010-2011 Annual costs.** Tuition/fees (projected): $40,392. Room/board: $9,600. Books/supplies: $275. Personal expenses: $750.

**2008-2009 Financial aid.** All financial aid based on need. 91 full-time freshmen applied for aid; 88 were judged to have need; 88 of these received aid. Average need met was 97%. Average scholarship/grant was $24,521; average loan $3,875. 78% of total undergraduate aid awarded as scholarships/grants, 22% as loans/jobs. **Additional information:** Families receive individual attention in determining need. Independent students must submit parental data. Financial aid information also required of noncustodial parent in cases of separation or divorce. Aid is awarded on a first-come, first-served basis until institutional money is exhausted. Apply by February 15; after April 1 aid is difficult to obtain.

**Application procedures. Admission:** Priority date 3/1; no deadline. No application fee. Admission notification on a rolling basis. Must reply by May 1 or within 2 week(s) if notified thereafter. Early application is encouraged. **Financial aid:** Priority date 2/15; no closing date. FAFSA, CSS PROFILE required. Applicants notified on a rolling basis starting 12/10; must reply by 5/1 or within 2 week(s) of notification.

**Academics. Special study options:** Accelerated study, internships. **Credit/placement by examination:** CLEP. **Support services:** Tutoring, writing center.

**Majors. Liberal arts:** Arts/sciences.

**Computing on campus.** 20 workstations in library, computer center. Dormitories wired for high-speed internet access and linked to campus network. Commuter students can connect to campus network. Helpline, wireless network available.

**Student life. Freshman orientation:** Mandatory. Four-day program held twice a year. Includes on-campus service day, student activities fair, numerous community meals, and formal welcoming ceremony. **Housing:** Guaranteed on-campus for freshmen. Coed dorms, single-sex dorms, special housing for disabled, apartments, wellness housing available. Pets allowed in dorm rooms. Single-sex suites available. **Activities:** Bands, choral groups, dance, drama, film society, literary magazine, music ensembles, musical theater, student government, student newspaper, peer counseling, Beneficial Farm, New Testament study group, Project Politae.

**Athletics. Intramural:** Badminton, basketball, boxing, fencing, football (non-tackle), handball, judo, racquetball, skiing, soccer, softball, squash, table tennis, tennis, volleyball.

**Student services.** Alcohol/substance abuse counseling, career counseling, student employment services, financial aid counseling, health services, personal counseling, placement for graduates, women's services.

**Contact.** E-mail: admissions@sjcsf.edu
Phone: (505) 984-6060 Toll-free number: (800) 331-5232
Fax: (505) 984-6162
Lawrence Clendenin, Director of Admissions, St. John's College, 1160 Camino Cruz Blanca, Santa Fe, NM 87505

## University of New Mexico

**Albuquerque, New Mexico**  **CB member**
**www.unm.edu**  **CB code: 4845**

- Public 4-year university
- Commuter campus in very large city
- 19,613 degree-seeking undergraduates: 19% part-time, 55% women, 3% African American, 4% Asian American, 37% Hispanic American, 7% Native American, 1% international
- 5,909 graduate students
- 62% of applicants admitted
- SAT or ACT (ACT writing recommended) required
- 43% graduate within 6 years

**General.** Founded in 1889. Regionally accredited. New Campus in Rio Rancho; branch campuses in Valencia County, Los Alamos, Gallup, and Taos. **Degrees:** 3,160 bachelor's, 11 associate awarded; master's, doctoral, professional offered. **ROTC:** Army, Naval, Air Force. **Location:** 2 miles from downtown. **Calendar:** Semester, limited summer session. **Full-time faculty:** 957 total; 84% have terminal degrees, 22% minority, 46% women. **Part-time faculty:** 524 total; 38% have terminal degrees, 20% minority, 52% women. **Class size:** 41% < 20, 40% 20-39, 5% 40-49, 10% 50-99, 4% >100. **Special facilities:** 5 museums; observatory; meteoritics institute; arboretum; teaching hospital; major research facilities in ceramics, optoelectronics, space nuclear power, high power devices and systems; institute of lithography; Latin American institute.

**Freshman class profile.** 10,743 applied, 6,614 admitted, 3,409 enrolled.

| Mid 50% test scores | | | |
|---|---|---|---|
| SAT critical reading: | 480-610 | GPA 3.0-3.49: | 36% |
| SAT math: | 480-610 | GPA 2.0-2.99: | 28% |
| ACT composite: | 19-25 | Rank in top quarter: | 47% |
| GPA 3.75 or higher: | 19% | Rank in top tenth: | 21% |
| GPA 3.50-3.74: | 17% | Return as sophomores: | 79% |
| | | Out-of-state: | 11% |

**Basis for selection.** School achievement record (2.25 GPA required in college-preparatory units) most important. Test scores, class rank second. Essays, recommendations considered. Essay is considered in student appeal process. **Homeschooled:** Applicants must either pass GED, submit SAT Subject Test scores, or have 2.25 GPA and complete 13 college prep academic units. **Learning Disabled:** Student who is not admissible according to numerical admissions and self-discloses disability can be admitted after being approved by Special Admissions Committee.

**High school preparation.** College-preparatory program required. 13 units required. Required units include English 4, mathematics 3, social studies 1, history 1, science 2 (laboratory 1) and foreign language 2. Foreign language requirements must be in same language. 1 science must be laboratory in biology, chemistry or physics. Math must be algebra I, geometry, algebra II, trigonometry or higher. 1 English must be 11th or 12th grade composition.

**2009-2010 Annual costs.** Tuition/fees: $5,101; $17,234 out-of-state. Room/board: $7,746. Books/supplies: $920. Personal expenses: $2,966.

**Financial aid.** **Non-need-based:** Scholarships awarded for academics, alumni affiliation, art, athletics, job skills, leadership, minority status, music/drama, religious affiliation, ROTC, state residency.

**Application procedures.** **Admission:** Priority date 6/15; no deadline. $20 fee, may be waived for applicants with need. Admission notification on a rolling basis. **Financial aid:** Priority date 3/1; no closing date. FAFSA required. Applicants notified on a rolling basis.

**Academics.** **Special study options:** Accelerated study, combined bachelor's/graduate degree, cooperative education, distance learning, double major, dual enrollment of high school students, ESL, exchange student, honors, independent study, internships, semester at sea, student-designed major, study abroad, teacher certification program, Washington semester, weekend college. **Credit/placement by examination:** AP, CLEP, IB, SAT, ACT, institutional tests. **Support services:** Learning center, reduced course load, remedial instruction, study skills assistance, tutoring.

**Majors.** **Architecture:** Architecture, environmental design. **Area/ethnic studies:** African-American, American, Asian, European, Latin American, Native American, Russian/Slavic, women's. **Biology:** General, biochemistry. **Business:** Business admin. **Communications:** General, journalism, media studies. **Computer sciences:** General. **Conservation:** Environmental science. **Education:** Art, early childhood, elementary, health, music, physical, secondary, special, technology/industrial arts. **Engineering:** Chemical, civil, computer, electrical, mechanical, nuclear, science. **Family/consumer sciences:** General, family studies, food/nutrition. **Foreign languages:** General, classics, comparative lit, French, German, linguistics, Portuguese, Russian, sign language interpretation, Spanish. **Health:** Audiology/speech pathology, clinical lab technology, dental hygiene, EMT paramedic, medical radiologic technology/radiation therapy, nursing (RN), physician assistant. **History:** General. **Liberal arts:** Arts/sciences, humanities. **Math:** General, statistics. **Philosophy/religion:** Philosophy, religion. **Physical sciences:** Astrophysics, chemistry, geology, physics. **Protective services:** Corrections. **Psychology:** General. **Public administration:** Community org/advocacy. **Social sciences:** Anthropology, economics, geography, political science, sociology. **Visual/performing arts:** Art, art history/conservation, dance, dramatic, film/cinema, music performance, theater design.

**Most popular majors.** Biology 7%, business/marketing 15%, education 13%, engineering/engineering technologies 6%, health sciences 8%, liberal arts 6%, psychology 8%, social sciences 9%, visual/performing arts 6%.

**Computing on campus.** 766 workstations in dormitories, library, computer center, student center. Dormitories wired for high-speed internet access and linked to campus network. Commuter students can connect to campus network. Online course registration, online library, helpline, student web hosting, wireless network available.

**Student life.** **Freshman orientation:** Mandatory, $125 fee. Preregistration for classes offered. Two-day sessions held June-August. **Housing:** Coed dorms, special housing for disabled, apartments, fraternity/sorority housing, wellness housing available. $300 deposit. Senior housing, academic floors, scholar's wing, global learning center, freshman living learning community, outdoors/wellness, major based units available. **Activities:** Bands, campus ministries, choral groups, dance, drama, film society, international student organizations, literary magazine, music ensembles, Model UN, musical theater, opera, radio station, student government, student newspaper, symphony orchestra, TV station, Panhellenic Council, black student union, MEChA, Hillel, Navigators, wilderness alliance, international center.

**Athletics.** NCAA. **Intercollegiate:** Baseball M, basketball, cross-country, diving W, football (tackle) M, golf, skiing, soccer, softball W, swimming W, tennis, track and field, volleyball W. **Intramural:** Archery, badminton, basketball, fencing, football (non-tackle), football (tackle) M, golf, racquetball, skiing, soccer, softball, swimming, tennis, triathlon, volleyball, water polo. **Team name:** Lobos.

**Student services.** Adult student services, alcohol/substance abuse counseling, career counseling, services for economically disadvantaged, student employment services, financial aid counseling, health services, legal services, minority student services, on-campus daycare, personal counseling, placement for graduates, veterans' counselor, women's services. **Physically disabled:** Services for visually, speech, hearing impaired.

**Contact.** E-mail: apply@unm.edu
Phone: (505) 277-8900 Toll-free number: (800) 225-5866
Fax: (505) 277-6686
Deborah Kieltyka, Associate Director of Admissions and Recruiting Services, University of New Mexico, Office of Admissions, Albuquerque, NM 87196-4895

## University of the Southwest

**Hobbs, New Mexico**  **CB member**
**www.usw.edu**  **CB code: 4116**

- Private 4-year liberal arts and teachers college
- Commuter campus in large town
- 267 degree-seeking undergraduates: 45% women, 3% African American, 1% Asian American, 45% Hispanic American, 1% international
- 193 degree-seeking graduate students
- 63% graduate within 6 years

**General.** Founded in 1956. Regionally accredited. **Degrees:** 82 bachelor's awarded; master's offered. **Location:** 110 miles from Lubbock, Texas. **Calendar:** Semester, extensive summer session. **Full-time faculty:** 14 total; 79% have terminal degrees, 14% minority, 50% women. **Part-time faculty:** 43 total; 16% have terminal degrees, 9% minority, 51% women. **Class size:** 81% < 20, 19% 20-39.

**Freshman class profile.** 213 applied, 128 admitted, 62 enrolled.

| Mid 50% test scores | | | |
|---|---|---|---|
| SAT critical reading: | 350-530 | GPA 3.0-3.49: | 40% |
| SAT math: | 390-550 | GPA 2.0-2.99: | 34% |
| SAT writing: | 360-470 | Rank in top quarter: | 24% |
| ACT composite: | 14-21 | End year in good standing: | 77% |
| GPA 3.75 or higher: | 7% | Return as sophomores: | 86% |
| GPA 3.50-3.74: | 17% | Out-of-state: | 11% |

**Basis for selection.** Open admission, but selective for some programs. Applicants must meet 2 of 3 criteria: ACT 19 or SAT 910 (exclusive of Writing), 2.0 GPA; top half of graduating class. **Homeschooled:** Statement describing homeschool structure and mission, transcript of courses and grades, state high school equivalency certificate required. **Learning Disabled:** Students with special needs are required to submit diagnostic test results in which special need was evaluated during last 3 years, Individual Education Plan (IEP), and other supporting documentation.

**2010-2011 Annual costs.** Tuition/fees (projected): $13,608. Books/supplies: $1,200. Personal expenses: $1,000.

**2008-2009 Financial aid. Need-based:** 59 full-time freshmen applied for aid; 50 were judged to have need; 50 of these received aid. Average need met was 70%. Average scholarship/grant was $3,051; average loan $2,481. 34% of total undergraduate aid awarded as scholarships/grants, 66% as loans/jobs. **Non-need-based:** Awarded to 241 full-time undergraduates, including 76 freshmen. Scholarships awarded for academics, alumni affiliation, athletics, leadership, religious affiliation, state residency.

**Application procedures. Admission:** No deadline. $25 fee, may be waived for applicants with need. Admission notification on a rolling basis beginning on or about 7/1. **Financial aid:** Priority date 4/1, closing date 6/1. FAFSA, institutional form required. Applicants notified on a rolling basis starting 4/1; must reply within 2 week(s) of notification.

**Academics.** 6 hours religious studies, 3 hours economics (free enterprise) is required of all students. **Special study options:** Combined bachelor's/graduate degree, distance learning, double major, dual enrollment of high school students, internships, teacher certification program. Internet program for criminal justice degree only. **Credit/placement by examination:** AP, CLEP, IB. 30 credit hours maximum toward bachelor's degree. **Support services:** Reduced course load, remedial instruction, study skills assistance, tutoring.

**Majors. Biology:** General. **Business:** Accounting, business admin, management information systems, marketing. **Education:** Bilingual, elementary, English, mathematics, physical, sales/marketing, science, secondary, social science, special. **History:** General. **Liberal arts:** Arts/sciences, humanities. **Philosophy/religion:** Religion. **Protective services:** Criminal justice. **Psychology:** General. **Social sciences:** General. **Theology:** Pastoral counseling, youth ministry.

**Most popular majors.** Business/marketing 19%, education 39%, liberal arts 8%, psychology 11%.

**Computing on campus.** 35 workstations in library, computer center. Dormitories wired for high-speed internet access. Online library, helpline, wireless network available.

**Student life. Freshman orientation:** Mandatory. Preregistration for classes offered. Held 1 week prior to beginning of classes. **Housing:** Single-sex dorms, apartments, wellness housing available. $300 fully refundable deposit. **Activities:** Campus ministries, literary magazine, student government, debate club, teaching club, Students in Free Enterprise, Alpha Phi Omega, Southwest Cultural Pride Club, Sigma Tau Delta, USW Alumni Association.

**Athletics.** NAIA. **Intercollegiate:** Baseball M, basketball M, cross-country, golf, soccer, softball W, tennis, track and field. **Intramural:** Badminton M, basketball, football (tackle) M, soccer W, table tennis, volleyball W. **Team name:** Mustangs.

**Student services.** Chaplain/spiritual director, student employment services, financial aid counseling, personal counseling, placement for graduates, veterans' counselor.

**Contact.** E-mail: admissions@usw.edu
Phone: (575) 392-6563 Toll-free number: (800) 530-4400 ext. 1007
Fax: (575) 392-6006
Ashley Taylor, Admissions Coordinator, University of the Southwest, 6610 Lovington Highway #506, Hobbs, NM 88240

---

## Western New Mexico University
Silver City, New Mexico     CB member
www.wnmu.edu     CB code: 4535

- Public 4-year university
- Commuter campus in large town
- 1,113 degree-seeking undergraduates

**General.** Founded in 1893. Regionally accredited. **Degrees:** 170 bachelor's, 77 associate awarded; master's offered. **Location:** 155 miles from El Paso, Texas, 193 miles from Tucson, Arizona. **Calendar:** Semester, extensive summer session. **Full-time faculty:** 100 total; 93% have terminal degrees. **Part-time faculty:** 140 total. **Class size:** 79% < 20, 19% 20-39, less than 1% 40-49, 1% 50-99. **Special facilities:** Museum specializing in Native American cultures, fine arts center and gallery, amphitheater.

**Freshman class profile.**

| Mid 50% test scores | | | |
|---|---|---|---|
| SAT critical reading: | 380-460 | ACT composite: | 16-21 |
| SAT math: | 390-500 | Out-of-state: | 17% |
| | | Live on campus: | 50% |

**Basis for selection.** Open admission. COMPASS test used for placement. **Homeschooled:** State high school equivalency certificate required. If state high school equivalency certificate not received, student must take GED.

**High school preparation.** Recommended units include English 4, mathematics 3, social studies 2, history 1 and science 2.

**2009-2010 Annual costs.** Tuition/fees: $3,589; $12,805 out-of-state. Room/board: $5,560. Books/supplies: $810. Personal expenses: $2,060.

**2008-2009 Financial aid. Non-need-based:** Scholarships awarded for academics, athletics, state residency.

**Application procedures. Admission:** Priority date 8/1; no deadline. No application fee. Admission notification on a rolling basis. **Financial aid:** Closing date 4/1. FAFSA, institutional form required. Applicants notified on a rolling basis starting 4/1; must reply within 2 week(s) of notification.

**Academics. Special study options:** Cooperative education, distance learning, double major, dual enrollment of high school students, honors, independent study, internships, liberal arts/career combination, teacher certification program. **Credit/placement by examination:** AP, CLEP, IB. 12 credit hours maximum toward associate degree, 32 toward bachelor's. **Support services:** Learning center, remedial instruction, study skills assistance, tutoring, writing center.

**Majors. Area/ethnic studies:** Chicano/Hispanic-American/Latino. **Biology:** General, botany, zoology. **Business:** General, accounting, business admin, managerial economics, marketing, operations. **Computer sciences:** General. **Conservation:** Wildlife. **Education:** General, art, biology, business, chemistry, elementary, ESL, health, mathematics, middle, music, physical, science, secondary, social science, social studies, Spanish, special, technology/industrial arts, voc/tech. **Foreign languages:** Spanish. **Health:** Clinical lab technology. **History:** General. **Liberal arts:** Arts/sciences. **Math:** General. **Physical sciences:** Chemistry. **Protective services:** Criminal justice, law enforcement admin. **Psychology:** General. **Public administration:** Social work. **Social sciences:** General, sociology. **Visual/performing arts:** Studio arts.

**Most popular majors.** Business/marketing 21%, education 20%, health sciences 9%, liberal arts 12%, security/protective services 8%.

**Computing on campus.** 150 workstations in dormitories, library, computer center. Dormitories linked to campus network. Commuter students can connect to campus network. Online course registration, online library, helpline available.

**Student life. Freshman orientation:** Available, $10 fee. Preregistration for classes offered. Two-day sessions held once a month from late May through mid-August. **Housing:** Guaranteed on-campus for all undergraduates. Coed dorms, single-sex dorms, special housing for disabled, apartments available. $75 deposit. **Activities:** Bands, campus ministries, choral groups, drama, music ensembles, musical theater, student government, student newspaper, symphony orchestra, Baptist student union, Society for the Advancement of Management, St. Francis Newman club, Chicano student organization, criminal justice, Native American club.

**Athletics.** NCAA. **Intercollegiate:** Basketball, cross-country, football (tackle) M, golf, softball W, tennis, volleyball W. **Intramural:** Basketball, racquetball, softball, swimming, tennis, volleyball. **Team name:** Mustangs.

**Student services.** Chaplain/spiritual director, career counseling, student employment services, financial aid counseling, health services, minority student services, on-campus daycare, personal counseling, placement for graduates. **Physically disabled:** Services for visually, speech, hearing impaired.

**Contact.** E-mail: tresslerd@wnmu.edu
Phone: (505) 538-6106 Toll-free number: (800) 872-9668
Fax: (505) 538-6127
Dan Tressler, Director of Admissions, Western New Mexico University, Castorena 106, Silver City, NM 88062

# New York

## Adelphi University
**Garden City, New York**
www.adelphi.edu

**CB member**
**CB code: 2003**

- Private 4-year university
- Commuter campus in large town
- 4,923 degree-seeking undergraduates: 13% part-time, 71% women, 11% African American, 6% Asian American, 7% Hispanic American, 3% international
- 2,934 degree-seeking graduate students
- 70% of applicants admitted
- SAT or ACT with writing, application essay required
- 62% graduate within 6 years; 44% enter graduate study

**General.** Founded in 1896. Regionally accredited. Program for students with learning disabilities. **Degrees:** 1,273 bachelor's, 8 associate awarded; master's, doctoral, professional offered. **ROTC:** Army, Air Force. **Location:** 20 miles from New York City. **Calendar:** Semester, limited summer session. **Full-time faculty:** 308 total; 86% have terminal degrees, 21% minority, 54% women. **Part-time faculty:** 585 total; 17% minority, 66% women. **Class size:** 46% < 20, 49% 20-39, 3% 40-49, 1% 50-99. **Special facilities:** Speech and hearing center, science library, observatory, arboretum.

**Freshman class profile.** 7,359 applied, 5,125 admitted, 1,005 enrolled.

| Mid 50% test scores | | GPA 2.0-2.99: | 22% |
|---|---|---|---|
| SAT critical reading: | 480-580 | Rank in top quarter: | 60% |
| SAT math: | 500-600 | Rank in top tenth: | 24% |
| SAT writing: | 500-590 | End year in good standing: | 91% |
| ACT composite: | 20-26 | Return as sophomores: | 80% |
| GPA 3.75 or higher: | 24% | Out-of-state: | 11% |
| GPA 3.50-3.74: | 23% | Live on campus: | 43% |
| GPA 3.0-3.49: | 30% | International: | 2% |

**Basis for selection.** 3.0 cumulative GPA, and combined critical reading, math and writing SAT score of 1500 or higher very important. Rank in top third of class, school and community activities, references also important. SAT/ACT scores accepted on rolling basis. SAT recommended for General Studies entrants, not required for adult academic programs in University College. Applicants to dance, drama, music, or art require audition and portfolio review, education majors must have 2.75 minimum GPA. **Home-schooled:** State high school equivalency certificate required. GED required if applicant not receiving diploma from accredited high school or academy. **Learning Disabled:** Fee-based learning disability program where students receive academic and counseling support, requires admission: interview required, SAT recommended, WAIS-III, WJ-III required.

**High school preparation.** College-preparatory program recommended. 16 units recommended. Recommended units include English 4, mathematics 3, science 3 and foreign language 2. 4 additional units recommended in either social studies, history, English, mathematics, science or foreign language.

**2009-2010 Annual costs.** Tuition/fees: $26,230. Room/board: $10,500. Books/supplies: $1,000. Personal expenses: $1,200.

**2009-2010 Financial aid. Need-based:** 864 full-time freshmen applied for aid; 718 were judged to have need; 696 of these received aid. Average need met was 38%. Average scholarship/grant was $6,340; average loan $3,979. 64% of total undergraduate aid awarded as scholarships/grants, 36% as loans/jobs. **Non-need-based:** Awarded to 4,705 full-time undergraduates, including 1,057 freshmen. Scholarships awarded for academics, alumni affiliation, art, athletics, leadership, minority status, music/drama, religious affiliation.

**Application procedures. Admission:** No deadline. $35 fee, may be waived for applicants with need. Admission notification on a rolling basis beginning on or about 10/1. **Financial aid:** Priority date 3/1; no closing date. FAFSA required. Applicants notified on a rolling basis starting 2/15.

**Academics. Special study options:** Accelerated study, combined bachelor's/graduate degree, cross-registration, distance learning, double major, dual enrollment of high school students, ESL, honors, independent study, internships, liberal arts/career combination, study abroad, teacher certification program, Washington semester, weekend college. Learning Disabilities program combining matriculation with support services; University College for adults 21 and over; 1-year intensive General Studies program for freshmen with HS records/SAT scores that do not meet school standards. Students who successfully complete this program invited to enroll in other school programs in their sophomore year. **Credit/placement by examination:** AP, CLEP, IB. 30 credit hours maximum toward bachelor's degree. **Support services:** Learning center, pre-admission summer program, reduced course load, study skills assistance, tutoring, writing center.

**Honors college/program.** SAT, 3.5 GPA, evidence of academic or creative writing and interview required. 60-90 freshmen admitted.

**Majors. Area/ethnic studies:** Latin American. **Biology:** General, biochemistry. **Business:** Accounting, business admin, finance. **Communications:** Journalism, media studies. **Computer sciences:** General, information systems. **Conservation:** Environmental studies. **Education:** Art, health, physical, secondary. **Foreign languages:** French, Spanish. **Health:** Audiology/speech pathology, nursing (RN). **History:** General. **Interdisciplinary:** Biological/physical sciences, global studies. **Liberal arts:** Humanities. **Math:** General. **Parks/recreation:** Health/fitness, sports admin. **Philosophy/religion:** Philosophy. **Physical sciences:** Chemistry, physics. **Protective services:** Law enforcement admin. **Psychology:** General. **Public administration:** Social work. **Social sciences:** General, anthropology, economics, political science, sociology. **Visual/performing arts:** Art history/conservation, dance, dramatic, studio arts.

**Most popular majors.** Business/marketing 13%, health sciences 31%, psychology 7%, social sciences 11%, visual/performing arts 7%.

**Computing on campus.** 680 workstations in dormitories, library, computer center, student center. Dormitories wired for high-speed internet access and linked to campus network. Commuter students can connect to campus network. Online course registration, online library, helpline, repair service, student web hosting, wireless network available.

**Student life. Freshman orientation:** Mandatory, $255 fee. Preregistration for classes offered. 3-day orientation held on Garden City campus. **Housing:** Coed dorms, special housing for disabled available. $300 nonrefundable deposit, deadline 5/1. Special housing available for students in Honors College, Performing Arts, and Excel Mentoring Program. **Activities:** Bands, campus ministries, choral groups, dance, drama, film society, international student organizations, literary magazine, music ensembles, Model UN, musical theater, opera, radio station, student government, student newspaper, symphony orchestra, Approximately 80 activities are offered.

**Athletics.** NCAA. **Intercollegiate:** Baseball M, basketball, bowling W, cross-country, golf M, lacrosse, soccer, softball W, swimming, tennis, track and field, volleyball W. **Intramural:** Badminton, basketball, cheerleading W, football (non-tackle), soccer, volleyball, weight lifting M. **Team name:** Panthers.

**Student services.** Adult student services, alcohol/substance abuse counseling, chaplain/spiritual director, career counseling, student employment services, financial aid counseling, health services, minority student services, on-campus daycare, personal counseling, placement for graduates, veterans' counselor. **Physically disabled:** Services for visually, speech, hearing impaired. **Learning disabled:** Comprehensive services available.

**Contact.** E-mail: admissions@adelphi.edu
Phone: (516) 877-3050 Toll-free number: (800) 233-5744
Fax: (516) 877-3039
Christine Murphy, Director of Admissions, Adelphi University, One South Avenue, Levermore 110, Garden City, NY 11530-0701

## Albany College of Pharmacy and Health Sciences
**Albany, New York**
www.acphs.edu

**CB code: 2013**

- Private 4-year health science and pharmacy college
- Residential campus in small city
- 1,112 degree-seeking undergraduates: 1% part-time, 60% women, 3% African American, 14% Asian American, 2% Hispanic American, 8% international
- 452 degree-seeking graduate students
- 66% of applicants admitted
- SAT or ACT with writing, application essay required
- 71% graduate within 6 years

**General.** Founded in 1881. Regionally accredited. **Degrees:** 17 bachelor's awarded; master's, professional offered. **ROTC:** Army, Naval, Air Force. **Location:** 200 miles from New York City. **Calendar:** Semester, limited summer session. **Full-time faculty:** 94 total; 85% have terminal degrees, 13% minority, 45% women. **Part-time faculty:** 28 total; 54% have terminal degrees, 4% minority, 61% women. **Class size:** 38% < 20, 38% 20-39, less than 1% 40-49, 7% 50-99, 17% >100. **Special facilities:** Turn-of-the-century antique pharmacy.

**Freshman class profile.** 1,060 applied, 702 admitted, 193 enrolled.

| Mid 50% test scores | | GPA 2.0-2.99: | 7% |
|---|---|---|---|
| SAT critical reading: | 510-620 | Rank in top quarter: | 88% |
| SAT math: | 580-660 | Rank in top tenth: | 53% |
| SAT writing: | 500-620 | End year in good standing: | 97% |
| ACT composite: | 25-28 | Return as sophomores: | 90% |
| GPA 3.75 or higher: | 41% | Out-of-state: | 18% |
| GPA 3.50-3.74: | 24% | Live on campus: | 96% |
| GPA 3.0-3.49: | 28% | International: | 8% |

**Basis for selection.** High school record, test scores, essay, letters of recommendation, New York State Regents Examinations considered. Special emphasis on science and mathematics grades.

**High school preparation.** College-preparatory program required. 17 units required; 21 recommended. Required and recommended units include English 4, mathematics 3-4, social studies 3, science 4 (laboratory 4) and academic electives 6.

**2009-2010 Annual costs.** Tuition/fees: $26,410. Required fees includes cost of laptop ($2,000). Room/board: $8,300. Books/supplies: $800. Personal expenses: $700.

**2009-2010 Financial aid.** **Need-based:** 195 full-time freshmen applied for aid; 177 were judged to have need; 146 of these received aid. Average need met was 51%. Average scholarship/grant was $9,280; average loan $3,618. 32% of total undergraduate aid awarded as scholarships/grants, 68% as loans/jobs. **Non-need-based:** Awarded to 186 full-time undergraduates, including 43 freshmen. Scholarships awarded for academics, alumni affiliation.

**Application procedures. Admission:** Priority date 2/1; no deadline. $75 fee, may be waived for applicants with need. Admission notification on a rolling basis beginning on or about 3/1. Must reply by May 1 or within 2 week(s) if notified thereafter. **Financial aid:** Priority date 2/1, closing date 5/1. FAFSA, CSS PROFILE required. Applicants notified by 3/25; must reply within 2 week(s) of notification.

**Academics. Special study options:** Combined bachelor's/graduate degree, cross-registration, independent study. **Credit/placement by examination:** AP, CLEP. **Support services:** Study skills assistance, tutoring, writing center.

**Majors. Health:** Clinical lab science, cytotechnology, health services, pharmaceutical sciences.

**Computing on campus.** PC or laptop required. 30 workstations in library. Dormitories wired for high-speed internet access and linked to campus network. Commuter students can connect to campus network. Online library, helpline, repair service, wireless network available.

**Student life. Freshman orientation:** Mandatory, $250 fee. Usually held over first weekend prior to class start. **Policies:** College observes honor code. Residency required in first 2 years of study except for students living within 30-mile radius of campus. **Housing:** Guaranteed on-campus for freshmen. Coed dorms, apartments available. $250 nonrefundable deposit, deadline 6/1. **Activities:** Choral groups, dance, international student organizations, literary magazine, student government, student newspaper, Academy of Student Pharmacists, student pharmaceutical society of state of NY, Phi Lambda Sigma.

**Athletics. Intercollegiate:** Basketball, soccer. **Intramural:** Basketball, football (non-tackle), tennis, volleyball. **Team name:** Panthers.

**Student services.** Alcohol/substance abuse counseling, chaplain/spiritual director, career counseling, student employment services, financial aid counseling, health services, minority student services, personal counseling, placement for graduates.

**Contact.** E-mail: admissions@acphs.edu
Phone: (518) 694-7221 Toll-free number: (888) 203-8010
Fax: (518) 694-7322
Matthew Stever, Director of Admissions, Albany College of Pharmacy and Health Sciences, 106 New Scotland Avenue, Albany, NY 12208-3492

---

## Alfred University
**Alfred, New York**
www.alfred.edu
**CB member**
**CB code: 2005**

- Private 4-year university
- Residential campus in rural community
- 1,846 degree-seeking undergraduates: 1% part-time, 51% women, 5% African American, 2% Asian American, 3% Hispanic American, 2% international
- 386 degree-seeking graduate students
- 70% of applicants admitted
- SAT or ACT (ACT writing optional), application essay required
- 69% graduate within 6 years; 26% enter graduate study

**General.** Founded in 1836. Regionally accredited. **Degrees:** 399 bachelor's awarded; master's, doctoral offered. **ROTC:** Army. **Location:** 75 miles from Rochester, 65 miles from Elmira. **Calendar:** Semester, limited summer session. **Full-time faculty:** 165 total. **Part-time faculty:** 34 total. **Class size:** 62% < 20, 33% 20-39, 2% 40-49, 2% 50-99, 1% >100. **Special facilities:** Observatory, memorial carillon, art galleries, ceramics museum and library, equestrian center.

**Freshman class profile.** 2,579 applied, 1,816 admitted, 465 enrolled.

| Mid 50% test scores | | GPA 2.0-2.99: | 29% |
|---|---|---|---|
| SAT critical reading: | 490-600 | Rank in top quarter: | 54% |
| SAT math: | 510-600 | Rank in top tenth: | 22% |
| SAT writing: | 470-590 | Return as sophomores: | 71% |
| ACT composite: | 22-27 | Out-of-state: | 25% |
| GPA 3.75 or higher: | 14% | Live on campus: | 98% |
| GPA 3.50-3.74: | 18% | International: | 4% |
| GPA 3.0-3.49: | 38% | | |

**Basis for selection.** Rigor of high school curriculum, grades, class rank, standardized ACT or SAT test results, extracurricular involvement, letters of recommendation, and character are all factors. International students required to submit TOEFL if they do not take the SAT or ACT. Interview recommended. Portfolio required for students seeking admission to School of Art & Design. **Homeschooled:** Advise students to document courses taken and provide reading list. SAT or ACT mandatory and relied on heavily.

**High school preparation.** College-preparatory program recommended. 16 units required. Required units include English 4, mathematics 2, social studies 2, science 2 (laboratory 2). 3-4 math for business college, 2-3 math for liberal arts and science college, 2 math for art and design college, 4 math for engineering school.

**2010-2011 Annual costs.** Tuition/fees (projected): $25,976. Tuition info provided is for students enrolling in the College of Business or the College of Liberal Arts and Sciences. Costs for students enrolling in the School of Engineering vary by program and/or residency. Costs for students enrolling in the School of Art and Design vary by residency. Room/board: $11,364. Books/supplies: $1,000. Personal expenses: $1,150.

**2008-2009 Financial aid. Non-need-based:** Scholarships awarded for academics, art, leadership, music/drama.

**Application procedures. Admission:** Priority date 2/1; deadline 8/1 (postmark date). $50 fee, may be waived for applicants with need. Admission notification on a rolling basis beginning on or about 11/15. Must reply by May 1 or within 2 week(s) if notified thereafter. **Financial aid:** Closing date 3/15. FAFSA, institutional form required. Applicants notified on a rolling basis starting 2/15; must reply by 5/1 or within 2 week(s) of notification.

**Academics.** Credit hours needed for graduation vary from 120-138 depending on major. Physical education requirement for all students. Additional graduation requirements vary by college/school. Preadmission summer program is required for students enrolling at AU through Opportunity Programs (EOP or HEOP). **Special study options:** Combined bachelor's/graduate degree, cooperative education, cross-registration, double major, ESL, exchange student, honors, independent study, internships, liberal arts/career combination, New York semester, semester at sea, student-designed major, study abroad, teacher certification program, United Nations semester, Washington semester. **Credit/placement by examination:** AP, CLEP, IB, SAT, ACT, institutional tests. **Support services:** Reduced course load, study skills assistance, tutoring, writing center.

**Majors. Biology:** General. **Business:** Accounting, business admin, finance, marketing. **Communications:** General. **Conservation:** Environmental studies. **Education:** Art, biology, business, chemistry, elementary, English, French, mathematics, middle, physics, social studies, Spanish. **Engineering:** Biomedical, ceramic, electrical, materials, materials science, mechanical. **Foreign languages:** French, German, Spanish. **Health:** Athletic training, predental, premedicine, preveterinary. **History:** General. **Interdisciplinary:** Biological/physical sciences, gerontology, intercultural. **Liberal arts:** Arts/sciences. **Math:** General. **Philosophy/religion:** Philosophy. **Physical sciences:** Chemistry, geology, physics. **Protective services:** Criminal justice. **Psychology:** General. **Social sciences:** Economics, political science, sociology. **Visual/performing arts:** Ceramics, dramatic, studio arts. **Other:** Glass science engineering.

**Most popular majors.** Business/marketing 14%, education 6%, engineering/engineering technologies 14%, psychology 9%, visual/performing arts 31%.

**Computing on campus.** 450 workstations in dormitories, library, computer center, student center. Dormitories wired for high-speed internet access and linked to campus network. Commuter students can connect to campus network. Online course registration, online library, helpline, student web hosting, wireless network available.

**Student life. Freshman orientation:** Mandatory. Preregistration for classes offered. Starts the Wednesday before classes begin in the fall. **Policies:** Students must abide by Code of Honor. Policies against hazing and sexual harassment. All students required to live in residence halls 6 semesters. Students in poor academic standing required to live on campus. Exceptions granted for married students, students 23 and older, students living with parents/legal guardian and commuting from home, students with dependents, and veterans. **Housing:** Guaranteed on-campus for freshmen. Coed dorms, apartments, wellness housing available. $300 nonrefundable deposit, deadline 5/1. Experiential living available. **Activities:** Bands, choral groups, dance, drama, film society, international student organizations, literary magazine, music ensembles, musical theater, radio station, student government, student newspaper, symphony orchestra, TV station, Hillel, Brothers and Sisters in Christ, Spectrum, Student Volunteers for Community Action, Alpha Phi Omega, Habitat for Humanity, Students Acting for Equality, Umoja, Omicron Delta Kappa, Poder Latino.

**Athletics.** NCAA. **Intercollegiate:** Basketball, cross-country, diving, equestrian, football (tackle) M, lacrosse, skiing, soccer, softball W, swimming, tennis, track and field, volleyball W. **Intramural:** Basketball, football (nontackle), lacrosse M, racquetball, skiing, soccer, softball, squash, tennis, volleyball. **Team name:** Saxons.

**Student services.** Alcohol/substance abuse counseling, chaplain/spiritual director, career counseling, services for economically disadvantaged, student employment services, financial aid counseling, health services, minority student services, personal counseling, placement for graduates, women's services. **Physically disabled:** Services for visually, speech, hearing impaired.

**Contact.** E-mail: admissions@alfred.edu
Phone: (607) 871-2115 Toll-free number: (800) 541-9229
Fax: (607) 871-2198
Jeremy Spencer, Director of Admissions, Alfred University, Alumni Hall, Alfred, NY 14802-1205

## Bard College
**Annandale-on-Hudson, New York**          CB member
**www.bard.edu**          CB code: 2037

- Private 4-year liberal arts college affiliated with Episcopal Church
- Residential campus in small town
- 1,900 degree-seeking undergraduates: 2% part-time, 57% women, 2% African American, 3% Asian American, 3% Hispanic American, 1% Native American, 12% international
- 295 degree-seeking graduate students
- 33% of applicants admitted
- Application essay required
- 79% graduate within 6 years

**General.** Founded in 1860. Regionally accredited. **Degrees:** 404 bachelor's awarded; master's, doctoral offered. **Location:** 90 miles from New York City, 50 miles from Albany. **Calendar:** Semester. **Full-time faculty:** 145 total; 96% have terminal degrees, 15% minority, 44% women. **Part-time faculty:** 92 total; 86% have terminal degrees, 14% minority, 54% women. **Class size:** 69% < 20, 31% 20-39, less than 1% 40-49. **Special facilities:** Ecology field station contiguous to Hudson River Estuary Preserves; curatorial studies and art center; museum of late 20th-century art; archaeological field school; economics institute; center for studies in decorative arts, design and culture; performing arts center; science center.

**Freshman class profile.** 5,510 applied, 1,826 admitted, 505 enrolled.

| Mid 50% test scores | | End year in good standing: | 90% |
|---|---|---|---|
| SAT critical reading: | 680-740 | Return as sophomores: | 87% |
| SAT math: | 650-680 | Out-of-state: | 56% |
| Rank in top quarter: | 95% | Live on campus: | 99% |
| Rank in top tenth: | 64% | International: | 15% |

**Basis for selection.** School transcripts and achievement record, rigor of high school program, essays, academic recommendations, talents and dedication to activities, love of learning, and personal ambition important. Campus tour and information session recommended. Tape or CD, brief musical autobiography, and audition required of conservatory applicants. **Homeschooled:** Statement describing homeschool structure and mission, transcript of courses and grades required.

**High school preparation.** College-preparatory program required. 24 units recommended. Recommended units include English 4, mathematics 4, social studies 4, history 4, science 4 (laboratory 3) and foreign language 4.

**2009-2010 Annual costs.** Tuition/fees: $39,880. Room/board: $11,300. Books/supplies: $850. Personal expenses: $600.

**2009-2010 Financial aid. Need-based:** 362 full-time freshmen applied for aid; 336 were judged to have need; 336 of these received aid. Average need met was 90%. Average scholarship/grant was $31,540; average loan $3,547. 82% of total undergraduate aid awarded as scholarships/grants, 18% as loans/jobs. **Non-need-based:** Awarded to 35 full-time undergraduates, including 7 freshmen. Scholarships awarded for academics. **Additional information:** Excellence and Equal Cost Program for students who graduate in top 10 of public high school class lowers fees to levels equivalent to those at home state university or college.

**Application procedures. Admission:** Closing date 1/15 (receipt date). $50 fee, may be waived for applicants with need. Application must be submitted on paper. Admission notification on a rolling basis beginning on or about 4/1. Must reply by May 1 or within 2 week(s) if notified thereafter. Applicants may be admitted through early action, regular procedure, or Immediate Decision Plan, which gives next-day decision after day-long program and individual interview. Sessions scheduled in early fall. **Financial aid:** Priority date 2/1, closing date 2/15. FAFSA, CSS PROFILE required. Applicants notified by 4/1; must reply by 5/1.

**Academics.** Strong tradition of independent study and tutorial work with faculty member. Writing-intensive, multidisciplinary programs. Extensive programs in languages, human rights and globalization and international affairs. Unique collaboration with The Rockefeller University. **Special study options:** Combined bachelor's/graduate degree, cross-registration, double major, dual enrollment of high school students, ESL, independent study, internships, New York semester, student-designed major, study abroad, Washington semester. Intensive language studies in Italy, Germany, France, Mexico, Russia, China, program in International Education (Central and Eastern Europe and Southern Africa). **Credit/placement by examination:** AP, CLEP, IB. **Support services:** Learning center, reduced course load, remedial instruction, study skills assistance, tutoring, writing center.

**Majors. Area/ethnic studies:** African, American, Asian, French, German, Italian, Latin American, Near/Middle Eastern, Russian/Slavic, Spanish/Iberian. **Biology:** General. **Computer sciences:** Computer science. **Foreign languages:** General, ancient Greek, Arabic, Chinese, comparative lit, French, German, Hebrew, Italian, Japanese, Latin, Russian, Sanskrit, Spanish, translation. **Health:** Premedicine. **History:** General, American, Asian, European. **Interdisciplinary:** Global studies, medieval/Renaissance, neuroscience. **Legal studies:** Prelaw. **Liberal arts:** Arts/sciences. **Math:** General. **Philosophy/religion:** Judaic, philosophy, religion. **Physical sciences:** Chemistry, physics. **Psychology:** General. **Social sciences:** General, anthropology, archaeology, economics, political science, sociology. **Visual/performing arts:** General, acting, art history/conservation, cinematography, conducting, dance, directing/producing, dramatic, film/cinema, jazz, multimedia, music history, music performance, music theory/composition, photography, piano/organ, play/screenwriting, stringed instruments, studio arts, theater history, voice/opera. **Other:** Gender and sexuality, Human rights.

**Most popular majors.** English 15%, foreign language 8%, history 9%, social sciences 15%, visual/performing arts 32%.

**Computing on campus.** 425 workstations in library, computer center, student center. Dormitories wired for high-speed internet access and linked to campus network. Commuter students can connect to campus network. Online course registration, online library, helpline, student web hosting, wireless network available.

**Student life. Freshman orientation:** Mandatory, $660 fee. 3-week writing-intensive Workshop in Language and Thinking held on campus in August immediately prior to fall semester; coincides with Bard Music Festival. **Policies:** All students members of the student government association, a democratic forum that allocates funds, takes action on campus issues, and provides student representation on administrative and faculty committees. **Housing:**

Guaranteed on-campus for freshmen. Coed dorms, single-sex dorms, cooperative housing, wellness housing available. Pets allowed in dorm rooms. **Activities:** Bands, campus ministries, choral groups, dance, drama, film society, international student organizations, literary magazine, music ensembles, Model UN, musical theater, opera, radio station, student government, student newspaper, symphony orchestra, over 120 clubs and organizations available.

**Athletics.** NCAA. **Intercollegiate:** Basketball, cross-country, soccer, squash M, tennis, track and field, volleyball. **Intramural:** Basketball, bowling, soccer, softball, squash. **Team name:** Raptors.

**Student services.** Adult student services, alcohol/substance abuse counseling, chaplain/spiritual director, career counseling, services for economically disadvantaged, student employment services, financial aid counseling, health services, legal services, minority student services, personal counseling, placement for graduates, women's services. **Physically disabled:** Services for visually, hearing impaired.

**Contact.** E-mail: admissions@bard.edu
Phone: (845) 758-7472 Fax: (845) 758-5208
Mary Backlund, Director of Admission, Bard College, 30 Campus Road, Annandale-on-Hudson, NY 12504-5000

---

## Barnard College
**New York, New York**  
**www.barnard.edu**  
CB member  
CB code: 2038

- Private 4-year liberal arts college for women
- Residential campus in very large city
- 2,417 degree-seeking undergraduates: 3% part-time, 100% women, 4% African American, 16% Asian American, 9% Hispanic American, 5% international
- 31% of applicants admitted
- SAT and SAT Subject Tests or ACT with writing, application essay required
- 91% graduate within 6 years; 21% enter graduate study

**General.** Founded in 1889. Regionally accredited. Cross-registration and shared facilities with Columbia University. Students receive Columbia University degrees. **Degrees:** 633 bachelor's awarded. **Calendar:** Semester. **Full-time faculty:** 208 total; 94% have terminal degrees, 15% minority, 58% women. **Part-time faculty:** 141 total; 86% have terminal degrees, 12% minority, 74% women. **Class size:** 71% <20, 18% 20-39, 4% 40-49, 6% 50-99, 2% >100. **Special facilities:** Black box theater, center for toddler development, center for research on women, theater, dance studios, access to 3,600-acre nature preserve in upstate New York, greenhouse, access to geological observatory.

**Freshman class profile.** 4,174 applied, 1,295 admitted, 577 enrolled.

| Mid 50% test scores | | | |
|---|---|---|---|
| SAT critical reading: | 630-730 | Rank in top quarter: | 93% |
| SAT math: | 620-710 | Rank in top tenth: | 75% |
| SAT writing: | 660-740 | Return as sophomores: | 93% |
| ACT composite: | 28-32 | Out-of-state: | 67% |
| GPA 3.75 or higher: | 70% | Live on campus: | 99% |
| GPA 3.50-3.74: | 20% | International: | 6% |
| GPA 3.0-3.49: | 10% | | |

**Basis for selection.** High school record most important. Depth and difficulty of high school program considered. Test scores, recommendations, involvement in school and community activities, special talents, skills considered. Interview recommended.

**High school preparation.** College-preparatory program required. 16 units recommended. Recommended units include English 4, mathematics 3, science 3 (laboratory 2) and foreign language 3. Additional units in social sciences, art, music also recommended.

**2009-2010 Annual costs.** Tuition/fees: $38,650. Room/board: $12,319. Books/supplies: $1,146. Personal expenses: $1,366.

**2009-2010 Financial aid.** All financial aid based on need. 308 full-time freshmen applied for aid; 231 were judged to have need; 231 of these received aid. Average need met was 100%. Average scholarship/grant was $33,153; average loan $3,257. 85% of total undergraduate aid awarded as scholarships/grants, 15% as loans/jobs. **Additional information:** HEOP for NY residents only; no loan. Pell eligible students: no loan for first-year students, loan reduced to $2,000 for sophomores, juniors and seniors.

**Application procedures. Admission:** Closing date 1/1 (postmark date). $55 fee, may be waived for applicants with need. Application must be submitted on paper. Admission notification 4/1. Must reply by May 1 or within 2 week(s) if notified thereafter. **Financial aid:** Closing date 2/1. FAFSA,

institutional form, CSS PROFILE required. Applicants notified by 3/31; must reply by 5/1.

**Academics.** Interdisciplinary first-year seminar; coursework in global cultures, which may also fulfill other degree requirements. **Special study options:** Accelerated study, combined bachelor's/graduate degree, cross-registration, double major, dual enrollment of high school students, exchange student, honors, independent study, internships, liberal arts/career combination, student-designed major, study abroad, teacher certification program. Independent scholars program, BA/BS in engineering and applied science. **Credit/placement by examination:** AP, CLEP, IB, institutional tests. 30 credit hours maximum toward bachelor's degree. **Support services:** Pre-admission summer program, tutoring, writing center.

**Majors. Architecture:** Architecture, history/criticism. **Area/ethnic studies:** African, American, Asian, European, French, German, Latin American, Near/Middle Eastern, Russian/Slavic, Slavic, Spanish/Iberian, women's. **Biology:** General, biochemistry, biophysics, environmental. **Computer sciences:** General, computer science. **Conservation:** Environmental science, environmental studies. **Engineering:** Physics. **Foreign languages:** Ancient Greek, classics, comparative lit, French, German, Italian, Latin, linguistics, modern Greek, Russian, Spanish. **History:** General. **Interdisciplinary:** Ancient studies, biopsychology, medieval/Renaissance. **Math:** General, applied, statistics. **Philosophy/religion:** Philosophy, religion. **Physical sciences:** Astronomy, astrophysics, chemical physics, chemistry, geology, physics. **Psychology:** General. **Social sciences:** Anthropology, economics, geography, political science, sociology, urban studies. **Visual/performing arts:** General, art history/conservation, dance, dramatic, film/cinema, jazz.

**Most popular majors.** Area/ethnic studies 10%, biology 8%, English 12%, history 6%, psychology 7%, social sciences 29%, visual/performing arts 13%.

**Computing on campus.** 210 workstations in dormitories, library, computer center, student center. Dormitories wired for high-speed internet access and linked to campus network. Commuter students can connect to campus network. Online course registration, online library, helpline, repair service, wireless network available.

**Student life. Freshman orientation:** Mandatory. Week-long program that begins August 27. **Housing:** Guaranteed on-campus for all undergraduates. Special housing for disabled, apartments available. $400 nonrefundable deposit, deadline 6/15. Coed dorms offered through Columbia University. **Activities:** Bands, campus ministries, choral groups, dance, drama, film society, literary magazine, music ensembles, musical theater, opera, radio station, student government, student newspaper, symphony orchestra, TV station, more than 100 organizations.

**Athletics.** NCAA. **Intercollegiate:** Archery W, basketball W, cross-country W, diving W, fencing W, field hockey W, golf W, lacrosse W, rowing (crew) W, soccer W, softball W, swimming W, tennis W, track and field W, volleyball W. **Intramural:** Archery W, badminton W, basketball W, bowling W, cross-country W, fencing W, racquetball W, sailing W, soccer W, softball W, swimming W, tennis W, volleyball W. **Team name:** Lions.

**Student services.** Alcohol/substance abuse counseling, career counseling, student employment services, financial aid counseling, health services, personal counseling, placement for graduates, women's services. **Physically disabled:** Services for visually, speech, hearing impaired.

**Contact.** E-mail: admissions@barnard.edu
Phone: (212) 854-2014 Fax: (212) 854-6220
Jennifer Fondiller, Dean of Admissions, Barnard College, 3009 Broadway, New York, NY 10027-6598

---

## Beis Medrash Heichal Dovid
**Far Rockaway, New York**

- Private 4-year rabbinical college for men affiliated with Jewish faith
- Residential campus in large city
- 116 degree-seeking undergraduates
- 15 degree-seeking graduate students

**General.** Accredited by AARTS. **Degrees:** 2 bachelor's awarded; master's offered. **Calendar:** Semester. **Full-time faculty:** 4 total. **Part-time faculty:** 4 total.

**Basis for selection.** Religious faith most important criteria. **Home-schooled:** Transcript of courses and grades, state high school equivalency certificate, interview, letter of recommendation (nonparent) required.

**2010-2011 Annual costs.** Tuition/fees: $8,450. Room/board: $4,500.

**Application procedures. Admission:** No deadline. $250 fee. Admission notification on a rolling basis.

**Academics. Credit/placement by examination:** CLEP.

**Majors. Theology:** Talmudic.

**Contact.** Phone: (718) 868-2300 ext. 360 Fax: (718) 406-8359
Aaron Steinberg, Admin. Assist., Beis Medrash Heichal Dovid, 211 Beach
17th Street, Far Rockaway, NY 11691

## Berkeley College
**White Plains, New York**
www.berkeleycollege.edu                    **CB code: 2064**

- For-profit 4-year business college
- Commuter campus in small city
- 718 degree-seeking undergraduates: 4% part-time, 63% women, 36%
  African American, 3% Asian American, 26% Hispanic American, 6%
  international

**General.** Founded in 1945. Regionally accredited. **Degrees:** 85 bachelor's,
25 associate awarded. **Location:** 28 miles from New York City. **Calendar:**
Quarter, extensive summer session. **Full-time faculty:** 20 total. **Part-time
faculty:** 30 total. **Class size:** 39% < 20, 61% 20-39. **Special facilities:** Access to Manhattanville College facilities.

**Freshman class profile.**

| Out-of-state: | 18% | International: | 4% |
|---|---|---|---|

**Basis for selection.** Class rank, high school record, interview most important. Passing grade on school entrance examination required. SAT/ACT
considered if submitted. Interviews strongly recommended.

**2010-2011 Annual costs.** Tuition/fees (projected): $20,700. Room only:
$8,300. Books/supplies: $1,360. Personal expenses: $3,000.

**Financial aid. Non-need-based:** Scholarships awarded for academics, alumni
affiliation. **Additional information:** Alumni scholarship examination given
in November and December. Full and partial scholarships awarded.

**Application procedures. Admission:** No deadline. $50 fee. Admission
notification on a rolling basis. Admitted applicants must reply within 2 weeks
of notification. **Financial aid:** No deadline. FAFSA required. Applicants
notified on a rolling basis starting 3/1; must reply within 6 week(s) of notification.

**Academics. Special study options:** Accelerated study, distance learning,
ESL, internships, New York semester, study abroad. **Credit/placement by
examination:** AP, CLEP, SAT, ACT, institutional tests. **Support services:**
Learning center, remedial instruction, study skills assistance, tutoring, writing center.

**Majors. Business:** Accounting, business admin, fashion, financial planning, international, management information systems, marketing. **Health:**
Health care admin. **Protective services:** Law enforcement admin.

**Computing on campus.** 150 workstations in library, computer center.
Dormitories linked to campus network. Commuter students can connect to
campus network. Online library, helpline, wireless network available.

**Student life. Freshman orientation:** Mandatory. **Housing:** Coed dorms
available. $400 fully refundable deposit. **Activities:** Student government,
accounting club, Berkeley club, Phi Beta Lambda, Phi Theta Kappa, international club, fashion club, paralegal club.

**Athletics. Intramural:** Basketball, cheerleading, soccer. **Team name:** Knights.

**Student services.** Adult student services, career counseling, student employment services, financial aid counseling, personal counseling, placement
for graduates.

**Contact.** E-mail: info@berkeleycollege.edu
Phone: (914) 694-1122 Toll-free number: (800) 446-5400
Fax: (914) 328-9469
Linda Pinsky, AVP Enrollment, NY, Berkeley College, 99 Church Street,
White Plains, NY 10601

## Berkeley College of New York City
**New York, New York**
www.berkeleycollege.edu                    **CB code: 0954**

- For-profit 4-year business college
- Commuter campus in very large city
- 3,672 degree-seeking undergraduates: 13% part-time, 69% women

**General.** Founded in 1936. Regionally accredited. Extension center located in Lower Manhattan (Financial District) and a branch campus located
in Westchester County (White Plains). **Degrees:** 435 bachelor's, 145 associate awarded. **Location:** Midtown Manhattan. **Calendar:** Quarter, extensive summer session. **Full-time faculty:** 83 total. **Part-time faculty:** 150
total. **Class size:** 11% < 20, 89% 20-39.

**Basis for selection.** High school record and interview most important.
Institutional entrance tests required of all applicants. SAT or ACT accepted
in lieu of institutional entrance exam.

**2010-2011 Annual costs.** Tuition/fees (projected): $20,700. Books/
supplies: $1,360. Personal expenses: $3,000.

**Financial aid. Non-need-based:** Scholarships awarded for academics, alumni
affiliation. **Additional information:** Alumni scholarship examination given
in November and December. Full and partial scholarships awarded.

**Application procedures. Admission:** No deadline. $50 fee. Admission
notification on a rolling basis. Admitted applicants must reply within 2 weeks
of notification. **Financial aid:** No deadline. FAFSA required. Applicants
notified on a rolling basis starting 3/1; must reply within 6 week(s) of notification.

**Academics. Special study options:** Accelerated study, distance learning,
ESL, internships, study abroad. **Credit/placement by examination:** AP,
CLEP, SAT, ACT, institutional tests. **Support services:** Learning center,
remedial instruction, study skills assistance, tutoring, writing center.

**Majors. Business:** Accounting, business admin, fashion, financial planning, international, management information systems, marketing. **Health:**
Health care admin. **Protective services:** Law enforcement admin.

**Computing on campus.** 200 workstations in library, computer center.
Commuter students can connect to campus network. Online library, helpline, wireless network available.

**Student life. Freshman orientation:** Mandatory. **Housing:** $400 deposit.
**Activities:** Student government, international club, multicultural club, fashion club, accounting club, paralegal club, student government.

**Athletics. Intramural:** Basketball, cheerleading, soccer. **Team name:** Knights.

**Student services.** Adult student services, alcohol/substance abuse counseling, career counseling, student employment services, financial aid counseling, personal counseling, placement for graduates.

**Contact.** E-mail: info@berkeleycollege.edu
Phone: (212) 986-4343 Toll-free number: (800) 446-5400
Fax: (212) 818-1079
Linda Pinsky, AVP, Enrollment NY, Berkeley College of New York City, 3
East 43rd Street, New York, NY 10017

## Beth Hamedrash Shaarei Yosher Institute
**Brooklyn, New York**
                                             **CB code: 0731**

- Private 5-year rabbinical college for men affiliated with Jewish faith
- Very large city
- 41 degree-seeking undergraduates

**General.** Founded in 1962. Accredited by AARTS. First Talmudic degree
and ordination available. **Degrees:** 4 bachelor's awarded; doctoral offered.
**Calendar:** Semester.

**Basis for selection.** Test scores most important. High school record considered.

**2009-2010 Annual costs.** Personal expenses: $1,600.

**Application procedures. Admission:** No deadline.

**Academics. Credit/placement by examination:** CLEP.

**Majors. Philosophy/religion:** Judaic.

**Contact.** Phone: (718) 854-2290
Director of Student Financial Aid, Beth Hamedrash Shaarei Yosher
Institute, 4102-10 16th Avenue, Brooklyn, NY 11204

## Beth Hatalmud Rabbinical College
### Brooklyn, New York
CB code: 7317

- Private 4-year rabbinical college for men affiliated with Jewish faith
- Very large city
- 66 degree-seeking undergraduates

**General.** Founded in 1950. Accredited by AARTS. Ordination and First Rabbinic degree available. **Calendar:** Semester.

**Basis for selection.** Institutional examination.

**2009-2010 Annual costs.** Tuition/fees: $6,100.

**Application procedures. Admission:** Closing date 9/1. Admission notification on a rolling basis.

**Academics. Credit/placement by examination:** CLEP.

**Majors. Philosophy/religion:** Judaic.

**Student life. Policies:** Religious observance required.

**Contact.** Phone: (718) 259-2525
Director of Admissions, Beth Hatalmud Rabbinical College, 2127 82nd Street, Brooklyn, NY 11214

## Boricua College
### New York, New York
### www.boricuacollege.edu
CB code: 2901

- Private 4-year liberal arts college
- Commuter campus in very large city
- 993 degree-seeking undergraduates
- 42 degree-seeking graduate students
- 66% of applicants admitted
- Application essay, interview required

**General.** Founded in 1974. Regionally accredited. Boricua College has four centers: one each in Manhattan and the Bronx, and two in Brooklyn. **Degrees:** 140 bachelor's, 139 associate awarded; master's offered. **Calendar:** Semester, limited summer session. **Full-time faculty:** 47 total; 32% have terminal degrees, 40% women. **Part-time faculty:** 58 total; 22% women. **Class size:** 100% 20-39.

**Freshman class profile.** 562 applied, 371 admitted, 179 enrolled.

**End year in good standing:** 43%    **Return as sophomores:** 45%

**Basis for selection.** Entrance examination, academic records, interview by the faculty, 2 letters of recommendation. Institutional tests required for admissions and placement. Final interview and approval by the faculty is required. **Learning Disabled:** Evaluation is done based on individual needs of the candidate.

**2009-2010 Annual costs.** Tuition/fees: $9,500. Books/supplies: $400. Personal expenses: $3,625.

**Application procedures. Admission:** No deadline. $25 fee, may be waived for applicants with need. Admission notification on a rolling basis. **Financial aid:** Priority date 4/30; no closing date. FAFSA required. Applicants notified on a rolling basis; must reply within 3 week(s) of notification.

**Academics.** Academic load consists of 5 courses per semester: 3 applied studies courses (individualized instruction, colloquium, experiential), 1 theoretical, and 1 cultural class. Academic support services are available at different hours upon request. **Special study options:** Accelerated study, independent study, internships, liberal arts/career combination, teacher certification program. **Credit/placement by examination:** CLEP, institutional tests. 30 credit hours maximum toward bachelor's degree. **Support services:** Reduced course load, tutoring.

**Majors. Area/ethnic studies:** Latin American. **Business:** Business admin. **Education:** Elementary. **Liberal arts:** Arts/sciences. **Public administration:** Human services.

**Computing on campus.** 120 workstations in library, computer center, student center. Online library, helpline, wireless network available.

**Student life. Freshman orientation:** Mandatory. Preregistration for classes offered. Based on appointments. **Policies:** Student regulations include a sexual harassment policy. **Activities:** Choral groups, dance, drama, opera, student government, student newspaper.

**Athletics. Intramural:** Basketball, volleyball.

**Student services.** Adult student services, career counseling, student employment services, personal counseling, placement for graduates.

**Contact.** E-mail: acruz@boricuacollege.edu
Phone: (212) 694-1000 ext. 650 Fax: (212) 694-1015
Miriam Pfeffer, Director of Admissions, Boricua College, 3755 Broadway, New York, NY 10032

## Briarcliffe College
### Bethpage, New York
### www.briarcliffe.edu
CB code: 3108

- For-profit 4-year business and technical college
- Commuter campus in large town
- 1,503 degree-seeking undergraduates

**General.** Founded in 1966. Regionally accredited. **Degrees:** 238 bachelor's, 461 associate awarded. **Location:** 20 miles from New York City. **Calendar:** Semester, extensive summer session. **Full-time faculty:** 65 total. **Part-time faculty:** 128 total.

**Basis for selection.** School achievement record important, recommendations suggested. Interviews recommended. **Homeschooled:** Not accepted.

**High school preparation.** Recommended units include English 4, mathematics 2, social studies 4 and science 1.

**2009-2010 Annual costs.** Tuition/fees: $18,592.

**Financial aid. Non-need-based:** Scholarships awarded for academics.

**Application procedures. Admission:** No deadline. $35 fee. Admission notification on a rolling basis. **Financial aid:** No deadline. FAFSA, institutional form required. Applicants notified on a rolling basis.

**Academics. Special study options:** Distance learning, independent study, internships. **Credit/placement by examination:** AP, CLEP, institutional tests. **Support services:** Learning center, reduced course load, remedial instruction, study skills assistance, tutoring.

**Majors. Business:** Accounting, business admin, marketing. **Computer sciences:** Information technology, networking, programming. **Visual/performing arts:** General.

**Computing on campus.** 400 workstations in library, computer center. Commuter students can connect to campus network. Online library available.

**Student life. Freshman orientation:** Mandatory. Preregistration for classes offered. **Housing:** Coed dorms available. **Activities:** Student government.

**Athletics.** USCAA. **Intercollegiate:** Baseball M, basketball W, bowling, lacrosse M, soccer M, softball W, volleyball W.

**Student services.** Financial aid counseling, placement for graduates.

**Contact.** E-mail: info@bcl.edu
Phone: (516) 918-3600 Fax: (516) 470-6020
Alan Shikowitz, Vice President of Enrollment Management, Briarcliffe College, 1055 Stewart Avenue, Bethpage, NY 11714

## Canisius College
### Buffalo, New York
### www.canisius.edu
CB member
CB code: 2073

- Private 4-year liberal arts and teachers college affiliated with Roman Catholic Church
- Residential campus in large city
- 3,105 degree-seeking undergraduates: 3% part-time, 53% women, 6% African American, 1% Asian American, 2% Hispanic American, 4% international
- 1,572 degree-seeking graduate students
- 77% of applicants admitted
- SAT or ACT (ACT writing optional) required
- 69% graduate within 6 years

**General.** Founded in 1870. Regionally accredited. Campus connected by underground tunnel system, rapid transit stations near campus. **Degrees:** 824 bachelor's, 13 associate awarded; master's offered. **ROTC:** Army. **Calendar:** Semester, limited summer session. **Full-time faculty:** 230 total; 94% have terminal degrees, 7% minority, 37% women. **Part-time faculty:** 233 total; 22% have terminal degrees, 6% minority, 51% women. **Class size:** 46% < 20, 50% 20-39, 3% 40-49, 1% 50-99. **Special facilities:** Mini-planetarium, seismograph station, rare book room, digital media lab, human performance lab, animal care unit.

**Freshman class profile.** 3,996 applied, 3,084 admitted, 758 enrolled.

| Mid 50% test scores | | | |
|---|---|---|---|
| SAT critical reading: | 500-600 | GPA 2.0-2.99: | 14% |
| SAT math: | 510-620 | Rank in top quarter: | 57% |
| ACT composite: | 23-29 | Rank in top tenth: | 27% |
| GPA 3.75 or higher: | 37% | Return as sophomores: | 82% |
| GPA 3.50-3.74: | 19% | Out-of-state: | 8% |
| GPA 3.0-3.49: | 30% | Live on campus: | 69% |
| | | International: | 3% |

**Basis for selection.** Primary emphasis placed on strength of academic record, achievement, class rank and SAT/ACT scores. Essays, recommendations important. Extracurricular activities, alumni affiliation factors. Interview and essay recommended.

**High school preparation.** College-preparatory program required. 17 units required; 26 recommended. Required and recommended units include English 4, mathematics 3-4, social studies 4, science 2-4 (laboratory 2), foreign language 2-4 and academic electives 4.

**2009-2010 Annual costs.** Tuition/fees: $29,512. Room/board: $10,556.

**2009-2010 Financial aid. Need-based:** 641 full-time freshmen applied for aid; 584 were judged to have need; 579 of these received aid. Average need met was 86%. Average scholarship/grant was $20,026; average loan $3,294. 72% of total undergraduate aid awarded as scholarships/grants, 28% as loans/jobs. **Non-need-based:** Awarded to 1,352 full-time undergraduates, including 375 freshmen. Scholarships awarded for academics, alumni affiliation, art, athletics, job skills, music/drama, religious affiliation, ROTC.

**Application procedures. Admission:** Priority date 3/1; deadline 5/1. $40 fee, may be waived for applicants with need, free for online applicants. Admission notification on a rolling basis beginning on or about 12/15. Must reply by 5/1. **Financial aid:** Priority date 2/15; no closing date. FAFSA required. Applicants notified on a rolling basis starting 3/1; must reply within 2 week(s) of notification.

**Academics.** Pre-professional programs include pre-engineering, prelaw, premedical, predentistry, preveterinary medicine, prepharmacy. **Special study options:** Combined bachelor's/graduate degree, cooperative education, cross-registration, distance learning, double major, dual enrollment of high school students, ESL, exchange student, honors, independent study, internships, study abroad, teacher certification program. Early assurance for medical and dental school with SUNY Buffalo Medical and Dental Schools (New York state residents only), and the Upstate Medical School at Syracuse; 7-year joint degree programs with SUNY Buffalo Dental School, the Ohio College of Podiatric Medicine, the New York College of Podiatric Medicine and SUNY State College of Optometry in NYC; AS/BS with Fashion Institute of Technology. **Credit/placement by examination:** AP, CLEP, IB, SAT, ACT, institutional tests. 30 credit hours maximum toward bachelor's degree. **Support services:** Learning center, pre-admission summer program, reduced course load, remedial instruction, study skills assistance, tutoring, writing center.

**Majors. Area/ethnic studies:** European. **Biology:** General, animal behavior, biochemistry, bioinformatics. **Business:** Accounting, accounting technology, entrepreneurial studies, finance, international, management information systems, management science, marketing. **Communications:** General, digital media. **Computer sciences:** Computer science. **Conservation:** Environmental science. **Education:** Early childhood, early childhood special, elementary, physical, secondary. **Foreign languages:** French, Germanic, Spanish. **Health:** Athletic training, clinical lab science. **History:** General. **Liberal arts:** Arts/sciences, humanities. **Math:** General. **Philosophy/religion:** Philosophy, religion. **Physical sciences:** Chemistry, physics. **Protective services:** Criminal justice. **Psychology:** General. **Social sciences:** Anthropology, economics, international relations, political science, sociology, urban studies. **Visual/performing arts:** Art history/conservation.

**Most popular majors.** Biology 8%, business/marketing 29%, communications/journalism 12%, education 11%, parks/recreation 7%, psychology 10%, social sciences 10%.

**Computing on campus.** 500 workstations in dormitories, library, computer center, student center. Dormitories wired for high-speed internet access and linked to campus network. Commuter students can connect to campus network. Online course registration, online library, helpline, repair service, student web hosting, wireless network available.

**Student life. Freshman orientation:** Mandatory, $125 fee. Preregistration for classes offered. Program includes testing, advisement, registration, introduction to student services. **Policies:** Religious observance required. **Housing:** Coed dorms, special housing for disabled, apartments, wellness housing available. $200 fully refundable deposit, deadline 5/1. Science and honors housing, townhouses. **Activities:** Bands, campus ministries, choral groups, dance, drama, film society, international student organizations, literary magazine, music ensembles, Model UN, musical theater, radio station, student government, student newspaper, TV station, political science association, ethnic and social service organizations, international affairs society, social justice club, Circle K, Global Horizons, German club, Italian club, Little Theater.

**Athletics.** NCAA. **Intercollegiate:** Baseball M, basketball, cross-country, golf M, ice hockey M, lacrosse, soccer, softball W, swimming, synchronized swimming W, volleyball W. **Intramural:** Cheerleading, golf M, rowing (crew) W, rugby. **Team name:** Golden Griffins.

**Student services.** Adult student services, alcohol/substance abuse counseling, chaplain/spiritual director, career counseling, services for economically disadvantaged, student employment services, financial aid counseling, health services, minority student services, personal counseling, placement for graduates, veterans' counselor. **Physically disabled:** Services for visually, speech, hearing impaired. **Learning disabled:** Comprehensive services available.

**Contact.** E-mail: admissions@canisius.edu
Phone: (716) 888-2200 Toll-free number: (800) 843-1517
Fax: (716) 888-3230
Ann Marie Moscovic, Director of Admissions, Canisius College, 2001 Main Street, Buffalo, NY 14208-1098

## Cazenovia College
**Cazenovia, New York**
www.cazenovia.edu                    **CB code: 2078**

- Private 4-year liberal arts college
- Residential campus in small town
- 1,073 degree-seeking undergraduates: 10% part-time, 73% women, 4% African American, 3% Hispanic American
- 74% of applicants admitted

**General.** Founded in 1824. Regionally accredited. **Degrees:** 210 bachelor's, 5 associate awarded. **ROTC:** Army, Air Force. **Location:** 20 miles from Syracuse. **Calendar:** Semester, limited summer session. **Full-time faculty:** 56 total; 79% have terminal degrees, 4% minority, 61% women. **Part-time faculty:** 90 total; 36% have terminal degrees, 3% minority, 60% women. **Class size:** 75% < 20, 24% 20-39, less than 1% 50-99. **Special facilities:** 160-acre farm and equine center, art and design facility and gallery.

**Freshman class profile.** 2,075 applied, 1,528 admitted, 272 enrolled.

| Mid 50% test scores | | | |
|---|---|---|---|
| SAT critical reading: | 440-540 | GPA 2.0-2.99: | 33% |
| SAT math: | 440-550 | Rank in top quarter: | 32% |
| ACT composite: | 17-24 | Rank in top tenth: | 12% |
| GPA 3.75 or higher: | 17% | End year in good standing: | 93% |
| GPA 3.50-3.74: | 14% | Return as sophomores: | 72% |
| GPA 3.0-3.49: | 36% | Out-of-state: | 21% |
| | | Live on campus: | 100% |

**Basis for selection.** Rigor of secondary school record very important; interview, recommendations, school activities important. SAT or ACT recommended. Portfolio recommended for art, graphic and interior design, photography programs.

**High school preparation.** 16 units recommended. Recommended units include English 4, mathematics 2, social studies 4 and science 2. Art courses recommended for art and design majors.

**2009-2010 Annual costs.** Tuition/fees: $24,152. Room/board: $10,476. Books/supplies: $1,000. Personal expenses: $100.

**2009-2010 Financial aid. Need-based:** 265 full-time freshmen applied for aid; 234 were judged to have need; 234 of these received aid. Average need met was 77%. Average scholarship/grant was $14,711; average loan $3,067. 66% of total undergraduate aid awarded as scholarships/grants, 34% as loans/jobs. **Non-need-based:** Awarded to 186 full-time undergraduates, including 55 freshmen. Scholarships awarded for academics.

**Application procedures. Admission:** Priority date 3/1; no deadline. $30 fee, may be waived for applicants with need, free for online applicants. Admission notification on a rolling basis beginning on or about 11/1. Must reply by May 1 or within 2 week(s) if notified thereafter. **Financial aid:** Priority date 3/1; no closing date. FAFSA required. Applicants notified on a rolling basis starting 11/1; must reply by 5/1 or within 2 week(s) of notification.

**Academics. Special study options:** Combined bachelor's/graduate degree, double major, exchange student, honors, independent study, internships, student-designed major, study abroad, teacher certification program, Washington semester. **Credit/placement by examination:** AP, CLEP, IB, institutional tests. **Support services:** Learning center, pre-admission summer program, reduced course load, remedial instruction, study skills assistance, tutoring, writing center.

**Majors. Agriculture:** Equine science. **Business:** Accounting, business admin, fashion. **Communications:** General. **Conservation:** Environmental studies. **Education:** Early childhood, special. **Liberal arts:** Arts/sciences. **Parks/recreation:** Sports admin. **Protective services:** Criminal justice. **Psychology:** General. **Public administration:** Human services. **Social sciences:** General. **Visual/performing arts:** Design, fashion design, interior design, photography, studio arts.

**Most popular majors.** Business/marketing 31%, education 6%, public administration/social services 7%, security/protective services 8%, visual/performing arts 33%.

**Computing on campus.** 250 workstations in dormitories, library, computer center. Dormitories wired for high-speed internet access and linked to campus network. Commuter students can connect to campus network. Online library, helpline, wireless network available.

**Student life. Freshman orientation:** Mandatory. Preregistration for classes offered. **Housing:** Coed dorms, single-sex dorms, special housing for disabled available. $200 nonrefundable deposit, deadline 5/1. Single room suites available. **Activities:** Jazz band, campus ministries, choral groups, dance, drama, film society, musical theater, radio station, student government, student newspaper, human services club, overseas travel club, Young Democrats, Young Republicans, Cazventures outdoor club, Certified Peer Educators, You Are Not Alone-LGBT, Student Organization of Ethnic Diversity.

**Athletics.** NCAA. **Intercollegiate:** Baseball M, basketball, cheerleading, cross-country, equestrian, golf M, lacrosse, rowing (crew), soccer, softball W, volleyball W. **Intramural:** Basketball, bowling, equestrian, football (non-tackle), rowing (crew), skiing, soccer, softball, swimming, volleyball, weight lifting. **Team name:** Wildcats.

**Student services.** Alcohol/substance abuse counseling, chaplain/spiritual director, career counseling, services for economically disadvantaged, student employment services, financial aid counseling, health services, personal counseling, placement for graduates. **Physically disabled:** Services for visually, speech, hearing impaired.

**Contact.** E-mail: admission@cazenovia.edu
Phone: (315) 655-7208 Toll-free number: (800) 654-3210
Fax: (315) 655-4860
Robert Croot, Vice President for Enrollment Management and Dean for Admissions and Financial Aid, Cazenovia College, 3 Sullivan Street, Cazenovia, NY 13035

## Central Yeshiva Tomchei Tmimim-Lubavitch
**Brooklyn, New York**

**CB code: 0549**

▶ Private 4-year rabbinical college for men affiliated with Jewish faith
▶ Very large city
▶ 605 degree-seeking undergraduates
▶ 75 graduate students

**General.** Accredited by AARTS. **Degrees:** 105 bachelor's awarded; master's offered. **Calendar:** Continuous.

**Application procedures. Admission:** No deadline.

**Academics. Credit/placement by examination:** CLEP.

**Majors. Philosophy/religion:** Judaic. **Theology:** Talmudic.

**Contact.** E-mail: uofiop@juno.com
Phone: (718) 859-7600
Central Yeshiva Tomchei Tmimim-Lubavitch, 841-853 Ocean Parkway, Brooklyn, NY 11230

## City University of New York: Baruch College
**New York, New York**  **CB member**
**www.baruch.cuny.edu**  **CB code: 2034**

▶ Public 4-year business and liberal arts college
▶ Commuter campus in very large city
▶ 12,080 degree-seeking undergraduates: 22% part-time, 51% women, 10% African American, 32% Asian American, 16% Hispanic American, 12% international
▶ 3,853 degree-seeking graduate students
▶ 23% of applicants admitted
▶ SAT or ACT (ACT writing optional) required
▶ 60% graduate within 6 years

**General.** Founded in 1919. Regionally accredited. **Degrees:** 2,710 bachelor's awarded; master's offered. **ROTC:** Army. **Calendar:** Semester, extensive summer session. **Full-time faculty:** 498 total; 97% have terminal degrees, 26% minority, 37% women. **Part-time faculty:** 668 total; 60% have terminal degrees, 29% minority, 41% women. **Class size:** 27% < 20, 56% 20-39, 5% 40-49, 10% 50-99, 2% >100. **Special facilities:** Performing arts center (black box theater, gallery, various theaters and recital halls).

**Freshman class profile.** 19,775 applied, 4,476 admitted, 1,442 enrolled.

| Mid 50% test scores | | Rank in top tenth: | 34% |
|---|---|---|---|
| SAT critical reading: | 490-590 | End year in good standing: | 89% |
| SAT math: | 560-670 | Return as sophomores: | 88% |
| GPA 3.75 or higher: | 13% | Out-of-state: | 4% |
| GPA 3.50-3.74: | 14% | International: | 7% |
| GPA 3.0-3.49: | 34% | Fraternities: | 1% |
| GPA 2.0-2.99: | 36% | Sororities: | 1% |
| Rank in top quarter: | 61% | | |

**Basis for selection.** Overall high school performance and 82 average or combined SAT score of 1200 required. Students who did not score a minimum of 480 on the verbal and math SAT are required to take a skills assessment test. **Homeschooled:** 1200 SAT required. **Learning Disabled:** No special requirements; recommended that students call Disability Service Office to discuss available services.

**High school preparation.** 16 units required. Required and recommended units include English 4, mathematics 3-4, social studies 4, science 2 (laboratory 2), foreign language 2 and academic electives 1.

**2009-2010 Annual costs.** Tuition/fees: $4,970; $12,820 out-of-state. Books/supplies: $1,070. Personal expenses: $1,734.

**2009-2010 Financial aid. Need-based:** 82% of total undergraduate aid awarded as scholarships/grants, 18% as loans/jobs. **Non-need-based:** Scholarships awarded for academics, state residency.

**Application procedures. Admission:** Priority date 12/1; deadline 2/1 (postmark date). $65 fee, may be waived for applicants with need. Admission notification 5/15. Admission notification on a rolling basis. Must reply by May 1 or within 2 week(s) if notified thereafter. **Financial aid:** Priority date 3/15, closing date 4/30. FAFSA required. Applicants notified on a rolling basis starting 4/1; must reply by 6/1 or within 6 week(s) of notification.

**Academics.** 120 credit hours required for BA/BS degrees, 124 for BBA. Optional humanities seminar examining 2 or more disciplines in arts and sciences; joint business/liberal arts and science majors; programs in arts administration, management of musical enterprise, real estate, and metropolitan development. **Special study options:** Accelerated study, combined bachelor's/graduate degree, cross-registration, distance learning, double major, ESL, exchange student, honors, independent study, internships, liberal arts/career combination, student-designed major, study abroad. **Credit/placement by examination:** AP, CLEP, IB, SAT, institutional tests. 21 credit hours maximum toward bachelor's degree. No more than 21 credits through AP and/or college courses taken in high school. **Support services:** Learning center, pre-admission summer program, reduced course load, study skills assistance, tutoring, writing center.

**Honors college/program.** Applicants must have high standardized test scores (1300+ on the SAT, exclusive of Writing) and high school averages (90+). Leadership potential and community involvement sought. Applicants must supply teacher recommendations and essay.

**Majors. Architecture:** Urban/community planning. **Biology:** General. **Business:** General, accounting, actuarial science, business admin, communications, finance, human resources, labor relations, management information systems, managerial economics, operations, real estate, sales/distribution. **Communications:** General, advertising, journalism. **Computer sciences:**

General, computer science, information systems. **Engineering:** Operations research. **Foreign languages:** Comparative lit, Spanish. **History:** General. **Interdisciplinary:** Biological/physical sciences. **Liberal arts:** Arts/sciences. **Math:** General, statistics. **Philosophy/religion:** Philosophy. **Psychology:** General. **Public administration:** General. **Social sciences:** Economics, political science, sociology. **Visual/performing arts:** Arts management, design, music management.

**Most popular majors.** Business/marketing 75%, communications/journalism 6%.

**Computing on campus.** 1,300 workstations in library, computer center, student center. Online course registration, online library, helpline, wireless network available.

**Student life. Freshman orientation:** Mandatory. Half day-long, on-campus session offered on multiple days. **Activities:** Campus ministries, choral groups, dance, drama, film society, literary magazine, Model UN, musical theater, radio station, student government, student newspaper, Hillel, National Association of Black Accountants, Golden Key, International Honor Society, Asian student association, Muslim student association, United International Student Body, Pre-Law Society, Caribbean student association.

**Athletics.** NCAA. **Intercollegiate:** Baseball M, basketball, cheerleading, cross-country, diving W, soccer M, softball W, swimming, tennis, volleyball. **Intramural:** Badminton, basketball, cross-country, racquetball, swimming, table tennis, volleyball. **Team name:** Bearcats.

**Student services.** Adult student services, alcohol/substance abuse counseling, chaplain/spiritual director, career counseling, student employment services, financial aid counseling, health services, legal services, personal counseling, placement for graduates, veterans' counselor. **Physically disabled:** Services for visually, speech, hearing impaired.

**Contact.** Phone: (646) 312-1400 Fax: (646) 312-1363
Jimmy Jung, Vice President for Enrollment Management Services, City University of New York: Baruch College, One Bernard Baruch Way, Box H-0720, New York, NY 10010-5585

## City University of New York: Brooklyn College

**Brooklyn, New York**  **CB member**
www.brooklyn.cuny.edu  **CB code: 2046**

- Public 4-year liberal arts college
- Commuter campus in very large city
- 12,021 degree-seeking undergraduates: 23% part-time, 59% women, 25% African American, 16% Asian American, 12% Hispanic American, 6% international
- 3,504 degree-seeking graduate students
- 28% of applicants admitted
- SAT or ACT (ACT writing optional) required
- 43% graduate within 6 years

**General.** Founded in 1930. Regionally accredited. **Degrees:** 2,200 bachelor's awarded; master's offered. **Location:** 10 miles from Manhattan. **Calendar:** Semester, extensive summer session. **Full-time faculty:** 557 total; 93% have terminal degrees, 22% minority, 44% women. **Part-time faculty:** 844 total; 22% minority, 49% women. **Class size:** 40% < 20, 53% 20-39, 5% 40-49, 2% 50-99, less than 1% >100. **Special facilities:** Astronomical observatory, greenhouse, applied sciences institute, institute for the humanities, infant study center, Brooklyn Center for the Performing Arts, particle accelerator.

**Freshman class profile.** 17,497 applied, 4,873 admitted, 977 enrolled.

| Mid 50% test scores | | Rank in top quarter: | 56% |
|---|---|---|---|
| SAT critical reading: | 470-580 | Rank in top tenth: | 19% |
| SAT math: | 510-610 | Return as sophomores: | 78% |
| GPA 3.75 or higher: | 8% | Out-of-state: | 1% |
| GPA 3.50-3.74: | 25% | International: | 5% |
| GPA 3.0-3.49: | 61% | Fraternities: | 1% |
| GPA 2.0-2.99: | 6% | Sororities: | 1% |

**Basis for selection.** Students accepted based on SAT scores and academic average. Essay required for BA/MD, CHC and Scholars, interview recommended for scholars program. Audition required for music conservatory, theater programs; portfolio required for fine arts program.

**High school preparation.** College-preparatory program recommended. 21 units recommended. Recommended units include English 4, mathematics 3, social studies 4, science 3, foreign language 3 and academic electives 4.

**2009-2010 Annual costs.** Tuition/fees: $5,051; $12,901 out-of-state. Books/supplies: $1,146. Personal expenses: $1,744.

**2009-2010 Financial aid. Need-based:** 852 full-time freshmen applied for aid; 754 were judged to have need; 750 of these received aid. Average need met was 99%. Average scholarship/grant was $3,600; average loan $3,500. 61% of total undergraduate aid awarded as scholarships/grants, 39% as loans/jobs. **Non-need-based:** Awarded to 2,841 full-time undergraduates, including 431 freshmen. Scholarships awarded for academics, art, leadership, music/drama, state residency.

**Application procedures. Admission:** Priority date 2/1; no deadline. $65 fee. Admission notification on a rolling basis beginning on or about 2/1. Must reply by May 1 or within 3 week(s) if notified thereafter. **Financial aid:** Priority date 4/1; no closing date. FAFSA required. Applicants notified on a rolling basis starting 5/1.

**Academics. Special study options:** Accelerated study, combined bachelor's/graduate degree, distance learning, double major, dual enrollment of high school students, ESL, honors, independent study, internships, student-designed major, study abroad, teacher certification program, Washington semester, weekend college. **Credit/placement by examination:** AP, CLEP, IB, SAT, ACT, institutional tests. 35 credit hours maximum toward bachelor's degree. **Support services:** Learning center, pre-admission summer program, reduced course load, study skills assistance, tutoring, writing center.

**Majors. Area/ethnic studies:** African-American, American, Caribbean, Chicano/Hispanic-American/Latino, Latin American, women's. **Biology:** General. **Business:** Accounting, business admin. **Communications:** General, broadcast journalism, journalism, radio/tv. **Communications technology:** Radio/tv. **Computer sciences:** General, information systems, web page design. **Conservation:** Environmental studies. **Education:** General, bilingual, biology, chemistry, early childhood, elementary, English, French, kindergarten/preschool, mathematics, music, physical, physics, social studies, Spanish, special. **Family/consumer sciences:** Food/nutrition. **Foreign languages:** Classics, comparative lit, French, Italian, linguistics, Russian, Spanish. **Health:** Audiology/speech pathology, speech pathology. **History:** General. **Interdisciplinary:** Biological/physical sciences, math/computer science. **Liberal arts:** Arts/sciences. **Math:** General, algebra, computational. **Parks/recreation:** Exercise sciences, health/fitness. **Philosophy/religion:** Judaic, philosophy, religion. **Physical sciences:** Chemistry, geology, physics. **Psychology:** General. **Public administration:** Community org/advocacy. **Social sciences:** Anthropology, economics, political science, sociology. **Visual/performing arts:** Art, art history/conservation, cinematography, dramatic, music performance, music theory/composition, studio arts.

**Most popular majors.** Business/marketing 33%, education 13%, health sciences 7%, psychology 12%, social sciences 6%, visual/performing arts 6%.

**Computing on campus.** 2,000 workstations in library, computer center, student center. Online library, wireless network available.

**Student life. Freshman orientation:** Available. **Activities:** Dance, drama, film society, international student organizations, literary magazine, music ensembles, musical theater, radio station, student government, student newspaper, symphony orchestra, TV station; Hillel, Newman Club, student Christian association, Alpha Phi Omega, Christian fellowship, Islamic society, Caribbean student union, accounting society, lesbian/gay/bisexual/transgender alliance.

**Athletics.** NCAA. **Intercollegiate:** Basketball, cross-country, soccer M, softball W, tennis, track and field, volleyball. **Intramural:** Badminton W, basketball, racquetball, soccer M, softball W, tennis, track and field, volleyball. **Team name:** Bulldogs.

**Student services.** Adult student services, alcohol/substance abuse counseling, career counseling, services for economically disadvantaged, student employment services, financial aid counseling, health services, on-campus daycare, personal counseling, placement for graduates, veterans' counselor, women's services. **Physically disabled:** Services for visually, speech, hearing impaired. **Learning disabled:** Comprehensive services available.

**Contact.** E-mail: adminqry@brooklyn.cuny.edu
Phone: (718) 951-5001 Fax: (718) 951-4506
Penelope Ferry, Director of Undergraduate Admissions, City University of New York: Brooklyn College, 2900 Bedford Avenue, Brooklyn, NY 11210

## City University of New York: City College

**New York, New York**  **CB member**
www.ccny.cuny.edu  **CB code: 2083**

- Public 4-year university
- Commuter campus in very large city

- 12,340 degree-seeking undergraduates: 22% part-time, 51% women, 23% African American, 22% Asian American, 36% Hispanic American, 10% international
- 2,969 degree-seeking graduate students
- 38% of applicants admitted
- SAT or ACT required
- 33% graduate within 6 years; 16% enter graduate study

**General.** Founded in 1847. Regionally accredited. **Degrees:** 1,414 bachelor's awarded; master's, professional offered. **Calendar:** Semester, extensive summer session. **Full-time faculty:** 584 total; 96% have terminal degrees, 18% minority, 39% women. **Part-time faculty:** 1,111 total; 18% have terminal degrees, 25% minority, 46% women. **Class size:** 43% < 20, 52% 20-39, 4% 40-49, less than 1% 50-99, less than 1% >100. **Special facilities:** Planetarium, weather station, ultra-fast laser spectroscopy laboratory, microwave laboratory, computer-aided design facilities, slide library, darkroom facilities, sonic music arts facility, structural biology center.

**Freshman class profile.** 22,159 applied, 8,339 admitted, 1,770 enrolled.

| Mid 50% test scores | | Rank in top quarter: | 36% |
|---|---|---|---|
| SAT critical reading: | 440-550 | Rank in top tenth: | 30% |
| SAT math: | 470-600 | End year in good standing: | 86% |
| GPA 3.75 or higher: | 7% | Return as sophomores: | 79% |
| GPA 3.50-3.74: | 17% | Out-of-state: | 9% |
| GPA 3.0-3.49: | 27% | Live on campus: | 3% |
| GPA 2.0-2.99: | 47% | International: | 8% |

**Basis for selection.** Academic average and number of academic units achieved in high school, SAT, or GED score of 325 or better important. Units recommended for admission must be acquired before graduation from any CUNY senior college. SAT section test scores of 450 or 20 ACT on math and verbal exempt student from taking placement exam. Interview required for biomedical education, audition required for music program; portfolio required for electronic design and multimedia. **Homeschooled:** Applicants must obtain GED or diploma through regionally accredited program.

**High school preparation.** College-preparatory program recommended. 16 units recommended. Recommended units include English 4, mathematics 2, social studies 4, science 2 (laboratory 2) and foreign language 2. One unit of art or music recommended. For science and engineering students, 3 units of mathematics required.

**2009-2010 Annual costs.** Tuition/fees: $4,929; $12,779 out-of-state. Some student housing available, rates vary by apartment size. Books/supplies: $1,070. Personal expenses: $3,672.

**2008-2009 Financial aid. Need-based:** 1,596 full-time freshmen applied for aid; 1,560 were judged to have need; 1,535 of these received aid. Average need met was 80%. Average scholarship/grant was $6,103; average loan $1,859. 67% of total undergraduate aid awarded as scholarships/grants, 33% as loans/jobs. **Non-need-based:** Awarded to 2,852 full-time undergraduates, including 986 freshmen. Scholarships awarded for academics, alumni affiliation, leadership.

**Application procedures. Admission:** Priority date 3/15; no deadline. $65 fee. Admission notification on a rolling basis beginning on or about 1/15. **Financial aid:** Priority date 4/15; no closing date. FAFSA required. Applicants notified on a rolling basis starting 4/15.

**Academics. Special study options:** Accelerated study, combined bachelor's/graduate degree, cooperative education, cross-registration, distance learning, double major, dual enrollment of high school students, ESL, exchange student, honors, independent study, internships, liberal arts/career combination, student-designed major, study abroad, teacher certification program. Center for Worker Education, doctoral degrees through CUNY Graduate Center. **Credit/placement by examination:** AP, CLEP, IB, ACT, institutional tests. **Support services:** Learning center, pre-admission summer program, reduced course load, study skills assistance, tutoring, writing center.

**Honors college/program.** Admits only new first-year students, who must apply by special application. Application deadline November 1 for early admission, December 15 for regular admission. For the class admitted fall 2005 (Class of 2009), the average high school GPA was 93.7 (on a scale of 100) and the average SAT was 1371 (exclusive of Writing). Students are expected to achieve an overall 3.3 GPA by the end of their first year and a 3.5 GPA by the end of their second year, which must be maintained until graduation in four years. Detailed information about additional benefits, including full-tuition scholarships and opportunity grants, and requirements of the Macaulay Honors College can be accessed on the college's or the Macaulay Honors College website.

**Majors. Architecture:** Architecture. **Area/ethnic studies:** African-American, Asian, Caribbean, Latin American. **Biology:** General, biochemistry. **Business:** General. **Communications:** General, advertising, journalism,

public relations. **Computer sciences:** Computer science. **Education:** Art, bilingual, biology, chemistry, early childhood, elementary, English, foreign languages, French, history, mathematics, music, physics, science, secondary, social studies, Spanish. •**Engineering:** Biomedical, chemical, civil, computer, electrical, mechanical. **Foreign languages:** General, comparative lit, French, Spanish. **Health:** Physician assistant, premedicine, prepharmacy, preveterinary. **History:** General. **Interdisciplinary:** Global studies. **Legal studies:** Prelaw. **Math:** General. **Philosophy/religion:** Judaic, philosophy. **Physical sciences:** Chemistry, geology, physics, planetary. **Psychology:** General. **Social sciences:** Anthropology, economics, international relations, political science, sociology. **Visual/performing arts:** General, art, art history/conservation, cinematography, commercial/advertising art, dramatic, film/cinema, graphic design, jazz, music performance, music theory/composition, studio arts.

**Most popular majors.** Biology 6%, education 6%, engineering/engineering technologies 16%, liberal arts 10%, psychology 13%, social sciences 9%, visual/performing arts 12%.

**Computing on campus.** 2,000 workstations in library, computer center, student center. Dormitories wired for high-speed internet access and linked to campus network. Commuter students can connect to campus network. Online course registration, online library, helpline, repair service, wireless network available.

**Student life. Freshman orientation:** Mandatory. Full-day program, including registration, held in spring and summer. **Housing:** Apartments, wellness housing available. $400 nonrefundable deposit. **Activities:** Jazz band, choral groups, dance, drama, film society, international student organizations, literary magazine, music ensembles, Model UN, musical theater, radio station, student government, student newspaper, TV station, numerous religious, political, ethnic, and social service organizations.

**Athletics.** NCAA. **Intercollegiate:** Baseball M, basketball, cross-country, fencing, lacrosse M, soccer, tennis, track and field, volleyball. **Intramural:** Badminton M, basketball, fencing, soccer M, softball W, swimming, tennis, track and field, volleyball. **Team name:** Beavers.

**Student services.** Alcohol/substance abuse counseling, chaplain/spiritual director, career counseling, services for economically disadvantaged, student employment services, financial aid counseling, health services, minority student services, on-campus daycare, personal counseling, placement for graduates, veterans' counselor, women's services. **Physically disabled:** Services for visually, speech, hearing impaired. **Learning disabled:** Comprehensive services available.

**Contact.** E-mail: admissions@ccny.cuny.edu
Phone: (212) 650-6977 Fax: (212) 650-6417
Joseph Fatozzi, Director of Admissions, City University of New York: City College, 160 Convent Avenue, New York, NY 10031

---

## City University of New York: College of Staten Island

**Staten Island, New York** — CB member
**www.csi.cuny.edu** — CB code: 2778

- Public 4-year liberal arts college
- Commuter campus in very large city
- 12,578 degree-seeking undergraduates: 27% part-time, 58% women, 6% African American, 6% Asian American, 8% Hispanic American, 3% international
- 897 degree-seeking graduate students
- 100% of applicants admitted
- Application essay, interview required
- 41% graduate within 6 years

**General.** Founded in 1955. Regionally accredited. **Degrees:** 1,085 bachelor's, 659 associate awarded; master's offered. **Location:** 10 miles from downtown Manhattan. **Calendar:** Semester, extensive summer session. **Full-time faculty:** 348 total; 83% have terminal degrees, 22% minority, 42% women. **Part-time faculty:** 596 total; 27% have terminal degrees, 16% minority, 50% women. **Class size:** 30% < 20, 52% 20-39, 15% 40-49, 3% 50-99, less than 1% >100. **Special facilities:** Astrophysical observatory, archives and special collections, artificial intelligence laboratory, center for developmental neuroscience and developmental disabilities, center for engineered polymeric materials, center for environmental science, nuclear magnetic resonance spectrometer, CUNY High Performance Computational Facility.

**Freshman class profile.** 9,730 applied, 9,730 admitted, 2,685 enrolled.

| Mid 50% test scores | | | |
|---|---|---|---|
| SAT critical reading: | 440-530 | GPA 3.0-3.49: | 30% |
| SAT math: | 460-550 | GPA 2.0-2.99: | 54% |
| SAT writing: | 430-520 | End year in good standing: | 71% |
| GPA 3.75 or higher: | 2% | Return as sophomores: | 80% |
| GPA 3.50-3.74: | 11% | Out-of-state: | 1% |
| | | International: | 2% |

**Basis for selection.** Applicants to the baccalaureate program considered on the basis of high school academic record and SAT scores. Open admission policy for associate degree programs; additional requirements including essays and recommendations for selective programs. SAT or ACT recommended. **Homeschooled:** State high school equivalency certificate required.

**High school preparation.** College-preparatory program recommended. 15 units required; 16 recommended. Required and recommended units include English 4, mathematics 2-3, social studies 4, science 2-3, foreign language 2-3, visual/performing arts .5.

**2009-2010 Annual costs.** Tuition/fees: $4,978; $12,828 out-of-state. Books/supplies: $1,070. Personal expenses: $1,734.

**2009-2010 Financial aid.** **Non-need-based:** Scholarships awarded for academics, art, leadership, minority status, music/drama.

**Application procedures. Admission:** Priority date 2/1; no deadline. $65 fee, may be waived for applicants with need. Application must be submitted online. Admission notification on a rolling basis beginning on or about 12/15. **Financial aid:** Priority date 3/31; no closing date. FAFSA required. Applicants notified on a rolling basis starting 6/1.

**Academics.** Baccalaureate for Unique and Interdisciplinary Studies available, CUNY's individualized, university-wide BA/BS degree, where students formulate proposals for unique areas of concentration, then collaborate with CUNY faculty members to design their degrees. **Special study options:** Accelerated study, cooperative education, cross-registration, distance learning, double major, dual enrollment of high school students, ESL, honors, independent study, internships, liberal arts/career combination, New York semester, study abroad, teacher certification program, United Nations semester, urban semester, Washington semester, weekend college. Cross-registration at any CUNY. **Credit/placement by examination:** AP, CLEP, IB, SAT, ACT, institutional tests. 30 credit hours maximum toward associate degree, 30 toward bachelor's. **Support services:** Learning center, pre-admission summer program, remedial instruction, study skills assistance, tutoring.

**Honors college/program.** Admission open to prospective first-semester freshmen only. Minimum 1200 SAT (exclusive of Writing) and 90 high school average. 40 seats available. High school transcript, SAT or ACT score, essay, and letters of recommendation required. Personal interview may be requested. Accepted students receive free tuition, lap top, and access to funds to support enrichment opportunities, including study abroad, unpaid internships.

**Majors. Area/ethnic studies:** African-American, American, women's. **Biology:** General, biochemistry. **Business:** General, accounting. **Communications:** General. **Computer sciences:** Computer science, information systems. **Education:** Biology, chemistry, English, history, mathematics, Spanish. **Engineering:** General. **Foreign languages:** Spanish. **Health:** Clinical lab science, nursing (RN). **History:** General. **Liberal arts:** Arts/sciences. **Math:** General. **Philosophy/religion:** Philosophy. **Physical sciences:** Chemistry, physics. **Psychology:** General. **Public administration:** Social work. **Social sciences:** Economics, international relations, political science. **Visual/performing arts:** Dramatic, film/cinema, studio arts. **Other:** Art/Photography.

**Most popular majors.** Business/marketing 24%, English 6%, liberal arts 10%, psychology 10%, social sciences 18%.

**Computing on campus.** 1,254 workstations in library, computer center, student center. Online course registration, online library, helpline, student web hosting, wireless network available.

**Student life. Freshman orientation:** Mandatory. Scheduled at beginning of each semester, after or during time periods devoted to testing, advisement, and registration. Students with less than 6 credits are required to complete the orientation requirement during the first semester prior to completing 12 credits. **Activities:** Jazz band, campus ministries, choral groups, dance, drama, film society, international student organizations, literary magazine, music ensembles, radio station, student government, student newspaper, Muslim student association, Israel club, Colleges Against Cancer, Chi Alpha Christian club, Hillel, armed forces club, international cultural dance club, Sri Lankan student association, South Asian student association, Love Thy Neighbor, College Republicans.

**Athletics.** NCAA. **Intercollegiate:** Baseball M, basketball, cross-country, diving, soccer, softball W, swimming, tennis, volleyball W. **Intramural:** Basketball, cricket, handball, racquetball, tennis, volleyball. **Team name:** Dolphins.

**Student services.** Adult student services, alcohol/substance abuse counseling, chaplain/spiritual director, career counseling, services for economically disadvantaged, student employment services, financial aid counseling, health services, minority student services, on-campus daycare, personal counseling, placement for graduates, veterans' counselor, women's services. **Physically disabled:** Services for visually, speech, hearing impaired.

**Contact.** E-mail: admissions@mail.cuny.csi.edu
Phone: (718) 982-2010 Fax: (718) 982-2500
Emmanuel Esperance, Director of Recruitment & Admissions, City University of New York: College of Staten Island, 2800 Victory Boulevard 2A-104, Staten Island, NY 10314

## City University of New York: CUNY Online
New York, New York
www.online.sps.cuny.edu/

- Public 4-year virtual university
- Very large city
- 744 degree-seeking undergraduates
- 62 graduate students
- Application essay required

**General.** Regionally accredited. CUNY Online offers fully asynchronous online bachelor's degree programs for students who have at least 30 earned credits, an MS in Business Management and Leadership, or a graduate certificate program in Immigration Law Studies. **Degrees:** 72 bachelor's awarded; master's offered. **Calendar:** Semester, limited summer session. **Part-time faculty:** 134 total; 78% have terminal degrees, 19% minority, 53% women. **Class size:** 59% < 20, 41% 20-39.

**Basis for selection.** Open admission, but selective for some programs. Accept only transfer applicants with at least 30 credits earned. SAT or ACT recommended. **Homeschooled:** State high school equivalency certificate required.

**2009-2010 Annual costs.** Tuition/fees: $4,980; $4,980 out-of-state. Books/supplies: $1,016.

**Application procedures. Admission:** Closing date 8/1 (receipt date). $70 fee, may be waived for applicants with need. Application must be submitted online. Admission notification on a rolling basis. **Financial aid:** Closing date 8/1.

**Academics. Special study options:** Distance learning. **Credit/placement by examination:** AP, CLEP, IB, SAT, ACT. 45 credit hours maximum toward bachelor's degree. **Support services:** Study skills assistance, tutoring.

**Majors. Business:** General. **Communications:** General.

**Most popular majors.** Business/marketing 10%, liberal arts 90%.

**Computing on campus.** PC or laptop required. Commuter students can connect to campus network. Helpline, student web hosting available.

**Student services.** Adult student services, financial aid counseling, veterans' counselor. **Physically disabled:** Services for visually, speech, hearing impaired.

**Contact.** E-mail: onlineba@mail.cuny.edu
Otilia Abraham, Coordinator of Admissions, City University of New York: CUNY Online, 101 West 31st Street, 7th Floor, New York, NY 10001-3507

## City University of New York: Hunter College
New York, New York                                      CB member
www.hunter.cuny.edu/                                   CB code: 2301

- Public 4-year liberal arts college
- Commuter campus in very large city
- 14,806 degree-seeking undergraduates: 25% part-time, 67% women, 11% African American, 19% Asian American, 18% Hispanic American, 9% international
- 5,133 degree-seeking graduate students
- 26% of applicants admitted
- SAT or ACT required
- 44% graduate within 6 years

**General.** Founded in 1870. Regionally accredited. **Degrees:** 2,620 bachelor's awarded; master's offered. **Calendar:** Semester, limited summer session. **Full-time faculty:** 691 total; 82% have terminal degrees, 20% minority, 50% women. **Part-time faculty:** 953 total; 24% have terminal degrees, 18% minority, 62% women. **Class size:** 42% < 20, 48% 20-39, 4% 40-49, 5% 50-99, less than 1% >100. **Special facilities:** Mathematics learning center, on-campus elementary and secondary schools.

**Freshman class profile.** 30,528 applied, 7,892 admitted, 2,022 enrolled.

| Mid 50% test scores | | GPA 3.0-3.49: | 36% |
|---|---|---|---|
| SAT critical reading: | 510-610 | GPA 2.0-2.99: | 32% |
| SAT math: | 520-620 | Return as sophomores: | 84% |
| GPA 3.75 or higher: | 13% | Out-of-state: | 5% |
| GPA 3.50-3.74: | 15% | | |

**Basis for selection.** Requirements vary by program. Indexing formula using weighted averages, high school academic units, and SAT scores for admission to some programs. SAT or ACT not required, but recommended, of first-time freshmen who graduated high school more than a year preceding admission.

**High school preparation.** 16 units recommended. Required and recommended units include English 2-4, mathematics 2-3, social studies 4, science 1-2 (laboratory 1), foreign language 2 and academic electives 1. 1 fine art or performing art recommended.

**2009-2010 Annual costs.** Tuition/fees: $4,999; $12,849 out-of-state. Room-only rates by room size and semester. Room only: $3,726. Books/supplies: $1,070. Personal expenses: $4,526.

**2008-2009 Financial aid.** **Need-based:** 1,563 full-time freshmen applied for aid; 1,436 were judged to have need; 1,216 of these received aid. Average need met was 77%. Average scholarship/grant was $5,571; average loan $2,732. 82% of total undergraduate aid awarded as scholarships/grants, 18% as loans/jobs. **Non-need-based:** Awarded to 2,953 full-time undergraduates, including 1,165 freshmen. Scholarships awarded for academics.

**Application procedures.** **Admission:** Closing date 3/15 (postmark date). $65 fee, may be waived for applicants with need. Admission notification on a rolling basis beginning on or about 1/15. **Financial aid:** Priority date 5/1; no closing date. FAFSA required. Applicants notified on a rolling basis starting 5/15.

**Academics.** **Special study options:** Accelerated study, combined bachelor's/ graduate degree, cross-registration, distance learning, double major, dual enrollment of high school students, exchange student, honors, independent study, internships, liberal arts/career combination, student-designed major, study abroad, teacher certification program. BA/MA/MS programs in anthropology, biology/EOPS, economics, English, history, math, music, physics, social research (MS). **Credit/placement by examination:** AP, CLEP, IB, institutional tests. 30 credit hours maximum toward bachelor's degree. **Support services:** Learning center, reduced course load, remedial instruction, study skills assistance, tutoring, writing center.

**Majors.** **Area/ethnic studies:** African-American, Latin American, Near/ Middle Eastern, women's. **Biology:** General, pharmacology. **Business:** Accounting. **Communications:** Media studies. **Computer sciences:** General. **Education:** General, art, biology, chemistry, drama/dance, early childhood, elementary, English, foreign languages, French, geography, German, health, history, Latin, mathematics, music, physical, physics, secondary, social studies, Spanish. **Family/consumer sciences:** Food/nutrition. **Foreign languages:** General, ancient Greek, Chinese, classics, comparative lit, French, German, Hebrew, Italian, Latin, Romance, Russian, Spanish. **Health:** Adult health nursing, clinical lab science, clinical lab technology, maternal/child health nursing, nurse practitioner, nursing (RN), pediatric nursing, psychiatric nursing, public health nursing, speech pathology. **History:** General. **Liberal arts:** Humanities. **Math:** General, statistics. **Philosophy/religion:** Judaic, philosophy, religion. **Physical sciences:** Chemistry, physics. **Psychology:** General. **Social sciences:** Anthropology, archaeology, economics, geography, international relations, political science, sociology, urban studies. **Visual/ performing arts:** Art history/conservation, cinematography, dance, dramatic, film/cinema, music performance, music theory/composition, studio arts.

**Most popular majors.** Business/marketing 8%, communications/ journalism 8%, English 15%, psychology 15%, social sciences 23%, visual/ performing arts 9%.

**Computing on campus.** 1,280 workstations in dormitories, library, computer center, student center. Commuter students can connect to campus network. Online course registration, online library, helpline, repair service, student web hosting, wireless network available.

**Student life.** **Freshman orientation:** Available. Preregistration for classes offered. **Housing:** Coed dorms, wellness housing available. **Activities:** Bands, choral groups, dance, drama, film society, literary magazine, music ensembles, musical theater, radio station, student government, student newspaper, symphony orchestra, TV station, over 100 political, ethnic, social, and religious organizations.

**Athletics.** NCAA. **Intercollegiate:** Basketball, cross-country, fencing, football (non-tackle) W, soccer M, softball W, swimming W, tennis, track and field, volleyball, wrestling M. **Intramural:** Basketball, bowling, football (non-tackle), racquetball, swimming, table tennis, tennis, volleyball. **Team name:** Hawks.

**Student services.** Adult student services, alcohol/substance abuse counseling, chaplain/spiritual director, career counseling, services for economically disadvantaged, student employment services, financial aid counseling, health services, legal services, minority student services, on-campus daycare, personal counseling, placement for graduates, veterans' counselor, women's services. **Physically disabled:** Services for visually, speech, hearing impaired.

**Contact.** E-mail: admissions@hunter.cuny.edu
Phone: (212) 772-4490
William Zlata, Director of Admissions, City University of New York:
Hunter College, 695 Park Avenue, New York, NY 10065

---

## City University of New York: John Jay College of Criminal Justice

**New York, New York**       **CB member**
www.jjay.cuny.edu/       **CB code: 2115**

◗ Public 4-year College of criminal justice and public safety.
◗ Commuter campus in very large city
◗ 13,170 degree-seeking undergraduates: 21% part-time, 57% women, 24% African American, 8% Asian American, 41% Hispanic American, 3% international
◗ 1,873 degree-seeking graduate students
◗ 63% of applicants admitted
◗ SAT or ACT with writing required
◗ 42% graduate within 6 years; 14% enter graduate study

**General.** Founded in 1964. Regionally accredited. **Degrees:** 1,801 bachelor's, 206 associate awarded; master's offered. **Calendar:** Semester, limited summer session. **Full-time faculty:** 418 total; 81% have terminal degrees, 34% minority, 44% women. **Part-time faculty:** 596 total; 33% minority, 45% women. **Class size:** 20% < 20, 79% 20-39, 1% 40-49, less than 1% 50-99, less than 1% >100. **Special facilities:** Security laboratory, fire science laboratory, explosion-proof toxicology research laboratory.

**Freshman class profile.** 11,603 applied, 7,285 admitted, 2,873 enrolled.

| Mid 50% test scores | | GPA 3.0-3.49: | 15% |
|---|---|---|---|
| SAT critical reading: | 400-490 | GPA 2.0-2.99: | 58% |
| SAT math: | 410-510 | End year in good standing: | 76% |
| SAT writing: | 390-490 | Return as sophomores: | 74% |
| GPA 3.75 or higher: | 1% | Out-of-state: | 4% |
| GPA 3.50-3.74: | 4% | International: | 2% |

**Basis for selection.** Admission to baccalaureate degree program requires minimum SAT score from 960 to 1020 and minimum high school average of 80. **Homeschooled:** State high school equivalency certificate required. Applicants must have diploma issued by local registered high school, and minimum SAT of 1100.

**High school preparation.** College-preparatory program recommended. 14 units required; 19 recommended. Required and recommended units include English 4, mathematics 3-4, social studies 2-4, (laboratory 2-3), foreign language 2-3 and visual/performing arts 1. One unit in fine arts required/ recommended.

**2009-2010 Annual costs.** Tuition/fees: $4,929; $12,779 out-of-state. Books/ supplies: $1,070. Personal expenses: $4,754.

**2008-2009 Financial aid.** **Need-based:** 2,099 full-time freshmen applied for aid; 1,784 were judged to have need; 1,469 of these received aid. Average need met was 85%. Average scholarship/grant was $2,926; average loan $2,331. 67% of total undergraduate aid awarded as scholarships/grants, 33% as loans/jobs. **Non-need-based:** Awarded to 300 full-time undergraduates, including 212 freshmen. Scholarships awarded for academics, leadership, minority status.

**Application procedures.** **Admission:** Priority date 2/1; deadline 5/31 (postmark date). $65 fee. Application must be submitted online. Admission notification on a rolling basis beginning on or about 1/15. Centralized application processing allows students to apply to 6 academic programs within CUNY system at same time. Admission to John Jay on space-available basis. **Financial aid:** Priority date 4/30; no closing date. FAFSA required. Applicants notified on a rolling basis starting 4/1; must reply within 2 week(s) of notification.

**Academics.** Degree requirements and curriculum combine professional education with the liberal arts. The Baccalaureate for Unique and Interdisciplinary Studies (CUNY BA), is CUNY's individualized, university-wide BA/BS degree, where students formulate proposals for unique areas of concentration, then collaborate with CUNY faculty members to design their degrees. **Special study options:** Combined bachelor's/graduate degree, cooperative education, cross-registration, distance learning, dual enrollment of high school students, ESL, exchange student, honors, independent study, internships, liberal arts/career combination, student-designed major, study abroad, weekend college. **Credit/placement by examination:** AP, CLEP, IB, SAT, ACT, institutional tests. 30 credit hours maximum toward associate degree, 30 toward bachelor's. **Support services:** Learning center, pre-admission summer program, reduced course load, remedial instruction, tutoring, writing center.

**Majors. Computer sciences:** General. **Physical sciences:** General. **Protective services:** Law enforcement admin. **Psychology:** General. **Public administration:** General, community org/advocacy. **Social sciences:** Criminology, economics, political science.

**Most popular majors.** Psychology 21%, public administration/social services 12%, security/protective services 50%, social sciences 14%.

**Computing on campus.** 1,800 workstations in library, computer center. Commuter students can connect to campus network. Online course registration, helpline available.

**Student life. Freshman orientation:** Available. Preregistration for classes offered. **Policies:** Students represented on college committees. **Activities:** Choral groups, dance, drama, musical theater, radio station, student government, student newspaper, law society, Irish club, Students Against War and Racism, Haitian club, Christian Seekers Fellowship, Jewish students society, Newman club, Betances Society, Black student society, ethnic organizations.

**Athletics.** NCAA. **Intercollegiate:** Baseball M, basketball, cross-country, diving W, rifle, soccer M, softball W, swimming W, tennis, volleyball W. **Intramural:** Basketball, rifle, soccer M, swimming. **Team name:** Bloodhounds.

**Student services.** Career counseling, services for economically disadvantaged, student employment services, financial aid counseling, health services, minority student services, on-campus daycare, personal counseling, placement for graduates, veterans' counselor, women's services. **Physically disabled:** Services for visually, speech, hearing impaired.

**Contact.**  E-mail: admiss@jjay.cuny.edu
Phone: (212) 237-8865 Fax: (212) 237-8777
Sandra Palleja, Director of Admissions, City University of New York: John Jay College of Criminal Justice, 445 West 59th Street, New York, NY 10019

## City University of New York: Lehman College

Bronx, New York                                   CB member
www.lehman.cuny.edu                          CB code: 2312

- Public 4-year liberal arts college
- Commuter campus in very large city
- 8,819 degree-seeking undergraduates: 33% part-time, 69% women
- 2,170 degree-seeking graduate students
- 26% of applicants admitted
- SAT or ACT (ACT writing optional) required
- 31% graduate within 6 years

**General.** Founded in 1931. Regionally accredited. **Degrees:** 1,458 bachelor's awarded; master's offered. **ROTC:** Army. **Location:** 8 miles from Manhattan. **Calendar:** Semester, limited summer session. **Full-time faculty:** 371 total; 75% have terminal degrees, 28% minority, 50% women. **Part-time faculty:** 401 total; 23% have terminal degrees, 37% minority, 53% women. **Class size:** 42% < 20, 57% 20-39, less than 1% 40-49, less than 1% 50-99. **Special facilities:** 2,500-seat performing arts center.

**Freshman class profile.** 15,291 applied, 3,915 admitted, 774 enrolled.

| Mid 50% test scores | | End year in good standing: | 82% |
|---|---|---|---|
| SAT critical reading: | 440-520 | Return as sophomores: | 77% |
| SAT math: | 460-530 | Out-of-state: | 1% |
| SAT writing: | 430-520 | | |

**Basis for selection.** High school record, GPA, and college preparatory courses most important. Tests are used to exempt students from placement tests. **Homeschooled:** State high school equivalency certificate required.

**High school preparation.** 16 units required. Required units include English 4, mathematics 3, social studies 4, science 2 (laboratory 1), foreign language 2 and visual/performing arts 1.

**2009-2010 Annual costs.** Tuition/fees: $4,940; $12,790 out-of-state. Books/supplies: $1,016. Personal expenses: $2,717.

**2008-2009 Financial aid.** All financial aid based on need.

**Application procedures. Admission:** $65 fee. Admission notification on a rolling basis. **Financial aid:** No deadline. FAFSA required. Applicants notified on a rolling basis starting 3/1.

**Academics. Special study options:** Accelerated study, cooperative education, cross-registration, distance learning, double major, dual enrollment of high school students, ESL, honors, independent study, internships, student-designed major, study abroad, teacher certification program. **Credit/placement by examination:** CLEP, IB, institutional tests. 30 credit hours maximum toward bachelor's degree. **Support services:** Learning center, pre-admission summer program, reduced course load, remedial instruction, study skills assistance, tutoring, writing center.

**Honors college/program.** Criteria for selection include high school academic record, SAT/ACT scores, essay, 2 letters of recommendation and interview.

**Majors. Area/ethnic studies:** African-American, Latin American. **Biology:** General. **Business:** Accounting, business admin. **Communications:** General. **Computer sciences:** General, information systems. **Education:** Health, mathematics, physical. **Family/consumer sciences:** Food/nutrition. **Foreign languages:** Comparative lit, French, Italian, linguistics, Spanish. **Health:** Audiology/speech pathology, facilities admin, nursing (RN). **History:** General. **Liberal arts:** Arts/sciences. **Math:** General. **Philosophy/religion:** Philosophy. **Physical sciences:** Chemistry, geology, physics. **Psychology:** General. **Public administration:** Social work. **Social sciences:** Anthropology, economics, geography, political science, sociology. **Visual/performing arts:** Art history/conservation, commercial/advertising art, music performance.

**Most popular majors.** Business/marketing 15%, education 24%, health sciences 20%, public administration/social services 8%, social sciences 11%.

**Computing on campus.** 88 workstations in library, computer center, student center. Commuter students can connect to campus network. Online library, helpline, repair service, student web hosting, wireless network available.

**Student life. Freshman orientation:** Mandatory. Preregistration for classes offered. **Activities:** Bands, choral groups, dance, drama, film society, literary magazine, music ensembles, musical theater, opera, radio station, student government, student newspaper, symphony orchestra, TV station, various religious, political, ethnic, and social service organizations.

**Athletics.** NCAA. **Intercollegiate:** Baseball M, basketball, cross-country, diving, softball W, swimming, tennis, track and field, volleyball. **Intramural:** Badminton, basketball, racquetball, soccer, softball, swimming, table tennis, tennis, volleyball. **Team name:** Lightning.

**Student services.** Adult student services, chaplain/spiritual director, career counseling, services for economically disadvantaged, student employment services, financial aid counseling, health services, on-campus daycare, personal counseling, placement for graduates, veterans' counselor, women's services. **Physically disabled:** Services for visually, speech, hearing impaired.

**Contact.**  E-mail: enroll@lehman.cuny.edu
Phone: (718) 960-8713 Toll-free number: (877) 534-6261
Fax: (718) 960-8712
Laurie Austin, Director of Admissions, City University of New York: Lehman College, 250 Bedford Park Boulevard West, Bronx, NY 10468

## City University of New York: Medgar Evers College

**Brooklyn, New York**
**www.mec.cuny.edu**

CB member
CB code: 2460

- Public 4-year liberal arts college
- Commuter campus in very large city
- 6,757 degree-seeking undergraduates: 31% part-time, 75% women, 88% African American, 1% Asian American, 6% Hispanic American, 2% international

**General.** Founded in 1969. Regionally accredited. **Degrees:** 329 bachelor's, 397 associate awarded. **Calendar:** Semester, extensive summer session. **Full-time faculty:** 179 total; 55% have terminal degrees, 84% minority, 46% women. **Part-time faculty:** 397 total; 86% minority, 45% women. **Class size:** 18% < 20, 80% 20-39, 2% 40-49, less than 1% 50-99.

**Freshman class profile.** 7,178 applied, 7,178 admitted, 1,378 enrolled.

| Mid 50% test scores | | | |
|---|---|---|---|
| SAT critical reading: | 340-440 | GPA 3.0-3.49: | 6% |
| SAT math: | 330-430 | GPA 2.0-2.99: | 69% |
| SAT writing: | 340-430 | End year in good standing: | 61% |
| GPA 3.75 or higher: | 1% | Return as sophomores: | 69% |
| GPA 3.50-3.74: | 1% | Out-of-state: | 1% |
| | | International: | 1% |

**Basis for selection.** Open admission, but selective for some programs. Special requirements for nursing and baccalaureate programs with school record, class rank, and test scores considered. Discretionary policy admits 25 students each semester without high school diplomas. Must be 21 years old, legal residents of New York City.

**High school preparation.** 15 units recommended. Recommended units include English 4, mathematics 3, history 2, science 2 and academic electives 4.

**2009-2010 Annual costs.** Tuition/fees: $4,902; $12,752 out-of-state. Books/supplies: $1,070. Personal expenses: $2,754.

**2009-2010 Financial aid. Need-based:** 92% of total undergraduate aid awarded as scholarships/grants, 8% as loans/jobs. **Non-need-based:** Scholarships awarded for academics, leadership.

**Application procedures. Admission:** Priority date 7/8; no deadline. $65 fee, may be waived for applicants with need. Admission notification on a rolling basis. **Financial aid:** Priority date 1/2, closing date 6/1. FAFSA required. Applicants notified on a rolling basis; must reply within 3 week(s) of notification.

**Academics. Special study options:** Cross-registration, distance learning, ESL, honors, independent study, internships, liberal arts/career combination, student-designed major, study abroad, teacher certification program. 2-year bachelor's program in nursing for RNs. **Credit/placement by examination:** AP, CLEP, IB, institutional tests. 15 credit hours maximum toward associate degree, 30 toward bachelor's. **Support services:** Learning center, pre-admission summer program, reduced course load, remedial instruction, tutoring, writing center.

**Majors. Biology:** General. **Business:** General, accounting, business admin. **Computer sciences:** Information systems. **Conservation:** Environmental studies. **Education:** Elementary, special. **Health:** Nursing (RN). **Liberal arts:** Arts/sciences. **Math:** General. **Psychology:** General. **Public administration:** General.

**Most popular majors.** Biology 9%, business/marketing 48%, health sciences 7%, psychology 15%.

**Computing on campus.** 250 workstations in library, computer center, student center. Online course registration, online library, wireless network available.

**Student life. Freshman orientation:** Available. Preregistration for classes offered. **Activities:** Jazz band, choral groups, dance, drama, literary magazine, radio station, student government, student newspaper, TV station, numerous religious, political, ethnic, and social service clubs.

**Athletics.** NCAA. **Intercollegiate:** Basketball, cross-country, soccer, softball W, track and field, volleyball. **Intramural:** Basketball, bowling, cheerleading W, soccer M, swimming, track and field W. **Team name:** Cougar.

**Student services.** Career counseling, student employment services, financial aid counseling, health services, on-campus daycare, personal counseling, placement for graduates, veterans' counselor, women's services. **Physically disabled:** Services for visually, speech, hearing impaired.

**Contact.** E-mail: enroll@mec.cuny.edu
Phone: (718) 270-6024 Fax: (718) 270-6411
Julie Augustine, Director of Admissions, City University of New York: Medgar Evers College, 1665 Bedford Avenue, Brooklyn, NY 11225-2201

## City University of New York: New York City College of Technology

**Brooklyn, New York**
**www.citytech.cuny.edu**

CB member
CB code: 2550

- Public 4-year technical college
- Commuter campus in very large city
- 14,366 degree-seeking undergraduates: 37% part-time, 47% women, 36% African American, 18% Asian American, 27% Hispanic American, 6% international

**General.** Founded in 1946. Regionally accredited. **Degrees:** 647 bachelor's, 878 associate awarded. **Calendar:** Semester, extensive summer session. **Full-time faculty:** 346 total; 66% have terminal degrees, 33% minority, 44% women. **Part-time faculty:** 645 total; 13% have terminal degrees, 39% minority, 40% women. **Class size:** 34% < 20, 62% 20-39, 4% 40-49, less than 1% 50-99. **Special facilities:** Ophthalmic dispensing and dental clinics, laboratory kitchens and dining room, immigration clinic, theater.

**Freshman class profile.** 14,419 applied, 12,105 admitted, 3,251 enrolled.

| Mid 50% test scores | | | |
|---|---|---|---|
| SAT critical reading: | 350-440 | Return as sophomores: | 80% |
| SAT math: | 370-470 | Out-of-state: | 1% |
| SAT writing: | 350-430 | International: | 5% |

**Basis for selection.** Open admission, but selective for some programs.

**High school preparation.** 14 units required; 19 recommended. Required and recommended units include English 4, mathematics 2-3, social studies 2-3, science 2-3 (laboratory 1-2), foreign language 1-2, visual/performing arts 1 and academic electives 1-2.

**2009-2010 Annual costs.** Tuition/fees: $4,939; $12,789 out-of-state. Books/supplies: $879. Personal expenses: $2,710.

**2009-2010 Financial aid. Need-based:** 2,530 full-time freshmen applied for aid; 2,241 were judged to have need; 2,165 of these received aid. Average need met was 59%. Average scholarship/grant was $6,442; average loan $564. 86% of total undergraduate aid awarded as scholarships/grants, 14% as loans/jobs. **Non-need-based:** Awarded to 551 full-time undergraduates, including 402 freshmen. Scholarships awarded for state residency. **Additional information:** Foreign students applying for aid must have resided in New York for at least 1 year.

**Application procedures. Admission:** Priority date 3/15; no deadline. $65 fee, may be waived for applicants with need. Admission notification on a rolling basis. **Financial aid:** Priority date 5/15; no closing date. FAFSA required.

**Academics.** Students in health science programs work under supervision with patients in clinical settings. Industry standard facilities used in hospitality management program. **Special study options:** Cross-registration, distance learning, dual enrollment of high school students, ESL, honors, independent study, internships, student-designed major, study abroad, teacher certification program. Bridge programs to higher education or careers in engineering technology, alternate format program for those out of high school 5 years with or without diploma. **Credit/placement by examination:** CLEP, IB, institutional tests. Students can earn credit by successfully completing examinations offered for certain courses. Eligibility and the nature, content and grading of each exam are determined by the departmental faculty and must be approved by the provost. **Support services:** Learning center, pre-admission summer program, remedial instruction, study skills assistance, tutoring, writing center.

**Majors. Business:** Hospitality admin, tourism/travel. **Communications technology:** Graphic/printing. **Computer sciences:** General. **Construction:** Maintenance. **Education:** Technology/industrial arts. **Engineering technology:** Electromechanical, telecommunications. **Health:** Health services admin. **Legal studies:** Paralegal. **Math:** Applied. **Public administration:** Human services. **Visual/performing arts:** Commercial/advertising art, theater design. **Other:** Architectural technology.

**Most popular majors.** Architecture 8%, business/marketing 17%, computer/information sciences 20%, engineering/engineering technologies 8%, health sciences 6%, legal studies 8%, public administration/social services 12%, visual/performing arts 15%.

**Computing on campus.** 391 workstations in library, computer center, student center. Online course registration, online library, helpline, wireless network available.

**Student life. Freshman orientation:** Available. Held the week before classes begin. **Housing:** Some housing available at nearby university. **Activities:** Drama, musical theater, student government, student newspaper, full range of student clubs.

**Athletics.** NCAA. **Intercollegiate:** Basketball, cross-country, soccer M, softball W, tennis, volleyball. **Intramural:** Basketball, handball, soccer M, table tennis, track and field, volleyball. **Team name:** Yellow Jackets.

**Student services.** Adult student services, career counseling, services for economically disadvantaged, student employment services, financial aid counseling, health services, minority student services, on-campus daycare, personal counseling. **Physically disabled:** Services for visually, speech, hearing impaired.

**Contact.**   E-mail: admissions@citytech.cuny.edu
Phone: (718) 260-5500 Fax: (718) 260-5504
Alexis Chaconis, Director of Admissions, City University of New York: New York City College of Technology, 300 Jay Street Namm G17, Brooklyn, NY 11201

## City University of New York: Queens College
**Flushing, New York**
**www.qc.cuny.edu**                    **CB code: 2750**

- Public 4-year liberal arts college
- Commuter campus in very large city
- 15,270 degree-seeking undergraduates: 23% part-time, 59% women
- 4,191 degree-seeking graduate students
- 33% of applicants admitted
- SAT or ACT (ACT writing optional) required
- 52% graduate within 6 years

**General.** Founded in 1937. Regionally accredited. **Degrees:** 2,646 bachelor's awarded; master's offered. **ROTC:** Army, Naval. **Location:** 17 miles from Manhattan. **Calendar:** Semester, extensive summer session. **Full-time faculty:** 636 total; 85% have terminal degrees, 20% minority, 44% women. **Part-time faculty:** 766 total; 22% minority, 50% women. **Class size:** 32% < 20, 53% 20-39, 5% 40-49, 9% 50-99, 1% >100. **Special facilities:** Louis Armstrong archives, center for the performing arts, center for Byzantine and Modern Greek studies, neuroscience research center, museum.

**Freshman class profile.** 18,028 applied, 5,878 admitted, 1,712 enrolled.

| Mid 50% test scores | | | |
|---|---|---|---|
| SAT critical reading: | 490-550 | GPA 2.0-2.99: | 3% |
| SAT math: | 490-580 | Return as sophomores: | 86% |
| SAT writing: | 490-550 | Out-of-state: | 1% |
| GPA 3.75 or higher: | 5% | Live on campus: | 2% |
| GPA 3.50-3.74: | 21% | Fraternities: | 1% |
| GPA 3.0-3.49: | 71% | Sororities: | 1% |

**Basis for selection.** Factors include high school grades, strength of academic program, and test scores. Successful candidates will have chosen well-rounded program of study and attained at least B+ average. SAT scores on Critical Reading and Mathematics are considered. SAT Subject Tests recommended. SAT and SAT Subject Test required of scholarship and honors college applicants. Essay and interview required for scholarship, honors program; audition recommended for music, performance; portfolio recommended for bachelor of fine arts. Other criteria considered for appeals. **Homeschooled:** Transcript of courses and grades, state high school equivalency certificate required. Students must submit a letter from the superintendent of their school district confirming that all high school graduation requirements of the district have been met through home schooling. If students cannot obtain the letter from the high school district, they must obtain a General Equivalency Development Diploma (GED). **Learning Disabled:** Untimed SAT/ACT accepted.

**High school preparation.** College-preparatory program required. 16 units required; 17 recommended. Required and recommended units include English 4, mathematics 3, social studies 4, science 2-3 (laboratory 2-3) and foreign language 3.

**2009-2010 Annual costs.** Tuition/fees: $5,047; $12,897 out-of-state. Books/supplies: $1,070. Personal expenses: $3,672.

**2008-2009 Financial aid. Non-need-based:** Scholarships awarded for academics, athletics, music/drama, state residency.

**Application procedures. Admission:** Priority date 1/1; deadline 5/15. $65 fee, may be waived for applicants with need. Application must be submitted online. Admission notification 5/30. Admission notification on a rolling basis. Must reply by May 1 or within 4 week(s) if notified thereafter. Admitted applicants must reply by May 1 for some programs, within 4 weeks after notification for others. **Financial aid:** Priority date 2/1; no closing date. FAFSA, institutional form required. Applicants notified on a rolling basis starting 3/1; must reply within 3 week(s) of notification.

**Academics.** Required core liberal arts curriculum includes courses in the humanities, physical and biological sciences, scientific methodology and quantitative reasoning, social sciences, and pre-industrial/non-western civilization. **Special study options:** Accelerated study, cross-registration, double major, dual enrollment of high school students, ESL, honors, independent study, internships, liberal arts/career combination, student-designed major, study abroad, teacher certification program, weekend college. **Credit/placement by examination:** AP, CLEP, IB, SAT, ACT, institutional tests. 24 credit hours maximum toward bachelor's degree. **Support services:** Learning center, pre-admission summer program, study skills assistance, tutoring, writing center.

**Honors college/program.** 40 students, average SAT of 1300 (exclusive of Writing) or higher, high school average 95 or higher, required to submit SAT Subject Test scores, interview required.

**Majors. Area/ethnic studies:** African, American, East Asian, Latin American, women's. **Biology:** General. **Business:** Accounting, actuarial science, finance, international, labor studies. **Communications:** Media studies. **Computer sciences:** Computer science. **Conservation:** Environmental science, environmental studies. **Education:** Art, early childhood, elementary, ESL, family/consumer sciences, music, physical, physics. **Family/consumer sciences:** General. **Foreign languages:** Ancient Greek, Chinese, comparative lit, French, German, Hebrew, Italian, Latin, linguistics, Russian, Spanish. **Health:** Communication disorders. **History:** General. **Liberal arts:** Arts/sciences. **Math:** General. **Parks/recreation:** Exercise sciences. **Philosophy/religion:** Judaic, philosophy, religion. **Physical sciences:** Chemistry, geology, physics. **Psychology:** General. **Social sciences:** General, anthropology, economics, political science, sociology, urban studies. **Visual/performing arts:** Art history/conservation, dramatic, film/cinema, graphic design, music performance, studio arts. **Other:** Byzantine and Modern Greek studies, Multi-/Interdisciplinary studies.

**Most popular majors.** Business/marketing 21%, education 7%, English 7%, psychology 13%, social sciences 25%.

**Computing on campus.** 2,300 workstations in library, computer center, student center. Commuter students can connect to campus network. Online course registration, online library, helpline, repair service, student web hosting, wireless network available.

**Student life. Freshman orientation:** Mandatory. Preregistration for classes offered. Held in June, July, August. **Policies:** Students found guilty of any form of academic dishonesty, such as plagiarism or cheating on an examination, are subject to discipline, including suspension or dismissal from the college. **Housing:** Coed dorms, apartments, wellness housing available. $400 partly refundable deposit, deadline 6/1. Dormitories available on a first-come, first-served basis. Disabled and international students do not have separate accommodations. **Activities:** Bands, campus ministries, choral groups, dance, drama, film society, international student organizations, literary magazine, music ensembles, Model UN, musical theater, radio station, student government, student newspaper, symphony orchestra, TV station, Catholic, Protestant, Hindu, Jewish, Greek Orthodox, Muslim, African American, Asian, Bangladeshi, Guyanese, Haitian, Hispanic, Italian, Irish, lesbian, and gay student organizations; honor societies; various clubs; political student associations.

**Athletics.** NCAA. **Intercollegiate:** Baseball M, basketball, cross-country, diving, fencing W, lacrosse W, soccer, softball W, swimming, table tennis W, tennis, track and field, volleyball W, water polo M. **Intramural:** Basketball, cross-country, football (non-tackle), soccer, softball, table tennis, tennis, track and field, volleyball. **Team name:** Knights.

**Student services.** Adult student services, alcohol/substance abuse counseling, career counseling, services for economically disadvantaged, student employment services, financial aid counseling, health services, minority student services, on-campus daycare, personal counseling, placement for graduates, veterans' counselor, women's services. **Physically disabled:** Services for visually, speech, hearing impaired.

**Contact.**   E-mail: vincent.angrisani@qc.cuny.edu
Phone: (718) 997-5600 Fax: (718) 997-5617
Vincent Angrisani, Executive Director of Admissions and Enrollment Management, City University of New York: Queens College, 6530 Kissena Boulevard, Jefferson 117, Flushing, NY 11367-1597

## City University of New York: York College
Jamaica, New York      CB member
www.york.cuny.edu      CB code: 2992

- Public 4-year liberal arts college
- Commuter campus in very large city
- 6,915 degree-seeking undergraduates: 30% part-time, 66% women, 35% African American, 9% Asian American, 14% Hispanic American
- 48 degree-seeking graduate students
- SAT or ACT (ACT writing recommended) required

**General.** Founded in 1966. Regionally accredited. **Degrees:** 763 bachelor's awarded; master's offered. **Location:** 14 miles from midtown Manhattan. **Calendar:** Semester, limited summer session. **Full-time faculty:** 210 total; 42% minority, 55% women. **Part-time faculty:** 276 total; 53% minority, 56% women. **Class size:** 21% < 20, 38% 20-39, 6% 40-49, 14% 50-99, 20% >100. **Special facilities:** Theater, cardio-pneumo-simulator, flight simulator.

**Freshman class profile.** 1,045 enrolled.

| | | | |
|---|---|---|---|
| End year in good standing: | 80% | Out-of-state: | 1% |
| Return as sophomores: | 75% | | |

**Basis for selection.** 75 average with 12 high school academic units basic admission requirement; allowance made for higher average or test scores. Units recommended for admission must be acquired before graduation from any CUNY senior college. Admission requirements for CUNY senior colleges will be automatically satisfied with completion of our core requirement. Interview required for occupational therapy, nursing, physician assistant, and social work or for appeal.

**High school preparation.** College-preparatory program recommended. 12 units required; 20 recommended. Required and recommended units include English 4, mathematics 2, social studies 2, science 2, foreign language 2 and academic electives 8-10.

**2009-2010 Annual costs.** Tuition/fees: $4,912; $12,762 out-of-state. Books/supplies: $1,016. Personal expenses: $4,526.

**2009-2010 Financial aid.** **Need-based:** 888 full-time freshmen applied for aid; 837 were judged to have need; 756 of these received aid. Average need met was 69%. Average scholarship/grant was $2,595; average loan $2,686. 85% of total undergraduate aid awarded as scholarships/grants, 15% as loans/jobs. **Non-need-based:** Awarded to 526 full-time undergraduates, including 317 freshmen. Scholarships awarded for academics.

**Application procedures.** Admission: Closing date 1/9. $65 fee. Admission notification on a rolling basis beginning on or about 1/1. Centralized application processing allows students to apply to 6 schools within CUNY system at same time. **Financial aid:** Priority date 5/1; no closing date. FAFSA required. Applicants notified on a rolling basis starting 3/1.

**Academics.** **Special study options:** Combined bachelor's/graduate degree, cooperative education, distance learning, double major, dual enrollment of high school students, ESL, honors, independent study, internships, liberal arts/career combination, student-designed major, study abroad, teacher certification program. Co-op programs in business, computer science, health professions. **Credit/placement by examination:** AP, CLEP, IB, institutional tests. 16 credit hours maximum toward bachelor's degree. Students with SAT/ACT scores exempt from CUNY skills assessment tests. **Support services:** Learning center, pre-admission summer program, remedial instruction, study skills assistance, tutoring, writing center.

**Majors.** **Area/ethnic studies:** African-American. **Biology:** General, biotechnology. **Business:** Accounting, business admin, management information systems, marketing. **Communications:** General. **Communications technology:** General. **Computer sciences:** General, computer science. **Education:** Health, physical. **Family/consumer sciences:** Aging. **Foreign languages:** French, Spanish. **Health:** Clinical lab science, clinical lab technology, environmental health, health services, movement therapy, nursing (RN), physician assistant, public health ed. **History:** General. **Interdisciplinary:** Gerontology. **Liberal arts:** Arts/sciences. **Math:** General. **Philosophy/religion:** Philosophy. **Physical sciences:** Chemistry, geology, physics. **Psychology:** General. **Public administration:** Social work. **Social sciences:** Anthropology, economics, political science, sociology. **Transportation:** Aviation management. **Visual/performing arts:** Art history/conservation, dramatic. **Other:** Multi/Interdisciplinary studies.

**Most popular majors.** Business/marketing 30%, health sciences 18%, psychology 16%, public administration/social services 8%, social sciences 8%.

**Computing on campus.** 650 workstations in library, computer center, student center. Online library, helpline, wireless network available.

**Student life.** Freshman orientation: Available. Preregistration for classes offered. **Activities:** Jazz band, choral groups, drama, film society, literary magazine, musical theater, student government, student newspaper, TV station, 48 organizations.

**Athletics.** NCAA. **Intercollegiate:** Basketball, cheerleading, cross-country, soccer, softball W, swimming, tennis, track and field, volleyball, weight lifting. **Intramural:** Badminton, basketball, soccer M, softball W, swimming, table tennis, tennis, track and field, volleyball, weight lifting. **Team name:** Cardinals.

**Student services.** Adult student services, chaplain/spiritual director, career counseling, student employment services, financial aid counseling, health services, on-campus daycare, personal counseling, placement for graduates, veterans' counselor. **Physically disabled:** Services for visually, speech, hearing impaired.

**Contact.** E-mail: admissions@york.cuny.edu
Phone: (718) 262-2165 Fax: (718) 262-2601
Diane Warmsley, Director of Admissions/Enrollment, City University of New York: York College, 94-20 Guy R. Brewer Boulevard, Jamaica, NY 11451-9989

## Clarkson University
Potsdam, New York      CB member
www.clarkson.edu      CB code: 2084

- Private 4-year university
- Residential campus in small town
- 2,717 degree-seeking undergraduates: 27% women, 3% African American, 4% Asian American, 3% Hispanic American, 1% Native American, 3% international
- 434 degree-seeking graduate students
- 73% of applicants admitted
- SAT or ACT (ACT writing optional), application essay required
- 72% graduate within 6 years; 23% enter graduate study

**General.** Founded in 1896. Regionally accredited. **Degrees:** 587 bachelor's awarded; master's, doctoral, professional offered. **ROTC:** Army, Air Force. **Location:** 85 miles from Ottawa, Canada, 69 miles from Olympic Village in Lake Placid. **Calendar:** Semester, extensive summer session. **Full-time faculty:** 204 total; 86% have terminal degrees, 21% minority, 26% women. **Part-time faculty:** 22 total; 32% have terminal degrees, 4% minority, 46% women. **Class size:** 47% < 20, 29% 20-39, 6% 40-49, 14% 50-99, 4% >100. **Special facilities:** Design, prototyping and testing facilities for SPEED Team competitions (Student Projects for Engineering Experience and Design); center for the environment; center for sustainable energy systems; center for air resources engineering and science; center for advanced materials processing; great rivers center; center for rehabilitation engineering, science, and technology; center for innovation.

**Freshman class profile.** 4,125 applied, 2,998 admitted, 777 enrolled.

| Mid 50% test scores | | GPA 2.0-2.99: | 11% |
|---|---|---|---|
| SAT critical reading: | 500-610 | Rank in top quarter: | 67% |
| SAT math: | 560-660 | Rank in top tenth: | 34% |
| SAT writing: | 490-580 | End year in good standing: | 85% |
| ACT composite: | 23-27 | Return as sophomores: | 87% |
| GPA 3.75 or higher: | 30% | Out-of-state: | 30% |
| GPA 3.50-3.74: | 26% | Live on campus: | 98% |
| GPA 3.0-3.49: | 33% | International: | 2% |

**Basis for selection.** Secondary school transcripts, test scores, recommendations, school and community involvement all given strong consideration. SAT Subject Tests recommended. Interview recommended. **Homeschooled:** Transcript of courses and grades required. **Learning Disabled:** Documented information on disabilities is necessary.

**High school preparation.** College-preparatory program recommended. 16 units required. Required and recommended units include English 4, mathematics 3-4 and science 3-4.

**2009-2010 Annual costs.** Tuition/fees: $32,910. Room/board: $11,118.

**2009-2010 Financial aid.** **Need-based:** 733 full-time freshmen applied for aid; 641 were judged to have need; 641 of these received aid. Average need met was 85%. Average scholarship/grant was $24,862; average loan $4,066. 76% of total undergraduate aid awarded as scholarships/grants, 24% as loans/jobs. **Non-need-based:** Awarded to 755 full-time undergraduates, including 271 freshmen. Scholarships awarded for academics, alumni affiliation, leadership, minority status, ROTC.

**Application procedures. Admission:** Closing date 1/15 (postmark date). $50 fee, may be waived for applicants with need, free for online applicants. Admission notification on a rolling basis beginning on or about 2/1. Must reply by May 1 or within 2 week(s) if notified thereafter. Candidates encouraged to submit completed applications between October 1 and March 1 of their final year in high school. **Financial aid:** Priority date 2/15; no closing date. FAFSA required. Applicants notified on a rolling basis starting 3/19; must reply by 5/1 or within 2 week(s) of notification.

**Academics.** All students in the School of Business programs must complete a study-abroad experience; all students must fulfill the learning outcomes of the Clarkson Common Experience; a BS degree may be earned in 3 years by motivated, high-achieving high school students. **Special study options:** Accelerated study, combined bachelor's/graduate degree, cooperative education, cross-registration, distance learning, double major, dual enrollment of high school students, ESL, honors, independent study, liberal arts/career combination, semester at sea, student-designed major, study abroad, Washington semester. Women In Science and Engineering (WISE) Living/Learning Community; interdisciplinary degree programs that combine Engineering and Business, Business and Liberal Arts, and Environmental Science and Policy; a large number of 3+2 and 2+2 articulation agreements that facilitate transfer to Clarkson from community colleges and other baccalaureate institutions; business students experience a unique introduction to entrepreneurship through working with the Shipley Center for Innovation, the Clarkson Entrepreneurs Organization (CEO) and the Clarkson Center for Global Competitiveness. **Credit/placement by examination:** AP, CLEP, IB, institutional tests. 30 credit hours maximum toward bachelor's degree. **Support services:** Study skills assistance, tutoring, writing center.

**Majors. Area/ethnic studies:** American. **Biology:** General, environmental toxicology, molecular biochemistry. **Business:** Accounting/finance, business admin, entrepreneurial studies, logistics, management information systems. **Communications:** General, digital media. **Computer sciences:** Computer science. **Conservation:** Environmental science. **Engineering:** General, aerospace, chemical, civil, computer, electrical, environmental, mechanical, software. **Engineering technology:** Industrial management. **History:** General. **Liberal arts:** Arts/sciences, humanities. **Math:** General, applied. **Physical sciences:** Chemistry, physics. **Psychology:** General. **Social sciences:** General, political science, sociology. **Other:** Professional studies.

**Most popular majors.** Biology 7%, business/marketing 17%, engineering/engineering technologies 58%.

**Computing on campus.** 350 workstations in library, computer center. Dormitories wired for high-speed internet access and linked to campus network. Commuter students can connect to campus network. Online course registration, online library, helpline, repair service, student web hosting, wireless network available.

**Student life. Freshman orientation:** Available. **Housing:** Guaranteed on-campus for freshmen. Coed dorms, single-sex dorms, special housing for disabled, apartments, fraternity/sorority housing, wellness housing available. **Activities:** Bands, choral groups, drama, international student organizations, literary magazine, musical theater, radio station, student government, student newspaper, symphony orchestra, TV station, Alpha Phi Omega, America Indian Science and Engineering Society, Circle K, College Republicans, Hillel Club, Intervarsity Christian Fellowship, Muslim students association, National Society of Black Engineers, Society of Hispanic Professional Engineers, Young Democrats.

**Athletics.** NCAA. **Intercollegiate:** Baseball M, basketball, cross-country, diving, golf M, ice hockey, lacrosse, skiing, soccer, swimming, volleyball W. **Intramural:** Basketball, football (non-tackle), ice hockey, soccer, softball, volleyball. **Team name:** Golden Knights.

**Student services.** Alcohol/substance abuse counseling, career counseling, services for economically disadvantaged, student employment services, financial aid counseling, health services, minority student services, personal counseling, placement for graduates, veterans' counselor, women's services. **Physically disabled:** Services for visually, speech, hearing impaired. **Learning disabled:** Comprehensive services available.

**Contact.** E-mail: admission@clarkson.edu
Phone: (315) 268-6480 Toll-free number: (800) 527-6577
Fax: (315) 268-7647
Brian Grant, Director of Admission, Clarkson University, Holcroft House, Potsdam, NY 13699-5605

## Colgate University
Hamilton, New York
www.colgate.edu

CB member
CB code: 2086

- Private 4-year liberal arts college
- Residential campus in small town

- 2,799 degree-seeking undergraduates: 53% women, 6% African American, 5% Asian American, 6% Hispanic American, 1% Native American, 5% international
- 9 degree-seeking graduate students
- 32% of applicants admitted
- SAT or ACT (ACT writing optional), application essay required
- 90% graduate within 6 years; 20% enter graduate study

**General.** Founded in 1819. Regionally accredited. **Degrees:** 704 bachelor's awarded; master's offered. **ROTC:** Army. **Location:** 38 miles from Syracuse, 25 miles from Utica. **Calendar:** Semester. **Full-time faculty:** 266 total; 96% have terminal degrees, 21% minority, 40% women. **Part-time faculty:** 49 total; 57% have terminal degrees, 14% minority, 61% women. **Class size:** 61% < 20, 36% 20-39, 1% 40-49, 2% 50-99, less than 1% >100. **Special facilities:** Anthropology museum, center for learning, teaching, and research, life sciences complex, geology/fossil collection, observatory, electron microscopes, laser lab, weather lab, geographic information system, center for outreach volunteerism and education.

**Freshman class profile.** 7,816 applied, 2,464 admitted, 750 enrolled.

| Mid 50% test scores | | | |
|---|---|---|---|
| SAT critical reading: | 630-730 | GPA 2.0-2.99: | 6% |
| SAT math: | 640-730 | Rank in top quarter: | 89% |
| ACT composite: | 29-32 | Rank in top tenth: | 65% |
| GPA 3.75 or higher: | 39% | Return as sophomores: | 95% |
| GPA 3.50-3.74: | 28% | Out-of-state: | 74% |
| GPA 3.0-3.49: | 27% | Live on campus: | 100% |
| | | International: | 6% |

**Basis for selection.** School achievement record of primary importance. Teacher/counselor recommendations, test scores, and major talent or personal accomplishment considered. Disadvantaged, nontraditional, and minority applicants given special consideration. **Homeschooled:** Statement describing homeschool structure and mission, transcript of courses and grades, letter of recommendation (nonparent) required. **Learning Disabled:** Optional self-disclosure of disabilities in admissions process.

**High school preparation.** College-preparatory program recommended. 16 units required; 20 recommended. Required and recommended units include English 4, mathematics 3-4, social studies 3-4, science 3-4 (laboratory 2-3) and foreign language 3-4. Foreign language units should be in 1 language.

**2009-2010 Annual costs.** Tuition/fees: $40,970. Room/board: $9,970. Books/supplies: $1,940.

**2009-2010 Financial aid. Need-based:** 318 full-time freshmen applied for aid; 252 were judged to have need; 252 of these received aid. Average need met was 100%. Average scholarship/grant was $35,526; average loan $2,107. 89% of total undergraduate aid awarded as scholarships/grants, 11% as loans/jobs. **Non-need-based:** Awarded to 164 full-time undergraduates, including 47 freshmen. Scholarships awarded for athletics.

**Application procedures. Admission:** Closing date 1/15 (postmark date). $55 fee, may be waived for applicants with need, free for online applicants. Admission notification 4/1. Must reply by 5/1. **Financial aid:** Closing date 1/15. CSS PROFILE required. Applicants notified by 4/1; must reply by 5/1 or within 2 week(s) of notification.

**Academics. Special study options:** Combined bachelor's/graduate degree, cross-registration, double major, honors, independent study, internships, semester at sea, student-designed major, study abroad, teacher certification program, urban semester, Washington semester. 3-4 architecture program with Washington University (MO), 3-2 program in engineering with Columbia University, Rensselaer Polytechnic Institute, and Washington University; Early Assurance Medical School program with American University; extended study program during winter or summer breaks offer academic work in a variety of locations around world. **Credit/placement by examination:** AP, CLEP, IB, SAT, institutional tests. **Support services:** Learning center, pre-admission summer program, reduced course load, study skills assistance, tutoring, writing center.

**Majors. Area/ethnic studies:** African, African-American, Asian, Latin American, Native American, Russian/Slavic, women's. **Biology:** General, biochemistry, molecular. **Computer sciences:** General, computer science. **Conservation:** General, environmental studies. **Education:** General. **Foreign languages:** Classics, French, German, Japanese, Latin, modern Greek, Russian, Spanish. **Health:** Predental, premedicine, preveterinary. **History:** General. **Interdisciplinary:** Biological/physical sciences, math/computer science, natural sciences, neuroscience, peace/conflict. **Liberal arts:** Arts/sciences. **Math:** General. **Philosophy/religion:** Philosophy, religion. **Physical sciences:** Astronomy, astrophysics, chemistry, geology, physics. **Psychology:** General. **Social sciences:** General, anthropology, economics, geography, international economic development, international relations, political science, sociology. **Visual/performing arts:** Art, art history/conservation, dramatic, studio arts.

**Most popular majors.** Biology 9%, English 8%, foreign language 10%, history 9%, psychology 6%, social sciences 33%, visual/performing arts 7%.

**Computing on campus.** 848 workstations in dormitories, library, computer center, student center. Dormitories wired for high-speed internet access and linked to campus network. Commuter students can connect to campus network. Online course registration, online library, helpline, repair service, student web hosting, wireless network available.

**Student life. Freshman orientation:** Mandatory. Preregistration for classes offered. 4-day program held 4 days before first day of classes. **Policies:** All students required to read, sign, and abide by Academic Honor Code. **Housing:** Guaranteed on-campus for all undergraduates. Coed dorms, special housing for disabled, apartments, cooperative housing, fraternity/sorority housing, wellness housing available. $500 nonrefundable deposit, deadline 5/1. Accommodations for students with special needs, townhouses for small groups of students available. **Activities:** Bands, choral groups, dance, drama, film society, literary magazine, music ensembles, musical theater, radio station, student government, student newspaper, symphony orchestra, TV station, over 180 campus organizations.

**Athletics.** NCAA. **Intercollegiate:** Basketball, cheerleading, cross-country, diving, field hockey W, football (tackle) M, golf M, ice hockey, lacrosse, rowing (crew), soccer, softball W, swimming, tennis, track and field, volleyball W. **Intramural:** Basketball, bowling, football (non-tackle), golf, ice hockey, racquetball, rifle, soccer, softball, squash, table tennis, tennis, volleyball. **Team name:** Raiders.

**Student services.** Alcohol/substance abuse counseling, chaplain/spiritual director, career counseling, services for economically disadvantaged, student employment services, financial aid counseling, health services, minority student services, personal counseling, placement for graduates, women's services. **Physically disabled:** Services for visually, hearing impaired.

**Contact.** E-mail: admission@mail.colgate.edu
Phone: (315) 228-7401 Fax: (315) 228-7544
Gary Ross, Dean of Admission, Colgate University, 13 Oak Drive, Hamilton, NY 13346-1383

---

## College of Mount St. Vincent
**Riverdale, New York**                                       **CB member**
**www.mountsaintvincent.edu**                                 **CB code: 2088**

- Private 4-year liberal arts college affiliated with Roman Catholic Church
- Residential campus in very large city
- 1,504 degree-seeking undergraduates: 10% part-time, 74% women, 12% African American, 10% Asian American, 30% Hispanic American
- 131 degree-seeking graduate students
- 72% of applicants admitted
- SAT or ACT (ACT writing optional), application essay required
- 55% graduate within 6 years; 20% enter graduate study

**General.** Founded in 1847. Regionally accredited. Dual certification in elementary and special education and secondary and special education. 5-year program for master of science in education. **Degrees:** 277 bachelor's awarded; master's offered. **ROTC:** Air Force. **Location:** 12 miles from midtown Manhattan. **Calendar:** Semester, limited summer session. **Full-time faculty:** 73 total; 82% have terminal degrees, 10% minority, 62% women. **Part-time faculty:** 92 total. **Class size:** 50% < 20, 49% 20-39, 2% 40-49. **Special facilities:** NMR spectrometer, computer graphics and animation center, computer classrooms, forensic science equipment.

**Freshman class profile.** 2,057 applied, 1,472 admitted, 391 enrolled.

| Mid 50% test scores | | GPA 2.0-2.99: | 55% |
|---|---|---|---|
| SAT critical reading: | 410-520 | End year in good standing: | 80% |
| SAT math: | 400-510 | Return as sophomores: | 74% |
| GPA 3.75 or higher: | 5% | Out-of-state: | 11% |
| GPA 3.50-3.74: | 6% | Live on campus: | 59% |
| GPA 3.0-3.49: | 28% | International: | 1% |

**Basis for selection.** School achievement record (rank in top half of class, 3.0 high school GPA) most important, test scores and recommendations important, school and community activities considered. Interview recommended. **Homeschooled:** Transcript of courses and grades required. **Learning Disabled:** Must submit IEP or other certification to receive service.

**High school preparation.** College-preparatory program recommended. 16 units required; 20 recommended. Required and recommended units include English 4, mathematics 2-3, social studies 2-3, science 2-3 and foreign language 2-3. 3 math for nursing, science, and math majors; 3 science with lab for nursing and science majors.

---

**2009-2010 Annual costs.** Tuition/fees: $25,710. Room/board: $9,900. Books/supplies: $900. Personal expenses: $900.

**2008-2009 Financial aid. Non-need-based:** Scholarships awarded for academics, alumni affiliation, leadership.

**Application procedures. Admission:** No deadline. $35 fee, may be waived for applicants with need, free for online applicants. Admission notification on a rolling basis beginning on or about 2/1. Must reply by May 1 or within 3 week(s) if notified thereafter. **Financial aid:** Priority date 3/1; no closing date. FAFSA required. Applicants notified on a rolling basis starting 3/1; must reply by 5/1 or within 3 week(s) of notification.

**Academics. Special study options:** Accelerated study, combined bachelor's/graduate degree, double major, honors, independent study, internships, liberal arts/career combination, study abroad, teacher certification program. 3-2 occupational therapy program with Columbia University, 3-2 physical therapy with New York Medical College. **Credit/placement by examination:** AP, CLEP, IB, institutional tests. 18 credit hours maximum toward bachelor's degree. **Support services:** Learning center, pre-admission summer program, reduced course load, remedial instruction, study skills assistance, tutoring, writing center.

**Majors. Biology:** General, biochemistry. **Business:** General, business admin. **Communications:** General. **Foreign languages:** General, French, Spanish. **Health:** Nursing (RN), preop/surgical nursing. **History:** General. **Liberal arts:** Arts/sciences. **Math:** General. **Philosophy/religion:** Philosophy, religion. **Physical sciences:** Chemistry. **Psychology:** General. **Social sciences:** Economics, sociology.

**Most popular majors.** Biology 6%, business/marketing 18%, communications/journalism 13%, health sciences 23%, liberal arts 12%, psychology 10%.

**Computing on campus.** 323 workstations in library, computer center. Dormitories wired for high-speed internet access and linked to campus network. Commuter students can connect to campus network. Online course registration, online library, helpline, repair service, wireless network available.

**Student life. Freshman orientation:** Mandatory, $125 fee. Preregistration for classes offered. 3 days with overnight for all freshmen; parent participation overnight optional. **Housing:** Guaranteed on-campus for all undergraduates. Coed dorms, single-sex dorms, special housing for disabled available. $200 fully refundable deposit, deadline 5/1. **Activities:** Campus ministries, choral groups, dance, drama, international student organizations, literary magazine, musical theater, radio station, student government, student newspaper, TV station, Culturally Aware Students of Today, Latino club, student nurses association, Circle-K, Student Action for Viable Earth, black student union, pep club, communications club.

**Athletics.** NCAA. **Intercollegiate:** Baseball M, basketball, cross-country, lacrosse, soccer, softball W, swimming, tennis, track and field W, volleyball. **Team name:** Dolphins.

**Student services.** Adult student services, chaplain/spiritual director, career counseling, student employment services, financial aid counseling, health services, personal counseling, placement for graduates. **Physically disabled:** Services for visually, hearing impaired.

**Contact.** E-mail: admissions.office@mountsaintvincent.edu
Phone: (718) 405-3267 Toll-free number: (800) 665-2678
Fax: (718) 549-7945
Roland Pinzon, Director of Admission, College of Mount St. Vincent, 6301 Riverdale Avenue, Riverdale, NY 10471-1093

---

## College of New Rochelle
**New Rochelle, New York**                                    **CB member**
**www.cnr.edu**                                               **CB code: 2089**

- Private 4-year nursing and liberal arts college for women affiliated with Roman Catholic Church
- Residential campus in small city
- 811 degree-seeking undergraduates
- 31% of applicants admitted
- SAT or ACT (ACT writing optional) required

**General.** Founded in 1904. Regionally accredited. Independent institution in Roman Catholic tradition. Coeducational school of nursing and graduate school. **Degrees:** 240 bachelor's awarded; master's offered. **ROTC:** Army, Naval. **Location:** 14 miles from New York City. **Calendar:** Semester, limited summer session. **Full-time faculty:** 84 total. **Part-time faculty:** 127 total. **Class size:** 73% < 20, 27% 20-39, less than 1% 50-99. **Special facilities:** 2 learning skills centers (including 1 for nursing), electron microscope, institute for entrepreneurial studies, computer graphics laboratory, model classroom, rare book collections of James Joyce, Thomas More, Ursuline Order.

**Freshman class profile.** 984 applied, 302 admitted, 88 enrolled.

| Mid 50% test scores | | | |
|---|---|---|---|
| SAT critical reading: | 460-540 | GPA 3.0-3.49: | 57% |
| SAT math: | 450-540 | GPA 2.0-2.99: | 3% |
| ACT composite: | 20-24 | Rank in top quarter: | 62% |
| GPA 3.75 or higher: | 4% | Rank in top tenth: | 17% |
| GPA 3.50-3.74: | 36% | Out-of-state: | 16% |
| | | Live on campus: | 93% |

**Basis for selection.** Admissions based on secondary school record. Class rank and standardized test scores also important. Essay, interview recommended; portfolio required for art program.

**High school preparation.** 16 units required. Required and recommended units include English 4, mathematics 3, social studies 3, science 3 (laboratory 2) and foreign language 2. Biology, chemistry, 3 math required for nursing and physical therapy.

**2009-2010 Annual costs.** Tuition/fees: $26,426. All incoming freshmen given laptop at no additional cost. Room/board: $9,600. Books/supplies: $600. Personal expenses: $1,000.

**2008-2009 Financial aid.** **Non-need-based:** Scholarships awarded for academics, art, leadership.

**Application procedures.** **Admission:** No deadline. $35 fee, may be waived for applicants with need. Admission notification on a rolling basis beginning on or about 11/1. Must reply by May 1 or within 3 week(s) if notified thereafter. **Financial aid:** Priority date 3/1; no closing date. FAFSA, institutional form required. Applicants notified on a rolling basis starting 1/1; must reply within 2 week(s) of notification.

**Academics.** Laptop computers given to all undergraduate students. **Special study options:** Accelerated study, combined bachelor's/graduate degree, cooperative education, cross-registration, double major, exchange student, honors, independent study, internships, liberal arts/career combination, study abroad, teacher certification program, United Nations semester, Washington semester. Preprofessional programs in law, medicine, health. **Credit/placement by examination:** AP, CLEP, institutional tests. 15 credit hours maximum toward bachelor's degree. **Support services:** Learning center, reduced course load, remedial instruction, study skills assistance, tutoring, writing center.

**Majors.** **Area/ethnic studies:** American, women's. **Biology:** General. **Business:** General. **Communications:** Broadcast journalism, media studies. **Conservation:** Environmental studies. **Education:** General, art, elementary, special. **Foreign languages:** Classics, French, Latin, Spanish. **Health:** Art therapy, nursing (RN). **History:** General. **Interdisciplinary:** Biological/physical sciences, global studies. **Legal studies:** Prelaw. **Math:** General. **Philosophy/religion:** Philosophy, religion. **Physical sciences:** Chemistry. **Psychology:** General. **Public administration:** Social work. **Social sciences:** Economics, political science, sociology. **Visual/performing arts:** Art history/conservation, studio arts.

**Most popular majors.** Health sciences 67%, psychology 9%.

**Computing on campus.** 223 workstations in dormitories, library, computer center. Dormitories wired for high-speed internet access and linked to campus network. Commuter students can connect to campus network. Online course registration, online library, helpline, wireless network available.

**Student life.** **Freshman orientation:** Available. Preregistration for classes offered. **Housing:** Guaranteed on-campus for all undergraduates. Wellness housing available. $100 deposit. **Activities:** Campus ministries, choral groups, dance, drama, film society, literary magazine, musical theater, student government, student newspaper, community services, Latin American Women Society, Black Student Union, CNR Drama, nurses gospel choir.

**Athletics.** NCAA. **Intercollegiate:** Basketball W, cross-country W, softball W, swimming W, tennis W, volleyball W. **Team name:** Blue Angels.

**Student services.** Adult student services, alcohol/substance abuse counseling, chaplain/spiritual director, career counseling, services for economically disadvantaged, student employment services, financial aid counseling, health services, personal counseling, placement for graduates, women's services. **Physically disabled:** Services for visually, speech, hearing impaired.

**Contact.** E-mail: admission@cnr.edu
Phone: (914) 654-5452 Toll-free number: (800) 933-5923
Fax: (914) 654-5464
Ellen Lockamy, Director of Admissions, College of New Rochelle, 29 Castle Place, New Rochelle, NY 10805-2339

## College of Saint Rose
Albany, New York
www.strose.edu

CB member
CB code: 2091

- Private 4-year liberal arts and teachers college
- Commuter campus in small city
- 2,993 degree-seeking undergraduates: 5% part-time, 70% women, 4% African American, 2% Asian American, 5% Hispanic American, 1% international
- 2,113 degree-seeking graduate students
- 72% of applicants admitted
- SAT or ACT (ACT writing optional) required

**General.** Founded in 1920. Regionally accredited. **Degrees:** 690 bachelor's awarded; master's offered. **ROTC:** Army, Naval, Air Force. **Location:** 140 miles from New York City. **Calendar:** Semester, limited summer session. **Full-time faculty:** 213 total; 87% have terminal degrees, 13% minority, 55% women. **Part-time faculty:** 228 total; 4% minority, 62% women. **Class size:** 65% < 20, 35% 20-39, less than 1% 40-49, less than 1% 50-99. **Special facilities:** Communications and interactive media center, center for the arts, performance hall, personal studio spaces, center for technology and teaching.

**Freshman class profile.** 4,025 applied, 2,882 admitted, 583 enrolled.

| Mid 50% test scores | | | |
|---|---|---|---|
| SAT critical reading: | 460-570 | Rank in top quarter: | 43% |
| SAT math: | 470-570 | Rank in top tenth: | 13% |
| ACT composite: | 19-25 | End year in good standing: | 91% |
| GPA 3.75 or higher: | 24% | Return as sophomores: | 80% |
| GPA 3.50-3.74: | 20% | Out-of-state: | 10% |
| GPA 3.0-3.49: | 30% | Live on campus: | 84% |
| GPA 2.0-2.99: | 26% | International: | 1% |

**Basis for selection.** High school transcript and SAT/ACT scores most important. Strongly consider extracurricular activities, overall academic rigor of high school work (Honors, AP, University in the High School courses). Interview, essay recommended. Portfolio review required for potential art majors, audition required for music majors.

**High school preparation.** College-preparatory program required. Required and recommended units include English 4, mathematics 3-4, social studies 4, history 4, science 3-4 (laboratory 2), foreign language 3-4, computer science 2, visual/performing arts 2 and academic electives 4.

**2009-2010 Annual costs.** Tuition/fees: $23,092. Room/board: $9,454. Books/supplies: $1,200. Personal expenses: $1,500.

**2008-2009 Financial aid.** **Need-based:** 540 full-time freshmen applied for aid; 537 were judged to have need; 536 of these received aid. Average need met was 11%. Average scholarship/grant was $4,098; average loan $1,638. 58% of total undergraduate aid awarded as scholarships/grants, 42% as loans/jobs. **Non-need-based:** Awarded to 298 full-time undergraduates, including 69 freshmen. Scholarships awarded for academics, alumni affiliation, art, athletics, minority status, music/drama, state residency.

**Application procedures.** **Admission:** Priority date 12/1; no deadline. $40 fee, may be waived for applicants with need, free for online applicants. Admission notification on a rolling basis beginning on or about 11/1. **Financial aid:** Priority date 3/1; no closing date. FAFSA required. Applicants notified on a rolling basis starting 2/15; must reply by 5/1 or within 2 week(s) of notification.

**Academics.** **Special study options:** Accelerated study, combined bachelor's/graduate degree, cross-registration, double major, exchange student, independent study, internships, liberal arts/career combination, student-designed major, study abroad, teacher certification program. **Credit/placement by examination:** AP, CLEP, IB, institutional tests. 15 credit hours maximum toward bachelor's degree. **Support services:** Learning center, preadmission summer program, reduced course load, remedial instruction, study skills assistance, tutoring, writing center.

**Majors.** **Area/ethnic studies:** American, women's. **Biology:** General, biochemistry, cell/histology. **Business:** Accounting, business admin. **Communications:** Media studies. **Computer sciences:** General. **Education:** Art, biology, chemistry, early childhood, elementary, English, kindergarten/preschool, mathematics, music, science, secondary, social studies, Spanish, trade/industrial. **Foreign languages:** Spanish. **Health:** Audiology/speech pathology, clinical lab science. **History:** American. **Legal studies:** General, prelaw. **Liberal arts:** Arts/sciences. **Math:** General. **Philosophy/religion:** Philosophy, religion. **Physical sciences:** Chemistry, geochemistry. **Protective services:** Forensics, law enforcement admin. **Psychology:** General. **Public administration:** Social work. **Social sciences:** Political science, sociology. **Visual/performing arts:** Commercial/advertising art, music performance. **Other:** Fine arts and art studies.

**Most popular majors.** Business/marketing 14%, communication technologies 6%, education 44%, visual/performing arts 7%.

**Computing on campus.** 550 workstations in dormitories, library, computer center, student center. Dormitories wired for high-speed internet access and linked to campus network. Commuter students can connect to campus network. Online course registration, online library, helpline, student web hosting, wireless network available.

**Student life. Freshman orientation:** Mandatory, $265 fee. Two-part orientation: 2-day overnight summer program and week-long program that begins 2 days prior to start of fall classes. **Policies:** Sanctions for plagiarism, cheating, academic misconduct, or any other submission of another's work as one's own. Use of alcohol by underage students prohibited, with limits on amounts students 21 and over can possess. Use of drugs prohibited. Sexual violence not tolerated. No smoking in any campus building or within 20 feet of any building entrance and in any college-owned vehicle. **Housing:** Coed dorms, single-sex dorms, special housing for disabled, apartments available. $150 nonrefundable deposit, deadline 5/1. **Activities:** Bands, campus ministries, choral groups, dance, drama, international student organizations, literary magazine, music ensembles, musical theater, radio station, student government, student newspaper, symphony orchestra, TV station, Brothers and Sisters in Christ, College Republicans, ALANA Steppers, Best Buddies, Big Brothers, Big Sisters, Habitat for Humanity, social work organization.

**Athletics.** NCAA. **Intercollegiate:** Baseball M, basketball, cross-country, golf M, soccer, softball W, swimming, tennis W, track and field, volleyball W. **Intramural:** Basketball, football (non-tackle) M, soccer, volleyball. **Team name:** Golden Knights.

**Student services.** Adult student services, alcohol/substance abuse counseling, chaplain/spiritual director, career counseling, services for economically disadvantaged, student employment services, financial aid counseling, health services, legal services, minority student services, personal counseling, placement for graduates. **Physically disabled:** Services for visually, speech, hearing impaired.

**Contact.** E-mail: admit@strose.edu
Phone: (518) 454-5111 Toll-free number: (800) 637-8556
Fax: (518) 454-2013
Mary Grondahl, Associate Vice President for Enrollment Planning and Undergraduate Admissions, College of Saint Rose, 432 Western Avenue, Albany, NY 12203

---

## Columbia University

**New York, New York**      **CB member**
**www.columbia.edu**      **CB code: 2116**

- Private 4-year university
- Residential campus in very large city
- 5,766 degree-seeking undergraduates: 48% women, 11% African American, 18% Asian American, 13% Hispanic American, 1% Native American, 10% international
- 10% of applicants admitted
- SAT or ACT with writing, SAT Subject Tests, application essay required
- 96% graduate within 6 years

**General.** Founded in 1754. Regionally accredited. **Degrees:** 1,427 bachelor's awarded; master's, doctoral, professional offered. **ROTC:** Army, Naval, Air Force. **Calendar:** Semester, extensive summer session. **Full-time faculty:** 1,444 total; 100% have terminal degrees, 23% minority, 32% women. **Part-time faculty:** 352 total; 100% have terminal degrees, 20% minority, 39% women. **Class size:** 79% < 20, 11% 20-39, 3% 40-49, 6% 50-99, 2% >100. **Special facilities:** Art and architecture galleries, cinemas, theaters, geological observatory, interactive graphics laboratory, telecommunications research center, plasma laboratory, materials laboratory, astronomical observatory.

**Freshman class profile.** 25,427 applied, 2,501 admitted, 1,419 enrolled.

| Mid 50% test scores | | Return as sophomores: | 99% |
|---|---|---|---|
| SAT critical reading: | 680-770 | Out-of-state: | 75% |
| SAT math: | 690-780 | Live on campus: | 99% |
| SAT writing: | 680-770 | International: | 11% |
| ACT composite: | 31-34 | | |

**Basis for selection.** School achievement record most important. Test scores, recommendations, essay, extracurricular activities also important. TOEFL or IELTS exam required of all non-native speakers. Interview recommended

for all; audition required for Julliard program. **Homeschooled:** 2 additional SAT Subject Tests.

**High school preparation.** Recommended units include English 4, mathematics 4, history 4, science 4 (laboratory 4), foreign language 4 and academic electives 4.

**2009-2010 Annual costs.** Tuition/fees: $41,316. Room/board: $10,228. Books/supplies: $2,100.

**2009-2010 Financial aid.** All financial aid based on need. 908 full-time freshmen applied for aid; 774 were judged to have need; 774 of these received aid. Average need met was 100%. Average scholarship/grant was $36,464; average loan $2,698. 95% of total undergraduate aid awarded as scholarships/grants, 5% as loans/jobs. **Additional information:** We have eliminated student loans for those receiving Columbia need-based aid and replaced them with additional University grants, and significantly reduced the parent contribution for families making less than $100,000 per year.

**Application procedures. Admission:** Closing date 1/1 (postmark date). $75 fee, may be waived for applicants with need. Admission notification 4/1. Must reply by 5/1. **Financial aid:** Closing date 3/2. FAFSA, CSS PROFILE required. Applicants notified by 4/1; must reply by 5/1.

**Academics. Special study options:** Accelerated study, combined bachelor's/graduate degree, cooperative education, cross-registration, double major, dual enrollment of high school students, ESL, exchange student, independent study, internships, liberal arts/career combination, student-designed major, study abroad, teacher certification program. Combined 3-2 program with engineering with over 100 liberal arts colleges around the country. **Credit/placement by examination:** AP, CLEP, IB, institutional tests. 16 credit hours maximum toward bachelor's degree. **Support services:** Pre-admission summer program, study skills assistance, tutoring, writing center.

**Majors. Architecture:** Architecture. **Area/ethnic studies:** African, African-American, American, Asian, Asian-American, Central/Eastern European, Chicano/Hispanic-American/Latino, Chinese, East Asian, European, French, German, Italian, Japanese, Korean, Latin American, Near/Middle Eastern, Polish, regional, Russian/Slavic, Slavic, Spanish/Iberian, women's. **Biology:** General, biochemistry, biophysics, ecology, environmental, evolutionary. **Computer sciences:** Computer science. **Conservation:** General, environmental science. **Education:** General. **Engineering:** Biomedical, chemical, civil, computer, electrical, environmental, geological, materials, materials science, mechanical, mechanics, metallurgical, mining, operations research. **Engineering technology:** Industrial management. **Foreign languages:** Ancient Greek, Biblical, Chinese, classics, comparative lit, East Asian, French, German, Germanic, Italian, Japanese, Korean, Latin, linguistics, modern Greek, Russian, Slavic, Spanish. **History:** General. **Interdisciplinary:** Ancient studies, classical/archaeology, intercultural, medieval/Renaissance, neuroscience. **Math:** General, applied, statistics. **Philosophy/religion:** Philosophy, religion. **Physical sciences:** Astronomy, astrophysics, chemical physics, chemistry, geochemistry, geology, geophysics, physics, planetary. **Psychology:** General. **Social sciences:** Anthropology, archaeology, economics, political science, sociology, urban studies. **Visual/performing arts:** General, art history/conservation, dance, dramatic, film/cinema, jazz, studio arts, theater history.

**Most popular majors.** Biology 6%, engineering/engineering technologies 22%, history 8%, social sciences 24%.

**Computing on campus.** 150 workstations in dormitories, library, computer center, student center. Dormitories wired for high-speed internet access and linked to campus network. Commuter students can connect to campus network. Online course registration, online library, helpline, student web hosting, wireless network available.

**Student life. Freshman orientation:** Mandatory, $495 fee. Preregistration for classes offered. A one-week program offering academic advising sessions, cultural events, parents orientation sessions, and more. Students may also choose to participate in pre-orientation programs like the Columbia Outdoor Orientation Program or the Columbia Urban Experience. **Housing:** Guaranteed on-campus for all undergraduates. Coed dorms, special housing for disabled, fraternity/sorority housing available. Special interest (group) housing available. **Activities:** Bands, campus ministries, choral groups, dance, drama, film society, international student organizations, literary magazine, music ensembles, Model UN, musical theater, opera, radio station, student government, student newspaper, symphony orchestra, TV station, African-American, Hispanic, Native American, Asian-American, Gay/Lesbian student organizations, community service groups, religious groups of all denominations.

**Athletics.** NCAA. **Intercollegiate:** Archery W, baseball M, basketball, cross-country, diving, fencing, field hockey W, football (tackle) M, golf, lacrosse W, rowing (crew), soccer, softball W, swimming, tennis, track and field, volleyball W, wrestling M. **Intramural:** Basketball, football (non-tackle), racquetball, soccer, softball, squash, tennis, volleyball. **Team name:** Lions.

**Student services.** Alcohol/substance abuse counseling, chaplain/spiritual director, career counseling, services for economically disadvantaged, student employment services, financial aid counseling, health services, minority student services, personal counseling, placement for graduates, women's services. **Physically disabled:** Services for visually, speech, hearing impaired.

**Contact.** E-mail: ugrad-ask@columbia.edu
Phone: (212) 854-2522 Fax: (212) 854-1209
Jessica Marinaccio, Dean of Undergraduate Admissions, Columbia University, 1130 Amsterdam Avenue, New York, NY 10027

## Columbia University: School of General Studies
### New York, New York
www.gs.columbia.edu                    CB code: 2095

- Private 4-year university and liberal arts college
- Residential campus in very large city
- 1,351 degree-seeking undergraduates: 40% part-time, 50% women
- 37% of applicants admitted
- SAT or ACT (ACT writing optional), application essay required

**General.** Founded in 1947. Regionally accredited. Liberal arts division of university for nontraditional students whose undergraduate study has been interrupted or postponed for at least 1 year. Postbaccalaureate premedical program offered. **Degrees:** 271 bachelor's awarded. **ROTC:** Army, Air Force. **Calendar:** Semester, extensive summer session. **Full-time faculty:** 777 total; 100% have terminal degrees, 23% minority, 36% women. **Part-time faculty:** 247 total; 100% have terminal degrees, 22% minority, 41% women. **Special facilities:** Earth Institute, observatory.

**Freshman class profile.** 249 applied, 92 admitted, 56 enrolled.

**Basis for selection.** Maturity and varied backgrounds of students considered. Aptitude and motivation important together with academic performance and test scores. Interview requested when needed. **Learning Disabled:** Registration with the Office of Disability Services recommended.

**High school preparation.** College-preparatory program recommended.

**2009-2010 Annual costs.** Tuition/fees: $39,910. First-year students also pay a one-time transcript fee of $95. Room/board: $12,020. Books/supplies: $2,000.

**2009-2010 Financial aid.** All financial aid based on need. 63% of total undergraduate aid awarded as scholarships/grants, 37% as loans/jobs.

**Application procedures. Admission:** Closing date 6/1 (postmark date). $65 fee. Admission notification on a rolling basis beginning on or about 2/1. Must reply by May 1 or within 2 week(s) if notified thereafter. For both regular and early action deadlines, notification within six weeks after completed application is submitted. **Financial aid:** Priority date 4/15, closing date 6/1. FAFSA, institutional form required. Applicants notified on a rolling basis; must reply within 3 week(s) of notification.

**Academics. Special study options:** Accelerated study, combined bachelor's/graduate degree, cross-registration, double major, dual enrollment of high school students, ESL, exchange student, honors, independent study, internships, student-designed major, study abroad, teacher certification program. Dual degree program with Jewish Theological Seminary, List College. **Credit/placement by examination:** AP, CLEP, SAT, ACT, institutional tests. 30 credit hours maximum toward bachelor's degree. **Support services:** Learning center, pre-admission summer program, reduced course load, remedial instruction, study skills assistance, tutoring, writing center.

**Majors. Architecture:** Architecture. **Area/ethnic studies:** African, African-American, American, Asian, Chicano/Hispanic-American/Latino, East Asian, Latin American, Near/Middle Eastern, Russian/Slavic, women's. **Biology:** General, evolutionary. **Computer sciences:** General, computer science. **Conservation:** General, environmental studies. **Education:** Elementary, secondary. **Foreign languages:** Classics, comparative lit, French, German, Italian, Portuguese, Russian, Spanish. **Health:** Premedicine. **History:** General. **Math:** General, applied, statistics. **Philosophy/religion:** Philosophy, religion. **Physical sciences:** Astronomy, astrophysics, chemistry, geochemistry, geology, geophysics, oceanography, physics. **Psychology:** General. **Public administration:** Human services. **Social sciences:** Economics, political science, sociology, urban studies. **Visual/performing arts:** General, art history/conservation, dance, dramatic, film/cinema, music performance, musicology, painting, sculpture, voice/opera.

**Most popular majors.** English 13%, history 11%, interdisciplinary studies 6%, philosophy/religious studies 6%, social sciences 37%.

**Computing on campus.** 347 workstations in dormitories, library, computer center, student center. Dormitories wired for high-speed internet access and linked to campus network. Commuter students can connect to campus network. Online course registration, online library, helpline, repair service, student web hosting, wireless network available.

**Student life. Freshman orientation:** Mandatory, $135 fee. Preregistration for classes offered. Generally held 1 week before classes start. Academic planning session (held prior to beginning of semester) required of all new students. **Housing:** Coed dorms, single-sex dorms, special housing for disabled, apartments, cooperative housing, fraternity/sorority housing available. $400 nonrefundable deposit, deadline 8/1. Limited on-campus housing available. Off-campus housing registry provides listings of Columbia-affiliated apartments. **Activities:** Bands, campus ministries, choral groups, dance, drama, film society, international student organizations, literary magazine, music ensembles, Model UN, musical theater, opera, radio station, student government, student newspaper, symphony orchestra, TV station, many religious, political, and ethnic organizations.

**Athletics.** NCAA. **Intercollegiate:** Archery W, baseball M, basketball, cross-country, diving, fencing, field hockey W, football (tackle) M, golf, lacrosse W, rowing (crew), soccer, softball W, swimming, tennis, track and field, volleyball W, wrestling M. **Intramural:** Baseball M, basketball, boxing, cricket M, diving, fencing, lacrosse, racquetball, skiing, soccer, softball, squash, swimming, tennis, volleyball. **Team name:** Lions.

**Student services.** Adult student services, alcohol/substance abuse counseling, chaplain/spiritual director, career counseling, services for economically disadvantaged, student employment services, financial aid counseling, health services, minority student services, personal counseling, placement for graduates, veterans' counselor, women's services. **Physically disabled:** Services for visually impaired. **Learning disabled:** Comprehensive services available.

**Contact.** E-mail: gsdegree@columbia.edu
Phone: (212) 854-2772 Toll-free number: (800) 895-1169
Fax: (212) 854-6316
Curtis Rodgers, Dean of Enrollment Management, Columbia University: School of General Studies, 408 Lewisohn Hall, Mail Code 4101, New York, NY 10027

## Concordia College
### Bronxville, New York                    CB member
www.concordia-ny.edu                    CB code: 2096

- Private 4-year liberal arts college affiliated with Lutheran Church - Missouri Synod
- Residential campus in small town
- 734 degree-seeking undergraduates: 13% part-time, 64% women
- 69% of applicants admitted
- SAT or ACT (ACT writing recommended), application essay required

**General.** Founded in 1881. Regionally accredited. Christian principles central to program of study. **Degrees:** 160 bachelor's, 3 associate awarded. **Location:** 14 miles from New York City. **Calendar:** Semester, limited summer session. **Full-time faculty:** 33 total; 67% have terminal degrees, 18% minority, 46% women. **Part-time faculty:** 44 total; 18% minority, 41% women. **Class size:** 62% < 20, 37% 20-39, 1% 40-49. **Special facilities:** Electric-piano laboratory, distance learning classroom, media electronic and digital learning center.

**Freshman class profile.** 691 applied, 474 admitted, 101 enrolled.

| Mid 50% test scores | | | |
|---|---|---|---|
| SAT critical reading: | 410-490 | GPA 3.0-3.49: | 23% |
| SAT math: | 390-490 | GPA 2.0-2.99: | 54% |
| SAT writing: | 400-500 | Rank in top quarter: | 27% |
| ACT composite: | 16-19 | Rank in top tenth: | 13% |
| GPA 3.75 or higher: | 6% | Return as sophomores: | 68% |
| GPA 3.50-3.74: | 10% | Out-of-state: | 26% |
| | | International: | 7% |

**Basis for selection.** Test scores, school achievement record, interview important; community and church involvement considered. Interview required for some, recommended for others; audition required for music program. **Homeschooled:** Statement describing homeschool structure and mission, transcript of courses and grades, interview, letter of recommendation (nonparent) required. Show explanation of all course work studied and grades obtained. **Learning Disabled:** Students required to meet with learning specialist and submit most recent psychological assessment.

**High school preparation.** 15 units recommended. Recommended units include English 4, mathematics 3, social studies 2, science 2 (laboratory 2) and foreign language 2.

**2009-2010 Annual costs.** Tuition/fees: $24,700. Room/board: $9,125. Books/supplies: $1,000. Personal expenses: $950.

**Financial aid. Non-need-based:** Scholarships awarded for academics, athletics, leadership, music/drama.

**Application procedures. Admission:** Closing date 3/15 (postmark date). $50 fee, may be waived for applicants with need. Admission notification on a rolling basis beginning on or about 12/1. Must reply by May 1 or within 4 week(s) if notified thereafter. **Financial aid:** Priority date 4/1; no closing date. FAFSA required. Applicants notified on a rolling basis starting 4/1; must reply by 5/1 or within 3 week(s) of notification.

**Academics. Special study options:** Combined bachelor's/graduate degree, cooperative education, cross-registration, distance learning, double major, ESL, exchange student, honors, independent study, internships, liberal arts/career combination, student-designed major, study abroad, teacher certification program. **Credit/placement by examination:** AP, CLEP, IB, institutional tests. 30 credit hours maximum toward associate degree, 30 toward bachelor's. **Support services:** Reduced course load, remedial instruction, study skills assistance, tutoring, writing center.

**Majors. Biology:** General, ecology. **Business:** General, accounting, business admin, finance, international. **Education:** General, elementary. **Health:** Nursing (RN), premedicine. **History:** General. **Interdisciplinary:** Behavioral sciences. **Legal studies:** Prelaw. **Liberal arts:** Arts/sciences. **Math:** General. **Philosophy/religion:** Religion. **Physical sciences:** Geology. **Psychology:** General. **Public administration:** Social work. **Social sciences:** General. **Theology:** Religious ed, sacred music.

**Computing on campus.** 30 workstations in library, computer center. Dormitories wired for high-speed internet access and linked to campus network. Commuter students can connect to campus network. Online course registration, online library, helpline, repair service, wireless network available.

**Student life. Freshman orientation:** Mandatory. Preregistration for classes offered. Held at beginning of semester with adviser. **Housing:** Guaranteed on-campus for all undergraduates. Single-sex dorms available. $300 deposit, deadline 5/1. **Activities:** Jazz band, campus ministries, choral groups, drama, music ensembles, musical theater, student government, student newspaper, Christian service organizations, Afro-Latino American club, social work club, Prayer Partners, environmental club, In His Name, Lutheran Women League, Rotaract club.

**Athletics. NCAA. Intercollegiate:** Baseball M, basketball, cross-country, golf, soccer, softball W, tennis, volleyball. **Intramural:** Basketball, football (non-tackle), softball W, squash, tennis, volleyball. **Team name:** Clippers.

**Student services.** Adult student services, alcohol/substance abuse counseling, chaplain/spiritual director, career counseling, student employment services, financial aid counseling, health services, minority student services, personal counseling, placement for graduates. **Learning disabled:** Comprehensive services available.

**Contact.** E-mail: admission@concordia-ny.edu
Phone: (914) 337-9300 ext. 2155 Toll-free number: (800) 937-2655
Fax: (914) 395-4636
Robert Piurowski, Director of Admission, Concordia College, 171 White Plains Road, Bronxville, NY 10708

---

## Cooper Union for the Advancement of Science and Art

**New York, New York**
www.cooper.edu

**CB member**
**CB code: 2097**

▶ Private 4-year visual arts and engineering college
▶ Commuter campus in very large city
▶ 880 degree-seeking undergraduates: 38% women, 5% African American, 19% Asian American, 8% Hispanic American, 1% Native American, 15% international
▶ 93 degree-seeking graduate students
▶ 7% of applicants admitted
▶ SAT or ACT (ACT writing optional), application essay required
▶ 89% graduate within 6 years; 60% enter graduate study

**General.** Founded in 1859. Regionally accredited. Full-tuition scholarship school of architecture, art, and engineering. **Degrees:** 202 bachelor's awarded; master's offered. **Calendar:** Semester, limited summer session. **Full-time faculty:** 55 total; 87% have terminal degrees, 13% minority, 26% women. **Part-time faculty:** 173 total; 62% have terminal degrees, 14% minority, 29% women. **Class size:** 72% < 20, 27% 20-39, less than 1% 40-49, less than 1% 50-99. **Special facilities:** Special labs in: biomechanics, materials,

soils, hydraulics, design systems, computers, circuits, signal processing, acoustics and audio engineering, combustion research and demonstration, robotic theater studio, rapid prototyping, energy reclamation and innovation, materials and micro/nano engineering, mechatronics, thermal/fluid/engines, tissue engineering.

**Freshman class profile.** 3,387 applied, 249 admitted, 193 enrolled.

| Mid 50% test scores | | | |
|---|---|---|---|
| SAT critical reading: | 590-710 | Rank in top quarter: | 98% |
| SAT math: | 600-770 | Rank in top tenth: | 93% |
| ACT composite: | 29-33 | End year in good standing: | 92% |
| GPA 3.75 or higher: | 41% | Return as sophomores: | 94% |
| GPA 3.50-3.74: | 16% | Out-of-state: | 40% |
| GPA 3.0-3.49: | 35% | Live on campus: | 80% |
| GPA 2.0-2.99: | 8% | International: | 13% |

**Basis for selection.** Engineering applicants reviewed on high school record and program, essays, SAT, and required SAT Subject Test scores. Art and architecture applicants selected on basis of home test, high school record and program, SAT. All international students must apply by using an address within the United States. 2 SAT Subject Tests required for engineering applicants: 1 math and 1 chemistry or 1 math and 1 physics. Portfolios required for art applicants. All art and architecture applicants must complete a home test. **Homeschooled:** Statement describing homeschool structure and mission, transcript of courses and grades, letter of recommendation (nonparent) required. Must present proof of high school graduation certification (national) or equivalent.

**High school preparation.** College-preparatory program recommended. 16 units required; 18 recommended. Required and recommended units include English 4, mathematics 1-4, social studies 1-4, history 1, science 1-4 (laboratory 3) and academic electives 8. 1 science required for architecture and art. 2 science and 4 math required for engineering including physics, chemistry, and precalculus; calculus preferred. 1 math required for art, 3 math for architecture including trigonometry or precalculus. 18 total units recommended for engineering.

**2009-2010 Annual costs.** Tuition/fees: $36,650. All students receive a full-tuition scholarship (covering tuition only) for the duration of their enrollment. Room only: $9,900. Books/supplies: $1,600. Personal expenses: $1,575.

**2008-2009 Financial aid. Need-based:** 117 full-time freshmen applied for aid; 88 were judged to have need; 88 of these received aid. Average need met was 92%. Average scholarship/grant was $3,309; average loan $2,972. 64% of total undergraduate aid awarded as scholarships/grants, 36% as loans/jobs. **Non-need-based:** Awarded to 888 full-time undergraduates, including 252 freshmen. Scholarships awarded for academics. **Additional information:** All students receive full-tuition scholarships. Students able to document need receive financial aid package that may include combination of grants, loans, work-study, internships. Late financial aid applications processed on rolling basis.

**Application procedures. Admission:** Priority date 12/1; deadline 1/1 (postmark date). $65 fee, may be waived for applicants with need. Admission notification 4/1. Must reply by May 1 or within 4 week(s) if notified thereafter. Regular application closing date for architecture January 1, for fine arts January 10, for engineering February 1. **Financial aid:** Priority date 4/15, closing date 6/1. FAFSA, CSS PROFILE required. Applicants notified by 6/1; must reply by 6/30 or within 2 week(s) of notification.

**Academics.** Engineering tutorials and engineering mentor program available. All freshman engineering majors required to prove or acquire computer literacy. 128 credit hours required for graduation in art program, 135 in engineering, and 160 in architecture. Students may take classes in all 3 schools. Art students encouraged to take courses throughout 7 disciplines. Architecture students take 5 years of design culminating in thesis year. Engineering students encouraged to take coursework in other majors. **Special study options:** Combined bachelor's/graduate degree, cross-registration, exchange student, independent study, internships, student-designed major, study abroad. Research opportunities. Students may take up to 1 year off between studies to pursue related experiences. **Credit/placement by examination:** AP, CLEP, institutional tests. Varies depending upon school and department. **Support services:** Tutoring, writing center.

**Majors. Architecture:** Architecture. **Engineering:** General, chemical, civil, electrical, mechanical. **Visual/performing arts:** Graphic design, studio arts. **Other:** Interdisciplinary engineering.

**Most popular majors.** Architecture 14%, engineering/engineering technologies 59%, visual/performing arts 27%.

**Computing on campus.** 650 workstations in dormitories, library, computer center. Dormitories linked to campus network. Commuter students can connect to campus network. Online library, helpline, repair service, student web hosting, wireless network available.

**Student life. Freshman orientation:** Available, $100 fee. 2.5 days, part of which is spent off-campus. **Housing:** Coed dorms, wellness housing available. $500 fully refundable deposit, deadline 6/1. **Activities:** Bands, choral groups, dance, drama, film society, literary magazine, music ensembles, musical theater, student government, student newspaper, symphony orchestra, 90 registered clubs available.

**Athletics. Intercollegiate:** Basketball, cross-country, equestrian W, lacrosse M, soccer M, tennis, volleyball. **Intramural:** Badminton, baseball M, basketball, bowling, cross-country, fencing, golf, judo, soccer, softball, table tennis, tennis, volleyball. **Team name:** Pioneers.

**Student services.** Alcohol/substance abuse counseling, career counseling, student employment services, financial aid counseling, minority student services, personal counseling, placement for graduates, veterans' counselor. **Physically disabled:** Services for visually, hearing impaired.

**Contact.** E-mail: admissions@cooper.edu
Phone: (212) 353-4120 Fax: (212) 353-4342
Mitchell Lipton, Dean of Admissions and Records/Registrar, Cooper Union for the Advancement of Science and Art, 30 Cooper Square, Suite 300, New York, NY 10003-7183

## Cornell University
Ithaca, New York
www.cornell.edu

CB member
CB code: 2098

- Private 4-year university
- Residential campus in large town
- 13,882 degree-seeking undergraduates: 49% women, 5% African American, 17% Asian American, 6% Hispanic American, 8% international
- 6,640 degree-seeking graduate students
- 19% of applicants admitted
- SAT or ACT with writing, application essay required
- 92% graduate within 6 years

**General.** Founded in 1865. Regionally accredited. 7 undergraduate colleges: Agriculture And Life Sciences; Architecture, Art, and Planning; Arts and Sciences; Engineering; Hotel Administration; Human Ecology; Industrial and Labor Relations. 6 graduate/professional colleges. **Degrees:** 3,456 bachelor's awarded; master's, doctoral, professional offered. **ROTC:** Army, Naval, Air Force. **Location:** 60 miles from Syracuse. **Calendar:** Semester, extensive summer session. **Full-time faculty:** 1,685 total; 93% have terminal degrees, 17% minority, 30% women. **Part-time faculty:** 163 total; 74% have terminal degrees, 7% minority, 30% women. **Class size:** 56% < 20, 20% 20-39, 6% 40-49, 12% 50-99, 6% >100. **Special facilities:** Art museum, Africana studies/research center, arboretum, particle accelerator, biotechnology institute, supercomputer, national research centers, center for performing arts, observatory, marine laboratory, woods sanctuary, ornithology laboratory, vertebrates museum.

**Freshman class profile.** 34,371 applied, 6,565 admitted, 3,181 enrolled.

| Mid 50% test scores | | | |
|---|---|---|---|
| SAT critical reading: | 630-730 | Rank in top tenth: | 86% |
| SAT math: | 660-770 | Return as sophomores: | 96% |
| ACT composite: | 29-33 | Out-of-state: | 69% |
| Rank in top quarter: | 98% | Live on campus: | 100% |
| | | International: | 10% |

**Basis for selection.** School achievement record (difficulty of courses, grades earned), test scores, preparation and background for specific programs especially important. Essays, recommendations considered. Subject Test requirements depend upon college/school. Please consult admissions office. Interview required for architecture, hotel administration programs; portfolio required for design programs. **Homeschooled:** Well-documented coursework required.

**High school preparation.** College-preparatory program recommended. 16 units required. Required and recommended units include English 4, mathematics 3, social studies 3, history 3, science 3 (laboratory 3) and foreign language 3. Requirements vary by college.

**2009-2010 Annual costs.** Tuition/fees: $37,954. Tuition amounts listed are for Endowed/Private colleges only: Architecture, Art & Planning; Arts & Sciences; Engineering; Hotel Administration. Contract/State college amounts differ and vary by residency and program. Room/board: $12,160.

**2009-2010 Financial aid.** All financial aid based on need. 2,223 full-time freshmen applied for aid; 1,647 were judged to have need; 1,647 of these received aid. Average need met was 100%. Average scholarship/grant was $32,614; average loan $2,944. 86% of total undergraduate aid awarded

as scholarships/grants, 14% as loans/jobs. **Additional information:** No parental contribution for students from families with incomes below $60,000 and assets below $100,000; need-based student loans capped at $7,500 annually whose families have annual incomes above $120,000; parental contribution reduced for selected students who have financial need and whose families have annual incomes above $60,000.

**Application procedures. Admission:** Closing date 1/2 (postmark date). $70 fee, may be waived for applicants with need. Early April. Must reply by May 1 or within 2 week(s) if notified thereafter. **Financial aid:** Closing date 1/2. FAFSA, institutional form, CSS PROFILE required. Applicants notified by 4/1; must reply by 5/1.

**Academics.** Cornell/Hughes Scholars program for independent research in neurobiology, physiology, genetics and development, and biochemistry (molecular and cell biology), Cornell in Rome program for studies in architecture and fine arts, undergraduate research opportunities in traditional majors as well as in many interdisciplinary fields including American Indian studies, cognitive studies, agriculture, food and society, FALCON language programs. **Special study options:** Accelerated study, cooperative education, cross-registration, distance learning, double major, ESL, exchange student, honors, independent study, internships, liberal arts/career combination, New York semester, semester at sea, student-designed major, study abroad, teacher certification program, urban semester, Washington semester. **Credit/placement by examination:** AP, CLEP, IB, institutional tests. No limit is set to the hours of credit examination that may be counted toward a bachelor's degree. **Support services:** Learning center, pre-admission summer program, reduced course load, study skills assistance, tutoring, writing center.

**Majors. Agriculture:** General, agribusiness operations, agronomy, animal sciences, business, food science, horticultural science, international, ornamental horticulture, plant protection, plant sciences. **Architecture:** Architecture, landscape, urban/community planning. **Area/ethnic studies:** African-American, American, Asian, gay/lesbian, German, Near/Middle Eastern, Russian/Slavic, women's. **Biology:** General, animal genetics, animal physiology, bacteriology, biochemistry, biometrics, ecology, entomology, plant pathology. **Business:** Hotel/motel admin, labor relations, restaurant/food services. **Communications:** General. **Computer sciences:** Computer science, information technology. **Conservation:** General, economics. **Education:** General, agricultural, biology, chemistry, family/consumer sciences, mathematics, physics, science. **Engineering:** General, agricultural, chemical, civil, electrical, environmental, materials, mechanical, operations research, physics. **Family/consumer sciences:** General, consumer economics, family studies, food/nutrition. **Foreign languages:** Classics, comparative lit, French, German, Italian, linguistics, Russian, Spanish. **Health:** Premedicine. **History:** General. **Interdisciplinary:** Neuroscience, science/society. **Liberal arts:** Arts/sciences. **Math:** General. **Philosophy/religion:** Philosophy, religion. **Physical sciences:** Astronomy, atmospheric science, chemistry, geology, physics. **Psychology:** General. **Public administration:** General, community org/advocacy, policy analysis. **Social sciences:** General, anthropology, archaeology, economics, political science, sociology. **Visual/performing arts:** Art history/conservation, dance, dramatic, fiber arts, film/cinema, studio arts, theater design.

**Most popular majors.** Agriculture 13%, biology 12%, business/marketing 14%, engineering/engineering technologies 18%, social sciences 10%.

**Computing on campus.** 2,650 workstations in dormitories, library, computer center, student center. Dormitories wired for high-speed internet access and linked to campus network. Commuter students can connect to campus network. Online course registration, online library, helpline, repair service, student web hosting, wireless network available.

**Student life. Freshman orientation:** Mandatory. Preregistration for classes offered. Six days and nights immediately prior to start of classes in August. Over 500 upper-level student Orientation Volunteers participate. All seven undergraduate colleges/schools provide orientations that include academic advising, information sessions, and a number of other programs. **Housing:** Guaranteed on-campus for freshmen. Coed dorms, single-sex dorms, special housing for disabled, apartments, cooperative housing, fraternity/sorority housing available. **Activities:** Bands, campus ministries, choral groups, dance, drama, film society, international student organizations, literary magazine, music ensembles, Model UN, musical theater, radio station, student government, student newspaper, symphony orchestra, TV station, Hillel, Campus Crusade for Christ, La Asociacion Latina, African, Native American, Caribbean, Vietnamese, international, and lesbian/gay/bisexual groups, debate.

**Athletics.** NCAA. **Intercollegiate:** Baseball M, basketball, cross-country, diving, equestrian W, fencing W, field hockey W, football (tackle) M, golf M, gymnastics W, ice hockey, lacrosse, rowing (crew), soccer, softball W, squash, swimming, tennis, track and field, volleyball W, wrestling M. **Intramural:** Badminton, basketball, bowling, cross-country, football (non-tackle), golf, ice hockey, skiing, soccer, softball, squash, table tennis, tennis, volleyball, water polo, wrestling. **Team name:** Big Red.

**Student services.** Alcohol/substance abuse counseling, chaplain/spiritual director, career counseling, student employment services, financial aid counseling, health services, minority student services, on-campus daycare, personal counseling, placement for graduates, veterans' counselor, women's services. **Physically disabled:** Services for visually, speech, hearing impaired.

**Contact.** E-mail: admissions@cornell.edu
Phone: (607) 255-5241 Fax: (607) 255-0659
Jason Locke, Director of Undergraduate Admissions, Cornell University, 410 Thurston Avenue, Ithaca, NY 14850-2488

## Culinary Institute of America
Hyde Park, New York — CB member
www.ciachef.edu — CB code: 3301

- Private 4-year culinary school
- Residential campus in large town
- 2,824 degree-seeking undergraduates: 44% women
- 87% of applicants admitted
- Application essay required
- 49% graduate within 6 years

**General.** Founded in 1946. Candidate for regional accreditation.; also accredited by ACCSC. **Degrees:** 321 bachelor's, 1,078 associate awarded. **Location:** 80 miles from New York City. **Calendar:** Semester. **Special facilities:** 41 teaching kitchens and bakeshops, 5 restaurants, theaters.

**Freshman class profile.** 957 applied, 828 admitted, 566 enrolled.

| | | | |
|---|---|---|---|
| Rank in top quarter: | 35% | Return as sophomores: | 79% |
| Rank in top tenth: | 9% | Out-of-state: | 77% |
| End year in good standing: | 92% | International: | 5% |

**Basis for selection.** School achievement record, 6 months work experience (particularly in hands-on food preparation), and interview important. SAT/ACT not used for admissions, but if tests taken recommended that students submit scores.

**High school preparation.** Recommended units include English 4, mathematics 3, social studies 2, history 2 and science 2.

**2009-2010 Annual costs.** Tuition/fees: $24,630. Room and board costs shown for typical undergraduate; costs may vary. Room/board: $8,110. Books/supplies: $1,550. Personal expenses: $5,000.

**2008-2009 Financial aid. Need-based:** 31% of total undergraduate aid awarded as scholarships/grants, 69% as loans/jobs. **Non-need-based:** Scholarships awarded for academics, alumni affiliation, job skills, leadership, minority status.

**Application procedures. Admission:** No deadline. $50 fee, may be waived for applicants with need. Admission notification on a rolling basis. **Financial aid:** Priority date 12/15; no closing date. FAFSA required. Applicants notified by 4/1; must reply by 5/1 or within 4 week(s) of notification.

**Academics.** Curriculum devoted exclusively to culinary arts and baking and pastry arts education. Freshmen may enroll in one of 4 enrollment seasons throughout the year. All students complete 18-week paid externship program. Two-thirds of class time involves hands-on cooking, baking, table service, and dining room operations management in kitchens, bakeshops, and 5 student-staffed public restaurants. **Special study options:** Cross-registration, distance learning, internships. **Credit/placement by examination:** CLEP, institutional tests. **Support services:** Learning center, reduced course load, remedial instruction, study skills assistance, tutoring, writing center.

**Majors. Business:** Restaurant/food services.

**Computing on campus.** 218 workstations in dormitories, library, computer center, student center. Dormitories wired for high-speed internet access and linked to campus network. Commuter students can connect to campus network. Online library, helpline, repair service, wireless network available.

**Student life. Freshman orientation:** Mandatory. **Housing:** Guaranteed on-campus for freshmen. Coed dorms, special housing for disabled, wellness housing available. Hearing impaired student housing available. **Activities:** International student organizations, literary magazine, student government, student newspaper, Alliance, Eta Sigma Delta Honor Society, Baking and Pastry Arts Society, Black Culinarian Society, Chefs Supporting Agriculture, Culinary Christian Fellowship, Ice Carving Society, Global Culinary Society, Garden Society, Oye Me.

**Athletics. Intercollegiate:** Basketball, cross-country, soccer, tennis. **Intramural:** Basketball, football (non-tackle), soccer, softball, volleyball. **Team name:** Flames.

**Student services.** Alcohol/substance abuse counseling, chaplain/spiritual director, career counseling, student employment services, financial aid counseling, health services, personal counseling, placement for graduates, veterans' counselor. **Physically disabled:** Services for visually, speech, hearing impaired.

**Contact.** E-mail: admissions@culinary.edu
Phone: (845) 452-9430 Toll-free number: (800) 285-4627
Fax: (845) 451-1068
Rachel Birchwood, Director of Admissions, Culinary Institute of America, 1946 Campus Drive, Hyde Park, NY 12538-1499

## Daemen College
Amherst, New York — CB member
www.daemen.edu — CB code: 2762

- Private 4-year liberal arts college
- Residential campus in small city
- 1,750 degree-seeking undergraduates: 14% part-time, 74% women, 10% African American, 1% Asian American, 3% Hispanic American, 1% international
- 882 degree-seeking graduate students
- 62% of applicants admitted
- Application essay required
- 49% graduate within 6 years; 39% enter graduate study

**General.** Founded in 1947. Regionally accredited. **Degrees:** 304 bachelor's awarded; master's, professional offered. **ROTC:** Army. **Location:** 9 miles from downtown Buffalo. **Calendar:** Semester, limited summer session. **Full-time faculty:** 100 total; 80% have terminal degrees, 6% minority, 59% women. **Part-time faculty:** 158 total; 21% have terminal degrees, 9% minority, 61% women. **Class size:** 56% < 20, 38% 20-39, 3% 40-49, 2% 50-99, less than 1% >100. **Special facilities:** Natural and health science research center, video-conference center, center for sustainable communities and civic engagement, center for special education and after-school programs.

**Freshman class profile.** 1,964 applied, 1,219 admitted, 402 enrolled.

| Mid 50% test scores | | GPA 3.0-3.49: | 35% |
|---|---|---|---|
| SAT critical reading: | 440-550 | GPA 2.0-2.99: | 30% |
| SAT math: | 450 580 | Rank in top quarter: | 51% |
| SAT writing: | 430-540 | Rank in top tenth: | 17% |
| ACT composite: | 19-25 | Return as sophomores: | 72% |
| GPA 3.75 or higher: | 19% | International: | 1% |
| GPA 3.50-3.74: | 15% | Fraternities: | 1% |

**Basis for selection.** Emphasis on rigor of high school academic program and test scores with secondary consideration given to school activities and recommendations. Work experience also considered for entry into physician assistant program. 30 credit hour transfer limit on International Baccalaureate coursework. SAT or ACT recommended. Applicants who have been out of high school for more than 2 years not required to submit SAT or ACT scores. Submission of tests are optional for all. If opting out of tests, must provide high school transcript, grades and rigor of courses, class rank, writing sample, teacher/counselor recommendation, and extracurricular activities. Essay and interview required for physician assistant program; portfolio required for art program. High school counselor completes recommendation section of the application. **Homeschooled:** State high school equivalency certificate required. Applicants should provide evidence of equivalency of high school education by GED or attestation of equivalency by superintendent of schools in student's public school district of residence. This documentation needed for financial aid eligibility. **Learning Disabled:** Bring to the attention of Admission Office need for special accommodations and submit current medical evidence of disability and limitations that require accommodations. Feasibility determined by nature and cost of accommodation, availability of funding, and whether accommodation will impact fundamental nature of course or program, among other factors.

**High school preparation.** College-preparatory program recommended. 16 units recommended. Recommended units include English 4, mathematics 4, social studies 4, science 4 (laboratory 1). All science and allied health programs require 3 math and 3 science units. Business program requires 3 math. Foreign language programs require 3 foreign language units.

**2009-2010 Annual costs.** Tuition/fees: $20,720. Room/board: $9,450. Books/supplies: $800. Personal expenses: $800.

**2008-2009 Financial aid. Need-based:** 367 full-time freshmen applied for aid; 358 were judged to have need; 358 of these received aid. Average

scholarship/grant was $7,130; average loan $3,789. 56% of total undergraduate aid awarded as scholarships/grants, 44% as loans/jobs. **Non-need-based:** Awarded to 1,119 full-time undergraduates, including 324 freshmen. Scholarships awarded for academics, art, athletics, leadership.

**Application procedures. Admission:** No deadline. $25 fee, may be waived for applicants with need, free for online applicants. Admission notification on a rolling basis beginning on or about 10/15. Must reply by May 1 or within 2 week(s) if notified thereafter. **Financial aid:** Priority date 2/15; no closing date. FAFSA required. Applicants notified on a rolling basis starting 2/1; must reply within 2 week(s) of notification.

**Academics.** All professional programs require internships or field placements. There is a general service-learning graduation requirement for all students. **Special study options:** Accelerated study, combined bachelor's/graduate degree, cross-registration, distance learning, double major, dual enrollment of high school students, exchange student, honors, independent study, internships, liberal arts/career combination, student-designed major, study abroad, teacher certification program, Washington semester, weekend college. Post-RN BS program in nursing and the 1-2-1 nursing program with RN and BS degree. Dual degree (BS/MS) in Physician Assistant Studies and Accounting/Professional Accountancy. **Credit/placement by examination:** AP, CLEP, IB, SAT, ACT, institutional tests. Veterans may receive credit for military educational experiences. Freshmen with transfer credits must take 9 credits in writing intensive courses, 3 credits in service learning, and 3 credits in quantitative literacy. **Support services:** Learning center, pre-admission summer program, remedial instruction, study skills assistance, tutoring, writing center.

**Majors. Biology:** General, biochemistry. **Business:** Accounting, business admin. **Education:** Art, early childhood, elementary, special. **Foreign languages:** French, Spanish. **Health:** Nursing (RN). **History:** General. **Interdisciplinary:** Natural sciences. **Math:** General. **Philosophy/religion:** Religion. **Psychology:** General. **Public administration:** Social work. **Social sciences:** Political science. **Visual/performing arts:** Art, arts management, graphic design, printmaking, studio arts. **Other:** Health care studies.

**Most popular majors.** Biology 14%, business/marketing 9%, education 13%, health sciences 38%, psychology 7%, visual/performing arts 8%.

**Computing on campus.** 146 workstations in library, computer center, student center. Dormitories wired for high-speed internet access and linked to campus network. Commuter students can connect to campus network. Online course registration, online library, repair service, wireless network available.

**Student life. Freshman orientation:** Mandatory, $105 fee. Preregistration for classes offered. Two sessions (2 days each) offered in July for incoming freshmen. One day in mid-August for new transfer students. **Housing:** Guaranteed on-campus for freshmen. Coed dorms, wellness housing available. $200 fully refundable deposit, deadline 5/1. Coed apartment-style residence halls; some apartments are handicapped accessible. **Activities:** Choral groups, dance, drama, literary magazine, student government, student newspaper, multicultural association, Students without Borders, environmental club, Voices of Zion, One World Alliance.

**Athletics.** NAIA. **Intercollegiate:** Basketball, cross-country, golf M, soccer, volleyball W. **Intramural:** Basketball, football (non-tackle) M, softball. **Team name:** Wildcats.

**Student services.** Alcohol/substance abuse counseling, chaplain/spiritual director, career counseling, student employment services, financial aid counseling, personal counseling, placement for graduates, veterans' counselor. **Physically disabled:** Services for hearing impaired.

**Contact.** E-mail: admissions@daemen.edu
Phone: (716) 839-8225 Toll-free number: (800) 462-7652
Fax: (716) 839-8229
Donna Shaffner, Dean of Admissions, Daemen College, 4380 Main Street, Amherst, NY 14226-3592

## Davis College
**Johnson City, New York**
**www.davisny.edu**                                    CB code: 2233

- Private 4-year Bible college affiliated with nondenominational tradition
- Residential campus in large town
- 223 degree-seeking undergraduates
- SAT or ACT (ACT writing optional), application essay required

**General.** Regionally accredited; also accredited by ABHE. **Degrees:** 30 bachelor's, 11 associate awarded. **Location:** 2 miles from Binghamton. **Calendar:** Semester, limited summer session. **Full-time faculty:** 11 total. **Part-time faculty:** 13 total.

**Basis for selection.** Pastor recommendation and high school record most important. Must give evidence of personal knowledge of the Lord Jesus Christ as Savior. Applicant lifestyle consistency with biblical principles is important. **Homeschooled:** Must submit evidence of completion of high school requirements such as a high school transcript, home school transcript or GED.

**2009-2010 Annual costs.** Tuition/fees: $12,600. Room/board: $6,000.

**Application procedures. Admission:** No deadline. $45 fee. Admission notification on a rolling basis. Dual credit opportunities for high school juniors and seniors through on-campus and online courses. Possible for high school students to complete all freshman requirements prior to high school graduation. **Financial aid:** No deadline. FAFSA, institutional form required. Applicants notified on a rolling basis.

**Academics. Special study options:** Distance learning, dual enrollment of high school students, independent study, internships, student-designed major. **Credit/placement by examination:** CLEP, SAT, ACT. **Support services:** Reduced course load, study skills assistance, tutoring.

**Majors. Theology:** Religious ed.

**Computing on campus.** Dormitories linked to campus network. Commuter students can connect to campus network. Wireless network available.

**Student life. Freshman orientation:** Mandatory. Preregistration for classes offered. **Housing:** Single-sex dorms, apartments available. **Activities:** Campus ministries, choral groups, international student organizations, music ensembles, student government.

**Athletics.** NCCAA. **Intercollegiate:** Basketball, soccer. **Intramural:** Soccer, volleyball. **Team name:** Falcons.

**Student services.** Financial aid counseling, health services, personal counseling.

**Contact.** E-mail: admissions@davisny.edu
Phone: (607) 729-1581 ext. 406 Toll-free number: (800) 331-4137 ext. 406
Fax: (607) 798-7754
Rick Cramer, Admissions Director, Davis College, 400 Riverside Drive, Johnson City, NY 13790

## DeVry College of New York
**Long Island City, New York**
**www.devry.edu**                                    CB code: 4276

- For-profit 4-year business and technical college
- Commuter campus in very large city
- 1,166 degree-seeking undergraduates: 22% part-time, 28% women, 36% African American, 10% Asian American, 32% Hispanic American, 1% international
- 224 degree-seeking graduate students
- Interview required

**General.** Regionally accredited. **Degrees:** 132 bachelor's, 30 associate awarded; master's offered. **Calendar:** Semester, extensive summer session. **Full-time faculty:** 39 total; 41% minority, 13% women. **Part-time faculty:** 71 total; 44% minority, 28% women.

**Freshman class profile.** 285 enrolled.

| | | | |
|---|---|---|---|
| Out-of-state: | 5% | International: | 1% |

**Basis for selection.** Applicants must have high school diploma or equivalent, or degree from an accredited postsecondary institution. Must demonstrate proficiency in basic college-level skills through test scores and/or institutionally administered placement examinations, and be at least 17 years of age on the first day of classes. New students may enter at beginning of any semester. SAT/ACT considered but not required for admission. If applicant chooses not to submit either, must take institution-administered admissions test.

**High school preparation.** College-preparatory program recommended.

**2009-2010 Annual costs.** Tuition/fees: $14,800. Books/supplies: $1,310. Personal expenses: $3,574.

**2008-2009 Financial aid.** All financial aid based on need.

**Application procedures. Admission:** No deadline. $50 fee. Admission notification on a rolling basis. **Financial aid:** No deadline. Applicants notified on a rolling basis.

**Academics. Special study options:** Accelerated study, distance learning. **Credit/placement by examination:** CLEP, institutional tests. **Support services:** Learning center, remedial instruction, tutoring.

**Majors. Business:** Business admin. **Computer sciences:** Networking, systems analysis. **Engineering technology:** Biomedical, computer, electrical. **Other:** Technical management.

**Most popular majors.** Business/marketing 53%, computer/information sciences 29%, engineering/engineering technologies 18%.

**Computing on campus.** 394 workstations in library, computer center. Online course registration, online library, helpline available.

**Student life. Freshman orientation:** Mandatory. **Activities:** Muslim student association, martial arts club.

**Student services.** Career counseling, student employment services, financial aid counseling, placement for graduates, veterans' counselor. **Physically disabled:** Services for visually, hearing impaired.

**Contact.** Phone: (718) 472-2728
Newton Myvett, Director of Admissions, DeVry College of New York, 3020 Thomson Avenue, Long Island City, NY 11101-3051

## Dominican College of Blauvelt
**Orangeburg, New York**
www.dc.edu
CB member
CB code: 2190

- Private 4-year The College has six divisions: Allied Health, Arts & Sciences, Business, Nursing, Social Sciences, and Teacher Education.
- Residential campus in small town
- 1,637 degree-seeking undergraduates: 17% part-time, 68% women, 17% African American, 9% Asian American, 20% Hispanic American, 1% international
- 337 degree-seeking graduate students
- 73% of applicants admitted
- SAT or ACT with writing required
- 33% graduate within 6 years

**General.** Founded in 1952. Regionally accredited. Private non-affiliated institution, Catholic in origin and Dominican in tradition. **Degrees:** 304 bachelor's, 2 associate awarded; master's, professional offered. **Location:** 17 miles from midtown Manhattan. **Calendar:** Differs by program, limited summer session. **Full-time faculty:** 72 total; 56% have terminal degrees, 6% minority, 74% women. **Part-time faculty:** 163 total; 19% have terminal degrees, 12% minority, 61% women. **Class size:** 56% < 20, 44% 20-39.

**Freshman class profile.** 1,474 applied, 1,072 admitted, 375 enrolled.

| Mid 50% test scores | | | |
|---|---|---|---|
| SAT critical reading: | 390-490 | GPA 3.0-3.49: | 31% |
| SAT math: | 400-500 | GPA 2.0-2.99: | 58% |
| SAT writing: | 400-490 | End year in good standing: | 83% |
| ACT composite: | 17-20 | Return as sophomores: | 65% |
| GPA 3.75 or higher: | 5% | Out-of-state: | 33% |
| GPA 3.50-3.74: | 6% | Live on campus: | 82% |
| | | International: | 2% |

**Basis for selection.** Admissions based on secondary school records and standardized test scores. Interviews and written essays required in some cases. Meeting with admissions counselor not always required for admission but always desirable. Some applicants may be asked to meet with member of admissions staff. **Learning Disabled:** Students with current professional documentation of disabilities will be provided with reasonable accommodations to assure access to and full participation in mainstream of educational process.

**High school preparation.** College-preparatory program recommended. 16 units required; 18 recommended. Required and recommended units include English 4, mathematics 3, social studies 3-4, science 3 (laboratory 1), foreign language 1-2 and academic electives 2.

**2009-2010 Annual costs.** Tuition/fees: $21,120. Room/board: $9,730. Books/supplies: $1,500.

**2009-2010 Financial aid. Need-based:** 350 full-time freshmen applied for aid; 335 were judged to have need; 335 of these received aid. Average need met was 78%. Average scholarship/grant was $11,829; average loan $3,270. 55% of total undergraduate aid awarded as scholarships/grants, 45% as loans/jobs. **Non-need-based:** Awarded to 265 full-time undergraduates, including 124 freshmen. Scholarships awarded for academics, athletics. **Additional information:** Individual financial aid counseling available.

**Application procedures. Admission:** No deadline. $35 fee, may be waived for applicants with need. Admission notification on a rolling basis. **Financial aid:** Priority date 2/15; no closing date. FAFSA required. Applicants notified on a rolling basis starting 2/1; must reply within 2 week(s) of notification.

**Academics. Special study options:** Accelerated study, combined bachelor's/graduate degree, cooperative education, distance learning, dual enrollment of high school students, honors, independent study, internships, study abroad, teacher certification program, weekend college. Accelerated Bachelor of Science in Nursing for college graduates. **Credit/placement by examination:** AP, CLEP, IB, SAT, ACT, institutional tests. 30 credit hours maximum toward associate degree, 60 toward bachelor's. **Support services:** Learning center, remedial instruction, study skills assistance, tutoring, writing center.

**Majors. Biology:** General. **Business:** Accounting, business admin, finance, human resources, international, management information systems, marketing. **Communications:** Media studies. **Computer sciences:** General. **Education:** General, biology, elementary, English, mathematics, multiple handicapped, secondary, social science, special. **Foreign languages:** Spanish. **Health:** Athletic training, health services, nursing (RN). **History:** General. **Legal studies:** Prelaw. **Liberal arts:** Humanities. **Math:** General. **Psychology:** General. **Public administration:** Social work. **Social sciences:** General, criminology, economics.

**Most popular majors.** Business/marketing 24%, education 7%, English 7%, health sciences 33%, social sciences 15%.

**Computing on campus.** 140 workstations in dormitories, library, computer center. Dormitories wired for high-speed internet access and linked to campus network. Commuter students can connect to campus network. Online library, repair service, wireless network available.

**Student life. Freshman orientation:** Mandatory. **Policies:** Alcohol-free campus. **Housing:** Guaranteed on-campus for all undergraduates. Coed dorms, wellness housing available. $200 deposit. Suites with multiple bedrooms, a bathroom and kitchen available for upperclass students. **Activities:** Campus ministries, choral groups, dance, drama, literary magazine, Model UN, musical theater, student government, student newspaper, Dominicans Uniting Latinos for Cultural Education, Helping Hands, Bridges International Service Project, Campus Compact for Community Service and Civic Engagement, Students Against the Abuse of Women, United Nations Committee.

**Athletics.** NAIA, NCAA. **Intercollegiate:** Baseball M, basketball, cross-country W, golf M, lacrosse, soccer, softball W, track and field W, volleyball W. **Intramural:** Basketball, football (non-tackle), handball, rowing (crew), softball, volleyball. **Team name:** Chargers.

**Student services.** Alcohol/substance abuse counseling, chaplain/spiritual director, career counseling, student employment services, financial aid counseling, health services, personal counseling, placement for graduates. **Physically disabled:** Services for visually, hearing impaired.

**Contact.** E-mail: admissions@dc.edu
Phone: (845) 848-7900 Toll-free number: (866) 432-4636
Fax: (845) 365-3150
Joyce Elbe, Director of Admissions, Dominican College of Blauvelt, 470 Western Highway, Orangeburg, NY 10962-1210

## Dowling College
**Oakdale, New York**
www.dowling.edu
CB member
CB code: 2011

- Private 4-year business and liberal arts college
- Commuter campus in large town
- 2,681 degree-seeking undergraduates: 21% part-time, 56% women
- 2,167 degree-seeking graduate students
- 86% of applicants admitted
- Application essay required
- 36% graduate within 6 years

**General.** Founded in 1955. Regionally accredited. School of Aviation situated at Brookhaven Airport. **Degrees:** 579 bachelor's awarded; master's, doctoral offered. **ROTC:** Army, Air Force. **Location:** 50 miles from New York City. **Calendar:** Semester, extensive summer session. **Full-time faculty:** 119 total; 95% have terminal degrees, 12% minority, 35% women. **Part-time faculty:** 339 total; 26% have terminal degrees, 20% minority, 42% women. **Class size:** 65% < 20, 35% 20-39, less than 1% 40-49, less than 1% 50-99. **Special facilities:** College-owned fleet of aircraft, FRASCA flight simulators, virtual airport.

**Freshman class profile.** 2,221 applied, 1,918 admitted, 544 enrolled.

| Mid 50% test scores | | | |
|---|---|---|---|
| SAT critical reading: | 410-510 | Rank in top quarter: | 28% |
| SAT math: | 420-540 | Rank in top tenth: | 8% |
| GPA 3.75 or higher: | 3% | Return as sophomores: | 66% |
| GPA 3.50-3.74: | 10% | Out-of-state: | 7% |
| GPA 3.0-3.49: | 40% | Live on campus: | 11% |
| GPA 2.0-2.99: | 40% | International: | 5% |

**Basis for selection.** Program of study, recent achievement, academic rank, school record, standardized test scores, counselor's recommendation considered. Letter of recommendation required.

**High school preparation.** College-preparatory program recommended. 16 units required. Required units include English 4, mathematics 3, social studies 4, science 2, foreign language 2 and academic electives 1. 4 additional units recommended.

**2009-2010 Annual costs.** Tuition/fees: $22,850. Room/board: $10,200. Books/supplies: $1,000. Personal expenses: $1,842.

**2009-2010 Financial aid.** **Non-need-based:** Scholarships awarded for academics, alumni affiliation, athletics.

**Application procedures.** **Admission:** Closing date 5/15. $35 fee, may be waived for applicants with need. Admission notification on a rolling basis beginning on or about 11/15. Application deadline for spring semester is 11/15. **Financial aid:** Priority date 4/30; no closing date. FAFSA required. Applicants notified on a rolling basis starting 3/1.

**Academics.** Optional winter term enables students to take 2 additional courses. **Special study options:** Accelerated study, combined bachelor's/graduate degree, cooperative education, double major, ESL, honors, independent study, internships, liberal arts/career combination, student-designed major, study abroad, teacher certification program, weekend college. Federal Aviation Administration cooperative program, Higher Education Opportunity Program (HEOP). **Credit/placement by examination:** AP, CLEP, IB, SAT, ACT, institutional tests. 30 credit hours maximum toward bachelor's degree. **Support services:** Learning center, pre-admission summer program, reduced course load, remedial instruction, study skills assistance, tutoring.

**Majors. Biology:** General. **Business:** Accounting, business admin, finance. **Computer sciences:** General, computer science. **Conservation:** Environmental science. **Education:** General, art, biology, business, chemistry, early childhood, elementary, English, foreign languages, mathematics, middle, multilevel teacher, music, physical, science, social science, social studies, Spanish, special. **History:** General. **Liberal arts:** Arts/sciences, humanities. **Math:** General, applied. **Philosophy/religion:** Philosophy. **Physical sciences:** Chemistry. **Psychology:** General. **Social sciences:** General, anthropology, economics, political science, sociology. **Transportation:** Aviation, aviation management. **Visual/performing arts:** General, dramatic, graphic design. **Other:** Communications arts, Marine studies, Natural science and math, Romance languages, Sport management.

**Most popular majors.** Business/marketing 29%, education 20%, liberal arts 6%, psychology 10%, social sciences 9%, trade and industry 6%.

**Computing on campus.** 180 workstations in library, computer center. Dormitories wired for high-speed internet access and linked to campus network. Online course registration, online library, helpline, wireless network available.

**Student life. Freshman orientation:** Available. Preregistration for classes offered. **Housing:** Coed dorms available. $500 nonrefundable deposit. **Activities:** Jazz band, choral groups, drama, international student organizations, literary magazine, music ensembles, musical theater, student government, student newspaper, symphony orchestra, 23 clubs and organizations related to academics, honor societies in business, education, economics, and psychology, Circle-K, computer science, scholarship society.

**Athletics.** NCAA. **Intercollegiate:** Baseball M, basketball, cross-country W, equestrian W, golf M, lacrosse M, rowing (crew), soccer, softball W, tennis, volleyball W. **Intramural:** Basketball, bowling, soccer, softball. **Team name:** Golden Lions.

**Student services.** Adult student services, alcohol/substance abuse counseling, chaplain/spiritual director, career counseling, services for economically disadvantaged, student employment services, financial aid counseling, health services, personal counseling, placement for graduates. **Physically disabled:** Services for visually, speech, hearing impaired.

**Contact.** E-mail: admissions@dowling.edu
Phone: (631) 244-3030 Toll-free number: (800) 369-5464
Fax: (631) 244-1059
Glenn Berman, Assistant VP for Enrollment Services/Dean of Admissions, Dowling College, 150 Idle Hour Boulevard, Oakdale, NY 11769-1999

## D'Youville College

**Buffalo, New York**
www.dyc.edu

**CB member**
**CB code: 2197**

- Private 4-year health science and liberal arts college
- Commuter campus in large city
- 1,709 degree-seeking undergraduates: 14% part-time, 73% women, 11% African American, 2% Asian American, 4% Hispanic American, 1% Native American, 9% international
- 1,103 degree-seeking graduate students
- 83% of applicants admitted
- SAT or ACT (ACT writing optional) required
- 63% graduate within 6 years

**General.** Founded in 1908. Regionally accredited. **Degrees:** 318 bachelor's awarded; master's, doctoral, professional offered. **ROTC:** Army. **Location:** 1 mile from downtown. **Calendar:** Semester, extensive summer session. **Full-time faculty:** 144 total; 6% minority, 60% women. **Part-time faculty:** 178 total; 5% minority, 42% women. **Class size:** 65% < 20, 32% 20-39, 2% 40-49, less than 1% 50-99, less than 1% >100. **Special facilities:** Equipment for blind and visually impaired including computer system with speech synthesizer, Braille printer, Versabraille and print enhancer, professional theater, gross anatomy lab.

**Freshman class profile.** 949 applied, 791 admitted, 155 enrolled.

| Mid 50% test scores | | | |
|---|---|---|---|
| SAT critical reading: | 470-560 | Rank in top tenth: | 13% |
| SAT math: | 490-580 | Return as sophomores: | 73% |
| SAT writing: | 460-460 | Out-of-state: | 8% |
| ACT composite: | 21-25 | Live on campus: | 41% |
| Rank in top quarter: | 50% | International: | 2% |

**Basis for selection.** High school GPA, class rank, test scores, type of high school program important. Interview, essay, letters of recommendation optional. 3 recommendations required for physician's assistant program. Interview required for physician's assistant and chiropractic programs. **Homeschooled:** Transcript of courses and grades, state high school equivalency certificate, letter of recommendation (nonparent) required.

**High school preparation.** College-preparatory program recommended. 16 units recommended. Recommended units include English 4, mathematics 3, social studies 3, science 3 and foreign language 3. Biology and chemistry required for nursing, occupational therapy, physical therapy, dietetics, chiropractic and physician's assistant programs. 3 units of math required for accounting.

**2009-2010 Annual costs.** Tuition/fees: $20,030. Substantial scholarships available depending on SAT/ACT scores. Room/board: $9,800. Books/supplies: $1,200. Personal expenses: $800.

**2008-2009 Financial aid.** **Need-based:** 207 full-time freshmen applied for aid; 183 were judged to have need; 183 of these received aid. Average need met was 80%. Average scholarship/grant was $13,679; average loan $3,993. 46% of total undergraduate aid awarded as scholarships/grants, 54% as loans/jobs. **Non-need-based:** Awarded to 148 full-time undergraduates, including 49 freshmen. Scholarships awarded for academics, leadership, religious affiliation, ROTC.

**Application procedures.** **Admission:** No deadline. $25 fee, may be waived for applicants with need, free for online applicants. Admission notification on a rolling basis. Must reply by May 1 or within 2 week(s) if notified thereafter. **Financial aid:** Priority date 3/1; no closing date. FAFSA required. Applicants notified on a rolling basis starting 4/1; must reply within 2 week(s) of notification.

**Academics.** **Special study options:** Accelerated study, combined bachelor's/graduate degree, cross-registration, distance learning, double major, dual enrollment of high school students, exchange student, independent study, internships, liberal arts/career combination, study abroad, teacher certification program, weekend college. Career Discovery Program for undecided students; teacher certification at the graduate level only. **Credit/placement by examination:** CLEP, IB, institutional tests. 15 credit hours maximum toward bachelor's degree. Life experience may be granted credit through local Challenge Examinations. Prior to entering D'Youville, up to 15 credits may be earned via standardized examinations; additional 15 credits may be earned via standardized examinations after enrolling. **Support services:** Learning center, pre-admission summer program, reduced course load, remedial instruction, study skills assistance, tutoring, writing center.

**Majors. Biology:** General. **Business:** General, accounting, business admin, international. **Computer sciences:** Information technology. **Health:** Health care admin, nursing (RN), physician assistant, predental, premedicine, preop/surgical nursing, prepharmacy, preveterinary. **History:** General. **Interdisciplinary:** Global studies. **Legal studies:** Prelaw. **Math:** General. **Philosophy/religion:** Philosophy. **Physical sciences:** Chemistry. **Psychology:** General. **Social sciences:** Sociology.

**Most popular majors.** Biology 7%, business/marketing 14%, health sciences 56%, interdisciplinary studies 8%.

**Computing on campus.** 100 workstations in dormitories, library, computer center, student center, student center. Dormitories wired for high-speed internet access and linked to campus network. Commuter students can connect to campus network. Online library, helpline, repair service, student web hosting, wireless network available.

**Student life. Freshman orientation:** Mandatory, $60 fee. Preregistration for classes offered. Programs vary for traditional, transfer, and graduate students. **Housing:** Guaranteed on-campus for freshmen. Coed dorms, special housing for disabled, apartments, wellness housing available. $100 fully refundable deposit. Quiet floors for upper level students. **Activities:** Campus ministries, choral groups, drama, international student organizations, literary magazine, Model UN, student government, student newspaper, black student union, Latin American club, Lambda Sigma, writers club, student nurses association, Asian student union.

**Athletics.** NCAA. **Intercollegiate:** Baseball M, basketball, cross-country, golf, rowing (crew) W, soccer, softball W, tennis, volleyball. **Intramural:** Basketball, cheerleading W, table tennis, volleyball. **Team name:** Spartans.

**Student services.** Adult student services, alcohol/substance abuse counseling, chaplain/spiritual director, career counseling, services for economically disadvantaged, student employment services, financial aid counseling, health services, minority student services, personal counseling, placement for graduates, veterans' counselor. **Physically disabled:** Services for visually, speech, hearing impaired.

**Contact.** E-mail: admissions@dyc.edu
Phone: (716) 829-7600 Toll-free number: (800) 777-3921
Fax: (716) 829-7900
Steve Smith, Director of Admissions, D'Youville College, 320 Porter Avenue, Buffalo, NY 14201-1084

---

## Eastman School of Music of the University of Rochester
### Rochester, New York
**www.esm.rochester.edu**                    **CB code: 2224**

- Private 4-year music and performing arts college
- Residential campus in large city
- 500 degree-seeking undergraduates
- 28% of applicants admitted
- Application essay, interview required

**General.** Founded in 1921. Regionally accredited. Professional school within University of Rochester. Eastman students may take non-music classes, earn BA or BS degree, and attend social events at University of Rochester's River Campus. **Degrees:** 111 bachelor's awarded; master's, doctoral offered. **ROTC:** Naval. **Location:** 357 miles from New York City, 80 miles from Niagara Falls. **Calendar:** Semester, limited summer session. **Full-time faculty:** 96 total. **Part-time faculty:** 46 total. **Class size:** 89% < 20, 9% 20-39, 1% 40-49, less than 1% 50-99. **Special facilities:** 4 performance halls including 3094-seat theater, computers for synthesis and analysis of music, complete analog and digital recording studios, music library containing over 700,000 items, over 135 practice rooms.

**Freshman class profile.** 950 applied, 270 admitted, 135 enrolled.

| | | | |
|---|---|---|---|
| Out-of-state: | 75% | Fraternities: | 7% |
| Live on campus: | 99% | Sororities: | 11% |

**Basis for selection.** Proficiency in major area most important, in addition to academic record, test scores, interview, recommendations. Composition majors submit portfolio of scores. Some areas (jazz, composition, voice, piano, flute, clarinet, violin, cello) prescreened in advance of live audition. Candidates encouraged to audition at Eastman in the spring on designated audition dates, but auditions are held at regional sites in January, and auditions by recording are also possible in most areas. SAT and SAT Subject Tests or ACT recommended. Candidates who come to Eastman for a live

audition are also give a musicianship test, and a music theory test. Audition required for all; research/term paper required for theory majors; portfolio required for composition majors. Interview recommended for all, required for composition, music education, musical arts, theory majors. **Homeschooled:** Statement describing homeschool structure and mission, transcript of courses and grades, state high school equivalency certificate, interview, letter of recommendation (nonparent) required. SAT or ACT, at least 2 SAT Subject Tests required. Taking college credit classes also encouraged. **Learning Disabled:** To facilitate a smooth audition day experience, Admissions Office requests advance notice of any special considerations.

**High school preparation.** 16 units required. Required units include English 4.

**2009-2010 Annual costs.** Tuition/fees: $38,936. Room/board: $11,920. Books/supplies: $650. Personal expenses: $1,500.

**2008-2009 Financial aid. Non-need-based:** Scholarships awarded for academics, alumni affiliation, job skills, leadership, minority status, music/drama, state residency.

**Application procedures. Admission:** Closing date 12/1 (postmark date). $100 fee, may be waived for applicants with need. Application must be submitted online. Admission notification on a rolling basis beginning on or about 3/15. Must reply by May 1 or within 2 week(s) if notified thereafter. Admission review occurs following candidate's audition/interview. Regional auditions in Asia occur in fall, regional auditions in United States typically occur in January, auditions at Eastman School of Music occur in February and early March; typically, admission review and decisions following final audition date in Rochester. Separate (additional) application required for dual degree program. **Financial aid:** Closing date 2/28. FAFSA, institutional form required. Applicants notified on a rolling basis starting 3/15; must reply by 5/1 or within 2 week(s) of notification.

**Academics.** Arts leadership programs; orchestral studies and sacred music diploma programs. **Special study options:** Double major, ESL, independent study, internships, student-designed major, study abroad, teacher certification program. **Credit/placement by examination:** AP, CLEP, institutional tests. **Support services:** Pre-admission summer program, remedial instruction, study skills assistance, tutoring, writing center.

**Majors. Education:** Music. **Visual/performing arts:** Jazz, music performance, music theory/composition, piano/organ, voice/opera.

**Most popular majors.** Education 16%, visual/performing arts 84%.

**Computing on campus.** 50 workstations in dormitories, library, computer center, student center. Dormitories wired for high-speed internet access and linked to campus network. Commuter students can connect to campus network. Online course registration, online library, helpline, repair service, student web hosting, wireless network available.

**Student life. Freshman orientation:** Mandatory, $195 fee. Includes mandatory placement testing. **Policies:** Undergraduates required to live in college housing for first 3 years unless released by Assistant Dean of Residential Life. **Housing:** Guaranteed on-campus for freshmen. Coed dorms, single-sex dorms, special housing for disabled, fraternity/sorority housing, wellness housing available. **Activities:** Bands, choral groups, literary magazine, music ensembles, opera, radio station, student government, student newspaper, symphony orchestra, international students association, Amnesty International, Intervarsity Christian Fellowship, Jewish students, Lambda, student association, graduate student association, musical organizations.

**Student services.** Adult student services, alcohol/substance abuse counseling, chaplain/spiritual director, career counseling, student employment services, financial aid counseling, health services, personal counseling, placement for graduates. **Physically disabled:** Services for visually, speech impaired.

**Contact.** E-mail: admissions@esm.rochester.edu
Phone: (585) 274-1060 Toll-free number: (800) 388-9695
Fax: (585) 232-8601
Matthew Ardizzone, Director of Admissions, Eastman School of Music of the University of Rochester, 26 Gibbs Street, Rochester, NY 14604-2599

---

## Elmira College
### Elmira, New York
**www.elmira.edu**                    **CB member**
**CB code: 2226**

- Private 4-year liberal arts college
- Residential campus in large town
- 1,277 degree-seeking undergraduates: 18% part-time, 73% women, 3% African American, 1% Asian American, 2% Hispanic American, 1% international

- 275 degree-seeking graduate students
- 79% of applicants admitted
- SAT or ACT (ACT writing optional), application essay required
- 66% graduate within 6 years; 52% enter graduate study

**General.** Founded in 1855. Regionally accredited. **Degrees:** 311 bachelor's, 4 associate awarded; master's offered. **ROTC:** Army, Air Force. **Location:** 106 miles from Rochester, 90 miles from Syracuse, 50 miles from Binghamton. **Calendar:** 4-4-1. Limited summer session. **Full-time faculty:** 82 total; 1% minority. **Part-time faculty:** 119 total; 51% have terminal degrees, 3% minority, 63% women. **Class size:** 81% < 20, 19% 20-39, less than 1% 40-49. **Special facilities:** Center for Mark Twain Studies.

**Freshman class profile.** 2,083 applied, 1,648 admitted, 430 enrolled.

| Mid 50% test scores | | Rank in top quarter: | 56% |
|---|---|---|---|
| SAT critical reading: | 490-600 | Rank in top tenth: | 31% |
| SAT math: | 470-590 | End year in good standing: | 90% |
| ACT composite: | 21-26 | Return as sophomores: | 73% |
| GPA 3.75 or higher: | 22% | Out-of-state: | 48% |
| GPA 3.50-3.74: | 13% | Live on campus: | 97% |
| GPA 3.0-3.49: | 32% | International: | 3% |
| GPA 2.0-2.99: | 33% | | |

**Basis for selection.** GED not accepted. School academic record primary. Test scores, recommendations, essay, character and extracurricular activities important. Interview highly recommended. **Homeschooled:** Statement describing homeschool structure and mission, transcript of courses and grades, interview, letter of recommendation (nonparent) required.

**High school preparation.** College-preparatory program recommended. 16 units required. Required and recommended units include English 4, mathematics 3, social studies 3, history 1, science 3 (laboratory 2), foreign language 2 and academic electives 2. 1 additional unit of foreign language recommended for foreign language, education, and international business programs.

**2009-2010 Annual costs.** Tuition/fees: $34,800. Room/board: $10,800. Books/supplies: $600. Personal expenses: $550.

**2009-2010 Financial aid. Need-based:** 277 full-time freshmen applied for aid; 252 were judged to have need; 252 of these received aid. Average need met was 80%. Average scholarship/grant was $23,653; average loan $3,266. 74% of total undergraduate aid awarded as scholarships/grants, 26% as loans/jobs. **Non-need-based:** Awarded to 312 full-time undergraduates, including 87 freshmen. Scholarships awarded for academics, leadership, ROTC, state residency. **Additional information:** Sibling Scholarship program provides 50% discounts on second immediate family member's room and board, regardless of need.

**Application procedures. Admission:** Priority date 2/1; deadline 3/1 (postmark date). $50 fee, may be waived for applicants with need. Admission notification on a rolling basis beginning on or about 10/15. Must reply by May 1 or within 2 week(s) if notified thereafter. **Financial aid:** Priority date 2/1; no closing date. FAFSA required. Applicants notified on a rolling basis starting 2/1; must reply by 5/1 or within 2 week(s) of notification.

**Academics.** Mandatory writing program for all freshmen. 7.5-credit internship/community service, often done during 6-week spring term, required of all students. International study emphasized. **Special study options:** Accelerated study, combined bachelor's/graduate degree, double major, dual enrollment of high school students, ESL, exchange student, independent study, internships, liberal arts/career combination, student-designed major, study abroad, teacher certification program. **Credit/placement by examination:** AP, CLEP, IB, institutional tests. 30 credit hours maximum toward bachelor's degree. **Support services:** Reduced course load, study skills assistance, tutoring, writing center.

**Majors. Area/ethnic studies:** American. **Biology:** General, biochemistry. **Business:** Accounting, business admin, international, managerial economics, marketing. **Conservation:** Environmental studies. **Education:** Art, biology, chemistry, elementary, English, foreign languages, French, history, mathematics, middle, multi-level teacher, science, secondary, social science, social studies, Spanish, speech, speech impaired. **Foreign languages:** General, ancient Greek, classics, French, Latin, Spanish. **Health:** Audiology/speech pathology, clinical lab science, nursing (RN), predental, premedicine, preveterinary. **History:** General. **Legal studies:** Prelaw. **Math:** General. **Philosophy/religion:** Philosophy, religion. **Physical sciences:** Chemistry. **Protective services:** Criminal justice. **Psychology:** General. **Public administration:** General, human services. **Social sciences:** General, anthropology, economics, international relations, political science, sociology. **Visual/performing arts:** Art, dramatic.

**Most popular majors.** Business/marketing 19%, education 19%, health sciences 9%, psychology 10%, security/protective services 6%, social sciences 16%.

**Computing on campus.** 145 workstations in library, computer center. Dormitories wired for high-speed internet access and linked to campus network. Commuter students can connect to campus network. Wireless network available.

**Student life. Freshman orientation:** Mandatory, $350 fee. Preregistration for classes offered. 2-day summer registration program for course registration, assessments, and get-acquainted activities. 4-day orientation program in the fall. **Housing:** Guaranteed on-campus for all undergraduates. Coed dorms, single-sex dorms, special housing for disabled, apartments, wellness housing available. Quiet floors. All undergraduates required to live in college housing unless living with family or over the age of 25. **Activities:** Concert band, campus ministries, choral groups, dance, drama, international student organizations, literary magazine, music ensembles, Model UN, musical theater, radio station, student government, student newspaper, More than 100 student interest groups including Christian Fellowship, Hillel, international student club, Habitat for Humanity, ski club, College Democrats, College Republicans, equestrian club, and sports medicine club.

**Athletics.** NCAA. **Intercollegiate:** Basketball, cheerleading M, equestrian, field hockey W, golf, ice hockey, lacrosse, soccer, softball W, tennis, volleyball. **Intramural:** Badminton, basketball, bowling, football (nontackle), handball, ice hockey, racquetball, skiing, skin diving, soccer, softball, squash, swimming, table tennis, tennis, volleyball. **Team name:** Soaring Eagles.

**Student services.** Alcohol/substance abuse counseling, chaplain/spiritual director, career counseling, student employment services, financial aid counseling, health services, personal counseling, placement for graduates, veterans' counselor, women's services. **Physically disabled:** Services for visually, speech, hearing impaired.

**Contact.** E-mail: admissions@elmira.edu
Phone: (607) 735-1724 Toll-free number: (800) 935-6472
Fax: (607) 735-1718
Brett Moore, Director of Admissions, Elmira College, One Park Place, Elmira, NY 14901

---

## Eugene Lang College The New School for Liberal Arts

**New York, New York**
www.lang.edu

**CB member**
**CB code: 2521**

- Private 4-year liberal arts college
- Commuter campus in very large city
- 1,439 degree-seeking undergraduates: 6% part-time, 67% women, 5% African American, 5% Asian American, 9% Hispanic American, 4% international
- 68% of applicants admitted
- SAT or ACT, application essay, interview required
- 63% graduate within 6 years

**General.** Founded in 1978. Regionally accredited. Students design academic programs with advisers. Students can select courses within The New School and Cooper Union. **Degrees:** 253 bachelor's awarded. **Location:** Located in Manhattan. **Calendar:** Semester, limited summer session. **Full-time faculty:** 70 total; 79% have terminal degrees, 24% minority, 53% women. **Part-time faculty:** 73 total; 8% minority, 52% women. **Class size:** 87% < 20, 13% 20-39, less than 1% 40-49. **Special facilities:** Photography labs, screening rooms, art galleries, art and sound space, environment and design center, center for art and politics.

**Freshman class profile.** 1,682 applied, 1,141 admitted, 298 enrolled.

| Mid 50% test scores | | GPA 2.0-2.99: | 34% |
|---|---|---|---|
| SAT critical reading: | 530-640 | Rank in top quarter: | 63% |
| SAT math: | 480-580 | Rank in top tenth: | 23% |
| SAT writing: | 540-640 | End year in good standing: | 91% |
| ACT composite: | 22-27 | Return as sophomores: | 67% |
| GPA 3.75 or higher: | 12% | Out-of-state: | 77% |
| GPA 3.50-3.74: | 13% | Live on campus: | 82% |
| GPA 3.0-3.49: | 41% | International: | 4% |

**Basis for selection.** Success in college preparatory studies most important supplemented by writing ability, intellectual curiosity, interview. Extracurricular/community activities, evidence of special talents, recommendations important. Telephone interviews available to students who cannot travel to New York. Essay required for BA/BFA; audition required for jazz, BA/BFA; portfolio required for art, BA/BFA.

**High school preparation.** College-preparatory program recommended. 16 units required; 18 recommended. Required and recommended units include English 4, mathematics 3, social studies 3, history 2, science 3 and foreign language 2. Honors/AP courses recommended.

**2009-2010 Annual costs.** Tuition/fees: $34,550. Room/board: $15,260. Books/supplies: $1,475. Personal expenses: $1,550.

**2009-2010 Financial aid. Need-based:** 201 full-time freshmen applied for aid; 173 were judged to have need; 173 of these received aid. Average need met was 75%. Average scholarship/grant was $23,130; average loan $9,913. 75% of total undergraduate aid awarded as scholarships/grants, 25% as loans/jobs. **Non-need-based:** Awarded to 79 full-time undergraduates, including 42 freshmen. Scholarships awarded for academics, leadership, music/drama.

**Application procedures. Admission:** Closing date 2/1 (postmark date). $50 fee, may be waived for applicants with need. Admission notification on a rolling basis beginning on or about 3/25. Must reply by May 1 or within 3 week(s) if notified thereafter. **Financial aid:** Priority date 3/1; no closing date. FAFSA required. Applicants notified on a rolling basis starting 3/1; must reply within 4 week(s) of notification.

**Academics.** Students map out individual program of study within 5 broad areas of concentration. Seminars rather than lecture classes. **Special study options:** Accelerated study, combined bachelor's/graduate degree, cross-registration, distance learning, double major, dual enrollment of high school students, ESL, exchange student, independent study, internships, liberal arts/career combination, student-designed major, study abroad, urban semester. Five-year combined BA/BFA. **Credit/placement by examination:** CLEP, IB. **Support services:** Tutoring, writing center.

**Majors. Education:** General. **Foreign languages:** General, comparative lit. **History:** General. **Liberal arts:** Arts/sciences. **Philosophy/religion:** Judaic, philosophy, religion. **Psychology:** General. **Social sciences:** General, economics, urban studies. **Visual/performing arts:** General. **Other:** Gender studies.

**Computing on campus.** 1,200 workstations in library, computer center, student center. Dormitories wired for high-speed internet access and linked to campus network. Commuter students can connect to campus network. Online course registration, online library, helpline, student web hosting, wireless network available.

**Student life. Freshman orientation:** Mandatory. Preregistration for classes offered. One week before classes begin. **Housing:** Guaranteed on-campus for all undergraduates. Coed dorms, special housing for disabled, apartments, wellness housing available. $250 nonrefundable deposit, deadline 7/1. **Activities:** Jazz band, choral groups, dance, drama, international student organizations, literary magazine, music ensembles, opera, radio station, student government, student newspaper, symphony orchestra, Students for a Democratic Society, various international clubs, sketch comedy group, theatre collective, student sustainability committee, Proud Environment at The New School (OPEN), Adventure Force, Women of Color, philosophy club.

**Student services.** Career counseling, student employment services, financial aid counseling, health services, minority student services, personal counseling. **Learning disabled:** Comprehensive services available.

**Contact.** E-mail: lang@newschool.edu
Phone: (212) 229-5665 Toll-free number: (877) 528-3321
Fax: (212) 229-5355
Karen Williams, Director of Admissions, Eugene Lang College The New School for Liberal Arts, 72 Fifth Avenue, New York, NY 10011

## Excelsior College
**Albany, New York**
**www.excelsior.edu**                   CB code: 0759

- Private 4-year virtual liberal arts college
- Commuter campus in small city
- 30,780 degree-seeking undergraduates: 100% part-time, 56% women, 20% African American, 5% Asian American, 7% Hispanic American, 1% Native American
- 1,144 degree-seeking graduate students

**General.** Founded in 1970. Regionally accredited. Ranked as a military-friendly college. **Degrees:** 2,698 bachelor's, 2,906 associate awarded; master's offered. **Calendar:** Continuous, extensive summer session. **Full-time faculty:** 35 total; 94% women. **Part-time faculty:** 369 total. **Class size:** 81% < 20, 19% 20-39. **Special facilities:** Virtual library in collaboration with the Sheridan Libraries at Johns Hopkins University, student section of American Nuclear Society.

**Basis for selection.** Open admission, but selective for some programs. Admission to the associate degree nursing program is limited to students with specified health care background.

**2009-2010 Annual costs.** Students charged $895 enrollment fee and $315 per credit hour. Because of nontraditional pricing, school does not charge set tuition based on 15 credit hours per semester.

**2008-2009 Financial aid.** All financial aid based on need. 45% of total undergraduate aid awarded as scholarships/grants, 55% as loans/jobs. **Additional information:** Excelsior College is Title IV eligible for certain degree programs. College approved for all veterans educational benefit programs.

**Application procedures. Admission:** No deadline. $75 fee. Admission notification on a rolling basis. Students may enroll at year-round, and credit accepted in transfer determines classification (freshman, sophomore, junior, senior). Applicants without high school diploma admitted as special students. **Financial aid:** Priority date 7/1; no closing date. FAFSA, institutional form required. Applicants notified on a rolling basis starting 8/1; must reply within 2 week(s) of notification.

**Academics.** Portfolio assessment option in subject areas where proficiency or performance examinations unavailable. **Special study options:** Accelerated study, combined bachelor's/graduate degree, distance learning, external degree, honors, independent study. Master of Arts in Liberal Studies students may design their thesis around career and/or personal interests. **Credit/placement by examination:** CLEP, institutional tests. Some degrees can be earned entirely by examination. **Support services:** Reduced course load, study skills assistance, tutoring, writing center.

**Majors. Biology:** General. **Business:** General, accounting, business admin, finance, hospitality admin, human resources, insurance, international, management information systems, marketing, operations. **Communications:** General. **Computer sciences:** General, information systems, information technology. **Engineering technology:** Nuclear. **Foreign languages:** General. **Health:** Health care admin, health services, nursing (RN). **History:** General. **Interdisciplinary:** Gerontology. **Liberal arts:** Arts/sciences. **Math:** General. **Philosophy/religion:** Philosophy. **Physical sciences:** Chemistry, geology, optics, physics. **Protective services:** Correctional facilities, emergency management/homeland security, law enforcement admin, police science. **Psychology:** General. **Social sciences:** Economics, geography, political science, sociology. **Other:** Area studies, Electronics engineering technology, End of life care.

**Most popular majors.** Business/marketing 11%, liberal arts 70%.

**Computing on campus.** Commuter students can connect to campus network. Online course registration, online library, helpline available.

**Student life. Freshman orientation:** Available. Orientation conducted online. **Activities:** Student newspaper.

**Student services.** Adult student services, career counseling, financial aid counseling, veterans' counselor.

**Contact.** E-mail: admissions@excelsior.edu
Phone: (518) 464-8500 Toll-free number: (888) 647-2388
Fax: (518) 464-8777
Annette Jeffes, Assistant VP for Enrollment Management, Admissions, Excelsior College, 7 Columbia Circle, Albany, NY 12203-5159

## Fashion Institute of Technology
**New York, New York**
**www.fitnyc.edu**                    CB code: 2257

- Public 4-year visual arts and business college
- Commuter campus in very large city
- 7,989 degree-seeking undergraduates: 12% part-time, 85% women
- 203 degree-seeking graduate students
- 40% of applicants admitted
- Application essay required

**General.** Founded in 1944. Regionally accredited. SUNY institution. Specialized 2-year and 4-year programs provide professional preparation for fashion and design industries. **Degrees:** 1,185 bachelor's, 1,927 associate awarded; master's offered. **Calendar:** Semester, extensive summer session. **Full-time faculty:** 253 total; 53% women. **Part-time faculty:** 754 total; 53% women. **Class size:** 35% < 20, 65% 20-39. **Special facilities:** Textile and costume collection, fragrance laboratory, computer-aided design, textile, knitting, communications facility.

**Freshman class profile.** 3,973 applied, 1,605 admitted, 1,068 enrolled.

| Return as sophomores: | 86% | Live on campus: | 64% |
|---|---|---|---|
| Out-of-state: | 35% | | |

**Basis for selection.** Rank in class, portfolio, essay, community service, work experience, awards and honors considered. Portfolio required for art and design.

**High school preparation.** College-preparatory program recommended.

**2009-2010 Annual costs.** Tuition/fees: $4,164; $11,592 out-of-state. Room/board: $11,248. Books/supplies: $1,600. Personal expenses: $1,500.

**2009-2010 Financial aid.** All financial aid based on need.

**Application procedures. Admission:** Priority date 1/1; deadline 2/1. $40 fee. Admission notification on a rolling basis. Must reply by May 1 or within 2 week(s) if notified thereafter. **Financial aid:** Priority date 2/1; no closing date. FAFSA, institutional form required. Applicants notified on a rolling basis starting 4/15; must reply within 2 week(s) of notification.

**Academics. Special study options:** Distance learning, ESL, exchange student, honors, internships, study abroad. One-year programs, evening/weekend programs. **Credit/placement by examination:** AP, CLEP, IB, SAT, ACT, institutional tests. See FIT's website for transfer credit policies. **Support services:** Learning center, remedial instruction, study skills assistance, tutoring, writing center.

**Majors. Business:** Fashion, international marketing, market research, special products marketing. **Communications:** Advertising. **Communications technology:** Animation/special effects. **Family/consumer sciences:** Clothing/textiles, textile manufacture. **Visual/performing arts:** Arts management, commercial photography, commercial/advertising art, fashion design, graphic design, illustration, industrial design, interior design, studio arts.

**Most popular majors.** Business/marketing 39%, communications/journalism 14%, visual/performing arts 42%.

**Computing on campus.** 1,500 workstations in dormitories, library, computer center, student center. Dormitories wired for high-speed internet access and linked to campus network. Commuter students can connect to campus network. Online course registration, helpline, repair service, student web hosting, wireless network available.

**Student life. Freshman orientation:** Mandatory. Preregistration for classes offered. **Housing:** Coed dorms, single-sex dorms, special housing for disabled, apartments, wellness housing available. **Activities:** Campus ministries, choral groups, drama, international student organizations, literary magazine, radio station, student government, student newspaper, TV station, more than 60 groups and organizations available.

**Athletics.** NJCAA. **Intercollegiate:** Basketball, cheerleading M, cross-country, swimming, tennis, volleyball W. **Team name:** Tigers.

**Student services.** Alcohol/substance abuse counseling, chaplain/spiritual director, career counseling, services for economically disadvantaged, student employment services, financial aid counseling, health services, personal counseling, placement for graduates. **Physically disabled:** Services for visually, speech, hearing impaired.

**Contact.** Phone: (212) 217-3760
Yamiley Saintvil, Director of Admissions, Fashion Institute of Technology, Seventh Avenue at 27th Street, New York, NY 10001-5992

---

### Five Towns College
**Dix Hills, New York**
www.ftc.edu                                   CB code: 3142

- For-profit 4-year music and liberal arts college
- Commuter campus in large town
- 997 degree-seeking undergraduates
- 185 graduate students
- SAT or ACT with writing, application essay required

**General.** Founded in 1972. Regionally accredited. **Degrees:** 202 bachelor's, 6 associate awarded; master's, professional offered. **Location:** 40 miles from New York City. **Calendar:** Semester, limited summer session. **Full-time faculty:** 33 total. **Part-time faculty:** 96 total. **Class size:** 51% < 20, 43% 20-39, 6% 40-49, less than 1% 50-99. **Special facilities:** 24-, 48- and 72-track recording studios with ProTools and surround sound, SSL9000J Board, Korg MIDI technology studio with G-5 iMacs, AVID system, professional film/video arts studio with HD filming equipment and editing labs, theater technology labs.

---

**Freshman class profile.**

| Mid 50% test scores | | | |
|---|---|---|---|
| SAT critical reading: | 400-510 | ACT composite: | 18-22 |
| SAT math: | 390-520 | Out-of-state: | 9% |
| SAT writing: | 400-510 | Live on campus: | 20% |

**Basis for selection.** Minimum 2.5 GPA required. Applicants for music and theater programs must pass audition and demonstrate competency in music, math, and English. SAT/ACT recommended but not required for transfer students. Audition required for music, theater, musical theatrer programs. Placement exams, interviews required for some. **Learning Disabled:** Provide recent copy of individualized educational program and psychological report.

**High school preparation.** 18 units recommended. Recommended units include English 4, mathematics 3, social studies 4, science 3 and foreign language 2. Music harmony and other applied music classes recommended for music students.

**2009-2010 Annual costs.** Tuition/fees: $17,750. Room/board: $12,650. Books/supplies: $1,000. Personal expenses: $3,200.

**2009-2010 Financial aid. Need-based:** Average need met was 48%. Average scholarship/grant was $7,800; average loan $3,500. 65% of total undergraduate aid awarded as scholarships/grants, 35% as loans/jobs. **Non-need-based:** Scholarships awarded for academics, music/drama.

**Application procedures. Admission:** No deadline. $35 fee, may be waived for applicants with need. Application must be submitted on paper. Admission notification on a rolling basis beginning on or about 11/1. **Financial aid:** Priority date 3/31; no closing date. FAFSA, institutional form required. Applicants notified on a rolling basis; must reply within 4 week(s) of notification.

**Academics.** Number of credit hours required for students in major field of study varies by program. **Special study options:** Combined bachelor's/graduate degree, distance learning, dual enrollment of high school students, independent study, internships, liberal arts/career combination, teacher certification program. **Credit/placement by examination:** AP, CLEP, institutional tests. **Support services:** Learning center, pre-admission summer program, reduced course load, remedial instruction, tutoring.

**Majors. Business:** Business admin. **Communications:** General, broadcast journalism, journalism, media studies, radio/tv. **Communications technology:** Recording arts. **Education:** Elementary, music. **Visual/performing arts:** Acting, cinematography, dramatic, film/cinema, jazz, music performance, music theory/composition, piano/organ, stringed instruments, voice/opera.

**Most popular majors.** Business/marketing 59%, education 8%, visual/performing arts 29%.

**Computing on campus.** 84 workstations in library, computer center, student center. Dormitories wired for high-speed internet access and linked to campus network. Commuter students can connect to campus network. Helpline, repair service, wireless network available.

**Student life. Freshman orientation:** Mandatory. Preregistration for classes offered. **Housing:** Coed dorms, wellness housing available. $250 fully refundable deposit. **Activities:** Bands, choral groups, dance, drama, film society, music ensembles, musical theater, radio station, student government, student newspaper, TV station.

**Student services.** Alcohol/substance abuse counseling, career counseling, services for economically disadvantaged, student employment services, financial aid counseling, health services, personal counseling, placement for graduates. **Learning disabled:** Comprehensive services available.

**Contact.** E-mail: admissions@ftc.edu
Phone: (631) 424-7000 ext. 2110 Fax: (631) 656-3199
Jerry Cohen, Dean of Enrollment, Five Towns College, 305 North Service Road, Dix Hills, NY 11746-6055

---

### Fordham University
**Bronx, New York**                           CB member
www.fordham.edu                               CB code: 2259

- Private 4-year university affiliated with Roman Catholic Church
- Residential campus in very large city
- 7,873 degree-seeking undergraduates: 7% part-time, 53% women, 5% African American, 8% Asian American, 13% Hispanic American, 3% international
- 6,227 degree-seeking graduate students
- 50% of applicants admitted

◆ SAT or ACT (ACT writing optional), application essay required
◆ 79% graduate within 6 years

**General.** Founded in 1841. Regionally accredited. Rose Hill campus in Bronx, Lincoln Center campus in Manhattan. **Degrees:** 1,885 bachelor's awarded; master's, doctoral, professional offered. **ROTC:** Army, Naval, Air Force. **Calendar:** Semester, extensive summer session. **Full-time faculty:** 667 total; 96% have terminal degrees, 16% minority, 40% women. **Part-time faculty:** 736 total; 46% have terminal degrees, 13% minority, 47% women. **Class size:** 49% < 20, 48% 20-39, 1% 40-49, less than 1% 50-99, less than 1% >100. **Special facilities:** Environmental center in Armonk, seismic station, Fordham Hispanic Research, Third Age Center addressing issues of older population.

**Freshman class profile.** 24,557 applied, 12,181 admitted, 1,835 enrolled.

| Mid 50% test scores | | GPA 3.0-3.49: | 31% |
|---|---|---|---|
| SAT critical reading: | 570-670 | GPA 2.0-2.99: | 8% |
| SAT math: | 570-670 | Rank in top quarter: | 78% |
| SAT writing: | 570-670 | Rank in top tenth: | 42% |
| ACT composite: | 26-30 | Out-of-state: | 52% |
| GPA 3.75 or higher: | 35% | Live on campus: | 76% |
| GPA 3.50-3.74: | 25% | International: | 3% |

**Basis for selection.** School achievement record most important followed by test scores, class rank, extracurricular activities, recommendations, essay, personal characteristics. Special consideration given to children of alumni. SAT Subject Tests recommended. Audition required for dance and theater programs.

**High school preparation.** College-preparatory program required. 22 units required; 25 recommended. Required and recommended units include English 4, mathematics 3-4, social studies 2, history 2, science 3-4, foreign language 2-3 and academic electives 6.

**2009-2010 Annual costs.** Tuition/fees: $36,882. Room/board: $13,716. Books/supplies: $840. Personal expenses: $1,540.

**2008-2009 Financial aid.** **Non-need-based:** Scholarships awarded for academics, athletics, ROTC.

**Application procedures.** **Admission:** Closing date 1/15 (postmark date). $50 fee, may be waived for applicants with need. Admission notification 4/1. Must reply by May 1 or within 2 week(s) if notified thereafter. **Financial aid:** Closing date 2/1. FAFSA, CSS PROFILE required. Applicants notified by 3/31; must reply by 5/1 or within 2 week(s) of notification.

**Academics.** **Special study options:** Combined bachelor's/graduate degree, distance learning, double major, ESL, exchange student, honors, independent study, internships, student-designed major, study abroad, teacher certification program, United Nations semester. Global Program in International Business. **Credit/placement by examination:** AP, CLEP, IB, institutional tests. 32 credit hours maximum toward bachelor's degree. Credit for CLEP examination only offered for liberal studies, adult continuing education school. **Support services:** Pre-admission summer program, tutoring, writing center.

**Majors.** **Area/ethnic studies:** African, African-American, American, Latin American, Near/Middle Eastern, Russian/Slavic, women's. **Biology:** General. **Business:** General, accounting, business admin, finance, international, management information systems, managerial economics, market research. **Communications:** General. **Computer sciences:** General. **Foreign languages:** Ancient Greek, classics, comparative lit, French, German, Italian, Latin, modern Greek, Russian, Spanish. **Health:** Predental, premedicine, prepharmacy, preveterinary. **History:** General. **Interdisciplinary:** Intercultural. **Legal studies:** Prelaw. **Math:** General. **Philosophy/religion:** Philosophy, religion. **Physical sciences:** Chemistry, physics. **Protective services:** Criminal justice. **Psychology:** General. **Public administration:** General, social work. **Social sciences:** Anthropology, economics, political science, sociology, urban studies. **Visual/performing arts:** Art, art history/conservation, dance, dramatic, film/cinema, photography, studio arts, theater design.

**Most popular majors.** Business/marketing 27%, communications/journalism 12%, English 6%, psychology 7%, social sciences 20%.

**Computing on campus.** 900 workstations in dormitories, library, computer center. Dormitories wired for high-speed internet access and linked to campus network. Commuter students can connect to campus network. Online course registration, online library, helpline, repair service, wireless network available.

**Student life.** **Freshman orientation:** Mandatory, $110 fee. Comprehensive academic and social orientation 3 days prior to start of classes. **Housing:** Guaranteed on-campus for all undergraduates. Coed dorms, apartments available. **Activities:** Bands, campus ministries, choral groups, dance, drama,

film society, international student organizations, literary magazine, music ensembles, musical theater, radio station, student government, student newspaper, symphony orchestra, TV station, Rose Hill Ambassadors, international black student union, Progressive Students for Justice, Circle-K, commuter student association, Emerging Leaders, weekend activities committee.

**Athletics.** NCAA. **Intercollegiate:** Baseball M, basketball, cross-country, diving, football (tackle) M, golf M, rowing (crew) W, soccer, softball W, squash M, swimming, tennis, track and field, volleyball W, water polo M. **Intramural:** Basketball, football (tackle), golf W, handball, racquetball, soccer, softball, swimming, tennis, triathlon, volleyball. **Team name:** Rams.

**Student services.** Adult student services, alcohol/substance abuse counseling, chaplain/spiritual director, career counseling, student employment services, financial aid counseling, health services, personal counseling, placement for graduates. **Physically disabled:** Services for visually, hearing impaired.

**Contact.** E-mail: enroll@fordham.edu
Phone: (718) 817-4000 Toll-free number: (800) 367-3426
Peter Farrell, Director of Admissions, Fordham University, East 441
Fordham Road, Bronx, NY 10458-9993

---

## Globe Institute of Technology
**New York, New York**
**www.globe.edu**                              CB code: 3333

◆ For-profit 4-year university and business college
◆ Commuter campus in very large city
◆ 542 undergraduates

**General.** Regionally accredited. **Degrees:** 141 bachelor's, 295 associate awarded. **Calendar:** Semester, extensive summer session. **Full-time faculty:** 45 total. **Part-time faculty:** 170 total. **Class size:** 55% < 20, 40% 20-39, 5% 40-49.

**Freshman class profile.**

| Mid 50% test scores | | SAT math: | 500-600 |
|---|---|---|---|
| SAT critical reading: | 500-600 | SAT writing: | 500-600 |

**Basis for selection.** Open admission, but selective for some programs. Special requirements for video game development program. Interviews strongly recommended. **Learning Disabled:** Student should meet with school psychologist to discuss needs.

**2009-2010 Annual costs.** Tuition/fees: $11,040. Room/board: $4,500. Books/supplies: $800.

**2009-2010 Financial aid.** **Non-need-based:** Scholarships awarded for academics, athletics.

**Application procedures.** **Admission:** No deadline. $50 fee, may be waived for applicants with need. Admission notification on a rolling basis. Housing deposit required 30 days before first day of the semester. **Financial aid:** No deadline. FAFSA, institutional form required. Applicants notified on a rolling basis.

**Academics.** **Special study options:** Combined bachelor's/graduate degree, distance learning, ESL, independent study, internships, liberal arts/career combination, weekend college. Video Game Development program admits only students in top 15% of graduating class and students with combined SAT score greater than 1950. **Credit/placement by examination:** AP, CLEP, institutional tests. 30 credit hours maximum toward associate degree, 60 toward bachelor's. **Support services:** Learning center, pre-admission summer program, reduced course load, remedial instruction, study skills assistance, tutoring, writing center.

**Majors.** **Business:** General, accounting, accounting technology, accounting/business management, accounting/finance, banking/financial services, business admin, customer service, finance, hospitality admin, hotel/motel admin, management information systems, nonprofit/public, office management, operations, resort management, restaurant/food services, small business admin, tourism/travel. **Computer sciences:** General, a.i./robotics, applications programming, computer graphics, computer science, database management, information technology, LAN/WAN management, networking, programming, security, system admin, systems analysis, vendor certification, web page design, webmaster. **Health:** Facilities admin, health care admin, office admin. **Legal studies:** Legal secretary, paralegal.

**Most popular majors.** Business/marketing 60%, computer/information sciences 20%, health sciences 10%, legal studies 10%.

**Computing on campus.** 200 workstations in library, computer center, student center. Dormitories wired for high-speed internet access. Commuter students can connect to campus network. Online course registration, online library, helpline, student web hosting, wireless network available.

**Student life. Freshman orientation:** Mandatory. Preregistration for classes offered. **Housing:** Guaranteed on-campus for all undergraduates. Coed dorms, apartments available. **Activities:** Dance, film society, literary magazine, student government, student newspaper, international club, Chinese club, Russian club, Latino club, Wall Street club, Carib club, film club, African club, dance club.

**Athletics.** NJCAA. **Intercollegiate:** Baseball M, basketball, football (tackle) M, soccer, volleyball W. **Team name:** Knights.

**Student services.** Adult student services, alcohol/substance abuse counseling, career counseling, services for economically disadvantaged, student employment services, financial aid counseling, minority student services, personal counseling, placement for graduates, women's services.

**Contact.** E-mail: admissions@globe.edu
Phone: (212) 349-4330 Toll-free number: (877) 394-5623
Fax: (212) 302-9242
Michael Scalice, Admissions Director, Globe Institute of Technology, 500 Seventh Ave, 2nd Floor, New York, NY 10018

---

## Hamilton College
**Clinton, New York**
www.hamilton.edu

CB member
CB code: 2286

- Private 4-year liberal arts college
- Residential campus in rural community
- 1,851 degree-seeking undergraduates: 53% women, 4% African American, 8% Asian American, 5% Hispanic American, 1% Native American, 5% international
- 30% of applicants admitted
- SAT and SAT Subject Tests or ACT (ACT writing optional), application essay required
- 86% graduate within 6 years

**General.** Founded in 1812. Regionally accredited. **Degrees:** 472 bachelor's awarded. **ROTC:** Army, Air Force. **Location:** 10 miles from Utica, 50 miles from Syracuse. **Calendar:** Semester. **Full-time faculty:** 177 total; 97% have terminal degrees, 16% minority, 41% women. **Part-time faculty:** 42 total; 52% have terminal degrees, 10% minority, 52% women. **Class size:** 73% < 20, 24% 20-39, 3% 40-49, less than 1% 50-99. **Special facilities:** Observatory, nature preserve, electron microscope.

**Freshman class profile.** 4,661 applied, 1,390 admitted, 466 enrolled.

| Mid 50% test scores | | | |
|---|---|---|---|
| SAT critical reading: | 660-740 | Rank in top tenth: | 80% |
| SAT math: | 650-730 | Return as sophomores: | 96% |
| SAT writing: | 650-740 | Out-of-state: | 65% |
| ACT composite: | 28-31 | Live on campus: | 100% |
| Rank in top quarter: | 97% | International: | 6% |

**Basis for selection.** School achievement record, rank in high school class, school and community activities, application essay, graded example of expository writing, recommendations important. Test scores and interview also considered. Some preference given children of alumni. Special consideration given students from minority groups, disadvantaged backgrounds, and certain geographic regions. Several options for meeting standardized test requirement: SAT; or ACT; or 3 exams of student's choice, must include a quantitative test, a verbal or writing test, and a third test student chooses. Acceptable quantitative tests: SAT Math, SAT Subject Tests in math, chemistry, or physics; AP Computer Science, Chemistry, Economics, Math, or Physics; IB Chemistry, Computing Studies, Economics, Math, Physics, or Physical and Chemical Systems. Acceptable verbal/writing tests: SAT Critical Reading; SAT Writing; ACT Writing; AP English Language and Composition; IB Language (A1, A2, or B English). Interview recommended for all; expository prose required; audition tape recommended for music applicants; audition DVD recommended for theater and dance applicants; portfolio recommended for studio art applicants. **Homeschooled:** Statement describing homeschool structure and mission required.

**High school preparation.** College-preparatory program recommended. 16 units recommended. Recommended units include English 4, mathematics 3, social studies 3, science 3 and foreign language 3.

**2009-2010 Annual costs.** Tuition/fees: $39,760. Room/board: $10,100. Books/supplies: $1,300. Personal expenses: $1,000.

**2009-2010 Financial aid.** All financial aid based on need. 269 full-time freshmen applied for aid; 207 were judged to have need; 207 of these received aid. Average need met was 100%. Average scholarship/grant was $34,004; average loan $2,914. 88% of total undergraduate aid awarded as scholarships/grants, 12% as loans/jobs. **Additional information:** Will meet demonstrated need of all aided applicants. Incoming students no longer awarded merit scholarships.

**Application procedures. Admission:** Closing date 1/1 (postmark date). $75 fee, may be waived for applicants with need, free for online applicants. Admission notification 4/1. Must reply by 5/1. **Financial aid:** Closing date 2/8. FAFSA, institutional form, CSS PROFILE required. Applicants notified by 4/1; must reply by 5/1.

**Academics.** Sophomores may attain guaranteed early admission to a participating New York State medical school. Students must complete senior program or project in their concentration. May participate in Williams College Mystic Seaport Program. **Special study options:** Accelerated study, combined bachelor's/graduate degree, cross-registration, double major, ESL, independent study, internships, New York semester, student-designed major, study abroad, Washington semester. 3-2 program in engineering with Columbia University, Rensselaer Polytechnic Institute, Washington University (St. Louis); 3-3 program in law at Columbia University. **Credit/placement by examination:** AP, CLEP, IB, institutional tests. **Support services:** Learning center, pre-admission summer program, reduced course load, study skills assistance, tutoring, writing center.

**Majors. Area/ethnic studies:** African-American, American, Asian, German, Russian/Slavic, women's. **Biology:** General, biochemistry, molecular. **Communications:** General. **Computer sciences:** General. **Conservation:** Environmental studies. **Foreign languages:** General, Chinese, classics, comparative lit, French, Spanish. **History:** General. **Interdisciplinary:** Neuroscience. **Liberal arts:** Arts/sciences. **Math:** General. **Philosophy/religion:** Philosophy, religion. **Physical sciences:** Chemical physics, chemistry, geology, physics. **Psychology:** General. **Public administration:** Policy analysis. **Social sciences:** Anthropology, archaeology, economics, international relations, political science, sociology. **Visual/performing arts:** Art history/conservation, dance, dramatic, studio arts.

**Most popular majors.** English 6%, foreign language 10%, mathematics 6%, psychology 8%, social sciences 31%, visual/performing arts 6%.

**Computing on campus.** 625 workstations in library, computer center, student center. Dormitories wired for high-speed internet access and linked to campus network. Commuter students can connect to campus network. Online course registration, online library, helpline, repair service, student web hosting, wireless network available.

**Student life. Freshman orientation:** Mandatory. One week prior to start of classes. **Policies:** Honor code covers all examinations, papers, research, and use of library. **Housing:** Guaranteed on-campus for all undergraduates. Coed dorms, special housing for disabled, apartments, cooperative housing, wellness housing available. Special interest housing available including language houses and international house, quiet areas. **Activities:** Bands, campus ministries, choral groups, dance, drama, film society, international student organizations, literary magazine, music ensembles, Model UN, musical theater, radio station, student government, student newspaper, symphony orchestra, Newman Council, Jewish student organization, Black and Latin student union, Christian Fellowship, La Vanguardia, Amnesty International, Muslim students association, Asian cultural society, West Indian and African association, Women's Center.

**Athletics.** NCAA. **Intercollegiate:** Baseball M, basketball, cross-country, diving, field hockey W, football (tackle) M, golf M, ice hockey, lacrosse, rowing (crew), soccer, softball W, squash, swimming, tennis, track and field, volleyball W. **Intramural:** Badminton, basketball, cross-country, diving, football (non-tackle), golf, ice hockey, racquetball, skiing, soccer, softball, squash, swimming, tennis, volleyball, water polo. **Team name:** Continentals.

**Student services.** Adult student services, alcohol/substance abuse counseling, chaplain/spiritual director, career counseling, student employment services, financial aid counseling, health services, minority student services, on-campus daycare, personal counseling, placement for graduates, women's services. **Physically disabled:** Services for visually, speech, hearing impaired.

**Contact.** E-mail: admission@hamilton.edu
Phone: (315) 859-4421 Toll-free number: (800) 843-2655
Fax: (315) 859-4457
Monica Inzer, Vice President and Dean of Admission and Financial Aid, Hamilton College, 198 College Hill Road, Clinton, NY 13323-1293

---

## Hartwick College
**Oneonta, New York**
www.hartwick.edu

CB member
CB code: 2288

- Private 4-year liberal arts college
- Residential campus in large town

- 1,455 degree-seeking undergraduates: 2% part-time, 59% women, 4% African American, 2% Asian American, 4% Hispanic American, 3% international
- 91% of applicants admitted
- Application essay required
- 55% graduate within 6 years; 97% enter graduate study

**General.** Founded in 1797. Regionally accredited. Additional campus for recreation, research, student residences. **Degrees:** 283 bachelor's awarded. **Location:** 68 miles from Binghamton, 75 miles from Albany. **Calendar:** 4-1-4, limited summer session. **Full-time faculty:** 103 total; 80% have terminal degrees, 5% minority, 41% women. **Part-time faculty:** 92 total; 21% have terminal degrees, 2% minority, 53% women. **Class size:** 62% < 20, 35% 20-39, 2% 40-49, less than 1% 50-99. **Special facilities:** Environmental field station, museum, Native American artifact and library collections, tissue culture laboratory, electron microscope, 16-inch telescope and observatory, nuclear magnetic resonance spectrometer, fine and performing arts center.

**Freshman class profile.** 2,385 applied, 2,177 admitted, 402 enrolled.

| Mid 50% test scores | | | |
|---|---|---|---|
| SAT critical reading: | 480-600 | Rank in top quarter: | 42% |
| SAT math: | 490-600 | Rank in top tenth: | 17% |
| SAT writing: | 480-580 | Return as sophomores: | 75% |
| ACT composite: | 23-27 | Out-of-state: | 33% |
| GPA 3.75 or higher: | 9% | Live on campus: | 98% |
| GPA 3.50-3.74: | 22% | International: | 3% |
| GPA 3.0-3.49: | 31% | Fraternities: | 8% |
| GPA 2.0-2.99: | 36% | Sororities: | 10% |

**Basis for selection.** School achievement record, class rank, personal qualities, extracurricular activities, and recommendations considered. Test scores optional except for students applying to nursing program. SAT/ACT score submission not required for admission except for nursing majors and homeschooled candidates. Interview recommended for all; audition required for music program; portfolio recommended for art program. **Homeschooled:** Transcript of courses and grades, letter of recommendation (nonparent) required. Must meet all stated application requirements and submit SAT or ACT test score. At least 3 SAT Subject Tests strongly recommended. Transcripts should be submitted with course description and/or syllabi.

**High school preparation.** College-preparatory program recommended. 19 units recommended. Recommended units include English 4, mathematics 3, social studies 2, history 2, science 3 (laboratory 2) and foreign language 3.

**2009-2010 Annual costs.** Tuition/fees: $33,330. Room/board: $9,075. Books/supplies: $700. Personal expenses: $400.

**2008-2009 Financial aid. Non-need-based:** Scholarships awarded for academics, alumni affiliation, athletics, leadership, state residency.

**Application procedures. Admission:** Closing date 2/15 (postmark date). $35 fee, may be waived for applicants with need, free for online applicants. Admission notification on a rolling basis. Must reply by 5/1. **Financial aid:** Priority date 2/15; no closing date. FAFSA required. Applicants notified by 3/15; must reply within 2 week(s) of notification.

**Academics.** Curriculum includes first-year seminar, core requirements and contemporary issues seminar. Senior thesis required. First-year students provided with notebook-sized personal computer. **Special study options:** Accelerated study, combined bachelor's/graduate degree, cross-registration, double major, exchange student, honors, independent study, internships, liberal arts/career combination, semester at sea, student-designed major, study abroad, teacher certification program, urban semester, Washington semester. Off-campus January term in England, France, Ghana, Madagascar, South Africa; Philadelphia Urban Semester; Boston Semester; Outward Bound, NOLS programs; cooperative program in law with Albany Law School; 3-2 engineering with Clarkson University, Columbia University; 3-year accelerated bachelor's degree. **Credit/placement by examination:** AP, CLEP, IB, institutional tests. **Support services:** Reduced course load, study skills assistance, tutoring, writing center.

**Majors. Biology:** General, biochemistry. **Business:** Accounting, business admin. **Computer sciences:** General, information systems. **Education:** Music. **Foreign languages:** French, German, Spanish. **Health:** Clinical lab science, nursing (RN). **History:** General. **Liberal arts:** Arts/sciences. **Math:** General. **Philosophy/religion:** Philosophy, religion. **Physical sciences:** Chemistry, geology, physics. **Psychology:** General. **Social sciences:** Anthropology, economics, political science, sociology. **Visual/performing arts:** Art, art history/conservation, dramatic.

**Most popular majors.** Biology 8%, business/marketing 16%, health sciences 9%, psychology 7%, social sciences 22%, visual/performing arts 10%.

**Computing on campus.** 56 workstations in library, computer center. Dormitories wired for high-speed internet access and linked to campus network. Commuter students can connect to campus network. Online course registration, online library, helpline, repair service, student web hosting, wireless network available.

**Student life. Freshman orientation:** Mandatory, $300 fee. Preregistration for classes offered. Summer registration/parent orientation and 4-day pre-semester in-residence program. **Housing:** Guaranteed on-campus for freshmen. Coed dorms, single-sex dorms, special housing for disabled, apartments, fraternity/sorority housing, wellness housing available. Housing at environmental campus available. **Activities:** Pep band, campus ministries, choral groups, dance, drama, literary magazine, music ensembles, radio station, student government, student newspaper, 70 academic and social organizations available.

**Athletics.** NCAA. **Intercollegiate:** Basketball, cheerleading M, cross-country, diving, equestrian W, field hockey W, football (tackle) M, lacrosse, soccer, swimming, tennis, volleyball W, water polo W. **Intramural:** Basketball, football (non-tackle), racquetball, soccer, volleyball. **Team name:** Hawks.

**Student services.** Alcohol/substance abuse counseling, chaplain/spiritual director, career counseling, financial aid counseling, health services, personal counseling, placement for graduates. **Physically disabled:** Services for visually, hearing impaired.

**Contact.** E-mail: admissions@hartwick.edu
Phone: (607) 431-4150 Toll-free number: (888) 427-8942
Fax: (607) 431-4154
David Conway, VP Enrollment Management, Hartwick College, Box 4022, Oneonta, NY 13820-4022

## Hilbert College
**Hamburg, New York**
**www.hilbert.edu**                    **CB code: 2334**

- Private 4-year liberal arts college affiliated with Roman Catholic Church
- Commuter campus in large town
- 959 degree-seeking undergraduates: 19% part-time, 63% women, 10% African American, 4% Hispanic American, 1% Native American
- 96% of applicants admitted
- 51% graduate within 6 years

**General.** Founded in 1957. Regionally accredited. Affiliated with Franciscan Sisters of St. Joseph. Legal assistant program approved by American Bar Association. **Degrees:** 193 bachelor's, 30 associate awarded. **ROTC:** Army. **Location:** 10 miles from Buffalo. **Calendar:** Semester, limited summer session. **Full-time faculty:** 46 total; 46% have terminal degrees, 4% minority, 50% women. **Part-time faculty:** 80 total; 19% have terminal degrees, 1% minority, 38% women. **Class size:** 90% < 20, 9% 20-39, less than 1% 40-49. **Special facilities:** Comprehensive law library.

**Freshman class profile.** 990 applied, 950 admitted, 214 enrolled.

| Mid 50% test scores | | | |
|---|---|---|---|
| SAT critical reading: | 390-500 | Rank in top quarter: | 19% |
| SAT math: | 410-540 | Rank in top tenth: | 4% |
| ACT composite: | 17-23 | End year in good standing: | 85% |
| GPA 3.75 or higher: | 4% | Return as sophomores: | 65% |
| GPA 3.50-3.74: | 24% | Out-of-state: | 4% |
| GPA 3.0-3.49: | 71% | Live on campus: | 44% |
| GPA 2.0-2.99: | 1% | International: | 1% |

**Basis for selection.** School achievement record and course selection important. Candidates must meet minimum academic criteria including high school GPA. SAT or ACT recommended. Essay, interview recommended. **Homeschooled:** Transcript of courses and grades, state high school equivalency certificate required. **Learning Disabled:** Separate statement directly to academic services required.

**High school preparation.** 16 units required; 21 recommended. Required and recommended units include English 4, mathematics 3-4, social studies 3-4, science 2-3 (laboratory 1-2) and foreign language 1-2.

**2009-2010 Annual costs.** Tuition/fees: $17,950. Room/board: $7,700. Books/supplies: $750. Personal expenses: $800.

**2008-2009 Financial aid. Need-based:** 225 full-time freshmen applied for aid; 208 were judged to have need; 208 of these received aid. Average need met was 69%. Average scholarship/grant was $8,520; average loan $3,994. 52% of total undergraduate aid awarded as scholarships/grants, 48% as loans/jobs. **Non-need-based:** Awarded to 99 full-time undergraduates,

including 26 freshmen. Scholarships awarded for academics, alumni affiliation, leadership, minority status, state residency.

**Application procedures. Admission:** Priority date 6/30; deadline 9/1 (receipt date). $20 fee, may be waived for applicants with need. Admission notification on a rolling basis beginning on or about 6/30. **Financial aid:** Priority date 3/1; no closing date. FAFSA required. Applicants notified on a rolling basis starting 3/1; must reply within 2 week(s) of notification.

**Academics. Special study options:** Combined bachelor's/graduate degree, cooperative education, cross-registration, distance learning, dual enrollment of high school students, honors, independent study, internships, study abroad, Washington semester. Member of Western New York consortium. **Credit/placement by examination:** AP, CLEP, IB, SAT, institutional tests. 18 credit hours maximum toward associate degree, 32 toward bachelor's. **Support services:** Learning center, reduced course load, study skills assistance, tutoring, writing center.

**Majors. Business:** Accounting, business admin. **Communications:** Digital media. **Communications technology:** Photo/film/video. **Health:** Health services. **Legal studies:** Paralegal. **Liberal arts:** Arts/sciences. **Protective services:** Criminal justice, forensics, police science. **Psychology:** General. **Public administration:** Human services. **Social sciences:** Political science.

**Most popular majors.** Business/marketing 18%, legal studies 7%, psychology 8%, security/protective services 49%.

**Computing on campus.** 146 workstations in dormitories, library, computer center, student center. Dormitories wired for high-speed internet access. Online course registration, online library, helpline, wireless network available.

**Student life. Freshman orientation:** Mandatory, $25 fee. 1-day programs held in June, July or August. **Housing:** Guaranteed on-campus for all undergraduates. Coed dorms, apartments available. $50 nonrefundable deposit, deadline 8/1. **Activities:** Campus ministries, choral groups, drama, literary magazine, student government, student newspaper, SADD, Human Service Association, Psychology Club, Great Expectations, Criminal Justice Club, Students in Free Enterprise, Common Grounds, Economic Crime Investigation Club.

**Athletics.** NCAA. **Intercollegiate:** Baseball M, basketball, cross-country, golf, soccer, softball W, volleyball. **Intramural:** Basketball, football (non-tackle), soccer, softball, table tennis, volleyball. **Team name:** Hawks.

**Student services.** Adult student services, alcohol/substance abuse counseling, chaplain/spiritual director, career counseling, student employment services, financial aid counseling, minority student services, personal counseling, placement for graduates, veterans' counselor. **Physically disabled:** Services for visually, hearing impaired.

**Contact.** E-mail: admissions@hilbert.edu
Phone: (716) 649-7900 ext. 211 Toll-free number: (800) 649-8003
Fax: (716) 649-1152
Timothy Lee, Director of Admissions, Hilbert College, 5200 South Park Avenue, Hamburg, NY 14075-1597

## Hobart and William Smith Colleges

Geneva, New York — CB member
www.hws.edu — CB code: 2294

- Private 4-year liberal arts college
- Residential campus in large town
- 2,093 degree-seeking undergraduates: 54% women
- 8 degree-seeking graduate students
- 56% of applicants admitted
- Application essay required
- 79% graduate within 6 years

**General.** Founded in 1822. Regionally accredited. Hobart and William Smith are coordinate colleges. All classes coeducational with one faculty, one President, one Board of Trustees, and one campus, but with separate deans, student governments, and athletic departments. **Degrees:** 418 bachelor's awarded; master's offered. **ROTC:** Army, Naval, Air Force. **Location:** 50 miles from Syracuse, 40 miles from Rochester. **Calendar:** Semester. **Full-time faculty:** 195 total; 97% have terminal degrees, 15% minority, 42% women. **Part-time faculty:** 15 total; 93% have terminal degrees, 13% minority, 47% women. **Class size:** 64% < 20, 33% 20-39, 1% 40-49, less than 1% 50-99. **Special facilities:** 70-foot research vessel, 100-acre nature preserve, Finger Lakes Institute.

**Freshman class profile.** 5,207 applied, 2,918 admitted, 549 enrolled.

| Mid 50% test scores | | | |
|---|---|---|---|
| SAT critical reading: | 570-660 | GPA 3.0-3.49: | 29% |
| SAT math: | 580-650 | GPA 2.0-2.99: | 21% |
| SAT writing: | 560-650 | Rank in top quarter: | 73% |
| ACT composite: | 25-30 | Rank in top tenth: | 41% |
| GPA 3.75 or higher: | 31% | Return as sophomores: | 86% |
| GPA 3.50-3.74: | 19% | Out-of-state: | 56% |
| | | Live on campus: | 100% |

**Basis for selection.** High school record, school and community activities, recommendations, interview and talents all considered as part of the admissions decision. Economically and educationally disadvantaged NY state residents may apply through the Higher Education Opportunity Program. Standardized tests only required for those applying for the Trustee or Blackwell scholarships, those who come from a high school without a traditionally graded transcript, or those for whom English is not a first language (TOEFL exam is acceptable for non-native English speakers). Interview strongly encouraged for all and required for trustee scholar applicants. Candidates for arts scholars program must submit portfolio. **Homeschooled:** Students without a traditional, graded transcript must submit standardized test scores.

**High school preparation.** College-preparatory program required. 20 units required. Required and recommended units include English 4, mathematics 3, social studies 2-3, science 3 (laboratory 2), foreign language 2-3 and academic electives 2-4. Mathematics must include algebra, geometry, and trigonometry sequence.

**2009-2010 Annual costs.** Tuition/fees: $40,221. Room/board: $10,024. Books/supplies: $1,000. Personal expenses: $600.

**2008-2009 Financial aid. Need-based:** 400 full-time freshmen applied for aid; 328 were judged to have need; 323 of these received aid. Average need met was 81%. Average scholarship/grant was $25,109; average loan $3,043. 77% of total undergraduate aid awarded as scholarships/grants, 23% as loans/jobs. **Non-need-based:** Awarded to 555 full-time undergraduates, including 159 freshmen. Scholarships awarded for academics, art, leadership, music/drama.

**Application procedures. Admission:** Closing date 2/1 (postmark date). $45 fee, may be waived for applicants with need, free for online applicants. Admission notification 4/1. Must reply by 5/1. **Financial aid:** Closing date 2/15. FAFSA, CSS PROFILE required. Applicants notified by 4/1; must reply by 5/1 or within 2 week(s) of notification.

**Academics.** All students must complete a major and a minor or a second major, 1 of which must be interdisciplinary. **Special study options:** Combined bachelor's/graduate degree, double major, ESL, exchange student, honors, independent study, internships, liberal arts/career combination, semester at sea, student-designed major, study abroad, teacher certification program, United Nations semester, Washington semester. **Credit/placement by examination:** AP, CLEP, IB, institutional tests. Credit by examination counted toward degree limited to equivalent of 7 courses. **Support services:** Learning center, pre-admission summer program, reduced course load, remedial instruction, study skills assistance, tutoring, writing center.

**Majors. Architecture:** Architecture. **Area/ethnic studies:** African, African-American, American, Asian, Chicano/Hispanic-American/Latino, European, gay/lesbian, Latin American, Russian/Slavic, women's. **Biology:** General, biochemistry. **Communications:** Media studies. **Computer sciences:** General, computer science. **Conservation:** Environmental studies. **Foreign languages:** Chinese, classics, comparative lit, French, Japanese, Latin, Russian, Spanish. **Health:** Predental, premedicine, preveterinary. **History:** General. **Interdisciplinary:** Math/computer science. **Math:** General. **Philosophy/religion:** Philosophy, religion. **Physical sciences:** Chemistry, geology, physics. **Psychology:** General. **Public administration:** Policy analysis. **Social sciences:** Anthropology, economics, international relations, political science, sociology, urban studies. **Visual/performing arts:** Art history/conservation, dance, dramatic, studio arts.

**Computing on campus.** 150 workstations in dormitories, library, computer center, student center. Dormitories wired for high-speed internet access and linked to campus network. Commuter students can connect to campus network. Online course registration, online library, helpline, repair service, student web hosting, wireless network available.

**Student life. Freshman orientation:** Mandatory. Preregistration for classes offered. 3-day program in late August with optional pre-orientation adventure program. **Housing:** Guaranteed on-campus for all undergraduates. Coed dorms, single-sex dorms, special housing for disabled, apartments, cooperative housing, fraternity/sorority housing, wellness housing available. **Activities:** Bands, campus ministries, choral groups, dance, drama, film society, international student organizations, literary magazine, music ensembles, musical theater, radio station, student government, student newspaper, symphony orchestra, Literary Corps, international students club, black student union, PRIDE Alliance, Hillel, Geneva Heroes (service), College Republicans, College Democrats, Caribbean student association, Latin American organization.

**Athletics.** NCAA. **Intercollegiate:** Basketball, cross-country, diving W, field hockey W, football (tackle) M, golf, ice hockey M, lacrosse, rowing (crew), sailing, soccer, squash, swimming W, tennis. **Intramural:** Badminton, basketball, bowling, cross-country, football (non-tackle), golf, ice hockey, lacrosse, racquetball, skiing, soccer, softball, squash, swimming, table tennis, tennis, track and field, volleyball, water polo. **Team name:** Statesmen (Hobart); Herons (William Smith).

**Student services.** Alcohol/substance abuse counseling, chaplain/spiritual director, career counseling, services for economically disadvantaged, student employment services, financial aid counseling, health services, minority student services, personal counseling, placement for graduates, veterans' counselor, women's services. **Physically disabled:** Services for visually, speech, hearing impaired. **Learning disabled:** Comprehensive services available.

**Contact.** E-mail: admissions@hws.edu
Phone: (315) 781-3622 Toll-free number: (800) 852-2256
Fax: (315) 781-3914
John Young, Director of Admissions, Hobart and William Smith Colleges, 629 South Main Street, Geneva, NY 14456

---

## Hofstra University
**Hempstead, New York**
**www.hofstra.edu**

**CB member**
**CB code: 2295**

- Private 4-year university
- Residential campus in large city
- 7,756 degree-seeking undergraduates: 6% part-time, 52% women, 9% African American, 5% Asian American, 9% Hispanic American, 2% international
- 3,945 degree-seeking graduate students
- 57% of applicants admitted
- Application essay required
- 55% graduate within 6 years; 31% enter graduate study

**General.** Founded in 1935. Regionally accredited. **Degrees:** 1,750 bachelor's awarded; master's, doctoral, professional offered. **ROTC:** Army. **Location:** 25 miles from New York City. **Calendar:** 4-1-4, extensive summer session. **Full-time faculty:** 544 total; 91% have terminal degrees, 17% minority, 40% women. **Part-time faculty:** 636 total; 38% have terminal degrees, 11% minority, 48% women. **Class size:** 48% < 20, 45% 20-39, 3% 40-49, 3% 50-99. **Special facilities:** Financial trading room, comprehensive media production facility, converged newsroom learning center, linux beowolf cluster, digital language lab, technology, science and engineering labs, rooftop observatory, 7 theaters, assessment centers for client observation and counseling, child care institute, cultural center, museum, arboretum, bird sanctuary.

**Freshman class profile.** 20,829 applied, 11,801 admitted, 1,568 enrolled.

| Mid 50% test scores | | | |
|---|---|---|---|
| SAT critical reading: | 540-630 | Rank in top quarter: | 59% |
| SAT math: | 560-640 | Rank in top tenth: | 31% |
| ACT composite: | 24-28 | End year in good standing: | 88% |
| GPA 3.75 or higher: | 28% | Return as sophomores: | 76% |
| GPA 3.50-3.74: | 16% | Out-of-state: | 45% |
| GPA 3.0-3.49: | 32% | Live on campus: | 73% |
| GPA 2.0-2.99: | 24% | International: | 2% |

**Basis for selection.** Holistic review of each applicant. Secondary school record, standardized test scores (SAT or ACT, required for some), TOEFL scores for international applicants, personal essay and letters of recommendation most important. SAT Subject Tests recommended. No deadline (rolling) for SAT or ACT test scores. Standardized tests not required for admission to New Opportunities at Hofstra (NOAH), School of University Studies, Program for Academic Learning Skills (PALS) or International Applicants (TOEFL is required). Interview required of HEOP, School for University Studies and Program for Academic Learning Skills applicants. Audition recommended for music, theater programs; portfolio recommended for fine arts program. **Homeschooled:** Statement describing homeschool structure and mission, transcript of courses and grades, state high school equivalency certificate required. Must provide at least 2 recommendations, including 1 from primary instructor or person who has primary responsibility for assessing applicant's academic performance. School required to certify completion of secondary school for all enrolled students prior to graduation. **Learning Disabled:** Students may apply to the Program for Academic Learning Skills. Application includes copy of psychological testing, WAISR or WISC.

**High school preparation.** College-preparatory program required. 16 units required. Required and recommended units include English 4, mathematics 3-4, social studies 3-4, science 3-4 (laboratory 1-2) and foreign language 2-3. Social studies includes history; 4 math, 1 chemistry, and 1 physics required for engineering.

**2009-2010 Annual costs.** Tuition/fees: $30,130. Room/board: $11,330. Books/supplies: $1,000. Personal expenses: $1,242.

**2008-2009 Financial aid. Need-based:** 1,338 full-time freshmen applied for aid; 1,048 were judged to have need; 1,037 of these received aid. Average need met was 55%. Average scholarship/grant was $11,578; average loan $3,393. 43% of total undergraduate aid awarded as scholarships/grants, 57% as loans/jobs. **Non-need-based:** Awarded to 1,856 full-time undergraduates, including 483 freshmen. Scholarships awarded for academics, art, athletics, leadership, music/drama, ROTC, state residency.

**Application procedures. Admission:** No deadline. $70 fee, may be waived for applicants with need. Admission notification on a rolling basis beginning on or about 2/1. Must reply by May 1 or within 2 week(s) if notified thereafter. **Financial aid:** Priority date 2/15; no closing date. FAFSA required. Applicants notified on a rolling basis starting 3/1; must reply by 5/1 or within 2 week(s) of notification.

**Academics. Special study options:** Accelerated study, combined bachelor's/graduate degree, cross-registration, distance learning, double major, dual enrollment of high school students, ESL, external degree, honors, independent study, internships, liberal arts/career combination, student-designed major, study abroad, teacher certification program, Washington semester. **Credit/placement by examination:** AP, CLEP, IB, institutional tests. 30 credit hours maximum toward bachelor's degree. **Support services:** Learning center, pre-admission summer program, reduced course load, study skills assistance, tutoring, writing center.

**Honors college/program.** Students invited to join when applying for admission. Typically only the top 10% of all admits offered invitation. During first year, students enroll in small multidisciplinary courses. After first year, students choose from wide range of honors-level courses in all academic areas of study.

**Majors. Area/ethnic studies:** African, American, Asian, Caribbean, Chicano/Hispanic-American/Latino, Latin American, women's. **Biology:** General, biochemistry. **Business:** General, accounting, business admin, entrepreneurial studies, finance, international, labor studies, management information systems, managerial economics, marketing. **Communications:** General, journalism, media studies, public relations, radio/tv. **Computer sciences:** Computer science. **Conservation:** Environmental studies. **Education:** Art, biology, business, chemistry, early childhood, elementary, English, foreign languages, French, German, health, mathematics, multi-level teacher, music, physical, physics, science, secondary, social studies, Spanish. **Engineering:** Biomedical, civil, computer, electrical, environmental, industrial, manufacturing, mechanical, science. **Foreign languages:** Chinese, classics, comparative lit, French, German, Hebrew, Italian, Latin, linguistics, Russian, Spanish. **Health:** Athletic training, audiology/speech pathology, community health, health services, physician assistant, predental, premedicine, preveterinary. **History:** General. **Interdisciplinary:** Math/computer science, natural sciences. **Legal studies:** Prelaw. **Liberal arts:** Arts/sciences, humanities. **Math:** General, applied. **Philosophy/religion:** Judaic, philosophy, religion. **Physical sciences:** Chemistry, geology, physics. **Protective services:** Forensics. **Psychology:** General. **Social sciences:** General, anthropology, econometrics, economics, geography, political science, sociology. **Visual/performing arts:** Acting, art history/conservation, ceramics, dance, directing/producing, dramatic, jazz, metal/jewelry, music history, music management, music performance, music theory/composition, painting, photography, studio arts.

**Most popular majors.** Business/marketing 33%, communications/journalism 16%, education 8%, health sciences 6%, psychology 8%, social sciences 8%.

**Computing on campus.** 1,628 workstations in dormitories, library, computer center. Dormitories wired for high-speed internet access and linked to campus network. Commuter students can connect to campus network. Online course registration, online library, helpline, repair service, student web hosting, wireless network available.

**Student life. Freshman orientation:** Mandatory, $200 fee. Preregistration for classes offered. Several orientation programs. Summer orientation is a 3-day/2-night program in which new students live on campus and begin preparation for the fall semester. The program extends into the entire first year beginning with the full array of programs five days prior to the start of classes and then throughout the year with programs and events designed to acclimate students to student life. **Housing:** Guaranteed on-campus for all undergraduates. Coed dorms, special housing for disabled, apartments, wellness housing available. $300 nonrefundable deposit, deadline 5/1. Honors housing, living-learning community, quiet floors, women's floors. **Activities:** Bands, campus ministries, choral groups, dance, drama, film society, international student organizations, literary magazine, music ensembles, musical theater, opera, radio station, student government, student newspaper, symphony orchestra, TV station, African people's organization, College Republicans, Entertainment Unlimited, Hillel, Muslim student association, Hofstra Democrats, Hofstra Organization of Latin Americans, Hofstra Pride Network, progressive students union, Women of Action.

**Athletics.** NCAA. **Intercollegiate:** Baseball M, basketball, cross-country, field hockey W, golf, lacrosse, soccer, softball W, tennis, volleyball W, wrestling M. **Intramural:** Badminton, basketball, football (non-tackle) M, soccer, softball, table tennis, tennis, volleyball. **Team name:** Pride.

**Student services.** Adult student services, alcohol/substance abuse counseling, chaplain/spiritual director, career counseling, student employment services, financial aid counseling, health services, minority student services, on-campus daycare, personal counseling, placement for graduates, veterans' counselor. **Physically disabled:** Services for visually, speech, hearing impaired. **Learning disabled:** Comprehensive services available.

**Contact.** E-mail: admission@hofstra.edu
Phone: (516) 463-6700 Toll-free number: (800) 463-7872
Fax: (516) 463-5100
Sunil Samuel, Director of Admission, Hofstra University, Admissions Center, 100 Hofstra University, Hempstead, NY 11549

## Holy Trinity Orthodox Seminary
**Jordanville, New York**
www.hts.edu                                    CB code: 2298

- Private 5-year seminary college for men affiliated with Russian Orthodox Church
- Residential campus in rural community
- 25 degree-seeking undergraduates
- Application essay required

**General.** Founded in 1948. Regionally accredited. **Degrees:** 9 bachelor's awarded. **Location:** 20 miles from Utica. **Calendar:** Semester, limited summer session. **Full-time faculty:** 6 total; 17% have terminal degrees, 17% women. **Part-time faculty:** 13 total; 8% have terminal degrees, 8% women. **Class size:** 100% < 20. **Special facilities:** Museum of Russian history, archives, icon painting studio.

**Freshman class profile.** 5 enrolled.

| Out-of-state: | 50% | Live on campus: | 100% |
|---|---|---|---|

**Basis for selection.** Orthodoxy/Orthodox baptism, entrance exam required. Recommendation from spiritual father or parish priest important. **Homeschooled:** Letter of recommendation (nonparent) required.

**2009-2010 Annual costs.** Tuition/fees: $3,000. Room/board: $2,500. Books/supplies: $200.

**Financial aid. Additional information:** Work-study program can reasonably pay for room and board over the course of the academic year.

**Application procedures. Admission:** Closing date 5/1 (postmark date). No application fee.

**Academics. Special study options:** Distance learning, ESL. **Credit/placement by examination:** CLEP, institutional tests. **Support services:** Remedial instruction, tutoring.

**Majors. Theology:** Theology.

**Computing on campus.** 8 workstations in dormitories, library.

**Student life. Freshman orientation:** Mandatory. **Policies:** Closed campus. Religious observance required. **Housing:** Guaranteed on-campus for all undergraduates. Wellness housing available. **Activities:** Choral groups, student newspaper.

**Contact.** E-mail: info@hts.edu
Phone: (315) 858-0945
Dc. Vladimir Tsurikov, Dean, Holy Trinity Orthodox Seminary, Box 36, Jordanville, NY 13361

## Houghton College
**Houghton, New York**                        CB member
www.houghton.edu                              CB code: 2299

- Private 4-year liberal arts college affiliated with Wesleyan Church
- Residential campus in rural community

- 1,270 degree-seeking undergraduates: 2% part-time, 66% women, 2% African American, 2% Asian American, 1% Hispanic American, 4% international
- 23 degree-seeking graduate students
- 82% of applicants admitted
- SAT or ACT (ACT writing optional), application essay required
- 70% graduate within 6 years

**General.** Founded in 1883. Regionally accredited. All students receive laptop computer as part of tuition. Extension campuses in suburban Buffalo and in the Adirondack State Park. Study abroad programs in London, Tanzania, and Australia. School of Music accredited by National Association of Schools of Music. **Degrees:** 381 bachelor's, 4 associate awarded; master's offered. **ROTC:** Army. **Location:** 60 miles from Buffalo, 70 miles from Rochester. **Calendar:** Semester, limited summer session. **Full-time faculty:** 88 total; 88% have terminal degrees, 6% minority, 31% women. **Part-time faculty:** 56 total; 16% have terminal degrees, 11% minority, 52% women. **Class size:** 65% < 20, 28% 20-39, 4% 40-49, 3% 50-99. **Special facilities:** Equestrian center with indoor riding ring, ropes/initiatives course, downhill and cross-country skiing facilities, media arts computer lab, hiking and biking trails.

**Freshman class profile.** 1,080 applied, 889 admitted, 287 enrolled.

| Mid 50% test scores | | GPA 2.0-2.99: | 10% |
|---|---|---|---|
| SAT critical reading: | 520-650 | Rank in top quarter: | 66% |
| SAT math: | 510-620 | Rank in top tenth: | 39% |
| SAT writing: | 500-640 | Return as sophomores: | 86% |
| ACT composite: | 23-29 | Out-of-state: | 47% |
| GPA 3.75 or higher: | 39% | Live on campus: | 97% |
| GPA 3.50-3.74: | 31% | International: | 4% |
| GPA 3.0-3.49: | 20% | | |

**Basis for selection.** Student's high school transcript and standardized test scores of the utmost importance. Application essays, Christian character recommendation, other intangibles also considered. Interview recommended for all applicants. Audition and separate application required for entrance into the School of Music. **Learning Disabled:** Students must provide an IEP to receive services.

**High school preparation.** College-preparatory program recommended. 16 units recommended. Recommended units include English 4, mathematics 3, social studies 1, history 2, science 2 (laboratory 2) and foreign language 2.

**2009-2010 Annual costs.** Tuition/fees: $24,440. Tuition includes laptop computer, fees. Room/board: $7,000. Books/supplies: $900. Personal expenses: $2,250.

**2009-2010 Financial aid. Need-based:** 259 full-time freshmen applied for aid; 230 were judged to have need; 230 of these received aid. Average need met was 79%. Average scholarship/grant was $15,549; average loan $4,482. 60% of total undergraduate aid awarded as scholarships/grants, 40% as loans/jobs. **Non-need-based:** Awarded to 327 full-time undergraduates, including 92 freshmen. Scholarships awarded for academics, alumni affiliation, art, athletics, music/drama, religious affiliation, ROTC, state residency. **Additional information:** Wesley Full Tuition Grant offered to 25 new students each year. Covers the balance of tuition after all state and federal aid is awarded.

**Application procedures. Admission:** No deadline. $40 fee, may be waived for applicants with need. Admission notification on a rolling basis. Must reply by May 1 or within 4 week(s) if notified thereafter. **Financial aid:** Priority date 3/1; no closing date. FAFSA required. Applicants notified on a rolling basis starting 3/15; must reply by 5/1.

**Academics. Special study options:** Combined bachelor's/graduate degree, cross-registration, double major, exchange student, honors, independent study, internships, liberal arts/career combination, study abroad, teacher certification program, Washington semester. **Credit/placement by examination:** AP, CLEP, IB, SAT, ACT, institutional tests. 16 credit hours maximum toward associate degree, 32 toward bachelor's. **Support services:** Learning center, reduced course load, study skills assistance, tutoring, writing center.

**Honors college/program.** Admission to the First-Year Honors Program requires separate application, academic reference, writing sample, and interview.

**Majors. Agriculture:** Equestrian studies. **Biology:** General, biochemistry, environmental. **Business:** General, accounting, business admin. **Communications:** General, digital media, public relations. **Computer sciences:** Computer science, information technology. **Education:** General, biology, chemistry, elementary, English, ESL, foreign languages, history, mathematics, music, physical, physics, secondary, social studies, Spanish. **Engineering:**

Physics. **Foreign languages:** Spanish. **Health:** Predental, premedicine, prepharmacy, preveterinary. **History:** General. **Liberal arts:** Humanities. **Math:** General. **Parks/recreation:** General, health/fitness. **Philosophy/religion:** Philosophy, religion. **Physical sciences:** Chemistry, physics. **Psychology:** General. **Social sciences:** International relations, political science, sociology. **Theology:** Bible, preministerial. **Visual/performing arts:** Art, music performance, music theory/composition, piano/organ, stringed instruments, studio arts, voice/opera. **Other:** Ethnic, cultural minority, and gender studies, other.

**Most popular majors.** Biology 6%, business/marketing 26%, education 16%, English 6%, visual/performing arts 8%.

**Computing on campus.** PC or laptop required. 15 workstations in library, computer center, student center. Dormitories wired for high-speed internet access and linked to campus network. Commuter students can connect to campus network. Online library, helpline, repair service, wireless network available.

**Student life. Freshman orientation:** Mandatory. Preregistration for classes offered. **Policies:** Drinking of alcoholic beverages and smoking on or off campus prohibited. Religious observance required. **Housing:** Guaranteed on-campus for freshmen. Single-sex dorms, special housing for disabled, apartments, wellness housing available. $300 nonrefundable deposit, deadline 5/1. **Activities:** Bands, campus ministries, choral groups, drama, international student organizations, literary magazine, music ensembles, musical theater, opera, student government, student newspaper, symphony orchestra, Allegany County Outreach, Global Christian Fellowship, Habitat for Humanity, Youth for Christ, Fellowship of Christian Athletes, Intercultural Student Organization.

**Athletics.** NAIA. **Intercollegiate:** Basketball, cross-country, field hockey W, soccer, track and field, volleyball W. **Intramural:** Basketball, equestrian, football (non-tackle) M, racquetball, soccer, table tennis, volleyball, water polo. **Team name:** Highlanders.

**Student services.** Chaplain/spiritual director, career counseling, student employment services, financial aid counseling, health services, personal counseling, placement for graduates. **Physically disabled:** Services for visually impaired. **Learning disabled:** Comprehensive services available.

**Contact.** E-mail: admission@houghton.edu
Phone: (585) 567-9353 Toll-free number: (800) 777-2556
Fax: (585) 567-9522
Matt Reitnour, Director of Admission, Houghton College, 1 Willard Avenue/PO Box 128, Houghton, NY 14744-0128

---

## Iona College
**New Rochelle, New York**  **CB member**
**www.iona.edu**  **CB code: 2324**

▶ Private 4-year business and liberal arts college affiliated with Roman Catholic Church

▶ Residential campus in small city

▶ 3,314 degree-seeking undergraduates: 2% part-time, 56% women, 5% African American, 2% Asian American, 12% Hispanic American, 1% international

▶ 896 degree-seeking graduate students

▶ 58% of applicants admitted

▶ SAT or ACT (ACT writing optional), application essay required

▶ 62% graduate within 6 years; 70% enter graduate study

**General.** Founded in 1940. Regionally accredited. Independent institution in Roman Catholic, Christian Brothers tradition. **Degrees:** 643 bachelor's awarded; master's offered. **ROTC:** Army, Air Force. **Location:** 20 miles from New York City. **Calendar:** Semester, extensive summer session. **Full-time faculty:** 183 total; 92% have terminal degrees, 14% minority, 34% women. **Part-time faculty:** 207 total. **Class size:** 41% < 20, 52% 20-39, 6% 40-49, less than 1% 50-99. **Special facilities:** Extensive Irish and rare books collection.

**Freshman class profile.** 7,313 applied, 4,242 admitted, 792 enrolled.

| Mid 50% test scores | | | |
|---|---|---|---|
| SAT critical reading: | 540-640 | Rank in top quarter: | 54% |
| SAT math: | 550-650 | Rank in top tenth: | 31% |
| GPA 3.75 or higher: | 5% | Return as sophomores: | 85% |
| GPA 3.50-3.74: | 15% | Out-of-state: | 24% |
| GPA 3.0-3.49: | 56% | Live on campus: | 64% |
| GPA 2.0-2.99: | 24% | International: | 2% |

**Basis for selection.** High school curriculum and GPA most important, followed by test scores, recommendations, interview, extracurricular activities, essays, grade trends. Interviews recommended. **Homeschooled:** Transcript of courses and grades, interview, letter of recommendation (nonparent) required.

**High school preparation.** College-preparatory program recommended. 16 units required; 20 recommended. Required and recommended units include English 4, mathematics 3-4, social studies 1-2, history 1-2, science 2-3 (laboratory 2), foreign language 2 and academic electives 1-3.

**2010-2011 Annual costs.** Tuition/fees: $28,850. Room/board: $11,800. Books/supplies: $1,500. Personal expenses: $1,250.

**2009-2010 Financial aid. Need-based:** 783 full-time freshmen applied for aid; 630 were judged to have need; 630 of these received aid. Average need met was 31%. Average scholarship/grant was $6,039; average loan $3,077. 60% of total undergraduate aid awarded as scholarships/grants, 40% as loans/jobs. **Non-need-based:** Awarded to 3,238 full-time undergraduates, including 821 freshmen. Scholarships awarded for academics, alumni affiliation, athletics, ROTC.

**Application procedures. Admission:** Closing date 2/15 (postmark date). $50 fee, may be waived for applicants with need. Admission notification 3/20. Must reply by 5/1. **Financial aid:** Closing date 4/15. FAFSA, institutional form required. Applicants notified on a rolling basis starting 12/20; must reply by 5/1 or within 2 week(s) of notification.

**Academics. Special study options:** Accelerated study, combined bachelor's/graduate degree, distance learning, double major, honors, independent study, internships, liberal arts/career combination, study abroad, teacher certification program, weekend college. **Credit/placement by examination:** AP, CLEP, IB, SAT, ACT. 60 credit hours maximum toward bachelor's degree. **Support services:** Learning center, pre-admission summer program, reduced course load, tutoring, writing center.

**Majors. Biology:** General, biochemistry, environmental. **Business:** Accounting, business admin, finance, international, management information systems, marketing. **Communications:** General, advertising, journalism, media studies, public relations, radio/tv. **Computer sciences:** Computer science, networking, web page design. **Education:** Biology, early childhood, elementary, English, French, mathematics, secondary, social studies, Spanish. **Foreign languages:** French, Italian, Spanish. **Health:** Audiology/speech pathology, clinical lab science, health care admin. **History:** General. **Interdisciplinary:** Global studies. **Liberal arts:** Arts/sciences. **Math:** General, applied. **Philosophy/religion:** Philosophy, religion. **Physical sciences:** Chemistry, physics. **Protective services:** Law enforcement admin. **Psychology:** General. **Public administration:** Social work. **Social sciences:** Economics, political science, sociology. **Visual/performing arts:** Dramatic. **Other:** Italian teacher education.

**Most popular majors.** Business/marketing 33%, communications/journalism 19%, education 8%, psychology 10%, security/protective services 8%.

**Computing on campus.** 627 workstations in dormitories, library, computer center, student center. Dormitories wired for high-speed internet access and linked to campus network. Commuter students can connect to campus network. Online course registration, online library, helpline, repair service, wireless network available.

**Student life. Freshman orientation:** Mandatory. Preregistration for classes offered. Overnight summer program in June and July; 1-day welcome program. **Housing:** Coed dorms, special housing for disabled, apartments, wellness housing available. $400 nonrefundable deposit, deadline 5/1. Living-learning communities. **Activities:** Pep band, campus ministries, choral groups, dance, drama, film society, international student organizations, literary magazine, Model UN, musical theater, radio station, student government, student newspaper, TV station, Gaelic Society, Council of Multicultural Leaders, Italian club, Students of Caribbean Ancestry, Hispanic Organization for Latin Awareness, Amnesty International, Democrats, Republicans, Hellenic Society, Asian student association, Students for American Awareness.

**Athletics.** NCAA. **Intercollegiate:** Baseball M, basketball, cross-country, diving, golf M, lacrosse W, rowing (crew), soccer, softball W, swimming, track and field, volleyball W, water polo. **Intramural:** Basketball, football (non-tackle), soccer, table tennis, volleyball. **Team name:** Gaels.

**Student services.** Adult student services, alcohol/substance abuse counseling, chaplain/spiritual director, career counseling, student employment services, financial aid counseling, health services, minority student services, personal counseling, placement for graduates, veterans' counselor, women's services. **Physically disabled:** Services for speech impaired. **Learning disabled:** Comprehensive services available.

**Contact.** E-mail: icad@iona.edu
Phone: (914) 633-2502 Toll-free number: (800) 231-4662
Fax: (914) 633-2182
Kevin Cavanagh, Assistant VP for College Admissions, Iona College, 715
North Avenue, New Rochelle, NY 10801-1890

## Ithaca College
**Ithaca, New York**
**www.ithaca.edu**
**CB member**
**CB code: 2325**

- Private 4-year health science and liberal arts college
- Residential campus in large town
- 6,400 degree-seeking undergraduates: 1% part-time, 57% women, 3% African American, 4% Asian American, 4% Hispanic American, 1% Native American, 2% international
- 445 degree-seeking graduate students
- 79% of applicants admitted
- SAT or ACT with writing, application essay required
- 77% graduate within 6 years; 40% enter graduate study

**General.** Founded in 1892. Regionally accredited. **Degrees:** 1,403 bachelor's awarded; master's, professional offered. **ROTC:** Army, Air Force. **Location:** 250 miles from New York City, 60 miles from Syracuse. **Calendar:** Semester, extensive summer session. **Full-time faculty:** 461 total; 95% have terminal degrees, 8% minority, 46% women. **Part-time faculty:** 241 total; 69% have terminal degrees, 8% minority, 52% women. **Class size:** 53% < 20, 39% 20-39, 4% 40-49, 3% 50-99, less than 1% >100. **Special facilities:** Digital audio/video labs, photography labs, cinematography post-production studio, film animation lab, lighting studio, physical therapy and occupational therapy clinics, speech and hearing clinic, exercise science labs, greenhouse, tissue culture laboratory, simulated trading room, recording and electroacoustic music studio, observatory.

**Freshman class profile.** 11,916 applied, 9,471 admitted, 2,027 enrolled.

| Mid 50% test scores | | End year in good standing: | 93% |
|---|---|---|---|
| SAT critical reading: | 530-630 | Return as sophomores: | 86% |
| SAT math: | 530-640 | Out-of-state: | 57% |
| SAT writing: | 530-630 | Live on campus: | 99% |
| Rank in top quarter: | 67% | International: | 1% |
| Rank in top tenth: | 27% | | |

**Basis for selection.** School achievement record, test scores most important. School and community activities, accomplishments, special talents, interview also important. Audition required for music, theater arts programs; portfolio recommended for BFA program. **Homeschooled:** Transcript of courses and grades, letter of recommendation (nonparent) required. Applicants encouraged to provide in-depth information regarding academic preparation.

**High school preparation.** College-preparatory program required. 16 units required; 19 recommended. Required and recommended units include English 4, mathematics 3-4, social studies 3-4, science 3-4, foreign language 2 and academic electives 1.

**2009-2010 Annual costs.** Tuition/fees: $32,060. Room/board: $11,780. Books/supplies: $1,200. Personal expenses: $1,552.

**2009-2010 Financial aid. Need-based:** 1,777 full-time freshmen applied for aid; 1,497 were judged to have need; 1,497 of these received aid. Average need met was 93%. Average scholarship/grant was $19,799; average loan $5,746. 71% of total undergraduate aid awarded as scholarships/grants, 29% as loans/jobs. **Non-need-based:** Awarded to 2,225 full-time undergraduates, including 857 freshmen. Scholarships awarded for academics, alumni affiliation, leadership, minority status, music/drama, ROTC.

**Application procedures. Admission:** Closing date 2/1. $60 fee, may be waived for applicants with need. Application must be submitted online. Admission notification 4/15. Admission notification on a rolling basis. Must reply by May 1 or within 2 week(s) if notified thereafter. **Financial aid:** Priority date 2/1; no closing date. FAFSA, CSS PROFILE required. Applicants notified on a rolling basis starting 2/15.

**Academics.** Over 70 minors available. **Special study options:** Accelerated study, combined bachelor's/graduate degree, cross-registration, distance learning, double major, dual enrollment of high school students, honors, independent study, internships, liberal arts/career combination, student-designed major, study abroad, teacher certification program, Washington semester. London Center (England), Los Angeles program, Washington semester, study opportunities in over 50 countries. **Credit/placement by examination:** AP, CLEP, IB, institutional tests. 90 credit hours maximum toward bachelor's degree. **Support services:** Study skills assistance, tutoring, writing center.

**Majors. Biology:** General, biochemistry. **Business:** General, accounting, business admin, finance, international, managerial economics, market research, marketing. **Communications:** General, broadcast journalism, journalism, media studies, organizational, radio/tv. **Communications technology:** Recording arts. **Computer sciences:** General, computer science, information systems, information technology, programming. **Conservation:** General, environmental studies. **Education:** Art, biology, chemistry, Deaf/hearing impaired, English, foreign languages, French, German, health, history, mathematics, multi-level teacher, music, physical, physics, science, secondary, social studies, Spanish, speech impaired. **Foreign languages:** General, French, German, Italian, Spanish. **Health:** Athletic training, facilities admin, occupational therapy assistant, predental, premedicine, preveterinary, public health ed, recreational therapy, speech pathology. **History:** General. **Interdisciplinary:** Gerontology, intercultural, nutrition sciences. **Legal studies:** General, prelaw. **Liberal arts:** Arts/sciences. **Math:** General. **Parks/recreation:** Exercise sciences, health/fitness, sports admin. **Philosophy/religion:** Philosophy. **Physical sciences:** Chemistry, physics. **Psychology:** General, industrial. **Social sciences:** General, anthropology, applied economics, econometrics, economics, political science, sociology. **Visual/performing arts:** General, acting, art, art history/conservation, arts management, cinematography, dance, dramatic, film/cinema, jazz, music performance, music theory/composition, photography, studio arts, theater arts management, theater design. **Other:** Documentary studies and production, Sport studies.

**Most popular majors.** Business/marketing 11%, communications/journalism 19%, English 7%, health sciences 14%, parks/recreation 6%, social sciences 7%, visual/performing arts 19%.

**Computing on campus.** 640 workstations in library, computer center. Dormitories wired for high-speed internet access and linked to campus network. Commuter students can connect to campus network. Online course registration, online library, helpline, repair service, student web hosting, wireless network available.

**Student life. Freshman orientation:** Available, $265 fee. Preregistration for classes offered. 2.5 days in summer and 4 days before school highlighted by placement tests and registration. Separate parent orientation program offered in summer. **Housing:** Guaranteed on-campus for all undergraduates. Coed dorms, single-sex dorms, special housing for disabled, apartments, fraternity/sorority housing available. **Activities:** Bands, campus ministries, choral groups, dance, drama, film society, international student organizations, literary magazine, music ensembles, musical theater, opera, radio station, student government, student newspaper, symphony orchestra, TV station, Jewish, Christian, Catholic, Muslim, and Christian Science organizations, African-Latino society, Amnesty International, BiGayla, community service network, Habitat for Humanity, Sex and Gender Education, Asia Society, Friends of Israel.

**Athletics.** NCAA. **Intercollegiate:** Baseball M, basketball, cross-country, diving, field hockey W, football (tackle) M, golf W, gymnastics W, lacrosse, rowing (crew), soccer, softball W, swimming, tennis, track and field, volleyball W, wrestling M. **Intramural:** Basketball, bowling, football (non-tackle) M, soccer, softball, table tennis, tennis, volleyball, weight lifting. **Team name:** Bombers.

**Student services.** Adult student services, alcohol/substance abuse counseling, chaplain/spiritual director, career counseling, student employment services, financial aid counseling, health services, minority student services, personal counseling, placement for graduates, veterans' counselor. **Physically disabled:** Services for visually, speech, hearing impaired.

**Contact.** E-mail: admission@ithaca.edu
Phone: (607) 274-3124 Toll-free number: (800) 429-4274
Fax: (607) 274-1900
Gerard Turbide, Director of Admission, Ithaca College, 953 Danby Road, Ithaca, NY 14850-7000

## Jewish Theological Seminary of America
**New York, New York**
**www.jtsa.edu**
**CB code: 2339**

- Private 4-year rabbinical and seminary college affiliated with Jewish faith
- Residential campus in very large city
- 177 degree-seeking undergraduates: 6% part-time, 54% women, 1% Hispanic American, 3% international
- 319 degree-seeking graduate students
- 62% of applicants admitted
- SAT or ACT with writing, application essay required
- 87% graduate within 6 years

**General.** Founded in 1886. Regionally accredited. **Degrees:** 48 bachelor's awarded; master's, doctoral offered. **ROTC:** Army, Naval, Air Force. **Calendar:** Semester, extensive summer session. **Full-time faculty:** 52 total; 29% women. **Part-time faculty:** 70 total; 53% women. **Class size:** 86% < 20, 13% 20-39, 1% 40-49. **Special facilities:** Jewish museum containing over 27,000 objects (paintings, sculptures, works on paper, artifacts, etc.), library containing largest collection of Hebraica and Judaica outside of Israel.

**Freshman class profile.** 102 applied, 63 admitted, 41 enrolled.

| Mid 50% test scores | | | |
|---|---|---|---|
| SAT critical reading: | 640-700 | GPA 3.50-3.74: | 40% |
| SAT math: | 620-660 | GPA 3.0-3.49: | 10% |
| SAT writing: | 620-720 | Return as sophomores: | 89% |
| ACT composite: | 30-32 | Out-of-state: | 87% |
| GPA 3.75 or higher: | 50% | International: | 5% |

**Basis for selection.** GED not accepted. School achievement record, interest in Jewish studies, test scores, recommendations important; leadership potential considered. Interview recommended for residents in the New York area (within 100 mile radius).

**High school preparation.** Recommended units include English 4, mathematics 4, social studies 1, history 3, science 4, foreign language 4 and academic electives 4. Additional courses in Judaic studies, when available.

**2009-2010 Annual costs.** Tuition/fees: $15,000. Costs quoted paid to school only; separate costs assessed for dual-degree enrollment at Columbia University/Barnard College. Room only: $9,200. Books/supplies: $500.

**2009-2010 Financial aid. Non-need-based:** Scholarships awarded for academics, alumni affiliation, leadership.

**Application procedures. Admission:** Closing date 2/15 (postmark date). $65 fee, may be waived for applicants with need. Application must be submitted on paper. Admission notification 4/1. Must reply by 5/1. Application deadline January 1 for double degree program with Barnard College, February 15 for joint program with Columbia University. **Financial aid:** Priority date 2/1, closing date 3/1. FAFSA, institutional form, CSS PROFILE required. Applicants notified on a rolling basis starting 4/1; must reply within 4 week(s) of notification.

**Academics. Special study options:** Cross-registration, distance learning, double major, exchange student, honors, independent study, liberal arts/career combination, student-designed major, study abroad. BA/MA program with The Graduate School or William Davidson School of Jewish Education. **Credit/placement by examination:** AP, CLEP, institutional tests. 6 credit hours maximum toward bachelor's degree. **Support services:** Pre-admission summer program, remedial instruction, tutoring, writing center.

**Majors. Foreign languages:** General. **Philosophy/religion:** Judaic. **Theology:** Sacred music. **Visual/performing arts:** Music performance, music theory/composition.

**Computing on campus.** 50 workstations in dormitories, library, computer center. Dormitories wired for high-speed internet access and linked to campus network. Commuter students can connect to campus network. Online course registration, online library, helpline, wireless network available.

**Student life. Freshman orientation:** Mandatory. **Policies:** Student life centers around supportive Jewish community. Undergraduates enrolled in joint degree programs with Barnard and Columbia participate in their extracurricular activities. **Housing:** Coed dorms, special housing for disabled available. **Activities:** Concert band, choral groups, dance, musical theater, student government, student newspaper, community service organization.

**Athletics. Intramural:** Basketball, bowling, field hockey W, lacrosse M, softball, volleyball.

**Student services.** Career counseling, student employment services, health services, personal counseling, placement for graduates.

**Contact.** E-mail: lcadmissions@jtsa.edu
Phone: (212) 678-8832 Fax: (212) 280-6022
Melissa Present, Director of Admissions, Jewish Theological Seminary of America, 3080 Broadway, New York, NY 10027

## Juilliard School
**New York, New York**
**www.juilliard.edu**
CB code: 2340

- Private 4-year music and performing arts college
- Commuter campus in very large city

- 489 degree-seeking undergraduates: 48% women
- 344 degree-seeking graduate students
- 7% of applicants admitted
- Application essay, interview required
- 84% graduate within 6 years

**General.** Founded in 1905. Regionally accredited. **Degrees:** 108 bachelor's awarded; master's, doctoral offered. **Calendar:** Semester. **Full-time faculty:** 116 total; 10% minority, 37% women. **Part-time faculty:** 176 total; 19% minority, 29% women. **Class size:** 88% < 20, 12% 20-39. **Special facilities:** Media center, over 100 practice rooms with over 200 pianos, scenery and costume shops, 15 2-story rehearsal studios, 5 theaters, 2 recital halls.

**Freshman class profile.** 2,151 applied, 153 admitted, 108 enrolled.

| | | | |
|---|---|---|---|
| Return as sophomores: | 93% | Live on campus: | 100% |
| Out-of-state: | 85% | International: | 20% |

**Basis for selection.** Quality of performance at audition most important. Foreign students given English proficiency examination at time of audition or may present TOEFL. Audition required. **Homeschooled:** Transcript of courses and grades, letter of recommendation (nonparent) required.

**High school preparation.** Extensive previous study in major field of dance, drama, or music required.

**2009-2010 Annual costs.** Tuition/fees: $30,500. Room/board: $11,810. Books/supplies: $700. Personal expenses: $3,400.

**2009-2010 Financial aid. Need-based:** 101 full-time freshmen applied for aid; 80 were judged to have need; 80 of these received aid. Average need met was 75%. Average scholarship/grant was $22,359; average loan $3,333. 73% of total undergraduate aid awarded as scholarships/grants, 27% as loans/jobs. **Non-need-based:** Awarded to 27 full-time undergraduates, including 5 freshmen. Scholarships awarded for music/drama.

**Application procedures. Admission:** Closing date 12/1. $100 fee, may be waived for applicants with need. Admission notification 4/1. Must reply by May 1 or within 2 week(s) if notified thereafter. Music auditions held in March. Drama auditions in January and February. Dance auditions in February and March. Application closing date December 1; notification by April 1 or one month after audition. **Financial aid:** Closing date 3/1. FAFSA, institutional form required. Applicants notified by 4/1; must reply by 5/1.

**Academics.** 3-year diploma program available in performing arts. **Credit/placement by examination:** AP, CLEP, institutional tests. **Support services:** Tutoring.

**Majors. Visual/performing arts:** Dance, dramatic, jazz, music performance, music theory/composition, piano/organ, stringed instruments.

**Computing on campus.** 65 workstations in dormitories, library, computer center. Dormitories wired for high-speed internet access. Online library, wireless network available.

**Student life. Freshman orientation:** Mandatory, $200 fee. For all new students, begins 10 days before first day of classes. **Housing:** Guaranteed on-campus for freshmen. Coed dorms available. $150 nonrefundable deposit, deadline 5/15. **Activities:** Student government, student newspaper, ArtREACH, Korea Campus Crusade for Christ, Christian Fellowship, Amnesty Juilliard.

**Student services.** Alcohol/substance abuse counseling, career counseling, student employment services, financial aid counseling, health services, minority student services, personal counseling, placement for graduates.

**Contact.** E-mail: admissions@juilliard.edu
Phone: (212) 799-5000 ext. 223 Fax: (212) 769-6420
Lee Cioppa, Associate Dean for Admissions, Juilliard School, 60 Lincoln Center Plaza, New York, NY 10023-6588

## Kehilath Yakov Rabbinical Seminary
**Brooklyn, New York**
CB code: 0619

- Private 4-year rabbinical college for men affiliated with Jewish faith
- Very large city
- 106 degree-seeking undergraduates

**General.** Accredited by AARTS. **Degrees:** 11 bachelor's awarded. **Calendar:** Continuous.

**2009-2010 Annual costs.** Tuition/fees: $5,200. Room/board: $2,200.

**Application procedures. Admission:** No deadline.

**Academics. Credit/placement by examination:** CLEP.

**Majors. Philosophy/religion:** Judaic. **Theology:** Talmudic.

**Contact.** Phone: (718) 963-3940 Fax: (718) 387-8586
Kehilath Yakov Rabbinical Seminary, 206 Wilson Street, Brooklyn, NY 11211

## Keuka College
**Keuka Park, New York**
**www.keuka.edu**

**CB member**
**CB code: 2350**

◗ Private 4-year liberal arts college affiliated with American Baptist Churches in the USA
◗ Residential campus in rural community
◗ 1,522 degree-seeking undergraduates: 20% part-time, 75% women, 7% African American, 2% Asian American, 3% Hispanic American, 2% Native American
◗ 154 degree-seeking graduate students
◗ 77% of applicants admitted
◗ Application essay required
◗ 52% graduate within 6 years; 36% enter graduate study

**General.** Founded in 1890. Regionally accredited. **Degrees:** 286 bachelor's awarded; master's offered. **Location:** 50 miles from Rochester, 60 miles from Syracuse. **Calendar:** 4-1-4, limited summer session. **Full-time faculty:** 69 total; 86% have terminal degrees, 4% minority, 64% women. **Part-time faculty:** 106 total; 26% have terminal degrees, 59% women. **Class size:** 54% < 20, 45% 20-39, 1% 40-49. **Special facilities:** Lakefront for boating, sailing and science projects and research.

**Freshman class profile.** 867 applied, 666 admitted, 253 enrolled.

| Mid 50% test scores | | | |
|---|---|---|---|
| SAT critical reading: | 410-550 | GPA 2.0-2.99: | 28% |
| SAT math: | 430-510 | Rank in top quarter: | 38% |
| SAT writing: | 410-520 | Rank in top tenth: | 11% |
| ACT composite: | 18-24 | End year in good standing: | 87% |
| GPA 3.75 or higher: | 10% | Return as sophomores: | 64% |
| GPA 3.50-3.74: | 19% | Out-of-state: | 6% |
| GPA 3.0-3.49: | 41% | Live on campus: | 97% |

**Basis for selection.** Overall GPA, extracurricular activities, community service, leadership experience, letter of recommendation, quality of essay, SAT/ACT scores considered by committee. Interview recommended for all, required for some.

**High school preparation.** College-preparatory program recommended. 18 units recommended. Recommended units include English 4, mathematics 3, social studies 3, history 2, science 3 (laboratory 2) and foreign language 3.

**2009-2010 Annual costs.** Tuition/fees: $22,830. Room/board: $9,160. Books/supplies: $1,200. Personal expenses: $1,000.

**2009-2010 Financial aid. Need-based:** 240 full-time freshmen applied for aid; 225 were judged to have need; 225 of these received aid. Average need met was 70%. Average scholarship/grant was $14,052; average loan $5,087. 53% of total undergraduate aid awarded as scholarships/grants, 47% as loans/jobs. **Non-need-based:** Awarded to 161 full-time undergraduates, including 32 freshmen. Scholarships awarded for academics, alumni affiliation, leadership, minority status, religious affiliation.

**Application procedures. Admission:** No deadline. $30 fee, may be waived for applicants with need. Admission notification on a rolling basis beginning on or about 9/1. **Financial aid:** Priority date 3/15; no closing date. FAFSA required. Applicants notified on a rolling basis starting 3/1; must reply by 5/1 or within 2 week(s) of notification.

**Academics.** All students must complete 1 field period or internship each year, every 30 credit hours (experiential education). Field Period enables students to spend 4 weeks a year participating in an internship or international travel, or undertaking an independent project. **Special study options:** Accelerated study, combined bachelor's/graduate degree, cooperative education, cross-registration, double major, dual enrollment of high school students, independent study, internships, student-designed major, study abroad, teacher certification program. Albany semester; 3-1 in clinical science with New York Chiropractic College. **Credit/placement by examination:** AP, CLEP, SAT, ACT, institutional tests. 12 credit hours maximum toward bachelor's degree. **Support services:** Learning center, reduced course load, remedial instruction, study skills assistance, tutoring, writing center.

**Majors. Biology:** General, biochemistry. **Business:** Accounting, business admin, marketing. **Communications:** General. **Conservation:** Environmental science. **Education:** Biology, early childhood, English, mathematics, secondary, social studies, special. **Foreign languages:** American Sign Language, sign language interpretation. **Health:** Clinical lab science, nursing (RN). **Legal studies:** Prelaw. **Liberal arts:** Arts/sciences. **Math:** General. **Protective services:** Law enforcement admin. **Psychology:** General. **Public administration:** Social work. **Social sciences:** General, criminology, sociology.

**Most popular majors.** Business/marketing 21%, education 19%, health sciences 23%, security/protective services 17%.

**Computing on campus.** 140 workstations in dormitories, library, computer center. Dormitories wired for high-speed internet access and linked to campus network. Helpline, repair service, wireless network available.

**Student life. Freshman orientation:** Mandatory, $150 fee. Preregistration for classes offered. 2-session summer program. **Policies:** No smoking allowed in any campus building, including residence halls. **Housing:** Guaranteed on-campus for all undergraduates. Coed dorms, single-sex dorms, special housing for disabled, apartments, cooperative housing, wellness housing available. $150 deposit. Leadership and management housing. **Activities:** Bands, campus ministries, choral groups, dance, drama, film society, international student organizations, literary magazine, musical theater, radio station, student government, student newspaper, social work club, Keuka Leaders club, Keuka Circle (community service), Newman Club, minority support group, political action coalition, Student Nurse Association.

**Athletics.** NCAA. **Intercollegiate:** Baseball M, basketball, cross-country, golf, lacrosse, soccer, softball W, synchronized swimming W, tennis, volleyball W. **Intramural:** Basketball, football (non-tackle), soccer, softball, volleyball. **Team name:** Storm.

**Student services.** Adult student services, alcohol/substance abuse counseling, chaplain/spiritual director, career counseling, student employment services, financial aid counseling, health services, minority student services, personal counseling, placement for graduates, women's services. **Physically disabled:** Services for visually, speech, hearing impaired.

**Contact.** E-mail: admissions@mail.keuka.edu
Phone: (315) 279-5254 Toll-free number: (800) 335-3852
Fax: (315) 279-5386
Carolanne Marquis, Executive Vice President, Keuka College, 141 Cental Avenue, Keuka Park, NY 14478-0098

## King's College
**New York, New York**
**www.tkc.edu**

**CB code: 2871**

◗ Private 4-year liberal arts college affiliated with nondenominational tradition
◗ Residential campus in very large city
◗ 298 degree-seeking undergraduates: 3% part-time, 61% women, 1% African American, 3% Asian American, 6% Hispanic American, 2% international
◗ 74% of applicants admitted
◗ SAT or ACT (ACT writing optional), interview required
◗ 69% graduate within 6 years; 5% enter graduate study

**General.** Regionally accredited. **Degrees:** 47 bachelor's awarded. **Calendar:** Semester, limited summer session. **Full-time faculty:** 16 total; 88% have terminal degrees, 12% women. **Part-time faculty:** 16 total; 62% have terminal degrees, 19% minority, 56% women. **Class size:** 55% < 20, 35% 20-39, 5% 40-49, 5% 50-99.

**Freshman class profile.** 663 applied, 490 admitted, 103 enrolled.

| Mid 50% test scores | | | |
|---|---|---|---|
| SAT critical reading: | 610-700 | GPA 3.0-3.49: | 22% |
| SAT math: | 540-630 | GPA 2.0-2.99: | 11% |
| SAT writing: | 590-680 | Rank in top quarter: | 57% |
| ACT composite: | 24-27 | Rank in top tenth: | 22% |
| GPA 3.75 or higher: | 45% | Return as sophomores: | 68% |
| GPA 3.50-3.74: | 22% | Out-of-state: | 96% |
| | | Live on campus: | 96% |

**Basis for selection.** Admissions based on academic preparedness and leadership qualities, primarily assessed through transcript, SAT or ACT scores, and entrance interview. **Learning Disabled:** Documentation required of any learning disabilities that will require special accommodation.

**High school preparation.** Required and recommended units include English 4, mathematics 3-4, social studies 2, history 2, science 3-4, foreign language 1-2 and academic electives 2.

**2009-2010 Annual costs.** Tuition/fees: $25,000. Room only: $9,000.

**2009-2010 Financial aid. Need-based:** 91 full-time freshmen applied for aid; 78 were judged to have need; 78 of these received aid. Average need met was 63%. Average scholarship/grant was $17,776; average loan $3,500. 69% of total undergraduate aid awarded as scholarships/grants, 31% as loans/jobs. **Non-need-based:** Awarded to 286 full-time undergraduates, including 103 freshmen. Scholarships awarded for academics, leadership.

**Application procedures. Admission:** Priority date 11/15; no deadline. $30 fee, may be waived for applicants with need. Admission notification on a rolling basis beginning on or about 9/15. Must reply by May 1 or within 4 week(s) if notified thereafter. **Financial aid:** No deadline. FAFSA required. Applicants notified on a rolling basis starting 2/15.

**Academics.** Bibically-based curriculum with a common core in politics, philosophy, economics. **Special study options:** Independent study, internships, New York semester, study abroad. **Credit/placement by examination:** AP, CLEP, IB, SAT, ACT, institutional tests. **Support services:** Learning center.

**Majors. Business:** Business admin. **Other:** Politics, philosophy, and economics.

**Most popular majors.** Business/marketing 70%, interdisciplinary studies 29%.

**Computing on campus.** PC or laptop required. 8 workstations in library. Dormitories wired for high-speed internet access and linked to campus network. Commuter students can connect to campus network. Wireless network available.

**Student life. Freshman orientation:** Mandatory. Preregistration for classes offered. Held two days prior to first day of class. **Policies:** No alcoholic beverages/drug usage permitted on campus or in housing. **Housing:** Guaranteed on-campus for all undergraduates. Apartments available. $600 non-refundable deposit. **Activities:** Campus ministries, dance, drama, film society, literary magazine, music ensembles, student government, student newspaper.

**Athletics. Team name:** Pride.

**Student services.** Chaplain/spiritual director, career counseling, student employment services, financial aid counseling.

**Contact.** E-mail: admissions@tkc.edu
Phone: (212) 659-3610 Toll-free number: (888) 969-7200 ext. 3610
Fax: (212) 659-3611
Brian Parker, Vice President of Admissions, King's College, 350 Fifth Avenue, Lower Lobby, New York, NY 10118

## Laboratory Institute of Merchandising
**New York, New York**
www.limcollege.edu
**CB member**
**CB code: 2380**

- For-profit 4-year college of fashion business
- Commuter campus in very large city
- 1,357 degree-seeking undergraduates
- 65% of applicants admitted
- SAT or ACT (ACT writing optional), application essay, interview required

**General.** Founded in 1939. Regionally accredited. **Degrees:** 222 bachelor's, 28 associate awarded; master's offered. **Location:** Located in midtown Manhattan. **Calendar:** Semester, limited summer session. **Full-time faculty:** 24 total. **Part-time faculty:** 145 total. **Class size:** 66% < 20, 34% 20-39.

**Freshman class profile.** 1,110 applied, 717 admitted, 259 enrolled.

| Mid 50% test scores | | | |
|---|---|---|---|
| SAT critical reading: | 430-520 | GPA 3.0-3.49: | 29% |
| SAT math: | 420-510 | GPA 2.0-2.99: | 52% |
| ACT composite: | 19-23 | Rank in top quarter: | 17% |
| GPA 3.75 or higher: | 11% | Rank in top tenth: | 3% |
| GPA 3.50-3.74: | 5% | Out-of-state: | 58% |
| | | Live on campus: | 66% |

**Basis for selection.** Interview, high school transcript, SAT/ACT score, letters of recommendation and college transcripts important. **Home-schooled:** Transcript of courses and grades, state high school equivalency certificate, interview, letter of recommendation (nonparent) required.

**High school preparation.** College-preparatory program recommended.

**2009-2010 Annual costs.** Tuition/fees: $20,425. Room/board: $19,400. Books/supplies: $1,100. Personal expenses: $2,000.

**2008-2009 Financial aid.** All financial aid based on need.

**Application procedures. Admission:** No deadline. $40 fee, may be waived for applicants with need. Admission notification on a rolling basis beginning on or about 12/15. **Financial aid:** Priority date 4/1; no closing date. FAFSA, institutional form required. Applicants notified on a rolling basis starting 2/15; must reply within 2 week(s) of notification.

**Academics.** Associate degree program distributed among liberal arts, business, and professional courses, including 2 work projects of 3 credits and 5 weeks each. Bachelor's degree programs distributed among liberal arts, business, and professional courses with a semester-long, 13-credit cooperative work project. Freshmen and sophomores participate in 3-credit, 5-week work project. Seniors participate in 16-week full-semester co-op. Curriculum also includes weekly field trips into fashion industry and guest lecturer series featuring fashion professionals. **Special study options:** Combined bachelor's/graduate degree, cooperative education, internships, study abroad. 3-credit trip to Europe in winter/summer. **Credit/placement by examination:** AP, CLEP, SAT, ACT, institutional tests. **Support services:** Learning center, pre-admission summer program, reduced course load, remedial instruction, study skills assistance, tutoring, writing center.

**Majors. Business:** Business admin, fashion, management science, marketing. **Family/consumer sciences:** Apparel marketing. **Other:** Visual merchandising.

**Most popular majors.** Business/marketing 40%, family/consumer sciences 51%, visual/performing arts 9%.

**Computing on campus.** 270 workstations in library, computer center, student center. Dormitories wired for high-speed internet access. Commuter students can connect to campus network. Online library, helpline available.

**Student life. Freshman orientation:** Mandatory. **Housing:** Coed dorms available. $700 partly refundable deposit. Affiliated with local YW-YMHA and Educational Housing Inc. in which traditional residence life experience available. **Activities:** Student government.

**Student services.** Alcohol/substance abuse counseling, career counseling, student employment services, financial aid counseling, personal counseling, placement for graduates.

**Contact.** E-mail: admissions@limcollege.edu
Phone: (212) 752-1530 ext. 289 Toll-free number: (800) 677-1323
Fax: (212) 750-3432
Kristina Ortiz, Director of Admissions, Laboratory Institute of Merchandising, 12 East 53rd Street, New York, NY 10022

## Le Moyne College
**Syracuse, New York**
www.lemoyne.edu
**CB member**
**CB code: 2366**

- Private 4-year liberal arts college affiliated with Roman Catholic Church
- Residential campus in small city
- 2,465 degree-seeking undergraduates: 6% part-time, 61% women, 4% African American, 2% Asian American, 5% Hispanic American, 1% Native American, 1% international
- 572 degree-seeking graduate students
- 67% of applicants admitted
- SAT or ACT (ACT writing optional), application essay required
- 71% graduate within 6 years; 40% enter graduate study

**General.** Founded in 1946. Regionally accredited. **Degrees:** 593 bachelor's awarded; master's offered. **ROTC:** Army, Air Force. **Location:** 2 miles from downtown. **Calendar:** Semester, extensive summer session. **Full-time faculty:** 158 total; 94% have terminal degrees, 15% minority, 43% women. **Part-time faculty:** 167 total; 30% have terminal degrees, 4% minority, 50% women. **Class size:** 41% < 20, 56% 20-39, 1% 40-49, 1% 50-99. **Special facilities:** Performing arts center.

**Freshman class profile.** 4,526 applied, 3,023 admitted, 608 enrolled.

| Mid 50% test scores | | | |
|---|---|---|---|
| SAT critical reading: | 490-580 | Rank in top quarter: | 58% |
| SAT math: | 510-610 | Rank in top tenth: | 22% |
| ACT composite: | 20-26 | End year in good standing: | 94% |
| GPA 3.75 or higher: | 22% | Return as sophomores: | 85% |
| GPA 3.50-3.74: | 22% | Out-of-state: | 6% |
| GPA 3.0-3.49: | 35% | Live on campus: | 84% |
| GPA 2.0-2.99: | 21% | International: | 1% |

**Basis for selection.** High school courses and performance most important; class rank, test scores, recommendations, essay, interview, extracurricular activities also important. Students from underrepresented populations encouraged. February 1 priority date by which SAT scores must be received for fall term admission. Interview recommended. **Homeschooled:** Statement describing homeschool structure and mission, transcript of courses and grades, interview, letter of recommendation (nonparent) required. **Learning Disabled:** Interview strongly recommended.

**High school preparation.** College-preparatory program recommended. 17 units required. Required and recommended units include English 4, mathematics 3-4, social studies 4, science 3-4 (laboratory 3) and foreign language 3. 4 math required for science and math majors.

**2009-2010 Annual costs.** Tuition/fees: $25,780. Room/board: $9,990. Books/supplies: $1,230. Personal expenses: $900.

**2008-2009 Financial aid. Need-based:** 511 full-time freshmen applied for aid; 451 were judged to have need; 451 of these received aid. Average need met was 81%. Average scholarship/grant was $11,013; average loan $3,588. 62% of total undergraduate aid awarded as scholarships/grants, 38% as loans/jobs. **Non-need-based:** Awarded to 814 full-time undergraduates, including 232 freshmen. Scholarships awarded for academics, alumni affiliation, athletics, leadership, minority status, ROTC. **Additional information:** Parent loan program at low interest, monthly payment plans and alternative loans for students.

**Application procedures. Admission:** Priority date 2/1; no deadline. $35 fee, may be waived for applicants with need, free for online applicants. Admission notification on a rolling basis beginning on or about 1/1. Must reply by May 1 or within 4 week(s) if notified thereafter. **Financial aid:** Priority date 2/1; no closing date. FAFSA, institutional form required. Applicants notified by 3/15; must reply by 5/1 or within 2 week(s) of notification.

**Academics.** Academic accommodations and services for students with documented disabilities. **Special study options:** Accelerated study, combined bachelor's/graduate degree, double major, dual enrollment of high school students, honors, independent study, internships, liberal arts/career combination, semester at sea, study abroad, teacher certification program, Washington semester. Certificate of Advanced Studies in Educational Leadership and Certificate of Advanced Studies in Nursing. **Credit/placement by examination:** AP, CLEP, IB. **Support services:** Learning center, remedial instruction, study skills assistance, tutoring, writing center.

**Majors. Biology:** General, biochemistry, ecology. **Business:** Accounting, business admin, finance, labor studies, management information systems, marketing, operations. **Communications:** General. **Computer sciences:** General. **Conservation:** Environmental studies. **Foreign languages:** French, Spanish. **Health:** Nursing (RN), predental, premedicine, prepharmacy, preveterinary. **History:** General. **Interdisciplinary:** Biological/physical sciences, peace/conflict. **Legal studies:** Prelaw. **Math:** General. **Philosophy/religion:** Philosophy, religion. **Physical sciences:** Chemistry, physics. **Psychology:** General. **Social sciences:** Criminology, economics, political science, sociology. **Visual/performing arts:** Dramatic. **Other:** Engineering, Health/Medical preparatory programs.

**Most popular majors.** Biology 11%, business/marketing 30%, communications/journalism 7%, English 8%, psychology 16%, social sciences 14%.

**Computing on campus.** 325 workstations in dormitories, library, computer center, student center. Dormitories wired for high-speed internet access and linked to campus network. Commuter students can connect to campus network. Online course registration, online library, helpline, repair service, student web hosting, wireless network available.

**Student life. Freshman orientation:** Mandatory, $200 fee. Preregistration for classes offered. 3 summer orientation sessions of 2 days each and one fall orientation. **Housing:** Guaranteed on-campus for all undergraduates. Coed dorms, single-sex dorms, special housing for disabled, apartments available. Living/Learning communities available. **Activities:** Bands, campus ministries, choral groups, dance, drama, film society, international student organizations, literary magazine, music ensembles, Model UN, musical theater, radio station, student government, student newspaper, TV station, international club, Amnesty International, Habitat for Humanity, Democrats Club, Republican Club, Gaelic Society, El Progreso, Pride in Our Work Ethnicity and Race, Muslim student association.

**Athletics.** NCAA. **Intercollegiate:** Baseball M, basketball, cross-country, diving, golf, lacrosse, soccer, softball W, swimming, tennis, volleyball W. **Intramural:** Basketball, football (non-tackle) M, racquetball, soccer, softball, volleyball. **Team name:** Dolphins.

**Student services.** Adult student services, alcohol/substance abuse counseling, chaplain/spiritual director, career counseling, student employment services, financial aid counseling, health services, minority student services,

personal counseling, placement for graduates, veterans' counselor. **Physically disabled:** Services for visually, speech, hearing impaired.

**Contact.** E-mail: admission@lemoyne.edu
Phone: (315) 445-4300 Toll-free number: (800) 333-4733
Fax: (315) 445-4711
Dennis Nicholson, Director of Admission, Le Moyne College, 1419 Salt Springs Road, Syracuse, NY 13214-1301

## Long Island University: Brooklyn Campus
**Brooklyn, New York**    CB member
**www.liu.edu**    CB code: 2369

- Private 4-year university and liberal arts college
- Commuter campus in very large city
- 4,873 degree-seeking undergraduates: 14% part-time, 71% women, 31% African American, 15% Asian American, 11% Hispanic American, 1% international
- 3,305 degree-seeking graduate students
- 73% of applicants admitted

**General.** Founded in 1926. Regionally accredited. **Degrees:** 590 bachelor's, 34 associate awarded; master's, doctoral, professional offered. **ROTC:** Army. **Calendar:** Semester, extensive summer session. **Full-time faculty:** 304 total; 52% women. **Part-time faculty:** 414 total.

**Freshman class profile.** 4,543 applied, 3,329 admitted, 1,042 enrolled.

| Mid 50% test scores | | | |
|---|---|---|---|
| SAT critical reading: | 400-500 | Rank in top quarter: | 33% |
| SAT math: | 400-560 | Rank in top tenth: | 12% |
| ACT composite: | 17-23 | Return as sophomores: | 60% |
| GPA 3.75 or higher: | 12% | Out-of-state: | 21% |
| GPA 3.50-3.74: | 12% | Live on campus: | 25% |
| GPA 3.0-3.49: | 19% | International: | 1% |
| GPA 2.0-2.99: | 42% | | |

**Basis for selection.** Rigor of secondary school record, class rank, academic GPA, recommendations, test scores, essay considered. ACT or SAT required for admission to computer science, molecular biology, nursing, pharmacy, pre-athletic training, pre-occupational therapy, and pre-physician assistant majors. Interview, audition, and/or personal statement may be required for particular programs.

**High school preparation.** College-preparatory program recommended. 16 units recommended. Recommended units include English 4, mathematics 2, social studies 3 and academic electives 4. Academic electives include any electives from fields of foreign languages, social studies, mathematics or natural science. Other electives include 3 credits of any studies except physical education and military science that lead to graduation from accredited high school.

**2009-2010 Annual costs.** Tuition/fees: $28,730. Room/board: $10,450.

**Application procedures. Admission:** Priority date 6/1; no deadline. $30 fee, may be waived for applicants with need. Admission notification on a rolling basis. Some programs have February 1 application deadline. **Financial aid:** Priority date 3/15, closing date 5/1. FAFSA required. Applicants notified on a rolling basis.

**Academics. Special study options:** Accelerated study, combined bachelor's/graduate degree, cooperative education, double major, ESL, honors, independent study, internships, student-designed major, study abroad, teacher certification program, United Nations semester. **Credit/placement by examination:** AP, CLEP, IB, institutional tests. **Support services:** Learning center, pre-admission summer program, reduced course load, remedial instruction, study skills assistance, tutoring, writing center.

**Majors. Biology:** General, biochemistry, molecular. **Business:** Accounting, business admin, finance, sales/distribution. **Communications:** General, journalism. **Computer sciences:** General. **Education:** Art, biology, chemistry, elementary, English, mathematics, music, physical, secondary, Spanish, speech impaired. **Foreign languages:** General. **Health:** Audiology/speech pathology, clinical lab science, cytotechnology, nuclear medical technology, nursing (RN), physician assistant, respiratory therapy assistant. **History:** General. **Liberal arts:** Arts/sciences, humanities. **Math:** General. **Parks/recreation:** Exercise sciences. **Philosophy/religion:** Philosophy. **Physical sciences:** Chemistry. **Psychology:** General. **Public administration:** Social work. **Social sciences:** General, economics, political science, sociology. **Visual/performing arts:** General, commercial/advertising art, dance, jazz, music performance, studio arts.

**Most popular majors.** Biology 6%, business/marketing 14%, health sciences 47%.

**Computing on campus.** 600 workstations in dormitories, library, computer center, student center. Dormitories wired for high-speed internet access and linked to campus network. Commuter students can connect to campus network. Repair service, wireless network available.

**Student life. Freshman orientation:** Available. Preregistration for classes offered. **Housing:** Coed dorms, special housing for disabled available. $150 deposit. **Activities:** Jazz band, choral groups, dance, drama, literary magazine, music ensembles, musical theater, radio station, student government, student newspaper, TV station, American Pharmacists Association, Hillel Jewish students organization, student activities board, Society of Health Systems Pharmacists.

**Athletics.** NCAA. **Intercollegiate:** Baseball M, basketball, cross-country, golf, lacrosse W, soccer, softball W, tennis W, track and field, volleyball W. **Team name:** Blackbirds.

**Student services.** Chaplain/spiritual director, career counseling, student employment services, financial aid counseling, health services, personal counseling, placement for graduates. **Physically disabled:** Services for visually, speech, hearing impaired.

**Contact.** E-mail: admissions@brooklyn.liu.edu
Phone: (718) 488-1011 Toll-free number: (800) 548-7526
Fax: (718) 797-2399
Elizabeth Storinge, Dean of Admissions, Long Island University: Brooklyn Campus, 1 University Plaza, Brooklyn, NY 11201-8423

---

## Long Island University: C. W. Post Campus

**Brookville, New York**      **CB member**
**www.liu.edu**      **CB code: 2070**

- Private 4-year university and liberal arts college
- Commuter campus in small town
- 4,558 degree-seeking undergraduates: 11% part-time, 60% women, 9% African American, 4% Asian American, 8% Hispanic American, 6% international
- 3,274 degree-seeking graduate students
- 82% of applicants admitted
- SAT or ACT (ACT writing optional), application essay required
- 42% graduate within 6 years

**General.** Founded in 1954. Regionally accredited. **Degrees:** 960 bachelor's, 2 associate awarded; master's, doctoral, professional offered. **ROTC:** Army. **Location:** 25 miles from New York City. **Calendar:** Semester, extensive summer session. **Full-time faculty:** 324 total; 45% women. **Part-time faculty:** 565 total. **Special facilities:** Tilles center for the performing arts.

**Freshman class profile.** 4,923 applied, 4,052 admitted, 855 enrolled.

| Mid 50% test scores | | GPA 2.0-2.99: | 51% |
|---|---|---|---|
| SAT critical reading: | 440-530 | Rank in top quarter: | 25% |
| SAT math: | 440-550 | Rank in top tenth: | 10% |
| ACT composite: | 19-23 | Return as sophomores: | 68% |
| GPA 3.75 or higher: | 9% | Out-of-state: | 13% |
| GPA 3.50-3.74: | 12% | Live on campus: | 57% |
| GPA 3.0-3.49: | 25% | International: | 4% |

**Basis for selection.** Rigor of secondary school record, class rank, GPA, recommendations, test scores, essay considered. Audition required for dance, music, and theater programs; interview recommended for communication arts, dance, and theater/film programs; portfolio required for art programs.

**High school preparation.** 16 units recommended. Recommended units include English 4, mathematics 3, social studies 4, science 3 (laboratory 3) and foreign language 2.

**2009-2010 Annual costs.** Tuition/fees: $28,768. Room/board: $10,942. Books/supplies: $675.

**Application procedures. Admission:** Priority date 3/1; no deadline. $30 fee, may be waived for applicants with need. Admission notification on a rolling basis. **Financial aid:** Priority date 3/1; no closing date. FAFSA required. Applicants notified on a rolling basis starting 3/1; must reply by 5/1.

**Academics. Special study options:** Accelerated study, combined bachelor's/graduate degree, cooperative education, cross-registration, double major, dual enrollment of high school students, ESL, honors, independent study, internships, student-designed major, study abroad, teacher certification program, United Nations semester, Washington semester, weekend college. **Credit/placement by examination:** AP, CLEP, IB, institutional tests. **Support services:** Learning center, pre-admission summer program, reduced course load, remedial instruction, study skills assistance, tutoring, writing center.

**Majors. Area/ethnic studies:** American. **Biology:** General, cell/histology. **Business:** Accounting, business admin, finance. **Communications:** Advertising, journalism, public relations. **Communications technology:** Radio/tv. **Computer sciences:** Computer science, information systems, information technology. **Conservation:** Environmental science. **Education:** Art, biology, chemistry, elementary, English, foreign languages, French, health, kindergarten/preschool, mathematics, music, physical, social studies, Spanish. **Foreign languages:** General, French, Italian, Spanish. **Health:** Art therapy, audiology/speech pathology, clinical lab science, cytotechnology, facilities admin, medical radiology technology/radiation therapy, medical records admin, nursing (RN), prepharmacy. **History:** General. **Interdisciplinary:** Nutrition sciences. **Liberal arts:** Arts/sciences. **Math:** General, applied. **Philosophy/religion:** Philosophy. **Physical sciences:** Chemistry, geology, physics. **Protective services:** Forensics, law enforcement admin. **Psychology:** General. **Public administration:** General, social work. **Social sciences:** Economics, geography, international relations, political science, sociology. **Visual/performing arts:** Art history/conservation, arts management, cinematography, commercial/advertising art, dance, digital art, dramatic, multimedia, music performance, photography, studio arts. **Other:** Earth science education.

**Most popular majors.** Business/marketing 20%, education 19%, health sciences 12%, psychology 6%, security/protective services 7%, social sciences 6%, visual/performing arts 13%.

**Computing on campus.** Dormitories wired for high-speed internet access and linked to campus network. Commuter students can connect to campus network. Repair service, wireless network available.

**Student life. Freshman orientation:** Available, $120 fee. Preregistration for classes offered. 2-day sessions for freshmen held in July and August prior to start of fall classes. **Housing:** Guaranteed on-campus for freshmen. Coed dorms, single-sex dorms available. $300 deposit, deadline 5/1. 24-hour intensified study housing available. **Activities:** Bands, choral groups, dance, drama, film society, literary magazine, music ensembles, musical theater, radio station, student government, student newspaper, TV station, association for campus programming, African People's Organization, resident student association, Newman club.

**Athletics.** NCAA. **Intercollegiate:** Baseball M, basketball, cross-country, field hockey W, football (tackle) M, lacrosse, soccer, softball W, swimming W, tennis W, volleyball W. **Team name:** Pioneers.

**Student services.** Adult student services, alcohol/substance abuse counseling, chaplain/spiritual director, career counseling, student employment services, financial aid counseling, health services, personal counseling, placement for graduates, veterans' counselor. **Physically disabled:** Services for visually, speech, hearing impaired. **Learning disabled:** Comprehensive services available.

**Contact.** E-mail: enroll@cwpost.liu.edu
Phone: (516) 299-2900 Toll-free number: (800) 548-7526
Fax: (516) 299-2137
Joanne Graziano, Admissions Director, Long Island University: C. W. Post Campus, 720 Northern Boulevard, Brookville, NY 11548-1300.

---

## Machzikei Hadath Rabbinical College

**Brooklyn, New York**

**CB code: 0726**

- Private 5-year rabbinical and seminary college for men affiliated with Jewish faith
- Commuter campus in very large city
- 116 degree-seeking undergraduates
- Interview required

**General.** Founded in 1956. Accredited by AARTS. First Talmudic degree and ordination available. **Degrees:** 18 bachelor's awarded. **Calendar:** Semester. **Full-time faculty:** 8 total. **Part-time faculty:** 3 total.

**Basis for selection.** Interview most important. Essay recommended.

**2009-2010 Annual costs.** Tuition/fees: $7,350.

**Application procedures. Admission:** Priority date 6/1; deadline 7/1. $150 fee, may be waived for applicants with need. Admission notification on a rolling basis. **Financial aid:** No deadline. Applicants notified on a rolling basis.

**Academics. Special study options:** Independent study, study abroad. **Credit/placement by examination:** CLEP. **Support services:** Pre-admission summer program, remedial instruction.

**Majors. Theology:** Talmudic.

**Student life. Policies:** Religious observance required.

**Contact.** Phone: (718) 854-8777 ext. 23 Fax: (718) 851-1265
Rabbi A.M. Leizerowitz, Director of Admissions, Machzikei Hadath
Rabbinical College, 5407 16th Avenue, Brooklyn, NY 11204

## Manhattan College
Riverdale, New York                                    CB member
www.manhattan.edu                                      CB code: 2395

- Private 4-year engineering and liberal arts college affiliated with
  Roman Catholic Church
- Residential campus in very large city
- 3,049 degree-seeking undergraduates: 3% part-time, 47% women
- 413 degree-seeking graduate students
- 65% of applicants admitted
- SAT or ACT with writing required

**General.** Founded in 1853. Regionally accredited. Independent institution
in the Roman Catholic tradition sponsored by De La Salle Christian Brothers. **Degrees:** 723 bachelor's awarded; master's offered. **ROTC:** Army, Air
Force. **Location:** 10 miles from midtown Manhattan. **Calendar:** Semester,
extensive summer session. **Full-time faculty:** 191 total; 96% have terminal
degrees, 15% minority, 36% women. **Part-time faculty:** 180 total; 38%
have terminal degrees, 38% women. **Class size:** 45% < 20, 54% 20-39, 1%
40-49. **Special facilities:** Plant morphogenesis laboratory.

**Freshman class profile.** 5,055 applied, 3,300 admitted, 693 enrolled.

| Mid 50% test scores | | | |
|---|---|---|---|
| SAT critical reading: | 500-590 | Rank in top quarter: | 59% |
| SAT math: | 510-620 | Rank in top tenth: | 21% |
| ACT composite: | 22-26 | End year in good standing: | 96% |
| GPA 3.75 or higher: | 25% | Out-of-state: | 33% |
| GPA 3.50-3.74: | 15% | Live on campus: | 80% |
| GPA 3.0-3.49: | 40% | Fraternities: | 1% |
| GPA 2.0-2.99: | 20% | Sororities: | 1% |

**Basis for selection.** School achievement record and test scores most
important. Essay, recommendations, and extracurricular activities also reviewed. Interview recommended. **Homeschooled:** State high school equivalency certificate, letter of recommendation (nonparent) required.

**High school preparation.** College-preparatory program recommended.
16 units required; 17 recommended. Required and recommended units include English 4, mathematics 3-4, social studies 3, science 2-3, foreign
language 2-3 and academic electives 2. 4 mathematics, 4 science (including
precalculus, chemistry, and physics) recommended of engineering majors
and most science majors.

**2009-2010 Annual costs.** Tuition/fees: $26,000. Program fees range from
$1,700 to $2,700 depending on program. Room/board: $10,160. Books/
supplies: $750. Personal expenses: $1,000.

**2009-2010 Financial aid.** All financial aid based on need.

**Application procedures. Admission:** Priority date 3/1; no deadline. $60
fee, may be waived for applicants with need. Admission notification on a
rolling basis beginning on or about 12/15. **Financial aid:** Priority date 3/1,
closing date 4/1. FAFSA required. Applicants notified on a rolling basis
starting 2/15; must reply by 5/1.

**Academics. Special study options:** Accelerated study, combined bachelor's/
graduate degree, cooperative education, cross-registration, distance learning, double major, ESL, exchange student, honors, independent study, internships, liberal arts/career combination, student-designed major, study abroad,
teacher certification program, Washington semester. **Credit/placement by
examination:** AP, CLEP, institutional tests. 30 credit hours maximum toward bachelor's degree. **Support services:** Learning center, reduced course
load, remedial instruction, study skills assistance, tutoring, writing center.

**Majors. Biology:** General, biochemistry. **Business:** General, accounting,
finance, international, management information systems, managerial economics, statistics. **Communications:** General, broadcast journalism, journalism. **Computer sciences:** General, computer science, information systems. **Education:** General, biology, chemistry, computer, early childhood,
elementary, English, foreign languages, French, health, history, mathematics, middle, physical, physics, science, secondary, social science, social studies, Spanish, special. **Engineering:** Chemical, civil, computer, electrical,
mechanical. **Foreign languages:** French, Spanish. **Health:** Nuclear medical
technology, predental, premedicine, preveterinary. **History:** General. **Interdisciplinary:** Peace/conflict. **Legal studies:** Prelaw. **Math:** General. **Phi-
losophy/religion:** Philosophy, religion. **Physical sciences:** Chemistry, physics. **Psychology:** General. **Social sciences:** Economics, sociology.

**Most popular majors.** Business/marketing 32%, communications/
journalism 9%, education 17%, engineering/engineering technologies 19%.

**Computing on campus.** 320 workstations in library, computer center,
student center. Dormitories wired for high-speed internet access and linked
to campus network. Commuter students can connect to campus network.
Online course registration, online library, helpline, repair service available.

**Student life. Freshman orientation:** Mandatory, $165 fee. **Housing:** Guar-
anteed on-campus for all undergraduates. Coed dorms available. $700 de-
posit, deadline 5/1. **Activities:** Bands, campus ministries, choral groups,
dance, drama, international student organizations, literary magazine, music
ensembles, Model UN, musical theater, radio station, student government,
student newspaper, symphony orchestra, TV station, African American club,
Caribbean society, Chinese student association, Circle-K, Gaelic society,
Young Conservatives, Democrats, Republicans, multicultural student union.

**Athletics.** NCAA. **Intercollegiate:** Baseball M, basketball, cheerleading,
cross-country, golf M, lacrosse, soccer, softball W, swimming W, tennis,
track and field, volleyball W. **Intramural:** Baseball M, basketball, cross-
country, soccer, softball, track and field, volleyball. **Team name:** Jaspers.

**Student services.** Alcohol/substance abuse counseling, chaplain/
spiritual director, career counseling, student employment services, financial
aid counseling, health services, personal counseling, placement for graduates, veterans' counselor. **Physically disabled:** Services for visually, hearing impaired.

**Contact.** E-mail: admit@manhattan.edu
Phone: (718) 862-7200 Toll-free number: (800) 622-9235
Fax: (718) 862-8019
William Bissett, Vice President for Enrollment Management, Manhattan
College, 4513 Manhattan College Parkway, Riverdale, NY 10471

## Manhattan School of Music
New York, New York
www.msmnyc.edu                                         CB code: 2396

- Private 4-year music college
- Residential campus in very large city
- 392 degree-seeking undergraduates: 1% part-time, 48% women, 3%
  African American, 10% Asian American, 5% Hispanic American, 27%
  international
- 538 degree-seeking graduate students
- 35% of applicants admitted
- Application essay required
- 62% graduate within 6 years

**General.** Founded in 1917. Regionally accredited. Extensive performance
opportunities on campus and off. **Degrees:** 87 bachelor's awarded; master's, doctoral offered. **Calendar:** Semester. **Full-time faculty:** 71 total;
75% have terminal degrees, 8% minority, 32% women. **Part-time faculty:**
301 total; 11% have terminal degrees, 17% minority, 41% women. **Class
size:** 81% < 20, 16% 20-39, 1% 50-99, 2% >100. **Special facilities:** 850-
seat concert hall, recital halls, state-of-the art-performance spaces, distance
learning center, electronic music studios, recording studio, performance library.

**Freshman class profile.** 990 applied, 345 admitted, 80 enrolled.

| GPA | | | |
|---|---|---|---|
| GPA 3.75 or higher: | 42% | Return as sophomores: | 84% |
| GPA 3.50-3.74: | 24% | Out-of-state: | 58% |
| GPA 3.0-3.49: | 24% | Live on campus: | 76% |
| GPA 2.0-2.99: | 8% | International: | 23% |

**Basis for selection.** Audition, availability of space in specific performance area, and academic record most important. Audition required. **Homeschooled:** Statement describing homeschool structure and mission, transcript of courses and grades, letter of recommendation (nonparent) required.
GED accepted, but if no GED, SAT or ACT required.

**High school preparation.** College-preparatory program recommended.
Recommended units include English 4, mathematics 3, social studies 4,
history 4, science 3 and foreign language 4. Extensive music training required.

**2009-2010 Annual costs.** Tuition/fees: $31,900. Health fees approxi-
mately $2,300 additional unless already insured. Room/board: $14,280. Books/
supplies: $1,000. Personal expenses: $1,600.

**2008-2009 Financial aid. Need-based:** 64 full-time freshmen applied
for aid; 51 were judged to have need; 51 of these received aid. Average
need met was 36%. Average scholarship/grant was $12,572; average loan
$3,873. 58% of total undergraduate aid awarded as scholarships/grants, 42%

as loans/jobs. **Non-need-based:** Awarded to 113 full-time undergraduates, including 35 freshmen. Scholarships awarded for academics, alumni affiliation, leadership, music/drama.

**Application procedures. Admission:** Closing date 12/1 (receipt date). $100 fee, may be waived for applicants with need. Application must be submitted online. Admission notification 4/1. Must reply by May 1 or within 2 week(s) if notified thereafter. **Financial aid:** Closing date 3/1. FAFSA, institutional form, CSS PROFILE required. Applicants notified by 4/1; must reply by 5/1 or within 2 week(s) of notification.

**Academics. Special study options:** Cross-registration, ESL, independent study, study abroad. **Credit/placement by examination:** CLEP, institutional tests. 60 credit hours maximum toward bachelor's degree. **Support services:** Reduced course load, remedial instruction, tutoring.

**Majors. Visual/performing arts:** Music performance, music theory/composition.

**Computing on campus.** 20 workstations in library, computer center. Dormitories wired for high-speed internet access and linked to campus network. Online library, helpline, wireless network available.

**Student life. Freshman orientation:** Mandatory. Preregistration for classes offered. 1-2 weeks before classes start. Placement exams, orchestra and opera auditions held. **Policies:** Undergraduates required to live in residence hall for first 2 years. Alcohol allowed only for those over 21 and only in designated areas. No smoking in the building. **Housing:** Guaranteed on-campus for freshmen. Coed dorms available. $500 nonrefundable deposit, deadline 6/15. Housing guaranteed only to students who submit documents and pay deposit by set deadline. **Activities:** Bands, choral groups, international student organizations, music ensembles, musical theater, opera, student government, student newspaper, symphony orchestra, Pan-African student union, international student organization, resident community council, student council, GLBT student group, chess club, soccer club.

**Student services.** Career counseling, student employment services, financial aid counseling, personal counseling. **Physically disabled:** Services for visually impaired.

**Contact.** E-mail: admission@msmnyc.edu
Phone: (212) 749-2802 ext. 4436 Fax: (212) 749-3025
Amy Anderson, Associate Dean for Enrollment Management, Manhattan School of Music, 120 Claremont Avenue, New York, NY 10027-4698

## Manhattanville College
**Purchase, New York**
www.manhattanville.edu
**CB member**
**CB code: 2397**

- Private 4-year liberal arts and teachers college
- Residential campus in small town
- 1,781 degree-seeking undergraduates: 4% part-time, 65% women, 8% African American, 2% Asian American, 16% Hispanic American, 13% international
- 661 degree-seeking graduate students
- 53% of applicants admitted
- Application essay required
- 58% graduate within 6 years

**General.** Founded in 1841. Regionally accredited. Strong relationship with United Nations. **Degrees:** 345 bachelor's awarded; master's offered. **Location:** 25 miles from New York City. **Calendar:** Semester, extensive summer session. **Full-time faculty:** 100 total; 100% have terminal degrees, 13% minority, 52% women. **Part-time faculty:** 166 total; 98% have terminal degrees, 12% minority, 51% women. **Class size:** 73% < 20, 25% 20-39, 2% 40-49. **Special facilities:** Photography laboratory, observatory, environmental biology laboratory, TV production studio, blackbox theater.

**Freshman class profile.** 4,502 applied, 2,370 admitted, 568 enrolled.

| Mid 50% test scores | | GPA 2.0-2.99: | 43% |
|---|---|---|---|
| SAT critical reading: | 520-640 | Rank in top quarter: | 47% |
| SAT math: | 510-610 | Rank in top tenth: | 22% |
| ACT composite: | 22-26 | Return as sophomores: | 75% |
| GPA 3.75 or higher: | 9% | Out-of-state: | 45% |
| GPA 3.50-3.74: | 12% | Live on campus: | 85% |
| GPA 3.0-3.49: | 36% | International: | 13% |

**Basis for selection.** School achievement record, recommendations, test scores or samples of academic work most important. Essay, school and community activities. Interview strongly recommended. Portfolio required for fine arts program; audition recommended for dance, music and theater programs.

**High school preparation.** 16 units required. Required units include English 4, mathematics 3, social studies 2, science 2 and academic electives 5.

**2010-2011 Annual costs.** Tuition/fees (projected): $34,350. Room/board: $13,500. Books/supplies: $800. Personal expenses: $1,550.

**2008-2009 Financial aid. Need-based:** 377 full-time freshmen applied for aid; 346 were judged to have need; 346 of these received aid. Average need met was 99%. Average scholarship/grant was $18,740; average loan $3,927. 63% of total undergraduate aid awarded as scholarships/grants, 37% as loans/jobs. **Non-need-based:** Awarded to 1,348 full-time undergraduates, including 380 freshmen. Scholarships awarded for academics, alumni affiliation, art, leadership, music/drama. **Additional information:** Upper level students may earn additional money and academic credit through internship program.

**Application procedures. Admission:** Closing date 3/1 (postmark date). $70 fee, may be waived for applicants with need. Admission notification on a rolling basis beginning on or about 1/2. Must reply by May 1 or within 2 week(s) if notified thereafter. **Financial aid:** Closing date 3/1. FAFSA required. Applicants notified on a rolling basis starting 2/1; must reply by 5/1 or within 2 week(s) of notification.

**Academics.** Students must complete portfolio before graduation, which is individualized academic plan and profile. **Special study options:** Accelerated study, combined bachelor's/graduate degree, cooperative education, cross-registration, distance learning, double major, dual enrollment of high school students, ESL, exchange student, external degree, honors, independent study, internships, liberal arts/career combination, student-designed major, study abroad, teacher certification program, weekend college. Study abroad programs in Oxford, Paris, Tokyo, Osaka, Madrid, Seville, Florence, Rome, Berlin, Galway and the world capitals program in Jerusalem, Santiago, Brussels, Buenos Aires, Prague, Moscow, and South Africa. **Credit/placement by examination:** AP, CLEP, IB, institutional tests. Up to 60 transfer credits allowed: up to 30 AP credits, up to 18 IB credits, no CLEP limit. **Support services:** Learning center, reduced course load, remedial instruction, study skills assistance, tutoring, writing center.

**Majors. Area/ethnic studies:** American, Asian, French. **Biology:** General, biochemistry. **Business:** Business admin, finance. **Communications:** General. **Computer sciences:** General. **Education:** General. **Foreign languages:** Romance. **History:** General. **Interdisciplinary:** Neuroscience. **Liberal arts:** Arts/sciences. **Math:** General. **Philosophy/religion:** Philosophy, religion. **Physical sciences:** Chemistry, physics. **Psychology:** General. **Social sciences:** Economics, political science, sociology. **Visual/performing arts:** Art history/conservation, dance, dramatic.

**Most popular majors.** Business/marketing 22%, communications/journalism 11%, English 8%, history 8%, psychology 11%, social sciences 13%, visual/performing arts 13%.

**Computing on campus.** 270 workstations in dormitories, library, computer center, student center. Dormitories wired for high-speed internet access and linked to campus network. Commuter students can connect to campus network. Online course registration, online library, helpline, repair service, student web hosting, wireless network available.

**Student life. Freshman orientation:** Mandatory. Preregistration for classes offered. **Housing:** Coed dorms, wellness housing available. $385 deposit, deadline 5/1. **Activities:** Bands, campus ministries, choral groups, dance, drama, film society, international student organizations, literary magazine, music ensembles, Model UN, musical theater, opera, radio station, student government, student newspaper, symphony orchestra, TV station, language and culture clubs, Students Organized Against Racism, women's resource center, gay/straight coalition, political science association, multicultural advisory board, Black student union.

**Athletics.** NCAA. **Intercollegiate:** Baseball M, basketball, cheerleading M, field hockey W, golf M, ice hockey, lacrosse, soccer, softball W, tennis. **Intramural:** Basketball. **Team name:** Valiants.

**Student services.** Adult student services, alcohol/substance abuse counseling, chaplain/spiritual director, career counseling, services for economically disadvantaged, student employment services, financial aid counseling, health services, minority student services, personal counseling, placement for graduates, women's services. **Physically disabled:** Services for visually, speech, hearing impaired. **Learning disabled:** Comprehensive services available.

**Contact.** E-mail: admissions@mville.edu
Phone: (914) 323-5464 Toll-free number: (800) 328-4553
Fax: (914) 694-1732
Erica Padilla, Director of Admissions, Manhattanville College, 2900 Purchase Street, Purchase, NY 10577

## Mannes College The New School for Music
**New York, New York**
www.mannes.edu                                    CB code: 2398

- Private 4-year music college
- Commuter campus in very large city
- 207 degree-seeking undergraduates: 8% part-time, 57% women, 4% African American, 11% Asian American, 3% Hispanic American, 39% international
- 174 degree-seeking graduate students
- 35% of applicants admitted
- 67% graduate within 6 years

**General.** Founded in 1916. Regionally accredited. Division of The New School. **Degrees:** 21 bachelor's awarded; master's offered. **Location:** Located in Manhattan. **Calendar:** Semester, limited summer session. **Full-time faculty:** 6 total; 17% have terminal degrees, 17% women. **Part-time faculty:** 138 total; 13% minority, 38% women. **Class size:** 99% < 20, less than 1% 20-39, less than 1% 40-49, less than 1% 50-99. **Special facilities:** 2 concert halls.

**Freshman class profile.** 442 applied, 153 admitted, 52 enrolled.

| | | | |
|---|---|---|---|
| GPA 3.75 or higher: | 28% | Return as sophomores: | 86% |
| GPA 3.50-3.74: | 20% | Out-of-state: | 56% |
| GPA 3.0-3.49: | 40% | Live on campus: | 37% |
| GPA 2.0-2.99: | 12% | International: | 46% |
| End year in good standing: | 100% | | |

**Basis for selection.** In order of importance: specific talent for major as evidenced by audition in major instrument or evaluation of previous accomplishment for composers and theory majors, general musicianship skills (ear, theory, etc.), academic record. Institutionally designed entrance examination, including major audition. Written examinations in music theory, dictation, ear training, and English usage. Audition required, essay recommended. Placement exams and interviews required for all Bachelor of Music, Bachelor of Science, Undergraduate Diploma, and Master of Music applicants. If applicant does not complete all sessions, application incomplete and will not be considered for acceptance. Tapes may be submitted for advisory opinion.

**High school preparation.** Required and recommended units include English 4, mathematics 4, social studies 2, science 4 (laboratory 2) and foreign language 2.

**2009-2010 Annual costs.** Tuition/fees: $33,600. Room/board: $15,260. Books/supplies: $1,475. Personal expenses: $1,550.

**2009-2010 Financial aid. Need-based:** 13 full-time freshmen applied for aid; 11 were judged to have need; 11 of these received aid. Average need met was 54%. Average scholarship/grant was $12,079; average loan $10,636. 61% of total undergraduate aid awarded as scholarships/grants, 39% as loans/jobs. **Non-need-based:** Awarded to 15 full-time undergraduates, including 3 freshmen. Scholarships awarded for music/drama. **Additional information:** Closing date for scholarship applications 2 weeks prior to audition date.

**Application procedures. Admission:** Closing date 12/1 (postmark date). $100 fee. Admission notification on a rolling basis beginning on or about 4/1. Must reply by May 1 or within 3 week(s) if notified thereafter. **Financial aid:** Priority date 3/1; no closing date. FAFSA required. Applicants notified on a rolling basis starting 3/1; must reply within 4 week(s) of notification.

**Academics. Special study options:** Accelerated study, double major, ESL, independent study, internships. **Credit/placement by examination:** CLEP, institutional tests. **Support services:** Remedial instruction, tutoring, writing center.

**Majors. Visual/performing arts:** Conducting, music performance, music theory/composition, piano/organ, stringed instruments, studio arts, voice/opera.

**Computing on campus.** 15 workstations in library, computer center. Dormitories wired for high-speed internet access and linked to campus network. Commuter students can connect to campus network. Online course registration, helpline, student web hosting, wireless network available.

**Student life. Freshman orientation:** Mandatory. **Housing:** Guaranteed on-campus for all undergraduates. Coed dorms, special housing for disabled, apartments available. $250 nonrefundable deposit, deadline 7/1. **Activities:** Jazz band, choral groups, dance, drama, international student organizations, literary magazine, music ensembles, opera, radio station, student

government, student newspaper, symphony orchestra, student government group, Students for a Democratic Society, various international clubs, sketch comedy group, theatre collective, student sustainability committee, Out, Proud Environment at The New School (OPEN), Adventure Force, Women of Color, The New Tunes.

**Student services.** Career counseling, student employment services, financial aid counseling, health services, personal counseling. **Learning disabled:** Comprehensive services available.

**Contact.** E-mail: mannesadmissions@newschool.edu
Phone: (212) 580-0210 ext. 4862 Toll-free number: (800) 292-3040
Fax: (212) 580-1738
Georgia Schmitt, Director of Admissions, Mannes College The New School for Music, 150 West 85th Street, New York, NY 10024

## Marist College
**Poughkeepsie, New York**                         CB member
www.marist.edu                                     CB code: 2400

- Private 4-year liberal arts college
- Residential campus in small city
- 4,837 degree-seeking undergraduates: 6% part-time, 58% women, 3% African American, 2% Asian American, 6% Hispanic American
- 840 degree-seeking graduate students
- 36% of applicants admitted
- SAT or ACT with writing, application essay required
- 83% graduate within 6 years

**General.** Founded in 1929. Regionally accredited. Substantial internship opportunities for all majors. Students participate in community service program. **Degrees:** 1,077 bachelor's awarded; master's offered. **ROTC:** Army. **Location:** 75 miles from New York City, 75 miles from Albany. **Calendar:** Semester, limited summer session. **Full-time faculty:** 220 total; 75% have terminal degrees, 10% minority, 44% women. **Part-time faculty:** 377 total; 7% minority, 47% women. **Class size:** 50% < 20, 50% 20-39, less than 1% 40-49. **Special facilities:** Bureau of economic research, laboratory for environmental studies, management studies center, institute for public opinion, on-campus arboretum, online journalism laboratory.

**Freshman class profile.** 10,004 applied, 3,601 admitted, 1,041 enrolled.

| Mid 50% test scores | | | |
|---|---|---|---|
| SAT critical reading: | 520-620 | GPA 2.0-2.99: | 22% |
| SAT math: | 540-640 | Rank in top quarter: | 70% |
| SAT writing: | 530-640 | Rank in top tenth: | 27% |
| ACT composite: | 23-28 | Return as sophomores: | 88% |
| GPA 3.75 or higher: | 17% | Out-of-state: | 52% |
| GPA 3.50-3.74: | 15% | Live on campus: | 94% |
| GPA 3.0-3.49: | 45% | International: | 1% |

**Basis for selection.** Secondary school achievement record, rank in top third of class primary consideration. Test scores, recommendations, activities, personal and leadership qualities also important. Campus visits and information sessions with admission counselors strongly recommended. **Homeschooled:** Transcript of courses and grades, letter of recommendation (nonparent) required.

**High school preparation.** College-preparatory program required. 17 units required. Required and recommended units include English 4, mathematics 3-4, social studies 2, history 1, science 3-4 (laboratory 2-3), foreign language 2-3 and academic electives 2. 1 U.S. history required. 4 math recommended for computer science and physical science majors, 2 social studies required, 2 social science recommended.

**2009-2010 Annual costs.** Tuition/fees: $26,605. Room/board: $11,225.

**2009-2010 Financial aid. Need-based:** 865 full-time freshmen applied for aid; 632 were judged to have need; 632 of these received aid. Average need met was 67%. Average scholarship/grant was $12,758; average loan $5,049. 67% of total undergraduate aid awarded as scholarships/grants, 33% as loans/jobs. **Non-need-based:** Awarded to 2,709 full-time undergraduates, including 807 freshmen. Scholarships awarded for academics, athletics, music/drama, ROTC, state residency.

**Application procedures. Admission:** Closing date 2/15 (postmark date). $50 fee, may be waived for applicants with need. Admission notification 3/30. Must reply by 5/1. **Financial aid:** Priority date 2/15, closing date 5/1. FAFSA, institutional form required. Applicants notified on a rolling basis starting 3/15; must reply by 5/1 or within 2 week(s) of notification.

**Academics.** Paralegal certificates offered. **Special study options:** Accelerated study, combined bachelor's/graduate degree, cooperative education, cross-registration, distance learning, double major, dual enrollment of high school students, ESL, honors, independent study, internships, liberal arts/career combination, semester at sea, study abroad, teacher certification program, United Nations semester, Washington semester, weekend college. Undergraduates may take graduate classes. Cooperative education in arts, business, computer science, education, humanities, natural science, social/behavioral science, technologies. **Credit/placement by examination:** AP, CLEP, IB, SAT, ACT, institutional tests. ACT-PEP accepted on individual basis. **Support services:** Learning center, reduced course load, study skills assistance, tutoring, writing center.

**Majors. Area/ethnic studies:** American. **Biology:** General, biochemistry, biomedical sciences. **Business:** Accounting, business admin, fashion, finance, human resources, international, marketing. **Communications:** Advertising, journalism, media studies, public relations, radio/tv. **Computer sciences:** Computer science, game design, information systems, information technology, programming. **Conservation:** Environmental science. **Education:** Biology, chemistry, English, French, mathematics, social studies, Spanish, special. **Foreign languages:** French, Spanish. **Health:** Athletic training, clinical lab science. **History:** General. **Math:** General, applied, computational. **Philosophy/religion:** Philosophy. **Physical sciences:** Chemistry. **Protective services:** Law enforcement admin. **Psychology:** General. **Public administration:** Social work. **Social sciences:** Economics, political science. **Visual/performing arts:** Art, art history/conservation, fashion design, studio arts. **Other:** Environmental policy, Theater.

**Most popular majors.** Business/marketing 30%, communications/journalism 20%, education 13%, psychology 6%.

**Computing on campus.** 646 workstations in dormitories, library, computer center, student center. Dormitories wired for high-speed internet access and linked to campus network. Commuter students can connect to campus network. Online course registration, online library, helpline, repair service, student web hosting, wireless network available.

**Student life. Freshman orientation:** Mandatory, $90 fee. 1-day orientation in June. **Housing:** Guaranteed on-campus for freshmen. Coed dorms, special housing for disabled, apartments, wellness housing available. $500 nonrefundable deposit, deadline 5/1. Garden apartments, townhouses, suites available. **Activities:** Bands, campus ministries, choral groups, dance, drama, film society, literary magazine, music ensembles, musical theater, radio station, student government, student newspaper, TV station, black student union, Asian Alliance, Circle K, ARCO, community service programs, Habitat for Humanity, political science club, council on theatre arts, social action clubs.

**Athletics.** NCAA. **Intercollegiate:** Baseball M, basketball, cross-country, diving, football (tackle) M, lacrosse, rowing (crew), soccer, softball W, swimming, tennis, track and field, volleyball W, water polo W. **Intramural:** Basketball, soccer, softball, volleyball. **Team name:** Red Foxes.

**Student services.** Adult student services, alcohol/substance abuse counseling, chaplain/spiritual director, career counseling, student employment services, financial aid counseling, health services, personal counseling, placement for graduates, veterans' counselor. **Physically disabled:** Services for visually, hearing impaired. **Learning disabled:** Comprehensive services available.

**Contact.** E-mail: admission@marist.edu
Phone: (845) 575-3226 Toll-free number: (800) 436-5483
Fax: (845) 575-3215
Kent Rinehart, Dean of Undergraduate Admission, Marist College, 3399 North Road, Poughkeepsie, NY 12601-1387

## Marymount Manhattan College

**New York, New York**     **CB member**
**www.mmm.edu**     **CB code: 2405**

- Private 4-year liberal arts college
- Residential campus in very large city
- 1,979 degree-seeking undergraduates: 13% part-time, 76% women, 12% African American, 3% Asian American, 14% Hispanic American, 3% international
- 70% of applicants admitted
- SAT or ACT (ACT writing optional), application essay required
- 49% graduate within 6 years

**General.** Founded in 1936. Regionally accredited. **Degrees:** 338 bachelor's, 5 associate awarded. **Calendar:** Semester, limited summer session. **Full-time faculty:** 96 total; 91% have terminal degrees, 12% minority, 57% women. **Part-time faculty:** 214 total; 18% have terminal degrees, 14% minority, 45% women. **Class size:** 69% <20, 31% 20-39, less than 1% 40-49. **Special facilities:** Communications and learning center, communication arts multimedia suite, center for science education.

**Freshman class profile.** 3,447 applied, 2,419 admitted, 516 enrolled.

| Mid 50% test scores | | | |
|---|---|---|---|
| SAT critical reading: | 490-600 | GPA 3.0-3.49: | 44% |
| SAT math: | 460-560 | GPA 2.0-2.99: | 32% |
| SAT writing: | 490-590 | Return as sophomores: | 62% |
| ACT composite: | 22-26 | Out-of-state: | 67% |
| GPA 3.75 or higher: | 10% | Live on campus: | 77% |
| GPA 3.50-3.74: | 14% | International: | 2% |

**Basis for selection.** High school GPA of 3.0 and SAT verbal and math scores of 450 each recommended. Letters of recommendation from teachers and administrators, extracurricular and community activities important. Rolling deadline for SAT/ACT score receipt. Interview recommended for all; audition required for acting, dance, and theater programs; portfolio recommended for art program. **Homeschooled:** Transcript of courses and grades required. Must submit official high school transcripts if high school attended before withdrawing. **Learning Disabled:** Interview and Wechsler Delta Adult Intelligence Scale test required.

**High school preparation.** College-preparatory program recommended. 17 units required. Required and recommended units include English 4, mathematics 3, social studies 3, science 3 (laboratory 2), foreign language 2 and academic electives 4.

**2009-2010 Annual costs.** Tuition/fees: $22,656. Room/board: $12,874. Books/supplies: $1,000. Personal expenses: $2,400.

**2009-2010 Financial aid. Need-based:** 411 full-time freshmen applied for aid; 343 were judged to have need; 343 of these received aid. Average need met was 50%. Average scholarship/grant was $11,158; average loan $3,388. 56% of total undergraduate aid awarded as scholarships/grants, 44% as loans/jobs. **Non-need-based:** Awarded to 326 full-time undergraduates, including 90 freshmen. Scholarships awarded for academics, art, leadership, state residency. **Additional information:** Limited international scholarships for top applicants.

**Application procedures. Admission:** Priority date 3/15; no deadline. $60 fee, may be waived for applicants with need. Admission notification on a rolling basis beginning on or about 9/1. Must reply by May 1 or within 3 week(s) if notified thereafter. **Financial aid:** Priority date 3/15; no closing date. FAFSA required. Applicants notified on a rolling basis starting 3/15; must reply by 5/1 or within 2 week(s) of notification.

**Academics. Special study options:** Accelerated study, distance learning, double major, dual enrollment of high school students, exchange student, independent study, internships, liberal arts/career combination, study abroad, teacher certification program. 5-year bachelor's/master's program in computer science with Polytechnic University, programs with Laboratory Institute of Merchandising, New York School of Interior Design, Deutsches Haus at New York University, China Institute, New York Institute of Finance, American Institute of Banking, Hunter College of CUNY, Martha Graham School of Dance, HEOP. **Credit/placement by examination:** AP, CLEP, IB, SAT, institutional tests. 30 credit hours maximum toward bachelor's degree. Maximum of 12 credits for language proficiency. SAT Subject used for placement if submitted. **Support services:** Learning center, reduced course load, remedial instruction, study skills assistance, tutoring, writing center.

**Majors. Biology:** General. **Business:** Accounting, business admin. **Communications:** General. **Health:** Audiology/speech pathology. **History:** General. **Liberal arts:** Humanities. **Philosophy/religion:** Philosophy, religion. **Psychology:** General. **Social sciences:** International relations, political science, sociology. **Visual/performing arts:** Acting, art, art history/conservation, dance, dramatic, graphic design, studio arts.

**Most popular majors.** Communications/journalism 27%, psychology 7%, social sciences 12%, visual/performing arts 37%.

**Computing on campus.** 215 workstations in library, computer center, student center. Dormitories wired for high-speed internet access and linked to campus network. Commuter students can connect to campus network. Wireless network available.

**Student life. Freshman orientation:** Mandatory. Preregistration for classes offered. 3 days of introductions, information, activities, and social engagements. **Housing:** Coed dorms available. $500 nonrefundable deposit, deadline 5/1. **Activities:** Choral groups, dance, drama, international student organizations, literary magazine, musical theater, radio station, student government, student newspaper, ethnic, religious, political, women's, environmental, and cultural groups, student professional organizations, and honor societies.

**Student services.** Adult student services, alcohol/substance abuse counseling, chaplain/spiritual director, career counseling, student employment services, financial aid counseling, health services, personal counseling, placement for graduates. **Physically disabled:** Services for speech, hearing impaired. **Learning disabled:** Comprehensive services available.

**Contact.** E-mail: admissions@mmm.edu
Phone: (212) 517-0430 Toll-free number: (800) 627-9668
Fax: (212) 517-0448
Jim Rogers, Dean of Admissions, Marymount Manhattan College, 221 East 71st Street, New York, NY 10021-4597

## Medaille College
### Buffalo, New York
### www.medaille.edu
**CB code: 2422**

- Private 4-year liberal arts college
- Commuter campus in large city
- 1,750 degree-seeking undergraduates: 2% part-time, 63% women, 11% African American, 1% Hispanic American
- 1,110 degree-seeking graduate students
- 72% of applicants admitted
- SAT or ACT with writing, application essay required
- 39% graduate within 6 years; 27% enter graduate study

**General.** Founded in 1875. Regionally accredited. **Degrees:** 318 bachelor's, 94 associate awarded; master's offered. **ROTC:** Army. **Location:** 3 miles from downtown. **Calendar:** Semester, limited summer session. **Full-time faculty:** 84 total; 68% have terminal degrees, 12% minority, 48% women. **Part-time faculty:** 238 total; 22% minority, 49% women. **Class size:** 40% < 20, 58% 20-39, less than 1% 40-49, less than 1% 50-99, less than 1% >100. **Special facilities:** New media institute.

**Freshman class profile.** 1,340 applied, 965 admitted, 411 enrolled.

| Mid 50% test scores | | | |
|---|---|---|---|
| | | ACT composite: | 18-22 |
| SAT critical reading: | 400-500 | Return as sophomores: | 68% |
| SAT math: | 420-520 | Live on campus: | 51% |

**Basis for selection.** Motivation and maturity, as well as academic record and test scores, considered. SAT recommended. Interview strongly recommended.

**High school preparation.** College-preparatory program recommended. 12 units required; 20 recommended. Required and recommended units include English 4, mathematics 2-3, social studies 4, history 2, science 2-3 (laboratory 2) and foreign language 2. 3 math, 3 science recommended for veterinary technology.

**2009-2010 Annual costs.** Tuition/fees: $19,590. Tuition for students admitted in Fall 2008 is $19,140; tuition for students admitted before Fall 2008 is $18,290. Room/board: $9,288. Books/supplies: $1,100. Personal expenses: $1,100.

**2008-2009 Financial aid. Need-based:** 360 full-time freshmen applied for aid; 360 were judged to have need; 360 of these received aid. Average need met was 70%. Average scholarship/grant was $8,000; average loan $5,000. 58% of total undergraduate aid awarded as scholarships/grants, 42% as loans/jobs. **Non-need-based:** Awarded to 1,254 full-time undergraduates, including 368 freshmen. Scholarships awarded for academics, leadership.

**Application procedures. Admission:** Priority date 8/1; no deadline. $25 fee, may be waived for applicants with need, free for online applicants. Admission notification on a rolling basis beginning on or about 10/1. Must reply by May 1 or within 4 week(s) if notified thereafter. **Financial aid:** Priority date 3/1; no closing date. FAFSA required. Applicants notified on a rolling basis starting 3/1; must reply within 2 week(s) of notification.

**Academics.** All pre-professional programs require participation in at least 1 internship. Branch campuses in Amherst and Rochester. **Special study options:** Accelerated study, combined bachelor's/graduate degree, cross-registration, double major, honors, independent study, internships, liberal arts/career combination, student-designed major, teacher certification program, weekend college. Module system for full-time evening students and for full-time weekend students. **Credit/placement by examination:** AP, CLEP, IB, SAT. 30 credit hours maximum toward associate degree, 60 toward bachelor's. **Support services:** Learning center, reduced course load, remedial instruction, study skills assistance, tutoring.

**Majors. Biology:** General. **Business:** General, business admin, management information systems. **Communications:** Media studies. **Computer sciences:** General. **Education:** General, biology, elementary, English, mathematics, middle, secondary, social studies. **Family/consumer sciences:** Child care. **Health:** Veterinary technology/assistant. **Interdisciplinary:** Biopsychology. **Liberal arts:** Arts/sciences. **Math:** General. **Parks/recreation:** Sports admin. **Protective services:** Police science. **Psychology:** General. **Visual/performing arts:** General.

**Most popular majors.** Business/marketing 40%, communications/journalism 7%, education 8%, health sciences 7%, parks/recreation 12%.

**Computing on campus.** 120 workstations in dormitories, library, computer center, student center. Dormitories wired for high-speed internet access and linked to campus network. Commuter students can connect to campus network. Online library, wireless network available.

**Student life. Freshman orientation:** Mandatory. Preregistration for classes offered. **Housing:** Coed dorms, single-sex dorms, apartments, wellness housing available. $100 deposit, deadline 9/1. **Activities:** Drama, film society, literary magazine, musical theater, radio station, student government, student newspaper, TV station, African American student union, child and youth services club, student volunteer center, multicultural association, SADD, international student society, resident student council.

**Athletics.** NCAA. **Intercollegiate:** Baseball M, basketball, bowling W, cross-country, golf, lacrosse, soccer, softball W, volleyball. **Team name:** Mavericks.

**Student services.** Adult student services, career counseling, student employment services, financial aid counseling, health services, personal counseling, placement for graduates, veterans' counselor. **Physically disabled:** Services for visually, speech, hearing impaired.

**Contact.** E-mail: admissionsug@medaille.edu
Phone: (716) 880-2200 Toll-free number: (800) 292-1582
Fax: (716) 880-2007
Greg Florczak, Director of Undergraduate Admissions, Medaille College, 18 Agassiz Circle, Buffalo, NY 14214

## Medaille College: Amherst
### Williamsville, New York
### www.medaille.edu

- Private 4-year liberal arts college
- Commuter campus in small town

**General. Calendar:** Semester.

**Annual costs/financial aid.** Tuition/fees (2009-2010): $19,510.

**Contact.** Phone: (716) 631-1061
Registrar, 30 Wilson Road, Williamsville, NY 14221

## Medaille College: Rochester
### Rochester, New York
### www.medaille.edu

- Private 4-year liberal arts college
- Small city

**General. Calendar:** Semester.

**Annual costs/financial aid.** Tuition/fees (2009-2010): $19,510.

**Contact.** Phone: (585) 272-0030
Registrar, 1880 South Winton Road, Rochester, NY 14618

## Mercy College
### Dobbs Ferry, New York
### www.mercy.edu
**CB code: 2409**

- Private 4-year liberal arts college
- Commuter campus in large town
- 5,516 degree-seeking undergraduates: 26% part-time, 67% women, 27% African American, 3% Asian American, 30% Hispanic American, 1% international
- 3,427 degree-seeking graduate students
- 59% of applicants admitted

**General.** Founded in 1950. Regionally accredited. Main campus in Dobbs Ferry plus additional campus locations in Bronx, Manhattan, White Plains, and Yorktown Heights. **Degrees:** 1,071 bachelor's, 104 associate awarded; master's, doctoral offered. **ROTC:** Army, Air Force. **Location:** 22 miles from New York City. **Calendar:** Semester, extensive summer session. **Full-time faculty:** 193 total; 79% have terminal degrees, 21% minority, 56% women. **Part-time faculty:** 635 total; 25% minority, 55% women. **Class**

**size:** 70% < 20, 29% 20-39, less than 1% 40-49, less than 1% 50-99. **Special facilities:** Music and recording studios, biological research labs, Roy Disney digital arts studio.

**Freshman class profile.** 4,355 applied, 2,558 admitted, 926 enrolled.

| | | | |
|---|---|---|---|
| Return as sophomores: | 57% | **Live on campus:** | 6% |
| Out-of-state: | 7% | | |

**Basis for selection.** SAT/ACT optional. SAT or ACT, SAT Subject Tests recommended. Additional interview with Program Director required for Nursing, Occupational Therapy, Physical Therapy, Social Work, Veterinary Technology, Computer Arts programs. **Homeschooled:** State high school equivalency certificate required.

**High school preparation.** College-preparatory program required. 21 units required. Required units include English 4, mathematics 4, social studies 2, history 2, science 3 (laboratory 1), foreign language 3 and academic electives 3.

**2009-2010 Annual costs.** Tuition/fees: $16,490. Room/board: $10,812. Books/supplies: $1,320. Personal expenses: $1,580.

**2008-2009 Financial aid. Need-based:** 647 full-time freshmen applied for aid; 604 were judged to have need; 582 of these received aid. Average need met was 53%. Average scholarship/grant was $8,713; average loan $3,125. 68% of total undergraduate aid awarded as scholarships/grants, 32% as loans/jobs. **Non-need-based:** Awarded to 1,051 full-time undergraduates, including 357 freshmen. Scholarships awarded for academics, athletics.

**Application procedures. Admission:** No deadline. $40 fee, may be waived for applicants with need. Admission notification on a rolling basis beginning on or about 12/1. Must reply by May 1 or within 3 week(s) if notified thereafter. **Financial aid:** Priority date 2/15; no closing date. FAFSA required. Applicants notified on a rolling basis starting 4/1; must reply within 2 week(s) of notification.

**Academics.** Some graduate programs on trimester and quarter schedule. Programs leading to provisional state certification offered in education. **Special study options:** Accelerated study, combined bachelor's/graduate degree, cooperative education, distance learning, double major, dual enrollment of high school students, honors, independent study, internships, study abroad, teacher certification program, weekend college. Program for college students with learning disabilities. **Credit/placement by examination:** CLEP, SAT, ACT, institutional tests. 30 credit hours maximum toward associate degree, 30 toward bachelor's. **Support services:** Learning center, pre-admission summer program, reduced course load, remedial instruction, study skills assistance, tutoring, writing center.

**Honors college/program.** Minimum 90 or above high school average required. Approximately 65 freshmen admitted. Students take honors English, speech and math freshmen year and additional four academic honors courses for total of 24 credits.

**Majors. Agriculture:** Animal sciences. **Biology:** General. **Business:** Accounting, accounting/business management, business admin. **Communications:** Media studies. **Computer sciences:** General, information systems, security. **Foreign languages:** Spanish. **Health:** Audiology/speech pathology, clinical lab science, health services, nursing admin. **History:** General. **Legal studies:** General. **Liberal arts:** Arts/sciences. **Math:** General. **Protective services:** Law enforcement admin. **Psychology:** General. **Public administration:** Social work. **Social sciences:** General, political science, sociology. **Visual/performing arts:** Commercial/advertising art. **Other:** Homeland security, Music industry and technology.

**Most popular majors.** Business/marketing 23%, health sciences 16%, psychology 10%, social sciences 32%.

**Computing on campus.** 708 workstations in dormitories, library, computer center, student center. Dormitories wired for high-speed internet access and linked to campus network. Commuter students can connect to campus network. Online course registration, online library, helpline, repair service, wireless network available.

**Student life. Freshman orientation:** Available. Preregistration for classes offered. **Policies:** Student services geared to commuter population with midday activities and programs. **Housing:** Coed dorms available. $300 nonrefundable deposit, deadline 5/1. **Activities:** Campus ministries, dance, Model UN, student government, student newspaper, Reporter's Impact, Military Veterans club, Green club, Dance Off Society Showstoppers, chess club, Latin American student association, Mercy College Models, Veterinary Technology club, Italian club, Accounting Society, Creative Minds poetry club.

**Athletics.** NCAA. **Intercollegiate:** Baseball M, basketball, cross-country, lacrosse, soccer, softball W, tennis M, track and field, volleyball W. **Intramural:** Baseball M, basketball, softball. **Team name:** Mavericks.

**Student services.** Adult student services, alcohol/substance abuse counseling, career counseling, services for economically disadvantaged, student employment services, financial aid counseling, health services, minority student services, on-campus daycare, personal counseling, placement for graduates, veterans' counselor. **Physically disabled:** Services for visually, speech, hearing impaired. **Learning disabled:** Comprehensive services available.

**Contact.** E-mail: admissions@mercy.edu
Phone: (914) 674-7324 Toll-free number: (877) 637-2946
Fax: (914) 674-7608
Deirdre Whitman, Vice President for Enrollment Management, Mercy College, 555 Broadway, Dobbs Ferry, NY 10522

## Mesivta Torah Vodaath Seminary
### Brooklyn, New York
**CB code: 0636**

- Private 5-year rabbinical college for men affiliated with Jewish faith
- Very large city
- 131 degree-seeking undergraduates
- 119 graduate students
- 84% of applicants admitted

**General.** Founded in 1918. Accredited by AARTS. First Talmudic degree and ordination available. **Degrees:** 17 bachelor's awarded; doctoral offered. **ROTC:** Naval, Air Force. **Calendar:** Semester.

**Freshman class profile.** 31 applied, 26 admitted, 26 enrolled.

**Basis for selection.** Religious affiliation or commitment very important. Test scores, interview, school and community activities, recommendations, alumni relation important. School achievement record considered. Interview recommended.

**2009-2010 Annual costs.** Tuition/fees: $7,050. Room/board: $4,500.

**Application procedures. Admission:** No deadline. $200 fee.

**Academics. Special study options:** Independent study. **Credit/placement by examination:** CLEP, institutional tests. **Support services:** Tutoring.

**Majors. Theology:** Talmudic.

**Student life. Activities:** Dance.

**Student services.** Career counseling, personal counseling, placement for graduates.

**Contact.** Phone: (718) 941-8000
Aaron Braun, Director of Admissions, Mesivta Torah Vodaath Seminary, 425 East Ninth Street, Brooklyn, NY 11218

## Metropolitan College of New York
### New York, New York
### www.metropolitan.edu
**CB member**
**CB code: 4802**

- Private 4-year business and liberal arts college
- Commuter campus in very large city
- 676 degree-seeking undergraduates
- 51% of applicants admitted
- Application essay, interview required

**General.** Founded in 1964. Regionally accredited. Students attend 3-semester full year with 1-month break. Off-site extensions for human services program in the Bronx, Staten Island and northeastern Queens. Students receive credit for applying studies to jobs or internship sites. **Degrees:** 166 bachelor's, 59 associate awarded; master's offered. **Location:** In downtown Manhattan. **Calendar:** Semester, extensive summer session. **Full-time faculty:** 24 total. **Part-time faculty:** 157 total. **Class size:** 73% < 20, 27% 20-39.

**Freshman class profile.** 502 applied, 256 admitted, 121 enrolled.

**Basis for selection.** Academic record, test scores, previous volunteer experience, school and community activities, professional recommendations, motivation and communication skills as demonstrated in interviews considered. Combined SAT score of 1050 (exclusive of Writing) or higher can be substituted for institution-administered Test of Adult Basic Education or ACCUPLACER required for admission.

**High school preparation.** 16 units required. Required units include English 4, mathematics 2, social studies 2, science 1 and foreign language 4.

**2009-2010 Annual costs.** Tuition/fees: $16,750. Tuition reported is for undergraduate business program; costs for other programs may vary. Books/supplies: $1,500. Personal expenses: $726.

**2008-2009 Financial aid. Non-need-based:** Scholarships awarded for academics. **Additional information:** Limited merit scholarships.

**Application procedures. Admission:** Priority date 8/15; no deadline. $30 fee, may be waived for applicants with need. Admission notification on a rolling basis beginning on or about 3/15. **Financial aid:** Priority date 3/15; no closing date. FAFSA required. Applicants notified on a rolling basis.

**Academics.** Class work integrated with field work. Class learning applied, documented and assessed in internship or employment setting. **Special study options:** Accelerated study, cooperative education, honors, internships, liberal arts/career combination, study abroad, teacher certification program, weekend college. **Credit/placement by examination:** CLEP, IB. 32 credit hours maximum toward bachelor's degree. **Support services:** Learning center, remedial instruction, tutoring.

**Majors. Area/ethnic studies:** African-American. **Business:** General, business admin, communications, managerial economics. **Communications:** General. **Education:** General. **Legal studies:** Prelaw. **Public administration:** Community org/advocacy, human services, social work. **Social sciences:** General, sociology, urban studies.

**Most popular majors.** Business/marketing 30%, public administration/social services 70%.

**Computing on campus.** 130 workstations in library, computer center.

**Student life. Freshman orientation:** Mandatory. **Activities:** Drama, student government, student newspaper, honor societies, networking club, dance committee.

**Student services.** Adult student services, career counseling, student employment services, financial aid counseling, personal counseling, placement for graduates, veterans' counselor. **Physically disabled:** Services for visually, hearing impaired.

**Contact.** Phone: (212) 343-1234 ext. 5001 Toll-free number: (800) 338-4465 Fax: (212) 343-8470
Steven Lenhart, Vice President of Enrollment Management, Metropolitan College of New York, 431 Canal Street, New York, NY 10013-1919

## Mirrer Yeshiva Central Institute
### Brooklyn, New York
**CB code: 0661**

- Private 4-year rabbinical college for men affiliated with Jewish faith
- Very large city
- 248 degree-seeking undergraduates
- 58 graduate students

**General.** Accredited by AARTS. **Degrees:** 32 bachelor's awarded; master's, doctoral offered. **Calendar:** Continuous. **Full-time faculty:** 16 total.

**2009-2010 Annual costs.** Tuition/fees: $4,700. Room/board: $4,000.

**Application procedures. Admission:** No deadline.

**Academics. Credit/placement by examination:** CLEP.

**Majors. Theology:** Talmudic.

**Contact.** Phone: (718) 645-0536
Rabbi Pincus Hecht, Admissions Director, Mirrer Yeshiva Central Institute, 1795 Ocean Parkway, Brooklyn, NY 11223

## Molloy College
### Rockville Centre, New York
### www.molloy.edu
**CB member**
**CB code: 2415**

- Private 4-year liberal arts college affiliated with Roman Catholic Church
- Commuter campus in large town
- 2,969 degree-seeking undergraduates: 23% part-time, 78% women, 15% African American, 7% Asian American, 11% Hispanic American, 1% international
- 919 degree-seeking graduate students
- 59% of applicants admitted

- SAT or ACT with writing, application essay required
- 59% graduate within 6 years

**General.** Founded in 1955. Regionally accredited. Independent institution in Dominican tradition. **Degrees:** 576 bachelor's, 46 associate awarded; master's offered. **ROTC:** Army, Naval. **Location:** 20 miles from New York City. **Calendar:** 4-1-4, limited summer session. **Full-time faculty:** 169 total; 68% have terminal degrees, 14% minority, 73% women. **Part-time faculty:** 350 total; 67% have terminal degrees, 15% minority, 65% women. **Class size:** 64% < 20, 35% 20-39, less than 1% 40-49. **Special facilities:** Weather station at Jones Beach, international business center.

**Freshman class profile.** 1,803 applied, 1,064 admitted, 417 enrolled.

| Mid 50% test scores | | | |
|---|---|---|---|
| SAT critical reading: | 460-560 | GPA 3.50-3.74: | 8% |
| SAT math: | 480-570 | GPA 3.0-3.49: | 28% |
| SAT writing: | 470-560 | GPA 2.0-2.99: | 52% |
| ACT composite: | 22-27 | Rank in top quarter: | 50% |
| GPA 3.75 or higher: | 9% | Rank in top tenth: | 30% |
| | | Return as sophomores: | 87% |

**Basis for selection.** Secondary school achievement with particular attention to grade 11 performance most important. Test scores also important. Recommendations, school and community activities, interview considered. Audition required for music program; portfolio required for art program. **Homeschooled:** State high school equivalency certificate required. **Learning Disabled:** Applicants reviewed by separate committee.

**High school preparation.** College-preparatory program required. 20.5 units required. Required units include English 4, mathematics 3, social studies 4, science 3, foreign language 3, academic electives 3.5. Science, math, and nursing majors must have 1 biology, 1 chemistry, and 3 math.

**2009-2010 Annual costs.** Tuition/fees: $21,070. Books/supplies: $1,412. Personal expenses: $2,438.

**2008-2009 Financial aid. Need-based:** 389 full-time freshmen applied for aid; 324 were judged to have need; 323 of these received aid. Average need met was 61%. Average scholarship/grant was $10,102; average loan $4,308. 40% of total undergraduate aid awarded as scholarships/grants, 60% as loans/jobs. **Non-need-based:** Awarded to 394 full-time undergraduates, including 117 freshmen. Scholarships awarded for academics, alumni affiliation, art, athletics, leadership, music/drama, religious affiliation.

**Application procedures. Admission:** No deadline. $30 fee, may be waived for applicants with need. Admission notification on a rolling basis beginning on or about 10/15. Must reply by May 1 or within 2 week(s) if notified thereafter. **Financial aid:** Priority date 4/15, closing date 5/1. FAFSA required. Applicants notified on a rolling basis starting 3/1; must reply within 5 week(s) of notification.

**Academics. Special study options:** Combined bachelor's/graduate degree, double major, ESL, honors, independent study, internships, liberal arts/career combination, student-designed major, study abroad, teacher certification program. **Credit/placement by examination:** AP, CLEP, IB, institutional tests. 15 credit hours maximum toward associate degree, 30 toward bachelor's. **Support services:** Learning center, pre-admission summer program, reduced course load, remedial instruction, study skills assistance, tutoring, writing center.

**Majors. Biology:** General, ecology. **Business:** Accounting, business admin. **Communications:** General. **Computer sciences:** Computer science, information systems. **Education:** General, art, biology, elementary, English, history, mathematics, music, secondary, social studies, Spanish, special. **Foreign languages:** Spanish. **Health:** Audiology/speech pathology, health services admin, music therapy, nursing (RN). **History:** General. **Liberal arts:** Arts/sciences. **Math:** General. **Philosophy/religion:** Philosophy. **Protective services:** Law enforcement admin. **Psychology:** General. **Public administration:** Social work. **Social sciences:** Political science, sociology. **Visual/performing arts:** General, art, music performance.

**Most popular majors.** Business/marketing 9%, education 14%, health sciences 48%.

**Computing on campus.** 420 workstations in library, computer center, student center. Commuter students can connect to campus network. Online course registration, online library, helpline, wireless network available.

**Student life. Freshman orientation:** Mandatory. **Activities:** Jazz band, campus ministries, choral groups, dance, drama, literary magazine, music ensembles, student government, student newspaper, African American and Caribbean organization, Gaelic society, Out for Acceptance, social work club, Union Hispana de Molloy, Youth for Christ, HOPE Team.

**Athletics.** NCAA. **Intercollegiate:** Baseball M, basketball, cross-country, equestrian, lacrosse, soccer, softball W, tennis W, volleyball W. **Team name:** Lions.

**Student services.** Adult student services, alcohol/substance abuse counseling, chaplain/spiritual director, career counseling, services for economically disadvantaged, student employment services, financial aid counseling, health services, personal counseling, veterans' counselor. **Physically disabled:** Services for visually, hearing impaired.

**Contact.** E-mail: admissions@molloy.edu
Phone: (516) 678-5000 ext. 6240 Toll-free number: (888) 466-5569
Fax: (516) 256-2247
Marguerite Lane, Director of Admissions, Molloy College, PO Box 5002, Rockville Centre, NY 11570

---

## Monroe College
### Bronx, New York
**www.monroecollege.edu**　　　　　　　**CB code: 2463**

◗ For-profit 4-year business and health science college
◗ Commuter campus in very large city
◗ 6,674 degree-seeking undergraduates: 22% part-time, 71% women, 46% African American, 1% Asian American, 42% Hispanic American, 5% international
◗ 467 degree-seeking graduate students
◗ 61% of applicants admitted
◗ Application essay, interview required
◗ 51% graduate within 6 years

**General.** Founded in 1933. Regionally accredited. Branch campus in New Rochelle offers all programs, courses, and services available at main campus. **Degrees:** 1,019 bachelor's, 1,390 associate awarded; master's offered. **ROTC:** Army. **Calendar:** Semester, extensive summer session. **Full-time faculty:** 79 total; 38% have terminal degrees, 77% minority, 53% women. **Part-time faculty:** 258 total; 10% have terminal degrees, 58% minority, 42% women. **Class size:** 44% < 20, 55% 20-39, less than 1% 50-99.

**Freshman class profile.** 2,914 applied, 1,780 admitted, 1,367 enrolled.

| | | | |
|---|---|---|---|
| Return as sophomores: | 79% | Live on campus: | 25% |
| Out-of-state: | 1% | International: | 3% |

**Basis for selection.** Interview, school achievement record, test scores required. Modified open admissions for students who pass admissions test.

**2009-2010 Annual costs.** Tuition/fees: $11,744. Room/board: $7,540. Books/supplies: $1,000. Personal expenses: $5,990.

**2008-2009 Financial aid.** All financial aid based on need.

**Application procedures. Admission:** No deadline. $35 fee. Admission notification on a rolling basis. **Financial aid:** Closing date 3/31. FAFSA required. Applicants notified on a rolling basis starting 7/1.

**Academics. Special study options:** Cooperative education, distance learning, dual enrollment of high school students, honors, internships, liberal arts/career combination, study abroad, weekend college. **Credit/placement by examination:** AP, CLEP, IB, institutional tests. 30 credit hours maximum toward associate degree, 30 toward bachelor's. **Support services:** Learning center, pre-admission summer program, remedial instruction, study skills assistance, tutoring, writing center.

**Majors. Business:** Accounting, business admin, hospitality admin. **Computer sciences:** General. **Health:** Health services admin. **Protective services:** Law enforcement admin.

**Most popular majors.** Business/marketing 32%, computer/information sciences 11%, health sciences 38%, security/protective services 19%.

**Computing on campus.** 800 workstations in dormitories, library, computer center. Dormitories wired for high-speed internet access and linked to campus network. Commuter students can connect to campus network. Online course registration, online library, helpline, wireless network available.

**Student life. Freshman orientation:** Mandatory. Preregistration for classes offered. **Housing:** Coed dorms available. $100 deposit. Assistance for foreign students in securing local housing. Student apartments available near New Rochelle campus. On-campus housing at New Rochelle campus. **Activities:** Dance, international student organizations, Students in Free Enterprise, NABA.

**Athletics.** NJCAA. **Intercollegiate:** Baseball M, basketball, soccer M, volleyball W. **Intramural:** Basketball, softball W. **Team name:** Mustangs.

**Student services.** Adult student services, career counseling, student employment services, financial aid counseling, personal counseling, placement

---

for graduates, veterans' counselor. **Physically disabled:** Services for visually, speech, hearing impaired.

**Contact.** E-mail: ejerome@monroecollege.edu
Phone: (718) 933-6700 Toll-free number: (800) 556-6676
Fax: (718) 364-3552
Evan Jerome, Director of Admissions, Monroe College, Monroe College Way, Bronx, NY 10468

---

## Mount Saint Mary College
### Newburgh, New York　　　　　　　**CB member**
**www.msmc.edu**　　　　　　　　　　　**CB code: 2423**

◗ Private 4-year liberal arts college affiliated with Roman Catholic Church
◗ Residential campus in large town
◗ 2,214 degree-seeking undergraduates: 16% part-time, 75% women, 7% African American, 2% Asian American, 10% Hispanic American
◗ 450 degree-seeking graduate students
◗ 72% of applicants admitted
◗ SAT or ACT with writing required
◗ 51% graduate within 6 years; 28% enter graduate study

**General.** Founded in 1954. Regionally accredited. Independent institution in Judeo-Christian tradition, founded by Dominican Sisters of Newburgh. **Degrees:** 466 bachelor's awarded; master's offered. **Location:** 58 miles from New York City. **Calendar:** Semester, limited summer session. **Full-time faculty:** 81 total; 85% have terminal degrees, 9% minority, 58% women. **Part-time faculty:** 138 total; 21% have terminal degrees, 11% minority, 54% women. **Class size:** 41% < 20, 55% 20-39, 2% 40-49, 2% 50-99. **Special facilities:** Elementary school on campus.

**Freshman class profile.** 2,612 applied, 1,877 admitted, 478 enrolled.

| Mid 50% test scores | | | |
|---|---|---|---|
| SAT critical reading: | 450-540 | Rank in top quarter: | 33% |
| SAT math: | 460-560 | Rank in top tenth: | 9% |
| SAT writing: | 450-540 | End year in good standing: | 82% |
| ACT composite: | 19-23 | Return as sophomores: | 72% |
| GPA 3.75 or higher: | 9% | Out-of-state: | 20% |
| GPA 3.50-3.74: | 16% | Live on campus: | 77% |
| GPA 3.0-3.49: | 46% | | |
| GPA 2.0-2.99: | 28% | | |

**Basis for selection.** Admissions decisions based on total admission score which weighs high school average, class rank, and test scores as well as teacher/counselor recommendations. Interviews are by invitation only after completed application is received. Personal essay required for transfer students. **Homeschooled:** State high school equivalency certificate, interview required. Need SAT or ACT. **Learning Disabled:** Must include IEP with application. Must meet with Director of Counseling and Coordinator of Services for Persons with Disabilities.

**High school preparation.** College preparatory program recommended. 21 units recommended. Recommended units include English 4, mathematics 3, social studies 3, history 2, science 3, foreign language 2, computer science 1 and academic electives 3. Biology and chemistry required for nursing majors.

**2009-2010 Annual costs.** Tuition/fees: $21,930. Room/board: $11,584. Books/supplies: $1,100. Personal expenses: $1,000.

**2009-2010 Financial aid. Need-based:** 443 full-time freshmen applied for aid; 364 were judged to have need; 364 of these received aid. Average need met was 66%. Average scholarship/grant was $11,818; average loan $3,144. 50% of total undergraduate aid awarded as scholarships/grants, 50% as loans/jobs. **Non-need-based:** Awarded to 338 full-time undergraduates, including 137 freshmen. Scholarships awarded for academics, ROTC.

**Application procedures. Admission:** Closing date 8/15 (postmark date). $45 fee, may be waived for applicants with need. Admission notification on a rolling basis beginning on or about 9/15. **Financial aid:** Priority date 2/15, closing date 3/1. FAFSA required. Applicants notified on a rolling basis starting 3/15; must reply by 5/1.

**Academics. Special study options:** Accelerated study, combined bachelor's/graduate degree, cooperative education, cross-registration, distance learning, double major, dual enrollment of high school students, exchange student, honors, independent study, internships, liberal arts/career combination, student-designed major, study abroad, teacher certification program. **Credit/placement by examination:** AP, CLEP, IB, SAT, ACT, institutional tests. 45 credit hours maximum toward bachelor's degree. **Support services:** Learning center, pre-admission summer program, reduced course load, remedial instruction, study skills assistance, tutoring, writing center.

**Majors. Biology:** General. **Business:** Accounting, business admin. **Communications:** Media studies, public relations. **Computer sciences:** Information technology. **Education:** Early childhood, multi-level teacher, secondary. **Foreign languages:** Spanish. **Health:** Clinical lab science, nursing (RN). **History:** General. **Interdisciplinary:** Natural sciences. **Math:** General. **Physical sciences:** Chemistry. **Psychology:** General. **Public administration:** Human services. **Social sciences:** General, sociology.

**Most popular majors.** Business/marketing 24%, English 10%, health sciences 13%, history 13%, mathematics 7%, psychology 10%.

**Computing on campus.** 580 workstations in dormitories, library, computer center, student center. Dormitories wired for high-speed internet access and linked to campus network. Commuter students can connect to campus network. Online course registration, online library, helpline, repair service, student web hosting, wireless network available.

**Student life. Freshman orientation:** Mandatory, $225 fee. Preregistration for classes offered. Two sessions held in July. **Housing:** Coed dorms, single-sex dorms, special housing for disabled available. $450 nonrefundable deposit, deadline 5/1. **Activities:** Concert band, campus ministries, choral groups, dance, drama, film society, literary magazine, music ensembles, musical theater, radio station, student government, student newspaper, black student union, Habitat for Humanity, Big Brothers/Big Sisters, Christian fellowship, Latin student union.

**Athletics.** NCAA. **Intercollegiate:** Baseball M, basketball, cross-country, lacrosse, soccer, softball W, swimming, tennis, volleyball W. **Intramural:** Basketball, bowling, football (non-tackle) M, golf, soccer, softball, swimming, table tennis, volleyball. **Team name:** Blue Knights.

**Student services.** Adult student services, alcohol/substance abuse counseling, chaplain/spiritual director, career counseling, services for economically disadvantaged, student employment services, financial aid counseling, health services, personal counseling, placement for graduates. **Physically disabled:** Services for visually impaired.

**Contact.** E-mail: admissions@msmc.edu
Phone: (845) 569-3248 Toll-free number: (888) 937-6762
Fax: (845) 562-6762
Rodney Morrison, Director of Admissions, Mount Saint Mary College, 330 Powell Avenue, Newburgh, NY 12550

## Nazareth College
**Rochester, New York**
**www.naz.edu**

**CB member**
**CB code: 2511**

- Private 4-year liberal arts college
- Residential campus in large city
- 2,189 degree-seeking undergraduates: 6% part-time, 76% women, 4% African American, 2% Asian American, 4% Hispanic American, 1% international
- 1,033 degree-seeking graduate students
- 77% of applicants admitted
- Application essay required
- 72% graduate within 6 years

**General.** Founded in 1924. Regionally accredited. **Degrees:** 499 bachelor's awarded; master's, professional offered. **ROTC:** Army, Air Force. **Location:** 7 miles from downtown. **Calendar:** Semester, extensive summer session. **Full-time faculty:** 156 total; 93% have terminal degrees, 13% minority, 62% women. **Part-time faculty:** 258 total; 28% have terminal degrees, 9% minority, 72% women. **Class size:** 60% < 20, 40% 20-39, less than 1% 40-49, less than 1% 50-99. **Special facilities:** Arts center, psychology research facility, speech clinic, physical therapy clinic, center for service learning, center for interfaith studies and dialogue.

**Freshman class profile.** 2,221 applied, 1,710 admitted, 492 enrolled.

| Mid 50% test scores | | GPA 2.0-2.99: | 26% |
|---|---|---|---|
| SAT critical reading: | 540-610 | Rank in top quarter: | 64% |
| SAT math: | 530-620 | Rank in top tenth: | 31% |
| ACT composite: | 23-27 | Return as sophomores: | 86% |
| GPA 3.75 or higher: | 25% | Out-of-state: | 8% |
| GPA 3.50-3.74: | 21% | Live on campus: | 87% |
| GPA 3.0-3.49: | 27% | | |

**Basis for selection.** School achievement record, strength of high school academic program, class rank, recommendations, extracurricular activities most important. Standardized test optional. Interview recommended for all; audition required for music and theater arts programs; portfolio required for art programs.

**High school preparation.** College-preparatory program required. 16 units required; 20 recommended. Required and recommended units include English 4, mathematics 3-4, social studies 3-4, science 3-4 (laboratory 2) and foreign language 3-4.

**2009-2010 Annual costs.** Tuition/fees: $25,186. Room/board: $10,304. Books/supplies: $1,100.

**2008-2009 Financial aid. Need-based:** 430 full-time freshmen applied for aid; 365 were judged to have need; 365 of these received aid. Average need met was 77%. Average scholarship/grant was $13,635; average loan $3,629. 58% of total undergraduate aid awarded as scholarships/grants, 42% as loans/jobs. **Non-need-based:** Awarded to 1,095 full-time undergraduates, including 272 freshmen. Scholarships awarded for academics, alumni affiliation, art, leadership, minority status, music/drama, ROTC, state residency.

**Application procedures. Admission:** Priority date 12/15; deadline 2/15 (postmark date). $40 fee, may be waived for applicants with need, free for online applicants. Admission notification on a rolling basis beginning on or about 3/1. Must reply by May 1 or within 4 week(s) if notified thereafter. **Financial aid:** Priority date 2/15; no closing date. FAFSA required. CSS PROFILE required of early decision applicants only. Applicants notified on a rolling basis starting 2/1; must reply by 5/1.

**Academics. Special study options:** Combined bachelor's/graduate degree, cross-registration, distance learning, double major, exchange student, honors, independent study, internships, study abroad, teacher certification program, Washington semester. 2-2 bachelor's degree completion program for registered nurses and Monroe Community College graduates. **Credit/placement by examination:** AP, CLEP, IB, SAT, ACT. 30 credit hours maximum toward bachelor's degree. **Support services:** Reduced course load, remedial instruction, study skills assistance, tutoring, writing center.

**Majors. Area/ethnic studies:** American. **Biology:** General, biochemistry. **Business:** General, accounting, human resources, international, marketing. **Communications:** General. **Computer sciences:** Information systems. **Conservation:** Environmental science. **Education:** Art, biology, business, chemistry, elementary, English, foreign languages, history, mathematics, music, secondary, special, speech, speech impaired. **Foreign languages:** French, German, Italian, Spanish. **Health:** Communication disorders, music therapy, nursing (RN), speech pathology. **History:** General. **Interdisciplinary:** Global studies, peace/conflict. **Math:** General. **Philosophy/religion:** Philosophy, religion. **Physical sciences:** Chemistry. **Psychology:** General. **Public administration:** Social work. **Social sciences:** General, anthropology, economics, political science, sociology. **Visual/performing arts:** Art, art history/conservation, dramatic, music history, music management, music performance, music theory/composition, musical theater, studio arts.

**Most popular majors.** Business/marketing 12%, education 6%, English 7%, health sciences 19%, history 7%, psychology 9%, public administration/social services 6%, social sciences 7%, visual/performing arts 9%.

**Computing on campus.** 240 workstations in dormitories, library, computer center. Dormitories wired for high-speed internet access and linked to campus network. Commuter students can connect to campus network. Online course registration, online library, helpline, wireless network available.

**Student life. Freshman orientation:** Mandatory, $100 fee. Preregistration for classes offered. Orientation charge included in first-year fees. 3-day weekend program includes community service. **Policies:** First- and second-year students are required to live on campus, unless living with family. **Housing:** Guaranteed on-campus for all undergraduates. Coed dorms, special housing for disabled, apartments, wellness housing available. $100 nonrefundable deposit, deadline 5/1. Foreign language houses, special interest housing available. **Activities:** Bands, campus ministries, choral groups, dance, drama, international student organizations, music ensembles, musical theater, radio station, student government, student newspaper, symphony orchestra, Amnesty International, Inter-Ethnic Nazareth Coalition, Center for Spirituality Council, Go Green!, undergraduate association, Rotaract, Students for Political Action and Awareness, French club, German club, Italian club.

**Athletics.** NCAA. **Intercollegiate:** Basketball, cross-country, diving, equestrian, field hockey W, golf, lacrosse, soccer, softball W, swimming, tennis, track and field, volleyball. **Intramural:** Basketball, racquetball, soccer, softball, swimming, tennis, volleyball. **Team name:** Golden Flyers.

**Student services.** Adult student services, alcohol/substance abuse counseling, chaplain/spiritual director, career counseling, services for economically disadvantaged, student employment services, financial aid counseling, health services, minority student services, on-campus daycare, personal counseling, placement for graduates, women's services. **Physically disabled:** Services for visually, speech, hearing impaired.

**Contact.** E-mail: admissions@naz.edu
Phone: (585) 389-2860 Toll-free number: (800) 462-3944
Fax: (585) 389-2826
Thomas DaRin, Vice President for Enrollment Management, Nazareth College, 4245 East Avenue, Rochester, NY 14618-3790

## New York Institute of Technology
### Old Westbury, New York
**www.nyit.edu**                                    **CB code: 2561**

- Private 4-year university and health science college
- Commuter campus in large town
- 4,927 degree-seeking undergraduates: 14% part-time, 38% women, 9% African American, 12% Asian American, 10% Hispanic American, 11% international
- 3,327 degree-seeking graduate students
- 74% of applicants admitted
- SAT or ACT (ACT writing recommended), application essay required
- 48% graduate within 6 years

**General.** Founded in 1955. Regionally accredited. Multiple sites, including campuses on Long Island, Manhattan, online, and at sites throughout the world. **Degrees:** 1,909 bachelor's, 45 associate awarded; master's, professional offered. **ROTC:** Army, Air Force. **Location:** 15 miles from New York City. **Calendar:** Semester, extensive summer session. **Full-time faculty:** 303 total; 64% have terminal degrees, 24% minority, 39% women. **Part-time faculty:** 610 total; 17% minority, 42% women. **Class size:** 63% < 20, 32% 20-39, 3% 40-49, 2% 50-99, less than 1% >100. **Special facilities:** Center for urban/suburban studies, center for neighborhood revitalization, Parkinson's disease treatment center, center for labor and industrial relations, center for energy, environment and economics, center for teaching and learning with technology, culinary arts center, center for entrepreneurial and small business services, center for business information technologies, motion graphics laboratory.

**Freshman class profile.** 4,650 applied, 3,455 admitted, 1,103 enrolled.

| Mid 50% test scores | | Rank in top quarter: | 45% |
|---|---|---|---|
| SAT critical reading: | 470-560 | Rank in top tenth: | 19% |
| SAT math: | 540-640 | Return as sophomores: | 70% |
| ACT composite: | 21-26 | Out-of-state: | 12% |
| GPA 3.75 or higher: | 16% | Live on campus: | 19% |
| GPA 3.50-3.74: | 29% | International: | 6% |
| GPA 3.0-3.49: | 44% | Fraternities: | 2% |
| GPA 2.0-2.99: | 11% | Sororities: | 1% |

**Basis for selection.** 2 letters of recommendation required for 4-year nursing, occupational therapy, physical therapy, physician assistant and all education programs. Proof of 100 hours of volunteer or work experience required for physical therapy, physician assistant, occupational therapy programs. SAT important, minimum scores vary with program. Interview required for occupational therapy, physician assistant, physical therapy, BS/doctor of osteopathic medicine, and BS/Juris Doctor program applicants. Portfolio required for fine arts program. **Homeschooled:** State high school equivalency certificate required.

**High school preparation.** 17 units required. Required and recommended units include English 4, mathematics 3, social studies 3-4, science 3 (laboratory 1) and academic electives 7. Freshmen in selected majors required to prove or acquire computer literacy.

**2009-2010 Annual costs.** Tuition/fees: $24,140. Room only charges apply to Manhattan campus; board charges vary on other campuses. Tuition/fee costs reported for nontechnology majors, vary for other programs. Room only: $10,310. Books/supplies: $1,400. Personal expenses: $2,550.

**2008-2009 Financial aid. Need-based:** 1,103 full-time freshmen applied for aid; 965 were judged to have need; 960 of these received aid. Average scholarship/grant was $4,227; average loan $3,859. 58% of total undergraduate aid awarded as scholarships/grants, 42% as loans/jobs. **Non-need-based:** Awarded to 3,007 full-time undergraduates, including 1,133 freshmen. Scholarships awarded for academics, athletics.

**Application procedures. Admission:** Closing date 3/1. $50 fee, may be waived for applicants with need. Admission notification on a rolling basis beginning on or about 1/1. Must reply by 5/1. Application closing date for nursing, occupational therapy, physical therapy and physician assistant programs February 1. Notification to applicants to these programs sent March 1. Applicants to these programs must reply by May 1 or within 30 days if notified thereafter. No deferred admission to these programs. **Financial aid:** Priority date 3/1; no closing date. FAFSA required. Applicants notified on a rolling basis starting 3/15; must reply by 5/1 or within 2 week(s) of notification.

**Academics.** School focuses on career-oriented professional education, applications-oriented research and service in public interest. **Special study options:** Accelerated study, combined bachelor's/graduate degree, cooperative education, cross-registration, distance learning, double major, dual enrollment of high school students, ESL, honors, independent study, internships, liberal arts/career combination, study abroad, teacher certification program, weekend college. Combined bachelor's/professional degree program in life sciences/osteopathic medicine, architectural technology/energy management, architectural technology/MBA, mechanical engineering/energy management, life sciences/physical therapy, life sciences/occupational therapy, behavioral sciences/law at Touro College Law Center. **Credit/placement by examination:** AP, CLEP, IB, institutional tests. 30 credit hours maximum toward associate degree, 60 toward bachelor's. **Support services:** Learning center, pre-admission summer program, reduced course load, remedial instruction, study skills assistance, tutoring, writing center.

**Majors. Architecture:** Architecture, technology. **Biology:** General. **Business:** Accounting, business admin, finance, hotel/motel admin, human resources, management information systems, marketing, tourism/travel. **Communications:** General, advertising, broadcast journalism, radio/tv. **Computer sciences:** General, computer graphics, computer science, networking. **Education:** Art, biology, business, chemistry, elementary, English, health occupations, mathematics, middle, physics, sales/marketing, science, social science, social studies, technology/industrial arts, trade/industrial, voc/tech. **Engineering:** Biomedical, computer, electrical, mechanical. **Engineering technology:** Aerospace, electrical, energy systems, environmental, mechanical. **Health:** Nursing (RN), physician assistant, premedicine. **Interdisciplinary:** Nutrition sciences. **Physical sciences:** Chemistry. **Protective services:** Law enforcement admin. **Psychology:** General. **Social sciences:** Political science, sociology. **Visual/performing arts:** Commercial/advertising art, interior design, studio arts.

**Most popular majors.** Architecture 8%, business/marketing 35%, communications/journalism 6%, interdisciplinary studies 14%.

**Computing on campus.** PC or laptop required. 1,210 workstations in dormitories, library, computer center, student center. Dormitories wired for high-speed internet access and linked to campus network. Commuter students can connect to campus network. Online course registration, online library, helpline, student web hosting, wireless network available.

**Student life. Freshman orientation:** Available. Preregistration for classes offered. One day at end of August. **Housing:** Guaranteed on-campus for all undergraduates. Coed dorms, special housing for disabled, apartments available. $300 nonrefundable deposit. Central Islip campus fully residential, special housing for graduate, architecture students. Off-campus housing available for Manhattan campus. **Activities:** Choral groups, dance, drama, film society, literary magazine, musical theater, radio station, student government, student newspaper, TV station, American Institute of Architecture Students, biomedical society, National Society of Black Engineers, Newman Club, Christian fellowship, Jewish student union, African people's organization, Community Connection, South Asian student association, Chinese student association.

**Athletics.** NCAA. **Intercollegiate:** Baseball M, basketball, cross-country, lacrosse M, soccer, softball W, volleyball W. **Intramural:** Basketball, football (non-tacklc), golf, socccr, softball, swimming, table tennis, tennis, volleyball, weight lifting. **Team name:** Bears.

**Student services.** Adult student services, alcohol/substance abuse counseling, chaplain/spiritual director, career counseling, student employment services, financial aid counseling, health services, personal counseling, placement for graduates, veterans' counselor. **Physically disabled:** Services for hearing impaired.

**Contact.** E-mail: admissions@nyit.edu
Phone: (516) 686-7520 Toll-free number: (800) 345-6948
Fax: (516) 686-7613
Jacquelyn Nealon, Vice President for Enrollment, New York Institute of Technology, Box 8000, Old Westbury, NY 11568

## New York School of Interior Design
### New York, New York
**www.nysid.edu**                                    **CB code: 0333**

- Private 4-year visual arts college
- Commuter campus in very large city
- 533 degree-seeking undergraduates: 63% part-time, 89% women, 5% African American, 13% Asian American, 9% Hispanic American, 1% international
- 58 degree-seeking graduate students
- 52% of applicants admitted
- Application essay required
- 75% graduate within 6 years; 10% enter graduate study

**General.** Founded in 1916. The college is devoted exclusively to interior design education. **Degrees:** 48 bachelor's, 70 associate awarded; master's offered. **Location:** Located in Manhattan. **Calendar:** Semester, extensive summer session. **Full-time faculty:** 8 total; 62% women. **Part-time faculty:** 72 total; 86% have terminal degrees, 42% women. **Class size:** 91% < 20, 9% 50-99. **Special facilities:** Three galleries for architecture and interior design exhibits, lighting laboratory.

**Freshman class profile.** 191 applied, 99 admitted, 28 enrolled.

| | | | |
|---|---|---|---|
| GPA 3.75 or higher: | 15% | End year in good standing: | 65% |
| GPA 3.50-3.74: | 15% | Return as sophomores: | 60% |
| GPA 3.0-3.49: | 40% | Live on campus: | 49% |
| GPA 2.0-2.99: | 30% | | |

**Basis for selection.** High school transcripts, 2 letters of recommendation, essay, and portfolio in art/design. Portfolio required, interview recommended. **Homeschooled:** State high school equivalency certificate required.

**High school preparation.** 16 units recommended. Recommended units include English 4, mathematics 2, social studies 2, history 2, science 2 and foreign language 2. Studio art or drafting is recommended.

**2010-2011 Annual costs.** Tuition/fees: $22,895. Books/supplies: $1,000. Personal expenses: $900.

**2009-2010 Financial aid.** All financial aid based on need. 9 full-time freshmen applied for aid; 9 were judged to have need; 9 of these received aid. Average need met was 30%. Average scholarship/grant was $2,500; average loan $3,500. 29% of total undergraduate aid awarded as scholarships/grants, 71% as loans/jobs.

**Application procedures. Admission:** Priority date 3/1; no deadline. $50 fee, may be waived for applicants with need. Admission notification on a rolling basis beginning on or about 4/1. Must reply by May 1 or within 4 week(s) if notified thereafter. **Financial aid:** Priority date 5/1; no closing date. FAFSA required. Applicants notified on a rolling basis starting 2/1; must reply within 2 week(s) of notification.

**Academics. Special study options:** Independent study, internships, study abroad, weekend college. **Credit/placement by examination:** AP, CLEP, IB, institutional tests. 17 credit hours maximum toward associate degree, 41 toward bachelor's. **Support services:** Study skills assistance, tutoring, writing center.

**Majors. Visual/performing arts:** Interior design.

**Computing on campus.** 125 workstations in library, computer center. Dormitories wired for high-speed internet access and linked to campus network. Commuter students can connect to campus network. Online course registration, helpline available.

**Student life. Freshman orientation:** Available. Preregistration for classes offered. General orientation is held the week before classes begin. **Housing:** Coed dorms available. **Activities:** Student chapter of American Society of Interior Designers.

**Student services.** Adult student services, career counseling, student employment services, financial aid counseling, personal counseling, placement for graduates.

**Contact.**   E-mail: admissions@nysid.edu
Phone: (212) 472-1500 ext. 204 Toll-free number: (800) 336-9743 ext. 204
Fax: (212) 472-1867
David Sprouls, Director of Admissions, New York School of Interior Design, 170 East 70th Street, New York, NY 10021-5110

## New York University
**New York, New York**   **CB member**
**www.nyu.edu**   **CB code: 2562**

- Private 4-year university
- Residential campus in very large city
- 21,227 degree-seeking undergraduates: 6% part-time, 61% women, 4% African American, 20% Asian American, 8% Hispanic American, 8% international
- 20,578 degree-seeking graduate students
- 38% of applicants admitted
- SAT and SAT Subject Tests or ACT with writing, application essay required
- 85% graduate within 6 years

**General.** Founded in 1831. Regionally accredited. School of Continuing and Professional Studies also available for adult degree and noncredit programs. **Degrees:** 6,059 bachelor's, 319 associate awarded; master's, doctoral, professional offered. **ROTC:** Army, Naval, Air Force. **Calendar:** Semester, extensive summer session. **Class size:** 60% < 20, 25% 20-39, 3% 40-49, 6% 50-99, 5% >100. **Special facilities:** Special academic facilities for arts, business, culture, education, international relations, language, law, media, music, public service, research, and social policy.

**Freshman class profile.** 37,462 applied, 14,159 admitted, 5,000 enrolled.

| Mid 50% test scores | | | |
|---|---|---|---|
| SAT critical reading: | 610-710 | GPA 2.0-2.99: | 1% |
| SAT math: | 600-720 | Rank in top quarter: | 92% |
| SAT writing: | 620-710 | Rank in top tenth: | 64% |
| ACT composite: | 27-31 | Return as sophomores: | 91% |
| GPA 3.75 or higher: | 32% | Out-of-state: | 72% |
| GPA 3.50-3.74: | 37% | Live on campus: | 87% |
| GPA 3.0-3.49: | 30% | International: | 11% |

**Basis for selection.** School achievement record most important. Standardized test scores, activities, essay, recommendations also important. Audition and/or submission of creative materials required for applicants to either Tisch School of the Arts or art and music programs within the School of Education. For admissions decisions, students have several testing options. All students must provide either a) The SAT Reasoning Test and two SAT Subject Tests; or b) The ACT (with Writing Test); or c) The SAT Reasoning Test and two AP exam scores; or d) Three SAT Subject Test scores in non-language tests (one in literature or the humanities, one in math or science; and one of the student's choice); or e) Three AP exam scores in non-language tests (one in literature or the humanities, one in math or science, and one of the student's choice). Audition required for dance, drama, and music programs; portfolio required for art, theater design, photography, cinema studies, film, television, radio, and dramatic writing programs. Portfolios may include writing, photography, film or other creative work. **Homeschooled:** Transcript of courses and grades, letter of recommendation (nonparent) required. Homeschooled applicants must submit official score reports from either the SAT Reasoning Test (including the Writing section), or the ACT with the ACT Writing Test, and at least two SAT Subject Test scores or two Advanced Placement test scores. Students must either be able to provide a homeschool diploma or certificate of completion that is considered the equivalent of a high school diploma in the applicant's home state, or they must be willing, if admitted, to apply for a New York State equivalency diploma upon the completion of twenty-four college credits.

**High school preparation.** College-preparatory program required. Required and recommended units include English 4, mathematics 3-4, history 4, science 3-4 and foreign language 2-3.

**2009-2010 Annual costs.** Tuition/fees: $38,765. Room/board: $13,228. Books/supplies: $950. Personal expenses: $1,000.

**2008-2009 Financial aid. Need-based:** 3,004 full-time freshmen applied for aid; 2,390 were judged to have need; 2,342 of these received aid. Average need met was 71%. Average scholarship/grant was $19,120; average loan $4,947. 57% of total undergraduate aid awarded as scholarships/grants, 43% as loans/jobs. **Non-need-based:** Awarded to 1,574 full-time undergraduates, including 244 freshmen. Scholarships awarded for academics.

**Application procedures. Admission:** Closing date 1/1 (postmark date). $65 fee, may be waived for applicants with need. Application must be submitted online. Admission notification 4/1. Must reply by 5/1. **Financial aid:** Closing date 2/15. FAFSA required. Applicants notified on a rolling basis starting 4/1; must reply by 5/1.

**Academics. Special study options:** Combined bachelor's/graduate degree, cross-registration, double major, honors, independent study, internships, liberal arts/career combination, student-designed major, study abroad, teacher certification program, Washington semester. NYU offers an exchange program with several historically black colleges including Spelman College, Morehouse College, and Xavier University of Louisiana. **Credit/placement by examination:** AP, CLEP, IB. 32 credit hours maximum toward bachelor's degree. 8 to 32 hours of credit may be awarded for International Baccalaureate. **Support services:** Learning center, pre-admission summer program, reduced course load, study skills assistance, tutoring, writing center.

**Majors. Architecture:** Urban/community planning. **Area/ethnic studies:** African-American, East Asian, European, Latin American, Near/Middle Eastern. **Biology:** General, biochemistry. **Business:** General, accounting, finance, hotel/motel admin, international, labor relations, managerial economics, real estate, restaurant/food services. **Communications:** General, journalism, radio/tv. **Communications technology:** Radio/tv. **Computer sciences:** General, computer science. **Education:** Art, business, elementary, ESL, kindergarten/

preschool, mathematics, music, social studies, special, speech impaired. **Engineering:** Operations research. **Family/consumer sciences:** Food/nutrition. **Foreign languages:** General, classics, comparative lit, French, German, Hebrew, Italian, linguistics, Russian, Spanish. **Health:** Audiology/speech pathology, dental hygiene, nursing (RN). **History:** General. **Interdisciplinary:** Neuroscience. **Liberal arts:** Arts/sciences, humanities. **Math:** General. **Parks/recreation:** Facilities management. **Philosophy/religion:** Philosophy, religion. **Physical sciences:** Chemistry, physics. **Psychology:** General. **Public administration:** General, community org/advocacy, social work. **Social sciences:** General, anthropology, economics, international relations, political science, sociology, urban studies. **Visual/performing arts:** Cinematography, commercial/advertising art, dance, dramatic, music performance, photography, studio arts. **Other:** Fundraising.

**Most popular majors.** Business/marketing 18%, communications/journalism 7%, liberal arts 7%, social sciences 16%, visual/performing arts 21%.

**Computing on campus.** Dormitories wired for high-speed internet access and linked to campus network. Commuter students can connect to campus network. Online course registration, online library, helpline, repair service, student web hosting, wireless network available.

**Student life. Freshman orientation:** Available. Preregistration for classes offered. Each undergraduate college handles its own orientation. Charges and program vary by school. **Housing:** Guaranteed on-campus for all undergraduates. Coed dorms, special housing for disabled, apartments, fraternity/sorority housing, wellness housing available. $300 nonrefundable deposit, deadline 5/1. First-Year Residential Experience program available for new students. **Activities:** Bands, campus ministries, choral groups, dance, drama, film society, international student organizations, literary magazine, music ensembles, Model UN, musical theater, opera, radio station, student government, student newspaper, symphony orchestra, TV station, over 400 clubs and organizations available.

**Athletics. NCAA. Intercollegiate:** Basketball, cross-country, diving, fencing, golf, soccer, swimming, tennis, track and field, volleyball, wrestling M. **Intramural:** Basketball, bowling, cross-country, football (non-tackle), soccer, volleyball, weight lifting. **Team name:** Violets.

**Student services.** Adult student services, alcohol/substance abuse counseling, chaplain/spiritual director, career counseling, services for economically disadvantaged, student employment services, financial aid counseling, health services, minority student services, personal counseling, placement for graduates, women's services. **Physically disabled:** Services for visually, speech, hearing impaired.

**Contact.** E-mail: admissions@nyu.edu
Phone: (212) 998-4500 Fax: (212) 995-4902
Randall Deike, Vice President for Enrollment Management and University Institutional Research, New York University, 665 Broadway, 11th floor, New York, NY 10012-2339

---

## Niagara University
**Niagara University, New York**
**www.niagara.edu**
**CB member**
**CB code: 2558**

- Private 4-year university affiliated with Roman Catholic Church
- Residential campus in small city
- 3,224 degree-seeking undergraduates: 8% part-time, 63% women, 4% African American, 1% Asian American, 2% Hispanic American, 1% Native American, 16% international
- 842 degree-seeking graduate students
- 80% of applicants admitted
- SAT or ACT (ACT writing optional) required
- 66% graduate within 6 years; 47% enter graduate study

**General.** Founded in 1856. Regionally accredited. Independent institution in the Vincentian tradition. **Degrees:** 691 bachelor's, 2 associate awarded; master's offered. **ROTC:** Army. **Location:** 20 miles from Buffalo; 90 miles from Toronto, Canada. **Calendar:** Semester, extensive summer session. **Full-time faculty:** 149 total; 92% have terminal degrees, 15% minority, 39% women. **Part-time faculty:** 205 total; 10% minority, 48% women. **Class size:** 44% < 20, 50% 20-39, 6% 40-49, less than 1% 50-99. **Special facilities:** Art museum, ice arena.

**Freshman class profile.** 2,942 applied, 2,362 admitted, 677 enrolled.

| Mid 50% test scores | | | |
|---|---|---|---|
| SAT critical reading: | 490-590 | Rank in top quarter: | 41% |
| SAT math: | 470-570 | Rank in top tenth: | 13% |
| ACT composite: | 19-25 | End year in good standing: | 96% |
| GPA 3.75 or higher: | 13% | Return as sophomores: | 76% |
| GPA 3.50-3.74: | 30% | Out-of-state: | 11% |
| GPA 3.0-3.49: | 51% | Live on campus: | 76% |
| GPA 2.0-2.99: | 6% | International: | 3% |

**Basis for selection.** School achievement record, class rank, test scores most important. School recommendation also important. Character, personality, and extracurricular activities considered. Alumni relationship also considered. Interview, essay recommended for all; audition recommended for theater program. **Homeschooled:** Transcript of courses and grades required. Letter from district superintendent or local district official confirming that the student has received an education "substantially equivalent" to instruction given to students graduating from the public high school in that district.

**High school preparation.** College-preparatory program recommended. 16 units required. Required units include English 4, mathematics 2, social studies 2, science 2, foreign language 2 and academic electives 4. 3 science (biology, chemistry mandatory, physics recommended) for math, science, nursing applicants. 2 foreign language required of all except business applicants. 3 math required for math, biology, business, biochemistry, chemistry, computer and information sciences, natural sciences, and nursing applicants. 3 social studies required for prospective social studies majors.

**2009-2010 Annual costs.** Tuition/fees: $24,825. Room/board: $10,250. Books/supplies: $1,050. Personal expenses: $750.

**2009-2010 Financial aid. Need-based:** 644 full-time freshmen applied for aid; 573 were judged to have need; 573 of these received aid. Average need met was 85%. Average scholarship/grant was $16,843; average loan $4,116. 65% of total undergraduate aid awarded as scholarships/grants, 35% as loans/jobs. **Non-need-based:** Awarded to 1,598 full-time undergraduates, including 467 freshmen. Scholarships awarded for academics, athletics, music/drama, ROTC. **Additional information:** Opportunity program available for academically and economically disadvantaged students.

**Application procedures. Admission:** Closing date 8/1 (receipt date). $30 fee, may be waived for applicants with need. Admission notification on a rolling basis. Must reply by May 1 or within 4 week(s) if notified thereafter. **Financial aid:** Priority date 2/15; no closing date. FAFSA required. Applicants notified on a rolling basis starting 3/1; must reply within 3 week(s) of notification.

**Academics.** Academic exploration program for students undecided about their choice of major. **Special study options:** Accelerated study, combined bachelor's/graduate degree, cooperative education, cross-registration, double major, dual enrollment of high school students, ESL, exchange student, honors, independent study, internships, liberal arts/career combination, New York semester, study abroad, teacher certification program, Washington semester. **Credit/placement by examination:** AP, CLEP, institutional tests. 15 credit hours maximum toward associate degree, 15 toward bachelor's. **Support services:** Learning center, pre-admission summer program, reduced course load, remedial instruction, study skills assistance, tutoring, writing center.

**Majors. Biology:** General, biochemistry. **Business:** Accounting, finance, hospitality admin, hotel/motel admin, human resources, international, logistics, managerial economics, marketing, restaurant/food services, tourism/travel, training/development. **Communications:** General. **Computer sciences:** General, computer science, information systems. **Education:** General, biology, business, chemistry, early childhood, elementary, English, French, mathematics, secondary, social studies, Spanish, special. **Foreign languages:** French, Spanish. **Health:** Nursing (RN), predental, premedicine, preveterinary. **History:** General. **Legal studies:** Prelaw. **Liberal arts:** Arts/sciences. **Math:** General. **Philosophy/religion:** Philosophy, religion. **Physical sciences:** Chemistry. **Protective services:** Criminal justice. **Psychology:** General. **Public administration:** Social work. **Science technology:** Biological. **Social sciences:** General, criminology, political science, sociology. **Transportation:** General. **Visual/performing arts:** Dramatic.

**Most popular majors.** Business/marketing 24%, education 18%, security/protective services 8%, social sciences 8%.

**Computing on campus.** 150 workstations in dormitories, library, computer center, student center. Dormitories wired for high-speed internet access and linked to campus network. Commuter students can connect to campus network. Online course registration, online library, helpline, repair service, wireless network available.

**Student life. Freshman orientation:** Available. Preregistration for classes offered. **Policies:** Freshmen not within reasonable commuting distance required to live on campus for 2 years. **Housing:** Guaranteed on-campus for all undergraduates. Coed dorms, apartments, wellness housing available. $100 nonrefundable deposit, deadline 5/1. **Activities:** Pep band, campus ministries, choral groups, dance, drama, international student organizations, musical theater, radio station, student government, student newspaper, ethnic awareness society, Knights of Columbus, community action program, Muscular Dystrophy Association, foreign student council, St. Vincent DePaul Society, Black Student Union.

**Athletics.** NCAA. **Intercollegiate:** Baseball M, basketball, cross-country, diving, golf, ice hockey, lacrosse, soccer, softball W, swimming, tennis, volleyball W. **Intramural:** Baseball M, basketball, bowling, golf, racquetball, skiing, softball, volleyball W, water polo. **Team name:** Purple Eagles.

**Student services.** Adult student services, alcohol/substance abuse counseling, chaplain/spiritual director, career counseling, services for economically disadvantaged, student employment services, financial aid counseling, health services, minority student services, personal counseling, placement for graduates, veterans' counselor.

**Contact.** E-mail: admissions@niagara.edu
Phone: (716) 286-8700 Fax: (716) 286-8733
Harry Gong, Director of Admissions, Niagara University, Niagara University, NY 14109

## Nyack College
**Nyack, New York**
www.nyack.edu                    CB code: 2560

- Private 4-year liberal arts college affiliated with Christian and Missionary Alliance
- Residential campus in large town
- 1,994 degree-seeking undergraduates: 18% part-time, 58% women, 36% African American, 7% Asian American, 23% Hispanic American, 1% Native American, 3% international
- 1,070 degree-seeking graduate students
- 99% of applicants admitted
- Application essay required

**General.** Founded in 1882. Regionally accredited. Extension center in Manhattan. **Degrees:** 426 bachelor's, 16 associate awarded; master's offered. **Location:** 25 miles from New York City. **Calendar:** Differs by program, limited summer session. **Full-time faculty:** 148 total. **Part-time faculty:** 190 total.

**Freshman class profile.** 640 applied, 635 admitted, 262 enrolled.

| Mid 50% test scores | | GPA 3.0-3.49: | 23% |
|---|---|---|---|
| SAT critical reading: | 400-530 | GPA 2.0-2.99: | 42% |
| SAT math: | 380-530 | Rank in top quarter: | 29% |
| ACT composite: | 18-25 | Rank in top tenth: | 12% |
| GPA 3.75 or higher: | 11% | Live on campus: | 85% |
| GPA 3.50-3.74: | 11% | International: | 1% |

**Basis for selection.** Applicants must have Christian commitment and sign agreement to abide by community life standards. Academic record, class rank, and test scores most important. Pastor's recommendation required for students applying to traditional undergraduate program. Interview recommended for those with unsatisfactory recommendations or academic concerns; audition required for music program. **Homeschooled:** Transcript of courses and grades required. **Learning Disabled:** Students should inform their admissions counselors.

**High school preparation.** 16 units required. Required and recommended units include English 4, foreign language 2 and academic electives 4. 3 in any combination of math and science and 3 in any combination of history and social science recommended.

**2010-2011 Annual costs.** Tuition/fees (projected): $20,500. Room/board: $8,200. Books/supplies: $750. Personal expenses: $2,250.

**2008-2009 Financial aid. Need-based:** 246 full-time freshmen applied for aid; 228 were judged to have need; 228 of these received aid. Average need met was 71%. Average scholarship/grant was $12,464; average loan $4,225. 48% of total undergraduate aid awarded as scholarships/grants, 52% as loans/jobs. **Non-need-based:** Awarded to 330 full-time undergraduates, including 85 freshmen. Scholarships awarded for academics, alumni affiliation, art, athletics, leadership, minority status, music/drama, religious affiliation, state residency.

**Application procedures. Admission:** No deadline. $25 fee, may be waived for applicants with need. Admission notification on a rolling basis. **Financial aid:** Priority date 3/1; no closing date. FAFSA required. Applicants notified on a rolling basis starting 3/1; must reply by 4/1 or within 4 week(s) of notification.

**Academics.** Adult degree completion program offers accelerated study option for adult students, with classes held throughout the New York metropolitan and lower Hudson Valley regions, Washington, DC and Dayton, Ohio. **Special study options:** Accelerated study, distance learning, double major, ESL, honors, independent study, internships, liberal arts/career combination, study abroad, teacher certification program, Washington semester. Adult degree completion program. **Credit/placement by examination:** AP, CLEP, SAT, institutional tests. 30 credit hours maximum toward bachelor's degree. **Support services:** Learning center, pre-admission summer program, reduced course load, remedial instruction, study skills assistance, tutoring, writing center.

**Majors. Business:** Accounting, business admin. **Communications:** General. **Computer sciences:** General. **Education:** Elementary, ESL, music. **History:** General. **Liberal arts:** Arts/sciences. **Math:** General. **Philosophy/religion:** Philosophy, religion. **Psychology:** General. **Public administration:** Social work. **Social sciences:** General. **Theology:** Religious ed, sacred music, theology. **Visual/performing arts:** Music performance, music theory/composition.

**Most popular majors.** Business/marketing 54%, interdisciplinary studies 9%, psychology 6%, theological studies 9%.

**Computing on campus.** 124 workstations in dormitories, library, computer center, student center. Commuter students can connect to campus network. Online course registration, online library, helpline, wireless network available.

**Student life. Freshman orientation:** Mandatory, $100 fee. Preregistration for classes offered. Usually 4 days the week prior to classes starting. **Policies:** Alcohol, tobacco, and narcotic drug use and possession prohibited on and off campus. Religious observance required. **Housing:** Single-sex dorms, apartments, wellness housing available. $150 deposit. **Activities:** Choral groups, drama, literary magazine, music ensembles, musical theater, radio station, student government, student newspaper, symphony orchestra, African American Association of Cultural Exchange, missions committee, drama ensemble, Association of Latin American Students, Asian student organization, mime and interpretive dance group, business club, WNYK Radio, Student Chapter of Music Educators National Conference.

**Athletics.** NCAA, NCCAA. **Intercollegiate:** Baseball M, basketball, cheerleading, cross-country, golf M, soccer, softball W, volleyball W. **Team name:** Warriors.

**Student services.** Adult student services, alcohol/substance abuse counseling, chaplain/spiritual director, career counseling, services for economically disadvantaged, student employment services, financial aid counseling, health services, personal counseling, placement for graduates. **Physically disabled:** Services for visually, hearing impaired.

**Contact.** E-mail: admissions@nyack.edu
Phone: (845) 358-1710 ext. 4401 Toll-free number: (800) 336-9225 ext. 4401 Fax: (845) 358-3047
Dinesh Mahtani, Director of Admissions, Nyack College, 1 South Boulevard, Nyack, NY 10960-3698

## Ohr Somayach Tanenbaum Education Center
**Monsey, New York**
www.os.edu                    CB code: 3357

- Private 4-year rabbinical college for men affiliated with Jewish faith
- Residential campus in large town
- 91 degree-seeking undergraduates: 11% part-time
- 11 degree-seeking graduate students
- Interview required

**General.** Founded in 1979. Accredited by AARTS. First and Second Talmudic degrees offered. **Degrees:** 12 bachelor's awarded; master's offered. **Location:** Half a mile from Spring Valley, 33 miles from New York City. **Calendar:** Semester, extensive summer session. **Full-time faculty:** 3 total. **Part-time faculty:** 2 total; 100% have terminal degrees.

**Basis for selection.** Potential for scholastic and character achievement evaluated through personal interview, recommendations, departmental examinations, and prior religious and secular studies. Essay recommended.

**2009-2010 Annual costs.** Tuition/fees: $7,000. Room/board: $7,000. Books/supplies: $300. Personal expenses: $725.

**Application procedures. Admission:** No deadline. $75 fee, may be waived for applicants with need. Admission notification on a rolling basis. **Financial aid:** No deadline. Applicants notified on a rolling basis starting 7/1; must reply within 4 week(s) of notification.

**Academics. Special study options:** Accelerated study, cross-registration, independent study, study abroad, teacher certification program. **Credit/ placement by examination:** CLEP, institutional tests. **Support services:** Pre-admission summer program, reduced course load, tutoring.

**Majors. Philosophy/religion:** Judaic. **Theology:** Talmudic.

**Computing on campus.** 3 workstations in computer center. Repair service available.

**Student life. Policies:** Religious observance required. **Housing:** Apartments available. $100 deposit. Students above age 30 must arrange own housing off campus. Assistance provided in locating housing. **Activities:** Singing group, community volunteers.

**Athletics. Intramural:** Baseball M, basketball M, skiing M, swimming M.

**Student services.** Career counseling, student employment services, personal counseling, placement for graduates.

**Contact.** E-mail: ohr@os.edu
Phone: (845) 425-1370 Fax: (845) 425-8865
Avrohom Braun, Dean of Students, Ohr Somayach Tanenbaum Education Center, 244 Route 306, Monsey, NY 10952

---

## Pace University
### New York, New York
**CB member**
### www.pace.edu
**CB code: 2635**

- Private 4-year university
- Residential campus in very large city
- 7,411 degree-seeking undergraduates: 13% part-time, 60% women, 11% African American, 9% Asian American, 13% Hispanic American, 5% international
- 4,648 degree-seeking graduate students
- 78% of applicants admitted
- SAT or ACT (ACT writing optional), application essay required
- 61% graduate within 6 years

**General.** Founded in 1906. Regionally accredited. Four schools and one college of the University are located on New York City and Pleasantville campuses: Dyson College of Arts and Sciences, Lienhard School of Nursing, School of Education, Lubin School of Business, and Seidenberg School of Computer Science and Information Systems. The School of Law and Lubin Graduate Center are located in White Plains. **Degrees:** 1,638 bachelor's, 83 associate awarded; master's, professional offered. **ROTC:** Army, Air Force. **Calendar:** Semester, limited summer session. **Full-time faculty:** 452 total; 86% have terminal degrees, 15% minority, 44% women. **Part-time faculty:** 666 total; 24% have terminal degrees, 15% minority, 51% women. **Class size:** 51% < 20, 46% 20-39, 2% 40-49, less than 1% 50-99, less than 1% >100. **Special facilities:** Art galleries, multimedia language laboratories, speech and hearing center, studio theater.

**Freshman class profile.** 10,985 applied, 8,587 admitted, 1,672 enrolled.

| Mid 50% test scores | | | |
|---|---|---|---|
| SAT critical reading: | 490-590 | Rank in top tenth: | 14% |
| SAT math: | 500-600 | End year in good standing: | 97% |
| ACT composite: | 20-26 | Return as sophomores: | 78% |
| GPA 3.75 or higher: | 21% | Out-of-state: | 40% |
| GPA 3.50-3.74: | 13% | Live on campus: | 75% |
| GPA 3.0-3.49: | 36% | International: | 5% |
| GPA 2.0-2.99: | 30% | Fraternities: | 2% |
| Rank in top quarter: | 39% | Sororities: | 2% |

**Basis for selection.** 85 high school GPA, rank in top half of class, test scores, recommendations, personal statement important. Extracurricular activities also considered. Non-native speakers of English required to take TOEFL. Official scores must be sent directly to school. Notarized copies not acceptable. Interviews strongly recommended; audition required for dance, dramatic arts, theater; portfolio recommended for art programs. Applicants to Lienhard School of Nursing must be certified in CPR. **Learning Disabled:** Diagnostic tests recommended.

**High school preparation.** College-preparatory program recommended. 16 units required; 20 recommended. Required and recommended units include English 4, mathematics 3-4, social studies 1-2, history 2-3, science 2 (laboratory 2), foreign language 2-3 and academic electives 2.

**2009-2010 Annual costs.** Tuition/fees: $32,926. Room/board: $11,560. Books/supplies: $800. Personal expenses: $1,248.

**2009-2010 Financial aid. Need-based:** 1,446 full-time freshmen applied for aid; 1,310 were judged to have need; 1,309 of these received aid. Average need met was 76%. Average scholarship/grant was $22,683; average loan $3,923. 77% of total undergraduate aid awarded as scholarships/grants, 23% as loans/jobs. **Non-need-based:** Awarded to 1,586 full-time undergraduates, including 423 freshmen. Scholarships awarded for academics, athletics, leadership, music/drama.

**Application procedures. Admission:** Closing date 3/1 (postmark date). $50 fee, may be waived for applicants with need. Admission notification on a rolling basis beginning on or about 12/15. Must reply by May 1 or within 2 week(s) if notified thereafter. **Financial aid:** Priority date 2/15; no closing date. FAFSA required. Applicants notified on a rolling basis starting 3/1; must reply by 5/1 or within 2 week(s) of notification.

**Academics.** Adult undergraduate degrees in liberal/general studies, business and computer science. **Special study options:** Accelerated study, combined bachelor's/graduate degree, cooperative education, cross-registration, distance learning, double major, dual enrollment of high school students, ESL, honors, independent study, internships, study abroad, teacher certification program. Evening and freshman studies programs, pre-freshman summer program, learning communities and service learning. **Credit/ placement by examination:** AP, CLEP, IB, institutional tests. 30 credit hours maximum toward associate degree, 96 toward bachelor's. **Support services:** Learning center, reduced course load, remedial instruction, study skills assistance, tutoring, writing center.

**Honors college/program.** Honors Program requires entering freshmen have 90 or higher high school GPA, SAT verbal minimum of 550, SAT math minimum of 550 and a combined SAT score of 1200 (exclusive of Writing). Honors program students may be enrolled in any of undergraduate schools at University.

**Majors. Area/ethnic studies:** American, women's. **Biology:** General; biochemistry. **Business:** General, accounting, business admin, e-commerce, entrepreneurial studies, finance, hotel/motel admin, human resources, international, international marketing, management science, marketing. **Communications:** General, advertising. **Computer sciences:** General, computer science, information systems, systems analysis. **Conservation:** Environmental science, environmental studies. **Education:** Biology, chemistry, early childhood, elementary, English, history, mathematics, science, social studies, Spanish, special, speech impaired. **Foreign languages:** General, Spanish. **Health:** Clinical lab science, communication disorders, nursing (RN). **History:** General. **Liberal arts:** Arts/sciences. **Math:** General. **Philosophy/religion:** Philosophy, religion. **Physical sciences:** Chemistry. **Protective services:** Forensics, law enforcement admin. **Psychology:** General. **Public administration:** Community org/advocacy. **Social sciences:** General, economics, political science. **Visual/performing arts:** Acting, art, art history/conservation, commercial/advertising art, dramatic, film/cinema, studio arts. **Other:** E-business and interactive media, Modern languages and cultures.

**Most popular majors.** Business/marketing 40%, communications/ journalism 10%, computer/information sciences 7%, health sciences 13%, psychology 6%.

**Computing on campus.** 282 workstations in library, computer center. Dormitories linked to campus network. Commuter students can connect to campus network. Online library, helpline, wireless network available.

**Student life. Freshman orientation:** Mandatory, $100 fee. Preregistration for classes offered. 2 days for freshmen and international students, 1 day for transfer students. **Housing:** Coed dorms, apartments, wellness housing available. $500 nonrefundable deposit, deadline 5/1. Apartment style housing for upperclassmen available. **Activities:** Choral groups, dance, drama, film society, international student organizations, literary magazine, Model UN, musical theater, radio station, student government, student newspaper, TV station, Collegiate Italian American Organization, Asian Cultural Society, International Student Club, Hillel, Pace Christian Fellowship, Caribbean Students Association, African Students Association at Pace, Sabor Latino, Project Pericles, NATURE (environmental club).

**Athletics.** NCAA. **Intercollegiate:** Baseball M, basketball, cross-country, equestrian W, football (tackle) M, golf M, lacrosse M, soccer W, softball W, swimming, tennis, track and field, volleyball W. **Intramural:** Football (nontackle), soccer, softball, volleyball. **Team name:** Setters.

**Student services.** Adult student services, career counseling, student employment services, health services, personal counseling, placement for graduates, veterans' counselor. **Physically disabled:** Services for visually, speech, hearing impaired.

**Contact.** E-mail: infoctr@pace.edu
Phone: (212) 346-1323 Toll-free number: (800) 874-7223
Fax: (212) 346-1040
Donna Hoyt, Dean of Admissions, Pace University, 1 Pace Plaza, New York, NY 10038-1598

## Pace University: Pleasantville/Briarcliff
**Pleasantville, New York**
www.pace.edu                                    CB code: 2685

◗ Private 4-year university
◗ Residential campus in small town

**General.** Regionally accredited. **Location:** 7 miles from White Plains, 30 miles from New York City. **Calendar:** Semester.

**Annual costs/financial aid.** Tuition/fees (2009-2010): $32,926. Room/board: $11,560. Books/supplies: $800. Personal expenses: $1,248. Need-based financial aid available to full-time and part-time students.

**Contact.**  Phone: (914) 773-3746
Director of Admission, 861 Bedford Road, Pleasantville, NY 10570

## Parsons The New School for Design
**New York, New York**
www.parsons.edu                                 CB code: 2638

◗ Private 4-year visual arts college
◗ Commuter campus in very large city
◗ 4,107 degree-seeking undergraduates: 10% part-time, 78% women, 4% African American, 16% Asian American, 8% Hispanic American, 32% international
◗ 491 degree-seeking graduate students
◗ 62% of applicants admitted
◗ SAT or ACT required
◗ 71% graduate within 6 years

**General.** Founded in 1896. Regionally accredited. Division of The New School. **Degrees:** 567 bachelor's, 410 associate awarded; master's offered. **Location:** Located in Manhattan. **Calendar:** Semester, extensive summer session. **Full-time faculty:** 148 total; 57% have terminal degrees, 14% minority, 48% women. **Part-time faculty:** 917 total; 17% minority, 52% women. **Class size:** 90% < 20, 10% 20-39, less than 1% 50-99, less than 1% >100. **Special facilities:** Architecture studio, labs, galleries, Parsons Institute for Information Mapping, Tishman Environment and Design Center, Vera List Center for Art and Politics.

**Freshman class profile.** 2,719 applied, 1,690 admitted, 752 enrolled.

| Mid 50% test scores | | | |
|---|---|---|---|
| SAT critical reading: | 470-600 | Rank in top quarter: | 42% |
| SAT math: | 490-610 | Rank in top tenth: | 17% |
| SAT writing: | 480-600 | End year in good standing: | 93% |
| ACT composite: | 21-26 | Return as sophomores: | 84% |
| GPA 3.75 or higher: | 16% | Out-of-state: | 74% |
| GPA 3.50-3.74: | 19% | Live on campus: | 75% |
| GPA 3.0-3.49: | 36% | International: | 27% |
| GPA 2.0-2.99: | 27% | | |

**Basis for selection.** Portfolio and home examination most important, followed by school achievement record and test scores. Activities, leadership, motivation considered. Applicants required to complete home examination of 4 specific art and design problems as supplement to portfolio. Portfolio required, essay recommended for all; interview recommended, required for those geographically close.

**High school preparation.** College-preparatory program recommended.

**2009-2010 Annual costs.** Tuition/fees: $36,010. Room/board: $15,260. Books/supplies: $2,050. Personal expenses: $1,550.

**2009-2010 Financial aid. Need-based:** 513 full-time freshmen applied for aid; 470 were judged to have need; 452 of these received aid. Average need met was 71%. Average scholarship/grant was $16,029; average loan $11,300. 60% of total undergraduate aid awarded as scholarships/grants, 40% as loans/jobs. **Non-need-based:** Awarded to 142 full-time undergraduates, including 51 freshmen. Scholarships awarded for academics, art.

**Application procedures. Admission:** $50 fee, may be waived for applicants with need. Admission notification on a rolling basis. Must reply by May 1 or within 3 week(s) if notified thereafter. **Financial aid:** Priority date 3/1; no closing date. FAFSA required. Applicants notified on a rolling basis starting 3/1; must reply within 4 week(s) of notification.

**Academics. Special study options:** Accelerated study, cross-registration, distance learning, double major, ESL, exchange student, independent study, internships, liberal arts/career combination, student-designed major, study abroad. Five-year combined BA/BFA, New York Studio Program. **Credit/**

**placement by examination:** CLEP, IB. **Support services:** Pre-admission summer program, remedial instruction, tutoring, writing center.

**Majors. Architecture:** Architecture, environmental design, interior, landscape. **Business:** Fashion. **Conservation:** Environmental studies. **Visual/performing arts:** Design, fashion design, illustration, industrial design, interior design, photography, studio arts. **Other:** Design and technology.

**Most popular majors.** Visual/performing arts 96%.

**Computing on campus.** 1,200 workstations in library, computer center. Dormitories wired for high-speed internet access and linked to campus network. Commuter students can connect to campus network. Online course registration, helpline, student web hosting, wireless network available.

**Student life. Freshman orientation:** Mandatory. Orientation to school, programs, services, and New York City. **Housing:** Guaranteed on-campus for all undergraduates. Coed dorms, special housing for disabled, apartments available. $250 nonrefundable deposit, deadline 7/1. **Activities:** Jazz band, choral groups, dance, drama, international student organizations, literary magazine, music ensembles, opera, radio station, student government, student newspaper, symphony orchestra, Students for a Democratic Society, various international clubs, sketch comedy group, theater collective, student sustainability committee, Out, Proud Environment at The New School (OPEN), Adventure Force, Women of Color, philosophy club.

**Student services.** Career counseling, services for economically disadvantaged, student employment services, financial aid counseling, health services, minority student services, personal counseling, placement for graduates. **Learning disabled:** Comprehensive services available.

**Contact.**  E-mail: parsadm@newschool.edu
Phone: (212) 229-8989 Toll-free number: (877) 528-3321
Fax: (212) 229-8975
David Norris, Director of Admission, Parsons The New School for Design, 72 Fifth Avenue, New York, NY 10011

## Paul Smith's College
**Paul Smiths, New York**
www.paulsmiths.edu                              CB code: 2640

◗ Private 4-year liberal arts college
◗ Residential campus in rural community
◗ 915 degree-seeking undergraduates

**General.** Founded in 1937. Regionally accredited. Hands-on experience in major, internship programs within college, and externships with leading companies. **Degrees:** 136 bachelor's, 118 associate awarded. **Location:** 25 miles from Lake Placid, 143 miles from Albany. **Calendar:** Semester, limited summer session. **Full-time faculty:** 54 total. **Part-time faculty:** 21 total. **Class size:** 60% < 20, 31% 20-39, 5% 40-49, 4% 50-99. **Special facilities:** Sugar maple plantation, sawmill, on-campus restaurant, 14,200-acre forest, on-campus retail bakery.

**Freshman class profile.**

| Mid 50% test scores | | | |
|---|---|---|---|
| | | ACT composite: | 17-23 |
| SAT critical reading: | 410-530 | Out-of-state: | 35% |
| SAT math: | 410-540 | Live on campus: | 97% |

**Basis for selection.** Most consideration given to high school or college course work as well as SAT/ACT scores. Personal essays, letters of recommendation, relevant experience and SAT/ACT scores highly encouraged. Interview recommended. **Homeschooled:** Statement describing homeschool structure and mission, transcript of courses and grades, interview, letter of recommendation (nonparent) required.

**High school preparation.** College-preparatory program recommended. 4 units required; 8 recommended. Required and recommended units include English 4, mathematics 2, science 2 (laboratory 2) and foreign language 2. High school subject requirements vary according to program.

**2010-2011 Annual costs.** Tuition/fees: $20,865. Program fees range from $660 to $2,120 depending on program. Room/board: $9,350. Books/supplies: $1,000. Personal expenses: $1,000.

**2008-2009 Financial aid. Need-based:** 290 full-time freshmen applied for aid; 273 were judged to have need; 273 of these received aid. Average need met was 73%. Average scholarship/grant was $11,113; average loan $4,447. 55% of total undergraduate aid awarded as scholarships/grants, 45% as loans/jobs. **Non-need-based:** Awarded to 137 full-time undergraduates, including 44 freshmen. Scholarships awarded for academics. **Additional information:** Merit aid only for international students; no financial aid application required.

**Application procedures. Admission:** No deadline. $30 fee, may be waived for applicants with need. Admission notification on a rolling basis beginning on or about 10/1. **Financial aid:** Priority date 3/31; no closing date. FAFSA required. Applicants notified on a rolling basis starting 3/5; must reply within 4 week(s) of notification.

**Academics. Special study options:** Combined bachelor's/graduate degree, double major, honors, independent study, internships, liberal arts/career combination, study abroad. **Credit/placement by examination:** AP, CLEP, IB, institutional tests. 15 credit hours maximum toward associate degree, 15 toward bachelor's. **Support services:** Learning center, reduced course load, remedial instruction, study skills assistance, tutoring, writing center.

**Majors. Biology:** General. **Business:** General, business admin, entrepreneurial studies, hospitality admin, hospitality/recreation, hotel/motel admin, resort management, restaurant/food services, tourism promotion, tourism/travel. **Conservation:** General, environmental science, fisheries, forest management, forest resources, forest sciences, forestry, management/policy, wildlife. **Health:** Predental, premedicine, preveterinary. **Interdisciplinary:** Biological/physical sciences. **Liberal arts:** Arts/sciences. **Parks/recreation:** General, facilities management. **Personal/culinary services:** Chef training, culinary arts, restaurant/catering.

**Most popular majors.** Business/marketing 17%, natural resources/environmental science 41%, parks/recreation 12%, personal/culinary services 27%.

**Computing on campus.** 140 workstations in library, computer center. Dormitories wired for high-speed internet access and linked to campus network. Commuter students can connect to campus network. Online library, helpline, student web hosting, wireless network available.

**Student life. Freshman orientation:** Mandatory, $125 fee. **Housing:** Guaranteed on-campus for all undergraduates. Coed dorms, single-sex dorms, wellness housing available. $100 nonrefundable deposit, deadline 5/1. **Activities:** Choral groups, literary magazine, radio station, student government, student newspaper, outing club, gaming and Anime club, conservation club, Junior American Culinary Federation, Christian Fellowship, fiber arts, fish and game club, ski and snowboard club, campus council.

**Athletics.** NAIA. **Intercollegiate:** Basketball, cross-country, rugby, soccer, volleyball W. **Intramural:** Basketball, ice hockey M, rugby, skiing, soccer, softball, volleyball, water polo. **Team name:** Bobcats.

**Student services.** Adult student services, alcohol/substance abuse counseling, chaplain/spiritual director, career counseling, services for economically disadvantaged, student employment services, financial aid counseling, health services, personal counseling, placement for graduates, veterans' counselor. **Physically disabled:** Services for visually, hearing impaired.

**Contact.** E-mail: admissions@paulsmiths.edu
Phone: (518) 327-6227 Toll-free number: (800) 421-2605
Fax: (518) 327-6016
Kathy Fitzgerald, Vice President of Enrollment Management, Paul Smith's College, PO Box 265, Routes 30 & 86, Paul Smiths, NY 12970-0265

---

## Polytechnic Institute of New York University
**Brooklyn, New York**  **CB member**
**www.poly.edu**  **CB code: 2668**

- Private 4-year university
- Commuter campus in very large city
- 1,632 degree-seeking undergraduates: 4% part-time, 20% women, 10% African American, 28% Asian American, 11% Hispanic American, 12% international
- 2,627 degree-seeking graduate students
- 55% of applicants admitted
- SAT or ACT, application essay required
- 54% graduate within 6 years

**General.** Founded in 1854. Regionally accredited. **Degrees:** 247 bachelor's awarded; master's, doctoral, professional offered. **ROTC:** Army, Air Force. **Location:** 2 miles from New York City. **Calendar:** Semester, extensive summer session. **Full-time faculty:** 152 total; 89% have terminal degrees, 24% minority, 18% women. **Part-time faculty:** 189 total; 57% have terminal degrees, 21% minority, 19% women. **Class size:** 52% < 20, 41% 20-39, 4% 40-49, 3% 50-99, less than 1% >100. **Special facilities:** Library of science and technology, center for advanced technology in telecommunications, institute of imaging sciences, center for construction management technology, transportation research institute, wireless research institute, urban infrastructure institute.

**Freshman class profile.** 3,897 applied, 2,145 admitted, 366 enrolled.

| Mid 50% test scores | | | |
|---|---|---|---|
| SAT critical reading: | 560-640 | Rank in top tenth: | 36% |
| SAT math: | 630-720 | End year in good standing: | 79% |
| GPA 3.75 or higher: | 29% | Return as sophomores: | 85% |
| GPA 3.50-3.74: | 24% | Out-of-state: | 27% |
| GPA 3.0-3.49: | 26% | Live on campus: | 51% |
| GPA 2.0-2.99: | 20% | International: | 7% |
| Rank in top quarter: | 69% | Fraternities: | 6% |
| | | Sororities: | 3% |

**Basis for selection.** School achievement record, class rank, test scores, recommendations required. Special emphasis on mathematics and science areas. Interview recommended.

**High school preparation.** College-preparatory program required. Required and recommended units include English 4, mathematics 4, social studies 3, science 4, foreign language 2 and academic electives 2. Requirements include 1 chemistry, pre-calculus, calculus.

**2009-2010 Annual costs.** Tuition/fees: $34,420. Room/board: $9,000. Books/supplies: $1,000. Personal expenses: $1,575.

**2008-2009 Financial aid. Need-based:** 288 full-time freshmen applied for aid; 217 were judged to have need; 217 of these received aid. Average need met was 95%. Average scholarship/grant was $12,293; average loan $4,729. 62% of total undergraduate aid awarded as scholarships/grants, 38% as loans/jobs. **Non-need-based:** Awarded to 1,101 full-time undergraduates, including 236 freshmen. Scholarships awarded for academics.

**Application procedures. Admission:** Priority date 2/1; no deadline. $50 fee, may be waived for applicants with need, free for online applicants. Admission notification on a rolling basis beginning on or about 2/1. Must reply by May 1 or within 4 week(s) if notified thereafter. **Financial aid:** Priority date 3/1; no closing date. FAFSA, institutional form, CSS PROFILE required. Applicants notified on a rolling basis starting 3/15; must reply within 2 week(s) of notification.

**Academics. Special study options:** Accelerated study, combined bachelor's/graduate degree, cooperative education, distance learning, double major, honors, internships, study abroad. Joint master's degree program in dental materials science with New York University. **Credit/placement by examination:** AP, CLEP, IB, institutional tests. 16 credit hours maximum toward bachelor's degree. Students with outstanding record or specialized competence may establish 16 credits maximum toward baccalaureate degree by passing comprehensive examinations. Each department determines courses in which examination available and examination format. **Support services:** Learning center, pre-admission summer program, remedial instruction, study skills assistance, tutoring, writing center.

**Honors college/program.** Students selected for Honors College must have superior high school academic records and interview with member of Honors College Faculty Governing Board.

**Majors. Biology:** Molecular biochemistry. **Business:** Construction management, management information systems. **Computer sciences:** Computer science, web page design. **Engineering:** Chemical, civil, computer, electrical, mechanical. **Engineering technology:** Industrial management. **History:** Science/technology. **Interdisciplinary:** Science/society. **Liberal arts:** Arts/sciences. **Math:** Applied. **Physical sciences:** Chemistry, physics. **Social sciences:** Urban studies. **Other:** Sustainable urban environments.

**Most popular majors.** Business/marketing 9%, computer/information sciences 11%, engineering/engineering technologies 66%, physical sciences 7%.

**Computing on campus.** PC or laptop required. 104 workstations in dormitories, library, computer center, student center. Dormitories linked to campus network. Commuter students can connect to campus network. Online library, helpline, repair service, student web hosting, wireless network available.

**Student life. Freshman orientation:** Available. **Housing:** Guaranteed on-campus for freshmen. Coed dorms, fraternity/sorority housing, wellness housing available. $300 nonrefundable deposit. **Activities:** Film society, literary magazine, radio station, student government, student newspaper, Society of Women Engineers, Society of Black Engineers, Ambassador Society, ethnic and service organizations, Society of Hispanic Professional Engineers, Alpha Phi Omega service fraternity.

**Athletics.** NCAA. **Intercollegiate:** Baseball M, basketball, cross-country, judo, soccer, softball W, tennis, track and field, volleyball. **Intramural:** Basketball, bowling, football (non-tackle), golf, handball M, ice hockey M, racquetball, skiing, soccer, softball W, table tennis, track and field, volleyball, weight lifting. **Team name:** Blue Jays.

**Student services.** Career counseling, student employment services, placement for graduates.

**Contact.**  E-mail: uadmit@poly.edu
Phone: (718) 260-3100 Toll-free number: (800) 765-9832
Fax: (718) 260-3446
Joy Colelli, Dean of Admissions and New Students, Polytechnic Institute of
New York University, 6 Metrotech Center, Brooklyn, NY 11201-2999

## Pratt Institute
### Brooklyn, New York
**www.pratt.edu**

**CB member**
**CB code: 2669**

- Private 4-year university and visual arts college
- Residential campus in very large city
- 2,973 degree-seeking undergraduates: 5% part-time, 62% women, 5% African American, 15% Asian American, 9% Hispanic American, 13% international
- 1,689 degree-seeking graduate students
- 41% of applicants admitted
- SAT or ACT with writing, application essay required
- 57% graduate within 6 years

**General.** Founded in 1887. Regionally accredited. Additional campus located in Manhattan with associate degree programs, bachelor's degree in construction management program, and various graduate programs. **Degrees:** 630 bachelor's, 57 associate awarded; master's offered. **Location:** 2 miles from Manhattan. **Calendar:** Semester, extensive summer session. **Full-time faculty:** 120 total; 68% have terminal degrees, 13% minority, 38% women. **Part-time faculty:** 877 total; 15% minority, 42% women. **Class size:** 87% < 20, 13% 20-39, less than 1% 40-49, less than 1% 50-99. **Special facilities:** Wood and metal workshops, ceramics kiln studios and casting foundry, digital arts labs, printmaking workshop, fine arts center, center for community development.

**Freshman class profile.** 5,471 applied, 2,268 admitted, 629 enrolled.

| Mid 50% test scores | | | |
|---|---|---|---|
| SAT critical reading: | 530-640 | GPA 3.0-3.49: | 29% |
| SAT math: | 520-650 | GPA 2.0-2.99: | 14% |
| SAT writing: | 530-630 | Return as sophomores: | 83% |
| ACT composite: | 22-28 | Out-of-state: | 73% |
| GPA 3.75 or higher: | 35% | Live on campus: | 88% |
| GPA 3.50-3.74: | 22% | International: | 14% |

**Basis for selection.** Admissions committee considers overall academic record which includes academic performance, portfolio, curriculum, test scores, recommendation, and essay. SAT Subject Tests recommended for applicants to architecture program. Interview not required. Letter of recommendation required for all applicants. Portfolio required for architecture, art and design programs.

**High school preparation.** 16 units recommended. Recommended units include English 4, mathematics 4, social studies 1, science 2 and academic electives 5. 4 math required for architecture and construction management applicants.

**2009-2010 Annual costs.** Tuition/fees: $34,880. All architecture students required to purchase laptop and software (discounted) during summer. All sophomore interior design majors required to purchase laptop computer. Laptop costs approximately $3,600. Room/board: $9,765. Books/supplies: $3,000. Personal expenses: $1,000.

**2009-2010 Financial aid.** **Non-need-based:** Scholarships awarded for academics, art.

**Application procedures.** **Admission:** Closing date 1/5 (postmark date). $50 fee, may be waived for applicants with need. Admission notification 4/1. Must reply by May 1 or within 2 week(s) if notified thereafter. **Financial aid:** Closing date 2/1. FAFSA, institutional form required. Applicants notified on a rolling basis starting 3/11; must reply within 2 week(s) of notification.

**Academics.** **Special study options:** ESL, exchange student, independent study, internships, study abroad, teacher certification program. **Credit/placement by examination:** AP, CLEP, institutional tests. **Support services:** Learning center, pre-admission summer program, reduced course load, study skills assistance, tutoring, writing center.

**Majors.** **Architecture:** Architecture. **Business:** Construction management. **Communications technology:** Animation/special effects. **Computer sciences:** Computer graphics. **Construction:** Site management. **Education:** Art. **Visual/performing arts:** Art history/conservation, cinematography, design, digital art, fashion design, industrial design, interior design, photography, studio arts. **Other:** Critical and visual studies.

**Most popular majors.** Architecture 16%, visual/performing arts 69%.

**Computing on campus.** 300 workstations in dormitories, library, computer center, student center. Dormitories wired for high-speed internet access and linked to campus network. Commuter students can connect to campus network. Online course registration, helpline, repair service, student web hosting, wireless network available.

**Student life.** **Freshman orientation:** Available. Preregistration for classes offered. **Housing:** Guaranteed on-campus for freshmen. Coed dorms, special housing for disabled, apartments, wellness housing available. $300 fully refundable deposit, deadline 5/1. Healthy choice and quiet floors. **Activities:** Campus ministries, film society, international student organizations, literary magazine, music ensembles, radio station, student government, student newspaper, TV station, Christian Fellowship, Jewish student union, Muslim student association, Asian student organization, The Agenda, Korean student association, environmental resource group, Gay/Lesbian at Pratt, New York Public Interest Research Group, Pratt Projects (socially conscious project design and creation).

**Athletics.** NCAA. **Intercollegiate:** Basketball M, cross-country, soccer, tennis, track and field, volleyball W. **Intramural:** Badminton, basketball, football (non-tackle) M, weight lifting. **Team name:** Canonneers.

**Student services.** Alcohol/substance abuse counseling, chaplain/spiritual director, career counseling, student employment services, financial aid counseling, health services, minority student services, personal counseling, placement for graduates, veterans' counselor. **Physically disabled:** Services for visually, speech, hearing impaired.

**Contact.**  E-mail: visit@pratt.edu
Phone: (718) 636-3514 Toll-free number: (800) 331-0834
Fax: (718) 636-3670
William Swan, Director of Admissions, Pratt Institute, 200 Willoughby
Avenue, Brooklyn, NY 11205-3817

## Rabbinical Academy Mesivta Rabbi Chaim Berlin
### Brooklyn, New York

**CB code: 0719**

- Private 4-year rabbinical college for men affiliated with Jewish faith
- Very large city
- 222 degree-seeking undergraduates
- 108 graduate students

**General.** Accredited by AARTS. **Degrees:** 27 bachelor's awarded; master's offered. **Calendar:** Continuous. **Full-time faculty:** 12 total. **Part-time faculty:** 3 total.

**2009-2010 Annual costs.** Tuition/fees: $9,750. Room/board: $3,000.

**Application procedures.** **Admission:** No deadline. No application fee.

**Academics.** **Credit/placement by examination:** CLEP.

**Majors.** **Theology:** Talmudic.

**Contact.**  Phone: (718) 377-0777
Eli Rabinowitz, Admissions Director, Rabbinical Academy Mesivta Rabbi
Chaim Berlin, 1605 Coney Island Avenue, Brooklyn, NY 11230

## Rabbinical College Beth Shraga
### Monsey, New York

- Private 4-year rabbinical college for men affiliated with Jewish faith
- Commuter campus in large town
- 35 degree-seeking undergraduates

**General.** **Calendar:** Continuous.

**2009-2010 Annual costs.** Tuition/fees: $9,100. Tuition includes fees. Room/board: $4,200.

**Application procedures.** **Admission:** No deadline.

**Academics.** **Credit/placement by examination:** CLEP.

**Majors.** **Theology:** Talmudic.

**Contact.**  Phone: (845) 356-1980
Schraga Schiff, Admissions Director, Rabbinical College Beth Shraga, PO
Box 412, Monsey, NY 10952

## Rabbinical College Bobover Yeshiva B'nei Zion
### Brooklyn, New York
CB code: 7011

◆ Private 5-year rabbinical college for men affiliated with Jewish faith
◆ Very large city
◆ 199 degree-seeking undergraduates
◆ 53 graduate students

**General.** Accredited by AARTS. **Degrees:** 49 bachelor's awarded; doctoral offered. **Calendar:** Continuous.

**Basis for selection.** Approximately 150 folio pages of Talmud, courses on Pentateuch with commentaries, Orach Cham Codes of Jewish Law.

**2009-2010 Annual costs.** Tuition/fees: $6,160. Room/board: $4,300. Books/supplies: $400. Personal expenses: $500.

**Application procedures. Admission:** No deadline.

**Academics. Credit/placement by examination:** CLEP.

**Majors. Theology:** Talmudic.

**Contact.**  Phone: (718) 438-2018
Rabbinical College Bobover Yeshiva B'nei Zion, 1577 48th Street,
Brooklyn, NY 11219

## Rabbinical College Ch'san Sofer of New York
### Brooklyn, New York
CB code: 0714

◆ Private 4-year rabbinical college for men affiliated with Jewish faith
◆ Very large city
◆ 40 degree-seeking undergraduates
◆ 14 graduate students
◆ Interview required

**General.** Founded in 1940. Accredited by AARTS. Ordination and First Talmudic degree available. **Degrees:** 1 bachelor's awarded; master's offered. **Calendar:** Semester.

**Basis for selection.** Religious commitment, school achievement record, and interview most important.

**2009-2010 Annual costs.** Tuition/fees: $7,000.

**Application procedures. Admission:** Closing date 9/1. Admission notification on a rolling basis.

**Academics. Credit/placement by examination:** CLEP.

**Majors. Theology:** Talmudic.

**Student life. Policies:** Religious observance required.

**Contact.**  Phone: (718) 236-1171
Rabbinical College Ch'san Sofer of New York, 1876 50th Street, Brooklyn, NY 11204

## Rabbinical College of Long Island
### Long Beach, New York
CB code: 0675

◆ Private 4-year rabbinical and teachers college for men affiliated with Jewish faith
◆ Large town
◆ 121 degree-seeking undergraduates
◆ Interview required

**General.** Founded in 1965. Accredited by AARTS. Ordination and First Talmudic degree available. **Calendar:** Trimester. **Full-time faculty:** 4 total. **Part-time faculty:** 2 total.

**Basis for selection.** Religious commitment, interview, and recommendations most important.

**Application procedures. Admission:** No deadline. No application fee. Admission notification on a rolling basis.

**Academics. Credit/placement by examination:** CLEP.

**Majors. Theology:** Talmudic.

**Student life. Policies:** Religious observance required.

**Contact.**  Phone: (516) 431-7414
Rabbi. Chaim Hoberman, Director of Admissions, Rabbinical College of Long Island, 205 West Beech Street, Long Beach, NY 11561

## Rabbinical College of Ohr Shimon Yisroel
### Brooklyn, New York

◆ Private 4-year rabbinical college for men
◆ Very large city
◆ 159 degree-seeking undergraduates

**General.** Accredited by AARTS. **Degrees:** 34 bachelor's awarded. **Calendar:** Semester.

**2009-2010 Annual costs.** Tuition/fees: $6,600.

**Application procedures. Admission:** No deadline.

**Academics. Credit/placement by examination:** CLEP.

**Majors. Theology:** Talmudic.

**Contact.**  Phone: (718) 855-4092
Rabbinical College of Ohr Shimon Yisroel, 215-217 Hewes Street, Brooklyn, NY 11211

## Rabbinical Seminary of America
### Flushing, New York
CB code: 2776

◆ Private 5-year rabbinical and seminary college for men affiliated with Jewish faith
◆ Very large city
◆ 300 degree-seeking undergraduates
◆ 231 graduate students
◆ 95% of applicants admitted
◆ Interview required

**General.** Founded in 1933. Accredited by AARTS. Ordination available. 4-and 5-year undergraduate programs as well as graduate study. Campus in Jerusalem enrolls 50 students. **Degrees:** 44 bachelor's awarded; master's, doctoral offered. **Calendar:** Semester.

**Freshman class profile.** 98 applied, 93 admitted, 91 enrolled.

Out-of-state: 40%  Live on campus: 70%

**Basis for selection.** Interview most important. School record and test scores considered.

**High school preparation.** Diploma from Hebrew high school required.

**2009-2010 Annual costs.** Tuition/fees: $6,000. Room/board: $5,000.

**Application procedures. Admission:** Closing date 7/1. Admission notification on a rolling basis. **Financial aid:** No deadline. Applicants notified on a rolling basis.

**Academics. Special study options:** Independent study, internships. **Credit/placement by examination:** CLEP.

**Majors. Theology:** Talmudic.

**Contact.**  E-mail: registrar@rabbinical.org
Phone: (718) 268-4700 Fax: (718) 268-4684
Abraham Semmel, Registrar, Rabbinical Seminary of America, 76-01 147th Street, Flushing, NY 11367

## Rensselaer Polytechnic Institute
**Troy, New York** — **CB member**
**www.rpi.edu** — **CB code: 2757**

- Private 4-year university
- Residential campus in small city
- 5,539 degree-seeking undergraduates: 28% women, 3% African American, 11% Asian American, 6% Hispanic American, 1% Native American, 3% international
- 1,930 degree-seeking graduate students
- 43% of applicants admitted
- SAT or ACT with writing, application essay required
- 82% graduate within 6 years; 25% enter graduate study

**General.** Founded in 1824. Regionally accredited. **Degrees:** 1,076 bachelor's awarded; master's, doctoral offered. **ROTC:** Army, Naval, Air Force. **Location:** 10 miles from Albany, 150 miles from New York City. **Calendar:** Semester, extensive summer session. **Full-time faculty:** 383 total; 100% have terminal degrees, 23% minority, 21% women. **Part-time faculty:** 89 total; 70% have terminal degrees, 6% minority, 21% women. **Class size:** 53% < 20, 30% 20-39, 7% 40-49, 9% 50-99, 1% >100. **Special facilities:** Spectrometer; performing arts center with concert hall; computational center for nanotechnology innovations; wind tunnel; geotechnical centrifuge; clean room; electron linear accelerator; plasma dynamics lab, lighting research center; athletic village; center for terahertz research; nanoscale science and engineering center; linear accelerator lab; astronomical observatory; business incubation center; fresh water institute; social and behavioral research lab; center for game studies research; artificial intelligence and reasoning lab; human-level intelligence lab.

**Freshman class profile.** 12,350 applied, 5,291 admitted, 1,337 enrolled.

| Mid 50% test scores | | | |
|---|---|---|---|
| SAT critical reading: | 610-700 | Rank in top quarter: | 80% |
| SAT math: | 660-750 | Rank in top tenth: | 61% |
| SAT writing: | 580-680 | End year in good standing: | 95% |
| ACT composite: | 25-30 | Return as sophomores: | 91% |
| GPA 3.75 or higher: | 39% | Out-of-state: | 70% |
| GPA 3.50-3.74: | 35% | Live on campus: | 98% |
| GPA 3.0-3.49: | 25% | International: | 4% |
| GPA 2.0-2.99: | 1% | Fraternities: | 21% |
| | | Sororities: | 13% |

**Basis for selection.** School achievement record important, test scores and essay required, activities considered. SAT Subject Tests in a math and a science required for accelerated program applicants only, or ACT (which must include the optional writing component in lieu of SAT and SAT Subject Tests); students applying from countries (such as China) that do not offer our required standardized tests will be considered without testing on a case-by-case basis. Portfolio required for electronic arts, highly recommended for architecture.

**High school preparation.** College-preparatory program required. 15 units required. Required and recommended units include English 4, mathematics 4, social studies 2-3 and science 3-4. Best suited applicants will have completed 4 math through pre-calculus, 3 science, and 2 social studies and/or history.

**2009-2010 Annual costs.** Tuition/fees: $39,165. Room/board: $11,145. Books/supplies: $1,850.

**2008-2009 Financial aid.** **Need-based:** 1,097 full-time freshmen applied for aid; 877 were judged to have need; 877 of these received aid. Average need met was 88%. Average scholarship/grant was $22,418; average loan $5,741. 76% of total undergraduate aid awarded as scholarships/grants, 24% as loans/jobs. **Non-need-based:** Awarded to 2,438 full-time undergraduates, including 691 freshmen. Scholarships awarded for academics, alumni affiliation, art, athletics, leadership, minority status, music/drama, ROTC.

**Application procedures.** **Admission:** Closing date 1/15 (postmark date). $70 fee, may be waived for applicants with need. Admission notification 3/13. Must reply by 5/1. **Financial aid:** Closing date 2/15. FAFSA, CSS PROFILE required. Applicants notified by 3/25.

**Academics.** Extensive accelerated program offerings available in virtually all Science departments including Computer Science, Physics, Applied Physics, Biology, Biochemistry and Biophysics, Geology and Hydrology, leading to the BS-PhD. **Special study options:** Accelerated study, combined bachelor's/graduate degree, cooperative education, cross-registration, double major, dual enrollment of high school students, exchange student, honors, independent study, internships, liberal arts/career combination, student-designed major, study abroad. BS/MD with Albany Medical College; BS/JD with Columbia University and Albany Law School. **Credit/placement by examination:** AP, CLEP, IB. **Support services:** Learning center, pre-admission summer program, reduced course load, remedial instruction, study skills assistance, tutoring, writing center.

**Majors. Architecture:** Architecture. **Biology:** General, Biochemistry/biophysics and molecular biology, bioinformatics. **Business:** Business admin. **Communications:** General, digital media. **Computer sciences:** Computer science, information technology. **Conservation:** Environmental science. **Engineering:** General, aerospace, biomedical, chemical, civil, computer, electrical, environmental, materials, mechanical, nuclear, physics, science. **Engineering technology:** Industrial management. **Health:** Premedicine. **Interdisciplinary:** Biological/physical sciences, science/society. **Legal studies:** Prelaw. **Math:** General. **Philosophy/religion:** Philosophy. **Physical sciences:** Chemistry, geology, hydrology, physics. **Psychology:** General. **Social sciences:** Economics. **Visual/performing arts:** Studio arts. **Other:** Games & Simulation Arts and Sciences/Human Computer Interaction.

**Most popular majors.** Biology 6%, business/marketing 10%, computer/information sciences 8%, engineering/engineering technologies 53%.

**Computing on campus.** PC or laptop required. 916 workstations in dormitories, library, computer center, student center. Dormitories wired for high-speed internet access and linked to campus network. Commuter students can connect to campus network. Online course registration, online library, helpline, repair service, student web hosting, wireless network available.

**Student life. Freshman orientation:** Mandatory, $175 fee. Preregistration for classes offered. Held over 2-day period in July or August. **Policies:** College housing required of all freshmen unless student lives within 50-mile radius of campus with parent(s) or legal guardian(s). **Housing:** Guaranteed on-campus for freshmen. Coed dorms, special housing for disabled, apartments, fraternity/sorority housing available. **Activities:** Bands, campus ministries, choral groups, dance, drama, film society, international student organizations, literary magazine, music ensembles, musical theater, radio station, student government, student newspaper, symphony orchestra, TV station, student-run union; more than 160 athletic, service, media, multicultural, performing arts, visual arts, religious clubs and organizations.

**Athletics.** NCAA. **Intercollegiate:** Baseball M, basketball, cross-country, diving, field hockey W, football (tackle) M, golf M, ice hockey, lacrosse, soccer, softball W, swimming, tennis, track and field. **Intramural:** Badminton, basketball, bowling, football (non-tackle), golf, racquetball, soccer, softball, swimming, tennis, track and field, volleyball. **Team name:** Redhawks, Engineers.

**Student services.** Alcohol/substance abuse counseling, chaplain/spiritual director, career counseling, services for economically disadvantaged, student employment services, financial aid counseling, health services, legal services, minority student services, personal counseling, placement for graduates, women's services. **Physically disabled:** Services for visually, speech, hearing impaired. **Learning disabled:** Comprehensive services available.

**Contact.** E-mail: admissions@rpi.edu
Phone: (518) 276-6216 Fax: (518) 276-4072
Paul Marthers, Vice President for Enrollment, Rensselaer Polytechnic Institute, 110 Eighth Street, Troy, NY 12180-3590

## Roberts Wesleyan College
**Rochester, New York** — **CB member**
**www.roberts.edu** — **CB code: 2759**

- Private 4-year liberal arts college affiliated with Free Methodist Church of North America
- Residential campus in large city
- 1,388 degree-seeking undergraduates: 9% part-time, 69% women, 9% African American, 1% Asian American, 4% Hispanic American, 1% international
- 540 degree-seeking graduate students
- SAT or ACT (ACT writing recommended), application essay required
- 67% graduate within 6 years

**General.** Founded in 1866. Regionally accredited. **Degrees:** 361 bachelor's awarded; master's offered. **ROTC:** Army, Air Force. **Location:** 8 miles from downtown. **Calendar:** Semester, limited summer session. **Full-time faculty:** 102 total; 66% have terminal degrees, 9% minority, 47% women. **Part-time faculty:** 146 total; 20% have terminal degrees, 8% minority, 58% women. **Class size:** 62% < 20, 33% 20-39, 3% 40-49, 2% 50-99.

**Freshman class profile.** 886 admitted, 264 enrolled.

| Mid 50% test scores | | | |
|---|---|---|---|
| SAT critical reading: | 470-590 | GPA 3.0-3.49: | 29% |
| SAT math: | 480-610 | GPA 2.0-2.99: | 17% |
| SAT writing: | 450-560 | Rank in top quarter: | 56% |
| ACT composite: | 21-27 | Rank in top tenth: | 28% |
| GPA 3.75 or higher: | 32% | Return as sophomores: | 86% |
| GPA 3.50-3.74: | 21% | Out-of-state: | 12% |
| | | Live on campus: | 84% |

**Basis for selection.** Rank in top 30% of high school class, 2.9 GPA, recommendations, test scores, and interview important. Students expected to recognize Christian perspectives and values college upholds. Audition required for music program; portfolio required for art education, studio art. **Homeschooled:** Transcript of courses and grades, state high school equivalency certificate, letter of recommendation (nonparent) required. Strongly recommend applicants visit.

**High school preparation.** College-preparatory program recommended. 12 units required. Required and recommended units include English 4, mathematics 2-4, social studies 2-3, history 3, science 4 (laboratory 3) and foreign language 3. Biology and chemistry required of nursing applicants.

**2009-2010 Annual costs.** Tuition/fees: $23,780. Room/board: $8,520. Books/supplies: $1,000. Personal expenses: $1,800.

**2008-2009 Financial aid. Need-based:** 210 full-time freshmen applied for aid; 199 were judged to have need; 199 of these received aid. Average need met was 79%. Average scholarship/grant was $14,411; average loan $5,149. 55% of total undergraduate aid awarded as scholarships/grants, 45% as loans/jobs. **Non-need-based:** Awarded to 191 full-time undergraduates, including 54 freshmen. Scholarships awarded for academics, alumni affiliation, art, athletics, music/drama, religious affiliation, ROTC, state residency. **Additional information:** Dollars for Scholars offer matching grants of up to $750.

**Application procedures. Admission:** Priority date 2/1; deadline 8/15 (postmark date). $35 fee, may be waived for applicants with need, free for online applicants. Admission notification on a rolling basis. Must reply by May 1 or within 2 week(s) if notified thereafter. **Financial aid:** Priority date 3/15; no closing date. FAFSA required. Applicants notified on a rolling basis starting 3/15; must reply by 5/1 or within 2 week(s) of notification.

**Academics. Special study options:** Combined bachelor's/graduate degree, cross-registration, distance learning, double major, ESL, honors, independent study, internships, study abroad, teacher certification program, Washington semester. **Credit/placement by examination:** AP, CLEP, IB. 30 credit hours maximum toward bachelor's degree. **Support services:** Learning center, reduced course load, remedial instruction, study skills assistance, tutoring, writing center.

**Majors. Biology:** General, biochemistry. **Business:** Accounting, business admin, human resources, marketing. **Communications:** General. **Computer sciences:** General, computer science. **Education:** Art, biology, chemistry, early childhood, early childhood special, English, history, mathematics, music, physical, physics, science, social science, social studies, Spanish, special. **Foreign languages:** Spanish. **Health:** Health care admin, nursing (RN), preop/surgical nursing. **History:** General. **Interdisciplinary:** Biological/physical sciences. **Liberal arts:** Arts/sciences, humanities. **Math:** General. **Physical sciences:** Chemistry, physics. **Protective services:** Forensics, law enforcement admin. **Psychology:** General. **Public administration:** Social work. **Social sciences:** General, sociology. **Theology:** Bible, preministerial. **Visual/performing arts:** Piano/organ, studio arts, voice/opera. **Other:** Economic crime investigation, Music performance instrumental, Nursing, Philosophy/religion.

**Most popular majors.** Business/marketing 26%, education 20%, health sciences 19%, visual/performing arts 6%.

**Computing on campus.** 250 workstations in library, computer center, student center. Dormitories wired for high-speed internet access and linked to campus network. Commuter students can connect to campus network. Online course registration, online library, helpline, wireless network available.

**Student life. Freshman orientation:** Mandatory. Preregistration for classes offered. **Policies:** Religious observance required. **Housing:** Guaranteed on-campus for freshmen. Single-sex dorms, special housing for disabled, apartments, wellness housing available. $100 nonrefundable deposit, deadline 5/1. **Activities:** Bands, campus ministries, choral groups, dance, drama, international student organizations, music ensembles, musical theater, opera, radio station, student government, student newspaper, symphony orchestra, Chapel, mission trips, At the Foot of the Cross service, Habitat for Humanity, In Jesus' Name, Bible studies, SIFE (Student in Free Enterprise), Acting on Aids, senate, Celebration of Diversity.

**Athletics.** NAIA, NCCAA. **Intercollegiate:** Basketball, cross-country, golf, soccer, tennis, track and field, volleyball W. **Intramural:** Basketball, cross-country, football (non-tackle), racquetball, skiing, soccer, softball, table tennis, tennis, track and field, volleyball, water polo. **Team name:** Raiders.

**Student services.** Adult student services, alcohol/substance abuse counseling, chaplain/spiritual director, career counseling, student employment services, financial aid counseling, health services, personal counseling, placement for graduates, veterans' counselor. **Physically disabled:** Services for visually, hearing impaired.

**Contact.** E-mail: admissions@roberts.edu
Phone: (585) 594-6400 Toll-free number: (800) 777-4792
Fax: (585) 594-6371
Linda Hoffman, Vice President for Admissions and Marketing, Roberts Wesleyan College, 2301 Westside Drive, Rochester, NY 14624-1997

## Rochester Institute of Technology
**Rochester, New York**
www.rit.edu

CB member
CB code: 2760

- Private 4-year university
- Residential campus in large city
- 13,260 degree-seeking undergraduates: 7% part-time, 33% women, 5% African American, 5% Asian American, 4% Hispanic American, 11% international
- 2,728 graduate students
- 61% of applicants admitted
- SAT or ACT (ACT writing optional), application essay required
- 68% graduate within 6 years; 12% enter graduate study

**General.** Founded in 1829. Regionally accredited. University comprised of 8 colleges, including National Technical Institute for the Deaf. RIT also maintains campuses in Croatia, Dubai, and Kosovo. **Degrees:** 2,483 bachelor's, 321 associate awarded; master's, doctoral offered. **ROTC:** Army, Naval, Air Force. **Location:** 5 miles from downtown, 70 miles from Buffalo. **Calendar:** Quarter, extensive summer session. **Full-time faculty:** 945 total; 18% minority, 32% women. **Part-time faculty:** 481 total; 5% minority, 40% women. **Class size:** 38% < 20, 37% 20-39, 11% 40-49, 13% 50-99, 2% >100. **Special facilities:** Laser optics laboratory, observatory, animal care facility, color and black-and-white photography darkrooms, electronic prepress and publishing equipment, ceramic kilns, glass furnaces, blacksmithing area, student-operated restaurant, computer graphics and robotic labs, microelectronic, telecommunications, and computer engineering facilities, access to Internet 2 research network.

**Freshman class profile.** 12,994 applied, 7,988 admitted, 2,611 enrolled.

| Mid 50% test scores | | | |
|---|---|---|---|
| SAT critical reading: | 530-640 | Rank in top quarter: | 67% |
| SAT math: | 560-670 | Rank in top tenth: | 33% |
| SAT writing: | 520-620 | Return as sophomores: | 88% |
| ACT composite: | 25-30 | Out-of-state: | 51% |
| | | Live on campus: | 88% |

**Basis for selection.** Primary emphasis on high school grades in required courses, which vary by major. SAT or ACT given considerable weight. Class rank important. Candidates allowed to apply for up to 3 majors. ACT preferred for applicants to National Technical Institute for the Deaf. Interview recommended for all; portfolio required for art, crafts, and design programs. **Homeschooled:** Transcript of courses and grades required. Applicants should provide state certification of graduation if available.

**High school preparation.** College-preparatory program required. 22 units required. Required and recommended units include English 4, mathematics 2-3, social studies 4, science 2-3 (laboratory 1-2), foreign language 2 and academic electives 10. Units required for social studies may be met with history courses. College of Engineering requires 4 math including precalculus.

**2009-2010 Annual costs.** Tuition/fees: $29,283. Tuition for students matriculated full-time at the National Technical Institute for the Deaf (NTID) is $10,233. Room/board: $9,642. Books/supplies: $900. Personal expenses: $725.

**2008-2009 Financial aid. Need-based:** 2,305 full-time freshmen applied for aid; 1,945 were judged to have need; 1,945 of these received aid. Average need met was 88%. Average scholarship/grant was $15,000; average loan $5,100. 66% of total undergraduate aid awarded as scholarships/grants, 34% as loans/jobs. **Non-need-based:** Awarded to 3,451 full-time

815

undergraduates, including 861 freshmen. Scholarships awarded for academics, art, leadership, ROTC. **Additional information:** Most juniors and seniors participate in cooperative education program, earning an average $4,500-$6,500 per 3-month employment period through paid employment in jobs related to major.

**Application procedures. Admission:** Priority date 2/1; no deadline. $50 fee, may be waived for applicants with need. Admission notification on a rolling basis beginning on or about 3/1. Must reply by May 1 or within 2 week(s) if notified thereafter. Applications received after March 15 will be processed if space available. **Financial aid:** Priority date 3/1; no closing date. FAFSA required. Applicants notified on a rolling basis starting 3/15; must reply by 5/1.

**Academics. Special study options:** Accelerated study, combined bachelor's/graduate degree, cooperative education, cross-registration, distance learning, double major, ESL, exchange student, honors, independent study, internships, liberal arts/career combination, student-designed major, study abroad, teacher certification program, weekend college. Accelerated bachelor's/master's degree programs, England semester, Japan semester, summer program in Croatia. **Credit/placement by examination:** AP, CLEP, IB, SAT, ACT, institutional tests. 45 credit hours maximum toward associate degree. **Support services:** Learning center, pre-admission summer program, reduced course load, study skills assistance, tutoring, writing center.

**Majors. Biology:** General, biochemistry, bioinformatics, biomedical sciences, biotechnology. **Business:** General, accounting, accounting/business management, business admin, finance, hospitality admin, hotel/motel admin, international, management information systems, market research, marketing, resort management, restaurant/food services, special products marketing, statistics, tourism promotion, tourism/travel, travel services. **Communications:** General, advertising, digital media, journalism, photojournalism, public relations. **Communications technology:** Animation/special effects, desktop publishing, graphics, photo/film/video, printing management. **Computer sciences:** General, computer graphics, computer science, database management, game design, information technology, LAN/WAN management, networking, security, system admin, systems analysis, web page design, webmaster. **Conservation:** Environmental science. **Engineering:** Aerospace, biomedical, chemical, computer, electrical, industrial, manufacturing, mechanical, polymer, software, systems. **Engineering technology:** Civil, computer, electrical, electromechanical, environmental, manufacturing, mechanical, occupational safety, telecommunications. **Family/consumer sciences:** Consumer economics, food/nutrition, human nutrition. **Foreign languages:** American Sign Language, sign language interpretation. **Health:** Medical illustrating, physician assistant, predental, premedicine, prepharmacy, preveterinary, sonography. **Interdisciplinary:** Math/computer science. **Legal studies:** Prelaw. **Math:** Applied, computational, probability, statistics. **Personal/culinary services:** Restaurant/catering. **Philosophy/religion:** Philosophy. **Physical sciences:** Chemistry, physics, polymer chemistry. **Production:** Furniture, woodworking. **Protective services:** Law enforcement admin. **Psychology:** General. **Public administration:** Policy analysis. **Social sciences:** Economics, international relations, urban studies. **Visual/performing arts:** Ceramics, cinematography, commercial photography, commercial/advertising art, crafts, design, graphic design, illustration, industrial design, interior design, metal/jewelry, multimedia, painting, photography, printmaking, sculpture, studio arts.

**Most popular majors.** Biology 6%, business/marketing 11%, computer/information sciences 16%, engineering/engineering technologies 27%, interdisciplinary studies 9%, visual/performing arts 15%.

**Computing on campus.** 2,500 workstations in dormitories, library, computer center. Dormitories wired for high-speed internet access and linked to campus network. Commuter students can connect to campus network. Online course registration, online library, helpline, repair service, student web hosting, wireless network available.

**Student life. Freshman orientation:** Mandatory, $165 fee. Preregistration for classes offered. Orientation in September prior to start of classes. **Policies:** Alcohol prohibited in campus residence halls. **Housing:** Guaranteed on-campus for freshmen. Coed dorms, special housing for disabled, apartments, fraternity/sorority housing, wellness housing available. $300 non-refundable deposit, deadline 5/1. Special interest houses for students in selected majors or groups, single-sex floors within coed dorms, special honors program floor available. **Activities:** Bands, campus ministries, choral groups, dance, drama, film society, international student organizations, literary magazine, music ensembles, musical theater, radio station, student government, student newspaper, Asian Culture Society, Electronic Gaming Society, Gospel Ensemble, Society of Women Engineers, Society of Hispanic Engineers, National Society of Black Engineers, Emerging Black Artists, Feminist Action, Catholic Newman Network, Outing club.

**Athletics.** NCAA. **Intercollegiate:** Baseball M, basketball, cheerleading, cross-country, diving, ice hockey, lacrosse, rowing (crew), soccer, softball W, swimming, tennis, track and field, volleyball W, wrestling M. **Intramural:** Badminton, basketball, bowling, football (non-tackle) M, golf, ice hockey,

racquetball, soccer, softball, table tennis, tennis, volleyball. **Team name:** Tigers.

**Student services.** Adult student services, alcohol/substance abuse counseling, chaplain/spiritual director, career counseling, services for economically disadvantaged, student employment services, financial aid counseling, health services, legal services, minority student services, on-campus daycare, personal counseling, placement for graduates, veterans' counselor, women's services. **Physically disabled:** Services for visually, speech, hearing impaired. **Learning disabled:** Comprehensive services available.

**Contact.** E-mail: admissions@rit.edu
Phone: (585) 475-6631 Fax: (585) 475-7424
Daniel Shelley, Assistant Vice President and Director of Undergraduate Admissions, Rochester Institute of Technology, 60 Lomb Memorial Drive, Rochester, NY 14623-5604

## Russell Sage College
**Troy, New York**     CB member
www.sage.edu/rsc     CB code: 2764

▶ Private 4-year liberal arts college for women
▶ Residential campus in small city
▶ 704 degree-seeking undergraduates: 3% part-time, 99% women, 7% African American, 3% Asian American, 3% Hispanic American
▶ 76% of applicants admitted
▶ Application essay required
▶ 70% graduate within 6 years; 34% enter graduate study

**General.** Founded in 1916. Regionally accredited. Russell Sage College offers liberal arts and professional degree programs in business, nursing and health sciences, education, performing arts. RSC is a member of The Sage Colleges, including the coeducational Sage College of Albany and Sage Graduate School. **Degrees:** 219 bachelor's awarded. **ROTC:** Army, Naval, Air Force. **Location:** 10 miles from Albany, 150 miles from New York City. **Calendar:** Semester, extensive summer session. **Full-time faculty:** 56 total; 75% have terminal degrees, 4% minority, 68% women. **Part-time faculty:** 18 total; 83% have terminal degrees, 17% minority, 44% women. **Class size:** 57% < 20, 42% 20-39, 1% 40-49. **Special facilities:** Center for women's studies, New York State Theater Institute, INVEST nanotechnology business incubator.

**Freshman class profile.** 486 applied, 371 admitted, 128 enrolled.

| Mid 50% test scores | | | |
|---|---|---|---|
| SAT critical reading: | 550-590 | GPA 2.0-2.99: | 16% |
| SAT math: | 530-590 | Rank in top quarter: | 69% |
| ACT composite: | 24-25 | Rank in top tenth: | 24% |
| GPA 3.75 or higher: | 29% | End year in good standing: | 90% |
| GPA 3.50-3.74: | 18% | Return as sophomores: | 84% |
| GPA 3.0-3.49: | 35% | Out-of-state: | 16% |
| | | Live on campus: | 88% |

**Basis for selection.** High school record, standardized test scores most important. Recommendations of school officials, intended major, school and community activities considered. Results from SAT or ACT examinations optional for applicants whose secondary school rank is in top 20% of graduating class. Interview recommended. **Homeschooled:** Statement describing homeschool structure and mission, transcript of courses and grades, interview, letter of recommendation (nonparent) required. **Learning Disabled:** The Sage Colleges promote self-advocacy for students with disabilities and facilitates a positive and adaptive learning environment for such students. Students seeking accommodations are required to present a recent evaluation of their disability conducted by a licensed professional. Upon admission, those requesting accommodations must contact the Coordinator of Disability Services in the Campus Life Office.

**High school preparation.** College-preparatory program required. 16 units required. Required and recommended units include English 4, mathematics 3-4, social studies 4, science 3-4 (laboratory 2-3) and foreign language 2-3. Nursing program applicants must have 6 math/science combination including chemistry. Physical and occupational therapy students must have 4 math/science.

**2009-2010 Annual costs.** Tuition/fees: $27,790. Room/board: $9,670. Books/supplies: $1,200. Personal expenses: $1,225.

**2009-2010 Financial aid. Need-based:** 128 full-time freshmen applied for aid; 123 were judged to have need; 123 of these received aid. Average scholarship/grant was $9,190; average loan $4,595. 60% of total undergraduate aid awarded as scholarships/grants, 40% as loans/jobs. **Non-need-based:** Awarded to 611 full-time undergraduates, including 112 freshmen. Scholarships awarded for academics, alumni affiliation, leadership, music/drama.

**Application procedures. Admission:** Priority date 3/1; no deadline. $30 fee, may be waived for applicants with need. Admission notification on a rolling basis beginning on or about 12/15. Must reply by May 1 or within 2 week(s) if notified thereafter. **Financial aid:** Priority date 3/1; no closing date. FAFSA required. Applicants notified on a rolling basis starting 3/1; must reply by 5/1 or within 2 week(s) of notification.

**Academics.** All students complete internship, field experience, or clinical experience. All students engage in service learning through 2 required courses: Women in the World (first year) and Women Changing the World (senior year). **Special study options:** Accelerated study, combined bachelor's/graduate degree, cross-registration, distance learning, double major, honors, independent study, internships, liberal arts/career combination, student-designed major, study abroad, teacher certification program. Early College for high school juniors, combined bachelor's/master's, bachelor's/doctoral programs with Sage Graduate School, 3+3 BA/JD with Albany Law School, 3+2 BS/BSE with Rensselaer Polytechnic Institute, BA/MS Accelerated Physician Assistant Program with Albany Medical College, BA/MS Early Assurance Program with Albany Medical College, BA/MD Early Assurance Program with Albany Medical College. **Credit/placement by examination:** AP, CLEP, IB, SAT, ACT, institutional tests. 30 credit hours maximum toward bachelor's degree. **Support services:** Learning center, preadmission summer program, reduced course load, remedial instruction, study skills assistance, tutoring, writing center.

**Majors. Biology:** General, biochemistry. **Business:** Business admin. **Communications:** Media studies. **Conservation:** Environmental science. **Education:** Elementary. **Family/consumer sciences:** Human nutrition. **Foreign languages:** Spanish. **Health:** Health services, nursing (RN). **History:** General. **Interdisciplinary:** Global studies. **Liberal arts:** Arts/sciences. **Math:** General. **Physical sciences:** Chemistry. **Protective services:** Criminal justice, forensics. **Psychology:** General. **Social sciences:** Political science, sociology. **Visual/performing arts:** Dramatic, musical theater.

**Most popular majors.** Education 9%, health sciences 43%, liberal arts 8%, psychology 6%.

**Computing on campus.** 164 workstations in library, computer center, student center. Dormitories wired for high-speed internet access and linked to campus network. Commuter students can connect to campus network. Online course registration, online library, helpline, wireless network available.

**Student life. Freshman orientation:** Available, $200 fee. Preregistration for classes offered. 1-day welcome programs offered in June. 4-day orientation in September. **Policies:** Zero tolerance for drugs, harassment, or violence on campus. **Housing:** Guaranteed on-campus for all undergraduates. Wellness housing available. $100 partly refundable deposit, deadline 5/1. Special houses available for honor students and students interested in language/international awareness activities. Over-21 residence hall available for seniors. 19th-century brownstone residences available. **Activities:** Campus ministries, choral groups, dance, drama, literary magazine, music ensembles, musical theater, student government, student newspaper, Black and Latina student alliance, gay and lesbian alliance, Fellowship of Christian Athletes, Hillel, Newman Community, Rotaract Club, Key Club, Sage Votes.

**Athletics.** NCAA. **Intercollegiate:** Basketball W, soccer W, softball W, tennis W, volleyball W. **Intramural:** Volleyball W. **Team name:** Gators.

**Student services.** Adult student services, alcohol/substance abuse counseling, chaplain/spiritual director, career counseling, services for economically disadvantaged, student employment services, financial aid counseling, health services, minority student services, personal counseling, placement for graduates, women's services.

**Contact.** E-mail: rscadm@sage.edu
Phone: (518) 244-2217 Toll-free number: (888) 837-9724
Fax: (518) 244-6880
Kathy Rusch, Director of Admission, Russell Sage College, 45 Ferry Street, Troy, NY 12180-4115

---

## Sage College of Albany
**Albany, New York**
**www.sage.edu**                                          CB code: 2343

- Private 4-year business and liberal arts college
- Commuter campus in small city
- 806 degree-seeking undergraduates: 31% part-time, 66% women, 14% African American, 2% Asian American, 4% Hispanic American
- 65% of applicants admitted
- Application essay required
- 42% graduate within 6 years; 35% enter graduate study

---

**General.** Founded in 1957. Regionally accredited. **Degrees:** 220 bachelor's, 22 associate awarded. **ROTC:** Army, Air Force. **Location:** 150 miles from New York City. **Calendar:** Semester, extensive summer session. **Full-time faculty:** 40 total; 70% have terminal degrees, 8% minority, 58% women. **Part-time faculty:** 60 total; 48% have terminal degrees, 45% women. **Class size:** 75% < 20, 25% 20-39. **Special facilities:** Fine arts studio, graphic design and interior design studios, award-winning Opalka Gallery.

**Freshman class profile.** 529 applied, 342 admitted, 105 enrolled.

| Mid 50% test scores | | | |
|---|---|---|---|
| SAT critical reading: | 460-510 | GPA 2.0-2.99: | 52% |
| SAT math: | 480-530 | Rank in top quarter: | 26% |
| ACT composite: | 20-22 | Rank in top tenth: | 7% |
| GPA 3.75 or higher: | 5% | End year in good standing: | 63% |
| GPA 3.50-3.74: | 18% | Return as sophomores: | 63% |
| GPA 3.0-3.49: | 17% | Out-of-state: | 12% |
| | | Live on campus: | 80% |

**Basis for selection.** Recommendation of high school guidance counselor or teacher and academic record considered for all applicants. Applications reviewed on individual basis. SAT or ACT optional for applicants with secondary school rank in top 20% of graduating class. Interview recommended for all; portfolio required for art and design programs. **Homeschooled:** Statement describing homeschool structure and mission, transcript of courses and grades, interview, letter of recommendation (nonparent) required.

**High school preparation.** College-preparatory program required. 16 units required. Required and recommended units include English 4, mathematics 2-3, social studies 4, science 2-3 and foreign language 2.

**2009-2010 Annual costs.** Tuition/fees: $27,790. Room/board: $9,830. Books/supplies: $1,200. Personal expenses: $1,225.

**2009-2010 Financial aid. Need-based:** 104 full-time freshmen applied for aid; 104 were judged to have need; 104 of these received aid. Average scholarship/grant was $9,615; average loan $6,780. 68% of total undergraduate aid awarded as scholarships/grants, 32% as loans/jobs. **Non-need-based:** Scholarships awarded for academics, art, leadership.

**Application procedures. Admission:** Priority date 3/1; no deadline. $30 fee, may be waived for applicants with need. Admission notification on a rolling basis beginning on or about 11/1. Must reply by May 1 or within 2 week(s) if notified thereafter. **Financial aid:** Priority date 3/1; no closing date. FAFSA required. Applicants notified on a rolling basis starting 3/1; must reply by 5/1 or within 2 week(s) of notification.

**Academics.** College of Applied Studies offers specialties in art and design, business and communications, computer technologies, legal studies, creative studies. Four programs in fine arts (photography, graphic design, interior design, and fine arts) accredited by National Association of Schools of Art and Design. Transfer-friendly "two plus two" curriculum with professional study beginning in first 2 years; joint degrees in clinical biology and cytotechnology with Albany College of Pharmacy. Ease of transfer for community college graduates. **Special study options:** Combined bachelor's/graduate degree, cross-registration, distance learning, double major, honors, independent study, internships, liberal arts/career combination, student-designed major, study abroad. **Credit/placement by examination:** AP, CLEP, IB, SAT, ACT, institutional tests. 30 credit hours maximum toward associate degree, 30 toward bachelor's. **Support services:** Learning center, preadmission summer program, reduced course load, remedial instruction, study skills assistance, tutoring, writing center.

**Majors. Biology:** General. **Business:** Accounting, business admin. **Communications:** Digital media. **Computer sciences:** General, networking, webmaster. **Education:** Physical. **Health:** Cytotechnology, nursing (RN). **Legal studies:** General. **Liberal arts:** Arts/sciences. **Protective services:** Law enforcement admin. **Psychology:** General. **Public administration:** Policy analysis. **Social sciences:** General. **Visual/performing arts:** Graphic design, interior design, studio arts.

**Most popular majors.** Business/marketing 23%, computer/information sciences 7%, education 10%, health sciences 6%, liberal arts 11%, social sciences 11%, visual/performing arts 15%.

**Computing on campus.** 196 workstations in library, computer center. Dormitories wired for high-speed internet access and linked to campus network. Commuter students can connect to campus network. Online course registration, online library, helpline, wireless network available.

**Student life. Freshman orientation:** Available, $200 fee. Preregistration for classes offered. New students may receive academic advising and register for classes (summer, fall, spring) beginning March 1st each year. One-day welcome programs offered in June. 4-day orientation in September. **Policies:** Zero tolerance for drugs, harassment or violence on campus. **Housing:** Guaranteed on-campus for freshmen. Coed dorms, apartments, wellness housing available. $100 partly refundable deposit, deadline 5/1. Apartment-style suites available on adjacent campus. **Activities:** Literary magazine, student government, student newspaper, ALDANA (African American, Latino, Desi's, Asian, Native American Alliance), Sage Votes, Association of Campus Events, Gay Straight Alliance.

**Athletics.** NCAA. **Intercollegiate:** Basketball, cross-country M, golf M, lacrosse W, soccer, softball W, tennis, volleyball. **Intramural:** Badminton, football (non-tackle). **Team name:** Gators.

**Student services.** Adult student services, alcohol/substance abuse counseling, chaplain/spiritual director, career counseling, services for economically disadvantaged, student employment services, financial aid counseling, health services, minority student services, personal counseling, placement for graduates, veterans' counselor.

**Contact.** E-mail: scaadm@sage.adm
Phone: (518) 292-1730 Toll-free number: (888) 837-9724
Fax: (518) 292-1912
Andrew Palumbo, Director of Undergraduate Admission, Sage College of Albany, 140 New Scotland Avenue, Albany, NY 12208

---

## Saint Bonaventure University
St. Bonaventure, New York — CB member
www.sbu.edu — CB code: 2793

- Private 4-year university affiliated with Roman Catholic Church
- Residential campus in large town
- 1,878 degree-seeking undergraduates: 1% part-time, 52% women, 4% African American, 2% Asian American, 3% Hispanic American, 2% international
- 480 degree-seeking graduate students
- 84% of applicants admitted
- SAT or ACT (ACT writing optional) required
- 67% graduate within 6 years

**General.** Founded in 1858. Regionally accredited. Catholic institution in Franciscan tradition. **Degrees:** 381 bachelor's awarded; master's offered. **ROTC:** Army. **Location:** 75 miles from Buffalo. **Calendar:** Semester, limited summer session. **Full-time faculty:** 154 total; 79% have terminal degrees, 4% minority, 36% women. **Part-time faculty:** 82 total; 18% have terminal degrees, 2% minority, 37% women. **Class size:** 57% < 20, 42% 20-39, less than 1% 40-49, less than 1% 50-99. **Special facilities:** Observatory, digital media laboratory, permanent art collection, retreat facility, rare books collection.

**Freshman class profile.** 1,927 applied, 1,617 admitted, 466 enrolled.

| Mid 50% test scores | | GPA 2.0-2.99: | 17% |
|---|---|---|---|
| SAT critical reading: | 460-560 | Rank in top quarter: | 41% |
| SAT math: | 460-570 | Rank in top tenth: | 13% |
| SAT writing: | 450-560 | Return as sophomores: | 82% |
| ACT composite: | 20-25 | Out-of-state: | 24% |
| GPA 3.75 or higher: | 14% | Live on campus: | 96% |
| GPA 3.50-3.74: | 19% | International: | 2% |
| GPA 3.0-3.49: | 50% | | |

**Basis for selection.** Interview, high school GPA and curriculum most important. Recommendation, class rank, test scores, extracurricular activities also considered. Applicants to dual admission premed program with George Washington University or SUNY Upstate Medical University must submit Biology SAT Subject Test score. Essay recommended for all. **Homeschooled:** Statement describing homeschool structure and mission, transcript of courses and grades, letter of recommendation (nonparent) required. Course syllabus, book titles, and all course evaluations required to be considered for admission.

**High school preparation.** College-preparatory program required. 19 units recommended. Recommended units include English 4, mathematics 3, social studies 4, science 3 and foreign language 2. Science majors must have 4 science, 4 math. Business majors need 4 math. Recommend 3 science lab.

**2009-2010 Annual costs.** Tuition/fees: $25,885. Room/board: $9,015. Books/supplies: $700. Personal expenses: $650.

**Financial aid. Non-need-based:** Scholarships awarded for academics, art, athletics, leadership, minority status, music/drama, religious affiliation, ROTC, state residency.

**Application procedures. Admission:** Priority date 2/15; deadline 7/1 (postmark date). $30 fee, may be waived for applicants with need, free for online applicants. Admission notification on a rolling basis beginning on or about 10/1. Must reply by May 1 or within 1 week(s) if notified thereafter. Applications considered until housing is closed. **Financial aid:** Priority date

2/1; no closing date. FAFSA, institutional form required. Applicants notified on a rolling basis starting 4/1; must reply by 5/1 or within 3 week(s) of notification.

**Academics. Special study options:** Accelerated study, combined bachelor's/graduate degree, cross-registration, distance learning, double major, dual enrollment of high school students, exchange student, honors, independent study, internships, liberal arts/career combination, student-designed major, study abroad, teacher certification program, Washington semester. **Credit/placement by examination:** AP, CLEP, IB, SAT, ACT. 30 credit hours maximum toward bachelor's degree. **Support services:** Learning center, pre-admission summer program, reduced course load, remedial instruction, study skills assistance, tutoring, writing center.

**Majors. Area/ethnic studies:** Women's. **Biology:** General, biochemistry, bioinformatics. **Business:** Accounting, finance, management information systems, management science. **Communications:** Journalism, media studies. **Computer sciences:** General, computer science. **Conservation:** General. **Education:** Elementary, physical, special. **Foreign languages:** Classics, French, Latin, Spanish. **History:** General. **Interdisciplinary:** Gerontology, global studies. **Math:** General. **Parks/recreation:** Sports admin. **Philosophy/religion:** Philosophy. **Physical sciences:** Chemistry, physics. **Psychology:** General. **Social sciences:** General, political science, sociology. **Theology:** Theology. **Visual/performing arts:** General, art history/conservation, dramatic. **Other:** Childhood studies.

**Most popular majors.** Business/marketing 38%, communications/journalism 17%, education 12%, social sciences 11%.

**Computing on campus.** 321 workstations in dormitories, library, computer center. Dormitories wired for high-speed internet access and linked to campus network. Commuter students can connect to campus network. Online course registration, helpline, repair service, student web hosting, wireless network available.

**Student life. Freshman orientation:** Mandatory, $150 fee. Preregistration for classes offered. 2-day session held in July. **Policies:** Students must live on campus until they are seniors or 21 years old unless they live within commuting distance. **Housing:** Guaranteed on-campus for all undergraduates. Single-sex dorms, special housing for disabled, apartments available. $200 partly refundable deposit, deadline 5/1. **Activities:** Bands, campus ministries, choral groups, dance, drama, international student organizations, literary magazine, music ensembles, Model UN, radio station, student government, student newspaper, TV station, Students in Free Enterprise, College Republicans, College Democrats, Alpha Phi Omega, BonaResponds, Students for the Mountain, Center for Community Engagement.

**Athletics.** NCAA. **Intercollegiate:** Baseball M, basketball, cross-country, diving, golf M, lacrosse W, soccer, softball W, swimming, tennis. **Intramural:** Basketball, football (non-tackle) M, golf, racquetball, skiing, soccer, softball, swimming, table tennis, tennis, volleyball. **Team name:** Bonnies.

**Student services.** Alcohol/substance abuse counseling, chaplain/spiritual director, career counseling, services for economically disadvantaged, student employment services, financial aid counseling, health services, personal counseling, placement for graduates, veterans' counselor.

**Contact.** E-mail: admissions@sbu.edu
Phone: (716) 375-2400 Toll-free number: (800) 462-5050
Fax: (716) 375-4005
James DiRisio, Director of Admissions, Saint Bonaventure University, Route 417, St. Bonaventure, NY 14778-2284

---

## St. Francis College
Brooklyn Heights, New York — CB member
www.stfranciscollege.edu — CB code: 2796

- Private 4-year liberal arts college affiliated with Roman Catholic Church
- Commuter campus in very large city
- 2,451 degree-seeking undergraduates: 10% part-time, 54% women
- 30 degree-seeking graduate students
- 78% of applicants admitted
- SAT, application essay required
- 50% graduate within 6 years

**General.** Founded in 1884. Regionally accredited. **Degrees:** 386 bachelor's, 10 associate awarded; master's offered. **ROTC:** Army, Air Force. **Location:** 5 minutes from Manhattan by subway. **Calendar:** Semester, limited summer session. **Full-time faculty:** 80 total; 89% have terminal degrees, 11% minority, 46% women. **Part-time faculty:** 163 total; 20% have terminal degrees, 18% minority, 39% women. **Class size:** 47% < 20, 52%

20-39, less than 1% 40-49, less than 1% 50-99. **Special facilities:** Television production and editing facility with 3 Ikegami cameras and 17 Mac G5 digital editing stations.

**Freshman class profile.** 1,944 applied, 1,513 admitted, 591 enrolled.

| Mid 50% test scores | | | |
|---|---|---|---|
| SAT critical reading: | 420-510 | GPA 3.0-3.49: | 21% |
| SAT math: | 400-520 | GPA 2.0-2.99: | 47% |
| SAT writing: | 410-500 | Return as sophomores: | 80% |
| GPA 3.75 or higher: | 6% | Out-of-state: | 2% |
| GPA 3.50-3.74: | 8% | Live on campus: | 3% |
| | | International: | 4% |

**Basis for selection.** Academic achievement, test scores, counselor's recommendation, school and community activities, admissions interview important. Degree-seeking students who do not meet criteria may be admitted after review and assessment of their educational background. SAT/ACT scores must be received by first day of class for fall-term admission. Interview required of academically weak applicants. **Homeschooled:** Statement describing homeschool structure and mission, state high school equivalency certificate required.

**High school preparation.** 18.5 units recommended. Recommended units include English 4, mathematics 2, social studies 4, science 2, visual/performing arts 1, academic electives 5.5.

**2009-2010 Annual costs.** Tuition/fees: $16,480. Books/supplies: $1,000. Personal expenses: $4,000.

**2009-2010 Financial aid. Non-need-based:** Scholarships awarded for academics, athletics.

**Application procedures. Admission:** No deadline. $35 fee, may be waived for applicants with need. Admission notification on a rolling basis. Must reply by May 1 or within 2 week(s) if notified thereafter. **Financial aid:** Priority date 2/15; no closing date. FAFSA required. Applicants notified on a rolling basis starting 3/15; must reply within 2 week(s) of notification.

**Academics. Special study options:** Accelerated study, combined bachelor's/graduate degree, cooperative education, cross-registration, double major, dual enrollment of high school students, ESL, exchange student, honors, independent study, internships, student-designed major, study abroad, teacher certification program, Washington semester. Accelerated biomedical science program with New York College of Podiatric Medicine, medical technology program with St. Vincent Catholic Medical Centers of New York and New York Methodist Hospital, joint affiliation program with St. Vincent Catholic Medical Centers of New York in radiologic sciences. **Credit/placement by examination:** AP, CLEP, IB, SAT, ACT, institutional tests. 32 credit hours maximum toward associate degree, 98 toward bachelor's. **Support services:** Learning center, pre-admission summer program, remedial instruction, study skills assistance, tutoring, writing center.

**Majors. Biology:** General, biomedical sciences. **Business:** Accounting, business admin. **Communications:** General, digital media, public relations, radio/tv. **Computer sciences:** System admin. **Education:** Biology, chemistry, elementary, English, mathematics, physical, social studies, visually handicapped. **Foreign languages:** Spanish. **Health:** Clinical lab science, medical radiologic technology/radiation therapy, nursing (RN), physician assistant. **History:** General. **Liberal arts:** Arts/sciences. **Math:** General. **Philosophy/religion:** Philosophy, religion. **Physical sciences:** Chemistry. **Protective services:** Criminal justice. **Psychology:** General. **Social sciences:** Economics, political science, sociology. **Other:** Health promotion and science, International cultural studies.

**Most popular majors.** Business/marketing 18%, communications/journalism 12%, education 8%, health sciences 12%, liberal arts 13%, psychology 7%, social sciences 8%.

**Computing on campus.** 600 workstations in library, computer center, student center. Commuter students can connect to campus network. Helpline, wireless network available.

**Student life. Freshman orientation:** Mandatory. Preregistration for classes offered. **Housing:** St. Francis has partnered with Educational Housing Services and offers a limited amount of student housing. **Activities:** Campus ministries, choral groups, dance, drama, literary magazine, Model UN, student government, student newspaper, Latin American Society, Haitian Alliance, Caribbean student association, Christian club, Arab-American Society, French club, College Republicans, History and Political Science Society, Italian Historical Society.

**Athletics.** NCAA. **Intercollegiate:** Basketball, cross-country, diving, soccer M, swimming, tennis, track and field, volleyball W, water polo. **Intramural:** Basketball, football (tackle) M, soccer M, volleyball. **Team name:** Terriers.

**Student services.** Adult student services, chaplain/spiritual director, career counseling, services for economically disadvantaged, student employment services, financial aid counseling, health services, personal counseling, placement for graduates, veterans' counselor. **Physically disabled:** Services for visually, speech, hearing impaired.

**Contact.** E-mail: admissions@stfranciscollege.edu
Phone: (718) 489-3473 Fax: (718) 802-0453
John McAuliffe, Director of Admissions, St. Francis College, 180 Remsen Street, Brooklyn Heights, NY 11201-9902

---

## St. John Fisher College
**Rochester, New York**  CB member
**www.sjfc.edu**  CB code: 2798

- Private 4-year liberal arts college affiliated with Roman Catholic Church
- Residential campus in large town
- 2,810 degree-seeking undergraduates: 7% part-time, 59% women, 5% African American, 2% Asian American, 3% Hispanic American
- 1,051 degree-seeking graduate students
- 65% of applicants admitted
- SAT or ACT (ACT writing optional), application essay required
- 74% graduate within 6 years; 39% enter graduate study

**General.** Founded in 1948. Regionally accredited. **Degrees:** 764 bachelor's awarded; master's, doctoral, professional offered. **ROTC:** Army, Naval, Air Force. **Location:** 6 miles from downtown. **Calendar:** Semester, extensive summer session. **Full-time faculty:** 201 total; 89% have terminal degrees, 13% minority, 49% women. **Part-time faculty:** 174 total; 5% minority, 68% women. **Class size:** 42% < 20, 53% 20-39, 4% 40-49, less than 1% 50-99. **Special facilities:** Cyber cafe.

**Freshman class profile.** 3,440 applied, 2,237 admitted, 558 enrolled.

| Mid 50% test scores | | | |
|---|---|---|---|
| SAT critical reading: | 480-570 | GPA 2.0-2.99: | 16% |
| SAT math: | 510-600 | Rank in top quarter: | 55% |
| SAT writing: | 460-560 | Rank in top tenth: | 23% |
| ACT composite: | 22-26 | End year in good standing: | 90% |
| GPA 3.75 or higher: | 28% | Return as sophomores: | 82% |
| GPA 3.50-3.74: | 23% | Out-of-state: | 3% |
| GPA 3.0-3.49: | 33% | Live on campus: | 89% |

**Basis for selection.** GED not accepted. Admission based primarily on student's high school record, SAT or ACT scores, course curriculum, extracurricular activities, counselor and teacher recommendations, and personal statement or essay or graded paper. Interview recommended for all. **Homeschooled:** Transcript of courses and grades, letter of recommendation (nonparent) required. **Learning Disabled:** Admission standards and procedures for students with disabilities are the same as for all applicants.

**High school preparation.** College-preparatory program required. 16 units required. Required and recommended units include English 4, mathematics 4, social studies 4, science 4 and foreign language 3.

**2009-2010 Annual costs.** Tuition/fees: $24,280. Room/board: $10,090. Books/supplies: $900. Personal expenses: $600.

**2008-2009 Financial aid. Need-based:** 543 full-time freshmen applied for aid; 457 were judged to have need; 457 of these received aid. Average need met was 84%. Average scholarship/grant was $14,893; average loan $4,030. 55% of total undergraduate aid awarded as scholarships/grants, 45% as loans/jobs. **Non-need-based:** Awarded to 1,387 full-time undergraduates, including 409 freshmen. Scholarships awarded for academics, leadership.

**Application procedures. Admission:** Priority date 12/1; no deadline. $30 fee, may be waived for applicants with need. Admission notification on a rolling basis beginning on or about 12/1. Must reply by May 1 or within 3 week(s) if notified thereafter. **Financial aid:** Priority date 2/15; no closing date. FAFSA required. Applicants notified on a rolling basis starting 3/22; must reply by 5/1 or within 3 week(s) of notification.

**Academics.** All entering first-year students participate in integrative learning community designed to examine a topic from multiple perspectives, discover connections between different disciplines and develop close working relationships with other students and faculty. **Special study options:** Accelerated study, cross-registration, distance learning, double major, exchange student, honors, independent study, internships, liberal arts/career combination, student-designed major, study abroad, teacher certification program, Washington semester, weekend college. 3-4 optometry program with Pennsylvania College of Optometry, 2-2 environmental science and forestry program with SUNY, 3-2 pre-engineering program with affiliated engineering schools, 2-2 pre-engineering program with University of Detroit and Manhattan College, 4-2 pre-engineering program with Columbia University. **Credit/placement by examination:** AP, CLEP, IB, institutional tests. 66 credit hours maximum toward bachelor's degree. **Support services:** Reduced course load, study skills assistance, tutoring, writing center.

**Majors. Area/ethnic studies:** American. **Biology:** General. **Business:** Accounting, business admin, finance. **Communications:** General. **Computer sciences:** General, computer science. **Education:** General, biology, chemistry, elementary, English, French, history, mathematics, physics, secondary, social studies, Spanish, special. **Foreign languages:** French, Spanish. **Health:** Nursing (RN). **History:** General. **Liberal arts:** Arts/sciences. **Math:** General, statistics. **Parks/recreation:** Sports admin. **Philosophy/religion:** Philosophy, religion. **Physical sciences:** Chemistry, physics. **Psychology:** General. **Social sciences:** Anthropology, economics, international relations, political science, sociology.

**Most popular majors.** Business/marketing 26%, communications/journalism 9%, education 21%, health sciences 11%, social sciences 7%.

**Computing on campus.** 525 workstations in library, computer center, student center. Dormitories wired for high-speed internet access and linked to campus network. Commuter students can connect to campus network. Online course registration, online library, helpline, student web hosting, wireless network available.

**Student life. Freshman orientation:** Available. Preregistration for classes offered. 3-day program in late August. **Policies:** All housing is smoke-free. **Housing:** Guaranteed on-campus for freshmen. Coed dorms, single-sex dorms, special housing for disabled available. $300 nonrefundable deposit, deadline 5/1. All residence halls accessible to students with disabilities. **Activities:** Campus ministries, choral groups, dance, drama, literary magazine, musical theater, student government, student newspaper, TV station, Circle K, Latino student union, Black student union, Asian student union, Fisher Players, gospel choir, resident student association, commuter council, student activities board, Fisher Pride.

**Athletics.** NCAA. **Intercollegiate:** Baseball M, basketball, football (tackle) M, golf, lacrosse, soccer, softball W, tennis, volleyball W. **Intramural:** Basketball, football (non-tackle) M, soccer, volleyball. **Team name:** Cardinals.

**Student services.** Adult student services, chaplain/spiritual director, career counseling, services for economically disadvantaged, student employment services, financial aid counseling, health services, on-campus daycare, personal counseling, placement for graduates. **Physically disabled:** Services for visually, hearing impaired.

**Contact.** E-mail: admissions@sjfc.edu
Phone: (585) 385-8064 Toll-free number: (800) 444-4640
Fax: (585) 385-8386
Stacy Ledermann, Director of Freshman Admissions, St. John Fisher College, 3690 East Avenue, Rochester, NY 14618-3597

## St. John's University
Queens, New York — CB member
www.stjohns.edu — CB code: 2799

- Private 4-year university affiliated with Roman Catholic Church
- Commuter campus in very large city
- 12,115 degree-seeking undergraduates: 3% part-time, 54% women, 18% African American, 18% Asian American, 15% Hispanic American, 5% international
- 5,239 degree-seeking graduate students
- 43% of applicants admitted
- SAT or ACT (ACT writing optional) required
- 58% graduate within 6 years; 20% enter graduate study

**General.** Founded in 1870. Regionally accredited. Branch campuses in Staten Island, Manhattan, and Oakdale; graduate center in Rome. Study abroad opportunities in Paris, Dublin, and Salamanca, Spain. Summer study abroad programs in Korea, Vietnam, China, Dubai, Bermuda, London, Argentina, Spain, the South of France. Winter study abroad programs: Galapagos Islands, Puerto Rico, Italy. **Degrees:** 2,180 bachelor's, 37 associate awarded; master's, doctoral, professional offered. **ROTC:** Army. **Location:** 10 miles from midtown Manhattan. **Calendar:** Semester, extensive summer session. **Full-time faculty:** 669 total; 87% have terminal degrees, 20% minority, 42% women. **Part-time faculty:** 771 total; 36% have terminal degrees, 17% minority, 38% women. **Class size:** 34% < 20, 54% 20-39, 6% 40-49, 5% 50-99, less than 1% >100. **Special facilities:** Speech and hearing clinic, instructional media center, health dducation resource center, writing institute, institute of Asian studies.

**Freshman class profile.** 52,980 applied, 22,788 admitted, 3,108 enrolled.

| Mid 50% test scores | | | |
|---|---|---|---|
| SAT critical reading: | 480-590 | Rank in top quarter: | 50% |
| SAT math: | 490-620 | Rank in top tenth: | 24% |
| GPA 3.75 or higher: | 22% | Return as sophomores: | 78% |
| GPA 3.50-3.74: | 13% | Out-of-state: | 32% |
| GPA 3.0-3.49: | 33% | Live on campus: | 56% |
| GPA 2.0-2.99: | 30% | International: | 4% |

**Basis for selection.** School achievement record, standardized test scores, counselor/teacher recommendations, extracurricular activities, personal essay used. SAT or ACT scores are received on a rolling basis with the exception of SAT Subject Tests for pharmacy students, which must be received by February 1. Personal statement, essay recommended for all; portfolio required for creative photography, fine art, graphic design, illustration programs. **Homeschooled:** Statement describing homeschool structure and mission, transcript of courses and grades, state high school equivalency certificate required.

**High school preparation.** College-preparatory program recommended. 4 units required; 12 recommended. Required and recommended units include English 4, mathematics 3, social studies 2, history 2, science 2 (laboratory 2) and foreign language 2. Additional math/science classes highly recommended or required for certain majors.

**2009-2010 Annual costs.** Tuition/fees: $30,040. Tuition may vary by program and class year. Four-year fixed rate tuition plan available for incoming freshmen. Room/board: $13,140. Books/supplies: $1,000. Personal expenses: $2,700.

**2008-2009 Financial aid. Need-based:** 2,866 full-time freshmen applied for aid; 2,634 were judged to have need; 2,622 of these received aid. Average need met was 71%. Average scholarship/grant was $13,428; average loan $4,190. 59% of total undergraduate aid awarded as scholarships/grants, 41% as loans/jobs. **Non-need-based:** Awarded to 7,529 full-time undergraduates, including 2,362 freshmen. Scholarships awarded for academics, alumni affiliation, art, athletics, leadership, music/drama, religious affiliation, ROTC.

**Application procedures. Admission:** No deadline. $50 fee, may be waived for applicants with need, free for online applicants. Admission notification on a rolling basis beginning on or about 12/1. Must reply by May 1 or within 2 week(s) if notified thereafter. Application closing date for pharmacy students February 1. **Financial aid:** Priority date 2/1; no closing date. FAFSA required. Applicants notified on a rolling basis starting 3/15; must reply within 2 week(s) of notification.

**Academics. Special study options:** Accelerated study, combined bachelor's/graduate degree, cross-registration, distance learning, double major, dual enrollment of high school students, ESL, honors, independent study, internships, liberal arts/career combination, study abroad, teacher certification program, weekend college. **Credit/placement by examination:** AP, CLEP, IB, SAT, ACT, institutional tests. Students must complete at least 50 percent of major courses and at least 30 credits on campus. **Support services:** Learning center, pre-admission summer program, reduced course load, study skills assistance, tutoring, writing center.

**Majors. Area/ethnic studies:** Asian. **Biology:** General, toxicology. **Business:** Accounting, actuarial science, business admin, finance, hospitality admin, insurance, management information systems, marketing. **Communications:** General, advertising, journalism, public relations. **Communications technology:** Photo/film/video. **Computer sciences:** General, security. **Conservation:** Environmental studies. **Education:** Biology, elementary, English, mathematics, physics, social studies, Spanish, special. **Engineering technology:** Telecommunications. **Foreign languages:** French, Italian, Spanish. **Health:** Audiology/speech pathology, clinical lab science, health care admin, medical records technology, pathology assistant, physician assistant, radiologic technology/medical imaging. **History:** General. **Legal studies:** General. **Liberal arts:** Arts/sciences. **Math:** General. **Parks/recreation:** Sports admin. **Personal/culinary services:** Mortuary science. **Philosophy/religion:** Philosophy. **Physical sciences:** General, chemistry, physics. **Protective services:** Law enforcement admin, security management. **Psychology:** General. **Public administration:** General, human services. **Social sciences:** General, anthropology, economics, political science, sociology. **Theology:** Theology. **Visual/performing arts:** Graphic design, illustration, photography, studio arts. **Other:** Programs for foreign lawyers.

**Most popular majors.** Business/marketing 26%, communications/journalism 11%, education 6%, health sciences 7%, legal studies 6%, psychology 7%, security/protective services 8%.

**Computing on campus.** PC or laptop required. 1,245 workstations in dormitories, library, computer center, student center. Dormitories wired for high-speed internet access and linked to campus network. Commuter students can connect to campus network. Online course registration, online library, helpline, repair service, student web hosting, wireless network available.

**Student life. Freshman orientation:** Mandatory, $250 fee. 3-day orientation program includes trip to Manhattan. **Housing:** Coed dorms, apartments available. $300 nonrefundable deposit, deadline 5/1. Limited off-campus apartments available. **Activities:** Bands, campus ministries, choral groups, dance, drama, literary magazine, music ensembles, Model UN, musical theater, radio station, student government, student newspaper, TV station, over 180 organizations on all campuses.

**Athletics.** NCAA. **Intercollegiate:** Baseball M, basketball, cross-country W, fencing, golf, lacrosse M, soccer, softball W, tennis, track and field W, volleyball W. **Intramural:** Badminton, basketball, cheerleading, football (non-tackle), soccer, softball, table tennis, tennis, volleyball, weight lifting. **Team name:** Red Storm.

**Student services.** Adult student services, alcohol/substance abuse counseling, chaplain/spiritual director, career counseling, services for economically disadvantaged, student employment services, financial aid counseling, health services, minority student services, personal counseling, placement for graduates, veterans' counselor. **Physically disabled:** Services for visually, speech, hearing impaired.

**Contact.** E-mail: admhelp@stjohns.edu
Phone: (718) 990-2000 Toll-free number: (888) 978-5646
Fax: (718) 990-5827
Karen Vahey, Director of Admission, St. John's University, 8000 Utopia Parkway, Queens, NY 11439

---

## St. Joseph's College

**Brooklyn, New York**  **CB member**
**www.sjcny.edu**  **CB code: 2802**

- Private 4-year liberal arts and teachers college
- Commuter campus in very large city
- 1,133 degree-seeking undergraduates: 27% part-time, 75% women, 35% African American, 6% Asian American, 16% Hispanic American
- 207 degree-seeking graduate students
- 53% of applicants admitted
- SAT or ACT (ACT writing recommended) required
- 79% graduate within 6 years

**General.** Founded in 1916. Regionally accredited. **Degrees:** 221 bachelor's awarded; master's offered. **Location:** 8 miles from Manhattan. **Calendar:** Semester, limited summer session. **Full-time faculty:** 52 total; 81% have terminal degrees, 19% minority, 54% women. **Part-time faculty:** 87 total; 31% minority, 51% women. **Class size:** 76% < 20, 23% 20-39, 1% 40-49. **Special facilities:** On-campus laboratory preschool for children 3-6 years old, model school for prospective teachers.

**Freshman class profile.** 729 applied, 385 admitted, 204 enrolled.

| Mid 50% test scores | | | |
|---|---|---|---|
| SAT critical reading: | 440-540 | GPA 2.0-2.99: | 5% |
| SAT math: | 440-540 | Rank in top quarter: | 99% |
| GPA 3.75 or higher: | 32% | Rank in top tenth: | 30% |
| GPA 3.50-3.74: | 25% | Return as sophomores: | 85% |
| GPA 3.0-3.49: | 38% | Live on campus: | 5% |

**Basis for selection.** High school achievement record, SAT/ACT scores, class rank, activities, recommendations important. Personal statements encouraged. Essay, interview recommended.

**High school preparation.** 18 units required. Required and recommended units include English 4, mathematics 3, social studies 4, science 2, foreign language 2-3 and academic electives 3. 3 units science recommended for science majors. No specific course requirements for general studies applicants.

**2009-2010 Annual costs.** Tuition/fees: $16,763. Books/supplies: $1,000. Personal expenses: $600.

**2009-2010 Financial aid. Need-based:** 198 full-time freshmen applied for aid; 163 were judged to have need; 163 of these received aid. Average need met was 76%. Average scholarship/grant was $11,009; average loan $3,147. 67% of total undergraduate aid awarded as scholarships/grants, 33% as loans/jobs. **Non-need-based:** Awarded to 154 full-time undergraduates, including 63 freshmen. Scholarships awarded for academics, alumni affiliation, leadership, minority status.

**Application procedures. Admission:** No deadline. $25 fee, may be waived for applicants with need. Admission notification on a rolling basis.

---

**Financial aid:** Priority date 2/25; no closing date. FAFSA required. Applicants notified on a rolling basis starting 3/15; must reply by 5/1 or within 2 week(s) of notification.

**Academics. Special study options:** Accelerated study, honors, independent study, internships, teacher certification program, weekend college. Accelerated biomedical program with New York College of Podiatric Medicine. **Credit/placement by examination:** AP, CLEP, institutional tests. 30 credit hours maximum toward bachelor's degree. **Support services:** Reduced course load, tutoring, writing center.

**Majors. Biology:** General. **Business:** General, accounting, business admin, human resources. **Education:** General, early childhood, elementary, mathematics, middle, science, secondary, social studies, special. **Foreign languages:** General. **Health:** Health care admin, prenursing. **History:** General. **Liberal arts:** Arts/sciences. **Math:** General. **Physical sciences:** Chemistry. **Psychology:** General. **Social sciences:** General, sociology.

**Most popular majors.** Business/marketing 28%, English 6%, family/consumer sciences 18%, health sciences 26%, social sciences 7%.

**Computing on campus.** 90 workstations in library, computer center. Dormitories wired for high-speed internet access. Commuter students can connect to campus network. Online course registration, online library available.

**Student life. Freshman orientation:** Mandatory. Preregistration for classes offered. **Housing:** Coed dorms available. **Activities:** Jazz band, campus ministries, choral groups, dance, drama, film society, literary magazine, music ensembles, musical theater, student government, symphony orchestra, Gaelic society, Hispanic awareness club, heritage gallery, Asian awareness, Japanese animation, political affairs, student ambassador club.

**Athletics.** USCAA. **Intercollegiate:** Basketball, cross-country, softball W, swimming W, tennis M, volleyball. **Intramural:** Basketball, table tennis, volleyball. **Team name:** Bears.

**Student services.** Adult student services, chaplain/spiritual director, career counseling, student employment services, financial aid counseling, personal counseling, placement for graduates.

**Contact.** E-mail: asinfob@sjcny.edu
Phone: (718) 940-5800 Fax: (718) 636-8303
Theresa LaRocca-Meyer, Vice President for Enerollment Management, St. Joseph's College, 245 Clinton Avenue, Brooklyn, NY 11205-3688

---

## St. Joseph's College: Suffolk Campus

**Patchogue, New York**
**www.sjcny.edu**  **CB code: 2841**

- Private 4-year branch campus and liberal arts college
- Commuter campus in large town
- 3,828 degree-seeking undergraduates: 19% part-time, 72% women, 4% African American, 1% Asian American, 8% Hispanic American
- 469 degree-seeking graduate students
- 52% of applicants admitted
- SAT or ACT (ACT writing recommended) required
- 72% graduate within 6 years

**General.** Founded in 1916. Regionally accredited. **Degrees:** 756 bachelor's awarded; master's offered. **ROTC:** Air Force. **Location:** 60 miles from New York City. **Calendar:** Semester, extensive summer session. **Full-time faculty:** 115 total; 74% have terminal degrees, 10% minority, 59% women. **Part-time faculty:** 291 total; 6% minority, 49% women. **Class size:** 59% < 20, 41% 20-39, less than 1% 40-49. **Special facilities:** Playhouse.

**Freshman class profile.** 1,743 applied, 915 admitted, 485 enrolled.

| Mid 50% test scores | | | |
|---|---|---|---|
| SAT critical reading: | 440-540 | GPA 3.0-3.49: | 39% |
| SAT math: | 440-540 | GPA 2.0-2.99: | 5% |
| GPA 3.75 or higher: | 31% | Rank in top quarter: | 55% |
| GPA 3.50-3.74: | 25% | Rank in top tenth: | 19% |
| | | Return as sophomores: | 81% |

**Basis for selection.** Grades in high school academic classes, GPA and rank in class most important. Performance on standardized tests important. Strongly factored in are letters of recommendation, personal statement and school/community activities. Interview recommended. Essays required of scholarship candidates, strongly recommended for all others. **Homeschooled:** Transcript of courses and grades required. SAT or ACT required. Interview strongly recommended.

**High school preparation.** 19 units required. Required and recommended units include English 4, mathematics 3, social studies 4, science 3 (laboratory 3), foreign language 2 and academic electives 2. Social science unit must be American history.

**2009-2010 Annual costs.** Tuition/fees: $16,763. Books/supplies: $1,000. Personal expenses: $600.

**2009-2010 Financial aid. Need-based:** 477 full-time freshmen applied for aid; 330 were judged to have need; 325 of these received aid. Average need met was 83%. Average scholarship/grant was $9,477; average loan $3,109. 58% of total undergraduate aid awarded as scholarships/grants, 42% as loans/jobs. **Non-need-based:** Awarded to 636 full-time undergraduates, including 181 freshmen. Scholarships awarded for academics, alumni affiliation, leadership, minority status.

**Application procedures. Admission:** No deadline. $25 fee, may be waived for applicants with need. Application must be submitted on paper. Admission notification on a rolling basis. **Financial aid:** Priority date 2/25; no closing date. FAFSA required. Applicants notified on a rolling basis starting 3/15; must reply by 5/1 or within 2 week(s) of notification.

**Academics. Special study options:** Accelerated study, combined bachelor's/graduate degree, honors, independent study, internships, teacher certification program, weekend college. Bio-medical program with New York College of Pediatric Medicine. **Credit/placement by examination:** AP, CLEP, IB, institutional tests. 30 credit hours maximum toward bachelor's degree. **Support services:** Learning center, reduced course load, study skills assistance, tutoring, writing center.

**Majors. Biology:** General. **Business:** Accounting, business admin. **Communications:** General. **Computer sciences:** Computer science, information technology. **Education:** General, biology, early childhood, elementary, English, history, kindergarten/preschool, mathematics, middle, science, secondary, social studies, Spanish, special. **Foreign languages:** Spanish. **Health:** Facilities admin, predental, premedicine, preveterinary, recreational therapy. **History:** General. **Liberal arts:** Arts/sciences. **Math:** General. **Parks/recreation:** General. **Psychology:** General. **Social sciences:** General, criminology, economics, political science, sociology.

**Most popular majors.** Business/marketing 20%, English 14%, family/consumer sciences 31%, history 7%, mathematics 6%, social sciences 8%.

**Computing on campus.** 223 workstations in library, computer center. Commuter students can connect to campus network. Online course registration, online library, helpline, wireless network available.

**Student life. Freshman orientation:** Mandatory, $50 fee. Preregistration for classes offered. 1-day orientation in August just prior to start of classes. **Policies:** 2.7 average required to run for student government. **Activities:** Jazz band, campus ministries, choral groups, dance, drama, literary magazine, music ensembles, musical theater, student government, student newspaper, symphony orchestra, Amnesty International, student volunteer services, Circle K, Students Taking an Active Role in Society, Spanish club, Diversity Union, Habitat for Humanity, social sciences club, Lion's Club.

**Athletics.** NCAA. **Intercollegiate:** Baseball M, basketball, cross-country, equestrian, golf M, soccer, softball W, swimming, tennis, track and field, volleyball W. **Intramural:** Football (non-tackle). **Team name:** Golden Eagles.

**Student services.** Adult student services, alcohol/substance abuse counseling, chaplain/spiritual director, career counseling, student employment services, financial aid counseling, minority student services, personal counseling, veterans' counselor. **Physically disabled:** Services for visually, hearing impaired.

**Contact.** E-mail: asinfob@sjcny.edu
Phone: (631) 447-3219 Fax: (631) 447-3601
Gigi Lamens, Director of Admissions and Enrollment Planning, St. Joseph's College: Suffolk Campus, 155 West Roe Boulevard, Patchogue, NY 11772-2603

---

## St. Lawrence University

**Canton, New York**
www.stlawu.edu

CB member
CB code: 2805

- Private 4-year liberal arts college
- Residential campus in small town
- 2,271 degree-seeking undergraduates: 55% women, 3% African American, 2% Asian American, 4% Hispanic American, 1% Native American, 6% international
- 92 degree-seeking graduate students
- 39% of applicants admitted
- Application essay required
- 81% graduate within 6 years; 25% enter graduate study

**General.** Founded in 1856. Regionally accredited. **Degrees:** 444 bachelor's awarded; master's offered. **ROTC:** Army, Air Force. **Location:** 70 miles from Ottawa, Canada. **Calendar:** Semester, limited summer session. **Full-time faculty:** 170 total; 98% have terminal degrees, 14% minority, 49% women. **Part-time faculty:** 29 total; 59% have terminal degrees, 7% minority, 55% women. **Class size:** 64% < 20, 34% 20-39, less than 1% 40-49, 1% 50-99, less than 1% >100. **Special facilities:** 1,000 contiguous acres include woods and river habitat for conducting primary research; science facility; center for arts technology; golf course; crew boathouse; Adirondack Semester yurt village.

**Freshman class profile.** 4,715 applied, 1,848 admitted, 580 enrolled.

| Mid 50% test scores | | | |
|---|---|---|---|
| SAT critical reading: | 570-640 | Rank in top quarter: | 81% |
| SAT math: | 570-650 | Rank in top tenth: | 41% |
| SAT writing: | 560-640 | End year in good standing: | 92% |
| ACT composite: | 25-29 | Return as sophomores: | 92% |
| GPA 3.75 or higher: | 30% | Out-of-state: | 56% |
| GPA 3.50-3.74: | 26% | Live on campus: | 100% |
| GPA 3.0-3.49: | 31% | International: | 5% |
| GPA 2.0-2.99: | 13% | | |

**Basis for selection.** Academic record most important; test scores, extracurricular activities, seriousness of purpose and intellectual promise important. Students for whom English is not the native language must submit official TOEFL results and are encouraged to submit SAT or ACT. Interview recommended.

**High school preparation.** College-preparatory program required. 20 units recommended. Recommended units include English 4, mathematics 4, social studies 2, history 2, science 4 and foreign language 4.

**2009-2010 Annual costs.** Tuition/fees: $39,765. Room/board: $10,160. Books/supplies: $750.

**2009-2010 Financial aid. Need-based:** 446 full-time freshmen applied for aid; 384 were judged to have need; 384 of these received aid. Average need met was 92%. Average scholarship/grant was $27,822; average loan $3,223. 86% of total undergraduate aid awarded as scholarships/grants, 14% as loans/jobs. **Non-need-based:** Awarded to 602 full-time undergraduates, including 159 freshmen. Scholarships awarded for academics, alumni affiliation, athletics, minority status, ROTC, state residency.

**Application procedures. Admission:** Closing date 2/1 (postmark date). $60 fee, may be waived for applicants with need. Admission notification 3/31. Must reply by May 1 or within 2 week(s) if notified thereafter. **Financial aid:** Closing date 2/1. FAFSA required. Applicants notified by 3/31; must reply by 5/1 or within 2 week(s) of notification.

**Academics.** Quantitative Resource Center for math assistance. **Special study options:** Combined bachelor's/graduate degree, cross-registration, double major, exchange student, independent study, internships, student-designed major, study abroad, teacher certification program, Washington semester. Community-based learning; 3-2 program in engineering with Clarkson University, Columbia University, Rensselaer Polytechnic Institute, University of Rochester, University of Southern California, Washington University in St. Louis; early assurance programs in medicine with SUNY Health Science Center at Syracuse and in dentistry with SUNY at Buffalo; combined bachelor's/graduate degree program in business administration with Clarkson University, Union College and Rochester Institute of Technology; 15 study abroad programs in Australia, Europe, Kenya, Japan, Costa Rica, India, Canada, Trinidad and Tobago, China, Thailand. **Credit/placement by examination:** AP, CLEP, IB, institutional tests. 60 credit hours maximum toward bachelor's degree. **Support services:** Pre-admission summer program, reduced course load, study skills assistance, tutoring, writing center.

**Majors. Area/ethnic studies:** African, Asian, Canadian. **Biology:** General, biochemistry, biophysics, conservation, neurobiology/physiology. **Computer sciences:** Computer science. **Conservation:** Environmental studies. **Foreign languages:** General, French, German, Spanish. **History:** General. **Interdisciplinary:** Global studies, neuroscience. **Math:** General. **Philosophy/religion:** Philosophy, religion. **Physical sciences:** Chemistry, geology, geophysics, physics. **Psychology:** General. **Social sciences:** Anthropology, economics, political science, sociology. **Visual/performing arts:** Dramatic, studio arts.

**Most popular majors.** Biology 7%, English 6%, mathematics 6%, psychology 14%, social sciences 30%, visual/performing arts 11%.

**Computing on campus.** 608 workstations in dormitories, library, computer center, student center. Dormitories wired for high-speed internet access and linked to campus network. Commuter students can connect to campus network. Online course registration, helpline, repair service, student web hosting, wireless network available.

**Student life. Freshman orientation:** Mandatory. Preregistration for classes offered. Orientation is three days preceding the start of fall classes. Programs are focused on academic introductions to the liberal arts, to the living-learning community concept, and St. Lawrence traditions. **Policies:** First-Year Program requires freshmen to reside in college with academic/administrative staff. **Housing:** Guaranteed on-campus for all undergraduates. Coed dorms, apartments, fraternity/sorority housing, wellness housing available. Townhouse apartments for senior leaders, some suites available. Students can petition to have quiet or single-sex halls within dormitory. **Activities:** Concert band, campus ministries, choral groups, dance, drama, film society, international student organizations, literary magazine, music ensembles, radio station, student government, student newspaper, TV station, Jewish Student organization, black student union, Muslim students organization, environmental awareness organization, Habitat for Humanity, outing club, academic honorary societies, Circle K, Amnesty International.

**Athletics.** NCAA. **Intercollegiate:** Baseball M, basketball, cross-country, diving, equestrian, field hockey W, football (tackle) M, golf, ice hockey, lacrosse, rowing (crew), skiing, soccer, softball W, squash, swimming, tennis, track and field, volleyball W. **Intramural:** Basketball, football (non-tackle) M, football (tackle) M, ice hockey, soccer, softball W, triathlon. **Team name:** Saints.

**Student services.** Alcohol/substance abuse counseling, chaplain/spiritual director, career counseling, services for economically disadvantaged, student employment services, financial aid counseling, health services, minority student services, personal counseling, placement for graduates. **Physically disabled:** Services for visually, hearing impaired.

**Contact.** E-mail: admissions@stlawu.edu
Phone: (315) 229-5261 Toll-free number: (800) 285-1856
Fax: (315) 229-5818
Terry Cowdrey, Vice President and Dean of Admissions and Financial Aid, St. Lawrence University, Payson Hall, Canton, NY 13617

---

## St. Thomas Aquinas College

**Sparkill, New York**                                    **CB member**
**www.stac.edu**                                          **CB code: 2807**

- Private 4-year liberal arts college
- Commuter campus in large town
- 1,414 degree-seeking undergraduates: 6% part-time, 55% women, 6% African American, 3% Asian American, 16% Hispanic American, 1% international
- 210 degree-seeking graduate students
- 84% of applicants admitted
- SAT or ACT (ACT writing optional) required
- 56% graduate within 6 years

**General.** Founded in 1952. Regionally accredited. **Degrees:** 307 bachelor's, 7 associate awarded; master's offered. **ROTC:** Air Force. **Location:** 15 miles from New York City. **Calendar:** Semester, extensive summer session. **Full-time faculty:** 66 total; 86% have terminal degrees, 8% minority, 47% women. **Part-time faculty:** 74 total; 16% have terminal degrees, 11% minority, 53% women. **Class size:** 48% < 20, 52% 20-39. **Special facilities:** Arts, sciences and technology center, digital imaging laboratory.

**Freshman class profile.** 1,357 applied, 1,140 admitted, 295 enrolled.

| Mid 50% test scores | | GPA 2.0-2.99: | 58% |
|---|---|---|---|
| SAT critical reading: | 420-510 | Rank in top quarter: | 12% |
| SAT math: | 420-540 | Rank in top tenth: | 5% |
| SAT writing: | 420-520 | Return as sophomores: | 77% |
| ACT composite: | 17-24 | Out-of-state: | 19% |
| GPA 3.75 or higher: | 7% | Live on campus: | 64% |
| GPA 3.50-3.74: | 10% | International: | 1% |
| GPA 3.0-3.49: | 15% | | |

**Basis for selection.** School achievement record, test scores, recommendation, and interview considered. Applicants should be in top half of class and have GPA above 3.0. Essay, interview recommended for all; portfolio recommended for art program. **Homeschooled:** Statement describing home-school structure and mission, transcript of courses and grades, state high school equivalency certificate, letter of recommendation (nonparent) required.

**High school preparation.** 20 units required. Required units include English 4, mathematics 3, social studies 4, science 3 (laboratory 2) and foreign language 3.

**2010-2011 Annual costs.** Tuition/fees: $22,410. Room/board: $10,300. Books/supplies: $1,000. Personal expenses: $1,500.

**2008-2009 Financial aid. Need-based:** 316 full-time freshmen applied for aid; 227 were judged to have need; 220 of these received aid. Average need met was 58%. Average scholarship/grant was $10,809; average loan $3,544. 89% of total undergraduate aid awarded as scholarships/grants, 11% as loans/jobs. **Non-need-based:** Awarded to 289 full-time undergraduates, including 72 freshmen. Scholarships awarded for academics, athletics.

**Application procedures. Admission:** No deadline. $30 fee. Admission notification on a rolling basis beginning on or about 10/1. **Financial aid:** Priority date 2/15; no closing date. FAFSA required. Applicants notified on a rolling basis starting 3/1; must reply by 5/1 or within 4 week(s) of notification.

**Academics. Special study options:** Accelerated study, combined bachelor's/graduate degree, cooperative education, cross-registration, double major, dual enrollment of high school students, ESL, exchange student, honors, independent study, internships, liberal arts/career combination, study abroad, teacher certification program, Washington semester. **Credit/placement by examination:** AP, CLEP, IB, SAT, ACT, institutional tests. 15 credit hours maximum toward associate degree, 30 toward bachelor's. **Support services:** Learning center, pre-admission summer program, reduced course load, remedial instruction, study skills assistance, tutoring, writing center.

**Majors. Biology:** General. **Business:** General, accounting, business admin, finance, international marketing, marketing. **Communications:** General, broadcast journalism, journalism. **Computer sciences:** General. **Education:** General, art, biology, chemistry, elementary, English, foreign languages, history, mathematics, multi-level teacher, physics, science, secondary, social studies, Spanish, special. **Engineering:** General. **Foreign languages:** General, French, Spanish. **Health:** Art therapy, predental, premedicine, prenursing, prepharmacy, preveterinary. **History:** General. **Interdisciplinary:** Biological/physical sciences, math/computer science. **Legal studies:** Prelaw. **Liberal arts:** Arts/sciences. **Math:** General, applied. **Parks/recreation:** Facilities management. **Philosophy/religion:** Philosophy, religion. **Physical sciences:** Chemistry, physics. **Protective services:** Forensics, law enforcement admin. **Psychology:** General. **Social sciences:** General. **Visual/performing arts:** Art, commercial/advertising art, graphic design, studio arts.

**Most popular majors.** Business/marketing 21%, communications/journalism 8%, education 13%, parks/recreation 6%, psychology 9%, security/protective services 8%, social sciences 11%, visual/performing arts 7%.

**Computing on campus.** 200 workstations in dormitories, library, computer center, student center. Dormitories wired for high-speed internet access and linked to campus network. Commuter students can connect to campus network. Online library, helpline, wireless network available.

**Student life. Freshman orientation:** Mandatory, $75 fee. Preregistration for classes offered. **Housing:** Guaranteed on-campus for freshmen. Single-sex dorms, apartments, wellness housing available. $250 nonrefundable deposit, deadline 5/1. **Activities:** Choral groups, dance, drama, literary magazine, music ensembles, musical theater, opera, radio station, student government, student newspaper, TV station, political union, business association, community service organization.

**Athletics.** NAIA, NCAA. **Intercollegiate:** Baseball M, basketball, cross-country, golf, lacrosse W, soccer, softball W, tennis, track and field. **Intramural:** Basketball, skiing, softball, tennis. **Team name:** Spartans.

**Student services.** Adult student services, alcohol/substance abuse counseling, chaplain/spiritual director, career counseling, student employment services, financial aid counseling, health services, personal counseling, placement for graduates, veterans' counselor, women's services. **Physically disabled:** Services for visually, speech, hearing impaired. **Learning disabled:** Comprehensive services available.

**Contact.** E-mail: admissions@stac.edu
Phone: (845) 398-4100 Toll-free number: (800) 999-7822
Fax: (845) 398-4114
Danielle Mac Kay, Director of Admissions, St. Thomas Aquinas College, 125 Route 340, Sparkill, NY 10976

---

## Sarah Lawrence College

**Bronxville, New York**                                  **CB member**
**www.slc.edu**                                           **CB code: 2810**

- Private 4-year liberal arts college
- Residential campus in small city
- 1,295 degree-seeking undergraduates: 3% part-time, 73% women, 3% African American, 5% Asian American, 5% Hispanic American, 4% international
- 334 degree-seeking graduate students
- 58% of applicants admitted

- Application essay required
- 73% graduate within 6 years; 70% enter graduate study

**General.** Founded in 1926. Regionally accredited. **Degrees:** 321 bachelor's awarded; master's offered. **Location:** 15 miles from midtown Manhattan. **Calendar:** Semester, limited summer session. **Full-time faculty:** 107 total; 21% minority, 50% women. **Part-time faculty:** 203 total; 47% minority, 51% women. **Class size:** 94% < 20, 3% 20-39, less than 1% 40-49, 2% 50-99. **Special facilities:** Visual arts center, student-run theater, early childhood center, greenhouse.

**Freshman class profile.** 2,126 applied, 1,239 admitted, 365 enrolled.

| | | | |
|---|---|---|---|
| GPA 3.75 or higher: | 39% | End year in good standing: | 100% |
| GPA 3.50-3.74: | 29% | Return as sophomores: | 82% |
| GPA 3.0-3.49: | 25% | Out-of-state: | 78% |
| GPA 2.0-2.99: | 7% | Live on campus: | 100% |
| Rank in top quarter: | 79% | International: | 4% |
| Rank in top tenth: | 46% | | |

**Basis for selection.** Student essays (one of which is a graded, analytical writing sample) and transcript most important. Letters of recommendation and extracurricular commitments also important. Interview considered. Students interested in visual art or music encouraged to submit slides, cassette tapes, or compositions. If on-campus interview not possible, applicant may arrange interview with an alumna/us or counselor.

**High school preparation.** College-preparatory program required. Required and recommended units include English 4, mathematics 2-4, social studies 4, history 2-4, science 2-4 and foreign language 2-4.

**2009-2010 Annual costs.** Tuition/fees: $41,968. Room/board: $13,820. Books/supplies: $600. Personal expenses: $800.

**2009-2010 Financial aid.** All financial aid based on need. 261 full-time freshmen applied for aid; 235 were judged to have need; 235 of these received aid. Average need met was 96%. Average scholarship/grant was $32,318; average loan $2,590, 83% of total undergraduate aid awarded as scholarships/grants, 17% as loans/jobs.

**Application procedures. Admission:** Closing date 1/1 (postmark date). $60 fee, may be waived for applicants with need. Admission notification 4/1. Must reply by 5/1. **Financial aid:** Closing date 2/1. FAFSA, CSS PROFILE required. Applicants notified by 4/1; must reply by 5/1.

**Academics.** 90% of classes are seminars with 11-12 students. Individual biweekly conferences with professors and self-designed independent study available. Students design own course of study with advisor. Although there are no formal majors, students may de facto create double majors. Course work required in 3 of 4 divisions: humanities, history and the social sciences, natural sciences and mathematics, creative and performing arts. **Special study options:** Combined bachelor's/graduate degree, double major, exchange student, independent study, internships, student-designed major, study abroad, teacher certification program. Academic year in Oxford, Paris, Florence, Catania (Sicily), Havana (Cuba), theater year with British American Drama Academy in London; guest year at Reed College (OR), Eugene Lang College The New School (NY), Spelman College (GA), Pitzer College (CA), California Institute of the Arts, or Dartington College of Art at the University of Falmouth, England. **Credit/placement by examination:** AP, CLEP, IB. **Support services:** Tutoring, writing center.

**Majors. Liberal arts:** Arts/sciences.

**Computing on campus.** 110 workstations in library, computer center. Dormitories wired for high-speed internet access and linked to campus network. Commuter students can connect to campus network. Online library, helpline, student web hosting, wireless network available.

**Student life. Freshman orientation:** Mandatory. 9-day program held just before fall semester. **Housing:** Guaranteed on-campus for all undergraduates. Coed dorms, single-sex dorms, wellness housing available. $500 nonrefundable deposit, deadline 5/1. First-year students required to live on campus unless living at home. **Activities:** Jazz band, campus ministries, choral groups, dance, drama, film society, international student organizations, literary magazine, music ensembles, Model UN, musical theater, radio station, student government, student newspaper, symphony orchestra, Amnesty International, Harambe (students of African descent), Hillel, Queer Voice Coalition, Beyond Compliance, Asian-Pacific Islander Coalition to Advance Diversity, Unidad (students of Latino descent), FLUX (Feminist Liberation Union), Transaction, Sarah Lawrence Christian Union.

**Athletics. Intercollegiate:** Basketball M, cross-country, equestrian, rowing (crew), soccer M, softball W, swimming W, tennis, volleyball W. **Intramural:** Basketball W. **Team name:** Gryphons.

**Student services.** Adult student services, alcohol/substance abuse counseling, career counseling, student employment services, financial aid counseling, health services, minority student services, personal counseling, placement for graduates, veterans' counselor. **Physically disabled:** Services for visually, speech, hearing impaired.

**Contact.** E-mail: slcadmit@sarahlawrence.edu
Phone: (914) 395-2510 Toll-free number: (800) 888-2858
Fax: (914) 395-2515
Amy Abrams, Dean of Admission and Financial Aid, Sarah Lawrence College, 1 Mead Way, Bronxville, NY 10708-5999

## School of Visual Arts
**New York, New York** — CB member
**www.sva.edu** — CB code: 2835

- For-profit 4-year visual arts college
- Commuter campus in very large city
- 3,379 degree-seeking undergraduates: 4% part-time, 57% women, 3% African American, 13% Asian American, 10% Hispanic American, 19% international
- 522 degree-seeking graduate students
- 69% of applicants admitted
- SAT or ACT (ACT writing optional), application essay required
- 66% graduate within 6 years

**General.** Founded in 1947. Regionally accredited. Faculty composed entirely of working professionals. **Degrees:** 687 bachelor's awarded; master's offered. **Calendar:** Semester, limited summer session. **Full-time faculty:** 138 total; 6% minority, 38% women. **Part-time faculty:** 811 total; 11% minority, 37% women. **Class size:** 56% < 20, 42% 20-39, 1% 40-49, less than 1% 50-99. **Special facilities:** Visual arts museum, Milton Glaser design study center and archives, 8 student galleries including 9,000-square-foot gallery.

**Freshman class profile.** 3,048 applied, 2,098 admitted, 652 enrolled.

| Mid 50% test scores | | | |
|---|---|---|---|
| SAT critical reading: | 460-580 | GPA 3.50-3.74: | 14% |
| SAT math: | 450-580 | GPA 3.0-3.49: | 34% |
| SAT writing: | 460-570 | GPA 2.0-2.99: | 42% |
| ACT composite: | 19-25 | Out-of-state: | 60% |
| GPA 3.75 or higher: | 8% | Live on campus: | 69% |
| | | International: | 16% |

**Basis for selection.** Portfolio, academic record, interview important. Character and professional recommendations optional. Interview optional. Portfolio required for all programs. **Homeschooled:** Statement describing homeschool structure and mission, transcript of courses and grades, state high school equivalency certificate, interview, letter of recommendation (nonparent) required. GED.

**High school preparation.** College-preparatory program recommended. Recommended units include English 4, social studies 4, history 4 and visual/performing arts 2.

**2009-2010 Annual costs.** Tuition/fees: $26,800. Additional fees vary by department. Room only: $12,700. Books/supplies: $2,100. Personal expenses: $1,600.

**2009-2010 Financial aid. Need-based:** 452 full-time freshmen applied for aid; 396 were judged to have need; 386 of these received aid. Average need met was 41%. Average scholarship/grant was $9,473; average loan $3,581. 36% of total undergraduate aid awarded as scholarships/grants, 64% as loans/jobs. **Non-need-based:** Scholarships awarded for art.

**Application procedures. Admission:** No deadline. $50 fee, may be waived for applicants with need. Admission notification on a rolling basis beginning on or about 2/1. Admitted applicants are encouraged to reply by May 1. **Financial aid:** Priority date 2/1, closing date 3/1. FAFSA required. Applicants notified on a rolling basis starting 2/15; must reply within 4 week(s) of notification.

**Academics.** Curriculum designed to prepare students to graduate as working professionals in the arts. **Special study options:** ESL, exchange student, honors, independent study, internships, liberal arts/career combination, study abroad. **Credit/placement by examination:** AP, CLEP, IB. **Support services:** Learning center, pre-admission summer program, reduced course load, remedial instruction, study skills assistance, tutoring, writing center.

**Honors college/program.** Additional application component.

**Majors. Communications technology:** Animation/special effects. **Visual/performing arts:** Art history/conservation, commercial/advertising art, interior design, photography, studio arts.

**Most popular majors.** Communication technologies 6%, computer/information sciences 8%, visual/performing arts 81%.

**Computing on campus.** 728 workstations in library, computer center, student center. Dormitories wired for high-speed internet access and linked to campus network. Commuter students can connect to campus network. Online library, helpline, wireless network available.

**Student life. Freshman orientation:** Mandatory. Comprehensive 5-day program. **Housing:** Coed dorms, single-sex dorms, wellness housing available. $800 nonrefundable deposit, deadline 5/1. **Activities:** Film society, literary magazine, radio station, student government, student newspaper, Korean Christian, animal rights, international film club, Campus Crusade for Christ, political, anime film club, fine art club, MFA Speakers, wrestling club.

**Athletics. Intramural:** Baseball, tennis.

**Student services.** Alcohol/substance abuse counseling, career counseling, student employment services, financial aid counseling, health services, personal counseling, placement for graduates, veterans' counselor, women's services. **Physically disabled:** Services for hearing impaired.

**Contact.** E-mail: admissions@sva.edu
Phone: (212) 592-2100 Toll-free number: (800) 436-4204
Fax: (212) 592-2116
Adam Rogers, Director of Admissions, School of Visual Arts, 209 East 23rd Street, New York, NY 10010-3994

## Shor Yoshuv Rabbinical College
**Lawrence, New York**
**www.shoryoshuv.org**          CB code: 7129

▶ Private 4-year rabbinical college for men affiliated with Jewish faith
▶ Very large city
▶ 197 degree-seeking undergraduates
▶ 9 graduate students

**General.** Accredited by AARTS. **Degrees:** 6 bachelor's awarded; master's offered. **Calendar:** Continuous. **Full-time faculty:** 23 total.

**2009-2010 Annual costs.** Tuition/fees: $9,460. Room/board: $6,000.

**Application procedures. Admission:** Priority date 8/1; no deadline. $360 fee.

**Academics. Credit/placement by examination:** CLEP.

**Majors. Theology:** Talmudic.

**Contact.** E-mail: info@shoryoshuv.org
Phone: (516) 239-9002
Shlomo Krasnow, Admissions Director, Shor Yoshuv Rabbinical College, One Cedar Lawn Avenue, Lawrence, NY 11559

## Siena College
**Loudonville, New York**          CB member
**www.siena.edu**          CB code: 2814

▶ Private 4-year liberal arts college affiliated with Roman Catholic Church
▶ Residential campus in large town
▶ 3,220 degree-seeking undergraduates: 4% part-time, 53% women, 2% African American, 3% Asian American, 4% Hispanic American
▶ 20 degree-seeking graduate students
▶ 53% of applicants admitted
▶ SAT or ACT with writing, application essay required
▶ 80% graduate within 6 years; 27% enter graduate study

**General.** Founded in 1937. Regionally accredited. Affiliated with the Franciscan Friars. **Degrees:** 769 bachelor's awarded; master's offered. **ROTC:** Army, Naval, Air Force. **Location:** 2 miles from Albany. **Calendar:** Semester, limited summer session. **Full-time faculty:** 194 total; 91% have terminal degrees, 12% minority, 36% women. **Part-time faculty:** 136 total; 44% have terminal degrees, 7% minority, 46% women. **Class size:** 37% < 20, 63% 20-39, less than 1% 40-49. **Special facilities:** Financial technology center featuring real-time capital market trading room, accounting lab, stock ticker, plasma data screens, 24 multimedia workstations.

**Freshman class profile.** 7,282 applied, 3,889 admitted, 783 enrolled.

| Mid 50% test scores | | | |
|---|---|---|---|
| SAT critical reading: | 500-600 | GPA 2.0-2.99: | 13% |
| SAT math: | 530-630 | Rank in top quarter: | 61% |
| SAT writing: | 500-600 | Rank in top tenth: | 28% |
| ACT composite: | 22-27 | Return as sophomores: | 89% |
| GPA 3.75 or higher: | 31% | Out-of-state: | 22% |
| GPA 3.50-3.74: | 22% | Live on campus: | 94% |
| GPA 3.0-3.49: | 34% | International: | 1% |

**Basis for selection.** School achievement record most important, priority given to students with challenging courses. Test scores, activities, recommendations also important. Interview required for Albany Medical School program finalists; recommended for all others. **Homeschooled:** Transcript of courses and grades required.

**High school preparation.** College-preparatory program required. 13 units required; 19 recommended. Required and recommended units include English 4, mathematics 3-4, social studies 1, history 2-3, science 3-4 (laboratory 3-4) and foreign language 3.

**2009-2010 Annual costs.** Tuition/fees: $25,285. Room/board: $9,930.

**2008-2009 Financial aid. Need-based:** 737 full-time freshmen applied for aid; 583 were judged to have need; 581 of these received aid. Average need met was 77%. Average scholarship/grant was $14,505; average loan $3,307. 77% of total undergraduate aid awarded as scholarships/grants, 23% as loans/jobs. **Non-need-based:** Awarded to 2,015 full-time undergraduates, including 604 freshmen. Scholarships awarded for academics, athletics, leadership, minority status, ROTC, state residency.

**Application procedures. Admission:** Closing date 3/1 (postmark date). $50 fee, may be waived for applicants with need. Admission notification 3/15. Must reply by 5/1. **Financial aid:** Priority date 2/15, closing date 5/1. FAFSA required. Applicants notified by 4/1; must reply by 5/1.

**Academics.** Extensive internship program in capital district with state legislature, businesses, social agencies, libraries, and museums. **Special study options:** Accelerated study, combined bachelor's/graduate degree, cross-registration, double major, ESL, honors, independent study, internships, liberal arts/career combination, study abroad, teacher certification program, Washington semester. Semester in Washington, Gettysburg semester. **Credit/placement by examination:** AP, CLEP, IB, institutional tests. 36 credit hours maximum toward bachelor's degree. 36 total credits permitted by proficiency examination, non-collegiate-sponsored instructional/experiential learning combined. **Support services:** Tutoring, writing center.

**Majors. Area/ethnic studies:** American. **Biology:** General, biochemistry. **Business:** Accounting, actuarial science, business admin, finance, marketing. **Computer sciences:** General. **Conservation:** Environmental studies. **Foreign languages:** Classics, French, Spanish. **History:** General. **Math:** General. **Philosophy/religion:** Philosophy, religion. **Physical sciences:** Chemistry, physics. **Psychology:** General. **Public administration:** Social work. **Social sciences:** Economics, political science, sociology. **Visual/performing arts:** General. **Other:** Computational science.

**Most popular majors.** Biology 9%, business/marketing 44%, English 8%, history 6%, psychology 11%, social sciences 10%.

**Computing on campus.** 456 workstations in library, computer center. Dormitories wired for high-speed internet access and linked to campus network. Commuter students can connect to campus network. Online course registration, online library, helpline, wireless network available.

**Student life. Freshman orientation:** Mandatory, $220 fee. Preregistration for classes offered. 3-day summer program. **Housing:** Guaranteed on-campus for freshmen. Coed dorms, special housing for disabled, apartments, wellness housing available. On-campus townhouses, quiet living area. **Activities:** Pep band, campus ministries, choral groups, dance, drama, literary magazine, Model UN, musical theater, opera, radio station, student government, student newspaper, symphony orchestra, TV station, approximately 70 clubs and organizations.

**Athletics.** NCAA. **Intercollegiate:** Baseball M, basketball, cross-country, diving W, field hockey W, golf, lacrosse, soccer, softball W, swimming W, tennis, volleyball W, water polo W. **Intramural:** Basketball, football (non-tackle), golf, soccer, softball, volleyball. **Team name:** Saints.

**Student services.** Alcohol/substance abuse counseling, chaplain/spiritual director, career counseling, services for economically disadvantaged, student employment services, financial aid counseling, health services, minority student services, personal counseling, placement for graduates, women's services. **Physically disabled:** Services for visually, speech, hearing impaired.

**Contact.** E-mail: admit@siena.edu
Phone: (518) 783-2423 Toll-free number: (888) 287-4362
Fax: (518) 783-2436
Heather Renault, Assistant Vice President for Admissions, Siena College, 515 Loudon Road, Loudonville, NY 12211-1462

## Skidmore College
### Saratoga Springs, New York
www.skidmore.edu

CB member
CB code: 2815

- Private 4-year liberal arts college
- Residential campus in large town
- 2,630 degree-seeking undergraduates
- 42% of applicants admitted
- SAT or ACT with writing, application essay required

**General.** Founded in 1903. Regionally accredited. **Degrees:** 681 bachelor's awarded; master's offered. **ROTC:** Army, Air Force. **Location:** 30 miles from Albany. **Calendar:** Semester, limited summer session. **Full-time faculty:** 248 total. **Part-time faculty:** 89 total. **Class size:** 72% < 20, 27% 20-39, 1% 50-99, less than 1% >100. **Special facilities:** Fine and performing arts facilities, equestrian center, 400 acres of woodlands and trails, teaching museum.

**Freshman class profile.** 6,371 applied, 2,693 admitted, 664 enrolled.

| Mid 50% test scores | | | |
|---|---|---|---|
| SAT critical reading: | 570-680 | GPA 3.0-3.49: | 44% |
| SAT math: | 580-670 | GPA 2.0-2.99: | 14% |
| SAT writing: | 580-680 | Rank in top quarter: | 79% |
| ACT composite: | 26-30 | Rank in top tenth: | 37% |
| GPA 3.75 or higher: | 20% | Out-of-state: | 66% |
| GPA 3.50-3.74: | 22% | Live on campus: | 100% |

**Basis for selection.** Rigor of school record very important. Class rank, GPA, recommendations, and test scores also important. SAT Subject Tests recommended. 2 SAT Subject Tests recommended of all applicants. Interview recommended for all.

**High school preparation.** College-preparatory program required. Recommended units include English 4, mathematics 4, social studies 4, science 4 (laboratory 3) and foreign language 4.

**2009-2010 Annual costs.** Tuition/fees: $40,420. Room/board: $10,776. Books/supplies: $1,304. Personal expenses: $1,200.

**2009-2010 Financial aid. Non-need-based:** Scholarships awarded for music/drama.

**Application procedures. Admission:** Closing date 1/15 (postmark date). $60 fee, may be waived for applicants with need. Admission notification 4/1. Must reply by 5/1. Enrollment deposit of $500 required on or before May 1. **Financial aid:** Closing date 1/15. FAFSA, CSS PROFILE required. Applicants notified by 4/1; must reply by 5/1.

**Academics. Special study options:** Accelerated study, combined bachelor's/graduate degree, cross-registration, distance learning, double major, dual enrollment of high school students, exchange student, external degree, honors, independent study, internships, liberal arts/career combination, student-designed major, study abroad, teacher certification program, Washington semester. 3+2 programs in engineering with Dartmouth College and Clarkson University, 4+1 MAT with Union College, 4+1 MBA with Clarkson University and the Graduate College at Union University. **Credit/placement by examination:** AP, CLEP, IB, SAT, ACT, institutional tests. Up to 60 hours may be counted toward degree. Maximum of 12 semester hours may be granted in credit through CLEP subject examinations. **Support services:** Pre-admission summer program, study skills assistance, tutoring, writing center.

**Majors. Area/ethnic studies:** American, Asian, French, women's. **Biology:** General. **Business:** General. **Computer sciences:** General. **Conservation:** Environmental studies. **Education:** Elementary. **Foreign languages:** Classics, French, German, Spanish. **History:** General. **Interdisciplinary:** Biopsychology, neuroscience. **Liberal arts:** Arts/sciences. **Math:** General. **Parks/recreation:** Exercise sciences. **Philosophy/religion:** Philosophy, religion. **Physical sciences:** Chemistry, geology, physics. **Psychology:** General. **Public administration:** Social work. **Social sciences:** Anthropology, economics, international relations, political science, sociology. **Visual/performing arts:** Art history/conservation, dance, dramatic, music history. **Other:** Biology/philosophy.

**Most popular majors.** Business/marketing 12%, English 8%, liberal arts 6%, psychology 8%, social sciences 17%, visual/performing arts 16%.

**Computing on campus.** Dormitories wired for high-speed internet access and linked to campus network. Commuter students can connect to campus network. Online course registration, online library, helpline, student web hosting, wireless network available.

**Student life. Freshman orientation:** Mandatory. Programs on and off campus. Fee for off-campus programs. **Housing:** Guaranteed on-campus for all undergraduates. Coed dorms, single-sex dorms, special housing for disabled, apartments available. $500 nonrefundable deposit, deadline 5/1. There is a gender neutral wing. Townhouse clusters available for upperclassmen. **Activities:** Bands, campus ministries, choral groups, dance, drama, international student organizations, literary magazine, music ensembles, Model UN, musical theater, opera, radio station, student government, student newspaper, symphony orchestra, TV station, 80 clubs and organizations.

**Athletics.** NCAA. **Intercollegiate:** Baseball M, basketball, diving, equestrian W, field hockey W, golf M, ice hockey M, lacrosse, rowing (crew), soccer, softball W, swimming, tennis, volleyball W. **Intramural:** Basketball, football (tackle) M, racquetball, soccer, softball, tennis, volleyball, water polo. **Team name:** Thoroughbreds.

**Student services.** Alcohol/substance abuse counseling, chaplain/spiritual director, career counseling, services for economically disadvantaged, student employment services, financial aid counseling, health services, minority student services, on-campus daycare, personal counseling, placement for graduates, veterans' counselor. **Physically disabled:** Services for visually, speech, hearing impaired.

**Contact.** E-mail: admissions@skidmore.edu
Phone: (518) 580-5570 Toll-free number: (800) 867-6007
Fax: (518) 580-5584
Mary Lou Bates, Dean of Admissions and Financial Aid, Skidmore College, 815 North Broadway, Saratoga Springs, NY 12866

## State University of New York at Albany
### Albany, New York
www.albany.edu

CB member
CB code: 2532

- Public 4-year university
- Residential campus in small city
- 12,797 degree-seeking undergraduates: 4% part-time, 48% women, 10% African American, 6% Asian American, 9% Hispanic American, 3% international
- 4,478 degree-seeking graduate students
- 47% of applicants admitted
- SAT or ACT with writing, application essay required
- 63% graduate within 6 years; 51% enter graduate study

**General.** Founded in 1844. Regionally accredited. Extensive internships in New York's Capital Region. International center for research and development in nanotechnology. **Degrees:** 2,896 bachelor's awarded; master's, doctoral offered. **ROTC:** Army, Air Force. **Location:** 4 miles from downtown. **Calendar:** Semester, extensive summer session. **Full-time faculty:** 637 total; 95% have terminal degrees, 17% minority, 36% women. **Part-time faculty:** 631 total; 12% minority, 47% women. **Class size:** 20% < 20, 44% 20-39, 11% 40-49, 10% 50-99, 14% >100. **Special facilities:** Northeast Regional Forensic Institute; atmospheric science research center and Whiteface Mountain observation facility, microbeam analysis facility, large fine arts work areas, peptide synthesis facility, recombinant DNA sequencing laboratories, nanoscale science and engineering facilities.

**Freshman class profile.** 22,188 applied, 10,442 admitted, 2,333 enrolled.

| Mid 50% test scores | | | |
|---|---|---|---|
| SAT critical reading: | 500-590 | GPA 2.0-2.99: | 12% |
| SAT math: | 530-620 | Rank in top quarter: | 60% |
| ACT composite: | 22-27 | Rank in top tenth: | 21% |
| GPA 3.75 or higher: | 15% | Return as sophomores: | 85% |
| GPA 3.50-3.74: | 22% | Out-of-state: | 6% |
| GPA 3.0-3.49: | 51% | Live on campus: | 98% |
| | | International: | 3% |

**Basis for selection.** High school record, class rank, GPA, standardized test scores very important; essay, recommendations important. **Homeschooled:** Statement describing homeschool structure and mission, state high school equivalency certificate required.

**High school preparation.** College-preparatory program required. 18 units required. Required and recommended units include English 4, mathematics 2-4, social studies 3, history 2, science 2-3 (laboratory 2-3), foreign language 1-3 and academic electives 4.

**2009-2010 Annual costs.** Tuition/fees: $6,748; $14,648 out-of-state. Room/board: $10,238. Books/supplies: $1,600. Personal expenses: $1,142.

**2008-2009 Financial aid. Need-based:** 2,012 full-time freshmen applied for aid; 1,338 were judged to have need; 1,303 of these received aid. Average need met was 71%. Average scholarship/grant was $6,331; average loan $3,878. 54% of total undergraduate aid awarded as scholarships/grants, 46% as loans/jobs. **Non-need-based:** Awarded to 1,006 full-time undergraduates, including 309 freshmen. Scholarships awarded for academics, athletics, state residency.

**Application procedures. Admission:** Closing date 3/1 (receipt date). $50 fee, may be waived for applicants with need. Admission notification on a rolling basis beginning on or about 1/15. Must reply by May 1 or within 2 week(s) if notified thereafter. **Financial aid:** Priority date 3/15; no closing date. FAFSA required. Applicants notified on a rolling basis starting 3/20; must reply by 5/1.

**Academics.** Project Renaissance year-long program for first-year students offers interdisciplinary course of study, close acquaintance with faculty in program, and community living. Participation open to all freshmen on first-come, first-served basis. **Special study options:** Accelerated study, combined bachelor's/graduate degree, cross-registration, distance learning, double major, dual enrollment of high school students, ESL, honors, independent study, internships, liberal arts/career combination, student-designed major, study abroad, Washington semester. Accelerated 5-year bachelor's/master's in 40 fields, internships with New York State Legislature, 3+3 program with Albany Law School, biology/dental program with Boston University Goldman School of Dental Medicine, bachelor's/doctor of optometry with SUNY State College, early assurance program with Albany Medical College and SUNY Upstate Medical University. **Credit/placement by examination:** AP, CLEP, IB. 60 credit hours maximum toward bachelor's degree. **Support services:** Pre-admission summer program, remedial instruction, study skills assistance, tutoring, writing center.

**Honors college/program.** Applicants admitted as Presidential Scholars & Frederick Douglass Scholars invited to apply to the Honors College. Approximately 125 freshmen will be admitted each fall. An additional 25 current University at Albany students will be admitted at the end of their first year.

**Majors. Area/ethnic studies:** African-American, Asian, Caribbean, Central/Eastern European, Chinese, East Asian, Japanese, Latin American, Russian/Slavic, women's. **Biology:** General, biochemistry, environmental, molecular. **Business:** Accounting, business admin. **Communications:** General. **Computer sciences:** General, information systems. **Conservation:** Environmental science. **Engineering:** Materials science. **Foreign languages:** Classics, French, Italian, linguistics, Russian, Spanish. **Health:** Predental, premedicine, prepharmacy, preveterinary. **History:** General. **Interdisciplinary:** Classical/archaeology, global studies, medieval/Renaissance. **Math:** General, applied. **Philosophy/religion:** Judaic, philosophy, religion. **Physical sciences:** Atmospheric science, chemistry, physics. **Protective services:** Criminal justice. **Psychology:** General. **Public administration:** Social work. **Social sciences:** Anthropology, economics, geography, political science, sociology, urban studies. **Visual/performing arts:** Art history/conservation, dramatic, music performance, music theory/composition, studio arts. **Other:** Document studies.

**Most popular majors.** Business/marketing 16%, communications/journalism 10%, English 6%, history 7%, psychology 12%, social sciences 23%.

**Computing on campus.** 500 workstations in library. Dormitories wired for high-speed internet access and linked to campus network. Commuter students can connect to campus network. Online course registration, online library, helpline, student web hosting, wireless network available.

**Student life. Freshman orientation:** Mandatory, $200 fee. Preregistration for classes offered. 2 days in summer with parental participation, 2 days in fall without parental participation. **Housing:** Guaranteed on-campus for freshmen. Coed dorms, apartments, wellness housing available. $125 fully refundable deposit. Individualized services for disabled students available, including accessible housing information. **Activities:** Bands, campus ministries, choral groups, dance, drama, film society, international student organizations, literary magazine, music ensembles, musical theater, radio station, student government, student newspaper, symphony orchestra, over 200 student groups.

**Athletics.** NCAA. **Intercollegiate:** Baseball M, basketball, cross-country, field hockey W, football (tackle) M, golf W, lacrosse, rugby, soccer, softball W, tennis W, track and field, volleyball W. **Intramural:** Basketball, football (non-tackle), racquetball, soccer, softball, tennis, track and field, volleyball. **Team name:** Great Danes.

**Student services.** Alcohol/substance abuse counseling, chaplain/spiritual director, career counseling, services for economically disadvantaged, student employment services, financial aid counseling, health services, legal services, minority student services, on-campus daycare, personal counseling, placement for graduates, women's services. **Physically disabled:** Services for visually, speech, hearing impaired. **Learning disabled:** Comprehensive services available.

**Contact.** E-mail: ugadmissions@albany.edu
Phone: (518) 442-5435 Fax: (518) 442-5383
Robert Andrea, Director of Undergraduate Admissions, State University of New York at Albany, Office of Undergraduate Admissions, University Hall 112, Albany, NY 12222

## State University of New York at Binghamton
**Binghamton, New York**  CB member
**www.binghamton.edu**  CB code: 2535

- Public 4-year university
- Residential campus in small city
- 11,646 degree-seeking undergraduates: 3% part-time, 47% women, 5% African American, 12% Asian American, 7% Hispanic American, 10% international
- 2,825 degree-seeking graduate students
- 33% of applicants admitted
- SAT or ACT with writing, application essay required
- 81% graduate within 6 years; 38% enter graduate study

**General.** Founded in 1946. Regionally accredited. **Degrees:** 2,742 bachelor's awarded; master's, doctoral offered. **ROTC:** Army, Air Force. **Location:** 50 miles from Ithaca, 70 miles from Syracuse. **Calendar:** Semester, extensive summer session. **Full-time faculty:** 596 total; 91% have terminal degrees, 24% minority, 38% women. **Part-time faculty:** 275 total; 12% minority, 52% women. **Class size:** 40% < 20, 37% 20-39, 9% 40-49, 8% 50-99, 7% >100. **Special facilities:** 190-acre nature preserve, 4-climate greenhouse, performing arts center (5 theaters), art/dance studios, sculpture foundry, research centers, electron microcopy laboratories, geographic information systems core facility, public archeology facility, integrated electronics engineering center, institute for child development, information commons, events center, kosher kitchen.

**Freshman class profile.** 29,061 applied, 9,692 admitted, 2,123 enrolled.

| Mid 50% test scores | | | |
|---|---|---|---|
| SAT critical reading: | 580-670 | Rank in top quarter: | 84% |
| SAT math: | 620-710 | Rank in top tenth: | 51% |
| ACT composite: | 27-30 | End year in good standing: | 91% |
| GPA 3.75 or higher: | 59% | Return as sophomores: | 90% |
| GPA 3.50-3.74: | 19% | Out-of-state: | 17% |
| GPA 3.0-3.49: | 19% | Live on campus: | 97% |
| GPA 2.0-2.99: | 3% | International: | 14% |

**Basis for selection.** Quality of courses, grades and grade trend, and test scores. Evidence of intellectual curiosity, interest in others, and nonacademic pursuits sought through application. Geographic, socioeconomic, and ethnic diversity considered. SAT or ACT scores accepted on a rolling basis for fall term admissions. Audition offered for music; portfolio review offered for art; theater talent also considered. **Homeschooled:** State high school equivalency certificate required. Students required to obtain documentation of equivalency from local school boards.

**High school preparation.** College-preparatory program required. 16 units required. Required and recommended units include English 4, mathematics 3-4, social studies 2-4, history 4, science 2-4 and foreign language 3. 3 units of 1 foreign language or 2 each of 2 foreign languages required of liberal arts applicants.

**2009-2010 Annual costs.** Tuition/fees: $6,761; $14,661 out-of-state. Room/board: $10,614. Books/supplies: $800. Personal expenses: $750.

**2009-2010 Financial aid. Need-based:** 1,626 full-time freshmen applied for aid; 902 were judged to have need; 902 of these received aid. Average need met was 79%. Average scholarship/grant was $7,395; average loan $3,791. 38% of total undergraduate aid awarded as scholarships/grants, 62% as loans/jobs. **Non-need-based:** Awarded to 1,139 full-time undergraduates, including 204 freshmen. Scholarships awarded for academics, art, athletics, leadership, minority status, music/drama, state residency.

**Application procedures. Admission:** Priority date 1/15; no deadline. $40 fee, may be waived for applicants with need. Admission notification on a rolling basis beginning on or about 4/1. Must reply by May 1 or within 4 week(s) if notified thereafter. **Financial aid:** Priority date 2/1; no closing date. FAFSA required. Applicants notified on a rolling basis starting 4/1; must reply within 2 week(s) of notification.

**Academics. Special study options:** Accelerated study, combined bachelor's/graduate degree, cross-registration, distance learning, double major, dual enrollment of high school students, ESL, exchange student, honors, independent study, internships, liberal arts/career combination, student-designed major, study abroad, teacher certification program, Washington semester. Individualized majors programs; pre-health program prepares students for careers in medicine, dentistry, optometry, veterinary medicine, podiatry, nutrition, physical or occupational therapy and chiropractic; early assurance program guarantees graduate admission at partner SUNY schools: Buffalo, Upstate Medical-Syracuse and College of Optometry; 3-2 and 4-1 combined BA or BS/MA, MS, MAT, MBA, or MPA degree programs; teacher certification program is graduate only. **Credit/placement by examination:** AP, CLEP, IB, institutional tests. 32 credit hours maximum toward bachelor's degree. **Support services:** Learning center, pre-admission summer program, study skills assistance, tutoring, writing center.

**Majors. Area/ethnic studies:** African-American, Asian, East Asian, Latin American, South Asian. **Biology:** General, biochemistry, cellular/molecular. **Business:** Accounting, actuarial science, business admin, entrepreneurial studies, finance, international, logistics, management information systems, marketing. **Computer sciences:** General, computer science. **Conservation:** Environmental studies. **Engineering:** General, computer, electrical, industrial, mechanical. **Foreign languages:** Arabic, classics, comparative lit, French, German, Hebrew, Italian, Latin, linguistics, Spanish. **Health:** Nursing (RN), premedicine, preveterinary. **History:** General. **Interdisciplinary:** Medieval/Renaissance. **Legal studies:** Prelaw. **Math:** General. **Philosophy/religion:** Judaic, philosophy. **Physical sciences:** Chemistry, geology, physics. **Psychology:** General, psychobiology. **Social sciences:** General, anthropology, applied economics, cartography, economics, geography, international relations, political science, sociology. **Visual/performing arts:** Acting, art, art history/conservation, cinematography, directing/producing, dramatic, music performance, theater design. **Other:** Asian and Asian American studies, Bioengineering, Health/Medicinal prepatory programs, Human development, Literature and rhetoric, Multi/Interdisciplinary studies.

**Most popular majors.** Biology 7%, business/marketing 14%, engineering/engineering technologies 7%, English 9%, health sciences 7%, psychology 9%, social sciences 23%.

**Computing on campus.** 1,116 workstations in dormitories, library, computer center, student center. Dormitories wired for high-speed internet access and linked to campus network. Commuter students can connect to campus network. Online course registration, online library, helpline, student web hosting, wireless network available.

**Student life. Freshman orientation:** Available, $205 fee. Preregistration for classes offered. 2-day session held in summer for fall semester. Parents invited to participate. 2-day session held in January for students entering spring semester. **Housing:** Guaranteed on-campus for freshmen. Coed dorms, special housing for disabled, apartments, wellness housing available. $200 nonrefundable deposit, deadline 5/1. **Activities:** Bands, campus ministries, choral groups, dance, drama, film society, international student organizations, literary magazine, music ensembles, Model UN, musical theater, opera, radio station, student government, student newspaper, symphony orchestra, TV station, College Democrats, College Republicans, College Libertarians, Hillel, gospel choir, Asian student union, black student union, Campus Climate Challenge, Circle K, Engineers Without Borders.

**Athletics.** NCAA. **Intercollegiate:** Baseball M, basketball, cross-country, diving, golf M, lacrosse, soccer, softball W, swimming, tennis, track and field, volleyball W, wrestling M. **Intramural:** Basketball, bowling, football (non-tackle), racquetball, soccer, softball, table tennis, tennis, volleyball. **Team name:** Bearcats.

**Student services.** Adult student services, alcohol/substance abuse counseling, chaplain/spiritual director, career counseling, services for economically disadvantaged, student employment services, financial aid counseling, health services, legal services, minority student services, on-campus daycare, personal counseling, placement for graduates, veterans' counselor, women's services. **Physically disabled:** Services for visually, speech, hearing impaired. **Learning disabled:** Comprehensive services available.

**Contact.** E-mail: admit@binghamton.edu
Phone: (607) 777-2171 Fax: (607) 777-4445
Cheryl Brown, Director of Admissions, State University of New York at Binghamton, Box 6001, Binghamton, NY 13902-6001

---

## State University of New York at Buffalo
**Buffalo, New York**                                **CB member**
**www.buffalo.edu**                                  **CB code: 2925**

- Public 4-year university
- Commuter campus in large city

---

- 19,149 degree-seeking undergraduates: 6% part-time, 46% women, 7% African American, 10% Asian American, 3% Hispanic American, 13% international
- 9,063 degree-seeking graduate students
- 52% of applicants admitted
- SAT or ACT with writing required
- 66% graduate within 6 years; 41% enter graduate study

**General.** Founded in 1846. Regionally accredited. SUNY Buffalo is the largest and most comprehensive in the 64-campus State University of New York system. **Degrees:** 4,036 bachelor's awarded; master's, doctoral, professional offered. **ROTC:** Army. **Location:** 10 miles from downtown. **Calendar:** Semester, extensive summer session. **Full-time faculty:** 1,209 total; 94% have terminal degrees, 24% minority, 35% women. **Part-time faculty:** 528 total; 80% have terminal degrees, 11% minority, 49% women. **Class size:** 32% < 20, 35% 20-39, 9% 40-49, 14% 50-99, 9% >100. **Special facilities:** Center for the arts, concert hall, anthropology research museum, multidisciplinary center for earthquake engineering research, New York State Center of Excellence in Bioinformatics and Life Sciences, center for computational research, poetry and rare books collection, Center of Excellence for Document Analysis and Recognition, New York State Center for Engineering Design and Industrial Innovation, pharmacy museum, virtual site museum, electronic poetry center, archaeological survey center, numerous other research centers.

**Freshman class profile.** 21,137 applied, 10,913 admitted, 3,194 enrolled.

| Mid 50% test scores | | GPA 2.0-2.99: | 25% |
|---|---|---|---|
| SAT critical reading: | 510-600 | Rank in top quarter: | 65% |
| SAT math: | 550-650 | Rank in top tenth: | 28% |
| ACT composite: | 23-28 | Return as sophomores: | 89% |
| GPA 3.75 or higher: | 16% | Out-of-state: | 6% |
| GPA 3.50-3.74: | 14% | Live on campus: | 72% |
| GPA 3.0-3.49: | 45% | International: | 13% |

**Basis for selection.** Freshmen evaluated based on secondary school performance, strength of curriculum, standardized test scores, and, in some cases, supplemental application. SAT Subject Test considered for placement for foreign language. Audition required for music. **Homeschooled:** Transcript of courses and grades, letter of recommendation (nonparent) required. Essay describing educational program, special projects, extracurricular activities, and special accomplishments required as well as 2 letters of recommendation: 1 from parent or other person providing education, 1 from person involved with other activities. If admitted, will need to submit letter from superintendent of local school district attesting to completion of program of home instruction meeting requirements of Section 100.10 of the Regulations of the Commissioner of Education, or passing score on GED. **Learning Disabled:** No separate admissions process: eligibility for services must be established by provision of disability documentation that meets institutional standards.

**High school preparation.** College-preparatory program recommended. 17 units recommended. Recommended units include English 4, mathematics 3, social studies 4, science 3 and foreign language 3.

**2009-2010 Annual costs.** Tuition/fees: $7,013; $14,913 out-of-state. Room/board: $9,648. Books/supplies: $947. Personal expenses: $1,109.

**2008-2009 Financial aid. Need-based:** 2,588 full-time freshmen applied for aid; 1,692 were judged to have need; 1,687 of these received aid. Average need met was 64%. Average scholarship/grant was $1,014; average loan $2,715. 37% of total undergraduate aid awarded as scholarships/grants, 63% as loans/jobs. **Non-need-based:** Awarded to 1,212 full-time undergraduates, including 347 freshmen. Scholarships awarded for academics, athletics, minority status, music/drama, state residency.

**Application procedures. Admission:** Priority date 11/1; no deadline. $40 fee, may be waived for applicants with need. Admission notification on a rolling basis beginning on or about 2/1. Must reply by May 1 or within 2 week(s) if notified thereafter. **Financial aid:** Priority date 3/1; no closing date. FAFSA required. Applicants notified on a rolling basis starting 2/1; must reply by 5/1.

**Academics.** Over 300 baccalaureate, master's and doctoral degree programs. Comprehensive College of Arts and Sciences plus 11 professional schools including Law, Medicine and Dentistry. **Special study options:** Accelerated study, combined bachelor's/graduate degree, cooperative education, cross-registration, distance learning, double major, dual enrollment of high school students, ESL, exchange student, honors, independent study, internships, liberal arts/career combination, student-designed major, study abroad, teacher certification program, Washington semester. Certificate programs, combined degree programs, early assurance program with School of Medicine and Dentistry, Honors College and Learning Communities. **Credit/**

**placement by examination:** CLEP, IB, SAT, ACT, institutional tests. Maximum of 30 credits from International Baccalaureate. **Support services:** Learning center, pre-admission summer program, reduced course load, remedial instruction, study skills assistance, tutoring, writing center.

**Honors college/program.** Minimum 93 high school average, 1300 SAT combined reading and math, 29 ACT. Enroll approximately 325 freshmen a year. Program requirements include completion of colloquium and two honors seminars plus six advanced study opportunities.

**Majors. Architecture:** Architecture, environmental design. **Area/ethnic studies:** African-American, American, Asian, women's. **Biology:** General, biochemistry, bioinformatics, biomedical sciences, biophysics, biostatistics, biotechnology, exercise physiology, pharmacology/toxicology. **Business:** Business admin. **Communications:** General, media studies. **Computer sciences:** Computer science, information systems. **Engineering:** General, aerospace, chemical, civil, computer, electrical, environmental, industrial, mechanical, physics, structural. **Foreign languages:** Classics, French, German, Italian, linguistics, Spanish. **Health:** Audiology/speech pathology, clinical lab science, nuclear medical technology, nursing (RN). **History:** General. **Math:** General, applied. **Philosophy/religion:** Philosophy. **Physical sciences:** Chemistry, geology, physics, theoretical physics. **Psychology:** General. **Social sciences:** General, anthropology, economics, geography, political science, sociology. **Visual/performing arts:** Art, art history/conservation, dance, dramatic, film/cinema, music performance, studio arts. **Other:** Dramatic/Theatre arts and stagecraft, Multi/Interdisciplinary studies.

**Most popular majors.** Biology 9%, business/marketing 21%, communications/journalism 8%, engineering/engineering technologies 10%, health sciences 7%, psychology 10%, social sciences 15%.

**Computing on campus.** 2,450 workstations in dormitories, library, computer center, student center. Dormitories wired for high-speed internet access and linked to campus network. Commuter students can connect to campus network. Online course registration, online library, helpline, repair service, student web hosting, wireless network available.

**Student life. Freshman orientation:** Available, $190 fee. Preregistration for classes offered. One-and-a-half-day program. **Policies:** University standards, administrative regulations and student conduct rules apply. **Housing:** Guaranteed on-campus for all undergraduates. Coed dorms, special housing for disabled, apartments, wellness housing available. $300 fully refundable deposit, deadline 5/1. Academic interest, honors, freshman. **Activities:** Bands, campus ministries, choral groups, dance, drama, film society, international student organizations, literary magazine, music ensembles, musical theater, radio station, student government, student newspaper, symphony orchestra, TV station, over 300 registered organizations.

**Athletics. NCAA. Intercollegiate:** Baseball M, basketball, cross-country, diving, football (tackle) M, rowing (crew) W, soccer, softball W, swimming, tennis, track and field, volleyball W, wrestling M. **Intramural:** Badminton, basketball, cross-country, football (non-tackle), racquetball, soccer, softball, tennis, volleyball. **Team name:** Bulls.

**Student services.** Adult student services, alcohol/substance abuse counseling, chaplain/spiritual director, career counseling, services for economically disadvantaged, student employment services, financial aid counseling, health services, legal services, minority student services, on-campus daycare, personal counseling, placement for graduates, veterans' counselor. **Physically disabled:** Services for visually, speech, hearing impaired.

**Contact.** E-mail: ub-admissions@buffalo.edu
Phone: (716) 645-6900 Toll-free number: (888) 822-3648
Fax: (716) 645-6411
Patricia Armstrong, Director of Admissions, State University of New York at Buffalo, 12 Capen Hall, Buffalo, NY 14260-1660

---

## State University of New York at Farmingdale

| Farmingdale, New York | CB member |
| --- | --- |
| www.farmingdale.edu | CB code: 2526 |

◗ Public 4-year technical college
◗ Commuter campus in large town
◗ 6,147 degree-seeking undergraduates: 21% part-time, 42% women, 7% African American, 3% Asian American, 8% Hispanic American, 1% international
◗ 40% of applicants admitted
◗ 37% graduate within 6 years; 25% enter graduate study

**General.** Founded in 1912. Regionally accredited. **Degrees:** 695 bachelor's, 497 associate awarded. **Location:** 30 miles from New York City.

**Calendar:** Semester, extensive summer session. **Full-time faculty:** 191 total; 56% have terminal degrees, 18% minority, 46% women. **Part-time faculty:** 364 total; 16% have terminal degrees, 13% minority, 47% women. **Class size:** 29% < 20, 58% 20-39, 12% 40-49, 2% 50-99. **Special facilities:** CAD/CAM laboratory, fleet of single-engine and multi-engine aircraft, dental and health care laboratories, bioscience labs, Cold Spring Harbor Research lab on campus, manufacturing labs with plasmajet and advanced robotic technology, solar cell and hydrogen fuel cell research.

**Freshman class profile.** 5,714 applied, 2,312 admitted, 1,355 enrolled.

| Mid 50% test scores | | Rank in top quarter: | 31% |
| --- | --- | --- | --- |
| SAT critical reading: | 440-520 | Rank in top tenth: | 8% |
| SAT math: | 510-570 | End year in good standing: | 80% |
| SAT writing: | 450-530 | Return as sophomores: | 81% |
| GPA 3.75 or higher: | 5% | Out-of-state: | 1% |
| GPA 3.50-3.74: | 15% | Live on campus: | 5% |
| GPA 3.0-3.49: | 35% | International: | 1% |
| GPA 2.0-2.99: | 45% | | |

**Basis for selection.** School achievement record of primary importance. Applicants apply to and are accepted into a specific curriculum. Requirements vary according to program. SAT required for bachelor's degree students. Interview and portfolio required for advertising art and design, visual communications programs.

**High school preparation.** 20.5 units required. Required and recommended units include English 4, mathematics 2-4, social studies 4, science 2-4 and foreign language 2. Requirements vary by curriculum.

**2009-2010 Annual costs.** Tuition/fees: $6,030; $13,930 out-of-state. Room/board: $11,618. Books/supplies: $1,200. Personal expenses: $900.

**Financial aid. Non-need-based:** Scholarships awarded for academics.

**Application procedures. Admission:** No deadline. $40 fee, may be waived for applicants with need. Admission notification on a rolling basis beginning on or about 11/1. Must reply by May 1 or within 4 week(s) if notified thereafter. Priority given to applications received by January 15 for dental hygiene program and nursing program. **Financial aid:** Priority date 4/1; no closing date. FAFSA, institutional form required. Applicants notified on a rolling basis starting 4/1.

**Academics. Special study options:** Distance learning, double major, honors, internships, study abroad. **Credit/placement by examination:** AP, CLEP, institutional tests. **Support services:** Learning center, remedial instruction, study skills assistance, tutoring, writing center.

**Majors. Agriculture:** Horticulture. **Biology:** General. **Business:** Business admin, operations. **Communications:** Media studies. **Computer sciences:** Programming. **Construction:** Maintenance. **Engineering technology:** Architectural, automotive, computer, computer systems, electrical, industrial, manufacturing, mechanical. **Health:** Dental hygiene, nursing (RN). **Interdisciplinary:** Science/society. **Math:** Applied. **Protective services:** Security management, security services. **Psychology:** Industrial. **Social sciences:** Applied economics. **Transportation:** Airline/commercial pilot, aviation management. **Other:** Software technology.

**Most popular majors.** Biology 9%, business/marketing 37%, communications/journalism 9%, computer/information sciences 8%, engineering/engineering technologies 14%, security/protective services 8%, trade and industry 7%.

**Computing on campus.** 950 workstations in dormitories, library, computer center, student center. Dormitories wired for high-speed internet access and linked to campus network. Commuter students can connect to campus network. Online course registration, online library, wireless network available.

**Student life. Freshman orientation:** Mandatory, $125 fee. Preregistration for classes offered. **Housing:** Coed dorms available. $125 deposit. **Activities:** Choral groups, drama, international student organizations, literary magazine, radio station, student government, student newspaper, African student association, Asian student alliance, Caribbean student organization, Christian fellowship.

**Athletics. NCAA. Intercollegiate:** Baseball M, basketball, cross-country, golf M, lacrosse, soccer, softball W, tennis M, track and field, volleyball W. **Intramural:** Basketball, golf, racquetball, soccer, softball, squash, swimming, tennis, volleyball, weight lifting. **Team name:** Rams.

**Student services.** Alcohol/substance abuse counseling, career counseling, services for economically disadvantaged, student employment services, financial aid counseling, health services, on-campus daycare, personal counseling, placement for graduates, veterans' counselor. **Physically disabled:** Services for visually, speech, hearing impaired.

**Contact.** E-mail: admissions@farmingdale.edu
Phone: (631) 420-2200 Toll-free number: (800) 432-7646
Fax: (631) 420-2633
Jim Hall, Director of Admissions, State University of New York at
Farmingdale, 2350 Broadhollow Road, Farmingdale, NY 11735-1021

## State University of New York at New Paltz
**New Paltz, New York**          **CB member**
**www.newpaltz.edu**          **CB code: 2541**

- Public 4-year liberal arts college
- Residential campus in large town
- 6,308 degree-seeking undergraduates: 8% part-time, 66% women, 6% African American, 4% Asian American, 10% Hispanic American, 3% international
- 1,228 degree-seeking graduate students
- 34% of applicants admitted
- SAT or ACT with writing, application essay required
- 69% graduate within 6 years; 25% enter graduate study

**General.** Founded in 1828. Regionally accredited. More than 16 percent of undergraduates participate in international education each academic year. **Degrees:** 1,572 bachelor's awarded; master's offered. **Location:** 65 miles from Albany, 96 miles from New York City. **Calendar:** Semester, extensive summer session. **Full-time faculty:** 325 total; 83% have terminal degrees, 16% minority, 51% women. **Part-time faculty:** 343 total; 25% have terminal degrees, 12% minority, 59% women. **Class size:** 34% < 20, 58% 20-39, 6% 40-49, 2% 50-99, less than 1% >100. **Special facilities:** 3 theaters, recital hall, speech and hearing clinical center, music therapy training center, observatory, planetarium, theater collection, electronic classrooms.

**Freshman class profile.** 15,426 applied, 5,240 admitted, 1,054 enrolled.

| Mid 50% test scores | | | |
|---|---|---|---|
| SAT critical reading: | 520-610 | Rank in top quarter: | 70% |
| SAT math: | 520-610 | Rank in top tenth: | 24% |
| SAT writing: | 520-620 | End year in good standing: | 89% |
| GPA 3.75 or higher: | 9% | Return as sophomores: | 88% |
| GPA 3.50-3.74: | 36% | Out-of-state: | 6% |
| GPA 3.0-3.49: | 44% | Live on campus: | 96% |
| GPA 2.0-2.99: | 11% | International: | 1% |

**Basis for selection.** Secondary school curriculum and achievement, standardized test scores most important. Applicants, especially academically marginal, encouraged to send personal statements regarding academic work, recommendations from academic teachers, and any other pertinent information. One letter of recommendation required; audition required for music, music therapy, theater arts programs; portfolio required for art education, scenography, studio art, and visual arts programs. **Homeschooled:** Must submit all data as required by NYS Commissioner of Education's regulations (Section 100.10).

**High school preparation.** College-preparatory program required. 17 units required; 21 recommended. Required and recommended units include English 4, mathematics 3-4, social studies 4, history 1, science 3-4 (laboratory 2-4) and foreign language 2-4.

**2009-2010 Annual costs.** Tuition/fees: $6,081; $13,981 out-of-state. Room/board: $9,242.

**2009-2010 Financial aid.** All financial aid based on need. 928 full-time freshmen applied for aid; 554 were judged to have need; 552 of these received aid. Average need met was 57%. Average scholarship/grant was $5,214; average loan $3,546. 52% of total undergraduate aid awarded as scholarships/grants, 48% as loans/jobs.

**Application procedures. Admission:** Closing date 4/1 (receipt date). $40 fee, may be waived for applicants with need. Admission notification on a rolling basis beginning on or about 1/15. Must reply by May 1 or within 2 week(s) if notified thereafter. **Financial aid:** Priority date 3/15; no closing date. FAFSA required. Applicants notified on a rolling basis starting 4/1; must reply within 6 week(s) of notification.

**Academics. Special study options:** Combined bachelor's/graduate degree, cooperative education, cross-registration, distance learning, double major, dual enrollment of high school students, ESL, exchange student, honors, independent study, internships, liberal arts/career combination, New York semester, student-designed major, study abroad, teacher certification program, United Nations semester. Student exchange programs in Australia, Brazil, Cuba, Czech Republic, Denmark, Ecuador, England, France, Greece, Ireland, Italy, Japan, The Netherlands, New Zealand, Spain, Uzbekistan, U.S. Virgin Islands and Zimbabwe. **Credit/placement by examination:** AP,

CLEP, IB, SAT, institutional tests. 30 credit hours maximum toward bachelor's degree. **Support services:** Learning center, reduced course load, remedial instruction, study skills assistance, tutoring, writing center.

**Majors. Area/ethnic studies:** African-American, Asian, Latin American, women's. **Biology:** General. **Business:** General, accounting, business admin, finance, international. **Communications:** General, broadcast journalism, journalism. **Computer sciences:** General. **Education:** Art, biology, chemistry, early childhood, early childhood special, elementary, English, foreign languages, French, history, mathematics, middle, physics, science, secondary, social science, social studies, Spanish. **Engineering:** Computer, electrical. **Foreign languages:** French, Spanish. **Health:** Communication disorders. **History:** General. **Liberal arts:** Arts/sciences. **Math:** General. **Philosophy/religion:** Philosophy. **Physical sciences:** Chemistry, geology, physics. **Psychology:** General. **Social sciences:** Anthropology, economics, geography, international relations, political science, sociology. **Visual/performing arts:** General, art, art history/conservation, ceramics, commercial/advertising art, dramatic, metal/jewelry, painting, photography, printmaking, sculpture, studio arts. **Other:** Environmental geochemical science.

**Most popular majors.** Business/marketing 11%, education 34%, English 8%, psychology 6%, social sciences 8%, visual/performing arts 10%.

**Computing on campus.** 950 workstations in dormitories, library, computer center, student center. Dormitories wired for high-speed internet access and linked to campus network. Commuter students can connect to campus network. Online course registration, online library, helpline, student web hosting, wireless network available.

**Student life. Freshman orientation:** Available, $175 fee. Preregistration for classes offered. 3-day academic and transition program. **Housing:** Guaranteed on-campus for freshmen. Coed dorms, single-sex dorms, special housing for disabled available. $100 fully refundable deposit, deadline 5/1. First-year initiative, honors, art, nursing program housing. **Activities:** Bands, campus ministries, choral groups, dance, drama, international student organizations, literary magazine, music ensembles, Model UN, musical theater, radio station, student government, student newspaper, symphony orchestra, TV station, Jewish Action Movement, Black Student Union, Habitat for Humanity, Circle K International, equestrian club, NAACP, philosophy club, Korean culture union.

**Athletics.** NCAA. **Intercollegiate:** Baseball M, basketball, cross-country, diving, field hockey W, lacrosse W, soccer, softball W, swimming, tennis, volleyball. **Intramural:** Badminton, basketball, field hockey, football (non-tackle), golf, handball, racquetball, soccer, softball, tennis, volleyball. **Team name:** Hawks.

**Student services.** Alcohol/substance abuse counseling, chaplain/spiritual director, career counseling, services for economically disadvantaged, student employment services, financial aid counseling, health services, legal services, minority student services, on-campus daycare, personal counseling, placement for graduates, veterans' counselor, women's services. **Physically disabled:** Services for visually, speech, hearing impaired.

**Contact.** E-mail: admissions@newpaltz.edu
Phone: (845) 257-3200 Toll-free number: (888) 639-7589
Fax: (845) 257-3209
Kimberly Strano, Director of Freshmen Admissions, State University of New York at New Paltz, 100 Hawk Drive, New Paltz, NY 12561-2443

## State University of New York at Oswego
**Oswego, New York**          **CB member**
**www.oswego.edu**          **CB code: 2543**

- Public 4-year university
- Residential campus in large town
- 7,145 degree-seeking undergraduates: 5% part-time, 52% women, 4% African American, 2% Asian American, 5% Hispanic American, 1% international
- 698 degree-seeking graduate students
- 47% of applicants admitted
- SAT or ACT (ACT writing optional), application essay required
- 60% graduate within 6 years; 22% enter graduate study

**General.** Founded in 1861. Regionally accredited. **Degrees:** 1,489 bachelor's awarded; master's offered. **ROTC:** Army, Air Force. **Location:** 35 miles from Syracuse, 65 miles from Rochester. **Calendar:** Semester, limited summer session. **Full-time faculty:** 312 total; 79% have terminal degrees, 20% minority, 40% women. **Part-time faculty:** 199 total; 23% have terminal degrees, 8% minority, 48% women. **Class size:** 50% < 20, 33% 20-39, 9% 40-49, 5% 50-99, 3% >100. **Special facilities:** Weather facsimile machine, planetarium, cross-country ski facilities, advanced technology classrooms, biological field station.

**Freshman class profile.** 10,464 applied, 4,899 admitted, 1,391 enrolled.

| Mid 50% test scores | | | |
|---|---|---|---|
| SAT critical reading: | 530-590 | Rank in top tenth: | 15% |
| SAT math: | 520-600 | End year in good standing: | 92% |
| ACT composite: | 21-25 | Return as sophomores: | 81% |
| GPA 3.75 or higher: | 20% | Out-of-state: | 2% |
| GPA 3.50-3.74: | 22% | Live on campus: | 88% |
| GPA 3.0-3.49: | 44% | International: | 1% |
| GPA 2.0-2.99: | 14% | Fraternities: | 6% |
| Rank in top quarter: | 54% | Sororities: | 5% |

**Basis for selection.** High school GPA and curriculum most important, followed by test scores, supplemental portion of application and letters of recommendation. Special talents considered. Applicants recommended to send both SAT and ACT; higher score accepted. Interview recommended for all; portfolio required for graphic design and fine arts (BFA). **Home-schooled:** Proof of high school graduation or GED recognized by state of residency required. **Learning Disabled:** Advised to contact Office of Learning Services and/or Disability Services with copy of IEP if applicable.

**High school preparation.** College-preparatory program required. 18 units required; 20 recommended. Required and recommended units include English 4, mathematics 3-4, social studies 4, science 3-4 (laboratory 2-3) and foreign language 2-4. Combined minimum of 7 units of college prep math and science recommended.

**2009-2010 Annual costs.** Tuition/fees: $6,256; $14,156 out-of-state. Room/board: $10,870. Books/supplies: $800. Personal expenses: $850.

**2009-2010 Financial aid. Need-based:** 1,264 full-time freshmen applied for aid; 912 were judged to have need; 873 of these received aid. Average need met was 84%. Average scholarship/grant was $5,263; average loan $5,812. 42% of total undergraduate aid awarded as scholarships/grants, 58% as loans/jobs. **Non-need-based:** Awarded to 1,451 full-time undergraduates, including 375 freshmen. Scholarships awarded for academics, state residency.

**Application procedures. Admission:** Priority date 1/15; no deadline. $40 fee, may be waived for applicants with need. Admission notification on a rolling basis beginning on or about 1/15. Must reply by May 1 or within 4 week(s) if notified thereafter. **Financial aid:** Priority date 3/1; no closing date. FAFSA required. Applicants notified on a rolling basis starting 3/1; must reply by 5/1 or within 3 week(s) of notification.

**Academics. Special study options:** Accelerated study, combined bachelor's/graduate degree, cross-registration, distance learning, double major, dual enrollment of high school students, ESL, exchange student, external degree, honors, independent study, internships, liberal arts/career combination, study abroad, teacher certification program, Washington semester. **Credit/placement by examination:** AP, CLEP, IB, SAT. 30 credit hours maximum toward bachelor's degree. **Support services:** Learning center, pre-admission summer program, reduced course load, remedial instruction, study skills assistance, tutoring, writing center.

**Honors college/program.** Approximately 80 freshmen enroll annually, distinct program of general education classes held in small class settings.

**Majors. Area/ethnic studies:** American, women's. **Biology:** General, zoology. **Business:** Accounting, business admin, finance, human resources, management science. **Communications:** General, broadcast journalism, journalism, public relations. **Computer sciences:** Computer science, information systems. **Education:** Agricultural, biology, business, chemistry, elementary, English, French, German, health occupations, history, mathematics, physics, science, secondary, social studies, Spanish, technology/industrial arts, trade/industrial, voc/tech. **Engineering:** Software. **Family/consumer sciences:** Child development. **Foreign languages:** French, German, linguistics, Spanish. **Health:** Medical radiologic technology/radiation therapy, perfusion technology, public health ed. **History:** General. **Interdisciplinary:** Cognitive science, global studies. **Legal studies:** Prelaw. **Math:** General, applied. **Philosophy/religion:** Philosophy. **Physical sciences:** Chemistry, geochemistry, geology, meteorology, physics. **Psychology:** General. **Social sciences:** Anthropology, econometrics, economics, political science, sociology. **Visual/performing arts:** Art, commercial/advertising art, dramatic.

**Most popular majors.** Business/marketing 21%, communications/journalism 12%, education 27%, psychology 7%, security/protective services 6%, visual/performing arts 6%.

**Computing on campus.** 900 workstations in dormitories, library, computer center, student center. Dormitories wired for high-speed internet access and linked to campus network. Commuter students can connect to campus network. Online course registration, online library, helpline, student web hosting, wireless network available.

**Student life. Freshman orientation:** Mandatory, $180 fee. Preregistration for classes offered. 2-day program for incoming students and families. **Housing:** Guaranteed on-campus for all undergraduates. Coed dorms, wellness housing available. $100 fully refundable deposit, deadline 5/1. Pets allowed in dorm rooms. Global living and learning center, suites for upperclassmen, nontraditional student housing, first-year experience residence hall for incoming freshmen only, housing for 21 and over single suites available. **Activities:** Bands, choral groups, dance, drama, film society, international student organizations, literary magazine, music ensembles, musical theater, radio station, student government, student newspaper, symphony orchestra, TV station, Christian, Jewish, Catholic, and Baptist groups, black student union, Latin student union, Caribbean student association, international student association, Native American Heritage Association, Students Educating Everyone About Disabilities.

**Athletics.** NCAA. **Intercollegiate:** Baseball M, basketball, cross-country, diving, field hockey W, golf M, ice hockey, lacrosse, soccer, softball W, swimming, tennis, track and field, volleyball W, wrestling M. **Intramural:** Badminton, basketball, football (non-tackle), golf, racquetball, skiing, soccer, softball, swimming, table tennis, tennis, volleyball. **Team name:** Lakers.

**Student services.** Adult student services, alcohol/substance abuse counseling, career counseling, services for economically disadvantaged, student employment services, financial aid counseling, health services, minority student services, on-campus daycare, personal counseling, placement for graduates, veterans' counselor, women's services. **Physically disabled:** Services for visually, speech, hearing impaired.

**Contact.** E-mail: admiss@oswego.edu
Phone: (315) 312-2250 Fax: (315) 312-3260
Joseph Grant, Vice President for Student Affairs and Enrollment, State University of New York at Oswego, 229 Sheldon Hall, Oswego, NY 13126-3599

## State University of New York at Purchase
**Purchase, New York**
**www.purchase.edu**      **CB code: 2878**

- Public 4-year university
- Residential campus in large town
- 3,830 degree-seeking undergraduates: 6% part-time, 56% women, 7% African American, 3% Asian American, 12% Hispanic American, 2% international
- 127 degree-seeking graduate students
- 27% of applicants admitted
- SAT or ACT (ACT writing optional) required
- 49% graduate within 6 years

**General.** Founded in 1967. Regionally accredited. **Degrees:** 905 bachelor's awarded; master's offered. **Location:** 25 miles from New York City, 5 miles from White Plains. **Calendar:** Semester, extensive summer session. **Full-time faculty:** 150 total; 49% have terminal degrees, 17% minority, 51% women. **Part-time faculty:** 234 total; 17% have terminal degrees, 11% minority, 47% women. **Class size:** 70% < 20, 23% 20-39, 4% 40-49, 3% 50-99, less than 1% >100. **Special facilities:** Performing arts center, children's center, electron microscope, Neuberger Museum of Art.

**Freshman class profile.** 8,620 applied, 2,300 admitted, 694 enrolled.

| Mid 50% test scores | | | |
|---|---|---|---|
| SAT critical reading: | 510-630 | GPA 2.0-2.99: | 31% |
| SAT math: | 490-580 | Rank in top quarter: | 38% |
| SAT writing: | 500-620 | Rank in top tenth: | 11% |
| ACT composite: | 21-25 | Return as sophomores: | 82% |
| GPA 3.75 or higher: | 9% | Out-of-state: | 23% |
| GPA 3.50-3.74: | 19% | Live on campus: | 92% |
| GPA 3.0-3.49: | 41% | International: | 1% |

**Basis for selection.** For liberal arts and sciences programs, high school achievement record or test scores important. For conservatory, performing arts and visual arts applicants, audition, interview, or portfolio most important. SAT recommended. Interview and essay required for film, theater design/technology programs; audition required for acting, dance, music programs; portfolio required for visual arts program.

**High school preparation.** College-preparatory program recommended.

**2009-2010 Annual costs.** Tuition/fees: $6,475; $14,375 out-of-state. Room/board: $10,270. Books/supplies: $1,100. Personal expenses: $700.

**2009-2010 Financial aid. Need-based:** 567 full-time freshmen applied for aid; 378 were judged to have need; 378 of these received aid. Average

need met was 53%. Average scholarship/grant was $6,067; average loan $3,586. 40% of total undergraduate aid awarded as scholarships/grants, 60% as loans/jobs. **Non-need-based:** Awarded to 163 full-time undergraduates, including 36 freshmen. Scholarships awarded for academics, art, minority status, music/drama. **Additional information:** All applicants automatically considered for scholarship upon review of applications, essays, auditions, and/or portfolio.

**Application procedures. Admission:** Priority date 3/1; deadline 7/15 (postmark date). $40 fee, may be waived for applicants with need. Admission notification 5/1. Must reply by May 1 or within 2 week(s) if notified thereafter. Application deadlines vary by program. Priority date of 1/30 for students applying to acting, design/technology, and film programs. **Financial aid:** Priority date 2/1; no closing date. FAFSA required. Applicants notified on a rolling basis starting 3/1; must reply within 2 week(s) of notification.

**Academics. Special study options:** Cross-registration, distance learning, double major, ESL, independent study, internships, liberal arts/career combination, student-designed major, study abroad. Conservatory master-apprentice training in dance, music, acting, film, theater design technology, visual arts. **Credit/placement by examination:** AP, CLEP, institutional tests. 30 credit hours maximum toward bachelor's degree. **Support services:** Learning center, pre-admission summer program, remedial instruction, tutoring, writing center.

**Majors. Area/ethnic studies:** Women's. **Biology:** General, ecology. **Communications:** Journalism, media studies. **Conservation:** Environmental science, environmental studies. **Foreign languages:** General. **History:** General. **Interdisciplinary:** Math/computer science. **Liberal arts:** Arts/sciences. **Math:** General. **Philosophy/religion:** Philosophy. **Physical sciences:** Chemistry. **Psychology:** General. **Social sciences:** Anthropology, economics, political science, sociology. **Visual/performing arts:** Art history/conservation, arts management, cinematography, commercial/advertising art, dance, dramatic, drawing, graphic design, music performance, music theory/composition, painting, photography, play/screenwriting, printmaking, sculpture, theater design, theater history.

**Most popular majors.** English 6%, liberal arts 25%, social sciences 10%, visual/performing arts 35%.

**Computing on campus.** 600 workstations in dormitories, library, computer center. Dormitories wired for high-speed internet access and linked to campus network. Commuter students can connect to campus network. Online course registration, online library, helpline, repair service, wireless network available.

**Student life. Freshman orientation:** Mandatory, $120 fee. Preregistration for classes offered. **Housing:** Coed dorms, special housing for disabled, apartments, wellness housing available. $100 fully refundable deposit. Freshman residence, non-traditional age hall, presidential scholars, learning community. **Activities:** Jazz band, choral groups, dance, drama, film society, international student organizations, literary magazine, music ensembles, musical theater, radio station, student government, student newspaper, TV station, philosophy club, chemistry society, literature club, dance club, ski club, Purchase Experimental Theatre, Organization of African People in America (OAPIA), Latinos Unidos, Gay/Lesbian/Bisexual and Transgendered Union.

**Athletics.** NCAA. **Intercollegiate:** Baseball M, basketball, cross-country, golf M, soccer, softball W, swimming W, tennis, volleyball. **Intramural:** Badminton, basketball, bowling, cross-country, fencing, golf, racquetball, skiing, soccer, softball, squash, swimming, table tennis, tennis, volleyball, water polo, weight lifting. **Team name:** Panthers.

**Student services.** Adult student services, alcohol/substance abuse counseling, career counseling, services for economically disadvantaged, student employment services, financial aid counseling, health services, on-campus daycare, personal counseling, placement for graduates, veterans' counselor, women's services. **Physically disabled:** Services for visually, hearing impaired.

**Contact.** E-mail: admissn@purchase.edu
Phone: (914) 251-6300 Fax: (914) 251-6314
Stephanie McCaine, Admissions Director, State University of New York at Purchase, 735 Anderson Hill Road, Purchase, NY 10577-1400

---

## State University of New York at Stony Brook
**Stony Brook, New York**      **CB member**
**www.stonybrook.edu**      **CB code: 2548**

- Public 4-year university
- Residential campus in large town
- 16,034 degree-seeking undergraduates: 6% part-time, 48% women, 7% African American, 23% Asian American, 9% Hispanic American, 7% international

- 7,042 degree-seeking graduate students
- 40% of applicants admitted
- SAT or ACT with writing, application essay required
- 66% graduate within 6 years

**General.** Founded in 1957. Regionally accredited. **Degrees:** 3,264 bachelor's awarded; master's, doctoral, professional offered. **ROTC:** Army, Air Force. **Location:** 60 miles from New York City. **Calendar:** Semester, limited summer session. **Full-time faculty:** 938 total; 97% have terminal degrees, 19% minority, 35% women. **Part-time faculty:** 716 total; 14% minority, 46% women. **Class size:** 37% < 20, 36% 20-39, 7% 40-49, 13% 50-99, 8% >100. **Special facilities:** Nuclear accelerator, natural science museum, 3-theater fine arts center, nature preserve, working arrangements with Cold Spring Harbor Laboratory and Brookhaven National Laboratory.

**Freshman class profile.** 28,547 applied, 11,387 admitted, 2,806 enrolled.

| Mid 50% test scores | | GPA 2.0-2.99: | 4% |
|---|---|---|---|
| SAT critical reading: | 520-620 | Rank in top quarter: | 72% |
| SAT math: | 580-670 | Rank in top tenth: | 38% |
| SAT writing: | 520-620 | End year in good standing: | 89% |
| ACT composite: | 24-28 | Return as sophomores: | 89% |
| GPA 3.75 or higher: | 37% | Out-of-state: | 11% |
| GPA 3.50-3.74: | 25% | Live on campus: | 81% |
| GPA 3.0-3.49: | 34% | International: | 6% |

**Basis for selection.** High school GPA, test scores and level of high school curriculum most important factors. One letter of recommendation and supplemental application, including an essay, are required. Class rank, interview, extracurricular activities, considered. SAT Subject Tests recommended. Audition and musicianship examination required for major in music. Two essays required for admission to Scholars for Medicine, Engineering Scholars for Medicine, and Scholar for Dental Medicine. **Homeschooled:** State high school equivalency certificate required. Applicants required to take 5 Regents exams through their home district or have their home district verify that they have fulfilled high school graduation requirements. **Learning Disabled:** Applicants required to submit documentation of learning disability. Psychological and educational evaluation also required.

**High school preparation.** College-preparatory program required. 16 units required; 19 recommended. Required and recommended units include English 4, mathematics 3-4, social studies 4, science 3-4 and foreign language 2-3. 4 math and 4 science recommended for applicants to science, engineering, and math programs.

**2009-2010 Annual costs.** Tuition/fees: $6,489; $14,389 out-of-state. Room/board: $10,018. Books/supplies: $900. Personal expenses: $1,292.

**2008-2009 Financial aid. Need-based:** 2,318 full-time freshmen applied for aid; 1,521 were judged to have need; 1,468 of these received aid. Average need met was 67%. Average scholarship/grant was $6,849; average loan $4,557. 54% of total undergraduate aid awarded as scholarships/grants, 46% as loans/jobs. **Non-need-based:** Awarded to 1,449 full-time undergraduates, including 538 freshmen. Scholarships awarded for academics, alumni affiliation, art, athletics, job skills, leadership, music/drama.

**Application procedures. Admission:** Priority date 12/1; no deadline. $40 fee, may be waived for applicants with need. Admission notification on a rolling basis beginning on or about 3/1. Must reply by May 1 or within 2 week(s) if notified thereafter. **Financial aid:** Priority date 3/1; no closing date. FAFSA required. Applicants notified on a rolling basis starting 3/1; must reply by 5/1 or within 2 week(s) of notification.

**Academics. Special study options:** Combined bachelor's/graduate degree, cross-registration, distance learning, double major, dual enrollment of high school students, ESL, exchange student, honors, independent study, internships, New York semester, student-designed major, study abroad, teacher certification program, Washington semester. Sequential and combined Bachelor/Master degree programs. **Credit/placement by examination:** AP, CLEP, IB, SAT, ACT, institutional tests. 30 credit hours maximum toward bachelor's degree. **Support services:** Learning center, reduced course load, remedial instruction, tutoring, writing center.

**Honors college/program.** High grades in major subject areas, minimum cumulative unweighted high school average of 93, minimum combined SAT (exclusive of Writing) of 1300 or ACT score of 30, record of advanced or college-level course work, and evidence of writing ability required.

**Majors. Area/ethnic studies:** African-American, American, Asian, European, women's. **Biology:** General, biochemistry, marine, pharmacology. **Business:** Business admin. **Communications:** Journalism. **Computer sciences:** Computer science, information systems. **Conservation:** Environmental studies, water/wetlands/marine. **Engineering:** General, biomedical, computer hardware, electrical, mechanical. **Foreign languages:** Comparative lit, French,

German, Italian, linguistics, Russian, Spanish. **Health:** Clinical lab science, cytotechnology, nursing (RN), respiratory therapy technology. **History:** General. **Liberal arts:** Humanities. **Math:** General, applied. **Philosophy/religion:** Philosophy, religion. **Physical sciences:** Astronomy, chemistry, geology, physics. **Psychology:** General. **Public administration:** Social work. **Social sciences:** General, anthropology, economics, political science, sociology. **Visual/performing arts:** Art history/conservation, dramatic, studio arts. **Other:** Technological management systems.

**Most popular majors.** Biology 12%, business/marketing 8%, health sciences 19%, psychology 13%, social sciences 15%.

**Computing on campus.** 2,300 workstations in dormitories, library, computer center, student center. Dormitories wired for high-speed internet access and linked to campus network. Commuter students can connect to campus network. Online course registration, online library, helpline, repair service, student web hosting, wireless network available.

**Student life. Freshman orientation:** Mandatory, $180 fee. Preregistration for classes offered. 1-day session held in June through August. 1 day program prior to 1st day of classes. **Housing:** Coed dorms, special housing for disabled, apartments, wellness housing available. $200 fully refundable deposit, deadline 5/1. Single sex floors in coed dorms available. **Activities:** Bands, choral groups, dance, drama, film society, literary magazine, music ensembles, musical theater, opera, radio station, student government, student newspaper, symphony orchestra, Jewish, Protestant, Catholic, Islamic Society, Baha'i religious organizations, Inter-Varsity Christian Fellowship, international club, Chinese association, Indian student association, Pakistan club, African students association.

**Athletics.** NCAA. **Intercollegiate:** Baseball M, basketball, cross-country, diving, football (tackle) M, lacrosse, soccer, softball W, swimming, tennis, track and field, volleyball W. **Intramural:** Basketball, softball. **Team name:** Seawolves.

**Student services.** Adult student services, alcohol/substance abuse counseling, chaplain/spiritual director, career counseling, services for economically disadvantaged, student employment services, financial aid counseling, health services, minority student services, on-campus daycare, personal counseling, placement for graduates, veterans' counselor, women's services. **Physically disabled:** Services for visually, speech, hearing impaired.

**Contact.** E-mail: enroll@stonybrook.edu
Phone: (631) 632-6868 Toll-free number: (800) 872-7869
Fax: (631) 632-9898
Judith Burke-Berhannan, Dean of Admissions, State University of New York at Stony Brook, 118 Administration Building, Stony Brook, NY 11794-1901

## State University of New York College at Brockport

Brockport, New York                          CB member
www.brockport.edu                            CB code: 2537

- Public 4-year liberal arts college
- Residential campus in small town
- 7,052 degree-seeking undergraduates
- 1,371 graduate students
- SAT or ACT (ACT writing optional) required

**General.** Founded in 1867. Regionally accredited. **Degrees:** 1,663 bachelor's awarded; master's offered. **ROTC:** Army, Naval, Air Force. **Location:** 16 miles from Rochester. **Calendar:** Semester, limited summer session. **Full-time faculty:** 316 total; 84% have terminal degrees, 17% minority, 47% women. **Part-time faculty:** 274 total; 32% have terminal degrees, 8% minority, 52% women. **Class size:** 44% < 20, 49% 20-39, 4% 40-49, 3% 50-99, less than 1% >100. **Special facilities:** Aquaculture ponds, unidata weather information system, weather radio receiver, nuclear laboratory, high resolution germanium detector, research vessel on Lake Ontario, electron microscope, two supercomputers, Doppler radar system, hydrotherapy room, parallel supercomputer, ultramodern dance facilities including green room.

**Freshman class profile.**

| Mid 50% test scores | | GPA 3.0-3.49: | 37% |
|---|---|---|---|
| SAT critical reading: | 480-570 | GPA 2.0-2.99: | 13% |
| SAT math: | 500-590 | Rank in top quarter: | 50% |
| ACT composite: | 21-26 | Rank in top tenth: | 15% |
| GPA 3.75 or higher: | 28% | Out-of-state: | 2% |
| GPA 3.50-3.74: | 22% | Live on campus: | 89% |

**Basis for selection.** High school academic record including number of academic units, GPA, class rank, test scores important. Recommendations, essay, extracurricular activities strongly recommended. Recommend student

take SAT or ACT for the first time in junior year of high school. Interview required in some cases; auditions required for dance and theater acting. **Homeschooled:** Statement describing homeschool structure and mission, transcript of courses and grades, state high school equivalency certificate, letter of recommendation (nonparent) required. Outline of courses completed at high school level, official test scores (SAT/ACT), personal essay, 2 letters of recommendation, and biography of books read during high school program required.

**High school preparation.** College-preparatory program recommended. 18 units required. Required and recommended units include English 4, mathematics 3-4, social studies 4, science 3-4 (laboratory 1), foreign language 3, computer science 1, visual/performing arts 1 and academic electives 4.

**2009-2010 Annual costs.** Tuition/fees: $6,108; $14,008 out-of-state. Room/board: $9,200. Books/supplies: $3,202. Personal expenses: $1,621.

**2008-2009 Financial aid. Non-need-based:** Scholarships awarded for academics, alumni affiliation, art, leadership, minority status, ROTC, state residency.

**Application procedures. Admission:** Priority date 2/1; no deadline. $40 fee, may be waived for applicants with need. Admission notification on a rolling basis beginning on or about 11/15. Must reply by May 1 or within 3 week(s) if notified thereafter. **Financial aid:** Priority date 2/15; no closing date. FAFSA required. Applicants notified on a rolling basis starting 3/15; must reply by 5/1 or within 4 week(s) of notification.

**Academics.** Time/credit-shortened B.S. degree, experiential learning, domestic and international internships through Delta College. 3-1-3 program allows 30 college credits to be earned during student's senior year of high school. **Special study options:** Accelerated study, combined bachelor's/graduate degree, cross-registration, distance learning, double major, dual enrollment of high school students, honors, independent study, internships, New York semester, semester at sea, student-designed major, study abroad, teacher certification program, Washington semester. **Credit/placement by examination:** AP, CLEP, IB, institutional tests. 90 credit hours maximum toward bachelor's degree. **Support services:** Learning center, pre-admission summer program, reduced course load, study skills assistance, tutoring, writing center.

**Honors college/program.** Freshman applicants should have high school average of at least a 91 and SAT of 1150 (exclusive of Writing) or ACT of 25. The average honors student has a 93 GPA and a 1220 SAT and/or 27 ACT.

**Majors. Area/ethnic studies:** African, African-American, women's. **Biology:** General, aquatic, biochemistry, biotechnology, cellular/molecular, environmental, exercise physiology. **Business:** Accounting, business admin, finance, international, international marketing. **Communications:** General, broadcast journalism, journalism, media studies. **Computer sciences:** General, computer science. **Conservation:** General, environmental science, environmental studies. **Education:** General, bilingual, biology, chemistry, developmentally delayed, elementary, English, health, history, mathematics, physical, physics, science, secondary, social studies, Spanish, special. **Foreign languages:** General, French, Spanish. **Health:** Athletic training, clinical lab technology, health care admin, nursing (RN), predental, premedicine, preveterinary. **History:** General. **Math:** General. **Parks/recreation:** General, facilities management, sports admin. **Philosophy/religion:** Philosophy. **Physical sciences:** Atmospheric science, chemistry, geology, hydrology, meteorology, physics, planetary. **Protective services:** Police science, security management. **Psychology:** General. **Public administration:** Social work. **Science technology:** Biological. **Social sciences:** Anthropology, international relations, political science, sociology. **Visual/performing arts:** General, art, dance, dramatic, studio arts.

**Computing on campus.** 750 workstations in dormitories, library, computer center, student center. Dormitories wired for high-speed internet access and linked to campus network. Commuter students can connect to campus network. Online course registration, online library, helpline, wireless network available.

**Student life. Freshman orientation:** Available, $145 fee. Preregistration for classes offered. 24-hour program held in late June and early July. Students are given their course schedule and take a required Computer Skills Exam. A parent/family program runs parallel to the student orientation. **Housing:** Guaranteed on-campus for freshmen. Coed dorms, special housing for disabled, apartments, wellness housing available. $100 nonrefundable deposit, deadline 5/1. Special living options available include freshman first-year experience program, transfer student program, health club, scholar floors, single-sex areas, adult, 24-hour quiet, academic excellence floors. **Activities:** Campus ministries, choral groups, dance, drama, international student organizations, literary magazine, musical theater, radio station, student government, student newspaper, TV station, Organization for Students of African Descent, Association of Latin American Students, Alpha Chi Honor

Society, Caribbean club, women's center, Brockport Adult Student Organization, peer counseling, student alumni association, Native American student organization.

**Athletics.** NCAA. **Intercollegiate:** Baseball M, basketball, cross-country, diving, field hockey W, football (tackle) M, gymnastics W, ice hockey M, lacrosse, soccer, softball W, swimming, tennis W, track and field, volleyball W, wrestling M. **Intramural:** Badminton, basketball, bowling, football (nontackle), racquetball, soccer, softball, table tennis, volleyball. **Team name:** Golden Eagles.

**Student services.** Alcohol/substance abuse counseling, chaplain/spiritual director, career counseling, services for economically disadvantaged, student employment services, financial aid counseling, health services, legal services, minority student services, on-campus daycare, personal counseling, placement for graduates, veterans' counselor, women's services. **Physically disabled:** Services for visually, speech, hearing impaired.

**Contact.** E-mail: admit@brockport.edu
Phone: (585) 395-2751 Fax: (585) 395-5452
Bernard Valento, Director of Undergraduate Admissions, State University of New York College at Brockport, 350 New Campus Drive, Brockport, NY 14420-2915

## State University of New York College at Buffalo

**Buffalo, New York** — CB member
www.buffalostate.edu — CB code: 2533

- Public 4-year liberal arts and teachers college
- Commuter campus in large city
- 9,626 degree-seeking undergraduates
- 1,892 graduate students
- 43% of applicants admitted
- SAT or ACT (ACT writing optional), SAT Subject Tests required

**General.** Founded in 1867. Regionally accredited. **Degrees:** 1,768 bachelor's awarded; master's offered. **ROTC:** Army. **Location:** 450 miles from New York City, 250 miles from Cleveland. **Calendar:** Semester, limited summer session. **Full-time faculty:** 425 total; 84% have terminal degrees, 18% minority, 46% women. **Part-time faculty:** 453 total; 19% have terminal degrees, 8% minority, 52% women. **Special facilities:** Planetarium, performing arts center, center for environmental research and education, child care center, art center, Great Lakes research facility.

**Freshman class profile.** 11,132 applied, 4,749 admitted, 1,530 enrolled.

| Mid 50% test scores | | GPA 2.0-2.99: | 30% |
|---|---|---|---|
| SAT critical reading: | 440-530 | Rank in top quarter: | 32% |
| SAT math: | 450-540 | Rank in top tenth: | 8% |
| GPA 3.75 or higher: | 8% | Out-of-state: | 2% |
| GPA 3.50-3.74: | 13% | Fraternities: | 1% |
| GPA 3.0-3.49: | 49% | Sororities: | 1% |

**Basis for selection.** High school GPA, class rank, test scores important. Recommendations, essay, interview, volunteer work, work experience and extracurricular activities also considered. Portfolio required for fine arts program.

**High school preparation.** 17 units recommended. Required and recommended units include English 4, mathematics 2-3, science 2-3, foreign language 3 and academic electives 4.

**2009-2010 Annual costs.** Tuition/fees: $6,007; $13,907 out-of-state. Room/board: $9,186. Books/supplies: $900. Personal expenses: $1,000.

**2008-2009 Financial aid.** All financial aid based on need.

**Application procedures. Admission:** No deadline. $40 fee, may be waived for applicants with need. Admission notification on a rolling basis beginning on or about 12/15. Must reply by May 1 or within 4 week(s) if notified thereafter. **Financial aid:** Priority date 3/15, closing date 5/1. FAFSA required. Applicants notified on a rolling basis starting 5/1; must reply within 4 week(s) of notification.

**Academics. Special study options:** Cooperative education, cross-registration, distance learning, double major, dual enrollment of high school students, ESL, exchange student, honors, independent study, internships, liberal arts/career combination, New York semester, study abroad, teacher certification program, Washington semester. **Credit/placement by examination:** AP, CLEP, IB, institutional tests. 30 credit hours maximum toward

bachelor's degree. **Support services:** Learning center, pre-admission summer program, reduced course load, remedial instruction, study skills assistance, tutoring.

**Honors college/program.** High school students must have GPA of 90 or higher (or rank within the top 10 percent of their graduating class) and SAT scores of 1100 (exclusive of Writing) or higher. Advanced Placement courses with grades of B or better, cocurricular activities, and community involvement also considered.

**Majors. Architecture:** Urban/community planning. **Biology:** General. **Business:** General, business admin, fashion, hospitality admin, hospitality/recreation, office management. **Communications:** General, broadcast journalism, journalism, media studies. **Computer sciences:** General, information systems, programming. **Education:** General, art, biology, business, chemistry, early childhood, elementary, emotionally handicapped, English, foreign languages, French, health occupations, kindergarten/preschool, mathematics, mentally handicapped, music, physical, physically handicapped, physics, reading, sales/marketing, science, secondary, social studies, Spanish, speech impaired, technology/industrial arts, trade/industrial, voc/tech. **Engineering technology:** Electrical, electromechanical, industrial, mechanical. **Family/consumer sciences:** Clothing/textiles, food/nutrition. **Foreign languages:** French, Spanish. **Health:** Speech pathology. **History:** General. **Liberal arts:** Humanities. **Math:** General. **Parks/recreation:** Health/fitness. **Philosophy/religion:** Philosophy. **Physical sciences:** Chemistry, geology, physics, planetary. **Protective services:** Criminal justice, forensics. **Psychology:** General. **Public administration:** Social work. **Social sciences:** Anthropology, economics, geography, political science, sociology. **Visual/performing arts:** General, art history/conservation, commercial/advertising art, dramatic, fashion design, fiber arts, interior design, metal/jewelry, painting, photography, printmaking, sculpture, studio arts, theater arts management.

**Most popular majors.** Business/marketing 13%, communications/journalism 8%, education 24%, public administration/social services 6%, social sciences 9%, visual/performing arts 6%.

**Computing on campus.** 900 workstations in dormitories, library, computer center, student center. Dormitories wired for high-speed internet access and linked to campus network. Commuter students can connect to campus network. Online course registration, online library, helpline, repair service, wireless network available.

**Student life. Freshman orientation:** Mandatory, $175 fee. Preregistration for classes offered. **Housing:** Coed dorms, apartments, wellness housing available. $100 fully refundable deposit, deadline 7/1. Apartments for students with dependent children available. **Activities:** Bands, campus ministries, choral groups, dance, drama, film society, international student organizations, literary magazine, music ensembles, radio station, student government, student newspaper, Newman Club, Amnesty International, public interest groups, African American student organization, Adelante Estudiantes, Native American student organization, Muslim student organization, Caribbean student organization.

**Athletics.** NCAA. **Intercollegiate:** Basketball, cross-country, diving, football (tackle) M, ice hockey M, lacrosse W, soccer, softball W, swimming, tennis W, track and field, volleyball W. **Intramural:** Basketball, football (tackle) M, racquetball, soccer, softball, volleyball. **Team name:** Bengals.

**Student services.** Adult student services, career counseling, student employment services, health services, minority student services, on-campus daycare, personal counseling, placement for graduates, veterans' counselor. **Physically disabled:** Services for visually, speech, hearing impaired.

**Contact.** E-mail: admissions@buffalostate.edu
Phone: (716) 878-4017 Fax: (716) 878-6100
Carmela Thompson, Director of Admissions, State University of New York College at Buffalo, 1300 Elmwood Avenue, Moot Hall, Buffalo, NY 14222-1095

## State University of New York College at Cortland

**Cortland, New York** — CB member
www.cortland.edu — CB code: 2538

- Public 4-year liberal arts and teachers college
- Residential campus in large town
- 6,131 degree-seeking undergraduates: 1% part-time, 57% women, 3% African American, 2% Asian American, 6% Hispanic American, 1% Native American, 1% international
- 948 degree-seeking graduate students
- 39% of applicants admitted
- SAT or ACT (ACT writing recommended), application essay required
- 67% graduate within 6 years

**General.** Founded in 1868. Regionally accredited. **Degrees:** 1,354 bachelor's awarded; master's offered. **ROTC:** Army, Air Force. **Location:** 35 miles from Syracuse, 20 miles from Ithaca. **Calendar:** Semester, limited summer session. **Full-time faculty:** 336 total; 55% have terminal degrees, 12% minority, 48% women. **Part-time faculty:** 261 total; 14% have terminal degrees, 4% minority, 54% women. **Class size:** 44% < 20, 47% 20-39, 4% 40-49, 4% 50-99, 1% >100. **Special facilities:** Raquette Lake outdoor education complex, education center (geology field station), Hoxie Gorge Nature Preserve, science museum, ethnographic teaching museum, center for speech and hearing disorders.

**Freshman class profile.** 11,968 applied, 4,679 admitted, 1,167 enrolled.

| Mid 50% test scores | | Rank in top quarter: | 45% |
|---|---|---|---|
| SAT critical reading: | 510-590 | Rank in top tenth: | 10% |
| SAT math: | 480-560 | Return as sophomores: | 83% |
| GPA 3.75 or higher: | 24% | Out-of-state: | 3% |
| GPA 3.50-3.74: | 19% | Live on campus: | 98% |
| GPA 3.0-3.49: | 42% | International: | 2% |
| GPA 2.0-2.99: | 14% | | |

**Basis for selection.** Primary consideration given to course selection and performance. SAT/ACT scores, class rank, extracurricular activities, personal statement/essay, recommendations also enter into decision. Additional consideration for special talents, interview, alumni relation, geographical residence, minority status, volunteer work, work experience. Audition required for musical theater program; portfolio required for art studio program.

**High school preparation.** College-preparatory program required. Required and recommended units include English 4, mathematics 3-4, social studies 4, science 3-4 (laboratory 3) and foreign language 3-4. 2 units in math, science, or foreign language can be compensated for by 4+ units or advanced course work in another one of the three areas.

**2009-2010 Annual costs.** Tuition/fees: $6,145; $14,045 out-of-state. Room/board: $9,790. Books/supplies: $1,000. Personal expenses: $1,665.

**2008-2009 Financial aid. Non-need-based:** Scholarships awarded for academics, art, leadership, minority status, music/drama, state residency.

**Application procedures. Admission:** Priority date 3/1; no deadline. $40 fee. Admission notification on a rolling basis beginning on or about 1/2. Must reply by May 1 or within 4 week(s) if notified thereafter. **Financial aid:** Priority date 3/1; no closing date. FAFSA required. Applicants notified on a rolling basis starting 3/15; must reply by 5/1 or within 4 week(s) of notification.

**Academics. Special study options:** Combined bachelor's/graduate degree, cooperative education, cross-registration, distance learning, double major, dual enrollment of high school students, exchange student, honors, independent study, internships, liberal arts/career combination, student-designed major, study abroad, teacher certification program, Washington semester. **Credit/placement by examination:** AP, CLEP, IB, institutional tests. 30 credit hours maximum toward bachelor's degree. **Support services:** Learning center, pre-admission summer program, reduced course load, study skills assistance, tutoring, writing center.

**Honors college/program.** Open to entering fall freshmen and rising sophomores. Applicants should have exceptional academic record based on grades, standardized tests, course selection and extracurricular activities. To complete Honors Program, students must take at least 24 credits of honors-level courses, by taking combination of specially designated honors courses, contract courses and a course in which they complete the required honors thesis. Students also may use maximum of 2 Writing Intensive (WRIT) courses beyond the all-college requirements toward completion of the honors program.

**Majors. Area/ethnic studies:** African-American. **Biology:** General, biomedical sciences. **Communications:** General, organizational. **Education:** Biology, chemistry, elementary, English, ESL, French, health, kindergarten/preschool, mathematics, physical, physics, science, social studies, Spanish, special, speech impaired. **Foreign languages:** French, Spanish. **Health:** Athletic training, audiology/speech pathology, health services, recreational therapy. **History:** General. **Math:** General. **Parks/recreation:** General, exercise sciences, facilities management, sports admin. **Philosophy/religion:** Philosophy. **Physical sciences:** Chemistry, geology, physics. **Psychology:** General. **Public administration:** Community org/advocacy. **Social sciences:** Anthropology, criminology, economics, geography, international relations, political science, sociology. **Visual/performing arts:** Art, commercial/advertising art, studio arts.

**Most popular majors.** Education 54%, parks/recreation 13%, social sciences 10%.

**Computing on campus.** 838 workstations in dormitories, library, computer center, student center. Dormitories wired for high-speed internet access and linked to campus network. Commuter students can connect to campus network. Online course registration, online library, helpline, repair service, wireless network available.

**Student life. Freshman orientation:** Mandatory, $140 fee. Preregistration for classes offered. 1-1/2 day program during the summer includes overnight with faculty, staff and other students. **Policies:** All students must agree to abide by Code of Student Conduct. Freshmen/sophomores/transfers required to live on campus. **Housing:** Guaranteed on-campus for freshmen. Coed dorms, special housing for disabled, apartments, cooperative housing, wellness housing available. $150 deposit, deadline 5/1. Leadership house, quiet atmosphere, transfer floor. **Activities:** Campus ministries, choral groups, dance, drama, film society, international student organizations, literary magazine, music ensembles, Model UN, musical theater, radio station, student government, student newspaper, symphony orchestra, TV station, Agape, Hillel, Black student union, Caribbean student association, La Familia Latina, Habitat for Humanity, AIDS Prevention & Awareness, Colleges Against Cancer, Cortland Against All Rape, New York public interest research group.

**Athletics.** NCAA. **Intercollegiate:** Baseball M, basketball, cross-country, diving, field hockey W, football (non-tackle) M, football (tackle) M, golf W, gymnastics W, ice hockey, lacrosse, racquetball, soccer, softball W, swimming, tennis W, track and field, volleyball W, wrestling M. **Intramural:** Archery, badminton, basketball, bowling, football (non-tackle), golf, racquetball, soccer, softball, table tennis, tennis, volleyball, water polo, weight lifting. **Team name:** Red Dragons.

**Student services.** Adult student services, alcohol/substance abuse counseling, chaplain/spiritual director, career counseling, student employment services, financial aid counseling, health services, on-campus daycare, personal counseling, placement for graduates, veterans' counselor. **Physically disabled:** Services for visually, speech, hearing impaired.

**Contact.** E-mail: admissions@cortland.edu
Phone: (607) 753-4712 Fax: (607) 753-5998
Mark Yacavone, Director of Admissions, State University of New York College at Cortland, PO Box 2000, Cortland, NY 13045-0900

## State University of New York College at Fredonia

Fredonia, New York      CB member
www.fredonia.edu      CB code: 2539

▶ Public 4-year liberal arts college
▶ Residential campus in large town
▶ 5,321 degree-seeking undergraduates: 2% part-time, 56% women
▶ 383 degree-seeking graduate students
▶ 49% of applicants admitted
▶ SAT or ACT (ACT writing optional), application essay required
▶ 63% graduate within 6 years

**General.** Founded in 1826. Regionally accredited. **Degrees:** 1,102 bachelor's awarded; master's offered. **ROTC:** Army. **Location:** 45 miles from Buffalo, 50 miles from Erie, Pennsylvania. **Calendar:** Semester, limited summer session. **Full-time faculty:** 258 total; 90% have terminal degrees, 13% minority, 44% women. **Part-time faculty:** 186 total; 20% have terminal degrees, 8% minority, 48% women. **Class size:** 57% < 20, 34% 20-39, 4% 40-49, 4% 50-99, 2% >100. **Special facilities:** Arts center, theater, communication lab, sound recording studios, education and local history museums.

**Freshman class profile.** 6,632 applied, 3,281 admitted, 1,148 enrolled.

| Mid 50% test scores | | Rank in top quarter: | 49% |
|---|---|---|---|
| SAT critical reading: | 500-590 | Rank in top tenth: | 15% |
| SAT math: | 510-600 | End year in good standing: | 82% |
| ACT composite: | 21-25 | Return as sophomores: | 87% |
| GPA 3.75 or higher: | 25% | Out-of-state: | 2% |
| GPA 3.50-3.74: | 14% | Live on campus: | 96% |
| GPA 3.0-3.49: | 48% | Fraternities: | 2% |
| GPA 2.0-2.99: | 13% | Sororities: | 3% |

**Basis for selection.** Academic achievement, test results, and subjects taken given priority. Counselor recommendations, resume with supporting materials important when priority credentials marginal. Audition required for acting, music, musical performance, musical theater, production design. Portfolio required for all Visual Arts and New Media programs. **Home-schooled:** State high school equivalency certificate required. Letter from superintendent of school district in which the student resides, attesting to the student's completion of program of home instruction meeting requirements of Section 100.10 of the Regulations of the Commission of Education.

**High school preparation.** College-preparatory program recommended. 20 units required; 23 recommended. Required and recommended units include English 4, mathematics 3-4, social studies 4, science 3-4 (laboratory 3), foreign language 3-4, computer science 1, visual/performing arts 1 and academic electives 1.

**2009-2010 Annual costs.** Tuition/fees: $6,259; $14,159 out-of-state. Room/board: $9,630. Books/supplies: $1,100. Personal expenses: $692.

**2009-2010 Financial aid. Need-based:** 989 full-time freshmen applied for aid; 690 were judged to have need; 684 of these received aid. Average need met was 68%. Average scholarship/grant was $4,047; average loan $3,717. 50% of total undergraduate aid awarded as scholarships/grants, 50% as loans/jobs. **Non-need-based:** Awarded to 956 full-time undergraduates, including 314 freshmen. Scholarships awarded for academics, alumni affiliation, art, athletics, leadership, minority status, music/drama.

**Application procedures. Admission:** No deadline. $40 fee, may be waived for applicants with need. Admission notification on a rolling basis beginning on or about 12/1. Must reply by May 1 or within 4 week(s) if notified thereafter. **Financial aid:** Priority date 2/1, closing date 5/15. FAFSA required. Applicants notified on a rolling basis starting 3/10; must reply within 4 week(s) of notification.

**Academics.** Extensive interdisciplinary studies degree programs offered. **Special study options:** Accelerated study, combined bachelor's/graduate degree, cooperative education, distance learning, double major, honors, independent study, internships, student-designed major, study abroad, teacher certification program, Washington semester. Albany semester, over 90 exchange programs within SUNY system, 13 universities in engineering. **Credit/placement by examination:** AP, CLEP, IB. 30 credit hours maximum toward bachelor's degree. **Support services:** Learning center, study skills assistance, tutoring.

**Majors. Area/ethnic studies:** American. **Biology:** General, biochemistry, biotechnology, human/medical genetics, molecular genetics. **Business:** Accounting, business admin, communications, finance, management information systems, management science. **Communications:** General, broadcast journalism, public relations. **Communications technology:** Recording arts. **Computer sciences:** General. **Conservation:** Environmental studies. **Education:** General, biology, chemistry, early childhood, elementary, English, foreign languages, French, mathematics, music, physics, secondary, social studies, Spanish, speech impaired. **Foreign languages:** French, Spanish. **Health:** Audiology/speech pathology, clinical lab technology, communication disorders, music therapy. **History:** General. **Interdisciplinary:** Global studies. **Legal studies:** General, prelaw. **Math:** General. **Parks/recreation:** Sports admin. **Philosophy/religion:** Philosophy. **Physical sciences:** Chemistry, geochemistry, geology, geophysics, physics, planetary. **Protective services:** Criminal justice. **Psychology:** General. **Public administration:** Social work. **Social sciences:** Economics, political science, sociology. **Visual/performing arts:** Art, art history/conservation, ceramics, commercial/advertising art, dance, dramatic, drawing, music history, music management, music performance, music theory/composition, painting, piano/organ, printmaking, sculpture, studio arts, theater design, voice/opera.

**Most popular majors.** Business/marketing 13%, communications/journalism 10%, education 28%, psychology 6%, social sciences 7%, visual/performing arts 11%.

**Computing on campus.** 500 workstations in dormitories, library, computer center. Dormitories wired for high-speed internet access and linked to campus network. Commuter students can connect to campus network. Online course registration, online library, helpline, repair service, wireless network available.

**Student life. Freshman orientation:** Available, $140 fee. Preregistration for classes offered. 2-day program with students and parents held late June and early July; attendance strongly recommended. Fee includes cost of program, meals, housing, entertainment, orientation materials. **Housing:** Guaranteed on-campus for all undergraduates. Coed dorms, single-sex dorms, apartments, wellness housing available. $50 fully refundable deposit, deadline 5/1. **Activities:** Bands, campus ministries, choral groups, dance, drama, film society, international student organizations, literary magazine, music ensembles, musical theater, opera, radio station, student government, student newspaper, symphony orchestra, TV station, Newman Club, Black student union, Young Republicans, service fraternities and sororities, Jewish student union, Young Democrats, Native American Student Association, Latinos Unidos, Intervarsity Christian Fellowship, Strive Ministries, Inner Room, Alpha Phi Omega.

**Athletics.** NCAA. **Intercollegiate:** Baseball M, basketball, cheerleading M, cross-country, ice hockey M, lacrosse W, soccer, softball W, swimming, tennis W, track and field, volleyball W. **Intramural:** Basketball, field hockey

W, handball, ice hockey, lacrosse M, racquetball, soccer, softball, volleyball, water polo. **Team name:** Blue Devils.

**Student services.** Alcohol/substance abuse counseling, chaplain/spiritual director, career counseling, student employment services, financial aid counseling, health services, legal services, minority student services, on-campus daycare, personal counseling, placement for graduates, veterans' counselor. **Physically disabled:** Services for visually, speech, hearing impaired.

**Contact.**   E-mail: admissions.office@fredonia.edu
Phone: (716) 673-3251 Toll-free number: (800) 252-1212
Fax: (716) 673-3249
Christopher Dearth, Director of Admissions, State University of New York College at Fredonia, 178 Central Avenue, Fredonia, NY 14063-1136

---

**State University of New York College at Geneseo**
Geneseo, New York                                    CB member
www.geneseo.edu                                      CB code: 2540

- Public 4-year liberal arts college
- Residential campus in small town
- 5,488 degree-seeking undergraduates: 2% part-time, 57% women
- 148 degree-seeking graduate students
- 35% of applicants admitted
- SAT or ACT (ACT writing optional), application essay required
- 77% graduate within 6 years; 36% enter graduate study

**General.** Founded in 1871. Regionally accredited. **Degrees:** 1,332 bachelor's awarded; master's offered. **ROTC:** Army, Air Force. **Location:** 30 miles from Rochester. **Calendar:** Semester, limited summer session. **Full-time faculty:** 252 total; 84% have terminal degrees, 15% minority, 42% women. **Part-time faculty:** 101 total; 15% have terminal degrees, 8% minority, 50% women. **Class size:** 28% < 20, 55% 20-39, 9% 40-49, 5% 50-99, 3% >100. **Special facilities:** Nuclear accelerator, planetarium, 4 theaters, ice arena, arboretum.

**Freshman class profile.** 10,412 applied, 3,631 admitted, 948 enrolled.

| Mid 50% test scores | | | |
|---|---|---|---|
| SAT critical reading: | 610-700 | GPA 2.0-2.99: | 1% |
| SAT math: | 630-690 | Rank in top quarter: | 88% |
| ACT composite: | 28-30 | Rank in top tenth: | 56% |
| GPA 3.75 or higher: | 55% | End year in good standing: | 96% |
| GPA 3.50-3.74: | 33% | Return as sophomores: | 90% |
| GPA 3.0-3.49: | 11% | Out-of-state: | 2% |
| | | Live on campus: | 99% |

**Basis for selection.** Rigor of high school preparation, high school GPA, class rank, test scores, school and community activities, special talent, leadership, personal essay important. Special consideration given to minority applicants, children and grandchildren of alumni. Audition required for dramatic arts, music programs; portfolio required for art programs. **Homeschooled:** Statement describing homeschool structure and mission, transcript of courses and grades, state high school equivalency certificate, letter of recommendation (nonparent) required. Letter from high school offical or home school agency indicating the student is meeting production requirements.

**High school preparation.** College-preparatory program recommended. 20 units recommended. Recommended units include English 4, mathematics 4, social studies 4, science 4 and foreign language 4. Music, art also recommended. 4 math required for computer science and business majors.

**2009-2010 Annual costs.** Tuition/fees: $6,326; $14,226 out-of-state. Room/board: $9,550. Books/supplies: $900. Personal expenses: $950.

**2009-2010 Financial aid. Need-based:** 798 full-time freshmen applied for aid; 394 were judged to have need; 394 of these received aid. Average need met was 70%. Average scholarship/grant was $3,846; average loan $3,870. 51% of total undergraduate aid awarded as scholarships/grants, 49% as loans/jobs. **Non-need-based:** Awarded to 1,345 full-time undergraduates, including 192 freshmen. Scholarships awarded for academics, art, leadership, minority status, music/drama, religious affiliation, ROTC, state residency.

**Application procedures. Admission:** Closing date 1/1 (postmark date). $40 fee, may be waived for applicants with need. Admission notification on a rolling basis beginning on or about 3/1. Must reply by 5/1. **Financial aid:** Closing date 2/15. FAFSA required. Applicants notified on a rolling basis starting 3/15; must reply by 5/1.

**Academics.** **Special study options:** Combined bachelor's/graduate degree, cross-registration, double major, dual enrollment of high school students, ESL, honors, independent study, internships, study abroad, teacher certification program, Washington semester. Albany semester, 3-2 engineering, 3-3 engineering, 4-1 MBA, 3-4 dentistry, 3-4 optometry, 3-4 osteopathic medicine, 3-2 or 3-1 nursing, 3-3 physical therapy, pre-med and pre-law advisory program. **Credit/placement by examination:** AP, CLEP, IB, SAT, ACT, institutional tests. 30 credit hours maximum toward bachelor's degree. **Support services:** Learning center, pre-admission summer program, reduced course load, study skills assistance, tutoring, writing center.

**Majors.** **Area/ethnic studies:** African-American, American. **Biology:** General, biochemistry, biophysics. **Business:** General, accounting, business admin. **Communications:** General. **Computer sciences:** General. **Education:** Biology, chemistry, early childhood, elementary, English, French, mathematics, physics, science, social studies, Spanish, special, speech impaired. **Foreign languages:** Comparative lit, French, Spanish. **Health:** Communication disorders, speech pathology. **History:** General. **Math:** General. **Philosophy/religion:** Philosophy. **Physical sciences:** Chemistry, geochemistry, geology, geophysics, physics. **Psychology:** General. **Social sciences:** Anthropology, economics, geography, international relations, political science, sociology. **Visual/performing arts:** Art history/conservation, dramatic, music performance, studio arts.

**Most popular majors.** Biology 11%, business/marketing 13%, communications/journalism 8%, education 24%, English 6%, psychology 9%, social sciences 14%.

**Computing on campus.** PC or laptop required. 900 workstations in dormitories, library, computer center, student center. Dormitories wired for high-speed internet access and linked to campus network. Commuter students can connect to campus network. Online course registration, helpline, student web hosting, wireless network available.

**Student life.** **Freshman orientation:** Available, $145 fee. Preregistration for classes offered. 5 sessions, 2 days each, during June and July. **Housing:** Guaranteed on-campus for all undergraduates. Coed dorms, special housing for disabled, wellness housing available. $150 fully refundable deposit, deadline 5/1. Special interest housing available. Some fraternities/sororities have housing independent of college. **Activities:** Bands, campus ministries, choral groups, dance, drama, international student organizations, literary magazine, music ensembles, Model UN, musical theater, radio station, student government, student newspaper, symphony orchestra, TV station, 187 organizations and clubs, interfaith center.

**Athletics.** NCAA. **Intercollegiate:** Basketball, cross-country, diving, equestrian W, field hockey W, ice hockey W, lacrosse, soccer, softball W, swimming, tennis W, track and field, volleyball W. **Intramural:** Badminton, basketball, football (non-tackle), racquetball, skiing, soccer, softball, squash, table tennis, tennis, volleyball, water polo M. **Team name:** Blue Knights, Lady Knights.

**Student services.** Alcohol/substance abuse counseling, chaplain/spiritual director, career counseling, services for economically disadvantaged, student employment services, financial aid counseling, health services, legal services, minority student services, on-campus daycare, personal counseling, placement for graduates, veterans' counselor, women's services. **Physically disabled:** Services for visually, speech, hearing impaired.

**Contact.** E-mail: admissions@geneseo.edu
Phone: (585) 245-5571 Toll-free number: (866) 245-5211
Fax: (585) 245-5550
Kristine Shay, Director of Admissions, State University of New York College at Geneseo, 1 College Circle, Geneseo, NY 14454-1471

---

## State University of New York College at Old Westbury

**Old Westbury, New York**
**www.oldwestbury.edu**

**CB member**
**CB code: 2866**

◗ Public 4-year business and liberal arts college
◗ Commuter campus in small city
◗ 3,696 degree-seeking undergraduates: 14% part-time, 59% women, 33% African American, 8% Asian American, 19% Hispanic American, 1% Native American, 2% international
◗ 80 degree-seeking graduate students
◗ 51% of applicants admitted
◗ SAT or ACT with writing required
◗ 36% graduate within 6 years; 79% enter graduate study

**General.** Founded in 1965. Regionally accredited. Curricular focus on interdisciplinary and multicultural academic programs. **Degrees:** 723 bachelor's awarded; master's offered. **ROTC:** Army, Air Force. **Location:** 25 miles from New York City. **Calendar:** Semester, extensive summer session. **Full-time faculty:** 131 total; 84% have terminal degrees, 36% minority, 50% women. **Part-time faculty:** 120 total; 25% have terminal degrees, 26% minority, 53% women. **Class size:** 23% < 20, 75% 20-39, less than 1% 40-49, less than 1% 50-99. **Special facilities:** Language lab, performing arts theatre, recital hall, science laboratories, athletic center.

**Freshman class profile.** 3,610 applied, 1,830 admitted, 421 enrolled.

| Mid 50% test scores | | | |
|---|---|---|---|
| SAT critical reading: | 450-530 | GPA 2.0-2.99: | 55% |
| SAT math: | 460-550 | Return as sophomores: | 75% |
| SAT writing: | 430-520 | Out-of-state: | 3% |
| ACT composite: | 20-24 | Live on campus: | 59% |
| GPA 3.75 or higher: | 3% | International: | 1% |
| GPA 3.50-3.74: | 10% | Fraternities: | 1% |
| GPA 3.0-3.49: | 28% | Sororities: | 1% |

**Basis for selection.** High school GPA, SAT scores, letters of recommendation, interview, personal essay important. SAT Subject Tests recommended. Essay and interview recommended for academically weak students. **Homeschooled:** Statement describing homeschool structure and mission required. Letter from superintendent of local school district verifying home schooling equivalent to high school curriculum required.

**High school preparation.** College-preparatory program recommended. 18 units required; 21 recommended. Required and recommended units include English 4, mathematics 3, social studies 4, science 3 (laboratory 2-3), foreign language 2-3, computer science 1 and academic electives 2-3. Health and physical education.

**2009-2010 Annual costs.** Tuition/fees: $5,797; $13,697 out-of-state. Room/board: $9,032. Books/supplies: $1,000. Personal expenses: $1,210.

**2008-2009 Financial aid.** **Need-based:** 283 full-time freshmen applied for aid; 281 were judged to have need; 239 of these received aid. Average need met was 44%. Average scholarship/grant was $5,909; average loan $1,845. 49% of total undergraduate aid awarded as scholarships/grants, 51% as loans/jobs. **Non-need-based:** Awarded to 72 full-time undergraduates, including 18 freshmen. Scholarships awarded for academics, alumni affiliation, state residency.

**Application procedures.** **Admission:** Priority date 12/1; no deadline. $40 fee, may be waived for applicants with need. Admission notification on a rolling basis beginning on or about 1/7. Must reply by May 1 or within 2 week(s) if notified thereafter. **Financial aid:** Priority date 4/1; no closing date. FAFSA, institutional form required. Applicants notified on a rolling basis starting 4/15; must reply within 2 week(s) of notification.

**Academics.** All freshmen enroll in First-Year Experience program. **Special study options:** Combined bachelor's/graduate degree, cross-registration, distance learning, double major, ESL, exchange student, honors, independent study, internships, liberal arts/career combination, study abroad, teacher certification program, Washington semester. Minority access to research centers, Minority biomedical research. **Credit/placement by examination:** AP, CLEP, IB, SAT, institutional tests. 30 credit hours maximum toward bachelor's degree. Each department has own policy for accepting credit by examination in fulfillment of departmental requirements. 8 credits awarded for minimum of 2 years of active duty in any branch of military service. Veterans may also apply for credit based on specific formal courses of instruction given by military services. **Support services:** Learning center, pre-admission summer program, reduced course load, remedial instruction, study skills assistance, tutoring, writing center.

**Honors college/program.** High school GPA 90 or above, SAT scores 1100 or higher. The Honors curriculum will be comprised of 24 credits: First-year Seminar; Gen Ed Linked Course; English Composition 2; Internship or Study Abroad or Directed Research (Independent Study) or Civic Engagement Honors Course; Major Course Requirement with Research Component and Capstone Honors Course.

**Majors.** **Area/ethnic studies:** American. **Biology:** General, biochemistry. **Business:** Accounting, business admin, finance, labor relations, marketing. **Communications:** General. **Computer sciences:** General, information systems. **Education:** Bilingual, biology, chemistry, elementary, mathematics, middle, science, secondary, social studies, Spanish, special. **Foreign languages:** Comparative lit, Spanish. **Liberal arts:** Arts/sciences, humanities. **Math:** General. **Philosophy/religion:** Philosophy. **Physical sciences:** Chemistry. **Psychology:** General. **Social sciences:** General, criminology, sociology. **Visual/performing arts:** General.

**Most popular majors.** Business/marketing 33%, communications/journalism 8%, education 16%, psychology 11%, social sciences 17%.

**Computing on campus.** 450 workstations in library, computer center, student center. Dormitories wired for high-speed internet access. Online course registration, online library, helpline, wireless network available.

**Student life. Freshman orientation:** Mandatory, $110 fee. Preregistration for classes offered. Held prior to fall term for 3 days; for new students and parents. A one-day orientation is held prior to the spring term for all new students. **Housing:** Guaranteed on-campus for all undergraduates. Coed dorms, wellness housing available. $50 fully refundable deposit, deadline 5/1. Honors wing. **Activities:** Campus ministries, choral groups, dance, drama, film society, international student organizations, radio station, student government, student newspaper, women's center, Alianza Latina, African People's Organization, Big Brother/Big Sister club, Asian club, Access for All, Council for Unity, Shekinah Chorale.

**Athletics.** NCAA. **Intercollegiate:** Baseball M, basketball, cross-country, golf M, soccer, softball W, swimming, volleyball W. **Intramural:** Badminton, basketball, racquetball, soccer, softball W, squash, volleyball, weight lifting. **Team name:** Panthers.

**Student services.** Alcohol/substance abuse counseling, chaplain/spiritual director, career counseling, services for economically disadvantaged, student employment services, financial aid counseling, health services, on-campus daycare, personal counseling, women's services. **Physically disabled:** Services for visually, hearing impaired.

**Contact.** E-mail: enroll@oldwestbury.edu
Phone: (516) 876-3073 Fax: (516) 876-3307
Mary Marquez Bell, Vice President of Enrollment Services, State University of New York College at Old Westbury, Box 307, Old Westbury, NY 11568-0307

---

## State University of New York College at Oneonta

Oneonta, New York
www.oneonta.edu

CB member
CB code: 2542

- Public 4-year liberal arts college
- Residential campus in large town
- 5,650 degree-seeking undergraduates: 2% part-time, 57% women
- 141 degree-seeking graduate students
- 39% of applicants admitted
- SAT or ACT (ACT writing optional), application essay required
- 64% graduate within 6 years; 49% enter graduate study

**General.** Founded in 1887. Regionally accredited. **Degrees:** 1,356 bachelor's awarded; master's offered. **Location:** 75 miles from Albany, 175 miles from New York City. **Calendar:** Semester, extensive summer session. **Full-time faculty:** 261 total; 80% have terminal degrees, 18% minority, 46% women. **Part-time faculty:** 238 total; 18% have terminal degrees, 12% minority, 49% women. **Class size:** 43% < 20, 41% 20-39, 12% 40-49, 3% 50-99, less than 1% >100. **Special facilities:** Digital planetarium/theater, observatory, biological field station in Cooperstown, science discovery center, children's center, music recording studio with tunable walls, computer art lab, DNA computing and genomics lab.

**Freshman class profile.** 12,688 applied, 4,972 admitted, 1,109 enrolled.

| Mid 50% test scores | | | |
|---|---|---|---|
| SAT critical reading: | 520-590 | GPA 2.0-2.99: | 2% |
| SAT math: | 540-620 | Rank in top quarter: | 66% |
| ACT composite: | 23-26 | Rank in top tenth: | 24% |
| GPA 3.75 or higher: | 11% | End year in good standing: | 95% |
| GPA 3.50-3.74: | 18% | Return as sophomores: | 83% |
| GPA 3.0-3.49: | 69% | Out-of-state: | 2% |
| | | Live on campus: | 98% |

**Basis for selection.** School achievement record, curriculum, test scores most important. Personal experiences, motivations, awards, honors and recommendations considered. Students scoring below 420 on SAT math or below 450 on SAT verbal must take placement tests. High school writing sample can be submitted in place of essay; interview recommended. **Homeschooled:** Statement describing homeschool structure and mission, transcript of courses and grades, state high school equivalency certificate, interview, letter of recommendation (nonparent) required.

**High school preparation.** College-preparatory program recommended. 16 units required. Required and recommended units include English 4, mathematics 2-3, social studies 3, science 2-3 (laboratory 2) and foreign language 2-3. 15 specific units and 1 additional unit required in math, science, or foreign language.

**2009-2010 Annual costs.** Tuition/fees: $6,185; $14,085 out-of-state. Room/board: $8,900. Books/supplies: $900. Personal expenses: $1,070.

**2009-2010 Financial aid. Need-based:** 996 full-time freshmen applied for aid; 629 were judged to have need; 605 of these received aid. Average need met was 60%. Average scholarship/grant was $5,131; average loan

$3,685. 58% of total undergraduate aid awarded as scholarships/grants, 42% as loans/jobs. **Non-need-based:** Awarded to 1,061 full-time undergraduates, including 263 freshmen. Scholarships awarded for academics, alumni affiliation, leadership, minority status, music/drama, state residency.

**Application procedures. Admission:** Priority date 2/1; no deadline. $40 fee, may be waived for applicants with need. Admission notification on a rolling basis beginning on or about 12/1. Must reply by May 1 or within 4 week(s) if notified thereafter. **Financial aid:** Priority date 3/15; no closing date. FAFSA required. Applicants notified on a rolling basis starting 3/1; must reply by 5/1 or within 4 week(s) of notification.

**Academics. Special study options:** Combined bachelor's/graduate degree, cross-registration, distance learning, double major, ESL, honors, independent study, internships, liberal arts/career combination, New York semester, study abroad, teacher certification program, Washington semester. 3-1 program in fashion with Fashion Institute of Technology; 3-2 program in engineering with Alfred University, Clarkson University, Georgia Institute of Technology, Polytechnic Institute of New York, Rensselaer Polytechnic Institute, SUNY at Binghamton, SUNY Buffalo, Syracuse University; 2-2 program in forestry with SUNY College of Environmental Science and Forestry; 2-2 programs in physical therapy, medical technology, respiratory care, and cytotechnology with SUNY Upstate Medical University, combined bachelor's/graduate degree programs in accounting and management with SUNY Binghamton; 4-1 MBA program with Rochester Institute of Technology; 2-3 option in physical therapy with SUNY Upstate Medical University; 3-1 option in fashion marketing and 2-2 option in fashion design with American Intercontinental University in London. **Credit/placement by examination:** AP, CLEP, IB. 36 credit hours maximum toward bachelor's degree. **Support services:** Learning center, pre-admission summer program, reduced course load, remedial instruction, study skills assistance, tutoring, writing center.

**Majors. Area/ethnic studies:** African-American, Chicano/Hispanic-American/Latino. **Biology:** General, biochemistry. **Business:** Accounting, fashion, managerial economics. **Communications:** General, media studies. **Communications technology:** Animation/special effects. **Computer sciences:** General, computer graphics, computer science. **Conservation:** Environmental science. **Education:** Biology, chemistry, early childhood, elementary, English, family/consumer sciences, foreign languages, French, history, mathematics, multi-level teacher, physics, science, social science, Spanish. **Family/consumer sciences:** General, child development, clothing/textiles, family studies, food/nutrition. **Foreign languages:** French, Spanish. **History:** General. **Interdisciplinary:** Gerontology. **Math:** General, statistics. **Philosophy/religion:** Philosophy. **Physical sciences:** Atmospheric science, chemistry, geology, hydrology, physics. **Protective services:** Criminal justice. **Psychology:** General. **Social sciences:** Anthropology, economics, geography, political science, sociology. **Visual/performing arts:** Art history/conservation, digital art, dramatic, multimedia, music management, studio arts.

**Most popular majors.** Business/marketing 8%, communications/journalism 12%, education 18%, family/consumer sciences 9%, psychology 7%, visual/performing arts 18%.

**Computing on campus.** 700 workstations in dormitories, library, computer center, student center. Dormitories wired for high-speed internet access and linked to campus network. Commuter students can connect to campus network. Online course registration, online library, helpline, student web hosting, wireless network available.

**Student life. Freshman orientation:** Available, $100 fee. Preregistration for classes offered. Meet adviser, select courses, register for classes. **Housing:** Guaranteed on-campus for freshmen. Coed dorms, wellness housing available. $100 fully refundable deposit, deadline 5/1. Special interest housing options and apartment-style suites available within residence halls. **Activities:** Bands, campus ministries, choral groups, dance, drama, film society, international student organizations, literary magazine, music ensembles, Model UN, musical theater, opera, radio station, student government, student newspaper, symphony orchestra, TV station, Campus Ambassadors, Newman Club, Hillel, HOLA Hispanic/Latino Organization, Indian cultural club, Muslim student association, Students of Color Coalition, international students organization, Democracy Matters, Center for Social Responsibility and Community.

**Athletics.** NCAA. **Intercollegiate:** Baseball M, basketball, cross-country, field hockey W, lacrosse, soccer, softball W, swimming, tennis, track and field, volleyball W, wrestling M. **Intramural:** Basketball, football (non-tackle) W, soccer, softball, volleyball. **Team name:** Red Dragons.

**Student services.** Adult student services, alcohol/substance abuse counseling, chaplain/spiritual director, career counseling, services for economically disadvantaged, student employment services, financial aid counseling, health services, minority student services, on-campus daycare, personal counseling, placement for graduates, veterans' counselor, women's services. **Physically disabled:** Services for visually, speech, hearing impaired.

**Contact.** E-mail: admissions@oneonta.edu
Phone: (607) 436-2524 Toll-free number: (800) 786-9123
Fax: (607) 436-3074
Karen Brown, Director of Admissions, State University of New York
College at Oneonta, Admissions Office, 116 Alumni Hall, Oneonta, NY
13820-4016

## State University of New York College at Plattsburgh

| Plattsburgh, New York | CB member |
|---|---|
| www.plattsburgh.edu | CB code: 2544 |

- Public 4-year liberal arts and teachers college
- Residential campus in large town
- 5,810 degree-seeking undergraduates: 5% part-time, 55% women, 5% African American, 2% Asian American, 5% Hispanic American, 1% Native American, 7% international
- 499 degree-seeking graduate students
- 48% of applicants admitted
- SAT or ACT (ACT writing optional), application essay required
- 58% graduate within 6 years

**General.** Founded in 1889. Regionally accredited. Residential satellite campus for biotechnology and environmental science majors. **Degrees:** 1,172 bachelor's awarded; master's offered. **ROTC:** Army. **Location:** 60 miles from Montreal, Canada, 30 miles from Burlington, Vermont. **Calendar:** Semester, limited summer session. **Full-time faculty:** 285 total; 79% have terminal degrees, 12% minority, 42% women. **Part-time faculty:** 220 total; 18% have terminal degrees, 6% minority, 61% women. **Class size:** 44% < 20, 40% 20-39, 11% 40-49, 5% 50-99, less than 1% >100. **Special facilities:** Center for art, music, and theater, wilderness tract, planetarium, electron microscope, remote sensing laboratory, NMR spectrophotometer, computer operated infrared spectrophotometer, liquid scintillation counter, auditory research labs, speech and hearing clinic, Alzheimer's disease assistance center, virtual reality simulator lab, traumatic brain injury center.

**Freshman class profile.** 6,719 applied, 3,245 admitted, 1,066 enrolled.

| Mid 50% test scores | | GPA 2.0-2.99: | 35% |
|---|---|---|---|
| SAT critical reading: | 480-570 | Rank in top quarter: | 34% |
| SAT math: | 500-580 | Rank in top tenth: | 10% |
| ACT composite: | 20-24 | Return as sophomores: | 82% |
| GPA 3.75 or higher: | 3% | Out-of-state: | 6% |
| GPA 3.50-3.74: | 15% | Live on campus: | 91% |
| GPA 3.0-3.49: | 47% | International: | 6% |

**Basis for selection.** Curriculum, high school GPA, class rank, test scores most important. Trend of grades, school and community activities, personal interview, and recommendations also considered. Equal opportunity program for academically and financially disadvantaged students. Interview recommended; audition required for music programs; portfolio required for bachelor of fine arts programs. **Homeschooled:** Letter of recommendation (nonparent) required. Letter from superintendent of the school district in which the student resides attesting to the completion of program of home instruction meeting the requirements of the state of residence.

**High school preparation.** College-preparatory program required. 14 units required; 21 recommended. Required and recommended units include English 4, mathematics 3-4, social studies 3, history 1, science 3-4, foreign language 3 and academic electives 2.

**2009-2010 Annual costs.** Tuition/fees: $6,100; $14,000 out-of-state. Room/board: $8,600.

**2008-2009 Financial aid. Need-based:** 891 full-time freshmen applied for aid; 609 were judged to have need; 604 of these received aid. Average need met was 92%. Average scholarship/grant was $5,811; average loan $5,375. 41% of total undergraduate aid awarded as scholarships/grants, 59% as loans/jobs. **Non-need-based:** Awarded to 2,710 full-time undergraduates, including 582 freshmen. Scholarships awarded for academics, alumni affiliation, art, leadership, minority status, music/drama, ROTC, state residency.

**Application procedures. Admission:** Priority date 12/1; no deadline. $40 fee, may be waived for applicants with need. Admission notification on a rolling basis beginning on or about 1/15. Must reply by May 1 or within 4 week(s) if notified thereafter. **Financial aid:** Priority date 2/15; no closing date. FAFSA required. Applicants notified on a rolling basis starting 3/1; must reply by 5/1.

**Academics.** Credit for military experience, pass/fail option. **Special study options:** Combined bachelor's/graduate degree, cooperative education, cross-registration, distance learning, double major, dual enrollment of high school

students, ESL, exchange student, honors, independent study, internships, liberal arts/career combination, student-designed major, study abroad, teacher certification program. Semester and academic year programs in Canada, study opportunities abroad in Argentina, Australia, Chile, Uruguay, England, 3-2 program in engineering with Clarkson University, SUNY Stony Brook and Binghamton, Syracuse University, McGill University and University of Vermont, 3-4 BA/OD with SUNY College of Optometry, 4-1 BS/MBA with Clarkson University. **Credit/placement by examination:** AP, CLEP, IB, SAT, ACT, institutional tests. 30 credit hours maximum toward bachelor's degree. **Support services:** Learning center, pre-admission summer program, reduced course load, remedial instruction, study skills assistance, tutoring, writing center.

**Majors. Area/ethnic studies:** Canadian, Latin American, women's. **Biology:** General, biochemistry, cell/histology, ecology. **Business:** General, accounting, business admin, entrepreneurial studies, finance, hotel/motel admin, international, management information systems, marketing, restaurant/food services, tourism/travel. **Communications:** Journalism, media studies, organizational, radio/tv. **Computer sciences:** General. **Conservation:** General, environmental science. **Education:** Biology, chemistry, computer, early childhood, elementary, English, foreign languages, French, history, mathematics, multi-level teacher, physics, science, social science, social studies, Spanish, special. **Family/consumer sciences:** Family studies, food/nutrition. **Foreign languages:** French, Spanish. **Health:** Audiology/speech pathology, clinical lab science, cytotechnology, nursing (RN). **History:** General. **Liberal arts:** Arts/sciences. **Math:** General. **Parks/recreation:** General. **Philosophy/religion:** Philosophy. **Physical sciences:** Chemistry, geology, physics. **Protective services:** Criminal justice. **Psychology:** General. **Public administration:** Social work. **Social sciences:** Anthropology, economics, geography, political science, sociology. **Visual/performing arts:** General, art, dramatic. **Other:** Fitness and wellness, Global supply chain management.

**Most popular majors.** Business/marketing 19%, communications/journalism 9%, education 13%, health sciences 7%, psychology 8%, security/protective services 8%, social sciences 6%.

**Computing on campus.** 566 workstations in dormitories, library, computer center, student center. Dormitories wired for high-speed internet access and linked to campus network. Commuter students can connect to campus network. Online course registration, online library, helpline, repair service, student web hosting, wireless network available.

**Student life. Freshman orientation:** Available, $75 fee. Preregistration for classes offered. 2-night stay with meals included; simultaneous program for parents; includes course selection and registration. **Housing:** Guaranteed on-campus for all undergraduates. Coed dorms, special housing for disabled, wellness housing available. $50 fully refundable deposit. Living/learning communities available. **Activities:** Bands, choral groups, dance, drama, film society, literary magazine, music ensembles, musical theater, radio station, student government, student newspaper, TV station, Akeba, El Pueblo, environmental action committee, Hillel, Inter-Varsity Christian Fellowship, Newman Association, Points of View, College Democrats, College Republicans.

**Athletics.** NCAA. **Intercollegiate:** Baseball M, basketball, cross-country, ice hockey, lacrosse M, soccer, softball W, tennis W, track and field, volleyball W. **Intramural:** Basketball, field hockey, football (non-tackle) M, racquetball, softball, tennis, volleyball. **Team name:** Cardinals.

**Student services.** Adult student services, alcohol/substance abuse counseling, chaplain/spiritual director, career counseling, services for economically disadvantaged, student employment services, financial aid counseling, health services, legal services, minority student services, on-campus daycare, personal counseling, placement for graduates, veterans' counselor, women's services. **Physically disabled:** Services for visually, speech, hearing impaired.

**Contact.** E-mail: admissions@plattsburgh.edu
Phone: (518) 564-2040 Toll-free number: (888) 673-0012
Fax: (518) 564-2045
Richard Higgins, Associate Vice President for Enrollment Management, State University of New York College at Plattsburgh, Kehoe Administration Building, Plattsburgh, NY 12901

## State University of New York College at Potsdam

| Potsdam, New York | CB member |
|---|---|
| www.potsdam.edu | CB code: 2545 |

- Public 4-year liberal arts and teachers college
- Residential campus in large town
- 3,691 degree-seeking undergraduates: 2% part-time, 57% women
- 539 degree-seeking graduate students

- 66% of applicants admitted
- 58% graduate within 6 years; 47% enter graduate study

**General.** Founded in 1816. Regionally accredited. **Degrees:** 661 bachelor's awarded; master's offered. **ROTC:** Army, Air Force. **Location:** 150 miles from Syracuse, 80 miles from Montreal, Canada. **Calendar:** Semester, limited summer session. **Full-time faculty:** 262 total; 78% have terminal degrees, 9% minority, 43% women. **Part-time faculty:** 100 total; 12% have terminal degrees, 3% minority, 61% women. **Class size:** 64% < 20, 31% 20-39, 2% 40-49, 2% 50-99, less than 1% >100. **Special facilities:** Electronic music and recording studios, planetarium, seismographic laboratory, 24-hour computer laboratory, concert hall, music theater, anthropology museum, biology museum, teaching resource center, six fine arts studios, art gallery, ice rink.

**Freshman class profile.** 4,525 applied, 2,970 admitted, 835 enrolled.

| Mid 50% test scores | | | |
|---|---|---|---|
| SAT critical reading: | 470-570 | GPA 2.0-2.99: | 31% |
| SAT math: | 470-570 | Rank in top quarter: | 31% |
| ACT composite: | 20-24 | Rank in top tenth: | 7% |
| GPA 3.75 or higher: | 17% | End year in good standing: | 79% |
| GPA 3.50-3.74: | 17% | Return as sophomores: | 77% |
| GPA 3.0-3.49: | 34% | Live on campus: | 91% |

**Basis for selection.** Admissions decisions based on secondary school record and standardized test scores. Class rank, talent, ability, activities and community service also important. Most applicants will not need to submit a standardized test score for admission consideration. Essays and interviews required for some. Auditions required for music majors. Auditions encouraged for dance and theater majors. Portfolios encouraged for art majors. **Homeschooled:** GED required. SAT or ACT required.

**High school preparation.** College-preparatory program recommended. 13 units required; 21 recommended. Required and recommended units include English 4, mathematics 2-4, social studies 4, science 2-4 (laboratory 1-2), foreign language 4 and visual/performing arts 1.

**2009-2010 Annual costs.** Tuition/fees: $6,124; $14,024 out-of-state. Room/board: $9,270. Books/supplies: $1,200. Personal expenses: $1,100.

**2009-2010 Financial aid. Need-based:** 766 full-time freshmen applied for aid; 584 were judged to have need; 579 of these received aid. Average need met was 87%. Average scholarship/grant was $6,536; average loan $3,843. 59% of total undergraduate aid awarded as scholarships/grants, 41% as loans/jobs. **Non-need-based:** Awarded to 1,037 full-time undergraduates, including 309 freshmen. Scholarships awarded for academics, art, leadership, minority status, music/drama, ROTC. **Additional information:** Apply early to access limited, need-based awards.

**Application procedures. Admission:** No deadline. $40 fee, may be waived for applicants with need. Admission notification on a rolling basis beginning on or about 10/1. Must reply by May 1 for guaranteed enrollment. **Financial aid:** Priority date 3/1; no closing date. FAFSA required. Applicants notified on a rolling basis starting 2/1; must reply by 5/1 or within 4 week(s) of notification.

**Academics. Special study options:** Combined bachelor's/graduate degree, cross-registration, distance learning, double major, dual enrollment of high school students, exchange student, honors, independent study, internships, liberal arts/career combination, student-designed major, study abroad, teacher certification program. First-year students may enroll in interdisciplinary program to study art, literature, science, and sociology of the Adirondacks. Extension offers undergraduate and graduate courses with emphasis on teacher education. Combined degree options in engineering with Clarkson University and SUNY Binghamton; accounting, engineering or management with SUNY Institute of Technology. **Credit/placement by examination:** AP, CLEP, IB. Credit awarded for International Baccalaureate on course-by-course evaluation. **Support services:** Learning center, pre-admission summer program, reduced course load, study skills assistance, tutoring, writing center.

**Majors. Area/ethnic studies:** Women's. **Biology:** General, biochemistry. **Business:** Business admin, labor relations. **Computer sciences:** General. **Conservation:** Environmental studies. **Education:** Biology, chemistry, early childhood, elementary, English, foreign languages, French, mathematics, music, physics, science, social studies, Spanish. **Foreign languages:** French, Spanish. **Health:** Health services. **History:** General. **Interdisciplinary:** Biological/physical sciences. **Liberal arts:** Arts/sciences, humanities. **Math:** General. **Philosophy/religion:** Philosophy. **Physical sciences:** Chemistry, geology, physics. **Protective services:** Law enforcement admin. **Psychology:** General. **Social sciences:** Anthropology, archaeology, economics, political science, sociology. **Visual/performing arts:** Art history/conservation, commercial/advertising art, dance, dramatic, music performance, music theory/composition, studio arts.

**Most popular majors.** Business/marketing 10%, education 28%, English 7%, psychology 8%, social sciences 10%, visual/performing arts 11%.

**Computing on campus.** 690 workstations in dormitories, library, computer center, student center. Dormitories wired for high-speed internet access and linked to campus network. Commuter students can connect to campus network. Online course registration, online library, helpline, student web hosting, wireless network available.

**Student life. Freshman orientation:** Available, $180 fee. Preregistration for classes offered. Two-day program. **Policies:** Academic honor code outlines expectations for academic honesty and integrity; code of student rights, responsibilities, and conduct can be found in student handbook. **Housing:** Guaranteed on-campus for all undergraduates. Coed dorms, special housing for disabled, apartments, wellness housing available. $50 fully refundable deposit, deadline 5/1. First-year experience, quiet study, international house, transfer student housing, sustainability housing. **Activities:** Bands, campus ministries, choral groups, dance, drama, international student organizations, literary magazine, music ensembles, musical theater, opera, radio station, student government, student newspaper, symphony orchestra, Intervarsity Christian Fellowship, Black Student Alliance, Potsdam Association of Native Americans, Caribbean Latin American Student Society, Politics Association, Circle K, Lesbian, Gay, Bisexual and Transgender Association, Students for Peaceful Alternatives, Philosophy Forum, Pagan Studies.

**Athletics.** NCAA. **Intercollegiate:** Basketball, cross-country, equestrian, golf M, ice hockey, lacrosse, soccer, softball W, swimming, volleyball W. **Intramural:** Basketball, football (non-tackle), racquetball, soccer, softball, volleyball, water polo, weight lifting. **Team name:** Bears.

**Student services.** Adult student services, alcohol/substance abuse counseling, chaplain/spiritual director, career counseling, services for economically disadvantaged, student employment services, financial aid counseling, health services, legal services, minority student services, on-campus daycare, personal counseling, placement for graduates, veterans' counselor, women's services. **Physically disabled:** Services for visually, speech, hearing impaired.

**Contact.** E-mail: admissions@potsdam.edu
Phone: (315) 267-2180 Toll-free number: (877) 768-7326
Fax: (315) 267-2163
Thomas Nesbitt, Director of Admissions, State University of New York College at Potsdam, 44 Pierrepont Avenue, Potsdam, NY 13676

---

**State University of New York College of Environmental Science and Forestry**
Syracuse, New York                                    CB member
www.esf.edu                                           CB code: 2530

- Public 4-year university
- Residential campus in small city
- 1,561 degree-seeking undergraduates: 2% part-time, 40% women, 1% African American, 4% Asian American, 3% Hispanic American, 1% Native American, 1% international
- 502 degree-seeking graduate students
- 43% of applicants admitted
- SAT or ACT (ACT writing recommended), application essay required
- 65% graduate within 6 years; 38% enter graduate study

**General.** Founded in 1911. Regionally accredited. Doctoral granting; focused on the science, engineering, design and management of the environment and natural resources. **Degrees:** 316 bachelor's, 33 associate awarded; master's, doctoral offered. **ROTC:** Army, Air Force. **Location:** 1 mile from downtown. **Calendar:** Semester, limited summer session. **Full-time faculty:** 146 total; 96% have terminal degrees, 12% minority, 24% women. **Part-time faculty:** 27 total; 85% have terminal degrees, 4% minority, 41% women. **Class size:** 77% < 20, 12% 20-39, 4% 40-49, 4% 50-99, 3% >100. **Special facilities:** Six regional campuses and field stations used for field study and research, 25,000-acre multi-campus forest system, ecological center, wildlife collection, semi-commercial paper mill.

**Freshman class profile.** 1,677 applied, 723 admitted, 283 enrolled.

| Mid 50% test scores | | | |
|---|---|---|---|
| SAT critical reading: | 520-610 | End year in good standing: | 92% |
| SAT math: | 540-630 | Return as sophomores: | 88% |
| ACT composite: | 22-27 | Out-of-state: | 22% |
| Rank in top quarter: | 77% | Live on campus: | 90% |
| Rank in top tenth: | 39% | International: | 1% |

**Basis for selection.** High school record most important, test scores, essay, and recommendations also important. Applicant should have strong college preparatory program with focus on mathematics and science for most programs and design background preferred for Landscape Architecture. Interview or participation in informational program recommended for all; portfolio required for some landscape architecture applicants. **Homeschooled:** Statement describing homeschool structure and mission required. If no superintendent's statement provided, student must have GED to enroll.

**High school preparation.** College-preparatory program required. 14 units required; 19 recommended. Required and recommended units include English 4, mathematics 3-4, social studies 3, history 1, science 3-4 (laboratory 3-4) and foreign language 3.

**2009-2010 Annual costs.** Tuition/fees: $5,829; $13,729 out-of-state. Room and board available through Syracuse University at $11,920 per year. Books/supplies: $1,200. Personal expenses: $450.

**2009-2010 Financial aid. Need-based:** 260 full-time freshmen applied for aid; 166 were judged to have need; 166 of these received aid. Average need met was 100%. Average scholarship/grant was $4,000; average loan $5,500. 48% of total undergraduate aid awarded as scholarships/grants, 52% as loans/jobs. **Non-need-based:** Awarded to 410 full-time undergraduates, including 174 freshmen. Scholarships awarded for academics, alumni affiliation, leadership, minority status, ROTC, state residency.

**Application procedures. Admission:** Priority date 9/15; deadline 1/15. $40 fee, may be waived for applicants with need. Application must be submitted online. Admission notification 4/1. Must reply by May 1 or within 4 week(s) if notified thereafter. Applications submitted after the 1/15 regular closing date will be considered on a space-available basis. **Financial aid:** Priority date 3/1; no closing date. FAFSA required. Applicants notified on a rolling basis starting 3/15; must reply within 2 week(s) of notification.

**Academics. Special study options:** Combined bachelor's/graduate degree, cooperative education, cross-registration, dual enrollment of high school students, ESL, honors, independent study, internships, study abroad, teacher certification program. Associate degree programs in forestry technology and land surveying technology offered through The Ranger School in Adirondack Mountains. **Credit/placement by examination:** AP, CLEP, IB, institutional tests. **Support services:** Learning center, pre-admission summer program, reduced course load, study skills assistance, tutoring, writing center.

**Majors. Agriculture:** Animal sciences, plant protection. **Architecture:** Landscape. **Biology:** Aquatic, biochemistry, biotechnology, conservation, environmental, wildlife. **Business:** Construction management. **Conservation:** General, environmental science, environmental studies, fisheries, forest management, forest resources, forest sciences, forestry, management/policy, wildlife, wood science. **Education:** Biology, chemistry, science. **Engineering:** General, environmental. **Physical sciences:** Chemistry. **Other:** Bioprocess engineering, paper science and engineering, wood products engineering, Natural history and interpretation.

**Most popular majors.** Architecture 8%, biology 41%, engineering/engineering technologies 16%, natural resources/environmental science 29%, physical sciences 6%.

**Computing on campus.** 250 workstations in dormitories, library, computer center, student center. Dormitories wired for high-speed internet access and linked to campus network. Commuter students can connect to campus network. Online course registration, online library, helpline, repair service, student web hosting, wireless network available.

**Student life. Freshman orientation:** Mandatory, $50 fee. Preregistration for classes offered. 4-day program prior to start of fall classes. **Policies:** Freshmen are required to live on campus (in Syracuse University housing) unless they live within commuting distance. **Housing:** Guaranteed on-campus for freshmen. Coed dorms, special housing for disabled, apartments, fraternity/sorority housing, wellness housing available. $400 nonrefundable deposit, deadline 5/1. All on-campus housing available through Syracuse University. SUNY-ESF is located on the campus of Syracuse University. **Activities:** Bands, campus ministries, choral groups, dance, drama, film society, international student organizations, literary magazine, music ensembles, musical theater, radio station, student government, student newspaper, symphony orchestra, undergraduate student association, Alpha Xi Sigma honor society, Wildlife Society, multicultural organization, environmental action coalition, woodsmen's team, creative minds club, green campus initiative, soccer teams, golf team.

**Athletics. Intercollegiate:** Golf, soccer. **Intramural:** Basketball, football (non-tackle), racquetball, soccer, softball, tennis. **Team name:** The Mighty Oaks.

**Student services.** Alcohol/substance abuse counseling, chaplain/spiritual director, career counseling, services for economically disadvantaged, student employment services, financial aid counseling, health services, legal services, minority student services, personal counseling, placement for graduates, veterans' counselor, women's services. **Physically disabled:**

Services for visually, speech, hearing impaired. **Learning disabled:** Comprehensive services available.

**Contact.** E-mail: esfinfo@esf.edu
Phone: (315) 470-6600 Fax: (315) 470-6933
Susan Sanford, Director of Admissions & Inter-Institutional Relations, State University of New York College of Environmental Science and Forestry, 106 Bray Hall, Syracuse, NY 13210

---

## State University of New York Downstate Medical Center
**Brooklyn, New York**
www.downstate.edu                                    CB code: 2534

▶ Public two-year upper-division health science and nursing college
▶ Commuter campus in very large city

**General.** Founded in 1858. Regionally accredited. **Location:** 4 miles from downtown Brooklyn, 6 miles from downtown Manhattan. **Calendar:** Semester.

**Annual costs/financial aid.** Tuition/fees (2009-2010): $5,493; $13,393 out-of-state. Reported room-only price is for double standard; other room-only prices vary by accommodation and can range up to $8,504. Room: $4,668. Books/supplies: $1,358. Need-based financial aid available to full-time and part-time students.

**Contact.** Phone: (718) 270-2446
Director of Admissions & Enrollment, 450 Clarkson Avenue, Box 60, Brooklyn, NY 11203-2098

---

## State University of New York Empire State College
**Saratoga Springs, New York**                       CB member
www.esc.edu                                          CB code: 2214

▶ Public 4-year liberal arts college
▶ Commuter campus in large town
▶ 11,893 degree-seeking undergraduates: 60% part-time, 60% women, 14% African American, 2% Asian American, 8% Hispanic American, 1% Native American, 5% international
▶ 885 degree-seeking graduate students
▶ 78% of applicants admitted
▶ Application essay required

**General.** Founded in 1971. Regionally accredited. No campus or classrooms; students meet with faculty and use facilities at regional centers and units throughout state. Centers in Genesee Valley (Rochester), Long Island (Old Westbury), Metropolitan New York, Hudson Valley (Hartsdale), and Buffalo. Coordinating center at Saratoga Springs. Units in Binghamton, Ithaca, Mid-Hudson (New Paltz), Mohawk Valley (Utica-Rome), North Country (Plattsburgh), Onondaga (Syracuse), Saratoga Springs, Watertown, and International Programs in Athens, Prague, the Dominican Republic and several other locations. **Degrees:** 2,006 bachelor's, 503 associate awarded; master's offered. **Calendar:** Continuous, extensive summer session. **Full-time faculty:** 181 total; 97% have terminal degrees, 15% minority, 64% women. **Part-time faculty:** 1,266 total.

**Freshman class profile.** 1,023 applied, 800 admitted, 555 enrolled.

**Basis for selection.** Requirements for undergraduate admission: completed application, possession of high school diploma or equivalent, ability to pursue college-level work, payment of nonrefundable orientation fee, and completion of the college's orientation process.

**2009-2010 Annual costs.** Tuition/fees: $5,195; $13,095 out-of-state. Books/supplies: $1,502. Personal expenses: $1,000.

**2008-2009 Financial aid.** All financial aid based on need. 36% of total undergraduate aid awarded as scholarships/grants, 64% as loans/jobs.

**Application procedures. Admission:** Priority date 6/1; no deadline. No application fee. Admission notification on a rolling basis. **Financial aid:** Priority date 4/1; no closing date. FAFSA required. Applicants notified on a rolling basis; must reply within 3 week(s) of notification.

**Academics. Special study options:** Accelerated study, combined bachelor's/graduate degree, cross-registration, distance learning, double major, external degree, independent study, internships, student-designed major, teacher certification program. Weekend residencies for some specialized programs.

**Credit/placement by examination:** AP, CLEP, IB. 40 credit hours maximum toward associate degree, 96 toward bachelor's. **Support services:** Study skills assistance, tutoring, writing center.

**Majors. Business:** General, labor relations. **Education:** General. **Health:** Nursing (RN). **History:** General. **Interdisciplinary:** Biological/physical sciences. **Liberal arts:** Arts/sciences. **Psychology:** General. **Public administration:** Community org/advocacy. **Social sciences:** General, economics. **Visual/performing arts:** Studio arts.

**Most popular majors.** Business/marketing 41%, English 6%, physical sciences 7%, psychology 7%, public administration/social services 22%.

**Computing on campus.** 100 workstations in computer center. Commuter students can connect to campus network. Online course registration, online library, helpline available.

**Student life. Freshman orientation:** Mandatory, $50 fee.

**Student services.** Adult student services, career counseling, student employment services, veterans' counselor. **Physically disabled:** Services for visually, speech, hearing impaired.

**Contact.** E-mail: admissions@esc.edu
Phone: (518) 587-2100 Toll-free number: (800) 847-3000
Fax: (518) 587-9759
Jennifer D'Agostino, Director of Admissions, State University of New York Empire State College, Two Union Avenue, Saratoga Springs, NY 12866

---

## State University of New York Institute of Technology at Utica/Rome

**Utica, New York**  **CB member**
www.sunyit.edu  **CB code: 0755**

- Public 4-year business, engineering, nursing and liberal arts college
- Commuter campus in small city
- 2,003 degree-seeking undergraduates: 24% part-time, 43% women
- 522 degree-seeking graduate students
- 38% of applicants admitted
- SAT or ACT (ACT writing optional) required
- 53% graduate within 6 years

**General.** Founded in 1966. Regionally accredited. **Degrees:** 435 bachelor's awarded; master's offered. **ROTC:** Army. **Location:** 50 miles from Syracuse, 90 miles from Albany. **Calendar:** Semester, limited summer session. **Full-time faculty:** 96 total; 79% have terminal degrees, 24% minority, 38% women. **Part-time faculty:** 104 total; 21% have terminal degrees, 6% minority, 52% women. **Class size:** 59% < 20, 40% 20-39, less than 1% 40-49, less than 1% 50-99.

**Freshman class profile.** 1,770 applied, 678 admitted, 203 enrolled.

| Mid 50% test scores | | | |
|---|---|---|---|
| SAT critical reading: | 480-570 | Rank in top quarter: | 33% |
| SAT math: | 520-600 | Rank in top tenth: | 10% |
| ACT composite: | 22-25 | End year in good standing: | 78% |
| GPA 3.75 or higher: | 12% | Return as sophomores: | 70% |
| GPA 3.50-3.74: | 17% | Live on campus: | 77% |
| GPA 3.0-3.49: | 65% | | |
| GPA 2.0-2.99: | 6% | | |

**Basis for selection.** Students must meet minimum SAT/ACT score ranges with competitive high school averages as well as minimum high school unit requirements. Interview, essay required for some applicants; recommended for all. **Homeschooled:** Statement describing homeschool structure and mission, transcript of courses and grades, state high school equivalency certificate required. Statement from local public school superintendent that verifies home school curriculum matches NYS Regents Curriculum required.

**High school preparation.** College-preparatory program required. 17 units required; 25 recommended. Required and recommended units include English 4, mathematics 3-4, social studies 2, history 2, science 3-4 (laboratory 3-4), foreign language 3 and academic electives 2.

**2009-2010 Annual costs.** Tuition/fees: $6,090; $13,990 out-of-state. Room/board: $8,750. Books/supplies: $1,000. Personal expenses: $900.

**2009-2010 Financial aid. Need-based:** 179 full-time freshmen applied for aid; 146 were judged to have need; 145 of these received aid. Average scholarship/grant was $6,232; average loan $3,187. 47% of total undergraduate aid awarded as scholarships/grants, 53% as loans/jobs. **Non-need-based:** Awarded to 40 full-time undergraduates, including 15 freshmen. Scholarships awarded for academics.

**Application procedures. Admission:** Priority date 3/1; deadline 8/1 (receipt date). $40 fee, may be waived for applicants with need. Admission notification on a rolling basis beginning on or about 1/15. Must reply by May 1 or within 4 week(s) if notified thereafter. **Financial aid:** Priority date 3/15; no closing date. FAFSA required. Applicants notified on a rolling basis starting 3/17; must reply within 2 week(s) of notification.

**Academics.** SUNYIT has four schools that offer professional and technical and liberal arts programs: School of Business, School of Nursing & Health Systems, School of Arts & Sciences and School of Information Systems & Engineering Technologies. **Special study options:** Accelerated study, combined bachelor's/graduate degree, cross-registration, distance learning, double major, dual enrollment of high school students, independent study, internships, liberal arts/career combination, study abroad. Study abroad is coordinated through SUNY Study Abroad, offering 500 overseas programs in more than 51 countries. **Credit/placement by examination:** AP, CLEP, IB, SAT, ACT, institutional tests. Credit awarded for International Baccalaureate varies by academic department. **Support services:** Learning center, remedial instruction, study skills assistance, tutoring, writing center.

**Majors. Business:** General, accounting, business admin, finance. **Computer sciences:** General, information systems. **Engineering:** Electrical. **Engineering technology:** Civil, computer, electrical, industrial, mechanical. **Health:** Health care admin, medical records admin, nursing (RN). **Math:** Applied. **Protective services:** Criminal justice. **Psychology:** General. **Social sciences:** Sociology.

**Most popular majors.** Business/marketing 26%, communications/journalism 6%, computer/information sciences 14%, engineering/engineering technologies 24%, health sciences 16%, psychology 7%.

**Computing on campus.** 212 workstations in dormitories, library, computer center, student center. Dormitories wired for high-speed internet access and linked to campus network. Commuter students can connect to campus network. Online course registration, online library, helpline, student web hosting, wireless network available.

**Student life. Freshman orientation:** Mandatory, $150 fee. Preregistration for classes offered. **Housing:** Guaranteed on-campus for freshmen. Coed dorms, special housing for disabled available. $150 fully refundable deposit, deadline 5/1. **Activities:** Jazz band, international student organizations, radio station, student government, student newspaper, TV station, black student union, Latino student association.

**Athletics.** NCAA. **Intercollegiate:** Baseball M, basketball, bowling, cross-country, golf M, soccer, softball W, swimming, volleyball. **Intramural:** Badminton, basketball, bowling, cricket, golf, racquetball, soccer, softball, tennis W, volleyball. **Team name:** Wildcats.

**Student services.** Adult student services, alcohol/substance abuse counseling, chaplain/spiritual director, career counseling, services for economically disadvantaged, student employment services, financial aid counseling, health services, legal services, minority student services, personal counseling, placement for graduates, veterans' counselor, women's services. **Physically disabled:** Services for visually, speech, hearing impaired. **Learning disabled:** Comprehensive services available.

**Contact.** E-mail: admissions@sunyit.edu
Phone: (315) 792-7500 Toll-free number: (866) 278-6948
Fax: (315) 792-7837
Jennifer Phelan-Ninh, Director of Admissions, State University of New York Institute of Technology at Utica/Rome, 100 Seymour Road, Utica, NY 13502

---

## State University of New York Maritime College

**Throggs Neck, New York**  **CB member**
www.sunymaritime.edu  **CB code: 2536**

- Public 4-year maritime college
- Residential campus in very large city
- 1,562 degree-seeking undergraduates: 6% part-time, 10% women, 6% African American, 4% Asian American, 9% Hispanic American, 7% international
- 148 degree-seeking graduate students
- 63% of applicants admitted
- SAT or ACT (ACT writing optional) required
- 57% graduate within 6 years; 5% enter graduate study

**General.** Founded in 1874. Regionally accredited. Graduates eligible for commission as officers in Navy, Marine Corps, Coast Guard, Air Force, and commissioned Corps of the National Oceanic and Atmospheric Administration. 3 summer semesters at sea and regiment option required for students interested in obtaining U.S. Merchant Marine Officer's License. **Degrees:** 220 bachelor's, 7 associate awarded; master's offered. **ROTC:** Army, Naval. **Location:** 10 miles from New York City. **Calendar:** Semester, limited summer session. **Full-time faculty:** 70 total; 49% have terminal degrees, 6% minority, 21% women. **Part-time faculty:** 59 total; 24% have terminal degrees, 22% minority, 27% women. **Class size:** 31% < 20, 61% 20-39, 6% 40-49, 1% 50-99, 2% >100. **Special facilities:** 565-foot training ship, training tanker, Center for Simulated Marine Operations, bridge simulator, model basin and towing tank, CAD-CAM facilities, 2 diesel propulsion simulators, maritime museum, sailing center including several 1-ton ocean racers.

**Freshman class profile.** 1,386 applied, 874 admitted, 355 enrolled.

| Mid 50% test scores | | GPA 2.0-2.99: | 44% |
|---|---|---|---|
| SAT critical reading: | 460-550 | Rank in top quarter: | 60% |
| SAT math: | 510-600 | Rank in top tenth: | 12% |
| ACT composite: | 20-24 | Return as sophomores: | 76% |
| GPA 3.75 or higher: | 7% | Out-of-state: | 26% |
| GPA 3.50-3.74: | 16% | Live on campus: | 94% |
| GPA 3.0-3.49: | 31% | International: | 2% |

**Basis for selection.** Quality and strength of preparation, school achievement record, including first semester senior grades, class rank, test scores, extracurricular activities considered. Interview and essay recommended. Interviews and essays are not required but highly recommended. **Home-schooled:** Statement describing homeschool structure and mission, transcript of courses and grades, state high school equivalency certificate, letter of recommendation (nonparent) required. Accreditation of home school.

**High school preparation.** College-preparatory program recommended. 18 units required. Required and recommended units include English 3-4, mathematics 3-4, social studies 3, history 3, science 3-4 (laboratory 1) and foreign language 1-3. Math requirement includes algebra, geometry, trigonometry; math beyond trigonometry recommended. Chemistry or physics required; both strongly recommended.

**2009-2010 Annual costs.** Tuition/fees: $6,090; $13,990 out-of-state. Additional fees required for students in the regiment. Room/board: $9,930. Books/supplies: $1,200. Personal expenses: $1,910.

**2008-2009 Financial aid.** **Need-based:** 212 full-time freshmen applied for aid; 198 were judged to have need; 187 of these received aid. Average need met was 58%. Average scholarship/grant was $4,344; average loan $3,155. 36% of total undergraduate aid awarded as scholarships/grants, 64% as loans/jobs. **Non-need-based:** Awarded to 313 full-time undergraduates, including 107 freshmen. Scholarships awarded for academics, leadership, ROTC, state residency. **Additional information:** All cadets who are United States citizens, physically qualified for Merchant Marine license, and not yet 25 at time of enrollment eligible to apply for Student Incentive Payment (SIP) of $3,000 per year from Maritime Administration of the Department of Transportation. Out-of-state students who elect to participate in SIP pay in-state tuition fees.

**Application procedures.** **Admission:** Priority date 3/15; no deadline. $40 fee, may be waived for applicants with need. Admission notification on a rolling basis beginning on or about 9/15. Waitlist begins March 1st. **Financial aid:** Priority date 3/15, closing date 7/15. FAFSA, institutional form required. Applicants notified on a rolling basis starting 3/15.

**Academics.** Cadets acquire technical, professional, and leadership experience on training cruises to foreign and domestic ports during annual summer sea terms, while preparing for U.S. Merchant Marine Officer's License. **Special study options:** Cooperative education, distance learning, double major, dual enrollment of high school students, ESL, honors, independent study, internships, semester at sea. United States Coast Guard-issued deck and engine license program. **Credit/placement by examination:** AP, CLEP, IB, institutional tests. 18 credit hours maximum toward associate degree, 18 toward bachelor's. **Support services:** Learning center, pre-admission summer program, reduced course load, remedial instruction, study skills assistance, tutoring, writing center.

**Majors.** **Business:** General, business admin, marketing, tourism/travel. **Engineering:** General, electrical, industrial, marine, mechanical. **Liberal arts:** Arts/sciences. **Physical sciences:** Atmospheric science.

**Most popular majors.** Business/marketing 53%, engineering/ engineering technologies 40%, physical sciences 7%.

**Computing on campus.** 140 workstations in dormitories, library, computer center, student center. Dormitories wired for high-speed internet access and linked to campus network. Online course registration, online library, helpline, student web hosting, wireless network available.

**Student life.** **Freshman orientation:** Mandatory, $110 fee. Preregistration for classes offered. 2-day, overnight program held in July and August, focusing on small group interaction (each session limited to 85 participants) with the goals of campus knowledge, student networking, and registration.

Parents and families can attend an informational brunch. Regimental students required to additionally attend INDOC, a two-week long training period prior to the start of classes. **Policies:** Students can choose from two lifestyle options on campus, either traditional college or Regiment of Cadets. All students governed by the College Code of Conduct and within that all Cadets are governed by the Regimental Rules and Regulations. All students have access to and can participate in student organizations, athletics, student government, and recreation facilities. **Housing:** Coed dorms, special housing for disabled available. $100 fully refundable deposit, deadline 5/1. Most undergraduates required to live in on-campus housing. **Activities:** Bands, campus ministries, choral groups, international student organizations, music ensembles, student government, Newman Club, Eagle Scout Fraternity, culture club, Afro-Caribbean club, Emerald Society, Pershing Rifles, honor guard, Turkish club, Jewish club.

**Athletics.** NCAA. **Intercollegiate:** Baseball M, basketball, cross-country, football (tackle) M, ice hockey M, lacrosse, rifle, rowing (crew) W, sailing, soccer, softball W, swimming, volleyball W. **Intramural:** Basketball, cross-country, football (tackle) M, soccer, softball, volleyball. **Team name:** Privateers.

**Student services.** Alcohol/substance abuse counseling, chaplain/ spiritual director, career counseling, services for economically disadvantaged, student employment services, financial aid counseling, health services, legal services, personal counseling, placement for graduates, veterans' counselor, women's services. **Physically disabled:** Services for visually, speech, hearing impaired.

**Contact.** E-mail: admissions@sunymaritime.edu
Phone: (718) 409-7221 Toll-free number: (800) 654-1874
Fax: (718) 409-7465
Jonathan White, Dean of Admissions, State University of New York
Maritime College, 6 Pennyfield Avenue, Throggs Neck, NY 10465-4198

---

## State University of New York Upstate Medical University

**Syracuse, New York**
**www.upstate.edu**                              CB code: 2547

- Public two-year upper-division health science and nursing college
- Residential campus in small city
- 31% of applicants admitted
- Application essay, interview required

**General.** Founded in 1834. Regionally accredited. Undergraduate level consists of upper-division programs. Affiliated with Crouse-Irving Memorial Hospital, Veteran's Administration Medical Center, Community General Hospital of Greater Syracuse, St. Joseph's Hospital Health Center, Hutchings Psychiatric Center. **Degrees:** 107 bachelor's awarded; master's, doctoral, professional offered. **Articulation:** Agreements with SUNY Alfred, SUNY Canton, SUNY Cobleskill, SUNY Cortland, SUNY Delhi, SUNY Geneseo, SUNY Morrisville, SUNY Oswego, SUNY Oneonta, Cayuga CC, Columbia-Greene CC, Finger Lakes CC, Genesee CC, Jefferson CC, Mohawk Valley CC, Monroe CC, Niagara County CC, North Country CC, Onondaga CC, Sullivan CC, Tompkins Cortland CC. **ROTC:** Army. **Location:** 250 miles from New York City, 150 miles from Buffalo. **Calendar:** Semester, limited summer session. **Full-time faculty:** 40 total. **Part-time faculty:** 32 total. **Class size:** 87% < 20, 11% 20-39, less than 1% 40-49, less than 1% 50-99. **Special facilities:** Institutionally owned and operated 350-bed teaching hospital and Level 1 trauma center.

**Student profile.** 277 degree-seeking undergraduates, 1,121 degree-seeking graduate students. 538 applied as first time-transfer students, 165 admitted, 121 enrolled. 100% entered as juniors. 74% transferred from two-year, 26% transferred from four-year institutions.

| Women: | 76% | Part-time: | 46% |
|---|---|---|---|
| African American: | 10% | Out-of-state: | 6% |
| Asian American: | 4% | Live on campus: | 56% |
| Hispanic American: | 1% | 25 or older: | 57% |
| International: | 3% | | |

**Basis for selection.** High school transcript, college transcript, application essay, interview required. Evaluation of academic performance in courses required for admission. Personal interviews, recommendations, and essay also important. Applicants must complete admissions course requirements prior to admission. Final decision made at discretion of admissions committee, regardless of applicant's prior academic standing. Transfer accepted as juniors, seniors.

**2009-2010 Annual costs.** Tuition/fees: $5,522; $13,422 out-of-state. Room only: $4,127. Books/supplies: $975. Personal expenses: $1,416.

**Financial aid.** All financial aid based on need. Average need met was 100%. 35% of total undergraduate aid awarded as scholarships/grants, 65% as loans/jobs.

**Application procedures. Admission:** Rolling admission. $40 fee, may be waived for applicants with need. Application deadline for physical therapy program February 1. Cardiovascular perfusion program completes admission process March 1. Preference to New York residents. High school seniors may apply for admission 2 years prior to intended date of entry. Transfer students apply in fall 1 year prior to intended date of entry. **Financial aid:** Applicants notified on a rolling basis; must reply within 2 weeks of notification. FAFSA required.

**Academics. Special study options:** Accelerated study, combined bachelor's/graduate degree, distance learning, independent study. Distance Learning available for the Respiratory Therapy program at the SUNY Jefferson Community College campus. Accelerated 3+3 Doctor of Physical Therapy program available in conjunction with SUNY Brockport, SUNY Oneonta, SUNY Geneseo, SUNY Oswego, SUNY ESF, Syracuse University and LeMoyne College. **Credit/placement by examination:** AP, CLEP, institutional tests. 60 credit hours maximum toward bachelor's degree. **Support services:** Reduced course load, tutoring.

**Majors. Health:** Clinical lab science, nursing (RN), perfusion technology, respiratory therapy technology, sonography. **Other:** Medical imaging / X-ray / MRI / CT.

**Computing on campus.** 50 workstations in dormitories, library, computer center, student center. Dormitories wired for high-speed internet access and linked to campus network. Commuter students can connect to campus network. Helpline, student web hosting, wireless network available.

**Student life. Policies:** Students under 21 required to live on campus unless living at home. **Housing:** Guaranteed on-campus for all undergraduates. Coed dorms, apartments available. $150 nonrefundable deposit, deadline 8/1. **Activities:** Dance, international student organizations, student government, campus activities governing board, Chinese student association, Adopt-a-School, Christian medical fellowship, Community Outreach Preventive Education (COPE), Jewish medical association, Muslim student association.

**Athletics. Intramural:** Basketball, racquetball, soccer, softball, table tennis, tennis, volleyball.

**Student services.** Alcohol/substance abuse counseling, career counseling, financial aid counseling, health services, minority student services, on-campus daycare, personal counseling, placement for graduates, veterans' counselor.

**Contact.**  E-mail: admiss@upstate.edu
Phone: (315) 464-4570 Toll-free number: (800) 736-2171
Fax: (315) 464-8867
Jennifer Welch, Director of Admissions, State University of New York Upstate Medical University, 766 Irving Avenue, Syracuse, NY 13210

---

## Syracuse University

**Syracuse, New York**                                    **CB member**
www.syr.edu                                               **CB code: 2823**

- Private 4-year university
- Residential campus in small city
- 13,243 degree-seeking undergraduates: 4% part-time, 56% women, 8% African American, 9% Asian American, 7% Hispanic American, 1% Native American, 5% international
- 5,486 degree-seeking graduate students
- 60% of applicants admitted
- SAT or ACT with writing, application essay required
- 80% graduate within 6 years; 23% enter graduate study

**General.** Founded in 1870. Regionally accredited. **Degrees:** 2,670 bachelor's, 7 associate awarded; master's, doctoral, professional offered. **ROTC:** Army, Air Force. **Location:** 150 miles from Albany, 250 miles from New York City. **Calendar:** Semester, extensive summer session. **Full-time faculty:** 962 total; 87% have terminal degrees, 19% minority, 37% women. **Part-time faculty:** 545 total; 8% minority, 48% women. **Class size:** 63% < 20, 25% 20-39, 5% 40-49, 5% 50-99, 3% >100. **Special facilities:** Global collaboratory; life sciences complex; media laboratories; digital convergence center; technology center; environmental and energy facility; advanced flight simulator; art studios; film, video, photo, and computer graphic labs; darkrooms; theater; child development laboratory school; audio laboratory and archive; speech, language, and hearing clinic.

**Freshman class profile.** 20,951 applied, 12,596 admitted, 3,261 enrolled.

| Mid 50% test scores | | | |
|---|---|---|---|
| SAT critical reading: | 510-620 | Rank in top quarter: | 73% |
| SAT math: | 540-650 | Rank in top tenth: | 39% |
| SAT writing: | 520-630 | Return as sophomores: | 91% |
| ACT composite: | 23-28 | Out-of-state: | 55% |
| GPA 3.75 or higher: | 41% | Live on campus: | 99% |
| GPA 3.50-3.74: | 21% | International: | 5% |
| GPA 3.0-3.49: | 30% | Fraternities: | 12% |
| GPA 2.0-2.99: | 8% | Sororities: | 22% |

**Basis for selection.** Most important: strong performance in challenging, rigorous college preparatory curriculum from accredited secondary school, high school GPA and other qualitative factors, personal characteristics and talents, good citizenship. Other items of importance, but not strongest: secondary school counselor evaluation, 2 academic recommendations, standardized test scores. Applicants not admitted to their first-choice program may be considered for alternate programs on a space-available basis only if they checked this option on the admissions application. Priority given to those applying to first-choice programs. TOEFL exam is required of all applicants whose native language is not English. Portfolio required for art, architecture programs; audition required for drama, music programs. Interviews recommended for all. **Homeschooled:** Transcript of courses and grades, interview, letter of recommendation (nonparent) required. Submit detailed course descriptions/syllabus used. 2 recommendations from someone outside home required. For financial aid eligibility, letter from local school district must be submitted acknowledging that curriculum taught at home is substantially equivalent to that of the school district, or GED. **Learning Disabled:** No special admission requirements or procedures, but families should contact the Office of Disability Services with any questions.

**High school preparation.** College-preparatory program required. 19 units required. Required units include English 4, mathematics 4, social studies 4, science 4 (laboratory 4) and foreign language 3.

**2009-2010 Annual costs.** Tuition/fees: $34,926. Room/board: $12,374. Books/supplies: $1,306. Personal expenses: $892.

**2009-2010 Financial aid. Need-based:** 2,524 full-time freshmen applied for aid; 1,983 were judged to have need; 1,983 of these received aid. Average need met was 95%. Average scholarship/grant was $24,300; average loan $6,280. 72% of total undergraduate aid awarded as scholarships/grants, 28% as loans/jobs. **Non-need-based:** Awarded to 2,465 full-time undergraduates, including 503 freshmen. Scholarships awarded for academics, art, athletics, music/drama, ROTC, state residency.

**Application procedures. Admission:** Closing date 1/1 (postmark date). $70 fee, may be waived for applicants with need. Admission notification on a rolling basis beginning on or about 3/15. Must reply by May 1 or within 2 week(s) if notified thereafter. **Financial aid:** Closing date 2/2. FAFSA, CSS PROFILE required. Applicants notified by 3/15; must reply by 5/1.

**Academics. Special study options:** Accelerated study, combined bachelor's/graduate degree, cooperative education, distance learning, double major, dual enrollment of high school students, ESL, honors, independent study, internships, liberal arts/career combination, student-designed major, study abroad, teacher certification program. Syracuse offers many undergraduate research opportunities, pre-professional programs, and minors. **Credit/placement by examination:** AP, CLEP, IB, institutional tests. 30 credit hours maximum toward bachelor's degree. Maximum of 30 semester hours of credit may be accepted from all forms of extra-institutional, experiential learning, and examination programs. **Support services:** Learning center, pre-admission summer program, study skills assistance, tutoring, writing center.

**Majors. Architecture:** Architecture, interior. **Area/ethnic studies:** African-American, American, Latin American, Near/Middle Eastern, Russian/Slavic. **Biology:** General, biochemistry. **Business:** Accounting, business admin, entrepreneurial studies, finance, marketing, sales/distribution. **Communications:** General, advertising, journalism, radio/tv. **Computer sciences:** General, information systems. **Education:** Art, biology, chemistry, elementary, English, mathematics, music, physical, physics, social studies, special. **Engineering:** General, aerospace, biomedical, chemical, civil, computer, electrical, environmental, mechanical. **Family/consumer sciences:** Family studies, food/nutrition, institutional food production. **Foreign languages:** General, classics, French, German, Italian, linguistics, Russian, Spanish. **Health:** Audiology/speech pathology, predental, premedicine, preveterinary. **History:** General. **Legal studies:** Prelaw. **Liberal arts:** Arts/sciences, humanities. **Math:** General. **Parks/recreation:** Exercise sciences, sports admin. **Philosophy/religion:** Philosophy, religion. **Physical sciences:** Chemistry, geology, physics. **Psychology:** General. **Public administration:** General, social work. **Social sciences:** General, anthropology, economics, geography, international relations, political science, sociology. **Visual/performing arts:** Art history/conservation, cinematography, commercial/advertising art, dramatic, music history, music management, music performance, music theory/

composition, painting, photography, sculpture, studio arts. **Other:** Biophysical Science, Classical civilization, Earth science teacher education, Health and wellness, Supply chain management.

**Most popular majors.** Business/marketing 21%, engineering/ engineering technologies 6%, psychology 7%, social sciences 13%, visual/ performing arts 12%.

**Computing on campus.** 3,427 workstations in dormitories, library, computer center, student center. Dormitories wired for high-speed internet access and linked to campus network. Commuter students can connect to campus network. Online course registration, online library, helpline, repair service, student web hosting, wireless network available.

**Student life. Freshman orientation:** Mandatory. Preregistration for classes offered. Offered twice a year, August (4 to 5 days) and January (2 days) and provides both traditional programming (convocations, course registration and advising) as well as activities designed to build community. **Policies:** Freshmen and sophomores required to live on campus. Students must adhere to the Code of Student Conduct. **Housing:** Guaranteed on-campus for freshmen. Coed dorms, special housing for disabled, apartments, fraternity/ sorority housing, wellness housing available. $400 fully refundable deposit, deadline 5/1. International living center, single-sex floors and wings of residence halls, numerous learning communities, and interest housing available. **Activities:** Bands, campus ministries, choral groups, dance, drama, film society, international student organizations, literary magazine, music ensembles, musical theater, radio station, student government, student newspaper, symphony orchestra, TV station, more than 300 student organizations, offering involvement opportunities in arts, cultural, entertainment, environmental, governance, media, political, professional, service, social interests.

**Athletics.** NCAA. **Intercollegiate:** Basketball, cheerleading, cross-country, diving, field hockey W, football (tackle) M, ice hockey W, lacrosse, rowing (crew), soccer, softball W, swimming, tennis W, track and field, volleyball W. **Intramural:** Basketball, football (non-tackle), racquetball, soccer, softball, tennis, volleyball. **Team name:** Orange.

**Student services.** Adult student services, alcohol/substance abuse counseling, chaplain/spiritual director, career counseling, services for economically disadvantaged, student employment services, financial aid counseling, health services, legal services, minority student services, on-campus daycare, personal counseling, placement for graduates, veterans' counselor, women's services. **Physically disabled:** Services for visually, speech, hearing impaired.

**Contact.** E-mail: orange@syr.edu
Phone: (315) 443-3611 Fax: (315) 443-4226
Susan Donovan, Dean of Admissions, Syracuse University, 100 Crouse-Hinds Hall, Syracuse, NY 13244-2130

## Talmudical Institute of Upstate New York
**Rochester, New York**
www.tiuny.org                                      CB code: 1426

- Private 5-year rabbinical and seminary college for men affiliated with Jewish faith
- Residential campus in large city
- 27 degree-seeking undergraduates
- 6 graduate students
- Interview required

**General.** Founded in 1974. Accredited by AARTS. First Talmudic degree offered. **Degrees:** 2 bachelor's awarded; doctoral offered. **Calendar:** Semester. **Full-time faculty:** 3 total. **Part-time faculty:** 3 total.

**Freshman class profile.**

| | | | |
|---|---|---|---|
| Out-of-state: | 35% | Live on campus: | 100% |

**Basis for selection.** Interview and school achievement record important.

**Application procedures. Admission:** Closing date 9/1. Admission notification on a rolling basis. **Financial aid:** No deadline. Applicants notified on a rolling basis.

**Academics. Special study options:** Dual enrollment of high school students. **Credit/placement by examination:** CLEP.

**Majors. Philosophy/religion:** Judaic. **Theology:** Talmudic.

**Computing on campus.** 2 workstations in computer center.

**Student life. Policies:** Religious observance required. **Housing:** Guaranteed on-campus for all undergraduates.

**Contact.** Phone: (585) 473-2810 Fax: (585) 442-0417
Talmudical Institute of Upstate New York, 769 Park Avenue, Rochester, NY 14607

## Talmudical Seminary Oholei Torah
**Brooklyn, New York**
                                                   CB code: 0712

- Private 4-year rabbinical and seminary college for men affiliated with Jewish faith
- Very large city
- 301 degree-seeking undergraduates
- Interview required

**General.** Founded in 1956. Accredited by AARTS. First Talmudic degree offered. **Degrees:** 4 bachelor's awarded. **ROTC:** Army, Naval. **Calendar:** Semester, limited summer session.

**Basis for selection.** Interview and institutional entrance examinations important.

**2009-2010 Annual costs.** Tuition/fees: $6,600. Room/board: $3,200.

**Application procedures. Admission:** No deadline. Admission notification on a rolling basis. **Financial aid:** No deadline. Applicants notified on a rolling basis starting 5/21.

**Academics. Credit/placement by examination:** CLEP, institutional tests. **Support services:** Tutoring.

**Majors. Theology:** Talmudic.

**Student life. Policies:** Religious observance required. **Activities:** TV station, Lubavitcher Youth Organization.

**Student services.** Career counseling, personal counseling.

**Contact.** Phone: (718) 774-5215
Talmudical Seminary Oholei Torah, 667 Eastern Parkway, Brooklyn, NY 11213-3397

## Torah Temimah Talmudical Seminary
**Brooklyn, New York**
                                                   CB code: 7132

- Private 4-year rabbinical and seminary college for men affiliated with Jewish faith
- Very large city
- 175 degree-seeking undergraduates

**General.** Accredited by AARTS. **Degrees:** 2 bachelor's awarded. **Calendar:** Continuous.

**2009-2010 Annual costs.** Tuition/fees: $8,950. Room/board: $3,000.

**Application procedures. Admission:** No deadline.

**Academics. Credit/placement by examination:** CLEP.

**Majors. Theology:** Talmudic.

**Contact.** Phone: (718) 853-8500
Torah Temimah Talmudical Seminary, 555 Ocean Parkway, Brooklyn, NY 11218

## Touro College
**New York, New York**
www.touro.edu                                      CB code: 2902

- Private 4-year liberal arts college
- Commuter campus in very large city
- 8,484 degree-seeking undergraduates: 20% part-time, 69% women
- 9,624 degree-seeking graduate students
- 56% of applicants admitted

**General.** Founded in 1970. Regionally accredited. School of General Studies provides programs for part-time and adult students. **Degrees:** 1,506 bachelor's, 780 associate awarded; master's, professional offered. **Calendar:** Semester, limited summer session. **Full-time faculty:** 619 total; 50% women.

**Part-time faculty:** 970 total; 50% women. **Class size:** 84% < 20, 15% 20-39, less than 1% 40-49, less than 1% 50-99.

**Freshman class profile.** 4,942 applied, 2,746 admitted, 2,081 enrolled.

**Basis for selection.** For College of Liberal Arts and Sciences, 3.0 high school GPA, SAT verbal and math scores of 500 preferred. Recommendations from high school teachers and counselors and motivation important. High school experience less important for applicants to associate degree programs who take institutional admissions test. SAT or ACT recommended. SAT or ACT required for applicants to school of Health Sciences. Essay and interview recommended for College of Liberal Arts and Sciences.

**High school preparation.** 17 units recommended. Recommended units include English 4, mathematics 3, social studies 3, science 3 and foreign language 3. Requirements may vary by division.

**2009-2010 Annual costs.** Tuition/fees: $11,400. Tuition and fees vary by program. Reported costs are for the New York School of Career and Applied Studies. Room and board available only for students in the Lander College of Arts and Sciences. Room/board: $6,600. Books/supplies: $750. Personal expenses: $1,764.

**Application procedures.** Admission: No deadline. $50 fee, may be waived for applicants with need. Admission notification on a rolling basis. Financial aid: Priority date 5/15, closing date 6/1. FAFSA required. Applicants notified by 8/15.

**Academics.** Special study options: Accelerated study, combined bachelor's/graduate degree, distance learning, dual enrollment of high school students, ESL, honors, independent study, internships, liberal arts/career combination, student-designed major, study abroad, teacher certification program. **Credit/placement by examination:** AP, CLEP, institutional tests. **Support services:** Learning center, reduced course load, remedial instruction, tutoring.

**Majors.** Biology: General. **Business:** General, accounting, business admin, management information systems, managerial economics, marketing. **Communications:** General. **Computer sciences:** General. **Education:** Special. **Foreign languages:** General, Hebrew. **Health:** Communication disorders, medical records technology, nursing (RN), physician assistant, predental, premedicine, prepharmacy, preveterinary. **History:** General. **Interdisciplinary:** Biological/physical sciences. **Liberal arts:** Arts/sciences. **Math:** General. **Philosophy/religion:** Judaic, philosophy. **Physical sciences:** Chemistry. **Psychology:** General. **Social sciences:** General, economics, political science, sociology.

**Computing on campus.** 400 workstations in library, computer center.

**Student life. Freshman orientation:** Available. **Housing:** Single-sex dorms available. $50 deposit. No board or meal plan available. Kitchen facilities in student housing. **Activities:** Literary magazine, student government, student newspaper, accounting and business society, biology club, debating society, Jewish Affairs Committee, foreign students association, Omicron Delta.

**Student services.** Adult student services, career counseling, student employment services, personal counseling, placement for graduates, veterans' counselor.

**Contact.** E-mail: lasadmit@adminm.touro.edu
Phone: (718) 252-7800 ext. 299 Fax: (718) 253-9455
Arthur Wigfall, Director of Admissions, Touro College, 1602 Avenue J, Brooklyn, NY 11230

## U.T.A. Mesivta-Kiryas Jocl
Monroe, New York

- Private 4-year rabbinical college for men affiliated with Jewish faith
- Large town
- 1,180 degree-seeking undergraduates

**General.** Accredited by AARTS. **Degrees:** 161 bachelor's awarded. **Calendar:** Semester. **Full-time faculty:** 120 total.

**Basis for selection.** Religious commitment most important.

**2009-2010 Annual costs.** Tuition/fees: $5,500. Room/board: $3,500.

**Application procedures.** Admission: No deadline.

**Academics.** Credit/placement by examination: CLEP.

**Majors.** Theology: Talmudic.

**Contact.** Phone: (845) 783-9901
U.T.A. Mesivta-Kiryas Jocl, 9 Nickelsburg Road, #312, Monroe, NY 10950-2169

## Union College
Schenectady, New York      **CB member**
www.union.edu      **CB code: 2920**

- Private 4-year engineering and liberal arts college
- Residential campus in small city
- 2,141 degree-seeking undergraduates: 49% women, 5% African American, 7% Asian American, 5% Hispanic American, 3% international
- 41% of applicants admitted
- Application essay required
- 86% graduate within 6 years; 35% enter graduate study

**General.** Founded in 1795. Regionally accredited. **Degrees:** 530 bachelor's awarded. **ROTC:** Army, Naval, Air Force. **Location:** 15 miles from Albany, 175 miles from New York City. **Calendar:** Trimester, limited summer session. **Full-time faculty:** 199 total; 96% have terminal degrees, 13% minority, 43% women. **Part-time faculty:** 29 total; 48% have terminal degrees, 7% minority, 59% women. **Class size:** 70% < 20, 28% 20-39, 1% 40-49, less than 1% 50-99. **Special facilities:** Horticultural garden, superconducting nuclear magnetic resonance spectrometer, electron scanning microscope, tandem pelletron positive ion accelerator, X-ray diffraction equipment, remote-controlled telescope.

**Freshman class profile.** 4,829 applied, 1,987 admitted, 520 enrolled.

| Mid 50% test scores | | | |
|---|---|---|---|
| SAT critical reading: | 590-670 | GPA 2.0-2.99: | 10% |
| SAT math: | 620-700 | Rank in top quarter: | 84% |
| SAT writing: | 580-670 | Rank in top tenth: | 58% |
| ACT composite: | 27-30 | End year in good standing: | 99% |
| GPA 3.75 or higher: | 35% | Return as sophomores: | 91% |
| GPA 3.50-3.74: | 22% | Out-of-state: | 57% |
| GPA 3.0-3.49: | 32% | Live on campus: | 99% |
| | | International: | 4% |

**Basis for selection.** GED not accepted. Course selection and grades closely considered along with recommendations from high school and extracurricular record. Ethnic and geographic diversity sought in student body. Testing optional except for combined programs. Applicants for leadership in medicine, and law and public policy programs required to submit the SAT and 2 SAT Subject Tests and must complete necessary tests no later than December of senior year. Portfolio recommended for art programs. **Homeschooled:** Interview required.

**High school preparation.** College-preparatory program required. 16 units required; 24 recommended. Required and recommended units include English 4, mathematics 3-4, social studies 1-2, history 1-2, science 2-4 (laboratory 2-4) and foreign language 2-4.

**2009-2010 Annual costs.** Comprehensive fee: $50,439. Rebates offered to students living off-campus and/or not using a meal plan. Books/supplies: $485. Personal expenses: $1,136.

**2009-2010 Financial aid. Need-based:** 342 full-time freshmen applied for aid; 279 were judged to have need; 277 of these received aid. Average need met was 99%. Average scholarship/grant was $32,597; average loan $2,670. 87% of total undergraduate aid awarded as scholarships/grants, 13% as loans/jobs. **Non-need-based:** Awarded to 394 full-time undergraduates, including 81 freshmen. Scholarships awarded for academics, ROTC. **Additional information:** Cancellable loans given to eligible students who engage in public service work after graduation. Loans cancellable at rate of 20% for each year of service.

**Application procedures.** Admission: Closing date 1/15 (postmark date). $50 fee, may be waived for applicants with need, free for online applicants. Admission notification 4/1. Must reply by 5/1. If application filed online, supplemental graded, written essay from 11th or 12th grade required to complete application. **Financial aid:** Closing date 2/1. FAFSA, CSS PROFILE required. Applicants notified by 4/1; must reply by 5/1.

**Academics.** Special study options: Accelerated study, combined bachelor's/graduate degree, cross-registration, double major, dual enrollment of high school students, honors, independent study, internships, liberal arts/career combination, student-designed major, study abroad, teacher certification program. **Credit/placement by examination:** AP, CLEP, IB, institutional tests. 4 credit hours maximum toward bachelor's degree. **Support services:** Study skills assistance, tutoring, writing center.

**Majors. Area/ethnic studies:** American, Asian, Latin American. **Biology:** General, biochemistry. **Computer sciences:** General. **Engineering:** Biomedical, electrical, mechanical. **Foreign languages:** General, classics, French, German, Spanish. **History:** General. **Interdisciplinary:** Biological/physical sciences, neuroscience, science/society. **Liberal arts:** Arts/sciences, humanities. **Math:** General. **Philosophy/religion:** Philosophy, religion. **Physical sciences:** General, astronomy, chemistry, geology, physics. **Psychology:** General. **Social sciences:** General, anthropology, economics, political science, sociology. **Visual/performing arts:** General. **Other:** Geological and related sciences.

**Most popular majors.** Biology 11%, engineering/engineering technologies 10%, English 8%, history 6%, liberal arts 8%, psychology 8%, social sciences 29%.

**Computing on campus.** 504 workstations in dormitories, library, computer center, student center. Dormitories wired for high-speed internet access and linked to campus network. Commuter students can connect to campus network. Online course registration, online library, helpline, repair service, student web hosting, wireless network available.

**Student life. Freshman orientation:** Mandatory, $250 fee. Preregistration for classes offered. Begins Thursday and ends Sunday before classes begin. Orientation fee included in Admission and Security deposit. **Policies:** All students expected to live on campus during undergraduate years, provided housing is available. **Housing:** Guaranteed on-campus for freshmen. Coed dorms, apartments, fraternity/sorority housing, wellness housing available. Minerva Houses. Up to 45 students live in each. All students and faculty members have house affiliations. Each house contributes intellectual, cultural, and social events to the campus. **Activities:** Bands, campus ministries, choral groups, dance, drama, film society, international student organizations, literary magazine, music ensembles, Model UN, radio station, student government, student newspaper, symphony orchestra, TV station, African and Latino Alliance of Students, Asian Student Union, Big Brothers/Big Sisters, College Republicans, Intervarsity Christian Fellowship, Jewish Student Union, Middle Eastern Civilization and Culture Association, Newman Club, UCARE-a community action club, Union College Democrats.

**Athletics.** NCAA. **Intercollegiate:** Baseball M, basketball, cross-country, diving, field hockey W, football (tackle) M, ice hockey, lacrosse, rowing (crew), soccer, softball W, swimming, tennis, track and field, volleyball W. **Intramural:** Basketball, football (non-tackle) M, ice hockey, lacrosse M, soccer M, softball, tennis, volleyball. **Team name:** Dutchmen, Dutchwomen.

**Student services.** Alcohol/substance abuse counseling, chaplain/spiritual director, career counseling, services for economically disadvantaged, student employment services, financial aid counseling, health services, minority student services, personal counseling, placement for graduates. **Physically disabled:** Services for visually, hearing impaired.

**Contact.** E-mail: admissions@union.edu
Phone: (518) 388-6112 Toll-free number: (888) 843-6688
Fax: (518) 388-6986
Ann Brown, Director of Admissions, Union College, Grant Hall, Schenectady, NY 12308-3107

## United States Merchant Marine Academy

**Kings Point, New York** — CB member
www.usmma.edu — CB code: 2923

- Public 4-year military and maritime college
- Residential campus in large town
- 975 degree-seeking undergraduates
- 20 graduate students
- 25% of applicants admitted
- SAT or ACT (ACT writing optional), application essay required

**General.** Founded in 1943. Regionally accredited. Accepted applicants appointed to academy as midshipmen, USNR. **Degrees:** 198 bachelor's awarded; master's offered. **Location:** 20 miles from midtown Manhattan. **Calendar:** Trimester, limited summer session. **Full-time faculty:** 88 total. **Part-time faculty:** 1 total. **Class size:** 45% < 20, 54% 20-39, less than 1% 40-49, less than 1% 50-99. **Special facilities:** US Merchant Marine Museum, computer-aided operational research facility, T/V Kings Pointer docked on campus.

**Freshman class profile.** 1,823 applied, 450 admitted, 291 enrolled.

| Mid 50% test scores | | | |
|---|---|---|---|
| SAT critical reading: | 540-640 | Rank in top quarter: | 23% |
| SAT math: | 590-660 | Rank in top tenth: | 18% |
| ACT composite: | 25-29 | Out-of-state: | 86% |
| | | Live on campus: | 100% |

**Basis for selection.** Nomination by U.S. representatives or senators. Competitive standing determined by test scores, high school GPA, class rank, motivation, extracurricular activities, interest in academy, industry, citizenship, and recommendations from counselors, teachers, school principal. Must also meet medical requirements and pass physical fitness exercise regimen. Untimed test results not acceptable. Interview recommended. **Homeschooled:** Letter of recommendation (nonparent) required. Must have completed chemistry with lab or physics with lab through state-certified instructor.

**High school preparation.** 18 units required. Required and recommended units include English 4, mathematics 3-4, social studies 4, science 3-4 (laboratory 1-2), foreign language 2 and academic electives 8.

**2009-2010 Annual costs.** All midshipmen receive full tuition, room, board, and medical and dental expenses from the federal government. Total required freshman fees ($2,828) include purchase of laptop computer, color printer, and PDA. International freshman students pay required fees plus additional international student fee ($13,003 total). Books/supplies: $692.

**2008-2009 Financial aid. Additional information:** Students paid by steamship companies while at sea.

**Application procedures. Admission:** Closing date 3/1 (postmark date). No application fee. Admission notification on a rolling basis beginning on or about 11/1. Must reply by May 1 or within 2 week(s) if notified thereafter. **Financial aid:** Closing date 5/1. FAFSA, institutional form required. Applicants notified on a rolling basis starting 1/31.

**Academics. Special study options:** Honors, independent study, internships, semester at sea, study abroad. Sea training on merchant vessels. **Credit/placement by examination:** CLEP, institutional tests. **Support services:** Learning center, remedial instruction, study skills assistance, tutoring.

**Majors. Engineering:** Marine, systems. **Engineering technology:** Industrial management. **Mechanic/repair:** Marine. **Transportation:** General, maritime/Merchant Marine.

**Most popular majors.** Engineering/engineering technologies 39%, trade and industry 61%.

**Computing on campus.** PC or laptop required. 1,200 workstations in dormitories, library. Dormitories wired for high-speed internet access and linked to campus network. Helpline, repair service, wireless network available.

**Student life. Freshman orientation:** Mandatory. 2-week orientation starting in early July. **Housing:** Guaranteed on-campus for all undergraduates. Coed dorms, wellness housing available. Students required to live on campus. **Activities:** Bands, choral groups, drama, musical theater, student government, student newspaper, Christian Fellowship Community, Newman Club.

**Athletics.** NCAA. **Intercollegiate:** Baseball M, basketball, cross-country, diving, football (tackle) M, golf, lacrosse M, rowing (crew), sailing, soccer M, softball W, swimming, tennis, track and field, volleyball W, wrestling M. **Intramural:** Baseball M, basketball, boxing, cross-country, football (tackle) M, racquetball, rowing (crew), soccer, softball, tennis, track and field, volleyball, water polo, weight lifting. **Team name:** Mariners.

**Student services.** Alcohol/substance abuse counseling, chaplain/spiritual director, career counseling, student employment services, financial aid counseling, health services, personal counseling, placement for graduates.

**Contact.** E-mail: admissions@usmma.edu
Phone: (516) 773-5391 Toll-free number: (866) 546-4778
Fax: (516) 773-5390
CAPT. Robert Johnson, Director of Admissions, United States Merchant Marine Academy, 300 Steamboat Road, Admissions Center, Kings Point, NY 11024-1699

## United States Military Academy

**West Point, New York** — CB member
www.westpoint.edu — CB code: 2924

- Public 4-year military college
- Residential campus in small town
- 4,621 degree-seeking undergraduates: 15% women, 6% African American, 7% Asian American, 9% Hispanic American, 1% Native American, 1% international
- 14% of applicants admitted
- SAT or ACT with writing, application essay required
- 82% graduate within 6 years; 2% enter graduate study

**General.** Founded in 1802. Regionally accredited. **Degrees:** 989 bachelor's awarded. **Location:** 50 miles from New York City. **Calendar:** Semester, limited summer session. **Full-time faculty:** 625 total; 45% have terminal degrees, 11% minority, 18% women. **Class size:** 96% < 20, 3% 20-39, less than 1% 40-49. **Special facilities:** West Point Museum, American Revolutionary-era Fort Putnam, 4,500-seat Eisenhower Hall, 18-hole golf course, ski slope, 500,000 square-foot physical development center.

**Freshman class profile.** 11,107 applied, 1,570 admitted, 1,262 enrolled.

| Mid 50% test scores | | |
|---|---|---|
| SAT critical reading: | 560-660 | |
| SAT math: | 580-670 | |
| SAT writing: | 540-640 | |
| ACT composite: | 25-29 | |
| Rank in top quarter: | 70% | |

| | |
|---|---|
| Rank in top tenth: | 42% |
| End year in good standing: | 94% |
| Return as sophomores: | 92% |
| Out-of-state: | 94% |
| Live on campus: | 100% |
| International: | 1% |

**Basis for selection.** ACT/SAT, rigor of high school record, class rank, and faculty recommendations used to determine academic qualification. Demonstrated leadership potential, physical ability, medical exam and Candidate Fitness Assessment also important. Must be U.S. citizen, at least 17 but not yet 23 by July 1 of year admitted, unmarried, not pregnant, and without legal child support obligations. Naturalized citizens must provide documentation. Nomination by member of Congress required. Consideration also given to percentage of students from school who attend 4-year colleges after high school. The number of cadets at the Military Academy and the sources from which they may be nominated and appointed are prescribed in Sections 4341a, 4342-4344, and 4347, Title 10, United States Code (10 USC 4341a, 4342-4344, and 4347). Interview recommended. **Learning Disabled:** West Point does not accept students with learning disabilities. All students must be in good physical and mental health and pass a Department of Defense qualifying medical examination.

**High school preparation.** 19 units recommended. Recommended units include English 4, mathematics 4, social studies 1, history 1, science 4 (laboratory 2), foreign language 2 and academic electives 3. English units should have strong emphasis on composition, grammar, literature and speech; math should include algebra, geometry, intermediate algebra, and trigonometry; U.S. history should include courses in geography, government and economics. Precalculus, calculus and basic computing course helpful.

**2010-2011 Annual costs.** Tuition is covered by a full scholarship. All students are on Active Duty as members of the U.S. Army and receive an annual salary of approximately $10,150. Room and board, medical and dental care are provided by the U.S. Army; however, a one-time deposit of $2,000 is required upon admission to defray the initial cost of uniforms, books, supplies, equipment and fees. If needed, loans of $100 to $2,000 are available for the deposit.

**2008-2009 Financial aid. Additional information:** Cadets permitted to receive scholarships, but since there are no tuition, room or board charges, scholarships stipulated for tuition, room or board that are based only on need rather than merit cannot be accepted. Scholarships may be used for textbooks, uniforms and other expenses, or used dollar for dollar to offset initial $2,000 deposit.

**Application procedures. Admission:** Closing date 2/28 (receipt date). No application fee. Application must be submitted online. Admission notification on a rolling basis beginning on or about 11/15. Must reply by 5/1.

**Academics.** Cadets receive Bachelor of Science degree designed specifically to meet intellectual requirements of a commissioned officer in the Army. Cadets must complete minimum basic requirement of 40 academic courses. 8 semesters of physical education and 4 military science courses required. Cumulative GPA of at least 2.0 required, while meeting appropriate physical fitness and proper conduct standards. **Special study options:** Double major, exchange student, honors, independent study, internships, study abroad, Washington semester. Opportunities to attend Army Schools (Airborne, Air Assault, etc.) to learn special skills and to intern with an Army organization during the summer. **Credit/placement by examination:** AP, CLEP, institutional tests. Entering freshmen may be excused from certain core courses if they have sufficient knowledge of a subject to meet the appropriate department's standards. Credit earned at other colleges, Advanced Placement examination scores, and tests administered at West Point are considered in the validation decision. Validation of a course allows a student to substitute an additional elective in place of the validated course. If a student shows unusual ability or has prior knowledge of a subject but cannot validate it, he or she may be enrolled in an advanced or accelerated program. **Support services:** Learning center, reduced course load, remedial instruction, study skills assistance, tutoring.

**Majors. Area/ethnic studies:** African, East Asian, European, Latin American, Near/Middle Eastern, regional, Russian/Slavic. **Biology:** General. **Business:** Business admin, organizational behavior. **Computer sciences:** General, information systems, information technology. **Conservation:** Environmental science, environmental studies. **Engineering:** Chemical, civil, electrical, environmental, mechanical, nuclear, operations research, systems. **Engineering technology:** Civil, environmental, industrial management, mechanical, nuclear. **Foreign languages:** Arabic, Chinese, French, German, Portuguese, Russian, Spanish. **History:** American, European. **Interdisciplinary:** Cognitive science, global studies, systems science. **Legal studies:** General. **Liberal arts:** Humanities. **Math:** General. **Military:** General. **Parks/recreation:** Exercise sciences. **Physical sciences:** General, chemistry, physics. **Psychology:** General. **Social sciences:** Economics, geography, international relations, political science, sociology, U.S. government. **Other:** Applied statistics, Military history, Terrorism studies.

**Most popular majors.** Business/marketing 9%, engineering/engineering technologies 27%, foreign language 10%, history 6%, social sciences 19%.

**Computing on campus.** PC or laptop required. 1,000 workstations in dormitories, library, computer center. Dormitories wired for high-speed internet access and linked to campus network. Commuter students can connect to campus network. Online library, helpline, repair service, wireless network available.

**Student life. Freshman orientation:** Mandatory. Orientation takes place over the summer during 6-week Cadet Basic Training Program. **Policies:** Honor code. Cadets administer honor system with power to recommend dismissal. Military dress required. All cadets participate in intercollegiate, club or intramural level sport each semester. Seniors and juniors (after spring break) permitted to maintain cars. **Housing:** Guaranteed on-campus for all undergraduates. Coed dorms, wellness housing available. **Activities:** Pep band, campus ministries, choral groups, dance, drama, film society, international student organizations, literary magazine, music ensembles, Model UN, musical theater, radio station, student government, TV station, Arabic language club, Asian-Pacific club, Catholic Cadet Catechists, Big Brothers & Big Sisters, Cadet Alcohol & Drug Intervention Council, Jewish chapel choir, cultural affairs group, domestic affairs forum, Student Conference on US Affairs, Scoutmaster's Council.

**Athletics.** NCAA. **Intercollegiate:** Baseball M, basketball, cheerleading, cross-country, diving, football (tackle) M, golf M, gymnastics M, ice hockey M, lacrosse M, rifle, soccer, softball W, swimming, tennis, track and field, volleyball W, wrestling M. **Intramural:** Basketball, boxing M, football (tackle) M, rugby, soccer, squash, swimming, wrestling M. **Team name:** Black Knights.

**Student services.** Alcohol/substance abuse counseling, chaplain/spiritual director, career counseling, health services, legal services, personal counseling, placement for graduates, women's services.

**Contact.** E-mail: admissions@usma.edu
Phone: (845) 938-5760
Col. Deborah McDonald, Director of Admissions, United States Military Academy, 646 Swift Road, West Point, NY 10996-1905

## United Talmudical Seminary
### Brooklyn, New York
CB code: 0696

▶ Private 5-year rabbinical college for men affiliated with Jewish faith
▶ Very large city
▶ 1,566 degree-seeking undergraduates
▶ 60 graduate students

**General.** Founded in 1949. Accredited by AARTS. First Talmudic degree and ordination available. **Degrees:** 224 bachelor's awarded; master's offered. **Calendar:** Semester.

**Basis for selection.** Institutional examination.

**2009-2010 Annual costs.** Tuition/fees: $7,000. Room/board: $3,000.

**Application procedures. Admission:** No deadline.

**Academics. Credit/placement by examination:** CLEP.

**Majors. Theology:** Talmudic.

**Contact.** Phone: (718) 963-9260
Moses Greenfield, Director of Admissions, United Talmudical Seminary, 82 Lee Avenue, Brooklyn, NY 11211

## University of Rochester
### Rochester, New York
CB member
www.rochester.edu
CB code: 2928

▶ Private 4-year university
▶ Residential campus in large city

- 5,291 degree-seeking undergraduates: 2% part-time, 51% women, 4% African American, 10% Asian American, 4% Hispanic American, 8% international
- 4,092 degree-seeking graduate students
- 39% of applicants admitted
- SAT or ACT (ACT writing optional), application essay required
- 85% graduate within 6 years

**General.** Founded in 1850. Regionally accredited. **Degrees:** 1,253 bachelor's awarded; master's, doctoral, professional offered. **ROTC:** Army, Naval, Air Force. **Location:** 2 miles from downtown. **Calendar:** Semester, extensive summer session. **Full-time faculty:** 524 total; 90% have terminal degrees, 14% minority, 27% women. **Part-time faculty:** 280 total; 6% minority, 53% women. **Class size:** 58% < 20, 25% 20-39, 4% 40-49, 9% 50-99, 4% >100. **Special facilities:** Theater, music library, laboratory for laser energetics, nuclear structure research lab, institute for African and African-American studies, institute for gender and women's studies, observatory, Strong Memorial Hospital, Wilmot Cancer Center, Galisano Children's Hospital, Eastman Dental Center, center for visual science, Institute of Optics, VR lab, MRI scanner.

**Freshman class profile.** 12,111 applied, 4,686 admitted, 1,087 enrolled.

| Mid 50% test scores | | | |
|---|---|---|---|
| SAT critical reading: | 590-690 | GPA 2.0-2.99: | 2% |
| SAT math: | 640-720 | Rank in top quarter: | 91% |
| SAT writing: | 590-690 | Rank in top tenth: | 76% |
| ACT composite: | 28-33 | End year in good standing: | 96% |
| GPA 3.75 or higher: | 54% | Return as sophomores: | 96% |
| GPA 3.50-3.74: | 25% | Out-of-state: | 53% |
| GPA 3.0-3.49: | 19% | Live on campus: | 100% |
| | | International: | 8% |

**Basis for selection.** School achievement record, personal qualities, recommendations most important. Test scores, academic GPA, extracurricular activities important. Alumni relationship, minority status, special talents considered. An audition is required for music programs at Eastman School of Music. **Homeschooled:** Statement describing homeschool structure and mission, transcript of courses and grades, interview, letter of recommendation (nonparent) required. Must submit comprehensive description of the program of study (including syllabi with textbooks, where applicable), complete list of all literary texts completed, method of instruction (specifically for laboratory sciences) and assessment (written essays/multiple choice examinations, homework, etc.), and a personal statement reflecting on the value of the homeschooling experience. Most students who successfully gain admission to the University of Rochester have completed four years of English, four years of mathematics, four years of history/social studies, three years of laboratory science, and three years of foreign language study.

**High school preparation.** College-preparatory program required. 32 units required.

**2009-2010 Annual costs.** Tuition/fees: $38,690. Room/board: $11,200.

**2009-2010 Financial aid. Non-need-based:** Scholarships awarded for academics, alumni affiliation, leadership, music/drama, ROTC, state residency. **Additional information:** Alternative loans and financing information available.

**Application procedures. Admission:** Closing date 1/1 (postmark date). $60 fee, may be waived for applicants with need. Admission notification 4/1. Must reply by 5/1. **Financial aid:** Closing date 2/1. FAFSA, CSS PROFILE required. Applicants notified by 4/1; must reply by 5/1.

**Academics.** Rochester Curriculum: imposes minimal requirements, students can take advantage of flexibility in the curriculum to complete an education that reflects their interests and passions. Senior Scholars Program: allows selected undergraduates to devote their entire final year to work on a single intellectual project--a year-long independent study. Take Five Scholars Program: provides additional semester or year, tuition-free, where students can explore offerings of another department. **Special study options:** Accelerated study, combined bachelor's/graduate degree, cooperative education, cross-registration, double major, dual enrollment of high school students, ESL, honors, independent study, internships, liberal arts/career combination, New York semester, semester at sea, student-designed major, study abroad, teacher certification program, urban semester, Washington semester. **Credit/placement by examination:** AP, CLEP, IB, institutional tests. Students who prepare a course by independent study without registering for it and who pass an examination in that course may receive degree credit for it upon petition to their Administrative Committee. A letter of support from the chair of the department, or from his or her authorized delegate, is required. **Support services:** Learning center, pre-admission summer program, reduced course load, study skills assistance, tutoring, writing center.

**Majors. Area/ethnic studies:** African-American, Russian/Slavic, women's. **Biology:** General, biochemistry, cell/histology, ecology, embryology,

evolutionary, microbiology, molecular genetics. **Business:** Managerial economics. **Computer sciences:** Computer science. **Conservation:** Environmental science, environmental studies. **Engineering:** General, biomedical, chemical, electrical, geological, mechanical, science. **Foreign languages:** General, American Sign Language, classics, comparative lit, French, German, Japanese, linguistics, Russian, Spanish. **Health:** Nursing (RN). **History:** General. **Interdisciplinary:** Neuroscience. **Liberal arts:** Arts/sciences. **Math:** General, applied, statistics. **Philosophy/religion:** Philosophy, religion. **Physical sciences:** Chemistry, geology, optics, physics. **Psychology:** General, experimental. **Social sciences:** Anthropology, economics, international relations, political science. **Visual/performing arts:** Art history/conservation, film/cinema, jazz, music performance, music theory/composition, studio arts. **Other:** Clinical investigation, Economics and business strategies, Health policy, Health, behavior, and society, Mathematics and statistics, Physics and astronomy.

**Most popular majors.** Biology 12%, engineering/engineering technologies 7%, health sciences 9%, psychology 11%, social sciences 19%, visual/performing arts 11%.

**Computing on campus.** 447 workstations in dormitories, library, computer center, student center. Dormitories wired for high-speed internet access. Commuter students can connect to campus network. Online course registration, online library, helpline, repair service, wireless network available.

**Student life. Freshman orientation:** Mandatory. Preregistration for classes offered. Held 1 week prior to first day of classes. **Housing:** Guaranteed on-campus for freshmen. Coed dorms, single-sex dorms, special housing for disabled, apartments, fraternity/sorority housing, wellness housing available. Freshman housing, special-interest floors, suite-style living, single-gender floors. **Activities:** Bands, choral groups, dance, drama, film society, international student organizations, literary magazine, music ensembles, Model UN, musical theater, opera, radio station, student government, student newspaper, symphony orchestra, TV station, campus activities board, Black student union, Grassroots (environmental group), womens caucus, Hillel, Catholic Newman Society, debate union, UR Bhangra, Charles Drew Pre-Health Society, Colleges Against Cancer.

**Athletics.** NCAA. **Intercollegiate:** Baseball M, basketball, cross-country, diving, field hockey W, football (tackle) M, golf M, lacrosse W, rowing (crew), soccer, softball W, squash, swimming, tennis, track and field, volleyball W. **Intramural:** Basketball, bowling, boxing, fencing, football (tackle) M, golf M, judo, racquetball, rugby, soccer, softball, squash, table tennis, tennis, volleyball, weight lifting. **Team name:** Yellowjackets.

**Student services.** Adult student services, alcohol/substance abuse counseling, chaplain/spiritual director, career counseling, services for economically disadvantaged, student employment services, financial aid counseling, health services, minority student services, personal counseling, placement for graduates, veterans' counselor, women's services. **Physically disabled:** Services for visually, hearing impaired.

**Contact.** E-mail: admit@admissions.rochester.edu
Phone: (585) 275-3221 Toll-free number: (888) 822-2256
Fax: (585) 461-4595
Jonathan Burdick, Dean of Admissions and Financial Aid, University of Rochester, 300 Wilson Boulevard, Rochester, NY 14627-0251

---

## Utica College
**Utica, New York**
www.utica.edu

**CB member**
**CB code: 2932**

- Private 4-year liberal arts college
- Residential campus in small city
- 2,478 degree-seeking undergraduates: 17% part-time, 57% women, 11% African American, 2% Asian American, 4% Hispanic American, 1% Native American, 2% international
- 720 degree-seeking graduate students
- 78% of applicants admitted
- Application essay required
- 49% graduate within 6 years; 46% enter graduate study

**General.** Founded in 1946. Regionally accredited. **Degrees:** 432 bachelor's awarded; master's, professional offered. **ROTC:** Army, Air Force. **Location:** 50 miles from Syracuse. **Calendar:** Semester, limited summer session. **Full-time faculty:** 131 total; 86% have terminal degrees, 5% minority, 50% women. **Part-time faculty:** 212 total; 43% women. **Class size:** 74% < 20, 26% 20-39, less than 1% 40-49, less than 1% 50-99.

**Freshman class profile.** 2,930 applied, 2,297 admitted, 565 enrolled.

| Mid 50% test scores | | | |
|---|---|---|---|
| SAT critical reading: | 410-510 | GPA 2.0-2.99: | 39% |
| SAT math: | 420-520 | Rank in top quarter: | 30% |
| SAT writing: | 390-490 | Rank in top tenth: | 8% |
| ACT composite: | 18-23 | End year in good standing: | 87% |
| GPA 3.75 or higher: | 9% | Return as sophomores: | 64% |
| GPA 3.50-3.74: | 8% | Out-of-state: | 18% |
| GPA 3.0-3.49: | 42% | Live on campus: | 79% |
| | | International: | 3% |

**Basis for selection.** Academic record, high school course of study, rank in class most important. Extracurricular activities, essay, interview, recommendations also important. SAT or ACT scores required only for freshmen applying to BS Health Studies/DPT Physical Therapy, BS Health Studies/MS Occupational Therapy, Nursing, or joint health professions programs, Higher Education Opportunity Program (HEOP), or for academic merit scholarships. Interview recommended. **Homeschooled:** Applicants must receive GED within first year of attendance. **Learning Disabled:** Written evaluation required, including discrepancy analysis completed by licensed psychologist or certified learning disability specialist indicating specific learning disability or disabilities.

**High school preparation.** College-preparatory program recommended. 16 units required. Required units include English 4, mathematics 3, social studies 3, science 3, foreign language 2 and academic electives 1.

**2009-2010 Annual costs.** Tuition/fees: $27,284. Room/board: $10,850. Books/supplies: $984. Personal expenses: $832.

**2009-2010 Financial aid. Need-based:** 535 full-time freshmen applied for aid; 504 were judged to have need; 504 of these received aid. Average need met was 70%. Average scholarship/grant was $8,635; average loan $3,444. 67% of total undergraduate aid awarded as scholarships/grants, 33% as loans/jobs. **Non-need-based:** Awarded to 246 full-time undergraduates, including 54 freshmen. Scholarships awarded for academics.

**Application procedures. Admission:** No deadline. $40 fee, may be waived for applicants with need. Admission notification on a rolling basis beginning on or about 9/1. January 15 application deadline for all joint medical programs, BS in Health Studies/ MS in Occupational Therapy program, and BS in Health Studies/DPT in Physical Therapy program. February 15 application deadline for nursing program. **Financial aid:** Priority date 2/15; no closing date. FAFSA required. Applicants notified on a rolling basis starting 2/1; must reply by 5/1 or within 4 week(s) of notification.

**Academics. Special study options:** Accelerated study, combined bachelor's/graduate degree, cooperative education, cross-registration, distance learning, double major, dual enrollment of high school students, exchange student, honors, independent study, internships, liberal arts/career combination, study abroad, teacher certification program, United Nations semester, Washington semester, weekend college. BS Health Studies/MS Occupational Therapy weekend program; Economic Crime Investigation online program for transfer students. **Credit/placement by examination:** AP, CLEP, IB, SAT, institutional tests. 30 credit hours maximum toward bachelor's degree. **Support services:** Learning center, pre-admission summer program, reduced course load, remedial instruction, study skills assistance, tutoring, writing center.

**Majors. Biology:** General. **Business:** Accounting, business admin, managerial economics. **Communications:** General, journalism, public relations. **Computer sciences:** General. **Education:** Early childhood, elementary, ESL, secondary, special. **Foreign languages:** General. **Health:** Facilities admin, health services, nursing (RN), recreational therapy. **History:** General. **Liberal arts:** Arts/sciences. **Math:** General. **Philosophy/religion:** Philosophy. **Physical sciences:** Chemistry, physics. **Protective services:** Criminal justice. **Psychology:** General. **Social sciences:** Economics, international relations, political science, sociology.

**Most popular majors.** Business/marketing 14%, communications/journalism 8%, health sciences 22%, psychology 11%, security/protective services 20%.

**Computing on campus.** 227 workstations in library, computer center, student center. Dormitories wired for high-speed internet access and linked to campus network. Helpline available.

**Student life. Freshman orientation:** Available, $50 fee. Preregistration for classes offered. Summer program for freshmen and parents held during the third week of July. **Policies:** All freshmen required to live in college residence for first 2 years, unless residing at home. **Housing:** Guaranteed on-campus for freshmen. Coed dorms, special housing for disabled, apartments, wellness housing available. $200 deposit, deadline 5/1. Separate floors for men and women available in select residence halls. **Activities:** Concert band, choral groups, dance, drama, film society, literary magazine, radio station, student government, student newspaper, Latin American student union, Jewish student union, College Republicans, Women's resource center, Asian association, gospel choir, Africa in Motion, Christian Fellowship, West Indian Connection, UC Pride.

**Athletics.** NCAA. **Intercollegiate:** Baseball M, basketball, cross-country, diving, field hockey W, football (tackle) M, golf M, ice hockey, lacrosse, soccer, softball W, swimming, tennis, track and field, volleyball W, water polo W. **Intramural:** Basketball, bowling, football (non-tackle), racquetball, soccer, softball, tennis, volleyball, water polo. **Team name:** Pioneers.

**Student services.** Adult student services, alcohol/substance abuse counseling, chaplain/spiritual director, career counseling, services for economically disadvantaged, student employment services, financial aid counseling, health services, minority student services, personal counseling, placement for graduates, veterans' counselor, women's services. **Physically disabled:** Services for visually, speech, hearing impaired.

**Contact.** E-mail: admiss@utica.edu
Phone: (315) 792-3006 Toll-free number: (800) 782-8884
Fax: (315) 792-3003
Patrick Quinn, Vice President for Enrollment Management, Utica College, 1600 Burrstone Road, Utica, NY 13502-4892

---

## Vassar College
**Poughkeepsie, New York**
**www.vassar.edu**
**CB member**
**CB code: 2956**

- Private 4-year liberal arts college
- Residential campus in small city
- 2,394 degree-seeking undergraduates: 59% women, 5% African American, 11% Asian American, 7% Hispanic American, 6% international
- 1 degree-seeking graduate students
- 25% of applicants admitted
- SAT and SAT Subject Tests or ACT with writing, application essay required
- 92% graduate within 6 years; 17% enter graduate study

**General.** Founded in 1861. Regionally accredited. **Degrees:** 616 bachelor's awarded; master's offered. **Location:** 75 miles from New York City. **Calendar:** Semester, limited summer session. **Full-time faculty:** 296 total; 89% have terminal degrees, 25% minority, 48% women. **Part-time faculty:** 32 total; 62% have terminal degrees, 6% minority, 59% women. **Class size:** 67% < 20, 31% 20-39, 2% 40-49, less than 1% 50-99. **Special facilities:** Environmental nature center, observatory, electron microscope, nursery school, experimental theater, art center and geology museum, intercultural center and outdoor amphitheater.

**Freshman class profile.** 7,577 applied, 1,873 admitted, 660 enrolled.

| Mid 50% test scores | | | |
|---|---|---|---|
| SAT critical reading: | 660-750 | Rank in top quarter: | 95% |
| SAT math: | 640-720 | Rank in top tenth: | 67% |
| SAT writing: | 660-750 | End year in good standing: | 98% |
| ACT composite: | 29-32 | Return as sophomores: | 96% |
| GPA 3.75 or higher: | 58% | Out-of-state: | 76% |
| GPA 3.50-3.74: | 26% | Live on campus: | 99% |
| GPA 3.0-3.49: | 16% | International: | 6% |

**Basis for selection.** Academic credentials most important. Personal achievements, essay, and recommendations also considered carefully. Evidence that students have elected most demanding program available crucial. Disadvantaged status considered. 2 SAT Subject Tests of student's choice required. Optional interviews available with alumni.

**High school preparation.** College-preparatory program recommended. 20 units recommended. Recommended units include English 4, mathematics 4, social studies 2, history 2, science 4 (laboratory 3) and foreign language 4. Advanced and accelerated courses recommended whenever possible. Minimum of 20 units recommended with additional unit in science, foreign language, and studies.

**2009-2010 Annual costs.** Tuition/fees: $41,930. Room/board: $9,370. Books/supplies: $860. Personal expenses: $1,200.

**2009-2010 Financial aid.** All financial aid based on need. 478 full-time freshmen applied for aid; 399 were judged to have need; 399 of these received aid. Average need met was 100%. Average scholarship/grant was $35,696; average loan $1,754. 92% of total undergraduate aid awarded as scholarships/grants, 8% as loans/jobs. **Additional information:** No loans in the initial financial aid packages for students from families with total income used in need analysis of $60,000 or less.

**Application procedures. Admission:** Closing date 1/1 (receipt date). $60 fee, may be waived for applicants with need. Admission notification 4/1. Must reply by 5/1. **Financial aid:** Closing date 2/1. FAFSA, CSS PRO-FILE required. Applicants notified by 3/30; must reply by 5/1.

**Academics.** Introductory-level college course emphasizing written and oral communication required for freshmen. Majors declared through department, interdepartmental programs, multidisciplinary programs, and independent programs. Summer research with faculty. **Special study options:** Combined bachelor's/graduate degree, cooperative education, cross-registration, double major, exchange student, independent study, internships, liberal arts/career combination, student-designed major, study abroad, teacher certification program, urban semester, Washington semester. Independently designed junior year abroad programs; exchange programs with institutions in 12-college exchange as well as Fisk University, Hampton Institute, Howard University, Morehouse College, and Spelman College; 3-2 engineering program with Dartmouth College. **Credit/placement by examination:** AP, CLEP, IB, institutional tests. 4 credit hours maximum toward bachelor's degree. **Support services:** Learning center, reduced course load, study skills assistance, tutoring, writing center.

**Majors. Area/ethnic studies:** African, American, Asian, Latin American, women's. **Biology:** General, biochemistry. **Communications:** Media studies. **Computer sciences:** General. **Conservation:** Environmental studies. **Foreign languages:** Ancient Greek, Chinese, French, German, Italian, Japanese, Latin, Russian, Spanish. **History:** General. **Interdisciplinary:** Ancient studies, cognitive science, medieval/Renaissance, neuroscience, science/society. **Liberal arts:** Arts/sciences. **Math:** General. **Philosophy/religion:** Judaic, philosophy, religion. **Physical sciences:** Astronomy, chemistry, geology, physics. **Psychology:** General. **Social sciences:** Anthropology, economics, geography, international relations, political science, sociology, urban studies. **Visual/performing arts:** Art, dramatic, film/cinema.

**Most popular majors.** English 8%, foreign language 9%, interdisciplinary studies 6%, psychology 8%, social sciences 28%, visual/performing arts 13%.

**Computing on campus.** 432 workstations in dormitories, library, computer center, student center. Dormitories wired for high-speed internet access and linked to campus network. Commuter students can connect to campus network. Online course registration, helpline, repair service, student web hosting, wireless network available.

**Student life. Freshman orientation:** Mandatory. Preregistration for classes offered. Held one week prior to start of classes. **Housing:** Guaranteed on-campus for all undergraduates. Coed dorms, single-sex dorms, special housing for disabled, apartments, cooperative housing, wellness housing available. Quiet housing. **Activities:** Bands, campus ministries, choral groups, dance, drama, film society, international student organizations, literary magazine, music ensembles, Model UN, musical theater, opera, radio station, student government, student newspaper, symphony orchestra, TV station, Catholic community, Jewish union, Promoting Equality and Community Everywhere, Amnesty International, Young Socialists, Republican/Libertarian Coalition, AIDS education committee, Habitat for Humanity, Step Beyond (community service), African students union.

**Athletics.** NCAA. **Intercollegiate:** Baseball M, basketball, cross-country, diving, fencing, field hockey W, golf W, lacrosse, rowing (crew), soccer, squash, swimming, tennis, track and field, volleyball. **Intramural:** Badminton, basketball, bowling, football (non-tackle), golf, handball, soccer, softball, squash, tennis, volleyball, water polo. **Team name:** Brewers.

**Student services.** Alcohol/substance abuse counseling, chaplain/spiritual director, career counseling, student employment services, financial aid counseling, health services, minority student services, on-campus daycare, personal counseling, placement for graduates, veterans' counselor, women's services. **Physically disabled:** Services for visually, hearing impaired.

**Contact.** E-mail: admissons@vassar.edu
Phone: (845) 437-7300 Toll-free number: (800) 827-7270
Fax: (845) 437-7063
David Borus, Dean of Admission and Financial Aid, Vassar College, Box 10, 124 Raymond Avenue, Poughkeepsie, NY 12604-0077

## Vaughn College of Aeronautics and Technology

**Flushing, New York**
www.vaughn.edu

**CB member**
**CB code: 2001**

- Private 4-year engineering college
- Commuter campus in very large city
- 1,283 degree-seeking undergraduates: 27% part-time, 11% women, 21% African American, 12% Asian American, 38% Hispanic American, 1% Native American, 2% international
- 16 degree-seeking graduate students
- 92% of applicants admitted
- SAT or ACT (ACT writing recommended), application essay required
- 41% graduate within 6 years; 9% enter graduate study

**General.** Founded in 1932. Regionally accredited. Engineering technology programs accredited by the Accreditation Board for Engineering and Technology. Management programs accredited by the International Assembly of Collegiate Business Education. **Degrees:** 108 bachelor's, 136 associate awarded; master's offered. **ROTC:** Army, Air Force. **Location:** 5 miles from Manhattan. **Calendar:** Semester, extensive summer session. **Full-time faculty:** 39 total; 33% have terminal degrees, 28% minority, 10% women. **Part-time faculty:** 94 total; 6% have terminal degrees, 48% minority, 17% women. **Class size:** 60% < 20, 40% 20-39. **Special facilities:** Fiber optic Unix-Novell computer system, 65-foot tower overlooking LaGuardia Airport, Frasca 142 flight simulator, nondestructive testing laboratory, composite materials laboratory and computerized engine test-cell.

**Freshman class profile.** 492 applied, 454 admitted, 262 enrolled.

| Mid 50% test scores | | | |
|---|---|---|---|
| SAT critical reading: | 440-540 | GPA 2.0-2.99: | 58% |
| SAT math: | 470-550 | End year in good standing: | 69% |
| GPA 3.75 or higher: | 3% | Return as sophomores: | 88% |
| GPA 3.50-3.74: | 13% | Out-of-state: | 10% |
| GPA 3.0-3.49: | 26% | Live on campus: | 14% |
| | | International: | 1% |

**Basis for selection.** High school transcripts or GED scores most important followed by SAT, ACT, or TOEFL. B.S. programs require strong performance in high school math and sciences courses. Open admissions to associate degree programs. SAT or ACT with Writing exam required for all first-time, first-year applicants to BS program. Interview recommended. **Homeschooled:** Statement describing homeschool structure and mission, transcript of courses and grades, state high school equivalency certificate required. **Learning Disabled:** IEP documentation required.

**High school preparation.** College-preparatory program recommended. 14 units required; 18 recommended. Required and recommended units include English 4, mathematics 3-4, social studies 1-4 and science 2-4.

**2010-2011 Annual costs.** Tuition/fees (projected): $17,515. Room/board: $11,025. Books/supplies: $1,050. Personal expenses: $1,200.

**2009-2010 Financial aid. Need-based:** 239 full-time freshmen applied for aid; 239 were judged to have need; 239 of these received aid. Average need met was 85%. Average scholarship/grant was $1,100; average loan $1,750. 56% of total undergraduate aid awarded as scholarships/grants, 44% as loans/jobs. **Non-need-based:** Awarded to 410 full-time undergraduates, including 94 freshmen. Scholarships awarded for academics, alumni affiliation, job skills, leadership, ROTC, state residency.

**Application procedures. Admission:** Priority date 3/1; no deadline. $40 fee, may be waived for applicants with need. Admission notification on a rolling basis beginning on or about 2/1. **Financial aid:** Priority date 3/1; no closing date. FAFSA required. Applicants notified by 4/15; must reply within 2 week(s) of notification.

**Academics. Special study options:** Accelerated study, distance learning, double major, independent study, internships, liberal arts/career combination. **Credit/placement by examination:** AP, CLEP, IB, SAT, ACT, institutional tests. 30 credit hours maximum toward associate degree, 60 toward bachelor's. **Support services:** Learning center, pre-admission summer program, reduced course load, remedial instruction, study skills assistance, tutoring, writing center.

**Majors. Business:** General. **Engineering technology:** Electrical, mechanical. **Mechanic/repair:** Aircraft, aircraft powerplant, avionics, communications systems. **Transportation:** Airline/commercial pilot, aviation, aviation management. **Other:** Mechatronic engineering.

**Most popular majors.** Business/marketing 51%, engineering/engineering technologies 28%, trade and industry 21%.

**Computing on campus.** 95 workstations in dormitories, library, computer center, student center. Dormitories wired for high-speed internet access and linked to campus network. Commuter students can connect to campus network. Online library, helpline, repair service, wireless network available.

**Student life. Freshman orientation:** Mandatory, $160 fee. Preregistration for classes offered. Two-day orientation with one-night stay in residence hall. Offered on several dates throughout the summer. **Housing:** Coed dorms, wellness housing available. $250 partly refundable deposit, deadline 6/15. **Activities:** Dance, drama, international student organizations, student government, American Institute of Aeronautics and Astronautics, Society of Automotive Engineers, Institute of Electrical and Electronics Engineers, flying club, Women in Aviation-International.

**Athletics. Intercollegiate:** Basketball M, soccer M, tennis W. **Intramural:** Basketball, soccer, table tennis, tennis. **Team name:** Warriors.

**Student services.** Alcohol/substance abuse counseling, chaplain/spiritual director, career counseling, services for economically disadvantaged, student employment services, financial aid counseling, minority student services, personal counseling, placement for graduates, veterans' counselor.

**Contact.** E-mail: admitme@vaughn.edu
Phone: (718) 429-6600 ext. 118 Toll-free number: (800) 866-6828
Fax: (718) 779-2231
Vincent Papandrea, Assistant Vice President of Enrollment, Vaughn College of Aeronautics and Technology, 86-01 23rd Avenue, Flushing, NY 11369

## Wagner College
### Staten Island, New York
www.wagner.edu
CB member
CB code: 2966

- Private 4-year liberal arts college affiliated with Lutheran Church in America
- Residential campus in very large city
- 1,861 degree-seeking undergraduates: 3% part-time, 63% women, 5% African American, 2% Asian American, 6% Hispanic American, 1% international
- 391 degree-seeking graduate students
- 70% of applicants admitted
- SAT or ACT (ACT writing optional), application essay required
- 68% graduate within 6 years

**General.** Founded in 1883. Regionally accredited. **Degrees:** 475 bachelor's awarded; master's offered. **ROTC:** Army. **Location:** 10 miles from New York City. **Calendar:** Semester, limited summer session. **Full-time faculty:** 99 total; 89% have terminal degrees, 9% minority, 48% women. **Part-time faculty:** 139 total; 12% minority, 47% women. **Class size:** 56% < 20, 43% 20-39, less than 1% 40-49. **Special facilities:** Planetarium, electron microscopes.

**Freshman class profile.** 2,661 applied, 1,853 admitted, 519 enrolled.

| Mid 50% test scores | | | |
|---|---|---|---|
| SAT critical reading: | 520-640 | GPA 2.0-2.99: | 10% |
| SAT math: | 530-650 | Rank in top quarter: | 70% |
| SAT writing: | 520-640 | Rank in top tenth: | 15% |
| ACT composite: | 23-28 | Return as sophomores: | 78% |
| GPA 3.75 or higher: | 18% | Out-of-state: | 56% |
| GPA 3.50-3.74: | 24% | Live on campus: | 80% |
| GPA 3.0-3.49: | 48% | International: | 1% |

**Basis for selection.** School achievement, test scores, recommendations, interview, special talents, essay all considered. Interview recommended for all; audition required for music, theater programs; portfolio recommended for art programs. Interview required for Physician Assistant program. **Homeschooled:** Transcript of courses and grades required.

**High school preparation.** College-preparatory program required. 21 units required. Required units include English 4, mathematics 3, social studies 1, history 3, science 2 (laboratory 1), foreign language 2 and academic electives 6. 4 economics, arts, computers, or other elective areas of study required.

**2009-2010 Annual costs.** Tuition/fees: $32,580. Room/board: $9,700. Books/supplies: $745. Personal expenses: $1,295.

**2009-2010 Financial aid. Need-based:** 430 full-time freshmen applied for aid; 356 were judged to have need; 356 of these received aid. Average need met was 74%. Average scholarship/grant was $12,489; average loan $3,808. 56% of total undergraduate aid awarded as scholarships/grants, 44% as loans/jobs. **Non-need-based:** Awarded to 636 full-time undergraduates, including 150 freshmen. Scholarships awarded for academics, athletics, music/drama.

**Application procedures. Admission:** Priority date 2/1; deadline 2/15 (postmark date). $50 fee, may be waived for applicants with need. Admission notification on a rolling basis beginning on or about 3/1. Must reply by May 1 or within 2 week(s) if notified thereafter. **Financial aid:** Priority date 2/15; no closing date. FAFSA, institutional form required. Applicants notified on a rolling basis starting 3/1; must reply within 3 week(s) of notification.

**Academics. Special study options:** Combined bachelor's/graduate degree, double major, exchange student, honors, independent study, internships, New York semester, study abroad, teacher certification program, United Nations semester, Washington semester. Learning community. **Credit/**

**placement by examination:** AP, CLEP, IB, institutional tests. 9 credit hours maximum toward bachelor's degree. Up to 9 units may be awarded for credit by exam and prior experience. Each unit is equivalent to 3.3 credit hours. **Support services:** Reduced course load, study skills assistance, tutoring, writing center.

**Majors. Biology:** General, bacteriology. **Business:** Accounting, business admin, finance, international, managerial economics, marketing. **Computer sciences:** Computer science. **Education:** General, early childhood, middle, secondary. **Foreign languages:** French, Spanish. **Health:** Nursing (RN), physician assistant, predental, premedicine. **History:** General. **Liberal arts:** Arts/sciences. **Math:** General. **Philosophy/religion:** Philosophy. **Physical sciences:** Chemistry, physics. **Psychology:** General. **Public administration:** Policy analysis. **Social sciences:** Anthropology, economics, political science, sociology. **Visual/performing arts:** Arts management, dramatic, music performance, studio arts, theater design.

**Most popular majors.** Business/marketing 21%, education 7%, health sciences 12%, psychology 11%, social sciences 10%, visual/performing arts 19%.

**Computing on campus.** 230 workstations in dormitories, library, computer center. Dormitories wired for high-speed internet access and linked to campus network. Commuter students can connect to campus network. Online course registration, online library, helpline, wireless network available.

**Student life. Freshman orientation:** Mandatory. Freshmen move on-campus 3 days prior to start of fall semester. Orientation involves academic advisement and registration, social activities, and trip to Manhattan. **Housing:** Guaranteed on-campus for all undergraduates. Coed dorms, fraternity/sorority housing, wellness housing available. $300 nonrefundable deposit, deadline 5/1. **Activities:** Bands, campus ministries, choral groups, dance, drama, international student organizations, literary magazine, music ensembles, musical theater, radio station, student government, student newspaper, Lutheran student club, Newman Society, Hillel, national honor societies, Amnesty International, Young Democrats, Young Republicans, Nubian Society, Muslim student association, Habitat for Humanity.

**Athletics.** NCAA. **Intercollegiate:** Baseball M, basketball, cross-country, football (tackle) M, golf, lacrosse, soccer W, softball W, swimming W, tennis, track and field, water polo W. **Intramural:** Basketball, bowling, cheerleading W, football (tackle) M, soccer, softball, table tennis, tennis. **Team name:** Seahawks.

**Student services.** Alcohol/substance abuse counseling, chaplain/spiritual director, career counseling, student employment services, financial aid counseling, health services, personal counseling, placement for graduates, women's services. **Physically disabled:** Services for visually, hearing impaired.

**Contact.** E-mail: adm@wagner.edu
Phone: (718) 390-3411 Toll-free number: (800) 221-1010
Fax: (718) 390-3105
Leigh-Ann Nowicki, Dean of Admissions, Wagner College, One Campus Road, Staten Island, NY 10301-4495

## Webb Institute
### Glen Cove, New York
www.webb-institute.edu
CB member
CB code: 2970

- Private 4-year engineering and maritime college
- Residential campus in large town
- 89 degree-seeking undergraduates: 13% women, 8% Asian American, 4% Hispanic American
- 35% of applicants admitted
- SAT, SAT Subject Tests, interview required
- 81% graduate within 6 years; 28% enter graduate study

**General.** Founded in 1889. Regionally accredited. All students participate in 2-month paid winter work program in marine industry each year. **Degrees:** 17 bachelor's awarded. **Location:** 22 miles from New York City. **Calendar:** Semester. **Full-time faculty:** 11 total; 54% have terminal degrees, 9% women. **Part-time faculty:** 3 total; 67% have terminal degrees, 33% women. **Class size:** 100% 20-39. **Special facilities:** Adjoining nature preserve, model testing tank.

**Freshman class profile.** 68 applied, 24 admitted, 19 enrolled.

| Mid 50% test scores | | | |
|---|---|---|---|
| SAT critical reading: | 640-680 | GPA 2.0-2.99: | 9% |
| SAT math: | 700-740 | Rank in top quarter: | 83% |
| SAT writing: | 610-670 | Rank in top tenth: | 67% |
| GPA 3.75 or higher: | 46% | End year in good standing: | 92% |
| GPA 3.50-3.74: | 36% | Return as sophomores: | 92% |
| GPA 3.0-3.49: | 9% | Out-of-state: | 74% |
| | | Live on campus: | 100% |

**Basis for selection.** GED not accepted. High school record, class rank, test scores, and interview with President of college most important. Character, motivation, and outside activities considered. **Homeschooled:** Statement describing homeschool structure and mission, transcript of courses and grades, letter of recommendation (nonparent) required.

**High school preparation.** College-preparatory program recommended. 16 units required. Required units include English 4, mathematics 4, social studies 2, science 2 (laboratory 2) and academic electives 4.

**2010-2011 Annual costs.** All students receive 4-year, full-tuition scholarships. Room/board: $12,000. Books/supplies: $750. Personal expenses: $3,700.

**2008-2009 Financial aid.** All financial aid based on need.

**Application procedures. Admission:** Closing date 2/15 (postmark date). $25 fee, may be waived for applicants with need. Application must be submitted on paper. Admission notification on a rolling basis beginning on or about 3/15. Must reply by May 1 or within 2 week(s) if notified thereafter. **Financial aid:** Closing date 7/1. FAFSA required. Applicants notified by 8/1; must reply within 2 week(s) of notification.

**Academics.** Intensive single curriculum program demands high career motivation. **Special study options:** Double major, independent study, internships, study abroad. **Credit/placement by examination:** CLEP. **Support services:** Study skills assistance.

**Majors. Engineering:** Marine.

**Computing on campus.** PC or laptop required. 25 workstations in dormitories, library, computer center, student center. Dormitories wired for high-speed internet access and linked to campus network. Commuter students can connect to campus network. Repair service, wireless network available.

**Student life. Freshman orientation:** Mandatory. Held 1 week before classes start. **Housing:** Guaranteed on-campus for all undergraduates. Coed dorms, single-sex dorms, wellness housing available. $150 deposit. **Activities:** Choral groups, drama, music ensembles, student government, free membership available to local YMCA, women engineers, society of American naval engineers, WebbWomen, society of naval architects and marine engineers.

**Athletics. Intercollegiate:** Basketball, cross-country, sailing, soccer, tennis, track and field, volleyball. **Intramural:** Basketball, cross-country, soccer, triathlon, volleyball.

**Student services.** Alcohol/substance abuse counseling, career counseling, student employment services, financial aid counseling, health services, personal counseling, placement for graduates.

**Contact.** E-mail: admissions@webb-institute.edu
Phone: (516) 671-2213 Toll-free number: (866) 708-9322
Fax: (516) 674-9838
William Murray, Director of Enrollment Management, Webb Institute, 298 Crescent Beach Road, Glen Cove, NY 11542-1398

---

## Wells College

**Aurora, New York**
www.wells.edu

CB member
CB code: 2971

- Private 4-year liberal arts college
- Residential campus in rural community
- 552 degree-seeking undergraduates: 1% part-time, 71% women, 6% African American, 2% Asian American, 4% Hispanic American, 1% Native American, 2% international
- 67% of applicants admitted
- SAT or ACT (ACT writing recommended), application essay required
- 54% graduate within 6 years

**General.** Founded in 1868. Regionally accredited. **Degrees:** 100 bachelor's awarded. **ROTC:** Army, Air Force. **Location:** 30 miles from Ithaca, 50 miles from Syracuse. **Calendar:** Semester. **Full-time faculty:** 39 total; 95% have terminal degrees, 18% minority, 54% women. **Part-time faculty:** 19 total; 21% have terminal degrees, 10% minority, 47% women. **Class**

**size:** 85% < 20, 14% 20-39, 1% 40-49. **Special facilities:** Book arts center, lithography presses, digital imaging laboratory, boathouse with access to Cayuga Lake, indoor tennis courts, 9-hole golf course, science facility with growth chamber, cold room.

**Freshman class profile.** 1,673 applied, 1,124 admitted, 145 enrolled.

| Mid 50% test scores | | | |
|---|---|---|---|
| SAT critical reading: | 500-630 | GPA 2.0-2.99: | 23% |
| SAT math: | 480-600 | Rank in top quarter: | 65% |
| SAT writing: | 480-590 | Rank in top tenth: | 31% |
| ACT composite: | 22-27 | End year in good standing: | 88% |
| GPA 3.75 or higher: | 11% | Return as sophomores: | 76% |
| GPA 3.50-3.74: | 40% | Out-of-state: | 36% |
| GPA 3.0-3.49: | 26% | Live on campus: | 98% |
| | | International: | 3% |

**Basis for selection.** Academic achievement record most important. Test scores, class rank, recommendations, essay, school and community extracurricular activities also important. Evidence of leadership ability through academic and cocurricular activities also considered. Interviews highly recommended. **Homeschooled:** Statement describing homeschool structure and mission, transcript of courses and grades, state high school equivalency certificate required. Please contact Admissions Office for additional information.

**High school preparation.** College-preparatory program recommended. 17 units required; 23 recommended. Required and recommended units include English 4, mathematics 3-4, social studies 1, history 3, science 2-3 (laboratory 2-3), foreign language 1-2 and academic electives 2-3. Students encouraged to take 2 computer science, art, and/or music. AP and honors courses recommended.

**2009-2010 Annual costs.** Tuition/fees: $29,680. Room/board: $9,000. Books/supplies: $800. Personal expenses: $800.

**2009-2010 Financial aid. Need-based:** 136 full-time freshmen applied for aid; 125 were judged to have need; 125 of these received aid. Average need met was 79%. Average scholarship/grant was $21,320; average loan $3,680. 77% of total undergraduate aid awarded as scholarships/grants, 23% as loans/jobs. **Non-need-based:** Awarded to 333 full-time undergraduates, including 99 freshmen. Scholarships awarded for academics, alumni affiliation, leadership.

**Application procedures. Admission:** Priority date 12/15; deadline 3/1 (postmark date). $40 fee, may be waived for applicants with need. Admission notification 4/1. Must reply by 5/1. **Financial aid:** Priority date 2/15; no closing date. FAFSA required. CSS PROFILE required of early decision candidates only. Applicants notified on a rolling basis starting 3/1; must reply by 5/1.

**Academics.** Experiential learning integrated through internship and off-campus study programs, study abroad, research with professors, and community service. **Special study options:** Accelerated study, combined bachelor's/graduate degree, cross-registration, double major, independent study, internships, student-designed major, study abroad, teacher certification program, Washington semester. **Credit/placement by examination:** AP, CLEP, IB, SAT, ACT, institutional tests. 6 credit hours maximum toward bachelor's degree. **Support services:** Learning center, reduced course load, study skills assistance, tutoring, writing center.

**Majors. Area/ethnic studies:** African-American, American, women's. **Biology:** General, biochemistry, molecular. **Business:** General, managerial economics. **Computer sciences:** Computer science. **Conservation:** General, environmental science, environmental studies. **Foreign languages:** General, comparative lit, French, German, Spanish. **Health:** Predental, premedicine, preveterinary. **History:** General. **Interdisciplinary:** Global studies. **Legal studies:** Prelaw. **Liberal arts:** Humanities. **Math:** General. **Philosophy/religion:** Ethics, philosophy, religion. **Physical sciences:** Chemistry, physics. **Psychology:** General. **Public administration:** Policy analysis. **Social sciences:** Anthropology, economics, international relations, political science, sociology, U.S. government. **Visual/performing arts:** General, art, art history/conservation, dance, dramatic, studio arts.

**Most popular majors.** Biology 10%, English 11%, history 8%, psychology 15%, public administration/social services 7%, social sciences 14%, visual/performing arts 12%.

**Computing on campus.** 85 workstations in dormitories, library, computer center. Dormitories wired for high-speed internet access and linked to campus network. Commuter students can connect to campus network. Online course registration, online library, repair service, wireless network available.

**Student life. Freshman orientation:** Mandatory. Preregistration for classes offered. General introduction held during 5-day orientation before classes begin. **Policies:** Honor code governs academic and co-curricular life. **Housing:** Guaranteed on-campus for all undergraduates. Coed dorms, single-sex dorms, wellness housing available. $300 nonrefundable deposit, deadline 5/1. **Activities:** Choral groups, dance, drama, literary magazine, music ensembles, Model UN, student government, student newspaper, Amnesty International, American Red Cross Club, College Democrats, College Republicans, Praising Our Work, social and cultural organization, Women in Life-Long Learning.

**Athletics.** NCAA. **Intercollegiate:** Basketball, cross-country, field hockey W, golf, lacrosse, soccer, softball W, swimming, tennis W. **Intramural:** Basketball, field hockey, golf, sailing, skiing, soccer, tennis, volleyball. **Team name:** Express.

**Student services.** Adult student services, chaplain/spiritual director, career counseling, financial aid counseling, health services, minority student services, personal counseling, women's services.

**Contact.** E-mail: admissions@wells.edu
Phone: (315) 364-3264 Toll-free number: (800) 952-9355
Fax: (315) 364-3227
Susan Sloan, Director of Admissions, Wells College, 170 Main Street, Aurora, NY 13026

## Yeshiva and Kolel Bais Medrash Elyon
### Monsey, New York

- Private 4-year rabbinical college for men affiliated with Jewish faith
- Small city
- 24 degree-seeking undergraduates
- 2 graduate students
- 100% of applicants admitted

**General.** Accredited by AARTS. **Degrees:** 2 bachelor's awarded; doctoral offered. **Calendar:** Semester. **Full-time faculty:** 3 total. **Part-time faculty:** 2 total.

**Freshman class profile.** 1 applied, 1 admitted, 1 enrolled.

**Basis for selection.** Commitment to Jewish tenet.

**2009-2010 Annual costs.** Tuition/fees: $7,800. Cost of tuition includes room and board.

**Application procedures. Admission:** No deadline. No application fee. Admission notification on a rolling basis.

**Academics. Credit/placement by examination:** CLEP.

**Majors. Theology:** Talmudic.

**Contact.** Phone: (845) 356-7064
Rabbi. Israel Falk, Admissions Director, Yeshiva and Kolel Bais Medrash Elyon, 73 Main Street, Monsey, NY 10952

## Yeshiva and Kollel Harbotzas Torah
### Brooklyn, New York

- Private 4-year rabbinical college for men affiliated with Jewish faith
- Very large city
- 16 degree-seeking undergraduates
- 16 graduate students

**General.** Accredited by AARTS. **Degrees:** 4 bachelor's awarded; doctoral offered. **Calendar:** Semester.

**2009-2010 Annual costs.** Tuition/fees: $6,050.

**Application procedures. Admission:** No deadline.

**Academics. Credit/placement by examination:** CLEP.

**Majors. Theology:** Talmudic.

**Contact.** Phone: (718) 692-0208
Yeshiva and Kollel Harbotzas Torah, 1049 East 15th Street, Brooklyn, NY 11230

## Yeshiva Derech Chaim
### Brooklyn, New York

**CB code: 0552**

- Private 5-year rabbinical college for men affiliated with Jewish faith
- Very large city
- 110 degree-seeking undergraduates
- 66 graduate students
- Interview required

**General.** Founded in 1975. Accredited by AARTS. First and advanced Talmudic degrees available. **Degrees:** 12 bachelor's awarded; doctoral offered. **Calendar:** Semester. **Full-time faculty:** 12 total. **Part-time faculty:** 7 total.

**Basis for selection.** Dean interviews each applicant. Recommendations very important. Applicants without high school diplomas may be admitted on basis of national AARTS exam.

**2009-2010 Annual costs.** Tuition includes board expenses. Books/supplies: $400.

**Financial aid. Additional information:** Financial aid interview held with each admitted student.

**Application procedures. Admission:** Priority date 8/20; no deadline. No application fee. Admission notification on a rolling basis. **Financial aid:** No deadline. Applicants notified on a rolling basis.

**Academics. Credit/placement by examination:** CLEP.

**Majors. Theology:** Talmudic. **Other:** Rabbinical studies.

**Student life. Policies:** Religious observance required. **Activities:** Choral groups, TV station.

**Contact.** Phone: (718) 438-3070
Rabbi. Mordechai Rennert, Admissions Director, Yeshiva Derech Chaim, 1573 39th Street, Brooklyn, NY 11218

## Yeshiva D'Monsey Rabbinical College
### Monsey, New York

- Private 4-year rabbinical college for men affiliated with Jewish faith
- Large town
- 69 degree-seeking undergraduates

**General.** Accredited by AARTS. **Degrees:** 1 bachelor's awarded. **Calendar:** Semester.

**2009-2010 Annual costs.** Tuition/fees: $4,000. Room/board: $3,000.

**Application procedures. Admission:** No deadline.

**Academics. Credit/placement by examination:** CLEP.

**Majors. Theology:** Talmudic.

**Contact.** Phone: (845) 352-5852
Yeshiva D'Monsey Rabbinical College, 2 Roman Boulevard, Monsey, NY 10952

## Yeshiva Gedolah Imrei Yosef D'Spinka
### Brooklyn, New York

- Private 4-year rabbinical college for men affiliated with Jewish faith
- Very large city
- 106 degree-seeking undergraduates

**General.** Accredited by AARTS. **Degrees:** 37 bachelor's awarded. **Calendar:** Semester. **Full-time faculty:** 9 total.

**2009-2010 Annual costs.** Tuition/fees: $6,100.

**Application procedures. Admission:** Priority date 8/18; deadline 9/28. No application fee.

**Academics. Credit/placement by examination:** CLEP.

**Majors. Theology:** Talmudic.

**Contact.** Phone: (718) 851-1600
Yeshiva Gedolah Imrei Yosef D'Spinka, 1466 56th Street, Brooklyn, NY 11219

## Yeshiva Gedolah Zichron Moshe
**South Fallsburg, New York**

CB code: 0750

- Private 4-year rabbinical college for men affiliated with Jewish faith
- Small town
- 180 degree-seeking undergraduates
- 21 graduate students

**General.** Founded in 1969. Accredited by AARTS. First Talmudic degree and ordination available. **Degrees:** 3 bachelor's awarded; doctoral offered. **Calendar:** Semester.

**Basis for selection.** Institutional examination.

**2009-2010 Annual costs.** Tuition/fees: $10,100. Room/board: $3,000. Books/supplies: $200. Personal expenses: $3,003.

**Application procedures.** Admission: No deadline.

**Academics.** Credit/placement by examination: CLEP.

**Majors.** Theology: Talmudic.

**Contact.** Phone: (845) 434-5240 Fax: (845) 434-1009
Abba Gorelick, Dean of Admissions, Yeshiva Gedolah Zichron Moshe, 84 Laurel Park Road, South Fallsburg, NY 12779

## Yeshiva Karlin Stolin
**Brooklyn, New York**

CB code: 1582

- Private 4-year rabbinical college for men affiliated with Jewish faith
- Very large city
- 77 degree-seeking undergraduates

**General.** Accredited by AARTS. **Degrees:** 9 bachelor's awarded. **Calendar:** Semester.

**2009-2010 Annual costs.** Tuition/fees: $6,200. Room/board: $3,200.

**Application procedures.** Admission: No deadline.

**Academics.** Credit/placement by examination: CLEP.

**Majors.** Theology: Talmudic.

**Contact.** Phone: (718) 232-7800
Yeshiva Karlin Stolin, 1818 54th Street, Brooklyn, NY 11204-1545

## Yeshiva of Nitra
**Mount Kisco, New York**

CB code: 7131

- Private 4-year rabbinical college for men affiliated with Jewish faith
- Small city
- 213 degree-seeking undergraduates

**General.** Accredited by AARTS. **Degrees:** 12 bachelor's awarded; master's offered. **Calendar:** Continuous.

**2009-2010 Annual costs.** Tuition/fees: $6,700. Room/board: $3,300.

**Application procedures.** Admission: No deadline.

**Academics.** Credit/placement by examination: CLEP.

**Majors.** Theology: Talmudic.

**Contact.** Phone: (718) 387-0422
Yeshiva of Nitra, Pine Bridge Road, Mount Kisco, NY 10549

## Yeshiva of the Telshe Alumni
**Riverdale, New York**

- Private 4-year rabbinical college for men affiliated with Jewish faith
- Very large city
- 93 degree-seeking undergraduates

**General.** Accredited by AARTS. **Calendar:** Semester.

**2009-2010 Annual costs.** Tuition/fees: $7,900. Room/board: $4,600.

**Application procedures.** Admission: No deadline. $50 fee.

**Academics.** Credit/placement by examination: CLEP.

**Majors.** Theology: Talmudic.

**Contact.** Phone: (718) 601-3523
Yeshiva of the Telshe Alumni, 4904 Independence Avenue, Riverdale, NY 10471

## Yeshiva Shaar Hatorah
**Kew Gardens, New York**

CB code: 0743

- Private 4-year rabbinical college for men affiliated with Jewish faith
- Very large city
- 92 degree-seeking undergraduates
- 13 graduate students
- Interview required

**General.** Founded in 1976. Accredited by AARTS. Ordination and first rabbinic degree available. **Degrees:** 21 bachelor's awarded; master's offered. **Calendar:** Semester. **Full-time faculty:** 1 total. **Part-time faculty:** 1 total.

**Basis for selection.** Religious commitment, school achievement record, recommendations, and interview most important.

**2009-2010 Annual costs.** Comprehensive fee: $14,500.

**Application procedures.** Admission: No deadline. $100 fee.

**Academics.** Special study options: Double major. **Credit/placement by examination:** CLEP.

**Majors.** Theology: Talmudic.

**Student life. Policies:** Religious observance required.

**Contact.** Phone: (718) 846-1940
Yoel Yankelewitz, Admissions Director, Yeshiva Shaar Hatorah, 117-06 84th Avenue, Kew Gardens, NY 11418

## Yeshiva Shaarei Torah of Rockland
**Suffern, New York**

- Private 4-year rabbinical college for men affiliated with Jewish faith
- Commuter campus in large town
- 21 degree-seeking undergraduates

**General.** Accredited by AARTS. **Degrees:** 26 bachelor's awarded. **Calendar:** Semester. **Full-time faculty:** 7 total. **Part-time faculty:** 4 total.

**2009-2010 Annual costs.** Tuition/fees: $9,000. Room/board: $3,000.

**Application procedures.** Admission: No deadline. $250 fee.

**Academics.** Credit/placement by examination: CLEP.

**Majors.** Theology: Talmudic.

**Contact.** Phone: (845) 352-3431
Rabbi. Avraham Posner, Admissions Director, Yeshiva Shaarei Torah of Rockland, 91 West Carlton Road, Suffern, NY 10901

## Yeshiva University
**New York, New York**
www.yu.edu

**CB member**
**CB code: 2990**

- Private 4-year university
- Residential campus in very large city
- 2,848 degree-seeking undergraduates: 2% part-time, 46% women, 2% Hispanic American, 12% international
- 3,375 degree-seeking graduate students
- 63% of applicants admitted
- SAT or ACT with writing, application essay, interview required
- 80% graduate within 6 years

**General.** Founded in 1886. Regionally accredited. Campus locations in Manhattan and the Bronx. **Degrees:** 652 bachelor's, 315 associate awarded; master's, doctoral, professional offered. **Calendar:** Semester, limited summer session. **Full-time faculty:** 1,051 total; 20% minority, 36% women. **Part-time faculty:** 402 total; 7% minority, 39% women. **Class size:** 69% < 20, 28% 20-39, 1% 40-49, 1% 50-99.

**Freshman class profile.** 2,027 applied, 1,269 admitted, 819 enrolled.

| Mid 50% test scores | | | |
|---|---|---|---|
| SAT critical reading: | 550-690 | GPA 3.0-3.49: | 25% |
| SAT math: | 550-680 | GPA 2.0-2.99: | 15% |
| ACT composite: | 22-28 | Return as sophomores: | 90% |
| GPA 3.75 or higher: | 38% | Out-of-state: | 34% |
| GPA 3.50-3.74: | 21% | Live on campus: | 90% |
| | | International: | 7% |

**Basis for selection.** Equal weight given to high school GPA, test scores, ability and motivation as indicated in interview, school and community activities, recommendations of principal, guidance counselor, and/or employer. **Homeschooled:** Statement describing homeschool structure and mission, transcript of courses and grades, state high school equivalency certificate, interview required.

**High school preparation.** College-preparatory program required. 16 units recommended. Recommended units include English 4, mathematics 2, social studies 2, science 2 and foreign language 2.

**2009-2010 Annual costs.** Tuition/fees: $32,094. Room/board: $10,380. Books/supplies: $1,166. Personal expenses: $3,101.

**2009-2010 Financial aid. Additional information:** Essays required of Distinguished Scholarship applicants.

**Application procedures. Admission:** Priority date 2/1; no deadline. $65 fee, may be waived for applicants with need. Admission notification on a rolling basis beginning on or about 12/15. Must reply by May 1 or within 2 week(s) if notified thereafter. **Financial aid:** Priority date 4/15, closing date 5/1. FAFSA, institutional form required. Applicants notified on a rolling basis starting 4/1.

**Academics. Special study options:** Combined bachelor's/graduate degree, cross-registration, double major, dual enrollment of high school students, exchange student, honors, independent study, internships, student-designed major, study abroad, teacher certification program. **Credit/placement by examination:** CLEP, institutional tests. 44 credit hours maximum toward bachelor's degree. **Support services:** Reduced course load, tutoring, writing center.

**Honors college/program.** 1400 SAT (exclusive of Writing) or ACT equivalent, 2 nominations, interview required.

**Majors. Biology:** General. **Business:** Accounting, business admin. **Computer sciences:** General, computer science. **Education:** Elementary, foreign languages. **Engineering:** General. **Foreign languages:** Classics, French, Hebrew. **Health:** Audiology/speech pathology, premedicine. **History:** General. **Math:** General. **Philosophy/religion:** Judaic, philosophy. **Physical sciences:** Chemistry, physics. **Psychology:** General. **Social sciences:** Economics, political science, sociology.

**Most popular majors.** Biology 15%, business/marketing 16%, English 8%, psychology 16%.

**Computing on campus.** 350 workstations in library, computer center, student center. Dormitories wired for high-speed internet access and linked to campus network. Online library, helpline, repair service, wireless network available.

**Student life. Freshman orientation:** Mandatory. Held the week before classes. **Policies:** Students participate in university governance through college senates. **Housing:** Guaranteed on-campus for all undergraduates. Single-sex dorms, apartments available. $250 nonrefundable deposit, deadline 6/1.

**Activities:** Jazz band, choral groups, drama, literary magazine, music ensembles, musical theater, radio station, student government, student newspaper, neighborhood social service, pre-professional, special interest, and political clubs.

**Athletics.** NCAA. **Intercollegiate:** Baseball M, basketball, cross-country M, fencing M, golf M, soccer M, tennis M, volleyball M, wrestling M. **Intramural:** Basketball, tennis M, volleyball W. **Team name:** Macs.

**Student services.** Career counseling, student employment services, health services, personal counseling, placement for graduates.

**Contact.** E-mail: yuadmit@yu.edu
Phone: (212) 960-5277 Fax: (212) 960-0086
Michael Kranzler, Director of Undergraduate Admissions, Yeshiva University, 500 West 185th Street, New York, NY 10033

## Yeshivas Novominsk
**Brooklyn, New York**

- Private 4-year rabbinical college for men affiliated with Jewish faith
- Very large city
- 125 degree-seeking undergraduates

**General.** Accredited by AARTS. **Calendar:** Semester.

**2009-2010 Annual costs.** Tuition/fees: $8,400. Room/board: $3,500.

**Application procedures. Admission:** No deadline. $100 fee.

**Academics. Credit/placement by examination:** CLEP.

**Majors. Theology:** Talmudic.

**Contact.** Phone: (718) 438-2727
Yeshivas Novominsk, 1569 47th Street, Brooklyn, NY 11219

## Yeshivat Mikdash Melech
**Brooklyn, New York**
www.mikdashmelech.net

**CB code: 1432**

- Private 5-year rabbinical college for men affiliated with Jewish faith
- Residential campus in very large city
- 93 degree-seeking undergraduates: 10% international
- 19 degree-seeking graduate students
- Interview required

**General.** Accredited by AARTS. **Degrees:** 5 bachelor's awarded; master's offered. **Calendar:** Semester, extensive summer session. **Full-time faculty:** 6 total; 67% have terminal degrees. **Class size:** 100% < 20.

**Freshman class profile.**

| | | | |
|---|---|---|---|
| Out-of-state: | 47% | International: | 14% |
| Live on campus: | 70% | | |

**Basis for selection.** Open admission, but selective for some programs. Recommendations, school record, test scores, and class rank considered. **Homeschooled:** Statement describing homeschool structure and mission required.

**High school preparation.** Required units include English 3, mathematics 3, social studies 1, history 1, science 2 (laboratory 1), foreign language 1 and academic electives 1.

**2010-2011 Annual costs.** Tuition/fees: $6,500. Room/board: $3,800.

**2008-2009 Financial aid. Need-based:** 98% of total undergraduate aid awarded as scholarships/grants, 2% as loans/jobs. **Non-need-based:** Scholarships awarded for academics, leadership, religious affiliation.

**Application procedures. Admission:** No deadline. $400 fee, may be waived for applicants with need. Application must be submitted on paper. Admission notification on a rolling basis. **Financial aid:** No deadline. FAFSA, institutional form required. Applicants notified on a rolling basis starting 5/1.

**Academics. Special study options:** Independent study, study abroad. **Credit/placement by examination:** CLEP. **Support services:** Remedial instruction, tutoring.

**Majors. Philosophy/religion:** Judaic. **Theology:** Talmudic.

**Computing on campus.** Wireless network available.

**Student life. Freshman orientation:** Available. Preregistration for classes offered. **Policies:** Religious observance required. **Housing:** Guaranteed on-campus for freshmen. Wellness housing available.

**Student services.** Adult student services, chaplain/spiritual director, financial aid counseling.

**Contact.** E-mail: mikdashmelech@verizon.net
Phone: (718) 339-1090 Fax: (718) 998-9321
Rabbi. Shmuel Beyda, Admissions Director, Yeshivat Mikdash Melech, 1326 Ocean Parkway, Brooklyn, NY 11230

## Yeshivath Viznitz
### Monsey, New York

▶  Private 4-year rabbinical college for men
▶  Large town
▶  340 degree-seeking undergraduates

**General.** Accredited by AARTS. **Degrees:** 58 bachelor's awarded; doctoral offered. **Calendar:** Semester.

**2009-2010 Annual costs.** Tuition/fees: $5,250. Room/board: $1,650.

**Application procedures. Admission:** No deadline.

**Academics. Credit/placement by examination:** CLEP.

**Majors. Theology:** Talmudic.

**Contact.** Phone: (914) 356-1010
Yeshivath Viznitz, 25 Phyllis Terrace, Monsey, NY 10952

# North Carolina

## Apex School of Theology
**Durham, North Carolina**
**www.apexsot.edu**

- Public 4-year Bible college
- Small city
- 188 degree-seeking undergraduates
- 100 graduate students

**General.** Regionally accredited; also accredited by TRACS. **Degrees:** 12 bachelor's, 2 associate awarded; master's, doctoral offered. **Calendar:** Semester. **Full-time faculty:** 4 total. **Part-time faculty:** 15 total.

**Freshman class profile.** 60 applied, 60 admitted, 22 enrolled.

**Basis for selection.** Open admission.

**2009-2010 Annual costs.** Tuition/fees: $6,435.

**Application procedures. Admission:** No deadline. $25 fee.

**Academics. Credit/placement by examination:** CLEP.

**Majors. Theology:** Theology.

**Contact.** Carrol Cotten, Director of Admissions, Apex School of Theology, 2945 South Miami Boulevard, Suite 114, Durham, NC 27703

## Appalachian State University
**Boone, North Carolina**
**www.appstate.edu**

**CB member**
**CB code: 5010**

- Public 4-year university
- Residential campus in large town
- 14,698 degree-seeking undergraduates: 4% part-time, 52% women, 3% African American, 1% Asian American, 3% Hispanic American
- 1,916 degree-seeking graduate students
- 63% of applicants admitted
- SAT or ACT with writing required
- 64% graduate within 6 years

**General.** Founded in 1899. Regionally accredited. **Degrees:** 2,812 bachelor's awarded; master's, doctoral offered. **ROTC:** Army. **Location:** 87 miles from Winston-Salem. **Calendar:** Semester, extensive summer session. **Full-time faculty:** 824 total; 99% have terminal degrees, 10% minority, 44% women. **Part-time faculty:** 320 total; 79% have terminal degrees, 6% minority, 48% women. **Class size:** 38% < 20, 46% 20-39, 7% 40-49, 7% 50-99, 1% >100. **Special facilities:** Observatory, cultural museum, visual arts center, year round outdoor adventure camp.

**Freshman class profile.** 13,039 applied, 8,224 admitted, 2,743 enrolled.

| Mid 50% test scores | | | |
|---|---|---|---|
| SAT critical reading: | 530-620 | Rank in top quarter: | 62% |
| SAT math: | 540-630 | Rank in top tenth: | 22% |
| SAT writing: | 510-600 | Return as sophomores: | 86% |
| ACT composite: | 22-26 | Out-of-state: | 12% |
| GPA 3.75 or higher: | 66% | Live on campus: | 98% |
| GPA 3.50-3.74: | 17% | International: | 1% |
| GPA 3.0-3.49: | 14% | Fraternities: | 11% |
| GPA 2.0-2.99: | 3% | Sororities: | 11% |

**Basis for selection.** GED not accepted. Satisfactory combination of grades and/or class rank and required test scores. SAT Math used for placement; CE clarification: no date, but on space basis. Audition required for music majors; portfolio required for art majors.

**High school preparation.** College-preparatory program required. 13 units required. Required units include English 4, mathematics 4, social studies 1, history 1, science 3 (laboratory 1) and foreign language 2. Specific math units required.

**2009-2010 Annual costs.** Tuition/fees: $4,425; $15,046 out-of-state. Room/board: $6,240. Books/supplies: $700. Personal expenses: $1,400.

**2009-2010 Financial aid. Need-based:** 2,046 full-time freshmen applied for aid; 1,116 were judged to have need; 1,067 of these received aid. Average need met was 82%. Average scholarship/grant was $6,194; average loan $3,666. 55% of total undergraduate aid awarded as scholarships/grants, 45% as loans/jobs. **Non-need-based:** Awarded to 5,899 full-time undergraduates, including 1,104 freshmen. Scholarships awarded for academics, alumni affiliation, art, athletics, job skills, leadership, minority status, music/drama, religious affiliation, ROTC, state residency.

**Application procedures. Admission:** No deadline. $50 fee, may be waived for applicants with need. Must reply by 5/1. Postponement allowed on individual basis for one term during academic year. **Financial aid:** Priority date 3/15; no closing date. FAFSA required. Applicants notified on a rolling basis starting 4/1; must reply within 3 week(s) of notification.

**Academics. Special study options:** Distance learning, double major, dual enrollment of high school students, ESL, exchange student, honors, independent study, internships, liberal arts/career combination, student-designed major, study abroad, teacher certification program. **Credit/placement by examination:** AP, CLEP, IB, SAT, ACT, institutional tests. **Support services:** Learning center, pre-admission summer program, remedial instruction, study skills assistance, tutoring, writing center.

**Majors. Architecture:** Urban/community planning. **Area/ethnic studies:** Women's. **Biology:** General, ecology. **Business:** Accounting, actuarial science, business admin, construction management, finance, hospitality admin, insurance, international, management information systems, marketing. **Communications:** General, advertising, journalism, public relations, radio/tv. **Computer sciences:** Computer science. **Conservation:** Environmental science, environmental studies. **Education:** Art, biology, business, chemistry, drama/dance, elementary, English, family/consumer sciences, French, health, history, kindergarten/preschool, learning disabled, mathematics, middle, music, physical, physics, social studies, Spanish, technology/industrial arts. **Engineering technology:** Solar energy. **Family/consumer sciences:** Child development, clothing/textiles, food/nutrition. **Foreign languages:** French, Spanish. **Health:** Athletic training, communication disorders, health care admin, music therapy, nursing (RN), public health ed. **History:** General. **Interdisciplinary:** Global studies. **Liberal arts:** Arts/sciences. **Math:** General, statistics. **Parks/recreation:** Exercise sciences, facilities management. **Philosophy/religion:** Philosophy, religion. **Physical sciences:** Chemistry, geology, physics. **Protective services:** Criminal justice. **Psychology:** General. **Public administration:** Social work. **Social sciences:** Anthropology, economics, geography, political science, sociology. **Visual/performing arts:** Art, arts management, commercial photography, dance, dramatic, graphic design, industrial design, interior design, music management, music performance, studio arts. **Other:** Appalachian studies, Geology, secondary education.

**Most popular majors.** Business/marketing 20%, communications/journalism 8%, education 19%, psychology 6%, social sciences 8%, visual/performing arts 7%.

**Computing on campus.** 2,500 workstations in dormitories, library, computer center, student center. Dormitories wired for high-speed internet access and linked to campus network. Commuter students can connect to campus network. Online course registration, online library, helpline, repair service, wireless network available.

**Student life. Freshman orientation:** Mandatory. Preregistration for classes offered. 2-day program throughout summer and at beginning of each semester and summer school session. **Policies:** Student must be full-time and live on campus to join a fraternity or sorority. **Housing:** Guaranteed on-campus for freshmen. Coed dorms, single-sex dorms, special housing for disabled, apartments, wellness housing available. $100 nonrefundable deposit, deadline 5/1. Sorority housing available. **Activities:** Bands, campus ministries, choral groups, dance, drama, film society, international student organizations, literary magazine, music ensembles, Model UN, musical theater, opera, radio station, student government, student newspaper, symphony orchestra, Campus Crusade for Christ, Habitat for Humanity, Order of the Black and Gold, ACLU, College Democrats/Republicans, Wesley Foundation, Westminster Canterbury Fellowship, Circle K.

**Athletics.** NCAA. **Intercollegiate:** Baseball M, basketball, cross-country, field hockey W, football (tackle) M, golf, soccer, softball W, tennis, track and field, volleyball W, wrestling M. **Intramural:** Badminton, basketball, football (non-tackle), golf, racquetball, soccer, softball, swimming, table tennis, tennis, triathlon, volleyball. **Team name:** Mountaineers.

**Student services.** Adult student services, alcohol/substance abuse counseling, chaplain/spiritual director, career counseling, student employment services, financial aid counseling, health services, minority student services, on-campus daycare, personal counseling, placement for graduates, veterans' counselor, women's services. **Physically disabled:** Services for visually, speech, hearing impaired. **Learning disabled:** Comprehensive services available.

**Contact.** E-mail: admissions@appstate.edu
Phone: (828) 262-2000 Fax: (828) 262-3296
Misti Reese, Director of Admissions, Appalachian State University, ASU Box 32004, Boone, NC 28608

## Art Institute of Charlotte
**Charlotte, North Carolina**
www.artinstitutes.edu/charlotte          CB code: 3834

◆ For-profit 4-year visual arts and career college
◆ Commuter campus in very large city
◆ 1,024 degree-seeking undergraduates: 24% part-time, 66% women, 37% African American, 2% Asian American, 6% Hispanic American, 1% Native American
◆ Application essay, interview required

**General.** Accredited by ACICS. **Degrees:** 80 bachelor's, 104 associate awarded. **Location:** 8 miles from Center City. **Calendar:** Quarter, extensive summer session. **Full-time faculty:** 41 total; 17% have terminal degrees, 32% minority, 46% women. **Part-time faculty:** 30 total; 10% have terminal degrees, 13% minority, 57% women. **Class size:** 75% < 20, 25% 20-39. **Special facilities:** Computer labs, interior design lighting laboratory, photography studio, audio/video production studios, teaching restaurant open to the public.

**Basis for selection.** Open admission, but selective for some programs. Interviews required. Applicant must provide a written essay and high school transcripts with minimum 2.0 GPA. Students with a 2.0 average or lower required to take Accuplacer placement test. **Homeschooled:** Statement describing homeschool structure and mission, transcript of courses and grades, interview required.

**2009-2010 Annual costs.** Tuition/fees: $22,188. Fees for culinary students $300; fees for all other students $150. Housing cost is for four-person, furnished apartment and includes utilities (elect/water), washer/dryer, and free transportation between housing and campus. Room only: $4,950.

**2009-2010 Financial aid. Need-based:** 21% of total undergraduate aid awarded as scholarships/grants, 79% as loans/jobs.

**Application procedures. Admission:** No deadline. $150 fee. Admission notification on a rolling basis. **Financial aid:** No deadline. FAFSA required. Applicants notified on a rolling basis starting 7/1; must reply within 1 week(s) of notification.

**Academics.** Students begin studies in the majors alongside general education classes from the first quarter. **Special study options:** Distance learning, internships, study abroad. **Credit/placement by examination:** CLEP. **Support services:** Learning center, remedial instruction, study skills assistance, tutoring, writing center.

**Majors. Business:** Apparel. **Computer sciences:** Web page design. **Personal/ culinary services:** Culinary arts. **Visual/performing arts:** Graphic design, interior design.

**Computing on campus.** 224 workstations in library, computer center, student center. Commuter students can connect to campus network. Online library, helpline, student web hosting, wireless network available.

**Student life. Freshman orientation:** Mandatory. Preregistration for classes offered. Orientation is held the Saturday prior to the first day of classes which is typically on Monday. **Policies:** No weapons, drugs, or alcohol permitted on campus or in on-campus housing. **Housing:** Apartments available. $450 fully refundable deposit. **Activities:** Campus ministries, choral groups, student newspaper, VerseOne.

**Student services.** Alcohol/substance abuse counseling, career counseling, student employment services, financial aid counseling, personal counseling, placement for graduates, veterans' counselor.

**Contact.** E-mail: aichadm@aii.edu
Phone: (704) 357-8020 Toll-free number: (800) 872-4417
Fax: (704) 357-1133
Michelle Idle, Senior Director of Admissions, Art Institute of Charlotte, Three LakePointe Plaza, Charlotte, NC 28217-4536

## Barton College
**Wilson, North Carolina**          CB member
www.barton.edu          CB code: 5016

◆ Private 4-year liberal arts college affiliated with Christian Church (Disciples of Christ)
◆ Residential campus in large town

◆ 1,126 degree-seeking undergraduates: 22% part-time, 71% women, 26% African American, 2% Asian American, 2% Hispanic American, 1% Native American, 1% international
◆ 51% of applicants admitted
◆ SAT or ACT (ACT writing optional) required
◆ 40% graduate within 6 years

**General.** Founded in 1902. Regionally accredited. **Degrees:** 230 bachelor's awarded. **Location:** 45 miles from Raleigh. **Calendar:** 4-1-4, limited summer session. **Full-time faculty:** 68 total; 69% have terminal degrees, 9% minority, 47% women. **Part-time faculty:** 49 total; 8% have terminal degrees, 8% minority, 74% women. **Class size:** 64% < 20, 35% 20-39, less than 1% 40-49. **Special facilities:** Lula E. Rackley Gallery and the Virginia Thompson Graves Gallery of the Barton Museum, greenhouse, TV and music recording studios, photo developing labs and darkroom.

**Freshman class profile.** 2,681 applied, 1,360 admitted, 231 enrolled.

| Mid 50% test scores | | | |
|---|---|---|---|
| SAT critical reading: | 390-570 | GPA 2.0-2.99: | 46% |
| SAT math: | 400-590 | Rank in top quarter: | 31% |
| SAT writing: | 380-540 | Rank in top tenth: | 5% |
| ACT composite: | 16-24 | Return as sophomores: | 67% |
| GPA 3.75 or higher: | 9% | Out-of-state: | 18% |
| GPA 3.50-3.74: | 11% | Live on campus: | 91% |
| GPA 3.0-3.49: | 34% | International: | 1% |

**Basis for selection.** High school GPA, test scores, strong academic course study important. Interview recommended for marginal students; portfolio recommended for art students. **Homeschooled:** State high school equivalency certificate required.

**High school preparation.** 13 units required. Required and recommended units include English 4, mathematics 3, social studies 2, science 2 (laboratory 1), foreign language 2 and academic electives 1.

**2009-2010 Annual costs.** Tuition/fees: $20,648. Room/board: $7,012.

**2009-2010 Financial aid. Need-based:** 217 full-time freshmen applied for aid; 204 were judged to have need; 204 of these received aid. Average need met was 76%. Average scholarship/grant was $6,347; average loan $4,927. 47% of total undergraduate aid awarded as scholarships/grants, 53% as loans/jobs. **Non-need-based:** Awarded to 880 full-time undergraduates, including 235 freshmen. Scholarships awarded for academics, alumni affiliation, art, athletics, leadership, minority status, music/drama, religious affiliation, state residency.

**Application procedures. Admission:** No deadline. $25 fee, may be waived for applicants with need, free for online applicants. Admission notification on a rolling basis. Must reply by May 1 or within 2 week(s) if notified thereafter. **Financial aid:** Priority date 4/1; no closing date. FAFSA required. Applicants notified on a rolling basis starting 5/1; must reply within 2 week(s) of notification.

**Academics. Special study options:** Cooperative education, double major, ESL, honors, independent study, internships, liberal arts/career combination, study abroad, teacher certification program, Washington semester, weekend college. **Credit/placement by examination:** AP, CLEP, IB, SAT, ACT, institutional tests. 30 credit hours maximum toward bachelor's degree. **Support services:** Remedial instruction, study skills assistance, tutoring, writing center.

**Majors. Biology:** General. **Business:** Accounting, business admin, human resources. **Communications:** Media studies. **Computer sciences:** General. **Conservation:** Environmental science. **Education:** Art, Deaf/hearing impaired, elementary, learning disabled, middle, physical, social studies. **Foreign languages:** Spanish. **Health:** Athletic training, nursing (RN). **History:** General. **Interdisciplinary:** Gerontology. **Liberal arts:** Arts/sciences. **Math:** General. **Parks/recreation:** Health/fitness, sports admin. **Philosophy/ religion:** Religion. **Physical sciences:** Chemistry. **Protective services:** Criminal justice. **Psychology:** General. **Public administration:** Social work. **Social sciences:** Political science. **Visual/performing arts:** Dramatic, studio arts.

**Most popular majors.** Business/marketing 26%, education 17%, health sciences 19%, public administration/social services 6%, social sciences 7%.

**Computing on campus.** 176 workstations in dormitories, library, computer center, student center. Dormitories wired for high-speed internet access and linked to campus network. Commuter students can connect to campus network. Online library, helpline, wireless network available.

**Student life. Freshman orientation:** Mandatory, $75 fee. Preregistration for classes offered. Two-day sessions held during June. **Housing:** Guaranteed on-campus for freshmen. Coed dorms, single-sex dorms, special housing for disabled, fraternity/sorority housing, wellness housing available. $150 nonrefundable deposit, deadline 5/1. Full-time freshmen and sophomores not living with parents required to live on campus. Special permission required for students under 23 to live off-campus. **Activities:** Pep band, campus ministries, choral groups, dance, drama, literary magazine, musical theater, student government, student newspaper, symphony orchestra, TV station, Disciples on Campus, Fellowship of Christian Athletes, Habitat for Humanity, Alpha Phi Omega, Campus Conservatives, College Democrats, diversity education team, political science club, Campus Crusade for Christ.

**Athletics.** NCAA. **Intercollegiate:** Baseball M, basketball, cross-country, golf M, soccer, softball W, tennis, volleyball W. **Intramural:** Badminton, basketball, football (non-tackle), soccer, softball, tennis, volleyball. **Team name:** Bulldogs.

**Student services.** Adult student services, chaplain/spiritual director, career counseling, student employment services, financial aid counseling, health services, personal counseling, placement for graduates. **Physically disabled:** Services for visually, speech, hearing impaired.

**Contact.** E-mail: enroll@barton.edu
Phone: (252) 399-6317 Toll-free number: (800) 345-4973
Fax: (252) 399-6572
Amanda Metts, Director of Admissions, Barton College, Box 5000, Wilson, NC 27893-7000

## Belmont Abbey College
**Belmont, North Carolina**  **CB member**
**www.belmontabbeycollege.edu**  **CB code: 5055**

- Private 4-year liberal arts college affiliated with Roman Catholic Church
- Residential campus in small town
- 1,625 degree-seeking undergraduates: 6% part-time, 63% women
- 75% of applicants admitted
- SAT or ACT with writing required

**General.** Founded in 1876. Regionally accredited. **Degrees:** 219 bachelor's awarded. **ROTC:** Army, Naval, Air Force. **Location:** 10 miles from Charlotte. **Calendar:** Semester, limited summer session. **Full-time faculty:** 69 total; 64% have terminal degrees, 3% minority. **Part-time faculty:** 69 total; 96% have terminal degrees, 4% minority. **Class size:** 66% < 20, 33% 20-39, less than 1% 40-49, less than 1% 50-99.

**Freshman class profile.** 1,762 applied, 1,321 admitted, 403 enrolled.

| Mid 50% test scores | | | |
|---|---|---|---|
| SAT critical reading: | 450-570 | GPA 2.0-2.99: | 52% |
| SAT math: | 460-550 | Rank in top quarter: | 29% |
| ACT composite: | 17-23 | Rank in top tenth: | 10% |
| GPA 3.75 or higher: | 12% | Out-of-state: | 43% |
| GPA 3.50-3.74: | 13% | Live on campus: | 90% |
| GPA 3.0-3.49: | 22% | Fraternities: | 20% |
| | | Sororities: | 20% |

**Basis for selection.** GPA, class rank, high school curriculum, and test scores most important. Personal accomplishments, extracurricular activities, and letters of recommendation strongly considered.

**High school preparation.** College-preparatory program recommended. 16 units required. Required and recommended units include English 4, mathematics 3-4, social studies 1, history 1, science 2, foreign language 2-3 and academic electives 3. For science majors 4 math, 1 chemistry, 1 physics, 1 additional science recommended.

**2009-2010 Annual costs.** Tuition/fees: $22,512. Room/board: $9,702. Books/supplies: $1,000. Personal expenses: $2,000.

**2009-2010 Financial aid. Non-need-based:** Scholarships awarded for academics, athletics, leadership, religious affiliation, state residency.

**Application procedures. Admission:** Closing date 8/1 (postmark date). $35 fee, may be waived for applicants with need, free for online applicants. Admission notification on a rolling basis beginning on or about 9/15. Must reply by May 1 or within 3 week(s) if notified thereafter. **Financial aid:** Priority date 4/1; no closing date. FAFSA required. Applicants notified on a rolling basis starting 3/1; must reply within 2 week(s) of notification.

**Academics. Special study options:** Accelerated study, double major, dual enrollment of high school students, honors, independent study, internships, liberal arts/career combination, study abroad, teacher certification program, weekend college. **Credit/placement by examination:** AP, CLEP, IB, institutional tests. 30 credit hours maximum toward bachelor's degree. **Support services:** Learning center, study skills assistance, tutoring, writing center.

**Honors college/program.** Students with the following considered for The Honors Institute: 3.70 or higher high school GPA (unweighted); 1200 SAT score (minimum verbal score of 600); Honors Institute application including an essay and personal interview. Honors Institute includes expanded 4-year core curriculum based on Great Books, $3,500 travel stipend for summer study in Europe or The Washington Experience, a week in the nation's capital, beach/mountain retreats with faculty, and extensive cultural appreciation opportunities.

**Majors. Biology:** General. **Business:** Accounting, business admin. **Computer sciences:** Programming. **Education:** General, elementary. **Health:** Predental, premedicine, prepharmacy, preveterinary. **History:** General. **Legal studies:** Prelaw. **Liberal arts:** Arts/sciences. **Math:** General. **Philosophy/religion:** Philosophy, religion. **Protective services:** Criminal justice. **Psychology:** General. **Social sciences:** General, criminology, economics, political science, sociology. **Other:** Applied psychology.

**Most popular majors.** Biology 9%, business/marketing 49%, education 17%, social sciences 6%.

**Computing on campus.** 56 workstations in library, computer center, student center. Dormitories wired for high-speed internet access and linked to campus network. Commuter students can connect to campus network. Online course registration, online library, helpline, wireless network available.

**Student life. Freshman orientation:** Mandatory. Preregistration for classes offered. 4 days prior to class start. **Housing:** Guaranteed on-campus for all undergraduates. Coed dorms, single-sex dorms, special housing for disabled, apartments available. $400 deposit, deadline 8/24. 24-hour quiet (honors) dorm available. **Activities:** Campus ministries, choral groups, drama, international student organizations, literary magazine, musical theater, student government, student newspaper, BAC College Republicans, Belmont Abbey College Democrats, Delta Psi Theta Sorority, International Club, Association of Latino Professionals in Finance & Accounting.

**Athletics.** NCAA. **Intercollegiate:** Baseball M, basketball, cheerleading, cross-country, golf, lacrosse, soccer, softball W, volleyball W, wrestling M. **Intramural:** Basketball, bowling, cross-country, football (non-tackle) M, golf, softball, table tennis, volleyball. **Team name:** Crusaders.

**Student services.** Adult student services, alcohol/substance abuse counseling, chaplain/spiritual director, career counseling, student employment services, financial aid counseling, health services, personal counseling, placement for graduates, veterans' counselor. **Physically disabled:** Services for visually, speech, hearing impaired.

**Contact.** E-mail: admissions@bac.edu
Phone: (704) 461-6665 Toll-free number: (888) 222-0110
Fax: (704) 461-6220
Roger Jones, Director of Admissions, Belmont Abbey College, 100 Belmont - Mt. Holly Road, Belmont, NC 28012-2795

## Bennett College for Women
**Greensboro, North Carolina**  **CB member**
**www.bennett.edu**  **CB code: 5058**

- Private 4-year liberal arts college for women affiliated with United Methodist Church
- Residential campus in small city
- 711 degree-seeking undergraduates: 1% part-time, 100% women, 96% African American, 1% Hispanic American, 1% international
- 54% of applicants admitted
- Application essay required
- 48% graduate within 6 years

**General.** Founded in 1873. Regionally accredited. **Degrees:** 99 bachelor's awarded. **ROTC:** Army, Air Force. **Location:** 26 miles from Winston-Salem, 80 miles from Raleigh. **Calendar:** Semester, limited summer session. **Full-time faculty:** 56 total; 61% have terminal degrees, 64% minority, 71% women. **Part-time faculty:** 26 total; 8% have terminal degrees, 73% minority, 69% women. **Class size:** 68% < 20, 23% 20-39, 2% 40-49, 4% 50-99, 1% >100. **Special facilities:** Women's Leadership Institute, Carnegie Negro Library.

**Freshman class profile.** 1,676 applied, 905 admitted, 232 enrolled.

| Mid 50% test scores | | | |
|---|---|---|---|
| SAT critical reading: | 350-450 | GPA 2.0-2.99: | 69% |
| SAT math: | 320-420 | Rank in top quarter: | 10% |
| ACT composite: | 15-18 | Rank in top tenth: | 3% |
| GPA 3.75 or higher: | 1% | End year in good standing: | 87% |
| GPA 3.50-3.74: | 4% | Return as sophomores: | 75% |
| GPA 3.0-3.49: | 9% | Out-of-state: | 67% |
| | | Live on campus: | 98% |

**Basis for selection.** School achievement record, test scores, recommendations of counselors, and applicant's personal statement important. SAT or ACT recommended. Interview recommended for borderline students. **Homeschooled:** Transcript of courses and grades, letter of recommendation (nonparent) required.

**High school preparation.** College-preparatory program recommended. 18 units required. Required units include English 4, mathematics 3, social studies 2, science 2, foreign language 2 and academic electives 5.

**2009-2010 Annual costs.** Tuition/fees: $15,234. Room/board: $6,736. Books/supplies: $1,200. Personal expenses: $3,000.

**2009-2010 Financial aid. Need-based:** 221 full-time freshmen applied for aid; 214 were judged to have need; 214 of these received aid. Average need met was 49%. Average scholarship/grant was $10,070; average loan $3,468. 49% of total undergraduate aid awarded as scholarships/grants, 51% as loans/jobs. **Non-need-based:** Awarded to 23 full-time undergraduates, including 4 freshmen. Scholarships awarded for state residency.

**Application procedures. Admission:** No deadline. $30 fee, may be waived for applicants with need. Admission notification on a rolling basis. **Financial aid:** Closing date 4/15. FAFSA, institutional form required. Applicants notified by 7/15.

**Academics.** Accepted students who do not meet required SAT or ACT score admitted to Academic Enrichment Program which provides tutoring, counseling and other support services. **Special study options:** Accelerated study, cooperative education, cross-registration, double major, dual enrollment of high school students, exchange student, honors, independent study, internships, liberal arts/career combination, student-designed major, study abroad, teacher certification program, Washington semester. Bennett offers dual degree programs in engineering with North Carolina Agricultural and Technical State University. A calloborative program with Howard University in nursing is also available. **Credit/placement by examination:** AP, CLEP, SAT, ACT, institutional tests. **Support services:** Learning center, pre-admission summer program, reduced course load, remedial instruction, tutoring, writing center.

**Majors. Biology:** General. **Business:** Accounting, business admin. **Communications:** Media studies. **Computer sciences:** General. **Education:** Elementary, English, mathematics, mentally handicapped, middle, music. **Math:** General. **Physical sciences:** Chemistry. **Psychology:** General. **Public administration:** Social work. **Social sciences:** Political science, sociology. **Visual/performing arts:** General, arts management. **Other:** Interdisciplinary studies/special studies.

**Most popular majors.** Biology 9%, business/marketing 11%, communications/journalism 13%, education 8%, English 8%, interdisciplinary studies 8%, psychology 15%, public administration/social services 15%, social sciences 8%.

**Computing on campus.** 130 workstations in dormitories, library, computer center. Dormitories wired for high-speed internet access and linked to campus network. Commuter students can connect to campus network. Online library, wireless network available.

**Student life. Freshman orientation:** Mandatory, $100 fee. Preregistration for classes offered. **Housing:** Guaranteed on-campus for all undergraduates. Wellness housing available. $100 deposit. Students with GPA of 3.0 may reside in honor residence hall. **Activities:** Campus ministries, choral groups, dance, drama, film society, international student organizations, literary magazine, music ensembles, radio station, student government, student newspaper, TV station, Student Christian Fellowship, NAACP, social work club, Women in Communications, student teachers association, psychology club, political science club.

**Athletics.** NCAA. **Intercollegiate:** Basketball W. **Intramural:** Basketball W, softball W, swimming W, tennis W, volleyball W. **Team name:** Belles.

**Student services.** Chaplain/spiritual director, career counseling, student employment services, financial aid counseling, health services, on-campus daycare, personal counseling, placement for graduates.

**Contact.** E-mail: admiss@bennett.edu
Phone: (336) 370-8624 Toll-free number: (800) 413-5323
Fax: (336) 517-2166
Jocelyn Biggs, Director of Admissions, Bennett College for Women, 900 East Washington Street, Greensboro, NC 27401-3239

---

## Brevard College

Brevard, North Carolina
www.brevard.edu

**CB member**
**CB code: 5067**

- Private 4-year liberal arts college affiliated with United Methodist Church
- Residential campus in small town

---

- 651 degree-seeking undergraduates: 1% part-time, 43% women, 11% African American, 2% Hispanic American, 1% Native American, 3% international
- 54% of applicants admitted
- SAT or ACT (ACT writing recommended), application essay required
- 33% graduate within 6 years

**General.** Founded in 1853. Regionally accredited. **Degrees:** 107 bachelor's awarded. **Location:** 33 miles from Asheville. **Calendar:** Semester. **Full-time faculty:** 55 total; 67% have terminal degrees, 40% women. **Part-time faculty:** 35 total; 43% have terminal degrees, 43% women. **Class size:** 75% < 20, 25% 20-39. **Special facilities:** Mountain climbing wall, ropes challenge course, Appalachian center for environmental education, fitness appraisal lab, forest institute, performing arts center, academic enrichment center.

**Freshman class profile.** 1,191 applied, 640 admitted, 191 enrolled.

| Mid 50% test scores | | | |
|---|---|---|---|
| SAT critical reading: | 420-540 | Rank in top quarter: | 22% |
| SAT math: | 430-550 | Rank in top tenth: | 7% |
| ACT composite: | 16-21 | End year in good standing: | 77% |
| GPA 3.75 or higher: | 5% | Return as sophomores: | 58% |
| GPA 3.50-3.74: | 7% | Out-of-state: | 48% |
| GPA 3.0-3.49: | 27% | Live on campus: | 93% |
| GPA 2.0-2.99: | 57% | International: | 1% |

**Basis for selection.** High school record, class rank, SAT/ACT scores, references, extracurricular activities, recommendations, essay, interview, talent/ability, character/personal qualities, volunteer work important. Essay, interview recommended for all students; portfolio required for art students; audition required for music students. **Homeschooled:** Statement describing homeschool structure and mission, transcript of courses and grades required. Legal documentation from homeschool agency, local school district, or State Department of Education and admissions interview required. **Learning Disabled:** Evaluation by licensed professional within past 3 years.

**High school preparation.** 22 units recommended. Recommended units include English 4, mathematics 3, social studies 4, history 1, science 3 (laboratory 1), foreign language 2 and academic electives 4. Math units should include 2 algebra and 1 geometry.

**2009-2010 Annual costs.** Tuition/fees: $20,900. Room/board: $7,850. Books/supplies: $1,000. Personal expenses: $1,000.

**2009-2010 Financial aid. Need-based:** 150 full-time freshmen applied for aid; 132 were judged to have need; 132 of these received aid. Average need met was 81%. Average scholarship/grant was $13,500; average loan $3,850. 68% of total undergraduate aid awarded as scholarships/grants, 32% as loans/jobs. **Non-need-based:** Awarded to 245 full-time undergraduates, including 64 freshmen. Scholarships awarded for academics, art, athletics, leadership, music/drama, religious affiliation, state residency.

**Application procedures. Admission:** No deadline. $30 fee, may be waived for applicants with need, free for online applicants. Admission notification on a rolling basis beginning on or about 7/1. **Financial aid:** Priority date 4/15; no closing date. FAFSA required. Applicants notified on a rolling basis starting 2/1; must reply within 4 week(s) of notification.

**Academics. Special study options:** Double major, dual enrollment of high school students, honors, independent study, internships, student-designed major, study abroad, teacher certification program. **Credit/placement by examination:** AP, CLEP, IB, SAT, ACT, institutional tests. 92 credit hours maximum toward bachelor's degree. **Support services:** Learning center, reduced course load, remedial instruction, study skills assistance, tutoring, writing center.

**Majors. Biology:** Ecology. **Business:** Business admin. **Conservation:** Environmental science, environmental studies. **Education:** General, art, drama/dance, elementary, English, mathematics, multi-level teacher, music, physical, science, secondary, social studies. **Health:** Health services, predental, premedicine, prenursing, preveterinary. **History:** General. **Interdisciplinary:** Biological/physical sciences. **Liberal arts:** Arts/sciences. **Math:** General. **Parks/recreation:** Exercise sciences, facilities management. **Philosophy/religion:** Religion. **Protective services:** Law enforcement admin. **Psychology:** General. **Visual/performing arts:** Art, dramatic, music performance.

**Most popular majors.** Business/marketing 12%, health sciences 8%, interdisciplinary studies 28%, parks/recreation 19%, visual/performing arts 11%.

**Computing on campus.** 100 workstations in dormitories, library, computer center, student center. Dormitories wired for high-speed internet access and linked to campus network. Online library, helpline, wireless network available.

**Student life. Freshman orientation:** Mandatory, $95 fee. Preregistration for classes offered. Orientations held in August prior to start of classes. **Housing:** Guaranteed on-campus for all undergraduates. Coed dorms, single-sex dorms, special housing for disabled, wellness housing available. All non-county or non-adjacent-county residents required to live on campus until age 21. **Activities:** Bands, campus ministries, choral groups, dance, drama, literary magazine, music ensembles, musical theater, opera, student government, student newspaper, Recycling Club, Fellowship of Christian Athletes, Omicron Delta Kappa, Outing Club, Environmental Educators, History Club, Young Politicians of America, Business Club, Debate Society.

**Athletics. NCAA. Intercollegiate:** Baseball M, basketball, cheerleading M, cross-country, football (tackle) M, golf, soccer, softball W, tennis, track and field, volleyball W. **Intramural:** Archery, badminton, basketball, bowling, cross-country, equestrian, football (tackle) M, golf, skiing, soccer, softball, swimming, tennis, track and field, volleyball. **Team name:** Tornados.

**Student services.** Alcohol/substance abuse counseling, chaplain/spiritual director, career counseling, student employment services, financial aid counseling, health services, personal counseling, placement for graduates, veterans' counselor. **Physically disabled:** Services for visually, speech, hearing impaired.

**Contact.** E-mail: admissions@brevard.edu
Phone: (828) 883-8292 Toll-free number: (800) 527-9090
Fax: (828) 884-3790
Mathew Cox, Vice President of Admissions, Brevard College, One Brevard College Drive, Brevard, NC 28712

## Cabarrus College of Health Sciences
**Concord, North Carolina**
www.cabarruscollege.edu                                    CB code: 5136

- Private 4-year health science and nursing college
- Commuter campus in small city
- 407 degree-seeking undergraduates: 48% part-time, 89% women, 9% African American, 2% Asian American, 3% Hispanic American, 1% Native American
- 88% of applicants admitted
- Application essay required

**General.** Regionally accredited. **Degrees:** 14 bachelor's, 105 associate awarded. **Location:** 25 miles from Charlotte. **Calendar:** Semester, limited summer session. **Full-time faculty:** 36 total; 8% have terminal degrees, 6% minority, 94% women. **Part-time faculty:** 25 total; 24% have terminal degrees, 8% minority, 64% women. **Class size:** 64% < 20, 27% 20-39, 2% 40-49, 8% 50-99.

**Freshman class profile.** 49 applied, 43 admitted, 21 enrolled.

| Mid 50% test scores | | | |
|---|---|---|---|
| SAT critical reading: | 480-560 | GPA 3.50-3.74: | 14% |
| SAT math: | 450-520 | GPA 3.0-3.49: | 19% |
| ACT composite: | 19-21 | GPA 2.0-2.99: | 10% |
| GPA 3.75 or higher: | 57% | Rank in top quarter: | 52% |
| | | Rank in top tenth: | 19% |

**Basis for selection.** School record, class rank, essay, test scores, and recommendations most important.

**High school preparation.** Required and recommended units include English 4, mathematics 3, science 2 (laboratory 2) and foreign language 2.

**2009-2010 Annual costs.** Tuition/fees: $9,950. Books/supplies: $1,300.

**Application procedures. Admission:** Priority date 3/1; no deadline. $50 fee, may be waived for applicants with need.

**Academics. Special study options:** Cross-registration, distance learning, liberal arts/career combination. **Credit/placement by examination:** AP, CLEP, institutional tests. 15 credit hours maximum toward associate degree, 15 toward bachelor's. **Support services:** Learning center, study skills assistance.

**Majors. Health:** Health care admin, health services admin, nursing (RN).

**Computing on campus.** 24 workstations in library, computer center, student center. Commuter students can connect to campus network. Online library, wireless network available.

**Student life. Freshman orientation:** Mandatory. Preregistration for classes offered. 2-day orientation before start of first semester. **Activities:** Student government, student newspaper, Christian student union, association of nursing students, Rotaract.

**Student services.** Career counseling, financial aid counseling, on-campus daycare, personal counseling. **Physically disabled:** Services for hearing impaired.

**Contact.** E-mail: admissions@cabarruscollege.edu
Phone: (704) 403-1556 Fax: (704) 403-2077
Mark Ellison, Director of Admissions, Cabarrus College of Health Sciences, 401 Medical Park Drive, Concord, NC 28025-2405

## Campbell University
**Buies Creek, North Carolina**                            CB member
www.campbell.edu                                            CB code: 5100

- Private 4-year university and liberal arts college
- Residential campus in small town
- 2,755 degree-seeking undergraduates
- 35% of applicants admitted
- SAT or ACT (ACT writing recommended) required

**General.** Founded in 1887. Regionally accredited. **Degrees:** 953 bachelor's, 144 associate awarded; master's, professional offered. **ROTC:** Army. **Location:** 30 miles from Raleigh, 30 miles from Fayetteville. **Calendar:** Semester, extensive summer session. **Full-time faculty:** 196 total; 90% have terminal degrees, 36% women. **Part-time faculty:** 109 total; 50% have terminal degrees, 50% women. **Class size:** 55% < 20, 27% 20-39, 7% 40-49, 10% 50-99, less than 1% >100. **Special facilities:** Golf course, animal museum, drug information center, nature trail.

**Freshman class profile.** 5,115 applied, 1,790 admitted, 912 enrolled.

| Mid 50% test scores | | | |
|---|---|---|---|
| SAT critical reading: | 440-560 | GPA 3.0-3.49: | 20% |
| SAT math: | 460-580 | GPA 2.0-2.99: | 6% |
| SAT writing: | 430-550 | Rank in top quarter: | 81% |
| ACT composite: | 19-24 | Rank in top tenth: | 41% |
| GPA 3.75 or higher: | 63% | Out-of-state: | 20% |
| GPA 3.50-3.74: | 11% | Live on campus: | 80% |

**Basis for selection.** SAT, GPA, course selection, class rank, and standardized test scores considered. Students with less than the acceptable threshold may be considered for probational admission. Candidates reviewed on an individual basis. Interview recommended on a case by case basis. Essay recommended for all students; audition recommended for music programs.

**High school preparation.** College-preparatory program recommended. 13 units recommended. Recommended units include English 4, mathematics 3, social studies 2, science 2 (laboratory 1) and foreign language 2. One social science should be U.S. History. Math units must include algebra I and II as well as geometry.

**2010-2011 Annual costs.** Tuition/fees: $22,520. Room/board: $7,800. Books/supplies: $1,500.

**2009-2010 Financial aid. Non-need-based:** Scholarships awarded for academics, athletics, music/drama, ROTC, state residency.

**Application procedures. Admission:** No deadline. $35 fee, may be waived for applicants with need. Admission notification on a rolling basis. **Financial aid:** Priority date 3/15; no closing date. FAFSA required. Applicants notified on a rolling basis.

**Academics. Special study options:** Accelerated study, combined bachelor's/graduate degree, cooperative education, distance learning, double major, dual enrollment of high school students, exchange student, honors, independent study, internships, liberal arts/career combination, study abroad, teacher certification program, Washington semester. **Credit/placement by examination:** AP, CLEP, IB, SAT, ACT. **Support services:** Reduced course load, remedial instruction, study skills assistance, tutoring, writing center.

**Majors. Biology:** General, biochemistry. **Business:** General, accounting, business admin, communications, financial planning, international, management information systems. **Communications:** Advertising, broadcast journalism, journalism, public relations, radio/tv. **Computer sciences:** Computer graphics, computer science, information systems. **Education:** General, biology, early childhood, elementary, English, French, history, mathematics, middle, music, physical, secondary, social studies, Spanish. **Family/consumer sciences:** Child development, family studies. **Foreign languages:** French, Spanish. **Health:** Athletic training, predental, premedicine, prepharmacy, preveterinary. **History:** General. **Legal studies:** Prelaw. **Math:** General. **Parks/recreation:** Exercise sciences, health/fitness, sports admin. **Philosophy/religion:** Religion. **Physical sciences:** Chemistry. **Protective services:** Criminal justice. **Psychology:** General. **Public administration:** General, social work. **Social sciences:** Economics, international relations, political science. **Theology:** Religious ed, sacred music. **Visual/**

**performing arts:** Commercial/advertising art, dramatic, piano/organ, studio arts, voice/opera.

**Most popular majors.** Business/marketing 28%, health sciences 6%, liberal arts 12%, psychology 10%, social sciences 6%.

**Computing on campus.** Dormitories wired for high-speed internet access and linked to campus network. Commuter students can connect to campus network. Helpline, wireless network available.

**Student life. Freshman orientation:** Mandatory, $50 fee. Two weekend sessions in summer available to incoming freshmen and their families for students entering in Fall. Short program before classes start for students entering in Spring. **Policies:** Religious observance required. **Housing:** Guaranteed on-campus for freshmen. Single-sex dorms, special housing for disabled, apartments available. $100 fully refundable deposit. **Activities:** Bands, campus ministries, choral groups, drama, international student organizations, literary magazine, music ensembles, musical theater, student government, student newspaper, Baptist Student Union, College Democrats/Republicans, Fellowship of Christian Athletes, North Carolina Student Legislators, Campus Crusade, Christians in Action, Campbell Catholic Community, Circle K.

**Athletics.** NCAA. **Intercollegiate:** Baseball M, basketball, cheerleading, cross-country, football (tackle) M, golf, soccer, softball W, swimming W, tennis, track and field, volleyball W, wrestling M. **Intramural:** Basketball, football (non-tackle), soccer, softball, swimming, table tennis, tennis, volleyball, water polo. **Team name:** Fighting Camels.

**Student services.** Adult student services, alcohol/substance abuse counseling, chaplain/spiritual director, career counseling, student employment services, financial aid counseling, health services, personal counseling, placement for graduates, veterans' counselor. **Physically disabled:** Services for visually, speech, hearing impaired.

**Contact.** E-mail: buildyourfuture@campbell.edu
Phone: (910) 893-1290 ext. 1290 Toll-free
number: (800) 334-4111 ext. 1290 Fax: (910) 893-1288
Jason Hall, Assistant Vice President for Admissions, Campbell University, PO Box 546, Buies Creek, NC 27506

## Carolina Christian College
### Winston-Salem, North Carolina
### www.carolina.edu

- Private 4-year Bible college affiliated with Church of Christ
- Commuter campus in large city
- 41 degree-seeking undergraduates
- Application essay required

**General.** Accredited by ABHE. **Degrees:** 10 bachelor's awarded. **Calendar:** Differs by program, limited summer session. **Full-time faculty:** 1 total. **Part-time faculty:** 7 total; 29% have terminal degrees, 71% minority, 71% women.

**Freshman class profile.** 18 applied, 18 admitted, 18 enrolled.

**Basis for selection.** Open admission. COMPASS test required.

**2009-2010 Annual costs.** Tuition/fees: $4,700. Books/supplies: $500.

**Application procedures. Admission:** No deadline. $50 fee, may be waived for applicants with need. Application must be submitted on paper. Admission notification on a rolling basis. **Financial aid:** No deadline. FAFSA required. Applicants notified on a rolling basis.

**Academics. Special study options:** Accelerated study, independent study. **Credit/placement by examination:** CLEP. 12 credit hours maximum toward associate degree, 24 toward bachelor's. **Support services:** Remedial instruction.

**Majors. Theology:** Bible.

**Computing on campus.** 8 workstations in library. Wireless network available.

**Student life. Freshman orientation:** Available. **Activities:** Campus ministries, student government.

**Contact.** Phone: (336) 744-0900 ext. 103 Fax: (336) 744-0901
LaTanya Lucas, Academic Dean, Carolina Christian College, Box 777, Winston-Salem, NC 27102

## Catawba College
### Salisbury, North Carolina
CB member
### www.catawba.edu
CB code: 5103

- Private 4-year liberal arts college affiliated with United Church of Christ
- Residential campus in large town
- 1,324 degree-seeking undergraduates: 4% part-time, 52% women, 18% African American, 1% Asian American, 1% Hispanic American, 2% international
- 34 degree-seeking graduate students
- 70% of applicants admitted
- SAT or ACT (ACT writing recommended), application essay required
- 58% graduate within 6 years; 13% enter graduate study

**General.** Founded in 1851. Regionally accredited. **Degrees:** 257 bachelor's awarded; master's offered. **ROTC:** Army. **Location:** 30 miles from Charlotte, 50 miles from Greensboro. **Calendar:** Semester, limited summer session. **Full-time faculty:** 71 total; 87% have terminal degrees, 7% minority, 42% women. **Part-time faculty:** 35 total; 29% have terminal degrees, 3% minority, 51% women. **Class size:** 53% < 20, 44% 20-39, 2% 40-49, less than 1% 50-99. **Special facilities:** Comprehensive three-manual Casavant pipe-organ, observatory, 45-acre outdoor biological laboratory, nature preserve.

**Freshman class profile.** 1,104 applied, 768 admitted, 308 enrolled.

| Mid 50% test scores | | | |
|---|---|---|---|
| SAT critical reading: | 440-580 | GPA 2.0-2.99: | 22% |
| SAT math: | 470-520 | Rank in top quarter: | 43% |
| ACT composite: | 18-25 | Rank in top tenth: | 17% |
| GPA 3.75 or higher: | 36% | Return as sophomores: | 71% |
| GPA 3.50-3.74: | 12% | Out-of-state: | 30% |
| GPA 3.0-3.49: | 30% | Live on campus: | 87% |
| | | International: | 1% |

**Basis for selection.** School achievement record, class rank, standardized test scores, school recommendations important. SAT preferred, but ACT also accepted. Interview recommended for all students; audition recommended for drama, music programs.

**High school preparation.** College-preparatory program recommended. 16 units required. Required and recommended units include English 4, mathematics 3, social studies 3, science 3 (laboratory 3) and foreign language 2. Required credits must be academic subjects at college preparatory level.

**2009-2010 Annual costs.** Tuition/fees: $23,740. Room/board: $8,200. Books/supplies: $1,000. Personal expenses: $1,200.

**2008-2009 Financial aid. Need-based:** 207 full-time freshmen applied for aid; 171 were judged to have need; 171 of these received aid. Average need met was 96%. Average scholarship/grant was $5,629; average loan $4,336. 50% of total undergraduate aid awarded as scholarships/grants, 50% as loans/jobs. **Non-need-based:** Awarded to 1,252 full-time undergraduates, including 292 freshmen. Scholarships awarded for academics, athletics, music/drama, state residency.

**Application procedures. Admission:** Priority date 8/1; no deadline. $25 fee, may be waived for applicants with need. Admission notification on a rolling basis beginning on or about 10/1. **Financial aid:** Priority date 3/15; no closing date. FAFSA required. Applicants notified on a rolling basis starting 11/1; must reply within 2 week(s) of notification.

**Academics. Special study options:** Cross-registration, double major, dual enrollment of high school students, honors, independent study, internships, liberal arts/career combination, student-designed major, study abroad, teacher certification program. **Credit/placement by examination:** AP, CLEP, IB, institutional tests. 30 credit hours maximum toward bachelor's degree. **Support services:** Learning center, study skills assistance, tutoring, writing center.

**Majors. Biology:** General. **Business:** Accounting, business admin, management information systems. **Communications:** General. **Conservation:** Environmental science, environmental studies. **Education:** Elementary, gifted/talented, middle, music, physical. **Foreign languages:** French, Spanish. **Health:** Athletic training, recreational therapy. **History:** General. **Legal studies:** Prelaw. **Math:** General. **Parks/recreation:** General, health/fitness, sports admin. **Philosophy/religion:** Religion. **Physical sciences:** Chemistry. **Protective services:** Law enforcement admin. **Psychology:** General. **Public administration:** General. **Social sciences:** Political science, sociology. **Visual/performing arts:** Arts management, dramatic, music performance.

**Most popular majors.** Business/marketing 38%, education 14%, visual/performing arts 11%.

**Computing on campus.** 100 workstations in dormitories, library, computer center. Dormitories wired for high-speed internet access and linked to campus network. Commuter students can connect to campus network. Helpline, repair service, wireless network available.

**Student life. Freshman orientation:** Mandatory. Orientation program week prior to start of fall classes includes advising and registration for classes. Optional summer orientation programs for students and parents at additional cost. **Housing:** Guaranteed on-campus for all undergraduates. Coed dorms, single-sex dorms, wellness housing available. $200 nonrefundable deposit. **Activities:** Bands, campus ministries, choral groups, dance, drama, international student organizations, literary magazine, music ensembles, musical theater, student government, student newspaper, symphony orchestra, Alpha program, Athenian society, Helen Foil Beard Society, political science association, environmental service clubs, Fellowship of Christian Athletes, multi-cultural club, Philomathean club, volunteer club.

**Athletics.** NCAA. **Intercollegiate:** Baseball M, basketball, cross-country, football (tackle) M, golf, lacrosse M, soccer, softball W, swimming, tennis, volleyball W. **Intramural:** Basketball, cross-country, football (tackle) M, golf, handball, racquetball, soccer, softball, table tennis, tennis, volleyball. **Team name:** Catawba Indians.

**Student services.** Adult student services, alcohol/substance abuse counseling, chaplain/spiritual director, career counseling, student employment services, financial aid counseling, health services, personal counseling, placement for graduates. **Physically disabled:** Services for hearing impaired.

**Contact.** E-mail: admission@catawba.edu
Phone: (704) 637-4402 Toll-free number: (800) 228-2922
Fax: (704) 637-4422
Lois Williams, Vice President for Enrollment Services, Catawba College, 2300 West Innes Street, Salisbury, NC 28144-2488

## Chowan University
**Murfreesboro, North Carolina**    **CB member**
**www.chowan.edu**    **CB code: 5107**

- Private 4-year university and liberal arts college affiliated with Southern Baptist Convention
- Residential campus in rural community
- 1,080 degree-seeking undergraduates
- 59% of applicants admitted
- SAT or ACT (ACT writing optional) required

**General.** Founded in 1848. Regionally accredited. **Degrees:** 91 bachelor's, 9 associate awarded; master's offered. **Calendar:** Semester, limited summer session. **Full-time faculty:** 50 total. **Part-time faculty:** 20 total. **Class size:** 64% < 20, 33% 20-39, 2% 40-49, less than 1% 50-99. **Special facilities:** Graphic communications center.

**Freshman class profile.** 2,507 applied, 1,476 admitted, 480 enrolled.

| Mid 50% test scores | | | |
|---|---|---|---|
| SAT critical reading: | 380-470 | Out-of-state: | 55% |
| SAT math: | 380-480 | Live on campus: | 84% |
| SAT writing: | 380-470 | Fraternities: | 11% |
| ACT composite: | 15-21 | Sororities: | 20% |

**Basis for selection.** School achievement record, standardized test score (SAT or ACT score), student "fit" with the institution as determined by information from the application for admission. Interview and campus visit is recommended for all students; audition required for music majors; portfolio required for graphic design and studio art majors. **Homeschooled:** State high school equivalency certificate required.

**High school preparation.** College-preparatory program recommended. Recommended units include English 4, mathematics 3, social studies 2, science 2 (laboratory 2) and academic electives 7.

**2009-2010 Annual costs.** Tuition/fees: $19,065. Room/board: $7,310. Books/supplies: $864. Personal expenses: $1,000.

**2009-2010 Financial aid. Non-need-based:** Scholarships awarded for academics, athletics, leadership, music/drama, religious affiliation, state residency.

**Application procedures. Admission:** No deadline. $20 fee, may be waived for applicants with need. Admission notification on a rolling basis. **Financial aid:** Priority date 3/1; no closing date. FAFSA required. Applicants notified on a rolling basis starting 3/1; must reply within 2 week(s) of notification.

**Academics. Special study options:** Distance learning, double major, dual enrollment of high school students, honors, independent study, internships, liberal arts/career combination, study abroad, teacher certification program. **Credit/placement by examination:** CLEP, IB, SAT. 15 credit hours maximum toward associate degree, 15 toward bachelor's. **Support services:** Learning center, reduced course load, study skills assistance, tutoring.

**Majors. Biology:** General. **Business:** Accounting/business management, business admin, information resources management, marketing, small business admin. **Communications technology:** Graphics. **Education:** General, elementary, English, history, music, physical, secondary. **Health:** Athletic training, predental, premedicine, prenursing, prepharmacy, preveterinary. **History:** General. **Legal studies:** Prelaw. **Liberal arts:** Arts/sciences. **Parks/recreation:** Exercise sciences, health/fitness, sports admin. **Philosophy/religion:** Religion. **Physical sciences:** General. **Protective services:** Law enforcement admin. **Psychology:** General. **Social sciences:** General. **Visual/performing arts:** Graphic design, music performance, studio arts.

**Most popular majors.** Biology 12%, business/marketing 11%, communications/journalism 12%, education 17%, history 8%, parks/recreation 7%, psychology 7%, security/protective services 10%, visual/performing arts 10%.

**Computing on campus.** 219 workstations in library, computer center. Dormitories wired for high-speed internet access and linked to campus network. Commuter students can connect to campus network. Online course registration, online library, helpline, repair service, wireless network available.

**Student life. Freshman orientation:** Mandatory. Preregistration for classes offered. **Policies:** No alcohol on campus; restricted dorm visitation; academic honor code. Religious observance required. **Housing:** Guaranteed on-campus for all undergraduates. Single-sex dorms, wellness housing available. $100 nonrefundable deposit. **Activities:** Bands, campus ministries, choral groups, drama, international student organizations, literary magazine, music ensembles, student government, Christian student union, Student National Education Association, Fellowship of Christian Athletes, Rotaract, international student association, Voices of Inspiration, College Democrats, College Republicans, history club, women's club.

**Athletics.** NCAA, NCCAA. **Intercollegiate:** Baseball M, basketball, cheerleading, football (tackle) M, golf M, soccer, softball W, tennis, volleyball W. **Intramural:** Basketball, football (non-tackle) M, soccer, softball, table tennis, tennis, volleyball W. **Team name:** Hawks.

**Student services.** Alcohol/substance abuse counseling, chaplain/spiritual director, career counseling, student employment services, financial aid counseling, health services, personal counseling, placement for graduates, veterans' counselor.

**Contact.** E-mail: enroll@chowan.edu
Phone: (252) 398-1235 Toll-free number: (888) 424-6926
Fax: (252) 398-1190
R. Chad Holt, Vice President for Enrollment Management, Chowan University, One University Place, Murfreesboro, NC 27855-9901

## Davidson College
**Davidson, North Carolina**    **CB member**
**www.davidson.edu**    **CB code: 5150**

- Private 4-year liberal arts college affiliated with Presbyterian Church (USA)
- Residential campus in small town
- 1,739 degree-seeking undergraduates: 51% women, 7% African American, 5% Asian American, 5% Hispanic American, 1% Native American, 3% international
- 26% of applicants admitted
- SAT or ACT (ACT writing optional), application essay required
- 91% graduate within 6 years; 25% enter graduate study

**General.** Founded in 1837. Regionally accredited. **Degrees:** 429 bachelor's awarded. **ROTC:** Army, Air Force. **Location:** 19 miles from Charlotte. **Calendar:** Semester. **Full-time faculty:** 164 total; 97% have terminal degrees, 15% minority, 38% women. **Part-time faculty:** 5 total; 40% have terminal degrees, 20% minority, 80% women. **Class size:** 72% < 20, 28% 20-39, less than 1% 40-49. **Special facilities:** Laser facility, electron microscope, campus arboretum.

**Freshman class profile.** 4,494 applied, 1,175 admitted, 491 enrolled.

| Mid 50% test scores | | | |
|---|---|---|---|
| SAT critical reading: | 630-730 | **GPA 3.0-3.49:** | 7% |
| SAT math: | 630-710 | **Rank in top quarter:** | 97% |
| SAT writing: | 640-720 | **Rank in top tenth:** | 82% |
| ACT composite: | 28-32 | **Return as sophomores:** | 97% |
| **GPA 3.75 or higher:** | 78% | **Out-of-state:** | 77% |
| **GPA 3.50-3.74:** | 15% | **Live on campus:** | 100% |
| | | **International:** | 3% |

**Basis for selection.** GED not accepted. Course selection, rigor of program, grades, recommendations, essays, test scores, class rank considered. SAT and SAT Subject Tests or ACT recommended. Campus visit strongly recommended.

**High school preparation.** College-preparatory program required. 16 units required. Required and recommended units include English 4, mathematics 3-4, science 2-4 and foreign language 2-4. Foreign language units should be in same language. 2 required, 4 recommended for social studies or history units.

**2009-2010 Annual costs.** Tuition/fees: $35,124. Room/board: $9,906. Books/supplies: $1,000. Personal expenses: $1,325.

**2008-2009 Financial aid. Need-based:** 306 full-time freshmen applied for aid; 211 were judged to have need; 203 of these received aid. Average need met was 100%. Average scholarship/grant was $23,853; average loan $2,313. 94% of total undergraduate aid awarded as scholarships/grants, 6% as loans/jobs. **Non-need-based:** Awarded to 775 full-time undergraduates, including 191 freshmen. Scholarships awarded for academics, art, athletics, leadership, minority status, music/drama, ROTC. **Additional information:** The college has increased the money it provides for grants in financial aid packages and eliminated mandatory loans.

**Application procedures. Admission:** Closing date 1/2 (postmark date). $50 fee, may be waived for applicants with need. Admission notification 4/1. Must reply by 5/1. **Financial aid:** Closing date 2/15. FAFSA, CSS PROFILE required. Applicants notified by 4/1; must reply by 5/1.

**Academics.** 2-year interdisciplinary course in humanities available for freshmen and sophomores. Center for Special Studies supervises student-designed majors. **Special study options:** Cross-registration, double major, exchange student, honors, independent study, student-designed major, study abroad, teacher certification program, Washington semester. Visiting student program with Howard University and Morehouse College; Dean Rusk program in International Studies; Philadelphia Center Pro-School for Field Studies. **Credit/placement by examination:** AP, CLEP, IB, institutional tests. **Support services:** Tutoring, writing center.

**Majors. Biology:** General. **Foreign languages:** Classics, French, German, Spanish. **History:** General. **Math:** General. **Philosophy/religion:** Philosophy, religion. **Physical sciences:** Chemistry, physics. **Psychology:** General. **Social sciences:** Anthropology, economics, political science, sociology. **Visual/performing arts:** Art, dramatic. **Other:** Student-designed major through Center for Interdisciplinary Studies.

**Most popular majors.** Biology 8%, English 11%, foreign language 9%, history 12%, psychology 10%, social sciences 30%, visual/performing arts 6%.

**Computing on campus.** 142 workstations in dormitories, library, computer center, student center. Dormitories wired for high-speed internet access and linked to campus network. Commuter students can connect to campus network. Online course registration, helpline, repair service, wireless network available.

**Student life. Freshman orientation:** Mandatory, $100 fee. Preregistration for classes offered. **Housing:** Guaranteed on-campus for freshmen. Coed dorms, apartments, cooperative housing, wellness housing available. Substance-free, suite/apartment-style housing available. **Activities:** Bands, campus ministries, choral groups, dance, drama, international student organizations, literary magazine, music ensembles, musical theater, radio station, student government, student newspaper, symphony orchestra, black student coalition, Amnesty International, Young Democrats, College Republicans, Habitat for Humanity, Asia 3D, gender resource center.

**Athletics.** NCAA. **Intercollegiate:** Baseball M, basketball, cross-country, diving, field hockey W, football (tackle) M, golf M, lacrosse W, soccer, swimming, tennis, track and field, volleyball W, wrestling M. **Intramural:** Basketball, football (non-tackle), soccer, softball, volleyball. **Team name:** Wildcats.

**Student services.** Alcohol/substance abuse counseling, chaplain/spiritual director, career counseling, financial aid counseling, health services, minority student services, personal counseling, placement for graduates. **Physically disabled:** Services for visually, hearing impaired.

**Contact.** E-mail: admission@davidson.edu
Phone: (704) 894-2230 Toll-free number: (800) 768-0380
Fax: (704) 894-2016
Christopher Gruber, Vice President and Dean of Admission and Financial Aid, Davidson College, Box 7156, Davidson, NC 28035-7156

## DeVry University: Charlotte
**Charlotte, North Carolina**
**www.devry.edu**

- For-profit 4-year university
- Commuter campus in very large city
- 249 degree-seeking undergraduates: 42% part-time, 49% women, 64% African American, 1% Asian American, 6% Hispanic American
- 143 degree-seeking graduate students
- Interview required

**General. Degrees:** 31 bachelor's awarded; master's offered. **Calendar:** Semester. **Full-time faculty:** 2 total; 50% minority. **Part-time faculty:** 5 total; 60% minority, 20% women.

**Freshman class profile.** 68 enrolled.

**Basis for selection.** Academic record considered.

**High school preparation.** College-preparatory program recommended.

**2009-2010 Annual costs.** Tuition/fees: $14,160. Books/supplies: $1,310. Personal expenses: $3,574.

**2008-2009 Financial aid. Non-need-based:** Scholarships awarded for academics.

**Application procedures. Admission:** No deadline. $50 fee. Admission notification on a rolling basis. **Financial aid:** No deadline. FAFSA required. Applicants notified on a rolling basis.

**Academics. Special study options:** Accelerated study, distance learning. **Credit/placement by examination:** CLEP.

**Majors. Business:** Business admin. **Computer sciences:** General. **Other:** Technology management.

**Most popular majors.** Business/marketing 97%.

**Contact.** Phone: (704) 362-2345
DeVry University: Charlotte, 4521 Sharon Road, Charlotte, NC 28211

## Duke University
**Durham, North Carolina**            **CB member**
**www.duke.edu**                     **CB code: 5156**

- Private 4-year university affiliated with United Methodist Church
- Residential campus in small city
- 6,416 degree-seeking undergraduates: 49% women, 10% African American, 22% Asian American, 7% Hispanic American, 7% international
- 7,629 degree-seeking graduate students
- 19% of applicants admitted
- SAT and SAT Subject Tests or ACT with writing, application essay required
- 95% graduate within 6 years

**General.** Founded in 1838. Regionally accredited. **Degrees:** 1,625 bachelor's awarded; master's, doctoral, professional offered. **ROTC:** Army, Naval, Air Force. **Location:** 30 miles from Raleigh, 170 miles from Richmond, Virginia. **Calendar:** Semester, extensive summer session. **Full-time faculty:** 1,083 total; 96% have terminal degrees, 19% minority. **Class size:** 69% < 20, 21% 20-39, 3% 40-49, 4% 50-99, 2% >100. **Special facilities:** 4,500-square-foot residence/laboratory, marine laboratory, museum of art, Duke forest, teaching and research center, herbarium, science research center, French science center, global health institute, institute for genome sciences and policy, humanities institute, institute for ethics, Duke phytotron, institute for public policy, institute for environmental policy solutions, social science research institute, center for black culture.

**Freshman class profile.** 22,280 applied, 4,219 admitted, 1,723 enrolled.

| Mid 50% test scores | | | |
|---|---|---|---|
| SAT critical reading: | 660-750 | Rank in top tenth: | 90% |
| SAT math: | 680-780 | Return as sophomores: | 97% |
| SAT writing: | 660-760 | Out-of-state: | 85% |
| ACT composite: | 30-34 | Live on campus: | 100% |
| Rank in top quarter: | 97% | International: | 7% |

**Basis for selection.** GED not accepted. Courses, school achievement record, school and community activities, essays, recommendations, test scores considered. Special consideration to alumni children and minority applicants. Applicants requesting alumni interview must submit Part I of application by 10/1 for Early Decision or by 12/1 for regular decision. Students using ACT for admission need to submit SAT Subject Tests or AP scores for foreign language and mathematics placement. Applicants to Arts and Sciences submitting SAT must submit 2 SAT Subject Tests. Applicants to School of Engineering submitting SAT must take SAT Subject Test in mathematics and 1 other subject. Interview with alumnus/a in student's home area recommended, but not required; audition recommended for drama, music majors; portfolio recommended for art majors. **Homeschooled:** Transcript of courses and grades, letter of recommendation (nonparent) required.

**High school preparation.** College-preparatory program required. Recommended units include English 4, mathematics 4, social studies 4, science 4 and foreign language 4. 4 math and 1 physics or chemistry required for engineering applicants, with calculus required before enrolling.

**2010-2011 Annual costs.** Tuition/fees: $40,243. Room/board: $11,622. Books/supplies: $1,230. Personal expenses: $1,920.

**Financial aid. Non-need-based:** Scholarships awarded for academics, alumni affiliation, art, athletics, leadership, minority status, religious affiliation, ROTC, state residency.

**Application procedures. Admission:** Closing date 1/2 (postmark date). $75 fee, may be waived for applicants with need. Admission notification 4/1. Must reply by 5/1. **Financial aid:** Closing date 3/1. FAFSA, CSS PROFILE required. Applicants notified by 4/1; must reply by 5/1 or within 4 week(s) of notification.

**Academics.** International comparative studies with an emphasis in one or more areas. Special Focus Program for freshmen: engineering frontiers, evolution and humankind, forging social ideals, genome revolution, global health, memory and invention, visions of freedom. **Special study options:** Combined bachelor's/graduate degree, cross-registration, distance learning, double major, ESL, exchange student, honors, independent study, internships, New York semester, semester at sea, student-designed major, study abroad, teacher certification program, Washington semester. Art program/internship in New York City, marine biology semester in Beaufort. **Credit/placement by examination:** AP, CLEP, IB. **Support services:** Learning center, pre-admission summer program, tutoring, writing center.

**Majors. Area/ethnic studies:** African-American, Asian, women's. **Biology:** General, anatomy. **Computer sciences:** General. **Conservation:** General. **Engineering:** Biomedical, civil, electrical, mechanical. **Foreign languages:** Ancient Greek, classics, East Asian, French, German, Italian, Latin, Russian, Slavic, Spanish. **History:** General. **Interdisciplinary:** Medieval/Renaissance, neuroscience. **Math:** General. **Philosophy/religion:** Philosophy, religion. **Physical sciences:** Chemistry, geology, physics. **Psychology:** General. **Public administration:** Policy analysis. **Social sciences:** Anthropology, economics, political science, sociology. **Visual/performing arts:** Art history/conservation, design, dramatic.

**Most popular majors.** Biology 10%, engineering/engineering technologies 17%, psychology 11%, public administration/social services 9%, social sciences 27%.

**Computing on campus.** 450 workstations in dormitories, library, computer center, student center. Dormitories wired for high-speed internet access and linked to campus network. Commuter students can connect to campus network. Online course registration, online library, helpline, repair service, student web hosting, wireless network available.

**Student life. Freshman orientation:** Mandatory. Preregistration for classes offered. Held week prior to start of classes. **Housing:** Guaranteed on-campus for freshmen. Coed dorms, single-sex dorms, special housing for disabled, apartments, wellness housing available. $300 nonrefundable deposit, deadline 5/1. Special interest housing available for students in women's studies, the arts, languages, service (Alpha Phi Omega). All first-year students live together on East Campus. Most first-year residence halls have a faculty member in residence. All sophomores must live on West Campus. **Activities:** Bands, campus ministries, choral groups, dance, drama, film society, international student organizations, literary magazine, music ensembles, musical theater, opera, radio station, student government, student

newspaper, symphony orchestra, TV station, Black Student Alliance, Hillel, Newman Club, Spanish American-Latin Student Association, Volunteers for Youth, Big Brother/Big Sister, Campus Crusade for Christ, Duke Democrats, College Republicans, Habitat for Humanity.

**Athletics.** NCAA. **Intercollegiate:** Baseball M, basketball, cross-country, diving, fencing, field hockey W, football (tackle) M, golf, lacrosse, rowing (crew) W, soccer, swimming, tennis, track and field, volleyball W, wrestling M. **Intramural:** Badminton, baseball, basketball, football (tackle) M, golf, racquetball, soccer M, softball, squash, swimming, table tennis, tennis, volleyball. **Team name:** Blue Devils.

**Student services.** Adult student services, alcohol/substance abuse counseling, chaplain/spiritual director, career counseling, student employment services, financial aid counseling, health services, minority student services, on-campus daycare, personal counseling, placement for graduates, veterans' counselor, women's services. **Physically disabled:** Services for visually, speech, hearing impaired.

**Contact.** Phone: (919) 684-3214 Fax: (919) 681-8941
Christoph Guttentag, Dean of Undergraduate Admissions, Duke University, 2138 Campus Drive, Durham, NC 27708

---

## East Carolina University
**Greenville, North Carolina**
www.ecu.edu

CB member
CB code: 5180

- Public 4-year university
- Residential campus in small city
- 20,571 degree-seeking undergraduates: 11% part-time, 58% women, 14% African American, 2% Asian American, 2% Hispanic American, 1% Native American, 1% international
- 5,507 degree-seeking graduate students
- 67% of applicants admitted
- SAT or ACT with writing required
- 57% graduate within 6 years

**General.** Founded in 1907. Regionally accredited. **Degrees:** 3,606 bachelor's awarded; master's, doctoral, professional offered. **ROTC:** Army, Air Force. **Location:** 80 miles from Raleigh. **Calendar:** Semester, extensive summer session. **Full-time faculty:** 1,234 total; 80% have terminal degrees, 11% minority, 46% women. **Part-time faculty:** 240 total; 41% have terminal degrees, 10% minority, 54% women. **Class size:** 35% < 20, 41% 20-39, 10% 40-49, 10% 50-99, 4% >100. **Special facilities:** 2 accelerators, climbing wall, ropes course, global classroom, field station.

**Freshman class profile.** 15,221 applied, 10,196 admitted, 3,956 enrolled.

| Mid 50% test scores | | | |
|---|---|---|---|
| SAT critical reading: | 470-550 | GPA 3.0-3.49: | 36% |
| SAT math: | 490-570 | GPA 2.0-2.99: | 16% |
| SAT writing: | 450-540 | Rank in top quarter: | 42% |
| ACT composite: | 19-23 | Rank in top tenth: | 13% |
| GPA 3.75 or higher: | 29% | Return as sophomores: | 79% |
| GPA 3.50-3.74: | 19% | Out-of-state: | 19% |
| | | Live on campus: | 84% |

**Basis for selection.** Freshman admission decisions based on a formula that weighs class rank, high school GPA (unweighted), and standardized test scores. GED accepted for non-traditional freshmen. SAT preferred, ACT also accepted. Audition, statement of purpose and letter of recommendation required for music programs. **Homeschooled:** Transcript of courses and grades required.

**High school preparation.** College-preparatory program required. Required units include English 4, mathematics 4, social studies 2, history 1, science 3 (laboratory 1), foreign language 2, computer science 1 and visual/performing arts 1.

**2009-2010 Annual costs.** Tuition/fees: $4,271; $15,105 out-of-state. Room/board: $7,490. Books/supplies: $1,094. Personal expenses: $2,814.

**2009-2010 Financial aid. Need-based:** 3,008 full-time freshmen applied for aid; 1,919 were judged to have need; 1,855 of these received aid. Average need met was 78%. Average scholarship/grant was $7,943; average loan $2,833. 48% of total undergraduate aid awarded as scholarships/grants, 52% as loans/jobs. **Non-need-based:** Awarded to 1,810 full-time undergraduates, including 285 freshmen. Scholarships awarded for academics, alumni affiliation, art, athletics, music/drama, ROTC.

**Application procedures. Admission:** Closing date 3/15 (postmark date). $60 fee, may be waived for applicants with need. Admission notification on a rolling basis beginning on or about 9/8. Out-of-state freshman enrollment limited to 18% of incoming freshman class, and processed on space-available basis. Applications received prior to December 31 receive priority. **Financial aid:** Priority date 3/1; no closing date. FAFSA required. Applicants notified by 4/1; Applicants notified on a rolling basis starting 4/1; must reply within 3 week(s) of notification.

**Academics. Special study options:** Accelerated study, combined bachelor's/graduate degree, cooperative education, distance learning, double major, dual enrollment of high school students, exchange student, honors, independent study, internships, student-designed major, study abroad, teacher certification program, Washington semester. **Credit/placement by examination:** AP, CLEP, IB, SAT, ACT, institutional tests. **Support services:** Learning center, reduced course load, remedial instruction, study skills assistance, tutoring, writing center.

**Majors: Architecture:** Urban/community planning. **Area/ethnic studies:** African-American, women's. **Biology:** General, biochemistry, exercise physiology. **Business:** Accounting, accounting/business management, business admin, finance, hotel/motel admin, management information systems, marketing, office technology. **Communications:** General, broadcast journalism. **Computer sciences:** Computer science, information technology. **Education:** Art, business, drama/dance, elementary, English, family/consumer sciences, French, German, health, kindergarten/preschool, learning disabled, mathematics, middle, music, physical, sales/marketing, science, social studies, Spanish, special. **Engineering:** General. **Engineering technology:** Construction, drafting, industrial, manufacturing. **Family/consumer sciences:** Child development, clothing/textiles, family/community services. **Foreign languages:** French, German, Spanish. **Health:** Athletic training, audiology/speech pathology, clinical lab science, clinical nutrition, dietetics, environmental health, health services, marriage/family therapy, medical records admin, music therapy, nursing (RN), public health ed, recreational therapy, vocational rehab counseling. **History:** General, public archives. **Liberal arts:** Arts/sciences. **Math:** General. **Parks/recreation:** Exercise sciences, facilities management, sports admin. **Philosophy/religion:** Philosophy. **Physical sciences:** Chemistry, geology, physics. **Protective services:** Criminal justice. **Psychology:** General. **Public administration:** Social work. **Social sciences:** Anthropology, economics, geography, political science, sociology. **Visual/performing arts:** Acting, art, art history/conservation, ceramics, cinematography, dance, directing/producing, dramatic, drawing, fiber arts, graphic design, illustration, interior design, jazz, metal/jewelry, music performance, music theory/composition, painting, photography, piano/organ, printmaking, sculpture, stringed instruments, studio arts, voice/opera.

**Most popular majors.** Business/marketing 16%, communications/journalism 7%, education 14%, engineering/engineering technologies 9%, health sciences 17%.

**Computing on campus.** 2,188 workstations in dormitories, library, computer center, student center. Dormitories wired for high-speed internet access and linked to campus network. Commuter students can connect to campus network. Online course registration, online library, helpline, repair service, student web hosting, wireless network available.

**Student life. Freshman orientation:** Mandatory, $100 fee. Preregistration for classes offered. 2-phase program: 1 summer session (overnight stay) and 1 session the day prior to start of classes. **Housing:** Guaranteed on-campus for freshmen. Coed dorms, single-sex dorms, special housing for disabled, fraternity/sorority housing available. First-year student floor, leadership hall, extended quiet-hours floor, academic year residence halls available. **Activities:** Bands, campus ministries, choral groups, dance, drama, film society, international student organizations, literary magazine, music ensembles, Model UN, musical theater, opera, radio station, student government, student newspaper, symphony orchestra, TV station, 280 registered organizations.

**Athletics.** NCAA. **Intercollegiate:** Baseball M, basketball, cheerleading, cross-country, diving, football (tackle) M, golf, soccer W, softball W, swimming, tennis, track and field, volleyball. **Intramural:** Basketball, bowling, cross-country, football (non-tackle), golf, racquetball, softball, table tennis, tennis, volleyball. **Team name:** Pirates.

**Student services.** Adult student services, alcohol/substance abuse counseling, chaplain/spiritual director, career counseling, student employment services, financial aid counseling, health services, minority student services, personal counseling, placement for graduates, veterans' counselor. **Physically disabled:** Services for visually, speech, hearing impaired.

**Contact.** E-mail: admis@ecu.edu
Phone: (252) 328-6640 Fax: (252) 328-6945
Donald Joyner, Director of Admissions, East Carolina University, Office of Undergraduate Admissions, Greenville, NC 27858-4353

---

## Elizabeth City State University

**Elizabeth City, North Carolina**
www.ecsu.edu

**CB member**
**CB code: 5629**

▸ Public 4-year liberal arts college
▸ Residential campus in large town

▸ 3,045 degree-seeking undergraduates: 7% part-time, 61% women, 81% African American, 1% Hispanic American
▸ 56 degree-seeking graduate students
▸ 71% of applicants admitted
▸ SAT or ACT (ACT writing optional) required

**General.** Founded in 1891. Regionally accredited. **Degrees:** 397 bachelor's awarded; master's offered. **ROTC:** Army. **Location:** 50 miles from Norfolk, Virginia. **Calendar:** Semester, extensive summer session. **Full-time faculty:** 161 total; 53% have terminal degrees, 44% minority. **Part-time faculty:** 80 total; 6% have terminal degrees, 60% minority. **Class size:** 61% < 20, 31% 20-39, 7% 40-49, less than 1% 50-99. **Special facilities:** Recording studio, boardwalk in nature preserves/wetlands, golf driving range.

**Freshman class profile.** 1,976 applied, 1,407 admitted, 666 enrolled.

| Mid 50% test scores | | Rank in top quarter: | 13% |
|---|---|---|---|
| SAT critical reading: | 380-460 | Rank in top tenth: | 8% |
| SAT math: | 380-460 | Out-of-state: | 15% |
| GPA 3.75 or higher: | 6% | Live on campus: | 79% |
| GPA 3.50-3.74: | 6% | Fraternities: | 3% |
| GPA 3.0-3.49: | 23% | Sororities: | 6% |
| GPA 2.0-2.99: | 60% | | |

**Basis for selection.** GPA and test scores considered. Special consideration given to residents from 21 neighboring counties. All applicants to any campus in the UNC system, except those exempted by current campus policies, must submit standardized test scores. SAT preferred, ACT accepted. **Homeschooled:** Statement describing homeschool structure and mission, transcript of courses and grades, letter of recommendation (nonparent) required. **Learning Disabled:** Important to ascertain in advance the extent of the learning disability in order to provide the available service(s).

**High school preparation.** College-preparatory program recommended. 20 units required. Required units include English 4, mathematics 3, social studies 2, science 2 (laboratory 1) and foreign language 2. One additional laboratory science also required. Mathematics must include 1 algebra and 1 geometry. Social science must include 1 history.

**2009-2010 Annual costs.** Tuition/fees: $3,031; $12,080 out-of-state. Room/board: $5,495. Books/supplies: $620. Personal expenses: $1,500.

**Financial aid. Non-need-based:** Scholarships awarded for academics, athletics, minority status, ROTC, state residency.

**Application procedures. Admission:** Priority date 5/1; deadline 6/30. $30 fee. Admission notification on a rolling basis. **Financial aid:** Closing date 3/15. FAFSA required. Applicants notified on a rolling basis starting 6/1; must reply within 3 week(s) of notification.

**Academics. Special study options:** Combined bachelor's/graduate degree, cooperative education, distance learning, double major, honors, independent study, internships, liberal arts/career combination, teacher certification program, weekend college. **Credit/placement by examination:** AP, CLEP, IB, SAT. 48 credit hours maximum toward bachelor's degree. **Support services:** Learning center, pre-admission summer program, reduced course load, remedial instruction, study skills assistance, tutoring, writing center.

**Majors. Biology:** General. **Business:** Accounting, business admin. **Computer sciences:** Computer science. **Education:** Art, business, chemistry, elementary, English, history, learning disabled, mathematics, middle, physical, special, technology/industrial arts. **Engineering technology:** Industrial. **History:** General. **Math:** General. **Physical sciences:** Chemistry, geology, oceanography, physics. **Protective services:** Criminal justice. **Psychology:** General. **Public administration:** Social work. **Social sciences:** General, political science, sociology. **Transportation:** Aviation. **Visual/performing arts:** Music management, studio arts.

**Computing on campus.** 350 workstations in dormitories, library, computer center, student center. Dormitories wired for high-speed internet access and linked to campus network. Commuter students can connect to campus network. Online course registration, online library, helpline, repair service, wireless network available.

**Student life. Freshman orientation:** Mandatory, $100 fee. Preregistration for classes offered. Three sessions held during summer months covering 2 1/2 days each. **Housing:** Guaranteed on-campus for freshmen. Coed dorms, single-sex dorms, apartments, wellness housing available. $100 deposit, deadline 8/1. College-leased housing available. **Activities:** Bands, choral groups, dance, drama, literary magazine, music ensembles, radio station, student government, student newspaper, symphony orchestra, TV station, United Campus Religious Fellowship, honor and recognition societies in education, science, dramatics, journalism, student union program.

**Athletics.** NCAA. **Intercollegiate:** Baseball M, basketball, bowling W, boxing W, cheerleading, cross-country, football (tackle) M, golf, softball W, tennis, track and field, volleyball W, wrestling M. **Intramural:** Baseball M, basketball, boxing, football (non-tackle) M, softball, volleyball. **Team name:** Vikings.

**Student services.** Alcohol/substance abuse counseling, chaplain/spiritual director, career counseling, student employment services, financial aid counseling, health services, personal counseling, placement for graduates, veterans' counselor. **Physically disabled:** Services for visually, speech, hearing impaired.

**Contact.** E-mail: mdwilliams2@mail.ecsu.edu
Phone: (252) 335-3305 Toll-free number: (800) 347-3278
Fax: (252) 335-3537
Monette Williams, Director of Enrollment Management, Elizabeth City State University, 1704 Weeksville Road, Campus Box 901, Elizabeth City, NC 27909

## Elon University
**Elon, North Carolina**
www.elon.edu

**CB member**
**CB code: 5183**

- Private 4-year university and liberal arts college affiliated with United Church of Christ
- Residential campus in large town
- 4,995 degree-seeking undergraduates: 2% part-time, 59% women
- 671 degree-seeking graduate students
- 48% of applicants admitted
- SAT or ACT with writing, application essay required
- 78% graduate within 6 years; 16% enter graduate study

**General.** Founded in 1889. Regionally accredited. **Degrees:** 1,231 bachelor's awarded; master's, professional offered. **ROTC:** Army, Air Force. **Location:** 15 miles from Greensboro. **Calendar:** 4-1-4, extensive summer session. **Full-time faculty:** 343 total; 87% have terminal degrees, 9% minority, 46% women. **Part-time faculty:** 143 total; 46% have terminal degrees, 46% women. **Class size:** 51% < 20, 48% 20-39, less than 1% 40-49, less than 1% 50-99. **Special facilities:** Fine arts center, science center, academic pavilions.

**Freshman class profile.** 9,041 applied, 4,365 admitted, 1,291 enrolled.

| Mid 50% test scores | | | |
|---|---|---|---|
| SAT critical reading: | 570-660 | GPA 2.0-2.99: | 7% |
| SAT math: | 570-660 | Rank in top quarter: | 70% |
| SAT writing: | 570-660 | Rank in top tenth: | 32% |
| ACT composite: | 25-29 | End year in good standing: | 97% |
| GPA 3.75 or higher: | 64% | Return as sophomores: | 89% |
| GPA 3.50-3.74: | 10% | Out-of-state: | 75% |
| GPA 3.0-3.49: | 19% | Live on campus: | 100% |
| | | International: | 3% |

**Basis for selection.** School achievement record most important, followed by test scores. Class rank, school and community activities, personal statement, recommendations also considered. Audition required for all performing arts programs. **Homeschooled:** Statement describing homeschool structure and mission, transcript of courses and grades, state high school equivalency certificate, letter of recommendation (nonparent) required.

**High school preparation.** College-preparatory program required. Required and recommended units include English 4, mathematics 3-4, social studies 1, history 2-3, science 3 (laboratory 1) and foreign language 2-3. Algebra I, II and geometry required.

**2009-2010 Annual costs.** Tuition/fees: $25,489. Room/board: $8,236. Books/supplies: $900. Personal expenses: $1,500.

**2009-2010 Financial aid. Need-based:** 776 full-time freshmen applied for aid; 456 were judged to have need; 453 of these received aid. Average need met was 86%. Average scholarship/grant was $13,887; average loan $4,100. 69% of total undergraduate aid awarded as scholarships/grants, 31% as loans/jobs. **Non-need-based:** Awarded to 1,547 full-time undergraduates, including 408 freshmen. Scholarships awarded for academics, art, athletics, leadership, music/drama, ROTC, state residency.

**Application procedures. Admission:** Priority date 11/1; deadline 1/10 (postmark date). $50 fee, may be waived for applicants with need. Admission notification 3/15. Must reply by May 1 or within 1 week(s) if notified thereafter. **Financial aid:** Priority date 2/15; no closing date. FAFSA, institutional form, CSS PROFILE required. Applicants notified on a rolling basis starting 3/30.

**Academics. Special study options:** Accelerated study, combined bachelor's/graduate degree, cross-registration, distance learning, double major, dual

enrollment of high school students, ESL, exchange student, honors, independent study, internships, liberal arts/career combination, student-designed major, study abroad, teacher certification program, Washington semester. **Credit/placement by examination:** AP, CLEP, IB, SAT, ACT, institutional tests. **Support services:** Learning center, reduced course load, remedial instruction, study skills assistance, tutoring, writing center.

**Majors. Biology:** General. **Business:** Accounting, business admin, entrepreneurial studies, finance, international, management information systems, marketing. **Communications:** General, broadcast journalism, journalism. **Computer sciences:** General, computer science, information systems. **Conservation:** Environmental studies. **Education:** General, curriculum, elementary, middle, secondary, special. **Engineering:** General, chemical, computer, environmental, physics. **Engineering technology:** Environmental. **Foreign languages:** General, French, Spanish. **Health:** Predental, premedicine, staff services technology. **History:** General. **Legal studies:** Prelaw. **Math:** General, applied. **Parks/recreation:** Exercise sciences, facilities management, sports admin. **Philosophy/religion:** Philosophy, religion. **Physical sciences:** Chemistry, physics. **Protective services:** Criminal justice. **Psychology:** General. **Public administration:** General, human services. **Social sciences:** Anthropology, economics, international relations, political science, sociology. **Visual/performing arts:** Art, art history/conservation, ceramics, dance, digital art, dramatic, music performance, musical theater, painting, photography, theater design. **Other:** Cinema, Music technology, Professional writing and rhetoric.

**Most popular majors.** Business/marketing 21%, communications/journalism 17%, education 7%, parks/recreation 7%, social sciences 12%, visual/performing arts 7%.

**Computing on campus.** 850 workstations in dormitories, library, computer center, student center. Dormitories wired for high-speed internet access and linked to campus network. Commuter students can connect to campus network. Online course registration, online library, helpline, repair service, student web hosting, wireless network available.

**Student life. Freshman orientation:** Mandatory. Preregistration for classes offered. Optional orientation during spring of high school senior year. Required orientation in August. **Policies:** Freshmen and sophomores are required to live on campus; housing is guaranteed. **Housing:** Guaranteed on-campus for freshmen. Coed dorms, single-sex dorms, apartments, fraternity/sorority housing, wellness housing available. $500 fully refundable deposit, deadline 5/1. **Activities:** Bands, campus ministries, choral groups, dance, drama, film society, international student organizations, literary magazine, music ensembles, Model UN, musical theater, radio station, student government, student newspaper, symphony orchestra, TV station, Intervarsity Christian Fellowship, Young Republicans, Black cultural society, Epsilon Sigma Alpha, liberal arts forum, Hillel, student media, Habitat for Humanity.

**Athletics.** NCAA. **Intercollegiate:** Baseball M, basketball, cheerleading, cross-country, football (tackle) M, golf, soccer, softball W, tennis, track and field W, volleyball W. **Intramural:** Basketball, bowling, football (non-tackle), golf, racquetball, soccer, table tennis, tennis, volleyball. **Team name:** Phoenix.

**Student services.** Adult student services, alcohol/substance abuse counseling, chaplain/spiritual director, career counseling, student employment services, financial aid counseling, health services, minority student services, personal counseling, placement for graduates, veterans' counselor, women's services. **Physically disabled:** Services for visually, speech, hearing impaired.

**Contact.** E-mail: admissions@elon.edu
Phone: (336) 278-3566 Toll-free number: (800) 334-8448
Fax: (336) 278-7699
Greg Zaiser, Dean of Admissions, Elon University, 2700 Campus Box, Elon, NC 27244-2010

## Fayetteville State University
**Fayetteville, North Carolina**
www.uncfsu.edu

**CB member**
**CB code: 5212**

- Public 4-year university
- Commuter campus in small city
- 5,259 degree-seeking undergraduates: 21% part-time, 68% women, 74% African American, 1% Asian American, 4% Hispanic American, 1% Native American
- 390 degree-seeking graduate students
- SAT or ACT with writing required
- 32% graduate within 6 years

**General.** Founded in 1867. Regionally accredited. Courses leading to bachelor's degree also available at the Fort Bragg/Pope AFB Center, Seymour

Johnson AFB, and online. **Degrees:** 773 bachelor's awarded; master's, doctoral offered. **ROTC:** Army, Air Force. **Location:** 60 miles from Raleigh. **Calendar:** Semester, limited summer session. **Full-time faculty:** 245 total; 83% have terminal degrees, 64% minority, 40% women. **Part-time faculty:** 70 total; 53% have terminal degrees, 71% minority, 49% women. **Class size:** 44% < 20, 55% 20-39, 1% 40-49, less than 1% 50-99. **Special facilities:** Greenhouse, observatory, planetarium.

**Freshman class profile.**

| Mid 50% test scores | | Rank in top tenth: | 5% |
|---|---|---|---|
| SAT critical reading: | 370-440 | End year in good standing: | 62% |
| SAT math: | 380-460 | Return as sophomores: | 74% |
| SAT writing: | 350-430 | Out-of-state: | 7% |
| ACT composite: | 15-19 | Live on campus: | 79% |
| Rank in top quarter: | 21% | | |

**Basis for selection.** 2.0 GPA, SAT scores, completion of 18 prescribed high school units required. All applicants, except those exempted by current campus policies, must submit a standardized test score. SAT preferred, ACT also accepted.

**High school preparation.** 19 units required. Required and recommended units include English 4, mathematics 4, social studies 2, history 1, science 3, foreign language 2 and academic electives 6. Foreign language units can be used as academic elective units.

**2009-2010 Annual costs.** Tuition/fees: $3,177; $13,520 out-of-state. Car registration $45, insurance $378, room breakage deposit $125, late registration $20. Room/board: $5,421. Books/supplies: $350. Personal expenses: $750.

**Financial aid. Need-based:** 553 full-time freshmen applied for aid; 509 were judged to have need; 506 of these received aid. Average need met was 86%. Average scholarship/grant was $8,691; average loan $2,914. **Non-need-based:** Awarded to 2,612 full-time undergraduates, including 406 freshmen. Scholarships awarded for academics, alumni affiliation, athletics, music/drama, ROTC, state residency.

**Application procedures. Admission:** Closing date 7/1 (postmark date). $35 fee, may be waived for applicants with need. Admission notification on a rolling basis beginning on or about 1/15. Must reply by 7/1. **Financial aid:** Priority date 3/1, closing date 4/1. FAFSA required. Applicants notified on a rolling basis starting 4/15; must reply within 2 week(s) of notification.

**Academics. Special study options:** Accelerated study, combined bachelor's/graduate degree, cooperative education, distance learning, double major, dual enrollment of high school students, honors, independent study, internships, study abroad, teacher certification program, weekend college. **Credit/placement by examination:** AP, CLEP, institutional tests. 30 credit hours maximum toward bachelor's degree. **Support services:** Learning center, pre-admission summer program, remedial instruction, tutoring.

**Majors. Biology:** General. **Business:** Accounting, business admin, office management. **Computer sciences:** General. **Education:** Business, English, health, mathematics, middle, music, physical, secondary, social science. **History:** General. **Math:** General. **Physical sciences:** Chemistry. **Protective services:** Criminal justice. **Psychology:** General. **Public administration:** General. **Social sciences:** General, geography, political science, sociology. **Visual/performing arts:** General, dramatic.

**Most popular majors.** Business/marketing 17%, education 11%, psychology 15%, security/protective services 17%, social sciences 14%.

**Computing on campus.** 600 workstations in dormitories, library, computer center, student center. Dormitories wired for high-speed internet access and linked to campus network. Commuter students can connect to campus network. Online course registration, online library, helpline, wireless network available.

**Student life. Freshman orientation:** Mandatory, $45 fee. 3 Saturdays in July and August. **Housing:** Single-sex dorms available. $125 nonrefundable deposit, deadline 7/1. **Activities:** Bands, choral groups, drama, music ensembles, radio station, student government, student newspaper, TV station, Baptist student union, Federation of Young Democrats, NAACP, NCNW, Honda Campus All-Stars, art guild, Illusions modeling club.

**Athletics.** NCAA. **Intercollegiate:** Basketball, bowling W, cross-country, football (tackle) M, golf, softball W, tennis, track and field, volleyball W. **Intramural:** Baseball M, basketball, bowling, football (tackle) M, golf, gymnastics, swimming, tennis M, volleyball. **Team name:** Broncos.

**Student services.** Alcohol/substance abuse counseling, career counseling, student employment services, financial aid counseling, health services, on-campus daycare, personal counseling, placement for graduates, veterans' counselor. **Physically disabled:** Services for visually impaired.

**Contact.** E-mail: admissions@uncfsu.edu
Phone: (910) 672-1371 Toll-free number: (800) 222-2594
Fax: (910) 672-1414
Ulisa Bowles, Director of Admissions, Fayetteville State University, 1200 Murchison Road, Fayetteville, NC 28301-4298

## Gardner-Webb University
**Boiling Springs, North Carolina**     **CB member**
www.gardner-webb.edu     **CB code: 5242**

- Private 4-year university and liberal arts college affiliated with Southern Baptist Convention
- Residential campus in small town
- 2,640 degree-seeking undergraduates: 15% part-time, 65% women, 19% African American, 2% Hispanic American, 1% Native American
- 1,215 degree-seeking graduate students
- 62% of applicants admitted
- SAT or ACT (ACT writing optional) required
- 47% graduate within 6 years

**General.** Founded in 1905. Regionally accredited. **Degrees:** 673 bachelor's, 60 associate awarded; master's, professional offered. **ROTC:** Army, Air Force. **Location:** 45 miles from Charlotte, 60 miles from Greenville, SC. **Calendar:** Semester, extensive summer session. **Full-time faculty:** 140 total; 80% have terminal degrees, 4% minority, 46% women. **Class size:** 69% < 20, 30% 20-39, less than 1% 40-49. **Special facilities:** Observatory, adventure and ropes course, Lake Hollifield and Carillon.

**Freshman class profile.** 3,277 applied, 2,016 admitted, 448 enrolled.

| Mid 50% test scores | | GPA 2.0-2.99: | 25% |
|---|---|---|---|
| SAT critical reading: | 440-560 | Rank in top quarter: | 49% |
| SAT math: | 420-550 | Rank in top tenth: | 32% |
| ACT composite: | 18-23 | Return as sophomores: | 74% |
| GPA 3.75 or higher: | 37% | Out-of-state: | 40% |
| GPA 3.50-3.74: | 13% | Live on campus: | 95% |
| GPA 3.0-3.49: | 25% | | |

**Basis for selection.** School achievement record most important, followed by test scores, recommendations, and school and community activities. Expected 2.5 GPA. The Accuplacer placement test is required of students whose SAT or ACT scores fall below a certain minimum. This test will be used to determine whether the student is to be placed in remedial courses or college level English and Math courses. Interview, portfolio, essay recommended for all students; audition required for music scholarships. Interview may be required for conditionally admitted students.

**High school preparation.** College-preparatory program recommended. Recommended units include English 4, mathematics 3, social studies 1, science 3 (laboratory 2) and foreign language 2.

**2009-2010 Annual costs.** Tuition/fees: $21,170. Room/board: $6,810. Books/supplies: $1,000.

**2008-2009 Financial aid. Need-based:** 419 full-time freshmen applied for aid; 339 were judged to have need; 339 of these received aid. Average need met was 76%. Average scholarship/grant was $9,624; average loan $3,463. 57% of total undergraduate aid awarded as scholarships/grants, 43% as loans/jobs. **Non-need-based:** Awarded to 1,176 full-time undergraduates, including 373 freshmen. Scholarships awarded for academics, athletics, leadership, music/drama, religious affiliation, ROTC, state residency.

**Application procedures. Admission:** No deadline. $40 fee, may be waived for applicants with need, free for online applicants. Admission notification on a rolling basis. **Financial aid:** Priority date 3/15; no closing date. FAFSA required. Applicants notified on a rolling basis starting 3/1; must reply within 2 week(s) of notification.

**Academics.** Special program offerings possible (including interpreters, notetakers) for students who have tested learning disabled or physically disabled. **Special study options:** Accelerated study, combined bachelor's/graduate degree, distance learning, double major, dual enrollment of high school students, ESL, honors, independent study, internships, liberal arts/career combination, study abroad, teacher certification program. Spring break in New York; Fall break in Washington; Summer in Costa Rica and Quebec for language trips. **Credit/placement by examination:** AP, CLEP, IB, SAT, ACT, institutional tests. 64 credit hours maximum toward bachelor's degree. **Support services:** Learning center, pre-admission summer program, reduced course load, remedial instruction, study skills assistance, tutoring, writing center.

**Honors college/program.** Students participating in the Honors program have an average SAT of 1850 and an average GPA of 3.8. Students must complete 24 semester hours of course work designated as honors (six of which is comprised of an Honors Thesis during the junior and/or senior year).

**Majors. Biology:** General, ecology. **Business:** General, accounting, business admin, finance, international, management information systems. **Communications:** General, broadcast journalism, journalism, public relations. **Computer sciences:** General, computer science. **Education:** General, biology, chemistry, elementary, English, foreign languages, French, health, history, mathematics, middle, multi-level teacher, music, physical, science, secondary, social science, Spanish. **Foreign languages:** General, American Sign Language, French, sign language interpretation, Spanish. **Health:** Athletic training, health care admin, nursing (RN), predental, premedicine, prepharmacy, preveterinary. **History:** General. **Interdisciplinary:** Math/computer science. **Legal studies:** Prelaw. **Math:** General. **Parks/recreation:** Health/fitness. **Philosophy/religion:** Philosophy, religion. **Physical sciences:** Chemistry. **Psychology:** General. **Social sciences:** General, political science, sociology. **Theology:** Missionary, religious ed, sacred music, youth ministry. **Visual/performing arts:** Art, ceramics, dramatic, drawing, music management, music performance, music theory/composition, painting, photography, piano/organ, printmaking, sculpture, stringed instruments, studio arts, voice/opera. **Other:** Biblical languages and literature, Electronic publishing, English as a second language with teacher licensure, Health and wellness.

**Most popular majors.** Business/marketing 34%, health sciences 13%, social sciences 28%.

**Computing on campus.** 150 workstations in library, computer center. Dormitories wired for high-speed internet access and linked to campus network. Commuter students can connect to campus network. Online course registration, online library, helpline, wireless network available.

**Student life. Freshman orientation:** Mandatory, $100 fee. Three-day program typically held near the end of August just before fall semester commences. **Policies:** Limited visitation hours: noon to midnight in dorm rooms. Lobbies open for visitation until 2:00 am., no alcohol or tobacco allowed on campus, quiet hours observed from 10 pm through 10 am. **Housing:** Guaranteed on-campus for all undergraduates. Single-sex dorms, special housing for disabled, apartments, wellness housing available. $150 nonrefundable deposit. Honors student residence hall available. **Activities:** Bands, campus ministries, choral groups, dance, drama, international student organizations, literary magazine, music ensembles, musical theater, opera, radio station, student government, student newspaper, symphony orchestra, Fellowship of Christian Athletes, student volunteer groups, prison ministry, student YMCA, gospel choir, Bible studies, College Republicans, College Democrats.

**Athletics.** NCAA. **Intercollegiate:** Baseball M, basketball, cheerleading, cross-country, football (tackle) M, golf, soccer, softball W, swimming, tennis, track and field, volleyball W, wrestling M. **Intramural:** Badminton, baseball, basketball, football (non-tackle), racquetball, skiing, soccer, softball, swimming, table tennis, tennis, volleyball. **Team name:** Runnin' Bulldogs.

**Student services.** Alcohol/substance abuse counseling, chaplain/spiritual director, career counseling, student employment services, financial aid counseling, personal counseling, placement for graduates, veterans' counselor. **Physically disabled:** Services for visually, speech, hearing impaired. **Learning disabled:** Comprehensive services available.

**Contact.** E-mail: admissions@gardner-webb.edu
Phone: (704) 406-4498 Toll-free number: (800) 253-6472
Fax: (704) 406-4488
Nathan Alexander, Assistant Vice President of Enrollment Management and Admissions, Gardner-Webb University, P.O. Box 817, Boiling Springs, NC 28017

---

## Greensboro College

**Greensboro, North Carolina**
www.greensborocollege.edu

CB member
CB code: 5260

- Private 4-year liberal arts college affiliated with United Methodist Church
- Residential campus in large city
- 931 degree-seeking undergraduates: 4% part-time, 48% women, 21% African American, 2% Hispanic American
- 76 degree-seeking graduate students
- 58% of applicants admitted
- SAT or ACT with writing, application essay required
- 45% graduate within 6 years

**General.** Founded in 1838. Regionally accredited. **Degrees:** 191 bachelor's awarded; master's offered. **ROTC:** Army, Air Force. **Location:** 90

miles from Charlotte, 75 miles from Raleigh. **Calendar:** Semester, limited summer session. **Full-time faculty:** 68 total; 7% minority, 48% women. **Part-time faculty:** 79 total. **Class size:** 83% < 20, 17% 20-39. **Special facilities:** Historical museum, computerized music laboratories.

**Freshman class profile.** 1,796 applied, 1,050 admitted, 241 enrolled.

| Mid 50% test scores | | |
|---|---|---|
| SAT critical reading: | 420-550 | |
| SAT math: | 520-580 | |
| SAT writing: | 410-520 | |
| ACT composite: | 16-21 | |

| | |
|---|---|
| End year in good standing: | 84% |
| Return as sophomores: | 62% |
| Out-of-state: | 27% |
| Live on campus: | 93% |

**Basis for selection.** High school curriculum most important, followed by grades, class rank, test scores, personal statement, school and community activities, high school caliber. Recommendations, interview considered. Interview recommended for all students. Audition required for music, theater majors; portfolio required for art majors. **Homeschooled:** Interview highly recommended and SAT/ACT required. **Learning Disabled:** Students wishing to receive accommodations facilitated by the Office of Disability Services are responsible for disclosure of physical, psychological, and learning disabilities. Accommodation of learning and psychological disabilities must be accompanied by appropriate documentation that includes professional evaluation, diagnosis, and recommendations.

**High school preparation.** College-preparatory program recommended. Recommended units include English 4, mathematics 3, history 2, science 2 (laboratory 1) and foreign language 2. Remaining units must be selected from art, music, social science and physical education.

**2009-2010 Annual costs.** Tuition/fees: $23,346. Room/board: $8,721. Books/supplies: $900. Personal expenses: $900.

**2009-2010 Financial aid. Non-need-based:** Scholarships awarded for academics, alumni affiliation, art, leadership, music/drama, religious affiliation, state residency.

**Application procedures. Admission:** Priority date 12/15; no deadline. $35 fee, may be waived for applicants with need. Admission notification on a rolling basis. Must reply by May 1 or within 4 week(s) if notified thereafter. **Financial aid:** Priority date 4/15; no closing date. FAFSA, institutional form required. Applicants notified on a rolling basis starting 2/1; must reply within 2 week(s) of notification.

**Academics. Special study options:** Accelerated study, cross-registration, double major, dual enrollment of high school students, ESL, honors, independent study, internships, liberal arts/career combination, student-designed major, study abroad, teacher certification program, weekend college. Academic success program, minor in ethics across the curriculum, minor in women's and gender studies, minor in computer science. **Credit/placement by examination:** AP, CLEP, IB, institutional tests. 45 credit hours maximum toward bachelor's degree. **Support services:** Learning center, reduced course load, study skills assistance, tutoring, writing center.

**Majors. Biology:** General. **Business:** Accounting, managerial economics. **Communications:** General. **Education:** General, art, biology, drama/dance, early childhood, elementary, emotionally handicapped, English, history, learning disabled, mathematics, mentally handicapped, middle, multiple handicapped, music, physical, social studies, Spanish, special. **Foreign languages:** French, Spanish. **Health:** Athletic training. **History:** General. **Liberal arts:** Arts/sciences. **Math:** General. **Parks/recreation:** Exercise sciences, health/fitness, sports admin. **Philosophy/religion:** Religion. **Physical sciences:** Chemistry. **Psychology:** General. **Social sciences:** Political science, sociology. **Visual/performing arts:** Dramatic, music performance, studio arts, theater design.

**Most popular majors.** Biology 7%, business/marketing 25%, education 15%, social sciences 12%, visual/performing arts 16%.

**Computing on campus.** 152 workstations in dormitories, library, computer center, student center. Dormitories wired for high-speed internet access and linked to campus network. Commuter students can connect to campus network. Online library, helpline, repair service, wireless network available.

**Student life. Freshman orientation:** Mandatory. Preregistration for classes offered. Orientations held in May, June, July and August. **Housing:** Guaranteed on-campus for all undergraduates. Coed dorms, single-sex dorms, apartments, wellness housing available. $200 partly refundable deposit. All students who have earned less than 58 credit hours required to live in college housing unless married, veterans, or residing with parents. All students encouraged to do so. **Activities:** Bands, choral groups, dance, drama, international student organizations, literary magazine, music ensembles, Model UN, musical theater, opera, student government, student newspaper, Student Christian Fellowship, United African American Society, Student National Education Association, campus activity board, Fellowship of Christian Athletes, Los Amigos.

**Athletics.** NCAA. **Intercollegiate:** Baseball M, basketball, cheerleading, cross-country, football (tackle) M, golf M, lacrosse, soccer, softball W, swimming W, tennis, volleyball W. **Intramural:** Baseball M, basketball, football (non-tackle), skiing. **Team name:** The Pride.

**Student services.** Adult student services, alcohol/substance abuse counseling, chaplain/spiritual director, career counseling, student employment services, financial aid counseling, health services, personal counseling, placement for graduates. **Physically disabled:** Services for visually, speech, hearing impaired.

**Contact.** E-mail: admissions@greensborocollege.edu
Phone: (336) 272-7102 ext. 211 Toll-free number: (800) 346-8226
Fax: (336) 378-0154
Tim Jackson, Director of Admissions, Greensboro College, 815 West Market Street, Greensboro, NC 27401-1875

## Guilford College
**Greensboro, North Carolina**
www.guilford.edu
CB member
CB code: 5261

- Private 4-year liberal arts college affiliated with Society of Friends (Quaker)
- Residential campus in small city
- 2,681 degree-seeking undergraduates: 18% part-time, 59% women, 25% African American, 1% Asian American, 3% Hispanic American, 1% Native American, 1% international
- 62% of applicants admitted
- Application essay required
- 61% graduate within 6 years; 25% enter graduate study

**General.** Founded in 1837. Regionally accredited. **Degrees:** 505 bachelor's awarded. **ROTC:** Army, Naval, Air Force. **Location:** 90 miles from Raleigh, 100 miles from Charlotte. **Calendar:** Semester, limited summer session. **Full-time faculty:** 126 total; 86% have terminal degrees, 16% minority, 48% women. **Part-time faculty:** 119 total; 50% have terminal degrees, 11% minority, 57% women. **Class size:** 60% < 20, 39% 20-39, 1% 40-49, less than 1% 50-99. **Special facilities:** Observatory, multimedia learning center for cultures and languages, telecommunications center, photography studio, outdoor sculpture studio, computer visualization laboratory.

**Freshman class profile.** 3,780 applied, 2,356 admitted, 448 enrolled.

| Mid 50% test scores | | GPA 2.0-2.99: | 37% |
|---|---|---|---|
| SAT critical reading: | 460-600 | Rank in top quarter: | 39% |
| SAT math: | 460-590 | Rank in top tenth: | 16% |
| SAT writing: | 440-590 | End year in good standing: | 82% |
| ACT composite: | 20-26 | Return as sophomores: | 80% |
| GPA 3.75 or higher: | 10% | Out-of-state: | 49% |
| GPA 3.50-3.74: | 14% | Live on campus: | 98% |
| GPA 3.0-3.49: | 39% | | |

**Basis for selection.** School achievement record and essay most important. Test scores, interview, recommendations, interests, leadership ability also important. Minimum SAT composite score of 1000 (exclusive of Writing) or ACT score of 22 recommended. SAT or ACT recommended. Applicant may choose to submit portfolio instead of standardized test scores. Portfolio should reflect student's academic, creative, and personal interests and accomplishments. It must include, but is not limited to, 3-5 writing samples (at least one should be a graded expository written work) and, if available, a junior/senior reading list. Auditions and portfolios recommended in music, theater and art. **Homeschooled:** Interview required. Provide reason for homeschooling.

**High school preparation.** 12 units recommended. Recommended units include English 4, mathematics 3, social studies 3, history 3, science 3 and foreign language 2.

**2010-2011 Annual costs.** Tuition/fees: $28,800. Room/board: $7,950. Books/supplies: $900. Personal expenses: $1,200.

**2009-2010 Financial aid.** **Need-based:** 398 full-time freshmen applied for aid; 343 were judged to have need; 343 of these received aid. Average scholarship/grant was $10,642; average loan $5,854. 70% of total undergraduate aid awarded as scholarships/grants, 30% as loans/jobs. **Non-need-based:** Awarded to 446 full-time undergraduates, including 121 freshmen. Scholarships awarded for academics.

**Application procedures. Admission:** Priority date 2/15; deadline 8/15 (postmark date). $25 fee, may be waived for applicants with need, free for online applicants. Admission notification on a rolling basis beginning on or about 10/1. Must reply by May 1 or within 4 week(s) if notified thereafter.

**Financial aid:** Priority date 3/1; no closing date. FAFSA required. Applicants notified on a rolling basis starting 2/15; must reply within 2 week(s) of notification.

**Academics.** Faculty tutoring for skills development and student tutoring for course-specific help available. Assistance available for non-remedial writing, organizational/time-management skills, and students with learning disabilities. Remedial assistance and reader service for the blind available. **Special study options:** Accelerated study, combined bachelor's/graduate degree, cooperative education, cross-registration, double major, ESL, exchange student, honors, independent study, internships, liberal arts/career combination, student-designed major, study abroad, teacher certification program, Washington semester, weekend college. 3-2 degree programs available in forestry and environmental studies with Duke University, and in physician assistant training with Bowman Gray School of Medicine at Wake Forest University. Many internships, work-study programs, accelerated degree programs in business management, computer information systems, psychology, and biology, dual majors, student-designed majors, study abroad in 9 countries, and cross-registration with members of the Greater Greensboro Consortium (8 colleges/universities). **Credit/placement by examination:** AP, CLEP, IB, SAT, ACT, institutional tests. 32 credit hours maximum toward bachelor's degree. **Support services:** Learning center, pre-admission summer program, reduced course load, remedial instruction, study skills assistance, tutoring, writing center.

**Majors. Area/ethnic studies:** African-American, German, women's. **Biology:** General, biomedical sciences. **Business:** Accounting, business admin. **Computer sciences:** General, information systems, information technology. **Conservation:** Environmental studies. **Education:** Elementary, physical, secondary. **Foreign languages:** French, German, Germanic, Spanish. **Health:** Athletic training. **History:** General. **Interdisciplinary:** Peace/conflict. **Math:** General. **Parks/recreation:** Exercise sciences, health/fitness, sports admin. **Philosophy/religion:** Philosophy, religion. **Physical sciences:** Chemistry, geology, physics. **Protective services:** Criminal justice, forensics. **Psychology:** General. **Social sciences:** Economics, international relations, political science, sociology. **Visual/performing arts:** Art, dramatic, theater arts management. **Other:** Forensic accounting, Health sciences.

**Most popular majors.** Biology 9%, business/marketing 17%, history 7%, psychology 9%, security/protective services 12%, social sciences 11%, visual/performing arts 6%.

**Computing on campus.** 348 workstations in dormitories, library, computer center, student center. Dormitories wired for high-speed internet access and linked to campus network. Commuter students can connect to campus network. Online course registration, helpline, repair service, wireless network available.

**Student life. Freshman orientation:** Mandatory, $75 fee. Preregistration for classes offered. One-day event in Spring; parents invited. **Policies:** Consistent with its Quaker heritage, college promotes and encourages student involvement in community service projects. **Housing:** Guaranteed on-campus for freshmen. Coed dorms, single-sex dorms, special housing for disabled, apartments, cooperative housing, wellness housing available. $400 fully refundable deposit, deadline 5/1. Special interest housing available. **Activities:** Bands, campus ministries, choral groups, dance, drama, film society, international student organizations, literary magazine, music ensembles, musical theater, radio station, student government, student newspaper, African American cultural society, Amnesty International, Project Community, community senate, Christian fellowship, Native American club, Hillel, Quaker Concerns, Guilford Action Network.

**Athletics.** NCAA. **Intercollegiate:** Baseball, basketball, cross-country, football (tackle) M, golf M, lacrosse, rugby, soccer, softball W, swimming W, tennis, volleyball W. **Intramural:** Baseball, basketball, cheerleading W, football (non-tackle), soccer, softball, table tennis, tennis, volleyball, water polo. **Team name:** Quakers.

**Student services.** Adult student services, alcohol/substance abuse counseling, chaplain/spiritual director, career counseling, student employment services, financial aid counseling, health services, minority student services, personal counseling, placement for graduates, veterans' counselor, women's services. **Physically disabled:** Services for visually, speech, hearing impaired. **Learning disabled:** Comprehensive services available.

**Contact.** E-mail: admission@guilford.edu
Phone: (336) 316-2100 Toll-free number: (800) 992-7759
Fax: (336) 316-2954
Randy Doss, Vice President for Enrollment Services, Guilford College, Admissions, New Garden Hall, Greensboro, NC 27410-4108

## High Point University
**High Point, North Carolina**
www.highpoint.edu
CB member
CB code: 5293

- Private 4-year university and liberal arts college affiliated with United Methodist Church
- Residential campus in small city

- 3,248 degree-seeking undergraduates: 3% part-time, 62% women, 13% African American, 2% Asian American, 2% Hispanic American, 1% international
- 324 degree-seeking graduate students
- 71% of applicants admitted
- SAT or ACT (ACT writing optional) required
- 56% graduate within 6 years; 40% enter graduate study

**General.** Founded in 1924. Regionally accredited. High Point University in England (at Leeds University); exchange program in Oxford Brookes University (Oxford, England); opportunities for study abroad in Canada, Ecuador, England, France, Germany, Italy, Mexico, Scotland, Spain, and Wales. **Degrees:** 513 bachelor's awarded; master's offered. **ROTC:** Army, Air Force. **Location:** 15 miles from Greensboro, 15 miles from Winston Salem. **Calendar:** Semester, limited summer session. **Full-time faculty:** 158 total; 77% have terminal degrees. **Part-time faculty:** 125 total; 50% women. **Class size:** 60% < 20, 39% 20-39, less than 1% 40-49, less than 1% 50-99, less than 1% >100.

**Freshman class profile.** 4,529 applied, 3,228 admitted, 1,030 enrolled.

| Mid 50% test scores | | Rank in top quarter: | 41% |
|---|---|---|---|
| SAT critical reading: | 480-580 | Rank in top tenth: | 17% |
| SAT math: | 490-600 | Return as sophomores: | 79% |
| SAT writing: | 480-580 | Out-of-state: | 76% |
| ACT composite: | 20-25 | Live on campus: | 97% |
| GPA 3.75 or higher: | 9% | International: | 1% |
| GPA 3.50-3.74: | 11% | Fraternities: | 25% |
| GPA 3.0-3.49: | 35% | Sororities: | 15% |
| GPA 2.0-2.99: | 44% | | |

**Basis for selection.** The most important factors are the academic transcript, including grades received and course selection, followed by standardized test scores (SAT or ACT). Other important factors are demonstrated leadership, extracurricular and community involvement, and special talent. Students who speak English as a second language must demonstrate proficiency in English. TOEFL preferred, other instruments considered. International students may submit TOEFL in lieu of SAT or ACT, unless they wish to play on intercollegiate athletic teams in which case either SAT or ACT required. Interview strongly encouraged. Applicants asked to provide short essay answers to specific questions, but personal essays invited and considered. **Learning Disabled:** Regardless of disability status, a person must meet the academic and technical standards required for admission.

**High school preparation.** 14 units required. Required and recommended units include English 4, mathematics 3, social studies 3, science 2 (laboratory 1), foreign language 2 and academic electives 2.

**2010-2011 Annual costs.** Comprehensive fee: $35,400. Books/supplies: $1,500. Personal expenses: $2,000.

**2008-2009 Financial aid. Non-need-based:** Scholarships awarded for academics, alumni affiliation, art, athletics, leadership, music/drama, religious affiliation, state residency.

**Application procedures. Admission:** Priority date 11/3; deadline 3/14 (postmark date). $40 fee, may be waived for applicants with need. Admission notification on a rolling basis beginning on or about 1/1. Must reply by May 1 or within 4 week(s) if notified thereafter. **Financial aid:** Priority date 3/1; no closing date. FAFSA required. Applicants notified on a rolling basis starting 4/1; must reply within 3 week(s) of notification.

**Academics. Special study options:** Accelerated study, combined bachelor's/graduate degree, cooperative education, cross-registration, double major, dual enrollment of high school students, ESL, honors, independent study, internships, liberal arts/career combination, student-designed major, study abroad, teacher certification program. Dual degree programs with Duke University (forestry and environmental science) and Wake Forest University School of Medicine (medical technology). **Credit/placement by examination:** AP, CLEP, IB, SAT, ACT, institutional tests. 31 credit hours maximum toward bachelor's degree. **Support services:** Learning center, pre-admission summer program, reduced course load, study skills assistance, tutoring, writing center.

**Majors. Area/ethnic studies:** American. **Biology:** General. **Business:** Accounting, business admin, entrepreneurial studies, human resources, international, management information systems, marketing, organizational behavior. **Communications:** General, digital media, journalism. **Computer sciences:** General, computer science, security. **Conservation:** Forestry. **Education:** Art, early childhood, elementary, middle, physical, secondary, special. **Foreign languages:** General, French, Spanish. **Health:** Athletic training, clinical lab science. **History:** General. **Interdisciplinary:** Global studies. **Math:** General. **Parks/recreation:** Exercise sciences, facilities management, sports admin. **Philosophy/religion:** Philosophy, religion. **Physical sciences:** Chemistry. **Protective services:** Criminal justice. **Psychology:** General. **Social**

**sciences:** Political science, sociology. **Visual/performing arts:** Art, dramatic, interior design, theater design. **Other:** Games design and interactive communication, Home furnishings marketing.

**Most popular majors.** Business/marketing 41%, education 9%, psychology 6%, social sciences 8%.

**Computing on campus.** 950 workstations in library, computer center, student center. Dormitories wired for high-speed internet access and linked to campus network. Commuter students can connect to campus network. Online course registration, online library, helpline, repair service, student web hosting, wireless network available.

**Student life. Freshman orientation:** Mandatory. Preregistration for classes offered. **Housing:** Guaranteed on-campus for freshmen. Coed dorms, single-sex dorms, special housing for disabled, apartments, cooperative housing, fraternity/sorority housing, wellness housing available. $200 fully refundable deposit, deadline 5/1. **Activities:** Bands, choral groups, dance, drama, international student organizations, literary magazine, music ensembles, Model UN, musical theater, radio station, student government, student newspaper, TV station, Alpha Phi Omega, black cultural awareness, Board of Stewards, College Republicans, College Democrats, Fellowship of Christian Athletes, Phi Theta Kappa Alumni Association, volunteer center.

**Athletics.** NCAA. **Intercollegiate:** Baseball M, basketball, cheerleading, cross-country, golf, soccer, tennis, track and field, volleyball W. **Intramural:** Badminton, basketball, bowling, golf, racquetball, soccer, softball, swimming, table tennis, tennis, track and field M, volleyball, water polo. **Team name:** Panthers.

**Student services.** Adult student services, alcohol/substance abuse counseling, chaplain/spiritual director, career counseling, student employment services, financial aid counseling, health services, personal counseling, placement for graduates, veterans' counselor.

**Contact.**  E-mail: admiss@highpoint.edu
Phone: (336) 841-9216 Toll-free number: (800) 345-6993
Fax: (336) 888-6382
Andy Bills, Vice President for Enrollment, High Point University, 833 Montlieu Avenue, High Point, NC 27262-3598

---

## John Wesley College
### High Point, North Carolina
www.johnwesley.edu                              CB code: 5348

- Private 4-year Bible college affiliated with interdenominational tradition
- Commuter campus in small city
- 93 degree-seeking undergraduates: 28% part-time, 46% women
- 68% of applicants admitted
- Application essay, interview required

**General.** Founded in 1932. Accredited by ABHE. **Degrees:** 36 bachelor's, 2 associate awarded. **Location:** 15 miles from Greensboro, 60 miles from Charlotte. **Calendar:** Semester, limited summer session. **Full-time faculty:** 3 total; 100% have terminal degrees. **Part-time faculty:** 25 total. **Class size:** 98% < 20, 2% 20-39.

**Freshman class profile.** 19 applied, 13 admitted, 10 enrolled.

| Out-of-state: | 25% | Live on campus: | 50% |
|---|---|---|---|

**Basis for selection.** Future career in church-related vocations and motivation; religious commitment and personal statement very important. Positive personal testimony required. Finding and following God's will foremost. **Homeschooled:** Transcript of courses and grades required. Junior or higher standing, GPA 3.2 or higher, 16 or older, and recommendation from high school administrator or guidance counselor required.

**High school preparation.** 20 units recommended. Recommended units include English 4, mathematics 3, social studies 2, science 2 (laboratory 2).

**2009-2010 Annual costs.** Tuition/fees: $10,730. Room only: $2,344. Books/supplies: $1,200. Personal expenses: $2,700.

**2008-2009 Financial aid. Additional information:** Early Acceptance Scholarships, Academic Honor Scholarships, Married Student Credit and Minister/Missionary Dependent Scholarship available.

**Application procedures. Admission:** Closing date 8/8 (postmark date). $35 fee, may be waived for applicants with need. Admission notification on a rolling basis. **Financial aid:** Priority date 3/15; no closing date. FAFSA required. Applicants notified on a rolling basis starting 6/1; must reply within 3 week(s) of notification.

**Academics.** All students major in Bible; second major optional. **Special study options:** Accelerated study, cooperative education, distance learning, double major, dual enrollment of high school students, independent study, internships, student-designed major. **Credit/placement by examination:** AP, CLEP, IB, institutional tests. 15 credit hours maximum toward associate degree, 30 toward bachelor's. **Support services:** Reduced course load.

**Majors. Business:** Business admin. **Education:** Elementary. **Theology:** Pastoral counseling, religious ed, theology.

**Most popular majors.** Business/marketing 33%, philosophy/religious studies 67%.

**Computing on campus.** 6 workstations in library, computer center. Dormitories wired for high-speed internet access. Online library available.

**Student life. Freshman orientation:** Mandatory. Preregistration for classes offered. Orientation activities held 2 business days before classes begin. **Policies:** Religious observance required. **Housing:** Apartments, wellness housing available. $50 deposit, deadline 7/15. **Activities:** Campus ministries, drama, literary magazine, student government, evangelistic ministries, prison ministry, gospel music team, foreign missions involvement team.

**Athletics. Intramural:** Basketball, bowling, golf, table tennis, volleyball.

**Student services.** Chaplain/spiritual director, student employment services, financial aid counseling, personal counseling, veterans' counselor.

**Contact.** E-mail: admissions@johnwesley.edu
Phone: (336) 889-2262 ext. 127 Fax: (336) 889-2261
Jeremy Reese, Admissions Counselor, John Wesley College, 2314 North Centennial, High Point, NC 27265-3197

## Johnson & Wales University: Charlotte
**Charlotte, North Carolina**
www.jwu.edu                              CB code: 4360

▸ Private 4-year university
▸ Residential campus in very large city
▸ 2,451 degree-seeking undergraduates: 1% part-time, 58% women, 24% African American, 2% Asian American, 3% Hispanic American, 1% Native American, 1% international
▸ 62% of applicants admitted

**General. Degrees:** 312 bachelor's, 678 associate awarded. **Location:** Downtown. **Calendar:** Quarter. **Full-time faculty:** 83 total; 45% women. **Part-time faculty:** 19 total; 58% women. **Class size:** 33% < 20, 61% 20-39, 6% 40-49, less than 1% 50-99.

**Freshman class profile.** 6,178 applied, 3,806 admitted, 682 enrolled.

| Mid 50% test scores | | | |
|---|---|---|---|
| SAT critical reading: | 410-520 | GPA 3.0-3.49: | 32% |
| SAT math: | 410-540 | GPA 2.0-2.99: | 48% |
| SAT writing: | 390-510 | Return as sophomores: | 75% |
| GPA 3.75 or higher: | 11% | Out-of-state: | 68% |
| GPA 3.50-3.74: | 8% | Live on campus: | 85% |
| | | International: | 1% |

**Basis for selection.** Academic record, secondary school curriculum, class rank, GPA, test scores and interview important. Student motivation and interest given strong consideration. SAT or ACT required for applicants to the honors programs. **Homeschooled:** Transcript of courses and grades, state high school equivalency certificate required. SAT (verbal and math) or ACT required.

**High school preparation.** Required units include English 4, mathematics 3, social studies 2 and science 3.

**2010-2011 Annual costs.** Tuition/fees: $24,429. Room/board: $9,918. Books/supplies: $1,500. Personal expenses: $594.

**2009-2010 Financial aid. Non-need-based:** Scholarships awarded for academics, alumni affiliation, job skills, leadership, state residency.

**Application procedures. Admission:** No deadline. No application fee. Admission notification on a rolling basis beginning on or about 11/1. Must reply by May 1 or within 2 week(s) if notified thereafter. **Financial aid:** No deadline. FAFSA required. Applicants notified on a rolling basis starting 3/1.

**Academics.** Math center. **Special study options:** Accelerated study, cooperative education, dual enrollment of high school students, ESL, exchange student, honors, independent study, internships, study abroad. **Credit/placement by examination:** CLEP, institutional tests. **Support services:**

Learning center, pre-admission summer program, reduced course load, remedial instruction, study skills assistance, tutoring, writing center.

**Majors. Business:** Accounting, business admin, fashion, hotel/motel admin, management science, marketing, restaurant/food services. **Parks/recreation:** Facilities management, sports admin. **Personal/culinary services:** Chef training, restaurant/catering. **Other:** Food service.

**Most popular majors.** Business/marketing 37%, family/consumer sciences 49%, parks/recreation 14%.

**Computing on campus.** 160 workstations in library. Dormitories wired for high-speed internet access and linked to campus network. Commuter students can connect to campus network. Online library, helpline, wireless network available.

**Student life. Freshman orientation:** Available. **Housing:** Coed dorms available. $200 fully refundable deposit. **Activities:** Campus ministries, international student organizations, student government, student newspaper.

**Athletics. Team name:** Wildcats.

**Student services.** Career counseling, student employment services, financial aid counseling, health services, personal counseling, veterans' counselor. **Physically disabled:** Services for visually, speech, hearing impaired.

**Contact.** E-mail: admissions.clt@jwu.edu
Phone: (980) 598-1100 Toll-free number: (866) 598-2427
Fax: (980) 598-1111
Joseph Campos, Director of Admissions, Johnson & Wales University: Charlotte, 801 West Trade Street, Charlotte, NC 28202

## Johnson C. Smith University
**Charlotte, North Carolina**                    CB member
www.jcsu.edu                                      CB code: 5333

▸ Private 4-year university and liberal arts college
▸ Residential campus in very large city
▸ 1,466 degree-seeking undergraduates: 3% part-time, 59% women, 97% African American, 1% international
▸ 30% of applicants admitted
▸ SAT or ACT (ACT writing optional), application essay required
▸ 39% graduate within 6 years; 9% enter graduate study

**General.** Founded in 1867. Regionally accredited. **Degrees:** 211 bachelor's awarded. **ROTC:** Army, Air Force. **Location:** 244 miles from Atlanta. **Calendar:** Semester, limited summer session. **Full-time faculty:** 100 total; 81% have terminal degrees, 70% minority, 52% women. **Part-time faculty:** 31 total; 13% have terminal degrees, 81% minority, 55% women. **Class size:** 49% < 20, 49% 20-39, 2% 40-49.

**Freshman class profile.** 5,430 applied, 1,645 admitted, 282 enrolled.

| Mid 50% test scores | | | |
|---|---|---|---|
| SAT critical reading: | 400-460 | Rank in top quarter: | 21% |
| SAT math: | 400-470 | Rank in top tenth: | 6% |
| ACT composite: | 16-19 | End year in good standing: | 86% |
| GPA 3.75 or higher: | 4% | Return as sophomores: | 68% |
| GPA 3.50-3.74: | 6% | Out-of-state: | 76% |
| GPA 3.0-3.49: | 31% | Live on campus: | 95% |
| GPA 2.0-2.99: | 57% | International: | 1% |

**Basis for selection.** Competitive test scores and grade point averages (GPA) taken into account in admissions decisions. Two letters of recommendations, a resume or list of extra-curricular activities, and a personal statement explaining how Johnson C. Smith University can help them achieve their goals required. **Homeschooled:** Statement describing homeschool structure and mission required.

**High school preparation.** College-preparatory program required. 16 units required. Required units include English 4, mathematics 3, social studies 2, science 2 (laboratory 1), foreign language 2 and academic electives 3.

**2009-2010 Annual costs.** Tuition/fees: $15,754. Room/board: $6,132. Books/supplies: $1,750. Personal expenses: $3,250.

**2009-2010 Financial aid. Need-based:** 269 full-time freshmen applied for aid; 259 were judged to have need; 259 of these received aid. Average need met was 51%. Average scholarship/grant was $10,086; average loan $3,676. 44% of total undergraduate aid awarded as scholarships/grants, 56% as loans/jobs. **Non-need-based:** Awarded to 100 full-time undergraduates, including 23 freshmen. Scholarships awarded for academics, athletics, ROTC, state residency.

873

**Application procedures. Admission:** Closing date 3/15 (postmark date). $25 fee, may be waived for applicants with need. Admission notification on a rolling basis beginning on or about 4/1. Must reply by 5/1. **Financial aid:** Priority date 3/1; no closing date. FAFSA required. Applicants notified on a rolling basis starting 3/1; must reply within 2 week(s) of notification.

**Academics. Special study options:** Accelerated study, cooperative education, cross-registration, double major, exchange student, honors, independent study, internships, liberal arts/career combination, study abroad, teacher certification program. **Credit/placement by examination:** AP, CLEP, institutional tests. **Support services:** Learning center, pre-admission summer program, reduced course load, study skills assistance, tutoring, writing center.

**Majors. Biology:** General. **Business:** Business admin. **Communications:** Media studies. **Computer sciences:** General, information technology. **Education:** Elementary, health, mathematics, physical. **Engineering:** Computer. **Foreign languages:** French, Spanish. **Health:** Community health services. **History:** General. **Interdisciplinary:** Natural sciences. **Liberal arts:** Arts/sciences. **Math:** General. **Parks/recreation:** Sports admin. **Physical sciences:** Chemistry. **Psychology:** General. **Public administration:** Social work. **Social sciences:** General, criminology, economics, political science. **Visual/performing arts:** General.

**Most popular majors.** Business/marketing 20%, communications/journalism 13%, computer/information sciences 12%, liberal arts 6%, parks/recreation 7%, social sciences 12%.

**Computing on campus.** PC or laptop required. 335 workstations in dormitories, library, computer center. Dormitories wired for high-speed internet access and linked to campus network. Commuter students can connect to campus network. Online course registration, online library, helpline, repair service, wireless network available.

**Student life. Freshman orientation:** Available, $100 fee. Preregistration for classes offered. Three-day program in July for students and parents. **Housing:** Guaranteed on-campus for freshmen. Coed dorms, single-sex dorms available. $150 nonrefundable deposit, deadline 5/1. **Activities:** Bands, campus ministries, choral groups, dance, drama, international student organizations, music ensembles, student government, student newspaper, Alpha Phi Omega National Service Fraternity, Collegiate 100, Driven to Witness, For Your Brother, International Club, National Council of Negro Women, Political Science Club, Religious Life Program, Students in Free Enterprise.

**Athletics. NCAA. Intercollegiate:** Basketball, bowling W, cross-country, football (tackle) M, golf M, softball W, tennis, track and field, volleyball W. **Intramural:** Basketball, football (non-tackle), table tennis. **Team name:** Golden Bulls.

**Student services.** Adult student services, alcohol/substance abuse counseling, career counseling, services for economically disadvantaged, student employment services, financial aid counseling, health services, minority student services, personal counseling, veterans' counselor. **Physically disabled:** Services for visually, speech, hearing impaired.

**Contact.** E-mail: admissions@jcsu.edu
Phone: (704) 378-1010 Toll-free number: (800) 782-7303
Fax: (704) 378-1242
Ronice Johnson, Associate Director of Admissions, Johnson C. Smith University, 100 Beatties Ford Road, Charlotte, NC 28216-5398

## Lees-McRae College

**Banner Elk, North Carolina**
www.lmc.edu

**CB member**
**CB code: 5364**

- Private 4-year liberal arts college affiliated with Presbyterian Church (USA)
- Residential campus in rural community
- 906 degree-seeking undergraduates: 1% part-time, 62% women, 8% African American, 3% Hispanic American, 3% international
- 53% of applicants admitted
- SAT or ACT (ACT writing optional) required
- 46% graduate within 6 years

**General.** Founded in 1900. Regionally accredited. **Degrees:** 192 bachelor's awarded. **Location:** 17 miles from Boone, 40 miles from Johnson City, Tennessee. **Calendar:** Semester, limited summer session. **Full-time faculty:** 52 total; 58% have terminal degrees, 6% minority, 56% women. **Part-time faculty:** 2 total. **Class size:** 67% < 20, 33% 20-39, less than 1% 40-49, less than 1% 50-99. **Special facilities:** Wireless campus, biology field station, Blue Ridge Wildlife Rehabilitation Institute.

**Freshman class profile.** 1,287 applied, 677 admitted, 163 enrolled.

| Mid 50% test scores | | | |
|---|---|---|---|
| SAT critical reading: | 440-660 | GPA 2.0-2.99: | 46% |
| SAT math: | 420-480 | Rank in top quarter: | 41% |
| ACT composite: | 14-28 | Rank in top tenth: | 33% |
| GPA 3.75 or higher: | 15% | Return as sophomores: | 66% |
| GPA 3.50-3.74: | 16% | Out-of-state: | 44% |
| GPA 3.0-3.49: | 20% | Live on campus: | 98% |
| | | International: | 4% |

**Basis for selection.** High school record and rank in top half of class preferred. Test scores optional. Recommendations considered. Interview recommended for all students; portfolio recommended for performing arts programs. Audition required for athletic, performing arts programs.

**High school preparation.** College-preparatory program recommended. 18 units required; 19 recommended. Required and recommended units include English 4, mathematics 2-3, history 1, science 2, foreign language 1 and academic electives 8.

**2009-2010 Annual costs.** Tuition/fees: $21,625. Room/board: $7,400. Books/supplies: $950. Personal expenses: $1,945.

**2008-2009 Financial aid. Need-based:** 136 full-time freshmen applied for aid; 115 were judged to have need; 115 of these received aid. Average need met was 73%. Average scholarship/grant was $9,500; average loan $3,500. 72% of total undergraduate aid awarded as scholarships/grants, 28% as loans/jobs. **Non-need-based:** Awarded to 903 full-time undergraduates, including 189 freshmen. Scholarships awarded for academics, athletics, music/drama, religious affiliation, state residency.

**Application procedures. Admission:** Priority date 5/1; no deadline. No application fee. Admission notification on a rolling basis beginning on or about 11/1. **Financial aid:** Priority date 4/15; no closing date. FAFSA required. Applicants notified on a rolling basis starting 3/1; must reply within 2 week(s) of notification.

**Academics. Special study options:** Accelerated study, cross-registration, distance learning, double major, dual enrollment of high school students, ESL, exchange student, honors, independent study, internships, student-designed major, study abroad, teacher certification program. 3-2 program Environmental Science/Forestry with Duke University. **Credit/placement by examination:** AP, CLEP, IB, SAT, ACT, institutional tests. 16 credit hours maximum toward bachelor's degree. **Support services:** Learning center, remedial instruction, study skills assistance, tutoring, writing center.

**Majors. Biology:** General. **Business:** Business admin. **Communications:** General. **Computer sciences:** Computer science, information systems. **Education:** Drama/dance, elementary, physical. **Health:** Predental, premedicine, preveterinary. **Liberal arts:** Arts/sciences. **Math:** General. **Philosophy/religion:** Religion. **Protective services:** Criminal justice. **Psychology:** General. **Social sciences:** International relations, sociology. **Visual/performing arts:** General, art, arts management, dramatic, musical theater, theater design.

**Most popular majors.** Business/marketing 9%, education 45%, health sciences 7%, social sciences 15%, visual/performing arts 7%.

**Computing on campus.** 125 workstations in dormitories, library, computer center, student center. Dormitories wired for high-speed internet access and linked to campus network. Commuter students can connect to campus network. Online course registration, online library, helpline, wireless network available.

**Student life. Freshman orientation:** Mandatory. Preregistration for classes offered. 6 summer Freshmen Experience sessions (1 required) followed by August orientation. **Housing:** Guaranteed on-campus for freshmen. Coed dorms, single-sex dorms, apartments available. $250 nonrefundable deposit. **Activities:** Pep band, campus ministries, dance, drama, international student organizations, musical theater, student government, Order of the Tower, student ambassadors, residence hall association, sports medicine club, Phi Beta Lambda, Circle K, campus after the class hours, EMS club.

**Athletics. NCAA. Intercollegiate:** Basketball, cheerleading, cross-country, golf M, lacrosse, soccer, softball W, tennis, track and field, volleyball. **Intramural:** Basketball, cross-country, football (non-tackle), golf, skiing, soccer, softball, table tennis, tennis, volleyball. **Team name:** Bobcats.

**Student services.** Alcohol/substance abuse counseling, chaplain/spiritual director, career counseling, student employment services, financial aid counseling, health services, personal counseling, veterans' counselor.

**Contact.** E-mail: keener@lmc.edu
Phone: (828) 898-8723 Toll-free number: (800) 280-4562
Fax: (828) 898-8814
Frank OHagan, Director of Admissions, Lees-McRae College, Box 128, Banner Elk, NC 28604

## Lenoir-Rhyne University

**Hickory, North Carolina**
www.lr.edu

**CB member**
**CB code: 5365**

- Private 4-year liberal arts college affiliated with Evangelical Lutheran Church in America
- Residential campus in large town
- 1,387 degree-seeking undergraduates
- 78% of applicants admitted
- SAT or ACT with writing required

**General.** Founded in 1891. Regionally accredited. **Degrees:** 250 bachelor's awarded; master's offered. **ROTC:** Army, Naval. **Location:** 50 miles from Charlotte. **Calendar:** Semester, limited summer session. **Full-time faculty:** 89 total; 84% have terminal degrees, 4% minority. **Part-time faculty:** 53 total; 58% have terminal degrees, 8% minority. **Class size:** 68% < 20, 30% 20-39, 1% 40-49, less than 1% 50-99. **Special facilities:** Observatory, multimedia classrooms, outdoor classroom.

**Freshman class profile.** 2,574 applied, 1,998 admitted, 363 enrolled.

| Mid 50% test scores | | | |
|---|---|---|---|
| SAT critical reading: | 440-540 | GPA 3.0-3.49: | 22% |
| SAT math: | 450-570 | GPA 2.0-2.99: | 19% |
| SAT writing: | 460-550 | Rank in top quarter: | 48% |
| ACT composite: | 19-24 | Rank in top tenth: | 19% |
| GPA 3.75 or higher: | 43% | Out-of-state: | 22% |
| GPA 3.50-3.74: | 16% | Live on campus: | 78% |

**Basis for selection.** School achievement record and courses taken most important. Interview recommended for all students; audition required for music majors. **Homeschooled:** Transcript of courses and grades required.

**High school preparation.** 12 units required. Required units include English 4, mathematics 3, history 1, science 1 (laboratory 1) and foreign language 2. Chemistry required for nursing program. History refers to U.S. History; mathematics needs to include algebra I, algebra II, geometry.

**2010-2011 Annual costs.** Tuition/fees: $25,290. Room/board: $8,930. Books/supplies: $1,100. Personal expenses: $1,500.

**2008-2009 Financial aid. Non-need-based:** Scholarships awarded for academics, athletics, job skills, leadership, minority status, music/drama, ROTC, state residency.

**Application procedures. Admission:** No deadline. $35 fee, may be waived for applicants with need. Admission notification on a rolling basis beginning on or about 6/1. Must reply by May 1 or within 2 week(s) if notified thereafter. Students will not be put on the housing roster until the deposit is received. **Financial aid:** Priority date 3/1, closing date 8/1. FAFSA required. Applicants notified on a rolling basis starting 3/1; must reply within 2 week(s) of notification.

**Academics.** Special program for deaf, hearing-impaired and disabled students. **Special study options:** Accelerated study, combined bachelor's/graduate degree, cross-registration, distance learning, double major, dual enrollment of high school students, ESL, exchange student, external degree, honors, independent study, internships, liberal arts/career combination, student-designed major, study abroad, teacher certification program, Washington semester. **Credit/placement by examination:** AP, CLEP, IB, SAT, ACT, institutional tests. 16 credit hours maximum toward bachelor's degree. **Support services:** Learning center, pre-admission summer program, remedial instruction, study skills assistance, tutoring, writing center.

**Majors. Area/ethnic studies:** American. **Biology:** General. **Business:** Accounting, finance, international, management information systems, management science, marketing. **Communications:** General. **Computer sciences:** General, information systems. **Conservation:** Environmental studies, forestry. **Education:** Art, biology, chemistry, Deaf/hearing impaired, early childhood, elementary, English, ESL, history, mathematics, middle, music, physical, psychology, science, social science, social studies. **Engineering technology:** General. **Family/consumer sciences:** Child development. **Foreign languages:** French, German, Latin, Spanish. **Health:** Athletic training, clinical lab science, nursing (RN), premedicine. **History:** General. **Legal studies:** Prelaw. **Liberal arts:** Arts/sciences. **Math:** General. **Parks/recreation:** Sports admin. **Philosophy/religion:** Philosophy, religion. **Physical sciences:** Chemistry, physics. **Psychology:** General. **Public administration:** Human services. **Science technology:** Chemical. **Social sciences:** Economics, international relations, political science, sociology. **Theology:** Sacred music. **Visual/performing arts:** Arts management, dramatic, graphic design, music performance.

**Most popular majors.** Business/marketing 14%, education 18%, health sciences 24%, psychology 8%.

**Computing on campus.** 112 workstations in library, computer center, student center. Dormitories wired for high-speed internet access and linked to campus network. Commuter students can connect to campus network. Online library, helpline, wireless network available.

**Student life. Freshman orientation:** Mandatory. Preregistration for classes offered. Held 2 days before start of classes. **Housing:** Guaranteed on-campus for all undergraduates. Coed dorms, special housing for disabled, fraternity/sorority housing available. $200 deposit. **Activities:** Bands, campus ministries, choral groups, dance, drama, literary magazine, music ensembles, Model UN, musical theater, radio station, student government, student newspaper, symphony orchestra, Black Student Alliance, Campus Crusade for Christ, Fellowship of Christian Athletes, North Carolina Student Legislature, Intervarsity Christian Fellowship, College Democrats, Lutheran Student Movement, Student Occupational Therapy Association, Gay Straight Alliance, College Republicans, College Democrats.

**Athletics.** NCAA. **Intercollegiate:** Baseball M, basketball, cheerleading, cross-country, football (tackle) M, golf, soccer, softball W, swimming W, tennis, track and field, volleyball W. **Intramural:** Basketball, football (non-tackle), lacrosse M, soccer, softball, volleyball. **Team name:** Bears.

**Student services.** Adult student services, chaplain/spiritual director, career counseling, student employment services, financial aid counseling, health services, minority student services, personal counseling, veterans' counselor. **Physically disabled:** Services for hearing impaired.

**Contact.** E-mail: admission@lr.edu
Phone: (828) 328-7300 Toll-free number: (800) 277-5721
Fax: (828) 328-7378
Karen Feezor, Director of Admissions, Lenoir-Rhyne University, PO Box 7227, Hickory, NC 28603

## Livingstone College

**Salisbury, North Carolina**
www.livingstone.edu

**CB member**
**CB code: 5367**

- Private 4-year liberal arts college affiliated with African Methodist Episcopal Zion Church
- Residential campus in large town
- 1,082 degree-seeking undergraduates
- SAT or ACT (ACT writing optional) required

**General.** Founded in 1879. Regionally accredited. **Degrees:** 145 bachelor's awarded. **ROTC:** Army. **Location:** 44 miles from Charlotte. **Calendar:** Semester. **Full-time faculty:** 54 total. **Part-time faculty:** 11 total. **Class size:** 64% < 20, 28% 20-39, 4% 40-49, 1% 50-99, 2% >100. **Special facilities:** Center for Negro and African life, literature and international studies.

**Freshman class profile.**

| Mid 50% test scores | | | |
|---|---|---|---|
| SAT critical reading: | 330-420 | Rank in top quarter: | 6% |
| SAT math: | 330-430 | Rank in top tenth: | 4% |
| SAT writing: | 320-420 | Out-of-state: | 59% |
| ACT composite: | 13-16 | Live on campus: | 85% |

**Basis for selection.** School achievement record, test scores, recommendations important. College's placement test, instead of ELPT, used for advising and placement. Audition required for music majors; interview recommended for academically weak students.

**High school preparation.** 10 units required. Required and recommended units include English 4, mathematics 3, social studies 2, history 1, science 2 and foreign language 2.

**2009-2010 Annual costs.** Tuition/fees: $13,358. Room/board: $6,342. Books/supplies: $800. Personal expenses: $3,000.

**2008-2009 Financial aid. Non-need-based:** Scholarships awarded for academics, alumni affiliation, athletics, leadership, music/drama, religious affiliation, ROTC, state residency.

**Application procedures. Admission:** Priority date 5/15; no deadline. $25 fee, may be waived for applicants with need. Admission notification on a rolling basis. Must reply by May 1 or within 4 week(s) if notified thereafter. **Financial aid:** Priority date 3/15, closing date 6/30. FAFSA required. Applicants notified by 5/1; must reply within 4 week(s) of notification.

**Academics. Special study options:** Accelerated study, cross-registration, double major, independent study, internships, teacher certification program. **Credit/placement by examination:** CLEP, institutional tests. **Support services:** Learning center, reduced course load, study skills assistance, tutoring.

**Majors.** **Biology:** General. **Business:** Accounting, business admin. **Computer sciences:** General. **Education:** Elementary. **Engineering:** General. **Health:** Predental, prepharmacy. **History:** General. **Legal studies:** General. **Math:** General. **Parks/recreation:** Sports admin. **Physical sciences:** Chemistry. **Protective services:** Criminal justice. **Psychology:** General. **Public administration:** Social work. **Social sciences:** General, political science, sociology. **Theology:** Theology. **Visual/performing arts:** Dramatic.

**Most popular majors.** Business/marketing 25%, parks/recreation 9%, psychology 17%, security/protective services 15%, social sciences 13%.

**Computing on campus.** 200 workstations in dormitories, library, computer center. Dormitories wired for high-speed internet access and linked to campus network.

**Student life. Freshman orientation:** Mandatory, $100 fee. Preregistration for classes offered. **Housing:** Single-sex dorms, special housing for disabled, apartments available. $100 deposit. **Activities:** Bands, choral groups, dance, drama, film society, music ensembles, musical theater, radio station, student government, pre-theological union, AME Zion Council.

**Athletics.** NCAA. **Intercollegiate:** Basketball, bowling, cross-country, football (tackle) M, softball W, tennis, track and field, volleyball W. **Intramural:** Basketball. **Team name:** Blue Bears.

**Student services.** Career counseling, student employment services, health services, personal counseling, placement for graduates, veterans' counselor.

**Contact.** Phone: (704) 216-6001 Toll-free number: (800) 835-3435 Fax: (704) 216-6215
Nicole Daniels, Director of Enrollment Management and Admission, Livingstone College, 701 West Monroe Street, Salisbury, NC 28144-5213

---

## Mars Hill College
**Mars Hill, North Carolina**  **CB member**
**www.mhc.edu**  **CB code: 5395**

- Private 4-year liberal arts college affiliated with Baptist faith
- Residential campus in small town
- 1,213 degree-seeking undergraduates: 6% part-time, 51% women, 15% African American, 2% Asian American, 3% Hispanic American, 1% Native American, 3% international
- 57% of applicants admitted
- SAT or ACT (ACT writing optional) required
- 39% graduate within 6 years; 20% enter graduate study

**General.** Founded in 1856. Regionally accredited. **Degrees:** 231 bachelor's awarded. **Location:** 17 miles from Asheville. **Calendar:** Semester, extensive summer session. **Full-time faculty:** 71 total; 59% have terminal degrees, 3% minority, 44% women. **Part-time faculty:** 86 total. **Class size:** 71% < 20, 28% 20-39, less than 1% 40-49, less than 1% 50-99. **Special facilities:** Satellite receiver for foreign language study, Appalachian archives and artifacts museum.

**Freshman class profile.** 2,026 applied, 1,155 admitted, 297 enrolled.

| Mid 50% test scores | | | |
|---|---|---|---|
| SAT critical reading: | 420-530 | GPA 2.0-2.99: | 40% |
| SAT math: | 430-530 | Rank in top quarter: | 25% |
| ACT composite: | 17-24 | Rank in top tenth: | 6% |
| GPA 3.75 or higher: | 19% | End year in good standing: | 77% |
| GPA 3.50-3.74: | 12% | Return as sophomores: | 60% |
| GPA 3.0-3.49: | 28% | Out-of-state: | 34% |
| | | International: | 7% |

**Basis for selection.** School achievement record, test scores, school and community activities, recommendations from school officials all important. Students interested in early admission must apply as full-time students, achieve A average in courses, minimum SAT 1000 (exclusive of Writing) or ACT 22, and submit 2 recommendations from high school personnel. Audition required for music, theater programs. Essay, portfolio recommended; interview recommended for students who do not meet other admissions criteria. **Homeschooled:** Transcript of courses and grades required. **Learning Disabled:** Letter of documentation required.

**High school preparation.** 11 units required. Required and recommended units include English 4, mathematics 3, social studies 2, history 2, science 2, foreign language 2 and computer science 1.

**2010-2011 Annual costs.** Tuition/fees: $21,997. Room/board: $7,632. Books/supplies: $1,300. Personal expenses: $1,100.

**2008-2009 Financial aid. Need-based:** 293 full-time freshmen applied for aid; 265 were judged to have need; 265 of these received aid. Average need met was 79%. Average scholarship/grant was $14,116; average loan

$2,827. 68% of total undergraduate aid awarded as scholarships/grants, 32% as loans/jobs. **Non-need-based:** Awarded to 311 full-time undergraduates, including 91 freshmen. Scholarships awarded for academics, alumni affiliation, art, athletics, leadership, music/drama, religious affiliation, state residency.

**Application procedures. Admission:** No deadline. $25 fee, may be waived for applicants with need. Admission notification on a rolling basis. **Financial aid:** Priority date 3/15; no closing date. FAFSA required. Applicants notified on a rolling basis; must reply within 2 week(s) of notification.

**Academics. Special study options:** Accelerated study, cross-registration, distance learning, double major, dual enrollment of high school students, ESL, exchange student, independent study, internships, liberal arts/career combination, student-designed major, study abroad, teacher certification program. **Credit/placement by examination:** AP, CLEP, IB, SAT, ACT, institutional tests. 32 credit hours maximum toward bachelor's degree. **Support services:** Learning center, reduced course load, remedial instruction, study skills assistance, tutoring, writing center.

**Majors. Biology:** General, botany, zoology. **Business:** General, accounting, business admin, finance, international. **Communications:** General. **Computer sciences:** Computer science. **Education:** General, art, elementary, English, middle, music, physical, secondary. **Foreign languages:** Spanish. **Health:** Athletic training, clinical lab assistant, physician assistant, predental, premedicine, prepharmacy, preveterinary. **History:** General. **Interdisciplinary:** Biological/physical sciences. **Legal studies:** Prelaw. **Liberal arts:** Arts/sciences. **Math:** General. **Parks/recreation:** Facilities management, health/fitness. **Philosophy/religion:** Religion. **Physical sciences:** Chemistry. **Psychology:** General. **Public administration:** Social work. **Social sciences:** International relations, political science, sociology. **Visual/performing arts:** Art, dramatic, fashion design, music performance.

**Most popular majors.** Biology 6%, business/marketing 25%, education 31%, psychology 6%, visual/performing arts 6%.

**Computing on campus.** 180 workstations in library, computer center, student center. Dormitories wired for high-speed internet access and linked to campus network. Commuter students can connect to campus network. Online library, helpline, repair service, wireless network available.

**Student life. Freshman orientation:** Mandatory. Preregistration for classes offered. **Housing:** Guaranteed on-campus for all undergraduates. Single-sex dorms, special housing for disabled, apartments available. $250 deposit. College townhouses and apartments available to upperclassmen. **Activities:** Bands, campus ministries, choral groups, dance, drama, literary magazine, music ensembles, musical theater, student government, student newspaper, Christian Student Movement, Fellowship of Christian Athletes, The Refuge, Ladies of Distinction, Black Student Alliance, health care society, Green Students United, Bailey Mountain Cloggers.

**Athletics.** NCAA. **Intercollegiate:** Baseball M, basketball, cross-country, football (tackle) M, golf, lacrosse M, soccer, softball W, swimming, tennis, track and field, volleyball W. **Intramural:** Badminton, basketball, football (non-tackle), soccer, softball, tennis, volleyball, water polo M. **Team name:** Lions.

**Student services.** Adult student services, chaplain/spiritual director, career counseling, services for economically disadvantaged, student employment services, financial aid counseling, health services, personal counseling, veterans' counselor.

**Contact.** E-mail: admissions@mhc.edu
Phone: (828) 689-1201 Toll-free number: (866) 642-4968
Fax: (828) 689-1473
Ed Hoffmeyer, Dean of Admissions, Mars Hill College, Blackwell Hall, Box 370, Mars Hill, NC 28754

---

## Meredith College
**Raleigh, North Carolina**  **CB member**
**www.meredith.edu**  **CB code: 5410**

- Private 4-year liberal arts college for women
- Residential campus in large city
- 1,889 degree-seeking undergraduates: 7% part-time, 100% women, 11% African American, 3% Asian American, 3% Hispanic American, 1% Native American, 1% international
- 257 degree-seeking graduate students
- 65% of applicants admitted
- SAT or ACT (ACT writing optional) required
- 66% graduate within 6 years

**General.** Founded in 1891. Regionally accredited. **Degrees:** 430 bachelor's awarded; master's offered. **ROTC:** Army, Air Force. **Location:** 250 miles from Washington, DC, 375 miles from Atlanta. **Calendar:** Semester, limited summer session. **Full-time faculty:** 138 total; 91% have terminal degrees, 9% minority, 66% women. **Part-time faculty:** 142 total; 37% have terminal degrees, 8% minority, 75% women. **Class size:** 63% < 20, 35% 20-39, 2% 40-49. **Special facilities:** Amphitheatre, child care laboratory, experimental and clinical psychology laboratories, autism laboratory, astronomy observation deck, electron microscope suite, 15 student/faculty research laboratories, greenhouse.

**Freshman class profile.** 1,614 applied, 1,047 admitted, 481 enrolled.

| Mid 50% test scores | | | |
|---|---|---|---|
| SAT critical reading: | 460-570 | GPA 2.0-2.99: | 26% |
| SAT math: | 460-570 | Rank in top quarter: | 50% |
| ACT composite: | 18-24 | Rank in top tenth: | 22% |
| GPA 3.75 or higher: | 14% | Return as sophomores: | 76% |
| GPA 3.50-3.74: | 21% | Out-of-state: | 10% |
| GPA 3.0-3.49: | 39% | Live on campus: | 93% |
| | | International: | 2% |

**Basis for selection.** GED not accepted. School record (courses taken, grades on academic subjects, and class rank), test scores, and recommendations important. Meredith seeks to enroll qualified students of varying backgrounds, interests and talents and has a need-blind admission policy. Essay and/or interview may be required of some; audition recommended for music majors; portfolio recommended for art majors. **Homeschooled:** SAT Reasoning and SAT Subject Tests (English, math, and foreign language or one of applicant's choice) required.

**High school preparation.** 16 units required. Required units include English 4, mathematics 3, science 3 and foreign language 2. 3 units required in social studies or history. At least 1 elective required, preferably from core academic subjects.

**2009-2010 Annual costs.** Tuition/fees: $24,490. Tuition includes a new laptop computer for each full-time freshman, which will be replaced with a new laptop during her junior year. Upon graduation from Meredith, the laptop remains the property of the student. Room/board: $7,020. Books/supplies: $750. Personal expenses: $1,250.

**2009-2010 Financial aid.** **Non-need-based:** Scholarships awarded for academics, art, leadership, minority status, music/drama, religious affiliation, state residency.

**Application procedures.** **Admission:** Priority date 2/15; no deadline. $40 fee, may be waived for applicants with need. Admission notification on a rolling basis beginning on or about 11/1. Must reply by May 1 or within 2 week(s) if notified thereafter. **Financial aid:** Priority date 2/15; no closing date. FAFSA required. Applicants notified on a rolling basis starting 3/15; must reply by 5/1 or within 2 week(s) of notification.

**Academics.** Undergraduate research program available to students in all disciplines. Post-baccalaureate dietetic internship program and post-baccalaureate certificate in paralegal studies available. **Special study options:** Accelerated study, combined bachelor's/graduate degree, cooperative education, cross-registration, double major, dual enrollment of high school students, honors, independent study, internships, liberal arts/career combination, New York semester, student-designed major, study abroad, teacher certification program, United Nations semester, Washington semester. Study Abroad includes summer programs, semester/year abroad opportunities, and individually-tailored semesters. 3-2 in engineering with N.C. State University. **Credit/placement by examination:** AP, CLEP, IB, institutional tests. **Support services:** Learning center, reduced course load, remedial instruction, study skills assistance, tutoring, writing center.

**Majors. Biology:** General, molecular. **Business:** Accounting, business admin, fashion. **Communications:** General, media studies. **Computer sciences:** General, computer science. **Conservation:** Environmental science, environmental studies. **Education:** Art, drama/dance, music, physical. **Family/consumer sciences:** General, child development. **Foreign languages:** Spanish. **Health:** Dietetics. **History:** General. **Interdisciplinary:** Global studies. **Math:** General. **Parks/recreation:** Exercise sciences, health/fitness. **Philosophy/religion:** Religion. **Physical sciences:** Chemistry. **Psychology:** General. **Public administration:** Social work. **Social sciences:** Economics, international relations, political science, sociology, U.S. government. **Visual/performing arts:** Dance, dramatic, fashion design, graphic design, interior design, music pedagogy, music performance, studio arts.

**Most popular majors.** Business/marketing 17%, communications/journalism 7%, family/consumer sciences 8%, health sciences 6%, psychology 10%, social sciences 6%, visual/performing arts 17%.

**Computing on campus.** PC or laptop required. 145 workstations in dormitories, library, computer center, student center. Dormitories wired for high-speed internet access and linked to campus network. Commuter students can connect to campus network. Online course registration, online library, helpline, repair service, wireless network available.

**Student life. Freshman orientation:** Mandatory. Preregistration for classes offered. 4-day program before start of classes with extra day for athletes, international students, and students with disabilities. **Policies:** Honor Code is a longstanding tradition that requires individual integrity and community responsibility of all students. Traditional-aged freshmen and sophomores must live on campus except if married or living with parents or other relatives by special permission. **Housing:** Guaranteed on-campus for freshmen. Apartments, wellness housing available. $100 nonrefundable deposit, deadline 5/1. Pets allowed in dorm rooms. Campus housing available for all 4 years. All on-campus housing is wellness housing. **Activities:** Concert band, choral groups, dance, drama, international student organizations, literary magazine, music ensembles, Model UN, musical theater, student government, student newspaper, symphony orchestra, association for cultural awareness, unity council, service council, Habitat for Humanity, Angels for the Environment, College Democrats, College Republicans, Christian Association, Catholic Angels.

**Athletics.** NCAA. **Intercollegiate:** Basketball W, cross-country W, soccer W, softball W, tennis W, volleyball W. **Team name:** Avenging Angels.

**Student services.** Adult student services, alcohol/substance abuse counseling, chaplain/spiritual director, career counseling, student employment services, financial aid counseling, health services, minority student services, personal counseling, placement for graduates. **Physically disabled:** Services for visually, speech, hearing impaired.

**Contact.** E-mail: admissions@meredith.edu
Phone: (919) 760-8581 Toll-free number: (800) 637-3348
Fax: (919) 760-2348
Cristan Harris, Director of Admissions, Meredith College, 3800 Hillsborough Street, Raleigh, NC 27607-5298

---

## Methodist University
**Fayetteville, North Carolina**
**www.methodist.edu**                     **CB code: 5426**

- Private 4-year liberal arts college affiliated with United Methodist Church
- Residential campus in small city
- 1,965 degree-seeking undergraduates
- 48% of applicants admitted
- SAT or ACT (ACT writing optional) required

**General.** Founded in 1956. Regionally accredited. **Degrees:** 336 bachelor's, 15 associate awarded; master's offered. **ROTC:** Army, Air Force. **Location:** 50 miles from Raleigh-Durham. **Calendar:** Semester, extensive summer session. **Full-time faculty:** 131 total; 75% have terminal degrees, 12% minority. **Part-time faculty:** 89 total; 88% have terminal degrees, 17% minority. **Class size:** 74% < 20, 25% 20-39, less than 1% 40-49, less than 1% 50-99. **Special facilities:** Computer-assisted English composition laboratory, psychology computer-experimental laboratory, nature trail, professional golf and tennis management center, 18-hole golf course and driving range, environmental simulation center (virtual reality laboratory).

**Freshman class profile.**

| Mid 50% test scores | | | |
|---|---|---|---|
| SAT critical reading: | 430-540 | GPA 2.0-2.99: | 35% |
| SAT math: | 450-570 | Rank in top quarter: | 33% |
| SAT writing: | 440-520 | Rank in top tenth: | 12% |
| ACT composite: | 18-23 | Out-of-state: | 47% |
| GPA 3.75 or higher: | 22% | Live on campus: | 91% |
| GPA 3.50-3.74: | 10% | Fraternities: | 3% |
| GPA 3.0-3.49: | 33% | Sororities: | 3% |

**Basis for selection.** High school record (GPA), curriculum, test scores carefully considered. All prospective student files reviewed on individual basis. Extracurricular achievements and teacher/counselor recommendations also considered. Students who transfer English 101 credits must take institutional English Placement Exam. SAT/ACT scores not required of transfer students with more than 31 semester hours of transferable credit. Essay and interview recommended for all students; audition recommended for drama and music majors; portfolio recommended for art majors. **Homeschooled:** Transcript of courses and grades required.

**High school preparation.** College-preparatory program required. 16 units required; 20 recommended. Required and recommended units include English 4, mathematics 3-4, social studies 2, history 1-2, science 2-3 (laboratory 1-2), foreign language 2 and academic electives 4.

**2009-2010 Annual costs.** Tuition/fees: $23,038. Professional golf management, professional tennis management, and music students have additional fees. Room/board: $8,400. Books/supplies: $1,000. Personal expenses: $1,500.

**2008-2009 Financial aid. Non-need-based:** Scholarships awarded for academics, alumni affiliation, leadership, music/drama, religious affiliation, ROTC, state residency.

**Application procedures. Admission:** No deadline. $25 fee, may be waived for applicants with need, free for online applicants. Admission notification on a rolling basis beginning on or about 9/1. Must reply by May 1 or within 2 week(s) if notified thereafter. **Financial aid:** Priority date 5/1, closing date 7/1. FAFSA required. Applicants notified on a rolling basis starting 3/1; must reply within 2 week(s) of notification.

**Academics. Special study options:** Accelerated study, distance learning, double major, dual enrollment of high school students, ESL, exchange student, honors, independent study, internships, liberal arts/career combination, student-designed major, study abroad, teacher certification program, Washington semester, weekend college. **Credit/placement by examination:** AP, CLEP, IB, SAT, ACT, institutional tests. 45 credit hours maximum toward associate degree, 45 toward bachelor's. **Support services:** Learning center, reduced course load, remedial instruction, study skills assistance, tutoring, writing center.

**Majors. Biology:** General, botany, cellular/molecular, conservation, ecology, exercise physiology, microbiology, zoology. **Business:** Accounting, business admin, finance, golf management, hospitality admin, hospitality/recreation, management information systems, marketing, resort management, tourism/travel. **Communications:** General, journalism, media studies, organizational. **Computer sciences:** General, computer graphics, computer science, web page design. **Education:** General, art, biology, chemistry, elementary, English, foreign languages, mathematics, middle, music, physical, secondary, social studies, special. **Engineering technology:** Occupational safety. **Foreign languages:** French, Spanish. **Health:** Athletic training, facilities admin, health care admin, physician assistant, predental, premedicine, prenursing, prepharmacy, preveterinary. **History:** General. **Legal studies:** Prelaw. **Liberal arts:** Arts/sciences. **Math:** General. **Parks/recreation:** Exercise sciences, facilities management, health/fitness, sports admin. **Philosophy/religion:** Philosophy, religion. **Physical sciences:** Chemistry, forensic chemistry. **Protective services:** Criminal justice, emergency management/homeland security, forensics, law enforcement admin. **Psychology:** General. **Public administration:** Social work. **Social sciences:** Political science, sociology. **Theology:** Religious ed. **Visual/performing arts:** General, art, ceramics, graphic design, music performance, painting, printmaking, sculpture, studio arts. **Other:** Professional tennis management.

**Most popular majors.** Biology 6%, business/marketing 44%, education 7%, parks/recreation 8%, social sciences 8%.

**Computing on campus.** 220 workstations in library, computer center, student center. Dormitories wired for high-speed internet access and linked to campus network. Commuter students can connect to campus network. Online course registration, online library, helpline, wireless network available.

**Student life. Freshman orientation:** Available. Preregistration for classes offered. Typically held the weekend before classes begin in Fall. **Housing:** Guaranteed on-campus for all undergraduates. Coed dorms, single-sex dorms, apartments, wellness housing available. $100 nonrefundable deposit, deadline 5/1. Health/wellness hall, first-year experience hall available. **Activities:** Bands, campus ministries, choral groups, dance, drama, international student organizations, literary magazine, music ensembles, Model UN, musical theater, radio station, student government, student newspaper, symphony orchestra, Fellowship of Christian Athletes, Young Democrats/Republicans, African American culture society, student activities committee, commuting student organization.

**Athletics.** NCAA. **Intercollegiate:** Baseball M, basketball, cheerleading, cross-country, football (tackle) M, golf, lacrosse W, soccer, softball W, tennis, track and field, volleyball W. **Intramural:** Basketball, cheerleading W, football (non-tackle), golf, racquetball, soccer, softball, table tennis, tennis, volleyball. **Team name:** Monarchs.

**Student services.** Alcohol/substance abuse counseling, chaplain/spiritual director, career counseling, student employment services, financial aid counseling, health services, personal counseling, placement for graduates, veterans' counselor, women's services. **Physically disabled:** Services for visually impaired.

**Contact.** E-mail: admissions@methodist.edu
Phone: (910) 630-7027 Toll-free number: (800) 488-7110
Fax: (910) 630-7285
Jamie Legg, Director of Admissions, Methodist University, 5400 Ramsey Street, Fayetteville, NC 28311-1498

## Mid-Atlantic Christian University
Elizabeth City, North Carolina
www.macuniversity.edu          CB code: 5597

- Private 4-year university and Bible college affiliated with Church of Christ
- Residential campus in large town
- 159 degree-seeking undergraduates: 18% part-time, 43% women
- 40% of applicants admitted
- SAT or ACT (ACT writing optional), application essay required
- 46% graduate within 6 years

**General.** Founded in 1948. Regionally accredited; also accredited by ABHE. **Degrees:** 17 bachelor's, 10 associate awarded. **ROTC:** Army. **Location:** 50 miles from Norfolk, Virginia. **Calendar:** Semester, limited summer session. **Full-time faculty:** 8 total; 38% have terminal degrees, 38% women. **Part-time faculty:** 23 total; 22% have terminal degrees, 30% women. **Class size:** 82% < 20, 13% 20-39, 4% 40-49, 2% 50-99.

**Freshman class profile.** 135 applied, 54 admitted, 34 enrolled.

| Mid 50% test scores | | | |
|---|---|---|---|
| SAT critical reading: | 480-550 | Rank in top quarter: | 29% |
| SAT math: | 430-560 | Rank in top tenth: | 13% |
| SAT writing: | 480-550 | Return as sophomores: | 59% |
| ACT composite: | 18-22 | Out-of-state: | 11% |
| GPA 3.75 or higher: | 10% | Live on campus: | 94% |
| GPA 3.50-3.74: | 10% | International: | 3% |
| GPA 3.0-3.49: | 14% | | |
| GPA 2.0-2.99: | 56% | | |

**Basis for selection.** Evidence of Christian character, school achievement record, test scores, school and community activities, recommendations important. Interview recommended if questions arise from references or academic record. **Homeschooled:** Transcript of courses and grades, state high school equivalency certificate required.

**High school preparation.** 20 units required. Required and recommended units include English 4, mathematics 3, social studies 2, history 2, science 3 (laboratory 2), foreign language 6, computer science 1 and academic electives 4.

**2009-2010 Annual costs.** Tuition/fees: $9,700. Room/board: $6,790. Books/supplies: $900. Personal expenses: $2,500.

**2008-2009 Financial aid. Need-based:** 37 full-time freshmen applied for aid; 37 were judged to have need; 37 of these received aid. Average need met was 80%. Average scholarship/grant was $3,895; average loan $6,326. 38% of total undergraduate aid awarded as scholarships/grants, 62% as loans/jobs. **Non-need-based:** Awarded to 54 full-time undergraduates, including 13 freshmen. Scholarships awarded for academics, alumni affiliation, leadership, music/drama, religious affiliation.

**Application procedures. Admission:** No deadline. $50 fee, may be waived for applicants with need. Admission notification on a rolling basis beginning on or about 9/1. Must reply by May 1 or within 2 week(s) if notified thereafter. **Financial aid:** Priority date 2/1; no closing date. FAFSA, institutional form required. Applicants notified on a rolling basis starting 5/1; must reply within 2 week(s) of notification.

**Academics. Special study options:** Distance learning, double major, dual enrollment of high school students, internships. Semester-long mission intern class overseas. **Credit/placement by examination:** AP, CLEP, institutional tests. 8 credit hours maximum toward associate degree, 16 toward bachelor's. **Support services:** Learning center, reduced course load, remedial instruction, study skills assistance, writing center.

**Majors. Business:** Nonprofit/public. **Foreign languages:** Linguistics. **Philosophy/religion:** Religion. **Theology:** Bible, missionary, pastoral counseling, religious ed, theology, youth ministry.

**Most popular majors.** Business/marketing 17%, foreign language 17%, theological studies 66%.

**Computing on campus.** 24 workstations in dormitories, library, computer center. Dormitories wired for high-speed internet access and linked to campus network. Commuter students can connect to campus network.

**Student life. Freshman orientation:** Mandatory, $130 fee. Preregistration for classes offered. **Policies:** All students have opportunity to travel in choral group throughout country. Religious observance required. **Housing:** Guaranteed on-campus for all undergraduates. Single-sex dorms, special housing for disabled, apartments, wellness housing available. $75 nonrefundable deposit, deadline 4/1. **Activities:** Campus ministries, choral groups, drama, music ensembles, musical theater, student government.

**Athletics.** **Intercollegiate:** Basketball, volleyball. **Intramural:** Basketball, football (non-tackle), golf, soccer, softball, table tennis, tennis, volleyball. **Team name:** Mustangs.

**Student services.** Career counseling, student employment services, financial aid counseling, personal counseling, placement for graduates. **Physically disabled:** Services for hearing impaired.

**Contact.** E-mail: admissions@macuniversity.edu
Phone: (252) 334-2028 Toll-free number: (866) 996-MACU
Fax: (252) 334-2064
Garrett Lewis, Director of Enrollment Management, Mid-Atlantic Christian University, 715 North Poindexter Street, Elizabeth City, NC 27909

## Miller-Motte Technical College
**Wilmington, North Carolina**
www.miller-motte.edu                               CB code: 3342

◗ For-profit 4-year business and technical college
◗ Commuter campus in small city
◗ 842 degree-seeking undergraduates
◗ Interview required

**General.** Accredited by ACICS. **Degrees:** 18 bachelor's, 119 associate awarded. **Location:** 145 miles from Raleigh. **Calendar:** Quarter, extensive summer session. **Full-time faculty:** 35 total. **Part-time faculty:** 30 total.

**Basis for selection.** Open admission, but selective for some programs. Minimum test score of 15 on Wonderlic test for admission, 18 for Medical Assisting, 21 for Surgical Technology, 20 for Computer Systems Network Administrator, 18 for Criminal Justice, 18 for Paralegal, and 18 for Dental Assisting. **Homeschooled:** Transcript of courses and grades required.

**High school preparation.** 17 units recommended. Recommended units include English 4, mathematics 4, social studies 4, science 4 (laboratory 1).

**2010-2011 Annual costs.** Tuition/fees (projected): $13,650. Books/supplies: $2,000. Personal expenses: $3,350.

**2009-2010 Financial aid.** All financial aid based on need.

**Application procedures.** **Admission:** No deadline. $35 fee. Application must be submitted on paper. Admission notification on a rolling basis. **Financial aid:** No deadline. FAFSA, institutional form required.

**Academics.** **Special study options:** Distance learning, double major, internships. **Credit/placement by examination:** CLEP, institutional tests. 46 credit hours maximum toward associate degree. **Support services:** Learning center, reduced course load, remedial instruction, study skills assistance, tutoring.

**Majors.** **Business:** Business admin. **Health:** Health services. **Protective services:** Law enforcement admin.

**Most popular majors.** Business/marketing 50%, health sciences 50%.

**Computing on campus.** 120 workstations in library, computer center. Commuter students can connect to campus network. Online library, repair service, student web hosting available.

**Student life.** **Freshman orientation:** Mandatory. Preregistration for classes offered. **Activities:** Student newspaper.

**Athletics.** **Team name:** Marlin.

**Student services.** Career counseling, financial aid counseling, placement for graduates.

**Contact.** Phone: (910) 392-4660 Toll-free number: (800) 784-2110
Fax: (910) 799-6224
Jean Vokes, Director of Admissions, Miller-Motte Technical College, 5000 Market Street, Wilmington, NC 28405

## Montreat College
**Montreat, North Carolina**                      CB member
www.montreat.edu                                   CB code: 5423

◗ Private 4-year liberal arts college affiliated with Presbyterian Church Reformed and Independent
◗ Residential campus in small town
◗ 934 degree-seeking undergraduates
◗ SAT or ACT (ACT writing recommended), application essay required

**General.** Founded in 1916. Regionally accredited. North Carolina's only member institute of the Council for Christian Colleges and Universities. **Degrees:** 193 bachelor's, 68 associate awarded; master's offered. **Location:** 16 miles from Asheville. **Calendar:** Semester, limited summer session. **Full-time faculty:** 43 total; 72% have terminal degrees, 14% minority. **Part-time faculty:** 102 total. **Class size:** 72% < 20, 26% 20-39, 2% 40-49. **Special facilities:** Ropes course, climbing wall, chapel of the prodigal, Black Mountain Campus.

**Freshman class profile.** 676 applied, 315 admitted, 103 enrolled.

| Mid 50% test scores | | ACT composite: | 19-26 |
|---|---|---|---|
| SAT critical reading: | 450-560 | Out-of-state: | 31% |
| SAT math: | 450-560 | Live on campus: | 100% |
| SAT writing: | 420-540 | | |

**Basis for selection.** Open admission, but selective for some programs. Decisions are criteria-based, using GPA and SAT/ACT scores as initial qualifiers. Essay, recommendation, and extracurricular activities also considered. Interview required for students who do not meet standard admission requirements. **Homeschooled:** Transcript of courses and grades, letter of recommendation (nonparent) required. **Learning Disabled:** Students with documented learning disabilities are referred to the Director of Student Success before an admissions decision is made.

**High school preparation.** College-preparatory program required. 16 units required. Required units include English 4, mathematics 3, social studies 3, science 3, foreign language 1 and academic electives 2.

**2009-2010 Annual costs.** Tuition/fees: $20,576. Room/board: $6,541. Books/supplies: $975. Personal expenses: $1,910.

**2008-2009 Financial aid.** **Non-need-based:** Scholarships awarded for academics, alumni affiliation, athletics, leadership, music/drama, religious affiliation, state residency.

**Application procedures.** **Admission:** Closing date 8/13 (postmark date). $30 fee, may be waived for applicants with need. Admission notification on a rolling basis beginning on or about 9/15. **Financial aid:** Priority date 3/15; no closing date. FAFSA, institutional form required. Applicants notified on a rolling basis starting 1/15; must reply within 2 week(s) of notification.

**Academics.** **Special study options:** Accelerated study, double major, dual enrollment of high school students, independent study, internships, student-designed major, study abroad, teacher certification program, Washington semester. **Credit/placement by examination:** AP, CLEP, IB, institutional tests. 15 credit hours maximum toward associate degree, 30 toward bachelor's. **Support services:** Reduced course load, study skills assistance, tutoring, writing center.

**Majors.** **Area/ethnic studies:** American. **Biology:** General. **Business:** Accounting, business admin, international, marketing. **Communications:** Media studies. **Computer sciences:** General. **Conservation:** Environmental studies. **Education:** Elementary. **History:** General, American. **Parks/recreation:** General. **Philosophy/religion:** Christian. **Psychology:** General. **Public administration:** Human services. **Theology:** Bible, missionary, religious ed, youth ministry. **Visual/performing arts:** Music management, music performance.

**Most popular majors.** Business/marketing 72%.

**Computing on campus.** 60 workstations in library, computer center, student center. Dormitories wired for high-speed internet access and linked to campus network. Helpline, repair service, wireless network available.

**Student life.** **Freshman orientation:** Mandatory. Preregistration for classes offered. 5 days before classes start. There is also a pre-orientation program, Wilderness Journey, available at extra cost. **Policies:** No alcohol on campus. Religious observance required. **Housing:** Guaranteed on-campus for all undergraduates. Single-sex dorms, wellness housing available. $100 nonrefundable deposit, deadline 4/1. 351 spaces available for undergraduate students. **Activities:** Choral groups, dance, drama, music ensembles, musical theater, student government, student newspaper, missions club, Fellowship of Christian Athletes, Young Life.

**Athletics.** NAIA. **Intercollegiate:** Baseball M, basketball, cross-country, golf, soccer, softball W, track and field, volleyball W. **Intramural:** Basketball, football (non-tackle), soccer, softball, table tennis, tennis, volleyball. **Team name:** Cavaliers.

**Student services.** Adult student services, alcohol/substance abuse counseling, chaplain/spiritual director, career counseling, student employment services, financial aid counseling, health services, personal counseling, placement for graduates, veterans' counselor. **Physically disabled:** Services for visually, speech, hearing impaired.

**Contact.** E-mail: admissions@montreat.edu
Phone: (828) 669-8012 ext. 3781 Toll-free number: (800) 622-6968
Fax: (828) 669-0120
Tony Robinson, Director of Enrollment Development & Outreach,
Montreat College, Box 1267, Montreat, NC 28757-1267

## Mount Olive College
**Mount Olive, North Carolina**      **CB member**
**www.moc.edu**      **CB code: 5435**

- Private 4-year liberal arts college affiliated with Free Will Baptists
- Residential campus in small town
- 3,569 degree-seeking undergraduates

**General.** Founded in 1951. Regionally accredited. **Degrees:** 627 bachelor's, 206 associate awarded. **Location:** 13 miles from Goldsboro. **Calendar:** Semester, extensive summer session. **Full-time faculty:** 89 total; 86% have terminal degrees, 16% minority, 33% women. **Part-time faculty:** 233 total; 24% have terminal degrees, 13% minority, 46% women. **Class size:** 71% < 20, 29% 20-39, less than 1% >100.

**Freshman class profile.**

| Mid 50% test scores | | | |
|---|---|---|---|
| SAT critical reading: | 420-510 | GPA 3.0-3.49: | 28% |
| SAT math: | 430-530 | GPA 2.0-2.99: | 40% |
| ACT composite: | 15-21 | Rank in top quarter: | 36% |
| GPA 3.75 or higher: | 21% | Rank in top tenth: | 9% |
| GPA 3.50-3.74: | 8% | Out-of-state: | 11% |

**Basis for selection.** Open admission, but selective for some programs. School record, test scores, class rank important. Personal recommendations considered. Interview recommended for all students; portfolio recommended for art majors. Audition required for music majors.

**High school preparation.** College-preparatory program recommended. 17 units required. Required units include English 4, mathematics 3, social studies 3, science 3 (laboratory 1) and academic electives 3.

**2009-2010 Annual costs.** Tuition/fees: $13,776. Room/board: $5,540. Books/supplies: $1,400.

**2008-2009 Financial aid.** **Non-need-based:** Scholarships awarded for academics, art, athletics, leadership, music/drama, religious affiliation.

**Application procedures.** **Admission:** No deadline. $20 fee, may be waived for applicants with need, free for online applicants. Admission notification on a rolling basis beginning on or about 10/1. **Financial aid:** No deadline. FAFSA required. Applicants notified on a rolling basis starting 2/14; must reply within 2 week(s) of notification.

**Academics.** **Special study options:** Accelerated study, cooperative education, distance learning, double major, dual enrollment of high school students, external degree, honors, independent study, internships, liberal arts/career combination, teacher certification program. Accelerated extension program at Seymour Johnson Air Force Base in Goldsboro; 55-week degree completion program in business offered in New Bern, Wilmington, and Raleigh-Research Triangle Park. **Credit/placement by examination:** AP, CLEP, institutional tests. 15 credit hours maximum toward associate degree, 30 toward bachelor's. **Support services:** Learning center, reduced course load, remedial instruction, study skills assistance, tutoring, writing center.

**Majors.** **Biology:** General. **Business:** Accounting, business admin, human resources, management information systems, organizational behavior. **Communications:** General. **Computer sciences:** General. **History:** General. **Liberal arts:** Arts/sciences. **Math:** General. **Parks/recreation:** General. **Philosophy/religion:** Religion. **Protective services:** Criminal justice. **Psychology:** General. **Visual/performing arts:** Design, studio arts.

**Most popular majors.** Business/marketing 49%, education 16%, security/protective services 16%.

**Computing on campus.** 50 workstations in library, computer center. Dormitories wired for high-speed internet access and linked to campus network. Commuter students can connect to campus network. Online library, repair service, wireless network available.

**Student life.** **Freshman orientation:** Available. **Policies:** Religious observance required. **Housing:** Guaranteed on-campus for freshmen. Single-sex dorms, apartments available. $50 nonrefundable deposit, deadline 2/26. **Activities:** Concert band, campus ministries, choral groups, international student organizations, music ensembles, musical theater, student government, English society, political forum, recreation majors club, Fellowship of Christian Athletes, Phi Beta Lambda, minority students' organization, Fellowship of Christian Students, Free Spirit.

**Athletics.** NCAA. **Intercollegiate:** Baseball M, basketball, cross-country, golf, soccer, softball W, tennis, volleyball. **Intramural:** Badminton, baseball M, basketball, football (tackle) M, handball, racquetball, softball, table tennis, tennis, volleyball.

**Student services.** Adult student services, career counseling, student employment services, health services, personal counseling, placement for graduates, veterans' counselor.

**Contact.** E-mail: admissions@moc.edu
Phone: (919) 658-2502 Toll-free number: (800) 653-0854
Fax: (919) 658-9816
Tim Woodard, Director of Admissions, Mount Olive College, 634
Henderson Street, Mount Olive, NC 28365

## North Carolina Agricultural and Technical State University
**Greensboro, North Carolina**      **CB member**
**www.ncat.edu**      **CB code: 5003**

- Public 4-year university
- Residential campus in small city
- 8,669 degree-seeking undergraduates: 9% part-time, 53% women, 89% African American, 1% Asian American, 1% Hispanic American, 1% international
- 1,550 degree-seeking graduate students
- 65% of applicants admitted
- SAT or ACT with writing, SAT Subject Tests required

**General.** Founded in 1891. Regionally accredited. **Degrees:** 1,372 bachelor's awarded; master's, doctoral offered. **ROTC:** Army, Air Force. **Location:** 91 miles from Charlotte. **Calendar:** Semester. **Full-time faculty:** 520 total. **Part-time faculty:** 138 total. **Special facilities:** African heritage center, planetarium, herbarium, Olympic track.

**Freshman class profile.** 5,713 applied, 3,728 admitted, 1,898 enrolled.

| Mid 50% test scores | | | |
|---|---|---|---|
| SAT critical reading: | 400-500 | GPA 3.50-3.74: | 15% |
| SAT math: | 410-500 | GPA 3.0-3.49: | 30% |
| SAT writing: | 370-470 | GPA 2.0-2.99: | 50% |
| ACT composite: | 16-21 | Rank in top quarter: | 6% |
| GPA 3.75 or higher: | 5% | Rank in top tenth: | 6% |
| | | International: | 1% |

**Basis for selection.** High school GPA, class rank, test scores, recommendations, course selection reviewed. SAT preferred, but ACT accepted. Audition recommended for music programs; portfolio recommended for art programs.

**High school preparation.** 19 units required. Required units include English 4, mathematics 4, social studies 1, history 1, science 3 (laboratory 1), foreign language 2 and academic electives 4.

**2009-2010 Annual costs.** Tuition/fees: $3,696; $13,138 out-of-state. Room/board: $5,659. Books/supplies: $1,400. Personal expenses: $1,500.

**2009-2010 Financial aid.** **Non-need-based:** Scholarships awarded for academics, athletics, music/drama, ROTC.

**Application procedures.** **Admission:** Priority date 6/1; no deadline. $45 fee. Admission notification on a rolling basis beginning on or about 9/15. Must reply by May 1 or within 2 week(s) if notified thereafter. **Financial aid:** Priority date 3/15; no closing date. FAFSA required. Applicants notified on a rolling basis starting 4/1; must reply within 2 week(s) of notification.

**Academics.** **Special study options:** Cooperative education, cross-registration, distance learning, double major, dual enrollment of high school students, honors, internships, study abroad, teacher certification program, weekend college. **Credit/placement by examination:** AP, CLEP, SAT, ACT, institutional tests. **Support services:** Learning center, reduced course load, remedial instruction, study skills assistance, tutoring, writing center.

**Majors.** **Agriculture:** Animal sciences, business, economics, plant sciences. **Architecture:** Landscape. **Biology:** General. **Business:** General, accounting, business admin, finance, managerial economics, marketing, transportation. **Communications:** General, broadcast journalism, journalism, public relations. **Computer sciences:** General. **Education:** General, agricultural, biology, business, chemistry, driver/safety, early childhood, elementary, English, family/consumer sciences, foreign languages, French, history, mathematics, music, physical, physics, social science, special, speech, technology/industrial arts, trade/industrial. **Engineering:** Agricultural, architectural, chemical, civil, electrical, materials, mechanical. **Engineering technology:**

Industrial management, occupational safety. **Family/consumer sciences:** General, clothing/textiles, family studies, family/community services, food/nutrition. **Foreign languages:** French. **Health:** Occupational health. **History:** General. **Math:** General. **Parks/recreation:** Facilities management, health/fitness. **Physical sciences:** Chemistry, physics. **Psychology:** General. **Public administration:** Social work. **Social sciences:** General, political science, sociology. **Visual/performing arts:** General, art, dramatic.

**Most popular majors.** Business/marketing 14%, communications/journalism 7%, engineering/engineering technologies 20%, liberal arts 7%, psychology 8%.

**Computing on campus.** 675 workstations in library, computer center. Dormitories wired for high-speed internet access and linked to campus network. Commuter students can connect to campus network. Online course registration, helpline available.

**Student life. Freshman orientation:** Mandatory. Preregistration for classes offered. **Housing:** Guaranteed on-campus for freshmen. Coed dorms, single-sex dorms, wellness housing available. $150 deposit. **Activities:** Bands, choral groups, dance, drama, international student organizations, music ensembles, radio station, student government, student newspaper, symphony orchestra, TV station.

**Athletics.** NCAA. **Intercollegiate:** Baseball M, basketball, bowling W, cross-country, football (tackle) M, softball W, swimming W, tennis W, track and field, volleyball W, wrestling M. **Intramural:** Badminton, baseball M, basketball, bowling W, cross-country, football (tackle) M, golf, handball, racquetball, soccer, softball, swimming, table tennis, tennis, track and field, volleyball. **Team name:** Aggies.

**Student services.** Adult student services, alcohol/substance abuse counseling, career counseling, student employment services, financial aid counseling, health services, minority student services, personal counseling, placement for graduates, veterans' counselor. **Physically disabled:** Services for visually, speech, hearing impaired.

**Contact.** E-mail: uadmit@ncat.edu
Phone: (336) 334-7946 Toll-free number: (800) 443-8964
Fax: (336) 334-7478
Yvette Underdue-Murph, Associate Vice Chancellor for Enrollment Management, North Carolina Agricultural and Technical State University, Webb Hall, Greensboro, NC 27411-0001

## North Carolina Central University
**Durham, North Carolina**  CB member
www.nccu.edu  CB code: 5495

◗ Public 4-year university
◗ Commuter campus in small city
◗ 5,885 degree-seeking undergraduates
◗ 81% of applicants admitted
◗ SAT or ACT with writing required

**General.** Founded in 1910. Regionally accredited. Historically, the majority of students have been African American. **Degrees:** 832 bachelor's awarded; master's, professional offered. **ROTC:** Army, Air Force. **Location:** 23 miles from Raleigh. **Calendar:** Semester, extensive summer session. **Full-time faculty:** 409 total. **Part-time faculty:** 199 total. **Class size:** 36% < 20, 47% 20-39, 11% 40-49, 6% 50-99, less than 1% >100. **Special facilities:** Collection of primary resources on black life and culture, art museum with works of Afro-American culture.

**Freshman class profile.** 4,402 applied, 3,567 admitted, 1,358 enrolled.

| Mid 50% test scores | | | |
|---|---|---|---|
| SAT critical reading: | 380-460 | GPA 3.0-3.49: | 20% |
| SAT math: | 380-460 | GPA 2.0-2.99: | 60% |
| SAT writing: | 370-450 | Rank in top quarter: | 16% |
| ACT composite: | 15-18 | Rank in top tenth: | 5% |
| GPA 3.75 or higher: | 7% | Out-of-state: | 16% |
| GPA 3.50-3.74: | 5% | Live on campus: | 80% |

**Basis for selection.** Academic achievement, class rank, test scores important. SAT preferred, ACT also accepted. Audition required for music programs. **Homeschooled:** Transcript of courses and grades, state high school equivalency certificate required.

**High school preparation.** 14 units required. Required units include English 4, mathematics 4, social studies 2, history 1, science 3 (laboratory 2) and foreign language 2. Social studies units must include 1 U.S. history. One foreign language, and 1 math recommended during 12th grade. Students who graduate high school in and after 2006 must have one additional math course from the following: pre-calculus, AP statistics, AP calculus, IB

math level II, integrated math IV, discrete math, advanced models and functions.

**2009-2010 Annual costs.** Tuition/fees: $3,862; $13,931 out-of-state. Room/board: $6,540. Books/supplies: $1,500. Personal expenses: $1,575.

**Financial aid. Non-need-based:** Scholarships awarded for academics, alumni affiliation, athletics, minority status, music/drama, state residency. **Additional information:** Departmental grants based on need plus other available criteria.

**Application procedures. Admission:** Closing date 8/6. $40 fee. Admission notification on a rolling basis. Early admission available with permission from high school principal and academic dean. **Financial aid:** Priority date 4/1; no closing date. FAFSA required. Applicants notified by 5/1; must reply within 2 week(s) of notification.

**Academics. Special study options:** Cooperative education, distance learning, double major, ESL, honors, independent study, internships, study abroad, teacher certification program. **Credit/placement by examination:** AP, CLEP, SAT, ACT, institutional tests. 30 credit hours maximum toward bachelor's degree. **Support services:** Learning center, remedial instruction, study skills assistance, tutoring, writing center.

**Majors. Biology:** General. **Business:** Accounting, business admin, hospitality admin. **Communications:** Media studies. **Computer sciences:** Computer science, information systems. **Conservation:** Environmental science. **Education:** Art, biology, chemistry, drama/dance, elementary, English, family/consumer sciences, French, health, history, kindergarten/preschool, mathematics, middle, music, physical, physics, Spanish. **Family/consumer sciences:** General. **Foreign languages:** French, Spanish. **Health:** Athletic training, nursing (RN), public health ed. **History:** General. **Math:** General. **Parks/recreation:** Facilities management, health/fitness. **Physical sciences:** Chemistry, physics. **Protective services:** Law enforcement admin. **Psychology:** General. **Public administration:** Social work. **Social sciences:** Geography, political science, sociology. **Visual/performing arts:** Art, dramatic, jazz.

**Most popular majors.** Business/marketing 18%, education 9%, family/consumer sciences 6%, health sciences 6%, psychology 7%, security/protective services 10%, social sciences 11%.

**Computing on campus.** 400 workstations in dormitories, library, computer center. Dormitories wired for high-speed internet access and linked to campus network. Commuter students can connect to campus network. Online course registration, online library, helpline, repair service, wireless network available.

**Student life. Freshman orientation:** Mandatory, $125 fee. Preregistration for classes offered. **Housing:** Coed dorms, single-sex dorms available. $100 deposit, deadline 6/1. Coed honors dormitory available. **Activities:** Bands, choral groups, dance, drama, literary magazine, radio station, student government, student newspaper.

**Athletics.** NAIA, NCAA. **Intercollegiate:** Basketball, bowling, cheerleading W, cross-country, football (tackle) M, golf, softball W, tennis, track and field, volleyball W. **Team name:** Eagles.

**Student services.** Career counseling, student employment services, health services, on-campus daycare, personal counseling, placement for graduates, veterans' counselor.

**Contact.** E-mail: admissions@nccu.edu
Phone: (919) 560-6298 Toll-free number: (877) 667-7533
Fax: (919) 530-7625
Anthony Brooks, Director of Admissions, North Carolina Central University, PO Box 19717, Durham, NC 27707

## North Carolina State University
**Raleigh, North Carolina**  CB member
www.ncsu.edu  CB code: 5496

◗ Public 4-year university
◗ Residential campus in large city
◗ 23,361 degree-seeking undergraduates: 7% part-time, 43% women, 9% African American, 5% Asian American, 3% Hispanic American, 1% Native American, 2% international
◗ 4,435 degree-seeking graduate students
◗ 55% of applicants admitted
◗ SAT or ACT with writing required
◗ 70% graduate within 6 years

**General.** Founded in 1887. Regionally accredited. **Degrees:** 4,623 bachelor's, 182 associate awarded; master's, doctoral, professional offered. **ROTC:**

Army, Naval, Air Force. **Location:** One mile from downtown. **Calendar:** Semester, extensive summer session. **Full-time faculty:** 1,773 total; 87% have terminal degrees, 20% minority, 31% women. **Part-time faculty:** 172 total; 64% have terminal degrees, 12% minority, 43% women. **Class size:** 29% < 20, 43% 20-39, 9% 40-49, 12% 50-99, 8% >100. **Special facilities:** 3 electron microscopes, phytotron, research farms, 2 campus theaters, craft center, stable isotope laboratory, teaching forest, wood products laboratory, coastal marine science laboratory, 80,000 acres of research forests and research farm lands, fiber, fabric, and garment manufacturing equipment.

**Freshman class profile.** 18,782 applied, 10,252 admitted, 4,638 enrolled.

| Mid 50% test scores | | | |
|---|---|---|---|
| SAT critical reading: | 520-620 | Rank in top quarter: | 83% |
| SAT math: | 560-660 | Rank in top tenth: | 41% |
| SAT writing: | 510-610 | Return as sophomores: | 91% |
| ACT composite: | 23-28 | Out-of-state: | 9% |
| GPA 3.75 or higher: | 91% | Live on campus: | 74% |
| GPA 3.50-3.74: | 6% | International: | 3% |
| GPA 3.0-3.49: | 3% | Fraternities: | 6% |
| | | Sororities: | 17% |

**Basis for selection.** GED not accepted. School academic record, standardized test scores important. Counselor evaluations, extracurricular activities also considered. Preference given to students with exceptionally strong high school record. Level and difficulty of courses considered. Weighted grades for advanced, honors, AP courses considered. All applicants to the UNC system, except those exempted by current campus policies, must submit standardized test scores. SAT preferred, ACT also accepted. Essay recommended for all students. Interview and portfolio required for College of Design applicants. Verification of golf playing ability required for Professional Golf Management Program.

**High school preparation.** 16 units required; 20 recommended. Required and recommended units include English 4, mathematics 4, social studies 1, history 1, science 3-4 (laboratory 1-2), foreign language 2 and academic electives 1-4. Science units should include 1 life or biological science, 1 physical science, and 1 laboratory science. Honors, advanced, AP and IB courses given extra weight.

**2009-2010 Annual costs.** Tuition/fees: $5,474; $17,959 out-of-state. Room/board: $7,966. Books/supplies: $950. Personal expenses: $1,450.

**2009-2010 Financial aid. Need-based:** 3,529 full-time freshmen applied for aid; 2,190 were judged to have need; 2,167 of these received aid. Average need met was 89%. Average scholarship/grant was $9,356; average loan $2,174. 73% of total undergraduate aid awarded as scholarships/grants, 27% as loans/jobs. **Non-need-based:** Awarded to 2,103 full-time undergraduates, including 488 freshmen. Scholarships awarded for academics, alumni affiliation, athletics, leadership, ROTC, state residency. **Additional information:** Freshman Merit Scholarships; students submitting complete admissions application by the November 1 Early Action deadline automatically considered, additional information may be required after initial review.

**Application procedures. Admission:** Priority date 11/1; deadline 2/1 (postmark date). $70 fee, may be waived for applicants with need. Must reply by 5/1. Students applying under regular admission to College of Design must submit application by 12/1. Selected candidates will be invited to interview. **Financial aid:** Priority date 3/1; no closing date. FAFSA, institutional form required. CSS PROFILE recommended for early scholarship consideration. Applicants notified on a rolling basis starting 4/1.

**Academics. Special study options:** Accelerated study, combined bachelor's/graduate degree, cooperative education, cross-registration, distance learning, double major, dual enrollment of high school students, ESL, exchange student, external degree, honors, independent study, internships, liberal arts/career combination, student-designed major, study abroad, teacher certification program. 2+2 Engineering with University of North Carolina-Asheville and selected community colleges. **Credit/placement by examination:** AP, CLEP, IB, SAT, ACT, institutional tests. **Support services:** Learning center, pre-admission summer program, reduced course load, remedial instruction, study skills assistance, tutoring, writing center.

**Majors. Agriculture:** Agribusiness operations, agronomy, animal sciences, education services, food science, horticultural science, mechanization, poultry. **Architecture:** Architecture, environmental design, landscape. **Area/ethnic studies:** African-American, women's. **Biology:** General, biochemistry, botany, microbiology, zoology. **Business:** Accounting, business admin, managerial economics. **Communications:** General. **Computer sciences:** Computer science. **Conservation:** General, environmental science, forest management, management/policy, wood science. **Education:** General, agricultural, elementary, English, French, health occupations, mathematics, middle, sales/marketing, science, social studies, Spanish, technology/industrial arts. **Engineering:** General, aerospace, agricultural, biomedical, chemical, civil, computer, construction, electrical, environmental, industrial, materials, mechanical, nuclear, textile. **Engineering technology:** Environmental. **Family/consumer sciences:** Apparel marketing, clothing/

textiles. **Foreign languages:** French, Spanish. **History:** General. **Interdisciplinary:** Global studies, science/society. **Liberal arts:** Arts/sciences. **Math:** General, applied, statistics. **Parks/recreation:** Facilities management, sports admin. **Philosophy/religion:** Philosophy, religion. **Physical sciences:** Atmospheric science, chemistry, geology, oceanography, physics, polymer chemistry. **Psychology:** General. **Public administration:** Social work. **Social sciences:** Anthropology, criminology, geography, political science, sociology. **Visual/performing arts:** Arts management, design, graphic design, industrial design.

**Most popular majors.** Agriculture 7%, biology 10%, business/marketing 15%, communications/journalism 6%, engineering/engineering technologies 23%, social sciences 6%.

**Computing on campus.** 3,000 workstations in dormitories, library, computer center, student center. Dormitories wired for high-speed internet access and linked to campus network. Commuter students can connect to campus network. Online course registration, helpline, repair service, student web hosting, wireless network available.

**Student life. Freshman orientation:** Mandatory, $141 fee. Preregistration for classes offered. 2-day program. **Housing:** Coed dorms, single-sex dorms, special housing for disabled, apartments, fraternity/sorority housing, wellness housing available. International student dormitory, Residential Scholars Program, residence hall for students interested in computers and visual and performing arts, first year college living and learning experience. **Activities:** Bands, campus ministries, choral groups, dance, drama, international student organizations, literary magazine, music ensembles, musical theater, radio station, student government, student newspaper, symphony orchestra, Alpha Phi Omega, Baptist Student Union, Campus Crusade for Christ, Circle-K, international student board, Young Democrats, Young Republicans, Society of Afro-American Culture, YMCA.

**Athletics.** NCAA. **Intercollegiate:** Baseball M, basketball, cheerleading, cross-country, diving, football (tackle) M, golf, gymnastics W, rifle, soccer, softball W, swimming, tennis, track and field, volleyball W, wrestling M. **Intramural:** Archery, badminton, baseball M, basketball, bowling, cross-country, fencing, field hockey W, football (non-tackle), golf, gymnastics, handball, ice hockey M, lacrosse M, racquetball, rugby M, sailing, skiing, skin diving, soccer, softball, squash, swimming, table tennis, tennis, track and field, volleyball, wrestling M. **Team name:** Wolfpack.

**Student services.** Adult student services, alcohol/substance abuse counseling, chaplain/spiritual director, career counseling, student employment services, financial aid counseling, health services, legal services, minority student services, on-campus daycare, personal counseling, placement for graduates, veterans' counselor, women's services. **Physically disabled:** Services for visually, speech, hearing impaired.

**Contact.** E-mail: undergrad_admissions@ncsu.edu
Phone: (919) 515-2434 Fax: (919) 515-5039
Thomas Griffin, Director of Undergraduate Admissions, North Carolina State University, 203 Peele Hall, Box 7103, Raleigh, NC 27695-7103

## North Carolina Wesleyan College
**Rocky Mount, North Carolina**
**www.ncwc.edu**                                   **CB code: 5501**

- Private 4-year liberal arts college affiliated with United Methodist Church
- Residential campus in small city
- 1,577 degree-seeking undergraduates
- SAT or ACT (ACT writing optional) required

**General.** Founded in 1956. Regionally accredited. Adult students, 22 and older, can attend classes at sites in Raleigh, Goldsboro, and Rocky Mount. There is a free Silver Scholars Program for age 60 and above. **Degrees:** 318 bachelor's awarded. **ROTC:** Army. **Location:** 57 miles from Raleigh. **Calendar:** Semester, extensive summer session. **Full-time faculty:** 49 total; 76% have terminal degrees, 4% minority, 45% women. **Part-time faculty:** 107 total; 48% have terminal degrees, 20% minority. **Class size:** 82% < 20, 18% 20-39. **Special facilities:** Black Mountain archival collection, center for the performing arts.

**Freshman class profile.**

| Mid 50% test scores | | | |
|---|---|---|---|
| SAT critical reading: | 410-520 | Rank in top quarter: | 18% |
| SAT math: | 420-550 | Rank in top tenth: | 8% |
| SAT writing: | 400-510 | Out-of-state: | 42% |
| ACT composite: | 16-22 | Live on campus: | 85% |

**Basis for selection.** High school GPA most important, followed by SAT or ACT score, rigor of high school curriculum, and recommendations. Essay, school and community activities considered. SAT preferred. Essay, interview recommended for all students. **Homeschooled:** Statement describing homeschool structure and mission, interview required.

**High school preparation.** College-preparatory program recommended. Recommended units include English 4, mathematics 3, social studies 2, science 2 (laboratory 2) and foreign language 2.

**2009-2010 Annual costs.** Tuition/fees: $20,790. Room/board: $7,380. Books/supplies: $1,000. Personal expenses: $1,200.

**2009-2010 Financial aid.** All financial aid based on need. **Additional information:** Scholarships based on GPA. Various scholarship and leadership awards available.

**Application procedures. Admission:** No deadline. $25 fee, may be waived for applicants with need. Admission notification on a rolling basis. **Financial aid:** Priority date 3/1; no closing date. FAFSA required. Applicants notified on a rolling basis starting 1/1; must reply within 2 week(s) of notification.

**Academics. Special study options:** Accelerated study, cooperative education, cross-registration, distance learning, double major, dual enrollment of high school students, honors, independent study, internships, liberal arts/career combination, teacher certification program, weekend college. **Credit/placement by examination:** AP, CLEP, institutional tests. **Support services:** Learning center, pre-admission summer program, reduced course load, remedial instruction, study skills assistance, tutoring, writing center.

**Majors. Biology:** General. **Business:** Accounting, business admin. **Computer sciences:** Information systems. **Conservation:** General. **Education:** Elementary, middle, physical. **Health:** Premedicine. **History:** General. **Math:** General. **Philosophy/religion:** Religion. **Physical sciences:** Chemistry. **Protective services:** Criminal justice. **Psychology:** General. **Social sciences:** Political science, sociology. **Visual/performing arts:** Dramatic.

**Computing on campus.** 223 workstations in dormitories, library, computer center, student center. Dormitories wired for high-speed internet access and linked to campus network. Commuter students can connect to campus network. Online course registration, helpline, repair service available.

**Student life. Freshman orientation:** Mandatory. Preregistration for classes offered. Takes place prior to start of fall classes. **Housing:** Guaranteed on-campus for freshmen. Coed dorms, single-sex dorms, special housing for disabled, wellness housing available. $100 deposit, deadline 7/15. **Activities:** Bands, choral groups, drama, literary magazine, music ensembles, student government, student newspaper, Black Student Association, Fellowship of Christian Athletes, College Republicans, Wesleyan Christian Fellowship.

**Athletics.** NCAA. **Intercollegiate:** Baseball M, basketball, cheerleading M, cross-country W, football (tackle) M, golf M, lacrosse W, soccer, softball W, tennis, volleyball W. **Intramural:** Basketball, football (tackle) M, lacrosse W, soccer, softball, table tennis, tennis, volleyball. **Team name:** Bishops.

**Student services.** Adult student services, alcohol/substance abuse counseling, chaplain/spiritual director, career counseling, student employment services, financial aid counseling, health services, personal counseling, placement for graduates, veterans' counselor. **Physically disabled:** Services for visually, hearing impaired.

**Contact.** E-mail: adm@ncwc.edu
Phone: (252) 985-5200 Toll-free number: (800) 488-6292
Fax: (252) 985-5295
Gary Sherman, Director of Admissions, North Carolina Wesleyan College, 3400 North Wesleyan Boulevard, Rocky Mount, NC 27804

## Peace College
**Raleigh, North Carolina**
www.peace.edu

CB member
CB code: 5533

- Private 4-year liberal arts college for women affiliated with Presbyterian Church (USA)
- Residential campus in large city
- 692 degree-seeking undergraduates: 5% part-time, 99% women, 19% African American, 2% Asian American, 5% Hispanic American, 2% Native American, 1% international
- 64% of applicants admitted
- SAT or ACT (ACT writing optional), interview required

**General.** Founded in 1857. Regionally accredited. **Degrees:** 113 bachelor's awarded. **ROTC:** Army, Naval, Air Force. **Location:** Downtown.

**Calendar:** Semester, limited summer session. **Full-time faculty:** 44 total; 77% have terminal degrees, 11% minority, 68% women. **Part-time faculty:** 32 total; 34% have terminal degrees, 19% minority, 59% women. **Class size:** 74% < 20, 25% 20-39, less than 1% 50-99.

**Freshman class profile.** 994 applied, 635 admitted, 152 enrolled.

| Mid 50% test scores | | | |
|---|---|---|---|
| SAT critical reading: | 410-520 | GPA 2.0-2.99: | 42% |
| SAT math: | 400-500 | Rank in top quarter: | 23% |
| ACT composite: | 16-18 | Rank in top tenth: | 4% |
| GPA 3.75 or higher: | 15% | Out-of-state: | 12% |
| GPA 3.50-3.74: | 11% | Live on campus: | 89% |
| GPA 3.0-3.49: | 29% | International: | 1% |

**Basis for selection.** School achievement record, test scores, 2.0 GPA on college preparatory courses recommended. SAT combined score of 800 (exclusive of Writing) and above preferred or ACT of 17 minimum. Interview recommended for all students. Audition required for theater, drama, and music majors; portfolio required for art programs. **Homeschooled:** Statement describing homeschool structure and mission required. **Learning Disabled:** Students with learning disabilities are encouraged to contact disabilities resource center regarding their needs.

**High school preparation.** College-preparatory program recommended. 15 units required; 17 recommended. Required and recommended units include English 4, mathematics 3-4, social studies 2, history 2, science 3 and foreign language 2.

**2009-2010 Annual costs.** Tuition/fees: $24,133. Room/board: $8,250. Books/supplies: $1,300. Personal expenses: $2,400.

**2009-2010 Financial aid. Need-based:** 140 full-time freshmen applied for aid; 129 were judged to have need; 129 of these received aid. Average need met was 77%. Average scholarship/grant was $20,112; average loan $3,290. 67% of total undergraduate aid awarded as scholarships/grants, 33% as loans/jobs. **Non-need-based:** Awarded to 170 full-time undergraduates, including 29 freshmen. Scholarships awarded for academics, art, leadership, music/drama, state residency.

**Application procedures. Admission:** Priority date 4/1; no deadline. $25 fee, may be waived for applicants with need. Admission notification on a rolling basis beginning on or about 8/1. Must reply by May 1 or within 2 week(s) if notified thereafter. Prefer early admission candidates with SAT 1100 or above, 3.5 GPA in college preparatory courses, and rank in top 25% of class. On-campus interview required. **Financial aid:** Priority date 3/15; no closing date. FAFSA required. Applicants notified on a rolling basis starting 3/1; must reply within 4 week(s) of notification.

**Academics. Special study options:** Cooperative education, cross-registration, double major, dual enrollment of high school students, honors, independent study, internships, liberal arts/career combination, study abroad, teacher certification program. Adult degree evening program in Business and Human Services. Human Resources certificate. **Credit/placement by examination:** AP, CLEP, IB, SAT, ACT, institutional tests. 6 credit hours maximum toward bachelor's degree. CLEP credit is granted to students who have achieved the minimum score in designated subject tests. Students may petition program coordinators for additional or alternative credit, if warranted. **Support services:** Learning center, reduced course load, remedial instruction, study skills assistance, tutoring, writing center.

**Majors. Biology:** General. **Business:** Business admin, human resources. **Communications:** General. **Education:** Early childhood, multi-level teacher. **Family/consumer sciences:** Child development. **Foreign languages:** Spanish. **History:** General. **Liberal arts:** Arts/sciences. **Psychology:** General. **Social sciences:** Anthropology, political science. **Visual/performing arts:** Design, music performance. **Other:** Leadership studies.

**Most popular majors.** Biology 6%, business/marketing 21%, communications/journalism 14%, liberal arts 6%, psychology 10%, social sciences 10%.

**Computing on campus.** 180 workstations in dormitories, library, computer center, student center. Dormitories wired for high-speed internet access and linked to campus network. Commuter students can connect to campus network. Online course registration, online library, helpline, repair service, student web hosting, wireless network available.

**Student life. Freshman orientation:** Mandatory, $150 fee. Preregistration for classes offered. 2-day program offered prior to start of classes, during the summer and a four day program at the beginning with move-in. **Policies:** Honor Code and Student Code of Conduct. Religious observance required. **Housing:** Guaranteed on-campus for freshmen. Special housing for disabled available. $150 nonrefundable deposit, deadline 7/1. Freshmen and sophomores required to live on campus unless living with relatives in area. **Activities:** Campus ministries, choral groups, dance, drama, literary magazine, music ensembles, musical theater, opera, student government, student newspaper, Christian Association, honor societies, recreation association, Young Democrats/Republicans, Phi Theta Kappa, Green Team, Helping Hands, Home Sweet Homes, Politics Club.

**Athletics.** NCAA. **Intercollegiate:** Basketball W, cross-country W, soccer W, softball W, tennis W, volleyball W. **Intramural:** Tennis W. **Team name:** Peace Pacers.

**Student services.** Adult student services, chaplain/spiritual director, career counseling, student employment services, financial aid counseling, health services, personal counseling, placement for graduates.

**Contact.** E-mail: admissions@peace.edu
Phone: (919) 508-2000 Toll-free number: (800) 732-2347
Fax: (919) 508-2306
Matt Green, Dean of Enrollment, Peace College, 15 East Peace Street, Raleigh, NC 27604-1194

---

## Pfeiffer University
### Misenheimer, North Carolina
**CB member**
www.pfeiffer.edu — **CB code: 5536**

- Private 4-year university and liberal arts college affiliated with United Methodist Church
- Residential campus in rural community
- 1,066 degree-seeking undergraduates: 12% part-time, 55% women, 20% African American, 1% Asian American, 3% Hispanic American, 1% Native American, 4% international
- 946 degree-seeking graduate students
- SAT or ACT (ACT writing optional) required
- 57% graduate within 6 years

**General.** Founded in 1885. Regionally accredited. **Degrees:** 264 bachelor's awarded; master's offered. **ROTC:** Army. **Location:** 35 miles from Charlotte, 60 miles from Winston-Salem. **Calendar:** Semester, limited summer session. **Full-time faculty:** 73 total; 74% have terminal degrees, 14% minority, 37% women. **Part-time faculty:** 60 total; 7% minority, 38% women. **Class size:** 77% < 20, 22% 20-39, less than 1% 40-49, less than 1% 50-99. **Special facilities:** Retreat center.

**Freshman class profile.** 240 enrolled.

| Mid 50% test scores | | | |
|---|---|---|---|
| SAT critical reading: | 440-530 | Rank in top quarter: | 35% |
| SAT math: | 440-540 | Rank in top tenth: | 15% |
| GPA 3.75 or higher: | 24% | Return as sophomores: | 59% |
| GPA 3.50-3.74: | 12% | Out-of-state: | 37% |
| GPA 3.0-3.49: | 26% | Live on campus: | 79% |
| GPA 2.0-2.99: | 37% | International: | 5% |

**Basis for selection.** School achievement record, class rank, recommendations, and test scores reviewed. Essay tests for both SAT and ACT are used in scholarship/merit competitions. Interview recommended for all students; audition required for music programs.

**High school preparation.** College-preparatory program recommended. 12 units required; 16 recommended. Required and recommended units include English 4, mathematics 3, social studies 2-4, history 2, science 2-3 (laboratory 1) and foreign language 2. Math should include algebra I and geometry.

**2009-2010 Annual costs.** Tuition/fees: $19,215. Room/board: $7,928. Books/supplies: $1,000. Personal expenses: $1,000.

**2008-2009 Financial aid. Need-based:** 181 full-time freshmen applied for aid; 152 were judged to have need; 152 of these received aid. Average need met was 81%. Average scholarship/grant was $14,860; average loan $2,868. 67% of total undergraduate aid awarded as scholarships/grants, 33% as loans/jobs. **Non-need-based:** Awarded to 359 full-time undergraduates, including 79 freshmen. Scholarships awarded for academics, alumni affiliation, athletics, leadership, music/drama, religious affiliation, state residency.

**Application procedures. Admission:** No deadline. $35 fee, may be waived for applicants with need. Admission notification on a rolling basis beginning on or about 9/1. **Financial aid:** Priority date 5/1; no closing date. FAFSA required. Applicants notified on a rolling basis starting 3/1; must reply within 2 week(s) of notification.

**Academics. Special study options:** Accelerated study, combined bachelor's/graduate degree, cooperative education, distance learning, double major, dual enrollment of high school students, honors, independent study, internships, liberal arts/career combination, study abroad, teacher certification program,

---

Washington semester, weekend college. **Credit/placement by examination:** AP, CLEP, IB, SAT, ACT, institutional tests. **Support services:** Learning center, reduced course load, remedial instruction, study skills assistance, tutoring, writing center.

**Majors. Biology:** General. **Business:** General, accounting, business admin. **Communications:** General. **Computer sciences:** General. **Conservation:** Environmental studies. **Education:** Elementary, music, physical, secondary, social science, special. **Engineering:** General. **Health:** Athletic training, health care admin, predental, premedicine, preveterinary. **History:** General. **Legal studies:** Prelaw. **Liberal arts:** Arts/sciences. **Math:** General. **Parks/recreation:** Facilities management, sports admin. **Philosophy/religion:** Religion. **Physical sciences:** Chemistry. **Protective services:** Criminal justice, police science. **Psychology:** General. **Social sciences:** Economics, sociology. **Theology:** Missionary, religious ed, sacred music, youth ministry. **Visual/performing arts:** Arts management, dramatic.

**Most popular majors.** Business/marketing 33%, education 11%, parks/recreation 9%, security/protective services 11%.

**Computing on campus.** 120 workstations in library, computer center, student center. Dormitories wired for high-speed internet access and linked to campus network. Commuter students can connect to campus network. Online course registration, online library, helpline, repair service, wireless network available.

**Student life. Freshman orientation:** Available, $35 fee. **Housing:** Guaranteed on-campus for all undergraduates. Coed dorms, single-sex dorms, special housing for disabled, apartments, wellness housing available. $150 deposit. Apartment-style housing with shared kitchen and bath available for older students not married. **Activities:** Bands, campus ministries, choral groups, dance, drama, literary magazine, music ensembles, musical theater, student government, student newspaper, religious organizations, political groups, service clubs, professional clubs.

**Athletics.** NCAA. **Intercollegiate:** Baseball M, basketball, cross-country, golf, lacrosse, soccer, softball W, swimming, tennis, volleyball. **Intramural:** Basketball, lacrosse, soccer, softball, table tennis, tennis, volleyball. **Team name:** Falcons.

**Student services.** Alcohol/substance abuse counseling, chaplain/spiritual director, career counseling, student employment services, financial aid counseling, health services, personal counseling, placement for graduates, veterans' counselor.

**Contact.** E-mail: admiss@pfeiffer.edu
Phone: (704) 463-1360 ext. 2060 Toll-free number: (800) 338-2060
Fax: (704) 463-1363
Steven Cumming, Director of Admissions, Pfeiffer University, Box 960, Misenheimer, NC 28109

---

## Piedmont Baptist College
### Winston-Salem, North Carolina
www.pbc.edu — **CB code: 5555**

- Private 4-year Bible and seminary college affiliated with Baptist faith
- Small city
- 262 degree-seeking undergraduates
- ACT (writing optional), application essay required

**General.** Founded in 1945. Regionally accredited; also accredited by TRACS. **Degrees:** 44 bachelor's, 3 associate awarded; master's offered. **Location:** 75 miles from Charlotte, 100 miles from Raleigh. **Calendar:** Semester, limited summer session. **Full-time faculty:** 20 total. **Part-time faculty:** 15 total. **Class size:** 77% < 20, 17% 20-39, 4% 40-49, 1% 50-99. **Special facilities:** Restored 18th Century Moravian community, Old Salem.

**Freshman class profile.**

| | | | |
|---|---|---|---|
| Out-of-state: | 55% | Live on campus: | 44% |

**Basis for selection.** Student's life objectives and previous academic record important. Interview recommended for all students; audition required for music program.

**High school preparation.** Recommended units include English 4, mathematics 3, social studies 3, science 3 and foreign language 2.

**2009-2010 Annual costs.** Tuition/fees: $11,565. Room/board: $5,760. Books/supplies: $600. Personal expenses: $600.

**Application procedures. Admission:** Priority date 7/31; no deadline. $60 fee. Admission notification on a rolling basis beginning on or about

12/1. Must reply by May 1 or within 2 week(s) if notified thereafter. **Financial aid:** No deadline. Institutional form required. Applicants notified on a rolling basis starting 3/1.

**Academics. Special study options:** Cooperative education, distance learning, double major, dual enrollment of high school students, independent study, internships, teacher certification program. **Credit/placement by examination:** AP, CLEP, institutional tests. **Support services:** Learning center, reduced course load, remedial instruction, study skills assistance, tutoring.

**Majors. Education:** Elementary, English, music, physical. **Theology:** Bible, missionary, youth ministry.

**Most popular majors.** Education 33%, philosophy/religious studies 60%.

**Computing on campus.** 26 workstations in library, computer center, student center. Dormitories linked to campus network. Commuter students can connect to campus network. Online course registration, online library, helpline, wireless network available.

**Student life. Freshman orientation:** Mandatory. Preregistration for classes offered. Held 2 days prior to registration, overviews basic rules and guidelines. **Policies:** Religious observance required. **Housing:** Guaranteed on-campus for freshmen. Single-sex dorms, apartments available. **Activities:** Choral groups, drama, music ensembles, student government, student newspaper, missions fellowship, preachers' fellowship, youth leaders' fellowship, educators' fellowship, music fellowship.

**Athletics.** NCCAA. **Intercollegiate:** Basketball, soccer M, volleyball W. **Team name:** Conquerors.

**Student services.** Chaplain/spiritual director, career counseling, financial aid counseling, health services, personal counseling, placement for graduates, veterans' counselor.

**Contact.** E-mail: admissions@pbc.edu
Phone: (336) 725-8344 ext. 7900 Toll-free number: (800) 937-5097
Fax: (336) 725-5522
Angela Hoover, Director of Admissions, Piedmont Baptist College, 420 South Boad Street, Winston-Salem, NC 27101-5133

---

## Queens University of Charlotte
**Charlotte, North Carolina**
www.queens.edu

**CB member**
**CB code: 5560**

▶ Private 4-year university affiliated with Presbyterian Church (USA)
▶ Residential campus in very large city
▶ 1,880 degree-seeking undergraduates: 30% part-time, 78% women, 18% African American, 2% Asian American, 5% Hispanic American, 5% international
▶ 574 degree-seeking graduate students
▶ 76% of applicants admitted
▶ SAT or ACT with writing required
▶ 62% graduate within 6 years

**General.** Founded in 1857. Regionally accredited. **Degrees:** 277 bachelor's, 130 associate awarded; master's offered. **ROTC:** Army, Air Force. **Calendar:** Semester, limited summer session. **Full-time faculty:** 109 total; 70% have terminal degrees, 7% minority, 68% women. **Part-time faculty:** 107 total; 30% have terminal degrees, 13% minority, 61% women. **Class size:** 70% < 20, 27% 20-39, 2% 40-49, less than 1% 50-99. **Special facilities:** Rare books museum, recital hall.

**Freshman class profile.** 1,701 applied, 1,289 admitted, 315 enrolled.

| Mid 50% test scores | | | |
|---|---|---|---|
| SAT critical reading: | 470-580 | GPA 2.0-2.99: | 18% |
| SAT math: | 480-580 | Rank in top quarter: | 54% |
| SAT writing: | 470-570 | Rank in top tenth: | 43% |
| ACT composite: | 20-26 | Out-of-state: | 43% |
| GPA 3.75 or higher: | 40% | Live on campus: | 70% |
| GPA 3.50-3.74: | 13% | International: | 2% |
| GPA 3.0-3.49: | 29% | Fraternities: | 19% |
| | | Sororities: | 16% |

**Basis for selection.** High school courses taken, school achievement record, class rank, test scores important. Extracurricular activities, recommendations also considered. Official test scores must be received prior to admission. Interview recommended for all students. Audition required for drama, music, music therapy programs; portfolio recommended for art program. **Homeschooled:** Transcript of courses and grades required. Evidence of Home School registration in the home state (copy of Home School License) required.

**High school preparation.** College-preparatory program required. Required units include English 4, mathematics 3, social studies 2, science 2 (laboratory 1) and foreign language 2. Chemistry recommended for nursing majors.

**2009-2010 Annual costs.** Tuition/fees: $22,730. Room/board: $8,236. Books/supplies: $1,200. Personal expenses: $1,500.

**2009-2010 Financial aid. Need-based:** 263 full-time freshmen applied for aid; 225 were judged to have need; 225 of these received aid. Average need met was 76%. Average scholarship/grant was $15,556; average loan $3,287. 58% of total undergraduate aid awarded as scholarships/grants, 42% as loans/jobs. **Non-need-based:** Awarded to 546 full-time undergraduates, including 142 freshmen. Scholarships awarded for academics, art, athletics, leadership, minority status, music/drama, religious affiliation.

**Application procedures. Admission:** Priority date 12/1; no deadline. $40 fee, may be waived for applicants with need, free for online applicants. Admission notification on a rolling basis beginning on or about 10/1. Must reply by May 1 or within 3 week(s) if notified thereafter. Admission can be deferred up to one year. **Financial aid:** Priority date 3/1; no closing date. FAFSA required. Applicants notified on a rolling basis starting 3/15; must reply by 5/1 or within 3 week(s) of notification.

**Academics.** 6 credit hours of internships required to enhance job placement and career opportunities. **Special study options:** Cross-registration, double major, dual enrollment of high school students, honors, independent study, internships, student-designed major, study abroad, teacher certification program, Washington semester, weekend college. John Belk International Program (3-week study tours in Europe and Asia), interdisciplinary core curriculum, professional golf management, Harvard Model UN, European internship program offered. **Credit/placement by examination:** AP, CLEP, IB, institutional tests. 43 credit hours maximum toward bachelor's degree. **Support services:** Learning center, reduced course load, study skills assistance, tutoring, writing center.

**Majors. Area/ethnic studies:** American, European. **Biology:** General, biochemistry, environmental. **Business:** Business admin, golf management, international, marketing. **Communications:** General, journalism, media studies, organizational. **Computer sciences:** Information systems. **Conservation:** Environmental science, environmental studies. **Education:** General, elementary, English, foreign languages. **Foreign languages:** General. **Health:** Music therapy, nursing (RN), predental, premedicine, preop/surgical nursing, prepharmacy, preveterinary. **History:** General. **Interdisciplinary:** Global studies. **Legal studies:** Prelaw. **Math:** General, statistics. **Philosophy/religion:** Religion. **Physical sciences:** Chemistry. **Psychology:** General. **Social sciences:** Political science, sociology. **Visual/performing arts:** Dramatic, music performance, studio arts.

**Most popular majors.** Business/marketing 17%, communications/journalism 14%, health sciences 23%, psychology 8%, social sciences 7%.

**Computing on campus.** Dormitories wired for high-speed internet access and linked to campus network. Commuter students can connect to campus network. Online library, helpline, wireless network available.

**Student life. Freshman orientation:** Mandatory. Preregistration for classes offered. 2-day program held at beginning of academic year. Pre-orientation held in spring for all deposited freshmen. **Housing:** Guaranteed on-campus for freshmen. Coed dorms, special housing for disabled, wellness housing available. $300 fully refundable deposit, deadline 5/1. Apartment style residence hall available for traditional undergraduates only. **Activities:** Pep band, campus ministries, choral groups, dance, drama, international student organizations, literary magazine, music ensembles, Model UN, musical theater, student government, student newspaper, Students for Black Awareness, College Republicans, College Democrats, North Carolina Student Legislature, Justinian Society.

**Athletics.** NCAA. **Intercollegiate:** Basketball, cheerleading, cross-country, golf, lacrosse, soccer, softball W, tennis, track and field, volleyball W. **Intramural:** Basketball, football (non-tackle) M, soccer, softball, volleyball. **Team name:** Royals.

**Student services.** Alcohol/substance abuse counseling, chaplain/spiritual director, career counseling, student employment services, financial aid counseling, health services, minority student services, personal counseling, placement for graduates. **Physically disabled:** Services for visually impaired.

**Contact.** E-mail: admissions@queens.edu
Phone: (704) 337-2212 Toll-free number: (800) 849-0202
Fax: (704) 337-2403
William Lee, Director of Admissions, Queens University of Charlotte, 1900 Selwyn Ave, Charlotte, NC 28274

## St. Andrews Presbyterian College
**Laurinburg, North Carolina**     **CB member**
www.sapc.edu     **CB code: 5214**

- Private 4-year liberal arts college affiliated with Presbyterian Church (USA)
- Residential campus in large town
- 579 degree-seeking undergraduates: 4% part-time, 57% women, 10% African American, 1% Asian American, 3% Hispanic American, 1% Native American, 2% international
- 76% of applicants admitted
- SAT or ACT (ACT writing optional) required
- 45% graduate within 6 years

**General.** Founded in 1958. Regionally accredited. **Degrees:** 135 bachelor's awarded. **Location:** 40 miles from Fayetteville, 20 miles from Pinehurst. **Calendar:** Semester, limited summer session. **Full-time faculty:** 34 total; 76% have terminal degrees, 44% women. **Part-time faculty:** 41 total; 32% have terminal degrees, 5% minority, 49% women. **Class size:** 74% < 20, 25% 20-39, 1% 40-49. **Special facilities:** Psychology laboratory complex, equestrian facilities, nature preserve, electronic fine arts center.

**Freshman class profile.** 743 applied, 566 admitted, 147 enrolled.

| Mid 50% test scores | | | |
|---|---|---|---|
| SAT critical reading: | 430-520 | Rank in top quarter: | 23% |
| SAT math: | 450-550 | Rank in top tenth: | 4% |
| GPA 3.75 or higher: | 4% | End year in good standing: | 78% |
| GPA 3.50-3.74: | 14% | Return as sophomores: | 78% |
| GPA 3.0-3.49: | 39% | Out-of-state: | 63% |
| GPA 2.0-2.99: | 40% | Live on campus: | 95% |
| | | International: | 4% |

**Basis for selection.** High school GPA, test scores, curriculum, type of high school very important. Recommendations important. Interview required for academically weak students, recommended for all other applicants. **Homeschooled:** Transcript of courses and grades, state high school equivalency certificate required. Standardized test scores and interview required.

**High school preparation.** College-preparatory program recommended. Required units include English 3, mathematics 3, social studies 3, science 3, foreign language 1 and academic electives 2.

**2010-2011 Annual costs.** Tuition/fees: $21,614. Room/board: $8,938. Books/supplies: $1,300. Personal expenses: $2,000.

**2008-2009 Financial aid. Need-based:** 120 full-time freshmen applied for aid; 106 were judged to have need; 106 of these received aid. Average need met was 74%. Average scholarship/grant was $11,798; average loan $3,621. 82% of total undergraduate aid awarded as scholarships/grants, 18% as loans/jobs. **Non-need-based:** Awarded to 286 full-time undergraduates, including 63 freshmen. Scholarships awarded for academics, alumni affiliation, art, athletics, leadership, music/drama.

**Application procedures. Admission:** Priority date 5/1; no deadline. $30 fee, may be waived for applicants with need. Admission notification on a rolling basis beginning on or about 9/1. Housing deposit fully refundable until May 1st. **Financial aid:** Priority date 5/1; no closing date. FAFSA required. Applicants notified on a rolling basis starting 10/1; must reply within 2 week(s) of notification.

**Academics.** Academic programs include St. Andrew's General Education. **Special study options:** Double major, honors, independent study, internships, student-designed major, study abroad, teacher certification program, weekend college. Courses offered abroad during winter or summer in Britain, Greece, India, Switzerland, Venezuela, China, Hawaii, former Soviet Union; exchange programs with Stirling University, Scotland and Kansai Gaidai University, Japan; study at Brunnenburg Castle, Italy, and Beijing Normal College of Foreign Languages. **Credit/placement by examination:** AP, CLEP, IB, institutional tests. 30 credit hours maximum toward bachelor's degree. **Support services:** Reduced course load, tutoring, writing center.

**Majors. Agriculture:** Equestrian studies. **Area/ethnic studies:** Asian. **Biology:** General. **Business:** General, business admin, international. **Communications:** Media studies. **Education:** Elementary, physical. **Health:** Premedicine, preveterinary, recreational therapy. **History:** General, public archives. **Legal studies:** Prelaw. **Liberal arts:** Arts/sciences. **Math:** General. **Parks/recreation:** Health/fitness. **Philosophy/religion:** Philosophy, religion. **Physical sciences:** Chemistry. **Psychology:** General. **Social sciences:** Political science. **Visual/performing arts:** General, art.

**Most popular majors.** Biology 8%, business/marketing 26%, education 17%, English 6%, liberal arts 7%, parks/recreation 10%, psychology 14%.

**Computing on campus.** 100 workstations in library, computer center, student center. Dormitories wired for high-speed internet access and linked to campus network. Online library, repair service available.

**Student life. Freshman orientation:** Mandatory, $100 fee. 3 days prior to start of fall term. **Policies:** Honor code enforced. **Housing:** Guaranteed on-campus for all undergraduates. Coed dorms, single-sex dorms available. $250 deposit, deadline 8/25. **Activities:** Campus ministries, choral groups, drama, literary magazine, student government, student newspaper, Christian Student Fellowship, black student union, women's issues group, writer's forum, world culture club, Eco-Action, student activities union.

**Athletics.** NCAA. **Intercollegiate:** Baseball M, basketball, cross-country, equestrian, golf, lacrosse, soccer, softball W, tennis, track and field, volleyball W. **Intramural:** Basketball, bowling, racquetball, soccer, softball W, table tennis, volleyball. **Team name:** Knights.

**Student services.** Adult student services, alcohol/substance abuse counseling, career counseling, student employment services, financial aid counseling, health services, personal counseling, placement for graduates, women's services. **Physically disabled:** Services for visually, speech, hearing impaired.

**Contact.** E-mail: admissions@sapc.edu
Phone: (910) 277-5555 Toll-free number: (800) 763-0198
Fax: (910) 277-5087
Kirsten Simmons, Director of Admission, St. Andrews Presbyterian College, 1700 Dogwood Mile, Laurinburg, NC 28352

## St. Augustine's College
**Raleigh, North Carolina**     **CB member**
www.st-aug.edu     **CB code: 5596**

- Private 4-year liberal arts college affiliated with Episcopal Church
- Residential campus in large city
- 1,527 degree-seeking undergraduates
- Interview required

**General.** Founded in 1867. Regionally accredited. Home to historic St. Augustine's College Chapel and St. Agnes Hospital. **Degrees:** 168 bachelor's awarded. **ROTC:** Army, Air Force. **Location:** One mile from downtown. **Calendar:** Semester, limited summer session. **Full-time faculty:** 78 total. **Part-time faculty:** 42 total. **Class size:** 65% < 20, 33% 20-39, 2% 40-49, less than 1% 50-99. **Special facilities:** Archival collection tracing history of African-Americans in North Carolina and Delaney family.

**Freshman class profile.**

| Mid 50% test scores | | | |
|---|---|---|---|
| SAT critical reading: | 330-420 | Rank in top tenth: | 15% |
| SAT math: | 330-420 | Out-of-state: | 65% |
| ACT composite: | 15-19 | Live on campus: | 92% |
| Rank in top quarter: | 44% | Fraternities: | 6% |
| | | Sororities: | 12% |

**Basis for selection.** High school record (GPA and rank), standardized test scores and letters of recommendation reviewed. Alumni affiliation also considered. SAT or ACT recommended. Institutionally administered Accuplacer test is used for pre- and post-testing evaluation and placement purposes. Essay recommended. Auditions and interviews required of music majors. **Learning Disabled:** Students must self-identify. ADA Coordinator will assess level of disability and arrange for student to access the needed equipment or tutorials.

**High school preparation.** 20 units required. Required units include English 4, mathematics 3, social studies 2, science 2 and academic electives 9. One unit of algebra required, 2 units of laboratory recommended.

**2009-2010 Annual costs.** Tuition/fees: $15,690. Required fees include books. $250 is for supplies only. Room/board: $6,918. Books/supplies: $250. Personal expenses: $1,530.

**2009-2010 Financial aid. Non-need-based:** Scholarships awarded for academics, art, athletics, leadership, minority status, music/drama, religious affiliation, ROTC, state residency.

**Application procedures. Admission:** Closing date 8/1 (postmark date). $25 fee, may be waived for applicants with need. Admission notification on a rolling basis beginning on or about 1/1. **Financial aid:** Closing date 3/15. FAFSA, institutional form required. Applicants notified on a rolling basis starting 5/1; must reply within 2 week(s) of notification.

**Academics.** Required Learning Community program for all new freshmen and transfers. First-year program includes skills enhancement, college survival tips. Community service requirement part of course. **Special study options:** Accelerated study, cooperative education, cross-registration, double major, dual enrollment of high school students, honors, independent study, internships, liberal arts/career combination, study abroad, teacher certification program, weekend college. **Credit/placement by examination:** CLEP, IB, institutional tests. 15 credit hours maximum toward bachelor's degree. **Support services:** Learning center, pre-admission summer program, reduced course load, remedial instruction, study skills assistance, tutoring, writing center.

**Majors. Area/ethnic studies:** African-American. **Biology:** General, biomedical sciences. **Business:** Accounting, business admin, management science, real estate. **Communications:** General. **Computer sciences:** General, computer science. **Education:** Elementary. **Engineering:** General. **Health:** Occupational health, premedicine. **History:** General. **Legal studies:** Prelaw. **Math:** General. **Parks/recreation:** Health/fitness, sports admin. **Philosophy/religion:** Religion. **Physical sciences:** Chemistry. **Protective services:** Criminal justice, forensics. **Psychology:** General. **Social sciences:** Political science, sociology. **Visual/performing arts:** General, art, cinematography, music performance.

**Most popular majors.** Business/marketing 35%, communications/journalism 7%, computer/information sciences 12%, security/protective services 10%, social sciences 14%.

**Computing on campus.** 250 workstations in dormitories, library, computer center. Dormitories wired for high-speed internet access and linked to campus network. Commuter students can connect to campus network. Online course registration, online library, helpline, repair service available.

**Student life. Freshman orientation:** Mandatory, $60 fee. Preregistration for classes offered. 2-day orientations held in June, July, and August with students and parents. **Policies:** Alcohol and drug-free campus. No tolerance policy. No firearm policy. No smoking policy for all campus administrative buildings. Religious observance required. **Housing:** Guaranteed on-campus for freshmen. Single-sex dorms, wellness housing available. $150 deposit. **Activities:** Bands, choral groups, dance, drama, film society, music ensembles, musical theater, radio station, student government, student newspaper, symphony orchestra, TV station, Christian Fellowship Organization, Young Democrats of America, Falcons for the Cause, NAACP, foreign language club, Falcon Battalion/Army ROTC, Student Service Corps, SAC Association for Black Journalists, International student association, Latin American students organization.

**Athletics. NCAA. Intercollegiate:** Baseball M, basketball, bowling W, cheerleading W, cross-country, football (tackle) M, golf, softball W, tennis, track and field, volleyball W. **Intramural:** Baseball M, basketball, softball W, volleyball. **Team name:** Falcons.

**Student services.** Adult student services, alcohol/substance abuse counseling, chaplain/spiritual director, career counseling, services for economically disadvantaged, student employment services, financial aid counseling, health services, minority student services, personal counseling, placement for graduates, veterans' counselor. **Physically disabled:** Services for visually impaired.

**Contact.** E-mail: admissions@st-aug.edu
Phone: (919) 516-4012 Toll-free number: (800) 948-1126
Fax: (919) 516-5805
Jorge Sousa, Director of Admissions, St. Augustine's College, 1315 Oakwood Avenue, Raleigh, NC 27610-2298

## Salem College

**Winston-Salem, North Carolina**      **CB member**
**www.salem.edu**      **CB code: 5607**

- Private 4-year liberal arts college for women affiliated with Moravian Church in America
- Residential campus in small city
- 729 degree-seeking undergraduates: 16% part-time, 97% women, 19% African American, 1% Asian American, 5% Hispanic American, 6% international
- 212 degree-seeking graduate students
- 59% of applicants admitted
- SAT or ACT (ACT writing optional), application essay required
- 61% graduate within 6 years; 35% enter graduate study

**General.** Founded in 1772. Regionally accredited. Male students age 23 and over may enroll in adult program only; male students may not reside at the college. **Degrees:** 173 bachelor's awarded; master's offered. **ROTC:** Army. **Location:** 80 miles from Charlotte, 25 miles from Greensboro. **Calendar:** 4-1-4, limited summer session. **Full-time faculty:** 56 total; 89% have terminal degrees, 9% minority, 61% women. **Part-time faculty:** 49 total; 37% have terminal degrees, 12% minority, 63% women. **Class size:** 84% < 20, 16% 20-39. **Special facilities:** Center for women writers.

**Freshman class profile.** 580 applied, 342 admitted, 149 enrolled.

| Mid 50% test scores | | | |
|---|---|---|---|
| SAT critical reading: | 480-610 | GPA 2.0-2.99: | 6% |
| SAT math: | 470-580 | Rank in top quarter: | 67% |
| SAT writing: | 480-590 | Rank in top tenth: | 39% |
| ACT composite: | 22-28 | End year in good standing: | 93% |
| GPA 3.75 or higher: | 48% | Return as sophomores: | 74% |
| GPA 3.50-3.74: | 22% | Out-of-state: | 35% |
| GPA 3.0-3.49: | 24% | Live on campus: | 98% |

**Basis for selection.** School achievement record, essay or personal statement, test scores important. Recommendations, interview, extracurricular and community activities, talent, minority status considered. Interview recommended for all students. Audition required for music program; portfolio recommended for art program.

**High school preparation.** College-preparatory program required. 16 units required. Required units include English 4, mathematics 3, social studies 2, science 3, foreign language 2 and academic electives 3. Math requirement includes 2 algebra and 1 geometry. On a case by case basis, a portion of this requirement may be waived for adult students.

**2010-2011 Annual costs.** Tuition/fees: $21,948. Traditional-age students must enroll full-time. Students registering through the Fleer Center for Adult Education pay $1,074 tuition per course. Graduate students pay $302 per credit hour. Room/board: $11,520. Books/supplies: $960. Personal expenses: $910.

**2008-2009 Financial aid. Need-based:** 71% of total undergraduate aid awarded as scholarships/grants, 29% as loans/jobs. **Non-need-based:** Scholarships awarded for academics, alumni affiliation, leadership, minority status, music/drama, state residency.

**Application procedures. Admission:** Priority date 3/1; no deadline. $30 fee, may be waived for applicants with need, free for online applicants. Admission notification on a rolling basis beginning on or about 10/1. Must reply by May 1 or within 2 week(s) if notified thereafter. **Financial aid:** Priority date 3/1; no closing date. FAFSA required. Applicants notified on a rolling basis starting 3/1; must reply by 5/1 or within 2 week(s) of notification.

**Academics. Special study options:** Accelerated study, cross-registration, double major, dual enrollment of high school students, exchange student, honors, independent study, internships, liberal arts/career combination, student-designed major, study abroad, teacher certification program, Washington semester. 3-1 clinical laboratory sciences/medical technology program with Wake Forest University's Baptist Medical Center; various study abroad options available through Brethren Colleges of America (BCA); St. Peters, Oxford; and St. Clare's, Oxford. **Credit/placement by examination:** AP, CLEP, IB, SAT, institutional tests. **Support services:** Learning center, reduced course load, study skills assistance, tutoring, writing center.

**Majors. Area/ethnic studies:** American. **Biology:** General. **Business:** Accounting, business admin, international, nonprofit/public. **Communications:** General. **Education:** Elementary, music, secondary. **Foreign languages:** French, Spanish. **Health:** Clinical lab technology. **History:** General. **Math:** General. **Philosophy/religion:** Philosophy, religion. **Physical sciences:** Chemistry. **Psychology:** General. **Social sciences:** Economics, international relations, sociology. **Visual/performing arts:** Art history/conservation, arts management, interior design, music performance, studio arts.

**Most popular majors.** Biology 9%, business/marketing 12%, communications/journalism 9%, English 12%, foreign language 7%, psychology 9%, social sciences 18%, visual/performing arts 9%.

**Computing on campus.** 54 workstations in library, computer center. Dormitories wired for high-speed internet access and linked to campus network. Commuter students can connect to campus network. Online library, helpline, wireless network available.

**Student life. Freshman orientation:** Mandatory. Preregistration for classes offered. 3 days before fall term begins. Separate orientation program for adult students. **Housing:** Guaranteed on-campus for freshmen. Apartments, wellness housing available. $250 nonrefundable deposit, deadline 5/1. All full-time students under 23 years required to reside on-campus unless they reside with family within a 30 mile radius of the college. **Activities:** Marching band, campus ministries, choral groups, dance, drama, international student organizations, literary magazine, music ensembles, Model UN, musical theater, student government, student newspaper, College Democrats, College Republicans, Green Party, Catholic Student Association, Campus Activities Council, Intervarsity Fellowship, Habitat for Humanity.

**Athletics. NCAA. Intercollegiate:** Basketball W, cross-country W, soccer W, swimming W, tennis W, volleyball W. **Team name:** Spirits.

**Student services.** Adult student services, chaplain/spiritual director, career counseling, financial aid counseling, health services, personal counseling, placement for graduates, women's services.

**Contact.** E-mail: admissions@salem.edu
Phone: (336) 721-2621 Toll-free number: (800) 327-2536
Fax: (336) 917-5572
Katherine Watts, Dean of Admissions and Financial Aid, Salem College, 601 South Church Street, Winston-Salem, NC 27108

---

## Shaw University
**Raleigh, North Carolina**
**www.shawuniversity.edu**
**CB member**
**CB code: 5612**

▶ Private 4-year university and liberal arts college affiliated with Baptist faith
▶ Residential campus in large city
▶ 2,331 degree-seeking undergraduates: 8% part-time, 63% women, 86% African American, 1% international
▶ 196 degree-seeking graduate students
▶ 44% of applicants admitted
▶ SAT or ACT (ACT writing optional), application essay required
▶ 34% graduate within 6 years

**General.** Founded in 1865. Regionally accredited. **Degrees:** 394 bachelor's, 8 associate awarded; master's offered. **ROTC:** Army, Air Force. **Location:** 139 miles from Charlotte. **Calendar:** Semester, limited summer session. **Full-time faculty:** 105 total; 72% have terminal degrees, 85% minority, 35% women. **Part-time faculty:** 131 total; 39% have terminal degrees, 88% minority, 42% women. **Class size:** 69% < 20, 26% 20-39, 3% 40-49, 2% 50-99.

**Freshman class profile.** 6,067 applied, 2,668 admitted, 612 enrolled.

| Mid 50% test scores | | | |
|---|---|---|---|
| SAT critical reading: | 330-430 | GPA 3.0-3.49: | 11% |
| SAT math: | 320-420 | GPA 2.0-2.99: | 74% |
| SAT writing: | 320-420 | Rank in top quarter: | 12% |
| ACT composite: | 11-16 | Rank in top tenth: | 3% |
| GPA 3.75 or higher: | 2% | Out-of-state: | 52% |
| GPA 3.50-3.74: | 2% | Live on campus: | 72% |
| | | International: | 1% |

**Basis for selection.** 2.0 high school GPA desired. Interview, portfolio recommended for some. **Homeschooled:** Transcript of courses and grades, state high school equivalency certificate required.

**High school preparation.** 18 units required. Required units include English 3, mathematics 2, social studies 2, science 2 and academic electives 9. 9 electives in English, foreign language, mathematics, science.

**2009-2010 Annual costs.** Tuition/fees: $11,696. Room/board: $7,200. Books/supplies: $1,100. Personal expenses: $2,040.

**2008-2009 Financial aid. Non-need-based:** Scholarships awarded for academics, alumni affiliation, art, athletics, music/drama, religious affiliation.

**Application procedures. Admission:** Closing date 7/30. $25 fee, may be waived for applicants with need. Admission notification on a rolling basis beginning on or about 8/1. **Financial aid:** Priority date 3/1; no closing date. FAFSA required. Applicants notified on a rolling basis starting 3/15; must reply within 2 week(s) of notification.

**Academics. Special study options:** Accelerated study, cross-registration, distance learning, double major, dual enrollment of high school students, honors, independent study, internships, liberal arts/career combination, student-designed major, study abroad, teacher certification program. **Credit/placement by examination:** CLEP, SAT, ACT, institutional tests. 30 credit hours maximum toward associate degree, 60 toward bachelor's. **Support services:** Learning center, reduced course load, study skills assistance, tutoring, writing center.

**Majors. Biology:** General. **Business:** Business admin, international. **Communications:** Media studies. **Computer sciences:** General, computer science. **Conservation:** General. **Education:** Elementary, English, mathematics. **Foreign languages:** Spanish. **Health:** Athletic training, audiology/speech pathology, recreational therapy. **Liberal arts:** Arts/sciences. **Math:** General. **Parks/recreation:** General, exercise sciences. **Philosophy/religion:** Religion. **Physical sciences:** Chemistry, physics. **Protective services:** Criminal justice. **Psychology:** General. **Public administration:** General, social work. **Social sciences:** International relations, political science, sociology. **Visual/performing arts:** Dramatic.

**Most popular majors.** Business/marketing 27%, communications/journalism 7%, philosophy/religious studies 7%, psychology 6%, public administration/social services 13%, security/protective services 12%, social sciences 8%.

**Computing on campus.** 150 workstations in dormitories, library, computer center, student center. Dormitories wired for high-speed internet access and linked to campus network. Commuter students can connect to campus network. Online course registration, online library, helpline, repair service, student web hosting, wireless network available.

**Student life. Freshman orientation:** Available. **Housing:** Single-sex dorms, wellness housing available. $100 deposit. **Activities:** Bands, campus ministries, choral groups, dance, drama, international student organizations, music ensembles, musical theater, radio station, student government, student newspaper, NAACP, business, sociology, criminal justice, accounting clubs, Christian Fellowship, northern exposure, Order of the Eastern Star.

**Athletics.** NCAA. **Intercollegiate:** Baseball M, basketball, bowling W, cross-country, football (tackle) M, softball W, tennis, track and field, volleyball W. **Intramural:** Basketball, tennis, volleyball. **Team name:** Bears.

**Student services.** Adult student services, alcohol/substance abuse counseling, chaplain/spiritual director, career counseling, student employment services, financial aid counseling, health services, personal counseling, placement for graduates, veterans' counselor. **Physically disabled:** Services for visually, speech, hearing impaired.

**Contact.** E-mail: admissions@shawu.edu
Phone: (919) 546-8275 Toll-free number: (800) 214-6683
Fax: (919) 546-8271
Cassandra Clifton, Interim Director of Admissions and International Counselor, Shaw University, 118 East South Street, Raleigh, NC 27601

---

## Southeastern Baptist Theological Seminary
**Wake Forest, North Carolina**
**www.sebts.edu**
**CB code: 7050**

▶ Private 4-year Bible and seminary college affiliated with Southern Baptist Convention
▶ Small town
▶ 393 degree-seeking undergraduates

**General.** Founded in 1950. Regionally accredited. **Degrees:** 47 bachelor's, 3 associate awarded; master's, doctoral, professional offered. **Location:** 20 miles from Raleigh, 30 miles from Durham. **Calendar:** Semester, limited summer session. **Full-time faculty:** 48 total. **Part-time faculty:** 35 total.

**Freshman class profile.**

| Out-of-state: | 40% | Live on campus: | 80% |
|---|---|---|---|

**Basis for selection.** Open admission. Applicants must be 30 years of age or older. Recommendations most important. Perdue high school English test required.

**2009-2010 Annual costs.** Tuition/fees: $6,860. Non-Southern Baptist students per credit hour charge is $437. Books/supplies: $400.

**Financial aid. Additional information:** Special endowment awards $300 to all freshmen.

**Application procedures. Admission:** No deadline.

**Academics. Special study options:** Internships. **Credit/placement by examination:** CLEP. **Support services:** Remedial instruction.

**Majors. Theology:** Bible.

**Computing on campus.** 4 workstations in library.

**Student life. Activities:** Concert band, choral groups, music ensembles, student government, student newspaper.

**Athletics. Intramural:** Basketball, golf, racquetball, softball, tennis, volleyball.

**Student services.** Adult student services, career counseling, student employment services, health services, on-campus daycare, personal counseling, placement for graduates, veterans' counselor.

**Contact.** E-mail: admissions@sebts.edu
Phone: (919) 761-2280 Toll-free number: (800) 284-6317
Fax: (919) 556-0998
Allan Moseley, Dean of Students, Southeastern Baptist Theological Seminary, PO Box 1889, Wake Forest, NC 27588

# University of North Carolina at Asheville
**Asheville, North Carolina**     **CB member**
**www.unca.edu**     **CB code: 5013**

- Public 4-year university and liberal arts college
- Residential campus in small city
- 3,320 degree-seeking undergraduates: 9% part-time, 57% women, 2% African American, 1% Asian American, 3% Hispanic American, 1% international
- 36 degree-seeking graduate students
- 77% of applicants admitted
- SAT or ACT with writing, application essay required
- 59% graduate within 6 years; 20% enter graduate study

**General.** Founded in 1927. Regionally accredited. **Degrees:** 606 bachelor's awarded; master's offered. **Location:** 130 miles from Charlotte, 200 miles from Atlanta. **Calendar:** Semester, limited summer session. **Full-time faculty:** 208 total; 85% have terminal degrees, 11% minority, 44% women. **Part-time faculty:** 92 total; 47% have terminal degrees, 6% minority, 53% women. **Class size:** 54% < 20, 43% 20-39, 1% 40-49, 2% 50-99. **Special facilities:** Botanical gardens, Jewish studies center, arboretum, distance learning facility, music recording studio, National Environmental Modeling and Analysis Center (NEMAC), astronomical research institute, National Climatic Data Center.

**Freshman class profile.** 2,510 applied, 1,921 admitted, 641 enrolled.

| Mid 50% test scores | | | |
|---|---|---|---|
| SAT critical reading: | 540-640 | Rank in top tenth: | 22% |
| SAT math: | 530-630 | End year in good standing: | 92% |
| SAT writing: | 510-630 | Return as sophomores: | 82% |
| ACT composite: | 23-27 | Out-of-state: | 17% |
| GPA 3.75 or higher: | 65% | Live on campus: | 91% |
| GPA 3.50-3.74: | 19% | International: | 1% |
| GPA 3.0-3.49: | 16% | Fraternities: | 2% |
| Rank in top quarter: | 60% | Sororities: | 1% |

**Basis for selection.** GED not accepted. High school curriculum, GPA, and class rank (top third), most important. Test scores important. Counselor recommendation and essay question required. Interview, extracurricular activities that support academic achievement considered. Students expected to have completed advanced coursework. Personal statements helpful. Interviews recommended. **Homeschooled:** Must provide a transcript documenting all courses taken, particularly UNC system minimum admissions requirements, units of credit received. Transcript must be signed by homeschool administrator, and notorized. For North Carolina residents, a copy of the school's registration with the North Carolina Department of Non-Public Instruction is required. **Learning Disabled:** Untimed SAT accepted.

**High school preparation.** College-preparatory program required. 15 units required. Required and recommended units include English 4, mathematics 4, social studies 1, history 1, science 3 (laboratory 1), foreign language 2 and academic electives 4. Science units should include biology and physical science such as chemistry or physics. One unit US history, 1 unit other social studies required. Math must include algebra I, II and geometry and 1 math course with algebra II as pre-requisite.

**2009-2010 Annual costs.** Tuition/fees: $4,411; $16,128 out-of-state. Room/board: $6,890. Books/supplies: $850. Personal expenses: $1,400.

**2008-2009 Financial aid. Need-based:** 457 full-time freshmen applied for aid; 264 were judged to have need; 262 of these received aid. Average need met was 91%. Average scholarship/grant was $6,339; average loan $4,957. 59% of total undergraduate aid awarded as scholarships/grants, 41% as loans/jobs. **Non-need-based:** Awarded to 420 full-time undergraduates, including 107 freshmen. Scholarships awarded for academics, alumni affiliation, art, athletics, job skills, leadership, minority status, music/drama, state residency.

**Application procedures. Admission:** Priority date 11/15; deadline 2/15 (postmark date). $50 fee, may be waived for applicants with need. Admission notification on a rolling basis beginning on or about 3/15. Must reply by 5/1. **Financial aid:** Priority date 3/1; no closing date. FAFSA required. Applicants notified on a rolling basis starting 3/15.

**Academics. Special study options:** Cross-registration, distance learning, double major, dual enrollment of high school students, exchange student, honors, independent study, internships, liberal arts/career combination, semester at sea, student-designed major, study abroad, teacher certification program, Washington semester. **Credit/placement by examination:** AP, CLEP, IB, institutional tests. 30 credit hours maximum toward bachelor's degree.

AP and CLEP exam grades required for credit are subject to change. **Support services:** Learning center, reduced course load, remedial instruction, study skills assistance, tutoring, writing center.

**Majors. Area/ethnic studies:** Women's. **Biology:** General. **Business:** Accounting, business admin, operations. **Communications:** Media studies. **Computer sciences:** Computer science, web page design. **Conservation:** Environmental studies. **Engineering:** General. **Foreign languages:** Classics, French, German, Spanish. **Health:** Public health ed. **History:** General. **Liberal arts:** Arts/sciences. **Math:** General. **Philosophy/religion:** Philosophy, religion. **Physical sciences:** Atmospheric science, chemistry, physics. **Psychology:** General. **Social sciences:** Economics, political science, sociology. **Visual/performing arts:** Art, dramatic, studio arts.

**Most popular majors.** Business/marketing 7%, communications/journalism 6%, English 7%, foreign language 6%, natural resources/environmental science 6%, psychology 13%, social sciences 13%, visual/performing arts 10%.

**Computing on campus.** 216 workstations in dormitories, library, computer center, student center. Dormitories wired for high-speed internet access and linked to campus network. Commuter students can connect to campus network. Online course registration, online library, helpline, repair service, student web hosting, wireless network available.

**Student life. Freshman orientation:** Mandatory, $55 fee. Preregistration for classes offered. 2-day program for incoming freshmen held in June; 1-day program for transfer students held in June and August. Additional 3-day orientation conducted immediately prior to the start of classes. **Housing:** Guaranteed on-campus for freshmen. Coed dorms, single-sex dorms, special housing for disabled, wellness housing available. $150 deposit, deadline 5/1. 24-hour quiet, substance free floors available. **Activities:** Bands, campus ministries, choral groups, dance, drama, international student organizations, literary magazine, music ensembles, musical theater, radio station, student government, student newspaper, Baptist student union, international student association, InterVarsity Christian Fellowship, African American student association, Active Students for a Healthy Environment, University Ambassadors, Jewish student association, Asian Students in Asheville.

**Athletics.** NCAA. **Intercollegiate:** Baseball M, basketball, cheerleading, cross-country, soccer, tennis, track and field, volleyball W. **Intramural:** Basketball, football (non-tackle), racquetball, soccer, softball, table tennis, tennis, volleyball, water polo. **Team name:** Bulldogs.

**Student services.** Adult student services, alcohol/substance abuse counseling, chaplain/spiritual director, career counseling, student employment services, financial aid counseling, health services, minority student services, personal counseling, placement for graduates, veterans' counselor, women's services. **Physically disabled:** Services for visually, hearing impaired.

**Contact.** E-mail: admissions@unca.edu
Phone: (828) 251-6481 Toll-free number: (800) 531-9842
Fax: (828) 251-6482
Patrice Mitchell, Dean of Admissions and Financial Aid, University of North Carolina at Asheville, CPO#1320, UNCA, Asheville, NC 28804-8502

# University of North Carolina at Chapel Hill
**Chapel Hill, North Carolina**     **CB member**
**www.unc.edu**     **CB code: 5816**

- Public 4-year university
- Residential campus in large town
- 17,565 degree-seeking undergraduates: 2% part-time, 59% women, 11% African American, 7% Asian American, 5% Hispanic American, 1% Native American, 2% international
- 9,596 degree-seeking graduate students
- 32% of applicants admitted
- SAT or ACT with writing, application essay required
- 87% graduate within 6 years; 28% enter graduate study

**General.** Founded in 1789. Regionally accredited. **Degrees:** 4,319 bachelor's awarded; master's, doctoral, professional offered. **ROTC:** Army, Naval, Air Force. **Location:** 8 miles from Durham, 26 miles from Raleigh. **Calendar:** Semester, extensive summer session. **Full-time faculty:** 1,629 total; 84% have terminal degrees, 22% minority, 41% women. **Part-time faculty:** 136 total; 60% have terminal degrees, 7% minority, 48% women. **Class size:** 39% < 20, 43% 20-39, 7% 40-49, 6% 50-99, 5% >100. **Special facilities:** Planetarium, observatory, arboretum, botanical garden, art museum.

**Freshman class profile.** 23,224 applied, 7,345 admitted, 3,960 enrolled.

| Mid 50% test scores | | | |
|---|---|---|---|
| SAT critical reading: | 590-700 | Rank in top quarter: | 96% |
| SAT math: | 620-710 | Rank in top tenth: | 80% |
| SAT writing: | 580-680 | End year in good standing: | 99% |
| ACT composite: | 26-31 | Return as sophomores: | 96% |
| GPA 3.75 or higher: | 95% | Out-of-state: | 17% |
| GPA 3.50-3.74: | 2% | Live on campus: | 85% |
| GPA 3.0-3.49: | 2% | International: | 2% |
| GPA 2.0-2.99: | 1% | Fraternities: | 12% |
| | | Sororities: | 16% |

**Basis for selection.** GED not accepted. High school record, including course selection and performance, very important. Test scores, essays, activities, and recommendations also receive strong consideration. Separate consideration given to out-of-state children of alumni. Audition required for drama and music programs; portfolio recommended for art program. **Home-schooled:** SAT Subject Tests recommended. Students should follow curriculum equivalent to that of high school students taking Advanced Placement and honors courses. **Learning Disabled:** Students may voluntarily supply documentation regarding disability and impact on educational experiences with application.

**High school preparation.** College-preparatory program required. 16 units required. Required units include English 4, mathematics 4, social studies 2, science 3 (laboratory 1), foreign language 2 and academic electives 1. One social studies must be U.S. history. Both foreign language units must be for the same language.

**2009-2010 Annual costs.** Tuition/fees: $5,625; $23,513 out-of-state. Fees may be higher for dental programs. Room/board: $8,671. Books/supplies: $1,000. Personal expenses: $1,250.

**2008-2009 Financial aid. Need-based:** 2,878 full-time freshmen applied for aid; 1,218 were judged to have need; 1,208 of these received aid. Average need met was 100%. Average scholarship/grant was $10,996; average loan $3,065. 73% of total undergraduate aid awarded as scholarships/grants, 27% as loans/jobs. **Non-need-based:** Awarded to 4,452 full-time undergraduates, including 1,512 freshmen. Scholarships awarded for academics, alumni affiliation, art, athletics, leadership, music/drama, religious affiliation, state residency. **Additional information:** Carolina meets 100% of all need documented for both resident and non-resident undergraduates who quality for need based aid, with a favorable mix of approximately 2/3 grants and scholarships and 1/3 loans and work study.

**Application procedures. Admission:** Closing date 1/15 (postmark date). $70 fee, may be waived for applicants with need. Notification on or around 1/30 for early notification; on or around 3/20 for regular notification. Must reply by 5/1. **Financial aid:** Priority date 3/1; no closing date. FAFSA, CSS PROFILE required. Applicants notified on a rolling basis starting 3/15; must reply by 5/1.

**Academics.** Entering freshmen required to own laptop meeting university specifications, as a part of the Carolina Computing Initiative; qualified students will receive special loans or grants. **Special study options:** Combined bachelor's/graduate degree, cross-registration, distance learning, double major, dual enrollment of high school students, honors, independent study, internships, student-designed major, study abroad, teacher certification program, Washington semester. **Credit/placement by examination:** AP, CLEP, IB, SAT, ACT, institutional tests. Credit by examination is non-transferable. **Support services:** Learning center, pre-admission summer program, reduced course load, study skills assistance, tutoring, writing center.

**Majors. Area/ethnic studies:** African-American, American, Asian, European, Latin American, Russian/Slavic, women's. **Biology:** General, biostatistics, pathology. **Business:** Business admin, human resources. **Communications:** General, media studies. **Computer sciences:** Computer science, information systems. **Conservation:** Environmental science, environmental studies. **Education:** Early childhood, elementary, middle. **Family/consumer sciences:** Food/nutrition. **Foreign languages:** Classics, comparative lit, French, German, Italian, linguistics, Portuguese, Romance, Slavic, Spanish. **Health:** Clinical lab science, dental hygiene, environmental health, health care admin, medical radiologic technology/radiation therapy, nursing (RN), pharmaceutical sciences. **History:** General. **Interdisciplinary:** Global studies, peace/conflict. **Liberal arts:** Arts/sciences. **Math:** General, applied. **Parks/recreation:** Facilities management, health/fitness. **Philosophy/religion:** Philosophy, religion. **Physical sciences:** Chemistry, geology, physics. **Psychology:** General. **Public administration:** Policy analysis. **Social sciences:** Anthropology, archaeology, economics, geography, political science, sociology. **Visual/performing arts:** Art history/conservation, dramatic, music performance, studio arts. **Other:** Applied science.

**Most popular majors.** Area/ethnic studies 6%, biology 8%, business/marketing 8%, communications/journalism 12%, health sciences 7%, psychology 9%, social sciences 16%.

**Computing on campus.** PC or laptop required. 800 workstations in dormitories, library, computer center, student center. Dormitories wired for high-speed internet access and linked to campus network. Commuter students can connect to campus network. Online course registration, online library, helpline, repair service, student web hosting, wireless network available.

**Student life. Freshman orientation:** Mandatory, $160 fee. Preregistration for classes offered. **Policies:** Policies exist regarding: illegal drugs, honor code, student organizations, non-discrimination policy, no smoking policy, student possession and consumption of alcoholic beverages in facilities, harassment, facilities use policy, student grievance policy, and FERPA. **Housing:** Coed dorms, single-sex dorms, special housing for disabled, apartments, fraternity/sorority housing, wellness housing available. Special options: Learning communities such as RELIC (Religion as Explorative Learning Integrated in our Community), language houses, The Carolina Experience, Men@Carolina, W.E.L.L. (Women's Experiences: Learning and Leadership), Connected Learning Program, service and leadership, substance free environments, sustainability, UNITAS. **Activities:** Bands, campus ministries, choral groups, dance, drama, film society, international student organizations, literary magazine, music ensembles, Model UN, musical theater, opera, radio station, student government, student newspaper, symphony orchestra, TV station, Alpha Phi Omega co-ed service fraternity, Asian students association, Black Student Movement, Campus Crusade for Christ, Carolina Cancer Focus, Carolina Hispanic Association, College Republicans, Habitat for Humanity, Young Democrats.

**Athletics.** NCAA. **Intercollegiate:** Baseball M, basketball, cross-country, diving, fencing, field hockey W, football (tackle) M, golf, gymnastics W, lacrosse, rowing (crew) W, soccer, softball W, swimming, tennis, track and field, volleyball W, wrestling M. **Intramural:** Badminton, basketball, football (non-tackle), golf, racquetball, soccer, softball, swimming, table tennis, tennis, triathlon, volleyball, water polo. **Team name:** Tarheels.

**Student services.** Alcohol/substance abuse counseling, chaplain/spiritual director, career counseling, student employment services, financial aid counseling, health services, legal services, minority student services, on-campus daycare, personal counseling, placement for graduates, veterans' counselor, women's services. **Physically disabled:** Services for visually, speech, hearing impaired. **Learning disabled:** Comprehensive services available.

**Contact.** E-mail: unchelp@admissions.unc.edu
Phone: (919) 966-3621 Fax: (919) 962-3045
Stephen Farmer, Assistant Provost and Director of Undergraduate Admissions, University of North Carolina at Chapel Hill, Jackson Hall, Chapel Hill, NC 27599-2200

## University of North Carolina at Charlotte
**Charlotte, North Carolina**    CB member
www.uncc.edu    CB code: 5105

- Public 4-year university
- Residential campus in very large city
- 19,263 degree-seeking undergraduates: 14% part-time, 51% women, 16% African American, 5% Asian American, 5% Hispanic American, 3% international
- 3,814 degree-seeking graduate students
- 76% of applicants admitted
- SAT or ACT with writing required
- 54% graduate within 6 years

**General.** Founded in 1946. Regionally accredited. **Degrees:** 3,455 bachelor's awarded; master's, doctoral offered. **ROTC:** Army, Air Force. **Location:** 8 miles from downtown. **Calendar:** Semester, limited summer session. **Full-time faculty:** 981 total; 7% have terminal degrees, 16% minority, 42% women. **Part-time faculty:** 344 total; 2% have terminal degrees, 15% minority, 59% women. **Class size:** 29% < 20, 40% 20-39, 9% 40-49, 14% 50-99, 8% >100. **Special facilities:** Botanical and horticultural complex with controlled environment, 100-acre experimental ecological reserve, tropical rain forest conservatory, 46-acre wildlife refuge, 9,600-seat multipurpose student activity center.

**Freshman class profile.** 10,702 applied, 8,158 admitted, 3,187 enrolled.

| Mid 50% test scores | | | |
|---|---|---|---|
| SAT critical reading: | 470-550 | GPA 2.0-2.99: | 8% |
| SAT math: | 490-590 | Rank in top quarter: | 41% |
| SAT writing: | 460-550 | Rank in top tenth: | 12% |
| ACT composite: | 20-24 | End year in good standing: | 78% |
| GPA 3.75 or higher: | 36% | Return as sophomores: | 78% |
| GPA 3.50-3.74: | 21% | Out-of-state: | 9% |
| GPA 3.0-3.49: | 35% | Live on campus: | 73% |
| | | International: | 3% |

**Basis for selection.** Overall performance in high school academic courses, senior year academic courses in progress, and SAT scores considered. SAT preferred, but ACT also accepted. Audition required for music; interview required for art, architecture, and music programs; portfolio required for art, architecture programs. **Learning Disabled:** Students can submit documentation of their learning disability in the admissions process if they choose to disclose.

**High school preparation.** College-preparatory program required. 16 units required. Required units include English 4, mathematics 4, social studies 2, history 1, science 3 (laboratory 1), foreign language 2 and academic electives 1. English should emphasize grammar, composition & literature; science should include at least 1 unit in a life or biological science and at least 1 unit in a physical science and 1 lab; foreign language units should be in same language. 1 social studies unit must be in U.S. history. Health education and a computer course are also recommended.

**2009-2010 Annual costs.** Tuition/fees: $4,427; $15,039 out-of-state. Room/board: $6,796.

**2008-2009 Financial aid. Need-based:** 2,283 full-time freshmen applied for aid; 1,504 were judged to have need; 1,463 of these received aid. Average need met was 78%. Average scholarship/grant was $6,911; average loan $2,969. 44% of total undergraduate aid awarded as scholarships/grants, 56% as loans/jobs. **Non-need-based:** Awarded to 1,164 full-time undergraduates, including 188 freshmen. Scholarships awarded for academics, athletics, leadership, music/drama.

**Application procedures. Admission:** Closing date 7/1 (postmark date). $50 fee, may be waived for applicants with need. Admission notification 5/1. Admission notification on a rolling basis. Must reply by May 1 or within 2 week(s) if notified thereafter. **Financial aid:** Priority date 4/1; no closing date. FAFSA required. Applicants notified on a rolling basis starting 4/1; must reply within 3 week(s) of notification.

**Academics. Special study options:** Accelerated study, cooperative education, cross-registration, distance learning, double major, dual enrollment of high school students, ESL, honors, independent study, internships, study abroad, teacher certification program, Washington semester, weekend college. Wilderness exploration program. **Credit/placement by examination:** AP, CLEP, IB, institutional tests. 30 credit hours maximum toward bachelor's degree. **Support services:** Learning center, pre-admission summer program, reduced course load, study skills assistance, tutoring, writing center.

**Honors college/program.** Minimum GPA 3.0 or high school rank and SAT scores predictive of 3.0 GPA. Must submit 2-3 page essay describing educational goals and objectives, as well as one letter of recommendation from a person who can address potential for success in Honors Program. Brief interview may be scheduled.

**Majors. Architecture:** Architecture. **Area/ethnic studies:** African-American, Latin American. **Biology:** General. **Business:** Accounting, business admin, finance, international, management information systems, managerial economics, marketing, operations. **Communications:** General, organizational. **Computer sciences:** Computer science. **Education:** Art, chemistry, drama/dance, elementary, English, French, German, history, kindergarten/preschool, mathematics, mentally handicapped, middle, music, Spanish, special. **Engineering:** Civil, computer, electrical, mechanical, systems. **Engineering technology:** Civil, electrical, mechanical. **Family/consumer sciences:** Family studies. **Foreign languages:** French, German, Spanish. **Health:** Athletic training, clinical lab science, nursing (RN), public health ed, respiratory therapy technology. **History:** General. **Interdisciplinary:** Global studies. **Math:** General. **Parks/recreation:** Health/fitness. **Philosophy/religion:** Philosophy, religion. **Physical sciences:** Chemistry, geology, meteorology, physics. **Protective services:** Criminal justice, fire services admin. **Psychology:** General. **Public administration:** Social work. **Social sciences:** Anthropology, economics, geography, political science, sociology. **Visual/performing arts:** Art, art history/conservation, dance, dramatic, music performance, studio arts. **Other:** Engineering technologies, other, Mathematics and statistics, other.

**Most popular majors.** Business/marketing 21%, communications/journalism 6%, education 10%, engineering/engineering technologies 10%, health sciences 7%, psychology 8%, social sciences 6%.

**Computing on campus.** 1,500 workstations in dormitories, library, computer center, student center. Dormitories wired for high-speed internet access and linked to campus network. Commuter students can connect to campus network. Online course registration, online library, helpline, student web hosting, wireless network available.

**Student life. Freshman orientation:** Available, $85 fee. Preregistration for classes offered. 2-day program for freshmen and parents. Parents fee $32. **Policies:** Students must follow code of student responsibility, code of student academic integrity, and university policy statements. **Housing:** Coed dorms, single-sex dorms, special housing for disabled, apartments, fraternity/sorority housing, wellness housing available. $200 deposit. Housing for disabled students limited. Suite housing, honors housing, learning communities, and Greek village housing available. **Activities:** Bands, campus ministries, choral groups, dance, drama, international student organizations, literary magazine, music ensembles, musical theater, opera, radio station, student government, student newspaper, symphony orchestra, TV station, Campus Crusade for Christ, Hillel, College Democrats, College Republicans, feminist union, black student union, Latin American student organization, Muslim student association, Native American student organization, Asian student union.

**Athletics.** NCAA. **Intercollegiate:** Baseball M, basketball, cross-country, golf M, soccer, softball W, tennis, track and field, volleyball W. **Intramural:** Badminton, basketball, bowling, field hockey, football (non-tackle), golf, handball, lacrosse, racquetball, rugby, soccer, softball, swimming, table tennis, tennis, track and field, volleyball, water polo. **Team name:** Fortyniners.

**Student services.** Adult student services, alcohol/substance abuse counseling, chaplain/spiritual director, career counseling, services for economically disadvantaged, student employment services, financial aid counseling, health services, minority student services, personal counseling, placement for graduates, veterans' counselor, women's services. **Physically disabled:** Services for visually, speech, hearing impaired.

**Contact.** E-mail: unccadm@uncc.edu
Phone: (704) 687-2213 Fax: (704) 687-6483
Tina McEntire, Director of Admissions, University of North Carolina at Charlotte, Undergraduate Admissions- Cato Hall, Charlotte, NC 28223-0001

---

## University of North Carolina at Greensboro
**Greensboro, North Carolina**  **CB member**
**www.uncg.edu**  **CB code: 5913**

- Public 4-year university
- Commuter campus in small city
- 14,275 degree-seeking undergraduates: 11% part-time, 67% women, 23% African American, 4% Asian American, 2% Hispanic American, 1% international
- 2,366 degree-seeking graduate students
- 73% of applicants admitted
- SAT or ACT with writing required
- 52% graduate within 6 years

**General.** Founded in 1891. Regionally accredited. **Degrees:** 2,441 bachelor's awarded; master's, doctoral offered. **ROTC:** Army, Air Force. **Location:** 90 miles from Raleigh. **Calendar:** Semester, extensive summer session. **Full-time faculty:** 789 total; 80% have terminal degrees, 34% minority, 50% women. **Part-time faculty:** 466 total; 38% have terminal degrees, 37% minority, 62% women. **Class size:** 39% < 20, 41% 20-39, 6% 40-49, 3% 50-99, 11% >100. **Special facilities:** Observatory, Silva cello music collection, Randall Jarrell collection, women's studies collection.

**Freshman class profile.** 9,104 applied, 6,616 admitted, 2,511 enrolled.

| Mid 50% test scores | | | |
|---|---|---|---|
| SAT critical reading: | 460-560 | GPA 2.0-2.99: | 7% |
| SAT math: | 470-570 | Rank in top quarter: | 43% |
| SAT writing: | 450-540 | Rank in top tenth: | 14% |
| GPA 3.75 or higher: | 39% | Return as sophomores: | 77% |
| GPA 3.50-3.74: | 21% | Out-of-state: | 7% |
| GPA 3.0-3.49: | 33% | Live on campus: | 80% |
| | | International: | 1% |

**Basis for selection.** GED not accepted. Combined test scores and high school GPA based on academic courses most important. High school recommendations and activities considered. SAT preferred, but ACT accepted. Audition required for music program.

**High school preparation.** College-preparatory program recommended. 15 units required. Required units include English 4, mathematics 4, social studies 2, science 3 (laboratory 1) and foreign language 2.

**2009-2010 Annual costs.** Tuition/fees: $4,234; $15,995 out-of-state. Room/board: $6,507. Books/supplies: $1,662. Personal expenses: $2,196.

**2009-2010 Financial aid.** **Need-based:** 2,144 full-time freshmen applied for aid; 1,936 were judged to have need; 1,935 of these received aid. Average need met was 62%. Average scholarship/grant was $7,805; average loan $2,625. 58% of total undergraduate aid awarded as scholarships/grants, 42% as loans/jobs. **Non-need-based:** Awarded to 7,211 full-time undergraduates, including 1,530 freshmen. Scholarships awarded for academics, alumni affiliation, art, athletics, leadership, music/drama, state residency.

**Application procedures.** **Admission:** Priority date 11/1; deadline 3/1 (postmark date). $45 fee, may be waived for applicants with need. Application must be submitted on paper. Admission notification on a rolling basis beginning on or about 3/1. Must reply by May 1 or within 4 week(s) if notified thereafter. **Financial aid:** Priority date 3/1; no closing date. FAFSA required. Applicants notified on a rolling basis starting 3/15; must reply within 3 week(s) of notification.

**Academics.** **Special study options:** Accelerated study, combined bachelor's/graduate degree, cross-registration, distance learning, double major, dual enrollment of high school students, honors, independent study, internships, study abroad, teacher certification program, Washington semester. Evening university. **Credit/placement by examination:** AP, CLEP, IB, institutional tests. Up to 64 semester hours of any combination of transfer, correspondence, examination or other will be accepted. SAT Subject Test scores in some subjects may qualify for credit. **Support services:** Learning center, reduced course load, remedial instruction, study skills assistance, tutoring, writing center.

**Majors.** **Area/ethnic studies:** African-American, women's. **Biology:** General, biochemistry. **Business:** Accounting, business admin, finance, hospitality admin, international, managerial economics. **Communications:** Media studies. **Computer sciences:** Computer science, networking. **Education:** Art, biology, Deaf/hearing impaired, drama/dance, early childhood, elementary, English, French, mathematics, middle, music, physical, social science, social studies, Spanish, special. **Family/consumer sciences:** Child development, clothing/textiles, family studies. **Foreign languages:** Classics, French, German, Spanish. **Health:** Audiology/speech pathology, clinical lab science, nursing (RN), public health ed. **History:** General. **Interdisciplinary:** Nutrition sciences. **Liberal arts:** Arts/sciences. **Math:** General. **Parks/recreation:** General, exercise sciences. **Philosophy/religion:** Philosophy, religion. **Physical sciences:** Chemistry, physics. **Psychology:** General. **Public administration:** Social work. **Social sciences:** Anthropology, economics, geography, political science, sociology. **Visual/performing arts:** Art, dance, dramatic, interior design, music performance, music theory/composition, studio arts.

**Most popular majors.** Business/marketing 16%, education 13%, English 9%, family/consumer sciences 6%, health sciences 9%, parks/recreation 6%, social sciences 8%, visual/performing arts 9%.

**Computing on campus.** 600 workstations in dormitories, library, computer center, student center. Dormitories wired for high-speed internet access and linked to campus network. Commuter students can connect to campus network. Online course registration, online library, helpline, wireless network available.

**Student life.** **Freshman orientation:** Mandatory. Preregistration for classes offered. **Housing:** Coed dorms, single-sex dorms, apartments available. $150 nonrefundable deposit, deadline 5/1. Residential college (academic/residential program), International House available. **Activities:** Bands, choral groups, dance, drama, film society, international student organizations, literary magazine, music ensembles, Model UN, musical theater, opera, radio station, student government, student newspaper, symphony orchestra, neo-black society, environmental awareness foundation, political awareness club, Habitat for Humanity, Rotaract Club, gay, lesbian and bisexual student association.

**Athletics.** NCAA. **Intercollegiate:** Baseball M, basketball, cross-country, golf, soccer, softball W, tennis, volleyball W, wrestling M. **Intramural:** Badminton, basketball, bowling, golf, racquetball, soccer, softball, swimming, table tennis, tennis, track and field, volleyball. **Team name:** Spartans.

**Student services.** Adult student services, chaplain/spiritual director, career counseling, student employment services, financial aid counseling, health services, personal counseling, placement for graduates, veterans' counselor. **Physically disabled:** Services for visually, speech, hearing impaired.

**Contact.** E-mail: admissions@uncg.edu
Phone: (336) 334-5243 Fax: (336) 334-4180
Lise Keller, Director of Admissions, University of North Carolina at Greensboro, 1400 Spring Garden Street, Greensboro, NC 27402-6170

---

## University of North Carolina at Pembroke
**Pembroke, North Carolina**    **CB member**
**www.uncp.edu**    **CB code: 5534**

- Public 4-year university and liberal arts college
- Commuter campus in small town

- 5,631 degree-seeking undergraduates: 17% part-time, 61% women
- 713 degree-seeking graduate students
- 79% of applicants admitted
- SAT or ACT with writing required
- 34% graduate within 6 years; 22% enter graduate study

**General.** Founded in 1887. Regionally accredited. UNC Pembroke was founded in 1887, is part of the University of North Carolina state supported system. It provides a liberal arts education that includes art, business, health sciences, music, teacher preparation, and professional studies. **Degrees:** 739 bachelor's awarded; master's offered. **ROTC:** Army, Air Force. **Location:** 31 miles from Fayetteville, 100 miles from Raleigh. **Calendar:** Semester, limited summer session. **Full-time faculty:** 293 total; 74% have terminal degrees, 25% minority, 47% women. **Part-time faculty:** 107 total; 24% have terminal degrees, 22% minority, 60% women. **Class size:** 39% < 20, 52% 20-39, 8% 40-49. **Special facilities:** Native American resource center, performing arts center.

**Freshman class profile.** 3,031 applied, 2,392 admitted, 1,219 enrolled.

| Mid 50% test scores | | | |
|---|---|---|---|
| SAT critical reading: | 410-500 | Rank in top quarter: | 31% |
| SAT math: | 430-510 | Rank in top tenth: | 9% |
| SAT writing: | 390-480 | End year in good standing: | 73% |
| ACT composite: | 16-19 | Return as sophomores: | 68% |
| GPA 3.75 or higher: | 14% | Out-of-state: | 4% |
| GPA 3.50-3.74: | 10% | International: | 1% |
| GPA 3.0-3.49: | 31% | | |
| GPA 2.0-2.99: | 45% | | |

**Basis for selection.** High school record, class standing, GPA, test scores, and college preparatory courses important. Auditions and interviews may be required for acceptance to obtain entry into certain programs.

**High school preparation.** College-preparatory program required. 15 units required. Required units include English 4, mathematics 4, social studies 1, history 1, science 3 (laboratory 1) and foreign language 2.

**2009-2010 Annual costs.** Tuition/fees: $3,737; $12,944 out-of-state. Room/board: $6,490. Books/supplies: $1,184.

**2009-2010 Financial aid.** **Non-need-based:** Scholarships awarded for academics, alumni affiliation, art, athletics, music/drama, state residency.

**Application procedures.** **Admission:** Priority date 7/15; deadline 7/31. $40 fee, may be waived for applicants with need. Admission notification on a rolling basis beginning on or about 9/15. **Financial aid:** Priority date 3/15; no closing date. FAFSA required. Applicants notified on a rolling basis starting 4/15; must reply within 2 week(s) of notification.

**Academics.** Certification on secondary teaching level in English, biology, mathematics, social studies, and science education. **Special study options:** Accelerated study, cooperative education, cross-registration, distance learning, double major, dual enrollment of high school students, ESL, exchange student, external degree, honors, independent study, internships, study abroad, teacher certification program, Washington semester. **Credit/placement by examination:** AP, CLEP, SAT, ACT, institutional tests. 30 credit hours maximum toward bachelor's degree. **Support services:** Learning center, pre-admission summer program, reduced course load, remedial instruction, tutoring, writing center.

**Honors college/program.** Approximately 35 students are chosen yearly to participate. Selected students have distinguished themselves through academic achievement, leadership, and community involvement. These students do have additional acceptance requirements, which includes average SAT score of 1150 and GPA above 3.5. Academic program offers interdisciplinary educational opportunities that enhance the general curriculum as well as social and cultural opportunities.

**Majors.** **Area/ethnic studies:** American, Native American. **Biology:** General, biotechnology. **Business:** Accounting, business admin. **Communications:** Media studies. **Computer sciences:** Computer science, information technology. **Conservation:** Environmental science. **Education:** Art, biology, elementary, English, kindergarten/preschool, mathematics, middle, music, physical, science, social studies, special. **Foreign languages:** Spanish. **Health:** Athletic training, nursing (RN), public health ed. **History:** General. **Math:** General. **Parks/recreation:** Facilities management, health/fitness. **Physical sciences:** Chemistry, physics. **Protective services:** Criminal justice. **Psychology:** General. **Public administration:** Social work. **Social sciences:** Political science, sociology. **Visual/performing arts:** Dramatic, music performance, studio arts. **Other:** Multi-interdisciplinary studies, Philosophy and religion.

**Most popular majors.** Biology 12%, business/marketing 12%, education 13%, health sciences 8%, parks/recreation 7%, public administration/social services 6%, security/protective services 7%, social sciences 13%.

**Computing on campus.** 875 workstations in dormitories, library, computer center, student center. Dormitories wired for high-speed internet access and linked to campus network. Commuter students can connect to campus network. Online course registration, online library, helpline, wireless network available.

**Student life. Freshman orientation:** Mandatory, $50 fee. Preregistration for classes offered. 3-day orientation session held in Fall, Spring, Summer with campus tours, advising. **Housing:** Coed dorms, single-sex dorms, apartments available. $125 fully refundable deposit, deadline 7/15. Freshmen given preference for on-campus housing. Apartments available. **Activities:** Bands, campus ministries, choral groups, dance, drama, film society, international student organizations, literary magazine, music ensembles, Model UN, musical theater, radio station, student government, student newspaper, TV station, Native American Organization, African American Student Organization, Baptist Student Union, Methodist Campus Ministry, Fellowship of Christian Athletes, Campus Association of Social Workers, American Medical Student Association, criminal justice club.

**Athletics.** NCAA. **Intercollegiate:** Baseball M, basketball, cheerleading, cross-country, football (tackle) M, golf, soccer, softball W, tennis W, track and field, volleyball W, wrestling M. **Intramural:** Basketball, bowling, football (tackle) M, golf M, racquetball, soccer M, softball, volleyball, wrestling M. **Team name:** Braves.

**Student services.** Chaplain/spiritual director, career counseling, student employment services, financial aid counseling, health services, personal counseling, veterans' counselor. **Physically disabled:** Services for visually, hearing impaired. **Learning disabled:** Comprehensive services available.

**Contact.** E-mail: admissons@uncp.edu
Phone: (910) 521-6262 Toll-free number: (800) 949-8627
Fax: (910) 521-6497
Jackie Clark, Vice Chancellor for Enrollment Management, University of North Carolina at Pembroke, Box 1510, Pembroke, NC 28372

---

## University of North Carolina at Wilmington
**Wilmington, North Carolina**  CB member
**www.uncw.edu**  CB code: 5907

- Public 4-year university
- Commuter campus in small city
- 10,761 degree-seeking undergraduates: 7% part-time, 58% women, 4% African American, 2% Asian American, 4% Hispanic American, 1% Native American
- 1,112 degree-seeking graduate students
- 58% of applicants admitted
- SAT or ACT with writing, application essay required
- 70% graduate within 6 years

**General.** Founded in 1947. Regionally accredited. **Degrees:** 2,457 bachelor's awarded; master's, doctoral offered. **Location:** 125 miles from Raleigh. **Calendar:** Semester, extensive summer session. **Full-time faculty:** 587 total; 86% have terminal degrees, 14% minority, 43% women. **Part-time faculty:** 220 total; 30% have terminal degrees, 11% minority, 54% women. **Class size:** 31% <20, 53% 20-39, 9% 40-49, 6% 50-99, 1% >100. **Special facilities:** Wildlife preserve, research vessel for marine biology laboratory.

**Freshman class profile.** 9,283 applied, 5,402 admitted, 1,949 enrolled.

| Mid 50% test scores | | | |
|---|---|---|---|
| SAT critical reading: | 530-620 | GPA 2.0-2.99: | 2% |
| SAT math: | 550-630 | Rank in top quarter: | 62% |
| SAT writing: | 520-610 | Rank in top tenth: | 24% |
| ACT composite: | 22-27 | End year in good standing: | 99% |
| GPA 3.75 or higher: | 66% | Return as sophomores: | 85% |
| GPA 3.50-3.74: | 18% | Out-of-state: | 15% |
| GPA 3.0-3.49: | 14% | Live on campus: | 93% |

**Basis for selection.** High school record; rank in class, if provided; standardized test scores; and rigor of courses completed in high school are very important. SAT or ACT with writing required. Auditions for Music majors required. **Homeschooled:** Statement describing homeschool structure and mission, transcript of courses and grades, letter of recommendation (nonparent) required.

**High school preparation.** College-preparatory program required. Required units include English 4, mathematics 4, social studies 2, history 1, science 3 (laboratory 1) and foreign language 2. Of the 2 social studies units, 1 unit must be U.S. history.

**2009-2010 Annual costs.** Tuition/fees: $4,874; $15,756 out-of-state. Room/board: $7,620. Books/supplies: $934. Personal expenses: $1,053.

**2009-2010 Financial aid. Need-based:** 1,476 full-time freshmen applied for aid; 838 were judged to have need; 831 of these received aid. Average need met was 85%. Average scholarship/grant was $6,208; average loan $2,688. 55% of total undergraduate aid awarded as scholarships/grants, 45% as loans/jobs. **Non-need-based:** Awarded to 2,237 full-time undergraduates, including 439 freshmen. Scholarships awarded for academics, alumni affiliation, art, athletics, leadership, music/drama, state residency.

**Application procedures. Admission:** Priority date 11/1; deadline 2/1 (postmark date). $60 fee, may be waived for applicants with need. Admission notification 4/1. Must reply by May 1 or within 4 week(s) if notified thereafter. **Financial aid:** Priority date 4/1; no closing date. FAFSA, institutional form required. Applicants notified on a rolling basis starting 4/1; must reply within 3 week(s) of notification.

**Academics. Special study options:** Accelerated study, cooperative education, cross-registration, distance learning, double major, dual enrollment of high school students, ESL, exchange student, honors, independent study, internships, study abroad, teacher certification program. 2+2 Pre-Engineering programs. **Credit/placement by examination:** AP, CLEP, IB, SAT, institutional tests. **Support services:** Learning center, reduced course load, remedial instruction, study skills assistance, tutoring, writing center.

**Honors college/program.** 125 students admitted. Average SAT is 1300 (exclusive of Writing) and average high school GPA is 3.9.

**Majors. Biology:** General, marine. **Business:** Accounting, business admin, finance, management information systems, managerial economics, marketing. **Communications:** General. **Computer sciences:** Computer science. **Conservation:** Environmental science, environmental studies. **Education:** Biology, chemistry, elementary, emotionally handicapped, English, French, German, history, kindergarten/preschool, learning disabled, mathematics, mentally handicapped, middle, multiple handicapped, music, physical, Spanish, special. **Foreign languages:** French, German, Spanish. **Health:** Athletic training, nursing (RN), public health ed, recreational therapy. **History:** General. **Math:** General, statistics. **Parks/recreation:** Facilities management, health/fitness. **Philosophy/religion:** Philosophy, religion. **Physical sciences:** Chemistry, geology, physics. **Protective services:** Criminal justice. **Psychology:** General. **Public administration:** Social work. **Social sciences:** Anthropology, economics, geography, political science, sociology. **Visual/performing arts:** Art history/conservation, cinematography, dramatic, music performance, studio arts. **Other:** Health professions and related clinical sciences, Teacher education and professional development.

**Most popular majors.** Biology 7%, business/marketing 24%, communications/journalism 7%, education 11%, health sciences 6%, psychology 8%, social sciences 6%, visual/performing arts 6%.

**Computing on campus.** 1,111 workstations in dormitories, library, computer center, student center. Dormitories wired for high-speed internet access and linked to campus network. Commuter students can connect to campus network. Online course registration, online library, helpline, repair service, student web hosting, wireless network available.

**Student life. Freshman orientation:** Mandatory, $130 fee. Preregistration for classes offered. **Housing:** Coed dorms, single-sex dorms, apartments, wellness housing available. $105 nonrefundable deposit, deadline 5/1. **Activities:** Bands, campus ministries, choral groups, dance, drama, film society, international student organizations, literary magazine, music ensembles, Model UN, radio station, student government, student newspaper, symphony orchestra, TV station, black student union, surf club, Young Life, non-traditional student organization, SCUBA, Hillel, Amnesty International, PRIDE, Asian student association, environmental concerns organization.

**Athletics.** NCAA. **Intercollegiate:** Baseball M, basketball, cheerleading, cross-country, diving, golf, soccer, softball W, swimming, tennis, track and field, volleyball W. **Intramural:** Basketball, football (non-tackle), golf, soccer, softball, tennis, volleyball. **Team name:** Seahawks.

**Student services.** Adult student services, alcohol/substance abuse counseling, chaplain/spiritual director, career counseling, student employment services, financial aid counseling, health services, legal services, minority student services, personal counseling, placement for graduates, veterans' counselor. **Physically disabled:** Services for visually, speech, hearing impaired.

**Contact.** E-mail: admissions@uncw.edu
Phone: (910) 962-3243 Toll-free number: (800) 228-5571
Fax: (910) 962-3038
Janice Rockwell, Director, University of North Carolina at Wilmington, 601 South College Road, Wilmington, NC 28403-5904

## University of North Carolina School of the Arts

**Winston-Salem, North Carolina**                     CB member
www.uncsa.edu                                          CB code: 5512

- Public 4-year visual arts and performing arts college
- Residential campus in small city
- 736 degree-seeking undergraduates: 40% women
- 112 degree-seeking graduate students
- 45% of applicants admitted
- Interview required

**General.** Founded in 1963. Regionally accredited. State Conservatory with high school, undergraduate and graduate facilities. **Degrees:** 144 bachelor's awarded; master's offered. **Location:** 90 miles from Charlotte, 75 miles from Raleigh. **Calendar:** Trimester, limited summer session. **Full-time faculty:** 144 total; 38% have terminal degrees, 1% minority, 33% women. **Part-time faculty:** 39 total; 15% have terminal degrees, 46% women. **Class size:** 84% < 20, 14% 20-39, less than 1% 40-49, 1% 50-99. **Special facilities:** Stage production shop, film village with sound and recording stages.

**Freshman class profile.** 676 applied, 305 admitted, 179 enrolled.

| Mid 50% test scores | | | |
|---|---|---|---|
| | | **SAT writing:** | 510-610 |
| **SAT critical reading:** | 520-630 | **Out-of-state:** | 62% |
| **SAT math:** | 490-590 | **Live on campus:** | 95% |

**Basis for selection.** Talent, achievement, career potential most important. Admission heavily dependent on audition. SAT combined score of 800 (exclusive of Writing) or ACT composite score of 19, school record, recommendations important. SAT or ACT recommended. Interview recommended for all students. Audition required for dance, drama, music programs; portfolio required for design, filmmaking, production programs.

**High school preparation.** College-preparatory program recommended. 20 units required. Required and recommended units include English 4, mathematics 3, social studies 2, history 1, science 3 (laboratory 1), foreign language 2 and academic electives 4.

**2009-2010 Annual costs.** Tuition/fees: $5,278; $17,224 out-of-state. Required fees may vary by program. Room/board: $7,256. Books/supplies: $865. Personal expenses: $1,889.

**2008-2009 Financial aid.** Non-need-based: Scholarships awarded for academics, art, leadership, music/drama, state residency.

**Application procedures. Admission:** Priority date 3/1; no deadline. $60 fee, may be waived for applicants with need. Admission notification on a rolling basis beginning on or about 4/1. Must reply by May 1 or within 3 week(s) if notified thereafter. Application closing date dependent upon audition. Applications must be submitted at least 2 weeks before audition date. Dance, drama and filmmaking interviews begin in January and end in early March. Music and technical theater auditions begin in November and end in early March. Decisions generally are made by April 1, or about 2 weeks after audition if later than April 1. **Financial aid:** Priority date 3/1; no closing date. FAFSA required. Applicants notified on a rolling basis starting 4/1; must reply within 2 week(s) of notification.

**Academics.** Professional training supplemented by strong general studies curriculum, small classes 7:1 student-teacher ratio. **Special study options:** Independent study, internships. **Credit/placement by examination:** AP, CLEP. **Support services:** Remedial instruction, study skills assistance, tutoring, writing center.

**Majors. Liberal arts:** Arts/sciences. **Visual/performing arts:** Cinematography, dance, dramatic, music performance, theater design.

**Computing on campus.** 28 workstations in dormitories, library, student center. Dormitories wired for high-speed internet access and linked to campus network. Online course registration available.

**Student life. Freshman orientation:** Mandatory, $75 fee. Orientation is the first three days in the academic year. All art schools have separate orientations which include academic assessment. **Housing:** Guaranteed on-campus for freshmen. Coed dorms, single-sex dorms, apartments available. $200 deposit, deadline 5/1. **Activities:** Literary magazine, student government, student newspaper, spirituality committee, ADAPT-drug prevention team, C.A.R.E.-AIDS awareness and prevention team, Awareness for Gay and Lesbian Equality, Artists for Christ, Awareness of Black Arts, Minorities on the Move.

**Athletics. Team name:** Fighting Pickles.

**Student services.** Alcohol/substance abuse counseling, career counseling, student employment services, financial aid counseling, health services, personal counseling.

**Contact.** E-mail: admissions@uncsa.edu
Phone: (336) 770-3291 Fax: (336) 770-3370
Sheeler Lawson, Director of Admissions, University of North Carolina School of the Arts, 1533 South Main Street, Winston-Salem, NC 27127-2188

## Wake Forest University

**Winston-Salem, North Carolina**                     CB member
www.wfu.edu                                            CB code: 5885

- Private 4-year university
- Residential campus in small city
- 4,560 degree-seeking undergraduates: 1% part-time, 51% women, 7% African American, 6% Asian American, 4% Hispanic American, 2% international
- 2,462 degree-seeking graduate students
- 38% of applicants admitted
- Application essay required
- 90% graduate within 6 years

**General.** Founded in 1834. Regionally accredited. All freshmen receive a personal computer and a color printer/scanner/copier. **Degrees:** 1,063 bachelor's awarded; master's, doctoral, professional offered. **ROTC:** Army. **Location:** 4 miles from downtown. **Calendar:** Semester, limited summer session. **Full-time faculty:** 476 total; 90% have terminal degrees, 16% minority, 39% women. **Part-time faculty:** 149 total; 45% have terminal degrees, 6% minority, 36% women. **Class size:** 57% < 20, 36% 20-39, 4% 40-49, 3% 50-99, less than 1% >100. **Special facilities:** Museum of anthropology, center for nanotechnology and molecular materials, Reynolda house museum of American art, art gallery, archaeology laboratory, biomechanics laboratory, laser physics laboratory.

**Freshman class profile.** 10,553 applied, 3,959 admitted, 1,200 enrolled.

| Mid 50% test scores | | | |
|---|---|---|---|
| | | **Return as sophomores:** | 95% |
| **SAT critical reading:** | 580-690 | **Out-of-state:** | 74% |
| **SAT math:** | 600-700 | **Live on campus:** | 99% |
| **ACT composite:** | 27-31 | **International:** | 2% |
| **Rank in top quarter:** | 89% | **Fraternities:** | 33% |
| **Rank in top tenth:** | 75% | **Sororities:** | 46% |

**Basis for selection.** High school curriculum and achievement, test scores, school and community activities, essay, personal recommendations, special talents all important. Audition recommended for those competing for a Presidential Scholarship (for students with special talents in music, theater, art, dance, and debate).

**High school preparation.** College-preparatory program required. 16 units required; 20 recommended. Required and recommended units include English 4, mathematics 3-4, social studies 2-4, science 1-4 and foreign language 2-4.

**2010-2011 Annual costs.** Tuition/fees: $39,970. Room/board: $11,010. Books/supplies: $930. Personal expenses: $1,540.

**2009-2010 Financial aid. Need-based:** 432 full-time freshmen applied for aid; 354 were judged to have need; 349 of these received aid. Average need met was 100%. Average scholarship/grant was $28,085; average loan $8,028. 66% of total undergraduate aid awarded as scholarships/grants, 34% as loans/jobs. **Non-need-based:** Awarded to 1,699 full-time undergraduates, including 331 freshmen. Scholarships awarded for academics, alumni affiliation, art, athletics, leadership, music/drama, religious affiliation, ROTC, state residency. **Additional information:** In fall 2008, freshmen with an annual family income of less than $40,000 will have their student loans capped at $4,000 per year during their college years. Other financial aid to the students will come from grant and scholarship increases and work-study opportunities.

**Application procedures. Admission:** Closing date 1/1. $50 fee, may be waived for applicants with need. Admission notification 4/1. Must reply by 5/1. **Financial aid:** Priority date 2/15, closing date 3/1. FAFSA, CSS PROFILE required. Applicants notified on a rolling basis starting 4/1; must reply by 5/1 or within 4 week(s) of notification.

**Academics.** Language courses at all levels in Russian, Greek, Italian, Hebrew; elementary and intermediate courses in Chinese, Japanese and Arabic; elementary courses in Hindi, Portuguese. **Special study options:** Combined bachelor's/graduate degree, cross-registration, double major, dual enrollment of high school students, honors, independent study, internships, study abroad, teacher certification program, Washington semester. Semester in London, Venice, or Vienna and semester at universities in Dijon, Salamanca, Berlin, Moscow, Beijing, and Japan. **Credit/placement by examination:** AP, CLEP, IB, institutional tests. **Support services:** Learning center, reduced course load, study skills assistance, tutoring, writing center.

**Majors. Biology:** General, bacteriology. **Business:** General, accounting, finance, management science. **Communications:** General. **Computer sciences:** Computer science. **Education:** Elementary, social studies. **Foreign languages:** Ancient Greek, Chinese, classics, French, German, Japanese, Latin, Russian, Spanish. **Health:** Clinical lab science. **History:** General. **Math:** General. **Parks/recreation:** Exercise sciences. **Philosophy/religion:** Philosophy, religion. **Physical sciences:** Chemistry, physics. **Psychology:** General. **Social sciences:** Anthropology, econometrics, economics, political science, sociology. **Visual/performing arts:** Art history/conservation, dramatic, music history, music performance, studio arts.

**Most popular majors.** Biology 6%, business/marketing 18%, communications/journalism 7%, foreign language 7%, history 7%, psychology 6%, social sciences 25%.

**Computing on campus.** PC or laptop required. 4,412 workstations in dormitories, library, computer center, student center. Dormitories wired for high-speed internet access and linked to campus network. Commuter students can connect to campus network. Online course registration, online library, helpline, repair service, student web hosting, wireless network available.

**Student life. Freshman orientation:** Mandatory. Preregistration for classes offered. Six days before Fall classes start. **Policies:** First- and second-year students with residential status required to live on campus. **Housing:** Guaranteed on-campus for all undergraduates. Coed dorms, apartments, fraternity/sorority housing, wellness housing available. $500 deposit, deadline 5/1. **Activities:** Bands, campus ministries, choral groups, dance, drama, film society, international student organizations, literary magazine, music ensembles, Model UN, radio station, student government, student newspaper, symphony orchestra, TV station, Black Student Alliance, College Democrats, College Republicans, Alpha Phi Omega, InterVarsity Christian Fellowship, Amnesty International, Habitat for Humanity, volunteer service corps.

**Athletics.** NCAA. **Intercollegiate:** Baseball M, basketball, cheerleading, cross-country, field hockey W, football (tackle) M, golf, soccer, tennis, track and field, volleyball W. **Intramural:** Basketball, bowling, cross-country, diving, equestrian W, football (non-tackle), golf, racquetball, soccer, softball, table tennis, tennis, volleyball, water polo, wrestling M. **Team name:** Demon Deacons.

**Student services.** Alcohol/substance abuse counseling, chaplain/spiritual director, career counseling, student employment services, financial aid counseling, health services, minority student services, personal counseling, placement for graduates. **Physically disabled:** Services for visually, speech, hearing impaired.

**Contact.** E-mail: admissions@wfu.edu
Phone: (336) 758-5201 Fax: (336) 758-4324
Martha Allman, Director of Admissions, Wake Forest University, PO Box 7305, Winston-Salem, NC 27109-7305

## Warren Wilson College

**Asheville, North Carolina**  **CB member**
**www.warren-wilson.edu**  **CB code: 5886**

- Private 4-year liberal arts college affiliated with Presbyterian Church (USA)
- Residential campus in small city
- 941 degree-seeking undergraduates
- SAT or ACT (ACT writing optional), application essay required

**General.** Founded in 1894. Regionally accredited. **Degrees:** 153 bachelor's awarded; master's offered. **Location:** One mile from Asheville. **Calendar:** 4 consecutive 8-week terms. **Full-time faculty:** 62 total; 94% have terminal degrees, 11% minority, 48% women. **Part-time faculty:** 14 total; 71% have terminal degrees, 14% minority, 50% women. **Class size:** 81% < 20, 19% 20-39, less than 1% 40-49. **Special facilities:** 300-acre college farm, archaeological site, climbing wall, adventure challenge course, hiking trails.

**Freshman class profile.**

| Mid 50% test scores | | | |
|---|---|---|---|
| SAT critical reading: | 540-670 | Rank in top quarter: | 42% |
| SAT math: | 500-610 | Rank in top tenth: | 21% |
| SAT writing: | 530-610 | Out-of-state: | 80% |
| ACT composite: | 22-27 | Live on campus: | 98% |

**Basis for selection.** In order of importance: high school achievement, class rank, personal statement, recommendations, test scores, school and community activities. All records of examinations taken overseas plus TOEFL required of foreign applicants. Interview, portfolio recommended. **Home-schooled:** Submit transcript listing course titles and content, partial portfolio of sample work completed (graded papers), document that serves as diploma, copy of state rules under which school was formed or is recognized.

**High school preparation.** Required and recommended units include English 4, mathematics 3, history 3, science 2 (laboratory 2) and foreign language 2. Math requirement includes algebra I, II and geometry. Sciences must include 2 laboratories.

**2009-2010 Annual costs.** Tuition/fees: $24,196. All resident students required to work 15 hours per week in college's work program. $3,480 earnings credited toward tuition costs. Room/board: $7,770. Books/supplies: $900. Personal expenses: $1,509.

**2009-2010 Financial aid. Non-need-based:** Scholarships awarded for academics, art, job skills, leadership, religious affiliation, state residency.

**Application procedures. Admission:** Priority date 1/15; deadline 3/15 (receipt date). No application fee. Admission notification on a rolling basis beginning on or about 2/1. Must reply by 5/1. **Financial aid:** Priority date 4/1; no closing date. FAFSA, institutional form required. Applicants notified on a rolling basis starting 3/1; must reply within 3 week(s) of notification.

**Academics. Special study options:** Cross-registration, double major, dual enrollment of high school students, ESL, exchange student, honors, independent study, internships, liberal arts/career combination, student-designed major, study abroad, teacher certification program, Washington semester. **Credit/placement by examination:** AP, CLEP, institutional tests. **Support services:** Reduced course load, study skills assistance, tutoring, writing center.

**Majors. Biology:** General. **Business:** Business admin. **Conservation:** General. **Education:** General, early childhood, elementary, middle, secondary. **Foreign languages:** General. **Health:** Premedicine, preveterinary. **History:** General. **Liberal arts:** Arts/sciences. **Math:** General. **Parks/recreation:** General. **Philosophy/religion:** Philosophy, religion. **Physical sciences:** Chemistry. **Psychology:** General. **Public administration:** Social work. **Social sciences:** Anthropology, economics, political science, sociology. **Visual/performing arts:** Art.

**Most popular majors.** Biology 7%, education 8%, history 8%, interdisciplinary studies 14%, natural resources/environmental science 16%, psychology 8%, social sciences 14%.

**Computing on campus.** 91 workstations in library, computer center, student center. Dormitories wired for high-speed internet access and linked to campus network. Commuter students can connect to campus network. Online course registration, online library, helpline, wireless network available.

**Student life. Freshman orientation:** Mandatory, $200 fee. 7-day orientation (late August) includes full day community service, dinner/discussion with faculty. **Policies:** Triad program requires students to work 15 hours/week at an on-campus job and do 100 hours community service by graduation, in addition to academics. **Housing:** Guaranteed on-campus for all undergraduates. Coed dorms, single-sex dorms, apartments, cooperative housing, wellness housing available. **Activities:** Jazz band, choral groups, dance, drama, international student organizations, literary magazine, music ensembles, musical theater, student government, student newspaper, Amnesty International, Emmaus, Interfaith, Jewish student group, Buddhist experience, earth first, sustainable living.

**Athletics.** USCAA. **Intercollegiate:** Basketball, cross-country, soccer, swimming. **Intramural:** Basketball, football (non-tackle), soccer, table tennis, tennis, triathlon, volleyball. **Team name:** Owls.

**Student services.** Alcohol/substance abuse counseling, chaplain/spiritual director, career counseling, student employment services, financial aid counseling, health services, minority student services, personal counseling, placement for graduates.

**Contact.** E-mail: admit@warren-wilson.edu
Phone: (828) 771-2073 Toll-free number: (800) 934-3536
Fax: (828) 298-1440
Richard Blomgren, Dean of Admission, Warren Wilson College, Office of Admission, Asheville, NC 28815-9000

## Western Carolina University
**Cullowhee, North Carolina**          **CB member**
**www.wcu.edu**                         **CB code: 5897**

- Public 4-year university
- Residential campus in small town
- 7,205 degree-seeking undergraduates: 14% part-time, 53% women, 6% African American, 1% Asian American, 2% Hispanic American, 1% Native American, 3% international
- 1,748 degree-seeking graduate students
- 44% of applicants admitted
- SAT or ACT with writing required
- 50% graduate within 6 years

**General.** Founded in 1889. Regionally accredited. **Degrees:** 1,547 bachelor's awarded; master's, doctoral offered. **Location:** 53 miles from Asheville, 157 miles from Atlanta, GA. **Calendar:** Semester, extensive summer session. **Full-time faculty:** 474 total; 77% have terminal degrees, 5% minority, 46% women. **Part-time faculty:** 166 total; 28% have terminal degrees, 2% minority, 54% women. **Class size:** 33% < 20, 57% 20-39, 7% 40-49, 3% 50-99, less than 1% >100. **Special facilities:** Center for applied technology, fine and performing arts center, collection of historical Native American artifacts and documents, center for the advancement of teaching, public policy institute, mountain heritage center.

**Freshman class profile.** 12,325 applied, 5,441 admitted, 1,555 enrolled.

| Mid 50% test scores | | | |
|---|---|---|---|
| SAT critical reading: | 460-560 | GPA 2.0-2.99: | 19% |
| SAT math: | 480-560 | Rank in top quarter: | 43% |
| SAT writing: | 440-540 | Rank in top tenth: | 15% |
| ACT composite: | 18-23 | Return as sophomores: | 76% |
| GPA 3.75 or higher: | 31% | Out-of-state: | 8% |
| GPA 3.50-3.74: | 15% | Live on campus: | 98% |
| GPA 3.0-3.49: | 35% | International: | 1% |

**Basis for selection.** The most important admission factors are secondary school record, class rank, GPA, standardized test scores, talent/ability, and applicant's interest. SAT recommended. All applicants, except those exempted by current campus policies, must submit standardized test scores. SAT preferred, ACT also accepted. Essays not required but will be considered if submitted. Auditions and/or portfolios are required for some art/music/theater programs. **Homeschooled:** Must submit official transcript of all work completed and meet standards equivalent to those used for applicants from approved secondary schools.

**High school preparation.** College-preparatory program required. 20 units required; 24 recommended. Required and recommended units include English 4, mathematics 4, social studies 2, history 1, science 3 (laboratory 3), foreign language 2 and academic electives 4-8.

**2009-2010 Annual costs.** Tuition/fees: $4,330; $13,927 out-of-state. Room/board: $5,912. Books/supplies: $606. Personal expenses: $1,396.

**2009-2010 Financial aid. Need-based:** 1,341 full-time freshmen applied for aid; 926 were judged to have need; 921 of these received aid. Average need met was 81%. Average scholarship/grant was $7,351; average loan $3,963. 60% of total undergraduate aid awarded as scholarships/grants, 40% as loans/jobs. **Non-need-based:** Awarded to 932 full-time undergraduates, including 230 freshmen. Scholarships awarded for academics, art, athletics, leadership, music/drama, state residency.

**Application procedures. Admission:** Priority date 2/1; deadline 3/1 (postmark date). $45 fee, may be waived for applicants with need. Admission notification on a rolling basis beginning on or about 1/15. Must reply by 5/1. Housing deposit due upon receipt of student's acceptance. **Financial aid:** Priority date 3/15; no closing date. FAFSA, institutional form required. Applicants notified on a rolling basis starting 4/1.

**Academics. Special study options:** Accelerated study, combined bachelor's/graduate degree, cooperative education, distance learning, double major, dual enrollment of high school students, exchange student, honors, independent study, internships, student-designed major, study abroad, teacher certification program. Service learning. **Credit/placement by examination:** AP, CLEP, IB, institutional tests. Student may apply to be examined in any course identified by department head as available for credit by exam. Credit by

exam attempts must be completed prior to semester of graduation. Catalog does not specify maximum number of hours. **Support services:** Learning center, pre-admission summer program, reduced course load, study skills assistance, tutoring, writing center.

**Honors college/program.** For first-year students to be considered, must meet at least one of the following: 1875 SAT or 30 ACT, 4.0 weighted cumulative high school GPA, rank in the top 10% of class. Other requirements apply to transfer students and students currently enrolled.

**Majors. Biology:** General. **Business:** Accounting, business admin, entrepreneurial studies, finance, hospitality admin, international, management information systems, marketing. **Communications:** General. **Computer sciences:** Computer science. **Conservation:** Environmental science, management/policy. **Education:** Art, elementary, English, German, kindergarten/preschool, mathematics, middle, music, physical, science, social studies, Spanish, special. **Engineering:** Electrical. **Engineering technology:** General, construction, electrical, industrial, manufacturing. **Foreign languages:** French, German, Spanish. **Health:** Athletic training, clinical lab science, communication disorders, dietetics, EMT paramedic, environmental health, health care admin, medical records admin, nursing (RN), recreational therapy. **History:** General. **Liberal arts:** Arts/sciences. **Math:** General. **Parks/recreation:** Facilities management, sports admin. **Philosophy/religion:** Philosophy. **Physical sciences:** Chemistry, geology. **Protective services:** Criminal justice, forensics. **Psychology:** General. **Public administration:** General, social work. **Social sciences:** General, anthropology, geography, political science, sociology. **Visual/performing arts:** Art, dramatic, interior design, music performance, studio arts. **Other:** French, secondary education, Motion picture and television production.

**Most popular majors.** Business/marketing 17%, education 16%, engineering/engineering technologies 9%, health sciences 13%, security/protective services 7%.

**Computing on campus.** PC or laptop required. 107 workstations in library, computer center, student center. Dormitories wired for high-speed internet access and linked to campus network. Commuter students can connect to campus network. Online course registration, online library, helpline, repair service, student web hosting, wireless network available.

**Student life. Freshman orientation:** Mandatory, $115 fee. Preregistration for classes offered. 2-day orientation sessions are held in June and July. Sessions are for both students and parents. **Housing:** Guaranteed on-campus for freshmen. Coed dorms, single-sex dorms, special housing for disabled, apartments, fraternity/sorority housing, wellness housing available. $150 nonrefundable deposit, deadline 5/1. **Activities:** Bands, campus ministries, choral groups, dance, drama, film society, international student organizations, literary magazine, music ensembles, Model UN, musical theater, radio station, student government, student newspaper, TV station, finance club, Fellowship of Christian Athletes, black theater ansemble, Japanese animation society, Organization of Ebony Students, College Republicans, College Democrats, La Voz Latina, Pagan Student Association.

**Athletics.** NCAA. **Intercollegiate:** Baseball M, basketball, cheerleading, cross-country, football (tackle) M, golf, soccer W, softball W, tennis W, track and field, volleyball W. **Intramural:** Badminton, basketball, bowling, cross-country, football (non-tackle), football (tackle), racquetball, soccer, softball, swimming, table tennis, tennis, volleyball, water polo, weight lifting, wrestling. **Team name:** Catamounts.

**Student services.** Alcohol/substance abuse counseling, chaplain/spiritual director, career counseling, services for economically disadvantaged, student employment services, financial aid counseling, health services, minority student services, on-campus daycare, personal counseling, placement for graduates, women's services. **Physically disabled:** Services for visually, speech, hearing impaired.

**Contact.** E-mail: admiss@wcu.edu
Phone: (828) 227-7317 Toll-free number: (877) 928-4968
Fax: (828) 227-7319
Fred Hinson, Senior Associate Vice Chancellor for Academic Affairs, Western Carolina University, 102 Camp Building, Cullowhee, NC 28723

## Wingate University
**Wingate, North Carolina**          **CB member**
**www.wingate.edu**                   **CB code: 5908**

- Private 4-year university affiliated with Baptist faith
- Residential campus in small town
- 1,409 degree-seeking undergraduates: 3% part-time, 54% women, 10% African American, 2% Asian American, 3% Hispanic American, 1% Native American, 4% international
- 660 degree-seeking graduate students

◆ 52% of applicants admitted
◆ 54% graduate within 6 years

**General.** Founded in 1896. Regionally accredited. **Degrees:** 270 bachelor's awarded; master's, professional offered. **ROTC:** Army, Air Force. **Location:** 25 miles from Charlotte. **Calendar:** Semester, limited summer session. **Full-time faculty:** 119 total; 93% have terminal degrees, 3% minority, 48% women. **Part-time faculty:** 73 total; 15% have terminal degrees, 6% minority, 42% women. **Class size:** 59% < 20, 40% 20-39, 1% 40-49. **Special facilities:** Outdoor recreation laboratory, 11-acre lake, performing arts center.

**Freshman class profile.** 4,840 applied, 2,519 admitted, 375 enrolled.

| Mid 50% test scores | | Rank in top tenth: | 23% |
|---|---|---|---|
| SAT critical reading: | 440-550 | End year in good standing: | 94% |
| SAT math: | 460-570 | Return as sophomores: | 68% |
| ACT composite: | 19-25 | Out-of-state: | 20% |
| GPA 3.75 or higher: | 45% | Live on campus: | 91% |
| GPA 3.50-3.74: | 15% | International: | 3% |
| GPA 3.0-3.49: | 24% | Fraternities: | 10% |
| GPA 2.0-2.99: | 16% | Sororities: | 15% |
| Rank in top quarter: | 54% | | |

**Basis for selection.** Decisions based on secondary school record (GPA, class rank) and the rigor of secondary school record. Test scores are considered. SAT/ACT not required, but strongly recommended. SAT or ACT recommended. Interview recommended for all students; portfolio recommended for art majors; audition required for music majors.

**High school preparation.** College-preparatory program recommended. 13 units recommended. Recommended units include English 4, mathematics 3, social studies 2, science 2 (laboratory 1) and foreign language 2.

**2009-2010 Annual costs.** Tuition/fees: $20,140. Some music and art courses carry a fee. Room/board: $8,050. Books/supplies: $1,900. Personal expenses: $900.

**2009-2010 Financial aid. Need-based:** 342 full-time freshmen applied for aid; 301 were judged to have need; 301 of these received aid. Average need met was 86%. Average scholarship/grant was $9,405; average loan $2,948. 55% of total undergraduate aid awarded as scholarships/grants, 45% as loans/jobs. **Non-need-based:** Awarded to 1,625 full-time undergraduates, including 440 freshmen. Scholarships awarded for academics, alumni affiliation, art, athletics, music/drama, religious affiliation, state residency. **Additional information:** Institutional aid may not be available after June 1.

**Application procedures. Admission:** Priority date 4/1; no deadline. $30 fee, may be waived for applicants with need. Admission notification on a rolling basis beginning on or about 9/15. Must reply by May 1 or within 4 week(s) if notified thereafter. **Financial aid:** Priority date 5/1; no closing date. FAFSA required. Applicants notified on a rolling basis starting 3/15; must reply within 2 week(s) of notification.

**Academics.** Attendance at cultural events required as part of Lyceum program. Travel abroad available. Internships and undergraduate research under faculty supervision available. **Special study options:** Combined bachelor's/graduate degree, cross-registration, double major, dual enrollment of high school students, honors, independent study, internships, study abroad, teacher certification program. Adult Completion Program at the Wingate University School of Graduate Programs and Adult Education in downtown Matthews, NC. The program offers undergraduate courses in the evening for working adults. **Credit/placement by examination:** AP, CLEP, IB, SAT, ACT, institutional tests. 30 credit hours maximum toward bachelor's degree. **Support services:** Learning center, reduced course load, study skills assistance, tutoring, writing center.

**Majors. Area/ethnic studies:** American. **Biology:** General, environmental. **Business:** Accounting, business admin, finance, marketing. **Communications:** General, journalism, public relations. **Computer sciences:** Computer science. **Education:** Art, biology, elementary, English, mathematics, middle, music, physical, reading, social studies. **Foreign languages:** Spanish. **Health:** Athletic training, predental, premedicine, prepharmacy, preveterinary. **History:** General. **Interdisciplinary:** Math/computer science. **Legal studies:** Prelaw. **Liberal arts:** Arts/sciences. **Math:** General. **Parks/recreation:** Facilities management, sports admin. **Philosophy/religion:** Philosophy, religion. **Physical sciences:** Chemistry. **Psychology:** General. **Public administration:** Human services. **Social sciences:** Sociology. **Visual/performing arts:** Art, music performance, studio arts. **Other:** Pre-engineering studies.

**Most popular majors.** Biology 9%, business/marketing 18%, communications/journalism 19%, education 7%, liberal arts 8%, philosophy/religious studies 6%.

**Computing on campus.** 75 workstations in library, computer center, student center. Dormitories wired for high-speed internet access. Commuter students can connect to campus network. Wireless network available.

**Student life. Freshman orientation:** Mandatory. Preregistration for classes offered. Begins 4 days before classes. **Policies:** Honor Code. **Housing:** Guaranteed on-campus for all undergraduates. Single-sex dorms, special housing for disabled, apartments, wellness housing available. $300 deposit. **Activities:** Bands, campus ministries, choral groups, drama, international student organizations, literary magazine, music ensembles, musical theater, student government, student newspaper, TV station, academic honors societies, Greek life, Christian Student Union, minority student association, university and community assistance network, gospel choir, College Republicans, outdoor recreation and adventure club, running club.

**Athletics.** NCAA. **Intercollegiate:** Baseball M, basketball, cross-country, football (tackle) M, golf, lacrosse M, soccer, softball W, swimming, tennis, volleyball W. **Intramural:** Basketball, bowling, diving, football (tackle) M, golf, lacrosse W, racquetball, soccer, softball, swimming, table tennis, tennis, volleyball, water polo. **Team name:** Bulldogs.

**Student services.** Chaplain/spiritual director, career counseling, student employment services, financial aid counseling, health services, minority student services, personal counseling, placement for graduates.

**Contact.** E-mail: admit@wingate.edu
Phone: (704) 233-8200 Toll-free number: (800) 755-5550
Fax: (704) 233-8110
Thomas Brown, Dean of Enrollment Management, Wingate University, Campus Box 3059, Wingate, NC 28174-0157

## Winston-Salem State University
**Winston-Salem, North Carolina**  **CB member**
**www.wssu.edu**  **CB code: 5909**

◆ Public 4-year university and health science college
◆ Commuter campus in small city
◆ 5,914 degree-seeking undergraduates: 10% part-time, 70% women, 81% African American, 1% Asian American, 1% Hispanic American, 1% international
◆ 455 degree-seeking graduate students
◆ 57% of applicants admitted
◆ SAT or ACT with writing required
◆ 37% graduate within 6 years

**General.** Founded in 1892. Regionally accredited. **Degrees:** 1,012 bachelor's awarded; master's offered. **ROTC:** Army. **Location:** 28 miles from Greensboro, 75 miles from Charlotte. **Calendar:** Semester, limited summer session. **Full-time faculty:** 420 total; 48% minority. **Part-time faculty:** 69 total; 44% minority. **Class size:** 42% < 20, 50% 20-39, 6% 40-49, 2% 50-99.

**Freshman class profile.** 3,490 applied, 1,979 admitted, 795 enrolled.

| Mid 50% test scores | | Rank in top tenth: | 1% |
|---|---|---|---|
| SAT critical reading: | 390-470 | Return as sophomores: | 78% |
| SAT math: | 400-480 | Out-of-state: | 12% |
| ACT composite: | 16-19 | Live on campus: | 82% |
| Rank in top quarter: | 3% | International: | 1% |

**Basis for selection.** Admissions based on secondary school record, class rank, and standardized tests scores. Campus interview very important. Extracurricular activities also important. SAT preferred. Interview recommended for all students; audition required for music program.

**High school preparation.** 15 units required. Required units include English 4, mathematics 4, social studies 1, history 1, science 3 and foreign language 2. Mathematics units must include or exceed algebra I, geometry and algebra II.

**2009-2010 Annual costs.** Tuition/fees: $3,522; $12,508 out-of-state. Room/board: $6,362. Personal expenses: $2,100.

**2008-2009 Financial aid. Need-based:** 1,312 full-time freshmen applied for aid; 1,145 were judged to have need; 1,143 of these received aid. Average need met was 79%. Average scholarship/grant was $3,211; average loan $1,474. 58% of total undergraduate aid awarded as scholarships/grants, 42% as loans/jobs. **Non-need-based:** Awarded to 1,179 full-time undergraduates, including 327 freshmen. Scholarships awarded for academics, athletics, ROTC, state residency.

**Application procedures. Admission:** Closing date 2/16. $40 fee, may be waived for applicants with need. Admission notification on a rolling basis. **Financial aid:** Priority date 5/1; no closing date. FAFSA required. Applicants notified by 5/15; must reply within 2 week(s) of notification.

**Academics. Special study options:** Accelerated study, cross-registration, distance learning, double major, ESL, honors, independent study, internships, liberal arts/career combination, study abroad, teacher certification program, Washington semester, weekend college. **Credit/placement by examination:** AP, CLEP, IB, institutional tests. 33 credit hours maximum toward bachelor's degree. **Support services:** Learning center, reduced course load, remedial instruction, study skills assistance, tutoring, writing center.

**Majors. Area/ethnic studies:** African-American. **Biology:** General, biotechnology, molecular. **Business:** Accounting, business admin, managerial economics. **Communications:** Media studies. **Computer sciences:** Computer science, information technology. **Education:** Art, early childhood, elementary, English, mathematics, middle, music, physical, social studies, Spanish, special. **Foreign languages:** Spanish. **Health:** Clinical lab science, nursing (RN), recreational therapy, vocational rehab counseling. **History:** General. **Interdisciplinary:** Gerontology. **Liberal arts:** Arts/sciences. **Math:** General. **Parks/recreation:** Exercise sciences, sports admin. **Physical sciences:** Chemistry. **Protective services:** Criminal justice. **Psychology:** General. **Public administration:** Social work. **Social sciences:** Political science, sociology. **Visual/performing arts:** Art, music management.

**Most popular majors.** Business/marketing 13%, health sciences 42%, parks/recreation 7%, social sciences 7%.

**Computing on campus.** PC or laptop required. 500 workstations in dormitories, library, computer center, student center. Dormitories wired for high-speed internet access and linked to campus network. Commuter students can connect to campus network. Online course registration, online library, wireless network available.

**Student life. Freshman orientation:** Available, $300 fee. Preregistration for classes offered. Held on a summer weekend. **Housing:** Coed dorms, single-sex dorms available. $75 nonrefundable deposit, deadline 5/14. **Activities:** Bands, dance, drama, radio station, student government, student newspaper, TV station, student religious council.

**Athletics.** NCAA. **Intercollegiate:** Basketball, bowling W, cheerleading M, cross-country, football (tackle) M, golf M, softball W, tennis, track and field, volleyball W. **Intramural:** Basketball M. **Team name:** Rams.

**Student services.** Adult student services, career counseling, student employment services, financial aid counseling, health services, personal counseling, veterans' counselor. **Physically disabled:** Services for visually impaired.

**Contact.** E-mail: admissions@wssu.edu
Phone: (336) 750-2070 Toll-free number: (800) 257-4052
Fax: (336) 750-2079
Tomikia Legrande, Director of Admissions, Winston-Salem State University, 601 Martin Luther King Jr Drive, Winston-Salem, NC 27110

# North Dakota

## Dickinson State University
**Dickinson, North Dakota**
www.dsu.nodak.edu                                    CB code: 6477

▶ Public 4-year university
▶ Residential campus in large town
▶ 2,767 degree-seeking undergraduates: 35% part-time, 62% women, 1% African American, 1% Asian American, 2% Hispanic American, 2% Native American, 14% international
▶ 31% graduate within 6 years

**General.** Founded in 1918. Regionally accredited. **Degrees:** 511 bachelor's, 59 associate awarded. **Location:** 100 miles from Bismarck, 300 miles from Billings, Montana. **Calendar:** Semester, limited summer session. **Full-time faculty:** 89 total; 53% have terminal degrees, 4% minority, 49% women. **Part-time faculty:** 154 total; 8% have terminal degrees, 1% minority, 62% women. **Class size:** 64% < 20, 29% 20-39, 4% 40-49, 3% 50-99. **Special facilities:** Nature preserve.

**Freshman class profile.** 649 applied, 336 admitted, 325 enrolled.

| Mid 50% test scores | | |
|---|---|---|
| SAT critical reading: | 430-530 | Rank in top quarter: | 15% |
| SAT math: | 470-590 | Rank in top tenth: | 5% |
| ACT composite: | 18-23 | Return as sophomores: | 63% |
| | | Out-of-state: | 45% |

**Basis for selection.** Open admission, but selective for some programs. Minimum 20 ACT composite or minimum 2.0 GPA required for nursing program. To be accepted into our Honors Leadership Program students must have a 3.5 high school GPA and/or a 26 on ACT. **Homeschooled:** Transcript of courses and grades, letter of recommendation (nonparent) required.

**High school preparation.** College-preparatory program required. 13 units recommended. Recommended units include English 4, mathematics 3, social studies 3 and science 3. One algebra, 1 chemistry required for nursing program.

**2009-2010 Annual costs.** Tuition/fees: $5,249; $12,195 out-of-state. Tuition for South Dakota, Montana, Manitoba, Saskatchewan residents: $5,024. Room/board: $4,494. Books/supplies: $900. Personal expenses: $1,325.

**2008-2009 Financial aid.** **Non-need-based:** Scholarships awarded for academics, alumni affiliation, art, athletics, job skills, leadership, minority status, music/drama, religious affiliation, state residency. **Additional information:** Scholarships available to new students, priority deadline December 1.

**Application procedures.** **Admission:** No deadline. $35 fee. Admission notification on a rolling basis. **Financial aid:** Priority date 3/15; no closing date. FAFSA required. Must reply within 2 week(s) of notification.

**Academics.** Limited evening classes available. **Special study options:** Accelerated study, combined bachelor's/graduate degree, cooperative education, distance learning, double major, dual enrollment of high school students, ESL, honors, independent study, internships, liberal arts/career combination, student-designed major, study abroad, teacher certification program. **Credit/placement by examination:** CLEP, institutional tests. 8 credit hours maximum toward associate degree, 15 toward bachelor's. **Support services:** Learning center, remedial instruction, study skills assistance, tutoring, writing center.

**Honors college/program.** Must submit a resume, essay and two letters of recommendation; 25 freshmen admitted each fall; includes special academic track that concludes with a leadership minor.

**Majors.** **Agriculture:** Business. **Biology:** General. **Business:** General, accounting, administrative services, business admin, finance, management information systems, office management. **Communications:** General. **Computer sciences:** Computer science. **Education:** Art, biology, business, chemistry, computer, drama/dance, early childhood, elementary, English, foreign languages, health, history, mathematics, middle, music, physical, reading, science, secondary, social science, Spanish, speech. **Foreign languages:** Spanish. **Health:** Nursing (RN), predental, premedicine, preveterinary. **History:** General. **Interdisciplinary:** Behavioral sciences, natural sciences. **Legal studies:** Prelaw. **Liberal arts:** Arts/sciences. **Math:** General. **Parks/recreation:** Health/fitness. **Physical sciences:** Chemistry. **Psychology:** General. **Social sciences:** General, political science. **Visual/performing arts:** Art, dramatic, studio arts, theater design.

**Most popular majors.** Biology 6%, business/marketing 36%, education 16%, health sciences 7%, liberal arts 13%.

**Computing on campus.** 235 workstations in dormitories, library, computer center, student center. Dormitories wired for high-speed internet access and linked to campus network. Commuter students can connect to campus network. Online course registration, online library, helpline, repair service, wireless network available.

**Student life.** **Freshman orientation:** Mandatory, $35 fee. Preregistration for classes offered. **Housing:** Guaranteed on-campus for all undergraduates. Coed dorms, single-sex dorms, special housing for disabled, apartments, wellness housing available. $50 fully refundable deposit. **Activities:** Bands, choral groups, dance, drama, film society, literary magazine, music ensembles, musical theater, student government, student newspaper.

**Athletics.** NAIA. **Intercollegiate:** Baseball M, basketball, cross-country, football (tackle) M, golf, rodeo, softball W, track and field, volleyball W, wrestling M. **Intramural:** Basketball, football (non-tackle), soccer, softball, volleyball. **Team name:** Blue Hawks.

**Student services.** Adult student services, career counseling, services for economically disadvantaged, student employment services, financial aid counseling, health services, minority student services, personal counseling, placement for graduates. **Physically disabled:** Services for visually, speech, hearing impaired. **Learning disabled:** Comprehensive services available.

**Contact.** E-mail: dsu.hawks@dickinsonstate.edu
Phone: (701) 483-2175 Toll-free number: (800) 279-4295
Fax: (701) 483-2409
Norman Coley, Director of Enrollment Services, Dickinson State University, 291 Campus Drive, Dickinson, ND 58601-4896

## Jamestown College
**Jamestown, North Dakota**
www.jc.edu                                          CB code: 6318

▶ Private 4-year liberal arts college affiliated with Presbyterian Church (USA)
▶ Residential campus in large town
▶ 965 degree-seeking undergraduates: 4% part-time, 53% women, 1% African American, 2% Asian American, 2% Hispanic American, 1% Native American, 4% international
▶ 67% of applicants admitted
▶ SAT or ACT (ACT writing optional) required
▶ 51% graduate within 6 years; 7% enter graduate study

**General.** Founded in 1883. Regionally accredited. **Degrees:** 170 bachelor's awarded. **Location:** 100 miles from Fargo and Bismarck. **Calendar:** Semester, limited summer session. **Full-time faculty:** 57 total; 54% have terminal degrees, 7% minority, 46% women. **Part-time faculty:** 26 total; 8% have terminal degrees, 4% minority, 46% women. **Class size:** 55% < 20, 38% 20-39, 5% 40-49, 2% 50-99, less than 1% >100.

**Freshman class profile.** 898 applied, 602 admitted, 239 enrolled.

| Mid 50% test scores | | | |
|---|---|---|---|
| SAT critical reading: | 400-520 | GPA 2.0-2.99: | 22% |
| SAT math: | 400-570 | Rank in top quarter: | 37% |
| ACT composite: | 20-25 | Rank in top tenth: | 13% |
| GPA 3.75 or higher: | 22% | Return as sophomores: | 70% |
| GPA 3.50-3.74: | 17% | Out-of-state: | 56% |
| GPA 3.0-3.49: | 39% | Live on campus: | 95% |
| | | International: | 4% |

**Basis for selection.** Applicants with minimum 2.5 high school GPA or 18 ACT or 850 SAT (exclusive of Writing) generally accepted. Applicants may be admitted on standard, conditional, or probationary basis. Interview recommended for all students. Audition required for music program; portfolio recommended for art program. **Homeschooled:** Letter of recommendation (nonparent) required.

**High school preparation.** College-preparatory program recommended. Recommended units include English 4, mathematics 3, social studies 3, science 4 and foreign language 2.

**2009-2010 Annual costs.** Tuition/fees: $16,006. Room/board: $5,156. Books/supplies: $1,000. Personal expenses: $1,300.

**2009-2010 Financial aid.** **Need-based:** 208 full-time freshmen applied for aid; 164 were judged to have need; 164 of these received aid. Average need met was 77%. Average scholarship/grant was $9,709; average loan $3,566. 55% of total undergraduate aid awarded as scholarships/grants, 45% as loans/jobs. **Non-need-based:** Awarded to 561 full-time undergraduates, including 179 freshmen. Scholarships awarded for academics, alumni affiliation, art, athletics, job skills, leadership, music/drama, religious affiliation. **Additional information:** FAFSA must be received by March 15th for North Dakota residents to be considered for North Dakota state grants.

**Application procedures. Admission:** Priority date 7/1; no deadline. $35 fee, may be waived for applicants with need, free for online applicants. Admission notification on a rolling basis. **Financial aid:** Priority date 3/15; no closing date. FAFSA required. Applicants notified on a rolling basis starting 2/1; must reply within 2 week(s) of notification.

**Academics. Special study options:** Combined bachelor's/graduate degree, cooperative education, double major, dual enrollment of high school students, honors, independent study, internships, liberal arts/career combination, student-designed major, study abroad, teacher certification program. **Credit/placement by examination:** AP, CLEP, IB, SAT, ACT, institutional tests. Unlimited number of hours of credit by examination may be counted toward degree. **Support services:** Learning center, reduced course load, remedial instruction, study skills assistance, tutoring, writing center.

**Majors. Biology:** General, biochemistry. **Business:** Accounting, business admin, finance, financial planning, hospitality admin, international, management information systems, managerial economics, marketing, tourism/travel. **Communications:** General. **Computer sciences:** Computer science, information technology. **Education:** Biology, chemistry, early childhood, elementary, English, history, mathematics, music, physical, secondary, special. **Foreign languages:** French, German, Spanish. **Health:** Clinical lab science, nursing (RN), radiologic technology/medical imaging. **History:** General. **Math:** General, applied. **Parks/recreation:** Sports admin. **Philosophy/religion:** Religion. **Physical sciences:** Chemistry. **Protective services:** Criminal justice. **Psychology:** General. **Social sciences:** Political science. **Visual/performing arts:** Dramatic, music performance, studio arts.

**Most popular majors.** Business/marketing 20%, education 17%, health sciences 26%.

**Computing on campus.** 359 workstations in dormitories, library, computer center, student center. Dormitories wired for high-speed internet access and linked to campus network. Commuter students can connect to campus network. Online course registration, online library, helpline, repair service, student web hosting, wireless network available.

**Student life. Freshman orientation:** Mandatory. 3 days prior to classes. **Policies:** Weekly chapel service available on campus. Non-alcoholic nightclub available. **Housing:** Guaranteed on-campus for all undergraduates. Coed dorms, special housing for disabled, apartments, wellness housing available. $100 fully refundable deposit. **Activities:** Bands, campus ministries, choral groups, dance, drama, international student organizations, music ensembles, musical theater, student government, student newspaper, TV station, honor societies, Students of Service, Fellowship of Christian Athletes, Jimmie Janes, Jimmie Ambassadors, Ignition.

**Athletics. NAIA. Intercollegiate:** Baseball M, basketball, cross-country, football (tackle) M, golf, soccer, softball W, track and field, volleyball W, wrestling. **Intramural:** Basketball, bowling, football (non-tackle), racquetball, soccer, softball, volleyball. **Team name:** Jimmies.

**Student services.** Alcohol/substance abuse counseling, chaplain/spiritual director, career counseling, student employment services, financial aid counseling, personal counseling, placement for graduates, veterans' counselor.

**Contact.**  E-mail: admissions@jc.edu
Phone: (701) 252-3467 ext. 5562 Toll-free number: (800) 336-2554
Fax: (701) 253-4318
Tena Lawrence, Director of Admissions, Jamestown College, 6081 College Lane, Jamestown, ND 58405

---

## Mayville State University
### Mayville, North Dakota
**www.mayvillestate.edu**                    CB code: 6478

- Public 4-year business and teachers college
- Residential campus in small town
- 887 degree-seeking undergraduates: 39% part-time, 57% women, 6% African American, 1% Asian American, 4% Hispanic American, 2% Native American, 3% international
- 40% graduate within 6 years; 10% enter graduate study

**General.** Founded in 1889. Regionally accredited. Every student issued laptop computer. All students complete an Information Technology Certificate as part of their bachelor's degree. **Degrees:** 117 bachelor's, 3 associate awarded. **ROTC:** Army, Air Force. **Location:** 60 miles from Fargo, 40 miles from Grand Forks. **Calendar:** Semester, limited summer session. **Full-time faculty:** 36 total; 42% have terminal degrees, 3% minority, 39% women. **Part-time faculty:** 35 total; 11% have terminal degrees, 6% minority, 63% women. **Class size:** 65% < 20, 33% 20-39, 2% 40-49. **Special facilities:** Nature area, business incubation technology center, head start and child development center, undergraduate research labs.

**Freshman class profile.**

| | | | |
|---|---|---|---|
| GPA 3.75 or higher: | 14% | End year in good standing: | 84% |
| GPA 3.50-3.74: | 11% | Return as sophomores: | 61% |
| GPA 3.0-3.49: | 25% | Out-of-state: | 50% |
| GPA 2.0-2.99: | 47% | Live on campus: | 96% |
| Rank in top quarter: | 17% | International: | 2% |
| Rank in top tenth: | 2% | | |

**Basis for selection.** Open admission, but selective for some programs. Admission to teacher education programs based on meeting GPA criteria, completion of PPST, and specific prerequisites. ACT math scores used for placement. Interview recommended. **Homeschooled:** Transcript of courses and grades required. Must provide documentation equivalent to high school diploma.

**High school preparation.** College-preparatory program required. 17 units required; 18 recommended. Required and recommended units include English 4, mathematics 3, social studies 3, science 3 (laboratory 3) and foreign language 2. One unit of computer studies recommended.

**2009-2010 Annual costs.** Tuition/fees: $5,793; $7,849 out-of-state. Full-time tuition for South Dakota, Montana, Kansas, Michigan, Missouri, Nebraska, Manitoba, and Saskatchewan residents: $5,156. Full-time tuition for Minnesota residents: $4,307. All other states and Canadian provinces: $6,180. Room/board: $4,488. Books/supplies: $900. Personal expenses: $2,800.

**2009-2010 Financial aid. Need-based:** Average need met was 91%. Average scholarship/grant was $5,015; average loan $3,310. 40% of total undergraduate aid awarded as scholarships/grants, 60% as loans/jobs. **Non-need-based:** Scholarships awarded for academics, athletics, leadership, minority status, music/drama, state residency.

**Application procedures. Admission:** No deadline. $35 fee. Admission notification on a rolling basis beginning on or about 1/1. **Financial aid:** Priority date 2/15; no closing date. FAFSA required. Applicants notified on a rolling basis starting 5/1; must reply within 2 week(s) of notification.

**Academics. Special study options:** Accelerated study, cooperative education, distance learning, double major, dual enrollment of high school students, internships, student-designed major, teacher certification program. 3-year business administration degree with cooperative education internship. **Credit/placement by examination:** AP, CLEP, institutional tests. 30 credit hours maximum toward bachelor's degree. **Support services:** Learning center, pre-admission summer program, remedial instruction, study skills assistance, tutoring.

**Majors. Biology:** General. **Business:** Business admin. **Communications:** General. **Computer sciences:** General. **Education:** Biology, chemistry, early childhood, elementary, English, geography, health, history, mathematics, physical, social science. **Family/consumer sciences:** Child care. **Health:** Athletic training, clinical lab science, predental, premedicine, prenursing, prepharmacy, preveterinary. **Legal studies:** Prelaw. **Math:** General. **Parks/recreation:** Health/fitness, sports admin. **Physical sciences:** Chemistry. **Psychology:** General. **Social sciences:** General. **Other:** Health education.

**Most popular majors.** Business/marketing 31%, education 36%, family/consumer sciences 8%, parks/recreation 9%.

**Computing on campus.** PC or laptop required. Dormitories wired for high-speed internet access and linked to campus network. Commuter students can connect to campus network. Online course registration, online library, helpline, repair service, wireless network available.

**Student life. Freshman orientation:** Mandatory, $35 fee. Preregistration for classes offered. Half-day events held in June and July. **Housing:** Guaranteed on-campus for all undergraduates. Single-sex dorms, apartments, wellness housing available. $50 nonrefundable deposit. **Activities:** Bands, choral groups, drama, international student organizations, music ensembles, musical theater, radio station, student government, student newspaper, Campus Crusade, student education association, residence hall association, health and physical education club, student activities council, alumni ambassadors, minority/international student association, business administration club, psychology club.

**Athletics.** NAIA. **Intercollegiate:** Baseball M, basketball, football (tackle) M, softball W, volleyball W. **Intramural:** Badminton, basketball, bowling, football (non-tackle), golf, ice hockey M, racquetball, soccer, softball, table tennis, tennis, track and field, volleyball, weight lifting. **Team name:** Comets.

**Student services.** Adult student services, career counseling, student employment services, financial aid counseling, health services, on-campus daycare, personal counseling, placement for graduates, veterans' counselor. **Physically disabled:** Services for visually, hearing impaired.

**Contact.** E-mail: admit@mayvillestate.edu
Phone: (701) 788-4842 Toll-free number: (800) 437-4104
Fax: (701) 788-4748
Misti Wuori, Director of Admissions and Extended Learning, Mayville State University, 330 Third Street, NE, Mayville, ND 58257-1299

## Medcenter One College of Nursing
### Bismarck, North Dakota
www.medcenterone.com/collegeofnursing   CB code: 7051

▶ Private two-year upper-division nursing college
▶ Commuter campus in small city
▶ 58% of applicants admitted
▶ Application essay, interview required

**General.** Founded in 1988. Regionally accredited. Small college affiliated with Medcenter One health system. **Degrees:** 44 bachelor's awarded. **Articulation:** Agreement with Bismarck State College. **Location:** 190 miles from Fargo, 105 miles from Minot. **Calendar:** Semester, limited summer session. **Full-time faculty:** 10 total; 10% have terminal degrees, 10% minority, 100% women. **Part-time faculty:** 3 total; 100% women. **Class size:** 17% < 20, 17% 20-39, 67% 40-49.

**Student profile.** 89 degree-seeking undergraduates. 101 applied as first time-transfer students, 59 admitted, 45 enrolled. 100% entered as juniors. 91% transferred from two-year, 9% transferred from four-year institutions.

| | | | |
|---|---|---|---|
| Women: | 93% | Out-of-state: | 7% |
| African American: | 2% | 25 or older: | 36% |
| Native American: | 2% | | |

**Basis for selection.** High school transcript, college transcript, application essay, interview required. All students must transfer with minimum 65 credits of general education prerequisites, including 5 prerequisite science courses. Students not required to complete all prerequisites prior to applying but must have a minimum of 2 required sciences completed. Credits not completed at time of application must be completed prior to starting 300 level nursing courses fall semester. Overall college GPA, science GPA important. Transfer accepted as sophomores, juniors, seniors.

**2009-2010 Annual costs.** Tuition/fees: $10,294. Books/supplies: $1,069. Personal expenses: $1,000.

**Financial aid. Need-based:** 71 applied for aid; 54 were judged to have need; 54 of these received aid. Average need met was 97%. 40% of total undergraduate aid awarded as scholarships/grants, 60% as loans/jobs. **Non-need-based:** Awarded to 29 undergraduates.

**Application procedures. Admission:** Priority date 11/7. $40 fee. Application must be submitted on paper. **Financial aid:** No deadline. Applicants notified on a rolling basis starting 6/1; must reply within 2 weeks of notification.

**Academics. Special study options:** Internships. **Credit/placement by examination:** CLEP, institutional tests. 30 credit hours maximum toward bachelor's degree.

**Majors. Health:** Nursing (RN).

**Computing on campus.** 17 workstations in library, computer center. Online library, wireless network available.

**Student life. Activities:** Student government, Student Nurse Association, Student Organization.

**Student services.** Financial aid counseling, health services, personal counseling, placement for graduates.

**Contact.** E-mail: msmith@mohs.org
Phone: (701) 323-6833 Fax: (701) 323-6289
Mary Smith, Director of Student Services, Medcenter One College of Nursing, 512 North 7th Street, Bismarck, ND 58501-4425

## Minot State University
### Minot, North Dakota
www.minotstateu.edu                    CB code: 6479

▶ Public 4-year university and liberal arts college
▶ Commuter campus in large town
▶ 3,345 degree-seeking undergraduates: 31% part-time, 62% women
▶ 420 graduate students
▶ 82% of applicants admitted
▶ SAT or ACT (ACT writing optional) required
▶ 31% graduate within 6 years

**General.** Founded in 1913. Regionally accredited. **Degrees:** 564 bachelor's awarded; master's offered. **Location:** 105 miles from Bismarck, 225 miles from Grand Forks. **Calendar:** Semester, limited summer session. **Full-time faculty:** 170 total. **Part-time faculty:** 80 total. **Special facilities:** Natural history museum, center for persons with disabilities, Native American collection, observatory, rural crime and justice center, Center for Extended Teaching and Learning.

**Freshman class profile.** 724 applied, 595 admitted, 438 enrolled.

| Mid 50% test scores | | | |
|---|---|---|---|
| | | ACT composite: | 19-24 |
| SAT critical reading: | 430-510 | Return as sophomores: | 70% |
| SAT math: | 420-530 | Out-of-state: | 12% |
| SAT writing: | 410-510 | | |

**Basis for selection.** Secondary school record very important; ACT/SAT test scores, ACT composite score must be no less than 17; those below the recommended composite score are reviewed on an individual basis.

**High school preparation.** 13 units required. Required units include English 4, mathematics 3, social studies 3, science 3 (laboratory 3). Science should include at least 3 units of biology, chemistry, physics, or physical science. Social science should not include consumer education, cooperative marketing, orientation to social science, or marriage/family. Math must be algebra I or above.

**2009-2010 Annual costs.** Tuition/fees: $5,389; $5,389 out-of-state. Room/board: $4,602. Books/supplies: $1,000.

**2008-2009 Financial aid. Non-need-based:** Scholarships awarded for academics, alumni affiliation, art, athletics, minority status, music/drama, state residency. **Additional information:** Scholarship application deadline is 2/15.

**Application procedures. Admission:** Priority date 4/1; no deadline. $35 fee. Admission notification on a rolling basis. **Financial aid:** Priority date 3/15; no closing date. FAFSA, institutional form required. Applicants notified on a rolling basis starting 5/1; must reply within 2 week(s) of notification.

**Academics.** Wide variety of distance courses offered. **Special study options:** Cooperative education, distance learning, double major, dual enrollment of high school students, ESL, external degree, honors, independent study, internships, liberal arts/career combination, student-designed major, study abroad, teacher certification program. **Credit/placement by examination:** AP, CLEP, institutional tests. **Support services:** Learning center, reduced course load, remedial instruction, study skills assistance, tutoring, writing center.

**Majors. Biology:** General. **Business:** Accounting, business admin, finance, international, management information systems, marketing. **Communications:** Broadcast journalism, radio/tv. **Communications technology:** General. **Computer sciences:** General. **Education:** Art, biology, business, chemistry, Deaf/hearing impaired, elementary, English, foreign languages, French, German, history, mathematics, mentally handicapped, music, physical, physics, science, social science, Spanish, speech impaired. **Foreign languages:** General, French, German, Spanish. **Health:** Clinical lab science, communication disorders, health care admin, medical radiologic technology/radiation therapy, nursing (RN), substance abuse counseling. **History:** General. **Liberal arts:** Arts/sciences. **Math:** General. **Parks/recreation:** Sports admin. **Physical sciences:** General, chemistry, geology, physics. **Protective services:** Criminal justice. **Psychology:** General. **Public administration:** Social work. **Social sciences:** General, economics, geography, sociology. **Visual/performing arts:** Art, arts management, dramatic, music performance.

**Most popular majors.** Business/marketing 19%, health sciences 6%.

**Computing on campus.** 300 workstations in dormitories, library, computer center, student center. Dormitories wired for high-speed internet access and linked to campus network. Commuter students can connect to campus network. Online course registration, online library, helpline, repair service, wireless network available.

**Student life. Freshman orientation:** Mandatory, $35 fee. Preregistration for classes offered. **Policies:** First-year students required to live in university housing (exceptions exist). **Housing:** Guaranteed on-campus for freshmen. Coed dorms, single-sex dorms, apartments, wellness housing available. $100 deposit. **Activities:** Marching band, campus ministries, choral groups, drama, international student organizations, music ensembles, musical theater, radio station, student government, student newspaper, TV station, disability awareness organization, Democratic Party, Republican Party, Intervarsity Christian Fellowship, Native American cultural awareness club, United Campus Ministries, Catholic student association, international awareness club, Student Education of Hard of Hearing/Deaf, National Student Speech/Hearing Association.

**Athletics.** NAIA. **Intercollegiate:** Baseball M, basketball, cheerleading M, cross-country, football (tackle) M, golf, softball W, track and field, volleyball W. **Intramural:** Basketball, bowling, ice hockey M, racquetball, softball, track and field, volleyball. **Team name:** Beavers.

**Student services.** Adult student services, alcohol/substance abuse counseling, chaplain/spiritual director, career counseling, services for economically disadvantaged, student employment services, financial aid counseling, health services, minority student services, personal counseling, placement for graduates, veterans' counselor, women's services. **Physically disabled:** Services for visually, speech, hearing impaired.

**Contact.** E-mail: askmsu@minotstateu.edu
Phone: (701) 858-3350 Toll-free number: (800) 777-0750
Fax: (701) 839-6933
Kevin Harmon, Dean of Admissions, Minot State University, 500 University Avenue West, Minot, ND 58707-5002

---

## North Dakota State University

| Fargo, North Dakota | CB member |
|---|---|
| www.ndsu.edu | CB code: 6474 |

- ▶ Public 4-year university
- ▶ Residential campus in small city
- ▶ 11,733 degree-seeking undergraduates: 9% part-time, 43% women
- ▶ 2,456 degree-seeking graduate students
- ▶ 79% of applicants admitted
- ▶ SAT or ACT (ACT writing optional) required
- ▶ 55% graduate within 6 years

**General.** Founded in 1890. Regionally accredited. **Degrees:** 1,821 bachelor's awarded; master's, doctoral, professional offered. **ROTC:** Army, Air Force. **Location:** 250 miles from Minneapolis-St. Paul. **Calendar:** Semester, limited summer session. **Full-time faculty:** 647 total; 74% have terminal degrees, 18% minority, 34% women. **Part-time faculty:** 134 total; 26% have terminal degrees, 9% minority, 47% women. **Class size:** 45% < 20, 36% 20-39, 8% 40-49, 7% 50-99, 4% >100. **Special facilities:** Fine arts center, regional studies institute, biotechnology institute, engineering computer center, center for writers, wellness center, technology park, downtown campus for art and architecture, business and agribusiness, equine center.

**Freshman class profile.** 5,646 applied, 4,473 admitted, 2,459 enrolled.

| Mid 50% test scores | | Rank in top tenth: | 17% |
|---|---|---|---|
| SAT critical reading: | 470-610 | End year in good standing: | 78% |
| SAT math: | 490-650 | Return as sophomores: | 78% |
| ACT composite: | 20-26 | Out-of-state: | 60% |
| GPA 3.75 or higher: | 26% | Live on campus: | 88% |
| GPA 3.50-3.74: | 19% | International: | 2% |
| GPA 3.0-3.49: | 33% | Fraternities: | 6% |
| GPA 2.0-2.99: | 21% | Sororities: | 3% |
| Rank in top quarter: | 42% | | |

**Basis for selection.** All applicants must have completed college preparatory program in high school. Admission based on overall performance in high school, performance in college preparatory courses and standardized test scores. Admission to electrical engineering and mechanical engineering programs based on academic record and test scores. Campus visit recommended for all students. Audition required for music programs. Secondary admission requirements for many programs. **Homeschooled:** Applicants advised to work with local school district for issuance of a Certificate of Graduation.

**High school preparation.** College-preparatory program required. 13 units required. Required units include English 4, mathematics 3, social studies 3, science 3 (laboratory 3).

**2009-2010 Annual costs.** Tuition/fees: $6,455; $15,554 out-of-state. Tuition for South Dakota, Montana, Manitoba, Saskatchewan residents: $8,172. Room/board: $6,568. Books/supplies: $950. Personal expenses: $3,500.

**2008-2009 Financial aid.** Need-based: 2,086 full-time freshmen applied for aid; 1,343 were judged to have need; 1,297 of these received aid. Average need met was 66%. Average scholarship/grant was $3,636; average loan $3,639. 28% of total undergraduate aid awarded as scholarships/grants, 72% as loans/jobs. **Non-need-based:** Awarded to 2,608 full-time undergraduates, including 1,059 freshmen. Scholarships awarded for academics, alumni affiliation, art, athletics, leadership, minority status, music/drama, ROTC, state residency.

**Application procedures. Admission:** Closing date 8/15 (receipt date). $35 fee. Admission notification on a rolling basis. **Financial aid:** Closing date 3/15. FAFSA required. Applicants notified on a rolling basis starting 3/15.

**Academics. Special study options:** Combined bachelor's/graduate degree, cooperative education, cross-registration, distance learning, double major, dual enrollment of high school students, ESL, honors, independent study, internships, student-designed major, study abroad, teacher certification program. Tri-college, collaborative enrollment (ND University System) Pathway program with ND partner institution with remedial coursework for students not meeting admission requirements. **Credit/placement by examination:** CLEP, IB, ACT, institutional tests. **Support services:** Reduced course load, remedial instruction, study skills assistance, tutoring, writing center.

**Majors. Agriculture:** General, agribusiness operations, animal sciences, communications, crop production, economics, equestrian studies, food science, horticultural science, mechanization, plant protection, soil science, turf management. **Architecture:** Environmental design, landscape. **Area/ethnic studies:** Women's. **Biology:** General, Biochemistry/biophysics and molecular biology, biotechnology, botany, microbiology, zoology. **Business:** Accounting, business admin, communications, construction management, finance, hospitality admin, management information systems, marketing. **Communications:** Health, journalism, public relations. **Computer sciences:** Computer science. **Conservation:** Management/policy. **Education:** Agricultural, biology, chemistry, elementary, English, family/consumer sciences, French, health, history, mathematics, music, physical, physics, science, social science, social studies, Spanish. **Engineering:** Agricultural, civil, computer, construction, electrical, industrial, manufacturing, mechanical. **Family/consumer sciences:** Clothing/textiles, family studies. **Foreign languages:** Classics, French, Spanish. **Health:** Clinical lab science, dietetics, nursing (RN), preveterinary, radiologic technology/medical imaging, respiratory therapy technology, veterinary technology/assistant. **History:** General, public archives. **Interdisciplinary:** Global studies. **Legal studies:** Prelaw. **Liberal arts:** Humanities. **Math:** General, statistics. **Parks/recreation:** General, sports admin. **Philosophy/religion:** Philosophy. **Physical sciences:** Chemistry, geology, physics. **Protective services:** Criminal justice, emergency management/homeland security. **Psychology:** General, psychometrics. **Social sciences:** General, anthropology, economics, political science, sociology. **Visual/performing arts:** Art, dramatic, interior design. **Other:** Food safety.

**Most popular majors.** Agriculture 7%, biology 6%, business/marketing 18%, engineering/engineering technologies 14%, health sciences 13%.

**Computing on campus.** 500 workstations in dormitories, library, computer center, student center. Dormitories wired for high-speed internet access. Online course registration, online library, helpline, repair service, student web hosting, wireless network available.

**Student life. Freshman orientation:** Available, $10 fee. Offered in June, July or August and day before classes. **Policies:** No alcoholic beverages allowed on campus, code of student conduct. **Housing:** Guaranteed on-campus for freshmen. Coed dorms, single-sex dorms, apartments, fraternity/sorority housing, wellness housing available. $50 partly refundable deposit. Housing is handicap accessible. **Activities:** Bands, choral groups, dance, drama, international student organizations, music ensembles, radio station, student government, student newspaper, Newman Center, Lutheran Student Fellowship, United Campus Ministry, College Republicans, College Democrats, Circle-K, Mortar Board, Black Student Alliance, Native American student association.

**Athletics.** NCAA. **Intercollegiate:** Baseball M, basketball, cross-country, football (tackle) M, golf, soccer W, softball W, track and field, volleyball W, wrestling M. **Intramural:** Basketball, football (non-tackle), softball, volleyball. **Team name:** Bison.

**Student services.** Adult student services, alcohol/substance abuse counseling, career counseling, services for economically disadvantaged, student employment services, financial aid counseling, health services, minority student services, on-campus daycare, personal counseling, veterans' counselor. **Physically disabled:** Services for visually, speech, hearing impaired. **Learning disabled:** Comprehensive services available.

**Contact.** E-mail: ndsu.admission@ndsu.edu
Phone: (701) 231-8643 Toll-free number: (800) 488-6378
Fax: (701) 231-8802
Jobey Lichtblau, Director of Admission, North Dakota State University, Ceres Hall 114, Fargo, ND 58108-6050

## Rasmussen College: Fargo
**Fargo, North Dakota**
**www.rasmussen.edu**   **CB code: 3343**

▶ For-profit 4-year career college
▶ Commuter campus in small city
▶ 510 full-time, degree-seeking undergraduates

**General. Degrees:** 1 bachelor's, 164 associate awarded. **Calendar:** Quarter, extensive summer session. **Full-time faculty:** 18 total. **Part-time faculty:** 22 total.

**Basis for selection.** Open admission, but selective for some programs. Some programs require placement examinations.

**2009-2010 Annual costs.** Per-credit tuition ranges from $365 to $450 depending on course level. Personal expenses: $2,214.

**Application procedures. Admission:** No deadline. $60 fee. Admission notification on a rolling basis. **Financial aid:** No deadline. FAFSA, institutional form required. Applicants notified on a rolling basis.

**Academics. Special study options:** Distance learning, double major, independent study, internships, liberal arts/career combination. **Credit/placement by examination:** AP, CLEP, IB, institutional tests. 45 credit hours maximum toward associate degree, 90 toward bachelor's. 50% of a student's program must be completed through coursework at Rasmussen College. **Support services:** Learning center, remedial instruction, study skills assistance, tutoring, writing center.

**Majors. Business:** Accounting, business admin. **Protective services:** Criminal justice.

**Computing on campus.** 100 workstations in library, computer center, student center. Online course registration, online library, helpline, wireless network available.

**Student life. Freshman orientation:** Mandatory. **Activities:** Student government.

**Student services.** Adult student services, career counseling, services for economically disadvantaged, student employment services, financial aid counseling, placement for graduates.

**Contact.** E-mail: peter.limvere@rasmussen.edu
Phone: (701) 277-3889 Toll-free number: (800) 817-0009
Fax: (701) 277-5604
Peter Limvere, Director of Admissions, Rasmussen College: Fargo, 4012 19th Avenue SW, Fargo, ND 58103

## Trinity Bible College
**Ellendale, North Dakota**
**www.trinitybiblecollege.edu**   **CB code: 0356**

▶ Private 4-year Bible college affiliated with Assemblies of God
▶ Residential campus in rural community
▶ 296 undergraduates
▶ ACT (writing optional), application essay required

**General.** Founded in 1948. Regionally accredited; also accredited by ABHE. **Degrees:** 42 bachelor's, 15 associate awarded. **Location:** 60 miles from Jamestown, 38 miles from Aberdeen. **Calendar:** Semester, limited summer session. **Full-time faculty:** 30 total. **Part-time faculty:** 10 total. **Special facilities:** Pentecostal heritage collection of rare and out-of-print works, teacher education laboratory.

**Freshman class profile.**

Out-of-state:  77%   Live on campus:  85%

**Basis for selection.** Criteria include ACT scores and GPA references, school record, evidence of Christian testimony and lifestyle. Interview recommended. **Homeschooled:** Statement describing homeschool structure and mission, transcript of courses and grades, letter of recommendation (nonparent) required. Minimum ACT scores of 14 English, 15 math required.

**2009-2010 Annual costs.** Tuition/fees: $13,000. Room/board: $4,900. Books/supplies: $800. Personal expenses: $1,636.

**2009-2010 Financial aid. Non-need-based:** Scholarships awarded for academics, alumni affiliation, art, leadership, music/drama, religious affiliation.

**Application procedures. Admission:** No deadline. $25 fee, may be waived for applicants with need. Admission notification on a rolling basis. **Financial aid:** Priority date 3/1, closing date 9/1. FAFSA required. Applicants notified on a rolling basis starting 3/1; must reply within 3 week(s) of notification.

**Academics.** All students major or minor in Biblical studies in conjunction with another major or minor of their choice. **Special study options:** Distance learning, double major, dual enrollment of high school students, independent study, internships, liberal arts/career combination, teacher certification program. **Credit/placement by examination:** AP, CLEP, IB, SAT, ACT, institutional tests. 30 credit hours maximum toward associate degree, 30 toward bachelor's. **Support services:** Learning center, reduced course load, remedial instruction, tutoring.

**Majors. Business:** General. **Education:** Elementary. **Philosophy/religion:** Religion. **Theology:** Bible, missionary, religious ed, theology. **Visual/performing arts:** Dramatic.

**Most popular majors.** Business/marketing 10%, education 20%, philosophy/religious studies 25%, theological studies 40%.

**Computing on campus.** 30 workstations in dormitories, library, computer center. Dormitories wired for high-speed internet access and linked to campus network. Online library, helpline, wireless network available.

**Student life. Freshman orientation:** Mandatory. Preregistration for classes offered. **Policies:** Religious observance required. **Housing:** Single-sex dorms, apartments, wellness housing available. $150 deposit, deadline 8/31. **Activities:** Bands, choral groups, drama, music ensembles, radio station, student government, missions, photography, ministry clubs.

**Athletics.** NCCAA. **Intercollegiate:** Basketball, football (tackle) M. **Intramural:** Basketball, football (tackle) M, volleyball. **Team name:** Lions.

**Student services.** Chaplain/spiritual director, career counseling, student employment services, financial aid counseling, personal counseling, placement for graduates, veterans' counselor.

**Contact.** E-mail: admissions@trinitybiblecollege.edu
Phone: (701) 349-3621 Toll-free number: (888) 822-2329
Fax: (701) 349-5786
Elise Hess, Director of Admissions, Trinity Bible College, 50 6th Avenue South, Ellendale, ND 58436-7150

## University of Mary
**Bismarck, North Dakota**
**www.umary.edu**   **CB code: 6428**

▶ Private 4-year university affiliated with Roman Catholic Church
▶ Residential campus in small city
▶ 1,994 degree-seeking undergraduates: 20% part-time, 62% women, 2% African American, 1% Asian American, 2% Hispanic American, 4% Native American, 1% international
▶ 813 degree-seeking graduate students
▶ 78% of applicants admitted
▶ SAT or ACT (ACT writing optional) required
▶ 51% graduate within 6 years; 22% enter graduate study

**General.** Founded in 1959. Regionally accredited. Additional centers in Bismarck, Fargo, Grand Forks, ND, Billiings, MT, Kansas City, and Phoenix. **Degrees:** 495 bachelor's awarded; master's, professional offered. **Location:** 6 miles from downtown. **Calendar:** Semester, limited summer session. **Full-time faculty:** 93 total; 50% have terminal degrees, 1% minority, 55% women. **Part-time faculty:** 180 total; 20% have terminal degrees, 11% minority, 49% women. **Class size:** 57% < 20, 32% 20-39, 2% 40-49, 7% 50-99, 1% >100. **Special facilities:** Climbing wall, 3 art galleries.

**Freshman class profile.** 924 applied, 723 admitted, 313 enrolled.

| Mid 50% test scores | | | |
|---|---|---|---|
| SAT critical reading: | 410-500 | Rank in top quarter: | 45% |
| SAT math: | 440-560 | Rank in top tenth: | 6% |
| ACT composite: | 20-25 | End year in good standing: | 94% |
| GPA 3.75 or higher: | 37% | Return as sophomores: | 75% |
| GPA 3.50-3.74: | 16% | Out-of-state: | 38% |
| GPA 3.0-3.49: | 26% | Live on campus: | 85% |
| GPA 2.0-2.99: | 21% | International: | 1% |

**Basis for selection.** Automatic acceptance for applicants in top half of class with 2.5 GPA and 19 ACT. Applicants not meeting these standards may be admitted with specific conditions for enrollment. Audition required for music program; interview recommended for academically weak students. **Homeschooled:** State high school equivalency certificate required.

**High school preparation.** College-preparatory program recommended. Recommended units include English 4, mathematics 3, social studies 4 and science 3.

**2010-2011 Annual costs.** Tuition/fees (projected): $13,126. Room/board: $5,150. Books/supplies: $1,100. Personal expenses: $1,056.

**2009-2010 Financial aid. Need-based:** 38% of total undergraduate aid awarded as scholarships/grants, 62% as loans/jobs. **Non-need-based:** Scholarships awarded for academics, athletics, leadership, music/drama, religious affiliation, state residency.

**Application procedures. Admission:** No deadline. $25 fee, may be waived for applicants with need. Admission notification on a rolling basis. Must reply by May 1 or within 4 week(s) if notified thereafter. **Financial aid:** Priority date 3/15; no closing date. FAFSA required. Applicants notified on a rolling basis starting 2/1; must reply within 2 week(s) of notification.

**Academics. Special study options:** Accelerated study, combined bachelor's/graduate degree, cooperative education, distance learning, double major, dual enrollment of high school students, external degree, honors, independent study, internships, liberal arts/career combination, semester at sea, study abroad, teacher certification program. **Credit/placement by examination:** AP, CLEP, IB, SAT, ACT. **Support services:** Learning center, reduced course load, remedial instruction, study skills assistance, tutoring, writing center.

**Majors. Biology:** General. **Business:** Accounting, business admin, communications, finance, management information systems, marketing. **Communications:** Public relations. **Computer sciences:** General, information systems. **Education:** Biology, business, early childhood, elementary, English, history, mathematics, mentally handicapped, music, physical, reading, social science. **Engineering:** General. **Health:** Athletic training, clinical lab science, nursing (RN), radiologic technology/medical imaging, respiratory therapy technology, substance abuse counseling. **Math:** General. **Parks/recreation:** Exercise sciences, health/fitness, sports admin. **Philosophy/religion:** Religion. **Protective services:** Criminal justice, law enforcement admin. **Psychology:** General. **Public administration:** Social work. **Social sciences:** General. **Theology:** Sacred music, theology. **Visual/performing arts:** Music performance.

**Most popular majors.** Business/marketing 39%, education 12%, health sciences 22%, liberal arts 8%.

**Computing on campus.** 100 workstations in dormitories, library, computer center. Dormitories wired for high-speed internet access and linked to campus network. Commuter students can connect to campus network. Online course registration, online library, helpline, student web hosting, wireless network available.

**Student life. Freshman orientation:** Mandatory. Preregistration for classes offered. Three-day program immediately prior to the first day of classes. **Policies:** Freshmen and sophomores have an on-campus residency requirement. **Housing:** Guaranteed on-campus for freshmen. Single-sex dorms, special housing for disabled, apartments, wellness housing available. $100 fully refundable deposit. **Activities:** Bands, campus ministries, choral groups, dance, drama, international student organizations, music ensembles, musical theater, student government, student newspaper, Circle-K, Young Democrats, College Republicans, Fellowship of Christian Athletes, Lions Club, Spanish Club, International Club, Collegians for Life, Optimist Club.

**Athletics.** NCAA. **Intercollegiate:** Baseball M, basketball, cross-country, football (tackle) M, golf, soccer, softball W, tennis, track and field, volleyball W, wrestling M. **Intramural:** Badminton, basketball, football (non-tackle), golf, racquetball, soccer, softball, swimming, table tennis, tennis, triathlon, volleyball, water polo, weight lifting. **Team name:** Marauders.

**Student services.** Adult student services, chaplain/spiritual director, career counseling, services for economically disadvantaged, student employment services, financial aid counseling, health services, minority student services, personal counseling, placement for graduates, veterans' counselor. **Physically disabled:** Services for visually, hearing impaired.

**Contact.** E-mail: marauder@umary.edu
Phone: (701) 355-8030 Toll-free number: (800) 288-6279
Fax: (701) 255-7687
Mike Heitkamp, Director of Admissions, University of Mary, 7500 University Drive, Bismarck, ND 58504-9652

## University of North Dakota
**Grand Forks, North Dakota**
**www.und.edu**

CB code: 6878

- Public 4-year university
- Residential campus in small city

- 10,440 degree-seeking undergraduates: 16% part-time, 45% women, 1% African American, 1% Asian American, 1% Hispanic American, 3% Native American, 5% international
- 2,732 degree-seeking graduate students
- 73% of applicants admitted
- SAT or ACT (ACT writing optional) required
- 54% graduate within 6 years; 18% enter graduate study

**General.** Founded in 1883. Regionally accredited. **Degrees:** 1,859 bachelor's awarded; master's, doctoral, professional offered. **ROTC:** Army, Air Force. **Location:** 320 miles from Minneapolis-St. Paul, 150 miles from Winnipeg, Canada. **Calendar:** Semester, extensive summer session. **Full-time faculty:** 594 total; 80% have terminal degrees, 12% minority, 39% women. **Part-time faculty:** 70 total; 30% have terminal degrees, 6% minority, 61% women. **Class size:** 39% < 20, 46% 20-39, 6% 40-49, 6% 50-99, 3% >100. **Special facilities:** Art museum, atmospherium, supercomputing center, native media center, American Indian center, biomedical research center, climate change and CO2 center, instructional and learning technologies center, peace studies center, renewable energy center, rural health center, children and family services training center, clinical education center, environmental training institute, ecological studies institute, hydrogen technology center, Native American aging resource center, behavioral research center, Indian law center, wellness center.

**Freshman class profile.** 4,111 applied, 3,003 admitted, 1,992 enrolled.

| Mid 50% test scores | | | |
|---|---|---|---|
| ACT composite: | 20-25 | End year in good standing: | 81% |
| GPA 3.75 or higher: | 28% | Return as sophomores: | 77% |
| GPA 3.50-3.74: | 19% | Out-of-state: | 62% |
| GPA 3.0-3.49: | 32% | Live on campus: | 87% |
| GPA 2.0-2.99: | 21% | International: | 1% |
| Rank in top quarter: | 40% | Fraternities: | 5% |
| Rank in top tenth: | 17% | Sororities: | 8% |

**Basis for selection.** High school record and test scores most important. **Homeschooled:** Transcript of courses and grades required.

**High school preparation.** College-preparatory program required. 13 units required. Required and recommended units include English 4, mathematics 3, social studies 3, science 3 (laboratory 3) and foreign language 1. Math must be algebra I and above.

**2009-2010 Annual costs.** Tuition/fees: $6,726; $15,845 out-of-state. Tuition for South Dakota, Montana, Saskatchewan, Manitoba residents: $8,191. Room/board: $5,978.

**2009-2010 Financial aid. Need-based:** 1,616 full-time freshmen applied for aid; 997 were judged to have need; 991 of these received aid. Average need met was 69%. Average scholarship/grant was $4,159; average loan $3,507. 29% of total undergraduate aid awarded as scholarships/grants, 71% as loans/jobs. **Non-need-based:** Awarded to 2,526 full-time undergraduates, including 880 freshmen. Scholarships awarded for academics, alumni affiliation, art, athletics, job skills, leadership, music/drama, religious affiliation, ROTC.

**Application procedures. Admission:** No deadline. $35 fee. Admission notification on a rolling basis beginning on or about 9/1. **Financial aid:** Priority date 3/15; no closing date. FAFSA required. Applicants notified on a rolling basis starting 5/15; must reply within 4 week(s) of notification.

**Academics. Special study options:** Accelerated study, combined bachelor's/graduate degree, cooperative education, cross-registration, distance learning, double major, dual enrollment of high school students, ESL, exchange student, external degree, honors, independent study, internships, liberal arts/career combination, semester at sea, student-designed major, study abroad, teacher certification program, weekend college. **Credit/placement by examination:** AP, CLEP, IB, ACT, institutional tests. **Support services:** Learning center, pre-admission summer program, reduced course load, remedial instruction, study skills assistance, tutoring, writing center.

**Majors. Area/ethnic studies:** Chinese, Native American. **Biology:** General, animal behavior, wildlife. **Business:** Accounting, accounting/finance, business admin, entrepreneurial studies, finance, human resources, managerial economics, marketing, operations. **Communications:** General. **Communications technology:** Graphics. **Computer sciences:** General, systems analysis. **Education:** Business, early childhood, elementary, middle, music, physical, science, social science. **Engineering:** Chemical, civil, electrical, environmental, geological, mechanical. **Engineering technology:** Industrial, occupational safety. **Family/consumer sciences:** Food/nutrition. **Foreign languages:** General, classics, French, German, Scandinavian, Spanish. **Health:** Athletic training, clinical lab science, clinical nutrition, communication disorders, cytotechnology, dietetics, music therapy, nursing (RN), vocational rehab counseling. **History:** General. **Interdisciplinary:** Global studies. **Math:**

General. **Parks/recreation:** Facilities management. **Philosophy/religion:** Philosophy, religion. **Physical sciences:** General, atmospheric science, chemistry, geology, physics. **Protective services:** Criminal justice, forensics. **Psychology:** General. **Public administration:** General, social work. **Social sciences:** General, anthropology, economics, geography, political science, sociology. **Transportation:** Air traffic control, airline/commercial pilot, aviation management, flight instructor. **Visual/performing arts:** Art, dramatic, graphic design, music performance.

**Most popular majors.** Business/marketing 14%, education 7%, engineering/engineering technologies 8%, health sciences 12%, trade and industry 15%.

**Computing on campus.** 1,100 workstations in dormitories, library, computer center, student center. Dormitories wired for high-speed internet access and linked to campus network. Commuter students can connect to campus network. Online course registration, online library, helpline, student web hosting, wireless network available.

**Student life. Freshman orientation:** Available, $15 fee. Preregistration for classes offered. Held weekend before school opens in August. **Housing:** Guaranteed on-campus for freshmen. Coed dorms, single-sex dorms, special housing for disabled, apartments, fraternity/sorority housing, wellness housing available. $250 partly refundable deposit, deadline 5/1. **Activities:** Bands, campus ministries, choral groups, dance, drama, film society, international student organizations, literary magazine, music ensembles, musical theater, opera, radio station, student government, student newspaper, symphony orchestra, TV station, over 230 organizations available.

**Athletics.** NCAA. **Intercollegiate:** Baseball M, basketball, cross-country, diving, football (tackle) M, golf, ice hockey, soccer W, softball W, swimming, tennis W, track and field, volleyball W. **Intramural:** Badminton, basketball, cross-country, golf, ice hockey, racquetball, soccer W, softball W, swimming, tennis W, track and field, volleyball W. **Team name:** Fighting Sioux.

**Student services.** Adult student services, alcohol/substance abuse counseling, chaplain/spiritual director, career counseling, services for economically disadvantaged, student employment services, financial aid counseling, health services, legal services, minority student services, on-campus daycare, personal counseling, placement for graduates, veterans' counselor, women's services. **Physically disabled:** Services for visually, speech, hearing impaired.

**Contact.** E-mail: enrollmentservices@mail.und.nodak.edu
Phone: (701) 777-3821 Toll-free number: (800) 225-5863
Fax: (701) 777-2721
Deborah Melby, Director, University of North Dakota, Twamley Hall Room 205 264 Centennial Drive Stop 8357, Grand Forks, ND 58202-8357

## Valley City State University
**Valley City, North Dakota**
www.vcsu.edu                    CB code: 6480

‣ Public 4-year liberal arts and teachers college
‣ Residential campus in small town

**General.** Founded in 1889. Regionally accredited. **Location:** 60 miles from Fargo. **Calendar:** Semester.

**Annual costs/financial aid.** Tuition/fees (2009-2010): $5,926; $13,077 out-of-state. Full-time tuition for South Dakota, Montana, Manitoba, Saskatchewan residents: $5,353. Full-time tuition for WUE students: $6,424. Room/board: $4,726. Books/supplies: $800. Personal expenses: $1,827. Need-based financial aid available to full-time and part-time students.

**Contact.** Phone: (701) 845-7101
Director of Enrollment Services, 101 College Street SW, Valley City, ND 58072-4098

Four-Year Colleges

# Ohio

## Allegheny Wesleyan College
Salem, Ohio
www.awc.edu
CB code: 4120

- Private 4-year Bible college affiliated with Allegheny Wesleyan Methodist Connection
- Residential campus in small town
- 61 degree-seeking undergraduates

**General.** Accredited by ABHE. Beautiful country setting on 45 acres. **Degrees:** 3 bachelor's awarded. **Location:** 2 miles from Salem. **Calendar:** Semester. **Full-time faculty:** 8 total. **Part-time faculty:** 5 total.

**Basis for selection.** Open admission.

**2009-2010 Annual costs.** Tuition/fees: $5,550. Room/board: $3,300. Books/supplies: $550. Personal expenses: $800.

**Application procedures. Admission:** Priority date 4/25; deadline 8/26. $35 fee. Admission notification on a rolling basis. **Financial aid:** Priority date 8/26; no closing date.

**Academics. Special study options:** Double major, internships. **Credit/placement by examination:** AP, CLEP, institutional tests. 12 credit hours maximum toward associate degree, 12 toward bachelor's. **Support services:** Reduced course load, remedial instruction, tutoring.

**Majors. Theology:** Theology.

**Computing on campus.** 10 workstations in library, computer center. Online library, repair service available.

**Student life. Housing:** Coed dorms available. **Activities:** Student newspaper.

**Contact.** E-mail: college@awc.edu
Phone: (330) 337-6403 Toll-free number: (800) 292-3153 ext. 10
Fax: (330) 337-6255
Jeanne Zvaritch, Director of Admissions, Allegheny Wesleyan College, 2161 Woodside Road, Salem, OH 44460-9598

## Antioch University McGregor
Yellow Springs, Ohio
www.mcgregor.edu
CB code: 4527

- Private 4-year university and branch campus college
- Commuter campus in small town
- 176 degree-seeking undergraduates: 50% part-time, 77% women, 23% African American, 1% Hispanic American, 1% Native American
- 522 degree-seeking graduate students
- Application essay, interview required

**General.** Founded in 1988. Regionally accredited. **Degrees:** 36 bachelor's awarded; master's offered. **Location:** 18 miles from Dayton. **Calendar:** Quarter, limited summer session. **Full-time faculty:** 20 total; 50% women. **Part-time faculty:** 46 total; 46% women. **Special facilities:** Nature reserve.

**Basis for selection.** Applicants must be over 21. Recommendations and motivation most important.

**2009-2010 Annual costs.** Tuition/fees: $15,720. Books/supplies: $1,800.

**Application procedures. Admission:** Closing date 9/30 (postmark date). $45 fee, may be waived for applicants with need. Admission notification on a rolling basis. **Financial aid:** No deadline. Applicants notified on a rolling basis.

**Academics. Special study options:** Combined bachelor's/graduate degree, double major, independent study, student-designed major, teacher certification program, weekend college. **Credit/placement by examination:** CLEP. 45 credit hours maximum toward bachelor's degree. **Support services:** Reduced course load, writing center.

**Majors. Business:** Business admin, human resources. **Education:** General, early childhood. **Health:** Health services. **Liberal arts:** Arts/sciences, humanities. **Math:** General. **Public administration:** Human services.

**Most popular majors.** Business/marketing 45%, liberal arts 37%, psychology 14%.

**Computing on campus.** PC or laptop required. 35 workstations in computer center. Commuter students can connect to campus network. Online course registration, online library, helpline, wireless network available.

**Student life. Freshman orientation:** Mandatory, $25 fee. **Activities:** Radio station, student newspaper.

**Student services.** Adult student services, financial aid counseling.

**Contact.** E-mail: sas@mcgregor.edu
Phone: (937) 769-1818 Fax: (937) 769-1804
Oscar Robinson, Director of Admissions, Antioch University McGregor, 900 Dayton Street, Yellow Springs, OH 45387

## Art Academy of Cincinnati
Cincinnati, Ohio
www.artacademy.edu
CB code: 1002

- Private 4-year visual arts college
- Commuter campus in large city
- 183 degree-seeking undergraduates
- 18% of applicants admitted
- SAT or ACT (ACT writing optional), application essay required

**General.** Founded in 1869. Regionally accredited. **Degrees:** 30 bachelor's awarded; master's offered. **Location:** One mile from downtown. **Calendar:** Semester, limited summer session. **Full-time faculty:** 14 total; 57% women. **Part-time faculty:** 30 total. **Special facilities:** Glass-blowing facility, three art galleries.

**Freshman class profile.** 550 applied, 97 admitted, 56 enrolled.

| Mid 50% test scores | | ACT composite: | 18-24 |
|---|---|---|---|
| SAT critical reading: | 480-600 | Out-of-state: | 36% |
| SAT math: | 420-570 | Live on campus: | 51% |

**Basis for selection.** Academic background based upon GPA and ACT/SAT scores; portfolio review and interview very important; 1-page artist statement and 1 letter of recommendation required. Portfolio required for all; interview required for those within 150 miles of campus. **Home-schooled:** Transcript of courses and grades, state high school equivalency certificate required.

**High school preparation.** 12 units recommended. Recommended units include English 4, mathematics 3, social studies 1 and science 2. 3-4 units art recommended.

**2009-2010 Annual costs.** Tuition/fees: $21,880. Room only: $6,000. Books/supplies: $1,200.

**Financial aid. Non-need-based:** Scholarships awarded for academics, art.

**Application procedures. Admission:** Priority date 3/1; deadline 6/30 (postmark date). No application fee. Admission notification on a rolling basis. **Financial aid:** Priority date 4/1; no closing date. FAFSA required. Applicants notified on a rolling basis starting 3/1.

**Academics. Special study options:** Cross-registration, double major, exchange student, independent study, internships, New York semester, student-designed major, study abroad. **Credit/placement by examination:** AP, CLEP, institutional tests. **Support services:** Learning center, study skills assistance, tutoring, writing center.

**Majors. Visual/performing arts:** Art history/conservation, design, digital art, drawing, illustration, painting, photography, printmaking, sculpture, studio arts.

**Computing on campus.** 40 workstations in computer center. Dormitories wired for high-speed internet access.

**Student life. Freshman orientation:** Mandatory. Preregistration for classes offered. Held 5 days before school begins. **Housing:** Coed dorms available. $250 nonrefundable deposit, deadline 6/1. **Activities:** Film society, literary magazine, student government.

**Student services.** Career counseling, student employment services, financial aid counseling, personal counseling, placement for graduates, veterans' counselor. **Physically disabled:** Services for hearing impaired.

**Contact.** E-mail: admissions@artacademy.edu
Phone: (513) 562-8740 Toll-free number: (800) 323-5692
Fax: (513) 562-8778
John Cooper, Vice President of Enrollment Management, Art Academy of
Cincinnati, 1212 Jackson Street, Cincinnati, OH 45202

## Ashland University
Ashland, Ohio
www.ashland.edu                                        CB code: 1021

- Private 4-year university and liberal arts college affiliated with
  Brethren Church
- Residential campus in large town
- 2,612 degree-seeking undergraduates: 15% part-time, 52% women
- 2,652 degree-seeking graduate students
- 94% of applicants admitted
- SAT or ACT (ACT writing optional) required
- 61% graduate within 6 years

**General.** Founded in 1878. Regionally accredited. **Degrees:** 501 bachelor's, 11 associate awarded; master's, doctoral offered. **Location:** 60 miles from Cleveland, 80 miles from Columbus. **Calendar:** Semester, limited summer session. **Full-time faculty:** 234 total; 84% have terminal degrees, 6% minority, 42% women. **Part-time faculty:** 347 total; 33% have terminal degrees, 4% minority, 53% women. **Class size:** 63% < 20, 35% 20-39, 1% 40-49, less than 1% 50-99. **Special facilities:** Centers for public affairs, business and economic research, convocation, numismatic, nonviolence, educational improvement, entrepreneurial studies; institute for middle level education.

**Freshman class profile.** 2,903 applied, 2,742 admitted, 622 enrolled.

| Mid 50% test scores | | | |
|---|---|---|---|
| SAT critical reading: | 460-560 | Rank in top quarter: | 47% |
| SAT math: | 470-570 | Rank in top tenth: | 18% |
| SAT writing: | 440-550 | Return as sophomores: | 71% |
| ACT composite: | 20-24 | Out-of-state: | 8% |
| GPA 3.75 or higher: | 24% | Live on campus: | 87% |
| GPA 3.50-3.74: | 18% | International: | 1% |
| GPA 3.0-3.49: | 31% | Fraternities: | 8% |
| GPA 2.0-2.99: | 26% | Sororities: | 18% |

**Basis for selection.** School achievement record most important; test scores also important. Counselor's recommendation considered. Interview recommended for all; audition recommended for music, theater programs; portfolio recommended for art. **Homeschooled:** Transcript of courses and grades required.

**High school preparation.** College-preparatory program recommended. Required and recommended units include English 3-4, mathematics 2-3, social studies 2-3, history 1, science 2-3, foreign language 2 and academic electives 1.

**2009-2010 Annual costs.** Tuition/fees: $25,646. Room/board: $9,352. Books/supplies: $900. Personal expenses: $1,801.

**2009-2010 Financial aid. Need-based:** 605 full-time freshmen applied for aid; 521 were judged to have need; 521 of these received aid. Average need met was 90%. Average scholarship/grant was $16,963; average loan $4,044. 54% of total undergraduate aid awarded as scholarships/grants, 46% as loans/jobs. **Non-need-based:** Awarded to 2,061 full-time undergraduates, including 598 freshmen. Scholarships awarded for academics, alumni affiliation, art, athletics, job skills, leadership, minority status, music/drama, religious affiliation.

**Application procedures. Admission:** Priority date 8/15; no deadline. No application fee. Admission notification on a rolling basis beginning on or about 10/15. Must reply by May 1 or within 4 week(s) if notified thereafter. **Financial aid:** Priority date 3/15; no closing date. FAFSA, institutional form required. Applicants notified on a rolling basis starting 3/15; must reply within 3 week(s) of notification.

**Academics. Special study options:** Double major, ESL, honors, independent study, internships, student-designed major, study abroad, teacher certification program, weekend college. Pre-MBA courses for graduated nonbusiness majors, bachelor's degree completion program for RNs, teacher licensure for those with non-teaching degrees, pre-seminary. **Credit/placement by examination:** AP, CLEP, IB, SAT, ACT, institutional tests. 32 credit hours maximum toward associate degree, 32 toward bachelor's. **Support services:** Learning center, study skills assistance, tutoring, writing center.

**Majors. Area/ethnic studies:** American. **Biology:** General. **Business:** General, accounting, business admin, finance, franchise operations, management information systems, marketing, purchasing. **Communications:** General, journalism, radio/tv. **Computer sciences:** Computer science. **Conservation:** Environmental science. **Education:** Art, biology, business, chemistry, drama/dance, early childhood, English, family/consumer sciences, French, kindergarten/preschool, mathematics, middle, music, physical, science, social studies, Spanish, special. **Family/consumer sciences:** Family systems, food/nutrition. **Foreign languages:** French, Spanish. **Health:** Athletic training, nursing admin, recreational therapy. **History:** General. **Legal studies:** Prelaw. **Liberal arts:** Arts/sciences. **Math:** General. **Parks/recreation:** General, facilities management, sports admin. **Philosophy/religion:** Philosophy, religion. **Physical sciences:** Chemistry, geology, physics, planetary. **Protective services:** Law enforcement admin. **Psychology:** General. **Public administration:** Social work. **Social sciences:** Economics, political science, sociology. **Theology:** Bible, missionary, religious ed. **Visual/performing arts:** Commercial/advertising art, dramatic, music performance, music theory/composition, studio arts.

**Most popular majors.** Business/marketing 25%, education 30%, social sciences 7%.

**Computing on campus.** 1,500 workstations in dormitories, library, computer center, student center. Dormitories wired for high-speed internet access and linked to campus network. Commuter students can connect to campus network. Online course registration, online library, helpline, repair service, wireless network available.

**Student life. Freshman orientation:** Available, $100 fee. Preregistration for classes offered. One-day program usually held in June and July. **Housing:** Guaranteed on-campus for all undergraduates. Coed dorms, single-sex dorms, apartments, fraternity/sorority housing, wellness housing available. $200 fully refundable deposit, deadline 8/15. Scholar hall available. Apartments available to seniors. **Activities:** Bands, campus ministries, choral groups, dance, drama, international student organizations, literary magazine, music ensembles, musical theater, radio station, student government, student newspaper, symphony orchestra, TV station, Christian Fellowship, Newman Club, Fellowship of Christian Athletes, international club, black student union, campus activities board, community care, adventure club, Republican/Democratic club.

**Athletics.** NCAA. **Intercollegiate:** Baseball M, basketball, cheerleading, cross-country, diving, football (tackle) M, golf, soccer, softball W, swimming, tennis W, track and field, volleyball W, wrestling M. **Intramural:** Badminton, basketball, bowling, football (non-tackle), golf, racquetball, soccer, softball, swimming, table tennis, tennis, volleyball, wrestling M. **Team name:** Eagles.

**Student services.** Adult student services, alcohol/substance abuse counseling, chaplain/spiritual director, career counseling, student employment services, financial aid counseling, health services, minority student services, personal counseling, placement for graduates, veterans' counselor. **Physically disabled:** Services for visually, speech, hearing impaired.

**Contact.** E-mail: enrollme@ashland.edu
Phone: (419) 289-5052 Toll-free number: (800) 882-1548 ext. 5052
Fax: (419) 289-5999
Thomas Mansperger, Director of Admissions, Ashland University, 401
College Avenue, Ashland, OH 44805-9981

## Baldwin-Wallace College
Berea, Ohio                                          CB member
www.bw.edu                                           CB code: 1050

- Private 4-year liberal arts college affiliated with United Methodist
  Church
- Residential campus in large town
- 3,561 degree-seeking undergraduates: 11% part-time, 57% women, 7%
  African American, 1% Asian American, 3% Hispanic American, 2%
  international
- 688 degree-seeking graduate students
- 67% of applicants admitted
- Application essay required
- 68% graduate within 6 years

**General.** Founded in 1845. Regionally accredited. Campus in Beachwood, offering evening and Saturday classes for bachelor's and master's degrees in business, professional development and executive education. **Degrees:** 720 bachelor's awarded; master's offered. **ROTC:** Army, Air Force. **Location:** 15 miles from Cleveland. **Calendar:** Semester, limited summer session. **Full-time faculty:** 167 total; 79% have terminal degrees, 8% minority, 41% women. **Part-time faculty:** 251 total; 18% have terminal degrees, 10% minority, 48% women. **Class size:** 56% < 20, 42% 20-39, less than

1% 40-49, less than 1% 50-99. **Special facilities:** Observatory, 2 art galleries, 2 theaters, conservatory of music, 2 dance studios, cybercafe, arboretum, Lyceum Square (historical site).

**Freshman class profile.** 3,498 applied, 2,335 admitted, 755 enrolled.

| Mid 50% test scores | | | |
|---|---|---|---|
| SAT critical reading: | 480-610 | Rank in top quarter: | 54% |
| SAT math: | 490-590 | Rank in top tenth: | 28% |
| SAT writing: | 470-600 | End year in good standing: | 93% |
| ACT composite: | 21-26 | Return as sophomores: | 85% |
| GPA 3.75 or higher: | 32% | Out-of-state: | 14% |
| GPA 3.50-3.74: | 18% | Live on campus: | 84% |
| GPA 3.0-3.49: | 27% | International: | 1% |
| GPA 2.0-2.99: | 22% | Fraternities: | 15% |
| | | Sororities: | 20% |

**Basis for selection.** Academic achievement (preferably 3.2 GPA) and class rank (preferably top 30%) most important. Test scores used to support data from high school record. 23 ACT, 550 SAT verbal, 550 SAT math recommended. Applicants must be graduates of accredited secondary school. Test optional for full-time, first-time freshmen. In lieu of test scores, copy of recent graded school paper required. Interview recommended for all; audition required for music, music education, music theater, and music therapy programs; portfolio recommended for art program. **Homeschooled:** Statement describing homeschool structure and mission, transcript of courses and grades, letter of recommendation (nonparent) required.

**High school preparation.** College-preparatory program required. 16 units required; 23 recommended. Required and recommended units include English 4, mathematics 3-4, social studies 2-3, history 1, science 3-4 (laboratory 2), foreign language 1-2 and computer science 3. Some flexibility in choice of subjects permitted.

**2009-2010 Annual costs.** Tuition/fees: $24,230. Conservatory tuition is higher. Room/board: $7,960. Books/supplies: $1,220. Personal expenses: $2,150.

**2009-2010 Financial aid. Need-based:** 681 full-time freshmen applied for aid; 603 were judged to have need; 603 of these received aid. Average need met was 86%. Average scholarship/grant was $14,542; average loan $3,891. 69% of total undergraduate aid awarded as scholarships/grants, 31% as loans/jobs. **Non-need-based:** Awarded to 954 full-time undergraduates, including 203 freshmen. Scholarships awarded for academics, alumni affiliation, minority status, music/drama, religious affiliation, state residency.

**Application procedures. Admission:** Priority date 3/1; no deadline. $25 fee, may be waived for applicants with need, free for online applicants. Admission notification on a rolling basis beginning on or about 11/1. Must reply by May 1 or within 3 week(s) if notified thereafter. New Student Fee of $200 refundable until May 1. **Financial aid:** Priority date 5/1, closing date 9/1. FAFSA required. Applicants notified on a rolling basis starting 2/14.

**Academics.** Weekend classes limited to nontraditional students. **Special study options:** Accelerated study, combined bachelor's/graduate degree, cross-registration, distance learning, double major, dual enrollment of high school students, ESL, exchange student, honors, independent study, internships, liberal arts/career combination, semester at sea, student-designed major, study abroad, teacher certification program, Washington semester, weekend college. 3-2 in engineering with Case Western Reserve University and Columbia University (NY); 3-2 in Social Work with Case Western Reserve University; 3/2 Accounting MBA, 3/2 Human Resources MBA and 3/2 Computer Science/Info. Systems MBA Programs. **Credit/placement by examination:** AP, CLEP, IB, SAT, ACT, institutional tests. **Support services:** Learning center, reduced course load, remedial instruction, study skills assistance, tutoring, writing center.

**Majors. Biology:** General, exercise physiology. **Business:** Accounting, business admin, finance, human resources, international, marketing, nonprofit/public. **Communications:** General, media studies, public relations. **Computer sciences:** Computer science, networking, systems analysis. **Conservation:** Economics. **Education:** General, early childhood, learning disabled, middle, music. **Foreign languages:** French, German, Spanish. **Health:** Athletic training, communication disorders, health care admin, music therapy, predental, premedicine, prepharmacy, preveterinary. **History:** General. **Interdisciplinary:** Biological/physical sciences, global studies, neuroscience. **Math:** General. **Parks/recreation:** Health/fitness, sports admin. **Philosophy/religion:** Philosophy, religion. **Physical sciences:** Chemistry, physics. **Protective services:** Criminal justice. **Psychology:** General. **Social sciences:** Econometrics, economics, political science, sociology. **Visual/performing arts:** Art, art history/conservation, film/cinema, music history, music performance, music theory/composition, musical theater, piano/organ, studio arts, voice/opera. **Other:** Pre-Engineering.

**Most popular majors.** Biology 7%, business/marketing 30%, communications/journalism 8%, education 10%, psychology 6%, visual/performing arts 10%.

**Computing on campus.** 561 workstations in dormitories, library, computer center, student center. Dormitories wired for high-speed internet access and linked to campus network. Commuter students can connect to campus network. Online course registration, online library, helpline, repair service, student web hosting, wireless network available.

**Student life. Freshman orientation:** Mandatory, $75 fee. Preregistration for classes offered. Two-day program held in June, July, August. **Policies:** All full-time students required to live on campus first and second year. Residency exemptions made for commuting students living with families. **Housing:** Guaranteed on-campus for freshmen. Coed dorms, single-sex dorms, special housing for disabled, apartments, fraternity/sorority housing available. Housing for single mothers and children; living and learning center. **Activities:** Bands, campus ministries, choral groups, dance, drama, film society, international student organizations, literary magazine, music ensembles, Model UN, musical theater, opera, radio station, student government, student newspaper, symphony orchestra, TV station, Campus Crusade for Christ, Hillel, Newman student organization, College Democrats, College Republicans, black student alliance, Hispanic American student association, Middle Eastern student alliance, peer educators, Habitat for Humanity.

**Athletics.** NCAA. **Intercollegiate:** Baseball M, basketball, cross-country, diving, football (tackle) M, golf, soccer, softball W, swimming, tennis, track and field, volleyball W, wrestling M. **Intramural:** Badminton, basketball, football (non-tackle), football (tackle) M, golf, racquetball, soccer, softball, tennis, volleyball, wrestling M. **Team name:** Yellow Jackets.

**Student services.** Adult student services, alcohol/substance abuse counseling, chaplain/spiritual director, career counseling, student employment services, financial aid counseling, health services, minority student services, personal counseling. **Physically disabled:** Services for visually, speech, hearing impaired.

**Contact.** E-mail: admission@bw.edu
Phone: (440) 826-2222 Toll-free number: (877) 292-7759
Fax: (440) 826-3830
Susan Dileno, Vice President of Enrollment Management, Baldwin-Wallace College, 275 Eastland Road, Berea, OH 44017-2088

## Bluffton University
**Bluffton, Ohio**
www.bluffton.edu                                      **CB code: 1067**

- Private 4-year liberal arts college affiliated with Mennonite Church
- Residential campus in small town
- 943 degree-seeking undergraduates: 4% part-time, 51% women, 7% African American, 1% Asian American, 2% Hispanic American, 2% international
- 48 degree-seeking graduate students
- 66% of applicants admitted
- SAT or ACT (ACT writing optional) required
- 64% graduate within 6 years

**General.** Founded in 1899. Regionally accredited. Christian faith, values, and service to others in the Anabaptist, peace church tradition. **Degrees:** 216 bachelor's awarded; master's offered. **Location:** 15 miles from Lima, 65 miles from Toledo. **Calendar:** Semester, limited summer session. **Full-time faculty:** 62 total; 73% have terminal degrees, 2% minority, 34% women. **Part-time faculty:** 47 total; 11% have terminal degrees, 6% minority, 45% women. **Class size:** 58% < 20, 34% 20-39, 7% 40-49, less than 1% 50-99, less than 1% >100. **Special facilities:** Nature preserve.

**Freshman class profile.** 1,674 applied, 1,113 admitted, 257 enrolled.

| Mid 50% test scores | | | |
|---|---|---|---|
| | | GPA 2.0-2.99: | 40% |
| SAT critical reading: | 420-570 | Rank in top quarter: | 33% |
| SAT math: | 450-600 | Rank in top tenth: | 14% |
| ACT composite: | 19-24 | Return as sophomores: | 75% |
| GPA 3.75 or higher: | 20% | Out-of-state: | 16% |
| GPA 3.50-3.74: | 11% | Live on campus: | 96% |
| GPA 3.0-3.49: | 29% | International: | 1% |

**Basis for selection.** Class rank, school achievement record, and test scores very important. Campus visit and interview strongly recommended. Essay required for academically weak students; audition and portfolio required for scholarships in music and art. **Homeschooled:** Interview required.

**High school preparation.** College-preparatory program recommended. 16 units recommended. Recommended units include English 4, mathematics 3, social studies 3, science 3 and foreign language 3.

**2009-2010 Annual costs.** Tuition/fees: $24,044. Room/board: $7,970. Books/supplies: $1,150. Personal expenses: $1,430.

**Application procedures. Admission:** Priority date 5/1; deadline 8/15 (receipt date). $20 fee, may be waived for applicants with need, free for online applicants. Admission notification on a rolling basis beginning on or about 6/1.

**Academics. Special study options:** Accelerated study, distance learning, double major, dual enrollment of high school students, honors, independent study, internships, liberal arts/career combination, student-designed major, study abroad, teacher certification program, Washington semester. Degree-completion program for working adults 25 years and older. **Credit/placement by examination:** AP, CLEP, SAT, ACT, institutional tests. 20 credit hours maximum toward bachelor's degree. **Support services:** Learning center, reduced course load, remedial instruction, study skills assistance, tutoring, writing center.

**Majors. Biology:** General. **Business:** Accounting, business admin, management information systems, organizational behavior. **Communications:** General. **Computer sciences:** Information technology. **Education:** General, art, biology, business, chemistry, early childhood, elementary, English, health, history, kindergarten/preschool, mathematics, mentally handicapped, middle, music, physical, physics, science, secondary, social studies, special. **Family/consumer sciences:** Clothing/textiles, food/nutrition. **Foreign languages:** Spanish. **Health:** Premedicine. **History:** General. **Math:** General. **Parks/recreation:** Facilities management, health/fitness, sports admin. **Philosophy/religion:** Religion. **Physical sciences:** Chemistry, physics. **Protective services:** Criminal justice. **Psychology:** General. **Public administration:** Social work. **Social sciences:** General, economics, sociology. **Theology:** Youth ministry. **Visual/performing arts:** Art.

**Most popular majors.** Business/marketing 32%, education 19%, parks/recreation 8%, public administration/social services 8%.

**Computing on campus.** 125 workstations in dormitories, library, computer center, student center. Dormitories wired for high-speed internet access and linked to campus network. Commuter students can connect to campus network. Online course registration, online library, helpline, repair service, student web hosting, wireless network available.

**Student life. Freshman orientation:** Mandatory. Preregistration for classes offered. Fall orientation begins Friday before classes and continues through first week of classes. Additional 1-day event held over summer; students can choose 1 of 4 dates. **Policies:** No alcoholic beverages or tobacco allowed on campus. Honor system applies to all student activities. Students should feel comfortable with emphasis on faith and values. Voluntary chapel service once each week. All traditional undergraduate students required to live on campus or commute from home. **Housing:** Guaranteed on-campus for all undergraduates. Coed dorms, single-sex dorms available. **Activities:** Bands, campus ministries, choral groups, dance, drama, international student organizations, literary magazine, music ensembles, musical theater, radio station, student government, student newspaper, departmental clubs, Brothers and Sisters in Christ, peace club, Habitat for Humanity, Fellowship of Christian Athletes, African American student organization, peer awareness leaders, College Republicans, Young Democrats.

**Athletics.** NCAA. **Intercollegiate:** Baseball M, basketball, cheerleading M, cross-country, football (tackle) M, soccer, softball W, track and field, volleyball W. **Intramural:** Basketball, bowling, football (non-tackle), softball, volleyball. **Team name:** Beavers.

**Student services.** Alcohol/substance abuse counseling, chaplain/spiritual director, career counseling, student employment services, financial aid counseling, health services, minority student services, personal counseling, placement for graduates. **Physically disabled:** Services for visually, hearing impaired.

**Contact.** E-mail: admissions@bluffton.edu
Phone: (419) 358-3257 Toll-free number: (800) 488-3257
Fax: (419) 358-3081
Chris Jebsen, Director of Admissions, Bluffton University, 1 University Drive, Bluffton, OH 45817-2104

## Bowling Green State University
**Bowling Green, Ohio** — CB member
**www.bgsu.edu** — CB code: 1069

- Public 4-year university
- Residential campus in large town
- 14,023 degree-seeking undergraduates: 7% part-time, 53% women, 11% African American, 1% Asian American, 3% Hispanic American, 1% Native American, 2% international
- 2,564 degree-seeking graduate students

- 89% of applicants admitted
- SAT or ACT (ACT writing optional) required
- 60% graduate within 6 years

**General.** Founded in 1910. Regionally accredited. **Degrees:** 3,265 bachelor's awarded; master's, doctoral offered. **ROTC:** Army, Air Force. **Location:** 23 miles from Toledo. **Calendar:** Semester, limited summer session. **Full-time faculty:** 795 total; 75% have terminal degrees, 18% minority, 45% women. **Part-time faculty:** 157 total; 7% minority, 53% women. **Class size:** 32% < 20, 55% 20-39, 6% 40-49, 5% 50-99, 2% >100. **Special facilities:** Planetarium, film theater, sound recording archives, popular culture library, marine biology laboratory, educational memorabilia center.

**Freshman class profile.** 10,418 applied, 9,253 admitted, 3,163 enrolled.

| Mid 50% test scores | | | |
|---|---|---|---|
| SAT critical reading: | 450-580 | GPA 2.0-2.99: | 35% |
| SAT math: | 450-570 | Rank in top quarter: | 35% |
| SAT writing: | 450-550 | Rank in top tenth: | 12% |
| ACT composite: | 19-24 | End year in good standing: | 75% |
| GPA 3.75 or higher: | 16% | Return as sophomores: | 75% |
| GPA 3.50-3.74: | 14% | Out-of-state: | 11% |
| GPA 3.0-3.49: | 35% | Live on campus: | 88% |
| | | International: | 2% |

**Basis for selection.** Admissions decision based on high school sixth semester GPA and ACT or SAT test scores. Interview recommended for all; audition required for music; portfolio required for art programs. Essays required for honors program. **Homeschooled:** Transcript of courses and grades required. **Learning Disabled:** Prospective students encouraged to arrange an interview with Disability Services.

**High school preparation.** College-preparatory program recommended. Recommended units include English 4, mathematics 3, social studies 3, science 3 (laboratory 2), foreign language 2 and visual/performing arts 1.

**2009-2010 Annual costs.** Tuition/fees: $9,060; $16,368 out-of-state. Room/board: $7,670. Books/supplies: $1,216. Personal expenses: $2,422.

**2008-2009 Financial aid. Need-based:** 2,659 full-time freshmen applied for aid; 2,098 were judged to have need; 2,087 of these received aid. Average met was 77%. Average scholarship/grant was $6,058; average loan $5,924. 36% of total undergraduate aid awarded as scholarships/grants, 64% as loans/jobs. **Non-need-based:** Awarded to 2,837 full-time undergraduates, including 820 freshmen. Scholarships awarded for academics, alumni affiliation, art, athletics, leadership, minority status, music/drama, ROTC, state residency.

**Application procedures. Admission:** Priority date 2/1; deadline 7/15 (postmark date). $40 fee, may be waived for applicants with need. Admission notification on a rolling basis beginning on or about 10/1. Must reply by 5/1. **Financial aid:** No deadline. FAFSA required. Applicants notified on a rolling basis starting 4/15; must reply within 3 week(s) of notification.

**Academics.** Evening degree programs and career counseling offered for adults in the greater community. **Special study options:** Accelerated study, combined bachelor's/graduate degree, cooperative education, cross-registration, distance learning, double major, dual enrollment of high school students, ESL, exchange student, honors, independent study, internships, liberal arts/career combination, student-designed major, study abroad, teacher certification program, Washington semester. **Credit/placement by examination:** AP, CLEP, SAT, ACT, institutional tests. 30 hours toward bachelor's degree through portfolio program. **Support services:** Learning center, pre-admission summer program, reduced course load, remedial instruction, study skills assistance, tutoring, writing center.

**Majors. Architecture:** Environmental design, interior. **Area/ethnic studies:** African, African-American, American, Asian, Chicano/Hispanic-American/Latino, European, Latin American, Russian/Slavic, women's. **Biology:** General, bacteriology, biochemistry, parasitology. **Business:** General, accounting, actuarial science, business admin, executive assistant, fashion, finance, hospitality admin, human resources, insurance, international, labor relations, logistics, management information systems, market research, office management, operations, organizational behavior, real estate, retailing, sales/distribution, tourism promotion, tourism/travel. **Communications:** General, advertising, broadcast journalism, journalism, public relations, radio/tv. **Computer sciences:** General. **Conservation:** Management/policy. **Education:** General, art, biology, business, chemistry, college student counseling, computer, Deaf/hearing impaired, drama/dance, elementary, English, family/consumer sciences, foreign languages, health, history, instructional media, kindergarten/preschool, learning disabled, mathematics, mentally handicapped, middle, multi-level teacher, multiple handicapped, music, physical, physics, sales/marketing, science, social science, social studies, special, speech, technology/industrial arts, trade/industrial, voc/tech. **Engineering:** Operations research. **Engineering technology:** Aerospace, construction, electrical, electromechanical, environmental, industrial, mechanical, quality control. **Family/consumer sciences:** General, aging, child development, clothing/

textiles, family studies, family systems, family/community services, food/nutrition. **Foreign languages:** Classics, French, German, Latin, Russian, Spanish. **Health:** Art therapy, athletic training, audiology/speech pathology, clinical lab science, communication disorders, dietetics, environmental health, health care admin, medical records admin, nursing (RN), predental, premedicine, vocational rehab counseling. **History:** General. **Interdisciplinary:** Gerontology, neuroscience. **Legal studies:** Prelaw. **Liberal arts:** Arts/sciences. **Math:** General, statistics. **Parks/recreation:** General, sports admin. **Personal/culinary services:** Restaurant/catering. **Philosophy/religion:** Philosophy. **Physical sciences:** Chemistry, geochemistry, geology, geophysics, paleontology, physics. **Protective services:** Corrections, criminal justice, law enforcement admin, police science. **Psychology:** General. **Public administration:** General, social work. **Social sciences:** General, economics, geography, international relations, political science, sociology. **Theology:** Sacred music. **Visual/performing arts:** Art, art history/conservation, ceramics, commercial/advertising art, crafts, design, dramatic, drawing, fashion design, fiber arts, film/cinema, jazz, metal/jewelry, music history, music performance, music theory/composition, musicology, painting, photography, piano/organ, printmaking, sculpture, studio arts, voice/opera. **Other:** Business operations support and secretarial services, Exercise, movement, Family and consumer economics and related services, Physical therapy/therapist, Popular culture.

**Most popular majors.** Business/marketing 15%, education 22%, English 6%, health sciences 7%, visual/performing arts 8%.

**Computing on campus.** 1,500 workstations in dormitories, library, computer center, student center. Dormitories wired for high-speed internet access and linked to campus network. Commuter students can connect to campus network. Online course registration, online library, helpline, repair service, student web hosting, wireless network available.

**Student life. Freshman orientation:** Available. Preregistration for classes offered. Normally held in summer. **Housing:** Guaranteed on-campus for freshmen. Coed dorms, fraternity/sorority housing, wellness housing available. $200 deposit, deadline 5/1. No-alcohol wings, nonsmoking areas, residential housing communities available. **Activities:** Bands, choral groups, dance, drama, film society, international student organizations, literary magazine, music ensembles, musical theater, radio station, student government, student newspaper, symphony orchestra, TV station, Active Christians Today, African Peoples Association, Asian Communities, United Latino Student Union, World Student Association, Women's Group, College Democrats, College Republicans, Habitat for Humanity, Environmental Action Group.

**Athletics.** NCAA. **Intercollegiate:** Baseball M, basketball, cross-country, football (tackle) M, golf, gymnastics W, ice hockey M, soccer, softball W, swimming W, tennis W, track and field W, volleyball W. **Intramural:** Basketball, football (non-tackle), golf, racquetball, soccer, softball, swimming W, tennis W, track and field W, volleyball. **Team name:** Falcons.

**Student services.** Adult student services, alcohol/substance abuse counseling, career counseling, services for economically disadvantaged, student employment services, financial aid counseling, health services, legal services, minority student services, personal counseling, placement for graduates, veterans' counselor, women's services. **Physically disabled:** Services for visually, speech, hearing impaired.

**Contact.** E-mail: choosebgsu@bgsu.edu
Phone: (419) 372-2478 Toll-free number: (866) Cho-osebgsu
Fax: (419) 372-6955
Gary Swegan, Assistant Vice President/Director of Admissions, Bowling Green State University, 110 McFall Center, Bowling Green, OH 43403-0085

## Bryant & Stratton College: Eastlake
Eastlake, Ohio
www.bryantstratton.edu                    CB code: 3251

- For-profit 4-year business college
- Commuter campus in small town
- 806 degree-seeking undergraduates: 84% women
- Interview required

**General. Degrees:** 2 bachelor's, 10 associate awarded. **Location:** 15 miles from downtown Cleveland. **Calendar:** Continuous, limited summer session. **Full-time faculty:** 20 total. **Part-time faculty:** 35 total.

**Basis for selection.** Open admission. Student's evaluation and diagnostic tests must show qualification for at least pre-college, preparatory math and English courses. **Learning Disabled:** Students with learning disability must provide instructional effectiveness plan from high school counselor.

**2009-2010 Annual costs.** Books/supplies: $1,800. Personal expenses: $300.

**2008-2009 Financial aid. Non-need-based:** Scholarships awarded for academics.

**Application procedures. Admission:** Closing date 9/12 (receipt date). $35 fee. Admission notification on a rolling basis. **Financial aid:** No deadline. FAFSA required. Applicants notified on a rolling basis.

**Academics.** ACTIVUM learning system facilitates students in developing technical and career-based skills through field trips, portfolio presentations, computer simulations and internship opportunities. **Special study options:** Accelerated study, distance learning, double major, dual enrollment of high school students, independent study, internships. Professional skills center offers medical coding courses and computer certification. **Credit/placement by examination:** AP, CLEP, institutional tests. 12 credit hours maximum toward associate degree, 12 toward bachelor's. **Support services:** Remedial instruction, study skills assistance, tutoring.

**Majors. Business:** Business admin.

**Computing on campus.** 400 workstations in library, computer center. Commuter students can connect to campus network. Online library, helpline, repair service, wireless network available.

**Student life. Freshman orientation:** Mandatory. Preregistration for classes offered. Various 4-hour sessions over 1-2 days prior to start of each term. **Activities:** Student government, student newspaper, student council, Institute of Management Accountants, PC users group, campus ambassador society.

**Athletics.** NJCAA. **Intercollegiate:** Soccer M. **Team name:** Bobcats.

**Student services.** Adult student services, student employment services, financial aid counseling, placement for graduates. **Physically disabled:** Services for visually, speech, hearing impaired.

**Contact.** E-mail: mejohnson@bryantstratton.edu
Phone: (440) 510-1112 Fax: (440) 306-2015
Melanie Johnson, Director of Admissions, Bryant & Stratton College: Eastlake, 35350 Curtis Boulevard, Eastlake, OH 44095

## Bryant & Stratton College: Parma
Parma, Ohio
www.bryantstratton.edu                    CB code: 0577

- For-profit 4-year nursing and junior college
- Commuter campus in small city
- 662 degree-seeking undergraduates: 39% part-time, 82% women, 21% African American, 10% Hispanic American
- Interview required

**General.** Founded in 1854. Regionally accredited. On-line classes available. **Degrees:** 10 bachelor's, 100 associate awarded. **Location:** 10 miles from Cleveland. **Calendar:** Semester, extensive summer session. **Full-time faculty:** 17 total; 12% have terminal degrees, 47% women. **Part-time faculty:** 40 total; 50% women. **Class size:** 81% < 20, 18% 20-39, less than 1% 40-49.

**Freshman class profile.** 416 applied, 245 admitted, 221 enrolled.

**Basis for selection.** Open admission, but selective for some programs. Test of Adult Basic Education required; high school transcript preferred. Portfolio recommended. **Learning Disabled:** IEP plan required.

**2009-2010 Annual costs.** Books/supplies: $1,600. Personal expenses: $3,111.

**2008-2009 Financial aid.** All financial aid based on need.

**Application procedures. Admission:** No deadline. No application fee. Application must be submitted on paper. Admission notification on a rolling basis. **Financial aid:** No deadline. FAFSA required. Applicants notified on a rolling basis starting 6/1.

**Academics. Special study options:** Combined bachelor's/graduate degree, distance learning, internships. **Credit/placement by examination:** AP, CLEP, IB, institutional tests. **Support services:** Learning center, remedial instruction, study skills assistance, tutoring.

**Majors. Business:** Business admin.

**Computing on campus.** 86 workstations in library, computer center. Online library, wireless network available.

**Student life. Freshman orientation:** Mandatory. Preregistration for classes offered.

**Student services.** Adult student services, career counseling, student employment services, financial aid counseling, placement for graduates.

**Contact.** E-mail: atinman@bryantstratton.edu
Phone: (216) 265-3151 ext. 229 Fax: (216) 265-0325
Adriane Inman, Director of Admissions, Bryant & Stratton College: Parma, 12955 Snow Road, Parma, OH 44130-1013

## Capital University
**Columbus, Ohio**      **CB member**
**www.capital.edu**      **CB code: 1099**

▶ Private 4-year university affiliated with Evangelical Lutheran Church in America

▶ Residential campus in very large city

▶ 2,519 degree-seeking undergraduates: 8% part-time, 59% women, 9% African American, 2% Asian American, 2% Hispanic American, 1% international

▶ 901 degree-seeking graduate students

▶ 75% of applicants admitted

▶ SAT or ACT (ACT writing optional) required

▶ 64% graduate within 6 years; 16% enter graduate study

**General.** Founded in 1830. Regionally accredited. **Degrees:** 572 bachelor's awarded; master's, professional offered. **ROTC:** Army, Air Force. **Location:** 5 miles from downtown. **Calendar:** Semester, limited summer session. **Full-time faculty:** 203 total; 68% have terminal degrees, 12% minority, 49% women. **Part-time faculty:** 189 total; 24% have terminal degrees, 12% minority, 42% women. **Class size:** 60% < 20, 38% 20-39, less than 1% 40-49, less than 1% 50-99.

**Freshman class profile.** 3,510 applied, 2,631 admitted, 610 enrolled.

| Mid 50% test scores | | GPA 2.0-2.99: | 18% |
|---|---|---|---|
| SAT critical reading: | 480-590 | Rank in top quarter: | 52% |
| SAT math: | 480-600 | Rank in top tenth: | 22% |
| SAT writing: | 460-580 | Return as sophomores: | 74% |
| ACT composite: | 21-27 | Out-of-state: | 10% |
| GPA 3.75 or higher: | 31% | Live on campus: | 88% |
| GPA 3.50-3.74: | 18% | International: | 1% |
| GPA 3.0-3.49: | 33% | | |

**Basis for selection.** Academic achievement in college-preparatory curriculum most important. Recommendations, test scores, and extracurricular activities considered. Talent/ability are considered for admission into the Conservatory of Music. Interview recommended for all; audition required for music program; portfolio recommended for art, art therapy programs. **Homeschooled:** Statement describing homeschool structure and mission, transcript of courses and grades, letter of recommendation (nonparent) required.

**High school preparation.** College-preparatory program recommended. 18 units recommended. Recommended units include English 4, mathematics 3, social studies 3, science 3 (laboratory 2), foreign language 2 and visual/performing arts 1. Chemistry and algebra II for nursing applicants. One fine arts recommended.

**2009-2010 Annual costs.** Tuition/fees: $28,480. Room/board: $7,510. Books/supplies: $1,000. Personal expenses: $1,730.

**2008-2009 Financial aid. Non-need-based:** Scholarships awarded for academics, alumni affiliation, art, minority status, music/drama, religious affiliation, ROTC, state residency.

**Application procedures. Admission:** No deadline. $25 fee, may be waived for applicants with need, free for online applicants. Admission notification on a rolling basis beginning on or about 9/30. Must reply by May 1 or within 2 week(s) if notified thereafter. **Financial aid:** Priority date 2/28; no closing date. FAFSA required. Applicants notified on a rolling basis starting 3/1; must reply by 5/1.

**Academics.** Teacher certification for learning disabilities and reading. Paralegal certification available from law school. **Special study options:** Accelerated study, combined bachelor's/graduate degree, cooperative education, cross-registration, double major, dual enrollment of high school students, ESL, exchange student, external degree, honors, independent study, internships, liberal arts/career combination, student-designed major, study abroad, teacher certification program, Washington semester. Dual degree engineering program with Washington University, St. Louis, and Case Western Reserve; 3-2 occupational therapy program with Washington University, St.

Louis. **Credit/placement by examination:** AP, CLEP, IB, SAT, ACT, institutional tests. 27 credit hours maximum toward bachelor's degree. **Support services:** Learning center, reduced course load, remedial instruction, study skills assistance, tutoring, writing center.

**Majors. Biology:** General, biochemistry. **Business:** Accounting, business admin, managerial economics, marketing. **Communications:** General, organizational, public relations, radio/tv. **Computer sciences:** Computer science. **Conservation:** Environmental science. **Education:** Early childhood, middle, music, physical, special. **Engineering:** Computer. **Foreign languages:** French, Spanish. **Health:** Art therapy, athletic training, nursing (RN), nursing admin. **History:** General. **Math:** General. **Parks/recreation:** Exercise sciences, health/fitness. **Philosophy/religion:** Philosophy, religion. **Physical sciences:** Chemistry. **Psychology:** General. **Public administration:** General, social work. **Social sciences:** Criminology, economics, international relations, political science, sociology. **Visual/performing arts:** Art, dramatic, jazz, music management, music performance, music theory/composition, piano/organ, voice/opera.

**Most popular majors.** Business/marketing 13%, education 14%, health sciences 24%, public administration/social services 8%, social sciences 7%.

**Computing on campus.** 454 workstations in dormitories, library, computer center, student center. Dormitories wired for high-speed internet access and linked to campus network. Commuter students can connect to campus network. Online course registration, online library, helpline, wireless network available.

**Student life. Freshman orientation:** Mandatory, $200 fee. One-day program in summer, 5-day program before start of classes. **Housing:** Guaranteed on-campus for freshmen. Coed dorms, special housing for disabled, apartments, fraternity/sorority housing, wellness housing available. $100 non-refundable deposit, deadline 5/1. Honors housing, self-governing areas, and group cluster housing available. **Activities:** Bands, campus ministries, choral groups, dance, drama, international student organizations, literary magazine, music ensembles, musical theater, radio station, student government, student newspaper, symphony orchestra, TV station, black student union, Young Republicans, Campus Democrats, Circle K, Ebony Brotherhood Association, international student association, Capateers (volunteers), Habitat for Humanity, university programming.

**Athletics.** NCAA. **Intercollegiate:** Baseball M, basketball, cross-country, football (tackle) M, golf, soccer, softball W, tennis, track and field, volleyball W. **Intramural:** Basketball, bowling, football (non-tackle), softball, volleyball. **Team name:** Crusaders.

**Student services.** Chaplain/spiritual director, career counseling, student employment services, financial aid counseling, health services, minority student services, personal counseling, placement for graduates, veterans' counselor.

**Contact.** E-mail: admissions@capital.edu
Phone: (614) 236-6101 Toll-free number: (866) 544-6175
Fax: (614) 236-6926
Amanda Steiner, Director of Admission, Capital University, 1 College and Main, Columbus, OH 43209-2394

## Case Western Reserve University
**Cleveland, Ohio**      **CB member**
**www.case.edu**      **CB code: 1105**

▶ Private 4-year university

▶ Residential campus in very large city

▶ 4,145 degree-seeking undergraduates: 2% part-time, 43% women, 5% African American, 16% Asian American, 3% Hispanic American, 5% international

▶ 5,329 degree-seeking graduate students

▶ 70% of applicants admitted

▶ SAT or ACT with writing, application essay required

▶ 80% graduate within 6 years; 44% enter graduate study

**General.** Founded in 1826. Regionally accredited. **Degrees:** 958 bachelor's awarded; master's, doctoral, professional offered. **ROTC:** Army, Air Force. **Location:** 4 miles from downtown. **Calendar:** Semester, extensive summer session. **Full-time faculty:** 746 total; 90% have terminal degrees, 18% minority, 42% women. **Part-time faculty:** 171 total; 63% have terminal degrees, 8% minority, 39% women. **Class size:** 61% < 20, 25% 20-39, 4% 40-49, 6% 50-99, 4% >100. **Special facilities:** Biology field station, observatory, interdisciplinary research centers, natural history museum, historical society, botanical garden.

**Freshman class profile.** 7,998 applied, 5,599 admitted, 966 enrolled.

| Mid 50% test scores | | | |
|---|---|---|---|
| SAT critical reading: | 590-700 | Return as sophomores: | 91% |
| SAT math: | 650-740 | Out-of-state: | 53% |
| SAT writing: | 590-690 | Live on campus: | 97% |
| ACT composite: | 28-32 | International: | 9% |
| Rank in top quarter: | 87% | Fraternities: | 30% |
| Rank in top tenth: | 65% | Sororities: | 25% |

**Basis for selection.** School achievement record and test scores most important. School and community activities, essays, recommendations, and interview also considered. Special consideration to applicants from culturally, educationally, or economically disadvantaged backgrounds. IELTS, AP International English test, or TOEFL required for all international students. Interview recommended for all; audition required for music, music education programs; portfolio required for art education program. Writing sample required. **Homeschooled:** Transcript of courses and grades, interview required. At least 3 SAT Subject Tests highly recommended. Students encouraged to submit at least 2 letters from outside instructors or employers.

**High school preparation.** College-preparatory program required. 16 units required. Required and recommended units include English 4, mathematics 3-4, social studies 3-4, science 3 (laboratory 2-3) and foreign language 2-3. 3 laboratory science recommended. 4 math, 1 chemistry and physics recommended for engineering. 3 laboratory science (1 chemistry) recommended for science, math, and premedical.

**2009-2010 Annual costs.** Tuition/fees: $36,238. Room/board: $10,890. Books/supplies: $1,125. Personal expenses: $1,325.

**2009-2010 Financial aid. Need-based:** 749 full-time freshmen applied for aid; 617 were judged to have need; 617 of these received aid. Average need met was 80%. Average scholarship/grant was $25,196; average loan $6,869. 66% of total undergraduate aid awarded as scholarships/grants, 34% as loans/jobs. **Non-need-based:** Awarded to 3,288 full-time undergraduates, including 782 freshmen. Scholarships awarded for academics, art, leadership, music/drama.

**Application procedures. Admission:** Closing date 1/15 (postmark date). No application fee. Application must be submitted online. Admission notification 4/1. Must reply by 5/1. **Financial aid:** Priority date 2/15; no closing date. FAFSA, institutional form required. Applicants notified on a rolling basis starting 3/15; must reply by 5/1 or within 2 week(s) of notification.

**Academics.** Preprofessional Scholars Program gives talented undergraduates conditional acceptances to graduate schools of medicine, dentistry, law, and social work. Most programs allow students to pursue combined bachelor's/master's. **Special study options:** Accelerated study, combined bachelor's/graduate degree, cooperative education, cross-registration, double major, dual enrollment of high school students, ESL, exchange student, honors, independent study, internships, liberal arts/career combination, student-designed major, study abroad, teacher certification program, Washington semester. Exchange program with Fisk University, 3-2 binary program in engineering, biochemistry, and astronomy. **Credit/placement by examination:** AP, CLEP, IB, institutional tests. **Support services:** Learning center, pre-admission summer program, reduced course load, study skills assistance, tutoring, writing center.

**Majors. Area/ethnic studies:** American, Asian, French, German, Japanese, women's. **Biology:** General, biochemistry, evolutionary. **Business:** Accounting, business admin. **Computer sciences:** General, computer science. **Conservation:** Environmental studies. **Education:** Art, music. **Engineering:** General, aerospace, biomedical, chemical, civil, computer, electrical, materials, materials science, mechanical, physics, polymer, systems. **Family/consumer sciences:** Human nutrition. **Foreign languages:** Classics, comparative lit, French, German, Spanish. **Health:** Communication disorders, dietetics, nursing (RN). **History:** General, science/technology. **Interdisciplinary:** Cognitive science, gerontology, natural sciences, nutrition sciences. **Math:** General, applied, statistics. **Philosophy/religion:** Philosophy, religion. **Physical sciences:** Astronomy, chemistry, geology, physics. **Psychology:** General. **Social sciences:** Anthropology, economics, international relations, political science, sociology. **Visual/performing arts:** Art history/conservation, dramatic. **Other:** Pre-architecture, Systems biology.

**Most popular majors.** Biology 11%, business/marketing 8%, engineering/engineering technologies 24%, health sciences 10%, physical sciences 6%, psychology 8%, social sciences 12%.

**Computing on campus.** 415 workstations in dormitories, library, computer center, student center. Dormitories wired for high-speed internet access and linked to campus network. Commuter students can connect to campus network. Online course registration, online library, helpline, repair service, student web hosting, wireless network available.

**Student life. Freshman orientation:** Mandatory, $370 fee. Preregistration for classes offered. Four 3-day sessions beginning in July. **Housing:**

Guaranteed on-campus for freshmen. Coed dorms, apartments, fraternity/sorority housing, wellness housing available. Residential colleges for first-year students. Secured female-only floor available. Special-interest housing available. **Activities:** Bands, campus ministries, choral groups, dance, drama, film society, international student organizations, literary magazine, music ensembles, Model UN, musical theater, radio station, student government, student newspaper, symphony orchestra, University Christian Movement, Hillel Foundation, InterVarsity Christian Fellowship, African-American society, College Democrats, College Republicans, Habitat for Humanity, animal rights & ethics society.

**Athletics.** NCAA. **Intercollegiate:** Baseball M, basketball, cross-country, football (tackle) M, soccer, softball W, swimming, tennis, track and field, volleyball W, wrestling M. **Intramural:** Badminton, basketball, bowling, cross-country, football (non-tackle), football (tackle) M, golf, racquetball, soccer, softball, squash, swimming, table tennis, tennis, track and field, volleyball, water polo, weight lifting, wrestling M. **Team name:** Spartans.

**Student services.** Adult student services, alcohol/substance abuse counseling, chaplain/spiritual director, career counseling, student employment services, financial aid counseling, health services, legal services, minority student services, personal counseling, placement for graduates, veterans' counselor, women's services. **Physically disabled:** Services for visually, speech, hearing impaired.

**Contact.** E-mail: admission@case.edu
Phone: (216) 368-4450 Fax: (216) 368-5111
Robert McCullough, Director, Case Western Reserve University, Wolstein Hall, Cleveland, OH 44106-7055

## Cedarville University
**Cedarville, Ohio**
**www.cedarville.edu** — CB code: 1151

- Private 4-year university and liberal arts college affiliated with Baptist faith
- Residential campus in small town
- 2,926 degree-seeking undergraduates: 3% part-time, 54% women, 2% African American, 1% Asian American, 3% Hispanic American, 1% international
- 41 degree-seeking graduate students
- 76% of applicants admitted
- SAT or ACT (ACT writing recommended), application essay required
- 70% graduate within 6 years

**General.** Founded in 1887. Regionally accredited. **Degrees:** 646 bachelor's awarded; master's offered. **ROTC:** Army, Air Force. **Location:** 12 miles from Springfield, 20 miles from Dayton. **Calendar:** Semester, limited summer session. **Full-time faculty:** 212 total; 58% have terminal degrees, 6% minority, 27% women. **Part-time faculty:** 20 total; 5% minority, 60% women. **Class size:** 64% < 20, 27% 20-39, 3% 40-49, 5% 50-99, 1% >100.

**Freshman class profile.** 2,949 applied, 2,229 admitted, 729 enrolled.

| Mid 50% test scores | | | |
|---|---|---|---|
| SAT critical reading: | 530-650 | GPA 2.0-2.99: | 7% |
| SAT math: | 530-640 | Rank in top quarter: | 21% |
| SAT writing: | 520-630 | End year in good standing: | 93% |
| ACT composite: | 23-29 | Return as sophomores: | 82% |
| GPA 3.75 or higher: | 40% | Out-of-state: | 63% |
| GPA 3.50-3.74: | 32% | Live on campus: | 98% |
| GPA 3.0-3.49: | 21% | International: | 1% |

**Basis for selection.** Clear testimony of personal faith in Jesus Christ, evidence of consistent Christian lifestyle, above-average academic performance (academic records, class rank, test scores), personal references considered. Applications reviewed on a rolling basis. SAT and SAT Subject Tests or ACT recommended. Audition required for music majors; interview recommended for academically marginal students. Interview required for pre-pharmacy students. **Learning Disabled:** Students encouraged to contact Coordinator of Disabilities Services.

**High school preparation.** College-preparatory program required. Recommended units include English 4, mathematics 4, social studies 3, science 3 (laboratory 3) and foreign language 3. Additional math and science recommended for nursing, science, engineering, and math applicants.

**2009-2010 Annual costs.** Tuition/fees: $22,304. Room/board: $5,006. Books/supplies: $900. Personal expenses: $1,450.

**2008-2009 Financial aid. Need-based:** 685 full-time freshmen applied for aid; 549 were judged to have need; 548 of these received aid. Average need met was 38%. Average scholarship/grant was $3,316; average loan

$4,761. 49% of total undergraduate aid awarded as scholarships/grants, 51% as loans/jobs. **Non-need-based:** Awarded to 2,192 full-time undergraduates, including 714 freshmen. Scholarships awarded for academics, alumni affiliation, athletics, leadership, minority status, music/drama, ROTC, state residency.

**Application procedures. Admission:** Priority date 3/1; no deadline. $30 fee, may be waived for applicants with need. Admission notification on a rolling basis beginning on or about 8/1. Must reply by May 1 or within 2 week(s) if notified thereafter. **Financial aid:** Priority date 3/1; no closing date. FAFSA required. Applicants notified on a rolling basis starting 3/1; must reply within 4 week(s) of notification.

**Academics. Special study options:** Accelerated study, cooperative education, distance learning, double major, dual enrollment of high school students, honors, independent study, internships, liberal arts/career combination, student-designed major, study abroad, teacher certification program, Washington semester. **Credit/placement by examination:** AP, CLEP, IB, SAT, ACT, institutional tests. 40 credit hours maximum toward bachelor's degree. **Support services:** Reduced course load, remedial instruction, study skills assistance, tutoring, writing center.

**Majors. Area/ethnic studies:** American. **Biology:** General, cellular/molecular. **Business:** Accounting, business admin, finance, international, management information systems, marketing. **Communications:** General, journalism, media studies, organizational, political, radio/tv. **Communications technology:** General. **Computer sciences:** General, computer science. **Conservation:** Environmental science. **Education:** Biology, chemistry, early childhood, elementary, English, mathematics, middle, music, physical, physics, science, social studies, Spanish, special. **Engineering:** Computer, electrical, mechanical. **Foreign languages:** Spanish. **Health:** Athletic training, clinical lab science, nursing (RN), predental, premedicine, preveterinary. **History:** General. **Interdisciplinary:** Global studies. **Legal studies:** Prelaw. **Math:** General. **Parks/recreation:** Exercise sciences, health/fitness, sports admin. **Philosophy/religion:** Philosophy. **Physical sciences:** Chemistry, geology, physics. **Protective services:** Forensics, law enforcement admin. **Psychology:** General. **Public administration:** General, social work. **Social sciences:** General, political science, sociology. **Theology:** Missionary, pastoral counseling, religious ed, sacred music, theology, youth ministry. **Visual/performing arts:** Dramatic, graphic design, music pedagogy, music performance, music theory/composition, studio arts.

**Most popular majors.** Business/marketing 10%, education 13%, engineering/engineering technologies 6%, health sciences 11%, theological studies 9%, visual/performing arts 6%.

**Computing on campus.** 1,800 workstations in dormitories, library, student center. Dormitories linked to campus network. Commuter students can connect to campus network. Online course registration, helpline, repair service, wireless network available.

**Student life. Freshman orientation:** Mandatory, $105 fee. **Policies:** Alcohol, tobacco, and drugs prohibited. Religious observance required. **Housing:** Guaranteed on-campus for all undergraduates. Single-sex dorms, apartments available. $250 nonrefundable deposit, deadline 5/1. **Activities:** Bands, campus ministries, choral groups, drama, music ensembles, musical theater, radio station, student government, student newspaper, symphony orchestra, College Republicans, Emergency Medical Squad, Earth Stewardship Organization, Fellowship for World Missions, Students for Social Justice, Society for Technical Communicators, Society of Automotive Engineers International.

**Athletics.** NAIA, NCCAA. **Intercollegiate:** Baseball M, basketball, cheerleading, cross-country, golf M, soccer, softball W, tennis, track and field, volleyball W. **Intramural:** Badminton, basketball, bowling, cross-country, football (tackle) M, golf, racquetball, soccer, softball, table tennis, tennis, volleyball. **Team name:** Yellow Jackets.

**Student services.** Chaplain/spiritual director, career counseling, student employment services, financial aid counseling, health services, personal counseling, placement for graduates, veterans' counselor. **Physically disabled:** Services for visually impaired.

**Contact.** E-mail: admissions@cedarville.edu
Phone: (937) 766-7700 Toll-free number: (800) 233-2784
Fax: (937) 766-7575
Mark Weinstein, Director of Admissions, Cedarville University, 251 North Main Street, Cedarville, OH 45314-0601

## Central State University
**Wilberforce, Ohio**
www.centralstate.edu

CB member
CB code: 1107

- Public 4-year university and liberal arts college
- Residential campus in rural community

- 2,362 degree-seeking undergraduates: 6% part-time, 49% women, 96% African American, 1% Hispanic American
- 36 degree-seeking graduate students
- 39% of applicants admitted
- SAT or ACT (ACT writing optional) required

**General.** Founded in 1887. Regionally accredited. Ohio's only public historically black university. **Degrees:** 182 bachelor's awarded; master's offered. **ROTC:** Army, Air Force. **Location:** 18 miles from Dayton. **Calendar:** Semester, limited summer session. **Full-time faculty:** 113 total; 69% have terminal degrees, 68% minority, 34% women. **Part-time faculty:** 85 total; 79% minority, 48% women. **Class size:** 53% < 20, 42% 20-39, 3% 40-49, 2% 50-99. **Special facilities:** Afro-American museum, hydraulics laboratory, computer numerically controlled equipment for machining and robotic welding, business incubator.

**Freshman class profile.** 6,948 applied, 2,703 admitted, 713 enrolled.

| Mid 50% test scores | | | |
|---|---|---|---|
| SAT critical reading: | 340-430 | GPA 3.0-3.49: | 9% |
| SAT math: | 320-420 | GPA 2.0-2.99: | 66% |
| ACT composite: | 14-17 | End year in good standing: | 73% |
| GPA 3.75 or higher: | 1% | Return as sophomores: | 57% |
| GPA 3.50-3.74: | 2% | Out-of-state: | 50% |
| | | Live on campus: | 90% |

**Basis for selection.** Out-of-state residents must have 2.5 GPA and 19 ACT or 910 SAT. Ohio residents must have 2.0 GPA and 15 ACT or 720 SAT. Interview recommended. Personal essay required for admissions appeal process. **Homeschooled:** Transcript of courses and grades, state high school equivalency certificate, interview, letter of recommendation (nonparent) required. Ohio students need ONGP test results or OGT.

**High school preparation.** 16 units recommended. Recommended units include English 4, mathematics 3, social studies 3, science 3 and foreign language 2. 1 art recommended.

**2009-2010 Annual costs.** Tuition/fees: $5,294; $11,806 out-of-state. Room/board: $7,920. Books/supplies: $1,200. Personal expenses: $1,500.

**2009-2010 Financial aid. Non-need-based:** Scholarships awarded for academics, alumni affiliation, art, athletics, leadership, music/drama, religious affiliation, ROTC.

**Application procedures. Admission:** No deadline. $20 fee, may be waived for applicants with need. Admission notification on a rolling basis. **Financial aid:** Priority date 2/15; no closing date. FAFSA, institutional form required. Applicants notified on a rolling basis starting 5/1.

**Academics. Special study options:** Cooperative education, cross-registration, double major, honors, independent study, internships, study abroad, teacher certification program. **Credit/placement by examination:** AP, CLEP, SAT, ACT, institutional tests. 30 credit hours maximum toward bachelor's degree. **Support services:** Learning center, pre-admission summer program, reduced course load, tutoring, writing center.

**Majors. Biology:** General. **Business:** General, accounting. **Communications:** Broadcast journalism, journalism. **Computer sciences:** Computer science. **Education:** Early childhood, middle, multi-level teacher, secondary, special. **Engineering:** Environmental, manufacturing, water resource. **Engineering technology:** Industrial. **History:** General. **Math:** General. **Parks/recreation:** General. **Physical sciences:** Chemistry, geology. **Protective services:** Criminal justice. **Psychology:** General. **Public administration:** Social work. **Social sciences:** Economics, political science, sociology. **Visual/performing arts:** Art, jazz, music performance.

**Most popular majors.** Business/marketing 29%, communications/journalism 14%, education 18%, engineering/engineering technologies 6%, psychology 7%.

**Computing on campus.** 400 workstations in library, computer center, student center. Dormitories wired for high-speed internet access and linked to campus network. Online course registration, online library, helpline, repair service, wireless network available.

**Student life. Freshman orientation:** Mandatory, $125 fee. Preregistration for classes offered. **Housing:** Guaranteed on-campus for freshmen. Coed dorms, single-sex dorms available. $195 fully refundable deposit, deadline 8/1. **Activities:** Bands, campus ministries, choral groups, dance, drama, music ensembles, radio station, student government, student newspaper, TV station.

**Athletics.** NCAA. **Intercollegiate:** Basketball, cross-country, football (tackle) M, golf, tennis, track and field, volleyball. **Intramural:** Basketball, cross-country, football (non-tackle) M, racquetball, tennis. **Team name:** Marauders.

**Student services.** Alcohol/substance abuse counseling, chaplain/spiritual director, career counseling, services for economically disadvantaged, student employment services, financial aid counseling, health services, on-campus daycare, personal counseling, placement for graduates.

**Contact.** E-mail: admissions@centralstate.edu
Phone: (937) 376-6348 Toll-free number: (800) 388-2781
Fax: (937) 376-6648
Robin Rucker, Associate Director of Admissions, Central State University, PO Box 1004, Wilberforce, OH 45384-1004

---

## Chancellor University
Cleveland, Ohio
www.myers.edu                                    CB code: 1178

▶ Private 4-year university
▶ Commuter campus in very large city

**General.** Founded in 1848. Regionally accredited. **Location:** Downtown. **Calendar:** Semester.

**Annual costs/financial aid.** Books/supplies: $1,250. Personal expenses: $2,596.

**Contact.** Phone: (216) 432-8992
Vice President for Enrollment Management, 3921 Chester Avenue, Cleveland, OH 44114

---

## Cincinnati Christian University
Cincinnati, Ohio
www.ccuniversity.edu                             CB code: 1091

▶ Private 4-year university affiliated with Church of Christ/Christian Church
▶ Residential campus in very large city
▶ 779 degree-seeking undergraduates: 12% part-time, 43% women, 13% African American, 1% Hispanic American, 1% international
▶ 226 degree-seeking graduate students
▶ 99% of applicants admitted
▶ SAT or ACT (ACT writing optional), application essay required
▶ 42% graduate within 6 years

**General.** Founded in 1924. Regionally accredited; also accredited by ABHE. Member of Greater Cincinnati Consortium of Colleges and Universities. **Degrees:** 151 bachelor's, 14 associate awarded; master's offered. **Location:** 10 miles from downtown. **Calendar:** Semester, limited summer session. **Full-time faculty:** 34 total; 62% have terminal degrees, 9% minority, 21% women. **Part-time faculty:** 44 total; 18% have terminal degrees, 4% minority, 25% women. **Class size:** 69% < 20, 21% 20-39, 3% 40-49, 7% 50-99.

**Freshman class profile.** 258 applied, 256 admitted, 152 enrolled.

| Mid 50% test scores | | | |
|---|---|---|---|
| SAT critical reading: | 470-580 | GPA 2.0-2.99: | 45% |
| SAT math: | 430-560 | Rank in top quarter: | 21% |
| SAT writing: | 450-560 | Rank in top tenth: | 7% |
| ACT composite: | 18-23 | Return as sophomores: | 61% |
| GPA 3.75 or higher: | 11% | Out-of-state: | 30% |
| GPA 3.50-3.74: | 15% | Live on campus: | 59% |
| GPA 3.0-3.49: | 21% | International: | 1% |

**Basis for selection.** High school academic record and standardized test scores important. 2.5 GPA, 17 ACT/1215 SAT required for unconditional admission. Applicants age 25 or older can substitute English proficiency test and essay for SAT/ACT requirement. Audition required for music programs.

**2009-2010 Annual costs.** Tuition/fees: $12,380. Room/board: $6,470. Books/supplies: $800. Personal expenses: $1,950.

**2008-2009 Financial aid. Non-need-based:** Scholarships awarded for academics, athletics, leadership, music/drama, religious affiliation, state residency.

**Application procedures. Admission:** Priority date 3/1; deadline 7/1 (postmark date). $40 fee, may be waived for applicants with need. Admission notification on a rolling basis. **Financial aid:** Priority date 3/1; no closing date. FAFSA required. Applicants notified on a rolling basis starting 4/1; must reply within 2 week(s) of notification.

**Academics. Special study options:** Cooperative education, cross-registration, distance learning, double major, honors, independent study, internships, teacher certification program. Adult degree completion program. **Credit/placement by examination:** AP, CLEP, IB, institutional tests. 15 credit hours maximum toward associate degree, 30 toward bachelor's. **Support services:** Learning center, reduced course load, remedial instruction, study skills assistance, tutoring, writing center.

**Majors. Computer sciences:** Data processing, information technology, LAN/WAN management, programming. **Education:** Early childhood, elementary, middle, secondary, special. **Philosophy/religion:** Christian. **Psychology:** General. **Theology:** Bible, missionary, religious ed, sacred music.

**Most popular majors.** Business/marketing 6%, education 6%, psychology 9%, theological studies 79%.

**Computing on campus.** 57 workstations in dormitories, library, computer center, student center. Dormitories wired for high-speed internet access and linked to campus network. Online library, helpline, repair service, wireless network available.

**Student life. Freshman orientation:** Mandatory. Preregistration for classes offered. **Housing:** Guaranteed on-campus for all undergraduates. Single-sex dorms, apartments, wellness housing available. $35 nonrefundable deposit, deadline 7/1. **Activities:** Concert band, campus ministries, choral groups, drama, international student organizations, music ensembles, musical theater, student government.

**Athletics.** NCCAA. **Intercollegiate:** Baseball M, basketball, soccer, volleyball W. **Intramural:** Basketball, cheerleading, football (tackle) M, soccer, track and field, volleyball. **Team name:** Eagles.

**Student services.** Career counseling, student employment services, financial aid counseling, health services, personal counseling. **Physically disabled:** Services for hearing impaired.

**Contact.** E-mail: cbcadmission@ccuniversity.edu
Phone: (513) 244-8141 Toll-free number: (800) 949-4228
Fax: (513) 244-8140
Jenny Baker, Admissions Director, Cincinnati Christian University, 2700 Glenway Avenue, Cincinnati, OH 45204-3200

---

## Cincinnati College of Mortuary Science
Cincinnati, Ohio
www.ccms.edu                                     CB code: 0945

▶ Private 4-year school of mortuary science
▶ Commuter campus in large city
▶ 77 degree-seeking undergraduates: 39% women, 8% African American, 1% Hispanic American

**General.** Founded in 1882. Regionally accredited. **Degrees:** 43 bachelor's, 21 associate awarded. **Location:** 5 miles from downtown. **Calendar:** Quarter, extensive summer session. **Full-time faculty:** 6 total. **Part-time faculty:** 6 total. **Class size:** 100% 50-99.

**Basis for selection.** 2.0 GPA and test scores important. **Homeschooled:** Transcript of courses and grades, state high school equivalency certificate required. **Learning Disabled:** Documentation of the disability.

**High school preparation.** College-preparatory program recommended. 15 units recommended. Recommended units include English 3, mathematics 1, social studies 2 and science 2.

**2009-2010 Annual costs.** Tuition for 4-qtr. A.A.S. $16,875; 5-qtr. B.M.S. $20,250; 6-qtr. A.A.S. $22,275. Books and supplies for 4 quarter students $1,400; 6 quarter students $1,800; 5th quarter only $100.

**2009-2010 Financial aid.** All financial aid based on need.

**Application procedures. Admission:** Closing date 8/31 (postmark date). $40 fee. Application must be submitted on paper. Admission notification 9/15. Admission notification on a rolling basis. **Financial aid:** Priority date 7/1; no closing date. FAFSA required. Applicants notified on a rolling basis starting 3/1; must reply within 2 week(s) of notification.

**Academics.** Program of study contingent on licensing requirements of state in which student will practice. **Special study options:** Cooperative education. **Credit/placement by examination:** AP, CLEP, institutional tests.

**Majors. Personal/culinary services:** Mortuary science.

**Computing on campus.** 12 workstations in library.

**Student life. Freshman orientation:** Mandatory. **Housing:** Some housing available in local funeral homes.

**Contact.** E-mail: psullivan@ccms.edu
Phone: (513) 761-2020 Toll-free number: (888) 377-8433
Fax: (513) 761-3333
Pat Sullivan, Executive Director Enrollment Management, Cincinnati College of Mortuary Science, 645 West North Bend Road, Cincinnati, OH 45224-1428

## Cleveland Institute of Art
**Cleveland, Ohio**                                        **CB member**
**www.cia.edu**                                            **CB code: 1152**

- Private 4-year visual arts college
- Commuter campus in very large city
- 495 degree-seeking undergraduates: 1% part-time, 52% women, 6% African American, 5% Asian American, 5% Hispanic American, 2% international
- 79% of applicants admitted
- SAT or ACT (ACT writing optional), application essay required
- 54% graduate within 6 years

**General.** Founded in 1882. Regionally accredited. **Degrees:** 112 bachelor's awarded. **ROTC:** Army, Naval, Air Force. **Location:** 5 miles from downtown. **Calendar:** Semester, limited summer session. **Full-time faculty:** 47 total; 81% have terminal degrees, 8% minority, 45% women. **Part-time faculty:** 36 total; 39% have terminal degrees, 11% minority, 50% women. **Class size:** 74% < 20, 26% 20-39. **Special facilities:** Individual studio spaces, wood shop, metal shop, art galleries.

**Freshman class profile.** 457 applied, 362 admitted, 112 enrolled.

| Mid 50% test scores | | Rank in top quarter: | 32% |
|---|---|---|---|
| SAT critical reading: | 490-600 | Rank in top tenth: | 18% |
| SAT math: | 440-570 | End year in good standing: | 76% |
| ACT composite: | 20-26 | Return as sophomores: | 81% |
| GPA 3.75 or higher: | 18% | Out-of-state: | 39% |
| GPA 3.50-3.74: | 12% | Live on campus: | 80% |
| GPA 3.0-3.49: | 39% | International: | 1% |
| GPA 2.0-2.99: | 31% | | |

**Basis for selection.** Portfolio of 12 to 20 pieces, high school transcripts, statement of purpose, test scores, and 1 letter of recommendation required. Interview strongly recommended. **Homeschooled:** Transcript of courses and grades, state high school equivalency certificate, letter of recommendation (nonparent) required. GED required.

**High school preparation.** 20 units recommended. Recommended units include English 4, mathematics 3, social studies 3, science 3 and academic electives 6. 2 years of art recommended.

**2009-2010 Annual costs.** Tuition/fees: $31,904. Room/board: $10,536. Books/supplies: $2,000. Personal expenses: $1,940.

**2009-2010 Financial aid. Need-based:** Average need met was 41%. Average scholarship/grant was $13,447; average loan $3,860. 62% of total undergraduate aid awarded as scholarships/grants, 38% as loans/jobs. **Non-need-based:** Scholarships awarded for academics, art.

**Application procedures. Admission:** Priority date 7/1; no deadline. $30 fee, may be waived for applicants with need. Admission notification on a rolling basis beginning on or about 10/1. Must reply by May 1 or within 2 week(s) if notified thereafter. **Financial aid:** Priority date 3/15; no closing date. FAFSA, institutional form required. Applicants notified on a rolling basis starting 3/16; must reply within 4 week(s) of notification.

**Academics. Special study options:** Cooperative education, cross-registration, double major, exchange student, independent study, internships, New York semester, study abroad. Study for up to 2 semesters at any Alliance of Independent Colleges of Art and Design. **Credit/placement by examination:** AP, CLEP, IB. 63 credit hours maximum toward bachelor's degree. **Support services:** Reduced course load, study skills assistance, tutoring, writing center.

**Majors. Health:** Medical illustrating. **Visual/performing arts:** Ceramics, commercial/advertising art, digital art, drawing, fiber arts, illustration, industrial design, interior design, metal/jewelry, painting, photography, printmaking, sculpture.

**Computing on campus.** 303 workstations in dormitories, library, computer center. Dormitories wired for high-speed internet access. Online course registration, online library, student web hosting, wireless network available.

**Student life. Freshman orientation:** Mandatory, $165 fee. Preregistration for classes offered. Summer overnight program for students/parents and fall orientation for students only. **Housing:** Coed dorms, apartments, fraternity/sorority housing available. $150 nonrefundable deposit, deadline 6/1. **Activities:** Campus ministries, film society, student government, student newspaper, student artist association, student leadership council, student activities program board, student independent exhibition committee, gay/lesbian association, Artists for Christ, cinema club, community service club.

**Athletics. Intramural:** Basketball, bowling, football (non-tackle), softball, volleyball.

**Student services.** Alcohol/substance abuse counseling, chaplain/spiritual director, career counseling, student employment services, financial aid counseling, health services, legal services, personal counseling. **Learning disabled:** Comprehensive services available.

**Contact.** E-mail: admiss@cia.edu
Phone: (216) 421-7418 Toll-free number: (800) 223-4700
Fax: (216) 754-3634
Robert Borden, Dean of Admissions and Financial Aid, Cleveland Institute of Art, 11141 East Boulevard, Cleveland, OH 44106-1710

## Cleveland Institute of Music
**Cleveland, Ohio**
**www.cim.edu**                                           **CB code: 1124**

- Private 4-year music college
- Residential campus in very large city
- 253 degree-seeking undergraduates
- 35% of applicants admitted
- SAT or ACT (ACT writing optional), application essay required

**General.** Founded in 1920. Regionally accredited. **Degrees:** 40 bachelor's awarded; master's, doctoral offered. **Location:** 5 miles from downtown. **Calendar:** Semester, limited summer session. **Full-time faculty:** 37 total; 30% have terminal degrees, 11% minority, 40% women. **Part-time faculty:** 46 total; 9% have terminal degrees, 6% minority, 28% women. **Special facilities:** Electronic music studios, audio recording and distance learning facilities, large CD/DVD, record, and tape library, technology learning center.

**Freshman class profile.** 1,016 applied, 352 admitted, 200 enrolled.

| Out-of-state: | 77% | Live on campus: | 100% |
|---|---|---|---|

**Basis for selection.** Audition most important. High school record, test scores, and letters of recommendation also reviewed. Required institutional examinations include ear training and theory. Additional testing includes sight singing and keyboard proficiency. Audition required.

**High school preparation.** College-preparatory program recommended. 16 units recommended. Recommended units include English 4, mathematics 3, social studies 3, science 3 and foreign language 3.

**2009-2010 Annual costs.** Tuition/fees: $36,590. Room/board: $10,567. Books/supplies: $600. Personal expenses: $1,254.

**2008-2009 Financial aid. Need-based:** 31 full-time freshmen applied for aid; 27 were judged to have need; 27 of these received aid. Average need met was 81%. Average scholarship/grant was $16,870; average loan $5,126. 67% of total undergraduate aid awarded as scholarships/grants, 33% as loans/jobs. **Non-need-based:** Awarded to 113 full-time undergraduates, including 25 freshmen. Scholarships awarded for academics, music/drama.

**Application procedures. Admission:** Closing date 12/1 (receipt date). $100 fee. Application must be submitted online. Admission notification 4/1. Admission notification on a rolling basis. Must reply by 5/1. Deferred admission from fall to spring semesters is dependent upon space availability. **Financial aid:** Priority date 2/15; no closing date. FAFSA required. Applicants notified on a rolling basis starting 4/1; must reply by 5/1 or within 2 week(s) of notification.

**Academics. Special study options:** Cross-registration, double major, ESL, independent study, study abroad. **Credit/placement by examination:** AP, CLEP, IB, SAT, ACT, institutional tests. **Support services:** Learning center, reduced course load, remedial instruction, study skills assistance, tutoring, writing center.

**Majors. Communications technology:** Recording arts. **Visual/performing arts:** Music performance, music theory/composition, voice/opera.

**Computing on campus.** 36 workstations in dormitories, library, computer center, student center. Dormitories wired for high-speed internet access and linked to campus network. Helpline, repair service, wireless network available.

**Student life. Freshman orientation:** Mandatory. Held before the start of classes. **Policies:** Library privileges available through Case Western Reserve University. **Housing:** Coed dorms, wellness housing available. **Activities:** Jazz band, choral groups, dance, drama, music ensembles, opera, student government, student newspaper, symphony orchestra, most student activities, athletics and student services available through Case Western Reserve University.

**Student services.** Alcohol/substance abuse counseling, career counseling, student employment services, financial aid counseling, health services, personal counseling, placement for graduates, veterans' counselor.

**Contact.** E-mail: admission@cim.edu
Phone: (216) 795-3107 Fax: (216) 795-3161
William Fay, Director of Admission, Cleveland Institute of Music, 11021 East Boulevard, Cleveland, OH 44106

## Cleveland State University
Cleveland, Ohio — CB member
www.csuohio.edu — CB code: 1221

- Public 4-year university
- Commuter campus in large city
- 9,805 degree-seeking undergraduates: 24% part-time, 55% women, 21% African American, 3% Asian American, 4% Hispanic American, 2% international
- 5,019 degree-seeking graduate students
- 64% of applicants admitted
- SAT or ACT (ACT writing optional) required

**General.** Founded in 1964. Regionally accredited. **Degrees:** 1,732 bachelor's awarded; master's, doctoral, professional offered. **ROTC:** Army, Air Force. **Location:** Downtown. **Calendar:** Semester, extensive summer session. **Full-time faculty:** 537 total; 90% have terminal degrees, 22% minority, 40% women. **Part-time faculty:** 487 total; 11% have terminal degrees, 15% minority, 48% women. **Class size:** 41% < 20, 44% 20-39, 7% 40-49, 7% 50-99, less than 1% >100. **Special facilities:** Poetry center, bioethics center, rooftop garden, Center for Healing Across Cultures, Center for Poverty Studies.

**Freshman class profile.** 4,584 applied, 2,946 admitted, 1,185 enrolled.

| | | | |
|---|---|---|---|
| GPA 3.75 or higher: | 15% | Return as sophomores: | 66% |
| GPA 3.50-3.74: | 11% | Out-of-state: | 6% |
| GPA 3.0-3.49: | 28% | Live on campus: | 31% |
| GPA 2.0-2.99: | 45% | International: | 3% |
| Rank in top quarter: | 33% | Fraternities: | 2% |
| Rank in top tenth: | 12% | Sororities: | 2% |

**Basis for selection.** 2.3 GPA, 16 ACT/750 SAT, and successful completion of 13 core academic units required. 2.5 GPA and 20 ACT/950 SAT required for education applicants; 2.7 GPA and 23 ACT/1070 SAT required for engineering applicants. SAT scores exclusive of Writing. Audition required for music majors.

**High school preparation.** College-preparatory program required. 13 units required. Required and recommended units include English 4, mathematics 3, social studies 3, science 3, foreign language 2 and visual/performing arts 1.

**2010-2011 Annual costs.** Tuition/fees (projected): $8,196; $11,026 out-of-state. Room/board: $10,250. Books/supplies: $800. Personal expenses: $4,300.

**2009-2010 Financial aid. Need-based:** 811 full-time freshmen applied for aid; 746 were judged to have need; 728 of these received aid. Average need met was 52%. Average scholarship/grant was $7,106; average loan $3,286. 37% of total undergraduate aid awarded as scholarships/grants, 63% as loans/jobs. **Non-need-based:** Awarded to 669 full-time undergraduates, including 88 freshmen. Scholarships awarded for academics, alumni affiliation, art, athletics, leadership, minority status, music/drama, religious affiliation, ROTC.

**Application procedures. Admission:** Priority date 7/15; deadline 8/15. $30 fee, may be waived for applicants with need. Admission notification on a rolling basis beginning on or about 9/1. **Financial aid:** Priority date 2/15; no closing date. FAFSA required. Applicants notified on a rolling basis starting 3/15; must reply within 4 week(s) of notification.

**Academics. Special study options:** Accelerated study, combined bachelor's/graduate degree, cooperative education, cross-registration, distance learning, double major, dual enrollment of high school students, ESL, exchange student, honors, independent study, internships, liberal arts/career combination, student-designed major, study abroad, teacher certification program, weekend college. **Credit/placement by examination:** AP, CLEP, IB, SAT, ACT, institutional tests. 90 credit hours maximum toward bachelor's degree. Unlimited AP exam credits accepted. **Support services:** Learning center, reduced course load, remedial instruction, study skills assistance, tutoring, writing center.

**Majors. Area/ethnic studies:** Women's. **Biology:** General. **Business:** Accounting, finance, international, labor relations, management information systems, managerial economics, marketing, statistics. **Communications:** General, public relations. **Computer sciences:** General. **Conservation:** Environmental science, environmental studies. **Education:** General, early childhood, elementary, kindergarten/preschool, middle, physical, special. **Engineering:** Chemical, civil, computer, electrical, industrial, mechanical, metallurgical, science. **Engineering technology:** General, electrical. **Foreign languages:** French, Germanic, linguistics, Spanish. **Health:** Audiology/hearing, music therapy, nursing (RN), physician assistant. **History:** General. **Liberal arts:** Arts/sciences. **Math:** General. **Philosophy/religion:** Philosophy, religion. **Physical sciences:** Chemistry, geology, physics. **Psychology:** General. **Public administration:** Social work. **Science technology:** Biological. **Social sciences:** General, anthropology, criminology, economics, international relations, political science, sociology, urban studies. **Visual/performing arts:** Art, cinematography, dramatic.

**Most popular majors.** Business/marketing 21%, communications/journalism 8%, education 8%, engineering/engineering technologies 6%, health sciences 14%, psychology 7%, public administration/social services 6%, social sciences 11%.

**Computing on campus.** 711 workstations in dormitories, library, computer center, student center. Dormitories wired for high-speed internet access and linked to campus network. Commuter students can connect to campus network. Online course registration, online library, helpline, repair service, wireless network available.

**Student life. Freshman orientation:** Available, $25 fee. Preregistration for classes offered. All-day program during summer. **Housing:** Coed dorms, special housing for disabled, apartments, fraternity/sorority housing available. $150 nonrefundable deposit, deadline 1/19. **Activities:** Bands, choral groups, dance, drama, film society, international student organizations, literary magazine, music ensembles, musical theater, opera, radio station, student government, student newspaper, symphony orchestra, Newman Center, Los Latinos Unidos, Hillel, University Christian Movement, Organization for Afro-American Unity, NAACP, environmental action group, College Democrats and Republicans.

**Athletics.** NCAA. **Intercollegiate:** Baseball M, basketball, cross-country W, diving, fencing, golf, soccer, softball W, swimming, tennis, track and field W, volleyball W, wrestling M. **Intramural:** Badminton, basketball, bowling, cross-country, fencing, field hockey W, golf, handball, racquetball, rowing (crew), sailing, soccer, squash, swimming, table tennis, tennis, track and field, volleyball, water polo, wrestling M. **Team name:** Vikings.

**Student services.** Adult student services, alcohol/substance abuse counseling, career counseling, services for economically disadvantaged, student employment services, financial aid counseling, health services, legal services, minority student services, on-campus daycare, personal counseling, placement for graduates, veterans' counselor, women's services. **Physically disabled:** Services for visually, speech, hearing impaired. **Learning disabled:** Comprehensive services available.

**Contact.** E-mail: admissions@csuohio.edu
Phone: (216) 687-2100 Toll-free number: (800) 278-6446
Robert Spademan, Assistant Vice-President, Marketing & Admissions, Cleveland State University, 2121 Euclid Avenue, Cleveland, OH 44115-2214

## College of Mount St. Joseph
Cincinnati, Ohio — CB member
www.msj.edu — CB code: 1129

- Private 4-year liberal arts college affiliated with Roman Catholic Church
- Commuter campus in very large city
- 1,860 degree-seeking undergraduates: 28% part-time, 63% women, 10% African American, 1% Hispanic American
- 412 degree-seeking graduate students
- 70% of applicants admitted
- SAT or ACT (ACT writing recommended) required
- 55% graduate within 6 years

**General.** Founded in 1920. Regionally accredited. **Degrees:** 359 bachelor's, 11 associate awarded; master's, professional offered. **ROTC:** Army, Air Force. **Location:** 7 miles from downtown. **Calendar:** Semester, extensive summer session. **Full-time faculty:** 117 total; 74% have terminal degrees, 3% minority, 59% women. **Part-time faculty:** 119 total; 34% have terminal degrees, 3% minority, 68% women. **Class size:** 55% < 20, 43% 20-39, less than 1% 40-49, less than 1% 50-99.

**Freshman class profile.** 1,417 applied, 996 admitted, 368 enrolled.

| Mid 50% test scores | | GPA 2.0-2.99: | 32% |
|---|---|---|---|
| SAT critical reading: | 430-520 | Rank in top quarter: | 35% |
| SAT math: | 430-540 | Rank in top tenth: | 11% |
| ACT composite: | 19-24 | Return as sophomores: | 72% |
| GPA 3.75 or higher: | 16% | Out-of-state: | 20% |
| GPA 3.50-3.74: | 14% | Live on campus: | 61% |
| GPA 3.0-3.49: | 36% | | |

**Basis for selection.** Criteria for admission include college prep high school curriculum, strong GPA, standardized test scores, evidence of leadership and extracurricular involvement, and personal background. Essays, recommendations and interviews may be required for some students. Audition required for music programs. Portfolio recommended for art programs. **Homeschooled:** Letter of recommendation (nonparent) required. Transcripts required along with any documentation from state or national home schooling accreditation agency. Description of completed courses required.

**High school preparation.** College-preparatory program recommended. 17 units required; 23 recommended. Required and recommended units include English 4, mathematics 3-4, social studies 1-2, history 1-2, science 3-4 (laboratory 1-2), foreign language 2, visual/performing arts 1 and academic electives 1-2. Math must include a minimum of 1 year each of algebra and geometry. 1 fine arts required. May substitute 2 additional credits from other subjects in place of foreign language.

**2009-2010 Annual costs.** Tuition/fees: $22,800. Room/board: $7,152. Books/supplies: $800. Personal expenses: $600.

**2009-2010 Financial aid. Need-based:** 343 full-time freshmen applied for aid; 307 were judged to have need; 307 of these received aid. Average need met was 81%. Average scholarship/grant was $14,456; average loan $4,035. 53% of total undergraduate aid awarded as scholarships/grants, 47% as loans/jobs. **Non-need-based:** Awarded to 273 full-time undergraduates, including 77 freshmen. Scholarships awarded for academics, alumni affiliation, art, leadership, music/drama, ROTC, state residency.

**Application procedures. Admission:** Priority date 4/1; deadline 8/15 (postmark date). $25 fee, may be waived for applicants with need. Admission notification on a rolling basis beginning on or about 10/1. Must reply by May 1 or within 4 week(s) if notified thereafter. **Financial aid:** Priority date 3/1; no closing date. FAFSA required. Applicants notified on a rolling basis starting 1/31; must reply by 5/1 or within 4 week(s) of notification.

**Academics. Special study options:** Accelerated study, cooperative education, cross-registration, distance learning, double major, dual enrollment of high school students, honors, independent study, internships, liberal arts/career combination, study abroad, teacher certification program. **Credit/placement by examination:** AP, CLEP, IB, SAT, ACT, institutional tests. 32 credit hours maximum toward associate degree, 64 toward bachelor's. **Support services:** Learning center, reduced course load, remedial instruction, study skills assistance, tutoring, writing center.

**Majors. Biology:** General, biochemistry. **Business:** Accounting, business admin. **Communications:** General. **Computer sciences:** General. **Education:** Art, early childhood, middle, special. **Health:** Athletic training, nursing (RN). **History:** General. **Interdisciplinary:** Natural sciences. **Legal studies:** Paralegal. **Liberal arts:** Arts/sciences. **Math:** General. **Parks/recreation:** Sports admin. **Philosophy/religion:** Religion. **Physical sciences:** Chemistry. **Psychology:** General. **Public administration:** Social work. **Social sciences:** Criminology, sociology. **Theology:** Pastoral counseling, religious ed. **Visual/performing arts:** Art, graphic design, interior design, studio arts.

**Most popular majors.** Business/marketing 17%, education 8%, health sciences 28%, liberal arts 8%, social sciences 6%, visual/performing arts 9%.

**Computing on campus.** 278 workstations in library, computer center, student center. Commuter students can connect to campus network. Online course registration, online library, helpline, repair service, student web hosting, wireless network available.

**Student life. Freshman orientation:** Mandatory, $150 fee. Preregistration for classes offered. Two-part orientation: summer session, which includes a 2-day, 1-night stay in dorms, and welcome weekend consisting of service learning event and river cruise over the weekend before start of

classes. **Policies:** Smoke-free campus. All unmarried freshmen and sophomores under age 21 who live outside 35-mile radius of college required to live on campus and participate in meal program. **Housing:** Guaranteed on-campus for freshmen. Coed dorms, special housing for disabled available. $100 fully refundable deposit, deadline 8/15. **Activities:** Bands, campus ministries, choral groups, dance, drama, international student organizations, literary magazine, music ensembles, musical theater, student government, student newspaper, Circle K International, environmental awareness club, Japanese cultural appreciation club, black student union, Alpha Phi Omega service organization, Lions for Life, Habitat for Humanity.

**Athletics.** NCAA. **Intercollegiate:** Baseball M, basketball, cheerleading M, cross-country, football (tackle) M, golf, lacrosse, soccer, softball W, tennis, track and field, volleyball, wrestling M. **Intramural:** Basketball, football (non-tackle), handball, racquetball, soccer, softball, tennis, volleyball. **Team name:** Lions.

**Student services.** Adult student services, alcohol/substance abuse counseling, chaplain/spiritual director, career counseling, services for economically disadvantaged, student employment services, financial aid counseling, health services, minority student services, on-campus daycare, personal counseling, placement for graduates, veterans' counselor, women's services. **Physically disabled:** Services for visually, speech, hearing impaired. **Learning disabled:** Comprehensive services available.

**Contact.** E-mail: admissions@mail.msj.edu
Phone: (513) 244-4531 Toll-free number: (800) 654-9314
Fax: (513) 244-4629
Peggy Minnich, Director of Admission, College of Mount St. Joseph, 5701 Delhi Road, Cincinnati, OH 45233-1670

---

## College of Wooster

| Wooster, Ohio | CB member |
|---|---|
| www.wooster.edu | CB code: 1134 |

▶ Private 4-year liberal arts college
▶ Residential campus in large town
▶ 1,815 degree-seeking undergraduates: 1% part-time, 54% women, 6% African American, 3% Asian American, 2% Hispanic American, 5% international
▶ 59% of applicants admitted
▶ SAT or ACT with writing, application essay required
▶ 75% graduate within 6 years; 43% enter graduate study

**General.** Founded in 1866. Regionally accredited. **Degrees:** 435 bachelor's awarded. **Location:** 55 miles from Cleveland, 30 miles from Akron. **Calendar:** Semester, limited summer session. **Full-time faculty:** 131 total; 13% minority, 49% women. **Part-time faculty:** 29 total; 55% women. **Class size:** 64% < 20, 32% 20-39, 4% 40-49, less than 1% >100.

**Freshman class profile.** 4,752 applied, 2,795 admitted, 481 enrolled.

| Mid 50% test scores | | GPA 2.0-2.99: | 9% |
|---|---|---|---|
| SAT critical reading: | 540-660 | Rank in top quarter: | 74% |
| SAT math: | 540-650 | Rank in top tenth: | 36% |
| SAT writing: | 540-660 | End year in good standing: | 88% |
| ACT composite: | 24-29 | Return as sophomores: | 87% |
| GPA 3.75 or higher: | 41% | Out-of-state: | 58% |
| GPA 3.50-3.74: | 20% | Live on campus: | 100% |
| GPA 3.0-3.49: | 30% | International: | 2% |

**Basis for selection.** Course pattern and academic performance most important. Recommendations, extracurricular activities, class rank, test scores, interview considered. Interview recommended for all; audition recommended for music; portfolio recommended for art programs. **Homeschooled:** Statement describing homeschool structure and mission, interview, letter of recommendation (nonparent) required.

**High school preparation.** College-preparatory program required. Required and recommended units include English 4, mathematics 3-4, social studies 3-4, science 3-4, foreign language 2-3 and academic electives 2. Math recommendation includes 2 algebra.

**2009-2010 Annual costs.** Tuition/fees: $34,950. Room/board: $8,950. Books/supplies: $900. Personal expenses: $600.

**2009-2010 Financial aid. Need-based:** 385 full-time freshmen applied for aid; 313 were judged to have need; 313 of these received aid. Average need met was 89%. Average scholarship/grant was $23,066; average loan $3,511. 81% of total undergraduate aid awarded as scholarships/grants, 19% as loans/jobs. **Non-need-based:** Awarded to 778 full-time undergraduates, including 192 freshmen. Scholarships awarded for academics, minority status, music/drama, religious affiliation, state residency.

**Application procedures. Admission:** Closing date 2/15 (postmark date). $40 fee, may be waived for applicants with need, free for online applicants. Admission notification 4/1. Admission notification on a rolling basis. Must reply by May 1 or within 2 week(s) if notified thereafter. **Financial aid:** Priority date 2/15; no closing date. FAFSA, institutional form required. Either CSS PROFILE or institution application from prospective students. Applicants notified by 4/1; must reply by 5/1.

**Academics. Special study options:** Combined bachelor's/graduate degree, cooperative education, double major, exchange student, independent study, internships, New York semester, student-designed major, study abroad, teacher certification program, United Nations semester, urban semester, Washington semester. **Credit/placement by examination:** AP, CLEP, IB, institutional tests. 32 credit hours maximum toward bachelor's degree. **Support services:** Learning center, study skills assistance, tutoring, writing center.

**Majors. Area/ethnic studies:** African, African-American, East Asian, Latin American, Near/Middle Eastern, Russian/Slavic, South Asian, Western European, women's. **Biology:** General, biochemistry, Biochemistry/biophysics and molecular biology, molecular. **Business:** Managerial economics. **Communications:** General. **Computer sciences:** General. **Education:** Music. **Foreign languages:** General, classics, comparative lit, French, German, Russian, Spanish. **Health:** Audiology/speech pathology, music therapy. **History:** General. **Interdisciplinary:** Neuroscience. **Math:** General. **Philosophy/religion:** Philosophy, religion. **Physical sciences:** Chemical physics, chemistry, geology, molecular physics, physics. **Psychology:** General. **Public administration:** Social work. **Social sciences:** Anthropology, archaeology, economics, international relations, political science, sociology, urban studies. **Visual/performing arts:** Art history/conservation, dance, dramatic, music history, music performance, music theory/composition, studio arts. **Other:** Classical studies.

**Most popular majors.** Biology 8%, English 9%, history 9%, philosophy/religious studies 8%, physical sciences 6%, psychology 8%, social sciences 27%, visual/performing arts 7%.

**Computing on campus.** 275 workstations in dormitories, library, computer center, student center. Dormitories wired for high-speed internet access and linked to campus network. Commuter students can connect to campus network. Online course registration, online library, helpline, repair service, student web hosting, wireless network available.

**Student life. Freshman orientation:** Mandatory. Preregistration for classes offered. Held during the summer prior to start of classes. **Housing:** Guaranteed on-campus for all undergraduates. Coed dorms, single-sex dorms, fraternity/sorority housing, wellness housing available. Special housing for students participating in volunteer activities. **Activities:** Bands, campus ministries, choral groups, dance, drama, film society, international student organizations, literary magazine, music ensembles, Model UN, musical theater, radio station, student government, student newspaper, symphony orchestra, variety of religious, ethnic, and social service organizations available.

**Athletics.** NCAA. **Intercollegiate:** Baseball M, basketball, cross-country, diving, field hockey W, football (tackle) M, golf, lacrosse, soccer, softball W, swimming, tennis, track and field, volleyball W. **Intramural:** Badminton, basketball, bowling, football (non-tackle), golf, racquetball, soccer, softball, swimming, tennis, volleyball, water polo M. **Team name:** Fighting Scots.

**Student services.** Alcohol/substance abuse counseling, chaplain/spiritual director, career counseling, student employment services, financial aid counseling, health services, minority student services, personal counseling, placement for graduates. **Physically disabled:** Services for visually impaired.

**Contact.** E-mail: admissions@wooster.edu
Phone: (330) 263-2322 Toll-free number: (800) 877-9905
Fax: (330) 263-2621
Mary Karen Vellines, Vice President for Enrollment Management, College of Wooster, 847 College Avenue, Wooster, OH 44691-2363

**General.** Founded in 1879. Regionally accredited. **Degrees:** 304 bachelor's awarded. **Location:** Downtown. **Calendar:** Semester, limited summer session. **Full-time faculty:** 78 total; 68% have terminal degrees, 9% minority, 33% women. **Part-time faculty:** 105 total; 25% have terminal degrees, 9% minority, 49% women. **Class size:** 75% < 20, 25% 20-39. **Special facilities:** Student exhibition hall.

**Freshman class profile.** 625 applied, 453 admitted, 296 enrolled.

| Mid 50% test scores | | | |
|---|---|---|---|
| SAT critical reading: | 450-580 | GPA 3.0-3.49: | 31% |
| SAT math: | 420-550 | GPA 2.0-2.99: | 58% |
| SAT writing: | 440-570 | Rank in top quarter: | 15% |
| ACT composite: | 18-23 | Rank in top tenth: | 3% |
| GPA 3.75 or higher: | 8% | Return as sophomores: | 77% |
| GPA 3.50-3.74: | 3% | Out-of-state: | 18% |
| | | Live on campus: | 74% |

**Basis for selection.** Portfolio and 2.0 GPA important. Portfolio required; interview recommended.

**High school preparation.** Recommended units include English 4, mathematics 2, science 2 and foreign language 2. 4 units art recommended.

**2009-2010 Annual costs.** Tuition/fees: $24,648. Room/board: $8,630. Books/supplies: $3,000. Personal expenses: $200.

**2009-2010 Financial aid. Need-based:** Average need met was 56%. Average scholarship/grant was $13,293; average loan $3,792. 55% of total undergraduate aid awarded as scholarships/grants, 45% as loans/jobs. **Non-need-based:** Scholarships awarded for academics, art, ROTC, state residency.

**Application procedures. Admission:** No deadline. $30 fee, may be waived for applicants with need. Admission notification on a rolling basis. **Financial aid:** Priority date 2/15, closing date 2/15. FAFSA required. Applicants notified on a rolling basis starting 3/15; must reply within 2 week(s) of notification.

**Academics. Special study options:** Accelerated study, cooperative education, cross-registration, distance learning, double major, ESL, honors, independent study, internships, New York semester, study abroad. **Credit/placement by examination:** AP, CLEP, SAT, ACT, institutional tests. **Support services:** Learning center, reduced course load, remedial instruction, study skills assistance, tutoring.

**Majors. Visual/performing arts:** Commercial/advertising art, fashion design, illustration, industrial design, interior design, photography, studio arts.

**Computing on campus.** 485 workstations in dormitories, library, computer center, student center. Dormitories wired for high-speed internet access. Online library, wireless network available.

**Student life. Freshman orientation:** Mandatory. Three 2 day sessions in June, 1 day session in August. **Housing:** Guaranteed on-campus for freshmen. Coed dorms, special housing for disabled, apartments, wellness housing available. $225 fully refundable deposit, deadline 5/11. **Activities:** Choral groups, drama, film society, international student organizations, student government, student newspaper, student Bible study, gay/lesbian/bisexual group, environmental awareness group, black student organization, international student organization.

**Student services.** Adult student services, alcohol/substance abuse counseling, career counseling, student employment services, financial aid counseling, minority student services, personal counseling. **Physically disabled:** Services for visually, speech, hearing impaired. **Learning disabled:** Comprehensive services available.

**Contact.** E-mail: admissions@ccad.edu
Phone: (614) 224-9101 ext. 3261 Toll-free number: (877) 997-2223
Fax: (614) 232-8344
Thomas Green, Director of Admissions, Columbus College of Art and Design, 60 Cleveland Avenue, Columbus, OH 43215-3875

## Columbus College of Art and Design
### Columbus, Ohio
www.ccad.edu                                    CB code: 1085

- Private 4-year visual arts college
- Commuter campus in very large city
- 1,302 degree-seeking undergraduates: 5% part-time, 59% women, 7% African American, 4% Asian American, 4% Hispanic American, 3% international
- 72% of applicants admitted
- SAT or ACT (ACT writing optional), application essay required
- 65% graduate within 6 years

## Defiance College
### Defiance, Ohio                               CB member
www.defiance.edu                                CB code: 1162

- Private 4-year liberal arts college affiliated with United Church of Christ
- Residential campus in large town
- 944 degree-seeking undergraduates: 20% part-time, 52% women, 7% African American, 1% Asian American, 4% Hispanic American, 1% Native American
- 112 degree-seeking graduate students

- 74% of applicants admitted
- SAT or ACT (ACT writing optional) required
- 58% graduate within 6 years; 25% enter graduate study

**General.** Founded in 1850. Regionally accredited. **Degrees:** 148 bachelor's, 8 associate awarded; master's offered. **Location:** 55 miles from Toledo; 45 miles from Fort Wayne, Indiana. **Calendar:** Semester, extensive summer session. **Full-time faculty:** 44 total; 54% have terminal degrees, 7% minority, 41% women. **Part-time faculty:** 57 total; 16% have terminal degrees, 4% minority, 42% women. **Class size:** 69% < 20, 29% 20-39, 1% 40-49, less than 1% 50-99. **Special facilities:** Wildlife sanctuary.

**Freshman class profile.** 1,258 applied, 937 admitted, 216 enrolled.

| Mid 50% test scores | | | |
|---|---|---|---|
| SAT critical reading: | 400-540 | GPA 2.0-2.99: | 43% |
| SAT math: | 460-550 | Rank in top quarter: | 29% |
| SAT writing: | 380-510 | Rank in top tenth: | 9% |
| ACT composite: | 19-24 | End year in good standing: | 87% |
| GPA 3.75 or higher: | 15% | Return as sophomores: | 65% |
| GPA 3.50-3.74: | 16% | Out-of-state: | 21% |
| GPA 3.0-3.49: | 25% | Live on campus: | 91% |

**Basis for selection.** School achievement record, test scores, college preparatory curriculum important. 2.25 GPA, 18 ACT or 870 SAT (exclusive of Writing) required.

**High school preparation.** College-preparatory program recommended. 16 units recommended. Recommended units include English 4, mathematics 3, social studies 2, science 3, foreign language 2 and visual/performing arts 2. One unit fine arts and 1 unit of computer proficiency recommended.

**2010-2011 Annual costs.** Tuition/fees (projected): $24,320. Room/board: $8,120. Books/supplies: $1,350. Personal expenses: $1,200.

**2008-2009 Financial aid.** **Non-need-based:** Scholarships awarded for academics, leadership.

**Application procedures.** **Admission:** No deadline. $25 fee, may be waived for applicants with need, free for online applicants. Admission notification on a rolling basis beginning on or about 9/1. Must reply by May 1 or within 4 week(s) if notified thereafter. **Financial aid:** Priority date 3/1; no closing date. FAFSA required. Applicants notified on a rolling basis starting 3/15; must reply within 3 week(s) of notification.

**Academics.** Evening sessions available in many areas. Weekend college program for nontraditional students to pursue bachelor's or master's degree in several business majors. **Special study options:** Accelerated study, cooperative education, distance learning, double major, dual enrollment of high school students, honors, independent study, internships, student-designed major, study abroad, teacher certification program, weekend college. **Credit/placement by examination:** AP, CLEP, IB, institutional tests. 15 credit hours maximum toward associate degree, 30 toward bachelor's. **Support services:** Learning center, reduced course load, study skills assistance, tutoring, writing center.

**Majors. Biology:** General. **Business:** General, accounting, business admin, management information systems. **Communications:** General, journalism, public relations. **Computer sciences:** Computer forensics. **Conservation:** General, environmental studies. **Education:** General, art, biology, business, chemistry, early childhood, elementary, English, health, history, mathematics, middle, multi-level teacher, physical, science, secondary, social science, social studies, speech. **Health:** Athletic training, clinical lab technology, health services, predental, premedicine, preveterinary. **History:** General. **Interdisciplinary:** Biological/physical sciences, math/computer science, natural sciences. **Legal studies:** Prelaw. **Liberal arts:** Arts/sciences. **Math:** General. **Parks/recreation:** Health/fitness, sports admin. **Philosophy/religion:** Religion. **Protective services:** Forensics. **Psychology:** General. **Public administration:** Social work. **Social sciences:** General, criminology. **Theology:** Religious ed. **Visual/performing arts:** Art, commercial/advertising art, graphic design.

**Most popular majors.** Business/marketing 20%, education 24%, parks/recreation 10%, public administration/social services 10%, security/protective services 12%, visual/performing arts 6%.

**Computing on campus.** 150 workstations in dormitories, library, computer center, student center. Dormitories wired for high-speed internet access and linked to campus network. Commuter students can connect to campus network. Online library, helpline, wireless network available.

**Student life. Freshman orientation:** Mandatory. Preregistration for classes offered. One-day sessions held in April, May, June, and August. **Policies:** Students must live and take meals on campus unless they are seniors, married, veterans, or living with parents or close relatives within approved commuting distance. **Housing:** Guaranteed on-campus for freshmen. Coed dorms,

single-sex dorms, apartments, wellness housing available. ADA-compliant rooms available. **Activities:** Bands, campus ministries, choral groups, dance, drama, literary magazine, music ensembles, musical theater, student government, student newspaper, American Marketing Association, Black Action student association, campus activities board, criminal justice society, Fellowship of Christian Athletes, student ecology club, Habitat for Humanity.

**Athletics.** NCAA. **Intercollegiate:** Baseball M, basketball, cross-country, football (tackle) M, golf, soccer, softball W, tennis, track and field, volleyball W. **Intramural:** Basketball, football (non-tackle), football (tackle) M, racquetball, volleyball. **Team name:** Yellow Jackets.

**Student services.** Adult student services, alcohol/substance abuse counseling, chaplain/spiritual director, career counseling, student employment services, financial aid counseling, health services, minority student services, personal counseling, placement for graduates. **Physically disabled:** Services for hearing impaired.

**Contact.** E-mail: admissions@defiance.edu
Phone: (419) 783-2359 Toll-free number: (800) 520-4632
Fax: (419) 783-2468
Brad Harsha, Director of Admissions, Defiance College, 701 North Clinton Street, Defiance, OH 43512-1695

---

## Denison University
**Granville, Ohio**       **CB member**
**www.denison.edu**   •   **CB code: 1164**

- Private 4-year liberal arts college
- Residential campus in small town
- 2,240 degree-seeking undergraduates: 56% women, 6% African American, 2% Asian American, 3% Hispanic American, 6% international
- 2,267 graduate students
- 50% of applicants admitted
- Application essay required
- 83% graduate within 6 years

**General.** Founded in 1831. Regionally accredited. **Degrees:** 502 bachelor's awarded. **ROTC:** Army. **Location:** 27 miles from Columbus. **Calendar:** Semester. **Full-time faculty:** 197 total; 98% have terminal degrees, 16% minority, 44% women. **Part-time faculty:** 20 total; 45% have terminal degrees, 25% minority, 50% women. **Class size:** 65% < 20, 35% 20-39. **Special facilities:** Field research station in 350-acre biological reserve, high resolution spectrometer lab, nuclear magnetic resonance spectrometer, planetarium, economics computer lab, harmonic systems lab, digital media lab, fine and performing arts MIX lab (intermedia experimental lab), geographic information systems lab.

**Freshman class profile.** 5,002 applied, 2,509 admitted, 649 enrolled.

| Mid 50% test scores | | | |
|---|---|---|---|
| SAT critical reading: | 600-700 | Rank in top quarter: | 85% |
| SAT math: | 600-680 | Rank in top tenth: | 54% |
| ACT composite: | 27-30 | Return as sophomores: | 90% |
| GPA 3.75 or higher: | 36% | Out-of-state: | 68% |
| GPA 3.50-3.74: | 23% | Live on campus: | 99% |
| GPA 3.0-3.49: | 33% | International: | 7% |
| GPA 2.0-2.99: | 8% | Fraternities: | 18% |
| | | Sororities: | 19% |

**Basis for selection.** Academic record, recommendations, talent and ability, character and personal qualities most important. School and community activities, essay and personal potential also important. Test scores considered. Interview recommended for all; audition required for visual and performing arts program; portfolio recommended for studio art programs.

**High school preparation.** College-preparatory program required. 19 units required. Required units include English 4, mathematics 4, social studies 2, history 1, science 4, foreign language 3 and academic electives 1.

**2009-2010 Annual costs.** Tuition/fees: $36,560. Room/board: $9,160.

**2009-2010 Financial aid.** **Need-based:** 434 full-time freshmen applied for aid; 344 were judged to have need; 344 of these received aid. Average need met was 94%. Average scholarship/grant was $27,128; average loan $3,954. 67% of total undergraduate aid awarded as scholarships/grants, 33% as loans/jobs. **Non-need-based:** Awarded to 1,932 full-time undergraduates, including 546 freshmen. Scholarships awarded for academics, alumni affiliation, art, leadership, minority status, music/drama, state residency.

**Application procedures.** **Admission:** Closing date 1/15 (postmark date). $40 fee, may be waived for applicants with need, free for online applicants. Admission notification 4/1. Must reply by May 1 or within 2 week(s) if notified thereafter. **Financial aid:** No deadline. Applicants notified on a rolling basis starting 3/28.

**Academics. Special study options:** Double major, honors, independent study, internships, New York semester, semester at sea, student-designed major, study abroad, teacher certification program, Washington semester. 3-2 Duke U. Environmental Management; 3-2 U. of Michigan Natural Resources; 3-4 Case Western Reserve Dental; 3-2 Rensselaer Poly., Washington U. (St. Louis), Case Western Reserve, Columbia U. Engineering; Washington U. (St. Louis) Occupational Therapy. **Credit/placement by examination:** AP, CLEP, IB, institutional tests. **Support services:** Learning center, reduced course load, study skills assistance, tutoring, writing center.

**Majors. Area/ethnic studies:** African-American, East Asian, gay/lesbian, Latin American, Western European, women's. **Biology:** General, biochemistry. **Business:** Organizational behavior. **Communications:** General, digital media. **Computer sciences:** General. **Conservation:** General. **Education:** General, physical. **Foreign languages:** Classics, French, German, Spanish. **History:** General. **Math:** General. **Philosophy/religion:** Philosophy, religion. **Physical sciences:** Chemistry, geology, physics. **Psychology:** General. **Social sciences:** Anthropology, economics, political science, sociology. **Visual/performing arts:** Art history/conservation, dance, dramatic, film/cinema, studio arts.

**Most popular majors.** Biology 10%, communications/journalism 12%, English 8%, foreign language 6%, history 6%, psychology 8%, social sciences 22%, visual/performing arts 10%.

**Computing on campus.** Dormitories wired for high-speed internet access and linked to campus network. Commuter students can connect to campus network. Online library, helpline, student web hosting, wireless network available.

**Student life. Freshman orientation:** Mandatory. Preregistration for classes offered. Mandatory no-fee August orientation program and optional but highly recommended June program costing $175. **Housing:** Guaranteed on-campus for all undergraduates. Coed dorms, single-sex dorms, apartments, cooperative housing, wellness housing available. **Activities:** Jazz band, campus ministries, choral groups, dance, drama, film society, international student organizations, literary magazine, music ensembles, musical theater, radio station, student government, student newspaper, TV station, over 130 organizations available.

**Athletics. NCAA. Intercollegiate:** Baseball M, basketball, cross-country, diving, field hockey W, football (tackle) M, golf M, lacrosse, soccer, softball W, swimming, tennis, track and field, volleyball W. **Intramural:** Basketball, equestrian, football (non-tackle), golf, ice hockey M, lacrosse M, racquetball, rifle, rugby, skiing, soccer, softball, squash, tennis, volleyball, water polo, wrestling M. **Team name:** Big Red.

**Student services.** Alcohol/substance abuse counseling, chaplain/spiritual director, career counseling, student employment services, financial aid counseling, health services, minority student services, personal counseling, placement for graduates.

**Contact.** E-mail: admissions@denison.edu
Phone: (740) 587-6276 Toll-free number: (800) 336-4766
Fax: (740) 587-6306
Perry Robinson, Vice President and Director of Admissions, Denison University, 100 West College PO Box B, Granville, OH 43023

## DeVry University: Columbus
**Columbus, Ohio**      **CB member**
**www.devry.edu**      **CB code: 1605**

- For-profit 4-year university
- Commuter campus in very large city
- 2,697 degree-seeking undergraduates: 47% part-time, 42% women, 23% African American, 2% Asian American, 2% Hispanic American
- 306 degree-seeking graduate students
- Interview required
- 36% graduate within 6 years

**General.** Founded in 1952. Regionally accredited. **Degrees:** 379 bachelor's, 166 associate awarded; master's offered. **ROTC:** Army. **Location:** 5 miles from downtown. **Calendar:** Semester, extensive summer session. **Full-time faculty:** 44 total; 16% minority, 23% women. **Part-time faculty:** 198 total; 17% minority, 36% women.

**Freshman class profile.** 500 enrolled.

**Basis for selection.** Applicants must have high school diploma or equivalent, demonstrate proficiency in basic college-level skills through SAT or ACT scores or institution-administered placement examinations, and be 17

years of age. New students may enter at beginning of any semester. SAT or ACT recommended. CPT also accepted.

**High school preparation.** Required units include mathematics 1. Math unit must be algebra or higher.

**2009-2010 Annual costs.** Tuition/fees: $14,160. Books/supplies: $1,300. Personal expenses: $3,574.

**2008-2009 Financial aid.** All financial aid based on need.

**Application procedures. Admission:** No deadline. $50 fee. Admission notification on a rolling basis. **Financial aid:** No deadline. FAFSA required. Applicants notified on a rolling basis.

**Academics. Special study options:** Accelerated study, distance learning. **Credit/placement by examination:** CLEP, institutional tests. **Support services:** Learning center, tutoring.

**Majors. Business:** Business admin. **Computer sciences:** Networking, systems analysis. **Engineering technology:** Biomedical, computer, electrical. **Other:** Technical management.

**Most popular majors.** Business/marketing 49%, computer/information sciences 35%, engineering/engineering technologies 16%.

**Computing on campus.** 408 workstations in library, computer center, student center. Online course registration, online library, helpline available.

**Student life. Freshman orientation:** Mandatory. **Housing:** Private apartments, student-plan housing, private rooms available. **Activities:** Student association, Tau Alpha Pi, Christian Alliance, Asian American student association, Future Accounting Society, Institute of Electrical and Electronics Engineers, Association of IT Professionals, minority student union.

**Athletics. Intramural:** Basketball, soccer, volleyball.

**Student services.** Career counseling, student employment services, financial aid counseling, placement for graduates, veterans' counselor. **Physically disabled:** Services for visually, hearing impaired.

**Contact.** E-mail: admissions@devry.edu
Phone: (614) 253-1525 Toll-free number: (800) 426-2206
Fax: (614) 253-0843
Bill Holtry, Dean of Admissions, DeVry University: Columbus, 1350 Alum Creek Drive, Columbus, OH 43209-2705

## Franciscan University of Steubenville
**Steubenville, Ohio**      **CB member**
**www.franciscan.edu**      **CB code: 1133**

- Private 4-year university affiliated with Roman Catholic Church
- Residential campus in large town
- 2,034 degree-seeking undergraduates
- 72% of applicants admitted
- SAT or ACT (ACT writing optional), application essay required

**General.** Founded in 1946. Regionally accredited. **Degrees:** 478 bachelor's, 29 associate awarded; master's offered. **ROTC:** Army. **Location:** 40 miles from Pittsburgh. **Calendar:** Semester, limited summer session. **Full-time faculty:** 112 total. **Part-time faculty:** 111 total. **Class size:** 48% < 20, 37% 20-39, 11% 40-49, 3% 50-99, less than 1% >100. **Special facilities:** Replica of Portiuncula (St. Mary of the Angels) Chapel as rebuilt by St. Francis of Assisi in 1207, Tomb of the Unborn Child.

**Freshman class profile.** 1,450 applied, 1,040 admitted, 445 enrolled.

| Mid 50% test scores | | | |
|---|---|---|---|
| SAT critical reading: | 540-650 | GPA 3.0-3.49: | 25% |
| SAT math: | 500-630 | GPA 2.0-2.99: | 12% |
| SAT writing: | 510-630 | Rank in top quarter: | 56% |
| ACT composite: | 23-28 | Rank in top tenth: | 33% |
| GPA 3.75 or higher: | 44% | Out-of-state: | 80% |
| GPA 3.50-3.74: | 19% | Live on campus: | 88% |
| | | Sororities: | 1% |

**Basis for selection.** Admission requirements include 2.4 GPA, recommendations, interview when available, 1000 SAT (exclusive of Writing) or 21 ACT. Interview recommended. **Homeschooled:** Applicants should contact Admissions Office for requirements.

**High school preparation.** 15 units required. Required and recommended units include English 4, mathematics 3, social studies 2, history 2, science 3, foreign language 3 and academic electives 1. 10 units in 4 of the following fields: English, foreign language, social science, math, natural sciences. Remaining 5 units may be in other subjects counted toward graduation. Majors in chemistry, engineering science, or math should have 2 units algebra and 2 units geometry/trigonometry.

**2009-2010 Annual costs.** Tuition/fees: $19,650. Room/board: $6,750. Books/supplies: $1,200. Personal expenses: $1,200.

**2008-2009 Financial aid. Non-need-based:** Scholarships awarded for academics, leadership, religious affiliation.

**Application procedures. Admission:** Priority date 1/31; no deadline. $20 fee, may be waived for applicants with need, free for online applicants. Admission notification on a rolling basis beginning on or about 9/1. **Financial aid:** No deadline. FAFSA required. Applicants notified on a rolling basis starting 3/15; must reply within 3 week(s) of notification.

**Academics.** Students encouraged to spend 1 semester of sophomore year in study abroad program in Gaming, Austria. **Special study options:** Accelerated study, combined bachelor's/graduate degree, distance learning, double major, honors, independent study, internships, liberal arts/career combination, study abroad, teacher certification program. **Credit/placement by examination:** AP, CLEP, IB, institutional tests. 30 credit hours maximum toward associate degree, 30 toward bachelor's. **Support services:** Learning center, reduced course load, study skills assistance, tutoring, writing center.

**Honors college/program.** 1180 SAT (exclusive of Writing) or 26 ACT, 3.4 GPA, and series of essays required. 40 freshmen admitted. Academic program consists of a great books seminar sequence.

**Majors. Biology:** General. **Business:** Accounting, business admin. **Communications:** General. **Computer sciences:** General, computer science. **Education:** Elementary. **Foreign languages:** Classics, French, German, Spanish. **Health:** Mental health services, nursing (RN). **History:** General. **Legal studies:** General. **Liberal arts:** Humanities. **Math:** General. **Philosophy/religion:** Philosophy. **Physical sciences:** Chemistry. **Psychology:** General. **Public administration:** Social work. **Social sciences:** Anthropology, economics, political science, sociology. **Theology:** Religious ed, sacred music, theology. **Visual/performing arts:** Dramatic.

**Most popular majors.** Business/marketing 11%, education 9%, health sciences 15%, theological studies 27%.

**Computing on campus.** 126 workstations in library, computer center. Commuter students can connect to campus network. Online library, helpline available.

**Student life. Freshman orientation:** Mandatory, $150 fee. Preregistration for classes offered. Held weekend before fall classes begin, from Friday morning to Sunday afternoon. **Housing:** Guaranteed on-campus for freshmen. Single-sex dorms available. $300 nonrefundable deposit. Household groups of 10-20 students in residence halls may develop distinctive environment for their group within the context of Christian and Franciscan perspective. **Activities:** Campus ministries, choral groups, drama, international student organizations, literary magazine, music ensembles, radio station, student government, student newspaper, international student organization, Human Life Concerns (pro-life), Works of Mercy Program, leadership development.

**Athletics. Intercollegiate:** Baseball M, basketball, cross-country, rugby M, soccer, tennis M, volleyball W. **Intramural:** Basketball, bowling, football (non-tackle), racquetball, soccer, softball, tennis, volleyball, weight lifting, wrestling M. **Team name:** Barons.

**Student services.** Adult student services, chaplain/spiritual director, career counseling, student employment services, financial aid counseling, health services, personal counseling, veterans' counselor. **Physically disabled:** Services for visually, speech, hearing impaired.

**Contact.** E-mail: admissions@franciscan.edu
Phone: (740) 283-6226 Toll-free number: (800) 783-6220
Fax: (740) 284-5456
Margaret Weber, Director of Admissions, Franciscan University of Steubenville, 1235 University Boulevard, Steubenville, OH 43952-1763

## Franklin University
### Columbus, Ohio
www.franklin.edu
CB code: 1229

- Private 4-year university and business college
- Commuter campus in very large city
- 7,014 degree-seeking undergraduates: 63% part-time, 59% women, 21% African American, 2% Asian American, 2% Hispanic American, 2% international
- 885 degree-seeking graduate students

**General.** Founded in 1902. Regionally accredited. Credit courses offered at suburban campuses and online. **Degrees:** 1,599 bachelor's, 85 associate awarded; master's offered. **ROTC:** Army. **Location:** Downtown. **Calendar:** Trimester, extensive summer session. **Full-time faculty:** 59 total; 83% have terminal degrees, 29% minority, 34% women. **Part-time faculty:** 636 total; 20% have terminal degrees, 15% minority, 45% women. **Class size:** 75% < 20, 24% 20-39, less than 1% 40-49. **Special facilities:** Student learning center.

**Freshman class profile.**

| | | | |
|---|---|---|---|
| Return as sophomores: | 52% | Out-of-state: | 24% |

**Basis for selection.** Open admission, but selective for some programs. Admission tests not required but considered for placement if submitted. Selective admission for international (nonresident alien) students.

**High school preparation.** Recommended units include mathematics 3.

**2009-2010 Annual costs.** Tuition/fees: $8,940. Books/supplies: $900. Personal expenses: $2,150.

**2008-2009 Financial aid. Non-need-based:** Scholarships awarded for academics, leadership, minority status.

**Application procedures. Admission:** No deadline. No application fee. Admission notification on a rolling basis. **Financial aid:** Priority date 6/15; no closing date. FAFSA required. Applicants notified on a rolling basis; must reply within 2 week(s) of notification.

**Academics.** Accelerated 6-week course offerings in addition to 12- and 15-week formats. **Special study options:** Accelerated study, combined bachelor's/graduate degree, cooperative education, cross-registration, distance learning, double major, dual enrollment of high school students, ESL, independent study, internships, study abroad, weekend college. **Credit/placement by examination:** AP, CLEP, institutional tests. 32 credit hours maximum toward associate degree, 84 toward bachelor's. **Support services:** Learning center, reduced course load, remedial instruction, study skills assistance, tutoring, writing center.

**Majors. Business:** General, accounting, finance, human resources, management information systems, management science, marketing, nonprofit/public, operations. **Communications:** Digital media. **Computer sciences:** General, computer science, information technology, web page design. **Health:** Health care admin, medical records technology.

**Most popular majors.** Business/marketing 49%, computer/information sciences 45%.

**Computing on campus.** 370 workstations in library, computer center, student center. Commuter students can connect to campus network. Online course registration, online library, helpline, wireless network available.

**Student life. Freshman orientation:** Available. **Activities:** International student association.

**Student services.** Adult student services, career counseling, financial aid counseling, veterans' counselor. **Physically disabled:** Services for visually, speech, hearing impaired.

**Contact.** E-mail: info@franklin.edu
Phone: (614) 797-4700 Toll-free number: (877) 341-6300
Fax: (614) 224-8027
Wendi Robinson, Director of Undergraduate Student Services, Franklin University, 201 South Grant Avenue, Columbus, OH 43215-5399

## God's Bible School and College
### Cincinnati, Ohio
www.gbs.edu
CB code: 1238

- Private 4-year Bible college affiliated with interdenominational tradition
- Residential campus in large city
- 264 degree-seeking undergraduates

**General.** Founded in 1900. Accredited by ABHE. **Degrees:** 30 bachelor's, 15 associate awarded. **Location:** One mile from downtown. **Calendar:** Semester. **Full-time faculty:** 13 total. **Part-time faculty:** 14 total.

**Basis for selection.** Three references recommended (two required); SAT required for placement.

**High school preparation.** 17 units recommended. Recommended units include English 3, mathematics 2, social studies 2 and science 2.

**2009-2010 Annual costs.** Tuition/fees: $5,580. Room/board: $3,450. Books/supplies: $650. Personal expenses: $2,600.

**2009-2010 Financial aid. Non-need-based:** Scholarships awarded for academics, leadership, music/drama, religious affiliation. **Additional information:** Institutional work scholarships available.

**Application procedures. Admission:** Priority date 6/1; no deadline. $50 fee. Application must be submitted on paper. Admission notification on a rolling basis. **Financial aid:** Priority date 4/30; no closing date. FAFSA required. Applicants notified on a rolling basis.

**Academics. Special study options:** Distance learning, double major, independent study, internships, liberal arts/career combination. **Credit/placement by examination:** CLEP, SAT, institutional tests. **Support services:** Learning center.

**Majors. Education:** Elementary, English, music. **Theology:** Missionary, pastoral counseling, religious ed, sacred music, theology, youth ministry. **Other:** Church/family ministry.

**Computing on campus.** Dormitories wired for high-speed internet access. Wireless network available.

**Student life. Freshman orientation:** Mandatory. Preregistration for classes offered. Takes place week before classes begin, lasting for several days. **Policies:** Students agree to follow all rules, policies and regulations by matriculating. Please contact Office of Student Affairs for specific information. Religious observance required. **Housing:** Guaranteed on-campus for freshmen. Single-sex dorms, wellness housing available. **Activities:** Choral groups, drama, music ensembles, student government, student newspaper, symphony orchestra.

**Athletics. Intramural:** Basketball, volleyball.

**Student services.** Chaplain/spiritual director, student employment services, financial aid counseling, health services, personal counseling, placement for graduates, veterans' counselor.

**Contact.** E-mail: sbuckland@gbs.edu
Phone: (513) 721-7944 ext. 205 Toll-free number: (800) 486-4637 ext. 205
Fax: (513) 721-1357
Steve Buckland, Director of Admissions, God's Bible School and College, 1810 Young Street, Cincinnati, OH 45202-6838

---

## Heidelberg University

Tiffin, Ohio
www.heidelberg.edu

CB member
CB code: 1292

- Private 4-year liberal arts college affiliated with United Church of Christ
- Residential campus in large town
- 1,271 degree-seeking undergraduates: 7% part-time, 48% women, 10% African American, 1% Asian American, 3% Hispanic American, 1% international
- 184 degree-seeking graduate students
- 69% of applicants admitted
- SAT or ACT (ACT writing optional) required
- 54% graduate within 6 years

**General.** Founded in 1850. Regionally accredited. **Degrees:** 262 bachelor's awarded; master's offered. **ROTC:** Army, Air Force. **Location:** 52 miles from Toledo, 80 miles from Cleveland. **Calendar:** Semester, limited summer session. **Full-time faculty:** 70 total; 81% have terminal degrees, 11% minority, 43% women. **Part-time faculty:** 93 total; 28% have terminal degrees, 10% minority, 46% women. **Class size:** 61% < 20, 35% 20-39, 3% 40-49, 1% 50-99. **Special facilities:** National center for water quality research, cadaver laboratory, four wooded lots for science research, archaeology laboratory, historic and military archaeology center.

**Freshman class profile.** 2,209 applied, 1,527 admitted, 381 enrolled.

| Mid 50% test scores | | | |
|---|---|---|---|
| SAT critical reading: | 420-560 | GPA 2.0-2.99: | 42% |
| SAT math: | 450-560 | Rank in top quarter: | 34% |
| SAT writing: | 440-560 | Rank in top tenth: | 16% |
| ACT composite: | 18-24 | Return as sophomores: | 65% |
| GPA 3.75 or higher: | 20% | Out-of-state: | 20% |
| GPA 3.50-3.74: | 11% | Live on campus: | 91% |
| GPA 3.0-3.49: | 26% | Fraternities: | 11% |
| | | Sororities: | 18% |

**Basis for selection.** School achievement record most important, followed by test scores. Positive trend in grades and college prep coursework

also important. Special talents, community activities, and leadership qualities considered. Audition required for music; interview recommended for academically challanged students. **Learning Disabled:** Students with learning disabilities are strongly encouraged to self-report to the Academic Success Center after acceptance to the University. Appointments to discuss possible services/accommodations are welcome.

**High school preparation.** College-preparatory program recommended. 21 units recommended. Recommended units include English 4, mathematics 3, social studies 3, history 2, science 3 (laboratory 1), foreign language 2 and academic electives 3.

**2010-2011 Annual costs.** Tuition/fees (projected): $22,780. Room/board: $8,636. Books/supplies: $1,500. Personal expenses: $500.

**2009-2010 Financial aid. Need-based:** 356 full-time freshmen applied for aid; 327 were judged to have need; 327 of these received aid. Average need met was 80%. Average scholarship/grant was $14,695; average loan $4,143. 61% of total undergraduate aid awarded as scholarships/grants, 39% as loans/jobs. **Non-need-based:** Awarded to 780 full-time undergraduates, including 338 freshmen. Scholarships awarded for academics, music/drama, religious affiliation, state residency.

**Application procedures. Admission:** Priority date 1/1; deadline 8/1. $25 fee, may be waived for applicants with need, free for online applicants. Admission notification on a rolling basis beginning on or about 10/15. Must reply by May 1 or within 2 week(s) if notified thereafter. **Financial aid:** Priority date 3/1; no closing date. FAFSA required. Applicants notified on a rolling basis starting 3/1; must reply by 5/1 or within 2 week(s) of notification.

**Academics. Special study options:** Accelerated study, combined bachelor's/graduate degree, cooperative education, cross-registration, double major, dual enrollment of high school students, ESL, exchange student, honors, independent study, internships, liberal arts/career combination, study abroad, teacher certification program, Washington semester. **Credit/placement by examination:** AP, CLEP, IB, SAT, ACT, institutional tests. 30 credit hours maximum toward bachelor's degree. **Support services:** Learning center, reduced course load, study skills assistance, tutoring.

**Majors. Biology:** General, environmental. **Business:** Accounting, business admin, management science. **Communications:** General, public relations. **Computer sciences:** General, computer science. **Conservation:** Management/policy. **Education:** Music, physical. **Foreign languages:** German, Spanish. **Health:** Athletic training, health care admin, predental, premedicine, prenursing, preveterinary. **History:** General. **Interdisciplinary:** Biological/physical sciences. **Legal studies:** Prelaw. **Math:** General. **Parks/recreation:** Sports admin. **Philosophy/religion:** Religion. **Physical sciences:** Chemistry, physics. **Protective services:** Law enforcement admin. **Psychology:** General. **Public administration:** General. **Social sciences:** General, anthropology, economics, political science. **Visual/performing arts:** Music management, music performance, music theory/composition, musical theater.

**Most popular majors.** Business/marketing 23%, education 19%, parks/recreation 13%, psychology 10%.

**Computing on campus.** 125 workstations in dormitories, library, computer center, student center. Dormitories wired for high-speed internet access and linked to campus network. Online course registration, helpline, repair service, wireless network available.

**Student life. Freshman orientation:** Mandatory. Preregistration for classes offered. Five 2-day summer sessions offered. **Housing:** Guaranteed on-campus for all undergraduates. Coed dorms, single-sex dorms, special housing for disabled, apartments, cooperative housing, wellness housing available. $250 fully refundable deposit, deadline 8/1. Undergraduate specialty houses by major, interest, service groups available. **Activities:** Bands, campus ministries, choral groups, dance, drama, film society, international student organizations, literary magazine, music ensembles, Model UN, musical theater, opera, radio station, student government, student newspaper, symphony orchestra, TV station, campus fellowship, black student union, Young Democrats, Young Republicans, world student union, Alpha Phi Omega, political science organization, Amigos de ARISE.

**Athletics. NCAA. Intercollegiate:** Baseball M, basketball, cheerleading, cross-country, football (tackle) M, golf, soccer, softball W, tennis, track and field, volleyball W, wrestling M. **Intramural:** Archery, baseball M, basketball, bowling, golf, soccer, softball, table tennis, volleyball. **Team name:** Student Princes.

**Student services.** Adult student services, alcohol/substance abuse counseling, chaplain/spiritual director, career counseling, student employment services, financial aid counseling, health services, minority student services, personal counseling, placement for graduates, women's services. **Physically disabled:** Services for visually, hearing impaired.

**Contact.** E-mail: adminfo@heidelberg.edu
Phone: (419) 448-2330 Toll-free number: (800) 434-3352
Fax: (419) 448-2334
Lindsay Sooy, Director of Admission, Heidelberg University, 310 East
Market Street, Tiffin, OH 44883-2462

## Hiram College

**Hiram, Ohio**
**www.hiram.edu**

**CB member**
**CB code: 1297**

- Private 4-year liberal arts college affiliated with Christian Church (Disciples of Christ)
- Residential campus in rural community
- 1,339 degree-seeking undergraduates: 11% part-time, 55% women, 10% African American, 1% Asian American, 2% Hispanic American, 6% international
- 28 degree-seeking graduate students
- 88% of applicants admitted
- SAT or ACT (ACT writing optional), application essay required
- 69% graduate within 6 years

**General.** Founded in 1850. Regionally accredited. Affiliated with John Cabot University in Rome (Italy), Shoals Marine Laboratory (Appledore Island near Maine/New Hampshire coast), Institute of European Studies (Chicago). Exchange programs with Kansai University of Foreign Studies in Osaka (Japan) and Bosphorus University in Istanbul (Turkey). **Degrees:** 230 bachelor's awarded; master's offered. **Location:** 35 miles from Cleveland. **Calendar:** Semester, limited summer session. **Full-time faculty:** 79 total; 96% have terminal degrees, 2% minority, 48% women. **Part-time faculty:** 60 total; 28% have terminal degrees, 8% minority, 48% women. **Class size:** 74% < 20, 23% 20-39, 3% 40-49, less than 1% 50-99. **Special facilities:** 2 nature/science field research stations, observatory, center for literature and medicine.

**Freshman class profile.** 1,269 applied, 1,112 admitted, 293 enrolled.

| Mid 50% test scores | | | |
|---|---|---|---|
| SAT critical reading: | 440-600 | Rank in top quarter: | 46% |
| SAT math: | 450-590 | Rank in top tenth: | 20% |
| GPA 3.75 or higher: | 24% | Return as sophomores: | 78% |
| GPA 3.50-3.74: | 15% | Out-of-state: | 17% |
| GPA 3.0-3.49: | 28% | Live on campus: | 93% |
| GPA 2.0-2.99: | 33% | International: | 8% |

**Basis for selection.** School record, test scores, counselor and teacher recommendations emphasized. Extracurricular participation, alumni relationship considered. Interview required for scholarship candidates or academically marginal applicants; recommended for all others.

**High school preparation.** College-preparatory program recommended. 20 units required; 21 recommended. Required and recommended units include English 4, mathematics 3, social studies 3, history 1, science 3 (laboratory 2), foreign language 2-3 and academic electives 2. One course in fine arts recommended.

**2009-2010 Annual costs.** Tuition/fees: $27,135. Room/board: $9,010. Books/supplies: $700. Personal expenses: $1,404.

**2009-2010 Financial aid.** **Non-need-based:** Scholarships awarded for academics, alumni affiliation, music/drama, religious affiliation, state residency.

**Application procedures. Admission:** Priority date 2/15; no deadline. $35 fee, may be waived for applicants with need, free for online applicants. Admission notification on a rolling basis beginning on or about 10/1. Must reply by May 1 or within 2 week(s) if notified thereafter. **Financial aid:** Priority date 2/15; no closing date. FAFSA required. Applicants notified on a rolling basis starting 2/15; must reply by 5/1 or within 2 week(s) of notification.

**Academics.** Prelaw, premed and preveterinary programs offered. **Special study options:** Accelerated study, combined bachelor's/graduate degree, cross-registration, distance learning, double major, ESL, exchange student, independent study, internships, student-designed major, study abroad, teacher certification program, Washington semester, weekend college. **Credit/placement by examination:** AP, CLEP, IB, institutional tests. 60 credit hours maximum toward bachelor's degree. **Support services:** Reduced course load, study skills assistance, tutoring, writing center.

**Majors. Biology:** General, biochemistry, biomedical sciences. **Business:** Accounting/finance, business admin. **Communications:** General. **Computer sciences:** General, computer science. **Conservation:** Environmental studies. **Education:** General, elementary. **Foreign languages:** Classics, French, German, Spanish. **History:** General. **Interdisciplinary:** Math/computer science. **Legal studies:** Prelaw. **Math:** General. **Philosophy/religion:** Philosophy, religion. **Physical sciences:** Chemistry, physics. **Psychology:** General. **Social sciences:** General, economics, political science, sociology. **Visual/performing arts:** Art history/conservation, dramatic, studio arts.

**Most popular majors.** Biology 15%, business/marketing 22%, English 6%, social sciences 18%, visual/performing arts 6%.

**Computing on campus.** 100 workstations in dormitories, library, computer center, student center. Dormitories wired for high-speed internet access and linked to campus network. Commuter students can connect to campus network. Online course registration, online library, helpline, student web hosting, wireless network available.

**Student life. Freshman orientation:** Mandatory, $240 fee. Preregistration for classes offered. Several orientation sessions held throughout late spring and summer. **Housing:** Guaranteed on-campus for all undergraduates. Coed dorms, single-sex dorms, special housing for disabled, wellness housing available. $200 nonrefundable deposit, deadline 5/1. Dormitories include 24-hour and 12-hour quiet floors. **Activities:** Bands, campus ministries, choral groups, dance, drama, international student organizations, literary magazine, music ensembles, Model UN, opera, radio station, student government, student newspaper, symphony orchestra, African-American Students United, environmental awareness club, Christian Fellowship, Network for Progressive Action, conservative student forum, volunteer association, international organization, Intercultural Forum, Newman Club, Islamic Society.

**Athletics.** NCAA. **Intercollegiate:** Baseball M, basketball, cross-country, diving, football (tackle) M, golf, soccer, softball W, swimming, tennis, track and field, volleyball W. **Intramural:** Archery, basketball, football (non-tackle), soccer, softball, tennis, volleyball, water polo. **Team name:** Terriers.

**Student services.** Chaplain/spiritual director, career counseling, student employment services, health services, minority student services, personal counseling, placement for graduates, veterans' counselor.

**Contact.** E-mail: admission@hiram.edu
Phone: (330) 569-5169 Toll-free number: (800) 362-5280
Fax: (330) 569-5944
Sherman Dean, Director of Admission, Hiram College, Teachout Price Hall, Hiram, OH 44234

## John Carroll University

**University Heights, Ohio**
**www.jcu.edu**

**CB member**
**CB code: 1342**

- Private 4-year university affiliated with Roman Catholic Church
- Residential campus in large town
- 2,957 degree-seeking undergraduates: 2% part-time, 51% women, 6% African American, 2% Asian American, 3% Hispanic American
- 693 degree-seeking graduate students
- 81% of applicants admitted
- SAT or ACT (ACT writing recommended), application essay required
- 87% graduate within 6 years; 74% enter graduate study

**General.** Founded in 1886. Regionally accredited. **Degrees:** 700 bachelor's awarded; master's offered. **ROTC:** Army. **Location:** 9 miles from Cleveland. **Calendar:** Semester, extensive summer session. **Full-time faculty:** 212 total; 91% have terminal degrees, 12% minority, 41% women. **Part-time faculty:** 153 total; 37% have terminal degrees, 42% women. **Class size:** 45% < 20, 55% 20-39, less than 1% 40-49. **Special facilities:** Science and technology center.

**Freshman class profile.** 3,411 applied, 2,763 admitted, 661 enrolled.

| Mid 50% test scores | | | |
|---|---|---|---|
| SAT critical reading: | 480-580 | Rank in top quarter: | 49% |
| SAT math: | 480-600 | Rank in top tenth: | 20% |
| SAT writing: | 470-580 | End year in good standing: | 90% |
| ACT composite: | 21-26 | Return as sophomores: | 83% |
| GPA 3.75 or higher: | 24% | Out-of-state: | 31% |
| GPA 3.50-3.74: | 17% | Live on campus: | 92% |
| GPA 3.0-3.49: | 33% | Fraternities: | 4% |
| GPA 2.0-2.99: | 26% | Sororities: | 10% |

**Basis for selection.** High school academic record, rigor of curricula most important. Other criteria include test scores, extracurricular activities, essay. **Homeschooled:** State high school equivalency certificate, interview, letter of recommendation (nonparent) required. Extra emphasis placed on standardized testing. Encourage SAT subject testing if possible.

**High school preparation.** College-preparatory program required. 16 units required; 21 recommended. Required and recommended units include English 4, mathematics 3-4, social studies 2-4, science 2-3 (laboratory 2-3), foreign language 2-3 and academic electives 3. 2-4 units among social studies, history, social science, or religion.

**2009-2010 Annual costs.** Tuition/fees: $28,840. Room/board: $8,330. Books/supplies: $1,200. Personal expenses: $1,000.

**2009-2010 Financial aid. Need-based:** 563 full-time freshmen applied for aid; 491 were judged to have need; 491 of these received aid. Average need met was 85%. Average scholarship/grant was $17,877; average loan $3,975. 59% of total undergraduate aid awarded as scholarships/grants, 41% as loans/jobs. **Non-need-based:** Awarded to 701 full-time undergraduates, including 214 freshmen. Scholarships awarded for academics, alumni affiliation, leadership, minority status, ROTC, state residency. **Additional information:** Institutional form for need analysis required from upperclassmen and transfer students only.

**Application procedures. Admission:** Priority date 12/1; deadline 2/1 (postmark date). No application fee. Admission notification on a rolling basis beginning on or about 12/1. Must reply by May 1 or within 4 week(s) if notified thereafter. **Financial aid:** Priority date 2/15, closing date 3/15. FAFSA required. Applicants notified on a rolling basis starting 2/1; must reply by 5/1 or within 4 week(s) of notification.

**Academics. Special study options:** Accelerated study, combined bachelor's/graduate degree, cooperative education, cross-registration, double major, dual enrollment of high school students, exchange student, honors, independent study, internships, liberal arts/career combination, student-designed major, study abroad, teacher certification program, Washington semester. **Credit/placement by examination:** AP, CLEP, IB, institutional tests. 30 credit hours maximum toward bachelor's degree. **Support services:** Learning center, reduced course load, study skills assistance, tutoring, writing center.

**Majors. Biology:** General, biochemistry. **Business:** Accounting, business admin, finance, logistics, managerial economics. **Communications:** General. **Computer sciences:** General, computer science. **Conservation:** Environmental science, environmental studies. **Education:** Elementary, physical. **Engineering:** Physics. **Foreign languages:** Ancient Greek, comparative lit, French, German, Latin, Spanish. **Health:** Predental, premedicine, preveterinary. **History:** General. **Interdisciplinary:** Gerontology. **Legal studies:** Prelaw. **Liberal arts:** Arts/sciences. **Math:** General. **Philosophy/religion:** Philosophy, religion. **Physical sciences:** Chemistry, physics. **Psychology:** General. **Social sciences:** Economics, political science, sociology. **Visual/performing arts:** Art history/conservation.

**Most popular majors.** Biology 9%, business/marketing 31%, communications/journalism 15%, education 6%, psychology 9%, social sciences 9%.

**Computing on campus.** 200 workstations in dormitories, library, computer center, student center. Dormitories wired for high-speed internet access and linked to campus network. Commuter students can connect to campus network. Online course registration, online library, helpline, repair service, student web hosting, wireless network available.

**Student life. Freshman orientation:** Mandatory, $325 fee. Two-day, one overnight for parents and students. Students take placement tests. **Policies:** Students must adhere to the Student Code of Conduct. All incoming freshman students required to live on campus freshman and sophomore years. **Housing:** Guaranteed on-campus for all undergraduates. Coed dorms, single-sex dorms, special housing for disabled, apartments, fraternity/sorority housing, wellness housing available. $300 fully refundable deposit, deadline 5/1. Suite-style housing available. **Activities:** Pep band, campus ministries, choral groups, dance, drama, international student organizations, literary magazine, music ensembles, radio station, student government, student newspaper, TV station, Christian Life Community, African American Alliance, EMS Association, Habitat for Humanity, Labre Project, Students in Free Enterprise, Public Relations Student Society of America.

**Athletics.** NCAA. **Intercollegiate:** Baseball M, basketball, cheerleading M, cross-country, diving, football (tackle) M, golf, soccer, softball W, swimming, tennis, track and field, volleyball W, wrestling M. **Intramural:** Basketball, football (non-tackle), golf, racquetball, soccer, softball, table tennis, tennis, volleyball, water polo. **Team name:** Blue Streaks.

**Student services.** Adult student services, alcohol/substance abuse counseling, chaplain/spiritual director, career counseling, student employment services, financial aid counseling, health services, minority student services, personal counseling, placement for graduates, veterans' counselor, women's services. **Physically disabled:** Services for visually, speech, hearing impaired.

**Contact.** E-mail: admission@jcu.edu
Phone: (216) 397-4294 Toll-free number: (888) 335-6800
Fax: (216) 397-4981
Steven Vitatoe, Executive Director of Enrollment, John Carroll University, 20700 North Park Boulevard, University Heights, OH 44118-4581

---

## Kent State University

Kent, Ohio
www.kent.edu

CB member
CB code: 1367

- Public 4-year university
- Residential campus in large town
- 19,337 degree-seeking undergraduates: 10% part-time, 58% women
- 4,758 degree-seeking graduate students
- 72% of applicants admitted
- SAT or ACT (ACT writing recommended) required

**General.** Founded in 1910. Regionally accredited. **Degrees:** 3,879 bachelor's awarded; master's, doctoral offered. **ROTC:** Army, Air Force. **Location:** 50 miles from Cleveland, 11 miles from Akron. **Calendar:** Semester, extensive summer session. **Full-time faculty:** 888 total; 18% minority, 49% women. **Part-time faculty:** 652 total; 12% minority, 54% women. **Class size:** 46% < 20, 42% 20-39, 4% 40-49, 5% 50-99, 3% >100. **Special facilities:** 287-acre airport, liquid crystal institute, fashion museum, planetarium, ice arena, 18-hole golf course.

**Freshman class profile.** 14,933 applied, 10,735 admitted, 4,151 enrolled.

| Mid 50% test scores | | | |
|---|---|---|---|
| SAT critical reading: | 460-560 | GPA 3.0-3.49: | 34% |
| SAT math: | 460-580 | GPA 2.0-2.99: | 33% |
| SAT writing: | 440-560 | Rank in top quarter: | 37% |
| ACT composite: | 20-25 | Rank in top tenth: | 13% |
| GPA 3.75 or higher: | 15% | Return as sophomores: | 78% |
| GPA 3.50-3.74: | 17% | Out-of-state: | 17% |
| | | Live on campus: | 80% |

**Basis for selection.** Academic record, course work, test scores important. Varying criteria for nursing, education, flight, fashion design and merchandising, architecture, interior design, journalism and mass communication, 6-year medical program, music, dance, and honors college applicants. Interview required for 6-year medical program, recommended for all others. Audition required for dance, music, and musical theater students.

**High school preparation.** College-preparatory program recommended. 16 units recommended. Recommended units include English 4, mathematics 3, social studies 3, science 3 (laboratory 2), foreign language 2 and visual/performing arts 1. One fine arts or third unit of foreign language recommended.

**2009-2010 Annual costs.** Tuition/fees: $8,726; $16,418 out-of-state. Room/board: $7,940. Books/supplies: $1,280. Personal expenses: $2,430.

**2009-2010 Financial aid. Need-based:** 3,347 full-time freshmen applied for aid; 2,648 were judged to have need; 2,642 of these received aid. Average need met was 56%. Average scholarship/grant was $6,248; average loan $3,217. 53% of total undergraduate aid awarded as scholarships/grants, 47% as loans/jobs. **Non-need-based:** Awarded to 3,735 full-time undergraduates, including 1,360 freshmen. Scholarships awarded for academics, alumni affiliation, art, athletics, leadership, minority status, music/drama, ROTC, state residency. **Additional information:** Participant in US Department of Education's Quality Assurance Program and Experimental Sites Program.

**Application procedures. Admission:** Priority date 1/15; deadline 8/1 (postmark date). $40 fee, may be waived for applicants with need. Admission notification on a rolling basis beginning on or about 10/1. **Financial aid:** Priority date 3/1; no closing date. FAFSA required. Applicants notified on a rolling basis starting 3/15; must reply within 2 week(s) of notification.

**Academics. Special study options:** Accelerated study, combined bachelor's/graduate degree, cooperative education, cross-registration, distance learning, double major, dual enrollment of high school students, ESL, exchange student, external degree, honors, independent study, internships, liberal arts/career combination, New York semester, student-designed major, study abroad, teacher certification program, Washington semester, weekend college. BS/MD. **Credit/placement by examination:** AP, CLEP, IB, SAT, ACT, institutional tests. 30 credit hours maximum toward bachelor's degree. **Support services:** Learning center, pre-admission summer program, reduced course load, remedial instruction, study skills assistance, tutoring, writing center.

**Honors college/program.** Approximately 250 incoming freshman admitted; based on class rank within top 10%; 3.5 GPA; 25 ACT/1140 SAT (exclusive of Writing); small interactive classes (20 maximum); eight courses culminating with thesis project, portfolio, or course; two study abroad programs.

**Majors. Architecture:** Architecture. **Area/ethnic studies:** African-American, American, Latin American, Russian/Slavic. **Biology:** General, biotechnology, botany, zoology. **Business:** Accounting, business admin, fashion, finance, management information systems, management science, managerial economics, marketing. **Communications:** General, advertising, broadcast journalism, digital media, journalism, photojournalism, public relations, radio/tv. **Computer sciences:** Systems analysis. **Conservation:** General. **Education:** General, art, business, chemistry, early childhood, health, mathematics, middle, music, physical, science, social studies, special, technology/industrial arts, trade/industrial. **Engineering:** General, industrial. **Family/consumer sciences:** Family studies, food/nutrition. **Foreign languages:** French, German, Latin, Russian, sign language interpretation, Spanish. **Health:** Athletic training, audiology/speech pathology, clinical lab science, nursing (RN), predental, premedicine, preveterinary. **History:** General. **Interdisciplinary:** Peace/conflict. **Legal studies:** Paralegal. **Liberal arts:** Arts/sciences, humanities. **Math:** General, applied. **Parks/recreation:** Facilities management. **Philosophy/religion:** Philosophy. **Physical sciences:** Chemistry, geology, physics. **Protective services:** Criminal justice. **Psychology:** General. **Social sciences:** Anthropology, geography, international relations, political science, sociology. **Transportation:** Aviation. **Visual/performing arts:** Art history/conservation, commercial/advertising art, crafts, dance, dramatic, fashion design, interior design, painting. **Other:** Ethnic Heritage.

**Most popular majors.** Business/marketing 21%, communications/journalism 8%, education 10%, health sciences 12%, psychology 7%, visual/performing arts 6%.

**Computing on campus.** 2,100 workstations in dormitories, library, computer center, student center. Dormitories wired for high-speed internet access and linked to campus network. Commuter students can connect to campus network. Online course registration, online library, helpline, repair service, student web hosting, wireless network available.

**Student life. Freshman orientation:** Mandatory, $100 fee. Preregistration for classes offered. **Housing:** Guaranteed on-campus for freshmen. Coed dorms, single-sex dorms, special housing for disabled, apartments, fraternity/sorority housing available. $200 fully refundable deposit, deadline 6/1. Single undergraduate students must live in college housing first 4 semesters with some exemptions granted. Learning communities available. **Activities:** Bands, campus ministries, choral groups, dance, drama, international student organizations, literary magazine, music ensembles, musical theater, radio station, student government, student newspaper, TV station, social service, political and religious organizations available.

**Athletics.** NCAA. **Intercollegiate:** Baseball M, basketball, cross-country, field hockey W, football (tackle) M, golf, gymnastics W, soccer W, softball W, track and field, volleyball W, wrestling M. **Intramural:** Badminton, basketball, bowling, football (non-tackle), golf, racquetball, soccer, softball, table tennis, tennis, water polo, wrestling M. **Team name:** Golden Flashes.

**Student services.** Adult student services, alcohol/substance abuse counseling, chaplain/spiritual director, career counseling, services for economically disadvantaged, student employment services, financial aid counseling, health services, legal services, minority student services, personal counseling, placement for graduates, veterans' counselor, women's services. **Physically disabled:** Services for visually, speech, hearing impaired.

**Contact.** E-mail: admissions@kent.edu
Phone: (330) 672-2444 Toll-free number: (800) 988-5368
Fax: (330) 672-2499
Nancy DellaVecchia, Director of Admissions, Kent State University, PO Box 5190, Kent, OH 44242-0001

---

## Kenyon College

**Gambier, Ohio**
**www.kenyon.edu**

**CB member**
**CB code: 1370**

- Private 4-year liberal arts college
- Residential campus in rural community
- 1,616 degree-seeking undergraduates: 52% women, 4% African American, 6% Asian American, 3% Hispanic American, 1% Native American, 4% international
- 39% of applicants admitted
- SAT or ACT (ACT writing optional), application essay required
- 89% graduate within 6 years; 17% enter graduate study

**General.** Founded in 1824. Regionally accredited. **Degrees:** 386 bachelor's awarded. **Location:** 50 miles from Columbus. **Calendar:** Semester. **Full-time faculty:** 156 total; 99% have terminal degrees, 14% minority, 44% women. **Part-time faculty:** 46 total; 59% have terminal degrees, 15% minority, 48% women. **Class size:** 70% < 20, 27% 20-39, 2% 40-49, 1% 50-99, less than 1% >100. **Special facilities:** Observatory, environmental center and nature preserve, science center.

**Freshman class profile.** 3,992 applied, 1,538 admitted, 469 enrolled.

| Mid 50% test scores | | | |
|---|---|---|---|
| SAT critical reading: | 630-720 | GPA 2.0-2.99: | 2% |
| SAT math: | 600-680 | Rank in top quarter: | 87% |
| SAT writing: | 620-730 | Rank in top tenth: | 56% |
| ACT composite: | 28-32 | End year in good standing: | 99% |
| GPA 3.75 or higher: | 60% | Return as sophomores: | 91% |
| GPA 3.50-3.74: | 16% | Out-of-state: | 84% |
| GPA 3.0-3.49: | 22% | Live on campus: | 100% |
| | | International: | 5% |

**Basis for selection.** Secondary school record and personal character most important followed by test scores, class rank, recommendations, essay, talent, activities and interview. Alumni relationship, ethnicity, geographical residence and work experience considered. Non-native speakers of English required to submit TOEFL results. **Homeschooled:** Provide complete curriculum with texts and books used.

**High school preparation.** College-preparatory program required. 21 units required; 24 recommended. Required and recommended units include English 4, mathematics 3-4, social studies 1, history 2-3, science 3-4 (laboratory 3), foreign language 3-4 and academic electives 3. 1 fine arts recommended.

**2009-2010 Annual costs.** Tuition/fees: $40,980. Room/board: $7,260. Books/supplies: $1,300.

**2009-2010 Financial aid. Need-based:** 281 full-time freshmen applied for aid; 212 were judged to have need; 212 of these received aid. Average need met was 98%. Average scholarship/grant was $28,858; average loan $3,389. 86% of total undergraduate aid awarded as scholarships/grants, 14% as loans/jobs. **Non-need-based:** Scholarships awarded for academics, leadership, minority status.

**Application procedures. Admission:** Closing date 1/15 (postmark date). $45 fee, may be waived for applicants with need, free for online applicants. Admission notification 4/1. Must reply by 5/1. **Financial aid:** Closing date 2/15. FAFSA, CSS PROFILE required. Applicants notified by 4/1; must reply by 5/1.

**Academics. Special study options:** Accelerated study, combined bachelor's/graduate degree, double major, exchange student, honors, independent study, liberal arts/career combination, semester at sea, student-designed major, study abroad, urban semester, Washington semester. Cooperative 3-2 or 4-1 masters and teacher certification program with Bank Street College of Education; 3-2 engineering program with Case Western Reserve, Rensselaer Polytechnic Institute and Washington University; 3-2 environmental studies program with Duke University. Special off-campus semester programs: Historically Black Colleges; Boston University Marine Program (BUMP); The International Partnership for Service Learning: Appalachia, South Dakota; Marine Laboratory; National Theater Institute; Newberry Library Program in the Humanities; New York Arts Program; Oak Ridge Science Semester, Tennessee; The Philadelphia Center; SEA Semester; Semester in Environmental Science; Washington Semester Programs. **Credit/placement by examination:** AP, CLEP, IB, institutional tests. 3 credit hours maximum toward bachelor's degree. Credit determined for AP, IB or School Articulation Program (SCAP) counts toward 16 units required for graduation. No diversification requirements may be satisfied with AP credit. Maximum of 3 units of advanced placement credit is accepted by Kenyon. **Support services:** Study skills assistance, tutoring, writing center.

**Majors. Area/ethnic studies:** American, women's. **Biology:** General, biochemistry, molecular. **Foreign languages:** General, ancient Greek, classics, French, German, Latin, Spanish. **History:** General. **Interdisciplinary:** Neuroscience. **Math:** General. **Philosophy/religion:** Philosophy, religion. **Physical sciences:** Chemistry, physics. **Psychology:** General. **Social sciences:** Anthropology, economics, international relations, political science, sociology. **Visual/performing arts:** Art history/conservation, dance, dramatic, studio arts.

**Most popular majors.** Biology 11%, English 14%, history 7%, psychology 7%, social sciences 32%, visual/performing arts 12%.

**Computing on campus.** 400 workstations in dormitories, library, computer center. Dormitories wired for high-speed internet access and linked to campus network. Commuter students can connect to campus network. Online library, helpline, student web hosting, wireless network available.

**Student life. Freshman orientation:** Mandatory. Held 4 days prior to start of classes. **Housing:** Guaranteed on-campus for all undergraduates. Coed dorms, single-sex dorms, special housing for disabled, apartments, fraternity/sorority housing, wellness housing available. $350 nonrefundable deposit, deadline 5/1. Special accommodations can be made for married, international and disabled students. Fraternity and sorority housing available in room blocks only. Wellness and community service and social group halls on campus. **Activities:** Bands, campus ministries, choral groups, dance, drama, film society, international student organizations, literary magazine, music ensembles, Model UN, musical theater, opera, radio station, student government, student newspaper, symphony orchestra, black student union, Saturday Night Fellowship, Hillel, Asian awareness club, community service organization, allied sexual orientations, Amnesty International, Zen meditation group, political affairs clubs, Circle K.

**Athletics.** NCAA. **Intercollegiate:** Baseball M, basketball, cross-country, diving, field hockey W, football (tackle) M, golf M, lacrosse, soccer, softball W, swimming, tennis, track and field, volleyball W. **Intramural:** Basketball, football (non-tackle), racquetball, soccer, softball W, squash, volleyball. **Team name:** Lords/Ladies.

**Student services.** Alcohol/substance abuse counseling, chaplain/spiritual director, career counseling, student employment services, financial aid counseling, health services, minority student services, personal counseling, placement for graduates, women's services. **Physically disabled:** Services for visually, hearing impaired.

**Contact.** E-mail: admissions@kenyon.edu
Phone: (740) 427-5776 Toll-free number: (800) 848-2468
Fax: (740) 427-5770
Jennifer Delahunty, Dean of Admissions, Kenyon College, Ransom Hall, Gambier, OH 43022-9623

## Kettering College of Medical Arts
### Kettering, Ohio
www.kcma.edu
**CB code: 0602**

◆ Private 4-year health science and nursing college affiliated with Seventh-day Adventists
◆ Commuter campus in large city
◆ 785 degree-seeking undergraduates: 40% part-time, 79% women, 8% African American, 3% Asian American, 2% Hispanic American
◆ 92 degree-seeking graduate students
◆ 52% of applicants admitted
◆ Application essay required
◆ 96% graduate within 6 years

**General.** Founded in 1967. Regionally accredited. **Degrees:** 50 bachelor's, 193 associate awarded; master's offered. **Location:** 5 miles from Dayton. **Calendar:** Semester, limited summer session. **Full-time faculty:** 52 total; 56% have terminal degrees, 10% minority, 64% women. **Part-time faculty:** 18 total; 22% have terminal degrees, 6% minority, 78% women. **Class size:** 58% < 20, 27% 20-39, 7% 40-49, 7% 50-99.

**Freshman class profile.** 164 applied, 86 admitted, 56 enrolled.

| Mid 50% test scores | | | | |
|---|---|---|---|---|
| SAT critical reading: | 370-580 | Rank in top quarter: | 52% |
| SAT math: | 450-490 | Rank in top tenth: | 22% |
| SAT writing: | 300-510 | End year in good standing: | 83% |
| ACT composite: | 20-25 | Return as sophomores: | 83% |
| GPA 3.75 or higher: | 23% | Out-of-state: | 12% |
| GPA 3.50-3.74: | 24% | Live on campus: | 40% |
| GPA 3.0-3.49: | 30% | | |
| GPA 2.0-2.99: | 23% | | |

**Basis for selection.** High school GPA, test scores, personal statements important. Essay required for all applicants; interview required for physician assistant applicants.

**High school preparation.** 14 units recommended. Recommended units include English 4, mathematics 2 and science 3. Strong mathematics and science background recommended.

**2010-2011 Annual costs.** Tuition/fees (projected): $10,980. $175 program fee per semester for areas of study with clinical requirements. Room only: $3,140. Books/supplies: $1,067. Personal expenses: $2,809.

**Financial aid.** **Non-need-based:** Scholarships awarded for academics.

**Application procedures.** **Admission:** No deadline. $25 fee, may be waived for applicants with need. Application must be submitted online. Admission notification on a rolling basis. **Financial aid:** Priority date 3/31; no closing date. FAFSA, institutional form required. Applicants notified on a rolling basis starting 5/15; must reply within 3 week(s) of notification.

**Academics.** **Special study options:** Accelerated study, cross-registration, distance learning, double major, dual enrollment of high school students, honors. **Credit/placement by examination:** AP, CLEP, SAT, ACT, institutional tests. **Support services:** Learning center, reduced course load, study skills assistance, tutoring, writing center.

**Majors.** **Health:** Nursing (RN), predental, premedicine, sonography.

**Computing on campus.** 32 workstations in library, computer center. Dormitories wired for high-speed internet access and linked to campus network. Online library, helpline, wireless network available.

**Student life.** **Freshman orientation:** Mandatory. **Policies:** Religious observance required. **Housing:** Single-sex dorms, wellness housing available. $75 nonrefundable deposit. **Activities:** Campus ministries, religious life organizations.

**Student services.** Chaplain/spiritual director, career counseling, student employment services, financial aid counseling, health services, personal counseling, placement for graduates, veterans' counselor.

**Contact.** E-mail: studentadmissions@kcma.edu
Phone: (937) 395-8628 Toll-free number: (800) 433-5262
Fax: (937) 395-8338
Becky McDonald, Director of Enrollment Services, Kettering College of Medical Arts, 3737 Southern Boulevard, Kettering, OH 45429-1299

## Lake Erie College
### Painesville, Ohio
www.lec.edu
**CB member**
**CB code: 1391**

◆ Private 4-year liberal arts college
◆ Residential campus in large town

**General.** Founded in 1856. Regionally accredited. **Location:** 30 miles from Cleveland. **Calendar:** Semester.

**Annual costs/financial aid.** Tuition/fees (2009-2010): $25,296. Equestrian fee $1,039 per course. Room/board: $8,072. Books/supplies: $900. Personal expenses: $1,304. Need-based financial aid available to full-time and part-time students.

**Contact.** Phone: (440) 375-7050
Director of Admissions, 391 West Washington Street, Painesville, OH 44077-3389

## Laura and Alvin Siegal College of Judaic Studies
### Cleveland, Ohio
www.siegalcollege.edu
**CB code: 1190**

◆ Private 4-year liberal arts and teachers college affiliated with Jewish faith
◆ Commuter campus in large town

**General.** Founded in 1963. Regionally accredited. **Location:** 10 miles from Cleveland. **Calendar:** Semester.

**Annual costs/financial aid.** Books/supplies: $500. Need-based financial aid available to full-time and part-time students.

**Contact.** Phone: (216) 464-4050
Director of Student Services, 26500 Shaker Boulevard, Cleveland, OH 44122

## Lourdes College
### Sylvania, Ohio
www.lourdes.edu
**CB member**
**CB code: 1427**

◆ Private 4-year liberal arts college affiliated with Roman Catholic Church
◆ Commuter campus in large town
◆ 1,789 degree-seeking undergraduates: 44% part-time, 82% women, 16% African American, 1% Asian American, 5% Hispanic American
◆ 241 degree-seeking graduate students
◆ 80% of applicants admitted
◆ 43% graduate within 6 years

**General.** Founded in 1958. Regionally accredited. **Degrees:** 247 bachelor's, 37 associate awarded; master's offered. **ROTC:** Army, Air Force. **Location:** 10 miles from Toledo. **Calendar:** Semester, limited summer session. **Full-time faculty:** 80 total; 51% have terminal degrees, 10% minority, 72% women. **Part-time faculty:** 153 total; 19% have terminal degrees, 6% minority, 71% women. **Class size:** 59% < 20, 41% 20-39. **Special facilities:** Planetarium, life lab.

**Freshman class profile.** 390 applied, 312 admitted, 129 enrolled.

| Mid 50% test scores | | | |
|---|---|---|---|
| SAT critical reading: | 370-530 | GPA 2.0-2.99: | 52% |
| SAT math: | 420-570 | Rank in top quarter: | 21% |
| ACT composite: | 17-21 | Rank in top tenth: | 7% |
| GPA 3.75 or higher: | 12% | End year in good standing: | 80% |
| GPA 3.50-3.74: | 14% | Return as sophomores: | 58% |
| GPA 3.0-3.49: | 16% | Out-of-state: | 7% |

**Basis for selection.** Academic GPA very important, recommendations and interview considered. Conditional admission may be granted at discretion of the Director of Admission to high school graduates with no prior college experience who have below a 2.0 GPA on a 4.0 scale. **Homeschooled:** Transcript of courses and grades required.

**High school preparation.** College-preparatory program recommended. 17 units recommended. Recommended units include English 4, mathematics 3, social studies 3, science 3 (laboratory 2), foreign language 2 and visual/performing arts 1.

**2009-2010 Annual costs.** Tuition/fees: $15,300. Books/supplies: $1,008. Personal expenses: $3,578.

**2009-2010 Financial aid. Need-based:** 109 full-time freshmen applied for aid; 92 were judged to have need; 92 of these received aid. Average scholarship/grant was $6,269; average loan $3,378. 34% of total undergraduate aid awarded as scholarships/grants, 66% as loans/jobs. **Non-need-based:** Awarded to 459 full-time undergraduates, including 64 freshmen. Scholarships awarded for academics, art, minority status, state residency.

**Application procedures. Admission:** No deadline. $25 fee, may be waived for applicants with need, free for online applicants. Admission notification on a rolling basis. **Financial aid:** Priority date 3/1; no closing date. FAFSA required. Applicants notified on a rolling basis starting 3/1; must reply within 4 week(s) of notification.

**Academics. Special study options:** Distance learning, double major, dual enrollment of high school students, independent study, internships, liberal arts/career combination, student-designed major, study abroad, teacher certification program. **Credit/placement by examination:** AP, CLEP, institutional tests. 15 credit hours maximum toward associate degree, 30 toward bachelor's. **Support services:** Learning center, reduced course load, remedial instruction, study skills assistance, tutoring, writing center.

**Majors. Biology:** General. **Business:** Accounting/finance, business admin, human resources, management science, marketing. **Conservation:** Environmental science. **Education:** Early childhood, middle, secondary. **Health:** Health care admin, nursing (RN). **History:** General. **Philosophy/religion:** Religion. **Protective services:** Criminal justice. **Psychology:** General. **Public administration:** Social work. **Social sciences:** Sociology. **Visual/performing arts:** Art, art history/conservation. **Other:** Interdisciplinary Studies.

**Most popular majors.** Business/marketing 23%, education 12%, health sciences 33%, interdisciplinary studies 9%.

**Computing on campus.** 181 workstations in library, computer center, student center. Commuter students can connect to campus network. Online course registration, helpline, wireless network available.

**Student life. Freshman orientation:** Mandatory. Preregistration for classes offered. **Activities:** Campus ministries, choral groups, drama, literary magazine, student government, black student union, Latino student union, Young Democrats.

**Athletics. Intercollegiate:** Basketball M, golf, volleyball W. **Intramural:** Basketball, volleyball. **Team name:** Gray Wolves.

**Student services.** Adult student services, alcohol/substance abuse counseling, chaplain/spiritual director, career counseling, services for economically disadvantaged, financial aid counseling, personal counseling, veterans' counselor. **Physically disabled:** Services for visually, speech, hearing impaired.

**Contact.** E-mail: lcadmits@lourdes.edu
Phone: (419) 885-5291 ext. 3680 Toll-free
number: (800) 878-3210 ext. 3680 Fax: (419) 882-3987
Amy Mergen, Director of Admissions, Lourdes College, 6832 Convent Boulevard, Sylvania, OH 43560-2898

## Malone University
### Canton, Ohio
www.malone.edu
CB code: 1439

- Private 4-year university affiliated with Evangelical Friends Church-Eastern Region
- Residential campus in small city

- 2,097 degree-seeking undergraduates: 12% part-time, 59% women, 8% African American, 1% Asian American, 1% Hispanic American, 1% international
- 424 degree-seeking graduate students
- 71% of applicants admitted
- SAT or ACT (ACT writing optional) required
- 61% graduate within 6 years; 22% enter graduate study

**General.** Founded in 1892. Regionally accredited. Interdenominational Christian environment. **Degrees:** 483 bachelor's awarded; master's offered. **ROTC:** Army, Air Force. **Location:** 55 miles from Cleveland. **Calendar:** Semester, limited summer session. **Full-time faculty:** 110 total; 69% have terminal degrees, 4% minority, 49% women. **Part-time faculty:** 108 total; 19% have terminal degrees, 4% minority, 53% women. **Class size:** 52% < 20, 40% 20-39, 6% 40-49, 3% 50-99, less than 1% >100. **Special facilities:** Child development center.

**Freshman class profile.** 1,641 applied, 1,157 admitted, 482 enrolled.

| Mid 50% test scores | | | |
|---|---|---|---|
| SAT critical reading: | 470-590 | Rank in top quarter: | 48% |
| SAT math: | 460-590 | Rank in top tenth: | 23% |
| ACT composite: | 19-26 | End year in good standing: | 82% |
| GPA 3.75 or higher: | 30% | Return as sophomores: | 70% |
| GPA 3.50-3.74: | 16% | Out-of-state: | 16% |
| GPA 3.0-3.49: | 29% | Live on campus: | 86% |
| GPA 2.0-2.99: | 23% | International: | 1% |

**Basis for selection.** High school record, test scores and recommendations most important. Interview considered and encouraged. Audition required for entrance into music programs; portfolio required during first semester for art programs. **Homeschooled:** Transcript of courses and grades required. **Learning Disabled:** Students disclosing learning disabilities must interview with Director of Student Accessibility Services.

**High school preparation.** College-preparatory program required. 18 units required. Required units include English 4, mathematics 3, social studies 2, history 1, science 3 (laboratory 1), foreign language 2, visual/performing arts 1 and academic electives 2.

**2010-2011 Annual costs.** Tuition/fees (projected): $22,444. Room/board: $7,548. Books/supplies: $930. Personal expenses: $1,250.

**2009-2010 Financial aid. Need-based:** 445 full-time freshmen applied for aid; 414 were judged to have need; 414 of these received aid. Average need met was 78%. Average scholarship/grant was $15,254; average loan $3,701. 52% of total undergraduate aid awarded as scholarships/grants, 48% as loans/jobs. **Non-need-based:** Awarded to 1,419 full-time undergraduates, including 476 freshmen. Scholarships awarded for academics, alumni affiliation, athletics, leadership, music/drama, religious affiliation. **Additional information:** Prepayment discounts and employer deferred payments available for students in adult degree-completion programs. Employer deferred payment plan is available for traditional undergraduate students.

**Application procedures. Admission:** Closing date 7/1 (postmark date). $20 fee, may be waived for applicants with need, free for online applicants. Admission notification on a rolling basis beginning on or about 9/1. **Financial aid:** Priority date 3/1, closing date 7/31. FAFSA required. Applicants notified on a rolling basis starting 3/1; must reply within 2 week(s) of notification.

**Academics.** 50-56 hours of general education courses organized under the 3 areas of Foundations of Faith and Learning, Foundational Skills, and Engaging God's World. **Special study options:** Accelerated study, cross-registration, distance learning, double major, dual enrollment of high school students, exchange student, honors, independent study, internships, student-designed major, study abroad, teacher certification program, Washington semester, weekend college. 2 degree-completion programs for adult students in management, nursing; American Studies Program (Washington, D.C.), Australia Studies Centre (Sydney), China Studies Program (Shanghai), Latin American Studies Program (San Jose, Costa Rica), Middle East Studies Program (Cairo, Egypt), Russian Studies Program, Ugandan Studies Program, Los Angeles Film Studies Center, Contemporary Music Center (Martha's Vineyard), Washington Journalism Center, Daystar University in Kenya, Malone University Teacher Education semester in Guatemala. **Credit/placement by examination:** AP, CLEP, SAT, ACT, institutional tests. 62 credit hours maximum toward bachelor's degree. External credit by exam limit is 20, excluding AP credit for which an additional 30 credits are available. Other credits available by in house exams. **Support services:** Reduced course load, remedial instruction, study skills assistance, tutoring, writing center.

**Majors. Biology:** General, zoology. **Business:** Accounting, business admin. **Communications:** General, journalism, public relations, radio/tv. **Communications technology:** Recording arts. **Computer sciences:** Computer science. **Education:** Art, early childhood, English, health, learning disabled, middle, music, physical, science, social studies, Spanish. **Foreign languages:** Spanish. **Health:** Clinical lab science, nursing (RN), public health ed. **History:** General. **Liberal arts:** Arts/sciences. **Math:** General. **Parks/recreation:** Exercise sciences, sports admin. **Philosophy/religion:** Philosophy. **Physical sciences:** Chemistry. **Psychology:** General. **Public administration:** Social work. **Social sciences:** Political science. **Theology:** Bible, pastoral counseling, sacred music, theology, youth ministry. **Visual/performing arts:** Dramatic, studio arts.

**Most popular majors.** Business/marketing 36%, education 13%, health sciences 21%, theological studies 7%.

**Computing on campus.** 195 workstations in dormitories, library, computer center. Dormitories wired for high-speed internet access and linked to campus network. Commuter students can connect to campus network. Online course registration, online library, helpline, student web hosting, wireless network available.

**Student life. Freshman orientation:** Mandatory. Preregistration for classes offered. Held 5 days prior to start of semester; some on-campus events, community service, relationship-building activities. **Policies:** Christian institution with conservative campus lifestyle. Full-time students required to live on campus unless 22 or older, holding senior status, married or commuting from home; exceptions considered. Religious observance required. **Housing:** Single-sex dorms, special housing for disabled, wellness housing available. $100 nonrefundable deposit. **Activities:** Bands, campus ministries, choral groups, dance, drama, film society, international student organizations, literary magazine, music ensembles, musical theater, radio station, student government, student newspaper, TV station, Campus Crusade for Christ, Habitat for Humanity, Helping Hands, multicultural student union, Nurses Christian Fellowship, Rotoract, spiritual life committee, One Voice Gospel Choir, Fellowship of Christian Athletes, Worldview Forum Council.

**Athletics.** NAIA, NCCAA. **Intercollegiate:** Baseball M, basketball, cheerleading, cross-country, diving, football (tackle) M, golf, soccer, softball W, swimming, tennis, track and field, volleyball W. **Intramural:** Basketball, bowling, football (non-tackle), skiing, soccer, softball, table tennis, volleyball, weight lifting. **Team name:** Pioneers.

**Student services.** Adult student services, chaplain/spiritual director, career counseling, student employment services, financial aid counseling, health services, minority student services, personal counseling, placement for graduates. **Physically disabled:** Services for visually, speech, hearing impaired.

**Contact.** E-mail: admissions@malone.edu
Phone: (330) 471-8100 ext. 8145 Toll-free number: (800) 521-1146
Fax: (330) 471-8149
Brock Schroeder, Vice President for Enrollment Management, Malone University, 2600 Cleveland Avenue NW, Canton, OH 44709-3897

## Marietta College
Marietta, Ohio  **CB member**
www.marietta.edu  **CB code: 1444**

- Private 4-year liberal arts college
- Residential campus in large town
- 1,470 degree-seeking undergraduates: 3% part-time, 49% women, 4% African American, 1% Asian American, 1% Hispanic American, 10% international
- 82 degree-seeking graduate students
- 90% of applicants admitted
- SAT or ACT (ACT writing optional) required
- 59% graduate within 6 years; 32% enter graduate study

**General.** Founded in 1835. Regionally accredited. **Degrees:** 274 bachelor's, 1 associate awarded; master's offered. **Location:** 120 miles from Columbus, 110 miles from Pittsburgh. **Calendar:** Semester, limited summer session. **Full-time faculty:** 105 total; 78% have terminal degrees, 7% minority, 46% women. **Part-time faculty:** 41 total; 34% have terminal degrees, 2% minority. **Class size:** 76% < 20, 23% 20-39, less than 1% 40-49, less than 1% 50-99. **Special facilities:** Observatory, center for leadership development, greenhouse, cadaver lab, extensive fossil collection, many historically important documents from the beginning of the old Northwest Territory, planetarium.

**Freshman class profile.** 2,145 applied, 1,921 admitted, 386 enrolled.

| Mid 50% test scores | | | |
|---|---|---|---|
| SAT critical reading: | 480-600 | Rank in top tenth: | 32% |
| SAT math: | 490-610 | End year in good standing: | 70% |
| ACT composite: | 21-27 | Return as sophomores: | 77% |
| GPA 3.75 or higher: | 36% | Out-of-state: | 28% |
| GPA 3.50-3.74: | 16% | Live on campus: | 94% |
| GPA 3.0-3.49: | 30% | International: | 9% |
| GPA 2.0-2.99: | 18% | Fraternities: | 12% |
| Rank in top quarter: | 58% | Sororities: | 22% |

**Basis for selection.** High school curriculum, GPA, test scores most important. Recommendations and essay important. Interview recommended for all. Portfolio recommended for arts programs. Auditions required for some music programs. **Homeschooled:** Statement describing homeschool structure and mission, transcript of courses and grades, interview required. Chronicle of study required.

**High school preparation.** College-preparatory program recommended. 16 units required. Required units include English 4, mathematics 3, social studies 2, history 2, science 3 (laboratory 2), foreign language 2 and academic electives 1.

**2009-2010 Annual costs.** Tuition/fees: $27,066. Room/board: $8,046. Books/supplies: $720. Personal expenses: $648.

**2009-2010 Financial aid. Need-based:** 371 full-time freshmen applied for aid; 320 were judged to have need; 320 of these received aid. Average need met was 94%. Average scholarship/grant was $14,468; average loan $2,705. 74% of total undergraduate aid awarded as scholarships/grants, 26% as loans/jobs. **Non-need-based:** Awarded to 998 full-time undergraduates, including 255 freshmen. Scholarships awarded for academics, alumni affiliation, art, leadership, minority status, music/drama, state residency. **Additional information:** Auditions/portfolios for art, creative writing, music and theater required for competitive fine art scholarships.

**Application procedures. Admission:** Priority date 3/1; deadline 5/1 (postmark date). $25 fee, may be waived for applicants with need, free for online applicants. Admission notification on a rolling basis beginning on or about 9/1. Must reply by May 1 or within 2 week(s) if notified thereafter. **Financial aid:** Priority date 3/1, closing date 4/15. FAFSA, institutional form required. Applicants notified on a rolling basis starting 3/15; must reply by 5/1 or within 2 week(s) of notification.

**Academics.** Early Alert Program whereby professors can contact the Academic Resource Center to assist those students demonstrating need for additional academic support. **Special study options:** Combined bachelor's/graduate degree, double major, dual enrollment of high school students, ESL, exchange student, honors, independent study, internships, liberal arts/career combination, student-designed major, study abroad, teacher certification program, Washington semester. Leadership program, investigative studies. **Credit/placement by examination:** AP, CLEP, IB, SAT, ACT, institutional tests. 36 credit hours maximum toward bachelor's degree. **Support services:** Reduced course load, remedial instruction, study skills assistance, tutoring, writing center.

**Majors. Biology:** General, biochemistry. **Business:** Accounting, communications, finance, human resources, international, management information systems, marketing. **Communications:** General, advertising, broadcast journalism, journalism, organizational, public relations, radio/tv. **Computer sciences:** General, computer science, information systems. **Conservation:** Environmental science, environmental studies. **Education:** General, early childhood, elementary, middle, multi-level teacher, secondary. **Engineering:** Petroleum. **Foreign languages:** Spanish. **Health:** Athletic training. **History:** General. **Math:** General. **Physical sciences:** Chemistry, geology, physics. **Psychology:** General. **Social sciences:** Economics, political science. **Visual/performing arts:** Commercial/advertising art, dramatic, studio arts.

**Most popular majors.** Biology 7%, business/marketing 26%, communications/journalism 13%, education 6%, engineering/engineering technologies 7%, health sciences 6%, psychology 6%, social sciences 6%, visual/performing arts 8%.

**Computing on campus.** 350 workstations in library, computer center, student center. Dormitories wired for high-speed internet access and linked to campus network. Commuter students can connect to campus network. Online library, helpline, wireless network available.

**Student life. Freshman orientation:** Mandatory, $250 fee. Preregistration for classes offered. Four-and-one-half day program. Culminating event either white-water rafting trip or dinner theater production. **Policies:** Student code of conduct, judicial system, no alcohol policy for students under age of 21. **Housing:** Guaranteed on-campus for freshmen. Coed dorms, single-sex dorms, special housing for disabled, apartments, fraternity/sorority housing, wellness housing available. $200 deposit, deadline 5/1.

Special interest theme housing (honors, arts and humanities house) available. **Activities:** Bands, campus ministries, choral groups, dance, drama, international student organizations, literary magazine, music ensembles, Model UN, musical theater, radio station, student government, student newspaper, TV station, InterVarsity Christian Fellowship, Circle K, MC Democrats, MC Republicans, Rotoract, Feminist Rainbow Alliance, VOICE, American International Association, student global AIDS campaign.

**Athletics.** NCAA. **Intercollegiate:** Baseball M, basketball, cross-country, football (tackle) M, rowing (crew), soccer, softball W, tennis, track and field, volleyball W. **Intramural:** Badminton, basketball, bowling, football (non-tackle), golf, handball, racquetball, soccer, softball, table tennis, tennis, volleyball. **Team name:** Pioneers.

**Student services.** Adult student services, alcohol/substance abuse counseling, career counseling, student employment services, financial aid counseling, health services, minority student services, personal counseling, placement for graduates. **Physically disabled:** Services for visually, speech, hearing impaired. **Learning disabled:** Comprehensive services available.

**Contact.** E-mail: admit@marietta.edu
Phone: (740) 376-4600 Toll-free number: (800) 331-7896
Fax: (740) 376-8888
Jason Turley, Director of Admission, Marietta College, 215 Fifth Street, Marietta, OH 45750-4005

## MedCentral College of Nursing
Mansfield, Ohio
www.medcentral.edu                         CB code: 3935

▶ Private 4-year nursing college
▶ Commuter campus in small city
▶ 373 degree-seeking undergraduates: 4% part-time, 84% women, 2% African American, 1% Asian American, 1% Hispanic American
▶ SAT or ACT (ACT writing recommended) required

**General.** Regionally accredited. General electives taken at the Ohio State University-Mansfield. **Degrees:** 120 bachelor's awarded. **Location:** 60 miles from Cleveland, 60 miles from Columbus. **Calendar:** Quarter, limited summer session. **Full-time faculty:** 24 total; 17% have terminal degrees, 75% women.

**Freshman class profile.**

| Mid 50% test scores | | | |
|---|---|---|---|
| ACT composite: | 18-28 | GPA 3.0-3.49: | 61% |
| GPA 3.75 or higher: | 8% | GPA 2.0-2.99: | 10% |
| GPA 3.50-3.74: | 21% | Rank in top quarter: | 80% |
| | | Rank in top tenth: | 5% |

**Basis for selection.** Previous high school and college academic credentials very important. Co-curricular activities, work experience, students character also considered. **Homeschooled:** Transcript of courses and grades required. ACT/SAT required.

**High school preparation.** College-preparatory program recommended. 17 units required; 20 recommended. Required and recommended units include English 4, mathematics 3-4, social studies 2, history 1, science 3-4 (laboratory 2-3), foreign language 2, computer science 1 and academic electives 2.

**2009-2010 Annual costs.** Tuition/fees: $13,765. Room only: $5,385. Books/supplies: $2,000. Personal expenses: $3,000.

**2008-2009 Financial aid. Need-based:** 29% of total undergraduate aid awarded as scholarships/grants, 71% as loans/jobs. **Non-need-based:** Scholarships awarded for academics, leadership.

**Application procedures. Admission:** Priority date 5/1; deadline 7/1 (postmark date). $50 fee, may be waived for applicants with need. Application must be submitted on paper. Admission notification on a rolling basis beginning on or about 10/1. Must reply by 8/5. **Financial aid:** Priority date 4/2, closing date 9/15. FAFSA, institutional form required. Applicants notified on a rolling basis starting 4/1; must reply by 5/1 or within 2 week(s) of notification.

**Academics. Special study options:** Accelerated study, combined bachelor's/graduate degree, dual enrollment of high school students, independent study. **Credit/placement by examination:** AP, CLEP, SAT, ACT, institutional tests. 48 credit hours maximum toward bachelor's degree. **Support services:** Learning center, remedial instruction, study skills assistance, tutoring, writing center.

**Majors. Health:** Nursing (RN).

**Computing on campus.** 150 workstations in library, computer center. Dormitories wired for high-speed internet access and linked to campus network. Commuter students can connect to campus network. Online course registration, online library, helpline, wireless network available.

**Student life. Freshman orientation:** Mandatory. Held the beginning of academic quarter. **Housing:** Guaranteed on-campus for freshmen. Coed dorms, apartments, wellness housing available. $100 nonrefundable deposit, deadline 6/15. **Activities:** Choral groups, drama, musical theater, student government, National Student Nurses Association, student government association, SCRUBS Society, Sigma Theta, Tau International.

**Student services.** Adult student services, alcohol/substance abuse counseling, chaplain/spiritual director, career counseling, student employment services, financial aid counseling, health services, on-campus daycare, personal counseling.

**Contact.** E-mail: admissions@medcentral.edu
Phone: (419) 520-2600 Toll-free number: (877) 645-4360
Fax: (419) 520-2662
Tiffany Miller, Director of Admissions, MedCentral College of Nursing, 335 Glessner Avenue, Mansfield, OH 44903-2265

## Mercy College of Northwest Ohio
Toledo, Ohio
www.mercycollege.edu                       CB code: 4685

▶ Private 4-year health science and nursing college affiliated with Roman Catholic Church
▶ Commuter campus in large city
▶ 1,042 degree-seeking undergraduates: 48% part-time, 85% women, 8% African American, 1% Asian American, 2% Hispanic American
▶ 49% of applicants admitted
▶ 38% graduate within 6 years

**General. Degrees:** 58 bachelor's, 165 associate awarded. **Calendar:** Semester, limited summer session. **Full-time faculty:** 60 total; 30% have terminal degrees, 3% minority, 88% women. **Part-time faculty:** 63 total; 10% have terminal degrees, 8% minority, 71% women. **Class size:** 50% < 20, 37% 20-39, 8% 40-49, 5% 50-99.

**Freshman class profile.** 167 applied, 82 admitted, 67 enrolled.

| | | | |
|---|---|---|---|
| GPA 3.75 or higher: | 5% | End year in good standing: | 94% |
| GPA 3.50-3.74: | 7% | Return as sophomores: | 80% |
| GPA 3.0-3.49: | 76% | Out-of-state: | 11% |
| GPA 2.0-2.99: | 12% | Live on campus: | 41% |

**Basis for selection.** Students reviewed by admission, progression and graduation committee. 2.3 GPA required. Admission to programs of study may have higher GPA and specific course grade requirements.

**High school preparation.** College-preparatory program recommended. 11 units required; 23 recommended. Required and recommended units include English 3-4, mathematics 2-4, social studies 2-3, history 1, science 2-4 (laboratory 2-3), foreign language 2, computer science 1 and visual/performing arts 1.

**2009-2010 Annual costs.** Tuition/fees: $9,500. Books/supplies: $1,422. Personal expenses: $3,368.

**2008-2009 Financial aid. Need-based:** 54 full-time freshmen applied for aid; 47 were judged to have need; 44 of these received aid. Average need met was 53%. Average scholarship/grant was $5,739; average loan $3,310. 39% of total undergraduate aid awarded as scholarships/grants, 61% as loans/jobs. **Non-need-based:** Awarded to 202 full-time undergraduates, including 39 freshmen. Scholarships awarded for academics, alumni affiliation, leadership, religious affiliation, state residency.

**Application procedures. Admission:** Priority date 1/1; no deadline. $25 fee, may be waived for applicants with need. Application must be submitted on paper. Admission notification on a rolling basis beginning on or about 9/1. Must reply by May 1 or within 2 week(s) if notified thereafter. **Financial aid:** Priority date 3/1; no closing date. FAFSA required. Applicants notified on a rolling basis starting 3/1; must reply within 2 week(s) of notification.

**Academics. Special study options:** Combined bachelor's/graduate degree, distance learning, double major, independent study, internships. **Credit/placement by examination:** AP, CLEP, institutional tests. **Support services:** Learning center, reduced course load, remedial instruction, study skills assistance, tutoring, writing center.

**Majors. Health:** Health care admin, nursing (RN).

**Computing on campus.** 24 workstations in library, computer center, student center. Online course registration, online library, wireless network available.

**Student life. Freshman orientation:** Mandatory. Preregistration for classes offered. **Housing:** Apartments available. $100 fully refundable deposit. **Activities:** Campus ministries, student government, student newspaper, Student Senate, Phi Theta Kappa, national student nurses association, Sigma Theta Tau, College Ambassadors, American Society of Radiologic Technologists.

**Student services.** Adult student services, alcohol/substance abuse counseling, chaplain/spiritual director, career counseling, services for economically disadvantaged, student employment services, financial aid counseling, personal counseling. **Physically disabled:** Services for visually, hearing impaired.

**Contact.** E-mail: admissions@mercycollege.edu
Phone: (419) 251-1313 Toll-free number: (888) 806-3729
Fax: (419) 251-1462
Shelly McCoy Grissom, Chief Admissions Officer, Mercy College of Northwest Ohio, 2221 Madison Avenue, Toledo, OH 43604

---

## Miami University: Oxford Campus

Oxford, Ohio   CB member
www.muohio.edu   CB code: 1463

- Public 4-year university
- Residential campus in large town
- 14,553 degree-seeking undergraduates: 1% part-time, 53% women
- 1,512 degree-seeking graduate students
- 79% of applicants admitted
- SAT or ACT with writing, application essay required
- 82% graduate within 6 years

**General.** Founded in 1809. Regionally accredited. Associate degree programs and certificates offered at regional campuses in Hamilton and Middletown, with degrees conferred by main (Oxford) campus. **Degrees:** 3,605 bachelor's, 289 associate awarded; master's, doctoral offered. **ROTC:** Army, Naval, Air Force. **Location:** 35 miles from Cincinnati, 46 miles from Dayton. **Calendar:** Semester, extensive summer session. **Full-time faculty:** 827 total; 89% have terminal degrees, 17% minority, 41% women. **Part-time faculty:** 361 total; 24% have terminal degrees, 12% minority, 49% women. **Class size:** 32% < 20, 49% 20-39, 7% 40-49, 8% 50-99, 4% >100. **Special facilities:** Zoology museum.

**Freshman class profile.** 16,772 applied, 13,223 admitted, 3,236 enrolled.

| Mid 50% test scores | | GPA 2.0-2.99: | 6% |
|---|---|---|---|
| SAT critical reading: | 530-630 | Rank in top quarter: | 74% |
| SAT math: | 560-660 | Rank in top tenth: | 39% |
| ACT composite: | 24-29 | Return as sophomores: | 89% |
| GPA 3.75 or higher: | 38% | Out-of-state: | 30% |
| GPA 3.50-3.74: | 25% | Live on campus: | 98% |
| GPA 3.0-3.49: | 31% | | |

**Basis for selection.** Admission based upon academic performance, test scores, secondary school experience, community activities, and recommendations from the high school. Diversity of student body, applicant's special abilities, talents and achievements also considered. Audition required for music, theater programs; portfolio required for art, architecture programs. **Homeschooled:** Students who have not earned GED may present credentials that demonstrate levels of academic achievement, ability, and performance equivalent to that of high school graduates. Applicants may be requested to submit samples of work in various areas.

**High school preparation.** College-preparatory program recommended. 16 units recommended. Recommended units include English 4, mathematics 3, social studies 3, science 3, foreign language 2 and visual/performing arts 1.

**2009-2010 Annual costs.** Tuition/fees: $11,910; $26,670 out-of-state. Reported in-state tuition represents maximum range that freshmen will be charged. Room/board: $9,458.

**2008-2009 Financial aid. Need-based:** 2,538 full-time freshmen applied for aid; 1,505 were judged to have need; 1,492 of these received aid. Average need met was 72%. Average scholarship/grant was $6,716; average loan $5,571. 49% of total undergraduate aid awarded as scholarships/grants, 51% as loans/jobs. **Non-need-based:** Awarded to 5,456 full-time undergraduates, including 1,645 freshmen. Scholarships awarded for academics, art, athletics, leadership, minority status, music/drama, ROTC, state residency.

**Application procedures. Admission:** Priority date 12/1; deadline 2/1 (postmark date). $50 fee, may be waived for applicants with need. Admission notification 3/15. Must reply by 5/1. **Financial aid:** Priority date 2/15; no closing date. FAFSA required. Applicants notified on a rolling basis starting 3/20; must reply by 5/1 or within 3 week(s) of notification.

**Academics. Special study options:** Combined bachelor's/graduate degree, cooperative education, cross-registration, distance learning, double major, exchange student, honors, independent study, internships, liberal arts/career combination, semester at sea, student-designed major, study abroad, teacher certification program, Washington semester. Undergraduate associates, undergraduate research program, science and engineering research semester, 3-2 engineering with Case Western Reserve University and Columbia University, 3-2 forestry/environmental studies with Duke University, 3-1 and 4-1 in Clinical Laboratory Science, 3-1 Arts/Professional A.B./Professional degree. **Credit/placement by examination:** AP, CLEP, IB, institutional tests. 32 credit hours maximum toward associate degree, 32 toward bachelor's. **Support services:** Learning center, study skills assistance, tutoring, writing center.

**Majors. Architecture:** History/criticism, interior, urban/community planning. **Area/ethnic studies:** African-American, American, East Asian, Italian, Latin American, women's. **Biology:** Biochemistry, botany, zoology. **Business:** Accounting, business admin, finance, management information systems, managerial economics, marketing, operations. **Communications:** Digital media, journalism, media studies, public relations. **Computer sciences:** General, systems analysis. **Conservation:** Environmental science, environmental studies, wood science. **Education:** Art, biology, chemistry, early childhood, English, foreign languages, French, German, health, Latin, mathematics, middle, music, physical, physics, science, secondary, social studies, Spanish, special. **Engineering:** General, chemical, computer, electrical, manufacturing, mechanical, physics. **Engineering technology:** General, industrial management. **Family/consumer sciences:** Family studies. **Foreign languages:** Classics, French, German, linguistics, Spanish. **Health:** Athletic training, clinical lab science, nursing (RN), speech pathology. **History:** General. **Interdisciplinary:** Gerontology. **Liberal arts:** Arts/sciences. **Math:** General, statistics. **Parks/recreation:** Exercise sciences, health/fitness, sports admin. **Philosophy/religion:** Philosophy, religion. **Physical sciences:** Chemistry, geology, physics. **Psychology:** General. **Public administration:** General, social work. **Social sciences:** Anthropology, economics, geography, international relations, political science, sociology. **Visual/performing arts:** Art, art history/conservation, commercial/advertising art, dramatic, music performance.

**Most popular majors.** Biology 8%, business/marketing 26%, communications/journalism 6%, education 10%, English 6%, psychology 6%, social sciences 11%.

**Computing on campus.** 1,200 workstations in dormitories, library, computer center, student center. Dormitories wired for high-speed internet access and linked to campus network. Commuter students can connect to campus network. Online course registration, online library, helpline, repair service, student web hosting, wireless network available.

**Student life. Freshman orientation:** Mandatory, $80 fee. Preregistration for classes offered. Held for 2 days during June and July. **Housing:** Guaranteed on-campus for freshmen. Coed dorms, single-sex dorms, special housing for disabled, apartments, cooperative housing, fraternity/sorority housing, wellness housing available. $425 nonrefundable deposit, deadline 5/1. Special arrangements include sorority suites in residence halls. **Activities:** Bands, campus ministries, choral groups, dance, drama, film society, international student organizations, literary magazine, music ensembles, Model UN, musical theater, opera, radio station, student government, student newspaper, symphony orchestra, TV station, service network, black student action association, Campus Crusade for Christ, Jewish students association, College Democrats/College Republicans, Asian-American association, Alpha Phi Omega.

**Athletics.** NCAA. **Intercollegiate:** Baseball M, basketball, cross-country, diving, field hockey W, football (tackle) M, golf M, ice hockey M, soccer W, softball W, swimming, tennis W, track and field, volleyball W. **Intramural:** Baseball, basketball, football (non-tackle), ice hockey, racquetball, soccer, softball, tennis, volleyball. **Team name:** Red Hawks.

**Student services.** Alcohol/substance abuse counseling, chaplain/spiritual director, career counseling, services for economically disadvantaged, student employment services, financial aid counseling, health services, legal services, minority student services, on-campus daycare, personal counseling, placement for graduates, veterans' counselor, women's services. **Physically disabled:** Services for visually, speech, hearing impaired. **Learning disabled:** Comprehensive services available.

**Contact.** E-mail: admission@muohio.edu
Phone: (513) 529-2531 Fax: (513) 529-1550
Laurie Koehler, Director of Admissions, Miami University: Oxford Campus, 301 South Campus Avenue, Oxford, OH 45056

## Mount Carmel College of Nursing
**Columbus, Ohio**
**www.mccn.edu**
**CB member**
**CB code: 1502**

- Private 4-year nursing college affiliated with Roman Catholic Church
- Very large city
- 721 degree-seeking undergraduates: 17% part-time, 89% women, 6% African American, 2% Asian American, 2% Hispanic American
- 55 degree-seeking graduate students
- 86% of applicants admitted
- 69% graduate within 6 years

**General.** Regionally accredited. **Degrees:** 236 bachelor's awarded; master's offered. **ROTC:** Army, Air Force. **Location:** Downtown. **Calendar:** Semester, limited summer session. **Full-time faculty:** 35 total; 14% have terminal degrees, 20% minority, 91% women. **Part-time faculty:** 46 total; 17% have terminal degrees, 4% minority, 85% women. **Class size:** 36% < 20, 33% 20-39, 21% 40-49, 9% 50-99, 1% >100.

**Freshman class profile.** 169 applied, 146 admitted, 103 enrolled.

| Mid 50% test scores | | | |
|---|---|---|---|
| ACT composite: | 19-23 | Rank in top quarter: | 40% |
| GPA 3.75 or higher: | 16% | Rank in top tenth: | 23% |
| GPA 3.50-3.74: | 30% | Return as sophomores: | 79% |
| GPA 3.0-3.49: | 49% | Out-of-state: | 1% |
| GPA 2.0-2.99: | 5% | Live on campus: | 28% |

**Basis for selection.** High school record and standardized test score most important.

**High school preparation.** College-preparatory program required. 16 units required. Required units include English 4, mathematics 3, social studies 3, science 3 (laboratory 3) and foreign language 2.

**2009-2010 Annual costs.** Tuition/fees: $8,897. Books/supplies: $600. Personal expenses: $1,614.

**Application procedures. Admission:** Priority date 2/1; deadline 4/1. $30 fee. Must reply by 5/1. **Financial aid:** Priority date 3/1; no closing date. FAFSA, institutional form required. Applicants notified on a rolling basis.

**Academics. Special study options:** Accelerated study, cross-registration, honors. **Credit/placement by examination:** CLEP.

**Majors. Health:** Nursing (RN).

**Student life. Housing:** Apartments available. $200 nonrefundable deposit. **Activities:** Campus ministries, student government.

**Contact.** E-mail: mccnadmissions@mchs.com
Phone: (614) 234-1085 Toll-free number: (800) 556-6942
Fax: (614) 234-2875
Kim Campbell, Director of Admissions, Mount Carmel College of Nursing, 127 South Davis Avenue, Columbus, OH 43222-1589

## Mount Union College
**Alliance, Ohio**
**www.muc.edu**
**CB member**
**CB code: 1492**

- Private 4-year liberal arts college affiliated with United Methodist Church
- Residential campus in large town
- 2,187 degree-seeking undergraduates: 2% part-time, 50% women
- 19 degree-seeking graduate students
- 75% of applicants admitted
- SAT or ACT (ACT writing optional), application essay required
- 63% graduate within 6 years; 21% enter graduate study

**General.** Founded in 1846. Regionally accredited. **Degrees:** 346 bachelor's awarded; master's offered. **ROTC:** Army, Air Force. **Location:** 55 miles from Cleveland, 75 miles from Pittsburgh. **Calendar:** Semester, limited summer session. **Full-time faculty:** 124 total; 85% have terminal degrees, 11% minority, 36% women. **Part-time faculty:** 104 total; 5% minority, 50% women. **Class size:** 54% < 20, 43% 20-39, 2% 40-49, less than 1% 50-99, less than 1% >100. **Special facilities:** 2 astronomical observatories, 141-acre nature center for ecological studies, bird observatory, scanning electron microscope facility.

**Freshman class profile.** 2,320 applied, 1,747 admitted, 578 enrolled.

| Mid 50% test scores | | | |
|---|---|---|---|
| SAT critical reading: | 430-540 | GPA 2.0-2.99: | 34% |
| SAT math: | 440-590 | Rank in top quarter: | 40% |
| ACT composite: | 19-25 | Rank in top tenth: | 13% |
| GPA 3.75 or higher: | 15% | Return as sophomores: | 78% |
| GPA 3.50-3.74: | 19% | Out-of-state: | 14% |
| GPA 3.0-3.49: | 32% | Live on campus: | 96% |
| | | International: | 2% |

**Basis for selection.** Class rank, rigor of secondary school record, standardized test scores, academic GPA very important. Rolling deadline for SAT, ACT scores. Interview recommended for all. Audition recommended for communications, music, and theater programs. Portfolio recommended for art and communications programs. **Homeschooled:** Statement describing homeschool structure and mission required.

**High school preparation.** 18 units recommended. Recommended units include English 4, mathematics 3, social studies 3, science 3 (laboratory 2), foreign language 2 and academic electives 1.

**2009-2010 Annual costs.** Tuition/fees: $24,130. Room/board: $7,420. Books/supplies: $1,100. Personal expenses: $800.

**2008-2009 Financial aid. Need-based:** 547 full-time freshmen applied for aid; 480 were judged to have need; 479 of these received aid. Average need met was 83%. Average scholarship/grant was $13,776; average loan $5,071. 67% of total undergraduate aid awarded as scholarships/grants, 33% as loans/jobs. **Non-need-based:** Awarded to 460 full-time undergraduates, including 140 freshmen. Scholarships awarded for academics, alumni affiliation, art, job skills, leadership, music/drama, religious affiliation, ROTC, state residency.

**Application procedures. Admission:** Priority date 3/1; no deadline. No application fee. Admission notification on a rolling basis beginning on or about 10/1. Admission determined by space availability after May 1. **Financial aid:** Priority date 4/1; no closing date. FAFSA required. Applicants notified on a rolling basis starting 3/15; must reply within 4 week(s) of notification.

**Academics.** All freshmen must take Liberal Arts Experience course. **Special study options:** Accelerated study, cooperative education, double major, ESL, honors, independent study, internships, student-designed major, study abroad, teacher certification program. **Credit/placement by examination:** AP, CLEP, IB, institutional tests. 15 credit hours maximum toward bachelor's degree. **Support services:** Learning center, study skills assistance, tutoring, writing center.

**Majors. Area/ethnic studies:** American, Asian. **Biology:** General, biochemistry. **Business:** Accounting, business admin, international. **Communications:** General. **Computer sciences:** Programming, web page design. **Conservation:** Environmental science. **Education:** Early childhood, health, middle, music, physical, special. **Foreign languages:** French, German, Japanese, Spanish. **Health:** Athletic training, clinical lab science. **History:** General. **Interdisciplinary:** Neuroscience. **Math:** General. **Parks/recreation:** Exercise sciences, sports admin. **Philosophy/religion:** Philosophy, religion. **Physical sciences:** Chemistry, geology, physics. **Protective services:** Criminalistics. **Psychology:** General. **Social sciences:** Criminology, economics, international relations, political science, sociology. **Visual/performing arts:** Dramatic, music performance, studio arts.

**Most popular majors.** Biology 7%, business/marketing 22%, computer/information sciences 6%, education 13%, parks/recreation 11%, psychology 7%, social sciences 6%.

**Computing on campus.** 220 workstations in dormitories, library, computer center, student center. Dormitories wired for high-speed internet access and linked to campus network. Commuter students can connect to campus network. Online course registration, online library, helpline, repair service, student web hosting, wireless network available.

**Student life. Freshman orientation:** Available. Preregistration for classes offered. Two-day summer orientation includes program for parents. Fall orientation held week before registration for students only. **Housing:** Guaranteed on-campus for all undergraduates. Coed dorms, single-sex dorms, special housing for disabled, fraternity/sorority housing, wellness housing available. **Activities:** Bands, choral groups, dance, drama, literary magazine, music ensembles, musical theater, radio station, student government, student newspaper, academic clubs, academic honoraries, religious clubs, service organizations, Alpha Phi Omega, black student union, international students association, women students association, religious life council, student activities council.

**Athletics.** NCAA. **Intercollegiate:** Baseball M, basketball, cheerleading, cross-country, diving, football (tackle) M, golf, soccer, softball W, swimming, tennis, track and field, volleyball W, wrestling M. **Intramural:** Badminton, basketball, bowling, diving, football (non-tackle), golf, gymnastics, racquetball, soccer, softball, swimming, tennis, volleyball, water polo, weight lifting. **Team name:** Purple Raiders.

**Student services.** Adult student services, alcohol/substance abuse counseling, chaplain/spiritual director, career counseling, student employment services, financial aid counseling, health services, minority student services, personal counseling, placement for graduates. **Physically disabled:** Services for visually impaired.

**Contact.** E-mail: admission@muc.edu
Phone: (330) 823-2590 Toll-free number: (800) 334-6682
Fax: (330) 823-5097
Grace Chalker, Director of Admissions, Mount Union College, 1972 Clark Avenue, Alliance, OH 44601-3993

## Mount Vernon Nazarene University

**Mount Vernon, Ohio**  **CB member**
**www.mvnu.edu**  **CB code: 1531**

- Private 4-year university affiliated with Church of the Nazarene
- Residential campus in large town
- 1,939 degree-seeking undergraduates: 11% part-time, 62% women, 5% African American, 1% Asian American, 2% Hispanic American
- 540 degree-seeking graduate students
- 72% of applicants admitted
- SAT or ACT (ACT writing optional), application essay required
- 51% graduate within 6 years; 16% enter graduate study

**General.** Founded in 1964. Regionally accredited. **Degrees:** 473 bachelor's, 7 associate awarded; master's offered. **Location:** 45 miles from Columbus. **Calendar:** 4-1-4, limited summer session. **Full-time faculty:** 108 total; 64% have terminal degrees, 5% minority, 34% women. **Part-time faculty:** 159 total; 14% have terminal degrees, 4% minority, 43% women. **Class size:** 71% < 20, 24% 20-39, 3% 40-49, 2% 50-99. **Special facilities:** 70-acre biological research area and nature center, weather station.

**Freshman class profile.** 875 applied, 628 admitted, 303 enrolled.

| Mid 50% test scores | | GPA 2.0-2.99: | 26% |
|---|---|---|---|
| SAT critical reading: | 470-570 | Rank in top quarter: | 47% |
| SAT math: | 470-590 | Rank in top tenth: | 21% |
| ACT composite: | 19-25 | End year in good standing: | 83% |
| GPA 3.75 or higher: | 27% | Return as sophomores: | 73% |
| GPA 3.50-3.74: | 18% | Out-of-state: | 12% |
| GPA 3.0-3.49: | 28% | Live on campus: | 91% |

**Basis for selection.** High school record, ACT or SAT scores, recommendations important. Interview recommended. **Homeschooled:** Transcript of courses and grades, letter of recommendation (nonparent) required. Family members cannot complete either academic or character references. Employer can complete academic reference. Students who participate in accredited program must provide transcript from accrediting agency; otherwise, must provide a list of classes completed.

**High school preparation.** College-preparatory program recommended. 21 units recommended. Required and recommended units include English 4, mathematics 3, social studies 3, science 3 (laboratory 3), foreign language 2-3, visual/performing arts 1 and academic electives 3. 1 health and physical education.

**2010-2011 Annual costs.** Tuition/fees (projected): $21,330. Room/board: $6,180. Books/supplies: $1,200. Personal expenses: $1,964.

**2009-2010 Financial aid. Need-based:** 302 full-time freshmen applied for aid; 277 were judged to have need; 277 of these received aid. Average need met was 70%. Average scholarship/grant was $11,360; average loan $3,703. 50% of total undergraduate aid awarded as scholarships/grants, 50% as loans/jobs. **Non-need-based:** Awarded to 327 full-time undergraduates, including 75 freshmen. Scholarships awarded for academics, athletics, minority status, music/drama, religious affiliation, state residency.

**Application procedures. Admission:** Priority date 3/15; deadline 7/15 (receipt date). $25 fee, may be waived for applicants with need. Admission notification on a rolling basis beginning on or about 9/1. **Financial aid:** Priority date 3/15; no closing date. FAFSA, institutional form required. Applicants notified on a rolling basis starting 3/15; must reply within 2 week(s) of notification.

**Academics.** Off-campus January term offers unique educational opportunities, including urban and international studies. **Special study options:** Combined bachelor's/graduate degree, cooperative education, cross-registration, distance learning, double major, dual enrollment of high school

students, honors, independent study, internships, liberal arts/career combination, study abroad, teacher certification program, Washington semester. Cooperative pre-engineering program with Olivet Nazarene University, cooperative pre-occupational therapy/physical therapy/physician's assistant programs with Chatham College, and articulation agreements with Zane State College, Central Ohio Technical College, and North Central State College. Several opportunities for students to participate in service learning or mission trips. During the academic year, students may participate in one of the following trips: Germany, Hungary, Venezuela, Costa Rica, Nicaragua, Belize, Benin, Romania, or several out-of-state USA trips. **Credit/placement by examination:** AP, CLEP, IB, SAT, ACT, institutional tests. 30 credit hours maximum toward bachelor's degree. **Support services:** Reduced course load, study skills assistance.

**Majors. Biology:** General. **Business:** Accounting, administrative services, business admin, finance, international, management information systems, marketing, office management, organizational behavior. **Communications:** General, broadcast journalism, journalism, public relations. **Computer sciences:** General, computer science. **Education:** General, art, biology, business, chemistry, early childhood, elementary, English, family/consumer sciences, health, history, mathematics, middle, music, physical, physics, science, secondary, social studies, Spanish, special. **Family/consumer sciences:** General. **Foreign languages:** Spanish. **Health:** Clinical lab science, nursing (RN). **History:** General. **Math:** General. **Parks/recreation:** Exercise sciences, health/fitness, sports admin. **Philosophy/religion:** Philosophy, religion. **Physical sciences:** General, chemistry, physics. **Protective services:** Criminal justice, law enforcement admin. **Psychology:** General. **Public administration:** Social work. **Social sciences:** Sociology. **Theology:** Bible, missionary, pastoral counseling, religious ed, sacred music, youth ministry. **Visual/performing arts:** Art, dramatic, graphic design, music performance. **Other:** Applied business technology, Intercultural studies, Video and radio broadcasting.

**Most popular majors.** Business/marketing 52%, education 9%.

**Computing on campus.** 232 workstations in dormitories, library, computer center, student center. Dormitories wired for high-speed internet access and linked to campus network. Commuter students can connect to campus network. Online course registration, online library, helpline, wireless network available.

**Student life. Freshman orientation:** Mandatory, $25 fee. Preregistration for classes offered. Sessions held in June, July, and August. **Policies:** Students expected to comply with university's published lifestyle guidelines. Religious observance required. **Housing:** Guaranteed on-campus for freshmen. Single-sex dorms, special housing for disabled, apartments, wellness housing available. $150 fully refundable deposit, deadline 5/1. **Activities:** Bands, campus ministries, choral groups, drama, international student organizations, literary magazine, music ensembles, musical theater, opera, radio station, student government, student newspaper, Students in Free Enterprise, Fellowship of Christian Athletes, Young Republicans club, Young Democratic club, men's association, women's association, computing machinery association, American Sign Language club, Students with Concern, Mandate.

**Athletics.** NAIA, NCCAA. **Intercollegiate:** Baseball M, basketball, cross-country, golf M, soccer, softball W, volleyball W. **Intramural:** Basketball, bowling, football (non-tackle), soccer, softball, volleyball. **Team name:** Cougars.

**Student services.** Adult student services, alcohol/substance abuse counseling, chaplain/spiritual director, career counseling, student employment services, financial aid counseling, health services, minority student services, personal counseling, placement for graduates. **Physically disabled:** Services for visually, speech, hearing impaired.

**Contact.** E-mail: admissions@mvnu.edu
Phone: (740) 392-6868 ext. 4510 Toll-free number: (866) 462-6868
Fax: (740) 393-0511
James Smith, Director of Admissions, Mount Vernon Nazarene University, 800 Martinsburg Road, Mount Vernon, OH 43050

## Muskingum University

**New Concord, Ohio**  **CB member**
**www.muskingum.edu**  **CB code: 1496**

- Private 4-year liberal arts college affiliated with Presbyterian Church (USA)
- Residential campus in small town
- 1,661 degree-seeking undergraduates: 6% part-time, 52% women, 6% African American, 1% Asian American, 1% Hispanic American, 2% international
- 370 degree-seeking graduate students
- 79% of applicants admitted

♦ SAT or ACT (ACT writing optional) required

♦ 56% graduate within 6 years; 16% enter graduate study

**General.** Founded in 1837. Regionally accredited. **Degrees:** 336 bachelor's awarded; master's offered. **Location:** 70 miles from Columbus, 125 miles from Pittsburgh. **Calendar:** Semester, limited summer session. **Full-time faculty:** 101 total; 85% have terminal degrees, 10% minority, 44% women. **Part-time faculty:** 36 total; 11% have terminal degrees, 6% minority, 58% women. **Class size:** 63% < 20, 35% 20-39, 2% 40-49. **Special facilities:** Biology field station, conservation facility.

**Freshman class profile.** 2,042 applied, 1,603 admitted, 473 enrolled.

| Mid 50% test scores | | | |
|---|---|---|---|
| SAT critical reading: | 430-580 | Rank in top quarter: | 48% |
| SAT math: | 430-560 | Rank in top tenth: | 28% |
| SAT writing: | 420-570 | End year in good standing: | 80% |
| ACT composite: | 19-24 | Return as sophomores: | 75% |
| GPA 3.75 or higher: | 19% | Out-of-state: | 10% |
| GPA 3.50-3.74: | 16% | Live on campus: | 92% |
| GPA 3.0-3.49: | 30% | International: | 4% |
| GPA 2.0-2.99: | 35% | Fraternities: | 20% |
| | | Sororities: | 25% |

**Basis for selection.** School achievement record most important. Test scores, recommendations, extracurricular activities, interview considered. Special consideration to children of alumni. Essay and interview recommended for all; audition recommended for music programs; portfolio recommended for art programs. **Homeschooled:** Transcript of courses and grades, state high school equivalency certificate required. Portfolio of curriculum; statement of compliance with state truancy laws in cases where state certificate is not issued. **Learning Disabled:** PLUS Program available for students with disabilities that affect learning. Students must indicate interest in program when applying for admission, and must submit psychoeducational evaluations to complete application process. Application preferred filing date of March 1.

**High school preparation.** College-preparatory program required. 12 units required; 15 recommended. Required and recommended units include English 4, mathematics 2-3, social studies 2-3, science 2-3 (laboratory 2) and foreign language 2-3.

**2009-2010 Annual costs.** Tuition/fees: $19,990. Room/board: $7,740. Books/supplies: $1,000. Personal expenses: $900.

**2009-2010 Financial aid. Non-need-based:** Scholarships awarded for academics, alumni affiliation, art, leadership, minority status, music/drama, religious affiliation, state residency. **Additional information:** Scholarship priority date February 1.

**Application procedures. Admission:** Closing date 8/1. No application fee. Admission notification on a rolling basis beginning on or about 10/1. Must reply by May 1 or within 2 week(s) if notified thereafter. **Financial aid:** Priority date 3/15, closing date 8/1. FAFSA required. Applicants notified on a rolling basis starting 3/1; must reply by 5/1 or within 2 week(s) of notification.

**Academics. Special study options:** Accelerated study, distance learning, double major, dual enrollment of high school students, ESL, exchange student, honors, independent study, internships, liberal arts/career combination, student-designed major, study abroad, teacher certification program, United Nations semester, Washington semester. **Credit/placement by examination:** AP, CLEP, IB, SAT, ACT, institutional tests. **Support services:** Learning center, pre-admission summer program, reduced course load, study skills assistance, tutoring, writing center.

**Majors. Biology:** General, conservation, molecular. **Business:** General, accounting, international marketing, managerial economics. **Communications:** General, digital media, journalism. **Computer sciences:** General, computer science. **Conservation:** Environmental science. **Education:** Early childhood, elementary, middle, secondary, special. **Engineering:** General, science. **Foreign languages:** French, German, Spanish. **Health:** Clinical lab technology, nursing (RN), predental, premedicine, prepharmacy, preveterinary, speech pathology. **History:** General. **Interdisciplinary:** Neuroscience. **Legal studies:** Prelaw. **Liberal arts:** Humanities. **Math:** General. **Philosophy/religion:** Philosophy, religion. **Physical sciences:** Chemistry, geology, physics, planetary. **Protective services:** Police science. **Psychology:** General. **Social sciences:** Anthropology, economics, international relations, political science, sociology. **Theology:** Religious ed. **Visual/performing arts:** Art, dramatic.

**Most popular majors.** Biology 7%, business/marketing 21%, communications/journalism 7%, education 23%, psychology 8%, social sciences 8%.

**Computing on campus.** 217 workstations in dormitories, library, computer center, student center. Dormitories wired for high-speed internet access and linked to campus network. Commuter students can connect to campus network. Online course registration, online library, helpline, repair service, student web hosting, wireless network available.

**Student life. Freshman orientation:** Available. Preregistration for classes offered. Six 1-day sessions held on weekdays in May and June. **Housing:** Guaranteed on-campus for freshmen. Coed dorms, single-sex dorms, apartments, fraternity/sorority housing, wellness housing available. $150 deposit, deadline 5/1. **Activities:** Bands, campus ministries, choral groups, dance, drama, international student organizations, literary magazine, music ensembles, Model UN, musical theater, radio station, student government, student newspaper, symphony orchestra, TV station, Christian Fellowship, Fellowship of Christian Athletes, political awareness program, SADD, Habitat for Humanity, Young Democrats, Young Republicans.

**Athletics.** NCAA. **Intercollegiate:** Baseball M, basketball, cheerleading, cross-country, football (tackle) M, golf, soccer, softball W, tennis, track and field, volleyball W, wrestling M. **Intramural:** Basketball, bowling, cross-country, football (non-tackle), golf, lacrosse, racquetball, rugby, soccer, softball, table tennis M, tennis, track and field, volleyball, wrestling M. **Team name:** Muskies.

**Student services.** Alcohol/substance abuse counseling, chaplain/spiritual director, career counseling, student employment services, financial aid counseling, health services, on-campus daycare, personal counseling, placement for graduates, veterans' counselor. **Physically disabled:** Services for visually, hearing impaired. **Learning disabled:** Comprehensive services available.

**Contact.** E-mail: adminfo@muskingum.edu
Phone: (740) 826-8137 Toll-free number: (800) 752-6082
Fax: (740) 826-8100
Beth DaLonzo, Senior Director of Admissions and Student Financial Services, Muskingum University, 163 Stormont Street, New Concord, OH 43762-1199

## Notre Dame College
Cleveland, Ohio    CB member
www.notredamecollege.edu    CB code: 1566

♦ Private 4-year liberal arts college affiliated with Roman Catholic Church

♦ Commuter campus in very large city

♦ 1,584 degree-seeking undergraduates

♦ 50% of applicants admitted

♦ SAT or ACT, application essay required

**General.** Founded in 1922. Regionally accredited. Weekend college for adults who have graduated from high school 5 or more years prior to their first term of enrollment. **Degrees:** 102 bachelor's awarded; master's offered. **ROTC:** Army. **Location:** 10 miles from downtown Cleveland. **Calendar:** Semester, limited summer session. **Full-time faculty:** 50 total. **Part-time faculty:** 80 total. **Special facilities:** Science research center.

**Freshman class profile.** 2,386 applied, 1,193 admitted, 345 enrolled.

| Mid 50% test scores | | | |
|---|---|---|---|
| SAT critical reading: | 420-520 | Rank in top quarter: | 20% |
| SAT math: | 430-560 | Rank in top tenth: | 6% |
| ACT composite: | 17-22 | Out-of-state: | 17% |
| | | Live on campus: | 70% |

**Basis for selection.** School achievement record and test scores most important. Applicants should be in top half of class and have 2.5 high school GPA for unconditional admission. Extracurricular activities also considered. Interview recommended.

**High school preparation.** Recommended units include English 4, mathematics 3, social studies 2, history 1, science 3 (laboratory 3) and foreign language 3.

**2009-2010 Annual costs.** Tuition/fees: $22,742. Room/board: $7,592. Books/supplies: $2,058. Personal expenses: $808.

**Financial aid. Non-need-based:** Scholarships awarded for academics, state residency.

**Application procedures. Admission:** No deadline. $30 fee, may be waived for applicants with need, free for online applicants. Admission notification on a rolling basis. **Financial aid:** Closing date 5/1. FAFSA required. Applicants notified on a rolling basis starting 1/1; must reply within 2 week(s) of notification.

**Academics. Special study options:** Cooperative education, cross-registration, distance learning, double major, dual enrollment of high school students, exchange student, independent study, internships, student-designed major, study abroad, teacher certification program, weekend college. **Credit/placement by examination:** AP, CLEP, SAT, ACT, institutional tests. **Support services:** Learning center, reduced course load, remedial instruction, tutoring, writing center.

**Majors. Biology:** General, biochemistry, environmental. **Business:** Accounting, business admin, human resources, international, management information systems, marketing. **Communications:** General, digital media, public relations. **Communications technology:** Graphics. **Education:** Early childhood, elementary, secondary. **Health:** Nursing (RN), prenursing. **History:** General. **Math:** General. **Physical sciences:** Chemistry. **Psychology:** General. **Social sciences:** Criminology, political science. **Theology:** Theology. **Visual/performing arts:** General, graphic design, studio arts. **Other:** Public administration.

**Most popular majors.** Business/marketing 41%, education 25%, psychology 14%.

**Computing on campus.** 67 workstations in dormitories, library, computer center.

**Student life. Freshman orientation:** Mandatory, $100 fee. Preregistration for classes offered. Three 2-day sessions held in June, July, and August. Evening orientation sessions held in August and January for adult students. **Housing:** Coed dorms, wellness housing available. $150 deposit. **Activities:** Pep band, choral groups, drama, literary magazine, music ensembles, student government, student newspaper, campus ministry board, Black Scholars, multicultural student advisory board, St. Julie Scholars, psychology council, science and business clubs, Achievement in Research and Scholarship.

**Athletics.** NAIA. **Intercollegiate:** Baseball M, basketball, cross-country, diving W, field hockey W, golf, lacrosse W, soccer, softball W, swimming W, tennis M, track and field, volleyball W, wrestling M. **Intramural:** Soccer W, softball W, tennis, volleyball W. **Team name:** Falcons.

**Student services.** Adult student services, alcohol/substance abuse counseling, chaplain/spiritual director, career counseling, student employment services, financial aid counseling, health services, personal counseling, placement for graduates. **Learning disabled:** Comprehensive services available.

**Contact.** E-mail: admissions@ndc.edu
Phone: (216) 373-5355 Toll-free number: (877) 632-6446 ext. 5355
Fax: (216) 381-3802
David Armstrong, Vice President for Enrollment, Notre Dame College, 4545 College Road, Cleveland, OH 44121-4293

---

## Oberlin College
**Oberlin, Ohio**

**CB member**

**www.oberlin.edu**

**CB code: 1587**

- Private 4-year music and liberal arts college
- Residential campus in small town
- 2,888 degree-seeking undergraduates: 2% part-time, 55% women, 7% African American, 7% Asian American, 5% Hispanic American, 1% Native American, 6% international
- 31 graduate students
- 34% of applicants admitted
- SAT or ACT with writing required
- 86% graduate within 6 years

**General.** Founded in 1833. Regionally accredited. **Degrees:** 708 bachelor's awarded; master's offered. **Location:** 34 miles from Cleveland. **Calendar:** 4-1-4. **Full-time faculty:** 285 total; 96% have terminal degrees, 11% minority, 39% women. **Class size:** 72% < 20, 23% 20-39, 2% 40-49, 3% 50-99, less than 1% >100. **Special facilities:** Observatory, art museum, environmental studies building, arboretum.

**Freshman class profile.** 7,227 applied, 2,434 admitted, 809 enrolled.

| Mid 50% test scores | | GPA 2.0-2.99: | 3% |
|---|---|---|---|
| SAT critical reading: | 640-740 | Rank in top quarter: | 89% |
| SAT math: | 620-710 | Rank in top tenth: | 69% |
| SAT writing: | 640-730 | Return as sophomores: | 93% |
| ACT composite: | 27-32 | Out-of-state: | 91% |
| GPA 3.75 or higher: | 37% | Live on campus: | 100% |
| GPA 3.50-3.74: | 28% | International: | 7% |
| GPA 3.0-3.49: | 32% | | |

**Basis for selection.** GED not accepted. For college of arts and sciences: school achievement record, test scores, school and community leadership activities, recommendations, and interview important. Special consideration to applicants from minority and first generation college families and to foreign applicants. For conservatory: audition most important factor; admission selective. SAT Subject Tests recommended. Interview required for early admission candidates; recommended for all others. Audition required of applicants to conservatory; essay required of applicants to college of arts and sciences. **Homeschooled:** Interview required. SAT Subject Tests, detailed portfolio also required.

**High school preparation.** College-preparatory program required. Required units include English 4, mathematics 4, social studies 3, science 3 and foreign language 3.

**2009-2010 Annual costs.** Tuition/fees: $40,004. Room/board: $10,480. Books/supplies: $830. Personal expenses: $978.

**2009-2010 Financial aid. Need-based:** 544 full-time freshmen applied for aid; 472 were judged to have need; 472 of these received aid. Average need met was 100%. Average scholarship/grant was $27,888; average loan $4,448. 79% of total undergraduate aid awarded as scholarships/grants, 21% as loans/jobs. **Non-need-based:** Scholarships awarded for academics, music/drama.

**Application procedures. Admission:** Closing date 1/15 (postmark date). $35 fee, may be waived for applicants with need. Admission notification 4/1. Must reply by May 1 or within 2 week(s) if notified thereafter. 12/1 application closing date for Conservatory of Music; $100 application fee. **Financial aid:** Priority date 1/15, closing date 2/1. FAFSA, institutional form, CSS PROFILE required. Applicants notified by 4/1; must reply by 5/1 or within 2 week(s) of notification.

**Academics.** No core curriculum. Students required to take 9 credit hours in each academic division (Humanities, Social Sciences, and Math and Natural Science) and 9 hours related to cultural diversity. **Special study options:** Cross-registration, double major, dual enrollment of high school students, ESL, exchange student, honors, independent study, internships, New York semester, student-designed major, study abroad, teacher certification program, urban semester, Washington semester. 5-year dual degree program with music conservatory and liberal arts college, 3-2 engineering. **Credit/placement by examination:** AP, CLEP, IB, institutional tests. 30 credit hours maximum toward bachelor's degree. **Support services:** Learning center, remedial instruction, study skills assistance, tutoring, writing center.

**Majors. Area/ethnic studies:** African, African-American, American, East Asian, Latin American, Russian/Slavic, women's. **Biology:** General, biochemistry. **Computer sciences:** General. **Conservation:** Environmental studies. **Education:** Music. **Foreign languages:** Ancient Greek, classics, comparative lit, French, German, Latin, Russian, Spanish. **Health:** Predental, premedicine, preveterinary. **History:** General. **Interdisciplinary:** Neuroscience. **Legal studies:** Prelaw. **Math:** General. **Philosophy/religion:** Judaic, philosophy, religion. **Physical sciences:** Chemistry, geology, physics. **Psychology:** General. **Social sciences:** Anthropology, economics, political science, sociology. **Visual/performing arts:** Art history/conservation, conducting, dance, dramatic, film/cinema, jazz, music history, music theory/composition, piano/organ, stringed instruments, studio arts, voice/opera.

**Most popular majors.** Area/ethnic studies 8%, biology 10%, English 9%, history 7%, philosophy/religious studies 6%, social sciences 12%, visual/performing arts 26%.

**Computing on campus.** 340 workstations in dormitories, library, computer center. Dormitories wired for high-speed internet access and linked to campus network. Commuter students can connect to campus network. Online course registration, online library, helpline, repair service, student web hosting, wireless network available.

**Student life. Freshman orientation:** Mandatory. Preregistration for classes offered. Held week prior to fall classes. Includes day of service. **Policies:** Students agree to follow honor code. **Housing:** Guaranteed on-campus for all undergraduates. Coed dorms, single-sex dorms, apartments, cooperative housing, wellness housing available. **Activities:** Bands, campus ministries, choral groups, dance, drama, film society, international student organizations, literary magazine, music ensembles, musical theater, opera, radio station, student government, student newspaper, symphony orchestra, religious, political, inter-cultural, ethnic, social service, and gay/lesbian/bisexual organizations.

**Athletics.** NCAA. **Intercollegiate:** Baseball M, basketball, cross-country, diving, field hockey W, football (tackle) M, golf M, lacrosse, soccer, softball W, swimming, tennis, track and field, volleyball W. **Intramural:** Baseball M, basketball, bowling, football (non-tackle), handball, racquetball, rugby M, skin diving, soccer, softball, squash, table tennis, tennis, track and field, volleyball, weight lifting. **Team name:** Yeomen & Yeowomen.

**Student services.** Alcohol/substance abuse counseling, chaplain/spiritual director, career counseling, services for economically disadvantaged, student employment services, financial aid counseling, health services, minority student services, personal counseling, placement for graduates, women's services. **Physically disabled:** Services for visually, speech, hearing impaired.

**Contact.** E-mail: college.admissions@oberlin.edu
Phone: (440) 775-8411 Toll-free number: (800) 622-6243
Fax: (440) 775-6905
Debra Chermonte, Dean of Admissions and Financial Aid, Oberlin College, Carnegie Building, 101 North Professor Street, Oberlin, OH 44074

## Ohio Christian University
### Circleville, Ohio
### www.ohiochristian.edu
**CB code: 1088**

- Private 4-year university, Bible and teachers college affiliated with Churches of Christ in Christian Union
- Residential campus in large town
- 846 degree-seeking undergraduates
- 33% of applicants admitted
- SAT or ACT (ACT writing optional), application essay required

**General.** Founded in 1948. Candidate for regional accreditation.; also accredited by ABHE. **Degrees:** 73 bachelor's, 11 associate awarded. **Location:** 25 miles from Columbus. **Calendar:** Semester, limited summer session. **Full-time faculty:** 24 total. **Part-time faculty:** 111 total. **Class size:** 74% < 20, 22% 20-39, 2% 40-49, 3% 50-99.

**Freshman class profile.** 368 applied, 121 admitted, 121 enrolled.

| Mid 50% test scores | | | |
|---|---|---|---|
| | | ACT composite: | 17-21 |
| SAT critical reading: | 400-440 | Out-of-state: | 15% |
| SAT math: | 360-420 | Live on campus: | 37% |
| SAT writing: | 410-470 | | |

**Basis for selection.** Positive Christian testimony, potential for Christian service, sound academic performance, and personal character references important. Students without SAT or ACT may be admitted conditionally but must meet test requirement at earliest opportunity. Interview recommended for all; audition required for music majors.

**High school preparation.** 15 units recommended. Recommended units include English 4, mathematics 3, social studies 3, science 3 and foreign language 2.

**2009-2010 Annual costs.** Tuition/fees: $14,650. Room/board: $5,990. Books/supplies: $600. Personal expenses: $2,606.

**2008-2009 Financial aid.** All financial aid based on need. **Additional information:** Religious affiliation tuition discount.

**Application procedures. Admission:** Priority date 4/1; no deadline. $25 fee, may be waived for applicants with need. Admission notification on a rolling basis. Must reply by May 1 or within 2 week(s) if notified thereafter. **Financial aid:** Priority date 5/7; no closing date. FAFSA, institutional form required. Applicants notified on a rolling basis starting 5/1; must reply within 2 week(s) of notification.

**Academics.** Every student required to complete minimum of 30 hours in Bible and theology courses. **Special study options:** Accelerated study, combined bachelor's/graduate degree, distance learning, double major, dual enrollment of high school students, honors, independent study, internships, liberal arts/career combination, self-designed major, study abroad. **Credit/placement by examination:** AP, CLEP, ACT, institutional tests. **Support services:** Reduced course load, remedial instruction, study skills assistance, tutoring, writing center.

**Majors. Business:** General, accounting, accounting/business management, business admin. **Education:** General, early childhood, elementary, music, secondary. **Philosophy/religion:** Religion. **Psychology:** General. **Theology:** Missionary, pastoral counseling, religious ed, sacred music, theology, youth ministry.

**Most popular majors.** Education 8%, psychology 11%.

**Computing on campus.** 58 workstations in dormitories, library, computer center. Dormitories wired for high-speed internet access and linked to campus network. Online library, helpline, repair service, wireless network available.

**Student life. Freshman orientation:** Mandatory. Preregistration for classes offered. Held 2-days prior to start of classes. **Policies:** Curfew of 11:30 pm (Monday-Thursday), 1:00 am (Friday), 12:00 am (Saturday-Sunday); dress code. Religious observance required. **Housing:** Guaranteed on-campus for freshmen. Single-sex dorms, apartments available. $50 deposit, deadline 8/1. **Activities:** Choral groups, music ensembles, student government, ministerial association, prison ministries, S.H.I.N.E., world gospel mission student involvement, summer camp ministries.

**Athletics.** NCCAA. **Intercollegiate:** Archery, baseball M, basketball, soccer M, softball W, volleyball W. **Intramural:** Basketball, golf, skiing, soccer, table tennis, volleyball. **Team name:** Trailblazers.

**Student services.** Adult student services, chaplain/spiritual director, career counseling, student employment services, financial aid counseling, health services, minority student services, personal counseling, veterans' counselor. **Physically disabled:** Services for visually impaired.

**Contact.** E-mail: enroll@ohiochristian.edu
Phone: (740) 477-7701 Toll-free number: (877) 762-8669
Fax: (740) 477-7755
Mike Egenreider, Director of Admissions, Ohio Christian University, 1476 Lancaster Pike, Circleville, OH 43113

## Ohio Dominican University
### Columbus, Ohio
### www.ohiodominican.edu
**CB member**
**CB code: 1131**

- Private 4-year university and liberal arts college affiliated with Roman Catholic Church
- Commuter campus in very large city
- 1,882 degree-seeking undergraduates: 20% part-time, 60% women, 21% African American, 1% Asian American, 2% Hispanic American, 1% international
- 772 degree-seeking graduate students
- 59% of applicants admitted
- SAT or ACT (ACT writing optional), application essay required
- 45% graduate within 6 years

**General.** Founded in 1911. Regionally accredited. **Degrees:** 456 bachelor's, 75 associate awarded; master's offered. **ROTC:** Army. **Location:** 4 miles from downtown. **Calendar:** Semester, limited summer session. **Full-time faculty:** 72 total; 90% have terminal degrees, 8% minority, 56% women. **Part-time faculty:** 130 total; 28% have terminal degrees, 8% minority, 46% women. **Class size:** 55% < 20, 45% 20-39, less than 1% 40-49.

**Freshman class profile.** 2,367 applied, 1,404 admitted, 283 enrolled.

| Mid 50% test scores | | | |
|---|---|---|---|
| ACT composite: | 18-23 | Rank in top quarter: | 28% |
| GPA 3.75 or higher: | 13% | Rank in top tenth: | 9% |
| GPA 3.50-3.74: | 12% | Return as sophomores: | 61% |
| GPA 3.0-3.49: | 29% | Out-of-state: | 7% |
| GPA 2.0-2.99: | 46% | Live on campus: | 79% |

**Basis for selection.** High school GPA, curriculum most important, followed by class rank, test scores, interview, recommendations, and activities. Interview required for in-state applicants; recommended for out-of-state. **Homeschooled:** Transcript of courses and grades, state high school equivalency certificate required.

**High school preparation.** College-preparatory program recommended. 16 units recommended.

**2009-2010 Annual costs.** Tuition/fees: $24,558. Room/board: $7,900. Books/supplies: $1,000. Personal expenses: $1,500.

**Financial aid. Non-need-based:** Scholarships awarded for academics, athletics, state residency.

**Application procedures. Admission:** Priority date 4/1; no deadline. $25 fee. Admission notification on a rolling basis beginning on or about 9/1. **Financial aid:** Priority date 4/1; no closing date. FAFSA required. Applicants notified on a rolling basis starting 3/1; must reply within 2 week(s) of notification.

**Academics. Special study options:** Cross-registration, distance learning, double major, dual enrollment of high school students, honors, independent study, internships, study abroad, teacher certification program, Washington semester. **Credit/placement by examination:** AP, CLEP, IB, ACT. No limit on credit hours by examination, but residency requirement must be met. **Support services:** Learning center, reduced course load, remedial instruction, study skills assistance, tutoring.

**Majors. Biology:** General. **Business:** Accounting, business admin, communications, finance, international. **Communications:** General, public relations. **Computer sciences:** Information systems. **Education:** Art, biology, chemistry, elementary, English, mathematics, middle, multiple handicapped, physics, science, secondary, social studies, special. **History:** General. **Liberal arts:** Arts/sciences. **Math:** General. **Philosophy/religion:** Philosophy. **Physical sciences:** Chemistry. **Protective services:** Criminal justice. **Psychology:** General. **Public administration:** Social work. **Social sciences:** Economics, political science, sociology. **Theology:** Theology. **Visual/performing arts:** Art, graphic design.

**Most popular majors.** Business/marketing 50%, education 16%, social sciences 9%.

**Computing on campus.** 380 workstations in dormitories, library, computer center, student center. Dormitories wired for high-speed internet access and linked to campus network. Commuter students can connect to campus network. Online course registration, online library, helpline, student web hosting available.

**Student life. Freshman orientation:** Mandatory, $125 fee. Preregistration for classes offered. Held 2 days in August. **Housing:** Coed dorms available. $150 partly refundable deposit, deadline 8/15. **Activities:** Bands, campus ministries, choral groups, drama, literary magazine, music ensembles, radio station, student government, student newspaper, black student union, resident student association, commuter student association, social work club, psychology club, association of commuter students, association of resident students.

**Athletics.** NAIA. **Intercollegiate:** Baseball M, basketball, cheerleading, cross-country, football (tackle) M, golf, soccer, softball W, tennis, volleyball W. **Intramural:** Badminton, basketball, golf, soccer, table tennis, tennis, volleyball. **Team name:** Panthers.

**Student services.** Adult student services, chaplain/spiritual director, career counseling, student employment services, financial aid counseling, health services, minority student services, personal counseling, placement for graduates, veterans' counselor.

**Contact.** E-mail: admissions@ohiodominican.edu
Phone: (614) 251-4500 Toll-free number: (800) 955-6446
Fax: (614) 251-4772
Nicole Evans, Director of Admissions, Ohio Dominican University, 1216 Sunbury Road, Columbus, OH 43219

---

## Ohio Northern University

| | |
|---|---|
| Ada, Ohio | CB member |
| www.onu.edu | CB code: 1591 |

- Private 4-year university affiliated with United Methodist Church
- Residential campus in small town
- 2,445 degree-seeking undergraduates: 2% part-time, 46% women, 4% African American, 2% Asian American, 2% Hispanic American, 2% international
- 951 degree-seeking graduate students
- 89% of applicants admitted
- SAT or ACT (ACT writing optional) required
- 67% graduate within 6 years

**General.** Founded in 1871. Regionally accredited. **Degrees:** 511 bachelor's awarded; master's, professional offered. **ROTC:** Army, Air Force. **Location:** 15 miles from Lima, 80 miles from Columbus. **Calendar:** Quarter, limited summer session. **Full-time faculty:** 242 total; 75% have terminal degrees, 11% minority, 36% women. **Part-time faculty:** 72 total; 22% have terminal degrees, 4% minority, 53% women. **Class size:** 57% < 20, 38% 20-39, 2% 40-49, 1% 50-99, 2% >100. **Special facilities:** Nature center, drug information center (College of Pharmacy), pharmacy museum.

**Freshman class profile.** 2,917 applied, 2,592 admitted, 641 enrolled.

| Mid 50% test scores | | | |
|---|---|---|---|
| SAT critical reading: | 510-630 | Rank in top quarter: | 66% |
| SAT math: | 560-650 | Rank in top tenth: | 42% |
| SAT writing: | 510-620 | Return as sophomores: | 83% |
| ACT composite: | 23-29 | Out-of-state: | 14% |
| GPA 3.75 or higher: | 51% | Live on campus: | 96% |
| GPA 3.50-3.74: | 14% | International: | 2% |
| GPA 3.0-3.49: | 24% | Fraternities: | 19% |
| GPA 2.0-2.99: | 11% | Sororities: | 19% |

**Basis for selection.** 20 ACT preferred; secondary school record very important. Colleges of Pharmacy and Engineering have higher test score credentials for consideration. GPA, class rank, test scores, college prep curriculum, extracurricular activities considered in admission decisions. Essay required for all freshmen. Interview recommended for all. Audition required for music, performing arts programs. Portfolio recommended for art program. **Homeschooled:** Statement describing homeschool structure and mission required.

**High school preparation.** College-preparatory program required. 16 units required; 24 recommended. Required and recommended units include English 4, mathematics 2-4, social studies 2-3, history 2, science 2-3 (laboratory 2), foreign language 2, computer science 1, visual/performing arts 1 and academic electives 4. 4 units math and science required for engineering and pharmacy applicants.

**2009-2010 Annual costs.** Tuition/fees: $31,866. Room/board: $8,280. Books/supplies: $1,500. Personal expenses: $1,229.

**2009-2010 Financial aid. Non-need-based:** Scholarships awarded for academics, alumni affiliation, art, leadership, minority status, music/drama, ROTC, state residency.

**Application procedures. Admission:** Priority date 12/1; deadline 8/15 (receipt date). $30 fee, may be waived for applicants with need. Admission notification on a rolling basis. Must reply by 5/1. Priority date for scholarship eligibility December 1. Pharmacy deadline is November 1 of senior year. **Financial aid:** Priority date 4/15; no closing date. FAFSA, institutional form required. Applicants notified on a rolling basis starting 2/15; must reply within 2 week(s) of notification.

**Academics.** Pharmacy students admitted directly to 6-year PharmD. program. **Special study options:** Combined bachelor's/graduate degree, cooperative education, distance learning, double major, dual enrollment of high school students, ESL, exchange student, honors, independent study, internships, liberal arts/career combination, study abroad, teacher certification program, Washington semester. **Credit/placement by examination:** AP, CLEP, IB, SAT, ACT, institutional tests. 45 credit hours maximum toward bachelor's degree. **Support services:** Pre-admission summer program, reduced course load, remedial instruction, study skills assistance, tutoring, writing center.

**Majors. Biology:** General, biochemistry, exercise physiology, molecular. **Business:** Accounting, business admin, finance, international, management science, marketing. **Communications:** General, broadcast journalism, journalism, organizational, public relations. **Computer sciences:** Computer science. **Conservation:** General, environmental studies. **Construction:** Site management. **Education:** General, art, biology, chemistry, early childhood, elementary, English, foreign languages, French, health, history, mathematics, middle, music, physical, physics, science, secondary, social studies, Spanish, technology/industrial arts. **Engineering:** General, civil, computer, electrical, mechanical. **Engineering technology:** General, manufacturing. **Foreign languages:** French, German, Germanic, Spanish. **Health:** Athletic training, clinical lab assistant, nursing (RN), physician assistant, predental, premedicine, preveterinary. **History:** General. **Liberal arts:** Arts/sciences. **Math:** General, statistics. **Parks/recreation:** Health/fitness, sports admin. **Philosophy/religion:** Philosophy, religion. **Physical sciences:** Astronomy, chemistry, physics. **Protective services:** Criminal justice, forensics, law enforcement admin, police science. **Psychology:** General. **Social sciences:** General, international relations, political science, sociology. **Theology:** Youth ministry. **Visual/performing arts:** Art, commercial/advertising art, dramatic, music management, music performance, music theory/composition, studio arts. **Other:** Pharmacy business.

**Most popular majors.** Biology 11%, business/marketing 22%, education 6%, engineering/engineering technologies 20%, health sciences 8%, visual/performing arts 9%.

**Computing on campus.** 550 workstations in dormitories, library, computer center, student center. Dormitories wired for high-speed internet access and linked to campus network. Commuter students can connect to campus network. Online course registration, online library, helpline, repair service, wireless network available.

**Student life. Freshman orientation:** Mandatory. Preregistration for classes offered. Three 1-day held in June and July on Fridays. **Policies:** All students must reside on campus until 135 credit hours completed. No smoking in residence halls. **Housing:** Guaranteed on-campus for freshmen. Coed dorms, single-sex dorms, special housing for disabled, apartments, cooperative housing, fraternity/sorority housing, wellness housing available. $200 fully refundable deposit, deadline 5/1. Honors residence halls available. **Activities:** Bands, campus ministries, choral groups, dance, drama, international student organizations, literary magazine, music ensembles, Model UN, musical theater, opera, radio station, student government, student newspaper, symphony orchestra, TV station, Christian legal society, Fellowship of Christian Athletes, university religious association council, black student union, Amnesty International, College Republicans, black law student association, Habitat for Humanity, world student organization.

**Athletics.** NCAA. **Intercollegiate:** Baseball M, basketball, cross-country, diving, football (tackle) M, golf, soccer, softball W, swimming, tennis, track and field, volleyball W, wrestling M. **Intramural:** Badminton, basketball, bowling, football (non-tackle) M, racquetball, soccer, softball, swimming, table tennis M, tennis, track and field, volleyball, wrestling M. **Team name:** Polar Bears.

**Student services.** Alcohol/substance abuse counseling, chaplain/spiritual director, career counseling, student employment services, financial aid counseling, health services, legal services, minority student services, on-campus daycare, personal counseling, placement for graduates. **Physically disabled:** Services for visually, speech, hearing impaired.

**Contact.** E-mail: admissions-ug@onu.edu
Phone: (419) 772-2260 Toll-free number: (888) 408-4668
Fax: (419) 772-2821
Deborah Miller, Director of Admissions, Ohio Northern University, 525
South Main Street, Ada, OH 45810

## Ohio State University: Columbus Campus

**Columbus, Ohio** — **CB member**
**www.osu.edu** — **CB code: 1592**

- Public 4-year university
- Residential campus in very large city
- 40,178 degree-seeking undergraduates: 6% part-time, 46% women, 7% African American, 5% Asian American, 3% Hispanic American, 4% international
- 13,666 degree-seeking graduate students
- 76% of applicants admitted
- SAT or ACT with writing, application essay required
- 75% graduate within 6 years

**General.** Founded in 1870. Regionally accredited. Additional campuses in Wooster, Marion, Lima, Newark, Mansfield. **Degrees:** 9,329 bachelor's, 444 associate awarded; master's, doctoral, professional offered. **ROTC:** Army, Naval, Air Force. **Location:** 2 miles from downtown. **Calendar:** Quarter, extensive summer session. **Full-time faculty:** 3,310 total; 99% have terminal degrees, 20% minority, 32% women. **Part-time faculty:** 1,158 total; 14% minority, 49% women. **Class size:** 32% < 20, 38% 20-39, 9% 40-49, 13% 50-99, 8% >100. **Special facilities:** Radio telescope, dance notation bureau, extension center for educational research, biological science laboratory on Lake Erie, campus airport, environmental studies center, research vessel on Lake Erie, nuclear research reactor, supercomputer facility, arts center, cultural center, public service and public policy institute, polar research center, health policy studies center, mapping center, materials research center.

**Freshman class profile.** 18,256 applied, 13,822 admitted, 6,739 enrolled.

| Mid 50% test scores | | | |
|---|---|---|---|
| SAT critical reading: | 540-650 | Rank in top tenth: | 49% |
| SAT math: | 580-690 | Return as sophomores: | 93% |
| SAT writing: | 540-640 | Out-of-state: | 15% |
| ACT composite: | 25-30 | Live on campus: | 91% |
| Rank in top quarter: | 85% | International: | 4% |

**Basis for selection.** Secondary school record, class rank, test scores most important. Audition required for dance, music programs; portfolio required for art programs. **Homeschooled:** May be required to provide GED.

**High school preparation.** College-preparatory program recommended. Required and recommended units include English 4, mathematics 3-4, social studies 2-3, science 2-3 (laboratory 2-3), foreign language 2-3, visual/performing arts 1 and academic electives 1.

**2009-2010 Annual costs.** Tuition/fees: $8,706; $22,278 out-of-state. Room/board: $8,409. Books/supplies: $1,440. Personal expenses: $4,392.

**2009-2010 Financial aid. Need-based:** 5,464 full-time freshmen applied for aid; 3,619 were judged to have need; 3,603 of these received aid. Average need met was 58%. Average scholarship/grant was $8,430; average loan $3,445. 24% of total undergraduate aid awarded as scholarships/grants, 76% as loans/jobs. **Non-need-based:** Awarded to 10,090 full-time undergraduates, including 2,769 freshmen. Scholarships awarded for academics, alumni affiliation, art, athletics, job skills, leadership, minority status, music/drama, ROTC, state residency.

**Application procedures. Admission:** Closing date 2/1 (postmark date). $40 fee, may be waived for applicants with need. Admission notification on a rolling basis beginning on or about 12/1. Must reply by May 1 or within 4 week(s) if notified thereafter. **Financial aid:** Priority date 2/15; no closing date. FAFSA required. Applicants notified by 4/15; must reply by 5/1 or within 4 week(s) of notification.

**Academics. Special study options:** Accelerated study, combined bachelor's/graduate degree, cooperative education, cross-registration, distance learning, double major, dual enrollment of high school students, ESL, exchange student, honors, independent study, internships, liberal arts/career combination, semester at sea, student-designed major, study abroad, teacher certification program, Washington semester. **Credit/placement by examination:** AP, CLEP, IB, SAT, ACT, institutional tests. 45 credit hours maximum toward bachelor's degree. **Support services:** Learning center, pre-admission summer program, reduced course load, remedial instruction, study skills assistance, tutoring, writing center.

**Majors. Agriculture:** Agronomy, animal sciences, business, communications, economics, food processing, food science, landscaping, plant protection, plant sciences, turf management. **Architecture:** Architecture, environmental design, interior, landscape. **Area/ethnic studies:** African, African-American, Central/Eastern European, East Asian, Latin American, Near/Middle Eastern, Russian/Slavic, Western European, women's. **Biology:** General, biochemistry, botany, ecology, entomology, genetics, microbiology, molecular genetics, zoology. **Business:** General, accounting, actuarial science, fashion, finance, hospitality admin, hospitality/recreation, human resources, insurance, international, logistics, management information systems, managerial economics, marketing, operations, real estate, transportation. **Communications:** General, journalism, public relations. **Computer sciences:** General, computer science, information systems. **Conservation:** General, fisheries, forestry, management/policy, wildlife. **Education:** Agricultural, art, music, physical, special, technology/industrial arts, trade/industrial. **Engineering:** Aerospace, agricultural, ceramic, chemical, civil, computer, electrical, industrial, materials, materials science, mechanical, metallurgical, physics, systems. **Engineering technology:** Construction, surveying. **Family/consumer sciences:** General, clothing/textiles, family resources, family studies, family/community services, food/nutrition. **Foreign languages:** Arabic, Chinese, classics, comparative lit, French, German, Hebrew, Italian, Japanese, Latin, linguistics, modern Greek, Portuguese, Russian, Spanish. **Health:** Audiology/hearing, audiology/speech pathology, clinical lab science, dental hygiene, dietetics, medical radiologic technology/radiation therapy, medical records admin, perfusion technology, respiratory therapy technology. **History:** General. **Interdisciplinary:** Ancient studies, medieval/Renaissance, nutrition sciences, peace/conflict. **Liberal arts:** Arts/sciences. **Math:** General. **Parks/recreation:** Exercise sciences, facilities management, health/fitness, sports admin. **Philosophy/religion:** Islamic, Judaic, philosophy, religion. **Physical sciences:** Astronomy, chemistry, geology, geophysics, physics. **Production:** Welding. **Psychology:** General. **Public administration:** Social work. **Social sciences:** General, anthropology, criminology, economics, geography, international relations, political science, sociology, urban studies. **Transportation:** Aviation. **Visual/performing arts:** Art, art history/conservation, ceramics, dance, design, dramatic, drawing, industrial design, interior design, jazz, music history, music performance, music theory/composition, painting, photography, piano/organ, printmaking, sculpture, studio arts, voice/opera.

**Most popular majors.** Biology 6%, business/marketing 16%, communications/journalism 6%, engineering/engineering technologies 7%, family/consumer sciences 9%, health sciences 8%, psychology 6%, social sciences 14%.

**Computing on campus.** 800 workstations in dormitories, library, computer center, student center. Dormitories wired for high-speed internet access and linked to campus network. Commuter students can connect to campus network. Online course registration, online library, helpline, wireless network available.

**Student life. Freshman orientation:** Mandatory, $50 fee. Preregistration for classes offered. 2-day programs held June-August. **Policies:** Student organizations need to have 5 student members, faculty or staff advisor, constitution, and purpose statement to register. **Housing:** Guaranteed on-campus for freshmen. Coed dorms, single-sex dorms, special housing for disabled, apartments, cooperative housing, fraternity/sorority housing, wellness housing available. $200 partly refundable deposit. **Activities:** Bands, choral groups, dance, drama, film society, international student organizations, literary magazine, musical theater, opera, radio station, student government, student newspaper, symphony orchestra, TV station, over 950 organizations.

**Athletics.** NCAA. **Intercollegiate:** Baseball M, basketball, cheerleading, cross-country, diving, fencing, field hockey W, football (tackle) M, golf, gymnastics, ice hockey, lacrosse, rifle, soccer, softball W, swimming, synchronized swimming W, tennis, track and field, volleyball, wrestling M. **Intramural:** Badminton, baseball M, basketball, cricket, cross-country, football (non-tackle), golf, ice hockey, racquetball, soccer, softball, swimming, table tennis, tennis, volleyball, wrestling. **Team name:** Buckeyes.

**Student services.** Adult student services, alcohol/substance abuse counseling, career counseling, services for economically disadvantaged, student employment services, financial aid counseling, health services, legal services, minority student services, on-campus daycare, personal counseling, veterans' counselor, women's services. **Physically disabled:** Services for visually, speech, hearing impaired.

**Contact.** E-mail: askabuckeye@osu.edu
Phone: (614) 292-3980 Fax: (614) 292-4818
Mabel Freeman, Assistant Vice President for Undergraduate Admissions and First Year Experience, Ohio State University: Columbus Campus, 110 Enarson Hall, Columbus, OH 43210

## Ohio State University: Lima Campus

**Lima, Ohio**
**www.lima.ohio-state.edu** — **CB code: 1541**

- Public 4-year branch campus college
- Commuter campus in large town

- 1,342 degree-seeking undergraduates: 11% part-time, 53% women, 4% African American, 2% Asian American, 2% Hispanic American, 1% Native American
- 106 degree-seeking graduate students
- Application essay required
- 35% graduate within 6 years

**General.** Founded in 1960. Regionally accredited. Branch campus of Ohio State University; all degrees awarded through main campus. **Degrees:** 75 bachelor's, 42 associate awarded; master's offered. **ROTC:** Army, Naval, Air Force. **Location:** 78 miles from Toledo. **Calendar:** Quarter, limited summer session. **Full-time faculty:** 39 total; 97% have terminal degrees, 13% minority, 36% women. **Part-time faculty:** 48 total; 12% minority, 58% women. **Class size:** 35% < 20, 49% 20-39, 10% 40-49, 6% 50-99. **Special facilities:** Greenhouse, nature trails, dinosaur museum.

**Freshman class profile.**

| Mid 50% test scores | | | |
|---|---|---|---|
| | | ACT composite: | 19-24 |
| SAT critical reading: | 470-570 | Rank in top quarter: | 22% |
| SAT math: | 490-640 | Rank in top tenth: | 7% |
| SAT writing: | 430-560 | Return as sophomores: | 66% |

**Basis for selection.** Open admission, but selective for out-of-state students. Out-of-state students evaluated on basis of GPA, class rank, principal/counselor recommendation, and SAT/ACT scores. **Homeschooled:** May be required to provide GED.

**High school preparation.** College-preparatory program recommended. Recommended units include English 4, mathematics 4, social studies 3, science 3 (laboratory 2), foreign language 3, visual/performing arts 1 and academic electives 1.

**2009-2010 Annual costs.** Tuition/fees: $5,664; $19,233 out-of-state. Books/supplies: $1,440. Personal expenses: $3,960.

**2009-2010 Financial aid. Need-based:** 428 full-time freshmen applied for aid; 346 were judged to have need; 343 of these received aid. Average need met was 50%. Average scholarship/grant was $3,710; average loan $3,334. 32% of total undergraduate aid awarded as scholarships/grants, 68% as loans/jobs. **Non-need-based:** Awarded to 171 full-time undergraduates, including 104 freshmen. Scholarships awarded for academics, alumni affiliation, art, athletics, job skills, leadership, minority status, music/drama, ROTC, state residency.

**Application procedures. Admission:** Closing date 7/1 (postmark date). $40 fee, may be waived for applicants with need. Admission notification on a rolling basis beginning on or about 12/1. Must reply by May 1 or within 4 week(s) if notified thereafter. **Financial aid:** Priority date 3/1; no closing date. FAFSA required. Applicants notified on a rolling basis starting 4/1; must reply within 4 week(s) of notification.

**Academics.** Students often leave campus after 1-3 years and complete bachelor's degree on Columbus campus. **Special study options:** Accelerated study, cooperative education, cross-registration, distance learning, double major, dual enrollment of high school students, ESL, exchange student, honors, independent study, internships, liberal arts/career combination, student-designed major, study abroad, teacher certification program, weekend college. **Credit/placement by examination:** AP, CLEP, SAT, ACT, institutional tests. 45 credit hours maximum toward bachelor's degree. **Support services:** Learning center, remedial instruction, tutoring, writing center.

**Majors. Biology:** General. **Business:** General, financial planning, hospitality admin. **Education:** General. **Health:** Health services. **History:** General. **Math:** General. **Psychology:** General.

**Computing on campus.** 150 workstations in library, computer center. Commuter students can connect to campus network. Online course registration, online library, helpline, wireless network available.

**Student life. Freshman orientation:** Mandatory. Preregistration for classes offered. Orientation services available throughout year, days and evenings. **Activities:** Pep band, campus ministries, choral groups, dance, drama, film society, international student organizations, musical theater, student government, Campus Crusade for Christ, College Republicans, Students for Obama, Newman Club, veterans club, human service club, multicultural club, French and Japanese club, global club.

**Athletics. Intramural:** Baseball M, basketball, football (non-tackle), volleyball. **Team name:** Barons.

**Student services.** Adult student services, chaplain/spiritual director, career counseling, student employment services, financial aid counseling, on-campus daycare, personal counseling, placement for graduates. **Physically disabled:** Services for visually, speech, hearing impaired.

**Contact.** E-mail: admissions@lima.ohio-state.edu
Phone: (419) 995-8396 Fax: (419) 995-8483
Beth Keehn, Director of Admissions, Ohio State University: Lima Campus, 4240 Campus Drive, Lima, OH 45804-3596

## Ohio State University: Mansfield Campus
### Mansfield, Ohio
www.mansfield.ohio-state.edu                CB code: 0744

- Public 4-year branch campus college
- Commuter campus in large town
- 1,274 degree-seeking undergraduates: 13% part-time, 54% women, 7% African American, 2% Asian American, 2% Hispanic American, 1% Native American
- 63 degree-seeking graduate students
- Application essay required
- 33% graduate within 6 years

**General.** Founded in 1958. Regionally accredited. Branch campus of Ohio State University; all degrees awarded through main campus. **Degrees:** 73 bachelor's, 87 associate awarded; master's offered. **ROTC:** Army, Naval, Air Force. **Location:** 67 miles from Columbus. **Calendar:** Quarter, limited summer session. **Full-time faculty:** 46 total; 98% have terminal degrees, 9% minority, 46% women. **Part-time faculty:** 47 total; 8% minority, 62% women. **Class size:** 43% < 20, 45% 20-39, 5% 40-49, 7% 50-99, less than 1% >100. **Special facilities:** Archives and reading room, educational enrichment laboratory, language laboratory, elementary education suite.

**Freshman class profile.**

| Mid 50% test scores | | | |
|---|---|---|---|
| SAT critical reading: | 450-560 | Rank in top quarter: | 29% |
| SAT math: | 460-580 | Rank in top tenth: | 8% |
| SAT writing: | 440-540 | Return as sophomores: | 69% |
| ACT composite: | 20-24 | Out-of-state: | 1% |
| | | Live on campus: | 35% |

**Basis for selection.** Open admission, but selective for out-of-state students. Out-of-state applicants evaluated on basis of GPA, class rank, principal/counselor recommendations and SAT/ACT scores.

**High school preparation.** College-preparatory program recommended. Recommended units include English 4, mathematics 4, social studies 3, science 3 (laboratory 3), foreign language 3, visual/performing arts 1 and academic electives 1.

**2009-2010 Annual costs.** Tuition/fees: $5,664; $19,233 out-of-state. Room/board: $4,440. Books/supplies: $1,440. Personal expenses: $7,164.

**2009-2010 Financial aid. Need-based:** 412 full-time freshmen applied for aid; 338 were judged to have need; 335 of these received aid. Average need met was 52%. Average scholarship/grant was $4,681; average loan $3,496. 35% of total undergraduate aid awarded as scholarships/grants, 65% as loans/jobs. **Non-need-based:** Awarded to 96 full-time undergraduates, including 44 freshmen. Scholarships awarded for academics, alumni affiliation, art, athletics, job skills, leadership, minority status, music/drama, ROTC, state residency.

**Application procedures. Admission:** Closing date 7/1 (postmark date). $40 fee, may be waived for applicants with need. Admission notification on a rolling basis beginning on or about 12/1. Must reply by May 1 or within 4 week(s) if notified thereafter. **Financial aid:** Priority date 3/1; no closing date. FAFSA required. Applicants notified on a rolling basis starting 4/5; must reply within 4 week(s) of notification.

**Academics.** Students often leave campus after 1-3 years and complete bachelor's degree on Columbus campus. **Special study options:** Accelerated study, cooperative education, cross-registration, distance learning, double major, dual enrollment of high school students, ESL, exchange student, honors, independent study, internships, liberal arts/career combination, student-designed major, study abroad, teacher certification program. **Credit/placement by examination:** AP, CLEP, SAT, ACT, institutional tests. 45 credit hours maximum toward bachelor's degree. **Support services:** Learning center, remedial instruction, tutoring, writing center.

**Majors. Business:** Business admin. **Education:** Elementary. **History:** General. **Psychology:** General.

**Computing on campus.** 260 workstations in library, computer center, student center. Commuter students can connect to campus network. Online course registration, online library, helpline, wireless network available.

**Student life. Freshman orientation:** Mandatory. Preregistration for classes offered. **Housing:** Special housing for disabled, apartments, wellness housing available. $200 partly refundable deposit. **Activities:** Choral groups, dance, drama, film society, student newspaper, African American student union, campus acitivities board, College Crusade for Christ, College Democrats/ Republicans, Diversity Alliance, economics and business club, Habitat for Humanity, single parent network, Spanish club, Theta Alpha Pi.

**Athletics. Intercollegiate:** Soccer. **Intramural:** Basketball, bowling, golf, softball, table tennis, volleyball.

**Student services.** Adult student services, career counseling, student employment services, financial aid counseling, minority student services, personal counseling, placement for graduates. **Physically disabled:** Services for visually, speech, hearing impaired.

**Contact.** E-mail: admissions@mansfield.ohio-state.edu
Phone: (419) 755-4226 Fax: (419) 755-4241
Henry Thomas, Coordinator of Admissions and Financial Aid, Ohio State University: Mansfield Campus, 1680 University Drive, Mansfield, OH 44906

## Ohio State University: Marion Campus
Marion, Ohio
www.marion.ohio-state.edu                    CB code: 0752

- Public 4-year branch campus college
- Commuter campus in large town
- 1,681 degree-seeking undergraduates: 12% part-time, 46% women, 8% African American, 5% Asian American, 2% Hispanic American, 1% Native American
- 83 degree-seeking graduate students
- Application essay required
- 38% graduate within 6 years

**General.** Founded in 1958. Regionally accredited. Branch campus of Ohio State University; all degrees awarded through main campus. **Degrees:** 74 bachelor's, 159 associate awarded; master's offered. **ROTC:** Army, Naval, Air Force. **Location:** 44 miles from Columbus. **Calendar:** Quarter, limited summer session. **Full-time faculty:** 38 total; 97% have terminal degrees, 10% minority, 37% women. **Part-time faculty:** 79 total; 11% minority, 49% women. **Class size:** 28% < 20, 55% 20-39, 12% 40-49, 4% 50-99, 1% >100.

**Freshman class profile.** 980 applied, 957 admitted, 496 enrolled.

| Mid 50% test scores | | | |
|---|---|---|---|
| SAT critical reading: | 440-550 | ACT composite: | 19-24 |
| SAT math: | 470-590 | Rank in top quarter: | 28% |
| SAT writing: | 440-540 | Rank in top tenth: | 7% |
| | | Return as sophomores: | 75% |

**Basis for selection.** Open admission, but selective for out-of-state students. Out-of-state students evaluated on basis of GPA class rank, principal/ counselor recommendation, and SAT/ACT scores.

**High school preparation.** College-preparatory program recommended. Recommended units include English 4, mathematics 4, social studies 3, science 3 (laboratory 3), foreign language 3, visual/performing arts 1 and academic electives 1.

**2009-2010 Annual costs.** Tuition/fees: $5,664; $19,233 out-of-state. Books/ supplies: $1,440. Personal expenses: $3,960.

**2009-2010 Financial aid. Need-based:** 465 full-time freshmen applied for aid; 368 were judged to have need; 363 of these received aid. Average need met was 54%. Average scholarship/grant was $5,102; average loan $3,385. 37% of total undergraduate aid awarded as scholarships/grants, 63% as loans/jobs. **Non-need-based:** Awarded to 134 full-time undergraduates, including 65 freshmen. Scholarships awarded for academics, alumni affiliation, art, athletics, job skills, leadership, minority status, music/drama, ROTC, state residency.

**Application procedures. Admission:** Closing date 7/1 (postmark date). $40 fee, may be waived for applicants with need. Admission notification on a rolling basis beginning on or about 12/1. Must reply by May 1 or within 4 week(s) if notified thereafter. **Financial aid:** Priority date 3/1; no closing date. FAFSA required. Applicants notified on a rolling basis starting 5/1; must reply within 4 week(s) of notification.

**Academics.** Students often leave campus after 1-3 years and complete bachelor's degree on Columbus campus. **Special study options:** Accelerated study, cooperative education, cross-registration, distance learning, double major, dual enrollment of high school students, ESL, exchange student, honors, independent study, internships, liberal arts/career combination, student-designed major, study abroad, teacher certification program. **Credit/ placement by examination:** AP, CLEP, SAT, ACT, institutional tests. 45

credit hours maximum toward bachelor's degree. **Support services:** Learning center, reduced course load, remedial instruction, tutoring, writing center.

**Majors. Business:** Business admin. **Education:** Elementary. **History:** General. **Psychology:** General.

**Computing on campus.** 163 workstations in library, computer center. Commuter students can connect to campus network. Online course registration, online library, helpline, wireless network available.

**Student life. Freshman orientation:** Mandatory. Preregistration for classes offered. **Activities:** Campus ministries, choral groups, literary magazine, music ensembles, student government, Buckeye Ambassador, Christian and Pagan religious organizations, Democratic/Republican political organizations, education society, honors organizations, language organizations, theater and improv troupe, diversity student organization.

**Athletics. Intercollegiate:** Basketball M, golf M, gymnastics M, soccer M, softball, volleyball W. **Intramural:** Basketball, bowling, cheerleading M, football (non-tackle), golf, handball, racquetball, rugby, skiing, soccer, softball, table tennis, volleyball. **Team name:** Scarlet Wave.

**Student services.** Career counseling, student employment services, financial aid counseling, legal services, on-campus daycare, personal counseling, placement for graduates. **Physically disabled:** Services for visually, speech, hearing impaired.

**Contact.** E-mail: moreau.1@osu.edu
Phone: (740) 389-6786 ext. 6242 Fax: (740) 386-2439
Matt Moreau, Coordinator of Admissions, Ohio State University: Marion Campus, 1465 Mount Vernon Avenue, Marion, OH 43302

## Ohio State University: Newark Campus
Newark, Ohio
www.newark.osu.edu                    CB code: 0824

- Public 4-year branch campus college
- Commuter campus in large town
- 2,321 degree-seeking undergraduates: 11% part-time, 50% women, 11% African American, 3% Asian American, 2% Hispanic American
- 104 degree-seeking graduate students
- Application essay required
- 31% graduate within 6 years

**General.** Founded in 1957. Regionally accredited. Branch campus of Ohio State University; all degrees awarded through main campus. **Degrees:** 114 bachelor's, 156 associate awarded; master's offered. **ROTC:** Army, Naval, Air Force. **Location:** 28 miles from Columbus. **Calendar:** Quarter, limited summer session. **Full-time faculty:** 53 total; 98% have terminal degrees, 13% minority, 40% women. **Part-time faculty:** 83 total; 6% minority, 54% women. **Class size:** 35% < 20, 51% 20-39, 12% 40-49, 3% 50-99. **Special facilities:** Math laboratory, writing laboratory.

**Freshman class profile.**

| Mid 50% test scores | | | |
|---|---|---|---|
| SAT critical reading: | 440-540 | Rank in top quarter: | 21% |
| SAT math: | 450-560 | Rank in top tenth: | 4% |
| SAT writing: | 440-540 | Return as sophomores: | 64% |
| ACT composite: | 19-23 | Out-of-state: | 3% |
| | | Live on campus: | 15% |

**Basis for selection.** Open admission, but selective for out-of-state students. Out-of-state applicants evaluated based on GPA, class rank, recommendation by principal/counselor, and SAT/ACT score. **Homeschooled:** A GED may be required.

**High school preparation.** College-preparatory program recommended. Recommended units include English 4, mathematics 4, social studies 3, science 3 (laboratory 3), foreign language 3, visual/performing arts 1 and academic electives 1.

**2009-2010 Annual costs.** Tuition/fees: $5,664; $19,233 out-of-state. Room only: $6,105. Books/supplies: $1,440. Personal expenses: $7,164.

**2009-2010 Financial aid. Need-based:** 909 full-time freshmen applied for aid; 716 were judged to have need; 701 of these received aid. Average need met was 52%. Average scholarship/grant was $4,976; average loan $3,361. 33% of total undergraduate aid awarded as scholarships/grants, 67% as loans/jobs. **Non-need-based:** Awarded to 61 full-time undergraduates, including 28 freshmen. Scholarships awarded for academics, alumni affiliation, art, athletics, job skills, leadership, minority status, music/drama, ROTC, state residency.

**Application procedures. Admission:** Closing date 7/1 (postmark date). $40 fee, may be waived for applicants with need. Admission notification on a rolling basis beginning on or about 12/1. Must reply by May 1 or within 4 week(s) if notified thereafter. **Financial aid:** Priority date 3/1; no closing date. FAFSA required. Applicants notified on a rolling basis starting 5/1; must reply within 4 week(s) of notification.

**Academics.** Students often leave campus after 1-3 years and complete bachelor's degree on Columbus campus. **Special study options:** Accelerated study, cooperative education, cross-registration, distance learning, double major, dual enrollment of high school students, ESL, exchange student, honors, independent study, internships, liberal arts/career combination, student-designed major, study abroad, teacher certification program, weekend college. **Credit/placement by examination:** AP, CLEP, SAT, ACT, institutional tests. 45 credit hours maximum toward bachelor's degree. **Support services:** Learning center, remedial instruction, tutoring, writing center.

**Majors. Business:** Business admin. **Education:** General. **Psychology:** General.

**Computing on campus.** 1,100 workstations in library, computer center. Dormitories wired for high-speed internet access and linked to campus network. Commuter students can connect to campus network. Online course registration, online library, helpline, wireless network available.

**Student life. Freshman orientation:** Mandatory. Preregistration for classes offered. **Housing:** Coed dorms, apartments, wellness housing available. University-owned student apartments within 2-minute walk from campus. **Activities:** Campus ministries, choral groups, literary magazine, music ensembles, Model UN, student government, support groups, minority organization, international multicultural association, ski club, gay/straight alliance, academic and honors organizations.

**Athletics. Intercollegiate:** Baseball M, basketball, golf, soccer, softball W, volleyball W. **Intramural:** Badminton, baseball M, basketball, football (non-tackle), golf, table tennis, volleyball. **Team name:** Titans.

**Student services.** Career counseling, student employment services, financial aid counseling, minority student services, on-campus daycare, personal counseling, placement for graduates. **Physically disabled:** Services for visually, speech, hearing impaired.

**Contact.** E-mail: barclay.3@osu.edu
Phone: (740) 366-9333 Fax: (740) 364-9645
Ann Donahue, Coordinator of Admissions, Ohio State University: Newark Campus, 1179 University Drive, Newark, OH 43055

## Ohio University
**Athens, Ohio**
**www.ohio.edu**

**CB member**
**CB code: 1593**

◗ Public 4-year university

◗ Residential campus in large town

◗ 18,005 degree-seeking undergraduates: 9% part-time, 52% women, 5% African American, 1% Asian American, 2% Hispanic American, 3% international

◗ 3,956 degree-seeking graduate students

◗ 82% of applicants admitted

◗ SAT or ACT (ACT writing optional) required

◗ 70% graduate within 6 years; 28% enter graduate study

**General.** Founded in 1804. Regionally accredited. **Degrees:** 3,918 bachelor's, 620 associate awarded; master's, doctoral, professional offered. **ROTC:** Army, Air Force. **Location:** 75 miles from Columbus. **Calendar:** Quarter, extensive summer session. **Full-time faculty:** 881 total; 87% have terminal degrees, 19% minority, 37% women. **Part-time faculty:** 297 total; 56% have terminal degrees, 6% minority, 46% women. **Class size:** 45% < 20, 40% 20-39, 5% 40-49, 6% 50-99, 4% >100. **Special facilities:** University airport, nuclear accelerator, biotechnology research center, greenhouse, cartography center, meteorology center, contemporary history institute.

**Freshman class profile.** 14,204 applied, 11,591 admitted, 4,072 enrolled.

| Mid 50% test scores | | | |
|---|---|---|---|
| SAT critical reading: | 480-600 | Rank in top quarter: | 44% |
| SAT math: | 490-600 | Rank in top tenth: | 16% |
| SAT writing: | 470-580 | End year in good standing: | 84% |
| ACT composite: | 21-26 | Return as sophomores: | 82% |
| GPA 3.75 or higher: | 19% | Out-of-state: | 9% |
| GPA 3.50-3.74: | 19% | Live on campus: | 97% |
| GPA 3.0-3.49: | 44% | International: | 2% |
| GPA 2.0-2.99: | 18% | Fraternities: | 14% |
| | | Sororities: | 14% |

**Basis for selection.** High school record as represented by rank in class, GPA, and curriculum completed most important. Secondary criteria test scores and recommendation. Rank in top third of class preferred. Audition required for dance and music programs. Interview required for Honors Tutorial College. **Homeschooled:** Statement describing homeschool structure and mission, transcript of courses and grades required. Copy of academic assessment report, curriculum outline, and documentation from school district.

**High school preparation.** College-preparatory program required. 16 units required. Required units include English 4, mathematics 3, social studies 3, science 3, foreign language 2 and visual/performing arts 1.

**2009-2010 Annual costs.** Tuition/fees: $8,973; $17,937 out-of-state. Room/board: $9,408. Books/supplies: $873. Personal expenses: $990.

**2009-2010 Financial aid. Need-based:** 3,685 full-time freshmen applied for aid; 2,453 were judged to have need; 2,411 of these received aid. Average need met was 58%. Average scholarship/grant was $6,589; average loan $3,457. 38% of total undergraduate aid awarded as scholarships/grants, 62% as loans/jobs. **Non-need-based:** Awarded to 5,849 full-time undergraduates, including 1,973 freshmen. Scholarships awarded for academics, art, athletics, minority status, music/drama, religious affiliation, ROTC.

**Application procedures. Admission:** Closing date 2/1 (receipt date). $45 fee, may be waived for applicants with need. Admission notification on a rolling basis beginning on or about 9/15. Must reply by 5/1. **Financial aid:** Priority date 3/15, closing date 4/1. FAFSA required. Applicants notified on a rolling basis starting 4/1; must reply within 3 week(s) of notification.

**Academics.** Extensive learning community opportunities. **Special study options:** Accelerated study, combined bachelor's/graduate degree, cooperative education, cross-registration, distance learning, double major, dual enrollment of high school students, ESL, external degree, honors, independent study, internships, liberal arts/career combination, student-designed major, study abroad, teacher certification program. **Credit/placement by examination:** AP, CLEP, IB, ACT, institutional tests. Sophomore standing available by earning 45 quarter hours of credit based on AP scores. **Support services:** Learning center, pre-admission summer program, remedial instruction, study skills assistance, tutoring, writing center.

**Honors college/program.** Honors Tutorial College application deadline December 15, interview required.

**Majors. Area/ethnic studies:** African, African-American, Asian, European, Latin American, women's. **Biology:** General, botany, cellular/molecular, microbiology, wildlife, zoology. **Business:** Accounting, actuarial science, business admin, finance, human resources, international, management information systems, managerial economics, marketing. **Communications:** General, broadcast journalism, digital media, journalism, photojournalism, radio/tv. **Computer sciences:** General, computer science, information technology, networking. **Education:** Art, early childhood, family/consumer sciences, French, German, physical, secondary, Spanish, special. **Engineering:** Chemical, civil, electrical, industrial, mechanical. **Engineering technology:** Industrial. **Family/consumer sciences:** Child development, clothing/textiles, family resources, family studies, food/nutrition, housing, institutional food production. **Foreign languages:** Ancient Greek, classics, French, German, Latin, linguistics, Russian, Spanish. **Health:** Athletic training, audiology/speech pathology, community health services, dietetics, environmental health, health care admin, nursing (RN), occupational health. **History:** General. **Interdisciplinary:** Neuroscience. **Math:** General, applied. **Parks/recreation:** General, exercise sciences, health/fitness. **Philosophy/religion:** Philosophy, religion. **Physical sciences:** Astrophysics, atmospheric science, chemistry, geology, physics. **Psychology:** General. **Public administration:** Social work. **Social sciences:** Anthropology, criminology, economics, geography, political science, sociology, urban studies. **Transportation:** Aviation, aviation management. **Visual/performing arts:** Acting, art, art history/conservation, ceramics, cinematography, dance, dramatic, graphic design, music history, music performance, music theory/composition, painting, photography, piano/organ, play/screenwriting, printmaking, sculpture, studio arts, theater arts management, voice/opera.

**Most popular majors.** Business/marketing 12%, communications/journalism 14%, education 10%, health sciences 9%, liberal arts 6%, parks/recreation 6%, social sciences 7%.

**Computing on campus.** 1,000 workstations in library, computer center, student center. Dormitories wired for high-speed internet access and linked to campus network. Commuter students can connect to campus network. Online course registration, online library, helpline, repair service, student web hosting, wireless network available.

**Student life. Freshman orientation:** Mandatory. Preregistration for classes offered. Weekends in summer. **Housing:** Guaranteed on-campus for freshmen. Coed dorms, single-sex dorms, special housing for disabled, apartments, wellness housing available. $200 nonrefundable deposit, deadline 5/1. International, intensive-study residence halls available. **Activities:** Bands, campus ministries, choral groups, dance, drama, film society, literary magazine, music ensembles, musical theater, opera, radio station, student government, student newspaper, symphony orchestra, TV station, over 300 professional, religious, ethnic, political, and social service organizations.

**Athletics. NCAA. Intercollegiate:** Baseball M, basketball, cheerleading, cross-country, diving W, field hockey W, football (tackle) M, golf, soccer W, softball W, swimming W, track and field W, volleyball W, wrestling M. **Intramural:** Basketball, football (non-tackle), golf, racquetball, soccer, softball, table tennis, tennis, volleyball, wrestling. **Team name:** Bobcats.

**Student services.** Adult student services, alcohol/substance abuse counseling, career counseling, services for economically disadvantaged, student employment services, financial aid counseling, health services, legal services, minority student services, personal counseling, placement for graduates, veterans' counselor, women's services. **Physically disabled:** Services for visually, hearing impaired.

**Contact.** E-mail: admissions@ohio.edu
Phone: (740) 593-4100 Fax: (740) 593-0560
Melanie Hayden, Undergraduate Admissions, Ohio University, 120 Chubb Hall, Athens, OH 45701-2979

## Ohio University: Chillicothe Campus
Chillicothe, Ohio
www.chillicothe.ohiou.edu                    CB code: 0775

- Public 4-year branch campus college
- Commuter campus in large town

**General.** Founded in 1946. Regionally accredited. **Location:** 45 miles from Columbus. **Calendar:** Quarter.

**Annual costs/financial aid.** Tuition/fees (2009-2010): $4,647; $8,970 out-of-state. Books/supplies: $848. Need-based financial aid available to full-time and part-time students.

**Contact.** Phone: (740) 774-7240
Coordinator of Enrollment Services, 101 University Drive, Chillicothe, OH 45601

## Ohio University: Eastern Campus
St. Clairsville, Ohio
www.eastern.ohiou.edu                    CB code: 0828

- Public 4-year branch campus college
- Commuter campus in small town

**General.** Founded in 1957. Regionally accredited. **Location:** 7 miles from downtown; 14 miles from Wheeling, West Virginia. **Calendar:** Quarter.

**Annual costs/financial aid.** Tuition/fees (2009-2010): $4,461; $5,781 out-of-state. Need-based financial aid available to full-time and part-time students.

**Contact.** Phone: (740) 695-1720
Student Services Manager, 45425 National Road West, St. Clairsville, OH 43950-9724

## Ohio University: Lancaster Campus
Lancaster, Ohio
www.lancaster.ohiou.edu                    CB code: 0826

- Public 4-year branch campus college
- Large town

**General.** Founded in 1968. Regionally accredited. **Location:** 30 miles from Columbus. **Calendar:** Quarter.

**Annual costs/financial aid.** Tuition/fees (2009-2010): $4,647; $8,970 out-of-state. Books/supplies: $500. Need-based financial aid available to full-time and part-time students.

**Contact.** Phone: (740) 654-6711 ext. 215
Enrollment Manager, 1570 Granville Pike, Lancaster, OH 43130

## Ohio University: Southern Campus at Ironton
Ironton, Ohio
www.southern.ohiou.edu                    CB code: 1912

- Public 4-year branch campus college
- Commuter campus in large town
- 2,138 undergraduates

**General.** Founded in 1956. Regionally accredited. Student body reflects both traditional (65%) and non-traditional (45%) students who commute to classes from 3-state area (OH, KY, WV). **Degrees:** 133 associate awarded; master's offered. **Location:** 20 miles from Huntington, West Virginia. **Calendar:** Quarter. **Full-time faculty:** 32 total. **Part-time faculty:** 122 total. **Special facilities:** Microwave link with main campus and other regional campuses, Ohio horse park, nature center, Proctorville center.

**Basis for selection.** Open admission. **Homeschooled:** Transcript of courses and grades, state high school equivalency certificate required. Written verification from appropriate school district excusing attendance, personal statement discussing academic preparation for college, ACT, SAT required.

**High school preparation.** College-preparatory program recommended.

**2009-2010 Annual costs.** Tuition/fees: $4,461; $5,781 out-of-state. Books/supplies: $600. Personal expenses: $1,200.

**Financial aid. Non-need-based:** Scholarships awarded for academics, state residency.

**Application procedures. Admission:** No deadline. $20 fee, may be waived for applicants with need. Admission notification on a rolling basis. **Financial aid:** Priority date 3/15; no closing date. FAFSA required. Applicants notified on a rolling basis starting 4/1.

**Academics. Special study options:** Double major, dual enrollment of high school students, student-designed major, teacher certification program. **Credit/placement by examination:** CLEP, institutional tests. **Support services:** Learning center, remedial instruction, study skills assistance, tutoring, writing center.

**Majors. Business:** Business admin. **Communications:** General, health, organizational, political. **Health:** Health services, nursing (RN). **History:** General. **Protective services:** Criminal justice. **Other:** Long term health care administration, Specialized studies.

**Computing on campus.** Online course registration, online library, helpline, wireless network available.

**Student life. Freshman orientation:** Mandatory. Preregistration for classes offered. Summer and online orientations available. **Activities:** Concert band, international student organizations, literary magazine, music ensembles, radio station, student government, TV station, Phi Alpha Xi service honor society, Los Amigos Internacionales club, diversity student council, student nurses association, psychology club, art club.

**Athletics. Intercollegiate:** Equestrian.

**Student services.** Career counseling, financial aid counseling, personal counseling.

**Contact.** E-mail: askousc@ohiou.edu
Phone: (740) 533-4600 Toll-free number: (800) 626-0513
Fax: (740) 533-4632
Robert Pleasant, Director of Enrollment and Student Services, Ohio University: Southern Campus at Ironton, 1804 Liberty Avenue, Ironton, OH 45638

## Ohio University: Zanesville Campus
Zanesville, Ohio
www.zanesville.ohiou.edu                    CB code: 0846

- Public 4-year branch campus college
- Commuter campus in large town
- 1,871 degree-seeking undergraduates: 39% part-time, 71% women, 4% African American, 1% Hispanic American

**General.** Founded in 1946. Regionally accredited. **Degrees:** 179 associate awarded; master's offered. **Location:** 55 miles from Columbus. **Calendar:** Quarter, limited summer session. **Full-time faculty:** 35 total. **Part-time faculty:** 75 total.

**Basis for selection.** Open admission, but selective for some programs. Nursing admissions based on National League for Nursing test scores, high school GPA, and class rank. Admission to Colleges of Business, Engineering, and Communication based on high school rank and ACT scores. Essay, audition, and portfolio recommended for all; interview recommended for nursing program.

**High school preparation.** Recommended units include English 4, mathematics 3, social studies 3, science 3 and foreign language 2. One year of visual or performing arts recommended.

**2009-2010 Annual costs.** Tuition/fees: $4,647; $8,970 out-of-state. Books/supplies: $1,000. Personal expenses: $879.

**Application procedures. Admission:** No deadline. $20 fee, may be waived for applicants with need. Admission notification on a rolling basis beginning on or about 1/1. **Financial aid:** Priority date 3/15; no closing date. FAFSA required. Applicants notified on a rolling basis starting 4/15; must reply within 2 week(s) of notification.

**Academics. Special study options:** Cross-registration, double major, dual enrollment of high school students, independent study, student-designed major, study abroad, teacher certification program. **Credit/placement by examination:** AP, CLEP, institutional tests. **Support services:** Learning center, reduced course load, remedial instruction, tutoring.

**Majors. Business:** General. **Communications:** Health, organizational. **Education:** Early childhood, middle. **Public administration:** Human services.

**Computing on campus.** 50 workstations in library, computer center. Commuter students can connect to campus network. Online course registration, online library, wireless network available.

**Student life. Freshman orientation:** Mandatory. Preregistration for classes offered. **Activities:** Literary magazine, radio station, student government, cultural events committee, student nursing association.

**Athletics. Intercollegiate:** Baseball M, basketball, golf, tennis, volleyball W. **Intramural:** Badminton, basketball, bowling, golf, skiing, table tennis, tennis, volleyball. **Team name:** Tracers.

**Student services.** Chaplain/spiritual director, career counseling, student employment services, personal counseling, placement for graduates, veterans' counselor.

**Contact.** E-mail: ouzservices@ohio.edu
Phone: (740) 588-1439 Fax: (740) 588-1444
Jason Howard, Director of Student Services, Ohio University: Zanesville Campus, 1425 Newark Road, Zanesville, OH 43701

---

## Ohio Wesleyan University

| Delaware, Ohio | CB member |
| --- | --- |
| www.owu.edu | CB code: 1594 |

- Private 4-year liberal arts college affiliated with United Methodist Church
- Residential campus in large town
- 1,880 degree-seeking undergraduates: 1% part-time, 54% women, 5% African American, 2% Asian American, 2% Hispanic American, 1% Native American, 9% international
- 64% of applicants admitted
- SAT or ACT (ACT writing optional), application essay required
- 60% graduate within 6 years

**General.** Founded in 1842. Regionally accredited. **Degrees:** 394 bachelor's awarded. **ROTC:** Army, Air Force. **Location:** 25 miles from Columbus. **Calendar:** Semester, limited summer session. **Full-time faculty:** 138 total; 99% have terminal degrees, 6% minority, 38% women. **Part-time faculty:** 76 total; 34% have terminal degrees, 5% minority, 49% women. **Class size:** 68% < 20, 30% 20-39, 1% 40-49. **Special facilities:** 2 observatories, US Department of Agriculture laboratories, 2 nature field study preserves, science center, art museum.

**Freshman class profile.** 4,210 applied, 2,691 admitted, 498 enrolled.

| Mid 50% test scores | | | |
| --- | --- | --- | --- |
| SAT critical reading: | 520-660 | GPA 2.0-2.99: | 21% |
| SAT math: | 520-660 | Rank in top quarter: | 63% |
| ACT composite: | 23-29 | Rank in top tenth: | 38% |
| GPA 3.75 or higher: | 35% | Return as sophomores: | 81% |
| GPA 3.50-3.74: | 15% | Out-of-state: | 48% |
| GPA 3.0-3.49: | 28% | Live on campus: | 97% |
| | | International: | 9% |

**Basis for selection.** High school record (level of challenge and success) most important, followed by class rank, recommendations, test scores, essay, extracurricular activities, general aptitude, character, volunteerism, alumni affiliation. Special consideration given to music, fine art and theater talent. Interview recommended for all. Audition required for music programs. Portfolio recommended for art programs. Essay required of all applicants. **Homeschooled:** Statement describing homeschool structure and mission, state high school equivalency certificate, letter of recommendation (nonparent) required.

**High school preparation.** College-preparatory program required. 15 units required. Required and recommended units include English 4, mathematics 3-4, social studies 3-4, science 3-4 and foreign language 2-3.

**2009-2010 Annual costs.** Tuition/fees: $35,030. Room/board: $9,224. Books/supplies: $2,100.

**2009-2010 Financial aid. Non-need-based:** Scholarships awarded for academics, alumni affiliation, art, leadership, minority status, music/drama, religious affiliation, state residency.

**Application procedures. Admission:** Priority date 3/1; deadline 5/1 (postmark date). $35 fee, may be waived for applicants with need, free for online applicants. Admission notification on a rolling basis beginning on or about 10/1. Must reply by May 1 or within 2 week(s) if notified thereafter. **Financial aid:** Priority date 3/1, closing date 5/1. FAFSA, institutional form required. Applicants notified on a rolling basis starting 2/15; must reply by 5/1 or within 2 week(s) of notification.

**Academics.** Quantitative Skills Center provides individualized and alternative modes of instruction and tutoring to students who need assistance with math skills in any area of study. **Special study options:** Double major, dual enrollment of high school students, exchange student, honors, independent study, internships, New York semester, student-designed major, study abroad, teacher certification program, United Nations semester, urban semester, Washington semester. 3-2 engineering programs with Washington University (MO), Case Western Reserve University, California Institute of Technology (CA), Rensselaer Polytechnic Institute (NY), Alfred College of Ceramics (NY), and Polytechnic Institute of New York. **Credit/placement by examination:** AP, CLEP, IB, SAT, ACT, institutional tests. International Baccalaureate credit given for specific performance levels on higher exams. Students may receive exemption from certain requirements for test scores on SAT, SAT Subject Tests or ACT. **Support services:** Learning center, reduced course load, study skills assistance, tutoring, writing center.

**Majors. Area/ethnic studies:** African-American, East Asian, women's. **Biology:** General, bacteriology, biochemistry, botany, genetics, microbiology, zoology. **Business:** Accounting, international, managerial economics. **Communications:** Broadcast journalism, journalism. **Computer sciences:** General, computer science. **Conservation:** Environmental studies. **Education:** General, art, biology, chemistry, drama/dance, early childhood, elementary, foreign languages, French, German, health, kindergarten/preschool, Latin, mathematics, middle, multi-level teacher, music, physical, physics, science, secondary, social science, social studies, Spanish. **Foreign languages:** Biblical, classics, comparative lit, French, German, Latin, Spanish. **Health:** Predental, premedicine, preveterinary. **History:** General. **Interdisciplinary:** Ancient studies, medieval/Renaissance, neuroscience. **Legal studies:** Prelaw. **Liberal arts:** Arts/sciences. **Math:** General, statistics. **Philosophy/religion:** Philosophy, religion. **Physical sciences:** Astronomy, chemistry, geology, physics. **Psychology:** General. **Social sciences:** Anthropology, economics, geography, international relations, political science, sociology, U.S. government, urban studies. **Theology:** Preministerial. **Visual/performing arts:** Art history/conservation, dance, dramatic, music performance, studio arts.

**Most popular majors.** Biology 13%, business/marketing 11%, foreign language 6%, parks/recreation 7%, psychology 9%, social sciences 18%, visual/performing arts 7%.

**Computing on campus.** 300 workstations in dormitories, library, computer center, student center. Dormitories wired for high-speed internet access and linked to campus network. Commuter students can connect to campus network. Online library, helpline, repair service, student web hosting, wireless network available.

**Student life. Freshman orientation:** Mandatory. Preregistration for classes offered. Two-day session held in June and during the week before classes begin in August. **Housing:** Guaranteed on-campus for all undergraduates. Coed dorms, single-sex dorms, apartments, fraternity/sorority housing, wellness housing available. $400 nonrefundable deposit, deadline 5/1. Pets allowed in dorm rooms. Small living units for groups of 10-15 students. **Activities:** Bands, campus ministries, choral groups, dance, drama, international student organizations, literary magazine, music ensembles, Model UN, musical theater, opera, radio station, student government, student newspaper, symphony orchestra, B'nai B'rith Hillel Chapter, Christian Fellowship, Young Democrats, College Republicans, student union on black awareness, Sisters United, Tauheed, gay/lesbian/bisexual/transgender center, women's resource center, Habitat for Humanity.

**Athletics.** NCAA. **Intercollegiate:** Baseball M, basketball, cross-country, diving, field hockey W, football (tackle) M, golf M, lacrosse, soccer, softball W, swimming, tennis, track and field, volleyball W. **Intramural:** Badminton, basketball, equestrian, football (non-tackle) M, golf, handball, lacrosse, racquetball, soccer, softball, squash, swimming, tennis, track and field, volleyball, water polo. **Team name:** Battling Bishops.

**Student services.** Alcohol/substance abuse counseling, chaplain/spiritual director, career counseling, student employment services, financial aid counseling, health services, minority student services, on-campus daycare, personal counseling.

**Contact.** E-mail: owuadmit@owu.edu
Phone: (740) 368-3020 Toll-free number: (800) 922-8953
Fax: (740) 368-3314
Carol DelPropost, Assistant Vice President of Admission and Financial Aid, Ohio Wesleyan University, 75 South Sandusky Street, Delaware, OH 43015-2398

## Otterbein College

Westerville, Ohio
www.otterbein.edu

CB member
CB code: 1597

- Private 4-year liberal arts college affiliated with United Methodist Church
- Residential campus in large town
- 2,616 degree-seeking undergraduates: 13% part-time, 64% women
- 421 degree-seeking graduate students
- 78% of applicants admitted
- SAT or ACT (ACT writing optional) required
- 62% graduate within 6 years

**General.** Founded in 1847. Regionally accredited. **Degrees:** 552 bachelor's awarded; master's offered. **ROTC:** Army, Air Force. **Location:** 12 miles from Columbus. **Calendar:** Quarter, limited summer session. **Full-time faculty:** 164 total; 85% have terminal degrees, 12% minority, 53% women. **Part-time faculty:** 157 total; 8% minority, 66% women. **Class size:** 78% < 20, 18% 20-39, 2% 40-49, 2% 50-99, less than 1% >100. **Special facilities:** Observatory, 3 performance stages, stables, 3 art galleries.

**Freshman class profile.** 3,653 applied, 2,859 admitted, 643 enrolled.

| Mid 50% test scores | | | |
|---|---|---|---|
| SAT critical reading: | 470-600 | GPA 3.0-3.49: | 28% |
| SAT math: | 480-590 | GPA 2.0-2.99: | 21% |
| SAT writing: | 460-600 | Rank in top quarter: | 55% |
| ACT composite: | 19-25 | Rank in top tenth: | 24% |
| GPA 3.75 or higher: | 30% | Return as sophomores: | 76% |
| GPA 3.50-3.74: | 21% | Live on campus: | 80% |

**Basis for selection.** School achievement record most important; test scores also important. Recommendations, essay, interview, and extracurricular activities considered. Students applying between May 1 and June 1 accepted on space-available basis. Visit recommended for all; audition required for music and theater programs; portfolio recommended for visual art program. Essays required for scholarships. **Homeschooled:** Statement describing homeschool structure and mission, transcript of courses and grades required. Submit written documentation of successful completion of college preparatory high school equivalency. Transcripts from cooperating school district preferred. **Learning Disabled:** Students with diagnosed learning disabilities recommended to send documentation with admission application.

**High school preparation.** College-preparatory program recommended. Recommended units include English 4, mathematics 3, social studies 3, science 3 and foreign language 2. One unit in fine arts recommended.

**2009-2010 Annual costs.** Tuition/fees: $27,321. Room/board: $7,605. Books/supplies: $1,068. Personal expenses: $1,509.

**2009-2010 Financial aid.** **Non-need-based:** Scholarships awarded for academics, alumni affiliation, art, leadership, minority status, music/drama, state residency.

**Application procedures.** **Admission:** Priority date 2/1; no deadline. $25 fee, may be waived for applicants with need, free for online applicants. Admission notification on a rolling basis beginning on or about 10/1. Must reply by May 1 or within 4 week(s) if notified thereafter. **Financial aid:** Priority date 4/1; no closing date. FAFSA required. Applicants notified on a rolling basis starting 2/15.

**Academics.** **Special study options:** Accelerated study, combined bachelor's/graduate degree, cross-registration, double major, dual enrollment of high school students, exchange student, honors, independent study, internships, liberal arts/career combination, student-designed major, study abroad, teacher certification program, Washington semester, weekend college. BA/BS in engineering with Washington University (MO) or Case Western Reserve University. **Credit/placement by examination:** AP, CLEP, IB, SAT, ACT, institutional tests. 60 credit hours maximum toward bachelor's degree. **Support services:** Learning center, reduced course load, remedial instruction, study skills assistance, tutoring, writing center.

**Honors college/program.** Presidential Scholars or must be in top 10% of high school class and have 25 ACT.

**Majors.** **Agriculture:** Equestrian studies. **Biology:** General, biochemistry, molecular. **Business:** General, accounting, actuarial science, business admin, finance, managerial economics. **Communications:** General, broadcast journalism, journalism, organizational, public relations. **Computer sciences:** Computer science. **Conservation:** General, environmental studies, management/policy. **Education:** General, art, biology, chemistry, early childhood, elementary, English, foreign languages, French, health, history, mathematics, middle, multi-level teacher, music, physical, physics, science, secondary, social studies, Spanish, special. **Foreign languages:** French, Spanish. **Health:** Athletic training, nursing (RN), predental, premedicine, prepharmacy, preveterinary. **History:** General. **Legal studies:** Prelaw. **Math:** General. **Parks/recreation:** Health/fitness, sports admin. **Philosophy/religion:** Philosophy, religion. **Physical sciences:** Chemistry, physics. **Psychology:** General. **Social sciences:** Economics, international relations, political science, sociology. **Visual/performing arts:** General, acting, art, dramatic, music history, music performance, music theory/composition, theater design.

**Most popular majors.** Biology 6%, business/marketing 12%, communications/journalism 10%, education 16%, health sciences 18%, social sciences 6%, visual/performing arts 9%.

**Computing on campus.** 124 workstations in dormitories, library, computer center. Dormitories wired for high-speed internet access and linked to campus network. Commuter students can connect to campus network. Online course registration, helpline, wireless network available.

**Student life.** **Freshman orientation:** Mandatory. Preregistration for classes offered. One-day orientation held in July or August. **Housing:** Guaranteed on-campus for freshmen. Coed dorms, single-sex dorms, apartments, fraternity/sorority housing available. **Activities:** Bands, choral groups, dance, drama, international student organizations, literary magazine, music ensembles, musical theater, opera, radio station, student government, student newspaper, symphony orchestra, TV station, Fellowship of Christian Athletes, Christian support group, Afro-American student union, Asian American student union, international students association, religious life council.

**Athletics.** NCAA. **Intercollegiate:** Baseball M, basketball, cross-country, equestrian, football (tackle) M, golf, lacrosse M, soccer, softball W, tennis, track and field, volleyball W. **Intramural:** Basketball, bowling, football (non-tackle) M, handball, racquetball, soccer, softball, volleyball. **Team name:** Cardinals.

**Student services.** Adult student services, chaplain/spiritual director, career counseling, student employment services, financial aid counseling, health services, minority student services, personal counseling, placement for graduates, veterans' counselor. **Physically disabled:** Services for visually, hearing impaired.

**Contact.** E-mail: uotterb@otterbein.edu
Phone: (614) 823-1500 Toll-free number: (800) 488-8144
Fax: (614) 823-1200
Cass Johnson, Director of Admission, Otterbein College, One Otterbein College, Westerville, OH 43081

## Pontifical College Josephinum

Columbus, Ohio
www.pcj.edu

CB code: 1348

- Private 4-year liberal arts and seminary college for men affiliated with Roman Catholic Church
- Residential campus in very large city

- 78 degree-seeking undergraduates: 1% Asian American, 10% Hispanic American, 1% Native American, 8% international
- 41 degree-seeking graduate students
- 87% of applicants admitted
- SAT or ACT (ACT writing optional), application essay, interview required

**General.** Founded in 1892. Regionally accredited; also accredited by ATS. **Degrees:** 31 bachelor's awarded; master's offered. **Location:** 11 miles from downtown. **Calendar:** Semester. **Full-time faculty:** 12 total; 50% have terminal degrees, 33% women. **Part-time faculty:** 9 total; 44% have terminal degrees, 33% women. **Class size:** 98% < 20, 2% 20-39.

**Freshman class profile.** 15 applied, 13 admitted, 11 enrolled.

| Mid 50% test scores | | | |
|---|---|---|---|
|  | | ACT composite: | 17-31 |
| SAT critical reading: | 510-670 | Out-of-state: | 56% |
| SAT math: | 340-700 | Live on campus: | 100% |
| SAT writing: | 450-560 | | |

**Basis for selection.** School achievement record, recommendations from pastor and director of vocations required. **Homeschooled:** Transcript of courses and grades required.

**High school preparation.** College-preparatory program recommended. 10 units required; 18 recommended. Required and recommended units include English 4, mathematics 2-4, social studies 2-4, science 1-4 and foreign language 1-2.

**2009-2010 Annual costs.** Tuition/fees: $17,417. Room/board: $7,908. Books/supplies: $1,200.

**2009-2010 Financial aid.** All financial aid based on need.

**Application procedures.** Admission: Priority date 8/1; no deadline. $25 fee, may be waived for applicants with need. Application must be submitted on paper. Admission notification on a rolling basis beginning on or about 5/1. **Financial aid:** Priority date 9/2; no closing date. FAFSA, institutional form required. Applicants notified on a rolling basis starting 8/15; must reply within 2 week(s) of notification.

**Academics.** Students participate in supervised field experience and clinical pastoral education. **Special study options:** Double major, ESL, honors, independent study. **Credit/placement by examination:** AP, CLEP, IB, institutional tests. 30 credit hours maximum toward bachelor's degree. **Support services:** Learning center, reduced course load, remedial instruction, tutoring, writing center.

**Majors.** **Area/ethnic studies:** Chicano/Hispanic-American/Latino, Latin American. **History:** General. **Liberal arts:** Humanities. **Philosophy/religion:** Philosophy, religion.

**Most popular majors.** English 7%, history 7%, philosophy/religious studies 83%.

**Computing on campus.** 16 workstations in library, computer center. Dormitories wired for high-speed internet access and linked to campus network. Online library, wireless network available.

**Student life.** **Freshman orientation:** Mandatory. **Policies:** Daily chapel, morning and evening prayer. Religious observance required. **Activities:** Choral groups, music ensembles, student government, Latin American studies organization.

**Athletics.** **Intramural:** Basketball M, soccer M, softball M.

**Student services.** Chaplain/spiritual director, career counseling, financial aid counseling, health services, personal counseling.

**Contact.**  Phone: (614) 985-2241 Toll-free number: (888) 252-5812 Fax: (614) 885-2307
Perry Cahall, Director of Admissions, Pontifical College Josephinum, 7625 North High Street, Columbus, OH 43235-1499

## Rabbinical College of Telshe
### Wickliffe, Ohio
**CB code: 1660**

- Private 4-year rabbinical and teachers college for men affiliated with Jewish faith
- Small city
- 38 degree-seeking undergraduates

**General.** Founded in 1941. Accredited by AARTS. **Degrees:** 1 bachelor's awarded; master's offered. **Calendar:** Semester. **Full-time faculty:** 10 total. **Part-time faculty:** 15 total.

**Basis for selection.** GED not accepted. Personal interview and religious commitment most important. **Homeschooled:** Interview required.

**2009-2010 Annual costs.** Books/supplies: $300.

**Application procedures.** Admission: Closing date 8/15. $100 fee.

**Academics.** Credit/placement by examination: CLEP.

**Majors.** Theology: Talmudic.

**Student life.** Freshman orientation: Mandatory. Preregistration for classes offered.

**Contact.**  Phone: (440) 943-5300 ext. 17 Fax: (440) 943-5303
Rabbi Abraham Matitia, Registrar, Rabbinical College of Telshe, 28400 Euclid Avenue, Wickliffe, OH 44092-2584

## Shawnee State University
### Portsmouth, Ohio
www.shawnee.edu

**CB member**
**CB code: 1790**

- Public 4-year university
- Commuter campus in large town
- 4,027 degree-seeking undergraduates: 14% part-time, 58% women, 4% African American, 1% Native American, 1% international
- 80 degree-seeking graduate students
- 28% graduate within 6 years; 25% enter graduate study

**General.** Founded in 1986. Regionally accredited. **Degrees:** 371 bachelor's, 213 associate awarded; master's offered. **Location:** 90 miles from Columbus, 90 miles from Cincinnati. **Calendar:** Semester, extensive summer session. **Full-time faculty:** 151 total; 57% have terminal degrees, 9% minority, 44% women. **Part-time faculty:** 171 total; 51% women. **Class size:** 57% < 20, 37% 20-39, 2% 40-49, 3% 50-99, less than 1% >100. **Special facilities:** Planetarium.

**Freshman class profile.**

| | | | |
|---|---|---|---|
| Rank in top quarter: | 34% | Live on campus: | 42% |
| Rank in top tenth: | 12% | International: | 1% |
| End year in good standing: | 47% | Fraternities: | 1% |
| Return as sophomores: | 53% | Sororities: | 1% |
| Out-of-state: | 8% | | |

**Basis for selection.** Open admission, but selective for some programs. ACT required, interview recommended for admission to allied health programs. **Homeschooled:** State high school equivalency certificate required. GED required.

**High school preparation.** College-preparatory program recommended. 16 units recommended. Recommended units include English 4, mathematics 3, social studies 3, science 3 and foreign language 2. Algebra, biology, chemistry required for allied health programs.

**2009-2010 Annual costs.** Tuition/fees: $5,832; $10,176 out-of-state. Room/board: $8,046. Books/supplies: $1,440. Personal expenses: $2,174.

**Financial aid.** **Non-need-based:** Scholarships awarded for academics. **Additional information:** ACT recommended for scholarship applicants.

**Application procedures.** Admission: No deadline. No application fee. Admission notification on a rolling basis. Applicants to allied health programs advised to apply by February 1. **Financial aid:** Priority date 6/15; no closing date. FAFSA, institutional form required. Applicants notified on a rolling basis starting 5/1; must reply within 4 week(s) of notification.

**Academics.** **Special study options:** Cross-registration, distance learning, double major, dual enrollment of high school students, ESL, honors, independent study, internships, student-designed major, study abroad, teacher certification program, Washington semester. **Credit/placement by examination:** AP, CLEP, institutional tests. SAT or ACT may be used in lieu of university-developed placement test. **Support services:** Learning center, preadmission summer program, reduced course load, remedial instruction, study skills assistance, tutoring, writing center.

**Majors.** **Biology:** General. **Business:** Business admin, management information systems. **Education:** General, biology, chemistry, early childhood, history, kindergarten/preschool, mathematics, multi-level teacher, science, social science. **Engineering technology:** Computer, electrical, environmental, plastics. **Health:** Athletic training, nursing (RN), premedicine, prepharmacy, preveterinary. **History:** General. **Math:** General. **Parks/recreation:** Health/fitness, sports admin. **Physical sciences:** Atmospheric science, chemistry. **Psychology:** General. **Social sciences:** General, international relations, sociology. **Visual/performing arts:** General, ceramics, drawing, painting, photography, studio arts.

**Most popular majors.** Biology 6%, business/marketing 16%, education 9%, health sciences 10%, liberal arts 8%, parks/recreation 8%, psychology 8%, social sciences 10%, visual/performing arts 9%.

**Computing on campus.** 620 workstations in library, computer center, student center. Dormitories wired for high-speed internet access. Commuter students can connect to campus network. Online course registration, helpline, wireless network available.

**Student life. Freshman orientation:** Mandatory. Preregistration for classes offered. One-day programs held throughout the summer. **Housing:** Coed dorms available. $150 partly refundable deposit. **Activities:** Campus ministries, choral groups, drama, literary magazine, music ensembles, musical theater, student government, student newspaper, health executives and administrators learning society, student programming board, Habitat for Humanity.

**Athletics.** NAIA. **Intercollegiate:** Baseball M, basketball, cross-country, golf M, soccer, softball W, tennis W, volleyball W. **Intramural:** Basketball, bowling, golf, racquetball, softball M, swimming, table tennis, tennis, volleyball. **Team name:** Bears.

**Student services.** Alcohol/substance abuse counseling, career counseling, services for economically disadvantaged, student employment services, financial aid counseling, health services, on-campus daycare, personal counseling, placement for graduates, veterans' counselor. **Physically disabled:** Services for visually, speech, hearing impaired.

**Contact.** E-mail: to_ssu@shawnee.edu
Phone: (740) 351-4778 Toll-free number: (800) 959-2778
Fax: (740) 351-3111
Bob Trusz, Director of Admissions, Shawnee State University, 940 Second Street, Portsmouth, OH 45662

## Temple Baptist College
Cincinnati, Ohio
www.templebaptist.edu

- Private 4-year liberal arts college
- Very large city
- 93 degree-seeking undergraduates

**General.** Regionally accredited; also accredited by TRACS. **Degrees:** 5 bachelor's awarded. **Calendar:** Quarter. **Full-time faculty:** 12 total. **Part-time faculty:** 19 total.

**Basis for selection.** Letter of recommendation from pastor required.

**2009-2010 Annual costs.** Tuition/fees: $11,655.

**Application procedures. Admission:** No deadline. $50 fee. **Financial aid:** Closing date 10/1.

**Academics. Credit/placement by examination:** CLEP.

**Majors. Business:** Business admin. **Education:** General, elementary. **Theology:** Religious ed. **Other:** Christian ministries.

**Student life. Freshman orientation:** Mandatory.

**Contact.** E-mail: infotbc@templebaptist.edu
Phone: (513) 851-3800
Tanmay Pramanik, Vice President of Student Affairs, Temple Baptist College, 11965 Kenn Road, Cincinnati, OH 45240

## Tiffin University
Tiffin, Ohio
www.tiffin.edu

CB member
CB code: 1817

- Private 4-year university, business and liberal arts college
- Residential campus in large town
- 2,277 degree-seeking undergraduates: 19% part-time, 55% women, 19% African American, 1% Asian American, 3% Hispanic American, 3% international

- 1,054 degree-seeking graduate students
- 60% of applicants admitted
- SAT or ACT (ACT writing optional) required
- 43% graduate within 6 years

**General.** Founded in 1888. Regionally accredited. Off-campus courses offered in Cleveland, Lorain, Columbus, Elyria, Toledo, Fremont, and Cincinnati. **Degrees:** 362 bachelor's, 5 associate awarded; master's offered. **ROTC:** Army, Air Force. **Location:** 50 miles from Toledo, 90 miles from Columbus. **Calendar:** Semester, limited summer session. **Full-time faculty:** 68 total; 63% have terminal degrees, 12% minority, 47% women. **Part-time faculty:** 226 total; 26% have terminal degrees, 16% minority, 47% women. **Class size:** 67% < 20, 30% 20-39, 4% 40-49. **Special facilities:** Nature preserve.

**Freshman class profile.** 3,526 applied, 2,101 admitted, 673 enrolled.

| Mid 50% test scores | | | |
|---|---|---|---|
| SAT critical reading: | 430-530 | End year in good standing: | 85% |
| SAT math: | 430-530 | Return as sophomores: | 63% |
| ACT composite: | 18-23 | Out-of-state: | 46% |
| GPA 3.75 or higher: | 9% | Live on campus: | 60% |
| GPA 3.50-3.74: | 12% | International: | 1% |
| GPA 3.0-3.49: | 33% | Fraternities: | 1% |
| GPA 2.0-2.99: | 45% | Sororities: | 1% |

**Basis for selection.** Test scores, GPA very important. Students with below 2.0 GPA may be admitted conditionally into Learning Assistance Program. Interview required for academically weak applicants.

**High school preparation.** College-preparatory program recommended. Required and recommended units include English 4, mathematics 3, social studies 3, science 3 and foreign language 2.

**2010-2011 Annual costs.** Tuition/fees (projected): $18,390. Room/board: $8,340. Books/supplies: $1,500. Personal expenses: $2,700.

**2009-2010 Financial aid. Need-based:** 501 full-time freshmen applied for aid; 496 were judged to have need; 496 of these received aid. Average need met was 8%. Average scholarship/grant was $5,647; average loan $3,209. 46% of total undergraduate aid awarded as scholarships/grants, 54% as loans/jobs. **Non-need-based:** Awarded to 1,075 full-time undergraduates, including 358 freshmen. Scholarships awarded for academics, alumni affiliation, athletics, leadership, music/drama, state residency.

**Application procedures. Admission:** No deadline. $20 fee, may be waived for applicants with need, free for online applicants. Admission notification on a rolling basis beginning on or about 9/15. **Financial aid:** No deadline. FAFSA required. Applicants notified on a rolling basis starting 1/15; must reply within 2 week(s) of notification.

**Academics. Special study options:** Accelerated study, cross-registration, distance learning, double major, dual enrollment of high school students, ESL, exchange student, external degree, honors, independent study, internships, study abroad, teacher certification program, Washington semester. **Credit/placement by examination:** AP, CLEP, IB, SAT, ACT, institutional tests. 15 credit hours maximum toward associate degree, 30 toward bachelor's. **Support services:** Learning center, pre-admission summer program, reduced course load, remedial instruction, study skills assistance, tutoring, writing center.

**Majors. Agriculture:** Equine science. **Business:** Accounting, business admin, e-commerce, finance, hospitality admin, human resources, international, logistics, marketing, nonprofit/public, operations, organizational behavior. **Communications:** General, digital media, journalism, media studies, public relations. **Computer sciences:** General, information systems, information technology. **Education:** General, English, history. **Health:** Substance abuse counseling. **History:** General. **Liberal arts:** Arts/sciences. **Parks/recreation:** Sports admin. **Protective services:** Corrections, emergency management/homeland security, forensics, law enforcement admin. **Psychology:** General, experimental, forensic, industrial. **Public administration:** Human services. **Social sciences:** Criminology, international relations. **Visual/performing arts:** Art, arts management. **Other:** Interdisciplinary studies.

**Most popular majors.** Business/marketing 51%, psychology 6%, security/protective services 33%.

**Computing on campus.** 100 workstations in dormitories, library, computer center, student center. Dormitories wired for high-speed internet access and linked to campus network. Commuter students can connect to campus network. Online course registration, online library, helpline, repair service, wireless network available.

**Student life. Freshman orientation:** Available, $25 fee. Preregistration for classes offered. Three-part program; first part occurs on a Saturday in

April or May, or on a Friday in June; second part is a weekend in late July; third part occurs during first weekend of classes. **Policies:** Lower-division residential students required to be on meal plan. All undergraduates complete 26 hours of co-curricular credit. **Housing:** Guaranteed on-campus for freshmen. Coed dorms, single-sex dorms, special housing for disabled, apartments, fraternity/sorority housing available. $49 partly refundable deposit, deadline 4/9. Theme housing, performing arts, leadership society, house units, junior/senior house units. **Activities:** Bands, campus ministries, choral groups, dance, drama, international student organizations, literary magazine, music ensembles, musical theater, student government, student newspaper, black united students, World Student Organization, Greek council, Campus Crusade for Christ, Delta Sigma Kappa, gospel choir, Circle K.

**Athletics.** NCAA. **Intercollegiate:** Baseball M, basketball, cross-country, equestrian, football (tackle) M, golf, lacrosse W, soccer, softball W, tennis, track and field, volleyball W. **Intramural:** Basketball, cross-country. **Team name:** Dragons.

**Student services.** Adult student services, career counseling, student employment services, financial aid counseling, health services, minority student services, personal counseling, placement for graduates, veterans' counselor.

**Contact.** E-mail: admissions@tiffin.edu
Phone: (419) 447-6443 ext. 3423 Toll-free
number: (800) 968-6446 ext. 3423 Fax: (419) 443-5006
Cam Cruickshank, Vice President for Enrollment Management, Tiffin University, 155 Miami Street, Tiffin, OH 44883

## Tri-State Bible College
### South Point, Ohio
### www.tsbc.edu

◗ Private 4-year Bible college
◗ Commuter campus in rural community

**General.** Accredited by ABHE. **Location:** 150 miles from Cincinnati, 150 miles from Columbus, 50 miles from Charleston, WV. **Calendar:** Semester.

**Annual costs/financial aid.** Tuition/fees (2009-2010): $5,710. Books/supplies: $530. Personal expenses: $2,016.

**Contact.** Phone: (740) 377-2520
Director of Admission, 506 Margaret Street, South Point, OH 45680-0445

## Union Institute & University
### Cincinnati, Ohio                  CB member
### www.myunion.edu                   CB code: 0732

◗ Private 4-year university
◗ Commuter campus in very large city
◗ 920 degree-seeking undergraduates
◗ Application essay, interview required

**General.** Founded in 1964. Regionally accredited. Academic centers in Montpelier and Brattleboro, Vermont; North Miami Beach, Florida; Los Angeles and Sacramento, California. **Degrees:** 470 bachelor's awarded; master's, doctoral offered. **Location:** 2 miles from downtown. **Calendar:** Differs by program, extensive summer session. **Full-time faculty:** 35 total; 89% have terminal degrees, 11% minority, 46% women. **Part-time faculty:** 280 total; 47% have terminal degrees, 29% minority, 61% women. **Special facilities:** Courses may be offered at workplace or online.

**Basis for selection.** Maturity and evidence of ability to engage in self-directed learning is important. Programs designed for adult learners; majority are over age 25.

**2009-2010 Annual costs.** Tuition/fees: $11,012.

**2008-2009 Financial aid. Non-need-based:** Scholarships awarded for academics, state residency.

**Application procedures. Admission:** No deadline. $35 fee, may be waived for applicants with need. Admission notification on a rolling basis. **Financial aid:** No deadline. FAFSA required. Must reply within 4 week(s) of notification.

**Academics.** Many courses available through online learning. Serves adult learners, and offers both standardized curricula (B.S.) and individualized learning (B.A.) programs. Some courses may be individualized and engaged through faculty-mentored independent study. **Special study options:** Distance learning, external degree, independent study, internships, teacher

certification program, weekend college. **Credit/placement by examination:** CLEP, IB. 30 credit hours maximum toward bachelor's degree. **Support services:** Reduced course load.

**Majors. Business:** Business admin. **Education:** General, early childhood, elementary, ESL, mathematics, multi-level teacher, physical, reading, secondary, social studies, special. **Family/consumer sciences:** Child development. **Health:** Maternal/child health. **Liberal arts:** Arts/sciences. **Protective services:** Correctional facilities, criminal justice, emergency management/homeland security, law enforcement admin. **Psychology:** General. **Public administration:** General, social work. **Other:** Leadership.

**Computing on campus.** 60 workstations in library, computer center. Commuter students can connect to campus network. Online course registration, online library, helpline, wireless network available.

**Student life. Policies:** Programs for working adults. **Housing:** Short term on-campus housing provided for B.A. program in Montpelier, Vermont for students participating in brief residencies.

**Student services.** Adult student services, career counseling, financial aid counseling. **Physically disabled:** Services for visually, speech, hearing impaired.

**Contact.** E-mail: admissions@myunion.edu
Phone: (800) 486-3116 Toll-free number: (800) 486-3116
Fax: (802) 828-8565
Gregory Stewart, Vice President, Enrollment Management, Union Institute & University, 440 East McMillan Street, Cincinnati, OH 45206

## University of Akron
### Akron, Ohio                       CB member
### www.uakron.edu                    CB code: 1829

◗ Public 4-year university
◗ Commuter campus in small city
◗ 19,864 degree-seeking undergraduates: 18% part-time, 48% women, 15% African American, 2% Asian American, 1% Hispanic American, 1% international
◗ 4,343 degree-seeking graduate students
◗ 76% of applicants admitted
◗ SAT or ACT (ACT writing optional) required
◗ 33% graduate within 6 years

**General.** Founded in 1870. Regionally accredited. **Degrees:** 2,359 bachelor's, 375 associate awarded; master's, doctoral, professional offered. **ROTC:** Army, Air Force. **Location:** 40 miles from Cleveland. **Calendar:** Semester, limited summer session. **Full-time faculty:** 768 total; 82% have terminal degrees, 16% minority, 42% women. **Part-time faculty:** 904 total; 30% have terminal degrees, 7% minority, 53% women. **Class size:** 39% < 20, 48% 20-39, 6% 40-49, 4% 50-99, 2% >100. **Special facilities:** Polymer training center, bath nature preserve field station, gas turbine testing facility, training center for fire and hazardous materials.

**Freshman class profile.** 13,492 applied, 10,243 admitted, 4,252 enrolled.

| Mid 50% test scores | | | |
|---|---|---|---|
| SAT critical reading: | 430-560 | GPA 2.0-2.99: | 42% |
| SAT math: | 430-590 | Rank in top quarter: | 28% |
| ACT composite: | 18-24 | Rank in top tenth: | 11% |
| GPA 3.75 or higher: | 14% | Return as sophomores: | 69% |
| GPA 3.50-3.74: | 11% | Out-of-state: | 4% |
| GPA 3.0-3.49: | 24% | Live on campus: | 45% |
| | | International: | 1% |

**Basis for selection.** School record, class rank, GPA, and test scores most important. Open access to Summit College Student Success Program and Wayne College. Essay, interview required for honors program; audition required for dance, music programs. **Homeschooled:** Students required to obtain letter of exemption from school district.

**High school preparation.** College-preparatory program recommended. 15 units recommended. Recommended units include English 4, mathematics 3, social studies 3, science 3 and foreign language 2.

**2009-2010 Annual costs.** Tuition/fees: $8,752; $18,000 out-of-state. Room/board: $8,697. Books/supplies: $900. Personal expenses: $1,520.

**2008-2009 Financial aid. Need-based:** 3,458 full-time freshmen applied for aid; 2,713 were judged to have need; 2,713 of these received aid. Average need met was 53%. Average scholarship/grant was $5,471; average loan $3,488. 40% of total undergraduate aid awarded as scholarships/grants,

60% as loans/jobs. **Non-need-based:** Awarded to 5,974 full-time undergraduates, including 1,983 freshmen. Scholarships awarded for academics, art, athletics, leadership, music/drama, ROTC, state residency.

**Application procedures. Admission:** Closing date 8/11 (receipt date). $30 fee, may be waived for applicants with need. Admission notification on a rolling basis beginning on or about 9/15. **Financial aid:** Priority date 2/1; no closing date. FAFSA, institutional form required. Applicants notified on a rolling basis starting 4/1; must reply within 2 week(s) of notification.

**Academics. Special study options:** Accelerated study, combined bachelor's/graduate degree, cooperative education, distance learning, double major, ESL, external degree, honors, independent study, internships, student-designed major, study abroad, teacher certification program, weekend college. Undergraduates may take graduate level classes. Co-op programs in arts, business, computer science, engineering, family & consumer sciences, humanities, natural science, technologies. Dual enrollment offered for select graduate level programs. **Credit/placement by examination:** AP, CLEP, IB, SAT, ACT, institutional tests. 38 credit hours maximum toward associate degree, 38 toward bachelor's. **Support services:** Learning center, reduced course load, remedial instruction, study skills assistance, tutoring, writing center.

**Honors college/program.** Must have 2 out of 3 of following criteria: 3.5 GPA; high school class rank in highest 10%; 27 ACT or 1200 SAT (exclusive of Writing). Some students with other unique qualifications may be admitted.

**Majors. Architecture:** Urban/community planning. **Biology:** General, animal physiology, biochemistry, botany, ecology, microbiology, zoology. **Business:** Accounting, business admin, e-commerce, financial planning, hotel/motel admin, human resources, international, management information systems, marketing, operations, sales/distribution. **Communications:** General, organizational, public relations, radio/tv. **Computer sciences:** Computer science, networking. **Education:** Art, drama/dance, early childhood, early childhood special, English, family/consumer sciences, French, mathematics, middle, music, physical, science, social studies, Spanish, special, voc/tech. **Engineering:** General, biomedical, chemical, civil, computer, electrical, mechanical, polymer. **Engineering technology:** Construction, electrical, manufacturing, mechanical, surveying. **Family/consumer sciences:** Child development, clothing/textiles, family systems, housing. **Foreign languages:** Classics, French, Spanish. **Health:** Athletic training, audiology/speech pathology, communication disorders, dietetics, licensed practical nurse, nursing (RN), recreational therapy, respiratory therapy technology. **History:** General. **Liberal arts:** Arts/sciences, humanities. **Math:** General, applied, statistics. **Parks/recreation:** Exercise sciences, sports admin. **Philosophy/religion:** Philosophy. **Physical sciences:** Chemistry, geology, geophysics, physics, polymer chemistry. **Protective services:** Criminal justice, fire safety technology. **Psychology:** General. **Public administration:** Social work. **Social sciences:** General, anthropology, cartography, criminology, economics, geography, international relations, sociology, U.S. government. **Visual/performing arts:** Art history/conservation, ceramics, dance, dramatic, graphic design, jazz, metal/jewelry, music history, music performance, music theory/composition, photography, piano/organ, printmaking, sculpture, stringed instruments, studio arts, voice/opera.

**Most popular majors.** Business/marketing 20%, communications/journalism 10%, education 11%, engineering/engineering technologies 10%, health sciences 16%.

**Computing on campus.** 3,100 workstations in dormitories, library, student center. Dormitories wired for high-speed internet access and linked to campus network. Commuter students can connect to campus network. Online course registration, online library, helpline, repair service, student web hosting, wireless network available.

**Student life. Freshman orientation:** Mandatory, $50 fee. Preregistration for classes offered. One-day program. **Policies:** All student organizations make own criteria for members, but some criteria stipulated through university, such as 2.0 GPA requirement and good standing within university. **Housing:** Coed dorms, single-sex dorms, special housing for disabled, fraternity/sorority housing available. $150 nonrefundable deposit, deadline 2/1. Honors student dormitory. **Activities:** Bands, campus ministries, choral groups, dance, drama, international student organizations, music ensembles, musical theater, radio station, student government, student newspaper, symphony orchestra, TV station, Chinese students and scholars association, Indian students association, Muslim students association, black united students, H.O.L.A., Hillel, College Republicans, College Democrats, Campus Focus, gospel choir.

**Athletics.** NCAA. **Intercollegiate:** Baseball M, basketball, cheerleading, cross-country, diving W, football (tackle) M, golf M, rifle, soccer, softball W, swimming W, tennis W, track and field, volleyball W. **Intramural:** Badminton, basketball, bowling, cross-country, golf, racquetball, skiing, soccer, softball, swimming, table tennis, track and field, volleyball W, wrestling M. **Team name:** Zips.

**Student services.** Adult student services, alcohol/substance abuse counseling, career counseling, student employment services, financial aid counseling, health services, minority student services, on-campus daycare, personal counseling, placement for graduates, veterans' counselor, women's

services. **Physically disabled:** Services for visually, speech, hearing impaired.

**Contact.** E-mail: admissions@uakron.edu
Phone: (330) 972-7100 Toll-free number: (800) 655-4884
Fax: (330) 972-7022
Diane Raybuck, Director of Admissions, University of Akron, Simmons Hall, Akron, OH 44325-2001

## University of Cincinnati
**Cincinnati, Ohio** — CB member
**www.uc.edu** — CB code: 1833

- Public 4-year university
- Commuter campus in large city
- 21,339 degree-seeking undergraduates: 15% part-time, 50% women, 10% African American, 3% Asian American, 2% Hispanic American, 2% international
- 8,521 degree-seeking graduate students
- 67% of applicants admitted
- SAT or ACT with writing, application essay required
- 55% graduate within 6 years

**General.** Founded in 1819. Regionally accredited. **Degrees:** 3,766 bachelor's, 95 associate awarded; master's, doctoral, professional offered. **ROTC:** Army, Air Force. **Location:** 2 miles from downtown. **Calendar:** Quarter, extensive summer session. **Full-time faculty:** 1,187 total; 55% have terminal degrees, 16% minority, 42% women. **Part-time faculty:** 38 total; 10% have terminal degrees, 10% minority, 60% women. **Class size:** 39% < 20, 46% 20-39, 6% 40-49, 7% 50-99, 3% >100.

**Freshman class profile.** 15,088 applied, 10,086 admitted, 3,647 enrolled.

| Mid 50% test scores | | | |
|---|---|---|---|
| SAT critical reading: | 490-610 | GPA 2.0-2.99: | 16% |
| SAT math: | 520-640 | Rank in top quarter: | 49% |
| SAT writing: | 480-600 | Rank in top tenth: | 22% |
| ACT composite: | 22-27 | Return as sophomores: | 85% |
| GPA 3.75 or higher: | 27% | Out-of-state: | 8% |
| GPA 3.50-3.74: | 20% | Live on campus: | 69% |
| GPA 3.0-3.49: | 37% | International: | 1% |

**Basis for selection.** Secondary school record, test scores most important. Interview required for music programs; audition required for dance, music programs. **Homeschooled:** Transcript of courses and grades required. Release for home schooling from local Board of Education required.

**High school preparation.** College-preparatory program recommended. 16 units required. Required and recommended units include English 4, mathematics 3-4, social studies 2, history 1, science 2-3, foreign language 2 and academic electives 2. Specific requirements may vary for each college.

**2009-2010 Annual costs.** Tuition/fees: $9,399; $23,922 out-of-state. Room/board: $9,702. Books/supplies: $1,275. Personal expenses: $3,725.

**2009-2010 Financial aid. Need-based:** 3,566 full-time freshmen applied for aid; 2,680 were judged to have need; 2,653 of these received aid. Average need met was 64%. Average scholarship/grant was $6,342; average loan $3,365. 42% of total undergraduate aid awarded as scholarships/grants, 58% as loans/jobs. **Non-need-based:** Awarded to 6,775 full-time undergraduates, including 1,824 freshmen. Scholarships awarded for academics, alumni affiliation, art, athletics, leadership, minority status, music/drama, ROTC, state residency.

**Application procedures. Admission:** Priority date 1/15; deadline 9/1 (postmark date). $40 fee, may be waived for applicants with need. Admission notification on a rolling basis beginning on or about 10/1. **Financial aid:** No deadline. FAFSA required. Applicants notified on a rolling basis starting 3/12; must reply within 2 week(s) of notification.

**Academics.** Some engineering programs require students to acquire personal computers. **Special study options:** Accelerated study, combined bachelor's/graduate degree, cooperative education, distance learning, double major, ESL, honors, independent study, internships, liberal arts/career combination, study abroad, teacher certification program, Washington semester, weekend college. Learning at Large (students earn college credit without attending regularly scheduled classes). **Credit/placement by examination:** AP, CLEP, institutional tests. **Support services:** Pre-admission summer program, remedial instruction, study skills assistance, tutoring, writing center.

**Majors. Architecture:** Architecture, urban/community planning. **Area/ethnic studies:** African-American, Asian, French, German, Latin American,

Spanish/Iberian. **Biology:** General. **Business:** Accounting, business admin, finance, management information systems, management science, operations, real estate. **Communications:** General, radio/tv. **Computer sciences:** General. **Education:** Art, early childhood, elementary, health, music, secondary. **Engineering:** General, aerospace, chemical, civil, computer, electrical, mechanical, mechanics, metallurgical, nuclear. **Family/consumer sciences:** Food/nutrition. **Foreign languages:** Classics, comparative lit, French, German, Latin, linguistics, Spanish. **Health:** Audiology/speech pathology, clinical lab science, health care admin, nuclear medical technology, nursing (RN), predental, premedicine, prepharmacy, preveterinary. **History:** General. **Interdisciplinary:** Neuroscience. **Liberal arts:** Arts/sciences. **Math:** General. **Philosophy/religion:** Judaic, philosophy. **Physical sciences:** Chemistry, geology, physics. **Protective services:** Criminal justice. **Psychology:** General. **Public administration:** Social work. **Social sciences:** Anthropology, economics, geography, international relations, political science, sociology, urban studies. **Visual/performing arts:** Art history/conservation, commercial/advertising art, conducting, dance, dramatic, fashion design, industrial design, interior design, jazz, music history, music performance, music theory/composition, piano/organ, studio arts, theater design, voice/opera. **Other:** Electronic media.

**Most popular majors.** Business/marketing 17%, education 7%, engineering/engineering technologies 11%, English 7%, health sciences 17%, visual/performing arts 10%.

**Computing on campus.** 560 workstations in library, computer center. Dormitories wired for high-speed internet access and linked to campus network. Commuter students can connect to campus network. Online course registration, helpline, repair service, student web hosting, wireless network available.

**Student life. Freshman orientation:** Available. Preregistration for classes offered. **Housing:** Guaranteed on-campus for freshmen. Coed dorms, single-sex dorms, apartments, fraternity/sorority housing available. **Activities:** Bands, choral groups, dance, drama, film society, music ensembles, musical theater, opera, radio station, student government, student newspaper, symphony orchestra, women's initiative network, College Democrats, College Republicans.

**Athletics.** NCAA. **Intercollegiate:** Baseball M, basketball, cross-country, diving, football (tackle) M, golf, lacrosse W, soccer, swimming, tennis W, track and field, volleyball W. **Intramural:** Basketball, football (non-tackle), racquetball, soccer, softball, volleyball. **Team name:** Bearcats.

**Student services.** Adult student services, alcohol/substance abuse counseling, career counseling, services for economically disadvantaged, student employment services, financial aid counseling, health services, minority student services, on-campus daycare, personal counseling, placement for graduates, women's services. **Physically disabled:** Services for visually, speech, hearing impaired.

**Contact.** E-mail: admissions@uc.edu
Phone: (513) 556-1100 Toll-free number: (800) 827-8728
Fax: (513) 556-1105
Thomas Canepa, Associate Vice President, Admissions, University of Cincinnati, PO Box 210091, Cincinnati, OH 45221-0091

---

## University of Dayton
**Dayton, Ohio**  **CB member**
www.udayton.edu  **CB code: 1834**

- Private 4-year university affiliated with Roman Catholic Church
- Residential campus in small city
- 7,183 degree-seeking undergraduates: 4% part-time, 49% women, 3% African American, 1% Asian American, 2% Hispanic American, 2% international
- 2,839 degree-seeking graduate students
- 73% of applicants admitted
- SAT or ACT (ACT writing optional), application essay required
- 78% graduate within 6 years

**General.** Founded in 1850. Regionally accredited. **Degrees:** 1,738 bachelor's awarded; master's, doctoral, professional offered. **ROTC:** Army, Air Force. **Location:** 2 miles from downtown, 50 miles from Cincinnati. **Calendar:** Semester, extensive summer session. **Full-time faculty:** 475 total; 91% have terminal degrees, 14% minority, 36% women. **Part-time faculty:** 462 total; 6% minority, 43% women. **Class size:** 35% < 20, 54% 20-39, 7% 40-49, 3% 50-99, less than 1% >100. **Special facilities:** Research institute, portfolio management center, learning-teaching center, information sciences center, student-operated stores and coffee bars.

**Freshman class profile.** 12,212 applied, 8,938 admitted, 1,707 enrolled.

| Mid 50% test scores | | | |
|---|---|---|---|
| SAT critical reading: | 510-610 | Rank in top quarter: | 58% |
| SAT math: | 520-640 | Rank in top tenth: | 27% |
| ACT composite: | 23-28 | End year in good standing: | 92% |
| GPA 3.75 or higher: | 37% | Return as sophomores: | 87% |
| GPA 3.50-3.74: | 20% | Out-of-state: | 45% |
| GPA 3.0-3.49: | 33% | Live on campus: | 95% |
| GPA 2.0-2.99: | 10% | International: | 1% |

**Basis for selection.** Selection of courses in preparation for college, grade record and pattern in high school, class rank, SAT or ACT, character, and record of leadership and service. Will review PAA if presented. Interview recommended for all; audition required for all music programs. **Home-schooled:** Transcript of courses and grades required. Description of courses taken required, including bibliography of texts used for instruction. Examples of projects, homework or writing samples helpful. **Learning Disabled:** Prefer applicant provide documentation explaining disability for assessment.

**High school preparation.** College-preparatory program recommended. 16 units recommended. Recommended units include English 4, mathematics 3, social studies 3, science 2 (laboratory 1) and academic electives 4. 2 units of foreign language required for admission to the College of Arts and Sciences.

**2009-2010 Annual costs.** Tuition/fees: $28,690. $1,299 additional cost to all new incoming students for purchase of computer from university. International students pay additional $75 per month for health and accident insurance. Engineering majors required to pay additional $870 per semester in fees. Room/board: $8,290.

**2008-2009 Financial aid. Need-based:** 1,540 full-time freshmen applied for aid; 1,116 were judged to have need; 1,112 of these received aid. Average need met was 98%. Average scholarship/grant was $18,956; average loan $6,962. 58% of total undergraduate aid awarded as scholarships/grants, 42% as loans/jobs. **Non-need-based:** Awarded to 6,750 full-time undergraduates, including 1,953 freshmen. Scholarships awarded for academics, alumni affiliation, art, leadership, music/drama, ROTC, state residency.

**Application procedures. Admission:** Priority date 12/15; no deadline. $50 fee, may be waived for applicants with need. Application must be submitted online. Admission notification on a rolling basis beginning on or about 10/31. Must reply by May 1 or within 2 week(s) if notified thereafter. **Financial aid:** Priority date 3/31; no closing date. FAFSA required. Applicants notified on a rolling basis starting 3/15; must reply by 5/1 or within 3 week(s) of notification.

**Academics. Special study options:** Accelerated study, combined bachelor's/graduate degree, cooperative education, cross-registration, distance learning, double major, dual enrollment of high school students, ESL, exchange student, honors, independent study, internships, liberal arts/career combination, semester at sea, student-designed major, study abroad, teacher certification program, Washington semester. Domestic exchange program with other Marianist institutions; student-designed major in general studies only. **Credit/placement by examination:** AP, CLEP, IB, SAT, ACT, institutional tests. 24 credit hours maximum toward bachelor's degree. **Support services:** Learning center, pre-admission summer program, reduced course load, remedial instruction, study skills assistance, tutoring, writing center.

**Majors. Area/ethnic studies:** American. **Biology:** General, biochemistry, environmental. **Business:** General, accounting, business admin, entrepreneurial studies, finance, international, management information systems, managerial economics, marketing, operations. **Communications:** General, digital media, journalism, media studies, public relations. **Computer sciences:** General, computer science. **Conservation:** Environmental science. **Education:** Art, early childhood, foreign languages, French, German, middle, multilevel teacher, music, physical, secondary, Spanish, special. **Engineering:** Chemical, civil, computer, electrical, mechanical. **Engineering technology:** General, computer, electrical, industrial, manufacturing, mechanical. **Family/consumer sciences:** Food/nutrition. **Foreign languages:** French, German, Spanish. **Health:** Dietetics, music therapy, predental, premedicine. **History:** General. **Interdisciplinary:** Global studies. **Legal studies:** Prelaw. **Math:** General. **Parks/recreation:** Exercise sciences, facilities management, sports admin. **Philosophy/religion:** Philosophy, religion. **Physical sciences:** General, chemistry, geology, physics. **Protective services:** Criminal justice. **Psychology:** General. **Social sciences:** Econometrics, economics, political science, sociology. **Visual/performing arts:** Art history/conservation, design, dramatic, music performance, music theory/composition, photography, studio arts. **Other:** Human rights.

**Most popular majors.** Business/marketing 23%, communications/journalism 11%, education 11%, engineering/engineering technologies 14%.

**Computing on campus.** PC or laptop required. Dormitories wired for high-speed internet access and linked to campus network. Commuter students can connect to campus network. Online course registration, online library, helpline, repair service, student web hosting, wireless network available.

**Student life. Freshman orientation:** Mandatory, $115 fee. Preregistration for classes offered. Held 2-3 days preceding the first day of classes. Virtual orientation also available online. **Housing:** Guaranteed on-campus for freshmen. Coed dorms, single-sex dorms, special housing for disabled, apartments, fraternity/sorority housing, wellness housing available. $400 non-refundable deposit, deadline 5/1. University-owned houses available. **Activities:** Bands, campus ministries, choral groups, dance, drama, international student organizations, literary magazine, music ensembles, Model UN, musical theater, opera, radio station, student government, student newspaper, symphony orchestra, TV station, Catholic Life, Campus Crusade for Christ, College Democrats, College Republicans, diversity discussion group, Indian student association, NAACP, Irish club, Italian club.

**Athletics.** NCAA. **Intercollegiate:** Baseball M, basketball, cheerleading, cross-country, football (tackle) M, golf, rowing (crew) W, soccer, softball W, tennis, track and field W, volleyball W. **Intramural:** Badminton, basketball, bowling, football (non-tackle), golf, racquetball, soccer, softball, tennis, volleyball, water polo, wrestling. **Team name:** Flyers.

**Student services.** Adult student services, alcohol/substance abuse counseling, chaplain/spiritual director, career counseling, services for economically disadvantaged, student employment services, financial aid counseling, health services, minority student services, on-campus daycare, personal counseling, placement for graduates, women's services. **Physically disabled:** Services for visually, speech, hearing impaired. **Learning disabled:** Comprehensive services available.

**Contact.** E-mail: admission@udayton.edu
Phone: (937) 229-4411 Toll-free number: (800) 837-7433
Fax: (937) 229-4729
Robert Durkle, Dean of Admission, University of Dayton, 300 College Park, Dayton, OH 45469-1300

## University of Findlay
Findlay, Ohio
www.findlay.edu                                CB code: 1223

- Private 4-year university and health science college affiliated with Church of God
- Residential campus in large town
- 2,944 degree-seeking undergraduates: 11% part-time, 64% women, 3% African American, 1% Asian American, 1% Hispanic American, 5% international
- 1,069 degree-seeking graduate students
- 68% of applicants admitted
- SAT or ACT (ACT writing optional) required
- 55% graduate within 6 years

**General.** Founded in 1882. Regionally accredited. **Degrees:** 510 bachelor's, 53 associate awarded; master's, professional offered. **ROTC:** Army, Air Force. **Location:** 45 miles from Toledo, 90 miles from Columbus. **Calendar:** Semester, limited summer session. **Full-time faculty:** 195 total; 60% have terminal degrees, 12% minority, 48% women. **Part-time faculty:** 125 total; 18% have terminal degrees, 10% minority, 53% women. **Class size:** 55% < 20, 36% 20-39, 6% 40-49, 4% 50-99. **Special facilities:** Two equestrian farms, animal science facility, cadaver lab, environmental resource training center, planetarium, Center for Habitat Studies, museum.

**Freshman class profile.** 2,791 applied, 1,902 admitted, 642 enrolled.

| Mid 50% test scores | | Rank in top quarter: | 56% |
|---|---|---|---|
| SAT critical reading: | 460-570 | Rank in top tenth: | 30% |
| SAT math: | 480-590 | End year in good standing: | 87% |
| SAT writing: | 480-580 | Return as sophomores: | 74% |
| ACT composite: | 20-26 | Out-of-state: | 22% |
| GPA 3.75 or higher: | 34% | Live on campus: | 92% |
| GPA 3.50-3.74: | 18% | Fraternities: | 2% |
| GPA 3.0-3.49: | 30% | Sororities: | 2% |
| GPA 2.0-2.99: | 18% | | |

**Basis for selection.** School achievement record, curriculum, class rank, and recommendations. Essay required for special admissions program and interview is recommended. **Homeschooled:** Statement describing homeschool structure and mission, state high school equivalency certificate, letter of recommendation (nonparent) required. Greater weight placed on standardized entrance exam scores for admission, evaluation of GED if taken. **Learning Disabled:** Strongly encourage interview or campus visit.

**High school preparation.** College-preparatory program recommended. 16 units recommended. Recommended units include English 4, mathematics 3, social studies 3, history 1, science 4, foreign language 3 and academic electives 1. One fine arts unit recommended. Additional 1 math and 1 science for preveterinary and environmental programs.

**2009-2010 Annual costs.** Tuition/fees: $25,774. Pre-veterinary and equestrian students pay higher tuition in years one and two; pharmacy students pay higher tuition throughout the program. Room/board: $8,554. Books/supplies: $1,700.

**2008-2009 Financial aid. Need-based:** 585 full-time freshmen applied for aid; 462 were judged to have need; 462 of these received aid. Average need met was 71%. Average scholarship/grant was $12,371; average loan $2,828. 51% of total undergraduate aid awarded as scholarships/grants, 49% as loans/jobs. **Non-need-based:** Awarded to 2,506 full-time undergraduates, including 621 freshmen. Scholarships awarded for academics, alumni affiliation, athletics, music/drama, state residency.

**Application procedures. Admission:** Closing date 6/1 (receipt date). No application fee. Admission notification on a rolling basis beginning on or about 9/1. Must reply by May 1 or within 4 week(s) if notified thereafter. Part-time applicants may be admitted year round to any of the six different program start dates. **Financial aid:** Priority date 8/1, closing date 9/1. FAFSA required. Applicants notified on a rolling basis starting 3/1; must reply within 2 week(s) of notification.

**Academics. Special study options:** Accelerated study, combined bachelor's/graduate degree, cooperative education, distance learning, double major, dual enrollment of high school students, ESL, external degree, honors, independent study, internships, liberal arts/career combination, semester at sea, student-designed major, study abroad, teacher certification program, Washington semester, weekend college. BS in nursing with Mount Carmel College of Nursing and Lourdes College, 3-1 BA prgram with Art Institute Consortium. **Credit/placement by examination:** AP, CLEP, institutional tests. 15 credit hours maximum toward associate degree, 30 toward bachelor's. **Support services:** Learning center, reduced course load, remedial instruction, study skills assistance, tutoring, writing center.

**Majors. Agriculture:** Animal sciences, equestrian studies, farm/ranch. **Biology:** General. **Business:** General, accounting, business admin, entrepreneurial studies, finance, hospitality admin, hospitality/recreation, human resources, international, marketing. **Communications:** General, journalism, public relations. **Computer sciences:** General, computer science, systems analysis. **Education:** General, art, bilingual, biology, curriculum, developmentally delayed, drama/dance, driver/safety, early childhood, early childhood special, emotionally handicapped, English, ESL, evaluation, foreign languages, foundations, geography, health, history, kindergarten/preschool, learning disabled, mathematics, mentally handicapped, middle, multi-level teacher, multicultural, multiple handicapped, physical, psychology, reading, science, secondary, social science, social studies, Spanish, special, speech, testing/assessment. **Engineering technology:** Hazardous materials. **Foreign languages:** Japanese, Spanish. **Health:** Athletic training, environmental health, health care admin, nuclear medical technology, occupational health, prenursing, preveterinary. **History:** General. **Legal studies:** Prelaw. **Math:** General. **Parks/recreation:** Exercise sciences, health/fitness, sports admin. **Philosophy/religion:** Philosophy, religion. **Protective services:** Law enforcement admin. **Psychology:** General. **Public administration:** Social work. **Social sciences:** General, economics, political science, sociology. **Theology:** Theology. **Visual/performing arts:** Art, commercial/advertising art, dramatic, theater design.

**Most popular majors.** Agriculture 8%, business/marketing 22%, education 9%, health sciences 29%.

**Computing on campus.** 400 workstations in dormitories, library, computer center, student center. Dormitories wired for high-speed internet access and linked to campus network. Commuter students can connect to campus network. Online course registration, online library, helpline, repair service, student web hosting, wireless network available.

**Student life. Freshman orientation:** Mandatory, $100 fee. Preregistration for classes offered. One-day registrations for students and orientation for parents during summer. 2-day orientation for students 2 days before classes begin. **Policies:** All freshmen, sophomores, and juniors under the age of 22 required to live on-campus. **Housing:** Guaranteed on-campus for freshmen. Coed dorms, single-sex dorms, special housing for disabled, apartments, fraternity/sorority housing, wellness housing available. $150 nonrefundable deposit, deadline 7/1. Honors house and special interest houses. **Activities:** Bands, campus ministries, choral groups, dance, drama, international student organizations, literary magazine, music ensembles, musical theater, opera, radio station, student government, student newspaper, symphony orchestra, TV station, Circle-K, black student union, wilderness club, Campus Compact, College Democrats, College Republicans, Fellowship of Christian Athletes, Habitat for Humanity, international club, student government association.

**Athletics.** NCAA. **Intercollegiate:** Baseball M, basketball, cheerleading, cross-country, diving, equestrian, football (tackle) M, golf, soccer, softball W, swimming, tennis, track and field, volleyball W, wrestling M. **Intramural:** Basketball, bowling, cricket, football (non-tackle), golf, skiing, soccer, softball, table tennis, tennis, volleyball, water polo. **Team name:** Oilers.

**Student services.** Adult student services, alcohol/substance abuse counseling, chaplain/spiritual director, career counseling, services for economically disadvantaged, student employment services, financial aid counseling, health services, minority student services, personal counseling, placement for graduates, veterans' counselor, women's services. **Physically disabled:** Services for visually, speech, hearing impaired.

**Contact.** E-mail: admissions@findlay.edu
Phone: (419) 434-4540 Toll-free number: (800) 548-0932
Fax: (419) 434-4898
Donna Gruber, Director of Undergraduate Admissions, University of Findlay, 1000 North Main Street, Findlay, OH 45840-3653

## University of Rio Grande
Rio Grande, Ohio
www.rio.edu                               CB code: 1663

- Private 4-year community and liberal arts college
- Commuter campus in rural community
- 1,534 degree-seeking undergraduates: 20% part-time, 61% women, 4% African American, 1% Hispanic American, 1% international
- 104 degree-seeking graduate students
- 37% graduate within 6 years

**General.** Founded in 1876. Regionally accredited. Institution is both public and private. First 2 years are state subsidized, second 2 years are private, with higher tuition. Affiliated with Rio Grande Community College. **Degrees:** 201 bachelor's, 261 associate awarded; master's offered. **Location:** 12 miles from Gallipolis. **Calendar:** Semester, limited summer session. **Full-time faculty:** 105 total; 37% have terminal degrees, 7% minority, 55% women. **Part-time faculty:** 54 total; 4% have terminal degrees, 2% minority, 46% women. **Class size:** 73% < 20, 22% 20-39, 3% 40-49, 2% 50-99. **Special facilities:** Early childhood care center.

**Freshman class profile.** 2,733 applied, 2,192 admitted, 488 enrolled.

| | | | |
|---|---|---|---|
| GPA 3.75 or higher: | 8% | End year in good standing: | 66% |
| GPA 3.50-3.74: | 7% | Return as sophomores: | 56% |
| GPA 3.0-3.49: | 22% | Out-of-state: | 3% |
| GPA 2.0-2.99: | 51% | Live on campus: | 32% |
| Rank in top quarter: | 16% | International: | 2% |
| Rank in top tenth: | 6% | | |

**Basis for selection.** Open admission, but selective for some programs. ACT required for nursing, medical laboratory technician, radiologic technology, diagnostic medical sonography, respiratory therapy, and education programs. Deferred admission for students demonstrating need for remedial work. Acceptance to Education department occurs at end of sophomore year. **Learning Disabled:** Students with any kind of special needs asked to meet with Director of Accessibility to determine education plan and for academic advising purposes.

**High school preparation.** College-preparatory program recommended. 21 units recommended. Recommended units include English 4, mathematics 3, social studies 3, history 2, science 3 (laboratory 2), foreign language 2 and academic electives 9. Chemistry, algebra, biology required for nursing applicants.

**2009-2010 Annual costs.** Tuition/fees: $18,260. Tuition reported is for private university sector of institution. Public community college in-state in-district tuition: $2,970 ($96 per credit hour); in-state out-of-district, $3,450 ($115 per credit hour). All public community college undergraduates pay $632 in required fees. Out-of-state community college students charged private tuition rate. Room/board: $7,600. Books/supplies: $1,000. Personal expenses: $1,571.

**2008-2009 Financial aid. Need-based:** 296 full-time freshmen applied for aid; 225 were judged to have need; 225 of these received aid. Average scholarship/grant was $4,670; average loan $1,622. 49% of total undergraduate aid awarded as scholarships/grants, 51% as loans/jobs. **Non-need-based:** Awarded to 813 full-time undergraduates, including 48 freshmen. Scholarships awarded for academics, alumni affiliation, athletics, leadership, music/drama, state residency.

**Application procedures. Admission:** No deadline. $25 fee, may be waived for applicants with need, free for online applicants. Admission notification on a rolling basis. **Financial aid:** Priority date 3/15; no closing date. FAFSA, institutional form required. Applicants notified on a rolling basis starting 1/15; must reply within 3 week(s) of notification.

**Academics. Special study options:** Accelerated study, combined bachelor's/graduate degree, cooperative education, distance learning, double major, dual enrollment of high school students, ESL, honors, independent study, internships, liberal arts/career combination, student-designed major, study abroad, teacher certification program. **Credit/placement by examination:** AP, CLEP, institutional tests. **Support services:** Learning center, pre-admission summer program, reduced course load, remedial instruction, tutoring.

**Majors. Area/ethnic studies:** American. **Biology:** General. **Business:** General, accounting, accounting technology, business admin, entrepreneurial studies, marketing, office management, office technology, operations, real estate, retailing. **Communications:** General, journalism, media studies, public relations. **Computer sciences:** General, applications programming, computer science. **Conservation:** General, environmental studies, wildlife. **Education:** General, art, biology, business, chemistry, early childhood, elementary, English, health, history, mathematics, middle, multi-level teacher, music, physical, physics, reading, science, secondary, social science, special, speech. **Engineering technology:** Manufacturing. **Foreign languages:** Spanish. **Health:** Clinical lab science, health care admin, nursing (RN), premedicine. **History:** General. **Legal studies:** Prelaw. **Liberal arts:** Humanities. **Math:** General. **Parks/recreation:** Sports admin. **Physical sciences:** General, chemistry. **Psychology:** General. **Public administration:** General, social work. **Social sciences:** General, archaeology, economics. **Theology:** Preministerial. **Visual/performing arts:** Graphic design, multimedia, music management.

**Most popular majors.** Business/marketing 9%, education 31%, health sciences 8%, natural resources/environmental science 9%, parks/recreation 6%, public administration/social services 7%.

**Computing on campus.** 300 workstations in library, computer center, student center. Dormitories wired for high-speed internet access and linked to campus network. Online course registration, online library, repair service, student web hosting, wireless network available.

**Student life. Freshman orientation:** Available, $50 fee. Preregistration for classes offered. Offered 4 times during the summer. **Policies:** Smoke free dorms and buildings. **Housing:** Guaranteed on-campus for all undergraduates. Coed dorms, single-sex dorms, wellness housing available. $200 fully refundable deposit, deadline 7/15. **Activities:** Bands, choral groups, dance, drama, literary magazine, music ensembles, radio station, student government, student newspaper, TV station, international student organization, Valley Artist Services, Handicapped Coalition, Young Republicans, Rio Christian Fellowship, Student Ambassadors, Students in Free Enterprise.

**Athletics.** NAIA. **Intercollegiate:** Baseball M, basketball, cheerleading, cross-country, soccer, softball W, track and field, volleyball W. **Intramural:** Archery, badminton, basketball, equestrian, handball, racquetball, softball, swimming, tennis, water polo, wrestling M. **Team name:** Redstorm.

**Student services.** Career counseling, student employment services, financial aid counseling, health services, on-campus daycare, personal counseling, placement for graduates, veterans' counselor. **Physically disabled:** Services for visually, speech, hearing impaired.

**Contact.** E-mail: admissions@rio.edu
Phone: (740) 245-7206 Toll-free number: (800) 282-7201
Fax: (740) 245-7260
Rebecca Long, Director of Admissions, University of Rio Grande, 218 North College Avenue, Rio Grande, OH 45674

## University of Toledo
Toledo, Ohio                                    CB member
www.utoledo.edu                                 CB code: 1845

- Public 4-year university
- Commuter campus in large city
- 17,545 degree-seeking undergraduates: 15% part-time, 49% women, 16% African American, 2% Asian American, 3% Hispanic American, 3% international
- 4,645 degree-seeking graduate students
- 45% graduate within 6 years

**General.** Founded in 1872. Regionally accredited. **Degrees:** 2,489 bachelor's, 166 associate awarded; master's, doctoral, professional offered. **ROTC:** Army, Air Force. **Location:** 6 miles from downtown. **Calendar:** Semester, extensive summer session. **Full-time faculty:** 809 total; 40% women. **Part-time faculty:** 461 total; 50% women. **Class size:** 32% < 20, 40% 20-39, 13% 40-49, 9% 50-99, 5% >100. **Special facilities:** 2 observatories, ion accelerator, arboretum, planetarium, linear laser and nuclear physics laboratory, Lake Erie Research Center.

**Freshman class profile.** 12,713 applied, 11,446 admitted, 4,371 enrolled.

| GPA 3.75 or higher: | 18% | Return as sophomores: | 68% |
| GPA 3.50-3.74: | 13% | Out-of-state: | 10% |
| GPA 3.0-3.49: | 27% | Live on campus: | 62% |
| GPA 2.0-2.99: | 34% | International: | 2% |
| Rank in top quarter: | 37% | Fraternities: | 5% |
| Rank in top tenth: | 15% | Sororities: | 3% |

**Basis for selection.** Open admission, but selective for some programs and for out-of-state students. Out-of-state students need 2.0 GPA and 21 ACT or 980 SAT. Applicants to BS program in engineering need 3.0 GPA and 22 ACT or 1020 SAT. For admission to premedicine, predentistry, or preveterinary programs, 3.0 GPA and 25 ACT or 1130 SAT required. Applicants to computer science-engineering program need 3.0 GPA and 25 ACT or 1130 SAT, engineering technology 2.0 GPA and 21 ACT or 980 SAT, business college 2.25 GPA and 25 ACT or 1130 SAT. All SAT scores exclusive of Writing. Audition required for music program. **Homeschooled:** Official recognized transcript required. **Learning Disabled:** Registering with the Office of Accessibility recommended.

**High school preparation.** College-preparatory program required. Recommended units include English 4, mathematics 3, social studies 3 and science 3.

**2009-2010 Annual costs.** Tuition/fees: $7,926; $16,738 out-of-state. Room/board: $8,814. Books/supplies: $750. Personal expenses: $2,204.

**2009-2010 Financial aid.** **Need-based:** 3,826 full-time freshmen applied for aid; 3,139 were judged to have need; 3,132 of these received aid. Average need met was 60%. Average scholarship/grant was $7,294; average loan $3,585. 47% of total undergraduate aid awarded as scholarships/grants, 53% as loans/jobs. **Non-need-based:** Awarded to 3,876 full-time undergraduates, including 1,250 freshmen. Scholarships awarded for academics, alumni affiliation, art, athletics, leadership, minority status, music/drama, ROTC, state residency. **Additional information:** March priority date for federal aid. Students encouraged to apply as early as December for priority consideration for institutional aid.

**Application procedures.** **Admission:** No deadline. $40 fee, may be waived for applicants with need. Admission notification on a rolling basis beginning on or about 10/1. Freshman applicants desiring on-campus housing encouraged to apply early. **Financial aid:** Priority date 4/1; no closing date. FAFSA required. Applicants notified on a rolling basis starting 4/1.

**Academics.** **Special study options:** Accelerated study, combined bachelor's/graduate degree, cooperative education, cross-registration, distance learning, double major, dual enrollment of high school students, ESL, exchange student, external degree, honors, independent study, internships, liberal arts/career combination, student-designed major, study abroad, teacher certification program, weekend college. **Credit/placement by examination:** AP, CLEP, institutional tests. 30 credit hours maximum toward associate degree, 30 toward bachelor's. **Support services:** Learning center, pre-admission summer program, reduced course load, remedial instruction, study skills assistance, tutoring, writing center.

**Majors.** **Area/ethnic studies:** African-American, American, Asian, European, Latin American, Near/Middle Eastern, women's. **Biology:** General. **Business:** General, accounting, business admin, entrepreneurial studies, finance, human resources, international, logistics, management information systems, management science, market research, marketing, operations, organizational behavior. **Communications:** General, media studies. **Computer sciences:** Information systems, information technology. **Conservation:** Environmental studies. **Education:** General, art, business, English, French, German, health, kindergarten/preschool, mathematics, music, physical, science, secondary, social studies, Spanish, speech impaired, trade/industrial. **Engineering:** General, biomedical, chemical, civil, computer, electrical, industrial, mechanical. **Engineering technology:** Civil, electromechanical, mechanical. **Foreign languages:** French, German, linguistics, Spanish. **Health:** Facilities admin, medical records admin, nursing (RN), pharmaceutical sciences, predental, premedicine, preveterinary, public health ed, recreational therapy, respiratory therapy technology. **History:** General. **Interdisciplinary:** Medieval/Renaissance. **Legal studies:** Paralegal, prelaw. **Liberal arts:** Arts/sciences, humanities. **Math:** General. **Parks/recreation:** General, exercise sciences, health/fitness. **Philosophy/religion:** Philosophy, religion. **Physical sciences:** Astronomy, chemistry, geology, physics. **Protective services:** Criminal justice. **Psychology:** General. **Public administration:** Social work. **Social sciences:** Anthropology, economics, geography, international relations, political science, sociology, urban studies. **Visual/performing arts:** Art, art history/conservation, dramatic, film/cinema, studio arts.

**Most popular majors.** Business/marketing 20%, education 8%, engineering/engineering technologies 15%, health sciences 16%, interdisciplinary studies 6%.

**Computing on campus.** 5,000 workstations in dormitories, library, computer center, student center. Dormitories linked to campus network. Commuter students can connect to campus network. Online course registration, online library, helpline, repair service, wireless network available.

**Student life.** **Freshman orientation:** Mandatory, $60 fee. **Housing:** Coed dorms, special housing for disabled, fraternity/sorority housing available. $200 partly refundable deposit, deadline 4/1. **Activities:** Bands, campus ministries, choral groups, dance, drama, international student organizations, literary magazine, music ensembles, radio station, student government, student newspaper, TV station, black student union, Campus Crusade for Christ, Hillel, Latino student union, University YMCA, gay and lesbian student union, international student association, Habitat for Humanity, Toledo Campus Ministry Fellowship.

**Athletics.** NCAA. **Intercollegiate:** Baseball M, basketball, cross-country, diving W, football (tackle) M, golf, soccer W, softball W, swimming W, tennis, track and field W, volleyball W. **Intramural:** Badminton, basketball, bowling, cheerleading W, diving W, fencing, football (tackle), golf, lacrosse, racquetball, soccer, softball, swimming W, table tennis, tennis, track and field W, volleyball, weight lifting. **Team name:** Rockets.

**Student services.** Adult student services, alcohol/substance abuse counseling, chaplain/spiritual director, career counseling, services for economically disadvantaged, student employment services, financial aid counseling, health services, legal services, minority student services, on-campus daycare, personal counseling, placement for graduates, veterans' counselor, women's services. **Physically disabled:** Services for visually, speech, hearing impaired.

**Contact.** E-mail: enroll@utnet.utoledo.edu
Phone: (419) 530-8700 Toll-free number: (800) 586-5336
Fax: (419) 530-4504
William Pierce, Director of Admission, University of Toledo, 2801 West Bancroft Street, Toledo, OH 43606-3398

## Urbana University
Urbana, Ohio
www.urbana.edu                                CB code: 1847

- Private 4-year liberal arts college
- Commuter campus in large town
- 787 full-time, degree-seeking undergraduates
- 68% of applicants admitted
- SAT or ACT (ACT writing optional) required

**General.** Founded in 1850. Regionally accredited. **Degrees:** 208 bachelor's, 59 associate awarded; master's offered. **ROTC:** Army, Air Force. **Location:** 42 miles from Columbus, 49 miles from Dayton. **Calendar:** Semester, limited summer session. **Full-time faculty:** 50 total. **Part-time faculty:** 70 total. **Special facilities:** Johnny Appleseed museum.

**Freshman class profile.** 783 applied, 533 admitted, 190 enrolled.

| Mid 50% test scores | | ACT composite: | 18-21 |
| SAT critical reading: | 400-520 | Out-of-state: | 1% |
| SAT math: | 420-530 | Live on campus: | 50% |

**Basis for selection.** School achievement record, class rank, GPA, test scores, extra-curricular activities and honors important. Special consideration given to children of alumni. Recommendations and interviews encouraged. **Homeschooled:** Transcript of courses and grades, state high school equivalency certificate required.

**High school preparation.** College-preparatory program required. 15 units recommended. Required and recommended units include English 4, mathematics 2, social studies 2, science 2, foreign language 1 and academic electives 2.

**2009-2010 Annual costs.** Tuition/fees: $20,410. Room/board: $8,000. Books/supplies: $1,000. Personal expenses: $666.

**2008-2009 Financial aid.** **Need-based:** 174 full-time freshmen applied for aid; 161 were judged to have need; 161 of these received aid. Average need met was 73%. Average scholarship/grant was $2,547; average loan $3,695. 36% of total undergraduate aid awarded as scholarships/grants, 64% as loans/jobs. **Non-need-based:** Awarded to 201 full-time undergraduates, including 42 freshmen. Scholarships awarded for academics, alumni affiliation, athletics, music/drama.

**Application procedures.** **Admission:** No deadline. $25 fee, may be waived for applicants with need. Admission notification on a rolling basis. **Financial aid:** Closing date 4/15. FAFSA required. Applicants notified on a rolling basis starting 3/1; must reply within 4 week(s) of notification.

**Academics.** **Special study options:** Accelerated study, combined bachelor's/graduate degree, cooperative education, cross-registration, double major, honors, independent study, internships, liberal arts/career combination, student-designed major, study abroad, teacher certification program. **Credit/**

**placement by examination:** AP, CLEP, SAT, ACT, institutional tests. 15 credit hours maximum toward associate degree, 15 toward bachelor's. **Support services:** Learning center, pre-admission summer program, reduced course load, remedial instruction, study skills assistance, tutoring, writing center.

**Majors. Business:** Accounting, accounting/business management, business admin, communications, e-commerce, human resources, managerial economics, marketing, organizational behavior. **Communications:** General, journalism. **Computer sciences:** Information systems. **Education:** General, biology, elementary, English, mathematics, middle, science, secondary, social studies, special. **Health:** Athletic training, health services, predental, premedicine. **History:** General. **Interdisciplinary:** Biological/physical sciences. **Legal studies:** Prelaw. **Liberal arts:** Arts/sciences. **Math:** General. **Parks/recreation:** General, exercise sciences, sports admin. **Philosophy/religion:** Philosophy, religion. **Protective services:** Criminal justice, law enforcement admin. **Psychology:** General. **Public administration:** Community org/advocacy. **Social sciences:** General, political science, sociology.

**Computing on campus.** 60 workstations in dormitories, library, computer center, student center. Dormitories wired for high-speed internet access and linked to campus network. Commuter students can connect to campus network. Online course registration, online library, helpline, repair service, wireless network available.

**Student life. Freshman orientation:** Mandatory. Held during the summer. **Housing:** Guaranteed on-campus for freshmen. Single-sex dorms available. $125 deposit, deadline 5/1. **Activities:** Bands, choral groups, drama, literary magazine, music ensembles, musical theater, student government, student newspaper, black student union, College Against Cancer, commuter club, gay/straight alliacnce, Knights for Christ, sports medicine association, student activities committee, student business association, Univeristy Players theatre group, University Singers.

**Athletics.** NAIA, NCAA. **Intercollegiate:** Baseball M, basketball, cross-country, football (tackle) M, golf M, soccer, softball W, swimming, volleyball W. **Intramural:** Basketball, racquetball, swimming, table tennis, volleyball, weight lifting. **Team name:** Blue Knights.

**Student services.** Adult student services, alcohol/substance abuse counseling, career counseling, student employment services, financial aid counseling, health services, personal counseling, placement for graduates, veterans' counselor.

**Contact.** E-mail: admissions@urbana.edu
Phone: (937) 484-1356 Toll-free number: (800) 787-2262 ext. 1356
Fax: (937) 652-6871
Brian Kesse, Director of Admissions, Urbana University, 579 College Way, Urbana, OH 43078

---

## Ursuline College
**Pepper Pike, Ohio**
www.ursuline.edu

**CB member**
**CB code: 1848**

- Private 4-year liberal arts college for women affiliated with Roman Catholic Church
- Residential campus in small town
- 1,062 degree-seeking undergraduates: 35% part-time, 91% women, 26% African American, 1% Asian American, 2% Hispanic American
- 415 degree-seeking graduate students
- 90% of applicants admitted
- SAT or ACT (ACT writing optional), application essay required
- 46% graduate within 6 years; 32% enter graduate study

**General.** Founded in 1871. Regionally accredited. Primarily women's college, but some men admitted. **Degrees:** 231 bachelor's awarded; master's offered. **ROTC:** Army. **Location:** 10 miles from Cleveland. **Calendar:** Semester, limited summer session. **Full-time faculty:** 70 total; 64% have terminal degrees, 6% minority, 86% women. **Part-time faculty:** 118 total; 24% have terminal degrees, 11% minority, 73% women. **Class size:** 80% < 20, 20% 20-39.

**Freshman class profile.** 248 applied, 222 admitted, 95 enrolled.

| Mid 50% test scores | | | |
|---|---|---|---|
| SAT critical reading: | 410-510 | Rank in top quarter: | 14% |
| SAT math: | 400-530 | Rank in top tenth: | 5% |
| SAT writing: | 400-500 | End year in good standing: | 75% |
| ACT composite: | 19-23 | Return as sophomores: | 68% |
| GPA 3.75 or higher: | 8% | Out-of-state: | 8% |
| GPA 3.50-3.74: | 14% | Live on campus: | 65% |
| GPA 3.0-3.49: | 38% | | |
| GPA 2.0-2.99: | 39% | | |

**Basis for selection.** Secondary school record, recommendations, standardized test scores and essay very important. Community activities considered. Interview recommended for all. **Homeschooled:** Transcript of courses and grades, state high school equivalency certificate, interview, letter of recommendation (nonparent) required. Official transcript from accrediting agency needed.

**High school preparation.** College-preparatory program recommended. 18 units recommended. Recommended units include English 4, mathematics 3, social studies 3, science 3 (laboratory 2), foreign language 2 and visual/performing arts 1. One physical education unit recommended. Nursing students should have chemistry.

**2009-2010 Annual costs.** Tuition/fees: $23,000. Room/board: $7,664. Books/supplies: $1,100. Personal expenses: $716.

**2008-2009 Financial aid. Need-based:** 109 full-time freshmen applied for aid; 104 were judged to have need; 104 of these received aid. Average need met was 86%. Average scholarship/grant was $15,692; average loan $4,416. 45% of total undergraduate aid awarded as scholarships/grants, 55% as loans/jobs. **Non-need-based:** Awarded to 113 full-time undergraduates, including 15 freshmen. Scholarships awarded for academics, art, athletics, leadership, religious affiliation, ROTC.

**Application procedures. Admission:** No deadline. $25 fee, may be waived for applicants with need, free for online applicants. Applicants notified within 3 weeks of application. Must reply by May 1 or within 4 week(s) if notified thereafter. **Financial aid:** Priority date 3/15; no closing date. FAFSA required. Applicants notified on a rolling basis starting 3/1; must reply within 2 week(s) of notification.

**Academics. Special study options:** Accelerated study, combined bachelor's/graduate degree, cooperative education, cross-registration, distance learning, double major, independent study, internships, liberal arts/career combination, New York semester, teacher certification program, weekend college. Optional junior year program in fashion merchandising or design at Fashion Institute of Technology in New York City for enrichment electives only. **Credit/placement by examination:** AP, CLEP, SAT, ACT, institutional tests. 43 credit hours maximum toward bachelor's degree. **Support services:** Learning center, reduced course load, remedial instruction, study skills assistance, tutoring, writing center.

**Majors. Area/ethnic studies:** American. **Biology:** General, biomedical sciences, biotechnology, environmental. **Business:** Accounting, business admin, fashion, human resources, management information systems, marketing. **Communications:** Public relations. **Education:** Art, early childhood, English, mathematics, middle, science, social studies, special. **Family/consumer sciences:** Work/family studies. **Health:** Facilities admin, health care admin, health services, nursing (RN), prenursing, preop/surgical nursing. **History:** General. **Interdisciplinary:** Historic preservation. **Legal studies:** Paralegal. **Liberal arts:** Humanities. **Math:** General. **Philosophy/religion:** Christian, philosophy. **Psychology:** General. **Public administration:** Social work. **Social sciences:** Sociology. **Visual/performing arts:** Art history/conservation, fashion design, graphic design, interior design, studio arts.

**Most popular majors.** Business/marketing 13%, health sciences 55%, psychology 6%, visual/performing arts 8%.

**Computing on campus.** 72 workstations in dormitories, library, computer center, student center. Dormitories wired for high-speed internet access and linked to campus network. Online library, wireless network available.

**Student life. Freshman orientation:** Available. Preregistration for classes offered. Three-day program offered prior to start of fall semester. **Housing:** Coed dorms available. $100 fully refundable deposit. **Activities:** Choral groups, drama, literary magazine, student government, student nurses, education association, campus service and spiritual life committees, ethnic groups, public relations society, peer mentors.

**Athletics.** NAIA. **Intercollegiate:** Basketball W, bowling W, cross-country W, golf W, soccer W, softball W, swimming W, tennis W, track and field W, volleyball W. **Team name:** Arrows.

**Student services.** Adult student services, chaplain/spiritual director, career counseling, student employment services, financial aid counseling, minority student services, personal counseling. **Physically disabled:** Services for visually, speech, hearing impaired.

**Contact.** E-mail: admission@ursuline.edu
Phone: (440) 449-4203 Toll-free number: (888) 877-8546
Fax: (440) 684-6138
Kimberly Shepherd, Director of Admissions, Ursuline College, 2550 Lander Road, Pepper Pike, OH 44124-4398

## Walsh University

**North Canton, Ohio** **CB member**
**www.walsh.edu** **CB code: 1926**

- Private 4-year university and liberal arts college affiliated with Roman Catholic Church
- Residential campus in small city
- 2,278 degree-seeking undergraduates: 17% part-time, 63% women, 4% African American, 1% Asian American, 1% Hispanic American, 1% international
- 434 degree-seeking graduate students
- 81% of applicants admitted
- 53% graduate within 6 years; 17% enter graduate study

**General.** Founded in 1958. Regionally accredited. **Degrees:** 431 bachelor's, 3 associate awarded; master's, professional offered. **Location:** 20 miles from Akron, 55 miles from Cleveland. **Calendar:** Semester, limited summer session. **Full-time faculty:** 108 total; 75% have terminal degrees, 8% minority, 53% women. **Part-time faculty:** 158 total; 12% have terminal degrees, 3% minority, 49% women. **Class size:** 62% < 20, 37% 20-39, less than 1% 40-49, less than 1% 50-99. **Special facilities:** Bioinformatics laboratory, prayer garden.

**Freshman class profile.** 1,466 applied, 1,191 admitted, 489 enrolled.

| Mid 50% test scores | | | |
|---|---|---|---|
| SAT critical reading: | 440-530 | Rank in top quarter: | 41% |
| SAT math: | 460-560 | Rank in top tenth: | 16% |
| ACT composite: | 19-24 | End year in good standing: | 92% |
| GPA 3.75 or higher: | 21% | Return as sophomores: | 71% |
| GPA 3.50-3.74: | 18% | Out-of-state: | 19% |
| GPA 3.0-3.49: | 33% | Live on campus: | 74% |
| GPA 2.0-2.99: | 28% | International: | 1% |

**Basis for selection.** Secondary school record and standardized test scores very important; class rank, recommendations, essay, and character important. Essay, interview recommended for all. **Homeschooled:** Transcript of courses and grades required.

**High school preparation.** College-preparatory program recommended. 16 units recommended. Recommended units include English 4, mathematics 3, social studies 3, science 3, foreign language 2 and academic electives 1. Algebra, biology, and chemistry required for nursing applicants.

**2010-2011 Annual costs.** Tuition/fees (projected): $22,280. Room/board: $8,360. Books/supplies: $1,062. Personal expenses: $1,212.

**2009-2010 Financial aid. Need-based:** 471 full-time freshmen applied for aid; 409 were judged to have need; 409 of these received aid. Average need met was 77%. Average scholarship/grant was $5,918; average loan $3,960. 58% of total undergraduate aid awarded as scholarships/grants, 42% as loans/jobs. **Non-need-based:** Awarded to 1,689 full-time undergraduates, including 613 freshmen. Scholarships awarded for academics, alumni affiliation, athletics, music/drama, religious affiliation, state residency.

**Application procedures. Admission:** Closing date 8/15 (postmark date). $25 fee, may be waived for applicants with need. Admission notification on a rolling basis beginning on or about 10/1. Must reply by 8/15. **Financial aid:** Priority date 2/14; no closing date. FAFSA, institutional form required. Applicants notified on a rolling basis starting 2/15.

**Academics.** Accelerated degree completion program for adults with evening and weekend classes, multiple locations. Structured first semester available for selected students. **Special study options:** Accelerated study, combined bachelor's/graduate degree, distance learning, double major, dual enrollment of high school students, ESL, exchange student, external degree, honors, independent study, internships, liberal arts/career combination, study abroad, teacher certification program, Washington semester. CCSA Consortium for Study Abroad, Rome Experience. **Credit/placement by examination:** AP, CLEP, SAT, ACT, institutional tests. 45 credit hours maximum toward bachelor's degree. Credit and placement are based on each division's evaluation of test information. **Support services:** Learning center, reduced course load, remedial instruction, study skills assistance, tutoring, writing center.

**Honors college/program.** 3.75 high school GPA, 27 ACT or 1200 SAT (exclusive of Writing), writing sample and interview required. Special English and history courses, upper-level seminar and thesis courses.

**Majors. Biology:** General. **Business:** General, accounting, business admin, finance, management information systems, marketing. **Communications:** General. **Computer sciences:** General. **Education:** Early childhood, elementary, emotionally handicapped, English, mathematics, mentally handicapped, middle, multiple handicapped, physical, reading, science, secondary, social science, social studies. **Foreign languages:** French, Spanish. **Health:** Clinical lab science, nursing (RN), predental, premedicine, preveterinary. **History:** General. **Interdisciplinary:** Biological/physical sciences, natural sciences. **Math:** General. **Philosophy/religion:** Philosophy. **Physical sciences:** Chemistry. **Psychology:** General. **Social sciences:** Political science, sociology. **Theology:** Theology.

**Most popular majors.** Biology 7%, business/marketing 36%, communications/journalism 8%, education 17%, health sciences 11%, psychology 8%.

**Computing on campus.** 335 workstations in dormitories, library, student center. Dormitories wired for high-speed internet access and linked to campus network. Online course registration, online library, helpline, repair service, wireless network available.

**Student life. Freshman orientation:** Mandatory, $200 fee. Preregistration for classes offered. Held 5 weekends before classes begin in August. **Policies:** All full-time undergraduate students 23 and younger must live on campus (some exceptions permitted). **Housing:** Guaranteed on-campus for all undergraduates. Coed dorms, special housing for disabled, apartments, wellness housing available. $200 deposit, deadline 8/15. **Activities:** Pep band, campus ministries, choral groups, dance, drama, international student organizations, literary magazine, music ensembles, radio station, student government, student newspaper, Circle-K, Black student union, Habitat for Humanity, College Democrats, College Republicans, international club, Students for Life.

**Athletics.** NAIA. **Intercollegiate:** Baseball M, basketball, cheerleading, cross-country, football (tackle) M, golf, soccer, softball W, tennis, track and field, volleyball W. **Intramural:** Basketball, bowling, football (non-tackle), golf, soccer, softball, swimming, table tennis, tennis, volleyball. **Team name:** Cavaliers.

**Student services.** Adult student services, alcohol/substance abuse counseling, chaplain/spiritual director, career counseling, student employment services, financial aid counseling, health services, minority student services, personal counseling, placement for graduates, veterans' counselor. **Physically disabled:** Services for visually, speech, hearing impaired.

**Contact.** E-mail: admissions@walsh.edu
Phone: (330) 490-7172 Toll-free number: (800) 362-9846
Fax: (330) 490-7165
Brett Freshour, Vice President for Enrollment Management, Walsh University, 2020 East Maple Street NW, North Canton, OH 44720-3396

## Wilberforce University

**Wilberforce, Ohio** **CB member**
**www.wilberforce.edu** **CB code: 1906**

- Private 4-year liberal arts college affiliated with African Methodist Episcopal Church
- Residential campus in rural community
- 733 degree-seeking undergraduates
- 8 graduate students

**General.** Founded in 1856. Regionally accredited. Cooperative education program required of all students. **Degrees:** 153 bachelor's awarded; master's offered. **ROTC:** Army, Air Force. **Location:** 18 miles from Dayton. **Calendar:** Semester, extensive summer session. **Full-time faculty:** 35 total. **Part-time faculty:** 39 total. **Special facilities:** African Methodist Episcopal Church archives.

**Freshman class profile.**

| | | | |
|---|---|---|---|
| Out-of-state: | 67% | Live on campus: | 94% |

**Basis for selection.** Class rank (top two-thirds), high school GPA, test scores most important. SAT or ACT recommended. Essay, interview recommended.

**High school preparation.** 15 units required. Required and recommended units include English 4, mathematics 2-3, social studies 2, science 2-3 and foreign language 2.

**2009-2010 Annual costs.** Tuition/fees: $12,470. Room/board: $5,700. Books/supplies: $1,000. Personal expenses: $1,500.

**Application procedures. Admission:** Priority date 1/1; deadline 4/1. $25 fee, may be waived for applicants with need. Admission notification on a rolling basis. **Financial aid:** Priority date 3/15, closing date 6/1. FAFSA, institutional form required. Applicants notified on a rolling basis starting 3/15; must reply within 2 week(s) of notification.

**Academics. Special study options:** Cooperative education, cross-registration, honors, internships, study abroad. **Credit/placement by examination:** AP, CLEP, institutional tests. 30 credit hours maximum toward bachelor's degree. **Support services:** Remedial instruction, tutoring.

**Majors. Biology:** General. **Business:** Accounting, business admin, finance, managerial economics. **Communications:** Journalism. **Computer sciences:** General, information systems. **Engineering:** Chemical, civil, electrical, mechanical. **Foreign languages:** Comparative lit. **Health:** Health care admin. **Interdisciplinary:** Biological/physical sciences. **Liberal arts:** Arts/sciences. **Math:** General. **Physical sciences:** Chemistry. **Psychology:** General. **Social sciences:** Economics, political science, sociology. **Visual/performing arts:** Studio arts.

**Computing on campus.** 49 workstations in library, computer center.

**Student life. Housing:** Guaranteed on-campus for freshmen. Single-sex dorms, apartments available. **Activities:** Choral groups, dance, drama, music ensembles, radio station, student government, student newspaper, Inter-Faith Fellowship, Interdenominational Ministerial Alliance, Alpha-Omega.

**Athletics.** NAIA. **Intercollegiate:** Basketball, cross-country, golf, track and field. **Intramural:** Baseball M, basketball, softball, table tennis, tennis, volleyball.

**Student services.** Career counseling, student employment services, health services, personal counseling, placement for graduates, veterans' counselor.

**Contact.** E-mail: admissions@wilberforce.edu
Phone: (937) 708-5721 Toll-free number: (800) 367-8568
Fax: (937) 376-4751
Juan Alexander, Wilberforce University, 1055 North Bickett Road, Wilberforce, OH 45384-1001

---

## Wilmington College
**Wilmington, Ohio**
www.wilmington.edu

CB member
CB code: 1909

- Private 4-year liberal arts college affiliated with Society of Friends (Quaker)
- Residential campus in large town
- 1,395 degree-seeking undergraduates: 17% part-time, 56% women, 9% African American, 1% Hispanic American, 1% Native American, 1% international
- 48 graduate students
- 93% of applicants admitted
- SAT or ACT (ACT writing optional) required
- 62% graduate within 6 years

**General.** Founded in 1870. Regionally accredited. Affiliated with Wilmington Yearly Meeting of the Religious Society of Friends. Branch campuses in Cincinnati and other locations. BA in business offered at Cincinnati branch and Wilmington evening program. **Degrees:** 308 bachelor's awarded; master's offered. **Location:** 50 miles from Cincinnati, 60 miles from Columbus. **Calendar:** Semester, limited summer session. **Full-time faculty:** 72 total; 69% have terminal degrees, 1% minority, 43% women. **Part-time faculty:** 50 total; 52% women. **Class size:** 65% < 20, 33% 20-39, 2% 40-49. **Special facilities:** Greenhouse, herbarium, observatory, electron microscope, live animal area, sports medicine center, Peace Resource Center containing Hiroshima/Nagasaki Memorial collection.

**Freshman class profile.** 1,700 applied, 1,577 admitted, 337 enrolled.

| Mid 50% test scores | | | |
|---|---|---|---|
| SAT critical reading: | 430-540 | GPA 2.0-2.99: | 35% |
| SAT math: | 430-570 | Rank in top quarter: | 38% |
| ACT composite: | 17-23 | Rank in top tenth: | 13% |
| GPA 3.75 or higher: | 20% | Return as sophomores: | 68% |
| GPA 3.50-3.74: | 14% | Out-of-state: | 2% |
| GPA 3.0-3.49: | 31% | Live on campus: | 80% |
| | | International: | 2% |

**Basis for selection.** Previous academic record, test scores, counselor recommendation, and interview important. Essay, interview recommended for all.

**High school preparation.** College-preparatory program recommended. 16 units required. Required and recommended units include English 4, mathematics 2, social studies 2, science 2 (laboratory 2), foreign language 2 and academic electives 4. 6 art units recommended.

**2009-2010 Annual costs.** Tuition/fees: $24,286. Room/board: $8,272. Books/supplies: $500. Personal expenses: $450.

**Financial aid. Non-need-based:** Scholarships awarded for academics, alumni affiliation, religious affiliation, state residency.

**Application procedures. Admission:** Closing date 8/1. $25 fee, may be waived for applicants with need, free for online applicants. Admission notification on a rolling basis beginning on or about 12/1. Online application does not require application fee. **Financial aid:** Priority date 3/31, closing date 6/1. FAFSA required. Applicants notified on a rolling basis starting 3/1; must reply by 5/1 or within 2 week(s) of notification.

**Academics. Special study options:** Cross-registration, double major, dual enrollment of high school students, honors, independent study, internships, liberal arts/career combination, student-designed major, study abroad, teacher certification program, Washington semester, weekend college. **Credit/placement by examination:** AP, CLEP, IB, SAT, ACT, institutional tests. 30 credit hours maximum toward bachelor's degree. **Support services:** Learning center, reduced course load, remedial instruction, study skills assistance, tutoring, writing center.

**Majors. Agriculture:** Agribusiness operations, agronomy, animal sciences, business, equine science, farm/ranch, production. **Biology:** General, bacteriology, biochemistry, environmental. **Business:** Accounting, business admin, management science, marketing, sales/distribution. **Communications:** General, journalism, media studies, public relations. **Computer sciences:** General, computer science. **Education:** General, agricultural, biology, chemistry, early childhood, elementary, English, health, history, mathematics, middle, multi-level teacher, physical, science, secondary, social science, social studies. **Foreign languages:** Spanish. **History:** General. **Legal studies:** Prelaw. **Liberal arts:** Arts/sciences. **Math:** General. **Parks/recreation:** Sports admin. **Physical sciences:** Astronomy, chemistry, geology, planetary. **Protective services:** Criminal justice. **Psychology:** General. **Public administration:** Social work. **Social sciences:** General, economics, political science, sociology. **Visual/performing arts:** Art, commercial/advertising art, dramatic.

**Most popular majors.** Agriculture 7%, business/marketing 28%, education 20%, psychology 7%.

**Computing on campus.** 156 workstations in library, computer center. Dormitories wired for high-speed internet access and linked to campus network. Commuter students can connect to campus network. Online course registration, helpline, student web hosting available.

**Student life. Freshman orientation:** Mandatory. Held 3 days prior to start of fall semester. **Housing:** Guaranteed on-campus for all undergraduates. Coed dorms, single-sex dorms, apartments, fraternity/sorority housing available. $100 nonrefundable deposit, deadline 8/15. Living/learning units available. **Activities:** Campus ministries, choral groups, drama, international student organizations, literary magazine, music ensembles, musical theater, student government, student newspaper, social service, international club, education club, agriculture club, Christian Students, Young Friends (Quaker-Christian group), sports medicine association.

**Athletics.** NCAA. **Intercollegiate:** Baseball M, basketball, cheerleading, cross-country, football (tackle), golf, soccer, softball W, swimming, tennis, track and field, volleyball W, wrestling M. **Intramural:** Basketball, football (non-tackle), racquetball, soccer, softball, squash, table tennis, tennis, volleyball, weight lifting. **Team name:** Quakers.

**Student services.** Adult student services, alcohol/substance abuse counseling, chaplain/spiritual director, career counseling, student employment services, financial aid counseling, health services, minority student services, personal counseling, placement for graduates, veterans' counselor.

**Contact.** E-mail: admissions@wilmington.edu
Phone: (800) 341-9318 ext. 260 Fax: (937) 382-7077
Tina Garland, Director of Admission, Wilmington College, Box 1325 Pyle Center, Wilmington, OH 45177

---

## Wittenberg University
**Springfield, Ohio**
www.wittenberg.edu

CB member
CB code: 1922

- Private 4-year liberal arts college affiliated with Evangelical Lutheran Church in America
- Residential campus in small city
- 1,745 degree-seeking undergraduates: 57% women
- 8 degree-seeking graduate students
- 72% of applicants admitted
- Application essay required
- 66% graduate within 6 years

**General.** Founded in 1845. Regionally accredited. **Degrees:** 416 bachelor's awarded; master's offered. **ROTC:** Army, Air Force. **Location:** 25 miles from Dayton, 45 miles from Columbus. **Calendar:** Semester, limited summer session. **Full-time faculty:** 140 total; 93% have terminal degrees, 9% minority, 41% women. **Part-time faculty:** 57 total; 28% have terminal degrees, 7% minority, 54% women. **Class size:** 66% < 20, 33% 20-39, less than 1% 40-49, less than 1% 50-99, less than 1% >100. **Special facilities:** Observatory, East Asian art collection, Martin Luther library collection, humanities and technology center.

**Freshman class profile.** 3,222 applied, 2,321 admitted, 488 enrolled.

| Mid 50% test scores | | | |
|---|---|---|---|
| SAT critical reading: | 500-620 | GPA 2.0-2.99: | 22% |
| SAT math: | 500-620 | Rank in top quarter: | 50% |
| ACT composite: | 22-28 | Rank in top tenth: | 27% |
| GPA 3.75 or higher: | 32% | Return as sophomores: | 78% |
| GPA 3.50-3.74: | 15% | Out-of-state: | 30% |
| GPA 3.0-3.49: | 30% | Live on campus: | 94% |
| | | International: | 1% |

**Basis for selection.** In order of importance: school achievement record, courses taken, school attended, trend in work, test scores, counselor recommendation, extracurricular activities, and interview. Special consideration for children of alumni, minorities, Lutherans, residents of Clark County, and international students. Math and foreign language placement tests required. Interview recommended for all; portfolio required for art program; audition recommended for dance, music, theater programs. **Homeschooled:** On-campus interview.

**High school preparation.** College-preparatory program recommended. 16 units required; 21 recommended. Required and recommended units include English 4, mathematics 3-4, history 2-3, science 3-5 (laboratory 2) and foreign language 2-3.

**2009-2010 Annual costs.** Tuition/fees: $34,190. Room/board: $8,772.

**2009-2010 Financial aid.** All financial aid based on need. 432 full-time freshmen applied for aid; 376 were judged to have need; 376 of these received aid. Average need met was 88%. Average scholarship/grant was $24,377; average loan $4,147. 68% of total undergraduate aid awarded as scholarships/grants, 32% as loans/jobs. **Additional information:** Auditions required from applicants for music, theater, and dance scholarships. Portfolio required of applicants for art scholarships.

**Application procedures. Admission:** Priority date 3/15; no deadline. $40 fee, may be waived for applicants with need. Admission notification on a rolling basis. Must reply by May 1 or within 2 week(s) if notified thereafter. **Financial aid:** Priority date 3/1; no closing date. FAFSA required. Applicants notified on a rolling basis starting 3/1; must reply by 5/1 or within 2 week(s) of notification.

**Academics. Special study options:** Combined bachelor's/graduate degree, cross-registration, double major, dual enrollment of high school students, honors, independent study, internships, liberal arts/career combination, student-designed major, study abroad, teacher certification program, urban semester, Washington semester, weekend college. Semester programs with Duke University (marine biology), School of Visual Arts in New York, Camarillo Hospital in California, National Institutes of Health in Washington, D.C., Washington University (MO) (occupational therapy), Johns Hopkins Nursing Program; 3-2 engineering with Washington University (MO), Case Western Reserve University. **Credit/placement by examination:** AP, CLEP, IB, institutional tests. **Support services:** Learning center, pre-admission summer program, reduced course load, study skills assistance, tutoring, writing center.

**Majors. Area/ethnic studies:** American, East Asian, European, Russian/Slavic. **Biology:** General, biochemistry, molecular. **Business:** General, business admin, managerial economics, marketing. **Communications:** General. **Computer sciences:** Computer science. **Conservation:** Environmental studies. **Education:** General. **Foreign languages:** French, German, Spanish. **History:** General. **Interdisciplinary:** Biological/physical sciences, biopsychology, global studies, math/computer science. **Liberal arts:** Arts/sciences. **Math:** General. **Philosophy/religion:** Philosophy, religion. **Physical sciences:** General, chemistry, geology, physics. **Psychology:** General. **Social sciences:** General, economics, geography, political science, sociology, urban studies. **Visual/performing arts:** General, art.

**Most popular majors.** Biology 10%, business/marketing 12%, education 10%, English 10%, psychology 9%, social sciences 16%.

**Computing on campus.** 900 workstations in dormitories, library, computer center, student center. Dormitories wired for high-speed internet access and linked to campus network. Commuter students can connect to campus network. Online course registration, online library, helpline, student web hosting, wireless network available.

**Student life. Freshman orientation:** Mandatory. Preregistration for classes offered. Pre-orientation days offered 3 times during the summer. Full orientation held 3 days before the beginning of fall classes. **Housing:** Guaranteed on-campus for all undergraduates. Coed dorms, single-sex dorms, apartments, fraternity/sorority housing, wellness housing available. $400 deposit, deadline 7/1. Substance-free residence hall, honors residence hall, special theme halls available. **Activities:** Bands, campus ministries, choral groups, dance, drama, international student organizations, literary magazine, music ensembles, Model UN, musical theater, opera, radio station, student government, student newspaper, symphony orchestra, Newman club, Concerned Black Students, community volunteer service, Weaver Chapel Association, Project Woman, East Asian studies club, Hillel, Amnesty International, Habitat for Humanity.

**Athletics.** NCAA. **Intercollegiate:** Baseball M, basketball, cheerleading, cross-country, diving, field hockey W, football (tackle) M, golf, lacrosse, soccer, softball W, swimming, tennis, track and field, volleyball W. **Intramural:** Badminton, basketball, bowling, cricket M, diving, fencing, football (non-tackle), golf, gymnastics, handball M, ice hockey M, judo, racquetball, rugby, sailing, skiing, skin diving, soccer, softball, squash, swimming, table tennis, tennis, track and field, volleyball, water polo M, weight lifting. **Team name:** Tigers.

**Student services.** Adult student services, alcohol/substance abuse counseling, chaplain/spiritual director, career counseling, student employment services, financial aid counseling, health services, minority student services, personal counseling, placement for graduates, veterans' counselor, women's services.

**Contact.** E-mail: admission@wittenberg.edu
Phone: (937) 327-6314 Toll-free number: (877) 206-0332 ext. 6314
Fax: (937) 327-6379
Karen Hunt, Director of Admission, Wittenberg University, Ward Street and North Wittenberg, Springfield, OH 45501-0720

## Wright State University
Dayton, Ohio
www.wright.edu

CB member
CB code: 1179

- Public 4-year university
- Commuter campus in small city
- 13,024 degree-seeking undergraduates: 14% part-time, 55% women, 16% African American, 3% Asian American, 2% Hispanic American, 1% international
- 3,696 degree-seeking graduate students
- 84% of applicants admitted
- SAT or ACT (ACT writing optional) required
- 44% graduate within 6 years

**General.** Founded in 1964. Regionally accredited. **Degrees:** 2,254 bachelor's, 41 associate awarded; master's, professional offered. **ROTC:** Army, Air Force. **Location:** 10 miles from downtown. **Calendar:** Quarter, extensive summer session. **Full-time faculty:** 853 total; 44% women. **Part-time faculty:** 27 total; 41% women. **Class size:** 41% < 20, 45% 20-39, 6% 40-49, 7% 50-99, 2% >100. **Special facilities:** Biological preserve, disabled-accessible garden of the senses.

**Freshman class profile.** 6,188 applied, 5,214 admitted, 2,364 enrolled.

| Mid 50% test scores | | | |
|---|---|---|---|
| SAT critical reading: | 440-560 | Rank in top quarter: | 35% |
| SAT math: | 440-580 | Rank in top tenth: | 15% |
| SAT writing: | 430-550 | End year in good standing: | 68% |
| ACT composite: | 18-24 | Return as sophomores: | 70% |
| GPA 3.75 or higher: | 16% | Out-of-state: | 3% |
| GPA 3.50-3.74: | 11% | Live on campus: | 54% |
| GPA 3.0-3.49: | 27% | Fraternities: | 5% |
| GPA 2.0-2.99: | 42% | Sororities: | 3% |

**Basis for selection.** Liberal admission policy. College-preparatory curriculum, 2.0 GPA required. Test scores important for selected programs. Audition required for acting, dance, directing/stage management, music programs; portfolio required for art, art education programs. **Learning Disabled:** Students encouraged to contact Office of Disability Services to fill out application to qualify for support services.

**High school preparation.** College-preparatory program recommended. 16 units required. Required units include English 4, mathematics 3, social studies 3, science 3 (laboratory 3), foreign language 2 and visual/performing arts 1. Math requirement includes 2 algebra. Art, music or theater recommended. Students not meeting course recommendations must make up deficiency prior to admission to program.

**2009-2010 Annual costs.** Tuition/fees: $7,533; $14,595 out-of-state. Room/board: $7,829.

**2009-2010 Financial aid. Need-based:** 2,248 full-time freshmen applied for aid; 1,849 were judged to have need; 1,833 of these received aid. Average need met was 56%. Average scholarship/grant was $6,099; average loan $3,288. 34% of total undergraduate aid awarded as scholarships/grants, 66% as loans/jobs. **Non-need-based:** Awarded to 1,369 full-time undergraduates, including 406 freshmen. Scholarships awarded for academics, alumni affiliation, art, athletics, leadership, minority status, music/drama, ROTC.

**Application procedures. Admission:** No deadline. $30 fee. Admission notification on a rolling basis beginning on or about 10/1. Application by January recommended for students desiring on-campus housing. **Financial aid:** Priority date 2/15; no closing date. FAFSA required. Applicants notified on a rolling basis starting 3/15.

**Academics. Special study options:** Cooperative education, cross-registration, distance learning, double major, dual enrollment of high school students, ESL, honors, independent study, internships, student-designed major, study abroad, teacher certification program, weekend college. **Credit/placement by examination:** AP, CLEP, institutional tests. **Support services:** Learning center, pre-admission summer program, reduced course load, remedial instruction, tutoring, writing center.

**Majors. Area/ethnic studies:** African-American, women's. **Biology:** General, anatomy, biochemistry, pharmacology/toxicology. **Business:** Accounting, business admin, human resources, management information systems, management science, managerial economics, marketing, statistics. **Communications:** General, media studies, organizational. **Computer sciences:** General, computer science, information systems. **Education:** Art, business, early childhood, elementary, English, foreign languages, learning disabled, mathematics, mentally handicapped, multiple handicapped, music, physical, science, social studies. **Engineering:** General, biomedical, computer, electrical, materials, mechanical, physics, science, systems. **Engineering technology:** Biomedical, environmental. **Foreign languages:** General, classics, French, German, Latin, linguistics, modern Greek, Spanish. **Health:** Adult health nursing, clinical lab science, environmental health, nursing (RN), predental, premedicine, prepharmacy, preveterinary, vocational rehab counseling. **History:** General. **Interdisciplinary:** Systems science. **Legal studies:** Prelaw. **Liberal arts:** Arts/sciences. **Math:** General, applied, statistics. **Military:** General. **Philosophy/religion:** Philosophy, religion. **Physical sciences:** Chemistry, geology, physics. **Protective services:** Police science. **Psychology:** General. **Public administration:** General, social work. **Social sciences:** Anthropology, criminology, economics, geography, international relations, political science, sociology, urban studies. **Visual/performing arts:** Art, art history/conservation, arts management, dance, dramatic, drawing, film/cinema, music history, music performance, music theory/composition, photography, theater design.

**Most popular majors.** Business/marketing 28%, education 10%, engineering/engineering technologies 7%, health sciences 13%, psychology 7%, social sciences 8%.

**Computing on campus.** 600 workstations in dormitories, library, computer center, student center. Dormitories wired for high-speed internet access. Commuter students can connect to campus network. Online course registration, online library, helpline, repair service, student web hosting, wireless network available.

**Student life. Freshman orientation:** Available. Preregistration for classes offered. **Housing:** Coed dorms, special housing for disabled, apartments available. $150 fully refundable deposit. Honors dorm available. **Activities:** Bands, choral groups, dance, drama, literary magazine, music ensembles, Model UN, musical theater, opera, radio station, student government, student newspaper, symphony orchestra, TV station, black student union, Baptist student union, student association for escorts, College Students for Special Wish, Fellowship of Christian Students, Circle-K, Campus Crusade for Christ, Ohio College Democrats, Jewish student union.

**Athletics. NCAA. Intercollegiate:** Baseball M, basketball, cheerleading, cross-country, diving, golf M, soccer, softball W, swimming, tennis, track and field W, volleyball W. **Intramural:** Archery, baseball M, basketball, cricket M, cross-country, football (tackle), golf, handball, lacrosse M, soccer, softball, squash, tennis, volleyball W. **Team name:** Raiders.

**Student services.** Adult student services, chaplain/spiritual director, career counseling, student employment services, financial aid counseling, health services, legal services, minority student services, personal counseling, placement for graduates, veterans' counselor, women's services. **Physically disabled:** Services for visually, speech, hearing impaired.

**Contact.** E-mail: admissions@wright.edu
Phone: (937) 775-5700 Toll-free number: (800) 247-1770
Fax: (937) 775-5795
Cathy Davis, Director of Admissions, Wright State University, 3640 Colonel Glenn Highway, Dayton, OH 45435

## Xavier University

Cincinnati, Ohio     **CB member**
www.xavier.edu     **CB code: 1965**

- Private 4-year university affiliated with Roman Catholic Church
- Residential campus in large city
- 4,083 degree-seeking undergraduates: 9% part-time, 55% women, 12% African American, 2% Asian American, 3% Hispanic American, 1% international
- 2,512 degree-seeking graduate students
- 73% of applicants admitted
- SAT or ACT (ACT writing optional), application essay required
- 77% graduate within 6 years; 25% enter graduate study

**General.** Founded in 1831. Regionally accredited. **Degrees:** 798 bachelor's, 25 associate awarded; master's, professional offered. **ROTC:** Army, Air Force. **Location:** 5 miles from downtown. **Calendar:** Semester, limited summer session. **Full-time faculty:** 317 total; 77% have terminal degrees, 14% minority, 48% women. **Part-time faculty:** 308 total; 24% have terminal degrees, 10% minority, 53% women. **Class size:** 41% < 20, 56% 20-39, 1% 40-49, 2% 50-99, less than 1% >100.

**Freshman class profile.** 7,205 applied, 5,272 admitted, 1,183 enrolled.

| Mid 50% test scores | | | |
|---|---|---|---|
| SAT critical reading: | 530-620 | GPA 2.0-2.99: | 13% |
| SAT math: | 510-610 | Rank in top quarter: | 58% |
| SAT writing: | 500-600 | Rank in top tenth: | 24% |
| ACT composite: | 23-28 | End year in good standing: | 86% |
| GPA 3.75 or higher: | 34% | Return as sophomores: | 84% |
| GPA 3.50-3.74: | 22% | Out-of-state: | 47% |
| GPA 3.0-3.49: | 31% | Live on campus: | 90% |
| | | International: | 1% |

**Basis for selection.** Rigor of curriculum, class rank, grades, ACT or SAT scores, counselor recommendations, essay, and activities important. Campus visit recommended for all students.

**High school preparation.** College-preparatory program recommended. 21 units recommended. Recommended units include English 4, mathematics 3, social studies 3, science 3, foreign language 2 and academic electives 5. 1 health/physical education recommended.

**2009-2010 Annual costs.** Tuition/fees: $28,570. Room/board: $9,530.

**2009-2010 Financial aid. Need-based:** 977 full-time freshmen applied for aid; 776 were judged to have need; 775 of these received aid. Average need met was 80%. Average scholarship/grant was $14,659; average loan $4,165. 61% of total undergraduate aid awarded as scholarships/grants, 39% as loans/jobs. **Non-need-based:** Awarded to 1,526 full-time undergraduates, including 539 freshmen. Scholarships awarded for academics, alumni affiliation, art, athletics, leadership, music/drama, religious affiliation.

**Application procedures. Admission:** Closing date 2/1. $35 fee, may be waived for applicants with need, free for online applicants. Admission notification on a rolling basis beginning on or about 10/15. Must reply by May 1 or within 2 week(s) if notified thereafter. **Financial aid:** Priority date 2/15; no closing date. FAFSA required. Applicants notified on a rolling basis starting 2/15; must reply by 5/1.

**Academics.** Strong emphasis on ethics and values in core curriculum. **Special study options:** Combined bachelor's/graduate degree, cooperative education, cross-registration, double major, dual enrollment of high school students, ESL, honors, independent study, internships, study abroad, teacher certification program, urban semester, Washington semester, weekend college. Cooperative science-engineering program (physics and chemistry) with University of Cincinnati, forestry program and environmental management programs with Duke University, Service Learning Semester. **Credit/placement by examination:** AP, CLEP, IB, institutional tests. 30 credit hours maximum toward associate degree, 60 toward bachelor's. **Support services:** Learning center, pre-admission summer program, reduced course load, remedial instruction, study skills assistance, tutoring, writing center.

**Majors. Biology:** General. **Business:** General, accounting, business admin, entrepreneurial studies, finance, human resources, international, management information systems, managerial economics, marketing. **Communications:** Advertising, organizational, public relations, radio/tv. **Computer sciences:** Computer science. **Education:** General, biology, chemistry, early childhood, elementary, middle, Montessori teacher, music, physics, secondary, special. **Foreign languages:** Classics, French, German, Spanish. **Health:** Athletic training, clinical lab science, nursing (RN). **History:** General. **Interdisciplinary:** Natural sciences. **Liberal arts:** Arts/sciences. **Math:** General. **Parks/recreation:** Sports admin. **Philosophy/religion:** Philosophy. **Physical sciences:** Chemistry, physics. **Protective services:** Criminal justice.

**Psychology:** General. **Public administration:** Social work. **Social sciences:** Economics, international relations, political science, sociology. **Theology:** Theology. **Visual/performing arts:** Studio arts.

**Most popular majors.** Biology 6%, business/marketing 25%, communications/journalism 6%, health sciences 6%, liberal arts 15%, social sciences 8%.

**Computing on campus.** 250 workstations in dormitories, library, student center. Dormitories wired for high-speed internet access and linked to campus network. Commuter students can connect to campus network. Online course registration, online library, helpline, repair service, student web hosting, wireless network available.

**Student life. Freshman orientation:** Mandatory, $190 fee. Preregistration for classes offered. Held the weekend before the start of classes. **Policies:** Student handbook, responsible computer use, university alcohol policy, harassment code accountability procedures. **Housing:** Guaranteed on-campus for freshmen. Coed dorms, special housing for disabled, apartments available. $200 fully refundable deposit, deadline 5/1. **Activities:** Bands, campus ministries, choral groups, dance, drama, film society, international student organizations, literary magazine, music ensembles, musical theater, opera, radio station, student government, student newspaper, symphony orchestra, TV station, Life after Sunday, Xavier Interfaith, South Asian Society, St. Vincent DePaul Society, Natural Ties, Black student association, College Republicans, College Democrats, Voices of Solidarity, Student Organization of Latinos.

**Athletics.** NCAA. **Intercollegiate:** Baseball M, basketball, cheerleading, cross-country, golf, soccer, swimming, tennis, track and field, volleyball W. **Intramural:** Basketball, bowling, football (non-tackle), racquetball, soccer, softball, tennis, volleyball. **Team name:** Musketeers.

**Student services.** Adult student services, alcohol/substance abuse counseling, chaplain/spiritual director, career counseling, services for economically disadvantaged, student employment services, financial aid counseling, health services, minority student services, personal counseling, placement for graduates, veterans' counselor, women's services. **Physically disabled:** Services for visually, speech, hearing impaired. **Learning disabled:** Comprehensive services available.

**Contact.** E-mail: xuadmit@xavier.edu
Phone: (513) 745-3301 Toll-free number: (877) 982-3648
Fax: (513) 745-4319
Aaron Meis, Dean of Admissions, Xavier University, 3800 Victory Parkway, Cincinnati, OH 45207-5311

---

## Youngstown State University

Youngstown, Ohio     **CB member**
www.ysu.edu     **CB code: 1975**

▸ Public 4-year university
▸ Commuter campus in small city
▸ 13,035 degree-seeking undergraduates: 20% part-time, 52% women, 16% African American, 1% Asian American, 2% Hispanic American, 1% international
▸ 1,127 degree-seeking graduate students
▸ 35% graduate within 6 years

**General.** Founded in 1908. Regionally accredited. **Degrees:** 1,430 bachelor's, 221 associate awarded; master's, professional offered. **ROTC:** Army, Air Force. **Location:** 65 miles from Cleveland, 60 miles from Pittsburgh. **Calendar:** Semester, limited summer session. **Full-time faculty:** 447 total; 82% have terminal degrees, 15% minority, 40% women. **Part-time faculty:** 564 total; 5% minority, 53% women. **Class size:** 32% < 20, 50% 20-39, 9% 40-49, 7% 50-99, 2% >100. **Special facilities:** Planetarium, historic preservation center.

**Freshman class profile.** 5,057 applied, 3,931 admitted, 2,722 enrolled.

| Mid 50% test scores | | Rank in top quarter: | 22% |
|---|---|---|---|
| SAT critical reading: | 400-520 | Rank in top tenth: | 8% |
| SAT math: | 400-540 | End year in good standing: | 73% |
| SAT writing: | 380-510 | Return as sophomores: | 71% |
| ACT composite: | 17-23 | Out-of-state: | 10% |
| GPA 3.75 or higher: | 10% | Live on campus: | 19% |
| GPA 3.50-3.74: | 9% | International: | 1% |
| GPA 3.0-3.49: | 25% | Fraternities: | 2% |
| GPA 2.0-2.99: | 42% | Sororities: | 3% |

**Basis for selection.** Open admission, but selective for some programs and for out-of-state students. Out-of-state applicants must be in top two-thirds of class, or have 17 ACT or 820 SAT exclusive of Writing. Open admission policy for Ohio residents and Mercer and Lawrence County, Pennsylvania residents. Special requirements for nursing, engineering and some other programs. Interview required for BS/MD program; audition required for music, BFA theater programs. **Homeschooled:** Transcript of courses and grades required. ACT or SAT required unless out of high school 2 or more years. Official transcript showing documentation of coursework completed for grades 9-12 and indicating date of completion of studies or graduation must be send to Admissions. Any relevant supporting documents required by applicant's home state verifying homeschool curriculum required. Curriculum outline, detailing course content, textbooks used, any other relevant information regarding coursework must be submitted. Copy of the Superintendent's Exemption Notice showing the student is excused to receive homeschooling also required.

**High school preparation.** College-preparatory program recommended. 16 units recommended. Recommended units include English 4, mathematics 3, social studies 3, science 2 (laboratory 1), foreign language 2 and visual/performing arts 1. Recommended coursework includes English composition; algebra I and II, geometry; laboratory science; and US history and government.

**2009-2010 Annual costs.** Tuition/fees: $6,721; $12,394 out-of-state. Residents of any out-of-state area within 100 miles of campus are charged $9,414 yearly tuition. Per credit hour charge is $392. Room/board: $7,400. Books/supplies: $1,212. Personal expenses: $2,311.

**2008-2009 Financial aid. Need-based:** 1,839 full-time freshmen applied for aid; 1,528 were judged to have need; 1,528 of these received aid. Average scholarship/grant was $1,839; average loan $3,437. 51% of total undergraduate aid awarded as scholarships/grants, 49% as loans/jobs. **Non-need-based:** Awarded to 3,483 full-time undergraduates, including 760 freshmen. Scholarships awarded for academics, alumni affiliation, athletics, ROTC, state residency.

**Application procedures. Admission:** Priority date 2/15; deadline 8/15. $30 fee, may be waived for applicants with need. Admission notification on a rolling basis. Students who apply by February 15 eligible for early registration and orientation. **Financial aid:** Priority date 2/15; no closing date. FAFSA, institutional form required. Applicants notified on a rolling basis starting 5/30; must reply within 2 week(s) of notification.

**Academics. Special study options:** Accelerated study, combined bachelor's/graduate degree, cooperative education, cross-registration, distance learning, double major, ESL, exchange student, honors, internships, student-designed major, study abroad, teacher certification program, urban semester, Washington semester, weekend college. Off-campus study with Lorain County Community College. **Credit/placement by examination:** AP, CLEP, IB, institutional tests. In select CLEP and AP tests, higher grade may make student eligible for more credits. **Support services:** Learning center, pre-admission summer program, reduced course load, remedial instruction, study skills assistance, tutoring, writing center.

**Majors. Area/ethnic studies:** African-American, American. **Biology:** General. **Business:** General, accounting, apparel, banking/financial services, business admin, fashion, finance, financial planning, hospitality admin, hospitality/recreation, human resources, management information systems, managerial economics, marketing, merchandising, operations, public finance, retailing, sales/distribution, selling, tourism promotion, tourism/travel. **Communications:** General, advertising, journalism, public relations, radio/tv. **Computer sciences:** General, computer science, information systems, information technology, programming. **Conservation:** Environmental science. **Education:** General, art, autistic, biology, business, chemistry, computer, early childhood, elementary, emotionally handicapped, English, family/consumer sciences, foreign languages, French, health, history, kindergarten/preschool, learning disabled, mathematics, mentally handicapped, middle, multi-level teacher, multiple handicapped, music, physical, physics, science, secondary, social science, social studies, Spanish, special, speech. **Engineering:** General, chemical, civil, computer, electrical, industrial, materials, mechanical. **Engineering technology:** General, civil, electrical, mechanical. **Family/consumer sciences:** General, clothing/textiles, family studies, family/community services, food/nutrition, work/family studies. **Foreign languages:** General, French, German, Italian, Spanish. **Health:** Athletic training, clinical lab science, community health, community health services, dietetics, facilities admin, nursing (RN), predental, premedicine, prepharmacy, preveterinary, public health ed, respiratory therapy technology. **History:** General. **Interdisciplinary:** Gerontology. **Legal studies:** Prelaw. **Liberal arts:** Arts/sciences. **Math:** General. **Parks/recreation:** Exercise sciences, health/fitness, sports admin. **Philosophy/religion:** Philosophy, religion. **Physical sciences:** General, astronomy, chemistry, geology, physics, planetary. **Protective services:** Corrections, criminal justice, forensics, law enforcement admin, security services. **Psychology:** General. **Public administration:** General, social work. **Social sciences:** General, anthropology, econometrics, economics, geography, international economics, political science, sociology. **Visual/performing arts:** General, acting, art, art history/conservation, commercial/advertising art, dramatic, jazz, music history, music performance, music theory/composition, painting, photography, piano/organ, printmaking, stringed instruments, studio arts, theater design, voice/opera.

**Most popular majors.** Business/marketing 17%, education 18%, engineering/engineering technologies 7%, health sciences 11%.

**Computing on campus.** 170 workstations in dormitories, library, student center. Dormitories wired for high-speed internet access and linked to campus network. Commuter students can connect to campus network. Online course registration, online library, helpline, repair service, student web hosting, wireless network available.

**Student life. Freshman orientation:** Available, $50 fee. Orientation held in March, June, July, and August. **Housing:** Guaranteed on-campus for all undergraduates. Coed dorms, single-sex dorms, apartments, fraternity/sorority housing, wellness housing available. $200 deposit. University scholars program honors facility available. **Activities:** Bands, campus ministries, choral groups, dance, drama, film society, international student organizations, literary magazine, music ensembles, Model UN, musical theater, opera, radio station, student government, student newspaper, symphony orchestra, College Republicans, Student Democrats, Pan-African student union, National Panhellenic Council, Hispanic-American organization, student athlete advisory council, interfraternity council, Golden Key, Omicron Delta Kappa, gospel choir, Panhellenic Council.

**Athletics.** NCAA. **Intercollegiate:** Baseball M, basketball, cross-country, football (tackle) M, golf, soccer W, softball W, swimming W, tennis, track and field, volleyball W. **Intramural:** Badminton, basketball, football (nontackle), handball, racquetball, soccer, softball, swimming, table tennis, volleyball. **Team name:** Penguins.

**Student services.** Adult student services, alcohol/substance abuse counseling, chaplain/spiritual director, career counseling, student employment services, financial aid counseling, health services, minority student services, on-campus daycare, personal counseling, placement for graduates, veterans' counselor, women's services. **Physically disabled:** Services for visually, speech, hearing impaired.

**Contact.** E-mail: enroll@ysu.edu
Phone: (330) 941-2000 Toll-free number: (877) 468-6978
Fax: (330) 941-3674
Sue Davis, Director of Undergraduate Admissions, Youngstown State University, One University Plaza, Youngstown, OH 44555-0001

# Oklahoma

## Bacone College
### Muskogee, Oklahoma
### www.bacone.edu
### CB code: 6030

- Private 4-year liberal arts college affiliated with American Baptist Churches in the USA
- Residential campus in large town
- 1,021 degree-seeking undergraduates
- 78% of applicants admitted
- SAT or ACT required

**General.** Founded in 1880. Regionally accredited. American Indian heritage and commitment to serving Native Americans. Guided by Christian principles. **Degrees:** 47 bachelor's, 69 associate awarded. **Location:** 50 miles from Tulsa. **Calendar:** Semester, limited summer session. **Full-time faculty:** 23 total. **Part-time faculty:** 58 total. **Class size:** 70% < 20, 25% 20-39, 5% 40-49. **Special facilities:** Native American museum and collection.

**Freshman class profile.** 481 applied, 373 admitted, 222 enrolled.

| Mid 50% test scores | | | |
|---|---|---|---|
| SAT critical reading: | 400-470 | GPA 3.0-3.49: | 26% |
| SAT math: | 410-480 | GPA 2.0-2.99: | 56% |
| ACT composite: | 16-19 | Rank in top quarter: | 17% |
| GPA 3.75 or higher: | 6% | Rank in top tenth: | 5% |
| GPA 3.50-3.74: | 10% | Out-of-state: | 39% |
| | | Live on campus: | 78% |

**Basis for selection.** 2.0 GPA and 18 ACT required. Additional standards for admission to nursing and radiography programs. ACT results used as basis for counseling. Interview recommended for nursing, radiologic technology programs. **Homeschooled:** Official transcript from accredited homeschool organization or GED required.

**High school preparation.** College-preparatory program recommended. Recommended units include English 4, mathematics 3, history 2, science 2 (laboratory 2).

**2009-2010 Annual costs.** Tuition/fees: $11,700. Room/board: $7,400. Books/supplies: $1,000. Personal expenses: $500.

**2009-2010 Financial aid.** All financial aid based on need.

**Application procedures. Admission:** No deadline. $25 fee, may be waived for applicants with need, free for online applicants. Admission notification on a rolling basis. **Financial aid:** Priority date 3/31; no closing date. FAFSA required. Applicants notified on a rolling basis starting 4/1; must reply within 2 week(s) of notification.

**Academics. Special study options:** Accelerated study, cross-registration, double major, dual enrollment of high school students, independent study, internships, liberal arts/career combination, student-designed major, teacher certification program. **Credit/placement by examination:** AP, CLEP, SAT, ACT, institutional tests. 15 credit hours maximum toward associate degree. **Support services:** Learning center, pre-admission summer program, remedial instruction, study skills assistance, tutoring.

**Majors. Area/ethnic studies:** Native American. **Business:** Business admin. **Education:** Early childhood, elementary, health, physical. **Health:** Medical radiologic technology/radiation therapy, nursing (RN). **Parks/recreation:** Exercise sciences, facilities management, sports admin. **Protective services:** Criminal justice. **Other:** Christian ministry.

**Most popular majors.** Business/marketing 12%, education 61%, parks/recreation 13%, social sciences 11%.

**Computing on campus.** 84 workstations in library, computer center. Dormitories wired for high-speed internet access and linked to campus network. Commuter students can connect to campus network. Online library, wireless network available.

**Student life. Freshman orientation:** Mandatory, $100 fee. Preregistration for classes offered. **Policies:** No alcohol or tobacco products allowed on campus. **Housing:** Single-sex dorms available. $100 deposit. **Activities:** Campus ministries, choral groups, dance, drama, student government, student newspaper, Native learning work community, Native American students of promise, journalism club, praise team club, praise band, American Indian stickball club, criminal justice studies club, Native American student association, black student association, American Indian dance and song.

**Athletics.** NAIA. **Intercollegiate:** Baseball M, basketball, cheerleading, cross-country, football (tackle) M, golf, rodeo, soccer, softball W, tennis, track and field, volleyball W, wrestling M. **Intramural:** Basketball, football (tackle) M, soccer, softball, table tennis. **Team name:** Warriors.

**Student services.** Chaplain/spiritual director, career counseling, student employment services, financial aid counseling, health services, personal counseling, placement for graduates. **Physically disabled:** Services for visually, speech, hearing impaired.

**Contact.** E-mail: admissionsoffice@bacone.edu
Phone: (918) 683-4581 ext. 7342 Toll-free
number: (888) 682-5514 ext. 7342 Fax: (918) 781-7416
Harlan Johnson, Director of Admissions, Bacone College, 2299 Old Bacone Road, Muskogee, OK 74403

## Cameron University
### Lawton, Oklahoma
### CB member
### www.cameron.edu
### CB code: 6080

- Public 4-year university
- Commuter campus in small city
- 5,222 degree-seeking undergraduates: 29% part-time, 60% women
- 399 degree-seeking graduate students
- SAT or ACT required

**General.** Founded in 1909. Regionally accredited. **Degrees:** 523 bachelor's, 178 associate awarded; master's offered. **ROTC:** Army. **Location:** 90 miles from Oklahoma City. **Calendar:** Semester, limited summer session. **Full-time faculty:** 183 total; 72% have terminal degrees, 17% minority, 37% women. **Part-time faculty:** 183 total; 12% minority, 46% women. **Class size:** 48% < 20, 43% 20-39, 6% 40-49, 3% 50-99, less than 1% >100.

**Freshman class profile.** 2,070 applied, 2,067 admitted, 1,150 enrolled.

| Mid 50% test scores | | | |
|---|---|---|---|
| ACT composite: | 16-21 | Rank in top tenth: | 10% |
| GPA 3.75 or higher: | 18% | Return as sophomores: | 58% |
| GPA 3.50-3.74: | 20% | Out-of-state: | 16% |
| GPA 3.0-3.49: | 29% | Live on campus: | 14% |
| GPA 2.0-2.99: | 30% | Fraternities: | 1% |
| Rank ih top quarter: | 29% | Sororities: | 1% |

**Basis for selection.** Open admission. 2.7 GPA and rank in top half of class, or 20 ACT required for bachelor's degree, associate of science or associate of arts programs. Open admissions for associate of applied science degree candidates only. Those who do not meet bachelor's criteria admitted as associate degree candidates.

**High school preparation.** College-preparatory program required. 15 units required. Required and recommended units include English 4, mathematics 3, history 3, science 2-3 (laboratory 2), foreign language 1 and academic electives 3. One unit in government, geography, economics or non-Western culture.

**2009-2010 Annual costs.** Tuition/fees: $4,110; $9,975 out-of-state. Room/board: $3,576. Books/supplies: $1,050.

**2008-2009 Financial aid. Need-based:** 688 full-time freshmen applied for aid; 605 were judged to have need; 532 of these received aid. Average need met was 91%. Average scholarship/grant was $4,000; average loan $1,200. 63% of total undergraduate aid awarded as scholarships/grants, 37% as loans/jobs. **Non-need-based:** Awarded to 2,861 full-time undergraduates, including 850 freshmen. Scholarships awarded for academics, alumni affiliation, art, athletics, leadership, music/drama, ROTC.

**Application procedures. Admission:** Priority date 8/1; no deadline. $15 fee, may be waived for applicants with need. Admission notification on a rolling basis beginning on or about 6/10. **Financial aid:** Priority date 5/1; no closing date. FAFSA required. Applicants notified on a rolling basis starting 4/1; must reply by 8/7 or within 2 week(s) of notification.

**Academics. Special study options:** Accelerated study, combined bachelor's/graduate degree, cooperative education, distance learning, double major, dual enrollment of high school students, honors, independent study, internships, liberal arts/career combination, teacher certification program, weekend college. **Credit/placement by examination:** AP, CLEP, IB, institutional tests. **Support services:** Learning center, pre-admission summer program, reduced course load, remedial instruction, study skills assistance, tutoring, writing center.

**Majors. Agriculture:** General, agronomy, animal sciences, horticultural science. **Biology:** General. **Business:** Accounting, business admin. **Communications:** General, broadcast journalism, journalism, public relations. **Computer sciences:** General, computer science, web page design. **Education:** General, art, biology, chemistry, early childhood, elementary, English, history, mathematics, music, physical, science, secondary, social studies. **Engineering technology:** Electrical, mechanical drafting. **Family/consumer sciences:** General. **Foreign languages:** General, linguistics. **Health:** Clinical lab technology. **History:** General. **Interdisciplinary:** Biological/physical sciences, natural sciences. **Math:** General. **Parks/recreation:** Health/fitness. **Physical sciences:** Chemistry, physics. **Protective services:** Criminal justice. **Psychology:** General. **Science technology:** Biological. **Social sciences:** Political science, sociology. **Visual/performing arts:** Art, dramatic, studio arts.

**Most popular majors.** Business/marketing 19%, communications/journalism 6%, education 12%, interdisciplinary studies 7%, parks/recreation 6%, psychology 6%, security/protective services 11%.

**Computing on campus.** 450 workstations in dormitories, library, computer center. Dormitories wired for high-speed internet access and linked to campus network. Commuter students can connect to campus network. Online library, helpline, student web hosting, wireless network available.

**Student life. Freshman orientation:** Mandatory. 7 sessions annually, held June through August. **Policies:** Student code of conduct; no alcohol on campus. **Housing:** Guaranteed on-campus for all undergraduates. Single-sex dorms, special housing for disabled, apartments, wellness housing available. $200 fully refundable deposit, deadline 7/1. Quiet areas available. **Activities:** Bands, campus ministries, choral groups, drama, film society, international student organizations, literary magazine, music ensembles, musical theater, opera, radio station, student government, student newspaper, symphony orchestra, TV station, Ebony Society, Students of the Caribbean Alliance, American Indian student association, Latin alliance, Asian/Pacific Islander student association, Chi Alpha, Young Republicans.

**Athletics.** NCAA. **Intercollegiate:** Baseball M, basketball, cross-country M, golf, softball W, tennis, volleyball W. **Intramural:** Badminton, basketball, bowling, football (non-tackle), golf, racquetball, softball, tennis, volleyball. **Team name:** Aggies.

**Student services.** Chaplain/spiritual director, career counseling, services for economically disadvantaged, student employment services, financial aid counseling, minority student services, veterans' counselor. **Physically disabled:** Services for visually, speech, hearing impaired.

**Contact.** E-mail: zoed@cameron.edu
Phone: (580) 581-2200 Toll-free number: (888) 454-7600
Fax: (580) 581-5514
Zoe DuRant, Director of Admissions, Cameron University, 2800 West Gore Boulevard, Lawton, OK 73505-6377

## DeVry University: Oklahoma City Center
**Oklahoma City, Oklahoma**
**www.devry.edu**

- For-profit 4-year university and business college
- Very large city
- 111 degree-seeking undergraduates: 52% part-time, 41% women, 20% African American, 2% Asian American, 7% Hispanic American, 7% Native American
- 43 degree-seeking graduate students

**General.** Regionally accredited. **Degrees:** 8 bachelor's, 1 associate awarded; master's offered. **Calendar:** Semester. **Part-time faculty:** 10 total; 40% women.

**Freshman class profile.** 17 enrolled.

**Basis for selection.** Applicants must have high school diploma or equivalent, or degree from accredited post-secondary institution, demonstrate proficiency in basic college-level skills through SAT or ACT scores or institution-administered placement examinations, and be at least 17 years of age. DeVry-administered admissions test required if SAT or ACT test scores are not submitted.

**High school preparation.** College-preparatory program recommended.

**2009-2010 Annual costs.** Tuition/fees: $14,160. Books/supplies: $1,310. Personal expenses: $3,574.

**2008-2009 Financial aid. Non-need-based:** Scholarships awarded for academics.

**Application procedures. Admission:** No deadline. $50 fee. Admission notification on a rolling basis. **Financial aid:** No deadline. FAFSA required. Applicants notified on a rolling basis.

**Academics. Special study options:** Accelerated study, distance learning. **Credit/placement by examination:** CLEP.

**Majors. Business:** Business admin. **Computer sciences:** Networking, systems analysis, web page design. **Other:** Technical management.

**Most popular majors.** Business/marketing 88%, computer/information sciences 13%.

**Contact.** DeVry University: Oklahoma City Center, Lakepointe Towers, 4013 NW Expressway Street, Oklahoma City, OK 73116

## East Central University
**Ada, Oklahoma**
**www.ecok.edu**                                        **CB code: 6186**

- Public 4-year university
- Commuter campus in large town
- 3,730 degree-seeking undergraduates: 19% part-time, 58% women, 4% African American, 6% Hispanic American, 21% Native American, 3% international
- 876 degree-seeking graduate students
- 93% of applicants admitted
- SAT or ACT (ACT writing optional) required
- 35% graduate within 6 years

**General.** Founded in 1909. Regionally accredited. **Degrees:** 669 bachelor's awarded; master's offered. **Location:** 86 miles from Oklahoma City. **Calendar:** Semester, extensive summer session. **Full-time faculty:** 168 total; 64% have terminal degrees, 9% minority, 45% women. **Part-time faculty:** 110 total; 18% have terminal degrees, 12% minority, 60% women.

**Freshman class profile.** 915 applied, 852 admitted, 644 enrolled.

| Mid 50% test scores | | | |
|---|---|---|---|
| SAT critical reading: | 370-560 | GPA 2.0-2.99: | 25% |
| SAT math: | 390-570 | Rank in top quarter: | 39% |
| ACT composite: | 17-24 | Rank in top tenth: | 16% |
| GPA 3.75 or higher: | 24% | Return as sophomores: | 63% |
| GPA 3.50-3.74: | 18% | Out-of-state: | 6% |
| GPA 3.0-3.49: | 32% | Live on campus: | 72% |
| | | International: | 2% |

**Basis for selection.** Rank in top 50% of graduating class, 20 ACT or SAT equivalent, 2.7 GPA and required course work important.

**High school preparation.** 15 units required. Required and recommended units include English 4, mathematics 3, social studies 2, history 1, science 2 (laboratory 2) and academic electives 3. Additional courses from English, math, science, history, social sciences, foreign language, or computer science.

**2009-2010 Annual costs.** Tuition/fees: $4,221; $10,236 out-of-state. Room/board: $4,324. Books/supplies: $1,000. Personal expenses: $4,542.

**2008-2009 Financial aid. Need-based:** 429 full-time freshmen applied for aid; 341 were judged to have need; 327 of these received aid. Average need met was 56%. Average scholarship/grant was $5,297; average loan $3,705. 58% of total undergraduate aid awarded as scholarships/grants, 42% as loans/jobs. **Non-need-based:** Awarded to 978 full-time undergraduates, including 243 freshmen. Scholarships awarded for academics, athletics.

**Application procedures. Admission:** No deadline. $20 fee. Admission notification on a rolling basis. **Financial aid:** Closing date 3/1. FAFSA required. Applicants notified on a rolling basis starting 4/15; must reply within 2 week(s) of notification.

**Academics. Special study options:** Distance learning, double major, dual enrollment of high school students, exchange student, honors, independent study, internships, study abroad, teacher certification program. **Credit/placement by examination:** AP, CLEP, ACT, institutional tests. 94 credit hours maximum toward bachelor's degree. Students do not receive CLEP or AP credit until 12 hours completed in residence with 2.0 GPA. **Support services:** Learning center, pre-admission summer program, reduced course load, remedial instruction, study skills assistance, tutoring, writing center.

**Majors. Biology:** General. **Business:** General, accounting, administrative services, business admin, finance, managerial economics, marketing, office management, operations, sales/distribution. **Communications:** General, broadcast journalism, journalism. **Computer sciences:** General. **Education:** Agricultural, business, drama/dance, early childhood, elementary, English, family/

consumer sciences, history, mathematics, mentally handicapped, music, physical, physically handicapped, science, social studies, special, speech, technology/industrial arts, trade/industrial. **Family/consumer sciences:** General, clothing/textiles. **Foreign languages:** Comparative lit. **Health:** Athletic training, environmental health, medical records technology, predental, premedicine, prepharmacy, preveterinary, vocational rehab counseling. **History:** General. **Legal studies:** Paralegal, prelaw. **Math:** General, applied. **Parks/recreation:** General, exercise sciences, health/fitness. **Physical sciences:** Chemistry, physics. **Protective services:** Criminal justice, police science. **Psychology:** General. **Public administration:** Community org/advocacy, human services, social work. **Social sciences:** General, cartography, criminology, political science, sociology. **Visual/performing arts:** Art, dramatic, piano/organ, studio arts, voice/opera.

**Most popular majors.** Biology 7%, business/marketing 14%, education 21%, health sciences 12%, parks/recreation 6%, public administration/social services 12%.

**Computing on campus.** 750 workstations in library, computer center. Online library, helpline, repair service, wireless network available.

**Student life. Freshman orientation:** Mandatory. Preregistration for classes offered. **Housing:** Coed dorms, single-sex dorms, special housing for disabled, apartments, fraternity/sorority housing available. $40 nonrefundable deposit. **Activities:** Bands, choral groups, dance, drama, film society, literary magazine, music ensembles, musical theater, student government, student newspaper, association of black students, Native American student association, Baptist student union, united campus ministry, students with disabilities, Church of Christ Bible Chair, Life House, Sigma Society, Panhellenic, silent friends club.

**Athletics.** NCAA. **Intercollegiate:** Baseball M, basketball, cross-country, football (tackle) M, golf, soccer W, softball W, tennis, volleyball W. **Intramural:** Basketball, soccer, softball, volleyball. **Team name:** Tigers.

**Student services.** Adult student services, career counseling, student employment services, financial aid counseling, health services, minority student services, on-campus daycare, personal counseling, placement for graduates, veterans' counselor. **Physically disabled:** Services for visually, speech, hearing impaired.

**Contact.** E-mail: parmstro@ecok.edu
Phone: (580) 332-8000 Fax: (580) 559-5432
Pamla Armstrong, Registrar and Director of Admissions, East Central University, PMBJ8, 1100 East 14th Street, Ada, OK 74820

## Family of Faith College
**Shawnee, Oklahoma**
**www.familyoffaithcollege.edu**

- Private 4-year Bible college
- Residential campus in rural community
- 48 full-time, degree-seeking undergraduates
- SAT or ACT (ACT writing optional), application essay required

**General.** Regionally accredited; also accredited by ABHE. **Degrees:** 1 bachelor's awarded. **Location:** 6 miles from Shawnee, 30 miles from Oklahoma City. **Calendar:** Semester, limited summer session. **Full-time faculty:** 3 total; 33% have terminal degrees, 33% women. **Part-time faculty:** 12 total; 33% minority, 42% women.

**Freshman class profile.**

| Mid 50% test scores | | | |
|---|---|---|---|
| | | ACT composite: | 20-24 |
| SAT critical reading: | 500-550 | End year in good standing: | 75% |
| SAT math: | 400-450 | Return as sophomores: | 75% |

**Basis for selection.** SAT/ACT not required for certificate programs. Academic and personal references required. **Homeschooled:** Transcript of courses and grades, state high school equivalency certificate, letter of recommendation (nonparent) required.

**2009-2010 Annual costs.** Tuition/fees: $5,110. Room only: $1,600.

**Application procedures. Admission:** Closing date 6/1 (receipt date). $25 fee.

**Academics. Credit/placement by examination:** CLEP.

**Majors. Education:** Multi-level teacher. **Theology:** Bible, theology.

**Student life. Housing:** $50 fully refundable deposit.

**Contact.** E-mail: ffc@allegiance.tv
Phone: (405) 273-5331 Fax: (405) 273-8535
Rhonda Gaines, Vice President of Student Affairs, Family of Faith College, PO Box 1805, Shawnee, OK 74802-1805

## Hillsdale Free Will Baptist College
**Moore, Oklahoma**
**www.hc.edu**

- Private 4-year liberal arts college
- Residential campus in small city
- 229 degree-seeking undergraduates: 38% women
- 6 degree-seeking graduate students
- SAT or ACT (ACT writing recommended) required

**General.** Regionally accredited; also accredited by TRACS. **Degrees:** 25 bachelor's, 30 associate awarded; master's offered. **Location:** 2 miles from Oklahoma City, 2 miles from Norman. **Calendar:** Semester, limited summer session. **Full-time faculty:** 14 total. **Part-time faculty:** 29 total.

**Freshman class profile.** 82 enrolled.

**Basis for selection.** Academic GPA and test scores most important.

**2009-2010 Annual costs.** Tuition/fees: $11,100. Room/board: $5,200.

**Application procedures. Admission:** No deadline. $20 fee. **Financial aid:** Closing date 9/15.

**Academics. Special study options:** Distance learning, double major, independent study. **Credit/placement by examination:** AP, CLEP, ACT. **Support services:** Remedial instruction, tutoring.

**Majors. Biology:** Exercise physiology. **Business:** General. **Education:** Multi-level teacher. **Psychology:** General. **Theology:** Theology. **Other:** Christian education.

**Student life. Freshman orientation:** Mandatory, $100 fee. Preregistration for classes offered. **Housing:** Single-sex dorms, apartments available. **Activities:** Campus ministries, drama, music ensembles, student government.

**Athletics.** NCCAA. **Intercollegiate:** Baseball M, basketball, cross-country M, soccer M, softball W. **Team name:** Saints.

**Contact.** E-mail: recruitment@hc.edu
Phone: (415) 912-9011
Lyndsey Barentine, Admissions Counselor, Hillsdale Free Will Baptist College, PO Box 7208, Moore, OK 73153

## ITT Technical Institute: Tulsa
**Tulsa, Oklahoma**

- For-profit 4-year business and technical college
- Large city

**General.** Accredited by ACICS. **Calendar:** Quarter.

**Contact.** 4943 South 78th East Avenue, Tulsa, OK 74145

## Langston University
**Langston, Oklahoma**
**www.lunet.edu**

**CB member**
**CB code: 6361**

- Public 4-year university and liberal arts college
- Residential campus in rural community
- 2,390 degree-seeking undergraduates: 13% part-time, 59% women, 86% African American, 1% Asian American, 1% Hispanic American, 2% Native American, 2% international
- 342 degree-seeking graduate students
- 45% of applicants admitted
- SAT or ACT (ACT writing optional), application essay required

**General.** Founded in 1897. Regionally accredited. Branch campuses in Oklahoma City, Tulsa. **Degrees:** 363 bachelor's, 12 associate awarded; master's, doctoral offered. **ROTC:** Army, Air Force. **Location:** 40 miles from Oklahoma City, 90 miles from Tulsa. **Calendar:** Semester, limited summer session. **Full-time faculty:** 145 total; 74% minority, 46% women. **Part-time faculty:** 72 total; 72% minority, 61% women. **Class size:** 64% < 20,

29% 20-39, 3% 40-49, 3% 50-99. **Special facilities:** International dairy goat research facility.

**Freshman class profile.** 2,609 applied, 1,178 admitted, 889 enrolled.

| | | | |
|---|---|---|---|
| GPA 3.75 or higher: | 1% | Rank in top quarter: | 8% |
| GPA 3.50-3.74: | 2% | Rank in top tenth: | 2% |
| GPA 3.0-3.49: | 12% | Out-of-state: | 40% |
| GPA 2.0-2.99: | 63% | International: | 2% |

**Basis for selection.** 2.7 GPA, 20 ACT or SAT equivalent required. March 1 priority date for SAT or ACT scores. Audition recommended for music program.

**High school preparation.** 15 units required. Required and recommended units include English 4, mathematics 3, social studies 2, history 1, science 2-8 (laboratory 2), foreign language 1-4 and academic electives 4. Remaining units must be additional work in these areas or in computer science, speech, economics, geography, government, psychology, or sociology. Required units must begin with algebra I. Required social sciences units must include 1 US history.

**2009-2010 Annual costs.** Tuition/fees: $3,827; $9,407 out-of-state. Housing is apartment-style. Room/board: $7,120. Books/supplies: $800. Personal expenses: $2,037.

**2009-2010 Financial aid.** All financial aid based on need.

**Application procedures. Admission:** Priority date 3/1; no deadline. $25 fee. Admission notification on a rolling basis. **Financial aid:** Priority date 3/1, closing date 5/1. CSS PROFILE required. Applicants notified on a rolling basis starting 7/15; must reply within 2 week(s) of notification.

**Academics. Special study options:** Cooperative education, distance learning, double major, dual enrollment of high school students, honors, internships, liberal arts/career combination, study abroad, teacher certification program. **Credit/placement by examination:** AP, CLEP, SAT, ACT, institutional tests. 16 credit hours maximum toward associate degree, 30 toward bachelor's. **Support services:** Learning center, reduced course load, remedial instruction, tutoring.

**Majors. Agriculture:** Animal sciences, business, economics, farm/ranch. **Biology:** General, zoology. **Business:** Accounting, administrative services, business admin, human resources. **Communications:** General, broadcast journalism, journalism. **Communications technology:** General. **Computer sciences:** General. **Education:** General, business, elementary, family/consumer sciences, mathematics, music, physical, secondary, social studies, special, technology/industrial arts. **Family/consumer sciences:** General, clothing/textiles, family studies, food/nutrition. **Health:** Health care admin, preveterinary. **History:** General. **Legal studies:** Prelaw. **Math:** General. **Physical sciences:** Chemistry. **Protective services:** Corrections, police science. **Psychology:** General. **Social sciences:** General, economics, geography, sociology, urban studies. **Visual/performing arts:** Art, music performance.

**Most popular majors.** Business/marketing 23%, education 7%, health sciences 21%, liberal arts 9%, psychology 9%, security/protective services 8%, social sciences 6%.

**Computing on campus.** 300 workstations in library, computer center. Dormitories wired for high-speed internet access and linked to campus network.

**Student life. Freshman orientation:** Mandatory. Preregistration for classes offered. Begins 7 days prior to fall enrollment; includes social, cultural, and institutional activities along with registration and enrollment processes. **Policies:** All freshman and sophomore students required to live on campus. Students must have 2.0 GPA to join student organizations. Students must have 2.5 GPA to be in student government, campus royalty, or fraternities and sororities. **Housing:** Guaranteed on-campus for all undergraduates. Apartments available. $200 fully refundable deposit. **Activities:** Bands, choral groups, dance, drama, music ensembles, radio station, student government, student newspaper, TV station, Pan Hellenic fraternities and sororities, NAACP, NCNW.

**Athletics.** NAIA. **Intercollegiate:** Basketball, cheerleading, cross-country, football (tackle) M, softball W, track and field, volleyball W. **Intramural:** Basketball, football (non-tackle), track and field, volleyball. **Team name:** Lions.

**Student services.** Alcohol/substance abuse counseling, chaplain/spiritual director, career counseling, services for economically disadvantaged, student employment services, financial aid counseling, health services, on-campus daycare, personal counseling, placement for graduates, veterans' counselor. **Physically disabled:** Services for visually, speech, hearing impaired.

**Contact.** E-mail: gtrobertson@lunet.edu
Phone: (405) 466-3428 Fax: (405) 466-3391
Gayle Robertson, Director of Enrollment Management, Langston University, Box 728, Langston, OK 73050

## Mid-America Christian University
### Oklahoma City, Oklahoma
**www.macu.edu**  CB code: 0918

- Private 4-year university and liberal arts college affiliated with Church of God
- Residential campus in very large city
- 1,181 undergraduates
- SAT or ACT (ACT writing optional) required

**General.** Founded in 1953. Regionally accredited. **Degrees:** 147 bachelor's, 1 associate awarded; master's offered. **Location:** 10 miles from downtown. **Calendar:** Semester, limited summer session. **Full-time faculty:** 20 total; 35% have terminal degrees, 10% minority. **Part-time faculty:** 30 total; 20% minority. **Class size:** 67% < 20, 26% 20-39, 2% 40-49, 4% 50-99.

**Freshman class profile.**

| | | | |
|---|---|---|---|
| Out-of-state: | 64% | Live on campus: | 82% |

**Basis for selection.** Open admission. Applicants admitted who feel calling to full-time Christian vocations or seek God's will for their lives in a spiritual environment. 2 references required. Interview, audition recommended. **Homeschooled:** Applicants without GED must have 15 ACT English and 14 ACT math.

**High school preparation.** 16 units recommended. Recommended units include English 4, mathematics 2, social studies 2, science 2 and foreign language 2.

**2009-2010 Annual costs.** Tuition/fees: $13,480. Room/board: $5,560. Books/supplies: $800. Personal expenses: $660.

**2009-2010 Financial aid. Non-need-based:** Scholarships awarded for academics, leadership, minority status, music/drama.

**Application procedures. Admission:** Priority date 8/15; no deadline. $25 fee, may be waived for applicants with need, free for online applicants. Admission notification on a rolling basis beginning on or about 2/1. Students may provisionally enroll without graduation posted in senior year. **Financial aid:** Priority date 5/1; no closing date. FAFSA required. Applicants notified on a rolling basis starting 5/1.

**Academics.** Degree-completion program available for enrollees 25 years of age and above with approximately 2 years of college experience. Link program available for student lacking general education courses. **Special study options:** Combined bachelor's/graduate degree, distance learning, double major, dual enrollment of high school students, external degree, independent study, internships, liberal arts/career combination, teacher certification program, weekend college. **Credit/placement by examination:** AP, CLEP, SAT, ACT, institutional tests. 30 credit hours maximum toward associate degree, 30 toward bachelor's. Must be completed before accruing 30 credit hours. **Support services:** Remedial instruction, tutoring, writing center.

**Majors. Business:** Business admin, management information systems, management science, marketing. **Education:** Elementary, English, mathematics, music, secondary, social science, social studies. **Interdisciplinary:** Behavioral sciences. **Math:** General. **Philosophy/religion:** Religion. **Protective services:** Law enforcement admin. **Psychology:** Social. **Social sciences:** General. **Theology:** Bible, pastoral counseling, sacred music, theology. **Visual/performing arts:** Music performance.

**Most popular majors.** Computer/information sciences 7%, history 27%, philosophy/religious studies 15%, psychology 16%, theological studies 28%.

**Computing on campus.** 40 workstations in library, computer center, student center. Dormitories wired for high-speed internet access and linked to campus network. Online library, wireless network available.

**Student life. Freshman orientation:** Mandatory. Preregistration for classes offered. Held 1 day prior to start of classes. **Policies:** No smoking or drinking allowed on campus. Religious observance required. **Housing:** Guaranteed on-campus for freshmen. Single-sex dorms, wellness housing available. $50 deposit. **Activities:** Concert band, choral groups, drama, music ensembles, musical theater, student government, Missions Club, Student Ministerial Fellowship, Ministry Refresher Institute.

**Athletics.** NCCAA. **Intercollegiate:** Baseball M, basketball, golf, soccer M, softball W, volleyball W. **Intramural:** Basketball, bowling, softball W, table tennis, volleyball. **Team name:** Evangels.

**Student services.** Chaplain/spiritual director, career counseling, student employment services, financial aid counseling, health services, personal counseling, placement for graduates, veterans' counselor. **Physically disabled:** Services for speech impaired.

**Contact.** E-mail: info@macu.edu
Phone: (405) 692-3188 Toll-free number: (888) 436-3035
Fax: (405) 692-3165
Jason Duda, Director of Admissions, Mid-America Christian University, 3500 SW 119th Street, Oklahoma City, OK 73170

## Northeastern State University
Tahlequah, Oklahoma
www.nsuok.edu                                          CB code: 6485

- Public 4-year university
- Commuter campus in large town
- 8,092 degree-seeking undergraduates: 27% part-time, 60% women, 6% African American, 1% Asian American, 2% Hispanic American, 30% Native American, 3% international
- 1,218 degree-seeking graduate students
- 72% of applicants admitted
- ACT (writing optional) required

**General.** Founded in 1851. Regionally accredited. **Degrees:** 1,536 bachelor's awarded; master's, professional offered. **ROTC:** Army. **Location:** 60 miles from Tulsa, 30 miles from Muskogee. **Calendar:** Semester, extensive summer session. **Full-time faculty:** 299 total; 74% have terminal degrees, 13% minority, 48% women. **Part-time faculty:** 171 total; 26% have terminal degrees, 14% minority, 51% women. **Class size:** 43% < 20, 43% 20-39, 9% 40-49, 5% 50-99. **Special facilities:** Literacy study center, tribal studies center, Oklahoma Institute for Learning Styles.

**Freshman class profile.** 2,604 applied, 1,863 admitted, 1,113 enrolled.

| Mid 50% test scores | | End year in good standing: | 68% |
|---|---|---|---|
| ACT composite: | 18-23 | Return as sophomores: | 64% |
| GPA 3.75 or higher: | 19% | Out-of-state: | 6% |
| GPA 3.50-3.74: | 15% | Live on campus: | 79% |
| GPA 3.0-3.49: | 31% | International: | 1% |
| GPA 2.0-2.99: | 32% | Fraternities: | 12% |
| Rank in top quarter: | 39% | Sororities: | 14% |
| Rank in top tenth: | 16% | | |

**Basis for selection.** Admissions based on secondary school record, class rank, and standardized test scores. Audition required, interview recommended for music program. Interview recommended for drama program; portfolio recommended for graphic art program. Interview required for alternative admission. **Homeschooled:** Transcript of courses and grades required.

**High school preparation.** College-preparatory program required. 15 units required. Required and recommended units include English 4, mathematics 3, social studies 2, history 1, science 2 (laboratory 2) and foreign language 2. 3 from English, lab science, math, history, social studies, computer science, or foreign language.

**2009-2010 Annual costs.** Tuition/fees: $4,180; $10,270 out-of-state. Room/board: $4,966. Books/supplies: $1,155. Personal expenses: $1,080.

**2009-2010 Financial aid. Need-based:** 917 full-time freshmen applied for aid; 744 were judged to have need; 637 of these received aid. Average need met was 72%. Average scholarship/grant was $5,207; average loan $2,391. 88% of total undergraduate aid awarded as scholarships/grants, 12% as loans/jobs. **Non-need-based:** Awarded to 3,428 full-time undergraduates, including 711 freshmen. Scholarships awarded for academics, alumni affiliation, art, athletics, leadership, minority status, music/drama, religious affiliation, ROTC, state residency.

**Application procedures. Admission:** Priority date 8/1; no deadline. No application fee. Admission notification on a rolling basis. **Financial aid:** Priority date 3/15; no closing date. FAFSA, institutional form required. Applicants notified on a rolling basis starting 3/15.

**Academics.** NSU College of Optometry on campus. **Special study options:** Combined bachelor's/graduate degree, distance learning, double major, dual enrollment of high school students, honors, independent study, internships, student-designed major, teacher certification program, weekend college. **Credit/placement by examination:** AP, CLEP, IB, ACT, institutional tests. 30 credit hours maximum toward bachelor's degree. **Support services:** Learning center, pre-admission summer program, reduced course load, remedial instruction, study skills assistance, tutoring, writing center.

**Majors. Area/ethnic studies:** Native American. **Biology:** General, cell/histology, wildlife. **Business:** Accounting, business admin, entrepreneurial studies, finance, human resources, international, logistics, management information systems, marketing, nonprofit/public, operations, tourism/travel. **Communications:** General, advertising, journalism, public relations. **Computer sciences:** Computer science. **Conservation:** Environmental science. **Education:** Art, biology, chemistry, early childhood, elementary, English, learning disabled, mathematics, music, Native American, physical, physics, science, social studies, Spanish, speech. **Engineering:** Environmental. **Engineering technology:** Industrial safety. **Family/consumer sciences:** General, food/nutrition. **Foreign languages:** Spanish. **Health:** Audiology/speech pathology, clinical lab science, facilities admin, nursing (RN). **History:** General. **Math:** General. **Parks/recreation:** Exercise sciences. **Physical sciences:** Chemistry. **Protective services:** Law enforcement admin. **Psychology:** General, developmental. **Public administration:** Social work. **Social sciences:** Geography, political science, sociology. **Visual/performing arts:** Art, commercial/advertising art, design, dramatic, photography, studio arts. **Other:** Vision science.

**Most popular majors.** Business/marketing 22%, education 28%, psychology 6%, security/protective services 7%.

**Computing on campus.** 897 workstations in dormitories, library, computer center. Dormitories wired for high-speed internet access and linked to campus network. Commuter students can connect to campus network. Online library, helpline, student web hosting, wireless network available.

**Student life. Freshman orientation:** Mandatory. Preregistration for classes offered. **Housing:** Guaranteed on-campus for freshmen. Coed dorms, special housing for disabled, apartments, fraternity/sorority housing, wellness housing available. $75 fully refundable deposit, deadline 7/1. **Activities:** Bands, campus ministries, choral groups, dance, drama, international student organizations, literary magazine, music ensembles, Model UN, musical theater, student government, student newspaper, symphony orchestra, TV station, Native American student association, American Indian science and engineering society, Association of Black Collegians, government and international studies society, Christian Fellowship, Baptist campus ministries, Chi Alpha campus ministries, Habitat for Humanity, Sigma Theta Epsilon, RiverHawks for Christ.

**Athletics.** NCAA. **Intercollegiate:** Baseball M, basketball, football (tackle) M, golf, soccer, softball W, tennis W. **Intramural:** Basketball, football (non-tackle), golf, racquetball, soccer, softball, tennis, volleyball. **Team name:** RiverHawks.

**Student services.** Adult student services, alcohol/substance abuse counseling, career counseling, services for economically disadvantaged, student employment services, financial aid counseling, health services, personal counseling, placement for graduates, veterans' counselor. **Physically disabled:** Services for visually, speech, hearing impaired.

**Contact.** E-mail: nsuinfo@nsuok.edu
Phone: (918) 444-2200 Toll-free number: (800) 722-9614
Fax: (918) 458-2342
Dawn Cain, Director of Admissions, Northeastern State University, 600 North Grand Avenue, Tahlequah, OK 74464-2399

## Northwestern Oklahoma State University
Alva, Oklahoma
www.nwosu.edu                                          CB code: 6493

- Public 4-year university and teachers college
- Commuter campus in small town
- 1,906 degree-seeking undergraduates: 28% part-time, 56% women, 5% African American, 1% Asian American, 4% Hispanic American, 6% Native American, 2% international
- 180 degree-seeking graduate students
- 100% of applicants admitted
- SAT or ACT (ACT writing optional) required

**General.** Founded in 1897. Regionally accredited. **Degrees:** 305 bachelor's awarded; master's offered. **Location:** 160 miles from Oklahoma City, 70 miles from Enid. **Calendar:** Semester, limited summer session. **Full-time faculty:** 87 total; 42% have terminal degrees, 8% minority, 52% women. **Part-time faculty:** 59 total; 8% minority, 63% women. **Special facilities:** Farm, natural history museum.

*Four-Year Colleges*

**Freshman class profile.** 799 applied, 799 admitted, 406 enrolled.

| Mid 50% test scores | | | |
|---|---|---|---|
| SAT critical reading: | 390-490 | GPA 2.0-2.99: | 31% |
| SAT math: | 400-550 | Rank in top quarter: | 21% |
| ACT composite: | 17-22 | Rank in top tenth: | 3% |
| GPA 3.75 or higher: | 17% | Out-of-state: | 18% |
| GPA 3.50-3.74: | 16% | Live on campus: | 71% |
| GPA 3.0-3.49: | 34% | International: | 1% |

**Basis for selection.** Applicants with 2.7 GPA and in top 50% of class or with 19 ACT admitted unconditionally. Others admitted provisionally. Audition recommended for music program. **Homeschooled:** Transcript of courses and grades required.

**High school preparation.** 15 units required. Required and recommended units include English 4, mathematics 3, history 3, science 2 (laboratory 2), foreign language 2 and academic electives 3. 1 unit required from either government, economics, geography or non-Western culture.

**2009-2010 Annual costs.** Tuition/fees: $4,111; $10,141 out-of-state. Room/board: $3,700. Books/supplies: $1,200. Personal expenses: $2,000.

**2009-2010 Financial aid. Non-need-based:** Scholarships awarded for academics, alumni affiliation, art, athletics, leadership, music/drama.

**Application procedures. Admission:** No deadline. $15 fee. Admission notification on a rolling basis. **Financial aid:** No deadline. FAFSA required. Applicants notified on a rolling basis starting 5/1.

**Academics. Special study options:** Distance learning, double major, dual enrollment of high school students, honors, independent study, internships, study abroad, teacher certification program. 2-2 programs in many professional fields. **Credit/placement by examination:** AP, CLEP, SAT, ACT, institutional tests. **Support services:** Learning center, reduced course load, remedial instruction, tutoring, writing center.

**Majors. Agriculture:** General, business. **Biology:** General. **Business:** Accounting, business admin, e-commerce. **Communications:** Broadcast journalism, journalism, public relations. **Computer sciences:** General, information systems, programming. **Conservation:** Management/policy. **Education:** General, business, early childhood, elementary, English, health, learning disabled, mathematics, mentally handicapped, music, physical, science, social science, Spanish, special, technology/industrial arts. **Health:** Nursing (RN). **History:** General. **Legal studies:** Prelaw. **Math:** General. **Parks/recreation:** Health/fitness. **Physical sciences:** Chemistry. **Protective services:** Police science. **Psychology:** General. **Public administration:** Social work. **Social sciences:** General, political science, sociology. **Visual/performing arts:** Dramatic, music performance, piano/organ, voice/opera.

**Computing on campus.** 180 workstations in library, computer center, student center. Dormitories wired for high-speed internet access. Commuter students can connect to campus network. Online library, wireless network available.

**Student life. Freshman orientation:** Mandatory. Preregistration for classes offered. **Housing:** Single-sex dorms, special housing for disabled available. $75 fully refundable deposit. **Activities:** Bands, campus ministries, choral groups, drama, international student organizations, music ensembles, radio station, student government, student newspaper, TV station.

**Athletics.** NAIA. **Intercollegiate:** Baseball M, basketball, cross-country, football (tackle) M, golf, rodeo, soccer W, softball W. **Intramural:** Basketball, bowling, football (non-tackle), racquetball, softball, volleyball. **Team name:** Rangers.

**Student services.** Adult student services, career counseling, student employment services, financial aid counseling, health services, personal counseling, placement for graduates, veterans' counselor, women's services. **Physically disabled:** Services for visually, speech, hearing impaired.

**Contact.** E-mail: recruit@nwosu.edu
Phone: (580) 327-8546 Fax: (580) 327-8413
Matt Adair, Director of Recruitment, Northwestern Oklahoma State University, 709 Oklahoma Boulevard, Alva, OK 73717-2799

### Oklahoma Baptist University
Shawnee, Oklahoma
www.okbu.edu
CB member
CB code: 6541

- Private 4-year university and liberal arts college affiliated with Southern Baptist Convention
- Residential campus in large town

- 1,520 degree-seeking undergraduates: 5% part-time, 60% women, 7% African American, 1% Asian American, 4% Hispanic American, 8% Native American, 4% international
- 55 degree-seeking graduate students
- 66% of applicants admitted
- SAT or ACT (ACT writing optional) required
- 48% graduate within 6 years; 40% enter graduate study

**General.** Founded in 1910. Regionally accredited. Each summer approximately 250 students, faculty and staff serve in projects around the world. About 300 students participate in local service projects during the year. **Degrees:** 292 bachelor's, 2 associate awarded; master's offered. **ROTC:** Air Force. **Location:** 35 miles from Oklahoma City, 90 miles from Tulsa. **Calendar:** Semester, limited summer session. **Full-time faculty:** 105 total. **Part-time faculty:** 55 total. **Class size:** 62% < 20, 31% 20-39, 3% 40-49, 3% 50-99. **Special facilities:** Planetarium (operated by students), greenhouse, music technology laboratory, biblical research library.

**Freshman class profile.** 3,831 applied, 2,515 admitted, 368 enrolled.

| Mid 50% test scores | | | |
|---|---|---|---|
| SAT critical reading: | 480-590 | GPA 2.0-2.99: | 7% |
| SAT math: | 480-620 | Rank in top quarter: | 62% |
| ACT composite: | 21-26 | Rank in top tenth: | 30% |
| GPA 3.75 or higher: | 49% | End year in good standing: | 87% |
| GPA 3.50-3.74: | 18% | Return as sophomores: | 74% |
| GPA 3.0-3.49: | 26% | International: | 9% |

**Basis for selection.** 20 ACT or 950 SAT (exclusive of Writing), 3.0 GPA or class rank in top half required. Interview recommended for borderline applicants; audition recommended for drama, music programs; portfolio recommended for art program.

**High school preparation.** College-preparatory program recommended. 17 units recommended. Recommended units include English 4, mathematics 3, social studies 2, history 1, science 3 (laboratory 2), foreign language 2 and academic electives 2. Math recommendation includes 2 algebra and 1 plane geometry.

**2009-2010 Annual costs.** Tuition/fees: $17,624. Room/board: $5,510. Books/supplies: $1,100. Personal expenses: $1,660.

**2008-2009 Financial aid. Non-need-based:** Scholarships awarded for academics, alumni affiliation, art, athletics, job skills, leadership, music/drama, religious affiliation, ROTC, state residency.

**Application procedures. Admission:** Priority date 4/1; deadline 8/1 (postmark date). No application fee. Admission notification on a rolling basis beginning on or about 6/1. **Financial aid:** Priority date 3/1; no closing date. FAFSA, institutional form required. Applicants notified on a rolling basis starting 3/1; must reply by 5/1 or within 2 week(s) of notification.

**Academics.** Opportunities for January-term travel to Europe, Russia, South America; also opportunity to teach English in China and Hungary. **Special study options:** Accelerated study, combined bachelor's/graduate degree, cooperative education, double major, ESL, exchange student, honors, independent study, internships, liberal arts/career combination, student-designed major, study abroad, teacher certification program. Exchange program with Seinan Gakuin University, Japan, and Hong Kong Baptist College; opportunities for January-term travel to Europe, Russia, South America. **Credit/placement by examination:** AP, CLEP, IB, SAT, ACT, institutional tests. 32 credit hours maximum toward bachelor's degree. Essay required for English, government, history exams; oral exam required for French, German and Spanish; lab exam required for information systems. **Support services:** Learning center, reduced course load, remedial instruction, study skills assistance, tutoring, writing center.

**Majors. Biology:** General, biochemistry. **Business:** General, accounting, business admin, finance, international, international finance, management information systems, management science, marketing. **Communications:** General, broadcast journalism, journalism, public relations. **Computer sciences:** General, applications programming, computer science, information systems, systems analysis. **Education:** Art, biology, chemistry, early childhood, elementary, English, foreign languages, French, German, health, history, learning disabled, mathematics, mentally handicapped, music, physical, physics, science, secondary, social science, social studies, Spanish, special, speech. **Foreign languages:** General, French, German, Spanish. **Health:** Athletic training, nursing (RN). **History:** General. **Interdisciplinary:** Math/computer science. **Liberal arts:** Arts/sciences. **Math:** General. **Parks/recreation:** Exercise sciences, facilities management, health/fitness, sports admin. **Philosophy/religion:** Philosophy, religion. **Physical sciences:** Chemistry, physics. **Psychology:** General. **Public administration:** Social work. **Social sciences:** General, anthropology, political science, sociology. **Theology:** Bible, missionary, religious ed, sacred music, theology. **Visual/**

**performing arts:** Art, dramatic, music performance, music theory/composition, piano/organ, studio arts, voice/opera.

**Most popular majors.** Education 12%, health sciences 12%, philosophy/religious studies 6%, theological studies 11%.

**Computing on campus.** 200 workstations in dormitories, library, computer center, student center. Dormitories wired for high-speed internet access and linked to campus network. Commuter students can connect to campus network. Online course registration, online library, helpline, wireless network available.

**Student life. Freshman orientation:** Mandatory. Preregistration for classes offered. Held during the 3 days immediately prior to start of fall semester. **Policies:** Campus is alcohol/drug/smoke free. **Housing:** Guaranteed on-campus for all undergraduates. Single-sex dorms, apartments, wellness housing available. **Activities:** Bands, choral groups, drama, literary magazine, music ensembles, musical theater, opera, student government, student newspaper, symphony orchestra, TV station, Campus Crusade, FCA, Baptist Collegiate Ministries, Collegiate Republicans, Young Democrats, black student fellowship, international student union, Native American heritage association, residence hall association.

**Athletics.** NAIA. **Intercollegiate:** Baseball M, basketball, cross-country, golf, soccer, softball W, tennis, track and field. **Intramural:** Badminton, basketball, bowling, racquetball, soccer, softball, swimming, table tennis, tennis, volleyball. **Team name:** Bison.

**Student services.** Chaplain/spiritual director, career counseling, student employment services, financial aid counseling, health services, personal counseling, placement for graduates, veterans' counselor. **Physically disabled:** Services for visually, hearing impaired.

**Contact.** E-mail: admissions@mail.okbu.edu
Phone: (405) 878-2033 Toll-free number: (800) 654-3285
Fax: (405) 878-2068
Bruce Perkins, Director of Admissions, Oklahoma Baptist University, 500 West University, Shawnee, OK 74804

## Oklahoma Christian University
**Oklahoma City, Oklahoma**
**www.oc.edu**                                             CB code: 6086

▶ Private 4-year liberal arts college affiliated with Church of Christ
▶ Residential campus in very large city
▶ 1,918 degree-seeking undergraduates
▶ 254 graduate students
▶ 56% of applicants admitted
▶ SAT or ACT (ACT writing optional) required

**General.** Founded in 1950. Regionally accredited. Every student receives MacBook and choice of iPhone or iPod touch upon enrollment. **Degrees:** 328 bachelor's awarded; master's offered. **ROTC:** Army, Air Force. **Calendar:** Semester, extensive summer session. **Full-time faculty:** 110 total; 69% have terminal degrees, 6% minority, 29% women. **Part-time faculty:** 68 total; 15% have terminal degrees, 7% minority, 35% women. **Class size:** 53% < 20, 38% 20-39, 3% 40-49, 4% 50-99, less than 1% >100.

**Freshman class profile.** 1,718 applied, 970 admitted, 471 enrolled.

| Mid 50% test scores | | GPA 3.50-3.74: | 18% |
|---|---|---|---|
| SAT critical reading: | 470-640 | GPA 3.0-3.49: | 30% |
| SAT math: | 480-610 | GPA 2.0-2.99: | 15% |
| SAT writing: | 480-610 | Rank in top quarter: | 54% |
| ACT composite: | 20-27 | Rank in top tenth: | 30% |
| GPA 3.75 or higher: | 36% | Live on campus: | 96% |

**Basis for selection.** Students evaluated on both merit and character. Interview/campus visit strongly recommended.

**High school preparation.** College-preparatory program recommended. 15 units recommended. Required and recommended units include English 4, mathematics 4, social studies 3, science 4 (laboratory 2) and foreign language 2.

**2009-2010 Annual costs.** Tuition/fees: $16,366. Room/board: $6,630. Books/supplies: $800. Personal expenses: $1,360.

**2009-2010 Financial aid. Non-need-based:** Scholarships awarded for academics, art, athletics, leadership, music/drama, religious affiliation, ROTC.

**Application procedures. Admission:** Priority date 5/1; no deadline. $25 fee, may be waived for applicants with need. Admission notification on a rolling basis beginning on or about 9/1. Must reply by May 1 or within 2 week(s) if notified thereafter. **Financial aid:** Priority date 3/15, closing date 8/31. FAFSA required. Applicants notified on a rolling basis starting 1/15; must reply within 4 week(s) of notification.

**Academics. Special study options:** Accelerated study, combined bachelor's/graduate degree, cross-registration, distance learning, double major, dual enrollment of high school students, ESL, honors, independent study, internships, liberal arts/career combination, study abroad, teacher certification program. **Credit/placement by examination:** AP, CLEP, IB, SAT, ACT, institutional tests. 60 credit hours maximum toward bachelor's degree. **Support services:** Learning center, reduced course load, remedial instruction, study skills assistance, tutoring, writing center.

**Majors. Biology:** General, biochemistry. **Business:** General, accounting, business admin, management science, market research. **Communications:** General, advertising, broadcast journalism, journalism, media studies, public relations. **Communications technology:** Animation/special effects. **Computer sciences:** General, computer science, game design, information systems, programming. **Education:** Art, early childhood, elementary, English, ESL, mathematics, middle, music, physical, science, secondary, social studies, speech. **Engineering:** Computer, electrical, mechanical. **Family/consumer sciences:** Family studies. **Foreign languages:** Spanish. **Health:** Clinical lab science, predental, premedicine, prenursing, prepharmacy, pre-veterinary. **History:** General. **Interdisciplinary:** Biological/physical sciences, math/computer science. **Legal studies:** Prelaw. **Liberal arts:** Arts/sciences. **Math:** General. **Parks/recreation:** Health/fitness. **Philosophy/religion:** Christian, religion. **Physical sciences:** Chemistry, physics. **Psychology:** General. **Social sciences:** Political science. **Theology:** Bible, missionary, religious ed, theology, youth ministry. **Visual/performing arts:** Art, commercial/advertising art, design, dramatic, graphic design, interior design, music performance, piano/organ, studio arts, voice/opera.

**Computing on campus.** PC or laptop required. 1,850 workstations in dormitories, library, computer center, student center. Dormitories wired for high-speed internet access and linked to campus network. Commuter students can connect to campus network. Online course registration, online library, helpline, repair service, student web hosting, wireless network available.

**Student life. Freshman orientation:** Mandatory, $200 fee. Preregistration for classes offered. Two-part program includes 1-day summer event and week-long event the week before school starts. **Policies:** Single students must live on campus or with parents. Special arrangements considered. Religious observance required. **Housing:** Guaranteed on-campus for all undergraduates. Single-sex dorms, special housing for disabled, apartments, wellness housing available. $100 partly refundable deposit, deadline 5/1. **Activities:** Bands, campus ministries, choral groups, drama, international student organizations, literary magazine, music ensembles, musical theater, opera, radio station, student government, student newspaper, symphony orchestra, TV station.

**Athletics.** NAIA. **Intercollegiate:** Baseball M, basketball, cheerleading W, cross-country, golf M, soccer, softball W, tennis, track and field. **Intramural:** Basketball, bowling, cross-country, football (non-tackle), golf M, soccer, softball, swimming, table tennis, tennis, track and field, volleyball. **Team name:** Eagles.

**Student services.** Alcohol/substance abuse counseling, chaplain/spiritual director, career counseling, student employment services, financial aid counseling, health services, minority student services, personal counseling, placement for graduates, veterans' counselor, women's services. **Physically disabled:** Services for visually, speech, hearing impaired.

**Contact.** E-mail: info@oc.edu
Phone: (405) 425-5050 Toll-free number: (800) 877-5050
Fax: (405) 425-5069
Darci Thompson, Director of Admissions, Oklahoma Christian University, Box 11000, Oklahoma City, OK 73136-1100

## Oklahoma City University
**Oklahoma City, Oklahoma**                               CB member
**www.okcu.edu**                                           CB code: 6543

▶ Private 4-year university and liberal arts college affiliated with United Methodist Church
▶ Residential campus in very large city
▶ 2,283 degree-seeking undergraduates: 17% part-time, 60% women, 8% African American, 2% Asian American, 6% Hispanic American, 4% Native American, 18% international
▶ 1,527 degree-seeking graduate students
▶ 79% of applicants admitted
▶ SAT or ACT (ACT writing optional), application essay required
▶ 54% graduate within 6 years

**General.** Founded in 1904. Regionally accredited. **Degrees:** 513 bachelor's awarded; master's, professional offered. **ROTC:** Army, Air Force. **Location:** 180 miles from Dallas, 350 miles from Kansas City. **Calendar:** Semester, limited summer session. **Full-time faculty:** 198 total; 80% have terminal degrees, 11% minority, 45% women. **Part-time faculty:** 123 total; 65% have terminal degrees, 7% minority, 50% women. **Class size:** 72% < 20, 27% 20-39, less than 1% 40-49, less than 1% 50-99. **Special facilities:** Art center, entrepreneurship center, urban wilderness laboratory.

**Freshman class profile.** 1,185 applied, 931 admitted, 404 enrolled.

| Mid 50% test scores | | | |
|---|---|---|---|
| SAT critical reading: | 490-600 | Rank in top quarter: | 59% |
| SAT math: | 480-590 | Rank in top tenth: | 32% |
| ACT composite: | 22-27 | End year in good standing: | 85% |
| GPA 3.75 or higher: | 35% | Return as sophomores: | 76% |
| GPA 3.50-3.74: | 22% | Out-of-state: | 50% |
| GPA 3.0-3.49: | 33% | Live on campus: | 94% |
| GPA 2.0-2.99: | 10% | Fraternities: | 18% |
| | | Sororities: | 30% |

**Basis for selection.** School achievement record, which includes class rank, and test scores most important. Counselor recommendations, essays, and activities also considered. Interview recommended for all; audition required for dance, music programs; portfolio required for art, graphic design programs. **Homeschooled:** Must demonstrate that individual is graduating no earlier than their class in the public school system.

**High school preparation.** College-preparatory program recommended. 15 units required. Required units include English 4, mathematics 3, social studies 3, science 3 (laboratory 1) and foreign language 2. Math requirement includes 2 algebra and 1 geometry, trigonometry, math analysis, or calculus. Social studies requirement includes 1 world history, 1 state history or civics, and 1 U.S. history.

**2009-2010 Annual costs.** Tuition/fees: $24,350. Room/board: $7,160. Books/supplies: $1,500. Personal expenses: $1,000.

**2009-2010 Financial aid. Need-based:** Average need met was 91%. Average scholarship/grant was $17,731; average loan $3,826. 80% of total undergraduate aid awarded as scholarships/grants, 20% as loans/jobs. **Non-need-based:** Scholarships awarded for academics, alumni affiliation, art, athletics, leadership, music/drama, religious affiliation, ROTC, state residency.

**Application procedures. Admission:** Priority date 3/30; deadline 8/21 (postmark date). $40 fee, may be waived for applicants with need. Admission notification on a rolling basis beginning on or about 10/15. Must reply by May 1 or within 2 week(s) if notified thereafter. **Financial aid:** Priority date 3/1, closing date 6/30. FAFSA, institutional form required. Applicants notified on a rolling basis starting 2/20; must reply within 2 week(s) of notification.

**Academics. Special study options:** Accelerated study, combined bachelor's/graduate degree, cooperative education, distance learning, double major, dual enrollment of high school students, ESL, exchange student, external degree, honors, independent study, internships, liberal arts/career combination, New York semester, student-designed major, study abroad, teacher certification program, Washington semester. **Credit/placement by examination:** AP, CLEP, IB, SAT, ACT, institutional tests. 30 credit hours maximum toward bachelor's degree. **Support services:** Learning center, reduced course load, study skills assistance, tutoring, writing center.

**Majors. Area/ethnic studies:** American. **Biology:** General, biochemistry, biomedical sciences, cell/histology. **Business:** General, accounting, business admin, finance, international, management information systems, management science, managerial economics, marketing. **Communications:** Advertising, broadcast journalism, journalism, media studies, public relations, radio/tv. **Computer sciences:** General, computer science. **Education:** General, art, business, early childhood, elementary, English, foreign languages, French, German, health, history, mathematics, Montessori teacher, music, physical, science, secondary, social studies, Spanish, speech. **Foreign languages:** French, German, Spanish. **Health:** Athletic training, nursing (RN), predental, premedicine, prepharmacy, preveterinary. **History:** General. **Interdisciplinary:** Biological/physical sciences. **Legal studies:** Prelaw. **Liberal arts:** Arts/sciences, humanities. **Math:** General. **Parks/recreation:** Health/fitness. **Philosophy/religion:** Philosophy, religion. **Physical sciences:** Chemistry, physics. **Protective services:** Corrections, law enforcement admin, police science. **Psychology:** General. **Public administration:** Social work. **Social sciences:** Economics, political science, sociology. **Theology:** Bible, religious ed, sacred music, youth ministry. **Visual/performing arts:** General, acting, art, art history/conservation, arts management, cinematography, dance, dramatic, film/cinema, graphic design, music management, music performance, music theory/composition, photography, piano/organ, stringed instruments, studio arts, theater arts management, theater design, voice/opera. **Other:** Entertainment business, Justice studies, Kinesiology & exercise studies, World religions.

**Most popular majors.** Business/marketing 13%, health sciences 20%, liberal arts 26%, visual/performing arts 20%.

**Computing on campus.** 489 workstations in dormitories, library, computer center, student center. Dormitories wired for high-speed internet access and linked to campus network. Commuter students can connect to campus network. Online course registration, online library, helpline, repair service, student web hosting, wireless network available.

**Student life. Freshman orientation:** Mandatory, $50 fee. Preregistration for classes offered. **Housing:** Guaranteed on-campus for all undergraduates. Coed dorms, single-sex dorms, apartments, fraternity/sorority housing, wellness housing available. $100 deposit. Learning communities available. **Activities:** Bands, campus ministries, choral groups, dance, drama, international student organizations, literary magazine, music ensembles, musical theater, opera, student government, student newspaper, symphony orchestra, TV station, Kappa Phi, Sigma Theta Epsilon, association for people of color, United Methodist student fellowship, students of arts management, Alpha Phi sorority, Gamma Phi Beta sorority, Lambda Chi Alpha fraternity, Kappa Sigma fraternity.

**Athletics.** NAIA. **Intercollegiate:** Baseball M, basketball, cheerleading, cross-country, golf, soccer, softball W, track and field, volleyball W, wrestling. **Intramural:** Basketball, fencing, football (non-tackle) M, golf, softball, table tennis, volleyball. **Team name:** Stars.

**Student services.** Adult student services, chaplain/spiritual director, career counseling, services for economically disadvantaged, student employment services, financial aid counseling, health services, minority student services, personal counseling, placement for graduates, veterans' counselor. **Physically disabled:** Services for visually, hearing impaired.

**Contact.** E-mail: uadmissions@okcu.edu
Phone: (405) 208-5050 Toll-free number: (800) 633-7242
Fax: (405) 208-5916
Eduardo Prieto, Vice President of Enrollment Services, Oklahoma City University, 2501 North Blackwelder Avenue, Oklahoma City, OK 73106-1493

## Oklahoma Panhandle State University
**Goodwell, Oklahoma**
**www.opsu.edu**                    **CB code: 6571**

- Public 4-year university and liberal arts college
- Residential campus in rural community
- 1,177 degree-seeking undergraduates: 12% part-time, 48% women, 7% African American, 1% Asian American, 15% Hispanic American, 3% Native American, 4% international
- 100% of applicants admitted
- 38% graduate within 6 years

**General.** Founded in 1909. Regionally accredited. **Degrees:** 198 bachelor's, 41 associate awarded. **Location:** 110 miles from Amarillo, Texas, 10 miles from Guymon. **Calendar:** Semester, limited summer session. **Full-time faculty:** 67 total; 31% have terminal degrees, 2% minority, 37% women. **Part-time faculty:** 35 total; 43% women. **Class size:** 73% < 20, 22% 20-39, 2% 40-49, 2% 50-99, less than 1% >100. **Special facilities:** Agronomy experiment station, historical museum, livestock facilities, farming area, rodeo arena, meat lab.

**Freshman class profile.** 318 applied, 318 admitted, 298 enrolled.

| Mid 50% test scores | | | |
|---|---|---|---|
| SAT critical reading: | 370-410 | GPA 3.0-3.49: | 32% |
| SAT math: | 410-490 | GPA 2.0-2.99: | 33% |
| ACT composite: | 17-22 | Out-of-state: | 52% |
| GPA 3.75 or higher: | 18% | Live on campus: | 90% |
| GPA 3.50-3.74: | 12% | International: | 4% |

**Basis for selection.** Secondary school record, test scores and class rank most important. SAT or ACT recommended. Incoming students without ACT, or with score of 19 or below, must take ACCUPLACER test. **Homeschooled:** Transcript of courses and grades required.

**High school preparation.** 15 units required. Required units include English 4, mathematics 3, social studies 2, history 1, science 2 (laboratory 2) and academic electives 3.

**2009-2010 Annual costs.** Tuition/fees: $5,102; $10,442 out-of-state. Room/board: $3,370. Books/supplies: $240.

**2008-2009 Financial aid.** All financial aid based on need.

**Application procedures. Admission:** No deadline. No application fee. Admission notification on a rolling basis. **Financial aid:** Priority date 3/15; no closing date. FAFSA, institutional form required. Applicants notified by 5/1.

**Academics. Special study options:** Cooperative education, distance learning, double major, ESL, independent study, internships, teacher certification program. **Credit/placement by examination:** AP, CLEP, SAT, ACT, institutional tests. 34 credit hours maximum toward associate degree, 60 toward bachelor's. **Support services:** Learning center, reduced course load, remedial instruction, study skills assistance, tutoring, writing center.

**Majors. Agriculture:** Agribusiness operations, agronomy, animal sciences, equine science. **Biology:** General. **Business:** Accounting, business admin. **Computer sciences:** General. **Education:** Agricultural, business, elementary. **Engineering technology:** Industrial. **Health:** Nursing (RN). **History:** General. **Interdisciplinary:** Biological/physical sciences. **Math:** General. **Parks/recreation:** Health/fitness. **Physical sciences:** Chemistry. **Psychology:** General. **Social sciences:** General. **Visual/performing arts:** Art.

**Most popular majors.** Agriculture 18%, biology 14%, business/ marketing 12%, education 8%, parks/recreation 13%, psychology 8%.

**Computing on campus.** 150 workstations in dormitories, library, computer center, student center. Dormitories wired for high-speed internet access. Online library, wireless network available.

**Student life. Freshman orientation:** Mandatory. Preregistration for classes offered. **Housing:** Guaranteed on-campus for freshmen. Single-sex dorms, apartments available. **Activities:** Bands, choral groups, drama, music ensembles, musical theater, radio station, student government, student newspaper, Wesley Foundation, Baptist student union, Church of Christ student center, Circle-K, Newman club, Methodist student center.

**Athletics.** NCAA. **Intercollegiate:** Baseball M, basketball, cheerleading, cross-country, football (tackle) M, golf, softball W, volleyball W. **Intramural:** Basketball, football (non-tackle), golf, soccer, softball, table tennis, volleyball. **Team name:** Aggies.

**Student services.** Adult student services, alcohol/substance abuse counseling, chaplain/spiritual director, career counseling, student employment services, financial aid counseling, health services, minority student services, personal counseling, placement for graduates. **Physically disabled:** Services for visually, speech, hearing impaired.

**Contact.** E-mail: jolie@opsu.edu
Phone: (580) 349-1312 Toll-free number: (800) 664-6778
Fax: (580) 349-1371
Bobby Jenkins, Registrar and Director of Admissions, Oklahoma Panhandle State University, OPSU Admissions, Goodwell, OK 73939-0430

---

## Oklahoma State University

| Stillwater, Oklahoma | |
|---|---|
| http://osu.okstate.edu | CB member |
| | CB code: 6546 |

- Public 4-year university
- Residential campus in small city
- 17,606 degree-seeking undergraduates: 13% part-time, 48% women, 4% African American, 2% Asian American, 3% Hispanic American, 9% Native American, 2% international
- 4,606 degree-seeking graduate students
- 86% of applicants admitted
- SAT or ACT (ACT writing optional) required
- 60% graduate within 6 years

**General.** Founded in 1890. Regionally accredited. Campuses in Oklahoma City, Okmulgee, Tulsa and Center for Health Sciences (includes College of Osteopathic Medicine) at Tulsa. Stillwater campus includes the Center for Veterinary Health Sciences. **Degrees:** 3,833 bachelor's awarded; master's, doctoral, professional offered. **ROTC:** Army, Air Force. **Location:** 65 miles from Tulsa, 65 miles from Oklahoma City. **Calendar:** Semester, extensive summer session. **Full-time faculty:** 999 total; 92% have terminal degrees, 10% minority, 32% women. **Part-time faculty:** 274 total; 29% have terminal degrees, 10% minority, 55% women. **Class size:** 41% < 20, 35% 20-39, 11% 40-49, 9% 50-99, 4% >100. **Special facilities:** Laser research center with 8 laboratories and 30 laser systems, biotechnology and genetic engineering research center, telecommunication center.

**Freshman class profile.** 7,561 applied, 6,537 admitted, 3,148 enrolled.

| Mid 50% test scores | | | |
|---|---|---|---|
| SAT critical reading: | 480-600 | Rank in top quarter: | 55% |
| SAT math: | 500-640 | Rank in top tenth: | 27% |
| ACT composite: | 22-27 | Return as sophomores: | 79% |
| GPA 3.75 or higher: | 36% | Out-of-state: | 26% |
| GPA 3.50-3.74: | 21% | Live on campus: | 91% |
| GPA 3.0-3.49: | 33% | International: | 1% |
| GPA 2.0-2.99: | 10% | Fraternities: | 24% |
| | | Sororities: | 30% |

**Basis for selection.** Applicants must have 3.0 GPA and rank in top 33% of class, or 24 ACT/1090 SAT (exclusive of Writing), or 3.0 GPA in 15 required curricular units and 21 ACT/980 SAT(exclusive of Writing), or 3.0 GPA in 15 required curricular units, or 22 ACT/1020 SAT and answer 7 undergraduate application questions. Early application encouraged. Test scores must be received no later than Friday before classes begin for fall-term admission. Interview recommended for academically borderline students.

**High school preparation.** College-preparatory program required. 15 units required; 18 recommended. Required and recommended units include English 4, mathematics 3, social studies 2, history 1, science 2 (laboratory 2), foreign language 2, computer science 1 and academic electives 3.

**2009-2010 Annual costs.** Tuition/fees: $6,887; $17,241 out-of-state. Room/ board: $6,258. Books/supplies: $980. Personal expenses: $2,440.

**2008-2009 Financial aid. Need-based:** 2,018 full-time freshmen applied for aid; 1,484 were judged to have need; 1,444 of these received aid. Average need met was 72%. Average scholarship/grant was $5,866; average loan $3,145. 59% of total undergraduate aid awarded as scholarships/grants, 41% as loans/jobs. **Non-need-based:** Awarded to 6,915 full-time undergraduates, including 1,653 freshmen. Scholarships awarded for academics, alumni affiliation, art, athletics, leadership, minority status, music/drama, ROTC, state residency.

**Application procedures. Admission:** No deadline. $40 fee, may be waived for applicants with need. Admission notification on a rolling basis. Deferred admission allowed based on military deployments. **Financial aid:** Priority date 2/1; no closing date. FAFSA required. Applicants notified on a rolling basis starting 10/1; must reply within 4 week(s) of notification.

**Academics. Special study options:** Accelerated study, combined bachelor's/ graduate degree, cross-registration, distance learning, double major, dual enrollment of high school students, ESL, exchange student, honors, independent study, internships, semester at sea, student-designed major, study abroad, teacher certification program, Washington semester. **Credit/placement by examination:** AP, CLEP, IB, SAT, ACT. Maximum number of credit hours towards degree is subject to university "residence credit" policy. **Support services:** Learning center, pre-admission summer program, reduced course load, remedial instruction, study skills assistance, tutoring, writing center.

**Honors college/program.** 27 ACT/1220 SAT (exclusive of Writing) and 3.75 GPA required.

**Majors. Agriculture:** Animal sciences, business, communications, economics, food science, horticultural science, landscaping, soil science. **Architecture:** Architecture, landscape. **Area/ethnic studies:** American. **Biology:** General, biochemistry, botany, entomology, microbiology, physiology, zoology. **Business:** Accounting, business admin, entrepreneurial studies, finance, hospitality admin, international, management information systems, managerial economics, marketing. **Communications:** Journalism. **Computer sciences:** General. **Conservation:** Environmental science, forestry. **Education:** General, agricultural, elementary, music, physical, secondary, voc/tech. **Engineering:** Aerospace, agricultural, architectural, chemical, civil, computer, electrical, industrial, mechanical. **Engineering technology:** Construction, electrical, mechanical. **Family/consumer sciences:** Family studies, food/ nutrition, housing. **Foreign languages:** French, German, Russian, Spanish. **Health:** Athletic training, public health ed, speech pathology. **History:** General. **Liberal arts:** Arts/sciences. **Math:** General, statistics. **Parks/ recreation:** General. **Philosophy/religion:** Philosophy. **Physical sciences:** Chemistry, geology, physics. **Protective services:** Fire safety technology. **Psychology:** General. **Social sciences:** Economics, geography, political science, sociology. **Transportation:** Aviation. **Visual/performing arts:** Art, dramatic.

**Most popular majors.** Agriculture 7%, business/marketing 29%, education 7%, engineering/engineering technologies 10%, family/consumer sciences 8%.

**Computing on campus.** Dormitories wired for high-speed internet access and linked to campus network. Commuter students can connect to campus network. Online course registration, online library, helpline, repair service, wireless network available.

**Student life. Freshman orientation:** Mandatory. Preregistration for classes offered. One-day programs in June. Additional program held week before classes begin each fall semester for a fee. **Housing:** Guaranteed on-campus for freshmen. Coed dorms, single-sex dorms, special housing for disabled, apartments, fraternity/sorority housing, wellness housing available. $150 fully refundable deposit. **Activities:** Bands, campus ministries, choral groups, dance, drama, international student organizations, literary magazine, music ensembles, musical theater, opera, radio station, student government, student newspaper, symphony orchestra, TV station, Campus Crusade for Christ, Flying Aggies, rodeo club, Young Democrats, Young Republicans, fire protection society, Alpha Pi Omega, National Organization for Women, African American student association, Hispanic student association.

**Athletics.** NCAA. **Intercollegiate:** Baseball M, basketball, cross-country, equestrian W, football (tackle) M, golf, soccer W, softball W, tennis, track and field, wrestling M. **Intramural:** Archery, badminton, basketball, bowling, cross-country, football (tackle), golf, racquetball, soccer, softball, squash, swimming, table tennis, tennis, track and field, volleyball, water polo, weight lifting, wrestling M. **Team name:** Cowboys, Cowgirls.

**Student services.** Adult student services, alcohol/substance abuse counseling, career counseling, student employment services, financial aid counseling, health services, legal services, minority student services, personal counseling, placement for graduates, veterans' counselor, women's services. **Physically disabled:** Services for visually, speech, hearing impaired.

**Contact.** E-mail: admissions@okstate.edu
Phone: (405) 744-5358 Toll-free number: (800) 233-5019 ext. 1
Fax: (405) 744-7092
Christine Crenshaw, Director of Undergraduate Admissions, Oklahoma State University, 219 Student Union, Stillwater, OK 74078

---

## Oklahoma Wesleyan University
**Bartlesville, Oklahoma**                   CB member
www.okwu.edu                                 CB code: 6135

- Private 4-year university and liberal arts college affiliated with Wesleyan Church
- Residential campus in large town
- 1,031 degree-seeking undergraduates: 56% part-time, 62% women
- 59 degree-seeking graduate students
- SAT or ACT (ACT writing optional) required
- 36% graduate within 6 years

**General.** Founded in 1909. Regionally accredited. **Degrees:** 302 bachelor's, 58 associate awarded; master's offered. **Location:** 40 miles from Tulsa. **Calendar:** Differs by program, limited summer session. **Full-time faculty:** 29 total; 17% have terminal degrees, 3% minority, 28% women. **Part-time faculty:** 39 total; 67% women. **Class size:** 81% < 20, 18% 20-39, 1% 40-49. **Special facilities:** Historic mansion, fine arts center, city bike path.

**Freshman class profile.**

| Mid 50% test scores | | | |
|---|---|---|---|
| SAT critical reading: | 430-520 | GPA 3.0-3.49: | 26% |
| SAT math: | 420-550 | GPA 2.0-2.99: | 12% |
| ACT composite: | 19-25 | End year in good standing: | 17% |
| GPA 3.75 or higher: | 49% | Return as sophomores: | 65% |
| GPA 3.50-3.74: | 13% | Out-of-state: | 49% |
| | | Live on campus: | 81% |

**Basis for selection.** In addition to required high school study, students must fulfill 2 of the following: rank in top half of class, 2.0 GPA, 18 ACT. **Homeschooled:** Statement describing homeschool structure and mission, transcript of courses and grades required.

**High school preparation.** 15 units required. Required units include English 4, mathematics 2, social studies 2, science 1 (laboratory 1).

**2009-2010 Annual costs.** Tuition/fees: $17,770. Room/board: $6,288.

**2009-2010 Financial aid. Need-based:** 118 full-time freshmen applied for aid; 118 were judged to have need; 118 of these received aid. Average need met was 53%. Average scholarship/grant was $3,300; average loan $2,731. 54% of total undergraduate aid awarded as scholarships/grants, 46% as loans/jobs. **Non-need-based:** Scholarships awarded for academics, alumni affiliation, athletics, leadership, music/drama, religious affiliation, state residency.

**Application procedures. Admission:** No deadline. $25 fee, may be waived for applicants with need, free for online applicants. Admission notification on a rolling basis. Students must be accepted prior to beginning of classes. **Financial aid:** Priority date 4/1; no closing date. FAFSA, institutional form required. Applicants notified on a rolling basis starting 4/1; must reply by 5/1 or within 2 week(s) of notification.

---

**Academics. Special study options:** Distance learning, double major, dual enrollment of high school students, independent study, internships, student-designed major, study abroad, teacher certification program, Washington semester. **Credit/placement by examination:** AP, CLEP, SAT, ACT, institutional tests. 30 credit hours maximum toward associate degree, 36 toward bachelor's. **Support services:** Learning center, reduced course load, remedial instruction, study skills assistance, tutoring, writing center.

**Majors. Biology:** General. **Business:** General, business admin. **Communications:** General. **Computer sciences:** General, computer science. **Education:** Business, elementary, English, mathematics, music, physical, science, social studies. **History:** General. **Interdisciplinary:** Behavioral sciences. **Math:** General. **Parks/recreation:** Exercise sciences. **Philosophy/religion:** Christian. **Physical sciences:** Chemistry. **Psychology:** General. **Social sciences:** General, political science. **Theology:** Bible, missionary, sacred music, theology.

**Computing on campus.** 40 workstations in library, computer center, student center. Dormitories wired for high-speed internet access and linked to campus network. Online course registration, online library, helpline, repair service, wireless network available.

**Student life. Freshman orientation:** Mandatory, $100 fee. Preregistration for classes offered. **Policies:** Religious observance required. **Housing:** Guaranteed on-campus for all undergraduates. Single-sex dorms, apartments available. $200 fully refundable deposit. **Activities:** Bands, campus ministries, choral groups, music ensembles, student government, student newspaper, campus missionary fellowship, theology fellowship, Fellowship of Christian Athletes, Operation Saturation, Sudan fellowship, College Republicans.

**Athletics.** NAIA, NCCAA. **Intercollegiate:** Baseball M, basketball, cheerleading M, cross-country, golf M, soccer, tennis, track and field, volleyball W. **Intramural:** Basketball, football (non-tackle), racquetball, softball, table tennis, volleyball. **Team name:** Eagles.

**Student services.** Adult student services, chaplain/spiritual director, career counseling, student employment services, financial aid counseling, health services, placement for graduates, veterans' counselor.

**Contact.** E-mail: admissions@okwu.edu
Phone: (918) 335-6219 Toll-free number: (800) 468-6292
Fax: (918) 335-6229
John Means, Vice President of Enrollment Services, Oklahoma Wesleyan University, 2201 Silver Lake Road, Bartlesville, OK 74006

---

## Oral Roberts University
**Tulsa, Oklahoma**                          CB member
www.oru.edu                                  CB code: 6552

- Private 4-year university and liberal arts college affiliated with nondenominational tradition
- Residential campus in large city
- 2,558 degree-seeking undergraduates: 9% part-time, 58% women
- 365 graduate students
- 73% of applicants admitted
- SAT or ACT (ACT writing optional), application essay required
- 53% graduate within 6 years

**General.** Founded in 1965. Regionally accredited. Integrated math and science academy sponsored by Oklahoma State Regents for Higher Education. **Degrees:** 556 bachelor's awarded; master's, doctoral offered. **ROTC:** Air Force. **Location:** 7 miles from downtown. **Calendar:** Semester, limited summer session. **Full-time faculty:** 186 total; 64% have terminal degrees, 12% minority, 41% women. **Part-time faculty:** 105 total; 17% have terminal degrees, 17% minority, 49% women. **Class size:** 66% < 20, 27% 20-39, 3% 40-49, 5% 50-99, less than 1% >100. **Special facilities:** Prayer tower, mineralogical museum.

**Freshman class profile.** 1,127 applied, 819 admitted, 481 enrolled.

| Mid 50% test scores | | | |
|---|---|---|---|
| SAT critical reading: | 470-590 | GPA 2.0-2.99: | 24% |
| SAT math: | 460-570 | Rank in top quarter: | 45% |
| ACT composite: | 20-26 | Rank in top tenth: | 23% |
| GPA 3.75 or higher: | 31% | Return as sophomores: | 72% |
| GPA 3.50-3.74: | 16% | Out-of-state: | 68% |
| GPA 3.0-3.49: | 29% | Live on campus: | 75% |

**Basis for selection.** Academic record, test scores, personal essay, minister's recommendation, other recommendations, extracurricular activities considered. Students must provide immunization records. Interview recommended for all; audition required for music program; portfolio recommended for art program. **Homeschooled:** Under special circumstances, applicants may be required to submit additional curricular information and/or proof of high school equivalency.

**High school preparation.** College-preparatory program recommended. 16 units recommended. Recommended units include English 4, mathematics 2, social studies 2, science 1 (laboratory 1), foreign language 2 and academic electives 4. Students matriculating in bachelor of science program may substitute additional math units for foreign language.

**2009-2010 Annual costs.** Tuition/fees: $19,106. Room/board: $7,916. Books/supplies: $1,500. Personal expenses: $1,500.

**2008-2009 Financial aid. Need-based:** Average need met was 86%. Average scholarship/grant was $9,759; average loan $6,534. 18% of total undergraduate aid awarded as scholarships/grants, 82% as loans/jobs. **Non-need-based:** Awarded to 1,237 full-time undergraduates, including 168 freshmen. Scholarships awarded for academics, alumni affiliation, art, athletics, leadership, music/drama.

**Application procedures. Admission:** Priority date 11/15; no deadline. $35 fee, may be waived for applicants with need. Admission notification on a rolling basis. **Financial aid:** Priority date 3/15; no closing date. FAFSA required. Must reply by 7/15.

**Academics. Special study options:** Accelerated study, combined bachelor's/graduate degree, distance learning, double major, dual enrollment of high school students, ESL, external degree, honors, independent study, internships, liberal arts/career combination, student-designed major, study abroad, teacher certification program, Washington semester, weekend college. **Credit/placement by examination:** AP, CLEP, institutional tests. 30 credit hours maximum toward associate degree, 30 toward bachelor's. **Support services:** Learning center, reduced course load, remedial instruction, study skills assistance, tutoring.

**Majors. Biology:** General, biochemistry. **Business:** Accounting, business admin, finance, international, international marketing, management information systems, management science, marketing, organizational behavior. **Communications:** General. **Computer sciences:** General, computer science. **Education:** Art, business, early childhood, elementary, English, foreign languages, health, mathematics, music, physical, science, social studies, Spanish, special. **Engineering:** General, biomedical, computer, electrical, mechanical, physics. **Foreign languages:** French, German, Spanish. **Health:** Clinical lab science, nursing (RN). **History:** General. **Liberal arts:** Arts/sciences. **Math:** General. **Parks/recreation:** Exercise sciences, facilities management, health/fitness. **Physical sciences:** Chemistry, physics. **Psychology:** General. **Public administration:** Social work. **Social sciences:** International relations, political science. **Theology:** Bible, missionary, pastoral counseling, religious ed, sacred music, theology. **Visual/performing arts:** Acting, art, commercial/advertising art, dance, design, dramatic, music performance, music theory/composition, piano/organ, studio arts, theater design, voice/opera.

**Most popular majors.** Business/marketing 25%, communications/journalism 12%, education 9%, health sciences 6%, psychology 6%, theological studies 12%, visual/performing arts 6%.

**Computing on campus.** 382 workstations in library, computer center. Dormitories linked to campus network. Commuter students can connect to campus network. Online course registration, online library, wireless network available.

**Student life. Freshman orientation:** Mandatory. Preregistration for classes offered. **Policies:** Single undergraduate students under 25 years of age must live in university housing or with parents. Religious observance required. **Housing:** Guaranteed on-campus for all undergraduates. Single-sex dorms available. $125 nonrefundable deposit, deadline 8/8. **Activities:** Bands, campus ministries, choral groups, dance, drama, international student organizations, music ensembles, Model UN, musical theater, radio station, student government, student newspaper, TV station, community outreach, missions club, Young Republicans, Young Democrats, student activist society, Model United Nations.

**Athletics.** NCAA. **Intercollegiate:** Baseball M, basketball, cross-country, golf, soccer, tennis, track and field, volleyball W. **Intramural:** Badminton, basketball, bowling, cross-country, football (non-tackle), golf, racquetball, softball, swimming, table tennis, tennis, volleyball, wrestling M. **Team name:** Golden Eagles.

**Student services.** Chaplain/spiritual director, career counseling, student employment services, financial aid counseling, health services, personal counseling, placement for graduates, veterans' counselor. **Physically disabled:** Services for visually, speech, hearing impaired.

**Contact.** E-mail: admissions@oru.edu
Phone: (918) 496-6518 Toll-free number: (800) 678-8876
Fax: (918) 495-6222
Chris Belcher, Director of Admissions, Oral Roberts University, 7777 South Lewis Avenue, Tulsa, OK 74171

## Rogers State University
**Claremore, Oklahoma**
www.rsu.edu                                    CB code: 6545

- Public 4-year university
- Commuter campus in large town
- 4,115 degree-seeking undergraduates: 37% part-time, 63% women, 30% African American, 3% Asian American, 2% Hispanic American, 2% Native American, 1% international
- 58% of applicants admitted

**General.** Founded in 1909. Regionally accredited. **Degrees:** 189 bachelor's, 211 associate awarded. **Location:** 25 miles from Tulsa. **Calendar:** Semester, extensive summer session. **Full-time faculty:** 104 total; 64% have terminal degrees, 10% minority, 42% women. **Part-time faculty:** 141 total; 13% have terminal degrees, 12% minority, 65% women. **Class size:** 38% < 20, 59% 20-39, 3% 40-49, less than 1% 50-99. **Special facilities:** Conservation education reserve, Oklahoma military academy museum, innovation center.

**Freshman class profile.** 1,702 applied, 981 admitted, 849 enrolled.

| Mid 50% test scores | | Rank in top tenth: | 40% |
|---|---|---|---|
| ACT composite: | 17-22 | End year in good standing: | 67% |
| GPA 3.75 or higher: | 15% | Return as sophomores: | 54% |
| GPA 3.50-3.74: | 14% | Out-of-state: | 3% |
| GPA 3.0-3.49: | 30% | Live on campus: | 10% |
| GPA 2.0-2.99: | 37% | Fraternities: | 1% |
| Rank in top quarter: | 54% | Sororities: | 1% |

**Basis for selection.** Bachelor degree programs require 20 ACT and no curricular deficiencies. Open admission for associate degree programs. ACT recommended. Essay required for returning suspension students only.

**High school preparation.** College-preparatory program recommended. 15 units required; 19 recommended. Required and recommended units include English 4, mathematics 3-4, social studies 1, history 2, science 2-3 (laboratory 2-3), foreign language 2, computer science 1, visual/performing arts 2 and academic electives 3. Math should include algebra I and II; 1 computer science also recommended; history should include 1 unit of U.S. history and 1 of citizenship (government, geography, etc.).

**2009-2010 Annual costs.** Tuition/fees: $4,277; $9,734 out-of-state. Apartment-style housing. Room/board: $7,095. Books/supplies: $1,590. Personal expenses: $1,848.

**2009-2010 Financial aid. Need-based:** 677 full-time freshmen applied for aid; 472 were judged to have need; 470 of these received aid. Average need met was 27%. Average scholarship/grant was $5,049; average loan $2,962. 48% of total undergraduate aid awarded as scholarships/grants, 52% as loans/jobs. **Non-need-based:** Awarded to 66 full-time undergraduates, including 222 freshmen. Scholarships awarded for academics, art, athletics, leadership, music/drama, state residency.

**Application procedures. Admission:** No deadline. No application fee. Admission notification on a rolling basis beginning on or about 2/1. **Financial aid:** Priority date 6/1; no closing date. FAFSA, institutional form required. Applicants notified on a rolling basis starting 4/1; must reply within 1 week(s) of notification.

**Academics. Special study options:** Cooperative education, distance learning, honors, independent study, internships, study abroad, Washington semester. **Credit/placement by examination:** AP, CLEP, IB, SAT, ACT, institutional tests. 30 credit hours maximum toward associate degree, 45 toward bachelor's. **Support services:** Learning center, reduced course load, remedial instruction, study skills assistance, tutoring, writing center.

**Majors. Biology:** General. **Business:** Business admin, nonprofit/public. **Communications:** General. **Computer sciences:** General, computer graphics. **Health:** Nursing (RN). **Liberal arts:** Arts/sciences. **Parks/recreation:** Sports admin. **Protective services:** Law enforcement admin. **Psychology:** Community. **Public administration:** General. **Social sciences:** General. **Visual/performing arts:** General. **Other:** Applied technology, Business information technology.

**Most popular majors.** Biology 12%, business/marketing 36%, engineering/engineering technologies 16%, security/protective services 6%, social sciences 13%.

**Computing on campus.** 208 workstations in dormitories, library, student center. Dormitories wired for high-speed internet access and linked to campus network. Online library, helpline, wireless network available.

**Student life. Freshman orientation:** Available. Preregistration for classes offered. **Housing:** Coed dorms, special housing for disabled, apartments, wellness housing available. $200 fully refundable deposit. **Activities:** Jazz band, campus ministries, choral groups, drama, international student organizations, literary magazine, radio station, student government, student newspaper, TV station, Native American student association, Baptist collegiate ministry, student art association, criminal justice society, student nursing association, Students in Free Enterprise.

**Athletics.** NAIA. **Intercollegiate:** Baseball M, basketball, cheerleading, golf, rodeo, soccer, softball W. **Intramural:** Basketball, football (non-tackle), soccer, softball, volleyball. **Team name:** Hillcats.

**Student services.** Adult student services, alcohol/substance abuse counseling, career counseling, services for economically disadvantaged, student employment services, financial aid counseling, health services, on-campus daycare, personal counseling, veterans' counselor. **Physically disabled:** Services for visually, speech, hearing impaired. **Learning disabled:** Comprehensive services available.

**Contact.** E-mail: admissions@rsu.edu
Phone: (918) 343-7546 Toll-free number: (800) 256-7511
Fax: (918) 343-7595
Julie Rampey, Director of Admissions, Rogers State University, 1701 West Will Rogers Boulevard, Claremore, OK 74017

## St. Gregory's University
### Shawnee, Oklahoma
**www.stgregorys.edu**                  CB code: 6621

- Private 4-year university and liberal arts college affiliated with Roman Catholic Church
- Residential campus in large town
- 649 degree-seeking undergraduates: 49% part-time, 61% women
- 36 degree-seeking graduate students
- 61% of applicants admitted
- SAT or ACT (ACT writing optional), application essay required

**General.** Founded in 1875. Regionally accredited. Roman Catholic and Benedictine tradition. **Degrees:** 117 bachelor's, 37 associate awarded; master's offered. **ROTC:** Air Force. **Location:** 30 miles from Oklahoma City. **Calendar:** Semester, limited summer session. **Full-time faculty:** 39 total; 62% have terminal degrees, 5% minority, 46% women. **Part-time faculty:** 88 total; 23% have terminal degrees, 6% minority, 52% women. **Class size:** 93% < 20, 7% 20-39. **Special facilities:** Benedictine abbey, art museum.

**Freshman class profile.** 975 applied, 598 admitted, 90 enrolled.

**Basis for selection.** Core classes, GPA most important; test scores, class rank important. Interview required for students admitted on probation; audition required for dance, drama, and choral scholarships; portfolio required for art scholarships. **Homeschooled:** Interview required. **Learning Disabled:** Students with need beyond ADA standards may apply to Partners in Learning Program. Additional fee of approximately $7,000 required if admitted.

**High school preparation.** 17 units recommended. Recommended units include English 4, mathematics 3, social studies 2, history 2, science 2 (laboratory 2) and foreign language 2.

**2009-2010 Annual costs.** Tuition/fees: $16,294. Room/board: $6,404. Books/supplies: $900. Personal expenses: $2,000.

**2008-2009 Financial aid. Non-need-based:** Scholarships awarded for academics, alumni affiliation, art, athletics, job skills, leadership, music/drama, religious affiliation.

**Application procedures. Admission:** Priority date 8/1; no deadline. $25 fee, may be waived for applicants with need. Admission notification on a rolling basis. **Financial aid:** Priority date 4/1; no closing date. FAFSA, institutional form required. Applicants notified on a rolling basis starting 2/15; must reply within 3 week(s) of notification.

**Academics.** Discussion-based seminars on Western and Catholic intellectual traditions required of all freshmen and sophomore students. Special accelerated programs for non-traditional students in Shawnee, Oklahoma City, and Tulsa. **Special study options:** Accelerated study, cooperative education, double major, ESL, honors, independent study, internships, student-designed major, study abroad, teacher certification program. **Credit/placement by examination:** AP, CLEP, IB, SAT, ACT. 12 credit hours

maximum toward associate degree, 30 toward bachelor's. Course proficiency exams available in areas where no CLEP exams offered. **Support services:** Remedial instruction, study skills assistance, tutoring.

**Majors. Biology:** General, biomedical sciences. **Business:** Business admin. **Communications:** General. **Conservation:** General. **Education:** General, elementary, secondary. **History:** General. **Interdisciplinary:** Biological/physical sciences, natural sciences. **Liberal arts:** Arts/sciences, humanities. **Math:** General. **Parks/recreation:** Exercise sciences. **Protective services:** Criminal justice. **Psychology:** General. **Social sciences:** General, political science, sociology. **Theology:** Theology. **Visual/performing arts:** General, art, dance. **Other:** Fitness and health promotion.

**Most popular majors.** Biology 8%, business/marketing 59%, family/consumer sciences 13%, social sciences 8%.

**Computing on campus.** 60 workstations in dormitories, library, computer center, student center. Dormitories wired for high-speed internet access and linked to campus network. Commuter students can connect to campus network. Online library, helpline, repair service, student web hosting, wireless network available.

**Student life. Freshman orientation:** Mandatory. Preregistration for classes offered. Three-day program held prior to start of fall term, plus evenings in first week of fall semester. **Policies:** Smoke-free; alcohol/drug-free; on-campus residency required under age 22. **Housing:** Guaranteed on-campus for freshmen. Single-sex dorms, wellness housing available. $100 fully refundable deposit. **Activities:** Jazz band, campus ministries, choral groups, dance, drama, international student organizations, student government, Knights of Columbus, Fellowship of Christian Athletes, history club, student alumni council, Students in Free Enterprise, Hispanic awareness student association, human rights action committee, pro-life team.

**Athletics.** NAIA. **Intercollegiate:** Baseball M, basketball, soccer, softball W, volleyball W. **Intramural:** Basketball, football (non-tackle), football (tackle) M, racquetball, soccer, softball, table tennis, tennis, volleyball. **Team name:** Cavaliers.

**Student services.** Adult student services, alcohol/substance abuse counseling, chaplain/spiritual director, career counseling, services for economically disadvantaged, student employment services, financial aid counseling, minority student services, personal counseling, placement for graduates, veterans' counselor. **Learning disabled:** Comprehensive services available.

**Contact.** E-mail: admissions@stgregorys.edu
Phone: (405) 878-5444 Toll-free number: (888) 784-7347
Fax: (405) 878-5198
Director of Admissions, St. Gregory's University, 1900 West MacArthur Drive, Shawnee, OK 74804

## Southeastern Oklahoma State University
### Durant, Oklahoma
**www.sosu.edu**                  CB code: 6657

- Public 4-year liberal arts and teachers college
- Commuter campus in large town
- 3,730 degree-seeking undergraduates: 21% part-time, 54% women
- 360 degree-seeking graduate students
- 82% of applicants admitted
- SAT or ACT (ACT writing optional) required

**General.** Founded in 1909. Regionally accredited. Degree programs offered through satellite campus at Idabel and Higher Education Centers at Ardmore, McAlester, Tinker Air Force Base, Oklahoma City Community College, and Grayson County College. **Degrees:** 627 bachelor's awarded; master's offered. **Location:** 90 miles from Dallas. **Calendar:** Semester, extensive summer session. **Full-time faculty:** 143 total; 76% have terminal degrees, 38% minority, 41% women. **Part-time faculty:** 104 total; 17% have terminal degrees, 17% minority, 49% women. **Class size:** 47% < 20, 43% 20-39, 6% 40-49, 4% 50-99, less than 1% >100. **Special facilities:** Herbarium, equestrian facilities.

**Freshman class profile.** 1,083 applied, 890 admitted, 669 enrolled.

| Mid 50% test scores | | Rank in top quarter: | 43% |
|---|---|---|---|
| ACT composite: | 18-23 | Rank in top tenth: | 15% |
| GPA 3.75 or higher: | 20% | Out-of-state: | 24% |
| GPA 3.50-3.74: | 18% | Live on campus: | 57% |
| GPA 3.0-3.49: | 35% | Fraternities: | 1% |
| GPA 2.0-2.99: | 25% | Sororities: | 1% |

**Basis for selection.** High school transcript and test scores important. Must have 2.7 GPA and rank in top half of class, 20 ACT or 940 SAT (exclusive of Writing), score in top half of applicants on ACT scores, or attain 2.7 GPA in 15 core units. Audition required for drama, music programs. Interview required for alternative admissions. **Homeschooled:** 20 ACT required.

**High school preparation.** College-preparatory program recommended. 15 units required. Required and recommended units include English 4, mathematics 3, social studies 1, history 3, science 2 (laboratory 2), foreign language 1, computer science 1 and academic electives 3. 1 citizenship required.

**2009-2010 Annual costs.** Tuition/fees: $4,416; $10,887 out-of-state. Room/board: $4,900. Books/supplies: $800. Personal expenses: $1,447.

**2008-2009 Financial aid. Need-based:** 449 full-time freshmen applied for aid; 384 were judged to have need; 378 of these received aid. Average need met was 11%. Average scholarship/grant was $1,225; average loan $1,321. 60% of total undergraduate aid awarded as scholarships/grants, 40% as loans/jobs. **Non-need-based:** Awarded to 767 full-time undergraduates, including 223 freshmen. Scholarships awarded for academics, alumni affiliation, art, athletics, job skills, leadership, minority status, music/drama, state residency.

**Application procedures. Admission:** No deadline. $20 fee. Admission notification on a rolling basis. Open admission for adults over 21. **Financial aid:** Priority date 3/1; no closing date. FAFSA, institutional form required. Applicants notified on a rolling basis starting 4/15; must reply within 2 week(s) of notification.

**Academics.** Programs in aviation, ecology, energy, health-related sciences, and criminology. **Special study options:** Combined bachelor's/graduate degree, distance learning, double major, honors, independent study, internships, teacher certification program. **Credit/placement by examination:** AP, CLEP, IB, SAT, ACT, institutional tests. 60 credit hours maximum toward bachelor's degree. **Support services:** Learning center, pre-admission summer program, reduced course load, remedial instruction, study skills assistance, tutoring, writing center.

**Majors. Biology:** General, biotechnology. **Business:** Accounting, business admin, finance, management science, marketing. **Communications:** General. **Computer sciences:** General, information systems. **Conservation:** General. **Education:** Art, elementary, English, mathematics, music, physical, science, secondary, social studies, Spanish, special. **Engineering:** Aerospace. **Engineering technology:** Occupational safety. **Foreign languages:** Spanish. **History:** General. **Math:** General. **Mechanic/repair:** Aircraft. **Parks/recreation:** General. **Physical sciences:** Chemistry. **Protective services:** Criminal justice. **Psychology:** General. **Social sciences:** Political science, sociology. **Transportation:** Airline/commercial pilot. **Visual/performing arts:** Art, dramatic, graphic design, music performance.

**Most popular majors.** Biology 7%, business/marketing 9%, communications/journalism 8%, education 20%, engineering/engineering technologies 10%, liberal arts 12%, parks/recreation 6%, physical sciences 6%, trade and industry 7%.

**Computing on campus.** 2,138 workstations in dormitories, library, computer center, student center. Dormitories wired for high-speed internet access and linked to campus network. Commuter students can connect to campus network. Online course registration, online library, helpline, student web hosting, wireless network available.

**Student life. Freshman orientation:** Available, $20 fee. Preregistration for classes offered. **Policies:** No alcohol at university events on/off campus. **Housing:** Coed dorms, single-sex dorms, special housing for disabled available. $100 nonrefundable deposit. **Activities:** Bands, campus ministries, choral groups, dance, drama, international student organizations, literary magazine, music ensembles, musical theater, opera, radio station, student government, student newspaper, black American society, Wesley center, student Bible center, Chi Alpha, Young Democrats, College Republicans, Muslim student association.

**Athletics.** NCAA. **Intercollegiate:** Baseball M, basketball, cross-country W, football (tackle) M, golf M, rodeo, softball W, tennis, volleyball W. **Intramural:** Basketball, bowling, football (non-tackle), football (tackle) M, rodeo, soccer, softball, volleyball W. **Team name:** Savage Storm.

**Student services.** Adult student services, alcohol/substance abuse counseling, chaplain/spiritual director, career counseling, student employment services, financial aid counseling, health services, minority student services, personal counseling, placement for graduates, veterans' counselor. **Physically disabled:** Services for visually, speech, hearing impaired.

**Contact.** E-mail: admissions@se.edu
Phone: (580) 745-2060 Toll-free number: (800) 435-1327
Fax: (580) 745-7502
Kristie Luke, Associate Dean of Admissions and Records/Registrar, Southeastern Oklahoma State University, 1405 North Fourth Avenue, PMB 4225, Durant, OK 74701-0607

## Southern Nazarene University
**Bethany, Oklahoma**   **CB member**
www.snu.edu   **CB code: 6036**

- Private 4-year university and liberal arts college affiliated with Church of the Nazarene
- Residential campus in large town
- 1,653 degree-seeking undergraduates
- 457 graduate students
- SAT or ACT required

**General.** Founded in 1899. Regionally accredited. **Degrees:** 540 bachelor's, 2 associate awarded; master's offered. **ROTC:** Army, Air Force. **Location:** 10 miles from Oklahoma City. **Calendar:** Semester, limited summer session. **Full-time faculty:** 85 total. **Part-time faculty:** 60 total. **Special facilities:** Human cadaver laboratory, physics laser laboratory, laboratory school for children.

**Freshman class profile.**

| Mid 50% test scores | | | |
|---|---|---|---|
| ACT composite: | 18-26 | GPA 2.0-2.99: | 24% |
| GPA 3.75 or higher: | 32% | Rank in top quarter: | 45% |
| GPA 3.50-3.74: | 16% | Rank in top tenth: | 22% |
| GPA 3.0-3.49: | 27% | Live on campus: | 85% |

**Basis for selection.** 2.0 GPA and 19 ACT or SAT equivalent required for unconditional admissions. Students who do not meet requirements may be granted provisional acceptance by committee review. Interview recommended for all; audition recommended for music program. **Homeschooled:** Transcript of courses and grades required.

**High school preparation.** 13 units recommended. Recommended units include English 4, mathematics 3, social studies 2, science 2 and foreign language 2. One computer course recommended.

**2009-2010 Annual costs.** Tuition/fees: $17,664. Room/board: $6,550. Books/supplies: $600. Personal expenses: $1,200.

**2008-2009 Financial aid. Non-need-based:** Scholarships awarded for academics, athletics, ROTC, state residency.

**Application procedures. Admission:** Priority date 5/1; deadline 8/1. $35 fee, may be waived for applicants with need. Admission notification on a rolling basis. **Financial aid:** Priority date 3/1; no closing date. FAFSA, institutional form required. Applicants notified on a rolling basis starting 5/1; must reply within 2 week(s) of notification.

**Academics. Special study options:** Combined bachelor's/graduate degree, distance learning, double major, dual enrollment of high school students, external degree, honors, independent study, internships, liberal arts/career combination, student-designed major, study abroad, teacher certification program, urban semester, Washington semester. **Credit/placement by examination:** AP, CLEP, IB, institutional tests. 30 credit hours maximum toward bachelor's degree. **Support services:** Remedial instruction, study skills assistance, tutoring, writing center.

**Majors. Area/ethnic studies:** American. **Biology:** General, biochemistry. **Business:** General, accounting, business admin, finance, marketing. **Communications:** General, journalism. **Communications technology:** General. **Computer sciences:** General, networking. **Conservation:** General. **Education:** General, early childhood, elementary, English, history, mathematics, music, physical, reading, science, secondary, Spanish, speech. **Foreign languages:** Spanish. **Health:** Athletic training, clinical lab technology. **History:** General. **Interdisciplinary:** Behavioral sciences. **Legal studies:** Prelaw. **Liberal arts:** Arts/sciences. **Math:** General. **Parks/recreation:** Exercise sciences. **Philosophy/religion:** Philosophy, religion. **Physical sciences:** Chemistry, physics. **Protective services:** Criminal justice. **Psychology:** General. **Social sciences:** General, political science, sociology. **Theology:** Missionary, religious ed, sacred music, theology. **Transportation:** Aviation management. **Visual/performing arts:** General, graphic design.

**Most popular majors.** Business/marketing 54%, computer/information sciences 6%, education 6%, family/consumer sciences 9%, health sciences 7%.

**Computing on campus.** 120 workstations in library, computer center. Dormitories wired for high-speed internet access and linked to campus network. Helpline, repair service, wireless network available.

**Student life. Freshman orientation:** Mandatory. Preregistration for classes offered. **Policies:** Single students under 23 required to live on campus or with relatives. Religious observance required. **Housing:** Guaranteed on-campus for freshmen. Single-sex dorms, apartments available. $50 deposit, deadline 8/1. **Activities:** Bands, choral groups, drama, film society, music ensembles, student government, student newspaper, symphony orchestra, TV station, Gospel team, Mission Crusaders, Circle-K, Spanish club, Mortar Board.

**Athletics. NAIA. Intercollegiate:** Baseball M, basketball, cheerleading, cross-country, equestrian, football (tackle) M, golf, soccer, softball W, tennis, track and field, volleyball W. **Intramural:** Basketball, football (non-tackle), football (tackle) M, softball, tennis, track and field, volleyball. **Team name:** Crimson Storm.

**Student services.** Alcohol/substance abuse counseling, chaplain/spiritual director, career counseling, services for economically disadvantaged, student employment services, financial aid counseling, health services, personal counseling, placement for graduates. **Physically disabled:** Services for visually, speech, hearing impaired.

**Contact.** E-mail: wrogers@snu.edu
Phone: (405) 491-6324 Toll-free number: (800) 648-9899
Fax: (405) 491-6320
Warren Rogers, Director of Admissions, Southern Nazarene University, 6729 NW 39th Expressway, Bethany, OK 73008

---

## Southwestern Christian University
### Bethany, Oklahoma
**www.swcu.edu**                                    **CB code: 1433**

- Private 4-year liberal arts college affiliated with Pentecostal Holiness Church
- Residential campus in large town
- 230 degree-seeking undergraduates: 5% part-time, 48% women, 23% African American, 1% Asian American, 7% Hispanic American, 7% Native American, 2% international
- 88 degree-seeking graduate students
- 65% of applicants admitted
- SAT or ACT with writing, application essay, interview required
- 38% graduate within 6 years

**General.** Founded in 1946. Regionally accredited. Adult degree-completion program offered. Lockstep program allows for degree completion in 18 months or less. **Degrees:** 29 bachelor's, 4 associate awarded; master's offered. **ROTC:** Army. **Location:** 10 miles from Oklahoma City. **Calendar:** Semester, limited summer session. **Full-time faculty:** 8 total; 25% have terminal degrees, 12% minority, 62% women. **Part-time faculty:** 26 total; 38% have terminal degrees, 15% minority, 42% women.

**Freshman class profile.** 108 applied, 70 admitted, 48 enrolled.

| Mid 50% test scores | | Rank in top quarter: | 27% |
|---|---|---|---|
| ACT composite: | 17-21 | Rank in top tenth: | 8% |
| GPA 3.75 or higher: | 5% | End year in good standing: | 61% |
| GPA 3.50-3.74: | 25% | Return as sophomores: | 41% |
| GPA 3.0-3.49: | 32% | Out-of-state: | 4% |
| GPA 2.0-2.99: | 36% | Live on campus: | 48% |

**Basis for selection.** 2.5 GPA or 19 ACT required. Additional materials and interview may be requested.

**High school preparation.** Required units include English 4, mathematics 2, social studies 2, history 2, science 2 (laboratory 2).

**2009-2010 Annual costs.** Tuition/fees: $10,700. Adult education program $350 per credit hour. Room/board: $4,800. Books/supplies: $750. Personal expenses: $1,100.

**2009-2010 Financial aid. Need-based:** 48 full-time freshmen applied for aid; 48 were judged to have need; 48 of these received aid. Average need met was 95%. 37% of total undergraduate aid awarded as scholarships/grants, 63% as loans/jobs. **Non-need-based:** Awarded to 60 full-time undergraduates, including 47 freshmen. Scholarships awarded for academics, alumni affiliation, leadership, music/drama, religious affiliation.

**Application procedures. Admission:** No deadline. No application fee. Application must be submitted on paper. Admission notification on a rolling basis. **Financial aid:** Priority date 8/1; no closing date. FAFSA required. Applicants notified on a rolling basis starting 5/1; must reply within 2 week(s) of notification.

**Academics.** Applied Biblical Leadership Education (ABLE), an adult studies completion program. **Special study options:** Accelerated study, cross-registration, double major, dual enrollment of high school students, honors, independent study, internships, liberal arts/career combination. **Credit/placement by examination:** AP, CLEP, institutional tests. 30 credit hours

maximum toward bachelor's degree. **Support services:** Learning center, reduced course load, remedial instruction, tutoring.

**Majors. Business:** Business admin. **Philosophy/religion:** Religion. **Theology:** Bible, missionary, pastoral counseling, religious ed, sacred music, theology, youth ministry. **Visual/performing arts:** Music performance.

**Computing on campus.** 9 workstations in library. Dormitories wired for high-speed internet access and linked to campus network. Online library, wireless network available.

**Student life. Freshman orientation:** Mandatory. Preregistration for classes offered. Held the week prior to classes; includes academic, financial aid and spiritual life orientation. **Policies:** Extracurricular Christian programs and activities emphasized. Mandatory dress code. Students sign lifestyle covenant agreeing to certain behaviors. Religious observance required. **Housing:** Single-sex dorms available. $100 nonrefundable deposit, deadline 8/15. **Activities:** Campus ministries, choral groups, drama, music ensembles, musical theater, student government, student newspaper, Southwestern Ministerial Association, missionary society, Christian education association.

**Athletics. NCCAA. Intercollegiate:** Basketball M, cross-country, golf M, soccer M, softball, volleyball W. **Intramural:** Baseball M, basketball, cheerleading, football (non-tackle) M, softball, table tennis, volleyball. **Team name:** Eagles.

**Student services.** Adult student services, chaplain/spiritual director, career counseling, student employment services, financial aid counseling, personal counseling, veterans' counselor.

**Contact.** E-mail: admissions@swcu.edu
Phone: (405) 789-7661 ext. 3442 Toll-free number: (888) 418-9272
Fax: (405) 495-0078
Chad Pugh, Recruitment/Admissions, Southwestern Christian University, Box 340, Bethany, OK 73008

---

## Southwestern Oklahoma State University
### Weatherford, Oklahoma                          **CB member**
**www.swosu.edu**                                  **CB code: 6673**

- Public 4-year university
- Residential campus in large town
- 4,194 degree-seeking undergraduates: 13% part-time, 57% women, 5% African American, 2% Asian American, 5% Hispanic American, 9% Native American, 3% international
- 708 degree-seeking graduate students
- 92% of applicants admitted
- SAT or ACT (ACT writing optional) required

**General.** Founded in 1901. Regionally accredited. Campus at Sayre offers lower division and remedial courses, as well as associate degrees. **Degrees:** 626 bachelor's, 110 associate awarded; master's, professional offered. **Location:** 75 miles from Oklahoma City. **Calendar:** Semester, extensive summer session. **Full-time faculty:** 215 total; 59% have terminal degrees, 12% minority, 46% women. **Part-time faculty:** 15 total. **Class size:** 48% < 20, 40% 20-39, 7% 40-49, 6% 50-99.

**Freshman class profile.** 1,417 applied, 1,305 admitted, 927 enrolled.

| Mid 50% test scores | | Rank in top quarter: | 40% |
|---|---|---|---|
| ACT composite: | 18-24 | Rank in top tenth: | 18% |
| GPA 3.75 or higher: | 30% | Return as sophomores: | 66% |
| GPA 3.50-3.74: | 17% | Out-of-state: | 7% |
| GPA 3.0-3.49: | 29% | Live on campus: | 57% |
| GPA 2.0-2.99: | 24% | | |

**Basis for selection.** Bachelor degree programs require 19 ACT and no curricular deficiencies. Open admission for associate degree programs. Last date to submit test scores is first day of classes. Essay required for returning suspension students only.

**High school preparation.** College-preparatory program required. 15 units required; 17 recommended. Required and recommended units include English 4, mathematics 3, social studies 1, history 2, science 2 (laboratory 2), computer science 1 and academic electives 2-4. Social studies unit must be citizenship. Academic electives should be in fine arts. 3 units computer science or foreign language required.

**2009-2010 Annual costs.** Tuition/fees: $4,530; $9,870 out-of-state. Room/board: $4,400. Books/supplies: $1,230. Personal expenses: $996.

**2009-2010 Financial aid. Need-based:** 679 full-time freshmen applied for aid; 513 were judged to have need; 505 of these received aid. Average

need met was 87%. Average scholarship/grant was $1,282; average loan $1,397. 47% of total undergraduate aid awarded as scholarships/grants, 53% as loans/jobs. **Non-need-based:** Awarded to 2,514 full-time undergraduates, including 554 freshmen. Scholarships awarded for academics, alumni affiliation, art, athletics, leadership, music/drama, state residency.

**Application procedures. Admission:** No deadline. $15 fee. Admission notification on a rolling basis. **Financial aid:** Closing date 3/1. FAFSA, institutional form required. Applicants notified by 3/15.

**Academics. Special study options:** Accelerated study, combined bachelor's/graduate degree, distance learning, double major, independent study, internships, student-designed major, study abroad, teacher certification program, weekend college. Weekend college for nursing only. **Credit/placement by examination:** AP, CLEP, IB, ACT, institutional tests. 62 credit hours maximum toward bachelor's degree. **Support services:** Pre-admission summer program, reduced course load, remedial instruction, study skills assistance, tutoring, writing center.

**Majors. Biology:** General, biophysics. **Business:** General, accounting, business admin, human resources, management information systems. **Communications:** General. **Computer sciences:** General, computer science, information systems. **Education:** Art, early childhood, elementary, English, health, history, learning disabled, mathematics, mentally handicapped, music, physical, science, social science, special, technology/industrial arts. **Engineering:** General, physics. **Engineering technology:** Manufacturing. **Health:** Athletic training, clinical lab technology, health care admin, medical records admin, music therapy, nursing (RN). **History:** General. **Math:** General. **Parks/recreation:** General, facilities management. **Physical sciences:** Chemistry, physics. **Protective services:** Criminal justice. **Psychology:** General. **Public administration:** Social work. **Social sciences:** Political science, sociology. **Theology:** Sacred music. **Visual/performing arts:** Commercial/advertising art, music management, music performance, music theory/composition, piano/organ, voice/opera.

**Most popular majors.** Business/marketing 22%, education 17%, health sciences 20%, parks/recreation 7%, visual/performing arts 8%.

**Computing on campus.** 200 workstations in library, computer center. Dormitories wired for high-speed internet access. Commuter students can connect to campus network. Online library, wireless network available.

**Student life. Freshman orientation:** Mandatory, $60 fee. Preregistration for classes offered. **Housing:** Guaranteed on-campus for all undergraduates. Single-sex dorms, apartments available. $100 fully refundable deposit, deadline 8/1. **Activities:** Bands, campus ministries, choral groups, drama, international student organizations, literary magazine, music ensembles, Model UN, musical theater, opera, student government, student newspaper, symphony orchestra, 7 religious organizations, 4 political organizations, and approximately 75 social and professional clubs.

**Athletics.** NCAA. **Intercollegiate:** Baseball M, basketball, cheerleading, cross-country W, football (tackle) M, golf, rodeo, soccer, softball W. **Intramural:** Basketball, bowling, football (non-tackle), golf, racquetball, soccer, softball, swimming, tennis, volleyball. **Team name:** Bulldogs.

**Student services.** Adult student services, alcohol/substance abuse counseling, career counseling, student employment services, financial aid counseling, health services, personal counseling, placement for graduates, veterans' counselor. **Physically disabled:** Services for visually, hearing impaired.

**Contact.** E-mail: admissions@swosu.edu
Phone: (580) 774-3009 Fax: (580) 774-3795
Todd Boyd, Director of Admissions, Southwestern Oklahoma State University, 100 Campus Drive, Weatherford, OK 73096

## Spartan College of Aeronautics and Technology
**Tulsa, Oklahoma**
www.spartan.edu                                    CB code: 0336

- For-profit 4-year technical college
- Commuter campus in large city
- 1,084 degree-seeking undergraduates
- Interview required

**General.** Founded in 1928. Accredited by ACCSC. Multi-campus institution with technical campuses at Tulsa International Airport and R.L Jones Airport in South Tulsa. **Degrees:** 27 bachelor's, 143 associate awarded. **Location:** 100 miles from Oklahoma City. **Calendar:** Differs by program, extensive summer session. **Full-time faculty:** 63 total; 3% have terminal degrees, 13% women. **Part-time faculty:** 34 total; 3% have terminal degrees, 9% women. **Class size:** 62% < 20, 38% 20-39.

**Freshman class profile.**

| | | | |
|---|---|---|---|
| Out-of-state: | 81% | Live on campus: | 25% |

**Basis for selection.** Applicants must demonstrate proficiency in college-level skills by submission of examination scores deemed appropriate for the chosen program of study. Students wishing to attend flight training must obtain FAA Class II flight certificate and pass TSA screening. SAT or ACT recommended. **Homeschooled:** Statement describing homeschool structure and mission, transcript of courses and grades, state high school equivalency certificate, interview required.

**2010-2011 Annual costs.** Tuition/fees (projected): $15,000. Room only: $4,680.

**Application procedures. Admission:** No deadline. $100 fee. Admission notification on a rolling basis. **Financial aid:** No deadline. FAFSA, institutional form required. Applicants notified on a rolling basis starting 2/1; must reply within 2 week(s) of notification.

**Academics. Special study options:** Independent study. **Credit/placement by examination:** CLEP, institutional tests. No more than half of credits required for degree may be earned through examination. **Support services:** Remedial instruction, tutoring.

**Majors. Mechanic/repair:** Avionics. **Transportation:** Aviation management. **Other:** Aviation maintenance.technician.

**Computing on campus.** 100 workstations in library, student center. Dormitories wired for high-speed internet access. Online library, wireless network available.

**Student life. Freshman orientation:** Mandatory. Usually held on Friday immediately preceding start of classes. **Policies:** All students subject to random drug testing. **Housing:** Apartments, wellness housing available. **Activities:** Student government.

**Student services.** Career counseling, student employment services, financial aid counseling, personal counseling, placement for graduates, veterans' counselor.

**Contact.** E-mail: spartan@mail.spartan.edu
Phone: (918) 836-6886 Toll-free number: (800) 331-1204
Fax: (918) 831-5287
Damon Bowling, Vice President, Marketing, Spartan College of Aeronautics and Technology, Box 582833, Tulsa, OK 74158-2833

## University of Central Oklahoma
**Edmond, Oklahoma**                                    CB member
www.uco.edu                                            CB code: 6091

- Public 4-year university
- Commuter campus in small city
- 14,246 degree-seeking undergraduates: 31% part-time, 57% women, 10% African American, 4% Asian American, 4% Hispanic American, 6% Native American, 5% international
- 1,565 degree-seeking graduate students
- 75% of applicants admitted
- SAT or ACT (ACT writing optional) required
- 36% graduate within 6 years

**General.** Founded in 1890. Regionally accredited. **Degrees:** 2,318 bachelor's awarded; master's offered. **ROTC:** Army. **Location:** 12 miles from Oklahoma City. **Calendar:** Semester, extensive summer session. **Full-time faculty:** 434 total; 68% have terminal degrees, 15% minority, 48% women. **Part-time faculty:** 400 total; 14% have terminal degrees, 10% minority, 57% women. **Class size:** 31% < 20, 55% 20-39, 11% 40-49, 3% 50-99, less than 1% >100. **Special facilities:** Jazz lab.

**Freshman class profile.** 5,181 applied, 3,907 admitted, 3,177 enrolled.

| Mid 50% test scores | | | |
|---|---|---|---|
| ACT composite: | 19-24 | Rank in top tenth: | 13% |
| GPA 3.75 or higher: | 19% | Return as sophomores: | 61% |
| GPA 3.50-3.74: | 17% | Out-of-state: | 2% |
| GPA 3.0-3.49: | 38% | Live on campus: | 43% |
| GPA 2.0-2.99: | 25% | International: | 3% |
| Rank in top quarter: | 31% | Fraternities: | 12% |
| | | Sororities: | 9% |

**Basis for selection.** Must have 2.7 GPA and rank in top 50% of class, or 2.7 GPA in 15 unit high school core, or 20 ACT.

**High school preparation.** College-preparatory program recommended. 17 units required; 18 recommended. Required and recommended units include English 4, mathematics 3-4, social studies 1, history 2, science 2-3 (laboratory 2-3), foreign language 2 and academic electives 3.

**2009-2010 Annual costs.** Tuition/fees: $4,223; $10,652 out-of-state. Room/board: $5,942. Books/supplies: $1,000. Personal expenses: $2,000.

**2008-2009 Financial aid. Need-based:** 1,083 full-time freshmen applied for aid; 804 were judged to have need; 727 of these received aid. Average need met was 66%. Average scholarship/grant was $6,995; average loan $3,127. 37% of total undergraduate aid awarded as scholarships/grants, 63% as loans/jobs. **Non-need-based:** Awarded to 5,266 full-time undergraduates, including 208 freshmen. Scholarships awarded for academics, alumni affiliation, art, athletics, leadership, minority status, music/drama, ROTC, state residency.

**Application procedures. Admission:** No deadline. $25 fee. Admission notification on a rolling basis beginning on or about 4/1. **Financial aid:** Priority date 5/31; no closing date. FAFSA, institutional form required. Applicants notified on a rolling basis starting 5/1; must reply by 6/30 or within 4 week(s) of notification.

**Academics. Special study options:** Accelerated study, distance learning, double major, dual enrollment of high school students, ESL, honors, independent study, internships, teacher certification program. **Credit/placement by examination:** AP, CLEP, ACT, institutional tests. 94 credit hours maximum toward bachelor's degree. **Support services:** Learning center, reduced course load, remedial instruction, tutoring, writing center.

**Majors. Biology:** General. **Business:** Accounting, actuarial science, apparel, business admin, finance, human resources, insurance, management information systems, managerial economics, marketing, nonprofit/public, operations. **Communications:** General, advertising, broadcast journalism, journalism, photojournalism, public relations. **Computer sciences:** General, information technology. **Education:** General, art, biology, business, chemistry, curriculum, drama/dance, early childhood, elementary, ESL, family/consumer sciences, French, German, health occupations, history, instructional media, mathematics, music, physical, physics, reading, science, social studies, Spanish, special, technology/industrial arts. **Engineering:** Biomedical, physics. **Engineering technology:** General, industrial safety. **Family/consumer sciences:** General, aging, child development, family systems, food/nutrition. **Foreign languages:** French, German, Spanish. **Health:** Audiology/speech pathology, clinical lab science, nursing (RN), public health ed, speech pathology. **History:** General. **Liberal arts:** Arts/sciences. **Math:** General, applied, statistics. **Parks/recreation:** General, exercise sciences. **Personal/culinary services:** Mortuary science. **Philosophy/religion:** Philosophy. **Physical sciences:** Chemistry, physics. **Protective services:** Corrections, criminal justice, forensics, juvenile corrections, police science. **Psychology:** General. **Social sciences:** Applied economics, economics, geography, political science, sociology, urban studies. **Visual/performing arts:** Art, art history/conservation, dance, dramatic, graphic design, interior design, music performance, piano/organ, stringed instruments, voice/opera.

**Most popular majors.** Business/marketing 28%, communications/journalism 9%, education 9%, health sciences 6%, liberal arts 14%.

**Computing on campus.** 450 workstations in dormitories, library, computer center, student center. Dormitories wired for high-speed internet access. Commuter students can connect to campus network. Helpline, wireless network available.

**Student life. Freshman orientation:** Mandatory, $35 fee. Preregistration for classes offered. 3-day orientation held the week before classes start in August. **Housing:** Coed dorms, single-sex dorms, apartments, fraternity/sorority housing, wellness housing available. $150 fully refundable deposit. **Activities:** Bands, choral groups, dance, drama, international student organizations, music ensembles, musical theater, radio station, student government, student newspaper, symphony orchestra, TV station, Baptist student union, Fellowship of Christian Athletes, Young Democrats, Collegiate Republicans, black student association, Malaysian student association, association of women students, Webmasters.

**Athletics.** NCAA. **Intercollegiate:** Baseball M, basketball, cross-country, football (tackle) M, golf, ice hockey M, soccer W, softball W, tennis, track and field, volleyball W, wrestling M. **Intramural:** Badminton, baseball M, basketball, bowling, football (non-tackle), golf, handball, soccer, softball, swimming, table tennis, tennis, track and field, volleyball, wrestling M. **Team name:** Bronchos.

**Student services.** Career counseling, student employment services, health services, personal counseling, placement for graduates, veterans' counselor. **Physically disabled:** Services for visually, speech, hearing impaired.

**Contact.** E-mail: 4ucoinfo@uco.edu
Phone: (405) 974-2338 Fax: (405) 341-4964
Linda Lofton, Director, Admissions & Records, University of Central Oklahoma, 100 North University Drive, Edmond, OK 73034-0151

## University of Oklahoma
**Norman, Oklahoma**      CB member
www.ou.edu      CB code: 6879

- Public 4-year university
- Residential campus in small city
- 20,685 degree-seeking undergraduates: 13% part-time, 53% women, 6% African American, 6% Asian American, 5% Hispanic American, 7% Native American, 2% international
- 9,529 graduate students
- 93% of applicants admitted
- SAT or ACT (ACT writing optional) required
- 64% graduate within 6 years

**General.** Founded in 1890. Regionally accredited. Faculty-in-residence program has faculty live in student dorms and mix with students. **Degrees:** 4,471 bachelor's awarded; master's, doctoral, professional offered. **ROTC:** Army, Naval, Air Force. **Location:** 20 miles from Oklahoma City, 200 miles from Dallas. **Calendar:** Semester, extensive summer session. **Full-time faculty:** 1,442 total; 82% have terminal degrees, 18% minority, 41% women. **Part-time faculty:** 380 total; 51% have terminal degrees, 12% minority, 47% women. **Class size:** 46% < 20, 37% 20-39, 6% 40-49, 7% 50-99, 3% >100. **Special facilities:** Art museum, natural history museum, national weather center, national severe storms library, biological station, history of science collection, western history collection, Oklahoma geological survey.

**Freshman class profile.** 8,960 applied, 8,312 admitted, 3,760 enrolled.

| Mid 50% test scores | | | |
|---|---|---|---|
| SAT critical reading: | 510-640 | GPA 3.0-3.49: | 30% |
| SAT math: | 530-660 | GPA 2.0-2.99: | 5% |
| ACT composite: | 23-29 | Rank in top quarter: | 68% |
| GPA 3.75 or higher: | 39% | Rank in top tenth: | 34% |
| GPA 3.50-3.74: | 25% | International: | 2% |

**Basis for selection.** Standardized test scores, class rank, and secondary school record very important. Prescribed set of requirements for residents and nonresidents that guarantee admission. Applicants who do not meet requirements for guaranteed admission, but do meet certain performance minimums, will be placed on wait list and admitted on space-available basis, with preference given to most academically qualified. Audition required for dance, drama, music programs. **Homeschooled:** Transcript of courses and grades required. **Learning Disabled:** Students must self-identify after admission and provide documentation to receive special services.

**High school preparation.** College-preparatory program required. 15 units required. Required and recommended units include English 4, mathematics 3, social studies 2, history 1, science 3 (laboratory 3), foreign language 2, computer science 1 and academic electives 2. Must have 1 U.S. history and 2 additional units from history, economics, geography, government, or non-western culture.

**2009-2010 Annual costs.** Tuition/fees: $7,483; $17,464 out-of-state. Computer course fees and other college level fees vary by college. Room/board: $7,598. Books/supplies: $1,016. Personal expenses: $2,504.

**2008-2009 Financial aid. Need-based:** 2,406 full-time freshmen applied for aid; 2,305 were judged to have need; 2,305 of these received aid. Average need met was 95%. Average scholarship/grant was $5,978; average loan $3,648. 39% of total undergraduate aid awarded as scholarships/grants, 61% as loans/jobs. **Non-need-based:** Awarded to 7,879 full-time undergraduates, including 2,503 freshmen. Scholarships awarded for academics, alumni affiliation, art, athletics, leadership, minority status, music/drama, religious affiliation, ROTC.

**Application procedures. Admission:** Closing date 4/1 (receipt date). $40 fee, may be waived for applicants with need. Admission notification on a rolling basis. Freshman applicants encouraged to apply as soon as junior year in high school is completed or by scholarship deadline of February 1. Online application fee may be waived, with appropriate documentation, for applicants with financial need. **Financial aid:** Priority date 3/1; no closing date. FAFSA required. Applicants notified on a rolling basis starting 3/15; must reply within 6 week(s) of notification.

**Academics.** College of Liberal Studies through distance learning provides non-traditional students with coherent interdisciplinary liberal arts programs. **Special study options:** Accelerated study, combined bachelor's/graduate degree, cooperative education, distance learning, double major, dual enrollment of high school students, ESL, external degree, honors, independent study, internships, liberal arts/career combination, semester at sea, student-designed major, study abroad, teacher certification program, Washington semester, weekend college. **Credit/placement by examination:** AP, CLEP, IB, SAT, ACT, institutional tests. Credit for prior work/life experience awarded according to recommendations of American Council on Education. Applicability of credits toward a degree vary depending on the college. Credit by examination may be counted toward bachelor's degree, but total number of hours that may be applied vary depending on college. **Support services:** Learning center, pre-admission summer program, remedial instruction, study skills assistance, tutoring, writing center.

**Majors. Architecture:** Architecture, environmental design. **Area/ethnic studies:** African-American, Native American, women's. **Biology:** Biochemistry, botany, microbiology, zoology. **Business:** Accounting, business admin, construction management, finance, management information systems, management science, managerial economics, marketing. **Communications:** General, advertising, broadcast journalism, journalism. **Computer sciences:** Computer science, information systems. **Conservation:** Environmental science. **Education:** General, early childhood, elementary, English, foreign languages, mathematics, music, science, social studies, special. **Engineering:** General, aerospace, architectural, chemical, civil, computer, electrical, environmental, industrial, mechanical, petroleum, physics. **Foreign languages:** Chinese, classics, French, Germanic, Italian, linguistics, Russian, Spanish. **Health:** Clinical lab science, communication disorders, dental hygiene, medical radiologic technology/radiation therapy, nuclear medical technology, nursing (RN), sonography. **History:** General. **Interdisciplinary:** Global studies. **Liberal arts:** Arts/sciences, humanities. **Math:** General. **Parks/recreation:** Exercise sciences. **Philosophy/religion:** Judaic, philosophy, religion. **Physical sciences:** Astronomy, astrophysics, chemistry, geology, geophysics, meteorology, physics. **Psychology:** General. **Public administration:** General, social work. **Social sciences:** Anthropology, economics, geography, political science, sociology. **Transportation:** Aviation. **Visual/performing arts:** General, art history/conservation, dance, dramatic, film/cinema, interior design, music pedagogy, music performance, studio arts. **Other:** Geosciences, Human relations, Multidisciplinary studies.

**Most popular majors.** Biology 6%, business/marketing 16%, communications/journalism 10%, engineering/engineering technologies 6%, health sciences 13%, interdisciplinary studies 8%, social sciences 9%.

**Computing on campus.** 3,600 workstations in dormitories, library, computer center, student center. Dormitories wired for high-speed internet access and linked to campus network. Commuter students can connect to campus network. Online course registration, online library, helpline, repair service, student web hosting, wireless network available.

**Student life. Freshman orientation:** Available. Preregistration for classes offered. **Housing:** Guaranteed on-campus for freshmen. Coed dorms, single-sex dorms, special housing for disabled, apartments, fraternity/sorority housing, wellness housing available. $175 fully refundable deposit. Honors, cultural, scholastic, National Merit housing available. **Activities:** Bands, campus ministries, choral groups, dance, drama, film society, international student organizations, literary magazine, music ensembles, Model UN, musical theater, opera, radio station, student government, student newspaper, symphony orchestra, TV station, American Indian student association, black student association, Hispanic-American student association, Asian-American student association, College Republicans, Young Democrats, Hillel Jewish student organization, Chi Alpha Christian Fellowship, Muslim student association, Alpha Phi Omega.

**Athletics.** NCAA. **Intercollegiate:** Baseball M, basketball, cheerleading, cross-country, football (tackle) M, golf, gymnastics, rowing (crew) W, soccer W, softball W, tennis, track and field, volleyball W, wrestling M. **Intramural:** Badminton, basketball, football (non-tackle), golf, racquetball, soccer, softball, table tennis, tennis, volleyball, water polo. **Team name:** Sooners.

**Student services.** Adult student services, alcohol/substance abuse counseling, chaplain/spiritual director, career counseling, services for economically disadvantaged, student employment services, financial aid counseling, health services, legal services, minority student services, on-campus daycare, personal counseling, placement for graduates, veterans' counselor, women's services. **Physically disabled:** Services for visually, speech, hearing impaired.

**Contact.** E-mail: ou-pss@ou.edu
Phone: (405) 325-2252 Toll-free number: (800) 234-6868
Fax: (405) 325-7124
Craig Hayes, Executive Director of Recruitment Services, University of Oklahoma, 550 Parrington Oval, L-1, Norman, OK 73019-3032

## University of Science and Arts of Oklahoma
**Chickasha, Oklahoma**
www.usao.edu                                    CB code: 6544

- Public 4-year university and liberal arts college
- Residential campus in large town

- 1,013 degree-seeking undergraduates: 9% part-time, 64% women, 5% African American, 1% Asian American, 5% Hispanic American, 11% Native American, 6% international
- 74% of applicants admitted
- SAT or ACT (ACT writing optional) required

**General.** Founded in 1908. Regionally accredited. Offers trimester system classes, allowing for graduation in 3 years. **Degrees:** 200 bachelor's awarded. **Location:** 45 miles from Oklahoma City. **Calendar:** Trimester, extensive summer session. **Full-time faculty:** 55 total; 89% have terminal degrees, 11% minority, 49% women. **Part-time faculty:** 33 total; 18% have terminal degrees, 6% minority, 52% women. **Class size:** 62% < 20, 31% 20-39, 2% 40-49, 5% 50-99, less than 1% >100. **Special facilities:** Speech and hearing clinic, herbarium, child development center, school for the deaf.

**Freshman class profile.** 395 applied, 292 admitted, 187 enrolled.

| Mid 50% test scores | | Rank in top quarter: | 52% |
|---|---|---|---|
| SAT critical reading: | 380-480 | Rank in top tenth: | 21% |
| SAT math: | 480-570 | End year in good standing: | 84% |
| ACT composite: | 19-26 | Return as sophomores: | 72% |
| GPA 3.75 or higher: | 32% | Out-of-state: | 7% |
| GPA 3.50-3.74: | 22% | Live on campus: | 74% |
| GPA 3.0-3.49: | 33% | International: | 3% |
| GPA 2.0-2.99: | 12% | | |

**Basis for selection.** One of the following required: 24 ACT/1090 SAT (exclusive of Writing), OR 3.0 GPA and ranking in top 33% of high school graduating class, OR 3.0 GPA in the 15-unit high school core curriculum and 21 ACT/940 SAT. Students on active military duty are not required to take ACT or SAT. They must complete an academic readiness survey and assessment tests in English, math and science. **Homeschooled:** Transcript of courses and grades required.

**High school preparation.** College-preparatory program required. 15 units required; 20 recommended. Required and recommended units include English 4, mathematics 3-4, social studies 2, history 1, science 3 (laboratory 3), foreign language 2, computer science 1, visual/performing arts 2 and academic electives 2. 2 units of fine arts, drama and/or speech recommended.

**2009-2010 Annual costs.** Tuition/fees: $4,440; $10,560 out-of-state. Room/board: $5,000.

**2009-2010 Financial aid. Need-based:** 154 full-time freshmen applied for aid; 134 were judged to have need; 134 of these received aid. Average need met was 77%. Average scholarship/grant was $7,559; average loan $2,390. 63% of total undergraduate aid awarded as scholarships/grants, 37% as loans/jobs. **Non-need-based:** Awarded to 250 full-time undergraduates, including 41 freshmen. Scholarships awarded for academics, art, athletics, leadership, music/drama, state residency.

**Application procedures. Admission:** Closing date 9/1 (postmark date). $25 fee, may be waived for applicants with need, free for online applicants. Admission notification on a rolling basis beginning on or about 2/10. **Financial aid:** Priority date 3/15; no closing date. FAFSA, institutional form required. Applicants notified on a rolling basis starting 3/15.

**Academics. Special study options:** Accelerated study, double major, dual enrollment of high school students, honors, independent study, internships, student-designed major, study abroad, teacher certification program. **Credit/placement by examination:** AP, CLEP, SAT, ACT, institutional tests. 62 credit hours maximum toward bachelor's degree. **Support services:** Learning center, pre-admission summer program, reduced course load, remedial instruction, study skills assistance, tutoring, writing center.

**Majors. Area/ethnic studies:** Native American. **Biology:** General. **Business:** Business admin. **Communications:** General. **Computer sciences:** Computer science. **Education:** Deaf/hearing impaired, early childhood, elementary. **Health:** Speech pathology. **History:** General. **Interdisciplinary:** Natural sciences. **Math:** General. **Parks/recreation:** Health/fitness. **Physical sciences:** Chemistry, physics. **Psychology:** General. **Social sciences:** Economics, political science, sociology. **Visual/performing arts:** Art, dramatic, studio arts.

**Most popular majors.** Biology 7%, business/marketing 22%, education 18%, history 7%, psychology 9%, visual/performing arts 9%.

**Computing on campus.** 175 workstations in library, computer center, student center. Dormitories wired for high-speed internet access and linked to campus network. Online library, helpline, repair service, student web hosting, wireless network available.

**Student life. Freshman orientation:** Mandatory. Preregistration for classes offered. **Housing:** Guaranteed on-campus for freshmen. Coed dorms, apartments available. $300 nonrefundable deposit, deadline 5/1. **Activities:** Bands, campus ministries, choral groups, dance, drama, international student organizations, literary magazine, music ensembles, musical theater, student government, student newspaper, TV station, Ameslan culture club, Chi Alpha Christian Fellowship, College Democrats, College Republicans, African American student association, international student association, inter-tribal heritage club, student ambassadors, students with children club, feminist collective.

**Athletics.** NAIA. **Intercollegiate:** Baseball M, basketball, cheerleading, soccer, softball W. **Intramural:** Basketball, golf, softball M, volleyball. **Team name:** Drovers.

**Student services.** Alcohol/substance abuse counseling, career counseling, services for economically disadvantaged, student employment services, financial aid counseling, health services, minority student services, personal counseling, placement for graduates, veterans' counselor. **Physically disabled:** Services for visually, hearing impaired.

**Contact.** E-mail: usao-admissions@usao.edu
Phone: (405) 574-1357 Toll-free number: (800) 933-8726
Fax: (405) 574-1220
Kellee Johnson, Director of Admissions, University of Science and Arts of Oklahoma, 1727 West Alabama, Chickasha, OK 73018-5322

---

## University of Tulsa

Tulsa, Oklahoma

www.utulsa.edu

CB member
CB code: 6883

- Private 4-year university affiliated with Presbyterian Church (USA)
- Residential campus in large city
- 3,027 degree-seeking undergraduates: 4% part-time, 47% women, 6% African American, 3% Asian American, 4% Hispanic American, 4% Native American, 14% international
- 1,087 degree-seeking graduate students
- 50% of applicants admitted
- SAT or ACT (ACT writing optional) required
- 62% graduate within 6 years; 41% enter graduate study

**General.** Founded in 1894. Regionally accredited. **Degrees:** 619 bachelor's awarded; master's, doctoral, professional offered. **ROTC:** Air Force. **Location:** 100 miles from Oklahoma City. **Calendar:** Semester, limited summer session. **Full-time faculty:** 311 total; 96% have terminal degrees, 16% minority, 32% women. **Part-time faculty:** 78 total; 96% have terminal degrees, 14% minority, 44% women. **Class size:** 70% < 20, 25% 20-39, 4% 40-49, less than 1% 50-99. **Special facilities:** Biotechnology institute, center for communicative disorders, communication lab, tall grass prairie preserve.

**Freshman class profile.** 4,698 applied, 2,333 admitted, 690 enrolled.

| Mid 50% test scores | | | | |
|---|---|---|---|---|
| SAT critical reading: | 570-700 | Rank in top tenth: | 71% |
| SAT math: | 560-690 | End year in good standing: | 87% |
| ACT composite: | 25-32 | Return as sophomores: | 88% |
| GPA 3.75 or higher: | 53% | Out-of-state: | 48% |
| GPA 3.50-3.74: | 19% | Live on campus: | 90% |
| GPA 3.0-3.49: | 20% | International: | 12% |
| GPA 2.0-2.99: | 8% | Fraternities: | 21% |
| Rank in top quarter: | 89% | Sororities: | 23% |

**Basis for selection.** Primary requirements are school achievement records and test scores. High school guidance counselor recommendation required. Extracurricular activities, community involvement, and talents considered. Essays and interviews recommended for all; audition required for music, theater programs; portfolio required for art program. **Homeschooled:** Statement describing homeschool structure and mission, transcript of courses and grades, letter of recommendation (nonparent) required.

**High school preparation.** College-preparatory program recommended. 16 units recommended. Recommended units include English 4, mathematics 3, social studies 1, history 2, science 3 (laboratory 2), foreign language 2 and academic electives 1. 4 math and 4 physical science recommended for engineering and natural science students.

**2009-2010 Annual costs.** Tuition/fees: $26,812. A one-time $425 fee is charged first-time students for orientation, lifetime transcripts, course drop/add transactions, and graduation/commencement. Room/board: $8,544. Books/supplies: $1,200. Personal expenses: $2,875.

**2008-2009 Financial aid.** **Need-based:** 649 full-time freshmen applied for aid; 355 were judged to have need; 355 of these received aid. Average need met was 88%. Average scholarship/grant was $6,056; average loan $5,033. 34% of total undergraduate aid awarded as scholarships/grants, 66%

as loans/jobs. **Non-need-based:** Awarded to 2,526 full-time undergraduates, including 688 freshmen. Scholarships awarded for academics, alumni affiliation, art, athletics, leadership, minority status, music/drama, religious affiliation.

**Application procedures. Admission:** Priority date 2/1; no deadline. $35 fee, may be waived for applicants with need. Admission notification on a rolling basis beginning on or about 10/1. Must reply by May 1 or within 2 week(s) if notified thereafter. **Financial aid:** Priority date 4/1; no closing date. FAFSA, institutional form required. Applicants notified on a rolling basis starting 3/1; must reply by 5/1 or within 2 week(s) of notification.

**Academics. Special study options:** Accelerated study, combined bachelor's/graduate degree, double major, ESL, honors, independent study, internships, liberal arts/career combination, student-designed major, study abroad, teacher certification program, Washington semester. **Credit/placement by examination:** AP, CLEP, IB, SAT, ACT, institutional tests. 36 credit hours maximum toward bachelor's degree. **Support services:** Learning center, reduced course load, study skills assistance, tutoring, writing center.

**Majors. Area/ethnic studies:** Russian/Slavic. **Biology:** General, biochemistry. **Business:** Accounting, business admin, finance, international, management information systems, marketing, organizational behavior. **Communications:** General. **Computer sciences:** General, computer science, information technology. **Conservation:** Environmental studies. **Education:** Chemistry, Deaf/hearing impaired, early childhood, elementary, mathematics, music. **Engineering:** Chemical, electrical, mechanical, petroleum, physics. **Engineering technology:** Energy systems. **Foreign languages:** French, German, Spanish. **Health:** Athletic training, audiology/speech pathology, communication disorders, nursing (RN). **History:** General. **Interdisciplinary:** Global studies. **Legal studies:** General, prelaw. **Liberal arts:** Arts/sciences. **Math:** General, applied. **Parks/recreation:** Exercise sciences. **Philosophy/religion:** Philosophy, religion. **Physical sciences:** Chemistry, geology, geophysics, physics. **Psychology:** General. **Social sciences:** Anthropology, economics, political science, sociology. **Visual/performing arts:** Art, art history/conservation, arts management, dramatic, film/cinema, music performance, music theory/composition, piano/organ, voice/opera. **Other:** Biogeosciences.

**Most popular majors.** Business/marketing 19%, education 6%, engineering/engineering technologies 14%, social sciences 6%, visual/performing arts 8%.

**Computing on campus.** 900 workstations in dormitories, library, computer center, student center. Dormitories wired for high-speed internet access and linked to campus network. Commuter students can connect to campus network. Online course registration, online library, helpline, student web hosting, wireless network available.

**Student life. Freshman orientation:** Available. Preregistration for classes offered. Held the week prior to fall term. **Housing:** Guaranteed on-campus for freshmen. Coed dorms, single-sex dorms, special housing for disabled, apartments, fraternity/sorority housing, wellness housing available. $250 partly refundable deposit. Honors and language houses available. **Activities:** Bands, campus ministries, choral groups, dance, drama, international student organizations, literary magazine, music ensembles, Model UN, musical theater, opera, radio station, student government, student newspaper, symphony orchestra, TV station, Baptist student union, Fellowship of Christian Athletes, Jewish student association, Young Democrats, women's law caucus, Hispanic student association, College Republicans, International Fellowship House, Association of Black Collegians, volunteer income tax assistance project.

**Athletics.** NCAA. **Intercollegiate:** Basketball, cheerleading, cross-country, football (tackle) M, golf, rowing (crew) W, soccer, softball W, tennis, track and field, volleyball W. **Intramural:** Badminton, basketball, bowling, cross-country, diving, football (non-tackle), golf, racquetball, soccer, softball, squash, swimming, table tennis, tennis, track and field, volleyball, water polo, wrestling M. **Team name:** Golden Hurricane.

**Student services.** Adult student services, alcohol/substance abuse counseling, chaplain/spiritual director, career counseling, student employment services, financial aid counseling, health services, legal services, minority student services, on-campus daycare, personal counseling, placement for graduates, veterans' counselor, women's services. **Physically disabled:** Services for visually, speech, hearing impaired.

**Contact.** E-mail: admission@utulsa.edu
Phone: (918) 631-2307 Toll-free number: (800) 331-3050
Fax: (918) 631-5003
John Corso, Associate Vice President of Enrollment and Student Services, University of Tulsa, 800 South Tucker Drive, Tulsa, OK 74104-3189

# Oregon

## Art Institute of Portland
**Portland, Oregon**                    **CB member**
www.aipd.artinstitutes.edu          **CB code: 4231**

▶ For-profit 4-year visual arts and liberal arts college
▶ Commuter campus in large city
▶ 1,896 degree-seeking undergraduates
▶ 75% of applicants admitted
▶ Application essay, interview required

**General.** Founded in 1963. Regionally accredited. **Degrees:** 255 bachelor's, 40 associate awarded. **Calendar:** Quarter, extensive summer session. **Full-time faculty:** 39 total. **Part-time faculty:** 94 total. **Special facilities:** Specialized library, design laboratories, audio/visual laboratory.

**Freshman class profile.** 809 applied, 606 admitted, 586 enrolled.

**Basis for selection.** Proof of graduation from secondary school/GED required. Interview, essay, college transcripts, and/or English/math placement exam considered.

**2009-2010 Annual costs.** Tuition/fees: $21,195. Room only: $8,415. Books/supplies: $1,275. Personal expenses: $3,696.

**2009-2010 Financial aid. Non-need-based:** Scholarships awarded for art. **Additional information:** Applicants encouraged to apply early for financial aid. Scholarship deadlines range from January 1 to March 1.

**Application procedures. Admission:** No deadline. $50 fee. Admission notification on a rolling basis. **Financial aid:** Priority date 3/1; no closing date. FAFSA required. Applicants notified on a rolling basis starting 1/1; must reply within 5 week(s) of notification.

**Academics. Special study options:** Accelerated study, distance learning, honors, independent study, internships, liberal arts/career combination, study abroad. **Credit/placement by examination:** AP, CLEP, IB, SAT, ACT, institutional tests. Credit by examination only offered for courses in writing, computing, graphics, drawing, and math. **Support services:** Learning center, reduced course load, remedial instruction, study skills assistance, tutoring.

**Majors. Business:** Fashion. **Computer sciences:** Applications programming, computer graphics, web page design. **Visual/performing arts:** Art history/conservation, arts management, cinematography, commercial/advertising art, design, fashion design, graphic design, industrial design, interior design, multimedia.

**Most popular majors.** Computer/information sciences 24%, visual/performing arts 76%.

**Computing on campus.** 240 workstations in library, computer center. Dormitories wired for high-speed internet access. Commuter students can connect to campus network. Student web hosting, wireless network available.

**Student life. Freshman orientation:** Mandatory. Preregistration for classes offered. Held before each quarter-registration, advising and community services available. **Policies:** Student code of conduct published in catalog. No alcohol or drugs on campus or in housing. **Housing:** Special housing for disabled, apartments, wellness housing available. $250 partly refundable deposit. Apartments for 2 or 4 students. **Activities:** Film society, student government, student newspaper.

**Student services.** Alcohol/substance abuse counseling, career counseling, student employment services, financial aid counseling, personal counseling, placement for graduates, veterans' counselor. **Physically disabled:** Services for visually impaired, speech, hearing impaired.

**Contact.** E-mail: aipdadm@aii.edu
Phone: (503) 228-6528 Toll-free number: (888) 228-6528
Fax: (503) 227-1945
Alan Yanda, Director of Admissions, Art Institute of Portland, 1122 Northwest Davis Street, Portland, OR 97209-2911

## Concordia University
**Portland, Oregon**
www.cu-portland.edu                    **CB code: 4079**

▶ Private 4-year liberal arts and teachers college affiliated with Lutheran Church - Missouri Synod
▶ Commuter campus in very large city
▶ 1,073 degree-seeking undergraduates: 12% part-time, 64% women, 7% African American, 6% Asian American, 6% Hispanic American, 1% Native American, 1% international
▶ 648 degree-seeking graduate students
▶ 59% of applicants admitted
▶ SAT or ACT (ACT writing optional) required
▶ 41% graduate within 6 years

**General.** Founded in 1905. Regionally accredited. **Degrees:** 229 bachelor's awarded; master's offered. **ROTC:** Air Force. **Location:** 5 miles from downtown. **Calendar:** Semester, limited summer session. **Full-time faculty:** 52 total; 67% have terminal degrees, 4% minority, 48% women. **Part-time faculty:** 117 total; 21% have terminal degrees, 5% minority, 54% women. **Class size:** 66% < 20, 33% 20-39, less than 1% 40-49, less than 1% 50-99. **Special facilities:** Environmental research center, children's literature center, Shakespeare authorship research center.

**Freshman class profile.** 1,002 applied, 596 admitted, 191 enrolled.

| Mid 50% test scores | | GPA 2.0-2.99: | 25% |
|---|---|---|---|
| SAT critical reading: | 450-570 | Rank in top quarter: | 45% |
| SAT math: | 460-560 | Rank in top tenth: | 19% |
| ACT composite: | 18-24 | End year in good standing: | 85% |
| GPA 3.75 or higher: | 24% | Return as sophomores: | 74% |
| GPA 3.50-3.74: | 20% | Out-of-state: | 47% |
| GPA 3.0-3.49: | 31% | Live on campus: | 80% |

**Basis for selection.** 2.5 GPA, 480 SAT verbal, or 18 ACT required. **Homeschooled:** Statement describing homeschool structure and mission, state high school equivalency certificate, letter of recommendation (nonparent) required. Interview may be required.

**High school preparation.** College-preparatory program recommended. 19 units recommended. Recommended units include English 4, mathematics 3, social studies 3, science 3, foreign language 2 and academic electives 3. One computer/keyboarding recommended.

**2009-2010 Annual costs.** Tuition/fees: $23,400. Room/board: $6,800. Books/supplies: $800. Personal expenses: $1,600.

**2009-2010 Financial aid. Non-need-based:** Scholarships awarded for academics, athletics, leadership, music/drama, religious affiliation.

**Application procedures. Admission:** Priority date 3/1; deadline 7/1 (postmark date). $20 fee, may be waived for applicants with need, free for online applicants. Admission notification on a rolling basis beginning on or about 1/1. Must reply by May 1 or within 2 week(s) if notified thereafter. **Financial aid:** No deadline. FAFSA required. Applicants notified on a rolling basis starting 3/15; must reply by 5/1 or within 3 week(s) of notification.

**Academics. Special study options:** Accelerated study, cross-registration, distance learning, double major, dual enrollment of high school students, ESL, honors, independent study, internships, semester at sea, study abroad, teacher certification program. **Credit/placement by examination:** AP, CLEP, institutional tests. **Support services:** Learning center, remedial instruction, tutoring, writing center.

**Majors. Biology:** General. **Business:** General, business admin, international. **Education:** General, biology, business, chemistry, early childhood, elementary, English, health, history, mathematics, middle, multi-level teacher, physical, science, secondary, social studies. **Health:** Athletic training, health care admin, nursing (RN), premedicine. **History:** General. **Liberal arts:** Arts/sciences. **Parks/recreation:** Health/fitness, sports admin. **Philosophy/religion:** Religion. **Physical sciences:** Chemistry. **Psychology:** General. **Public administration:** Social work. **Social sciences:** General. **Theology:** Religious ed, theology.

**Most popular majors.** Business/marketing 32%, education 16%, health sciences 19%, public administration/social services 10%.

**Computing on campus.** PC or laptop required. 75 workstations in dormitories, library, computer center, student center. Dormitories wired for high-speed internet access and linked to campus network. Commuter students can connect to campus network. Online course registration, online library, helpline, repair service, wireless network available.

**Student life. Freshman orientation:** Mandatory. Preregistration for classes offered. Usually held the day before classes begin. **Policies:** Optional attendance for chapel services. Lutheran format, mixture of traditional and contemporary services offered. **Housing:** Guaranteed on-campus for freshmen. Coed dorms, apartments, wellness housing available. $50 deposit, deadline 5/1. Homestay option for international students. **Activities:** Campus ministries, choral groups, drama, international student organizations, literary magazine, music ensembles, student government, student newspaper, social service organization, Circle K, Spiritual Life, El Club Latino.

**Athletics. NAIA. Intercollegiate:** Baseball M, basketball, cross-country, golf, soccer, softball W, track and field, volleyball W. **Intramural:** Basketball, softball, tennis, volleyball. **Team name:** Cavaliers.

**Student services.** Adult student services, chaplain/spiritual director, career counseling, financial aid counseling, health services, personal counseling, placement for graduates, veterans' counselor.

**Contact.** E-mail: admissions@cu-portland.edu
Phone: (503) 280-8501 Toll-free number: (800) 321-9371
Fax: (503) 280-8531
Bobi Swan, Dean of Admission, Concordia University, 2811 Northeast Holman Street, Portland, OR 97211-6099

## Corban College
### Salem, Oregon
### www.corban.edu
**CB code: 4956**

- Private 4-year liberal arts college affiliated with Baptist faith
- Residential campus in small city
- 820 degree-seeking undergraduates: 8% part-time, 60% women
- 118 degree-seeking graduate students
- 57% of applicants admitted
- SAT or ACT (ACT writing recommended), application essay required
- 56% graduate within 6 years

**General.** Founded in 1935. Regionally accredited. **Degrees:** 203 bachelor's, 5 associate awarded; master's offered. **ROTC:** Army, Air Force. **Location:** 45 miles from Portland. **Calendar:** Semester, limited summer session. **Full-time faculty:** 45 total; 56% have terminal degrees, 2% minority, 24% women. **Part-time faculty:** 62 total; 14% have terminal degrees, 2% minority, 40% women. **Class size:** 61% < 20, 31% 20-39, 6% 40-49, 2% 50-99. **Special facilities:** Archaeological museum.

**Freshman class profile.** 907 applied, 518 admitted, 216 enrolled.

| Mid 50% test scores | | GPA 2.0-2.99: | 9% |
|---|---|---|---|
| SAT critical reading: | 500-630 | Rank in top quarter: | 61% |
| SAT math: | 490-610 | Rank in top tenth: | 31% |
| SAT writing: | 470-590 | Return as sophomores: | 72% |
| ACT composite: | 20-26 | Out-of-state: | 44% |
| GPA 3.75 or higher: | 45% | Live on campus: | 92% |
| GPA 3.50-3.74: | 21% | International: | 6% |
| GPA 3.0-3.49: | 25% | | |

**Basis for selection.** Commitment to Christianity, high school GPA, test scores, recommendations, essays, school and community activities considered. Audition required for music program. **Homeschooled:** Transcript of courses and grades, state high school equivalency certificate required.

**High school preparation.** College-preparatory program recommended. 14 units recommended. Recommended units include English 4, mathematics 3, social studies 3, science 2 and foreign language 2.

**2009-2010 Annual costs.** Tuition/fees: $23,220. Room/board: $7,520. Books/supplies: $900. Personal expenses: $1,602.

**2009-2010 Financial aid. Need-based:** 187 full-time freshmen applied for aid; 175 were judged to have need; 175 of these received aid. Average need met was 72%. Average scholarship/grant was $17,115; average loan $3,881. 65% of total undergraduate aid awarded as scholarships/grants, 35% as loans/jobs. **Non-need-based:** Scholarships awarded for academics, alumni affiliation, athletics, leadership, music/drama, ROTC.

**Application procedures. Admission:** Priority date 3/1; deadline 8/1 (receipt date). $35 fee, may be waived for applicants with need. Admission notification on a rolling basis beginning on or about 12/1. **Financial aid:** Priority date 2/15; no closing date. FAFSA required. Applicants notified on a rolling basis starting 3/1.

**Academics. Special study options:** Accelerated study, combined bachelor's/graduate degree, cooperative education, cross-registration, distance learning, double major, external degree, honors, independent study, internships,

liberal arts/career combination, student-designed major, study abroad, teacher certification program, Washington semester, weekend college. **Credit/placement by examination:** AP, CLEP, IB, institutional tests. 20 credit hours maximum toward associate degree, 32 toward bachelor's. **Support services:** Learning center, reduced course load, tutoring.

**Majors. Business:** General, accounting, accounting/business management, accounting/finance, business admin, communications, finance, information resources management, management information systems. **Communications:** General, journalism. **Education:** General, biology, business, elementary, English, history, mathematics, middle, multi-level teacher, music, physical, science, secondary, social science, social studies. **Health:** Predental, premedicine, prenursing, prepharmacy, preveterinary. **History:** General. **Legal studies:** Prelaw. **Liberal arts:** Arts/sciences, humanities. **Math:** General. **Parks/recreation:** Health/fitness, sports admin. **Philosophy/religion:** Religion. **Psychology:** General. **Public administration:** Community org/advocacy. **Social sciences:** General. **Theology:** Bible, missionary, pastoral counseling, preministerial, religious ed, sacred music, theology, youth ministry. **Visual/performing arts:** Music performance, piano/organ, voice/opera.

**Most popular majors.** Business/marketing 28%, education 19%, English 9%, liberal arts 7%, psychology 28%.

**Computing on campus.** 34 workstations in dormitories, library, computer center, student center. Dormitories wired for high-speed internet access and linked to campus network. Commuter students can connect to campus network. Online library, helpline, repair service, wireless network available.

**Student life. Freshman orientation:** Mandatory. Preregistration for classes offered. Students assigned to core group of 12-18 students, with adviser to answer questions and schedule classes for fall semester. Core group advisers often visit students in their homes. **Policies:** Religious observance required. **Housing:** Guaranteed on-campus for freshmen. Single-sex dorms, special housing for disabled, apartments available. $100 nonrefundable deposit, deadline 8/1. **Activities:** Bands, campus ministries, choral groups, drama, literary magazine, music ensembles, musical theater, radio station, student government, student newspaper, symphony orchestra, Christian fellowships.

**Athletics. NAIA, NCCAA. Intercollegiate:** Baseball M, basketball, cross-country, golf, soccer, softball W, volleyball W. **Intramural:** Basketball, football (non-tackle), soccer, softball, volleyball, weight lifting. **Team name:** Warriors.

**Student services.** Adult student services, chaplain/spiritual director, career counseling, student employment services, financial aid counseling, health services, personal counseling, placement for graduates. **Physically disabled:** Services for visually, hearing impaired.

**Contact.** E-mail: admissions@corban.edu
Phone: (503) 375-7005 Toll-free number: (800) 845-3005
Fax: (503) 585-4316
Marty Ziesemer, Director of Admissions, Corban College, 5000 Deer Park Drive SE, Salem, OR 97317-9392

## DeVry University: Portland
### Portland, Oregon
### www.devry.edu

- For-profit 4-year university
- Commuter campus in very large city
- 130 degree-seeking undergraduates: 50% part-time, 39% women, 9% African American, 2% Asian American, 8% Hispanic American, 2% Native American
- 86 degree-seeking graduate students

**General. Degrees:** 12 bachelor's awarded; master's offered. **Calendar:** Semester. **Part-time faculty:** 32 total; 9% minority, 12% women.

**Freshman class profile.** 29 enrolled.

**Basis for selection.** Applicants must have high school diploma or equivalent, or a degree from accredited postsecondary institution, demonstrate proficiency in basic college-level skills through SAT or ACT scores or institution-administered placement exams, and be at least 17 years of age on the first day of classes. If applicant chooses not to submit SAT/ACT, DeVry-administered admissions test will be given.

**High school preparation.** College-preparatory program recommended.

**2009-2010 Annual costs.** Tuition/fees: $14,160. Books/supplies: $1,310. Personal expenses: $3,574.

**2008-2009 Financial aid. Non-need-based:** Scholarships awarded for academics.

**Application procedures. Admission:** No deadline. $50 fee. Admission notification on a rolling basis. **Financial aid:** No deadline. FAFSA required. Applicants notified on a rolling basis.

**Academics. Special study options:** Accelerated study, distance learning. **Credit/placement by examination:** CLEP.

**Majors. Business:** Business admin. **Computer sciences:** Networking, systems analysis, web page design. **Other:** Technical management.

**Most popular majors.** Business/marketing 83%, computer/information sciences 17%.

**Student life. Housing:** Private apartments, student-plan housing, private rooms available.

**Contact.** Phone: (866) 543-3879
DeVry University: Portland, Peterkort Center II, Portland, OR 97225

---

## Eastern Oregon University
### La Grande, Oregon
**www.eou.edu**                    CB code: 4300

- Public 4-year university and liberal arts college
- Residential campus in large town
- 3,160 degree-seeking undergraduates: 34% part-time, 61% women, 2% African American, 2% Asian American, 4% Hispanic American, 3% Native American, 1% international
- 310 degree-seeking graduate students
- 78% of applicants admitted
- SAT or ACT (ACT writing optional) required

**General.** Founded in 1929. Regionally accredited. **Degrees:** 539 bachelor's awarded; master's offered. **ROTC:** Army. **Location:** 260 miles from Portland; 180 miles from Boise, Idaho. **Calendar:** Quarter, limited summer session. **Full-time faculty:** 115 total; 48% have terminal degrees, 46% women. **Part-time faculty:** 12 total; 25% have terminal degrees, 58% women. **Class size:** 66% < 20, 29% 20-39, 2% 40-49, 3% 50-99, less than 1% >100. **Special facilities:** Wildlife habitat laboratory, agriculture experiment station.

**Freshman class profile.** 977 applied, 765 admitted, 473 enrolled.

| Mid 50% test scores | | | |
|---|---|---|---|
| SAT critical reading: | 420-530 | GPA 3.0-3.49: | 32% |
| SAT math: | 410-520 | GPA 2.0-2.99: | 35% |
| SAT writing: | 390-500 | Rank in top quarter: | 31% |
| ACT composite: | 17-22 | Rank in top tenth: | 14% |
| GPA 3.75 or higher: | 17% | Return as sophomores: | 72% |
| GPA 3.50-3.74: | 12% | Out-of-state: | 32% |
| | | Live on campus: | 57% |

**Basis for selection.** Secondary school record most important; 3.0 GPA in 14 subject areas required. Students not meeting requirements must submit portfolio including essay and 2 letters of recommendation. Limited number of students not meeting requirements may be admitted. **Homeschooled:** State high school equivalency certificate, letter of recommendation (nonparent) required. Applicants must present certificate of completion and portfolio including essay, letters of recommendation, standardized test scores.

**High school preparation.** College-preparatory program required. Required and recommended units include English 4, mathematics 3, science 2 (laboratory 1) and foreign language 2.

**2009-2010 Annual costs.** Tuition/fees: $6,456; $6,456 out-of-state. Per Oregon statute, nonresident tuition rates same as resident rates. Room/board: $7,750. Books/supplies: $1,350. Personal expenses: $1,227.

**2009-2010 Financial aid. Need-based:** 406 full-time freshmen applied for aid; 326 were judged to have need; 326 of these received aid. Average need met was 53%. Average scholarship/grant was $5,901; average loan $2,570. 51% of total undergraduate aid awarded as scholarships/grants, 49% as loans/jobs. **Non-need-based:** Awarded to 668 full-time undergraduates, including 193 freshmen. Scholarships awarded for academics, art, leadership, minority status, music/drama, state residency.

**Application procedures. Admission:** Priority date 12/1; deadline 9/1 (postmark date). $50 fee, may be waived for applicants with need. Admission notification on a rolling basis beginning on or about 10/1. **Financial aid:** Priority date 3/1; no closing date. FAFSA required. Applicants notified on a rolling basis starting 4/1; must reply within 4 week(s) of notification.

---

**Academics.** Regional advisers for distance education students. **Special study options:** Combined bachelor's/graduate degree, cooperative education, cross-registration, distance learning, double major, dual enrollment of high school students, exchange student, external degree, honors, independent study, internships, liberal arts/career combination, semester at sea, student-designed major, study abroad, teacher certification program, weekend college. **Credit/placement by examination:** AP, CLEP, IB, institutional tests. 45 credit hours maximum toward bachelor's degree. **Support services:** Learning center, study skills assistance, tutoring, writing center.

**Majors. Agriculture:** Agronomy, business, economics, range science, soil science. **Biology:** General. **Business:** General, accounting, business admin, managerial economics. **Computer sciences:** General, computer science, web page design. **Conservation:** General. **Education:** General, early childhood, elementary, ESL, German, middle, science, secondary, social science, social studies, Spanish. **Health:** Nursing (RN), ophthalmic lab technology, predental, premedicine, preop/surgical nursing, prepharmacy, preveterinary. **History:** General. **Legal studies:** Prelaw. **Liberal arts:** Arts/sciences. **Math:** General. **Parks/recreation:** Health/fitness. **Physical sciences:** Chemistry, physics. **Protective services:** Fire services admin. **Psychology:** General. **Social sciences:** Anthropology, political science, sociology. **Visual/performing arts:** Dramatic, studio arts.

**Most popular majors.** Business/marketing 33%, education 17%, liberal arts 20%.

**Computing on campus.** 150 workstations in dormitories, library, computer center, student center. Dormitories wired for high-speed internet access and linked to campus network. Commuter students can connect to campus network. Online course registration, online library, helpline, repair service, wireless network available.

**Student life. Freshman orientation:** Available. Preregistration for classes offered. **Housing:** Guaranteed on-campus for freshmen. Coed dorms, apartments available. **Activities:** Bands, choral groups, dance, drama, international student organizations, literary magazine, music ensembles, Model UN, musical theater, radio station, student government, student newspaper, symphony orchestra, international relations club, outdoor club, biology club, Fellowship of Christian Athletes, Latter-day Saints student association.

**Athletics.** NAIA. **Intercollegiate:** Basketball, cheerleading, cross-country, football (tackle) M, rodeo, soccer W, softball W, track and field, volleyball W. **Intramural:** Badminton, basketball, football (non-tackle), racquetball, softball, swimming, tennis, volleyball. **Team name:** Mountaineers.

**Student services.** Alcohol/substance abuse counseling, career counseling, student employment services, financial aid counseling, health services, minority student services, personal counseling, placement for graduates, veterans' counselor, women's services. **Physically disabled:** Services for visually, hearing impaired.

**Contact.** E-mail: admissions@eou.edu
Phone: (541) 962-3393 Toll-free number: (800) 452-8639
Fax: (541) 962-3418
Michael Dannells, Director of Admissions, Eastern Oregon University, One University Boulevard, La Grande, OR 97850

---

## Eugene Bible College
### Eugene, Oregon
**www.ebc.edu**                    CB code: 4274

- Private 4-year Bible college affiliated with Open Bible Standard Churches
- Residential campus in small city
- 107 degree-seeking undergraduates
- 27% of applicants admitted
- Application essay required

**General.** Founded in 1925. Accredited by ABHE. **Degrees:** 28 bachelor's awarded. **Location:** 100 miles from Portland. **Calendar:** Quarter, extensive summer session. **Full-time faculty:** 6 total; 33% have terminal degrees, 50% minority, 33% women. **Part-time faculty:** 14 total. **Class size:** 54% < 20, 38% 20-39, 6% 40-49, 2% 50-99.

**Freshman class profile.** 149 applied, 40 admitted, 27 enrolled.

| Mid 50% test scores | | | |
|---|---|---|---|
| SAT critical reading: | 450-580 | GPA 3.0-3.49: | 34% |
| SAT math: | 430-610 | GPA 2.0-2.99: | 32% |
| ACT composite: | 19-24 | Rank in top quarter: | 40% |
| GPA 3.75 or higher: | 11% | Rank in top tenth: | 9% |
| GPA 3.50-3.74: | 16% | Out-of-state: | 26% |
| | | Live on campus: | 81% |

**Basis for selection.** School achievement and activities, test scores, recommendations, personal essay most important. Religious affiliation or commitment important factor. **Homeschooled:** CAT test, SAT Subject Test, or ITBS recommended.

**High school preparation.** College-preparatory program recommended.

**2009-2010 Annual costs.** Tuition/fees: $10,923. Room/board: $6,027. Books/supplies: $900. Personal expenses: $1,500.

**2008-2009 Financial aid. Non-need-based:** Scholarships awarded for academics, athletics, leadership, religious affiliation. **Additional information:** Some early acceptance awards possible for those admitted by May 15. Distance awards to those coming from over 1,000 miles away. Some awards for husbands and wives enrolled at same time.

**Application procedures. Admission:** Priority date 1/1; deadline 8/1 (receipt date). $30 fee, may be waived for applicants with need. Admission notification on a rolling basis beginning on or about 12/31. **Financial aid:** Priority date 5/1, closing date 9/1. FAFSA required. Applicants notified on a rolling basis starting 7/15; must reply within 4 week(s) of notification.

**Academics.** Transfer-track programs available in elementary education: first 2 years at college, final 2-3 years at other institutions. **Special study options:** Distance learning, double major, independent study, internships. **Credit/placement by examination:** AP, CLEP, institutional tests. **Support services:** Reduced course load, remedial instruction, study skills assistance, tutoring.

**Majors. Philosophy/religion:** Christian, religion. **Theology:** Bible, missionary, pastoral counseling, religious ed, sacred music, theology, youth ministry.

**Computing on campus.** 18 workstations in dormitories, library, computer center, student center. Dormitories wired for high-speed internet access. Repair service available.

**Student life. Freshman orientation:** Mandatory. Preregistration for classes offered. Week-long program ends with camping retreat to mountains with fellow students and faculty. **Policies:** Students required to sign Code of Conduct agreement. Student ministry/community service required. Religious observance required. **Housing:** Guaranteed on-campus for freshmen. Single-sex dorms, apartments available. $75 partly refundable deposit, deadline 9/1. **Activities:** Concert band, campus ministries, choral groups, drama, music ensembles, musical theater, student government.

**Athletics. Intramural:** Basketball, soccer, volleyball. **Team name:** Deacons.

**Student services.** Chaplain/spiritual director, student employment services, financial aid counseling, personal counseling, placement for graduates, veterans' counselor.

**Contact.** E-mail: admissions@ebc.edu
Phone: (541) 485-1780 Toll-free number: (800) 322-2638
Fax: (541) 343-5801
Sarah Maestas, Director of Admissions/Registrar, Eugene Bible College, 2155 Bailey Hill Road, Eugene, OR 97405

---

## George Fox University
**Newberg, Oregon**
**www.georgefox.edu**

**CB member**
**CB code: 4325**

◗ Private 4-year university and seminary college affiliated with Society of Friends (Quaker)
◗ Residential campus in large town
◗ 1,949 degree-seeking undergraduates: 14% part-time, 60% women, 2% African American, 5% Asian American, 5% Hispanic American, 2% Native American, 5% international
◗ 1,288 degree-seeking graduate students
◗ 69% of applicants admitted
◗ SAT or ACT (ACT writing optional), application essay required
◗ 64% graduate within 6 years; 14% enter graduate study

**General.** Founded in 1891. Regionally accredited. Volunteer service encouraged through all-campus Serve Day and serve trips during school breaks. Freshmen receive laptop computer to keep upon graduating. **Degrees:** 528 bachelor's awarded; master's, professional offered. **ROTC:** Air Force. **Location:** 23 miles from Portland. **Calendar:** Semester, limited summer session. **Full-time faculty:** 165 total; 67% have terminal degrees, 7% minority, 39% women. **Part-time faculty:** 199 total; 23% have terminal degrees, 4% minority, 50% women. **Class size:** 59% < 20, 35% 20-39, 5% 40-49, 1%

50-99. **Special facilities:** Center for retreats and outdoor ministries, electron microscope, art galleries.

**Freshman class profile.** 1,528 applied, 1,052 admitted, 413 enrolled.

| Mid 50% test scores | | | |
|---|---|---|---|
| SAT critical reading: | 490-610 | GPA 2.0-2.99: | 11% |
| SAT math: | 480-610 | Rank in top quarter: | 60% |
| SAT writing: | 480-590 | Rank in top tenth: | 29% |
| ACT composite: | 21-26 | End year in good standing: | 86% |
| GPA 3.75 or higher: | 41% | Return as sophomores: | 79% |
| GPA 3.50-3.74: | 22% | Out-of-state: | 38% |
| GPA 3.0-3.49: | 25% | Live on campus: | 98% |
| | | International: | 3% |

**Basis for selection.** Decision based on grade transcript; test scores; recommendations from teacher and counselor; church, school, and community activities. Interview recommended for all; audition recommended for drama, music programs. **Homeschooled:** Statement describing homeschool structure and mission, transcript of courses and grades, letter of recommendation (nonparent) required.

**High school preparation.** College-preparatory program recommended. 16 units recommended. Recommended units include English 4, mathematics 2, social studies 3, history 2, science 2 (laboratory 2) and foreign language 2.

**2010-2011 Annual costs.** Tuition/fees: $27,970. Room/board: $8,630. Books/supplies: $700. Personal expenses: $1,380.

**2009-2010 Financial aid. Need-based:** 360 full-time freshmen applied for aid; 319 were judged to have need; 319 of these received aid. Average need met was 90%. Average scholarship/grant was $10,215; average loan $3,155. 65% of total undergraduate aid awarded as scholarships/grants, 35% as loans/jobs. **Non-need-based:** Awarded to 1,094 full-time undergraduates, including 304 freshmen. Scholarships awarded for academics, alumni affiliation, art, job skills, leadership, minority status, music/drama, religious affiliation. **Additional information:** Audition required for music and drama scholarships.

**Application procedures. Admission:** Priority date 2/1; no deadline. $40 fee, may be waived for applicants with need. Admission notification on a rolling basis beginning on or about 10/1. Must reply by May 1 or within 2 week(s) if notified thereafter. **Financial aid:** Priority date 2/1; no closing date. FAFSA required. Applicants notified on a rolling basis starting 3/1; must reply within 6 week(s) of notification.

**Academics. Special study options:** Accelerated study, cross-registration, double major, dual enrollment of high school students, ESL, exchange student, honors, independent study, internships, student-designed major, study abroad, teacher certification program, Washington semester. **Credit/placement by examination:** AP, CLEP, IB, SAT, ACT, institutional tests. 32 credit hours maximum toward bachelor's degree. **Support services:** Learning center, reduced course load, remedial instruction, study skills assistance, tutoring, writing center.

**Majors. Biology:** General. **Business:** Accounting/business management, business admin, management information systems. **Communications:** General, journalism, organizational. **Computer sciences:** General, information systems. **Education:** Elementary, music. **Engineering:** General, civil, computer, electrical, mechanical. **Family/consumer sciences:** General. **Foreign languages:** Spanish. **Health:** Athletic training, nursing (RN). **History:** General. **Interdisciplinary:** Behavioral sciences, cognitive science, global studies. **Math:** General. **Parks/recreation:** Health/fitness. **Philosophy/religion:** Philosophy, religion. **Physical sciences:** Chemistry. **Psychology:** General. **Public administration:** Social work. **Social sciences:** Economics, political science, sociology. **Theology:** Bible, pastoral counseling. **Visual/performing arts:** Art, cinematography, dramatic.

**Most popular majors.** Business/marketing 28%, health sciences 7%, interdisciplinary studies 13%, visual/performing arts 7%.

**Computing on campus.** 141 workstations in dormitories, library, computer center, student center. Dormitories wired for high-speed internet access and linked to campus network. Commuter students can connect to campus network. Online course registration, online library, helpline, repair service, wireless network available.

**Student life. Freshman orientation:** Mandatory. Preregistration for classes offered. One-day programs available during summer. New students attend 3-day program at start of semester. **Policies:** Three-year residency requirement for undergraduates. Required spiritual formation program and chapel program. Religious observance required. **Housing:** Single-sex dorms, special housing for disabled, apartments, wellness housing available. Pets allowed in dorm rooms. **Activities:** Bands, campus ministries, choral groups, drama, international student organizations, literary magazine, music ensembles, musical theater, radio station, student government, student newspaper, symphony orchestra, Christian services committee, associated student community, multicultural club, Fellowship of Christian Athletes, Young

Life, leadership development program, Little Bruin, urban services, College Republicans, College Democrats.

**Athletics.** NCAA. **Intercollegiate:** Baseball M, basketball, cross-country, golf, soccer, softball W, tennis, track and field, volleyball W. **Intramural:** Badminton, basketball, football (non-tackle), golf, racquetball, skiing, soccer, table tennis, tennis, volleyball. **Team name:** Bruins.

**Student services.** Adult student services, alcohol/substance abuse counseling, chaplain/spiritual director, career counseling, student employment services, financial aid counseling, health services, minority student services, personal counseling, veterans' counselor. **Physically disabled:** Services for visually, speech, hearing impaired.

**Contact.** E-mail: admissions@georgefox.edu
Phone: (503) 554-2240 Toll-free number: (800) 765-4369 ext. 2240
Fax: (503) 554-3110
Ryan Dougherty, Director of Undergraduate Admissions, George Fox University, 414 North Meridian Street #6089, Newberg, OR 97132-2697

## Gutenberg College
**Eugene, Oregon**
www.gutenberg.edu                                    CB code: 2605

- Private 4-year liberal arts college
- Small city
- 37 degree-seeking undergraduates: 51% women
- SAT, application essay required

**General.** Candidate for regional accreditation.; also accredited by TRACS. "Great Books" education from a biblical worldview. **Degrees:** 10 bachelor's awarded. **Calendar:** Quarter. **Full-time faculty:** 8 total. **Part-time faculty:** 2 total.

**Freshman class profile.** 10 enrolled.

**Basis for selection.** Admissions decision based on application, essays, 2 references (academic and character), SAT, transcripts, and course of study. 2 written essays required.

**2009-2010 Annual costs.** Tuition/fees: $11,853. Estimated annual cost of on-campus room and meal program is $5,000. Books/supplies: $650. Personal expenses: $500.

**Application procedures. Admission:** Closing date 3/1. $40 fee. Late applications after 3/1 may be considered; application fee is $60 for late applicants. **Financial aid:** Closing date 6/1. CSS PROFILE required.

**Academics. Credit/placement by examination:** CLEP.

**Majors. Liberal arts:** Arts/sciences.

**Student life. Freshman orientation:** Mandatory. **Housing:** Single-sex dorms available.

**Contact.** E-mail: admissions@gutenberg.edu
Phone: (541) 683-5141
Kasey Pilcher, Director of Admissions, Gutenberg College, 1883 University Street, Eugene, OR 97403

## ITT Technical Institute: Portland
**Portland, Oregon**
www.itt-tech.edu                                     CB code: 0947

- For-profit 4-year technical college
- Commuter campus in large city

**General.** Founded in 1979. Accredited by ACICS. **Location:** 10 miles from downtown. **Calendar:** Quarter.

**Contact.** Phone: (503) 255-6500
Director of Recruitment, 6035 Northeast 78th Court, Portland, OR 97218

## Lewis & Clark College
**Portland, Oregon**                                  CB member
www.lclark.edu                                        CB code: 4384

- Private 4-year liberal arts college
- Residential campus in very large city

- 1,905 degree-seeking undergraduates: 1% part-time, 60% women, 2% African American, 7% Asian American, 5% Hispanic American, 1% Native American, 6% international
- 1,546 degree-seeking graduate students
- 65% of applicants admitted
- Application essay required
- 76% graduate within 6 years; 37% enter graduate study

**General.** Founded in 1867. Regionally accredited. **Degrees:** 413 bachelor's awarded; master's, doctoral, professional offered. **Calendar:** Semester, limited summer session. **Full-time faculty:** 231 total; 94% have terminal degrees, 9% minority, 46% women. **Part-time faculty:** 149 total; 52% have terminal degrees, 9% minority, 56% women. **Class size:** 66% < 20, 31% 20-39, 2% 40-49, 1% 50-99. **Special facilities:** DIC and fluorescence microscopes, time-lapse deconvolution microscope, high-resolution oxygen analyzer, carbon dioxide gas exchange analyzer, end-point and real-time PCR equipment, multi-capacity lyophilizer, gel electrophoresis and imaging facilities, solar telescope with spectrograph, imaging laboratory with high resolution optical microscope, research astronomical observatory, holographic laboratory, electro-acoustic music studio, 85-rank Casavant organ, multi-media foreign language lab, human-computer interaction laboratory, climate-controlled greenhouse, GIS lab running ArcGIS for environmental research.

**Freshman class profile.** 5,343 applied, 3,448 admitted, 498 enrolled.

| Mid 50% test scores | | GPA 2.0-2.99: | 3% |
|---|---|---|---|
| SAT critical reading: | 610-710 | Rank in top quarter: | 81% |
| SAT math: | 610-680 | Rank in top tenth: | 46% |
| SAT writing: | 590-690 | End year in good standing: | 90% |
| ACT composite: | 27-30 | Return as sophomores: | 83% |
| GPA 3.75 or higher: | 53% | Out-of-state: | 91% |
| GPA 3.50-3.74: | 21% | Live on campus: | 98% |
| GPA 3.0-3.49: | 23% | International: | 6% |

**Basis for selection.** School curriculum and achievement most important. Standardized tests, recommendations, extracurricular involvement, essay, and interview also considered. Students may apply using Portfolio Path, where test scores are optional. In addition to the Common Application and Supplement, Portfolio Path applicants submit 3 academic teacher recommendations and academic portfolio. Applicants may choose whether to submit standardized test scores. All other admission requirements remain the same. Interviews optional. Audition recommended for music scholarships. **Homeschooled:** School's Portfolio Path for admissions recommended. GED required, interview recommended.

**High school preparation.** College-preparatory program recommended. Recommended units include English 4, mathematics 4, social studies 4, science 3 (laboratory 2) and foreign language 3. One unit fine arts recommended.

**2009-2010 Annual costs.** Tuition/fees: $35,233. Room/board: $9,006. Books/supplies: $1,050. Personal expenses: $990.

**2009-2010 Financial aid. Need-based:** Average need met was 83%. Average scholarship/grant was $21,303; average loan $3,414. 80% of total undergraduate aid awarded as scholarships/grants, 20% as loans/jobs. **Non-need-based:** Awarded to 246 full-time undergraduates, including 56 freshmen. Scholarships awarded for academics.

**Application procedures. Admission:** Closing date 2/1 (postmark date). $50 fee, may be waived for applicants with need, free for online applicants. Admission notification 4/1. Must reply by 5/1. **Financial aid:** Priority date 2/15; no closing date. FAFSA, CSS PROFILE required. Applicants notified on a rolling basis starting 3/1.

**Academics. Special study options:** Accelerated study, combined bachelor's/graduate degree, cross-registration, double major, dual enrollment of high school students, ESL, honors, independent study, internships, New York semester, student-designed major, study abroad, Washington semester. 3-2 engineering program with Columbia University, University of Southern California, Oregon Graduate Institute of Science and Engineering at OHSU, Washington University (St. Louis). **Credit/placement by examination:** AP, CLEP, IB, institutional tests. Up to 24 semester hours awarded for International Baccalaureate full diploma with score of 36 (16 hours for diploma with 32-35). Scores of 5 on higher level AP exams get 4 credits. **Support services:** Learning center, reduced course load, study skills assistance, tutoring, writing center.

**Majors. Area/ethnic studies:** East Asian. **Biology:** General, biochemistry. **Communications:** General. **Computer sciences:** Computer science. **Conservation:** Environmental studies. **Foreign languages:** General, French, German, Spanish. **History:** General. **Interdisciplinary:** Math/computer science. **Liberal arts:** Arts/sciences. **Math:** General. **Philosophy/religion:** Philosophy, religion. **Physical sciences:** Chemistry, physics. **Psychology:** General. **Social sciences:** Anthropology, economics, international relations, political science, sociology. **Visual/performing arts:** Art, dramatic, music performance, studio arts.

**Most popular majors.** Biology 9%, English 7%, foreign language 10%, psychology 15%, social sciences 26%, visual/performing arts 11%.

**Computing on campus.** 158 workstations in library, computer center, student center. Dormitories wired for high-speed internet access and linked to campus network. Commuter students can connect to campus network. Online library, helpline, repair service, student web hosting, wireless network available.

**Student life. Freshman orientation:** Mandatory. Preregistration for classes offered. Held 4 days preceding class in late August. **Policies:** Students required to live on-campus for 2 years. **Housing:** Guaranteed on-campus for freshmen. Coed dorms, single-sex dorms available. Apartment-style residence halls available for upperclassmen. **Activities:** Bands, campus ministries, choral groups, dance, drama, international student organizations, literary magazine, music ensembles, Model UN, musical theater, radio station, student government, student newspaper, symphony orchestra, TV station, Jewish student union, InterVarsity Christian Fellowship, Fellowship of Christian Athletes, Hawaii club, Amnesty International, black student union, Circle K, forensics, Gringos y Latinos.

**Athletics.** NCAA. **Intercollegiate:** Baseball M, basketball, cross-country, football (tackle) M, golf, rowing (crew), soccer W, softball W, swimming, tennis, track and field, volleyball W. **Intramural:** Badminton, basketball, cross-country, softball, swimming, table tennis, tennis, volleyball, water polo. **Team name:** Pioneers, Pios.

**Student services.** Adult student services, alcohol/substance abuse counseling, chaplain/spiritual director, career counseling, services for economically disadvantaged, student employment services, financial aid counseling, health services, legal services, minority student services, personal counseling, placement for graduates, veterans' counselor, women's services. **Physically disabled:** Services for visually, speech, hearing impaired.

**Contact.** E-mail: admissions@lclark.edu
Phone: (503) 768-7040 Toll-free number: (800) 444-4111
Fax: (503) 768-7055
Mervyn Brockett, Associate Provost, Dean of Admissions, Lewis & Clark College, 0615 SW Palatine Hill Road, Portland, OR 97219-7899

---

## Linfield College
**McMinnville, Oregon**
**www.linfield.edu**

**CB member**
**CB code: 4387**

- Private 4-year liberal arts college affiliated with American Baptist Churches in the USA
- Residential campus in large town
- 1,625 degree-seeking undergraduates: 2% part-time, 57% women, 2% African American, 9% Asian American, 5% Hispanic American, 2% Native American, 5% international
- 82% of applicants admitted
- SAT or ACT (ACT writing optional), application essay required
- 73% graduate within 6 years; 30% enter graduate study

**General.** Founded in 1849. Regionally accredited. Students interested in nursing or health sciences major may begin studies on the McMinnville Campus and then transfer to the Portland Campus to complete their degrees. Part-time students who wish to complete bachelor's degree online are served through Division of Continuing Education. **Degrees:** 312 bachelor's awarded. **ROTC:** Air Force. **Location:** 38 miles from Portland. **Calendar:** 4-1-4, limited summer session. **Full-time faculty:** 112 total; 96% have terminal degrees, 45% women. **Part-time faculty:** 74 total; 23% have terminal degrees, 53% women. **Class size:** 68% < 20, 29% 20-39, 1% 40-49, 1% 50-99, less than 1% >100. **Special facilities:** Cadaver lab, anthropology museum, music technology lab, interactive writing laboratory, speaking center.

**Freshman class profile.** 1,692 applied, 1,381 admitted, 423 enrolled.

| Mid 50% test scores | | | |
|---|---|---|---|
| SAT critical reading: | 480-600 | Rank in top quarter: | 69% |
| SAT math: | 490-600 | Rank in top tenth: | 30% |
| SAT writing: | 460-580 | End year in good standing: | 95% |
| ACT composite: | 21-27 | Return as sophomores: | 81% |
| GPA 3.75 or higher: | 38% | Out-of-state: | 49% |
| GPA 3.50-3.74: | 24% | Live on campus: | 99% |
| GPA 3.0-3.49: | 30% | International: | 5% |
| GPA 2.0-2.99: | 8% | Fraternities: | 10% |
| | | Sororities: | 25% |

**Basis for selection.** High school academic performance, writing sample, recommendations from teachers and counselors, and pre-college test results

important. Non-academic community and school activities considered. Interview recommended. **Homeschooled:** Transcript of courses and grades required. Homeschool supplement to the Common Application required.

**High school preparation.** College-preparatory program recommended. 17 units recommended. Recommended units include English 4, mathematics 4, social studies 3, science 3 and foreign language 2.

**2009-2010 Annual costs.** Tuition/fees: $29,034. Room/board: $8,280. Books/supplies: $750. Personal expenses: $1,100.

**2009-2010 Financial aid. Need-based:** 299 full-time freshmen applied for aid; 299 were judged to have need; 266 of these received aid. Average need met was 84%. Average scholarship/grant was $13,361; average loan $3,320. 64% of total undergraduate aid awarded as scholarships/grants, 36% as loans/jobs. **Non-need-based:** Awarded to 1,131 full-time undergraduates, including 292 freshmen. Scholarships awarded for academics, minority status, music/drama.

**Application procedures. Admission:** Priority date 2/15; no deadline. $40 fee, may be waived for applicants with need. Must reply by May 1 or within 2 week(s) if notified thereafter. **Financial aid:** Priority date 2/1; no closing date. FAFSA required. Must reply by 5/1 or within 2 week(s) of notification.

**Academics. Special study options:** Cross-registration, distance learning, double major, ESL, external degree, independent study, internships, liberal arts/career combination, semester at sea, student-designed major, study abroad, teacher certification program, Washington semester. Semester abroad programs at Linfield centers in Australia, Austria, China (Beijing and Hong Kong), Costa Rica, Ecuador, England, France, Ireland, Japan, Korea, Mexico, New Zealand, and Norway; shorter term study abroad opportunities through one-month January term. **Credit/placement by examination:** AP, CLEP, IB, institutional tests. 30 credit hours maximum toward bachelor's degree. **Support services:** Learning center, reduced course load, study skills assistance, tutoring, writing center.

**Majors. Area/ethnic studies:** German. **Biology:** General. **Business:** General, accounting, finance, international. **Communications:** General, media studies. **Computer sciences:** Computer science. **Conservation:** Environmental studies. **Education:** Elementary, music. **Foreign languages:** French, German, Japanese, Spanish. **Health:** Athletic training, health services, nursing (RN). **History:** General. **Math:** General. **Parks/recreation:** Exercise sciences, health/fitness. **Philosophy/religion:** Philosophy, religion. **Physical sciences:** General, applied physics, chemistry, physics. **Psychology:** General. **Social sciences:** Anthropology, economics, political science, sociology. **Visual/performing arts:** Art, design, dramatic, music performance, music theory/composition, studio arts.

**Most popular majors.** Business/marketing 24%, communications/journalism 6%, education 9%, history 8%, parks/recreation 8%, psychology 7%, social sciences 10%.

**Computing on campus.** 250 workstations in dormitories, library, computer center, student center. Dormitories wired for high-speed internet access and linked to campus network. Commuter students can connect to campus network. Online course registration, online library, helpline, repair service, student web hosting, wireless network available.

**Student life. Freshman orientation:** Mandatory. Preregistration for classes offered. Four-day program held at beginning of fall semester; includes advising, peer mentoring. **Policies:** All students required to live on-campus unless they are of senior standing, married, or living with parents locally. **Housing:** Guaranteed on-campus for all undergraduates. Coed dorms, single-sex dorms, special housing for disabled, apartments, fraternity/sorority housing, wellness housing available. **Activities:** Bands, campus ministries, choral groups, dance, drama, international student organizations, literary magazine, music ensembles, musical theater, opera, radio station, student government, student newspaper, symphony orchestra, multicultural student club, Greenfield, Hawaiian club, Fellowship of Christian Athletes, progressive student union, Circle-K, Habitat for Humanity, gay straight alliance, Republican club.

**Athletics.** NCAA. **Intercollegiate:** Baseball M, basketball, cross-country, football (tackle) M, golf, lacrosse W, soccer, softball, swimming, tennis, track and field, volleyball W. **Intramural:** Basketball, bowling, soccer, softball, volleyball. **Team name:** Wildcats.

**Student services.** Adult student services, alcohol/substance abuse counseling, chaplain/spiritual director, career counseling, student employment services, financial aid counseling, health services, minority student services, personal counseling, placement for graduates, veterans' counselor, women's services. **Physically disabled:** Services for visually, speech, hearing impaired.

**Contact.** E-mail: admission@linfield.edu
Phone: (503) 883-2213 Toll-free number: (800) 640-2287
Fax: (503) 883-2472
Lisa Knodle-Bragiel, Director of Admission, Linfield College, 900
Southeast Baker Street, McMinnville, OR 97218-6894

## Marylhurst University
### Marylhurst, Oregon
### www.marylhurst.edu
**CB code: 0440**

- Private 4-year university and liberal arts college affiliated with Roman Catholic Church
- Commuter campus in large town
- 911 degree-seeking undergraduates: 70% part-time, 71% women, 5% African American, 1% Asian American, 3% Hispanic American, 1% international
- 889 degree-seeking graduate students

**General.** Founded in 1893. Regionally accredited. **Degrees:** 166 bachelor's awarded; master's, professional offered. **Location:** 10 miles from Portland. **Calendar:** Quarter, extensive summer session. **Full-time faculty:** 52 total. **Part-time faculty:** 201 total. **Class size:** 98% < 20, 2% 20-39.

**Freshman class profile.** 44 applied, 31 admitted, 23 enrolled.

End year in good standing: 92%    Return as sophomores: 58%

**Basis for selection.** Open admission, but selective for some programs. High school GPA, record and recommendations considered for selective programs. **Homeschooled:** Interview required.

**2009-2010 Annual costs.** Tuition/fees: $16,920. Personal expenses: $1,500.

**2008-2009 Financial aid. Need-based:** 7 full-time freshmen applied for aid; 5 were judged to have need; 4 of these received aid. Average need met was 35%. Average scholarship/grant was $5,804; average loan $2,896. 28% of total undergraduate aid awarded as scholarships/grants, 72% as loans/jobs. **Non-need-based:** Awarded to 14 full-time undergraduates, including 6 freshmen. Scholarships awarded for academics.

**Application procedures. Admission:** No deadline. $20 fee. Admission notification on a rolling basis. **Financial aid:** Priority date 3/1; no closing date. FAFSA, institutional form required. Applicants notified on a rolling basis starting 5/1.

**Academics. Special study options:** Accelerated study, cooperative education, cross-registration, distance learning, double major, dual enrollment of high school students, ESL, independent study, internships, liberal arts/career combination, student-designed major, teacher certification program, weekend college. **Credit/placement by examination:** AP, CLEP, IB, institutional tests. 45 credit hours maximum toward bachelor's degree. **Support services:** Learning center, reduced course load, study skills assistance, tutoring, writing center.

**Majors. Business:** General, business admin, communications, real estate. **Communications:** General. **Conservation:** Environmental studies. **Liberal arts:** Arts/sciences. **Philosophy/religion:** Philosophy, religion. **Psychology:** General. **Social sciences:** General. **Visual/performing arts:** Art, interior design, studio arts. **Other:** Cultural studies.

**Most popular majors.** Business/marketing 34%, communications/journalism 6%, English 6%, interdisciplinary studies 13%, visual/performing arts 17%.

**Computing on campus.** 41 workstations in library. Commuter students can connect to campus network. Online course registration, helpline, wireless network available.

**Student life. Activities:** Jazz band, campus ministries, choral groups, literary magazine, music ensembles, symphony orchestra.

**Student services.** Adult student services, career counseling, financial aid counseling, personal counseling, veterans' counselor. **Physically disabled:** Services for visually, hearing impaired.

**Contact.** E-mail: admissions@marylhurst.edu
Phone: (503) 699-6268 Toll-free number: (800) 634-9982 ext. 6268
Fax: (503) 635-6585
Gretchen Potter, Director of Admissions, Marylhurst University, PO Box 261, Marylhurst, OR 97036-0261

## Mount Angel Seminary
### St. Benedict, Oregon
### www.mtangel.edu
**CB code: 4491**

- Private 4-year seminary college for men affiliated with Roman Catholic Church
- Residential campus in small town
- 80 degree-seeking undergraduates
- 86 graduate students

**General.** Founded in 1887. Regionally accredited; also accredited by ATS. All undergraduates candidates for Roman Catholic priesthood. **Degrees:** 15 bachelor's awarded; master's, professional offered. **Location:** 40 miles from Portland. **Calendar:** Semester. **Full-time faculty:** 25 total. **Part-time faculty:** 15 total.

**Freshman class profile.**

Out-of-state: 75%    Live on campus: 100%

**Basis for selection.** Primarily recommendations from sponsoring dioceses or clergymen, personal interview important. Test scores considered. SAT or ACT recommended. Interview recommended.

**2009-2010 Annual costs.** Tuition/fees: $14,096. Formation fee of $3,267 per year. Room/board: $9,850. Books/supplies: $800. Personal expenses: $1,000.

**Application procedures. Admission:** Closing date 6/15. $27 fee, may be waived for applicants with need. Admission notification on a rolling basis beginning on or about 9/1. **Financial aid:** No deadline. Institutional form required. Applicants notified on a rolling basis; must reply within 2 week(s) of notification.

**Academics. Special study options:** Cross-registration, double major, ESL. Interdivisional program, 3-week full-time pursuit of single approved course of study. **Credit/placement by examination:** CLEP, institutional tests.

**Majors. Liberal arts:** Arts/sciences. **Philosophy/religion:** Philosophy. **Theology:** Theology.

**Computing on campus.** 10 workstations in dormitories, library, computer center.

**Student life. Policies:** All full-time students working toward priesthood required to live on campus. Religious observance required. **Housing:** Guaranteed on-campus for all undergraduates. **Activities:** Student government.

**Athletics. Intramural:** Basketball M, racquetball M, soccer M, swimming M, volleyball M.

**Student services.** Health services, personal counseling.

**Contact.** Phone: (503) 845-3951 Fax: (503) 845-3126
Admissions Director, Mount Angel Seminary, One Abbey Drive, St. Benedict, OR 97373

## Multnomah University
### Portland, Oregon
### www.multnomah.edu
**CB code: 4496**

- Private 4-year Bible and seminary college affiliated with interdenominational tradition
- Residential campus in very large city
- 578 degree-seeking undergraduates: 17% part-time, 42% women
- 280 degree-seeking graduate students
- 87% of applicants admitted
- SAT or ACT (ACT writing recommended), application essay required
- 37% graduate within 6 years

**General.** Founded in 1936. Regionally accredited; also accredited by ABHE. Emphasis on preparation for Christian ministries. **Degrees:** 130 bachelor's awarded; master's offered. **Location:** 5 miles from downtown. **Calendar:** Semester, limited summer session. **Full-time faculty:** 44 total; 80% have terminal degrees, 9% minority, 16% women. **Part-time faculty:** 65 total; 51% have terminal degrees, 5% minority, 20% women. **Class size:** 76% < 20, 16% 20-39, 4% 40-49, 4% 50-99, less than 1% >100.

**Freshman class profile.** 134 applied, 117 admitted, 62 enrolled.

| Mid 50% test scores | | | |
|---|---|---|---|
| SAT critical reading: | 530-620 | GPA 3.0-3.49: | 26% |
| SAT math: | 450-590 | GPA 2.0-2.99: | 24% |
| SAT writing: | 470-610 | Rank in top quarter: | 50% |
| ACT composite: | 19-27 | Rank in top tenth: | 27% |
| GPA 3.75 or higher: | 23% | Return as sophomores: | 73% |
| GPA 3.50-3.74: | 27% | Out-of-state: | 60% |
| | | Live on campus: | 59% |

**Basis for selection.** School achievement record, test scores, recommendations most important. **Homeschooled:** If official transcript cannot be supplied, parental statement verifying student has met high school graduation requirements for home schoolers for their home state or GED test scores required.

**High school preparation.** College-preparatory program recommended. Recommended units include English 4, mathematics 2, social studies 3, history 2, science 3 (laboratory 1) and foreign language 2.

**2009-2010 Annual costs.** Tuition/fees: $14,520. Cost of health insurance if student is not covered is approximately $1,200. Room/board: $6,150. Books/supplies: $1,000. Personal expenses: $3,200.

**2008-2009 Financial aid. Need-based:** 69 full-time freshmen applied for aid; 57 were judged to have need; 56 of these received aid. Average need met was 44%. Average scholarship/grant was $4,971; average loan $2,718. 40% of total undergraduate aid awarded as scholarships/grants, 60% as loans/jobs. **Non-need-based:** Awarded to 33 full-time undergraduates, including 6 freshmen. Scholarships awarded for academics, leadership, music/drama, religious affiliation.

**Application procedures. Admission:** Priority date 3/1; deadline 7/15 (postmark date). $40 fee. Admission notification on a rolling basis. Must reply by 8/15. **Financial aid:** Priority date 3/1, closing date 7/1. FAFSA, institutional form required. Applicants notified on a rolling basis starting 4/1; must reply within 2 week(s) of notification.

**Academics. Special study options:** Cooperative education, distance learning, double major, internships, liberal arts/career combination, teacher certification program. **Credit/placement by examination:** AP, CLEP, IB, institutional tests. 20 credit hours maximum toward bachelor's degree. **Support services:** Reduced course load, study skills assistance, tutoring, writing center.

**Majors. Communications:** General, journalism. **Education:** Elementary. **Foreign languages:** Ancient Greek, Hebrew. **History:** General. **Psychology:** General. **Theology:** Bible, missionary, pastoral counseling, religious ed, sacred music, theology, youth ministry.

**Computing on campus.** 42 workstations in dormitories, library, computer center, student center. Dormitories wired for high-speed internet access and linked to campus network. Commuter students can connect to campus network. Online course registration, online library, helpline, wireless network available.

**Student life. Freshman orientation:** Mandatory. Preregistration for classes offered. Held 3 days before start of classes. **Policies:** No alcohol, smoking, gambling. Religious observance required. **Housing:** Guaranteed on-campus for freshmen. Single-sex dorms, special housing for disabled, apartments available. $100 fully refundable deposit, deadline 7/15. Houses for students with spouses or dependents. **Activities:** Campus ministries, choral groups, drama, music ensembles, student government, student newspaper.

**Athletics.** NCCAA. **Intercollegiate:** Basketball, volleyball W. **Intramural:** Basketball, football (non-tackle), soccer, volleyball. **Team name:** Lions.

**Student services.** Chaplain/spiritual director, career counseling, student employment services, financial aid counseling, health services, personal counseling, placement for graduates, veterans' counselor.

**Contact.** E-mail: admiss@multnomah.edu
Phone: (503) 255-0332 ext. 485 Toll-free number: (800) 275-4672
Fax: (503) 254-1268
John Mayner, Director of Admissions, Multnomah University, 8435 Northeast Glisan Street, Portland, OR 97220-5898

## Northwest Christian University
### Eugene, Oregon
**www.northwestchristian.edu**                    **CB code: 4543**

- Private 4-year university affiliated with Christian Church (Disciples of Christ)
- Commuter campus in small city

- 443 degree-seeking undergraduates: 17% part-time, 59% women, 2% African American, 3% Asian American, 5% Hispanic American, 2% Native American
- 110 degree-seeking graduate students
- 95% of applicants admitted
- SAT or ACT (ACT writing recommended), application essay required
- 39% graduate within 6 years

**General.** Founded in 1895. Regionally accredited. **Degrees:** 120 bachelor's, 2 associate awarded; master's offered. **Location:** 110 miles from Portland. **Calendar:** Semester, limited summer session.

**Freshman class profile.** 596 applied, 568 admitted, 78 enrolled.

| Mid 50% test scores | | | |
|---|---|---|---|
| SAT critical reading: | 450-560 | GPA 3.0-3.49: | 37% |
| SAT math: | 450-550 | GPA 2.0-2.99: | 19% |
| SAT writing: | 450-530 | Rank in top quarter: | 45% |
| ACT composite: | 20-23 | Rank in top tenth: | 21% |
| GPA 3.75 or higher: | 41% | End year in good standing: | 95% |
| GPA 3.50-3.74: | 3% | Return as sophomores: | 78% |
| | | Out-of-state: | 29% |

**Basis for selection.** Overall grade performance; adherence to College Preparation Standards; content and difficulty of courses taken; standardized test scores; quality of involvement in applicant's church, community, and school activities important. Additional information may be requested, including updated transcripts, additional essays, and interview. Interview recommended, personal statement required.

**High school preparation.** College-preparatory program recommended. 14 units recommended. Recommended units include English 4, mathematics 3, social studies 3, science 2 (laboratory 1) and foreign language 2.

**2009-2010 Annual costs.** Tuition/fees: $22,900. Room/board: $6,800. Books/supplies: $900. Personal expenses: $2,340.

**2009-2010 Financial aid. Non-need-based:** Scholarships awarded for academics, athletics, leadership, music/drama, religious affiliation.

**Application procedures. Admission:** Priority date 7/1; no deadline. No application fee. Admission notification on a rolling basis beginning on or about 9/15. **Financial aid:** Priority date 3/1; no closing date. FAFSA required. Applicants notified on a rolling basis starting 3/1; must reply within 2 week(s) of notification.

**Academics. Special study options:** Accelerated study, cross-registration, distance learning, double major, dual enrollment of high school students, exchange student, independent study, internships, semester at sea, student-designed major, study abroad, teacher certification program. **Credit/placement by examination:** AP, CLEP, IB, SAT, ACT. No limit on credit by examination. **Support services:** Reduced course load, remedial instruction, study skills assistance, tutoring, writing center.

**Majors. Biology:** Exercise physiology. **Business:** Accounting, business admin. **Communications:** General. **Education:** Multi-level teacher. **Health:** Health services admin. **History:** General. **Interdisciplinary:** Global studies, intercultural. **Math:** General. **Psychology:** General. **Theology:** Bible, missionary, pastoral counseling, sacred music, theology, youth ministry. **Visual/performing arts:** Music management.

**Most popular majors.** Business/marketing 34%, computer/information sciences 6%, education 15%, health sciences 12%, public administration/social services 7%.

**Computing on campus.** 55 workstations in dormitories, library, computer center. Dormitories wired for high-speed internet access and linked to campus network. Commuter students can connect to campus network. Online library, helpline, wireless network available.

**Student life. Freshman orientation:** Mandatory. Preregistration for classes offered. 4-day program; includes excursion trip. **Policies:** Attendance at chapel required of all students. Religious observance required. **Housing:** Guaranteed on-campus for freshmen. Coed dorms, apartments available. $100 fully refundable deposit, deadline 5/1. Pets allowed in dorm rooms. **Activities:** Pep band, campus ministries, choral groups, dance, drama, literary magazine, music ensembles, student government, student newspaper, Parable, Circle K, Believers Building Bonds through Boardgames, community life groups.

**Athletics.** NAIA. **Intercollegiate:** Basketball, cross-country, golf, soccer, softball W, track and field, volleyball W. **Intramural:** Badminton, basketball, football (non-tackle) M, handball, skiing, volleyball. **Team name:** Beacons.

**Student services.** Adult student services, alcohol/substance abuse counseling, chaplain/spiritual director, career counseling, student employment services, financial aid counseling, personal counseling, placement for graduates, veterans' counselor. **Physically disabled:** Services for hearing impaired.

**Contact.** E-mail: admissions@northwestchristian.edu
Phone: (541) 684-7201 Toll-free number: (877) 463-6622
Fax: (541) 684-7317
Jennifer Samples, Director of Admissions, Northwest Christian University, 828 East 11th Avenue, Eugene, OR 97401-3745

## Oregon College of Art & Craft
### Portland, Oregon
### www.ocac.edu

- Private 4-year visual arts college
- Commuter campus in very large city
- 124 degree-seeking undergraduates: 29% part-time, 71% women, 2% Asian American, 2% Hispanic American, 5% Native American
- 88% of applicants admitted
- Application essay required
- 52% graduate within 6 years

**General.** Candidate for regional accreditation. **Degrees:** 28 bachelor's awarded. **Calendar:** Semester. **Full-time faculty:** 9 total; 89% have terminal degrees, 11% minority, 44% women. **Part-time faculty:** 19 total; 84% have terminal degrees, 5% minority, 63% women. **Class size:** 96% < 20, 4% 20-39.

**Freshman class profile.** 42 applied, 37 admitted, 14 enrolled.

| Mid 50% test scores | | | |
|---|---|---|---|
| SAT critical reading: | 470-630 | GPA 3.0-3.49: | 40% |
| SAT math: | 440-550 | GPA 2.0-2.99: | 39% |
| SAT writing: | 450-610 | Return as sophomores: | 68% |
| ACT composite: | 24-30 | Out-of-state: | 25% |
| GPA 3.75 or higher: | 15% | Live on campus: | 37% |

**Basis for selection.** Talent and ability, GPA, essay and interview very important. Portfolio required. **Homeschooled:** Statement describing home-school structure and mission required.

**High school preparation.** Recommended units include English 4, mathematics 3, social studies 1, history 3, science 3, foreign language 2 and visual/performing arts 2.

**2009-2010 Annual costs.** Tuition/fees: $21,610. Fees vary by area of concentration. Room/board: $9,500. Books/supplies: $1,800.

**2009-2010 Financial aid. Need-based:** Average need met was 36%. Average scholarship/grant was $7,111; average loan $3,500. 46% of total undergraduate aid awarded as scholarships/grants, 54% as loans/jobs. **Non-need-based:** Scholarships awarded for academics, art.

**Application procedures. Admission:** Priority date 3/1; no deadline. $35 fee, may be waived for applicants with need. Admission notification on a rolling basis beginning on or about 1/1. Must reply by May 1 or within 4 week(s) if notified thereafter. **Financial aid:** Priority date 3/1; no closing date. FAFSA required. Applicants notified on a rolling basis starting 3/15.

**Academics.** Tutor guided study groups held in the evenings for all students who want to participate. **Special study options:** Cross-registration, exchange student, independent study, internships, study abroad. **Credit/placement by examination:** AP, CLEP, IB, institutional tests. **Support services:** Study skills assistance, tutoring.

**Majors. Production:** Furniture, woodworking. **Visual/performing arts:** Ceramics, drawing, fiber arts, metal/jewelry, painting, photography. **Other:** Book arts.

**Computing on campus.** Dormitories wired for high-speed internet access. Helpline, wireless network available.

**Student life. Freshman orientation:** Mandatory. Preregistration for classes offered. Two-day orientation includes field trip to Portland Art Museum. Guided kayaking trip also offered. **Housing:** Cooperative housing available. $150 nonrefundable deposit, deadline 5/1. Small number of on-campus housing available for new students straight from high school. **Activities:** Student government, student newspaper.

**Student services.** Career counseling, financial aid counseling, personal counseling.

**Contact.** E-mail: admissions@ocac.edu
Phone: (503) 297-5544 ext. 129 Toll-free number: (800) 390-0632
Fax: (503) 297-9651
Devon Simpson, Assistant Director of Admissions, Oregon College of Art & Craft, 8245 SW Barnes Road, Portland, OR 97225-6349

## Oregon Health & Science University
### Portland, Oregon
**CB member**
### www.ohsu.edu
**CB code: 4900**

- Public 3-year university and health science college
- Commuter campus in very large city
- 728 degree-seeking undergraduates: 73% part-time, 83% women, 1% African American, 4% Asian American, 5% Hispanic American, 2% Native American, 1% international
- 1,803 degree-seeking graduate students

**General.** Founded in 1887. Regionally accredited. **Degrees:** 221 bachelor's awarded; master's, doctoral, professional offered. **Calendar:** Quarter, limited summer session. **Full-time faculty:** 2,215 total. **Part-time faculty:** 515 total.

**Basis for selection.** Admission requirements vary by program.

**2009-2010 Annual costs.** Tuition/fees: $18,724; $29,974 out-of-state. Tuition shown is for undergraduate nursing program; costs for other programs vary. Books/supplies: $1,368.

**2009-2010 Financial aid. Need-based:** 99% of total undergraduate aid awarded as scholarships/grants, 1% as loans/jobs. **Non-need-based:** Scholarships awarded for academics, minority status, state residency.

**Application procedures. Admission:** Closing date 1/15 (postmark date). $120 fee, may be waived for applicants with need. Application must be submitted online. Admission notification on a rolling basis. Must reply by 5/1. **Financial aid:** Priority date 3/1; no closing date.

**Academics. Special study options:** Accelerated study, distance learning. **Credit/placement by examination:** CLEP. **Support services:** Pre-admission summer program, study skills assistance, tutoring.

**Majors. Health:** Clinical lab science, EMT paramedic, medical radiologic technology/radiation therapy, nursing (RN).

**Computing on campus.** 60 workstations in library, computer center, student center. Commuter students can connect to campus network. Online library, helpline, wireless network available.

**Student life. Freshman orientation:** Mandatory. Orientation varies by program. **Activities:** Student government, student newspaper.

**Athletics. Intramural:** Basketball, soccer, swimming, table tennis, tennis, volleyball.

**Student services.** Career counseling, financial aid counseling, health services, personal counseling.

**Contact.** E-mail: proginfo@ohsu.edu
Phone: (503) 494-8311
Oregon Health & Science University, 3181 SW Sam Jackson Park Road, Portland, OR 97239-3098

## Oregon Institute of Technology
### Klamath Falls, Oregon
**CB member**
### www.oit.edu
**CB code: 4587**

- Public 4-year career college
- Commuter campus in small city
- 3,036 degree-seeking undergraduates
- 93% of applicants admitted
- SAT or ACT with writing required

**General.** Founded in 1947. Regionally accredited. Upper-division courses offered in electronics engineering technology, manufacturing engineering technology. Software engineering technology offered at OIT Portland West in Beaverton area. **Degrees:** 488 bachelor's, 72 associate awarded; master's offered. **ROTC:** Army. **Location:** 280 miles from Portland; 270 miles from Reno, Nevada. **Calendar:** Quarter, limited summer session. **Full-time faculty:** 134 total. **Part-time faculty:** 113 total. **Class size:** 54% < 20, 40% 20-39, 3% 40-49, 4% 50-99. **Special facilities:** Center for research on geothermal energy, renewable energy center, center for health professions.

**Freshman class profile.** 775 applied, 719 admitted, 368 enrolled.

| Mid 50% test scores | | | |
|---|---|---|---|
| SAT critical reading: | 440-560 | GPA 3.0-3.49: | 38% |
| SAT math: | 470-590 | GPA 2.0-2.99: | 17% |
| SAT writing: | 420-540 | Rank in top quarter: | 52% |
| ACT composite: | 21-27 | Rank in top tenth: | 18% |
| GPA 3.75 or higher: | 22% | Out-of-state: | 11% |
| GPA 3.50-3.74: | 23% | Live on campus: | 51% |

**Basis for selection.** Secondary school record and standardized test scores very important. Class rank, recommendations, essay, interview, character/personal qualities and work experience all considered. Applicants from nonstandard or unaccredited high schools must take 3 SAT Subject Tests: 1 English, 1 math, 1 other of student's choice. **Learning Disabled:** Tech opportunities available.

**High school preparation.** 14 units required. Required units include English 4, mathematics 3, social studies 3, science 2 (laboratory 1) and foreign language 2.

**2009-2010 Annual costs.** Tuition/fees: $6,570; $18,090 out-of-state. Room/board: $8,245. Books/supplies: $1,000. Personal expenses: $2,438.

**2008-2009 Financial aid.** **Non-need-based:** Scholarships awarded for academics, athletics, leadership, minority status.

**Application procedures.** **Admission:** Priority date 2/1; no deadline. $50 fee. Admission notification on a rolling basis beginning on or about 10/15. Must reply by May 1 or within 4 week(s) if notified thereafter. Application deadline for dual enrollment is 3 weeks before term starts. **Financial aid:** Priority date 3/1; no closing date. FAFSA required. Applicants notified on a rolling basis starting 4/1; must reply within 3 week(s) of notification.

**Academics.** **Special study options:** Combined bachelor's/graduate degree, cooperative education, cross-registration, distance learning, double major, dual enrollment of high school students, external degree, internships, liberal arts/career combination, study abroad. **Credit/placement by examination:** AP, CLEP, SAT, ACT, institutional tests. No more than 25% of credits submitted for graduation may be credit by examination. **Support services:** Learning center, reduced course load, remedial instruction, study skills assistance, tutoring.

**Majors. Biology:** General. **Business:** Accounting, management information systems, marketing, operations, small business admin. **Communications:** General. **Computer sciences:** Information technology. **Conservation:** Environmental science. **Engineering:** Civil, electrical, mechanical. **Engineering technology:** Computer, electrical, energy systems, manufacturing, mechanical, software, surveying. **Health:** Clinical lab science, dental hygiene, health care admin, health services, medical records admin, nuclear medical technology, radiologic technology/medical imaging, respiratory therapy technology, sonography. **Math:** Applied. **Psychology:** General. **Other:** Echocardiography, Embedded systems engineering technology.

**Most popular majors.** Business/marketing 17%, engineering/engineering technologies 33%, health sciences 31%, psychology 11%.

**Computing on campus.** 656 workstations in dormitories, library, computer center. Dormitories wired for high-speed internet access. Commuter students can connect to campus network. Online course registration, online library, helpline, repair service, student web hosting, wireless network available.

**Student life. Freshman orientation:** Mandatory. Preregistration for classes offered. **Housing:** Coed dorms available. $150 partly refundable deposit, deadline 5/1. **Activities:** Choral groups, radio station, student government, student newspaper, symphony orchestra, TV station, Newman club, Latterday Saints, Christian Fellowship, Native American club, international student club, Circle K, Latin American club, residence hall association, Phi Delta Theta, College Republicans.

**Athletics.** NAIA. **Intercollegiate:** Baseball M, basketball, cross-country, soccer W, softball W, track and field, volleyball W. **Intramural:** Basketball, cheerleading, cross-country, football (tackle) M, lacrosse M, soccer, softball, track and field, volleyball. **Team name:** Owls.

**Student services.** Adult student services, alcohol/substance abuse counseling, career counseling, student employment services, financial aid counseling, health services, personal counseling, placement for graduates, veterans' counselor. **Physically disabled:** Services for visually, hearing impaired.

**Contact.** E-mail: oit@oit.edu
Phone: (541) 885-1150 Toll-free number: (800) 422-2017
Fax: (541) 885-1115
Ginny Gardiner, Director of Admissions, Oregon Institute of Technology, 3201 Campus Drive, Klamath Falls, OR 97601

---

## Oregon State University
**Corvallis, Oregon**
www.oregonstate.edu

**CB member**
**CB code: 4586**

- Public 4-year university
- Residential campus in small city
- 17,139 degree-seeking undergraduates: 13% part-time, 47% women, 1% African American, 9% Asian American, 5% Hispanic American, 1% Native American, 2% international
- 3,317 degree-seeking graduate students
- 83% of applicants admitted
- SAT or ACT with writing, application essay required
- 60% graduate within 6 years

**General.** Founded in 1868. Regionally accredited. **Degrees:** 3,300 bachelor's awarded; master's, doctoral, professional offered. **ROTC:** Army, Naval, Air Force. **Location:** 80 miles from Portland, 45 miles from Eugene. **Calendar:** Quarter, extensive summer session. **Full-time faculty:** 838 total; 75% have terminal degrees, 14% minority, 41% women. **Part-time faculty:** 202 total; 46% have terminal degrees, 8% minority, 49% women. **Class size:** 37% < 20, 34% 20-39, 8% 40-49, 13% 50-99, 8% >100. **Special facilities:** Arboretum, 13,429-acre forest, radiation center (with TRIGA Mark II Nuclear Reactor), wave research facility, marine science center museum and aquarium.

**Freshman class profile.** 10,048 applied, 8,303 admitted, 3,436 enrolled.

| Mid 50% test scores | | | |
|---|---|---|---|
| SAT critical reading: | 460-580 | Rank in top quarter: | 52% |
| SAT math: | 480-610 | Rank in top tenth: | 24% |
| SAT writing: | 440-560 | Return as sophomores: | 83% |
| ACT composite: | 20-26 | Out-of-state: | 19% |
| GPA 3.75 or higher: | 29% | Live on campus: | 79% |
| GPA 3.50-3.74: | 23% | International: | 2% |
| GPA 3.0-3.49: | 37% | Fraternities: | 16% |
| GPA 2.0-2.99: | 11% | Sororities: | 11% |

**Basis for selection.** Secondary school record, GPA, essay most important. Students not meeting admission requirements may petition for exception. Students who do not meet subject requirements, who graduated from nonstandard or unaccredited high schools, or who graduated prior to 1987 must submit SAT Subject Test scores in addition to SAT or ACT. Applicants with GED not required to submit test scores. **Homeschooled:** Must submit SAT Subject Tests or GED.

**High school preparation.** College-preparatory program required. 14 units required. Required and recommended units include English 4, mathematics 3, social studies 3, science 2 (laboratory 1-2) and foreign language 2.

**2009-2010 Annual costs.** Tuition/fees: $6,727; $19,651 out-of-state. Room/board: $9,920.

**2009-2010 Financial aid.** **Need-based:** 2,565 full-time freshmen applied for aid; 1,740 were judged to have need; 1,698 of these received aid. Average need met was 65%. Average scholarship/grant was $2,669; average loan $3,207. 41% of total undergraduate aid awarded as scholarships/grants, 59% as loans/jobs. **Non-need-based:** Awarded to 718 full-time undergraduates, including 127 freshmen. Scholarships awarded for academics, athletics, job skills, leadership, minority status, ROTC, state residency.

**Application procedures.** **Admission:** Priority date 2/1; deadline 9/1. $50 fee. Admission notification on a rolling basis beginning on or about 10/1. Must reply by May 1 or within 3 week(s) if notified thereafter. **Financial aid:** Priority date 2/1, closing date 5/1. FAFSA required. Applicants notified on a rolling basis starting 4/1; must reply within 4 week(s) of notification.

**Academics.** **Special study options:** Accelerated study, cooperative education, cross-registration, distance learning, double major, dual enrollment of high school students, ESL, exchange student, external degree, honors, independent study, internships, liberal arts/career combination, student-designed major, study abroad, teacher certification program. **Credit/placement by examination:** AP, CLEP, IB, institutional tests. **Support services:** Learning center, remedial instruction, study skills assistance, tutoring.

**Majors. Agriculture:** General, agronomy, animal sciences, business, economics, food science, horticultural science, plant sciences, range science. **Area/ethnic studies:** American. **Biology:** General, bacteriology, biochemistry, biophysics, biotechnology, botany, entomology, zoology. **Business:** Business admin. **Computer sciences:** General. **Conservation:** General, environmental science, fisheries, forest management, forest resources, management/policy, wildlife. **Education:** Technology/industrial arts. **Engineering:**

Biomedical, chemical, civil, computer, construction, electrical, environmental, forest, industrial, manufacturing, mechanical, mining, nuclear, physics. **Family/consumer sciences:** Clothing/textiles, family studies, food/nutrition, housing, merchandising. **Foreign languages:** French, German, Spanish. **Health:** Clinical lab technology, environmental health, health care admin, physics/radiologic health, public health ed. **History:** General. **Interdisciplinary:** Biological/physical sciences, global studies. **Liberal arts:** Arts/sciences. **Math:** General. **Parks/recreation:** General, health/fitness. **Philosophy/religion:** Philosophy. **Physical sciences:** Chemistry, geology, physics. **Psychology:** General. **Social sciences:** Anthropology, economics, geography, political science, sociology. **Visual/performing arts:** General, art, fashion design, interior design.

**Most popular majors.** Agriculture 6%, biology 7%, business/marketing 16%, engineering/engineering technologies 16%, family/consumer sciences 10%, parks/recreation 6%.

**Computing on campus.** 1,660 workstations in dormitories, library, computer center. Dormitories wired for high-speed internet access and linked to campus network. Commuter students can connect to campus network. Online course registration, helpline, repair service, student web hosting, wireless network available.

**Student life. Freshman orientation:** Available. Preregistration for classes offered. **Housing:** Coed dorms, special housing for disabled, apartments, cooperative housing, fraternity/sorority housing available. $45 nonrefundable deposit. **Activities:** Bands, campus ministries, choral groups, dance, drama, film society, international student organizations, literary magazine, music ensembles, Model UN, musical theater, opera, radio station, student government, student newspaper, symphony orchestra, TV station, 253 student organizations, 47 student honor and recognition societies.

**Athletics.** NCAA. **Intercollegiate:** Baseball M, basketball, cheerleading, cross-country W, football (tackle) M, golf, gymnastics W, rowing (crew), soccer, softball W, swimming W, volleyball W, wrestling M. **Intramural:** Badminton, basketball, bowling, cross-country, football (tackle) M, golf, racquetball, soccer, softball, swimming, tennis, track and field, volleyball, water polo, wrestling M. **Team name:** Beavers.

**Student services.** Adult student services, career counseling, student employment services, financial aid counseling, health services, legal services, minority student services, on-campus daycare, personal counseling, placement for graduates, veterans' counselor, women's services. **Physically disabled:** Services for visually, speech, hearing impaired.

**Contact.** E-mail: osuadmit@orst.edu
Phone: (541) 737-4411 Toll-free number: (800) 291-4192
Fax: (541) 737-2482
Michele Sandlin, Director of Admissions, Oregon State University, 104 Kerr Administration Building, Corvallis, OR 97331-2130

## Pacific Northwest College of Art
**Portland, Oregon**
www.pnca.edu                          CB code: 4504

▶ Private 4-year visual arts college
▶ Commuter campus in large city
▶ 554 degree-seeking undergraduates: 7% part-time, 65% women, 1% African American, 3% Asian American, 4% Hispanic American, 2% Native American, 1% international
▶ 46 degree-seeking graduate students
▶ 53% of applicants admitted
▶ Application essay required
▶ 44% graduate within 6 years

**General.** Founded in 1909. Regionally accredited. **Degrees:** 58 bachelor's awarded; master's offered. **Calendar:** Semester, limited summer session. **Full-time faculty:** 25 total; 88% have terminal degrees, 20% minority, 48% women. **Part-time faculty:** 67 total; 48% women. **Class size:** 96% < 20, 4% 20-39. **Special facilities:** Student art galleries, printmaking center, individual studio spaces for seniors.

**Freshman class profile.** 445 applied, 238 admitted, 106 enrolled.

| | | | |
|---|---|---|---|
| GPA 3.75 or higher: | 15% | Return as sophomores: | 65% |
| GPA 3.50-3.74: | 15% | Out-of-state: | 52% |
| GPA 3.0-3.49: | 24% | Live on campus: | 58% |
| GPA 2.0-2.99: | 38% | International: | 3% |

**Basis for selection.** Portfolio, essays important. 2.0 GPA recommended for academic courses. Greater emphasis on portfolio. Interview recommended. **Homeschooled:** Statement describing homeschool structure and mission, transcript of courses and grades, state high school equivalency

certificate, letter of recommendation (nonparent) required. SAT/ACT exam recommended.

**High school preparation.** Recommended units include English 4, mathematics 3, social studies 3 and science 3. Visual arts classes recommended.

**2009-2010 Annual costs.** Tuition/fees: $23,304. Off-campus housing available, approximately one mile from campus. Cost is $4,090. Books/supplies: $985. Personal expenses: $615.

**2009-2010 Financial aid. Non-need-based:** Scholarships awarded for academics, art.

**Application procedures. Admission:** Priority date 3/1; no deadline. $35 fee, may be waived for applicants with need, free for online applicants. Admission notification on a rolling basis. Must reply by May 1 or within 4 week(s) if notified thereafter. **Financial aid:** Priority date 3/1; no closing date. FAFSA required. Applicants notified on a rolling basis starting 4/1; must reply by 5/1 or within 4 week(s) of notification.

**Academics.** Thesis required during fourth year. **Special study options:** Cooperative education, cross-registration, dual enrollment of high school students, exchange student, independent study, internships, New York semester, student-designed major, study abroad. 5-year BA/BFA program with Reed College. **Credit/placement by examination:** AP, CLEP. **Support services:** Study skills assistance, tutoring, writing center.

**Majors. Visual/performing arts:** Design, illustration, multimedia, painting, photography, printmaking, sculpture, studio arts.

**Computing on campus.** 130 workstations in library, computer center, student center. Commuter students can connect to campus network. Online library, wireless network available.

**Student life. Freshman orientation:** Available. Preregistration for classes offered. Three-day program held immediately prior to start of semester. **Housing:** Coed dorms available. $450 partly refundable deposit, deadline 6/15. Pets allowed in dorm rooms. Student housing available through partnership with College Housing Northwest. **Activities:** Film society, radio station, student government.

**Student services.** Career counseling, financial aid counseling, personal counseling.

**Contact.** E-mail: admissions@pnca.edu
Phone: (503) 821-8972 Fax: (503) 821-8978
Chris Sweet, Director of Admissions, Pacific Northwest College of Art, 1241 NW Johnson Street, Portland, OR 97209

## Pacific University
**Forest Grove, Oregon**
www.pacificu.edu                          CB code: 4601

▶ Private 4-year university affiliated with United Church of Christ
▶ Residential campus in large town
▶ 1,445 degree-seeking undergraduates: 4% part-time, 65% women, 1% African American, 23% Asian American, 5% Hispanic American, 1% Native American, 2% international
▶ 1,669 degree-seeking graduate students
▶ 78% of applicants admitted
▶ SAT or ACT (ACT writing optional), application essay required
▶ 60% graduate within 6 years

**General.** Founded in 1849. Regionally accredited. Branch campuses in Hillsboro, Portland, and Eugene for selected professional programs. **Degrees:** 309 bachelor's awarded; master's, professional offered. **ROTC:** Army, Air Force. **Location:** 25 miles from Portland. **Calendar:** Semester, limited summer session. **Full-time faculty:** 205 total; 83% have terminal degrees, 14% minority, 48% women. **Part-time faculty:** 148 total; 32% have terminal degrees, 12% minority, 59% women. **Class size:** 65% < 20, 31% 20-39, 1% 40-49, 3% 50-99. **Special facilities:** Permaculture project, wildlife refuge, performing arts center, arboretum, center for Internet studies, English language institute, humanitarian center, institute for ethics and social policy, center for gender equity.

**Freshman class profile.** 1,627 applied, 1,275 admitted, 349 enrolled.

| Mid 50% test scores | | | |
|---|---|---|---|
| SAT critical reading: | 500-600 | Rank in top quarter: | 69% |
| SAT math: | 510-620 | Rank in top tenth: | 39% |
| ACT composite: | 21-27 | Return as sophomores: | 76% |
| GPA 3.75 or higher: | 45% | Out-of-state: | 51% |
| GPA 3.50-3.74: | 24% | Live on campus: | 94% |
| GPA 3.0-3.49: | 27% | Fraternities: | 1% |
| GPA 2.0-2.99: | 4% | Sororities: | 5% |

**Basis for selection.** Strength of high school program, GPA, test scores, course selection, interview most important. 1000 SAT (exclusive of Writing) plus 3.0 GPA recommended. Recommendation, essay, extracurricular activities, leadership involvement also important. Audition required for music program; portfolio recommended for art program. **Homeschooled:** Statement describing homeschool structure and mission, transcript of courses and grades, state high school equivalency certificate, interview, letter of recommendation (nonparent) required.

**High school preparation.** College-preparatory program recommended. 21 units recommended. Recommended units include English 4, mathematics 3, social studies 3, history 1, science 3 (laboratory 1), foreign language 2 and academic electives 4.

**2009-2010 Annual costs.** Tuition/fees: $29,966. Room/board: $8,118. Books/supplies: $950. Personal expenses: $900.

**2009-2010 Financial aid. Need-based:** 316 full-time freshmen applied for aid; 272 were judged to have need; 272 of these received aid. Average need met was 88%. Average scholarship/grant was $16,292; average loan $3,344. 94% of total undergraduate aid awarded as scholarships/grants, 6% as loans/jobs. **Non-need-based:** Awarded to 357 full-time undergraduates, including 100 freshmen. Scholarships awarded for academics, alumni affiliation, art, music/drama.

**Application procedures. Admission:** Priority date 2/15; deadline 8/15. $40 fee, may be waived for applicants with need. Admission notification on a rolling basis beginning on or after 10/1. Must reply by May 1 or within 2 week(s) if notified thereafter. **Financial aid:** Priority date 3/1; no closing date. FAFSA required. Applicants notified on a rolling basis starting 3/1.

**Academics. Special study options:** Combined bachelor's/graduate degree, cross-registration, double major, ESL, independent study, internships, liberal arts/career combination, study abroad, teacher certification program, Washington semester. 3-2 engineering programs with Oregon Graduate Institute and Washington University, 3-2 applied physics program, 4-1 computer science, 4-1 environmental science programs with Oregon Graduate Institute, exchange programs with University of Vienna, Beijing Normal University, University of Edinburgh, other institutions in Europe and Asia; cooperative arrangement with Northwest Film Center. **Credit/placement by examination:** AP, CLEP, IB, SAT, ACT, institutional tests. **Support services:** Learning center, reduced course load, tutoring, writing center.

**Majors. Area/ethnic studies:** American, Asian, Latin American, Western European, women's. **Biology:** General, biochemistry, bioinformatics. **Business:** Business admin. **Communications:** General, journalism. **Computer sciences:** General. **Conservation:** Environmental science, environmental studies. **Education:** General. **Foreign languages:** General, Chinese, French, German, Japanese, Spanish. **History:** General. **Liberal arts:** Arts/sciences. **Math:** General. **Parks/recreation:** Exercise sciences. **Philosophy/religion:** Philosophy. **Physical sciences:** Chemistry, physics. **Psychology:** General. **Public administration:** Social work. **Social sciences:** Economics, international relations, political science, sociology. **Visual/performing arts:** General, art, dramatic, multimedia, music performance.

**Most popular majors.** Biology 8%, business/marketing 8%, communications/journalism 8%, education 7%, English 7%, health sciences 13%, parks/recreation 10%, social sciences 9%.

**Computing on campus.** 200 workstations in dormitories, library, computer center, student center. Dormitories wired for high-speed internet access and linked to campus network. Commuter students can connect to campus network. Online library, helpline, repair service, student web hosting, wireless network available.

**Student life. Freshman orientation:** Mandatory. Preregistration for classes offered. **Policies:** Unmarried freshmen and sophomores under age 21 must live on campus unless living near campus with family. **Housing:** Guaranteed on-campus for freshmen. Coed dorms, special housing for disabled, apartments available. $100 fully refundable deposit, deadline 5/1. 1 wing designated for females. **Activities:** Bands, campus ministries, choral groups, dance, drama, film society, international student organizations, literary magazine, music ensembles, radio station, student government, student newspaper, Hawaii club, Christian Fellowship, politics and law forum, Circle K, humanitarian center, gay and lesbian support group, ethnic diversity appreciation club, United Church of Christ student organization.

**Athletics.** NCAA. **Intercollegiate:** Baseball M, basketball, cheerleading, cross-country, golf, lacrosse W, soccer, softball W, swimming, tennis, track and field, volleyball W, wrestling. **Intramural:** Basketball, football (tackle), golf, handball, racquetball, soccer, softball, tennis, volleyball. **Team name:** Boxers.

**Student services.** Alcohol/substance abuse counseling, career counseling, student employment services, financial aid counseling, health services, minority student services, personal counseling, placement for graduates, veterans' counselor.

**Contact.** E-mail: admissions@pacificu.edu
Phone: (503) 352-2218 Toll-free number: (800) 677-6712
Fax: (503) 352-2975
Karen Dunston, Director of Undergraduate Admission, Pacific University, 2043 College Way, Forest Grove, OR 97116-1797

## Portland State University
**Portland, Oregon** — CB member
**www.pdx.edu** — CB code: 4610

- Public 4-year university
- Commuter campus in very large city
- 19,267 degree-seeking undergraduates
- 6,298 graduate students
- 79% of applicants admitted
- SAT or ACT with writing required

**General.** Founded in 1946. Regionally accredited. Courses offered at off-campus locations. **Degrees:** 3,321 bachelor's awarded; master's, doctoral offered. **ROTC:** Army, Air Force. **Location:** Downtown. **Calendar:** Quarter, extensive summer session. **Full-time faculty:** 837 total; 13% minority, 45% women. **Part-time faculty:** 617 total; 9% minority, 52% women. **Class size:** 30% < 20, 43% 20-39, 11% 40-49, 14% 50-99, 2% >100. **Special facilities:** Native American center.

**Freshman class profile.** 5,180 applied, 4,067 admitted, 1,649 enrolled.

| Mid 50% test scores | | | |
|---|---|---|---|
| SAT critical reading: | 460-600 | GPA 3.50-3.74: | 19% |
| SAT math: | 460-570 | GPA 3.0-3.49: | 42% |
| SAT writing: | 440-560 | GPA 2.0-2.99: | 25% |
| ACT composite: | 18-24 | Return as sophomores: | 69% |
| GPA 3.75 or higher: | 14% | Out-of-state: | 20% |

**Basis for selection.** 3.0 GPA or 1000 SAT (exclusive of Writing)/21 ACT required for automatic admission. Various combinations of test scores and GPA also qualify for automatic admissions. Others may qualify under special action by admissions committee. Interview recommended for those who do not meet regular admission requirement. **Homeschooled:** State high school equivalency certificate required.

**High school preparation.** 14 units required. Required and recommended units include English 4, mathematics 3, social studies 2, history 1, science 2 (laboratory 1) and foreign language 2. One unit laboratory science recommended.

**2009-2010 Annual costs.** Tuition/fees: $6,764; $21,198 out-of-state. Room/board: $9,135. Books/supplies: $1,854. Personal expenses: $1,932.

**2009-2010 Financial aid. Non-need-based:** Scholarships awarded for academics, art, athletics, music/drama, state residency.

**Application procedures. Admission:** Priority date 6/1; no deadline. $50 fee. Application must be submitted on paper. Admission notification on a rolling basis. **Financial aid:** Priority date 2/28; no closing date. FAFSA required. Applicants notified on a rolling basis; must reply within 4 week(s) of notification.

**Academics.** Community based service and research projects offered in Portland area. All students required to complete 45 credit hour multidisciplinary core curriculum, including community service learning experience. Teaching certification only offered at graduate level. **Special study options:** Accelerated study, combined bachelor's/graduate degree, cooperative education, distance learning, double major, ESL, exchange student, honors, independent study, internships, liberal arts/career combination, study abroad, teacher certification program, Washington semester. Haystack Summer Program in the arts and sciences. **Credit/placement by examination:** AP, CLEP, institutional tests. 45 credit hours maximum toward bachelor's degree. **Support services:** Pre-admission summer program, reduced course load, tutoring, writing center.

**Honors college/program.** Students with 1200 SAT (exclusive of Writing) and 3.5 GPA eligible to apply. Limited to 200 participants.

**Majors.** **Architecture:** Architecture, urban/community planning. **Area/ ethnic studies:** African, Central/Eastern European, East Asian, European, Latin American, Near/Middle Eastern, women's. **Biology:** General, biochemistry. **Business:** General, accounting, business admin, finance, human resources, logistics, management information systems, marketing. **Computer sciences:** Computer science. **Conservation:** General. **Education:** Health. **Engineering:** Civil, computer, electrical, mechanical. **Family/consumer sciences:** Family studies. **Foreign languages:** Chinese, French, German, Japanese, linguistics, Russian, Spanish. **Health:** Audiology/hearing, public health ed. **History:** General. **Interdisciplinary:** Biological/physical sciences. **Liberal arts:** Arts/sciences. **Math:** General. **Philosophy/religion:** Philosophy. **Physical sciences:** Chemistry, geology, physics. **Protective services:** Criminal justice, law enforcement admin. **Psychology:** General. **Public administration:** Social work. **Social sciences:** General, anthropology, economics, geography, international relations, political science, sociology, urban studies. **Visual/performing arts:** Art, art history/conservation, commercial/ advertising art, design, dramatic, drawing, music performance, painting, printmaking, sculpture, studio arts.

**Most popular majors.** Business/marketing 20%, liberal arts 9%, psychology 8%, social sciences 16%.

**Computing on campus.** 925 workstations in dormitories, library, computer center, student center. Dormitories wired for high-speed internet access and linked to campus network. Commuter students can connect to campus network. Online course registration, online library, helpline, repair service, student web hosting, wireless network available.

**Student life.** **Freshman orientation:** Available. Preregistration for classes offered. **Policies:** Dormitory and meal service not managed by University available on campus. **Housing:** Coed dorms, special housing for disabled, apartments, fraternity/sorority housing available. Pets allowed in dorm rooms. **Activities:** Bands, campus ministries, choral groups, dance, drama, film society, international student organizations, literary magazine, music ensembles, musical theater, opera, radio station, student government, student newspaper, symphony orchestra, student public interest research group, black cultural affairs board, United Indian Students in Higher Education, women's union, outdoor program, disabled student union, Hispanic student union.

**Athletics.** NCAA. **Intercollegiate:** Baseball M, basketball, cross-country, football (tackle) M, golf, soccer W, softball W, tennis, track and field, volleyball W. **Intramural:** Archery, basketball, football (tackle) M, golf, racquetball, soccer W, softball, volleyball. **Team name:** Vikings.

**Student services.** Adult student services, alcohol/substance abuse counseling, chaplain/spiritual director, career counseling, student employment services, financial aid counseling, health services, legal services, minority student services, on-campus daycare, personal counseling, placement for graduates, veterans' counselor, women's services. **Physically disabled:** Services for visually, speech, hearing impaired.

**Contact.** E-mail: admissions@pdx.edu
Phone: (503) 725-3511 Toll-free number: (800) 547-8887 ext. 3511
Fax: (503) 725-5525
Agnes Hoffman, Vice Provost for Enrollment Management, Portland State University, PO Box 751-ADM, Portland, OR 97207-0751

## Reed College

**Portland, Oregon**
**www.reed.edu**

**CB member**
**CB code: 4654**

- Private 4-year liberal arts college
- Residential campus in very large city
- 1,440 degree-seeking undergraduates: 2% part-time, 55% women, 3% African American, 9% Asian American, 7% Hispanic American, 1% Native American, 6% international
- 29 degree-seeking graduate students
- 41% of applicants admitted
- SAT or ACT (ACT writing optional), application essay required
- 78% graduate within 6 years; 13% enter graduate study

**General.** Founded in 1909. Regionally accredited. **Degrees:** 318 bachelor's awarded; master's offered. **Location:** 5 miles from downtown. **Calendar:** Semester. **Full-time faculty:** 121 total; 91% have terminal degrees, 12% minority, 38% women. **Part-time faculty:** 12 total; 83% have terminal degrees, 8% minority, 33% women. **Class size:** 72% < 20, 24% 20-39, less than 1% 40-49, 2% 50-99, 1% >100. **Special facilities:** Nuclear research reactor, wildlife refuge, fish ladder.

**Freshman class profile.** 3,161 applied, 1,281 admitted, 368 enrolled.

| Mid 50% test scores | | | |
|---|---|---|---|
| SAT critical reading: | 660-760 | GPA 2.0-2.99: | 1% |
| SAT math: | 620-710 | Rank in top quarter: | 86% |
| SAT writing: | 650-740 | Rank in top tenth: | 59% |
| ACT composite: | 29-33 | Return as sophomores: | 88% |
| GPA 3.75 or higher: | 70% | Out-of-state: | 92% |
| GPA 3.50-3.74: | 18% | Live on campus: | 98% |
| GPA 3.0-3.49: | 11% | International: | 6% |

**Basis for selection.** Academic achievement, essay, recommendations, test scores most important. Qualities of character, such as motivation, intellectual curiosity, individual responsibility, social consciousness are important. SAT Subject Tests recommended. Interview recommended. **Homeschooled:** Transcript of courses and grades, letter of recommendation (nonparent) required. High school diploma waived in some cases. Must be above age of compulsory education in home state, submit writing sample, essay.

**High school preparation.** College-preparatory program recommended. Recommended units include English 4, mathematics 3, social studies 1, history 3, science 3 and foreign language 3.

**2009-2010 Annual costs.** Tuition/fees: $39,700. Room/board: $10,250. Books/supplies: $950. Personal expenses: $900.

**2009-2010 Financial aid.** All financial aid based on need. 241 full-time freshmen applied for aid; 183 were judged to have need; 183 of these received aid. Average need met was 100%. Average scholarship/grant was $33,181; average loan $3,004. 86% of total undergraduate aid awarded as scholarships/grants, 14% as loans/jobs. **Additional information:** College meets demonstrated need of continuing students who have attended Reed minimum of 2 semesters, who file financial aid applications on time, and who maintain satisfactory academic progress. Institutional aid consideration is for total of 8 semesters.

**Application procedures.** **Admission:** Closing date 1/15 (postmark date). $50 fee, may be waived for applicants with need. Admission notification 4/1. Must reply by May 1 or within 2 week(s) if notified thereafter. **Financial aid:** Closing date 2/1. FAFSA, institutional form, CSS PROFILE required. Applicants notified by 4/1; must reply by 5/1 or within 2 week(s) of notification.

**Academics.** All students take a 1-year course in the humanities. After declaring their major, students must pass a junior qualifying examination prior to senior year. Seniors engage in a 1-year research project in their major field writing a senior thesis and orally defending it before a committee of faculty members. **Special study options:** Combined bachelor's/ graduate degree, cross-registration, double major, dual enrollment of high school students, exchange student, independent study, internships, liberal arts/career combination, study abroad. Computer science program with University of Washington; engineering arrangement with California Institute of Technology, Columbia University School of Engineering and Applied Sciences, Rensselaer Polytechnic Institute; forestry-environmental sciences degree arrangement with Nicholas School of the Environment of Duke University; joint 5-year art program with Pacific Northwest College of Art. **Credit/placement by examination:** AP, CLEP, IB, institutional tests. 30 credit hours maximum toward bachelor's degree. **Support services:** Learning center, study skills assistance, tutoring, writing center.

**Majors.** **Area/ethnic studies:** American. **Biology:** General, biochemistry, molecular. **Foreign languages:** Chinese, classics, comparative lit, French, German, linguistics, Russian, Spanish. **History:** General. **Math:** General. **Philosophy/religion:** Philosophy, religion. **Physical sciences:** Chemistry, physics. **Psychology:** General. **Social sciences:** Anthropology, economics, international relations, political science, sociology. **Visual/performing arts:** Art, dramatic. **Other:** Multi/Interdisciplinary Studies.

**Most popular majors.** Biology 11%, English 13%, foreign language 13%, history 7%, interdisciplinary studies 8%, physical sciences 8%, psychology 8%, social sciences 18%.

**Computing on campus.** 432 workstations in dormitories, library, computer center, student center. Dormitories wired for high-speed internet access and linked to campus network. Commuter students can connect to campus network. Online course registration, online library, helpline, repair service, student web hosting, wireless network available.

**Student life.** **Freshman orientation:** Mandatory. Preregistration for classes offered. Held 5 days before start of classes. **Policies:** Honor code in effect. First-year students required to live on campus. **Housing:** Guaranteed on-campus for freshmen. Coed dorms, single-sex dorms, special housing for disabled, apartments, cooperative housing, wellness housing available. $100 partly refundable deposit, deadline 6/15. Chinese, French, German, Russian, and Spanish language houses available for upper division students.

**Activities:** Campus ministries, choral groups, dance, drama, film society, international student organizations, literary magazine, music ensembles, Model UN, radio station, student government, student newspaper, symphony orchestra, Christian Fellowship, Jewish Student Union, women's center, environmental coalition, politically active student groups, volunteer tutoring, language and outing clubs, poetry forum.

**Athletics. Intramural:** Archery, badminton, basketball M, equestrian, fencing, golf, judo, rowing (crew), rugby, sailing, skiing, soccer, softball, squash, swimming, tennis, volleyball. **Team name:** Griffins.

**Student services.** Adult student services, alcohol/substance abuse counseling, career counseling, student employment services, financial aid counseling, health services, minority student services, personal counseling, placement for graduates. **Physically disabled:** Services for visually, speech, hearing impaired.

**Contact.** E-mail: admission@reed.edu
Phone: (503) 777-7511 Toll-free number: (800) 547-4750
Fax: (503) 777-7553
Kristine Sawicki, Dean of Admission, Reed College, 3203 SE Woodstock Boulevard, Portland, OR 97202-8199

## Southern Oregon University
**Ashland, Oregon**                               **CB member**
**www.sou.edu**                                   **CB code: 4702**

- Public 4-year university and liberal arts college
- Residential campus in large town
- 4,132 degree-seeking undergraduates: 19% part-time, 57% women, 2% African American, 5% Asian American, 5% Hispanic American, 2% Native American, 2% international
- 518 degree-seeking graduate students
- SAT or ACT (ACT writing recommended) required

**General.** Founded in 1926. Regionally accredited. Designated by National Aeronautical and Space Administration to cooperate in NASA-directed joint space research by undergraduates. **Degrees:** 666 bachelor's awarded; master's offered. **Location:** 180 miles from Eugene, 285 miles from Portland. **Calendar:** Quarter, extensive summer session. **Full-time faculty:** 207 total; 81% have terminal degrees. **Part-time faculty:** 104 total. **Class size:** 46% < 20, 42% 20-39, 6% 40-49, 5% 50-99, 1% >100. **Special facilities:** Herbarium, U.S. Fish and Wildlife forensics laboratory, public radio network studios, preschool and kindergarten, community television studio, center for visual arts, biotechnology center, institute for environmental economic and civic studies.

### Freshman class profile.

| Mid 50% test scores | | | |
|---|---|---|---|
| SAT critical reading: | 450-580 | GPA 3.50-3.74: | 18% |
| SAT math: | 460-570 | GPA 3.0-3.49: | 38% |
| ACT composite: | 20-25 | GPA 2.0-2.99: | 30% |
| GPA 3.75 or higher: | 14% | Out-of-state: | 24% |
| | | Live on campus: | 70% |

**Basis for selection.** Admission based on 2.75 GPA from regionally accredited high school, 21 ACT, 1010 SAT (exclusive of Writing), and 14 required high school academic units. For students from non-regionally accredited high schools and homeschooled students: 1010 combined scores on SAT Critical Reading and Math, 470 on SAT Writing, and two SAT Subject Tests (Math Level I or Math Level IIc and one other subject area of students choice). Requests for special admission for undergraduates reviewed individually.

**High school preparation.** College-preparatory program recommended. 14 units required. Required units include English 4, mathematics 3, social studies 3, science 2 (laboratory 1) and foreign language 2.

**2009-2010 Annual costs.** Tuition/fees: $6,252; $19,914 out-of-state. Room/board: $9,174. Books/supplies: $1,155. Personal expenses: $2,475.

**2009-2010 Financial aid. Non-need-based:** Scholarships awarded for academics, alumni affiliation, art, athletics, leadership, minority status, music/drama, religious affiliation, state residency.

**Application procedures. Admission:** No deadline. $50 fee, may be waived for applicants with need. Admission notification on a rolling basis. **Financial aid:** No deadline. FAFSA required. Applicants notified on a rolling basis starting 3/1; must reply within 2 week(s) of notification.

**Academics. Special study options:** Accelerated study, combined bachelor's/graduate degree, cooperative education, cross-registration, distance learning, double major, dual enrollment of high school students, ESL, exchange student, honors, independent study, internships, liberal arts/career combination, student-designed major, study abroad, teacher certification program. **Credit/placement by examination:** AP, CLEP, IB, institutional tests. 24 credit hours maximum toward bachelor's degree. **Support services:** Learning center, reduced course load, remedial instruction, study skills assistance, tutoring, writing center.

**Majors. Biology:** General. **Business:** General, accounting, business admin, hospitality admin, marketing. **Communications:** General, journalism, public relations. **Computer sciences:** General, computer science, programming, security. **Conservation:** Environmental studies. **Education:** General. **Foreign languages:** General, Spanish. **Health:** Athletic training, nursing (RN), predental, premedicine, preop/surgical nursing, prepharmacy, preveterinary. **History:** General. **Interdisciplinary:** Biological/physical sciences, math/computer science. **Legal studies:** Prelaw. **Math:** General. **Parks/recreation:** Health/fitness, sports admin. **Physical sciences:** Chemistry, geology, physics. **Protective services:** Criminal justice, law enforcement admin, police science. **Psychology:** General. **Social sciences:** General, anthropology, criminology, economics, geography, political science, sociology. **Visual/performing arts:** Art, dramatic, music management.

**Most popular majors.** Business/marketing 17%, communications/journalism 10%, psychology 12%, security/protective services 10%, social sciences 9%, visual/performing arts 10%.

**Computing on campus.** 750 workstations in dormitories, library, computer center, student center. Dormitories wired for high-speed internet access and linked to campus network. Commuter students can connect to campus network. Online course registration, online library, helpline, student web hosting, wireless network available.

**Student life. Freshman orientation:** Mandatory. Preregistration for classes offered. Early registration in July; orientation few days before start of classes. **Housing:** Guaranteed on-campus for freshmen. Coed dorms, special housing for disabled, apartments, wellness housing available. $50 deposit. Special quiet, nonsmoking, older student or freshmen residence halls available. **Activities:** Bands, campus ministries, choral groups, dance, drama, international student organizations, literary magazine, music ensembles, musical theater, opera, radio station, student government, student newspaper, symphony orchestra, TV station, 100 clubs available.

**Athletics.** NAIA. **Intercollegiate:** Basketball, cross-country, football (tackle) M, soccer W, softball W, tennis W, track and field, volleyball W, wrestling M. **Intramural:** Badminton, baseball M, basketball, bowling, golf, racquetball, rugby, sailing, skiing, soccer, softball, swimming, table tennis, tennis, track and field, volleyball, water polo. **Team name:** Raiders.

**Student services.** Adult student services, alcohol/substance abuse counseling, career counseling, services for economically disadvantaged, student employment services, financial aid counseling, health services, legal services, minority student services, on-campus daycare, personal counseling, placement for graduates, veterans' counselor, women's services. **Physically disabled:** Services for visually, speech, hearing impaired. **Learning disabled:** Comprehensive services available.

**Contact.** E-mail: admissions@sou.edu
Phone: (541) 552-6411 Toll-free number: (800) 482-7672 ext. 6411
Fax: (541) 552-8403
Mark Bottorff, Director of Admissions, Southern Oregon University, 1250 Siskiyou Boulevard, Ashland, OR 97520-5032

## University of Oregon
**Eugene, Oregon**                                **CB member**
**www.uoregon.edu**                               **CB code: 4846**

- Public 4-year university
- Residential campus in small city
- 18,213 degree-seeking undergraduates: 7% part-time, 51% women, 2% African American, 6% Asian American, 4% Hispanic American, 1% Native American, 6% international
- 3,438 degree-seeking graduate students
- 80% of applicants admitted
- SAT or ACT with writing, application essay required
- 67% graduate within 6 years; 28% enter graduate study

**General.** Founded in 1876. Regionally accredited. **Degrees:** 3,818 bachelor's awarded; master's, doctoral, professional offered. **ROTC:** Army, Air Force. **Location:** 110 miles from Portland. **Calendar:** Quarter, extensive summer session. **Full-time faculty:** 892 total; 73% have terminal degrees, 16% minority, 41% women. **Part-time faculty:** 382 total; 48% have terminal degrees, 11% minority, 51% women. **Class size:** 37% < 20, 42% 20-39, 5% 40-49, 10% 50-99, 7% >100. **Special facilities:** Art museum, natural and cultural history museum, sports marketing center, entrepreneurship center, Many Nations Longhouse, chemistry laboratory, instrumentation center, computer music center, mountain observatory, marine biology institute.

**Freshman class profile.** 16,780 applied, 13,367 admitted, 3,839 enrolled.

| Mid 50% test scores | | Rank in top tenth: | 26% |
|---|---|---|---|
| SAT critical reading: | 490-610 | End year in good standing: | 91% |
| SAT math: | 500-620 | Return as sophomores: | 84% |
| GPA 3.75 or higher: | 28% | Out-of-state: | 39% |
| GPA 3.50-3.74: | 26% | Live on campus: | 83% |
| GPA 3.0-3.49: | 42% | International: | 5% |
| GPA 2.0-2.99: | 4% | Fraternities: | 9% |
| Rank in top quarter: | 60% | Sororities: | 16% |

**Basis for selection.** 3.0 GPA, graduation from a standard or regionally accredited high school, C- or higher in 14 college preparatory courses, and SAT or ACT required. Strength of academic course work, grade trends, class rank, standardized test scores, academic motivation as demonstrated in the application essay, special talents, extracurricular activities, including community service or the need to work to assist your family financially, and ability to enhance the diversity of the university important. Extracurricular activities will be considered but will not compensate for low grades or weak course schedules. For automatic admission, 3.4 GPA and 16 college preparatory units with grades of C- required. Audition required for dance and music programs. Portfolio required for arts, architecture, and interior architecture programs. **Homeschooled:** 1540 SAT or 22 ACT with optional writing component and average score of 470 (940 total) for SAT Subject Tests in Math I or II and second test of choice required. Applicant must demonstrate proficiency in second language; test strongly recommended to meet second language proficiency requirements. **Learning Disabled:** If student does not meet admission requirements and has self-identified a documented disability, then a secondary review will take place by the disability review committee.

**High school preparation.** College-preparatory program required. 14 units required; 16 recommended. Required and recommended units include English 4, mathematics 3, social studies 3, science 2 (laboratory 1) and foreign language 2.

**2009-2010 Annual costs.** Tuition/fees: $7,428; $23,718 out-of-state. Additional program-specific fees may apply. Room/board: $10,645. Books/supplies: $1,050. Personal expenses: $2,412.

**2009-2010 Financial aid. Need-based:** 2,559 full-time freshmen applied for aid; 1,596 were judged to have need; 1,493 of these received aid. Average need met was 53%. Average scholarship/grant was $6,794; average loan $3,529. 47% of total undergraduate aid awarded as scholarships/grants, 53% as loans/jobs. **Non-need-based:** Awarded to 3,529 full-time undergraduates, including 1,287 freshmen. Scholarships awarded for academics, athletics, leadership, minority status, music/drama, ROTC, state residency.

**Application procedures. Admission:** Priority date 11/1; deadline 1/15 (postmark date). $50 fee, may be waived for applicants with need. Admission notification on a rolling basis beginning on or about 12/15. Must reply by May 1 or within 4 week(s) if notified thereafter. Additional academic deadlines: Architecture, 1/15 (priority deadline, 12/1); Interior Architecture, 1/15; Digital Arts, 2/1; Landscape Architecture, 1/15; Art, 2/1; Product Design, 1/15; School of Music and Dance, 1/15; Clark Honors College, 11/1 early notification, 1/15 standard notification. **Financial aid:** Priority date 3/1; no closing date. FAFSA required. Applicants notified on a rolling basis starting 4/15; must reply within 4 week(s) of notification.

**Academics. Special study options:** Cross-registration, distance learning, double major, ESL, exchange student, honors, independent study, internships, liberal arts/career combination, semester at sea, student-designed major, study abroad, teacher certification program. Dual enrollment with Lane Community College and Southwestern Oregon Community College. Professional distinctions program (certificate program) in which students gain direct professional preparation through internships, special courses, professional mentor, and development of electronic resume and portfolio. **Credit/placement by examination:** CLEP, IB, SAT, ACT, institutional tests. For some courses, departments have authorized the use of subject examinations prepared by the College Level Examination Program (CLEP). Once a student is admitted, successfully completed CLEP subject exams are accepted as transfer credit. **Support services:** Learning center, study skills assistance, tutoring.

**Honors college/program.** Short self-introduction, admission essay, teacher evaluations, description of accomplishments, SAT or ACT scores, GPA, depth and breadth of high school curriculum, and the ways in which the applicant will add to the diversity of the Clark Honors College community all considered; 175 admitted.

**Majors. Architecture:** Architecture, interior, landscape. **Area/ethnic studies:** Asian, Russian/Slavic, women's. **Biology:** General, biochemistry, marine, physiology. **Business:** General, accounting. **Communications:** Advertising, journalism, media studies, public relations. **Computer sciences:** General.

**Conservation:** Environmental science, environmental studies. **Education:** General, music. **Foreign languages:** Ancient Greek, Chinese, classics, comparative lit, French, German, Italian, Japanese, Latin, linguistics, Romance, Russian, Spanish. **Health:** Communication disorders. **History:** General. **Interdisciplinary:** Ancient studies, biological/physical sciences, global studies, math/computer science, medieval/Renaissance. **Liberal arts:** Humanities. **Math:** General. **Philosophy/religion:** Judaic, philosophy, religion. **Physical sciences:** Chemistry, geology, physics. **Psychology:** General. **Public administration:** General, human services. **Social sciences:** General, anthropology, economics, geography, political science, sociology. **Visual/performing arts:** Art, art history/conservation, ceramics, dance, digital art, dramatic, fiber arts, jazz, metal/jewelry, multimedia, music performance, music theory/composition, painting, photography, printmaking, sculpture, studio arts. **Other:** Product design.

**Most popular majors.** Biology 7%, business/marketing 12%, communications/journalism 8%, foreign language 8%, interdisciplinary studies 6%, psychology 7%, social sciences 21%, visual/performing arts 7%.

**Computing on campus.** 1,750 workstations in dormitories, library, computer center, student center. Dormitories wired for high-speed internet access and linked to campus network. Commuter students can connect to campus network. Online course registration, online library, helpline, repair service, student web hosting, wireless network available.

**Student life. Freshman orientation:** Mandatory. Preregistration for classes offered. 2-day session during summer for students and family members. **Housing:** Coed dorms, apartments, cooperative housing, fraternity/sorority housing, wellness housing available. $250 partly refundable deposit. Separate men's and women's floors, residential academic programs, family housing available. **Activities:** Bands, campus ministries, choral groups, dance, drama, film society, international student organizations, literary magazine, music ensembles, musical theater, opera, radio station, student government, student newspaper, symphony orchestra, Jewish student union, Muslim student association, College Democrats, College Republicans, black student union, Asian/Pacific American student union, non-traditional student union, Coalition Against Environmental Racism, international student association, service based fraternities and sororities.

**Athletics.** NCAA. **Intercollegiate:** Baseball M, basketball, cross-country, football (tackle) M, golf, gymnastics W, lacrosse W, soccer W, softball W, tennis, track and field, volleyball W. **Intramural:** Badminton, basketball, cross-country, football (non-tackle), golf, racquetball, soccer, softball, swimming, tennis, track and field, volleyball. **Team name:** Ducks.

**Student services.** Adult student services, alcohol/substance abuse counseling, career counseling, services for economically disadvantaged, student employment services, financial aid counseling, health services, legal services, minority student services, on-campus daycare, personal counseling, placement for graduates, veterans' counselor, women's services. **Physically disabled:** Services for visually, speech, hearing impaired. **Learning disabled:** Comprehensive services available.

**Contact.** E-mail: uoadmit@uoregon.edu
Phone: (541) 346-3201 Toll-free number: (800) 232-3825
Fax: (541) 346-5815
Brian Henley, Director of Admissions, University of Oregon, 1217
University of Oregon, Eugene, OR 97403-1217

---

## University of Portland
**Portland, Oregon**       **CB member**
**www.up.edu**       **CB code: 4847**

- Private 4-year university affiliated with Roman Catholic Church
- Residential campus in large city
- 3,077 degree-seeking undergraduates: 1% part-time, 61% women, 1% African American, 12% Asian American, 5% Hispanic American, 1% Native American, 2% international
- 520 degree-seeking graduate students
- 74% of applicants admitted
- SAT or ACT (ACT writing optional), application essay required
- 75% graduate within 6 years; 25% enter graduate study

**General.** Founded in 1901. Regionally accredited. **Degrees:** 744 bachelor's awarded; master's, professional offered. **ROTC:** Army, Air Force. **Calendar:** Semester, limited summer session. **Full-time faculty:** 207 total; 90% have terminal degrees, 4% minority, 44% women. **Part-time faculty:** 108 total; 9% have terminal degrees, 3% minority, 45% women. **Class size:** 36% < 20, 53% 20-39, 8% 40-49, 3% 50-99, less than 1% >100.

Four-Year Colleges

**Freshman class profile.** 7,096 applied, 5,220 admitted, 816 enrolled.

| Mid 50% test scores | | | |
|---|---|---|---|
| SAT critical reading: | 530-640 | Rank in top quarter: | 76% |
| SAT math: | 550-650 | Rank in top tenth: | 43% |
| GPA 3.75 or higher: | 46% | End year in good standing: | 92% |
| GPA 3.50-3.74: | 24% | Return as sophomores: | 86% |
| GPA 3.0-3.49: | 26% | Out-of-state: | 66% |
| GPA 2.0-2.99: | 4% | Live on campus: | 94% |
| | | International: | 3% |

**Basis for selection.** School achievement record, test scores, counselor recommendation, essay important. **Homeschooled:** Transcript of courses and grades required. Interview strongly encouraged.

**High school preparation.** College-preparatory program recommended. Required and recommended units include English 3-4, mathematics 2-3, social studies 2, history 2, science 2 and academic electives 7. Engineering, math, and some science majors require additional math and science courses.

**2010-2011 Annual costs.** Tuition/fees: $32,330. Room/board: $9,540. Books/supplies: $1,000. Personal expenses: $800.

**2009-2010 Financial aid. Need-based:** 676 full-time freshmen applied for aid; 549 were judged to have need; 548 of these received aid. Average need met was 77%. Average scholarship/grant was $8,897; average loan $3,436. 64% of total undergraduate aid awarded as scholarships/grants, 36% as loans/jobs. **Non-need-based:** Awarded to 2,853 full-time undergraduates, including 796 freshmen. Scholarships awarded for academics, alumni affiliation, athletics, music/drama, religious affiliation, ROTC.

**Application procedures. Admission:** Priority date 2/1; deadline 6/1 (postmark date). $50 fee, may be waived for applicants with need. Admission notification on a rolling basis beginning on or about 10/1. Must reply by May 1 or within 2 week(s) if notified thereafter. **Financial aid:** Priority date 3/1; no closing date. FAFSA required. Applicants notified on a rolling basis starting 3/15; must reply within 3 week(s) of notification.

**Academics. Special study options:** Cross-registration, double major, honors, independent study, internships, liberal arts/career combination, study abroad, teacher certification program, Washington semester. **Credit/placement by examination:** AP, CLEP, IB, institutional tests. 45 credit hours maximum toward bachelor's degree. **Support services:** Learning center, study skills assistance, tutoring, writing center.

**Majors. Biology:** General. **Business:** Accounting, business admin, finance, international, marketing. **Communications:** Media studies, organizational. **Computer sciences:** Computer science. **Conservation:** Environmental science, environmental studies. **Education:** Elementary, music, secondary. **Engineering:** Civil, computer, electrical, environmental, mechanical. **Foreign languages:** French, German, Spanish. **Health:** Nursing (RN). **History:** General. **Math:** General. **Philosophy/religion:** Philosophy. **Physical sciences:** Chemistry, physics. **Psychology:** General. **Public administration:** Social work. **Social sciences:** Political science, sociology. **Theology:** Theology. **Visual/performing arts:** Dramatic, theater arts management.

**Most popular majors.** Biology 10%, business/marketing 16%, communications/journalism 6%, engineering/engineering technologies 8%, foreign language 8%, health sciences 24%.

**Computing on campus.** 400 workstations in dormitories, library, computer center, student center. Dormitories wired for high-speed internet access and linked to campus network. Commuter students can connect to campus network. Online course registration, online library, helpline, student web hosting, wireless network available.

**Student life. Freshman orientation:** Available. Preregistration for classes offered. Held 3 days before classes begin. **Housing:** Guaranteed on-campus for freshmen. Coed dorms, single-sex dorms available. $100 nonrefundable deposit, deadline 5/1. Rental houses available. **Activities:** Bands, campus ministries, choral groups, dance, drama, film society, international student organizations, literary magazine, music ensembles, musical theater, radio station, student government, student newspaper, symphony orchestra, volunteer services, Black student union, international club, Hawaiian club, Engineeers Without Borders, feminist discussion group, Bible study group, Movimiento Estudiantil de Chicanos de Astlan, ecology club, Student Led Unity Garden (SLUG).

**Athletics.** NCAA. **Intercollegiate:** Baseball M, basketball, cross-country, golf, soccer, tennis, track and field, volleyball W. **Intramural:** Basketball, bowling, football (non-tackle), golf, skiing, soccer, softball, swimming, table tennis, tennis, volleyball, weight lifting. **Team name:** Pilots.

**Student services.** Adult student services, alcohol/substance abuse counseling, chaplain/spiritual director, career counseling, student employment services, financial aid counseling, health services, personal counseling, placement for graduates, veterans' counselor. **Physically disabled:** Services for visually, speech, hearing impaired.

**Contact.** E-mail: admissions@up.edu
Phone: (503) 943-7147 Toll-free number: (888) 627-5601
Fax: (503) 943-7315
Jason McDonald, Dean of Admissions, University of Portland, 5000 North Willamette Boulevard, Portland, OR 97203-5798

## Warner Pacific College
**Portland, Oregon**
www.warnerpacific.edu                     CB code: 4595

- Private 4-year liberal arts college affiliated with Church of God
- Residential campus in very large city
- 1,181 degree-seeking undergraduates: 1% part-time, 62% women, 4% African American, 3% Asian American, 4% Hispanic American
- 152 degree-seeking graduate students
- 63% of applicants admitted
- SAT or ACT (ACT writing recommended), application essay required
- 53% graduate within 6 years; 14% enter graduate study

**General.** Founded in 1937. Regionally accredited. **Degrees:** 198 bachelor's, 29 associate awarded; master's offered. **ROTC:** Army, Naval, Air Force. **Location:** 44 miles from Salem; 10 miles from Vancouver, Washington. **Calendar:** Semester, limited summer session. **Full-time faculty:** 24 total; 58% have terminal degrees, 8% minority, 29% women. **Part-time faculty:** 100 total; 11% have terminal degrees, 7% minority, 55% women. **Class size:** 80% < 20, 19% 20-39, 1% 40-49. **Special facilities:** Field station for wildlife observation and study.

**Freshman class profile.** 544 applied, 341 admitted, 101 enrolled.

| Mid 50% test scores | | | |
|---|---|---|---|
| SAT critical reading: | 440-580 | GPA 3.0-3.49: | 40% |
| SAT math: | 430-570 | GPA 2.0-2.99: | 38% |
| SAT writing: | 440-560 | End year in good standing: | 60% |
| ACT composite: | 17-25 | Return as sophomores: | 60% |
| GPA 3.75 or higher: | 16% | Out-of-state: | 26% |
| GPA 3.50-3.74: | 6% | Live on campus: | 69% |
| | | International: | 2% |

**Basis for selection.** High school GPA important; test scores, essay, and signed lifestyle agreement required. **Homeschooled:** Statement describing homeschool structure and mission, transcript of courses and grades, state high school equivalency certificate, interview, letter of recommendation (non-parent) required. **Learning Disabled:** Students are extended extra services to assist them to be successful.

**High school preparation.** 11 units recommended. Recommended units include English 4, mathematics 2, social studies 3 and science 2.

**2009-2010 Annual costs.** Tuition/fees: $17,110. Per-credit-hour charge: 1-5 credits, $475; 6-11 credits, $750. Room/board: $6,646. Books/supplies: $1,100. Personal expenses: $1,634.

**2008-2009 Financial aid. Need-based:** 90 full-time freshmen applied for aid; 79 were judged to have need; 79 of these received aid. Average need met was 71%. Average scholarship/grant was $5,130; average loan $3,462. 52% of total undergraduate aid awarded as scholarships/grants, 48% as loans/jobs. **Non-need-based:** Awarded to 404 full-time undergraduates, including 90 freshmen. Scholarships awarded for academics, alumni affiliation, athletics, leadership, minority status, music/drama, religious affiliation.

**Application procedures. Admission:** No deadline. $50 fee, may be waived for applicants with need. Admission notification on a rolling basis. **Financial aid:** Priority date 3/1, closing date 8/30. FAFSA required. Applicants notified on a rolling basis starting 3/1; must reply within 2 week(s) of notification.

**Academics. Special study options:** Accelerated study, cooperative education, cross-registration, double major, independent study, internships, liberal arts/career combination, student-designed major, study abroad, teacher certification program, Washington semester. 2-2 nursing program with Walla Walla School of Nursing. **Credit/placement by examination:** AP, CLEP, institutional tests. 30 credit hours maximum toward associate degree, 30 toward bachelor's. No more than 45 total alternative credits (maximum 30 of any one type). **Support services:** Learning center, reduced course load, remedial instruction, study skills assistance, tutoring.

**Majors. Area/ethnic studies:** American. **Biology:** General. **Business:** Business admin, international. **Communications:** General. **Education:** Elementary, music, physical, secondary. **Family/consumer sciences:** Family studies. **History:** General. **Interdisciplinary:** Accounting/computer science, biopsychology. **Liberal arts:** Arts/sciences. **Parks/recreation:** Exercise sciences, health/fitness, sports admin. **Philosophy/religion:** Religion. **Physical**

sciences: General. **Psychology:** General, developmental. **Public adminis-tration:** Social work. **Social sciences:** General, urban studies. **Theology:** Preministerial.

**Most popular majors.** Business/marketing 30%, education 15%, family/consumer sciences 39%.

**Computing on campus.** 30 workstations in dormitories, library, computer center. Dormitories wired for high-speed internet access and linked to campus network. Online library, helpline, wireless network available.

**Student life. Freshman orientation:** Available. Preregistration for classes offered. **Policies:** Religious observance required. **Housing:** Guaranteed on-campus for freshmen. Single-sex dorms, special housing for disabled, apartments available. $100 deposit. **Activities:** Bands, campus ministries, choral groups, drama, literary magazine, music ensembles, student government.

**Athletics.** NAIA, NCCAA. **Intercollegiate:** Basketball, cross-country, golf, soccer, track and field, volleyball W. **Intramural:** Badminton, basketball, football (non-tackle), volleyball. **Team name:** Knights.

**Student services.** Adult student services, chaplain/spiritual director, career counseling, student employment services, financial aid counseling, health services, minority student services, personal counseling, placement for graduates.

**Contact.** E-mail: admissions@warnerpacific.edu
Phone: (503) 517-1020 Toll-free number: (800) 804-1510
Fax: (503) 517-1352
Shannon Mackey, Executive Director of Enrollment Management, Warner Pacific College, 2219 SE 68th Avenue, Portland, OR 97215-4026

---

## Western Oregon University
**Monmouth, Oregon**      **CB member**
**www.wou.edu**      **CB code: 4585**

- Public 4-year liberal arts and teachers college
- Residential campus in small town
- 4,731 degree-seeking undergraduates: 11% part-time, 57% women, 3% African American, 4% Asian American, 9% Hispanic American, 2% Native American, 5% international
- 464 degree-seeking graduate students
- 89% of applicants admitted
- SAT or ACT with writing required
- 39% graduate within 6 years

**General.** Founded in 1856. Regionally accredited. **Degrees:** 776 bachelor's, 1 associate awarded; master's offered. **ROTC:** Army, Naval, Air Force. **Location:** 15 miles from Salem, 60 miles from Portland. **Calendar:** Quarter, limited summer session. **Full-time faculty:** 209 total; 72% have terminal degrees, 8% minority, 46% women. **Part-time faculty:** 150 total; 23% have terminal degrees, 7% minority, 53% women. **Special facilities:** Arctic museum, teaching research institute, early childhood and training development center.

**Freshman class profile.** 2,326 applied, 2,062 admitted, 1,013 enrolled.

| Mid 50% test scores | | | |
|---|---|---|---|
| SAT critical reading: | 420-540 | Rank in top quarter: | 37% |
| SAT math: | 350-610 | Rank in top tenth: | 12% |
| SAT writing: | 400-510 | End year in good standing: | 82% |
| ACT composite: | 17-22 | Return as sophomores: | 62% |
| GPA 3.75 or higher: | 15% | Out-of-state: | 27% |
| GPA 3.50-3.74: | 16% | Live on campus: | 88% |
| GPA 3.0-3.49: | 37% | International: | 1% |
| GPA 2.0-2.99: | 31% | | |

**Basis for selection.** 2.75 GPA required. 1000 SAT (exclusive of Writing) strongly recommended, but only used in admissions decision if applicant does not meet GPA or college preparation requirements. If applicant does not meet academic requirements, other evidence of potential in the form of interviews, portfolios, auditions, and essays considered. **Home-schooled:** 1000 SAT (exclusive of Writing) or 21 ACT or 1410 SAT Subject Tests combined score in 3 subjects required; must take 1 SAT Reasoning Test, 1 SAT Subject Test in math, and second exam in foreign language.

**High school preparation.** College-preparatory program required. 14 units required. Required and recommended units include English 4, mathematics 3, social studies 2, history 1, science 2 (laboratory 1) and foreign language 2.

**2009-2010 Annual costs.** Tuition/fees: $6,813; $17,868 out-of-state. Resident tuition reflects WOU "Promise 2009" which is a four-year tuition commitment for resident UG students. Nonresident rate shown is for non-Promise students. Room/board: $8,040. Books/supplies: $1,125. Personal expenses: $2,475.

**2009-2010 Financial aid. Need-based:** Average need met was 68%. Average scholarship/grant was $7,040; average loan $3,309. 42% of total undergraduate aid awarded as scholarships/grants, 58% as loans/jobs. **Non-need-based:** Scholarships awarded for academics, alumni affiliation, art, athletics, leadership, music/drama.

**Application procedures. Admission:** No deadline. $50 fee. Admission notification on a rolling basis. **Financial aid:** Priority date 3/1; no closing date. FAFSA required. Applicants notified on a rolling basis starting 2/28; must reply within 3 week(s) of notification.

**Academics. Special study options:** Combined bachelor's/graduate degree, distance learning, double major, dual enrollment of high school students, ESL, exchange student, honors, independent study, internships, student-designed major, study abroad, teacher certification program. Preprofessional studies, interdisciplinary studies, nondegree licensure programs, service learning and career development. **Credit/placement by examination:** AP, CLEP, IB, SAT, ACT, institutional tests. 48 credit hours maximum toward bachelor's degree. **Support services:** Learning center, remedial instruction, study skills assistance, tutoring, writing center.

**Majors. Biology:** General. **Business:** General. **Communications:** General. **Computer sciences:** General. **Education:** General, biology, chemistry, elementary, health, instructional media, middle, multi-level teacher, physical, reading, science, secondary, social studies, Spanish. **Foreign languages:** Sign language interpretation, Spanish. **History:** General. **Interdisciplinary:** Biological/physical sciences, math/computer science, natural sciences. **Liberal arts:** Arts/sciences. **Math:** General. **Philosophy/religion:** Philosophy. **Physical sciences:** Chemistry, geology, planetary. **Protective services:** Corrections, fire services admin, law enforcement admin. **Psychology:** General. **Public administration:** General. **Social sciences:** General, anthropology, economics, geography, political science, sociology. **Visual/performing arts:** General, art, dance, dramatic, studio arts, theater arts management.

**Most popular majors.** Business/marketing 15%, education 20%, interdisciplinary studies 9%, psychology 7%, social sciences 6%, visual/performing arts 6%.

**Computing on campus.** 411 workstations in dormitories, library, computer center, student center. Dormitories wired for high-speed internet access and linked to campus network. Commuter students can connect to campus network. Online course registration, online library, helpline, repair service, wireless network available.

**Student life. Freshman orientation:** Available. Held last weekend in June and 2nd and 3rd weekends in July on Friday and/or Saturday. **Policies:** No alcohol permitted in residence halls. **Housing:** Guaranteed on-campus for freshmen. Coed dorms, special housing for disabled, apartments, wellness housing available. Family housing, housing by learning communities, community living options available. **Activities:** Bands, campus ministries, choral groups, dance, drama, international student organizations, literary magazine, music ensembles, musical theater, student government, student newspaper, symphony orchestra, TV station, Baptist student union, Big Brother/Big Sister, multicultural student union, Campus Crusade for Christ, Circle K, environmental action committee.

**Athletics.** NCAA. **Intercollegiate:** Baseball M, basketball, cheerleading, cross-country, football (tackle) M, soccer W, softball W, track and field, volleyball W. **Intramural:** Basketball, bowling, cross-country, football (non-tackle), football (tackle) M, golf, racquetball, rifle, skiing, soccer, softball, swimming, table tennis, tennis, track and field, triathlon, volleyball, water polo, weight lifting, wrestling. **Team name:** Wolves.

**Student services.** Adult student services, alcohol/substance abuse counseling, chaplain/spiritual director, career counseling, services for economically disadvantaged, student employment services, financial aid counseling, health services, minority student services, on-campus daycare, personal counseling, placement for graduates, veterans' counselor, women's services. **Physically disabled:** Services for visually, speech, hearing impaired.

**Contact.** E-mail: wolfgram@wou.edu
Phone: (503) 838-8211 Toll-free number: (877) 877-1593
Fax: (503) 838-8067
Rob Findtner, Director of Admissions, Western Oregon University, 345 North Monmouth Avenue, Monmouth, OR 97361

## Willamette University

| | |
|---|---|
| Salem, Oregon | **CB member** |
| www.willamette.edu | **CB code: 4954** |

◆ Private 4-year university and liberal arts college affiliated with United Methodist Church

◆ Residential campus in small city

◆ 1,853 degree-seeking undergraduates: 1% part-time, 56% women, 2% African American, 7% Asian American, 6% Hispanic American, 1% Native American, 1% international

◆ 832 degree-seeking graduate students

◆ 60% of applicants admitted

◆ SAT or ACT with writing, application essay required

◆ 79% graduate within 6 years; 25% enter graduate study

**General.** Founded in 1842. Regionally accredited. Sister school to Tokyo International University of America. **Degrees:** 400 bachelor's awarded; master's, professional offered. **ROTC:** Army, Air Force. **Location:** 45 miles from Portland. **Calendar:** Semester. **Full-time faculty:** 213 total; 96% have terminal degrees, 17% minority, 45% women. **Part-time faculty:** 83 total; 69% have terminal degrees, 6% minority, 37% women. **Class size:** 69% < 20, 31% 20-39, less than 1% 40-49. **Special facilities:** Art museum, American headquarters for International Debate Education Association, papers and memorabilia of Senator Mark O. Hatfield, botanical gardens, Japanese gardens, rose gardens, rural retreat center, wildlife refuge field station, digital art and music studios, 2 electron microscopes (scanning and transmission), 500 MHz Nuclear Magnetic Resonance spectrometer, 305 acre Zena research forest.

**Freshman class profile.** 5,739 applied, 3,416 admitted, 541 enrolled.

| Mid 50% test scores | | GPA 3.0-3.49: | 28% |
|---|---|---|---|
| SAT critical reading: | 560-670 | Rank in top quarter: | 80% |
| SAT math: | 560-650 | Rank in top tenth: | 49% |
| SAT writing: | 550-660 | End year in good standing: | 97% |
| ACT composite: | 25-30 | Return as sophomores: | 88% |
| GPA 3.75 or higher: | 51% | Out-of-state: | 71% |
| GPA 3.50-3.74: | 21% | Live on campus: | 97% |

**Basis for selection.** School record most important, followed by test scores, essay, recommendations, school and community activities, and interview. Audition recommended for music, theater programs; portfolio recommended for art program. **Homeschooled:** Recommend submission of accredited transcript from governing agency, if available.

**High school preparation.** College-preparatory program recommended. 17 units required; 20 recommended. Required and recommended units include English 4, mathematics 4, social studies 1, history 2, science 3 (laboratory 3), foreign language 3-4 and computer science 2.

**2009-2010 Annual costs.** Tuition/fees: $35,610. Room/board: $8,350. Books/supplies: $900.

**2009-2010 Financial aid. Need-based:** 459 full-time freshmen applied for aid; 357 were judged to have need; 357 of these received aid. Average need met was 89%. Average scholarship/grant was $24,061; average loan $3,426. 76% of total undergraduate aid awarded as scholarships/grants, 24% as loans/jobs. **Non-need-based:** Awarded to 850 full-time undergraduates, including 304 freshmen. Scholarships awarded for academics, alumni affiliation, leadership, minority status, music/drama, religious affiliation.

**Application procedures. Admission:** Priority date 2/1; no deadline. $50 fee, may be waived for applicants with need, free for online applicants. Admission notification on a rolling basis beginning on or about 10/1. Must reply by May 1 or within 2 week(s) if notified thereafter. **Financial aid:** Priority date 2/1; no closing date. FAFSA required. CSS PROFILE recommended of early action applicants. Applicants notified on a rolling basis starting 4/1; must reply by 5/1 or within 2 week(s) of notification.

**Academics. Special study options:** Accelerated study, combined bachelor's/graduate degree, cross-registration, double major, dual enrollment of high school students, exchange student, independent study, internships, student-designed major, study abroad, teacher certification program, urban semester, Washington semester. Interdisciplinary freshman study program, undergraduate research grants, field studies program in ecology in Hawaii, Ecuador, American Southwest, Oregon; 3-2 program, master's degree in management; 3-2 program, bachelor's degree in computer science with Oregon Graduate Institute, University of Oregon; 3-2 program, master's degree in forestry with Duke University. **Credit/placement by examination:** AP, CLEP, IB, institutional tests. 32 credit hours maximum toward bachelor's degree. **Support services:** Reduced course load, study skills assistance, tutoring, writing center.

**Majors. Area/ethnic studies:** American, Asian, Japanese, Latin American, women's. **Biology:** General. **Computer sciences:** General. **Conservation:** Environmental science. **Education:** Music. **Foreign languages:** Classics, comparative lit, French, German, Spanish. **History:** General. **Interdisciplinary:** Global studies. **Liberal arts:** Humanities. **Math:** General. **Parks/recreation:** Exercise sciences. **Philosophy/religion:** Philosophy, religion. **Physical sciences:** Chemistry, physics. **Psychology:** General. **Social sciences:** Anthropology, economics, political science, sociology. **Visual/performing arts:** Art history/conservation, dramatic, film/cinema, music performance, music theory/composition, piano/organ, stringed instruments, studio arts, voice/opera. **Other:** Science studies.

**Most popular majors.** Biology 7%, English 11%, foreign language 9%, interdisciplinary studies 7%, physical sciences 6%, psychology 9%, social sciences 26%, visual/performing arts 6%.

**Computing on campus.** 400 workstations in dormitories, library, computer center, student center. Dormitories wired for high-speed internet access and linked to campus network. Commuter students can connect to campus network. Online course registration, online library, helpline, repair service, student web hosting, wireless network available.

**Student life. Freshman orientation:** Mandatory. Preregistration for classes offered. Five-day program before start of semester. **Housing:** Guaranteed on-campus for freshmen. Coed dorms, apartments, fraternity/sorority housing, wellness housing available. $400 nonrefundable deposit, deadline 5/1. Environmental, intensive study halls available. **Activities:** Bands, campus ministries, choral groups, dance, drama, film society, international student organizations, literary magazine, music ensembles, Model UN, musical theater, opera, student government, student newspaper, symphony orchestra. More than 100 student organizations available.

**Athletics.** NCAA. **Intercollegiate:** Baseball M, basketball, cross-country, football (tackle) M, golf, rowing (crew), soccer, softball W, swimming, tennis, track and field, volleyball W. **Intramural:** Badminton, basketball, bowling, football (non-tackle), racquetball, soccer, softball, table tennis, tennis, volleyball, water polo, weight lifting. **Team name:** Bearcats.

**Student services.** Alcohol/substance abuse counseling, chaplain/spiritual director, career counseling, student employment services, financial aid counseling, health services, minority student services, personal counseling, veterans' counselor, women's services. **Physically disabled:** Services for visually, speech, hearing impaired.

**Contact.** E-mail: libarts@willamette.edu
Phone: (503) 370-6303 Toll-free number: (877) 542-2787
Fax: (503) 375-5363
Madeleine Rhyneer, Vice President for Admissions and Financial Aid, Willamette University, 900 State Street, Salem, OR 97301-3922

# Pennsylvania

**Albright College**
Reading, Pennsylvania                  **CB member**
www.albright.edu                       **CB code: 2004**

- Private 4-year liberal arts college affiliated with United Methodist Church
- Residential campus in small city
- 2,259 degree-seeking undergraduates: 59% women, 11% African American, 1% Asian American, 6% Hispanic American, 6% international
- 22 degree-seeking graduate students
- 56% of applicants admitted
- Application essay required
- 62% graduate within 6 years

**General.** Founded in 1856. Regionally accredited. **Degrees:** 482 bachelor's awarded; master's offered. **Location:** 50 miles from Philadelphia. **Calendar:** 4-1-4, limited summer session. **Full-time faculty:** 114 total; 84% have terminal degrees, 12% minority, 49% women. **Part-time faculty:** 47 total; 23% have terminal degrees, 4% minority, 60% women. **Class size:** 66% < 20, 33% 20-39, less than 1% 40-49, less than 1% 50-99. **Special facilities:** Satellite dish for foreign language program, transmission and scanning electron microscopes, Holocaust resource center, center for local government, center for cultural ecology, center for Latin American studies.

**Freshman class profile.** 5,565 applied, 3,113 admitted, 541 enrolled.

| Mid 50% test scores | | | |
|---|---|---|---|
| SAT critical reading: | 480-570 | Rank in top tenth: | 23% |
| SAT math: | 480-570 | End year in good standing: | 95% |
| ACT composite: | 20-25 | Return as sophomores: | 73% |
| GPA 3.75 or higher: | 25% | Out-of-state: | 42% |
| GPA 3.50-3.74: | 18% | Live on campus: | 91% |
| GPA 3.0-3.49: | 27% | International: | 6% |
| GPA 2.0-2.99: | 30% | Fraternities: | 3% |
| Rank in top quarter: | 48% | Sororities: | 4% |

**Basis for selection.** High school performance (with emphasis on difficulty of curriculum pursued), personal statement, and recommendations most important. Community service, extracurricular activity and test scores considered. Interview recommended.

**High school preparation.** College-preparatory program required. 16 units required; 20 recommended. Required and recommended units include English 4, mathematics 2-3, social studies 2, history 1-2, science 3-4 (laboratory 1-2), foreign language 2-3 and academic electives 2. Bachelor of science applicants should have 1 additional unit in science and 1 in math. 2 units of laboratory science recommended.

**2009-2010 Annual costs.** Tuition/fees: $31,600. Room/board: $8,770. Books/supplies: $1,000. Personal expenses: $1,100.

**2009-2010 Financial aid. Need-based:** 490 full-time freshmen applied for aid; 455 were judged to have need; 451 of these received aid. Average need met was 81%. Average scholarship/grant was $21,335; average loan $4,849. 70% of total undergraduate aid awarded as scholarships/grants, 30% as loans/jobs. **Non-need-based:** Scholarships awarded for academics, alumni affiliation, art, leadership, minority status, music/drama, religious affiliation.

**Application procedures. Admission:** Priority date 3/1; no deadline. $25 fee, may be waived for applicants with need. Admission notification on a rolling basis beginning on or about 10/1. Must reply by May 1 or within 2 week(s) if notified thereafter. **Financial aid:** Priority date 3/1; no closing date. FAFSA required. Applicants notified on a rolling basis starting 2/15; must reply by 5/1 or within 2 week(s) of notification.

**Academics.** Flexible curriculum combines liberal arts education with hands-on experiences. Institution emphasizes faculty-student collaboration and has an active undergraduate research program, which also funds summer projects with faculty. **Special study options:** Accelerated study, combined bachelor's/graduate degree, cross-registration, double major, dual enrollment of high school students, ESL, exchange student, honors, independent study, internships, liberal arts/career combination, semester at sea, student-designed major, study abroad, teacher certification program, urban semester, Washington

semester. Interdisciplinary studies, student research. **Credit/placement by examination:** AP, CLEP, IB, SAT, ACT. 28 credit hours maximum toward bachelor's degree. **Support services:** Learning center, pre-admission summer program, reduced course load, study skills assistance, tutoring, writing center.

**Majors. Area/ethnic studies:** American, Latin American, women's. **Biology:** General, biochemistry. **Business:** Accounting, business admin, finance, international, marketing. **Communications:** General. **Computer sciences:** General, information systems. **Conservation:** General, environmental science, environmental studies. **Education:** Art, early childhood, elementary, secondary, special. **Family/consumer sciences:** Clothing/textiles. **Foreign languages:** French, Spanish. **Health:** Predental, premedicine, preveterinary. **History:** General. **Math:** General. **Philosophy/religion:** Philosophy, religion. **Physical sciences:** Chemistry, optics, physics. **Psychology:** General. **Social sciences:** Anthropology, criminology, economics, political science, sociology. **Visual/performing arts:** Dramatic, studio arts.

**Most popular majors.** Biology 6%, business/marketing 30%, psychology 16%, social sciences 10%, visual/performing arts 10%.

**Computing on campus.** 250 workstations in dormitories, library, computer center, student center. Dormitories wired for high-speed internet access and linked to campus network. Online course registration, online library, helpline, wireless network available.

**Student life. Freshman orientation:** Mandatory. Preregistration for classes offered. Held 4 days prior to start of fall classes. **Housing:** Guaranteed on-campus for all undergraduates. Coed dorms, wellness housing available. $100 nonrefundable deposit, deadline 6/1. Honors housing, break housing suite, all freshmen housing, all-female floors, all-male floors, single rooms, single-sex suites/apartments/wings. **Activities:** Bands, campus ministries, choral groups, dance, drama, international student organizations, literary magazine, music ensembles, musical theater, radio station, student government, student newspaper, TV station, Newman, Hillel, Christian Fellowship, African American society, Asian American society, environmental action group, American Association of University Women, human services organization.

**Athletics.** NCAA. **Intercollegiate:** Baseball M, basketball, cheerleading, cross-country, field hockey W, football (tackle) M, golf M, soccer, softball W, swimming, tennis, track and field, volleyball W. **Intramural:** Basketball, bowling, football (non-tackle), soccer, softball, volleyball. **Team name:** Lions.

**Student services.** Adult student services, chaplain/spiritual director, career counseling, student employment services, financial aid counseling, health services, minority student services, personal counseling, women's services. **Physically disabled:** Services for visually, hearing impaired.

**Contact.** E-mail: admission@albright.edu
Phone: (610) 921-7700 Toll-free number: (800) 252-1856
Fax: (610) 921-7729
Gregory Eichhorn, Vice-President for Enrollment Management & Dean of Admissions, Albright College, 13th & Bern Streets, Reading, PA 19612-5234

**Allegheny College**
Meadville, Pennsylvania                **CB member**
www.allegheny.edu                      **CB code: 2006**

- Private 4-year liberal arts college affiliated with United Methodist Church
- Residential campus in large town
- 2,099 degree-seeking undergraduates: 1% part-time, 55% women, 4% African American, 3% Asian American, 3% Hispanic American, 1% international
- 66% of applicants admitted
- SAT or ACT (ACT writing recommended), application essay required
- 74% graduate within 6 years; 43% enter graduate study

**General.** Founded in 1815. Regionally accredited. **Degrees:** 489 bachelor's awarded. **Location:** 90 miles from Pittsburgh and Cleveland. **Calendar:** Semester, limited summer session. **Full-time faculty:** 152 total; 93% have terminal degrees, 14% minority, 44% women. **Part-time faculty:** 33 total; 36% have terminal degrees, 52% women. **Class size:** 58% < 20, 38% 20-39, 2% 40-49, 1% 50-99. **Special facilities:** Science complex, planetarium, observatory, Geographic Information Systems (GIS) learning lab, smart classrooms, solid-volume glass sculpture grouping, environmental research preserve, 80-acre protected forest, seismographic network station, art studios, dance studio and performance area, Center for Political Participation, Center for Economic and Environmental Development, environmental roof garden, Center for Experiential Learning.

**Freshman class profile.** 3,916 applied, 2,594 admitted, 583 enrolled.

| Mid 50% test scores | | | |
|---|---|---|---|
| SAT critical reading: | 550-660 | Rank in top quarter: | 76% |
| SAT math: | 560-650 | Rank in top tenth: | 45% |
| SAT writing: | 550-640 | End year in good standing: | 99% |
| ACT composite: | 23-29 | Return as sophomores: | 88% |
| GPA 3.75 or higher: | 52% | Out-of-state: | 46% |
| GPA 3.50-3.74: | 21% | Live on campus: | 98% |
| GPA 3.0-3.49: | 21% | International: | 1% |
| GPA 2.0-2.99: | 6% | Fraternities: | 23% |
| | | Sororities: | 29% |

**Basis for selection.** Rigor of high school program most important, followed by high school achievement. Test scores important. Essay, minority status, alumni ties, geography considered. One recommendation from guidance counselor and one from teacher required. Interview recommended. **Homeschooled:** Campus visit and individual interview with admissions counselor to discuss portfolios recommended. Recommendation from a non-family member, description of the level of instruction. **Learning Disabled:** Recommended interview with Director of Student Support Services.

**High school preparation.** College-preparatory program required. 16 units required. Required units include English 4, mathematics 3, social studies 3, science 3, foreign language 2 and academic electives 1.

**2010-2011 Annual costs.** Tuition/fees: $34,810. Room/board: $8,790. Books/supplies: $1,000. Personal expenses: $800.

**2009-2010 Financial aid. Need-based:** 498 full-time freshmen applied for aid; 402 were judged to have need; 402 of these received aid. Average need met was 92%. Average scholarship/grant was $21,029; average loan $4,761. 77% of total undergraduate aid awarded as scholarships/grants, 23% as loans/jobs. **Non-need-based:** Awarded to 769 full-time undergraduates, including 243 freshmen. Scholarships awarded for academics, leadership, minority status, state residency.

**Application procedures. Admission:** Closing date 2/15 (postmark date). $35 fee, may be waived for applicants with need, free for online applicants. Admission notification 4/1. Must reply by 5/1. **Financial aid:** Priority date 2/15; no closing date. FAFSA required. Applicants notified on a rolling basis starting 3/1; must reply by 5/1 or within 4 week(s) of notification.

**Academics.** Teacher partnerships with Columbia University Teachers College, Xavier School of Education and University of Pittsburgh; business school partnership with Simon Graduate School of Business Administration at University of Rochester; medical school partnerships with Jefferson Medical College and Drexel College of Medicine; accelerated master's degree program with Carnegie Mellon University for public policy and management, arts management, health policy and management, information systems management, and information technology; accelerated master's degree program with Chatham College for physician assistant; marine biology study programs. **Special study options:** Combined bachelor's/graduate degree, double major, dual enrollment of high school students, ESL, exchange student, independent study, internships, student-designed major, study abroad, Washington semester. Graduate school partnerships, marine biology study program, combined degree programs (3-2, 3-4), Experiential Learning Term (summer study program), double minor, pre-professional programs, domestic off-campus semester away study programs. **Credit/placement by examination:** AP, CLEP, IB, institutional tests. 20 credit hours maximum toward bachelor's degree. **Support services:** Learning center, reduced course load, study skills assistance, tutoring, writing center.

**Majors. Area/ethnic studies:** Women's. **Biology:** General, biochemistry. **Business:** Managerial economics. **Communications:** General, journalism, media studies. **Computer sciences:** Computer science. **Conservation:** Environmental science, environmental studies. **Education:** General. **Engineering:** Software. **Foreign languages:** French, German, Spanish. **Health:** Predental, premedicine, prenursing, prepharmacy, preveterinary. **History:** General. **Interdisciplinary:** Neuroscience. **Legal studies:** Prelaw. **Math:** General. **Philosophy/religion:** Philosophy, religion. **Physical sciences:** Chemistry, geology, physics. **Psychology:** General. **Social sciences:** Applied economics, economics, international relations, political science. **Visual/performing arts:** Art, art history/conservation, dramatic, music performance, studio arts. **Other:** Art and technology, Environmental geology, Health/medical preparatory.

**Most popular majors.** Biology 14%, English 7%, interdisciplinary studies 7%, physical sciences 8%, psychology 17%, social sciences 20%.

**Computing on campus.** 185 workstations in library, computer center, student center. Dormitories wired for high-speed internet access and linked to campus network. Commuter students can connect to campus network. Online library, helpline, repair service, student web hosting, wireless network available.

**Student life. Freshman orientation:** Mandatory. 4-day session held 4 days directly before fall classes begin. **Policies:** Honor code. **Housing:** Guaranteed on-campus for all undergraduates. Coed dorms, single-sex dorms, special housing for disabled, apartments, fraternity/sorority housing, wellness housing available. Environmentally-sensitive townhouses, LEED certified, low fume material; quiet study floors. **Activities:** Bands, campus ministries, choral groups, dance, drama, international student organizations, literary magazine, music ensembles, Model UN, musical theater, radio station, student government, student newspaper, symphony orchestra, TV station, Association for Asian and Asian-American Awareness, Advancement of Black Culture, Union Latina, Habitat for Humanity, Newman Association, Hillel, Christian Outreach, Alpha Phi Omega, Americorps Bonner Leaders, College Democrats.

**Athletics.** NCAA. **Intercollegiate:** Baseball M, basketball, cross-country, diving, football (tackle) M, golf, lacrosse W, soccer, softball W, swimming, tennis, track and field, volleyball W. **Intramural:** Basketball, bowling, football (non-tackle), racquetball, soccer, softball, tennis, volleyball. **Team name:** Gators.

**Student services.** Adult student services, chaplain/spiritual director, career counseling, student employment services, financial aid counseling, health services, minority student services, personal counseling, placement for graduates. **Physically disabled:** Services for visually, hearing impaired.

**Contact.** E-mail: admissions@allegheny.edu
Phone: (814) 332-4351 Toll-free number: (800) 521-5293
Fax: (814) 337-0431
Jennifer Winge, Director of Admissions, Allegheny College, Box 5, 520 North Main Street, Meadville, PA 16335

## Alvernia University

Reading, Pennsylvania — CB member
www.alvernia.edu — CB code: 2431

- Private 4-year university and liberal arts college affiliated with Roman Catholic Church
- Residential campus in small city
- 1,990 degree-seeking undergraduates: 19% part-time, 68% women, 11% African American, 2% Asian American, 6% Hispanic American, 1% Native American, 1% international
- 628 degree-seeking graduate students
- 78% of applicants admitted
- SAT or ACT (ACT writing optional) required
- 56% graduate within 6 years

**General.** Founded in 1958. Regionally accredited. Affiliated with Bernardine Sisters, Third Order of St. Francis. **Degrees:** 415 bachelor's, 8 associate awarded; master's, doctoral offered. **ROTC:** Army. **Location:** 60 miles from Philadelphia. **Calendar:** Semester, limited summer session. **Full-time faculty:** 85 total; 60% have terminal degrees, 7% minority, 58% women. **Part-time faculty:** 212 total; 20% have terminal degrees, 27% minority, 48% women. **Class size:** 54% < 20, 46% 20-39, less than 1% 40-49, less than 1% 50-99.

**Freshman class profile.** 1,605 applied, 1,252 admitted, 328 enrolled.

| Mid 50% test scores | | | |
|---|---|---|---|
| SAT critical reading: | 440-540 | GPA 2.0-2.99: | 38% |
| SAT math: | 440-550 | Rank in top quarter: | 25% |
| SAT writing: | 420-530 | Rank in top tenth: | 6% |
| ACT composite: | 17-21 | End year in good standing: | 91% |
| GPA 3.75 or higher: | 13% | Return as sophomores: | 72% |
| GPA 3.50-3.74: | 16% | Out-of-state: | 27% |
| GPA 3.0-3.49: | 31% | Live on campus: | 75% |

**Basis for selection.** Important factors include academic performance, standardized test scores, class rank, extracurricular activities, and community involvement. Essay, interview recommended for all. Interview required of nursing, occupational therapy and physical therapist assistant applicants.

**High school preparation.** College-preparatory program recommended. 16 units recommended. Recommended units include English 4, mathematics 4, social studies 3, science 2, foreign language 2 and computer science 1.

**2009-2010 Annual costs.** Tuition/fees: $24,350. Room/board: $9,212. Books/supplies: $1,400. Personal expenses: $1,196.

**2008-2009 Financial aid. Need-based:** 364 full-time freshmen applied for aid; 323 were judged to have need; 323 of these received aid. Average need met was 75%. Average scholarship/grant was $11,728; average loan $5,698. 56% of total undergraduate aid awarded as scholarships/grants, 44% as loans/jobs. **Non-need-based:** Awarded to 213 full-time undergraduates, including 67 freshmen. Scholarships awarded for academics, state residency.

**Application procedures. Admission:** No deadline. $25 fee, may be waived for applicants with need. Admission notification on a rolling basis beginning on or about 10/1. Must reply by May 1 or within 2 week(s) if notified thereafter. **Financial aid:** Priority date 5/1; no closing date. FAFSA required. Applicants notified on a rolling basis starting 2/20; must reply within 2 week(s) of notification.

**Academics. Special study options:** Accelerated study, combined bachelor's/ graduate degree, cross-registration, distance learning, double major, dual enrollment of high school students, ESL, honors, independent study, internships, student-designed major, study abroad, teacher certification program, Washington semester. **Credit/placement by examination:** AP, CLEP, IB, institutional tests. 30 credit hours maximum toward associate degree, 30 toward bachelor's. Total of 30 credits allowed for all experiential credit, CLEP, life experience, challenge exam. **Support services:** Learning center, pre-admission summer program, reduced course load, remedial instruction, study skills assistance, tutoring, writing center.

**Majors. Biology:** General, biochemistry. **Business:** General, accounting, human resources, marketing. **Communications:** General. **Computer sciences:** General. **Education:** General, biology, chemistry, computer, early childhood, elementary, English, mathematics, science, social studies, special. **Health:** Athletic training, nursing (RN), substance abuse counseling. **History:** General. **Interdisciplinary:** Biological/physical sciences. **Liberal arts:** Arts/sciences. **Math:** General. **Parks/recreation:** Sports admin. **Philosophy/religion:** Religion. **Physical sciences:** Chemistry. **Protective services:** Forensics, law enforcement admin. **Psychology:** General. **Public administration:** Social work. **Social sciences:** General, political science. **Theology:** Theology.

**Most popular majors.** Business/marketing 18%, education 11%, health sciences 30%, security/protective services 14%.

**Computing on campus.** 324 workstations in dormitories, library, computer center, student center. Dormitories wired for high-speed internet access and linked to campus network. Commuter students can connect to campus network. Online course registration, online library, helpline, wireless network available.

**Student life. Freshman orientation:** Mandatory. Preregistration for classes offered. Held weekend before classes start. **Housing:** Guaranteed on-campus for freshmen. Coed dorms, special housing for disabled, apartments available. $250 nonrefundable deposit, deadline 6/1. Single-sex townhouses available. Single-sex floors in dorms. **Activities:** Concert band, campus ministries, choral groups, dance, drama, literary magazine, music ensembles, student government, student newspaper.

**Athletics.** NCAA. **Intercollegiate:** Baseball M, basketball, cross-country, field hockey W, golf M, ice hockey M, lacrosse, soccer, softball W, tennis, track and field, volleyball W. **Intramural:** Basketball, cheerleading W, football (non-tackle), soccer. **Team name:** Crusaders.

**Student services.** Adult student services, chaplain/spiritual director, career counseling, services for economically disadvantaged, student employment services, financial aid counseling, health services, minority student services, personal counseling, placement for graduates, veterans' counselor. **Physically disabled:** Services for visually impaired.

**Contact.** E-mail: admissions@alvernia.edu
Phone: (610) 796-8269 Toll-free number: (888) 258-3764
Fax: (610) 796-2873
Jeff Dittman, Dean of Undergraduate Admission, Alvernia University, 400 St. Bernardine Street, Reading, PA 19607-1799

---

## Arcadia University
**Glenside, Pennsylvania**  **CB member**
www.arcadia.edu  **CB code: 2039**

- Private 4-year university affiliated with Presbyterian Church (USA)
- Residential campus in large town
- 2,174 degree-seeking undergraduates: 7% part-time, 73% women, 8% African American, 3% Asian American, 4% Hispanic American, 1% international
- 1,512 degree-seeking graduate students
- 61% of applicants admitted
- SAT or ACT with writing, application essay required
- 61% graduate within 6 years

**General.** Founded in 1853. Regionally accredited. **Degrees:** 423 bachelor's awarded; master's, doctoral offered. **ROTC:** Army. **Location:** 10 miles from Philadelphia. **Calendar:** Semester, limited summer session. **Full-time faculty:** 107 total; 17% minority, 49% women. **Part-time faculty:** 308 total; 10% minority, 57% women. **Class size:** 73% < 20, 25% 20-39, 1%

40-49, 1% 50-99. **Special facilities:** Observatory housing 14-inch Schmidt-Cassegrain telescope with extensive astrophotography capabilities, Grey Towers Castle (national historic landmark) used as residence hall.

**Freshman class profile.** 5,175 applied, 3,151 admitted, 534 enrolled.

| Mid 50% test scores | | | |
|---|---|---|---|
| SAT critical reading: | 510-610 | GPA 2.0-2.99: | 14% |
| SAT math: | 500-600 | Rank in top quarter: | 58% |
| SAT writing: | 500-600 | Rank in top tenth: | 23% |
| ACT composite: | 21-27 | Return as sophomores: | 77% |
| GPA 3.75 or higher: | 35% | Out-of-state: | 48% |
| GPA 3.50-3.74: | 23% | Live on campus: | 86% |
| GPA 3.0-3.49: | 27% | International: | 1% |

**Basis for selection.** Emphasis placed on academic records, including type of program followed, courses taken, grades earned, class rank. Standardized test scores, counselor/ teacher recommendations, participation in school and community activities important. Character references also considered. Supplementary materials demonstrating student's talents and potential recommended. Portfolio review required for fine arts department. Auditions required for BFA in acting. **Homeschooled:** Statement describing homeschool structure and mission, letter of recommendation (nonparent) required. Portfolio representing academic record/work and level of achievement for grades 9-12 required.

**High school preparation.** College-preparatory program required. 19 units recommended. Recommended units include English 4, mathematics 3, social studies 2, history 2, science 3 (laboratory 3) and foreign language 2. Additional units in foreign language, math, and/or laboratory science recommended. Math includes algebra II and geometry.

**2009-2010 Annual costs.** Tuition/fees: $31,260. Room/board: $10,680. Books/supplies: $1,000. Personal expenses: $650.

**2009-2010 Financial aid. Need-based:** 508 full-time freshmen applied for aid; 485 were judged to have need; 485 of these received aid. Average need met was 75%. Average scholarship/grant was $19,403; average loan $3,834. 68% of total undergraduate aid awarded as scholarships/grants, 32% as loans/jobs. **Non-need-based:** Awarded to 617 full-time undergraduates, including 72 freshmen. Scholarships awarded for academics, alumni affiliation, art, leadership, music/drama.

**Application procedures. Admission:** Priority date 1/15; deadline 3/1. $30 fee, may be waived for applicants with need, free for online applicants. Admission notification on a rolling basis beginning on or about 9/1. Must reply by May 1 or within 2 week(s) if notified thereafter. **Financial aid:** Priority date 3/1; no closing date. FAFSA, institutional form required. Applicants notified on a rolling basis starting 2/15; must reply by 5/1.

**Academics. Special study options:** Accelerated study, combined bachelor's/ graduate degree, cooperative education, cross-registration, distance learning, double major, dual enrollment of high school students, exchange student, honors, independent study, internships, liberal arts/career combination, student-designed major, study abroad, teacher certification program, Washington semester. Combined programs leading to graduate degrees in physical therapy, physician assistant studies (option to combine with public health), forensic science, international peace and conflict resolution. Combined with other universities for degrees in engineering, nursing, optometry. **Credit/ placement by examination:** CLEP, IB, institutional tests. 64 credit hours maximum toward bachelor's degree. **Support services:** Learning center, pre-admission summer program, reduced course load, remedial instruction, study skills assistance, tutoring, writing center.

**Majors. Area/ethnic studies:** Italian, Spanish/Iberian. **Biology:** General. **Business:** General, accounting, business admin, finance, human resources, international, management information systems, management science, marketing. **Communications:** General, media studies, radio/tv. **Computer sciences:** General, computer science, programming. **Conservation:** Environmental studies. **Education:** General, art, biology, chemistry, early childhood, elementary, English, mathematics, multi-level teacher, science, secondary, social science, social studies, special. **Engineering:** General. **Foreign languages:** French, Spanish. **Health:** Art therapy, facilities admin, health care admin, health services admin, medical illustrating. **History:** General. **Interdisciplinary:** Biological/physical sciences. **Legal studies:** General. **Liberal arts:** Arts/sciences. **Math:** General. **Philosophy/religion:** Philosophy. **Physical sciences:** Chemistry, physics. **Psychology:** General. **Social sciences:** Criminology, international relations, political science, sociology. **Visual/ performing arts:** General, acting, art, art history/conservation, ceramics, commercial/advertising art, dramatic, graphic design, illustration, interior design, metal/jewelry, painting, photography, printmaking, studio arts, theater history. **Other:** Global legal studies, Sound and music, Sport psychology.

**Most popular majors.** Biology 10%, business/marketing 13%, education 10%, psychology 11%, social sciences 8%, visual/performing arts 15%.

**Computing on campus.** 200 workstations in library, computer center. Dormitories wired for high-speed internet access and linked to campus network. Commuter students can connect to campus network. Online course registration, helpline, repair service, wireless network available.

**Student life. Freshman orientation:** Mandatory. Preregistration for classes offered. **Housing:** Guaranteed on-campus for all undergraduates. Coed dorms, single-sex dorms, special housing for disabled, apartments, wellness housing available. $300 nonrefundable deposit, deadline 5/1. Living and learning community available. **Activities:** Choral groups, dance, drama, literary magazine, music ensembles, musical theater, radio station, student government, student newspaper, TV station, approximately 45 clubs and organizations.

**Athletics.** NCAA. **Intercollegiate:** Baseball M, basketball, equestrian, field hockey W, golf, lacrosse W, soccer, softball W, swimming, tennis, volleyball W. **Intramural:** Basketball, field hockey W, football (non-tackle), skiing, soccer, softball, swimming M, tennis, volleyball, weight lifting. **Team name:** Scarlet Knights.

**Student services.** Adult student services, alcohol/substance abuse counseling, career counseling, services for economically disadvantaged, student employment services, financial aid counseling, health services, minority student services, personal counseling, placement for graduates.

**Contact.** E-mail: admiss@arcadia.edu
Phone: (215) 572-2910 Toll-free number: (877) 272-2342
Fax: (215) 881-8767
Mark Lapreziosa, Associate Vice President of Enrollment Management, Arcadia University, 450 South Easton Road, Glenside, PA 19038-3295

## Art Institute of Philadelphia
**Philadelphia, Pennsylvania**
www.artinstitutes.edu/Philadelphia                    CB code: 2033

- For-profit 4-year visual arts college
- Commuter campus in very large city
- 3,500 degree-seeking undergraduates
- Application essay, interview required

**General.** Founded in 1966. Accredited by ACICS. **Degrees:** 459 bachelor's, 188 associate awarded. **Calendar:** Quarter, extensive summer session. **Full-time faculty:** 99 total. **Part-time faculty:** 120 total. **Special facilities:** Recording studio utilizing Pro-tools software, digital photography laboratory, nonlinear digital editing suites, and full-service chef instructor/student-run restaurant.

**Basis for selection.** High school transcript most important. Essay and interview required. Portfolio recommended. **Homeschooled:** Transcript of courses and grades, state high school equivalency certificate required.

**High school preparation.** Background or strong interest in chosen major preferred.

**2010-2011 Annual costs.** Tuition/fees (projected): $22,614. Books/supplies: $1,200.

**Financial aid. Additional information:** Institute-sponsored scholarships available.

**Application procedures. Admission:** No deadline. $50 fee. Admission notification on a rolling basis. **Financial aid:** No deadline. FAFSA, institutional form required. Applicants notified on a rolling basis starting 3/1; must reply within 2 week(s) of notification.

**Academics.** Academic program designed to simulate working environment, focusing course work on job-related skills. **Special study options:** Independent study, internships. **Credit/placement by examination:** CLEP, IB, SAT, ACT, institutional tests. **Support services:** Learning center, reduced course load, remedial instruction, study skills assistance, tutoring.

**Majors. Communications technology:** Animation/special effects. **Computer sciences:** Web page design. **Personal/culinary services:** Chef training. **Visual/performing arts:** Cinematography, commercial/advertising art, design, fashion design, industrial design, interior design, photography.

**Computing on campus.** 507 workstations in dormitories, library, computer center. Dormitories wired for high-speed internet access. Online library, student web hosting available.

**Student life. Freshman orientation:** Mandatory. **Housing:** Guaranteed on-campus for all undergraduates. Coed dorms, apartments available. **Activities:** Student government.

**Student services.** Career counseling, student employment services, financial aid counseling, personal counseling, placement for graduates.

**Contact.** E-mail: aiphadm@aii.edu
Phone: (215) 567-7080 Toll-free number: (800) 275-2474
Fax: (215) 405-6399
Larry McHugh, Director of Admissions, Art Institute of Philadelphia, 1622 Chestnut Street, Philadelphia, PA 19103-5198

## Art Institute of Pittsburgh
**Pittsburgh, Pennsylvania**
www.artinstitutes.edu/pittsburgh                    CB code: 2029

- For-profit 4-year visual arts and technical college
- Commuter campus in large city
- 2,765 degree-seeking undergraduates
- Application essay, interview required

**General.** Founded in 1921. Regionally accredited. **Degrees:** 486 bachelor's, 94 associate awarded. **Calendar:** Continuous, extensive summer session. **Full-time faculty:** 386 total. **Part-time faculty:** 798 total. **Special facilities:** Photography laboratory, art gallery, traveling exhibits, 24-track recording studio.

**Freshman class profile.**

| Out-of-state: | 50% | Live on campus: | 50% |
|---|---|---|---|

**Basis for selection.** High school transcript most important. Essay required. Interview required. Limited portfolio required for some programs. **Homeschooled:** Statement describing homeschool structure and mission, transcript of courses and grades, state high school equivalency certificate, letter of recommendation (nonparent) required.

**High school preparation.** Prefer students with demonstrated interest in chosen major.

**2009-2010 Annual costs.** Tuition/fees: $21,385. Culinary lab fee for food courses, $250; $100 lab fee per online course. Room only: $6,720. Books/supplies: $1,445.

**Application procedures. Admission:** No deadline. $50 fee. Admission notification on a rolling basis. **Financial aid:** No deadline. FAFSA, institutional form required. Applicants notified on a rolling basis starting 4/15.

**Academics. Special study options:** Distance learning, internships, study abroad. **Credit/placement by examination:** AP, CLEP, institutional tests. **Support services:** Learning center, remedial instruction, tutoring, writing center.

**Majors. Business:** Fashion. **Communications technology:** Animation/special effects. **Computer sciences:** Web page design. **Personal/culinary services:** Chef training, restaurant/catering. **Visual/performing arts:** Cinematography, commercial/advertising art, design, industrial design, interior design, photography.

**Computing on campus.** 225 workstations in dormitories, library, computer center. Dormitories wired for high-speed internet access and linked to campus network. Commuter students can connect to campus network. Online course registration, online library, helpline, student web hosting, wireless network available.

**Student life. Freshman orientation:** Mandatory. Preregistration for classes offered. One-day program held before start of classes. **Housing:** Coed dorms, apartments, wellness housing available. $100 deposit. **Activities:** Drama, film society, international student organizations, student government, student newspaper, community relations activities, student success task force, student council.

**Student services.** Alcohol/substance abuse counseling, career counseling, student employment services, financial aid counseling, personal counseling, placement for graduates, veterans' counselor. **Physically disabled:** Services for visually, speech, hearing impaired.

**Contact.** E-mail: aipadm@aii.edu
Phone: (412) 263-6600 Toll-free number: (800) 275-2470
Fax: (412) 263-6667
Melanie Gibson, Senior Director of Admissions, Art Institute of Pittsburgh, 420 Boulevard of the Allies, Pittsburgh, PA 15219-1328

## Art Institute of Pittsburgh - Online Division
**Pittsburgh, Pennsylvania**
www.aionline.edu                    CB code: 3835

- For-profit 4-year virtual college
- Large city

**General.** Accredited by ACICS. **Calendar:** Quarter.

**Annual costs/financial aid.** Tuition/fees (2009-2010): $19,665.

**Contact.** Phone: (877) 872-8869
Admissions Director, 1400 Penn Avenue, Pittsburgh, PA 15222

---

## Baptist Bible College of Pennsylvania
**Clarks Summit, Pennsylvania**
**www.bbc.edu**                                      **CB code: 2036**

- Private 4-year Bible and seminary college affiliated with Baptist faith
- Residential campus in small city
- 566 degree-seeking undergraduates
- 281 graduate students
- 64% of applicants admitted
- SAT or ACT (ACT writing optional), application essay required
- 50% graduate within 6 years

**General.** Founded in 1932. Regionally accredited; also accredited by ABHE. Part of each student's curriculum includes ministry/service experiences in churches or social agencies. **Degrees:** 127 bachelor's, 26 associate awarded; master's, doctoral, professional offered. **ROTC:** Army. **Location:** 7 miles from Scranton, 20 miles from Wilkes-Barre. **Calendar:** Semester, limited summer session. **Full-time faculty:** 38 total; 66% have terminal degrees, 26% women. **Part-time faculty:** 29 total; 31% have terminal degrees, 38% women. **Class size:** 70% < 20, 20% 20-39, 4% 40-49, 6% 50-99, 1% >100.

**Freshman class profile.** 272 applied, 175 admitted, 122 enrolled.

| Mid 50% test scores | | | |
|---|---|---|---|
| SAT critical reading: | 470-560 | GPA 3.50-3.74: | 24% |
| SAT math: | 430-550 | GPA 3.0-3.49: | 25% |
| SAT writing: | 430-550 | GPA 2.0-2.99: | 22% |
| ACT composite: | 19-25 | Return as sophomores: | 70% |
| GPA 3.75 or higher: | 24% | Out-of-state: | 70% |
| | | Live on campus: | 96% |

**Basis for selection.** Academic record, test scores, references/recommendations most important. Audition required, interview recommended for all; portfolio required for music programs.

**High school preparation.** College-preparatory program recommended.

**2010-2011 Annual costs.** Tuition/fees (projected): $17,285. Room/board: $6,450. Books/supplies: $600. Personal expenses: $1,770.

**2008-2009 Financial aid. Need-based:** 55% of total undergraduate aid awarded as scholarships/grants, 45% as loans/jobs. **Non-need-based:** Scholarships awarded for academics, leadership, music/drama, religious affiliation.

**Application procedures. Admission:** Priority date 5/1; deadline 8/15 (postmark date). $30 fee. Admission notification on a rolling basis. Must reply by May 1 or within 4 week(s) if notified thereafter. **Financial aid:** Closing date 5/1. FAFSA, institutional form required. Applicants notified on a rolling basis starting 4/1.

**Academics. Special study options:** Combined bachelor's/graduate degree, distance learning, double major, dual enrollment of high school students, independent study, internships, study abroad, teacher certification program. **Credit/placement by examination:** AP, CLEP, IB, SAT, ACT, institutional tests. **Support services:** Reduced course load, remedial instruction, study skills assistance, tutoring, writing center.

**Majors. Business:** Administrative services. **Communications:** General. **Education:** Early childhood, elementary, health, mathematics, multi-level teacher, music, physical, science, secondary, social studies. **Parks/recreation:** Health/fitness. **Theology:** Missionary, preministerial, sacred music, youth ministry.

**Most popular majors.** Education 18%, liberal arts 19%, philosophy/religious studies 18%, psychology 11%, trade and industry 18%, visual/performing arts 7%.

**Computing on campus.** 30 workstations in library, computer center. Dormitories wired for high-speed internet access and linked to campus network. Online course registration, online library, helpline, wireless network available.

**Student life. Freshman orientation:** Mandatory. Preregistration for classes offered. Parent and student orientation weekend includes sessions on academics, student life, finances, and interaction with faculty. **Policies:** Religious observance required. **Housing:** Guaranteed on-campus for all undergraduates. Single-sex dorms, special housing for disabled, wellness housing

available. $250 deposit, deadline 5/1. **Activities:** Choral groups, drama, music ensembles, student government, student newspaper, several religious and service groups.

**Athletics.** NCAA, NCCAA. **Intercollegiate:** Baseball M, basketball, cheerleading W, cross-country, golf M, soccer, softball W, tennis W, track and field, volleyball, wrestling M. **Intramural:** Basketball, soccer, softball M, volleyball. **Team name:** Defenders.

**Student services.** Adult student services, alcohol/substance abuse counseling, chaplain/spiritual director, career counseling, student employment services, financial aid counseling, health services, personal counseling, placement for graduates, women's services.

**Contact.** E-mail: admissions@bbc.edu
Phone: (570) 586-2400 ext. 9271 Toll-free number: (800) 451-7664
Fax: (570) 585-9299
Ken Shepard, Vice President for Enrollment and Marketing Services,
Baptist Bible College of Pennsylvania, 538 Venard Road, Clarks Summit,
PA 18411-1297

---

## Bloomsburg University of Pennsylvania
**Bloomsburg, Pennsylvania**                          **CB member**
**www.bloomu.edu**                                    **CB code: 2646**

- Public 4-year university and liberal arts college
- Residential campus in large town
- 8,377 degree-seeking undergraduates: 4% part-time, 58% women, 7% African American, 1% Asian American, 3% Hispanic American, 1% international
- 881 degree-seeking graduate students
- 64% of applicants admitted
- SAT or ACT (ACT writing optional) required
- 64% graduate within 6 years; 21% enter graduate study

**General.** Founded in 1839. Regionally accredited. **Degrees:** 1,565 bachelor's awarded; master's, professional offered. **ROTC:** Army, Air Force. **Location:** 40 miles from Wilkes-Barre, 80 miles from Harrisburg. **Calendar:** Semester, extensive summer session. **Full-time faculty:** 400 total; 84% have terminal degrees, 13% minority, 41% women. **Part-time faculty:** 91 total; 14% have terminal degrees, 1% minority, 66% women. **Class size:** 21% < 20, 65% 20-39, 7% 40-49, 3% 50-99, 4% >100.

**Freshman class profile.** 11,749 applied, 7,473 admitted, 2,040 enrolled.

| Mid 50% test scores | | | |
|---|---|---|---|
| SAT critical reading: | 450-540 | Rank in top tenth: | 12% |
| SAT math: | 460-560 | Return as sophomores: | 81% |
| SAT writing: | 440-540 | Out-of-state: | 13% |
| Rank in top quarter: | 36% | Live on campus: | 90% |

**Basis for selection.** School achievement record and class rank most important. School's recommendation considered in borderline cases. **Homeschooled:** Statement describing homeschool structure and mission, transcript of courses and grades, state high school equivalency certificate required.

**High school preparation.** College-preparatory program required. 16 units required; 19 recommended. Required and recommended units include English 4, mathematics 3-4, social studies 2, history 2, science 3-4, foreign language 2, computer science 1 and academic electives 2.

**2009-2010 Annual costs.** Tuition/fees: $7,110; $15,442 out-of-state. Room/board: $6,488. Books/supplies: $1,200. Personal expenses: $3,000.

**2009-2010 Financial aid. Need-based:** 1,882 full-time freshmen applied for aid; 1,788 were judged to have need; 1,667 of these received aid. Average need met was 74%. Average scholarship/grant was $6,609; average loan $3,395. 48% of total undergraduate aid awarded as scholarships/grants, 52% as loans/jobs. **Non-need-based:** Awarded to 1,573 full-time undergraduates, including 531 freshmen. Scholarships awarded for academics, art, athletics, job skills, leadership, minority status, music/drama, ROTC, state residency.

**Application procedures. Admission:** Priority date 12/1; no deadline. $30 fee, may be waived for applicants with need. Admission notification on a rolling basis beginning on or about 9/18. Must reply by May 1 or within 2 week(s) if notified thereafter. **Financial aid:** Priority date 3/15; no closing date. FAFSA required. Applicants notified on a rolling basis starting 4/1.

**Academics.** **Special study options:** Combined bachelor's/graduate degree, cooperative education, cross-registration, distance learning, double major, dual enrollment of high school students, ESL, exchange student, honors, independent study, internships, liberal arts/career combination, study abroad, teacher certification program. **Credit/placement by examination:** AP, CLEP, SAT, institutional tests. 64 credit hours maximum toward bachelor's degree. **Support services:** Learning center, pre-admission summer program, reduced course load, remedial instruction, study skills assistance, tutoring, writing center.

**Majors.** **Biology:** General. **Business:** General, accounting, business admin. **Communications:** General, media studies. **Computer sciences:** General, computer forensics, computer science. **Education:** Early childhood, middle, special. **Engineering:** Electrical. **Foreign languages:** French, German, sign language interpretation, Spanish. **Health:** Audiology/speech pathology, clinical lab science, medical radiologic technology/radiation therapy, nursing (RN), physics/radiologic health. **History:** General. **Math:** General. **Philosophy/religion:** Philosophy. **Physical sciences:** Chemistry, geology, physics. **Protective services:** Criminal justice. **Psychology:** General. **Public administration:** Social work. **Social sciences:** Anthropology, economics, geography, political science, sociology. **Visual/performing arts:** Art history/conservation, dramatic, studio arts. **Other:** Exercise science, Secondary education comprehensive social studies.

**Most popular majors.** Business/marketing 20%, education 16%, English 8%, health sciences 13%, social sciences 11%.

**Computing on campus.** 1,440 workstations in dormitories, library, computer center, student center. Dormitories wired for high-speed internet access and linked to campus network. Commuter students can connect to campus network. Online course registration, online library, helpline, wireless network available.

**Student life.** **Freshman orientation:** Mandatory, $77 fee. Preregistration for classes offered. One-day program in July and 3-day program prior to start of classes. **Housing:** Guaranteed on-campus for freshmen. Coed dorms, apartments, cooperative housing, wellness housing available. $100 partly refundable deposit, deadline 5/1. **Activities:** Bands, campus ministries, choral groups, dance, drama, international student organizations, literary magazine, music ensembles, Model UN, radio station, student government, student newspaper, symphony orchestra, TV station, Bloomsburg Christian Fellowship, Hillel, University Democrats, College Republicans, community government association, Black Cultural Society, Student Organization of Latinos, Habitat for Humanity.

**Athletics.** NCAA. **Intercollegiate:** Baseball M, basketball, cross-country, field hockey W, football (tackle) M, lacrosse W, soccer, softball W, swimming, tennis, track and field, wrestling M. **Intramural:** Basketball, field hockey W, football (non-tackle) M, racquetball, soccer, softball, tennis, volleyball, wrestling M. **Team name:** Huskies.

**Student services.** Adult student services, alcohol/substance abuse counseling, chaplain/spiritual director, career counseling, services for economically disadvantaged, student employment services, financial aid counseling, health services, legal services, minority student services, on-campus daycare, personal counseling, placement for graduates, veterans' counselor, women's services. **Physically disabled:** Services for visually, speech, hearing impaired.

**Contact.** E-mail: buadmiss@bloomu.edu
Phone: (570) 389-4316 Fax: (570) 389-4741
Christopher Keller, Director of Admissions and Records, Bloomsburg University of Pennsylvania, 104 Student Service Center, Bloomsburg, PA 17815

---

## Bryn Athyn College of the New Church
**Bryn Athyn, Pennsylvania**  **CB member**
www.brynathyn.edu  **CB code: 2002**

- Private 4-year liberal arts college affiliated with General Church of the New Jerusalem (Swedenborgian)
- Residential campus in small town
- 184 degree-seeking undergraduates: 4% part-time, 50% women, 7% African American, 2% Asian American, 21% international
- 23 degree-seeking graduate students
- 92% of applicants admitted
- SAT or ACT with writing, application essay required
- 31% graduate within 6 years

**General.** Founded in 1876. Regionally accredited. **Degrees:** 16 bachelor's, 13 associate awarded; master's offered. **ROTC:** Army, Air Force. **Location:** 15 miles from Philadelphia. **Calendar:** Trimester. **Full-time faculty:** 26 total; 62% have terminal degrees, 4% minority, 46% women. **Part-time**

**faculty:** 25 total; 20% have terminal degrees, 40% women. **Class size:** 89% < 20, 11% 20-39. **Special facilities:** Performing arts center, archives, ecological restoration trust.

**Freshman class profile.** 227 applied, 208 admitted, 70 enrolled.

| Mid 50% test scores | | | |
|---|---|---|---|
| SAT critical reading: | 490-630 | GPA 3.0-3.49: | 37% |
| SAT math: | 470-600 | GPA 2.0-2.99: | 15% |
| SAT writing: | 470-610 | Return as sophomores: | 74% |
| ACT composite: | 20-23 | Out-of-state: | 35% |
| GPA 3.75 or higher: | 23% | Live on campus: | 81% |
| GPA 3.50-3.74: | 25% | International: | 16% |

**Basis for selection.** Applicants expected to have interest in the New Church. School achievement record important; test scores considered. TOEFL required of non-native English speakers. SAT may be required of some Canadian applicants. Interview recommended; may be required. **Home-schooled:** SAT Subject Tests in literature and math recommended.

**High school preparation.** College-preparatory program recommended. 15 units recommended. Recommended units include English 4, mathematics 3, history 3, science 3 and foreign language 2. 3 units social studies and/or history required.

**2009-2010 Annual costs.** Tuition/fees: $11,991. Room/board: $6,300. Books/supplies: $950. Personal expenses: $700.

**2009-2010 Financial aid.** **Need-based:** Average need met was 94%. Average scholarship/grant was $10,645; average loan $1,974. 90% of total undergraduate aid awarded as scholarships/grants, 10% as loans/jobs. **Non-need-based:** Scholarships awarded for academics, leadership, religious affiliation.

**Application procedures.** **Admission:** Priority date 2/1; deadline 7/1 (receipt date). No application fee. Admission notification on a rolling basis beginning on or about 2/1. Must reply by 8/1. **Financial aid:** Closing date 6/1. FAFSA, institutional form required. Applicants notified on a rolling basis starting 4/30; must reply by 9/30.

**Academics.** **Special study options:** Accelerated study, cooperative education, cross-registration, distance learning, ESL, independent study, internships, student-designed major, study abroad, teacher certification program. Students can combine multiple curricular areas to design an educational program tailored to meet their particular interests, abilities, and needs. The areas which can be combined are the following: biological sciences, business, classical languages, computer science, education, English, history, mathematics, philosophy, physical sciences, psychology, religion, and social sciences. **Credit/placement by examination:** AP, CLEP, IB, institutional tests. **Support services:** Remedial instruction, study skills assistance, tutoring, writing center.

**Majors.** **Biology:** General. **Business:** General. **Computer sciences:** General. **Education:** General, biology, English, history. **History:** General. **Math:** General. **Philosophy/religion:** Religion. **Theology:** Theology.

**Most popular majors.** Education 7%, English 6%, history 20%, interdisciplinary studies 60%, theological studies 7%.

**Computing on campus.** 55 workstations in dormitories, library, computer center, student center. Dormitories wired for high-speed internet access and linked to campus network. Commuter students can connect to campus network. Online library, helpline, repair service, wireless network available.

**Student life.** **Freshman orientation:** Mandatory. **Policies:** No alcohol on campus, restricted dorm visiting, required chapel attendance. Religious observance required. **Housing:** Guaranteed on-campus for all undergraduates. Single-sex dorms available. $150 deposit, deadline 7/15. Satellite housing available. **Activities:** Choral groups, dance, drama, international student organizations, musical theater, student government, student newspaper, CARE.

**Athletics.** **Intercollegiate:** Badminton, ice hockey M, lacrosse, soccer, volleyball W. **Team name:** Blaze.

**Student services.** Chaplain/spiritual director, career counseling, student employment services, financial aid counseling, health services, personal counseling.

**Contact.** E-mail: admissions@brynathyn.edu
Phone: (267) 502-2511 Fax: (267) 502-2593
Stefanie Niles, Vice President for Enrollment Management, Bryn Athyn College of the New Church, PO Box 462, Bryn Athyn, PA 19009-0462

## Bryn Mawr College
**Bryn Mawr, Pennsylvania**
www.brynmawr.edu

**CB member**
**CB code: 2049**

◆ Private 4-year liberal arts college for women
◆ Residential campus in very large city
◆ 1,289 degree-seeking undergraduates: 1% part-time, 100% women, 6% African American, 12% Asian American, 5% Hispanic American, 10% international
◆ 435 degree-seeking graduate students
◆ 49% of applicants admitted
◆ SAT and SAT Subject Tests or ACT (ACT writing optional), application essay required
◆ 80% graduate within 6 years

**General.** Founded in 1885. Regionally accredited. Academic exchange with Haverford College, Swarthmore College, and University of Pennsylvania. Extracurricular and social coordination with Haverford. **Degrees:** 331 bachelor's awarded; master's, doctoral offered. **ROTC:** Air Force. **Location:** 11 miles from Philadelphia. **Calendar:** Semester, limited summer session. **Full-time faculty:** 158 total; 97% have terminal degrees, 16% minority, 50% women. **Part-time faculty:** 53 total; 60% have terminal degrees, 9% minority, 79% women. **Class size:** 72% < 20, 21% 20-39, 2% 40-49, 4% 50-99. **Special facilities:** Collections of minerals, archaeological and anthropological artifacts.

**Freshman class profile.** 2,276 applied, 1,107 admitted, 362 enrolled.

| Mid 50% test scores | | | |
|---|---|---|---|
| SAT critical reading: | 600-700 | Rank in top tenth: | 61% |
| SAT math: | 580-680 | Return as sophomores: | 93% |
| SAT writing: | 610-700 | Out-of-state: | 89% |
| ACT composite: | 26-30 | Live on campus: | 100% |
| Rank in top quarter: | 87% | International: | 17% |

**Basis for selection.** School achievement record, recommendations, essay most important. Test scores, school and community activities, extracurricular achievements important. For those submitting SAT, 2 SAT Subject Tests required. Interview recommended. **Homeschooled:** Statement describing homeschool structure and mission, transcript of courses and grades, state high school equivalency certificate, interview, letter of recommendation (nonparent) required. Interview required, but may be completed with admissions officer or alumna.

**High school preparation.** 16 units recommended. Required and recommended units include English 4, mathematics 3, social studies 2, history 2, science 2 (laboratory 1), foreign language 3 and academic electives 2.

**2010-2011 Annual costs.** Tuition/fees: $39,360. Room/board: $12,420.

**2009-2010 Financial aid.** All financial aid based on need. 278 full-time freshmen applied for aid; 249 were judged to have need; 249 of these received aid. Average need met was 100%. Average scholarship/grant was $33,108; average loan $3,330. 84% of total undergraduate aid awarded as scholarships/grants, 16% as loans/jobs.

**Application procedures. Admission:** Closing date 1/15 (postmark date). $50 fee, may be waived for applicants with need. Admission notification 4/1. Must reply by 5/1. **Financial aid:** Priority date 2/5, closing date 3/1. FAFSA, CSS PROFILE required. Applicants notified by 3/23; must reply by 5/1.

**Academics.** Most examinations self-scheduled. **Special study options:** Accelerated study, combined bachelor's/graduate degree, cross-registration, double major, dual enrollment of high school students, exchange student, independent study, internships, liberal arts/career combination, student-designed major, study abroad, teacher certification program. 3-2 Program in City and Regional Planning with the University of Pennsylvania. A.B./B.S. 3-2 engineering programs with University of Pennsylvania. **Credit/placement by examination:** AP, CLEP, IB, institutional tests. 32 credit hours maximum toward bachelor's degree. **Support services:** Preadmission summer program, reduced course load, study skills assistance, tutoring, writing center.

**Majors. Architecture:** Urban/community planning. **Area/ethnic studies:** East Asian. **Biology:** General. **Computer sciences:** Computer science. **Foreign languages:** Ancient Greek, classics, comparative lit, French, German, Italian, Latin, Russian, Spanish. **History:** General. **Interdisciplinary:** Classical/archaeology. **Math:** General. **Philosophy/religion:** Philosophy, religion. **Physical sciences:** Astronomy, chemistry, geology, physics. **Psychology:** General. **Social sciences:** Anthropology, archaeology, economics, political science, sociology, urban studies. **Visual/performing arts:** Art history/conservation, studio arts.

**Most popular majors.** Biology 8%, English 11%, foreign language 10%, history 6%, physical sciences 6%, psychology 10%, social sciences 29%, visual/performing arts 6%.

**Computing on campus.** 200 workstations in dormitories, library, computer center, student center. Dormitories linked to campus network. Commuter students can connect to campus network. Online course registration, online library, helpline, repair service, student web hosting, wireless network available.

**Student life. Freshman orientation:** Mandatory. Week-long program; students divided into groups of 10-20 students based on residence hall assignments. **Policies:** Self-governing student body, academic and social honor code, Customs and Traditions programs. **Housing:** Guaranteed on-campus for all undergraduates. Coed dorms, apartments, cooperative housing, wellness housing available. $200 fully refundable deposit, deadline 6/1. Students may live at Haverford. Foreign language houses available (Chinese, French, German, Hebrew, Italian, Russian, Spanish). Special housing available for non-traditional-aged students. **Activities:** Jazz band, campus ministries, choral groups, dance, drama, film society, international student organizations, literary magazine, music ensembles, Model UN, musical theater, radio station, student government, student newspaper, Mujeres, Rainbow Alliance, investment group, Jewish student union.

**Athletics.** NCAA. **Intercollegiate:** Badminton W, basketball W, cross-country W, field hockey W, lacrosse W, rowing (crew) W, soccer W, swimming W, tennis W, track and field W, volleyball W. **Intramural:** Tennis W, volleyball W. **Team name:** Owls.

**Student services.** Adult student services, alcohol/substance abuse counseling, chaplain/spiritual director, career counseling, services for economically disadvantaged, student employment services, financial aid counseling, health services, minority student services, personal counseling, placement for graduates, women's services. **Physically disabled:** Services for visually, speech, hearing impaired.

**Contact.** E-mail: admissions@brynmawr.edu
Phone: (610) 526-5152 Toll-free number: (800) 262-1885
Fax: (610) 526-7471
Jennifer Rickard, Dean of Admissions and Financial Aid, Bryn Mawr College, 101 North Merion Avenue, Bryn Mawr, PA 19010-2899

## Bucknell University
**Lewisburg, Pennsylvania**
www.bucknell.edu

**CB member**
**CB code: 2050**

◆ Private 4-year university
◆ Residential campus in small town
◆ 3,523 degree-seeking undergraduates: 51% women, 3% African American, 4% Asian American, 3% Hispanic American, 3% international
◆ 89 degree-seeking graduate students
◆ 30% of applicants admitted
◆ SAT or ACT with writing, application essay required
◆ 90% graduate within 6 years; 22% enter graduate study

**General.** Founded in 1846. Regionally accredited. **Degrees:** 865 bachelor's awarded; master's offered. **ROTC:** Army. **Location:** 75 miles from Harrisburg, 195 miles from Philadelphia. **Calendar:** Semester, limited summer session. **Full-time faculty:** 345 total; 97% have terminal degrees, 13% minority, 39% women. **Part-time faculty:** 22 total; 18% have terminal degrees, 36% women. **Class size:** 56% < 20, 40% 20-39, 2% 40-49, 1% 50-99, less than 1% >100. **Special facilities:** Observatory, 63-acre nature preserve, center for performing arts, poetry center, greenhouse, outdoor naturalistic primate facility, engineering structural test lab, gas chromatograph/mass spectrometer, nuclear magnetic resonance spectrometer, herbarium, 18-hole golf course, small business development center, environmental center, center for public policy, high ropes course.

**Freshman class profile.** 7,572 applied, 2,263 admitted, 920 enrolled.

| Mid 50% test scores | | | |
|---|---|---|---|
| SAT critical reading: | 600-680 | Rank in top tenth: | 59% |
| SAT math: | 630-720 | End year in good standing: | 97% |
| SAT writing: | 600-690 | Return as sophomores: | 94% |
| ACT composite: | 27-31 | Out-of-state: | 77% |
| Rank in top quarter: | 88% | Live on campus: | 99% |
| | | International: | 3% |

**Basis for selection.** Emphasis on school achievement. Test scores, recommendations, special talents and abilities, evidence of volunteer work, personal qualities important. If English is not student's first language and student submits SAT scores with Critical Reading score below 550, TOEFL required. Audition required for music program; portfolio recommended for art program. **Homeschooled:** Statement describing homeschool structure and mission, interview required. Interview, SAT, graded English paper, writing sample (not from English class), program description or certification from homeschooler's accrediting agency or school district, name/address/phone number of homeschool supervisor required.

**High school preparation.** College-preparatory program required. 16 units required; 20 recommended. Required and recommended units include English 4, mathematics 3-4, social studies 2, history 2, science 2-3, foreign language 2-4 and academic electives 1.

**2010-2011 Annual costs.** Tuition/fees: $42,342. Room/board: $9,938. Books/supplies: $880. Personal expenses: $1,000.

**2009-2010 Financial aid. Need-based:** 527 full-time freshmen applied for aid; 434 were judged to have need; 434 of these received aid. Average need met was 95%. Average scholarship/grant was $22,500; average loan $4,400. 76% of total undergraduate aid awarded as scholarships/grants, 24% as loans/jobs. **Non-need-based:** Awarded to 355 full-time undergraduates, including 126 freshmen. Scholarships awarded for academics, art, athletics, leadership, music/drama, ROTC.

**Application procedures. Admission:** Closing date 1/15 (postmark date). $60 fee, may be waived for applicants with need. Admission notification 4/1. Must reply by 5/1. **Financial aid:** Closing date 1/1. FAFSA, CSS PROFILE required. Applicants notified by 4/1; must reply by 5/1.

**Academics. Special study options:** Combined bachelor's/graduate degree, double major, dual enrollment of high school students, honors, independent study, internships, liberal arts/career combination, student-designed major, study abroad, teacher certification program, Washington semester. **Credit/placement by examination:** AP, CLEP, IB, institutional tests. No policy limit on number of credits; only a few courses offer this option. **Support services:** Learning center, study skills assistance, tutoring, writing center.

**Majors. Area/ethnic studies:** East Asian, Latin American, women's. **Biology:** General, animal behavior, biochemistry, cellular/molecular. **Business:** Accounting, business admin. **Computer sciences:** General. **Conservation:** Environmental studies. **Education:** General, early childhood, elementary, music, secondary. **Engineering:** Biomedical, chemical, civil, computer, electrical, mechanical. **Foreign languages:** Classics, French, German, Russian, Spanish. **History:** General. **Interdisciplinary:** Neuroscience. **Liberal arts:** Humanities. **Math:** General. **Philosophy/religion:** Philosophy, religion. **Physical sciences:** Chemistry, geology, physics. **Psychology:** General. **Social sciences:** Anthropology, econometrics, economics, geography, international relations, political science, sociology. **Visual/performing arts:** General, art history/conservation, dramatic, music history, music performance, music theory/composition, studio arts. **Other:** Economics and mathematics studies.

**Most popular majors.** Biology 9%, business/marketing 14%, engineering/engineering technologies 16%, English 6%, psychology 7%, social sciences 25%.

**Computing on campus.** 970 workstations in dormitories, library, computer center, student center. Dormitories wired for high-speed internet access and linked to campus network. Commuter students can connect to campus network. Online course registration, online library, helpline, repair service, wireless network available.

**Student life. Freshman orientation:** Mandatory, $100 fee. Preregistration for classes offered. Held 5 days prior to start of classes. **Policies:** All first-year students must sign statement of student responsibility. **Housing:** Guaranteed on-campus for all undergraduates. Coed dorms, single-sex dorms, special housing for disabled, apartments, cooperative housing, fraternity/sorority housing, wellness housing available. Seven residential colleges with themes: arts, humanities, global, environment, social justice, technology and society; language and culture; quiet floors available. **Activities:** Bands, campus ministries, choral groups, dance, drama, film society, international student organizations, literary magazine, music ensembles, Model UN, musical theater, opera, radio station, student government, student newspaper, symphony orchestra, Hillel, Chinese Culture Association, Brothers and Sisters Empowered, Japan Society, Muslim student association, O.H.L.A.S. (formerly Le Cumbre Hispanic), College Democrats, College Republicans, Habitat for Humanity.

**Athletics.** NCAA. **Intercollegiate:** Baseball M, basketball, cross-country, diving, field hockey W, football (tackle) M, golf, lacrosse, rowing (crew) W, soccer, softball W, swimming, tennis, track and field, volleyball W, water polo, wrestling M. **Intramural:** Badminton, basketball, bowling, cross-country, football (non-tackle), golf, racquetball, soccer, softball, squash, table tennis, tennis, volleyball, weight lifting M. **Team name:** Bison.

**Student services.** Alcohol/substance abuse counseling, chaplain/spiritual director, career counseling, financial aid counseling, health services, minority student services, personal counseling, placement for graduates, women's services. **Physically disabled:** Services for visually, hearing impaired.

**Contact.** E-mail: admissions@bucknell.edu
Phone: (570) 577-1101 Fax: (570) 577-3538
Robert Springall, Dean of Admissions, Bucknell University, Freas Hall, Lewisburg, PA 17837-9988

## Cabrini College
**Radnor, Pennsylvania**
www.cabrini.edu

**CB member**
**CB code: 2071**

- Private 4-year liberal arts college affiliated with Roman Catholic Church
- Residential campus in large town
- 1,538 degree-seeking undergraduates: 6% part-time, 64% women, 6% African American, 1% Asian American, 1% Hispanic American
- 1,729 degree-seeking graduate students
- 75% of applicants admitted
- SAT or ACT (ACT writing optional) required
- 52% graduate within 6 years

**General.** Founded in 1957. Regionally accredited. College sponsored by Missionary Sisters of the Sacred Heart (international religious order serving six continents). **Degrees:** 385 bachelor's awarded; master's offered. **ROTC:** Army, Air Force. **Location:** 18 miles from Philadelphia, 5 miles from King of Prussia. **Calendar:** Semester, limited summer session. **Full-time faculty:** 70 total; 83% have terminal degrees, 9% minority, 57% women. **Part-time faculty:** 254 total; 22% have terminal degrees, 9% minority, 59% women. **Class size:** 59% < 20, 41% 20-39, less than 1% 40-49. **Special facilities:** College-operated preschool (off-campus), human performance lab, video studio, graphic design lab.

**Freshman class profile.** 2,666 applied, 1,988 admitted, 359 enrolled.

| Mid 50% test scores | | Rank in top quarter: | 20% |
|---|---|---|---|
| SAT critical reading: | 430-520 | Rank in top tenth: | 4% |
| SAT math: | 430-510 | End year in good standing: | 88% |
| GPA 3.75 or higher: | 14% | Return as sophomores: | 66% |
| GPA 3.50-3.74: | 14% | Out-of-state: | 49% |
| GPA 3.0-3.49: | 30% | Live on campus: | 84% |
| GPA 2.0-2.99: | 42% | | |

**Basis for selection.** School achievement record, test scores, academic potential, and personal qualities most important. Special consideration for children of alumni and students with special backgrounds, skills or abilities. Community action required. Non-English-speaking international students may take TOEFL instead of SAT/ACT. Interview recommended for all. **Homeschooled:** Transcript of courses and grades, state high school equivalency certificate required. Provide as much external testing data as possible. Standardized test scores given more weight for homeschooled students.

**High school preparation.** College-preparatory program required. 17 units required; 21 recommended. Required and recommended units include English 4, mathematics 3-4, social studies 3, science 3, foreign language 2 and academic electives 2. Two arts and humanities also recommended. Additional math and science units recommended for science students.

**2009-2010 Annual costs.** Tuition/fees: $31,030. Room/board: $11,400. Books/supplies: $1,050. Personal expenses: $360.

**2009-2010 Financial aid. Need-based:** 315 full-time freshmen applied for aid; 280 were judged to have need; 280 of these received aid. Average need met was 71%. Average scholarship/grant was $9,890; average loan $3,696. 70% of total undergraduate aid awarded as scholarships/grants, 30% as loans/jobs. **Non-need-based:** Scholarships awarded for academics.

**Application procedures. Admission:** Priority date 5/1; no deadline. $35 fee, may be waived for applicants with need. Admission notification on a rolling basis. **Financial aid:** Closing date 4/1. FAFSA required. Applicants notified on a rolling basis starting 2/15.

**Academics.** Education fieldwork opportunities provided to education majors from sophomore to senior years. Students participate in community service. Internship or co-op programs offered in all majors. **Special study options:** Combined bachelor's/graduate degree, cooperative education, cross-registration, double major, honors, independent study, internships, liberal arts/career combination, student-designed major, study abroad, teacher certification program, Washington semester. Exchange programs with Eastern University, Rosemont College, Valley Forge Military College; cross-registration with Southeastern Pennsylvania Consortium for Higher Education (8-member consortium of private colleges/universities). **Credit/placement by examination:** AP, CLEP, IB, SAT, institutional tests. 30 credit hours maximum toward bachelor's degree. DANTES. **Support services:** Learning center, reduced course load, remedial instruction, study skills assistance, tutoring, writing center.

**Majors. Area/ethnic studies:** American. **Biology:** General. **Business:** Accounting, business admin, finance, human resources, management information systems, marketing. **Communications:** General. **Computer sciences:** General, information technology. **Education:** General, elementary, kindergarten/preschool, special. **Foreign languages:** French, Italian, Spanish. **Health:** Premedicine. **History:** General. **Liberal arts:** Arts/sciences. **Math:** General. **Parks/recreation:** Exercise sciences. **Philosophy/religion:** Philosophy, religion. **Physical sciences:** Chemistry. **Psychology:** General. **Public administration:** Social work. **Social sciences:** Criminology, political science, sociology. **Visual/performing arts:** Graphic design.

**Most popular majors.** Biology 6%, business/marketing 24%, communications/journalism 14%, education 18%, parks/recreation 6%.

**Computing on campus.** 426 workstations in dormitories, library, computer center. Dormitories wired for high-speed internet access and linked to campus network. Commuter students can connect to campus network. Online course registration, online library, helpline, student web hosting, wireless network available.

**Student life. Freshman orientation:** Mandatory, $210 fee. Preregistration for classes offered. 3-day program prior to the beginning of the fall semester. **Housing:** Coed dorms, single-sex dorms, special housing for disabled, apartments available. $350 fully refundable deposit, deadline 5/1. Special interest housing options designated for intensified study, honors, Hispanic culture and community service. **Activities:** Campus ministries, choral groups, dance, drama, film society, international student organizations, literary magazine, music ensembles, musical theater, radio station, student government, student newspaper, TV station, Black Student Union, Habitat for Humanity, Cavaliers for Life, La Raza, Up 'til Dawn, Search Club, Student Democratic Association.

**Athletics.** NCAA. **Intercollegiate:** Basketball, cross-country, field hockey W, golf M, lacrosse, soccer, softball W, swimming, tennis, track and field, volleyball W. **Intramural:** Basketball, cricket, football (non-tackle), soccer, squash, volleyball. **Team name:** Cavaliers.

**Student services.** Adult student services, alcohol/substance abuse counseling, chaplain/spiritual director, career counseling, student employment services, financial aid counseling, health services, minority student services, personal counseling, placement for graduates. **Physically disabled:** Services for visually, hearing impaired.

**Contact.** E-mail: admit@cabrini.edu
Phone: (610) 902-8552 Toll-free number: (800) 848-1003
Fax: (610) 902-8508
Stephen Colfer, Senior Associate Director of Admissions, Cabrini College, 610 King of Prussia Road, Radnor, PA 19087-3698

## California University of Pennsylvania
**California, Pennsylvania**  **CB member**
**www.cup.edu**  **CB code: 2647**

▸ Public 4-year university
▸ Commuter campus in small town
▸ 7,151 degree-seeking undergraduates
▸ 63% of applicants admitted
▸ SAT required

**General.** Founded in 1852. Regionally accredited. Green-oriented; utilizes geothermal technologies to reduce energy consumption. **Degrees:** 1,296 bachelor's, 47 associate awarded; master's offered. **ROTC:** Army, Air Force. **Location:** 38 miles from Pittsburgh. **Calendar:** Semester, limited summer session. **Full-time faculty:** 308 total. **Part-time faculty:** 99 total. **Class size:** 28% < 20, 50% 20-39, 11% 40-49, 10% 50-99, less than 1% >100. **Special facilities:** International corporate art collection, 98-acre farm with recreational facilities.

**Freshman class profile.** 4,706 applied, 2,965 admitted, 2,165 enrolled.

| Mid 50% test scores | | | |
|---|---|---|---|
| SAT critical reading: | 460-530 | GPA 3.0-3.49: | 36% |
| SAT math: | 470-540 | GPA 2.0-2.99: | 39% |
| SAT writing: | 450-540 | Rank in top quarter: | 28% |
| ACT composite: | 19-21 | Rank in top tenth: | 7% |
| GPA 3.75 or higher: | 11% | Out-of-state: | 7% |
| GPA 3.50-3.74: | 13% | Live on campus: | 75% |

**Basis for selection.** School achievement record, test scores, activities, recommendations, interview considered. Essay recommended. **Home-schooled:** Transcript of courses and grades required.

**High school preparation.** 19 units required; 21 recommended. Required and recommended units include English 4, mathematics 3, social studies 2, history 2, science 1 (laboratory 1), foreign language 2 and academic electives 6.

**2009-2010 Annual costs.** Tuition/fees: $7,676; $11,010 out-of-state. Room/board: $9,320. Books/supplies: $900. Personal expenses: $1,628.

**2009-2010 Financial aid. Non-need-based:** Scholarships awarded for academics, alumni affiliation, art, athletics, leadership, minority status, music/drama, religious affiliation, ROTC, state residency.

**Application procedures. Admission:** Priority date 5/1; no deadline. $25 fee, may be waived for applicants with need. Admission notification on a rolling basis. **Financial aid:** Priority date 5/1; no closing date. FAFSA required. Applicants notified on a rolling basis starting 4/1; must reply within 3 week(s) of notification.

**Academics. Special study options:** Accelerated study, combined bachelor's/graduate degree, cooperative education, cross-registration, distance learning, double major, dual enrollment of high school students, exchange student, external degree, honors, independent study, internships, liberal arts/career combination, student-designed major, study abroad, teacher certification program, urban semester, Washington semester, weekend college. **Credit/placement by examination:** AP, CLEP, IB, SAT, institutional tests. **Support services:** Learning center, pre-admission summer program, reduced course load, remedial instruction, study skills assistance, tutoring, writing center.

**Honors college/program.** Minimum 1100 SAT (exclusive of Writing), 3.0 GPA, letter of recommendation required. Admitted students work with adviser and dean to design course of study.

**Majors. Biology:** General. **Business:** Accounting, business admin. **Communications:** General. **Computer sciences:** General. **Conservation:** Environmental science. **Education:** General, elementary, kindergarten/preschool, special. **Engineering technology:** General, computer, electrical. **Foreign languages:** General, French, German, Russian, Spanish. **Health:** Athletic training, clinical lab technology, communication disorders, nursing (RN). **History:** General. **Interdisciplinary:** Gerontology. **Liberal arts:** Arts/sciences. **Math:** General. **Parks/recreation:** Facilities management, sports admin. **Philosophy/religion:** Philosophy. **Physical sciences:** General, chemistry, geology, physics. **Protective services:** Criminal justice. **Psychology:** General. **Public administration:** Social work. **Social sciences:** General, geography, political science. **Visual/performing arts:** Art, commercial/advertising art, dramatic, graphic design.

**Most popular majors.** Business/marketing 12%, education 21%, engineering/engineering technologies 8%, health sciences 8%, parks/recreation 6%, psychology 6%, security/protective services 8%.

**Computing on campus.** 1,220 workstations in dormitories, library, computer center, student center. Dormitories wired for high-speed internet access and linked to campus network. Commuter students can connect to campus network. Online course registration, online library, helpline available.

**Student life. Freshman orientation:** Mandatory. Preregistration for classes offered. One-day session held in July or August. **Policies:** Freshman students under 21 and not commuting from parental home required to live in dormitory. **Housing:** Coed dorms, special housing for disabled, fraternity/sorority housing, wellness housing available. $235 deposit. **Activities:** Bands, campus ministries, choral groups, dance, drama, film society, international student organizations, literary magazine, music ensembles, musical theater, opera, radio station, student government, student newspaper, symphony orchestra, TV station.

**Athletics.** NCAA. **Intercollegiate:** Baseball M, basketball, cheerleading, cross-country, football (tackle) M, golf, rugby, soccer, softball, swimming W, tennis W, track and field, volleyball. **Intramural:** Archery, badminton, baseball M, basketball, bowling, cheerleading, cross-country, fencing, football (non-tackle), football (tackle), golf, gymnastics, handball, ice hockey, judo, lacrosse, racquetball, rugby, skiing, skin diving M, soccer, softball W, swimming W, table tennis, tennis W, track and field, triathlon, volleyball, weight lifting, wrestling M. **Team name:** Vulcans.

**Student services.** Adult student services, alcohol/substance abuse counseling, chaplain/spiritual director, career counseling, services for economically disadvantaged, student employment services, financial aid counseling, health services, legal services, minority student services, personal counseling, placement for graduates, veterans' counselor, women's services. **Physically disabled:** Services for visually, speech, hearing impaired. **Learning disabled:** Comprehensive services available.

**Contact.** E-mail: inquiry@cup.edu
Phone: (724) 938-4404 Fax: (724) 938-4564
William Edmonds, Dean of Admissions, California University of Pennsylvania, 250 University Avenue, California, PA 15419-1394

## Carlow University
**Pittsburgh, Pennsylvania** — CB member
www.carlow.edu — CB code: 2421

- Private 4-year university and liberal arts college affiliated with Roman Catholic Church
- Commuter campus in large city
- 1,520 degree-seeking undergraduates: 27% part-time, 93% women, 17% African American, 1% Asian American, 1% Hispanic American, 1% Native American
- 722 degree-seeking graduate students
- 65% of applicants admitted
- SAT or ACT (ACT writing optional) required
- 45% graduate within 6 years; 28% enter graduate study

**General.** Founded in 1929. Regionally accredited. Founded by the Sisters of Mercy in 1929 and member of the Conference for Mercy Higher Education. **Degrees:** 350 bachelor's awarded; master's, professional offered. **ROTC:** Army, Naval, Air Force. **Location:** 3 miles from downtown. **Calendar:** Semester, limited summer session. **Full-time faculty:** 97 total; 72% have terminal degrees, 7% minority, 76% women. **Part-time faculty:** 185 total; 24% have terminal degrees, 8% minority, 71% women. **Class size:** 88% < 20, 11% 20-39, 1% 40-49, less than 1% 50-99. **Special facilities:** Early learning center and school, science and technology research labs, cadaver lab, communications lab, greenhouse, darkroom, biochamber, children's science lab, International Poetry Forum archives, Women of Spirit Institute.

**Freshman class profile.** 1,124 applied, 735 admitted, 257 enrolled.

| Mid 50% test scores | | | |
|---|---|---|---|
| SAT critical reading: | 440-530 | GPA 3.0-3.49: | 39% |
| SAT math: | 430-510 | GPA 2.0-2.99: | 26% |
| SAT writing: | 420-530 | Rank in top quarter: | 36% |
| ACT composite: | 18-24 | Rank in top tenth: | 16% |
| GPA 3.75 or higher: | 20% | Return as sophomores: | 69% |
| GPA 3.50-3.74: | 15% | Out-of-state: | 5% |
| | | Live on campus: | 67% |

**Basis for selection.** Secondary school GPA, rank, record, and course work most important. SAT or ACT also considered. 2.5 GPA and class ranking in upper two-fifths of graduating class strengthen the application. International students must take TOEFL and ACT or SAT exams. Essay, interview recommended for all and in some cases required. Portfolio recommended for all art programs. **Homeschooled:** Transcript of courses and grades required. Personal interview and portfolio from most recent year highly recommended.

**High school preparation.** College-preparatory program recommended. 18 units required. Required and recommended units include English 4, mathematics 3-4, social studies 2, history 2, science 3-4 (laboratory 2) and academic electives 4. Applicants to professional nursing programs must have 4 units English, 3 units social sciences, 2 units math (1 must be algebra), and 2 units laboratory science, including chemistry.

**2009-2010 Annual costs.** Tuition/fees: $21,720. Undergraduate adult students pay $520 per credit hour. Room/board: $8,552. Books/supplies: $1,020. Personal expenses: $1,300.

**2008-2009 Financial aid. Need-based:** 46% of total undergraduate aid awarded as scholarships/grants, 54% as loans/jobs.

**Application procedures. Admission:** No deadline. $20 fee, may be waived for applicants with need, free for online applicants. Admission notification on a rolling basis. **Financial aid:** Priority date 4/1; no closing date. FAFSA required. Applicants notified on a rolling basis starting 2/15; must reply within 4 week(s) of notification.

**Academics. Special study options:** Accelerated study, combined bachelor's/graduate degree, cross-registration, distance learning, double major, dual enrollment of high school students, honors, independent study, internships, liberal arts/career combination, semester at sea, student-designed major, study abroad, teacher certification program, weekend college. 3+2 programs: biology/environmental engineering, chemistry/chemical engineering, math/engineering with Carnegie Mellon University; Biology/environmental science and management, 3+3 JD Law Program with Duquesne University. First Year Experience for freshmen, graduate certificates and minors in nursing, social sciences, education, and accounting. **Credit/placement by examination:** AP, CLEP, IB, institutional tests. 30 credit hours maximum toward bachelor's degree. **Support services:** Learning center, reduced course load, remedial instruction, study skills assistance, tutoring, writing center.

**Majors. Biology:** General, environmental. **Business:** Accounting, auditing, business admin, human resources. **Communications:** General, media studies. **Conservation:** Environmental science. **Education:** Art, early childhood, elementary, middle, special. **Foreign languages:** Spanish. **Health:** Art therapy, nursing (RN), perfusion technology. **History:** General. **Liberal arts:** Arts/sciences. **Math:** General. **Philosophy/religion:** Philosophy. **Physical sciences:** Chemistry. **Psychology:** General. **Public administration:** Policy analysis, social work. **Social sciences:** Political science, sociology. **Theology:** Theology. **Visual/performing arts:** Studio arts. **Other:** Behavioral health service coordinator, Corporate communications, Management in health services, Scientific/medical marketing.

**Most popular majors.** Biology 10%, business/marketing 14%, education 13%, health sciences 31%, psychology 7%.

**Computing on campus.** 160 workstations in library, computer center, student center. Dormitories wired for high-speed internet access and linked to campus network. Commuter students can connect to campus network. Online course registration, online library, helpline, repair service, wireless network available.

**Student life. Freshman orientation:** Mandatory. Preregistration for classes offered. Held 2 days prior to semester, includes seminars, team-building activities, social events. **Housing:** Single-sex dorms available. $100 deposit. **Activities:** Pep band, campus ministries, choral groups, dance, drama, literary magazine, musical theater, student government, student newspaper, community outreach, Alpha Phi Omega, eco club, social work association, united Black students, Alternative Spring Break, FEMME, PRIDE, Chi Eta Phi.

**Athletics.** NAIA. **Intercollegiate:** Basketball W, soccer W, softball W, tennis W, volleyball W. **Team name:** Celtics.

**Student services.** Adult student services, alcohol/substance abuse counseling, chaplain/spiritual director, career counseling, student employment services, financial aid counseling, health services, minority student services, on-campus daycare, personal counseling, placement for graduates, women's services. **Physically disabled:** Services for visually, speech, hearing impaired.

**Contact.** E-mail: admissions@carlow.edu
Phone: (412) 578-6059 Toll-free number: (800) 333-2275
Fax: (412) 578-6321
Susan Winstel, Director of Admissions, Carlow University, 3333 Fifth Avenue, Pittsburgh, PA 15213-3165

## Carnegie Mellon University
**Pittsburgh, Pennsylvania** — CB member
www.cmu.edu — CB code: 2074

- Private 4-year university
- Residential campus in large city
- 5,951 degree-seeking undergraduates: 1% part-time, 41% women, 5% African American, 24% Asian American, 5% Hispanic American, 1% Native American, 15% international
- 5,420 degree-seeking graduate students
- 36% of applicants admitted
- SAT or ACT with writing, SAT Subject Tests, application essay required
- 85% graduate within 6 years

**General.** Founded in 1900. Regionally accredited. **Degrees:** 1,349 bachelor's awarded; master's, doctoral offered. **ROTC:** Army, Naval, Air Force. **Location:** 5 miles from downtown. **Calendar:** Semester, limited summer session. **Full-time faculty:** 883 total; 98% have terminal degrees, 16% minority, 26% women. **Part-time faculty:** 80 total; 99% have terminal degrees, 19% minority, 44% women. **Class size:** 62% < 20, 23% 20-39, 4% 40-49, 8% 50-99, 3% >100. **Special facilities:** Botanical institute, rare books collection, recording studios, design studios, photo shoot studio, music halls.

**Freshman class profile.** 14,153 applied, 5,132 admitted, 1,423 enrolled.

| Mid 50% test scores | | | |
|---|---|---|---|
| SAT critical reading: | 620-720 | GPA 2.0-2.99: | 3% |
| SAT math: | 670-780 | Rank in top quarter: | 93% |
| SAT writing: | 620-720 | Rank in top tenth: | 75% |
| ACT composite: | 28-34 | Return as sophomores: | 95% |
| GPA 3.75 or higher: | 46% | Out-of-state: | 83% |
| GPA 3.50-3.74: | 29% | Live on campus: | 99% |
| GPA 3.0-3.49: | 22% | International: | 12% |

**Basis for selection.** Academic and artistic potential, standardized tests, activities, jobs, interests, and other personalized information important. Applicants to art, architecture, design, drama, and music programs should submit Common Application and Carnegie Mellon Supplement by regular decision fine arts deadline of December 1. SAT subject tests are not required for drama, design, art, or music applicants. All other students/applicants must take appropriate tests, preferably by December, but no later than January. All other applicants must take appropriate tests, preferably by December, but no later than January. College of Fine Arts deadline for application December 1. CMU uses AP, SAT/ACT, SAT/ACT subject tests and institutional exams for placement. Interview recommended for all; audition required for drama, music programs; portfolio required for art, design programs. **Homeschooled:** Transcript of courses and grades, letter of recommendation (nonparent) required. Submit syllabus/course descriptions of work done; transcript of grades/evaluations; recommendation from counselor, representative of state board of education, homeschool association, or other person of authority.

**High school preparation.** College-preparatory program required. Required and recommended units include English 4, mathematics 4, science 3 (laboratory 3), foreign language 2 and academic electives 3-4. Requirements vary by program.

**2009-2010 Annual costs.** Tuition/fees: $40,920. Room/board: $10,340. Books/supplies: $1,000. Personal expenses: $1,400.

**2009-2010 Financial aid. Need-based:** 1,014 full-time freshmen applied for aid; 792 were judged to have need; 783 of these received aid. Average need met was 82%. Average scholarship/grant was $24,707; average loan $3,657. 73% of total undergraduate aid awarded as scholarships/grants, 27% as loans/jobs. **Non-need-based:** Awarded to 1,479 full-time undergraduates, including 416 freshmen. Scholarships awarded for academics, art, leadership, minority status, music/drama, state residency. **Additional information:** Early need analysis offered; merit awards available. Students notified within week to 10 days of receipt of financial aid application.

**Application procedures. Admission:** Closing date 1/1 (postmark date). $70 fee, may be waived for applicants with need. Admission notification 4/15. Admission notification on a rolling basis. Must reply by 5/1. **Financial aid:** Priority date 2/15, closing date 5/1. FAFSA, institutional form required. Applicants notified by 3/15.

**Academics. Special study options:** Combined bachelor's/graduate degree, cooperative education, cross-registration, distance learning, double major, dual enrollment of high school students, exchange student, independent study, internships, liberal arts/career combination, student-designed major, study abroad, teacher certification program, Washington semester. **Credit/placement by examination:** AP, CLEP, IB, SAT, ACT, institutional tests. **Support services:** Learning center, pre-admission summer program, study skills assistance, tutoring, writing center.

**Majors. Architecture:** Architecture, history/criticism, technology. **Area/ethnic studies:** European, Latin American, Russian/Slavic. **Biology:** General, biophysics. **Business:** Business admin, managerial economics. **Communications:** General. **Computer sciences:** Computer science, information systems. **Conservation:** Management/policy. **Engineering:** General, biomedical, chemical, civil, computer, electrical, environmental, materials, materials science, mechanical, operations research. **Foreign languages:** General, Chinese, French, German, Japanese, linguistics, Spanish. **History:** General, European. **Interdisciplinary:** Behavioral sciences, biopsychology, cognitive science, neuroscience, systems science. **Liberal arts:** Arts/sciences. **Math:** General, applied, computational, probability, statistics. **Philosophy/religion:** Ethics, logic, philosophy. **Physical sciences:** Astrophysics, chemical physics, chemistry, physics. **Psychology:** General, cognitive, psychobiology. **Public administration:** Policy analysis. **Social sciences:** General, anthropology, economics. **Visual/performing arts:** Art, dramatic, industrial design, jazz, music performance, music theory/composition, piano/organ, stringed instruments, voice/opera. **Other:** Architecture and related services, Communication design, Ethnic, cultural minority, and gender studies, History and policy/social and cultural history, Language and information technologies, Science and humanities scholars.

**Most popular majors.** Business/marketing 12%, computer/information sciences 11%, engineering/engineering technologies 27%, interdisciplinary studies 6%, visual/performing arts 10%.

**Computing on campus.** 444 workstations in dormitories, library. Dormitories wired for high-speed internet access and linked to campus network. Commuter students can connect to campus network. Online course registration, online library, helpline, repair service, student web hosting, wireless network available.

**Student life. Freshman orientation:** Mandatory, $192 fee. Week-long program held one week before start of classes. **Policies:** Freshmen required to live on campus. **Housing:** Guaranteed on-campus for freshmen. Coed dorms, single-sex dorms, special housing for disabled, apartments, fraternity/sorority housing, wellness housing available. $600 nonrefundable deposit, deadline 5/1. Special interest group housing available. **Activities:** Bands, campus ministries, choral groups, dance, drama, film society, international

student organizations, literary magazine, music ensembles, Model UN, musical theater, radio station, student government, student newspaper, symphony orchestra, TV station, Alpha Phi Omega, Hillel, minority women's club, service clubs, National Society of Black Engineers, Society of Women Engineers, Phi Beta Kappa.

**Athletics.** NCAA. **Intercollegiate:** Basketball, cheerleading, cross-country, diving, football (tackle) M, golf M, soccer, swimming, tennis, track and field, volleyball W. **Intramural:** Badminton, basketball, bowling, cross-country, fencing, football (non-tackle), golf, racquetball, soccer, softball, squash, swimming, table tennis, tennis, track and field, volleyball, water polo. **Team name:** Tartans.

**Student services.** Alcohol/substance abuse counseling, chaplain/spiritual director, career counseling, student employment services, financial aid counseling, health services, on-campus daycare, personal counseling, placement for graduates, women's services. **Physically disabled:** Services for visually, speech, hearing impaired. **Learning disabled:** Comprehensive services available.

**Contact.** E-mail: undergraduate-admissions@andrew.cmu.edu
Phone: (412) 268-2082 Fax: (412) 268-7838
Michael Steidel, Director of Admissions, Carnegie Mellon University, 5000 Forbes Avenue, Pittsburgh, PA 15213-3890

---

## Cedar Crest College
### Allentown, Pennsylvania
www.cedarcrest.edu

**CB member**
**CB code: 2079**

- Private 4-year liberal arts college for women
- Residential campus in small city
- 1,653 degree-seeking undergraduates: 42% part-time, 95% women, 8% African American, 3% Asian American, 7% Hispanic American, 1% international
- 195 degree-seeking graduate students
- 63% of applicants admitted
- SAT or ACT (ACT writing optional), application essay required
- 55% graduate within 6 years; 20% enter graduate study

**General.** Founded in 1867. Regionally accredited. Men admitted to evening and weekend classes and daytime programs in nursing and nuclear medicine. **Degrees:** 313 bachelor's awarded; master's offered. **ROTC:** Army. **Location:** 55 miles from Philadelphia, 100 miles from New York City. **Calendar:** Semester, extensive summer session. **Full-time faculty:** 90 total; 72% have terminal degrees, 4% minority, 63% women. **Part-time faculty:** 101 total; 16% have terminal degrees, 3% minority, 73% women. **Class size:** 68% <20, 27% 20-39, 2% 40-49, 3% 50-99, less than 1% >100. **Special facilities:** Wildlife sanctuary, outdoor Greek theater, arboretum, sculpture garden, aquatic center, college-operated museums.

**Freshman class profile.** 1,583 applied, 1,003 admitted, 196 enrolled.

| Mid 50% test scores | | | |
|---|---|---|---|
| SAT critical reading: | 490-590 | GPA 2.0-2.99: | 33% |
| SAT math: | 480-590 | Rank in top quarter: | 56% |
| SAT writing: | 480-570 | Rank in top tenth: | 26% |
| ACT composite: | 20-26 | End year in good standing: | 95% |
| GPA 3.75 or higher: | 13% | Return as sophomores: | 79% |
| GPA 3.50-3.74: | 16% | Out-of-state: | 46% |
| GPA 3.0-3.49: | 38% | Live on campus: | 82% |

**Basis for selection.** Secondary school curriculum and grades most important. Test scores important. Special talents, potential for academic and personal growth considered. Interview and essay recommended for all. **Homeschooled:** Transcript of courses and grades, letter of recommendation (nonparent) required.

**High school preparation.** College-preparatory program recommended. 16 units required. Required and recommended units include English 4, mathematics 3, social studies 3, science 2 (laboratory 2), foreign language 2 and academic electives 3. Special natural science requirements for nuclear medicine and nursing.

**2009-2010 Annual costs.** Tuition/fees: $28,135. On-campus students pay $350 resident communication fee; continuing education program's average per-credit-hour cost, $593. Room/board: $9,321. Books/supplies: $1,000. Personal expenses: $850.

**2009-2010 Financial aid. Need-based:** 194 full-time freshmen applied for aid; 183 were judged to have need; 183 of these received aid. Average need met was 79%. Average scholarship/grant was $19,347; average loan $3,552. 67% of total undergraduate aid awarded as scholarships/grants, 33%

as loans/jobs. **Non-need-based:** Scholarships awarded for academics, alumni affiliation, art, leadership, music/drama.

**Application procedures. Admission:** No deadline. $30 fee, may be waived for applicants with need, free for online applicants. Admission notification on a rolling basis beginning on or about 9/15. Must reply by May 1 or within 2 week(s) if notified thereafter. **Financial aid:** Priority date 5/1; no closing date. FAFSA required. Applicants notified on a rolling basis starting 1/1; must reply by 5/15.

**Academics. Special study options:** Accelerated study, combined bachelor's/graduate degree, cross-registration, distance learning, double major, dual enrollment of high school students, ESL, honors, independent study, internships, liberal arts/career combination, student-designed major, study abroad, teacher certification program, Washington semester, weekend college. **Credit/placement by examination:** AP, CLEP, IB. 18 credit hours maximum toward bachelor's degree. **Support services:** Learning center, pre-admission summer program, remedial instruction, study skills assistance, tutoring, writing center.

**Majors. Biology:** General, biochemistry, environmental, genetics. **Business:** Accounting, business admin, marketing. **Communications:** General. **Computer sciences:** General. **Education:** Elementary, secondary. **Family/consumer sciences:** Food/nutrition. **Foreign languages:** Spanish. **Health:** Nuclear medical technology. **History:** General. **Interdisciplinary:** Neuroscience. **Math:** General. **Physical sciences:** Chemistry. **Psychology:** General. **Public administration:** Social work. **Social sciences:** Criminology, political science. **Visual/performing arts:** General, art, dance, dramatic, studio arts.

**Most popular majors.** Biology 12%, business/marketing 12%, health sciences 30%, physical sciences 6%, psychology 12%.

**Computing on campus.** 195 workstations in dormitories, library, computer center, student center. Dormitories wired for high-speed internet access and linked to campus network. Online course registration, online library, helpline, repair service, wireless network available.

**Student life. Freshman orientation:** Mandatory. Preregistration for classes offered. 5-day academic and social program in August mandatory. 2-day academic testing and advising program in June mandatory. **Policies:** Drinking under age 21 prohibited; honor philosophy exists. **Housing:** Guaranteed on-campus for all undergraduates. Special housing for disabled available. $100 nonrefundable deposit. **Activities:** Campus ministries, choral groups, dance, drama, international student organizations, literary magazine, music ensembles, musical theater, radio station, student government, student newspaper, Amnesty International, Black Student Union, Best Buddies, Cedar Crest Christian Fellowship, Hillel Society, international student organization, Muslim student association, Sisters Inc, Global Eyes, Take Back the Night.

**Athletics.** NCAA. **Intercollegiate:** Basketball W, cross-country W, field hockey W, lacrosse W, soccer W, softball W, tennis W, volleyball W. **Intramural:** Badminton W, basketball W, football (non-tackle) W, soccer W, softball W, triathlon W. **Team name:** Falcons.

**Student services.** Adult student services, alcohol/substance abuse counseling, chaplain/spiritual director, career counseling, services for economically disadvantaged, student employment services, financial aid counseling, health services, minority student services, personal counseling, placement for graduates, women's services. **Physically disabled:** Services for visually, hearing impaired.

**Contact.** E-mail: admissions@cedarcrest.edu
Phone: (610) 740-3780 Toll-free number: (800) 360-1222
Fax: (610) 606-4647
Kimberly Owens, Senior Executive Vice President for Enrollment Management, Cedar Crest College, 100 College Drive, Allentown, PA 18104-6196

---

### Central Pennsylvania College
**Summerdale, Pennsylvania**
**www.centralpenn.edu**　　　　　　　　　**CB code: 1061**

- For-profit 4-year business and technical college
- Commuter campus in rural community
- 1,213 degree-seeking undergraduates: 44% part-time, 64% women, 23% African American, 2% Asian American, 6% Hispanic American, 1% Native American
- Application essay, interview required
- 61% graduate within 6 years

---

**General.** Founded in 1881. Regionally accredited. **Degrees:** 201 bachelor's, 96 associate awarded. **Location:** 5 miles from Harrisburg. **Calendar:** Trimester, extensive summer session. **Full-time faculty:** 24 total. **Part-time faculty:** 88 total. **Special facilities:** Student-staffed restaurant, travel agency, online campus store, mock courtroom, optometric room, multimedia lab, child-care facility, advanced technology education center, conference facility, crime lab.

**Freshman class profile.** 1,228 applied, 627 admitted, 146 enrolled.

| | | |
|---|---|---|
| **Out-of-state:** 20% | **Live on campus:** | 64% |

**Basis for selection.** Open admission, but selective for some programs. High school achievement record very important for admission to physical therapist assistant program. Minimum GPA of 2.5 (3.0 preferred) and two references required for entrance into the physical therapy assistant program. **Homeschooled:** Provide transcript of courses completed with grades and include parent/teacher/academy signatures. **Learning Disabled:** Students meet with academic dean to discuss provisions needed for individual learning experience.

**2009-2010 Annual costs.** Tuition/fees: $17,130. Room/board: $6,285. Books/supplies: $1,200. Personal expenses: $1,000.

**Financial aid. Non-need-based:** Scholarships awarded for academics, alumni affiliation, job skills, leadership, minority status, state residency.

**Application procedures. Admission:** Priority date 5/1; no deadline. No application fee. Admission notification on a rolling basis. **Financial aid:** Priority date 3/15; no closing date. FAFSA, institutional form required. Applicants notified on a rolling basis starting 2/1; must reply within 2 week(s) of notification.

**Academics. Special study options:** Distance learning, double major, dual enrollment of high school students, honors, independent study, internships, study abroad. **Credit/placement by examination:** AP, CLEP, IB, institutional tests. 15 credit hours maximum toward associate degree, 15 toward bachelor's. **Support services:** Learning center, reduced course load, remedial instruction, study skills assistance, tutoring, writing center.

**Majors. Business:** Accounting, business admin. **Communications:** General. **Computer sciences:** Computer science. **Legal studies:** General. **Protective services:** Criminal justice, emergency management/homeland security.

**Most popular majors.** Business/marketing 53%, computer/information sciences 15%, security/protective services 27%.

**Computing on campus.** 150 workstations in library, computer center. Dormitories wired for high-speed internet access and linked to campus network. Commuter students can connect to campus network. Online course registration, online library, helpline, wireless network available.

**Student life. Freshman orientation:** Mandatory. Preregistration for classes offered. **Policies:** Dress code, mandatory attendance, ethics policies, no alcohol or drugs. **Housing:** Guaranteed on-campus for freshmen. Apartments, wellness housing available. $250 deposit. All resident housing is either single-gender townhouses or apartments. **Activities:** Choral groups, literary magazine, student government, student newspaper, Gamma Beta Phi, Delta Epsilon Chi, technology club, Club MED, Toastmasters, Young Republicans.

**Athletics.** NJCAA. **Intercollegiate:** Basketball, bowling, golf. **Intramural:** Basketball, football (non-tackle), softball, tennis, volleyball. **Team name:** Silver Knights.

**Student services.** Adult student services, alcohol/substance abuse counseling, career counseling, student employment services, financial aid counseling, on-campus daycare, personal counseling, placement for graduates.

**Contact.** E-mail: admissions@centralpenn.edu
Phone: (717) 728-2201 Toll-free number: (800) 759-2727
Fax: (717) 732-5254
Stacy Scott, Director of Admissions, Central Pennsylvania College, College Hill & Valley Roads, Summerdale, PA 17093-0309

---

### Chatham University
**Pittsburgh, Pennsylvania**　　　　　　　**CB member**
**www.chatham.edu**　　　　　　　　　　**CB code: 2081**

- Private 4-year university and liberal arts college for women
- Residential campus in large city
- 771 degree-seeking undergraduates: 12% part-time, 99% women, 12% African American, 2% Asian American, 2% Hispanic American, 6% international
- 1,130 degree-seeking graduate students

- 68% of applicants admitted
- Application essay required
- 58% graduate within 6 years

**General.** Founded in 1869. Regionally accredited. **Degrees:** 172 bachelor's awarded; master's, professional offered. **ROTC:** Army, Naval, Air Force. **Location:** 5 miles from downtown. **Calendar:** Semester, limited summer session. **Full-time faculty:** 88 total; 97% have terminal degrees, 4% minority, 64% women. **Part-time faculty:** 150 total. **Class size:** 68% < 20, 30% 20-39, 1% 40-49, less than 1% 50-99. **Special facilities:** Broadcast studio, science complex and greenhouse, proscenium theater, arboretum.

**Freshman class profile.** 641 applied, 433 admitted, 131 enrolled.

| Mid 50% test scores | | | |
|---|---|---|---|
| SAT critical reading: | 480-600 | GPA 2.0-2.99: | 19% |
| SAT math: | 460-580 | Rank in top quarter: | 35% |
| SAT writing: | 470-600 | Rank in top tenth: | 15% |
| ACT composite: | 22-25 | Return as sophomores: | 71% |
| GPA 3.75 or higher: | 28% | Out-of-state: | 28% |
| GPA 3.50-3.74: | 14% | Live on campus: | 83% |
| GPA 3.0-3.49: | 38% | International: | 6% |

**Basis for selection.** School achievement record, essays, and test scores most important, though test scores are not required. Students who do not submit SAT/ACT scores required to submit a graded writing sample and resume/list of activities. Portfolios may also be submitted. Activities, talents, volunteer work, paid work, alumnae relationship, class rank, recommendations considered. TOEFL or IELTS required for international students. Campus visit or interviews recommended for all.

**High school preparation.** College-preparatory program recommended. 11 units required; 15 recommended. Required and recommended units include English 4, mathematics 2-3, science 2-3 and foreign language 2. Require 3 units of social science.

**2009-2010 Annual costs.** Tuition/fees: $28,290. Required fees ($1,020) cover technology fee, which includes cost of HP tablet computer (required for all first-time first-year students) and the campus fee. Room/board: $8,700. Books/supplies: $860. Personal expenses: $2,862.

**2009-2010 Financial aid. Need-based:** Average need met was 78%. Average scholarship/grant was $8,021; average loan $4,586. 57% of total undergraduate aid awarded as scholarships/grants, 43% as loans/jobs. **Non-need-based:** Scholarships awarded for academics, alumni affiliation, leadership, minority status.

**Application procedures. Admission:** Priority date 3/15; deadline 8/1. $35 fee, may be waived for applicants with need, free for online applicants. Admission notification on a rolling basis beginning on or about 10/15. Must reply by May 1 or within 2 week(s) if notified thereafter. **Financial aid:** Priority date 5/1; no closing date. FAFSA required. Applicants notified on a rolling basis starting 2/15; must reply by 5/1 or within 2 week(s) of notification.

**Academics.** All students eligible through PACE Center to receive free tutoring in every course offered. Specialized courses offered for students having academic difficulties, as well as career preparation courses to help students choose a career path. **Special study options:** Accelerated study, combined bachelor's/graduate degree, cooperative education, cross-registration, distance learning, double major, dual enrollment of high school students, ESL, exchange student, honors, independent study, internships, liberal arts/career combination, semester at sea, student-designed major, study abroad, teacher certification program, Washington semester. Five-year bachelor's/master's programs on campus and with other institutions. **Credit/placement by examination:** AP, CLEP, IB. 12 credit hours maximum toward bachelor's degree. **Support services:** Learning center, reduced course load, remedial instruction, study skills assistance, tutoring, writing center.

**Majors. Architecture:** Interior. **Area/ethnic studies:** Women's. **Biology:** General, biochemistry. **Business:** Accounting, business admin, international, managerial economics, marketing. **Communications:** General, broadcast journalism, journalism, public relations. **Conservation:** Environmental science, environmental studies. **Education:** Early childhood, elementary. **Engineering:** General. **Foreign languages:** French, Spanish. **Health:** Nursing (RN). **History:** General. **Legal studies:** Prelaw. **Liberal arts:** Arts/sciences. **Math:** General. **Parks/recreation:** Exercise sciences. **Physical sciences:** Chemistry, physics. **Protective services:** Forensics. **Psychology:** General. **Public administration:** Policy analysis, social work. **Social sciences:** Economics, international relations, political science. **Visual/performing arts:** Art history/conservation, arts management, photography, studio arts. **Other:** Film and digitial technology.

**Most popular majors.** Biology 14%, communications/journalism 6%, health sciences 13%, psychology 13%, social sciences 6%, visual/performing arts 11%.

**Computing on campus.** PC or laptop required. 300 workstations in dormitories, library, computer center. Dormitories wired for high-speed internet access and linked to campus network. Commuter students can connect to campus network. Online course registration, online library, helpline, repair service, student web hosting, wireless network available.

**Student life. Freshman orientation:** Mandatory. Preregistration for classes offered. Held immediately before classes begin in late August. Mini-orientations held during late spring and summer when students can register for courses. **Policies:** Honor code. **Housing:** Guaranteed on-campus for all undergraduates. Apartments, wellness housing available. $150 nonrefundable deposit, deadline 5/1. Intercultural residence hall, community service floor and environmental floor within larger residence hall available. **Activities:** Choral groups, dance, drama, international student organizations, literary magazine, music ensembles, musical theater, student government, student newspaper, Black student union, Christian Fellowship, Jewish organization, Feminist collective, Gateway student association, Green Horizons, Mortar Board, Students Against Sexual Oppression.

**Athletics.** NCAA. **Intercollegiate:** Basketball W, cross-country W, ice hockey W, soccer W, softball W, swimming W, tennis W, volleyball W, water polo W. **Team name:** Cougars.

**Student services.** Adult student services, chaplain/spiritual director, career counseling, services for economically disadvantaged, student employment services, financial aid counseling, health services, personal counseling, placement for graduates, women's services. **Physically disabled:** Services for visually, speech, hearing impaired.

**Contact.** E-mail: admissions@chatham.edu
Phone: (412) 365-1825 Toll-free number: (800) 837-1290
Fax: (412) 365-1609
Lisa Meyers, Director of Undergraduate Admissions, Chatham University, Woodland Road, Pittsburgh, PA 15232

## Chestnut Hill College
**Philadelphia, Pennsylvania**
www.chc.edu

CB member
CB code: 2082

- Private 4-year liberal arts college affiliated with Roman Catholic Church
- Residential campus in very large city
- 1,431 degree-seeking undergraduates: 20% part-time, 70% women
- 836 degree-seeking graduate students
- 73% of applicants admitted
- SAT or ACT (ACT writing optional), application essay required

**General.** Founded in 1924. Regionally accredited. Extended campus at adjacent Sugar Loaf Hill. **Degrees:** 237 bachelor's awarded; master's, professional offered. **Location:** 17 miles from Center City. **Calendar:** Semester, limited summer session. **Full-time faculty:** 76 total; 82% have terminal degrees, 8% minority, 70% women. **Part-time faculty:** 267 total; 30% have terminal degrees, 9% minority, 55% women. **Special facilities:** Observatory, planetarium, Irish literature collection, multimedia center, smart classrooms.

**Freshman class profile.** 2,519 applied, 1,846 admitted, 273 enrolled.

| Mid 50% test scores | | | |
|---|---|---|---|
| SAT critical reading: | 450-550 | GPA 3.0-3.49: | 38% |
| SAT math: | 450-540 | GPA 2.0-2.99: | 42% |
| SAT writing: | 440-550 | Rank in top quarter: | 28% |
| ACT composite: | 17-22 | Rank in top tenth: | 7% |
| GPA 3.75 or higher: | 10% | Out-of-state: | 33% |
| GPA 3.50-3.74: | 9% | Live on campus: | 70% |

**Basis for selection.** Secondary school record, essay very important. Standardized test scores, recommendations, character, interview, extracurricular activities important. Alumni connection, talent, volunteer activity, work experience considered. Open admissions to accelerated program in the School of Continuing and Professional Studies. Students are placed in writing, math, and language courses on basis of placement tests administered by the college. **Homeschooled:** Must subscribe to a homeschool agency.

**High school preparation.** College-preparatory program recommended. 16 units recommended. Recommended units include English 4, mathematics 3, social studies 4, science 3 and foreign language 2.

**2010-2011 Annual costs.** Tuition/fees (projected): $28,100. Room/board: $9,065. Books/supplies: $1,000. Personal expenses: $1,400.

**2009-2010 Financial aid. Need-based:** 268 full-time freshmen applied for aid; 225 were judged to have need; 223 of these received aid. Average

need met was 75%. Average scholarship/grant was $15,577; average loan $3,836. 60% of total undergraduate aid awarded as scholarships/grants, 40% as loans/jobs. **Non-need-based:** Awarded to 158 full-time undergraduates, including 72 freshmen. Scholarships awarded for academics, alumni affiliation, athletics, leadership, religious affiliation, **Additional information:** Application priority date 1/15 for merit-based scholarships.

**Application procedures. Admission:** Priority date 1/20; no deadline. $35 fee, may be waived for applicants with need. Admission notification on a rolling basis. Must reply by May 1 or within 3 week(s) if notified thereafter. **Financial aid:** Closing date 4/15. FAFSA required. Applicants notified on a rolling basis starting 1/31; must reply by 5/1 or within 3 week(s) of notification.

**Academics.** Montessori certification available with elementary and pre-elementary education. Secondary education certification available in major field of study. Interdisciplinary bachelor's degree in international business, language, and culture. **Special study options:** Combined bachelor's/graduate degree, cooperative education, cross-registration, double major, dual enrollment of high school students, ESL, exchange student, honors, independent study, internships, student-designed major, study abroad, teacher certification program. 2-2 double bachelor's program in biology or chemistry and medical technology with Thomas Jefferson University School of Allied Health Sciences, 3-2 BA/MS psychology, 3-2 BS/MS applied technology, 5-year BS/MEd elementary education with emphasis in special education, dual degree bachelor's in biology or chemistry, master's in physician assistant at Arcadia University, dual degree bachelor's in biology or chemistry, Doctor of Podiatric Medicine at Temple University. **Credit/placement by examination:** AP, CLEP, IB, institutional tests. 12 credit hours maximum toward bachelor's degree. **Support services:** Learning center, pre-admission summer program, reduced course load, remedial instruction, study skills assistance, tutoring, writing center.

**Majors. Biology:** General, biochemistry, molecular. **Business:** Accounting, accounting/business management, business admin, communications, human resources, international, marketing. **Communications:** General. **Communications technology:** General. **Computer sciences:** General, information technology. **Conservation:** Environmental science. **Education:** Early childhood, elementary, multi-level teacher, music. **Family/consumer sciences:** Child care. **Foreign languages:** French, Spanish. **Health:** Health care admin. **History:** General. **Interdisciplinary:** Math/computer science. **Liberal arts:** Arts/sciences. **Math:** General. **Physical sciences:** Chemistry. **Protective services:** Forensics, law enforcement admin. **Psychology:** General. **Public administration:** Human services. **Social sciences:** Political science, sociology.

**Most popular majors.** Business/marketing 20%, education 12%, psychology 9%, public administration/social services 17%, security/protective services 12%.

**Computing on campus.** PC or laptop required. 40 workstations in library, computer center. Commuter students can connect to campus network. Helpline, wireless network available.

**Student life. Freshman orientation:** Available. Preregistration for classes offered. Held 2 or 3 times during the summer. Additional program held the few days before classes begin. **Housing:** Coed dorms, wellness housing available. $200 nonrefundable deposit, deadline 5/1. **Activities:** Jazz band, campus ministries, choral groups, drama, international student organizations, literary magazine, music ensembles, musical theater, radio station, student government, student newspaper, symphony orchestra, TV station, African-American awareness society, Caribbean Culture Club, ecology club, gay/straight alliance, hospitality club, Hispanics in Action, Mosaic of Cultures club, Students for Peace and Justice, College Democrats, College Republicans.

**Athletics.** NCAA. **Intercollegiate:** Baseball M, basketball, cross-country, golf, lacrosse W, soccer, softball W, tennis, volleyball W. **Team name:** Griffins.

**Student services.** Adult student services, alcohol/substance abuse counseling, chaplain/spiritual director, career counseling, financial aid counseling, health services, personal counseling. **Physically disabled:** Services for visually impaired.

**Contact.** E-mail: chcapply@chc.edu
Phone: (215) 248-7001 Toll-free number: (800) 248-0052
Fax: (215) 248-7082
Mark Osborn, Assistant Dean for Admissions, School of Undergraduate Studies, Chestnut Hill College, 9601 Germantown Avenue, Philadelphia, PA 19118-2693

## Cheyney University of Pennsylvania
Cheyney, Pennsylvania
www.cheyney.edu

CB member
CB code: 2648

- Public 4-year university
- Residential campus in small town

- 1,339 degree-seeking undergraduates: 6% part-time, 53% women, 92% African American, 1% Hispanic American
- 81 degree-seeking graduate students
- 50% of applicants admitted
- SAT or ACT, application essay required
- 22% graduate within 6 years

**General.** Founded in 1837. Regionally accredited. Courses offered at Philadelphia Urban Center. **Degrees:** 167 bachelor's awarded; master's offered. **ROTC:** Army. **Location:** 25 miles from Philadelphia. **Calendar:** Semester, limited summer session. **Full-time faculty:** 75 total; 79% minority, 48% women. **Part-time faculty:** 24 total; 79% minority, 54% women. **Special facilities:** Planetarium, weather station, theater arts center.

**Freshman class profile.** 3,298 applied, 1,637 admitted, 607 enrolled.

| Mid 50% test scores | | | |
|---|---|---|---|
| SAT critical reading: | 330-420 | GPA 3.0-3.49: | 14% |
| SAT math: | 320-410 | GPA 2.0-2.99: | 64% |
| SAT writing: | 320-410 | Rank in top quarter: | 15% |
| ACT composite: | 14-21 | Rank in top tenth: | 6% |
| GPA 3.75 or higher: | 1% | Return as sophomores: | 60% |
| GPA 3.50-3.74: | 2% | Out-of-state: | 33% |
| | | Live on campus: | 89% |

**Basis for selection.** Test scores, class rank, GPA, counselor recommendation, extracurricular activities important. 830 SAT (exclusive of Writing) or 17 ACT required. SAT Subject Tests recommended. Interview recommended.

**High school preparation.** College-preparatory program recommended. 13 units required. Required units include English 4, mathematics 3, history 2, science 2 and foreign language 2.

**2009-2010 Annual costs.** Tuition/fees: $7,360; $15,692 out-of-state. Tuition for residents of MD, NY, NJ and DE is $11,108. Room/board: $7,746. Books/supplies: $1,300.

**Financial aid. Non-need-based:** Scholarships awarded for academics, athletics.

**Application procedures. Admission:** Closing date 3/31. $20 fee, may be waived for applicants with need. Admission notification on a rolling basis. Must reply by 3/31. **Financial aid:** Priority date 3/15; no closing date. FAFSA required. Applicants notified on a rolling basis starting 4/1; must reply within 2 week(s) of notification.

**Academics.** Health and physical education courses required of most students. **Special study options:** Cooperative education, cross-registration, distance learning, double major, honors, independent study, internships, study abroad, teacher certification program. **Credit/placement by examination:** AP, CLEP, institutional tests. 23 credit hours maximum toward bachelor's degree. **Support services:** Learning center, pre-admission summer program, reduced course load, remedial instruction, tutoring.

**Majors. Biology:** General. **Business:** Business admin, hospitality admin. **Communications:** General. **Computer sciences:** General. **Education:** Early childhood, elementary, special. **Family/consumer sciences:** Clothing/textiles. **Foreign languages:** French, Spanish. **Health:** Clinical lab science. **Interdisciplinary:** Biological/physical sciences. **Math:** General. **Parks/recreation:** Facilities management. **Physical sciences:** Chemistry. **Psychology:** General. **Social sciences:** General, economics, political science, sociology. **Visual/performing arts:** Art, dramatic. **Other:** Geographic information science.

**Most popular majors.** Biology 7%, business/marketing 25%, communications/journalism 7%, parks/recreation 7%, psychology 12%, social sciences 25%.

**Computing on campus.** 296 workstations in dormitories, library, computer center, student center. Dormitories wired for high-speed internet access and linked to campus network. Online course registration, helpline, repair service available.

**Student life. Freshman orientation:** Mandatory. **Policies:** Ecumenical services held on campus. **Housing:** Guaranteed on-campus for freshmen. Coed dorms, single-sex dorms available. $100 fully refundable deposit, deadline 5/11. Honors dorm. **Activities:** Bands, choral groups, drama, film society, music ensembles, radio station, student government, student newspaper, TV station, Shades of Unity, Toastmasters, business club, education club, NAACP, Latino Students in Action, LaOriginale, Commuter Students Association.

**Athletics.** NCAA. **Intercollegiate:** Basketball, bowling W, cross-country, football (tackle) M, tennis W, track and field, volleyball W. **Intramural:** Basketball, football (tackle) M. **Team name:** Wolves.

**Student services.** Career counseling, student employment services, health services, personal counseling, placement for graduates, veterans' counselor.

**Contact.** E-mail: abrown@cheyney.edu
Phone: (610) 399-2275 Toll-free number: (800) 243-9639
Fax: (610) 399-2099
Angela Brown, Director of Admissions, Cheyney University of Pennsylvania, 1837 University Circle, Cheyney, PA 19319-0019

## Clarion University of Pennsylvania

| Clarion, Pennsylvania | CB member |
|---|---|
| www.clarion.edu | CB code: 2649 |

▶ Public 4-year business and teachers college
▶ Residential campus in small town
▶ 5,929 degree-seeking undergraduates: 11% part-time, 60% women, 6% African American, 1% Asian American, 1% Hispanic American, 1% international
▶ 1,047 degree-seeking graduate students
▶ 68% of applicants admitted
▶ SAT or ACT (ACT writing optional) required
▶ 53% graduate within 6 years

**General.** Founded in 1867. Regionally accredited. **Degrees:** 854 bachelor's, 156 associate awarded; master's offered. **ROTC:** Army. **Location:** 85 miles from Pittsburgh, 75 miles from Erie. **Calendar:** Semester, limited summer session. **Full-time faculty:** 256 total; 10% minority, 49% women. **Part-time faculty:** 120 total; 2% minority, 53% women. **Class size:** 25% < 20, 55% 20-39, 12% 40-49, 7% 50-99, 2% >100. **Special facilities:** Planetarium.

**Freshman class profile.** 4,777 applied, 3,271 admitted, 1,449 enrolled.

| Mid 50% test scores | | | |
|---|---|---|---|
| SAT critical reading: | 410-520 | Rank in top quarter: | 22% |
| SAT math: | 420-530 | Rank in top tenth: | 6% |
| SAT writing: | 400-500 | Return as sophomores: | 72% |
| GPA 3.75 or higher: | 14% | Out-of-state: | 5% |
| GPA 3.50-3.74: | 19% | Live on campus: | 60% |
| GPA 3.0-3.49: | 28% | Fraternities: | 1% |
| GPA 2.0-2.99: | 34% | Sororities: | 6% |

**Basis for selection.** School achievement record, class rank, GPA, test scores considered. Audition required of music program applicants; Nursing students must complete NLN entrance exam. **Homeschooled:** Transcript of courses and grades required.

**High school preparation.** College-preparatory program required. 13 units required; 19 recommended. Required and recommended units include English 4, mathematics 3-4, social studies 3-4, science 3-4 (laboratory 1) and foreign language 2.

**2009-2010 Annual costs.** Tuition/fees: $7,380; $12,934 out-of-state. Tuition for incoming out-of-state residents with SAT of 1000 or higher and at least a 3.0 GPA or the top 30% of their graduating class is $8,331. Room/board: $6,390. Books/supplies: $850. Personal expenses: $2,200.

**2008-2009 Financial aid. Need-based:** 1,209 full-time freshmen applied for aid; 960 were judged to have need; 918 of these received aid. Average need met was 69%. Average scholarship/grant was $5,735; average loan $3,164. 48% of total undergraduate aid awarded as scholarships/grants, 52% as loans/jobs. **Non-need-based:** Awarded to 1,491 full-time undergraduates, including 446 freshmen. Scholarships awarded for academics, art, athletics, leadership, minority status, music/drama, state residency.

**Application procedures. Admission:** No deadline. $30 fee, may be waived for applicants with need. Admission notification on a rolling basis beginning on or about 9/1. **Financial aid:** Closing date 4/15. FAFSA required. Applicants notified on a rolling basis starting 3/1.

**Academics. Special study options:** Accelerated study, combined bachelor's/graduate degree, cooperative education, distance learning, double major, dual enrollment of high school students, honors, independent study, internships, liberal arts/career combination, study abroad, teacher certification program. Co-op program in engineering with two participating schools; co-op in speech pathology and audiology with Gallaudet University. Joint and collaborative programs in MSLS/JD, pharmacy, osteopathic medicine, nanotechnology, master of nursing, language, radiologic science, respiratory care and industrial technology. **Credit/placement by examination:** AP, CLEP, IB, institutional tests. 38 credit hours maximum toward bachelor's degree. **Support services:** Learning center, pre-admission summer program, remedial instruction, study skills assistance, tutoring, writing center.

**Majors. Biology:** General, molecular. **Business:** Accounting, business admin, finance, international, labor relations, managerial economics, marketing, real estate. **Communications:** General. **Computer sciences:** General, information systems. **Conservation:** Environmental science. **Education:** Early childhood, elementary, special. **Foreign languages:** French, Spanish. **Health:** Audiology/speech pathology, clinical lab technology, medical radiologic technology/radiation therapy, nursing (RN). **History:** General. **Interdisciplinary:** Biological/physical sciences. **Liberal arts:** Arts/sciences, library science. **Math:** General, applied. **Philosophy/religion:** Philosophy. **Physical sciences:** Chemistry, geology, physics. **Psychology:** General, social. **Social sciences:** Anthropology, economics, political science, sociology. **Visual/performing arts:** Art, dramatic, music management.

**Most popular majors.** Business/marketing 19%, communications/journalism 10%, education 17%, health sciences 12%, liberal arts 8%, social sciences 7%.

**Computing on campus.** 1,143 workstations in dormitories, library, computer center, student center. Dormitories wired for high-speed internet access and linked to campus network. Commuter students can connect to campus network. Online course registration, online library, helpline, student web hosting, wireless network available.

**Student life. Freshman orientation:** Mandatory, $150 fee. Preregistration for classes offered. One-day session held in January, spring and summer. **Policies:** Students who live on campus are guaranteed a room on campus the following year. **Housing:** Coed dorms, single-sex dorms, apartments, fraternity/sorority housing, wellness housing available. $100 nonrefundable deposit. **Activities:** Bands, choral groups, dance, drama, literary magazine, music ensembles, musical theater, radio station, student government, student newspaper, TV station, Koinonia Christian Fellowship, African American Caucus, Newman Association, Hip Hop Dance Team, NAACP, Young Democrats, Eagle Ambassadors, People Reaching Out and Understanding Disabilities, Students Together Against Rape, University Activities Board.

**Athletics.** NCAA. **Intercollegiate:** Baseball M, basketball, cross-country W, diving, football (tackle) M, golf M, soccer W, softball W, swimming, tennis W, track and field W, volleyball W, wrestling M. **Intramural:** Badminton, basketball, bowling, golf, racquetball, soccer, softball, swimming, table tennis, tennis, track and field, volleyball, water polo, wrestling. **Team name:** Golden Eagles.

**Student services.** Adult student services, alcohol/substance abuse counseling, chaplain/spiritual director, career counseling, services for economically disadvantaged, student employment services, financial aid counseling, health services, minority student services, on-campus daycare, personal counseling, placement for graduates, veterans' counselor, women's services. **Physically disabled:** Services for visually, speech, hearing impaired.

**Contact.** E-mail: admissions@clarion.edu
Phone: (814) 393-2306 Toll-free number: (800) 672-7171
Fax: (814) 393-2030
William Bailey, Dean of Enrollment Management, Clarion University of Pennsylvania, 840 Wood Street, Clarion, PA 16214

## Curtis Institute of Music

| Philadelphia, Pennsylvania | |
|---|---|
| www.curtis.edu | CB code: 2100 |

▶ Private 4-year music college
▶ Commuter campus in very large city
▶ 127 degree-seeking undergraduates: 50% women, 3% African American, 13% Asian American, 2% Hispanic American, 39% international
▶ 32 degree-seeking graduate students
▶ 4% of applicants admitted
▶ SAT required
▶ 92% graduate within 6 years

**General.** Founded in 1924. Regionally accredited. **Degrees:** 20 bachelor's awarded; master's offered. **Calendar:** Semester. **Full-time faculty:** 1 total; 100% women. **Part-time faculty:** 96 total; 8% have terminal degrees, 14% minority, 33% women. **Special facilities:** More than 82,000 titles in audiovisual materials, sheet music, and books.

**Freshman class profile.** 261 applied, 11 admitted, 11 enrolled.

| End year in good standing: | 100% | Out-of-state: | 81% |
|---|---|---|---|
| Return as sophomores: | 100% | International: | 9% |

**Basis for selection.** Admission based on audition. Test scores considered for applicants to bachelor's degree program. **Homeschooled:** Transcript of courses and grades, state high school equivalency certificate required.

**High school preparation.** Major emphasis on applied music activities.

**2009-2010 Annual costs.** All students awarded a full-tuition scholarship. Bachelor of Music students pay $2,290 (required fees) and $17,910 (additional expenses), which covers supplies, off-campus room/board, and miscellaneous expenses for the academic year. Students required to have adequate health insurance coverage. Books/supplies: $1,575.

**2009-2010 Financial aid.** All financial aid based on need. 9 full-time freshmen applied for aid; 7 were judged to have need; 5 of these received aid. Average need met was 91%. Average scholarship/grant was $4,187; average loan $3,500. 49% of total undergraduate aid awarded as scholarships/grants, 51% as loans/jobs. **Additional information:** All admitted students receive a full tuition scholarship. The estimated value of this scholarship is $33,500.

**Application procedures. Admission:** Closing date 12/11 (postmark date). $150 fee, may be waived for applicants with need. Application must be submitted on paper. Admission notification 4/1. Must reply by 5/1. **Financial aid:** Priority date 3/1; no closing date. FAFSA, institutional form required. Applicants notified by 4/1; must reply by 5/1 or within 2 week(s) of notification.

**Academics. Special study options:** Double major, ESL. **Credit/placement by examination:** AP, CLEP, SAT, institutional tests. **Support services:** Remedial instruction, study skills assistance, tutoring.

**Majors. Visual/performing arts:** Music performance, music theory/composition.

**Computing on campus.** 16 workstations in library, computer center, student center. Online library, repair service, wireless network available.

**Student life. Freshman orientation:** Mandatory. Preregistration for classes offered. Orientation for international students begins 2 weeks before classes start. The general orientation for all students (including international students) begins 1 week before classes begin. **Housing:** Apartments available. **Activities:** Music ensembles, opera, student government, symphony orchestra.

**Student services.** Alcohol/substance abuse counseling, career counseling, financial aid counseling, health services, personal counseling, veterans' counselor.

**Contact.** E-mail: admissions@curtis.edu
Phone: (215) 893-5262 Fax: (215) 893-7900
Christopher Hodges, Admissions Officer, Curtis Institute of Music, 1726 Locust Street, Philadelphia, PA 19103-6187

---

## Delaware Valley College
**Doylestown, Pennsylvania**
www.delval.edu

CB member
CB code: 2510

- Private 4-year agricultural and liberal arts college
- Residential campus in large town
- 1,877 degree-seeking undergraduates: 12% part-time, 58% women, 4% African American, 1% Asian American, 2% Hispanic American
- 246 degree-seeking graduate students
- 72% of applicants admitted
- SAT or ACT (ACT writing optional), application essay required
- 50% graduate within 6 years

**General.** Founded in 1896. Regionally accredited. **Degrees:** 374 bachelor's, 4 associate awarded; master's offered. **Location:** 20 miles from Philadelphia, 70 miles from New York City. **Calendar:** Semester, extensive summer session. **Full-time faculty:** 82 total; 57% have terminal degrees, 10% minority, 42% women. **Part-time faculty:** 118 total; 20% have terminal degrees, 3% minority, 33% women. **Class size:** 55% < 20, 37% 20-39, 5% 40-49, 3% 50-99. **Special facilities:** Equine facility with indoor and outdoor arenas, animal farms, dairy, farm market, arboretum greenhouses, tissue culture laboratories.

**Freshman class profile.** 1,770 applied, 1,266 admitted, 452 enrolled.

| Mid 50% test scores | | | | |
|---|---|---|---|---|
| SAT critical reading: | 450-550 | GPA 2.0-2.99: | | 17% |
| SAT math: | 460-560 | Rank in top quarter: | | 37% |
| SAT writing: | 430-550 | Rank in top tenth: | | 13% |
| ACT composite: | 20-25 | Return as sophomores: | | 76% |
| GPA 3.75 or higher: | 35% | Out-of-state: | | 48% |
| GPA 3.50-3.74: | 17% | Live on campus: | | 90% |
| GPA 3.0-3.49: | 31% | Fraternities: | | 4% |
| | | Sororities: | | 5% |

**Basis for selection.** Academic achievement, class rank, test scores, letters of recommendation from math or science teacher and guidance counselor, grades in math and science considered. Interview, essay recommended. **Homeschooled:** State high school equivalency certificate required.

**High school preparation.** College-preparatory program required. 15 units required. Required units include English 3, mathematics 2, social studies 2, science 2 (laboratory 1) and academic electives 6. Business administration computer information systems management, criminal justice, or English majors and students applying for the equine science program need only one unit of science: biology, chemistry or physics.

**2009-2010 Annual costs.** Tuition/fees: $27,742. Room/board: $9,836. Books/supplies: $1,000. Personal expenses: $900.

**2009-2010 Financial aid. Need-based:** 416 full-time freshmen applied for aid; 373 were judged to have need; 373 of these received aid. Average need met was 70%. Average scholarship/grant was $15,780; average loan $3,570. 65% of total undergraduate aid awarded as scholarships/grants, 35% as loans/jobs. **Non-need-based:** Awarded to 455 full-time undergraduates, including 124 freshmen. Scholarships awarded for academics, alumni affiliation, music/drama.

**Application procedures. Admission:** Closing date 5/1. $50 fee, may be waived for applicants with need, free for online applicants. Admission notification on a rolling basis beginning on or about 10/31. Must reply by May 1 or within 4 week(s) if notified thereafter. **Financial aid:** Priority date 4/1; no closing date. FAFSA required. Applicants notified on a rolling basis starting 2/1; must reply by 5/1 or within 2 week(s) of notification.

**Academics.** Students complete 500-hour employment program related to major. **Special study options:** Accelerated study, combined bachelor's/graduate degree, distance learning, double major, dual enrollment of high school students, honors, independent study, internships, study abroad, teacher certification program, weekend college. **Credit/placement by examination:** AP, CLEP, institutional tests. Credit for 5 courses may be granted through examination. **Support services:** Learning center, pre-admission summer program, reduced course load, remedial instruction, study skills assistance, tutoring, writing center.

**Majors. Agriculture:** Agribusiness operations, agronomy, animal sciences, crop production, dairy, food science, horticultural science, ornamental horticulture, turf management. **Biology:** General, zoology. **Business:** Accounting, business admin, management information systems, marketing. **Computer sciences:** General. **Conservation:** Wildlife. **Education:** Secondary. **Math:** General. **Physical sciences:** Chemistry. **Protective services:** Law enforcement admin. **Psychology:** Counseling.

**Most popular majors.** Agriculture 46%, biology 12%, business/marketing 18%, education 6%, natural resources/environmental science 8%.

**Computing on campus.** 150 workstations in dormitories, library, computer center, student center. Dormitories wired for high-speed internet access and linked to campus network. Online library, helpline, repair service, wireless network available.

**Student life. Freshman orientation:** Mandatory. **Housing:** Guaranteed on-campus for freshmen. Coed dorms, single-sex dorms available. $200 fully refundable deposit, deadline 5/1. **Activities:** Concert band, choral groups, drama, literary magazine, music ensembles, radio station, student government, student newspaper, Intervarsity Christian Fellowship, Hillel, Students for Diversity, Lions Club, Alpha Phi Omega, Habitat for Humanity, Project EARTH, Students in Free Enterprise, Animal Lifeline, Positive Awareness of Wildlife and Zoos.

**Athletics.** NCAA. **Intercollegiate:** Baseball M, basketball, cheerleading M, cross-country, equestrian, field hockey W, football (tackle) M, golf M, soccer, softball W, track and field, volleyball W, wrestling M. **Intramural:** Basketball, equestrian, football (tackle) M, softball, volleyball. **Team name:** Aggies.

**Student services.** Adult student services, career counseling, student employment services, health services, personal counseling, placement for graduates. **Physically disabled:** Services for visually, speech, hearing impaired.

**Contact.** E-mail: admitme@delval.edu
Phone: (215) 489-2211 Toll-free number: (800) 233-5825
Fax: (215) 230-2968
Stephen Zenko, Director of Admissions, Delaware Valley College, 700 East Butler Avenue, Doylestown, PA 18901-2697

---

## DeSales University
**Center Valley, Pennsylvania**
www.desales.edu

CB member
CB code: 2021

- Private 4-year university affiliated with Roman Catholic Church
- Residential campus in small town

- 2,333 degree-seeking undergraduates: 26% part-time, 59% women
- 817 degree-seeking graduate students
- 73% of applicants admitted
- SAT or ACT required
- 69% graduate within 6 years

**General.** Founded in 1964. Regionally accredited. **Degrees:** 518 bachelor's awarded; master's offered. **ROTC:** Army. **Location:** 7 miles from Allentown, 50 miles from Philadelphia. **Calendar:** Semester, limited summer session. **Full-time faculty:** 104 total; 69% have terminal degrees, 5% minority, 49% women. **Part-time faculty:** 184 total; 47% women. **Class size:** 40% < 20, 56% 20-39, 3% 40-49, 2% 50-99.

**Freshman class profile.** 1,998 applied, 1,465 admitted, 378 enrolled.

| Mid 50% test scores | | Rank in top quarter: | 49% |
|---|---|---|---|
| SAT critical reading: | 490-600 | Rank in top tenth: | 22% |
| SAT math: | 490-600 | Return as sophomores: | 82% |
| SAT writing: | 480-590 | Out-of-state: | 36% |
| ACT composite: | 19-25 | Live on campus: | 90% |

**Basis for selection.** High school achievement most important. Test scores and recommendations also considered. Essay, interview recommended for all; audition required for dance, theater programs. Interview required for physician assistant program.

**High school preparation.** College-preparatory program required. 16 units required; 18 recommended. Required and recommended units include English 4, mathematics 3-4, social studies 3-4, science 2 (laboratory 2) and foreign language 2. Biology, chemistry, 3 math recommended for biology major. 3 math, including 2 algebra, recommended for business major. Chemistry, physics, 3 math recommended for chemistry major. Biology, chemistry, physics, 2 math recommended for nursing major. 2 biology, chemistry, or physics, and 3 math recommended for pre-med major. 4 math recommended for math major.

**2009-2010 Annual costs.** Tuition/fees: $27,000. Room/board: $9,750. Books/supplies: $1,200. Personal expenses: $3,804.

**2009-2010 Financial aid. Need-based:** 347 full-time freshmen applied for aid; 294 were judged to have need; 294 of these received aid. Average need met was 70%. Average scholarship/grant was $15,482; average loan $3,352. 55% of total undergraduate aid awarded as scholarships/grants, 45% as loans/jobs. **Non-need-based:** Awarded to 1,118 full-time undergraduates, including 302 freshmen. Scholarships awarded for academics, leadership, music/drama.

**Application procedures. Admission:** Priority date 3/1; deadline 8/1. $30 fee, may be waived for applicants with need. Admission notification on a rolling basis. Must reply by May 1 or within 2 week(s) if notified thereafter. **Financial aid:** Priority date 2/1, closing date 5/1. FAFSA required. Applicants notified on a rolling basis starting 2/15; must reply by 5/1 or within 2 week(s) of notification.

**Academics. Special study options:** Accelerated study, combined bachelor's/graduate degree, cross-registration, distance learning, double major, dual enrollment of high school students, ESL, honors, independent study, internships, liberal arts/career combination, semester at sea, study abroad, teacher certification program, weekend college. BS in medical studies, MS in physician assistant studies; cross-registration at consortium schools: Cedar Crest, Moravian, Muhlenberg, Lafayette, Lehigh. **Credit/placement by examination:** AP, CLEP, institutional tests. 24 credit hours maximum toward bachelor's degree. For AP credit for Physics B must complete lab component. Must submit research paper for CLEP English Composition with Essay to obtain 6 credits. **Support services:** Learning center, pre-admission summer program, reduced course load, study skills assistance, tutoring.

**Majors. Biology:** General, biochemistry. **Business:** General, accounting, business admin, e-commerce, finance, human resources, management information systems, management science, marketing. **Communications:** General. **Computer sciences:** General, computer science. **Education:** Elementary, special. **Foreign languages:** Spanish. **Health:** Clinical lab science, nursing (RN). **History:** General. **Legal studies:** General. **Liberal arts:** Arts/sciences. **Math:** General. **Parks/recreation:** Exercise sciences, sports admin. **Philosophy/religion:** Philosophy. **Physical sciences:** Chemistry. **Protective services:** Criminal justice. **Psychology:** General. **Social sciences:** Political science. **Theology:** Theology. **Visual/performing arts:** Dance, dramatic, film/cinema.

**Most popular majors.** Business/marketing 23%, education 8%, health sciences 19%, parks/recreation 6%, security/protective services 8%, visual/performing arts 9%.

**Computing on campus.** 200 workstations in library, computer center, student center. Dormitories wired for high-speed internet access and linked to campus network. Commuter students can connect to campus network.

Online course registration, online library, helpline, student web hosting, wireless network available.

**Student life. Freshman orientation:** Mandatory, $200 fee. Preregistration for classes offered. One-day academic orientation in May or June; 4-day social and academic orientation in August. **Policies:** Students under 21 cannot possess or be in presence of alcohol. Access to dorm rooms of opposite sex restricted during certain hours. **Housing:** Guaranteed on-campus for all undergraduates. Single-sex dorms, wellness housing available. Town houses for upperclassmen, common-interest housing available. **Activities:** Pep band, campus ministries, choral groups, dance, drama, film society, international student organizations, literary magazine, music ensembles, Model UN, musical theater, radio station, student government, student newspaper, TV station, pro-life club, accounting and finance club, Habitat For Humanity, Spanish Alliance, Best Buddies, Esto Vir, Lion's Club, natural science club.

**Athletics.** NCAA. **Intercollegiate:** Baseball M, basketball, cross-country, field hockey W, golf M, lacrosse M, soccer, softball W, tennis, track and field, volleyball W. **Intramural:** Basketball, football (non-tackle), soccer, softball, volleyball. **Team name:** Bulldogs.

**Student services.** Adult student services, alcohol/substance abuse counseling, chaplain/spiritual director, career counseling, services for economically disadvantaged, student employment services, financial aid counseling, health services, minority student services, personal counseling, placement for graduates, veterans' counselor.

**Contact.** E-mail: admiss@desales.edu
Phone: (610) 282-4443 Toll-free number: (877) 433-7253
Fax: (610) 282-0131
Derrick Wetzell, Director of Admissions, DeSales University, 2755 Station Avenue, Center Valley, PA 18034-9568

## DeVry University: Fort Washington
**Fort Washington, Pennsylvania**
www.devry.edu
**CB code: 3866**

- For-profit 4-year university
- Commuter campus in large town
- 891 degree-seeking undergraduates: 51% part-time, 32% women, 33% African American, 4% Asian American, 8% Hispanic American, 1% Native American
- 157 degree-seeking graduate students
- Interview required
- 31% graduate within 6 years

**General. Degrees:** 91 bachelor's, 23 associate awarded; master's offered. **Location:** 35 miles from Philadelphia. **Calendar:** Semester, extensive summer session. **Full-time faculty:** 24 total; 33% minority, 33% women. **Part-time faculty:** 131 total; 11% minority, 41% women.

**Freshman class profile.** 196 enrolled.

**Basis for selection.** Applicants must have high school diploma or equivalent, or a degree from accredited postsecondary institution, demonstrate proficiency in basic college-level skills through SAT or ACT scores or institution-administered placement exams, and be at least 17 years of age on the first day of classes. New students may enter at beginning of any semester. CPT also accepted.

**High school preparation.** College-preparatory program recommended. Math unit must be algebra or higher.

**2009-2010 Annual costs.** Tuition/fees: $14,800. Books/supplies: $1,310. Personal expenses: $3,270.

**2008-2009 Financial aid.** All financial aid based on need.

**Application procedures. Admission:** No deadline. $50 fee. Admission notification on a rolling basis. **Financial aid:** No deadline. FAFSA required. Applicants notified on a rolling basis.

**Academics. Special study options:** Accelerated study, distance learning. **Credit/placement by examination:** CLEP. **Support services:** Learning center, remedial instruction, tutoring.

**Majors. Business:** Business admin. **Computer sciences:** Networking, systems analysis. **Engineering:** Software. **Engineering technology:** Biomedical, computer, electrical. **Other:** Technical management.

**Most popular majors.** Business/marketing 63%, computer/information sciences 28%, engineering/engineering technologies 10%.

**Computing on campus.** 407 workstations in library, computer center. Online course registration, online library, helpline available.

**Student life. Freshman orientation:** Mandatory. **Activities:** Campus Crusade for Christ, electronic gamers club, creative arts club.

**Athletics. Intramural:** Volleyball.

**Student services.** Career counseling, student employment services, financial aid counseling, placement for graduates, veterans' counselor. **Physically disabled:** Services for visually, hearing impaired.

**Contact.** E-mail: admissions@phi.devry.edu
Phone: (215) 591-5701 Toll-free number: (866) 303-3879
Fax: (215) 591-5745
Steve Cohen, Director of Admission, DeVry University: Fort Washington, 1140 Virginia Drive, Fort Washington, PA 19034-3204

## Dickinson College

**Carlisle, Pennsylvania**     **CB member**
**www.dickinson.edu**     **CB code: 2186**

- Private 4-year liberal arts college
- Residential campus in large town
- 2,330 degree-seeking undergraduates: 56% women, 4% African American, 4% Asian American, 5% Hispanic American, 6% international
- 49% of applicants admitted
- Application essay required
- 84% graduate within 6 years; 38% enter graduate study

**General.** Founded in 1783. Regionally accredited. **Degrees:** 576 bachelor's awarded. **ROTC:** Army. **Location:** 100 miles from Philadelphia, 90 miles from Washington, DC. **Calendar:** Semester, limited summer session. **Full-time faculty:** 193 total; 93% have terminal degrees, 10% minority, 44% women. **Part-time faculty:** 44 total; 48% have terminal degrees, 4% minority, 54% women. **Class size:** 71% < 20, 28% 20-39, 1% 40-49. **Special facilities:** Arts center, planetarium and multiple telescope observatory, intercontinental satellite communications for study-abroad programs, study of contemporary issues center.

**Freshman class profile.** 5,026 applied, 2,459 admitted, 581 enrolled.

| Mid 50% test scores | | Rank in top tenth: | 37% |
|---|---|---|---|
| SAT critical reading: | 600-690 | End year in good standing: | 99% |
| SAT math: | 590-680 | Return as sophomores: | 92% |
| SAT writing: | 590-690 | Out-of-state: | 77% |
| ACT composite: | 26-30 | Live on campus: | 100% |
| Rank in top quarter: | 71% | International: | 6% |

**Basis for selection.** Academic potential as shown by school achievement record most important. Extracurricular activities very important. Counselor recommendation required. Motivation, personal character considered. Special consideration given to applicants of color. Preference given to academically qualified children of alumni if they satisfy above criteria. Standardized tests optional. SAT or ACT recommended. Interview recommended.

**High school preparation.** College-preparatory program recommended. 16 units required. Required and recommended units include English 4, mathematics 3, social studies 2, science 3 (laboratory 2), foreign language 2-3 and academic electives 2.

**2010-2011 Annual costs.** Tuition/fees: $41,545. Room/board: $10,430. Books/supplies: $1,000. Personal expenses: $1,200.

**2009-2010 Financial aid. Need-based:** 393 full-time freshmen applied for aid; 323 were judged to have need; 320 of these received aid. Average need met was 97%. Average scholarship/grant was $28,583; average loan $4,026. 80% of total undergraduate aid awarded as scholarships/grants, 20% as loans/jobs. **Non-need-based:** Awarded to 250 full-time undergraduates, including 68 freshmen. Scholarships awarded for academics, leadership, ROTC.

**Application procedures. Admission:** Closing date 2/1 (postmark date). $65 fee, may be waived for applicants with need. Admission notification 3/31. Must reply by May 1 or within 2 week(s) if notified thereafter. **Financial aid:** Priority date 11/15, closing date 2/1. FAFSA, CSS PROFILE required. Applicants notified by 3/20; must reply by 5/1 or within 2 week(s) of notification.

**Academics.** Certificates in interdepartmental programs offered in Latin American studies in conjunction with bachelor's degree. Prebusiness, prelaw and premedical preparation available in conjunction with majors listed. **Special study options:** Accelerated study, combined bachelor's/graduate

degree, cross-registration, double major, ESL, exchange student, independent study, internships, liberal arts/career combination, student-designed major, study abroad, teacher certification program, Washington semester. 3-2 engineering programs with University of Pennsylvania, Case Western Reserve University, Rensselaer Polytechnic Institute; 3-3 law degree with Dickinson School of Law of Penn State University. **Credit/placement by examination:** AP, CLEP, IB, institutional tests. **Support services:** Tutoring, writing center.

**Majors. Area/ethnic studies:** African, American, East Asian, Italian, Near/Middle Eastern, women's. **Biology:** General, biochemistry. **Business:** International. **Computer sciences:** General. **Conservation:** Environmental science, environmental studies. **Foreign languages:** Classics, French, German, Italian, Russian, Spanish. **History:** General. **Interdisciplinary:** Medieval/Renaissance, neuroscience. **Legal studies:** General, prelaw. **Math:** General. **Philosophy/religion:** Judaic, philosophy, religion. **Physical sciences:** Chemistry, geology, physics. **Psychology:** General. **Public administration:** Policy analysis. **Social sciences:** Anthropology, archaeology, economics, international relations, political science, sociology. **Visual/performing arts:** Dramatic, studio arts. **Other:** Dance and music.

**Most popular majors.** Area/ethnic studies 7%, biology 7%, business/marketing 12%, English 6%, foreign language 8%, psychology 6%, social sciences 28%.

**Computing on campus.** 661 workstations in dormitories, library, computer center, student center. Dormitories wired for high-speed internet access and linked to campus network. Commuter students can connect to campus network. Online course registration, online library, helpline, repair service, wireless network available.

**Student life. Freshman orientation:** Mandatory. Preregistration for classes offered. **Housing:** Guaranteed on-campus for all undergraduates. Coed dorms, special housing for disabled, apartments, fraternity/sorority housing available. **Activities:** Bands, choral groups, dance, drama, film society, international student organizations, literary magazine, music ensembles, Model UN, musical theater, radio station, student government, student newspaper, symphony orchestra, public affairs, social service, religious, multicultural, College Democrats, Young Republicans, debate club.

**Athletics.** NCAA. **Intercollegiate:** Baseball M, basketball, cross-country, field hockey W, football (tackle) M, golf, lacrosse, soccer, softball W, swimming, tennis, track and field, volleyball W. **Intramural:** Badminton, basketball M, bowling M, field hockey W, football (non-tackle) M, football (tackle) M, golf, racquetball, soccer, softball, squash, table tennis, tennis, volleyball M. **Team name:** Red Devils.

**Student services.** Adult student services, alcohol/substance abuse counseling, career counseling, student employment services, financial aid counseling, health services, minority student services, on-campus daycare, personal counseling, placement for graduates. **Physically disabled:** Services for visually, speech, hearing impaired.

**Contact.** E-mail: admit@dickinson.edu
Phone: (717) 245-1231 Toll-free number: (800) 644-1773
Fax: (717) 245-1442
Stephanie Balmer, Vice President for Enrollment and Communications, Dickinson College, PO Box 1773, Carlisle, PA 17013-2896

## Drexel University

**Philadelphia, Pennsylvania**     **CB member**
**www.drexel.edu**     **CB code: 2194**

- Private 5-year university
- Commuter campus in very large city
- 13,069 degree-seeking undergraduates: 18% part-time, 45% women, 8% African American, 12% Asian American, 3% Hispanic American, 7% international
- 8,885 degree-seeking graduate students
- 55% of applicants admitted
- SAT or ACT (ACT writing optional) required

**General.** Founded in 1891. Regionally accredited. Most undergraduate programs require up to 18 months work experience within 5-year program of study. **Degrees:** 2,745 bachelor's, 20 associate awarded; master's, doctoral, professional offered. **ROTC:** Army, Naval, Air Force. **Calendar:** Quarter, extensive summer session. **Full-time faculty:** 928 total; 81% have terminal degrees, 17% minority, 42% women. **Part-time faculty:** 571 total; 81% have terminal degrees, 11% minority, 43% women. **Class size:** 51% < 20, 40% 20-39, 3% 40-49, 5% 50-99, 2% >100. **Special facilities:** Art collection, observatory, rifle range.

**Freshman class profile.** 39,827 applied, 21,729 admitted, 2,346 enrolled.

| Mid 50% test scores | | Rank in top tenth: | 30% |
|---|---|---|---|
| SAT critical reading: | 540-630 | Return as sophomores: | 83% |
| SAT math: | 570-670 | Out-of-state: | 49% |
| SAT writing: | 520-630 | Live on campus: | 87% |
| ACT composite: | 23-28 | International: | 10% |
| Rank in top quarter: | 63% | | |

**Basis for selection.** Academic average, counselor's recommendation and test scores most important, followed by class rank, school, community and church activities. Employment also considered. Essay required for most majors for media arts and design programs. Portfolio required for graphic design, music industry, photography and fashion design. Audition required for dance.

**High school preparation.** College-preparatory program required. Required and recommended units include mathematics 3, science 1 (laboratory 1) and foreign language 1. Engineering applicants required to have 4 units math (including algebra I and II, geometry, trigonometry, and pre-calculus) and 2 units lab science (including chemistry and physics). Science applicants required to have 4 units math (including algebra I and II, geometry, and trigonometry) and 2 units lab science (including biology, chemistry, or physics). Most other applicants must have algebra I and II and geometry as required math units and one lab science.

**2010-2011 Annual costs.** Tuition/fees: $33,005. Room/board: $13,125. Books/supplies: $1,950. Personal expenses: $3,000.

**2009-2010 Financial aid. Non-need-based:** Scholarships awarded for academics, alumni affiliation, art, athletics, leadership, music/drama, ROTC.

**Application procedures. Admission:** Closing date 3/1 (postmark date). $75 fee, may be waived for applicants with need, free for online applicants. Admission notification on a rolling basis. Must reply by May 1 or within 2 week(s) if notified thereafter. **Financial aid:** Closing date 3/1. FAFSA required. Applicants notified on a rolling basis starting 3/15.

**Academics. Special study options:** Accelerated study, combined bachelor's/graduate degree, cooperative education, distance learning, double major, dual enrollment of high school students, ESL, honors, independent study, internships, semester at sea, study abroad, teacher certification program, weekend college. 3-3 programs in engineering with Lincoln University and Indiana University of Pennsylvania. **Credit/placement by examination:** AP, CLEP, IB, institutional tests. 30 credit hours maximum toward bachelor's degree. **Support services:** Learning center, pre-admission summer program, reduced course load, remedial instruction, study skills assistance, tutoring, writing center.

**Majors. Architecture:** Architecture. **Biology:** General. **Business:** General, hotel/motel admin, managerial economics. **Computer sciences:** Computer science, information systems, security, web page design. **Conservation:** Environmental science, environmental studies. **Engineering:** Architectural, biomedical, chemical, civil, computer, construction, electrical, environmental, industrial, materials, mechanical, software. **Engineering technology:** General. **Health:** Clinical lab assistant, health care admin, nursing (RN), physician assistant, substance abuse counseling. **History:** General. **Interdisciplinary:** Biological/physical sciences, nutrition sciences. **Liberal arts:** Humanities. **Math:** General. **Parks/recreation:** Sports admin. **Personal/culinary services:** Chef training, restaurant/catering. **Physical sciences:** Chemistry, physics. **Protective services:** Law enforcement admin. **Psychology:** General. **Social sciences:** Anthropology, international relations, political science, sociology. **Visual/performing arts:** Cinematography, dance, design, fashion design, graphic design, interior design, photography, play/screenwriting, theater arts management. **Other:** Communications and applied technology, Design and merchandising.

**Most popular majors.** Business/marketing 23%, computer/information sciences 6%, engineering/engineering technologies 22%, health sciences 18%, visual/performing arts 10%.

**Computing on campus.** PC or laptop required. 610 workstations in dormitories, library, computer center, student center. Dormitories wired for high-speed internet access and linked to campus network. Commuter students can connect to campus network. Online course registration, online library, helpline, repair service, student web hosting, wireless network available.

**Student life. Freshman orientation:** Available. Preregistration for classes offered. 2-day overnight sessions held in July; 3-day program prior to start of classes. **Housing:** Guaranteed on-campus for freshmen. Coed dorms, special housing for disabled, apartments, fraternity/sorority housing available. $200 nonrefundable deposit, deadline 6/15. Freshmen required to live on campus unless living with parents. **Activities:** Bands, campus ministries, choral groups, dance, drama, film society, literary magazine, music ensembles, musical theater, radio station, student government, student newspaper, TV station, Newman Center, Hillel, Alpha Phi Omega, NAACP, Eye Openers, Disciples in Deed, Drexel Christian Fellowship, Jewish Heritage Program.

**Athletics.** NCAA. **Intercollegiate:** Basketball, cheerleading, diving, field hockey W, golf M, lacrosse, rowing (crew), soccer, softball W, swimming, tennis, wrestling M. **Intramural:** Badminton, basketball, football (non-tackle), soccer, softball, squash, table tennis, tennis, volleyball. **Team name:** Dragons.

**Student services.** Adult student services, career counseling, student employment services, financial aid counseling, health services, minority student services, personal counseling, placement for graduates. **Physically disabled:** Services for visually, speech, hearing impaired.

**Contact.** E-mail: enroll@drexel.edu
Phone: (215) 895-2400 Toll-free number: (800) 237-3935
Fax: (215) 895-5939
Joan McDonald, Senior Vice President of Enrollment Management, Drexel University, 3141 Chestnut Street, Philadelphia, PA 19104-2875

---

**Duquesne University**
Pittsburgh, Pennsylvania     CB member
www.duq.edu     CB code: 2196

- Private 4-year university affiliated with Roman Catholic Church
- Residential campus in large city
- 5,735 degree-seeking undergraduates: 3% part-time, 57% women, 4% African American, 2% Asian American, 2% Hispanic American, 2% international
- 4,503 graduate students
- 76% of applicants admitted
- SAT or ACT with writing, application essay required
- 72% graduate within 6 years; 37% enter graduate study

**General.** Founded in 1878. Regionally accredited. **Degrees:** 1,201 bachelor's awarded; master's, doctoral, professional offered. **ROTC:** Army, Naval, Air Force. **Calendar:** Semester, extensive summer session. **Full-time faculty:** 463 total; 85% have terminal degrees, 7% minority, 41% women. **Part-time faculty:** 483 total; 5% minority, 48% women. **Class size:** 48% < 20, 41% 20-39, 6% 40-49, 3% 50-99, 2% >100. **Special facilities:** Recording complex, recital hall, music electronic studio, keyboard lab, music technology center, music control lab, academic research center for pharmaceutical information, pharmaceutical technology center, pharmacy manufacturing lab, phenomenology center, health sciences cadaver lab, nurse managed wellness center, business school investment center, center for nursing research, confocal microscopes, mass spectrometry facilities, 400- and 500-MHZ NMR spectrometers, electron microscopes, x-ray diffraction spectrometers, research center for pharmacy care - pharmacy wellness and disease management program, patient simulation lab, digital media center, center for health care diversity.

**Freshman class profile.** 6,626 applied, 5,054 admitted, 1,432 enrolled.

| Mid 50% test scores | | Rank in top quarter: | 55% |
|---|---|---|---|
| SAT critical reading: | 510-600 | Rank in top tenth: | 24% |
| SAT math: | 520-610 | End year in good standing: | 98% |
| SAT writing: | 510-600 | Return as sophomores: | 86% |
| ACT composite: | 23-28 | Out-of-state: | 26% |
| GPA 3.75 or higher: | 39% | Live on campus: | 91% |
| GPA 3.50-3.74: | 21% | International: | 1% |
| GPA 3.0-3.49: | 31% | Fraternities: | 11% |
| GPA 2.0-2.99: | 9% | Sororities: | 15% |

**Basis for selection.** School achievement record, standardized test scores, recommendations, essay very important. Decisions based on overall GPA, standardized test scores, curriculum, volunteer activities, and leadership roles. Interview recommended for all; audition required for music program. **Homeschooled:** Transcript of courses and grades required. **Learning Disabled:** Documentation of learning disabilities may be required.

**High school preparation.** College-preparatory program required. 16 units recommended. Recommended units include English 4, mathematics 2, social studies 2, science 2, foreign language 2 and academic electives 4.

**2009-2010 Annual costs.** Tuition/fees: $26,468. Room/board: $9,200. Books/supplies: $1,000. Personal expenses: $600.

**2008-2009 Financial aid. Need-based:** 1,278 full-time freshmen applied for aid; 976 were judged to have need; 976 of these received aid. Average need met was 91%. Average scholarship/grant was $14,011; average loan $4,160. 47% of total undergraduate aid awarded as scholarships/

grants, 53% as loans/jobs. **Non-need-based:** Awarded to 1,668 full-time undergraduates, including 534 freshmen. Scholarships awarded for academics, athletics, music/drama, ROTC.

**Application procedures. Admission:** Priority date 11/1; deadline 7/1 (receipt date). $50 fee, may be waived for applicants with need. Admission notification on a rolling basis beginning on or about 9/15. Must reply by May 1 or within 2 week(s) if notified thereafter. **Financial aid:** Closing date 5/1. FAFSA, institutional form required. Applicants notified on a rolling basis starting 3/1; must reply by 5/1 or within 3 week(s) of notification.

**Academics. Special study options:** Accelerated study, combined bachelor's/graduate degree, cross-registration, distance learning, double major, dual enrollment of high school students, ESL, exchange student, external degree, honors, independent study, internships, liberal arts/career combination, semester at sea, student-designed major, study abroad, teacher certification program, Washington semester, weekend college. **Credit/placement by examination:** AP, CLEP, IB, institutional tests. 60 credit hours maximum toward bachelor's degree. **Support services:** Learning center, pre-admission summer program, reduced course load, remedial instruction, study skills assistance, tutoring, writing center.

**Honors college/program.** 1300 SAT (exclusive of Writing) or ACT equivalent, 3.5 GPA and ranking in the top 10% of graduating class (if high school ranks seniors). Other well qualified students may apply. Approximately 100 incoming freshmen admitted each year.

**Majors. Biology:** General, biochemistry. **Business:** General, accounting, business admin, communications, entrepreneurial studies, finance, international, investments/securities, logistics, management information systems, management science, managerial economics, marketing, nonprofit/public. **Communications:** General, journalism, public relations. **Computer sciences:** Computer science, programming, web page design, webmaster. **Conservation:** Environmental science. **Education:** General, early childhood, elementary, English, Latin, mathematics, multi-level teacher, music, secondary, social studies, Spanish, special. **Foreign languages:** General, ancient Greek, classics, Latin, Spanish. **Health:** Athletic training, health care admin, music therapy, nursing (RN), premedicine. **History:** General. **Liberal arts:** Arts/sciences. **Math:** General. **Philosophy/religion:** Philosophy. **Physical sciences:** Chemistry, physics. **Protective services:** Security management. **Psychology:** General. **Social sciences:** Economics, international relations, political science, sociology. **Theology:** Theology. **Visual/performing arts:** Art history/conservation, dramatic, music performance. **Other:** Computer software and media applications, Public relations, advertising, and applied communications.

**Most popular majors.** Business/marketing 25%, communications/journalism 7%, education 9%, health sciences 22%.

**Computing on campus.** 850 workstations in dormitories, library, computer center, student center. Dormitories wired for high-speed internet access and linked to campus network. Commuter students can connect to campus network. Online course registration, online library, helpline, repair service, student web hosting, wireless network available.

**Student life. Freshman orientation:** Mandatory, $150 fee. Preregistration for classes offered. 5-day program in August; includes volunteer opportunities. **Policies:** All recognized student organizations must have faculty or staff adviser, have purpose consistent with university mission, and abide by Code of Rights, Responsibilities and Conduct. **Housing:** Guaranteed on-campus for freshmen. Coed dorms, special housing for disabled, apartments, fraternity/sorority housing, wellness housing available. $300 nonrefundable deposit, deadline 5/1. Club wings available, fraternity and sorority wings available, and international wings available. **Activities:** Bands, campus ministries, choral groups, dance, drama, film society, international student organizations, literary magazine, music ensembles, Model UN, musical theater, opera, radio station, student government, student newspaper, symphony orchestra, TV station, Black student union, Duquesne University Volunteers, Latin American student association, Evergreen, Indian student association, St. Vincent de Paul Society, College Republicans, Asian student association, Young Democrats.

**Athletics.** NCAA. **Intercollegiate:** Baseball M, basketball, cheerleading, cross-country, football (tackle) M, golf M, lacrosse W, rowing (crew) W, soccer, swimming, tennis, track and field, volleyball W, wrestling M. **Intramural:** Basketball, football (non-tackle), racquetball, soccer, swimming, volleyball. **Team name:** Dukes.

**Student services.** Adult student services, alcohol/substance abuse counseling, chaplain/spiritual director, career counseling, services for economically disadvantaged, student employment services, financial aid counseling, health services, minority student services, on-campus daycare, personal counseling, placement for graduates, veterans' counselor, women's services. **Physically disabled:** Services for visually, speech, hearing impaired.

**Contact.** E-mail: admissions@duq.edu
Phone: (412) 396-6222 Toll-free number: (800) 456-0590
Fax: (412) 396-6223
Paul-James Cukanna, Associate Vice President, Enrollment Management, Duquesne University, 600 Forbes Avenue, Administration Building, Pittsburgh, PA 15282-0201

---

## East Stroudsburg University of Pennsylvania

**East Stroudsburg, Pennsylvania**
**www4.esu.edu**

CB member
CB code: 2650

- Public 4-year university
- Residential campus in large town
- 6,288 degree-seeking undergraduates: 8% part-time, 54% women, 6% African American, 2% Asian American, 6% Hispanic American, 1% international
- 943 degree-seeking graduate students
- SAT or ACT with writing required
- 59% graduate within 6 years

**General.** Founded in 1893. Regionally accredited. **Degrees:** 1,274 bachelor's, 1 associate awarded; master's offered. **ROTC:** Army, Air Force. **Location:** 40 miles from Allentown and Scranton. **Calendar:** Semester, extensive summer session. **Full-time faculty:** 311 total; 76% have terminal degrees, 13% minority, 47% women. **Part-time faculty:** 55 total; 29% have terminal degrees, 9% minority, 66% women. **Class size:** 25% < 20, 55% 20-39, 18% 40-49, 2% 50-99, less than 1% >100. **Special facilities:** 30-acre ecological studies area, business accelerator program.

**Freshman class profile.** 1,358 enrolled.

| Mid 50% test scores | | Rank in top tenth: | 6% |
|---|---|---|---|
| SAT critical reading: | 440-520 | Return as sophomores: | 77% |
| SAT math: | 450-540 | Out-of-state: | 32% |
| SAT writing: | 430-520 | Live on campus: | 82% |
| Rank in top quarter: | 27% | International: | 1% |

**Basis for selection.** Academic achievement primary factor in selection process. Whole-person assessment also used, taking into account school and community activities, achievements and aspirations. SAT recommended.

**High school preparation.** College-preparatory program recommended. 21 units recommended. Recommended units include English 4, mathematics 3, social studies 3, science 3 (laboratory 2) and foreign language 3.

**2009-2010 Annual costs.** Tuition/fees: $7,394; $15,726 out-of-state. Tuition for incoming out of state residents who are high achieving science and technology majors (biology, chemistry, computer science, mathematics, and physics) is $8,332. Room/board: $6,418. Books/supplies: $1,000. Personal expenses: $1,951.

**2008-2009 Financial aid. Need-based:** 1,045 full-time freshmen applied for aid; 725 were judged to have need; 599 of these received aid. Average need met was 80%. Average scholarship/grant was $4,497; average loan $3,334. 41% of total undergraduate aid awarded as scholarships/grants, 59% as loans/jobs. **Non-need-based:** Awarded to 1,391 full-time undergraduates, including 387 freshmen. Scholarships awarded for academics, alumni affiliation, art, athletics, leadership, minority status, music/drama, religious affiliation, state residency.

**Application procedures. Admission:** Priority date 3/1; deadline 4/1 (postmark date). $35 fee, may be waived for applicants with need. Admission notification on a rolling basis beginning on or about 12/1. **Financial aid:** Closing date 3/1. FAFSA required. Applicants notified by 4/1; must reply by 5/1.

**Academics. Special study options:** Accelerated study, combined bachelor's/graduate degree, cross-registration, distance learning, double major, dual enrollment of high school students, exchange student, honors, independent study, internships, student-designed major, study abroad, teacher certification program. **Credit/placement by examination:** AP, CLEP, SAT, ACT, institutional tests. 24 credit hours maximum toward bachelor's degree. **Support services:** Learning center, pre-admission summer program, reduced course load, remedial instruction, study skills assistance, tutoring, writing center.

**Majors. Biology:** General, biochemistry, biotechnology, ecology, marine. **Business:** Business admin, hospitality admin. **Communications:** General. **Communications technology:** General. **Computer sciences:** General, security. **Education:** Early childhood, elementary, health, physical, special. **Foreign languages:** French, Spanish. **Health:** Athletic training, audiology/speech pathology, clinical lab science, health services admin, nursing (RN).

**History:** General. **Interdisciplinary:** Biological/physical sciences. **Liberal arts:** Arts/sciences, humanities. **Math:** General. **Parks/recreation:** Exercise sciences, facilities management. **Philosophy/religion:** Philosophy. **Physical sciences:** General, chemistry, geology, physics. **Psychology:** General. **Social sciences:** General, economics, geography, political science, sociology. **Visual/performing arts:** General, dramatic, graphic design.

**Most popular majors.** Biology 7%, business/marketing 14%, education 22%, health sciences 9%, parks/recreation 10%, psychology 7%, social sciences 11%.

**Computing on campus.** 397 workstations in dormitories, library, computer center, student center. Dormitories linked to campus network. Online course registration, helpline, wireless network available.

**Student life. Freshman orientation:** Available, $65 fee. Preregistration for classes offered. 2-day event during summer with joint and separate sessions for parents. **Housing:** Guaranteed on-campus for freshmen. Coed dorms, single-sex dorms, special housing for disabled, apartments, wellness housing available. $150 nonrefundable deposit. **Activities:** Bands, campus ministries, choral groups, dance, drama, literary magazine, music ensembles, musical theater, radio station, student government, student newspaper, symphony orchestra, Latin American Students Association, Campus Democrats, Young Republicans, African American Student Alliance, Fellowship of Christian Athletes, Newman Club, Women for Awareness.

**Athletics.** NCAA. **Intercollegiate:** Baseball M, basketball, cross-country, field hockey W, football (tackle) M, lacrosse W, soccer, softball W, swimming W, tennis, track and field, wrestling M. **Intramural:** Badminton, basketball, football (non-tackle), racquetball, soccer, softball, tennis, water polo. **Team name:** Warriors.

**Student services.** Adult student services, chaplain/spiritual director, career counseling, student employment services, financial aid counseling, health services, minority student services, on-campus daycare, personal counseling, placement for graduates, veterans' counselor, women's services. **Physically disabled:** Services for visually, speech, hearing impaired.

**Contact.** E-mail: undergrads@po-box.esu.edu
Phone: (570) 422-3542 Toll-free number: (877) 230-5547
Fax: (570) 422-3933
Jeff Jones, Director of Admissions, East Stroudsburg University of Pennsylvania, 200 Prospect Street, East Stroudsburg, PA 18301-2999

## Eastern University
### St. Davids, Pennsylvania
**www.eastern.edu** **CB code: 2220**

- Private 4-year university affiliated with American Baptist Churches in the USA
- Residential campus in small town
- 2,564 degree-seeking undergraduates: 14% part-time, 69% women, 21% African American, 2% Asian American, 11% Hispanic American, 1% international
- 1,618 graduate students
- 71% of applicants admitted
- SAT or ACT (ACT writing recommended), application essay required
- 64% graduate within 6 years

**General.** Founded in 1952. Regionally accredited. **Degrees:** 580 bachelor's, 75 associate awarded; master's, doctoral offered. **ROTC:** Army, Air Force. **Location:** 10 miles from Philadelphia. **Calendar:** Semester, limited summer session. **Full-time faculty:** 115 total; 86% have terminal degrees, 22% minority, 42% women. **Part-time faculty:** 275 total; 28% have terminal degrees, 21% minority, 48% women. **Class size:** 70% < 20, 29% 20-39, less than 1% 40-49, less than 1% 50-99, less than 1% >100. **Special facilities:** Planetarium, observatory.

**Freshman class profile.** 1,416 applied, 1,002 admitted, 408 enrolled.

| Mid 50% test scores | | | |
|---|---|---|---|
| SAT critical reading: | 480-600 | GPA 2.0-2.99: | 22% |
| SAT math: | 480-590 | Rank in top quarter: | 53% |
| SAT writing: | 480-590 | Rank in top tenth: | 21% |
| ACT composite: | 19-23 | Return as sophomores: | 74% |
| GPA 3.75 or higher: | 30% | Out-of-state: | 43% |
| GPA 3.50-3.74: | 16% | Live on campus: | 94% |
| GPA 3.0-3.49: | 31% | International: | 1% |

**Basis for selection.** SAT, GPA, and class rank most important. Interest in school mission, slope of grades, attendance, interviews also evaluated. Interview recommended.

**High school preparation.** College-preparatory program required. Recommended units include English 4, mathematics 3, social studies 2, science 3 and foreign language 3.

**2009-2010 Annual costs.** Tuition/fees: $23,820. Room/board: $8,870. Books/supplies: $1,000. Personal expenses: $1,900.

**Application procedures. Admission:** No deadline. $25 fee, may be waived for applicants with need. Admission notification on a rolling basis. **Financial aid:** No deadline. FAFSA, institutional form required. Applicants notified on a rolling basis starting 4/1.

**Academics. Special study options:** Accelerated study, cross-registration, double major, honors, independent study, student-designed major, study abroad, teacher certification program, Washington semester. **Credit/placement by examination:** AP, CLEP, IB, SAT, ACT. 30 credit hours maximum toward associate degree, 60 toward bachelor's. **Support services:** Pre-admission summer program, remedial instruction, study skills assistance, tutoring, writing center.

**Honors college/program.** Students must be in top 9% of class and have 1300 SAT (exclusive of Writing) or 30 ACT, or have extraordinary leadership abilities with significant academic achievements.

**Majors. Biology:** General, biochemistry. **Business:** Accounting/finance, business admin, entrepreneurial studies, international, marketing, nonprofit/public. **Communications:** General. **Conservation:** General. **Education:** Elementary. **Foreign languages:** Spanish. **Health:** Athletic training, nursing (RN). **History:** General. **Math:** General. **Parks/recreation:** Exercise sciences. **Physical sciences:** Chemistry. **Psychology:** General. **Public administration:** Social work. **Social sciences:** Political science, sociology. **Theology:** Bible, missionary, theology, youth ministry. **Visual/performing arts:** Dance. **Other:** Economic development.

**Most popular majors.** Business/marketing 29%, education 14%, health sciences 12%, social sciences 8%, theological studies 7%.

**Computing on campus.** 131 workstations in dormitories, library, computer center, student center. Dormitories wired for high-speed internet access and linked to campus network. Commuter students can connect to campus network. Repair service, wireless network available.

**Student life. Freshman orientation:** Mandatory. Preregistration for classes offered. Held 3 days before fall semester. **Policies:** Smoke-free campus. **Housing:** Coed dorms, apartments, wellness housing available. $150 nonrefundable deposit, deadline 8/1. Students required to live on campus unless they receive permission from Dean of Students Office. **Activities:** Bands, choral groups, dance, drama, literary magazine, music ensembles, musical theater, student government, student newspaper, black student league, Penn State Education Association, yacht club, gospel outreach, Fellowship of Christian Athletes, Habitat for Humanity, Evangelicals for Social Action, students organized against racism, prison ministry, Latinos Unidos.

**Athletics.** NCAA. **Intercollegiate:** Baseball M, basketball, cross-country W, field hockey W, golf, lacrosse, soccer, softball W, tennis, volleyball W. **Intramural:** Basketball, cheerleading, golf, soccer, tennis, volleyball. **Team name:** Eagles.

**Student services.** Adult student services, alcohol/substance abuse counseling, chaplain/spiritual director, career counseling, financial aid counseling, health services, legal services, minority student services, personal counseling, veterans' counselor, women's services. **Physically disabled:** Services for visually, speech, hearing impaired.

**Contact.** E-mail: ugadm@eastern.edu
Phone: (610) 341-5967 Toll-free number: (800) 452-0996
Fax: (610) 341-1723
Michael Dziedziak, Director of Admissions, Eastern University, 1300 Eagle Road, St. Davids, PA 19087-3696

## Edinboro University of Pennsylvania
### Edinboro, Pennsylvania
**www.edinboro.edu** **CB member** **CB code: 2651**

- Public 4-year university
- Commuter campus in small town
- 6,301 degree-seeking undergraduates: 10% part-time, 56% women, 9% African American, 1% Asian American, 2% Hispanic American, 1% international
- 1,518 degree-seeking graduate students
- 73% of applicants admitted
- 47% graduate within 6 years

**General.** Founded in 1857. Regionally accredited. Extensive programs and services for physically and learning disabled students available. Credit courses, continuing education, workshops, and seminars offered at Porreco Extension Center in Erie. **Degrees:** 991 bachelor's, 82 associate awarded; master's offered. **ROTC:** Army. **Location:** 18 miles from Erie. **Calendar:** Semester, extensive summer session. **Full-time faculty:** 346 total; 7% minority, 46% women. **Part-time faculty:** 63 total; 2% minority, 35% women. **Class size:** 29% < 20, 54% 20-39, 10% 40-49, 7% 50-99, less than 1% >100. **Special facilities:** Observatory, planetarium, natural wildlife museum, robotics laboratory, center for performing arts, speech and hearing clinic, Ft. LeBoeuf Museum.

**Freshman class profile.** 4,411 applied, 3,238 admitted, 1,440 enrolled.

| Mid 50% test scores | | | |
|---|---|---|---|
| SAT critical reading: | 420-520 | Rank in top tenth: | 5% |
| SAT math: | 410-520 | End year in good standing: | 87% |
| ACT composite: | 17-22 | Return as sophomores: | 75% |
| GPA 3.75 or higher: | 18% | Out-of-state: | 16% |
| GPA 3.50-3.74: | 14% | Live on campus: | 77% |
| GPA 3.0-3.49: | 30% | International: | 1% |
| GPA 2.0-2.99: | 36% | Fraternities: | 1% |
| Rank in top quarter: | 20% | Sororities: | 2% |

**Basis for selection.** High school curriculum, test scores, GPA, and class rank most important. Recommendations and activities record also reviewed. Interview and essay recommended; audition required for music program. **Homeschooled:** Transcript of courses and grades, interview, letter of recommendation (nonparent) required. Students out of high school less than two years also need test scores.

**High school preparation.** College-preparatory program recommended. 15 units recommended. Recommended units include English 4, mathematics 3, social studies 4, science 3, foreign language 2 and computer science 1.

**2009-2010 Annual costs.** Tuition/fees: $7,316; $10,094 out-of-state. Room/board: $7,430.

**2008-2009 Financial aid. Need-based:** 1,174 full-time freshmen applied for aid; 965 were judged to have need; 936 of these received aid. Average need met was 59%. Average scholarship/grant was $2,586; average loan $2,924. 48% of total undergraduate aid awarded as scholarships/grants, 52% as loans/jobs. **Non-need-based:** Awarded to 4,356 full-time undergraduates, including 1,014 freshmen. Scholarships awarded for academics, alumni affiliation, art, athletics, job skills, leadership, minority status, music/drama, religious affiliation, ROTC, state residency.

**Application procedures. Admission:** No deadline. $30 fee, may be waived for applicants with need. Admission notification on a rolling basis beginning on or about 9/15. Must reply by May 1 or within 4 week(s) if notified thereafter. **Financial aid:** Priority date 3/15, closing date 5/1. FAFSA required. Applicants notified on a rolling basis starting 3/22; must reply within 2 week(s) of notification.

**Academics.** 60 credits of general education electives required for bachelor's degree. Associate degree counseling, peer tutoring, peer mentors, academic advising center, and trial admissions program offered. **Special study options:** Combined bachelor's/graduate degree, cooperative education, cross-registration, distance learning, double major, dual enrollment of high school students, honors, independent study, internships, liberal arts/career combination, student-designed major, study abroad, teacher certification program. **Credit/placement by examination:** AP, CLEP, SAT, ACT, institutional tests. 30 credit hours maximum toward associate degree, 30 toward bachelor's. **Support services:** Learning center, pre-admission summer program, reduced course load, remedial instruction, study skills assistance, tutoring, writing center.

**Majors. Area/ethnic studies:** Latin American, women's. **Biology:** General. **Business:** Accounting, business admin, marketing, operations. **Communications:** General, broadcast journalism, journalism, media studies. **Computer sciences:** General. **Conservation:** Environmental science. **Education:** Elementary, special. **Foreign languages:** German, Spanish. **Health:** Clinical lab technology, communication disorders, nursing (RN), predental, premedicine, preveterinary. **History:** General. **Interdisciplinary:** Biological/physical sciences. **Liberal arts:** Arts/sciences, humanities. **Math:** General. **Parks/recreation:** Health/fitness, sports admin. **Philosophy/religion:** Philosophy. **Physical sciences:** Chemistry, geology, physics, planetary. **Protective services:** Criminal justice. **Psychology:** General. **Public administration:** Social work. **Social sciences:** General, anthropology, economics, geography, political science, sociology. **Visual/performing arts:** Art, art history/conservation, ceramics, dramatic, drawing, fiber arts, graphic design, painting, photography, printmaking, sculpture.

**Most popular majors.** Business/marketing 9%, communications/journalism 8%, education 11%, health sciences 10%, liberal arts 6%, psychology 6%, security/protective services 8%, social sciences 7%, visual/performing arts 15%.

**Computing on campus.** 1,055 workstations in dormitories, library, computer center, student center. Dormitories wired for high-speed internet access and linked to campus network. Commuter students can connect to campus network. Online course registration, online library, helpline, repair service, student web hosting, wireless network available.

**Student life. Freshman orientation:** Mandatory. Preregistration for classes offered. Summer and spring programs. **Policies:** Zero tolerance policy for alcohol and drugs on campus. **Housing:** Guaranteed on-campus for freshmen. Coed dorms, special housing for disabled available. $75 fully refundable deposit, deadline 5/1. Living-learning and suite style housing available. **Activities:** Bands, campus ministries, choral groups, dance, drama, film society, international student organizations, literary magazine, music ensembles, opera, radio station, student government, student newspaper, TV station.

**Athletics.** NCAA. **Intercollegiate:** Basketball, cross-country, football (tackle) M, lacrosse W, soccer W, softball W, swimming, track and field, volleyball W, wrestling M. **Intramural:** Basketball, football (non-tackle), racquetball, soccer, softball, volleyball, wrestling M. **Team name:** The Fighting Scots.

**Student services.** Adult student services, alcohol/substance abuse counseling, chaplain/spiritual director, career counseling, student employment services, financial aid counseling, health services, minority student services, personal counseling, placement for graduates, veterans' counselor. **Physically disabled:** Services for visually, speech, hearing impaired. **Learning disabled:** Comprehensive services available.

**Contact.** E-mail: eup_admissions@edinboro.edu
Phone: (814) 732-2761 Toll-free number: (888) 846-2676
Fax: (814) 732-2420
James Cooney, Director of Undergraduate Admissions, Edinboro University of Pennsylvania, 200 East Normal Street, Edinboro, PA 16444

## Elizabethtown College
**Elizabethtown, Pennsylvania**   CB member
**www.etown.edu**   CB code: 2225

- Private 4-year liberal arts college affiliated with Church of the Brethren
- Residential campus in large town
- 2,243 degree-seeking undergraduates: 17% part-time, 64% women, 3% African American, 2% Asian American, 2% Hispanic American, 1% international
- 39 degree-seeking graduate students
- 75% of applicants admitted
- SAT or ACT (ACT writing optional), application essay required
- 73% graduate within 6 years

**General.** Founded in 1899. Regionally accredited. **Degrees:** 530 bachelor's, 25 associate awarded; master's offered. **Location:** 20 miles from Harrisburg, 90 miles from Philadelphia. **Calendar:** Semester, limited summer session. **Full-time faculty:** 125 total; 87% have terminal degrees, 5% minority, 42% women. **Part-time faculty:** 79 total; 20% have terminal degrees, 8% minority, 51% women. **Class size:** 67% < 20, 31% 20-39, less than 1% 40-49, less than 1% 50-99. **Special facilities:** Anabaptist and Pietist groups center, global citizenship center, Brethren Colleges Abroad headquarters.

**Freshman class profile.** 3,322 applied, 2,487 admitted, 568 enrolled.

| Mid 50% test scores | | | |
|---|---|---|---|
| SAT critical reading: | 500-600 | Rank in top tenth: | 33% |
| SAT math: | 510-630 | Return as sophomores: | 83% |
| ACT composite: | 20-27 | Out-of-state: | 36% |
| Rank in top quarter: | 63% | Live on campus: | 97% |
| | | International: | 3% |

**Basis for selection.** School achievement record most important. College preparatory program strongly recommended. Co-curricular activities also considered, particularly service-oriented activities. Applicants should be in top quarter of class. Students may waive SAT/ACT score from admissions and merit-based scholarship decisions if they are ranked in top 10% of class or have 3.5 GPA if school does not rank. Interview required for occupational therapy and honors program. For international business applicants, essay must demonstrate interest in that subject area. Audition required for music, music education, music therapy programs; portfolio required for art program. **Homeschooled:** Letter of recommendation (nonparent) required.

**High school preparation.** 15 units required; 20 recommended. Required and recommended units include English 4, mathematics 3-4, social studies 2, history 2, science 2-4 (laboratory 2-3), foreign language 2 and academic electives 2.

**2010-2011 Annual costs.** Tuition/fees: $33,250. Room/board: $8,500. Books/supplies: $800. Personal expenses: $700.

**2009-2010 Financial aid. Need-based:** 479 full-time freshmen applied for aid; 409 were judged to have need; 409 of these received aid. Average need met was 84%. Average scholarship/grant was $19,243; average loan $3,733. 70% of total undergraduate aid awarded as scholarships/grants, 30% as loans/jobs. **Non-need-based:** Awarded to 570 full-time undergraduates, including 206 freshmen. Scholarships awarded for academics, art, music/drama, religious affiliation.

**Application procedures. Admission:** Priority date 3/1; no deadline. $30 fee, may be waived for applicants with need, free for online applicants. Admission notification on a rolling basis beginning on or about 12/1. Must reply by May 1 or within 2 week(s) if notified thereafter. December 15 closing date for occupational therapy program. March 1 closing date for international business. January 15 closing date for honors program. **Financial aid:** Priority date 3/15; no closing date. FAFSA, institutional form required. Applicants notified on a rolling basis starting 3/1; must reply by 5/1 or within 2 week(s) of notification.

**Academics. Special study options:** Combined bachelor's/graduate degree, distance learning, double major, dual enrollment of high school students, ESL, exchange student, external degree, honors, independent study, internships, study abroad, teacher certification program, Washington semester. 3-3 program in physical therapy (DPT) with Thomas Jefferson University; 3-2 in engineering with Penn State; 3-2 with Duke University in forestry and environmental management; 3-3 in physical therapy with Widener University and University of Maryland, Baltimore; 3+4 in dentistry with Temple University; agreements for MBA programs at Lehigh University, Rutgers University, Loyola College (MD), Penn State University, Harrisburg. **Credit/placement by examination:** AP, CLEP, IB, SAT, ACT, institutional tests. Credit by examination unlimited provided student is able to fulfill residency requirement. Credit for International Baccalaureate awarded only for subject exams and only for earned scores from 4-7. **Support services:** Learning center, reduced course load, study skills assistance, tutoring, writing center.

**Majors. Biology:** General, biochemistry, biotechnology, environmental. **Business:** Accounting, accounting/finance, business admin, entrepreneurial studies, finance, international, management information systems, managerial economics, marketing. **Communications:** Public relations. **Computer sciences:** General, information systems. **Conservation:** Forest management. **Education:** Early childhood, elementary, middle, science. **Engineering:** General, computer, industrial. **Foreign languages:** General, French, German, Japanese, Spanish. **Health:** Music therapy. **History:** General. **Math:** General. **Philosophy/religion:** Christian, philosophy, religion. **Physical sciences:** Chemistry, physics. **Psychology:** General. **Public administration:** Social work. **Social sciences:** General, anthropology, criminology, economics, political science, sociology. **Visual/performing arts:** Dramatic, studio arts. **Other:** Actuarial science, Corporate communications, Ethics and society, Health and occupation.

**Most popular majors.** Biology 8%, business/marketing 27%, communications/journalism 10%, education 11%, health sciences 6%, social sciences 9%.

**Computing on campus.** 200 workstations in dormitories, library, computer center, student center. Dormitories wired for high-speed internet access and linked to campus network. Commuter students can connect to campus network. Online course registration, online library, helpline, student web hosting, wireless network available.

**Student life. Freshman orientation:** Mandatory. One-day summer program in June and multi-day program at beginning of fall semester. **Policies:** All residence halls are smoke-free. **Housing:** Guaranteed on-campus for all undergraduates. Coed dorms, single-sex dorms, special housing for disabled, apartments, wellness housing available. Special housing available for students involved in service learning and community service. **Activities:** Bands, campus ministries, choral groups, dance, drama, international student organizations, literary magazine, music ensembles, musical theater, radio station, student government, student newspaper, symphony orchestra, TV station, Newman club, Intervarsity Christian Fellowship, Hillel, Circle-K, Habitat for Humanity, Amnesty International, College Democrats, Republican club.

**Athletics.** NCAA. **Intercollegiate:** Baseball M, basketball, cross-country, field hockey W, golf M, lacrosse, soccer, softball W, swimming, tennis, track and field, volleyball W, wrestling M. **Intramural:** Badminton, basketball, racquetball, soccer, softball, tennis, volleyball. **Team name:** Blue Jays.

**Student services.** Adult student services, alcohol/substance abuse counseling, chaplain/spiritual director, career counseling, student employment services, financial aid counseling, health services, minority student services, personal counseling, placement for graduates, veterans' counselor, women's services. **Physically disabled:** Services for visually, hearing impaired.

**Contact.** E-mail: admissions@etown.edu
Phone: (717) 361-1400 Fax: (717) 361-1365
Debra Murray, Director of Admissions, Elizabethtown College, One Alpha Drive, Elizabethtown, PA 17022-2298

---

## Franklin & Marshall College
Lancaster, Pennsylvania
www.fandm.edu

CB member
CB code: 2261

- Private 4-year liberal arts college
- Residential campus in small city
- 2,137 degree-seeking undergraduates: 51% women, 4% African American, 4% Asian American, 5% Hispanic American, 1% Native American, 8% international
- 48% of applicants admitted
- Application essay required
- 85% graduate within 6 years; 25% enter graduate study

**General.** Founded in 1787. Regionally accredited. **Degrees:** 530 bachelor's awarded. **Location:** 60 miles from Philadelphia, 120 miles from Washington, DC. **Calendar:** Semester, limited summer session. **Full-time faculty:** 201 total; 94% have terminal degrees, 12% minority, 38% women. **Part-time faculty:** 49 total; 59% have terminal degrees, 4% minority, 47% women. **Class size:** 57% < 20, 42% 20-39, less than 1% 40-49, less than 1% 50-99. **Special facilities:** Observatory, science library, retail sales complex, bronze casting foundry, field house, planetarium, natural history museum, concert hall, performing arts center, Writers House.

**Freshman class profile.** 5,255 applied, 2,547 admitted, 629 enrolled.

| Mid 50% test scores | | | |
|---|---|---|---|
| SAT critical reading: | 600-690 | Return as sophomores: | 92% |
| SAT math: | 630-690 | Out-of-state: | 70% |
| Rank in top quarter: | 86% | Live on campus: | 99% |
| Rank in top tenth: | 63% | International: | 7% |

**Basis for selection.** School achievement record, test scores or graded writing samples, extracurricular activities, recommendations, essay considered. Submission of standardized test scores optional for all students. If students choose to omit scores, two recent graded writing samples must then be submitted. Interview required for early decision applicants, strongly recommended for others. Auditions and portfolios recommended for all students who wish to demonstrate particular talent. **Homeschooled:** Interview required. Interview, accrediting and evaluative documentation from home state, and SAT or ACT required. 3 SAT Subject Tests highly recommended.

**High school preparation.** College-preparatory program required. Required and recommended units include English 4, mathematics 3-4, social studies 1-3, history 2-3, science 2-3 (laboratory 2-3), foreign language 2-4 and visual/performing arts 1.

**2009-2010 Annual costs.** Tuition/fees: $39,980. Room/board: $10,430. Books/supplies: $700. Personal expenses: $950.

**2009-2010 Financial aid. Need-based:** 407 full-time freshmen applied for aid; 291 were judged to have need; 291 of these received aid. Average need met was 100%. Average scholarship/grant was $28,914; average loan $3,554. 75% of total undergraduate aid awarded as scholarships/grants, 25% as loans/jobs. **Non-need-based:** Scholarships awarded for academics, art, leadership, minority status, music/drama.

**Application procedures. Admission:** Closing date 2/1 (postmark date). $60 fee, may be waived for applicants with need. Admission notification 4/1. Must reply by May 1 or within 2 week(s) if notified thereafter. **Financial aid:** Priority date 2/1, closing date 3/1. FAFSA, CSS PROFILE required. Applicants notified by 4/1; must reply by 5/1.

**Academics. Special study options:** Accelerated study, combined bachelor's/graduate degree, cross-registration, double major, dual enrollment of high school students, exchange student, honors, independent study, internships, liberal arts/career combination, New York semester, student-designed major, study abroad, teacher certification program, Washington semester. 3-2 programs in forestry, engineering, environmental studies; Columbia University's New York/Paris program. **Credit/placement by examination:** AP, CLEP, IB, institutional tests. 64 credit hours maximum toward bachelor's degree. **Support services:** Pre-admission summer program, reduced course load, tutoring, writing center.

**Majors. Area/ethnic studies:** African, African-American, American. **Biology:** General, biochemistry. **Business:** Business admin. **Conservation:** Environmental science, environmental studies. **Foreign languages:** Ancient Greek, classics, French, German, Latin, Spanish. **History:** General. **Interdisciplinary:** Behavioral sciences, biopsychology, neuroscience. **Math:** General. **Philosophy/religion:** Philosophy, religion. **Physical sciences:** Astronomy, astrophysics, chemistry, geology, physics. **Psychology:** General. **Social sciences:** Anthropology, economics, political science, sociology. **Visual/performing arts:** Art history/conservation, dance, dramatic, studio arts.

**Most popular majors.** Biology 8%, business/marketing 13%, English 8%, foreign language 7%, interdisciplinary studies 11%, physical sciences 6%, social sciences 25%.

**Computing on campus.** 125 workstations in library, computer center. Dormitories wired for high-speed internet access and linked to campus network. Commuter students can connect to campus network. Online course registration, online library, helpline, repair service, student web hosting, wireless network available.

**Student life. Freshman orientation:** Mandatory, $200 fee. Preregistration for classes offered. 5 days prior to start of classes. **Policies:** All students required to live in college-approved housing. **Housing:** Guaranteed on-campus for freshmen. Coed dorms, special housing for disabled, apartments, wellness housing available. French house, arts house, international house available to upperclassmen, community outreach house, sustainability house, and men's and women's floors. **Activities:** Bands, campus ministries, choral groups, dance, drama, international student organizations, literary magazine, music ensembles, musical theater, opera, radio station, student government, student newspaper, symphony orchestra, TV station, East Asian society, Catholic Campus Community, Hillel, Christian Fellowship, Habitat for Humanity, Voices for Women, Coalition for Choice, Environmental Action Alliance, Black student union, Mi Gente Latina.

**Athletics.** NCAA. **Intercollegiate:** Baseball M, basketball, cross-country, field hockey W, football (tackle) M, golf, lacrosse, rowing (crew), soccer, softball W, squash, swimming, tennis, track and field, volleyball W, wrestling M. **Intramural:** Basketball, football (non-tackle), soccer, softball. **Team name:** Diplomats.

**Student services.** Alcohol/substance abuse counseling, chaplain/spiritual director, career counseling, student employment services, financial aid counseling, health services, minority student services, on-campus daycare, personal counseling, placement for graduates, women's services.

**Contact.** E-mail: admission@fandm.edu
Phone: (717) 291-3953 Fax: (717) 291-4389
Sara Shapiro Harberson, Dean of Admission, Franklin & Marshall College, PO Box 3003, Lancaster, PA 17604-3003

## Gannon University
**Erie, Pennsylvania**  CB member
www.gannon.edu  CB code: 2270

- Private 4-year university affiliated with Roman Catholic Church
- Residential campus in small city
- 2,593 degree-seeking undergraduates: 6% part-time, 59% women, 6% African American, 2% Asian American, 2% Hispanic American, 2% international
- 1,243 degree-seeking graduate students
- 84% of applicants admitted
- SAT or ACT (ACT writing optional) required
- 64% graduate within 6 years

**General.** Founded in 1925. Regionally accredited. **Degrees:** 454 bachelor's, 32 associate awarded; master's, doctoral, professional offered. **ROTC:** Army. **Location:** 120 miles from Pittsburgh, 90 miles from Cleveland. **Calendar:** Semester, extensive summer session. **Full-time faculty:** 200 total; 72% have terminal degrees, 12% minority, 45% women. **Part-time faculty:** 155 total; 22% have terminal degrees, 3% minority, 48% women. **Class size:** 52% < 20, 46% 20-39, less than 1% 40-49, less than 1% 50-99. **Special facilities:** Environmental studies center, computer integrated enterprise manufacturing center, floating laboratory providing hands-on environmental study on Lake Erie.

**Freshman class profile.** 3,019 applied, 2,527 admitted, 660 enrolled.

| Mid 50% test scores | | GPA 2.0-2.99: | 21% |
|---|---|---|---|
| SAT critical reading: | 440-560 | Rank in top quarter: | 50% |
| SAT math: | 450-590 | Rank in top tenth: | 28% |
| ACT composite: | 19-26 | Return as sophomores: | 82% |
| GPA 3.75 or higher: | 38% | Out-of-state: | 28% |
| GPA 3.50-3.74: | 15% | Live on campus: | 72% |
| GPA 3.0-3.49: | 25% | International: | 2% |

**Basis for selection.** High school record important, including course selection, GPA, class rank, standardized test scores, recommendations, personal statement. Admission requirements vary by program. Limited number of students who do not meet all admissions requirements may be accepted into General Studies program. **Homeschooled:** Interview required. **Learning Disabled:** Applicants screened through director must be interviewed.

**High school preparation.** College-preparatory program required. 16 units required. Required units include English 4, mathematics 2, social studies 2, history 1 and academic electives 3.

**2010-2011 Annual costs.** Tuition/fees: $24,582. Room/board: $9,720. Books/supplies: $1,200. Personal expenses: $1,359.

**2009-2010 Financial aid. Need-based:** 620 full-time freshmen applied for aid; 573 were judged to have need; 573 of these received aid. Average need met was 83%. Average scholarship/grant was $17,012; average loan $3,390. 72% of total undergraduate aid awarded as scholarships/grants, 28% as loans/jobs. **Non-need-based:** Awarded to 553 full-time undergraduates, including 145 freshmen. Scholarships awarded for academics, athletics, leadership, music/drama, religious affiliation, ROTC.

**Application procedures. Admission:** Priority date 1/15; no deadline. $25 fee, may be waived for applicants with need. Admission notification on a rolling basis beginning on or about 9/15. Early application especially recommended for health science programs since space is limited. Closing date for occupational therapy, physician's assistant, radiological science programs January 15. Closing date for medical program December 15. **Financial aid:** Priority date 3/15; no closing date. FAFSA, institutional form required. Applicants notified on a rolling basis starting 11/1; must reply by 5/1 or within 4 week(s) of notification.

**Academics.** Preferred admission to doctorate physical therapy program granted to students with bachelor's degree from Gannon in physical therapy. Occupational therapy and physician assistant programs are 5-year master's degree programs. **Special study options:** Accelerated study, combined bachelor's/graduate degree, cooperative education, distance learning, double major, dual enrollment of high school students, honors, independent study, internships, liberal arts/career combination, study abroad, teacher certification program, Washington semester. **Credit/placement by examination:** AP, CLEP, IB, institutional tests. 36 credit hours maximum toward bachelor's degree. **Support services:** Learning center, reduced course load, remedial instruction, study skills assistance, tutoring, writing center.

**Honors college/program.** Minimum 1150 SAT score (exclusive of Writing), 3.0 GPA, rank in top tenth of high school class, college preparatory curriculum, extracurricular activities, community service. Recommendation, interview and essay required. Approximately 50 freshmen admitted per year.

**Majors. Biology:** General, bioinformatics. **Business:** Accounting, business admin, entrepreneurial studies, finance, insurance, international, management information systems, marketing. **Communications:** Advertising, journalism. **Communications technology:** Radio/tv. **Computer sciences:** General, programming. **Conservation:** Environmental science. **Education:** Early childhood, elementary, foreign languages, secondary, social studies. **Engineering:** Chemical, electrical, environmental, mechanical. **Foreign languages:** General. **Health:** Clinical lab science, dietetics, nursing (RN), premedicine, respiratory therapy technology. **History:** General. **Interdisciplinary:** Global studies. **Legal studies:** Paralegal, prelaw. **Liberal arts:** Arts/sciences. **Math:** General. **Parks/recreation:** Exercise sciences, sports admin. **Personal/culinary services:** Mortuary science. **Philosophy/religion:** Philosophy. **Physical sciences:** Chemistry. **Protective services:** Criminal justice. **Psychology:** General. **Public administration:** Social work. **Science technology:** Biological. **Social sciences:** Political science. **Theology:** Theology. **Visual/performing arts:** General, dramatic. **Other:** Foreign language and international studies.

**Most popular majors.** Biology 11%, business/marketing 16%, education 6%, health sciences 27%.

**Computing on campus.** 380 workstations in dormitories, library, computer center, student center. Dormitories wired for high-speed internet access and linked to campus network. Commuter students can connect to campus network. Online library, helpline, wireless network available.

**Student life. Freshman orientation:** Mandatory, $60 fee. Preregistration for classes offered. 4 separate sessions during summer. Open to parents and students. **Housing:** Guaranteed on-campus for freshmen. Coed dorms, special housing for disabled, apartments available. $100 fully refundable deposit, deadline 5/1. **Activities:** Bands, campus ministries, choral groups, dance, drama, international student organizations, literary magazine, music ensembles, Model UN, musical theater, radio station, student government, student newspaper, Social Concerns, minority student union, College Democrats, College Republicans, activities programming board, debate, Vitality Through Exercise, residence union.

**Athletics.** NCAA. **Intercollegiate:** Baseball M, basketball, cross-country, diving, football (tackle) M, golf, lacrosse W, soccer, softball W, swimming, volleyball W, water polo, wrestling M. **Intramural:** Basketball, football (non-tackle), handball, racquetball, soccer, volleyball, wrestling M. **Team name:** Golden Knights.

**Student services.** Adult student services, alcohol/substance abuse counseling, chaplain/spiritual director, career counseling, services for economically disadvantaged, student employment services, financial aid counseling, health services, minority student services, personal counseling, placement for graduates, veterans' counselor. **Learning disabled:** Comprehensive services available.

**Contact.** E-mail: admissions@gannon.edu
Phone: (814) 871-7240 Toll-free number: (800) 426-6668
Fax: (814) 871-5803
Terrance Kizina, Director of Admissions, Gannon University, 109 University Square, Erie, PA 16541-0001

## Geneva College
**Beaver Falls, Pennsylvania**
www.geneva.edu

**CB member**
**CB code: 2273**

- Private 4-year liberal arts college affiliated with Reformed Presbyterian Church of North America
- Residential campus in large town
- 1,306 degree-seeking undergraduates: 1% part-time, 49% women
- 263 graduate students
- 80% of applicants admitted
- SAT or ACT (ACT writing optional), application essay required
- 59% graduate within 6 years

**General.** Founded in 1848. Regionally accredited. **Degrees:** 333 bachelor's, 3 associate awarded; master's offered. **ROTC:** Army. **Location:** 35 miles from Pittsburgh. **Calendar:** Semester, limited summer session. **Full-time faculty:** 74 total; 76% have terminal degrees, 8% minority, 35% women. **Part-time faculty:** 97 total; 5% minority, 38% women. **Class size:** 30% < 20, 51% 20-39, 8% 40-49, 10% 50-99, 1% >100. **Special facilities:** Collection of artifacts and records of Pittsburgh steel industry, technology development center, observatory, high adventure ropes course.

**Freshman class profile.** 1,158 applied, 932 admitted, 338 enrolled.

| Mid 50% test scores | | | |
|---|---|---|---|
| SAT critical reading: | 470-580 | Rank in top quarter: | 41% |
| SAT math: | 470-600 | Rank in top tenth: | 19% |
| ACT composite: | 19-25 | Return as sophomores: | 78% |
| GPA 3.75 or higher: | 32% | Out-of-state: | 34% |
| GPA 3.50-3.74: | 17% | Live on campus: | 88% |
| GPA 3.0-3.49: | 35% | International: | 1% |
| | | GPA 2.0-2.99: | 16% |

**Basis for selection.** Academic performance and test scores most important. Recommendations and extracurricular activities considered. Placement tests in English and math required if the student does not perform well enough on the relevant SAT or ACT examinations. For students with high SAT or ACT scores, placement tests used to determine if students should be placed in more advanced courses. Interview recommended for all; audition required for music program. **Homeschooled:** Transcript of courses and grades required. Help in preparing homeschooler's transcript available if necessary.

**High school preparation.** College-preparatory program required. 16 units required. Required units include English 4, mathematics 2, social studies 3, science 1, foreign language 2 and academic electives 4. Engineering students should have 1 unit of chemistry and physics, 4 units of college-preparatory mathematics including trigonometry or precalculus.

**2010-2011 Annual costs.** Tuition/fees (projected): $22,236. Room/board: $8,000. Books/supplies: $900. Personal expenses: $1,150.

**2009-2010 Financial aid. Need-based:** 301 full-time freshmen applied for aid; 278 were judged to have need; 278 of these received aid. Average need met was 85%. Average scholarship/grant was $15,253; average loan $3,954. 67% of total undergraduate aid awarded as scholarships/grants, 33% as loans/jobs. **Non-need-based:** Awarded to 277 full-time undergraduates, including 61 freshmen. Scholarships awarded for academics, alumni affiliation, music/drama, religious affiliation.

**Application procedures. Admission:** No deadline. $40 fee, may be waived for applicants with need, free for online applicants. Admission notification on a rolling basis beginning on or about 9/1. Must reply by May 1 or within 3 week(s) if notified thereafter. **Financial aid:** Priority date 3/15; no closing date. FAFSA required. Applicants notified on a rolling basis starting 3/1; must reply by 5/1 or within 4 week(s) of notification.

**Academics. Special study options:** Accelerated study, cooperative education, cross-registration, double major, dual enrollment of high school students, honors, independent study, internships, liberal arts/career combination, student-designed major, study abroad, teacher certification program, Washington semester. **Credit/placement by examination:** AP, CLEP, SAT,

ACT, institutional tests. 30 credit hours maximum toward bachelor's degree. **Support services:** Reduced course load, remedial instruction, study skills assistance, tutoring, writing center.

**Majors. Biology:** General. **Business:** Accounting, business admin, human resources. **Communications:** General. **Computer sciences:** General. **Education:** General, elementary, mathematics, music, special. **Engineering:** General, chemical. **Health:** Speech pathology. **History:** General. **Liberal arts:** Arts/sciences. **Math:** Applied. **Philosophy/religion:** Philosophy. **Physical sciences:** Chemistry, physics. **Psychology:** General. **Public administration:** Human services. **Social sciences:** Political science, sociology. **Theology:** Bible, youth ministry. **Visual/performing arts:** Music management, music performance.

**Most popular majors.** Business/marketing 18%, education 20%, engineering/engineering technologies 6%, English 6%, public administration/social services 7%, theological studies 13%.

**Computing on campus.** 150 workstations in dormitories, library, computer center, student center. Dormitories wired for high-speed internet access and linked to campus network. Commuter students can connect to campus network. Online course registration, online library, helpline, repair service, wireless network available.

**Student life. Freshman orientation:** Mandatory. Preregistration for classes offered. Held 5 days prior to start of classes. **Policies:** Smoking, drinking, social or ballroom dancing not permitted on campus. Students must live on campus unless married, commuting, or over age 24. Religious observance required. **Housing:** Guaranteed on-campus for all undergraduates. Single-sex dorms, apartments, wellness housing available. $150 fully refundable deposit. **Activities:** Bands, campus ministries, choral groups, drama, international student organizations, literary magazine, music ensembles, radio station, student government, student newspaper, Acting on Aids, American Society of Civil Engineering, American Society of Mechanical Engineers, black student organization, Business and Professional Women, Creation Stewardship Club, International Justice Mission, Young Republicans, Young Democrats.

**Athletics.** NCAA, NCCAA. **Intercollegiate:** Baseball M, basketball, cross-country, football (tackle) M, soccer, softball W, tennis W, track and field, volleyball W. **Intramural:** Basketball, football (non-tackle), racquetball, soccer, softball, volleyball. **Team name:** Golden Tornadoes.

**Student services.** Alcohol/substance abuse counseling, chaplain/spiritual director, career counseling, student employment services, financial aid counseling, health services, minority student services, personal counseling, placement for graduates. **Physically disabled:** Services for visually, hearing impaired. **Learning disabled:** Comprehensive services available.

**Contact.** E-mail: admissions@geneva.edu
Phone: (724) 847-6500 Toll-free number: (800) 847-8255
Fax: (724) 847-6776
Dave Layton, Dean of Undergraduate Enrollment, Geneva College, 3200 College Avenue, Beaver Falls, PA 15010

## Gettysburg College
**Gettysburg, Pennsylvania**
www.gettysburg.edu

**CB member**
**CB code: 2275**

- Private 4-year liberal arts college
- Residential campus in large town
- 2,692 degree-seeking undergraduates: 50% women, 4% African American, 1% Asian American, 3% Hispanic American, 2% international
- 40% of applicants admitted
- SAT or ACT (ACT writing optional), application essay required

**General.** Founded in 1832. Regionally accredited. **Degrees:** 632 bachelor's awarded. **ROTC:** Army. **Location:** 36 miles from Harrisburg, 80 miles from Washington, DC. **Calendar:** Semester. **Full-time faculty:** 204 total; 90% have terminal degrees, 17% minority, 44% women. **Part-time faculty:** 74 total; 8% have terminal degrees, 8% minority, 47% women. **Class size:** 69% < 20, 29% 20-39, 2% 40-49, less than 1% 50-99. **Special facilities:** Observatory, planetarium, intercultural resource center, women's resource center, child study center, public service center, optics and plasma physics laboratories, infrared and NMR spectrometers, proton accelerator, science center, outdoor climbing wall, Sunderman Conservatory of Music.

**Freshman class profile.** 5,448 applied, 2,201 admitted, 739 enrolled.

| Mid 50% test scores | | Out-of-state: | 74% |
|---|---|---|---|
| SAT critical reading: | 610-690 | Live on campus: | 94% |
| SAT math: | 610-690 | International: | 2% |
| Rank in top quarter: | 86% | Fraternities: | 40% |
| Rank in top tenth: | 68% | Sororities: | 26% |

**Basis for selection.** Academic record, recommendations, and activities most important. Audition required for the Sunderman Conservatory of Music; portfolio recommended for art program. Interview strongly recommended. **Homeschooled:** Statement describing homeschool structure and mission, transcript of courses and grades, interview, letter of recommendation (nonparent) required.

**High school preparation.** College-preparatory program required. Required and recommended units include English 4, mathematics 3-4, history 3-4, science 3-4 (laboratory 3-4) and foreign language 3-4. History requirement can be fulfilled with social studies units, depending on available high school courses.

**2009-2010 Annual costs.** Tuition/fees: $39,100. Room/board: $9,360. Books/supplies: $1,000.

**2009-2010 Financial aid. Need-based:** 574 full-time freshmen applied for aid; 438 were judged to have need; 433 of these received aid. Average need met was 100%. Average scholarship/grant was $24,791; average loan $3,701. 86% of total undergraduate aid awarded as scholarships/grants, 14% as loans/jobs. **Non-need-based:** Awarded to 1,061 full-time undergraduates, including 356 freshmen. Scholarships awarded for academics, music/drama, religious affiliation.

**Application procedures. Admission:** Closing date 2/1 (postmark date). $55 fee, may be waived for applicants with need. Admission notification 4/1. Must reply by May 1 or within 2 week(s) if notified thereafter. **Financial aid:** Closing date 2/15. FAFSA, CSS PROFILE required. Applicants notified by 3/26; must reply by 5/1.

**Academics. Special study options:** Combined bachelor's/graduate degree, double major, independent study, internships, semester at sea, student-designed major, study abroad, teacher certification program, United Nations semester, Washington semester. 3-2 programs in engineering with Columbia University, Rensselaer Polytechnic Institute, and Washington University in St. Louis; 3-2 program in nursing with Johns Hopkins University; pre-law and health professions advising available. **Credit/placement by examination:** AP, CLEP, IB, SAT, institutional tests. **Support services:** Study skills assistance, tutoring, writing center.

**Majors. Area/ethnic studies:** African-American, American, Asian, Asian-American, East Asian, Japanese, Latin American, women's. **Biology:** General, biochemistry, conservation, molecular. **Business:** Business admin, finance, international, management science, marketing, nonprofit/public. **Communications:** General, journalism. **Computer sciences:** General, computer science. **Conservation:** General, environmental science, environmental studies, forestry, management/policy, water/wetlands/marine. **Education:** Music. **Engineering:** General, biomedical, chemical, civil, computer, electrical, environmental, mechanical, mechanics, physics, science. **Foreign languages:** Classics, comparative lit, French, German, Japanese, Latin, Spanish. **Health:** Health services, nursing (RN), predental, premedicine, prepharmacy, preveterinary. **History:** General, American, Asian, European. **Interdisciplinary:** Behavioral sciences, biological/physical sciences, global studies, math/computer science, medieval/Renaissance, natural sciences, neuroscience, peace/conflict. **Legal studies:** Prelaw. **Liberal arts:** Arts/sciences. **Math:** General. **Parks/recreation:** Exercise sciences, health/fitness, sports admin. **Philosophy/religion:** Philosophy, religion. **Physical sciences:** Astronomy, chemistry, physics. **Psychology:** General. **Social sciences:** Anthropology, economics, international relations, political science, sociology, U.S. government. **Theology:** Preministerial. **Visual/performing arts:** General, art, art history/conservation, dramatic, film/cinema, music performance, music theory/composition, piano/organ, studio arts, theater arts management, voice/opera.

**Most popular majors.** Biology 14%, business/marketing 14%, English 9%, history 6%, psychology 9%, social sciences 20%.

**Computing on campus.** 620 workstations in library, computer center, student center. Dormitories wired for high-speed internet access and linked to campus network. Commuter students can connect to campus network. Online course registration, online library, helpline, repair service, student web hosting, wireless network available.

**Student life. Freshman orientation:** Mandatory. Preregistration for classes offered. Held 5 days prior to the start of fall semester. **Housing:** Guaranteed on-campus for all undergraduates. Coed dorms, single-sex dorms, apartments, fraternity/sorority housing, wellness housing available. $500 nonrefundable deposit, deadline 5/1. **Activities:** Bands, choral groups, dance, drama, film society, international student organizations, literary magazine, music

ensembles, musical theater, opera, radio station, student government, student newspaper, symphony orchestra, TV station, over 120 clubs available.

**Athletics.** NCAA. **Intercollegiate:** Baseball M, basketball, cheerleading, cross-country, field hockey W, football (tackle) M, golf, lacrosse, soccer, softball W, swimming, tennis, track and field, volleyball W, wrestling M. **Intramural:** Badminton, basketball, field hockey, football (non-tackle), golf, lacrosse W, skiing, soccer, softball, volleyball, weight lifting. **Team name:** Bullets.

**Student services.** Chaplain/spiritual director, career counseling, student employment services, financial aid counseling, health services, minority student services, personal counseling, placement for graduates, women's services.

**Contact.** E-mail: admiss@gettysburg.edu
Phone: (717) 337-6100 Toll-free number: (800) 431-0803
Fax: (717) 337-6145
Gail Sweezey, Director of Admissions, Gettysburg College, 300 North Washington Street, Gettysburg, PA 17325-1484

---

## Gratz College
**Melrose Park, Pennsylvania**
www.gratz.edu
**CB code: 2280**

▸ Private 4-year college of Jewish studies affiliated with Jewish faith
▸ Commuter campus in very large city

**General.** Founded in 1895. Regionally accredited. **Location:** 6 miles from Philadelphia. **Calendar:** Semester.

**Annual costs/financial aid.** Tuition/fees (2009-2010): $12,300. Undergraduate students may take as many as 18 hours per semester for the full-time (academic year) tuition rate of $12,200. Books/supplies: $1,000. Personal expenses: $3,000.

**Contact.** Phone: (215) 635-7300 ext. 140
Director of Student Life, 7605 Old York Road, Melrose Park, PA 19027

---

## Grove City College
**Grove City, Pennsylvania**
www.gcc.edu
**CB member**
**CB code: 2277**

▸ Private 4-year liberal arts college affiliated with Presbyterian Church (USA)
▸ Residential campus in small town
▸ 2,504 degree-seeking undergraduates: 1% part-time, 50% women, 1% African American, 2% Asian American, 2% Hispanic American
▸ 64% of applicants admitted
▸ SAT or ACT (ACT writing optional), application essay, interview required
▸ 83% graduate within 6 years; 25% enter graduate study

**General.** Founded in 1876. Regionally accredited. **Degrees:** 563 bachelor's awarded. **Location:** 60 miles from Pittsburgh. **Calendar:** Semester, extensive summer session. **Full-time faculty:** 128 total; 92% have terminal degrees, 2% minority, 26% women. **Part-time faculty:** 86 total; 16% have terminal degrees, 4% minority, 44% women. **Class size:** 42% < 20, 44% 20-39, 7% 40-49, 5% 50-99, 1% >100. **Special facilities:** Observatory.

**Freshman class profile.** 1,761 applied, 1,123 admitted, 633 enrolled.

| Mid 50% test scores | | GPA 2.0-2.99: | 2% |
|---|---|---|---|
| SAT critical reading: | 560-690 | Rank in top quarter: | 85% |
| SAT math: | 570-680 | Rank in top tenth: | 51% |
| ACT composite: | 25-30 | Return as sophomores: | 93% |
| GPA 3.75 or higher: | 55% | Out-of-state: | 53% |
| GPA 3.50-3.74: | 24% | Live on campus: | 94% |
| GPA 3.0-3.49: | 19% | | |

**Basis for selection.** High school record, GPA or class rank, test scores, recommendations, interview, character, and extracurricular activities very important. Audition required for music program. **Homeschooled:** Transcript of courses and grades, interview, letter of recommendation (nonparent) required. Outside activities important.

**High school preparation.** College-preparatory program recommended. 17 units recommended. Recommended units include English 4, mathematics 3, social studies 2, history 2, science 3 (laboratory 2) and foreign language 3. Engineering, science, and math applicants must have 4 math and 4 science.

**2010-2011 Annual costs.** Tuition/fees: $13,088. Room/board: $7,132. Books/supplies: $1,000. Personal expenses: $350.

**2009-2010 Financial aid. Need-based:** 373 full-time freshmen applied for aid; 285 were judged to have need; 275 of these received aid. Average need met was 53%. Average scholarship/grant was $6,024. 63% of total undergraduate aid awarded as scholarships/grants, 37% as loans/jobs. **Non-need-based:** Awarded to 408 full-time undergraduates, including 88 freshmen. Scholarships awarded for academics, leadership, minority status. **Additional information:** Institutional aid applications required for institutional scholarships, loans, and student employment.

**Application procedures. Admission:** Closing date 2/1 (postmark date). $50 fee, may be waived for applicants with need. Decision letters mailed 3/15. Must reply by 5/1. **Financial aid:** Closing date 4/15. Institutional form required. Applicants notified on a rolling basis starting 3/15; must reply by 5/1.

**Academics.** All students required to complete general education core that includes 3-year humanities sequence, with emphasis in religion, philosophy, history, philosophy of science, science/faith/technology, literature, art, and music, as well as courses in social sciences, quantitative/logical reasoning, natural sciences (with labs), physical education, and a foreign language. **Special study options:** Accelerated study, double major, independent study, internships, study abroad, teacher certification program, Washington semester. **Credit/placement by examination:** AP, CLEP, IB. **Support services:** Reduced course load, study skills assistance, tutoring.

**Majors. Biology:** General, biochemistry, molecular. **Business:** Accounting, business admin, communications, entrepreneurial studies, international, managerial economics, marketing. **Communications:** General. **Computer sciences:** General, applications programming, systems analysis. **Education:** Biology, chemistry, early childhood, elementary, English, French, history, mathematics, music, physics, science, secondary, social studies, Spanish. **Engineering:** Electrical, mechanical. **Engineering technology:** Industrial management. **Foreign languages:** French, Spanish. **Health:** Predental, premedicine, preveterinary. **History:** General. **Interdisciplinary:** Math/computer science. **Legal studies:** Prelaw. **Math:** General. **Philosophy/religion:** Philosophy, religion. **Physical sciences:** Chemistry, physics. **Psychology:** General. **Social sciences:** Economics, political science, sociology. **Visual/performing arts:** Music management, music performance.

**Most popular majors.** Biology 9%, business/marketing 18%, communications/journalism 6%, education 11%, engineering/engineering technologies 10%, English 7%, history 6%, social sciences 8%.

**Computing on campus.** PC or laptop required. 50 workstations in library, computer center. Dormitories wired for high-speed internet access and linked to campus network. Commuter students can connect to campus network. Online course registration, online library, helpline, repair service, student web hosting, wireless network available.

**Student life. Freshman orientation:** Available, $25 fee. Preregistration for classes offered. One-day programs in June and a 3-day program in August prior to fall semester. **Policies:** Alcohol not permitted on campus. Chapel program consists of lectures, vespers, and seminars. Students must attend 16 chapels per semester. Religious observance required. **Housing:** Guaranteed on-campus for all undergraduates. Single-sex dorms, apartments, wellness housing available. **Activities:** Bands, campus ministries, choral groups, dance, drama, international student organizations, literary magazine, music ensembles, musical theater, opera, radio station, student government, student newspaper, symphony orchestra, TV station, Fellowship of Christian Athletes, Salt Company, Warriors for Christ, Young Life, Newman club, College Republicans, College Democrats, outing club, orientation board, Life Advocates.

**Athletics.** NCAA. **Intercollegiate:** Baseball M, basketball, cheerleading M, cross-country, diving, football (tackle) M, golf, soccer, softball W, swimming, tennis, track and field, volleyball W, water polo W. **Intramural:** Badminton, basketball, bowling, football (non-tackle), football (tackle), golf M, handball M, racquetball, soccer W, softball, swimming W, tennis, volleyball. **Team name:** Wolverines.

**Student services.** Alcohol/substance abuse counseling, chaplain/spiritual director, career counseling, student employment services, financial aid counseling, health services, minority student services, personal counseling, placement for graduates.

**Contact.** E-mail: admissions@gcc.edu
Phone: (724) 458-2100 Fax: (724) 458-3395
Jeffrey Mincey, Director of Admissions, Grove City College, 100 Campus Drive, Grove City, PA 16127-2104

---

## Gwynedd-Mercy College
**Gwynedd Valley, Pennsylvania**
www.gmc.edu

**CB member**
**CB code: 2278**

- Private 4-year nursing and liberal arts college affiliated with Roman Catholic Church
- Residential campus in large town
- 2,130 degree-seeking undergraduates: 30% part-time, 74% women, 21% African American, 2% Asian American, 1% Hispanic American
- 421 degree-seeking graduate students
- 65% of applicants admitted
- SAT or ACT (ACT writing optional) required
- 69% graduate within 6 years

**General.** Founded in 1948. Regionally accredited. Affiliated with the Religious Sisters of Mercy. 8-week evening sessions running 12 months for business and accounting majors. Accelerated degree program begins every 6 weeks. **Degrees:** 358 bachelor's, 193 associate awarded; master's offered. **Location:** 20 miles from Philadelphia. **Calendar:** Semester, limited summer session. **Full-time faculty:** 75 total; 63% have terminal degrees, 71% women. **Part-time faculty:** 206 total; 23% have terminal degrees, 7% minority, 54% women. **Class size:** 65% < 20, 31% 20-39, less than 1% 40-49, 3% 50-99, less than 1% >100. **Special facilities:** Lincoln-era collection, nursery laboratory school for early childhood education.

**Freshman class profile.** 1,908 applied, 1,240 admitted, 319 enrolled.

| Mid 50% test scores | | | |
|---|---|---|---|
| SAT critical reading: | 440-530 | Return as sophomores: | 76% |
| SAT math: | 430-530 | Out-of-state: | 15% |
| | | Live on campus: | 78% |

**Basis for selection.** School achievement record most important, followed by test scores and recommendations. Extracurricular activities considered. Nursing program very competitive.

**High school preparation.** College-preparatory program recommended. 16 units required. Required units include English 4, mathematics 3, history 1, science 3 and academic electives 3. Chemistry required for applicants to nursing, cardiovascular, biology, medical technology programs. Biology required for cardiovascular, health information technology programs. Physics required for radiation therapy, medical technology, biology programs. Chemistry or physics required for respiratory therapy.

**2009-2010 Annual costs.** Tuition/fees: $24,180. Tuition and fees for nursing and allied health programs $25,230 for full-time, and $600 per credit hour for part-time. Room/board: $9,330. Books/supplies: $650. Personal expenses: $1,000.

**2008-2009 Financial aid. Need-based:** 318 full-time freshmen applied for aid; 257 were judged to have need; 257 of these received aid. Average need met was 75%. Average scholarship/grant was $12,479; average loan $4,210. 77% of total undergraduate aid awarded as scholarships/grants, 23% as loans/jobs. **Non-need-based:** Awarded to 1,006 full-time undergraduates, including 269 freshmen. Scholarships awarded for academics, leadership.

**Application procedures. Admission:** Closing date 8/20 (receipt date). $25 fee, may be waived for applicants with need, free for online applicants. Admission notification on a rolling basis beginning on or about 9/20. Must reply by May 1 or within 3 week(s) if notified thereafter. Nursing program usually filled by May 1. **Financial aid:** Priority date 3/15, closing date 7/15. FAFSA, institutional form required. Applicants notified on a rolling basis starting 3/1; must reply by 5/1 or within 2 week(s) of notification.

**Academics. Special study options:** Accelerated study, cooperative education, cross-registration, double major, dual enrollment of high school students, ESL, honors, independent study, internships, liberal arts/career combination, teacher certification program, weekend college. **Credit/placement by examination:** AP, CLEP, institutional tests. Credit by examination cannot be applied to open electives. **Support services:** Learning center, reduced course load, remedial instruction, study skills assistance, tutoring, writing center.

**Majors. Biology:** General. **Business:** Accounting, business admin. **Computer sciences:** General. **Education:** Biology, business, elementary, mathematics, special. **Family/consumer sciences:** Aging. **Health:** Cardiovascular technology, clinical lab science, medical radiologic technology/radiation therapy, medical records admin, nursing (RN), premedicine, preveterinary, respiratory therapy technology. **History:** General. **Math:** General. **Protective services:** Law enforcement admin. **Psychology:** General. **Social sciences:** Sociology.

**Most popular majors.** Business/marketing 34%, education 15%, health sciences 31%, psychology 6%.

**Computing on campus.** 217 workstations in library, computer center, student center. Dormitories wired for high-speed internet access and linked to campus network. Commuter students can connect to campus network. Online course registration, online library, helpline, wireless network available.

**Student life. Freshman orientation:** Available. Preregistration for classes offered. Multiple full-day sessions offered during the summer. **Housing:** Coed dorms, special housing for disabled available. $250 deposit, deadline 5/1. **Activities:** Campus ministries, choral groups, drama, literary magazine, musical theater, student government, student newspaper, Kappa Delta Pi, business society, honor societies, Mercy Corps, resident council, student nurses' association, education club, peer counseling, psychology/sociology club, biology student association,.

**Athletics.** NCAA. **Intercollegiate:** Baseball M, basketball, cross-country, field hockey W, golf M, lacrosse W, soccer, softball W, tennis, track and field, volleyball W. **Intramural:** Volleyball. **Team name:** Griffins.

**Student services.** Adult student services, chaplain/spiritual director, career counseling, student employment services, financial aid counseling, health services, minority student services, on-campus daycare, personal counseling, placement for graduates.

**Contact.** E-mail: admissions@gmc.edu
Phone: (215) 646-7300 ext. 530 Toll-free number: (800) 342-5462
Fax: (215) 641-5556
Michele Diehl, Director of Undergraduate Admissions, Gwynedd-Mercy College, 1325 Sumneytown Pike, Gwynedd Valley, PA 19437-0901

## Harrisburg University of Science and Technology
**Harrisburg, Pennsylvania**
**www.HarrisburgU.edu**

- Private 4-year university
- Commuter campus in small city
- 146 degree-seeking undergraduates: 16% part-time, 44% women
- 54 degree-seeking graduate students
- 56% of applicants admitted

**General.** Regionally accredited. **Degrees:** 9 bachelor's awarded; master's offered. **Calendar:** Trimester, limited summer session. **Full-time faculty:** 10 total; 90% have terminal degrees, 20% minority, 50% women. **Part-time faculty:** 25 total; 20% have terminal degrees, 28% women. **Class size:** 95% < 20, 5% 20-39.

**Freshman class profile.** 203 applied, 114 admitted, 45 enrolled.

| | | | |
|---|---|---|---|
| End year in good standing: | 65% | Out-of-state: | 10% |
| Return as sophomores: | 40% | | |

**Basis for selection.** Admissions based on high school record. SAT or ACT recommended. Interview and essay or personal statement strongly recommended. **Homeschooled:** Statement describing homeschool structure and mission required.

**2009-2010 Annual costs.** Tuition/fees: $18,000. Laptop required. Estimated Cost: $1,200. Books/supplies: $1,500. Personal expenses: $1,700.

**2009-2010 Financial aid. Need-based:** Average need met was 52%. Average scholarship/grant was $10,938; average loan $3,791. 57% of total undergraduate aid awarded as scholarships/grants, 43% as loans/jobs. **Non-need-based:** Scholarships awarded for academics, leadership, state residency.

**Application procedures. Admission:** No deadline. No application fee. Admission notification on a rolling basis. **Financial aid:** No deadline. FAFSA required. Applicants notified on a rolling basis; must reply within 2 week(s) of notification.

**Academics. Special study options:** Dual enrollment of high school students, internships. **Credit/placement by examination:** AP, CLEP, institutional tests. 18 credit hours maximum toward bachelor's degree. **Support services:** Reduced course load, remedial instruction, study skills assistance, tutoring.

**Majors. Biology:** Biotechnology. **Business:** E-commerce. **Computer sciences:** General, information technology. **Conservation:** Environmental science. **Physical sciences:** General, chemistry. **Science technology:** Biological. **Social sciences:** Geography. **Other:** Geospatial imaging.

**Most popular majors.** Computer/information sciences 37%, physical sciences 62%.

**Computing on campus.** PC or laptop required. 12 workstations in computer center. Commuter students can connect to campus network. Online library, wireless network available.

**Student life. Freshman orientation:** Mandatory. Preregistration for classes offered.

**Student services.** Financial aid counseling.

**Contact.** E-mail: admissions@HarrisburgU.edu
Phone: (717) 901-5160 Fax: (717) 901-3160
Timothy Dawson, Director of Admissions and Enrollment Systems, Harrisburg University of Science and Technology, 326 Market Street, Harrisburg, PA 17101-2208

## Haverford College
**Haverford, Pennsylvania**
**www.haverford.edu**

**CB member**
**CB code: 2289**

- Private 4-year liberal arts college
- Residential campus in large town
- 1,190 degree-seeking undergraduates: 55% women, 8% African American, 9% Asian American, 8% Hispanic American, 3% international
- 25% of applicants admitted
- SAT and SAT Subject Tests or ACT with writing, application essay required
- 92% graduate within 6 years; 17% enter graduate study

**General.** Founded in 1833. Regionally accredited. Founded by the Society of Friends (Quakers), but now independent. **Degrees:** 307 bachelor's awarded. **Location:** 10 miles from Philadelphia. **Calendar:** Semester. **Full-time faculty:** 121 total; 97% have terminal degrees, 26% minority, 46% women. **Part-time faculty:** 17 total; 76% have terminal degrees, 12% minority, 53% women. **Class size:** 76% < 20, 21% 20-39, 1% 40-49, 2% 50-99. **Special facilities:** Observatory, arboretum, fine arts foundry.

**Freshman class profile.** 3,403 applied, 862 admitted, 323 enrolled.

| Mid 50% test scores | | Rank in top tenth: | 94% |
|---|---|---|---|
| SAT critical reading: | 660-740 | Return as sophomores: | 95% |
| SAT math: | 640-740 | Out-of-state: | 87% |
| SAT writing: | 660-750 | Live on campus: | 100% |
| Rank in top quarter: | 99% | International: | 2% |

**Basis for selection.** School record, test scores, extracurricular achievements, and recommendations important. College seeks diversity of social, economic, and geographic backgrounds. Some preference given to children of alumni. First-year applicants must take SAT or ACT plus 2 SAT Subject Tests before deadline for decision plan chosen. Interview required of applicants living within 150 miles of college, recommended for others. **Homeschooled:** Statement describing homeschool structure and mission, transcript of courses and grades, interview, letter of recommendation (nonparent) required.

**High school preparation.** College-preparatory program recommended. No specific high school curriculum required, but recommend four years of English and at least three years of mathematics, the sciences, history and two years of social studies, and one or two foreign languages.

**2010-2011 Annual costs.** Tuition/fees: $40,624. Room/board: $12,346. Books/supplies: $1,194. Personal expenses: $1,468.

**2009-2010 Financial aid.** All financial aid based on need. 206 full-time freshmen applied for aid; 156 were judged to have need; 156 of these received aid. Average need met was 100%. Average scholarship/grant was $33,575; average loan $625. 93% of total undergraduate aid awarded as scholarships/grants, 7% as loans/jobs.

**Application procedures. Admission:** Closing date 1/15. $60 fee, may be waived for applicants with need. Admission notification 4/15. Must reply by May 1 or within 2 week(s) if notified thereafter. **Financial aid:** Closing date 2/1. FAFSA, CSS PROFILE required. Applicants notified by 4/1; must reply by 5/1.

**Academics.** Academic Flexibility Program allows for advanced independent work and interdepartmental majors. Ample opportunity for student-faculty research. Senior seminars, comprehensive examination and/or senior thesis required for completion of all major programs. **Special study options:** Combined bachelor's/graduate degree, cross-registration, double major, exchange student, independent study, internships, liberal arts/career combination, student-designed major, study abroad, teacher certification program. Exchange programs with Spelman College (GA), Claremont McKenna College and Pitzer College (CA), Fisk University (TN); cross-registration with Bryn Mawr College, Swarthmore College, noncredit internships also available; 3-2 engineering program with California Institute of Technology. **Credit/placement by examination:** AP, CLEP, IB, institutional tests. **Support services:** Learning center, study skills assistance, tutoring, writing center.

**Majors. Architecture:** Urban/community planning. **Area/ethnic studies:** East Asian. **Biology:** General. **Computer sciences:** General. **Foreign languages:** Ancient Greek, classics, comparative lit, French, German, Italian, Latin, Russian, Spanish. **History:** General. **Liberal arts:** Arts/sciences. **Math:** General. **Philosophy/religion:** Philosophy, religion. **Physical sciences:** Astronomy, chemistry, geology, physics. **Psychology:** General. **Social sciences:** Anthropology, archaeology, economics, political science, sociology, urban studies. **Visual/performing arts:** Art history/conservation, studio arts.

**Most popular majors.** Biology 13%, English 9%, foreign language 6%, mathematics 6%, physical sciences 7%, psychology 9%, social sciences 30%.

**Computing on campus.** 300 workstations in dormitories, library, computer center, student center. Dormitories wired for high-speed internet access and linked to campus network. Commuter students can connect to campus network. Online course registration, online library, helpline, student web hosting, wireless network available.

**Student life. Freshman orientation:** Mandatory, $200 fee. Preregistration for classes offered. Directly precedes the start of the fall semester. **Policies:** Student conduct regulated by academic and social honor code, which allows for unsupervised examinations. Students serve on campus governance and policy-making committees. **Housing:** Guaranteed on-campus for all undergraduates. Coed dorms, single-sex dorms, apartments, wellness housing available. Students may live at Bryn Mawr College through dormitory exchange program. Students at both colleges may eat meals on either campus. **Activities:** Campus ministries, choral groups, dance, drama, international student organizations, literary magazine, music ensembles, musical theater, radio station, student government, student newspaper, Quaker activities committee, Hillel, Christian Fellowship, environmental action committee, black students league, Puerto Rican students association, Asian students association, Bisexual/Gay/Lesbian alliance, Eighth Dimension Volunteer Service Program.

**Athletics.** NCAA. **Intercollegiate:** Baseball M, basketball, cricket M, cross-country, fencing, field hockey W, lacrosse, soccer, softball W, squash, tennis, track and field, volleyball W. **Intramural:** Basketball, soccer, tennis.

**Student services.** Alcohol/substance abuse counseling, career counseling, student employment services, financial aid counseling, health services, minority student services, personal counseling, placement for graduates, women's services. **Physically disabled:** Services for visually, speech, hearing impaired.

**Contact.** E-mail: admission@haverford.edu
Phone: (610) 896-1350 Fax: (610) 896-1338
Jess Lord, Dean of Admissions and Financial Aid, Haverford College, 370 Lancaster Avenue, Haverford, PA 19041-1392

## Holy Family University
**Philadelphia, Pennsylvania**
www.holyfamily.edu

CB member
CB code: 2297

- Private 4-year university and liberal arts college affiliated with Roman Catholic Church
- Commuter campus in very large city
- 2,084 degree-seeking undergraduates: 25% part-time, 74% women, 7% African American, 5% Asian American, 5% Hispanic American, 1% Native American, 1% international
- 1,074 degree-seeking graduate students
- 74% of applicants admitted
- SAT or ACT (ACT writing optional) required
- 64% graduate within 6 years; 5% enter graduate study

**General.** Founded in 1954. Regionally accredited. Additional campuses in Newtown and Bensalem. **Degrees:** 510 bachelor's, 25 associate awarded; master's offered. **Location:** 12 miles from downtown. **Calendar:** Semester, extensive summer session. **Full-time faculty:** 94 total; 85% have terminal degrees, 11% minority, 64% women. **Part-time faculty:** 260 total; 16% have terminal degrees, 4% minority, 48% women. **Class size:** 67% < 20, 33% 20-39. **Special facilities:** Early childhood center with nursery school and kindergarten.

**Freshman class profile.** 1,241 applied, 913 admitted, 380 enrolled.

| Mid 50% test scores | | | |
|---|---|---|---|
| SAT critical reading: | 420-510 | GPA 3.0-3.49: | 28% |
| SAT math: | 420-510 | GPA 2.0-2.99: | 46% |
| ACT composite: | 19-21 | End year in good standing: | 77% |
| GPA 3.75 or higher: | 10% | Return as sophomores: | 75% |
| GPA 3.50-3.74: | 14% | Out-of-state: | 15% |
| | | Live on campus: | 28% |

**Basis for selection.** High school record most important, followed by recommendations, interview and test scores. Motivation, schoolwork and community activities considered. Essay, interview recommended. **Home-schooled:** State-issued equivalency diploma required. **Learning Disabled:** Students must meet with Counseling Center to be evaluated. Results and formal report shared with Admission department and acceptance decision is made. Results discussed with student.

**High school preparation.** 16 units required. Required units include English 4, mathematics 3, history 2, science 2, foreign language 2 and academic electives 3. All students must have algebra I, algebra II, and geometry. Math majors need trigonometry. Nursing requires biology, chemistry, and science electives. Science requires biology, chemistry, and trigonometry.

**2009-2010 Annual costs.** Tuition/fees: $22,460. Room/board: $9,900. Books/supplies: $972. Personal expenses: $600.

**2009-2010 Financial aid. Need-based:** 363 full-time freshmen applied for aid; 318 were judged to have need; 318 of these received aid. Average need met was 89%. Average scholarship/grant was $14,220; average loan $3,468. 50% of total undergraduate aid awarded as scholarships/grants, 50% as loans/jobs. **Non-need-based:** Awarded to 284 full-time undergraduates, including 156 freshmen. Scholarships awarded for academics, alumni affiliation, athletics.

**Application procedures. Admission:** No deadline. $25 fee, may be waived for applicants with need. Admission notification on a rolling basis beginning on or about 9/15. Must reply by May 1 or within 2 week(s) if notified thereafter. **Financial aid:** Priority date 3/1; no closing date. FAFSA, institutional form required. Applicants notified on a rolling basis starting 3/15; must reply within 2 week(s) of notification.

**Academics. Special study options:** Accelerated study, cooperative education, cross-registration, distance learning, double major, honors, independent study, internships, liberal arts/career combination, teacher certification program, weekend college. **Credit/placement by examination:** AP, CLEP, SAT, ACT, institutional tests. 30 credit hours maximum toward bachelor's degree. **Support services:** Learning center, pre-admission summer program, reduced course load, remedial instruction, study skills assistance, tutoring, writing center.

**Majors. Biology:** General, biochemistry. **Business:** Accounting, accounting/finance, business admin, finance, human resources, international, management information systems. **Communications:** Media studies. **Education:** Art, biology, chemistry, early childhood, elementary, English, French, history, mathematics, social science, social studies, Spanish, special. **Foreign languages:** French, Spanish. **Health:** Clinical lab science, nursing (RN), radiologic technology/medical imaging. **History:** General. **Liberal arts:** Humanities. **Math:** General. **Parks/recreation:** Sports admin. **Philosophy/religion:** Religion. **Physical sciences:** Chemistry. **Protective services:** Criminal justice, fire services admin. **Psychology:** General, industrial. **Public administration:** Social work. **Social sciences:** Economics, sociology. **Visual/performing arts:** Studio arts.

**Most popular majors.** Business/marketing 17%, education 20%, health sciences 38%, psychology 8%.

**Computing on campus.** 450 workstations in dormitories, library, computer center. Dormitories wired for high-speed internet access and linked to campus network. Commuter students can connect to campus network. Online course registration, online library, helpline, repair service, wireless network available.

**Student life. Freshman orientation:** Mandatory. **Policies:** Mature and intelligent student conduct expected in accordance with college's interests, standards, and ideals. **Housing:** Guaranteed on-campus for freshmen. Coed dorms, special housing for disabled, apartments, wellness housing available. $300 fully refundable deposit, deadline 3/15. On-campus housing available for some athletes. **Activities:** Campus ministries, choral groups, drama, literary magazine, radio station, student government, student newspaper, TV station, community health and welfare organizations, social and departmental clubs, honor societies, ministry team, Habitat for Humanity.

**Athletics.** NCAA. **Intercollegiate:** Basketball, cross-country, golf M, lacrosse W, soccer, softball W, tennis W, track and field, volleyball W. **Intramural:** Basketball, bowling, cheerleading W, football (non-tackle), racquetball, table tennis, volleyball. **Team name:** Tigers.

**Student services.** Adult student services, alcohol/substance abuse counseling, chaplain/spiritual director, career counseling, student employment services, financial aid counseling, health services, minority student services, personal counseling, placement for graduates. **Physically disabled:** Services for visually, speech, hearing impaired. **Learning disabled:** Comprehensive services available.

**Contact.** E-mail: admissions@holyfamily.edu
Phone: (215) 637-3050 Fax: (215) 281-1022
Lauren Campbell, Director of Admissions, Holy Family University, 9801 Frankford Avenue, Philadelphia, PA 19114-2009

---

## Immaculata University
**Immaculata, Pennsylvania**  **CB member**
**www.immaculata.edu**  **CB code: 2320**

- Private 4-year university and liberal arts college affiliated with Roman Catholic Church
- Residential campus in large town
- 2,950 degree-seeking undergraduates: 64% part-time, 78% women, 13% African American, 2% Asian American, 2% Hispanic American, 1% Native American, 1% international
- 959 degree-seeking graduate students
- 80% of applicants admitted
- SAT or ACT (ACT writing recommended) required
- 62% graduate within 6 years

**General.** Founded in 1920. Regionally accredited. **Degrees:** 609 bachelor's, 21 associate awarded; master's, doctoral offered. **Location:** 20 miles from Philadelphia. **Calendar:** Semester, limited summer session. **Full-time faculty:** 103 total; 79% have terminal degrees, 9% minority, 74% women. **Part-time faculty:** 308 total; 24% have terminal degrees, 58% women. **Class size:** 80% < 20, 20% 20-39.

**Freshman class profile.** 1,216 applied, 975 admitted, 196 enrolled.

| Mid 50% test scores | | | |
|---|---|---|---|
| SAT critical reading: | 420-510 | GPA 3.50-3.74: | 12% |
| SAT math: | 410-510 | GPA 3.0-3.49: | 26% |
| SAT writing: | 420-520 | GPA 2.0-2.99: | 44% |
| ACT composite: | 17-21 | Return as sophomores: | 72% |
| GPA 3.75 or higher: | 14% | Out-of-state: | 39% |
| | | Live on campus: | 81% |

**Basis for selection.** Class rank, academic program, test scores, counselor recommendation important. Minimum 2.3 GPA preferred. Interviews, essay recommended. Audition required for music program. **Homeschooled:** Transcript of courses and grades required. **Learning Disabled:** Proof of psychological or educational testing date must be supplied.

**High school preparation.** College-preparatory program required. 16 units required; 20 recommended. Required and recommended units include English 4, mathematics 2-3, social studies 2-3, science 2-4 (laboratory 1), foreign language 2-3 and visual/performing arts 4. Music required for music majors.

**2010-2011 Annual costs.** Tuition/fees: $27,870. Room/board: $11,460. Books/supplies: $1,695. Personal expenses: $2,880.

**2009-2010 Financial aid. Non-need-based:** Scholarships awarded for academics, alumni affiliation, art, job skills, leadership, minority status, music/drama, religious affiliation, state residency.

**Application procedures. Admission:** Priority date 3/1; no deadline. $35 fee, may be waived for applicants with need. Admission notification on a rolling basis beginning on or about 9/15. Must reply by May 1 or within 2 week(s) if notified thereafter. **Financial aid:** Priority date 2/15, closing date 4/15. FAFSA required. Applicants notified on a rolling basis starting 2/1; must reply within 2 week(s) of notification.

**Academics. Special study options:** Accelerated study, combined bachelor's/graduate degree, cross-registration, distance learning, double major, dual enrollment of high school students, honors, independent study, internships, liberal arts/career combination, semester at sea, study abroad, teacher certification program, Washington semester. **Credit/placement by examination:** AP, CLEP, IB, SAT, ACT, institutional tests. 30 credit hours maximum toward associate degree, 63 toward bachelor's. **Support services:** Learning center, reduced course load, remedial instruction, study skills assistance, tutoring, writing center.

**Majors. Biology:** General. **Business:** Accounting, business admin, fashion, finance, human resources, marketing. **Communications:** General. **Computer sciences:** Information systems. **Conservation:** Environmental studies. **Education:** Business, elementary, family/consumer sciences, mathematics, music. **Foreign languages:** French, German, Spanish. **Health:** Dietetics,

health care admin, health services, music therapy, nursing (RN), premedicine. **History:** General. **Interdisciplinary:** Biological/physical sciences, biopsychology, math/computer science. **Liberal arts:** Arts/sciences. **Math:** General. **Parks/recreation:** Exercise sciences. **Personal/culinary services:** Institutional food service. **Physical sciences:** Chemistry. **Protective services:** Criminal justice. **Psychology:** General. **Public administration:** Policy analysis. **Social sciences:** Economics, international relations, political science, sociology. **Theology:** Theology. **Visual/performing arts:** Music performance. **Other:** Organizational dynamics, Spanish psychology.

**Most popular majors.** Business/marketing 30%, health sciences 40%, psychology 6%.

**Computing on campus.** 326 workstations in dormitories, library, computer center, student center. Dormitories wired for high-speed internet access and linked to campus network. Commuter students can connect to campus network. Online course registration, online library, helpline, wireless network available.

**Student life. Freshman orientation:** Mandatory. Preregistration for classes offered. 2-day session held in summer. **Housing:** Coed dorms, single-sex dorms, special housing for disabled, apartments available. $250 partly refundable deposit. **Activities:** Bands, campus ministries, choral groups, dance, drama, international student organizations, literary magazine, music ensembles, musical theater, student government, student newspaper, symphony orchestra, African American cultural society, American Music Therapy Association, Modern Foreign Language Association.

**Athletics.** NCAA. **Intercollegiate:** Basketball, cross-country W, field hockey W, golf, lacrosse, soccer, softball W, tennis, volleyball W. **Intramural:** Basketball, cross-country W, field hockey W, lacrosse W, soccer W, softball W, swimming W, tennis W, volleyball W. **Team name:** Mighty Macs.

**Student services.** Adult student services, alcohol/substance abuse counseling, chaplain/spiritual director, career counseling, student employment services, financial aid counseling, health services, minority student services, personal counseling, placement for graduates. **Physically disabled:** Services for visually, hearing impaired.

**Contact.** E-mail: admiss@immaculata.edu
Phone: (610) 647-4400 ext. 3060 Toll-free number: (877) 428-6329 Fax: (610) 640-0836
Rebecca Bowlby, Director of Admission, Immaculata University, PO Box 642, Immaculata, PA 19345-0642

---

## Indiana University of Pennsylvania
**Indiana, Pennsylvania**  **CB member**
**www.iup.edu**  **CB code: 2652**

- Public 4-year university
- Residential campus in large town
- 11,821 degree-seeking undergraduates: 5% part-time, 56% women, 11% African American, 1% Asian American, 2% Hispanic American, 1% international
- 2,247 degree-seeking graduate students
- 60% of applicants admitted
- SAT or ACT (ACT writing optional) required
- 51% graduate within 6 years

**General.** Founded in 1875. Regionally accredited. Branch campuses located in Punxsutawney and Armstrong County. **Degrees:** 2,079 bachelor's, 9 associate awarded; master's, doctoral offered. **ROTC:** Army. **Location:** 50 miles from Pittsburgh. **Calendar:** Semester, extensive summer session. **Full-time faculty:** 611 total; 13% minority, 49% women. **Part-time faculty:** 62 total; 5% minority, 63% women. **Class size:** 33% < 20, 44% 20-39, 10% 40-49, 11% 50-99, 1% >100. **Special facilities:** Museums, ski slopes, nature preserve, lodge, and sailing base.

**Freshman class profile.** 11,669 applied, 7,041 admitted, 3,008 enrolled.

| Mid 50% test scores | | | |
|---|---|---|---|
| SAT critical reading: | 440-540 | Rank in top tenth: | 8% |
| SAT math: | 440-540 | Return as sophomores: | 74% |
| SAT writing: | 430-520 | Out-of-state: | 7% |
| Rank in top quarter: | 26% | Live on campus: | 81% |
| | | International: | 1% |

**Basis for selection.** School achievement record, recommendations and extracurricular activities considered, test scores, and high school rank important. Audition required for music program; portfolio required for art program. **Homeschooled:** Transcript of courses and grades required.

**High school preparation.** 4 units recommended. Recommended units include English 3, mathematics 3, social studies 3, science 3 and foreign language 2. Additional .5 unit computer science recommended.

**2009-2010 Annual costs.** Tuition/fees: $7,209; $15,541 out-of-state. Additional fees of $104 for out-of-state students. Tuition is $8,332 for students in any of these categories: OH, VA, WV, IN and MI residents; branch campus students from any state; out-of-state students with high school GPA of at least 3.0; any transfer student with GPA of at least 3.0. Room/board: $6,278. Books/supplies: $1,100. Personal expenses: $2,828.

**2008-2009 Financial aid. Need-based:** 2,787 full-time freshmen applied for aid; 2,097 were judged to have need; 2,081 of these received aid. Average need met was 77%. Average scholarship/grant was $5,387; average loan $3,650. 43% of total undergraduate aid awarded as scholarships/grants, 57% as loans/jobs. **Non-need-based:** Awarded to 2,303 full-time undergraduates, including 986 freshmen. Scholarships awarded for academics, alumni affiliation, art, athletics, job skills, leadership, music/drama, ROTC, state residency.

**Application procedures. Admission:** Priority date 12/31; no deadline. $35 fee, may be waived for applicants with need. Admission notification on a rolling basis beginning on or about 9/1. Must reply by May 1 or within 2 week(s) if notified thereafter. **Financial aid:** Priority date 4/15; no closing date. FAFSA required. Applicants notified on a rolling basis starting 3/15.

**Academics. Special study options:** Accelerated study, combined bachelor's/graduate degree, cooperative education, cross-registration, distance learning, double major, dual enrollment of high school students, ESL, exchange student, external degree, honors, independent study, internships, liberal arts/career combination, student-designed major, study abroad, teacher certification program, urban semester, Washington semester, weekend college. **Credit/placement by examination:** AP, CLEP, IB, SAT, ACT, institutional tests. Unlimited number of hours of credit by examination may be counted toward degree. **Support services:** Learning center, pre-admission summer program, remedial instruction, study skills assistance, tutoring, writing center.

**Majors. Architecture:** Urban/community planning. **Biology:** General, biochemistry. **Business:** General, accounting, business admin, fashion, finance, hospitality admin, human resources, international, management information systems, marketing, office management. **Communications:** General, journalism. **Computer sciences:** General. **Education:** Deaf/hearing impaired, early childhood, elementary, physically handicapped, social science, special, speech impaired, trade/industrial. **Engineering technology:** Occupational safety. **Family/consumer sciences:** General, consumer economics, family studies, food/nutrition. **Foreign languages:** French, German, Spanish. **Health:** Clinical lab science, environmental health, nuclear medical technology, nursing (RN), respiratory therapy technology. **History:** General. **Interdisciplinary:** Biological/physical sciences. **Math:** General, applied. **Parks/recreation:** Health/fitness. **Philosophy/religion:** Philosophy, religion. **Physical sciences:** General, applied physics, chemistry, geology, physics. **Psychology:** General. **Social sciences:** Anthropology, criminology, economics, geography, international relations, political science, sociology. **Visual/performing arts:** Art, dramatic, multimedia, music performance, studio arts. **Other:** Disability services, Economics and mathematics, French for international trade.

**Most popular majors.** Business/marketing 24%, communications/journalism 7%, education 8%, family/consumer sciences 6%, health sciences 8%, parks/recreation 6%, social sciences 16%, visual/performing arts 8%.

**Computing on campus.** 3,500 workstations in dormitories, library, computer center. Dormitories wired for high-speed internet access and linked to campus network. Commuter students can connect to campus network. Online course registration, helpline, repair service, student web hosting, wireless network available.

**Student life. Freshman orientation:** Mandatory, $140 fee. Preregistration for classes offered. **Housing:** Guaranteed on-campus for freshmen. Coed dorms, special housing for disabled, apartments, wellness housing available. $80 nonrefundable deposit, deadline 5/15. Honors college dormitory, substance-free housing, academic specialty floors available. **Activities:** Bands, campus ministries, choral groups, dance, drama, international student organizations, music ensembles, musical theater, radio station, student government, student newspaper, symphony orchestra, TV station, Alpha Phi Omega National Service Fraternity (coeducational), Gamma Sigma Sigma Service Sorority, African American Cultural Center, Campus Crusade for Christ, Coalition for Christian Outreach, Newman Center, Panhellenic Association, NAACP.

**Athletics.** NCAA. **Intercollegiate:** Baseball M, basketball, cross-country, diving, field hockey W, football (tackle) M, golf M, lacrosse W, soccer W, softball W, swimming, tennis W, track and field, volleyball W. **Intramural:** Archery, badminton, basketball, bowling, cross-country, fencing, football (non-tackle), golf, racquetball, soccer, softball, table tennis, tennis, track

and field, volleyball, water polo, weight lifting, wrestling M. **Team name:** Crimson Hawks.

**Student services.** Adult student services, alcohol/substance abuse counseling, chaplain/spiritual director, career counseling, services for economically disadvantaged, student employment services, financial aid counseling, health services, legal services, minority student services, on-campus daycare, personal counseling, placement for graduates, veterans' counselor, women's services. **Physically disabled:** Services for visually, speech, hearing impaired.

**Contact.** E-mail: admissions_inquiry@iup.edu
Phone: (724) 357-2230 Toll-free number: (800) 442-6830
Fax: (724) 357-6281
Rhonda Luckey, Vice President for Student Affairs, Indiana University of Pennsylvania, 117 John Sutton Hall, 1011 South Drive, Indiana, PA 15705-1088

---

## Juniata College
**Huntingdon, Pennsylvania**
www.juniata.edu

CB member
CB code: 2341

- Private 4-year liberal arts college
- Residential campus in small town
- 1,360 degree-seeking undergraduates: 56% women, 2% African American, 2% Asian American, 2% Hispanic American, 7% international
- 72% of applicants admitted
- Application essay required
- 79% graduate within 6 years; 33% enter graduate study

**General.** Founded in 1876. Regionally accredited. **Degrees:** 332 bachelor's awarded. **Location:** 30 miles from Altoona and State College. **Calendar:** Semester, limited summer session. **Full-time faculty:** 100 total; 94% have terminal degrees, 6% minority, 39% women. **Part-time faculty:** 40 total; 12% have terminal degrees, 5% minority, 68% women. **Class size:** 76% < 20, 21% 20-39, 3% 40-49, 1% 50-99. **Special facilities:** Nature preserve, environmental studies field station, observatory, early childhood education center.

**Freshman class profile.** 1,964 applied, 1,410 admitted, 366 enrolled.

| Mid 50% test scores | | | |
|---|---|---|---|
| SAT critical reading: | 550-650 | Rank in top quarter: | 74% |
| SAT math: | 550-660 | Rank in top tenth: | 41% |
| GPA 3.75 or higher: | 53% | End year in good standing: | 95% |
| GPA 3.50-3.74: | 22% | Return as sophomores: | 85% |
| GPA 3.0-3.49: | 20% | Out-of-state: | 32% |
| GPA 2.0-2.99: | 5% | Live on campus: | 96% |
| | | International: | 4% |

**Basis for selection.** School achievement record most important. Standardized test scores, school and community activities, recommendations and essay also important. SAT or ACT recommended. Students may submit SAT or ACT scores either directly from the testing agency or from the guidance counselor. If a student chooses not to submit standardized test scores, then must submit two graded papers. Interview recommended. **Homeschooled:** Interview required.

**High school preparation.** College-preparatory program required. 16 units required; 18 recommended. Required and recommended units include English 4, mathematics 3-4, social studies 1, history 3, science 3-4 (laboratory 2) and foreign language 2.

**2010-2011 Annual costs.** Tuition/fees: $32,820. Room/board: $8,980. Books/supplies: $600. Personal expenses: $1,000.

**2009-2010 Financial aid. Need-based:** 305 full-time freshmen applied for aid; 262 were judged to have need; 262 of these received aid. Average need met was 86%. Average scholarship/grant was $21,571; average loan $3,847. 75% of total undergraduate aid awarded as scholarships/grants, 25% as loans/jobs. **Non-need-based:** Awarded to 545 full-time undergraduates, including 136 freshmen. Scholarships awarded for academics, art, leadership.

**Application procedures. Admission:** Priority date 12/1; deadline 3/15 (postmark date). $30 fee, may be waived for applicants with need, free for online applicants. Admission notification on a rolling basis beginning on or about 2/28. Must reply by May 1 or within 2 week(s) if notified thereafter. **Financial aid:** Closing date 3/1. FAFSA required. Applicants notified on a rolling basis starting 2/28; must reply by 5/1.

**Academics.** Majors replaced by Programs of Emphasis. Over 50% of students design individualized POE. **Special study options:** Combined bachelor's/graduate degree, double major, dual enrollment of high school students, ESL, exchange student, honors, independent study, internships, student-designed major, study abroad, teacher certification program, urban semester, Washington semester. Marine biology with Oregon Marine Program; 3-3 law with Duquesne University; 3-2 engineering with Columbia University, Pennsylvania State University, Clarkson University, Washington University; 3-4 dentistry with Temple University; 3-4 medicine with Tulane University School of Medicine, Lake Erie College of Osteopathic Medicine, Temple University School of Medicine; 3-4 optometry with Pennsylvania College of Optometry; 3-4 podiatry with Temple University School of Podiatric Medicine and Ohio College of Podiatric Medicine; nursing with Johns Hopkins University, Case Western Reserve University; biotechnology, cytotechnology with Jefferson College of Health Professions; physical therapy with Widener University, Drexel University, Jefferson College of Health Professions; medical technology with Jefferson College of Health Professions, Altoona Regional Health Systems, Lancaster General College of Nursing & Health Sciences. **Credit/placement by examination:** AP, CLEP, IB, institutional tests. Unlimited number of hours of credit by examination may be counted toward degree. **Support services:** Reduced course load, study skills assistance, tutoring, writing center.

**Majors.** **Biology:** General, biochemistry, botany, cell/histology, ecology, marine, microbiology, molecular, zoology. **Business:** General, accounting, business admin, entrepreneurial studies, finance, human resources, information resources management, international, marketing. **Communications:** General, digital media, health. **Computer sciences:** General, information technology. **Conservation:** Environmental science, environmental studies, wildlife. **Education:** General, biology, chemistry, early childhood, early childhood special, elementary, English, French, German, mathematics, multi-level teacher, physics, science, secondary, social studies, Spanish. **Engineering:** General, physics. **Foreign languages:** General, French, German, Russian, Spanish. **Health:** Predental, premedicine, prenursing, prepharmacy, preveterinary. **History:** General. **Interdisciplinary:** Global studies, museum, natural sciences, peace/conflict. **Legal studies:** Prelaw. **Liberal arts:** Arts/sciences, humanities. **Math:** General. **Philosophy/religion:** Philosophy, religion. **Physical sciences:** General, chemistry, geology, physics. **Psychology:** General. **Public administration:** General, social work. **Social sciences:** General, anthropology, criminology, international relations, political science, sociology. **Visual/performing arts:** Art history/conservation, dramatic, studio arts, theater arts management. **Other:** Pre-allied health, Professional writing.

**Most popular majors.** Biology 18%, business/marketing 15%, communications/journalism 7%, interdisciplinary studies 6%; liberal arts 6%, natural resources/environmental science 6%, psychology 8%, social sciences 8%.

**Computing on campus.** PC or laptop required. 340 workstations in library, computer center, student center. Dormitories wired for high-speed internet access and linked to campus network. Commuter students can connect to campus network. Online course registration, online library, helpline, repair service, wireless network available.

**Student life. Freshman orientation:** Available. Preregistration for classes offered. 2 days in summer, parallel programs for new students and their parents. **Housing:** Guaranteed on-campus for all undergraduates. Coed dorms, single-sex dorms, apartments, wellness housing available. $400 nonrefundable deposit, deadline 5/1. Special interest housing available. **Activities:** Bands, campus ministries, choral groups, dance, drama, international student organizations, literary magazine, music ensembles, Model UN, musical theater, radio station, student government, student newspaper, symphony orchestra, TV station, Christian Ministry Board, Catholic Council, Hillel, Muslim student association, United Spiritual Council, Brethren Student Fellowship, Habitat for Humanity, Colleges Against Cancer, African American Student Alliance.

**Athletics.** NCAA. **Intercollegiate:** Baseball M, basketball, cross-country, field hockey W, football (tackle) M, soccer, softball W, swimming W, tennis, track and field, volleyball. **Intramural:** Basketball, soccer, volleyball. **Team name:** Eagles.

**Student services.** Adult student services, alcohol/substance abuse counseling, chaplain/spiritual director, career counseling, student employment services, financial aid counseling, health services, minority student services, personal counseling, placement for graduates. **Physically disabled:** Services for visually, hearing impaired.

**Contact.** E-mail: admissions@juniata.edu
Phone: (814) 641-3420 Toll-free number: (877) 586-4282
Fax: (814) 641-3100
Michelle Bartol, Dean of Enrollment, Juniata College, 1700 Moore Street, Huntingdon, PA 16652-2196

---

## Keystone College
**La Plume, Pennsylvania**
www.keystone.edu

**CB member**
**CB code: 2351**

- Private 4-year liberal arts college
- Residential campus in small town
- 1,612 degree-seeking undergraduates: 21% part-time, 60% women
- 50 graduate students
- 95% of applicants admitted
- SAT or ACT (ACT writing optional), application essay required
- 36% graduate within 6 years; 7% enter graduate study

**General.** Founded in 1868. Regionally accredited. Students may enroll in up to 12 credits as nonmatriculating prior to making formal application to college. Trimester system for Adult Weekender Program. **Degrees:** 251 bachelor's, 72 associate awarded. **ROTC:** Army, Air Force. **Location:** 15 miles from Scranton. **Calendar:** Differs by program, limited summer session. **Full-time faculty:** 71 total; 41% have terminal degrees, 4% minority, 63% women. **Part-time faculty:** 206 total; 13% have terminal degrees, 2% minority, 53% women. **Class size:** 80% < 20, 20% 20-39, less than 1% 40-49, less than 1% 50-99. **Special facilities:** Observatory, children's center, Microsoft-certified systems engineer training site, Willary Water Resource center, U.S. Mid-Atlantic Urban Forestry Center, restaurant (operated by culinary students), delayed harvest trout stream, Countryside Conservancy, PRAXIS testing location, Nightshade Press, nature trails.

**Freshman class profile.** 778 applied, 739 admitted, 336 enrolled.

| Mid 50% test scores | | | |
|---|---|---|---|
| SAT critical reading: | 390-480 | Rank in top quarter: | 11% |
| SAT math: | 380-480 | Rank in top tenth: | 3% |
| SAT writing: | 380-470 | Return as sophomores: | 61% |
| ACT composite: | 15-18 | Out-of-state: | 16% |
| | | Live on campus: | 46% |

**Basis for selection.** School achievement record, extracurricular activities, test scores, recommendations, class rank, preparation in proposed major area of study considered. Portfolio and interview required for all art and art education applications. Admissions interview required for some on a case-by-case basis. **Homeschooled:** Statement describing homeschool structure and mission, interview required. Portfolio of high school level work also required. **Learning Disabled:** Current psychological report and Individualized Educational Program or 504 plan should be submitted at time of application. On-campus interview generally required to ensure that the college provides a level of support needed for the student to be academically successful.

**High school preparation.** College-preparatory program required. 16 units required; 20 recommended. Required and recommended units include English 4, mathematics 3-4, social studies 2, history 1, science 2-3 (laboratory 1), foreign language 2, computer science 1, visual/performing arts 1 and academic electives 2. Foreign language recommended for art, communications, and liberal arts curricula. 4 math and 3 science (including 2 lab) recommended for allied health, environmental science, biology, pre-medical tracks, and forensic biology.

**2009-2010 Annual costs.** Tuition/fees: $18,420. Room/board: $8,760. Books/supplies: $1,600.

**2008-2009 Financial aid. Need-based:** Average need met was 72%. Average scholarship/grant was $19,907; average loan $3,500. 55% of total undergraduate aid awarded as scholarships/grants, 45% as loans/jobs. **Non-need-based:** Awarded to 58 full-time undergraduates, including 17 freshmen. Scholarships awarded for academics, leadership.

**Application procedures. Admission:** Priority date 5/1; deadline 7/15 (receipt date). $30 fee, may be waived for applicants with need. Admission notification on a rolling basis beginning on or about 10/1. Must reply by May 1 or within 3 week(s) if notified thereafter. **Financial aid:** Priority date 5/1; no closing date. FAFSA required. Applicants notified on a rolling basis starting 2/1; must reply within 2 week(s) of notification.

**Academics.** Students in good academic and financial standing who have not received at least 1 job offer or acceptance into a transfer or graduate program within 6 months after graduating and fulfilling requirements of Career Development Center will be provided with additional courses and career counseling at no extra charge. **Special study options:** Combined bachelor's/graduate degree, cooperative education, cross-registration, distance learning, double major, dual enrollment of high school students, ESL, honors, independent study, internships, study abroad, teacher certification program, weekend college. 2+2, 2+3, 3+3, 4+3 programs with various 4-year institutions for students studying allied health, health sciences, and environmental sciences. **Credit/placement by examination:** AP, CLEP, IB, SAT, ACT, institutional tests. 12 credit hours maximum toward associate degree, 18 toward bachelor's. Maximum of 32 credits for associate degree-seekers and 64 credits for bachelor's degree-seekers awarded for prior work and/or life experience. **Support services:** Learning center, pre-admission summer program, reduced course load, remedial instruction, study skills assistance, tutoring, writing center.

**Majors. Biology:** General, biochemistry, biomedical sciences, environmental. **Business:** General, accounting, accounting/business management, business admin, management information systems, organizational behavior. **Communications:** General, advertising, journalism, public relations. **Communications technology:** Graphics. **Computer sciences:** General, information systems, information technology, LAN/WAN management, networking, systems analysis. **Conservation:** General, management/policy, water/wetlands/marine. **Education:** General, art, early childhood, elementary, mathematics, multi-level teacher, social studies. **Family/consumer sciences:** General, child care, child development, family systems. **Health:** Predental, premedicine, prepharmacy, preveterinary. **Interdisciplinary:** Biological/physical sciences, natural sciences. **Legal studies:** Prelaw. **Liberal arts:** Humanities. **Parks/recreation:** General, facilities management, sports admin. **Protective services:** Criminal justice, criminalistics, forensics, law enforcement admin. **Psychology:** General. **Social sciences:** General. **Visual/performing arts:** Art, ceramics, drawing, graphic design, illustration, painting, photography, printmaking, sculpture, studio arts.

**Most popular majors.** Business/marketing 25%, communications/journalism 9%, computer/information sciences 6%, education 18%, parks/recreation 9%, security/protective services 17%.

**Computing on campus.** 120 workstations in dormitories, library, computer center, student center. Dormitories wired for high-speed internet access and linked to campus network. Commuter students can connect to campus network. Online course registration, helpline, wireless network available.

**Student life. Freshman orientation:** Mandatory, $125 fee. Preregistration for classes offered. One-day program during summer for scheduling classes. 2-day overnight program prior to start of classes. **Policies:** Alcohol and drug-free campus. **Housing:** Guaranteed on-campus for freshmen. Coed dorms, single-sex dorms, special housing for disabled available. $100 fully refundable deposit, deadline 5/1. **Activities:** Campus ministries, choral groups, drama, international student organizations, literary magazine, musical theater, radio station, student government, student newspaper, Multicultural Affairs Student Association, Opposing Prejudice Ending Negativity (OPEN), Students in Free Enterprise, Keystone Service Club, Rotaract, Winner's Circle.

**Athletics.** NCAA. **Intercollegiate:** Baseball M, basketball, cross-country, field hockey W, golf M, soccer, softball W, tennis, track and field, volleyball W. **Intramural:** Basketball, football (non-tackle), soccer, softball, table tennis, tennis, volleyball. **Team name:** Giants.

**Student services.** Adult student services, alcohol/substance abuse counseling, chaplain/spiritual director, career counseling, services for economically disadvantaged, student employment services, financial aid counseling, health services, minority student services, on-campus daycare, personal counseling, placement for graduates, veterans' counselor, women's services.

**Contact.** E-mail: admissions@keystone.edu
Phone: (570) 945-8111 Toll-free number: (800) 824-2764
Fax: (570) 945-7916
Sarah Keating, Vice President for Enrollment and Director of Admissions, Keystone College, One College Green, La Plume, PA 18440-1099

## King's College

| Wilkes-Barre, Pennsylvania | CB member |
|---|---|
| www.kings.edu | CB code: 2353 |

◗ Private 4-year business and liberal arts college affiliated with Roman Catholic Church

◗ Residential campus in small city

◗ 2,042 degree-seeking undergraduates: 4% part-time, 49% women, 2% African American, 1% Asian American, 4% Hispanic American

◗ 251 degree-seeking graduate students

◗ 75% of applicants admitted

◗ 68% graduate within 6 years; 27% enter graduate study

**General.** Founded in 1946. Regionally accredited. **Degrees:** 438 bachelor's awarded; master's offered. **ROTC:** Army, Air Force. **Location:** 110 miles from Philadelphia, 140 miles from New York City. **Calendar:** Semester, extensive summer session. **Full-time faculty:** 129 total; 83% have terminal degrees, 5% minority, 40% women. **Part-time faculty:** 80 total; 20% have terminal degrees, 46% women. **Class size:** 59% < 20, 40% 20-39, less than 1% 40-49. **Special facilities:** Rooftop greenhouse, molecular biology laboratory.

**Freshman class profile.** 2,172 applied, 1,633 admitted, 496 enrolled.

| Mid 50% test scores | | | |
|---|---|---|---|
| SAT critical reading: | 460-550 | GPA 2.0-2.99: | 25% |
| SAT math: | 470-560 | Rank in top quarter: | 40% |
| SAT writing: | 450-550 | Rank in top tenth: | 15% |
| GPA 3.75 or higher: | 29% | Return as sophomores: | 74% |
| GPA 3.50-3.74: | 9% | Out-of-state: | 34% |
| GPA 3.0-3.49: | 37% | Live on campus: | 73% |

**Basis for selection.** Class rank and academic GPA very important. Standardized test scores important. SAT or ACT recommended. Students may choose a standardized test option/essay choice in which an official graded writing sample from either junior or senior year is submitted and notarized by the high school guidance office. Students choosing this option are required to notify the Office of Admission on the application. A student's decision is non-reversible and must be made prior to application review. Interview recommended. **Homeschooled:** Transcript of courses and grades, state high school equivalency certificate required. **Learning Disabled:** Learning-disabled students applying for the first-year academic studies program must submit supplemental application with appropriate documentation. Contact Director of Academic Skills Center during admission process.

**High school preparation.** College-preparatory program required. 16 units required; 24 recommended. Required and recommended units include English 4, mathematics 3-4, social studies 3-4, science 3-4 (laboratory 2), foreign language 2-3 and computer science 2.

**2009-2010 Annual costs.** Tuition/fees: $25,644. Room/board: $9,838. Books/supplies: $1,220. Personal expenses: $1,260.

**2009-2010 Financial aid. Need-based:** 474 full-time freshmen applied for aid; 427 were judged to have need; 427 of these received aid. Average need met was 73%. Average scholarship/grant was $16,246; average loan $4,129. 72% of total undergraduate aid awarded as scholarships/grants, 28% as loans/jobs. **Non-need-based:** Awarded to 515 full-time undergraduates, including 116 freshmen. Scholarships awarded for academics, leadership, ROTC. **Additional information:** Any minority student with financial need may receive some aid in the form of a diversity scholarship.

**Application procedures. Admission:** No deadline. $30 fee, may be waived for applicants with need, free for online applicants. Admission notification on a rolling basis beginning on or about 10/1. Must reply by May 1 or within 2 week(s) if notified thereafter. **Financial aid:** Priority date 2/15; no closing date. FAFSA, institutional form required. Applicants notified on a rolling basis starting 3/1; must reply within 2 week(s) of notification.

**Academics. Special study options:** Accelerated study, cross-registration, distance learning, double major, dual enrollment of high school students, ESL, honors, independent study, internships, student-designed major, study abroad, teacher certification program, Washington semester, weekend college. Preprofessional programs in dentistry, medicine, pharmacy, veterinary science. **Credit/placement by examination:** AP, CLEP, IB, SAT, ACT, institutional tests. 15 credit hours maximum toward associate degree, 30 toward bachelor's. **Support services:** Learning center, pre-admission summer program, reduced course load, study skills assistance, tutoring, writing center.

**Majors. Biology:** General. **Business:** Accounting, business admin, finance, human resources, international, marketing. **Communications:** Media studies. **Computer sciences:** General, computer science. **Conservation:** Environmental science, environmental studies. **Education:** Early childhood, elementary, special. **Foreign languages:** French, Spanish. **Health:** Athletic training, clinical lab science, health services. **History:** General. **Interdisciplinary:** Biological/physical sciences, neuroscience. **Math:** General. **Philosophy/religion:** Philosophy. **Physical sciences:** Chemistry. **Protective services:** Criminal justice. **Psychology:** General. **Social sciences:** Economics, political science, sociology. **Theology:** Theology. **Visual/performing arts:** Dramatic.

**Most popular majors.** Biology 6%, business/marketing 30%, communications/journalism 8%, education 10%, health sciences 6%, psychology 6%, security/protective services 10%.

**Computing on campus.** 470 workstations in dormitories, library, computer center, student center. Dormitories wired for high-speed internet access and linked to campus network. Commuter students can connect to campus network. Online course registration, helpline, repair service, student web hosting, wireless network available.

**Student life. Freshman orientation:** Mandatory, $160 fee. Preregistration for classes offered. Held the 4 days prior to start of fall classes. **Housing:** Guaranteed on-campus for all undergraduates. Coed dorms, single-sex dorms, apartments available. $200 nonrefundable deposit. **Activities:** Campus ministries, choral groups, dance, drama, literary magazine, music ensembles, radio station, student government, student newspaper, association of campus events, organizations of various majors, Campion Society, Blood Council, Circle K, politics society, environmental awareness and outdoors club, residence hall council, service fraternity and sorority.

**Athletics.** NCAA. **Intercollegiate:** Baseball M, basketball, cheerleading, cross-country, field hockey W, football (tackle) M, golf M, lacrosse, soccer, softball W, swimming, tennis, volleyball W, wrestling M. **Intramural:** Basketball, football (non-tackle) M, soccer. **Team name:** Monarchs.

**Student services.** Adult student services, chaplain/spiritual director, career counseling, student employment services, financial aid counseling, health services, on-campus daycare, personal counseling, placement for graduates.

**Contact.** E-mail: admissions@kings.edu
Phone: (570) 208-5858 Toll-free number: (888) 546-4772
Fax: (570) 208-5971
Michelle Lawrence-Schmude, Director of Admissions, King's College, 133 North River Street, Wilkes-Barre, PA 18711

---

### Kutztown University of Pennsylvania
**Kutztown, Pennsylvania**  CB member
**www.kutztown.edu**  CB code: 2653

- Public 4-year university
- Residential campus in small town
- 9,181 degree-seeking undergraduates: 5% part-time, 57% women, 6% African American, 1% Asian American, 5% Hispanic American, 1% international
- 789 degree-seeking graduate students
- 66% of applicants admitted
- SAT or ACT (ACT writing optional) required
- 51% graduate within 6 years; 21% enter graduate study

**General.** Founded in 1866. Regionally accredited. **Degrees:** 1,753 bachelor's awarded; master's offered. **ROTC:** Army. **Location:** 20 miles from Allentown and Reading. **Calendar:** Semester, extensive summer session. **Full-time faculty:** 461 total; 77% have terminal degrees, 15% minority, 46% women. **Part-time faculty:** 43 total; 19% have terminal degrees, 5% minority, 49% women. **Class size:** 27% < 20, 57% 20-39, 4% 40-49, 6% 50-99, 5% >100. **Special facilities:** Observatory, on-campus preschool, Pennsylvania German heritage cultural center, planetarium.

**Freshman class profile.** 9,540 applied, 6,301 admitted, 1,989 enrolled.

| Mid 50% test scores | | | |
|---|---|---|---|
| SAT critical reading: | 440-530 | Rank in top quarter: | 22% |
| SAT math: | 430-530 | Rank in top tenth: | 6% |
| SAT writing: | 430-520 | End year in good standing: | 80% |
| ACT composite: | 17-22 | Return as sophomores: | 78% |
| GPA 3.75 or higher: | 8% | Out-of-state: | 14% |
| GPA 3.50-3.74: | 11% | Live on campus: | 90% |
| GPA 3.0-3.49: | 32% | International: | 1% |
| GPA 2.0-2.99: | 49% | Fraternities: | 4% |
| | | Sororities: | 4% |

**Basis for selection.** School records and academic aptitude tests most important. Recommendations, essays, extracurricular activities considered. SAT Subject Tests (biology and chemistry) required for medical technology program. Audition required for music program; portfolio and/or art test required for art education, communication design, crafts, and fine arts programs. **Homeschooled:** Applicants must submit supporting data from Pennsylvania Home Schooling Association.

**High school preparation.** College-preparatory program recommended. 18 units recommended. Recommended units include English 4, mathematics 4, social studies 4, science 4 and foreign language 2. Course recommendations vary for specific programs.

**2009-2010 Annual costs.** Tuition/fees: $7,398; $15,730 out-of-state. Room/board: $7,698. Books/supplies: $1,100. Personal expenses: $2,600.

**2008-2009 Financial aid.** **Need-based:** 1,653 full-time freshmen applied for aid; 1,129 were judged to have need; 1,093 of these received aid. Average need met was 54%. Average scholarship/grant was $4,766; average loan $3,269. 34% of total undergraduate aid awarded as scholarships/grants, 66% as loans/jobs. **Non-need-based:** Awarded to 677 full-time undergraduates, including 137 freshmen. Scholarships awarded for academics, art, athletics, leadership, minority status, music/drama.

**Application procedures.** **Admission:** Priority date 12/1; no deadline. $35 fee, may be waived for applicants with need. Admission notification on a rolling basis beginning on or about 10/1. Must reply by May 1 or by date stated on notification letter. **Financial aid:** Priority date 3/1; no closing date. FAFSA required. Applicants notified on a rolling basis starting 3/30; must reply by 5/1 or within 4 week(s) of notification.

**Academics.** **Special study options:** Combined bachelor's/graduate degree, cross-registration, distance learning, double major, dual enrollment of high school students, honors, independent study, internships, liberal arts/career combination, student-designed major, study abroad, teacher certification program. **Credit/placement by examination:** AP, CLEP, IB, SAT, ACT, institutional tests. **Support services:** Learning center, pre-admission summer program, remedial instruction, study skills assistance, tutoring, writing center.

**Majors.** **Area/ethnic studies:** German. **Biology:** General, biochemistry. **Business:** Accounting, business admin, finance, human resources, international, marketing. **Communications:** Digital media. **Computer sciences:** Information technology. **Conservation:** Environmental science. **Education:** Elementary, kindergarten/preschool, special, speech impaired, visually handicapped. **Foreign languages:** French, German, Spanish. **Health:** Clinical lab science, nursing (RN). **History:** General. **Interdisciplinary:** Biological/physical sciences. **Liberal arts:** Library science. **Math:** General. **Parks/recreation:** General. **Philosophy/religion:** Philosophy. **Physical sciences:** Chemistry, geology, oceanography, physics. **Protective services:** Criminal justice. **Psychology:** General. **Public administration:** General, social work. **Social sciences:** General, anthropology, geography, political science, sociology. **Visual/performing arts:** Art, commercial/advertising art, crafts, dramatic, studio arts.

**Most popular majors.** Business/marketing 17%, education 19%, English 8%, psychology 10%, social sciences 6%, visual/performing arts 11%.

**Computing on campus.** 800 workstations in dormitories, library, computer center, student center. Dormitories wired for high-speed internet access and linked to campus network. Commuter students can connect to campus network. Online course registration, online library, helpline, student web hosting, wireless network available.

**Student life.** **Freshman orientation:** Mandatory, $115 fee. Preregistration for classes offered. 2-day, one overnight session in June, plus 1-day informational program preceding fall semester. **Policies:** No alcohol or drugs. **Housing:** Guaranteed on-campus for freshmen. Coed dorms, single-sex dorms, apartments, cooperative housing available. $125 fully refundable deposit, deadline 5/1. **Activities:** Bands, campus ministries, choral groups, dance, drama, film society, international student organizations, literary magazine, music ensembles, Model UN, musical theater, radio station, student government, student newspaper, symphony orchestra, TV station, Student Alliance for Learning, Success and Achievement, black student union, Minority Achievement Coalition, Brothers and Sisters Seeking Excellence, Feminist Majority Leadership Alliance, Circle K, volunteer center, social work club.

**Athletics.** NCAA. **Intercollegiate:** Baseball M, basketball, bowling W, cross-country, field hockey W, football (tackle) M, golf W, lacrosse W, soccer W, softball W, swimming W, tennis, track and field, volleyball W, wrestling M. **Intramural:** Basketball, football (non-tackle), racquetball, soccer, softball, table tennis, tennis, volleyball. **Team name:** Golden Bears.

**Student services.** Adult student services, alcohol/substance abuse counseling, career counseling, services for economically disadvantaged, student employment services, financial aid counseling, health services, minority student services, on-campus daycare, personal counseling, veterans' counselor, women's services. **Physically disabled:** Services for visually, speech, hearing impaired.

**Contact.** E-mail: admission@kutztown.edu
Phone: (610) 683-4060 Toll-free number: (877) 628-1915
Fax: (610) 683-1375
William Stahler, Director of Admissions, Kutztown University of Pennsylvania, Admissions Office, Kutztown, PA 19530-0730

---

### La Roche College
**Pittsburgh, Pennsylvania**  CB member
**www.laroche.edu**  CB code: 2379

- Private 4-year liberal arts college affiliated with Roman Catholic Church
- Commuter campus in large city
- 1,181 degree-seeking undergraduates: 17% part-time, 64% women, 6% African American, 1% Asian American, 1% Hispanic American, 11% international
- 126 degree-seeking graduate students
- 68% of applicants admitted
- SAT or ACT (ACT writing optional) required
- 59% graduate within 6 years

**General.** Founded in 1963. Regionally accredited. Founded and sponsored by Sisters of Divine Providence. **Degrees:** 265 bachelor's, 28 associate awarded; master's offered. **ROTC:** Army, Air Force. **Calendar:** Semester, limited summer session. **Full-time faculty:** 63 total; 76% have terminal degrees, 8% minority, 51% women. **Part-time faculty:** 110 total; 14% have terminal degrees, 54% women. **Class size:** 75% < 20, 25% 20-39.

**Freshman class profile.** 859 applied, 580 admitted, 193 enrolled.

| Mid 50% test scores | | | |
|---|---|---|---|
| SAT critical reading: | 380-500 | GPA 2.0-2.99: | 40% |
| SAT math: | 390-500 | Rank in top quarter: | 21% |
| SAT writing: | 400-510 | Rank in top tenth: | 3% |
| ACT composite: | 17-22 | Return as sophomores: | 60% |
| GPA 3.75 or higher: | 12% | Out-of-state: | 11% |
| GPA 3.50-3.74: | 11% | Live on campus: | 67% |
| GPA 3.0-3.49: | 36% | International: | 16% |

**Basis for selection.** Depth and rigor of curriculum considered. Standardized test scores considered in relation to other factors. Recommendation from guidance counselor important. Extracurricular involvement considered. Essay, interview recommended.

**High school preparation.** College-preparatory program recommended. 16 units required; 18 recommended. Required and recommended units include English 4, mathematics 3, social studies 3, history 3, science 3 (laboratory 2) and foreign language 2.

**2009-2010 Annual costs.** Tuition/fees: $21,638. Room/board: $8,756. Books/supplies: $1,000. Personal expenses: $1,376.

**2009-2010 Financial aid.** **Need-based:** 164 full-time freshmen applied for aid; 155 were judged to have need; 150 of these received aid. Average need met was 93%. Average scholarship/grant was $3,586; average loan $4,955. 50% of total undergraduate aid awarded as scholarships/grants, 50% as loans/jobs. **Non-need-based:** Awarded to 748 full-time undergraduates, including 156 freshmen. Scholarships awarded for academics.

**Application procedures.** **Admission:** No deadline. $50 fee, may be waived for applicants with need. Admission notification on a rolling basis beginning on or about 10/1. **Financial aid:** Priority date 2/15, closing date 5/1. FAFSA required. Applicants notified on a rolling basis starting 3/1; must reply within 2 week(s) of notification.

**Academics.** **Special study options:** Accelerated study, combined bachelor's/graduate degree, cross-registration, distance learning, double major, ESL, honors, independent study, internships, student-designed major, study abroad, teacher certification program, Washington semester. **Credit/placement by examination:** AP, CLEP, IB, institutional tests. 60 credit hours maximum toward bachelor's degree. **Support services:** Learning center, reduced course load, remedial instruction, study skills assistance, tutoring, writing center.

**Majors.** **Architecture:** Interior. **Biology:** General. **Business:** Accounting, finance, international, management science, marketing, real estate. **Communications:** General, media studies. **Computer sciences:** General, computer science, information technology. **Education:** Elementary, English. **Foreign languages:** Spanish. **Health:** Medical radiologic technology/radiation therapy, nursing (RN), respiratory therapy technology. **History:** General. **Liberal arts:** Arts/sciences. **Math:** General. **Philosophy/religion:** Religion. **Physical sciences:** Chemistry. **Protective services:** Criminal justice, emergency management/homeland security. **Psychology:** General. **Public administration:** Human services. **Social sciences:** International relations, political science, sociology. **Theology:** Religious ed. **Visual/performing arts:** Dance, design.

**Most popular majors.** Architecture 11%, business/marketing 29%, health sciences 6%, psychology 9%, security/protective services 6%, visual/performing arts 9%.

**Computing on campus.** 200 workstations in dormitories, library, computer center. Dormitories wired for high-speed internet access and linked to campus network. Commuter students can connect to campus network. Online course registration, online library, helpline, wireless network available.

**Student life.** **Freshman orientation:** Mandatory. Preregistration for classes offered. **Housing:** Coed dorms available. $100 nonrefundable deposit, deadline 5/1. **Activities:** Campus ministries, choral groups, dance, drama, international student organizations, literary magazine, radio station, student government, student newspaper, professional organizations, Project Achievement, environment club, Black student coalition, African Student Forum, Rotaract club, community service.

**Athletics.** NCAA. **Intercollegiate:** Baseball M, basketball, cross-country, golf M, soccer, softball W, tennis W, volleyball W. **Intramural:** Basketball, racquetball, soccer, softball, table tennis, tennis, volleyball. **Team name:** Redhawks.

**Student services.** Adult student services, alcohol/substance abuse counseling, chaplain/spiritual director, career counseling, services for economically disadvantaged, student employment services, financial aid counseling,

health services, minority student services, personal counseling, placement for graduates, veterans' counselor. **Physically disabled:** Services for visually impaired. **Learning disabled:** Comprehensive services available.

**Contact.** E-mail: admissions@laroche.edu
Phone: (412) 536-1271 Toll-free number: (800) 838-4572
Fax: (412) 536-1048
David McFarland, Director of Admissions, La Roche College, 9000 Babcock Boulevard, Pittsburgh, PA 15237

## La Salle University
**Philadelphia, Pennsylvania**
**www.lasalle.edu**

**CB member**
**CB code: 2363**

▶ Private 4-year university and liberal arts college affiliated with Roman Catholic Church
▶ Residential campus in very large city
▶ 4,206 degree-seeking undergraduates: 23% part-time, 63% women, 17% African American, 4% Asian American, 9% Hispanic American, 1% international
▶ 1,982 degree-seeking graduate students
▶ 65% of applicants admitted
▶ SAT or ACT (ACT writing optional), application essay required
▶ 74% graduate within 6 years

**General.** Founded in 1863. Regionally accredited. **Degrees:** 860 bachelor's, 26 associate awarded; master's, doctoral offered. **ROTC:** Army, Air Force. **Location:** 6 miles from downtown. **Calendar:** Semester, extensive summer session. **Full-time faculty:** 227 total; 78% have terminal degrees, 10% minority, 50% women. **Part-time faculty:** 168 total; 11% minority, 59% women. **Class size:** 46% < 20, 50% 20-39, 4% 40-49. **Special facilities:** Art museum, restored home and gardens of 18th-century American portrait painter Charles Wilson Peale.

**Freshman class profile.** 5,592 applied, 3,650 admitted, 1,009 enrolled.

| Mid 50% test scores | | | |
|---|---|---|---|
| SAT critical reading: | 450-560 | Rank in top tenth: | 14% |
| SAT math: | 450-560 | Return as sophomores: | 82% |
| GPA 3.75 or higher: | 23% | Out-of-state: | 38% |
| GPA 3.50-3.74: | 16% | Live on campus: | 79% |
| GPA 3.0-3.49: | 32% | International: | 1% |
| GPA 2.0-2.99: | 29% | Fraternities: | 7% |
| Rank in top quarter: | 37% | Sororities: | 18% |

**Basis for selection.** High school GPA and standardized test scores most important. Activities, recommendations considered. Admission through Academic Discovery Program provides counseling and tutorial support for students who need academic assistance and meet certain criteria of financial need. Interview recommended. **Homeschooled:** Statement describing home-school structure and mission required.

**High school preparation.** College-preparatory program required. 16 units required. Required units include English 4, mathematics 3, history 1, science 1 (laboratory 1), foreign language 2 and academic electives 5.

**2010-2011 Annual costs.** Tuition/fees: $33,700. Room/board: $11,230. Books/supplies: $500. Personal expenses: $1,119.

**2009-2010 Financial aid.** **Need-based:** 860 full-time freshmen applied for aid; 761 were judged to have need; 761 of these received aid. Average need met was 75%. Average scholarship/grant was $19,406; average loan $3,594. 68% of total undergraduate aid awarded as scholarships/grants, 32% as loans/jobs. **Non-need-based:** Awarded to 1,045 full-time undergraduates, including 313 freshmen. Scholarships awarded for academics, athletics, ROTC.

**Application procedures.** **Admission:** No deadline. $35 fee, may be waived for applicants with need, free for online applicants. Admission notification on a rolling basis beginning on or about 12/15. Must reply by May 1 or within 2 week(s) if notified thereafter. **Financial aid:** Priority date 2/15; no closing date. FAFSA required. Applicants notified on a rolling basis starting 3/15; must reply by 5/1 or within 2 week(s) of notification.

**Academics.** **Special study options:** Accelerated study, combined bachelor's/graduate degree, cooperative education, double major, dual enrollment of high school students, ESL, honors, independent study, internships, study abroad, teacher certification program. 3-2 with Thomas Jefferson University. **Credit/placement by examination:** AP, CLEP, SAT, ACT, institutional tests. 70 credit hours maximum toward bachelor's degree. **Support services:** Learning center, pre-admission summer program, reduced course load, remedial instruction, study skills assistance, tutoring, writing center.

**Majors. Area/ethnic studies:** Central/Eastern European, regional, Russian/Slavic. **Biology:** General, biochemistry. **Business:** General, accounting, banking/financial services, business admin, communications, finance, human resources, insurance, international, international marketing, labor relations, management science, managerial economics, market research, marketing, nonprofit/public, operations, organizational behavior, statistics. **Communications:** General, broadcast journalism, digital media, journalism, media studies, public relations, radio/tv. **Communications technology:** Desktop publishing, radio/tv. **Computer sciences:** General, applications programming, computer graphics, computer science, database management, information systems, information technology, programming, web page design. **Conservation:** General, environmental science. **Education:** General, bilingual, biology, chemistry, developmentally delayed, early childhood, early childhood special, elementary, emotionally handicapped, English, foreign languages, French, German, history, mathematics, mentally handicapped, middle, multi-level teacher, physically handicapped, science, secondary, social science, social studies, Spanish, special. **Foreign languages:** General, Biblical, classics, comparative lit, French, German, Italian, Latin, Spanish. **Health:** Audiology/hearing, audiology/speech pathology, nursing (RN), predental, premedicine, preveterinary, speech pathology. **History:** General, American. **Interdisciplinary:** Biological/physical sciences, math/computer science, nutrition sciences, peace/conflict, systems science. **Legal studies:** Prelaw. **Liberal arts:** Arts/sciences. **Math:** General, applied, statistics. **Philosophy/religion:** Philosophy, religion. **Physical sciences:** Chemistry, geology, planetary. **Protective services:** Criminal justice. **Psychology:** General. **Public administration:** General, social work. **Social sciences:** General, criminology, economics, international economics, international relations, political science, sociology, U.S. government. **Theology:** Religious ed. **Visual/performing arts:** Art history/conservation, cinematography, film/cinema, music history, studio arts.

**Most popular majors.** Business/marketing 20%, communications/journalism 9%, education 6%, health sciences 35%, psychology 7%, public administration/social services 7%.

**Computing on campus.** 181 workstations in library, computer center, student center. Dormitories wired for high-speed internet access and linked to campus network. Commuter students can connect to campus network. Online course registration, online library, helpline, repair service, student web hosting, wireless network available.

**Student life. Freshman orientation:** Mandatory, $100 fee. Preregistration for classes offered. **Policies:** Nonalcoholic nightclub and eatery available 7 days a week. **Housing:** Guaranteed on-campus for all undergraduates. Coed dorms, special housing for disabled, apartments, wellness housing available. $200 nonrefundable deposit, deadline 5/1. Campus owned and operated townhouses available. **Activities:** Jazz band, campus ministries, choral groups, dance, drama, film society, international student organizations, literary magazine, musical theater, radio station, student government, student newspaper, TV station, black student union, Hillel, women's center, social work association, veterans club, Young Socialist Alliance, student council for exceptional children, urban center.

**Athletics. NCAA. Intercollegiate:** Baseball M, basketball, cheerleading, cross-country, diving, field hockey W, golf, lacrosse W, rowing (crew), soccer, softball W, swimming, tennis, track and field, volleyball W. **Intramural:** Basketball, football (non-tackle), football (tackle), rugby M, softball, volleyball. **Team name:** Explorers.

**Student services.** Adult student services, alcohol/substance abuse counseling, chaplain/spiritual director, career counseling, services for economically disadvantaged, student employment services, health services, minority student services, on-campus daycare, personal counseling, placement for graduates, veterans' counselor.

**Contact.** E-mail: admiss@lasalle.edu
Phone: (215) 951-1500 Toll-free number: (800) 328-1910
Fax: (215) 951-1656
James Plunkett, Executive Director of Admission, La Salle University, 1900 West Olney Avenue, Philadelphia, PA 19141-1199

---

## Lafayette College
**Easton, Pennsylvania**
www.lafayette.edu

**CB member**
**CB code: 2361**

- Private 4-year engineering and liberal arts college affiliated with Presbyterian Church (USA)
- Residential campus in large town
- 2,378 degree-seeking undergraduates: 1% part-time, 47% women, 5% African American, 4% Asian American, 5% Hispanic American, 7% international
- 42% of applicants admitted
- SAT or ACT with writing, application essay required
- 90% graduate within 6 years

---

**General.** Founded in 1826. Regionally accredited. **Degrees:** 573 bachelor's awarded. **ROTC:** Army. **Location:** 80 miles from New York City, 60 miles from Philadelphia. **Calendar:** Semester, limited summer session. **Full-time faculty:** 208 total; 100% have terminal degrees, 13% minority, 35% women. **Part-time faculty:** 48 total; 46% have terminal degrees, 8% minority, 35% women. **Class size:** 57% < 20, 39% 20-39, 1% 40-49, 3% 50-99. **Special facilities:** Advanced computer-aided design laboratory, satellite downlink capability.

**Freshman class profile.** 5,635 applied, 2,387 admitted, 616 enrolled.

| Mid 50% test scores | | | |
|---|---|---|---|
| SAT critical reading: | 570-670 | GPA 2.0-2.99: | 10% |
| SAT math: | 600-710 | Rank in top quarter: | 87% |
| SAT writing: | 580-680 | Rank in top tenth: | 59% |
| ACT composite: | 26-30 | Return as sophomores: | 95% |
| GPA 3.75 or higher: | 26% | Out-of-state: | 79% |
| GPA 3.50-3.74: | 24% | Live on campus: | 100% |
| GPA 3.0-3.49: | 40% | International: | 7% |

**Basis for selection.** Academic performance, class rank, quality of courses taken, personal qualities, extracurricular record, recommendations, and standardized test results important. Special consideration to applicants who will contribute diversity to student body. SAT Subject Tests recommended. SAT Subject Tests, if submitted, may be considered for placement in math and foreign languages. Interview recommended for all; portfolio recommended for art program.

**High school preparation.** College-preparatory program recommended. 18 units recommended. Recommended units include English 4, mathematics 3, science 2 (laboratory 2), foreign language 2 and academic electives 5. 4 math, chemistry, physics required of bachelor of science degree candidates.

**2009-2010 Annual costs.** Tuition/fees: $38,490. Room/board: $11,799. Books/supplies: $1,000. Personal expenses: $900.

**2008-2009 Financial aid. Need-based:** 395 full-time freshmen applied for aid; 260 were judged to have need; 258 of these received aid. Average need met was 98%. Average scholarship/grant was $31,097; average loan $3,579. 87% of total undergraduate aid awarded as scholarships/grants, 13% as loans/jobs. **Non-need-based:** Awarded to 500 full-time undergraduates, including 111 freshmen. Scholarships awarded for academics, athletics, leadership, ROTC. **Additional information:** Parent loans, up to $7,500 annually, available with college absorbing interest while student is enrolled. Family has 8 years after graduation to repay. Not limited to those demonstrating need.

**Application procedures. Admission:** Closing date 1/1. $60 fee, may be waived for applicants with need. Admission notification 4/1. Must reply by May 1 or within 2 week(s) if notified thereafter. **Financial aid:** Priority date 2/15, closing date 3/15. FAFSA, CSS PROFILE required. Applicants notified by 4/1; must reply by 5/1.

**Academics.** Examples of students' self-designed interdisciplinary majors include Management Science, Studies in Human Rights, Asian Studies, Computational Biology, and Community Development among many others. Interdisciplinary minors also offered. **Special study options:** Cross-registration, double major, dual enrollment of high school students, exchange student, honors, independent study, internships, New York semester, semester at sea, student-designed major, study abroad, urban semester, Washington semester. Interim-session courses abroad and on campus. **Credit/placement by examination:** AP, CLEP, IB, institutional tests. **Support services:** Reduced course load, study skills assistance, tutoring, writing center.

**Majors. Area/ethnic studies:** African, American, Asian, Russian/Slavic. **Biology:** General, biochemistry. **Computer sciences:** General. **Engineering:** General, chemical, civil, electrical, mechanical. **Foreign languages:** French, German, Spanish. **History:** General. **Interdisciplinary:** Neuroscience. **Math:** General. **Philosophy/religion:** Philosophy, religion. **Physical sciences:** Chemistry, geology, physics. **Psychology:** General. **Public administration:** Policy analysis. **Social sciences:** Anthropology, econometrics, economics, international economics, international relations, political science, sociology. **Visual/performing arts:** Art, music history, studio arts.

**Most popular majors.** Biology 7%, engineering/engineering technologies 16%, English 7%, history 6%, psychology 9%, social sciences 35%.

**Computing on campus.** 600 workstations in library, computer center, student center. Dormitories wired for high-speed internet access and linked to campus network. Commuter students can connect to campus network. Online course registration, online library, helpline, repair service, student web hosting, wireless network available.

**Student life. Freshman orientation:** Mandatory. Preregistration for classes offered. 4-day program before fall classes begin. **Housing:** Guaranteed on-campus for all undergraduates. Coed dorms, single-sex dorms, special housing for disabled, apartments, fraternity/sorority housing, wellness housing available. Scholars houses, Hillel House, arts houses. **Activities:** Bands, campus ministries, choral groups, dance, drama, film society, international student organizations, literary magazine, music ensembles, Model UN, musical theater, radio station, student government, student newspaper, symphony orchestra, Hillel Society, Muslim student association, Newman Association, Association of Black Collegians, Association for Lafayette Feminists, Lafayette Environmental Awareness and Protection, College Democrats, College Republicans, Students for Social Justice.

**Athletics. NCAA. Intercollegiate:** Baseball M, basketball, cheerleading, cross-country, diving, fencing, field hockey W, football (tackle) M, golf, lacrosse, soccer, softball W, swimming, tennis, track and field, volleyball W. **Intramural:** Badminton, basketball, bowling, football (non-tackle), golf, racquetball, soccer, softball, squash, table tennis, tennis, volleyball, water polo. **Team name:** Leopards.

**Student services.** Adult student services, alcohol/substance abuse counseling, chaplain/spiritual director, career counseling, services for economically disadvantaged, student employment services, financial aid counseling, health services, minority student services, personal counseling, placement for graduates, women's services. **Physically disabled:** Services for visually impaired. **Learning disabled:** Comprehensive services available.

**Contact.** E-mail: admissions@lafayette.edu
Phone: (610) 330-5100 Fax: (610) 330-5355
Carol Rowlands, Director of Admissions, Lafayette College, 118 Markle Hall, Easton, PA 18042

## Lancaster Bible College
Lancaster, Pennsylvania
www.lbc.edu                                    CB code: 2388

- Private 4-year Bible college affiliated with nondenominational tradition
- Residential campus in small city
- 702 degree-seeking undergraduates: 16% part-time, 47% women, 3% African American, 1% Asian American, 1% Hispanic American, 1% international
- 155 degree-seeking graduate students
- 97% of applicants admitted
- SAT or ACT (ACT writing recommended), application essay required
- 58% graduate within 6 years

**General.** Founded in 1933. Regionally accredited; also accredited by ABHE. **Degrees:** 135 bachelor's, 21 associate awarded; master's offered. **Location:** 64 miles from Philadelphia. **Calendar:** Semester, limited summer session. **Full-time faculty:** 29 total; 55% have terminal degrees, 7% minority, 31% women. **Part-time faculty:** 55 total; 49% have terminal degrees, 34% women. **Class size:** 65% < 20, 29% 20-39, 5% 40-49, less than 1% 50-99.

**Freshman class profile.** 314 applied, 304 admitted, 134 enrolled.

| | | | |
|---|---|---|---|
| End year in good standing: | 92% | Live on campus: | 78% |
| Return as sophomores: | 77% | International: | 2% |
| Out-of-state: | 17% | | |

**Basis for selection.** Application must include personal spiritual testimony, academic transcripts, SAT or ACT scores, and 3 references. Interview recommended for all; audition required for music program. **Home-schooled:** Yearly evaluations should be included with application.

**2009-2010 Annual costs.** Tuition/fees: $15,840. Room/board: $6,780. Books/supplies: $1,000. Personal expenses: $1,500.

**2008-2009 Financial aid. Need-based:** 109 full-time freshmen applied for aid; 93 were judged to have need; 92 of these received aid. Average need met was 44%. Average scholarship/grant was $8,518; average loan $3,288. 51% of total undergraduate aid awarded as scholarships/grants, 49% as loans/jobs. **Non-need-based:** Awarded to 446 full-time undergraduates, including 112 freshmen. Scholarships awarded for academics, alumni affiliation, leadership, music/drama.

**Application procedures. Admission:** Priority date 8/1; no deadline. $25 fee, may be waived for applicants with need. Admission notification on a rolling basis. **Financial aid:** Priority date 5/1; no closing date. FAFSA required. Applicants notified on a rolling basis starting 3/1; must reply within 3 week(s) of notification.

**Academics. Special study options:** Accelerated study, distance learning, double major, independent study, internships, study abroad, teacher certification program. **Credit/placement by examination:** AP, CLEP, SAT, ACT, institutional tests. 15 credit hours maximum toward associate degree, 30 toward bachelor's. **Support services:** Learning center, reduced course load, remedial instruction, study skills assistance, tutoring, writing center.

**Majors. Education:** Elementary, physical. **Theology:** Bible.

**Most popular majors.** Education 6%, theological studies 94%.

**Computing on campus.** 35 workstations in dormitories, library, computer center, student center. Dormitories wired for high-speed internet access and linked to campus network. Commuter students can connect to campus network. Online course registration, online library, helpline, repair service, wireless network available.

**Student life. Freshman orientation:** Mandatory, $125 fee. Preregistration for classes offered. 2 days prior to start of classes. **Policies:** Religious observance required. **Housing:** Guaranteed on-campus for freshmen. Single-sex dorms available. **Activities:** Bands, choral groups, drama, international student organizations, music ensembles, musical theater, student government, student newspaper, Christian Counseling Fellowship, married couples fellowship, Helpers in Service teams, student missionary fellowship, resident affairs council, commuter affairs council.

**Athletics. NCAA, NCCAA. Intercollegiate:** Baseball M, basketball, cheerleading, cross-country, lacrosse W, soccer, tennis, volleyball. **Intramural:** Basketball, football (non-tackle) M, soccer, softball, table tennis, tennis, volleyball. **Team name:** Chargers.

**Student services.** Chaplain/spiritual director, career counseling, student employment services, financial aid counseling, health services, personal counseling, placement for graduates. **Learning disabled:** Comprehensive services available.

**Contact.** E-mail: admissions@lbc.edu
Phone: (717) 560-8271 Toll-free number: (866) 522-4968
Fax: (717) 560-8213
Scott Boyer, Director, Admissions, Lancaster Bible College, 901 Eden Road, Lancaster, PA 17601-5036

## Lebanon Valley College
Annville, Pennsylvania                         CB member
www.lvc.edu                                    CB code: 2364

- Private 4-year liberal arts college affiliated with United Methodist Church
- Residential campus in small town
- 1,650 degree-seeking undergraduates: 5% part-time, 56% women, 2% African American, 2% Asian American, 2% Hispanic American
- 251 degree-seeking graduate students
- 81% of applicants admitted
- 76% graduate within 6 years; 25% enter graduate study

**General.** Founded in 1866. Regionally accredited. **Degrees:** 424 bachelor's, 2 associate awarded; master's, professional offered. **ROTC:** Army. **Location:** 7 miles from Hershey, 25 miles from Harrisburg. **Calendar:** Semester, limited summer session. **Full-time faculty:** 100 total; 88% have terminal degrees, 7% minority, 37% women. **Part-time faculty:** 98 total; 24% have terminal degrees, 41% women. **Class size:** 55% < 20, 43% 20-39, less than 1% 40-49, 2% 50-99. **Special facilities:** Electronic pianos, sound recording studio, transmission electron microscope, scanning electron microscope, Fourier transform infrared spectrometer, atomic absorption spectrometer, nuclear magnetic resonance spectrometer, molecular modeling lab, arboretum, physical therapy wellness pool.

**Freshman class profile.** 1,698 applied, 1,368 admitted, 378 enrolled.

| Mid 50% test scores | | Rank in top tenth: | 34% |
|---|---|---|---|
| SAT critical reading: | 480-590 | End year in good standing: | 95% |
| SAT math: | 500-620 | Return as sophomores: | 86% |
| SAT writing: | 470-580 | Out-of-state: | 20% |
| ACT composite: | 19-25 | Live on campus: | 89% |
| Rank in top quarter: | 71% | International: | 1% |

**Basis for selection.** Record of high school achievement in challenging college prep courses is most important. Recommendations, test scores (optional), school and community activities evaluated. Submission of standardized test scores is optional for all applicants. Essay and interview recommended for all; audition required for music program.

**High school preparation.** College-preparatory program required. 16 units required. Required and recommended units include English 4, mathematics 3, social studies 1, history 2, science 2-3 (laboratory 2) and foreign language 2-3.

**2009-2010 Annual costs.** Tuition/fees: $30,490. Room/board: $8,080. Books/supplies: $1,000. Personal expenses: $1,200.

**2009-2010 Financial aid. Need-based:** 364 full-time freshmen applied for aid; 321 were judged to have need; 321 of these received aid. Average need met was 85%. Average scholarship/grant was $20,015; average loan $4,318. 76% of total undergraduate aid awarded as scholarships/grants, 24% as loans/jobs. **Non-need-based:** Awarded to 366 full-time undergraduates, including 87 freshmen. Scholarships awarded for academics, alumni affiliation, music/drama.

**Application procedures. Admission:** No deadline. $30 fee, may be waived for applicants with need. Admission notification on a rolling basis beginning on or about 10/15. Must reply by May 1 or within 2 week(s) if notified thereafter. For early admission of high school students, regular application procedures apply. Permission from school district necessary. **Financial aid:** Priority date 3/1; no closing date. FAFSA, institutional form required. Applicants notified on a rolling basis starting 3/1; must reply by 5/1 or within 2 week(s) of notification.

**Academics. Special study options:** Combined bachelor's/graduate degree, double major, dual enrollment of high school students, independent study, internships, liberal arts/career combination, student-designed major, study abroad, teacher certification program, urban semester, Washington semester. **Credit/placement by examination:** AP, CLEP, IB, institutional tests. 15 credit hours maximum toward associate degree, 30 toward bachelor's. **Support services:** Reduced course load, study skills assistance, tutoring, writing center.

**Majors. Area/ethnic studies:** American. **Biology:** General, Biochemistry/biophysics and molecular biology. **Business:** Accounting, actuarial science, business admin. **Communications:** Digital media. **Communications technology:** Recording arts. **Computer sciences:** Computer science. **Education:** Early childhood, elementary, music, special. **Foreign languages:** French, German, Spanish. **Health:** Clinical lab science, health care admin, health services. **History:** General. **Math:** General. **Philosophy/religion:** Philosophy, religion. **Physical sciences:** Chemistry, physics. **Psychology:** General, psychobiology. **Social sciences:** Criminology, economics, political science, sociology. **Visual/performing arts:** Music management, music performance, studio arts.

**Most popular majors.** Biology 6%, business/marketing 14%, education 17%, health sciences 8%, psychology 8%, social sciences 11%, visual/performing arts 11%.

**Computing on campus.** 199 workstations in library, computer center, student center. Dormitories wired for high-speed internet access and linked to campus network. Commuter students can connect to campus network. Online course registration, online library, helpline, student web hosting, wireless network available.

**Student life. Freshman orientation:** Mandatory. Preregistration for classes offered. One-day programs in May and July; 3-day program in August. **Housing:** Guaranteed on-campus for all undergraduates. Coed dorms, single-sex dorms, special housing for disabled, apartments available. Suites. **Activities:** Bands, campus ministries, choral groups, drama, international student organizations, literary magazine, music ensembles, musical theater, radio station, student government, student newspaper, symphony orchestra, College Republicans, College Democrats, Cornerstone, Best Buddies, Student Action for Earth, The F Word, Council of Christian Organizations, A.S.I.A., Habitat for Humanity.

**Athletics.** NCAA. **Intercollegiate:** Baseball M, basketball, cross-country, field hockey W, football (tackle) M, golf M, ice hockey M, lacrosse, soccer, softball W, swimming, tennis, track and field, volleyball W. **Intramural:** Basketball, football (non-tackle), racquetball, softball, volleyball. **Team name:** Flying Dutchmen.

**Student services.** Alcohol/substance abuse counseling, chaplain/spiritual director, career counseling, student employment services, financial aid counseling, health services, minority student services, personal counseling, placement for graduates. **Physically disabled:** Services for visually, speech impaired. **Learning disabled:** Comprehensive services available.

**Contact.** E-mail: admission@lvc.edu
Phone: (717) 867-6181 Toll-free number: (866) 582-4236
Fax: (717) 867-6026
Susan Jones, Director of Admission, Lebanon Valley College, 101 North College Avenue, Annville, PA 17003-1400

## Lehigh University
**Bethlehem, Pennsylvania**
www.lehigh.edu

CB member
CB code: 2365

- Private 4-year university
- Residential campus in small city

- 4,792 degree-seeking undergraduates: 1% part-time, 41% women, 4% African American, 6% Asian American, 6% Hispanic American, 4% international
- 2,010 degree-seeking graduate students
- 33% of applicants admitted
- SAT or ACT with writing, application essay required
- 86% graduate within 6 years; 31% enter graduate study

**General.** Founded in 1865. Regionally accredited. **Degrees:** 1,202 bachelor's awarded; master's, doctoral offered. **ROTC:** Army. **Location:** 50 miles from Philadelphia, 75 miles from New York City. **Calendar:** Semester, limited summer session. **Full-time faculty:** 464 total; 99% have terminal degrees, 16% minority, 28% women. **Part-time faculty:** 208 total; 5% minority, 44% women. **Class size:** 49% < 20, 36% 20-39, 5% 40-49, 6% 50-99, 4% >100. **Special facilities:** Two aberration-corrected electron microscopes, financial service laboratory, broadband seismic station, multidirectional experimental laboratory, electron optical labs, particle accelerator, rock climbing wall.

**Freshman class profile.** 11,170 applied, 3,662 admitted, 1,193 enrolled.

| Mid 50% test scores | | | |
|---|---|---|---|
| SAT critical reading: | 590-630 | Return as sophomores: | 94% |
| SAT math: | 630-710 | Out-of-state: | 78% |
| Rank in top quarter: | 99% | Live on campus: | 99% |
| Rank in top tenth: | 93% | International: | 5% |

**Basis for selection.** Recommendations and school record very important. All submitted material considered. SAT Subject Tests recommended. Applicants whose native language is not English must take the TOEFL. Minimum target score of 570 on the paper-pencil test, or 90 on the Internet-based TOEFL is recommended for admission. IELTS results accepted in place of TOEFL with a recommended minimum score of 7.0. Students scoring 570 or higher on the Critical Reading section of the SAT not required to submit TOEFL/IELTS scores, but it is highly recommended. Campus visit recommended.

**High school preparation.** 16 units required. Required units include English 4, mathematics 3, social studies 2, (laboratory 2), foreign language 2 and academic electives 3. Chemistry required, physics recommended for engineering and science candidates. Waivers in math granted by some departments to well-qualified candidates.

**2010-2011 Annual costs.** Tuition/fees: $39,780. Room/board: $10,520.

**2009-2010 Financial aid. Need-based:** 777 full-time freshmen applied for aid; 554 were judged to have need; 554 of these received aid. Average need met was 97%. Average scholarship/grant was $27,887; average loan $3,388. 82% of total undergraduate aid awarded as scholarships/grants, 18% as loans/jobs. **Non-need-based:** Awarded to 604 full-time undergraduates, including 142 freshmen. Scholarships awarded for academics, art, athletics, leadership, music/drama, ROTC. **Additional information:** Loans eliminated for students eligible for financial aid and whose family income is less than $50,000.

**Application procedures. Admission:** Closing date 1/1 (postmark date). $70 fee, may be waived for applicants with need. Admission notification 4/1. Must reply by 5/1. **Financial aid:** Closing date 2/15. FAFSA, CSS PROFILE required. Applicants notified by 3/30; must reply by 5/1 or within 3 week(s) of notification.

**Academics. Special study options:** Accelerated study, combined bachelor's/graduate degree, cooperative education, cross-registration, distance learning, double major, ESL, exchange student, external degree, honors, independent study, internships, liberal arts/career combination, study abroad, urban semester, Washington semester. **Credit/placement by examination:** AP, CLEP. **Support services:** Learning center, study skills assistance, tutoring, writing center.

**Majors. Architecture:** Architecture. **Area/ethnic studies:** African-American, American, Asian, women's. **Biology:** General, biochemistry, molecular. **Business:** Accounting, finance, logistics, management science, managerial economics, marketing. **Communications:** Journalism. **Computer sciences:** Computer science, information systems. **Conservation:** Environmental science. **Engineering:** Biomedical, chemical, civil, computer, electrical, environmental, industrial, manufacturing, materials, mechanical, mechanics, physics, structural, systems. **Foreign languages:** Classics, French, German, Spanish. **Health:** Pharmaceutical sciences, predental, premedicine. **History:** General. **Interdisciplinary:** Biological/physical sciences, cognitive science, global studies, science/society. **Math:** General, statistics. **Philosophy/religion:** Philosophy, religion. **Physical sciences:** Astronomy, astrophysics, chemistry, geology, physics. **Psychology:** General. **Social sciences:** Anthropology, international relations, political science, sociology. **Visual/performing arts:** Art, art history/conservation, design, dramatic, music history. **Other:** Classical civilization.

**Most popular majors.** Biology 6%, business/marketing 31%, engineering/engineering technologies 26%, psychology 6%, social sciences 6%.

**Computing on campus.** 638 workstations in dormitories, library, computer center. Dormitories wired for high-speed internet access and linked to campus network. Commuter students can connect to campus network. Online course registration, online library, helpline, repair service, student web hosting, wireless network available.

**Student life. Freshman orientation:** Mandatory, $240 fee. Preregistration for classes offered. Four-day program held prior to the first day of classes. **Housing:** Guaranteed on-campus for freshmen. Coed dorms, special housing for disabled, apartments, fraternity/sorority housing, wellness housing available. $500 nonrefundable deposit, deadline 5/1. Residential college (Taylor College) available. **Activities:** Bands, campus ministries, choral groups, dance, drama, film society, international student organizations, literary magazine, music ensembles, Model UN, musical theater, radio station, student government, student newspaper, symphony orchestra, Global Union, Asian cultural society, Fellowship of Christian Athletes, Omicron Delta Kappa, Chinese culture club, Black student union, Muslim students association, Alpha Phi Omega Service Fraternity, Best Buddies.

**Athletics.** NCAA. **Intercollegiate:** Baseball M, basketball, cross-country, diving, field hockey W, football (tackle) M, golf, lacrosse, rowing (crew) W, soccer, softball W, swimming, tennis, track and field, volleyball W, wrestling M. **Intramural:** Basketball, cross-country, football (non-tackle), soccer, softball, volleyball. **Team name:** Mountain Hawks.

**Student services.** Alcohol/substance abuse counseling, chaplain/spiritual director, career counseling, student employment services, financial aid counseling, health services, minority student services, on-campus daycare, personal counseling, placement for graduates, veterans' counselor, women's services.

**Contact.** E-mail: admissions@lehigh.edu
Phone: (610) 758-3100 Fax: (610) 758-4361
Bruce Gardiner, Director of Admissions, Lehigh University, 27 Memorial Drive West, Bethlehem, PA 18015-3094

---

## Lincoln University
**Lincoln University, Pennsylvania**
**www.lincoln.edu**                                   CB code: 2367

▶ Public 4-year university and liberal arts college
▶ Residential campus in small town
▶ 2,030 degree-seeking undergraduates: 1% part-time, 58% women, 79% African American, 2% international
▶ 614 degree-seeking graduate students
▶ 31% of applicants admitted
▶ SAT or ACT (ACT writing optional), application essay required
▶ 36% graduate within 6 years

**General.** Founded in 1854. Regionally accredited. **Degrees:** 254 bachelor's awarded; master's offered. **ROTC:** Army. **Location:** 45 miles from Philadelphia. **Calendar:** Semester, limited summer session. **Full-time faculty:** 101 total; 75% have terminal degrees, 67% minority, 37% women. **Part-time faculty:** 93 total. **Class size:** 44% < 20, 52% 20-39, 3% 40-49, less than 1% 50-99.

**Freshman class profile.** 7,432 applied, 2,303 admitted, 579 enrolled.

| Mid 50% test scores | | GPA 2.0-2.99: | 67% |
|---|---|---|---|
| SAT critical reading: | 370-450 | Rank in top quarter: | 19% |
| SAT math: | 360-440 | Rank in top tenth: | 6% |
| ACT composite: | 15-19 | Return as sophomores: | 78% |
| GPA 3.75 or higher: | 2% | Out-of-state: | 48% |
| GPA 3.50-3.74: | 5% | Live on campus: | 99% |
| GPA 3.0-3.49: | 19% | International: | 1% |

**Basis for selection.** Admissions based on secondary school record and class rank; recommendations, standardized test scores, talent, and ability also important.

**High school preparation.** 21 units required. Required units include English 4, mathematics 3, social studies 3, science 3 and academic electives 5. 2 arts or humanities required.

**2009-2010 Annual costs.** Tuition/fees: $8,718; $12,832 out-of-state. Out-of-state students pay additional $630 in fees, which are included in out-of-state tuition figure. Room/board: $7,890. Books/supplies: $1,430. Personal expenses: $1,240.

**2009-2010 Financial aid. Non-need-based:** Scholarships awarded for academics, alumni affiliation, leadership, music/drama.

**Application procedures. Admission:** Priority date 4/1; no deadline. $20 fee, may be waived for applicants with need. Admission notification on a rolling basis beginning on or about 2/15. **Financial aid:** Closing date 5/1. FAFSA required. Applicants notified on a rolling basis starting 4/1; must reply within 3 week(s) of notification.

**Academics. Special study options:** Exchange student, honors, independent study, internships, study abroad, teacher certification program. 3-2 in advanced science/engineering with Drexel University; Penn State University; Howard University; University of Delaware, Temple University, Widener University, and New Jersey Institute of Technology. **Credit/placement by examination:** AP, CLEP, IB, SAT, institutional tests. **Support services:** Learning center, reduced course load, remedial instruction, study skills assistance, tutoring, writing center.

**Majors. Biology:** General. **Business:** Accounting, actuarial science, business admin, finance, human resources. **Communications:** General, broadcast journalism, journalism. **Computer sciences:** General, information technology. **Conservation:** Environmental science. **Education:** Early childhood, elementary, English, mathematics, music, secondary, special. **Engineering:** General. **Foreign languages:** French, Spanish. **Health:** Recreational therapy. **History:** General. **Math:** General. **Parks/recreation:** Health/fitness. **Philosophy/religion:** Philosophy, religion. **Physical sciences:** General, chemistry, physics. **Protective services:** Criminal justice. **Psychology:** General, industrial, psychobiology. **Public administration:** General, human services. **Social sciences:** Anthropology, economics, international relations, political science, sociology. **Visual/performing arts:** Studio arts.

**Most popular majors.** Biology 7%, business/marketing 19%, communications/journalism 12%, psychology 8%, public administration/social services 7%, security/protective services 8%, social sciences 11%.

**Computing on campus.** 181 workstations in dormitories, library, computer center. Dormitories wired for high-speed internet access and linked to campus network. Commuter students can connect to campus network. Online library, repair service, wireless network available.

**Student life. Freshman orientation:** Mandatory, $169 fee. Preregistration for classes offered. **Housing:** Guaranteed on-campus for freshmen. Coed dorms, single-sex dorms, apartments available. $275 deposit. **Activities:** Jazz band, choral groups, dance, drama, international student organizations, music ensembles, radio station, student government, student newspaper, TV station, Music Educator National Conference, Mu Phi Alpha, Tolson Society, law society, Phi Kappa Epsilon honor society, fashion club, religious organizations, and social clubs.

**Athletics.** NCAA. **Intercollegiate:** Baseball M, basketball, bowling W, cross-country, football (tackle) M, soccer, softball, tennis, track and field, volleyball W. **Intramural:** Baseball M, basketball, boxing W, cheerleading W, cross-country, diving, softball, swimming, tennis, track and field, volleyball. **Team name:** Lions.

**Student services.** Alcohol/substance abuse counseling, chaplain/spiritual director, career counseling, student employment services, financial aid counseling, health services, personal counseling, women's services.

**Contact.** E-mail: admiss@lincoln.edu
Phone: (484) 365-7206 Toll-free number: (800) 790-0191
Fax: (484) 365-8109
Germel Eaton-Clarke, Director of Admissions, Lincoln University, 1570 Baltimore Pike, Lincoln University, PA 19352-0999

---

## Lock Haven University of Pennsylvania
**Lock Haven, Pennsylvania**                          CB member
**www.lhup.edu**                                      CB code: 2654

▶ Public 4-year university and liberal arts college
▶ Residential campus in small town
▶ 4,874 degree-seeking undergraduates: 5% part-time, 57% women, 7% African American, 1% Asian American, 2% Hispanic American, 1% international
▶ 258 degree-seeking graduate students
▶ 76% of applicants admitted
▶ SAT or ACT (ACT writing optional) required
▶ 53% graduate within 6 years

**General.** Founded in 1870. Regionally accredited. Branch campus in Clearfield. **Degrees:** 798 bachelor's, 89 associate awarded; master's offered. **ROTC:** Army. **Location:** 26 miles from Williamsport, 35 miles from State College. **Calendar:** Semester, limited summer session. **Full-time faculty:** 236 total; 74% have terminal degrees, 13% minority, 46% women.

**Part-time faculty:** 12 total; 42% women. **Class size:** 28% < 20, 46% 20-39, 15% 40-49, 9% 50-99, 1% >100. **Special facilities:** Rural retreat conference center, cadaver dissection laboratory, electron microscope, primate laboratory.

**Freshman class profile.** 4,499 applied, 3,438 admitted, 1,202 enrolled.

| Mid 50% test scores | | | |
|---|---|---|---|
| SAT critical reading: | 410-510 | GPA 2.0-2.99: | 30% |
| SAT math: | 420-520 | Rank in top quarter: | 25% |
| SAT writing: | 400-500 | Rank in top tenth: | 7% |
| ACT composite: | 17-21 | Return as sophomores: | 69% |
| GPA 3.75 or higher: | 15% | Out-of-state: | 9% |
| GPA 3.50-3.74: | 23% | Live on campus: | 79% |
| GPA 3.0-3.49: | 31% | International: | 1% |

**Basis for selection.** Course selection, grades received, and test scores most important. Preferred test score report date February 1. Interview required for nursing program; audition required for music programs. **Home-schooled:** Provide as much documentation as possible. Interview required.

**High school preparation.** College-preparatory program required. 16 units required; 21 recommended. Required and recommended units include English 4, mathematics 3-4, social studies 2, history 2, science 3-4 (laboratory 2-3) and foreign language 2. 4 units math required for math, computer science, biology, physics, and chemistry majors. 1 unit each biology, chemistry, physics required for health science majors. 1 unit each biology, anatomy and physiology, chemistry recommended for health and physical education majors.

**2009-2010 Annual costs.** Tuition/fees: $7,201; $13,533 out-of-state. All freshman students are required to have a laptop computer for use in the classroom. Computers can be purchased through the university; cost of computer is not included in mandatory fees. The university has a small number of laptops available to students who cannot afford to make such a purchase. Room/board: $6,736. Books/supplies: $1,139. Personal expenses: $1,844.

**2009-2010 Financial aid. Need-based:** 1,149 full-time freshmen applied for aid; 885 were judged to have need; 885 of these received aid. Average need met was 75%. Average scholarship/grant was $6,304; average loan $3,233. 50% of total undergraduate aid awarded as scholarships/grants, 50% as loans/jobs. **Non-need-based:** Awarded to 663 full-time undergraduates, including 114 freshmen. Scholarships awarded for academics, art, athletics, leadership, minority status, music/drama, ROTC, state residency.

**Application procedures. Admission:** Priority date 3/1; no deadline. $25 fee, may be waived for applicants with need. Admission notification on a rolling basis beginning on or about 10/1. Must reply by May 1 or within 2 week(s) if notified thereafter. **Financial aid:** Closing date 3/15. FAFSA required. Applicants notified on a rolling basis starting 4/1; must reply within 2 week(s) of notification.

**Academics. Special study options:** Combined bachelor's/graduate degree, cross-registration, distance learning, double major, dual enrollment of high school students, honors, independent study, internships, student-designed major, study abroad, teacher certification program. Exchange program with institutions in Taiwan, Russia, Australia, France, England, Poland, Germany, Scotland, Costa Rica, China, Japan, Croatia, Italy, Kenya, Mexico. 2-2 program in music education with Clarion University of Pennsylvania and Millersville University of Pennsylvania. **Credit/placement by examination:** AP, CLEP, IB, SAT, institutional tests. 30 credit hours maximum toward bachelor's degree. **Support services:** Learning center, preadmission summer program, reduced course load, remedial instruction, study skills assistance, tutoring, writing center.

**Majors. Biology:** General. **Business:** Accounting, business admin. **Communications:** Journalism. **Computer sciences:** General, computer science. **Education:** Elementary, kindergarten/preschool, special. **Foreign languages:** French, German, Spanish. **History:** General. **Interdisciplinary:** Biological/physical sciences. **Legal studies:** Paralegal. **Liberal arts:** Arts/sciences. **Math:** General. **Parks/recreation:** Facilities management, sports admin. **Philosophy/religion:** Philosophy. **Physical sciences:** Chemistry, geology, physics. **Protective services:** Law enforcement admin. **Psychology:** General. **Public administration:** Social work. **Social sciences:** General, economics, geography, international relations, political science, sociology. **Visual/performing arts:** Art, dramatic, studio arts. **Other:** Health and physical education.

**Most popular majors.** Business/marketing 13%, education 13%, health sciences 8%, parks/recreation 21%, security/protective services 9%.

**Computing on campus.** PC or laptop required. 290 workstations in dormitories, library, computer center, student center. Dormitories wired for high-speed internet access and linked to campus network. Commuter students can connect to campus network. Online course registration, online library, helpline, repair service, student web hosting, wireless network available.

**Student life. Freshman orientation:** Available, $75 fee. Overnight new student and parent programs, run concurrently, held during June. **Housing:** Guaranteed on-campus for freshmen. Coed dorms, apartments available. $200 nonrefundable deposit, deadline 5/1. **Activities:** Bands, campus ministries, choral groups, dance, drama, international student organizations, literary magazine, music ensembles, musical theater, radio station, student government, student newspaper, symphony orchestra, TV station, Newman Club, Black Cultural Society, Campus Crusade, Commonwealth Association of Students, Fellowship of Christian Athletes, social service society, Full Gospel Fellowship, New Life Student Fellowship.

**Athletics.** NCAA. **Intercollegiate:** Baseball M, basketball, boxing, cheerleading, cross-country, field hockey W, football (tackle) M, lacrosse W, soccer, softball W, swimming W, track and field, volleyball W, wrestling M. **Intramural:** Badminton, basketball, cross-country, field hockey W, golf, racquetball, skiing, soccer, softball, tennis, volleyball, water polo, wrestling M. **Team name:** Bald Eagles, Lady Eagles.

**Student services.** Adult student services, alcohol/substance abuse counseling, chaplain/spiritual director, career counseling, student employment services, financial aid counseling, health services, minority student services, personal counseling, placement for graduates, veterans' counselor, women's services. **Physically disabled:** Services for visually, speech impaired.

**Contact.** E-mail: admissions@lhup.edu
Phone: (570) 484-2027 Toll-free number: (800) 332-8900
Fax: (570) 484-2201
Stephen Lee, Director of Admissions, Lock Haven University of Pennsylvania, LHU Office of Admissions, Lock Haven, PA 17745

## Lycoming College
**Williamsport, Pennsylvania** — CB member
www.lycoming.edu — CB code: 2372

- Private 4-year liberal arts college affiliated with United Methodist Church
- Residential campus in small city
- 1,347 degree-seeking undergraduates: 1% part-time, 52% women, 3% African American, 1% Asian American, 2% Hispanic American, 1% Native American, 1% international
- 68% of applicants admitted
- SAT or ACT (ACT writing optional), application essay required
- 71% graduate within 6 years; 20% enter graduate study

**General.** Founded in 1812. Regionally accredited. **Degrees:** 281 bachelor's awarded. **ROTC:** Army. **Location:** 90 miles from Harrisburg, 170 miles from Philadelphia. **Calendar:** Semester, limited summer session. **Full-time faculty:** 89 total; 97% have terminal degrees, 7% minority, 37% women. **Part-time faculty:** 37 total; 16% have terminal degrees, 43% women. **Class size:** 65% < 20, 32% 20-39, 2% 40-49, less than 1% 50-99, less than 1% >100. **Special facilities:** Planetarium, clean water institute, graphics computer lab, polling institute.

**Freshman class profile.** 1,913 applied, 1,297 admitted, 772 enrolled.

| Mid 50% test scores | | | |
|---|---|---|---|
| SAT critical reading: | 470-580 | Rank in top tenth: | 19% |
| SAT math: | 470-580 | End year in good standing: | 90% |
| SAT writing: | 460-570 | Return as sophomores: | 78% |
| ACT composite: | 20-27 | Out-of-state: | 37% |
| Rank in top quarter: | 43% | Live on campus: | 90% |
| | | International: | 1% |

**Basis for selection.** Academic achievement as reflected in school record, class rank, and test scores most important. Curriculum, counselor and teacher recommendations also considered. Interview recommended for all; portfolio recommended for art program and creative writing program; audition recommended for music and theater programs.

**High school preparation.** College-preparatory program required. 16 units required; 21 recommended. Required and recommended units include English 4, mathematics 3-4, social studies 3-4, science 2-3 (laboratory 2-3), foreign language 2-3 and academic electives 2.

**2009-2010 Annual costs.** Tuition/fees: $29,894. Room/board: $8,134. Books/supplies: $900. Personal expenses: $1,000.

**2009-2010 Financial aid. Need-based:** 368 full-time freshmen applied for aid; 347 were judged to have need; 347 of these received aid. Average need met was 81%. Average scholarship/grant was $20,267; average loan $4,044. 73% of total undergraduate aid awarded as scholarships/grants, 27% as loans/jobs. **Non-need-based:** Awarded to 256 full-time undergraduates, including 67 freshmen. Scholarships awarded for academics, art, leadership, minority status, music/drama, religious affiliation, ROTC.

**Application procedures. Admission:** Priority date 4/1; deadline 7/1 (receipt date). $35 fee, may be waived for applicants with need, free for online applicants. Admission notification on a rolling basis beginning on or about 12/15. Must reply by May 1 or within 4 week(s) if notified thereafter. **Financial aid:** Priority date 3/1; no closing date. FAFSA, institutional form required. Applicants notified on a rolling basis starting 3/1; must reply by 5/1.

**Academics.** Teacher certification offered on elementary and secondary levels; special education certification as part of bachelor of arts program. **Special study options:** Accelerated study, combined bachelor's/graduate degree, cross-registration, double major, honors, independent study, internships, student-designed major, study abroad, teacher certification program, United Nations semester, urban semester, Washington semester. **Credit/placement by examination:** AP, CLEP, IB, institutional tests. 64 credit hours maximum toward bachelor's degree. **Support services:** Learning center, study skills assistance, tutoring, writing center.

**Majors. Area/ethnic studies:** American. **Biology:** General, anatomy, ecology, molecular. **Business:** Accounting, actuarial science, business admin, communications, finance, international finance, managerial economics, marketing. **Communications:** General, digital media. **Foreign languages:** French, German, Spanish. **History:** General, American, European. **Interdisciplinary:** Classical/archaeology. **Math:** General. **Philosophy/religion:** Philosophy, religion. **Physical sciences:** Astronomy, chemistry, physics. **Protective services:** Criminal justice. **Psychology:** General. **Social sciences:** Anthropology, archaeology, criminology, econometrics, economics, political science, sociology, U.S. government. **Visual/performing arts:** General, acting, art, art history/conservation, commercial/advertising art, directing/producing, dramatic, painting, photography, printmaking, sculpture, studio arts. **Other:** Actuarial mathematics.

**Most popular majors.** Biology 8%, business/marketing 19%, communications/journalism 7%, history 8%, interdisciplinary studies 6%, psychology 10%, social sciences 14%, visual/performing arts 8%.

**Computing on campus.** 137 workstations in library, computer center, student center. Dormitories wired for high-speed internet access and linked to campus network. Commuter students can connect to campus network. Online course registration, online library, helpline, repair service, student web hosting, wireless network available.

**Student life. Freshman orientation:** Mandatory, $200 fee. Preregistration for classes offered. 2-day, one-night event for students and parents. Choose one of 3 dates. **Policies:** Students must live in college-owned residence halls or apartments. **Housing:** Guaranteed on-campus for all undergraduates. Coed dorms, single-sex dorms, special housing for disabled, apartments, fraternity/sorority housing, wellness housing available. $100 nonrefundable deposit, deadline 5/1. Study-intensive housing, Creative Arts Society housing available. **Activities:** Bands, campus ministries, choral groups, dance, drama, film society, international student organizations, literary magazine, music ensembles, musical theater, radio station, student government, student newspaper, symphony orchestra, TV station, Circle K, Habitat for Humanity, College Democrats, College Republicans, environmental awareness foundation, Black Student Union, Big Brothers/Big Sisters, Colleges Against Cancer, Religious Experiences at Lycoming.

**Athletics.** NCAA. **Intercollegiate:** Basketball, cross-country, football (tackle) M, golf, lacrosse, soccer, softball W, swimming, tennis, volleyball W, wrestling M. **Intramural:** Basketball, football (non-tackle), soccer, softball, table tennis, volleyball. **Team name:** Warriors.

**Student services.** Alcohol/substance abuse counseling, chaplain/spiritual director, career counseling, student employment services, financial aid counseling, health services, personal counseling, placement for graduates, women's services. **Physically disabled:** Services for visually, hearing impaired.

**Contact.** E-mail: admissions@lycoming.edu
Phone: (570) 321-4026 Toll-free number: (800) 345-3920 ext. 4026
Fax: (570) 321-4317
James Spencer, Dean of Admissions and Financial Aid, Lycoming College, 700 College Place, Williamsport, PA 17701

---

## Mansfield University of Pennsylvania
### Mansfield, Pennsylvania
### www.mansfield.edu
CB code: 2655

- Public 4-year university
- Residential campus in small town
- 2,999 degree-seeking undergraduates: 6% part-time, 60% women, 7% African American, 1% Asian American, 2% Hispanic American, 1% Native American, 1% international
- 452 degree-seeking graduate students

- 75% of applicants admitted
- SAT or ACT (ACT writing optional) required
- 43% graduate within 6 years

**General.** Founded in 1857. Regionally accredited. **Degrees:** 554 bachelor's, 31 associate awarded; master's offered. **ROTC:** Army. **Location:** 50 miles from Williamsport, 30 miles from Corning, New York. **Calendar:** Semester, limited summer session. **Full-time faculty:** 156 total; 11% minority, 45% women. **Part-time faculty:** 67 total; 4% minority, 64% women. **Class size:** 32% < 20, 53% 20-39, 8% 40-49, 7% 50-99, less than 1% >100. **Special facilities:** Planetarium, solar collector, science museum, animal collection, fisheries research boat, leadership institute.

**Freshman class profile.** 2,800 applied, 2,108 admitted, 717 enrolled.

| Mid 50% test scores | | | |
|---|---|---|---|
| SAT critical reading: | 420-530 | Rank in top quarter: | 32% |
| SAT math: | 430-540 | Rank in top tenth: | 9% |
| SAT writing: | 410-520 | Return as sophomores: | 74% |
| ACT composite: | 18-23 | Out-of-state: | 16% |
| GPA 3.75 or higher: | 27% | Live on campus: | 86% |
| GPA 3.50-3.74: | 16% | International: | 1% |
| GPA 3.0-3.49: | 27% | Fraternities: | 7% |
| GPA 2.0-2.99: | 28% | Sororities: | 10% |

**Basis for selection.** Class rank, high school curriculum, test scores important; counselor's recommendation, extracurricular activities considered. Special consideration given to applicants eligible for Equal Education Opportunity Program. Entry competitive in X-ray technology, respiratory therapy, fisheries, music, art programs, premed, nursing, biology, chemistry. Essay recommended for all; interview required for radiology program; audition required for music program; portfolio required for art program. **Homeschooled:** Statement describing homeschool structure and mission, transcript of courses and grades required.

**High school preparation.** College-preparatory program recommended. 21 units required; 25 recommended. Required and recommended units include English 4, mathematics 3-4, history 4, science 2-3 (laboratory 2-3), foreign language 2-4 and academic electives 6.

**2009-2010 Annual costs.** Tuition/fees: $7,756; $16,088 out-of-state. Tuition for NY residents is $9,166; per-credit-hour charge for NY residents is $382. Room/board: $7,016. Books/supplies: $1,200. Personal expenses: $800.

**2008-2009 Financial aid. Need-based:** Average need met was 81%. Average scholarship/grant was $2,200; average loan $2,664. 48% of total undergraduate aid awarded as scholarships/grants, 52% as loans/jobs. **Non-need-based:** Awarded to 45 full-time undergraduates, including 17 freshmen. Scholarships awarded for academics, art, athletics, leadership, music/drama, state residency.

**Application procedures. Admission:** No deadline. $25 fee, may be waived for applicants with need. Admission notification on a rolling basis beginning on or about 7/1. Must reply by May 1 or within 2 week(s) if notified thereafter. Applicants to competitive programs should apply by January 15. **Financial aid:** Priority date 3/15; no closing date. FAFSA, institutional form required. Applicants notified on a rolling basis starting 3/15; must reply within 2 week(s) of notification.

**Academics. Special study options:** Cross-registration, distance learning, double major, dual enrollment of high school students, ESL, exchange student, honors, independent study, internships, liberal arts/career combination, student-designed major, study abroad, teacher certification program, Washington semester. Online programs. **Credit/placement by examination:** AP, CLEP, IB, SAT, ACT, institutional tests. **Support services:** Learning center, pre-admission summer program, reduced course load, remedial instruction, study skills assistance, tutoring, writing center.

**Majors. Architecture:** Urban/community planning. **Biology:** General, biochemistry, cell/histology, marine, molecular. **Business:** Accounting, actuarial science, business admin, human resources, international, marketing, tourism promotion, tourism/travel. **Communications:** General, broadcast journalism, journalism, public relations. **Computer sciences:** General, computer science, information systems. **Conservation:** General, environmental studies, fisheries. **Education:** Art, biology, chemistry, early childhood, elementary, English, foreign languages, French, German, history, mathematics, middle, multi-level teacher, music, physics, secondary, social studies, Spanish, special. **Foreign languages:** French, German, Spanish. **Health:** Clinical lab science, clinical lab technology, music therapy, predental, premedicine, preop/surgical nursing, prepharmacy, preveterinary. **History:** General. **Legal studies:** Prelaw. **Liberal arts:** Arts/sciences. **Math:** General. **Philosophy/religion:** Philosophy. **Physical sciences:** Chemistry, geology, physics. **Protective services:** Law enforcement admin. **Psychology:** General. **Public administration:** Social work. **Social sciences:** General, anthropology, economics, geography, political science, sociology. **Visual/performing arts:** Art, art history/conservation, dramatic, graphic design, music management, music performance, piano/organ, studio arts, voice/opera.

**Most popular majors.** Business/marketing 9%, communications/journalism 7%, education 13%, English 7%, health sciences 9%, psychology 8%, security/protective services 11%, social sciences 6%, visual/performing arts 11%.

**Computing on campus.** 840 workstations in dormitories, library, computer center, student center. Dormitories wired for high-speed internet access and linked to campus network. Commuter students can connect to campus network. Online course registration, online library, helpline, wireless network available.

**Student life. Freshman orientation:** Mandatory, $65 fee. Preregistration for classes offered. 2-day program for students and parents. **Housing:** Guaranteed on-campus for all undergraduates. Coed dorms, fraternity/sorority housing available. $200 partly refundable deposit. **Activities:** Bands, campus ministries, choral groups, dance, drama, international student organizations, literary magazine, music ensembles, Model UN, musical theater, radio station, student government, student newspaper, symphony orchestra, TV station, Black Awareness Association, Inter-Varsity Christian Fellowship, Commonwealth Association of Students.

**Athletics.** NCAA. **Intercollegiate:** Baseball M, basketball, cross-country, diving W, field hockey W, soccer W, softball W, swimming W, track and field. **Intramural:** Basketball, football (non-tackle) M, soccer, softball, tennis, volleyball, water polo. **Team name:** Mounties.

**Student services.** Adult student services, alcohol/substance abuse counseling, chaplain/spiritual director, career counseling, services for economically disadvantaged, student employment services, financial aid counseling, health services, minority student services, on-campus daycare, personal counseling, placement for graduates, veterans' counselor, women's services. **Physically disabled:** Services for visually, speech, hearing impaired.

**Contact.** E-mail: admissions@mansfield.edu
Phone: (570) 662-4243 Toll-free number: (800) 577-6826
Fax: (570) 662-4121
Brian Barden, Executive Director of Enrollment Services, Mansfield University of Pennsylvania, South Hall, Mansfield, PA 16933

---

## Marywood University

**Scranton, Pennsylvania**  **CB member**
www.marywood.edu  **CB code: 2407**

- Private 4-year university affiliated with Roman Catholic Church
- Residential campus in small city
- 2,147 degree-seeking undergraduates: 5% part-time, 70% women, 1% African American, 2% Asian American, 3% Hispanic American, 1% international
- 1,130 degree-seeking graduate students
- 72% of applicants admitted
- SAT or ACT (ACT writing optional) required
- 70% graduate within 6 years

**General.** Founded in 1915. Regionally accredited. **Degrees:** 400 bachelor's awarded; master's, doctoral, professional offered. **ROTC:** Army, Air Force. **Location:** 110 miles from Philadelphia, 120 miles from New York City. **Calendar:** Semester, extensive summer session. **Full-time faculty:** 142 total; 85% have terminal degrees, 5% minority, 56% women. **Part-time faculty:** 240 total; 8% minority, 55% women. **Class size:** 52% < 20, 45% 20-39, 1% 40-49, 1% 50-99. **Special facilities:** Arboretum, technology lab, science multimedia lab, interactive voice lab, music computer lab, video conferencing facility, speech and hearing clinic, healthy family center, early childhood center, center for athletics and wellness, dance studio, black box small venue theater, human performance lab, Wall St. learning center, studio arts center, psychology/education research lab, FAA approved aviation simulator lab, nursing simulation lab, graphics design lab, assistive technology labs, communication/disorders clinic, culinary labs, three art museums.

**Freshman class profile.** 1,923 applied, 1,392 admitted, 473 enrolled.

| Mid 50% test scores | | | |
|---|---|---|---|
| SAT critical reading: | 480-570 | GPA 3.0-3.49: | 32% |
| SAT math: | 480-570 | GPA 2.0-2.99: | 33% |
| SAT writing: | 470-570 | Rank in top quarter: | 56% |
| ACT composite: | 20-23 | Rank in top tenth: | 22% |
| GPA 3.75 or higher: | 17% | Out-of-state: | 31% |
| GPA 3.50-3.74: | 17% | Live on campus: | 70% |

**Basis for selection.** Class rank, high school achievement weighed alongside SAT/ACT scores. Course selection, achievement outside classroom,

involvement in activities in and out of school, and letters of recommendations also considered. TOEFL used for admission of non-native English speakers. Essay and interviews recommended for all. Audition for music program; portfolio for art program required after acceptance. **Learning Disabled:** Students may request accommodation by submitting documentation to admissions office or coordinator of services for students with disabilities.

**High school preparation.** College-preparatory program recommended. 16 units required. Required units include English 4, mathematics 2, social studies 3, science 1 (laboratory 1) and academic electives 6. Biological science must be laboratory science.

**2009-2010 Annual costs.** Tuition/fees: $26,270. Room/board: $11,498. Books/supplies: $900. Personal expenses: $800.

**2008-2009 Financial aid. Need-based:** 395 full-time freshmen applied for aid; 350 were judged to have need; 349 of these received aid. Average need met was 81%. Average scholarship/grant was $6,308; average loan $3,705. 57% of total undergraduate aid awarded as scholarships/grants, 43% as loans/jobs. **Non-need-based:** Awarded to 1,852 full-time undergraduates, including 404 freshmen. Scholarships awarded for academics, alumni affiliation, art, leadership, music/drama, ROTC.

**Application procedures. Admission:** No deadline. $35 fee, may be waived for applicants with need, free for online applicants. Admission notification on a rolling basis beginning on or about 10/1. Must reply by May 1 or within 3 week(s) if notified thereafter. Students applying for early admission must submit letter from their high school principal recommending them for early admission. **Financial aid:** Priority date 2/15; no closing date. FAFSA required. Applicants notified on a rolling basis starting 2/15; must reply by 5/1 or within 3 week(s) of notification.

**Academics.** Healthy Family Center provides opportunities for study and research in nutrition, dietetics, and athletic performance; Robert J. Mellow Center for Athletics and Wellness provides full support for athletic training program. **Special study options:** Combined bachelor's/graduate degree, cross-registration, distance learning, double major, dual enrollment of high school students, ESL, honors, independent study, internships, semester at sea, student-designed major, study abroad, teacher certification program. Students may study in any accredited school in any country that is approved by Marywood, or Marywood also has faculty-led, short-term study abroad programs. **Credit/placement by examination:** AP, CLEP, IB, institutional tests. 30 credit hours maximum toward associate degree, 66 toward bachelor's. **Support services:** Learning center, pre-admission summer program, reduced course load, remedial instruction, study skills assistance, tutoring, writing center.

**Majors. Architecture:** Architecture, environmental design. **Biology:** General, biotechnology. **Business:** Accounting, business admin, financial planning, hospitality admin, international, marketing. **Communications:** Digital media. **Conservation:** Environmental science. **Education:** Art, biology, early childhood, elementary, emotionally handicapped, ESL, family/consumer sciences, French, mathematics, music, science, social science, Spanish, special. **Foreign languages:** French, Spanish. **Health:** Art therapy, athletic training, audiology/speech pathology, clinical lab science, dietetics, health care admin, health services, music therapy, nursing (RN). **History:** General. **Math:** General. **Parks/recreation:** Health/fitness. **Philosophy/religion:** Philosophy, religion. **Protective services:** Criminal justice. **Psychology:** General, industrial. **Public administration:** Social work. **Social sciences:** General. **Transportation:** Aviation management. **Visual/performing arts:** Arts management, ceramics, dramatic, graphic design, illustration, interior design, music performance, painting, photography, sculpture. **Other:** History/political science, Musical theater.

**Most popular majors.** Business/marketing 11%, education 18%, health sciences 22%, psychology 7%, visual/performing arts 17%.

**Computing on campus.** 400 workstations in dormitories, library, computer center, student center. Dormitories wired for high-speed internet access and linked to campus network. Commuter students can connect to campus network. Online course registration, online library, helpline, repair service, student web hosting, wireless network available.

**Student life. Freshman orientation:** Mandatory, $200 fee. Preregistration for classes offered. 3-day program held in July, for student and family. Additional 3-day program prior to start of classes. **Policies:** First- and second-year students under 21 not living at home with families in area required to live on campus. **Housing:** Guaranteed on-campus for freshmen. Coed dorms, single-sex dorms, special housing for disabled, apartments, wellness housing available. Volunteer services residential community. **Activities:** Bands, campus ministries, choral groups, dance, drama, international student organizations, literary magazine, music ensembles, musical theater, radio station, student government, student newspaper, TV station, Amnesty International, collegiate volunteers, environmental club, Volunteers in Action, Psi Chi, Peer Mediators, Gay-Straight Alliance, Americorps.

**Athletics.** NCAA. **Intercollegiate:** Baseball M, basketball, cross-country, diving, field hockey W, lacrosse, soccer, softball W, swimming, tennis, volleyball W. **Intramural:** Badminton, basketball, football (non-tackle), racquetball, soccer, softball, table tennis, tennis, volleyball, water polo. **Team name:** Pacers.

**Student services.** Adult student services, alcohol/substance abuse counseling, chaplain/spiritual director, career counseling, services for economically disadvantaged, student employment services, financial aid counseling, health services, minority student services, on-campus daycare, personal counseling, placement for graduates, women's services. **Physically disabled:** Services for visually, speech, hearing impaired. **Learning disabled:** Comprehensive services available.

**Contact.** E-mail: yourfuture@marywood.edu
Phone: (570) 348-6234 Toll-free number: (866) 279-9663
Fax: (570) 961-4763
Christian DiGregorio, Director of University Admissions, Marywood University, 2300 Adams Avenue, Scranton, PA 18509-1598

---

## Mercyhurst College

| | |
|---|---|
| Erie, Pennsylvania | CB member |
| www.mercyhurst.edu | CB code: 2410 |

- Private 4-year liberal arts college affiliated with Roman Catholic Church
- Residential campus in small city
- 3,941 degree-seeking undergraduates: 12% part-time, 59% women, 6% African American, 1% Asian American, 2% Hispanic American, 5% international
- 348 degree-seeking graduate students
- 74% of applicants admitted
- SAT or ACT (ACT writing recommended), application essay required
- 68% graduate within 6 years; 31% enter graduate study

**General.** Founded in 1926. Regionally accredited. **Degrees:** 630 bachelor's, 201 associate awarded; master's offered. **ROTC:** Air Force. **Location:** 100 miles from Pittsburgh; 90 miles from Buffalo, New York. **Calendar:** Trimester, limited summer session. **Full-time faculty:** 186 total; 53% have terminal degrees, 4% minority, 50% women. **Part-time faculty:** 94 total; 7% have terminal degrees, 3% minority, 57% women. **Class size:** 52% < 20, 46% 20-39, less than 1% 40-49, less than 1% 50-99. **Special facilities:** Observatory, archaeological materials preservation laboratory.

**Freshman class profile.** 2,990 applied, 2,210 admitted, 669 enrolled.

| Mid 50% test scores | | GPA 2.0-2.99: | 19% |
|---|---|---|---|
| SAT critical reading: | 470-570 | Rank in top quarter: | 18% |
| SAT math: | 470-580 | Rank in top tenth: | 15% |
| SAT writing: | 460-560 | End year in good standing: | 94% |
| ACT composite: | 21-25 | Return as sophomores: | 81% |
| GPA 3.75 or higher: | 34% | Out-of-state: | 47% |
| GPA 3.50-3.74: | 17% | Live on campus: | 88% |
| GPA 3.0-3.49: | 30% | International: | 6% |

**Basis for selection.** Admissions based on secondary school record. Class rank, standardized test scores, talent, ability, character, and personal qualities also important. Audition required for dance and music programs; portfolio required for art program. **Homeschooled:** SAT/ACT and transcript preferred.

**High school preparation.** College-preparatory program recommended. 16 units required. Required and recommended units include English 4, mathematics 2-3, social studies 5, science 2-3 (laboratory 2) and foreign language 2-3.

**2010-2011 Annual costs.** Tuition/fees: $26,346. Room/board: $9,195. Books/supplies: $1,000. Personal expenses: $600.

**2009-2010 Financial aid. Non-need-based:** Scholarships awarded for academics, alumni affiliation, art, athletics, leadership, minority status, music/drama, religious affiliation, ROTC.

**Application procedures. Admission:** Priority date 3/15; no deadline. $30 fee, may be waived for applicants with need, free for online applicants. Admission notification on a rolling basis beginning on or about 11/15. Must reply by May 1 or within 2 week(s) if notified thereafter. **Financial aid:** Priority date 3/1; no closing date. FAFSA required. Applicants notified on a rolling basis starting 2/15; must reply by 5/1 or within 2 week(s) of notification.

**Academics.** Education department offers graduate student-taught special education programs for learning disabled students. **Special study options:**

Combined bachelor's/graduate degree, cooperative education, cross-registration, distance learning, double major, honors, independent study, internships, liberal arts/career combination, New York semester, semester at sea, student-designed major, study abroad, teacher certification program, Washington semester, weekend college. **Credit/placement by examination:** AP, CLEP, IB, SAT, ACT, institutional tests. 30 credit hours maximum toward bachelor's degree. **Support services:** Learning center, pre-admission summer program, reduced course load, remedial instruction, study skills assistance, tutoring, writing center.

**Majors. Biology:** General, biochemistry. **Business:** Accounting, business admin, fashion, finance, hospitality admin, international. **Communications:** General. **Computer sciences:** General. **Education:** Art, biology, business, chemistry, early childhood, elementary, English, family/consumer sciences, foreign languages, mathematics, music, science, secondary, social science, special. **Foreign languages:** General. **Health:** Art therapy, health services, medical records technology. **History:** General. **Interdisciplinary:** Global studies. **Math:** General. **Philosophy/religion:** Philosophy, religion. **Physical sciences:** Chemistry, geology. **Protective services:** Criminal justice, forensics. **Psychology:** General. **Public administration:** Social work. **Social sciences:** Anthropology, political science, sociology. **Theology:** Religious ed. **Visual/performing arts:** Dance, interior design, music performance, studio arts.

**Most popular majors.** Biology 6%, business/marketing 23%, education 12%, interdisciplinary studies 13%, security/protective services 11%, visual/performing arts 6%.

**Computing on campus.** 375 workstations in dormitories, library, computer center, student center. Dormitories wired for high-speed internet access and linked to campus network. Commuter students can connect to campus network. Online course registration, online library, helpline, repair service, student web hosting, wireless network available.

**Student life. Freshman orientation:** Mandatory, $150 fee. Preregistration for classes offered. 3 days prior to start of classes. **Housing:** Guaranteed on-campus for all undergraduates. Single-sex dorms, apartments, wellness housing available. $350 fully refundable deposit, deadline 8/1. **Activities:** Bands, campus ministries, choral groups, dance, drama, international student organizations, literary magazine, music ensembles, musical theater, opera, radio station, student government, student newspaper, symphony orchestra, Association of Black Collegians, Habitat for Humanity, Amnesty International, ambassadors club.

**Athletics.** NCAA. **Intercollegiate:** Baseball M, basketball, cheerleading, cross-country, field hockey W, football (tackle) M, golf, ice hockey, lacrosse, rowing (crew), soccer, softball W, tennis, volleyball W, water polo, wrestling M. **Intramural:** Basketball, bowling, football (non-tackle) M, ice hockey, skiing, soccer, softball. **Team name:** Lakers.

**Student services.** Adult student services, alcohol/substance abuse counseling, chaplain/spiritual director, career counseling, services for economically disadvantaged, student employment services, financial aid counseling, health services, personal counseling, placement for graduates, veterans' counselor. **Physically disabled:** Services for hearing impaired. **Learning disabled:** Comprehensive services available.

**Contact.** E-mail: admissions@mercyhurst.edu
Phone: (814) 824-2202 Toll-free number: (800) 825-1926
Fax: (814) 824-2071
Christopher Coons, Director of Undergraduate Admissions, Mercyhurst College, 501 East 38th Street, Erie, PA 16546-0001

---

## Messiah College

| | |
|---|---|
| Grantham, Pennsylvania | CB member |
| www.messiah.edu | CB code: 2411 |

- Private 4-year liberal arts college affiliated with interdenominational tradition
- Residential campus in small town
- 2,728 degree-seeking undergraduates: 1% part-time, 63% women, 2% African American, 2% Asian American, 2% Hispanic American, 2% international
- 35 degree-seeking graduate students
- 69% of applicants admitted
- Application essay required
- 78% graduate within 6 years; 18% enter graduate study

**General.** Founded in 1909. Regionally accredited. Students able to take coursework at Temple University. **Degrees:** 623 bachelor's awarded; master's offered. **Location:** 10 miles from Harrisburg, 20 miles from Gettysburg. **Calendar:** Semester, limited summer session. **Full-time faculty:** 170 total; 81% have terminal degrees, 8% minority, 38% women. **Part-time**

**faculty:** 109 total; 7% minority, 52% women. **Class size:** 45% < 20, 49% 20-39, 2% 40-49, 3% 50-99, 1% >100. **Special facilities:** Historical library and archives, natural history museum, service and learning center, Anabaptist, Pietist, Wesleyan studies institute, community-supported agriculture, solar panel array and pavilion.

**Freshman class profile.** 3,014 applied, 2,072 admitted, 698 enrolled.

| Mid 50% test scores | | | |
|---|---|---|---|
| SAT critical reading: | 510-620 | GPA 2.0-2.99: | 5% |
| SAT math: | 510-640 | Rank in top quarter: | 67% |
| SAT writing: | 510-620 | Rank in top tenth: | 35% |
| ACT composite: | 23-28 | End year in good standing: | 97% |
| GPA 3.75 or higher: | 59% | Return as sophomores: | 87% |
| GPA 3.50-3.74: | 17% | Out-of-state: | 44% |
| GPA 3.0-3.49: | 19% | Live on campus: | 97% |
| | | International: | 2% |

**Basis for selection.** Admitted students normally in top third of class and have B average or better. Statement of Christian commitment required. SAT or ACT recommended. Tests required of standard choice applicants. Students in the top 20% of high school class may apply without test scores, but must submit graded writing sample and have on-campus interview. Interview required for students who apply by the "Write Choice" application method, strongly recommended for all others. **Homeschooled:** Comprehensive transcript of senior year academic program as well as courses and course evaluations of 9th through 11th grades required. Include independent evaluation by qualified educator if available. **Learning Disabled:** Autobiographical statement required. Psychoeducational report (done within last 4 years) and interview required only after admissions decision. High school IEP recommended.

**High school preparation.** College-preparatory program required. 16 units required; 20 recommended. Required and recommended units include English 4, mathematics 2-3, social studies 2, history 2, science 2-3 (laboratory 2-3), foreign language 2 and academic electives 4.

**2010-2011 Annual costs.** Tuition/fees: $27,480. Room/board: $8,160. Books/supplies: $1,050. Personal expenses: $1,220.

**2009-2010 Financial aid. Need-based:** 609 full-time freshmen applied for aid; 527 were judged to have need; 527 of these received aid. Average need met was 72%. Average scholarship/grant was $13,875; average loan $3,719. 62% of total undergraduate aid awarded as scholarships/grants, 38% as loans/jobs. **Non-need-based:** Awarded to 877 full-time undergraduates, including 238 freshmen. Scholarships awarded for academics, art, leadership, music/drama, religious affiliation.

**Application procedures. Admission:** Priority date 5/1; no deadline. $30 fee, may be waived for applicants with need. Admission notification on a rolling basis beginning on or about 7/1. Must reply by May 1 or within 4 week(s) if notified thereafter. **Financial aid:** Priority date 4/1; no closing date. FAFSA required. Applicants notified on a rolling basis starting 3/15; must reply by 5/1 or within 4 week(s) of notification.

**Academics.** Supplemental instructional support available. **Special study options:** Accelerated study, double major, dual enrollment of high school students, ESL, exchange student, honors, independent study, internships, student-designed major, study abroad, teacher certification program, urban semester, Washington semester. Pass/Fail option. **Credit/placement by examination:** AP, CLEP, IB, institutional tests. 32 credit hours maximum toward bachelor's degree. **Support services:** Learning center, pre-admission summer program, reduced course load, remedial instruction, study skills assistance, tutoring, writing center.

**Majors. Biology:** General, biochemistry. **Business:** Accounting, business admin, e-commerce, entrepreneurial studies, human resources, international, managerial economics, marketing. **Communications:** General, journalism, radio/tv. **Computer sciences:** Computer science, information systems. **Conservation:** Environmental science, environmental studies. **Education:** Art, biology, chemistry, early childhood, elementary, English, family/consumer sciences, French, German, mathematics, music, physical, social studies, Spanish. **Engineering:** General. **Family/consumer sciences:** Family/community services. **Foreign languages:** French, German, Spanish. **Health:** Athletic training, clinical nutrition, nursing (RN). **History:** General. **Interdisciplinary:** Biopsychology, nutrition sciences. **Liberal arts:** Humanities. **Math:** General. **Parks/recreation:** General, exercise sciences, sports admin. **Philosophy/religion:** Philosophy. **Physical sciences:** Chemistry, physics. **Protective services:** Criminal justice. **Psychology:** General. **Public administration:** Social work. **Social sciences:** Economics, political science, sociology. **Theology:** Bible, religious ed. **Visual/performing arts:** Art history/conservation, arts management, dramatic, studio arts.

**Most popular majors.** Business/marketing 13%, communications/journalism 7%, education 14%, health sciences 10%, psychology 7%, visual/performing arts 6%.

**Computing on campus.** 571 workstations in dormitories, library, computer center, student center. Dormitories wired for high-speed internet access and linked to campus network. Commuter students can connect to campus network. Online course registration, online library, helpline, student web hosting, wireless network available.

**Student life. Freshman orientation:** Mandatory. Preregistration for classes offered. 4-day orientation for students and parents during fall welcome weekend; includes placement exams and service day. **Policies:** Students generally required to live on campus unless married or living with relatives. Religious observance required. **Housing:** Guaranteed on-campus for all undergraduates. Coed dorms, single-sex dorms, special housing for disabled, apartments, wellness housing available. $200 partly refundable deposit, deadline 5/1. **Activities:** Bands, campus ministries, choral groups, dance, drama, film society, international student organizations, literary magazine, music ensembles, musical theater, radio station, student government, student newspaper, symphony orchestra, outreach teams, World Christian Fellowship, Nurses Christian Fellowship, Newman Club, Powerhouse band, Acclamation dance, Alliance of Confessing Theologies.

**Athletics.** NCAA. **Intercollegiate:** Baseball M, basketball, cross-country, field hockey W, golf M, lacrosse, soccer, softball W, swimming, tennis, track and field, volleyball W, wrestling M. **Intramural:** Basketball, football (non-tackle), racquetball, soccer, softball, volleyball. **Team name:** Falcons.

**Student services.** Chaplain/spiritual director, career counseling, student employment services, financial aid counseling, health services, minority student services, on-campus daycare, personal counseling, placement for graduates. **Physically disabled:** Services for visually, speech, hearing impaired.

**Contact.** E-mail: admiss@messiah.edu
Phone: (717) 691-6000 Toll-free number: (800) 233-4220
Fax: (717) 691-2307
John Chopka, Vice President of Enrollment Management, Messiah College, PO Box 3005, Grantham, PA 17027-0800

## Millersville University of Pennsylvania

**Millersville, Pennsylvania**    **CB member**
**www.millersville.edu**    **CB code: 2656**

- Public 4-year university and liberal arts college
- Residential campus in small town
- 7,242 degree-seeking undergraduates: 8% part-time, 56% women, 7% African American, 1% Asian American, 4% Hispanic American
- 905 degree-seeking graduate students
- 53% of applicants admitted
- SAT or ACT (ACT writing recommended) required
- 61% graduate within 6 years

**General.** Founded in 1855. Regionally accredited. **Degrees:** 1,427 bachelor's, 1 associate awarded; master's offered. **ROTC:** Army. **Location:** 3 miles from Lancaster, 35 miles from Harrisburg. **Calendar:** 4-1-4, limited summer session. **Full-time faculty:** 305 total; 95% have terminal degrees, 16% minority, 47% women. **Part-time faculty:** 153 total; 29% have terminal degrees, 6% minority, 53% women. **Class size:** 17% < 20, 68% 20-39, 9% 40-49, 4% 50-99, 2% >100.

**Freshman class profile.** 7,241 applied, 3,849 admitted, 1,333 enrolled.

| Mid 50% test scores | | | |
|---|---|---|---|
| SAT critical reading: | 480-570 | Rank in top quarter: | 45% |
| SAT math: | 490-590 | Rank in top tenth: | 16% |
| SAT writing: | 460-560 | Return as sophomores: | 82% |
| ACT composite: | 20-24 | Out-of-state: | 6% |
| | | Live on campus: | 85% |

**Basis for selection.** High school record most important, followed by class rank, test scores, and recommendations. Special consideration to students with special talents. Educationally and economically disadvantaged students may be admitted to Aim for Success enrichment program if they demonstrate potential for college success. Applicants without SAT scores may enroll as non-degree students and be admitted to degree-seeking status after completing 12 credits with 2.0 GPA. Interview required for applicants to disadvantaged program; recommended for all others. Audition required for music applicants; portfolio required for art applicants. RN required for nursing program. Letters of reference and personal statement are recommended.

**High school preparation.** College-preparatory program required. 15 units required; 21 recommended. Required and recommended units include English 4, mathematics 3, social studies 3, history 2, science 3 (laboratory 1), foreign language 2 and academic electives 4.

**2009-2010 Annual costs.** Tuition/fees: $7,147; $15,479 out-of-state. Room/board: $7,766. Books/supplies: $1,000. Personal expenses: $1,745.

**2008-2009 Financial aid. Need-based:** 1,152 full-time freshmen applied for aid; 753 were judged to have need; 735 of these received aid. Average need met was 78%. Average scholarship/grant was $5,130; average loan $3,232. 44% of total undergraduate aid awarded as scholarships/grants,

56% as loans/jobs. **Non-need-based:** Awarded to 719 full-time undergraduates, including 197 freshmen. Scholarships awarded for academics, athletics, minority status.

**Application procedures. Admission:** Priority date 1/1; no deadline. $50 fee, may be waived for applicants with need. Admission notification on a rolling basis beginning on or about 9/15. Extensions of reply date for accepted applicants granted upon request until May 1. **Financial aid:** Closing date 3/15. FAFSA required. Applicants notified on a rolling basis starting 3/19; must reply within 2 week(s) of notification.

**Academics. Special study options:** Accelerated study, combined bachelor's/graduate degree, cooperative education, cross-registration, distance learning, double major, dual enrollment of high school students, honors, independent study, internships, study abroad, teacher certification program. Off-campus study, learning disabilities services, adult continuing education program. **Credit/placement by examination:** AP, CLEP, IB, institutional tests. **Support services:** Learning center, reduced course load, remedial instruction, study skills assistance, tutoring, writing center.

**Majors. Biology:** General. **Business:** Business admin. **Communications:** General. **Computer sciences:** General. **Education:** Elementary, secondary, special. **Engineering technology:** Industrial, occupational safety. **Foreign languages:** French, German, Spanish. **Health:** Nursing (RN). **History:** General. **Math:** General. **Philosophy/religion:** Philosophy. **Physical sciences:** Atmospheric science, chemistry, geology, oceanography, physics. **Psychology:** General. **Public administration:** Social work. **Social sciences:** Anthropology, economics, geography, international relations, political science, sociology. **Visual/performing arts:** Art. **Other:** International studies, Social studies, Technology education.

**Most popular majors.** Biology 6%, business/marketing 14%, communications/journalism 6%, education 18%, engineering/engineering technologies 7%, psychology 9%, social sciences 11%.

**Computing on campus.** 705 workstations in dormitories, library, computer center, student center. Dormitories wired for high-speed internet access and linked to campus network. Commuter students can connect to campus network. Online course registration, online library, helpline, repair service, wireless network available.

**Student life. Freshman orientation:** Mandatory, $290 fee. 6-day program in August includes parents. **Housing:** Guaranteed on-campus for freshmen. Coed dorms, apartments, wellness housing available. $125 partly refundable deposit, deadline 4/1. Academic interest housing available for several subject areas. University-affiliated apartments and dormitory for single students adjacent to campus. **Activities:** Bands, campus ministries, choral groups, dance, drama, international student organizations, literary magazine, music ensembles, musical theater, radio station, student government, student newspaper, symphony orchestra, TV station, Black Student Union, commuting student association, Circle-K, College Republicans, Marauder Graphics, Asian and Friends Affiliation, College Democrats, NAACP, Society on Latino Affairs.

**Athletics.** NCAA. **Intercollegiate:** Baseball M, basketball, cheerleading M, cross-country, field hockey W, football (tackle) M, golf M, lacrosse W, soccer, softball W, swimming W, tennis, track and field, volleyball W, wrestling M. **Intramural:** Badminton, basketball, golf, racquetball, soccer, softball, tennis, volleyball, water polo. **Team name:** Marauders.

**Student services.** Adult student services, alcohol/substance abuse counseling, chaplain/spiritual director, career counseling, services for economically disadvantaged, student employment services, financial aid counseling, health services, minority student services, personal counseling, placement for graduates, veterans' counselor, women's services. **Physically disabled:** Services for visually, speech, hearing impaired.

**Contact.** E-mail: admissions@millersville.edu
Phone: (717) 872-3371 Toll-free number: (800) 682-3648
Fax: (717) 871-2147
Douglas Zander, Associate Provost for Enrollment Management, Millersville University of Pennsylvania, PO Box 1002, Millersville, PA 17551-0302

---

**Misericordia University**
**Dallas, Pennsylvania**
www.misericordia.edu

CB member
CB code: 2087

- Private 4-year health science and liberal arts college affiliated with Roman Catholic Church
- Residential campus in large town
- 2,315 degree-seeking undergraduates: 28% part-time, 71% women, 1% African American, 1% Asian American, 2% Hispanic American
- 368 degree-seeking graduate students

- 69% of applicants admitted
- SAT or ACT (ACT writing optional) required
- 68% graduate within 6 years; 15% enter graduate study

**General.** Founded in 1924. Regionally accredited. Guaranteed Placement Program (within six months of graduation); Women with Children program for single women. **Degrees:** 410 bachelor's awarded; master's, professional offered. **ROTC:** Army, Air Force. **Location:** 9 miles from Wilkes-Barre, 20 miles from Scranton. **Calendar:** Semester, limited summer session. **Full-time faculty:** 96 total; 79% have terminal degrees, 6% minority, 54% women. **Part-time faculty:** 179 total; 16% have terminal degrees, 2% minority, 52% women. **Class size:** 54% < 20, 45% 20-39, 1% 40-49.

**Freshman class profile.** 1,533 applied, 1,060 admitted, 381 enrolled.

| Mid 50% test scores | | | |
|---|---|---|---|
| SAT critical reading: | 470-550 | GPA 2.0-2.99: | 26% |
| SAT math: | 480-570 | Rank in top quarter: | 49% |
| ACT composite: | 20-25 | Rank in top tenth: | 15% |
| GPA 3.75 or higher: | 14% | End year in good standing: | 91% |
| GPA 3.50-3.74: | 21% | Return as sophomores: | 85% |
| GPA 3.0-3.49: | 38% | Out-of-state: | 25% |
| | | Live on campus: | 81% |

**Basis for selection.** In order of importance: high school achievement, test scores, character, recommendations from school teachers or counselors. Test scores weighed more heavily for health science programs. Essay, interview recommended. Essay required for occupational therapy applicants. **Homeschooled:** Transcript of courses and grades required. If applicant not affiliated with specific organization, college will accept transcript from home schooling parent that shows course work completed and grades achieved. GED not required. **Learning Disabled:** Essay, 3 letters of recommendation, documentation of disability, test results (i.e., WAIS) required. SAT/ACT not required.

**High school preparation.** College-preparatory program recommended. 16 units required. Required units include English 4, mathematics 4, social studies 4 and science 4. 2 units science and algebra required for allied health applicants. Strong math background required for computer science, physical therapy, chemistry and biology applicants.

**2010-2011 Annual costs.** Tuition/fees: $24,990. Room/board: $10,410. Books/supplies: $800. Personal expenses: $500.

**2009-2010 Financial aid. Need-based:** 357 full-time freshmen applied for aid; 308 were judged to have need; 308 of these received aid. Average need met was 73%. Average scholarship/grant was $13,218; average loan $6,800. 60% of total undergraduate aid awarded as scholarships/grants, 40% as loans/jobs. **Non-need-based:** Awarded to 278 full-time undergraduates, including 81 freshmen. Scholarships awarded for academics, alumni affiliation, leadership, minority status, state residency.

**Application procedures. Admission:** No deadline. $25 fee, may be waived for applicants with need. Admission notification on a rolling basis beginning on or about 9/1. Must reply by May 1 or within 4 week(s) if notified thereafter. Essay required for applicants to 5-year occupational therapy bachelor's/master's program. Closing date for applications to 5-year physical therapy bachelor's/master's program is February 1. **Financial aid:** Priority date 3/1, closing date 5/1. FAFSA, institutional form required. Applicants notified on a rolling basis starting 3/15; must reply by 5/1.

**Academics. Special study options:** Accelerated study, combined bachelor's/graduate degree, cross-registration, distance learning, double major, dual enrollment of high school students, honors, independent study, internships, student-designed major, study abroad, teacher certification program, weekend college. **Credit/placement by examination:** AP, CLEP, IB, SAT, ACT, institutional tests. 40 credit hours maximum toward bachelor's degree. **Support services:** Learning center, pre-admission summer program, study skills assistance, tutoring, writing center.

**Majors. Biology:** General, biochemistry. **Business:** Accounting, business admin, management science, marketing. **Communications:** General. **Computer sciences:** General, information technology. **Education:** Elementary, special. **Health:** Clinical lab science, health care admin, medical radiologic technology/radiation therapy, nursing (RN). **History:** General. **Liberal arts:** Arts/sciences. **Math:** General. **Parks/recreation:** Sports admin. **Philosophy/religion:** Philosophy. **Physical sciences:** Chemistry. **Psychology:** General. **Public administration:** Social work.

**Most popular majors.** Business/marketing 19%, education 10%, health sciences 44%, liberal arts 6%.

**Computing on campus.** 100 workstations in dormitories, library, computer center, student center. Dormitories wired for high-speed internet access and linked to campus network. Commuter students can connect to campus network. Online course registration, online library, helpline, repair service, wireless network available.

**Student life. Freshman orientation:** Mandatory, $200 fee. Preregistration for classes offered. One-day testing for math and English placement. **Housing:** Coed dorms available. $100 nonrefundable deposit, deadline 5/1. Leadership house, apartment building for women with children located adjacent to campus. **Activities:** Jazz band, campus ministries, choral groups, dance, drama, literary magazine, music ensembles, radio station, student government, student newspaper, TV station, student nurses association, Council for Exceptional Children, Circle-K, Peer Associates, Diversity Institute.

**Athletics.** NCAA. **Intercollegiate:** Baseball M, basketball, cheerleading M, cross-country, field hockey W, golf M, lacrosse, soccer, softball W, swimming, tennis, track and field, volleyball W. **Intramural:** Basketball, cross-country, football (non-tackle), racquetball, soccer, softball, tennis, volleyball. **Team name:** Cougars.

**Student services.** Adult student services, alcohol/substance abuse counseling, chaplain/spiritual director, career counseling, services for economically disadvantaged, student employment services, financial aid counseling, health services, minority student services, personal counseling, placement for graduates, women's services. **Physically disabled:** Services for visually, speech, hearing impaired. **Learning disabled:** Comprehensive services available.

**Contact.** E-mail: admiss@misericordia.edu
Phone: (570) 674-6264 Toll-free number: (866) 262-6363
Fax: (570) 675-2441
Glenn Bozinski, Director of Admissions, Misericordia University, 301 Lake Street, Dallas, PA 18612-1098

## Moore College of Art and Design
**Philadelphia, Pennsylvania**
www.moore.edu                                  CB code: 2417

- Private 4-year visual arts college for women
- Commuter campus in very large city
- 527 degree-seeking undergraduates: 6% part-time, 100% women, 12% African American, 2% Asian American, 6% Hispanic American, 3% international
- 55 degree-seeking graduate students
- 64% of applicants admitted
- Interview required
- 56% graduate within 6 years

**General.** Founded in 1848. Regionally accredited. **Degrees:** 103 bachelor's awarded; master's offered. **Location:** 90 miles from New York City. **Calendar:** Semester, limited summer session. **Full-time faculty:** 24 total; 71% have terminal degrees, 8% minority, 50% women. **Part-time faculty:** 105 total; 11% minority, 66% women. **Class size:** 79% < 20, 21% 20-39. **Special facilities:** Professional and student galleries.

**Freshman class profile.** 536 applied, 344 admitted, 103 enrolled.

| Mid 50% test scores | | | |
|---|---|---|---|
| SAT critical reading: | 450-580 | GPA 3.0-3.49: | 45% |
| SAT math: | 420-530 | GPA 2.0-2.99: | 40% |
| ACT composite: | 19-25 | Return as sophomores: | 75% |
| GPA 3.75 or higher: | 6% | Out-of-state: | 46% |
| GPA 3.50-3.74: | 9% | International: | 5% |

**Basis for selection.** High school record, interview, portfolio, and test scores important. 850 SAT (exclusive of Writing) or 18 ACT and 2.5 GPA required. First-time degree seeking students must complete writing placement essay. Transfer students may participate in the Directed Self-Placement program for English courses. Portfolio required; essay recommended for all. **Homeschooled:** State high school equivalency certificate required. **Learning Disabled:** Students who request accommodations must provide qualifying documentation on professional letterhead and contain dates of assessment, signatures, titles, and license/certification numbers of diagnosing professionals. Documentation should be no more than 3 years old.

**High school preparation.** 14 units recommended. Recommended units include English 4, mathematics 2, social studies 4, science 2, foreign language 2 and visual/performing arts 3. Portfolio review required.

**2009-2010 Annual costs.** Tuition/fees: $29,240. Room/board: $11,026. Books/supplies: $2,060. Personal expenses: $2,000.

**2009-2010 Financial aid. Non-need-based:** Scholarships awarded for academics, art, leadership.

**Application procedures. Admission:** $40 fee, may be waived for applicants with need. Admission notification on a rolling basis beginning on or

about 11/15. Must reply by May 1 or within 3 week(s) if notified thereafter. **Financial aid:** Priority date 3/1, closing date 5/1. FAFSA required. Applicants notified on a rolling basis starting 2/15; must reply within 2 week(s) of notification.

**Academics. Special study options:** Double major, exchange student, independent study, internships, teacher certification program. **Credit/placement by examination:** AP, CLEP, IB, institutional tests. 6 credit hours maximum toward bachelor's degree. **Support services:** Pre-admission summer program, reduced course load, study skills assistance, tutoring.

**Majors. Education:** Art. **Interdisciplinary:** Museum. **Visual/performing arts:** Art history/conservation, fashion design, graphic design, illustration, interior design, photography, studio arts.

**Most popular majors.** Visual/performing arts 97%.

**Computing on campus.** PC or laptop required. 125 workstations in dormitories, library, computer center. Dormitories wired for high-speed internet access. Commuter students can connect to campus network. Online course registration, wireless network available.

**Student life. Freshman orientation:** Mandatory, $55 fee. Held 4 days prior to beginning of semester. **Housing:** Guaranteed on-campus for freshmen. $200 partly refundable deposit, deadline 7/15. **Activities:** Student government, student newspaper, student-run gallery, Emerging Leaders in the Arts, student judiciary committee, residence life staff, More Magazine, Business Scholars in the Arts.

**Student services.** Adult student services, career counseling, student employment services, financial aid counseling, health services, personal counseling.

**Contact.** E-mail: admiss@moore.edu
Phone: (215) 965-4014 Toll-free number: (800) 523-2025
Fax: (215) 568-3547
Heeseung Lee, Director of Admissions, Moore College of Art and Design, The Parkway at 20th Street, Philadelphia, PA 19103-1179

## Moravian College
**Bethlehem, Pennsylvania**                    CB member
www.moravian.edu                               CB code: 2418

- Private 4-year liberal arts college affiliated with Moravian Church in America
- Residential campus in small city
- 1,618 degree-seeking undergraduates: 5% part-time, 59% women, 3% African American, 2% Asian American, 6% Hispanic American, 1% international
- 159 degree-seeking graduate students
- 75% of applicants admitted
- SAT or ACT with writing, application essay required
- 75% graduate within 6 years

**General.** Founded in 1742. Regionally accredited. Member of Lehigh Valley Association of Independent Colleges Consortium. Sixth oldest college in country. **Degrees:** 338 bachelor's awarded; master's offered. **ROTC:** Army. **Location:** 60 miles from Philadelphia, 90 miles from New York City. **Calendar:** Semester, extensive summer session. **Full-time faculty:** 120 total; 91% have terminal degrees, 8% minority, 52% women. **Part-time faculty:** 79 total; 38% have terminal degrees, 2% minority, 53% women. **Class size:** 62% < 20, 36% 20-39, 2% 40-49, less than 1% 50-99.

**Freshman class profile.** 2,021 applied, 1,521 admitted, 380 enrolled.

| Mid 50% test scores | | | |
|---|---|---|---|
| SAT critical reading: | 490-590 | Rank in top tenth: | 28% |
| SAT math: | 490-600 | Return as sophomores: | 78% |
| SAT writing: | 480-590 | Out-of-state: | 42% |
| ACT composite: | 20-22 | Live on campus: | 87% |
| Rank in top quarter: | 51% | Fraternities: | 11% |
| | | Sororities: | 15% |

**Basis for selection.** High school record and standardized test scores important. Academic credentials, character, extracurricular involvement, volunteer work and potential for contribution considered. Interviews strongly recommended; audition required for music applicants; portfolio required for art applicants. **Homeschooled:** Letter of recommendation (nonparent) required. Interview strongly encouraged in order to share educational background in detail.

**High school preparation.** College-preparatory program required. 16 units required; 18 recommended. Required and recommended units include English 4, mathematics 3-4, social studies 4, science 3 (laboratory 2) and foreign language 2-3. 4 math units recommended for business, science, or math students.

**2009-2010 Annual costs.** Tuition/fees: $31,250. Room/board: $8,728. Books/supplies: $950. Personal expenses: $1,406.

**2009-2010 Financial aid. Need-based:** 355 full-time freshmen applied for aid; 320 were judged to have need; 320 of these received aid. Average need met was 80%. Average scholarship/grant was $20,141; average loan $4,148. 64% of total undergraduate aid awarded as scholarships/grants, 36% as loans/jobs. **Non-need-based:** Awarded to 304 full-time undergraduates, including 77 freshmen. Scholarships awarded for academics, alumni affiliation, leadership, minority status, music/drama, religious affiliation, ROTC.

**Application procedures. Admission:** Closing date 3/1 (postmark date). $40 fee, may be waived for applicants with need, free for online applicants. Admission notification 3/15. Must reply by 5/1. **Financial aid:** Priority date 2/14, closing date 3/15. FAFSA required. Applicants notified on a rolling basis starting 4/1; must reply by 5/1 or within 2 week(s) of notification.

**Academics.** Learning Center offers partial but responsive program for learning disabled students. **Special study options:** Combined bachelor's/graduate degree, cooperative education, cross-registration, double major, honors, independent study, internships, student-designed major, study abroad, teacher certification program, Washington semester. Allied health program with Thomas Jefferson University, forestry program cooperative with Duke University, engineering programs cooperative with Lehigh University and Washington University (MO), dental program cooperative with Temple University. **Credit/placement by examination:** AP, CLEP, IB, SAT, ACT, institutional tests. Some courses not included in credit-by-examination option. **Support services:** Learning center, study skills assistance, tutoring, writing center.

**Majors. Area/ethnic studies:** German. **Biology:** General, biochemistry. **Business:** Accounting, business admin, international. **Computer sciences:** Computer science. **Conservation:** Environmental science, environmental studies. **Education:** Music, science, social science. **Foreign languages:** Classics, French, German, Spanish. **Health:** Clinical lab science, nursing (RN). **History:** General. **Interdisciplinary:** Neuroscience. **Math:** General. **Philosophy/religion:** Philosophy, religion. **Physical sciences:** Chemistry, geology, physics. **Protective services:** Criminal justice. **Psychology:** General. **Social sciences:** Economics, political science, sociology. **Theology:** Sacred music. **Visual/performing arts:** Art, art history/conservation, dramatic, graphic design, music performance, music theory/composition, studio arts.

**Most popular majors.** Biology 8%, business/marketing 18%, English 11%, health sciences 6%, history 6%, psychology 10%, social sciences 17%, visual/performing arts 11%.

**Computing on campus.** 263 workstations in library, computer center. Dormitories wired for high-speed internet access and linked to campus network. Commuter students can connect to campus network. Online library, helpline, repair service, wireless network available.

**Student life. Freshman orientation:** Mandatory, $100 fee. Preregistration for classes offered. 3-day program held immediately prior to fall semester. **Housing:** Guaranteed on-campus for all undergraduates. Coed dorms, single-sex dorms, special housing for disabled, apartments, fraternity/sorority housing, wellness housing available. $400 nonrefundable deposit, deadline 5/1. Townhouses and suites available. **Activities:** Bands, campus ministries, choral groups, dance, drama, international student organizations, literary magazine, music ensembles, Model UN, musical theater, opera, radio station, student government, student newspaper, symphony orchestra, Hillel Society, Newman Association, Moravian College Christian Fellowship, Spectrum, Catacombs, Campus Community Connection, The Forum, multicultural club, The Learning Connection.

**Athletics.** NCAA. **Intercollegiate:** Baseball M, basketball, cross-country, field hockey W, football (tackle) M, golf M, lacrosse, soccer, softball W, tennis, track and field, volleyball W. **Intramural:** Basketball, football (non-tackle), soccer, softball, table tennis, tennis, volleyball. **Team name:** Greyhounds.

**Student services.** Adult student services, alcohol/substance abuse counseling, chaplain/spiritual director, career counseling, student employment services, financial aid counseling, health services, minority student services, personal counseling, placement for graduates. **Physically disabled:** Services for visually, speech, hearing impaired.

**Contact.** E-mail: admissions@moravian.edu
Phone: (610) 861-1320 Toll-free number: (800) 441-3191
Fax: (610) 625-7930
James Mackin, Director of Admission, Moravian College, 1200 Main Street, Bethlehem, PA 18018

---

## Mount Aloysius College
**Cresson, Pennsylvania**     **CB member**
**www.mtaloy.edu**     **CB code: 2420**

- Private 4-year liberal arts college affiliated with Roman Catholic Church
- Commuter campus in small town
- 1,482 degree-seeking undergraduates: 21% part-time, 73% women, 3% African American, 1% Hispanic American, 1% international
- 27 degree-seeking graduate students
- 80% of applicants admitted
- SAT or ACT (ACT writing optional), application essay required
- 32% graduate within 6 years

**General.** Founded in 1939. Regionally accredited. **Degrees:** 184 bachelor's, 189 associate awarded; master's offered. **Location:** 12 miles from Altoona, 90 miles from Pittsburgh. **Calendar:** Semester, limited summer session. **Full-time faculty:** 62 total; 47% have terminal degrees, 68% women. **Part-time faculty:** 116 total; 52% women. **Class size:** 63% < 20, 37% 20-39, less than 1% 40-49. **Special facilities:** Health and science center with mock operating room, telehealth/telenursing, ecumenical library.

**Freshman class profile.** 1,219 applied, 972 admitted, 360 enrolled.

| Mid 50% test scores | | | |
|---|---|---|---|
| SAT critical reading: | 420-510 | GPA 3.50-3.74: | 19% |
| SAT math: | 420-510 | GPA 3.0-3.49: | 38% |
| SAT writing: | 400-500 | GPA 2.0-2.99: | 28% |
| ACT composite: | 15-20 | Return as sophomores: | 59% |
| GPA 3.75 or higher: | 12% | Out-of-state: | 7% |
| | | Live on campus: | 57% |

**Basis for selection.** School record, test scores, activities, talent, and character most important. Nursing entrance test not required for students with SAT of 900 (exclusive of Writing) or higher. Placement test waived if student scores 500 or higher in either section. Interview required for students with lower SAT scores and GPA. Interviews and essays required for physical therapist assistant majors. **Learning Disabled:** Admission interview required.

**High school preparation.** College-preparatory program recommended. 16 units required. Required and recommended units include English 4, mathematics 3, social studies 3, history 3, science 3, foreign language 2 and academic electives 3. Algebra and 2 lab sciences required for nursing. Algebra, chemistry required for physical therapist assistant, radiography and medical imaging applicants. Biology required for occupational therapy assistant applicants.

**2010-2011 Annual costs.** Tuition/fees (projected): $18,000. Room/board: $7,660. Books/supplies: $2,000. Personal expenses: $3,000.

**2009-2010 Financial aid. Need-based:** 349 full-time freshmen applied for aid; 328 were judged to have need; 328 of these received aid. Average need met was 30%. Average scholarship/grant was $2,890; average loan $3,470. 51% of total undergraduate aid awarded as scholarships/grants, 49% as loans/jobs. **Non-need-based:** Awarded to 66 full-time undergraduates, including 42 freshmen. Scholarships awarded for academics, art, leadership, music/drama, religious affiliation.

**Application procedures. Admission:** No deadline. $30 fee, may be waived for applicants with need. Admission notification on a rolling basis beginning on or about 8/1. **Financial aid:** Priority date 4/1; no closing date. FAFSA required. Applicants notified on a rolling basis starting 3/15; must reply within 2 week(s) of notification.

**Academics. Special study options:** Accelerated study, combined bachelor's/graduate degree, distance learning, honors, independent study, internships, student-designed major, teacher certification program. **Credit/placement by examination:** AP, CLEP, SAT, institutional tests. 15 credit hours maximum toward associate degree, 30 toward bachelor's. **Support services:** Learning center, pre-admission summer program, reduced course load, remedial instruction, study skills assistance, tutoring, writing center.

**Majors. Business:** Accounting, accounting/business management, business admin. **Computer sciences:** General, information technology. **Education:** Early childhood, elementary. **Foreign languages:** Sign language interpretation. **Health:** Health services, nursing (RN), physician assistant, radiologic technology/medical imaging. **History:** General. **Interdisciplinary:** Behavioral sciences, math/computer science. **Legal studies:** Prelaw. **Liberal arts:** Arts/sciences, humanities. **Protective services:** Criminal justice. **Psychology:** General. **Social sciences:** General, criminology, political science.

**Most popular majors.** Business/marketing 19%, education 6%, foreign language 7%, health sciences 36%, liberal arts 13%, security/protective services 9%.

**Computing on campus.** 175 workstations in dormitories, library, computer center, student center. Dormitories linked to campus network. Helpline, repair service available.

**Student life. Freshman orientation:** Mandatory. **Housing:** Guaranteed on-campus for all undergraduates. Coed dorms available. **Activities:** Campus ministries, choral groups, drama, student government, student newspaper, nursing, occupational therapy assistant, business, Phi Theta Kappa, student programming council.

**Athletics.** NCAA. **Intercollegiate:** Baseball M, basketball, cross-country, golf, soccer, softball W, volleyball W. **Intramural:** Baseball M, basketball, football (tackle), golf, skiing, soccer, softball W, table tennis, tennis, volleyball. **Team name:** Mounties.

**Student services.** Alcohol/substance abuse counseling, chaplain/spiritual director, career counseling, student employment services, financial aid counseling, health services, on-campus daycare, personal counseling, placement for graduates, veterans' counselor. **Physically disabled:** Services for hearing impaired.

**Contact.** E-mail: admissions@mtaloy.edu
Phone: (814) 886-6383 Toll-free number: (888) 823-2220
Fax: (814) 886-6441
Frank Crouse, Vice President for Enrollment Management/Dean of Admissions, Mount Aloysius College, 7373 Admiral Peary Highway, Cresson, PA 16630

## Muhlenberg College
**Allentown, Pennsylvania**
www.muhlenberg.edu

**CB member**
**CB code: 2424**

- Private 4-year liberal arts college affiliated with Evangelical Lutheran Church in America
- Residential campus in small city
- 2,411 degree-seeking undergraduates: 4% part-time, 58% women, 2% African American, 2% Asian American, 3% Hispanic American
- 45% of applicants admitted
- Application essay required
- 85% graduate within 6 years; 32% enter graduate study

**General.** Founded in 1848. Regionally accredited. **Degrees:** 531 bachelor's awarded. **ROTC:** Army. **Location:** 55 miles from Philadelphia, 90 miles from New York City. **Calendar:** Semester, limited summer session. **Full-time faculty:** 166 total; 87% have terminal degrees, 7% minority, 51% women. **Part-time faculty:** 94 total; 22% have terminal degrees, 6% minority, 39% women. **Class size:** 64% < 20, 35% 20-39, less than 1% 40-49, less than 1% 50-99, less than 1% >100. **Special facilities:** 3-theater complex, electronic music studio, natural history museum, 38-acre environmental field station, greenhouse, two electron microscopes, isolation laboratories, DNA sequencer, 20-foot boat for marine studies, 60-acre arboretum.

**Freshman class profile.** 4,410 applied, 2,002 admitted, 577 enrolled.

| Mid 50% test scores | | | |
|---|---|---|---|
| SAT critical reading: | 560-660 | GPA 2.0-2.99: | 22% |
| SAT math: | 560-660 | Rank in top quarter: | 43% |
| SAT writing: | 560-660 | Rank in top tenth: | 41% |
| ACT composite: | 25-31 | End year in good standing: | 97% |
| GPA 3.75 or higher: | 18% | Return as sophomores: | 92% |
| GPA 3.50-3.74: | 21% | Out-of-state: | 72% |
| GPA 3.0-3.49: | 39% | Live on campus: | 99% |

**Basis for selection.** High school courses, grades, class rank, test scores, personal qualities, essay, recommendations, special talents and activities important. Interview strongly recommended. Test scores optional; SAT/ACT required for consideration for Assured Admission Medical and Dental Programs, merit scholarships, honors programs. Audition recommended for dance, drama, music programs; portfolio recommended for art program. **Homeschooled:** Statement describing homeschool structure and mission, transcript of courses and grades, state high school equivalency certificate, letter of recommendation (nonparent) required. Interview strongly recommended.

**High school preparation.** 16 units required; 20 recommended. Required and recommended units include English 4, mathematics 3-4, social studies 2, history 2-3, science 2-3 and foreign language 2-4. Advanced placement and accelerated courses encouraged.

**2009-2010 Annual costs.** Tuition/fees: $36,990. Room/board: $8,440. Books/supplies: $1,400. Personal expenses: $1,400.

**2009-2010 Financial aid. Need-based:** 80% of total undergraduate aid awarded as scholarships/grants, 20% as loans/jobs. **Non-need-based:** Scholarships awarded for academics, art, leadership, music/drama.

**Application procedures. Admission:** Closing date 2/15 (postmark date). $50 fee, may be waived for applicants with need. Admission notification 4/1. Must reply by 5/1. **Financial aid:** Closing date 2/15. FAFSA, institutional form, CSS PROFILE required. Applicants notified by 4/1; must reply by 5/1.

**Academics. Special study options:** Accelerated study, combined bachelor's/graduate degree, cross-registration, double major, exchange student, honors, independent study, internships, student-designed major, study abroad, teacher certification program, Washington semester. Study abroad with Lehigh Valley Association of Independent Colleges; over 60 agreements with foreign universities for study abroad; 3-2 or 4-2 combined Degree Program in Engineering with Columbia University or Washington University. MC/Penn Dental Program-University of Pennsylvania. Combined program with Drexel University College of Medicine. 7-year Optometry Program-State University of New York 3-2 or 4-2. Combined Degree Program in Environmental Science or Forestry. **Credit/placement by examination:** AP, CLEP, IB, SAT, ACT, institutional tests. 68 credit hours maximum toward bachelor's degree. 68 credit hours equivalent to 17 course units. **Support services:** Learning center, reduced course load, study skills assistance, tutoring, writing center.

**Majors. Area/ethnic studies:** American, German, Russian/Slavic. **Biology:** General, biochemistry. **Business:** Accounting, business admin, finance, human resources, management information systems. **Communications:** General. **Computer sciences:** General. **Conservation:** Environmental science. **Foreign languages:** General, French, German, Spanish. **History:** General. **Interdisciplinary:** Natural sciences, neuroscience. **Math:** General. **Philosophy/religion:** Philosophy, religion. **Physical sciences:** General, chemistry, physics. **Psychology:** General. **Social sciences:** Anthropology, economics, international relations, political science, sociology. **Visual/performing arts:** Art, dance, dramatic, film/cinema.

**Most popular majors.** Biology 6%, business/marketing 25%, communications/journalism 9%, English 6%, psychology 10%, social sciences 12%, visual/performing arts 17%.

**Computing on campus.** 490 workstations in dormitories, library, computer center. Dormitories wired for high-speed internet access and linked to campus network. Commuter students can connect to campus network. Online course registration, helpline, repair service, wireless network available.

**Student life. Freshman orientation:** Mandatory, $120 fee. Preregistration for classes offered. 3-day program prior to start of classes in August. **Policies:** Students share responsibility for maintaining high standards and must pledge to abide by Academic Behavior Code. **Housing:** Guaranteed on-campus for all undergraduates. Coed dorms, single-sex dorms, special housing for disabled, apartments, fraternity/sorority housing, wellness housing available. $400 deposit, deadline 5/1. College-owned houses in neighborhood surrounding campus. **Activities:** Bands, dance, drama, film society, literary magazine, music ensembles, musical theater, radio station, student government, student newspaper, symphony orchestra, TV station, over 100 clubs and organizations.

**Athletics.** NCAA. **Intercollegiate:** Baseball M, basketball, cheerleading, cross-country, field hockey W, football (tackle) M, golf, lacrosse, soccer, softball W, tennis, track and field, volleyball W, wrestling M. **Intramural:** Basketball, cross-country, football (non-tackle) M, racquetball, soccer, softball, swimming, tennis, volleyball. **Team name:** Mules.

**Student services.** Adult student services, alcohol/substance abuse counseling, chaplain/spiritual director, career counseling, student employment services, financial aid counseling, health services, minority student services, personal counseling, placement for graduates, women's services. **Physically disabled:** Services for visually, speech, hearing impaired.

**Contact.** E-mail: admissions@muhlenberg.edu
Phone: (484) 664-3200 Fax: (484) 664-3234
Christopher Hooker-Haring, Dean of Admission and Financial Aid, Muhlenberg College, 2400 Chew Street, Allentown, PA 18104

## Neumann University
**Aston, Pennsylvania**
www.neumann.edu

**CB member**
**CB code: 2628**

- Private 4-year university affiliated with Roman Catholic Church
- Residential campus in large town
- 2,501 degree-seeking undergraduates: 20% part-time, 65% women, 13% African American, 1% Asian American, 3% Hispanic American, 2% international
- 598 degree-seeking graduate students
- 94% of applicants admitted
- SAT or ACT required
- 56% graduate within 6 years; 20% enter graduate study

**General.** Founded in 1965. Regionally accredited. Provides Catholic education in Franciscan tradition. **Degrees:** 464 bachelor's, 28 associate awarded; master's, doctoral, professional offered. **ROTC:** Army. **Location:** 19 miles from Philadelphia. **Calendar:** Semester, limited summer session. **Full-time faculty:** 91 total; 66% have terminal degrees, 4% minority, 65% women. **Part-time faculty:** 195 total; 15% have terminal degrees, 5% minority, 67% women. **Class size:** 44% < 20, 54% 20-39, less than 1% 40-49, less than 1% 50-99, less than 1% >100. **Special facilities:** Franciscan studies institute, Betty Neumann archives.

**Freshman class profile.** 2,358 applied, 2,213 admitted, 520 enrolled.

| Mid 50% test scores | | | |
|---|---|---|---|
| SAT critical reading: | 400-490 | Rank in top quarter: | 50% |
| SAT math: | 400-490 | Rank in top tenth: | 30% |
| GPA 3.75 or higher: | 2% | End year in good standing: | 85% |
| GPA 3.50-3.74: | 3% | Return as sophomores: | 73% |
| GPA 3.0-3.49: | 45% | Out-of-state: | 32% |
| GPA 2.0-2.99: | 50% | Live on campus: | 72% |
| | | International: | 3% |

**Basis for selection.** Acceptance depends on major applied for, SAT scores and high school GPA. Interview recommended. **Homeschooled:** State high school equivalency certificate required.

**High school preparation.** College-preparatory program recommended. 16 units required; 17 recommended. Required and recommended units include English 4, mathematics 2, social studies 2, science 2-3, foreign language 2 and academic electives 4.

**2009-2010 Annual costs.** Tuition/fees: $21,360. Room/board: $9,718. Books/supplies: $1,200. Personal expenses: $2,000.

**2008-2009 Financial aid.** All financial aid based on need. 512 full-time freshmen applied for aid; 485 were judged to have need; 485 of these received aid. Average need met was 65%. Average scholarship/grant was $12,000; average loan $3,000. 57% of total undergraduate aid awarded as scholarships/grants, 43% as loans/jobs.

**Application procedures. Admission:** No deadline. $35 fee, may be waived for applicants with need, free for online applicants. Admission notification on a rolling basis. Must reply by May 1 or within 2 week(s) if notified thereafter. **Financial aid:** No deadline. FAFSA required. Applicants notified on a rolling basis; must reply within 2 week(s) of notification.

**Academics. Special study options:** Accelerated study, combined bachelor's/graduate degree, cooperative education, distance learning, double major, exchange student, honors, independent study, internships, liberal arts/career combination, student-designed major, study abroad, teacher certification program, weekend college. **Credit/placement by examination:** AP, CLEP, SAT, institutional tests. 15 credit hours maximum toward associate degree, 30 toward bachelor's. **Support services:** Learning center, pre-admission summer program, reduced course load, remedial instruction, study skills assistance, tutoring, writing center.

**Majors. Biology:** General. **Business:** Accounting, business admin, international, marketing. **Communications:** General. **Computer sciences:** General. **Conservation:** Environmental studies. **Education:** Early childhood, elementary. **Health:** Clinical lab technology, nursing (RN). **Liberal arts:** Arts/sciences. **Parks/recreation:** Health/fitness, sports admin. **Philosophy/religion:** Religion. **Protective services:** Criminal justice. **Psychology:** General. **Social sciences:** Political science.

**Most popular majors.** Business/marketing 11%, education 16%, health sciences 19%, liberal arts 25%.

**Computing on campus.** 400 workstations in dormitories, library, computer center. Dormitories wired for high-speed internet access and linked to campus network. Commuter students can connect to campus network. Online library, helpline, wireless network available.

**Student life. Freshman orientation:** Mandatory. Preregistration for classes offered. Held the last weekend before classes begin. **Policies:** Alcohol-free campus. **Housing:** Guaranteed on-campus for all undergraduates. Coed dorms, apartments available. $200 deposit, deadline 8/1. **Activities:** Jazz band, campus ministries, choral groups, dance, drama, international student organizations, literary magazine, music ensembles, musical theater, radio station, student government, student newspaper, TV station, Black student union, environmental club, bio/sci club, business association, professional education society, student nurses association, psychology club.

**Athletics.** NCAA. **Intercollegiate:** Baseball M, basketball, cross-country, field hockey W, golf M, ice hockey, lacrosse, soccer, softball W, tennis, volleyball W. **Intramural:** Basketball, lacrosse M, soccer, softball W, table tennis, tennis, volleyball. **Team name:** Knights.

**Student services.** Adult student services, alcohol/substance abuse counseling, chaplain/spiritual director, career counseling, services for economically disadvantaged, student employment services, financial aid counseling, health services, on-campus daycare, personal counseling, placement for graduates.

**Contact.** E-mail: neumann@neumann.edu
Phone: (610) 558-5616 Toll-free number: (800) 963-8626
Fax: (610) 558-5652
Dennis Murphy, Vice President for Enrollment Management, Neumann University, One Neumann Drive, Aston, PA 19014-1298

---

## Peirce College
**Philadelphia, Pennsylvania**
www.peirce.edu

**CB member**
**CB code: 2674**

- Private 4-year business and technical college
- Commuter campus in very large city
- 2,067 degree-seeking undergraduates: 60% part-time, 72% women, 60% African American, 1% Asian American, 5% Hispanic American, 2% international
- 100% graduate within 6 years; 17% enter graduate study

**General.** Founded in 1865. Regionally accredited. **Degrees:** 291 bachelor's, 202 associate awarded. **Calendar:** Semester, limited summer session. **Full-time faculty:** 30 total; 60% have terminal degrees, 33% minority, 53% women. **Part-time faculty:** 129 total; 24% have terminal degrees, 31% minority, 42% women. **Class size:** 81% < 20, 19% 20-39.

**Freshman class profile.**

| | | | |
|---|---|---|---|
| End year in good standing: | 79% | International: | 1% |
| Out-of-state: | 9% | | |

**Basis for selection.** Open admission.

**2009-2010 Annual costs.** Tuition/fees: $14,850.

**2008-2009 Financial aid. Need-based:** 15 full-time freshmen applied for aid; 14 were judged to have need; 14 of these received aid. Average need met was 47%. Average scholarship/grant was $4,699; average loan $4,107. 43% of total undergraduate aid awarded as scholarships/grants, 57% as loans/jobs. **Non-need-based:** Scholarships awarded for academics, alumni affiliation, leadership. **Additional information:** Tuition discounts available for US students serving in US military and in protect-and-serve fields.

**Application procedures. Admission:** No deadline. $50 fee, may be waived for applicants with need. Admission notification on a rolling basis. **Financial aid:** Priority date 5/1; no closing date. FAFSA required. Applicants notified on a rolling basis starting 5/1.

**Academics. Special study options:** Accelerated study, cooperative education, distance learning. **Credit/placement by examination:** CLEP, IB, institutional tests. 30 credit hours maximum toward associate degree, 90 toward bachelor's. **Support services:** Learning center, study skills assistance, tutoring.

**Majors. Business:** Business admin. **Computer sciences:** Information systems. **Legal studies:** Paralegal.

**Most popular majors.** Business/marketing 59%, computer/information sciences 25%, legal studies 16%.

**Computing on campus.** PC or laptop required. 37 workstations in library, student center. Commuter students can connect to campus network. Online course registration, online library, helpline, wireless network available.

**Student life. Freshman orientation:** Mandatory, $518 fee. Preregistration for classes offered. **Activities:** Chi Alpha Epsilon Honor Society, Delta Mu Delta Honor Society, paralegal student association, information technology student association, Students for Free Enterprise.

**Student services.** Adult student services, career counseling, services for economically disadvantaged, student employment services, financial aid counseling, health services. **Physically disabled:** Services for visually, hearing impaired.

**Contact.** E-mail: info@peirce.edu
Phone: (215) 670-9214 Toll-free number: (888) 467-3472 ext. 9214
Fax: (215) 670-9366
Nadine Maher, Dean of Enrollment Management, Peirce College, 1420 Pine Street, Philadelphia, PA 19102-4699

## Penn State Abington
### Abington, Pennsylvania
www.abington.psu.edu                    CB code: 2660

- Public 4-year branch campus college
- Commuter campus in small city
- 2,907 degree-seeking undergraduates: 10% part-time, 47% women, 13% African American, 15% Asian American, 7% Hispanic American, 1% international
- 27 graduate students
- 84% of applicants admitted
- SAT or ACT with writing required
- 46% graduate within 6 years

**General.** Founded in 1950. Regionally accredited. **Degrees:** 383 bachelor's, 39 associate awarded. **ROTC:** Army, Air Force. **Location:** 15 miles from Philadelphia. **Calendar:** Semester, limited summer session. **Full-time faculty:** 105 total; 59% have terminal degrees, 11% minority, 44% women. **Part-time faculty:** 132 total; 26% have terminal degrees, 11% minority, 44% women. **Class size:** 34% < 20, 55% 20-39, 5% 40-49, 4% 50-99, 1% >100.

**Freshman class profile.** 3,479 applied, 2,932 admitted, 843 enrolled.

| Mid 50% test scores | | | |
|---|---|---|---|
| SAT critical reading: | 410-520 | Rank in top quarter: | 23% |
| SAT math: | 430-550 | Rank in top tenth: | 6% |
| SAT writing: | 400-510 | Return as sophomores: | 72% |
| GPA 3.75 or higher: | 6% | Out-of-state: | 8% |
| GPA 3.50-3.74: | 11% | International: | 1% |
| GPA 3.0-3.49: | 31% | | |
| GPA 2.0-2.99: | 51% | | |

**Basis for selection.** Admission decisions based upon high school GPA, standardized test scores, class rank, personal statements, activities. Essay considered if submitted; portfolios required for select majors. **Home-schooled:** Provide complete documentation showing courses studied and all evaluations presented from home school evaluator or supervisor assigned to student in cooperation with local school district or evaluator approved through program.

**High school preparation.** College-preparatory program recommended. Required units include English 4, mathematics 3, social studies 3, science 3 and foreign language 2.

**2009-2010 Annual costs.** Tuition/fees: $12,250; $18,268 out-of-state. Books/supplies: $1,264. Personal expenses: $1,854.

**2008-2009 Financial aid.** **Need-based:** 705 full-time freshmen applied for aid; 539 were judged to have need; 519 of these received aid. Average need met was 66%. Average scholarship/grant was $6,764; average loan $3,287. 46% of total undergraduate aid awarded as scholarships/grants, 54% as loans/jobs. **Non-need-based:** Awarded to 510 full-time undergraduates, including 327 freshmen. Scholarships awarded for academics, alumni affiliation, athletics, ROTC.

**Application procedures.** **Admission:** Priority date 11/30; no deadline. $50 fee, may be waived for applicants with need. Admission notification on a rolling basis beginning on or about 11/1. Must reply by May 1 or within 2 week(s) if notified thereafter. All freshmen applications processed at University Park Campus. **Financial aid:** Priority date 2/15; no closing date. FAFSA required. Applicants notified on a rolling basis starting 3/1.

**Academics.** **Special study options:** Accelerated study, combined bachelor's/graduate degree, cooperative education, distance learning, double major, dual enrollment of high school students, ESL, exchange student, external degree, honors, independent study, internships, liberal arts/career combination, student-designed major, study abroad, teacher certification program, weekend college. **Credit/placement by examination:** AP, CLEP, IB, SAT. 60 credit hours maximum toward bachelor's degree. **Support services:** Learning center, pre-admission summer program, remedial instruction, study skills assistance, tutoring, writing center.

**Majors.** **Agriculture:** General, agribusiness operations, agronomy, animal sciences, education services, food science, horticultural science, landscaping, mechanization, soil science, turf management. **Area/ethnic studies:** African-American, American, East Asian, Latin American, women's. **Biology:** General, bacteriology, biochemistry, pathology, toxicology. **Business:** General, accounting, actuarial science, communications, finance, hospitality admin, labor relations, management information systems, managerial economics, marketing, organizational behavior. **Communications:** General, advertising, journalism. **Computer sciences:** General, information systems. **Conservation:** General, forest sciences, forest technology. **Education:** Art, elementary, foreign languages, secondary, special, testing/assessment. **Engineering:** Aerospace, architectural, biomedical, chemical, civil, computer,

electrical, environmental, industrial, materials science, mechanical, mining, nuclear, petroleum, science. **Engineering technology:** Electrical. **Family/consumer sciences:** Family studies, human nutrition. **Foreign languages:** Classics, comparative lit, French, German, Italian, Japanese, Russian, Spanish. **Health:** Communication disorders, health care admin, nursing (RN), premedicine. **History:** General. **Interdisciplinary:** Biological/physical sciences, medieval/Renaissance. **Liberal arts:** Arts/sciences. **Math:** General, statistics. **Parks/recreation:** General, exercise sciences. **Philosophy/religion:** Judaic, philosophy, religion. **Physical sciences:** Astronomy, atmospheric science, chemistry, geology, physics. **Protective services:** Criminal justice, forensics, law enforcement admin. **Psychology:** General, social. **Science technology:** Biological. **Social sciences:** Anthropology, archaeology, economics, geography, international economic development, international relations, political science, sociology. **Visual/performing arts:** General, acting, art, art history/conservation, design, film/cinema, graphic design, theater design. **Other:** Adult and continuing education, Biological and biomedical science, Rehabilitation and therapeutic studies, Security and protective services.

**Most popular majors.** Business/marketing 37%, computer/information sciences 6%, English 8%, interdisciplinary studies 8%, psychology 15%, security/protective services 13%.

**Computing on campus.** 150 workstations in library, computer center. Commuter students can connect to campus network. Online course registration, online library, helpline, repair service, student web hosting, wireless network available.

**Student life.** **Freshman orientation:** Mandatory, $30 fee. Preregistration for classes offered. 3-part process before classes start: one-day orientation, advising appointment, and new student day. **Policies:** Acts of intolerance and high-risk drinking discouraged at all locations. All facilities designated smoke-free. Students expected to abide by The Penn State Principles. **Activities:** Campus ministries, choral groups, dance, drama, film society, literary magazine, student government, student newspaper, Christian Fellowship, Asian club, black student union, Hillel, lesbian and gay alliance, Latino student association, Italian American organization, Muslim student association, Praise and Worship gospel association.

**Athletics.** USCAA. **Intercollegiate:** Baseball M, basketball, golf, lacrosse, soccer, softball, tennis, volleyball W. **Intramural:** Basketball, cross-country, football (non-tackle) M, handball, soccer, softball, tennis, volleyball. **Team name:** Nittany Lions.

**Student services.** Adult student services, alcohol/substance abuse counseling, career counseling, services for economically disadvantaged, student employment services, financial aid counseling, health services, minority student services, personal counseling, placement for graduates, veterans' counselor. **Physically disabled:** Services for visually, speech, hearing impaired.

**Contact.** E-mail: abingtonadmissions@psu.edu
Phone: (215) 881-7600 Fax: (215) 881-7655
Anne Rohrbach, Executive Director for Undergraduate Admissions, Penn State Abington, 201 Shields Building, University Park, PA 16802-1294

## Penn State Altoona
### Altoona, Pennsylvania
www.aa.psu.edu                    CB code: 2660

- Public 4-year branch campus college
- Residential campus in small city
- 4,017 degree-seeking undergraduates: 4% part-time, 47% women, 6% African American, 2% Asian American, 3% Hispanic American
- 35 graduate students
- 87% of applicants admitted
- SAT or ACT with writing required
- 68% graduate within 6 years

**General.** Founded in 1929. Regionally accredited. **Degrees:** 298 bachelor's, 74 associate awarded. **ROTC:** Army, Air Force. **Location:** 2 miles from downtown. **Calendar:** Semester, limited summer session. **Full-time faculty:** 184 total; 71% have terminal degrees, 9% minority, 45% women. **Part-time faculty:** 141 total; 22% have terminal degrees, 4% minority, 44% women. **Class size:** 40% < 20, 46% 20-39, 5% 40-49, 9% 50-99, less than 1% >100. **Special facilities:** MAC lab, CAD lab, robotics lab, manufacturing lab, automation lab, environmental studies lab, comprehensive art studio space.

**Freshman class profile.** 5,198 applied, 4,547 admitted, 1,587 enrolled.

| Mid 50% test scores | | | |
|---|---|---|---|
| SAT critical reading: | 440-540 | GPA 2.0-2.99: | 44% |
| SAT math: | 460-570 | Rank in top quarter: | 29% |
| SAT writing: | 440-540 | Rank in top tenth: | 6% |
| GPA 3.75 or higher: | 4% | Return as sophomores: | 85% |
| GPA 3.50-3.74: | 10% | Out-of-state: | 17% |
| GPA 3.0-3.49: | 42% | Fraternities: | 4% |
| | | Sororities: | 2% |

**Basis for selection.** Admission decisions based upon high school GPA, test scores, class rank, personal statements, and activities. Essay considered if submitted; portfolios required for select majors. **Homeschooled:** Provide complete documentation showing courses studied and all evaluations presented from home school evaluator or supervisor assigned to student in cooperation with local school district or evaluator approved through program.

**High school preparation.** College-preparatory program recommended. Required units include English 4, mathematics 3, social studies 3, science 3 and foreign language 2.

**2009-2010 Annual costs.** Tuition/fees: $12,750; $19,078 out-of-state. Room/board: $8,790. Books/supplies: $1,264. Personal expenses: $2,916.

**2008-2009 Financial aid. Need-based:** 1,238 full-time freshmen applied for aid; 967 were judged to have need; 923 of these received aid. Average need met was 61%. Average scholarship/grant was $5,588; average loan $3,387. 36% of total undergraduate aid awarded as scholarships/grants, 64% as loans/jobs. **Non-need-based:** Awarded to 821 full-time undergraduates, including 363 freshmen. Scholarships awarded for academics, alumni affiliation, athletics, ROTC.

**Application procedures. Admission:** Priority date 11/30; no deadline. $50 fee, may be waived for applicants with need. Admission notification on a rolling basis beginning on or about 11/1. Must reply by May 1 or within 2 week(s) if notified thereafter. All freshmen applications processed at University Park Campus. **Financial aid:** Priority date 2/15; no closing date. FAFSA required. Applicants notified on a rolling basis starting 3/1.

**Academics. Special study options:** Accelerated study, cooperative education, cross-registration, distance learning, double major, dual enrollment of high school students, ESL, exchange student, honors, independent study, internships, liberal arts/career combination, student-designed major, study abroad, teacher certification program, weekend college. **Credit/placement by examination:** AP, CLEP, IB, SAT. 60 credit hours maximum toward bachelor's degree. **Support services:** Learning center, remedial instruction, study skills assistance, tutoring, writing center.

**Majors. Agriculture:** General, agribusiness operations, agronomy, animal sciences, education services, food science, horticultural science, landscaping, mechanization, soil science, turf management. **Area/ethnic studies:** African-American, East Asian, Latin American, women's. **Biology:** General, bacteriology, biochemistry, pathology, toxicology. **Business:** General, accounting, actuarial science, finance, hospitality admin, labor relations, management information systems, managerial economics, marketing, organizational behavior. **Communications:** General, advertising, journalism. **Computer sciences:** General, information systems. **Conservation:** General, environmental studies, forest sciences, forest technology. **Education:** Art, elementary, foreign languages, secondary, special, testing/assessment. **Engineering:** Aerospace, architectural, biomedical, chemical, civil, computer, electrical, environmental, industrial, materials science, mechanical, mining, nuclear, petroleum, science. **Engineering technology:** Electrical. **Family/consumer sciences:** Family studies, human nutrition. **Foreign languages:** Classics, comparative lit, French, German, Italian, Japanese, Russian, Spanish. **Health:** Communication disorders, health care admin, nursing (RN), premedicine. **History:** General. **Interdisciplinary:** Biological/physical sciences, medieval/Renaissance. **Liberal arts:** Arts/sciences. **Math:** General, statistics. **Parks/recreation:** Exercise sciences, facilities management. **Philosophy/religion:** Judaic, philosophy, religion. **Physical sciences:** Astronomy, atmospheric science, chemistry, geology, physics. **Protective services:** Criminal justice, forensics, law enforcement admin. **Psychology:** General. **Science technology:** Biological. **Social sciences:** Anthropology, archaeology, economics, geography, international economic development, international relations, political science, sociology. **Visual/performing arts:** General, acting, art, art history/conservation, design, film/cinema, graphic design, theater design. **Other:** Adult and continuing education, Biological and biomedical science, Rehabilitation and therapeutic studies, Security and protective services, Visual and performing arts.

**Most popular majors.** Business/marketing 21%, communications/journalism 7%, education 14%, engineering/engineering technologies 8%, family/consumer sciences 7%, psychology 7%, security/protective services 13%.

**Computing on campus.** 450 workstations in dormitories, library, computer center. Dormitories wired for high-speed internet access and linked to campus network. Commuter students can connect to campus network. Online course registration, online library, helpline, student web hosting, wireless network available.

**Student life. Freshman orientation:** Mandatory. Preregistration for classes offered. Begins Saturday prior to start of classes and runs 2 weeks. **Policies:** Acts of intolerance and high-risk drinking discouraged at all locations. All facilities designated as smoke-free. **Housing:** Coed dorms, special housing for disabled, wellness housing available. $100 partly refundable deposit, deadline 5/1. Suites, special interest housing available. **Activities:** Bands, campus ministries, choral groups, dance, drama, film society, international student organizations, literary magazine, music ensembles, student government, student newspaper, black student union, Circle K, Latin American student association, Catholic campus community, Students About Living Truth, Jewish student association, Asian student association, German club, Eco-Action, Being United for Social Transformation.

**Athletics.** NCAA. **Intercollegiate:** Baseball M, basketball, cross-country, diving, golf, soccer, softball W, swimming, tennis, volleyball W. **Intramural:** Badminton, basketball, football (non-tackle), football (tackle), racquetball, soccer, softball, table tennis, track and field, triathlon, volleyball, weight lifting. **Team name:** Nittany Lions.

**Student services.** Adult student services, alcohol/substance abuse counseling, chaplain/spiritual director, career counseling, services for economically disadvantaged, student employment services, financial aid counseling, health services, minority student services, personal counseling, placement for graduates, veterans' counselor, women's services. **Physically disabled:** Services for visually, speech, hearing impaired.

**Contact.** E-mail: aaadmit@psu.edu
Phone: (814) 949-5466 Toll-free number: (800) 848-9843
Fax: (814) 949-5564
Anne Rohrbach, Executive Director of Undergraduate Admissions, Penn State Altoona, 201 Shields Building, University Park, PA 16802-1294

## Penn State Beaver
**Monaca, Pennsylvania**
**www.br.psu.edu**  CB code: 2660

- Public 4-year branch campus college
- Residential campus in small town
- 671 degree-seeking undergraduates: 5% part-time, 41% women, 8% African American, 7% Asian American, 3% Hispanic American
- 3 degree-seeking graduate students
- 93% of applicants admitted
- SAT or ACT with writing required
- 49% graduate within 6 years

**General.** Founded in 1964. Regionally accredited. **Degrees:** 58 bachelor's, 4 associate awarded; master's offered. **Location:** 30 miles from Pittsburgh. **Calendar:** Semester, limited summer session. **Full-time faculty:** 33 total; 67% have terminal degrees, 21% minority, 54% women. **Part-time faculty:** 25 total; 16% have terminal degrees, 4% minority, 48% women. **Class size:** 50% < 20, 44% 20-39, 4% 40-49, 2% 50-99.

**Freshman class profile.** 761 applied, 708 admitted, 250 enrolled.

| Mid 50% test scores | | | |
|---|---|---|---|
| SAT critical reading: | 410-530 | GPA 3.0-3.49: | 36% |
| SAT math: | 430-540 | GPA 2.0-2.99: | 49% |
| SAT writing: | 400-500 | Rank in top quarter: | 31% |
| GPA 3.75 or higher: | 2% | Rank in top tenth: | 6% |
| GPA 3.50-3.74: | 10% | Return as sophomores: | 69% |
| | | Out-of-state: | 12% |

**Basis for selection.** Admission decisions based upon high school GPA as well as other factors, including standardized verbal and math test scores, class rank, personal statements, activities lists. Essay considered if submitted; portfolios required for select majors. **Homeschooled:** Helpful if applicants provide complete documentation showing courses studied and all evaluations from home school evaluator or supervisor assigned to student in cooperation with local school district or evaluator approved through program.

**High school preparation.** College-preparatory program recommended. Required units include English 4, mathematics 3, social studies 3, science 3 and foreign language 2.

**2009-2010 Annual costs.** Tuition/fees: $12,250; $18,268 out-of-state. Room/board: $8,790. Books/supplies: $1,264. Personal expenses: $2,916.

**2008-2009 Financial aid. Need-based:** 269 full-time freshmen applied for aid; 210 were judged to have need; 207 of these received aid. Average need met was 67%. Average scholarship/grant was $5,591; average loan

$3,231. 41% of total undergraduate aid awarded as scholarships/grants, 59% as loans/jobs. **Non-need-based:** Awarded to 229 full-time undergraduates, including 148 freshmen. Scholarships awarded for academics, alumni affiliation, athletics, ROTC.

**Application procedures. Admission:** Priority date 11/30; no deadline. $50 fee, may be waived for applicants with need. Admission notification on a rolling basis beginning on or about 11/1. Must reply by May 1 or within 2 week(s) if notified thereafter. All freshmen applications processed at University Park Campus. **Financial aid:** Priority date 2/15; no closing date. FAFSA required. Applicants notified on a rolling basis starting 3/1.

**Academics. Special study options:** Cross-registration, distance learning, double major, dual enrollment of high school students, ESL, honors, independent study, internships, semester at sea, study abroad. **Credit/placement by examination:** AP, CLEP, IB, SAT. 60 credit hours maximum toward bachelor's degree. **Support services:** Learning center, pre-admission summer program, reduced course load, remedial instruction, study skills assistance, tutoring, writing center.

**Majors. Agriculture:** General, agribusiness operations, agronomy, animal sciences, education services, food science, horticultural science, landscaping, mechanization, soil science, turf management. **Area/ethnic studies:** African-American, East Asian, Latin American, women's. **Biology:** General, bacteriology, biochemistry, pathology, toxicology. **Business:** Accounting, actuarial science, business admin, finance, hospitality admin, labor relations, management information systems, managerial economics, marketing, organizational behavior. **Communications:** General, advertising, journalism. **Computer sciences:** General, information systems. **Conservation:** General, forest sciences, forest technology. **Education:** Art, elementary, evaluation, foreign languages, secondary, special, testing/assessment. **Engineering:** Aerospace, architectural, biomedical, chemical, civil, computer, electrical, environmental, industrial, materials science, mechanical, mining, nuclear, petroleum, science. **Engineering technology:** Electrical. **Family/consumer sciences:** Family studies, human nutrition. **Foreign languages:** Classics, comparative lit, French, German, Italian, Japanese, Russian, Spanish. **Health:** Communication disorders, health care admin, nursing (RN), premedicine. **History:** General. **Interdisciplinary:** Biological/physical sciences, medieval/Renaissance. **Liberal arts:** Arts/sciences. **Math:** General, statistics. **Parks/recreation:** Exercise sciences, facilities management. **Philosophy/religion:** Judaic, philosophy, religion. **Physical sciences:** Astronomy, atmospheric science, chemistry, geology, physics. **Protective services:** Forensics, law enforcement admin. **Psychology:** General. **Science technology:** Biological. **Social sciences:** Anthropology, archaeology, economics, geography, international economic development, international relations, political science, sociology. **Visual/performing arts:** General, acting, art, art history/conservation, design, film/cinema, graphic design, theater design. **Other:** Adult and continuing education, Biological and biomedical science, Rehabilitation and therapeutic studies, Security and protective services.

**Most popular majors.** Business/marketing 36%, communications/journalism 16%, computer/information sciences 21%, psychology 22%.

**Computing on campus.** 127 workstations in library, computer center, student center. Dormitories wired for high-speed internet access and linked to campus network. Commuter students can connect to campus network. Online course registration, online library, helpline, repair service, student web hosting, wireless network available.

**Student life. Freshman orientation:** Mandatory, $30 fee. Preregistration for classes offered. One-day orientation session just before classes begin. **Policies:** Acts of intolerance and high-risk drinking discouraged at all locations. All facilities designated as smoke-free. **Housing:** Coed dorms available. $100 partly refundable deposit, deadline 5/1. Townhouses available. **Activities:** Campus ministries, drama, film society, literary magazine, radio station, student government, student newspaper, Common Ground Christian club, Big Brothers/Big Sisters.

**Athletics.** USCAA. **Intercollegiate:** Baseball M, basketball, soccer M, softball W, volleyball W. **Intramural:** Basketball, bowling, football (non-tackle), table tennis, volleyball. **Team name:** Nittany Lions.

**Student services.** Adult student services, alcohol/substance abuse counseling, chaplain/spiritual director, career counseling, services for economically disadvantaged, student employment services, financial aid counseling, health services, personal counseling, placement for graduates, veterans' counselor. **Physically disabled:** Services for visually, speech, hearing impaired.

**Contact.** E-mail: br-admissions@psu.edu
Phone: (724) 773-3800 Fax: (724) 773-3658
Anne Rohrbach, Executive Director for Undergraduate Admissions, Penn State Beaver, 201 Shields Building, University Park, PA 16802-1294

## Penn State Berks
Reading, Pennsylvania
www.bk.psu.edu                                    CB code: 2660

- Public 4-year branch campus college
- Residential campus in small city
- 2,501 degree-seeking undergraduates: 8% part-time, 44% women, 7% African American, 4% Asian American, 6% Hispanic American, 1% international
- 112 graduate students
- 83% of applicants admitted
- SAT or ACT with writing required
- 64% graduate within 6 years

**General.** Founded in 1924. Regionally accredited. **Degrees:** 212 bachelor's, 57 associate awarded. **ROTC:** Army. **Location:** 5 miles from downtown. **Calendar:** Semester, limited summer session. **Full-time faculty:** 113 total; 64% have terminal degrees, 13% minority, 47% women. **Part-time faculty:** 87 total; 23% have terminal degrees, 3% minority, 51% women. **Class size:** 39% < 20, 44% 20-39, 8% 40-49, 10% 50-99.

**Freshman class profile.** 2,631 applied, 2,196 admitted, 794 enrolled.

| Mid 50% test scores | | | | |
|---|---|---|---|---|
| SAT critical reading: | 440-540 | GPA 2.0-2.99: | 52% |
| SAT math: | 460-570 | Rank in top quarter: | 28% |
| SAT writing: | 430-530 | Rank in top tenth: | 6% |
| GPA 3.75 or higher: | 4% | Return as sophomores: | 78% |
| GPA 3.50-3.74: | 9% | Out-of-state: | 11% |
| GPA 3.0-3.49: | 34% | International: | 2% |

**Basis for selection.** Admission decisions based upon high school GPA, test scores, class rank, personal statements, and activities. Essay considered if submitted; portfolios required for select majors. **Homeschooled:** Complete documentation showing courses studied and all evaluations presented from home school evaluator or supervisor assigned to student in cooperation with local school district or evaluator approved through program required.

**High school preparation.** College-preparatory program recommended. Required units include English 4, mathematics 3, social studies 3, science 3 and foreign language 2.

**2009-2010 Annual costs.** Tuition/fees: $12,750; $19,078 out-of-state. Room/board: $9,560. Books/supplies: $1,264. Personal expenses: $2,916.

**2008-2009 Financial aid. Need-based:** 840 full-time freshmen applied for aid; 621 were judged to have need; 594 of these received aid. Average need met was 58%. Average scholarship/grant was $5,799; average loan $3,389. 34% of total undergraduate aid awarded as scholarships/grants, 66% as loans/jobs. **Non-need-based:** Awarded to 375 full-time undergraduates, including 171 freshmen. Scholarships awarded for academics, alumni affiliation, athletics, ROTC.

**Application procedures. Admission:** Priority date 11/30; no deadline. $50 fee, may be waived for applicants with need. Admission notification on a rolling basis beginning on or about 11/1. Must reply by May 1 or within 2 week(s) if notified thereafter. All freshmen applications processed at University Park Campus. **Financial aid:** Priority date 2/15; no closing date. FAFSA required. Applicants notified on a rolling basis starting 3/1.

**Academics. Special study options:** Accelerated study, cooperative education, cross-registration, distance learning, dual enrollment of high school students, ESL, honors, independent study, internships, study abroad, teacher certification program. **Credit/placement by examination:** AP, CLEP, IB, SAT. 60 credit hours maximum toward bachelor's degree. **Support services:** Learning center, pre-admission summer program, remedial instruction, study skills assistance, tutoring, writing center.

**Majors. Agriculture:** General, agribusiness operations, agronomy, animal sciences, education services, food science, horticultural science, landscaping, mechanization, soil science, turf management. **Area/ethnic studies:** African-American, American, East Asian, Latin American, women's. **Biology:** General, bacteriology, biochemistry, pathology, toxicology. **Business:** General, accounting, actuarial science, finance, hospitality admin, labor relations, management information systems, managerial economics, marketing, organizational behavior. **Communications:** General, advertising, journalism. **Computer sciences:** General, information systems. **Conservation:** General, forest sciences, forest technology. **Education:** Art, elementary, foreign languages, secondary, special, testing/assessment. **Engineering:** Aerospace, architectural, biomedical, chemical, civil, computer, electrical, environmental, industrial, materials science, mechanical, mining, nuclear, petroleum, science. **Engineering technology:** Electrical. **Family/consumer sciences:**

Family studies, human nutrition. **Foreign languages:** General, classics, comparative lit, French, German, Italian, Japanese, Russian, Spanish. **Health:** Communication disorders, health care admin, nursing (RN), premedicine. **History:** General. **Interdisciplinary:** Biological/physical sciences, medieval/Renaissance. **Liberal arts:** Arts/sciences. **Math:** General, statistics. **Parks/recreation:** Exercise sciences, facilities management. **Philosophy/religion:** Judaic, philosophy, religion. **Physical sciences:** Astronomy, atmospheric science, chemistry, geology, physics. **Protective services:** Forensics, law enforcement admin. **Psychology:** General. **Science technology:** Biological. **Social sciences:** Anthropology, archaeology, economics, geography, international economic development, international relations, political science, sociology. **Visual/performing arts:** General, acting, art, art history/conservation, design, film/cinema, graphic design, theater design. **Other:** Adult and continuing education, Biological and biomedical science, Rehabilitation and therapeutic studies, Security and protective services.

**Most popular majors.** Business/marketing 36%, computer/information sciences 10%, education 11%, engineering/engineering technologies 9%, interdisciplinary studies 12%, parks/recreation 7%, psychology 9%.

**Computing on campus.** 311 workstations in dormitories, library, computer center, student center. Dormitories wired for high-speed internet access and linked to campus network. Commuter students can connect to campus network. Online course registration, online library, helpline, repair service, student web hosting, wireless network available.

**Student life. Freshman orientation:** Mandatory. Preregistration for classes offered. Week prior to the start of classes. **Policies:** All facilities smoke-free. **Housing:** Coed dorms, special housing for disabled available. $100 partly refundable deposit, deadline 5/1. Honor students, suites, special interest houses available. **Activities:** Pep band, choral groups, dance, drama, film society, literary magazine, radio station, student government, student newspaper, TV station, Christian fellowship, Dimensions-the Ethnic Society, multicultural dance group, Substance Free, Rainbow Alliance, political science club, Spiritual Praise Choir, yoga and meditation society.

**Athletics.** NCAA. **Intercollegiate:** Baseball M, basketball, cross-country, golf M, soccer, softball W, tennis, volleyball W. **Intramural:** Badminton, basketball, football (non-tackle), golf, table tennis, volleyball. **Team name:** NIttany Lions.

**Student services.** Adult student services, alcohol/substance abuse counseling, career counseling, services for economically disadvantaged, student employment services, financial aid counseling, health services, minority student services, personal counseling, placement for graduates, veterans' counselor. **Physically disabled:** Services for visually, speech, hearing impaired. **Learning disabled:** Comprehensive services available.

**Contact.** E-mail: admissionsbk@psu.edu
Phone: (610) 396-6060 Fax: (610) 396-6077
Annc Rohrbach, Executive Director for Undergraduate Admissions, Penn State Berks, 201 Shields Building, University Park, PA 16802-1294

## Penn State Brandywine
**Media, Pennsylvania**
**www.brandywine.psu.edu**          CB code: 2660

- Public 4-year branch campus college
- Commuter campus in small town
- 1,411 degree-seeking undergraduates: 10% part-time, 42% women, 12% African American, 7% Asian American, 3% Hispanic American
- 1 graduate students
- 85% of applicants admitted
- SAT or ACT with writing required
- 37% graduate within 6 years

**General.** Founded in 1966. Regionally accredited. **Degrees:** 182 bachelor's, 3 associate awarded. **ROTC:** Army, Air Force. **Location:** 20 miles from Philadelphia. **Calendar:** Semester, limited summer session. **Full-time faculty:** 59 total; 64% have terminal degrees, 14% minority, 49% women. **Part-time faculty:** 74 total; 23% have terminal degrees, 7% minority, 62% women. **Class size:** 42% < 20, 52% 20-39, 4% 40-49, 2% 50-99, less than 1% >100.

**Freshman class profile.** 1,277 applied, 1,089 admitted, 397 enrolled.

| Mid 50% test scores | | | |
|---|---|---|---|
| SAT critical reading: | 420-530 | GPA 3.0-3.49: | 29% |
| SAT math: | 430-550 | GPA 2.0-2.99: | 55% |
| SAT writing: | 410-520 | Rank in top quarter: | 22% |
| GPA 3.75 or higher: | 6% | Rank in top tenth: | 8% |
| GPA 3.50-3.74: | 9% | Return as sophomores: | 71% |
| | | Out-of-state: | 4% |

**Basis for selection.** Admission decisions based on high school GPA, as well as other factors, which may include standardized verbal and math test scores, class rank, personal statements, and list of activities. Essay considered if submitted; portfolios required for select majors. **Homeschooled:** Applicants should provide complete documentation showing courses studied and all evaluations presented from evaluator or supervisor assigned to student in cooperation with local school district or evaluator approved through program.

**High school preparation.** College-preparatory program recommended. Required units include English 4, mathematics 3, social studies 3, science 3 and foreign language 2.

**2009-2010 Annual costs.** Tuition/fees: $12,150; $18,168 out-of-state. Books/supplies: $1,264. Personal expenses: $1,854.

**2008-2009 Financial aid. Need-based:** 324 full-time freshmen applied for aid; 232 were judged to have need; 225 of these received aid. Average need met was 65%. Average scholarship/grant was $5,605; average loan $3,008. 43% of total undergraduate aid awarded as scholarships/grants, 57% as loans/jobs. **Non-need-based:** Awarded to 366 full-time undergraduates, including 172 freshmen. Scholarships awarded for academics, alumni affiliation, athletics, ROTC.

**Application procedures. Admission:** Priority date 11/30; no deadline. $50 fee, may be waived for applicants with need. Admission notification on a rolling basis beginning on or about 11/1. Must reply by May 1 or within 2 week(s) if notified thereafter. All freshmen applications processed at University Park Campus. **Financial aid:** Priority date 2/15; no closing date. FAFSA required. Applicants notified on a rolling basis starting 3/1.

**Academics. Special study options:** Combined bachelor's/graduate degree, distance learning, double major, dual enrollment of high school students, ESL, honors, independent study, internships, study abroad, teacher certification program. **Credit/placement by examination:** AP, CLEP, IB, SAT. 60 credit hours maximum toward bachelor's degree. **Support services:** Learning center, pre-admission summer program, reduced course load, remedial instruction, study skills assistance, tutoring, writing center.

**Majors. Agriculture:** General, agribusiness operations, agronomy, animal sciences, education services, food science, horticultural science, landscaping, mechanization, soil science, turf management. **Area/ethnic studies:** African-American, American, East Asian, Latin American, women's. **Biology:** General, bacteriology, biochemistry, pathology, toxicology. **Business:** Accounting, actuarial science, business admin, finance, hospitality admin, labor relations, management information systems, managerial economics, marketing, organizational behavior. **Communications:** General, advertising, journalism. **Computer sciences:** General, information systems. **Conservation:** General, forest sciences, forest technology. **Education:** Art, elementary, foreign languages, secondary, special, testing/assessment. **Engineering:** Aerospace, architectural, biomedical, chemical, civil, computer, electrical, environmental, industrial, materials science, mechanical, mining, nuclear, petroleum, science. **Engineering technology:** Electrical. **Family/consumer sciences:** Family studies, human nutrition. **Foreign languages:** Classics, comparative lit, French, German, Italian, Japanese, Russian, Spanish. **Health:** Communication disorders, health care admin, nursing (RN), premedicine. **History:** General. **Interdisciplinary:** Biological/physical sciences, medieval/Renaissance. **Liberal arts:** Arts/sciences. **Math:** General, statistics. **Parks/recreation:** Exercise sciences, facilities management. **Philosophy/religion:** Judaic, philosophy, religion. **Physical sciences:** Astronomy, atmospheric science, chemistry, geology, physics. **Protective services:** Forensics, law enforcement admin. **Psychology:** General. **Science technology:** Biological. **Social sciences:** Anthropology, archaeology, economics, geography, international economic development, international relations, political science, sociology. **Visual/performing arts:** General, acting, art, art history/conservation, design, film/cinema, graphic design, theater design. **Other:** Adult and continuing education, Rehabilitation and therapeutic studies, Security and protective services.

**Most popular majors.** Business/marketing 35%, communications/journalism 21%, computer/information sciences 8%, family/consumer sciences 21%, liberal arts 8%.

**Computing on campus.** 142 workstations in library, computer center, student center. Commuter students can connect to campus network. Online course registration, online library, helpline, repair service, student web hosting, wireless network available.

**Student life. Freshman orientation:** Available. Preregistration for classes offered. Held in summer, prior to fall semester. **Policies:** Acts of intolerance and high-risk drinking discouraged at all locations. All facilities designated smoke-free. **Activities:** Choral groups, dance, film society, literary magazine, student government, student newspaper, Black Student League, Nittany Christian Fellowship, Gay-Straight Alliance, gospel ensemble, Jewish Student League.

**Athletics.** USCAA. **Intercollegiate:** Baseball M, basketball, soccer, tennis, volleyball W. **Intramural:** Basketball, soccer. **Team name:** Nittany Lions.

**Student services.** Adult student services, alcohol/substance abuse counseling, career counseling, services for economically disadvantaged, student employment services, financial aid counseling, health services, minority student services, personal counseling, placement for graduates, veterans' counselor, women's services. **Physically disabled:** Services for visually, speech, hearing impaired.

**Contact.** E-mail: bwadmissions@psu.edu
Phone: (610) 892-1200 Fax: (610) 892-1320
Anne Rohrbach, Executive Director for Undergraduate Admissions, Penn State Brandywine, 201 Shields Building, University Park, PA 16802-1294

---

## Penn State DuBois
### DuBois, Pennsylvania
www.ds.psu.edu                                        CB code: 2660

- Public 4-year branch campus college
- Commuter campus in small town
- 774 degree-seeking undergraduates: 11% part-time, 49% women, 1% African American, 1% Asian American, 2% Hispanic American, 2% international
- 1 graduate students
- 92% of applicants admitted
- SAT or ACT with writing required
- 58% graduate within 6 years

**General.** Founded in 1935. Regionally accredited. **Degrees:** 49 bachelor's, 103 associate awarded; master's offered. **Location:** 120 miles from Pittsburgh. **Calendar:** Semester, limited summer session. **Full-time faculty:** 46 total; 65% have terminal degrees, 17% minority, 48% women. **Part-time faculty:** 48 total; 21% have terminal degrees, 48% women. **Class size:** 63% < 20, 33% 20-39, 2% 40-49, 2% 50-99, less than 1% >100.

**Freshman class profile.** 550 applied, 505 admitted, 243 enrolled.

| Mid 50% test scores | | GPA 2.0-2.99: | 60% |
|---|---|---|---|
| SAT critical reading: | 410-500 | Rank in top quarter: | 21% |
| SAT math: | 410-530 | Rank in top tenth: | 5% |
| SAT writing: | 380-480 | Return as sophomores: | 74% |
| GPA 3.75 or higher: | 1% | Out-of-state: | 1% |
| GPA 3.50-3.74: | 13% | International: | 2% |
| GPA 3.0-3.49: | 24% | | |

**Basis for selection.** Admission decisions based upon high school GPA, as well as other factors, which may include standardized verbal and math test scores, class rank, personal statements, and list of activities. Essay considered if submitted; portfolios required for select majors. **Homeschooled:** Applicants should provide complete documentation showing the courses studied and all evaluations presented from evaluator or supervisor assigned to student in cooperation with local school district or evaluator who is approved through the program.

**High school preparation.** College-preparatory program recommended. Required units include English 4, mathematics 3, social studies 3, science 3 and foreign language 2.

**2009-2010 Annual costs.** Tuition/fees: $12,130; $18,148 out-of-state. Books/supplies: $1,264. Personal expenses: $1,854.

**2008-2009 Financial aid. Need-based:** 220 full-time freshmen applied for aid; 182 were judged to have need; 181 of these received aid. Average need met was 70%. Average scholarship/grant was $6,046; average loan $3,283. 45% of total undergraduate aid awarded as scholarships/grants, 55% as loans/jobs. **Non-need-based:** Awarded to 186 full-time undergraduates, including 84 freshmen. Scholarships awarded for academics, alumni affiliation, athletics, ROTC.

**Application procedures. Admission:** Priority date 11/30; no deadline. $50 fee, may be waived for applicants with need. Admission notification on a rolling basis beginning on or about 11/1. Must reply by May 1 or within 2 week(s) if notified thereafter. All freshmen applications processed at University Park Campus. **Financial aid:** Priority date 2/15; no closing date. FAFSA required. Applicants notified on a rolling basis starting 3/1.

**Academics. Special study options:** Accelerated study, cross-registration, distance learning, double major, dual enrollment of high school students, honors, independent study, internships, student-designed major, study abroad. **Credit/placement by examination:** AP, CLEP, IB, SAT. 60 credit hours maximum toward bachelor's degree. **Support services:** Learning center,

reduced course load, remedial instruction, study skills assistance, tutoring, writing center.

**Majors. Agriculture:** General, agribusiness operations, agronomy, animal sciences, education services, food science, horticultural science, landscaping, mechanization, soil science, turf management. **Area/ethnic studies:** African-American, East Asian, Latin American, women's. **Biology:** General, bacteriology, biochemistry, pathology, toxicology. **Business:** Accounting, actuarial science, business admin, finance, hospitality admin, labor relations, management information systems, managerial economics, marketing, organizational behavior. **Communications:** General, advertising, journalism. **Computer sciences:** General, information systems. **Conservation:** General, forest sciences, forest technology. **Education:** Art, elementary, foreign languages, secondary, special, testing/assessment. **Engineering:** Aerospace, architectural, biomedical, chemical, civil, computer, electrical, environmental, industrial, materials science, mechanical, mining, nuclear, petroleum, science. **Engineering technology:** Electrical. **Family/consumer sciences:** Family studies, human nutrition. **Foreign languages:** Classics, comparative lit, French, German, Italian, Japanese, Russian, Spanish. **Health:** Communication disorders, health care admin, nursing (RN), premedicine. **History:** General. **Interdisciplinary:** Biological/physical sciences, medieval/Renaissance. **Liberal arts:** Arts/sciences. **Math:** General, statistics. **Parks/recreation:** Exercise sciences, facilities management. **Philosophy/religion:** Judaic, philosophy, religion. **Physical sciences:** Astronomy, atmospheric science, chemistry, geology, physics. **Protective services:** Forensics, law enforcement admin. **Psychology:** General. **Science technology:** Biological. **Social sciences:** Anthropology, archaeology, economics, geography, international economic development, international relations, political science, sociology. **Visual/performing arts:** General, acting, art, art history/conservation, design, film/cinema, graphic design, theater design. **Other:** Adult and continuing education, Rehabilitation and therapeutic studies, Security and protective services.

**Most popular majors.** Business/marketing 41%, family/consumer sciences 35%, liberal arts 25%.

**Computing on campus.** 212 workstations in computer center, student center. Commuter students can connect to campus network. Online course registration, online library, helpline, repair service, student web hosting available.

**Student life. Freshman orientation:** Available. Preregistration for classes offered. Both fall and spring orientations available. **Policies:** Acts of intolerance and high risk drinking discouraged at all locations. All facilities designated smoke free. Students expected to abide by The Penn State Principles. **Housing:** Independently owned housing available nearby. **Activities:** Choral groups, drama, film society, literary magazine, student government, student newspaper, diversity club, women's liaison committee, veterans club, adult learner student organization, environmental conservation and outing club, Campus Crusade for Christ, world cultures club.

**Athletics.** USCAA. **Intercollegiate:** Basketball M, cross-country, volleyball W. **Intramural:** Basketball, table tennis, volleyball. **Team name:** Nittany Lions.

**Student services.** Adult student services, alcohol/substance abuse counseling, career counseling, services for economically disadvantaged, student employment services, financial aid counseling, health services, personal counseling, placement for graduates, veterans' counselor, women's services. **Physically disabled:** Services for visually, speech, hearing impaired.

**Contact.** E-mail: duboisinfo@psu.edu
Phone: (814) 375-4720 Toll-free number: (800) 346-7627
Fax: (814) 375-4784
Anne Rohrbach, Executive Director for Undergraduate Admissions, Penn State DuBois, 201 Shields Building, University Park, PA 16802-1294

---

## Penn State Erie, The Behrend College
### Erie, Pennsylvania
www.erie.psu.edu                                        CB code: 2660

- Public 4-year branch campus college
- Residential campus in small city
- 4,099 degree-seeking undergraduates: 5% part-time, 37% women, 3% African American, 2% Asian American, 2% Hispanic American, 1% international
- 109 degree-seeking graduate students
- 87% of applicants admitted
- SAT or ACT with writing required
- 68% graduate within 6 years

**General.** Founded in 1926. Regionally accredited. **Degrees:** 648 bachelor's, 57 associate awarded; master's offered. **ROTC:** Army. **Calendar:**

Semester, limited summer session. **Full-time faculty:** 222 total; 62% have terminal degrees, 14% minority, 34% women. **Part-time faculty:** 66 total; 23% have terminal degrees, 2% minority, 38% women. **Class size:** 33% < 20, 43% 20-39, 19% 40-49, 4% 50-99, 1% >100. **Special facilities:** Observatory, natural area for science field trips and experimentation, hiking trails, cross-country skiing.

**Freshman class profile.** 3,217 applied, 2,791 admitted, 1,088 enrolled.

| Mid 50% test scores | | GPA 2.0-2.99: | 28% |
| --- | --- | --- | --- |
| SAT critical reading: | 450-550 | Rank in top quarter: | 44% |
| SAT math: | 480-600 | Rank in top tenth: | 14% |
| SAT writing: | 450-540 | Return as sophomores: | 85% |
| GPA 3.75 or higher: | 8% | Out-of-state: | 9% |
| GPA 3.50-3.74: | 17% | International: | 2% |
| GPA 3.0-3.49: | 47% | | |

**Basis for selection.** Admission decisions based on high school GPA, standardized test scores, class rank, personal statements, and activities. Essay considered if submitted; portfolios required for select majors. **Homeschooled:** Complete documentation helpful, showing courses studied and all evaluations presented from home school evaluator, supervisor assigned to student in cooperation with local school district, or evaluator approved through program.

**High school preparation.** College-preparatory program recommended. Required units include English 4, mathematics 3, social studies 3, science 3 and foreign language 2.

**2009-2010 Annual costs.** Tuition/fees: $12,750; $19,078 out-of-state. Room/board: $8,790. Books/supplies: $1,264. Personal expenses: $2,916.

**2008-2009 Financial aid. Need-based:** 975 full-time freshmen applied for aid; 787 were judged to have need; 766 of these received aid. Average need met was 63%. Average scholarship/grant was $5,483; average loan $3,493. 36% of total undergraduate aid awarded as scholarships/grants, 64% as loans/jobs. **Non-need-based:** Awarded to 933 full-time undergraduates, including 285 freshmen. Scholarships awarded for academics, alumni affiliation, athletics, ROTC.

**Application procedures. Admission:** Priority date 11/30; no deadline. $50 fee, may be waived for applicants with need. Admission notification on a rolling basis beginning on or about 11/1. Must reply by May 1 or within 2 week(s) if notified thereafter. All freshmen applications processed at University Park Campus. **Financial aid:** Priority date 2/15; no closing date. FAFSA required. Applicants notified on a rolling basis starting 3/1.

**Academics. Special study options:** Accelerated study, combined bachelor's/graduate degree, cooperative education, distance learning, double major, dual enrollment of high school students, honors, independent study, internships, liberal arts/career combination, semester at sea, study abroad, teacher certification program. **Credit/placement by examination:** AP, CLEP, IB, SAT, institutional tests. 60 credit hours maximum toward bachelor's degree. **Support services:** Learning center, pre-admission summer program, remedial instruction, study skills assistance, tutoring, writing center.

**Majors. Agriculture:** General, agribusiness operations, agronomy, animal sciences, education services, food science, horticultural science, landscaping, mechanization, soil science, turf management. **Area/ethnic studies:** African-American, East Asian, Latin American, women's. **Biology:** General, bacteriology, biochemistry, pathology, toxicology. **Business:** Accounting, actuarial science, business admin, finance, hospitality admin, international, labor relations, management information systems, managerial economics, marketing, organizational behavior. **Communications:** General, advertising, journalism. **Computer sciences:** General, computer science, information systems. **Conservation:** General, forest sciences, forest technology. **Education:** Art, elementary, foreign languages, secondary, special, testing/assessment. **Engineering:** Aerospace, architectural, biomedical, chemical, civil, computer, electrical, environmental, industrial, materials science, mechanical, mining, nuclear, petroleum, polymer, science, software. **Engineering technology:** Electrical, mechanical. **Family/consumer sciences:** Family studies, human nutrition. **Foreign languages:** Classics, comparative lit, French, German, Italian, Japanese, Russian, Spanish. **Health:** Communication disorders, health care admin, nursing (RN), premedicine. **History:** General. **Interdisciplinary:** Biological/physical sciences, medieval/Renaissance. **Liberal arts:** Arts/sciences. **Math:** General, statistics. **Parks/recreation:** Exercise sciences, facilities management. **Philosophy/religion:** Judaic, philosophy, religion. **Physical sciences:** General, astronomy, atmospheric science, chemistry, geology, physics. **Protective services:** Forensics, law enforcement admin. **Psychology:** General. **Science technology:** Biological. **Social sciences:** Anthropology, archaeology, economics, geography, international economic development, international relations, political science, sociology. **Visual/performing arts:** General, acting, art, art history/conservation, design, film/cinema, graphic design, theater design. **Other:** Adult and continuing education, Biological and biomedical science, Multi-/Interdisciplinary studies, Rehabilitation and therapeutic studies, Security and protective services.

**Most popular majors.** Biology 7%, business/marketing 37%, communications/journalism 6%, engineering/engineering technologies 27%, psychology 6%.

**Computing on campus.** 778 workstations in dormitories, library, computer center, student center. Dormitories wired for high-speed internet access and linked to campus network. Commuter students can connect to campus network. Online course registration, online library, helpline, repair service, student web hosting, wireless network available.

**Student life. Freshman orientation:** Mandatory. Preregistration for classes offered. Held during the 3 days before start of classes. **Policies:** Acts of intolerance and high-risk drinking discouraged at all locations. All facilities designated as smoke-free. **Housing:** Coed dorms, single-sex dorms, special housing for disabled, apartments available. $100 partly refundable deposit, deadline 5/1. Suites, special interest housing available. **Activities:** Bands, campus ministries, choral groups, dance, drama, film society, international student organizations, literary magazine, music ensembles, radio station, student government, student newspaper, Asian student organization, Association of Black Collegians, National Society of Black Engineers, human relations programming council, multicultural council, Irish American society, Women Today, College Republicans, InterVarsity Christian fellowship, gospel choir.

**Athletics.** NCAA. **Intercollegiate:** Baseball M, basketball, cross-country, golf, soccer, softball W, swimming, tennis, track and field, volleyball W, water polo. **Intramural:** Badminton, basketball, bowling, football (non-tackle), golf, soccer, softball, swimming, table tennis, track and field, triathlon, volleyball. **Team name:** Behrend Lions.

**Student services.** Adult student services, alcohol/substance abuse counseling, chaplain/spiritual director, career counseling, services for economically disadvantaged, student employment services, financial aid counseling, health services, minority student services, on-campus daycare, personal counseling, placement for graduates, veterans' counselor, women's services. **Physically disabled:** Services for visually, speech, hearing impaired.

**Contact.** E-mail: behrend.admissions@psu.edu
Phone: (814) 898-6100 Toll-free number: (866) 374-3378
Fax: (814) 898-6044
Anne Rohrbach, Executive Director for Undergraduate Admissions, Penn State Erie, The Behrend College, 201 Shields Building, University Park, PA 16801-1294

## Penn State Fayette, The Eberly Campus
**Uniontown, Pennsylvania**
www.fe.psu.edu                                        CB code: 2660

- Public 4-year branch campus college
- Commuter campus in large town
- 895 degree-seeking undergraduates: 19% part-time, 56% women, 5% African American, 1% Hispanic American, 1% international
- 93% of applicants admitted
- SAT or ACT with writing required
- 46% graduate within 6 years

**General.** Founded in 1934. Regionally accredited. **Degrees:** 60 bachelor's, 136 associate awarded. **Location:** 40 miles from Pittsburgh. **Calendar:** Semester, limited summer session. **Full-time faculty:** 54 total; 48% have terminal degrees, 6% minority, 37% women. **Part-time faculty:** 40 total; 30% have terminal degrees, 8% minority, 58% women. **Class size:** 54% < 20, 44% 20-39, 2% 40-49, less than 1% 50-99.

**Freshman class profile.** 574 applied, 531 admitted, 233 enrolled.

| Mid 50% test scores | | GPA 2.0-2.99: | 49% |
| --- | --- | --- | --- |
| SAT critical reading: | 400-500 | Rank in top quarter: | 32% |
| SAT math: | 400-530 | Rank in top tenth: | 12% |
| SAT writing: | 380-500 | Return as sophomores: | 78% |
| GPA 3.75 or higher: | 10% | Out-of-state: | 3% |
| GPA 3.50-3.74: | 12% | International: | 3% |
| GPA 3.0-3.49: | 27% | | |

**Basis for selection.** Admission decisions based on high school GPA, as well as other factors, which may include standardized verbal and math test scores, class rank, personal statements, and activities lists. Essay considered if submitted; portfolios required for select majors. **Homeschooled:** Complete documentation helpful, showing courses studied and all evaluations presented from home school evaluator, supervisor assigned to student in cooperation with local school district, or evaluator approved through program. **Learning Disabled:** Prospective students with disabilities are encouraged to contact or visit the Office for Disability Services in their junior or senior years in high school in order to find out more about disability services at the college level.

**High school preparation.** College-preparatory program recommended. Required units include English 4, mathematics 3, social studies 3, science 3 and foreign language 2.

**2009-2010 Annual costs.** Tuition/fees: $12,150; $18,168 out-of-state. Books/supplies: $1,264. Personal expenses: $1,854.

**2008-2009 Financial aid. Need-based:** 197 full-time freshmen applied for aid; 177 were judged to have need; 176 of these received aid. Average need met was 67%. Average scholarship/grant was $5,579; average loan $3,297. 42% of total undergraduate aid awarded as scholarships/grants, 58% as loans/jobs. **Non-need-based:** Awarded to 237 full-time undergraduates, including 78 freshmen. Scholarships awarded for academics, alumni affiliation, athletics, ROTC.

**Application procedures. Admission:** Priority date 11/30; no deadline. $50 fee, may be waived for applicants with need. Admission notification on a rolling basis beginning on or about 11/1. Must reply by May 1 or within 2 week(s) if notified thereafter. All freshmen applications processed at University Park Campus. **Financial aid:** Priority date 2/15; no closing date. FAFSA required. Applicants notified on a rolling basis starting 3/1.

**Academics. Special study options:** Accelerated study, cross-registration, distance learning, double major, dual enrollment of high school students, honors, independent study, internships, student-designed major, study abroad, weekend college. **Credit/placement by examination:** AP, CLEP, IB, SAT. 60 credit hours maximum toward bachelor's degree. **Support services:** Learning center, remedial instruction, study skills assistance, tutoring, writing center.

**Majors. Agriculture:** General, agribusiness operations, agronomy, animal sciences, education services, food science, horticultural science, landscaping, mechanization, soil science, turf management. **Area/ethnic studies:** African-American, East Asian, Latin American, women's. **Biology:** General, bacteriology, biochemistry, pathology, toxicology. **Business:** Accounting, actuarial science, business admin, finance, hospitality admin, labor relations, management information systems, managerial economics, marketing, organizational behavior. **Communications:** General, advertising, journalism. **Computer sciences:** General, information systems. **Conservation:** General, forest sciences, forest technology. **Education:** Art, elementary, foreign languages, secondary, special, testing/assessment. **Engineering:** Aerospace, architectural, biomedical, chemical, civil, computer, electrical, environmental, industrial, materials science, mechanical, mining, nuclear, petroleum, science. **Engineering technology:** Electrical. **Family/consumer sciences:** Family studies, human nutrition. **Foreign languages:** Classics, comparative lit, French, German, Italian, Japanese, Russian, Spanish. **Health:** Communication disorders, health care admin, nursing (RN), premedicine. **History:** General. **Interdisciplinary:** Biological/physical sciences, medieval/Renaissance. **Liberal arts:** Arts/sciences. **Math:** General, statistics. **Parks/recreation:** Exercise sciences, facilities management. **Philosophy/religion:** Judaic, philosophy, religion. **Physical sciences:** Astronomy, atmospheric science, chemistry, geology, physics. **Protective services:** Criminal justice, forensics, law enforcement admin. **Psychology:** General. **Science technology:** Biological. **Social sciences:** Anthropology, archaeology, economics, geography, international economic development, international relations, political science, sociology. **Visual/performing arts:** General, acting, art, art history/conservation, design, film/cinema, graphic design, theater design. **Other:** Adult and continuing education, Biological and biomedical science, Rehabilitation and therapeutic studies, Security and protective service.

**Most popular majors.** Business/marketing 22%, English 6%, family/consumer sciences 25%, liberal arts 8%, security/protective services 35%.

**Computing on campus.** 196 workstations in library, computer center, student center. Commuter students can connect to campus network. Online course registration, online library, helpline, repair service, student web hosting available.

**Student life. Freshman orientation:** Available. Preregistration for classes offered. **Policies:** Acts of intolerance and high-risk drinking discouraged at all locations. All facilities designated smoke-free. **Housing:** Privately owned, off-campus housing available. **Activities:** Drama, literary magazine, musical theater, student government, student newspaper, adult student organization, humanities society, Christian club, minority students association, Women in Science Engineering and Technology, Students Against Destructive Decisions.

**Athletics.** USCAA. **Intercollegiate:** Baseball M, basketball, golf M, softball W, volleyball W. **Intramural:** Basketball, football (non-tackle), racquetball, softball, tennis. **Team name:** Nittany Lions.

**Student services.** Adult student services, alcohol/substance abuse counseling, career counseling, services for economically disadvantaged, student employment services, financial aid counseling, health services, on-campus

daycare, personal counseling, placement for graduates, veterans' counselor. **Physically disabled:** Services for visually, speech, hearing impaired.

**Contact.** E-mail: feadm@psu.edu
Phone: (724) 430-4130 Toll-free number: (877) 568-4130
Fax: (724) 430-4175
Anne Rohrbach, Executive Director for Undergraduate Admissions, Penn State Fayette, The Eberly Campus, 201 Shields Building, University Park, PA 16802-1294

## Penn State Greater Allegheny
### McKeesport, Pennsylvania
### www.ga.psu.edu

- Public 4-year branch campus college
- Residential campus in large town
- 648 degree-seeking undergraduates: 5% part-time, 41% women, 25% African American, 4% Asian American, 4% Hispanic American
- 86% of applicants admitted
- SAT or ACT with writing required
- 47% graduate within 6 years

**General.** Founded in 1947. Regionally accredited. **Degrees:** 60 bachelor's, 7 associate awarded; master's offered. **Location:** 15 miles from Pittsburgh. **Calendar:** Semester, limited summer session. **Full-time faculty:** 36 total; 72% have terminal degrees, 22% minority, 47% women. **Part-time faculty:** 25 total; 16% have terminal degrees, 4% minority, 44% women. **Class size:** 53% < 20, 45% 20-39, 2% 40-49, 1% 50-99. **Special facilities:** Computer-based lab science equipment, special computer labs for systems integration and networking.

**Freshman class profile.** 710 applied, 611 admitted, 262 enrolled.

| Mid 50% test scores | | | |
|---|---|---|---|
| SAT critical reading: | 390-520 | GPA 2.0-2.99: | 57% |
| SAT math: | 400-540 | Rank in top quarter: | 31% |
| SAT writing: | 390-510 | Rank in top tenth: | 9% |
| GPA 3.75 or higher: | 4% | Return as sophomores: | 71% |
| GPA 3.50-3.74: | 9% | Out-of-state: | 15% |
| GPA 3.0-3.49: | 27% | Live on campus: | 43% |
| | | International: | 3% |

**Basis for selection.** Admission decisions based upon high school GPA, as well as other factors, which may include standardized verbal and math test scores, class rank, personal statements, and list of activities. Essay considered if submitted; portfolios required for select majors. **Homeschooled:** Complete documentation showing the courses studied and all evaluations presented from evaluator or supervisor assigned to student in cooperation with local school district or evaluator who is approved through the program.

**High school preparation.** College-preparatory program recommended. Required units include English 4, mathematics 3, social studies 3, science 3 and foreign language 2.

**2009-2010 Annual costs.** Tuition/fees: $12,250; $18,268 out-of-state. Room/board: $8,790. Books/supplies: $1,264. Personal expenses: $2,916.

**2008-2009 Financial aid. Need-based:** 212 full-time freshmen applied for aid; 186 were judged to have need; 185 of these received aid. Average need met was 70%. Average scholarship/grant was $6,374; average loan $3,361. 47% of total undergraduate aid awarded as scholarships/grants, 53% as loans/jobs. **Non-need-based:** Awarded to 237 full-time undergraduates, including 130 freshmen. Scholarships awarded for academics, alumni affiliation, athletics, ROTC.

**Application procedures. Admission:** Priority date 11/30; no deadline. $50 fee, may be waived for applicants with need. Admission notification on a rolling basis beginning on or about 11/1. Must reply by May 1 or within 2 week(s) if notified thereafter. **Financial aid:** Priority date 2/15; no closing date. FAFSA required. Applicants notified on a rolling basis starting 3/1.

**Academics. Special study options:** Cross-registration, distance learning, double major, dual enrollment of high school students, ESL, honors, independent study, internships, liberal arts/career combination, student-designed major, study abroad. **Credit/placement by examination:** AP, CLEP, IB, SAT. 60 credit hours maximum toward bachelor's degree. **Support services:** Learning center, pre-admission summer program, reduced course load, remedial instruction, study skills assistance, tutoring, writing center.

**Majors. Agriculture:** General, agribusiness operations, agronomy, animal sciences, education services, food science, horticultural science, landscaping, mechanization, soil science, turf management. **Area/ethnic studies:** African-American, East Asian, Latin American, women's. **Biology:** General, bacteriology, biochemistry, pathology, toxicology. **Business:** Accounting, actuarial science, business admin, finance, hospitality admin, labor relations, management information systems, managerial economics, marketing, organizational behavior. **Communications:** General, advertising, journalism. **Computer sciences:** General, information systems. **Conservation:** General, forest sciences, forest technology. **Education:** Art, elementary, foreign languages, secondary, special, testing/assessment. **Engineering:** Aerospace, architectural, biomedical, chemical, civil, computer, electrical, environmental, industrial, materials science, mechanical, mining, nuclear, petroleum, science. **Engineering technology:** Electrical. **Family/consumer sciences:** Family studies, human nutrition. **Foreign languages:** Classics, comparative lit, French, German, Italian, Japanese, Russian, Spanish. **Health:** Communication disorders, health care admin, nursing (RN), premedicine. **History:** General. **Interdisciplinary:** Biological/physical sciences, medieval/ Renaissance. **Liberal arts:** Arts/sciences. **Math:** General, statistics. **Parks/ recreation:** Exercise sciences, facilities management. **Philosophy/religion:** Judaic, philosophy, religion. **Physical sciences:** Astronomy, atmospheric science, chemistry, geology, physics. **Protective services:** Forensics, law enforcement admin. **Psychology:** General. **Science technology:** Biological. **Social sciences:** Anthropology, archaeology, economics, geography, international economic development, international relations, political science, sociology. **Visual/performing arts:** General, acting, art, art history/ conservation, design, film/cinema, graphic design, theater design. **Other:** Adult and continuing education, Biological and biomedical science, Rehabilitation and therapeutic studies, Security and protective services.

**Most popular majors.** Business/marketing 38%, communications/ journalism 18%, computer/information sciences 17%, psychology 25%.

**Computing on campus.** 203 workstations in dormitories, library, computer center, student center. Dormitories wired for high-speed internet access and linked to campus network. Commuter students can connect to campus network. Online course registration, online library, helpline, student web hosting, wireless network available.

**Student life. Freshman orientation:** Mandatory. Preregistration for classes offered. Orientation held prior to start of semester. **Policies:** Acts of intolerance and high-risk drinking discouraged at all locations. All facilities designated as smoke-free. Students expected to abide by The Penn State Principles. **Housing:** Coed dorms, special housing for disabled, wellness housing available. $100 partly refundable deposit, deadline 5/1. **Activities:** Campus ministries, choral groups, dance, drama, literary magazine, music ensembles, radio station, student government, student newspaper, TV station, black student union, Christian fellowship, gospel choir, Spanish club, multicultural organization.

**Athletics.** USCAA. **Intercollegiate:** Baseball M, basketball, golf, soccer M, softball W, volleyball W. **Intramural:** Basketball, football (non-tackle), soccer, softball, volleyball.

**Student services.** Adult student services, alcohol/substance abuse counseling, chaplain/spiritual director, career counseling, services for economically disadvantaged, student employment services, financial aid counseling, health services, minority student services, personal counseling, placement for graduates, veterans' counselor, women's services. **Physically disabled:** Services for visually, speech, hearing impaired.

**Contact.** E-mail: psuga@psu.edu
Phone: (412) 675-9010 Fax: (412) 675-9046
Anne Rohrbach, Executive Director for Undergraduate Admissions, Penn State Greater Allegheny, 101 Frable Building, McKeesport, PA 15132-7698

---

## Penn State Harrisburg
**Middletown, Pennsylvania**
www.hbg.psu.edu                                    CB code: 2660

- Public 4-year branch campus college
- Residential campus in small town
- 2,567 degree-seeking undergraduates: 15% part-time, 46% women, 8% African American, 7% Asian American, 4% Hispanic American, 3% international
- 1,223 degree-seeking graduate students
- 86% of applicants admitted
- SAT or ACT with writing required
- 67% graduate within 6 years

**General.** Founded in 1966. Regionally accredited. **Degrees:** 488 bachelor's, 14 associate awarded; master's, doctoral offered. **ROTC:** Army. **Location:** 8 miles from Harrisburg. **Calendar:** Semester, limited summer session. **Full-time faculty:** 200 total; 85% have terminal degrees, 29% minority, 40% women. **Part-time faculty:** 97 total; 33% have terminal degrees, 7% minority, 45% women. **Class size:** 44% < 20, 48% 20-39, 6% 40-49, 2% 50-99. **Special facilities:** Black cultural arts center, humanities gallery, American studies archives.

**Freshman class profile.** 2,431 applied, 2,096 admitted, 479 enrolled.

| Mid 50% test scores | | | |
|---|---|---|---|
| SAT critical reading: | 450-550 | GPA 2.0-2.99: | 43% |
| SAT math: | 470-590 | Rank in top quarter: | 33% |
| SAT writing: | 440-550 | Rank in top tenth: | 10% |
| GPA 3.75 or higher: | 4% | Return as sophomores: | 83% |
| GPA 3.50-3.74: | 10% | Out-of-state: | 23% |
| GPA 3.0-3.49: | 43% | International: | 8% |

**Basis for selection.** Admissions based on secondary school record and standardized test scores.

**High school preparation.** College-preparatory program recommended. Required units include English 4, mathematics 3, social studies 3, science 3 and foreign language 2.

**2009-2010 Annual costs.** Tuition/fees: $12,750; $19,078 out-of-state. Room/board: $9,080. Books/supplies: $1,264. Personal expenses: $2,916.

**2008-2009 Financial aid. Need-based:** 353 full-time freshmen applied for aid; 273 were judged to have need; 262 of these received aid. Average need met was 60%. Average scholarship/grant was $5,420; average loan $3,409. 32% of total undergraduate aid awarded as scholarships/grants, 68% as loans/jobs. **Non-need-based:** Awarded to 333 full-time undergraduates, including 95 freshmen. Scholarships awarded for academics, alumni affiliation, athletics, ROTC.

**Application procedures. Admission:** Priority date 11/30; no deadline. $50 fee, may be waived for applicants with need. Admission notification on a rolling basis beginning on or about 11/1. Must reply by May 1 or within 2 week(s) if notified thereafter. All freshmen applications processed at University Park Campus. **Financial aid:** Priority date 2/15; no closing date. FAFSA required. Applicants notified on a rolling basis starting 3/1.

**Academics. Special study options:** Cooperative education, cross-registration, distance learning, double major, dual enrollment of high school students, honors, independent study, internships, student-designed major, study abroad, teacher certification program. **Credit/placement by examination:** AP, CLEP, IB, SAT. 60 credit hours maximum toward bachelor's degree. **Support services:** Learning center, study skills assistance, tutoring, writing center.

**Majors. Area/ethnic studies:** American. **Business:** Business admin, finance, international, management information systems, marketing, organizational behavior. **Communications:** General. **Computer sciences:** General, information systems. **Education:** Elementary, social studies. **Engineering:** Civil, electrical, environmental, mechanical, structural. **Family/consumer sciences:** Family studies. **Health:** Nursing (RN). **Liberal arts:** Humanities. **Math:** Applied. **Protective services:** Criminal justice. **Psychology:** General. **Public administration:** Policy analysis. **Social sciences:** Sociology. **Other:** Multi-/Interdisciplinary studies, Security and protective services.

**Most popular majors.** Business/marketing 35%, communications/ journalism 7%, education 9%, engineering/engineering technologies 22%, psychology 7%.

**Computing on campus.** 520 workstations in library, computer center. Dormitories wired for high-speed internet access and linked to campus network. Commuter students can connect to campus network. Online course registration, online library, helpline, repair service, student web hosting, wireless network available.

**Student life. Freshman orientation:** Available. Preregistration for classes offered. Held 2 days prior to the start of classes. **Policies:** Acts of intolerance and high-risk drinking discouraged at all locations. All facilities designated smoke-free. **Housing:** Special housing for disabled, apartments available. $100 partly refundable deposit, deadline 5/1. Special interest housing available. **Activities:** Choral groups, dance, drama, literary magazine, music ensembles, radio station, student government, student newspaper, black student union, Christian Fellowship, resident community council.

**Athletics.** NCAA. **Intercollegiate:** Baseball M, basketball, cross-country, golf, soccer, softball W, tennis, volleyball W. **Intramural:** Badminton, basketball, racquetball, tennis. **Team name:** Nittany Lions.

**Student services.** Adult student services, alcohol/substance abuse counseling, career counseling, services for economically disadvantaged, student employment services, financial aid counseling, health services, minority student services, on-campus daycare, personal counseling, placement for graduates, veterans' counselor, women's services. **Physically disabled:** Services for visually, speech, hearing impaired.

**Contact.** E-mail: hbgadmit@psu.edu
Phone: (717) 948-6250 Toll-free number: (800) 222-2056
Fax: (717) 948-6325
Anne Rohrbach, Executive Director for Undergraduate Admissions, Penn State Harrisburg, 201 Shields Building, University Park, PA 16802-1294

## Penn State Hazleton
### Hazleton, Pennsylvania
www.hn.psu.edu                           CB code: 2660

- Public 4-year branch campus college
- Residential campus in large town
- 1,207 degree-seeking undergraduates: 3% part-time, 43% women, 11% African American, 4% Asian American, 13% Hispanic American
- 92% of applicants admitted
- SAT or ACT (ACT writing optional) required
- 52% graduate within 6 years

**General.** Founded in 1934. Regionally accredited. **Degrees:** 41 bachelor's, 39 associate awarded; master's offered. **ROTC:** Army, Air Force. **Location:** 4 miles from Hazleton. **Calendar:** Semester, limited summer session. **Full-time faculty:** 54 total; 59% have terminal degrees, 15% minority, 44% women. **Part-time faculty:** 31 total; 19% have terminal degrees, 6% minority, 48% women. **Class size:** 39% < 20, 51% 20-39, 4% 40-49, 5% 50-99. **Special facilities:** Weather station.

**Freshman class profile.** 1,514 applied, 1,391 admitted, 564 enrolled.

| Mid 50% test scores | | | |
|---|---|---|---|
| SAT critical reading: | 400-520 | GPA 2.0-2.99: | 61% |
| SAT math: | 410-530 | Rank in top quarter: | 25% |
| SAT writing: | 390-500 | Rank in top tenth: | 8% |
| GPA 3.75 or higher: | 2% | Return as sophomores: | 79% |
| GPA 3.50-3.74: | 5% | Out-of-state: | 33% |
| GPA 3.0-3.49: | 29% | International: | 1% |

**Basis for selection.** Admission decisions based on high school GPA, as well as other factors, which may include standardized verbal and math test scores, class rank, personal statements, and activities lists. Essay considered if submitted; portfolios required for select majors. **Homeschooled:** Complete documentation helpful, showing courses studied and all evaluations presented from home school evaluator, supervisor assigned to student in cooperation with local school district, or evaluator approved through program.

**High school preparation.** College-preparatory program recommended. Required units include English 4, mathematics 3, social studies 3, science 3 and foreign language 2.

**2009-2010 Annual costs.** Tuition/fees: $12,200; $18,218 out-of-state. Room/board: $8,790. Books/supplies: $1,264. Personal expenses: $2,916.

**2008-2009 Financial aid. Need-based:** 482 full-time freshmen applied for aid; 388 were judged to have need; 382 of these received aid. Average need met was 62%. Average scholarship/grant was $5,754; average loan $3,411. 39% of total undergraduate aid awarded as scholarships/grants, 61% as loans/jobs. **Non-need-based:** Awarded to 419 full-time undergraduates, including 249 freshmen. Scholarships awarded for academics, alumni affiliation, athletics, ROTC.

**Application procedures. Admission:** Priority date 11/30; no deadline. $50 fee, may be waived for applicants with need. Admission notification on a rolling basis beginning on or about 11/1. Must reply by May 1 or within 2 week(s) if notified thereafter. All freshman applications processed at University Park Campus. **Financial aid:** Priority date 2/15; no closing date. FAFSA required. Applicants notified on a rolling basis starting 3/1.

**Academics. Special study options:** Accelerated study, cross-registration, distance learning, double major, dual enrollment of high school students, ESL, honors, independent study, internships, student-designed major, study abroad. **Credit/placement by examination:** AP, CLEP, IB, SAT. 60 credit hours maximum toward bachelor's degree. **Support services:** Learning center, remedial instruction, study skills assistance, tutoring, writing center.

**Honors college/program.** 300 admitted university-wide each year.

**Majors. Agriculture:** General, agribusiness operations, agronomy, animal sciences, education services, food science, horticultural science, landscaping, mechanization, soil science, turf management. **Area/ethnic studies:** African-American, East Asian, Latin American, women's. **Biology:** General, bacteriology, biochemistry, pathology, toxicology. **Business:** Accounting, actuarial science, business admin, finance, hospitality admin, labor relations, management information systems, managerial economics, marketing,

organizational behavior. **Communications:** General, advertising, journalism. **Computer sciences:** General, information systems. **Conservation:** General, forest sciences, forest technology. **Education:** Art, elementary, foreign languages, secondary, special, testing/assessment. **Engineering:** Aerospace, architectural, biomedical, chemical, civil, computer, electrical, environmental, industrial, materials science, mechanical, mining, nuclear, petroleum, science. **Family/consumer sciences:** Family studies, human nutrition. **Foreign languages:** Classics, comparative lit, French, German, Italian, Japanese, Russian, Spanish. **Health:** Communication disorders, health care admin, nursing (RN), premedicine. **History:** General. **Interdisciplinary:** Biological/physical sciences, medieval/Renaissance. **Liberal arts:** Arts/sciences. **Math:** General, statistics. **Parks/recreation:** Exercise sciences, facilities management. **Philosophy/religion:** Judaic, philosophy, religion. **Physical sciences:** Astronomy, atmospheric science, chemistry, geology, physics. **Protective services:** Forensics, law enforcement admin. **Psychology:** General. **Science technology:** Biological. **Social sciences:** Anthropology, archaeology, economics, geography, international economic development, international relations, political science, sociology. **Visual/performing arts:** General, acting, art, art history/conservation, design, film/cinema, graphic design, theater design. **Other:** Biological and biomedical science, Rehabilitation and therapeutic studies, Security and protective services.

**Most popular majors.** Business/marketing 44%, computer/information sciences 32%, liberal arts 24%.

**Computing on campus.** 166 workstations in library, student center. Dormitories wired for high-speed internet access and linked to campus network. Commuter students can connect to campus network. Online course registration, online library, helpline, repair service, student web hosting, wireless network available.

**Student life. Freshman orientation:** Available. Preregistration for classes offered. Testing and academic advising in June; formal orientation in August and September. **Policies:** Acts of intolerance and high-risk drinking discouraged at all locations. All facilities designated as smoke-free. Students expected to abide by The Penn State Principles. **Housing:** Coed dorms available. $100 partly refundable deposit, deadline 5/1. Townhouses, suites available. **Activities:** Choral groups, dance, drama, literary magazine, radio station, student government, student newspaper, multicultural club, Circle K, Allies, Fellowship of Christian Athletes, Helping Hands.

**Athletics.** USCAA. **Intercollegiate:** Baseball M, basketball, cheerleading, golf, soccer M, softball W, tennis, volleyball W. **Intramural:** Rifle, softball, table tennis, tennis, volleyball. **Team name:** Nittany Lions.

**Student services.** Adult student services, alcohol/substance abuse counseling, chaplain/spiritual director, career counseling, services for economically disadvantaged, student employment services, financial aid counseling, health services, legal services, minority student services, personal counseling, placement for graduates, veterans' counselor, women's services. **Physically disabled:** Services for visually, speech, hearing impaired.

**Contact.** E-mail: admissions-hn@psu.edu
Phone: (570) 450-3142 Toll-free number: (800) 279-8495
Fax: (570) 450-3182
Anne Rohrbach, Executive Director for Undergraduate Admissions, Penn State Hazleton, 201 Shields Building, University Park, PA 16802-1294

## Penn State Lehigh Valley
### Center Valley, Pennsylvania
www.lv.psu.edu                           CB code: 2660

- Public 4-year branch campus college
- Commuter campus in rural community
- 649 degree-seeking undergraduates: 12% part-time, 41% women, 3% African American, 9% Asian American, 12% Hispanic American
- 16 graduate students
- 94% of applicants admitted
- SAT or ACT with writing required
- 47% graduate within 6 years

**General.** Regionally accredited. **Degrees:** 82 bachelor's, 6 associate awarded. **ROTC:** Army. **Location:** 15 miles from Allentown, 30 miles from Easton. **Calendar:** Semester, limited summer session. **Full-time faculty:** 35 total; 71% have terminal degrees, 14% minority, 51% women. **Part-time faculty:** 60 total; 22% have terminal degrees, 2% minority, 58% women. **Class size:** 60% < 20, 35% 20-39, 4% 40-49, less than 1% 50-99.

**Freshman class profile.** 797 applied, 746 admitted, 227 enrolled.

| Mid 50% test scores | | GPA 3.0-3.49: | 29% |
|---|---|---|---|
| SAT critical reading: | 430-530 | GPA 2.0-2.99: | 55% |
| SAT math: | 420-560 | Rank in top quarter: | 25% |
| SAT writing: | 410-520 | Rank in top tenth: | 8% |
| GPA 3.75 or higher: | 3% | Return as sophomores: | 78% |
| GPA 3.50-3.74: | 8% | Out-of-state: | 5% |

**Basis for selection.** Admission decisions based on high school GPA, standardized test scores, class rank, personal statements, and activities. Essay considered if submitted; portfolios required for select majors. **Homeschooled:** Applicants should provide complete documentation showing courses studied and all evaluations presented from evaluator or supervisor assigned to student in cooperation with local school district or evaluator approved through program.

**High school preparation.** College-preparatory program recommended. Required units include English 4, mathematics 3, social studies 3, science 3 and foreign language 2.

**2009-2010 Annual costs.** Tuition/fees: $12,250; $18,268 out-of-state. Books/supplies: $1,264. Personal expenses: $1,854.

**2008-2009 Financial aid. Need-based:** 176 full-time freshmen applied for aid; 125 were judged to have need; 121 of these received aid. Average need met was 59%. Average scholarship/grant was $6,036; average loan $3,270. 41% of total undergraduate aid awarded as scholarships/grants, 59% as loans/jobs. **Non-need-based:** Awarded to 122 full-time undergraduates, including 55 freshmen. Scholarships awarded for academics, alumni affiliation, athletics, ROTC.

**Application procedures. Admission:** Priority date 11/30; no deadline. $50 fee, may be waived for applicants with need. Admission notification on a rolling basis beginning on or about 11/1. Must reply by May 1 or within 2 week(s) if notified thereafter. All freshmen applications processed at University Park Campus. **Financial aid:** Priority date 2/15; no closing date. FAFSA required. Applicants notified on a rolling basis starting 3/1.

**Academics. Special study options:** Accelerated study, cooperative education, cross-registration, distance learning, dual enrollment of high school students, honors, independent study, internships, liberal arts/career combination, study abroad, teacher certification program. **Credit/placement by examination:** AP, CLEP, IB, SAT. 60 credit hours maximum toward bachelor's degree. **Support services:** Learning center, reduced course load, study skills assistance, tutoring, writing center.

**Majors. Agriculture:** General, agribusiness operations, agronomy, animal sciences, education services, food science, horticultural science, landscaping, mechanization, soil science, turf management. **Area/ethnic studies:** African-American, East Asian, Latin American, women's. **Biology:** General, bacteriology, biochemistry, pathology, toxicology. **Business:** General, accounting, actuarial science, business admin, finance, hospitality admin, labor relations, management information systems, managerial economics, marketing, organizational behavior. **Communications:** General, advertising, journalism. **Computer sciences:** General, information systems. **Conservation:** General, forest sciences, forest technology. **Education:** Art, elementary, foreign languages, secondary, special, testing/assessment. **Engineering:** Aerospace, architectural, biomedical, chemical, civil, computer, electrical, environmental, industrial, materials science, mechanical, mining, nuclear, petroleum, science. **Engineering technology:** Electrical. **Family/consumer sciences:** Family studies, human nutrition. **Foreign languages:** General, classics, comparative lit, French, German, Italian, Japanese, Russian, Spanish. **Health:** Communication disorders, health care admin, nursing (RN), premedicine. **History:** General. **Interdisciplinary:** Biological/physical sciences, medieval/Renaissance. **Liberal arts:** Arts/sciences. **Math:** General, statistics. **Parks/recreation:** Exercise sciences, facilities management. **Philosophy/religion:** Judaic, philosophy, religion. **Physical sciences:** Astronomy, atmospheric science, chemistry, geology, physics. **Protective services:** Forensics, law enforcement admin. **Psychology:** General. **Science technology:** Biological. **Social sciences:** Anthropology, archaeology, economics, geography, international economic development, international relations, political science, sociology. **Visual/performing arts:** General, acting, art, art history/conservation, design, film/cinema, graphic design, theater design. **Other:** Adult and continuing education, Biological and biomedical science, Engineering, Rehabilitation and therapeutic studies, Security and protective services.

**Most popular majors.** Business/marketing 50%, computer/information sciences 9%, education 22%, psychology 17%.

**Computing on campus.** 155 workstations in dormitories, library, computer center, student center. Commuter students can connect to campus network. Online course registration, online library, helpline, repair service, student web hosting, wireless network available.

**Student life. Freshman orientation:** Mandatory. Preregistration for classes offered. One-day program held prior to start of classes. **Policies:** Acts of

intolerance and high-risk drinking discouraged at all locations. All facilities designated as smoke-free. Students expected to abide by The Penn State Principles. **Activities:** Dance, drama, literary magazine, student government, student newspaper, Asian club, Christian Fellowship, Habitat for Humanity.

**Athletics.** USCAA. **Intercollegiate:** Golf, tennis. **Intramural:** Basketball, football (non-tackle), soccer. **Team name:** Nittany Lions.

**Student services.** Adult student services, alcohol/substance abuse counseling, career counseling, services for economically disadvantaged, student employment services, financial aid counseling, health services, minority student services, personal counseling, placement for graduates, veterans' counselor. **Physically disabled:** Services for visually, speech, hearing impaired. **Learning disabled:** Comprehensive services available.

**Contact.** E-mail: admissions-lv@psu.edu
Phone: (610) 285-5035 Fax: (610) 285-5220
Anne Rohrbach, Executive Director for Undergraduate Admissions, Penn State Lehigh Valley, 2809 Saucon Valley Road, Center Vally, PA 18034-8447

## Penn State Mont Alto
**Mont Alto, Pennsylvania**
**www.ma.psu.edu**        **CB code: 2660**

▶ Public 4-year branch campus college
▶ Residential campus in rural community
▶ 1,069 degree-seeking undergraduates: 20% part-time, 58% women, 13% African American, 3% Asian American, 4% Hispanic American
▶ 8 graduate students
▶ 90% of applicants admitted
▶ SAT or ACT with writing required
▶ 49% graduate within 6 years

**General.** Founded in 1929. Regionally accredited. **Degrees:** 29 bachelor's, 126 associate awarded. **ROTC:** Army. **Location:** 12 miles from Chambersburg. **Calendar:** Semester, limited summer session. **Full-time faculty:** 58 total; 52% have terminal degrees, 9% minority, 52% women. **Part-time faculty:** 59 total; 19% have terminal degrees, 2% minority, 64% women. **Class size:** 54% < 20, 41% 20-39, 4% 40-49, 2% 50-99.

**Freshman class profile.** 900 applied, 810 admitted, 426 enrolled.

| Mid 50% test scores | | GPA 3.0-3.49: | 36% |
|---|---|---|---|
| SAT critical reading: | 420-520 | GPA 2.0-2.99: | 49% |
| SAT math: | 420-550 | Rank in top quarter: | 36% |
| SAT writing: | 390-510 | Rank in top tenth: | 9% |
| GPA 3.75 or higher: | 3% | Return as sophomores: | 76% |
| GPA 3.50-3.74: | 9% | Out-of-state: | 27% |

**Basis for selection.** Admission decisions based upon high school GPA, as well as other factors, which may include standardized verbal and math test scores, class rank, personal statements, and list of activities. Essay considered if submitted; portfolios required for select majors. **Homeschooled:** Applicants should provide complete documentation showing courses studied and all evaluations presented from evaluator or supervisor assigned to student in cooperation with local school district or evaluator who is approved through the program.

**High school preparation.** College-preparatory program recommended. Required units include English 4, mathematics 3, social studies 3, science 3 and foreign language 2.

**2009-2010 Annual costs.** Tuition/fees: $12,250; $18,268 out-of-state. Room/board: $8,790. Books/supplies: $1,264. Personal expenses: $2,916.

**2008-2009 Financial aid. Need-based:** 334 full-time freshmen applied for aid; 261 were judged to have need; 258 of these received aid. Average need met was 66%. Average scholarship/grant was $5,325; average loan $3,324. 39% of total undergraduate aid awarded as scholarships/grants, 61% as loans/jobs. **Non-need-based:** Awarded to 294 full-time undergraduates, including 156 freshmen. Scholarships awarded for academics, alumni affiliation, athletics, ROTC.

**Application procedures. Admission:** Priority date 11/30; no deadline. $50 fee, may be waived for applicants with need. Admission notification on a rolling basis beginning on or about 11/1. Must reply by May 1 or within 2 week(s) if notified thereafter. All freshmen applications processed at University Park Campus. **Financial aid:** Priority date 2/15; no closing date. FAFSA required. Applicants notified on a rolling basis starting 3/1.

**Academics. Special study options:** Accelerated study, cross-registration, distance learning, double major, dual enrollment of high school students, honors, independent study, internships, study abroad. **Credit/placement by examination:** AP, CLEP, IB, SAT. 60 credit hours maximum toward bachelor's degree. **Support services:** Learning center, pre-admission summer program, remedial instruction, study skills assistance, tutoring, writing center.

**Majors. Agriculture:** General, agribusiness operations, agronomy, animal sciences, education services, food science, horticultural science, landscaping, mechanization, soil science, turf management. **Area/ethnic studies:** African-American, East Asian, Latin American, women's. **Biology:** General, bacteriology, biochemistry, pathology, toxicology. **Business:** Accounting, actuarial science, business admin, finance, hospitality admin, labor relations, management information systems, managerial economics, marketing, organizational behavior. **Communications:** General, advertising, journalism. **Computer sciences:** General, information systems. **Conservation:** General, forest sciences, forest technology. **Education:** Art, elementary, foreign languages, secondary, special, testing/assessment. **Engineering:** Aerospace, architectural, biomedical, chemical, civil, computer, electrical, environmental, industrial, materials science, mechanical, mining, nuclear, petroleum, science. **Engineering technology:** Electrical. **Family/consumer sciences:** Family studies, human nutrition. **Foreign languages:** Classics, comparative lit, French, German, Italian, Japanese, Russian, Spanish. **Health:** Communication disorders, health care admin, nursing (RN), premedicine. **History:** General. **Interdisciplinary:** Biological/physical sciences, medieval/Renaissance. **Liberal arts:** Arts/sciences. **Math:** General, statistics. **Parks/recreation:** Exercise sciences, facilities management. **Philosophy/religion:** Judaic, philosophy, religion. **Physical sciences:** Astronomy, atmospheric science, chemistry, geology, physics. **Protective services:** Forensics, law enforcement admin. **Psychology:** General. **Science technology:** Biological. **Social sciences:** Anthropology, archaeology, economics, geography, international economic development, international relations, political science, sociology. **Visual/performing arts:** General, acting, art, art history/conservation, design, film/cinema, graphic design, theater design. **Other:** Adult and continuing education, Rehabilitation and therapeutic studies, Security and protective services.

**Most popular majors.** Business/marketing 55%, English 10%, family/consumer sciences 21%, health sciences 7%, liberal arts 7%.

**Computing on campus.** 164 workstations in computer center, student center. Dormitories wired for high-speed internet access and linked to campus network. Commuter students can connect to campus network. Online course registration, online library, helpline, repair service, student web hosting, wireless network available.

**Student life. Freshman orientation:** Available. Preregistration for classes offered. **Policies:** Acts of intolerance and high-risk drinking discouraged at all locations. All facilities designated as smoke-free. **Housing:** Coed dorms, special housing for disabled available. $100 partly refundable deposit, deadline 5/1. Suites, special interest housing, townhouses available. **Activities:** Jazz band, dance, drama, student government, student newspaper, Christian fellowship, language club, multicultural club, volunteer club, black student union, Asian student association.

**Athletics.** USCAA. **Intercollegiate:** Basketball, cheerleading, cross-country, golf, soccer, softball W, tennis, volleyball W. **Intramural:** Badminton, basketball, racquetball, soccer, softball, volleyball. **Team name:** Nittany Lions.

**Student services.** Adult student services, alcohol/substance abuse counseling, chaplain/spiritual director, career counseling, services for economically disadvantaged, student employment services, financial aid counseling, health services, minority student services, placement for graduates, veterans' counselor, women's services. **Physically disabled:** Services for visually, speech, hearing impaired.

**Contact.** E-mail: psuma@psu.edu
Phone: (717) 749-6130 Toll-free number: (800) 392-6173
Fax: (717) 749-6132
Anne Rohrbach, Executive Director for Undergraduate Admissions, Penn State Mont Alto, 201 Shields Building, University Park, PA 16802-1294

## Penn State New Kensington
**New Kensington, Pennsylvania**
www.nk.psu.edu
**CB code: 2660**

- Public 4-year branch campus college
- Commuter campus in large town
- 711 degree-seeking undergraduates: 16% part-time, 38% women, 2% African American, 1% Asian American, 1% Hispanic American
- 1 graduate students
- 89% of applicants admitted
- SAT or ACT with writing required
- 49% graduate within 6 years

**General.** Founded in 1958. Regionally accredited. **Degrees:** 73 bachelor's, 37 associate awarded; master's offered. **Location:** 22 miles from Pittsburgh. **Calendar:** Semester, limited summer session. **Full-time faculty:** 39 total; 62% have terminal degrees, 15% minority, 41% women. **Part-time faculty:** 35 total; 23% have terminal degrees, 11% minority, 34% women. **Class size:** 66% < 20, 30% 20-39, 2% 40-49, 1% 50-99.

**Freshman class profile.** 476 applied, 422 admitted, 184 enrolled.

| Mid 50% test scores | | | |
|---|---|---|---|
| SAT critical reading: | 410-520 | GPA 2.0-2.99: | 56% |
| SAT math: | 440-550 | Rank in top quarter: | 24% |
| SAT writing: | 410-510 | Rank in top tenth: | 7% |
| GPA 3.75 or higher: | 4% | Return as sophomores: | 76% |
| GPA 3.50-3.74: | 6% | Out-of-state: | 2% |
| GPA 3.0-3.49: | 33% | International: | 1% |

**Basis for selection.** Admission decisions based upon high school GPA, as well as other factors, which may include standardized verbal and math test scores, class rank, personal statements, and list of activities. Essay considered if submitted; portfolios required for select majors. **Homeschooled:** Applicants should provide complete documentation showing the courses studied and all evaluations presented from evaluator or supervisor assigned to student in cooperation with local school district or evaluator who is approved through the program.

**High school preparation.** College-preparatory program recommended. Required units include English 4, mathematics 3, social studies 3, science 3 and foreign language 2.

**2009-2010 Annual costs.** Tuition/fees: $12,200; $18,218 out-of-state. Books/supplies: $1,264. Personal expenses: $1,854.

**2008-2009 Financial aid. Need-based:** 172 full-time freshmen applied for aid; 137 were judged to have need; 137 of these received aid. Average need met was 70%. Average scholarship/grant was $5,394; average loan $3,313. 40% of total undergraduate aid awarded as scholarships/grants, 60% as loans/jobs. **Non-need-based:** Awarded to 161 full-time undergraduates, including 88 freshmen. Scholarships awarded for academics, alumni affiliation, athletics, ROTC.

**Application procedures. Admission:** Priority date 11/30; no deadline. $50 fee, may be waived for applicants with need. Admission notification on a rolling basis beginning on or about 11/1. Must reply by May 1 or within 2 week(s) if notified thereafter. All freshmen applications processed at University Park Campus. **Financial aid:** Priority date 2/15; no closing date. FAFSA required. Applicants notified on a rolling basis starting 3/1.

**Academics. Special study options:** Cross-registration, distance learning, double major, dual enrollment of high school students, external degree, honors, independent study, internships, study abroad. **Credit/placement by examination:** AP, CLEP, IB, SAT. 60 credit hours maximum toward bachelor's degree. **Support services:** Learning center, pre-admission summer program, remedial instruction, study skills assistance, tutoring, writing center.

**Majors. Agriculture:** General, agribusiness operations, agronomy, animal sciences, education services, food science, horticultural science, landscaping, mechanization, soil science, turf management. **Area/ethnic studies:** African-American, East Asian, Latin American, women's. **Biology:** General, bacteriology, biochemistry, pathology, toxicology. **Business:** Accounting, actuarial science, business admin, finance, hospitality admin, labor relations, management information systems, managerial economics, marketing, organizational behavior. **Communications:** General, advertising, journalism. **Computer sciences:** General, information systems. **Conservation:** General, forest sciences, forest technology. **Education:** Art, elementary, evaluation, foreign languages, secondary, special, testing/assessment. **Engineering:** Aerospace, architectural, biomedical, chemical, civil, computer, electrical, environmental, industrial, materials science, mechanical, mining, nuclear, petroleum, science. **Engineering technology:** Electrical. **Family/consumer sciences:** Family studies, human nutrition. **Foreign languages:** Classics, comparative lit, French, German, Italian, Japanese, Russian, Spanish. **Health:** Communication disorders, health care admin, nursing (RN), premedicine. **History:** General. **Interdisciplinary:** Biological/physical sciences, medieval/Renaissance. **Liberal arts:** Arts/sciences. **Math:** General, statistics. **Parks/recreation:** Exercise sciences, facilities management. **Philosophy/religion:** Judaic, philosophy, religion. **Physical sciences:** Astronomy, atmospheric science, chemistry, geology, physics. **Protective services:** Forensics, law enforcement admin. **Psychology:** General. **Science technology:** Biological. **Social sciences:** Anthropology, archaeology, economics, geography, international economic development, international relations, political science, sociology. **Visual/performing arts:** General, acting, art, art history/conservation, design, film/cinema, graphic design, theater design. **Other:** Adult and continuing education, Biological and biomedical science, Rehabilitation and therapeutic studies, Security and protective services.

**Most popular majors.** Business/marketing 43%, communications/journalism 12%, computer/information sciences 15%, engineering/engineering technologies 7%, psychology 21%.

**Computing on campus.** 265 workstations in computer center. Commuter students can connect to campus network. Online course registration, online library, helpline, repair service, student web hosting, wireless network available.

**Student life. Freshman orientation:** Mandatory, $25 fee. Preregistration for classes offered. 2-day program held prior to beginning of classes. **Policies:** Acts of intolerance and high-risk drinking discouraged at all locations. All facilities designated as smoke-free. Students expected to abide by The Penn State Principles. **Housing:** Privately owned apartment complex adjacent to campus. Multiple single apartments available within 30 minutes. **Activities:** Jazz band, dance, drama, literary magazine, musical theater, student government, student newspaper, multicultural club, Society of Women Engineers, Spanish culture club.

**Athletics.** USCAA. **Intercollegiate:** Basketball, cheerleading, golf, volleyball W. **Intramural:** Basketball, football (non-tackle), racquetball, soccer, softball, table tennis, volleyball. **Team name:** Nittany Lions.

**Student services.** Adult student services, alcohol/substance abuse counseling, chaplain/spiritual director, career counseling, services for economically disadvantaged, student employment services, financial aid counseling, health services, minority student services, placement for graduates, veterans' counselor, women's services. **Physically disabled:** Services for visually, speech, hearing impaired.

**Contact.** E-mail: nkadmissions@psu.edu
Phone: (724) 334-5466 Toll-free number: (888) 968-7297
Fax: (724) 334-6111
Anne Rohrbach, Executive Director for Undergraduate Admissions, Penn State New Kensington, 201 Shields Building, University Park, PA 16802-1294

---

## Penn State Schuylkill
### Schuylkill Haven, Pennsylvania
**www.sl.psu.edu**  CB code: 2660

- Public 4-year branch campus college
- Residential campus in small town
- 908 degree-seeking undergraduates: 10% part-time, 56% women, 29% African American, 2% Asian American, 5% Hispanic American
- 1 degree-seeking graduate students
- 86% of applicants admitted
- SAT or ACT with writing required
- 49% graduate within 6 years

**General.** Founded in 1934. Regionally accredited. **Degrees:** 44 bachelor's, 27 associate awarded. **Location:** 4 miles from Pottsville. **Calendar:** Semester, limited summer session. **Full-time faculty:** 43 total; 74% have terminal degrees, 2% minority, 42% women. **Part-time faculty:** 34 total; 15% have terminal degrees, 6% minority, 59% women. **Class size:** 48% < 20, 46% 20-39, 5% 40-49, less than 1% 50-99, less than 1% >100.

**Freshman class profile.** 894 applied, 766 admitted, 348 enrolled.

| Mid 50% test scores | | | |
|---|---|---|---|
| SAT critical reading: | 370-480 | GPA 3.0-3.49: | 28% |
| SAT math: | 370-480 | GPA 2.0-2.99: | 60% |
| SAT writing: | 360-470 | Rank in top quarter: | 24% |
| GPA 3.75 or higher: | 2% | Rank in top tenth: | 5% |
| GPA 3.50-3.74: | 5% | Return as sophomores: | 79% |
| | | Out-of-state: | 19% |

**Basis for selection.** Admission decisions based upon high school GPA, standardized test scores, class rank, personal statements, and activities. Essay considered if submitted; portfolios required for select majors. **Homeschooled:** Complete documentation showing courses studied and all evaluations presented from evaluator or supervisor assigned to student in cooperation with local school district or evaluator approved through program.

**High school preparation.** College-preparatory program recommended. Required units include English 4, mathematics 3, social studies 3, science 3 and foreign language 2.

**2009-2010 Annual costs.** Tuition/fees: $12,150; $18,168 out-of-state. Books/supplies: $1,264. Personal expenses: $1,854.

**2008-2009 Financial aid. Need-based:** 356 full-time freshmen applied for aid; 317 were judged to have need; 313 of these received aid. Average need met was 71%. Average scholarship/grant was $6,638; average loan $3,407. 47% of total undergraduate aid awarded as scholarships/grants, 53%

as loans/jobs. **Non-need-based:** Awarded to 326 full-time undergraduates, including 205 freshmen. Scholarships awarded for academics, alumni affiliation, athletics, ROTC.

**Application procedures. Admission:** Priority date 11/30; no deadline. $50 fee, may be waived for applicants with need. Admission notification on a rolling basis beginning on or about 11/1. Must reply by May 1 or within 2 week(s) if notified thereafter. All freshmen applications processed at University Park Campus. **Financial aid:** Priority date 2/15; no closing date. FAFSA required. Applicants notified on a rolling basis starting 3/1.

**Academics. Special study options:** Accelerated study, cooperative education, distance learning, double major, dual enrollment of high school students, honors, independent study, internships, student-designed major, study abroad. **Credit/placement by examination:** AP, CLEP, IB, SAT. 60 credit hours maximum toward bachelor's degree. **Support services:** Learning center, remedial instruction, study skills assistance, tutoring, writing center.

**Majors. Agriculture:** General, agribusiness operations, agronomy, animal sciences, education services, food science, horticultural science, landscaping, mechanization, soil science, turf management. **Area/ethnic studies:** African-American, East Asian, Latin American, women's. **Biology:** General, bacteriology, biochemistry, pathology, toxicology. **Business:** Accounting, actuarial science, business admin, finance, hospitality admin, labor relations, management information systems, managerial economics, marketing, organizational behavior. **Communications:** General, advertising, journalism. **Computer sciences:** General, information systems. **Conservation:** General, forest sciences, forest technology. **Education:** Art, elementary, foreign languages, secondary, special, testing/assessment. **Engineering:** Aerospace, architectural, biomedical, chemical, civil, computer, electrical, environmental, industrial, materials science, mechanical, mining, nuclear, petroleum, science. **Engineering technology:** Electrical. **Family/consumer sciences:** Family studies, human nutrition. **Foreign languages:** Classics, comparative lit, French, German, Italian, Japanese, Russian, Spanish. **Health:** Communication disorders, health care admin, nursing (RN), premedicine. **History:** General. **Interdisciplinary:** Biological/physical sciences, medieval/Renaissance. **Liberal arts:** Arts/sciences, humanities. **Math:** General, statistics. **Parks/recreation:** Exercise sciences, facilities management. **Philosophy/religion:** Judaic, philosophy, religion. **Physical sciences:** Astronomy, atmospheric science, chemistry, geology, physics. **Protective services:** Criminal justice, forensics, law enforcement admin. **Psychology:** General. **Science technology:** Biological. **Social sciences:** Anthropology, archaeology, economics, geography, international economic development, international relations, political science, sociology. **Visual/performing arts:** General, acting, art, art history/conservation, design, film/cinema, graphic design, theater design. **Other:** Adult and continuing education, Rehabilitation and therapeutic studies, Security and protective services.

**Most popular majors.** Business/marketing 27%, computer/information sciences 9%, psychology 39%, security/protective services 25%.

**Computing on campus.** 165 workstations in computer center, student center. Dormitories wired for high-speed internet access and linked to campus network. Commuter students can connect to campus network. Online course registration, online library, helpline, repair service, student web hosting, wireless network available.

**Student life. Freshman orientation:** Available. Preregistration for classes offered. 3-day program held prior to start of classes. **Policies:** Acts of intolerance and high-risk drinking discouraged at all locations. All facilities designated as smoke-free. Students expected to abide by The Penn State Principles. **Housing:** Special housing for disabled, apartments available. $100 partly refundable deposit. **Activities:** Campus ministries, choral groups, dance, drama, musical theater, student government, student newspaper, Campus Crusade for Christ, criminal justice club, religious and philosophical forum, united minority leaders, Keystone honor society.

**Athletics.** USCAA. **Intercollegiate:** Basketball, cross-country, golf M, soccer M, softball W, volleyball W. **Intramural:** Basketball, football (non-tackle) M, soccer, softball, table tennis, volleyball. **Team name:** Nittany Lions.

**Student services.** Adult student services, career counseling, services for economically disadvantaged, student employment services, financial aid counseling, health services, minority student services, personal counseling, placement for graduates, veterans' counselor. **Physically disabled:** Services for visually, speech, hearing impaired.

**Contact.** E-mail: sl-admissions@psu.edu
Phone: (570) 385-6252 Fax: (570) 385-6272
Anne Rohrbach, Executive Director for Undergraduate Admissions, Penn State Schuylkill, 200 University Drive, Schuylkill Haven, PA 17972-2208

## Penn State Shenango
### Sharon, Pennsylvania
www.shenango.psu.edu                    CB code: 2660

- Public 4-year branch campus college
- Commuter campus in large town
- 661 degree-seeking undergraduates: 31% part-time, 69% women, 7% African American, 1% Asian American, 2% Hispanic American
- 77% of applicants admitted
- SAT or ACT with writing required
- 37% graduate within 6 years

**General.** Founded in 1965. Regionally accredited. **Degrees:** 69 bachelor's, 60 associate awarded. **Location:** 17 miles from Youngstown, Ohio. **Calendar:** Semester, limited summer session. **Full-time faculty:** 31 total; 52% have terminal degrees, 13% minority, 48% women. **Part-time faculty:** 42 total; 14% have terminal degrees, 2% minority, 48% women. **Class size:** 64% < 20, 28% 20-39, 5% 40-49, 3% 50-99. **Special facilities:** Scanning electron microscope.

**Freshman class profile.** 273 applied, 211 admitted, 139 enrolled.

| Mid 50% test scores | | | |
|---|---|---|---|
| SAT critical reading: | 410-530 | GPA 3.0-3.49: | 30% |
| SAT math: | 420-520 | GPA 2.0-2.99: | 58% |
| SAT writing: | 380-470 | Rank in top quarter: | 18% |
| GPA 3.75 or higher: | 2% | Rank in top tenth: | 3% |
| GPA 3.50-3.74: | 10% | Return as sophomores: | 57% |
| | | Out-of-state: | 13% |

**Basis for selection.** Admission decisions based upon GPA, as well as other factors which may include standardized verbal and math test scores, class rank, personal statements, and activities lists. Essay considered if submitted; portfolios required for select majors. **Homeschooled:** Complete documentation showing courses studied and all evaluations presented from home school evaluator or supervisor assigned to the student in cooperation with the local school district or evaluator who is approved through the program.

**High school preparation.** College-preparatory program recommended. Required units include English 4, mathematics 3, social studies 3, science 3 and foreign language 2.

**2009-2010 Annual costs.** Tuition/fees: $12,050; $18,068 out-of-state. Books/supplies: $1,264. Personal expenses: $1,854.

**2008-2009 Financial aid. Need-based:** 120 full-time freshmen applied for aid; 105 were judged to have need; 105 of these received aid. Average need met was 67%. Average scholarship/grant was $5,556; average loan $3,299. 42% of total undergraduate aid awarded as scholarships/grants, 58% as loans/jobs. **Non-need-based:** Awarded to 170 full-time undergraduates, including 72 freshmen. Scholarships awarded for academics, alumni affiliation, athletics, ROTC.

**Application procedures. Admission:** Priority date 11/30; no deadline. $50 fee, may be waived for applicants with need. Admission notification on a rolling basis beginning on or about 11/1. Must reply by May 1 or within 2 week(s) if notified thereafter. All freshmen applications processed at University Park Campus. **Financial aid:** Priority date 2/15; no closing date. FAFSA required. Applicants notified on a rolling basis starting 3/1.

**Academics. Special study options:** Accelerated study, cross-registration, distance learning, double major, dual enrollment of high school students, honors, independent study, internships, student-designed major, study abroad. **Credit/placement by examination:** AP, CLEP, IB, SAT. 60 credit hours maximum toward bachelor's degree. **Support services:** Learning center, remedial instruction, study skills assistance, tutoring, writing center.

**Majors. Agriculture:** General, agribusiness operations, agronomy, animal sciences, education services, food science, horticultural science, landscaping, mechanization, soil science, turf management. **Area/ethnic studies:** African-American, East Asian, Latin American, women's. **Biology:** General, bacteriology, biochemistry, pathology, toxicology. **Business:** Accounting, actuarial science, business admin, finance, hospitality admin, labor relations, management information systems, managerial economics, marketing, organizational behavior. **Communications:** General, advertising, journalism. **Computer sciences:** General, information systems. **Conservation:** General, forest sciences, forest technology. **Education:** Art, elementary, evaluation, foreign languages, secondary, special, testing/assessment. **Engineering:** Aerospace, architectural, biomedical, chemical, civil, computer, electrical, environmental, industrial, materials science, mechanical, mining, nuclear, petroleum, science. **Engineering technology:** Electrical. **Family/consumer sciences:** Family studies, human nutrition. **Foreign languages:** Classics, comparative lit, French, German, Italian, Japanese, Russian, Spanish. **Health:** Communication disorders, health care admin, nursing (RN), premedicine. **History:** General. **Interdisciplinary:** Biological/physical sciences, medieval/

Renaissance. **Liberal arts:** Arts/sciences. **Math:** General, statistics. **Parks/recreation:** Exercise sciences, facilities management. **Philosophy/religion:** Judaic, philosophy, religion. **Physical sciences:** Astronomy, atmospheric science, chemistry, geology, physics. **Protective services:** Forensics, law enforcement admin. **Psychology:** General. **Science technology:** Biological. **Social sciences:** Anthropology, archaeology, economics, geography, international economic development, international relations, political science, sociology. **Visual/performing arts:** General, acting, art, art history/conservation, design, film/cinema, graphic design, theater design. **Other:** Adult and continuing education, Rehabilitation and therapeutic studies, Security and protective services.

**Most popular majors.** Business/marketing 22%, family/consumer sciences 39%, health sciences 25%, liberal arts 15%.

**Computing on campus.** 132 workstations in library, computer center, student center. Commuter students can connect to campus network. Online course registration, online library, helpline, repair service, student web hosting, wireless network available.

**Student life. Freshman orientation:** Mandatory. Preregistration for classes offered. One-day program held prior to start of semester. **Policies:** Acts of intolerance and high-risk drinking discouraged at all locations. All facilities designated as smoke-free. Students expected to abide by The Penn State Principles. **Activities:** Choral groups, literary magazine, student government, environmental club, students for cultural diversity, Women in Transition, Word of God Bible study club, Adults Seeking Knowledge.

**Athletics.** USCAA. **Intramural:** Basketball, golf, softball, volleyball. **Team name:** Nittany Lions.

**Student services.** Adult student services, alcohol/substance abuse counseling, career counseling, student employment services, financial aid counseling, health services, minority student services, placement for graduates, veterans' counselor, women's services. **Physically disabled:** Services for visually, speech, hearing impaired.

**Contact.** E-mail: psushenango@psu.edu
Phone: (724) 983-2800 Fax: (724) 983-2820
Anne Rohrbach, Executive Director for Undergraduate Admissions, Penn State Shenango, 201 Shields Building, University Park, PA 16802-1294

## Penn State University Park
### University Park, Pennsylvania                    CB member
www.psu.edu                    CB code: 2660

- Public 4-year university
- Residential campus in large town
- 37,855 degree-seeking undergraduates: 2% part-time, 45% women, 4% African American, 5% Asian American, 4% Hispanic American, 4% international
- 6,332 degree-seeking graduate students
- 52% of applicants admitted
- SAT or ACT with writing required
- 85% graduate within 6 years

**General.** Founded in 1855. Regionally accredited. **Degrees:** 9,692 bachelor's, 122 associate awarded; master's, doctoral, professional offered. **ROTC:** Army, Naval, Air Force. **Location:** 90 miles from Harrisburg. **Calendar:** Semester, extensive summer session. **Full-time faculty:** 2,432 total; 78% have terminal degrees, 19% minority, 37% women. **Part-time faculty:** 365 total; 30% have terminal degrees, 10% minority, 50% women. **Class size:** 30% < 20, 41% 20-39, 10% 40-49, 10% 50-99, 8% >100. **Special facilities:** Art museum, earth and mineral science museum and art gallery, anthropology museum, entomological museum, sports museum, land-grant frescoes, agricultural museum, Pennsylvania space grant consortium.

**Freshman class profile.** 40,714 applied, 21,017 admitted, 6,560 enrolled.

| Mid 50% test scores | | | |
|---|---|---|---|
| SAT critical reading: | 530-630 | GPA 2.0-2.99: | 6% |
| SAT math: | 560-670 | Rank in top quarter: | 86% |
| SAT writing: | 540-640 | Rank in top tenth: | 50% |
| GPA 3.75 or higher: | 30% | Return as sophomores: | 93% |
| GPA 3.50-3.74: | 31% | Out-of-state: | 34% |
| GPA 3.0-3.49: | 33% | International: | 8% |

**Basis for selection.** Admission decisions based upon high school GPA, standardized test scores, class rank, personal statements, and activities. Essay considered if submitted; portfolios required for select majors. **Homeschooled:** Complete documentation showing courses studied and all evaluations presented from evaluator or supervisor assigned to student in cooperation with local school district or evaluator approved through program.

**High school preparation.** College-preparatory program recommended. Required units include English 4, mathematics 3, social studies 3, science 3 and foreign language 2. 3 units required in arts and humanities. Additional requirements for some programs.

**2009-2010 Annual costs.** Tuition/fees: $14,416; $25,946 out-of-state. Room/board: $8,790. Books/supplies: $1,264. Personal expenses: $2,916.

**2008-2009 Financial aid. Need-based:** 5,327 full-time freshmen applied for aid; 3,414 were judged to have need; 3,209 of these received aid. Average need met was 63%. Average scholarship/grant was $6,122; average loan $3,414. 33% of total undergraduate aid awarded as scholarships/grants, 67% as loans/jobs. **Non-need-based:** Awarded to 9,052 full-time undergraduates, including 2,048 freshmen. Scholarships awarded for academics, alumni affiliation, athletics, ROTC.

**Application procedures. Admission:** Priority date 11/30; no deadline. $50 fee, may be waived for applicants with need. Admission notification on a rolling basis beginning on or about 11/1. **Financial aid:** Priority date 2/15; no closing date. FAFSA required. Applicants notified on a rolling basis starting 3/1.

**Academics. Special study options:** Accelerated study, combined bachelor's/ graduate degree, cooperative education, cross-registration, distance learning, double major, dual enrollment of high school students, ESL, exchange student, external degree, honors, independent study, internships, liberal arts/ career combination, semester at sea, student-designed major, study abroad, teacher certification program, Washington semester, weekend college. **Credit/ placement by examination:** AP, CLEP, IB, SAT, institutional tests. 60 credit hours maximum toward bachelor's degree. **Support services:** Learning center, pre-admission summer program, study skills assistance, tutoring, writing center.

**Honors college/program.** Candidates will be assessed based on the academic and extracurricular documents submitted with the application, as well as responses to essay questions and letters of recommendation.

**Majors. Agriculture:** General, agribusiness operations, agronomy, animal sciences, education services, food science, horticultural science, landscaping, mechanization, soil science, turf management. **Architecture:** Architecture, landscape. **Area/ethnic studies:** African-American, East Asian, Latin American, women's. **Biology:** General, bacteriology, biochemistry, pathology, toxicology. **Business:** Accounting, actuarial science, finance, hospitality admin, labor relations, management information systems, managerial economics, marketing, organizational behavior. **Communications:** General, advertising, journalism. **Computer sciences:** General, information systems. **Conservation:** General, forest sciences, forest technology. **Education:** Adult/ continuing, art, elementary, foreign languages, secondary, special, testing/ assessment. **Engineering:** Aerospace, architectural, biomedical, chemical, civil, computer, electrical, environmental, industrial, materials science, mechanical, mining, nuclear, petroleum, science. **Engineering technology:** Environmental. **Family/consumer sciences:** Family studies, human nutrition. **Foreign languages:** Classics, comparative lit, French, German, Italian, Japanese, Russian, Spanish. **Health:** Communication disorders, health care admin, nursing (RN), premedicine. **History:** General. **Interdisciplinary:** Biological/physical sciences, medieval/Renaissance. **Liberal arts:** Arts/ sciences. **Math:** General, statistics. **Parks/recreation:** Exercise sciences, facilities management. **Philosophy/religion:** Judaic, philosophy, religion. **Physical sciences:** Astronomy, atmospheric science, chemistry, geology, physics. **Protective services:** Criminal justice, forensics, law enforcement admin, security management. **Psychology:** General. **Science technology:** Biological. **Social sciences:** Anthropology, archaeology, economics, geography, international economic development, international relations, political science, sociology. **Visual/performing arts:** General, acting, art, art history/ conservation, design, film/cinema, graphic design, music performance, theater design. **Other:** Rehabilitation.

**Most popular majors.** Business/marketing 18%, communications/ journalism 9%, computer/information sciences 7%, engineering/ engineering technologies 13%, social sciences 7%.

**Computing on campus.** 6,150 workstations in dormitories, library, computer center, student center. Dormitories wired for high-speed internet access and linked to campus network. Commuter students can connect to campus network. Online course registration, online library, helpline, repair service, student web hosting, wireless network available.

**Student life. Freshman orientation:** Mandatory. Preregistration for classes offered. Held the 2 days prior to start of classes. **Policies:** Acts of intolerance and high-risk drinking discouraged at all locations. All facilites designated as smoke-free. **Housing:** Coed dorms, single-sex dorms, special housing for disabled, apartments, fraternity/sorority housing available. $100 partly refundable deposit, deadline 5/1. Suites, special interest housing available. **Activities:** Bands, campus ministries, choral groups, dance, drama, film society, international student organizations, literary magazine, music ensembles, Model UN, musical theater, opera, radio station, student government, student newspaper, symphony orchestra, TV station, adult learners,

eco-action, Habitat for Humanity, minorities in agriculture and natural resources, National Society of Black Engineers, College Democrats, College Libertarians, Black Caucus, Alliance Christian Fellowship, Commission for Women.

**Athletics.** NCAA. **Intercollegiate:** Baseball M, basketball, cheerleading, cross-country, diving, fencing, field hockey W, football (tackle) M, golf, gymnastics, lacrosse, soccer, softball W, swimming, tennis, track and field, volleyball, wrestling M. **Intramural:** Badminton, basketball, bowling, crosscountry, diving, football (non-tackle), football (tackle), golf, gymnastics, racquetball, soccer, softball, squash, swimming, tennis, track and field, volleyball, wrestling. **Team name:** Nittany Lions.

**Student services.** Adult student services, alcohol/substance abuse counseling, chaplain/spiritual director, career counseling, services for economically disadvantaged, student employment services, financial aid counseling, health services, legal services, minority student services, on-campus daycare, personal counseling, placement for graduates, veterans' counselor, women's services. **Physically disabled:** Services for visually, speech, hearing impaired.

**Contact.** E-mail: admissions@psu.edu
Phone: (814) 865-5471 Fax: (814) 863-7590
Anne Rohrbach, Executive Director for Undergraduate Admissions, Penn State University Park, 201 Shields Building, University Park, PA 16802-1294

## Penn State Wilkes-Barre
**Lehman, Pennsylvania**
www.wb.psu.edu                    CB code: 2660

- Public 4-year branch campus college
- Commuter campus in small city
- 594 degree-seeking undergraduates: 7% part-time, 29% women, 3% African American, 1% Asian American, 2% Hispanic American
- 39 graduate students
- 91% of applicants admitted
- SAT or ACT with writing required
- 51% graduate within 6 years

**General.** Founded in 1916. Regionally accredited. **Degrees:** 40 bachelor's, 13 associate awarded. **ROTC:** Army, Air Force. **Location:** 10 miles from Wilkes-Barre. **Calendar:** Semester, limited summer session. **Full-time faculty:** 36 total; 61% have terminal degrees, 17% minority, 19% women. **Part-time faculty:** 20 total; 20% have terminal degrees, 45% women. **Class size:** 55% < 20, 42% 20-39, 2% 40-49, 2% 50-99.

**Freshman class profile.** 609 applied, 554 admitted, 204 enrolled.

| Mid 50% test scores | | | |
|---|---|---|---|
| SAT critical reading: | 430-530 | GPA 3.0-3.49: | 29% |
| SAT math: | 430-560 | GPA 2.0-2.99: | 53% |
| SAT writing: | 400-500 | Rank in top quarter: | 27% |
| GPA 3.75 or higher: | 4% | Rank in top tenth: | 4% |
| GPA 3.50-3.74: | 12% | Return as sophomores: | 73% |
| | | Out-of-state: | 6% |

**Basis for selection.** Admission decisions based upon high school GPA, standardized test scores, class rank, personal statements, and activities. Essay considered if submitted; portfolios required for select majors. **Homeschooled:** Complete documentation showing courses studied and all evaluations presented from evaluator or supervisor assigned to student in cooperation with local school district or evaluator approved through program. **Learning Disabled:** Prospective students with disabilities encouraged to contact or visit the Office for Disability Services in their junior or senior years in high school in order to find out more about disability services at the college level.

**High school preparation.** College-preparatory program recommended. Required units include English 4, mathematics 3, social studies 3, science 3 and foreign language 2.

**2009-2010 Annual costs.** Tuition/fees: $12,150; $18,168 out-of-state. Books/supplies: $1,264. Personal expenses: $1,854.

**2008-2009 Financial aid. Need-based:** 161 full-time freshmen applied for aid; 116 were judged to have need; 115 of these received aid. Average need met was 67%. Average scholarship/grant was $5,794; average loan $3,179. 45% of total undergraduate aid awarded as scholarships/grants, 55% as loans/jobs. **Non-need-based:** Awarded to 160 full-time undergraduates, including 71 freshmen. Scholarships awarded for academics, alumni affiliation, athletics, ROTC.

**Application procedures. Admission:** Priority date 11/30; no deadline. $50 fee, may be waived for applicants with need. Admission notification on a rolling basis beginning on or about 11/30. Must reply by May 1 or within 2 week(s) if notified thereafter. All freshmen applications processed at University Park Campus. **Financial aid:** Priority date 2/15; no closing date. FAFSA required. Applicants notified on a rolling basis starting 3/1.

**Academics. Special study options:** Accelerated study, cross-registration, distance learning, double major, dual enrollment of high school students, honors, independent study, internships, student-designed major, study abroad. **Credit/placement by examination:** AP, CLEP, IB, SAT. 60 credit hours maximum toward bachelor's degree. **Support services:** Learning center, study skills assistance, tutoring, writing center.

**Majors. Agriculture:** General, agribusiness operations, agronomy, animal sciences, education services, food science, horticultural science, landscaping, mechanization, soil science, turf management. **Area/ethnic studies:** African-American, East Asian, Latin American, women's. **Biology:** General, bacteriology, biochemistry, pathology, toxicology. **Business:** Accounting, actuarial science, business admin, finance, hospitality admin, labor relations, management information systems, managerial economics, marketing, organizational behavior. **Communications:** General, advertising, journalism. **Computer sciences:** General, information systems. **Conservation:** General, forest sciences, forest technology. **Education:** Art, elementary, foreign languages, secondary, special, testing/assessment. **Engineering:** Aerospace, architectural, biomedical, chemical, civil, computer, electrical, environmental, industrial, materials science, mechanical, mining, nuclear, petroleum, science, surveying. **Engineering technology:** Electrical. **Family/consumer sciences:** Family studies, human nutrition. **Foreign languages:** Classics, comparative lit, French, German, Italian, Japanese, Russian, Spanish. **Health:** Communication disorders, health care admin, nursing (RN), premedicine. **History:** General. **Interdisciplinary:** Biological/physical sciences, medieval/Renaissance. **Liberal arts:** Arts/sciences. **Math:** General, statistics. **Parks/recreation:** Exercise sciences, facilities management. **Philosophy/religion:** Judaic, philosophy, religion. **Physical sciences:** Astronomy, atmospheric science, chemistry, geology, physics. **Protective services:** Criminal justice, forensics, law enforcement admin. **Psychology:** General. **Science technology:** Biological. **Social sciences:** Anthropology, archaeology, economics, geography, international economic development, international relations, political science, sociology. **Visual/performing arts:** General, acting, art, art history/conservation, design, film/cinema, graphic design, theater design. **Other:** Adult and continuing education, Biological and biomedical science, Rehabilitation and therapeutic studies, Security and protective services.

**Most popular majors.** Business/marketing 35%, computer/information sciences 10%, English 18%, security/protective services 33%.

**Computing on campus.** 196 workstations in library, computer center, student center. Commuter students can connect to campus network. Online course registration, online library, helpline, repair service, student web hosting, wireless network available.

**Student life. Freshman orientation:** Mandatory. Preregistration for classes offered. One-day session held prior to start of classes. **Policies:** Acts of intolerance and high-risk drinking discouraged at all locations. All facilities designated smoke-free. Students expected to abide by The Penn State Principles. **Activities:** Dance, Model UN, radio station, student government, student newspaper, students for justice club.

**Athletics.** USCAA. **Intercollegiate:** Baseball M, basketball M, cross-country, golf, soccer, volleyball W. **Intramural:** Basketball, football (tackle), racquetball, softball, volleyball. **Team name:** Nittany Lions.

**Student services.** Adult student services, alcohol/substance abuse counseling, chaplain/spiritual director, career counseling, services for economically disadvantaged, student employment services, financial aid counseling, health services, minority student services, personal counseling, placement for graduates. **Physically disabled:** Services for visually, hearing impaired.

**Contact.** E-mail: wbadmissions@psu.edu
Phone: (570) 675-9238 Toll-free number: (800) 966-6613
Fax: (570) 675-9113
Anne Rohrbach, Executive Director for Undergraduate Admissions, Penn State Wilkes-Barre, 201 Shields Building, University Park, PA 16802-1294

---

## Penn State Worthington Scranton
**Dunmore, Pennsylvania**
www.sn.psu.edu                    CB code: 2660

- Public 4-year branch campus college
- Commuter campus in large town
- 1,224 degree-seeking undergraduates: 17% part-time, 53% women, 1% African American, 2% Asian American, 3% Hispanic American
- 89% of applicants admitted
- SAT or ACT with writing required
- 39% graduate within 6 years

---

**General.** Founded in 1923. Regionally accredited. **Degrees:** 129 bachelor's, 77 associate awarded. **ROTC:** Army, Air Force. **Location:** 1 mile from Scranton. **Calendar:** Semester, limited summer session. **Full-time faculty:** 57 total; 61% have terminal degrees, 16% minority, 54% women. **Part-time faculty:** 46 total; 17% have terminal degrees, 4% minority, 54% women. **Class size:** 42% < 20, 50% 20-39, 6% 40-49, 2% 50-99.

**Freshman class profile.** 915 applied, 812 admitted, 353 enrolled.

| Mid 50% test scores | | GPA 3.0-3.49: | 34% |
|---|---|---|---|
| SAT critical reading: | 400-510 | GPA 2.0-2.99: | 57% |
| SAT math: | 400-510 | Rank in top quarter: | 20% |
| SAT writing: | 390-500 | Rank in top tenth: | 4% |
| GPA 3.75 or higher: | 1% | Return as sophomores: | 74% |
| GPA 3.50-3.74: | 5% | Out-of-state: | 3% |

**Basis for selection.** Admission decisions based upon high school GPA, as well as other factors, which may include standardized verbal and math test scores, class rank, personal statements, and list of activities. Essay considered if submitted; portfolios required for select majors. **Homeschooled:** Provide complete documentation showing courses studied and all evaluations presented from evaluator or supervisor assigned to student in cooperation with local school district or evaluator who is approved through the program.

**High school preparation.** College-preparatory program recommended. Required units include English 4, mathematics 3, social studies 3, science 3 and foreign language 2.

**2009-2010 Annual costs.** Tuition/fees: $12,110; $18,128 out-of-state. Books/supplies: $1,168. Personal expenses: $1,854.

**2008-2009 Financial aid. Need-based:** 306 full-time freshmen applied for aid; 241 were judged to have need; 238 of these received aid. Average need met was 66%. Average scholarship/grant was $4,796; average loan $3,244. 37% of total undergraduate aid awarded as scholarships/grants, 63% as loans/jobs. **Non-need-based:** Awarded to 256 full-time undergraduates, including 125 freshmen. Scholarships awarded for academics, alumni affiliation, athletics, ROTC.

**Application procedures. Admission:** Priority date 11/30; no deadline. $50 fee, may be waived for applicants with need. Admission notification on a rolling basis beginning on or about 11/1. Must reply by May 1 or within 2 week(s) if notified thereafter. All freshmen applications processed at University Park Campus. **Financial aid:** Priority date 2/15; no closing date. FAFSA required. Applicants notified on a rolling basis starting 3/1.

**Academics. Special study options:** Accelerated study, cooperative education, cross-registration, distance learning, double major, dual enrollment of high school students, honors, independent study, internships, study abroad. **Credit/placement by examination:** AP, CLEP, IB, SAT. 60 credit hours maximum toward bachelor's degree. **Support services:** Learning center, remedial instruction, study skills assistance, tutoring, writing center.

**Majors. Agriculture:** General, agribusiness operations, agronomy, animal sciences, education services, food science, horticultural science, landscaping, mechanization, soil science, turf management. **Area/ethnic studies:** African-American, American, East Asian, Latin American, women's. **Biology:** General, bacteriology, biochemistry, pathology, toxicology. **Business:** Accounting, actuarial science, business admin, finance, hospitality admin, labor relations, management information systems, managerial economics, marketing, organizational behavior. **Communications:** General, advertising, journalism. **Computer sciences:** General, information systems. **Conservation:** General, forest sciences, forest technology. **Education:** Art, elementary, foreign languages, secondary, special, testing/assessment. **Engineering:** Aerospace, architectural, biomedical, chemical, civil, computer, electrical, environmental, industrial, materials science, mechanical, mining, nuclear, petroleum, science. **Engineering technology:** Construction. **Family/consumer sciences:** Family studies, human nutrition. **Foreign languages:** Classics, comparative lit, French, German, Italian, Japanese, Russian, Spanish. **Health:** Communication disorders, health care admin, nursing (RN), premedicine. **History:** General. **Interdisciplinary:** Biological/physical sciences, medieval/Renaissance. **Liberal arts:** Arts/sciences. **Math:** General, statistics. **Parks/recreation:** Exercise sciences, facilities management. **Philosophy/religion:** Judaic, philosophy, religion. **Physical sciences:** Astronomy, atmospheric science, chemistry, geology, physics. **Protective services:** Forensics, law enforcement admin. **Psychology:** General. **Science technology:** Biological. **Social sciences:** Anthropology, archaeology, economics, geography, international economic development, international relations, political science, sociology. **Visual/performing arts:** General, acting, art, art history/conservation, design, film/cinema, graphic design, theater design. **Other:** Adult and continuing education, Biological and biomedical science, Rehabilitation and therapeutic studies, Security and protective services.

**Most popular majors.** Business/marketing 43%, computer/information sciences 19%, family/consumer sciences 15%, health sciences 10%, liberal arts 11%.

**Computing on campus.** 180 workstations in library, computer center, student center. Commuter students can connect to campus network. Online course registration, online library, helpline, repair service, student web hosting, wireless network available.

**Student life. Freshman orientation:** Available. Preregistration for classes offered. **Policies:** Acts of intolerance and high-risk drinking discouraged at all locations. All facilities designated as smoke-free. Students expected to abide by The Penn State Principles. **Activities:** Jazz band, choral groups, drama, literary magazine, music ensembles, student government, student newspaper, community human service organization, Faith and Values, German club, lighthouse club, multicultural club, veterans club, public affairs club.

**Athletics.** USCAA. **Intercollegiate:** Baseball M, basketball, cross-country, soccer M, softball W. **Intramural:** Basketball, soccer, softball, volleyball, weight lifting. **Team name:** Nittany Lions.

**Student services.** Adult student services, alcohol/substance abuse counseling, career counseling, services for economically disadvantaged, student employment services, financial aid counseling, health services, personal counseling, placement for graduates, veterans' counselor, women's services. **Physically disabled:** Services for visually, speech, hearing impaired.

**Contact.** E-mail: wsadmissions@psu.edu
Phone: (570) 963-2500 Fax: (570) 963-2524
Anne Rohrbach, Executive Director for Undergraduate Admissions, Penn State Worthington Scranton, 201 Shields Building, University Park, PA 16802-1294

## Penn State York
**York, Pennsylvania**
www.yk.psu.edu
**CB code: 2660**

▶ Public 4-year branch campus college
▶ Commuter campus in large town
▶ 1,157 degree-seeking undergraduates: 21% part-time, 44% women, 6% African American, 5% Asian American, 6% Hispanic American
▶ 42 degree-seeking graduate students
▶ 87% of applicants admitted
▶ SAT or ACT with writing required
▶ 45% graduate within 6 years

**General.** Founded in 1926. Regionally accredited. **Degrees:** 86 bachelor's, 62 associate awarded; master's offered. **Calendar:** Semester, extensive summer session. **Full-time faculty:** 58 total; 64% have terminal degrees, 16% minority, 34% women. **Part-time faculty:** 50 total; 26% have terminal degrees, 2% minority, 44% women. **Class size:** 53% < 20, 43% 20-39, 3% 40-49, 1% 50-99.

**Freshman class profile.** 1,236 applied, 1,080 admitted, 313 enrolled.

| Mid 50% test scores | | GPA 3.0-3.49: | 32% |
|---|---|---|---|
| SAT critical reading: | 430-540 | GPA 2.0-2.99: | 54% |
| SAT math: | 430-570 | Rank in top quarter: | 29% |
| SAT writing: | 410-520 | Rank in top tenth: | 8% |
| GPA 3.75 or higher: | 5% | Return as sophomores: | 74% |
| GPA 3.50-3.74: | 7% | Out-of-state: | 16% |

**Basis for selection.** Admission decisions based upon high school GPA and other factors, which may include standardized verbal and math test scores, class rank, personal statements, activities lists. Essay considered if submitted; portfolios required for select majors. **Homeschooled:** Complete documentation showing courses studied and all evaluations from home school evaluator or supervisor assigned to student in cooperation with local school district or evaluator approved through program.

**High school preparation.** College-preparatory program recommended. Required units include English 4, mathematics 3, social studies 3, science 3 and foreign language 2.

**2009-2010 Annual costs.** Tuition/fees: $12,110; $18,128 out-of-state. Books/supplies: $1,264. Personal expenses: $1,854.

**2008-2009 Financial aid. Need-based:** 291 full-time freshmen applied for aid; 208 were judged to have need; 200 of these received aid. Average need met was 63%. Average scholarship/grant was $5,730; average loan $3,093. 39% of total undergraduate aid awarded as scholarships/grants, 61% as loans/jobs. **Non-need-based:** Awarded to 231 full-time undergraduates, including 116 freshmen. Scholarships awarded for academics, alumni affiliation, athletics, ROTC.

**Application procedures. Admission:** Priority date 11/30; no deadline. $50 fee, may be waived for applicants with need. Admission notification on

a rolling basis beginning on or about 11/1. Must reply by May 1 or within 2 week(s) if notified thereafter. All freshmen applications processed at University Park Campus. **Financial aid:** Priority date 2/15; no closing date. FAFSA required. Applicants notified on a rolling basis starting 3/1.

**Academics. Special study options:** Accelerated study, cross-registration, distance learning, double major, dual enrollment of high school students, ESL, honors, independent study, internships, student-designed major, study abroad. **Credit/placement by examination:** AP, CLEP, IB, SAT. 60 credit hours maximum toward bachelor's degree. **Support services:** Learning center, pre-admission summer program, reduced course load, remedial instruction, study skills assistance, tutoring, writing center.

**Majors. Agriculture:** General, agribusiness operations, agronomy, animal sciences, education services, food science, horticultural science, landscaping, mechanization, soil science, turf management. **Area/ethnic studies:** African-American, American, East Asian, Latin American, women's. **Biology:** General, bacteriology, biochemistry, pathology, toxicology. **Business:** Accounting, actuarial science, business admin, finance, hospitality admin, labor relations, management information systems, managerial economics, marketing, organizational behavior. **Communications:** General, advertising, journalism. **Computer sciences:** General, information systems. **Conservation:** General, forest sciences, forest technology. **Education:** Art, elementary, foreign languages, secondary, special, testing/assessment. **Engineering:** Aerospace, architectural, biomedical, chemical, civil, computer, electrical, environmental, industrial, materials science, mechanical, mining, nuclear, petroleum, science. **Engineering technology:** Electrical. **Family/consumer sciences:** Family studies, human nutrition. **Foreign languages:** Classics, comparative lit, French, German, Italian, Japanese, Russian, Spanish. **Health:** Communication disorders, health care admin, nursing (RN), premedicine. **History:** General. **Interdisciplinary:** Biological/physical sciences, medieval/Renaissance. **Liberal arts:** Arts/sciences. **Math:** General, statistics. **Parks/recreation:** Exercise sciences, facilities management. **Philosophy/religion:** Judaic, philosophy, religion. **Physical sciences:** Astronomy, atmospheric science, chemistry, geology, physics. **Protective services:** Forensics, law enforcement admin. **Psychology:** General. **Science technology:** Biological. **Social sciences:** Anthropology, archaeology, economics, geography, international economic development, international relations, political science, sociology. **Visual/performing arts:** General, acting, art, art history/conservation, design, film/cinema, graphic design, theater design. **Other:** Adult and continuing education, Rehabilitation and therapeutic studies, Security and protective services.

**Most popular majors.** Business/marketing 40%, computer/information sciences 12%, engineering/engineering technologies 6%, English 7%, family/consumer sciences 17%, interdisciplinary studies 8%, liberal arts 6%.

**Computing on campus.** 169 workstations in computer center. Commuter students can connect to campus network. Online course registration, online library, helpline, repair service, student web hosting, wireless network available.

**Student life. Freshman orientation:** Mandatory. Preregistration for classes offered. Full-day event in August. **Policies:** Acts of intolerance and high-risk drinking discouraged at all locations. All facilities designated as smoke-free. Students expected to abide by The Penn State Principles. **Housing:** Room, apartment, house rentals in the local community available. **Activities:** Dance, drama, literary magazine, student government, student newspaper, black student union, Christian fellowship, Hispanic students association, Rainbow Alliance, veterans club, Asian culture club, foreign policy club, debate club.

**Athletics. Intercollegiate:** Baseball M, basketball, soccer, tennis, volleyball. **Intramural:** Badminton, basketball, football (non-tackle) M, handball, soccer, softball, table tennis, tennis, volleyball. **Team name:** Nittany Lions.

**Student services.** Adult student services, alcohol/substance abuse counseling, chaplain/spiritual director, career counseling, services for economically disadvantaged, student employment services, financial aid counseling, health services, minority student services, personal counseling, placement for graduates, veterans' counselor, women's services. **Physically disabled:** Services for visually, speech, hearing impaired. **Learning disabled:** Comprehensive services available.

**Contact.** E-mail: ykadmissions@psu.edu
Phone: (717) 771-4040 Toll-free number: (800) 778-6227
Fax: (717) 771-4005
Anne Rohrbach, Executive Director for Undergraduate Admissions, Penn State York, 201 Shields Building, University Park, PA 16802-1294

## Pennsylvania College of Art and Design
**Lancaster, Pennsylvania**
www.pcad.edu
**CB code: 2681**

▶ Private 4-year visual arts college
▶ Commuter campus in small city

- 273 degree-seeking undergraduates: 8% part-time, 65% women
- 42% of applicants admitted
- Application essay, interview required
- 42% graduate within 6 years

**General.** Regionally accredited. **Degrees:** 47 bachelor's awarded. **Location:** 75 miles from Philadelphia, 75 miles from Baltimore. **Calendar:** Semester, limited summer session. **Full-time faculty:** 14 total; 36% women. **Part-time faculty:** 33 total; 33% women. **Class size:** 84% < 20, 16% 20-39. **Special facilities:** Visual arts gallery.

**Freshman class profile.** 342 applied, 145 admitted, 73 enrolled.

| | | | |
|---|---|---|---|
| GPA 3.75 or higher: | 13% | End year in good standing: | 88% |
| GPA 3.50-3.74: | 20% | Return as sophomores: | 61% |
| GPA 3.0-3.49: | 15% | Out-of-state: | 19% |
| GPA 2.0-2.99: | 50% | | |

**Basis for selection.** Portfolio review, interview, personal statement, and high school transcripts required. Students with GPA below 2.5 required to submit two letters of recommendation. Portfolio required. **Homeschooled:** Transcript of courses and grades, state high school equivalency certificate, interview required.

**High school preparation.** College-preparatory program recommended.

**2009-2010 Annual costs.** Tuition/fees: $17,280. Books/supplies: $1,265. Personal expenses: $971.

**2009-2010 Financial aid. Need-based:** 35% of total undergraduate aid awarded as scholarships/grants, 65% as loans/jobs.

**Application procedures. Admission:** No deadline. $40 fee, may be waived for applicants with need. Application must be submitted on paper. Admission notification on a rolling basis. Must reply by May 1 or within 2 week(s) if notified thereafter.

**Academics. Special study options:** Dual enrollment of high school students, internships. **Credit/placement by examination:** AP, CLEP, institutional tests.

**Majors. Visual/performing arts:** Graphic design, illustration, photography, studio arts.

**Computing on campus.** PC or laptop required. Online library, wireless network available.

**Student life. Freshman orientation:** Mandatory. **Housing:** Housing referral service available. **Activities:** Student government.

**Student services.** Career counseling, student employment services, financial aid counseling.

**Contact.** E-mail: admissions@pcad.edu
Phone: (717) 396-7833 Toll-free number: (800) 689-0379
Fax: (717) 396-1339
Natalie Lascek-Speakman, Director of Admission Marketing & Recruitment, Pennsylvania College of Art and Design, PO Box 59, Lancaster, PA 17608-0059

## Pennsylvania College of Technology
**Williamsport, Pennsylvania**     CB member
www.pct.edu     CB code: 2989

- Public 4-year technical college
- Commuter campus in small city
- 6,324 degree-seeking undergraduates: 14% part-time, 35% women, 3% African American, 1% Asian American, 2% Hispanic American
- 52% graduate within 6 years

**General.** Founded in 1965. Regionally accredited. **Degrees:** 569 bachelor's, 985 associate awarded. **ROTC:** Army. **Location:** 85 miles from Harrisburg, 70 miles from Wilkes-Barre. **Calendar:** Semester, limited summer session. **Full-time faculty:** 296 total; 3% minority, 28% women. **Part-time faculty:** 188 total; 3% minority, 53% women. **Special facilities:** Automotive technology center, aviation center, plastics manufacturing center, community arts center, earth science center.

**Freshman class profile.** 4,061 applied, 3,567 admitted, 2,347 enrolled.

**Basis for selection.** Open admission, but selective for some programs. Competitive admissions to health science programs, using GPA, SAT scores, high school rank, selected course grades, completed developmental course

work. Some programs have more specific requirements. SAT recommended for all bachelor's programs, dental hygiene, radiography, occupational therapy assistant, nursing applicants; college placement exams required for all applicants. **Homeschooled:** Transcript of courses and grades, state high school equivalency certificate required. Must provide proof of graduation from an organization governed by the State Board of Education, such as Pennsylvania Home Schoolers Accreditation Agency. Otherwise must present GED.

**2009-2010 Annual costs.** Tuition/fees: $12,480; $15,630 out-of-state. Room/board: $8,350. Books/supplies: $1,000. Personal expenses: $2,450.

**2008-2009 Financial aid. Non-need-based:** Scholarships awarded for academics, alumni affiliation.

**Application procedures. Admission:** Closing date 7/1 (postmark date). $50 fee, may be waived for applicants with need. Admission notification on a rolling basis. **Financial aid:** Priority date 4/1; no closing date. FAFSA, institutional form required. Applicants notified on a rolling basis starting 6/1; must reply by 7/1 or within 4 week(s) of notification.

**Academics. Special study options:** Accelerated study, cooperative education, cross-registration, distance learning, dual enrollment of high school students, exchange student, honors, independent study, internships, student-designed major, study abroad, weekend college. **Credit/placement by examination:** AP, CLEP, institutional tests. 30 credit hours maximum toward associate degree, 30 toward bachelor's. **Support services:** Learning center, pre-admission summer program, remedial instruction, study skills assistance, tutoring.

**Majors. Business:** Accounting, business admin, management information systems. **Communications technology:** Graphic/printing. **Computer sciences:** Networking, security, web page design. **Construction:** Masonry. **Engineering technology:** Architectural, automotive, civil, construction, electrical, energy systems, heat/ac/refrig, industrial, manufacturing, mechanical, plastics. **Health:** Adult health nursing, cardiovascular technology, dental hygiene, EMT paramedic, medical records admin, surgical technology. **Mechanic/repair:** Avionics, electronics/electrical, heating/ac/refrig, industrial electronics. **Parks/recreation:** Exercise sciences. **Personal/culinary services:** Restaurant/catering. **Visual/performing arts:** Commercial/advertising art.

**Most popular majors.** Business/marketing 17%, computer/information sciences 15%, engineering/engineering technologies 42%, health sciences 15%.

**Computing on campus.** 2,400 workstations in dormitories, library, computer center, student center. Dormitories wired for high-speed internet access and linked to campus network. Commuter students can connect to campus network. Online course registration, online library, helpline, repair service, student web hosting, wireless network available.

**Student life. Freshman orientation:** Available. Preregistration for classes offered. 2-day sessions offered throughout the summer. **Policies:** No alcohol or illegal drugs on campus. Smoke-free buildings and housing environments. **Housing:** Coed dorms, wellness housing available. $300 partly refundable deposit. Academic theme housing offers a living-learning atmosphere. **Activities:** Campus ministries, dance, international student organizations, radio station, student government, Alpha Omega Fellowship, Campus Crusade for Christ, Earth Smart, human services club, multicultural society, occupational therapy assistant club, physicians assistant club, Skills USA, student nurses association.

**Athletics.** USCAA. **Intercollegiate:** Archery, baseball M, basketball, bowling, cross-country, golf, soccer, softball W, tennis, volleyball. **Intramural:** Archery, badminton, basketball, bowling, football (non-tackle), golf, soccer, softball, table tennis, tennis, volleyball, weight lifting. **Team name:** Wildcats.

**Student services.** Adult student services, alcohol/substance abuse counseling, career counseling, student employment services, financial aid counseling, health services, on-campus daycare, personal counseling, placement for graduates. **Physically disabled:** Services for visually, speech, hearing impaired.

**Contact.** E-mail: admissions@pct.edu
Phone: (570) 327-4761 Toll-free number: (800) 367-9222
Fax: (570) 321-5551
Dennis Correll, Associate Dean for Admissions and Financial Aid, Pennsylvania College of Technology, One College Avenue, Williamsport, PA 17701

## Philadelphia Biblical University
**Langhorne, Pennsylvania**
www.pbu.edu     CB code: 2661

- Private 4-year university and Bible college affiliated with Protestant Evangelical tradition
- Residential campus in small town

- 1,044 degree-seeking undergraduates: 6% part-time, 53% women, 13% African American, 4% Asian American, 4% Hispanic American, 1% international
- 274 degree-seeking graduate students
- 77% of applicants admitted
- SAT or ACT (ACT writing optional), application essay required
- 55% graduate within 6 years; 30% enter graduate study

**General.** Founded in 1913. Regionally accredited; also accredited by ABHE. **Degrees:** 307 bachelor's awarded; master's offered. **ROTC:** Air Force. **Location:** 17 miles from Philadelphia; 5 miles from Trenton, New Jersey. **Calendar:** Semester, limited summer session. **Full-time faculty:** 51 total; 67% have terminal degrees, 14% minority, 31% women. **Part-time faculty:** 57 total; 19% have terminal degrees, 9% minority, 33% women. **Class size:** 61% < 20, 33% 20-39, 3% 40-49, 3% 50-99.

**Freshman class profile.** 465 applied, 356 admitted, 195 enrolled.

| Mid 50% test scores | | | |
|---|---|---|---|
| SAT critical reading: | 480-570 | Rank in top quarter: | 35% |
| SAT math: | 450-570 | Rank in top tenth: | 18% |
| ACT composite: | 19-26 | End year in good standing: | 99% |
| GPA 3.75 or higher: | 31% | Return as sophomores: | 82% |
| GPA 3.50-3.74: | 15% | Out-of-state: | 54% |
| GPA 3.0-3.49: | 25% | Live on campus: | 89% |
| GPA 2.0-2.99: | 28% | International: | 1% |

**Basis for selection.** High school GPA, pastor's references, writing sample, SAT or ACT scores required for some. Some applicants not meeting academic admissions requirements may be admitted and placed in a remedial program. Interview recommended for all; audition required for music program. **Homeschooled:** Letter of recommendation (nonparent) required.

**High school preparation.** College-preparatory program recommended. 15 units recommended. Recommended units include English 4, mathematics 1, social studies 3, science 2 and foreign language 2.

**2009-2010 Annual costs.** Tuition/fees: $19,272. Room/board: $7,650. Books/supplies: $1,000. Personal expenses: $1,600.

**2009-2010 Financial aid. Non-need-based:** Scholarships awarded for academics, leadership, minority status.

**Application procedures. Admission:** No deadline. $25 fee, may be waived for applicants with need. Admission notification on a rolling basis. **Financial aid:** Priority date 3/1; no closing date. FAFSA required. Applicants notified on a rolling basis starting 2/15.

**Academics.** Students may participate in semester studies in Israel or in the 'Best Semester' program. **Special study options:** Accelerated study, combined bachelor's/graduate degree, double major, honors, internships, study abroad, teacher certification program. **Credit/placement by examination:** CLEP, IB, SAT, ACT, institutional tests. 12 credit hours maximum toward bachelor's degree. **Support services:** Learning center, reduced course load, remedial instruction, study skills assistance, tutoring, writing center.

**Majors. Business:** Business admin. **Education:** Early childhood, elementary, English, mathematics, music, physical, social studies. **Parks/recreation:** Health/fitness. **Public administration:** Social work. **Theology:** Bible, missionary, pastoral counseling, religious ed, sacred music, theology. **Visual/performing arts:** Music performance, music theory/composition.

**Most popular majors.** Business/marketing 7%, education 12%, philosophy/religious studies 70%, public administration/social services 9%.

**Computing on campus.** 79 workstations in dormitories, library, student center. Dormitories wired for high-speed internet access and linked to campus network. Commuter students can connect to campus network. Online course registration, online library, helpline, wireless network available.

**Student life. Freshman orientation:** Mandatory. Preregistration for classes offered. **Policies:** Religious observance required. **Housing:** Guaranteed on-campus for freshmen. Single-sex dorms, special housing for disabled, apartments available. $250 deposit. **Activities:** Concert band, campus ministries, choral groups, drama, international student organizations, music ensembles, musical theater, opera, student government, student newspaper, symphony orchestra, student missionary fellowship, commuter council, resident council, student theological society, cultural awareness association, student business club, social committee.

**Athletics.** NCAA, NCCAA. **Intercollegiate:** Baseball M, basketball, cross-country, golf M, soccer, softball W, tennis W, volleyball. **Intramural:** Basketball, football (non-tackle), soccer, table tennis, tennis, volleyball. **Team name:** Eagles.

**Student services.** Alcohol/substance abuse counseling, chaplain/spiritual director, career counseling, student employment services, financial aid counseling, health services, personal counseling, placement for graduates. **Physically disabled:** Services for visually, hearing impaired.

**Contact.** E-mail: admissions@pbu.edu
Phone: (215) 702-4235 Toll-free number: (800) 366-0049
Fax: (215) 702-4248
Jamie Gleason, Director of Admissions, Philadelphia Biblical University, 200 Manor Avenue, Langhorne, PA 19047-2990

## Philadelphia University

**Philadelphia, Pennsylvania**    **CB member**
**www.philau.edu**    **CB code: 2666**

- Private 4-year university
- Residential campus in very large city
- 2,880 degree-seeking undergraduates: 7% part-time, 67% women
- 601 degree-seeking graduate students
- 71% of applicants admitted
- SAT or ACT (ACT writing optional) required
- 60% graduate within 6 years

**General.** Founded in 1884. Regionally accredited. **Degrees:** 561 bachelor's, 14 associate awarded; master's, doctoral offered. **Location:** 7 miles from Center City. **Calendar:** Semester, limited summer session. **Full-time faculty:** 110 total; 76% have terminal degrees, 13% minority, 42% women. **Part-time faculty:** 328 total; 11% minority, 42% women. **Class size:** 64% < 20, 35% 20-39, less than 1% 40-49, less than 1% 50-99, less than 1% >100. **Special facilities:** Computer-aided design laboratories in architecture, graphic design and fashion design; CAD facilities, university design center, rapid prototyping.

**Freshman class profile.** 3,800 applied, 2,707 admitted, 720 enrolled.

| Mid 50% test scores | | | |
|---|---|---|---|
| SAT critical reading: | 490-570 | GPA 2.0-2.99: | 19% |
| SAT math: | 490-600 | Rank in top quarter: | 45% |
| SAT writing: | 480-570 | Rank in top tenth: | 18% |
| ACT composite: | 21-26 | Return as sophomores: | 80% |
| GPA 3.75 or higher: | 25% | Out-of-state: | 54% |
| GPA 3.50-3.74: | 23% | Live on campus: | 95% |
| GPA 3.0-3.49: | 33% | Fraternities: | 1% |
| | | Sororities: | 1% |

**Basis for selection.** Academic record, GPA, and test scores most important. Extracurricular activities, counselor's recommendation and interview considered. Interview, essay recommended.

**High school preparation.** College-preparatory program recommended. 15 units required; 19 recommended. Required and recommended units include English 4, mathematics 3-4, social studies 2-3, history 1-2, science 3-4 (laboratory 2), foreign language 2 and academic electives 2.

**2009-2010 Annual costs.** Tuition/fees: $27,498. Room/board: $9,182. Books/supplies: $1,600. Personal expenses: $1,789.

**2009-2010 Financial aid. Need-based:** 653 full-time freshmen applied for aid; 561 were judged to have need; 561 of these received aid. Average need met was 76%. Average scholarship/grant was $16,233; average loan $4,011. 59% of total undergraduate aid awarded as scholarships/grants, 41% as loans/jobs. **Non-need-based:** Awarded to 934 full-time undergraduates, including 218 freshmen. Scholarships awarded for academics, athletics.

**Application procedures. Admission:** No deadline. $40 fee, may be waived for applicants with need. Admission notification on a rolling basis beginning on or about 11/1. Must reply by May 1 or within 1 week(s) if notified thereafter. **Financial aid:** Closing date 4/15. FAFSA required. Applicants notified on a rolling basis starting 2/10; must reply by 5/1.

**Academics. Special study options:** Accelerated study, combined bachelor's/graduate degree, cooperative education, distance learning, double major, honors, independent study, internships, liberal arts/career combination, semester at sea, study abroad. **Credit/placement by examination:** AP, CLEP, SAT, institutional tests. 60 credit hours maximum toward bachelor's degree. **Support services:** Learning center, reduced course load, remedial instruction, study skills assistance, tutoring, writing center.

**Majors. Architecture:** Architecture, interior, landscape. **Biology:** General, biochemistry, environmental. **Business:** Accounting, apparel, business admin, fashion, finance, international, management information systems, marketing. **Communications:** Digital media. **Communications technology:** Animation/special effects, graphics. **Conservation:** Environmental studies. **Engineering:** General, architectural, industrial, mechanical, textile. **Family/consumer sciences:** Apparel marketing, clothing/textiles, textile science.

**Health:** Health care admin, premedicine. **Interdisciplinary:** Biopsychology. **Legal studies:** Prelaw. **Physical sciences:** Chemistry. **Psychology:** General. **Visual/performing arts:** Fashion design, fiber arts, graphic design, industrial design, interior design. **Other:** Professional communications.

**Most popular majors.** Architecture 18%, business/marketing 41%, visual/performing arts 24%.

**Computing on campus.** PC or laptop required. 400 workstations in library, computer center, student center. Dormitories wired for high-speed internet access and linked to campus network. Commuter students can connect to campus network. Online course registration, online library, helpline, student web hosting, wireless network available.

**Student life. Freshman orientation:** Mandatory, $100 fee. Preregistration for classes offered. 3-day residential program in summer. **Housing:** Guaranteed on-campus for freshmen. Coed dorms, single-sex dorms, special housing for disabled, apartments, wellness housing available. $250 fully refundable deposit. Townhouses available. **Activities:** Campus ministries, choral groups, dance, drama, international student organizations, student government, student newspaper, professional (major-related) organizations, Black awareness society, Hillel, Christian fellowship, community service corps, Minaret, Gemini Theatre, Phila Capella, Gay Lesbian Bisexual Allies Coalition.

**Athletics.** NCAA. **Intercollegiate:** Baseball M, basketball, cross-country, golf M, lacrosse W, rowing (crew), soccer, softball W, tennis, volleyball W. **Intramural:** Basketball, cross-country, football (tackle) M, skiing, soccer, softball, swimming, tennis, volleyball W. **Team name:** Rams.

**Student services.** Adult student services, alcohol/substance abuse counseling, career counseling, student employment services, financial aid counseling, health services, personal counseling, placement for graduates. **Physically disabled:** Services for visually, hearing impaired. **Learning disabled:** Comprehensive services available.

**Contact.** E-mail: admissions@philau.edu
Phone: (215) 951-2800 Toll-free number: (800) 951-7287
Fax: (215) 951-2907
Greg Potts, Director of Admissions, Philadelphia University, School House Lane and Henry Avenue, Philadelphia, PA 19144-5497

## Point Park University
**Pittsburgh, Pennsylvania**
**www.pointpark.edu**

**CB member**
**CB code: 2676**

- Private 4-year university
- Commuter campus in large city
- 3,355 degree-seeking undergraduates: 22% part-time, 60% women, 19% African American, 1% Asian American, 2% Hispanic American, 1% international
- 566 degree-seeking graduate students
- 72% of applicants admitted
- SAT or ACT (ACT writing optional), application essay, interview required
- 53% graduate within 6 years

**General.** Founded in 1960. Regionally accredited. **Degrees:** 673 bachelor's, 3 associate awarded; master's offered. **ROTC:** Army, Air Force. **Location:** Downtown. **Calendar:** Semester, extensive summer session. **Full-time faculty:** 122 total; 62% have terminal degrees, 7% minority, 38% women. **Part-time faculty:** 310 total. **Class size:** 74% < 20, 26% 20-39, less than 1% 40-49, less than 1% 50-99, less than 1% >100. **Special facilities:** Children's school, Pittsburgh Playhouse, 3-theater performing arts center.

**Freshman class profile.** 3,089 applied, 2,235 admitted, 530 enrolled.

| Mid 50% test scores | | GPA 2.0-2.99: | 29% |
|---|---|---|---|
| SAT critical reading: | 470-570 | Rank in top quarter: | 41% |
| SAT math: | 450-560 | Rank in top tenth: | 16% |
| SAT writing: | 460-570 | Return as sophomores: | 77% |
| ACT composite: | 19-24 | Out-of-state: | 32% |
| GPA 3.75 or higher: | 15% | Live on campus: | 74% |
| GPA 3.50-3.74: | 19% | International: | 2% |
| GPA 3.0-3.49: | 37% | | |

**Basis for selection.** High school record, class rank, test scores most important. Recommendations, extracurricular activities, talent, character also important. Audition required for some majors, portfolio recommended for multimedia, technical theater, stage management programs.

**High school preparation.** College-preparatory program recommended. 15 units recommended. Recommended units include English 4, mathematics 4, social studies 4, history 4, science 4 and foreign language 2.

**2009-2010 Annual costs.** Tuition/fees: $21,334. Room/board: $9,020. Books/supplies: $1,000. Personal expenses: $1,100.

**2009-2010 Financial aid. Need-based:** 489 full-time freshmen applied for aid; 433 were judged to have need; 433 of these received aid. Average need met was 74%. Average scholarship/grant was $13,547; average loan $4,605. 48% of total undergraduate aid awarded as scholarships/grants, 52% as loans/jobs. **Non-need-based:** Awarded to 660 full-time undergraduates, including 302 freshmen. Scholarships awarded for academics, alumni affiliation, art, athletics, leadership, music/drama.

**Application procedures. Admission:** No deadline. $40 fee, may be waived for applicants with need, free for online applicants. Admission notification on a rolling basis beginning on or about 10/1. Must reply by May 1 or within 2 week(s) if notified thereafter. **Financial aid:** Priority date 4/15; no closing date. FAFSA required. Applicants notified on a rolling basis starting 2/15; must reply by 8/30 or within 2 week(s) of notification.

**Academics. Special study options:** Accelerated study, cooperative education, cross-registration, distance learning, double major, dual enrollment of high school students, ESL, exchange student, honors, independent study, internships, liberal arts/career combination, student-designed major, study abroad, teacher certification program, weekend college. Numerous off-campus programs for college credits. Several accelerated programs available. Offers professionally oriented programs in arts, business, communications, and technology. **Credit/placement by examination:** AP, CLEP, IB, institutional tests. 30 credit hours maximum toward associate degree, 60 toward bachelor's. **Support services:** Learning center, pre-admission summer program, reduced course load, remedial instruction, study skills assistance, tutoring.

**Majors. Biology:** General, biotechnology. **Business:** Accounting, business admin, human resources. **Communications:** Advertising, broadcast journalism, journalism, media studies, photojournalism. **Computer sciences:** Information technology. **Conservation:** Environmental science. **Education:** Biology, drama/dance, early childhood, elementary, English, mathematics. **Engineering technology:** Civil, mechanical. **History:** General. **Interdisciplinary:** Behavioral sciences. **Legal studies:** General. **Personal/culinary services:** Mortuary science. **Protective services:** Criminal justice, law enforcement admin. **Psychology:** General. **Public administration:** General. **Social sciences:** General, international relations, political science. **Visual/performing arts:** Cinematography, dance, dramatic, photography.

**Most popular majors.** Business/marketing 22%, communications/journalism 9%, education 7%, engineering/engineering technologies 6%, security/protective services 14%, visual/performing arts 25%.

**Computing on campus.** 285 workstations in library, computer center, student center. Dormitories wired for high-speed internet access and linked to campus network. Commuter students can connect to campus network. Online course registration, online library, helpline, repair service, student web hosting, wireless network available.

**Student life. Freshman orientation:** Mandatory. Preregistration for classes offered. Held in summer months, includes placement testing if needed for major. **Policies:** Policies regarding student conduct, plagiarism and resident life. **Housing:** Guaranteed on-campus for all undergraduates. Coed dorms, special housing for disabled, apartments available. $400 deposit. Living & learning communities; suite style housing. **Activities:** Choral groups, dance, drama, film society, international student organizations, literary magazine, musical theater, radio station, student government, student newspaper, TV station, black student union, Amnesty International.

**Athletics.** NAIA. **Intercollegiate:** Baseball M, basketball, cross-country, golf, soccer, softball W, volleyball W. **Intramural:** Basketball M, tennis, volleyball, weight lifting M. **Team name:** Pioneers.

**Student services.** Adult student services, alcohol/substance abuse counseling, career counseling, student employment services, financial aid counseling, health services, on-campus daycare, personal counseling, placement for graduates, veterans' counselor. **Physically disabled:** Services for visually, speech, hearing impaired.

**Contact.** E-mail: enroll@pointpark.edu
Phone: (412) 392-3430 Toll-free number: (800) 321-0129
Fax: (412) 392-3902
Joell Minford, Director of Admissions, Point Park University, 201 Wood Street, Pittsburgh, PA 15222-1984

## Restaurant School at Walnut Hill College
### Philadelphia, Pennsylvania
www.walnuthillcollege.edu                    CB code: 4883

- For-profit 4-year culinary school and business college
- Commuter campus in very large city
- 562 degree-seeking undergraduates
- 72% of applicants admitted
- Application essay, interview required

**General.** Accredited by ACCSC. Emphasis on fine dining and upscale hotels. **Degrees:** 52 bachelor's, 181 associate awarded. **Calendar:** Quarter. **Full-time faculty:** 21 total. **Part-time faculty:** 3 total. **Special facilities:** Students interact with numerous food and beverage outlets open to public. 4 uniquely themed restaurants and pastry shop/cafe.

**Freshman class profile.** 320 applied, 230 admitted, 192 enrolled.

| Out-of-state: | 51% | Live on campus: | 30% |
|---|---|---|---|

**Basis for selection.** All students must interview with admissions representative, submit two letters of reference, 250-word essay, SAT/ACT scores and/or take a basic skills evaluation. Decisions are based on all information received, however the interview is the most heavily weighted. SAT or ACT recommended. Students who score below 900 combined on SAT/ACT Math and Critical Reading, or who did not take either test, must take in-house assessment test. **Homeschooled:** Interview required.

**2009-2010 Annual costs.** Tuition/fees: $21,300. Room only: $5,875.

**Application procedures. Admission:** No deadline. $50 fee. Admission notification on a rolling basis. **Financial aid:** No deadline.

**Academics. Special study options:** Independent study, internships. **Credit/placement by examination:** CLEP. **Support services:** Study skills assistance, tutoring.

**Majors. Business:** Hotel/motel admin, restaurant/food services. **Personal/culinary services:** Baking, chef training, restaurant/catering.

**Computing on campus.** 48 workstations in library, computer center. Dormitories wired for high-speed internet access and linked to campus network. Online library, wireless network available.

**Student life. Freshman orientation:** Mandatory. 3-day orientation held week prior to start of classes. **Housing:** Guaranteed on-campus for all undergraduates. Coed dorms available. $850 fully refundable deposit. **Activities:** Literary magazine, music ensembles, student newspaper.

**Student services.** Career counseling, student employment services, financial aid counseling.

**Contact.** E-mail: info@walnuthillcollege.edu
Phone: (215) 222-4200 ext. 3011 Toll-free
number: (877) 925-6884 ext. 3011 Fax: (215) 222-2811
Becky Smith, Director of Admissions, Restaurant School at Walnut Hill College, 4207 Walnut Street, Philadelphia, PA 19104

## Robert Morris University
### Moon Township, Pennsylvania
www.rmu.edu                    CB member
                               CB code: 2769

- Private 4-year university
- Commuter campus in large town
- 3,587 degree-seeking undergraduates: 14% part-time, 44% women, 9% African American, 1% Asian American, 1% Hispanic American, 3% international
- 1,069 degree-seeking graduate students
- 92% of applicants admitted
- SAT or ACT (ACT writing optional) required
- 58% graduate within 6 years

**General.** Founded in 1921. Regionally accredited. **Degrees:** 865 bachelor's awarded; master's, professional offered. **ROTC:** Army, Air Force. **Location:** 17 miles from Pittsburgh. **Calendar:** Semester, limited summer session. **Full-time faculty:** 177 total; 81% have terminal degrees, 11% minority, 37% women. **Part-time faculty:** 202 total; 31% have terminal degrees, 5% minority, 52% women. **Class size:** 42% < 20, 50% 20-39, 7% 40-49, less than 1% 50-99.

**Freshman class profile.** 3,775 applied, 3,460 admitted, 726 enrolled.

| Mid 50% test scores | | Rank in top quarter: | 33% |
|---|---|---|---|
| SAT critical reading: | 450-540 | Rank in top tenth: | 9% |
| SAT math: | 460-580 | Return as sophomores: | 79% |
| SAT writing: | 440-540 | Out-of-state: | 22% |
| ACT composite: | 20-24 | Live on campus: | 79% |
| GPA 3.75 or higher: | 18% | International: | 4% |
| GPA 3.50-3.74: | 24% | Fraternities: | 3% |
| GPA 3.0-3.49: | 32% | Sororities: | 9% |
| GPA 2.0-2.99: | 26% | | |

**Basis for selection.** Academic potential, high school GPA, class rank, test scores, and evidence of motivation important. Interview required of restricted-status applicants, recommended for all others.

**High school preparation.** College-preparatory program required. 16 units required; 18 recommended. Required and recommended units include English 4, mathematics 3, social studies 4, science 2, foreign language 2 and academic electives 3.

**2010-2011 Annual costs.** Tuition/fees: $21,550. Room/board: $10,660. Books/supplies: $1,200. Personal expenses: $1,500.

**2009-2010 Financial aid. Need-based:** 647 full-time freshmen applied for aid; 577 were judged to have need; 577 of these received aid. Average need met was 75%. Average scholarship/grant was $13,211; average loan $3,960. 47% of total undergraduate aid awarded as scholarships/grants, 53% as loans/jobs. **Non-need-based:** Awarded to 764 full-time undergraduates, including 220 freshmen. Scholarships awarded for academics, athletics.

**Application procedures. Admission:** Priority date 12/1; deadline 7/1 (postmark date). $30 fee, may be waived for applicants with need, free for online applicants. Admission notification on a rolling basis beginning on or about 8/1. Must reply by May 1 or within 3 week(s) if notified thereafter. **Financial aid:** No deadline. FAFSA required. Applicants notified on a rolling basis starting 3/15.

**Academics. Special study options:** Cooperative education, cross-registration, distance learning, double major, honors, independent study, internships, study abroad, teacher certification program, weekend college. **Credit/placement by examination:** AP, CLEP, SAT, ACT, institutional tests. 30 credit hours maximum toward bachelor's degree. **Support services:** Pre-admission summer program, reduced course load, remedial instruction, study skills assistance, tutoring.

**Majors. Biology:** General. **Business:** Accounting, actuarial science, business admin, finance, hospitality admin, management information systems, marketing, organizational behavior. **Communications:** General. **Computer sciences:** Information systems. **Conservation:** Environmental science. **Education:** Business, elementary. **Engineering:** Manufacturing, software. **Health:** Health services admin, medical radiologic technology/radiation therapy, nursing (RN). **Math:** Applied. **Parks/recreation:** Sports admin. **Psychology:** General. **Social sciences:** General, economics. **Visual/performing arts:** Design. **Other:** Competitive intelligence systems, information technology project management, Professional communications.

**Most popular majors.** Business/marketing 54%, communications/journalism 9%, health sciences 6%, parks/recreation 7%.

**Computing on campus.** 300 workstations in dormitories, library, computer center, student center. Dormitories wired for high-speed internet access and linked to campus network. Commuter students can connect to campus network. Online course registration, online library, helpline, wireless network available.

**Student life. Freshman orientation:** Mandatory, $100 fee. Preregistration for classes offered. 3-day program. **Housing:** Coed dorms, single-sex dorms, special housing for disabled, apartments, wellness housing available. $100 nonrefundable deposit, deadline 5/1. **Activities:** Bands, campus ministries, choral groups, drama, international student organizations, literary magazine, musical theater, radio station, student government, student newspaper, TV station, minority student organizations, campus activities board, inter-residence hall council, inter-fraternity council/Panhellenic council, honor societies, major-related organizations, campus Republicans and Democrats, community service and volunteer organizations.

**Athletics.** NCAA. **Intercollegiate:** Basketball, field hockey W, football (tackle) M, golf, ice hockey, lacrosse, rowing (crew) W, soccer, softball W, tennis, track and field, volleyball W. **Intramural:** Basketball, football (non-tackle) M, softball, volleyball W. **Team name:** Colonials.

**Student services.** Adult student services, alcohol/substance abuse counseling, chaplain/spiritual director, career counseling, services for economically disadvantaged, student employment services, financial aid counseling, health services, minority student services, personal counseling, placement for graduates, veterans' counselor, women's services. **Physically disabled:** Services for visually, speech, hearing impaired. **Learning disabled:** Comprehensive services available.

**Contact.**   E-mail: admissionsoffice@rmu.edu
Phone: (412) 397-5200 Toll-free number: (800) 762-0097
Fax: (412) 397-2425
Kellie Laurenzi, Dean of Admissions, Robert Morris University, 6001 University Boulevard, Moon Township, PA 15108-1189

## Rosemont College
### Rosemont, Pennsylvania
**www.rosemont.edu**

CB member
CB code: 2763

- Private 4-year liberal arts college affiliated with Roman Catholic Church
- Residential campus in small town
- 543 degree-seeking undergraduates: 20% part-time, 80% women, 46% African American, 4% Asian American, 7% Hispanic American, 1% international
- 384 degree-seeking graduate students
- 54% of applicants admitted
- SAT or ACT required
- 59% graduate within 6 years

**General.** Founded in 1921. Regionally accredited. **Degrees:** 144 bachelor's awarded; master's offered. **ROTC:** Army, Air Force. **Location:** 11 miles from Philadelphia. **Calendar:** Semester, limited summer session. **Full-time faculty:** 29 total; 93% have terminal degrees, 62% women. **Part-time faculty:** 108 total; 83% have terminal degrees, 15% minority, 65% women. **Class size:** 82% < 20, 18% 20-39.

**Freshman class profile.** 1,104 applied, 595 admitted, 177 enrolled.

| Mid 50% test scores | | | |
|---|---|---|---|
| SAT critical reading: | 400-510 | GPA 2.0-2.99: | 48% |
| SAT math: | 400-490 | End year in good standing: | 95% |
| SAT writing: | 380-500 | Return as sophomores: | 63% |
| GPA 3.75 or higher: | 12% | Out-of-state: | 30% |
| GPA 3.50-3.74: | 10% | Live on campus: | 90% |
| GPA 3.0-3.49: | 30% | International: | 2% |

**Basis for selection.** School achievement record and curriculum, recommendations, test scores, extracurricular activities strongly considered. Interview recommended. **Homeschooled:** Statement describing homeschool structure and mission, transcript of courses and grades, letter of recommendation (nonparent) required.

**High school preparation.** College-preparatory program recommended. 18 units required. Required units include English 4, mathematics 2, social studies 2, history 2, science 2 (laboratory 2), foreign language 2 and academic electives 2.

**2009-2010 Annual costs.** Tuition/fees: $25,000. Room/board: $10,580. Books/supplies: $1,500. Personal expenses: $1,000.

**2009-2010 Financial aid. Need-based:** 168 full-time freshmen applied for aid; 165 were judged to have need; 165 of these received aid. Average need met was 75%. Average scholarship/grant was $22,462; average loan $3,323. 74% of total undergraduate aid awarded as scholarships/grants, 26% as loans/jobs. **Non-need-based:** Scholarships awarded for academics, art, religious affiliation.

**Application procedures. Admission:** No deadline. $35 fee, may be waived for applicants with need, free for online applicants. Admission notification on a rolling basis. Must reply by May 1 or within 2 week(s) if notified thereafter. $350 deposit required if student plans to live on campus. $200 deposit if student plans to commute to campus. **Financial aid:** Priority date 2/15; no closing date. FAFSA required. Applicants notified on a rolling basis starting 2/15; must reply within 4 week(s) of notification.

**Academics. Special study options:** Accelerated study, combined bachelor's/graduate degree, cross-registration, distance learning, double major, ESL, exchange student, honors, independent study, internships, liberal arts/career combination, student-designed major, study abroad, teacher certification program, Washington semester. **Credit/placement by examination:** AP, CLEP, IB, SAT, ACT, institutional tests. 30 credit hours maximum toward bachelor's degree. Students may be exempted if they demonstrate mastery of subject as determined by particular department. **Support services:** Learning center, pre-admission summer program, reduced course load, remedial instruction, study skills assistance, tutoring, writing center.

**Majors. Area/ethnic studies:** Women's. **Biology:** General, biochemistry. **Business:** General, accounting, business admin, communications, hospitality admin, human resources, management science, managerial economics, marketing, organizational behavior. **Communications:** General. **Education:** Elementary, secondary. **Foreign languages:** General, French, German, Italian, Spanish. **History:** General. **Liberal arts:** Arts/sciences, humanities. **Math:** General. **Philosophy/religion:** Philosophy, religion. **Physical sciences:** Chemistry. **Protective services:** Criminal justice. **Psychology:** General. **Social sciences:** General, economics, political science, sociology. **Visual/performing arts:** Art history/conservation, studio arts.

**Most popular majors.** Biology 6%, business/marketing 37%, psychology 7%, social sciences 15%, visual/performing arts 11%.

**Computing on campus.** 100 workstations in dormitories, library, computer center, student center. Dormitories wired for high-speed internet access and linked to campus network. Commuter students can connect to campus network. Online course registration, online library, helpline, student web hosting, wireless network available.

**Student life. Freshman orientation:** Mandatory, $280 fee. Preregistration for classes offered. Orientation approximately 3 days; includes academics component. **Housing:** Guaranteed on-campus for all undergraduates. Single-sex dorms, wellness housing available. $150 fully refundable deposit, deadline 5/1. **Activities:** Bands, campus ministries, choral groups, dance, drama, international student organizations, literary magazine, music ensembles, Model UN, musical theater, opera, radio station, student government, student newspaper, premed club, politics club, Rosemont Alcohol and Drug Awareness Resource, multicultural society, Best Buddies, Triad, art society.

**Athletics.** NCAA. **Intercollegiate:** Basketball, field hockey W, lacrosse W, soccer M, softball W, tennis, volleyball W. **Team name:** Ravens.

**Student services.** Adult student services, alcohol/substance abuse counseling, chaplain/spiritual director, career counseling, student employment services, financial aid counseling, health services, legal services, minority student services, on-campus daycare, personal counseling, placement for graduates, veterans' counselor, women's services. **Physically disabled:** Services for visually, speech, hearing impaired.

**Contact.**   E-mail: admissions@rosemont.edu
Phone: (610) 526-2966 Toll-free number: (800) 331-0708
Fax: (610) 520-4399
Chuck Walz, Vice President for Enrollment Management, Rosemont College, 1400 Montgomery Avenue, Rosemont, PA 19010-1699

## St. Charles Borromeo Seminary - Overbrook
### Wynnewood, Pennsylvania
**www.scs.edu**

CB code: 2794

- Private 4-year seminary college for men affiliated with Roman Catholic Church
- Residential campus in large town
- 57 degree-seeking undergraduates: 2% African American, 4% Asian American, 7% Hispanic American, 4% international
- 107 degree-seeking graduate students
- 100% of applicants admitted
- Application essay, interview required
- 33% graduate within 6 years

**General.** Founded in 1832. Regionally accredited; also accredited by ATS. College and theology divisions enroll full-time seminary students. Religious studies division enrolls part-time undergraduate and graduate students who wish to pursue theological studies. Part-time programs open to men and women. **Degrees:** 11 bachelor's awarded; master's offered. **Location:** 4 miles from central Philadelphia. **Calendar:** Semester, limited summer session. **Full-time faculty:** 10 total; 60% have terminal degrees, 30% women. **Part-time faculty:** 12 total; 8% have terminal degrees, 25% minority, 50% women. **Class size:** 100% < 20. **Special facilities:** Rare book and special collections.

**Freshman class profile.** 13 applied, 13 admitted, 13 enrolled.

| Mid 50% test scores | | | |
|---|---|---|---|
| SAT critical reading: | 460-660 | Rank in top tenth: | 28% |
| SAT math: | 410-580 | Return as sophomores: | 100% |
| SAT writing: | 410-670 | Out-of-state: | 15% |
| Rank in top quarter: | 42% | Live on campus: | 100% |

**Basis for selection.** Sponsorship by diocese or religious community required for admission to college and theology divisions. Seminary applicants holding bachelor's degree from accredited institution may enter special pretheology program. SAT or ACT recommended. **Homeschooled:** Transcript of courses and grades, letter of recommendation (nonparent) required.

**High school preparation.** College-preparatory program recommended. 20 units recommended. Recommended units include English 4, mathematics 3, social studies 3, science 3 and foreign language 3. 3 to 4 units of religious education recommended. GED accepted on individual basis.

**2009-2010 Annual costs.** Tuition/fees: $15,190. Room/board: $9,560. Books/supplies: $800. Personal expenses: $600.

**2009-2010 Financial aid. Need-based:** Average need met was 81%. Average scholarship/grant was $16,517; average loan $2,990. 93% of total undergraduate aid awarded as scholarships/grants, 7% as loans/jobs. **Non-need-based:** Scholarships awarded for religious affiliation.

**Application procedures. Admission:** Priority date 3/1; deadline 7/15. No application fee. Admission notification on a rolling basis beginning on or about 4/1. Level of admission dependent on academic background in philosophy, theology, and classical languages. **Financial aid:** No deadline. FAFSA, institutional form required. Applicants notified on a rolling basis starting 6/1; must reply within 4 week(s) of notification.

**Academics.** Strong emphasis on philosophy, theology, classical languages, and liberal arts. **Special study options:** Accelerated study, ESL, independent study. **Credit/placement by examination:** AP, CLEP, institutional tests. 12 credit hours maximum toward bachelor's degree. **Support services:** Reduced course load, study skills assistance, tutoring.

**Majors. Philosophy/religion:** Philosophy.

**Computing on campus.** 60 workstations in library, computer center. Online library available.

**Student life. Freshman orientation:** Mandatory. **Policies:** Religious observance required. **Housing:** Guaranteed on-campus for all undergraduates. Wellness housing available. On-campus housing available for seminarians in college and theology divisions. On-campus housing available to students in religious studies division during summer session. **Activities:** Choral groups, drama, music ensembles, student government, student newspaper, Seminarians for Life.

**Athletics. Intramural:** Basketball M, football (tackle) M, soccer M, volleyball M.

**Student services.** Chaplain/spiritual director, financial aid counseling, health services, personal counseling.

**Contact.** E-mail: frdd@adphila.org
Phone: (610) 785-6271 Fax: (610) 617-9267
Rev. David Diamond, Vice Rector, St. Charles Borromeo Seminary - Overbrook, 100 East Wynnewood Road, Wynnewood, PA 19096

---

## St. Francis University

**Loretto, Pennsylvania**                                   **CB member**
**www.francis.edu**                                         **CB code: 2797**

- Private 4-year university and liberal arts college affiliated with Roman Catholic Church
- Residential campus in rural community
- 1,643 degree-seeking undergraduates: 5% part-time, 60% women, 5% African American, 1% Asian American, 1% Hispanic American, 1% international
- 621 degree-seeking graduate students
- 77% of applicants admitted
- SAT or ACT (ACT writing recommended), application essay required
- 69% graduate within 6 years

**General.** Founded in 1847. Regionally accredited. **Degrees:** 310 bachelor's, 7 associate awarded; master's, professional offered. **ROTC:** Army. **Location:** 90 miles from Pittsburgh, 20 miles from Altoona. **Calendar:** Semester, limited summer session. **Full-time faculty:** 110 total; 58% have terminal degrees, 3% minority, 53% women. **Part-time faculty:** 115 total; 2% minority, 37% women. **Class size:** 48% < 20, 46% 20-39, 3% 40-49, 3% 50-99. **Special facilities:** Rural health and wellness institute, small business development center, global competitiveness center, Southern Alleghenies art museum, center for remote and medically underserved areas, nature trail.

**Freshman class profile.** 1,501 applied, 1,161 admitted, 433 enrolled.

| Mid 50% test scores | | | |
|---|---|---|---|
| SAT critical reading: | 450-560 | Rank in top quarter: | 54% |
| SAT math: | 470-580 | Rank in top tenth: | 26% |
| SAT writing: | 440-550 | Return as sophomores: | 88% |
| ACT composite: | 19-25 | Out-of-state: | 29% |
| GPA 3.75 or higher: | 36% | Live on campus: | 90% |
| GPA 3.50-3.74: | 21% | International: | 3% |
| GPA 3.0-3.49: | 27% | Fraternities: | 13% |
| GPA 2.0-2.99: | 16% | Sororities: | 10% |

**Basis for selection.** High school record most important, followed by test scores, counselor's recommendations, major area of interest, activities, honors. Relationship to alumni also considered. Campus visit highly recommended. Admission to professional track programs places more weight on test scores. Interview highly recommended. Physician assistant and physical therapy students must complete essay directed at their chosen discipline. **Learning Disabled:** Send documentation to the Academic Center for Enrichment.

**High school preparation.** College-preparatory program recommended. 16 units required. Required and recommended units include English 4, mathematics 2-4, social studies 2, history 1, science 1-4, foreign language 2, computer science 1, visual/performing arts 1 and academic electives 7. One natural science for nonscience majors, 2 for science majors also required. One science unit must include laboratory. Remaining units in academic electives. 4 math and 2 science required for physician assistant and occupational therapy. 4 math and 4 science required for physical therapy.

**2009-2010 Annual costs.** Tuition/fees: $25,554. Room/board: $8,716. Books/supplies: $1,500. Personal expenses: $3,050.

**2008-2009 Financial aid. Need-based:** 415 full-time freshmen applied for aid; 368 were judged to have need; 365 of these received aid. Average need met was 67%. Average scholarship/grant was $15,254; average loan $2,732. 61% of total undergraduate aid awarded as scholarships/grants, 39% as loans/jobs. **Non-need-based:** Awarded to 549 full-time undergraduates, including 155 freshmen. Scholarships awarded for academics, alumni affiliation, athletics, music/drama, religious affiliation.

**Application procedures. Admission:** Priority date 3/1; deadline 7/30 (postmark date). $30 fee, may be waived for applicants with need. Admission notification on a rolling basis. Application closing date for physical therapy, occupational therapy, and physician assistant programs January 15. Notification by February 1. **Financial aid:** Priority date 5/1; no closing date. FAFSA required. Applicants notified on a rolling basis starting 3/1.

**Academics. Special study options:** Combined bachelor's/graduate degree, cooperative education, distance learning, double major, honors, independent study, internships, liberal arts/career combination, semester at sea, student-designed major, study abroad, teacher certification program, Washington semester. **Credit/placement by examination:** AP, CLEP, IB, SAT, ACT, institutional tests. 15 credit hours maximum toward associate degree, 30 toward bachelor's. **Support services:** Learning center, pre-admission summer program, reduced course load, remedial instruction, study skills assistance, tutoring, writing center.

**Honors college/program.** 3.25 GPA, 1150 SAT (580 Critical Reading, exclusive of Writing), and position in top 20% of high school class required. About 40 applicants admitted.

**Majors. Area/ethnic studies:** American, French. **Biology:** General, marine. **Business:** Accounting, business admin, finance, management information systems, marketing. **Communications:** General, public relations. **Computer sciences:** General, computer science, information systems, programming. **Conservation:** Environmental science, environmental studies, forest management, forestry. **Education:** General, biology, chemistry, elementary, English, foreign languages, French, history, mathematics, multi-level teacher, psychology, secondary, social science, social studies, Spanish, speech. **Engineering:** General, environmental. **Foreign languages:** General, French, Spanish. **Health:** Clinical lab technology, nursing (RN), physician assistant. **History:** General. **Interdisciplinary:** Biological/physical sciences, math/computer science. **Math:** General. **Philosophy/religion:** Philosophy, religion. **Physical sciences:** Chemistry. **Psychology:** General. **Public administration:** General, social work. **Social sciences:** Economics, political science, sociology. **Other:** Exercise physiology.

**Most popular majors.** Biology 7%, business/marketing 25%, education 11%, health sciences 33%, psychology 7%.

**Computing on campus.** PC or laptop required. 40 workstations in dormitories, library, computer center, student center. Dormitories wired for high-speed internet access and linked to campus network. Commuter students can connect to campus network. Online library, helpline, repair service, wireless network available.

**Student life. Freshman orientation:** Mandatory. Preregistration for classes offered. Held at various times during spring and summer. **Policies:** All students required to live in campus-owned housing unless commuting from home. **Housing:** Guaranteed on-campus for all undergraduates. Coed dorms, single-sex dorms, special housing for disabled, apartments, fraternity/sorority housing, wellness housing available. $100 deposit, deadline 5/1. **Activities:** Bands, campus ministries, choral groups, drama, music ensembles, musical theater, radio station, student government, student newspaper, TV station, Secular Franciscan Order, student activities organization, multicultural awareness club, Historians' Round Table, Habitat for Humanity, Peace and Justice Center, current affairs club, prelaw club.

**Athletics.** NCAA. **Intercollegiate:** Basketball, bowling W, cross-country, field hockey W, football (tackle) M, golf, lacrosse W, soccer, softball W, swimming W, tennis, track and field, volleyball. **Intramural:** Basketball, cross-country, football (non-tackle), ice hockey, skiing, soccer, softball, swimming, table tennis, tennis, track and field, volleyball. **Team name:** Red Flash.

**Student services.** Adult student services, alcohol/substance abuse counseling, chaplain/spiritual director, career counseling, student employment services, financial aid counseling, health services, minority student services, personal counseling, placement for graduates, veterans' counselor.

**Contact.** E-mail: admissions@francis.edu
Phone: (814) 472-3100 Toll-free number: (800) 342-5732
Fax: (814) 472-3335
Erin McCloskey, Vice President for Enrollment Management, St. Francis University, Box 600, Loretto, PA 15940

## Saint Joseph's University
**Philadelphia, Pennsylvania**  CB member
www.sju.edu  CB code: 2801

- Private 4-year university affiliated with Roman Catholic Church
- Residential campus in very large city
- 5,188 degree-seeking undergraduates: 13% part-time, 52% women, 7% African American, 2% Asian American, 4% Hispanic American, 1% international
- 2,578 degree-seeking graduate students
- 82% of applicants admitted
- SAT or ACT (ACT writing optional), application essay required
- 78% graduate within 6 years

**General.** Founded in 1851. Regionally accredited. Founded by the Society of Jesus. **Degrees:** 1,108 bachelor's, 7 associate awarded; master's, doctoral offered. **ROTC:** Army, Naval, Air Force. **Location:** 8 miles from downtown. **Calendar:** Semester, extensive summer session. **Full-time faculty:** 284 total; 90% have terminal degrees, 13% minority, 39% women. **Part-time faculty:** 372 total; 9% minority, 42% women. **Class size:** 35% < 20, 54% 20-39, 9% 40-49, 1% 50-99.

**Freshman class profile.** 6,520 applied, 5,370 admitted, 1,192 enrolled.

| Mid 50% test scores | | | |
|---|---|---|---|
| SAT critical reading: | 510-600 | GPA 2.0-2.99: | 17% |
| SAT math: | 510-620 | Rank in top quarter: | 55% |
| SAT writing: | 510-610 | Rank in top tenth: | 23% |
| ACT composite: | 21-26 | Return as sophomores: | 86% |
| GPA 3.75 or higher: | 25% | Out-of-state: | 61% |
| GPA 3.50-3.74: | 19% | Live on campus: | 96% |
| GPA 3.0-3.49: | 39% | International: | 1% |

**Basis for selection.** GED not accepted. Careful consideration given to applicant's academic GPA and rigor of high school record. Important factors include application essay, counselor or teacher recommendations, character and personal qualities.

**High school preparation.** College-preparatory program recommended. 12 units required. Required units include English 4, mathematics 3, history 1, science 2 (laboratory 1) and foreign language 2.

**2009-2010 Annual costs.** Tuition/fees: $34,090. Room/board: $11,575. Books/supplies: $1,500. Personal expenses: $2,500.

**2009-2010 Financial aid. Need-based:** 888 full-time freshmen applied for aid; 650 were judged to have need; 650 of these received aid. Average need met was 83%. Average scholarship/grant was $16,206; average loan $4,063. 59% of total undergraduate aid awarded as scholarships/grants, 41% as loans/jobs. **Non-need-based:** Awarded to 3,976 full-time undergraduates, including 1,083 freshmen. Scholarships awarded for academics, alumni affiliation, art, athletics, minority status, music/drama, ROTC.

**Application procedures. Admission:** Closing date 2/1 (postmark date). $60 fee, may be waived for applicants with need. Admission notification 3/15. Must reply by May 1 or within 2 week(s) if notified thereafter. **Financial aid:** Priority date 2/15; no closing date. FAFSA required. Applicants notified on a rolling basis starting 3/1; must reply by 5/1.

**Academics. Special study options:** Accelerated study, combined bachelor's/graduate degree, cooperative education, distance learning, double major, dual enrollment of high school students, ESL, exchange student, honors, independent study, internships, student-designed major, study abroad, teacher certification program, Washington semester, weekend college. Jesuit student exchange. **Credit/placement by examination:** AP, CLEP, IB, institutional tests. **Support services:** Learning center, pre-admission summer program, reduced course load, study skills assistance, tutoring, writing center.

**Majors. Area/ethnic studies:** European, French. **Biology:** General, biochemistry. **Business:** Accounting, actuarial science, business admin, finance, international, international marketing, management information systems, marketing, merchandising, purchasing, special products marketing. **Communications:** General. **Computer sciences:** General, information systems. **Conservation:** Environmental studies. **Education:** Art, elementary, English, foreign languages, mathematics, science, secondary, social studies, special. **Foreign languages:** French, German, Italian, Latin, Spanish. **Health:** Facilities admin, health services. **History:** General. **Legal studies:** General. **Liberal arts:** Arts/sciences, humanities. **Math:** General. **Philosophy/religion:** Philosophy, religion. **Physical sciences:** Chemistry, physics. **Psychology:** General, industrial. **Public administration:** General. **Social sciences:** General, criminology, economics, international relations, political science, sociology. **Visual/performing arts:** General.

**Most popular majors.** Business/marketing 50%, education 6%, English 6%, psychology 6%, social sciences 11%.

**Computing on campus.** 725 workstations in dormitories, library, computer center, student center. Dormitories wired for high-speed internet access and linked to campus network. Commuter students can connect to campus network. Online course registration, online library, helpline, repair service, student web hosting, wireless network available.

**Student life. Freshman orientation:** Available, $225 fee. **Housing:** Guaranteed on-campus for freshmen. Coed dorms, single-sex dorms, special housing for disabled, apartments, wellness housing available. $250 nonrefundable deposit, deadline 5/1. **Activities:** Bands, campus ministries, choral groups, dance, drama, film society, international student organizations, literary magazine, music ensembles, musical theater, radio station, student government, student newspaper, Black student union, Caribbean students association, Hand-in-Hand, College Democrats, College Republicans, Habitat for Humanity, Students for Life, community service weekly programs.

**Athletics.** NCAA. **Intercollegiate:** Baseball M, basketball, cross-country, field hockey W, golf M, lacrosse, rowing (crew), soccer, softball W, tennis, track and field. **Intramural:** Basketball, football (non-tackle), racquetball, soccer, softball, tennis, volleyball. **Team name:** Hawks.

**Student services.** Adult student services, alcohol/substance abuse counseling, chaplain/spiritual director, career counseling, services for economically disadvantaged, student employment services, financial aid counseling, health services, minority student services, personal counseling, women's services. **Physically disabled:** Services for visually, speech, hearing impaired. **Learning disabled:** Comprehensive services available.

**Contact.** E-mail: admit@sju.edu
Phone: (610) 660-1300 Toll-free number: (888) 232-4295
Fax: (610) 660-1314
Maureen Mathis, Executive Director of Undergraduate Admissions, Saint Joseph's University, 5600 City Avenue, Philadelphia, PA 19131

## St. Vincent College
**Latrobe, Pennsylvania**  CB member
www.stvincent.edu  CB code: 2808

- Private 4-year liberal arts college affiliated with Roman Catholic Church
- Residential campus in large town
- 1,653 degree-seeking undergraduates: 2% part-time, 46% women, 6% African American, 1% Asian American, 2% Hispanic American, 1% international
- 232 degree-seeking graduate students
- 67% of applicants admitted
- SAT or ACT (ACT writing optional), application essay required
- 73% graduate within 6 years; 32% enter graduate study

**General.** Founded in 1846. Regionally accredited. Affiliated with Order of Saint Benedict. **Degrees:** 397 bachelor's awarded; master's offered. **ROTC:** Army, Air Force. **Location:** 35 miles from Pittsburgh. **Calendar:** Semester, extensive summer session. **Special facilities:** Planetarium, observatory, radio telescope, wetlands program, rare book collection, spectrophotometer, spectrometer, physiograph workstations, nature reserve, digital imaging lab, Fred Rogers archives.

**Freshman class profile.** 1,765 applied, 1,191 admitted, 448 enrolled.

| Mid 50% test scores | | | |
|---|---|---|---|
| SAT critical reading: | 480-590 | GPA 3.0-3.49: | 25% |
| SAT math: | 490-600 | GPA 2.0-2.99: | 17% |
| SAT writing: | 470-590 | Rank in top quarter: | 51% |
| ACT composite: | 20-26 | Rank in top tenth: | 17% |
| GPA 3.75 or higher: | 35% | Return as sophomores: | 86% |
| GPA 3.50-3.74: | 23% | Out-of-state: | 23% |
| | | Live on campus: | 88% |

**Basis for selection.** High school curriculum and grades most important; class rank, test scores, and essay important. Recommendations from school counselor considered. Interview recommended for all; audition required for music programs; portfolio required for art programs. **Learning Disabled:** All prior test results related to learning disability should be submitted.

**High school preparation.** College-preparatory program recommended. 16 units required; 20 recommended. Required and recommended units include English 4, mathematics 3, social studies 3, science 1-3 (laboratory 1), foreign language 2 and academic electives 5. One plane geometry, 1 intermediate algebra, .5 trigonometry, and 1 physics required for 3-2 engineering program applicants.

**2009-2010 Annual costs.** Tuition/fees: $26,146. Room/board: $8,184. Books/supplies: $1,200. Personal expenses: $1,600.

**2009-2010 Financial aid. Non-need-based:** Scholarships awarded for academics, alumni affiliation, leadership, minority status, religious affiliation.

**Application procedures. Admission:** Priority date 2/1; deadline 4/1 (postmark date). $25 fee, may be waived for applicants with need, free for online applicants. Admission notification on a rolling basis beginning on or about 10/1. Must reply by May 1 or within 3 week(s) if notified thereafter. **Financial aid:** Priority date 3/1, closing date 5/1. FAFSA required. Applicants notified on a rolling basis starting 3/1; must reply within 2 week(s) of notification.

**Academics.** College attempts to place career orientation in context of broader human and religious values with emphasis on liberal arts core curriculum. **Special study options:** Accelerated study, combined bachelor's/ graduate degree, cooperative education, cross-registration, double major, dual enrollment of high school students, external degree, honors, independent study, internships, study abroad, teacher certification program. 3-2 engineering BA/BS program with University of Pittsburgh, Catholic University of America, Pennsylvania State; 4-1 BS/MBA, 3-3 BA/JD, 3-2 occupational therapy, physical therapy, and physician's assistant, 2-4 pharmacy programs with Duquesne University; 3-4 podiatry with Ohio College of Pediatric Medicine and Pennsylvania College of Pediatric Medicine. **Credit/placement by examination:** AP, CLEP, IB, institutional tests. 62 credit hours maximum toward bachelor's degree. **Support services:** Learning center, preadmission summer program, remedial instruction, study skills assistance, tutoring, writing center.

**Majors. Biology:** General, biochemistry, bioinformatics. **Business:** Accounting, business admin, finance, international, marketing. **Communications:** General. **Computer sciences:** General. **Conservation:** Environmental science, management/policy. **Education:** Art, business, elementary, physics, psychology. **Engineering:** General. **Foreign languages:** French, Spanish. **Health:** Predental, premedicine, prepharmacy, preveterinary. **History:** General. **Liberal arts:** Arts/sciences. **Math:** General. **Philosophy/religion:** Philosophy. **Physical sciences:** Chemistry, physics. **Psychology:** General, educational. **Public administration:** Policy analysis. **Social sciences:** Anthropology, economics, political science, sociology. **Theology:** Religious ed, theology. **Visual/performing arts:** Art history/conservation, arts management, dramatic, graphic design, music performance, studio arts.

**Most popular majors.** Biology 10%, business/marketing 29%, communications/journalism 6%, education 6%, English 7%, history 8%, psychology 9%, social sciences 8%.

**Computing on campus.** 286 workstations in dormitories, library, computer center, student center. Dormitories wired for high-speed internet access and linked to campus network. Online course registration, helpline, repair service, wireless network available.

**Student life. Freshman orientation:** Mandatory, $125 fee. 4-weeks of activities are planned to acclimate students to college on academic and social levels. Upperclassmen volunteer to serve as mentors to first-year students through the program. **Housing:** Guaranteed on-campus for freshmen.

Coed dorms, apartments available. $200 nonrefundable deposit, deadline 5/1. **Activities:** Pep band, campus ministries, choral groups, dance, drama, international student organizations, literary magazine, music ensembles, musical theater, radio station, student government, student newspaper, TV station, Respect for Life club, Democrats club, College Republicans, Students for Social Justice, pre-law society, Student Council for Exceptional Children, Italian club, Habitat for Humanity.

**Athletics.** NCAA. **Intercollegiate:** Baseball M, basketball, cross-country, field hockey W, football (tackle) M, golf, lacrosse, soccer, softball W, swimming, tennis, track and field M, volleyball W. **Intramural:** Basketball, football (non-tackle), soccer, softball, table tennis, volleyball. **Team name:** Bearcats.

**Student services.** Adult student services, alcohol/substance abuse counseling, chaplain/spiritual director, career counseling, student employment services, financial aid counseling, health services, minority student services, personal counseling, placement for graduates. **Physically disabled:** Services for visually, speech, hearing impaired. **Learning disabled:** Comprehensive services available.

**Contact.** E-mail: admission@stvincent.edu
Phone: (724) 805-2500 Toll-free number: (800) 782-5549
Fax: (724) 532-5069
David Collins, Assistant Vice President of Admission and Financial Aid, St. Vincent College, 300 Fraser Purchase Road, Latrobe, PA 15650-2690

---

## Seton Hill University
**Greensburg, Pennsylvania**    CB member
**www.setonhill.edu**    CB code: 2812

- Private 4-year university and liberal arts college affiliated with Roman Catholic Church
- Residential campus in large town
- 1,483 degree-seeking undergraduates: 9% part-time, 62% women, 9% African American, 1% Asian American, 1% Hispanic American, 2% international
- 413 degree-seeking graduate students
- 66% of applicants admitted
- Application essay required
- 59% graduate within 6 years; 23% enter graduate study

**General.** Founded in 1918. Regionally accredited. **Degrees:** 272 bachelor's awarded; master's offered. **ROTC:** Army, Air Force. **Location:** 35 miles from Pittsburgh. **Calendar:** Semester, limited summer session. **Full-time faculty:** 78 total; 85% have terminal degrees, 6% minority, 54% women. **Part-time faculty:** 107 total; 33% have terminal degrees, less than 1% minority, 43% women. **Class size:** 54% < 20, 42% 20-39, 3% 40-49, less than 1% 50-99. **Special facilities:** Child development center, kindergarten, women in business center, Catholic Holocaust education center.

**Freshman class profile.** 1,729 applied, 1,143 admitted, 299 enrolled.

| Mid 50% test scores | | | |
|---|---|---|---|
| SAT critical reading: | 420-540 | GPA 2.0-2.99: | 33% |
| SAT math: | 430-560 | Rank in top quarter: | 44% |
| SAT writing: | 420-540 | Rank in top tenth: | 18% |
| ACT composite: | 17-24 | End year in good standing: | 94% |
| GPA 3.75 or higher: | 26% | Return as sophomores: | 77% |
| GPA 3.50-3.74: | 17% | Out-of-state: | 25% |
| GPA 3.0-3.49: | 22% | Live on campus: | 85% |
| | | International: | 3% |

**Basis for selection.** School achievement record most important, followed by test scores and recommendations. Applicants from minorities or low-income families encouraged, accepted on basis of motivation and potential. SAT or ACT recommended. Students who have not taken SAT or ACT may submit 2 graded writing samples for consideration. Interview recommended for all; audition required for music, theater programs; portfolio required for art program. Additional application required for physician assistant and BS/DO and BS/DPharm programs. **Homeschooled:** Must provide SAT/ACT scores and official transcript issued by a school district or agency approving the curriculum, or GED.

**High school preparation.** College-preparatory program recommended. 15 units required. Required and recommended units include English 4, mathematics 2, social studies 2, science 1 (laboratory 1), foreign language 2 and academic electives 4. 4 math units recommended for science majors.

**2009-2010 Annual costs.** Tuition/fees: $26,622. Room/board: $8,550. Books/supplies: $1,000. Personal expenses: $2,500.

**2009-2010 Financial aid. Need-based:** 260 full-time freshmen applied for aid; 239 were judged to have need; 238 of these received aid. Average need met was 80%. Average scholarship/grant was $19,367; average loan

$4,672. 68% of total undergraduate aid awarded as scholarships/grants, 32% as loans/jobs. **Non-need-based:** Awarded to 372 full-time undergraduates, including 101 freshmen. Scholarships awarded for academics, alumni affiliation, art, athletics, job skills, music/drama, religious affiliation, ROTC.

**Application procedures. Admission:** Priority date 5/1; deadline 8/15 (postmark date). $35 fee, may be waived for applicants with need, free for online applicants. Admission notification on a rolling basis beginning on or about 9/1. **Financial aid:** Priority date 5/1; no closing date. FAFSA, institutional form required. Applicants notified on a rolling basis starting 11/15; must reply by 5/1 or within 2 week(s) of notification.

**Academics. Special study options:** Accelerated study, combined bachelor's/graduate degree, cross-registration, distance learning, double major, ESL, exchange student, honors, independent study, internships, liberal arts/career combination, New York semester, semester at sea, student-designed major, study abroad, teacher certification program, United Nations semester, Washington semester, weekend college. **Credit/placement by examination:** AP, CLEP, IB, SAT, ACT. 30 credit hours maximum toward bachelor's degree. **Support services:** Learning center, pre-admission summer program, reduced course load, remedial instruction, study skills assistance, tutoring, writing center.

**Majors. Biology:** General, biochemistry. **Business:** Accounting, actuarial science, business admin, entrepreneurial studies, finance, hospitality admin, human resources, international, management information systems, marketing, sales/distribution. **Communications:** General, journalism. **Computer sciences:** Computer science. **Education:** Art, biology, chemistry, English, family/consumer sciences, foreign languages, mathematics, music, Spanish. **Engineering:** General. **Family/consumer sciences:** General, child care, child development. **Foreign languages:** Spanish. **Health:** Art therapy, clinical lab science, dietetics, music therapy, nursing (RN), physician assistant. **History:** General. **Legal studies:** Prelaw. **Math:** General. **Parks/recreation:** Sports admin. **Philosophy/religion:** Religion. **Physical sciences:** Chemistry. **Protective services:** Criminal justice, forensics. **Psychology:** General. **Public administration:** Human services, social work. **Social sciences:** Economics, international relations, political science, sociology. **Theology:** Sacred music. **Visual/performing arts:** Acting, art history/conservation, arts management, ceramics, commercial/advertising art, dramatic, drawing, metal/jewelry, music performance, painting, printmaking, sculpture, studio arts, theater arts management, theater design.

**Most popular majors.** Business/marketing 31%, health sciences 7%, psychology 6%, public administration/social services 8%, security/protective services 6%, social sciences 7%, visual/performing arts 11%.

**Computing on campus.** 350 workstations in dormitories, library, computer center, student center. Dormitories wired for high-speed internet access and linked to campus network. Commuter students can connect to campus network. Online course registration, helpline, repair service, student web hosting, wireless network available.

**Student life. Freshman orientation:** Mandatory, $25 fee. Preregistration for classes offered. One-day, on-campus family orientation in summer. Four-day orientation during weekend and weekdays prior to start of classes. **Policies:** Residence hall students involved in setting community standards. **Housing:** Guaranteed on-campus for all undergraduates. Coed dorms, single-sex dorms, wellness housing available. **Activities:** Bands, campus ministries, choral groups, dance, drama, international student organizations, literary magazine, music ensembles, musical theater, student government, student newspaper, symphony orchestra, social work club, liturgical groups, Respect Life, Operation Christmas Basket, Association of Black Collegians, National Coalition Building Institute, Helping Hands, Habitat for Humanity.

**Athletics.** NCAA. **Intercollegiate:** Baseball M, basketball, cross-country, equestrian W, field hockey W, football (tackle) M, golf W, lacrosse, soccer, softball W, tennis W, track and field, volleyball W, wrestling M. **Intramural:** Basketball W, equestrian W, soccer W, softball W, volleyball W. **Team name:** Griffins.

**Student services.** Adult student services, alcohol/substance abuse counseling, chaplain/spiritual director, career counseling, services for economically disadvantaged, student employment services, financial aid counseling, health services, minority student services, on-campus daycare, personal counseling, placement for graduates, veterans' counselor. **Physically disabled:** Services for visually, speech, hearing impaired.

**Contact.** E-mail: admit@setonhill.edu
Phone: (724) 838-4255 Toll-free number: (800) 826-6234
Fax: (724) 830-1294
Sherri Bett, Director of Admissions, Seton Hill University, 1 Seton Hill Drive, Greensburg, PA 15601

---

## Shippensburg University of Pennsylvania
Shippensburg, Pennsylvania  **CB member**
www.ship.edu  **CB code: 2657**

- Public 4-year university
- Residential campus in small town
- 6,861 degree-seeking undergraduates: 4% part-time, 53% women, 7% African American, 1% Asian American, 2% Hispanic American
- 1,071 degree-seeking graduate students
- 72% of applicants admitted
- SAT or ACT (ACT writing optional) required
- 63% graduate within 6 years

**General.** Founded in 1871. Regionally accredited. **Degrees:** 1,289 bachelor's awarded; master's offered. **ROTC:** Army. **Location:** 40 miles from Harrisburg. **Calendar:** Semester, extensive summer session. **Full-time faculty:** 329 total; 93% have terminal degrees, 14% minority, 43% women. **Part-time faculty:** 73 total; 20% have terminal degrees, 3% minority, 55% women. **Class size:** 22% < 20, 56% 20-39, 18% 40-49, 3% 50-99. **Special facilities:** On-campus elementary school for student teachers, planetarium, vertebrate museum, greenhouse, herbarium, electron microscope, NMR spectrometer, fashion archives, interfaith spiritual center, women's center, performing arts center, student recreation center.

**Freshman class profile.** 7,001 applied, 5,008 admitted, 1,679 enrolled.

| Mid 50% test scores | | | |
|---|---|---|---|
| SAT critical reading: | 440-530 | GPA 2.0-2.99: | 32% |
| SAT math: | 440-550 | Rank in top quarter: | 32% |
| ACT composite: | 18-22 | Rank in top tenth: | 9% |
| GPA 3.75 or higher: | 16% | End year in good standing: | 73% |
| GPA 3.50-3.74: | 15% | Return as sophomores: | 72% |
| GPA 3.0-3.49: | 37% | Out-of-state: | 7% |
| | | Live on campus: | 86% |

**Basis for selection.** Secondary school record and test scores important. Summer Bridge Program provides access and academic support to students who do not meet regular admission criteria but have demonstrated potential, desire, and motivation to succeed in college. Interviews advisable in some situations. **Homeschooled:** Transcript of courses and grades, state high school equivalency certificate required. Those working with accredited agency must submit copy of both annual evaluation and homeschool diploma. All others encouraged to schedule interview and present portfolio, and must provide GED results. Grade transcripts required (if available). **Learning Disabled:** Students must register with Office of Disability Services and provide documentation from qualified professional that verifies disability. Documentation must be less than 3 years old. Reasonable accommodations provided.

**High school preparation.** College-preparatory program required. 16 units recommended. Recommended units include English 4, mathematics 3, social studies 3, science 3 (laboratory 3) and foreign language 3.

**2009-2010 Annual costs.** Tuition/fees: $7,444; $15,776 out-of-state. Tuition for transfer students from five neighboring MD community colleges with dual admission agreements is $8,332. Tuition for all MD residents not covered by the aforementioned differential for transfer students is $12,498. Room/board: $7,086. Books/supplies: $1,100. Personal expenses: $414.

**2009-2010 Financial aid. Need-based:** 1,508 full-time freshmen applied for aid; 1,065 were judged to have need; 1,023 of these received aid. Average need met was 67%. Average scholarship/grant was $6,298; average loan $3,217. 42% of total undergraduate aid awarded as scholarships/grants, 58% as loans/jobs. **Non-need-based:** Awarded to 979 full-time undergraduates, including 287 freshmen. Scholarships awarded for academics, athletics.

**Application procedures. Admission:** No deadline. $30 fee, may be waived for applicants with need. Admission notification on a rolling basis. Must reply by April 1 or request a May 1 extension in writing. **Financial aid:** Priority date 3/15; no closing date. FAFSA required. Applicants notified on a rolling basis; must reply within 2 week(s) of notification.

**Academics.** Web-based online courses and programs also available. **Special study options:** Accelerated study, combined bachelor's/graduate degree, cooperative education, distance learning, double major, dual enrollment of high school students, honors, independent study, internships, semester at sea, study abroad, teacher certification program, Washington semester. **Credit/placement by examination:** AP, CLEP, IB, SAT, ACT, institutional tests. 30 credit hours maximum toward bachelor's degree. **Support services:** Learning center, pre-admission summer program, reduced course load, remedial instruction, study skills assistance, tutoring, writing center.

**Majors. Biology:** General. **Business:** Accounting, business admin, finance, logistics, management science, marketing. **Communications:** Journalism.

**Computer sciences:** General, systems analysis. **Conservation:** Environmental studies. **Education:** Early childhood, elementary, middle. **Foreign languages:** French, Spanish. **Health:** Health care admin. **History:** General. **Math:** General. **Parks/recreation:** Exercise sciences. **Physical sciences:** Chemistry, geology, physics. **Protective services:** Criminal justice. **Psychology:** General. **Public administration:** General, social work. **Social sciences:** Economics, geography, political science, sociology. **Visual/ performing arts:** Art.

**Most popular majors.** Business/marketing 25%, communications/ journalism 6%, education 14%, psychology 8%, security/protective services 7%, social sciences 7%.

**Computing on campus.** 800 workstations in library, computer center, student center. Dormitories wired for high-speed internet access and linked to campus network. Commuter students can connect to campus network. Online course registration, online library, helpline, repair service, student web hosting, wireless network available.

**Student life. Freshman orientation:** Mandatory, $80 fee. Orientation held in summer and prior to fall and spring semesters. **Policies:** University student code of conduct in effect. **Housing:** Guaranteed on-campus for freshmen. Coed dorms, apartments, wellness housing available. $100 partly refundable deposit, deadline 4/1. **Activities:** Bands, campus ministries, choral groups, dance, drama, international student organizations, literary magazine, music ensembles, musical theater, radio station, student government, student newspaper, symphony orchestra, TV station, African American organization, Fellowship of Christian Athletes, Christian Fellowship, College Republicans, Jewish student organization, Big Brother-Big Sister, nontraditional student organization, Latino student organization, Asian-American association, College Democrats.

**Athletics.** NCAA. **Intercollegiate:** Baseball M, basketball, cross-country, field hockey W, football (tackle) M, lacrosse W, soccer, softball W, swimming, tennis W, track and field, volleyball W, wrestling M. **Intramural:** Basketball, soccer, softball, volleyball. **Team name:** Raiders.

**Student services.** Adult student services, chaplain/spiritual director, career counseling, student employment services, financial aid counseling, health services, minority student services, on-campus daycare, personal counseling, placement for graduates, veterans' counselor, women's services. **Physically disabled:** Services for visually, hearing impaired.

**Contact.** E-mail: admiss@ship.edu
Phone: (717) 477-1231 Toll-free number: (800) 822-8028
Fax: (717) 477-4016
Thomas Speakman, Dean of Enrollment Services, Shippensburg University of Pennsylvania, 1871 Old Main Drive, Shippensburg, PA 17257-2299

---

## Slippery Rock University of Pennsylvania

| Slippery Rock, Pennsylvania | CB member |
|---|---|
| www.sru.edu | CB code: 2658 |

- Public 4-year university
- Residential campus in rural community
- 7,703 degree-seeking undergraduates: 6% part-time, 56% women, 5% African American, 1% Asian American, 1% Hispanic American, 1% international
- 761 degree-seeking graduate students
- 63% of applicants admitted
- SAT or ACT (ACT writing optional) required
- 58% graduate within 6 years; 22% enter graduate study

**General.** Founded in 1889. Regionally accredited. **Degrees:** 1,654 bachelor's awarded; master's, professional offered. **ROTC:** Army. **Location:** 50 miles from Pittsburgh. **Calendar:** Semester, extensive summer session. **Full-time faculty:** 348 total; 89% have terminal degrees, 18% minority, 46% women. **Part-time faculty:** 61 total; 26% have terminal degrees, 10% minority, 64% women. **Class size:** 16% < 20, 59% 20-39, 16% 40-49, 5% 50-99, 3% >100. **Special facilities:** Environmental education centers, crime scene investigation house, planetarium.

**Freshman class profile.** 5,928 applied, 3,718 admitted, 1,545 enrolled.

| Mid 50% test scores | | | |
|---|---|---|---|
| SAT critical reading: | 460-550 | Rank in top quarter: | 42% |
| SAT math: | 470-560 | Rank in top tenth: | 12% |
| SAT writing: | 450-540 | End year in good standing: | 86% |
| ACT composite: | 19-24 | Return as sophomores: | 81% |
| GPA 3.75 or higher: | 21% | Out-of-state: | 11% |
| GPA 3.50-3.74: | 22% | Live on campus: | 95% |
| GPA 3.0-3.49: | 40% | International: | 1% |
| GPA 2.0-2.99: | 17% | Fraternities: | 6% |
| | | Sororities: | 5% |

**Basis for selection.** Recommended minimum 2.5 GPA, or 76 percent or higher average. Minimum score of 900 SAT (exclusive of Writing) or 20 ACT recommended. Audition required for music and dance majors. **Home-schooled:** Documentation of homeschool diploma or certification information regarding how homeschool material was covered.

**High school preparation.** College-preparatory program recommended. 16 units recommended. Recommended units include English 4, mathematics 3, social studies 3, history 3, science 3 (laboratory 1) and foreign language 2.

**2009-2010 Annual costs.** Tuition/fees: $7,235; $10,012 out-of-state. Tuition for out-of-state students with at least 3.0 GPA is $8,331; all out-of-state undergraduates pay an additional $104 in required fees. Room/board: $8,332. Books/supplies: $1,363. Personal expenses: $1,880.

**2009-2010 Financial aid. Need-based:** 1,474 full-time freshmen applied for aid; 1,103 were judged to have need; 1,096 of these received aid. Average need met was 65%. Average scholarship/grant was $3,865; average loan $3,247. 46% of total undergraduate aid awarded as scholarships/grants, 54% as loans/jobs. **Non-need-based:** Awarded to 3,168 full-time undergraduates, including 859 freshmen. Scholarships awarded for academics, alumni affiliation, art, athletics, job skills, leadership, minority status, music/drama, ROTC, state residency. **Additional information:** May 1 closing date for Pennsylvania state grants.

**Application procedures. Admission:** No deadline. $30 fee, may be waived for applicants with need. Admission notification on a rolling basis beginning on or about 6/15. Must reply by May 1 or within 2 week(s) if notified thereafter. **Financial aid:** Priority date 5/1; no closing date. FAFSA required. Applicants notified on a rolling basis starting 3/15.

**Academics.** Exploratory Program for undecided majors, First Year Student Seminar, Living-Learning Environments in the Residence Halls, Learning Communities based on academic majors. **Special study options:** Combined bachelor's/graduate degree, distance learning, double major, dual enrollment of high school students, exchange student, honors, independent study, internships, liberal arts/career combination, student-designed major, study abroad, teacher certification program. **Credit/placement by examination:** AP, CLEP, IB, SAT, ACT, institutional tests. 45 credit hours maximum toward bachelor's degree. **Support services:** Learning center, pre-admission summer program, reduced course load, remedial instruction, study skills assistance, tutoring, writing center.

**Majors. Biology:** General, biochemistry, biomedical sciences. **Business:** Accounting, actuarial science, business admin, finance, international, marketing. **Communications:** General, digital media, journalism, public relations. **Computer sciences:** Computer science, information systems, information technology. **Education:** Elementary, special. **Engineering technology:** Occupational safety. **Foreign languages:** French, Spanish. **Health:** Athletic training, cytotechnology, health services admin, music therapy, nursing (RN), recreational therapy. **History:** General. **Interdisciplinary:** Science/society. **Math:** General, statistics. **Parks/recreation:** Exercise sciences, facilities management, health/fitness, sports admin. **Philosophy/religion:** Philosophy. **Physical sciences:** Chemistry, forensic chemistry, geology, physics. **Psychology:** General. **Public administration:** Social work. **Social sciences:** Criminology, economics, geography, political science. **Visual/performing arts:** Acting, art, dance, music performance, play/screenwriting, studio arts, theater arts management, theater design. **Other:** Chemistry, environmental, Spanish, business administration.

**Most popular majors.** Business/marketing 16%, education 23%, health sciences 15%, parks/recreation 10%.

**Computing on campus.** 1,323 workstations in dormitories, library, computer center, student center. Dormitories wired for high-speed internet access and linked to campus network. Commuter students can connect to campus network. Online course registration, online library, helpline, repair service, wireless network available.

**Student life. Freshman orientation:** Mandatory, $90 fee. Preregistration for classes offered. Several sessions held during summer months. **Housing:** Guaranteed on-campus for freshmen. Coed dorms, special housing for disabled, apartments available. $175 partly refundable deposit. Living-learning communities available. **Activities:** Bands, campus ministries, choral groups, dance, drama, film society, international student organizations, literary magazine, music ensembles, Model UN, musical theater, radio station, student government, student newspaper, symphony orchestra, TV station, Campus Crusade for Christ, Amnesty International, College Democrats, College Republicans, Black Action Society, Latino Student Organization, Council for Exceptional Children, American Sign Language Club, Adapted Physical Activity Council, RockOUT (formerly LGBTA).

**Athletics.** NCAA. **Intercollegiate:** Baseball M, basketball, cheerleading, cross-country, field hockey W, football (tackle) M, lacrosse W, soccer, softball W, tennis W, track and field, volleyball W. **Intramural:** Badminton, basketball, bowling, football (non-tackle), racquetball, soccer, softball, tennis, volleyball, water polo. **Team name:** The Rock.

**Student services.** Adult student services, alcohol/substance abuse counseling, chaplain/spiritual director, career counseling, services for economically disadvantaged, student employment services, financial aid counseling, health services, legal services, minority student services, on-campus daycare, personal counseling, placement for graduates, veterans' counselor, women's services. **Physically disabled:** Services for visually, speech, hearing impaired.

**Contact.** E-mail: asktherock@sru.edu
Phone: (724) 738-2015 Toll-free number: (800) 929-4778
Fax: (724) 738-2913
Mimi Campbell, Associate Director of Admissions, Slippery Rock University of Pennsylvania, 1 Morrow Way, Slippery Rock, PA 16057-1383

## Susquehanna University
**Selinsgrove, Pennsylvania** — CB member
**www.susqu.edu** — CB code: 2820

- Private 4-year university and liberal arts college affiliated with Evangelical Lutheran Church in America
- Residential campus in small town
- 2,170 degree-seeking undergraduates: 1% part-time, 53% women, 3% African American, 2% Asian American, 3% Hispanic American, 1% international
- 75% of applicants admitted
- Application essay required
- 81% graduate within 6 years; 20% enter graduate study

**General.** Founded in 1858. Regionally accredited. **Degrees:** 428 bachelor's, 2 associate awarded. **ROTC:** Army. **Location:** 50 miles from Harrisburg. **Calendar:** Semester, limited summer session. **Full-time faculty:** 133 total; 93% have terminal degrees, 16% minority, 46% women. **Part-time faculty:** 104 total; 31% have terminal degrees, 5% minority, 47% women. **Class size:** 51% < 20, 49% 20-39, less than 1% 40-49, less than 1% 50-99. **Special facilities:** Ecology field station, film library, music library, rare book room, 24-hour study center, arboretum, observatory, 450-seat teaching theater, child development center, satellite dishes, distribution system for foreign language broadcasts, video conferencing facility, high technology center for business and communications.

**Freshman class profile.** 2,954 applied, 2,212 admitted, 624 enrolled.

| Mid 50% test scores | | | |
|---|---|---|---|
| SAT critical reading: | 500-600 | GPA 2.0-2.99: | 28% |
| SAT math: | 510-610 | Rank in top quarter: | 51% |
| SAT writing: | 500-600 | Rank in top tenth: | 23% |
| ACT composite: | 23-27 | End year in good standing: | 91% |
| GPA 3.75 or higher: | 26% | Return as sophomores: | 87% |
| GPA 3.50-3.74: | 15% | Out-of-state: | 49% |
| GPA 3.0-3.49: | 30% | Live on campus: | 98% |
| | | International: | 1% |

**Basis for selection.** School record and class rank most important, test scores secondary. Application essay, interview, teacher and counselor evaluations, activities, and interest in the university considered. Students have option of submitting 2 graded writing samples in place of SAT or ACT scores. Interview highly recommended for all. Audition required for music majors. Portfolio required for writing and graphic design majors. **Home-schooled:** Student should have detailed description of course work taken.

**High school preparation.** College-preparatory program required. 18 units required; 25 recommended. Required and recommended units include English 4, mathematics 3-4, social studies 2-4, history 2, science 3-4 (laboratory 2-3), foreign language 2-4 and academic electives 2-3.

**2010-2011 Annual costs.** Tuition/fees: $34,070. Room/board: $9,230. Books/supplies: $850. Personal expenses: $750.

**2009-2010 Financial aid. Need-based:** Average need met was 82%. Average scholarship/grant was $19,942; average loan $3,545. 72% of total undergraduate aid awarded as scholarships/grants, 28% as loans/jobs. **Non-need-based:** Scholarships awarded for academics, alumni affiliation, leadership, minority status, music/drama, ROTC. **Additional information:** Graduated pay scale for federal work-study program.

**Application procedures. Admission:** Closing date 3/1 (postmark date). $35 fee, may be waived for applicants with need, free for online applicants. Admission notification 5/1. Admission notification on a rolling basis. Must reply by 5/1. **Financial aid:** Priority date 3/1, closing date 5/1. FAFSA, CSS PROFILE required. Applicants notified by 3/1; must reply by 5/1.

**Academics. Special study options:** Accelerated study, combined bachelor's/graduate degree, cross-registration, distance learning, double major, dual enrollment of high school students, exchange student, honors, independent study, internships, liberal arts/career combination, semester at sea, student-designed major, study abroad, teacher certification program, United Nations semester, urban semester, Washington semester. Internships abroad, 3-2 forestry or environmental management with Duke University, semester in London for junior business majors, 150-hour option in accounting to meet American Institute of CPA requirements, dentistry with Temple University, 2-2 allied health with Thomas Jefferson University. **Credit/placement by examination:** AP, CLEP, IB, SAT, ACT, institutional tests. 65 credit hours maximum toward bachelor's degree. **Support services:** Reduced course load, study skills assistance, tutoring, writing center.

**Majors. Biology:** General, biochemistry, ecology. **Business:** Accounting, business admin. **Communications:** General. **Computer sciences:** Computer science, information systems. **Conservation:** Environmental science. **Education:** Early childhood, elementary, music. **Foreign languages:** French, German, Spanish. **History:** General. **Interdisciplinary:** Global studies. **Liberal arts:** Arts/sciences. **Math:** General. **Philosophy/religion:** Philosophy, religion. **Physical sciences:** Chemistry, physics. **Psychology:** General. **Social sciences:** Economics, political science, sociology. **Visual/performing arts:** Art, art history/conservation, dramatic, graphic design, music performance.

**Most popular majors.** Biology 7%, business/marketing 27%, communications/journalism 12%, English 10%, liberal arts 6%, social sciences 9%, visual/performing arts 9%.

**Computing on campus.** 450 workstations in dormitories, library, computer center, student center. Dormitories wired for high-speed internet access and linked to campus network. Commuter students can connect to campus network. Online course registration, online library, helpline, student web hosting, wireless network available.

**Student life. Freshman orientation:** Mandatory. Preregistration for classes offered. 4-day program; includes community service projects. **Housing:** Guaranteed on-campus for all undergraduates. Coed dorms, special housing for disabled, apartments, fraternity/sorority housing available. $400 nonrefundable deposit, deadline 5/1. Volunteer services living groups, scholars' house, townhouses available. **Activities:** Bands, campus ministries, choral groups, dance, drama, film society, international student organizations, literary magazine, music ensembles, musical theater, opera, radio station, student government, student newspaper, symphony orchestra, TV station, volunteer services program, investment club, Habitat for Humanity, Student Environmental Action Coalition, Hispanic and Latino student organization, black student organization, Asian student organization, Big Brothers/Big Sisters, Hillel.

**Athletics.** NCAA. **Intercollegiate:** Baseball M, basketball, cheerleading, cross-country, field hockey W, football (tackle) M, golf, lacrosse, rowing (crew), soccer, softball W, swimming, tennis, track and field, volleyball W. **Intramural:** Baseball M, basketball, football (non-tackle), ice hockey M, racquetball, soccer, softball, tennis, volleyball. **Team name:** Crusaders.

**Student services.** Adult student services, alcohol/substance abuse counseling, chaplain/spiritual director, career counseling, student employment services, financial aid counseling, health services, minority student services, on-campus daycare, personal counseling, placement for graduates, veterans' counselor, women's services. **Physically disabled:** Services for visually, speech, hearing impaired.

**Contact.** E-mail: suadmiss@susqu.edu
Phone: (570) 372-4260 Toll-free number: (800) 326-9672
Fax: (570) 372-2722
Chris Markle, Director of Admissions, Susquehanna University, 514 University Avenue, Selinsgrove, PA 17870-1164

## Swarthmore College
**Swarthmore, Pennsylvania** — CB member
**www.swarthmore.edu** — CB code: 2821

- Private 4-year liberal arts college
- Residential campus in small town

- 1,505 degree-seeking undergraduates: 52% women, 10% African American, 16% Asian American, 11% Hispanic American, 1% Native American, 7% international
- 17% of applicants admitted
- SAT and SAT Subject Tests or ACT with writing, application essay required
- 93% graduate within 6 years; 21% enter graduate study

**General.** Founded in 1864. Regionally accredited. Quaker tradition. **Degrees:** 394 bachelor's awarded. **ROTC:** Army, Naval, Air Force. **Location:** 11 miles from Philadelphia. **Calendar:** Semester. **Full-time faculty:** 171 total; 100% have terminal degrees, 15% minority, 40% women. **Part-time faculty:** 40 total; 60% have terminal degrees, 20% minority, 52% women. **Class size:** 78% < 20, 18% 20-39, 2% 40-49, 1% 50-99, less than 1% >100. **Special facilities:** 399-acre arboretum, observatory, performing arts center, solar energy laboratory, Friends historical library, peace collection, LEED certified science center, 400-meter dual durometer track, civic and social responsibility center.

**Freshman class profile.** 5,575 applied, 969 admitted, 394 enrolled.

| Mid 50% test scores | | | |
|---|---|---|---|
| SAT critical reading: | 670-760 | Rank in top tenth: | 87% |
| SAT math: | 670-770 | End year in good standing: | 99% |
| SAT writing: | 670-760 | Return as sophomores: | 99% |
| ACT composite: | 30-33 | Out-of-state: | 89% |
| Rank in top quarter: | 99% | Live on campus: | 100% |
| | | International: | 7% |

**Basis for selection.** High school record, recommendations, class rank, test scores, essay, reading and experience in school and out, intellectual capacity and character important. Social responsibility considered. Interview strongly recommended. Both on and off-campus interviews are available to prospective students. Students may submit supplemental materials for review by the creative writing, dance, music, theater, and/or visual arts faculty. **Homeschooled:** Students should make every effort to complete the application, noting that it may need to be adapted to the specific experiences of the homeschooler. Information about the curricula used, including transcripts from any formal classes is requested. Examples of research projects, papers, etc. are very useful. Although not required, a personal interview is recommended for all applicants, and particularly for homeschoolers as it provides an additional opportunity for students to present their unique educational experience from a personal point of view. **Learning Disabled:** Proper documentation required.

**High school preparation.** Recommended units include English 4, mathematics 3 and science 3. 3 history/social studies, study of 1 or 2 foreign languages, and coursework in art and music recommended.

**2010-2011 Annual costs.** Tuition/fees: $39,600. Room/board: $11,900. Books/supplies: $1,150. Personal expenses: $1,120.

**2009-2010 Financial aid. Need-based:** 277 full-time freshmen applied for aid; 216 were judged to have need; 216 of these received aid. Average need met was 100%. Average scholarship/grant was $34,615. 95% of total undergraduate aid awarded as scholarships/grants, 5% as loans/jobs. **Non-need-based:** Awarded to 12 full-time undergraduates, including 4 freshmen. Scholarships awarded for academics, leadership, state residency. **Additional information:** Swarthmore maintains need-blind admissions policy for U.S. citizens and permanent residents, wherein admission and financial aid decisions are made independently. All Swarthmore aid awards are loan-free and are packaged to meet the full demonstrated need for admitted students.

**Application procedures. Admission:** Closing date 1/2 (postmark date). $60 fee, may be waived for applicants with need. Admission notification 4/1. Must reply by 5/1. **Financial aid:** Closing date 2/15. FAFSA, institutional form, CSS PROFILE required. Applicants notified by 4/1; must reply by 5/1.

**Academics. Special study options:** Accelerated study, cross-registration, double major, exchange student, honors, independent study, internships, student-designed major, study abroad, teacher certification program. Cooperative exchange programs with Rice and Tufts universities and Harvey Mudd, Pomona, Mills, and Middlebury colleges. **Credit/placement by examination:** AP, CLEP, IB, institutional tests. **Support services:** Study skills assistance, tutoring, writing center.

**Majors. Area/ethnic studies:** Asian, German, women's. **Biology:** General, biochemistry. **Computer sciences:** General. **Education:** General. **Engineering:** General. **Foreign languages:** Ancient Greek, Chinese, classics, comparative lit, French, German, Japanese, Latin, linguistics, Russian, Spanish. **History:** General. **Interdisciplinary:** Medieval/Renaissance. **Math:** General. **Philosophy/religion:** Islamic, philosophy, religion. **Physical sciences:** Astronomy, astrophysics, chemical physics, chemistry, physics. **Psychology:** General, psychobiology. **Social sciences:** Anthropology, economics, political science, sociology. **Visual/performing arts:** Art history/conservation, dance, dramatic, film/cinema, studio arts.

**Most popular majors.** Biology 9%, engineering/engineering technologies 6%, English 6%, foreign language 8%, history 8%, philosophy/religious studies 6%, psychology 8%, social sciences 25%, visual/performing arts 9%.

**Computing on campus.** 269 workstations in dormitories, library, computer center, student center. Dormitories wired for high-speed internet access and linked to campus network. Commuter students can connect to campus network. Online course registration, online library, helpline, repair service, student web hosting, wireless network available.

**Student life. Freshman orientation:** Mandatory. 4-day orientation program held in August. Optional pre-orientation programs available. **Policies:** New students are required to live on campus. **Housing:** Guaranteed on-campus for all undergraduates. Coed dorms, single-sex dorms available. Gender-neutral housing (sharing rooms and/or bathrooms). **Activities:** Jazz band, campus ministries, choral groups, dance, drama, film society, international student organizations, literary magazine, music ensembles, opera, radio station, student government, student newspaper, symphony orchestra, Earthlust, Hillel, Muslim students organization, Saturdays of Service, Swarthmore Christian Fellowship, Swarthmore Sudan, War News Radio.

**Athletics.** NCAA. **Intercollegiate:** Badminton W, baseball M, basketball, cross-country, field hockey W, golf M, lacrosse, soccer, softball W, swimming, tennis, track and field, volleyball W. **Intramural:** Basketball, football (non-tackle), soccer, softball, table tennis, tennis, volleyball. **Team name:** Garnet.

**Student services.** Alcohol/substance abuse counseling, chaplain/spiritual director, career counseling, services for economically disadvantaged, student employment services, financial aid counseling, health services, minority student services, personal counseling, placement for graduates, women's services. **Physically disabled:** Services for visually, speech, hearing impaired.

**Contact.** E-mail: admissions@swarthmore.edu
Phone: (610) 328-8300 Toll-free number: (800) 667-3110
Fax: (610) 328-8580
James Bock, Dean of Admissions and Financial Aid, Swarthmore College, 500 College Avenue, Swarthmore, PA 19081

## Talmudical Yeshiva of Philadelphia
### Philadelphia, Pennsylvania
**CB code: 1037**

- Private 4-year rabbinical college for men affiliated with Jewish faith
- Residential campus in very large city
- 116 degree-seeking undergraduates: 2% international
- 85% of applicants admitted
- Interview required

**General.** Founded in 1953. Accredited by AARTS. First Talmudic degree and ordination available. **Degrees:** 19 bachelor's awarded. **Calendar:** Trimester, extensive summer session. **Full-time faculty:** 5 total. **Part-time faculty:** 1 total.

**Freshman class profile.** 52 applied, 44 admitted, 38 enrolled.

| | | | |
|---|---|---|---|
| End year in good standing: | 97% | Out-of-state: | 92% |
| Return as sophomores: | 91% | Live on campus: | 100% |

**Basis for selection.** Institutional examinations required.

**High school preparation.** 20 units required. Required and recommended units include English 4, social studies 3, science 3 and foreign language 2.

**2009-2010 Annual costs.** Tuition/fees: $7,600. Room/board: $6,300. Books/supplies: $900.

**2008-2009 Financial aid.** All financial aid based on need. 21 full-time freshmen applied for aid; 21 were judged to have need; 21 of these received aid. 97% of total undergraduate aid awarded as scholarships/grants, 3% as loans/jobs.

**Application procedures. Admission:** Priority date 1/15; no deadline. No application fee. Admission notification on a rolling basis beginning on or about 7/15. **Financial aid:** Priority date 8/1, closing date 5/1. FAFSA, institutional form required. Applicants notified on a rolling basis starting 3/15; must reply within 2 week(s) of notification.

**Academics. Credit/placement by examination:** CLEP, IB, institutional tests. **Support services:** Tutoring.

**Majors. Theology:** Talmudic.

**Student life. Policies:** Religious observance required. **Housing:** Guaranteed on-campus for all undergraduates.

**Student services.** Career counseling, health services, personal counseling, placement for graduates.

**Contact.** Phone: (215) 473-1212 Fax: (215) 477-5065
Rabbi. Sholom Kamenetsky, Admissions Director, Talmudical Yeshiva of Philadelphia, 6063 Drexel Road, Philadelphia, PA 19131

## Temple University

| Philadelphia, Pennsylvania | |
|---|---|
| | CB member |
| www.temple.edu | CB code: 2906 |

- Public 4-year university
- Commuter campus in very large city
- 26,469 degree-seeking undergraduates: 9% part-time, 53% women, 16% African American, 10% Asian American, 4% Hispanic American, 3% international
- 8,145 degree-seeking graduate students
- 61% of applicants admitted
- SAT or ACT with writing, application essay required
- 67% graduate within 6 years

**General.** Founded in 1884. Regionally accredited. Campuses in Ambler, Fort Washington, downtown Philadelphia, Harrisburg, Rome, Japan and other international locations. **Degrees:** 5,238 bachelor's, 4 associate awarded; master's, doctoral, professional offered. **ROTC:** Army, Naval, Air Force. **Location:** 2 miles from downtown. **Calendar:** Semester, extensive summer session. **Full-time faculty:** 1,384 total; 76% have terminal degrees, 16% minority, 37% women. **Part-time faculty:** 1,506 total; 14% minority, 45% women. **Class size:** 34% < 20, 47% 20-39, 10% 40-49, 6% 50-99, 3% >100. **Special facilities:** Observatory, planetarium, arboretum, technology center.

**Freshman class profile.** 18,574 applied, 11,265 admitted, 4,203 enrolled.

| Mid 50% test scores | | | |
|---|---|---|---|
| SAT critical reading: | 490-600 | Rank in top quarter: | 57% |
| SAT math: | 510-610 | Rank in top tenth: | 21% |
| SAT writing: | 500-600 | Return as sophomores: | 88% |
| ACT composite: | 21-26 | Out-of-state: | 25% |
| GPA 3.75 or higher: | 22% | Live on campus: | 76% |
| GPA 3.50-3.74: | 22% | International: | 2% |
| GPA 3.0-3.49: | 43% | Fraternities: | 3% |
| GPA 2.0-2.99: | 13% | Sororities: | 3% |

**Basis for selection.** Admissions process holistic; every aspect of student's academic history considered. Interview and essay required for transfer nursing applicants. Audition required for dance, music programs; portfolio required for art. **Homeschooled:** Statement describing homeschool structure and mission, transcript of courses and grades, letter of recommendation (nonparent) required.

**High school preparation.** College-preparatory program required. 16 units required; 22 recommended. Required and recommended units include English 4, mathematics 3-4, social studies 2, history 1-2, science 2-3 (laboratory 1-2), foreign language 2 and academic electives 1-3.

**2009-2010 Annual costs.** Tuition/fees: $11,764; $21,044 out-of-state. Room/board: $9,198. Books/supplies: $1,000. Personal expenses: $4,436.

**2008-2009 Financial aid. Need-based:** 3,746 full-time freshmen applied for aid; 2,749 were judged to have need; 2,685 of these received aid. Average need met was 91%. Average scholarship/grant was $5,804; average loan $3,427. 54% of total undergraduate aid awarded as scholarships/grants, 46% as loans/jobs. **Non-need-based:** Awarded to 10,364 full-time undergraduates, including 2,233 freshmen. Scholarships awarded for academics, art, athletics, music/drama, ROTC.

**Application procedures. Admission:** Closing date 3/1 (postmark date). $50 fee, may be waived for applicants with need. Admission notification on a rolling basis beginning on or about 10/15. Must reply by May 1 or within 2 week(s) if notified thereafter. **Financial aid:** Closing date 3/1. FAFSA required. Applicants notified on a rolling basis starting 2/15; must reply by 5/1 or within 3 week(s) of notification.

**Academics. Special study options:** Combined bachelor's/graduate degree, cooperative education, cross-registration, distance learning, double major, dual enrollment of high school students, ESL, exchange student, honors, independent study, internships, liberal arts/career combination, student-designed major, study abroad, teacher certification program. Programs in Japan, Italy, Costa Rica, France, Germany, Ghana, India, Spain, Turkey, United Kingdom and Brazil. **Credit/placement by examination:** AP, CLEP, IB, institutional tests. **Support services:** Learning center, pre-admission summer program, reduced course load, remedial instruction, study skills assistance, tutoring, writing center.

**Majors. Agriculture:** Horticultural science. **Architecture:** Architecture, landscape, urban/community planning. **Area/ethnic studies:** African-American, American, Asian, Latin American, women's. **Biology:** General, biochemistry, biophysics. **Business:** Accounting, actuarial science, business admin, e-commerce, entrepreneurial studies, finance, hospitality admin, insurance, international, labor relations, management information systems, marketing, real estate. **Communications:** Advertising, broadcast journalism, journalism, organizational, public relations, radio/tv. **Computer sciences:** General, information technology. **Conservation:** Environmental science, environmental studies. **Education:** Art, business, elementary, English, foreign languages, mathematics, music, science, social studies, trade/industrial. **Engineering:** Civil, computer, electrical, mechanical. **Engineering technology:** General, civil, computer hardware, construction, electromechanical, energy systems, environmental, manufacturing. **Foreign languages:** Classics, French, German, Hebrew, Italian, linguistics, Russian, Spanish. **Health:** Athletic training, audiology/speech pathology, medical records admin, music therapy, nursing (RN), public health ed, recreational therapy. **History:** General. **Liberal arts:** Arts/sciences. **Math:** General. **Parks/recreation:** Exercise sciences, facilities management. **Philosophy/religion:** Judaic, philosophy, religion. **Physical sciences:** Chemistry, geology, physics. **Protective services:** Criminal justice. **Psychology:** General. **Public administration:** Social work. **Social sciences:** Anthropology, economics, international relations, political science, sociology, urban studies. **Visual/performing arts:** Acting, art, art history/conservation, ceramics, dance, dramatic, fiber arts, film/cinema, graphic design, jazz, metal/jewelry, music history, music pedagogy, music performance, music theory/composition, painting, photography, printmaking, sculpture, voice/opera. **Other:** Public communications.

**Most popular majors.** Business/marketing 22%, communications/journalism 11%, education 8%, health sciences 6%, psychology 6%, social sciences 6%, visual/performing arts 11%.

**Computing on campus.** 3,670 workstations in dormitories, library, computer center, student center. Dormitories wired for high-speed internet access and linked to campus network. Commuter students can connect to campus network. Online library, helpline, student web hosting, wireless network available.

**Student life. Freshman orientation:** Mandatory. Preregistration for classes offered. Includes placement testing. **Housing:** Guaranteed on-campus for freshmen. Coed dorms, special housing for disabled, apartments available. $250 fully refundable deposit, deadline 5/1. Living/learning centers available. **Activities:** Bands, campus ministries, choral groups, dance, drama, film society, international student organizations, literary magazine, music ensembles, musical theater, opera, radio station, student government, student newspaper, symphony orchestra, TV station, Newman Club, Hillel, Young Democrats, Young Republicans, professional organizations, public service organization, cultural organization.

**Athletics.** NCAA. **Intercollegiate:** Baseball M, basketball, cheerleading, cross-country, fencing W, field hockey W, football (tackle) M, golf M, gymnastics, lacrosse W, rowing (crew), soccer, softball W, tennis, track and field, volleyball W. **Intramural:** Basketball, football (non-tackle) M, soccer M, softball, volleyball. **Team name:** Owls.

**Student services.** Adult student services, alcohol/substance abuse counseling, career counseling, services for economically disadvantaged, student employment services, financial aid counseling, health services, personal counseling, placement for graduates, veterans' counselor. **Physically disabled:** Services for visually, speech, hearing impaired. **Learning disabled:** Comprehensive services available.

**Contact.** E-mail: tuadm@temple.edu
Phone: (215) 204-7200 Toll-free number: (888) 340-2222
Fax: (215) 204-5694
Karin Mormando, Director, Undergraduate Admissions, Temple University, 103 Conwell Hall, Philadelphia, PA 19122-6096

## Thiel College

| Greenville, Pennsylvania | |
|---|---|
| | CB member |
| www.thiel.edu | CB code: 2910 |

- Private 4-year liberal arts college affiliated with Evangelical Lutheran Church in America
- Residential campus in small town

- 962 degree-seeking undergraduates: 2% part-time, 46% women, 4% African American, 1% Hispanic American, 5% international
- 72% of applicants admitted
- SAT or ACT (ACT writing optional), application essay required
- 40% graduate within 6 years

**General.** Founded in 1866. Regionally accredited. **Degrees:** 253 bachelor's, 5 associate awarded. **Location:** 75 miles from Pittsburgh, 75 miles from Cleveland. **Calendar:** Semester, limited summer session. **Full-time faculty:** 61 total; 70% have terminal degrees, 8% minority, 38% women. **Part-time faculty:** 50 total; 10% have terminal degrees, 4% minority, 60% women. **Class size:** 65% < 20, 33% 20-39, 1% 40-49, less than 1% >100. **Special facilities:** Wildlife sanctuary, black box theater.

**Freshman class profile.** 1,265 applied, 907 admitted, 272 enrolled.

| Mid 50% test scores | | | |
|---|---|---|---|
| SAT critical reading: | 420-510 | Rank in top tenth: | 10% |
| SAT math: | 410-520 | End year in good standing: | 85% |
| ACT composite: | 17-23 | Return as sophomores: | 61% |
| GPA 3.75 or higher: | 12% | Out-of-state: | 39% |
| GPA 3.50-3.74: | 12% | Live on campus: | 95% |
| GPA 3.0-3.49: | 26% | International: | 4% |
| GPA 2.0-2.99: | 47% | Fraternities: | 11% |
| Rank in top quarter: | 31% | Sororities: | 18% |

**Basis for selection.** High school GPA, class rank, curriculum, and recommendation important. SAT or ACT scores received for fall admission on rolling basis. **Learning Disabled:** Students with disabilities must submit evidence of disability to Office of Special Needs.

**High school preparation.** College-preparatory program recommended. 16 units recommended. Recommended units include English 4, mathematics 2, social studies 3, science 2 (laboratory 2), foreign language 2 and academic electives 3. Engineering, math, and science majors should complete 3 years of college preparatory math and science.

**2009-2010 Annual costs.** Tuition/fees: $22,448. Room/board: $8,790. Books/supplies: $1,000. Personal expenses: $3,000.

**2009-2010 Financial aid. Need-based:** Average need met was 71%. Average scholarship/grant was $15,767; average loan $4,631. 65% of total undergraduate aid awarded as scholarships/grants, 35% as loans/jobs. **Non-need-based:** Scholarships awarded for academics, alumni affiliation, leadership, music/drama, religious affiliation.

**Application procedures. Admission:** Priority date 4/1; no deadline. No application fee. Admission notification on a rolling basis beginning on or about 8/1. Must reply by May 1 or within 2 week(s) if notified thereafter. **Financial aid:** Priority date 3/15; no closing date. FAFSA required. Applicants notified on a rolling basis starting 2/15; must reply within 2 week(s) of notification.

**Academics. Special study options:** Combined bachelor's/graduate degree, cooperative education, distance learning, double major, dual enrollment of high school students, honors, internships, liberal arts/career combination, semester at sea, study abroad, teacher certification program, United Nations semester, Washington semester. 3-2 engineering with Case Western Reserve University and University of Pittsburgh, 3-2 engineering technologies with Point Park College, Pittsburgh, cooperative program with Art Institute of Pittsburgh, cooperative engineering with Youngstown State University, exchange with Duke University in forestry. **Credit/placement by examination:** AP, CLEP, IB, SAT, ACT, institutional tests. 30 credit hours maximum toward bachelor's degree. **Support services:** Learning center, reduced course load, remedial instruction, study skills assistance, tutoring, writing center.

**Majors. Biology:** General. **Business:** Accounting, actuarial science, business admin, communications, international, management information systems. **Communications:** General. **Communications technology:** Radio/tv. **Computer sciences:** General, information systems. **Conservation:** General, environmental studies. **Education:** Biology, chemistry, elementary, English, history, mathematics, physics, science, social studies. **Health:** Audiology/speech pathology, clinical lab technology, cytotechnology. **History:** General. **Interdisciplinary:** Neuroscience. **Math:** General. **Personal/culinary services:** General, mortuary science. **Philosophy/religion:** Philosophy, religion. **Physical sciences:** Chemistry, physics. **Protective services:** Criminal justice. **Psychology:** General. **Social sciences:** Political science, sociology. **Theology:** Religious ed. **Visual/performing arts:** General, art, commercial/advertising art. **Other:** Binary engineering.

**Most popular majors.** Business/marketing 35%, education 6%, psychology 12%, security/protective services 7%, social sciences 6%.

**Computing on campus.** PC or laptop required. 300 workstations in dormitories, library, computer center, student center. Dormitories wired for high-speed internet access and linked to campus network. Commuter students can connect to campus network. Online course registration, helpline, wireless network available.

**Student life. Freshman orientation:** Mandatory, $275 fee. Preregistration for classes offered. Weekend before classes start. **Housing:** Guaranteed on-campus for all undergraduates. Coed dorms, apartments, fraternity/sorority housing, wellness housing available. $100 partly refundable deposit. Special interest housing, learning/living environment available. **Activities:** Bands, campus ministries, choral groups, dance, drama, international student organizations, literary magazine, music ensembles, musical theater, radio station, student government, student newspaper, symphony orchestra, TV station, Organization of Black Collegiates, Lutheran student movement, Circle K.

**Athletics.** NCAA. **Intercollegiate:** Baseball M, basketball, cheerleading, cross-country, football (tackle) M, golf, lacrosse, soccer, softball W, track and field, volleyball, wrestling M. **Intramural:** Badminton, basketball, softball, table tennis, volleyball. **Team name:** Tomcats.

**Student services.** Alcohol/substance abuse counseling, chaplain/spiritual director, career counseling, financial aid counseling, health services, minority student services, personal counseling, placement for graduates. **Physically disabled:** Services for visually, hearing impaired.

**Contact.** E-mail: admission@thiel.edu
Phone: (724) 589-2345 Toll-free number: (800) 248-4435
Fax: (724) 589-2013
Amy Becher, Director of Admissions, Thiel College, 75 College Avenue, Greenville, PA 16125-2181

## Thomas Jefferson University: College of Health Professions
### Philadelphia, Pennsylvania
www.jefferson.edu                                   CB code: 2903

- Private two-year upper-division health science and nursing college
- Residential campus in very large city
- Application essay required

**General.** Founded in 1824. Regionally accredited. Associate degree programs available in evening division. **Degrees:** 374 bachelor's, 99 associate awarded; master's, professional offered. **Articulation:** Agreements with Bloomsburg U of Pennsylvania, Bucks County CC, Cabrini College, CC of Philadelphia, Delaware County CC, Elizabethtown College, Juniata College, Keystone JC, La Salle U, Lebanon Valley College of Pennsylvania, Manor JC, Moravian College, Penn State: Delaware County Campus, St. Joseph's U, Shippensburg U of Pennsylvania, Susquehanna U, Villanova U, Gordon College, Burlington County College, Camden County College, Gloucester County College, Penn State: Abington Campus, Rider U, Muhlenberg College, Middlesex County College, Cumberland County College, Arcadia U. **ROTC:** Naval, Air Force. **Calendar:** Semester, limited summer session. **Full-time faculty:** 150 total. **Part-time faculty:** 55 total. **Special facilities:** Rare book collection, simulation labs, human performance lab (gait research), simulation building.

**Student profile.** 841 degree-seeking undergraduates. 80% entered as juniors, 20% entered as seniors. 55% transferred from two-year, 45% transferred from four-year institutions.

| | | | |
|---|---|---|---|
| Out-of-state: | 27% | Live on campus: | 30% |

**Basis for selection.** College transcript, application essay required. Decisions based on review of college transcripts, recommendations, written personal statement, and interview. Specific prerequisite credit requirements for each program. Volunteer experiences strongly recommended; 2 site visits required for OT applicants. Transfer accepted as sophomores, juniors, seniors.

**2009-2010 Annual costs.** Tuition/fees: $25,939. Books/supplies: $1,495. Personal expenses: $1,125.

**Financial aid. Non-need-based:** Scholarships awarded for academics, leadership, state residency.

**Application procedures. Admission:** Priority date 3/1. $50 fee, may be waived for applicants with need. **Financial aid:** Applicants notified on a rolling basis starting 11/15; must reply within 2 weeks of notification. FAFSA, institutional form required.

**Academics.** Plan College Education Program allows qualified high school seniors to reserve a place for future enrollment after completion of required college program. **Special study options:** Accelerated study, combined bachelor's/graduate degree, distance learning, independent study, internships, study abroad. **Credit/placement by examination:** AP, CLEP, institutional tests.

30 credit hours maximum toward bachelor's degree. **Support services:** Preadmission summer program, study skills assistance, tutoring, writing center.

**Majors. Biology:** Biotechnology. **Health:** Cardiovascular technology, clinical lab science, cytotechnology, nursing (RN), preop/surgical nursing, sonography. **Science technology:** Biological.

**Computing on campus.** 100 workstations in library, computer center, student center. Dormitories wired for high-speed internet access. Commuter students can connect to campus network. Online course registration, online library, helpline, wireless network available.

**Student life. Housing:** Guaranteed on-campus for all undergraduates. Coed dorms, special housing for disabled, apartments available. **Activities:** Choral groups, international student organizations, student government, African American student society, Chinese students and scholars society, Hands of Hope, Jewish student association, Medical Professionals for Choice, Asian professional society, Latino health organization, occupational therapy association, physical therapy association, Student Nurses Association of Pennsylvania.

**Athletics. Intramural:** Basketball, football (non-tackle) M, golf, racquetball, rugby, softball, squash, swimming, table tennis, tennis, volleyball, water polo.

**Student services.** Adult student services, alcohol/substance abuse counseling, career counseling, student employment services, financial aid counseling, health services, minority student services, on-campus daycare, personal counseling, placement for graduates, veterans' counselor.

**Contact.** Phone: (215) 503-8890 Toll-free number: (877) 533-3247 Fax: (215) 503-7241
Karen Astle, Assistant Dean for Admission, Thomas Jefferson University: College of Health Professions, 130 South Ninth Street, Edison Building, Suite 100, Philadelphia, PA 19107

## University of Pennsylvania

**Philadelphia, Pennsylvania**   **CB member**
www.upenn.edu   **CB code: 2926**

- Private 4-year university
- Residential campus in very large city
- 9,768 degree-seeking undergraduates: 3% part-time, 51% women, 8% African American, 19% Asian American, 6% Hispanic American, 10% international
- 9,543 degree-seeking graduate students
- 18% of applicants admitted
- SAT and SAT Subject Tests or ACT with writing, application essay required
- 95% graduate within 6 years; 20% enter graduate study

**General.** Founded in 1740. Regionally accredited. **Degrees:** 2,831 bachelor's, 1 associate awarded; master's, doctoral, professional offered. **ROTC:** Army, Naval, Air Force. **Location:** One mile from downtown. **Calendar:** Semester, extensive summer session. **Full-time faculty:** 1,411 total; 100% have terminal degrees, 18% minority, 36% women. **Part-time faculty:** 789 total; 100% have terminal degrees, 11% minority, 41% women. **Class size:** 72% < 20, 17% 20-39, 3% 40-49, 6% 50-99, 2% >100. **Special facilities:** Anthropology museum, contemporary art institute, arboretum, astronomical observatory, large animal research center, women's center, undergraduate research center, wind tunnel, Kelly Writer's House, Hillel Foundation.

**Freshman class profile.** 22,808 applied, 4,040 admitted, 2,475 enrolled.

| Mid 50% test scores | | Rank in top quarter: | 100% |
|---|---|---|---|
| SAT critical reading: | 660-750 | Rank in top tenth: | 96% |
| SAT math: | 690-780 | End year in good standing: | 99% |
| SAT writing: | 670-760 | Return as sophomores: | 98% |
| ACT composite: | 30-34 | Class size: | |
| GPA 3.75 or higher: | 77% | Out-of-state: | 83% |
| GPA 3.50-3.74: | 11% | Live on campus: | 100% |
| GPA 3.0-3.49: | 10% | International: | 11% |
| GPA 2.0-2.99: | 2% | Fraternities: | 29% |
| | | Sororities: | 26% |

**Basis for selection.** Transcript indicating rigor of course work and achievement/evaluation most important criteria. Co-curricular involvements and testing strongly considered, as are counselor and faculty recommendations. Personal commentary (essays) and interview considered as well. Entire ACT and/or SAT test score history required. Portfolio suggested for Architecture and Fine Arts programs. **Homeschooled:** Statement describing homeschool structure and mission, transcript of courses and grades, letter of recommendation (nonparent) required. Commentary from primary instructor most important, and at least 1 other academic reference highly recommended. SAT subject tests in major academic areas highly recommended.

**High school preparation.** College-preparatory program recommended. 20 units recommended. Recommended units include English 4, mathematics 4, social studies 2, history 3, science 3 (laboratory 3) and foreign language 4.

**2009-2010 Annual costs.** Tuition/fees: $38,970. Room/board: $11,016. Books/supplies: $1,042. Personal expenses: $2,067.

**2008-2009 Financial aid.** All financial aid based on need. 1,404 full-time freshmen applied for aid; 1,113 were judged to have need; 1,113 of these received aid. Average need met was 100%. Average scholarship/grant was $35,908; average loan $115. 90% of total undergraduate aid awarded as scholarships/grants, 10% as loans/jobs.

**Application procedures. Admission:** Closing date 1/1 (postmark date). $75 fee, may be waived for applicants with need. Admission notification 4/1. Must reply by 5/1. Rolling admission notification for Advanced Nursing Practitioner (ANP) applicants; notification begins on or about February 15. **Financial aid:** Priority date 2/15; no closing date. FAFSA, institutional form, CSS PROFILE required. Applicants notified by 4/1; must reply by 5/1.

**Academics. Special study options:** Accelerated study, combined bachelor's/graduate degree, cross-registration, double major, dual enrollment of high school students, ESL, exchange student, honors, independent study, internships, liberal arts/career combination, student-designed major, study abroad, teacher certification program, Washington semester. **Credit/placement by examination:** AP, CLEP, IB, institutional tests. No maximum number of semester hours of credit by examination counted toward degree. **Support services:** Learning center, pre-admission summer program, remedial instruction, study skills assistance, tutoring, writing center.

**Majors. Architecture:** Architecture, environmental design. **Area/ethnic studies:** African, African-American, American, East Asian, South Asian, women's. **Biology:** General, biochemistry, bioinformatics, biomedical sciences, biophysics. **Business:** Accounting, actuarial science, business admin, e-commerce, finance, human resources, insurance, international, management information systems, marketing, operations, real estate, sales/distribution, transportation. **Communications:** General. **Computer sciences:** General, computer graphics, networking. **Conservation:** Environmental studies. **Education:** General, elementary. **Engineering:** Biomedical, chemical, computer, electrical, environmental, materials, materials science, mechanical, systems. **Foreign languages:** Classics, comparative lit, East Asian, French, German, Italian, linguistics, Russian, Semitic, Spanish. **Health:** Community health services, health care admin, nursing (RN). **History:** General, science/technology. **Interdisciplinary:** Cognitive science, global studies, natural sciences, neuroscience. **Legal studies:** General. **Liberal arts:** Arts/sciences, humanities. **Math:** General, statistics. **Philosophy/religion:** Judaic, logic, philosophy, religion. **Physical sciences:** Chemistry, geology, physics. **Psychology:** General. **Public administration:** Policy analysis. **Social sciences:** General, anthropology, economics, international relations, political science, sociology, urban studies. **Visual/performing arts:** General, art history/conservation, dramatic, film/cinema, studio arts.

**Most popular majors.** Biology 6%, business/marketing 21%, engineering/engineering technologies 11%, health sciences 8%, social sciences 18%.

**Computing on campus.** 1,295 workstations in dormitories, library, computer center, student center. Dormitories wired for high-speed internet access and linked to campus network. Commuter students can connect to campus network. Online course registration, online library, helpline, repair service, student web hosting, wireless network available.

**Student life. Freshman orientation:** Mandatory. Preregistration for classes offered. **Housing:** Guaranteed on-campus for freshmen. Coed dorms, special housing for disabled, apartments, fraternity/sorority housing, wellness housing available. $200 nonrefundable deposit, deadline 5/1. Private off-campus housing available. **Activities:** Bands, campus ministries, choral groups, dance, drama, film society, international student organizations, literary magazine, music ensembles, Model UN, musical theater, opera, radio station, student government, student newspaper, symphony orchestra, TV station, various religious, political, ethnic, social service, performing arts, cultural, and sports organizations.

**Athletics.** NCAA. **Intercollegiate:** Baseball M, basketball, cross-country, diving, fencing, field hockey W, football (tackle) M, golf, gymnastics W, lacrosse, rowing (crew), soccer, softball W, squash, swimming, tennis, track and field, volleyball W, wrestling M. **Intramural:** Basketball, football (non-tackle), soccer, tennis, volleyball. **Team name:** Quakers.

**Student services.** Adult student services, alcohol/substance abuse counseling, chaplain/spiritual director, career counseling, services for economically disadvantaged, student employment services, financial aid counseling, health services, legal services, minority student services, on-campus day-care, personal counseling, placement for graduates, veterans' counselor, women's services. **Physically disabled:** Services for visually, speech, hearing impaired. **Learning disabled:** Comprehensive services available.

**Contact.** E-mail: info@admissions.ugao.upenn.edu
Phone: (215) 898-7507 Fax: (215) 898-9670
Eric Furda, Dean of Admissions, University of Pennsylvania, 1 College Hall, Philadelphia, PA 19104

## University of Pittsburgh
**Pittsburgh, Pennsylvania**     **CB member**
www.pitt.edu     **CB code: 2927**

- Public 4-year university
- Residential campus in large city
- 17,682 degree-seeking undergraduates: 6% part-time, 51% women, 8% African American, 5% Asian American, 1% Hispanic American, 1% international
- 9,957 degree-seeking graduate students
- 59% of applicants admitted
- SAT or ACT (ACT writing optional) required
- 76% graduate within 6 years; 39% enter graduate study

**General.** Founded in 1787. Regionally accredited. Regional campuses in Johnstown, Bradford, Titusville, and Greensburg. **Degrees:** 3,856 bachelor's awarded; master's, doctoral, professional offered. **ROTC:** Army, Naval, Air Force. **Location:** 3 miles from downtown. **Calendar:** Semester, extensive summer session. **Class size:** 40% < 20, 35% 20-39, 7% 40-49, 12% 50-99, 6% >100. **Special facilities:** Observatory, nationality rooms, performance hall, American music center, ecology laboratory.

**Freshman class profile.** 21,737 applied, 12,722 admitted, 3,642 enrolled.

| Mid 50% test scores | | | |
|---|---|---|---|
| SAT critical reading: | 570-680 | Rank in top quarter: | 86% |
| SAT math: | 590-680 | Rank in top tenth: | 49% |
| SAT writing: | 560-660 | Return as sophomores: | 93% |
| ACT composite: | 25-30 | Out-of-state: | 29% |
| GPA 3.75 or higher: | 65% | Live on campus: | 97% |
| GPA 3.50-3.74: | 17% | International: | 2% |
| GPA 3.0-3.49: | 16% | Fraternities: | 12% |
| GPA 2.0-2.99: | 2% | Sororities: | 10% |

**Basis for selection.** GED not accepted. High school record, class rank, test scores, and activities considered. College of General Studies applicants must apply directly to that college, not through Admissions and Financial Aid. Students admitted as freshmen into School of Arts and Sciences, School of Engineering, School of Nursing, and College of Business Administration. Students may be conditionally accepted into the School of Pharmacy, PharmD program with the provision that they successfully complete 4 terms (2 years) of preprofessional study in School of Arts and Sciences. Interview and essay recommended for all; audition required for music program; portfolio recommended for studio art program; essay required for pharmacy applicants. **Homeschooled:** Statement describing homeschool structure and mission, transcript of courses and grades required.

**High school preparation.** College-preparatory program required. 17 units required; 23 recommended. Required and recommended units include English 4, mathematics 3-4, social studies 2-3, science 3-4 (laboratory 3-4), foreign language 2-3 and academic electives 3-5.

**2009-2010 Annual costs.** Tuition/fees: $14,154; $23,852 out-of-state. Room/board: $8,900.

**2009-2010 Financial aid. Need-based:** 3,007 full-time freshmen applied for aid; 2,059 were judged to have need; 2,020 of these received aid. Average need met was 81%. Average scholarship/grant was $9,623; average loan $4,318. 56% of total undergraduate aid awarded as scholarships/grants, 44% as loans/jobs. **Non-need-based:** Awarded to 4,065 full-time undergraduates, including 1,116 freshmen. Scholarships awarded for academics, athletics.

**Application procedures. Admission:** No deadline. $45 fee, may be waived for applicants with need. Admission notification on a rolling basis beginning on or about 10/1. Must reply by May 1 or within 3 week(s) if notified thereafter. **Financial aid:** Priority date 3/1; no closing date. FAFSA required. Applicants notified on a rolling basis starting 3/15.

**Academics.** Accelerated high school program enables students to take courses in School of Arts and Sciences while in high school. **Special study**

**options:** Accelerated study, combined bachelor's/graduate degree, cooperative education, cross-registration, distance learning, double major, dual enrollment of high school students, ESL, exchange student, external degree, honors, independent study, internships, liberal arts/career combination, student-designed major, study abroad, teacher certification program. Freshman seminars, early admission to some graduate programs for exceptional students. **Credit/placement by examination:** AP, CLEP, IB, SAT, ACT, institutional tests. 60 credit hours maximum toward bachelor's degree. College of Arts and Sciences does not accept CLEP. **Support services:** Learning center, pre-admission summer program, reduced course load, remedial instruction, study skills assistance, tutoring, writing center.

**Majors. Area/ethnic studies:** African-American. **Biology:** General, ecology, microbiology, molecular. **Business:** Accounting, business admin, finance, marketing. **Communications:** Media studies. **Computer sciences:** Computer science, information systems. **Education:** Physical. **Engineering:** Biomedical, chemical, civil, computer, electrical, industrial, materials, mechanical, physics. **Foreign languages:** Chinese, classics, French, German, Italian, Japanese, linguistics, Polish, Russian, Slavic, Spanish. **Health:** Audiology/speech pathology, dental hygiene, dietetics, medical records admin, nursing (RN), orthotics/prosthetics. **History:** General, science/technology. **Interdisciplinary:** Biological/physical sciences, neuroscience. **Liberal arts:** Arts/sciences, humanities. **Math:** General, applied, statistics. **Philosophy/religion:** Philosophy, religion. **Physical sciences:** General, chemistry, geology, physics. **Protective services:** Corrections. **Psychology:** General, educational. **Public administration:** General, social work. **Social sciences:** General, anthropology, economics, political science, sociology, urban studies. **Visual/performing arts:** Art history/conservation, dramatic, film/cinema, studio arts.

**Most popular majors.** Business/marketing 14%, engineering/engineering technologies 9%, English 11%, health sciences 9%, psychology 9%, social sciences 14%.

**Computing on campus.** 2,000 workstations in library, computer center, student center. Dormitories wired for high-speed internet access and linked to campus network. Commuter students can connect to campus network. Online course registration, online library, helpline, repair service, student web hosting, wireless network available.

**Student life. Freshman orientation:** Available. Preregistration for classes offered. **Housing:** Guaranteed on-campus for freshmen. Coed dorms, single-sex dorms, special housing for disabled, apartments, fraternity/sorority housing, wellness housing available. $325 fully refundable deposit. Rooms can be adapted to meet disabled students' particular needs. **Activities:** Bands, campus ministries, choral groups, dance, drama, film society, international student organizations, literary magazine, music ensembles, Model UN, radio station, student government, student newspaper, TV station, approximately 400 student organizations.

**Athletics.** NCAA. **Intercollegiate:** Baseball M, basketball, cross-country, diving, football (tackle) M, gymnastics W, soccer, softball W, swimming, tennis W, track and field, volleyball W, wrestling M. **Intramural:** Badminton, basketball, football (tackle) M, handball, racquetball, soccer, squash, swimming, volleyball. **Team name:** Panthers.

**Student services.** Adult student services, alcohol/substance abuse counseling, chaplain/spiritual director, career counseling, student employment services, financial aid counseling, health services, personal counseling, placement for graduates, veterans' counselor. **Physically disabled:** Services for visually, speech, hearing impaired.

**Contact.** E-mail: oafa@pitt.edu
Phone: (412) 624-7488 Fax: (412) 648-8815
Betsy Porter, Director, Office of Admissions and Financial Aid, University of Pittsburgh, 4227 Fifth Avenue, 1st Floor, Alumni Hall, Pittsburgh, PA 15260

## University of Pittsburgh at Bradford
**Bradford, Pennsylvania**     **CB member**
www.upb.pitt.edu     **CB code: 2935**

- Public 4-year university
- Residential campus in large town
- 1,600 degree-seeking undergraduates: 9% part-time, 55% women, 6% African American, 2% Asian American, 1% Hispanic American, 1% Native American
- 83% of applicants admitted
- SAT or ACT (ACT writing optional) required
- 44% graduate within 6 years; 22% enter graduate study

**General.** Founded in 1963. Regionally accredited. **Degrees:** 236 bachelor's, 53 associate awarded. **ROTC:** Army. **Location:** 160 miles from Pittsburgh, 79 miles from Buffalo, New York. **Calendar:** Semester, extensive summer session. **Full-time faculty:** 72 total; 62% have terminal degrees, 15% minority, 32% women. **Part-time faculty:** 76 total; 14% have terminal degrees, 4% minority, 58% women. **Class size:** 48% < 20, 44% 20-39, 4% 40-49, 4% 50-99. **Special facilities:** Located in the Allegheny National Forest.

**Freshman class profile.** 987 applied, 816 admitted, 420 enrolled.

| Mid 50% test scores | | | |
|---|---|---|---|
| SAT critical reading: | 440-520 | GPA 3.0-3.49: | 33% |
| SAT math: | 450-550 | GPA 2.0-2.99: | 42% |
| SAT writing: | 430-530 | Rank in top quarter: | 6% |
| ACT composite: | 19-23 | End year in good standing: | 70% |
| GPA 3.75 or higher: | 12% | Return as sophomores: | 72% |
| GPA 3.50-3.74: | 12% | Out-of-state: | 17% |
| | | Live on campus: | 76% |

**Basis for selection.** School achievement record, test scores, interview most important. Essay and recommendations considered. **Homeschooled:** Required: Complete listing of courses taken/completed/in progress, syllabus for each course, textbook used, 1 recommendation from educator, 1 outside recommendation, personal essay, personal interview, state requirement satisfaction.

**High school preparation.** College-preparatory program recommended. 15 units required. Required and recommended units include English 4, mathematics 2-2.5, history 1, science 1-2 (laboratory 1-2), foreign language 2 and academic electives 5. Engineering and math students must have trigonometry and physics with a lab. Nursing majors must have 3 social science and 1 each of chemistry and biology with labs in both.

**2009-2010 Annual costs.** Tuition/fees: $11,722; $21,282 out-of-state. Room/board: $7,480. Books/supplies: $1,050. Personal expenses: $1,570.

**2009-2010 Financial aid. Need-based:** 412 full-time freshmen applied for aid; 358 were judged to have need; 358 of these received aid. Average need met was 95%. Average scholarship/grant was $5,482; average loan $3,408. 33% of total undergraduate aid awarded as scholarships/grants, 67% as loans/jobs. **Non-need-based:** Awarded to 675 full-time undergraduates, including 371 freshmen. Scholarships awarded for academics, alumni affiliation, ROTC, state residency.

**Application procedures. Admission:** Priority date 5/1; no deadline. $45 fee, may be waived for applicants with need. Admission notification on a rolling basis beginning on or about 11/1. Must reply by May 1 or within 2 week(s) if notified thereafter. **Financial aid:** Priority date 3/1; no closing date. FAFSA required. Applicants notified on a rolling basis starting 4/1; must reply within 2 week(s) of notification.

**Academics.** Student services include: on-going individual academic, personal and career counseling; strategies for maintaining and improving GPA; assistance with study skills and life management issues; cultural enrichment activities; computer learning lab services; graduate school assistance. **Special study options:** Combined bachelor's/graduate degree, cross-registration, distance learning, double major, dual enrollment of high school students, external degree, honors, independent study, internships, semester at sea, study abroad, teacher certification program. 3-4 pre-optometry program with Pennsylvania College of Optometry, 1-4 pharmacy program with Oakland campus, 3+4 program with LECOM in Osteopathic Medicine. **Credit/placement by examination:** AP, CLEP, IB, SAT, ACT, institutional tests. 30 credit hours maximum toward associate degree, 90 toward bachelor's. **Support services:** Learning center, reduced course load, remedial instruction, study skills assistance, tutoring.

**Majors. Biology:** General. **Business:** General, accounting, business admin, entrepreneurial studies, hospitality admin. **Communications:** Public relations, radio/tv. **Computer sciences:** Applications programming, computer science. **Conservation:** Environmental studies. **Education:** General, elementary, physical, secondary, social science. **Engineering:** General, chemical, civil, electrical, industrial, mechanical, science. **Engineering technology:** Petroleum. **Health:** Athletic training, nursing (RN), radiologic technology/medical imaging. **Interdisciplinary:** Biological/physical sciences. **Liberal arts:** Humanities. **Math:** Applied. **Parks/recreation:** Sports admin. **Physical sciences:** General, chemistry. **Protective services:** Corrections, law enforcement admin. **Psychology:** General. **Social sciences:** General, demography, economics, political science, sociology. **Visual/performing arts:** General.

**Most popular majors.** Business/marketing 18%, communications/journalism 6%, education 15%, health sciences 15%, security/protective services 8%, social sciences 18%.

**Computing on campus.** 120 workstations in library, computer center, student center. Dormitories wired for high-speed internet access and linked to campus network. Commuter students can connect to campus network. Online course registration, online library, helpline, repair service, student web hosting, wireless network available.

**Student life. Freshman orientation:** Mandatory, $90 fee. Preregistration for classes offered. 2-day program for students and parents in July; additional 3-day program immediately prior to start of classes. **Housing:** Guaranteed on-campus for freshmen. Coed dorms, special housing for disabled, apartments available. $125 nonrefundable deposit, deadline 5/1. Townhouse/apartment style housing available. **Activities:** Campus ministries, choral groups, dance, drama, literary magazine, radio station, student government, student newspaper, black action committee, Christ in Action, Collegiate Liberals of America, Conservative Union, Habitat for Humanity, ideology expression club.

**Athletics.** NCAA. **Intercollegiate:** Baseball M, basketball, cross-country, golf, soccer, softball W, swimming, volleyball W. **Intramural:** Basketball, football (non-tackle), golf, ice hockey, soccer, softball, swimming, table tennis, tennis, volleyball, water polo. **Team name:** Panthers.

**Student services.** Adult student services, alcohol/substance abuse counseling, chaplain/spiritual director, career counseling, student employment services, financial aid counseling, health services, personal counseling, placement for graduates, veterans' counselor.

**Contact.** E-mail: admissions@upb.pitt.edu
Phone: (814) 362-7555 Toll-free number: (800) 872-1787
Fax: (814) 362-5150
Alexander Nazemetz, Director of Admissions, University of Pittsburgh at Bradford, 300 Campus Drive, Bradford, PA 16701

## University of Pittsburgh at Greensburg
**Greensburg, Pennsylvania**
**www.upg.pitt.edu**                    **CB code: 2936**

- Public 4-year branch campus and liberal arts college
- Commuter campus in large town
- 1,785 degree-seeking undergraduates: 6% part-time, 49% women, 5% African American, 2% Asian American, 2% Hispanic American
- 74% of applicants admitted
- SAT or ACT with writing required
- 54% graduate within 6 years

**General.** Founded in 1963. Regionally accredited. **Degrees:** 285 bachelor's awarded. **ROTC:** Army, Air Force. **Location:** 35 miles from Pittsburgh. **Calendar:** Semester, limited summer session. **Full-time faculty:** 74 total. **Part-time faculty:** 60 total. **Class size:** 20% < 20, 50% 20-39, 18% 40-49, 7% 50-99, 5% >100. **Special facilities:** Wildlife sanctuary and nature trail, humanities village, behavioral science village, natural sciences and new technologies village, international village.

**Freshman class profile.** 1,276 applied, 942 admitted, 411 enrolled.

| Mid 50% test scores | | | |
|---|---|---|---|
| SAT critical reading: | 460-550 | GPA 2.0-2.99: | 15% |
| SAT math: | 470-570 | Rank in top quarter: | 38% |
| SAT writing: | 450-540 | Rank in top tenth: | 10% |
| ACT composite: | 19-23 | Return as sophomores: | 79% |
| GPA 3.75 or higher: | 20% | Out-of-state: | 2% |
| GPA 3.50-3.74: | 19% | Live on campus: | 64% |
| GPA 3.0-3.49: | 46% | International: | 1% |

**Basis for selection.** High school curriculum and grades most important, followed by class rank and SAT/ACT scores. Interviews, essays and letters of recommendation all optional. **Homeschooled:** Transcript of courses and grades required.

**High school preparation.** 15 units required; 20 recommended. Required and recommended units include English 4, mathematics 2-4, social studies 2, history 2, science 1-2 (laboratory 1), foreign language 3, computer science 1 and academic electives 1-3. If student is missing foreign language unit, must have enough academic elective units to meet the minimum total units required (15).

**2009-2010 Annual costs.** Tuition/fees: $11,852; $21,412 out-of-state. Room/board: $7,840. Books/supplies: $1,000. Personal expenses: $1,500.

**2009-2010 Financial aid. Need-based:** 383 full-time freshmen applied for aid; 324 were judged to have need; 320 of these received aid. Average need met was 48%. Average scholarship/grant was $4,601; average loan $3,606. 45% of total undergraduate aid awarded as scholarships/grants, 55% as loans/jobs. **Non-need-based:** Awarded to 175 full-time undergraduates, including 82 freshmen. Scholarships awarded for academics, leadership, minority status.

**Application procedures. Admission:** No deadline. $45 fee, may be waived for applicants with need. Admission notification on a rolling basis beginning on or about 9/1. Must reply by May 1 or within 3 week(s) if notified thereafter. **Financial aid:** Priority date 2/15; no closing date. FAFSA required. Applicants notified on a rolling basis starting 3/15; must reply within 3 week(s) of notification.

**Academics. Special study options:** Combined bachelor's/graduate degree, cross-registration, double major, dual enrollment of high school students, exchange student, independent study, internships, liberal arts/career combination, student-designed major, study abroad. **Credit/placement by examination:** AP, CLEP, SAT, ACT, institutional tests. 30 credit hours maximum toward bachelor's degree. **Support services:** Learning center, reduced course load, remedial instruction, study skills assistance, tutoring, writing center.

**Majors. Area/ethnic studies:** American. **Biology:** General. **Business:** Accounting, business admin, management information systems. **Communications:** General, journalism, public relations. **Computer sciences:** Information systems. **Health:** Predental, premedicine, prepharmacy, preveterinary. **History:** General. **Liberal arts:** Arts/sciences. **Math:** Applied. **Physical sciences:** Chemistry. **Protective services:** Law enforcement admin. **Psychology:** General. **Social sciences:** General, anthropology, criminology, political science.

**Most popular majors.** Biology 9%, business/marketing 31%, English 13%, psychology 24%, social sciences 6%.

**Computing on campus.** 400 workstations in dormitories, library, computer center. Dormitories wired for high-speed internet access and linked to campus network. Commuter students can connect to campus network. Online course registration, online library, helpline, repair service, student web hosting, wireless network available.

**Student life. Freshman orientation:** Mandatory, $55 fee. **Housing:** Coed dorms, wellness housing available. $150 fully refundable deposit, deadline 5/1. **Activities:** Choral groups, dance, drama, international student organizations, literary magazine, musical theater, radio station, student government, student newspaper, student activities board, honor societies, academic societies, Alpha Phi Omega, Circle K, Amnesty International, Christian fellowship club, College Republicans, College Democrats.

**Athletics.** NCAA. **Intercollegiate:** Baseball M, basketball, cross-country, golf, soccer, softball W, tennis, volleyball W. **Intramural:** Baseball M, basketball, golf, racquetball, skiing, soccer, softball, table tennis, tennis, volleyball. **Team name:** Bobcats.

**Student services.** Adult student services, alcohol/substance abuse counseling, career counseling, student employment services, financial aid counseling, health services, personal counseling, placement for graduates, veterans' counselor. **Physically disabled:** Services for visually, hearing impaired.

**Contact.** E-mail: upgadmit@pitt.edu
Phone: (724) 836-9880 Fax: (724) 836-7471
Heather Kabala, Director of Admissions, University of Pittsburgh at Greensburg, 150 Finoli Drive, Greensburg, PA 15601

## University of Pittsburgh at Johnstown

Johnstown, Pennsylvania                    CB member
www.upj.pitt.edu                           CB code: 2934

- Public 4-year engineering and liberal arts college
- Residential campus in small city
- 3,043 degree-seeking undergraduates: 4% part-time, 46% women, 2% African American, 2% Asian American, 1% Hispanic American, 1% international
- 89% of applicants admitted
- SAT or ACT (ACT writing recommended) required
- 63% graduate within 6 years

**General.** Founded in 1927. Regionally accredited. **Degrees:** 494 bachelor's, 15 associate awarded. **Location:** 70 miles from Pittsburgh. **Calendar:** Semester, limited summer session. **Class size:** 22% < 20, 63% 20-39, 11% 40-49, 3% 50-99, less than 1% >100. **Special facilities:** 40-acre nature preserve maintained by biology department, performing arts center.

**Freshman class profile.** 1,652 applied, 1,473 admitted, 822 enrolled.

| Mid 50% test scores | | | |
|---|---|---|---|
| SAT critical reading: | 450-540 | GPA 2.0-2.99: | 23% |
| SAT math: | 460-570 | Rank in top quarter: | 35% |
| SAT writing: | 440-540 | Rank in top tenth: | 10% |
| ACT composite: | 18-23 | Return as sophomores: | 73% |
| GPA 3.75 or higher: | 26% | Out-of-state: | 1% |
| GPA 3.50-3.74: | 17% | Live on campus: | 76% |
| GPA 3.0-3.49: | 34% | International: | 2% |

**Basis for selection.** College preparatory curriculum, high school achievement, test scores, and class rank very important. Recommendations and essay considered. Interview recommended.

**High school preparation.** 15 units required. Required and recommended units include English 4, mathematics 2-3, social studies 4, science 2 (laboratory 1) and foreign language 2. One each of trigonometry, physics, and chemistry required for engineering technology program.

**2009-2010 Annual costs.** Tuition/fees: $11,754; $21,314 out-of-state. Room/board: $7,370. Books/supplies: $1,030. Personal expenses: $1,550.

**2009-2010 Financial aid. Need-based:** 733 full-time freshmen applied for aid; 589 were judged to have need; 584 of these received aid. Average need met was 57%. Average scholarship/grant was $5,736; average loan $3,611. 47% of total undergraduate aid awarded as scholarships/grants, 53% as loans/jobs. **Non-need-based:** Awarded to 751 full-time undergraduates, including 246 freshmen. Scholarships awarded for academics, athletics, leadership, minority status, state residency.

**Application procedures. Admission:** No deadline. $45 fee, may be waived for applicants with need. Admission notification on a rolling basis beginning on or about 9/1. Must reply by May 1 or within 2 week(s) if notified thereafter. **Financial aid:** Priority date 4/1; no closing date. FAFSA required. Applicants notified on a rolling basis starting 3/15; must reply within 2 week(s) of notification.

**Academics. Special study options:** Accelerated study, combined bachelor's/graduate degree, cooperative education, cross-registration, distance learning, double major, dual enrollment of high school students, independent study, internships, liberal arts/career combination, student-designed major, study abroad, teacher certification program. **Credit/placement by examination:** AP, CLEP, IB, SAT, ACT, institutional tests. 90 credit hours maximum toward bachelor's degree. **Support services:** Learning center, reduced course load, study skills assistance, tutoring, writing center.

**Majors. Area/ethnic studies:** American. **Biology:** General. **Business:** General, accounting, finance, managerial economics, marketing. **Communications:** General, journalism. **Computer sciences:** General. **Conservation:** Environmental studies. **Education:** Biology, chemistry, elementary, English, mathematics, science, secondary, social science, social studies. **Engineering technology:** Civil, computer, electrical, mechanical. **Health:** Predental, premedicine, preveterinary. **History:** General. **Legal studies:** Prelaw. **Liberal arts:** Arts/sciences. **Math:** General. **Physical sciences:** Chemistry, geology. **Psychology:** General. **Social sciences:** General, economics, geography, political science, sociology. **Visual/performing arts:** Dramatic.

**Most popular majors.** Biology 8%, business/marketing 27%, communications/journalism 9%, education 16%, engineering/engineering technologies 10%, psychology 6%, social sciences 7%.

**Computing on campus.** 150 workstations in library, computer center. Dormitories wired for high-speed internet access and linked to campus network. Commuter students can connect to campus network. Online course registration, online library, helpline, student web hosting, wireless network available.

**Student life. Freshman orientation:** Mandatory, $55 fee. Preregistration for classes offered. One-day program. **Policies:** To be eligible to hold office within group or organization, student must be full-time and have minimum 2.0 GPA. **Housing:** Guaranteed on-campus for all undergraduates. Coed dorms, special housing for disabled, apartments, fraternity/sorority housing available. $150 fully refundable deposit, deadline 7/1. Townhouses, lodges, and single-sex residences available. **Activities:** Bands, campus ministries, choral groups, dance, drama, literary magazine, music ensembles, Model UN, musical theater, radio station, student government, student newspaper, TV station, Newman Association, Black Action Society, Student Outreach Through Service, Time Out Christian Fellowship, Student Council on World Affairs, political science club, Habitat for Humanity.

**Athletics.** NCAA. **Intercollegiate:** Baseball M, basketball, cross-country W, golf, soccer, track and field W, volleyball W, wrestling M. **Intramural:** Basketball, football (non-tackle), softball, volleyball. **Team name:** Mountain Cats.

**Student services.** Adult student services, alcohol/substance abuse counseling, chaplain/spiritual director, career counseling, student employment services, financial aid counseling, health services, personal counseling, placement for graduates, veterans' counselor. **Physically disabled:** Services for visually, speech, hearing impaired.

**Contact.** E-mail: upjadmit@pitt.edu
Phone: (814) 269-7050 Toll-free number: (800) 765-4875
Fax: (814) 269-7044
Bernard Sarneso, Director of Admissions, University of Pittsburgh at Johnstown, 450 Schoolhouse Road, 157 Blackington Hall, Johnstown, PA 15904-1200

---

## University of Scranton
### Scranton, Pennsylvania
**www.scranton.edu**

CB member
CB code: 2929

- Private 4-year university and liberal arts college affiliated with Roman Catholic Church
- Residential campus in small city
- 4,067 degree-seeking undergraduates: 3% part-time, 57% women, 1% African American, 3% Asian American, 4% Hispanic American, 1% international
- 1,598 degree-seeking graduate students
- 71% of applicants admitted
- SAT or ACT (ACT writing optional), application essay required
- 81% graduate within 6 years

**General.** Founded in 1888. Regionally accredited. **Degrees:** 822 bachelor's, 5 associate awarded; master's, professional offered. **ROTC:** Army, Air Force. **Location:** 125 miles from Philadelphia, 125 miles from New York City. **Calendar:** Semester, limited summer session. **Full-time faculty:** 267 total; 80% have terminal degrees, 11% minority, 40% women. **Part-time faculty:** 235 total; 24% have terminal degrees, 3% minority, 50% women. **Class size:** 45% < 20, 54% 20-39, 1% 40-49, less than 1% 50-99. **Special facilities:** 2 cyber-cafes, conference and retreat center at Chapman Lake, performing arts center with seating for 700.

**Freshman class profile.** 8,054 applied, 5,749 admitted, 1,038 enrolled.

| Mid 50% test scores | | GPA 2.0-2.99: | 19% |
|---|---|---|---|
| SAT critical reading: | 510-600 | Rank in top quarter: | 62% |
| SAT math: | 520-620 | Rank in top tenth: | 27% |
| GPA 3.75 or higher: | 18% | Return as sophomores: | 89% |
| GPA 3.50-3.74: | 23% | Out-of-state: | 59% |
| GPA 3.0-3.49: | 40% | Live on campus: | 86% |

**Basis for selection.** Program taken, GPA, SAT scores, class rank most important. Essay, extracurricular/leadership activities, recommendations important. **Homeschooled:** State high school equivalency certificate required.

**High school preparation.** College-preparatory program recommended. 16 units required. Required and recommended units include English 4, mathematics 3-4, social studies 2, science 3 (laboratory 1), foreign language 2 and academic electives 4. Science and business students should have 4 math; science students should have 4 science.

**2009-2010 Annual costs.** Tuition/fees: $33,124. Room/board: $11,440. Books/supplies: $1,150. Personal expenses: $1,150.

**2009-2010 Financial aid. Non-need-based:** Scholarships awarded for academics, minority status, ROTC.

**Application procedures. Admission:** Closing date 3/1 (postmark date). No application fee. Application must be submitted online. Admission notification on a rolling basis beginning on or about 1/15. Must reply by May 1 or within 2 week(s) if notified thereafter. **Financial aid:** Priority date 2/15; no closing date. FAFSA required. Applicants notified on a rolling basis starting 3/1; must reply by 5/1 or within 2 week(s) of notification.

**Academics. Special study options:** Accelerated study, combined bachelor's/graduate degree, cross-registration, distance learning, double major, dual enrollment of high school students, ESL, exchange student, honors, independent study, internships, semester at sea, study abroad, teacher certification program, United Nations semester, Washington semester. Baccalaureate/master's degree programs available. **Credit/placement by examination:** AP, CLEP, IB, SAT, ACT, institutional tests. 30 credit hours maximum toward bachelor's degree. **Support services:** Learning center, pre-admission summer program, remedial instruction, study skills assistance, tutoring, writing center.

**Majors. Biology:** General, biochemistry, biophysics, molecular. **Business:** Accounting, business admin, finance, human resources, international, management science, marketing, operations. **Communications:** General. **Computer sciences:** General, information systems. **Conservation:** General. **Education:** Early childhood, elementary, secondary, special. **Engineering:** Electrical. **Foreign languages:** Ancient Greek, classics, French, German, Latin, Spanish. **Health:** Clinical lab science, health care admin, nursing (RN). **History:** General. **Interdisciplinary:** Neuroscience. **Math:** General. **Philosophy/religion:** Philosophy, religion. **Physical sciences:** Chemistry, physics. **Protective services:** Criminal justice, forensics. **Psychology:** General. **Public administration:** Human services. **Social sciences:** Economics, international relations, political science, sociology. **Visual/performing arts:** Dramatic.

**Most popular majors.** Biology 10%, business/marketing 18%, communications/journalism 8%, education 10%, health sciences 14%, social sciences 6%.

**Computing on campus.** PC or laptop required. 972 workstations in dormitories, library, computer center, student center. Dormitories wired for high-speed internet access and linked to campus network. Commuter students can connect to campus network. Online course registration, online library, helpline, repair service, student web hosting, wireless network available.

**Student life. Freshman orientation:** Mandatory, $275 fee. Preregistration for classes offered. Overnight program (1.5 days) for students and parents, held between end of June and mid-July. **Housing:** Guaranteed on-campus for all undergraduates. Coed dorms, single-sex dorms, apartments, wellness housing available. $150 nonrefundable deposit, deadline 5/1. **Activities:** Bands, campus ministries, choral groups, dance, drama, international student organizations, literary magazine, music ensembles, radio station, student government, student newspaper, TV station, religious and social service organizations, veterans club, Young Democrats, Young Republicans, professional clubs, collegiate volunteers, multicultural club, debating club.

**Athletics.** NCAA. **Intercollegiate:** Baseball M, basketball, cross-country, field hockey W, golf M, ice hockey M, lacrosse, soccer, softball W, swimming, tennis, volleyball W, wrestling M. **Intramural:** Baseball M, basketball, bowling, cross-country, football (tackle) M, golf, handball, lacrosse, racquetball, rugby, skiing, soccer, softball, swimming, table tennis, tennis, track and field, volleyball, water polo M, wrestling M. **Team name:** Royals.

**Student services.** Adult student services, alcohol/substance abuse counseling, chaplain/spiritual director, career counseling, student employment services, health services, personal counseling, placement for graduates, veterans' counselor. **Physically disabled:** Services for visually, hearing impaired.

**Contact.** E-mail: admissions@scranton.edu
Phone: (570) 941-7540 Toll-free number: (888) 727-2686
Fax: (570) 941-5928
Joseph Roback, Assistant Vice President for Admissions and Enrollment, University of Scranton, 800 Linden Street, Scranton, PA 18510-4699

---

## University of the Arts
### Philadelphia, Pennsylvania
**www.uarts.edu**

CB member
CB code: 2664

- Private 4-year visual arts and performing arts college
- Residential campus in very large city
- 2,139 degree-seeking undergraduates: 1% part-time, 56% women, 11% African American, 3% Asian American, 5% Hispanic American, 1% Native American, 4% international
- 236 degree-seeking graduate students
- 50% of applicants admitted
- SAT or ACT (ACT writing optional), application essay required
- 64% graduate within 6 years

**General.** Founded in 1870. Regionally accredited. **Degrees:** 418 bachelor's awarded; master's offered. **Calendar:** Semester, limited summer session. **Full-time faculty:** 115 total; 86% have terminal degrees, 10% minority, 41% women. **Part-time faculty:** 352 total; 8% minority, 43% women. **Class size:** 79% < 20, 21% 20-39, less than 1% 50-99, less than 1% >100. **Special facilities:** Digital multimedia laboratories, Oxberry animation stand, MIDI and recording studios, analog and digital electronic music studios, music calligraphy laboratory, center for publication arts, industrial design computer-aided product design center, genre-specific art galleries.

**Freshman class profile.** 2,449 applied, 1,215 admitted, 473 enrolled.

| Mid 50% test scores | | | |
|---|---|---|---|
| SAT critical reading: | 460-590 | GPA 3.0-3.49: | 28% |
| SAT math: | 430-550 | GPA 2.0-2.99: | 53% |
| SAT writing: | 450-580 | Return as sophomores: | 79% |
| ACT composite: | 18-27 | Out-of-state: | 68% |
| GPA 3.75 or higher: | 8% | Live on campus: | 85% |
| GPA 3.50-3.74: | 9% | International: | 5% |

**Basis for selection.** Academic records, art work portfolio, audition very important. SAT or ACT scores considered in relation to the former. Statement of purpose and letters of recommendation also important. Class placement in English composition through SAT/ACT scores. August 15 score deadline for placement, counseling and/or credit. Interview recommended for all; audition required for performing arts programs; portfolio required for multimedia, visual arts, writing programs; essay required for media arts, performing arts, and visual arts programs. **Homeschooled:** Statement describing homeschool structure and mission, transcript of courses and grades, state high school equivalency certificate, letter of recommendation (nonparent) required. Interview not required but recommended; GED accepted in lieu of state high school equivalency certificate.

**High school preparation.** Required and recommended units include English 4, mathematics 3, social studies 2, history 2, science 2 and foreign language 2. Coursework in art, dance, music, creative writing, or theater as appropriate for specific programs recommended.

**2009-2010 Annual costs.** Tuition/fees: $31,000. Room only: $7,200. Books/supplies: $2,100. Personal expenses: $1,665.

**Financial aid.** Non-need-based: Scholarships awarded for academics, art, music/drama.

**Application procedures.** Admission: Priority date 3/1; no deadline. $60 fee, may be waived for applicants with need. Admission notification on a rolling basis beginning on or about 11/1. Must reply by May 1 or within 3 week(s) if notified thereafter. **Financial aid:** Priority date 3/1; no closing date. FAFSA required. Applicants notified on a rolling basis starting 3/15; must reply within 2 week(s) of notification.

**Academics.** Credit for course work may be given to entering freshmen by portfolio review (awarded after first year) or audition and placement testing. Art and design students declare major at end of first year, dance students at end of second year. **Special study options:** Accelerated study, cross-registration, double major, dual enrollment of high school students, ESL, exchange student, independent study, internships, liberal arts/career combination, study abroad, teacher certification program. **Credit/placement by examination:** AP, CLEP, IB, SAT, ACT, institutional tests. Credit by examination counted toward bachelor's degree varies by program. **Support services:** Learning center, pre-admission summer program, reduced course load, remedial instruction, study skills assistance, tutoring, writing center.

**Majors. Communications:** Digital media. **Communications technology:** Animation/special effects. **Education:** Drama/dance. **Visual/performing arts:** Acting, cinematography, crafts, dance, directing/producing, graphic design, illustration, industrial design, multimedia, music performance, music theory/composition, musical theater, painting, photography, play/screenwriting, printmaking, sculpture, studio arts, theater design.

**Most popular majors.** Visual/performing arts 95%.

**Computing on campus.** PC or laptop required. 400 workstations in library, computer center, student center. Dormitories wired for high-speed internet access and linked to campus network. Commuter students can connect to campus network. Online course registration, online library, helpline, wireless network available.

**Student life. Freshman orientation:** Available. Preregistration for classes offered. Includes educational sessions on various social issues of university life. **Policies:** Campus code of conduct. **Housing:** Coed dorms, apartments, wellness housing available. $300 deposit, deadline 6/1. All housing in apartment-style units. **Activities:** Jazz band, choral groups, dance, drama, film society, international student organizations, literary magazine, music ensembles, musical theater, radio station, student government, African American Student Union, GBLT Student Union, Global Exchange, JewArts, Latino Student Union, Remedy (student-driven green initiative), UArts Christian Fellowship, Student Council.

**Athletics. Intramural:** Volleyball.

**Student services.** Adult student services, alcohol/substance abuse counseling, career counseling, services for economically disadvantaged, student employment services, financial aid counseling, health services, personal counseling, placement for graduates, veterans' counselor. **Physically disabled:** Services for visually, speech, hearing impaired.

**Contact.** E-mail: admissions@uarts.edu
Phone: (215) 717-6030 Toll-free number: (800) 616-2787
Fax: (215) 717-6045
Susan Gandy, Director of Admission, University of the Arts, 320 South Broad Street, Philadelphia, PA 19102

## University of the Sciences in Philadelphia
**Philadelphia, Pennsylvania** — CB member
www.usp.edu — CB code: 2663

- Private 4-year health science and pharmacy college
- Residential campus in very large city
- 2,602 degree-seeking undergraduates: 1% part-time, 60% women, 4% African American, 38% Asian American, 2% Hispanic American, 1% international
- 307 degree-seeking graduate students
- 62% of applicants admitted
- SAT or ACT with writing required
- 60% graduate within 6 years

**General.** Founded in 1821. Regionally accredited. **Degrees:** 242 bachelor's awarded; master's, doctoral, professional offered. **ROTC:** Army, Air Force. **Calendar:** Semester, limited summer session. **Full-time faculty:** 157 total; 78% have terminal degrees, 15% minority, 46% women. **Part-time faculty:** 101 total; 14% minority, 60% women. **Class size:** 43% < 20, 41% 20-39, 4% 40-49, 4% 50-99, 8% >100. **Special facilities:** History of pharmacy museum, advanced pharmacy studies lab, research labs, science and technology center, wet labs.

**Freshman class profile.** 4,178 applied, 2,592 admitted, 513 enrolled.

| Mid 50% test scores | | | |
|---|---|---|---|
| SAT critical reading: | 520-600 | Rank in top quarter: | 78% |
| SAT math: | 560-650 | Rank in top tenth: | 47% |
| ACT composite: | 23-27 | End year in good standing: | 90% |
| GPA 3.75 or higher: | 36% | Return as sophomores: | 85% |
| GPA 3.50-3.74: | 30% | Out-of-state: | 55% |
| GPA 3.0-3.49: | 27% | Live on campus: | 88% |
| GPA 2.0-2.99: | 7% | International: | 2% |

**Basis for selection.** High school curriculum, GPA, class rank if provided by high school, and SAT or ACT test scores most important criteria. SAT recommended. SAT and ACT writing component required only for pharmacy applicants. Essay and/or letters of recommendation not required, but reviewed if provided. **Homeschooled:** Transcript of courses and grades, state high school equivalency certificate required. **Learning Disabled:** If admitted under current admission process, students will be provided with necessary additional services to assist in academic success.

**High school preparation.** College-preparatory program required. 16 units required; 19 recommended. Required and recommended units include English 4, mathematics 3-4, social studies 1, history 1, science 3-4 (laboratory 3), foreign language 1 and academic electives 4.

**2009-2010 Annual costs.** Tuition/fees: $29,630. Room/board: $11,582. Books/supplies: $1,050. Personal expenses: $2,660.

**2008-2009 Financial aid.** Need-based: 495 full-time freshmen applied for aid; 432 were judged to have need; 432 of these received aid. Average need met was 72%. Average scholarship/grant was $7,799; average loan $3,457. 78% of total undergraduate aid awarded as scholarships/grants, 22% as loans/jobs. **Non-need-based:** Scholarships awarded for academics, athletics.

**Application procedures.** Admission: No deadline. $45 fee, may be waived for applicants with need, free for online applicants. Admission notification on a rolling basis beginning on or about 10/1. Must reply by May 1 or within 2 week(s) if notified thereafter. **Financial aid:** Closing date 3/15. FAFSA required. Applicants notified on a rolling basis starting 1/15; must reply by 5/1 or within 2 week(s) of notification.

**Academics.** Direct-entry admission for freshman pharmacy, DPT and MPT physical therapy program, occupational therapy and physician assistant programs. Students not required to reapply to professional phase of their majors. **Special study options:** Combined bachelor's/graduate degree, double major, ESL, honors, internships, liberal arts/career combination, teacher certification program. **Credit/placement by examination:** AP, CLEP, IB, SAT, ACT, institutional tests. **Support services:** Learning center, pre-admission summer program, reduced course load, remedial instruction, study skills assistance, tutoring, writing center.

**Majors. Biology:** General, biochemistry, bioinformatics, microbiology, pharmacology/toxicology. **Business:** Marketing. **Computer sciences:** Computer science. **Conservation:** Environmental science. **Health:** Clinical lab science, health services, physician assistant. **Parks/recreation:** Sports admin. **Physical sciences:** Chemistry, physics. **Psychology:** General, medical. **Other:** Humanities and science, Pharmaceutical marketing and management.

**Most popular majors.** Biology 13%, health sciences 85%.

**Computing on campus.** 165 workstations in dormitories, library, computer center, student center. Dormitories wired for high-speed internet access and linked to campus network. Commuter students can connect to campus network. Online course registration, online library, helpline, repair service, wireless network available.

**Student life. Freshman orientation:** Mandatory. Programs for parents and students; placement testing. **Policies:** Campus alcohol free. **Housing:** Guaranteed on-campus for freshmen. Coed dorms, apartments, fraternity/sorority housing, wellness housing available. $200 nonrefundable deposit, deadline 5/1. Honor halls. **Activities:** Concert band, choral groups, dance, drama, literary magazine, musical theater, student government, student newspaper, professional organizations, Greek letter organizations, religious groups, honor societies, student community involvement program, ethnic/diversity groups, student chapters of scientific organizations, student publications.

**Athletics.** NAIA, NCAA. **Intercollegiate:** Baseball M, basketball, cross-country, golf, rifle, softball W, tennis, volleyball W. **Intramural:** Archery, badminton, basketball, bowling, rifle, table tennis, volleyball. **Team name:** Devils.

**Student services.** Adult student services, alcohol/substance abuse counseling, career counseling, student employment services, financial aid counseling, health services, personal counseling, placement for graduates, veterans' counselor. **Physically disabled:** Services for visually, speech, hearing impaired.

**Contact.** E-mail: admit@usp.edu
Phone: (215) 596-8810 Toll-free number: (888) 996-8747
Fax: (215) 596-8821
Dianna Collins, Executive Director of Admission and Enrollment Services, University of the Sciences in Philadelphia, 600 South 43rd Street, Philadelphia, PA 19104-4495

## Ursinus College
**Collegeville, Pennsylvania**   CB member
**www.ursinus.edu**   CB code: 2931

- Private 4-year liberal arts college
- Residential campus in small town
- 1,716 degree-seeking undergraduates: 54% women, 6% African American, 4% Asian American, 3% Hispanic American, 1% international
- 57% of applicants admitted
- Application essay required
- 83% graduate within 6 years; 34% enter graduate study

**General.** Founded in 1869. Regionally accredited. All freshmen receive laptop computers (updated at beginning of junior year). **Degrees:** 339 bachelor's awarded. **Location:** 28 miles from Philadelphia. **Calendar:** Semester. **Full-time faculty:** 125 total; 90% have terminal degrees, 14% minority, 48% women. **Part-time faculty:** 69 total; 41% have terminal degrees, 13% minority, 58% women. **Class size:** 75% < 20, 23% 20-39, less than 1% 40-49, less than 1% 50-99, less than 1% >100. **Special facilities:** Performing arts center, art museum, observatory, outdoor sculpture collection, public walking trails.

**Freshman class profile.** 6,125 applied, 3,471 admitted, 513 enrolled.

| Mid 50% test scores | | Rank in top quarter: | 77% |
|---|---|---|---|
| SAT critical reading: | 570-680 | Rank in top tenth: | 45% |
| SAT math: | 570-670 | End year in good standing: | 99% |
| SAT writing: | 560-660 | Return as sophomores: | 89% |
| ACT composite: | 25-29 | Out-of-state: | 47% |
| GPA 3.75 or higher: | 50% | Live on campus: | 98% |
| GPA 3.50-3.74: | 20% | Fraternities: | 20% |
| GPA 3.0-3.49: | 21% | Sororities: | 30% |
| GPA 2.0-2.99: | 9% | | |

**Basis for selection.** Academic achievement most important, including courses taken, grades received. Test scores also important. Motivation and activities considered. Rank in top fifth of class preferred. Alumni children and minorities receive special consideration. SAT/ACT optional for students ranking in top 10% of class, or with minimum 3.5 GPA from non-ranking school. Interview recommended.

**High school preparation.** College-preparatory program required. 17 units required; 22 recommended. Required and recommended units include English 4, mathematics 3-4, social studies 1-4, science 1-4 (laboratory 1-2), foreign language 2-4, academic electives 2.5. An additional 2.5 credits spread among academic or arts electives.

**2009-2010 Annual costs.** Tuition/fees: $38,670. Room/board: $9,250. Books/supplies: $1,000. Personal expenses: $1,200.

**2009-2010 Financial aid. Need-based:** 452 full-time freshmen applied for aid; 359 were judged to have need; 359 of these received aid. Average need met was 85%. Average scholarship/grant was $25,580; average loan $3,661. 77% of total undergraduate aid awarded as scholarships/grants, 23% as loans/jobs. **Non-need-based:** Awarded to 583 full-time undergraduates, including 178 freshmen. Scholarships awarded for academics, alumni affiliation, art, leadership, music/drama.

**Application procedures. Admission:** Closing date 2/15 (receipt date). No application fee. Admission notification 4/1. Must reply by 5/1. Rolling notification for Early Action within 7 weeks of receipt of application. **Financial aid:** Closing date 2/15. FAFSA, institutional form, CSS PROFILE required. Applicants notified by 4/1; must reply by 5/1 or within 2 week(s) of notification.

**Academics.** Summer undergraduate research fellowships available. Independent Learning Experience required of all. Study abroad encouraged. All first-year students complete overview of human thought, creativity, culture, history in a 2-semester seminar called the Common Intellectual Experience (CIE). **Special study options:** Combined bachelor's/graduate degree, double major, dual enrollment of high school students, ESL, exchange student, independent study, internships, semester at sea, student-designed major, study abroad, teacher certification program, United Nations semester, Washington semester. Howard University semester. **Credit/placement by examination:** AP, CLEP, IB, institutional tests. **Support services:** Pre-admission summer program, reduced course load, tutoring, writing center.

**Majors. Area/ethnic studies:** American, East Asian. **Biology:** General. **Communications:** General. **Computer sciences:** Computer science. **Conservation:** Environmental studies. **Foreign languages:** Classics, French, German, Spanish. **History:** General. **Interdisciplinary:** Biological/physical sciences, neuroscience. **Math:** General. **Parks/recreation:** Health/fitness. **Philosophy/religion:** Philosophy. **Physical sciences:** Chemistry, physics. **Psychology:** General. **Social sciences:** Anthropology, economics, international relations, political science, sociology. **Visual/performing arts:** Art, art history/conservation, dance, dramatic.

**Most popular majors.** Biology 16%, interdisciplinary studies 8%, parks/recreation 10%, psychology 8%, social sciences 23%.

**Computing on campus.** PC or laptop required. 1,655 workstations in dormitories, library, computer center, student center. Dormitories wired for high-speed internet access and linked to campus network. Commuter students can connect to campus network. Online course registration, online library, helpline, repair service, student web hosting, wireless network available.

**Student life. Freshman orientation:** Mandatory. Preregistration for classes offered. Two-day session in June and 4-day session in August before start of classes. **Housing:** Guaranteed on-campus for all undergraduates. Coed dorms, single-sex dorms, wellness housing available. $500 nonrefundable deposit, deadline 5/1. Multicultural, community service, art, physical science, literature houses and quiet halls available. **Activities:** Bands, campus ministries, choral groups, dance, drama, film society, literary magazine, music ensembles, Model UN, musical theater, radio station, student government, student newspaper, TV station, Relay for Life, Association of Latinos Motivated to Achieve, Best Buddies, College Democrats, College Republicans, Hillel, Inter-Faith Outreach, Buddhist meditation group.

**Athletics.** NCAA. **Intercollegiate:** Baseball M, basketball, cross-country, field hockey W, football (tackle) M, golf, gymnastics W, lacrosse, soccer, softball W, swimming, tennis, track and field, volleyball W, wrestling M. **Intramural:** Basketball, football (non-tackle) M, soccer, softball, squash, swimming, tennis, volleyball. **Team name:** Bears.

**Student services.** Adult student services, alcohol/substance abuse counseling, chaplain/spiritual director, career counseling, student employment services, financial aid counseling, health services, minority student services, personal counseling, placement for graduates. **Physically disabled:** Services for visually, speech, hearing impaired.

**Contact.** E-mail: admissions@ursinus.edu
Phone: (610) 409-3200 Fax: (610) 409-3662
Richard Floyd, Director of Admission, Ursinus College, PO Box 1000, Collegeville, PA 19426-1000

## Valley Forge Christian College
### Phoenixville, Pennsylvania
www.vfcc.edu                              CB code: 2579

- Private 4-year liberal arts college affiliated with Assemblies of God
- Residential campus in large town
- 927 degree-seeking undergraduates: 10% part-time, 52% women, 10% African American, 3% Asian American, 10% Hispanic American
- 20 degree-seeking graduate students
- 73% of applicants admitted
- SAT or ACT with writing, application essay required
- 51% graduate within 6 years

**General.** Founded in 1938. Regionally accredited. **Degrees:** 134 bachelor's, 12 associate awarded; master's offered. **Location:** 25 miles from Philadelphia. **Calendar:** Semester, limited summer session. **Full-time faculty:** 31 total; 55% have terminal degrees, 10% minority, 36% women. **Part-time faculty:** 49 total; 16% have terminal degrees, 8% minority, 31% women. **Class size:** 64% < 20, 25% 20-39, 3% 40-49, 5% 50-99, 3% >100.

**Freshman class profile.** 533 applied, 388 admitted, 232 enrolled.

| Mid 50% test scores | | | |
|---|---|---|---|
| SAT critical reading: | 420-540 | End year in good standing: | 77% |
| SAT math: | 390-540 | Return as sophomores: | 79% |
| SAT writing: | 350-580 | Out-of-state: | 8% |
| ACT composite: | 17-25 | Live on campus: | 85% |

**Basis for selection.** School achievement record, pastor recommendation, written essay, test scores important. Bible test required for all; music, computer, English, and math tests required for some. Interview recommended. **Homeschooled:** Statement describing homeschool structure and mission required. Student must sign and date a VFCC home schooled self-certification form. **Learning Disabled:** Academic recommendation from counselor IEP or other.

**High school preparation.** 16 units recommended. Recommended units include English 4, mathematics 2, social studies 4, science 4 and foreign language 2.

**2010-2011 Annual costs.** Tuition/fees: $16,250. Room/board: $7,096. Books/supplies: $794. Personal expenses: $1,764.

**2008-2009 Financial aid. Need-based:** 183 full-time freshmen applied for aid; 158 were judged to have need; 157 of these received aid. Average need met was 51%. Average scholarship/grant was $5,543; average loan $3,095. 40% of total undergraduate aid awarded as scholarships/grants, 60% as loans/jobs. **Non-need-based:** Awarded to 278 full-time undergraduates, including 190 freshmen. Scholarships awarded for academics, leadership, music/drama, religious affiliation, state residency.

**Application procedures. Admission:** Priority date 5/1; deadline 8/1 (receipt date). $25 fee, may be waived for applicants with need, free for online applicants. Admission notification 8/15. Admission notification on a rolling basis. **Financial aid:** Priority date 5/1; no closing date. FAFSA required. Applicants notified on a rolling basis starting 3/15; must reply within 3 week(s) of notification.

**Academics. Special study options:** Accelerated study, distance learning, dual enrollment of high school students, ESL, independent study, internships, liberal arts/career combination, study abroad, teacher certification program, weekend college. **Credit/placement by examination:** AP, CLEP, IB, SAT, ACT, institutional tests. 30 credit hours maximum toward associate degree, 30 toward bachelor's. **Support services:** Learning center, reduced course load, remedial instruction, study skills assistance, tutoring, writing center.

**Majors. Business:** Business admin. **Communications:** Digital media. **Education:** Early childhood, elementary, music. **Foreign languages:** Translation. **Public administration:** Social work. **Theology:** Bible, missionary, pastoral counseling, religious ed, sacred music, theology. **Visual/performing arts:** Music performance.

**Most popular majors.** Business/marketing 10%, education 18%, psychology 14%, theological studies 50%.

**Computing on campus.** PC or laptop required. 86 workstations in library, computer center. Dormitories wired for high-speed internet access and linked to campus network. Commuter students can connect to campus network. Online course registration, online library, helpline, repair service, student web hosting, wireless network available.

**Student life. Freshman orientation:** Mandatory, $55 fee. Preregistration for classes offered. 3-day program held weekend prior to beginning of classes.

**Policies:** Religious observance required. **Housing:** Guaranteed on-campus for all undergraduates. Single-sex dorms, apartments available. $100 nonrefundable deposit. **Activities:** Bands, campus ministries, choral groups, dance, drama, music ensembles, student government, student newspaper.

**Athletics.** NCCAA. **Intercollegiate:** Baseball M, basketball, soccer, volleyball W. **Intramural:** Basketball, bowling, football (non-tackle), soccer, softball. **Team name:** Patriots.

**Student services.** Chaplain/spiritual director, career counseling, student employment services, financial aid counseling, health services, personal counseling, placement for graduates.

**Contact.** E-mail: admission@vfcc.edu
Phone: (610) 935-0450 Toll-free number: (800) 432-8322
Fax: (610) 917-2069
Rev. William Chenco, Director of Admissions, Valley Forge Christian College, 1401 Charlestown Road, Phoenixville, PA 19460

## Villanova University
### Villanova, Pennsylvania
www.villanova.edu              CB member   CB code: 2959

- Private 4-year university affiliated with Roman Catholic Church
- Residential campus in large town
- 6,897 degree-seeking undergraduates: 4% part-time, 51% women, 5% African American, 7% Asian American, 7% Hispanic American, 3% international
- 3,061 degree-seeking graduate students
- 46% of applicants admitted
- SAT or ACT with writing, application essay required
- 89% graduate within 6 years

**General.** Founded in 1842. Regionally accredited. **Degrees:** 1,927 bachelor's awarded; master's, doctoral, professional offered. **ROTC:** Army, Naval, Air Force. **Location:** 12 miles from Philadelphia. **Calendar:** Semester, extensive summer session. **Full-time faculty:** 570 total; 89% have terminal degrees, 14% minority, 37% women. **Part-time faculty:** 339 total; 37% have terminal degrees, 6% minority, 45% women. **Class size:** 43% < 20, 53% 20-39, 1% 40-49, 2% 50-99, less than 1% >100. **Special facilities:** Astronomy and astrophysics observatories, electron microscope, research with NASA, structural engineering teaching and research laboratory.

**Freshman class profile.** 13,098 applied, 6,079 admitted, 1,643 enrolled.

| Mid 50% test scores | | | |
|---|---|---|---|
| SAT critical reading: | 580-680 | Rank in top tenth: | 58% |
| SAT math: | 620-710 | Return as sophomores: | 94% |
| GPA 3.75 or higher: | 61% | Out-of-state: | 79% |
| GPA 3.50-3.74: | 22% | Live on campus: | 97% |
| GPA 3.0-3.49: | 15% | International: | 2% |
| GPA 2.0-2.99: | 2% | Fraternities: | 15% |
| Rank in top quarter: | 88% | Sororities: | 25% |

**Basis for selection.** High school record, class rank, standardized test scores, counselor recommendation, essay, extracurricular activities considered. Interview required for finalists of health affiliation programs and Presidential Scholarship consideration. **Homeschooled:** Objective third-party evaluation (state high school association, for example), including syllabi, required.

**High school preparation.** College-preparatory program required. 22 units required. Required and recommended units include English 4, mathematics 4, science 4 (laboratory 2-3), foreign language 2-4 and academic electives 2. 4 social studies and/or history required. Total units required varies by academic college. 3 laboratory science recommended.

**2009-2010 Annual costs.** Tuition/fees: $38,820. Full-time tuition includes laptop for all students. Room/board: $10,510. Books/supplies: $950. Personal expenses: $950.

**2009-2010 Financial aid. Need-based:** 1,187 full-time freshmen applied for aid; 870 were judged to have need; 869 of these received aid. Average need met was 87%. Average scholarship/grant was $25,493; average loan $3,462. 64% of total undergraduate aid awarded as scholarships/grants, 36% as loans/jobs. **Non-need-based:** Awarded to 1,476 full-time undergraduates, including 414 freshmen. Scholarships awarded for academics, alumni affiliation, athletics, leadership, minority status, religious affiliation, ROTC.

**Application procedures. Admission:** Closing date 1/7 (receipt date). $75 fee, may be waived for applicants with need. Application must be submitted online. Admission notification 4/1. Must reply by 5/1. November 1 priority application date for scholarship consideration. **Financial aid:** Closing date 2/7. FAFSA, institutional form, CSS PROFILE required. Applicants notified by 4/1; must reply by 5/1 or within 2 week(s) of notification.

**Academics.** **Special study options:** Accelerated study, combined bachelor's/ graduate degree, cooperative education, cross-registration, distance learning, double major, dual enrollment of high school students, ESL, exchange student, honors, independent study, internships, liberal arts/career combination, study abroad, teacher certification program, Washington semester. Cooperative certification programs in elementary education with Rosemont College. **Credit/placement by examination:** AP, CLEP, IB, institutional tests. 30 credit hours maximum toward bachelor's degree. Deans make decisions regarding prior work and life experiences on individual basis. **Support services:** Reduced course load, study skills assistance, tutoring, writing center.

**Majors. Biology:** General. **Business:** Accounting, business admin, finance, management information systems, managerial economics, marketing. **Communications:** General. **Computer sciences:** General, information systems. **Education:** Elementary, secondary. **Engineering:** Chemical, civil, computer, electrical, mechanical. **Foreign languages:** Classics, French, German, Italian, Spanish. **Health:** Nursing (RN), predental, premedicine. **History:** General. **Interdisciplinary:** Biological/physical sciences. **Liberal arts:** Arts/sciences. **Math:** General. **Philosophy/religion:** Philosophy, religion. **Physical sciences:** Astronomy, astrophysics, chemistry, physics. **Protective services:** Law enforcement admin. **Psychology:** General. **Public administration:** Human services. **Social sciences:** Economics, geography, political science, sociology. **Visual/performing arts:** Art history/conservation.

**Most popular majors.** Business/marketing 31%, communications/ journalism 8%, engineering/engineering technologies 11%, health sciences 12%, social sciences 10%.

**Computing on campus.** PC or laptop required. 2,530 workstations in dormitories, library, computer center, student center. Dormitories wired for high-speed internet access and linked to campus network. Commuter students can connect to campus network. Online course registration, online library, helpline, repair service, student web hosting, wireless network available.

**Student life. Freshman orientation:** Mandatory, $125 fee. 4-day on-campus program prior to start of fall term. **Housing:** Guaranteed on-campus for freshmen. Coed dorms, single-sex dorms, apartments, wellness housing available. $700 nonrefundable deposit, deadline 5/1. On-campus housing available for transfer students on space-available basis; themed learning communities. **Activities:** Bands, campus ministries, choral groups, dance, drama, film society, international student organizations, literary magazine, music ensembles, Model UN, musical theater, radio station, student government, student newspaper, symphony orchestra, TV station, Special Olympics, Amnesty International, Villanovans for Life, Black Cultural Society, Big Brother/Sister, Committee for the Homeless, Project Sunshine, Habitat for Humanity, Blue Key Society.

**Athletics.** NCAA. **Intercollegiate:** Baseball M, basketball, bowling W, cheerleading, cross-country, diving, field hockey W, football (tackle) M, golf M, lacrosse, rowing (crew) W, soccer, softball W, swimming, tennis, track and field, volleyball W, water polo W. **Intramural:** Basketball, cross-country, field hockey W, football (non-tackle), skiing, soccer, softball, tennis, volleyball. **Team name:** Wildcats.

**Student services.** Adult student services, alcohol/substance abuse counseling, chaplain/spiritual director, career counseling, services for economically disadvantaged, student employment services, financial aid counseling, health services, minority student services, personal counseling, placement for graduates. **Physically disabled:** Services for visually, hearing impaired.

**Contact.** E-mail: gotovu@villanova.edu
Phone: (610) 519-4000 Fax: (610) 519-6450
Michael Gaynor, Director of University Admission, Villanova University, 800 Lancaster Avenue, Villanova, PA 19085-1672

---

## Washington & Jefferson College

**Washington, Pennsylvania**  **CB member**
**www.washjeff.edu**  **CB code: 2967**

- Private 4-year liberal arts college
- Residential campus in large town
- 1,479 degree-seeking undergraduates: 1% part-time, 47% women, 3% African American, 1% Asian American, 1% Hispanic American
- 42% of applicants admitted
- Application essay required
- 73% graduate within 6 years; 36% enter graduate study

---

**General.** Founded in 1781. Regionally accredited. **Degrees:** 320 bachelor's awarded. **ROTC:** Army, Air Force. **Location:** 27 miles from Pittsburgh. **Calendar:** 4-1-4, limited summer session. **Full-time faculty:** 116 total; 91% have terminal degrees, 13% minority, 40% women. **Part-time faculty:** 43 total; 33% have terminal degrees, 14% minority, 40% women. **Class size:** 70% < 20, 30% 20-39, less than 1% 40-49. **Special facilities:** Microplate reader, cell culture labs, isolator lab, X-ray diffraction unit, neuropsychology lab, atomic absorption unit, nuclear magnetic resonance lab, refrigerated centrifuge, global learning unit, language lab, spectrometers, laser scanning confocal microscope facility, Abernathy field station.

**Freshman class profile.** 6,658 applied, 2,777 admitted, 393 enrolled.

| Mid 50% test scores | | | |
|---|---|---|---|
| SAT critical reading: | 510-610 | GPA 2.0-2.99: | 22% |
| SAT math: | 520-620 | Rank in top quarter: | 71% |
| ACT composite: | 22-28 | Rank in top tenth: | 38% |
| GPA 3.75 or higher: | 24% | End year in good standing: | 92% |
| GPA 3.50-3.74: | 24% | Return as sophomores: | 86% |
| GPA 3.0-3.49: | 30% | Out-of-state: | 31% |
| | | Live on campus: | 96% |

**Basis for selection.** Entire high school record including difficulty of schedule, GPA, class rank, extracurricular activities, essay, letters of recommendation important. **Homeschooled:** Letter of recommendation (nonparent) required.

**High school preparation.** College-preparatory program required. 15 units required. Required units include English 3, mathematics 3, history 1, foreign language 2 and academic electives 6. Six or more academic elective courses from English, math, foreign language, history, and social or natural history required.

**2009-2010 Annual costs.** Tuition/fees: $32,895. Room/board: $9,110. Books/supplies: $800. Personal expenses: $700.

**2009-2010 Financial aid. Need-based:** 359 full-time freshmen applied for aid; 310 were judged to have need; 310 of these received aid. Average need met was 82%. Average scholarship/grant was $9,524; average loan $3,730. 68% of total undergraduate aid awarded as scholarships/grants, 32% as loans/jobs. **Non-need-based:** Awarded to 1,235 full-time undergraduates, including 361 freshmen. Scholarships awarded for academics, alumni affiliation.

**Application procedures. Admission:** Priority date 1/15; deadline 3/1 (postmark date). $25 fee, may be waived for applicants with need, free for online applicants. Admission notification on a rolling basis beginning on or about 10/1. Must reply by 5/1. **Financial aid:** Priority date 2/15; no closing date. FAFSA required. Applicants notified on a rolling basis starting 3/1; must reply by 5/1.

**Academics. Special study options:** Accelerated study, combined bachelor's/ graduate degree, double major, dual enrollment of high school students, honors, independent study, internships, student-designed major, study abroad, teacher certification program, Washington semester. **Credit/placement by examination:** AP, CLEP, IB, SAT, ACT, institutional tests. 68 credit hours maximum toward bachelor's degree. **Support services:** Learning center, reduced course load, study skills assistance, tutoring.

**Majors. Biology:** General, biochemistry, biophysics, cellular/anatomical. **Business:** General, accounting, international. **Computer sciences:** Information technology. **Conservation:** Environmental studies. **Education:** General, art. **Foreign languages:** French, German, Spanish. **History:** General. **Interdisciplinary:** Global studies. **Math:** General. **Philosophy/religion:** Philosophy, religion. **Physical sciences:** Chemistry, physics. **Psychology:** General. **Social sciences:** Economics, political science, sociology. **Visual/ performing arts:** Art, theater history. **Other:** Multi-/interdisciplinary studies.

**Most popular majors.** Biology 9%, business/marketing 27%, education 7%, English 9%, foreign language 7%, history 6%, psychology 13%, social sciences 11%.

**Computing on campus.** 450 workstations in library, computer center, student center. Dormitories wired for high-speed internet access and linked to campus network. Commuter students can connect to campus network. Online course registration, online library, helpline, repair service, student web hosting, wireless network available.

**Student life. Freshman orientation:** Mandatory. Preregistration for classes offered. 3-day series of sessions and activities to help students adjust to campus life and understand their roles as members of the campus community. **Policies:** All students required to live in campus housing unless granted written approval or living with parents 15 miles or less from the college. Students not permitted to smoke in rooms, hallways, or lounges. **Housing:** Guaranteed on-campus for all undergraduates. Coed dorms, single-sex dorms, special housing for disabled, apartments, fraternity/sorority housing, wellness housing available. Pets allowed in dorm rooms. On-campus suites available. **Activities:** Bands, campus ministries, choral groups, dance, drama, film society, international student organizations, literary magazine, music ensembles, Model UN, musical theater, radio station, student government, student newspaper, symphony orchestra, Newman Club, Hillel Society, Young Republicans, College Democrats, liberal student union, Black student union, Alpha Phi Omega, Get Involved in Volunteer Experiences, Asian culture association, Gay Straight Alliance.

**Athletics.** NCAA. **Intercollegiate:** Baseball M, basketball, cheerleading, cross-country, diving, field hockey W, football (tackle) M, golf, lacrosse, soccer, softball W, swimming, tennis, track and field, volleyball W, water polo, wrestling M. **Intramural:** Basketball, bowling, cross-country, football (non-tackle) M, racquetball, soccer, table tennis, tennis, triathlon, volleyball. **Team name:** Presidents.

**Student services.** Adult student services, alcohol/substance abuse counseling, chaplain/spiritual director, career counseling, student employment services, financial aid counseling, health services, minority student services, personal counseling, placement for graduates, women's services.

**Contact.** E-mail: admission@washjeff.edu
Phone: (724) 223-6025 Toll-free number: (888) 926-3529
Fax: (724) 223-6534
Alton Newell, Vice President for Enrollment, Washington & Jefferson College, 60 South Lincoln Street, Washington, PA 15301

## Waynesburg University
**Waynesburg, Pennsylvania**  **CB member**
**www.waynesburg.edu**  **CB code: 2969**

- Private 4-year liberal arts college affiliated with Presbyterian Church (USA)
- Residential campus in small town
- 1,533 degree-seeking undergraduates: 2% part-time, 59% women, 3% African American, 1% Hispanic American
- 803 degree-seeking graduate students
- 71% of applicants admitted
- SAT or ACT with writing required
- 59% graduate within 6 years

**General.** Founded in 1849. Regionally accredited. Member of the Council for Christian Colleges and Universities. **Degrees:** 372 bachelor's, 2 associate awarded; master's offered. **ROTC:** Army. **Location:** 50 miles from Pittsburgh. **Calendar:** Semester, limited summer session. **Full-time faculty:** 67 total; 61% have terminal degrees, 4% minority, 48% women. **Part-time faculty:** 99 total; 18% have terminal degrees, 48% women. **Class size:** 60% < 20, 36% 20-39, 3% 40-49, less than 1% 50-99. **Special facilities:** Geological museum, historical museum, constitutional studies and moral leadership center, research and economic development center, service leadership center.

**Freshman class profile.** 1,875 applied, 1,339 admitted, 386 enrolled.

| Mid 50% test scores | | GPA 2.0-2.99: | 13% |
|---|---|---|---|
| SAT critical reading: | 450-540 | Rank in top quarter: | 43% |
| SAT math: | 450-560 | Rank in top tenth: | 15% |
| GPA 3.75 or higher: | 28% | Return as sophomores: | 76% |
| GPA 3.50-3.74: | 18% | Out-of-state: | 19% |
| GPA 3.0-3.49: | 41% | Live on campus: | 86% |

**Basis for selection.** High school classes taken, grades, test scores, activities, community activities, interview, and recommendations considered. Essay, interview recommended. **Homeschooled:** Statement describing homeschool structure and mission, transcript of courses and grades, state high school equivalency certificate required. College should be apprised if applicant enrolled in program approved by state's department of education.

**High school preparation.** College-preparatory program required. 16 units required. Required and recommended units include English 4, mathematics 3, social studies 2, science 2-3, foreign language 2 and academic electives 5.

**2010-2011 Annual costs.** Tuition/fees: $18,410. Room/board: $7,580. Books/supplies: $1,300. Personal expenses: $170.

**2009-2010 Financial aid.** **Need-based:** Average need met was 81%. Average scholarship/grant was $12,105; average loan $3,286. 98% of total undergraduate aid awarded as scholarships/grants, 2% as loans/jobs. **Non-need-based:** Scholarships awarded for academics, alumni affiliation, job skills, leadership, religious affiliation, state residency.

**Application procedures.** **Admission:** No deadline. $20 fee, may be waived for applicants with need, free for online applicants. Admission notification on a rolling basis. Rolling date as specified in deposit letter. **Financial aid:** Priority date 3/15; no closing date. FAFSA required. Applicants

notified on a rolling basis starting 2/15; must reply within 2 week(s) of notification.

**Academics.** Nursing majors must complete 126 credit hours for bachelor of science degree. **Special study options:** Accelerated study, combined bachelor's/graduate degree, distance learning, double major, dual enrollment of high school students, ESL, honors, independent study, internships, liberal arts/career combination, study abroad, teacher certification program, Washington semester. 3-2 program in engineering with Penn State University in state College, PA and Washington University in St Louis; 3-1 program in marine biology with Florida Institute of Technology; 3-3 law program with Duquesne University. **Credit/placement by examination:** CLEP, IB, SAT, ACT, institutional tests. 15 credit hours maximum toward bachelor's degree. **Support services:** Learning center, reduced course load, study skills assistance, tutoring, writing center.

**Majors. Biology:** General, environmental, marine. **Business:** General, accounting, business admin, finance, international, international marketing. **Communications:** General, advertising, broadcast journalism, digital media, journalism, public relations. **Computer sciences:** General, computer science, information technology, networking. **Education:** Art, biology, chemistry, elementary, English, history, mathematics, science, secondary, social studies, special. **Family/consumer sciences:** Family studies. **Health:** Athletic training, nursing (RN), predental, premedicine, preveterinary. **History:** General. **Legal studies:** Prelaw. **Math:** General. **Parks/recreation:** Exercise sciences, sports admin. **Philosophy/religion:** Religion. **Physical sciences:** Chemistry. **Protective services:** Forensics, law enforcement admin. **Psychology:** General. **Public administration:** Human services. **Social sciences:** General, political science, sociology. **Theology:** Theology. **Visual/performing arts:** Art, arts management. **Other:** Forensic accounting.

**Most popular majors.** Business/marketing 16%, communications/journalism 6%, education 7%, health sciences 35%, public administration/social services 7%.

**Computing on campus.** 160 workstations in dormitories, library, computer center, student center. Dormitories wired for high-speed internet access and linked to campus network. Commuter students can connect to campus network. Online course registration, online library, helpline, wireless network available.

**Student life. Freshman orientation:** Mandatory. Preregistration for classes offered. One-day summer program for parents and students; 2-day program prior to start of classes. **Policies:** No alcohol or drugs permitted on campus. **Housing:** Guaranteed on-campus for all undergraduates. Coed dorms, single-sex dorms available. $150 partly refundable deposit. **Activities:** Bands, choral groups, dance, drama, literary magazine, music ensembles, musical theater, radio station, student government, student newspaper, TV station, Fellowship of Christian Athletes, Newman Club, black student union, Waynesburg Christian Fellowship, Bonner Scholars, Alpha Phi Omega, Habitat for Humanity, leadership program.

**Athletics.** NCAA. **Intercollegiate:** Baseball M, basketball, cross-country, football (tackle) M, golf, lacrosse W, soccer, softball W, tennis, track and field, volleyball W, wrestling M. **Intramural:** Basketball, bowling, football (non-tackle), racquetball, softball, table tennis, volleyball W. **Team name:** Yellow Jackets.

**Student services.** Adult student services, chaplain/spiritual director, career counseling, student employment services, financial aid counseling, health services, minority student services, personal counseling, placement for graduates.

**Contact.** E-mail: admissions@waynesburg.edu
Phone: (724) 852-3248 Toll-free number: (800) 225-7393
Fax: (724) 627-8124
Sarah Zwinger, Director of Admissions, Waynesburg University, 51 West College Street, Waynesburg, PA 15370-1222

## West Chester University of Pennsylvania
**West Chester, Pennsylvania**  **CB member**
**www.wcupa.edu**  **CB code: 2659**

- Public 4-year university
- Commuter campus in large town
- 11,561 degree-seeking undergraduates: 7% part-time, 60% women, 9% African American, 2% Asian American, 3% Hispanic American
- 1,692 degree-seeking graduate students
- 49% of applicants admitted
- SAT or ACT with writing, application essay required
- 65% graduate within 6 years

**General.** Founded in 1871. Regionally accredited. **Degrees:** 2,252 bachelor's awarded; master's offered. **ROTC:** Army, Air Force. **Location:** 23

miles from Philadelphia. **Calendar:** Semester, extensive summer session. **Full-time faculty:** 550 total; 14% minority, 51% women. **Part-time faculty:** 264 total; 8% minority, 53% women. **Class size:** 25% < 20, 65% 20-39, 5% 40-49, 4% 50-99, less than 1% >100. **Special facilities:** Herbarium, 151-acre natural area for environmental studies, planetarium, speech and hearing clinic, autism clinic, center for government and community affairs, mineral museum.

**Freshman class profile.** 13,619 applied, 6,667 admitted, 2,248 enrolled.

| Mid 50% test scores | | | |
|---|---|---|---|
| SAT critical reading: | 480-560 | Rank in top quarter: | 33% |
| SAT math: | 490-580 | Rank in top tenth: | 9% |
| SAT writing: | 480-570 | Return as sophomores: | 84% |
| GPA 3.75 or higher: | 18% | Out-of-state: | 15% |
| GPA 3.50-3.74: | 19% | Live on campus: | 92% |
| GPA 3.0-3.49: | 41% | Fraternities: | 7% |
| GPA 2.0-2.99: | 22% | Sororities: | 4% |

**Basis for selection.** College preparatory curriculum in high school, standardized test scores, and personal statement required. Specific course prerequisites depend on major selection. Additional documentation is required of candidates for the summer academic development program. Interview required for athletic training, premedical, and pharmaceutical product development programs. Audition required for music. **Homeschooled:** Students must have work certified by PA Homeschoolers' Association or their high school.

**High school preparation.** College-preparatory program required. 16 units required; 25 recommended. Required and recommended units include English 4, mathematics 3-4, social studies 2, history 2, science 2-3 (laboratory 1-2), foreign language 2, computer science 1, visual/performing arts 1 and academic electives 1-2.

**2009-2010 Annual costs.** Tuition/fees: $7,211; $15,543 out-of-state. Room/board: $7,214. Books/supplies: $1,320. Personal expenses: $2,072.

**Application procedures. Admission:** Priority date 1/1; no deadline. $35 fee, may be waived for applicants with need. Admission notification on a rolling basis beginning on or about 10/1. Must reply by May 1 or within 4 week(s) if notified thereafter. **Financial aid:** Priority date 3/1; no closing date. FAFSA required. Must reply within 4 week(s) of notification.

**Academics. Special study options:** Cooperative education, cross-registration, distance learning, double major, dual enrollment of high school students, ESL, exchange student, honors, independent study, internships, liberal arts/career combination, student-designed major, study abroad, teacher certification program, Washington semester. **Credit/placement by examination:** AP, CLEP, IB, SAT, institutional tests. 32 credit hours maximum toward bachelor's degree. **Support services:** Learning center, pre-admission summer program, reduced course load, remedial instruction, study skills assistance, tutoring, writing center.

**Majors. Area/ethnic studies:** American, women's. **Biology:** General, biochemistry. **Business:** General, accounting, business admin, finance, managerial economics, sales/distribution. **Computer sciences:** General. **Education:** Early childhood, elementary, middle, special. **Foreign languages:** French, German, Latin, Russian, Spanish. **Health:** Athletic training, audiology/speech pathology, dietetics, health care admin, nursing (RN), premedicine. **History:** General. **Liberal arts:** Arts/sciences. **Math:** General. **Parks/recreation:** Health/fitness. **Philosophy/religion:** Philosophy. **Physical sciences:** Analytical chemistry, chemistry, geology, physics. **Protective services:** Criminal justice. **Psychology:** General. **Public administration:** Social work. **Social sciences:** Anthropology, geography, political science, sociology. **Visual/performing arts:** Art, dance, dramatic, music performance, studio arts. **Other:** Pharmaceutical product development.

**Most popular majors.** Business/marketing 16%, education 17%, English 8%, health sciences 11%, liberal arts 10%, visual/performing arts 7%.

**Computing on campus.** 1,200 workstations in dormitories, library, computer center, student center. Dormitories wired for high-speed internet access and linked to campus network. Commuter students can connect to campus network. Online course registration, helpline, repair service, wireless network available.

**Student life. Freshman orientation:** Mandatory, $155 fee. One-day program in late June/early July followed by 3-day program prior to start of classes in August. **Policies:** Code of conduct applicable on and off campus. **Housing:** Coed dorms, single-sex dorms, special housing for disabled, apartments, fraternity/sorority housing, wellness housing available. $100 nonrefundable deposit, deadline 5/1. **Activities:** Bands, campus ministries, choral groups, dance, drama, international student organizations, literary magazine, music ensembles, musical theater, opera, radio station, student government, student newspaper, symphony orchestra, TV station, lesbian, gay, bisexual, and transgender association, Hillel, Newman Club, Crusade for Christ,

Black Student Union, Latino American student organization, College Democrats, College Republicans.

**Athletics.** NCAA. **Intercollegiate:** Baseball M, basketball, cheerleading M, cross-country, diving, field hockey W, football (tackle) M, golf, gymnastics W, lacrosse W, rugby W, soccer, softball W, swimming, tennis, track and field, volleyball W. **Intramural:** Basketball, field hockey, football (non-tackle), soccer, softball, tennis, volleyball. **Team name:** Golden Rams.

**Student services.** Adult student services, alcohol/substance abuse counseling, chaplain/spiritual director, career counseling, services for economically disadvantaged, student employment services, financial aid counseling, health services, legal services, minority student services, on-campus daycare, personal counseling, placement for graduates, veterans' counselor, women's services. **Physically disabled:** Services for visually, speech, hearing impaired. **Learning disabled:** Comprehensive services available.

**Contact.** E-mail: ugadmiss@wcupa.edu
Phone: (610) 436-3411 Toll-free number: (877) 315-2165
Fax: (610) 436-2907
Marsha Haug, Assistant Vice President for Admissions and Enrollment Services, West Chester University of Pennsylvania, Messikomer Hall, West Chester, PA 19383

## Westminster College

New Wilmington, Pennsylvania        CB member
www.westminster.edu                 CB code: 2975

- Private 4-year liberal arts college affiliated with Presbyterian Church (USA)
- Residential campus in small town
- 1,469 degree-seeking undergraduates
- 61% of applicants admitted
- Application essay required

**General.** Founded in 1852. Regionally accredited. General studies curriculum with a freshman common experience. Semester at Oxford. **Degrees:** 306 bachelor's awarded; master's offered. **ROTC:** Army. **Location:** 60 miles from Pittsburgh. **Calendar:** Semester, limited summer session. **Full-time faculty:** 106 total. **Part-time faculty:** 57 total. **Class size:** 63% < 20, 36% 20-39, less than 1% 40-49, less than 1% 50-99. **Special facilities:** Observatory, environmental outdoor laboratory, planetarium, electron microscopes, radar defractor.

**Freshman class profile.** 3,908 applied, 2,394 admitted, 451 enrolled.

| Mid 50% test scores | | | |
|---|---|---|---|
| SAT critical reading: | 480-570 | GPA 2.0-2.99: | 19% |
| SAT math: | 490-600 | Rank in top quarter: | 59% |
| SAT writing: | 480-580 | Rank in top tenth: | 26% |
| ACT composite: | 20-26 | Out-of-state: | 19% |
| GPA 3.75 or higher: | 29% | Live on campus: | 97% |
| GPA 3.50-3.74: | 20% | Fraternities: | 33% |
| GPA 3.0-3.49: | 32% | Sororities: | 35% |

**Basis for selection.** Class rank most important. Test scores also important. SAT or ACT recommended. Interview recommended for all; audition recommended for music; portfolio recommended for art.

**High school preparation.** 16 units required. Required units include English 4, mathematics 3, social studies 2, history 1, science 2 (laboratory 2), foreign language 2 and academic electives 3.

**2010-2011 Annual costs.** Tuition/fees: $29,150. Room/board: $8,840. Books/supplies: $1,000. Personal expenses: $1,250.

**2009-2010 Financial aid. Non-need-based:** Scholarships awarded for academics, athletics.

**Application procedures. Admission:** Closing date 5/1. $35 fee, may be waived for applicants with need. Admission notification on a rolling basis beginning on or about 11/1. **Financial aid:** Closing date 5/1. FAFSA, institutional form required. Applicants notified on a rolling basis starting 11/1; must reply by 5/1 or within 3 week(s) of notification.

**Academics. Special study options:** Double major, exchange student, honors, independent study, internships, liberal arts/career combination, semester at sea, student-designed major, study abroad, teacher certification program, Washington semester. 3-2 engineering programs with Case Western Reserve University (OH), Penn State, Washington University (MO), 3-2 law program with Duquesne University. **Credit/placement by examination:** AP, CLEP, institutional tests. **Support services:** Learning center, reduced course load, tutoring.

**Majors. Biology:** General, biochemistry, biophysics, ecology, molecular. **Business:** Accounting, business admin, finance, international, international finance, management science, managerial economics, organizational behavior. **Communications:** Broadcast journalism, public relations. **Computer sciences:** General, computer science, programming. **Education:** General, elementary, English, foreign languages, middle, multi-level teacher, secondary, social studies. **Engineering:** General. **Foreign languages:** General, classics, French, German, Latin, Spanish. **Health:** Predental, premedicine, prepharmacy, preveterinary. **History:** General. **Interdisciplinary:** Biopsychology, math/computer science. **Legal studies:** Prelaw. **Math:** General. **Philosophy/religion:** Philosophy, religion. **Physical sciences:** Chemistry, physics. **Protective services:** Criminal justice. **Psychology:** General. **Public administration:** Social work. **Social sciences:** Economics, international relations, political science, sociology. **Theology:** Religious ed. **Visual/performing arts:** Art, dramatic, music performance, music theory/composition, piano/organ, studio arts, voice/opera.

**Computing on campus.** 160 workstations in library, computer center. Dormitories linked to campus network. Commuter students can connect to campus network. Helpline available.

**Student life. Freshman orientation:** Mandatory, $105 fee. 4-day general social and academic orientation. **Housing:** Guaranteed on-campus for freshmen. Coed dorms, single-sex dorms, special housing for disabled, fraternity/sorority housing available. **Activities:** Bands, campus ministries, choral groups, dance, drama, film society, literary magazine, music ensembles, musical theater, radio station, student government, student newspaper, symphony orchestra, TV station, Fellowship of Christian Athletes, mock convention, service organizations, social awareness and action groups, Students in Action Who Value the Environment, Habitat for Humanity, Alpha Phi Omega.

**Athletics. NCAA. Intercollegiate:** Baseball M, basketball, cross-country, football (tackle) M, golf, soccer, softball W, swimming, tennis, track and field, volleyball W. **Intramural:** Archery, badminton, basketball, equestrian, racquetball, rugby M, softball, track and field W, volleyball. **Team name:** Titans.

**Student services.** Adult student services, career counseling, student employment services, health services, personal counseling, placement for graduates.

**Contact.** E-mail: admis@westminster.edu
Phone: (724) 946-7100 Fax: (724) 946-7171
Bradley Tokar, Dean of Admissions, Westminster College, Admissions, Westminster College, New Wilmington, PA 16172-0001

## Widener University

Chester, Pennsylvania       CB member
www.widener.edu       CB code: 2642

- Private 4-year university
- Residential campus in large town
- 3,247 degree-seeking undergraduates: 17% part-time, 55% women, 14% African American, 3% Asian American, 3% Hispanic American, 2% international
- 2,944 degree-seeking graduate students
- 70% of applicants admitted
- SAT or ACT (ACT writing optional) required
- 57% graduate within 6 years

**General.** Founded in 1821. Regionally accredited. **Degrees:** 605 bachelor's, 21 associate awarded; master's, doctoral, professional offered. **ROTC:** Army, Naval, Air Force. **Location:** 10 miles from Philadelphia. **Calendar:** Semester, limited summer session. **Full-time faculty:** 310 total; 89% have terminal degrees, 12% minority, 50% women. **Part-time faculty:** 353 total; 45% have terminal degrees, 11% minority, 46% women. **Class size:** 60% < 20, 39% 20-39, less than 1% 40-49, 1% 50-99. **Special facilities:** Astronomical observatory, rock climbing wall, restaurant lab, executive seminar facility, child development center, recording studio, education lab, commercial graphics lab, physical therapy lab.

**Freshman class profile.** 4,636 applied, 3,251 admitted, 720 enrolled.

| Mid 50% test scores | | | |
|---|---|---|---|
| SAT critical reading: | 440-540 | Rank in top tenth: | 13% |
| SAT math: | 460-560 | Return as sophomores: | 72% |
| GPA 3.75 or higher: | 22% | Out-of-state: | 44% |
| GPA 3.50-3.74: | 19% | Live on campus: | 85% |
| GPA 3.0-3.49: | 33% | International: | 1% |
| GPA 2.0-2.99: | 26% | Fraternities: | 9% |
| Rank in top quarter: | 39% | Sororities: | 8% |

**Basis for selection.** Strength of curriculum, GPA, standardized test scores, class rank most important; recommendations, strength of character important. Interview recommended. **Homeschooled:** Transcript of courses and grades required. Curriculum validation and interview with director of admissions required.

**High school preparation.** College-preparatory program required. 18 units required; 23 recommended. Required and recommended units include English 4, mathematics 3-4, social studies 3-4, science 3-4 (laboratory 2), foreign language 2 and academic electives 3.

**2010-2011 Annual costs.** Tuition/fees: $33,270. Room/board: $11,720. Books/supplies: $1,200. Personal expenses: $1,170.

**2009-2010 Financial aid. Need-based:** 667 full-time freshmen applied for aid; 622 were judged to have need; 621 of these received aid. Average need met was 77%. Average scholarship/grant was $9,460; average loan $4,130. 56% of total undergraduate aid awarded as scholarships/grants, 44% as loans/jobs. **Non-need-based:** Awarded to 2,036 full-time undergraduates, including 582 freshmen. Scholarships awarded for academics, leadership, music/drama, ROTC.

**Application procedures. Admission:** Priority date 2/15; no deadline. $35 fee, may be waived for applicants with need, free for online applicants. Admission notification on a rolling basis beginning on or about 10/1. Must reply by May 1 or within 2 week(s) if notified thereafter. **Financial aid:** Priority date 2/15; no closing date. FAFSA required. Applicants notified on a rolling basis starting 3/15; must reply within 4 week(s) of notification.

**Academics. Special study options:** Accelerated study, combined bachelor's/graduate degree, cooperative education, distance learning, double major, ESL, honors, independent study, internships, liberal arts/career combination, student-designed major, study abroad, teacher certification program, weekend college. **Credit/placement by examination:** AP, CLEP, IB, institutional tests. Students can earn up to 2 years of credit in some fields via CLEP, challenge exams, and Advanced Placement exams. **Support services:** Learning center, pre-admission summer program, reduced course load, remedial instruction, study skills assistance, tutoring, writing center.

**Majors. Area/ethnic studies:** Women's. **Biology:** General, biochemistry. **Business:** Accounting, business admin, finance, financial planning, hospitality admin, human resources, international, management information systems, managerial economics, operations. **Communications:** General. **Computer sciences:** General, computer science, information systems. **Education:** Early childhood, elementary, science, special. **Engineering:** General, chemical, civil, electrical, mechanical. **Foreign languages:** French, Spanish. **Health:** Health services, nursing (RN), predental, premedicine, prenursing, preveterinary. **History:** General. **Legal studies:** Prelaw. **Liberal arts:** Arts/sciences. **Math:** General. **Physical sciences:** Chemistry, physics. **Protective services:** Law enforcement admin. **Psychology:** General. **Public administration:** Social work. **Social sciences:** Anthropology, economics, international relations, political science, sociology. **Visual/performing arts:** Studio arts.

**Most popular majors.** Business/marketing 27%, engineering/engineering technologies 9%, health sciences 24%, psychology 10%.

**Computing on campus.** 720 workstations in library, student center. Dormitories wired for high-speed internet access and linked to campus network. Commuter students can connect to campus network. Online course registration, online library, helpline, repair service, student web hosting, wireless network available.

**Student life. Freshman orientation:** Mandatory. Preregistration for classes offered. **Housing:** Guaranteed on-campus for freshmen. Coed dorms, single-sex dorms, apartments, cooperative housing, fraternity/sorority housing, wellness housing available. $100 nonrefundable deposit, deadline 5/1. **Activities:** Bands, campus ministries, choral groups, dance, drama, film society, international student organizations, literary magazine, music ensembles, radio station, student government, student newspaper, TV station, Hillel, black student union, political affairs club, Young Republicans, Young Democrats, environmental society, Widener Big Friends, Crusade for Christ, Alpha Phi Omega, Asian student association, presidential service corps.

**Athletics. NCAA. Intercollegiate:** Baseball M, basketball, cheerleading M, cross-country, field hockey W, football (tackle) M, golf M, lacrosse, soccer, softball W, swimming, track and field, volleyball W. **Intramural:** Basketball, cricket M, football (non-tackle), skiing, soccer, softball, volleyball, water polo M. **Team name:** Pride.

**Student services.** Adult student services, alcohol/substance abuse counseling, chaplain/spiritual director, career counseling, services for economically disadvantaged, student employment services, financial aid counseling, health services, on-campus daycare, personal counseling, placement for graduates, veterans' counselor, women's services. **Physically disabled:** Services for visually, speech, hearing impaired. **Learning disabled:** Comprehensive services available.

**Contact.** E-mail: admissions.office@widener.edu
Phone: (610) 499-4126 Toll-free number: (888) 943-3637
Fax: (610) 499-4676
Edwin Wright, Director of Admissions, Widener University, One University Place, Chester, PA 19013

## Wilkes University
### Wilkes-Barre, Pennsylvania
www.wilkes.edu
**CB member**
**CB code: 2977**

- Private 4-year university
- Residential campus in small city
- 2,133 degree-seeking undergraduates: 6% part-time, 48% women, 3% African American, 2% Asian American, 2% Hispanic American, 2% international
- 3,999 degree-seeking graduate students
- 76% of applicants admitted
- SAT or ACT required
- 63% graduate within 6 years

**General.** Founded in 1933. Regionally accredited. **Degrees:** 491 bachelor's awarded; master's, doctoral, professional offered. **ROTC:** Army, Air Force. **Location:** 100 miles from Philadelphia, 140 miles from New York City. **Calendar:** Semester, extensive summer session. **Full-time faculty:** 149 total; 89% have terminal degrees, 8% minority, 47% women. **Part-time faculty:** 305 total; 3% minority, 47% women. **Class size:** 52% < 20, 42% 20-39, 2% 40-49, 5% 50-99, less than 1% >100. **Special facilities:** Performing arts center, field station, telecommunications center, indoor recreation and athletic center.

**Freshman class profile.** 2,641 applied, 1,995 admitted, 532 enrolled.

| Mid 50% test scores | | | |
|---|---|---|---|
| SAT critical reading: | 460-580 | Rank in top tenth: | 25% |
| SAT math: | 480-600 | Return as sophomores: | 80% |
| SAT writing: | 450-570 | Out-of-state: | 20% |
| Rank in top quarter: | 53% | Live on campus: | 73% |

**Basis for selection.** 920 SAT (exclusive of Writing) and/or rank in top 50% of high school class required for unconditional admission. Conditional admission may be offered to some applicants who do not meet these standards; must attend summer program prior to first semester. Interview recommended for all; audition required for theater arts programs.

**High school preparation.** Recommended units include English 4, mathematics 3, social studies 3, science 2 (laboratory 2) and computer science 1.

**2009-2010 Annual costs.** Tuition/fees: $26,010. Room/board: $11,100. Books/supplies: $1,100. Personal expenses: $1,400.

**2008-2009 Financial aid. Need-based:** 534 full-time freshmen applied for aid; 474 were judged to have need; 471 of these received aid. Average need met was 78%. Average scholarship/grant was $9,136; average loan $2,835. 56% of total undergraduate aid awarded as scholarships/grants, 44% as loans/jobs. **Non-need-based:** Awarded to 1,689 full-time undergraduates, including 466 freshmen. Scholarships awarded for academics, leadership, minority status, music/drama.

**Application procedures. Admission:** No deadline. $40 fee, may be waived for applicants with need. Admission notification on a rolling basis. Must reply by May 1 or within 2 week(s) if notified thereafter. **Financial aid:** Priority date 3/1; no closing date. FAFSA required. Applicants notified on a rolling basis starting 3/1.

**Academics. Special study options:** Combined bachelor's/graduate degree, cooperative education, cross-registration, distance learning, double major, dual enrollment of high school students, ESL, external degree, honors, independent study, internships, student-designed major, study abroad, teacher certification program, weekend college. **Credit/placement by examination:** AP, CLEP, institutional tests. Credit by examination may be given to within 30 credits of graduation. **Support services:** Learning center, preadmission summer program, reduced course load, remedial instruction, study skills assistance, tutoring, writing center.

**Majors. Biology:** General, biochemistry. **Business:** Accounting, business admin, entrepreneurial studies. **Communications:** General, digital media. **Computer sciences:** General, information systems. **Education:** Elementary, special. **Engineering:** Electrical, environmental, mechanical. **Engineering technology:** Industrial management. **Foreign languages:** Spanish. **Health:** Clinical lab science, nursing (RN), pharmaceutical sciences. **History:** General. **Liberal arts:** Arts/sciences. **Math:** General. **Philosophy/religion:** Philosophy. **Physical sciences:** Chemistry, geology. **Protective services:** Criminal justice. **Psychology:** General. **Social sciences:** International relations,

political science, sociology. **Visual/performing arts:** Dramatic, music performance.

**Most popular majors.** Biology 10%, business/marketing 15%, communications/journalism 7%, engineering/engineering technologies 10%, health sciences 11%, liberal arts 16%, psychology 9%.

**Computing on campus.** 565 workstations in library, computer center, student center. Dormitories wired for high-speed internet access and linked to campus network. Commuter students can connect to campus network. Online course registration, online library, helpline, wireless network available.

**Student life. Freshman orientation:** Mandatory, $135 fee. Preregistration for classes offered. **Housing:** Guaranteed on-campus for all undergraduates. Coed dorms, single-sex dorms, apartments available. $100 nonrefundable deposit. **Activities:** Bands, campus ministries, choral groups, dance, drama, international student organizations, literary magazine, music ensembles, musical theater, radio station, student government, student newspaper, TV station.

**Athletics.** NCAA. **Intercollegiate:** Baseball M, basketball, cross-country, field hockey W, football (tackle) M, golf M, lacrosse W, soccer, softball W, tennis, volleyball W, wrestling M. **Intramural:** Basketball M, bowling, football (tackle) M, ice hockey M, racquetball, rowing (crew), rugby M, skiing, softball, table tennis, volleyball. **Team name:** Colonels.

**Student services.** Adult student services, career counseling, student employment services, financial aid counseling, health services, personal counseling, placement for graduates, veterans' counselor. **Physically disabled:** Services for visually, hearing impaired.

**Contact.** E-mail: admissions@wilkes.edu
Phone: (570) 408-4400 Toll-free number: (800) 945-5378
Fax: (570) 408-4904
Melanie Mickelson, Vice President of Enrollment Services, Wilkes University, 84 West South Street, Wilkes-Barre, PA 18766

## Wilson College
### Chambersburg, Pennsylvania
www.wilson.edu
**CB member**
**CB code: 2979**

- Private 4-year liberal arts college for women affiliated with Presbyterian Church (USA)
- Residential campus in large town
- 525 degree-seeking undergraduates: 34% part-time, 93% women
- 31 degree-seeking graduate students
- 70% of applicants admitted
- Application essay required
- 60% graduate within 6 years; 20% enter graduate study

**General.** Founded in 1869. Regionally accredited. Men admitted to adult degree program, post-baccalaureate teacher intern program. Residential program for single mothers with children. **Degrees:** 93 bachelor's, 10 associate awarded; master's offered. **ROTC:** Army. **Location:** 90 miles from Washington, DC; 145 miles from Philadelphia. **Calendar:** 4-1-4, limited summer session. **Full-time faculty:** 45 total; 84% have terminal degrees, 7% minority, 53% women. **Part-time faculty:** 34 total; 21% have terminal degrees, 3% minority, 68% women. **Class size:** 82% < 20, 18% 20-39, less than 1% 40-49. **Special facilities:** Equestrian center, sustainable living center, veterinary medical center, archival center, science complex.

**Freshman class profile.** 566 applied, 394 admitted, 103 enrolled.

| Mid 50% test scores | | | |
|---|---|---|---|
| | | GPA 2.0-2.99: | 30% |
| SAT critical reading: | 440-550 | Rank in top quarter: | 40% |
| SAT math: | 420-560 | Rank in top tenth: | 8% |
| SAT writing: | 440-550 | End year in good standing: | 95% |
| ACT composite: | 16-21 | Return as sophomores: | 70% |
| GPA 3.75 or higher: | 18% | Out-of-state: | 47% |
| GPA 3.50-3.74: | 20% | Live on campus: | 87% |
| GPA 3.0-3.49: | 31% | International: | 3% |

**Basis for selection.** Admissions based on secondary school record. Class rank, recommendations, character, and personal qualities also important. SAT/ACT optional for students with 3.0 GPA in specified college prep curriculum from a regionally accredited secondary school. Interview recommended. **Homeschooled:** Transcript of courses and grades, letter of recommendation (nonparent) required.

**High school preparation.** College-preparatory program recommended. 15 units required. Required units include English 4, mathematics 3, social studies 4, science 2 (laboratory 2) and foreign language 2.

**2009-2010 Annual costs.** Tuition/fees: $26,930. Room/board: $9,070. Books/supplies: $1,000. Personal expenses: $800.

**2009-2010 Financial aid. Need-based:** 98 full-time freshmen applied for aid; 92 were judged to have need; 92 of these received aid. Average need met was 82%. Average scholarship/grant was $20,354; average loan $3,323. 66% of total undergraduate aid awarded as scholarships/grants, 34% as loans/jobs. **Non-need-based:** Awarded to 78 full-time undergraduates, including 24 freshmen. Scholarships awarded for academics, alumni affiliation, religious affiliation, state residency.

**Application procedures. Admission:** Priority date 4/30; no deadline. $35 fee, may be waived for applicants with need, free for online applicants. Admission notification on a rolling basis beginning on or about 9/15. Must reply by May 1 or within 3 week(s) if notified thereafter. **Financial aid:** Priority date 4/30; no closing date. FAFSA, institutional form required. Applicants notified on a rolling basis starting 2/15.

**Academics. Special study options:** Cooperative education, cross-registration, double major, ESL, honors, independent study, internships, liberal arts/career combination, student-designed major, study abroad, teacher certification program, Washington semester. **Credit/placement by examination:** AP, CLEP, IB, SAT, ACT, institutional tests. 4 credit hours maximum toward associate degree, 4 toward bachelor's. **Support services:** Learning center, reduced course load, remedial instruction, study skills assistance, tutoring, writing center.

**Majors. Agriculture:** Equestrian studies. **Biology:** General. **Business:** Accounting, business admin, management information systems. **Communications:** Media studies. **Conservation:** Environmental science, environmental studies. **Education:** Elementary. **Foreign languages:** French, Spanish. **Health:** Veterinary technology/assistant. **Math:** General. **Parks/recreation:** Exercise sciences, sports admin. **Philosophy/religion:** Philosophy, religion. **Physical sciences:** Chemistry. **Psychology:** General, psychobiology. **Social sciences:** General, economics, international relations, sociology. **Visual/performing arts:** Art. **Other:** Equine facilitated therapeutics, Equine journalism, Financial mathematics.

**Most popular majors.** Agriculture 13%, business/marketing 12%, education 18%, health sciences 28%, social sciences 10%.

**Computing on campus.** 105 workstations in dormitories, library, computer center, student center. Dormitories wired for high-speed internet access and linked to campus network. Commuter students can connect to campus network. Online course registration, online library, helpline, repair service, wireless network available.

**Student life. Freshman orientation:** Mandatory, $250 fee. Preregistration for classes offered. Held in August. **Policies:** Honor principle, shared governance. **Housing:** Guaranteed on-campus for all undergraduates. Wellness housing available. $300 nonrefundable deposit. Pets allowed in dorm rooms. Students of junior standing or above guaranteed single residence hall room. Housing for single mothers with children available. **Activities:** Campus ministries, choral groups, dance, drama, international student organizations, literary magazine, music ensembles, radio station, student government, student newspaper, religious activities committee, language clubs, interfaith support group, black student union, Curran Scholars, Alternative Spring Break, Agape Christian Fellowship, Habitat for Humanity, Muhibbah International Club, Political Science Association.

**Athletics.** NCAA. **Intercollegiate:** Basketball W, field hockey W, gymnastics W, lacrosse W, soccer W, softball W, tennis W. **Team name:** Phoenix.

**Student services.** Adult student services, alcohol/substance abuse counseling, chaplain/spiritual director, career counseling, student employment services, financial aid counseling, health services, on-campus daycare, personal counseling, placement for graduates, women's services.

**Contact.** E-mail: admissions@wilson.edu
Phone: (717) 262-2002 Toll-free number: (800) 421-8402
Fax: (717) 262-2546
Mary Ann Naso, Vice President for Enrollment and Admissions, Wilson College, 1015 Philadelphia Avenue, Chambersburg, PA 17201-1285

## Yeshivath Beth Moshe
**Scranton, Pennsylvania**

**CB code: 1657**

- Private 4-year rabbinical college for men affiliated with Jewish faith
- Small city

**General.** Founded in 1965. Accredited by AARTS. **Calendar:** Continuous.

**Contact.** Phone: (717) 346-1747
Admissions Director, 930 Hickory Street, Scranton, PA 18505

## York College of Pennsylvania
**York, Pennsylvania**      **CB member**
**www.ycp.edu**      **CB code: 2991**

- Private 4-year liberal arts college
- Residential campus in small city
- 5,086 degree-seeking undergraduates: 10% part-time, 55% women, 3% African American, 1% Asian American, 1% Hispanic American
- 281 degree-seeking graduate students
- 56% of applicants admitted
- SAT or ACT with writing required
- 65% graduate within 6 years

**General.** Founded in 1787. Regionally accredited. **Degrees:** 985 bachelor's, 24 associate awarded; master's offered. **ROTC:** Army. **Location:** 46 miles from Baltimore, 95 miles from Philadelphia. **Calendar:** Semester, extensive summer session. **Full-time faculty:** 156 total; 86% have terminal degrees, 42% women. **Part-time faculty:** 400 total; 19% have terminal degrees, 54% women. **Class size:** 47% < 20, 49% 20-39, 3% 40-49, less than 1% 50-99, less than 1% >100. **Special facilities:** Engineering innovation center, telecommunications center, rare books collection, oral history room, video production studios, nursing education center.

**Freshman class profile.** 11,048 applied, 6,197 admitted, 1,102 enrolled.

| Mid 50% test scores | | | |
|---|---|---|---|
| SAT critical reading: | 510-600 | GPA 3.0-3.49: | 29% |
| SAT math: | 500-570 | GPA 2.0-2.99: | 18% |
| SAT writing: | 470-560 | Rank in top quarter: | 41% |
| ACT composite: | 20-24 | Rank in top tenth: | 13% |
| GPA 3.75 or higher: | 37% | Return as sophomores: | 78% |
| GPA 3.50-3.74: | 16% | Out-of-state: | 45% |
| | | Live on campus: | 68% |

**Basis for selection.** High school record, standardized test results, personal qualities most important. Interviews, essays recommended for academically borderline students; audition required for music programs; portfolio recommended for art programs. **Homeschooled:** Statement describing homeschool structure and mission, transcript of courses and grades, state high school equivalency certificate, letter of recommendation (nonparent) required. Diploma required from home school association or local school district; portfolio evaluation conducted by certified teacher; syllabus for each course.

**High school preparation.** College-preparatory program recommended. 15 units required. Required and recommended units include English 4, mathematics 3-4, social studies 3, science 3 and foreign language 2. One biology, 2 chemistry, and 2 algebra required of nursing applicants.

**2010-2011 Annual costs.** Tuition/fees: $15,140. Room/board: $8,530. Books/supplies: $1,200. Personal expenses: $1,000.

**2009-2010 Financial aid. Need-based:** 996 full-time freshmen applied for aid; 703 were judged to have need; 698 of these received aid. Average need met was 74%. Average scholarship/grant was $5,659; average loan $4,822. 56% of total undergraduate aid awarded as scholarships/grants, 44% as loans/jobs. **Non-need-based:** Awarded to 1,434 full-time undergraduates, including 588 freshmen. Scholarships awarded for academics, alumni affiliation, music/drama.

**Application procedures. Admission:** No deadline. $30 fee, may be waived for applicants with need, free for online applicants. Admission notification on a rolling basis beginning on or about 10/1. **Financial aid:** No deadline. FAFSA required. Applicants notified on a rolling basis starting 3/1; must reply within 4 week(s) of notification.

**Academics. Special study options:** Combined bachelor's/graduate degree, cooperative education, double major, dual enrollment of high school students, honors, independent study, internships, liberal arts/career combination, student-designed major, study abroad, teacher certification program. **Credit/placement by examination:** AP, CLEP, IB, SAT, ACT, institutional tests. 30 credit hours maximum toward associate degree, 60 toward bachelor's. **Support services:** Learning center, reduced course load, remedial instruction, study skills assistance, tutoring, writing center.

**Majors. Biology:** General. **Business:** Accounting, business admin, entrepreneurial studies, finance, management information systems, marketing. **Communications:** General, media studies, public relations. **Communications technology:** Recording arts. **Computer sciences:** Computer science. **Education:** Biology, elementary, English, mathematics, music, science, social studies. **Engineering:** Computer, electrical, mechanical. **Engineering**

**technology:** Industrial management. **Foreign languages:** Spanish. **Health:** Clinical lab science, licensed practical nurse, nuclear medical technology, nursing (RN), respiratory therapy technology. **History:** General. **Interdisciplinary:** Behavioral sciences. **Math:** General. **Parks/recreation:** General, sports admin. **Philosophy/religion:** Philosophy. **Physical sciences:** Chemistry. **Protective services:** Forensics, law enforcement admin. **Psychology:** General. **Social sciences:** Economics, international relations, political science, sociology. **Visual/performing arts:** Commercial/advertising art, dramatic, studio arts. **Other:** Engineering management.

**Most popular majors.** Business/marketing 20%, communications/journalism 8%, education 12%, health sciences 13%, parks/recreation 6%, security/protective services 9%.

**Computing on campus.** 893 workstations in library, computer center. Dormitories wired for high-speed internet access and linked to campus network. Commuter students can connect to campus network. Online course registration, online library, helpline, wireless network available.

**Student life. Freshman orientation:** Mandatory. Preregistration for classes offered. 4-day program prior to fall semester. **Housing:** Guaranteed on-campus for freshmen. Coed dorms, single-sex dorms, special housing for disabled, apartments, fraternity/sorority housing, wellness housing available. $200 fully refundable deposit. Minidorms featuring units of 10 students, suites, sponsored houses, and apartments available. **Activities:** Bands, choral groups, dance, drama, literary magazine, music ensembles, Model UN, musical theater, radio station, student government, student newspaper, symphony orchestra, TV station, over 80 student organizations.

**Athletics.** NCAA. **Intercollegiate:** Baseball M, basketball, cheerleading, cross-country, field hockey W, golf M, lacrosse, soccer, softball W, swimming, tennis, track and field, volleyball W, wrestling M. **Intramural:** Badminton, basketball, football (non-tackle), lacrosse M, rugby M, skiing, soccer M, softball, swimming, tennis, track and field, volleyball, water polo M, wrestling M. **Team name:** Spartans.

**Student services.** Adult student services, alcohol/substance abuse counseling, chaplain/spiritual director, career counseling, services for economically disadvantaged, student employment services, financial aid counseling, health services, minority student services, personal counseling, placement for graduates, veterans' counselor. **Physically disabled:** Services for visually, hearing impaired.

**Contact.** E-mail: admissions@ycp.edu
Phone: (717) 849-1600 Toll-free number: (800) 455-8018
Fax: (717) 849-1607
Nancy Spataro, Director of Admissions, York College of Pennsylvania, 441 Country Club Road, York, PA 17403-3651

# Puerto Rico

**Contact.** Phone: (787) 720-1022 ext. 1027
Admissions Officer, PO Box 3918, Guaynabo, PR 00970

## American University of Puerto Rico
Bayamon, Puerto Rico        CB member
www.aupr.edu        CB code: 0961

- Private 4-year university and business college
- Commuter campus in large city
- 2,940 degree-seeking undergraduates

**General.** Founded in 1963. Regionally accredited. Branch campus at Manati. **Degrees:** 382 bachelor's, 39 associate awarded; master's offered. **ROTC:** Army. **Location:** 12 miles from San Juan. **Calendar:** Semester, limited summer session. **Full-time faculty:** 53 total. **Part-time faculty:** 123 total. **Special facilities:** Fully computerized classrooms.

**Basis for selection.** Open admission. SAT required for English-speaking applicants and NCAA student athletes. Interview recommended. **Homeschooled:** Transcript of courses and grades, state high school equivalency certificate required.

**High school preparation.** 18 units recommended. Recommended units include English 3, mathematics 2, social studies 2, history 1, science 2, foreign language 3 and academic electives 5.

**2009-2010 Annual costs.** Tuition/fees: $5,330. Books/supplies: $900.

**2009-2010 Financial aid.** All financial aid based on need.

**Application procedures. Admission:** No deadline. $25 fee, may be waived for applicants with need. Admission notification on a rolling basis. **Financial aid:** Priority date 4/30, closing date 5/31. FAFSA, institutional form required. Applicants notified by 6/1; must reply within 2 week(s) of notification.

**Academics. Special study options:** Honors, independent study, internships, liberal arts/career combination. **Credit/placement by examination:** AP, CLEP, institutional tests. **Support services:** Learning center, reduced course load, tutoring.

**Majors. Business:** General, accounting, administrative services, business admin, office technology, office/clerical, purchasing. **Communications:** General. **Communications technology:** General. **Education:** General, business, elementary, ESL, mathematics, physical, secondary, Spanish, special. **Social sciences:** General.

**Computing on campus.** 75 workstations in computer center.

**Student life. Freshman orientation:** Mandatory. Preregistration for classes offered. **Activities:** Student government.

**Athletics.** NCAA. **Intercollegiate:** Basketball, cross-country, swimming, tennis, track and field, volleyball. **Intramural:** Basketball, cross-country, softball M, table tennis, track and field, volleyball. **Team name:** Pirates.

**Student services.** Career counseling, student employment services, health services, personal counseling, veterans' counselor. **Physically disabled:** Services for speech impaired.

**Contact.** E-mail: oficinaadmisiones@aupr.edu
Phone: (787) 620-2040 ext. 2020 Fax: (787) 785-7377
Margarita Cruz, Director of Admissions, American University of Puerto Rico, PO Box 2037, Bayamon, PR 00960-2037

## Atlantic College
Guaynabo, Puerto Rico
www.atlanticcollege.edu        CB code: 7137

- Private 4-year liberal arts college
- Commuter campus in small city

**General.** Founded in 1983. Accredited by ACICS. **Location:** 20 miles from San Juan. **Calendar:** Quarter.

**Annual costs/financial aid.** Books/supplies: $800. Need-based financial aid available to full-time and part-time students.

## Bayamon Central University
Bayamon, Puerto Rico        CB member
www.ucb.edu.pr        CB code: 0840

- Private 4-year university affiliated with Roman Catholic Church
- Commuter campus in large city
- 1,832 degree-seeking undergraduates: 19% part-time, 69% women
- 393 degree-seeking graduate students
- 38% of applicants admitted
- 43% graduate within 6 years; 3% enter graduate study

**General.** Founded in 1970. Regionally accredited. Member of consortium of U.S. and South American universities. Virtually all students come from Spanish-speaking backgrounds. **Degrees:** 256 bachelor's, 30 associate awarded; master's offered. **ROTC:** Army, Air Force. **Location:** 9 miles from San Juan. **Calendar:** Semester, limited summer session. **Full-time faculty:** 49 total. **Part-time faculty:** 114 total. **Special facilities:** Library of Dominican Order.

**Freshman class profile.** 1,068 applied, 405 admitted, 282 enrolled.

| | | | |
|---|---|---|---|
| GPA 3.75 or higher: | 3% | GPA 3.0-3.49: | 27% |
| GPA 3.50-3.74: | 11% | GPA 2.0-2.99: | 50% |

**Basis for selection.** School achievement record and test scores most important. Minimum 2.0 high school GPA. Fluency in Spanish, basic knowledge of English necessary. Conditional admission to those identified as having underdeveloped academic potential. SAT or ACT accepted from English-speaking students. Score report must be received by 04/15. Essay recommended for all; interview recommended for academically weak. **Homeschooled:** Transcript of courses and grades required. **Learning Disabled:** Details of protocol for students with physical or learning disabilities available at the Admission Office and the Counseling and Orientation Office.

**High school preparation.** Required units include English 3, mathematics 3, social studies 3 and science 1. 3 units of Spanish required.

**2009-2010 Annual costs.** Tuition/fees: $7,250. Books/supplies: $1,250. Personal expenses: $3,036.

**2009-2010 Financial aid.** All financial aid based on need.

**Application procedures. Admission:** Priority date 12/6; deadline 5/6 (postmark date). $25 fee, may be waived for applicants with need. Application must be submitted on paper. Admission notification on a rolling basis beginning on or about 3/4. **Financial aid:** Priority date 5/31, closing date 7/2. FAFSA, institutional form required.

**Academics.** All classroom instruction conducted in Spanish. Core curriculum includes courses in Spanish. Course in methodology of learning must be satisfactorily completed. **Special study options:** Double major, independent study, teacher certification program. **Credit/placement by examination:** AP, CLEP. **Support services:** Learning center, reduced course load, remedial instruction, tutoring.

**Majors. Biology:** General. **Business:** General, accounting, administrative services, business admin, finance, human resources, management information systems, management science, marketing. **Communications:** Journalism. **Conservation:** General. **Education:** Early childhood, elementary, English, instructional media, mathematics, physical, science, secondary, Spanish, special. **Foreign languages:** Spanish. **Health:** Occupational health. **Interdisciplinary:** Biological/physical sciences, natural sciences. **Philosophy/religion:** Philosophy, religion. **Physical sciences:** Chemistry. **Psychology:** General. **Public administration:** General, social work.

**Most popular majors.** Business/marketing 26%, education 41%, public administration/social services 8%.

**Computing on campus.** 200 workstations in library, computer center, student center. Online library available.

**Student life. Freshman orientation:** Mandatory. Preregistration for classes offered. **Activities:** Drama, student government, student newspaper.

**Athletics. Intercollegiate:** Basketball, cross-country, swimming, table tennis, track and field, volleyball. **Intramural:** Basketball, track and field, volleyball. **Team name:** Halcones.

**Student services.** Alcohol/substance abuse counseling, chaplain/spiritual director, career counseling, student employment services, financial aid counseling, health services, on-campus daycare, personal counseling, placement for graduates. **Physically disabled:** Services for visually, speech, hearing impaired.

**Contact.** E-mail: chernandez@ucb.edu.pr
Phone: (787) 786-3030 ext. 2100 Fax: (787) 740-2200
Cristina Hernandez, Director of Admissions, Bayamon Central University, PO Box 1725, Bayamon, PR 00960-1725

## Caribbean University
**Bayamon, Puerto Rico**
www.caribbean.edu

**CB member**
**CB code: 0779**

◆ Private 4-year health science and liberal arts college
◆ Commuter campus in large city

**General.** Founded in 1969. Regionally accredited. Extension centers in Carolina, Vega Baja, and Ponce. **Degrees:** 219 bachelor's, 47 associate awarded; master's offered. **ROTC:** Army, Naval, Air Force. **Location:** 12 miles from San Juan. **Calendar:** Differs by program, limited summer session. **Full-time faculty:** 60 total. **Part-time faculty:** 80 total. **Special facilities:** College-operated museum program at Bayamon campus.

**Basis for selection.** Open admission. School achievement record, test scores important, and interview considered. SAT required of English-speaking applicants. PAA score reports by August 15. Interview recommended for academically weak. **Homeschooled:** State high school equivalency certificate required.

**High school preparation.** College-preparatory program recommended.

**2009-2010 Annual costs.** Tuition/fees: $4,520. Annual full-time tuition for engineering program: $3,960; per-credit-hour charge: $165. Books/supplies: $1,200. Personal expenses: $1,950.

**2008-2009 Financial aid.** All financial aid based on need.

**Application procedures. Admission:** No deadline. $25 fee, may be waived for applicants with need. Admission notification on a rolling basis beginning on or about 3/1. **Financial aid:** Priority date 5/30; no closing date. FAFSA required. Applicants notified on a rolling basis starting 7/30; must reply within 2 week(s) of notification.

**Academics. Special study options:** Combined bachelor's/graduate degree, distance learning, honors, liberal arts/career combination, teacher certification program, weekend college. **Credit/placement by examination:** CLEP, institutional tests. **Support services:** Learning center, remedial instruction, tutoring.

**Majors. Biology:** General. **Business:** Accounting, administrative services, business admin. **Computer sciences:** General. **Education:** Business, elementary, English, mathematics, science, secondary, special. **Engineering:** Civil, petroleum. **Foreign languages:** Spanish. **Health:** Nursing (RN), premedicine, speech pathology. **Legal studies:** Prelaw. **Parks/recreation:** General. **Public administration:** Social work. **Social sciences:** General, criminology.

**Computing on campus.** 100 workstations in library, computer center, student center. Online course registration, online library, student web hosting, wireless network available.

**Student life. Freshman orientation:** Mandatory. Preregistration for classes offered. **Activities:** Choral groups, drama, music ensembles, student government, student newspaper.

**Athletics. Intercollegiate:** Cheerleading. **Intramural:** Basketball, cross-country, football (tackle), gymnastics, judo, table tennis, tennis, track and field, volleyball. **Team name:** Gryphoms.

**Student services.** Alcohol/substance abuse counseling, career counseling, services for economically disadvantaged, student employment services, financial aid counseling, health services, personal counseling, placement for graduates, veterans' counselor. **Physically disabled:** Services for visually, speech, hearing impaired.

**Contact.** E-mail: admisiones@caribbean.edu
Phone: (787) 780-0070 ext. 1111 Toll-free number: (787) 780-0070
Fax: (787) 785-0101
Ida Alvarado, Admissions Coordinator, Caribbean University, PO Box 493, Bayamon, PR 00960-0493

## Carlos Albizu University: San Juan
**San Juan, Puerto Rico**
www.albizu.edu

**CB code: 2104**

◆ Private two-year upper-division university
◆ Large town

**General.** Regionally accredited. **Calendar:** Semester.

**Annual costs/financial aid.** Tuition/fees (2009-2010): $5,123. Books/supplies: $2,606. Personal expenses: $3,681.

**Contact.** Phone: (787) 725-6500 ext. 21
Director of Admissions, 151 Tanca Street, San Juan, PR 00902-3711

## Columbia Centro Universitario: Caguas
**Caguas, Puerto Rico**
www.columbiaco.edu

**CB code: 2315**

◆ For-profit 4-year business and technical college
◆ Commuter campus in small city
◆ 1,270 degree-seeking undergraduates: 44% part-time, 70% women
◆ 86 degree-seeking graduate students
◆ Interview required
◆ 12% graduate within 6 years

**General.** Founded in 1966. Regionally accredited. **Degrees:** 102 bachelor's, 148 associate awarded; master's offered. **Location:** 15 miles from San Juan. **Calendar:** Differs by program, extensive summer session. **Full-time faculty:** 14 total; 14% have terminal degrees, 50% women. **Part-time faculty:** 66 total; 17% have terminal degrees, 70% women. **Class size:** 54% < 20, 46% 20-39.

**Freshman class profile.** 969 applied, 518 admitted, 229 enrolled.

**Basis for selection.** Open admission, but selective for some programs. For nursing program, applicants must have 1.90 GPA. Otherwise, applicants will be admitted under the conditional enrollment option. Parent signature and vaccination certificate required for students under age 21. Portfolio required for adult education students. **Homeschooled:** Transcript of courses and grades, state high school equivalency certificate required.

**High school preparation.** 15 units required. Required units include English 3, mathematics 2, social studies 2, history 2, science 3 and academic electives 3.

**2009-2010 Annual costs.** Tuition/fees: $5,380. Books/supplies: $467. Personal expenses: $1,809.

**2008-2009 Financial aid.** All financial aid based on need.

**Application procedures. Admission:** No deadline. $50 fee. Application must be submitted on paper. Admission notification on a rolling basis.

**Academics. Credit/placement by examination:** AP, CLEP. **Support services:** Tutoring.

**Majors. Business:** Business admin. **Health:** Nursing (RN).

**Most popular majors.** Business/marketing 45%, health sciences 55%.

**Computing on campus.** 27 workstations in library, computer center.

**Student life. Freshman orientation:** Mandatory.

**Student services.** Career counseling, student employment services, financial aid counseling, personal counseling, placement for graduates, veterans' counselor.

**Contact.** E-mail: info@columbiaco.edu
Phone: (787) 743-4041 ext. 240 Toll-free number: (800) 981-4877 ext. 240
Fax: (787) 744-7031
Xiomara Sanchez, Admissions Coordinator, Columbia Centro Universitario: Caguas, PO Box 8517, Caguas, PR 00726

## Conservatory of Music of Puerto Rico
**San Juan, Puerto Rico**
www.cmpr.edu

**CB code: 1115**

◆ Public 4-year music college
◆ Commuter campus in large city
◆ 368 degree-seeking undergraduates: 22% part-time, 29% women, 91% Hispanic American, 9% international
◆ 28 degree-seeking graduate students
◆ 52% of applicants admitted
◆ Interview required
◆ 41% graduate within 6 years; 19% enter graduate study

**General.** Founded in 1959. Regionally accredited. **Degrees:** 45 bachelor's awarded; master's offered. **Calendar:** Semester, limited summer session. **Full-time faculty:** 54 total; 7% have terminal degrees, 96% minority, 22% women. **Part-time faculty:** 27 total; 26% have terminal degrees, 96% minority, 48% women. **Class size:** 96% < 20, 3% 20-39, less than 1% 40-49, less than 1% 50-99. **Special facilities:** Library with more than 26,000 musical scores, technology lab (computers applied to music), piano lab, theater.

**Freshman class profile.** 124 applied, 64 admitted, 45 enrolled.

| | | | |
|---|---|---|---|
| GPA 3.75 or higher: | 29% | End year in good standing: | 95% |
| GPA 3.50-3.74: | 19% | Return as sophomores: | 100% |
| GPA 3.0-3.49: | 35% | International: | 2% |
| GPA 2.0-2.99: | 17% | | |

**Basis for selection.** Musical ability very important. School achievement record, test scores important. Recommendations considered. Must take entrance examination in both theory and instrument. SAT is accepted from applicants from US mainland. Audition required for music performance. Essays and interview also required for music education. **Homeschooled:** State high school equivalency certificate required.

**High school preparation.** College-preparatory program recommended. Required and recommended units include English 3, mathematics 3, history 3, science 3, foreign language 3 and academic electives 3.

**2009-2010 Annual costs.** Tuition/fees: $2,750; $2,750 out-of-state. Education or instrument seminar, $150; piano accompanist (only for voice students in all four years of studies and performance students in their third and fourth year of studies), $150 for academic year. Books/supplies: $1,800. Personal expenses: $1,250.

**2008-2009 Financial aid.** All financial aid based on need. 50 full-time freshmen applied for aid; 50 were judged to have need; 50 of these received aid. Average need met was 40%. Average scholarship/grant was $4,500; average loan $2,342. 68% of total undergraduate aid awarded as scholarships/grants, 32% as loans/jobs.

**Application procedures. Admission:** Closing date 12/15 (receipt date). $35 fee. Application must be submitted on paper. Admission notification 4/30. **Financial aid:** Priority date 12/15; no closing date. FAFSA required. Applicants notified on a rolling basis starting 4/30.

**Academics. Special study options:** Cross-registration, dual enrollment of high school students, liberal arts/career combination, teacher certification program. **Credit/placement by examination:** AP, CLEP, institutional tests. 12 credit hours maximum toward bachelor's degree. **Support services:** Learning center, pre-admission summer program, reduced course load, remedial instruction, tutoring.

**Majors. Education:** Music. **Visual/performing arts:** Jazz, music performance, piano/organ, stringed instruments, voice/opera.

**Most popular majors.** Education 11%, visual/performing arts 89%.

**Computing on campus.** 17 workstations in library, computer center. Online library, wireless network available.

**Student life. Freshman orientation:** Mandatory. Preregistration for classes offered. **Activities:** Bands, choral groups, music ensembles, opera, student government, symphony orchestra.

**Student services.** Career counseling, student employment services, financial aid counseling, personal counseling, placement for graduates.

**Contact.** E-mail: esantiago@cmpr.gobierno.pr
Phone: (787) 751-0160 ext. 275 Fax: (787) 763-3886
Eutimia Santiago, Director, Admissions Office and Institutional Research, Conservatory of Music of Puerto Rico, 951 Ave. Ponce de Leon, San Juan, PR 00907-3373

## Electronic Data Processing College of Puerto Rico
### Hato Rey, Puerto Rico
www.edpcollege.edu                              CB code: 2243

▸ For-profit 4-year business and technical college
▸ Commuter campus in very large city

**General.** Founded in 1968. Candidate for regional accreditation. **Calendar:** Semester.

**Annual costs/financial aid.** Books/supplies: $465. Personal expenses: $1,455.

**Contact.** Phone: (787) 765-3560
Admissions Director, PO Box 1923, Hato Rey, PR 00919-2303

## Electronic Data Processing College: San Sebastian
### San Sebastian, Puerto Rico
www.edpcollege.edu                              CB code: 3219

▸ For-profit 4-year business and health science college
▸ Commuter campus in small city
▸ 221 degree-seeking undergraduates
▸ 90% of applicants admitted
▸ Interview required

**General. Degrees:** 39 bachelor's, 37 associate awarded. **Location:** 28 miles from Mayaguez. **Calendar:** Semester, extensive summer session. **Full-time faculty:** 21 total. **Part-time faculty:** 49 total. **Class size:** 78% < 20, 22% 20-39.

**Freshman class profile.** 210 applied, 188 admitted, 188 enrolled.

**Basis for selection.** Minimum 2.5 grade point average required for Health Academic Area Programs. Interview required for Physical Therapy Technology. Candidates for admission must take either College Entrance Examination Board tests or placement test offered by institution. **Learning Disabled:** Interview with student doctor, vocational rehabilitation program, or other government agencies required.

**High school preparation.** 18 units required. Required units include English 3, mathematics 3, history 3, science 3, foreign language 3 and academic electives 3.

**Application procedures. Admission:** No deadline. $15 fee.

**Academics. Special study options:** Cooperative education, internships. **Credit/placement by examination:** CLEP. **Support services:** Learning center, reduced course load, remedial instruction, tutoring.

**Computing on campus.** 103 workstations in library, computer center.

**Student life. Freshman orientation:** Mandatory.

**Athletics. Intercollegiate:** Softball M, volleyball. **Team name:** Zoros.

**Student services.** Alcohol/substance abuse counseling, career counseling, services for economically disadvantaged, student employment services, financial aid counseling, personal counseling, placement for graduates.

**Contact.** Phone: (787) 896-2252 ext. 225 Toll-free number: (888) 915-3372 ext. 225 Fax: (787) 896-0066
Zenuida Olavarria, Admissions Officer, Electronic Data Processing College: San Sebastian, PO Box 1674, San Sebastian, PR 00685

## Escuela de Artes Plasticas de Puerto Rico
### San Juan, Puerto Rico
www.eap.edu                                     CB code: 7036

▸ Public 4-year visual arts college
▸ Commuter campus in large city
▸ 530 degree-seeking undergraduates: 31% part-time, 57% women
▸ 50% of applicants admitted
▸ Interview required
▸ 31% graduate within 6 years; 6% enter graduate study

**General.** Founded in 1965. Regionally accredited. **Degrees:** 62 bachelor's awarded. **Location:** 12 miles from Carolina and Bayamon. **Calendar:** Semester, extensive summer session. **Full-time faculty:** 16 total; 62% have terminal degrees, 44% women. **Part-time faculty:** 48 total; 44% have terminal degrees, 60% women. **Class size:** 86% < 20, 14% 20-39. **Special facilities:** Art gallery and student design center.

**Freshman class profile.** 145 applied, 72 admitted, 71 enrolled.

| | | | |
|---|---|---|---|
| GPA 3.75 or higher: | 23% | GPA 2.0-2.99: | 31% |
| GPA 3.50-3.74: | 14% | End year in good standing: | 88% |
| GPA 3.0-3.49: | 32% | Return as sophomores: | 75% |

**Basis for selection.** Applicants must complete pre-admissions studio course during the summer. Admissions committee interviews each candidate and reviews portfolio. Test scores and high school GPA very important. SAT for mainland U.S. applicants. Portfolio or admission seminar required. **Homeschooled:** State high school equivalency certificate required.

**2009-2010 Annual costs.** Tuition/fees: $2,950; $5,650 out-of-state. Books/supplies: $2,500. Personal expenses: $1,760.

**2008-2009 Financial aid.** All financial aid based on need. 99% of total undergraduate aid awarded as scholarships/grants, 1% as loans/jobs.

**Application procedures. Admission:** Closing date 6/10 (receipt date). $25 fee. Application must be submitted on paper. Admission notification on a rolling basis. **Financial aid:** Priority date 4/25, closing date 5/23. FAFSA required. Applicants notified by 7/11.

**Academics. Special study options:** Internships, liberal arts/career combination, teacher certification program. **Credit/placement by examination:** CLEP, institutional tests. **Support services:** Learning center, reduced course load, study skills assistance.

**Majors. Education:** Art. **Visual/performing arts:** General, design, fashion design, industrial design, painting, printmaking, sculpture.

**Most popular majors.** Education 16%, visual/performing arts 84%.

**Computing on campus.** 102 workstations in library, computer center.

**Student life. Freshman orientation:** Mandatory. Preregistration for classes offered. **Policies:** Policies in effect regarding drugs and alcohol, academic progress, sexual harassment; security workshops; handicap policies. **Activities:** Literary magazine, music ensembles, student government.

**Student services.** Adult student services, alcohol/substance abuse counseling, career counseling, student employment services, financial aid counseling, personal counseling, placement for graduates. **Physically disabled:** Services for visually, speech, hearing impaired.

**Contact.** E-mail: admisiones@eap.edu
Phone: (787) 725-8120 ext. 319 Fax: (787) 721-3798
Litza Layer, Director of Admissions, Escuela de Artes Plasticas de Puerto Rico, PO Box 9021112, San Juan, PR 00902-1112

## Inter American University of Puerto Rico: Aguadilla Campus
**Aguadilla, Puerto Rico**
**www.aguadilla.inter.edu**                    CB code: 2042

- Private 4-year university and liberal arts college
- Commuter campus in small city
- 4,188 degree-seeking undergraduates: 16% part-time, 55% women, 100% Hispanic American
- 233 degree-seeking graduate students

**General.** Founded in 1957. Regionally accredited. Adult higher education program, continuing education program. **Degrees:** 266 bachelor's, 66 associate awarded; master's offered. **ROTC:** Army, Air Force. **Location:** 10 miles from Aguadilla City, 17 miles from Mayaguez. **Calendar:** Semester, extensive summer session. **Full-time faculty:** 77 total; 100% have terminal degrees, 60% women. **Part-time faculty:** 150 total; 100% have terminal degrees, 41% women. **Special facilities:** Manuel Mendez Bellester special collection.

**Freshman class profile.** 1,845 applied, 1,490 admitted, 911 enrolled.

**Basis for selection.** Open admission, but selective for some programs. Regular program requires minimum 2.0 GPA from accredited secondary school and combined score of 800 on SAT (exclusive of Writing) or PAA. SAT accepted for English-speaking applicants. School achievement record, test scores very important. Pilot Program requires minimum 1.75 GPA from accredited secondary school and College Board examination. Interview required for AVANCE, adult higher education, and Educational Services programs.

**High school preparation.** 18 units required. Required units include English 3, mathematics 2, history 2, science 2, foreign language 3 and academic electives 6.

**2009-2010 Annual costs.** Tuition/fees: $5,368. Students without health insurance coverage must pay an additional $1,395 in fees for the academic year. Books/supplies: $600.

**2009-2010 Financial aid. Need-based:** 64% of total undergraduate aid awarded as scholarships/grants, 36% as loans/jobs. **Non-need-based:** Scholarships awarded for academics.

**Application procedures. Admission:** Priority date 5/1; deadline 5/15 (receipt date). No application fee. Admission notification on a rolling basis. **Financial aid:** Closing date 4/30. FAFSA required. Applicants notified by 6/15; must reply by 8/8.

**Academics. Special study options:** Cross-registration, distance learning, dual enrollment of high school students, exchange student, honors, independent study, internships, teacher certification program. **Credit/placement by examination:** AP, CLEP. **Support services:** Learning center, remedial instruction, study skills assistance, tutoring.

**Majors. Biology:** General, biotechnology, microbiology. **Business:** Accounting, administrative services, business admin, hotel/motel admin, management information systems, marketing. **Computer sciences:** Computer science. **Education:** Early childhood, elementary, secondary. **Engineering technology:** Electrical. **Health:** Nursing (RN). **Mechanic/repair:** Computer. **Protective services:** Criminal justice. **Other:** Psychosocial human services.

**Most popular majors.** Biology 6%, business/marketing 23%, education 30%, health sciences 6%, legal studies 13%, psychology 12%.

**Computing on campus.** 708 workstations in library, computer center. Commuter students can connect to campus network. Online course registration, online library, wireless network available.

**Student life. Freshman orientation:** Mandatory. One-day program in August. **Activities:** Choral groups, drama, radio station, student government, student newspaper, Juventud Universitaria Catolica, Asociacion Evangelica Universitaria, Future Teachers Association, Criminal Justice Association, Secretarial Sciences Association, Psychosocial Human Services Association, Hotel Management Association, Marketing Association, Honors Society.

**Athletics. Intercollegiate:** Baseball M, basketball, cheerleading, cross-country, judo, soccer M, softball, table tennis, tennis, track and field, volleyball, weight lifting. **Intramural:** Basketball, cross-country, softball, table tennis, tennis, track and field, volleyball, weight lifting. **Team name:** Tigers.

**Student services.** Adult student services, chaplain/spiritual director, career counseling, student employment services, financial aid counseling, health services, personal counseling, placement for graduates, veterans' counselor.

**Contact.** Phone: (787) 891-0925 ext. 2101 Fax: (787) 882-3020
Doris Perez, Director of Admissions, Inter American University of Puerto Rico: Aguadilla Campus, Box 20000, Aguadilla, PR 00605

## Inter American University of Puerto Rico: Arecibo Campus
**Arecibo, Puerto Rico**
**www.arecibo.inter.edu**                    CB code: 1411

- Private 4-year liberal arts college
- Commuter campus in small city
- 4,528 degree-seeking undergraduates

**General.** Founded in 1957. Regionally accredited. **Degrees:** 467 bachelor's, 52 associate awarded; master's offered. **ROTC:** Army. **Location:** 45 miles from San Juan. **Calendar:** Semester, limited summer session. **Full-time faculty:** 88 total. **Part-time faculty:** 210 total.

**Basis for selection.** Minimum 2.0 high school GPA. Test scores important; minimum admission index of 800 required. Special admissions policies apply to adults 21 years or older. SAT required of English-speaking applicants. Score reports by August 3. Interview recommended for academically weak.

**High school preparation.** 15 units required. Required units include English 3, mathematics 3, social studies 3, science 3 and foreign language 3.

**2009-2010 Annual costs.** Tuition/fees: $5,406. Students without health insurance coverage must pay an additional $1,395 in fees for the academic year. Books/supplies: $890. Personal expenses: $880.

**2008-2009 Financial aid. Non-need-based:** Scholarships awarded for academics, athletics.

**Application procedures. Admission:** No application fee. Admission notification on a rolling basis. **Financial aid:** Priority date 5/1; no closing date. FAFSA, institutional form required. Applicants notified on a rolling basis.

**Academics. Special study options:** Cooperative education, distance learning, honors, independent study, internships, study abroad, teacher certification program. **Credit/placement by examination:** AP, CLEP, institutional tests. 15 credit hours maximum toward associate degree, 15 toward bachelor's. **Support services:** Pre-admission summer program, remedial instruction, study skills assistance, tutoring.

**Majors. Biology:** General, bacteriology. **Business:** Accounting, administrative services, business admin, management science. **Computer sciences:** General, computer science. **Education:** Biology, chemistry, early childhood, elementary, secondary, Spanish, special. **Health:** Nursing (RN). **Physical sciences:** Chemistry. **Protective services:** Criminal justice. **Public administration:** Social work.

**Computing on campus.** 350 workstations in library, computer center. Commuter students can connect to campus network. Helpline, wireless network available.

**Student life. Freshman orientation:** Mandatory. **Activities:** Drama, student government, Baptist Unity, Young Catholics Association, Criminal Justice Association, Haziel Evangelical Association, Future Social Workers Association, Bahai Association, Student Counseling Association, Society for Human Resources.

**Athletics. Intercollegiate:** Basketball, soccer, softball, table tennis, tennis, track and field, volleyball. **Intramural:** Basketball, cheerleading, soccer, softball, table tennis, tennis, track and field, volleyball. **Team name:** Tigers.

**Student services.** Adult student services, alcohol/substance abuse counseling, chaplain/spiritual director, career counseling, student employment services, health services, personal counseling, veterans' counselor. **Physically disabled:** Services for visually, hearing impaired.

**Contact.** E-mail: pmontalvo@arecibo.inter.edu
Phone: (787) 878-5195 Fax: (787) 880-1624
Provi Montalvo, Director of Admissions, Inter American University of Puerto Rico: Arecibo Campus, PO Box 4050, Arecibo, PR 00614-4050

---

## Inter American University of Puerto Rico: Barranquitas Campus
**Barranquitas, Puerto Rico**
www.br.inter.edu                    CB code: 2067

▸ Private 4-year university and branch campus college
▸ Commuter campus in large town

**General.** Founded in 1957. Regionally accredited. **Location:** 35 miles from San Juan. **Calendar:** Semester.

**Annual costs/financial aid.** Tuition/fees (2009-2010): $5,368. Students without health insurance coverage must pay an additional $1,395 in fees for the academic year. Books/supplies: $900. Personal expenses: $2,731. Need-based financial aid available to full-time and part-time students.

**Contact.** Phone: (787) 857-3600 ext. 2011
Director of Admissions, PO Box 517, Barranquitas, PR 00794

---

## Inter American University of Puerto Rico: Bayamon Campus
**Bayamon, Puerto Rico**
www.bc.inter.edu                    CB code: 2043

▸ Private 4-year university and engineering college
▸ Commuter campus in small city
▸ 5,075 degree-seeking undergraduates: 14% part-time, 44% women, 100% Hispanic American
▸ 62 degree-seeking graduate students
▸ 44% of applicants admitted
▸ 13% graduate within 6 years

**General.** Founded in 1912. Regionally accredited. **Degrees:** 502 bachelor's, 43 associate awarded; master's offered. **ROTC:** Army, Naval, Air Force. **Location:** 15 miles from San Juan. **Calendar:** Semester, limited summer session. **Full-time faculty:** 104 total; 36% have terminal degrees, 46% women. **Part-time faculty:** 249 total; 9% have terminal degrees, 47% women. **Special facilities:** Wetland used as a natural laboratory, mata de platano field station.

**Freshman class profile.** 2,953 applied, 1,309 admitted, 1,199 enrolled.

| | | | |
|---|---|---|---|
| GPA 3.75 or higher: | 8% | GPA 3.0-3.49: | 26% |
| GPA 3.50-3.74: | 11% | GPA 2.0-2.99: | 50% |

**Basis for selection.** High school GPA and test scores most important. Minimum GPA of 2.0, minimum admission index (based on college formula) of 800. Achievement tests required for placement in math, English, and Spanish. Interview recommended.

**High school preparation.** Required units include English 3, mathematics 3, social studies 1, history 2, science 3 and foreign language 3.

**2009-2010 Annual costs.** Tuition/fees: $5,406. Students without health insurance coverage must pay an additional $1,395 in fees for the academic year. Books/supplies: $993.

**2009-2010 Financial aid.** All financial aid based on need. 1,111 full-time freshmen applied for aid; 1,064 were judged to have need; 647 of these received aid. Average need met was 1%. Average scholarship/grant was $105; average loan $140. 30% of total undergraduate aid awarded as scholarships/grants, 70% as loans/jobs.

**Application procedures. Admission:** Closing date 5/1 (receipt date). No application fee. Admission notification on a rolling basis. Must reply by 8/1. **Financial aid:** Priority date 6/30; no closing date. FAFSA required. Applicants notified on a rolling basis starting 5/10.

**Academics. Special study options:** Accelerated study, cooperative education, distance learning, honors, independent study, internships, study abroad. **Credit/placement by examination:** AP, CLEP. 225 credit hours maximum toward associate degree, 225 toward bachelor's. **Support services:** Learning center, pre-admission summer program, study skills assistance, tutoring.

**Majors. Agriculture:** Food processing. **Biology:** General, biotechnology. **Business:** Accounting, auditing, business admin, entrepreneurial studies, finance, human resources, logistics, management information systems, managerial economics, marketing, office management. **Communications:** Digital media. **Communications technology:** General. **Computer sciences:** Computer science. **Conservation:** Environmental science. **Engineering:** Computer, electrical, industrial, mechanical. **Engineering technology:** Electrical. **Health:** Licensed practical nurse, nursing (RN). **Interdisciplinary:** Accounting/computer science. **Math:** General. **Mechanic/repair:** Computer. **Parks/recreation:** Sports admin. **Philosophy/religion:** Religion. **Physical sciences:** Chemistry. **Protective services:** Correctional facilities, criminal justice, forensics. **Psychology:** General. **Public administration:** General. **Transportation:** Aviation management.

**Computing on campus.** 510 workstations in library, computer center. Commuter students can connect to campus network. Online course registration, online library, repair service, wireless network available.

**Student life. Freshman orientation:** Mandatory. Preregistration for classes offered. **Housing:** Wellness housing available. **Activities:** Concert band, choral groups, drama, student council, business administration students association, Catholic students association, Christian university brotherhood association, society of joined students for science, photography club, AN-CLA group, senior class association, engineering students association.

**Athletics. Intercollegiate:** Baseball M, basketball, cross-country, soccer M, softball, swimming, table tennis, tennis, track and field, volleyball, wrestling M. **Intramural:** Basketball, cross-country, softball, swimming, table tennis, tennis, track and field, volleyball, wrestling M. **Team name:** Tigers.

**Student services.** Adult student services, alcohol/substance abuse counseling, chaplain/spiritual director, career counseling, student employment services, financial aid counseling, health services, on-campus daycare, personal counseling, placement for graduates, veterans' counselor. **Physically disabled:** Services for visually, speech, hearing impaired.

**Contact.** E-mail: calicea@bc.inter.edu
Phone: (787) 279-1912 ext. 2017 Fax: (787) 279-2205
Carlos Alicea, Director of Students Services, Inter American University of Puerto Rico: Bayamon Campus, 500 Dr. John Will Harris Road, Bayamon, PR 00957

---

## Inter American University of Puerto Rico: Fajardo Campus
**Fajardo, Puerto Rico**
www.fajardo.inter.edu                    CB code: 2065

▸ Private 4-year university and branch campus college
▸ Commuter campus in large town
▸ 2,223 degree-seeking undergraduates: 23% part-time, 66% women

◗  29 degree-seeking graduate students
◗  56% of applicants admitted

**General.** Regionally accredited. **Degrees:** 199 bachelor's, 16 associate awarded; master's offered. **ROTC:** Air Force. **Location:** 34 miles from San Juan. **Calendar:** Semester, limited summer session. **Full-time faculty:** 40 total; 32% have terminal degrees, 90% minority, 55% women. **Part-time faculty:** 102 total; 10% have terminal degrees, 90% minority, 59% women.

**Freshman class profile.** 970 applied, 547 admitted, 528 enrolled.

| | | | |
|---|---|---|---|
| GPA 3.50-3.74: | 14% | GPA 2.0-2.99: | 46% |
| GPA 3.0-3.49: | 29% | | |

**Basis for selection.** High school students must have 2.0 GPA and average of 400 on first three parts of PAA. Special admissions policies apply to adults age 21 or older. PAA test required for Spanish-speaking applicants; SAT or ACT required for English-speaking applicants. **Homeschooled:** Statement describing homeschool structure and mission required.

**High school preparation.** 15 units required. Required units include English 3, mathematics 2, social studies 2 and science 3. 3 units Spanish required for Puerto Rican students.

**2009-2010 Annual costs.** Tuition/fees: $5,406. Students without health insurance coverage must pay an additional $1,395 in fees for the academic year. Books/supplies: $985.

**Application procedures. Admission:** Closing date 5/15. No application fee. Admission notification on a rolling basis. **Financial aid:** Closing date 4/30. FAFSA, institutional form required. Applicants notified on a rolling basis.

**Academics. Special study options:** Cross-registration, distance learning, double major, dual enrollment of high school students, ESL, honors, independent study, internships, teacher certification program, Washington semester. Adult education program. **Credit/placement by examination:** CLEP, institutional tests. 15 credit hours maximum toward bachelor's degree. Maximum 24 credit hours counted for adult education students. **Support services:** Tutoring.

**Majors. Business:** General, accounting, administrative services, business admin. **Education:** General, biology, early childhood, elementary, ESL, secondary, social studies, Spanish. **Protective services:** Criminal justice.

**Most popular majors.** Business/marketing 28%, computer/information sciences 12%, education 36%, social sciences 24%.

**Computing on campus.** 188 workstations in library, computer center. Commuter students can connect to campus network. Online course registration, online library, wireless network available.

**Student life. Freshman orientation:** Mandatory. Preregistration for classes offered. **Activities:** Dance, drama, student government, student council, young Christian students fraternity, tourism student association, history club, human resources students association, future teachers association, criminal justice student association, multilingual student association, special education students association, computer science student association.

**Athletics. Intramural:** Baseball M, basketball, boxing M, cheerleading W, judo M, softball, table tennis, tennis, track and field, volleyball. **Team name:** Tigers.

**Student services.** Adult student services, chaplain/spiritual director, career counseling, student employment services, financial aid counseling, health services, personal counseling, placement for graduates, veterans' counselor.

**Contact.** E-mail: ada.caraballo@fajardo.inter.edu
Phone: (787) 860-3100 Fax: (787) 860-3470
Ada Caraballo, Admissions Director, Inter American University of Puerto Rico: Fajardo Campus, Call Box 70003, Fajardo, PR 00738-7003

## Inter American University of Puerto Rico: Guayama Campus
**Guayama, Puerto Rico**
**www.guayama.inter.edu**
**CB code: 2077**

◗  Private 4-year university
◗  Commuter campus in large town
◗  2,289 degree-seeking undergraduates: 18% part-time, 67% women, 100% Hispanic American
◗  67 degree-seeking graduate students

◗  39% of applicants admitted
◗  Interview required

**General.** Founded in 1957. Regionally accredited. **Degrees:** 216 bachelor's, 78 associate awarded; master's offered. **ROTC:** Army. **Location:** 18 miles from Ponce. **Calendar:** Semester, limited summer session. **Full-time faculty:** 46 total; 22% have terminal degrees, 54% women. **Part-time faculty:** 146 total; 8% have terminal degrees, 58% women. **Class size:** 40% < 20, 44% 20-39, 13% 40-49, 3% 50-99.

**Freshman class profile.** 757 applied, 294 admitted, 271 enrolled.

**Basis for selection.** High school graduates must have 2.0 GPA and 800 admission index.

**2009-2010 Annual costs.** Tuition/fees: $5,368. Students without health insurance coverage must pay an additional $1,395 in fees for the academic year. Books/supplies: $894. Personal expenses: $3,878.

**2009-2010 Financial aid.** All financial aid based on need. Average need met was 1%. Average scholarship/grant was $58; average loan $149. 11% of total undergraduate aid awarded as scholarships/grants, 89% as loans/jobs.

**Application procedures. Admission:** Priority date 5/15; no deadline. No application fee. Admission notification on a rolling basis beginning on or about 4/1. **Financial aid:** Closing date 4/29. FAFSA, institutional form required. Applicants notified by 6/15; must reply by 7/30.

**Academics. Special study options:** Accelerated study, distance learning, dual enrollment of high school students, exchange student, external degree, honors, internships, study abroad, teacher certification program, weekend college. **Credit/placement by examination:** CLEP. **Support services:** Learning center, remedial instruction, tutoring.

**Majors. Biology:** General, biotechnology. **Business:** Accounting, business admin, human resources, office management. **Education:** Early childhood special, elementary, ESL, kindergarten/preschool, physical. **Health:** Nursing (RN), respiratory therapy technology. **Mechanic/repair:** Computer. **Philosophy/religion:** Religion. **Protective services:** Law enforcement admin.

**Most popular majors.** Business/marketing 30%, computer/information sciences 6%, education 30%, health sciences 8%, security/protective services 13%, trade and industry 8%.

**Computing on campus.** 232 workstations in library, computer center, student center. Online course registration, online library, wireless network available.

**Student life. Freshman orientation:** Mandatory. **Activities:** Choral groups, dance, student government, religious circle.

**Athletics. Intercollegiate:** Baseball M, basketball, cross-country, soccer M. **Intramural:** Baseball M, basketball, cross-country M, softball, table tennis W, tennis W, track and field. **Team name:** Tigers.

**Student services.** Adult student services, chaplain/spiritual director, career counseling, student employment services, health services, personal counseling, placement for graduates, veterans' counselor. **Physically disabled:** Services for visually impaired.

**Contact.** E-mail: lferrer@inter.edu
Phone: (787) 864-7059 Fax: (787) 864-8232
Laura Ferrer-Sanchez, Director of Admissions, Inter American University of Puerto Rico: Guayama Campus, PO Box 10004, Guayama, PR 00785

## Inter American University of Puerto Rico: Metropolitan Campus
**San Juan, Puerto Rico**
**www.metro.inter.edu**
**CB member**
**CB code: 0873**

◗  Private 4-year branch campus college
◗  Commuter campus in large city
◗  6,518 degree-seeking undergraduates: 29% part-time, 54% women
◗  3,106 degree-seeking graduate students
◗  20% of applicants admitted
◗  20% graduate within 6 years

**General.** Founded in 1962. Regionally accredited. **Degrees:** 750 bachelor's, 78 associate awarded; master's, doctoral offered. **ROTC:** Army, Air Force. **Location:** 9 miles from San Juan. **Calendar:** Semester, limited summer session. **Full-time faculty:** 216 total; 57% have terminal degrees, 56%

women. **Part-time faculty:** 304 total; 38% have terminal degrees, 57% women. **Class size:** 31% < 20, 48% 20-39, 14% 40-49, 7% 50-99.

**Freshman class profile.** 4,968 applied, 1,008 admitted, 765 enrolled.

**Basis for selection.** School grade average and test scores important. Minimum GPA of 2.0 plus score average of 400 in SAT. Special admissions policies apply to adults 21 years of age or older. SAT required of English-speaking applicants.

**High school preparation.** Required units include English 3, mathematics 3 and science 3.

**2009-2010 Annual costs.** Tuition/fees: $5,406. Students without health insurance coverage must pay an additional $1,395 in fees for the academic year.

**2009-2010 Financial aid. Need-based:** Average scholarship/grant was $24; average loan $83. 45% of total undergraduate aid awarded as scholarships/grants, 55% as loans/jobs.

**Application procedures. Admission:** Closing date 5/15 (receipt date). No application fee. Admission notification on a rolling basis. Must reply by 8/15. **Financial aid:** Closing date 4/30. FAFSA required. Applicants notified on a rolling basis.

**Academics.** Adult education programs available. **Special study options:** Accelerated study, distance learning, ESL, honors, independent study, internships. **Credit/placement by examination:** AP, CLEP. 12 credit hours maximum toward associate degree, 12 toward bachelor's. Departmental convalidation test. **Support services:** Learning center, pre-admission summer program, remedial instruction, study skills assistance, tutoring, writing center.

**Majors. Biology:** General, biomedical sciences. **Business:** Accounting, administrative services, business admin, entrepreneurial studies, finance, human resources, management information systems, managerial economics, marketing, office management, office/clerical. **Computer sciences:** General. **Education:** Bilingual, chemistry, elementary, ESL, history, mathematics, physical, science, Spanish, special. **Foreign languages:** Spanish. **Health:** Clinical lab science, health care admin, nursing (RN). **History:** General. **Math:** General. **Physical sciences:** Chemistry. **Protective services:** Correctional facilities, criminal justice. **Psychology:** General. **Public administration:** Social work. **Social sciences:** General, political science, sociology. **Theology:** Religious ed. **Visual/performing arts:** Music performance.

**Computing on campus.** 799 workstations in library, computer center. Commuter students can connect to campus network. Online course registration, online library available.

**Student life. Freshman orientation:** Mandatory. Preregistration for classes offered. Held 2 weeks before regular classes begin. **Activities:** Choral groups, drama, international student organizations, student government, student newspaper, Future Teachers Association, Alpha Phi Omega fraternity, ROTARACT, student associations in following areas of interest: criminal justice, microbiology, chemistry, medical technology, nursing, psychology, counseling.

**Athletics. Intercollegiate:** Baseball M, basketball, judo M, softball, swimming, tennis, track and field, volleyball. **Intramural:** Basketball, softball, table tennis, tennis, volleyball. **Team name:** Tigres.

**Student services.** Adult student services, alcohol/substance abuse counseling, chaplain/spiritual director, career counseling, student employment services, financial aid counseling, health services, on-campus daycare, personal counseling, placement for graduates, veterans' counselor. **Physically disabled:** Services for visually, speech, hearing impaired.

**Contact.** E-mail: jolivieri@metro.inter.edu
Phone: (787) 250-1912 ext. 2188 Fax: (787) 250-1025
Janies Olivieri, Admissions Officer, Inter American University of Puerto Rico: Metropolitan Campus, Box 191293, San Juan, PR 00919-1293

---

## Inter American University of Puerto Rico: Ponce Campus
### Mercedita, Puerto Rico
www.ponce.inter.edu                          CB code: 3531

- Private 4-year university
- Large town
- 5,703 degree-seeking undergraduates: 14% part-time, 59% women, 100% Hispanic American
- 294 degree-seeking graduate students

---

- 58% of applicants admitted
- 20% graduate within 6 years

**General.** Regionally accredited. **Degrees:** 381 bachelor's, 134 associate awarded; master's offered. **ROTC:** Naval. **Calendar:** Semester. **Full-time faculty:** 93 total; 31% have terminal degrees, 54% women. **Part-time faculty:** 244 total; 10% have terminal degrees, 67% women. **Class size:** 22% < 20, 55% 20-39, 17% 40-49, 6% 50-99.

**Freshman class profile.** 3,940 applied, 2,290 admitted, 1,260 enrolled.

**Basis for selection.** 2.0 high school GPA and average of 400 on first three parts of PAA. Interview required for AVANCE program.

**High school preparation.** 18 units required. Required units include English 3, mathematics 3, social studies 1, history 3, science 3 (laboratory 1), foreign language 3 and academic electives 1.

**2009-2010 Annual costs.** Tuition/fees: $5,406. Students without health insurance coverage must pay an additional $1,395 in fees for the academic year. Books/supplies: $925. Personal expenses: $3,878.

**2009-2010 Financial aid.** All financial aid based on need. Average need met was 2%. Average scholarship/grant was $172; average loan $239. 22% of total undergraduate aid awarded as scholarships/grants, 78% as loans/jobs.

**Application procedures. Admission:** Closing date 5/15 (receipt date). No application fee. Admission notification on a rolling basis. **Financial aid:** No deadline. FAFSA required.

**Academics. Special study options:** Cooperative education, distance learning, honors, independent study, internships, study abroad, teacher certification program, weekend college. Adult programs (AVANCE), development programs, PREAD program. **Credit/placement by examination:** CLEP. **Support services:** Learning center, study skills assistance, tutoring.

**Majors. Biology:** General. **Business:** Accounting, administrative services, business admin, finance, hotel/motel admin, human resources, international, management information systems, management science, marketing, office technology, operations, training/development. **Communications:** Journalism, public relations. **Computer sciences:** Computer science, information systems. **Conservation:** General. **Education:** Biology, early childhood, elementary, ESL, secondary, special. **Health:** Nursing (RN). **Protective services:** Law enforcement admin.

**Most popular majors.** Biology 6%, business/marketing 33%, computer/information sciences 7%, education 22%, health sciences 11%, legal studies 15%.

**Computing on campus.** PC or laptop required. 983 workstations in library, computer center, student center. Commuter students can connect to campus network. Online course registration, online library, helpline available.

**Student life. Freshman orientation:** Available. Includes workshops, seminars, and social activities. **Activities:** Concert band, choral groups, dance, student government, student newspaper.

**Athletics. Intercollegiate:** Baseball M, basketball, cross-country M, judo, softball, table tennis M, track and field, weight lifting, wrestling. **Intramural:** Baseball M, basketball, cross-country M, softball, table tennis M, track and field, weight lifting, wrestling. **Team name:** Tigers.

**Student services.** Adult student services, alcohol/substance abuse counseling, chaplain/spiritual director, career counseling, student employment services, financial aid counseling, health services, on-campus daycare, personal counseling, placement for graduates, women's services. **Physically disabled:** Services for visually, speech, hearing impaired.

**Contact.** E-mail: fldiaz@poce.inter.edu
Phone: (787) 841-0110 Fax: (787) 841-0103
Franco Diaz Vega, Director of Admissions, Inter American University of Puerto Rico: Ponce Campus, 104 Turpo Industrial Park Road #1, Mercedita, PR 00715-1602

---

## Inter American University of Puerto Rico: San German Campus
### San German, Puerto Rico
www.sg.inter.edu                          CB code: 0946

- Private 4-year university
- Commuter campus in large town
- 4,800 degree-seeking undergraduates

- 84% of applicants admitted
- 31% graduate within 6 years

**General.** Founded in 1912. Regionally accredited. San German Inter American School (pre-school to grade 12). **Degrees:** 460 bachelor's, 40 associate awarded; master's, doctoral offered. **ROTC:** Army, Air Force. **Location:** 14 miles from Mayaguez, 104 miles from San Juan. **Calendar:** Semester, extensive summer session. **Full-time faculty:** 129 total; 48% have terminal degrees, 57% women. **Part-time faculty:** 178 total; 17% have terminal degrees, 53% women. **Class size:** 32% < 20, 62% 20-39, 5% 40-49, 1% 50-99. **Special facilities:** Nature preserve, museums.

**Freshman class profile.** 1,532 applied, 1,284 admitted, 955 enrolled.

| | | | |
|---|---|---|---|
| GPA 3.75 or higher: | 8% | GPA 2.0-2.99: | 45% |
| GPA 3.50-3.74: | 7% | Return as sophomores: | 75% |
| GPA 3.0-3.49: | 19% | Out-of-state: | 2% |

**Basis for selection.** High school GPA and test scores important. SAT or ACT recommended. SAT required of English-speaking applicants. Essay, interview recommended for all; audition recommended for music; portfolio recommended for art programs. **Homeschooled:** Statement describing homeschool structure and mission, transcript of courses and grades, state high school equivalency certificate required.

**High school preparation.** 11 units required; 18 recommended. Required and recommended units include English 3, mathematics 2-3, social studies 2-3, history 2-3, science 2-3, foreign language 3 and academic electives 3. 3 units of Spanish required of Spanish-speaking students.

**2009-2010 Annual costs.** Tuition/fees: $5,406. Students without health insurance coverage must pay an additional $1,395 in fees for the academic year. Room/board: $2,500. Books/supplies: $894. Personal expenses: $880.

**2008-2009 Financial aid. Need-based:** 1,092 full-time freshmen applied for aid; 1,065 were judged to have need; 751 of these received aid. Average need met was 2%. Average scholarship/grant was $293; average loan $258. 64% of total undergraduate aid awarded as scholarships/grants, 36% as loans/jobs. **Non-need-based:** Awarded to 120 full-time undergraduates, including 29 freshmen. Scholarships awarded for academics, athletics.

**Application procedures. Admission:** Closing date 5/15 (receipt date). No application fee. Admission notification on a rolling basis beginning on or about 2/15. **Financial aid:** Closing date 5/14. FAFSA, institutional form required. Applicants notified on a rolling basis; must reply by 8/1.

**Academics.** Bilingual program enables students to learn English or Spanish while taking courses in their native language. **Special study options:** Accelerated study, cooperative education, cross-registration, distance learning, double major, dual enrollment of high school students, ESL, honors, independent study, internships, liberal arts/career combination, study abroad, teacher certification program, weekend college. Weekend college in some graduate programs. **Credit/placement by examination:** AP, CLEP, institutional tests. 12 credit hours maximum toward associate degree, 18 toward bachelor's. **Support services:** Learning center, reduced course load, remedial instruction, tutoring.

**Majors. Architecture:** Architecture. **Biology:** General. **Business:** Accounting, administrative services, business admin, finance, human resources, management information systems, management science, marketing, office management. **Computer sciences:** General, computer science. **Education:** General, art, biology, chemistry, early childhood, elementary, English, ESL, history, kindergarten/preschool, mathematics, music, physical, secondary, social studies, Spanish, special, voc/tech. **Engineering technology:** Electrical. **Health:** Clinical lab science, licensed practical nurse, nursing (RN). **Math:** General. **Parks/recreation:** Health/fitness. **Physical sciences:** Chemistry. **Psychology:** General. **Public administration:** General. **Social sciences:** Political science, sociology. **Visual/performing arts:** General, ceramics, drawing, music performance, painting, photography, sculpture.

**Most popular majors.** Biology 14%, business/marketing 20%, education 32%, psychology 7%, visual/performing arts 6%.

**Computing on campus.** 1,200 workstations in dormitories, library, computer center, student center. Dormitories wired for high-speed internet access and linked to campus network. Commuter students can connect to campus network. Online course registration, online library, wireless network available.

**Student life. Freshman orientation:** Mandatory. Preregistration for classes offered. General orientation program offered in spring, summer, and fall. **Housing:** Single-sex dorms, apartments, wellness housing available. $25 fully refundable deposit, deadline 6/30. **Activities:** Bands, choral groups, dance, drama, international student organizations, music ensembles, student government, student newspaper, Student Bible Union, Bahai association, counselors student association, Catholic student organization, bilingual English-Spanish organization.

**Athletics. Intercollegiate:** Baseball M, basketball, cross-country, soccer M, softball, swimming, table tennis, tennis, track and field, volleyball, weight lifting. **Intramural:** Basketball, cross-country, softball, table tennis, tennis, track and field, volleyball. **Team name:** Tigers.

**Student services.** Adult student services, alcohol/substance abuse counseling, chaplain/spiritual director, career counseling, student employment services, financial aid counseling, health services, on-campus daycare, personal counseling, placement for graduates, veterans' counselor.

**Contact.** E-mail: milcama@sg.inter.edu
Phone: (787) 892-3090 Fax: (787) 892-6350
Mildred Camacho, Director of Admissions, Inter American University of Puerto Rico: San German Campus, Box 5100, San German, PR 00683-9801

## National College of Business and Technology: Arecibo
**Arecibo, Puerto Rico**
**www.nationalcollegepr.edu**                    **CB code: 3222**

- For-profit 3-year business and technical college
- Commuter campus in small city
- 2,015 degree-seeking undergraduates
- 89% of applicants admitted

**General.** Accredited by ACICS. **Degrees:** 84 bachelor's, 172 associate awarded. **Calendar:** Trimester. **Full-time faculty:** 38 total; 71% women. **Part-time faculty:** 55 total; 74% women. **Class size:** 42% < 20, 57% 20-39, less than 1% 40-49.

**Freshman class profile.** 520 applied, 463 admitted, 421 enrolled.

| | | | |
|---|---|---|---|
| GPA 3.0-3.49: | 20% | GPA 2.0-2.99: | 70% |

**Basis for selection.** Admissions based on high school record and institutional admissions test. College Entrance Examination Board test or institutional tests required for admissions. **Homeschooled:** Transcript of courses and grades, state high school equivalency certificate required.

**High school preparation.** 18 units required. Required units include English 3, mathematics 3, history 3, science 3, foreign language 3 and academic electives 3.

**2009-2010 Annual costs.** Tuition/fees: $7,260.

**2008-2009 Financial aid.** All financial aid based on need. 904 full-time freshmen applied for aid; 904 were judged to have need; 883 of these received aid. Average need met was 3%. Average scholarship/grant was $3,195; average loan $684. 94% of total undergraduate aid awarded as scholarships/grants, 6% as loans/jobs.

**Application procedures. Admission:** Priority date 8/8; deadline 3/9. $25 fee. Application must be submitted on paper. Admission notification on a rolling basis. **Financial aid:** Priority date 12/31, closing date 4/29. FAFSA required. Applicants notified on a rolling basis starting 5/2; must reply by 5/15 or within 2 week(s) of notification.

**Academics. Special study options:** Distance learning, independent study, internships. **Credit/placement by examination:** AP, CLEP, institutional tests. **Support services:** Tutoring.

**Majors. BACHELOR'S. Business:** Administrative services. **Computer sciences:** General, information technology. **Education:** Kindergarten/preschool. **Health:** Nursing (RN). **ASSOCIATE. Business:** Administrative services, business admin, tourism/travel. **Computer sciences:** General. **Engineering technology:** Electrical. **Health:** Dental assistant, medical secretary, nursing (RN), pharmacy assistant. **Legal studies:** Legal secretary.

**Most popular majors.** Business/marketing 16%, computer/information sciences 6%, education 46%, health sciences 31%.

**Computing on campus.** 175 workstations in library, computer center, student center. Online library, helpline, student web hosting, wireless network available.

**Student life. Freshman orientation:** Mandatory. Preregistration for classes offered. **Activities:** Student newspaper.

**Athletics. Intramural:** Basketball, softball, volleyball.

**Student services.** Alcohol/substance abuse counseling, career counseling, financial aid counseling, personal counseling, placement for graduates, veterans' counselor.

**Contact.** E-mail: aaviles@nationalcollegepr.edu
Phone: (787) 879-5044 ext. 5203 Toll-free number: (800) 780-5134
Fax: (787) 879-5047
Mercedes Pagan, Admissions Director, National College of Business and Technology: Arecibo, PO Box 4035, MSC 452, Arecibo, PR 00614

## National College of Business and Technology: Bayamon

**Bayamon, Puerto Rico**    CB member
**www.nationalcollegepr.edu**    CB code: 7135

- For-profit 3-year business and technical college
- Commuter campus in small city
- 2,500 degree-seeking undergraduates
- 91% of applicants admitted

**General.** Accredited by ACICS. **Degrees:** 97 bachelor's, 290 associate awarded. **Location:** 25 miles from San Juan. **Calendar:** Trimester. **Full-time faculty:** 51 total; 65% women. **Part-time faculty:** 70 total; 71% women. **Class size:** 38% < 20, 58% 20-39, 4% 40-49.

**Freshman class profile.** 950 applied, 865 admitted, 718 enrolled.

| | | | |
|---|---|---|---|
| GPA 3.75 or higher: | 6% | GPA 2.0-2.99: | 56% |
| GPA 3.50-3.74: | 8% | End year in good standing: | 56% |
| GPA 3.0-3.49: | 18% | | |

**Basis for selection.** High school transcript, College Entrance Examination Board test or institutional test required for admissions. **Homeschooled:** Transcript of courses and grades, state high school equivalency certificate required.

**High school preparation.** 18 units required. Required units include English 3, mathematics 3, history 3, science 3, foreign language 3 and academic electives 3.

**2009-2010 Annual costs.** Tuition/fees: $7,260.

**2008-2009 Financial aid.** All financial aid based on need. 1,012 full-time freshmen applied for aid; 1,012 were judged to have need; 975 of these received aid. Average need met was 2%. Average scholarship/grant was $3,195; average loan $684. 95% of total undergraduate aid awarded as scholarships/grants, 5% as loans/jobs.

**Application procedures. Admission:** $25 fee. Application must be submitted on paper. Admission notification 8/9. Admission notification on a rolling basis. **Financial aid:** Priority date 12/31, closing date 4/29. FAFSA required. Applicants notified on a rolling basis starting 5/2; must reply by 5/15 or within 2 week(s) of notification.

**Academics. Special study options:** Distance learning, independent study, internships. **Credit/placement by examination:** AP, CLEP. 15 credit hours maximum toward associate degree, 30 toward bachelor's. **Support services:** Tutoring.

**Majors. BACHELOR'S. Business:** Administrative services. **Computer sciences:** Information systems, programming. **Education:** Kindergarten/preschool, technology/industrial arts. **Health:** Nursing (RN). **ASSOCIATE. Business:** Accounting, administrative services, entrepreneurial studies, office technology, tourism/travel. **Computer sciences:** Information systems, programming. **Engineering technology:** Electrical. **Health:** Dental assistant, nursing (RN), pharmacy assistant. **Legal studies:** Legal secretary.

**Most popular majors.** Business/marketing 12%, computer/information sciences 19%, education 15%, health sciences 54%.

**Computing on campus.** 185 workstations in library, computer center, student center. Online library, student web hosting, wireless network available.

**Student life. Freshman orientation:** Mandatory. Preregistration for classes offered. **Housing:** Wellness housing available. **Activities:** Drama, student newspaper.

**Athletics. Intramural:** Basketball M, softball, table tennis, volleyball.

**Student services.** Alcohol/substance abuse counseling, career counseling, financial aid counseling, personal counseling, placement for graduates, veterans' counselor.

**Contact.** E-mail: mepagan@nationalcollegepr.edu
Phone: (787) 780-5134 ext. 4000 Toll-free number: (800) 780-5134
Fax: (787) 779-4909
Suzette Rubio, Admissions and Marketing Director, National College of Business and Technology: Bayamon, PO Box 2036, Bayamon, PR 00960

## National College of Business and Technology: Rio Grande

**Rio Grande, Puerto Rico**
**www.nationalcollegepr.edu**

- For-profit 3-year business and technical college
- Commuter campus in small town
- 1,550 degree-seeking undergraduates
- 79% of applicants admitted

**General.** Accredited by ACICS. **Degrees:** 27 bachelor's, 177 associate awarded. **Calendar:** Trimester. **Full-time faculty:** 18 total; 61% women. **Part-time faculty:** 72 total; 71% women. **Class size:** 52% < 20, 40% 20-39, 8% 40-49, less than 1% 50-99.

**Freshman class profile.** 1,214 applied, 960 admitted, 756 enrolled.

| | | | |
|---|---|---|---|
| GPA 3.75 or higher: | 6% | GPA 3.0-3.49: | 18% |
| GPA 3.50-3.74: | 8% | GPA 2.0-2.99: | 56% |

**Basis for selection.** College Entrance Examination Board test or institutional tests required for admissions. **Homeschooled:** Transcript of courses and grades, state high school equivalency certificate required.

**High school preparation.** 18 units required. Required units include English 3, mathematics 3, history 3, science 3, foreign language 3 and academic electives 3.

**2009-2010 Annual costs.** Tuition/fees: $7,260.

**2008-2009 Financial aid.** All financial aid based on need. 695 full-time freshmen applied for aid; 695 were judged to have need; 670 of these received aid. Average need met was 2%. Average scholarship/grant was $3,195; average loan $684. 91% of total undergraduate aid awarded as scholarships/grants, 9% as loans/jobs.

**Application procedures. Admission:** Priority date 8/15; deadline 3/21. $25 fee. Application must be submitted on paper. Admission notification 8/9. Admission notification on a rolling basis. **Financial aid:** FAFSA required. Must reply by 5/15 or within 2 week(s) of notification.

**Academics. Special study options:** ESL, independent study, internships, weekend college. **Credit/placement by examination:** AP, CLEP. **Support services:** Tutoring.

**Majors. BACHELOR'S. Computer sciences:** Information technology. **Health:** Nursing (RN). **ASSOCIATE. Business:** Accounting, entrepreneurial studies, tourism/travel. **Computer sciences:** Information technology. **Health:** Dental assistant, medical secretary, nursing (RN), pharmacy assistant. **Legal studies:** Legal secretary.

**Most popular majors.** Business/marketing 44%, health sciences 56%.

**Computing on campus.** 85 workstations in library, computer center. Online library, helpline, student web hosting, wireless network available.

**Student life. Freshman orientation:** Mandatory. Preregistration for classes offered. **Housing:** Wellness housing available. **Activities:** Dance, student newspaper.

**Athletics. Intramural:** Basketball, cross-country, softball, table tennis, volleyball.

**Student services.** Alcohol/substance abuse counseling, career counseling, financial aid counseling, personal counseling, placement for graduates.

**Contact.** E-mail: mepagan@nationalcollegepr.edu
Phone: (800) 981-0812 Fax: (787) 888-8280
Suzette Rubio, Admissions Director, National College of Business and Technology: Rio Grande, PO Box 3064, Rio Grande, PR 00745

## Pontifical Catholic University of Puerto Rico

**Ponce, Puerto Rico**    CB member
**www.pucpr.edu**    CB code: 0910

- Private 4-year university affiliated with Roman Catholic Church
- Commuter campus in small city

- 5,371 degree-seeking undergraduates
- 83% of applicants admitted
- SAT or ACT (ACT writing optional) required
- 38% graduate within 6 years

**General.** Founded in 1948. Regionally accredited. Branch campuses in Arecibo and Mayaguez. **Degrees:** 624 bachelor's, 11 associate awarded; master's, doctoral, professional offered. **ROTC:** Army, Air Force. **Location:** 60 miles from San Juan. **Calendar:** Semester, limited summer session. **Full-time faculty:** 191 total. **Part-time faculty:** 194 total.

**Freshman class profile.** 1,798 applied, 1,487 admitted, 1,001 enrolled.

| Mid 50% test scores | | | |
|---|---|---|---|
| SAT critical reading: | 400-530 | Live on campus: | 4% |
| SAT math: | 390-530 | Fraternities: | 1% |
| Return as sophomores: | 75% | Sororities: | 1% |

**Basis for selection.** School achievement record, test scores important. SAT required of English-speaking applicants. Interview required for special program; essay or personal statement for some programs. **Homeschooled:** Transcript of courses and grades, state high school equivalency certificate required.

**High school preparation.** 15 units required. Required units include English 4, mathematics 3, history 2, science 2 and foreign language 4. 3 units English, 3 units foreign language, 2 units mathematics, 1 unit science, 1 unit history required for 3-year high schools.

**2009-2010 Annual costs.** Tuition/fees: $5,318. Room only: $1,300. Books/supplies: $684. Personal expenses: $1,645.

**2009-2010 Financial aid. Non-need-based:** Scholarships awarded for academics, athletics.

**Application procedures. Admission:** Priority date 3/15; deadline 7/15 (receipt date). $15 fee, may be waived for applicants with need. Admission notification on a rolling basis beginning on or about 2/15. **Financial aid:** Closing date 5/30. FAFSA, institutional form required. Applicants notified by 6/15; must reply within 4 week(s) of notification.

**Academics. Special study options:** Accelerated study, combined bachelor's/graduate degree, double major, dual enrollment of high school students, ESL, exchange student, honors, independent study, internships, liberal arts/career combination, study abroad, teacher certification program. **Credit/placement by examination:** AP, CLEP, institutional tests. 30 credit hours maximum toward bachelor's degree. **Support services:** Learning center, pre-admission summer program, reduced course load, remedial instruction, tutoring.

**Majors. Area/ethnic studies:** Chicano/Hispanic-American/Latino. **Biology:** General. **Business:** General, accounting, administrative services, business admin, communications, entrepreneurial studies, finance, human resources, international, management information systems, managerial economics, marketing, tourism/travel, transportation. **Communications:** General. **Conservation:** General, environmental studies. **Education:** Art, biology, business, chemistry, early childhood, elementary, English, ESL, family/consumer sciences, history, mathematics, music, physical, science, secondary, social studies, Spanish, special. **Family/consumer sciences:** General. **Foreign languages:** Spanish. **Health:** Cardiovascular technology, clinical lab science, health services, nursing (RN), premedicine. **History:** General. **Interdisciplinary:** Gerontology. **Legal studies:** General, prelaw. **Liberal arts:** Arts/sciences. **Math:** General. **Philosophy/religion:** Philosophy. **Physical sciences:** Chemistry, physics. **Psychology:** General. **Public administration:** General, social work. **Social sciences:** Criminology, political science, sociology. **Transportation:** Maritime/Merchant Marine. **Visual/performing arts:** Studio arts.

**Most popular majors.** Business/marketing 17%, education 32%, health sciences 13%, liberal arts 7%, public administration/social services 8%.

**Computing on campus.** 448 workstations in library, computer center, student center. Commuter students can connect to campus network. Online course registration, online library, wireless network available.

**Student life. Freshman orientation:** Mandatory. **Housing:** Single-sex dorms available. $25 nonrefundable deposit. **Activities:** Choral groups, dance, drama, musical theater, radio station, student government, student newspaper, TV station, Pi Gamma Mu, Phi Alpha Theta, Beta Beta Beta, Alpha Beta Chi, Phi Delta Kappa, honor society for business students, Pioneer Students in Christ and Mary, Miles Jesu, Knights of Columbus, Phi Sigma Kappa.

**Athletics. Intercollegiate:** Basketball, cross-country, diving, judo, soccer, softball M, swimming, table tennis, tennis, track and field, volleyball, water polo M, wrestling M. **Intramural:** Archery, basketball, cross-country, diving, softball, swimming, table tennis, tennis, track and field, volleyball, wrestling M. **Team name:** Pioneers.

**Student services.** Chaplain/spiritual director, career counseling, student employment services, health services, on-campus daycare, personal counseling, placement for graduates, veterans' counselor. **Learning disabled:** Comprehensive services available.

**Contact.** E-mail: admisiones@pucpr.edu
Phone: (787) 841-2000 ext. 1000 Fax: (787) 840-4295
Ana Bonilla, Director of Admissions, Pontifical Catholic University of Puerto Rico, 2250 Las Americas Avenue, Suite 284, Ponce, PR 00717-9777

## Theological University of the Caribbean
### Saint Just, Puerto Rico
www.cbp.edu

- Private 4-year Bible and seminary college
- Small city

**General.** Accredited by ABHE. **Calendar:** Semester.

**Contact.** Phone: (787) 761-0808
Registrar, PO Box 901, Saint Just, PR 00978-0901

## Turabo University
### Gurabo, Puerto Rico
www.suagm.edu/ut          CB code: 0780

- Private 4-year university
- Commuter campus in small city
- 13,098 degree-seeking undergraduates: 21% part-time, 58% women, 100% Hispanic American
- 3,021 degree-seeking graduate students
- 13% graduate within 6 years

**General.** Founded in 1972. Regionally accredited. 5 off-campus sites. **Degrees:** 991 bachelor's, 119 associate awarded; master's, professional offered. **ROTC:** Army. **Location:** 17 miles from San Juan. **Calendar:** Semester, limited summer session. **Full-time faculty:** 165 total; 47% have terminal degrees, 47% women. **Part-time faculty:** 857 total; 14% have terminal degrees, 52% women. **Class size:** 49% < 20, 49% 20-39, 2% 40-49, less than 1% 50-99.

**Freshman class profile.** 6,113 applied, 2,975 admitted, 2,215 enrolled.

| | | | |
|---|---|---|---|
| GPA 3.75 or higher: | 6% | GPA 2.0-2.99: | 55% |
| GPA 3.50-3.74: | 7% | Return as sophomores: | 72% |
| GPA 3.0-3.49: | 24% | | |

**Basis for selection.** Open admission, but selective for some programs. SAT required for admission to honors and science programs.

**High school preparation.** 15 units required. Required units include English 3, mathematics 3, social studies 2, science 2 and foreign language 3.

**2009-2010 Annual costs.** Tuition/fees: $4,924. Books/supplies: $896. Personal expenses: $3,481.

**2009-2010 Financial aid.** All financial aid based on need.

**Application procedures. Admission:** No deadline. $15 fee, may be waived for applicants with need. Admission notification on a rolling basis beginning on or about 3/1. **Financial aid:** Priority date 5/30; no closing date. FAFSA required. Applicants notified by 8/30.

**Academics. Special study options:** Accelerated study, distance learning, honors, independent study, internships, liberal arts/career combination, weekend college. **Credit/placement by examination:** CLEP, institutional tests. **Support services:** Remedial instruction, study skills assistance, tutoring.

**Majors. Biology:** General. **Business:** Accounting, business admin, management information systems, marketing, office management. **Communications:** General. **Education:** Biology, chemistry, early childhood, elementary, English, history, mathematics, physical, science, social science, Spanish, special, trade/industrial. **Engineering:** Computer, electrical, mechanical. **Engineering technology:** Industrial management. **Foreign languages:** Sign language interpretation. **Health:** Nursing (RN), speech pathology. **Interdisciplinary:** Natural sciences. **Liberal arts:** Humanities. **Physical sciences:** Chemistry. **Public administration:** General, social work. **Social sciences:**

General, criminology, sociology. **Visual/performing arts:** Graphic design, industrial design, interior design.

**Most popular majors.** Business/marketing 39%, education 25%, engineering/engineering technologies 6%, health sciences 8%, social sciences 14%.

**Computing on campus.** Commuter students can connect to campus network. Helpline available.

**Student life. Freshman orientation:** Available. Preregistration for classes offered. **Activities:** Choral groups, dance, drama, music ensembles, radio station, student government, student newspaper, TV station.

**Athletics.** NAIA. **Intercollegiate:** Baseball M, basketball, cross-country, judo, soccer M, softball, swimming, tennis, track and field, volleyball, weight lifting. **Intramural:** Basketball, softball, table tennis, tennis W, volleyball, weight lifting. **Team name:** Tainos.

**Student services.** Adult student services, alcohol/substance abuse counseling, career counseling, services for economically disadvantaged, student employment services, financial aid counseling, health services, personal counseling, placement for graduates, veterans' counselor. **Physically disabled:** Services for visually, speech, hearing impaired.

**Contact.** Phone: (787) 746-3009 Toll-free number: (800) 747-8362 Fax: (787) 743-7940
Virginia Gonzalez, Associate Director of Admissions and Financial Aid, Turabo University, PO Box 3030, Gurabo, PR 00778

## Universidad Adventista de las Antillas
**Mayaguez, Puerto Rico**      **CB member**
**www.uaa.edu**      **CB code: 1020**

- Private 4-year university and liberal arts college affiliated with Seventh-day Adventists
- Commuter campus in small city
- 927 degree-seeking undergraduates: 6% part-time, 59% women
- 52 graduate students

**General.** Founded in 1957. Regionally accredited. **Degrees:** 106 bachelor's, 12 associate awarded; master's offered. **Location:** 100 miles from San Juan. **Calendar:** Semester, limited summer session. **Full-time faculty:** 41 total. **Part-time faculty:** 33 total. **Class size:** 30% < 20, 52% 20-39, 9% 40-49, 10% 50-99.

**Freshman class profile.** 199 enrolled.

| | | | |
|---|---|---|---|
| End year in good standing: | 67% | Out-of-state: | 20% |
| Return as sophomores: | 83% | | |

**Basis for selection.** Open admission, but selective for some programs. SAT or ACT recommended for English-speaking applicants. Interview required for nursing program. **Homeschooled:** Letter of recommendation (nonparent) required. Unless homeschool is accredited, applicant must take GED.

**High school preparation.** College-preparatory program recommended. 18 units recommended. Recommended units include English 3, mathematics 3, social studies 3, science 3 and academic electives 3. 3 Spanish units recommended.

**2009-2010 Annual costs.** Tuition/fees: $10,320. On-campus room/board figure ($3,800) includes most expensive meal plan ($1,200); less expensive meal plans are available for $300 or $600 for the academic year. Tuition for nonresident aliens is the sum of private tuition ($4,535 per semester) and the Form I-20 deposit ($4,000 only in the first year); after the first year, these students receive credit refund at registration ($500 per semester). Room/board: $3,800. Books/supplies: $1,000. Personal expenses: $750.

**2009-2010 Financial aid. Need-based:** Average need met was 100%. Average scholarship/grant was $3,375; average loan $2,250. 74% of total undergraduate aid awarded as scholarships/grants, 26% as loans/jobs.

**Application procedures. Admission:** No deadline. $20 fee, may be waived for applicants with need. Admission notification on a rolling basis. **Financial aid:** No deadline. FAFSA, institutional form required. Applicants notified on a rolling basis starting 8/15; must reply within 3 week(s) of notification.

**Academics. Special study options:** Combined bachelor's/graduate degree, cooperative education, double major, ESL, internships, liberal arts/career combination, teacher certification program. **Credit/placement by examination:** AP, CLEP, institutional tests. 12 credit hours maximum toward

associate degree, 12 toward bachelor's. **Support services:** Learning center, reduced course load, remedial instruction, tutoring.

**Majors. Biology:** General. **Business:** General, administrative services. **Computer sciences:** General, computer science, information systems. **Education:** Elementary, music, secondary. **Foreign languages:** Spanish. **Health:** Respiratory therapy technology. **History:** General. **Physical sciences:** Chemistry. **Psychology:** General. **Theology:** Theology.

**Most popular majors.** Business/marketing 12%, education 13%, health sciences 36%, theological studies 12%.

**Computing on campus.** 62 workstations in dormitories, library, computer center. Commuter students can connect to campus network. Online course registration, online library, repair service available.

**Student life. Freshman orientation:** Mandatory. Preregistration for classes offered. 2-day program at beginning of each semester. **Policies:** Religious environment designed for Seventh-day Adventist students. **Housing:** Guaranteed on-campus for freshmen. Single-sex dorms, apartments available. **Activities:** Concert band, choral groups, drama, music ensembles, student government, student newspaper, L.I.F.E., S.C.O.R., international club, ministerial club.

**Athletics. Intramural:** Basketball, bowling, gymnastics, soccer, softball M, swimming, table tennis, tennis, track and field, volleyball. **Team name:** Eagles Gym Team.

**Student services.** Alcohol/substance abuse counseling, chaplain/spiritual director, career counseling, student employment services, financial aid counseling, health services, personal counseling, veterans' counselor.

**Contact.** E-mail: admissions@uaa.edu
Phone: (787) 834-9595 ext. 2208 Fax: (787) 834-9597
Evelyn del Valle, Director of Admissions, Universidad Adventista de las Antillas, PO Box 118, Mayaguez, PR 00681-0118

## Universidad Central del Caribe
**Bayamon, Puerto Rico**
**www.uccaribe.edu/**      **CB code: 1549**

- Private 4-year university
- Small city

**General.** Regionally accredited. **Calendar:** Differs by program.

**Annual costs/financial aid.** Tuition/fees (2009-2010): $8,648. Books/supplies: $600.

**Contact.** Phone: (787) 740-1611
Dean for Student Affairs, Decanato de Admisiones y Asuntos Estudiantiles, Bayamon, PR 00960-6032

## Universidad del Este
**Carolina, Puerto Rico**      **CB member**
**www.suagm.edu/une**      **CB code: 0883**

- Private 4-year university and liberal arts college
- Commuter campus in small city
- 12,075 degree-seeking undergraduates: 26% part-time, 65% women, 100% Hispanic American
- 1,257 degree-seeking graduate students
- 15% graduate within 6 years

**General.** Founded in 1949. Regionally accredited. **Degrees:** 790 bachelor's, 168 associate awarded; master's offered. **ROTC:** Army. **Location:** 5 miles from San Juan. **Calendar:** Semester, limited summer session. **Full-time faculty:** 86 total; 37% have terminal degrees, 100% minority, 58% women. **Part-time faculty:** 993 total; 9% have terminal degrees, 100% minority, 58% women. **Class size:** 49% < 20, 47% 20-39, 3% 40-49, less than 1% 50-99.

**Freshman class profile.** 8,381 applied, 3,903 admitted, 2,574 enrolled.

| | | | |
|---|---|---|---|
| GPA 3.75 or higher: | 4% | GPA 2.0-2.99: | 57% |
| GPA 3.50-3.74: | 7% | Return as sophomores: | 73% |
| GPA 3.0-3.49: | 21% | | |

**Basis for selection.** Open admission, but selective for some programs. Special requirements for health and science programs; interview recommended. SAT required for English-speaking freshman applicants. **Home-schooled:** Statement describing homeschool structure and mission, letter of recommendation (nonparent) required.

**2009-2010 Annual costs.** Tuition/fees: $4,924. Books/supplies: $1,600.

**2009-2010 Financial aid. Need-based:** 76% of total undergraduate aid awarded as scholarships/grants, 24% as loans/jobs. **Non-need-based:** Scholarships awarded for academics, athletics.

**Application procedures. Admission:** Priority date 3/30; no deadline. $15 fee, may be waived for applicants with need. Admission notification on a rolling basis. **Financial aid:** Priority date 5/30; no closing date. FAFSA, institutional form required. Applicants notified by 7/30.

**Academics. Special study options:** Accelerated study, combined bachelor's/graduate degree, distance learning, honors, independent study, internships, liberal arts/career combination, teacher certification program, weekend college. **Credit/placement by examination:** CLEP. **Support services:** Reduced course load, remedial instruction, study skills assistance, tutoring.

**Majors. Biology:** General, biotechnology, microbiology. **Business:** Accounting, administrative services, business admin, hotel/motel admin, insurance, management information systems, marketing. **Conservation:** Environmental science. **Education:** Early childhood, English, health, physical, science, secondary, special. **Family/consumer sciences:** Facilities/event planning. **Health:** Critical care nursing, health care admin, medical radiologic technology/radiation therapy, nursing (RN), sonography. **Legal studies:** Paralegal. **Personal/culinary services:** Restaurant/catering. **Protective services:** Law enforcement admin. **Psychology:** General. **Public administration:** Social work. **Social sciences:** General.

**Most popular majors.** Business/marketing 52%, education 13%, health sciences 7%, public administration/social services 10%, security/protective services 14%.

**Computing on campus.** Commuter students can connect to campus network. Online library, helpline, repair service, wireless network available.

**Student life. Freshman orientation:** Available. **Activities:** Choral groups, dance, drama, international student organizations, student government, student newspaper, Phi Theta Kappa, Future Secretaries of America, nursing club.

**Athletics. Intercollegiate:** Baseball M, basketball, cross-country, softball W, track and field, volleyball, weight lifting. **Intramural:** Basketball, volleyball. **Team name:** Pitirre.

**Student services.** Adult student services, alcohol/substance abuse counseling, career counseling, services for economically disadvantaged, student employment services, financial aid counseling, health services, personal counseling, placement for graduates, veterans' counselor. **Physically disabled:** Services for visually, speech, hearing impaired.

**Contact.** E-mail: admisiones_une@suagm.edu
Phone: (787) 257-8080 Toll-free number: (800) 981-6570
Fax: (787) 257-8601 ext. 3307
Magda Ostolaza, Director of Marketing and Recruitment, Universidad del Este, PO Box 2010, Carolina, PR 00984-2010

## Universidad Metropolitana
**Rio Piedras, Puerto Rico**                     **CB member**
**www.suagm.edu/umet**                           **CB code: 1519**

- Private 4-year university and liberal arts college
- Commuter campus in large city
- 10,316 degree-seeking undergraduates: 20% part-time, 66% women, 100% Hispanic American
- 2,306 degree-seeking graduate students
- 52% of applicants admitted
- 19% graduate within 6 years

**General.** Founded in 1985. Regionally accredited. **Degrees:** 883 bachelor's, 73 associate awarded; master's, doctoral offered. **ROTC:** Army, Naval, Air Force. **Location:** 3 miles from San Juan. **Calendar:** Semester, limited summer session. **Full-time faculty:** 106 total; 40% have terminal degrees, 100% minority, 66% women. **Part-time faculty:** 890 total; 16% have terminal degrees, 100% minority, 54% women. **Class size:** 53% < 20, 46% 20-39, 1% 40-49, less than 1% 50-99.

**Freshman class profile.** 7,456 applied, 3,891 admitted, 2,003 enrolled.

| | | | |
|---|---|---|---|
| GPA 3.75 or higher: | 5% | GPA 2.0-2.99: | 54% |
| GPA 3.50-3.74: | 6% | Return as sophomores: | 71% |
| GPA 3.0-3.49: | 22% | | |

**Basis for selection.** School achievement record and test scores considered. SAT required of English-speaking applicants. Interview required for academically weak. **Homeschooled:** State high school equivalency certificate required.

**2009-2010 Annual costs.** Tuition/fees: $4,924. Books/supplies: $1,600.

**Financial aid.** All financial aid based on need.

**Application procedures. Admission:** Closing date 8/15 (receipt date). $15 fee, may be waived for applicants with need. Admission notification on a rolling basis. **Financial aid:** Priority date 5/30; no closing date. FAFSA required. Applicants notified by 7/30.

**Academics.** Flexible admissions policy allows Universidad Metropolitana to accept challenge of providing all students with increased opportunities for success. **Special study options:** Accelerated study, combined bachelor's/graduate degree, distance learning, honors, independent study, internships, liberal arts/career combination, teacher certification program, Washington semester, weekend college. Off-campus full-degree sites. **Credit/placement by examination:** CLEP. **Support services:** Learning center, pre-admission summer program, remedial instruction, tutoring.

**Majors. Biology:** General, molecular. **Business:** Accounting, banking/financial services, business admin, management information systems, managerial economics, marketing, office management, sales/distribution. **Communications:** Digital media, media studies. **Computer sciences:** Computer science. **Conservation:** Environmental science. **Education:** Early childhood, elementary, kindergarten/preschool, multi-level teacher, physical, secondary, special. **Health:** Environmental health, nursing (RN), nursing admin, respiratory therapy technology. **Interdisciplinary:** Natural sciences. **Physical sciences:** General, chemistry. **Protective services:** Criminal justice. **Psychology:** General. **Public administration:** Social work. **Social sciences:** General. **Other:** Natural resources law enforcement, Specialized merchandising, sales and operations.

**Most popular majors.** Business/marketing 44%, education 20%, health sciences 8%, public administration/social services 13%, security/protective services 8%.

**Computing on campus.** Commuter students can connect to campus network. Online library, helpline, repair service, wireless network available.

**Student life. Freshman orientation:** Mandatory. Preregistration for classes offered. Held 4 weeks before the beginning of the academic year. **Activities:** Choral groups, dance, drama, radio station, student government, student newspaper, TV station, Business Students Association, Social Work Students Association, Communication Students Association.

**Athletics. Intercollegiate:** Baseball M, basketball, cheerleading, cross-country, judo, soccer, softball W, table tennis, tennis, track and field, volleyball, weight lifting. **Intramural:** Basketball, cross-country, table tennis, volleyball. **Team name:** Cocodrilo.

**Student services.** Adult student services, alcohol/substance abuse counseling, career counseling, services for economically disadvantaged, student employment services, financial aid counseling, health services, on-campus daycare, personal counseling, placement for graduates, veterans' counselor, women's services. **Physically disabled:** Services for visually, hearing impaired.

**Contact.** E-mail: admisiones-umet@suagm.edu
Phone: (787) 766-1717 ext. 6587 Toll-free number: (787) 747-8362
Fax: (787) 751-0992
Julio Rodriguez, Director of Admission and Financial Aid, Universidad Metropolitana, Apartado 21150, San Juan, PR 00928

## Universidad Pentecostal Mizpa
**San Juan, Puerto Rico**
**www.colmizpa.edu**

- Private 4-year university and Bible college affiliated with Pentecostal Holiness Church
- Commuter campus in very large city
- 255 degree-seeking undergraduates: 56% part-time, 47% women, 100% Hispanic American
- 88% of applicants admitted
- Interview required

**General.** Accredited by ABHE. **Degrees:** 10 bachelor's, 14 associate awarded. **Calendar:** Semester, limited summer session. **Full-time faculty:** 1 total. **Part-time faculty:** 25 total. **Class size:** 88% < 20, 12% 20-39.

**Freshman class profile.** 17 applied, 15 admitted, 13 enrolled.

| | | | |
|---|---|---|---|
| GPA 3.75 or higher: | 3% | End year in good standing: | 59% |
| GPA 3.50-3.74: | 10% | Return as sophomores: | 57% |
| GPA 3.0-3.49: | 50% | Live on campus: | 4% |
| GPA 2.0-2.99: | 34% | | |

**Basis for selection.** Religious affiliation very important; rigor of secondary school record considered. **Homeschooled:** State high school equivalency certificate, interview required. **Learning Disabled:** Certified information concerning disability must be provided by student.

**2009-2010 Annual costs.** Tuition/fees: $3,530. Room only: $1,400. Books/supplies: $500. Personal expenses: $3,440.

**2009-2010 Financial aid.** All financial aid based on need. 9 full-time freshmen applied for aid; 9 were judged to have need; 9 of these received aid. 92% of total undergraduate aid awarded as scholarships/grants, 8% as loans/jobs.

**Application procedures. Admission:** No deadline. $40 fee ($40 out-of-state). Application must be submitted on paper. **Financial aid:** No deadline. FAFSA required.

**Academics. Special study options:** External degree, weekend college. **Credit/placement by examination:** CLEP, institutional tests. **Support services:** Learning center, writing center.

**Majors. Theology:** Bible, pastoral counseling, religious ed.

**Computing on campus.** Online library, wireless network available.

**Student life. Freshman orientation:** Mandatory. Preregistration for classes offered. **Policies:** Religious observance required. **Housing:** Single-sex dorms, wellness housing available. $125 fully refundable deposit. **Activities:** Radio station, student government, student newspaper, TV station.

**Athletics. Intramural:** Table tennis.

**Student services.** Adult student services, chaplain/spiritual director, career counseling, services for economically disadvantaged, student employment services, financial aid counseling, personal counseling.

**Contact.** E-mail: decanatoestudiante@colmizpa.edu
Phone: (787) 720-4476 Fax: (787) 720-2012
Jorge Burgos, Admissions Director and Dean of Students, Universidad Pentecostal Mizpa, PO Box 20966, San Juan, PR 00928-0966

## Universidad Politecnica de Puerto Rico
Hato Rey, Puerto Rico      CB member
www.pupr.edu      CB code: 0614

- Private 5-year university and engineering college
- Commuter campus in large city
- 4,853 degree-seeking undergraduates: 47% part-time, 23% women
- 674 graduate students
- 94% of applicants admitted

**General.** Founded in 1966. Regionally accredited. **Degrees:** 471 bachelor's awarded; master's offered. **ROTC:** Army, Air Force. **Location:** 3 miles from San Juan. **Calendar:** Trimester, extensive summer session. **Full-time faculty:** 154 total. **Part-time faculty:** 143 total.

**Freshman class profile.** 773 applied, 727 admitted, 559 enrolled.

**Basis for selection.** Minimum 2.5 high school GPA and PAA combined score of 1300 required. SAT in English or Spanish required. **Homeschooled:** Statement describing homeschool structure and mission, transcript of courses and grades, state high school equivalency certificate required.

**High school preparation.** 15 units required. Required units include English 3, mathematics 3, social studies 3, science 3, foreign language 3 and academic electives 3.

**2009-2010 Annual costs.** Books/supplies: $2,312.

**2008-2009 Financial aid. Non-need-based:** Scholarships awarded for academics, music/drama.

**Application procedures. Admission:** Closing date 8/1. $30 fee. Admission notification on a rolling basis. **Financial aid:** Priority date 5/15, closing date 6/30. FAFSA required. Applicants notified by 7/15.

**Academics. Special study options:** Cooperative education, distance learning, honors. **Credit/placement by examination:** AP, CLEP. **Support services:** Pre-admission summer program, remedial instruction, study skills assistance, tutoring.

**Majors. Architecture:** Architecture. **Business:** General, business admin. **Computer sciences:** Computer science. **Engineering:** Chemical, civil, computer, electrical, industrial, mechanical. **Engineering technology:** Surveying.

**Most popular majors.** Engineering/engineering technologies 90%.

**Computing on campus.** 550 workstations in library, computer center. Online library, wireless network available.

**Student life. Freshman orientation:** Available. Preregistration for classes offered. Week-long orientation offered every trimester. **Activities:** Choral groups, drama, student government, TV station, University Bible Association, drugs and alcohol committee.

**Athletics. Intercollegiate:** Baseball M, basketball, cross-country, soccer M, table tennis, tennis, track and field, volleyball. **Intramural:** Basketball, cross-country W, table tennis, tennis, track and field, volleyball. **Team name:** Beavers.

**Student services.** Alcohol/substance abuse counseling, career counseling, services for economically disadvantaged, student employment services, financial aid counseling, health services, personal counseling, placement for graduates, veterans' counselor. **Physically disabled:** Services for hearing impaired.

**Contact.** Phone: (787) 754-8000 ext. 309 Fax: (787) 764-8712
Teresa Cardona, Director of Admissions, Universidad Politecnica de Puerto Rico, PO Box 192017, San Juan, PR 00919-2017

## University College of San Juan
San Juan, Puerto Rico      CB member
www.cunisanjuan.edu      CB code: 0391

- Public 4-year community and technical college
- Commuter campus in very large city
- 100% of applicants admitted

**General.** Founded in 1972. Regionally accredited. **Degrees:** 76 bachelor's, 100 associate awarded. **Calendar:** Semester, limited summer session. **Full-time faculty:** 27 total. **Part-time faculty:** 73 total. **Class size:** 48% < 20, 50% 20-39, 2% 40-49. **Special facilities:** Language laboratory, learning resource center, amphitheater.

**Freshman class profile.** 548 applied, 548 admitted, 422 enrolled.

**Basis for selection.** Combined College Board PAA test scores of 2000 and 2.0 high school GPA required for regular students. Special consideration and priority to applicants from low-income families. SAT/ACT accepted from US applicants. Interview required for nursing program.

**High school preparation.** 16 units required. Required units include English 3, mathematics 2, social studies 2, history 2, science 1 and academic electives 2. 3 Spanish courses required.

**2009-2010 Annual costs.** Tuition/fees: $3,150. Books/supplies: $1,200. Personal expenses: $920.

**2008-2009 Financial aid.** All financial aid based on need.

**Application procedures. Admission:** Closing date 5/1. $15 fee. Admission notification 6/1. Admission after July 31 on space-available basis. **Financial aid:** Closing date 9/30. FAFSA, institutional form required. Applicants notified by 10/30.

**Academics. Special study options:** Cooperative education, double major, exchange student, honors, study abroad. **Credit/placement by examination:** AP, CLEP. **Support services:** Remedial instruction, tutoring.

**Majors. Business:** Accounting. **Computer sciences:** General. **Health:** Nursing (RN). **Protective services:** Police science.

**Most popular majors.** Business/marketing 13%, computer/information sciences 19%, health sciences 39%, security/protective services 29%.

**Computing on campus.** 240 workstations in library, computer center. Commuter students can connect to campus network. Online library, wireless network available.

**Student life. Freshman orientation:** Mandatory. One-day program in summer that offers opportunity to meet faculty and staff. **Activities:** Choral groups, dance, drama, student government.

**Athletics. Intercollegiate:** Basketball M, cross-country, softball, table tennis, tennis, track and field, volleyball, weight lifting. **Intramural:** Basketball, bowling, cross-country, handball, racquetball, softball M, table tennis, tennis, track and field, volleyball. **Team name:** Falcons.

**Student services.** Career counseling, student employment services, health services, personal counseling, placement for graduates, veterans' counselor. **Physically disabled:** Services for visually, speech, hearing impaired.

**Contact.** E-mail: admisiones@cts.sanjuancapital.com
Phone: (787) 250-7375 Fax: (787) 250-7395
Sandra Rivera, Admissions Officer, University College of San Juan, 180 Jose R. Oliver Avenue, San Juan, PR 00918

## University of Puerto Rico: Aguadilla
Aguadilla, Puerto Rico
www.uprag.edu                    CB code: 0983

- Public 4-year liberal arts and technical college
- Commuter campus in small city
- 2,997 degree-seeking undergraduates: 8% part-time, 62% women, 100% Hispanic American
- 89% of applicants admitted
- 42% graduate within 6 years

**General.** Founded in 1972. Regionally accredited. **Degrees:** 289 bachelor's, 29 associate awarded. **ROTC:** Army. **Location:** 81 miles from San Juan. **Calendar:** Semester, limited summer session. **Full-time faculty:** 127 total; 24% have terminal degrees, 98% minority, 54% women. **Part-time faculty:** 32 total; 22% have terminal degrees, 97% minority, 53% women. **Class size:** 13% < 20, 87% 20-39.

**Freshman class profile.** 901 applied, 804 admitted, 751 enrolled.

| | | | |
|---|---|---|---|
| GPA 3.75 or higher: | 36% | GPA 2.0-2.99: | 14% |
| GPA 3.50-3.74: | 20% | End year in good standing: | 76% |
| GPA 3.0-3.49: | 30% | Return as sophomores: | 76% |

**Basis for selection.** Admissions based on secondary school record and standardized test scores. Talent and ability considered. SAT and SAT Subject Tests in Spanish and math level I required of English-speaking applicants. **Homeschooled:** Copy of curriculum required.

**High school preparation.** Recommended units include English 3, mathematics 2 and social studies 2. 3 Spanish recommended.

**2009-2010 Annual costs.** Tuition/fees: $1,812; $4,226 out-of-state. Books/supplies: $1,825. Personal expenses: $1,200.

**2008-2009 Financial aid.** All financial aid based on need. 84% of total undergraduate aid awarded as scholarships/grants, 16% as loans/jobs.

**Application procedures. Admission:** Priority date 11/17; deadline 1/30 (receipt date). $20 fee, may be waived for applicants with need. Application must be submitted on paper. Admission notification 4/2. Admission notification on a rolling basis. Must reply by 4/30. **Financial aid:** Closing date 5/6. FAFSA, institutional form required. Applicants notified on a rolling basis starting 4/1; must reply within 1 week(s) of notification.

**Academics. Special study options:** Honors, liberal arts/career combination, teacher certification program. **Credit/placement by examination:** CLEP, institutional tests. **Support services:** Learning center, remedial instruction, tutoring.

**Majors. Biology:** General. **Business:** General, accounting, executive assistant, finance, human resources, management information systems, marketing. **Education:** Elementary, English. **Engineering technology:** Electrical, environmental.

**Most popular majors.** Biology 14%, business/marketing 46%, education 22%, engineering/engineering technologies 8%.

**Computing on campus.** 427 workstations in library, computer center, student center. Online library, student web hosting, wireless network available.

**Student life. Freshman orientation:** Available. **Housing:** Family community housing and private guest house available. **Activities:** Concert band, choral groups, drama, student government, Organizacion Juventud en Cristo, Estudiantes Orientadores, Teatro Experimental 80, Bio-Study, Kayukembo Association, Companeros Alertas Ante Un Mundo Buscando Alternativas, alcohol and drug prevention organization, Centro de Reciclaje y Orientacion Ambiental.

**Athletics. Intercollegiate:** Baseball M, basketball, cross-country, softball W, table tennis, tennis, track and field, volleyball, weight lifting. **Intramural:** Baseball M, basketball, cross-country, softball W, table tennis, tennis, track and field, volleyball, weight lifting. **Team name:** Tiburones.

**Student services.** Alcohol/substance abuse counseling, career counseling, student employment services, financial aid counseling, health services, personal counseling, placement for graduates. **Physically disabled:** Services for visually impaired.

**Contact.** E-mail: meserrano@uprag.edu
Phone: (787) 890-2681 ext. 280
Melba Serrano, Admissions Officer, University of Puerto Rico: Aguadilla, Box 6150, Aguadilla, PR 00604-6150

## University of Puerto Rico: Arecibo
Arecibo, Puerto Rico
www.upra.edu                    CB code: 0911

- Public 4-year university
- Commuter campus in small city
- 3,563 full-time, degree-seeking undergraduates
- 275 graduate students

**General.** Founded in 1967. Regionally accredited. **Degrees:** 468 bachelor's, 52 associate awarded; master's offered. **ROTC:** Army. **Location:** 48 miles from San Juan. **Calendar:** Semester, limited summer session. **Full-time faculty:** 217 total. **Part-time faculty:** 60 total. **Class size:** 25% < 20, 75% 20-39.

**Basis for selection.** Admissions considered according to admission index (defined and published for each academic program) based equally on high school GPA and SAT scores. Applicants must take Academic Aptitude Test and Achievement Test offered by the College Entrance Examination Board (CEEB). Interviews sometimes required. **Homeschooled:** State high school equivalency certificate required.

**2009-2010 Annual costs.** Tuition/fees: $1,812; $4,226 out-of-state. Books/supplies: $1,320. Personal expenses: $1,000.

**2008-2009 Financial aid.** All financial aid based on need.

**Application procedures. Admission:** Closing date 11/30. $20 fee. Admission notification 3/18. **Financial aid:** Closing date 4/27. FAFSA, institutional form required.

**Academics. Special study options:** ESL, exchange student, honors, internships, liberal arts/career combination, study abroad, Washington semester. Evening college, continuing education program, and professional improvement program. **Credit/placement by examination:** AP, CLEP, IB. **Support services:** Learning center, pre-admission summer program, remedial instruction, study skills assistance, tutoring, writing center.

**Majors. Biology:** Bacteriology. **Business:** Accounting, administrative services, business admin, finance, marketing. **Communications:** Radio/tv. **Communications technology:** Radio/tv. **Computer sciences:** Computer science. **Education:** Biology, elementary, ESL, mathematics, physical, Spanish. **Engineering technology:** Industrial. **Health:** Nursing (RN). **Psychology:** Industrial.

**Most popular majors.** Biology 9%, business/marketing 26%, communications/journalism 15%, education 25%, health sciences 9%, psychology 7%.

**Computing on campus.** 269 workstations in library, computer center. Commuter students can connect to campus network. Online library, student web hosting, wireless network available.

**Student life. Freshman orientation:** Mandatory. Preregistration for classes offered. 4-day program held (mornings) in summer. **Activities:** Concert band, choral groups, dance, drama, film society, music ensembles, student government, student newspaper, Cheerleaders UPRA, Rhythm Busters, Federacion de Estudiantes de Iberoamericana, Asociacion de Estudiantes Coro de Concierto, Asociacion Nacional de Estudiantes de Educacion, writers club, Capitulo de Estudiantes de Microbiologia, Asociacion Intercesores Cristiana, ACTRE.

**Athletics. Intercollegiate:** Baseball M, basketball, cross-country, judo, softball W, track and field, volleyball, weight lifting, wrestling M. **Intramural:** Basketball, softball W, volleyball. **Team name:** Los Lobos (Wolves).

**Student services.** Alcohol/substance abuse counseling, career counseling, services for economically disadvantaged, student employment services, financial aid counseling, health services, personal counseling, placement for graduates, women's services. **Physically disabled:** Services for visually, hearing impaired.

**Contact.** E-mail: mmendez@upra.edu
Phone: (787) 815-0000 ext. 4110 Fax: (787) 817-3461
Magaly Mendez, Admissions Officer, University of Puerto Rico: Arecibo, PO Box 4010, Arecibo, PR 00614-4010

## University of Puerto Rico: Bayamon University College
Bayamon, Puerto Rico
www.uprb.edu                                            CB code: 0852

▶ Public 4-year university and technical college
▶ Commuter campus in small city
▶ 5,184 degree-seeking undergraduates: 15% part-time, 53% women, 100% Hispanic American
▶ 22% of applicants admitted
▶ 31% graduate within 6 years

**General.** Founded in 1971. Regionally accredited. **Degrees:** 459 bachelor's, 53 associate awarded. **ROTC:** Army. **Location:** 9 miles from San Juan. **Calendar:** Semester, limited summer session. **Full-time faculty:** 191 total; 36% have terminal degrees, 100% minority, 54% women. **Part-time faculty:** 133 total; 21% have terminal degrees, 100% minority, 55% women. **Special facilities:** Multimedia laboratory.

**Freshman class profile.** 5,892 applied, 1,288 admitted, 1,213 enrolled.

| | | | |
|---|---|---|---|
| End year in good standing: | 78% | Out-of-state: | 1% |
| Return as sophomores: | 89% | | |

**Basis for selection.** High school GPA and test scores most important. Higher scores required of applicants to bachelor's programs. Special consideration given to applicants with special talents or handicaps. SAT and 2 SAT Subject Tests (Spanish, mathematics) accepted for English-speaking applicants from U.S. mainland. PAA required of Spanish-speaking applicants.

**High school preparation.** 12 units required. Required and recommended units include English 2, mathematics 2, social studies 1-2 and science 1. 3 units Spanish also required.

**2009-2010 Annual costs.** Tuition/fees: $1,812; $4,226 out-of-state. Books/supplies: $1,825. Personal expenses: $600.

**Financial aid.** All financial aid based on need.

**Application procedures. Admission:** Priority date 12/10; deadline 1/31 (receipt date). $15 fee. Application must be submitted on paper. Admission notification on a rolling basis beginning on or about 4/25. Must reply by 5/30. **Financial aid:** Closing date 6/15. Institutional form required. Applicants notified by 7/12; must reply within 4 week(s) of notification.

**Academics. Special study options:** Cooperative education, cross-registration, double major, ESL, exchange student, honors, internships. **Credit/placement by examination:** AP, CLEP. **Support services:** Pre-admission summer program, reduced course load, study skills assistance, tutoring.

**Majors. Biology:** General. **Business:** Accounting, business admin, executive assistant, finance, logistics, marketing. **Computer sciences:** General. **Education:** Multi-level teacher, physically handicapped. **Engineering technology:** Electrical.

**Most popular majors.** Biology 10%, business/marketing 50%, computer/information sciences 8%, education 25%, engineering/engineering technologies 6%.

**Computing on campus.** 370 workstations in computer center. Commuter students can connect to campus network. Wireless network available.

**Student life. Freshman orientation:** Available. **Activities:** Bands, choral groups, drama, student government, student newspaper, Confraternidad de Cristianos Unidos, Asociacion Juventud Catolica, Society for Human Resource Management, Asociacion de Estudiantes Orientadores, American Marketing Association, Asociacion de Estudiantes de Computadoras, Asociacion de Gerencia de Materiales.

**Athletics. NCAA. Intercollegiate:** Baseball M, basketball, cheerleading, cross-country, swimming, table tennis, tennis, track and field, volleyball, weight lifting, wrestling M. **Intramural:** Table tennis, tennis, volleyball. **Team name:** Vaqueros.

**Student services.** Adult student services, career counseling, student employment services, health services, personal counseling, placement for graduates.

**Contact.** E-mail: cmontes@uprb.edu
Phone: (787) 993-8952 Fax: (787) 993-8929
Carmen Montes, Director of Admissions, University of Puerto Rico: Bayamon University College, 174 Street #170 Minillas Industrial Park, Bayamon, PR 00959-1919

## University of Puerto Rico: Carolina Regional College
Carolina, Puerto Rico
www.uprc.edu                                            CB code: 3891

▶ Public 4-year university
▶ Commuter campus in small city
▶ 4,293 degree-seeking undergraduates: 24% part-time, 64% women
▶ 76% of applicants admitted
▶ 37% graduate within 6 years

**General.** Founded in 1974. Regionally accredited. **Degrees:** 474 bachelor's, 90 associate awarded. **Location:** 10 miles from San Juan. **Calendar:** Quarter, limited summer session. **Full-time faculty:** 144 total; 31% have terminal degrees, 51% women. **Part-time faculty:** 134 total; 19% have terminal degrees, 44% women.

**Freshman class profile.** 1,759 applied, 1,334 admitted, 1,143 enrolled.

| Mid 50% test scores | | | |
|---|---|---|---|
| SAT critical reading: | 470-580 | GPA 3.0-3.49: | 37% |
| SAT math: | 470-580 | GPA 2.0-2.99: | 20% |
| GPA 3.75 or higher: | 20% | End year in good standing: | 77% |
| GPA 3.50-3.74: | 23% | Return as sophomores: | 76% |

**Basis for selection.** High school GPA and test scores important. SAT and SAT Subject Tests in Spanish, Math Level 1 required of English-speaking applicants. Interview recommended for those with exceptional ability; portfolio recommended for art. **Homeschooled:** Transcript of courses and grades, state high school equivalency certificate required.

**High school preparation.** 15 units required; 17 recommended. Required and recommended units include English 3, mathematics 3, social studies 3, history 2, science 2, foreign language 3 and academic electives 1.

**2009-2010 Annual costs.** Tuition/fees: $3,012; $4,397 out-of-state. Books/supplies: $2,735. Personal expenses: $1,200.

**2008-2009 Financial aid.** All financial aid based on need.

**Application procedures. Admission:** Closing date 1/31 (receipt date). $20 fee ($20 out-of-state). Must reply by 6/12. **Financial aid:** Closing date 6/30. FAFSA, institutional form required. Applicants notified by 6/30; Applicants notified on a rolling basis starting 6/10.

**Academics. Special study options:** Honors, internships, liberal arts/career combination, study abroad. **Credit/placement by examination:** AP, CLEP, SAT. 12 credit hours maximum toward associate degree, 12 toward bachelor's. **Support services:** Learning center, pre-admission summer program, remedial instruction, study skills assistance, tutoring, writing center.

**Majors. Business:** Administrative services, business admin, finance, hotel/motel admin, tourism promotion. **Communications:** Advertising. **Communications technology:** Graphic/printing. **Protective services:** Forensics, law enforcement admin.

**Most popular majors.** Business/marketing 53%, communications/journalism 16%, communication technologies 8%, security/protective services 23%.

**Computing on campus.** 160 workstations in library, computer center. Online course registration, online library, wireless network available.

**Student life. Freshman orientation:** Mandatory. Preregistration for classes offered. **Activities:** Concert band, choral groups, dance, drama, international student organizations, student government, Asociacion estudiantil de coro y banda y circulo teatral, asociacion juvenil pro-ayuda social, coalicion de universitarios pro-ambiente, consejo de estudiantes, estudiantes de adm.

de hoteles y restaurantes, estudiantes de justicia criminal, estudiantes de medios graficos y de publicidad comercial, estudiantes turisticos universitarios (ESTU), innovative interior design association (IDEA), universitarios cristianos en accion (UCA).

**Athletics. Intercollegiate:** Baseball M, basketball, cheerleading, cross-country, soccer M, softball W, tennis, track and field, volleyball, weight lifting. **Intramural:** Basketball M. **Team name:** Jaguar.

**Student services.** Alcohol/substance abuse counseling, career counseling, services for economically disadvantaged, student employment services, financial aid counseling, health services, on-campus daycare, personal counseling, veterans' counselor. **Physically disabled:** Services for visually impaired.

**Contact.** Phone: (787) 757-1485 Fax: (787) 750-7940
Celia Mendez, Director of Admissions, University of Puerto Rico: Carolina Regional College, PO Box 4800, Carolina, PR 00984-4800

## University of Puerto Rico: Cayey University College

Cayey, Puerto Rico
www.cayey.upr.edu

CB member
CB code: 0981

- Public 4-year liberal arts and teachers college
- Commuter campus in large town
- 3,735 degree-seeking undergraduates: 9% part-time, 71% women, 100% Hispanic American
- 41% graduate within 6 years

**General.** Founded in 1967. Regionally accredited. **Degrees:** 497 bachelor's awarded. **ROTC:** Army. **Location:** 30 miles from San Juan. **Calendar:** Semester, limited summer session. **Full-time faculty:** 139 total. **Part-time faculty:** 35 total. **Class size:** 31% < 20, 68% 20-39, less than 1% 40-49. **Special facilities:** Museum, eco-park, ecological learning center, interdisciplinary research center, violence prevention center.

**Freshman class profile.**

| Mid 50% test scores | | | |
|---|---|---|---|
| SAT critical reading: | 470-600 | GPA 3.50-3.74: | 24% |
| SAT math: | 470-620 | GPA 3.0-3.49: | 25% |
| GPA 3.75 or higher: | 37% | GPA 2.0-2.99: | 14% |
| | | Return as sophomores: | 89% |

**Basis for selection.** School achievement record, test scores most important. SAT required for English-speaking applicants. Students from Puerto Rico must submit their CEEB test scores for math and verbal aptitude. SAT critical reading will be used to evaluate verbal aptitude. Audition, portfolio required for admission of candidates based on special talents such as sports; interview recommended for music, theater programs.

**High school preparation.** 18 units required. Required units include English 3, mathematics 3, social studies 3, history 3, science 2 and academic electives 3. 3 units of Spanish required.

**2009-2010 Annual costs.** Tuition/fees: $1,812; $4,226 out-of-state. Books/supplies: $2,735. Personal expenses: $1,000.

**2009-2010 Financial aid.** All financial aid based on need.

**Application procedures. Admission:** Closing date 11/30 (postmark date). $20 fee. Admission notification 4/4. Must reply by 5/4. **Financial aid:** Closing date 6/30. FAFSA required. Applicants notified by 7/30.

**Academics. Special study options:** Accelerated study, combined bachelor's/graduate degree, ESL, exchange student, honors, liberal arts/career combination, study abroad, teacher certification program. **Credit/placement by examination:** AP, CLEP, institutional tests. 72 credit hours maximum toward associate degree, 135 toward bachelor's. **Support services:** Preadmission summer program, remedial instruction, tutoring, writing center.

**Majors. Biology:** General. **Business:** General, accounting, administrative services, business admin, office management, office/clerical. **Education:** English, history, mathematics, physical, science, social science, social studies, Spanish, special. **Foreign languages:** Spanish. **History:** General. **Interdisciplinary:** Natural sciences. **Liberal arts:** Humanities. **Math:** General. **Physical sciences:** Chemistry. **Psychology:** General. **Social sciences:** General, economics, sociology. **Other:** Psychology and mental health.

**Most popular majors.** Biology 8%, business/marketing 26%, education 34%, interdisciplinary studies 8%, psychology 11%.

**Computing on campus.** 1,000 workstations in library, computer center. Online course registration, online library, wireless network available.

**Student life. Freshman orientation:** Mandatory. Preregistration for classes offered. **Housing:** Housing available for some athletes and exchange students. **Activities:** Bands, choral groups, dance, drama, student government, symphony orchestra, Asociacion de Estudiantes del Programa de Estudios de Honor, Asociacion de Estudiantes de Psicologia Psy-Chi, Circulo de Historia, The English Club, Circulo de Quimica, American Medical Student Association, GAIA, Circulo de Matematica, Asociacion de Estudiantes de Contabilidad, Club de Leones UPR de Cayey.

**Athletics.** NCAA. **Intercollegiate:** Baseball M, basketball, cross-country, soccer M, softball, swimming, table tennis, tennis, track and field, volleyball, weight lifting. **Intramural:** Baseball M, basketball, cross-country, soccer M, softball, swimming, table tennis, tennis, track and field, volleyball, weight lifting. **Team name:** Toritos.

**Student services.** Alcohol/substance abuse counseling, career counseling, services for economically disadvantaged, student employment services, financial aid counseling, health services, on-campus daycare, personal counseling, placement for graduates, veterans' counselor. **Physically disabled:** Services for visually impaired.

**Contact.** E-mail: admisiones@cayey.upr.edu
Phone: (787) 738-5633 Fax: (787) 738-5633
Wilfredo Lopez, Director of Admissions, University of Puerto Rico: Cayey University College, Oficina de Admisiones UPR- Cayey, Cayey, PR 00736

## University of Puerto Rico: Humacao

Humacao, Puerto Rico
www.uprh.edu

CB member
CB code: 0874

- Public 4-year university and liberal arts college
- Commuter campus in small city
- 4,510 degree-seeking undergraduates: 8% part-time, 67% women, 99% Hispanic American
- 37% of applicants admitted
- 42% graduate within 6 years

**General.** Founded in 1962. Regionally accredited. **Degrees:** 490 bachelor's, 110 associate awarded. **Location:** 30 miles from San Juan. **Calendar:** Semester, limited summer session. **Full-time faculty:** 279 total. **Part-time faculty:** 35 total. **Special facilities:** Observatory, census data center, communication competencies center.

**Freshman class profile.** 2,709 applied, 997 admitted, 945 enrolled.

| | | | |
|---|---|---|---|
| GPA 3.75 or higher: | 42% | GPA 2.0-2.99: | 7% |
| GPA 3.50-3.74: | 25% | Return as sophomores: | 88% |
| GPA 3.0-3.49: | 26% | Out-of-state: | 2% |

**Basis for selection.** High school achievement record, test scores important. Non-native speakers of Spanish required to prove fluency through institutional examinations, interviews. Applicants for admission must take the Spanish version of Puerto Rico CEEB of the College Board: aptitude test (verbal and mathematics) and achievement test battery (Spanish, English and mathematics). In lieu of the above, applicants make take SAT and SAT Subject Tests (Spanish Composition and Spanish Reading). SAT and SAT Subject Tests (Spanish and Mathematics Level I) required of English-speaking applicants. **Homeschooled:** Sworn statement indicating that student received formal education at home. **Learning Disabled:** Director of Disabled Students Services Office (SERPI) evaluates learning disabled students to determine if they qualify for special admission.

**High school preparation.** 18 units recommended. Recommended units include English 3, mathematics 3, social studies 1, history 2, science 3, foreign language 3 and academic electives 3. Foreign language must be Spanish.

**2009-2010 Annual costs.** Tuition/fees: $1,812; $4,226 out-of-state. Books/supplies: $1,825. Personal expenses: $1,200.

**2008-2009 Financial aid. Need-based:** 89% of total undergraduate aid awarded as scholarships/grants, 11% as loans/jobs. **Non-need-based:** Scholarships awarded for academics, athletics, music/drama.

**Application procedures. Admission:** Priority date 12/15; deadline 1/29 (receipt date). $20 fee. Admission notification 4/15. Admission notification on a rolling basis. Must reply by 5/1. **Financial aid:** Priority date 3/1, closing date 6/30. FAFSA, institutional form required. Applicants notified on a rolling basis starting 4/30; must reply by 7/31.

**Academics.** Course work conducted in Spanish. **Special study options:** Exchange student, honors, internships, teacher certification program. **Credit/placement by examination:** AP, CLEP. 40 credit hours maximum toward associate degree, 40 toward bachelor's. **Support services:** Learning center,

pre-admission summer program, reduced course load, remedial instruction, study skills assistance, tutoring, writing center.

**Majors. Biology:** General, marine, microbiology. **Business:** General, accounting, administrative services, business admin, human resources, international. **Conservation:** Wildlife. **Education:** Elementary, ESL. **Health:** Nursing (RN). **Math:** Computational. **Physical sciences:** Chemistry, physics. **Public administration:** Social work. **Social sciences:** General.

**Most popular majors.** Biology 12%, business/marketing 38%, education 23%, physical sciences 8%, public administration/social services 11%.

**Computing on campus.** 981 workstations in library, computer center. Commuter students can connect to campus network. Online course registration, online library, wireless network available.

**Student life. Freshman orientation:** Available. Preregistration for classes offered. One-day program. **Activities:** Pep band, choral groups, dance, student government, various religious and social service organizations.

**Athletics. Intercollegiate:** Baseball M, basketball, cheerleading, cross-country, judo, softball W, swimming, tennis W, track and field, volleyball, weight lifting, wrestling M. **Intramural:** Softball W, volleyball. **Team name:** Buhos.

**Student services.** Alcohol/substance abuse counseling, career counseling, student employment services, health services, personal counseling, women's services. **Physically disabled:** Services for visually, speech, hearing impaired.

**Contact.** E-mail: elizabeth.gerena@upr.edu
Phone: (787) 850-9301 Fax: (787) 850-9428
Elizabeth Gerena, Director of Admissions, University of Puerto Rico: Humacao, 100 Road 908 CUH Station, Humacao, PR 00791

## University of Puerto Rico: Mayaguez
**Mayaguez, Puerto Rico**
www.uprm.edu
CB member
CB code: 0912

- Public 5-year university
- Commuter campus in small city

**General.** Founded in 1911. Regionally accredited. **Location:** 100 miles from San Juan. **Calendar:** Semester.

**Annual costs/financial aid.** Tuition/fees (2009-2010): $1,812; $4,226 out-of-state. Books/supplies: $1,520. Personal expenses: $1,000. Need-based financial aid available to full-time and part-time students.

**Contact.** Phone: (787) 265-3811
Director of Admissions, Admissions Office, Mayaguez, PR 00681-9021

## University of Puerto Rico: Medical Sciences
**San Juan, Puerto Rico**
www.rcm.upr.edu
CB code: 0631

- Public 4-year university
- Commuter campus in large city
- 535 degree-seeking undergraduates: 8% part-time, 81% women, 100% Hispanic American
- 1,840 degree-seeking graduate students

**General.** Founded in 1950. Regionally accredited. First-time freshmen not admitted. **Degrees:** 101 bachelor's, 47 associate awarded; master's, doctoral, professional offered. **Calendar:** Differs by program, limited summer session. **Full-time faculty:** 705 total. **Part-time faculty:** 199 total. **Class size:** 69% < 20, 29% 20-39, 1% 40-49, 1% 50-99.

**Basis for selection.** Candidates are admitted on a competitive basis. Applicants must present evidence of successful completion of all admission requirements for the program in which they are interested. In most programs, an admissions committee will also consider nonacademic factors as additional criteria in screening applicants.

**2009-2010 Annual costs.** Tuition/fees: $1,812; $4,226 out-of-state. Books/supplies: $1,200. Personal expenses: $800.

**2009-2010 Financial aid.** All financial aid based on need.

**Application procedures. Admission:** No deadline. $20 fee. **Financial aid:** Priority date 4/30, closing date 6/15. FAFSA, institutional form required. Applicants notified on a rolling basis starting 8/1; must reply within 2 week(s) of notification.

**Academics. Special study options:** Combined bachelor's/graduate degree, exchange student, honors, internships. **Credit/placement by examination:** CLEP. **Support services:** Tutoring.

**Majors. Health:** Clinical lab science, clinical lab technology, nuclear medical technology, nursing (RN), public health ed, veterinary technology/assistant.

**Computing on campus.** 216 workstations in library, computer center. Commuter students can connect to campus network. Helpline, repair service available.

**Student life. Activities:** Choral groups, dance, drama, student government.

**Athletics. Intramural:** Basketball M, soccer M, softball M, volleyball.

**Student services.** Career counseling, student employment services, financial aid counseling, health services, legal services, personal counseling, women's services. **Physically disabled:** Services for visually impaired.

**Contact.** E-mail: margarita.rivera4@upr.edu
Phone: (787) 758-2525 ext. 5211 Fax: (787) 282-7117
Margarita Rivera, Director, Central Office of Admissions, University of Puerto Rico: Medical Sciences, PO Box 365067, San Juan, PR 00936-5067

## University of Puerto Rico: Ponce
**Ponce, Puerto Rico**
www.uprp.edu
CB code: 0836

- Public 4-year university and branch campus college
- Commuter campus in small city
- 3,438 degree-seeking undergraduates: 11% part-time, 59% women
- 43% of applicants admitted
- 41% graduate within 6 years

**General.** Founded in 1970. Regionally accredited. **Degrees:** 362 bachelor's, 90 associate awarded. **ROTC:** Army. **Location:** 68 miles from San Juan, 46 miles from Mayaguez. **Calendar:** Semester, limited summer session. **Full-time faculty:** 158 total. **Part-time faculty:** 39 total. **Class size:** 28% < 20, 72% 20-39.

**Freshman class profile.** 2,319 applied, 990 admitted, 862 enrolled.

| Mid 50% test scores | | GPA 3.0-3.49: | 29% |
|---|---|---|---|
| SAT critical reading: | 480-590 | GPA 2.0-2.99: | 5% |
| SAT math: | 490-620 | End year in good standing: | 83% |
| GPA 3.75 or higher: | 39% | Return as sophomores: | 83% |
| GPA 3.50-3.74: | 27% | | |

**Basis for selection.** Admission based on general application index (GAI), combination of high school GPA and College Board test scores (50% each). Programs have their own GAI requirements. Interview required for academically weak and special ability. **Homeschooled:** State high school equivalency certificate required.

**High school preparation.** 18 units required. Required units include English 3, mathematics 3, social studies 3, science 3 and academic electives 2. 3 units Spanish, 1 unit fine arts.

**2009-2010 Annual costs.** Tuition/fees: $1,812; $4,226 out-of-state. Books/supplies: $1,825. Personal expenses: $800.

**2008-2009 Financial aid.** All financial aid based on need. 85% of total undergraduate aid awarded as scholarships/grants, 15% as loans/jobs.

**Application procedures. Admission:** Closing date 11/30. $20 fee. Admission notification on a rolling basis beginning on or about 4/15. Must reply by May 1 or within 3 week(s) if notified thereafter. **Financial aid:** Closing date 5/30. FAFSA, institutional form required.

**Academics. Special study options:** Dual enrollment of high school students, honors, internships. **Credit/placement by examination:** CLEP. **Support services:** Remedial instruction, tutoring.

**Majors. Biology:** General. **Business:** Accounting, administrative services, business admin, finance, marketing. **Computer sciences:** General. **Education:** Elementary. **Health:** Athletic training. **Math:** General. **Protective services:** Forensics. **Psychology:** General.

**Most popular majors.** Biology 11%, business/marketing 38%, education 24%, psychology 19%.

**Computing on campus.** 344 workstations in library, computer center, student center. Wireless network available.

**Student life. Freshman orientation:** Mandatory. **Activities:** Bands, choral groups, dance, drama, student government, Christian youth organizations, including those devoted to Catholic and Baptist students.

**Athletics. Intercollegiate:** Basketball, cross-country, softball, table tennis, tennis, track and field, volleyball. **Intramural:** Basketball, cross-country, gymnastics, softball, table tennis, tennis, track and field, volleyball.

**Student services.** Career counseling, student employment services, health services, on-campus daycare, personal counseling, placement for graduates, veterans' counselor. **Physically disabled:** Services for visually impaired.

**Contact.** E-mail: avelazquez@uprp.edu
Phone: (787) 844-8181 ext. 2531 Fax: (787) 840-8108
Acmin Rivera, Director of Admissions, University of Puerto Rico: Ponce, Box 7186, Ponce, PR 00732

---

## University of Puerto Rico: Rio Piedras
**San Juan, Puerto Rico**                        **CB member**
**www.uprrp.edu**                                **CB code: 0979**

- Public 4-year university
- Commuter campus in large city
- 15,344 degree-seeking undergraduates: 13% part-time, 65% women
- 3,610 graduate students
- 36% of applicants admitted
- 47% graduate within 6 years

**General.** Founded in 1903. Regionally accredited. Most courses conducted in Spanish. Students must have working knowledge of Spanish and English. **Degrees:** 2,334 bachelor's awarded; master's, doctoral, professional offered. **ROTC:** Army, Air Force. **Calendar:** Semester, limited summer session. **Full-time faculty:** 1,022 total; 75% have terminal degrees, 50% women. **Part-time faculty:** 334 total; 26% have terminal degrees, 49% women. **Class size:** 41% < 20, 57% 20-39, 1% 40-49, less than 1% 50-99, less than 1% >100. **Special facilities:** Museum of history, anthropology and art, theater, warm-blooded animal house, herbarium, biology museum, high-technology microscopy, nanotechnology lasers, virtual astronomy lab.

**Freshman class profile.** 8,290 applied, 2,969 admitted, 2,868 enrolled.

| Mid 50% test scores | | GPA 3.0-3.49: | 25% |
|---|---|---|---|
| SAT critical reading: | 540-650 | GPA 2.0-2.99: | 7% |
| SAT math: | 540-680 | Return as sophomores: | 91% |
| GPA 3.75 or higher: | 44% | Live on campus: | 10% |
| GPA 3.50-3.74: | 24% | | |

**Basis for selection.** Admissions based on secondary school record and standardized test scores. Talent and ability considered. Applicants must take Academic Aptitude Test and Achievement Test offered by the College Board. Otherwise, SAT scores must be submitted. Environmental Design requires separate application form and school test; Fine Arts requires departmental test. **Homeschooled:** Notarized homeschooling certificate.

**High school preparation.** Required and recommended units include English 3, mathematics 2, social studies 1, history 1, science 2 and academic electives 6. 3 units Spanish required.

**2009-2010 Annual costs.** Tuition/fees: $1,812; $4,226 out-of-state. Room/board: $8,280. Books/supplies: $1,825. Personal expenses: $1,200.

**2009-2010 Financial aid.** All financial aid based on need. **Additional information:** Tuition waived for honor students, athletes, members of chorus, and others with special talents.

**Application procedures. Admission:** Closing date 12/15 (postmark date). $20 fee. Admission notification 4/15. Must reply by 3/1. **Financial aid:** FAFSA required.

**Academics. Special study options:** Combined bachelor's/graduate degree, cooperative education, double major, exchange student, external degree, honors, internships, liberal arts/career combination, semester at sea, student-designed major, study abroad, teacher certification program, Washington semester. **Credit/placement by examination:** AP, CLEP, institutional tests. 30 credit hours maximum toward bachelor's degree. **Support services:** Remedial instruction, study skills assistance, tutoring, writing center.

**Majors. Architecture:** Environmental design. **Biology:** General. **Business:** General, accounting, administrative services, finance, human resources, labor relations, management information systems, managerial economics, marketing, operations, statistics. **Communications:** Digital media, journalism, media studies, public relations. **Computer sciences:** Computer science. **Conservation:** Environmental science. **Education:** Elementary, family/consumer sciences, secondary. **Family/consumer sciences:** General, food/nutrition. **Foreign languages:** General, comparative lit, French, Spanish. **History:** American, European. **Interdisciplinary:** Intercultural, natural sciences. **Legal studies:** Prelaw. **Liberal arts:** Arts/sciences. **Math:** General. **Philosophy/religion:** Philosophy. **Physical sciences:** Chemistry, physics. **Psychology:** General. **Public administration:** Social work. **Social sciences:** General, anthropology, economics, geography, political science, sociology. **Visual/performing arts:** General, art, art history/conservation, dramatic, drawing, multimedia, painting, photography, sculpture, studio arts.

**Most popular majors.** Business/marketing 20%, communications/journalism 6%, education 19%, interdisciplinary studies 11%, psychology 7%, social sciences 11%.

**Computing on campus.** 154 workstations in dormitories, library, computer center, student center. Dormitories wired for high-speed internet access and linked to campus network. Commuter students can connect to campus network. Online library, wireless network available.

**Student life. Freshman orientation:** Available. Preregistration for classes offered. Session held for 1 day in summer. **Policies:** Students represented in university administration. **Housing:** Coed dorms, wellness housing available. $35 fully refundable deposit, deadline 5/30. **Activities:** Jazz band, choral groups, dance, drama, literary magazine, musical theater, opera, radio station, student government, Club Avanza, Confraternidad Universitaria de Avivamiento, Jovenes Cristianos Universitarios, Juventud Universitaria Popular, Club de la Cruz Roja Americana del Recinto de Rio Piedras.

**Athletics. NAIA, NCAA. Intercollegiate:** Basketball, cross-country, gymnastics, soccer M, softball, swimming, table tennis, tennis, track and field, volleyball, water polo M, wrestling M. **Intramural:** Basketball, cross-country, gymnastics, soccer M, softball, swimming, table tennis, tennis, track and field, volleyball, water polo, wrestling M. **Team name:** Gallitos/Jerezanas.

**Student services.** Adult student services, alcohol/substance abuse counseling, career counseling, student employment services, health services, on-campus daycare, personal counseling, placement for graduates, veterans' counselor. **Physically disabled:** Services for visually, speech, hearing impaired.

**Contact.** E-mail: admisiones@uprrp.edu
Phone: (787) 764-7290 Toll-free number: (888) 966-2877
Fax: (787) 763-4265
Cruz Valentin, Director of Admissions, University of Puerto Rico: Rio Piedras, Box 23344, San Juan, PR 00931-3344

---

## University of Puerto Rico: Utuado
**Utuado, Puerto Rico**                        **CB member**
**www.uprutuado.edu**                          **CB code: 3893**

- Public 4-year agricultural college
- Commuter campus in large town
- 1,544 degree-seeking undergraduates: 7% part-time, 56% women
- 45% of applicants admitted
- Interview required
- 28% graduate within 6 years

**General.** Founded in 1979. Regionally accredited. **Degrees:** 94 bachelor's, 59 associate awarded. **ROTC:** Army. **Location:** 20 miles from Arecibo. **Calendar:** Semester, limited summer session. **Full-time faculty:** 68 total; 54% have terminal degrees, 100% minority, 46% women. **Part-time faculty:** 39 total; 10% have terminal degrees, 100% minority, 44% women. **Special facilities:** 118-acre farm.

**Freshman class profile.** 1,854 applied, 840 admitted, 556 enrolled.

**Basis for selection.** GED not accepted. High school GPA, test scores important. SAT required of English-speaking students.

**High school preparation.** Required units include English 3, mathematics 2, history 3, science 2 and foreign language 3. 3 fine arts required.

**2009-2010 Annual costs.** Tuition/fees: $1,812; $4,226 out-of-state. Books/supplies: $1,825. Personal expenses: $1,200.

**Financial aid.** All financial aid based on need.

**Application procedures. Admission:** Priority date 11/15; no deadline. $20 fee, may be waived for applicants with need. Must reply by May 1 or within 2 week(s) if notified thereafter. **Financial aid:** Priority date 5/31; no closing date. FAFSA required. Applicants notified on a rolling basis starting 9/30; must reply within 4 week(s) of notification.

**Academics. Special study options:** Cooperative education, honors, internships, teacher certification program. **Credit/placement by examination:** AP, CLEP. **Support services:** Reduced course load, remedial instruction, tutoring.

**Majors. Business:** Accounting, office/clerical. **Education:** Elementary.

**Most popular majors.** Business/marketing 23%, education 77%.

**Computing on campus.** 90 workstations in library, computer center. Online library, wireless network available.

**Student life. Freshman orientation:** Mandatory. **Housing:** Wellness housing available. Private housing near college available. **Activities:** Choral groups, drama, student government.

**Athletics. Intercollegiate:** Baseball M, basketball, cross-country, soccer M, softball, table tennis, track and field, volleyball, weight lifting. **Intramural:** Baseball M, basketball, cross-country, soccer M, softball, table tennis, track and field, volleyball, weight lifting. **Team name:** Guaraguao.

**Student services.** Alcohol/substance abuse counseling, career counseling, financial aid counseling, health services, personal counseling, placement for graduates, veterans' counselor.

**Contact.** Phone: (787) 894-2316 Fax: (787) 894-2891
Eltie Perez, Admissions Officer, University of Puerto Rico: Utuado, PO Box 2500, Utuado, PR 00641

## University of the Sacred Heart
**Santurce, Puerto Rico**     **CB member**
**www.sagrado.edu**     **CB code: 0913**

▶ Private 4-year university and liberal arts college affiliated with Roman Catholic Church
▶ Commuter campus in large city
▶ 4,518 degree-seeking undergraduates: 14% part-time, 61% women, 100% Hispanic American
▶ 1,084 degree-seeking graduate students

**General.** Founded in 1935. Regionally accredited. **Degrees:** 460 bachelor's, 110 associate awarded; master's offered. **Location:** Located in the San Juan metropolitan area, near the Luis Munos Marin International Airport. **Calendar:** Semester, extensive summer session. **Full-time faculty:** 121 total. **Part-time faculty:** 243 total. **Class size:** 47% < 20, 53% 20-39. **Special facilities:** Jardin Escultorico, Museo de la Radio, Pabellon de las Artes, Patio de las Artes, Galeria Jose (Pepin) Mendez y Teatro Emilio S. Belaval.

### Freshman class profile.

| | | | |
|---|---|---|---|
| GPA 3.75 or higher: | 9% | GPA 2.0-2.99: | 49% |
| GPA 3.50-3.74: | 12% | Out-of-state: | 2% |
| GPA 3.0-3.49: | 29% | | |

**Basis for selection.** High school GPA and highest score CEEB important. SAT scores accepted in place of CEEB. Interview required for nursing program.

**High school preparation.** 15 units required. Required and recommended units include English 3, mathematics 3, social studies 2, science 3, foreign language 3 and academic electives 3.

**2009-2010 Annual costs.** Tuition/fees: $5,870. Room only: $2,500. Books/supplies: $1,806. Personal expenses: $4,192.

**Financial aid. Non-need-based:** Scholarships awarded for academics, athletics.

**Application procedures. Admission:** Priority date 12/15; deadline 6/30. $15 fee, may be waived for applicants with need. Admission notification on a rolling basis. **Financial aid:** Priority date 4/30, closing date 5/30. FAFSA, institutional form required. Applicants notified on a rolling basis starting 6/15; must reply by 8/30.

**Academics. Special study options:** Combined bachelor's/graduate degree, cooperative education, cross-registration, double major, dual enrollment of high school students, exchange student, external degree, honors,

independent study, internships, liberal arts/career combination, semester at sea, teacher certification program. International programs with universities in Mexico and Spain. **Credit/placement by examination:** AP, CLEP, institutional tests. **Support services:** Pre-admission summer program, reduced course load, remedial instruction, tutoring.

**Majors. Biology:** General. **Business:** Accounting, business admin, tourism promotion. **Communications:** General, advertising, journalism. **Computer sciences:** Computer science, information systems. **Education:** General, bilingual, elementary, secondary. **Health:** Nursing (RN). **Interdisciplinary:** Natural sciences. **Math:** General. **Parks/recreation:** Health/fitness. **Physical sciences:** Chemistry. **Psychology:** General. **Public administration:** Social work. **Social sciences:** General. **Visual/performing arts:** General, dramatic, photography.

**Most popular majors.** Business/marketing 17%, communications/journalism 46%, education 9%, psychology 7%, social sciences 7%.

**Computing on campus.** 500 workstations in dormitories, library, computer center, student center. Commuter students can connect to campus network. Repair service available.

**Student life. Freshman orientation:** Available. **Housing:** Single-sex dorms available. $150 deposit, deadline 6/15. **Activities:** Choral groups, drama, film society, literary magazine, radio station, student government, student newspaper, TV station, pastoral services organization, health and allied sciences organization, student council, senior class organization, judo club, soccer club, nursing club, Christian club, microbioloby club, psychology club, chemistry club, justice system, telecommunication club.

**Athletics. Intercollegiate:** Basketball M, cross-country, swimming, tennis M, track and field, volleyball, wrestling M. **Intramural:** Basketball M, softball M, swimming, table tennis, volleyball. **Team name:** Dolphins.

**Student services.** Alcohol/substance abuse counseling, career counseling, student employment services, financial aid counseling, health services, personal counseling, placement for graduates, veterans' counselor. **Physically disabled:** Services for visually, hearing impaired.

**Contact.** E-mail: admision@sagrado.edu
Phone: (787) 728-1515 ext. 3236 Fax: (787) 728-2066
Luis Henriquez, Director of Admissions and Promotion, University of the Sacred Heart, Universidad del Sagrado Corazon Oficina de Nuevo Ingreso, San Juan, PR 00914-0383

# Rhode Island

## Brown University
**Providence, Rhode Island**
www.brown.edu

**CB member**
**CB code: 3094**

- Private 4-year university and liberal arts college
- Residential campus in small city
- 6,013 degree-seeking undergraduates: 52% women, 6% African American, 16% Asian American, 9% Hispanic American, 9% international
- 1,832 degree-seeking graduate students
- 11% of applicants admitted
- SAT and SAT Subject Tests or ACT with writing, application essay required
- 95% graduate within 6 years; 27% enter graduate study

**General.** Founded in 1764. Regionally accredited. **Degrees:** 1,443 bachelor's awarded; master's, doctoral, professional offered. **ROTC:** Army. **Location:** 45 miles from Boston. **Calendar:** Semester, limited summer session. **Full-time faculty:** 689 total. **Part-time faculty:** 191 total. **Special facilities:** Museum of anthropology, observatory, center for the performing arts, center for information technology, institute for education, institute for international studies, center for the humanities.

**Freshman class profile.** 24,988 applied, 2,790 admitted, 1,495 enrolled.

| Mid 50% test scores | | | |
|---|---|---|---|
| SAT critical reading: | 650-760 | Rank in top tenth: | 92% |
| SAT math: | 670-780 | Return as sophomores: | 97% |
| SAT writing: | 660-770 | Out-of-state: | 86% |
| ACT composite: | 28-33 | Live on campus: | 100% |
| Rank in top quarter: | 99% | International: | 10% |

**Basis for selection.** GED not accepted. Strength of academic course load and student's achievement in courses most important. Extracurricular activities, recommendations, personal essay important; test scores strongly considered. Students submitting SAT should submit scores of any 2 SAT Subject Tests. Portfolio recommended for art, music programs. Alumni interviews available, but not required, for all applicants. **Learning Disabled:** Untimed standardized tests accepted.

**High school preparation.** 19 units recommended. Recommended units include English 4, mathematics 4, history 2, science 4 (laboratory 3), foreign language 4 and academic electives 1. At least 1 art unit (music or art) recommended. Familiarity with computers recommended. Physics, chemistry, and advanced mathematics recommended for prospective science or engineering majors.

**2009-2010 Annual costs.** Tuition/fees: $38,848. Part-time students pay $4,756 per course in tuition; most undergraduates take eight courses per academic year. Room/board: $10,280. Books/supplies: $2,902. Personal expenses: $1,636.

**2009-2010 Financial aid.** All financial aid based on need. 880 full-time freshmen applied for aid; 637 were judged to have need; 637 of these received aid. Average need met was 100%. Average scholarship/grant was $32,100; average loan $4,659. 88% of total undergraduate aid awarded as scholarships/grants, 12% as loans/jobs.

**Application procedures. Admission:** Closing date 1/1 (postmark date). $75 fee, may be waived for applicants with need. Admission notification 4/1. Must reply by 5/1. **Financial aid:** Closing date 2/1. FAFSA, CSS PROFILE required. Applicants notified by 4/1; must reply by 5/1.

**Academics.** Students must complete course requirements in major(s) of choice, but are free to choose courses without a core curriculum prior to designating a major. **Special study options:** Accelerated study, combined bachelor's/graduate degree, cross-registration, double major, exchange student, honors, independent study, internships, student-designed major, study abroad, teacher certification program. 8-year medical program, cross-registration with Rhode Island School of Design, early childhood certification (in teaching) program via Wheaton College courses. **Credit/placement by examination:** AP, CLEP, institutional tests. **Support services:** Reduced course load, study skills assistance, tutoring, writing center.

**Majors. Architecture:** History/criticism. **Area/ethnic studies:** African, African-American, American, Asian, Chicano/Hispanic-American/Latino, East Asian, European, French, German, Italian, Latin American, Near/Middle Eastern, Slavic, South Asian, women's. **Biology:** General, aquatic, biochemistry, biophysics, cell/histology, molecular. **Computer sciences:** Computer science. **Conservation:** Environmental science, environmental studies. **Education:** General. **Engineering:** Biomedical, chemical, civil, computer, electrical, materials, mechanical, physics. **Foreign languages:** Ancient Greek, classics, comparative lit, French, German, Italian, Latin, linguistics, Portuguese, Slavic, Spanish. **Health:** Community health services. **History:** General. **Interdisciplinary:** Ancient studies, biological/physical sciences, cognitive science, math/computer science, medieval/Renaissance, neuroscience. **Math:** General, applied, statistics. **Philosophy/religion:** Judaic, philosophy, religion. **Physical sciences:** Chemical physics, chemistry, geochemistry, geology, geophysics, physics. **Psychology:** General. **Public administration:** Policy analysis. **Social sciences:** Anthropology, archaeology, economics, international economic development, international relations, political science, sociology, urban studies. **Visual/performing arts:** General, art history/conservation, dramatic, musicology, studio arts.

**Most popular majors.** Biology 19%, physical sciences 11%, social sciences 45%.

**Computing on campus.** 500 workstations in dormitories, library, computer center, student center. Dormitories wired for high-speed internet access and linked to campus network. Commuter students can connect to campus network. Online course registration, online library, helpline, repair service, wireless network available.

**Student life. Freshman orientation:** Mandatory. Preregistration for classes offered. 5-day program, beginning Wednesday prior to Labor Day. **Policies:** Students must live in on-campus housing for first 3 years; those entering 7th semester may request off-campus residence. **Housing:** Guaranteed on-campus for all undergraduates. Coed dorms, single-sex dorms, cooperative housing, fraternity/sorority housing, wellness housing available. Language houses, social dormitories, cultural houses, special program housing (international students, technology students, environmental students) available. **Activities:** Bands, choral groups, dance, drama, film society, literary magazine, music ensembles, musical theater, radio station, student government, student newspaper, symphony orchestra, TV station, African students association, ACLU, Amnesty International, Asian American students association, Big Brothers, community outreach, Catholic pastoral council, Latino American students association, international organization, Canadian club.

**Athletics.** NCAA. **Intercollegiate:** Baseball M, basketball, cross-country, diving, equestrian W, fencing, field hockey W, football (tackle) M, golf, gymnastics W, ice hockey, lacrosse, rowing (crew), skiing M, soccer, softball W, squash, swimming, tennis, track and field, volleyball W, water polo, wrestling M. **Intramural:** Badminton, basketball, fencing, field hockey W, ice hockey, lacrosse, racquetball, rugby, soccer, softball, squash, swimming, tennis, volleyball, water polo. **Team name:** Bears.

**Student services.** Adult student services, alcohol/substance abuse counseling, chaplain/spiritual director, career counseling, student employment services, financial aid counseling, health services, minority student services, personal counseling, placement for graduates, women's services. **Physically disabled:** Services for visually, hearing impaired.

**Contact.** E-mail: admission_undergraduate@brown.edu
Phone: (401) 863-2378 Fax: (401) 863-9300
James Miller, Dean of Admission, Brown University, 45 Prospect Street, Providence, RI 02912

## Bryant University
**Smithfield, Rhode Island**
www.bryant.edu

**CB member**
**CB code: 3095**

- Private 4-year business and liberal arts college
- Residential campus in large town
- 3,367 degree-seeking undergraduates: 3% part-time, 43% women, 4% African American, 3% Asian American, 4% Hispanic American, 5% international
- 246 degree-seeking graduate students
- 53% of applicants admitted
- SAT or ACT (ACT writing optional), application essay required
- 69% graduate within 6 years

**General.** Founded in 1863. Regionally accredited. Students in the College of Business earn a liberal arts minor that complements their business background; students in the College of Arts and Sciences earn a business administration minor that enhances the value of their liberal arts education. **Degrees:** 774 bachelor's awarded; master's offered. **ROTC:** Army. **Location:**

12 miles from Providence, 40 miles from Boston. **Calendar:** Semester, extensive summer session. **Full-time faculty:** 158 total; 85% have terminal degrees, 10% minority, 38% women. **Part-time faculty:** 98 total; 20% have terminal degrees, 12% minority, 44% women. **Class size:** 27% < 20, 71% 20-39, 2% 40-49. **Special facilities:** Center for information and technology (housing library and financial markets center that features real-time stock market data and Reuters 3000); all-weather outdoor track, golf practice green and driving range; communications complex that features several computer labs, digital television studio, control room, and editing suite.

**Freshman class profile.** 5,393 applied, 2,870 admitted, 751 enrolled.

| Mid 50% test scores | | GPA 2.0-2.99: | 18% |
|---|---|---|---|
| SAT critical reading: | 510-590 | Rank in top quarter: | 58% |
| SAT math: | 550-630 | Rank in top tenth: | 25% |
| SAT writing: | 510-600 | Return as sophomores: | 87% |
| ACT composite: | 23-27 | Out-of-state: | 87% |
| GPA 3.75 or higher: | 17% | Live on campus: | 96% |
| GPA 3.50-3.74: | 23% | International: | 7% |
| GPA 3.0-3.49: | 42% | | |

**Basis for selection.** Secondary school curriculum, GPA, guidance counselor's recommendation, personal essay very important; class rank and test scores important. Evidence of math ability important for consideration by business programs. **Homeschooled:** Must complete a state-accredited program. Course descriptions and progress reports required as part of application process. **Learning Disabled:** Foreign language requirement may be waived.

**High school preparation.** College-preparatory program required. 16 units required; 18 recommended. Required and recommended units include English 4, mathematics 4, history 2-3, science 2-3 (laboratory 2) and foreign language 2. Mathematics must include a year beyond algebra II, with a preference for pre-calculus or calculus in senior year. History includes social sciences.

**2010-2011 Annual costs.** Tuition/fees: $33,357. Room/board: $12,458. Books/supplies: $1,300. Personal expenses: $1,000.

**2008-2009 Financial aid. Need-based:** 573 full-time freshmen applied for aid; 478 were judged to have need; 478 of these received aid. Average need met was 67%. Average scholarship/grant was $13,850; average loan $3,360. 68% of total undergraduate aid awarded as scholarships/grants, 32% as loans/jobs. **Non-need-based:** Awarded to 1,604 full-time undergraduates, including 384 freshmen. Scholarships awarded for academics, athletics, minority status, ROTC.

**Application procedures. Admission:** Closing date 2/1 (postmark date). $50 fee, may be waived for applicants with need. Admission notification 3/21. Must reply by 5/1. **Financial aid:** Closing date 2/15. FAFSA required. Applicants notified by 3/24; must reply by 5/1.

**Academics.** Business majors must minor in Arts & Sciences. Arts & Sciences majors must minor in Business. All students may select minors. New students complete a one-credit Foundations for Learning course. International Business majors share residence and must complete 12 credit hours in study abroad. **Special study options:** Double major, ESL, honors, independent study, internships, study abroad. **Credit/placement by examination:** AP, CLEP, IB, institutional tests. 30 credit hours maximum toward bachelor's degree. **Support services:** Learning center, study skills assistance, tutoring, writing center.

**Majors. Business:** Accounting, accounting technology, actuarial science, business admin, finance, financial planning, international, international finance, marketing. **Communications:** General. **Computer sciences:** General, information technology. **Conservation:** Environmental science. **History:** General. **Math:** Applied, statistics. **Psychology:** General. **Social sciences:** Applied economics, economics, international relations, sociology.

**Most popular majors.** Business/marketing 84%.

**Computing on campus.** PC or laptop required. 478 workstations in library, computer center. Dormitories wired for high-speed internet access and linked to campus network. Commuter students can connect to campus network. Online course registration, online library, helpline, repair service, student web hosting, wireless network available.

**Student life. Freshman orientation:** Mandatory, $75 fee. Preregistration for classes offered. 2-day program in June during which students and parents/guardians are housed in campus residence halls overnight. Students also take mathematics placement exam and register for elective courses. **Policies:** All residence halls are smoke free. Students 21 and over may drink in privacy of room. Quiet study hour policy in effect through academic year. **Housing:** Guaranteed on-campus for freshmen. Coed dorms, single-sex dorms, special housing for disabled, apartments available. Honors, international business communities. **Activities:** Bands, campus ministries, choral groups, dance,

drama, international student organizations, literary magazine, music ensembles, musical theater, radio station, student government, student newspaper, TV station, Christian fellowship, Hillel, College Democrats and Republicans, multicultural student union, Alliance for Women's Awareness, Amnesty International, Big Brothers/Big Sisters.

**Athletics.** NCAA. **Intercollegiate:** Baseball M, basketball, cross-country, field hockey W, football (tackle) M, golf M, lacrosse, soccer, softball W, swimming, tennis, track and field, volleyball W, wrestling M. **Intramural:** Basketball, football (non-tackle) M, soccer, softball, volleyball. **Team name:** Bulldogs.

**Student services.** Adult student services, alcohol/substance abuse counseling, chaplain/spiritual director, career counseling, services for economically disadvantaged, student employment services, financial aid counseling, health services, minority student services, personal counseling, placement for graduates, veterans' counselor, women's services. **Physically disabled:** Services for visually, hearing impaired.

**Contact.** E-mail: admission@bryant.edu
Phone: (401) 232-6100 Toll-free number: (800) 622-7001
Fax: (401) 232-6741
Michelle Beauregard, Director of Admission, Bryant University, 1150 Douglas Pike, Smithfield, RI 02917

---

## Johnson & Wales University: Providence

| Providence, Rhode Island | CB member |
|---|---|
| www.jwu.edu | CB code: 3465 |

- Private 4-year university
- Residential campus in small city
- 9,495 degree-seeking undergraduates: 8% part-time, 54% women, 7% African American, 2% Asian American, 6% Hispanic American, 8% international
- 1,214 degree-seeking graduate students
- 72% of applicants admitted

**General.** Founded in 1914. Regionally accredited. **Degrees:** 1,452 bachelor's, 1,735 associate awarded; master's, doctoral offered. **ROTC:** Army. **Location:** 200 miles from New York City, 50 miles from Boston. **Calendar:** Quarter, limited summer session. **Full-time faculty:** 292 total; 42% women. **Part-time faculty:** 182 total; 45% women. **Class size:** 45% < 20, 41% 20-39, 14% 40-49, less than 1% 50-99. **Special facilities:** 3 university-operated hotels and restaurants, banquet facilities, information kiosk, culinary museum, equine center.

**Freshman class profile.** 14,072 applied, 10,076 admitted, 2,299 enrolled.

| Mid 50% test scores | | GPA 3.0-3.49: | 29% |
|---|---|---|---|
| SAT critical reading: | 420-520 | GPA 2.0-2.99: | 50% |
| SAT math: | 420-540 | Out-of-state: | 89% |
| SAT writing: | 410-520 | Live on campus: | 86% |
| GPA 3.75 or higher: | 10% | International: | 6% |
| GPA 3.50-3.74: | 11% | | |

**Basis for selection.** Academic record, secondary school curriculum, GPA, class rank, test scores important; student motivation and interest given strong consideration. SAT or ACT required for admission to honors program. Interview and letter of recommendation generally required of students in bottom quarter of class; essay and interview recommended for others. **Homeschooled:** Transcript of courses and grades, state high school equivalency certificate required. SAT (Critical Reading and Math) or ACT required.

**High school preparation.** College-preparatory program recommended. Required units include English 4, mathematics 3, social studies 2 and science 3.

**2010-2011 Annual costs.** Tuition/fees (projected): $24,429. Room/board: $8,904. Books/supplies: $1,500. Personal expenses: $1,623.

**2009-2010 Financial aid. Non-need-based:** Scholarships awarded for academics, alumni affiliation, job skills, leadership, state residency.

**Application procedures. Admission:** No deadline. No application fee. Admission notification on a rolling basis beginning on or about 11/1. Must reply by May 1 or within 2 week(s) if notified thereafter. **Financial aid:** No deadline. FAFSA required. Applicants notified on a rolling basis starting 3/1; must reply within 2 week(s) of notification.

**Academics. Special study options:** Accelerated study, cooperative education, dual enrollment of high school students, ESL, exchange student, honors, independent study, internships, study abroad. Externships, practicums (hands-on learning). **Credit/placement by examination:** CLEP, institutional tests. **Support services:** Learning center, pre-admission summer program, reduced course load, remedial instruction, study skills assistance, tutoring, writing center.

**Majors. Agriculture:** Equestrian studies, equine science, farm/ranch. **Business:** Accounting, business admin, entrepreneurial studies, fashion, finance, hospitality admin, hotel/motel admin, international, investments/securities, marketing, public finance, tourism promotion, tourism/travel. **Communications:** Advertising. **Computer sciences:** Information systems, systems analysis, web page design, webmaster. **Engineering:** Computer, systems. **Engineering technology:** Drafting. **Interdisciplinary:** Nutrition sciences. **Parks/recreation:** Facilities management, sports admin. **Personal/culinary services:** Baking, chef training, culinary arts, food service, restaurant/catering. **Protective services:** Law enforcement admin.

**Most popular majors.** Business/marketing 44%, family/consumer sciences 13%, parks/recreation 10%, personal/culinary services 14%.

**Computing on campus.** 400 workstations in library, computer center. Dormitories wired for high-speed internet access and linked to campus network. Commuter students can connect to campus network. Online library, helpline, wireless network available.

**Student life. Freshman orientation:** Mandatory, $276 fee. Preregistration for classes offered. **Housing:** Guaranteed on-campus for freshmen. Coed dorms, wellness housing available. $300 deposit. **Activities:** Campus ministries, drama, international student organizations, student government, student newspaper, Hillel, Christian student union, ACLU, Latin-American club, Asian club, T.R.U.E. (Together Realizing Unity Can Exist), College Republicans.

**Athletics.** NCAA. **Intercollegiate:** Baseball M, basketball, cross-country, equestrian, golf M, ice hockey M, sailing, soccer, softball W, tennis, volleyball, wrestling M. **Intramural:** Basketball, soccer, softball, tennis. **Team name:** Wildcats.

**Student services.** Career counseling, student employment services, financial aid counseling, health services, personal counseling, placement for graduates, veterans' counselor, women's services. **Physically disabled:** Services for visually, speech, hearing impaired.

**Contact.** E-mail: admissions.pvd@jwu.edu
Phone: (401) 598-2310 Toll-free number: (800) 342-5598
Fax: (401) 598-2948
Amy Podbelski, Director of Admissions, Johnson & Wales University: Providence, 8 Abbott Park Place, Providence, RI 02903-3703

## New England Institute of Technology
Warwick, Rhode Island
www.neit.edu                              CB code: 0339

- Private 4-year technical college
- Commuter campus in small city
- 3,341 degree-seeking undergraduates: 11% part-time, 20% women, 7% African American, 2% Asian American, 5% Hispanic American, 1% Native American
- Interview required

**General.** Founded in 1940. Regionally accredited. **Degrees:** 224 bachelor's, 891 associate awarded. **Location:** 10 miles from Providence, 50 miles from Boston. **Calendar:** Quarter, extensive summer session. **Full-time faculty:** 99 total; 11% have terminal degrees. **Part-time faculty:** 145 total; 6% have terminal degrees.

**Basis for selection.** Open admission. Basic skills testing, Ronald P. Carver reading test used for placement. Portfolio recommended for drafting program.

**2009-2010 Annual costs.** Tuition/fees: $18,140. Books/supplies: $1,280. Personal expenses: $1,440.

**Financial aid. Non-need-based:** Scholarships awarded for academics. **Additional information:** Tuition at time of first enrollment guaranteed all students for 2 years.

**Application procedures. Admission:** No deadline. $25 fee. Admission notification on a rolling basis. Must reply by May 1 or within 4 week(s) if notified thereafter. **Financial aid:** Priority date 6/1; no closing date. FAFSA, institutional form required. Applicants notified on a rolling basis starting 6/15.

**Academics. Special study options:** Accelerated study, cooperative education, distance learning, double major, ESL, internships, student-designed major. **Credit/placement by examination:** AP, CLEP, institutional tests. 51 credit hours maximum toward associate degree. **Support services:** Learning center, pre-admission summer program, reduced course load, remedial instruction, study skills assistance, tutoring, writing center.

**Majors. Business:** General. **Communications technology:** Recording arts. **Computer sciences:** General, computer science, information technology, systems analysis. **Engineering:** Architectural, manufacturing, mechanical. **Engineering technology:** Electrical, manufacturing. **Visual/performing arts:** Interior design.

**Computing on campus.** 50 workstations in library, computer center. Online course registration, online library, wireless network available.

**Student life. Freshman orientation:** Mandatory. Preregistration for classes offered. **Activities:** Radio station, student newspaper, TV station, international student club.

**Student services.** Career counseling, student employment services, financial aid counseling, personal counseling, placement for graduates, veterans' counselor.

**Contact.** E-mail: neit@neit.edu
Phone: (401) 467-7744 Toll-free number: (800) 736-7744 ext. 3357
Fax: (401) 738-5122
Mark Blondin, Director of Admissions, New England Institute of Technology, 2500 Post Road, Warwick, RI 02886-2286

## Providence College
Providence, Rhode Island                        CB member
www.providence.edu                              CB code: 3693

- Private 4-year liberal arts college affiliated with Roman Catholic Church
- Residential campus in small city
- 3,829 degree-seeking undergraduates: 57% women, 3% African American, 2% Asian American, 4% Hispanic American, 1% international
- 465 degree-seeking graduate students
- 60% of applicants admitted
- Application essay required
- 88% graduate within 6 years

**General.** Founded in 1917. Regionally accredited. In addition to its traditional undergraduate college, Providence College has a community-oriented evening school that caters to part-time students. **Degrees:** 1,019 bachelor's, 2 associate awarded; master's offered. **ROTC:** Army. **Location:** 50 miles from Boston, 180 miles from New York City. **Calendar:** Semester, limited summer session. **Full-time faculty:** 297 total; 93% have terminal degrees, 10% minority, 34% women. **Part-time faculty:** 103 total; 33% have terminal degrees, 4% minority, 42% women. **Class size:** 48% < 20, 48% 20-39, less than 1% 40-49, 2% 50-99, less than 1% >100.

**Freshman class profile.** 8,376 applied, 5,008 admitted, 955 enrolled.

| Mid 50% test scores | | GPA 2.0-2.99: | 13% |
|---|---|---|---|
| SAT critical reading: | 530-630 | Rank in top quarter: | 72% |
| SAT math: | 530-640 | Rank in top tenth: | 37% |
| SAT writing: | 540-640 | End year in good standing: | 99% |
| ACT composite: | 23-28 | Return as sophomores: | 91% |
| GPA 3.75 or higher: | 17% | Out-of-state: | 88% |
| GPA 3.50-3.74: | 22% | Live on campus: | 97% |
| GPA 3.0-3.49: | 48% | International: | 1% |

**Basis for selection.** GED not accepted. Emphasis placed on scholastic ability, motivation, character, and seriousness of purpose. Recommendations and essay considered. Strength of curriculum and grades are the most important factors. Standardized tests scores are optional. Prospective students who choose not to submit standardized test scores will receive full consideration, without penalty, for admission. Audition recommended for music programs; portfolio recommended for art programs. **Homeschooled:** Statement describing homeschool structure and mission, transcript of courses and grades, state high school equivalency certificate, letter of recommendation (nonparent) required. If not associated with a particular program or institution, the applicant is encouraged to submit a descriptive resume that outlines the student's high school work, level of challenge, and depth and breadth of curriculum, including reading lists and a graded writing sample. **Learning Disabled:** Students must provide documentation of disability. Accommodations are then made as deemed appropriate.

**High school preparation.** College-preparatory program required. Required and recommended units include English 4, mathematics 4, social studies 2, history 2, science 3-4 (laboratory 2) and foreign language 3.

**2010-2011 Annual costs.** Tuition/fees: $39,435. Room/board: $11,690. Books/supplies: $800. Personal expenses: $1,500.

**2009-2010 Financial aid. Need-based:** 754 full-time freshmen applied for aid; 579 were judged to have need; 579 of these received aid. Average need met was 76%. Average scholarship/grant was $17,180; average loan $4,413. 68% of total undergraduate aid awarded as scholarships/grants, 32% as loans/jobs. **Non-need-based:** Awarded to 608 full-time undergraduates, including 173 freshmen. Scholarships awarded for academics, athletics, minority status, ROTC.

**Application procedures. Admission:** Closing date 1/15 (postmark date). $55 fee, may be waived for applicants with need. Admission notification 4/1. Must reply by 5/1. **Financial aid:** Closing date 2/1. FAFSA, CSS PROFILE required. Applicants notified by 4/1; must reply by 5/1.

**Academics. Special study options:** Combined bachelor's/graduate degree, cross-registration, distance learning, double major, dual enrollment of high school students, honors, independent study, internships, liberal arts/career combination, semester at sea, student-designed major, study abroad, teacher certification program, Washington semester. **Credit/placement by examination:** AP, CLEP, IB, SAT, ACT, institutional tests. International Baccalaureate credit restricted to 5-7 higher level exams. **Support services:** Learning center, reduced course load, study skills assistance, tutoring, writing center.

**Majors. Area/ethnic studies:** American, women's. **Biology:** General, biochemistry. **Business:** Accounting, business admin, finance, labor relations, marketing, organizational behavior. **Computer sciences:** Computer science. **Education:** Mathematics, music, secondary, special. **Engineering:** Physics, systems. **Foreign languages:** French, Italian, Spanish. **Health:** Health care admin. **History:** General. **Interdisciplinary:** Global studies. **Liberal arts:** Arts/sciences, humanities. **Math:** General. **Philosophy/religion:** Philosophy. **Physical sciences:** Chemistry. **Psychology:** General. **Public administration:** Community org/advocacy, social work. **Social sciences:** General, economics, political science, sociology. **Theology:** Theology. **Visual/performing arts:** General, art history/conservation, ceramics, digital art, drawing, painting, photography, sculpture, studio arts. **Other:** Global studies.

**Most popular majors.** Biology 8%, business/marketing 31%, education 8%, English 7%, history 6%, social sciences 14%.

**Computing on campus.** 338 workstations in dormitories, library, computer center, student center. Dormitories wired for high-speed internet access and linked to campus network. Commuter students can connect to campus network. Online course registration, online library, helpline, repair service, student web hosting, wireless network available.

**Student life. Freshman orientation:** Mandatory. Preregistration for classes offered. Six-day program. **Housing:** Guaranteed on-campus for freshmen. Coed dorms, single-sex dorms, special housing for disabled, wellness housing available. $200 nonrefundable deposit, deadline 5/1. **Activities:** Bands, campus ministries, choral groups, dance, drama, international student organizations, literary magazine, music ensembles, musical theater, radio station, student government, student newspaper, TV station, Afro-American society, Big Brothers and Sisters, Pastoral Service Organization, PC Pals, Best Buddies, College Democrats, College Republicans, Amigos Unidos, Asian American Club.

**Athletics.** NCAA. **Intercollegiate:** Basketball, cross-country, diving, field hockey W, ice hockey, lacrosse M, soccer, softball W, swimming, tennis W, track and field, volleyball W. **Intramural:** Basketball, field hockey W, football (non-tackle), ice hockey, lacrosse, racquetball, soccer, softball, tennis, volleyball. **Team name:** Friars.

**Student services.** Adult student services, alcohol/substance abuse counseling, chaplain/spiritual director, career counseling, services for economically disadvantaged, student employment services, financial aid counseling, health services, minority student services, personal counseling, placement for graduates. **Physically disabled:** Services for visually, hearing impaired.

**Contact.** E-mail: pcadmiss@providence.edu
Phone: (401) 865-2535 Toll-free number: (800) 721-6444
Fax: (401) 865-2826
Christopher Lydon, Associate Vice President for Admissions and Enrollment Planning, Providence College, Harkins Hall 222, 1 Cunningham Square, Providence, RI 02918-0001

---

## Rhode Island College
**Providence, Rhode Island**
www.ric.edu

**CB member**
**CB code: 3724**

- Public 4-year liberal arts college
- Commuter campus in small city
- 7,500 degree-seeking undergraduates: 24% part-time, 67% women
- 733 degree-seeking graduate students
- 77% of applicants admitted
- SAT or ACT with writing, application essay required
- 45% graduate within 6 years

**General.** Founded in 1854. Regionally accredited. **Degrees:** 1,228 bachelor's awarded; master's, doctoral offered. **ROTC:** Army. **Location:** 4 miles from downtown Providence. **Calendar:** Semester, extensive summer session. **Full-time faculty:** 311 total; 91% have terminal degrees, 11% minority, 54% women. **Part-time faculty:** 450 total; 58% women. **Class size:** 40% < 20, 59% 20-39, less than 1% 50-99, less than 1% >100. **Special facilities:** Center for the performing arts, art gallery.

**Freshman class profile.** 3,938 applied, 3,027 admitted, 1,253 enrolled.

| Mid 50% test scores | | Rank in top quarter: | 33% |
|---|---|---|---|
| SAT critical reading: | 420-520 | Rank in top tenth: | 11% |
| SAT math: | 420-520 | Return as sophomores: | 77% |
| SAT writing: | 420-530 | Out-of-state: | 20% |
| ACT composite: | 16-21 | Live on campus: | 43% |

**Basis for selection.** High school academic record and class rank most important, followed by test scores, essay, references. TOEFL required for all applicants who have been in the country for less than 5 years and are not native speakers of English. SAT scores required of non-native speakers of English who have been in the United States for more than five years. Interview available but not required; audition required for music performance, and portfolio required for bachelor of fine arts. **Homeschooled:** Transcript of courses and grades, state high school equivalency certificate, interview required. Must submit GED scores unless their homeschool curriculum is provided by an accredited agency.

**High school preparation.** College-preparatory program required. 18 units required. Required units include English 4, mathematics 3, social studies 2, science 2 (laboratory 2), foreign language 2 and academic electives 5. Biology and either chemistry or physics are recommended lab sciences. 2 years of the same foreign language required. Algebra I, II and geometry required. All units must be college-preparatory.

**2009-2010 Annual costs.** Tuition/fees: $6,408; $15,488 out-of-state. Permanent residents of Massachusetts and Connecticut communities within a 50-mile radius of Providence are eligible for Rhode Island's in-state tuition plus 50% of the in-state rate. Room/board: $8,818. Books/supplies: $1,000. Personal expenses: $1,000.

**2009-2010 Financial aid. Need-based:** 1,085 full-time freshmen applied for aid; 805 were judged to have need; 782 of these received aid. Average need met was 77%. Average scholarship/grant was $6,160; average loan $3,265. 43% of total undergraduate aid awarded as scholarships/grants, 57% as loans/jobs. **Non-need-based:** Awarded to 191 full-time undergraduates, including 75 freshmen. Scholarships awarded for academics, alumni affiliation, art, music/drama.

**Application procedures. Admission:** Closing date 3/15 (postmark date). $50 fee, may be waived for applicants with need. Admission notification on a rolling basis beginning on or about 12/15. Must reply by May 1 or within 2 week(s) if notified thereafter. **Financial aid:** Priority date 3/1; no closing date. FAFSA, institutional form required. Applicants notified on a rolling basis starting 3/15; must reply within 3 week(s) of notification.

**Academics. Special study options:** Combined bachelor's/graduate degree, double major, dual enrollment of high school students, ESL, exchange student, honors, independent study, internships, student-designed major, study abroad, teacher certification program. **Credit/placement by examination:** CLEP, SAT, ACT, institutional tests. **Support services:** Learning center, pre-admission summer program, reduced course load, remedial instruction, study skills assistance, tutoring, writing center.

**Majors. Area/ethnic studies:** African-American, Latin American, women's. **Biology:** General. **Business:** General, accounting, business admin, finance, labor studies, management information systems, managerial economics, marketing. **Communications:** General. **Computer sciences:** General, computer science. **Education:** Art, biology, chemistry, early childhood, elementary, English, foreign languages, French, geography, health, history, mathematics, multi-level teacher, music, physical, physics, science, secondary, social science, social studies, Spanish, special, technology/industrial arts, voc/tech. **Foreign languages:** French, Spanish. **Health:** Clinical lab science, nursing (RN), predental, premedicine, preveterinary, substance abuse counseling. **History:** General. **Legal studies:** Prelaw. **Liberal arts:** Arts/sciences. **Math:** General. **Philosophy/religion:** Philosophy. **Physical sciences:** Chemistry, physics. **Protective services:** Criminal justice. **Psychology:** General. **Public administration:** General, social work. **Social sciences:** General, anthropology, economics, geography, political science, sociology. **Visual/performing arts:** Art history/conservation, dance, dramatic, film/cinema, music performance, studio arts.

**Most popular majors.** Business/marketing 12%, communications/journalism 8%, education 22%, health sciences 10%, psychology 12%, social sciences 8%, visual/performing arts 7%.

**Computing on campus.** 690 workstations in library, computer center, student center. Dormitories wired for high-speed internet access and linked to campus network. Commuter students can connect to campus network. Online course registration, online library, helpline, repair service, student web hosting, wireless network available.

**Student life. Freshman orientation:** Available, $85 fee. Preregistration for classes offered. Held throughout July in 2-day cycles. Some single days are available. **Housing:** Coed dorms, single-sex dorms, special housing for disabled available. $220 partly refundable deposit, deadline 5/15. **Activities:** Bands, campus ministries, choral groups, dance, drama, film society, international student organizations, literary magazine, music ensembles, musical theater, radio station, student government, student newspaper, symphony orchestra, TV station, Amnesty International, Cape Verdean student association, Intra-Varsity Student Fellowship, Latin American student organization, RIC Angels, College Republicans, Political Science Club, Asian Student Association, Student for Justice in Palestine, Rainbow Alliance.

**Athletics.** NCAA. **Intercollegiate:** Baseball M, basketball, cross-country, golf M, gymnastics W, lacrosse W, soccer, softball W, tennis, track and field, volleyball W, wrestling M. **Intramural:** Badminton, basketball, football (non-tackle) M, golf, gymnastics W, sailing, skin diving, soccer, softball, swimming, tennis, volleyball, water polo. **Team name:** Anchormen, Anchorwomen.

**Student services.** Adult student services, alcohol/substance abuse counseling, chaplain/spiritual director, career counseling, student employment services, financial aid counseling, health services, minority student services, on-campus daycare, personal counseling, placement for graduates, veterans' counselor, women's services. **Physically disabled:** Services for visually, speech, hearing impaired. **Learning disabled:** Comprehensive services available.

**Contact.** E-mail: admissions@ric.edu
Phone: (401) 456-8234 Toll-free number: (800) 669-5760
Fax: (401) 456-8817
Deborah Johnson, Director of Admissions, Rhode Island College, 600 Mount Pleasant Avenue, Providence, RI 02908

---

### Rhode Island School of Design
**Providence, Rhode Island**  **CB member**
**www.risd.edu**  **CB code: 3726**

- Private 4-year visual arts college
- Residential campus in small city
- 1,940 degree-seeking undergraduates
- 420 graduate students
- 35% of applicants admitted
- SAT or ACT with writing, application essay required

**General.** Founded in 1877. Regionally accredited. **Degrees:** 494 bachelor's awarded; master's offered. **Location:** 52 miles from Boston, 180 miles from New York City. **Calendar:** 4-1-4, limited summer session. **Full-time faculty:** 146 total. **Part-time faculty:** 357 total. **Special facilities:** Fine art and design museum, extensive photograph and clipping collections, slide collection, recreational farm on Narragansett Bay, nature laboratory.

**Freshman class profile.** 2,819 applied, 987 admitted, 454 enrolled.

| Mid 50% test scores | | | |
|---|---|---|---|
| SAT critical reading: | 540-680 | Rank in top quarter: | 58% |
| SAT math: | 590-690 | Rank in top tenth: | 23% |
| SAT writing: | 560-680 | Out-of-state: | 96% |
| ACT composite: | 22-29 | Live on campus: | 98% |

**Basis for selection.** Academic history, visual portfolio, and 3 required drawings most important. Portfolio required for all applicants. **Homeschooled:** Proof of high school equivalency/GED required.

---

**High school preparation.** Architecture, interior architecture, landscape architecture, and industrial design applicants must have 2 algebra, .5 trigonometry, 1 science.

**2009-2010 Annual costs.** Tuition/fees: $36,659. Room/board: $10,846. Books/supplies: $2,600. Personal expenses: $2,415.

**Application procedures. Admission:** Closing date 2/15 (receipt date). $60 fee, may be waived for applicants with need. Admission notification 4/1. Must reply by 5/1. **Financial aid:** Closing date 2/15. FAFSA, CSS PROFILE required. Applicants notified by 4/1; must reply by 5/1.

**Academics. Special study options:** Cross-registration, double major, exchange student, independent study, internships, study abroad, teacher certification program. **Credit/placement by examination:** AP, CLEP, IB. **Support services:** Remedial instruction, tutoring, writing center.

**Majors. Architecture:** Architecture, interior, landscape. **Visual/performing arts:** Ceramics, cinematography, fashion design, fiber arts, graphic design, illustration, industrial design, metal/jewelry, painting, photography, printmaking, sculpture, studio arts.

**Most popular majors.** Architecture 9%, visual/performing arts 91%.

**Computing on campus.** 425 workstations in dormitories, library, computer center, student center. Dormitories wired for high-speed internet access and linked to campus network. Commuter students can connect to campus network. Online course registration, helpline, repair service, student web hosting, wireless network available.

**Student life. Freshman orientation:** Mandatory. **Housing:** Guaranteed on-campus for freshmen. Coed dorms, apartments, wellness housing available. $175 nonrefundable deposit, deadline 5/1. **Activities:** Dance, drama, film society, literary magazine, student government, student newspaper.

**Athletics. Intramural:** Baseball M, basketball, ice hockey, soccer, softball.

**Student services.** Alcohol/substance abuse counseling, chaplain/spiritual director, career counseling, financial aid counseling, health services, legal services, minority student services, personal counseling, placement for graduates. **Physically disabled:** Services for hearing impaired.

**Contact.** E-mail: admissions@risd.edu
Phone: (401) 454-6300 Toll-free number: (800) 364-7473
Fax: (401) 454-6309
Edward Newhall, Director of Admissions, Rhode Island School of Design, Two College Street, Providence, RI 02903-2791

---

### Roger Williams University
**Bristol, Rhode Island**  **CB member**
**www.rwu.edu**  **CB code: 3729**

- Private 4-year university and liberal arts college
- Residential campus in large town
- 4,267 degree-seeking undergraduates
- 74% of applicants admitted
- SAT or ACT (ACT writing recommended), application essay required

**General.** Founded in 1956. Regionally accredited. Certificate and associate programs offered only in School of Continuing Studies in Providence and Bristol. **Degrees:** 932 bachelor's awarded; master's, professional offered. **ROTC:** Army. **Location:** 18 miles from Providence, 10 miles from Newport. **Calendar:** Semester, limited summer session. **Full-time faculty:** 214 total. **Part-time faculty:** 331 total. **Class size:** 58% < 20, 42% 20-39, less than 1% 40-49, less than 1% 50-99. **Special facilities:** Marine and natural sciences building with marine biology wetlab.

**Freshman class profile.** 5,693 applied, 4,237 admitted, 1,026 enrolled.

| Mid 50% test scores | | GPA 2.0-2.99: | 29% |
|---|---|---|---|
| SAT critical reading: | 500-580 | Rank in top quarter: | 38% |
| SAT math: | 510-590 | Rank in top tenth: | 14% |
| GPA 3.75 or higher: | 14% | Out-of-state: | 91% |
| GPA 3.50-3.74: | 14% | Live on campus: | 96% |
| GPA 3.0-3.49: | 43% | | |

**Basis for selection.** Admissions based on high school performance and SAT or ACT scores. Audition required for dance; portfolio required for art, architecture programs. **Homeschooled:** State high school equivalency certificate required. Students must submit portfolio of their work.

**High school preparation.** College-preparatory program required. 22 units required; 26 recommended. Required and recommended units include English 4, mathematics 3-4, social studies 2-3, history 2-3, science 2-4 (laboratory 2), foreign language 2 and academic electives 2-3. Specific subject requirements vary with intended major.

**2009-2010 Annual costs.** Tuition/fees: $28,700. Tuition differential for architecture program. Room/board: $12,290. Books/supplies: $900. Personal expenses: $794.

**2009-2010 Financial aid. Non-need-based:** Scholarships awarded for academics, ROTC.

**Application procedures. Admission:** Closing date 2/1. $50 fee. Application must be submitted online. Admission notification on a rolling basis beginning on or about 3/15. Must reply by 5/1. **Financial aid:** Priority date 1/1, closing date 2/1. FAFSA, CSS PROFILE required. Applicants notified on a rolling basis starting 3/20; must reply by 5/1.

**Academics.** All students graduate with two areas of specialization: one in their major and a second in a liberal arts discipline; most students may complete two majors. **Special study options:** Combined bachelor's/ graduate degree, cooperative education, distance learning, double major, dual enrollment of high school students, ESL, exchange student, external degree, honors, independent study, internships, liberal arts/career combination, semester at sea, student-designed major, study abroad, teacher certification program, Washington semester, weekend college. **Credit/placement by examination:** AP, CLEP, IB, SAT, institutional tests. 15 credit hours maximum toward associate degree, 30 toward bachelor's. Students can test out of no more than 25% of the credits required for a degree. **Support services:** Learning center, reduced course load, study skills assistance, tutoring, writing center.

**Honors college/program.** Applicants must have 1250 SAT (exclusive of Writing) and 3.3 GPA; 1300 SAT required for architecture and marine biology. Application deadline, February 1st.

**Majors. Architecture:** Architecture, history/criticism. **Area/ethnic studies:** American. **Biology:** General, marine. **Business:** Accounting, business admin, finance, international, management information systems, marketing. **Communications:** Journalism, media studies. **Communications technology:** Graphics. **Computer sciences:** General, computer science. **Conservation:** General. **Construction:** Site management. **Education:** Elementary, secondary. **Engineering:** General. **Foreign languages:** General. **History:** General. **Interdisciplinary:** Historic preservation. **Legal studies:** General, paralegal. **Math:** General. **Philosophy/religion:** Philosophy. **Physical sciences:** Chemistry. **Protective services:** Law enforcement admin. **Psychology:** General. **Public administration:** General. **Social sciences:** Anthropology, economics, political science, sociology. **Visual/performing arts:** Art history/conservation, dance, dramatic, graphic design, studio arts.

**Most popular majors.** Architecture 6%, biology 6%, business/marketing 17%, communications/journalism 7%, education 6%, engineering/ engineering technologies 8%, psychology 10%, security/protective services 13%.

**Computing on campus.** 540 workstations in dormitories, library, computer center. Dormitories wired for high-speed internet access and linked to campus network. Commuter students can connect to campus network. Online course registration, online library, helpline, repair service, wireless network available.

**Student life. Freshman orientation:** Mandatory. Preregistration for classes offered. 2-day program with overnight stay on campus during summer; separate orientations for transfer and international students. **Housing:** Guaranteed on-campus for freshmen. Coed dorms, special housing for disabled, apartments, wellness housing available. $350 fully refundable deposit, deadline 5/1. Special interest academic and honors housing available. **Activities:** Choral groups, dance, drama, film society, international student organizations, literary magazine, Model UN, musical theater, radio station, student government, student newspaper, Hillel, Inter-Varsity Christian Fellowship, multicultural student union, College Democrats, College Republicans, environmental and animal rights club, Model UN, Best Buddies of Rhode Island, Habitat for Humanity, student volunteer association.

**Athletics.** NCAA. **Intercollegiate:** Baseball M, basketball, cross-country, diving, equestrian, lacrosse, sailing, soccer, softball W, swimming, tennis, volleyball W, wrestling M. **Intramural:** Basketball, field hockey, football (non-tackle), golf, racquetball, skiing, soccer, softball, squash, tennis, volleyball, water polo. **Team name:** Hawks.

**Student services.** Chaplain/spiritual director, career counseling, student employment services, financial aid counseling, health services, minority student services, personal counseling, women's services. **Physically disabled:** Services for visually, hearing impaired.

**Contact.** E-mail: admit@rwu.edu
Phone: (401) 254-3500 Toll-free number: (800) 458-7144 ext. 3500
Fax: (401) 254-3557
Didier Bouvet, Dean of Admissions, Roger Williams University, 1 Old Ferry Road, Bristol, RI 02809-2921

---

## Salve Regina University
### Newport, Rhode Island
**CB member**
www.salve.edu
**CB code: 3759**

- Private 4-year university and liberal arts college affiliated with Roman Catholic Church
- Residential campus in large town
- 1,976 degree-seeking undergraduates: 4% part-time, 69% women, 2% African American, 1% Asian American, 3% Hispanic American, 1% Native American, 1% international
- 451 degree-seeking graduate students
- 64% of applicants admitted
- SAT or ACT (ACT writing optional), application essay required
- 68% graduate within 6 years; 24% enter graduate study

**General.** Founded in 1934. Regionally accredited. Affiliated with Religious Sisters of Mercy. **Degrees:** 485 bachelor's awarded; master's, doctoral offered. **ROTC:** Army. **Location:** 30 miles from Providence. **Calendar:** Semester, limited summer session. **Full-time faculty:** 117 total; 78% have terminal degrees, 8% minority, 56% women. **Part-time faculty:** 131 total; 34% have terminal degrees, 6% minority, 48% women. **Class size:** 48% < 20, 51% 20-39, less than 1% 40-49. **Special facilities:** International relations and public policy center.

**Freshman class profile.** 5,256 applied, 3,385 admitted, 505 enrolled.

| Mid 50% test scores | | | |
|---|---|---|---|
| SAT critical reading: | 500-590 | GPA 2.0-2.99: | 19% |
| SAT math: | 500-590 | Rank in top quarter: | 57% |
| SAT writing: | 500-590 | Rank in top tenth: | 21% |
| ACT composite: | 22-26 | End year in good standing: | 97% |
| GPA 3.75 or higher: | 20% | Return as sophomores: | 76% |
| GPA 3.50-3.74: | 20% | Out-of-state: | 88% |
| GPA 3.0-3.49: | 41% | Live on campus: | 99% |
| | | International: | 1% |

**Basis for selection.** High school achievement most important, followed by rank in top half of high school class, test scores, recommendations, essay, activities, interview. Special consideration given to applicants from minority and low-income families. SAT or TOEFL required for international applicants. Audition and portfolio considered. **Homeschooled:** Statement describing homeschool structure and mission, transcript of courses and grades, letter of recommendation (nonparent) required. Require two recommendations, one of which must be academic. Course syllabus required for each course; results of SAT or ACT examinations; portfolio of academic accomplishments including a reading list, course descriptions and list of extracurricular/community involvement.

**High school preparation.** College-preparatory program required. 16 units required. Required units include English 4, mathematics 3, social studies 1, science 2 (laboratory 2), foreign language 2 and academic electives 4. Additional course work may be required of students who have not completed recommended units. Social studies includes history.

**2009-2010 Annual costs.** Tuition/fees: $32,350. Required fees include a one-time laptop fee of $2,350 for all first-year students. Room/board: $10,950. Books/supplies: $900. Personal expenses: $1,000.

**2009-2010 Financial aid. Non-need-based:** Scholarships awarded for academics, ROTC.

**Application procedures. Admission:** Priority date 2/1; no deadline. $50 fee, may be waived for applicants with need. Must reply by May 1 or within 2 week(s) if notified thereafter. **Financial aid:** Priority date 3/1; no closing date. FAFSA, CSS PROFILE required. Applicants notified by 4/1; must reply by 4/15 or within 2 week(s) of notification.

**Academics.** Credit may be awarded for learning associated with life experience. **Special study options:** Accelerated study, combined bachelor's/ graduate degree, distance learning, double major, dual enrollment of high school students, ESL, honors, independent study, internships, liberal arts/ career combination, semester at sea, study abroad, teacher certification program, Washington semester. **Credit/placement by examination:** AP, CLEP, IB, SAT, ACT, institutional tests. **Support services:** Learning center, reduced course load, study skills assistance, tutoring, writing center.

**Majors. Area/ethnic studies:** American. **Biology:** General. **Business:** Accounting, business admin, finance, management science, market research.

**Computer sciences:** Information systems. **Education:** Biology, drama/dance, early childhood, elementary, English, French, history, mathematics, music, Spanish, special. **Foreign languages:** French, Spanish. **Health:** Nursing (RN). **History:** American, European. **Interdisciplinary:** Historic preservation. **Liberal arts:** Arts/sciences. **Math:** General. **Philosophy/religion:** Philosophy, religion. **Physical sciences:** Chemistry. **Protective services:** Law enforcement admin. **Psychology:** General. **Public administration:** Social work. **Social sciences:** Economics, political science, sociology. **Visual/performing arts:** Art history/conservation, ceramics, dramatic, graphic design, painting, photography, studio arts. **Other:** Interactive communication technology.

**Most popular majors.** Business/marketing 23%, education 18%, English 6%, health sciences 14%, psychology 6%, security/protective services 10%.

**Computing on campus.** PC or laptop required. 300 workstations in library, computer center, student center. Dormitories wired for high-speed internet access and linked to campus network. Commuter students can connect to campus network. Online course registration, online library, helpline, repair service, student web hosting, wireless network available.

**Student life. Freshman orientation:** Mandatory, $300 fee. Preregistration for classes offered. 2-day sessions during June and July for full-time freshmen; separate sessions for international and transfer students. **Housing:** Guaranteed on-campus for freshmen. Coed dorms, single-sex dorms, special housing for disabled, apartments, wellness housing available. $500 nonrefundable deposit, deadline 5/1. Off-campus housing available to upperclassmen. **Activities:** Bands, campus ministries, choral groups, dance, drama, film society, international student organizations, literary magazine, music ensembles, Model UN, radio station, student government, student newspaper, Artist's Guild, Artist's Sanctuary, Circle K, environmental club, Student Outdoor Adventures, Volunteers Interested in Researching and Guiding, Women's Issues Now, Stagefright Theater Company.

**Athletics.** NCAA. **Intercollegiate:** Baseball M, basketball, cross-country, field hockey W, football (tackle) M, ice hockey, lacrosse, soccer, softball W, tennis, track and field W, volleyball W. **Intramural:** Basketball, field hockey W, football (non-tackle) W, football (tackle) M, racquetball, soccer, softball, tennis, track and field W, volleyball, weight lifting. **Team name:** Seahawks.

**Student services.** Alcohol/substance abuse counseling, chaplain/spiritual director, career counseling, student employment services, financial aid counseling, health services, minority student services, personal counseling, placement for graduates, veterans' counselor. **Physically disabled:** Services for visually, hearing impaired.

**Contact.** E-mail: sruadmis@salve.edu
Phone: (401) 341-2908 Toll-free number: (888) 467-2583
Fax: (401) 848-2823
Colleen Emerson, Dean of Undergraduate Admissions, Salve Regina University, 100 Ochre Point Avenue, Newport, RI 02840-4192

---

## University of Rhode Island
**Kingston, Rhode Island**                    **CB member**
**www.uri.edu**                               **CB code: 3919**

- Public 4-year university
- Commuter campus in small town
- 12,972 degree-seeking undergraduates: 10% part-time, 56% women, 5% African American, 3% Asian American, 6% Hispanic American
- 2,627 degree-seeking graduate students
- 84% of applicants admitted
- SAT or ACT (ACT writing recommended), application essay required
- 60% graduate within 6 years

**General.** Founded in 1892. Regionally accredited. College of Continuing Education in Providence offers credit-bearing courses for degree and non-degree students. **Degrees:** 2,276 bachelor's awarded; master's, doctoral, professional offered. **ROTC:** Army. **Location:** 30 miles from Providence. **Calendar:** Semester, extensive summer session. **Full-time faculty:** 679 total; 87% have terminal degrees, 15% minority, 42% women. **Part-time faculty:** 13 total; 46% have terminal degrees, 8% minority, 77% women. **Class size:** 35% < 20, 51% 20-39, 6% 40-49, 5% 50-99, 3% >100. **Special facilities:** Inner space center, center for robotics research, animal science farm, planetarium, marine sciences campus, American historic textiles museum, aquaculture center, fisheries and marine technology laboratory, biotechnology center, human performance laboratory.

**Freshman class profile.** 16,126 applied, 13,484 admitted, 3,055 enrolled.

| Mid 50% test scores | | | |
|---|---|---|---|
| SAT critical reading: | 480-580 | GPA 3.0-3.49: | 35% |
| SAT math: | 490-600 | GPA 2.0-2.99: | 32% |
| SAT writing: | 490-590 | Rank in top quarter: | 45% |
| ACT composite: | 21-26 | Rank in top tenth: | 17% |
| GPA 3.75 or higher: | 14% | Return as sophomores: | 79% |
| GPA 3.50-3.74: | 16% | Out-of-state: | 52% |
| | | Live on campus: | 85% |

**Basis for selection.** School record primary, test scores secondary; extracurricular activities considered. Economically and socially disadvantaged students from Rhode Island admitted through special program for talent development.

**High school preparation.** College-preparatory program required. 18 units required. Required units include English 4, mathematics 3, social studies 2, science 2 (laboratory 1), foreign language 2 and academic electives 5.

**2009-2010 Annual costs.** Tuition/fees: $9,528; $26,026 out-of-state. Room/board: $9,892. Books/supplies: $1,200. Personal expenses: $1,440.

**2009-2010 Financial aid. Need-based:** 2,577 full-time freshmen applied for aid; 2,033 were judged to have need; 1,754 of these received aid. Average need met was 59%. Average scholarship/grant was $7,501; average loan $4,191. 52% of total undergraduate aid awarded as scholarships/grants, 48% as loans/jobs. **Non-need-based:** Awarded to 949 full-time undergraduates, including 300 freshmen. Scholarships awarded for academics, alumni affiliation, art, athletics, music/drama, ROTC.

**Application procedures. Admission:** Closing date 2/1 (postmark date), $65 fee, may be waived for applicants with need. Admission notification 3/31. Admission notification on a rolling basis. Must reply by 5/1. **Financial aid:** Priority date 3/1; no closing date. FAFSA required. Applicants notified on a rolling basis starting 3/31; must reply by 5/1.

**Academics. Special study options:** Combined bachelor's/graduate degree, distance learning, double major, dual enrollment of high school students, exchange student, honors, independent study, internships, semester at sea, study abroad, teacher certification program, weekend college. **Credit/placement by examination:** AP, CLEP, IB, SAT, ACT, institutional tests. 45 credit hours maximum toward bachelor's degree. **Support services:** Learning center, pre-admission summer program, reduced course load, remedial instruction, study skills assistance, tutoring, writing center.

**Honors college/program.** Students who graduated in top 10% of high school class or those with 3.2 college GPA eligible to enroll.

**Majors. Agriculture:** Animal sciences, turf management. **Architecture:** Landscape. **Area/ethnic studies:** African-American, Latin American, women's. **Biology:** General, marine, microbiology, zoology. **Business:** General, accounting, apparel, business admin, entrepreneurial studies, finance, financial planning, international, management information systems, marketing. **Communications:** General, journalism, public relations. **Computer sciences:** General. **Conservation:** Environmental studies, fisheries, management/policy, water/wetlands/marine, wildlife. **Education:** Elementary, music, physical, secondary. **Engineering:** Biomedical, chemical, civil, computer, electrical, industrial, mechanical, ocean. **Family/consumer sciences:** Clothing/textiles, family studies, food/nutrition. **Foreign languages:** Classics, comparative lit, French, German, Italian, Spanish. **Health:** Clinical lab science, communication disorders, dietetics, health care admin, nursing (RN). **History:** General. **Math:** General. **Philosophy/religion:** Philosophy. **Physical sciences:** Chemistry, forensic chemistry, geology, oceanography, physics. **Psychology:** General. **Public administration:** Policy analysis. **Social sciences:** Anthropology, econometrics, economics, political science, sociology. **Visual/performing arts:** Art history/conservation, cinematography, dramatic, music performance, music theory/composition, studio arts. **Other:** Applied sociology, Chemical and ocean engineering, Environmental horticulture and turf management, Environmental plant biology, Human science and services, Human studies, Kinesiology.

**Most popular majors.** Biology 6%, business/marketing 16%, communications/journalism 10%, engineering/engineering technologies 8%, family/consumer sciences 7%, health sciences 10%, psychology 7%, social sciences 6%.

**Computing on campus.** Dormitories wired for high-speed internet access and linked to campus network. Commuter students can connect to campus network. Online course registration, online library, helpline, repair service, wireless network available.

**Student life. Freshman orientation:** Available, $160 fee. Preregistration for classes offered. Two-day programs throughout June. Family members may attend. **Housing:** Guaranteed on-campus for freshmen. Coed dorms, special housing for disabled, apartments, cooperative housing, fraternity/

sorority housing, wellness housing available. $200 partly refundable deposit, deadline 5/1. First-year focused residence halls, living/learning communities by academic college and program. **Activities:** Bands, campus ministries, choral groups, dance, drama, film society, international student organizations, literary magazine, music ensembles, musical theater, radio station, student government, student newspaper, TV station, student entertainment committee, Latin American student association, NAACP, gaming club, recreation club sports council.

**Athletics.** NCAA. **Intercollegiate:** Baseball M, basketball, cheerleading, cross-country, diving W, football (tackle) M, golf M, rowing (crew) W, soccer, softball W, swimming W, tennis W, track and field, volleyball W. **Team name:** Rams.

**Student services.** Adult student services, alcohol/substance abuse counseling, chaplain/spiritual director, career counseling, student employment services, financial aid counseling, health services, legal services, minority student services, on-campus daycare, personal counseling, placement for graduates, veterans' counselor, women's services. **Physically disabled:** Services for visually, speech, hearing impaired. **Learning disabled:** Comprehensive services available.

**Contact.**  E-mail: admission@uri.edu
Phone: (401) 874-7000 Fax: (401) 874-5523
Cynthia Bonn, Dean of Admission, University of Rhode Island, 14 Upper College Road, Kingston, RI 02881-1322

# South Carolina

## Allen University
**Columbia, South Carolina**
**www.allenuniversity.edu**                          **CB code: 5006**

◆ Private 4-year university and liberal arts college affiliated with African Methodist Episcopal Church
◆ Residential campus in large city
◆ 827 degree-seeking undergraduates: 3% part-time, 56% women, 99% African American
◆ 72% of applicants admitted

**General.** Founded in 1870. Regionally accredited. **Degrees:** 49 bachelor's awarded. **ROTC:** Army. **Location:** 112 miles from Charleston, 72 miles from Charlotte, North Carolina. **Calendar:** Semester, limited summer session. **Full-time faculty:** 29 total; 45% have terminal degrees, 38% women. **Part-time faculty:** 12 total; 75% women. **Class size:** 43% < 20, 45% 20-39, 2% 40-49, 4% 50-99, 7% >100.

**Freshman class profile.** 1,937 applied, 1,395 admitted, 242 enrolled.

| | | | |
|---|---|---|---|
| GPA 3.50-3.74: | 3% | GPA 2.0-2.99: | 69% |
| GPA 3.0-3.49: | 14% | | |

**Basis for selection.** Applicants reviewed by admission committee. Decision provided to applicant in writing. Interview, campus visit recommended. **Homeschooled:** Statement describing homeschool structure and mission, transcript of courses and grades, state high school equivalency certificate, interview, letter of recommendation (nonparent) required.

**High school preparation.** College-preparatory program recommended. Recommended units include English 4, mathematics 4, social studies 3, history 3, science 3, foreign language 1 and computer science 1.

**2009-2010 Annual costs.** Tuition/fees: $10,884. Room/board: $5,240. Books/supplies: $800. Personal expenses: $800.

**2009-2010 Financial aid. Need-based:** Average need met was 62%. Average scholarship/grant was $7,346; average loan $3,238. **Non-need-based:** Scholarships awarded for academics, athletics, music/drama, ROTC.

**Application procedures. Admission:** Priority date 6/30; deadline 7/31 (receipt date). No application fee. Admission notification on a rolling basis. Must reply by May 1 or within 2 week(s) if notified thereafter. **Financial aid:** Priority date 4/15, closing date 7/20. FAFSA required. Applicants notified on a rolling basis starting 4/1; must reply within 2 week(s) of notification.

**Academics. Special study options:** Cooperative education, honors, independent study, internships, teacher certification program, weekend college. Nontraditional program for returning students. **Credit/placement by examination:** CLEP, institutional tests. 3 credit hours maximum toward bachelor's degree. **Support services:** Learning center, pre-admission summer program, reduced course load, study skills assistance, tutoring, writing center.

**Majors. Biology:** General. **Business:** Business admin. **Math:** General. **Philosophy/religion:** Religion. **Physical sciences:** Chemistry. **Social sciences:** General.

**Most popular majors.** Biology 10%, business/marketing 34%, social sciences 32%.

**Computing on campus.** Dormitories wired for high-speed internet access and linked to campus network. Commuter students can connect to campus network. Online course registration, online library, helpline, wireless network available.

**Student life. Freshman orientation:** Mandatory. Preregistration for classes offered. Week-long session. Students complete financial aid forms, receive dorm assignments, and complete the registration process. **Housing:** Guaranteed on-campus for freshmen. Single-sex dorms, apartments available. $50 nonrefundable deposit, deadline 7/31. **Activities:** Campus ministries, choral groups, dance, international student organizations, student government, social science club, NAACP, BASIC, global ministries.

**Athletics.** NAIA. **Intercollegiate:** Basketball, cross-country, golf, track and field, volleyball W. **Team name:** Yellow Jackets.

**Student services.** Adult student services, chaplain/spiritual director, career counseling, student employment services, financial aid counseling, health services, personal counseling, placement for graduates.

**Contact.** Phone: (803) 376-5735 Toll-free number: (877) 625-5368 Fax: (803) 758-2704
Terri Parker, Director of Admissions, Allen University, 1530 Harden Street, Columbia, SC 29204

## Anderson University
**Anderson, South Carolina**                          **CB member**
**www.andersonuniversity.edu**                        **CB code: 5008**

◆ Private 4-year liberal arts and teachers college affiliated with Southern Baptist Convention
◆ Residential campus in large town
◆ 2,127 degree-seeking undergraduates: 21% part-time, 67% women
◆ 140 degree-seeking graduate students
◆ 68% of applicants admitted
◆ SAT or ACT (ACT writing optional) required
◆ 53% graduate within 6 years

**General.** Founded in 1911. Regionally accredited. **Degrees:** 337 bachelor's awarded; master's offered. **ROTC:** Army, Air Force. **Location:** 32 miles from Greenville, 100 miles from Atlanta. **Calendar:** Differs by program, limited summer session. **Full-time faculty:** 76 total; 74% have terminal degrees, 8% minority, 47% women. **Part-time faculty:** 106 total; 28% have terminal degrees, 3% minority, 51% women. **Class size:** 63% < 20, 36% 20-39, less than 1% 40-49, less than 1% 50-99, less than 1% >100. **Special facilities:** Fine arts center cultural program, on-campus audio recording studio, electronic classrooms.

**Freshman class profile.** 1,926 applied, 1,319 admitted, 494 enrolled.

| Mid 50% test scores | | | |
|---|---|---|---|
| SAT critical reading: | 410-560 | GPA 2.0-2.99: | 20% |
| SAT math: | 460-560 | Rank in top quarter: | 50% |
| SAT writing: | 450-570 | Rank in top tenth: | 28% |
| ACT composite: | 18-24 | Return as sophomores: | 74% |
| GPA 3.75 or higher: | 21% | Out-of-state: | 5% |
| GPA 3.50-3.74: | 23% | Live on campus: | 89% |
| GPA 3.0-3.49: | 35% | International: | 2% |

**Basis for selection.** High school achievement record, test scores important; recommendations considered. Minimum high school GPA of 2.5 and SAT (exclusive of Writing) combined score of 1000 preferred. Each applicant considered individually. Applicants not meeting these guidelines may be admitted into developmental studies program. Recommendations, further grades or interview may be required for academically weak applicants. Interview recommended for some; audition required for art, music, theater programs. **Learning Disabled:** Applicants with diagnosed learning disabilities must meet regular requirements and supply summary of recent (within 1 year of enrollment) diagnostic testing.

**High school preparation.** College-preparatory program recommended. 20 units required. Required and recommended units include English 4, mathematics 3-4, social studies 2, history 2, science 3-4 (laboratory 2), foreign language 2 and academic electives 4.

**2009-2010 Annual costs.** Tuition/fees: $19,212. Room/board: $7,600. Books/supplies: $1,650. Personal expenses: $2,450.

**Financial aid. Non-need-based:** Scholarships awarded for academics, alumni affiliation, art, athletics, leadership, minority status, music/drama, religious affiliation, state residency.

**Application procedures. Admission:** No deadline. No application fee. Admission notification on a rolling basis beginning on or about 9/1. **Financial aid:** Priority date 3/1, closing date 6/30. FAFSA required. Applicants notified on a rolling basis starting 3/15; must reply within 2 week(s) of notification.

**Academics. Special study options:** Accelerated study, cooperative education, distance learning, double major, dual enrollment of high school students, honors, independent study, internships, liberal arts/career combination, study abroad, teacher certification program, Washington semester. **Credit/placement by examination:** AP, CLEP, IB, institutional tests. 24 credit hours maximum toward bachelor's degree. **Support services:** Learning center, reduced course load, remedial instruction, study skills assistance, tutoring, writing center.

**Majors. Biology:** General. **Business:** General, business admin, finance, human resources, marketing, organizational behavior, retailing. **Communications:** General. **Education:** Art, early childhood, elementary, English, history, mathematics, music, physical, special. **Foreign languages:** Spanish. **History:** General. **Interdisciplinary:** Behavioral sciences. **Liberal arts:** Arts/sciences. **Math:** General. **Parks/recreation:** Exercise sciences. **Philosophy/religion:** Christian. **Protective services:** Law enforcement admin. **Psychology:** General. **Public administration:** Human services. **Visual/performing arts:** Art, dramatic, interior design, music performance, musical theater. **Other:** Mathematics Actuarial Science, Pre-engineering, Psychology Human Services.

**Most popular majors.** Business/marketing 33%, education 31%, psychology 6%, visual/performing arts 11%.

**Computing on campus.** 130 workstations in library, computer center, student center. Dormitories wired for high-speed internet access and linked to campus network. Commuter students can connect to campus network. Online course registration, online library, helpline, wireless network available.

**Student life. Freshman orientation:** Mandatory. Preregistration for classes offered. 2 orientation sessions held during summer. **Housing:** Guaranteed on-campus for freshmen. Single-sex dorms, apartments, wellness housing available. $250 fully refundable deposit, deadline 5/1. **Activities:** Bands, campus ministries, choral groups, dance, drama, literary magazine, music ensembles, musical theater, student government, student newspaper, symphony orchestra, Gamma Beta Phi, campus activities board, Fellowship of Christian Athletes, Minorities for Change, student alumni council, Reformed University Fellowship, Young Life.

**Athletics.** NCAA. **Intercollegiate:** Baseball M, basketball, cheerleading M, cross-country, golf, soccer, softball W, tennis, track and field, volleyball W, wrestling M. **Intramural:** Basketball, football (non-tackle), racquetball, softball, table tennis, tennis, volleyball, weight lifting M. **Team name:** Trojans.

**Student services.** Adult student services, chaplain/spiritual director, career counseling, student employment services, financial aid counseling, health services, on-campus daycare, personal counseling, placement for graduates. **Physically disabled:** Services for visually impaired.

**Contact.** E-mail: admissions@andersonuniversity.edu
Phone: (864) 231-2030 Toll-free number: (800) 542-3594
Fax: (864) 231-2033
Pam Bryant, Director of Admissions, Anderson University, 316 Boulevard, Anderson, SC 29621-4002

---

## Benedict College
**Columbia, South Carolina**
**www.benedict.edu**

**CB member**
**CB code: 5056**

- Private 4-year liberal arts college affiliated with American Baptist Churches in the USA
- Residential campus in very large city
- 2,984 degree-seeking undergraduates: 1% part-time, 51% women, 99% African American
- 78% of applicants admitted
- SAT or ACT required

**General.** Founded in 1870. Regionally accredited. Benedict College is a historically black institution. **Degrees:** 296 bachelor's awarded. **ROTC:** Army, Air Force. **Location:** 110 miles from Greenville, 120 miles from Charleston. **Calendar:** Semester, limited summer session. **Full-time faculty:** 132 total; 54% have terminal degrees, 86% minority, 46% women. **Part-time faculty:** 34 total; 12% have terminal degrees, 100% minority, 56% women. **Class size:** 46% < 20, 33% 20-39, 13% 40-49, 8% 50-99.

**Freshman class profile.** 6,328 applied, 4,912 admitted, 840 enrolled.

| Mid 50% test scores | | | |
|---|---|---|---|
| SAT critical reading: | 320-430 | GPA 2.0-2.99: | 51% |
| SAT math: | 320-430 | Rank in top quarter: | 15% |
| ACT composite: | 13-17 | Rank in top tenth: | 5% |
| GPA 3.75 or higher: | 4% | Return as sophomores: | 60% |
| GPA 3.50-3.74: | 6% | Out-of-state: | 50% |
| GPA 3.0-3.49: | 19% | Live on campus: | 93% |

**Basis for selection.** High school GPA and test scores important.

**High school preparation.** College-preparatory program recommended. 20 units recommended. Recommended units include English 4, mathematics 3, social studies 3 and science 2.

---

**2009-2010 Annual costs.** Tuition/fees: $15,590. Room/board: $7,172. Books/supplies: $1,000. Personal expenses: $1,400.

**Application procedures. Admission:** No deadline. $25 fee. Admission notification on a rolling basis. **Financial aid:** Priority date 4/15; no closing date. FAFSA required. Applicants notified on a rolling basis starting 4/15.

**Academics. Special study options:** Accelerated study, double major, dual enrollment of high school students, external degree, honors, internships, teacher certification program, weekend college. **Credit/placement by examination:** AP, CLEP, institutional tests. 24 credit hours maximum toward bachelor's degree. **Support services:** Learning center, pre-admission summer program, reduced course load, remedial instruction, study skills assistance, tutoring, writing center.

**Majors. Biology:** General. **Business:** Accounting, business admin. **Computer sciences:** General, computer science. **Conservation:** Environmental science. **Education:** Early childhood, elementary. **Engineering technology:** Electrical. **Family/consumer sciences:** Family studies. **History:** General. **Math:** General. **Parks/recreation:** Health/fitness. **Physical sciences:** Chemistry, physics. **Public administration:** Social work. **Social sciences:** Economics, political science. **Visual/performing arts:** Art, multimedia.

**Most popular majors.** Biology 10%, business/marketing 20%, communications/journalism 7%, family/consumer sciences 9%, health sciences 9%, liberal arts 6%, psychology 6%, public administration/social services 6%, security/protective services 10%.

**Computing on campus.** 385 workstations in dormitories, library, computer center, student center. Dormitories wired for high-speed internet access and linked to campus network. Commuter students can connect to campus network. Online library, helpline, repair service, wireless network available.

**Student life. Freshman orientation:** Mandatory. Preregistration for classes offered. **Housing:** Guaranteed on-campus for freshmen. Single-sex dorms available. **Activities:** Bands, choral groups, dance, drama, music ensembles, radio station, student government, student newspaper, Gordon-Jenkins Theological Association.

**Athletics.** NAIA. **Intercollegiate:** Baseball M, basketball, cross-country, football (tackle) M, golf, soccer M, softball, tennis, track and field, volleyball W, wrestling M. **Intramural:** Baseball M, basketball, softball W, volleyball W. **Team name:** Tigers.

**Student services.** Adult student services, chaplain/spiritual director, career counseling, student employment services, financial aid counseling, health services, minority student services, on-campus daycare, personal counseling, placement for graduates, veterans' counselor.

**Contact.** E-mail: admissions@benedict.edu
Phone: (803) 705-4491 Toll-free number: (800) 868-6598
Fax: (803) 253-5167
Phyllis Thompson, Director of Admissions, Benedict College, 1600 Harden Street, Columbia, SC 29204

---

## Bob Jones University
**Greenville, South Carolina**
**www.bju.edu**

- Private 4-year Bible and liberal arts college affiliated with Non-demoninational
- Residential campus in small city
- 3,432 degree-seeking undergraduates: 2% part-time, 55% women, 1% African American, 5% Asian American, 3% Hispanic American
- 470 degree-seeking graduate students
- 75% of applicants admitted
- Application essay required
- 64% graduate within 6 years

**General.** Regionally accredited; also accredited by TRACS. **Degrees:** 715 bachelor's, 60 associate awarded; master's, doctoral offered. **Location:** 100 miles from Charlotte, NC. **Calendar:** Semester, limited summer session. **Full-time faculty:** 228 total; 39% have terminal degrees, 3% minority, 41% women. **Part-time faculty:** 67 total; 31% have terminal degrees, 2% minority, 82% women.

**Freshman class profile.** 1,610 applied, 1,212 admitted, 860 enrolled.

| | | | |
|---|---|---|---|
| GPA 3.75 or higher: | 35% | End year in good standing: | 92% |
| GPA 3.50-3.74: | 21% | Return as sophomores: | 73% |
| GPA 3.0-3.49: | 25% | Out-of-state: | 75% |
| GPA 2.0-2.99: | 18% | Live on campus: | 85% |
| Rank in top quarter: | 38% | | |

**Basis for selection.** Prospective applicants whose admissions fall outside of the requirements will go to the Admissions Committee for a decision. Some graduate programs require interviews, auditions, and/or portfolios. **Homeschooled:** Achievement test scores. **Learning Disabled:** Students with documented learning disabilities are afforded help through the Learning Resource Center and the Academic Success Center.

**High school preparation.** College-preparatory program recommended. 16 units required. Required and recommended units include English 3, mathematics 2, social studies 2, science 1, foreign language 2 and academic electives 6.

**2009-2010 Annual costs.** Tuition/fees: $11,825.

**2009-2010 Financial aid. Need-based:** 38% of total undergraduate aid awarded as scholarships/grants, 62% as loans/jobs.

**Application procedures. Admission:** No deadline. $45 fee, may be waived for applicants with need. Admission notification on a rolling basis. Those admitted are asked to reply within three weeks of being notified by paying a deposit. **Financial aid:** No deadline. FAFSA, institutional form required. Applicants notified on a rolling basis.

**Academics. Special study options:** Accelerated study, combined bachelor's/graduate degree, distance learning, ESL, independent study, internships, teacher certification program. **Credit/placement by examination:** CLEP, institutional tests. **Support services:** Learning center, pre-admission summer program, reduced course load, remedial instruction, study skills assistance, tutoring, writing center.

**Majors. Biology:** General, biophysics. **Business:** General, accounting, actuarial science, business admin, human resources, international, office management. **Communications:** General, broadcast journalism, journalism, public relations, radio/tv. **Computer sciences:** Computer science, information technology. **Construction:** Carpentry. **Education:** Art, college student counseling, early childhood, elementary, English, mathematics, middle, music, science, social studies, special. **Engineering:** Computer, electrical, operations research, science. **Engineering technology:** Computer systems. **Family/consumer sciences:** General, clothing/textiles, food/nutrition. **Foreign languages:** French, German, Spanish. **Health:** Communication disorders, nursing (RN), premedicine, preveterinary, speech pathology. **History:** General. **Liberal arts:** Humanities. **Math:** General. **Parks/recreation:** Health/fitness. **Physical sciences:** Chemistry, physics. **Protective services:** Law enforcement admin. **Psychology:** Counseling. **Social sciences:** International relations, political science. **Theology:** Bible, missionary, religious ed, theology. **Transportation:** Aviation management. **Visual/performing arts:** Art, cinematography, commercial/advertising art, dramatic, music performance, piano/organ. **Other:** Automotive service, Interior design, Practical christian training, Pre-physical therapy, String pedagogy.

**Most popular majors.** Business/marketing 14%, education 13%, health sciences 10%, theological studies 12%, visual/performing arts 12%.

**Computing on campus.** 420 workstations in dormitories, library, computer center. Dormitories linked to campus network. Commuter students can connect to campus network. Online course registration, online library, helpline, repair service, wireless network available.

**Student life. Freshman orientation:** Mandatory. Preregistration for classes offered. **Policies:** Religious observance required. **Housing:** Single-sex dorms, special housing for disabled, apartments available. **Activities:** Concert band, campus ministries, choral groups, drama, music ensembles, opera, radio station, student government, student newspaper, symphony orchestra, TV station.

**Athletics. Intramural:** Baseball M, basketball, cheerleading W, soccer, softball W, volleyball W.

**Student services.** Chaplain/spiritual director, career counseling, student employment services, financial aid counseling, health services, on-campus daycare, personal counseling, placement for graduates. **Physically disabled:** Services for visually, speech, hearing impaired. **Learning disabled:** Comprehensive services available.

**Contact.** E-mail: admissions@bju.edu
Phone: (800) 252-6363 Toll-free number: (800) 252-6363
Fax: (800) 232-9258
Gary Deedrick, Director of Admissions, Bob Jones University, 1700 Wade Hampton Boulevard, Greenville, SC 29614

## Charleston Southern University
### Charleston, South Carolina
www.csuniv.edu     CB code: 5079

- Private 4-year university and liberal arts college affiliated with Southern Baptist Convention
- Commuter campus in large city
- 2,757 degree-seeking undergraduates: 14% part-time, 62% women, 29% African American, 1% Asian American, 3% Hispanic American, 1% international
- 443 degree-seeking graduate students
- SAT or ACT with writing required

**General.** Founded in 1964. Regionally accredited. **Degrees:** 475 bachelor's awarded; master's offered. **ROTC:** Army, Air Force. **Location:** 15 miles from downtown. **Calendar:** 4-1-4, limited summer session. **Full-time faculty:** 132 total; 5% minority, 48% women. **Part-time faculty:** 92 total. **Special facilities:** Earthquake research center.

**Freshman class profile.**

| Mid 50% test scores | | ACT composite: | 20-25 |
|---|---|---|---|
| SAT critical reading: | 470-560 | Out-of-state: | 23% |
| SAT math: | 480-580 | Live on campus: | 73% |

**Basis for selection.** School achievement record, academic coursework, test scores, GPA most important. Interview and recommendations considered. Students may be required to take institutional math test for acceptance and/or placement. Essay, interview recommended for all; audition recommended for music programs. **Learning Disabled:** Special needs allowances require documentation and interview with Director of Special Needs.

**High school preparation.** College-preparatory program recommended. 23 units required. Required and recommended units include English 4, mathematics 3-4, social studies 2, history 2, science 3 (laboratory 2) and foreign language 2.

**2009-2010 Annual costs.** Tuition/fees: $19,238. Room/board: $7,394. Books/supplies: $1,050.

**2008-2009 Financial aid. Non-need-based:** Scholarships awarded for academics, athletics, religious affiliation, ROTC.

**Application procedures. Admission:** No deadline. $40 fee, may be waived for applicants with need. Admission notification on a rolling basis beginning on or about 9/1. **Financial aid:** Priority date 4/15; no closing date. FAFSA required. Applicants notified on a rolling basis starting 3/1; must reply within 2 week(s) of notification.

**Academics. Special study options:** Accelerated study, combined bachelor's/graduate degree, cooperative education, cross-registration, distance learning, double major, dual enrollment of high school students, honors, internships, study abroad, teacher certification program. **Credit/placement by examination:** AP, CLEP, IB, SAT, ACT, institutional tests. 30 credit hours maximum toward associate degree, 30 toward bachelor's. **Support services:** Learning center, remedial instruction, study skills assistance, tutoring, writing center.

**Majors. Biology:** General, biochemistry. **Business:** Accounting, business admin, finance, management information systems, marketing. **Computer sciences:** Computer science. **Education:** Early childhood, elementary, English, mathematics, multi-level teacher, music, physical, science, social studies, Spanish. **Foreign languages:** Spanish. **Health:** Athletic training, music therapy, nursing (RN). **History:** General, American, European. **Liberal arts:** Humanities. **Math:** General, applied. **Parks/recreation:** Health/fitness. **Philosophy/religion:** Religion. **Physical sciences:** Chemistry. **Protective services:** Criminal justice. **Psychology:** General. **Social sciences:** General, economics, political science, sociology. **Theology:** Sacred music, youth ministry. **Visual/performing arts:** Music performance, voice/opera. **Other:** Biological and biomedical sciences, Business administration, management and operations, Dramatic/theatre arts and stagecraft, Science technologies/technicians.

**Most popular majors.** Biology 9%, business/marketing 30%, education 8%, health sciences 11%, psychology 8%, security/protective services 8%, social sciences 7%.

**Computing on campus.** 150 workstations in dormitories, library, computer center, student center. Dormitories wired for high-speed internet access. Commuter students can connect to campus network. Online library, helpline, student web hosting, wireless network available.

**Student life. Freshman orientation:** Available. Preregistration for classes offered. **Policies:** Religious observance required. **Housing:** Guaranteed on-campus for freshmen. Single-sex dorms available. $200 fully refundable deposit, deadline 8/15. **Activities:** Bands, choral groups, dance, drama, international student organizations, literary magazine, music ensembles, musical theater, student government, student newspaper, College Republicans, Young Democrats, Afro-American society, Baptist Student Union, Fellowship of Christian Athletes, Campus Crusade, future teachers society.

**Athletics.** NCAA. **Intercollegiate:** Baseball M, basketball, cross-country, football (tackle) M, golf, soccer, softball W, tennis, track and field, volleyball W. **Intramural:** Basketball, soccer, softball, volleyball. **Team name:** Buccaneer.

**Student services.** Adult student services, chaplain/spiritual director, career counseling, student employment services, financial aid counseling, health services, personal counseling, placement for graduates, veterans' counselor. **Physically disabled:** Services for visually, speech, hearing impaired.

**Contact.** E-mail: enroll@csuniv.edu
Phone: (843) 863-7050 Toll-free number: (800) 947-7474
Fax: (843) 863-7070
Jim Rhoton, Director of Admissions, Charleston Southern University, 9200 University Boulevard, Charleston, SC 29423-8087

## The Citadel

**Charleston, South Carolina**      **CB member**
www.citadel.edu      **CB code: 5108**

- Public 4-year military college
- Residential campus in large city
- 2,311 degree-seeking undergraduates: 3% part-time, 6% women, 7% African American, 3% Asian American, 5% Hispanic American, 1% international
- 792 degree-seeking graduate students
- 79% of applicants admitted
- SAT or ACT with writing required
- 68% graduate within 6 years; 17% enter graduate study

**General.** Founded in 1842. Regionally accredited. The Citadel, The Military College of South Carolina, is a unique public institution with the mission of educating principled leaders through its Corps of Cadets and Graduate College. **Degrees:** 483 bachelor's awarded; master's offered. **ROTC:** Army, Naval, Air Force. **Location:** 110 miles from Columbia; 120 miles from Savannah, Georgia. **Calendar:** Semester, extensive summer session. **Full-time faculty:** 172 total; 95% have terminal degrees, 12% minority, 30% women. **Part-time faculty:** 66 total; 41% have terminal degrees, 8% minority, 52% women. **Class size:** 42% < 20, 50% 20-39, 5% 40-49, 3% 50-99. **Special facilities:** Archives museum, beach house, boating center.

**Freshman class profile.** 2,165 applied, 1,717 admitted, 591 enrolled.

| Mid 50% test scores | | | |
|---|---|---|---|
| SAT critical reading: | 480-580 | GPA 2.0-2.99: | 27% |
| SAT math: | 510-600 | Rank in top quarter: | 33% |
| ACT composite: | 19-23 | Rank in top tenth: | 12% |
| GPA 3.75 or higher: | 23% | Return as sophomores: | 83% |
| GPA 3.50-3.74: | 16% | Out-of-state: | 54% |
| GPA 3.0-3.49: | 34% | Live on campus: | 100% |
| | | International: | 1% |

**Basis for selection.** Admissions based on class rank, test scores, GPA, alumni recommendations, extracurricular activities. Interview recommended.

**High school preparation.** College-preparatory program required. 20 units required. Required and recommended units include English 4, mathematics 3-4, social studies 2, history 1, science 3 (laboratory 3), foreign language 2 and academic electives 4. One physical education or ROTC required.

**2009-2010 Annual costs.** Tuition/fees: $8,735; $22,545 out-of-state. Freshmen also pay $5,940 deposit and upperclassmen pay $1,874 deposit for uniforms, laundry, dry cleaning charges, infirmary fees, books, and supplies. Room/board: $7,054.

**2009-2010 Financial aid. Need-based:** 497 full-time freshmen applied for aid; 371 were judged to have need; 359 of these received aid. Average need met was 69%. Average scholarship/grant was $12,229; average loan $3,537. 65% of total undergraduate aid awarded as scholarships/grants, 35% as loans/jobs. **Non-need-based:** Awarded to 930 full-time undergraduates, including 219 freshmen. Scholarships awarded for academics, alumni affiliation, athletics, leadership, ROTC, state residency.

**Application procedures. Admission:** No deadline. $40 fee. Admission notification on a rolling basis beginning on or about 7/15. **Financial aid:** Priority date 3/1; no closing date. FAFSA, institutional form required. Applicants notified on a rolling basis starting 4/1; must reply by 4/1 or within 2 week(s) of notification.

**Academics.** 4 years of ROTC required. **Special study options:** Cooperative education, distance learning, double major, ESL, honors, independent study, internships, study abroad, teacher certification program. **Credit/placement by examination:** AP, CLEP, SAT, institutional tests. **Support services:** Learning center, pre-admission summer program, study skills assistance, tutoring, writing center.

**Majors. Biology:** General. **Business:** Business admin. **Computer sciences:** General. **Education:** Physical, secondary. **Engineering:** Civil, electrical. **Foreign languages:** General. **History:** General. **Math:** General. **Physical sciences:** Chemistry, physics. **Protective services:** Law enforcement admin. **Psychology:** General. **Social sciences:** Political science.

**Most popular majors.** Business/marketing 33%, education 9%, engineering/engineering technologies 12%, history 7%, security/protective services 14%, social sciences 11%.

**Computing on campus.** 350 workstations in dormitories, library, computer center. Dormitories linked to campus network. Commuter students can connect to campus network. Online course registration, online library, helpline, repair service, wireless network available.

**Student life. Freshman orientation:** Mandatory. Preregistration for classes offered. **Housing:** Guaranteed on-campus for all undergraduates. Coed dorms available. **Activities:** Bands, campus ministries, choral groups, international student organizations, literary magazine, student government, student newspaper, African American Society, American Society of Civil Engineers, Association for Computing Machinery, Alpha Phi Omega, Summerall Guards, African Methodist Episcopal, Baptist Student Union, Campus Crusade for Christ, Knights of Columbus, Army Aviator Association of America.

**Athletics.** NCAA. **Intercollegiate:** Baseball M, basketball M, cross-country, football (tackle) M, golf W, rifle, soccer W, tennis M, track and field, volleyball W, wrestling M. **Intramural:** Badminton, basketball, diving, football (non-tackle), golf, handball, racquetball, soccer, softball, swimming, table tennis, tennis, track and field, triathlon, volleyball, weight lifting, wrestling. **Team name:** Bulldogs.

**Student services.** Alcohol/substance abuse counseling, chaplain/spiritual director, career counseling, student employment services, financial aid counseling, health services, minority student services, personal counseling, placement for graduates, veterans' counselor.

**Contact.** E-mail: admissions@citadel.edu
Phone: (843) 953-5230 Toll-free number: (800) 868-1842
Fax: (843) 953-7036
Lt. Col. John Powell, Director of Admissions, The Citadel, 171 Moultrie Street, Charleston, SC 29409

## Claflin University

**Orangeburg, South Carolina**      **CB member**
www.claflin.edu      **CB code: 5109**

- Private 4-year liberal arts college affiliated with United Methodist Church
- Residential campus in large town
- 1,735 degree-seeking undergraduates: 1% part-time, 66% women, 95% African American, 2% international
- 81 degree-seeking graduate students
- 35% of applicants admitted
- SAT or ACT (ACT writing optional) required
- 47% graduate within 6 years

**General.** Founded in 1869. Regionally accredited. **Degrees:** 267 bachelor's awarded; master's offered. **ROTC:** Army, Air Force. **Location:** 45 miles from Columbia. **Calendar:** Semester, limited summer session. **Full-time faculty:** 109 total; 77% have terminal degrees, 71% minority, 45% women. **Part-time faculty:** 29 total; 34% have terminal degrees, 76% minority, 45% women. **Class size:** 41% < 20, 56% 20-39, 2% 40-49, less than 1% 50-99. **Special facilities:** Center for excellence in science and math, center for excellence in mass communication, leadership development center, institute for the study of southern African American history, culture and policy, center for biotechnology.

**Freshman class profile.** 4,092 applied, 1,423 admitted, 468 enrolled.

| Mid 50% test scores | | | |
|---|---|---|---|
| SAT critical reading: | 410-500 | Rank in top quarter: | 45% |
| SAT math: | 390-490 | Rank in top tenth: | 9% |
| | | Return as sophomores: | 72% |
| GPA 3.75 or higher: | 7% | Out-of-state: | 24% |
| GPA 3.50-3.74: | 12% | Live on campus: | 94% |
| GPA 3.0-3.49: | 35% | International: | 1% |
| GPA 2.0-2.99: | 46% | | |

**Basis for selection.** School achievement record, test scores, recommendation of high school officials, personal background, experience, character traits, educational objectives important. Audition required; essay, interview, portfolio recommended.

**High school preparation.** 20 units required. Required units include English 4, mathematics 3, social studies 2, history 1, (laboratory 2) and academic electives 7. Physical education.

**2009-2010 Annual costs.** Tuition/fees: $12,768. Room/board: $6,806. Books/supplies: $1,000. Personal expenses: $1,600.

**Application procedures. Admission:** Closing date 8/1. $20 fee, may be waived for applicants with need. Admission notification on a rolling basis beginning on or about 10/1. **Financial aid:** Priority date 4/15; no closing date. FAFSA, institutional form required. Applicants notified on a rolling basis starting 5/15; must reply within 2 week(s) of notification.

**Academics. Special study options:** Accelerated study, combined bachelor's/graduate degree, cooperative education, cross-registration, double major, dual enrollment of high school students, honors, independent study, internships, liberal arts/career combination, study abroad, teacher certification program, weekend college. **Credit/placement by examination:** AP, CLEP, institutional tests. 18 credit hours maximum toward bachelor's degree. **Support services:** Learning center, pre-admission summer program, reduced course load, remedial instruction, tutoring, writing center.

**Honors college/program.** 30 to 35 students admitted annually based on academic achievement, leadership, and SAT scores.

**Majors. Area/ethnic studies:** African-American, American. **Biology:** General, biochemistry, bioinformatics, biotechnology. **Business:** Business admin, management information systems, marketing, organizational behavior. **Communications:** Media studies. **Computer sciences:** Computer science. **Conservation:** Environmental science. **Education:** Art, early childhood, elementary, English, mathematics, middle, music. **Engineering:** Software. **History:** General. **Math:** General. **Parks/recreation:** Health/fitness, sports admin. **Philosophy/religion:** Philosophy, religion. **Physical sciences:** Chemistry. **Protective services:** Law enforcement admin. **Social sciences:** Political science, sociology. **Visual/performing arts:** Art, studio arts.

**Most popular majors.** Biology 9%, business/marketing 29%, communications/journalism 8%, education 6%, security/protective services 12%, social sciences 21%.

**Computing on campus.** 500 workstations in dormitories, library, computer center, student center. Dormitories wired for high-speed internet access and linked to campus network. Commuter students can connect to campus network. Online course registration, online library, repair service, wireless network available.

**Student life. Freshman orientation:** Mandatory. Preregistration for classes offered. Early registration sessions held during summer, one-week orientation held during early fall, semester-long orientation seminars held during first academic year. **Housing:** Guaranteed on-campus for freshmen. Single-sex dorms available. $50 nonrefundable deposit, deadline 4/15. **Activities:** Bands, choral groups, dance, drama, film society, international student organizations, literary magazine, music ensembles, radio station, student government, student newspaper, TV station, Alpha Kappa Mu, Oxford Club, literature, art and film society, Phi Beta Lambda, Esquire XIII, Students in Free Enterprise, NAACP.

**Athletics.** NCAA. **Intercollegiate:** Baseball M, basketball, cross-country, softball W, track and field, volleyball W. **Intramural:** Basketball, softball W, volleyball W. **Team name:** Panthers.

**Student services.** Adult student services, chaplain/spiritual director, career counseling, student employment services, financial aid counseling, health services, minority student services, personal counseling, placement for graduates, veterans' counselor.

**Contact.** E-mail: admissions@claflin.edu
Phone: (803) 535-5339 Toll-free number: (800) 922-1276
Fax: (803) 535-5387
Claflin University, 400 Magnolia Street, Orangeburg, SC 29115

---

## Clemson University
**Clemson, South Carolina**
www.clemson.edu

CB member
CB code: 5111

- Public 4-year university and engineering college
- Residential campus in large town
- 15,247 degree-seeking undergraduates: 6% part-time, 46% women, 7% African American, 2% Asian American, 1% Hispanic American, 1% international
- 3,765 graduate students
- 63% of applicants admitted
- SAT or ACT with writing required
- 77% graduate within 6 years

**General.** Founded in 1889. Regionally accredited. **Degrees:** 3,198 bachelor's awarded; master's, doctoral offered. **ROTC:** Army, Air Force. **Location:** 17 miles from Anderson. **Calendar:** Semester, extensive summer session. **Full-time faculty:** 1,052 total; 88% have terminal degrees, 15% minority, 33% women. **Part-time faculty:** 130 total; 57% have terminal degrees, 8% minority, 40% women. **Class size:** 49% < 20, 32% 20-39, 8% 40-49, 8% 50-99, 3% >100. **Special facilities:** Planetarium, agricultural and forestry experimental facilities, geology museum, state botanical gardens, center for sustainable living, John C. Calhoun historical site and home, performing arts center.

**Freshman class profile.** 16,282 applied, 10,224 admitted, 3,386 enrolled.

| Mid 50% test scores | | | |
|---|---|---|---|
| SAT critical reading: | 550-640 | Rank in top quarter: | 81% |
| SAT math: | 590-680 | Rank in top tenth: | 50% |
| ACT composite: | 25-30 | Return as sophomores: | 91% |
| GPA 3.75 or higher: | 79% | Out-of-state: | 35% |
| GPA 3.50-3.74: | 10% | Live on campus: | 98% |
| GPA 3.0-3.49: | 10% | Fraternities: | 14% |
| GPA 2.0-2.99: | 1% | Sororities: | 27% |

**Basis for selection.** Admission competitive and based largely on high school curriculum, performance in that curriculum, peer comparison, SAT or ACT scores, and choice of major. Campus visit recommended for all. Interview, portfolio recommended for art applicants. Audition required for performing arts program. **Homeschooled:** Statement describing homeschool structure and mission, transcript of courses and grades required. Include copies of all secondary school transcripts and course descriptions of any courses different from those traditionally offered in public school settings.

**High school preparation.** College-preparatory program required. 19 units required. Required and recommended units include English 4, mathematics 3-4, social studies 3-4, history 1-2, science 3 (laboratory 3-4), foreign language 3-4 and academic electives 2. Also require physical education or ROTC. 3 foreign language units must be in same language.

**2009-2010 Annual costs.** Tuition/fees: $11,478; $25,388 out-of-state. Laptop computer required of all entering new students. This cost has been estimated at $1600. Room/board: $6,980. Books/supplies: $900. Personal expenses: $1,920.

**2008-2009 Financial aid. Non-need-based:** Scholarships awarded for academics, art, athletics, leadership, minority status, music/drama, ROTC, state residency.

**Application procedures. Admission:** Priority date 12/1; deadline 5/1 (receipt date). $60 fee, may be waived for applicants with need. Admission notification on a rolling basis beginning on or about 2/15. Must reply by 5/1. Scholarship candidates notified on rolling basis, beginning on or about October 1 for fall admission. Preferred application date of December 1. Those who apply by that date, and whose application file is complete, will receive an admission decision on or about the week of February 15 for fall admission. **Financial aid:** Priority date 4/1; no closing date. FAFSA required. Applicants notified on a rolling basis starting 4/1; must reply within 3 week(s) of notification.

**Academics. Special study options:** Combined bachelor's/graduate degree, cooperative education, distance learning, double major, dual enrollment of high school students, exchange student, honors, independent study, internships, study abroad, teacher certification program, Washington semester. Cooperative language center. **Credit/placement by examination:** AP, CLEP, IB, institutional tests. Challenge examinations offered by each academic department. **Support services:** Learning center, pre-admission summer program, study skills assistance, tutoring, writing center.

**Honors college/program.** Less than 10 percent of freshman class invited to enroll. Minimum peer comparison must show student in top 3 percent of graduating secondary school class.

**Majors. Agriculture:** Agronomy, animal sciences, aquaculture, business, economics, food science, horticultural science, horticulture, plant sciences. **Architecture:** Architecture, landscape. **Biology:** General, biochemistry, biomedical sciences, botany, entomology, genetics, microbiology, plant pathology, zoology. **Business:** General, accounting, construction management, finance, marketing, operations. **Computer sciences:** General, information systems. **Conservation:** General, forest management, forest sciences. **Education:** Agricultural, early childhood, elementary, mathematics, middle, science, secondary, special, technology/industrial arts. **Engineering:** Agricultural, biomedical, ceramic, chemical, civil, computer, electrical, industrial, mechanical. **Foreign languages:** General, Spanish. **Health:** Clinical lab science, nursing (RN), predental, premedicine, prepharmacy, preveterinary. **History:** General. **Interdisciplinary:** Nutrition sciences. **Math:** General. **Parks/recreation:** Facilities management. **Philosophy/religion:** Philosophy. **Physical sciences:** Chemistry, geology, physics. **Psychology:** General. **Social sciences:** Economics, political science, sociology. **Visual/performing arts:** Art, industrial design.

**Most popular majors.** Agriculture 7%, biology 6%, business/marketing 22%, education 6%, engineering/engineering technologies 14%, health sciences 8%, social sciences 9%.

**Computing on campus.** PC or laptop required. 875 workstations in library, computer center. Dormitories wired for high-speed internet access and linked to campus network. Commuter students can connect to campus network. Online course registration, online library, helpline, repair service, student web hosting, wireless network available.

**Student life. Freshman orientation:** Mandatory, $55 fee. Preregistration for classes offered. One and 1/2-day sessions held 8 times during June and July. Students must complete online mathematics placement exam prior to participating in orientation. **Policies:** All students required to submit proof of legal presence in the United States. **Housing:** Guaranteed on-campus for all undergraduates. Coed dorms, single-sex dorms, special housing for disabled, apartments, fraternity/sorority housing, wellness housing available. $50 nonrefundable deposit. Housing guaranteed so long as continuing in on-campus housing. **Activities:** Bands, choral groups, dance, drama, international student organizations, literary magazine, music ensembles, musical theater, radio station, student government, student newspaper, symphony orchestra, TV station, religious organizations, Young Democrats, Young Republicans, minority awareness organizations, Blue Key, Alpha Phi Omega, Mortarboard, Hillel, Fellowship of Christian Athletes.

**Athletics.** NCAA. **Intercollegiate:** Baseball M, basketball, cross-country, diving, football (tackle) M, golf M, rowing (crew) W, soccer, swimming, tennis, track and field, volleyball W. **Intramural:** Basketball, diving, fencing, field hockey W, football (non-tackle), golf, racquetball, soccer, softball, table tennis, tennis, track and field, volleyball. **Team name:** Tigers.

**Student services.** Alcohol/substance abuse counseling, chaplain/spiritual director, career counseling, student employment services, financial aid counseling, health services, minority student services, personal counseling, placement for graduates, veterans' counselor. **Physically disabled:** Services for visually, speech, hearing impaired.

**Contact.** E-mail: cuadmissions@clemson.edu
Phone: (864) 656-2287 Fax: (864) 656-2464
Robert Barkley, Director of Admissions, Clemson University, 105 Sikes Hall, Clemson, SC 29634-5124

---

## Coastal Carolina University

**Conway, South Carolina**  
**www.coastal.edu**

**CB member**  
**CB code: 5837**

- Public 4-year university
- Commuter campus in small city
- 7,544 degree-seeking undergraduates: 6% part-time, 53% women, 15% African American, 1% Asian American, 3% Hispanic American, 1% international
- 294 degree-seeking graduate students
- 74% of applicants admitted
- SAT or ACT (ACT writing optional) required
- 46% graduate within 6 years

**General.** Founded in 1954. Regionally accredited. Barrier-reef island used for marine science field studies and research. **Degrees:** 1,222 bachelor's awarded; master's offered. **ROTC:** Army. **Location:** 9 miles from Myrtle Beach. **Calendar:** Semester, extensive summer session. **Full-time faculty:**

316 total; 82% have terminal degrees, 10% minority, 41% women. **Part-time faculty:** 253 total; 25% have terminal degrees, 8% minority, 57% women. **Class size:** 36% < 20, 50% 20-39, 9% 40-49, 5% 50-99, less than 1% >100.

**Freshman class profile.** 8,706 applied, 6,438 admitted, 1,775 enrolled.

| Mid 50% test scores | | | |
|---|---|---|---|
| SAT critical reading: | 460-550 | Rank in top tenth: | 9% |
| SAT math: | 470-570 | End year in good standing: | 74% |
| ACT composite: | 19-22 | Return as sophomores: | 66% |
| GPA 3.75 or higher: | 23% | Out-of-state: | 55% |
| GPA 3.50-3.74: | 15% | Live on campus: | 82% |
| GPA 3.0-3.49: | 33% | International: | 1% |
| GPA 2.0-2.99: | 29% | Fraternities: | 7% |
| Rank in top quarter: | 32% | Sororities: | 9% |

**Basis for selection.** Secondary school record and test scores most important; class rank important. Applicants whose native language is not English must take TOEFL. Tests are not required for applicants 22 years or older. Interview recommended for all. **Homeschooled:** Transcript of courses and grades required. Copy of declaration of intent to home school as filed with local board of education. **Learning Disabled:** To become eligible for support services, students with disabilities must provide documentation of disability to Service for Students with Disabilities Office.

**High school preparation.** College-preparatory program required. 20 units required. Required and recommended units include English 4, mathematics 3-4, social studies 2, history 1, science 3 (laboratory 3), foreign language 2, computer science 1, visual/performing arts 1 and academic electives 4. 1 unit of physical education or ROTC.

**2009-2010 Annual costs.** Tuition/fees: $8,950; $18,470 out-of-state. Room/board: $7,200.

**2008-2009 Financial aid. Need-based:** 1,419 full-time freshmen applied for aid; 1,037 were judged to have need; 1,001 of these received aid. Average need met was 53%. Average scholarship/grant was $4,664; average loan $7,279. 36% of total undergraduate aid awarded as scholarships/grants, 64% as loans/jobs. **Non-need-based:** Awarded to 2,748 full-time undergraduates, including 895 freshmen. Scholarships awarded for academics, art, athletics, leadership, music/drama, ROTC, state residency.

**Application procedures. Admission:** Priority date 12/1; deadline 8/15 (receipt date). $45 fee, may be waived for applicants with need. Admission notification on a rolling basis beginning on or about 9/15. Must reply by May 1 or within 2 week(s) if notified thereafter. **Financial aid:** Priority date 3/1; no closing date. FAFSA required. Applicants notified on a rolling basis starting 3/1; must reply by 5/15.

**Academics.** Professional golf management specialization in any program in the Wall College of Business, accredited by PGA. International tourism management specialization in resort tourism management program. CPA/CMA option in accounting. **Special study options:** Accelerated study, combined bachelor's/graduate degree, cooperative education, distance learning, double major, dual enrollment of high school students, honors, independent study, internships, liberal arts/career combination, student-designed major, study abroad, teacher certification program. 3-2 engineering program with Clemson University. **Credit/placement by examination:** AP, CLEP, IB, SAT, institutional tests. Credit by examination must be obtained prior to reaching senior classification (90 credit hours). Will not be awarded for courses previously audited, or courses that have been previously failed. Cannot be used to raise a grade previously earned in a college course. **Support services:** Learning center, reduced course load, tutoring, writing center.

**Majors. Biology:** General, marine. **Business:** Accounting, business admin, finance, managerial economics, marketing, resort management. **Communications:** General. **Computer sciences:** General, information systems. **Education:** Early childhood, elementary, middle, physical, special. **Foreign languages:** Spanish. **Health:** Public health ed. **History:** General. **Liberal arts:** Arts/sciences. **Math:** Applied. **Parks/recreation:** Exercise sciences, sports admin. **Philosophy/religion:** Philosophy. **Physical sciences:** Chemistry, physics. **Psychology:** General. **Social sciences:** Political science, sociology. **Visual/performing arts:** Dramatic, graphic design, musical theater, studio arts.

**Most popular majors.** Biology 10%, business/marketing 31%, communications/journalism 6%, education 10%, health sciences 7%, psychology 7%, social sciences 6%, visual/performing arts 6%.

**Computing on campus.** 600 workstations in dormitories, library, computer center, student center. Dormitories wired for high-speed internet access and linked to campus network. Commuter students can connect to campus network. Online course registration, online library, helpline, student web hosting, wireless network available.

**Student life. Freshman orientation:** Mandatory, $90 fee. Preregistration for classes offered. 2-day programs. **Housing:** Coed dorms, special housing for disabled available. $150 partly refundable deposit, deadline 8/15. **Activities:** Bands, campus ministries, choral groups, dance, drama, international student organizations, literary magazine, music ensembles, musical theater, radio station, student government, student newspaper, Reformed University Fellowship, African American association, gospel choir, Society for Advancement of Management, Students Taking Active Responsibility, physical education club.

**Athletics.** NCAA. **Intercollegiate:** Baseball M, basketball, cheerleading, cross-country, football (tackle) M, golf, soccer, softball W, tennis, track and field, volleyball W. **Intramural:** Badminton, basketball, football (non-tackle), golf, soccer, softball, volleyball, water polo. **Team name:** Chanticleers.

**Student services.** Adult student services, alcohol/substance abuse counseling, career counseling, student employment services, financial aid counseling, health services, minority student services, personal counseling, placement for graduates, veterans' counselor, women's services. **Physically disabled:** Services for visually, speech, hearing impaired.

**Contact.** E-mail: admissions@coastal.edu
Phone: (843) 349-2170 Toll-free number: (800) 277-7000
Fax: (843) 349-2127
Judy Vogt, Vice President for Enrollment Services, Coastal Carolina University, PO Box 261954, Conway, SC 29528-6054

## Coker College
### Hartsville, South Carolina
**CB member**
**www.coker.edu**
**CB code: 5112**

- Private 4-year liberal arts college
- Residential campus in large town
- 653 degree-seeking undergraduates: 2% part-time, 62% women
- 56% of applicants admitted
- SAT or ACT (ACT writing optional) required

**General.** Founded in 1908. Regionally accredited. **Degrees:** 240 bachelor's awarded. **Location:** 70 miles from Columbia, 80 miles from Charlotte, North Carolina. **Calendar:** Semester, limited summer session. **Full-time faculty:** 55 total. **Part-time faculty:** 15 total. **Class size:** 92% < 20, 8% 20-39. **Special facilities:** Botanical gardens.

**Freshman class profile.** 1,112 applied, 624 admitted, 192 enrolled.

| Mid 50% test scores | | | |
|---|---|---|---|
| SAT critical reading: | 440-530 | Rank in top quarter: | 33% |
| SAT math: | 420-550 | Rank in top tenth: | 16% |
| ACT composite: | 18-23 | Out-of-state: | 21% |
| | | Live on campus: | 91% |

**Basis for selection.** Academic record, test scores, interview, school and community activities important. Recommendations also used to determine status. Applicants admitted on basis of test scores and GPA in academic core courses. Special talents and alumni relations important. Essay recommended for all; audition required for dance, music, theater programs; portfolio required for art programs.

**High school preparation.** 15 units required. Required units include English 4, mathematics 3, social studies 3, science 3 (laboratory 1) and foreign language 2.

**2009-2010 Annual costs.** Tuition/fees: $19,723. Room/board: $6,240. Books/supplies: $1,200. Personal expenses: $1,000.

**2009-2010 Financial aid. Non-need-based:** Scholarships awarded for academics, alumni affiliation, art, athletics, job skills, leadership, minority status, music/drama, religious affiliation, ROTC, state residency. **Additional information:** Endowed scholarship program for qualified applicants. June 1 deadline for filing South Carolina Tuition Grant forms.

**Application procedures. Admission:** Priority date 5/1; deadline 8/1. $15 fee, may be waived for applicants with need, free for online applicants. Admission notification on a rolling basis beginning on or about 9/1. Must reply by May 1 or within 8 week(s) if notified thereafter. Juniors allowed to apply and make admissions decision during summer prior to senior year. **Financial aid:** Priority date 4/1, closing date 6/1. FAFSA required. Applicants notified on a rolling basis starting 3/1; must reply by 5/1 or within 3 week(s) of notification.

**Academics. Special study options:** Cooperative education, double major, dual enrollment of high school students, honors, independent study, internships, student-designed major, study abroad, teacher certification program. 2-2 programs with two-year colleges, 3-1 program with regional medical facility. **Credit/placement by examination:** AP, CLEP, IB, institutional tests. Unlimited hours of credit by examination may be counted toward

degree. **Support services:** Reduced course load, remedial instruction, study skills assistance, tutoring, writing center.

**Majors. Biology:** General. **Business:** Business admin. **Communications:** General. **Computer sciences:** Computer science. **Education:** General, art, biology, business, chemistry, early childhood, elementary, English, history, mathematics, music, physical. **Foreign languages:** French, Spanish. **Health:** Clinical lab science, dance therapy, recreational therapy. **History:** General. **Math:** General. **Parks/recreation:** Exercise sciences, sports admin. **Physical sciences:** Chemistry. **Psychology:** General. **Public administration:** Social work. **Social sciences:** Criminology, political science, sociology. **Visual/performing arts:** Acting, art, commercial/advertising art, dance, dramatic, music performance, music theory/composition, photography, piano/organ, studio arts, theater design, voice/opera.

**Computing on campus.** 65 workstations in dormitories, library, computer center, student center. Dormitories wired for high-speed internet access and linked to campus network. Online library, student web hosting, wireless network available.

**Student life. Freshman orientation:** Mandatory. Preregistration for classes offered. 3-day session held immediately before fall classes begin. **Housing:** Guaranteed on-campus for freshmen. Coed dorms available. $100 fully refundable deposit, deadline 5/1. **Activities:** Choral groups, dance, drama, literary magazine, musical theater, student government, student newspaper, Campus Crusade, Psi Chi, African American Sisterhood, Helping: Our Way of Life, multicultural affairs committee.

**Athletics.** NCAA. **Intercollegiate:** Baseball M, basketball, cheerleading, cross-country, golf M, soccer, softball W, tennis, volleyball W. **Intramural:** Badminton, basketball, bowling, cross-country, football (non-tackle), handball, racquetball, rowing (crew) W, sailing, soccer, softball, swimming, table tennis, tennis, track and field, volleyball, water polo, weight lifting. **Team name:** Cobras.

**Student services.** Adult student services, chaplain/spiritual director, career counseling, student employment services, financial aid counseling, health services, personal counseling, placement for graduates.

**Contact.** E-mail: admissions@coker.edu
Phone: (843) 383-8050 Toll-free number: (800) 950-1908
Fax: (843) 383-8056
Perry Wilson, Director of Admissions, Coker College, 300 East College Avenue, Hartsville, SC 29550

## College of Charleston
### Charleston, South Carolina
**CB member**
**www.cofc.edu**
**CB code: 5113**

- Public 4-year liberal arts college
- Residential campus in large city
- 9,736 degree-seeking undergraduates: 5% part-time, 64% women, 5% African American, 2% Asian American, 2% Hispanic American, 1% international
- 525 degree-seeking graduate students
- 70% of applicants admitted
- SAT or ACT (ACT writing optional), application essay required
- 64% graduate within 6 years

**General.** Founded in 1770. Regionally accredited. **Degrees:** 2,212 bachelor's awarded; master's offered. **ROTC:** Air Force. **Calendar:** Semester, limited summer session. **Full-time faculty:** 523 total; 87% have terminal degrees, 10% minority, 43% women. **Part-time faculty:** 370 total; 36% have terminal degrees, 7% minority, 54% women. **Class size:** 27% < 20, 61% 20-39, 6% 40-49, 5% 50-99, less than 1% >100. **Special facilities:** Communications museum, early childhood development center, observatory, marine science laboratory, sculpture studio, sailing center, African-American history and culture research center, bilingual legal interpreting center, media and technology studio, center for entrepreneurship, real estate center, natural history museum.

**Freshman class profile.** 11,083 applied, 7,703 admitted, 2,143 enrolled.

| Mid 50% test scores | | | |
|---|---|---|---|
| SAT critical reading: | 560-650 | Rank in top quarter: | 68% |
| SAT math: | 560-640 | Rank in top tenth: | 31% |
| ACT composite: | 23-27 | Return as sophomores: | 83% |
| GPA 3.75 or higher: | 58% | Out-of-state: | 57% |
| GPA 3.50-3.74: | 20% | Live on campus: | 92% |
| GPA 3.0-3.49: | 20% | Fraternities: | 18% |
| GPA 2.0-2.99: | 2% | Sororities: | 24% |

**Basis for selection.** School grades, class rank, curriculum most important, then test scores. Recommendations and activities helpful in borderline cases. Personal essay optional. Writing portion of ACT required only if student does not also submit SAT (with mandatory Writing component). Interview recommended for all. **Homeschooled:** Students should indicate which school district syllabus was followed during home schooling.

**High school preparation.** College-preparatory program required. 20 units required. Required and recommended units include English 4, mathematics 3-4, social studies 3, history 2, science 3 (laboratory 3), foreign language 3 and academic electives 4. Mathematics requirement includes 2 algebra. Social science recommendation .5 economics and .5 government. 2 units of same foreign language, 1 additional unit of advanced mathematics, computer science, world history, world geography, or Western civilization required.

**2009-2010 Annual costs.** Tuition/fees: $8,988; $21,846 out-of-state. Room/board: $9,411. Books/supplies: $1,170. Personal expenses: $1,639.

**2008-2009 Financial aid. Need-based:** 1,192 full-time freshmen applied for aid; 763 were judged to have need; 733 of these received aid. Average need met was 66%. Average scholarship/grant was $3,052; average loan $3,336. 47% of total undergraduate aid awarded as scholarships/grants, 53% as loans/jobs. **Non-need-based:** Awarded to 2,706 full-time undergraduates, including 825 freshmen. Scholarships awarded for academics, alumni affiliation, art, athletics, music/drama.

**Application procedures. Admission:** Priority date 11/1; deadline 4/1. $50 fee, may be waived for applicants with need. Notification sent by mid April. Must reply by 5/1. March 1 application date recommended for residence hall students. Admissions deposit refundable until May 1 for fall semester, December 1 for spring semester. Written notice required. **Financial aid:** Priority date 3/15; no closing date. FAFSA required. Applicants notified on a rolling basis starting 4/10; must reply within 8 week(s) of notification.

**Academics. Special study options:** Accelerated study, combined bachelor's/graduate degree, cooperative education, cross-registration, distance learning, double major, dual enrollment of high school students, ESL, exchange student, honors, independent study, internships, liberal arts/career combination, semester at sea, study abroad, teacher certification program. Internships and courses in conjunction with Spoleto US (international arts festival); 3-2 engineering program with Case Western Reserve University, Clemson University, University of South Carolina; marine engineering option with University of Michigan. **Credit/placement by examination:** AP, CLEP, IB, SAT, institutional tests. 30 credit hours maximum toward bachelor's degree. **Support services:** Learning center, pre-admission summer program, reduced course load, study skills assistance, tutoring, writing center.

**Majors. Area/ethnic studies:** Latin American. **Biology:** General, biochemistry, marine. **Business:** Accounting, business admin, hospitality admin, international. **Communications:** General. **Computer sciences:** General, information systems. **Education:** Early childhood, elementary, middle, physical, secondary, special. **Foreign languages:** Classics, French, German, Spanish. **Health:** Athletic training, predental, premedicine. **History:** General. **Interdisciplinary:** Historic preservation. **Math:** General. **Philosophy/religion:** Philosophy, religion. **Physical sciences:** Astronomy, astrophysics, chemistry, geology, physics. **Psychology:** General. **Social sciences:** Anthropology, economics, political science, sociology, urban studies. **Visual/performing arts:** Art history/conservation, arts management, dramatic, studio arts. **Other:** Discovery informatics.

**Most popular majors.** Biology 10%, business/marketing 24%, communications/journalism 13%, education 8%, psychology 7%, social sciences 11%, visual/performing arts 9%.

**Computing on campus.** 2,500 workstations in dormitories, library, computer center, student center. Dormitories wired for high-speed internet access and linked to campus network. Commuter students can connect to campus network. Online course registration, helpline, wireless network available.

**Student life. Freshman orientation:** Mandatory. Preregistration for classes offered. **Policies:** Honor system, student code of conduct, alcohol and drug policies, students' rights and responsibilities, and other policies and guidelines. **Housing:** Coed dorms, single-sex dorms, apartments, fraternity/sorority housing available. $200 fully refundable deposit, deadline 5/1. Restored old Charleston houses used as residence halls, some with kitchen facilities in suite. **Activities:** Bands, campus ministries, choral groups, dance, drama, international student organizations, literary magazine, music ensembles, musical theater, radio station, student government, student newspaper, symphony orchestra, over 100 organizations available.

**Athletics.** NCAA. **Intercollegiate:** Baseball M, basketball, cross-country, diving, equestrian W, golf, sailing, soccer, softball W, swimming, tennis, track and field W, volleyball W. **Intramural:** Badminton, basketball, equestrian W, fencing, football (tackle), racquetball, rowing (crew), rugby W, soccer, softball, tennis, volleyball, weight lifting. **Team name:** Cougars.

**Student services.** Adult student services, alcohol/substance abuse counseling, chaplain/spiritual director, career counseling, student employment services, financial aid counseling, health services, legal services, minority student services, on-campus daycare, personal counseling, placement for graduates, veterans' counselor. **Physically disabled:** Services for visually, speech, hearing impaired.

**Contact.** E-mail: admissions@cofc.edu
Phone: (843) 953-5670 Fax: (843) 953-6322
Suzette Stille, Director of Admission, College of Charleston, Office of Admissions and Adult Student Services, Charleston, SC 29424-0001

## Columbia College
**Columbia, South Carolina**　　　　　**CB member**
**www.columbiasc.edu**　　　　　　　**CB code: 5117**

- Private 4-year liberal arts college for women affiliated with United Methodist Church
- Residential campus in large city
- 1,185 degree-seeking undergraduates: 19% part-time, 98% women
- 227 degree-seeking graduate students
- 74% of applicants admitted
- SAT or ACT with writing required
- 40% graduate within 6 years

**General. Founded** in 1854. Regionally accredited. **Degrees:** 221 bachelor's awarded; master's offered. **ROTC:** Army. **Location:** 70 miles from Charlotte, North Carolina. **Calendar:** Semester, limited summer session. **Full-time faculty:** 78 total; 80% have terminal degrees, 13% minority, 68% women. **Part-time faculty:** 65 total; 35% have terminal degrees, 11% minority, 68% women. **Class size:** 58% < 20, 42% 20-39, less than 1% 50-99. **Special facilities:** Leadership center for women.

**Freshman class profile.** 1,019 applied, 750 admitted, 219 enrolled.

| Mid 50% test scores | | GPA 2.0-2.99: | 20% |
|---|---|---|---|
| SAT critical reading: | 440-570 | Rank in top quarter: | 41% |
| SAT math: | 440-540 | Rank in top tenth: | 16% |
| SAT writing: | 430-550 | End year in good standing: | 80% |
| ACT composite: | 18-23 | Return as sophomores: | 64% |
| GPA 3.75 or higher: | 35% | Out-of-state: | 11% |
| GPA 3.50-3.74: | 14% | Live on campus: | 84% |
| GPA 3.0-3.49: | 29% | | |

**Basis for selection.** School record, test scores, recommendations most important. Audition recommended for dance, music programs; portfolio recommended for art programs; essay, interview recommended for borderline applicants.

**High school preparation.** 16 units recommended. Recommended units include English 4, mathematics 3, social studies 2, history 1, science 2 (laboratory 2), foreign language 2 and academic electives 2. 2.5 units in music, dance, art also recommended.

**2009-2010 Annual costs.** Tuition/fees: $23,480. Room/board: $6,510. Books/supplies: $800. Personal expenses: $2,750.

**2008-2009 Financial aid. Need-based:** 269 full-time freshmen applied for aid; 250 were judged to have need; 250 of these received aid. Average need met was 78%. Average scholarship/grant was $18,434; average loan $3,040. 69% of total undergraduate aid awarded as scholarships/grants, 31% as loans/jobs. **Non-need-based:** Awarded to 231 full-time undergraduates, including 95 freshmen. Scholarships awarded for academics, alumni affiliation, art, athletics, leadership, music/drama.

**Application procedures. Admission:** No deadline. $25 fee, may be waived for applicants with need, free for online applicants. Admission notification on a rolling basis beginning on or about 10/1. Must reply by May 1 or within 4 week(s) if notified thereafter. **Financial aid:** Priority date 4/1; no closing date. FAFSA required. Applicants notified on a rolling basis starting 3/15; must reply within 2 week(s) of notification.

**Academics. Special study options:** Double major, dual enrollment of high school students, exchange student, honors, independent study, internships, student-designed major, study abroad, teacher certification program, Washington semester. **Credit/placement by examination:** AP, CLEP, IB, SAT, ACT, institutional tests. **Support services:** Learning center, reduced course load, remedial instruction, study skills assistance, tutoring, writing center.

**Majors. Biology:** General. **Business:** Accounting, business admin. **Communications:** General, journalism. **Computer sciences:** General. **Education:** Drama/dance, early childhood, elementary, middle, music, special. **Family/**

consumer sciences: Family studies. **Foreign languages:** French, Spanish. **Health:** Speech pathology. **History:** General. **Interdisciplinary:** Behavioral sciences. **Liberal arts:** Arts/sciences. **Math:** General. **Philosophy/religion:** Religion. **Physical sciences:** Chemistry. **Psychology:** General. **Public administration:** Social work. **Social sciences:** Political science. **Theology:** Religious ed. **Visual/performing arts:** Art, dance, music performance, piano/organ, studio arts, voice/opera. **Other:** Public affairs.

**Most popular majors.** Biology 7%, business/marketing 25%, communications/journalism 7%, education 11%, health sciences 6%, interdisciplinary studies 6%, psychology 8%, public administration/social services 8%, visual/performing arts 6%.

**Computing on campus.** 165 workstations in dormitories, library, computer center, student center. Dormitories wired for high-speed internet access and linked to campus network. Online course registration, online library, helpline, repair service, wireless network available.

**Student life. Freshman orientation:** Available, $150 fee. Preregistration for classes offered. One-day program in June. 4-day program in August where students participate in community service project. **Policies:** All students required to live on campus during first 2 years unless living with parent or guardian. All residence halls nonsmoking. Chapel requirements in place for first-year, sophomore, and junior students. Religious observance required. **Housing:** Guaranteed on-campus for freshmen. Wellness housing available. $100 deposit, deadline 5/1. **Activities:** Concert band, choral groups, dance, drama, international student organizations, literary magazine, music ensembles, musical theater, student government, student newspaper, Young Republicans, Young Democrats, CC Serves, Sister to Sista, African-American student association, NAACP.

**Athletics.** NAIA. **Intercollegiate:** Basketball W, soccer W, softball W, tennis W, volleyball W. **Team name:** Koalas.

**Student services.** Adult student services, chaplain/spiritual director, career counseling, student employment services, financial aid counseling, health services, personal counseling, placement for graduates, veterans' counselor.

**Contact.** E-mail: admissions@columbiasc.edu
Phone: (803) 786-3871 Toll-free number: (800) 277-1301
Fax: (803) 786-3674
Ron White, Vice President of Enrollment Management, Columbia College, 1301 Columbia College Drive, Columbia, SC 29203

## Columbia International University
### Columbia, South Carolina
www.ciu.edu                           CB code: 5116

- Private 4-year university and Bible college affiliated with multidenominational/evangelical churches
- Residential campus in small city
- 505 degree-seeking undergraduates: 6% part-time, 54% women, 8% African American, 1% Asian American, 1% Hispanic American, 1% Native American, 3% international
- 392 degree-seeking graduate students
- 71% of applicants admitted
- SAT or ACT (ACT writing optional), application essay required
- 44% graduate within 6 years

**General.** Founded in 1923. Regionally accredited; also accredited by ABHE, ATS. **Degrees:** 104 bachelor's, 17 associate awarded; master's, doctoral offered. **Location:** 75 miles from Charlotte, NC, 225 miles from Atlanta. **Calendar:** Semester, limited summer session. **Full-time faculty:** 25 total. **Part-time faculty:** 26 total. **Class size:** 64% < 20, 23% 20-39, 1% 40-49, 8% 50-99, 4% >100. **Special facilities:** Prayer towers.

**Freshman class profile.** 199 applied, 141 admitted, 93 enrolled.

| Mid 50% test scores | | GPA 2.0-2.99: | 19% |
|---|---|---|---|
| SAT critical reading: | 510-630 | Rank in top quarter: | 44% |
| SAT math: | 470-570 | Rank in top tenth: | 11% |
| ACT composite: | 19-24 | Return as sophomores: | 80% |
| GPA 3.75 or higher: | 42% | Out-of-state: | 43% |
| GPA 3.50-3.74: | 18% | Live on campus: | 86% |
| GPA 3.0-3.49: | 20% | International: | 2% |

**Basis for selection.** School achievement, recommendations, test scores, essay, school and community activities, religious commitment important. Audition required for church music program. **Homeschooled:** Transcripts should include GPA.

**High school preparation.** Recommended units include English 4, mathematics 2, social studies 2, science 1 and foreign language 2. Thorough background in English grammar and composition required.

**2009-2010 Annual costs.** Tuition/fees: $16,875. Room/board: $6,210. Books/supplies: $600. Personal expenses: $2,000.

**2009-2010 Financial aid. Need-based:** 63 full-time freshmen applied for aid, 52 were judged to have need; 48 of these received aid. Average need met was 49%. Average scholarship/grant was $1,200; average loan $1,900. 33% of total undergraduate aid awarded as scholarships/grants, 67% as loans/jobs. **Non-need-based:** Awarded to 159 full-time undergraduates, including 32 freshmen. Scholarships awarded for academics, leadership, state residency. **Additional information:** Spouse scholarship program; special short quarter scholarships for missionaries on furlough.

**Application procedures. Admission:** Priority date 5/1; deadline 8/1 (postmark date). $45 fee, may be waived for applicants with need. Admission notification on a rolling basis. **Financial aid:** Priority date 1/31; no closing date. FAFSA, institutional form required. Applicants notified on a rolling basis starting 12/18; must reply within 4 week(s) of notification.

**Academics. Special study options:** Combined bachelor's/graduate degree, cross-registration, distance learning, double major, independent study, internships, liberal arts/career combination, study abroad, teacher certification program. **Credit/placement by examination:** AP, CLEP, IB. 15 credit hours maximum toward associate degree, 30 toward bachelor's. **Support services:** Learning center, reduced course load, remedial instruction, study skills assistance, tutoring.

**Majors. Area/ethnic studies:** Near/Middle Eastern. **Business:** Nonprofit/public. **Communications:** General. **Education:** Multi-level teacher. **Foreign languages:** Biblical. **Interdisciplinary:** Intercultural. **Liberal arts:** Humanities. **Psychology:** General. **Theology:** Bible, pastoral counseling, religious ed, sacred music, youth ministry.

**Most popular majors.** Communications/journalism 11%, education 6%, interdisciplinary studies 10%, liberal arts 22%, psychology 9%, theological studies 30%.

**Computing on campus.** 46 workstations in library, computer center. Dormitories wired for high-speed internet access and linked to campus network. Online course registration, online library, helpline, repair service available.

**Student life. Freshman orientation:** Mandatory, $40 fee. Preregistration for classes offered. 3 sessions held prior to start of fall semester; 1 session held 3 days prior to start of spring semester. **Policies:** Standards of Christian living are outlined in the Biblical Standards Handbook. Religious observance required. **Housing:** Guaranteed on-campus for all undergraduates. Single-sex dorms available. $100 partly refundable deposit. Mobile home park available for married students. **Activities:** Concert band, choral groups, drama, music ensembles, radio station, student government, student newspaper, symphony orchestra, student missions connection, African-American Fellowship, student senate, student union, grad life council.

**Athletics. Intramural:** Basketball, football (non-tackle), soccer M, softball, table tennis, volleyball.

**Student services.** Chaplain/spiritual director, career counseling, student employment services, financial aid counseling, health services, personal counseling, placement for graduates, veterans' counselor. **Physically disabled:** Services for visually, hearing impaired. **Learning disabled:** Comprehensive services available.

**Contact.** E-mail: yesciu@ciu.edu
Phone: (803) 754-4100 ext. 5024 Toll-free number: (800) 777-2227
Fax: (803) 786-4209
Dan Griffin, Director of Admissions, Columbia International University, PO Box 3122, Columbia, SC 29230-3122

## Converse College
### Spartanburg, South Carolina                  CB member
www.converse.edu                                 CB code: 5121

- Private 4-year music, liberal arts and performing arts college for women
- Residential campus in small city
- 720 degree-seeking undergraduates: 18% part-time, 100% women, 15% African American, 1% Asian American, 3% Hispanic American, 1% Native American, 2% international
- 536 degree-seeking graduate students
- 68% of applicants admitted
- SAT or ACT (ACT writing optional), application essay required
- 64% graduate within 6 years; 27% enter graduate study

**General.** Founded in 1889. Regionally accredited. Men admitted to graduate programs. **Degrees:** 183 bachelor's awarded; master's offered. **ROTC:** Army. **Location:** 70 miles from Charlotte, NC. **Calendar:** 4-1-4, limited summer session. **Full-time faculty:** 78 total; 96% have terminal degrees, 9% minority, 56% women. **Part-time faculty:** 9 total; 33% have terminal degrees, 56% women. **Class size:** 81% < 20, 19% 20-39. **Special facilities:** State of the art science educational facility, music library, music and performing arts auditorium,.

**Freshman class profile.** 602 applied, 409 admitted, 157 enrolled.

| Mid 50% test scores | | | |
|---|---|---|---|
| SAT critical reading: | 480-590 | GPA 2.0-2.99: | 8% |
| SAT math: | 480-580 | Rank in top quarter: | 64% |
| ACT composite: | 20-25 | Rank in top tenth: | 33% |
| GPA 3.75 or higher: | 62% | Return as sophomores: | 72% |
| GPA 3.50-3.74: | 13% | Out-of-state: | 26% |
| GPA 3.0-3.49: | 17% | Live on campus: | 90% |
| | | International: | 1% |

**Basis for selection.** School record, class rank, test scores, extracurricular activities, school recommendation considered. Interview recommended for all; audition required for music programs. **Homeschooled:** Statement describing homeschool structure and mission, interview, letter of recommendation (nonparent) required.

**High school preparation.** College-preparatory program required. 24 units recommended. Recommended units include English 4, mathematics 3, social studies 2, history 2, science 3 (laboratory 2), foreign language 3 and academic electives 5.

**2009-2010 Annual costs.** Tuition/fees: $25,230. Special fees for laboratory, studio art, computer programming, and other courses requiring special materials. Room/board: $7,760. Books/supplies: $750. Personal expenses: $1,500.

**2009-2010 Financial aid. Need-based:** 156 full-time freshmen applied for aid; 142 were judged to have need; 142 of these received aid. Average need met was 85.53%. Average scholarship/grant was $19,848; average loan $4,526. 70% of total undergraduate aid awarded as scholarships/grants, 30% as loans/jobs. **Non-need-based:** Awarded to 237 full-time undergraduates, including 72 freshmen. Scholarships awarded for academics, alumni affiliation, art, athletics, leadership, music/drama, ROTC, state residency.

**Application procedures. Admission:** Priority date 1/15; no deadline. No application fee. Admission notification on a rolling basis beginning on or about 10/1. Must reply by May 1 or within 2 week(s) if notified thereafter. **Financial aid:** Closing date 3/15. FAFSA required. Applicants notified on a rolling basis starting 3/1; must reply by 5/1 or within 2 week(s) of notification.

**Academics. Special study options:** Combined bachelor's/graduate degree, cross-registration, double major, ESL, honors, independent study, internships, liberal arts/career combination, student-designed major, study abroad, teacher certification program. Women's leadership program. **Credit/placement by examination:** AP, CLEP, IB, SAT, ACT, institutional tests. 30 credit hours maximum toward bachelor's degree. **Support services:** Learning center, remedial instruction, study skills assistance, tutoring, writing center.

**Majors. Biology:** General, biochemistry. **Business:** Accounting, finance, international, managerial economics, marketing, training/development. **Education:** General, Deaf/hearing impaired, early childhood, elementary, special. **Foreign languages:** General, Spanish. **Health:** Art therapy, music therapy. **History:** General. **Math:** General. **Philosophy/religion:** Religion. **Physical sciences:** Chemistry. **Psychology:** General. **Social sciences:** Economics, political science. **Visual/performing arts:** Art, art history/conservation, dramatic, interior design, music history, music pedagogy, music performance, music theory/composition, piano/organ, stringed instruments, studio arts, theater arts management, voice/opera.

**Most popular majors.** Education 22%, English 9%, foreign language 6%, health sciences 6%, psychology 13%, visual/performing arts 22%.

**Computing on campus.** 75 workstations in dormitories, library, computer center, student center. Dormitories wired for high-speed internet access and linked to campus network. Commuter students can connect to campus network. Online library, helpline, repair service, wireless network available.

**Student life. Freshman orientation:** Mandatory. Preregistration for classes offered. 3-day program. **Policies:** Strong honor tradition based on mutual trust and responsibility. **Housing:** Guaranteed on-campus for all undergraduates. Wellness housing available. $300 partly refundable deposit, deadline 5/1. **Activities:** Concert band, campus ministries, choral groups, dance, drama, international student organizations, literary magazine, music ensembles, Model UN, musical theater, opera, student government, student newspaper, symphony orchestra, Student Christian Association, student activities committee, Young Republicans, community service organizations, honor organizations, student volunteer services.

**Athletics.** NCAA. **Intercollegiate:** Basketball W, cross-country W, equestrian W, lacrosse W, soccer W, swimming W, tennis W, volleyball W. **Intramural:** Archery W, basketball W, football (non-tackle) W, soccer W, softball W, swimming W, synchronized swimming W, volleyball W. **Team name:** Valkyries.

**Student services.** Adult student services, alcohol/substance abuse counseling, chaplain/spiritual director, career counseling, student employment services, financial aid counseling, health services, personal counseling, placement for graduates. **Physically disabled:** Services for hearing impaired.

**Contact.** E-mail: admissions@converse.edu
Phone: (864) 596-9040 Toll-free number: (800) 766-1125
Fax: (864) 596-9225
April Lewis, Director of Admissions, Converse College, 580 East Main Street, Spartanburg, SC 29302-0006

## Erskine College
Due West, South Carolina    CB member
www.erskine.edu    CB code: 5188

- Private 4-year liberal arts and seminary college affiliated with Associate Reformed Presbyterian Church
- Residential campus in rural community
- 578 degree-seeking undergraduates: 2% part-time, 55% women, 7% African American, 1% Asian American, 1% Hispanic American, 3% international
- 287 degree-seeking graduate students
- 70% of applicants admitted
- SAT or ACT (ACT writing optional), application essay required
- 69% graduate within 6 years

**General.** Founded in 1839. Regionally accredited. Affiliated with Erskine Theological Seminary. **Degrees:** 115 bachelor's awarded; master's, doctoral offered. **Location:** 18 miles from Anderson, 45 miles from Greenville. **Calendar:** 4-1-4, limited summer session. **Full-time faculty:** 42 total; 86% have terminal degrees, 7% minority, 38% women. **Part-time faculty:** 25 total; 20% have terminal degrees, 4% minority, 32% women. **Class size:** 73% < 20, 27% 20-39. **Special facilities:** Arts center.

**Freshman class profile.** 589 applied, 415 admitted, 182 enrolled.

| Mid 50% test scores | | | |
|---|---|---|---|
| SAT critical reading: | 470-580 | Rank in top quarter: | 67% |
| SAT math: | 490-610 | Rank in top tenth: | 31% |
| ACT composite: | 23-27 | End year in good standing: | 78% |
| GPA 3.75 or higher: | 64% | Return as sophomores: | 63% |
| GPA 3.50-3.74: | 13% | Out-of-state: | 24% |
| GPA 3.0-3.49: | 17% | Live on campus: | 98% |
| GPA 2.0-2.99: | 5% | International: | 3% |

**Basis for selection.** High school transcript, testings and personal qualities considered in admissions decisions. Rigor of coursework most important. Grades, class rank, test scores, extracurricular activities, essay very important. Interview required for academically weak; audition required for music. **Homeschooled:** Transcript of courses and grades, letter of recommendation (nonparent) required. High school diploma, GED, or college preparatory diploma certification required. Portfolio showing courses studied, textbooks used, course outline and extracurricular activities may be requested in some instances.

**High school preparation.** College-preparatory program required. 14 units required. Required units include English 4, mathematics 2, science 2 (laboratory 2). 2 social sciences and at least 4 other units earned from these subject areas: history, science, Latin, modern foreign languages, advanced math and English.

**2009-2010 Annual costs.** Tuition/fees: $24,645. Room/board: $8,325. Books/supplies: $1,500. Personal expenses: $1,250.

**2008-2009 Financial aid. Non-need-based:** Scholarships awarded for academics, alumni affiliation, art, athletics, leadership, minority status, music/drama, religious affiliation, state-residency. **Additional information:** Filing deadline 5/1 for institutional form, 6/30 for state form.

**Application procedures. Admission:** No deadline. $25 fee, may be waived for applicants with need, free for online applicants. Admission notification on a rolling basis beginning on or about 11/15. **Financial aid:** Priority date 4/1; no closing date. FAFSA, institutional form required. Applicants notified on a rolling basis starting 12/15; must reply within 2 week(s) of notification.

**Academics.** **Special study options:** Double major, independent study, internships, study abroad, teacher certification program. **Credit/placement by examination:** AP, CLEP, IB, institutional tests. 18 credit hours maximum toward bachelor's degree. **Support services:** Pre-admission summer program, study skills assistance, tutoring, writing center.

**Majors.** **Area/ethnic studies:** American. **Biology:** General. **Business:** Business admin. **Education:** Early childhood, elementary, physical, secondary, social studies, special. **Foreign languages:** French, Spanish. **Health:** Athletic training, clinical lab technology. **History:** General. **Math:** General. **Parks/recreation:** Health/fitness, sports admin. **Philosophy/religion:** Philosophy, religion. **Physical sciences:** Chemistry, physics. **Psychology:** General. **Social sciences:** Political science. **Theology:** Religious ed. **Visual/performing arts:** Art.

**Most popular majors.** Biology 20%, business/marketing 17%, education 12%, parks/recreation 6%, philosophy/religious studies 9%, physical sciences 6%, psychology 10%.

**Computing on campus.** Dormitories wired for high-speed internet access and linked to campus network. Commuter students can connect to campus network. Helpline, repair service, student web hosting, wireless network available.

**Student life.** **Freshman orientation:** Mandatory. Preregistration for classes offered. Orientation held in August prior to first day of classes. **Policies:** Religious observance required. **Housing:** Guaranteed on-campus for all undergraduates. Single-sex dorms, wellness housing available. $300 deposit. **Activities:** Bands, campus ministries, choral groups, dance, drama, literary magazine, music ensembles, musical theater, radio station, student government, student newspaper, national honor societies for academics, drama, and leadership, association of minority students, denominational organizations, judicial council, Fellowship of Christian Athletes, Habitat for Humanity, council for exceptional children.

**Athletics.** NCAA. **Intercollegiate:** Baseball M, basketball, cross-country, golf, lacrosse W, soccer, softball W, tennis, volleyball W. **Intramural:** Basketball, football (non-tackle) W, football (tackle) M, racquetball, soccer, softball, tennis. **Team name:** Flying Fleet.

**Student services.** Alcohol/substance abuse counseling, chaplain/spiritual director, career counseling, financial aid counseling, health services, personal counseling, placement for graduates.

**Contact.** E-mail: admissions@erskine.edu
Phone: (864) 379-8838 Toll-free number: (800) 241-8721
Fax: (864) 379-2167
Woody O'Cain, Vice President for Enrollment, Erskine College, PO Box 176, Due West, SC 29639-0176

## Francis Marion University
**Florence, South Carolina**   CB member
**www.fmarion.edu**   CB code: 5442

- Public 4-year university and liberal arts college
- Commuter campus in small city
- 3,381 degree-seeking undergraduates: 4% part-time, 67% women, 48% African American, 1% Asian American, 1% Hispanic American, 1% Native American, 1% international
- 187 degree-seeking graduate students
- 56% of applicants admitted
- SAT or ACT (ACT writing optional) required
- 37% graduate within 6 years

**General.** Founded in 1970. Regionally accredited. **Degrees:** 496 bachelor's awarded; master's offered. **Location:** 7 miles from downtown, 80 miles from Columbia. **Calendar:** Semester, limited summer session. **Full-time faculty:** 200 total; 81% have terminal degrees, 9% minority, 43% women. **Part-time faculty:** 54 total; 43% have terminal degrees, 7% minority, 67% women. **Class size:** 46% < 20, 47% 20-39, 2% 40-49, 5% 50-99. **Special facilities:** Planetarium, observatory, arboretum, hewn timber cabins.

**Freshman class profile.** 3,432 applied, 1,930 admitted, 794 enrolled.

| Mid 50% test scores | | | |
|---|---|---|---|
| SAT critical reading: | 430-530 | Rank in top quarter: | 48% |
| SAT math: | 430-530 | Rank in top tenth: | 15% |
| SAT writing: | 400-500 | End year in good standing: | 66% |
| ACT composite: | 18-22 | Return as sophomores: | 68% |
| GPA 3.75 or higher: | 38% | Out-of-state: | 1% |
| GPA 3.50-3.74: | 16% | Live on campus: | 64% |
| GPA 3.0-3.49: | 30% | International: | 1% |
| GPA 2.0-2.99: | 16% | Fraternities: | 6% |
| | | Sororities: | 10% |

**Basis for selection.** Combination of standardized test scores and high school GPA important. Borderline cases may be admitted provisionally. Proficiency in math and English required. **Learning Disabled:** Accommodations provided with documentation.

**High school preparation.** 20 units required. Required and recommended units include English 4, mathematics 3-4, social studies 3, history 1, science 3 (laboratory 3), foreign language 2 and academic electives 4. Social studies should include 1 history; 2 units of same foreign language required.

**2009-2010 Annual costs.** Tuition/fees: $7,960; $15,585 out-of-state. Room/board: $6,024. Books/supplies: $1,700. Personal expenses: $4,764.

**2009-2010 Financial aid.** **Non-need-based:** Scholarships awarded for academics, music/drama.

**Application procedures.** **Admission:** No deadline. $30 fee, may be waived for applicants with need. Application must be submitted on paper. Admission notification on a rolling basis beginning on or about 9/1. April 1 reply date for dormitory students. **Financial aid:** Priority date 3/1; no closing date. FAFSA required. Applicants notified on a rolling basis starting 4/15.

**Academics.** **Special study options:** Double major, dual enrollment of high school students, honors, independent study, internships, study abroad, teacher certification program, Washington semester. **Credit/placement by examination:** AP, CLEP, institutional tests. **Support services:** Reduced course load, tutoring, writing center.

**Majors.** **Biology:** General. **Business:** Accounting, business admin, finance, management information systems, managerial economics, marketing. **Communications:** Media studies. **Computer sciences:** General. **Education:** Art, early childhood, English, history, mathematics, secondary, social studies. **Foreign languages:** French, German, Spanish. **Health:** Nursing (RN). **History:** General. **Liberal arts:** Arts/sciences. **Math:** General. **Physical sciences:** Chemistry, physics. **Psychology:** General. **Social sciences:** Economics, international relations, political science, sociology. **Visual/performing arts:** Art, dramatic.

**Most popular majors.** Biology 17%, business/marketing 25%, education 9%, health sciences 6%, psychology 9%, social sciences 14%.

**Computing on campus.** 551 workstations in dormitories, library, computer center, student center. Dormitories wired for high-speed internet access. Online course registration, online library available.

**Student life.** **Freshman orientation:** Mandatory, $46 fee. Preregistration for classes offered. Held in summer for fall term. Session in January for spring. **Housing:** Single-sex dorms, special housing for disabled, apartments, wellness housing available. $250 deposit. **Activities:** Jazz band, campus ministries, choral groups, drama, literary magazine, music ensembles, student government, student newspaper, TV station, College Democrats, Young Republicans, NAACP, Rotaract, minority student association, psychology club, education club, First Fellowship.

**Athletics.** NCAA. **Intercollegiate:** Baseball M, basketball, cross-country, golf M, soccer, softball W, tennis, track and field, volleyball W. **Intramural:** Basketball, bowling, football (non-tackle), golf, racquetball, soccer, softball, table tennis, tennis, track and field, volleyball. **Team name:** Patriots.

**Student services.** Adult student services, chaplain/spiritual director, career counseling, student employment services, health services, minority student services, personal counseling, placement for graduates, veterans' counselor. **Physically disabled:** Services for visually, speech, hearing impaired.

**Contact.** E-mail: admission@fmarion.edu
Phone: (843) 661-1231 Toll-free number: (800) 368-7551
Fax: (843) 661-4635
James Schlimmer, Director of Admissions, Francis Marion University, PO Box 100547, Florence, SC 29502-0547

## Furman University
Greenville, South Carolina     **CB member**
www.furman.edu     **CB code: 5222**

- Private 4-year liberal arts college
- Residential campus in small city
- 2,724 degree-seeking undergraduates: 4% part-time, 57% women, 7% African American, 2% Asian American, 2% Hispanic American, 1% international
- 125 degree-seeking graduate students
- 68% of applicants admitted
- Application essay required
- 86% graduate within 6 years; 41% enter graduate study

**General.** Founded in 1826. Regionally accredited. Abundant internship and collaborative research opportunities. **Degrees:** 647 bachelor's awarded; master's offered. **ROTC:** Army. **Location:** 100 miles from Charlotte, North Carolina, 140 miles from Atlanta. **Calendar:** Semester, extensive summer session. **Full-time faculty:** 234 total; 96% have terminal degrees, 12% minority, 32% women. **Part-time faculty:** 36 total; 64% have terminal degrees, 3% minority, 56% women. **Class size:** 57% < 20, 43% 20-39, less than 1% 40-49, less than 1% 50-99. **Special facilities:** Observatory, center for engaged learning, center for international education, center for collaborative learning and communication, center for sustainability.

**Freshman class profile.** 4,538 applied, 3,080 admitted, 656 enrolled.

| Mid 50% test scores | | | |
|---|---|---|---|
| SAT critical reading: | 580-690 | GPA 2.0-2.99: | 2% |
| SAT math: | 600-680 | Rank in top quarter: | 86% |
| SAT writing: | 580-680 | Rank in top tenth: | 61% |
| ACT composite: | 25-30 | Return as sophomores: | 92% |
| GPA 3.75 or higher: | 74% | Out-of-state: | 70% |
| GPA 3.50-3.74: | 14% | Live on campus: | 98% |
| GPA 3.0-3.49: | 10% | Fraternities: | 32% |
| | | Sororities: | 44% |

**Basis for selection.** High school record including courses taken and grades most important, then SAT or ACT scores. Special talents such as fine arts, athletic ability, writing ability considered. Special consideration given to children of alumni and minorities. SAT or ACT recommended. If ACT or SAT score is not submitted, the student must submit either AP, SAT Subject Test or IB scores in both Math and English. Audition required for music scholarship applicants; portfolio required for art scholarship applicants. **Homeschooled:** SAT Subject Tests including math, subject of student's choice recommended. Interview strongly recommended.

**High school preparation.** College-preparatory program recommended. 14 units required; 18 recommended. Required and recommended units include English 4, mathematics 3-4, social studies 3-4, science 2-3 (laboratory 2-3) and foreign language 2-3.

**2009-2010 Annual costs.** Tuition/fees: $36,656. Room/board: $9,170. Books/supplies: $110. Personal expenses: $900.

**2009-2010 Financial aid. Need-based:** 447 full-time freshmen applied for aid; 348 were judged to have need; 348 of these received aid. Average need met was 85.3%. Average scholarship/grant was $26,737; average loan $3,297. 76% of total undergraduate aid awarded as scholarships/grants, 24% as loans/jobs. **Non-need-based:** Awarded to 1,913 full-time undergraduates, including 541 freshmen. Scholarships awarded for academics, alumni affiliation, art, athletics, leadership, music/drama, religious affiliation, ROTC, state residency. **Additional information:** 5-point comprehensive education financing plan includes financial aid packaging, money management counseling, debt management counseling, outside scholarship coordination, summer job-match program.

**Application procedures. Admission:** Closing date 1/15 (postmark date). $50 fee, may be waived for applicants with need, free for online applicants. Admission notification 3/15. Must reply by 5/1. **Financial aid:** Closing date 1/15. FAFSA, institutional form, CSS PROFILE required. Applicants notified by 3/15; must reply by 5/1.

**Academics.** Strong emphasis on research, internships and other opportunities for engaged, hands-on learning. **Special study options:** Combined bachelor's/graduate degree, double major, independent study, internships, student-designed major, study abroad, teacher certification program, United Nations semester, Washington semester. Undergraduate research program, 3-2 engineering with Auburn University, Clemson University, Georgia Institute of Technology, North Carolina State, Washington University in St. Louis, 3-2 forestry program with Duke University, 3-1 dentistry and medicine programs with any accredited medical or dental school, 3-2 nursing, pharmacy, physical therapy, and physician assistant programs with any accredited medical school. **Credit/placement by examination:** AP, CLEP, IB, institutional tests. **Support services:** Learning center, reduced course load, study skills assistance, tutoring, writing center.

**Majors. Area/ethnic studies:** Asian. **Biology:** General. **Business:** Accounting, business admin, management information systems. **Communications:** General. **Computer sciences:** Computer science. **Education:** General, music. **Foreign languages:** Ancient Greek, French, German, Latin, Spanish. **Health:** Predental, premedicine, prenursing, prepharmacy, preveterinary. **History:** General. **Interdisciplinary:** Math/computer science. **Legal studies:** Prelaw. **Liberal arts:** Arts/sciences. **Math:** General. **Parks/recreation:** Exercise sciences, health/fitness. **Philosophy/religion:** Philosophy, religion. **Physical sciences:** Chemistry, geology, physics. **Psychology:** General. **Social sciences:** Economics, political science, sociology, urban studies. **Theology:** Sacred music. **Visual/performing arts:** Art, dramatic, music history, music performance, music theory/composition. **Other:** Mathematics economics.

**Most popular majors.** Biology 6%, business/marketing 15%, communications/journalism 7%, foreign language 7%, history 9%, physical sciences 6%, social sciences 16%, visual/performing arts 7%.

**Computing on campus.** 450 workstations in library, computer center, student center. Dormitories wired for high-speed internet access and linked to campus network. Commuter students can connect to campus network. Online course registration, helpline, student web hosting, wireless network available.

**Student life. Freshman orientation:** Mandatory. Preregistration for classes offered. 4-day session including academic placement testing, advisory services, entertainment, and recreation. **Housing:** Guaranteed on-campus for freshmen. Coed dorms, single-sex dorms, apartments, wellness housing available. $400 nonrefundable deposit, deadline 5/1. Lakeside cottages and environmentally equipped eco-cottage also available. **Activities:** Bands, campus ministries, choral groups, dance, drama, film society, international student organizations, literary magazine, music ensembles, musical theater, opera, radio station, student government, student newspaper, symphony orchestra, TV station, Collegiate Educational Service Corps, Young Democrats, College Republicans, Student League for Black Culture, Fellowship of Christian Athletes, Council for Exceptional Children, Habitat for Humanity, arts students league.

**Athletics.** NCAA. **Intercollegiate:** Baseball M, basketball, cheerleading, cross-country, football (tackle) M, golf, soccer, softball W, tennis, track and field, volleyball W. **Intramural:** Basketball, bowling, cross-country, football (non-tackle), golf, handball, racquetball, rowing (crew), soccer, softball, swimming, tennis, track and field, volleyball. **Team name:** Paladins.

**Student services.** Adult student services, alcohol/substance abuse counseling, chaplain/spiritual director, career counseling, student employment services, financial aid counseling, health services, minority student services, personal counseling, placement for graduates, veterans' counselor, women's services. **Physically disabled:** Services for visually, hearing impaired.

**Contact.** E-mail: admissions@furman.edu
Phone: (864) 294-2034 Fax: (864) 294-2018
Brad Pochard, Director of Admissions, Furman University, 3300 Poinsett Highway, Greenville, SC 29613

## ITT Technical Institute: Greenville
Greenville, South Carolina
www.itt-tech.edu     **CB code: 2708**

- For-profit 4-year technical college
- Commuter campus in large city

**General.** Accredited by ACICS. **Calendar:** Quarter.

**Contact.** Phone: (864) 288-0777
Director of Recruitment, 6 Independence Pointe, Greenville, SC 29615

## Lander University
Greenwood, South Carolina     **CB member**
www.lander.edu     **CB code: 5363**

- Public 4-year liberal arts and teachers college
- Residential campus in large town
- 2,760 degree-seeking undergraduates: 6% part-time, 66% women
- 17 degree-seeking graduate students
- 48% of applicants admitted
- SAT or ACT (ACT writing optional), interview required
- 41% graduate within 6 years

**General.** Founded in 1872. Regionally accredited. **Degrees:** 452 bachelor's awarded; master's offered. **ROTC:** Army. **Location:** 55 miles from Greenville, 75 miles from Columbia. **Calendar:** Semester, limited summer session. **Full-time faculty:** 138 total; 62% have terminal degrees, 6% minority, 49% women. **Part-time faculty:** 79 total; 19% have terminal degrees, 8% minority, 61% women. **Class size:** 44% < 20, 45% 20-39, 5% 40-49, 6% 50-99.

**Freshman class profile.** 2,739 applied, 1,305 admitted, 581 enrolled.

| Mid 50% test scores | | | |
|---|---|---|---|
| SAT critical reading: | 430-540 | GPA 3.0-3.49: | 27% |
| SAT math: | 450-550 | GPA 2.0-2.99: | 13% |
| ACT composite: | 18-22 | Return as sophomores: | 70% |
| GPA 3.75 or higher: | 43% | Out-of-state: | 4% |
| GPA 3.50-3.74: | 17% | Live on campus: | 80% |

**Basis for selection.** Test scores, class rank, curriculum, high school GPA important. Out-of-state students must rank in top half of high school class. Selectivity of students may be based on transcripts and GED score. Audition required for music programs; interview recommended for art, music programs; portfolio recommended for art programs.

**High school preparation.** 20 units recommended. Recommended units include English 4, mathematics 3, social studies 2, history 1, science 3 (laboratory 3), foreign language 2 and academic electives 4. One unit physical education or ROTC also recommended.

**2009-2010 Annual costs.** Tuition/fees: $8,920; $16,720 out-of-state. Room/board: $6,842. Books/supplies: $100. Personal expenses: $1,600.

**2008-2009 Financial aid. Non-need-based:** Scholarships awarded for academics, art, athletics, leadership, music/drama.

**Application procedures. Admission:** No deadline. $35 fee, may be waived for applicants with need. Admission notification on a rolling basis. **Financial aid:** Priority date 4/15; no closing date. FAFSA required. Applicants notified on a rolling basis starting 4/15; must reply within 4 week(s) of notification.

**Academics. Special study options:** Combined bachelor's/graduate degree, cooperative education, distance learning, double major, dual enrollment of high school students, honors, independent study, internships, liberal arts/career combination, student-designed major, study abroad, teacher certification program. Dual degree in engineering with Clemson University, nursing (RN to BSN completion) offered online, MBA and M.Ed. in counseling/school administration from Clemson University offered on campus. **Credit/placement by examination:** AP, CLEP, IB, institutional tests. 30 credit hours maximum toward bachelor's degree. **Support services:** Learning center, pre-admission summer program, reduced course load, remedial instruction, study skills assistance, tutoring, writing center.

**Majors. Biology:** General. **Business:** Business admin. **Computer sciences:** General. **Conservation:** Environmental science. **Education:** Early childhood, elementary, Montessori teacher, physical, secondary, special. **Foreign languages:** Spanish. **Health:** Athletic training, nursing (RN). **History:** General. **Liberal arts:** Arts/sciences, humanities. **Math:** General. **Parks/recreation:** Exercise sciences. **Physical sciences:** Chemistry. **Protective services:** Law enforcement admin. **Psychology:** General. **Social sciences:** Political science, sociology. **Visual/performing arts:** Art.

**Most popular majors.** Business/marketing 19%, education 15%, health sciences 10%, parks/recreation 6%, psychology 7%, social sciences 14%.

**Computing on campus.** PC or laptop required. 233 workstations in library, computer center. Dormitories linked to campus network. Commuter students can connect to campus network. Online course registration, online library, helpline, repair service, wireless network available.

**Student life. Freshman orientation:** Mandatory. Preregistration for classes offered. **Housing:** Coed dorms, single-sex dorms available. $175 partly refundable deposit, deadline 4/15. **Activities:** Bands, choral groups, dance, drama, literary magazine, music ensembles, student government, student newspaper, Baptist Student Union, Bible study, Young Democrats, College Republicans, Minorities on the Move, Blue Key and Alpha Kappa Gamma (honor societies).

**Athletics.** NCAA. **Intercollegiate:** Baseball M, basketball, golf M, soccer, softball W, tennis, volleyball W. **Intramural:** Basketball, football (non-tackle), golf, soccer, softball, volleyball. **Team name:** Bearcats.

**Student services.** Adult student services, alcohol/substance abuse counseling, career counseling, student employment services, financial aid counseling, health services, minority student services, personal counseling, placement for graduates, veterans' counselor. **Physically disabled:** Services for

visually, speech, hearing impaired. **Learning disabled:** Comprehensive services available.

**Contact.** E-mail: admissions@lander.edu
Phone: (864) 388 8307 Fax: (864) 388-8125
Jennifer Mathis, Director of Admissions, Lander University, Stanley Avenue, Greenwood, SC 29649-2099

## Limestone College
**Gaffney, South Carolina**
www.limestone.edu

CB code: 5366

- Private 4-year liberal arts college
- Residential campus in large town
- 805 degree-seeking undergraduates: 1% part-time, 42% women, 20% African American, 3% Hispanic American
- 71% of applicants admitted
- SAT or ACT (ACT writing optional) required
- 39% graduate within 6 years

**General.** Founded in 1845. Regionally accredited. Evening classes are located at eight sites throughout South Carolina and online. **Degrees:** 145 bachelor's, 1 associate awarded. **ROTC:** Army. **Location:** 25 miles from Spartanburg. **Calendar:** Semester, extensive summer session. **Full-time faculty:** 63 total; 81% have terminal degrees, 5% minority, 44% women. **Part-time faculty:** 16 total; 19% have terminal degrees, 12% minority, 69% women. **Class size:** 58% < 20, 41% 20-39, less than 1% 40-49. **Special facilities:** Computer graphics art lab.

**Freshman class profile.** 1,236 applied, 874 admitted, 257 enrolled.

| Mid 50% test scores | | | |
|---|---|---|---|
| SAT critical reading: | 410-490 | GPA 2.0-2.99: | 40% |
| SAT math: | 430-540 | Rank in top quarter: | 12% |
| ACT composite: | 15-26 | Rank in top tenth: | 3% |
| GPA 3.75 or higher: | 17% | End year in good standing: | 83% |
| GPA 3.50-3.74: | 13% | Return as sophomores: | 58% |
| GPA 3.0-3.49: | 29% | Out-of-state: | 41% |
| | | Live on campus: | 72% |

**Basis for selection.** SAT combined score of 900 (exclusive of Writing) or ACT score of 19 (exclusive of Writing) and GPA of 2.0. Admissions committee must approve all applicants who do not meet these standards. SAT requirement waived for freshmen 21 or older or in military service. The SAT or ACT requirement is waived for students admitted into the PALS (Program for Alternative Learning Styles) Program. Interview required for lower-ranking applicants; recommended for all others. Audition required of first-time, first-year freshmen for music, music education, theater programs; portfolio required for art education, studio art programs; essay required for honors program. **Learning Disabled:** Documentation required to be eligible for Program for Alternative Learning Styles (PALS).

**High school preparation.** 12 units required. Required units include English 4, mathematics 3, social studies 3, science 2 (laboratory 2).

**2010-2011 Annual costs.** Tuition/fees (projected): $19,200. Room/board: $7,000. Books/supplies: $1,870. Personal expenses: $1,640.

**2008-2009 Financial aid. Need-based:** 328 full-time freshmen applied for aid; 298 were judged to have need; 298 of these received aid. Average need met was 52%. Average scholarship/grant was $7,806; average loan $2,773. 31% of total undergraduate aid awarded as scholarships/grants, 69% as loans/jobs. **Non-need-based:** Awarded to 281 full-time undergraduates, including 71 freshmen. Scholarships awarded for academics, art, athletics, job skills, leadership, music/drama, religious affiliation, ROTC, state residency.

**Application procedures. Admission:** Priority date 8/1; deadline 8/26 (receipt date). $25 fee, may be waived for applicants with need, free for online applicants. Admission notification on a rolling basis beginning on or about 6/1. **Financial aid:** Priority date 2/1; no closing date. FAFSA required. Applicants notified on a rolling basis starting 1/15; must reply within 3 week(s) of notification.

**Academics. Special study options:** Accelerated study, distance learning, double major, honors, independent study, internships, liberal arts/career combination, student-designed major, teacher certification program. **Credit/placement by examination:** AP, CLEP, institutional tests. 15 credit hours maximum toward associate degree, 30 toward bachelor's. **Support services:** Learning center, reduced course load, remedial instruction, study skills assistance, tutoring, writing center.

**Majors. Biology:** General. **Business:** Managerial economics, marketing, training/development. **Computer sciences:** Programming, security. **Education:** Art, biology, elementary, English, mathematics, music, physical, social studies. **Health:** Athletic training, predental, premedicine, prenursing, prepharmacy, preveterinary. **History:** General. **Legal studies:** Prelaw. **Liberal arts:** Arts/sciences. **Math:** General. **Parks/recreation:** Sports admin. **Physical sciences:** Chemistry. **Protective services:** Law enforcement admin. **Psychology:** General. **Public administration:** Social work. **Visual/performing arts:** Dramatic, graphic design, music performance, studio arts. **Other:** Information science/studies, Pre-chiropractic.

**Most popular majors.** Business/marketing 20%, education 26%, history 6%, parks/recreation 13%, psychology 6%.

**Computing on campus.** 104 workstations in library, computer center. Dormitories wired for high-speed internet access and linked to campus network. Commuter students can connect to campus network. Online library, helpline, repair service, wireless network available.

**Student life. Freshman orientation:** Mandatory. Preregistration for classes offered. 5 days prior to start of semester. **Policies:** Alcohol-free campus. Students must live on campus unless age 21, or have attained 90 credit hours, or live with immediate family within 50 miles of campus. **Housing:** Guaranteed on-campus for freshmen. Single-sex dorms, wellness housing available. $50 fully refundable deposit. Off-campus apartments available. **Activities:** Bands, campus ministries, choral groups, drama, international student organizations, literary magazine, music ensembles, musical theater, student government, fellowship of Christian athletes, student alumni leadership council, student organization of social workers, Students in Free Enterprise, Christian education and leadership program, Phi Alpha Theta history honor society, outdoor recreation education club, Joyful Saints gospel choir.

**Athletics.** NCAA. **Intercollegiate:** Baseball M, basketball, cross-country, field hockey W, golf, lacrosse, soccer, softball W, swimming, tennis, track and field, volleyball, wrestling M. **Intramural:** Bowling, football (non-tackle), table tennis. **Team name:** Saints.

**Student services.** Adult student services, alcohol/substance abuse counseling, chaplain/spiritual director, career counseling, student employment services, financial aid counseling, health services, personal counseling, placement for graduates, veterans' counselor. **Learning disabled:** Comprehensive services available.

**Contact.** E-mail: cphenicie@limestone.edu
Phone: (864) 488-4554 Toll-free number: (800) 795-7151 ext. 4554
Fax: (864) 487-8706
Chris Phenicie, Vice President for Enrollment Services, Limestone College, 1115 College Drive, Gaffney, SC 29340-3799

## Medical University of South Carolina
**Charleston, South Carolina**
www.musc.edu　　　　　　　　　　　　**CB code: 5407**

▸ Public two-year upper-division university
▸ Commuter campus in large city

**General.** Founded in 1824. Regionally accredited. Upper division/graduate academic health center consisting of six colleges: dental medicine, graduate studies, health professions, medicine, nursing, and pharmacy. College offers only two undergraduate degrees. **Degrees:** 194 bachelor's awarded; master's, doctoral, professional offered. **ROTC:** Air Force. **Location:** 350 miles from Atlanta. **Calendar:** Semester, limited summer session. **Full-time faculty:** 133 total; 87% have terminal degrees, 7% minority, 59% women. **Part-time faculty:** 67 total; 58% have terminal degrees, 9% minority, 55% women. **Class size:** 50% < 20, 50% 50-99. **Special facilities:** Historical medical library, dental museum, pharmacy museum.

**Student profile.** 267 degree-seeking undergraduates, 2,223 degree-seeking graduate students. 100% entered as juniors.

| | | | |
|---|---|---|---|
| Women: | 83% | Native American: | 1% |
| African American: | 10% | Part-time: | 18% |
| Asian American: | 5% | Out-of-state: | 14% |
| Hispanic American: | 1% | 25 or older: | 59% |

**2009-2010 Annual costs.** Tuition and fees for BS in nursing for in-state $13,168 out-of-state $22,776; BS in cardiovascular perfusion for in-state is $13,496 out-of-state $34,240; BS in health professions, in-state $13,526, out-of-state $35,258. Books/supplies: $2,450.

**Financial aid. Need-based:** 210 applied for aid; 189 were judged to have need; 183 of these received aid. Average need met was 54%. 27% of total undergraduate aid awarded as scholarships/grants, 73% as loans/jobs. **Non-need-based:** Awarded to 35 undergraduates. Scholarships awarded for academics, alumni affiliation, minority status, state residency.

**Application procedures. Admission:** $85 fee. Application must be submitted online. All admission policies and dates vary by academic program and college. **Financial aid:** FAFSA, institutional form required.

**Academics. Special study options:** Cross-registration, distance learning. **Credit/placement by examination:** AP, CLEP, institutional tests.

**Majors. Health:** Cardiovascular technology, nursing (RN).

**Computing on campus.** 300 workstations in library, student center. Commuter students can connect to campus network. Online library, helpline, student web hosting, wireless network available.

**Student life. Activities:** Campus ministries, choral groups, dance, international student organizations, literary magazine, music ensembles, student government, Christian Medical Society, campus crusade, student union, community help initiative, South Carolina health initiative, minority student union, Student National Medical Association.

**Athletics. Intramural:** Basketball, football (non-tackle), softball, volleyball.

**Student services.** Alcohol/substance abuse counseling, chaplain/spiritual director, services for economically disadvantaged, financial aid counseling, health services, legal services, minority student services, personal counseling, veterans' counselor.

**Contact.** E-mail: oesadmis@musc.edu
Phone: (843) 792-3281 Fax: (843) 792-6615
Lyla Hudson, Director of Admissions, Medical University of South Carolina, 41 Bee Street, Charleston, SC 29425

## Morris College
**Sumter, South Carolina**　　　　　　　　**CB member**
www.morris.edu　　　　　　　　　　　　**CB code: 5418**

▸ Private 4-year liberal arts college affiliated with Baptist faith
▸ Residential campus in large town
▸ 966 degree-seeking undergraduates: 1% part-time, 58% women, 100% African American
▸ 91% of applicants admitted
▸ 30% graduate within 6 years; 17% enter graduate study

**General.** Founded in 1908. Regionally accredited. **Degrees:** 134 bachelor's awarded. **ROTC:** Army. **Location:** 45 miles from Columbia, 110 miles from Charlotte, North Carolina. **Calendar:** Semester, limited summer session. **Full-time faculty:** 48 total; 71% have terminal degrees, 62% minority, 46% women. **Part-time faculty:** 17 total; 24% have terminal degrees, 71% minority, 35% women. **Class size:** 54% < 20, 43% 20-39, 3% 40-49, less than 1% 50-99. **Special facilities:** Radio station/training lab, electronic learning lab, television production studio.

**Freshman class profile.** 2,350 applied, 2,140 admitted, 301 enrolled.

| | | | |
|---|---|---|---|
| GPA 3.75 or higher: | 2% | Rank in top tenth: | 2% |
| GPA 3.50-3.74: | 3% | End year in good standing: | 73% |
| GPA 3.0-3.49: | 15% | Return as sophomores: | 56% |
| GPA 2.0-2.99: | 63% | Out-of-state: | 24% |
| Rank in top quarter: | 8% | Live on campus: | 92% |

**Basis for selection.** High school record most important. Students with less than 2.0 high school GPA may be admitted on probation but limited to 13-credit-hour load during each of first 2 semesters and required to participate in tutorial and study sessions. SAT or ACT scores must be submitted for all degree-seeking students, except foreign students. Scores used for informational/advisement purposes only. Interview recommended.

**High school preparation.** 24 units required. Required and recommended units include English 4, mathematics 4, social studies 2, history 1, science 3, foreign language 1-2, computer science 1 and academic electives 7. Government 0.5, economics 0.5.

**2009-2010 Annual costs.** Tuition/fees: $9,901. Room/board: $4,386. Books/supplies: $1,900. Personal expenses: $1,200.

**2008-2009 Financial aid.** All financial aid based on need. 306 full-time freshmen applied for aid; 306 were judged to have need; 306 of these received aid. Average met was 85%. Average scholarship/grant was $9,500; average loan $4,500. 48% of total undergraduate aid awarded as scholarships/grants, 52% as loans/jobs.

**Application procedures. Admission:** Priority date 7/1; no deadline. $20 fee, may be waived for applicants with need. Application must be submitted on paper. Admission notification on a rolling basis beginning on or about 11/1. **Financial aid:** Priority date 3/30; no closing date. FAFSA, institutional form required. Applicants notified on a rolling basis starting 6/1; must reply within 2 week(s) of notification.

**Academics.** **Special study options:** Accelerated study, combined bachelor's/graduate degree, cooperative education, double major, honors, internships, liberal arts/career combination, study abroad, teacher certification program. Adult Degree Program in Organizational Management offered through evening courses; students must be at least 25 years old and have earned 60 credit hours. **Credit/placement by examination:** AP, CLEP. 30 credit hours maximum toward bachelor's degree. **Support services:** Learning center, reduced course load, remedial instruction, study skills assistance, tutoring, writing center.

**Majors.** **Biology:** General. **Business:** Business admin, operations. **Communications:** Media studies. **Education:** Biology, early childhood, elementary, English, mathematics, social studies. **Health:** Community health services. **History:** General. **Liberal arts:** Arts/sciences. **Math:** General. **Parks/recreation:** Facilities management. **Protective services:** Law enforcement admin. **Social sciences:** Political science, sociology. **Theology:** Religious ed, theology.

**Most popular majors.** Biology 7%, business/marketing 34%, communications/journalism 7%, health sciences 12%, parks/recreation 8%, security/protective services 7%, social sciences 8%.

**Computing on campus.** 252 workstations in dormitories, library, computer center. Dormitories wired for high-speed internet access and linked to campus network. Wireless network available.

**Student life.** **Freshman orientation:** Mandatory. Preregistration for classes offered. Held during first week of fall and spring semesters. **Policies:** College promotes drug-free, alcohol-free campus. Cigarette smoking prohibited in all buildings. **Housing:** Guaranteed on-campus for freshmen. Single-sex dorms available. $100 fully refundable deposit, deadline 8/1. **Activities:** Pep band, campus ministries, choral groups, dance, drama, radio station, student government, student newspaper, Baptist Student Union, NAACP, Alpha Phi Omega, Durham Ministerial Union, National Association of Blacks in Criminal Justice.

**Athletics.** NAIA. **Intercollegiate:** Baseball M, basketball, cheerleading, cross-country, golf M, softball W, tennis, track and field, volleyball W. **Intramural:** Basketball, football (non-tackle), table tennis. **Team name:** Hornets.

**Student services.** Adult student services, alcohol/substance abuse counseling, chaplain/spiritual director, career counseling, services for economically disadvantaged, student employment services, financial aid counseling, health services, personal counseling, placement for graduates, veterans' counselor. **Physically disabled:** Services for visually, hearing impaired.

**Contact.** E-mail: dcalhoun@morris.edu
Phone: (803) 934-3225 Toll-free number: (866) 853-1345
Fax: (803) 773-8241
Deborah Calhoun, Director of Admission and Records, Morris College, 100 West College Street, Sumter, SC 29150-3599

## Newberry College
**Newberry, South Carolina**
www.newberry.edu

**CB member**
**CB code: 5493**

▶ Private 4-year liberal arts college affiliated with Evangelical Lutheran Church in America

▶ Residential campus in small city

▶ 1,098 degree-seeking undergraduates: 1% part-time, 45% women, 27% African American, 1% Asian American, 2% Hispanic American, 3% international

▶ 69% of applicants admitted

▶ 42% graduate within 6 years

**General.** Founded in 1856. Regionally accredited. **Degrees:** 134 bachelor's awarded. **ROTC:** Army. **Location:** 40 miles from Columbia. **Calendar:** Semester, limited summer session. **Full-time faculty:** 52 total; 71% have terminal degrees, 6% minority, 48% women. **Part-time faculty:** 49 total; 12% have terminal degrees, 4% minority, 55% women. **Class size:** 61% < 20, 36% 20-39, 2% 40-49, less than 1% 50-99.

**Freshman class profile.** 1,516 applied, 1,045 admitted, 345 enrolled.

| Mid 50% test scores | | End year in good standing: | 85% |
|---|---|---|---|
| SAT critical reading: | 410-520 | Return as sophomores: | 62% |
| SAT math: | 430-560 | Out-of-state: | 12% |
| SAT writing: | 400-500 | Live on campus: | 95% |
| ACT composite: | 17-23 | International: | 1% |
| Rank in top quarter: | 30% | Fraternities: | 1% |
| Rank in top tenth: | 12% | Sororities: | 2% |

**Basis for selection.** High school record and test scores important; recommendations and interview considered. SAT or ACT recommended. Interview recommended for all; audition required for drama, music programs; portfolio required for art. **Homeschooled:** Statement describing home-school structure and mission, transcript of courses and grades, state high school equivalency certificate, interview, letter of recommendation (nonparent) required. Submit transcripts from HS or home school association. If unavailable, submit major essays and course descriptions. References necessary from primary instructor and another source.

**High school preparation.** College-preparatory program recommended. 14 units required. Required and recommended units include English 4, mathematics 3, social studies 2, history 1, science 2 (laboratory 2) and foreign language 2.

**2009-2010 Annual costs.** Tuition/fees: $21,470. Room/board: $7,750.

**2009-2010 Financial aid.** **Need-based:** 318 full-time freshmen applied for aid; 300 were judged to have need; 300 of these received aid. Average need met was 75%. Average scholarship/grant was $18,600; average loan $3,468. 71% of total undergraduate aid awarded as scholarships/grants, 29% as loans/jobs. **Non-need-based:** Scholarships awarded for academics, alumni affiliation, athletics, leadership, music/drama, religious affiliation, ROTC, state residency.

**Application procedures.** **Admission:** Priority date 1/30; no deadline. $30 fee. Admission notification on a rolling basis. **Financial aid:** Priority date 3/15; no closing date. FAFSA, institutional form required. Applicants notified on a rolling basis starting 3/1; must reply by 5/1 or within 2 week(s) of notification.

**Academics.** **Special study options:** Accelerated study, double major, dual enrollment of high school students, honors, independent study, internships, liberal arts/career combination, student-designed major, study abroad, teacher certification program, weekend college. Medical Technology Dual Degree Program with Palmetto Baptist Medical Center. Forest and Environmental Management Dual Degree Program with Duke University. **Credit/placement by examination:** AP, CLEP, IB, SAT, ACT, institutional tests. 30 credit hours maximum toward bachelor's degree. Sophomore standing available by earning 24 credit hours based on AP exam scores. **Support services:** Learning center, reduced course load, remedial instruction, tutoring, writing center.

**Majors.** **Biology:** General. **Business:** Business admin. **Communications:** General. **Education:** General, early childhood, elementary, music, physical. **History:** General. **Interdisciplinary:** Global studies. **Legal studies:** Pre-law. **Liberal arts:** Arts/sciences, humanities. **Math:** General. **Parks/recreation:** General, sports admin. **Philosophy/religion:** Philosophy, religion. **Physical sciences:** Chemistry. **Psychology:** General. **Social sciences:** International relations, political science, sociology. **Theology:** Sacred music. **Visual/performing arts:** Art, dramatic, music history, music performance, music theory/composition.

**Most popular majors.** Biology 8%, business/marketing 27%, communications/journalism 8%, education 11%, history 8%, parks/recreation 12%, social sciences 6%.

**Computing on campus.** PC or laptop required. 12 workstations in library. Dormitories wired for high-speed internet access and linked to campus network. Commuter students can connect to campus network. Online course registration, online library, helpline, repair service, student web hosting, wireless network available.

**Student life.** **Freshman orientation:** Mandatory, $100 fee. Preregistration for classes offered. 2-day event. Students stay overnight on campus. **Policies:** Residence halls are non-smoking. **Housing:** Guaranteed on-campus for freshmen. Coed dorms, single-sex dorms, fraternity/sorority housing available. $100 nonrefundable deposit. **Activities:** Bands, campus ministries, choral groups, drama, literary magazine, music ensembles, musical theater, radio station, student government, student newspaper, TV station, Lutheran Student Movement, Baptist student union, Young Republicans, Intervarsity Fellowship of Christian Athletes, Students Organized for Community Service, South Carolina State Student Legislature.

**Athletics.** NCAA. **Intercollegiate:** Baseball M, basketball, cheerleading, cross-country, football (tackle) M, golf, soccer, softball W, tennis, volleyball W, wrestling M. **Intramural:** Basketball, football (non-tackle).

**Student services.** Alcohol/substance abuse counseling, chaplain/spiritual director, career counseling, student employment services, financial aid counseling, health services, personal counseling, placement for graduates.

**Contact.** E-mail: admissions@newberry.edu
Phone: (803) 321-5127 Toll-free number: (800) 845-4955 ext. 5127
Fax: (803) 321-5138
Amanda Richardson, Director of Admissions, Newberry College, 2100 College Street, Newberry, SC 29108

# North Greenville University
Tigerville, South Carolina
www.ngu.edu
CB code: 5498

◗ Private 4-year liberal arts college affiliated with Southern Baptist Convention
◗ Residential campus in rural community
◗ 1,953 degree-seeking undergraduates: 3% part-time, 51% women, 8% African American, 1% Hispanic American, 1% international
◗ 130 graduate students
◗ 55% of applicants admitted
◗ SAT or ACT (ACT writing optional) required
◗ 48% graduate within 6 years; 10% enter graduate study

**General.** Founded in 1891. Regionally accredited. Off-site recreation and learning center for Outdoor Leadership major. **Degrees:** 312 bachelor's, 7 associate awarded; master's offered. **ROTC:** Army. **Location:** 18 miles from Greenville; 54 miles from Asheville, North Carolina. **Calendar:** Semester, limited summer session. **Full-time faculty:** 122 total; 68% have terminal degrees, 12% minority, 34% women. **Part-time faculty:** 63 total; 11% have terminal degrees, 5% minority, 41% women. **Class size:** 61% < 20, 38% 20-39, less than 1% 40-49, less than 1% 50-99. **Special facilities:** Bible museum.

**Freshman class profile.** 1,618 applied, 893 admitted, 498 enrolled.

| Mid 50% test scores | | | |
|---|---|---|---|
| SAT critical reading: | 440-660 | GPA 3.0-3.49: | 35% |
| SAT math: | 470-630 | GPA 2.0-2.99: | 15% |
| SAT writing: | 450-670 | Rank in top quarter: | 45% |
| ACT composite: | 21-29 | Rank in top tenth: | 20% |
| GPA 3.75 or higher: | 29% | Out-of-state: | 21% |
| GPA 3.50-3.74: | 21% | Live on campus: | 89% |

**Basis for selection.** High school record, standardized test scores, class rank most important. Require 2 of the following: SAT 820 (exclusive of Writing); ACT 16; GPA 2.0; class rank top 60 percent. Computerized Placement Test required for those with SAT verbal and math scores below 500. Portfolio recommended for all; audition required for music, theater programs; essay required for English-deficient; interview recommended for music, theater programs. **Learning Disabled:** Meet with Director of Disability Services.

**High school preparation.** College-preparatory program required. 12 units required; 18 recommended. Required and recommended units include English 4, mathematics 2-3, social studies 1, history 1, science 2-3 (laboratory 1), foreign language 2, computer science 1, visual/performing arts 1 and academic electives 2.

**2009-2010 Annual costs.** Tuition/fees: $12,264. Room/board: $7,056. Books/supplies: $1,800. Personal expenses: $3,000.

**2008-2009 Financial aid. Need-based:** 76% of total undergraduate aid awarded as scholarships/grants, 24% as loans/jobs. **Non-need-based:** Scholarships awarded for academics, athletics, leadership, music/drama, religious affiliation, state residency.

**Application procedures. Admission:** Priority date 6/1; deadline 8/26. $25 fee, may be waived for applicants with need. Admission notification on a rolling basis. **Financial aid:** Priority date 6/1, closing date 6/30. FAFSA required. Applicants notified on a rolling basis starting 8/1; must reply within 2 week(s) of notification.

**Academics. Special study options:** Cross-registration, double major, dual enrollment of high school students, ESL, honors, independent study, internships, student-designed major, study abroad, teacher certification program. **Credit/placement by examination:** AP, CLEP, IB, SAT, ACT, institutional tests. 16 credit hours maximum toward associate degree, 30 toward bachelor's. CLEP and other exam credits cannot exceed 25 percent of hours needed for degree. **Support services:** Learning center, reduced course load, remedial instruction, study skills assistance, tutoring, writing center.

**Majors. Biology:** General. **Business:** General, accounting, business admin, international, marketing. **Communications:** Broadcast journalism, journalism, media studies, radio/tv. **Education:** Biology, early childhood, elementary, English, mathematics, music, social studies. **Health:** Predental, premedicine, prepharmacy. **History:** General. **Legal studies:** Prelaw. **Liberal arts:** Arts/sciences. **Math:** General. **Parks/recreation:** General, sports admin. **Psychology:** General. **Theology:** Bible, missionary, sacred music, youth ministry. **Visual/performing arts:** Dramatic, music performance, piano/organ, studio arts, voice/opera. **Other:** Health promotion and wellness.

**Most popular majors.** Business/marketing 21%, communications/journalism 9%, education 14%, liberal arts 13%, parks/recreation 9%, theological studies 17%.

**Computing on campus.** 75 workstations in library, computer center, student center. Dormitories wired for high-speed internet access and linked to campus network. Commuter students can connect to campus network. Online library, helpline, wireless network available.

**Student life. Freshman orientation:** Mandatory. Preregistration for classes offered. Held in August. **Policies:** Religious observance required. **Housing:** Guaranteed on-campus for all undergraduates. Single-sex dorms, special housing for disabled, apartments, wellness housing available. $100 deposit, deadline 8/26. **Activities:** Bands, campus ministries, choral groups, drama, literary magazine, music ensembles, musical theater, radio station, student government, student newspaper, symphony orchestra, Baptist student union, athletic ministries, Etude music society, Fellowship of Christians in Service, College Republicans.

**Athletics.** NCAA, NCCAA. **Intercollegiate:** Baseball M, basketball, cheerleading, cross-country, football (tackle) M, golf, soccer, softball W, tennis, volleyball W. **Intramural:** Basketball, football (non-tackle) M, softball, table tennis, tennis, volleyball. **Team name:** Crusaders.

**Student services.** Chaplain/spiritual director, career counseling, student employment services, financial aid counseling, health services, on-campus daycare, personal counseling, placement for graduates. **Physically disabled:** Services for visually impaired.

**Contact.** E-mail: admissions@ngu.edu
Phone: (864) 977-7001 Toll-free number: (800) 468-6642
Fax: (864) 977-7177
Keli Sewell, Vice President for Admissions and Financial Aid, North Greenville University, PO Box 1892, Tigerville, SC 29688-1892

# Presbyterian College
Clinton, South Carolina
CB member
www.presby.edu
CB code: 5540

◗ Private 4-year liberal arts college affiliated with Presbyterian Church (USA)
◗ Residential campus in small town
◗ 1,200 degree-seeking undergraduates: 1% part-time, 51% women, 8% African American, 1% Asian American, 1% Hispanic American
◗ 70% of applicants admitted
◗ SAT or ACT (ACT writing optional), application essay required
◗ 68% graduate within 6 years; 30% enter graduate study

**General.** Founded in 1880. Regionally accredited. **Degrees:** 237 bachelor's awarded. **ROTC:** Army. **Location:** 40 miles from Greenville, 35 miles from Spartanburg. **Calendar:** Semester, limited summer session. **Full-time faculty:** 87 total; 92% have terminal degrees, 6% minority, 31% women. **Part-time faculty:** 61 total; 21% have terminal degrees, 10% minority, 41% women. **Class size:** 59% < 20, 41% 20-39, less than 1% 40-49, less than 1% 50-99. **Special facilities:** Scanning electron and transmission microscopes, ecological research center, Confucius Institute.

**Freshman class profile.** 1,455 applied, 1,017 admitted, 364 enrolled.

| Mid 50% test scores | | | |
|---|---|---|---|
| | | Rank in top tenth: | 35% |
| SAT critical reading: | 490-620 | End year in good standing: | 96% |
| SAT math: | 510-630 | Return as sophomores: | 85% |
| ACT composite: | 21-27 | Out-of-state: | 36% |
| GPA 3.75 or higher: | 37% | Live on campus: | 99% |
| GPA 3.50-3.74: | 17% | International: | 1% |
| GPA 3.0-3.49: | 23% | Fraternities: | 35% |
| GPA 2.0-2.99: | 23% | Sororities: | 38% |
| Rank in top quarter: | 69% | | |

**Basis for selection.** Rigor of high school curriculum most important, followed by test scores, high school GPA, and high school recommendation. Extracurricular involvement and interview considered in some cases. Interview recommended. **Homeschooled:** State high school equivalency certificate required.

**High school preparation.** College-preparatory program required. 18 units required. Required and recommended units include English 4, mathematics 4, social studies 2, history 2, science 2-4 (laboratory 2), foreign language 2-3 and academic electives 2. 2 or more units of laboratory science recommended for science majors.

**2009-2010 Annual costs.** Tuition/fees: $28,880. Room/board: $8,345.

**2009-2010 Financial aid. Need-based:** 314 full-time freshmen applied for aid; 264 were judged to have need; 264 of these received aid. Average need met was 91%. Average scholarship/grant was $29,691; average loan $3,384. 86% of total undergraduate aid awarded as scholarships/grants, 14% as loans/jobs. **Non-need-based:** Awarded to 1,120 full-time undergraduates, including 316 freshmen. Scholarships awarded for academics, alumni affiliation, athletics, job skills, leadership, minority status, music/drama, religious affiliation, ROTC.

**Application procedures. Admission:** Priority date 2/1; deadline 6/30 (postmark date). $40 fee, may be waived for applicants with need. Admission notification 3/15. Must reply by 5/1. **Financial aid:** Priority date 3/15, closing date 6/30. FAFSA required. Applicants notified by 3/1; must reply by 5/1.

**Academics. Special study options:** Combined bachelor's/graduate degree, double major, dual enrollment of high school students, exchange student, honors, independent study, internships, semester at sea, study abroad, teacher certification program, Washington semester. 3-2 environmental science program, 3-2 engineering program, religious educational program, dual degrees offered with Auburn University (AL), Clemson University, Vanderbilt University (TN), University of South Carolina. **Credit/placement by examination:** AP, CLEP, IB, SAT, ACT, institutional tests. 40 credit hours maximum toward bachelor's degree. **Support services:** Pre-admission summer program, reduced course load, study skills assistance, tutoring, writing center.

**Majors. Biology:** General. **Business:** Accounting, business admin. **Computer sciences:** Computer science. **Education:** Early childhood, middle, music, special. **Foreign languages:** General, French, German, Spanish. **History:** General. **Math:** General. **Philosophy/religion:** Philosophy, religion. **Physical sciences:** Chemistry, physics. **Psychology:** General. **Social sciences:** Economics, political science, sociology. **Theology:** Sacred music. **Visual/performing arts:** Art, art history/conservation, dramatic, music performance, studio arts. **Other:** Medical Physics, Religious Education.

**Most popular majors.** Biology 9%, business/marketing 26%, English 6%, history 6%, philosophy/religious studies 10%, psychology 10%, social sciences 11%.

**Computing on campus.** 100 workstations in dormitories, library, computer center, student center. Dormitories wired for high-speed internet access and linked to campus network. Commuter students can connect to campus network. Online course registration, online library, helpline, student web hosting, wireless network available.

**Student life. Freshman orientation:** Mandatory, $100 fee. Preregistration for classes offered. Orientation includes registration, placement testing and organization fair. **Policies:** Honor code governs conduct inside and outside classroom, on and off campus. Cultural Enrichment Program requires students to attend 40 on-campus cultural events as part of graduation requirement. **Housing:** Guaranteed on-campus for all undergraduates. Coed dorms, single-sex dorms, apartments, fraternity/sorority housing, wellness housing available. $400 nonrefundable deposit, deadline 5/1. All full-time students, except those commuting daily from family's residence, required to live on campus. Sorority housing not available. **Activities:** Bands, campus ministries, choral groups, dance, drama, international student organizations, literary magazine, music ensembles, musical theater, opera, radio station, student government, student newspaper, symphony orchestra, Volunteer organizations, multicultural student union, Young Democrats and Republicans, interdenominational organizations, Habitat for Humanity, Amnesty International, Fellowship of Christian Athletes.

**Athletics.** NCAA. **Intercollegiate:** Baseball M, basketball, cheerleading, cross-country, football (tackle) M, golf, lacrosse, soccer, softball W, tennis, volleyball W. **Intramural:** Basketball, football (non-tackle), golf, soccer, softball, tennis, volleyball. **Team name:** Blue Hose.

**Student services.** Chaplain/spiritual director, career counseling, student employment services, financial aid counseling, health services, minority student services, personal counseling, placement for graduates.

**Contact.** E-mail: admissions@presby.edu
Phone: (864) 833-8230 Toll-free number: (800) 960-7583
Fax: (864) 833-8195
Leni Patterson, Dean of Enrollment Management, Presbyterian College, 503 South Broad Street, Clinton, SC 29325

---

## South Carolina State University
**Orangeburg, South Carolina**
www.scsu.edu

CB member
CB code: 5618

- Public 4-year university
- Residential campus in large town

---

- 3,831 degree-seeking undergraduates: 7% part-time, 54% women, 96% African American, 1% Hispanic American
- 649 degree-seeking graduate students
- 78% of applicants admitted
- SAT or ACT (ACT writing optional) required
- 45% graduate within 6 years

**General.** Founded in 1896. Regionally accredited. **Degrees:** 521 bachelor's awarded; master's, doctoral offered. **ROTC:** Army, Air Force. **Location:** 40 miles from Columbia, 70 miles from Charleston. **Calendar:** Semester, limited summer session. **Full-time faculty:** 228 total; 80% have terminal degrees, 73% minority, 43% women. **Part-time faculty:** 61 total; 5% have terminal degrees, 87% minority, 52% women. **Special facilities:** Planetarium, laboratory school, child development learning center.

**Freshman class profile.** 3,715 applied, 2,906 admitted, 723 enrolled.

| Mid 50% test scores | | | |
|---|---|---|---|
| SAT critical reading: | 380-470 | GPA 2.0-2.99: | 51% |
| SAT math: | 390-480 | Rank in top quarter: | 43% |
| ACT composite: | 15-18 | Rank in top tenth: | 6% |
| GPA 3.75 or higher: | 8% | Return as sophomores: | 66% |
| GPA 3.50-3.74: | 8% | Out-of-state: | 30% |
| GPA 3.0-3.49: | 25% | Live on campus: | 90% |

**Basis for selection.** Admission decisions based primarily on high school record, class rank, and standardized test scores. Audition required for music education program; portfolio required for art education program. **Learning Disabled:** Student must submit documentation, which is sent to Student Health Services Center--Disabled Student Support Services.

**High school preparation.** College-preparatory program required. 20 units required. Required units include English 4, mathematics 3, social studies 3, science 3 (laboratory 3), foreign language 2 and academic electives 4. 1 physical education or ROTC required.

**2009-2010 Annual costs.** Tuition/fees: $8,462; $16,626 out-of-state. Room/board: $8,662. Books/supplies: $1,200. Personal expenses: $3,150.

**2008-2009 Financial aid. Non-need-based:** Scholarships awarded for academics, athletics, ROTC.

**Application procedures. Admission:** Closing date 7/31 (postmark date). $25 fee, may be waived for applicants with need. Admission notification on a rolling basis. **Financial aid:** Closing date 5/1. FAFSA required. Applicants notified on a rolling basis starting 4/15; must reply by 7/1 or within 2 week(s) of notification.

**Academics. Special study options:** Cooperative education, cross-registration, distance learning, double major, dual enrollment of high school students, exchange student, honors, independent study, internships, liberal arts/career combination, student-designed major, study abroad, teacher certification program, Washington semester. **Credit/placement by examination:** AP, CLEP, institutional tests. 30 credit hours maximum toward bachelor's degree. **Support services:** Learning center, pre-admission summer program, tutoring, writing center.

**Majors. Agriculture:** Agribusiness operations. **Biology:** General. **Business:** Accounting, business admin, managerial economics, marketing. **Communications:** Media studies. **Computer sciences:** General. **Education:** Art, business, early childhood, elementary, family/consumer sciences, middle, music, physical, special, technology/industrial arts. **Engineering:** Nuclear. **Engineering technology:** Civil, electrical, industrial, mechanical. **Family/consumer sciences:** General, food/nutrition. **Foreign languages:** General. **Health:** Audiology/speech pathology, nursing (RN). **History:** General. **Math:** General. **Parks/recreation:** Health/fitness. **Physical sciences:** Chemistry, physics. **Protective services:** Law enforcement admin. **Psychology:** General. **Public administration:** Social work. **Social sciences:** General, political science, sociology. **Visual/performing arts:** Dramatic, music management, music performance, studio arts.

**Most popular majors.** Biology 9%, business/marketing 18%, education 9%, engineering/engineering technologies 9%, family/consumer sciences 10%, health sciences 6%, psychology 8%, public administration/social services 6%.

**Computing on campus.** 300 workstations in dormitories, library, computer center, student center. Dormitories wired for high-speed internet access and linked to campus network. Commuter students can connect to campus network. Online course registration, online library, helpline, repair service, wireless network available.

**Student life. Freshman orientation:** Available, $100 fee. Preregistration for classes offered. **Housing:** Guaranteed on-campus for freshmen. Single-sex dorms, apartments available. $25 deposit. **Activities:** Bands, choral groups, dance, drama, international student organizations, music ensembles, radio station, student government, student newspaper.

**Athletics.** NCAA. **Intercollegiate:** Basketball, cheerleading, cross-country, football (tackle) M, golf, soccer W, softball W, tennis, track and field, volleyball W. **Intramural:** Basketball, bowling, softball. **Team name:** Bulldogs.

**Student services.** Adult student services, alcohol/substance abuse counseling, chaplain/spiritual director, career counseling, services for economically disadvantaged, student employment services, financial aid counseling, health services, minority student services, personal counseling, placement for graduates, veterans' counselor. **Physically disabled:** Services for visually, speech, hearing impaired.

**Contact.** E-mail: admissions@scsu.edu
Phone: (803) 536-7185 Toll-free number: (800) 260-5956
Fax: (803) 536-8990
Antonio Boyle, Assistant Vice President of Enrollment Management and Director of Admissions, South Carolina State University, 300 College Street NE, Orangeburg, SC 29117

## South University: Columbia
### Columbia, South Carolina
### www.southuniversity.edu          CB code: 5097

- For-profit 4-year university
- Commuter campus in small city
- 1,006 degree-seeking undergraduates: 37% part-time, 81% women
- 250 graduate students

**General.** Founded in 1935. Regionally accredited. **Degrees:** 49 bachelor's, 43 associate awarded; master's offered. **Location:** 5 miles from downtown. **Calendar:** Quarter, extensive summer session. **Full-time faculty:** 36 total; 3% have terminal degrees, 31% minority, 50% women. **Part-time faculty:** 57 total; 60% have terminal degrees, 56% minority, 63% women.

**Basis for selection.** Open admission, but selective for some programs. SAT or ACT may be submitted in place of required institutional tests for placement. Score report due by September 15. **Homeschooled:** Students must provide evidence that home schooling was conducted in accordance with state laws. A certificate of attendance or completion is not sufficient.

**2009-2010 Annual costs.** Tuition/fees: $14,985.

**Financial aid.** All financial aid based on need.

**Application procedures. Admission:** No deadline. $50 fee. Admission notification on a rolling basis. **Financial aid:** Priority date 5/30; no closing date. FAFSA required. Applicants notified on a rolling basis starting 5/30.

**Academics. Special study options:** Distance learning, internships, weekend college. **Credit/placement by examination:** AP, CLEP, institutional tests. **Support services:** Reduced course load, remedial instruction, study skills assistance, tutoring, writing center.

**Majors. Business:** Business admin. **Computer sciences:** Information technology. **Health:** Health care admin, health services, nursing (RN). **Legal studies:** Paralegal. **Protective services:** Police science. **Psychology:** General. **Visual/performing arts:** Graphic design.

**Most popular majors.** Business/marketing 27%, computer/information sciences 6%, health sciences 29%, legal studies 27%, security/protective services 12%.

**Computing on campus.** Commuter students can connect to campus network. Online library, helpline, wireless network available.

**Student life. Freshman orientation:** Mandatory. Preregistration for classes offered.

**Student services.** Adult student services, career counseling, student employment services, financial aid counseling, personal counseling, placement for graduates, veterans' counselor. **Physically disabled:** Services for visually, speech, hearing impaired.

**Contact.** Phone: (803) 799-9082 Toll-free number: (866) 629-3031
Fax: (803) 799-9038
Trisha Wade, Director of Admissions, South University: Columbia, 9 Science Court, Columbia, SC 29203

## Southern Methodist College
### Orangeburg, South Carolina
### www.smcollege.edu

- Private 4-year Bible college
- Large town
- 30 degree-seeking undergraduates

**General.** Regionally accredited; also accredited by TRACS. **Degrees:** 4 bachelor's, 6 associate awarded. **Calendar:** Semester. **Full-time faculty:** 5 total. **Part-time faculty:** 6 total.

**Basis for selection.** Open admission.

**2009-2010 Annual costs.** Tuition/fees: $7,520.

**Application procedures. Admission:** No deadline. $35 fee.

**Academics. Credit/placement by examination:** CLEP.

**Majors. Theology:** Bible.

**Contact.** E-mail: smcinfo@smcollege.edu
Phone: (803) 268-1322
Vic Reasoner, Director of Admissions, Southern Methodist College, 541 Broughton St., Orangeburg, SC 29115

## Southern Wesleyan University
### Central, South Carolina
### www.swu.edu          CB code: 5896

- Private 4-year university and liberal arts college affiliated with Wesleyan Church
- Commuter campus in small town
- 1,692 degree-seeking undergraduates: 1% part-time, 63% women, 29% African American, 2% Hispanic American, 1% Native American, 1% international
- 705 degree-seeking graduate students
- SAT or ACT (ACT writing optional), application essay required
- 43% graduate within 6 years

**General.** Founded in 1906. Regionally accredited. **Degrees:** 322 bachelor's, 103 associate awarded; master's offered. **ROTC:** Army, Air Force. **Location:** 25 miles from Greenville. **Calendar:** Semester, limited summer session. **Full-time faculty:** 50 total; 76% have terminal degrees, 18% minority, 30% women. **Part-time faculty:** 169 total; 34% have terminal degrees, 28% minority, 42% women.

**Freshman class profile.**

| Mid 50% test scores | | | |
|---|---|---|---|
| SAT critical reading: | 440-540 | GPA 2.0-2.99: | 14% |
| SAT math: | 440-550 | Rank in top quarter: | 36% |
| SAT writing: | 410-540 | Rank in top tenth: | 13% |
| ACT composite: | 18-22 | Return as sophomores: | 67% |
| GPA 3.75 or higher: | 40% | Out-of-state: | 21% |
| GPA 3.50-3.74: | 15% | Live on campus: | 73% |
| GPA 3.0-3.49: | 30% | International: | 1% |

**Basis for selection.** GPA, class rank, test scores, and religious commitment important. Recommendations considered. Students admitted conditionally if combined SAT score is less than 800 (exclusive of Writing) or high school GPA is less than 2.3, and rank in bottom half of class. Students admitted conditionally take limited number of course hours and are on academic warning. Audition required for music; interview recommended for applicants with special physical, emotional problems.

**High school preparation.** College-preparatory program recommended. 10 units required. Required units include English 4, mathematics 2, social studies 2 and science 2.

**2010-2011 Annual costs.** Tuition/fees (projected): $19,500. Room/board: $8,150. Books/supplies: $950. Personal expenses: $1,000.

**2009-2010 Financial aid. Need-based:** 162 full-time freshmen applied for aid; 154 were judged to have need; 153 of these received aid. Average need met was 81%. Average scholarship/grant was $15,065; average loan $3,106. 61% of total undergraduate aid awarded as scholarships/grants, 39% as loans/jobs. **Non-need-based:** Scholarships awarded for academics, athletics, music/drama.

**Application procedures. Admission:** Closing date 8/1 (postmark date). $25 fee, may be waived for applicants with need. Admission notification on a rolling basis beginning on or about 10/1. Must reply by 5/1. **Financial aid.** Priority date 3/31, closing date 6/30. FAFSA, institutional form required. Applicants notified on a rolling basis starting 2/1; must reply within 2 week(s) of notification.

**Academics. Special study options:** Cooperative education, cross-registration, distance learning, double major, dual enrollment of high school students, ESL, honors, independent study, internships, liberal arts/career combination, student-designed major, study abroad, teacher certification program, Washington semester. **Credit/placement by examination:** AP, CLEP, SAT, ACT, institutional tests. 48 credit hours maximum toward associate degree, 68 toward bachelor's. **Support services:** Learning center, reduced course load, remedial instruction, study skills assistance, tutoring, writing center.

**Majors. Biology:** General. **Business:** Accounting, business admin. **Communications:** General. **Computer sciences:** General, computer forensics. **Education:** Biology, early childhood, elementary, English, mathematics, music, physical, special. **Health:** Medical radiologic technology/radiation therapy, predental, premedicine. **History:** General. **Math:** General. **Parks/recreation:** General, sports admin. **Philosophy/religion:** Religion. **Physical sciences:** Chemistry. **Protective services:** Criminal justice, forensics. **Psychology:** General. **Public administration:** Human services. **Social sciences:** General.

**Most popular majors.** Business/marketing 69%, education 8%.

**Computing on campus.** 256 workstations in dormitories, library, computer center, student center. Dormitories wired for high-speed internet access and linked to campus network. Commuter students can connect to campus network. Online course registration, online library, helpline, repair service, wireless network available.

**Student life. Freshman orientation:** Mandatory. Preregistration for classes offered. Held at the beginning of fall and spring semesters. **Policies:** Students must agree to abide by lifestyle expectations of university. Religious observance required. **Housing:** Guaranteed on-campus for all undergraduates. Coed dorms, single-sex dorms, special housing for disabled, apartments, wellness housing available. $200 fully refundable deposit. **Activities:** Bands, campus ministries, choral groups, drama, literary magazine, music ensembles, musical theater, student government, Christian Service Organization, Student Missions Fellowship, Rotaract, Fellowship of Christian Athletes, student activities board, Habitat for Humanity.

**Athletics.** NAIA, NCCAA. **Intercollegiate:** Baseball M, basketball, cross-country, golf M, soccer, softball W, volleyball W. **Intramural:** Basketball, football (non-tackle), soccer, softball, table tennis, tennis, volleyball. **Team name:** Warriors.

**Student services.** Adult student services, alcohol/substance abuse counseling, chaplain/spiritual director, career counseling, financial aid counseling, health services, minority student services, personal counseling. **Physically disabled:** Services for visually, hearing impaired.

**Contact.** E-mail: admissions@swu.edu
Phone: (864) 644-5550 Toll-free number: (800) 282-8798
Fax: (864) 644-5972
Amanda Young, Director of Admissions, Southern Wesleyan University, PO Box 1020, Central, SC 29630-1020

---

## University of South Carolina
**Columbia, South Carolina**  **CB member**
**www.sc.edu**  **CB code: 5818**

- Public 4-year university
- Residential campus in small city
- 20,135 degree-seeking undergraduates: 6% part-time, 54% women
- 7,521 degree-seeking graduate students
- 64% of applicants admitted
- SAT or ACT with writing required
- 69% graduate within 6 years

**General.** Founded in 1801. Regionally accredited. **Degrees:** 4,060 bachelor's, 7 associate awarded; master's, doctoral, professional offered. **ROTC:** Army, Naval, Air Force. **Location:** 70 miles from Charlotte, North Carolina. **Calendar:** Semester, extensive summer session. **Full-time faculty:** 1,142 total; 84% have terminal degrees, 11% minority, 40% women. **Part-time faculty:** 518 total; 34% have terminal degrees, 10% minority, 49% women. **Class size:** 40% < 20, 43% 20-39, 6% 40-49, 8% 50-99, 3% >100. **Special facilities:** Observatory, arboretum, green dorm with learning center focusing on sustainability.

**Freshman class profile.** 17,694 applied, 11,262 admitted, 3,917 enrolled.

| Mid 50% test scores | | | |
|---|---|---|---|
| SAT critical reading: | 530-640 | Rank in top quarter: | 60% |
| SAT math: | 560-650 | Rank in top tenth: | 27% |
| ACT composite: | 24-29 | Return as sophomores: | 87% |
| GPA 3.75 or higher: | 58% | Out-of-state: | 37% |
| GPA 3.50-3.74: | 16% | Live on campus: | 94% |
| GPA 3.0-3.49: | 20% | Fraternities: | 23% |
| GPA 2.0-2.99: | 6% | Sororities: | 34% |

**Basis for selection.** Admission based on high school curriculum, grades in required high school courses, SAT and ACT scores. **Learning Disabled:** Diagnostic tests required for learning disabled students.

**High school preparation.** College-preparatory program required. 18 units required. Required units include English 4, mathematics 4, social studies 2, history 1, science 3 (laboratory 3), foreign language 2, visual/performing arts 1 and academic electives 1.

**2009-2010 Annual costs.** Tuition/fees: $9,156; $23,732 out-of-state. Health professions (pharmacy, health, nursing), law and medical professions have higher undergraduate and graduate fees. Room/board: $6,986. Books/supplies: $900. Personal expenses: $2,420.

**2009-2010 Financial aid. Need-based:** 2,699 full-time freshmen applied for aid; 1,560 were judged to have need; 1,539 of these received aid. Average need met was 75%. Average scholarship/grant was $4,650; average loan $2,703. 55% of total undergraduate aid awarded as scholarships/grants, 45% as loans/jobs. **Non-need-based:** Awarded to 11,623 full-time undergraduates, including 3,251 freshmen. Scholarships awarded for academics, alumni affiliation, art, athletics, job skills, leadership, minority status, music/drama, religious affiliation, ROTC, state residency.

**Application procedures. Admission:** Closing date 12/1 (postmark date). $50 fee. Application must be submitted on paper. Admission notification on a rolling basis beginning on or about 3/15. Must reply by May 1 or within 2 week(s) if notified thereafter. **Financial aid:** Priority date 4/1; no closing date. FAFSA required. Applicants notified on a rolling basis starting 4/1.

**Academics.** One-month May term focusing on specialized topics. **Special study options:** Accelerated study, combined bachelor's/graduate degree, cooperative education, cross-registration, distance learning, double major, dual enrollment of high school students, ESL, exchange student, external degree, honors, independent study, internships, student-designed major, study abroad, teacher certification program, weekend college. Alternative Spring Break, Dobson Volunteer Service Program, International Program for Students, Undergraduate Research, Magellan Scholars. **Credit/placement by examination:** AP, CLEP, IB, institutional tests. Maximum number of semester hours of credit by examination allowed varies according to degree and program of study. **Support services:** Learning center, reduced course load, study skills assistance, tutoring, writing center.

**Honors college/program.** To be competitive for admission, students must have minimum 1300 SAT score (exclusive of Writing) and minimum high school GPA of 3.5. 600 admitted to yield freshman class of 275. Academic program consists of 115-125 honors classes per semester across most disciplines and levels.

**Majors. Area/ethnic studies:** African-American, European, Latin American, women's. **Biology:** General, marine. **Business:** Accounting, business admin, finance, hospitality admin, insurance, management science, managerial economics, marketing, office management, real estate, retailing. **Communications:** Advertising, broadcast journalism, journalism, media studies, public relations. **Computer sciences:** General. **Conservation:** Environmental science. **Education:** Art, early childhood, physical. **Engineering:** Biomedical, chemical, civil, computer, electrical, mechanical. **Foreign languages:** Classics, French, German, Italian, Russian, Spanish. **Health:** Cardiovascular technology, nursing (RN). **History:** General. **Liberal arts:** Arts/sciences. **Math:** General, statistics. **Parks/recreation:** Exercise sciences, sports admin. **Philosophy/religion:** Philosophy, religion. **Physical sciences:** Chemistry, geology, geophysics, physics. **Protective services:** Law enforcement admin. **Psychology:** Experimental. **Social sciences:** Anthropology, economics, geography, international relations, political science, sociology. **Visual/performing arts:** Art history/conservation, dance, dramatic, film/cinema, studio arts. **Other:** Business and technology education, Technology support and training management, Visual communications.

**Most popular majors.** Business/marketing 27%, communications/journalism 7%, education 7%, health sciences 6%, parks/recreation 7%, social sciences 9%, visual/performing arts 6%.

**Computing on campus.** 2,800 workstations in dormitories, library, computer center, student center. Dormitories wired for high-speed internet access and linked to campus network. Commuter students can connect to campus network. Online course registration, online library, helpline, wireless network available.

**Student life. Freshman orientation:** Available, $70 fee. Preregistration for classes offered. Parents may also attend to view campus for $40 fee. **Housing:** Guaranteed on-campus for freshmen. Coed dorms, single-sex dorms, special housing for disabled, apartments, fraternity/sorority housing, wellness housing available. $145 partly refundable deposit, deadline 5/1. Honors housing, Preston Residential College, communities for pre-medical, engineering, athletic, teaching fellows, global, and environmentally friendly available. **Activities:** Bands, campus ministries, choral groups, dance, drama, film society, international student organizations, literary magazine, music ensembles, Model UN, musical theater, opera, radio station, student government, student newspaper, symphony orchestra, TV station, Baptist Collegiate Ministry, University Ambassadors, Association of African American Students, Habitat for Humanity, Dance Marathon, cultural exchange association, orientation leaders association, Hill of the Lord, BGLSA.

**Athletics.** NCAA. **Intercollegiate:** Baseball M, basketball, cross-country W, diving, equestrian W; football (tackle) M, golf, soccer, softball W, swimming, tennis, track and field, volleyball W. **Intramural:** Badminton, basketball, bowling, golf, racquetball, soccer, softball, swimming, table tennis, tennis, volleyball, weight lifting. **Team name:** Fighting Gamecocks.

**Student services.** Adult student services, alcohol/substance abuse counseling, career counseling, services for economically disadvantaged, student employment services, financial aid counseling, health services, minority student services, personal counseling, placement for graduates, veterans' counselor, women's services. **Physically disabled:** Services for visually, speech, hearing impaired. **Learning disabled:** Comprehensive services available.

**Contact.** E-mail: admissions-ugrad@sc.edu
Phone: (803) 777-7700 Toll-free number: (800) 868-5872
Fax: (803) 777-0101
Mary Wagner, Senior Associate Director of Undergraduate Admissions, University of South Carolina, Office of Undergraduate Admissions, Columbia, SC 29208

---

## University of South Carolina at Aiken

**Aiken, South Carolina** — **CB member**
web.usca.edu — **CB code: 5840**

- Public 4-year university and liberal arts college
- Commuter campus in large town
- 2,919 degree-seeking undergraduates: 16% part-time, 66% women, 28% African American, 1% Asian American, 3% Hispanic American, 1% international
- 67 degree-seeking graduate students
- 38% of applicants admitted
- SAT or ACT (ACT writing recommended) required
- 35% graduate within 6 years

**General.** Founded in 1961. Regionally accredited. **Degrees:** 461 bachelor's awarded; master's offered. **Location:** 55 miles from Columbia; 15 miles from Augusta, Georgia. **Calendar:** Semester, limited summer session. **Full-time faculty:** 150 total; 73% have terminal degrees, 8% minority, 47% women. **Part-time faculty:** 83 total; 24% have terminal degrees, 8% minority, 46% women. **Class size:** 54% < 20, 45% 20-39, less than 1% 40-49, less than 1% 50-99. **Special facilities:** Fine arts center, science center, natatorium, planetarium, convocation center.

**Freshman class profile.** 2,712 applied, 1,017 admitted, 689 enrolled.

| Mid 50% test scores | | | |
|---|---|---|---|
| SAT critical reading: | 430-540 | Rank in top quarter: | 43% |
| SAT math: | 450-550 | Rank in top tenth: | 15% |
| SAT writing: | 410-520 | End year in good standing: | 85% |
| ACT composite: | 18-23 | Return as sophomores: | 69% |
| GPA 3.75 or higher: | 40% | Out-of-state: | 9% |
| GPA 3.50-3.74: | 14% | Live on campus: | 55% |
| GPA 3.0-3.49: | 33% | International: | 1% |
| GPA 2.0-2.99: | 13% | Fraternities: | 5% |
| | | Sororities: | 9% |

**Basis for selection.** Test scores, high school core GPA important. Admission based on course selection, standardized test scores and a predicted college GPA. Audition, essay, interview, portfolio recommended.

**High school preparation.** 21 units required. Required units include English 4, mathematics 4, social studies 2, history 1, science 3 (laboratory 3), foreign language 2, computer science 1, visual/performing arts 1 and academic electives 4. Physical education or ROTC of 1 unit; elective college preparatory credits must come from 3 different fields.

**2009-2010 Annual costs.** Tuition/fees: $7,950; $15,682 out-of-state. Room/board: $6,400. Books/supplies: $1,080. Personal expenses: $1,690.

---

**2008-2009 Financial aid. Need-based:** 540 full-time freshmen applied for aid; 352 were judged to have need; 352 of these received aid. Average need met was 74%. Average scholarship/grant was $7,871; average loan $3,170. 43% of total undergraduate aid awarded as scholarships/grants, 57% as loans/jobs. **Non-need-based:** Awarded to 802 full-time undergraduates, including 218 freshmen. Scholarships awarded for academics, alumni affiliation, art, athletics, leadership, minority status, music/drama, state residency.

**Application procedures. Admission:** Priority date 7/1; deadline 8/1 (postmark date). $45 fee, may be waived for applicants with need. Admission notification on a rolling basis beginning on or about 9/1. Must reply by May 1 or within 3 week(s) if notified thereafter. **Financial aid:** Priority date 3/15; no closing date. FAFSA required. Applicants notified on a rolling basis starting 11/1; must reply within 2 week(s) of notification.

**Academics. Special study options:** Cooperative education, distance learning, double major, dual enrollment of high school students, ESL, honors, independent study, internships, student-designed major, study abroad, teacher certification program. **Credit/placement by examination:** AP, CLEP, IB, institutional tests. 30 credit hours maximum toward bachelor's degree. **Support services:** Learning center, study skills assistance, tutoring, writing center.

**Majors. Biology:** General. **Business:** General. **Communications:** General. **Computer sciences:** Computer science. **Education:** General, early childhood, elementary, English, mathematics, middle, music, science, secondary, social science, social studies, special. **Health:** Nursing (RN). **History:** General. **Interdisciplinary:** Math/computer science. **Math:** Applied. **Parks/recreation:** Exercise sciences. **Physical sciences:** Chemistry. **Psychology:** General. **Social sciences:** Political science, sociology. **Visual/performing arts:** Studio arts.

**Most popular majors.** Biology 8%, business/marketing 23%, communications/journalism 7%, education 12%, health sciences 14%, parks/recreation 7%, social sciences 12%.

**Computing on campus.** 577 workstations in dormitories, library, computer center, student center. Dormitories wired for high-speed internet access and linked to campus network. Commuter students can connect to campus network. Online course registration, online library, helpline, wireless network available.

**Student life. Freshman orientation:** Mandatory, $75 fee. Preregistration for classes offered. Held in June, July, and August. June and July orientations offer registration. **Housing:** Coed dorms, special housing for disabled, apartments, wellness housing available. $25 partly refundable deposit. **Activities:** Bands, campus ministries, dance, drama, international student organizations, music ensembles, musical theater, student government, student newspaper, symphony orchestra, Campus Crusade for Christ, honor societies, Association for Women's Issues, Pacer Union Board, High Adventure Club, African American Students' Alliance, Community Action Board, College Republicans.

**Athletics.** NCAA. **Intercollegiate:** Baseball M, basketball, cheerleading, cross-country W, golf M, soccer, softball W, tennis, volleyball W. **Intramural:** Badminton, baseball M, basketball, bowling, golf, soccer, softball, table tennis, tennis, volleyball. **Team name:** Pacers.

**Student services.** Adult student services, alcohol/substance abuse counseling, career counseling, student employment services, financial aid counseling, health services, minority student services, on-campus daycare, personal counseling, placement for graduates, veterans' counselor. **Physically disabled:** Services for visually, speech, hearing impaired.

**Contact.** E-mail: admit@usca.edu
Phone: (803) 641-3366 Toll-free number: (888) 969-8722
Fax: (803) 641-3727
Andrew Hendrix, Director of Admissions, University of South Carolina at Aiken, 471 University Parkway, Aiken, SC 29801-6399

---

## University of South Carolina at Beaufort

**Bluffton, South Carolina** — **CB member**
www.uscb.edu — **CB code: 5845**

- Public 4-year university and liberal arts college
- Commuter campus in large town
- 1,319 degree-seeking undergraduates: 23% part-time, 63% women, 17% African American, 1% Asian American, 6% Hispanic American, 1% Native American, 1% international
- SAT or ACT (ACT writing optional) required

**General.** Founded in 1959. Regionally accredited. South Campus located at Gateway to Hilton Head, North Campus located in Historic Beaufort.

**Degrees:** 116 bachelor's, 5 associate awarded. **Location:** 72 miles from Charleston, 42 miles from Savannah, Georgia. **Calendar:** Semester, limited summer session. **Full-time faculty:** 62 total; 76% have terminal degrees, 11% minority, 39% women. **Part-time faculty:** 91 total. **Class size:** 54% < 20, 41% 20-39, 2% 40-49, 2% 50-99. **Special facilities:** Performing arts center.

### Freshman class profile.

| | | | |
|---|---|---|---|
| Out-of-state: | 20% | International: | 1% |
| Live on campus: | 40% | | |

**Basis for selection.** Test scores, rigor of secondary school record important; academic GPA considered.

**High school preparation.** 20 units required. Required units include English 4, mathematics 3, social studies 2, history 1, science 3 (laboratory 3), foreign language 2 and academic electives 5. Electives must be from 3 areas. Computer Science course recommended. 1 PE or ROTC required.

**2009-2010 Annual costs.** Tuition/fees: $7,330; $15,180 out-of-state. Room/board: $6,100. Books/supplies: $975. Personal expenses: $1,512.

**2009-2010 Financial aid. Non-need-based:** Scholarships awarded for academics, state residency.

**Application procedures. Admission:** No deadline. $40 fee, may be waived for applicants with need. Admission notification on a rolling basis beginning on or about 2/1. **Financial aid:** Priority date 4/15; no closing date. FAFSA required. Applicants notified on a rolling basis starting 5/31; must reply within 2 week(s) of notification.

**Academics. Special study options:** Combined bachelor's/graduate degree, cooperative education, distance learning, dual enrollment of high school students, independent study, internships, student-designed major, study abroad, teacher certification program, weekend college. **Credit/placement by examination:** AP, CLEP, institutional tests. 15 credit hours maximum toward associate degree, 30 toward bachelor's. **Support services:** Learning center, reduced course load, study skills assistance, tutoring, writing center.

**Majors. Biology:** General. **Business:** Business admin, hospitality admin. **Education:** Early childhood. **Foreign languages:** Spanish. **Health:** Nursing (RN). **History:** General. **Liberal arts:** Arts/sciences. **Psychology:** General. **Social sciences:** General.

**Most popular majors.** Business/marketing 35%, education 10%, English 6%, psychology 16%, social sciences 19%.

**Computing on campus.** 114 workstations in library, computer center. Dormitories wired for high-speed internet access. Online course registration, online library available.

**Student life. Freshman orientation:** Mandatory. Preregistration for classes offered. **Housing:** Special housing for disabled, apartments, wellness housing available. **Activities:** Choral groups, drama, literary magazine, musical theater, student government, student newspaper, African American student association, Christian student fellowship, business club, veterans association, education club, Gamma Beta Phi honor society, psychology/sociology/anthropology club.

**Athletics.** NAIA. **Intercollegiate:** Baseball M, cross-country, golf. **Intramural:** Football (non-tackle), soccer. **Team name:** Sand Sharks.

**Student services.** Career counseling, services for economically disadvantaged, student employment services, financial aid counseling, personal counseling, veterans' counselor.

**Contact.** E-mail: admissions@uscb.edu
Phone: (843) 208-8000 Toll-free number: (877) 885-5271
Fax: (843) 208-8290
Joffery Blair, Director of Admissions, University of South Carolina at Beaufort, One University Boulevard, Bluffton, SC 29909

## University of South Carolina Upstate
### Spartanburg, South Carolina
www.uscupstate.edu                    **CB code: 5850**

- Public 4-year university
- Commuter campus in small city
- 5,001 degree-seeking undergraduates: 11% part-time, 65% women, 26% African American, 2% Asian American, 3% Hispanic American, 1% international
- 13 degree-seeking graduate students
- 78% of applicants admitted
- SAT or ACT (ACT writing optional) required
- 37% graduate within 6 years

**General.** Founded in 1967. Regionally accredited. **Degrees:** 997 bachelor's awarded; master's offered. **ROTC:** Army. **Location:** 30 miles from Greenville, 70 miles from Charlotte, North Carolina. **Calendar:** Semester, extensive summer session. **Full-time faculty:** 231 total; 74% have terminal degrees, 14% minority, 56% women. **Part-time faculty:** 171 total; 36% have terminal degrees, 9% minority, 54% women. **Class size:** 49% < 20, 47% 20-39, 3% 40-49, less than 1% 50-99. **Special facilities:** Center for international studies and language services, audiovisual production center, digital lab, centers for interdisciplinary studies, watershed ecology center.

**Freshman class profile.** 2,822 applied, 2,213 admitted, 875 enrolled.

| Mid 50% test scores | | Rank in top quarter: | 36% |
|---|---|---|---|
| SAT critical reading: | 420-520 | Rank in top tenth: | 11% |
| SAT math: | 430-520 | Return as sophomores: | 64% |
| SAT writing: | 420-500 | Out-of-state: | 4% |
| ACT composite: | 18-22 | Live on campus: | 53% |
| GPA 3.75 or higher: | 36% | International: | 1% |
| GPA 3.50-3.74: | 19% | Fraternities: | 1% |
| GPA 3.0-3.49: | 29% | Sororities: | 1% |
| GPA 2.0-2.99: | 16% | | |

**Basis for selection.** Cumulative average of C or better in preparatory courses and minimum 850 SAT (exclusive of Writing), or 18 ACT required. Higher grades may offset lower SAT/ACT scores, and higher SAT/ACT scores may offset lower grades. All applicants who are 21 years of age or younger, with the exception of transfer applicants who have completed at least 30 semester hours of college credit, must submit results of the SAT or the ACT. Applicants who are 22 years of age or older are not required to submit SAT/ACT scores. Interviews recommended.

**High school preparation.** College-preparatory program required. 20 units required; 22 recommended. Required and recommended units include English 4, mathematics 3-4, social studies 2, history 1, science 3 (laboratory 3), foreign language 2-3 and academic electives 4. Students who graduated from high school between 1988-2000 must meet above requirements. However, these students need 2 rather than 3 laboratory sciences and 1 rather than 4 electives.

**2009-2010 Annual costs.** Tuition/fees: $8,812; $17,454 out-of-state. Room/board: $6,580. Books/supplies: $1,000. Personal expenses: $200.

**2008-2009 Financial aid. Need-based:** 571 full-time freshmen applied for aid; 449 were judged to have need; 446 of these received aid. Average need met was 65%. Average scholarship/grant was $4,475; average loan $3,049. 42% of total undergraduate aid awarded as scholarships/grants, 58% as loans/jobs. **Non-need-based:** Awarded to 1,298 full-time undergraduates, including 446 freshmen. Scholarships awarded for academics, athletics, minority status, ROTC, state residency. **Additional information:** Out-of-state students who are recipients of financial aid may qualify for out-of-state fee waiver. Educational benefits available to veterans and children of deceased/disabled veterans.

**Application procedures. Admission:** Priority date 8/15; no deadline. $40 fee, may be waived for applicants with need. Admission notification on a rolling basis beginning on or about 9/15. **Financial aid:** Priority date 3/1, closing date 7/15. FAFSA, institutional form required. Applicants notified on a rolling basis starting 5/1; must reply within 2 week(s) of notification.

**Academics. Special study options:** Accelerated study, cooperative education, cross-registration, distance learning, double major, ESL, exchange student, honors, independent study, internships, liberal arts/career combination, student-designed major, study abroad, teacher certification program, Washington semester. **Credit/placement by examination:** AP, CLEP, IB, institutional tests. 30 credit hours maximum toward bachelor's degree. Credit also awarded for: American College Testing Program, Defense Activity for Nontraditional Education Support, Institution Credit by Examination, Military Service School Credit, Credit for Non-collegiate Programs, and Correspondence Course Credits. **Support services:** Learning center, reduced course load, remedial instruction, study skills assistance, tutoring, writing center.

**Majors. Biology:** General. **Business:** Business admin. **Communications:** General. **Computer sciences:** General, information systems, information technology. **Education:** Early childhood, elementary, physical, secondary, special. **Engineering technology:** Industrial management. **Foreign languages:** Spanish. **Health:** Nursing (RN). **History:** General. **Interdisciplinary:** Accounting/computer science. **Liberal arts:** Arts/sciences. **Math:** General, applied. **Physical sciences:** Chemistry. **Protective services:** Criminal justice. **Psychology:** General. **Social sciences:** Political science, sociology. **Visual/performing arts:** Commercial/advertising art, design.

**Most popular majors.** Business/marketing 17%, computer/information sciences 6%, education 16%, health sciences 27%, liberal arts 9%, psychology 6%.

**Computing on campus.** 600 workstations in dormitories, library, computer center, student center. Dormitories wired for high-speed internet access and linked to campus network. Commuter students can connect to campus network. Online course registration, online library, helpline, repair service, student web hosting, wireless network available.

**Student life. Freshman orientation:** Available. Preregistration for classes offered. **Housing:** Coed dorms, apartments, wellness housing available. $135 fully refundable deposit, deadline 6/1. **Activities:** Jazz band, campus ministries, choral groups, dance, drama, international student organizations, literary magazine, music ensembles, student government, student newspaper, African-American Association, Baptist student union, Campus Crusade for Christ, College Republicans, Young Democrats, student education association, campus activity board, Association for the Education of Young Children, environmental club.

**Athletics.** NCAA. **Intercollegiate:** Baseball M, basketball, cheerleading, cross-country, golf, soccer, softball W, tennis, track and field, volleyball W. **Intramural:** Basketball, bowling, football (non-tackle), soccer, softball, table tennis, tennis, track and field, volleyball. **Team name:** Spartans.

**Student services.** Adult student services, alcohol/substance abuse counseling, chaplain/spiritual director, career counseling, services for economically disadvantaged, student employment services, financial aid counseling, health services, minority student services, on-campus daycare, personal counseling, placement for graduates, veterans' counselor, women's services. **Physically disabled:** Services for visually, speech, hearing impaired. **Learning disabled:** Comprehensive services available.

**Contact.** E-mail: dstewart@uscupstate.edu
Phone: (864) 503-5246 Toll-free number: (800) 277-8727
Fax: (864) 503-5727
Donette Stewart, Assistant Vice Chancellor for Enrollment Services, University of South Carolina Upstate, 800 University Way, Spartanburg, SC 29303

---

## Voorhees College
**Denmark, South Carolina**
www.voorhees.edu
**CB member**
**CB code: 5863**

- Private 4-year liberal arts college affiliated with Episcopal Church
- Residential campus in small town

**General.** Founded in 1897. Regionally accredited. **Location:** 50 miles from Columbia and Augusta, Georgia. **Calendar:** Semester.

**Annual costs/financial aid.** Tuition/fees (2009-2010): $10,164. Room/board: $6,314. Books/supplies: $600. Personal expenses: $1,365. Need-based financial aid available to full-time and part-time students.

**Contact.** Phone: (803) 780-1031
Dean, Enrollment Management, 213 Wiggins Road, Denmark, SC 29042

---

## W.L. Bonner Bible College
**Columbia, South Carolina**
www.wlbonnercollege.org

- Private 4-year Bible college
- Small city

**General.** Accredited by ABHE. **Calendar:** Semester.

**Contact.** Phone: (803) 754-3950
Registrar, 4430 Argent Court, Columbia, SC 29203

---

## Winthrop University
**Rock Hill, South Carolina**
www.winthrop.edu
**CB member**
**CB code: 5910**

- Public 4-year university
- Residential campus in small city
- 4,770 degree-seeking undergraduates: 7% part-time, 68% women, 27% African American, 2% Asian American, 2% Hispanic American, 2% international
- 1,042 degree-seeking graduate students
- 65% of applicants admitted
- SAT or ACT (ACT writing optional) required
- 61% graduate within 6 years

**General.** Founded in 1886. Regionally accredited. **Degrees:** 879 bachelor's awarded; master's offered. **ROTC:** Army. **Location:** 20 miles from Charlotte, North Carolina. **Calendar:** Semester, extensive summer session. **Full-time faculty:** 276 total; 81% have terminal degrees, 14% minority, 50% women. **Part-time faculty:** 276 total; 24% have terminal degrees, 9% minority, 67% women. **Class size:** 35% < 20, 53% 20-39, 9% 40-49, 3% 50-99. **Special facilities:** Nursery laboratory, music conservatory.

**Freshman class profile.** 4,511 applied, 2,946 admitted, 1,060 enrolled.

| Mid 50% test scores | | | |
|---|---|---|---|
| SAT critical reading: | 470-580 | Rank in top quarter: | 55% |
| SAT math: | 480-570 | Rank in top tenth: | 22% |
| ACT composite: | 20-25 | Return as sophomores: | 67% |
| GPA 3.75 or higher: | 52% | Out-of-state: | 10% |
| GPA 3.50-3.74: | 19% | Live on campus: | 90% |
| GPA 3.0-3.49: | 26% | International: | 2% |
| GPA 2.0-2.99: | 3% | Sororities: | 3% |

**Basis for selection.** School achievement record, test scores, counselor recommendations important, school and community activities considered. Essay, interview recommended for all; audition recommended for dance, music, theater programs.

**High school preparation.** 20 units required. Required units include English 4, mathematics 3, social studies 2, history 1, science 3 (laboratory 3), foreign language 2 and academic electives 4. Physical education or ROTC required.

**2009-2010 Annual costs.** Tuition/fees: $11,586; $21,576 out-of-state. Room/board: $6,530.

**2008-2009 Financial aid. Need-based:** 897 full-time freshmen applied for aid; 683 were judged to have need; 680 of these received aid. Average need met was 72%. Average scholarship/grant was $8,347; average loan $3,391. 62% of total undergraduate aid awarded as scholarships/grants, 38% as loans/jobs. **Non-need-based:** Awarded to 670 full-time undergraduates, including 219 freshmen. Scholarships awarded for academics, art, athletics, leadership, music/drama. **Additional information:** Academic scholarships from $1,500 to full tuition and board awarded to approximately one-third of entering freshman class each year.

**Application procedures. Admission:** Closing date 5/1. $40 fee, may be waived for applicants with need. Application must be submitted on paper. Admission notification on a rolling basis beginning on or about 10/21. Must reply by May 1 or within 3 week(s) if notified thereafter. 8 monthly notification dates for fall between October and May on the 21st of the month. **Financial aid:** Priority date 3/1; no closing date. FAFSA required. Applicants notified on a rolling basis starting 3/15; must reply within 4 week(s) of notification.

**Academics. Special study options:** Cooperative education, cross-registration, distance learning, double major, dual enrollment of high school students, ESL, exchange student, honors, independent study, internships, liberal arts/career combination, study abroad, teacher certification program, United Nations semester. **Credit/placement by examination:** AP, CLEP, IB, SAT, ACT, institutional tests. 30 credit hours maximum toward bachelor's degree. **Support services:** Pre-admission summer program, study skills assistance, tutoring, writing center.

**Majors. Biology:** General. **Business:** Business admin, e-commerce. **Communications:** Journalism, public relations. **Computer sciences:** General. **Education:** Early childhood, elementary, middle, music, physical, special. **Family/consumer sciences:** Food/nutrition. **Foreign languages:** General. **Health:** Clinical lab science, communication disorders. **History:** General. **Math:** General. **Parks/recreation:** Sports admin. **Philosophy/religion:** Philosophy, religion. **Physical sciences:** Chemistry. **Psychology:** General. **Public administration:** Social work. **Social sciences:** Political science, sociology. **Visual/performing arts:** Art, art history/conservation, dance, dramatic, studio arts.

**Most popular majors.** Biology 7%, business/marketing 22%, communications/journalism 7%, education 17%, psychology 8%, social sciences 7%, visual/performing arts 12%.

**Computing on campus.** 584 workstations in dormitories, library, computer center, student center. Dormitories wired for high-speed internet access and linked to campus network. Commuter students can connect to campus network. Online course registration, helpline, student web hosting, wireless network available.

**Student life. Freshman orientation:** Available. 3-day session in June. **Policies:** First and second year students are required to live on campus unless living with parents within 50 miles. **Housing:** Guaranteed on-campus for freshmen. Coed dorms, single-sex dorms, apartments, fraternity/sorority housing available. $100 deposit. **Activities:** Bands, campus ministries, choral groups, dance, drama, international student organizations, literary magazine, music ensembles, Model UN, musical theater, opera, radio station, student government, student newspaper, TV station, 115 clubs and organizations.

**Athletics.** NCAA. **Intercollegiate:** Baseball M, basketball, cross-country, golf, soccer, softball W, tennis, track and field, volleyball W. **Intramural:** Badminton, basketball, cross-country, fencing, football (non-tackle), football (tackle) M, golf, handball, racquetball, soccer, softball, swimming, table tennis, tennis, volleyball. **Team name:** Eagles.

**Student services.** Adult student services, alcohol/substance abuse counseling, career counseling, student employment services, financial aid counseling, health services, minority student services, personal counseling, placement for graduates, veterans' counselor.

**Contact.** E-mail: admissions@winthrop.edu
Phone: (803) 323-2191 Toll-free number: (800) 946-8476
Fax: (803) 323-2137
Debi Barber, Director of Admissions, Winthrop University, 701 Oakland Avenue, Rock Hill, SC 29733

## Wofford College
**Spartanburg, South Carolina**   CB member
www.wofford.edu   CB code: 5912

- Private 4-year liberal arts college affiliated with United Methodist Church
- Residential campus in small city
- 1,429 degree-seeking undergraduates: 1% part-time, 50% women, 7% African American, 3% Asian American, 2% Hispanic American, 1% international
- 58% of applicants admitted
- SAT or ACT with writing, application essay required
- 82% graduate within 6 years; 49% enter graduate study

**General.** Founded in 1854. Regionally accredited. **Degrees:** 294 bachelor's awarded. **ROTC:** Army. **Location:** 70 miles from Charlotte, North Carolina, 180 miles from Atlanta. **Calendar:** 4-1-4, limited summer session. **Full-time faculty:** 117 total; 93% have terminal degrees, 10% minority, 38% women. **Part-time faculty:** 30 total; 40% have terminal degrees, 3% minority, 40% women. **Class size:** 62% < 20, 37% 20-39, less than 1% 40-49, 1% 50-99. **Special facilities:** Arboretum, environmental studies center, South Carolina Methodist archives.

**Freshman class profile.** 2,442 applied, 1,415 admitted, 392 enrolled.

| Mid 50% test scores | | | |
|---|---|---|---|
| SAT critical reading: | 560-670 | Rank in top quarter: | 87% |
| SAT math: | 580-680 | Rank in top tenth: | 57% |
| SAT writing: | 560-660 | End year in good standing: | 93% |
| ACT composite: | 22-29 | Return as sophomores: | 87% |
| GPA 3.75 or higher: | 70% | Out-of-state: | 39% |
| GPA 3.50-3.74: | 12% | Live on campus: | 98% |
| GPA 3.0-3.49: | 12% | International: | 2% |
| GPA 2.0-2.99: | 6% | Fraternities: | 40% |
| | | Sororities: | 52% |

**Basis for selection.** High school record, including AP courses, most important. Test scores important. School recommendation, leadership, extracurricular activities considered. Interview recommended. **Learning Disabled:** Prospective students with learning disabilities consult with the Dean of Health Services.

**High school preparation.** College-preparatory program recommended. 20 units recommended. Recommended units include English 4, mathematics 4, social studies 2, history 1, science 3 (laboratory 3), foreign language 3, computer science 1, visual/performing arts 1 and academic electives 1.

**2009-2010 Annual costs.** Tuition/fees: $30,280. Room/board: $8,480. Books/supplies: $1,050. Personal expenses: $1,232.

**2009-2010 Financial aid. Need-based:** 300 full-time freshmen applied for aid; 223 were judged to have need; 222 of these received aid. Average need met was 88%. Average scholarship/grant was $26,184; average loan $3,016. 84% of total undergraduate aid awarded as scholarships/grants, 16% as loans/jobs. **Non-need-based:** Awarded to 803 full-time undergraduates, including 211 freshmen. Scholarships awarded for academics, athletics, leadership, music/drama, religious affiliation, ROTC, state residency.

**Application procedures. Admission:** Closing date 2/1 (postmark date). $35 fee, may be waived for applicants with need. Admission notification 3/15. Must reply by 5/1. Must be admitted by December 5 to be eligible for Wofford Scholars (academic merit scholarship) program. **Financial aid:** Closing date 3/15. FAFSA required. Applicants notified on a rolling basis starting 4/1; must reply by 5/1.

**Academics.** January Interim program devoted to internships, foreign travel, independent study, and other nontraditional academic pursuits. **Special study options:** Accelerated study, combined bachelor's/graduate degree, cross-registration, double major, dual enrollment of high school students, independent study, internships, liberal arts/career combination, student-designed major, study abroad, teacher certification program, Washington semester. Opportunities for summer research "Community of Scholars," studies abroad, service learning, and environmental studies. **Credit/placement by examination:** CLEP, IB. 30 credit hours maximum toward bachelor's degree. **Support services:** Tutoring, writing center.

**Majors. Biology:** General. **Business:** Accounting, finance, international, managerial economics. **Computer sciences:** General, computer science. **Conservation:** Environmental studies. **Foreign languages:** Chinese, French, German, Spanish. **History:** General. **Liberal arts:** Arts/sciences. **Math:** General. **Philosophy/religion:** Philosophy, religion. **Physical sciences:** Chemistry, physics. **Psychology:** General. **Social sciences:** Economics, sociology, U.S. government. **Visual/performing arts:** Art history/conservation, theater design.

**Most popular majors.** Biology 18%, business/marketing 26%, English 7%, foreign language 13%, social sciences 14%.

**Computing on campus.** 250 workstations in library, computer center, student center. Dormitories wired for high-speed internet access and linked to campus network. Commuter students can connect to campus network. Online course registration, online library, helpline, student web hosting, wireless network available.

**Student life. Freshman orientation:** Mandatory. Preregistration for classes offered. Weekend in summer before the start of classes. **Policies:** Honor code and honor council. Students not living with immediate family member must secure permission to live off-campus. **Housing:** Guaranteed on-campus for all undergraduates. Coed dorms, apartments, wellness housing available. $300 nonrefundable deposit, deadline 5/1. **Activities:** Bands, campus ministries, choral groups, dance, drama, international student organizations, literary magazine, music ensembles, student government, student newspaper, Fellowship of Christian Athletes, Baptist Collegiate Ministry, Association of African-American Students, student volunteer services, Wesley Fellowship, Catholic Newman Club, College Republicans, College Democrats, Lion's Club, Rotaract Club.

**Athletics.** NCAA. **Intercollegiate:** Baseball M, basketball, cross-country, football (tackle) M, golf, rifle, soccer, tennis, track and field, volleyball W. **Intramural:** Basketball, football (non-tackle), soccer, softball, volleyball. **Team name:** Terriers.

**Student services.** Alcohol/substance abuse counseling, chaplain/spiritual director, career counseling, student employment services, financial aid counseling, health services, minority student services, personal counseling, placement for graduates. **Physically disabled:** Services for visually, speech, hearing impaired.

**Contact.** E-mail: admission@wofford.edu
Phone: (864) 597-4130 Fax: (864) 597-4147
S. Wells Shepard, Director of Admission, Wofford College, 429 North Church Street, Spartanburg, SC 29303-3663

# South Dakota

## Augustana College
### Sioux Falls, South Dakota
www.augie.edu

**CB member**
**CB code: 6015**

- Private 4-year liberal arts college affiliated with Evangelical Lutheran Church in America
- Residential campus in small city
- 1,771 degree-seeking undergraduates: 6% part-time, 63% women, 1% African American, 1% Asian American, 2% international
- 22 degree-seeking graduate students
- 81% of applicants admitted
- SAT or ACT (ACT writing optional), application essay required
- 67% graduate within 6 years; 21% enter graduate study

**General.** Founded in 1860. Regionally accredited. **Degrees:** 322 bachelor's awarded; master's offered. **ROTC:** Army, Air Force. **Location:** 160 miles from Omaha, NE; 230 miles from Minneapolis-St. Paul. **Calendar:** 4-1-4, limited summer session. **Full-time faculty:** 125 total; 79% have terminal degrees, 2% minority, 45% women. **Part-time faculty:** 56 total; 11% have terminal degrees, 70% women. **Class size:** 57% < 20, 39% 20-39, 2% 40-49, 2% 50-99. **Special facilities:** Western studies museum and archives, archeology lab, prairie garden, ASL laboratory, art gallery, model classroom.

**Freshman class profile.** 1,284 applied, 1,036 admitted, 432 enrolled.

| Mid 50% test scores | | Rank in top quarter: | 61% |
|---|---|---|---|
| ACT composite: | 22-28 | Rank in top tenth: | 29% |
| GPA 3.75 or higher: | 48% | Return as sophomores: | 82% |
| GPA 3.50-3.74: | 20% | Out-of-state: | 40% |
| GPA 3.0-3.49: | 23% | Live on campus: | 97% |
| GPA 2.0-2.99: | 9% | International: | 2% |

**Basis for selection.** 20 ACT (or equivalent SAT), 2.75 GPA, rank in top half of class, high school transcript, recommendation, and writing sample required. Interview recommended for all; supplementary essay questions/materials required for students who do not meet minimum admission requirements.

**High school preparation.** 16 units recommended. Recommended units include English 4, mathematics 4, social studies 3, science 3 (laboratory 2) and foreign language 2. 1 unit fine arts and 1/2 unit computer science also recommended.

**2010-2011 Annual costs.** Tuition/fees: $25,104. Room/board: $6,260. Books/supplies: $800. Personal expenses: $800.

**2009-2010 Financial aid. Non-need-based:** Scholarships awarded for academics, alumni affiliation, art, athletics, leadership, minority status, music/drama, religious affiliation, state residency.

**Application procedures. Admission:** Priority date 2/1; no deadline. No application fee. Admission notification on a rolling basis beginning on or about 10/1. Must reply by May 1 or within 3 week(s) if notified thereafter. **Financial aid:** Priority date 3/1; no closing date. FAFSA required. Applicants notified on a rolling basis starting 3/15; must reply within 3 week(s) of notification.

**Academics. Special study options:** Cooperative education, cross-registration, double major, dual enrollment of high school students, exchange student, external degree, honors, independent study, internships, liberal arts/career combination, study abroad, teacher certification program, urban semester, Washington semester. **Credit/placement by examination:** AP, CLEP, IB, SAT, ACT, institutional tests. 32 credit hours maximum toward bachelor's degree. **Support services:** Reduced course load, study skills assistance, tutoring, writing center.

**Majors. Biology:** General, biochemistry. **Business:** General, accounting, business admin, communications, management information systems. **Communications:** General, journalism. **Computer sciences:** Computer science. **Education:** Art, biology, Deaf/hearing impaired, elementary, emotionally handicapped, English, French, German, history, learning disabled, mathematics, mentally handicapped, multicultural, music, physical, physically handicapped, physics, psychology, secondary, social studies, Spanish, special, speech, speech impaired. **Engineering:** Physics. **Foreign languages:** General, American Sign Language, French, German, sign language interpretation, Spanish. **Health:** Athletic training, clinical lab science, clinical lab technology, communication disorders, nursing (RN), predental, premedicine, prepharmacy, preveterinary. **History:** General. **Interdisciplinary:** Global studies. **Math:** General. **Parks/recreation:** Exercise sciences, health/fitness, sports admin. **Philosophy/religion:** Philosophy, religion. **Physical sciences:** Chemistry, physics. **Psychology:** General. **Social sciences:** Anthropology, economics, political science, sociology. **Theology:** Sacred music. **Visual/performing arts:** Art, dramatic.

**Most popular majors.** Biology 7%, business/marketing 14%, education 18%, health sciences 16%, social sciences 7%.

**Computing on campus.** 255 workstations in dormitories, library, computer center, student center. Dormitories wired for high-speed internet access and linked to campus network. Commuter students can connect to campus network. Online library, helpline, repair service, wireless network available.

**Student life. Freshman orientation:** Mandatory. Preregistration for classes offered. Program begins at new student registration. **Housing:** Guaranteed on-campus for all undergraduates. Coed dorms, special housing for disabled, apartments available. $100 fully refundable deposit. **Activities:** Bands, campus ministries, choral groups, dance, drama, international student organizations, literary magazine, music ensembles, musical theater, student government, student newspaper, symphony orchestra, Lutheran-ELCA congregation, Fellowship of Christian Athletes, Circle K, Augie Democrats, College Republicans, Augie Green, Catholics in Action, Young Life, Colleges Against Cancer.

**Athletics.** NCAA. **Intercollegiate:** Baseball M, basketball, cheerleading M, cross-country, football (tackle) M, golf, soccer W, softball W, tennis, track and field, volleyball W, wrestling M. **Intramural:** Basketball, football (non-tackle), golf, racquetball, rugby W, soccer, softball, triathlon, volleyball. **Team name:** Vikings.

**Student services.** Adult student services, alcohol/substance abuse counseling, chaplain/spiritual director, career counseling, student employment services, financial aid counseling, health services, minority student services, on-campus daycare, personal counseling, placement for graduates, veterans' counselor. **Physically disabled:** Services for visually, hearing impaired.

**Contact.** E-mail: admission@augie.edu
Phone: (605) 274-5516 Toll-free number: (800) 727-2844
Fax: (605) 274-5518
Adam Heinitz, Director of Admission, Augustana College, 2001 South Summit Avenue, Sioux Falls, SD 57197-9990

## Black Hills State University
### Spearfish, South Dakota
www.bhsu.edu

**CB code: 6042**

- Public 4-year liberal arts and teachers college
- Commuter campus in large town
- 3,225 degree-seeking undergraduates: 22% part-time, 61% women, 1% African American, 1% Asian American, 2% Hispanic American, 4% Native American, 1% international
- 150 degree-seeking graduate students
- 93% of applicants admitted
- SAT or ACT (ACT writing optional) required

**General.** Founded in 1883. Regionally accredited. Evening degree program available at Ellsworth Air Force Base campus in Rapid City. **Degrees:** 440 bachelor's, 25 associate awarded; master's offered. **ROTC:** Army. **Location:** 45 miles from Rapid City. **Calendar:** Semester, extensive summer session. **Full-time faculty:** 117 total; 71% have terminal degrees, 8% minority, 39% women. **Part-time faculty:** 73 total; 34% have terminal degrees, 6% minority, 48% women. **Class size:** 39% < 20, 50% 20-39, 5% 40-49, 4% 50-99, less than 1% >100.

**Freshman class profile.** 1,003 applied, 932 admitted, 600 enrolled.

| Mid 50% test scores | | Rank in top quarter: | 28% |
|---|---|---|---|
| ACT composite: | 18-23 | Rank in top tenth: | 9% |
| GPA 3.75 or higher: | 13% | Return as sophomores: | 62% |
| GPA 3.50-3.74: | 14% | Out-of-state: | 23% |
| GPA 3.0-3.49: | 32% | Live on campus: | 72% |
| GPA 2.0-2.99: | 36% | International: | 1% |

**Basis for selection.** For bachelor's programs, requirements include 18 ACT or class rank in top 60% (in-state applicants), top half (out-of-state applicants) or 2.6 GPA in required courses. Portfolio recommended.

**High school preparation.** College-preparatory program recommended. 14 units required. Required units include English 4, mathematics 3, social studies 3, science 3 (laboratory 3) and visual/performing arts 1.

**2009-2010 Annual costs.** Tuition/fees: $6,227; $7,600 out-of-state. Reciprocity agreements reduce tuition for some out-of-state students . Room/board: $5,524. Books/supplies: $1,000. Personal expenses: $1,500.

**2008-2009 Financial aid.** All financial aid based on need.

**Application procedures. Admission:** Closing date 7/15. $20 fee. Admission notification on a rolling basis. **Financial aid:** Closing date 2/15. FAFSA required. Applicants notified on a rolling basis starting 5/15; must reply within 3 week(s) of notification.

**Academics. Special study options:** Cooperative education, distance learning, double major, dual enrollment of high school students, honors, independent study, internships, study abroad, teacher certification program. **Credit/placement by examination:** AP, CLEP, SAT, ACT, institutional tests. 32 credit hours maximum toward bachelor's degree. **Support services:** Learning center, remedial instruction, study skills assistance, tutoring, writing center.

**Majors. Area/ethnic studies:** Native American. **Biology:** General. **Business:** Accounting, business admin, entrepreneurial studies, human resources, marketing, office management, tourism/travel. **Communications:** Media studies. **Education:** Art, biology, business, chemistry, elementary, English, foreign languages, history, kindergarten/preschool, mathematics, middle, music, physical, science, social science, special, speech, technology/industrial arts. **Engineering technology:** Industrial. **Foreign languages:** Spanish. **Health:** Facilities admin. **History:** General. **Math:** General. **Parks/recreation:** General, exercise sciences, sports admin. **Physical sciences:** General, chemistry. **Psychology:** General. **Public administration:** Community org/advocacy. **Social sciences:** General, political science, sociology. **Visual/performing arts:** Art, commercial/advertising art.

**Most popular majors.** Biology 6%, business/marketing 20%, communications/journalism 7%, education 17%, English 6%, psychology 7%, public administration/social services 6%, social sciences 10%, visual/performing arts 6%.

**Computing on campus.** 500 workstations in dormitories, library, student center. Dormitories wired for high-speed internet access and linked to campus network. Commuter students can connect to campus network. Online course registration, online library, helpline, wireless network available.

**Student life. Freshman orientation:** Available. Preregistration for classes offered. **Housing:** Guaranteed on-campus for freshmen. Coed dorms, single-sex dorms, apartments available. $100 deposit. Married student housing. **Activities:** Bands, campus ministries, choral groups, drama, international student organizations, music ensembles, musical theater, radio station, student government, student newspaper, symphony orchestra, TV station, Native American special services, Inter-Greek council, United Ministry, Veterans club, Young Democrats, Young Republicans.

**Athletics.** NAIA. **Intercollegiate:** Basketball, cross-country, football (tackle) M, golf W, softball W, track and field, volleyball W. **Intramural:** Archery, badminton, basketball, bowling, golf, skiing, soccer, softball, swimming, table tennis, tennis, volleyball. **Team name:** Yellow Jackets.

**Student services.** Chaplain/spiritual director, career counseling, student employment services, financial aid counseling, health services, on-campus daycare, personal counseling, placement for graduates, veterans' counselor. **Physically disabled:** Services for visually, speech, hearing impaired.

**Contact.** E-mail: admissions@bhsu.edu
Phone: (605) 642-6343 Toll-free number: (800) 255-2478
Fax: (605) 642-6022
Beth Oaks, Director of Admissions, Black Hills State University, 1200 University Street Box 9502, Spearfish, SD 57799-9502

## Dakota State University
**Madison, South Dakota**
www.dsu.edu                    CB code: 6247

- Public 4-year university
- Residential campus in small town
- 1,450 degree-seeking undergraduates
- 379 graduate students
- 94% of applicants admitted
- SAT or ACT (ACT writing optional) required

**General.** Founded in 1881. Regionally accredited. **Degrees:** 190 bachelor's, 40 associate awarded; master's, doctoral offered. **ROTC:** Army, Air Force. **Location:** 45 miles from Sioux Falls. **Calendar:** Semester, limited summer session. **Full-time faculty:** 89 total; 71% have terminal degrees, 3% minority, 36% women. **Part-time faculty:** 32 total; 25% have terminal degrees, 50% women. **Class size:** 64% < 20, 33% 20-39, less than 1% 40-49, 2% 50-99, less than 1% >100. **Special facilities:** Smith-Zimmerman State Museum, technology building.

**Freshman class profile.** 672 applied, 630 admitted, 323 enrolled.

| Mid 50% test scores | | | |
|---|---|---|---|
| ACT composite: | 19-25 | Rank in top quarter: | 24% |
| GPA 3.75 or higher: | 15% | Rank in top tenth: | 7% |
| GPA 3.50-3.74: | 11% | End year in good standing: | 71% |
| GPA 3.0-3.49: | 33% | Out-of-state: | 26% |
| GPA 2.0-2.99: | 36% | Live on campus: | 87% |

**Basis for selection.** Top 60% of class or 18 ACT or 2.6 GPA in core courses required. Underqualified applicants considered for probational acceptance. **Homeschooled:** State high school equivalency certificate required. Equivalency certificate or ACT minimum scores required.

**High school preparation.** Recommended units include English 4, mathematics 3, social studies 3, science 3 (laboratory 3). 1 fine arts required, 0.5 computer studies.

**2009-2010 Annual costs.** Tuition/fees: $6,872; $8,245 out-of-state. Reciprocity agreements reduce tuition for some out-of-state students. Room/board: $4,890. Books/supplies: $900. Personal expenses: $2,291.

**2008-2009 Financial aid. Need-based:** 228 full-time freshmen applied for aid; 168 were judged to have need; 168 of these received aid. Average need met was 80%. Average scholarship/grant was $3,957; average loan $3,283. 27% of total undergraduate aid awarded as scholarships/grants, 73% as loans/jobs. **Non-need-based:** Awarded to 537 full-time undergraduates, including 176 freshmen. Scholarships awarded for academics, alumni affiliation, art, athletics, leadership, minority status, music/drama, state residency. **Additional information:** Application deadline for grants and scholarships March 1. No deadline for loan and job applications.

**Application procedures. Admission:** No deadline. $20 fee. Admission notification on a rolling basis. **Financial aid:** Priority date 3/1; no closing date. FAFSA required. Applicants notified on a rolling basis starting 4/1; must reply within 2 week(s) of notification.

**Academics. Special study options:** Cooperative education, cross-registration, distance learning, double major, dual enrollment of high school students, ESL, honors, independent study, internships, teacher certification program. **Credit/placement by examination:** AP, CLEP, IB, SAT, ACT, institutional tests. 16 credit hours maximum toward associate degree, 32 toward bachelor's. **Support services:** Learning center, reduced course load, remedial instruction, study skills assistance, tutoring, writing center.

**Majors. Biology:** General. **Business:** Accounting, business admin, finance, marketing. **Computer sciences:** General, computer graphics, information systems, security. **Education:** Biology, business, computer, elementary, English, mathematics, physical. **Health:** Medical records admin, respiratory therapy technology. **Parks/recreation:** Exercise sciences. **Physical sciences:** General. **Science technology:** Chemical. **Other:** Biology for information systems, Elementary education/special learning behavior, English for information systems, mathematics for information systems.

**Most popular majors.** Business/marketing 29%, computer/information sciences 30%, education 22%, parks/recreation 7%.

**Computing on campus.** PC or laptop required. Dormitories wired for high-speed internet access and linked to campus network. Commuter students can connect to campus network. Online course registration, online library, helpline, student web hosting, wireless network available.

**Student life. Freshman orientation:** Mandatory. Preregistration for classes offered. **Policies:** Alcohol/drug-free campus. 2-year live-in requirement, residence halls in 24/7 lockdown for student safety. Students living in residence halls required to have meal plan. **Housing:** Guaranteed on-campus for freshmen. Coed dorms, single-sex dorms, apartments, wellness housing available. $50 fully refundable deposit. **Activities:** Pep band, choral groups, dance, drama, international student organizations, literary magazine, music ensembles, musical theater, radio station, student government, student newspaper, InterVarsity Christian Fellowship, Colleges against Cancer.

**Athletics.** NAIA. **Intercollegiate:** Baseball M, basketball, cheerleading, cross-country, football (tackle) M, softball W, track and field, volleyball W. **Intramural:** Basketball, football (non-tackle), racquetball, softball, table tennis, tennis, volleyball. **Team name:** Trojans.

**Student services.** Alcohol/substance abuse counseling, chaplain/spiritual director, career counseling, student employment services, financial aid counseling, health services, minority student services, personal counseling, placement for graduates, veterans' counselor. **Physically disabled:** Services for visually, speech, hearing impaired.

**Contact.** E-mail: yourfuture@dsu.edu
Phone: (605) 256-5139 Toll-free number: (888) 378-9988
Fax: (605) 256-5020
Amy Crissinger, Director of Admission, Dakota State University, 820 North Washington Avenue, Madison, SD 57042

## Dakota Wesleyan University
### Mitchell, South Dakota
www.dwu.edu                                      CB code: 6155

- Private 4-year university and liberal arts college affiliated with United Methodist Church
- Residential campus in large town
- 724 degree-seeking undergraduates: 6% part-time, 58% women, 2% African American, 1% Asian American, 4% Hispanic American, 2% Native American, 1% international
- 26 degree-seeking graduate students
- 81% of applicants admitted
- 43% graduate within 6 years

**General.** Founded in 1885. Regionally accredited. **Degrees:** 98 bachelor's, 60 associate awarded; master's offered. **ROTC:** Army. **Location:** 70 miles from Sioux Falls. **Calendar:** Semester, limited summer session. **Full-time faculty:** 45 total; 78% have terminal degrees, 51% women. **Part-time faculty:** 32 total; 28% have terminal degrees, 62% women. **Class size:** 58% < 20, 34% 20-39, 6% 40-49, 2% 50-99. **Special facilities:** Observatory.

**Freshman class profile.** 538 applied, 434 admitted, 168 enrolled.

| Mid 50% test scores | | | |
|---|---|---|---|
| SAT critical reading: | 390-630 | GPA 3.0-3.49: | 29% |
| SAT math: | 410-580 | GPA 2.0-2.99: | 44% |
| SAT writing: | 320-540 | Rank in top quarter: | 19% |
| ACT composite: | 18-26 | Rank in top tenth: | 7% |
| GPA 3.75 or higher: | 15% | End year in good standing: | 89% |
| GPA 3.50-3.74: | 10% | Return as sophomores: | 64% |

**Basis for selection.** High school record, test scores, school activities considered. Recommendations and personal interview used for marginal students. **Homeschooled:** Transcript of courses and grades required. Meeting with admissions counselor and placement testing required when appropriate. ACT/SAT recommended. **Learning Disabled:** For special assistance, documentation of student's learning disability required.

**High school preparation.** Recommended units include English 4, mathematics 4, social studies 4, history 3, science 3 (laboratory 1) and foreign language 2.

**2009-2010 Annual costs.** Tuition/fees: $19,000. Room/board: $5,870. Books/supplies: $800. Personal expenses: $1,200.

**2009-2010 Financial aid. Need-based:** 159 full-time freshmen applied for aid; 141 were judged to have need; 141 of these received aid. Average need met was 66%. Average scholarship/grant was $10,600; average loan $3,300. 57% of total undergraduate aid awarded as scholarships/grants, 43% as loans/jobs. **Non-need-based:** Awarded to 157 full-time undergraduates, including 39 freshmen. Scholarships awarded for academics, alumni affiliation, art, athletics, leadership, minority status, music/drama, religious affiliation.

**Application procedures. Admission:** Closing date 8/25 (receipt date). $25 fee, may be waived for applicants with need. Admission notification on a rolling basis. **Financial aid:** Priority date 4/15; no closing date. FAFSA required. Applicants notified on a rolling basis starting 3/1; must reply within 2 week(s) of notification.

**Academics. Special study options:** Cross-registration, distance learning, double major, dual enrollment of high school students, exchange student, honors, independent study, internships, student-designed major, study abroad, teacher certification program, Washington semester. **Credit/placement by examination:** AP, CLEP, IB, institutional tests. 12 credit hours maximum toward associate degree, 63 toward bachelor's. **Support services:** Learning center, pre-admission summer program, reduced course load, remedial instruction, study skills assistance, tutoring, writing center.

**Majors. Biology:** General. **Business:** General, accounting. **Communications:** General, journalism. **Computer sciences:** Web page design. **Conservation:** Wildlife. **Education:** General, art, biology, business, elementary,

English, mathematics, music, physical, science, social science, social studies, special. **Health:** Athletic training, predental, premedicine, prepharmacy, preveterinary. **History:** General. **Interdisciplinary:** Behavioral sciences. **Legal studies:** Prelaw. **Math:** General. **Parks/recreation:** Exercise sciences, sports admin. **Philosophy/religion:** Religion. **Protective services:** Criminal justice. **Psychology:** General. **Public administration:** Human services. **Social sciences:** General, sociology. **Theology:** Sacred music. **Visual/performing arts:** Art, dramatic. **Other:** Public Service and Leadership.

**Most popular majors.** Biology 6%, business/marketing 22%, computer/information sciences 7%, education 20%, health sciences 7%, parks/recreation 6%, public administration/social services 6%, security/protective services 9%.

**Computing on campus.** 85 workstations in dormitories, library, computer center, student center. Dormitories wired for high-speed internet access and linked to campus network. Commuter students can connect to campus network. Online library, helpline, repair service, student web hosting, wireless network available.

**Student life. Freshman orientation:** Mandatory. Preregistration for classes offered. 2-day program held the weekend before classes begin. **Housing:** Guaranteed on-campus for freshmen. Coed dorms, single-sex dorms, apartments, wellness housing available. $50 fully refundable deposit. Honor housing available for upperclassmen; ADA rooms and apartments available. **Activities:** Concert band, campus ministries, choral groups, drama, literary magazine, music ensembles, student government, student newspaper, variety of organizations available.

**Athletics.** NAIA. **Intercollegiate:** Baseball M, basketball, cheerleading, cross-country, football (tackle) M, golf, soccer, softball W, track and field, volleyball W, wrestling M. **Intramural:** Basketball, softball, volleyball, weight lifting. **Team name:** Tigers.

**Student services.** Adult student services, alcohol/substance abuse counseling, chaplain/spiritual director, career counseling, services for economically disadvantaged, student employment services, financial aid counseling, health services, minority student services, on-campus daycare, personal counseling, placement for graduates. **Physically disabled:** Services for visually, hearing impaired.

**Contact.** E-mail: admissions@dwu.edu
Phone: (605) 995-2650 Toll-free number: (800) 333-8506
Fax: (605) 995-2699
Melissa Herr-Valburg, Director of Admissions, Dakota Wesleyan University, 1200 West University Avenue, Mitchell, SD 57301-4398

## Mount Marty College
### Yankton, South Dakota
www.mtmc.edu                                      CB code: 6416

- Private 4-year liberal arts college affiliated with Roman Catholic Church
- Residential campus in large town
- 833 degree-seeking undergraduates: 26% part-time, 61% women
- 133 graduate students
- 77% of applicants admitted
- 45% graduate within 6 years; 10% enter graduate study

**General.** Founded in 1936. Regionally accredited. **Degrees:** 149 bachelor's, 36 associate awarded; master's offered. **ROTC:** Army. **Location:** 75 miles from Sioux Falls, 60 miles from Sioux City, Iowa. **Calendar:** Semester, limited summer session. **Full-time faculty:** 44 total; 68% have terminal degrees, 43% women. **Part-time faculty:** 36 total; 14% have terminal degrees, 22% women. **Class size:** 80% < 20, 19% 20-39, less than 1% 40-49, less than 1% 50-99, less than 1% >100.

**Freshman class profile.** 336 applied, 259 admitted, 116 enrolled.

| Mid 50% test scores | | | |
|---|---|---|---|
| ACT composite: | 19-24 | Return as sophomores: | 86% |
| | | Out-of-state: | 60% |
| End year in good standing: | 98% | Live on campus: | 95% |

**Basis for selection.** Academic record, test scores, GPA very important. 2.0 GPA and 18 ACT required for consideration. Interview recommended for all; audition required for scholarship recipients, music and theater programs. **Learning Disabled:** Students requesting disability services must submit letter and documentation to support diagnosed disability.

**2009-2010 Annual costs.** Tuition/fees: $18,908. Room/board: $5,366. Books/supplies: $920. Personal expenses: $1,704.

**2009-2010 Financial aid. Non-need-based:** Scholarships awarded for academics, art, athletics, leadership, music/drama, religious affiliation. **Additional information:** Prestige scholarships application deadline 2/1.

**Application procedures. Admission:** Closing date 8/30 (receipt date). $35 fee, may be waived for applicants with need. Admission notification on a rolling basis. **Financial aid:** Priority date 3/1; no closing date. FAFSA, institutional form required. Applicants notified on a rolling basis starting 3/15; must reply within 2 week(s) of notification.

**Academics. Special study options:** Accelerated study, double major, dual enrollment of high school students, honors, independent study, internships, liberal arts/career combination, student-designed major, teacher certification program. **Credit/placement by examination:** AP, CLEP, IB, institutional tests. 88 credit hours maximum toward associate degree, 24 toward bachelor's. **Support services:** Learning center, reduced course load, remedial instruction, study skills assistance, tutoring, writing center.

**Majors. Biology:** General. **Business:** Accounting, business admin. **Communications:** Digital media. **Computer sciences:** Computer science, information technology, programming. **Education:** Biology, chemistry, elementary, English, health, history, mathematics, middle, music, physical, science, secondary, social science, special. **Health:** Clinical lab science, medical radiologic technology/radiation therapy, nursing (RN). **History:** General. **Liberal arts:** Arts/sciences. **Math:** General. **Parks/recreation:** Facilities management. **Philosophy/religion:** Religion. **Physical sciences:** Chemistry. **Protective services:** Criminal justice, forensics. **Psychology:** General. **Social sciences:** General. **Visual/performing arts:** Dramatic. **Other:** Exercise and wellness, IT management.

**Most popular majors.** Business/marketing 15%, education 17%, health sciences 23%, liberal arts 10%, social sciences 12%.

**Computing on campus.** PC or laptop required. 53 workstations in dormitories, library, computer center, student center. Dormitories wired for high-speed internet access and linked to campus network. Commuter students can connect to campus network. Online library, helpline, repair service, wireless network available.

**Student life. Freshman orientation:** Mandatory. Preregistration for classes offered. 3-day intensive orientation prior to beginning of fall semester. Orientation programs throughout academic year. **Policies:** Alcohol, tobacco and drug-free campus. Unmarried undergraduates under 21 required to live in college housing unless living with family. **Housing:** Guaranteed on-campus for freshmen. Single-sex dorms, special housing for disabled, wellness housing available. $50 partly refundable deposit. **Activities:** Bands, campus ministries, choral groups, drama, literary magazine, music ensembles, musical theater, student government, student newspaper, outreach team, Habitat for Humanity, education club, nursing club, English club.

**Athletics.** NAIA. **Intercollegiate:** Baseball M, basketball, cross-country, golf, soccer, softball W, track and field, volleyball W. **Intramural:** Basketball. **Team name:** Lancers.

**Student services.** Adult student services, alcohol/substance abuse counseling, chaplain/spiritual director, career counseling, student employment services, financial aid counseling, health services, on-campus daycare, personal counseling, placement for graduates, veterans' counselor. **Learning disabled:** Comprehensive services available.

**Contact.** E-mail: mmcadmit@mtmc.edu
Phone: (800) 658-4552 Toll-free number: (800) 658-4552
Fax: (605) 668-1607
Brandi Tschumper, Vice President of Enrollment Management, Mount Marty College, 1105 West Eighth Street, Yankton, SD 57078

## National American University: Rapid City
**Rapid City, South Dakota**
**www.national.edu**

**CB code: 6464**

- For-profit 4-year business and technical college
- Residential campus in small city
- 1,413 undergraduates

**General.** Founded in 1941. Regionally accredited. **Degrees:** 176 bachelor's, 80 associate awarded; master's offered. **ROTC:** Army. **Location:** 400 miles from Denver. **Calendar:** Quarter, extensive summer session. **Full-time faculty:** 13 total; 23% have terminal degrees, 46% women. **Part-time faculty:** 34 total; 15% have terminal degrees, 53% women. **Special facilities:** Animal health laboratories, athletic training facility.

**Basis for selection.** Open admission, but selective for some programs. All students required to complete university assessment testing prior to enrollment. Interview recommended for all. **Homeschooled:** Completion of GED or accredited high school correspondence required.

**High school preparation.** Algebra helpful for computer technology. Science recommended for health program.

**2009-2010 Annual costs.** Books/supplies: $1,200.

**Financial aid.** All financial aid based on need.

**Application procedures. Admission:** No deadline. $25 fee. Admission notification on a rolling basis. **Financial aid:** No deadline. FAFSA, institutional form required. Applicants notified on a rolling basis; must reply within 4 week(s) of notification.

**Academics.** Applied management program for students with associate degree in health or technical fields who desire to continue education in management. **Special study options:** Accelerated study, cooperative education, distance learning, double major, independent study, internships, liberal arts/career combination. **Credit/placement by examination:** AP, CLEP, IB, institutional tests. **Support services:** Learning center, reduced course load, remedial instruction, tutoring.

**Majors. Agriculture:** Animal training. **Business:** Accounting, business admin, management information systems, marketing, personal/financial services. **Computer sciences:** General, LAN/WAN management, programming, systems analysis, web page design, webmaster. **Health:** Athletic training, facilities admin. **Legal studies:** Paralegal, prelaw.

**Most popular majors.** Business/marketing 38%, computer/information sciences 7%, legal studies 6%.

**Computing on campus.** 77 workstations in dormitories, library, computer center. Wireless network available.

**Student life. Freshman orientation:** Mandatory. Preregistration for classes offered. **Housing:** Coed dorms available. $100 deposit. **Activities:** Student government, student newspaper.

**Athletics. Team name:** Mavericks.

**Student services.** Career counseling, student employment services, financial aid counseling, personal counseling, placement for graduates, veterans' counselor.

**Contact.** E-mail: rcadmissions@national.edu
Phone: (605) 394-4800 Toll-free number: (800) 209-0490
Fax: (605) 394-4871
Wanda Redlin, Director of Enrollment Management, National American University: Rapid City, 321 Kansas City Street, Rapid City, SD 57701

## Northern State University
**Aberdeen, South Dakota**
**www.northern.edu**

**CB code: 6487**

- Public 4-year university and liberal arts college
- Residential campus in large town
- 1,667 degree-seeking undergraduates: 16% part-time, 57% women
- 145 degree-seeking graduate students
- 93% of applicants admitted
- ACT (writing optional) required

**General.** Founded in 1901. Regionally accredited. Technology proficiency certification available for all degree programs. Emphasis on distance delivery technology in all degree programs, especially in teacher preparation. **Degrees:** 280 bachelor's, 15 associate awarded; master's offered. **Location:** 285 miles from Minneapolis-St. Paul. **Calendar:** Semester, limited summer session. **Full-time faculty:** 96 total; 77% have terminal degrees, 12% minority, 36% women. **Class size:** 42% < 20, 46% 20-39, 9% 40-49, 3% 50-99, less than 1% >100. **Special facilities:** E-learning center, center of excellence for international business.

**Freshman class profile.** 923 applied, 863 admitted, 329 enrolled.

| Mid 50% test scores | Out-of-state: | 25% |
|---|---|---|
| ACT composite: | 18-24 | |

**Basis for selection.** Applicants to 4-year programs should have 2.6 GPA or 18 ACT or rank in top 60% of class. C average required in core courses. Applicants not meeting requirements may apply. Applicants lacking required high school units admitted provisionally. Equivalent work must be completed within 2 years. Interview recommended for borderline applicants; portfolio recommended for art program.

**High school preparation.** 13 units required. Required units include English 4, mathematics 3, social studies 3, science 3 (laboratory 3). Mathematics units must be algebra or above; .5 fine arts required.

**2009-2010 Annual costs.** Tuition/fees: $6,063; $7,436 out-of-state. Reciprocity agreements reduce tuition for some out-of-state students. Room/board: $4,875. Books/supplies: $950. Personal expenses: $1,750.

**2008-2009 Financial aid. Need-based:** 32% of total undergraduate aid awarded as scholarships/grants, 68% as loans/jobs. **Non-need-based:** Scholarships awarded for academics, art, athletics, leadership, minority status, music/drama, state residency.

**Application procedures. Admission:** No deadline. $20 fee. Admission notification on a rolling basis. **Financial aid:** Priority date 3/1; no closing date. FAFSA required. Applicants notified by 4/15; must reply within 2 week(s) of notification.

**Academics. Special study options:** Accelerated study, cooperative education, cross-registration, distance learning, double major, dual enrollment of high school students, ESL, exchange student, external degree, honors, independent study, internships, liberal arts/career combination, student-designed major, study abroad, teacher certification program, Washington semester, weekend college. **Credit/placement by examination:** AP, CLEP, IB, institutional tests. 32 credit hours maximum toward bachelor's degree. **Support services:** Learning center, pre-admission summer program, reduced course load, remedial instruction, study skills assistance, tutoring, writing center.

**Majors. Biology:** General, ecology. **Business:** General, accounting, banking/financial services, business admin, finance, international, management information systems, marketing, office/clerical. **Communications:** General. **Computer sciences:** General. **Education:** General, art, business, early childhood, elementary, English, foreign languages, history, mathematics, multi-level teacher, music, physical, science, social science, special, speech. **Foreign languages:** French, German, Spanish. **Health:** Clinical lab science. **History:** General. **Math:** General. **Parks/recreation:** Health/fitness, sports admin. **Physical sciences:** Chemistry. **Psychology:** General. **Public administration:** Community org/advocacy, social work. **Social sciences:** Criminology, economics, political science, sociology. **Visual/performing arts:** Art, musical theater.

**Most popular majors.** Biology 7%, business/marketing 36%, education 24%, English 6%, parks/recreation 6%, social sciences 10%.

**Computing on campus.** 900 workstations in dormitories, library, computer center, student center. Dormitories wired for high-speed internet access and linked to campus network. Commuter students can connect to campus network. Online course registration, online library, helpline, repair service, student web hosting, wireless network available.

**Student life. Freshman orientation:** Mandatory. Preregistration for classes offered. **Housing:** Coed dorms, single-sex dorms, special housing for disabled, apartments available. $50 deposit. **Activities:** Bands, choral groups, dance, drama, literary magazine, music ensembles, musical theater, student government, student newspaper, symphony orchestra, TV station, over 100 student organizations.

**Athletics.** NCAA. **Intercollegiate:** Baseball M, basketball, cheerleading, cross-country, football (tackle) M, golf, rugby, soccer W, softball W, swimming W, tennis, track and field, volleyball W, wrestling M. **Intramural:** Badminton, baseball M, basketball, field hockey W, softball, swimming, table tennis, tennis, volleyball, weight lifting. **Team name:** Wolves.

**Student services.** Adult student services, alcohol/substance abuse counseling, chaplain/spiritual director, career counseling, services for economically disadvantaged, student employment services, financial aid counseling, health services, legal services, minority student services, on-campus daycare, personal counseling, placement for graduates, veterans' counselor, women's services. **Physically disabled:** Services for visually, speech, hearing impaired. **Learning disabled:** Comprehensive services available.

**Contact.** E-mail: admissions1@northern.edu
Phone: (605) 626-2544 Toll-free number: (800) 678-5330
Fax: (605) 626-2587
Allan Vogel, Director of Admissions, Northern State University, 1200 South Jay Street, Aberdeen, SD 57401-7198

## Oglala Lakota College
### Kyle, South Dakota
www.olc.edu                                             CB code: 1430

- Public 4-year liberal arts and teachers college
- Commuter campus in small town
- 1,804 degree-seeking undergraduates

**General.** Founded in 1971. Regionally accredited. Tribal College and founding member of American Indian Higher Education Consortium. Located on Pine Ridge Indian Reservation. **Degrees:** 40 bachelor's, 80 associate awarded;

master's offered. **Location:** 90 miles from Rapid City. **Calendar:** Semester, extensive summer session. **Full-time faculty:** 66 total; 12% have terminal degrees, 35% minority, 70% women. **Part-time faculty:** 89 total; 26% have terminal degrees, 29% minority, 36% women.

**Basis for selection.** Open admission. Testing for placement.

**2009-2010 Annual costs.** Tuition/fees: $2,900. Above rates for Native Americans. Non-Native American students pay tuition rate of $2,940 and $98 per credit hour. Books/supplies: $1,200. Personal expenses: $450.

**2008-2009 Financial aid. Additional information:** Deadline for applications for Bureau of Indian Affairs Higher Education Grants is 3/15; applicants notified early summer.

**Application procedures. Admission:** No deadline. No application fee. Application must be submitted on paper. **Financial aid:** No deadline. Applicants notified on a rolling basis.

**Academics. Special study options:** Distance learning, double major, independent study, internships, liberal arts/career combination, teacher certification program. **Credit/placement by examination:** CLEP, institutional tests. 13 credit hours maximum toward bachelor's degree. **Support services:** Learning center, reduced course load, remedial instruction, tutoring.

**Majors. Area/ethnic studies:** Native American. **Business:** Accounting, business admin, management information systems. **Computer sciences:** General. **Conservation:** General. **Education:** Elementary. **History:** General. **Liberal arts:** Arts/sciences. **Public administration:** Human services, social work. **Social sciences:** Sociology. **Other:** Life science.

**Computing on campus.** 175 workstations in library, student center. Dormitories wired for high-speed internet access. Wireless network available.

**Student life. Freshman orientation:** Available. Preregistration for classes offered. **Housing:** Coed dorms available. **Activities:** Student government, student newspaper, TV station.

**Athletics.** NJCAA. **Intercollegiate:** Basketball, cross-country, volleyball. **Team name:** Brave Hearts.

**Student services.** Career counseling, personal counseling.

**Contact.** Phone: (605) 455-6000 Fax: (605) 455-2787
Leslie Mesteth, Registrar, Oglala Lakota College, Box 490, Kyle, SD 57752-0490

## Presentation College
### Aberdeen, South Dakota
www.presentation.edu                                    CB code: 6582

- Private 4-year business and health science college affiliated with Roman Catholic Church
- Commuter campus in large town
- 614 degree-seeking undergraduates
- SAT or ACT (ACT writing optional) required

**General.** Founded in 1951. Regionally accredited. **Degrees:** 106 bachelor's, 29 associate awarded. **Location:** 200 miles from Sioux Falls, 280 miles from Minneapolis-St. Paul. **Calendar:** Semester, extensive summer session. **Full-time faculty:** 37 total. **Part-time faculty:** 50 total.

**Freshman class profile.**

| Mid 50% test scores | | GPA 3.0-3.49: | 29% |
|---|---|---|---|
| ACT composite: | 17-22 | GPA 2.0-2.99: | 33% |
| GPA 3.75 or higher: | 18% | Out-of-state: | 19% |
| GPA 3.50-3.74: | 10% | Live on campus: | 90% |

**Basis for selection.** GPA very important, followed by rigor of secondary school record and test scores. 18 ACT or 860 SAT (exclusive of Writing) required. ACT required for radiologic technology applicants. COMPASS assessment used for math placement. **Homeschooled:** Official transcript from local schooling guild, detailed course descriptions, list of textbooks, and letter of academic recommendation from primary educator required.

**High school preparation.** 16 units recommended. Recommended units include English 4, mathematics 3, social studies 2 and science 2. CPR certificate required of nursing and allied health applicants.

**2009-2010 Annual costs.** Tuition/fees: $14,250. Room/board: $5,500. Books/supplies: $1,300. Personal expenses: $620.

**Application procedures. Admission:** Priority date 4/1; deadline 9/1 (receipt date). $25 fee. Admission notification on a rolling basis. **Financial**

**aid:** Priority date 4/1; no closing date. FAFSA required. Applicants notified on a rolling basis starting 5/1; must reply within 2 week(s) of notification.

**Academics. Special study options:** Distance learning, double major, dual enrollment of high school students, external degree, internships, liberal arts/career combination. **Credit/placement by examination:** CLEP, ACT, institutional tests. 15 credit hours maximum toward associate degree, 30 toward bachelor's. **Support services:** Learning center, reduced course load, remedial instruction, study skills assistance, tutoring.

**Majors. Business:** Business admin. **Communications:** General. **Health:** Health care admin, medical radiologic technology/radiation therapy, nursing (RN). **Parks/recreation:** General. **Public administration:** Social work.

**Computing on campus.** 180 workstations in dormitories, library, computer center. Dormitories wired for high-speed internet access and linked to campus network.

**Student life. Freshman orientation:** Mandatory. Preregistration for classes offered. **Housing:** Coed dorms available. $250 deposit, deadline 7/15. **Activities:** Drama, student government, student newspaper, Native American club.

**Athletics.** NAIA. **Intercollegiate:** Baseball M, basketball, cross-country, golf, soccer, softball W, volleyball W. **Intramural:** Basketball, volleyball W. **Team name:** Saints.

**Student services.** Adult student services, career counseling, student employment services, health services, personal counseling, placement for graduates, veterans' counselor.

**Contact.** E-mail: admit@presentation.edu
Phone: (605) 229-8492 Toll-free number: (800) 437-6060
Fax: (605) 229-8425
JoEllen Lindner, Vice President for Enrollment and Student Retention Services, Presentation College, 1500 North Main Street, Aberdeen, SD 57401

## Sinte Gleska University
Mission, South Dakota
www.sintegleska.edu                    CB code: 7328

- Public 4-year university and liberal arts college
- Commuter campus in rural community
- 848 undergraduates
- 164 graduate students

**General.** Founded in 1970. Regionally accredited. College tribally controlled and charted by Rosebud Sicangu Lakota Tribe (Sioux). **Degrees:** 33 bachelor's, 54 associate awarded; master's offered. **Location:** 90 miles from Pierre, 240 miles from Sioux Falls. **Calendar:** Semester, limited summer session. **Full-time faculty:** 45 total.

**Basis for selection.** Open admission.

**2009-2010 Annual costs.** Tuition/fees: $3,590. Books/supplies: $500. Personal expenses: $500.

**Application procedures. Admission:** No deadline. No application fee. Admission notification on a rolling basis. **Financial aid:** No deadline. FAFSA required.

**Academics.** One of 18 colleges with membership in American Indian Higher Education Consortium. **Special study options:** Double major, dual enrollment of high school students, independent study, internships. **Credit/placement by examination:** CLEP. **Support services:** Learning center, reduced course load, remedial instruction, tutoring.

**Majors. Business:** Business admin, hospitality/recreation. **Computer sciences:** Computer science. **Education:** General, elementary, special. **Public administration:** Human services. **Social sciences:** General.

**Computing on campus.** 30 workstations in library, computer center.

**Student life. Activities:** Student government.

**Athletics. Intramural:** Basketball, football (tackle) M, softball, volleyball.

**Student services.** Adult student services, career counseling, personal counseling, veterans' counselor.

**Contact.** Phone: (605) 747-2263 Fax: (605) 747-4258
Jack Herman, Registrar, Sinte Gleska University, Box 105, Mission, SD 57555

## South Dakota School of Mines and Technology
Rapid City, South Dakota
www.sdsmt.edu                    CB code: 6652

- Public 4-year university
- Commuter campus in small city
- 1,632 degree-seeking undergraduates: 9% part-time, 22% women, 1% Asian American, 1% Hispanic American, 3% Native American, 3% international
- 262 degree-seeking graduate students
- 82% of applicants admitted
- SAT or ACT (ACT writing optional) required
- 35% graduate within 6 years; 25% enter graduate study

**General.** Founded in 1885. Regionally accredited. **Degrees:** 252 bachelor's, 9 associate awarded; master's, doctoral offered. **ROTC:** Army. **Location:** 222 miles from Cheyenne, Wyoming. **Calendar:** Semester, limited summer session. **Full-time faculty:** 121 total; 84% have terminal degrees, 13% minority, 17% women. **Part-time faculty:** 14 total; 36% have terminal degrees, 14% minority, 29% women. **Class size:** 38% < 20, 49% 20-39, 5% 40-49, 6% 50-99, 1% >100. **Special facilities:** Geology/paleontology museum, engineering/mining experiment station, atmospheric science institute, CAMP-center for advanced manufacturing and production, advanced materials processing and joining lab, analytical characterization and testing laboratory, additive manufacturing laboratory, center for accelerated applications at the nanoscale, center for bioenergy.

**Freshman class profile.** 975 applied, 801 admitted, 362 enrolled.

| Mid 50% test scores | | | |
|---|---|---|---|
| SAT critical reading: | 500-630 | GPA 2.0-2.99: | 12% |
| SAT math: | 550-670 | Rank in top quarter: | 55% |
| ACT composite: | 24-28 | Rank in top tenth: | 22% |
| GPA 3.75 or higher: | 35% | Return as sophomores: | 83% |
| GPA 3.50-3.74: | 22% | Out-of-state: | 49% |
| GPA 3.0-3.49: | 30% | Live on campus: | 84% |
| | | International: | 2% |

**Basis for selection.** Test scores, GPA or class rank very important. ACT and/or COMPASS used for placement. **Homeschooled:** 225 GED with 40 on each test (paper based); or 2250 GED with 410 on each test (computer based); or submit ACT/SAT and be reviewed by admissions review committee.

**High school preparation.** College-preparatory program recommended. 18.5 units required. Required units include English 4, mathematics 4, social studies 3, science 4 (laboratory 3), foreign language 2, computer science .5 and visual/performing arts 1. 1 unit of fine arts is art, theatre or music appreciation, analysis, or performance.

**2009-2010 Annual costs.** Tuition/fees: $6,830; $8,210 out-of-state. Reciprocity agreements reduce tuition for some out-of-state students. Room/board: $4,602. Books/supplies: $1,950. Personal expenses: $1,700.

**2009-2010 Financial aid. Need-based:** 348 full-time freshmen applied for aid; 207 were judged to have need; 207 of these received aid. Average need met was 70%. Average scholarship/grant was $4,290; average loan $3,018. 35% of total undergraduate aid awarded as scholarships/grants, 65% as loans/jobs. **Non-need-based:** Awarded to 672 full-time undergraduates, including 247 freshmen. Scholarships awarded for academics, athletics, leadership, ROTC. **Additional information:** Closing date for scholarship applications February 1.

**Application procedures. Admission:** No deadline. $20 fee. Admission notification on a rolling basis beginning on or about 11/1. High school students may be enrolled fulltime but as special (non-degree seeking) students prior to high school graduation. **Financial aid:** Priority date 3/15; no closing date. FAFSA required. Applicants notified on a rolling basis starting 5/1; must reply within 3 week(s) of notification.

**Academics.** Undergraduate teams compete in solar vehicle, ChemE Car, unmanned aero vehicle, SAE aero design, ASCE concrete canoe and bridge, SAE Formula SAE, SAE Mini Baja, ASME human-powered vehicle, SAE clean snowmobile challenge and SAMPE Composites national competitions. Site of 2 Research Experience for undergraduates programs funded by National Science Foundation. **Special study options:** Cooperative education, cross-registration, distance learning, dual enrollment of high school students, ESL, independent study, internships, liberal arts/career combination, study abroad. Web-based technical management masters program. **Credit/placement by examination:** AP, CLEP, IB, SAT, ACT, institutional tests. Credits obtained through validation other than nationally recognized exams are limited to 32 credit hours for bachelor's degrees and 16 credit hours for associate degrees. No limit to credits earned through nationally recognized exams such as CLEP, AP, or DANTES. **Support services:** Learning center, reduced course load, remedial instruction, study skills assistance, tutoring.

**Majors. Computer sciences:** Computer science. **Engineering:** Chemical, civil, computer, electrical, environmental, geological, industrial, mechanical, metallurgical, mining. **Interdisciplinary:** Science/society. **Math:** General. **Physical sciences:** Atmospheric science, chemistry, geology, physics. **Other:** Business applications in science and technology.

**Most popular majors.** Computer/information sciences 7%, engineering/engineering technologies 74%, interdisciplinary studies 8%, physical sciences 8%.

**Computing on campus.** PC or laptop required. 210 workstations in dormitories, library, computer center, student center. Dormitories wired for high-speed internet access and linked to campus network. Commuter students can connect to campus network. Online course registration, online library, helpline, repair service, student web hosting, wireless network available.

**Student life. Freshman orientation:** Available. Preregistration for classes offered. Held in April and May. Adventure weekends for various groups in summer. **Policies:** Dorm residents required to purchase meal plan each semester. **Housing:** Guaranteed on-campus for freshmen. Coed dorms, special housing for disabled, apartments, fraternity/sorority housing, wellness housing available. $100 nonrefundable deposit, deadline 8/15. **Activities:** Bands, campus ministries, choral groups, dance, drama, international student organizations, music ensembles, radio station, student government, student newspaper, Circle K, College Republicans, College Democrats, American Indian Science & Engineering Society, Habitat for Humanity, Muslim student association, Intervarsity Christian Fellowship.

**Athletics.** NAIA. **Intercollegiate:** Basketball, cross-country, football (tackle) M, golf, track and field, volleyball W. **Intramural:** Basketball, golf, racquetball, skiing, softball, swimming, track and field, volleyball. **Team name:** Hardrockers.

**Student services.** Adult student services, alcohol/substance abuse counseling, chaplain/spiritual director, career counseling, student employment services, financial aid counseling, health services, minority student services, on-campus daycare, personal counseling, placement for graduates, veterans' counselor, women's services. **Physically disabled:** Services for visually, speech, hearing impaired.

**Contact.** E-mail: admissions@sdsmt.edu
Phone: (605) 394-2414 Toll-free number: (877) 877-6044
Fax: (605) 394-1979
Tamara Martinez-Anderson, Director of Admissions, South Dakota School of Mines and Technology, 501 East St. Joseph Street, Rapid City, SD 57701

## South Dakota State University
**Brookings, South Dakota**
www.sdstate.edu                                CB code: 6653

- Public 4-year university
- Commuter campus in large town
- 9,786 degree-seeking undergraduates: 13% part-time, 51% women, 1% African American, 1% Asian American, 1% Hispanic American, 2% Native American, 1% international
- 1,582 graduate students
- 93% of applicants admitted
- SAT or ACT (ACT writing optional) required
- 54% graduate within 6 years

**General.** Founded in 1881. Regionally accredited. **Degrees:** 1,838 bachelor's, 24 associate awarded; master's, doctoral, professional offered. **ROTC:** Army, Air Force. **Location:** 50 miles from Sioux Falls. **Calendar:** Semester, limited summer session. **Full-time faculty:** 476 total; 72% have terminal degrees, 14% minority, 44% women. **Part-time faculty:** 203 total; 23% have terminal degrees, 4% minority, 71% women. **Class size:** 32% < 20, 49% 20-39, 7% 40-49, 9% 50-99, 3% >100. **Special facilities:** Water resources research center, agricultural experiment station, cooperative extension service, Northern Great Plains biostress center, agricultural heritage museum, animal disease research and diagnostic laboratory, entrepreneur institute, GIS center of excellence, innovation research park, performing arts center.

**Freshman class profile.** 4,191 applied, 3,917 admitted, 2,135 enrolled.

| Mid 50% test scores | | Rank in top quarter: | 37% |
|---|---|---|---|
| ACT composite: | 20-26 | Rank in top tenth: | 15% |
| GPA 3.75 or higher: | 25% | Return as sophomores: | 78% |
| GPA 3.50-3.74: | 17% | Out-of-state: | 33% |
| GPA 3.0-3.49: | 30% | Live on campus: | 97% |
| GPA 2.0-2.99: | 26% | International: | 1% |

**Basis for selection.** School achievement record and test scores most important. **Homeschooled:** Transcript of courses and grades required. Must take ACT and receive scores of 18 Comp, 18 English, 20 Math, 17 Social Studies/Reasoning, and 17 Science Reasoning.

**High school preparation.** College-preparatory program required. 14 units required. Required units include English 4, mathematics 3, social studies 3, science 3 (laboratory 3), computer science 1 and visual/performing arts 1. 1 fine arts required for students graduating from SD high school. Will accept noncredit fine arts activities in out-of-state schools that do not require it.

**2009-2010 Annual costs.** Tuition/fees: $6,155; $7,528 out-of-state. Reduced out-of-state tuition for Minnesota students. Room/board: $5,668. Books/supplies: $1,014. Personal expenses: $2,024.

**2009-2010 Financial aid. Non-need-based:** Scholarships awarded for academics, art, athletics, job skills, leadership, minority status, music/drama, ROTC, state residency.

**Application procedures. Admission:** No deadline. $20 fee. Admission notification on a rolling basis. **Financial aid:** Priority date 3/11; no closing date. FAFSA required. Applicants notified on a rolling basis starting 4/1; must reply within 3 week(s) of notification.

**Academics.** Evening, weekend and other condensed degree-awarding classes available at Sioux Falls Center for Public Higher Education. **Special study options:** Accelerated study, combined bachelor's/graduate degree, cooperative education, cross-registration, distance learning, double major, dual enrollment of high school students, exchange student, honors, independent study, internships, liberal arts/career combination, study abroad, teacher certification program. **Credit/placement by examination:** AP, CLEP, IB, SAT, ACT, institutional tests. 16 credit hours maximum toward associate degree, 32 toward bachelor's. **Support services:** Pre-admission summer program, reduced course load, remedial instruction, study skills assistance, tutoring, writing center.

**Majors. Agriculture:** General, agribusiness operations, agronomy, animal sciences, dairy, economics, horticulture, landscaping, mechanization, range science. **Biology:** General, biochemistry, microbiology. **Business:** Entrepreneurial studies, hotel/motel admin. **Communications:** Journalism. **Computer sciences:** General. **Conservation:** Management/policy, wildlife. **Education:** Agricultural, early childhood, music, secondary, voc/tech. **Engineering:** Agricultural, civil, electrical, mechanical, physics, software. **Engineering technology:** Construction, electrical, industrial management, industrial safety, manufacturing. **Family/consumer sciences:** Apparel marketing, consumer economics, family resources, family studies, food/nutrition. **Foreign languages:** French, German, Spanish. **Health:** Athletic training, clinical lab science, nursing (RN), pharmaceutical sciences. **History:** General. **Interdisciplinary:** Global studies. **Liberal arts:** Arts/sciences. **Math:** General. **Parks/recreation:** Facilities management, health/fitness. **Physical sciences:** Chemistry, physics. **Psychology:** General. **Social sciences:** Economics, geography, political science, sociology. **Transportation:** Aviation, aviation management, flight instructor. **Visual/performing arts:** General, graphic design, interior design, music management. **Other:** Health promotion.

**Most popular majors.** Agriculture 11%, biology 6%, engineering/engineering technologies 11%, family/consumer sciences 7%, health sciences 22%, social sciences 12%.

**Computing on campus.** 692 workstations in dormitories, library, computer center, student center. Dormitories wired for high-speed internet access and linked to campus network. Commuter students can connect to campus network. Online course registration, online library, helpline, repair service, wireless network available.

**Student life. Freshman orientation:** Mandatory. Preregistration for classes offered. 2-day programs in June, one-day programs later in the summer. **Policies:** Students out of high school for less than 2 years required to live in campus housing unless living with family. **Housing:** Guaranteed on-campus for freshmen. Coed dorms, special housing for disabled, apartments, fraternity/sorority housing, wellness housing available. $50 fully refundable deposit. Limited single rooms with optional meal plan available for upperclassmen. **Activities:** Bands, choral groups, dance, drama, literary magazine, music ensembles, musical theater, radio station, student government, student newspaper, symphony orchestra, University Program Council, Golden Key International Honor Society, Campus Crusade for Christ, Fellowship of Christian Athletes, Native American club, Circle K International, Black Student Alliance, geography club.

**Athletics.** NCAA. **Intercollegiate:** Baseball M, basketball, cross-country, equestrian W, football (tackle) M, golf, soccer W, softball W, swimming, tennis, track and field, volleyball W, wrestling M. **Intramural:** Badminton, basketball, football (non-tackle), golf, racquetball, soccer W, softball, swimming, table tennis, track and field, volleyball, wrestling M. **Team name:** Jackrabbits.

**Student services.** Adult student services, alcohol/substance abuse counseling, chaplain/spiritual director, career counseling, services for economically disadvantaged, student employment services, financial aid counseling, health services, legal services, minority student services, personal counseling, placement for graduates, veterans' counselor. **Physically disabled:** Services for visually, speech, hearing impaired.

**Contact.** E-mail: SDSU.Admissions@sdstate.edu
Phone: (605) 688-4121 Toll-free number: (800) 952-3541
Fax: (605) 688-6891
Tracy Welsh, Director of Admissions and High School Relations, South Dakota State University, Box 2201 SAD 200, Brookings, SD 57007-0649

## University of Sioux Falls
### Sioux Falls, South Dakota
www.usiouxfalls.edu                      CB code: 6651

- Private 4-year university and liberal arts college affiliated with American Baptist Churches in the USA
- Residential campus in small city
- 1,197 degree-seeking undergraduates: 15% part-time, 53% women
- 233 graduate students
- 97% of applicants admitted
- SAT or ACT (ACT writing optional) required

**General.** Founded in 1883. Regionally accredited. **Degrees:** 262 bachelor's, 1 associate awarded; master's offered. **ROTC:** Air Force. **Location:** 180 miles from Omaha, Nebraska. **Calendar:** 4-1-4, limited summer session. **Full-time faculty:** 65 total. **Part-time faculty:** 75 total. **Class size:** 57% < 20, 39% 20-39, 1% 40-49, 2% 50-99, less than 1% >100.

**Freshman class profile.** 705 applied, 682 admitted, 287 enrolled.

| Mid 50% test scores | | | |
|---|---|---|---|
| | | ACT composite: | 16-26 |
| SAT critical reading: | 390-480 | Out-of-state: | 40% |
| SAT math: | 430-470 | Live on campus: | 90% |

**Basis for selection.** ACT or SAT, GPA, and class rank important. Audition required for music, theater programs; portfolio recommended for art program. **Homeschooled:** Statement describing homeschool structure and mission, transcript of courses and grades required.

**High school preparation.** Recommended units include English 4, mathematics 3, social studies 3, history 3, science 2 and computer science 1.

**2009-2010 Annual costs.** Tuition/fees: $20,290. Room/board: $5,920. Books/supplies: $1,000. Personal expenses: $2,000.

**2008-2009 Financial aid. Non-need-based:** Scholarships awarded for academics, alumni affiliation, art, athletics, job skills, leadership, music/drama, religious affiliation, state residency.

**Application procedures. Admission:** No deadline. $25 fee, may be waived for applicants with need. Admission notification on a rolling basis. **Financial aid:** Priority date 3/1; no closing date. FAFSA required. Applicants notified on a rolling basis starting 3/1; must reply within 2 week(s) of notification.

**Academics.** Degree completion program offered for adults 25 and older with 64 hours previous college education. **Special study options:** Accelerated study, cross-registration, distance learning, double major, dual enrollment of high school students, honors, independent study, internships, liberal arts/career combination, student-designed major, study abroad, teacher certification program, Washington semester. **Credit/placement by examination:** AP, CLEP, IB, SAT, ACT. 16 credit hours maximum toward bachelor's degree. **Support services:** Learning center, reduced course load, study skills assistance, tutoring, writing center.

**Majors. Biology:** General. **Business:** Accounting, business admin, hospitality admin, organizational behavior. **Communications:** Journalism. **Computer sciences:** General, computer science. **Education:** Art, elementary, English, health, multi-level teacher, music. **Foreign languages:** Spanish. **Health:** Nursing (RN). **History:** General. **Liberal arts:** Arts/sciences. **Math:** General, applied. **Parks/recreation:** Exercise sciences. **Philosophy/religion:** Religion. **Physical sciences:** Chemistry. **Protective services:** Criminal justice, police science. **Psychology:** General. **Public administration:**

Social work. **Social sciences:** General, political science, sociology. **Theology:** Theology. **Visual/performing arts:** Art, dramatic.

**Most popular majors.** Business/marketing 36%, education 10%, public administration/social services 6%, security/protective services 7%, visual/performing arts 8%.

**Computing on campus.** 115 workstations in dormitories, library, computer center, student center. Dormitories wired for high-speed internet access and linked to campus network. Commuter students can connect to campus network. Online course registration, online library, helpline, repair service, student web hosting, wireless network available.

**Student life. Freshman orientation:** Available. Preregistration for classes offered. Held 2 days immediately preceding fall semester. **Policies:** No alcohol at university-sponsored events. Freshmen and sophomores required to live in college housing unless over 20 years of age or given permission by director of residence life. **Housing:** Coed dorms, single-sex dorms, apartments available. $50 deposit. **Activities:** Bands, campus ministries, choral groups, dance, drama, music ensembles, musical theater, opera, radio station, student government, student newspaper, symphony orchestra, TV station, nontraditional student association, student volunteer groups, religious organizations, Fellowship of Christian Athletes, Campus Crusade For Christ, Young Life.

**Athletics.** NAIA. **Intercollegiate:** Baseball M, basketball, cross-country, football (tackle) M, golf, soccer, softball W, tennis, track and field, volleyball W, wrestling M. **Intramural:** Basketball, golf, soccer, softball, table tennis, tennis, volleyball. **Team name:** Cougars.

**Student services.** Adult student services, alcohol/substance abuse counseling, chaplain/spiritual director, career counseling, student employment services, financial aid counseling, health services, personal counseling, placement for graduates, veterans' counselor, women's services. **Physically disabled:** Services for hearing impaired.

**Contact.** E-mail: admissions@usiouxfalls.edu
Phone: (605) 331-6600 Toll-free number: (800) 888-1047
Fax: (605) 331-6615
Jody Nour, Director of New Student Recruitment, University of Sioux Falls, 1101 West 22nd Street, Sioux Falls, SD 57105-1699

## University of South Dakota
### Vermillion, South Dakota
www.usd.edu                  CB member / CB code: 6881

- Public 4-year university
- Residential campus in large town
- 6,043 degree-seeking undergraduates: 28% part-time, 62% women, 2% African American, 1% Asian American, 1% Hispanic American, 2% Native American
- 2,114 degree-seeking graduate students
- 87% of applicants admitted
- SAT or ACT (ACT writing optional), interview required
- 48% graduate within 6 years; 96% enter graduate study

**General.** Founded in 1862. Regionally accredited. **Degrees:** 933 bachelor's, 310 associate awarded; master's, doctoral, professional offered. **ROTC:** Army. **Location:** 55 miles from Sioux Falls, 35 miles from Sioux City, Iowa. **Calendar:** Semester, extensive summer session. **Full-time faculty:** 367 total; 75% have terminal degrees, 13% minority, 50% women. **Part-time faculty:** 63 total; 2% minority, 95% women. **Class size:** 47% < 20, 40% 20-39, 6% 40-49, 4% 50-99, 2% >100. **Special facilities:** Center for instructional design and delivery, center for disabilities, governmental research bureau, state data center, federal technical procurement center, geological survey, archaeology lab, speech and hearing center, disaster mental health institute.

**Freshman class profile.** 3,129 applied, 2,721 admitted, 1,118 enrolled.

| Mid 50% test scores | | | |
|---|---|---|---|
| | | Rank in top quarter: | 38% |
| SAT critical reading: | 430-630 | Rank in top tenth: | 13% |
| SAT math: | 440-610 | End year in good standing: | 84% |
| ACT composite: | 20-26 | Return as sophomores: | 72% |
| GPA 3.75 or higher: | 22% | Out-of-state: | 29% |
| GPA 3.50-3.74: | 17% | Live on campus: | 82% |
| GPA 3.0-3.49: | 28% | Fraternities: | 20% |
| GPA 2.0-2.99: | 31% | Sororities: | 12% |

**Basis for selection.** Admission in good standing granted with 2.0 GPA in required courses or 2.6 overall, rank in top 60% of class, or 20 ACT.

Interview recommended for dental hygiene, nursing, physician assistant programs; audition recommended for music, theater programs; portfolio recommended for art program. **Homeschooled:** State high school equivalency certificate required.

**High school preparation.** College-preparatory program required. 14 units required; 18 recommended. Required and recommended units include English 4, mathematics 3-4, social studies 3, science 3-4 (laboratory 3) and foreign language 2. 1 fine arts required.

**2009-2010 Annual costs.** Tuition/fees: $6,468; $7,841 out-of-state. Reciprocity agreement in place for Minnesota residents. Reduced tuition for Iowa residents. Room/board: $5,787. Books/supplies: $900. Personal expenses: $2,000.

**2008-2009 Financial aid. Need-based:** Average need met was 75%. Average scholarship/grant was $4,176; average loan $3,360. 32% of total undergraduate aid awarded as scholarships/grants, 68% as loans/jobs. **Non-need-based:** Scholarships awarded for academics, art, athletics, leadership, minority status, music/drama, ROTC.

**Application procedures. Admission:** No deadline. $20 fee. Admission notification on a rolling basis beginning on or about 9/20. 2/15 closing date for dental hygiene and nursing programs. **Financial aid:** Priority date 3/15; no closing date. FAFSA required. Applicants notified on a rolling basis starting 5/5.

**Academics. Special study options:** Accelerated study, combined bachelor's/graduate degree, cross-registration, distance learning, double major, dual enrollment of high school students, ESL, exchange student, external degree, honors, independent study, internships, liberal arts/career combination, student-designed major, study abroad, teacher certification program. **Credit/placement by examination:** AP, CLEP, institutional tests. 15 credit hours maximum toward associate degree, 30 toward bachelor's. **Support services:** Pre-admission summer program, reduced course load, remedial instruction, tutoring.

**Honors college/program.** Honors program open to students in all majors who displayed potential for honors work in high school through good grades, college preparatory curriculum, high ACT scores, and participation in school and community activities.

**Majors. Area/ethnic studies:** Native American. **Biology:** General. **Business:** Accounting, business admin, finance, managerial economics. **Communications:** General, journalism, media studies. **Computer sciences:** General. **Education:** Biology, chemistry, drama/dance, early childhood, elementary, English, foreign languages, French, German, history, kindergarten/preschool, mathematics, music, physical, physics, science, social science, Spanish, special, speech. **Foreign languages:** French, German, Spanish. **Health:** Communication disorders, dental hygiene, health services admin, substance abuse counseling. **History:** General. **Interdisciplinary:** Global studies. **Liberal arts:** Arts/sciences. **Math:** General. **Parks/recreation:** General. **Philosophy/religion:** Philosophy. **Physical sciences:** Chemistry, geology, physics. **Protective services:** Criminal justice. **Psychology:** General. **Public administration:** Social work. **Social sciences:** Anthropology, economics, political science, sociology. **Visual/performing arts:** Art, arts management, dramatic, music performance, studio arts.

**Most popular majors.** Business/marketing 19%, communications/journalism 6%, education 14%, health sciences 14%, psychology 12%, security/protective services 6%, social sciences 9%.

**Computing on campus.** 885 workstations in dormitories, library, student center. Dormitories wired for high-speed internet access and linked to campus network. Commuter students can connect to campus network. Online course registration, online library, helpline, repair service, student web hosting, wireless network available.

**Student life. Freshman orientation:** Mandatory. Preregistration for classes offered. **Policies:** Students required to live in residence halls for first 2 years unless living in fraternity or sorority housing, or commuting from home. **Housing:** Guaranteed on-campus for freshmen. Coed dorms, special housing for disabled, apartments, fraternity/sorority housing, wellness housing available. $100 partly refundable deposit, deadline 9/1. Apartments available for students with dependent children. **Activities:** Bands, choral groups, dance, drama, international student organizations, literary magazine, music ensembles, musical theater, opera, radio station, student government, student newspaper, symphony orchestra, TV station, Young Democrats, College Republicans, Campus Crusade for Christ, Chinese student association, gay/lesbian/bisexual alliance, Habitat for Humanity, nontraditional student association, political science league.

**Athletics.** NCAA. **Intercollegiate:** Basketball, cross-country, diving, football (tackle) M, golf, soccer W, softball W, swimming, tennis W, track and field. **Intramural:** Badminton, basketball, bowling, cross-country, football (non-tackle), golf, racquetball, soccer, softball, swimming, table tennis, tennis, track and field, volleyball. **Team name:** Coyotes.

**Student services.** Adult student services, alcohol/substance abuse counseling, chaplain/spiritual director, career counseling, services for economically disadvantaged, student employment services, financial aid counseling, health services, legal services, minority student services, on-campus daycare, personal counseling, placement for graduates, veterans' counselor. **Physically disabled:** Services for visually, speech, hearing impaired.

**Contact.** E-mail: admission@usd.edu
Phone: (605) 677-5434 Toll-free number: (877) 269-6837
Fax: (605) 677-6753
Stephanie Moser, Director, University of South Dakota, 414 East Clark Street, Vermillion, SD 57069-2390

# Tennessee

## American Baptist College
**Nashville, Tennessee**
**www.abcnash.edu**                    CB code: 2401

♦ Private 4-year Bible college affiliated with Baptist faith
♦ Commuter campus in large city
♦ 84 degree-seeking undergraduates: 29% part-time, 32% women, 95% African American, 2% international
♦ Application essay required

**General.** Founded in 1924. Accredited by ABHE. **Degrees:** 16 bachelor's, 2 associate awarded. **Location:** 200 miles from Memphis. **Calendar:** Semester, limited summer session. **Full-time faculty:** 7 total. **Part-time faculty:** 8 total.

**Freshman class profile.**

| | | | |
|---|---|---|---|
| End year in good standing: | 73% | Live on campus: | 26% |
| Return as sophomores: | 75% | | |

**Basis for selection.** Recommendations, personal essay, religious commitment important. Admissions committee selects applicants best qualified to benefit from opportunities offered by college. **Homeschooled:** Transcript of courses and grades required.

**2009-2010 Annual costs.** Tuition/fees: $5,840. Room only: $1,800. Books/supplies: $900.

**Application procedures. Admission:** Closing date 7/1 (receipt date). $20 fee. Admission notification on a rolling basis. **Financial aid:** No deadline. FAFSA required. Applicants notified on a rolling basis; must reply within 2 week(s) of notification.

**Academics.** All students major in Bible studies or theology. Additional major in business administration optional. **Special study options:** Double major. **Credit/placement by examination:** CLEP, institutional tests.

**Majors. Area/ethnic studies:** African-American. **Business:** Business admin. **Education:** General, history, social science. **Liberal arts:** Arts/sciences. **Social sciences:** General. **Theology:** Bible, pastoral counseling, religious ed, theology.

**Computing on campus.** 15 workstations in library.

**Student life. Freshman orientation:** Mandatory. Preregistration for classes offered. **Housing:** Single-sex dorms, apartments available. **Activities:** Student government, student newspaper.

**Contact.** E-mail: mlockhart@abcnash.edu
Phone: (615) 256-1463 Fax: (615) 226-7855
Marcella Lockhart, Director of Enrollment Management, American Baptist College, 1800 Baptist World Center Drive, Nashville, TN 37207

## Aquinas College
**Nashville, Tennessee**                    CB member
**www.aquinascollege.edu**                    CB code: 7318

♦ Private 4-year nursing and liberal arts college affiliated with Roman Catholic Church
♦ Commuter campus in very large city
♦ 858 degree-seeking undergraduates
♦ 48% of applicants admitted
♦ Application essay required

**General.** Founded in 1961. Regionally accredited. **Degrees:** 67 bachelor's, 105 associate awarded. **Location:** 1 mile from downtown, 195 miles from Knoxville. **Calendar:** Semester, limited summer session. **Full-time faculty:** 36 total; 50% have terminal degrees, 67% women. **Part-time faculty:** 62 total; 27% have terminal degrees, 45% women.

**Freshman class profile.** 180 applied, 86 admitted, 29 enrolled.

| Mid 50% test scores | | | |
|---|---|---|---|
| SAT critical reading: | 560-660 | SAT writing: | 490-620 |
| SAT math: | 460-600 | ACT composite: | 18-25 |

**Basis for selection.** School achievement record, test scores important. **Homeschooled:** Transcript of courses and grades required. Must provide copy of transcript from accredited home school agency along with official ACT Report.

**High school preparation.** 20 units recommended. Recommended units include English 4, mathematics 3, social studies 3, science 3, foreign language 2 and academic electives 5.

**2010-2011 Annual costs.** Tuition/fees (projected): $18,330. Books/supplies: $1,000. Personal expenses: $1,500.

**2008-2009 Financial aid. Non-need-based:** Scholarships awarded for academics, alumni affiliation, leadership, religious affiliation.

**Application procedures. Admission:** Priority date 3/1; no deadline. $25 fee, may be waived for applicants with need. Admission notification on a rolling basis. **Financial aid:** Priority date 3/1; no closing date. FAFSA required. Applicants notified on a rolling basis starting 3/1; must reply within 2 week(s) of notification.

**Academics. Special study options:** Accelerated study, double major, dual enrollment of high school students, independent study, liberal arts/career combination, teacher certification program. **Credit/placement by examination:** AP, CLEP, SAT, ACT, institutional tests. 30 credit hours maximum toward associate degree, 60 toward bachelor's. **Support services:** Learning center, reduced course load, remedial instruction, study skills assistance, tutoring, writing center.

**Majors. Business:** Business admin, management information systems. **Education:** Elementary. **Health:** Nursing (RN). **Liberal arts:** Arts/sciences.

**Computing on campus.** 50 workstations in library, computer center. Online library, helpline available.

**Student life. Freshman orientation:** Mandatory. **Policies:** Drug-free/alcohol-free campus. **Activities:** Campus ministries, choral groups, student government, Phi Beta Lambda, Delta Epsilon Sigma, Association of Student Nurses, Association for Supervision and Curriculum Development student chapter, student affairs council, Frassati Society, Sigma Beta Delta.

**Student services.** Chaplain/spiritual director, financial aid counseling.

**Contact.** E-mail: admissions@aquinascollege.edu
Phone: (615) 297-7545 ext. 460 Toll-free number: (800) 649-9956
Fax: (615) 279-3893
Connie Hansom, Director of Admissions, Aquinas College, 4210 Harding Road, Nashville, TN 37205-2086

## Argosy University: Nashville
**Nashville, Tennessee**
**www.argosy.edu/nashville**

♦ For-profit 4-year university
♦ Very large city
♦ 51 degree-seeking undergraduates

**General.** Regionally accredited. **Degrees:** 6 bachelor's awarded; master's, doctoral, professional offered. **Calendar:** Continuous. **Full-time faculty:** 2 total. **Part-time faculty:** 32 total.

**Freshman class profile.** 5 enrolled.

**Basis for selection.** Open admission.

**Academics. Credit/placement by examination:** CLEP.

**Majors. Business:** Business admin. **Liberal arts:** Arts/sciences. **Protective services:** Police science. **Psychology:** General.

**Contact.** Phone: (615) 525-2800
Argosy University: Nashville, 100 Centerview Drive, Suite 225, Nashville, TN 37214

## Austin Peay State University
**Clarksville, Tennessee**
www.apsu.edu

**CB member**
**CB code: 1028**

- Public 4-year university and liberal arts college
- Commuter campus in small city
- 9,084 degree-seeking undergraduates: 23% part-time, 61% women
- 886 degree-seeking graduate students
- 90% of applicants admitted

**General.** Founded in 1927. Regionally accredited. **Degrees:** 1,180 bachelor's, 158 associate awarded; master's offered. **ROTC:** Army, Air Force. **Location:** 45 miles from Nashville. **Calendar:** Semester, limited summer session. **Full-time faculty:** 301 total; 11% minority, 45% women. **Part-time faculty:** 240 total; 10% minority, 58% women. **Class size:** 41% < 20, 48% 20-39, 6% 40-49, 4% 50-99, less than 1% >100. **Special facilities:** Zoological museum.

**Freshman class profile.** 3,111 applied, 2,802 admitted, 1,645 enrolled.

| Mid 50% test scores | | | |
|---|---|---|---|
| SAT critical reading: | 440-550 | Rank in top quarter: | 39% |
| SAT math: | 450-540 | Rank in top tenth: | 14% |
| ACT composite: | 19-23 | Return as sophomores: | 68% |
| GPA 3.75 or higher: | 15% | Out-of-state: | 7% |
| GPA 3.50-3.74: | 13% | Live on campus: | 39% |
| GPA 3.0-3.49: | 32% | Fraternities: | 9% |
| GPA 2.0-2.99: | 37% | Sororities: | 8% |

**Basis for selection.** Rigor of secondary school record, GPA, and test scores very important. ACT/SAT is required for all first time freshman applicants under age 21, except for active duty military. All first time freshman applicants 21 years of age and older, except for active duty military, must submit official COMPASS assessment scores prior to admission.

**High school preparation.** College-preparatory program required. 14 units required. Required units include English 4, mathematics 3, social studies 1, history 1, science 2 (laboratory 1) and foreign language 2. Mathematics units should be algebra I and II, 1 geometry or advanced mathematics. Social science units should be 1 social studies, 1 US history. Foreign language units must be in 1 language. 1 visual and/or performing arts also required.

**2009-2010 Annual costs.** Tuition/fees: $5,868; $17,946 out-of-state. Room/board: $6,120. Books/supplies: $1,550. Personal expenses: $2,000.

**2008-2009 Financial aid.** **Need-based:** 1,254 full-time freshmen applied for aid; 974 were judged to have need; 971 of these received aid. Average scholarship/grant was $5,319; average loan $3,383. 45% of total undergraduate aid awarded as scholarships/grants, 55% as loans/jobs. **Non-need-based:** Awarded to 2,758 full-time undergraduates, including 979 freshmen. Scholarships awarded for academics, art, athletics, leadership, music/drama, ROTC, state residency.

**Application procedures.** **Admission:** Closing date 7/25. $15 fee. Admission notification on a rolling basis. **Financial aid:** Priority date 4/1; no closing date. FAFSA required. Applicants notified on a rolling basis starting 5/1.

**Academics.** **Special study options:** Accelerated study, cooperative education, distance learning, double major, dual enrollment of high school students, ESL, honors, independent study, internships, study abroad, teacher certification program. Service Members Opportunity College (associate and bachelor's degrees). **Credit/placement by examination:** AP, CLEP, SAT, ACT, institutional tests. 32 credit hours maximum toward associate degree, 64 toward bachelor's. **Support services:** Learning center, remedial instruction, study skills assistance, tutoring, writing center.

**Honors college/program.** Rank in top 10% of class, 26 ACT, and commendable high school record required.

**Majors. Agriculture:** General. **Biology:** General. **Business:** General, nonprofit/public. **Communications:** Media studies. **Computer sciences:** General. **Education:** Health, special. **Engineering technology:** General. **Foreign languages:** General, Spanish. **Health:** Clinical lab science, medical radiologic technology/radiation therapy, nursing (RN). **History:** General. **Liberal arts:** Arts/sciences. **Math:** General. **Parks/recreation:** Health/fitness. **Philosophy/religion:** Philosophy. **Physical sciences:** Chemistry, geology, physics. **Protective services:** Law enforcement admin. **Psychology:** General. **Public administration:** Social work. **Social sciences:** Political science, sociology. **Visual/performing arts:** Art.

**Most popular majors.** Business/marketing 18%, communications/journalism 7%, health sciences 12%, interdisciplinary studies 7%, liberal arts 8%.

**Computing on campus.** 760 workstations in dormitories, library, computer center, student center. Dormitories wired for high-speed internet access and linked to campus network. Commuter students can connect to campus network. Online course registration, online library, helpline, wireless network available.

**Student life. Freshman orientation:** Mandatory, $60 fee. Preregistration for classes offered. **Policies:** Alcohol not permitted on campus. **Housing:** Coed dorms, single-sex dorms, special housing for disabled, apartments, fraternity/sorority housing available. $200 fully refundable deposit, deadline 8/15. **Activities:** Bands, campus ministries, choral groups, dance, drama, film society, international student organizations, literary magazine, music ensembles, musical theater, opera, radio station, student government, student newspaper, symphony orchestra, TV station, Wesley Foundation, Room In the Inn, Student Organization to Advance Renewable Energy, student art league.

**Athletics.** NCAA. **Intercollegiate:** Baseball M, basketball, cross-country, football (tackle) M, golf, rifle W, soccer W, softball W, tennis, track and field W, volleyball W. **Intramural:** Basketball, football (non-tackle), racquetball, soccer, table tennis, volleyball. **Team name:** Governors.

**Student services.** Adult student services, alcohol/substance abuse counseling, career counseling, student employment services, financial aid counseling, health services, on-campus daycare, personal counseling, veterans' counselor. **Physically disabled:** Services for visually, speech, hearing impaired.

**Contact.** E-mail: admissions@apsu.edu
Phone: (931) 221-7661 Toll-free number: (800) 844-2778
Fax: (931) 221-6168
Ryan Forsythe, Director of Admissions, Austin Peay State University, PO Box 4548, Clarksville, TN 37044

## Baptist College of Health Sciences
**Memphis, Tennessee**
www.bchs.edu

- Private 4-year health science and nursing college affiliated with Baptist faith
- Commuter campus in very large city
- 1,018 degree-seeking undergraduates: 45% part-time, 87% women, 33% African American, 2% Asian American, 2% Hispanic American
- 15% of applicants admitted
- SAT or ACT (ACT writing optional) required
- 42% graduate within 6 years

**General.** Regionally accredited. **Degrees:** 166 bachelor's awarded. **Calendar:** Trimester, limited summer session. **Full-time faculty:** 61 total. **Part-time faculty:** 46 total. **Class size:** 51% < 20, 48% 20-39, less than 1% 50-99.

**Freshman class profile.** 464 applied, 70 admitted, 69 enrolled.

| | | | |
|---|---|---|---|
| GPA 3.75 or higher: | 23% | GPA 2.0-2.99: | 6% |
| GPA 3.50-3.74: | 16% | End year in good standing: | 97% |
| GPA 3.0-3.49: | 55% | | |

**Basis for selection.** GED not accepted. Standardized test scores, GPA, rigor of secondary school record, recommendations very important. **Home-schooled:** Transcript of courses and grades, letter of recommendation (non-parent) required. Transcript must be from an accredited home school agency showing GPA, high school graduation date, and all courses and grades. **Learning Disabled:** With proper documentation, students may be allowed to take the entrance exam with pencil and paper instead of on computer.

**High school preparation.** College-preparatory program required. 10 units required; 15 recommended. Required and recommended units include English 4, mathematics 2, social studies 1, history 1, science 2 (laboratory 2), foreign language 2 and academic electives 1.

**2009-2010 Annual costs.** Tuition/fees: $9,730. Books/supplies: $1,100. Personal expenses: $4,350.

**2008-2009 Financial aid.** **Need-based:** 41% of total undergraduate aid awarded as scholarships/grants, 59% as loans/jobs.

**Application procedures. Admission:** Priority date 3/1; deadline 5/1 (postmark date). $25 fee, may be waived for applicants with need. Admission notification on a rolling basis beginning on or about 5/1. Must reply by 6/1.

**Academics. Special study options:** Accelerated study. **Credit/placement by examination:** AP, CLEP, institutional tests. 15 credit hours maximum toward bachelor's degree. **Support services:** Learning center, tutoring.

**Majors. Health:** Health care admin, medical radiologic technology/radiation therapy, nuclear medical technology, nursing (RN), radiologic technology/medical imaging, respiratory therapy technology, sonography.

**Computing on campus.** 57 workstations in library, computer center. Dormitories linked to campus network. Commuter students can connect to campus network. Online course registration, helpline, wireless network available.

**Student life. Freshman orientation:** Mandatory. Preregistration for classes offered. **Housing:** Coed dorms, wellness housing available. $100 fully refundable deposit. **Activities:** Campus ministries, student government.

**Student services.** Chaplain/spiritual director, financial aid counseling, health services, personal counseling.

**Contact.** E-mail: admissions@bchs.edu
Phone: (901) 575-2247 Toll-free number: (866) 575-2247
Fax: (901) 572-2461
Lissa Morgan, Manager, Admissions, Baptist College of Health Sciences, 1003 Monroe Avenue, Memphis, TN 38104

## Belmont University
### Nashville, Tennessee
### www.belmont.edu
**CB code: 1058**

▶ Private 4-year university
▶ Residential campus in very large city
▶ 4,339 degree-seeking undergraduates: 7% part-time, 57% women, 4% African American, 3% Asian American, 2% Hispanic American, 1% international
▶ 1,036 degree-seeking graduate students
▶ 77% of applicants admitted
▶ SAT or ACT (ACT writing optional), interview required
▶ 68% graduate within 6 years; 17% enter graduate study

**General.** Founded in 1951. Regionally accredited. **Degrees:** 975 bachelor's awarded; master's, doctoral offered. **ROTC:** Army, Naval, Air Force. **Location:** 2 miles from downtown. **Calendar:** Semester, limited summer session. **Full-time faculty:** 269 total; 80% have terminal degrees, 11% minority, 50% women. **Part-time faculty:** 336 total; 24% have terminal degrees, 6% minority, 56% women. **Class size:** 53% < 20, 46% 20-39, less than 1% 40-49, less than 1% 50-99. **Special facilities:** 22-track recording studio, Studio B on Music Row, 140-year-old antebellum mansion.

**Freshman class profile.** 3,220 applied, 2,466 admitted, 991 enrolled.

| Mid 50% test scores | | | |
|---|---|---|---|
| SAT critical reading: | 540-640 | Rank in top quarter: | 68% |
| SAT math: | 530-640 | Rank in top tenth: | 35% |
| ACT composite: | 23-29 | End year in good standing: | 91% |
| GPA 3.75 or higher: | 34% | Return as sophomores: | 82% |
| GPA 3.50-3.74: | 22% | Out-of-state: | 65% |
| GPA 3.0-3.49: | 34% | Live on campus: | 96% |
| GPA 2.0-2.99: | 10% | Fraternities: | 3% |
| | | Sororities: | 5% |

**Basis for selection.** Admissions based on test scores, course selection, GPA, class rank, recommendations, leadership activity. Interview required for music business; audition required for music programs.

**High school preparation.** College-preparatory program required. 18 units required. Required and recommended units include English 4, mathematics 3-4, social studies 3, science 2-4, foreign language 2 and academic electives 3.

**2010-2011 Annual costs.** Tuition/fees: $23,680. Room/board: $9,030. Books/supplies: $1,300. Personal expenses: $2,000.

**2008-2009 Financial aid. Need-based:** 859 full-time freshmen applied for aid; 464 were judged to have need; 450 of these received aid. Average need met was 89%. Average scholarship/grant was $5,175; average loan $3,524. 30% of total undergraduate aid awarded as scholarships/grants, 70% as loans/jobs. **Non-need-based:** Awarded to 1,818 full-time undergraduates, including 630 freshmen. Scholarships awarded for academics, art, athletics, leadership, music/drama, religious affiliation, state residency.

**Application procedures. Admission:** Priority date 12/1; deadline 8/1. $50 fee. Admission notification on a rolling basis beginning on or about 9/1. Must reply by May 1 or within 2 week(s) if notified thereafter. **Financial aid:** Priority date 3/1; no closing date. FAFSA required. Applicants notified

on a rolling basis starting 3/15; must reply by 5/1 or within 2 week(s) of notification.

**Academics. Special study options:** Accelerated study, combined bachelor's/graduate degree, cooperative education, distance learning, double major, dual enrollment of high school students, ESL, honors, independent study, internships, liberal arts/career combination, student-designed major, study abroad, teacher certification program, Washington semester. **Credit/placement by examination:** AP, CLEP, IB, SAT, ACT, institutional tests. 24 credit hours maximum toward bachelor's degree. **Support services:** Learning center, pre-admission summer program, reduced course load, tutoring, writing center.

**Majors. Biology:** General, environmental, molecular, molecular biochemistry. **Business:** General, accounting, entrepreneurial studies, finance, hospitality admin, management information systems, management science, managerial economics, marketing. **Communications:** General, broadcast journalism, journalism, media studies, public relations. **Computer sciences:** Computer science, information systems. **Education:** General, art, biology, chemistry, early childhood, elementary, English, French, health, health occupations, history, mathematics, middle, music, physical, physics, science, secondary, social science, social studies, Spanish. **Family/consumer sciences:** Child care. **Foreign languages:** French, German, Spanish. **Health:** Nursing (RN). **History:** General. **Liberal arts:** Arts/sciences. **Math:** General. **Parks/recreation:** Exercise sciences, health/fitness. **Philosophy/religion:** Philosophy, religion. **Physical sciences:** Chemistry, physics. **Psychology:** General. **Public administration:** Social work. **Social sciences:** Economics, political science, sociology. **Theology:** Sacred music. **Visual/performing arts:** Art, commercial/advertising art, dramatic, music management, music pedagogy, music performance, music theory/composition, piano/organ, voice/opera.

**Most popular majors.** Business/marketing 15%, communications/journalism 6%, health sciences 10%, visual/performing arts 41%.

**Computing on campus.** 500 workstations in dormitories, library, computer center, student center. Dormitories wired for high-speed internet access and linked to campus network. Commuter students can connect to campus network. Online course registration, online library, helpline, wireless network available.

**Student life. Freshman orientation:** Mandatory, $60 fee. Preregistration for classes offered. 2-day program in summer or 4-day program in fall before classes start. **Housing:** Guaranteed on-campus for freshmen. Single-sex dorms, apartments, wellness housing available. $100 nonrefundable deposit, deadline 5/1. **Activities:** Bands, campus ministries, choral groups, dance, drama, international student organizations, literary magazine, music ensembles, musical theater, opera, radio station, student government, student newspaper, symphony orchestra, TV station, Baptist student union, Christian music society, Campus Crusade for Christ, Fellowship of Christian Athletes, Black Student Alliance.

**Athletics.** NCAA. **Intercollegiate:** Baseball M, basketball, cross-country, golf, soccer, softball W, tennis, track and field, volleyball W. **Intramural:** Basketball, bowling, golf M, racquetball, softball, table tennis, tennis, volleyball. **Team name:** Bruins.

**Student services.** Adult student services, alcohol/substance abuse counseling, chaplain/spiritual director, career counseling, student employment services, financial aid counseling, health services, minority student services, personal counseling, placement for graduates, veterans' counselor.

**Contact.** E-mail: buadmission@mail.belmont.edu
Phone: (615) 460-6785 Fax: (615) 460-5434
Kathy Baugher, Dean of Enrollment Services, Belmont University, 1900 Belmont Boulevard, Nashville, TN 37212-3757

## Bethel University
### McKenzie, Tennessee
### www.bethelu.edu
**CB code: 1063**

▶ Private 4-year university and liberal arts college affiliated with Presbyterian Church (USA)
▶ Residential campus in small town
▶ 2,550 degree-seeking undergraduates: 1% part-time, 59% women, 37% African American, 1% Hispanic American, 2% international
▶ 591 graduate students
▶ 54% of applicants admitted
▶ SAT or ACT (ACT writing optional) required

**General.** Founded in 1842. Regionally accredited. Students are provided with a laptop computer upon full-time registration. **Degrees:** 425 bachelor's awarded; master's offered. **Location:** 115 miles from Nashville, 120 miles from Memphis. **Calendar:** Differs by program, limited summer session. **Full-time faculty:** 97 total; 46% have terminal degrees, 7% minority, 44%

women. **Part-time faculty:** 194 total. **Class size:** 72% < 20, 28% 20-39, less than 1% 40-49, less than 1% 50-99. **Special facilities:** Autism resource center.

**Freshman class profile.** 1,057 applied, 566 admitted, 350 enrolled.

| Mid 50% test scores | | | |
|---|---|---|---|
| SAT critical reading: | 420-530 | Return as sophomores: | 62% |
| SAT math: | 470-570 | Out-of-state: | 7% |
| ACT composite: | 17-23 | Live on campus: | 32% |

**Basis for selection.** GPA and academic units considered. Counselor recommendation and interview considered for academically marginal applicants. **Homeschooled:** 19 ACT and passing score on GED required.

**High school preparation.** College-preparatory program recommended. Required units include English 4, mathematics 2, social studies 2 and science 2.

**2010-2011 Annual costs.** Tuition/fees (projected): $12,242. Room/board: $6,926. Books/supplies: $1,000. Personal expenses: $1,750.

**2009-2010 Financial aid. Need-based:** 55% of total undergraduate aid awarded as scholarships/grants, 45% as loans/jobs. **Non-need-based:** Scholarships awarded for academics, athletics, music/drama, religious affiliation, state residency.

**Application procedures. Admission:** Priority date 2/3; no deadline. $30 fee. Admission notification on a rolling basis. **Financial aid:** Priority date 3/3, closing date 6/30. FAFSA, institutional form required. Applicants notified on a rolling basis starting 3/1.

**Academics. Special study options:** Accelerated study, combined bachelor's/graduate degree, double major, honors, independent study, internships, student-designed major, study abroad, teacher certification program, weekend college. **Credit/placement by examination:** AP, CLEP, SAT, ACT, institutional tests. 30 credit hours maximum toward bachelor's degree. Accepts CLEP, DANTES, institutional exams for credit. **Support services:** Remedial instruction, study skills assistance, tutoring.

**Majors. Biology:** General. **Business:** Accounting/business management, business admin, management information systems. **Education:** Elementary, music, physical, special. **Health:** Nursing (RN), premedicine, prepharmacy. **History:** General. **Math:** General. **Philosophy/religion:** Christian. **Physical sciences:** Chemistry. **Psychology:** General. **Public administration:** Human services. **Social sciences:** Sociology. **Visual/performing arts:** Dramatic, music management.

**Most popular majors.** Business/marketing 80%, education 6%.

**Computing on campus.** PC or laptop required. 650 workstations in dormitories, library. Dormitories wired for high-speed internet access and linked to campus network. Commuter students can connect to campus network. Online library, helpline, repair service, wireless network available.

**Student life. Freshman orientation:** Mandatory. Preregistration for classes offered. 1-day Saturday program held June-August. Week-long sessions held the week prior to start of classes. **Housing:** Guaranteed on-campus for freshmen. Coed dorms, single-sex dorms, apartments available. $175 nonrefundable deposit, deadline 8/18. **Activities:** Bands, choral groups, drama, music ensembles, musical theater, student government, Fellowship of Christian Athletes, honor societies, American Chemical Society, Student TN Education Association, art club, Students in Free Enterprise, Arete, Campus Crusade for Christ, Relay for Life.

**Athletics.** NAIA. **Intercollegiate:** Baseball M, basketball, bowling, cheerleading, cross-country, football (tackle) M, golf, rifle, soccer, softball W, tennis, track and field, volleyball W. **Intramural:** Basketball, football (non-tackle), football (tackle) M, golf, soccer, softball, swimming, table tennis, volleyball W. **Team name:** Wildcats.

**Student services.** Adult student services, alcohol/substance abuse counseling, chaplain/spiritual director, career counseling, student employment services, financial aid counseling, personal counseling, veterans' counselor.

**Contact.** E-mail: admissions@bethelu.edu
Phone: (731) 352-4030 Fax: (731) 352-4069
Tina Hodges, Enrollment Director of Admissions and Financial Aid, Bethel University, 325 Cherry Avenue, McKenzie, TN 38201

## Bryan College
**Dayton, Tennessee**
www.bryan.edu                    CB code: 1908

- Private 4-year liberal arts college affiliated with interdenominational tradition
- Residential campus in small town

- 1,011 degree-seeking undergraduates: 4% part-time, 54% women, 5% African American, 1% Asian American, 2% Hispanic American, 2% international
- 60 degree-seeking graduate students
- 75% of applicants admitted
- SAT or ACT (ACT writing recommended), application essay required
- 53% graduate within 6 years

**General.** Founded in 1930. Regionally accredited. All courses taught from Christian perspective. All faculty sign statement of faith annually. **Degrees:** 286 bachelor's, 5 associate awarded; master's offered. **Location:** 40 miles from Chattanooga. **Calendar:** Semester, limited summer session. **Full-time faculty:** 43 total; 79% have terminal degrees, 19% women. **Part-time faculty:** 23 total; 83% have terminal degrees, 4% minority, 17% women. **Class size:** 60% < 20, 33% 20-39, 3% 40-49, 4% 50-99, less than 1% >100. **Special facilities:** Natural history museum.

**Freshman class profile.** 459 applied, 344 admitted, 192 enrolled.

| Mid 50% test scores | | | |
|---|---|---|---|
| SAT critical reading: | 520-660 | GPA 3.0-3.49: | 23% |
| SAT math: | 480-610 | GPA 2.0-2.99: | 11% |
| SAT writing: | 490-660 | Return as sophomores: | 74% |
| ACT composite: | 20-28 | Out-of-state: | 51% |
| GPA 3.75 or higher: | 51% | Live on campus: | 94% |
| GPA 3.50-3.74: | 15% | International: | 1% |

**Basis for selection.** High school record, Christian character supported by references, and SAT or ACT scores important. 23 ACT/SAT equivalent or Pre-Professional Skills Test required of all teacher education applicants. Interview required for marginal applicants. **Homeschooled:** Detailed high school transcript of courses and grades required.

**High school preparation.** 18 units required. Required units include English 4, mathematics 3, social studies 3, science 3 and foreign language 2.

**2009-2010 Annual costs.** Tuition/fees: $17,860. Room/board: $5,309. Books/supplies: $1,400. Personal expenses: $1,500.

**2009-2010 Financial aid. Need-based:** 174 full-time freshmen applied for aid; 151 were judged to have need; 150 of these received aid. Average need met was 81%. Average scholarship/grant was $11,374; average loan $2,919. 63% of total undergraduate aid awarded as scholarships/grants, 37% as loans/jobs. **Non-need-based:** Awarded to 399 full-time undergraduates, including 129 freshmen. Scholarships awarded for academics, alumni affiliation, art, athletics, job skills, leadership, music/drama.

**Application procedures. Admission:** Priority date 5/1; no deadline. $35 fee, may be waived for applicants with need. Admission notification on a rolling basis. **Financial aid:** Priority date 2/15; no closing date. FAFSA required. Applicants notified on a rolling basis starting 1/1; must reply within 2 week(s) of notification.

**Academics. Special study options:** Combined bachelor's/graduate degree, distance learning, double major, dual enrollment of high school students, honors, independent study, internships, study abroad, teacher certification program, Washington semester. Adult degree completion program. **Credit/placement by examination:** AP, CLEP, IB, SAT, ACT, institutional tests. 30 credit hours maximum toward associate degree, 31 toward bachelor's. **Support services:** Reduced course load, remedial instruction, study skills assistance, tutoring, writing center.

**Majors. Biology:** General. **Business:** Business admin. **Communications:** General. **Computer sciences:** Computer science. **Education:** General. **Foreign languages:** Spanish. **History:** General. **Interdisciplinary:** Math/computer science. **Liberal arts:** Arts/sciences. **Math:** General. **Parks/recreation:** Exercise sciences. **Philosophy/religion:** Christian. **Psychology:** General. **Social sciences:** Political science. **Theology:** Bible, religious ed. **Visual/performing arts:** Dramatic.

**Most popular majors.** Business/marketing 61%, communications/journalism 8%, education 6%, psychology 6%.

**Computing on campus.** 100 workstations in dormitories, library, computer center, student center. Dormitories wired for high-speed internet access and linked to campus network. Commuter students can connect to campus network. Online library, helpline, student web hosting, wireless network available.

**Student life. Freshman orientation:** Mandatory. Preregistration for classes offered. **Policies:** No alcohol, tobacco, drugs. Curfew and dress code enforced. Religious observance required. **Housing:** Guaranteed on-campus for all undergraduates. Single-sex dorms, apartments available. $100 fully refundable deposit, deadline 8/10. **Activities:** Campus ministries, choral groups, drama, music ensembles, student government, student newspaper, Christian service organizations, community tutoring program, Students for Life, Fellowship of Christian Athletes.

**Athletics.** NAIA, NCCAA. **Intercollegiate:** Baseball M, basketball, cross-country, soccer, track and field, volleyball W. **Intramural:** Basketball, football (non-tackle) M, soccer, softball, table tennis, tennis, volleyball. **Team name:** Lions.

**Student services.** Adult student services, chaplain/spiritual director, career counseling, student employment services, financial aid counseling, health services, personal counseling, placement for graduates.

**Contact.** E-mail: admissions@bryan.edu
Phone: (423) 775-7204 Toll-free number: (800) 277-9522
Fax: (423) 775-7199
Michael Sapienza, Director of Enrollment Management, Bryan College, PO Box 7000, Dayton, TN 37321-7000

## Carson-Newman College
**Jefferson City, Tennessee**
www.cn.edu                                                CB code: 1102

- Private 4-year liberal arts college affiliated with Southern Baptist Convention
- Residential campus in small town
- 1,887 degree-seeking undergraduates: 7% part-time, 58% women, 8% African American, 1% Asian American, 1% Hispanic American, 2% international
- 248 degree-seeking graduate students
- 74% of applicants admitted
- SAT or ACT required
- 53% graduate within 6 years

**General.** Founded in 1851. Regionally accredited. **Degrees:** 323 bachelor's awarded; master's offered. **ROTC:** Army, Air Force. **Location:** 30 miles from Knoxville. **Calendar:** Semester, extensive summer session. **Full-time faculty:** 124 total; 77% have terminal degrees. **Part-time faculty:** 58 total. **Class size:** 63% < 20, 34% 20-39, 2% 40-49. **Special facilities:** Appalachia museum.

**Freshman class profile.** 3,031 applied, 2,236 admitted, 513 enrolled.

| Mid 50% test scores | | | |
|---|---|---|---|
| ACT composite: | 20-25 | Rank in top quarter: | 47% |
| GPA 3.75 or higher: | 31% | Rank in top tenth: | 27% |
| GPA 3.50-3.74: | 18% | Return as sophomores: | 66% |
| GPA 3.0-3.49: | 30% | Out-of-state: | 32% |
| GPA 2.0-2.99: | 21% | Live on campus: | 90% |
| | | International: | 1% |

**Basis for selection.** 2.5 GPA, 19 ACT or 920 SAT (exclusive of Writing), school and community activities, and recommendations important. Rank in top half of class considered. Essay required for marginal students; audition required for music; portfolio required for art; interview recommended for academically weak.

**High school preparation.** 20 units required. Required and recommended units include English 4, mathematics 2-3, social studies 3, history 2, science 2 (laboratory 1) and foreign language 2.

**2010-2011 Annual costs.** Tuition/fees (projected): $20,562. Room/board: $5,918. Books/supplies: $1,088. Personal expenses: $1,921.

**2009-2010 Financial aid.** **Non-need-based:** Scholarships awarded for academics, art, athletics, leadership, minority status, music/drama, religious affiliation, ROTC.

**Application procedures.** **Admission:** Priority date 12/31; deadline 8/1. $25 fee, may be waived for applicants with need. Admission notification on a rolling basis. Must reply by May 1 or within 4 week(s) if notified thereafter. **Financial aid:** Priority date 4/1; no closing date. FAFSA, institutional form required. Applicants notified on a rolling basis starting 2/1; must reply within 2 week(s) of notification.

**Academics.** 3-year pre-engineering programs available. **Special study options:** Accelerated study, double major, dual enrollment of high school students, ESL, exchange student, honors, independent study, internships, liberal arts/career combination, student-designed major, study abroad, teacher certification program, Washington semester, weekend college. **Credit/placement by examination:** AP, CLEP, institutional tests. 32 credit hours maximum toward associate degree, 32 toward bachelor's. **Support services:** Learning center, pre-admission summer program, reduced course load, remedial instruction, tutoring.

**Majors.** **Biology:** General. **Business:** General, accounting, business admin, managerial economics, small business admin. **Communications:** General, journalism. **Computer sciences:** General. **Education:** Early childhood, elementary, family/consumer sciences, middle, music, physical, secondary, special. **Family/consumer sciences:** Clothing/textiles, family/community services, food/nutrition. **Foreign languages:** French, Spanish. **Health:** Athletic training, health care admin, nursing (RN), predental, premedicine, prepharmacy. **History:** General. **Liberal arts:** Arts/sciences. **Math:** General. **Parks/recreation:** General, exercise sciences, health/fitness. **Philosophy/religion:** Philosophy, religion. **Physical sciences:** Applied physics, chemistry, physics. **Psychology:** General. **Social sciences:** Economics, political science, sociology. **Theology:** Sacred music, theology. **Visual/performing arts:** General, art, interior design, music performance, music theory/composition, painting, photography.

**Most popular majors.** Business/marketing 13%, communications/journalism 6%, education 19%, health sciences 21%, psychology 6%, social sciences 6%.

**Computing on campus.** 100 workstations in dormitories, library, computer center.

**Student life.** **Freshman orientation:** Available. Preregistration for classes offered. **Policies:** Religious observance required. **Housing:** Guaranteed on-campus for freshmen. Single-sex dorms, apartments available. $50 deposit, deadline 8/1. Honors house available. **Activities:** Bands, choral groups, dance, drama, film society, literary magazine, music ensembles, musical theater, radio station, student government, student newspaper, TV station, Baptist student union, Fellowship of Christian Athletes, honor societies, Appalachian Outreach, Bonners Scholars community service.

**Athletics.** NCAA. **Intercollegiate:** Baseball M, basketball, cross-country, football (tackle) M, golf M, soccer, softball W, tennis, track and field, volleyball W, wrestling M. **Intramural:** Badminton, basketball, bowling, golf, racquetball, soccer, softball, swimming, table tennis, tennis, volleyball. **Team name:** Eagles.

**Student services.** Adult student services, career counseling, health services, personal counseling, placement for graduates, veterans' counselor. **Physically disabled:** Services for visually, hearing impaired.

**Contact.** E-mail: mredding@cn.edu
Phone: (865) 471-3223 Fax: (865) 471-3502
Melanie Redding, Director of Admissions, Carson-Newman College, 1646 Russell Avenue, Jefferson City, TN 37760

## Christian Brothers University
**Memphis, Tennessee**                                   CB member
www.cbu.edu                                               CB code: 1121

- Private 4-year university affiliated with Roman Catholic Church
- Commuter campus in very large city
- 1,413 degree-seeking undergraduates: 11% part-time, 56% women
- 496 degree-seeking graduate students
- 49% of applicants admitted
- SAT or ACT (ACT writing optional), application essay required
- 56% graduate within 6 years

**General.** Founded in 1871. Regionally accredited. **Degrees:** 233 bachelor's awarded; master's offered. **ROTC:** Army, Naval, Air Force. **Location:** 200 miles from Nashville; 150 miles from Little Rock, AR. **Calendar:** Semester, limited summer session. **Full-time faculty:** 99 total; 87% have terminal degrees, 16% minority, 30% women. **Part-time faculty:** 60 total; 48% have terminal degrees, 17% minority, 53% women. **Class size:** 68% < 20, 32% 20-39. **Special facilities:** Center for life sciences.

**Freshman class profile.** 1,912 applied, 936 admitted, 301 enrolled.

| Mid 50% test scores | | | |
|---|---|---|---|
| ACT composite: | 21-26 | Out-of-state: | 20% |
| Rank in top quarter: | 73% | Live on campus: | 60% |
| Rank in top tenth: | 39% | International: | 2% |
| Return as sophomores: | 77% | Fraternities: | 26% |
| | | Sororities: | 21% |

**Basis for selection.** Graduation from approved secondary school or GED equivalent, 2.0 GPA, rank in upper 2/3 of graduating class, and satisfactory test scores required. SAT and ACT used for math placement. Audition required for some programs; interview recommended for all. **Homeschooled:** Must have standardized test scores.

**High school preparation.** Recommended units include English 4, mathematics 4 and science 4. College-preparatory program required of engineering applicants.

**2009-2010 Annual costs.** Tuition/fees: $23,730. Room/board: $6,320.

**2009-2010 Financial aid. Need-based:** 280 full-time freshmen applied for aid; 235 were judged to have need; 235 of these received aid. Average need met was 89%. Average scholarship/grant was $7,388; average loan $3,285. 57% of total undergraduate aid awarded as scholarships/grants, 43% as loans/jobs. **Non-need-based:** Awarded to 1,186 full-time undergraduates, including 320 freshmen. Scholarships awarded for academics, alumni affiliation, athletics, music/drama, state residency. **Additional information:** ROTC scholarships available to qualified applicants.

**Application procedures. Admission:** Priority date 12/1; no deadline. $25 fee, may be waived for applicants with need. Admission notification on a rolling basis beginning on or about 12/1. Must reply by May 1 or within 3 week(s) if notified thereafter. **Financial aid:** Priority date 2/15; no closing date. FAFSA required. Applicants notified on a rolling basis starting 3/1; must reply within 2 week(s) of notification.

**Academics. Special study options:** Accelerated study, cross-registration, distance learning, double major, dual enrollment of high school students, honors, independent study, internships, liberal arts/career combination, study abroad, teacher certification program. **Credit/placement by examination:** AP, CLEP, IB, SAT, ACT, institutional tests. 30 credit hours maximum toward bachelor's degree. **Support services:** Pre-admission summer program, reduced course load, tutoring, writing center.

**Majors. Biology:** General, biochemistry, biomedical sciences. **Business:** General, business admin. **Computer sciences:** Computer science. **Education:** Biology, chemistry, early childhood, elementary, English, history, mathematics, physics, secondary, special. **Engineering:** Chemical, civil, computer, electrical, mechanical, physics. **History:** General. **Interdisciplinary:** Biological/physical sciences, intercultural, math/computer science, natural sciences. **Liberal arts:** Arts/sciences. **Math:** General. **Philosophy/religion:** Philosophy, religion. **Physical sciences:** General, chemistry, physics. **Psychology:** General. **Visual/performing arts:** Studio arts.

**Most popular majors.** Biology 9%, business/marketing 34%, engineering/engineering technologies 9%, physical sciences 7%, psychology 24%.

**Computing on campus.** 310 workstations in dormitories, library, computer center, student center. Dormitories wired for high-speed internet access and linked to campus network. Commuter students can connect to campus network. Online course registration, online library, helpline, wireless network available.

**Student life. Freshman orientation:** Mandatory. Preregistration for classes offered. Held Friday-Monday before classes begin. **Housing:** Guaranteed on-campus for freshmen. Single-sex dorms, apartments available. $300 non-refundable deposit, deadline 5/1. Juniors and seniors may live in on-campus apartments. All Freshmen and Sophomores whose permanent address is beyond a 30 mile radius are required to live on campus. **Activities:** Choral groups, drama, literary magazine, musical theater, student government, black student association, The Chosen Generation, intercultural club, Lasallian Collegians, student peace association, Up 'Til Dawn.

**Athletics.** NCAA. **Intercollegiate:** Baseball M, basketball, cross-country, golf, soccer, softball W, tennis, volleyball W. **Intramural:** Basketball, bowling, football (non-tackle), soccer, softball, swimming, tennis, volleyball. **Team name:** Buccaneers.

**Student services.** Adult student services, alcohol/substance abuse counseling, chaplain/spiritual director, career counseling, student employment services, financial aid counseling, health services, minority student services, personal counseling, placement for graduates.

**Contact.** E-mail: admissions@cbu.edu
Phone: (901) 321-3205 Toll-free number: (800) 288-7576
Fax: (901) 321-3202
Tracey Dysart-Ford, Dean of Admissions, Christian Brothers University, 650 East Parkway South, Memphis, TN 38104-5519

## Crichton College
**Memphis, Tennessee**
**www.crichton.edu**                          CB code: 1782

- Private 4-year liberal arts college affiliated with nondenominational tradition
- Commuter campus in very large city
- 673 degree-seeking undergraduates: 28% part-time, 75% women, 79% African American, 1% Asian American, 1% Hispanic American, 1% international
- 42 graduate students
- SAT or ACT (ACT writing optional), application essay required

**General.** Founded in 1941. Regionally accredited. **Degrees:** 118 bachelor's awarded. **Location:** 7 miles from downtown. **Calendar:** Semester, extensive summer session. **Full-time faculty:** 23 total; 52% have terminal degrees, 30% minority, 44% women. **Part-time faculty:** 35 total; 11% have terminal degrees, 43% minority, 51% women. **Class size:** 64% < 20, 36% 20-39.

**Freshman class profile.**

| Mid 50% test scores | | | |
|---|---|---|---|
| ACT composite: | 14-18 | GPA 2.0-2.99: | 22% |
| GPA 3.75 or higher: | 11% | End year in good standing: | 73% |
| GPA 3.0-3.49: | 11% | Return as sophomores: | 26% |
| | | Out-of-state: | 11% |

**Basis for selection.** Official high school transcript with 2.0 GPA, 19 ACT, or 900 SAT required. **Homeschooled:** Transcript of courses and grades required. Homeschool must be accredited or affiliated with an accredited institution in order for student to be considered. **Learning Disabled:** Students who desire accommodation under ADA must demonstrate eligibility for accommodation by registering with Office of Student Success and providing current documentation of qualified disability.

**High school preparation.** College-preparatory program recommended. 14 units required. Required units include English 4, mathematics 3, social studies 3, science 3 and academic electives 1.

**2009-2010 Annual costs.** Tuition/fees: $9,750. Books/supplies: $1,608. Personal expenses: $6,651.

**2009-2010 Financial aid. Need-based:** Average scholarship/grant was $6,000; average loan $3,500. 58% of total undergraduate aid awarded as scholarships/grants, 42% as loans/jobs.

**Application procedures. Admission:** Priority date 1/1; no deadline. $25 fee, may be waived for applicants with need, free for online applicants. Admission notification on a rolling basis. **Financial aid:** Priority date 2/15; no closing date. FAFSA required. Applicants notified on a rolling basis starting 3/1; must reply within 2 week(s) of notification.

**Academics. Special study options:** Accelerated study, distance learning, double major, dual enrollment of high school students, independent study, internships, liberal arts/career combination, student-designed major, study abroad, teacher certification program. **Credit/placement by examination:** CLEP, IB, ACT, institutional tests. 30 credit hours maximum toward associate degree, 30 toward bachelor's. Maximum of 30 semester hours of continuing education units, credit for prior learning, correspondence, testing and /or non-accredited college credit may be applied toward degree. **Support services:** Learning center, reduced course load, remedial instruction, study skills assistance, tutoring, writing center.

**Majors. Biology:** General, biomedical sciences. **Business:** Business admin. **Education:** General, biology, business, chemistry, elementary, English, history, mathematics, middle, psychology. **History:** General. **Legal studies:** Prelaw. **Liberal arts:** Arts/sciences. **Psychology:** General. **Theology:** Preministerial.

**Computing on campus.** 31 workstations in library, computer center. Commuter students can connect to campus network. Online course registration, online library, helpline, wireless network available.

**Student life. Freshman orientation:** Mandatory. Preregistration for classes offered. **Policies:** Religious observance required. **Activities:** Campus ministries, choral groups, drama, international student organizations, musical theater, student government.

**Student services.** Adult student services, chaplain/spiritual director, career counseling, student employment services, financial aid counseling, personal counseling, placement for graduates.

**Contact.** E-mail: admissions@crichton.edu
Phone: (901) 320-9777 Toll-free number: (800) 960-9777
Fax: (901) 320-9791
Shelley Dunn, Director, Admission, Crichton College, 255 North Highland, Memphis, TN 38111-1375

## Cumberland University
**Lebanon, Tennessee**
**www.cumberland.edu**                          CB code: 1146

- Private 4-year university and liberal arts college
- Commuter campus in large town
- 990 degree-seeking undergraduates: 9% part-time, 56% women, 11% African American, 1% Asian American, 2% Hispanic American, 4% international
- 314 degree-seeking graduate students

- 57% of applicants admitted
- ACT (writing optional), application essay required
- 38% graduate within 6 years

**General.** Founded in 1842. Regionally accredited. **Degrees:** 213 bachelor's, 1 associate awarded; master's offered. **ROTC:** Army. **Location:** 30 miles from Nashville. **Calendar:** Semester, limited summer session. **Full-time faculty:** 39 total; 90% have terminal degrees, 10% minority, 44% women. **Part-time faculty:** 71 total; 17% have terminal degrees, 7% minority, 54% women. **Class size:** 56% < 20, 34% 20-39, 6% 40-49, 4% 50-99.

**Freshman class profile.** 675 applied, 384 admitted, 201 enrolled.

| Mid 50% test scores | | | |
|---|---|---|---|
| SAT critical reading: | 410-510 | Rank in top quarter: | 38% |
| SAT math: | 450-560 | Rank in top tenth: | 19% |
| SAT writing: | 420-530 | End year in good standing: | 62% |
| ACT composite: | 20-24 | Return as sophomores: | 62% |
| GPA 3.75 or higher: | 20% | Out-of-state: | 12% |
| GPA 3.50-3.74: | 14% | Live on campus: | 60% |
| GPA 3.0-3.49: | 31% | International: | 3% |
| GPA 2.0-2.99: | 34% | Fraternities: | 19% |
| | | Sororities: | 12% |

**Basis for selection.** High school academic record and standardized test scores most important. Audition, portfolio required for some programs; interview recommended for academically weak. **Homeschooled:** Transcript of courses and grades required.

**High school preparation.** College-preparatory program recommended. 16 units required; 19 recommended. Required and recommended units include English 4, mathematics 3-4, social studies 2, history 2, science 3 (laboratory 1-2) and foreign language 2.

**2009-2010 Annual costs.** Tuition/fees: $17,430. Room/board: $6,350. Books/supplies: $1,260. Personal expenses: $2,545.

**2009-2010 Financial aid.** **Non-need-based:** Scholarships awarded for academics, art, athletics, music/drama.

**Application procedures.** Admission: Priority date 2/15; no deadline. $25 fee, may be waived for applicants with need. Admission notification on a rolling basis beginning on or about 3/1. **Financial aid:** Priority date 2/1; no closing date. FAFSA, institutional form required. Applicants notified on a rolling basis starting 5/1; must reply within 2 week(s) of notification.

**Academics.** Selection of major or minor not required. **Special study options:** Accelerated study, combined bachelor's/graduate degree, cooperative education, distance learning, double major, dual enrollment of high school students, honors, independent study, internships, liberal arts/career combination, teacher certification program. **Credit/placement by examination:** AP, CLEP, ACT, institutional tests. 30 credit hours maximum toward bachelor's degree. **Support services:** Learning center, pre-admission summer program, reduced course load, remedial instruction, study skills assistance, tutoring, writing center.

**Majors.** **Area/ethnic studies:** American. **Biology:** General. **Business:** General, accounting, management science. **Education:** General, biology, early childhood, elementary, English, history, mathematics, middle, multi-level teacher, music, physical, secondary, social science, special. **Health:** Nursing (RN), predental, premedicine, prepharmacy, preveterinary. **History:** General. **Legal studies:** Prelaw. **Liberal arts:** Arts/sciences. **Math:** General. **Parks/recreation:** Health/fitness, sports admin. **Protective services:** Criminal justice. **Psychology:** General. **Public administration:** General. **Social sciences:** General, political science, sociology. **Visual/performing arts:** Studio arts.

**Most popular majors.** Business/marketing 16%, education 19%, health sciences 32%, parks/recreation 10%, security/protective services 6%.

**Computing on campus.** 60 workstations in library, computer center. Dormitories linked to campus network. Commuter students can connect to campus network. Online library, helpline, repair service, wireless network available.

**Student life.** Freshman orientation: Mandatory. Preregistration for classes offered. 1-1/2 day session held in August. **Housing:** Single-sex dorms, apartments, wellness housing available. $200 deposit, deadline 8/1. **Activities:** Bands, campus ministries, choral groups, dance, drama, music ensembles, musical theater, radio station, student government, student newspaper, Fellowship of Christian Athletes, African American student association, Campus Crusade for Christ, Champions for Christ.

**Athletics.** NAIA. **Intercollegiate:** Baseball M, basketball, bowling, cheerleading, cross-country, football (tackle) M, golf, soccer, softball W, tennis, volleyball W, wrestling M. **Intramural:** Basketball, football (non-tackle) M, softball, table tennis, volleyball. **Team name:** Bulldogs.

**Student services.** Adult student services, chaplain/spiritual director, career counseling, student employment services, financial aid counseling, health services, personal counseling, placement for graduates. **Physically disabled:** Services for visually impaired.

**Contact.** E-mail: admissions@cumberland.edu
Phone: (615) 444-2562 Toll-free number: (800) 467-0562
Fax: (615) 444-2569
Beatrice LaChance, Director of Enrollment Services, Cumberland University, One Cumberland Square, Lebanon, TN 37087

## DeVry University: Memphis
Memphis, Tennessee
www.devry.edu

- For-profit 4-year business and technical college
- Very large city
- 87 degree-seeking undergraduates: 49% part-time, 66% women, 75% African American, 1% Hispanic American
- 84 degree-seeking graduate students

**General.** Regionally accredited. **Degrees:** 9 associate awarded; master's offered. **Calendar:** Semester. **Part-time faculty:** 32 total; 47% minority, 41% women.

**Basis for selection.** Academic GPA important. Class rank considered. DeVry-administered admissions test required for applicants without SAT/ACT.

**2009-2010 Annual costs.** Tuition/fees: $14,160. Books/supplies: $1,300. Personal expenses: $3,574.

**2008-2009 Financial aid.** **Non-need-based:** Scholarships awarded for academics.

**Application procedures.** Admission: No deadline. $50 fee. Admission notification on a rolling basis. **Financial aid:** No deadline. FAFSA required. Applicants notified on a rolling basis.

**Academics.** **Special study options:** Accelerated study, distance learning. **Credit/placement by examination:** CLEP.

**Majors.** **Business:** Business admin. **Other:** Technical management.

**Contact.** DeVry University: Memphis, 6401 Poplar Avenue, Ste. 600, Memphis, TN 38119

## East Tennessee State University
Johnson City, Tennessee      CB member
www.etsu.edu      CB code: 1198

- Public 4-year university
- Commuter campus in small city
- 11,286 degree-seeking undergraduates: 13% part-time, 56% women, 5% African American, 2% Asian American, 1% Hispanic American, 1% Native American, 1% international
- 2,575 degree-seeking graduate students
- 85% of applicants admitted
- SAT or ACT (ACT writing optional) required
- 43% graduate within 6 years

**General.** Founded in 1911. Regionally accredited. Additional campuses in Kingsport, Bristol, and Greeneville. **Degrees:** 1,878 bachelor's awarded; master's, doctoral, professional offered. **ROTC:** Army. **Location:** 90 miles from Knoxville; 60 miles from Asheville, NC. **Calendar:** Semester, extensive summer session. **Full-time faculty:** 514 total. **Part-time faculty:** 296 total. **Class size:** 44% < 20, 40% 20-39, 7% 40-49, 7% 50-99, 2% >100. **Special facilities:** Appalachian archives, planetarium, observatory, arboretum.

**Freshman class profile.** 4,721 applied, 4,024 admitted, 2,099 enrolled.

| Mid 50% test scores | | | |
|---|---|---|---|
| SAT critical reading: | 420-550 | Rank in top quarter: | 44% |
| SAT math: | 430-560 | Rank in top tenth: | 19% |
| SAT writing: | 420-540 | Return as sophomores: | 70% |
| ACT composite: | 20-25 | Out-of-state: | 14% |
| GPA 3.75 or higher: | 21% | Live on campus: | 52% |
| GPA 3.50-3.74: | 19% | International: | 1% |
| GPA 3.0-3.49: | 32% | Fraternities: | 5% |
| GPA 2.0-2.99: | 25% | Sororities: | 5% |

**Basis for selection.** 2.3 GPA or 19 ACT/comparable SAT required. COMPASS may be required if ACT/SAT scores do not meet minimums. Interview recommended for dental hygiene, health-related professions, nursing, physical therapy programs; audition required for music; portfolio recommended for art. **Homeschooled:** Transcript of courses and grades required.

**High school preparation.** College-preparatory program required. 14 units required; 16 recommended. Required and recommended units include English 4, mathematics 3-4, social studies 1, history 1, science 2-3 (laboratory 1), foreign language 2 and visual/performing arts 1.

**2009-2010 Annual costs.** Tuition/fees: $5,588; $17,666 out-of-state. Room/board: $5,500. Books/supplies: $1,090. Personal expenses: $3,818.

**2008-2009 Financial aid. Need-based:** 54% of total undergraduate aid awarded as scholarships/grants, 46% as loans/jobs. **Non-need-based:** Scholarships awarded for academics, alumni affiliation, art, athletics, job skills, leadership, minority status, music/drama, religious affiliation, ROTC, state residency. **Additional information:** Housing costs payable by installment.

**Application procedures. Admission:** Priority date 7/1; no deadline. $15 fee, may be waived for applicants with need. Admission notification on a rolling basis beginning on or about 9/1. **Financial aid:** Priority date 4/15; no closing date. FAFSA required. Applicants notified on a rolling basis starting 4/15; must reply within 3 week(s) of notification.

**Academics. Special study options:** Combined bachelor's/graduate degree, cooperative education, distance learning, double major, dual enrollment of high school students, ESL, exchange student, external degree, honors, independent study, internships, student-designed major, study abroad, teacher certification program. **Credit/placement by examination:** CLEP, IB, SAT, ACT, institutional tests. **Support services:** Learning center, reduced course load, study skills assistance, tutoring, writing center.

**Honors college/program.** 29 ACT/comparable SAT and 3.5 GPA required; 20 new freshmen selected each year for specifically designed courses.

**Majors. Biology:** General. **Business:** Accounting, business admin, finance, managerial economics, marketing. **Communications:** Media studies. **Communications technology:** Animation/special effects. **Computer sciences:** General. **Education:** Special. **Engineering technology:** General, surveying. **Family/consumer sciences:** General, child development, family studies. **Foreign languages:** General. **Health:** Dental hygiene, environmental health, health services, nursing (RN). **History:** General. **Liberal arts:** Arts/sciences. **Math:** General. **Parks/recreation:** Health/fitness, sports admin. **Philosophy/religion:** Philosophy. **Physical sciences:** Chemistry, physics. **Protective services:** Law enforcement admin. **Psychology:** General. **Public administration:** Social work. **Social sciences:** Economics, geography, political science, sociology. **Visual/performing arts:** Art.

**Most popular majors.** Business/marketing 15%, health sciences 23%, liberal arts 6%.

**Computing on campus.** 1,400 workstations in dormitories, library, computer center, student center. Dormitories wired for high-speed internet access and linked to campus network. Commuter students can connect to campus network. Online course registration, online library, helpline, repair service, student web hosting, wireless network available.

**Student life. Freshman orientation:** Mandatory. Preregistration for classes offered. 5 sessions during summer, each for 1-2 days. **Housing:** Coed dorms, single-sex dorms, special housing for disabled, apartments, fraternity/sorority housing, wellness housing available. $100 fully refundable deposit. **Activities:** Bands, campus ministries, choral groups, drama, international student organizations, literary magazine, music ensembles, radio station, student government, student newspaper, TV station, Baptist student union, Campus Crusade, Catholic center, Christian student fellowship, Fellowship of Christian Athletes, Real Life Fellowship, Wesley Foundation, black affairs association.

**Athletics.** NCAA. **Intercollegiate:** Baseball M, basketball, cross-country, golf, soccer, softball W, tennis, track and field, volleyball W. **Intramural:** Basketball, cross-country, football (non-tackle), golf, handball, racquetball, softball, tennis, volleyball W, weight lifting M. **Team name:** Buccaneers.

**Student services.** Adult student services, alcohol/substance abuse counseling, chaplain/spiritual director, career counseling, services for economically disadvantaged, student employment services, financial aid counseling, health services, legal services, minority student services, on-campus daycare, personal counseling, placement for graduates, veterans' counselor, women's services. **Physically disabled:** Services for visually, speech, hearing impaired.

**Contact.** E-mail: go2etsu@etsu.edu
Phone: (423) 439-4213 Toll-free number: (800) 462-3878
Fax: (423) 439-4630
Michael Pitts, Director of Admissions, East Tennessee State University, ETSU Box 70731, Johnson City, TN 37614

## Fisk University
**Nashville, Tennessee**
www.fisk.edu

CB member
CB code: 1224

- Private 4-year liberal arts college affiliated with United Church of Christ
- Residential campus in very large city
- 593 degree-seeking undergraduates: 5% part-time, 65% women, 85% African American, 1% Asian American, 11% international
- 50 degree-seeking graduate students
- 64% of applicants admitted
- SAT or ACT with writing, interview required
- 57% graduate within 6 years; 33% enter graduate study

**General.** Founded in 1866. Regionally accredited. **Degrees:** 113 bachelor's awarded; master's offered. **ROTC:** Army, Naval. **Location:** 216 miles from Memphis, 225 miles from Atlanta. **Calendar:** Semester, limited summer session. **Full-time faculty:** 56 total; 75% have terminal degrees, 71% minority, 46% women. **Part-time faculty:** 30 total; 17% have terminal degrees, 83% minority, 33% women. **Class size:** 74% < 20, 23% 20-39, 1% 40-49, 1% 50-99.

**Freshman class profile.** 1,019 applied, 654 admitted, 95 enrolled.

| Mid 50% test scores | | | |
|---|---|---|---|
| SAT critical reading: | 430-560 | Rank in top quarter: | 40% |
| SAT math: | 420-540 | Rank in top tenth: | 17% |
| ACT composite: | 18-22 | End year in good standing: | 61% |
| GPA 3.75 or higher: | 13% | Return as sophomores: | 75% |
| GPA 3.50-3.74: | 15% | Out-of-state: | 70% |
| GPA 3.0-3.49: | 28% | Live on campus: | 92% |
| GPA 2.0-2.99: | 44% | International: | 5% |

**Basis for selection.** School achievement record, class rank, test scores, recommendations, activities important. Essay recommended for all; audition recommended for music. Interview required for scholarship nominees and must take place prior to 2/15.

**High school preparation.** 20 units recommended. Recommended units include English 4, mathematics 3, social studies 3, history 1, science 1, foreign language 1 and academic electives 6. 1 algebra and 1 geometry recommended.

**2009-2010 Annual costs.** Tuition/fees: $17,060. Room/board: $8,110. Books/supplies: $1,600. Personal expenses: $2,000.

**2009-2010 Financial aid.** All financial aid based on need. 95 full-time freshmen applied for aid; 95 were judged to have need; 86 of these received aid. Average need met was 54%. Average scholarship/grant was $13,688; average loan $2,310. 58% of total undergraduate aid awarded as scholarships/grants, 42% as loans/jobs.

**Application procedures. Admission:** Priority date 2/15; deadline 3/1 (receipt date). $50 fee, may be waived for applicants with need. Application must be submitted on paper. Admission notification on a rolling basis. Must reply by May 1 or within 2 week(s) if notified thereafter. **Financial aid:** Priority date 3/1, closing date 7/1. FAFSA required. Applicants notified on a rolling basis starting 4/1; must reply within 2 week(s) of notification.

**Academics. Special study options:** Combined bachelor's/graduate degree, cooperative education, cross-registration, double major, dual enrollment of high school students, exchange student, honors, independent study, internships, liberal arts/career combination, student-designed major, study abroad, teacher certification program. 2-2 program with Rush-Presbyterian-St. Luke's Medical Center in nursing, dual degree in science and engineering, dual degree in engineering and natural sciences in 5 years, 3-3 program with Howard University for Doctor of Pharmacy, 5-year MBA program with Vanderbilt University, 7-year MD, PhD, DDS programs with Meharry Medical College. **Credit/placement by examination:** AP, CLEP, IB, SAT,

ACT, institutional tests. 30 credit hours maximum toward bachelor's degree. **Support services:** Learning center, pre-admission summer program, tutoring, writing center.

**Majors. Biology:** General. **Business:** Business admin. **Computer sciences:** Computer science. **Education:** Music, special. **Foreign languages:** Spanish. **Health:** Nursing (RN). **History:** General. **Math:** General. **Physical sciences:** Chemistry, physics. **Psychology:** General. **Social sciences:** Political science, sociology. **Visual/performing arts:** Art, music performance. **Other:** Elected Studies.

**Most popular majors.** Biology 8%, business/marketing 12%, English 12%, psychology 27%, social sciences 15%.

**Computing on campus.** 100 workstations in dormitories, library, computer center. Dormitories wired for high-speed internet access and linked to campus network. Online course registration, helpline, student web hosting, wireless network available.

**Student life. Freshman orientation:** Available. Preregistration for classes offered. 3-5 day orientation held 1 week before classes. **Policies:** All students required to live on-campus, with few exceptions. Freshmen have 12 am curfew. **Housing:** Guaranteed on-campus for all undergraduates. Single-sex dorms, special housing for disabled available. $100 deposit, deadline 7/15. **Activities:** Jazz band, campus ministries, choral groups, dance, drama, literary magazine, music ensembles, radio station, student government, student newspaper, TV station, Baptist student union, Muslim student association, Nation of Islam, Carribean student union, African student association, race relations students organization.

**Athletics.** NAIA. **Intercollegiate:** Basketball. **Intramural:** Basketball, football (non-tackle). **Team name:** Bulldogs.

**Student services.** Career counseling, student employment services, financial aid counseling, health services, personal counseling, placement for graduates.

**Contact.** E-mail: admit@fisk.edu
Phone: (615) 329-8665 Toll-free number: (888) 702-0022
Fax: (615) 329-8774
Keith Chandler, Dean of Admissions, Fisk University, 1000 17th Avenue North, Nashville, TN 37208-3051

## Free Will Baptist Bible College
**Nashville, Tennessee**
www.fwbbc.edu
CB code: 1232

- Private 4-year Bible and teachers college affiliated with Free Will Baptists
- Residential campus in very large city
- 283 degree-seeking undergraduates: 19% part-time, 45% women, 9% African American, 1% Hispanic American, 2% international
- Application essay required
- 91% graduate within 6 years; 7% enter graduate study

**General.** Founded in 1942. Regionally accredited; also accredited by ABHE. **Degrees:** 41 bachelor's, 3 associate awarded. **ROTC:** Army, Air Force. **Location:** 3 miles from downtown. **Calendar:** Semester, limited summer session. **Full-time faculty:** 20 total. **Part-time faculty:** 28 total. **Class size:** 89% < 20, 8% 20-39, less than 1% 40-49, 3% 50-99.

**Freshman class profile.**

| | | | |
|---|---|---|---|
| Return as sophomores: | 61% | Live on campus: | 74% |
| Out-of-state: | 62% | International: | 2% |

**Basis for selection.** Open admission. Applicants without high school diploma or GED must pass GED prior to receiving degree.

**High school preparation.** 22 units recommended. Recommended units include English 4, mathematics 4, social studies 3, history 2, science 4, foreign language 3 and academic electives 2.

**2009-2010 Annual costs.** Tuition/fees: $13,534. Room/board: $5,700. Books/supplies: $600. Personal expenses: $820.

**2008-2009 Financial aid. Need-based:** 47% of total undergraduate aid awarded as scholarships/grants, 53% as loans/jobs. **Non-need-based:** Scholarships awarded for academics, art, music/drama.

**Application procedures. Admission:** Priority date 4/15; no deadline. $35 fee. Admission notification on a rolling basis. **Financial aid:** Priority date 4/15; no closing date. FAFSA, institutional form required. Applicants

notified on a rolling basis starting 7/1; must reply within 2 week(s) of notification.

**Academics. Special study options:** Distance learning, double major, dual enrollment of high school students, independent study, internships, teacher certification program. **Credit/placement by examination:** AP, CLEP, IB, institutional tests. 16 credit hours maximum toward bachelor's degree. **Support services:** Reduced course load, remedial instruction, tutoring.

**Majors. Business:** Business admin. **Education:** Early childhood, elementary, music, physical, secondary. **History:** General. **Parks/recreation:** Exercise sciences. **Psychology:** General. **Theology:** Bible, missionary, religious ed, theology.

**Most popular majors.** Business/marketing 16%, education 26%, English 13%, theological studies 29%.

**Computing on campus.** 42 workstations in library, computer center, student center. Commuter students can connect to campus network. Online library, repair service, wireless network available.

**Student life. Freshman orientation:** Mandatory. Preregistration for classes offered. **Policies:** Religious observance required. **Housing:** Single-sex dorms, apartments available. $100 fully refundable deposit, deadline 8/1. Single students required to live on campus unless living with parents or close relatives. **Activities:** Campus ministries, choral groups, drama, music ensembles, musical theater, student government, ministerial and missionary organizations, Christian service assignments, organization for business students, literary societies.

**Athletics.** NCCAA. **Intercollegiate:** Baseball M, basketball, volleyball W. **Intramural:** Basketball, softball, table tennis M, tennis, volleyball. **Team name:** Flames.

**Student services.** Career counseling, student employment services, financial aid counseling, personal counseling, placement for graduates, veterans' counselor.

**Contact.** E-mail: recruit@fwbbc.edu
Phone: (615) 844-5000 Toll-free number: (800) 763-9222
Fax: (615) 269-6028
Jeff Caudill, Director of Enrollment Services, Free Will Baptist Bible College, 3606 West End Avenue, Nashville, TN 37205-2403

## Freed-Hardeman University
**Henderson, Tennessee**
www.fhu.edu
CB member
CB code: 1230

- Private 4-year university and liberal arts college affiliated with Church of Christ
- Residential campus in small town
- 1,461 degree-seeking undergraduates: 4% part-time, 56% women, 5% African American, 1% Hispanic American, 3% international
- 531 degree-seeking graduate students
- 99% of applicants admitted
- SAT or ACT (ACT writing recommended) required
- 58% graduate within 6 years

**General.** Founded in 1869. Regionally accredited. Campus in Verviers, Belgium. **Degrees:** 265 bachelor's, 17 associate awarded; master's offered. **Location:** 15 miles from Jackson, 85 miles from Memphis. **Calendar:** Semester, limited summer session. **Full-time faculty:** 99 total; 70% have terminal degrees, 6% minority, 28% women. **Part-time faculty:** 47 total; 38% have terminal degrees, 6% minority, 38% women. **Class size:** 52% < 20, 36% 20-39, 7% 40-49, 5% 50-99.

**Freshman class profile.** 959 applied, 954 admitted, 408 enrolled.

| Mid 50% test scores | | GPA 2.0-2.99: | 20% |
|---|---|---|---|
| SAT critical reading: | 490-610 | Rank in top quarter: | 53% |
| SAT math: | 470-590 | Rank in top tenth: | 28% |
| ACT composite: | 20-26 | Return as sophomores: | 68% |
| GPA 3.75 or higher: | 39% | Out-of-state: | 50% |
| GPA 3.50-3.74: | 19% | Live on campus: | 90% |
| GPA 3.0-3.49: | 22% | International: | 2% |

**Basis for selection.** Admissions based on school achievement record, test scores, references. Applicants without minimum test score or high school GPA may be admitted with restrictions after further evaluation.

**High school preparation.** 20 units recommended. Recommended units include English 4, mathematics 2, social studies 2, science 2 and academic electives 10. Additional science and mathematics courses recommended.

**2009-2010 Annual costs.** Tuition/fees: $14,300. Room/board: $7,090. Books/supplies: $1,800. Personal expenses: $2,080.

**2009-2010 Financial aid. Need-based:** 383 full-time freshmen applied for aid; 319 were judged to have need; 318 of these received aid. Average need met was 72%. Average scholarship/grant was $11,779; average loan $3,395. 55% of total undergraduate aid awarded as scholarships/grants, 45% as loans/jobs. **Non-need-based:** Awarded to 539 full-time undergraduates, including 176 freshmen. Scholarships awarded for academics, art, athletics, leadership, minority status, music/drama.

**Application procedures. Admission:** No deadline. No application fee. Admission notification on a rolling basis. **Financial aid:** Priority date 2/1; no closing date. FAFSA required. Applicants notified on a rolling basis starting 3/10; must reply within 4 week(s) of notification.

**Academics.** Students enrolled for 12 or more undergraduate hours must register for Bible class. **Special study options:** Accelerated study, combined bachelor's/graduate degree, cooperative education, cross-registration, distance learning, double major, dual enrollment of high school students, honors, independent study, internships, liberal arts/career combination, student-designed major, study abroad, teacher certification program. 3-2 engineering co-op. **Credit/placement by examination:** AP, CLEP, IB, SAT, ACT, institutional tests. 33 credit hours maximum toward bachelor's degree. **Support services:** Learning center, reduced course load, remedial instruction, study skills assistance, tutoring.

**Honors college/program.** Approximately 5% of freshmen class admitted to honors course work as result of competitive application process.

**Majors. Biology:** General, biochemistry. **Business:** Accounting, business admin, finance, human resources, management information systems, marketing. **Communications:** General, journalism, media studies, public relations. **Computer sciences:** General. **Education:** Art, biology, curriculum, early childhood, elementary, English, history, mathematics, middle, multi-level teacher, music, physical, science, secondary, special. **Family/consumer sciences:** Family studies. **Health:** Health care admin. **History:** General. **Liberal arts:** Arts/sciences. **Math:** General. **Parks/recreation:** Exercise sciences. **Philosophy/religion:** Philosophy. **Physical sciences:** General, chemistry. **Protective services:** Criminal justice. **Psychology:** General. **Public administration:** Social work. **Social sciences:** General. **Theology:** Bible, missionary, theology. **Visual/performing arts:** Acting, art, design, interior design, theater design.

**Most popular majors.** Business/marketing 13%, education 12%, health sciences 11%, interdisciplinary studies 9%, parks/recreation 6%, theological studies 10%, visual/performing arts 8%.

**Computing on campus.** 238 workstations in dormitories, library, computer center, student center. Dormitories wired for high-speed internet access and linked to campus network. Commuter students can connect to campus network. Online course registration, online library, helpline, repair service, wireless network available.

**Student life. Freshman orientation:** Mandatory. Preregistration for classes offered. 4 days prior to start of classes in August. **Policies:** Daily chapel is mandatory. Nightly curfew enforced. Religious observance required. **Housing:** Guaranteed on-campus for freshmen. Single-sex dorms, apartments, wellness housing available. $100 nonrefundable deposit, deadline 4/1. Housing deposit refundable up to 30 days prior to term. Some student-teacher housing available for education majors. **Activities:** Bands, choral groups, drama, music ensembles, musical theater, radio station, student government, student newspaper, TV station, evangelism forum, preachers club, student-alumni association, university student ambassadors, university program council, youth workers club, Impact Team, Young Republicans, Young Democrats.

**Athletics.** NAIA. **Intercollegiate:** Baseball M, basketball, cheerleading W, soccer, softball W, volleyball W. **Intramural:** Badminton, basketball, cross-country, football (non-tackle), racquetball, soccer, softball, table tennis, tennis, volleyball. **Team name:** Lions.

**Student services.** Alcohol/substance abuse counseling, chaplain/spiritual director, career counseling, student employment services, financial aid counseling, health services, on-campus daycare, personal counseling, placement for graduates, veterans' counselor. **Physically disabled:** Services for visually, hearing impaired.

**Contact.** E-mail: admissions@fhu.edu
Phone: (731) 989-6651 Toll-free number: (800) 630-3480
Fax: (731) 989-6047
Belinda Anderson, Director of Admissions, Freed-Hardeman University, 158 East Main Street, Henderson, TN 38340

## International Academy of Design and Technology: Nashville
### Nashville, Tennessee
### www.iadtnashville.com

- For-profit 4-year branch campus and visual arts college
- Commuter campus in very large city
- 694 degree-seeking undergraduates

**General.** Accredited by ACICS. **Degrees:** 15 bachelor's, 87 associate awarded. **Calendar:** Quarter, extensive summer session. **Full-time faculty:** 10 total. **Part-time faculty:** 42 total.

**Basis for selection.** Open admission.

**2009-2010 Annual costs.** Tuition/fees: $15,750. Books/supplies: $1,800.

**Application procedures. Admission:** No deadline. $50 fee. **Financial aid:** No deadline.

**Academics. Credit/placement by examination:** CLEP.

**Majors. Business:** Fashion. **Visual/performing arts:** Fashion design, graphic design, interior design.

**Computing on campus.** Online library available.

**Student life. Freshman orientation:** Available.

**Student services.** Student employment services, financial aid counseling, placement for graduates.

**Contact.** E-mail: admissions@iadtnashville.com
Phone: (866) 302-4238
Sonya Flanagan-Ensign, Director of Admissions, International Academy of Design and Technology: Nashville, 1 Bridgestone Park, Nashville, TN 37214

## ITT Technical Institute: Knoxville
### Knoxville, Tennessee
### www.itt-tech.edu        CB code: 7139

- For-profit 4-year technical college
- Commuter campus in small city

**General.** Accredited by ACICS. **Calendar:** Quarter.

**Contact.** Phone: (865) 671-2800
Director of Recruitment, 10208 Technology Drive, Knoxville, TN 37932

## ITT Technical Institute: Memphis
### Cordova, Tennessee
### www.itt-tech.edu        CB code: 2731

- For-profit 4-year technical college
- Commuter campus in very large city

**General.** Accredited by ACICS. **Calendar:** Quarter.

**Contact.** Phone: (901) 762-0556
Director of Recruitment, 7260 Goodlett Farms Parkway, Cordova, TN 38016

## ITT Technical Institute: Nashville
### Nashville, Tennessee
### www.itt-tech.edu        CB code: 7025

- For-profit 4-year technical college
- Commuter campus in very large city

**General.** Accredited by ACICS. **Calendar:** Quarter.

**Contact.** Phone: (615) 889-8700
Director of Recruitment, 2845 Elm Hill Pike, Nashville, TN 37214

## Johnson Bible College
### Knoxville, Tennessee
### www.jbc.edu
**CB code: 1345**

- Private 4-year Bible college affiliated with Christian Church
- Residential campus in large city
- 672 degree-seeking undergraduates: 4% part-time, 47% women, 2% African American, 1% Asian American, 3% Hispanic American, 1% Native American, 1% international
- 103 degree-seeking graduate students
- SAT or ACT (ACT writing recommended), application essay required
- 60% graduate within 6 years

**General.** Founded in 1893. Regionally accredited; also accredited by ABHE. **Degrees:** 241 bachelor's, 33 associate awarded; master's offered. **Location:** 7 miles from Knoxville. **Calendar:** Semester, limited summer session. **Full-time faculty:** 29 total. **Part-time faculty:** 36 total. **Class size:** 38% < 20, 31% 20-39, 13% 40-49, 19% 50-99.

**Freshman class profile.**

| Mid 50% test scores | | Rank in top quarter: | 46% |
|---|---|---|---|
| ACT composite: | 19-26 | Rank in top tenth: | 20% |
| GPA 3.75 or higher: | 25% | Return as sophomores: | 73% |
| GPA 3.50-3.74: | 17% | Live on campus: | 96% |
| GPA 3.0-3.49: | 30% | International: | 1% |
| GPA 2.0-2.99: | 28% | | |

**Basis for selection.** High school transcript and 3 references, 1 from minister required. Combination of high school percentile rank and ACT score determines initial admission criteria. Interview recommended.

**High school preparation.** 16 units required. Required units include academic electives 4. 12 of the 16 units must be content courses such as English, history, mathematics, foreign language, and science.

**2009-2010 Annual costs.** Tuition/fees: $8,610. Part-time students pay mandatory fee of $35 per credit hour. Room/board: $5,350. Books/supplies: $900. Personal expenses: $2,060.

**2009-2010 Financial aid. Non-need-based:** Scholarships awarded for academics, leadership, minority status, music/drama, religious affiliation, state residency.

**Application procedures. Admission:** Closing date 7/1 (receipt date). $35 fee. Admission notification on a rolling basis. **Financial aid:** Priority date 5/1, closing date 8/1. FAFSA, institutional form required. Applicants notified on a rolling basis starting 4/30; must reply within 2 week(s) of notification.

**Academics.** Majors in Bible with double major in music, teacher education, counseling, preaching, or youth ministry/preaching offered. **Special study options:** Accelerated study, combined bachelor's/graduate degree, co-operative education, distance learning, double major, ESL, honors, independent study, internships, teacher certification program. **Credit/placement by examination:** CLEP, institutional tests. 32 credit hours maximum toward bachelor's degree. **Support services:** Learning center, remedial instruction, study skills assistance, tutoring.

**Majors. Business:** Nonprofit/public. **Theology:** Bible, sacred music.

**Most popular majors.** Education 13%, philosophy/religious studies 87%.

**Computing on campus.** 50 workstations in library, computer center. Dormitories linked to campus network. Commuter students can connect to campus network. Helpline, student web hosting, wireless network available.

**Student life. Freshman orientation:** Mandatory. Preregistration for classes offered. Weekend preceeding first semester. **Policies:** Religious observance required. **Housing:** Single-sex dorms, apartments, wellness housing available. $100 deposit, deadline 8/1. Mobile homes, duplex houses, available for family housing. **Activities:** Jazz band, campus ministries, choral groups, drama, literary magazine, music ensembles, musical theater, radio station, student government.

**Athletics.** NCCAA. **Intercollegiate:** Baseball M, basketball, soccer, volleyball W. **Intramural:** Basketball, softball, tennis, volleyball.

**Student services.** Alcohol/substance abuse counseling, chaplain/spiritual director, career counseling, student employment services, financial aid counseling, health services, on-campus daycare, personal counseling, placement for graduates. **Physically disabled:** Services for visually impaired.

**Contact.** E-mail: twingfield@jbc.edu
Phone: (865) 251-2233 Toll-free number: (800) 827-2122
Fax: (865) 251-2336
Tim Wingfield, Director of Admissions, Johnson Bible College, 7900 Johnson Drive, Knoxville, TN 37998-0001

## King College
### Bristol, Tennessee
### www.king.edu
**CB member**
**CB code: 1371**

- Private 4-year nursing and liberal arts college affiliated with Presbyterian Church (USA)
- Residential campus in large town
- 1,365 degree-seeking undergraduates: 2% part-time, 64% women, 3% African American, 2% Hispanic American, 1% Native American, 2% international
- 285 degree-seeking graduate students
- 62% of applicants admitted
- SAT or ACT (ACT writing optional), application essay required
- 54% graduate within 6 years

**General.** Founded in 1867. Regionally accredited. Christian values emphasized. **Degrees:** 440 bachelor's awarded; master's offered. **ROTC:** Army. **Location:** 110 miles from Knoxville, 95 miles from Asheville, North Carolina. **Calendar:** Semester, extensive summer session. **Full-time faculty:** 81 total; 74% have terminal degrees, 5% minority, 52% women. **Part-time faculty:** 71 total; 30% have terminal degrees, 1% minority, 61% women. **Class size:** 62% < 20, 31% 20-39, 4% 40-49, 3% 50-99. **Special facilities:** Observatory, nuclear physics laboratory.

**Freshman class profile.** 935 applied, 576 admitted, 207 enrolled.

| Mid 50% test scores | | GPA 2.0-2.99: | 21% |
|---|---|---|---|
| SAT critical reading: | 430-560 | Rank in top quarter: | 42% |
| SAT math: | 430-570 | Rank in top tenth: | 19% |
| ACT composite: | 20-25 | Return as sophomores: | 70% |
| GPA 3.75 or higher: | 24% | Out-of-state: | 41% |
| GPA 3.50-3.74: | 19% | Live on campus: | 78% |
| GPA 3.0-3.49: | 35% | International: | 1% |

**Basis for selection.** Qualified applicants should 2.4 GPA and 19 ACT/890 SAT (exclusive of Writing). Those who do not present this pattern may be conditionally accepted. SAT Writing used for financial aid eligibility purposes only. Interview recommended.

**High school preparation.** College-preparatory program required. 16 units required; 25 recommended. Required and recommended units include English 4, mathematics 3-4, social studies 1, history 1, science 1-2 (laboratory 1-2), foreign language 2 and academic electives 4. 2 Algebra (Algebra I and II); one unit of Geometry; 1 Natural Science required.

**2009-2010 Annual costs.** Tuition/fees: $21,880. Room/board: $7,418. Books/supplies: $600.

**2009-2010 Financial aid. Need-based:** Average need met was 78%. Average scholarship/grant was $17,190; average loan $3,690. 67% of total undergraduate aid awarded as scholarships/grants, 33% as loans/jobs. **Non-need-based:** Scholarships awarded for academics, athletics, music/drama.

**Application procedures. Admission:** No deadline. $20 fee, may be waived for applicants with need, free for online applicants. Admission notification on a rolling basis beginning on or about 8/15. **Financial aid:** Priority date 3/1; no closing date. FAFSA required. Applicants notified on a rolling basis starting 3/1; must reply within 2 week(s) of notification.

**Academics. Special study options:** Accelerated study, combined bachelor's/graduate degree, cross-registration, double major, dual enrollment of high school students, exchange student, honors, independent study, internships, student-designed major, study abroad, teacher certification program. **Credit/placement by examination:** AP, CLEP, SAT, ACT, institutional tests. 30 credit hours maximum toward bachelor's degree. **Support services:** Learning center, reduced course load, remedial instruction, study skills assistance, tutoring, writing center.

**Honors college/program.** Current students may be invited to join the Jack E. Snider Honors Center by invitation from a faculty member. Prospective students will meet entrance exam requirements.

**Majors. Area/ethnic studies:** American. **Biology:** General, biochemistry, biophysics. **Business:** Accounting, business admin, management information systems. **Communications:** Digital media. **Computer sciences:** Information technology. **Education:** Music, physical. **Foreign languages:** General, French, Spanish. **Health:** Athletic training, clinical lab science, nursing

(RN). **History:** General. **Interdisciplinary:** Neuroscience. **Math:** General. **Parks/recreation:** Health/fitness. **Philosophy/religion:** Religion. **Physical sciences:** Chemistry, physics. **Psychology:** General. **Social sciences:** Economics, political science. **Theology:** Bible, youth ministry. **Visual/performing arts:** General. **Other:** Forensic science, Health sciences chemistry, Interdisciplinary studies.

**Most popular majors.** Business/marketing 34%, health sciences 45%.

**Computing on campus.** PC or laptop required. 88 workstations in library, computer center, student center. Dormitories wired for high-speed internet access and linked to campus network. Commuter students can connect to campus network. Online library, helpline, repair service, wireless network available.

**Student life. Freshman orientation:** Available. Preregistration for classes offered. **Policies:** Traditional undergraduates participate in Chapel and Convocation series as part of service requirements necessary to fulfill degree requirements. Religious observance required. **Housing:** Guaranteed on-campus for all undergraduates. Single-sex dorms available. $250 partly refundable deposit. **Activities:** Bands, campus ministries, choral groups, dance, drama, international student organizations, music ensembles, musical theater, student government, student newspaper, Fellowship of Christian Athletes, Young Life Leadership, Student Life and Activities Committee at King, Students in Free Enterprise, King College Republicans, World Christian Fellowship, literary society.

**Athletics.** NCAA. **Intercollegiate:** Baseball M, basketball, cheerleading, cross-country, golf, soccer, softball W, swimming, tennis, track and field, volleyball W, wrestling. **Intramural:** Badminton, basketball, cross-country, football (non-tackle), golf, soccer, softball W, table tennis, track and field, volleyball. **Team name:** Tornado.

**Student services.** Adult student services, chaplain/spiritual director, career counseling, student employment services, financial aid counseling, health services, personal counseling, placement for graduates.

**Contact.** E-mail: admissions@king.edu
Phone: (423) 652-4861 Toll-free number: (800) 362-0014
Fax: (423) 652-4727
Micah Crews, Enrollment Management, King College, 1350 King College Road, Bristol, TN 37620-2699

## Lambuth University
**Jackson, Tennessee**
**www.lambuth.edu**                    **CB code: 1394**

- Private 4-year university and liberal arts college affiliated with United Methodist Church
- Residential campus in small city
- 573 degree-seeking undergraduates: 3% part-time, 37% women
- 51% of applicants admitted
- SAT or ACT (ACT writing optional), application essay required
- 39% graduate within 6 years; 21% enter graduate study

**General.** Founded in 1843. Regionally accredited. **Degrees:** 163 bachelor's awarded. **ROTC:** Army. **Location:** 80 miles from Memphis, 120 miles from Nashville. **Calendar:** Semester, limited summer session. **Full-time faculty:** 35 total; 71% have terminal degrees, 9% minority, 43% women. **Part-time faculty:** 50 total; 22% have terminal degrees, 8% minority, 50% women. **Class size:** 80% < 20, 18% 20-39, less than 1% 40-49, less than 1% 50-99, less than 1% >100. **Special facilities:** Planetarium, art and interior design complex, biological field station, education curriculum lab.

**Freshman class profile.** 693 applied, 356 admitted, 155 enrolled.

| Mid 50% test scores | | GPA 2.0-2.99: | 46% |
|---|---|---|---|
| SAT critical reading: | 370-520 | Rank in top quarter: | 26% |
| SAT math: | 410-550 | Rank in top tenth: | 8% |
| ACT composite: | 18-23 | End year in good standing: | 94% |
| GPA 3.75 or higher: | 12% | Return as sophomores: | 50% |
| GPA 3.50-3.74: | 13% | Out-of-state: | 18% |
| GPA 3.0-3.49: | 28% | Live on campus: | 82% |

**Basis for selection.** High school comprehensive record, test scores important. Audition required for drama, music programs; portfolio recommended for art program; tryouts required for athletes. **Learning Disabled:** Appropriate documentation supporting request for accommodations must be provided to director of student disabilities.

**High school preparation.** College-preparatory program recommended. 14 units recommended. Recommended units include English 4, mathematics 3, social studies 2, history 1, science 3 and foreign language 1.

**2009-2010 Annual costs.** Tuition/fees: $18,570. Room/board: $8,015. Books/supplies: $1,200. Personal expenses: $2,000.

**2009-2010 Financial aid. Non-need-based:** Scholarships awarded for academics, alumni affiliation, art, athletics, job skills, leadership, music/drama, religious affiliation, state residency. **Additional information:** Part-time students eligible for federal and state aid, but not institutional aid.

**Application procedures. Admission:** No deadline. $25 fee, may be waived for applicants with need. Admission notification on a rolling basis beginning on or about 10/1. Must reply by May 1 or within 2 week(s) if notified thereafter. **Financial aid:** Priority date 2/15; no closing date. FAFSA required. Applicants notified on a rolling basis starting 3/1; must reply by 5/1 or within 2 week(s) of notification.

**Academics.** Math and science study halls held 3 nights per week. **Special study options:** Combined bachelor's/graduate degree, cross-registration, double major, ESL, honors, independent study, internships, liberal arts/career combination, student-designed major, study abroad, teacher certification program, Washington semester. Legislative internships at state and national level. **Credit/placement by examination:** AP, CLEP, IB, SAT, ACT. 32 credit hours maximum toward bachelor's degree. **Support services:** Learning center, reduced course load, remedial instruction, study skills assistance, tutoring.

**Majors. Biology:** General. **Business:** General, accounting, accounting/business management, business admin, fashion, international, management information systems, managerial economics, marketing. **Communications:** General. **Computer sciences:** General. **Conservation:** Environmental science. **Education:** General, art, biology, business, chemistry, Deaf/hearing impaired, developmentally delayed, elementary, English, health, history, mathematics, mentally handicapped, middle, multiple handicapped, music, physical, secondary, special, speech impaired. **Family/consumer sciences:** General, clothing/textiles. **Foreign languages:** General, French, Germanic, Spanish. **Health:** Communication disorders. **History:** General. **Interdisciplinary:** Global studies. **Legal studies:** Prelaw. **Liberal arts:** Arts/sciences. **Math:** General. **Parks/recreation:** Facilities management, health/fitness, sports admin. **Philosophy/religion:** Philosophy, religion. **Physical sciences:** Chemistry. **Protective services:** Law enforcement admin. **Psychology:** General. **Public administration:** Social work. **Social sciences:** International relations, political science, sociology. **Theology:** Sacred music. **Visual/performing arts:** General, art, art history/conservation, design, dramatic, interior design, music performance, piano/organ, studio arts, voice/opera.

**Most popular majors.** Business/marketing 14%, education 14%, English 8%, parks/recreation 12%, psychology 10%, social sciences 8%, visual/performing arts 7%.

**Computing on campus.** 100 workstations in dormitories, library, computer center, student center. Dormitories wired for high-speed internet access and linked to campus network. Commuter students can connect to campus network. Online library, helpline, repair service, wireless network available.

**Student life. Freshman orientation:** Mandatory, $60 fee. Preregistration for classes offered. 1-day session held during summer followed by 3-4 day schedule of events just prior to beginning of classes. **Policies:** No alcohol, drug paraphernalia, hazing, fireworks, or firearms allowed. **Housing:** Guaranteed on-campus for freshmen. Coed dorms, single-sex dorms, special housing for disabled, apartments, fraternity/sorority housing, wellness housing available. $100 nonrefundable deposit, deadline 5/1. **Activities:** Bands, campus ministries, choral groups, drama, international student organizations, literary magazine, music ensembles, Model UN, musical theater, student government, student newspaper, black student union, Alpha Omega, Gamma Beta Phi, Fellowship of Christian Athletes, Best Buddies, Phi Sigma Eta, Religious Life Council, Companions in Christ, discipleship/accountability groups.

**Athletics.** NAIA. **Intercollegiate:** Baseball M, basketball, football (tackle) M, golf, soccer, softball W, tennis. **Intramural:** Basketball, football (non-tackle), softball, table tennis. **Team name:** Eagles.

**Student services.** Chaplain/spiritual director, career counseling, student employment services, financial aid counseling, health services, personal counseling, placement for graduates, veterans' counselor. **Physically disabled:** Services for visually, speech, hearing impaired.

**Contact.** E-mail: admit@lambuth.edu
Phone: (731) 425-3223 Toll-free number: (800) 526-2884
Fax: (731) 988-4600
Lisa Warmath, Associate Provost for Administrative Services, Lambuth University, 705 Lambuth Boulevard, Jackson, TN 38301-5296

## Lane College
**Jackson, Tennessee**
**www.lanecollege.edu**                    **CB code: 1395**

- Private 4-year liberal arts college affiliated with Christian Methodist Episcopal Church
- Residential campus in small city

◗ 2,146 degree-seeking undergraduates: 1% part-time, 53% women, 100% African American
◗ 37% of applicants admitted
◗ SAT or ACT (ACT writing optional) required

**General.** Founded in 1882. Regionally accredited. **Degrees:** 189 bachelor's awarded. **Location:** 80 miles from Memphis, 126 miles from Nashville. **Calendar:** Semester, limited summer session. **Full-time faculty:** 94 total. **Part-time faculty:** 8 total. **Class size:** 30% < 20, 68% 20-39, 1% 40-49, less than 1% 50-99.

**Freshman class profile.** 5,619 applied, 2,064 admitted, 692 enrolled.

| | | | |
|---|---|---|---|
| GPA 3.75 or higher: | 1% | Rank in top tenth: | 4% |
| GPA 3.50-3.74: | 1% | End year in good standing: | 62% |
| GPA 3.0-3.49: | 9% | Return as sophomores: | 62% |
| GPA 2.0-2.99: | 68% | Out-of-state: | 36% |
| Rank in top quarter: | 16% | Live on campus: | 97% |

**Basis for selection.** School achievement record and recommendations most important.

**High school preparation.** 16 units recommended. Recommended units include English 4, mathematics 2, social studies 2, science 2 and foreign language 2.

**2009-2010 Annual costs.** Tuition/fees: $8,000. Room/board: $5,520. Books/supplies: $1,000. Personal expenses: $650.

**2008-2009 Financial aid.** **Need-based:** 672 full-time freshmen applied for aid; 659 were judged to have need; 646 of these received aid. Average scholarship/grant was $1,253; average loan $3,120. 51% of total undergraduate aid awarded as scholarships/grants, 49% as loans/jobs. **Non-need-based:** Awarded to 27 full-time undergraduates, including 26 freshmen. Scholarships awarded for academics, athletics, religious affiliation.

**Application procedures.** **Admission:** Priority date 7/1; deadline 8/1 (postmark date). No application fee. Admission notification on a rolling basis beginning on or about 2/1. Must reply by May 1 or within 2 week(s) if notified thereafter. **Financial aid:** Priority date 3/1; no closing date. FAFSA required. Applicants notified on a rolling basis starting 3/31; must reply within 2 week(s) of notification.

**Academics.** **Special study options:** Accelerated study, independent study, internships, study abroad, teacher certification program. **Credit/placement by examination:** CLEP. **Support services:** Study skills assistance, tutoring, writing center.

**Majors.** **Biology:** General. **Business:** Business admin. **Communications:** General. **Computer sciences:** General. **Education:** Physical. **Foreign languages:** French. **History:** General. **Math:** General. **Philosophy/religion:** Religion. **Physical sciences:** Chemistry, physics. **Protective services:** Criminal justice. **Social sciences:** Sociology.

**Most popular majors.** Biology 11%, business/marketing 23%, communications/journalism 8%, computer/information sciences 6%, education 6%, interdisciplinary studies 16%, security/protective services 13%, social sciences 9%.

**Computing on campus.** 470 workstations in library, computer center. Dormitories wired for high-speed internet access and linked to campus network. Online library, helpline, wireless network available.

**Student life.** **Freshman orientation:** Mandatory. Preregistration for classes offered. Held during weekend in July. **Policies:** Religious observance required. **Housing:** Single-sex dorms available. $50 nonrefundable deposit. **Activities:** Bands, campus ministries, choral groups, dance, drama, music ensembles, student government, student newspaper, student ministerial alliance, student Christian association, pre-alumni council.

**Athletics.** NCAA. **Intercollegiate:** Baseball M, basketball, cheerleading M, cross-country, football (tackle) M, softball W, tennis, track and field, volleyball W. **Intramural:** Badminton, basketball, softball, swimming, table tennis, volleyball. **Team name:** Dragons.

**Student services.** Alcohol/substance abuse counseling, chaplain/spiritual director, career counseling, services for economically disadvantaged, student employment services, financial aid counseling, health services, personal counseling, placement for graduates, veterans' counselor.

**Contact.** E-mail: ebrown@lanecollege.edu
Phone: (731) 426-7533 Toll-free number: (800) 960-7533
Fax: (731) 426-7559
Evelyn Brown, Director of Admissions, Lane College, 545 Lane Avenue, Jackson, TN 38301-4598

## Lee University
### Cleveland, Tennessee
**www.leeuniversity.edu**      **CB code: 1401**

◗ Private 4-year university and liberal arts college affiliated with Church of God
◗ Residential campus in large town
◗ 3,602 degree-seeking undergraduates: 5% part-time, 56% women, 4% African American, 1% Asian American, 3% Hispanic American, 5% international
◗ 319 degree-seeking graduate students
◗ 65% of applicants admitted
◗ SAT or ACT (ACT writing optional) required
◗ 48% graduate within 6 years

**General.** Founded in 1918. Regionally accredited. **Degrees:** 643 bachelor's awarded; master's offered. **Location:** 20 miles from Chattanooga, 75 miles from Knoxville. **Calendar:** Semester, limited summer session. **Full-time faculty:** 149 total; 76% have terminal degrees, 15% minority, 34% women. **Part-time faculty:** 179 total; 28% have terminal degrees, 8% minority, 40% women. **Class size:** 46% < 20, 40% 20-39, 8% 40-49, 5% 50-99, 1% >100.

**Freshman class profile.** 1,768 applied, 1,142 admitted, 832 enrolled.

| | | | |
|---|---|---|---|
| Mid 50% test scores | | GPA 2.0-2.99: | 23% |
| SAT critical reading: | 480-610 | Rank in top quarter: | 46% |
| SAT math: | 460-600 | Rank in top tenth: | 25% |
| ACT composite: | 20-27 | Return as sophomores: | 73% |
| GPA 3.75 or higher: | 35% | Out-of-state: | 53% |
| GPA 3.50-3.74: | 16% | Live on campus: | 93% |
| GPA 3.0-3.49: | 24% | International: | 4% |

**Basis for selection.** School achievement record and test scores considered. Audition required for music program. **Homeschooled:** Must have high school transcript with date of graduation and 17 ACT or 860 SAT (exclusive of Writing).

**High school preparation.** College-preparatory program recommended. 13 units required; 14 recommended. Required and recommended units include English 4, mathematics 3, social studies 2, history 1, science 2, foreign language 1 and computer science 1.

**2009-2010 Annual costs.** Tuition/fees: $11,660. Room/board: $5,650. Books/supplies: $900. Personal expenses: $1,610.

**2009-2010 Financial aid.** **Need-based:** 724 full-time freshmen applied for aid; 542 were judged to have need; 534 of these received aid. Average need met was 69%. Average scholarship/grant was $9,509; average loan $3,307. 52% of total undergraduate aid awarded as scholarships/grants, 48% as loans/jobs. **Non-need-based:** Awarded to 951 full-time undergraduates, including 325 freshmen. Scholarships awarded for academics, alumni affiliation, athletics, leadership, minority status, music/drama, religious affiliation, state residency.

**Application procedures.** **Admission:** Closing date 9/1 (receipt date). $25 fee. Admission notification on a rolling basis beginning on or about 9/1. **Financial aid:** Priority date 3/15; no closing date. FAFSA required. Applicants notified on a rolling basis starting 2/1; must reply within 3 week(s) of notification.

**Academics.** **Special study options:** Distance learning, double major, dual enrollment of high school students, ESL, exchange student, external degree, honors, independent study, internships, liberal arts/career combination, study abroad, teacher certification program, Washington semester. **Credit/placement by examination:** AP, CLEP, IB, SAT, ACT, institutional tests. 32 credit hours maximum toward bachelor's degree. **Support services:** Learning center, pre-admission summer program, reduced course load, remedial instruction, tutoring, writing center.

**Majors.** **Biology:** General, biochemistry, environmental. **Business:** Accounting, business admin. **Communications:** General, advertising, digital media, journalism, public relations. **Computer sciences:** General. **Education:** General, biology, business, early childhood, elementary, English, foreign languages, health, history, mathematics, music, physical, psychology, secondary, Spanish, special. **Family/consumer sciences:** Family studies. **Foreign languages:** French, Spanish. **Health:** Athletic training, health services. **History:** General. **Math:** General. **Parks/recreation:** Health/fitness. **Physical sciences:** Chemistry. **Psychology:** General. **Social sciences:** Anthropology, political science, sociology. **Theology:** Bible, missionary, pastoral counseling, preministerial, religious ed, sacred music, theology, youth ministry. **Visual/performing arts:** Dramatic, music management, music performance. **Other:** Missiology/Intercultural Studies.

**Most popular majors.** Business/marketing 12%, communications/ journalism 9%, education 18%, psychology 13%, social sciences 6%, theological studies 20%.

**Computing on campus.** 470 workstations in dormitories, library, computer center, student center. Dormitories wired for high-speed internet access and linked to campus network. Online library, helpline, wireless network available.

**Student life. Freshman orientation:** Mandatory. Preregistration for classes offered. Held weekend before classes begin. **Policies:** Religious observance required. **Housing:** Guaranteed on-campus for freshmen. Single-sex dorms, apartments, wellness housing available. $200 fully refundable deposit, deadline 9/1. University leases apartments and houses for students. **Activities:** Bands, campus ministries, choral groups, drama, international student organizations, literary magazine, music ensembles, Model UN, musical theater, opera, student government, student newspaper, symphony orchestra, Greek councils, student leadership council, Collegiate Sertoma, married students fellowship, Pioneers for Christ, Fellowship of Christian Athletes, Missions Alive, deaf ministry association.

**Athletics.** NAIA, NCCAA. **Intercollegiate:** Baseball M, basketball, cross-country, golf M, soccer, softball W, tennis, volleyball W. **Intramural:** Basketball, bowling, football (non-tackle) M, racquetball, soccer, softball, table tennis, tennis, volleyball. **Team name:** Flames.

**Student services.** Alcohol/substance abuse counseling, chaplain/spiritual director, career counseling, student employment services, financial aid counseling, health services, personal counseling, placement for graduates, veterans' counselor.

**Contact.** E-mail: admissions@leeuniversity.edu
Phone: (423) 614-8500 Toll-free number: (800) 533-9930
Fax: (423) 614-8533
Phil Cook, Assistant Vice President for Enrollment, Lee University, 1120 North Ocoee Street, Cleveland, TN 37320-3450

## LeMoyne-Owen College
**Memphis, Tennessee**
www.loc.edu
CB member
CB code: 1403

- Private 4-year liberal arts college affiliated with United Church of Christ and Tennessee Baptist Convention
- Commuter campus in very large city
- 890 degree-seeking undergraduates
- 36% of applicants admitted
- SAT or ACT (ACT writing recommended) required

**General.** Founded in 1862. Regionally accredited. **Degrees:** 58 bachelor's awarded. **ROTC:** Army, Air Force. **Calendar:** Semester, extensive summer session. **Full-time faculty:** 53 total. **Part-time faculty:** 46 total. **Class size:** 82% < 20, 18% 20-39, less than 1% 40-49.

**Freshman class profile.** 955 applied, 344 admitted, 227 enrolled.

| Mid 50% test scores | | | |
|---|---|---|---|
| ACT composite: | 14-18 | Out-of-state: | 5% |
| | | Live on campus: | 10% |

**Basis for selection.** High school transcript, test scores, letter of recommendation, and interview important. Special consideration given to children of alumni. Essay, interview recommended.

**High school preparation.** 15 units required. Required units include English 4, mathematics 3, history 2, science 3, foreign language 2 and academic electives 1.

**2009-2010 Annual costs.** Tuition/fees: $10,318. Room/board: $4,852. Books/supplies: $750. Personal expenses: $1,800.

**2008-2009 Financial aid. Non-need-based:** Scholarships awarded for academics, athletics, music/drama.

**Application procedures. Admission:** Closing date 4/15. $25 fee. Admission notification on a rolling basis. Must reply by May 1 or within 2 week(s) if notified thereafter. **Financial aid:** Priority date 4/15; no closing date. FAFSA required. Applicants notified on a rolling basis starting 4/1.

**Academics. Special study options:** Accelerated study, cooperative education, cross-registration, distance learning, double major, dual enrollment of high school students, exchange student, honors, internships, liberal arts/career combination, student-designed major, study abroad, teacher certification program, weekend college. **Credit/placement by examination:** AP, CLEP, IB, ACT, institutional tests. 24 credit hours maximum toward bachelor's degree. **Support services:** Learning center, pre-admission summer program, reduced course load, remedial instruction, tutoring.

**Majors. Biology:** General. **Business:** Business admin. **Computer sciences:** Computer science, information technology. **Education:** Early childhood, English, mathematics, science, social studies, special. **History:** General. **Liberal arts:** Humanities. **Math:** General. **Physical sciences:** Chemistry. **Protective services:** Police science. **Public administration:** Social work. **Social sciences:** General, political science, sociology. **Visual/performing arts:** Art.

**Most popular majors.** Business/marketing 23%, security/protective services 6%.

**Computing on campus.** 223 workstations in library, computer center. Helpline, repair service available.

**Student life. Freshman orientation:** Mandatory. Preregistration for classes offered. **Housing:** Single-sex dorms, wellness housing available. $100 deposit. **Activities:** Jazz band, choral groups, dance, drama, music ensembles, student government, student newspaper, NAACP, social work club, Students for Free Enterprise, pre-alumni council, National Student Business Organization.

**Athletics.** NCAA. **Intercollegiate:** Baseball M, basketball, cross-country, golf, soccer, softball W, tennis, volleyball W. **Intramural:** Basketball. **Team name:** Magicians.

**Student services.** Adult student services, career counseling, student employment services, health services, personal counseling, placement for graduates, veterans' counselor.

**Contact.** E-mail: admission@loc.edu
Phone: (901) 435-1500 Fax: (901) 435-1524
June Chinn-Jointer, Director of Admissions/Recruitment, LeMoyne-Owen College, 807 Walker Avenue, Memphis, TN 38126

## Lincoln Memorial University
**Harrogate, Tennessee**
www.lmunet.edu
CB member
CB code: 1408

- Private 4-year university and liberal arts college
- Commuter campus in small town
- 1,464 degree-seeking undergraduates: 13% part-time, 72% women, 5% African American, 1% Asian American, 1% Hispanic American, 4% international
- 2,061 degree-seeking graduate students
- 69% of applicants admitted
- SAT or ACT (ACT writing optional) required
- 32% graduate within 6 years

**General.** Founded in 1897. Regionally accredited. **Degrees:** 172 bachelor's, 139 associate awarded; master's, doctoral, professional offered. **ROTC:** Army. **Location:** 50 miles from Knoxville. **Calendar:** Semester, limited summer session. **Full-time faculty:** 170 total; 74% have terminal degrees, 4% minority, 40% women. **Part-time faculty:** 56 total; 32% have terminal degrees, 2% minority, 38% women. **Class size:** 73% < 20, 26% 20-39, less than 1% 40-49, less than 1% 50-99. **Special facilities:** Abraham Lincoln library and museum, mountain research center.

**Freshman class profile.** 1,412 applied, 977 admitted, 318 enrolled.

| Mid 50% test scores | | | |
|---|---|---|---|
| SAT critical reading: | 420-550 | GPA 3.0-3.49: | 27% |
| SAT math: | 440-560 | GPA 2.0-2.99: | 25% |
| ACT composite: | 18-23 | Return as sophomores: | 65% |
| GPA 3.75 or higher: | 27% | Out-of-state: | 31% |
| GPA 3.50-3.74: | 20% | Live on campus: | 62% |
| | | International: | 3% |

**Basis for selection.** Academic record, ACT or SAT very important.

**High school preparation.** College-preparatory program recommended. Required and recommended units include English 4, mathematics 3-4, social studies 1-2, history 1, science 2, foreign language 2 and visual/performing arts 1.

**2009-2010 Annual costs.** Tuition/fees: $15,120. Room/board: $5,680. Books/supplies: $1,200.

**2009-2010 Financial aid. Need-based:** 306 full-time freshmen applied for aid; 285 were judged to have need; 285 of these received aid. Average need met was 78%. Average scholarship/grant was $14,047; average loan $3,487. 69% of total undergraduate aid awarded as scholarships/grants, 31% as loans/jobs. **Non-need-based:** Awarded to 208 full-time undergraduates, including 62 freshmen. Scholarships awarded for academics, alumni affiliation, athletics, music/drama, ROTC.

**Application procedures. Admission:** Priority date 6/1; no deadline. $25 fee, may be waived for applicants with need, free for online applicants. Admission notification on a rolling basis beginning on or about 9/1. **Financial aid:** Priority date 4/1; no closing date. FAFSA required. Applicants notified on a rolling basis starting 4/15; must reply within 3 week(s) of notification.

**Academics. Special study options:** Distance learning, double major, dual enrollment of high school students, ESL, internships, teacher certification program. **Credit/placement by examination:** CLEP, IB, SAT, ACT, institutional tests. 16 credit hours maximum toward associate degree, 32 toward bachelor's. **Support services:** Learning center, reduced course load, remedial instruction, study skills assistance, tutoring, writing center.

**Majors. Area/ethnic studies:** American. **Biology:** General. **Business:** General, accounting, business admin, management science, managerial economics, office/clerical. **Communications:** General. **Computer sciences:** General. **Conservation:** Environmental science, wildlife. **Education:** General, art, biology, business, chemistry, early childhood, elementary, English, health, history, mathematics, middle, physical, science, secondary, social science, social studies. **Health:** Athletic training, clinical lab science, clinical lab technology, nursing (RN), predental, premedicine, prepharmacy, preveterinary, veterinary technology/assistant. **History:** General. **Legal studies:** Prelaw. **Liberal arts:** Humanities. **Math:** General. **Parks/recreation:** Health/fitness. **Physical sciences:** Chemistry. **Psychology:** General. **Public administration:** Social work. **Social sciences:** General. **Visual/performing arts:** General, art.

**Most popular majors.** Biology 6%, business/marketing 27%, education 19%, health sciences 13%, security/protective services 6%.

**Computing on campus.** Dormitories wired for high-speed internet access and linked to campus network. Commuter students can connect to campus network. Online library, helpline, wireless network available.

**Student life. Freshman orientation:** Mandatory. Preregistration for classes offered. **Housing:** Guaranteed on-campus for all undergraduates. Coed dorms, single-sex dorms, special housing for disabled, apartments available. $200 fully refundable deposit. Housing deposit refundable in full until 7/1. **Activities:** Pep band, campus ministries, choral groups, dance, drama, international student organizations, literary magazine, music ensembles, radio station, student government, TV station, Baptist collegiate ministries, Students in Free Enterprise, international student union, All Beliefs in Action.

**Athletics.** NCAA. **Intercollegiate:** Baseball M, basketball, cheerleading, cross-country, golf, soccer, softball W, tennis, volleyball W. **Intramural:** Basketball, football (non-tackle), soccer, softball, swimming, table tennis, tennis, volleyball. **Team name:** Railsplitters.

**Student services.** Alcohol/substance abuse counseling, chaplain/spiritual director, career counseling, student employment services, financial aid counseling, health services, personal counseling, placement for graduates. **Physically disabled:** Services for visually, hearing impaired.

**Contact.** E-mail: admissions@lmunet.edu
Phone: (423) 869-3611 ext. 6280 Toll-free
number: (800) 325-0900 ext. 6280 Fax: (423) 869-6444
Lincoln Memorial University, 6965 Cumberland Gap Parkway, Harrogate, TN 37752-1901

## Lipscomb University
### Nashville, Tennessee
### www.lipscomb.edu
CB code: 1161

- Private 4-year university and liberal arts college affiliated with Church of Christ
- Residential campus in very large city
- 2,467 degree-seeking undergraduates: 6% part-time, 57% women, 6% African American, 3% Asian American, 2% Hispanic American, 3% international
- 785 degree-seeking graduate students
- 66% of applicants admitted
- SAT or ACT (ACT writing recommended), interview required
- 63% graduate within 6 years

**General.** Founded in 1891. Regionally accredited. **Degrees:** 490 bachelor's awarded; master's, professional offered. **ROTC:** Army, Air Force. **Location:** 4 miles from downtown. **Calendar:** Semester, extensive summer session. **Full-time faculty:** 147 total; 3% minority, 31% women. **Part-time faculty:** 196 total; 9% minority, 45% women. **Class size:** 56% < 20, 32% 20-39, 6% 40-49, 6% 50-99, less than 1% >100.

**Freshman class profile.** 2,683 applied, 1,783 admitted, 605 enrolled.

| Mid 50% test scores | | | |
|---|---|---|---|
| SAT critical reading: | 490-600 | GPA 2.0-2.99: | 20% |
| SAT math: | 490-610 | Rank in top quarter: | 48% |
| ACT composite: | 21-26 | Rank in top tenth: | 24% |
| GPA 3.75 or higher: | 34% | Return as sophomores: | 78% |
| GPA 3.50-3.74: | 15% | Out-of-state: | 35% |
| GPA 3.0-3.49: | 31% | Live on campus: | 84% |
| | | International: | 2% |

**Basis for selection.** School achievement record, test scores, educational and personal references required. Strong moral character desired. Audition required for music; portfolio required for art; interview recommended for art, honors, music programs.

**High school preparation.** College-preparatory program recommended. 14 units required. Required units include English 4, mathematics 2, social studies 2, science 2, foreign language 2 and academic electives 2. Math units preferably Algebra I, II. Foreign language units in the same language. 2 academic electives should be selected from natural sciences, mathematics, foreign languages, or social sciences.

**2009-2010 Annual costs.** Tuition/fees: $20,390. Room/board: $7,850. Books/supplies: $1,000. Personal expenses: $1,250.

**2009-2010 Financial aid. Non-need-based:** Scholarships awarded for academics, alumni affiliation, art, athletics, leadership, minority status, music/drama, religious affiliation, state residency.

**Application procedures. Admission:** Priority date 10/31; no deadline. $25 fee, may be waived for applicants with need. Admission notification on a rolling basis beginning on or about 8/15. **Financial aid:** Priority date 3/1; no closing date. FAFSA required. Applicants notified on a rolling basis starting 2/15.

**Academics. Special study options:** Combined bachelor's/graduate degree, cross-registration, distance learning, double major, dual enrollment of high school students, honors, independent study, internships, study abroad, teacher certification program, weekend college. **Credit/placement by examination:** AP, CLEP, IB, SAT, ACT, institutional tests. 30 credit hours maximum toward bachelor's degree. **Support services:** Learning center, pre-admission summer program, reduced course load, remedial instruction, study skills assistance, tutoring, writing center.

**Majors. Area/ethnic studies:** American. **Biology:** General, biochemistry. **Business:** Accounting, business admin, fashion, human resources, international, management information systems, managerial economics, marketing. **Communications:** Journalism, media studies, organizational, public relations. **Computer sciences:** Computer science, information technology. **Conservation:** Environmental science. **Education:** Art, biology, chemistry, drama/dance, elementary, English, ESL, French, German, history, mathematics, music, physical, physics, Spanish. **Engineering:** Computer, mechanical, mechanics, science. **Family/consumer sciences:** General, clothing/textiles, family systems, institutional food production. **Foreign languages:** French, German, Spanish. **Health:** Athletic training, dietetics, nursing (RN), predental, premedicine, prenursing, prepharmacy, preveterinary. **History:** General. **Interdisciplinary:** Peace/conflict. **Legal studies:** General, prelaw. **Math:** General. **Parks/recreation:** Exercise sciences. **Philosophy/religion:** Philosophy. **Physical sciences:** Chemistry, physics. **Psychology:** General. **Public administration:** General, social work. **Social sciences:** Political science, urban studies. **Theology:** Bible, missionary, youth ministry. **Visual/performing arts:** Commercial/advertising art, dramatic, music performance, music theory/composition, piano/organ, studio arts, voice/opera. **Other:** Pre-engineering.

**Most popular majors.** Biology 10%, business/marketing 24%, education 10%, English 6%, health sciences 9%, psychology 7%.

**Computing on campus.** 203 workstations in dormitories, library, computer center, student center. Dormitories wired for high-speed internet access and linked to campus network. Commuter students can connect to campus network. Online course registration, helpline, repair service, wireless network available.

**Student life. Freshman orientation:** Mandatory, $110 fee. Preregistration for classes offered. **Policies:** Daily chapel service and Bible studies required. Out-of-town undergraduates required to live on campus, except for seniors, students over age of 21, married students. Religious observance required. **Housing:** Single-sex dorms, apartments available. $125 fully refundable deposit. **Activities:** Bands, campus ministries, choral groups, drama, international student organizations, literary magazine, music ensembles, musical theater, radio station, student government, student newspaper, TV station, College Republicans, Young Democrats, honorary societies, multicultural association, Circle K, Fellowship of Christian Athletes, Youth Encouragement Services, men and women's service clubs, homeless ministry, DAC (ministry to the hearing impaired).

**Athletics.** NCAA. **Intercollegiate:** Baseball M, basketball, cross-country, golf, soccer, softball W, tennis, track and field, volleyball W. **Intramural:** Badminton, basketball, football (non-tackle), racquetball, soccer, softball, tennis, volleyball. **Team name:** Bisons.

**Student services.** Adult student services, chaplain/spiritual director, career counseling, student employment services, financial aid counseling, health services, minority student services, personal counseling, placement for graduates. **Physically disabled:** Services for visually, speech, hearing impaired.

**Contact.** E-mail: admissions@lipscomb.edu
Phone: (615) 966-1776 Toll-free number: (877) 582-4766
Fax: (615) 966-1804
Ricky Holaway, Director of Admissions, Lipscomb University, One University Park Drive, Nashville, TN 37204-3951

## Martin Methodist College
### Pulaski, Tennessee
www.martinmethodist.edu                    CB code: 1449

▶ Private 4-year liberal arts college affiliated with United Methodist Church
▶ Residential campus in small town
▶ 940 degree-seeking undergraduates
▶ 94% of applicants admitted

**General.** Founded in 1870. Regionally accredited. **Degrees:** 133 bachelor's, 13 associate awarded. **Location:** 70 miles from Nashville; 40 miles from Huntsville, AL. **Calendar:** Semester, limited summer session. **Full-time faculty:** 46 total; 50% have terminal degrees. **Part-time faculty:** 40 total; 20% have terminal degrees. **Class size:** 78% < 20, 21% 20-39, less than 1% 40-49.

**Freshman class profile.** 825 applied, 776 admitted, 248 enrolled.

| Mid 50% test scores | | | |
|---|---|---|---|
| SAT critical reading: | 410-460 | GPA 3.50-3.74: | 19% |
| SAT math: | 440-500 | GPA 3.0-3.49: | 34% |
| SAT writing: | 430-520 | GPA 2.0-2.99: | 28% |
| ACT composite: | 17-22 | Out-of-state: | 13% |
| GPA 3.75 or higher: | 15% | Live on campus: | 46% |

**Basis for selection.** High school record, interview, test scores important. Applicants must meet 2 of the following or apply for special circumstances admission status: 2.0 GPA, 18 ACT, or rank in upper 50% of class. Students conditionally admitted will be offered full enrollment after completion of a semester with 2.0 GPA. Audition recommended for music; portfolio recommended for art.

**High school preparation.** 13 units required. Required and recommended units include English 4, mathematics 2-3, social studies 2, history 1, science 2 (laboratory 2), foreign language 2, computer science 1 and academic electives 4.

**2009-2010 Annual costs.** Tuition/fees: $18,638. Room/board: $6,400. Books/supplies: $750. Personal expenses: $1,200.

**2008-2009 Financial aid. Non-need-based:** Scholarships awarded for academics, art, athletics, leadership, music/drama, religious affiliation, state residency.

**Application procedures. Admission:** Priority date 5/1; deadline 8/1 (postmark date). $30 fee. Admission notification on a rolling basis. **Financial aid:** No deadline. FAFSA, institutional form required. Applicants notified on a rolling basis starting 3/1; must reply within 2 week(s) of notification.

**Academics. Special study options:** Dual enrollment of high school students, ESL, honors, independent study, study abroad. **Credit/placement by examination:** AP, CLEP. 30 credit hours maximum toward associate degree. **Support services:** Learning center, pre-admission summer program, reduced course load, remedial instruction, study skills assistance, tutoring, writing center.

**Majors. Biology:** General. **Business:** General, accounting, business admin. **Education:** Elementary, middle, secondary. **Health:** Nursing (RN). **History:** General. **Parks/recreation:** Sports admin. **Philosophy/religion:** Religion. **Psychology:** General. **Public administration:** Human services. **Other:** Criminal justice, History and political science, Sport management.

**Most popular majors.** Biology 10%, business/marketing 15%, education 13%, liberal arts 13%, social sciences 22%.

**Computing on campus.** 150 workstations in library, computer center. Dormitories wired for high-speed internet access and linked to campus network. Commuter students can connect to campus network. Online course registration, online library, helpline, wireless network available.

**Student life. Freshman orientation:** Mandatory. Preregistration for classes offered. Held 3 days prior to other students' arrival. **Housing:** Guaranteed on-campus for all undergraduates. Single-sex dorms, apartments available. $125 fully refundable deposit, deadline 6/1. **Activities:** Campus ministries, choral groups, drama, international student organizations, music ensembles, student government, student newspaper, student Christian association, black student union, Fellowship of Christian Athletes.

**Athletics.** NAIA, NJCAA. **Intercollegiate:** Baseball M, basketball, bowling, cheerleading M, golf, soccer, softball W, tennis, volleyball W. **Intramural:** Basketball, football (non-tackle), racquetball, softball, swimming, table tennis, volleyball. **Team name:** RedHawks.

**Student services.** Adult student services, chaplain/spiritual director, career counseling, student employment services, financial aid counseling, personal counseling, placement for graduates, veterans' counselor.

**Contact.** E-mail: lsmith2@martinmethodist.edu
Phone: (931) 363-9868 Toll-free number: (800) 467-1273
Fax: (931) 363-9803
Lisa Smith, Director of Admissions, Martin Methodist College, 433 West Madison, Pulaski, TN 38478-2799

## Maryville College
### Maryville, Tennessee
www.maryvillecollege.edu        CB member
                                CB code: 1454

▶ Private 4-year liberal arts college affiliated with Presbyterian Church (USA)
▶ Residential campus in small city
▶ 1,103 degree-seeking undergraduates
▶ 73% of applicants admitted
▶ SAT or ACT (ACT writing optional) required

**General.** Founded in 1819. Regionally accredited. **Degrees:** 251 bachelor's awarded. **Location:** 15 miles from Knoxville. **Calendar:** 4-1-4, limited summer session. **Full-time faculty:** 79 total; 85% have terminal degrees, 6% minority, 54% women. **Part-time faculty:** 51 total. **Class size:** 73% < 20, 27% 20-39, less than 1% 40-49. **Special facilities:** Science center, fine arts center, college woods with ropes courses, equestrian center.

**Freshman class profile.** 1,563 applied, 1,143 admitted, 303 enrolled.

| Mid 50% test scores | | | |
|---|---|---|---|
| SAT critical reading: | 470-590 | GPA 3.0-3.49: | 31% |
| SAT math: | 470-580 | GPA 2.0-2.99: | 9% |
| SAT writing: | 460-580 | Rank in top quarter: | 65% |
| ACT composite: | 21-27 | Rank in top tenth: | 34% |
| GPA 3.75 or higher: | 39% | Out-of-state: | 23% |
| GPA 3.50-3.74: | 21% | Live on campus: | 87% |

**Basis for selection.** Admissions based on academic criteria, extracurricular involvement, and personal achievement. Successful students typically follow strong college preparatory curriculums and rank in top 25% of class. Writing samples encouraged. Essay, interview recommended for all; audition required for music; portfolio recommended for art. **Homeschooled:** Pursue rigorous curriculum that includes strong emphasis on writing and reasoning.

**High school preparation.** 15 units required. Required and recommended units include English 4, mathematics 3, social studies 2, history 1, science 2 (laboratory 1), foreign language 2 and academic electives 1.

**2009-2010 Annual costs.** Tuition/fees: $27,971. Room/board: $8,560. Books/supplies: $880. Personal expenses: $930.

**2009-2010 Financial aid. Non-need-based:** Scholarships awarded for academics, art, leadership, minority status, music/drama, religious affiliation, state residency.

**Application procedures. Admission:** Priority date 3/1; no deadline. No application fee. Admission notification on a rolling basis beginning on or about 10/1. Must reply by May 1 or within 2 week(s) if notified thereafter. **Financial aid:** Priority date 3/1; no closing date. FAFSA required. Applicants notified on a rolling basis starting 3/15; must reply within 4 week(s) of notification.

**Academics.** All students complete 6 credit-hour research project and comprehensive examination in their major area of study. **Special study options:**

Combined bachelor's/graduate degree, double major, ESL, honors, independent study, internships, liberal arts/career combination, student-designed major, study abroad, teacher certification program, Washington semester. **Credit/placement by examination:** AP, CLEP, IB, institutional tests. 32 credit hours maximum toward bachelor's degree. Students may petition individual departments for credit by examination. **Support services:** Learning center, reduced course load, remedial instruction, study skills assistance, tutoring, writing center.

**Majors. Biology:** General, biochemistry. **Business:** Business admin, international. **Computer sciences:** General. **Conservation:** Environmental studies. **Education:** General, biology, chemistry, English, ESL, health, history, mathematics, music, physical, social science, social studies, Spanish. **Engineering:** General. **Foreign languages:** American Sign Language, sign language interpretation, Spanish. **Health:** Nursing (RN), predental, premedicine, prenursing, prepharmacy, preveterinary. **History:** General. **Interdisciplinary:** Math/computer science. **Math:** General. **Parks/recreation:** General, health/fitness. **Philosophy/religion:** Philosophy, religion. **Physical sciences:** Chemical physics, chemistry. **Psychology:** General. **Social sciences:** Economics, international relations, political science, sociology. **Visual/performing arts:** Art, dramatic, music performance, studio arts.

**Most popular majors.** Biology 8%, business/marketing 24%, education 20%, English 6%, psychology 8%, social sciences 10%, visual/performing arts 6%.

**Computing on campus.** 265 workstations in library, computer center. Dormitories wired for high-speed internet access and linked to campus network. Commuter students can connect to campus network. Online course registration, online library, helpline, repair service, wireless network available.

**Student life. Freshman orientation:** Mandatory, $25 fee. Preregistration for classes offered. Held several days before registration; includes Mountain Challenge component. Optional 3-day wilderness experience. **Housing:** Guaranteed on-campus for all undergraduates. Coed dorms, single-sex dorms, special housing for disabled, apartments, wellness housing available. $200 fully refundable deposit, deadline 5/1. Housing deposit refundable before 5/1. **Activities:** Bands, campus ministries, choral groups, dance, drama, film society, international student organizations, literary magazine, music ensembles, Model UN, student government, student newspaper, symphony orchestra, Habitat for Humanity, Literary Corps, Fellowship of Christian Athletes, wellness council, student programming board, black student association.

**Athletics.** NCAA. **Intercollegiate:** Baseball M, basketball, cross-country, equestrian, football (tackle) M, soccer, softball W, tennis, volleyball W. **Intramural:** Archery, badminton, baseball M, basketball, bowling, football (non-tackle), golf, racquetball, rugby, skiing, soccer, softball, swimming, table tennis, tennis, track and field, volleyball, water polo. **Team name:** Scots.

**Student services.** Adult student services, alcohol/substance abuse counseling, chaplain/spiritual director, career counseling, student employment services, financial aid counseling, health services, minority student services, personal counseling, placement for graduates. **Physically disabled:** Services for visually, speech, hearing impaired.

**Contact.** E-mail: admissions@maryvillecollege.edu
Phone: (865) 981-8092 Toll-free number: (800) 597-2687
Fax: (865) 981-8005
Bill Sliwa, Vice President for Enrollment Management, Maryville College, 502 East Lamar Alexander Parkway, Maryville, TN 37804-5907

---

## Memphis College of Art
**Memphis, Tennessee**
www.mca.edu                                   **CB code: 1511**

- Private 4-year visual arts college
- Residential campus in very large city
- 356 degree-seeking undergraduates: 5% part-time, 60% women, 18% African American, 2% Asian American, 4% Hispanic American, 4% international
- 90 degree-seeking graduate students
- 47% of applicants admitted
- SAT or ACT (ACT writing optional) required
- 41% graduate within 6 years; 10% enter graduate study

**General.** Founded in 1936. Regionally accredited. Students have access to Memphis Brooks Museum of Art and Overton Park Zoo. Consortium with four other colleges. **Degrees:** 46 bachelor's awarded; master's offered. **Location:** 500 miles from New Orleans, 700 miles from Dallas. **Calendar:** Semester, limited summer session. **Full-time faculty:** 25 total; 84% have

terminal degrees, 8% minority, 52% women. **Part-time faculty:** 41 total; 27% have terminal degrees, 5% minority, 51% women. **Class size:** 86% < 20, 14% 20-39. **Special facilities:** 5 galleries.

**Freshman class profile.** 752 applied, 351 admitted, 100 enrolled.

| Mid 50% test scores | | | |
|---|---|---|---|
| ACT composite: | 19-25 | GPA 2.0-2.99: | 26% |
| GPA 3.75 or higher: | 25% | Return as sophomores: | 65% |
| GPA 3.50-3.74: | 18% | Out-of-state: | 68% |
| GPA 3.0-3.49: | 30% | Live on campus: | 75% |
| | | International: | 3% |

**Basis for selection.** Art portfolio, high school transcript, test scores required; letter of recommendation from art teacher and essay considered, but not required. Portfolio required; essay, interview recommended for all.

**High school preparation.** College-preparatory program recommended. Portfolio should include 10 to 20 pieces of work, originals or slides, with focus on direct observational drawing.

**2010-2011 Annual costs.** Tuition/fees (projected): $23,950. Room/board: $8,000. Books/supplies: $1,650. Personal expenses: $1,500.

**2009-2010 Financial aid. Need-based:** 92 full-time freshmen applied for aid; 86 were judged to have need; 86 of these received aid. Average need met was 80%. Average scholarship/grant was $6,252; average loan $3,500. 45% of total undergraduate aid awarded as scholarships/grants, 55% as loans/jobs. **Non-need-based:** Awarded to 309 full-time undergraduates, including 98 freshmen. Scholarships awarded for academics, art. **Additional information:** Students considered for institutional resources through admissions application process.

**Application procedures. Admission:** Priority date 3/31; no deadline. $25 fee, may be waived for applicants with need. Admission notification on a rolling basis beginning on or about 11/15. Must reply by May 1 or within 3 week(s) if notified thereafter. **Financial aid:** Priority date 2/15; no closing date. FAFSA required. Applicants notified on a rolling basis starting 3/15; must reply within 3 week(s) of notification.

**Academics. Special study options:** Combined bachelor's/graduate degree, cross-registration, double major, exchange student, independent study, internships, New York semester, study abroad. New York Studio Exchange Program. Mobility semester exchange at 30+ independent art colleges across the country (AICAD consortium). **Credit/placement by examination:** AP, CLEP, SAT, ACT, institutional tests. 15 credit hours maximum toward bachelor's degree. **Support services:** Reduced course load, remedial instruction, study skills assistance, tutoring, writing center.

**Majors. Computer sciences:** Computer graphics. **Visual/performing arts:** Art, commercial/advertising art, design, digital art, drawing, graphic design, illustration, metal/jewelry, multimedia, painting, photography, printmaking, sculpture, studio arts.

**Computing on campus.** 200 workstations in dormitories, library, computer center. Dormitories wired for high-speed internet access. Wireless network available.

**Student life. Freshman orientation:** Mandatory. Preregistration for classes offered. 4-day session includes parents. **Policies:** Considerable assistance available in matching roommates and helping students find affordable housing within walking distance. **Housing:** Coed dorms, apartments, wellness housing available. $300 deposit. **Activities:** International student organizations, student government, student newspaper, photography club, student alliance, multicultural student association, gay-straight alliance.

**Student services.** Adult student services, career counseling, student employment services, financial aid counseling, personal counseling, placement for graduates, veterans' counselor.

**Contact.** E-mail: info@mca.edu
Phone: (901) 272-5151 Toll-free number: (800) 727-1088
Fax: (901) 272-5158
Annette Moore, Dean of Admissions, Memphis College of Art, 1930 Poplar Avenue, Memphis, TN 38104-2764

---

## Middle Tennessee State University
**Murfreesboro, Tennessee**                    **CB member**
www.mtsu.edu                                   **CB code: 1466**

- Public 4-year university
- Commuter campus in small city
- 22,125 degree-seeking undergraduates: 15% part-time, 52% women, 16% African American, 3% Asian American, 3% Hispanic American
- 2,889 degree-seeking graduate students

- 70% of applicants admitted
- SAT or ACT (ACT writing optional) required

**General.** Founded in 1911. Regionally accredited. **Degrees:** 3,790 bachelor's awarded; master's, doctoral offered. **ROTC:** Army, Air Force. **Location:** 32 miles from Nashville. **Calendar:** Semester, extensive summer session. **Full-time faculty:** 931 total; 4% have terminal degrees, 16% minority, 44% women. **Part-time faculty:** 336 total; less than 1% have terminal degrees, 10% minority, 53% women. **Special facilities:** 3 recording studios, observatory, flight simulators, weather center, electronic music laboratory, digital audio edit laboratory, satellite mapping equipment, seismograph, 3 television studios, electronic newsroom, Centers for Historic Preservation and Popular Music.

**Freshman class profile.** 9,431 applied, 6,616 admitted, 3,596 enrolled.

| Mid 50% test scores | | ACT composite: | 20-25 |
|---|---|---|---|
| SAT critical reading: | 450-580 | Fraternities: | 5% |
| SAT math: | 460-580 | Sororities: | 7% |

**Basis for selection.** 3.0 GPA or 22 ACT or combination of 19 ACT and 2.7 GPA required. Personal statement required of students who do not meet standard requirements.

**High school preparation.** College-preparatory program recommended. 14 units required. Required units include English 4, mathematics 3, social studies 1, history 1, science 2 (laboratory 1), foreign language 2 and visual/performing arts 1. Foreign language units must be in single language. Mathematics units must include algebra I and II, geometry or other advanced mathematics. 1 US history, 1 global studies also required.

**2009-2010 Annual costs.** Tuition/fees: $6,048; $18,126 out-of-state. Room/board: $6,453. Books/supplies: $1,000. Personal expenses: $1,400.

**2009-2010 Financial aid.** **Non-need-based:** Scholarships awarded for academics, alumni affiliation, art, athletics, job skills, leadership, minority status, music/drama, religious affiliation, ROTC, state residency. **Additional information:** Application filing deadline for scholarships February 15.

**Application procedures.** **Admission:** Closing date 7/1 (postmark date). $25 fee. Admission notification on a rolling basis. **Financial aid:** Priority date 5/1; no closing date. FAFSA required. Applicants notified on a rolling basis starting 4/15; must reply within 2 week(s) of notification.

**Academics.** **Special study options:** Cooperative education, distance learning, double major, dual enrollment of high school students, honors, independent study, internships, study abroad, teacher certification program. Academic basic skills. **Credit/placement by examination:** CLEP, IB, SAT, ACT, institutional tests. 66 credit hours maximum toward bachelor's degree. Up to 66 semester hours from correspondence study, credit by-examination, credit for service-related experience, and flight training may be counted toward degree. **Support services:** Learning center, pre-admission summer program, reduced course load, remedial instruction, study skills assistance, tutoring, writing center.

**Honors college/program.** 26 ACT (1170 SAT, exclusive of Writing) and 3.0 GPA or 22 ACT (950 SAT) and 3.5 GPA required.

**Majors.** **Agriculture:** Agribusiness operations, animal sciences, plant sciences, soil science. **Biology:** General. **Business:** Accounting, business admin, finance, management information systems, managerial economics, marketing, office management, purchasing, sales/distribution. **Communications:** Media studies. **Computer sciences:** General, computer science. **Education:** Art, business, early childhood, health, kindergarten/preschool, sales/marketing, special, technology/industrial arts. **Engineering technology:** General, architectural, environmental, industrial, industrial management. **Family/consumer sciences:** Clothing/textiles, family resources, food/nutrition. **Foreign languages:** General. **Health:** Athletic training, nursing (RN). **History:** General. **Interdisciplinary:** Biological/physical sciences. **Liberal arts:** Arts/sciences. **Math:** General. **Parks/recreation:** Facilities management, health/fitness. **Philosophy/religion:** Philosophy. **Physical sciences:** Chemistry, geology, physics. **Protective services:** Law enforcement admin. **Psychology:** General. **Public administration:** Social work. **Social sciences:** Anthropology, economics, international relations, political science, sociology. **Transportation:** Aviation. **Visual/performing arts:** Art, art history/conservation, dramatic, interior design, music management.

**Most popular majors.** Business/marketing 20%, communications/journalism 8%, interdisciplinary studies 8%, liberal arts 7%, visual/performing arts 11%.

**Computing on campus.** 2,300 workstations in dormitories, library, computer center, student center. Dormitories wired for high-speed internet access and linked to campus network. Commuter students can connect to campus network. Online course registration, online library, helpline, wireless network available.

**Student life.** **Freshman orientation:** Mandatory, $45 fee. Preregistration for classes offered. Offered from mid-June to mid-July. **Policies:** Parents notified when student under age of 21 found responsible for use and/or possession of drugs or alcohol. **Housing:** Coed dorms, single-sex dorms, special housing for disabled, apartments, cooperative housing, fraternity/sorority housing available. $200 partly refundable deposit. **Activities:** Bands, campus ministries, choral groups, dance, drama, international student organizations, literary magazine, music ensembles, Model UN, musical theater, radio station, student government, student newspaper, symphony orchestra, TV station, Golden Key National Honor Society, African American student association, Fellowship of Christian Athletes, Collegiate Women International, Citizens for Action, Baptist student union, aerospace maintenance club, agricultural council, Student Tennessee Education Association.

**Athletics.** NCAA. **Intercollegiate:** Baseball M, basketball, cross-country, football (tackle) M, golf, soccer W, softball W, tennis, track and field, volleyball W. **Intramural:** Basketball M, boxing M, equestrian, football (tackle) M, racquetball, rugby M, soccer, softball, swimming, tennis, volleyball. **Team name:** Blue Raiders.

**Student services.** Adult student services, chaplain/spiritual director, career counseling, student employment services, financial aid counseling, health services, minority student services, on-campus daycare, personal counseling, placement for graduates, veterans' counselor, women's services. **Physically disabled:** Services for visually, speech, hearing impaired.

**Contact.** E-mail: admissions@mtsu.edu
Phone: (615) 898-2111 Fax: (615) 898-5478
Lynn Palmer, Director of Admissions, Middle Tennessee State University, 1301 East Main Street, Murfreesboro, TN 37132

## Milligan College
### Milligan College, Tennessee
### www.milligan.edu
**CB code: 1469**

- Private 4-year liberal arts college affiliated with Christian Churches/Churches of Christ
- Residential campus in small city
- 859 degree-seeking undergraduates: 6% part-time, 59% women, 7% African American, 3% Hispanic American, 3% international
- 196 degree-seeking graduate students
- 68% of applicants admitted
- SAT or ACT (ACT writing optional), application essay required

**General.** Founded in 1866. Regionally accredited. Weekly chapels, convocation programs, vespers. **Degrees:** 185 bachelor's awarded; master's offered. **ROTC:** Army. **Location:** 3 miles from Johnson City. **Calendar:** Semester, limited summer session. **Full-time faculty:** 67 total; 76% have terminal degrees, 3% minority, 51% women. **Part-time faculty:** 50 total; 44% have terminal degrees, 2% minority, 46% women. **Class size:** 71% < 20, 27% 20-39, less than 1% 40-49, less than 1% 50-99, less than 1% >100.

**Freshman class profile.** 643 applied, 438 admitted, 218 enrolled.

| Mid 50% test scores | | GPA 3.0-3.49: | 29% |
|---|---|---|---|
| SAT critical reading: | 480-580 | GPA 2.0-2.99: | 10% |
| SAT math: | 460-570 | Rank in top quarter: | 65% |
| SAT writing: | 450-570 | Rank in top tenth: | 37% |
| ACT composite: | 21-26 | Out-of-state: | 37% |
| GPA 3.75 or higher: | 39% | Live on campus: | 85% |
| GPA 3.50-3.74: | 22% | International: | 3% |

**Basis for selection.** Academic work, test scores, and references from minister/church leader and high school principal/counselor required. Audition required for music; interview recommended in some instances.

**High school preparation.** 17 units recommended. Recommended units include English 4, mathematics 3, social studies 2, history 3, science 3 and foreign language 2.

**2009-2010 Annual costs.** Tuition/fees: $21,860. Room/board: $5,850. Books/supplies: $800. Personal expenses: $1,132.

**2009-2010 Financial aid.** **Need-based:** Average need met was 83%. Average scholarship/grant was $15,919; average loan $3,525. 67% of total undergraduate aid awarded as scholarships/grants, 33% as loans/jobs. **Non-need-based:** Scholarships awarded for academics, alumni affiliation, art, athletics, job skills, minority status, music/drama, religious affiliation, state residency.

**Application procedures.** **Admission:** Priority date 4/1; deadline 8/1 (postmark date). $30 fee, may be waived for applicants with need. Admission notification on a rolling basis beginning on or about 10/1. Must reply by May 1 or within 2 week(s) if notified thereafter. **Financial aid:** Priority date

3/1; no closing date. FAFSA required. Applicants notified on a rolling basis starting 3/15; must reply within 2 week(s) of notification.

**Academics. Special study options:** Combined bachelor's/graduate degree, cross-registration, distance learning, double major, dual enrollment of high school students, independent study, internships, study abroad, teacher certification program, Washington semester. American Studies Program in Washington, DC; Australia Studies Center; China Studies Program; Contemporary Music Center in Martha's Vineyard; Latin American Studies Program in Costa Rica; Los Angeles Film Studies Center; Middle East Studies Program in Egypt; Russian Studies Program; Scholars' Semester in Oxford; Uganda Studies Program; Summer Institute of Journalism in Washington, DC; Oxford Summer Programme. **Credit/placement by examination:** AP, CLEP, IB, SAT, ACT, institutional tests. 32 credit hours maximum toward bachelor's degree. Students may not receive credit by examination upon achieving a total of 64 credit hours. **Support services:** Reduced course load, remedial instruction, study skills assistance, tutoring, writing center.

**Majors. Biology:** General. **Business:** Accounting, business admin. **Communications:** General. **Computer sciences:** General. **Education:** General, early childhood, music. **Health:** Nursing (RN). **History:** General. **Liberal arts:** Humanities. **Math:** General. **Parks/recreation:** Health/fitness. **Physical sciences:** Chemistry. **Psychology:** General. **Public administration:** Human services. **Social sciences:** Sociology. **Theology:** Bible. **Visual/performing arts:** General.

**Most popular majors.** Business/marketing 28%, communications/journalism 6%, education 11%, health sciences 18%, psychology 7%, theological studies 6%, visual/performing arts 6%.

**Computing on campus.** 102 workstations in library, computer center. Dormitories wired for high-speed internet access and linked to campus network. Commuter students can connect to campus network. Online library, helpline, repair service, student web hosting, wireless network available.

**Student life. Freshman orientation:** Available, $10 fee. Preregistration for classes offered. Weekend sessions available in April or June for students and parents. Abbreviated version offered weekend prior to first day of fall classes. **Policies:** Smoking and alcoholic beverages not permitted on-campus. Students must live in college housing unless married or living with members of immediate family. Religious observance required. **Housing:** Guaranteed on-campus for all undergraduates. Single-sex dorms, apartments, wellness housing available. $200 nonrefundable deposit, deadline 8/15. Housing deposit refundable until 5/1. **Activities:** Bands, choral groups, drama, literary magazine, music ensembles, musical theater, radio station, student government, student newspaper, symphony orchestra, Fellowship of Christian Athletes, missions club, service seekers, College Republicans, Habitat for Humanity, political awareness group, Roteract.

**Athletics.** NAIA. **Intercollegiate:** Baseball M, basketball, cross-country, golf M, soccer, softball W, swimming, tennis, track and field, volleyball W. **Intramural:** Basketball, football (non-tackle), softball, table tennis, tennis, volleyball. **Team name:** Buffaloes.

**Student services.** Adult student services, chaplain/spiritual director, career counseling, student employment services, financial aid counseling, health services, minority student services, personal counseling, placement for graduates.

**Contact.** E-mail: admissions@milligan.edu
Phone: (423) 461-8730 Toll-free number: (800) 262-8337
Fax: (423) 461-8982
Tracy Brinn, Director of Enrollment Management, Milligan College, Box 210, Milligan College, TN 37682

## O'More College of Design
**Franklin, Tennessee**
www.omorecollege.edu                     CB code: 1545

- Private 4-year visual arts college
- Commuter campus in large town
- 200 degree-seeking undergraduates
- SAT or ACT (ACT writing optional), application essay required

**General.** Founded in 1970. Accredited by ACCSC. **Degrees:** 50 bachelor's awarded. **Location:** 15 miles from Nashville. **Calendar:** Semester, limited summer session. **Full-time faculty:** 14 total; 21% have terminal degrees, 14% minority, 50% women. **Part-time faculty:** 33 total; 15% have terminal degrees, 3% minority, 64% women. **Class size:** 99% < 20, less than 1% 20-39. **Special facilities:** Sensory garden.

**Freshman class profile.**

| Mid 50% test scores | | | |
|---|---|---|---|
| SAT critical reading: | 560-680 | GPA 3.50-3.74: | 8% |
| SAT math: | 450-620 | GPA 3.0-3.49: | 48% |
| ACT composite: | 20-25 | GPA 2.0-2.99: | 16% |
| GPA 3.75 or higher: | 24% | Out-of-state: | 8% |

**Basis for selection.** High school record most important. Test scores, grades given equal weight. Portfolio of artwork or departmental home exam recommended for students not admitted automatically.

**High school preparation.** 18 units recommended. Recommended units include English 4, mathematics 3, social studies 1, history 2, science 3, foreign language 2 and academic electives 3. Art, mechanical drawing, and design courses are recommended.

**2009-2010 Annual costs.** Tuition/fees: $19,735. Books/supplies: $835.

**2009-2010 Financial aid.** All financial aid based on need.

**Application procedures. Admission:** Closing date 8/2 (postmark date). $50 fee, may be waived for applicants with need. Admission notification on a rolling basis. **Financial aid:** Priority date 4/1; no closing date. FAFSA required. Applicants notified on a rolling basis starting 8/1.

**Academics. Special study options:** Dual enrollment of high school students, independent study, internships, liberal arts/career combination, study abroad. Students may pick a minor at Belmont University. Annual study-abroad program in Ireland and annual international trip. **Credit/placement by examination:** AP, CLEP, institutional tests. 9 credit hours maximum toward bachelor's degree.

**Majors. Business:** Fashion. **Visual/performing arts:** Commercial/advertising art, design, fashion design, interior design.

**Computing on campus.** PC or laptop required. 30 workstations in library, computer center, student center. Student web hosting, wireless network available.

**Student life. Freshman orientation:** Mandatory. Preregistration for classes offered. **Activities:** Student government, student newspaper, student chapter of American Society of Interior Designers, O'More Fashion Merchandisers Association, Student Government Association, American Institute of Graphic Arts, International Interior Design Association.

**Student services.** Career counseling, student employment services, financial aid counseling.

**Contact.** E-mail: admissions@omorecollege.edu
Phone: (615) 794-4254 ext. 229 Toll-free number: (888) 662-1970 ext. 229
Fax: (615) 790-1662
Christopher Lee, VP of Enrollment, O'More College of Design, 423 South Margin Street, Franklin, TN 37064-0908

## Rhodes College
**Memphis, Tennessee**                     CB member
www.rhodes.edu                             CB code: 1730

- Private 4-year liberal arts college affiliated with Presbyterian Church (USA)
- Residential campus in very large city
- 1,659 degree-seeking undergraduates: 57% women, 7% African American, 5% Asian American, 2% Hispanic American, 1% Native American, 4% international
- 10 degree-seeking graduate students
- 42% of applicants admitted
- SAT or ACT (ACT writing optional), application essay required
- 82% graduate within 6 years; 35% enter graduate study

**General.** Founded in 1848. Regionally accredited. **Degrees:** 356 bachelor's awarded; master's offered. **ROTC:** Army, Air Force. **Location:** 4 miles from downtown. **Calendar:** Semester. **Full-time faculty:** 161 total; 98% have terminal degrees, 11% minority, 45% women. **Part-time faculty:** 32 total; 69% have terminal degrees, 6% minority, 41% women. **Class size:** 75% < 20, 23% 20-39, less than 1% 40-49, 1% 50-99. **Special facilities:** Arboretum, scanning electron microscope, rooftop observatory, cell culture facility, nuclear magnetic resonance instrument.

**Freshman class profile.** 5,039 applied, 2,113 admitted, 432 enrolled.

| Mid 50% test scores | | Rank in top quarter: | 81% |
|---|---|---|---|
| SAT critical reading: | 570-680 | Rank in top tenth: | 53% |
| SAT math: | 580-700 | Return as sophomores: | 88% |
| SAT writing: | 580-680 | Out-of-state: | 72% |
| ACT composite: | 26-30 | Live on campus: | 96% |
| GPA 3.75 or higher: | 56% | International: | 7% |
| GPA 3.50-3.74: | 19% | Fraternities: | 46% |
| GPA 3.0-3.49: | 20% | Sororities: | 53% |
| GPA 2.0-2.99: | 5% | | |

**Basis for selection.** Academic record, standardized test scores, class rank, recommendations, essay, school and community activities important. Applications sought from international students, minorities, and children of alumni. Interview recommended. **Homeschooled:** 2 SAT Subject Tests other than math or literature required.

**High school preparation.** 16 units required. Required units include English 4, mathematics 3, social studies 2, science 2 (laboratory 2), foreign language 2 and academic electives 3.

**2009-2010 Annual costs.** Tuition/fees: $33,710. Room/board: $8,314. Books/supplies: $1,020. Personal expenses: $1,350.

**2009-2010 Financial aid. Need-based:** Average need met was 87%. Average scholarship/grant was $21,487; average loan $4,510. 81% of total undergraduate aid awarded as scholarships/grants, 19% as loans/jobs. **Non-need-based:** Scholarships awarded for academics, art, minority status, music/drama, religious affiliation. **Additional information:** Auditions required for theater and music achievement awards and art achievement awards. Interviews recommended for merit scholarships. Notification of admissions decision for Bellingrath Scholarship applicants by 3/15; must reply by 5/01.

**Application procedures. Admission:** Priority date 1/15; no deadline. $45 fee, may be waived for applicants with need, free for online applicants. **Financial aid:** Closing date 3/1. FAFSA, CSS PROFILE required. Must reply by 5/1.

**Academics.** Expense-paid summer internships in businesses abroad. Model United Nations program, opportunities for participation in computer-simulated international negotiating, mock trial program. **Special study options:** Combined bachelor's/graduate degree, cooperative education, cross-registration, double major, dual enrollment of high school students, exchange student, honors, independent study, internships, liberal arts/career combination, student-designed major, study abroad, Washington semester. **Credit/placement by examination:** AP, CLEP, IB, institutional tests. 28 credit hours maximum toward bachelor's degree. **Support services:** Tutoring, writing center.

**Majors. Area/ethnic studies:** Latin American, Russian/Slavic. **Biology:** General, Biochemistry/biophysics and molecular biology. **Business:** Business admin, managerial economics. **Computer sciences:** Computer science. **Foreign languages:** Classics, French, German, modern Greek, Russian, Spanish. **History:** General. **Math:** General. **Philosophy/religion:** Philosophy, religion. **Physical sciences:** Chemistry, physics. **Psychology:** General. **Social sciences:** Anthropology, economics, international relations, political science, sociology, urban studies. **Visual/performing arts:** Art, dramatic.

**Most popular majors.** Biology 12%, business/marketing 10%, English 8%, history 11%, philosophy/religious studies 6%, physical sciences 8%, psychology 8%, social sciences 21%, visual/performing arts 8%.

**Computing on campus.** 220 workstations in library, computer center, student center. Dormitories wired for high-speed internet access and linked to campus network. Commuter students can connect to campus network. Online course registration, online library, helpline, repair service, wireless network available.

**Student life. Freshman orientation:** Mandatory, $110 fee. Preregistration for classes offered. 2-day summer program. **Policies:** Student-run honor system central to campus life. **Housing:** Guaranteed on-campus for freshmen. Coed dorms, single-sex dorms, apartments, wellness housing available. Special interest townhouses. **Activities:** Bands, campus ministries, choral groups, dance, drama, film society, international student organizations, literary magazine, music ensembles, Model UN, musical theater, radio station, student government, student newspaper, symphony orchestra, TV station, black student association, social service club, Inter-Varsity Christian Fellowship, international house, Habitat for Humanity, interfaith circle, diversity group, College Democrats, College Republicans.

**Athletics.** NCAA. **Intercollegiate:** Baseball M, basketball, cross-country, field hockey W, football (tackle) M, golf, soccer, softball W, swimming, tennis, track and field, volleyball W. **Intramural:** Basketball, football (non-tackle), football (tackle), racquetball, soccer, squash M, table tennis, tennis, volleyball. **Team name:** Lynx.

**Student services.** Alcohol/substance abuse counseling, chaplain/spiritual director, career counseling, student employment services, financial aid counseling, health services, minority student services, personal counseling, placement for graduates, women's services. **Physically disabled:** Services for visually, speech, hearing impaired.

**Contact.** E-mail: adminfo@rhodes.edu
Phone: (901) 843-3700 Toll-free number: (800) 844-5969
Fax: (901) 843-3631
David Wottle, Dean of Admissions and Financial Aid, Rhodes College, 2000 North Parkway, Memphis, TN 38112

## South College
**Knoxville, Tennessee**
**www.southcollegetn.edu**                    **CB code: 0711**

◆ For-profit 4-year liberal arts college
◆ Commuter campus in small city
◆ 1,033 degree-seeking undergraduates
◆ Interview required

**General.** Founded in 1882. Regionally accredited. **Degrees:** 44 bachelor's, 70 associate awarded. **Location:** Downtown. **Calendar:** Quarter, extensive summer session. **Full-time faculty:** 100 total. **Part-time faculty:** 50 total.

**Basis for selection.** CPTS examination required. SAT or ACT recommended. CPAt, SAT or ACT required.

**2009-2010 Annual costs.** Tuition/fees: $15,825. Reported annual costs are for programs in physical therapy assistance, radiography, health science. Costs of other programs vary by program. Books/supplies: $1,300. Personal expenses: $1,200.

**2008-2009 Financial aid.** All financial aid based on need.

**Application procedures. Admission:** No deadline. $50 fee. Admission notification on a rolling basis. **Financial aid:** No deadline. FAFSA, institutional form required. Applicants notified on a rolling basis.

**Academics. Special study options:** Accelerated study, double major, dual enrollment of high school students, internships, teacher certification program. **Credit/placement by examination:** CLEP, institutional tests. **Support services:** Learning center, reduced course load, study skills assistance, tutoring, writing center.

**Majors. Business:** Business admin. **Legal studies:** General.

**Computing on campus.** 85 workstations in library, computer center. Online library, wireless network available.

**Student life. Freshman orientation:** Mandatory. Preregistration for classes offered. **Activities:** Literary magazine, student government, student newspaper, Collegiate Secretaries International, paralegal association, student affairs advisory council, business club, students of medical assisting, movie club, community service club.

**Student services.** Career counseling, student employment services, financial aid counseling, placement for graduates, veterans' counselor.

**Contact.** E-mail: admissions@southcollegetn.edu
Phone: (865) 251-1800 Fax: (865) 470-8737
Walter Hosea, Admissions Director, South College, 3904 Lonas Drive, Knoxville, TN 37909

## Southern Adventist University
**Collegedale, Tennessee**
**www.southern.edu**                    **CB code: 1727**

◆ Private 4-year university and liberal arts college affiliated with Seventh-day Adventists
◆ Residential campus in small town
◆ 2,647 degree-seeking undergraduates
◆ 244 graduate students
◆ 71% of applicants admitted
◆ SAT or ACT (ACT writing optional) required
◆ 48% graduate within 6 years

**General.** Founded in 1892. Regionally accredited. **Degrees:** 371 bachelor's, 144 associate awarded; master's offered. **Location:** 18 miles from Chattanooga. **Calendar:** Semester, limited summer session. **Full-time faculty:** 139 total; 64% have terminal degrees, 13% minority, 40% women.

**Part-time faculty:** 118 total; 42% have terminal degrees, 9% minority, 38% women. **Special facilities:** Civil War collection, Lincoln collection, Anton Memorial Organ.

**Freshman class profile.** 1,513 applied, 1,074 admitted, 603 enrolled.

| Mid 50% test scores | | | |
|---|---|---|---|
| SAT critical reading: | 450-570 | GPA 3.0-3.49: | 32% |
| SAT math: | 430-560 | GPA 2.0-2.99: | 21% |
| ACT composite: | 19-26 | Return as sophomores: | 69% |
| GPA 3.75 or higher: | 30% | Out-of-state: | 78% |
| GPA 3.50-3.74: | 17% | Live on campus: | 89% |

**Basis for selection.** School achievement record and test scores important. SAT/ACT Writing component used in committee appeal. Interview recommended for all; audition required for music, gymnastics programs. **Homeschooled:** Transcript of courses and grades required. Home school organization must be academically accredited or student must take GED. Portfolio required and must include copy of original research paper and written statement reflecting on value student received from home school experience.

**High school preparation.** College-preparatory program recommended. 18 units required; 24 recommended. Required and recommended units include English 3-4, mathematics 2-3, social studies 1, history 1-2, science 2-3, foreign language 2 and academic electives 9. One unit chemistry (2.0 GPA or better) required for nursing majors. 2 units foreign language required for BA program applicants. Computer competency strongly recommended.

**2010-2011 Annual costs.** Tuition/fees (projected): $17,712. Room/board: $5,174. Books/supplies: $1,000. Personal expenses: $2,000.

**2009-2010 Financial aid. Need-based:** 476 full-time freshmen applied for aid; 282 were judged to have need; 280 of these received aid. Average need met was 82%. Average scholarship/grant was $1,272; average loan $3,963. 54% of total undergraduate aid awarded as scholarships/grants, 46% as loans/jobs. **Non-need-based:** Scholarships awarded for academics, alumni affiliation, art, leadership, music/drama.

**Application procedures. Admission:** Closing date 9/8 (receipt date). $25 fee, may be waived for applicants with need. Admission notification on a rolling basis. **Financial aid:** Priority date 3/1; no closing date. FAFSA required. Applicants notified on a rolling basis starting 2/15; must reply within 2 week(s) of notification.

**Academics. Special study options:** Combined bachelor's/graduate degree, double major, dual enrollment of high school students, ESL, honors, independent study, internships, study abroad, teacher certification program. **Credit/placement by examination:** CLEP, SAT, ACT, institutional tests. 12 credit hours maximum toward bachelor's degree. **Support services:** Learning center, reduced course load, remedial instruction, study skills assistance, tutoring, writing center.

**Majors. Biology:** General, biochemistry, biophysics. **Business:** Accounting, business admin, finance, human resources, international, management information systems, management science, marketing, nonprofit/public. **Communications:** Advertising, broadcast journalism, journalism, media studies, public relations. **Communications technology:** General. **Computer sciences:** Computer science, programming. **Education:** Art, biology, chemistry, elementary, English, French, history, mathematics, music, physical, physics, Spanish. **Family/consumer sciences:** Family systems. **Foreign languages:** General, French, Spanish. **Health:** Art therapy, clinical lab science, health care admin, nursing (RN). **History:** General, European. **Math:** General. **Parks/recreation:** Exercise sciences, sports admin. **Philosophy/religion:** Religion. **Physical sciences:** Chemistry, physics. **Psychology:** General. **Public administration:** Social work. **Social sciences:** Archaeology. **Theology:** Missionary, pastoral counseling, religious ed, theology. **Visual/performing arts:** Art, cinematography, commercial/advertising art, music performance, music theory/composition, photography. **Other:** Outdoor education.

**Most popular majors.** Biology 8%, business/marketing 15%, education 8%, health sciences 21%, psychology 6%, theological studies 6%.

**Computing on campus.** 200 workstations in dormitories, library, computer center. Dormitories wired for high-speed internet access and linked to campus network. Commuter students can connect to campus network. Online course registration, online library, helpline, repair service, student web hosting, wireless network available.

**Student life. Freshman orientation:** Mandatory. Preregistration for classes offered. Held prior to registration. Includes exams and instruction in course planning. **Policies:** Alcohol and drug free. Religious observance required. **Housing:** Guaranteed on-campus for all undergraduates. Single-sex dorms, apartments available. $250 fully refundable deposit, deadline 7/15. **Activities:** Bands, campus ministries, choral groups, drama, film society, music

ensembles, radio station, student government, student newspaper, symphony orchestra, TV station, African club, Black Christian Union, Partners at Wellness, Association of South East Asian Nation Students.

**Athletics. Intramural:** Badminton, basketball, racquetball, soccer, softball, table tennis, tennis, volleyball.

**Student services.** Chaplain/spiritual director, career counseling, student employment services, financial aid counseling, health services, personal counseling, placement for graduates, veterans' counselor.

**Contact.** E-mail: admissions@southern.edu
Phone: (423) 236-2844 Toll-free number: (800) 768-8437
Fax: (423) 236-1844
Marc Grundy, Director of Admissions, Southern Adventist University, Box 370, Collegedale, TN 37315-0370

---

## Tennessee State University
**Nashville, Tennessee**
www.tnstate.edu

CB member
CB code: 1803

- Public 4-year university
- Residential campus in very large city
- 6,660 degree-seeking undergraduates: 18% part-time, 63% women, 82% African American, 1% Asian American, 1% Hispanic American
- 1,735 degree-seeking graduate students
- 65% of applicants admitted
- SAT or ACT with writing required
- 38% graduate within 6 years; 9% enter graduate study

**General.** Founded in 1912. Regionally accredited. **Degrees:** 952 bachelor's, 112 associate awarded; master's, doctoral offered. **ROTC:** Air Force. **Location:** 115 miles from Chattanooga, 195 miles from Memphis. **Calendar:** Semester, limited summer session. **Full-time faculty:** 412 total; 84% have terminal degrees, 64% minority, 43% women. **Part-time faculty:** 167 total; 40% have terminal degrees, 48% minority, 56% women. **Class size:** 45% < 20, 49% 20-39, 4% 40-49, 3% 50-99, less than 1% >100.

**Freshman class profile.** 4,741 applied, 3,092 admitted, 1,338 enrolled.

| Mid 50% test scores | | | |
|---|---|---|---|
| SAT critical reading: | 400-500 | GPA 3.0-3.49: | 32% |
| SAT math: | 410-500 | GPA 2.0-2.99: | 54% |
| ACT composite: | 17-21 | End year in good standing: | 82% |
| GPA 3.75 or higher: | 5% | Return as sophomores: | 67% |
| GPA 3.50-3.74: | 8% | Out-of-state: | 42% |
| | | Live on campus: | 75% |

**Basis for selection.** School achievement record, test scores important. Interview required for health sciences, nursing, physical therapy programs. **Homeschooled:** State high school equivalency certificate required.

**High school preparation.** 14 units required. Required units include English 4, mathematics 3, social studies 2, science 2 (laboratory 1) and foreign language 2. One unit visual and/or performing arts recommended.

**2009-2010 Annual costs.** Tuition/fees: $5,444; $17,522 out-of-state. Room/board: $5,610. Books/supplies: $1,200. Personal expenses: $3,500.

**2008-2009 Financial aid. Non-need-based:** Scholarships awarded for academics.

**Application procedures. Admission:** Closing date 8/1. $25 fee. Application must be submitted on paper. Admission notification on a rolling basis. **Financial aid:** Priority date 4/1; no closing date. FAFSA required. Applicants notified on a rolling basis starting 4/15; must reply within 3 week(s) of notification.

**Academics. Special study options:** Combined bachelor's/graduate degree, cooperative education, cross-registration, distance learning, double major, ESL, exchange student, honors, independent study, internships, liberal arts/career combination, study abroad, teacher certification program. **Credit/placement by examination:** AP, CLEP, SAT, ACT, institutional tests. 33 credit hours maximum toward bachelor's degree. **Support services:** Learning center, remedial instruction, study skills assistance, tutoring, writing center.

**Majors. Agriculture:** Animal sciences. **Architecture:** Architecture. **Biology:** General, biochemistry. **Business:** Accounting, administrative services, business admin, managerial economics. **Communications:** General, journalism. **Computer sciences:** Computer science. **Education:** General, early childhood, physical, secondary, special. **Engineering:** General, architectural, civil, electrical. **Family/consumer sciences:** General, clothing/textiles, family studies, food/nutrition. **Foreign languages:** French, Spanish. **Health:** Audiology/

speech pathology, dental hygiene, health care admin, medical records admin. **History:** General. **Interdisciplinary:** Biological/physical sciences. **Liberal arts:** Arts/sciences. **Math:** General. **Physical sciences:** Chemistry, physics. **Protective services:** Criminal justice. **Psychology:** General. **Public administration:** Social work. **Social sciences:** General, political science, sociology, urban studies. **Visual/performing arts:** Art history/conservation, dramatic.

**Most popular majors.** Business/marketing 17%, health sciences 15%, liberal arts 20%, psychology 6%, visual/performing arts 7%.

**Computing on campus.** 450 workstations in dormitories, library, computer center, student center. Dormitories wired for high-speed internet access and linked to campus network. Commuter students can connect to campus network. Online course registration, online library, helpline, repair service, student web hosting, wireless network available.

**Student life. Freshman orientation:** Mandatory. Preregistration for classes offered. **Housing:** Coed dorms, single-sex dorms, apartments available. $100 fully refundable deposit, deadline 4/1. **Activities:** Bands, choral groups, dance, drama, film society, international student organizations, music ensembles, musical theater, radio station, student government, student newspaper, TV station, religious organizations, honor organization, literary organization.

**Athletics.** NCAA. **Intercollegiate:** Baseball M, basketball, cheerleading, cross-country, football (tackle) M, golf, softball W, tennis, track and field, volleyball W. **Intramural:** Basketball, bowling, football (non-tackle) M, racquetball, tennis, track and field, volleyball. **Team name:** Tigers.

**Student services.** Career counseling, student employment services, financial aid counseling, health services, minority student services, on-campus daycare, personal counseling, placement for graduates, veterans' counselor, women's services. **Physically disabled:** Services for visually, speech, hearing impaired.

**Contact.** Phone: (615) 963-5101 Fax: (615) 963-5108
Michael Freeman, Vice President of Student Affairs, Tennessee State University, 3500 John A. Merritt Boulevard, Nashville, TN 37209-1561

## Tennessee Technological University

| **Cookeville, Tennessee** | **CB member** |
|---|---|
| **www.tntech.edu** | **CB code: 1804** |

- Public 4-year university
- Residential campus in large town
- 8,676 degree-seeking undergraduates: 8% part-time, 47% women, 4% African American, 1% Asian American, 2% Hispanic American, 2% international
- 1,711 degree-seeking graduate students
- 84% of applicants admitted
- SAT or ACT (ACT writing recommended) required
- 53% graduate within 6 years

**General.** Founded in 1915. Regionally accredited. **Degrees:** 1,450 bachelor's awarded; master's offered. **ROTC:** Army, Air Force. **Location:** 80 miles from Nashville, 100 miles from Knoxville. **Calendar:** Semester, extensive summer session. **Full-time faculty:** 386 total; 72% have terminal degrees, 14% minority, 38% women. **Part-time faculty:** 262 total; 22% have terminal degrees, 5% minority, 64% women. **Class size:** 37% < 20, 44% 20-39, 9% 40-49, 7% 50-99, 3% >100. **Special facilities:** Center for crafts, cooperative fishery research unit, agricultural pavilion, center for energy systems research, center for manufacturing research, center for the management, utilization and protection of water resources, childcare resource center.

**Freshman class profile.** 4,486 applied, 3,786 admitted, 1,893 enrolled.

| Mid 50% test scores | | Rank in top quarter: | 53% |
|---|---|---|---|
| SAT critical reading: | 470-610 | Rank in top tenth: | 25% |
| SAT math: | 490-640 | Return as sophomores: | 72% |
| ACT composite: | 20-26 | Out-of-state: | 4% |
| GPA 3.75 or higher: | 31% | Live on campus: | 67% |
| GPA 3.50-3.74: | 19% | International: | 2% |
| GPA 3.0-3.49: | 30% | Fraternities: | 10% |
| GPA 2.0-2.99: | 20% | Sororities: | 10% |

**Basis for selection.** High school classes, GPA and test scores very important. Additional requirements for engineering, computer science, nursing and pre-professional majors. Interview recommended for all; audition recommended for music; portfolio recommended for arts, crafts. **Home-schooled:** 2.5 GPA and 19 ACT or GED required.

**High school preparation.** 14 units required. Required units include English 4, mathematics 3, social studies 1, history 1, science 2 (laboratory 1)

and foreign language 2. Math units must include algebra I and II and geometry or advanced math course. Science units must be biology, chemistry, or physics with laboratories (can include physical sciences). Foreign language units must be in single language. 1 U.S. history, 1 unit visual and/or performing arts also required. Social studies must be either world, ancient, modern, or European history, or world geography.

**2009-2010 Annual costs.** Tuition/fees: $5,586; $17,664 out-of-state. Room/board: $6,634. Books/supplies: $780. Personal expenses: $840.

**2008-2009 Financial aid. Non-need-based:** Scholarships awarded for academics, alumni affiliation, art, athletics, leadership, minority status, music/drama, ROTC, state residency. **Additional information:** Tuition and/or fee waivers available for children of Tennessee public school teachers.

**Application procedures. Admission:** Priority date 5/1; deadline 8/1 (postmark date). $15 fee. Admission notification on a rolling basis. **Financial aid:** Priority date 3/15; no closing date. FAFSA required. Applicants notified on a rolling basis starting 3/15; must reply within 2 week(s) of notification.

**Academics. Special study options:** Accelerated study, cooperative education, distance learning, double major, dual enrollment of high school students, ESL, honors, independent study, internships, liberal arts/career combination, study abroad, teacher certification program. **Credit/placement by examination:** AP, CLEP, IB, institutional tests. 33 credit hours maximum toward bachelor's degree. **Support services:** Learning center, pre-admission summer program, reduced course load, remedial instruction, study skills assistance, tutoring, writing center.

**Majors. Agriculture:** Agribusiness operations, agronomy, animal sciences, horticultural science, horticulture, landscaping, nursery operations, soil science. **Biology:** General, biochemistry. **Business:** General, accounting, finance, labor relations, management science, managerial economics, operations. **Communications:** General, journalism. **Communications technology:** General. **Computer sciences:** General, computer science, web page design. **Conservation:** General, fisheries, wildlife. **Education:** General, agricultural, early childhood, English, health, music, physical, secondary, special. **Engineering:** Chemical, civil, computer, electrical, industrial, mechanical. **Engineering technology:** Manufacturing. **Family/consumer sciences:** General, clothing/textiles, family/community services, food/nutrition, housing. **Foreign languages:** French, German, Spanish. **Health:** Nursing (RN), predental, premedicine, prepharmacy, preveterinary. **History:** General. **Math:** General. **Parks/recreation:** Health/fitness. **Physical sciences:** Chemistry, geology, physics. **Psychology:** General. **Social sciences:** Economics, political science, sociology. **Visual/performing arts:** Ceramics, drawing, fiber arts, music performance, painting, sculpture, studio arts.

**Most popular majors.** Business/marketing 18%, education 20%, engineering/engineering technologies 18%.

**Computing on campus.** 600 workstations in dormitories, library, computer center. Dormitories wired for high-speed internet access and linked to campus network. Commuter students can connect to campus network. Online course registration, online library, helpline, wireless network available.

**Student life. Freshman orientation:** Mandatory, $45 fee. Preregistration for classes offered. **Housing:** Guaranteed on-campus for freshmen. Coed dorms, single-sex dorms, special housing for disabled, apartments, fraternity/sorority housing available. $50 deposit. **Activities:** Bands, choral groups, dance, drama, literary magazine, music ensembles, musical theater, opera, radio station, student government, student newspaper, symphony orchestra, TV station, over 190 organizations.

**Athletics.** NCAA. **Intercollegiate:** Baseball M, basketball, cheerleading, cross-country, football (tackle) M, golf, rifle, soccer W, softball W, tennis, track and field W, volleyball W. **Intramural:** Basketball, bowling, golf M, handball, racquetball, rugby M, soccer, softball, tennis, volleyball, wrestling M. **Team name:** Golden Eagles.

**Student services.** Alcohol/substance abuse counseling, career counseling, student employment services, financial aid counseling, health services, minority student services, on-campus daycare, personal counseling, placement for graduates, veterans' counselor, women's services. **Physically disabled:** Services for visually, speech, hearing impaired. **Learning disabled:** Comprehensive services available.

**Contact.** E-mail: admissions@tntech.edu
Phone: (931) 372-3888 Toll-free number: (800) 255-8881
Fax: (931) 372-6250
Vanessa Palmer, Admissions, Tennessee Technological University, Office of Admissions, Cookeville, TN 38505-0001

## Tennessee Temple University
### Chattanooga, Tennessee
www.tntemple.edu                    CB code: 1818

◆ Private 4-year university and seminary college affiliated with Baptist faith

◆ Residential campus in small city

◆ 677 undergraduates

◆ 210 graduate students

◆ 41% of applicants admitted

◆ SAT or ACT with writing, application essay required

◆ 47% graduate within 6 years

**General.** Founded in 1946. Accredited by TRACS. **Degrees:** 67 bachelor's, 5 associate awarded; master's, professional offered. **Location:** 120 miles from Atlanta. **Calendar:** Semester, limited summer session. **Full-time faculty:** 22 total. **Part-time faculty:** 20 total. **Class size:** 77% < 20, 17% 20-39, 4% 40-49, less than 1% 50-99, less than 1% >100.

**Freshman class profile.** 241 applied, 98 admitted, 98 enrolled.

| Mid 50% test scores | | | |
|---|---|---|---|
| SAT critical reading: | 350-610 | Return as sophomores: | 41% |
| SAT math: | 340-530 | Out-of-state: | 26% |
| ACT composite: | 15-25 | Live on campus: | 72% |

**Basis for selection.** Test scores, personal reference, pastoral reference and written personal testimony about applicant's faith required. **Home-schooled:** Relevant experiences to support ability to succeed in college work may be substituted for high school diploma or GED. Submit transcript and other supporting information, such as course or curriculum descriptions, grades, graduation date, and the signatures of the instructor. Submit official transcripts from other secondary or post secondary institutions attended. **Learning Disabled:** Notification regarding disability and documentation to support the claim required.

**High school preparation.** College-preparatory program recommended. 10 units required; 15 recommended. Required and recommended units include English 4, mathematics 2-3, social studies 2-3, science 2-3 and foreign language 2. Computer fundamentals recommended.

**2009-2010 Annual costs.** Tuition/fees: $11,250. Room/board: $6,030. Books/supplies: $700. Personal expenses: $850.

**Financial aid. Non-need-based:** Scholarships awarded for academics, alumni affiliation, athletics, leadership, music/drama, state residency.

**Application procedures. Admission:** Priority date 3/31; deadline 8/1 (receipt date). $35 fee, may be waived for applicants with need. Admission notification on a rolling basis. **Financial aid:** Priority date 3/31; no closing date. FAFSA required. Applicants notified on a rolling basis starting 2/15; must reply within 2 week(s) of notification.

**Academics. Special study options:** Distance learning, double major, dual enrollment of high school students, external degree, independent study, internships, liberal arts/career combination, teacher certification program, Washington semester. **Credit/placement by examination:** AP, CLEP, IB, SAT, ACT, institutional tests. 16 credit hours maximum toward associate degree, 32 toward bachelor's. **Support services:** Reduced course load, remedial instruction, study skills assistance, tutoring, writing center.

**Majors. Biology:** General. **Business:** General, administrative services, business admin, office management. **Computer sciences:** Computer science. **Education:** Biology, Deaf/hearing impaired, elementary, English, history, mathematics, music, science, secondary, speech. **Health:** Premedicine. **History:** General. **Legal studies:** Prelaw. **Liberal arts:** Arts/sciences. **Math:** General. **Physical sciences:** General. **Psychology:** General. **Social sciences:** Political science. **Theology:** Bible, missionary, religious ed, sacred music, theology.

**Computing on campus.** 105 workstations in dormitories, library, computer center. Dormitories wired for high-speed internet access and linked to campus network. Commuter students can connect to campus network. Wireless network available.

**Student life. Freshman orientation:** Mandatory, $25 fee. Held 2-3 days prior to beginning of classes. **Policies:** Religious observance required. **Housing:** Guaranteed on-campus for all undergraduates. Single-sex dorms, apartments available. $100 deposit, deadline 5/31. **Activities:** Choral groups, drama, music ensembles, radio station, student government, student newspaper, Student Missions Fellowship, Student Preachers Fellowship.

**Athletics.** NCCAA. **Intercollegiate:** Baseball M, basketball, soccer M, volleyball W. **Intramural:** Basketball, football (tackle) M, soccer, softball, table tennis, tennis, volleyball, wrestling M. **Team name:** Crusaders.

**Student services.** Chaplain/spiritual director, student employment services, financial aid counseling, personal counseling, placement for graduates, veterans' counselor. **Physically disabled:** Services for visually, hearing impaired.

**Contact.** E-mail: ttuinfo@tntemple.edu
Phone: (423) 493-4371 Toll-free number: (800) 553-4050
Fax: (423) 493-4497
Diana Knowles, Director of Enrollment Services, Tennessee Temple University, 1815 Union Avenue, Chattanooga, TN 37404

## Tennessee Wesleyan College
### Athens, Tennessee
www.twcnet.edu                    CB code: 1805

◆ Private 4-year liberal arts and teachers college affiliated with United Methodist Church

◆ Commuter campus in large town

◆ 1,060 degree-seeking undergraduates: 12% part-time, 65% women

◆ 84% of applicants admitted

◆ SAT or ACT (ACT writing optional) required

◆ 52% graduate within 6 years

**General.** Founded in 1857. Regionally accredited. Baccalaureate programs in nursing and evening business school through Knoxville campus. **Degrees:** 212 bachelor's awarded. **ROTC:** Army, Naval, Air Force. **Location:** 50 miles from Chattanooga and Knoxville. **Calendar:** Semester, extensive summer session. **Full-time faculty:** 53 total; 68% have terminal degrees, 4% minority, 51% women. **Part-time faculty:** 34 total; 38% have terminal degrees, 3% minority, 32% women. **Class size:** 52% < 20, 39% 20-39, 7% 40-49, 3% 50-99.

**Freshman class profile.** 699 applied, 585 admitted, 249 enrolled.

| Mid 50% test scores | | | |
|---|---|---|---|
| SAT critical reading: | 400-530 | Rank in top quarter: | 55% |
| SAT math: | 400-510 | Rank in top tenth: | 29% |
| ACT composite: | 19-24 | Return as sophomores: | 63% |
| GPA 3.75 or higher: | 27% | Out-of-state: | 11% |
| GPA 3.50-3.74: | 17% | Live on campus: | 57% |
| GPA 3.0-3.49: | 31% | International: | 3% |
| GPA 2.0-2.99: | 24% | Fraternities: | 5% |
| | | Sororities: | 9% |

**Basis for selection.** Test scores, school records, recommendations and GPA very important. ACT/SAT not required if student has GED. Essay recommended for all; interview recommended for academically weak; audition required for music and theater.

**High school preparation.** College-preparatory program recommended. 10 units recommended. Recommended units include English 4, mathematics 2, social studies 1, history 1 and science 2.

**2009-2010 Annual costs.** Tuition/fees: $18,600. Room/board: $6,100. Books/supplies: $1,000. Personal expenses: $2,000.

**2008-2009 Financial aid. Need-based:** 250 full-time freshmen applied for aid; 207 were judged to have need; 204 of these received aid. Average need met was 77%. Average scholarship/grant was $13,070; average loan $2,731. 65% of total undergraduate aid awarded as scholarships/grants, 35% as loans/jobs. **Non-need-based:** Awarded to 339 full-time undergraduates, including 118 freshmen. Scholarships awarded for academics, alumni affiliation, athletics, minority status, music/drama, religious affiliation.

**Application procedures. Admission:** Closing date 8/15 (receipt date). $25 fee, may be waived for applicants with need. Admission notification on a rolling basis beginning on or about 9/1. **Financial aid:** No deadline. FAFSA, institutional form required. Applicants notified on a rolling basis starting 2/15; must reply within 2 week(s) of notification.

**Academics.** Study abroad opportunities available for students wishing to extend their learning globally. **Special study options:** Accelerated study, double major, exchange student, honors, independent study, internships, student-designed major, study abroad, teacher certification program. Member of the Private College Consortium for International Studies (semester in London program). **Credit/placement by examination:** AP, CLEP, IB, SAT, ACT, institutional tests. 12 credit hours maximum toward bachelor's degree. **Support services:** Learning center, reduced course load, remedial instruction, study skills assistance, tutoring, writing center.

**Majors. Area/ethnic studies:** American. **Biology:** General. **Business:** Accounting, business admin, finance, human resources. **Computer sciences:**

General. **Conservation:** Environmental studies. **Education:** Early childhood, elementary, multi-level teacher, secondary. **Health:** Nursing (RN), predental, premedicine, prenursing, prepharmacy, preveterinary. **History:** General. **Interdisciplinary:** Behavioral sciences, global studies, intercultural. **Legal studies:** Prelaw. **Math:** General. **Parks/recreation:** Health/fitness, sports admin. **Philosophy/religion:** Christian. **Physical sciences:** Chemistry. **Psychology:** General. **Public administration:** Human services. **Theology:** Preministerial.

**Most popular majors.** Business/marketing 28%, education 21%, health sciences 21%, interdisciplinary studies 6%.

**Computing on campus.** 133 workstations in dormitories, library, computer center, student center. Dormitories wired for high-speed internet access and linked to campus network. Online library, wireless network available.

**Student life. Freshman orientation:** Mandatory. Preregistration for classes offered. Held in August. **Policies:** All students required to live on-campus unless residing with relative within commuting distance, married, or have children. Visitation hours in dorms by opposite sex restricted. No alcohol allowed on campus. Religious observance required. **Housing:** Guaranteed on-campus for freshmen. Single-sex dorms, apartments, wellness housing available. **Activities:** Concert band, campus ministries, choral groups, drama, literary magazine, music ensembles, student government, student newspaper, Circle K, Hackberry and Oak Society, National Student Nurses Association, student activities board, Education Angels, Fellowship of Christian Athletes, Wesleyan Christian Fellowship, College Democrats.

**Athletics.** NAIA. **Intercollegiate:** Baseball M, basketball, cross-country, golf, soccer, softball W, tennis, volleyball W. **Team name:** Bulldogs.

**Student services.** Adult student services, alcohol/substance abuse counseling, chaplain/spiritual director, career counseling, student employment services, financial aid counseling, personal counseling, placement for graduates, veterans' counselor. **Physically disabled:** Services for visually, hearing impaired.

**Contact.** E-mail: admissions@twcnet.edu
Phone: (423) 745-7504 Toll-free number: (800) 742-5892
Fax: (423) 745-9335
Stan Harrison, Vice President Enrollment Management and Director of Athletics, Tennessee Wesleyan College, 204 East College Street, Athens, TN 37371-0040

## Trevecca Nazarene University
**Nashville, Tennessee**
www.trevecca.edu                    CB code: 1809

- Private 4-year university and liberal arts college affiliated with Church of the Nazarene
- Residential campus in very large city
- 1,234 degree-seeking undergraduates: 8% part-time, 55% women, 7% African American, 1% Asian American, 3% Hispanic American, 1% international
- 1,141 degree-seeking graduate students
- 69% of applicants admitted
- SAT or ACT (ACT writing optional) required
- 47% graduate within 6 years

**General.** Founded in 1901. Regionally accredited. **Degrees:** 352 bachelor's, 1 associate awarded; master's, doctoral offered. **ROTC:** Army. **Location:** 200 miles from Memphis, 175 miles from Knoxville. **Calendar:** Semester, limited summer session. **Full-time faculty:** 87 total; 83% have terminal degrees, 8% minority, 31% women. **Part-time faculty:** 135 total; 35% have terminal degrees, 2% minority, 44% women. **Class size:** 72% < 20, 23% 20-39, 3% 40-49, 2% 50-99.

**Freshman class profile.** 899 applied, 623 admitted, 244 enrolled.

| Mid 50% test scores | | | |
|---|---|---|---|
| SAT critical reading: | 440-570 | GPA 2.0-2.99: | 31% |
| SAT math: | 420-570 | Rank in top quarter: | 39% |
| ACT composite: | 19-25 | Rank in top tenth: | 17% |
| GPA 3.75 or higher: | 18% | Return as sophomores: | 71% |
| GPA 3.50-3.74: | 19% | Out-of-state: | 39% |
| GPA 3.0-3.49: | 29% | Live on campus: | 78% |
| | | International: | 1% |

**Basis for selection.** Must meet one of two conditions: 18 ACT (860 SAT, exclusive of Writing) or 2.5 GPA. **Homeschooled:** Transcript with all subjects and grades should be provided by correspondence-school based organization or by the parent depending on method of homeschooling. **Learning Disabled:** Students should contact Disability Services for information concerning documentation of disability and services available.

**High school preparation.** College-preparatory program recommended. 15 units recommended. Recommended units include English 4, mathematics 2, social studies 1, history 1, science 1, foreign language 2 and academic electives 4.

**2009-2010 Annual costs.** Tuition/fees: $16,776. Room/board: $7,348. Books/supplies: $1,100. Personal expenses: $405.

**2008-2009 Financial aid. Need-based:** 23% of total undergraduate aid awarded as scholarships/grants, 77% as loans/jobs. **Non-need-based:** Scholarships awarded for academics, alumni affiliation, art, athletics, leadership, minority status, music/drama, religious affiliation.

**Application procedures. Admission:** Priority date 4/1; deadline 8/1. $25 fee. Admission notification on a rolling basis. Must reply by May 1 or within 2 week(s) if notified thereafter. Enrollment deposit of $200 due by 5/1; refundable only if notification received by 5/1. **Financial aid:** Priority date 2/25, closing date 7/30. FAFSA required. Applicants notified by 3/1; Applicants notified on a rolling basis starting 3/1.

**Academics. Special study options:** Double major, internships, study abroad, teacher certification program. Adult degree completion program. **Credit/ placement by examination:** AP, CLEP, IB, SAT, ACT. 22 credit hours maximum toward associate degree, 45 toward bachelor's. Credit awarded after one semester and tuition paid. **Support services:** Learning center, remedial instruction, study skills assistance, tutoring.

**Majors. Biology:** General. **Business:** Accounting, business admin, e-commerce, management information systems, marketing. **Communications:** General, media studies, organizational. **Computer sciences:** Information technology, web page design. **Education:** Biology, business, chemistry, drama/dance, elementary, English, history, mathematics, music, physical, physics, secondary, special, speech. **Health:** Clinical lab science, nursing (RN). **History:** General. **Interdisciplinary:** Behavioral sciences, biological/ physical sciences. **Math:** General. **Parks/recreation:** Exercise sciences, sports admin. **Philosophy/religion:** Religion. **Physical sciences:** Chemistry, physics. **Protective services:** Law enforcement admin. **Psychology:** General. **Public administration:** Social work. **Social sciences:** Sociology. **Visual/ performing arts:** Dramatic, music management. **Other:** Christian ministries, Community development, Financial mathematics, Interpersonal communications, Mathematical biology, worship arts.

**Most popular majors.** Business/marketing 57%, education 7%, philosophy/ religious studies 7%.

**Computing on campus.** 200 workstations in dormitories, library, computer center, student center. Dormitories linked to campus network. Commuter students can connect to campus network. Helpline, wireless network available.

**Student life. Freshman orientation:** Mandatory. Preregistration for classes offered. **Policies:** Religious observance required. **Housing:** Single-sex dorms, apartments available. **Activities:** Bands, campus ministries, choral groups, drama, international student organizations, literary magazine, music ensembles, musical theater, radio station, student government, student newspaper, symphony orchestra, TV station, mission club, ministerial association, Phi Beta Lambda.

**Athletics.** NAIA. **Intercollegiate:** Baseball M, basketball, golf, soccer, softball W, volleyball W. **Intramural:** Badminton, basketball, football (tackle) M, golf, racquetball, softball, table tennis, track and field, volleyball. **Team name:** Trojans.

**Student services.** Chaplain/spiritual director, career counseling, student employment services, financial aid counseling, health services, personal counseling, placement for graduates.

**Contact.** E-mail: admissions_und@trevecca.edu
Phone: (615) 248-1320 Toll-free number: (888) 210-4868
Fax: (615) 248-7406
Michael Cantrell, Director of Admissions, Trevecca Nazarene University, 333 Murfreesboro Road, Nashville, TN 37210

## Tusculum College
**Greeneville, Tennessee**                    CB member
www.tusculum.edu                              CB code: 1812

- Private 4-year liberal arts college affiliated with Presbyterian Church (USA)
- Residential campus in large town
- 2,019 degree-seeking undergraduates: 3% part-time, 60% women, 11% African American, 1% Hispanic American, 2% international
- 184 degree-seeking graduate students
- 75% of applicants admitted

- SAT or ACT (ACT writing optional), application essay required
- 39% graduate within 6 years; 12% enter graduate study

**General.** Founded in 1794. Regionally accredited. Strong civic arts focus and service-learning curriculum. **Degrees:** 536 bachelor's awarded; master's offered. **Location:** 70 miles from Knoxville, 30 miles from Johnson City. **Calendar:** Differs by program, limited summer session. **Full-time faculty:** 73 total; 66% have terminal degrees, 51% women. **Part-time faculty:** 130 total. **Class size:** 65% < 20, 35% 20-39.

**Freshman class profile.** 2,437 applied, 1,836 admitted, 314 enrolled.

| Mid 50% test scores | | | |
|---|---|---|---|
| SAT critical reading: | 430-550 | Return as sophomores: | 62% |
| SAT math: | 470-560 | Out-of-state: | 33% |
| ACT composite: | 19-24 | Live on campus: | 71% |
| | | International: | 1% |

**Basis for selection.** Admissions based on secondary school record and standardized test scores. Essay also important. Math and English placement tests may be required based on ACT or SAT scores. Interview recommended. **Homeschooled:** Statement describing homeschool structure and mission, interview required. Syllabi for all courses taken and list of textbooks required.

**High school preparation.** College-preparatory program recommended. 12 units required. Required units include English 4, mathematics 3, social studies 3 and science 2.

**2010-2011 Annual costs.** Tuition/fees (projected): $19,920. Room/board: $8,000. Books/supplies: $960. Personal expenses: $1,400.

**Financial aid. Non-need-based:** Scholarships awarded for academics, athletics, leadership, religious affiliation, state residency.

**Application procedures. Admission:** No deadline. No application fee. Admission notification on a rolling basis. **Financial aid:** Closing date 2/15. FAFSA required. Applicants notified on a rolling basis starting 3/1; must reply within 3 week(s) of notification.

**Academics.** Semesters comprised of 4 blocks, each 3 1/2 weeks long. Students take one course per block. Intensive 16-month professional studies program designed for non-traditional students also offered. **Special study options:** Accelerated study, double major, honors, independent study, internships, student-designed major, study abroad, teacher certification program. **Credit/placement by examination:** CLEP, SAT, ACT, institutional tests. 30 credit hours maximum toward bachelor's degree. **Support services:** Learning center, pre-admission summer program, study skills assistance, tutoring, writing center.

**Majors. Biology:** General. **Business:** Accounting, business admin, entrepreneurial studies. **Communications:** Journalism. **Conservation:** General, environmental studies. **Education:** Art, biology, business, early childhood, elementary, English, health, history, mathematics, middle, physical, psychology, secondary, special. **Health:** Athletic training, clinical lab science, premedicine, prepharmacy. **History:** General. **Interdisciplinary:** Museum. **Legal studies:** Prelaw. **Math:** General. **Parks/recreation:** Health/fitness, sports admin. **Psychology:** General. **Social sciences:** Political science. **Visual/performing arts:** General.

**Most popular majors.** Business/marketing 55%, education 34%.

**Computing on campus.** 160 workstations in library, computer center, student center. Dormitories wired for high-speed internet access and linked to campus network. Commuter students can connect to campus network. Online library, helpline, repair service available.

**Student life. Freshman orientation:** Mandatory. Preregistration for classes offered. **Housing:** Guaranteed on-campus for freshmen. Single-sex dorms, apartments available. $200 nonrefundable deposit, deadline 6/1. Pets allowed in dorm rooms. **Activities:** Choral groups, drama, literary magazine, radio station, student government, student newspaper, TV station, Bonwandi, campus activities board, Fellowship of Christian Athletes.

**Athletics.** NCAA. **Intercollegiate:** Baseball M, basketball, cheerleading M, cross-country, football (tackle) M, golf, soccer, softball W, tennis, volleyball W. **Intramural:** Basketball, football (tackle), soccer, softball, table tennis, tennis, volleyball. **Team name:** Pioneers.

**Student services.** Adult student services, alcohol/substance abuse counseling, chaplain/spiritual director, career counseling, financial aid counseling, health services, personal counseling, placement for graduates, veterans' counselor.

**Contact.** E-mail: mripley@tusculum.edu
Phone: (423) 636-7300 Toll-free number: (800) 729-0256
Fax: (423) 638-7166
Melissa Ripley, Director of Admissions, Tusculum College, 60 Shiloh Road, Greeneville, TN 37743

---

## Union University
**Jackson, Tennessee**
**www.uu.edu**                                    CB code: 1826

- Private 4-year university and liberal arts college affiliated with Southern Baptist Convention
- Residential campus in small city
- 2,439 degree-seeking undergraduates: 10% part-time, 61% women, 11% African American, 1% Asian American, 1% Hispanic American, 2% international
- 1,075 degree-seeking graduate students
- 84% of applicants admitted
- 60% graduate within 6 years

**General.** Founded in 1823. Regionally accredited. **Degrees:** 598 bachelor's, 1 associate awarded; master's, doctoral, professional offered. **Location:** 80 miles from Memphis, 120 miles from Nashville. **Calendar:** Semester, extensive summer session. **Full-time faculty:** 177 total; 83% have terminal degrees, 6% minority, 44% women. **Part-time faculty:** 8 total; 25% minority, 75% women. **Class size:** 68% < 20, 27% 20-39, 4% 40-49, less than 1% 50-99. **Special facilities:** Aquatic center, creative communications center.

**Freshman class profile.** 1,526 applied, 1,278 admitted, 532 enrolled.

| Mid 50% test scores | | | |
|---|---|---|---|
| SAT critical reading: | 510-650 | Rank in top quarter: | 60% |
| SAT math: | 510-640 | Rank in top tenth: | 35% |
| ACT composite: | 21-29 | Return as sophomores: | 92% |
| GPA 3.75 or higher: | 52% | Out-of-state: | 36% |
| GPA 3.50-3.74: | 20% | Live on campus: | 83% |
| GPA 3.0-3.49: | 20% | International: | 1% |
| GPA 2.0-2.99: | 8% | Fraternities: | 29% |
| | | Sororities: | 20% |

**Basis for selection.** School achievement, recommendations, special talents, test scores important. 22 ACT or 1030 SAT (exclusive of Writing), top 50% of high school class, and 2.5 GPA required. Interview recommended for all; audition required for music; portfolio recommended for art, communications. Essay required for academic and leadership scholarships. **Homeschooled:** If class rank is unavailable, students may be admitted without conditions provided they meet minimum ACT/SAT scores and GPA requirements.

**High school preparation.** College-preparatory program required. 15 units required; 22 recommended. Required and recommended units include English 4, mathematics 3-4, social studies 2, history 1-2, science 3-4 (laboratory 2), foreign language 1-2, computer science 1, visual/performing arts 1 and academic electives 1-4.

**2009-2010 Annual costs.** Tuition/fees: $20,940. Room/board: $6,930. Books/supplies: $1,000. Personal expenses: $3,500.

**2009-2010 Financial aid. Non-need-based:** Scholarships awarded for academics, alumni affiliation, art, athletics, leadership, minority status, music/drama, religious affiliation, state residency.

**Application procedures. Admission:** Priority date 12/1; deadline 8/1 (postmark date). $35 fee, may be waived for applicants with need. Admission notification on a rolling basis beginning on or about 10/1. Must reply by May 1 or within 2 week(s) if notified thereafter. **Financial aid:** Priority date 2/15, closing date 3/1. FAFSA, institutional form required. Applicants notified on a rolling basis starting 2/15; must reply by 5/1 or within 2 week(s) of notification.

**Academics. Special study options:** Accelerated study, combined bachelor's/graduate degree, cooperative education, cross-registration, distance learning, double major, dual enrollment of high school students, ESL, exchange student, honors, independent study, internships, study abroad, teacher certification program, Washington semester. **Credit/placement by examination:** CLEP, IB, institutional tests. 32 credit hours maximum toward bachelor's degree. **Support services:** Learning center, pre-admission summer program, reduced course load, remedial instruction, study skills assistance, tutoring, writing center.

**Majors. Biology:** General, cellular/molecular, conservation, zoology. **Business:** Accounting, business admin, international, managerial economics, marketing. **Communications:** General, advertising, broadcast journalism, digital media, journalism, public relations. **Computer sciences:** Computer science, web page design. **Education:** General, art, biology, business, chemistry, early childhood special, elementary, English, ESL, foreign languages, French, history, kindergarten/preschool, mathematics, middle, music, physical, science, secondary, Spanish, special. **Engineering:** Electrical, mechanical, physics. **Family/consumer sciences:** Family systems. **Foreign languages:** French, Spanish. **Health:** Athletic training, clinical lab science, nursing (RN). **History:** General. **Interdisciplinary:** Intercultural. **Math:** General. **Parks/**

recreation: Exercise sciences, sports admin. **Philosophy/religion:** Christian, ethics, philosophy, religion. **Physical sciences:** General, chemical physics, chemistry, physics. **Psychology:** General. **Public administration:** Social work. **Social sciences:** Economics, political science, sociology. **Theology:** Sacred music, theology, youth ministry. **Visual/performing arts:** Dramatic, music performance, music theory/composition, studio arts.

**Most popular majors.** Business/marketing 9%, education 9%, health sciences 26%, interdisciplinary studies 16%, public administration/social services 6%.

**Computing on campus.** 300 workstations in dormitories, library, computer center, student center. Dormitories wired for high-speed internet access and linked to campus network. Commuter students can connect to campus network. Online course registration, online library, helpline, repair service, wireless network available.

**Student life. Freshman orientation:** Available, $70 fee. Preregistration for classes offered. Held 4 days before classes begin. **Policies:** Full-time resident students required to attend 14 chapel services per semester. Smoke and alcohol-free campus. Religious observance required. **Housing:** Guaranteed on-campus for all undergraduates. Single-sex dorms, special housing for disabled, apartments available. $100 nonrefundable deposit, deadline 5/1. **Activities:** Bands, campus ministries, choral groups, drama, film society, international student organizations, literary magazine, music ensembles, student government, student newspaper, Fellowship of Christian Athletes, ministerial association, student activity council, Mu Kappa, honors student association, Tennessee Intercollegiate State Legislature, LIFE Groups, Klemata.

**Athletics.** NAIA. **Intercollegiate:** Baseball M, basketball, cheerleading M, cross-country, golf M, soccer, softball W, tennis, volleyball W. **Intramural:** Basketball, cheerleading W, cross-country, football (non-tackle), golf, racquetball, softball, swimming, table tennis, tennis, volleyball, weight lifting. **Team name:** Bulldogs.

**Student services.** Adult student services, alcohol/substance abuse counseling, chaplain/spiritual director, career counseling, student employment services, financial aid counseling, health services, personal counseling, placement for graduates, veterans' counselor. **Physically disabled:** Services for visually, speech, hearing impaired.

**Contact.** E-mail: info@uu.edu
Phone: (731) 661-5000 Toll-free number: (800) 338-6466
Fax: (731) 661-5017
Rich Grimm, Vice President for Enrollment Services, Union University, 1050 Union University Drive, Jackson, TN 38305-3697

---

## University of Memphis
**Memphis, Tennessee**
**www.memphis.edu**　　　　　　　　　　**CB code: 1459**

- Public 4-year university
- Commuter campus in very large city
- 16,011 degree-seeking undergraduates: 22% part-time, 61% women, 39% African American, 3% Asian American, 2% Hispanic American, 1% international
- 3,955 degree-seeking graduate students
- 67% of applicants admitted
- SAT or ACT (ACT writing optional) required
- 39% graduate within 6 years

**General.** Founded in 1912. Regionally accredited. **Degrees:** 2,590 bachelor's awarded; master's, doctoral, professional offered. **ROTC:** Army, Naval, Air Force. **Location:** 10 miles from downtown. **Calendar:** Semester, extensive summer session. **Full-time faculty:** 840 total; 78% have terminal degrees, 21% minority, 41% women. **Part-time faculty:** 495 total; 34% have terminal degrees, 22% minority, 52% women. **Class size:** 38% < 20, 45% 20-39, 7% 40-49, 9% 50-99, 2% >100. **Special facilities:** Institute of Egyptian art and archaeology, speech and hearing center, earthquake research and information center, technology institute, Chucalissa Indian village and museum, Confucius institute.

**Freshman class profile.** 6,156 applied, 4,120 admitted, 2,256 enrolled.

| Mid 50% test scores | | | |
|---|---|---|---|
| ACT composite: | 19-24 | Rank in top quarter: | 42% |
| GPA 3.75 or higher: | 20% | Rank in top tenth: | 15% |
| GPA 3.50-3.74: | 14% | Return as sophomores: | 76% |
| GPA 3.0-3.49: | 34% | Out-of-state: | 10% |
| GPA 2.0-2.99: | 31% | Live on campus: | 44% |
| | | International: | 2% |

**Basis for selection.** GPA and test scores important. Admissions Index will be calculated for each applicant by first multiplying GPA by 30 and then adding ACT score. Admission competitive based on calculated index,

and includes evaluation of high school curriculum. Interview required for university college; audition required for music; portfolio required for fine arts. **Homeschooled:** Transcript of courses and grades required. Applicants must comply with state law by submitting proof of registration with the local education agency.

**High school preparation.** Required and recommended units include English 4, mathematics 3-4, social studies 2, history 1, science 2 (laboratory 1), foreign language 2 and visual/performing arts 1.

**2009-2010 Annual costs.** Tuition/fees: $6,524; $19,406 out-of-state. Room/board: $5,870. Books/supplies: $1,100. Personal expenses: $2,393.

**2009-2010 Financial aid. Need-based:** 2,076 full-time freshmen applied for aid; 1,578 were judged to have need; 1,339 of these received aid. Average need met was 82%. Average scholarship/grant was $6,987; average loan $3,382. 57% of total undergraduate aid awarded as scholarships/grants, 43% as loans/jobs. **Non-need-based:** Awarded to 6,964 full-time undergraduates, including 1,205 freshmen. Scholarships awarded for academics, alumni affiliation, art, athletics, leadership, minority status, music/drama, ROTC, state residency.

**Application procedures. Admission:** Closing date 7/1 (postmark date). $25 fee. Admission notification on a rolling basis. Must meet registration deadline. **Financial aid:** Priority date 3/1, closing date 6/1. FAFSA required. Applicants notified on a rolling basis starting 3/1; must reply within 2 week(s) of notification.

**Academics.** University enables students to create non-traditional degrees. **Special study options:** Accelerated study, cooperative education, cross-registration, distance learning, double major, dual enrollment of high school students, ESL, exchange student, external degree, honors, independent study, internships, liberal arts/career combination, student-designed major, study abroad, teacher certification program. **Credit/placement by examination:** AP, CLEP, IB, SAT, ACT, institutional tests. Number of credits awarded decided by individual departments. **Support services:** Learning center, pre-admission summer program, reduced course load, remedial instruction, study skills assistance, tutoring, writing center.

**Honors college/program.** 27 ACT or 1200 SAT (exclusive of Writing), 3.5 GPA required.

**Majors. Architecture:** Environmental design. **Area/ethnic studies:** African-American. **Biology:** General. **Business:** Accounting, business admin, finance, hotel/motel admin, international, logistics, management information systems, managerial economics, marketing, real estate, selling. **Communications:** Journalism, media studies. **Computer sciences:** Computer science. **Education:** Multi-level teacher, physical, special. **Engineering:** Biomedical, civil, computer, electrical, mechanical. **Engineering technology:** Computer, electrical, manufacturing. **Foreign languages:** General. **Health:** Nursing (RN). **History:** General. **Liberal arts:** Arts/sciences. **Math:** General. **Parks/recreation:** Exercise sciences, sports admin. **Philosophy/religion:** Philosophy. **Physical sciences:** Chemistry, geology, physics. **Protective services:** Law enforcement admin. **Psychology:** General. **Public administration:** Social work. **Social sciences:** Anthropology, economics, geography, international relations, political science, sociology. **Visual/performing arts:** Art, art history/conservation, dramatic.

**Most popular majors.** Business/marketing 20%, communications/journalism 6%, education 9%, health sciences 7%, interdisciplinary studies 13%, liberal arts 7%, visual/performing arts 6%.

**Computing on campus.** 2,000 workstations in dormitories, library, computer center, student center. Dormitories wired for high-speed internet access and linked to campus network. Commuter students can connect to campus network. Online course registration, online library, helpline, repair service, wireless network available.

**Student life. Freshman orientation:** Mandatory. Preregistration for classes offered. One or 2-day sessions, evening program for adult students. Fees vary by program. **Housing:** Coed dorms, single-sex dorms, special housing for disabled, apartments, fraternity/sorority housing available. **Activities:** Bands, campus ministries, choral groups, dance, drama, film society, literary magazine, music ensembles, musical theater, opera, radio station, student government, student newspaper, symphony orchestra.

**Athletics.** NCAA. **Intercollegiate:** Baseball M, basketball, cross-country, football (tackle) M, golf, rifle, soccer, softball W, tennis, track and field, volleyball W. **Intramural:** Basketball, bowling, cross-country, football (non-tackle), golf, racquetball, soccer, softball, table tennis, tennis, volleyball. **Team name:** Tigers.

**Student services.** Adult student services, alcohol/substance abuse counseling, career counseling, student employment services, financial aid counseling, health services, legal services, minority student services, on-campus daycare, personal counseling, placement for graduates, veterans' counselor, women's services. **Physically disabled:** Services for visually, speech, hearing impaired.

**Contact.** E-mail: recruitment@memphis.edu
Phone: (901) 678-2111 Toll-free number: (800) 669-2678
Fax: (901) 678-3053
Gloria Moore, Associate Director of Admissions, University of Memphis, 101 Wilder Tower, Memphis, TN 38152

## University of Tennessee Health Science Center
**Memphis, Tennessee**
www.uthsc.edu                          **CB code: 1850**

- Public two-year upper-division university and health science college
- Commuter campus in very large city
- Test scores, application essay, interview required

**General.** Founded in 1911. Regionally accredited. **Degrees:** 110 bachelor's awarded; master's, doctoral, professional offered. **Location:** 220 miles from Nashville; 299 miles from St. Louis, MO. **Calendar:** Semester. **Full-time faculty:** 1,033 total; 11% minority, 51% women. **Part-time faculty:** 227 total; 6% minority, 49% women. **Special facilities:** Computer laboratories, special laboratories for nursing, pharmacy, allied health, and dentistry instruction, simulated patients.

**Student profile.** 174 undergraduates. 58% entered as juniors, 42% entered as seniors. 58% transferred from two-year, 42% transferred from four-year institutions.

| Out-of-state: | 16% | 25 or older: | 50% |
|---|---|---|---|

**Basis for selection.** College transcript, application essay, interview, standardized test scores required. Students must have minimum 2 years of college and meet minimum requirements. Admissions based on GPA, test scores, consistency in achievement, course load and content, recommendations, extracurricular performance, motivation and goals, preprofessional evaluation, interview if required by program. Minimum GPA requirements and application closing dates vary by program. Transfer accepted as juniors, seniors.

**2009-2010 Annual costs.** Tuition/fees: $6,186; $14,166 out-of-state. Above cost are for bachelor's program in nursing. Other programs vary by cost. Books/supplies: $1,182.

**Financial aid. Need-based:** Average need met was 71%. 7% of total undergraduate aid awarded as scholarships/grants, 93% as loans/jobs. **Non-need-based:** Scholarships awarded for academics, leadership, minority status, state residency. **Additional information:** Scholarships available to defray out-of-state portion of fees charged to out-of-state minority students.

**Application procedures. Admission:** $75 fee. Application must be submitted online. **Financial aid:** No deadline. Applicants notified on a rolling basis starting 5/1; must reply within 2 weeks of notification. FAFSA required.

**Academics. Special study options:** Accelerated study, combined bachelor's/graduate degree, cooperative education, cross-registration, distance learning, double major, exchange student, independent study, internships. **Credit/placement by examination:** CLEP.

**Honors college/program.** Varies for each undergraduate program.

**Majors. Health:** Clinical lab science, cytotechnology, dental hygiene, medical records admin, nursing (RN).

**Computing on campus.** 100 workstations in library, computer center. Commuter students can connect to campus network. Online library, helpline, repair service, student web hosting, wireless network available.

**Student life. Housing:** Coed dorms, wellness housing available. $50 nonrefundable deposit. **Activities:** International student organizations, student government, student newspaper, Baptist student union, United Methodist fellowship, Catholic student association, black student association.

**Athletics. Intramural:** Badminton, basketball, bowling, golf, handball, racquetball, soccer, softball, squash, swimming, table tennis, tennis, volleyball, water polo.

**Student services.** Adult student services, alcohol/substance abuse counseling, career counseling, services for economically disadvantaged, student employment services, financial aid counseling, health services, legal services, minority student services, personal counseling, placement for graduates, veterans' counselor. **Physically disabled:** Services for visually, speech, hearing impaired. **Learning disabled:** Comprehensive services available.

**Contact.** E-mail: rpatte10@uthsc.edu
Phone: (901) 448-5560 Fax: (901) 448-7772
Ron Patterson, Director, University of Tennessee Health Science Center, 910 Madison Avenue, Memphis, TN 38163

## University of Tennessee: Chattanooga
**Chattanooga, Tennessee**
www.utc.edu                          **CB code: 1831**

- Public 4-year university
- Commuter campus in large city
- 8,855 degree-seeking undergraduates: 10% part-time, 56% women, 16% African American, 2% Asian American, 2% Hispanic American, 1% Native American, 1% international
- 1,389 degree-seeking graduate students
- 79% of applicants admitted
- SAT or ACT (ACT writing optional) required
- 42% graduate within 6 years

**General.** Founded in 1886. Regionally accredited. **Degrees:** 1,635 bachelor's awarded; master's, doctoral, professional offered. **ROTC:** Army. **Location:** 130 miles from Nashville, 118 miles from Atlanta. **Calendar:** Semester, extensive summer session. **Full-time faculty:** 411 total; 73% have terminal degrees, 12% minority, 45% women. **Part-time faculty:** 283 total; 22% have terminal degrees, 9% minority, 46% women. **Class size:** 30% < 20, 51% 20-39, 15% 40-49, 4% 50-99, less than 1% >100. **Special facilities:** Art galleries, theater, observatory, Challenger center.

**Freshman class profile.** 6,700 applied, 5,302 admitted, 2,209 enrolled.

| Mid 50% test scores | | | |
|---|---|---|---|
| ACT composite: | 20-25 | GPA 2.0-2.99: | 30% |
| GPA 3.75 or higher: | 18% | End year in good standing: | 75% |
| GPA 3.50-3.74: | 16% | Return as sophomores: | 67% |
| GPA 3.0-3.49: | 35% | Out-of-state: | 4% |
| | | Live on campus: | 77% |

**Basis for selection.** High school curriculum and GPA very important. 2.75 GPA with 17 ACT (830 SAT composite) or 2.0 GPA with 21 ACT (990 SAT) required. Test scores, special talents, recommendations, essay or personal statement considered. Essay recommended. **Homeschooled:** Transcript of courses and grades required. 2.75 HS GPA; 21 ACT or 980 SAT (excluding writing); and completion of all 14 high school units. **Learning Disabled:** Student may register for services with Office for Students with Disabilities after admissions.

**High school preparation.** College-preparatory program recommended. 14 units required. Required units include English 4, mathematics 3, social studies 1, history 1, science 2 (laboratory 2), foreign language 2 and visual/performing arts 1. Math units must include algebra I and II, and geometry. Foreign language units must be in same language. History unit should be US history. Social studies unit should be world history, European history or world geography.

**2009-2010 Annual costs.** Tuition/fees: $5,710; $16,954 out-of-state. Room/board: $8,056. Books/supplies: $1,000. Personal expenses: $1,430.

**2009-2010 Financial aid. Need-based:** 2,103 full-time freshmen applied for aid; 1,351 were judged to have need; 1,347 of these received aid. Average need met was 87%. Average scholarship/grant was $4,480; average loan $3,904. 60% of total undergraduate aid awarded as scholarships/grants, 40% as loans/jobs. **Non-need-based:** Awarded to 4,431 full-time undergraduates, including 1,429 freshmen. Scholarships awarded for academics, alumni affiliation, art, athletics, job skills, leadership, minority status, music/drama, religious affiliation, ROTC, state residency.

**Application procedures. Admission:** Closing date 8/1. $30 fee, may be waived for applicants with need. Admission notification on a rolling basis. **Financial aid:** Priority date 4/1; no closing date. FAFSA, institutional form required. Applicants notified on a rolling basis starting 3/1.

**Academics. Special study options:** Combined bachelor's/graduate degree, cooperative education, cross-registration, distance learning, double major, dual enrollment of high school students, ESL, honors, independent study, internships, study abroad, teacher certification program. Washington Center Internship, Southeastern Command and Leadership Academy (SECLA), Senator Tommy Burks Victim Assistance Academy,. **Credit/placement by examination:** AP, CLEP, SAT, ACT, institutional tests. 24 credit hours maximum toward bachelor's degree. May only be used for elective credit hours. **Support services:** Learning center, pre-admission summer program, reduced course load, remedial instruction, study skills assistance, tutoring, writing center.

---

**Honors college/program.** Based on application, teacher evaluations, essay, official high school transcript, and ACT or SAT; about 45 applicants admitted each year.

**Majors. Biology:** General. **Business:** Business admin. **Communications:** General. **Computer sciences:** Computer science. **Conservation:** Environmental science. **Education:** Art, early childhood, English, foreign languages, mathematics, middle, music, science, social studies, special. **Engineering:** General, electrical, mechanical. **Engineering technology:** Industrial management. **Family/consumer sciences:** General. **Foreign languages:** General. **Health:** Clinical lab science, nursing (RN). **History:** General. **Legal studies:** Paralegal. **Liberal arts:** Humanities. **Math:** General, applied. **Parks/recreation:** Exercise sciences. **Physical sciences:** Chemistry, geology, physics. **Protective services:** Law enforcement admin. **Psychology:** General. **Public administration:** Community org/advocacy, social work. **Social sciences:** General, economics, political science, sociology. **Visual/performing arts:** Art, dramatic, interior design. **Other:** Philosophy and religion, Sociology and anthropology.

**Most popular majors.** Business/marketing 27%, education 11%, health sciences 6%, parks/recreation 7%, psychology 7%, security/protective services 7%, social sciences 7%.

**Computing on campus.** 1,200 workstations in library, computer center, student center. Dormitories wired for high-speed internet access and linked to campus network. Commuter students can connect to campus network. Online course registration, online library, helpline, repair service, wireless network available.

**Student life. Freshman orientation:** Mandatory, $65 fee. Preregistration for classes offered. 2-day sessions held in summer. **Housing:** Guaranteed on-campus for freshmen. Coed dorms, apartments, fraternity/sorority housing available. $225 partly refundable deposit. **Activities:** Bands, campus ministries, choral groups, dance, drama, film society, international student organizations, literary magazine, music ensembles, Model UN, opera, radio station, student government, student newspaper, symphony orchestra, TV station, Bahai club, Baptist collegiate ministry, Campus Crusade for Christ, Fellowship of Christian Athletes, Omega Phi Alpha, Sigma Alpha Iota, Habitat for Humanity, College Democrats, College Republicans, National Society of Black Engineers.

**Athletics.** NCAA. **Intercollegiate:** Basketball, cross-country, football (tackle) M, golf, soccer W, softball W, tennis, track and field, volleyball W, wrestling M. **Intramural:** Badminton, basketball, cross-country, football (nontackle), racquetball, soccer, softball W, swimming, table tennis, tennis, volleyball, wrestling M. **Team name:** Mocs.

**Student services.** Adult student services, chaplain/spiritual director, career counseling, student employment services, financial aid counseling, health services, minority student services, on-campus daycare, personal counseling, placement for graduates, veterans' counselor, women's services. **Physically disabled:** Services for visually, speech, hearing impaired. **Learning disabled:** Comprehensive services available.

**Contact.** E-mail: yancy-freeman@utc.edu
Phone: (423) 425-4662 Toll-free number: (800) 882-6627
Fax: (423) 425-4157
Yancy Freeman, Director of Student Recruitment and Admissions, University of Tennessee: Chattanooga, 615 McCallie Avenue, Chattanooga, TN 37403

## University of Tennessee: Knoxville

Knoxville, Tennessee      **CB member**
www.utk.edu      **CB code: 1843**

- Public 4-year university
- Residential campus in large city
- 20,849 degree-seeking undergraduates: 6% part-time, 49% women, 8% African American, 3% Asian American, 2% Hispanic American, 1% Native American, 1% international
- 8,461 degree-seeking graduate students
- 73% of applicants admitted
- SAT or ACT (ACT writing optional) required
- 61% graduate within 6 years

**General.** Founded in 1794. Regionally accredited. **Degrees:** 4,205 bachelor's awarded; master's, doctoral, professional offered. **ROTC:** Army, Air Force. **Location:** 224 miles from Atlanta, 178 miles from Nashville. **Calendar:** Semester, extensive summer session. **Class size:** 31% < 20, 55% 20-39, 5% 40-49, 6% 50-99, 3% >100. **Special facilities:** 2 theaters, science/engineering research facility, international house, Olympic track, baseball stadium.

**Freshman class profile.** 12,234 applied, 8,892 admitted, 3,717 enrolled.

| Mid 50% test scores | | | |
|---|---|---|---|
| SAT critical reading: | 510-640 | Rank in top quarter: | 70% |
| SAT math: | 530-650 | Rank in top tenth: | 39% |
| ACT composite: | 24-29 | Return as sophomores: | 84% |
| GPA 3.75 or higher: | 58% | Out-of-state: | 10% |
| GPA 3.50-3.74: | 16% | Live on campus: | 92% |
| GPA 3.0-3.49: | 19% | International: | 1% |
| GPA 2.0-2.99: | 7% | Fraternities: | 22% |
| | | Sororities: | 23% |

**Basis for selection.** Admission based on high school grades in core academic subjects and standardized test scores. Other factors that indicate future academic success considered, as are special talents, student statement, extracurricular leadership, community involvement, class rank, and background. Essay not required but preferred; portfolio required for architecture and interior design; audition required for music.

**High school preparation.** College-preparatory program required. 14 units required. Required units include English 4, mathematics 3, social studies 1, history 1, science 2 (laboratory 1), foreign language 2 and visual/performing arts 1. Social science units must be 1 U.S. history and either world history, European history, or world geography. Mathematics units must include algebra I, algebra II, and 1 unit of either geometry, trigonometry, advanced mathematics, or calculus.

**2009-2010 Annual costs.** Tuition/fees: $6,855; $20,651 out-of-state. Out-of-state students pay additional required fees of $300. Room/board: $7,254. Books/supplies: $1,366. Personal expenses: $3,260.

**2009-2010 Financial aid.** All financial aid based on need. **Additional information:** Application priority date for scholarships 2/1.

**Application procedures. Admission:** Closing date 12/1 (postmark date). $30 fee, may be waived for applicants with need. Priority applicants notified in January. Regular applicants notified in March. Must reply by 5/1. **Financial aid:** Priority date 3/1; no closing date. FAFSA required. Applicants notified on a rolling basis starting 3/15; must reply within 3 week(s) of notification.

**Academics. Special study options:** Accelerated study, combined bachelor's/graduate degree, cooperative education, cross-registration, distance learning, double major, dual enrollment of high school students, ESL, exchange student, external degree, honors, independent study, internships, liberal arts/career combination, student-designed major, study abroad, teacher certification program. **Credit/placement by examination:** AP, CLEP, IB, institutional tests. Departmental proficiency available. Up to 50 hours of credit awarded for International Baccalaureate. **Support services:** Learning center, study skills assistance, tutoring, writing center.

**Majors. Agriculture:** Animal sciences, economics, food science, ornamental horticulture, plant sciences, soil chem/physics. **Architecture:** Architecture. **Area/ethnic studies:** African-American, American, Asian, Latin American, Russian/Slavic, women's. **Biology:** General. **Business:** General, accounting, business admin, finance, hotel/motel admin, human resources, logistics, managerial economics, marketing, tourism/travel. **Communications:** Advertising, journalism, public relations. **Computer sciences:** Computer science. **Conservation:** Forestry, wildlife. **Education:** Agricultural, art, Deaf/hearing impaired, elementary, middle, music, secondary, special. **Engineering:** Aerospace, agricultural, biomedical, chemical, civil, computer, electrical, industrial, materials, materials science, mechanical, nuclear, physics, science. **Family/consumer sciences:** Consumer economics, family studies, food/nutrition. **Foreign languages:** Ancient Greek, classics, comparative lit, French, German, Italian, Latin, Portuguese, Russian, Spanish. **Health:** Audiology/hearing, clinical lab science, nursing (RN), occupational health nursing, predental, premedicine, prepharmacy, preveterinary, speech pathology. **History:** General. **Interdisciplinary:** Medieval/Renaissance. **Legal studies:** Prelaw. **Math:** General, statistics. **Parks/recreation:** General, exercise sciences, sports admin. **Philosophy/religion:** Philosophy, religion. **Physical sciences:** Chemistry, geology, physics. **Psychology:** General. **Public administration:** General. **Social sciences:** Anthropology, economics, geography, political science, sociology. **Visual/performing arts:** Art, art history/conservation, commercial/advertising art, dramatic, interior design, music theory/composition, piano/organ, studio arts, voice/opera. **Other:** Journalism and electronic media.

**Most popular majors.** Business/marketing 18%, communications/journalism 10%, engineering/engineering technologies 8%, health sciences 6%, psychology 10%, social sciences 9%.

**Computing on campus.** 1,000 workstations in dormitories, library, computer center, student center. Dormitories wired for high-speed internet access and linked to campus network. Commuter students can connect to campus network. Online course registration, online library, helpline, repair service, student web hosting, wireless network available.

**Student life. Freshman orientation:** Mandatory, $99 fee. Preregistration for classes offered. 2-days session; parents may attend for $35 per parent and does not include housing. **Policies:** Freshmen must live on-campus unless residing with parent or legal guardian. **Housing:** Guaranteed on-campus for freshmen. Coed dorms, single-sex dorms, special housing for disabled, apartments, fraternity/sorority housing available. $100 fully refundable deposit. Transfer student floors available. **Activities:** Bands, campus ministries, choral groups, dance, drama, film society, international student organizations, literary magazine, music ensembles, Model UN, musical theater, opera, radio station, student government, student newspaper, symphony orchestra, TV station, black cultural center, women's center, various denomination student unions.

**Athletics.** NCAA. **Intercollegiate:** Baseball M, basketball, diving, football (tackle) M, golf, rowing (crew) W, soccer W, softball W, swimming, tennis, volleyball W. **Intramural:** Badminton, basketball, bowling, field hockey, football (tackle), golf, racquetball, soccer, softball, table tennis, tennis, volleyball, water polo, weight lifting. **Team name:** Volunteers.

**Student services.** Adult student services, alcohol/substance abuse counseling, chaplain/spiritual director, career counseling, student employment services, financial aid counseling, health services, minority student services, on-campus daycare, personal counseling, placement for graduates, veterans' counselor, women's services. **Physically disabled:** Services for visually, speech, hearing impaired.

**Contact.** E-mail: admissions@utk.edu
Phone: (865) 974-2184
Vern Granger, Director of Admissions, University of Tennessee: Knoxville, 320 Student Services Building, Circle Park, Knoxville, TN 37996-0230

## University of Tennessee: Martin
**Martin, Tennessee**
**www.utm.edu** CB code: 1844

- Public 4-year university
- Residential campus in small town
- 6,476 degree-seeking undergraduates: 10% part-time, 57% women, 16% African American, 1% Asian American, 1% Hispanic American, 2% international
- 430 degree-seeking graduate students
- 74% of applicants admitted
- SAT or ACT (ACT writing optional) required
- 49% graduate within 6 years; 24% enter graduate study

**General.** Founded in 1927. Regionally accredited. Coordinates online education for UT system. **Degrees:** 1,018 bachelor's awarded; master's offered. **ROTC:** Army. **Location:** 125 miles from Memphis, 150 miles from Nashville. **Calendar:** Semester, extensive summer session. **Full-time faculty:** 270 total; 75% have terminal degrees, 8% minority, 43% women. **Part-time faculty:** 263 total; 21% have terminal degrees, 9% minority, 51% women. **Class size:** 50% < 20, 37% 20-39, 7% 40-49, 6% 50-99, less than 1% >100. **Special facilities:** Teacher resource center, 680-acre agriculture, natural resources teaching, demonstration complex, teaching/research facility resort, international education center.

**Freshman class profile.** 3,581 applied, 2,657 admitted, 1,394 enrolled.

| Mid 50% test scores | | End year in good standing: | 76% |
|---|---|---|---|
| ACT composite: | 20-25 | Return as sophomores: | 72% |
| GPA 3.75 or higher: | 25% | Out-of-state: | 3% |
| GPA 3.50-3.74: | 19% | Live on campus: | 71% |
| GPA 3.0-3.49: | 37% | International: | 2% |
| GPA 2.0-2.99: | 19% | Fraternities: | 21% |
| Rank in top quarter: | 50% | Sororities: | 10% |
| Rank in top tenth: | 20% | | |

**Basis for selection.** 2.85 GPA with 18 ACT or 2.5 GPA with 21 ACT required. Students not meeting regular admission requirements may be considered for conditional admission. Auditions required in fine and performing arts. **Homeschooled:** 21 ACT and 2.85 GPA required.

**High school preparation.** College-preparatory program required. 14 units required. Required units include English 4, mathematics 3, history 2, science 2 (laboratory 1), foreign language 2 and visual/performing arts 1.

**2009-2010 Annual costs.** Tuition/fees: $5,769; $17,155 out-of-state. Room/board: $5,032. Books/supplies: $1,500. Personal expenses: $2,368.

**Application procedures. Admission:** Priority date 2/1; deadline 8/1. $30 fee. Admission notification on a rolling basis beginning on or about 9/1.

**Academics. Special study options:** Accelerated study, cooperative education, cross-registration, distance learning, double major, dual enrollment of high school students, ESL, exchange student, honors, independent study, internships, student-designed major, study abroad, teacher certification program. 3-1 pharmacy program, 3-1 veterinary medicine program, 3-1 dentistry program, 3-1 medicine program, 3-1 optometry program, 3-1 podiatry program, 3-1 chiropractory program. **Credit/placement by examination:** AP, CLEP, SAT, ACT, institutional tests. 30 credit hours maximum toward bachelor's degree. **Support services:** Remedial instruction, study skills assistance, tutoring, writing center.

**Majors. Agriculture:** General. **Biology:** General. **Business:** Accounting, business admin, finance, management information systems, managerial economics, marketing. **Communications:** General. **Computer sciences:** Computer science. **Conservation:** Management/policy. **Education:** Secondary, special. **Engineering:** General. **Family/consumer sciences:** General. **Foreign languages:** French, Spanish. **Health:** Nursing (RN). **History:** General. **Math:** General. **Parks/recreation:** Health/fitness. **Philosophy/religion:** Philosophy. **Physical sciences:** Chemistry, geology. **Protective services:** Law enforcement admin. **Psychology:** General. **Public administration:** Social work. **Social sciences:** International relations, political science, sociology. **Visual/performing arts:** General.

**Most popular majors.** Agriculture 6%, biology 7%, business/marketing 17%, interdisciplinary studies 21%, parks/recreation 6%.

**Computing on campus.** 254 workstations in dormitories, library, student center. Dormitories wired for high-speed internet access and linked to campus network. Commuter students can connect to campus network. Online course registration, online library, helpline, repair service, student web hosting, wireless network available.

**Student life. Freshman orientation:** Available, $165 fee. Preregistration for classes offered. 4-day program held in August. **Policies:** Freshmen must live on-campus. **Housing:** Guaranteed on-campus for freshmen. Coed dorms, single-sex dorms, special housing for disabled, apartments, fraternity/sorority housing available. $100 fully refundable deposit, deadline 8/1. **Activities:** Bands, campus ministries, choral groups, dance, drama, international student organizations, literary magazine, music ensembles, opera, radio station, student government, student newspaper, TV station, Chi Alpha Christian Fellowship, interfaith student center, Rotaract, Free Thinkers club, Fellowship of Christian Athletes, College Democrats, College Republicans, reformed university fellowship, Japanese animation research society.

**Athletics.** NCAA. **Intercollegiate:** Baseball M, basketball, cheerleading M, cross-country, equestrian W, football (tackle) M, golf M, rifle, rodeo, soccer W, softball W, tennis W, volleyball W. **Intramural:** Badminton, basketball, cross-country, football (non-tackle), racquetball, rugby, soccer, softball, swimming, table tennis, tennis, volleyball. **Team name:** Skyhawks.

**Student services.** Adult student services, alcohol/substance abuse counseling, chaplain/spiritual director, career counseling, services for economically disadvantaged, student employment services, financial aid counseling, health services, minority student services, on-campus daycare, personal counseling, placement for graduates, veterans' counselor. **Physically disabled:** Services for visually, speech, hearing impaired.

**Contact.** E-mail: admitme@utm.edu
Phone: (731) 881-7020 Toll-free number: (800) 829-8861
Fax: (731) 881-7029
Judy Rayburn, Director of Admissions, University of Tennessee: Martin, 200 Hall Moody Administration Building, Martin, TN 38238

## University of the South
**Sewanee, Tennessee** CB member
**www.sewanee.edu** CB code: 1842

- Private 4-year university affiliated with Episcopal Church
- Residential campus in rural community
- 1,450 degree-seeking undergraduates: 51% women, 5% African American, 3% Asian American, 3% Hispanic American, 1% Native American, 2% international
- 74 degree-seeking graduate students
- 68% of applicants admitted
- SAT or ACT with writing, application essay required
- 82% graduate within 6 years

**General.** Founded in 1857. Regionally accredited; also accredited by ATS. **Degrees:** 361 bachelor's awarded; master's, professional offered. **Location:** 45 miles from Chattanooga, 57 miles from Huntsville. **Calendar:** Semester, limited summer session. **Full-time faculty:** 136 total; 93% have terminal degrees, 9% minority, 35% women. **Part-time faculty:** 37 total; 68% have terminal degrees, 5% minority, 35% women. **Class size:** 72% < 20, 27%

20-39, less than 1% 40-49, less than 1% 50-99. **Special facilities:** Landscape analysis lab, observatory, materials analysis laboratory with electron microscopy, hiking and horseback riding trails, climbing.

**Freshman class profile.** 2,481 applied, 1,688 admitted, 402 enrolled.

| Mid 50% test scores | | | |
|---|---|---|---|
| SAT critical reading: | 570-690 | Rank in top quarter: | 67% |
| SAT math: | 580-670 | Rank in top tenth: | 43% |
| SAT writing: | 560-670 | Return as sophomores: | 90% |
| ACT composite: | 26-30 | Out-of-state: | 75% |
| GPA 3.75 or higher: | 38% | Live on campus: | 100% |
| GPA 3.50-3.74: | 22% | International: | 2% |
| GPA 3.0-3.49: | 30% | Fraternities: | 40% |
| GPA 2.0-2.99: | 10% | Sororities: | 52% |

**Basis for selection.** GED not accepted. School achievement record, recommendations, extracurricular activities, test scores, essay important. Children of alumni and minority applicants given special consideration. Interview recommended.

**High school preparation.** College-preparatory program required. 13 units required; 20 recommended. Required and recommended units include English 4, mathematics 3-4, social studies 1-2, history 1-2, science 2-4 (laboratory 2-3) and foreign language 2-4.

**2009-2010 Annual costs.** Tuition/fees: $34,172. Room/board: $9,760. Books/supplies: $800. Personal expenses: $900.

**2009-2010 Financial aid. Need-based:** 272 full-time freshmen applied for aid; 182 were judged to have need; 182 of these received aid. Average need met was 95%. Average scholarship/grant was $25,561; average loan $3,959. 84% of total undergraduate aid awarded as scholarships/grants, 16% as loans/jobs. **Non-need-based:** Awarded to 1,138 full-time undergraduates, including 299 freshmen. Scholarships awarded for academics, minority status, religious affiliation.

**Application procedures. Admission:** Closing date 2/1 (postmark date). $45 fee, may be waived for applicants with need, free for online applicants. Admission notification 3/17. Must reply by May 1 or within 2 week(s) if notified thereafter. **Financial aid:** Priority date 3/1; no closing date. FAFSA, institutional form required. Must reply within 4 week(s) of notification.

**Academics. Special study options:** Double major, independent study, internships, student-designed major, study abroad, Washington semester. **Credit/placement by examination:** AP, CLEP, IB, SAT, ACT, institutional tests. 60 credit hours maximum toward bachelor's degree. **Support services:** Tutoring.

**Majors. Area/ethnic studies:** American, Asian, French, German, Russian/Slavic. **Biology:** General, biochemistry. **Computer sciences:** General, computer science. **Conservation:** Environmental studies, forestry, management/policy. **Foreign languages:** Ancient Greek, comparative lit, French, German, Latin, modern Greek, Russian, Spanish. **History:** General. **Interdisciplinary:** Global studies, math/computer science, medieval/Renaissance. **Math:** General. **Philosophy/religion:** Philosophy, religion. **Physical sciences:** Chemistry, geology, physics. **Psychology:** General. **Social sciences:** Anthropology, economics, political science. **Visual/performing arts:** General, art history/conservation, studio arts.

**Most popular majors.** Biology 8%, English 16%, history 11%, natural resources/environmental science 6%, psychology 7%, social sciences 23%, visual/performing arts 6%.

**Computing on campus.** 200 workstations in dormitories, library, computer center. Dormitories wired for high-speed internet access and linked to campus network. Commuter students can connect to campus network. Online course registration, online library, helpline, repair service, student web hosting, wireless network available.

**Student life. Freshman orientation:** Mandatory. Preregistration for classes offered. Held several days before start of classes. **Policies:** Student-administered honor code strictly observed. **Housing:** Guaranteed on-campus for freshmen. Coed dorms, single-sex dorms, special housing for disabled, apartments, cooperative housing, fraternity/sorority housing, wellness housing available. $300 nonrefundable deposit, deadline 5/1. **Activities:** Bands, campus ministries, choral groups, dance, drama, film society, international student organizations, literary magazine, music ensembles, Model UN, musical theater, radio station, student government, student newspaper, symphony orchestra, tutoring center for disadvantaged youth, religious organizations, Big Brother-Big Sister program.

**Athletics.** NCAA. **Intercollegiate:** Baseball M, basketball, cross-country, diving, equestrian, fencing, field hockey W, football (tackle) M, golf, lacrosse, rowing (crew), rugby M, skiing, soccer, softball W, swimming, tennis, track and field, volleyball W. **Intramural:** Basketball, cross-country,

diving, golf, handball, racquetball, skin diving, soccer, softball, swimming, table tennis, tennis, track and field, volleyball, wrestling M. **Team name:** Tigers.

**Student services.** Chaplain/spiritual director, career counseling, student employment services, health services, minority student services, on-campus daycare, personal counseling, placement for graduates, women's services. **Physically disabled:** Services for visually, hearing impaired.

**Contact.** E-mail: admiss@sewanee.edu
Phone: (931) 598-1238 Toll-free number: (800) 522-2234
Fax: (931) 598-3248
Jay Fisher, Dean of Admission, University of the South, Office of Admission, Sewanee, TN 37383-1000

---

## Vanderbilt University

**Nashville, Tennessee**
www.vanderbilt.edu

CB member
CB code: 1871

- Private 4-year university
- Residential campus in very large city
- 6,764 degree-seeking undergraduates: 1% part-time, 52% women, 9% African American, 8% Asian American, 6% Hispanic American, 1% Native American, 4% international
- 5,584 degree-seeking graduate students
- 20% of applicants admitted
- SAT or ACT with writing, application essay required
- 91% graduate within 6 years; 38% enter graduate study

**General.** Founded in 1873. Regionally accredited. **Degrees:** 1,568 bachelor's awarded; master's, doctoral, professional offered. **ROTC:** Army, Naval, Air Force. **Location:** 240 miles from Atlanta, 300 miles from St. Louis. **Calendar:** Semester, limited summer session. **Full-time faculty:** 860 total. **Class size:** 65% < 20, 24% 20-39, 3% 40-49, 6% 50-99, 2% >100. **Special facilities:** Observatory, electron microscopes, television news archive, national arboretum, video productions, black cultural center, women's center, cinema and art museum.

**Freshman class profile.** 19,353 applied, 3,899 admitted, 1,599 enrolled.

| Mid 50% test scores | | | |
|---|---|---|---|
| SAT critical reading: | 660-750 | Rank in top quarter: | 97% |
| SAT math: | 690-770 | Rank in top tenth: | 86% |
| SAT writing: | 660-750 | Return as sophomores: | 96% |
| ACT composite: | 30-34 | Out-of-state: | 84% |
| GPA 3.75 or higher: | 49% | Live on campus: | 100% |
| GPA 3.50-3.74: | 28% | International: | 5% |
| GPA 3.0-3.49: | 22% | Fraternities: | 42% |
| GPA 2.0-2.99: | 1% | Sororities: | 53% |

**Basis for selection.** Academic achievement, recommendation, essay, test scores, activities important. Recommend SAT Subject tests and ACT exams but not required for admission. Audition required for music program. **Homeschooled:** Statement describing homeschool structure and mission required.

**High school preparation.** College-preparatory program required. 18 units required; 21 recommended. Required and recommended units include English 4, mathematics 3-4, social studies 2-3, history 1, science 3-4 (laboratory 2-3), foreign language 2 and academic electives 3. Additional unit in math and 2 in science recommended for engineering applicants. Music applicants do not require 2 units of science. Engineering program recommends 2 years of language. Education & Human Development program does not require language.

**2009-2010 Annual costs.** Tuition/fees: $38,578. Room/board: $12,650. Books/supplies: $1,208. Personal expenses: $2,062.

**2009-2010 Financial aid. Need-based:** 860 full-time freshmen applied for aid; 743 were judged to have need; 740 of these received aid. Average need met was 100%. Average scholarship/grant was $34,489; average loan $238. 96% of total undergraduate aid awarded as scholarships/grants, 4% as loans/jobs. **Non-need-based:** Awarded to 2,193 full-time undergraduates, including 598 freshmen. Scholarships awarded for academics, athletics, leadership, minority status, music/drama, ROTC, state residency. **Additional information:** Financial aid packages for incoming students do not include need-based loans. Need-based loans replaced with increased amounts of scholarship and/or grant assistance.

**Application procedures. Admission:** Priority date 1/3; deadline 3/1 (postmark date). $50 fee, may be waived for applicants with need. Admission notification 4/1. Must reply by 5/1. **Financial aid:** Priority date 2/1; no closing date. FAFSA, CSS PROFILE required. Applicants notified on a rolling basis starting 4/1.

**Academics.** All undergraduates take portion of coursework in College of Arts and Science. **Special study options:** Accelerated study, combined bachelor's/graduate degree, cooperative education, cross-registration, distance learning, double major, dual enrollment of high school students, ESL, honors, independent study, internships, student-designed major, study abroad, teacher certification program, Washington semester. **Credit/placement by examination:** AP, CLEP, IB, institutional tests. 30 credit hours maximum toward bachelor's degree. **Support services:** Learning center, study skills assistance, tutoring, writing center.

**Majors. Area/ethnic studies:** African-American, American, Central/Eastern European, East Asian, European, German, Latin American, regional, Russian/Slavic, Spanish/Iberian, Western European, women's. **Biology:** General, molecular. **Communications:** General. **Computer sciences:** Computer science. **Education:** General, early childhood, elementary, secondary, special. **Engineering:** Biomedical, chemical, civil, computer. **Foreign languages:** Classics, French, German, Romance, Russian, Spanish. **History:** General. **Interdisciplinary:** Classical/archaeology, cognitive science, natural sciences, neuroscience, science/society. **Math:** General. **Philosophy/religion:** Judaic, philosophy, religion. **Physical sciences:** Chemistry, geology, physics. **Psychology:** General. **Social sciences:** General, anthropology, applied economics, economics, international economic development, political science, sociology, urban studies. **Visual/performing arts:** Art, art history/conservation, dramatic, film/cinema, music performance, music theory/composition, piano/organ, stringed instruments, studio arts, voice/opera. **Other:** Language and literacy studies.

**Most popular majors.** Engineering/engineering technologies 13%, foreign language 6%, interdisciplinary studies 7%, psychology 6%, social sciences 31%.

**Computing on campus.** 400 workstations in library, computer center, student center. Dormitories wired for high-speed internet access and linked to campus network. Commuter students can connect to campus network. Online course registration, online library, helpline, repair service, student web hosting, wireless network available.

**Student life. Freshman orientation:** Mandatory, $20 fee. Preregistration for classes offered. **Housing:** Guaranteed on-campus for freshmen. Coed dorms, single-sex dorms, special housing for disabled, apartments, wellness housing available. **Activities:** Bands, campus ministries, choral groups, dance, drama, film society, international student organizations, literary magazine, music ensembles, Model UN, musical theater, opera, radio station, student government, student newspaper, symphony orchestra, TV station, over 400 clubs and organizations.

**Athletics.** NCAA. **Intercollegiate:** Baseball M, basketball, bowling W, cheerleading, cross-country, football (tackle) M, golf, lacrosse W, soccer W, swimming W, tennis, track and field W. **Intramural:** Badminton, basketball, bowling, football (non-tackle), golf, racquetball, soccer, softball, squash, swimming, table tennis, tennis, track and field, volleyball, water polo, wrestling. **Team name:** Commodores.

**Student services.** Alcohol/substance abuse counseling, chaplain/spiritual director, career counseling, student employment services, financial aid counseling, health services, minority student services, on-campus daycare, personal counseling, placement for graduates, women's services. **Physically disabled:** Services for visually, speech, hearing impaired.

**Contact.** E-mail: admissions@vanderbilt.edu
Phone: (615) 322-2561 Toll-free number: (800) 288-0432
Fax: (615) 343-7765
John Gaines, Director, Enrollment Management, Vanderbilt University, 2305 West End Avenue, Nashville, TN 37203-1727

## Visible School - Music and Worship Arts College
### Memphis, Tennessee
### www.visible.edu

- Private 3-year Bible and performing arts college affiliated with Christian Church
- Very large city
- 98 degree-seeking undergraduates
- SAT or ACT (ACT writing optional), application essay, interview required

**General.** Candidate for regional accreditation.; also accredited by TRACS. Provides practical ministry training and discipleship in addition to music education. **Degrees:** 14 bachelor's awarded. **Calendar:** Semester, limited summer session. **Full-time faculty:** 18 total. **Part-time faculty:** 2 total.

**Basis for selection.** Personal relationship with Jesus Christ required, having had a salvation experience. 18 ACT or 750 SAT (exclusive of Writing) or 1500 SAT (including Writing) required. Audition required for Modern Music Ministry program.

**2010-2011 Annual costs.** Tuition/fees (projected): $15,800. Room only: $3,400.

**Application procedures. Admission:** No deadline. $40 fee, may be waived for applicants with need. Admission notification on a rolling basis.

**Academics. Credit/placement by examination:** CLEP.

**Majors. Communications:** Digital media. **Theology:** Theology. **Visual/performing arts:** Music management, music performance.

**Contact.** E-mail: seeyourself@visibleschool.com
Phone: (901) 377-2992 Toll-free number: (877) 558-4742
Fax: (901) 377-0544
Heather Isaac, Admissions Coordinator, Visible School - Music and Worship Arts College, 1015 South Cooper Street, Memphis, TN 38104

## Watkins College of Art, Design and Film
### Nashville, Tennessee
### www.watkins.edu

- Private 4-year visual arts college
- Commuter campus in very large city
- 415 degree-seeking undergraduates
- 11 graduate students
- 80% of applicants admitted
- SAT or ACT (ACT writing optional), application essay required
- 40% graduate within 6 years; 15% enter graduate study

**General.** Candidate for regional accreditation. **Degrees:** 50 bachelor's, 1 associate awarded. **Location:** Located within city of Nashville Tennessee. **Calendar:** Semester, limited summer session. **Full-time faculty:** 19 total. **Part-time faculty:** 26 total. **Class size:** 90% < 20, 7% 20-39, 2% 40-49, less than 1% 50-99.

**Freshman class profile.** 125 applied, 100 admitted, 67 enrolled.

| Mid 50% test scores | | | |
|---|---|---|---|
| ACT composite: | 19-26 | GPA 3.0-3.49: | 33% |
| GPA 3.75 or higher: | 14% | GPA 2.0-2.99: | 35% |
| GPA 3.50-3.74: | 16% | End year in good standing: | 90% |
| | | Return as sophomores: | 90% |

**Basis for selection.** Admissions based on artistic exercises and academic essays, test scores, prior academic record and letter of recommendation. Artistic portfolio highly recommended. **Homeschooled:** Transcript of courses and grades, state high school equivalency certificate, letter of recommendation (nonparent) required.

**High school preparation.** Recommended units include English 4, mathematics 2, social studies 2, history 2, science 1, computer science 2 and visual/performing arts 4.

**2009-2010 Annual costs.** Tuition/fees: $18,600. Room only: $6,000.

**Application procedures. Admission:** Priority date 5/1; deadline 7/15 (postmark date). $50 fee, may be waived for applicants with need. Application must be submitted on paper. Admission notification on a rolling basis. Must reply by 7/31.

**Academics. Special study options:** Dual enrollment of high school students, internships. **Credit/placement by examination:** AP, CLEP, IB, institutional tests. **Support services:** Pre-admission summer program, study skills assistance, tutoring, writing center.

**Majors. Visual/performing arts:** Art, film/cinema, graphic design, interior design, photography, studio arts.

**Computing on campus.** 110 workstations in library, computer center. Dormitories wired for high-speed internet access. Wireless network available.

**Student life. Freshman orientation:** Mandatory. **Housing:** Guaranteed on-campus for freshmen. Coed dorms available. $300 fully refundable deposit, deadline 7/15. **Activities:** Film society, student government, student newspaper.

**Student services.** Alcohol/substance abuse counseling, career counseling, services for economically disadvantaged, financial aid counseling, personal counseling. **Physically disabled:** Services for visually, speech, hearing impaired.

**Contact.** E-mail: admissions@watkins.edu
Phone: (615) 383-4848 ext. 7418 Toll-free number: (866) 887-6395
Fax: (615) 383-4849
Linda Schwab, Director of Admissions, Watkins College of Art, Design and
Film, 2298 Rosa L. Parks Boulevard, Nashville, TN 37228

## Williamson Christian College
### Franklin, Tennessee
### www.williamsoncc.edu

- Private 4-year liberal arts college affiliated with interdenominational tradition
- Commuter campus in small city
- 70 degree-seeking undergraduates: 26% part-time, 43% women, 15% African American, 1% Asian American, 27% international

**General.** Accredited by ABHE. Accelerated degree completion programs available for working adults. **Degrees:** 10 bachelor's awarded. **Location:** 15 miles from downtown. **Calendar:** Semester, limited summer session. **Full-time faculty:** 5 total; 100% have terminal degrees, 40% women. **Part-time faculty:** 12 total; 17% have terminal degrees, 50% women. **Class size:** 100% < 20.

**Freshman class profile.**

| | | | |
|---|---|---|---|
| GPA 3.50-3.74: | 33% | End year in good standing: | 33% |
| GPA 3.0-3.49: | 34% | Return as sophomores: | 33% |
| GPA 2.0-2.99: | 33% | | |

**Basis for selection.** Open admission, but selective for some programs.

**2009-2010 Annual costs.** Tuition/fees: $9,550. Books/supplies: $900. Personal expenses: $3,843.

**2009-2010 Financial aid. Need-based:** 2 full-time freshmen applied for aid; 2 were judged to have need; 2 of these received aid. Average need met was 75%. Average scholarship/grant was $2,719; average loan $2,748. 47% of total undergraduate aid awarded as scholarships/grants, 53% as loans/jobs.

**Application procedures. Admission:** No deadline. $25 fee. Application must be submitted on paper. Admission notification on a rolling basis. **Financial aid:** No deadline. FAFSA required. Applicants notified on a rolling basis starting 7/1; must reply within 2 week(s) of notification.

**Academics. Special study options:** Accelerated study, distance learning, liberal arts/career combination, weekend college. **Credit/placement by examination:** AP, CLEP. 15 credit hours maximum toward associate degree, 32 toward bachelor's. **Support services:** Study skills assistance, tutoring.

**Majors. Business:** Nonprofit/public. **Philosophy/religion:** Religion.

**Most popular majors.** Business/marketing 50%, philosophy/religious studies 50%.

**Computing on campus.** 1 workstations in computer center. Wireless network available.

**Student life. Freshman orientation:** Mandatory. Preregistration for classes offered. **Activities:** Student government, student newspaper.

**Student services.** Adult student services, chaplain/spiritual director, financial aid counseling, personal counseling.

**Contact.** E-mail: mkelley@williamsoncc.edu
Phone: (615) 771-7821 Fax: (615) 771-7810
Michael Kelley, Director of Admissions, Williamson Christian College, 200 Seaboard Lane, Franklin, TN 37067

# Texas

## Abilene Christian University
**Abilene, Texas**
www.acu.edu

**CB member**
**CB code: 6001**

- Private 4-year university affiliated with Church of Christ
- Residential campus in small city
- 3,787 degree-seeking undergraduates: 6% part-time, 54% women, 8% African American, 1% Asian American, 8% Hispanic American, 1% Native American, 3% international
- 873 degree-seeking graduate students
- 49% of applicants admitted
- SAT or ACT (ACT writing recommended) required
- 62% graduate within 6 years

**General.** Founded in 1906. Regionally accredited. **Degrees:** 828 bachelor's, 1 associate awarded; master's, doctoral offered. **Location:** 150 miles from Dallas, Fort Worth. **Calendar:** Semester, limited summer session. **Full-time faculty:** 236 total; 82% have terminal degrees, 9% minority, 34% women. **Part-time faculty:** 135 total; 25% have terminal degrees, 6% minority, 42% women. **Class size:** 47% < 20, 41% 20-39, 6% 40-49, 5% 50-99, 2% >100. **Special facilities:** Converged media newsroom, Center for Restoration Studies, Voice Institute, demonstration farm and ranch, observatory.

**Freshman class profile.** 3,712 applied, 1,823 admitted, 983 enrolled.

| Mid 50% test scores | | | |
|---|---|---|---|
| SAT critical reading: | 480-600 | GPA 2.0-2.99: | 12% |
| SAT math: | 490-620 | Rank in top quarter: | 49% |
| ACT composite: | 21-27 | Rank in top tenth: | 23% |
| GPA 3.75 or higher: | 30% | Return as sophomores: | 75% |
| GPA 3.50-3.74: | 29% | Out-of-state: | 14% |
| GPA 3.0-3.49: | 29% | Live on campus: | 97% |
| | | International: | 2% |

**Basis for selection.** Rank in top half of class and/or 960 SAT (exclusive of Writing) or 20 ACT required. Audition required for music and theater programs. **Homeschooled:** Transcript of courses and grades required.

**High school preparation.** College-preparatory program required. 12 units recommended. Recommended units include English 4, mathematics 3, science 3 (laboratory 2) and foreign language 2.

**2009-2010 Annual costs.** Tuition/fees: $20,290. Room/board: $7,510. Books/supplies: $1,200. Personal expenses: $1,860.

**2008-2009 Financial aid. Need-based:** 832 full-time freshmen applied for aid; 630 were judged to have need; 629 of these received aid. Average need met was 73%. Average scholarship/grant was $10,654; average loan $3,287. 67% of total undergraduate aid awarded as scholarships/grants, 33% as loans/jobs. **Non-need-based:** Awarded to 2,720 full-time undergraduates, including 771 freshmen. Scholarships awarded for academics, art, athletics, leadership, minority status, music/drama, religious affiliation, state residency. **Additional information:** Early estimate service available.

**Application procedures. Admission:** Closing date 2/15 (postmark date). $50 fee, may be waived for applicants with need. Admission notification on a rolling basis beginning on or about 2/15. Must reply by 5/1. Admitted students should confirm the offer by submitting $250 enrollment deposit (non-refundable after May 1), along with letter of intent to the Admissions Office. Deposit is pre-payment toward total bill. **Financial aid:** Priority date 3/1; no closing date. FAFSA, institutional form required. Applicants notified on a rolling basis starting 4/1.

**Academics. Special study options:** Combined bachelor's/graduate degree, cross-registration, distance learning, double major, dual enrollment of high school students, ESL, honors, independent study, internships, student-designed major, study abroad, teacher certification program. **Credit/placement by examination:** AP, CLEP, IB, SAT, ACT, institutional tests. 15 credit hours maximum toward associate degree, 30 toward bachelor's. **Support services:** Pre-admission summer program, reduced course load, remedial instruction, study skills assistance, tutoring, writing center.

**Honors college/program.** Must have high school GPA of 3.75 or rank in top 10 percent of high school class; SAT of 1210 (exclusive of Writing)

or ACT of 27; submit satisfactory resume (achievements, awards, offices, etc.) and honor?s college application essay.

**Majors. Agriculture:** Agribusiness operations, animal sciences. **Biology:** General, biochemistry. **Business:** Accounting, business admin, finance, information resources management, management information systems, marketing. **Communications:** General, advertising, digital media, journalism. **Computer sciences:** Computer science, information technology. **Conservation:** Environmental science. **Education:** Art, biology, elementary, English, history, mathematics, middle, music, physical, science, secondary, social studies, Spanish, special. **Engineering:** Science. **Family/consumer sciences:** Family studies. **Foreign languages:** Spanish. **Health:** Clinical lab science, dietetics, nursing (RN), ophthalmic lab technology, predental, premedicine, prepharmacy, preveterinary, speech pathology. **History:** General. **Interdisciplinary:** Global studies. **Legal studies:** Prelaw. **Math:** General. **Parks/recreation:** Health/fitness, sports admin. **Physical sciences:** Chemistry, physics. **Protective services:** Law enforcement admin. **Psychology:** General. **Public administration:** Social work. **Social sciences:** Political science, sociology. **Theology:** Bible, missionary, preministerial, youth ministry. **Visual/performing arts:** Dramatic, graphic design, interior design, piano/organ, studio arts, voice/opera.

**Most popular majors.** Biology 6%, business/marketing 21%, communications/journalism 9%, education 10%, health sciences 7%, interdisciplinary studies 10%, psychology 6%, visual/performing arts 8%.

**Computing on campus.** 700 workstations in dormitories, library, computer center, student center. Dormitories wired for high-speed internet access and linked to campus network. Commuter students can connect to campus network. Online course registration, online library, helpline, student web hosting, wireless network available.

**Student life. Freshman orientation:** Mandatory, $115 fee. Preregistration for classes offered. Overnight program, held twice in summer; includes assessment testing and registration. **Policies:** Religious observance required. **Housing:** Guaranteed on-campus for freshmen. Single-sex dorms, special housing for disabled, apartments available. **Activities:** Bands, campus ministries, choral groups, dance, drama, international student organizations, literary magazine, music ensembles, Model UN, musical theater, opera, radio station, student government, student newspaper, symphony orchestra, TV station, student association, Seekers of the Word, campus activities team, Hispanos Unidos, College Democrats, African Missions Fellowship, Essence of Ebony, mission student committee, College Republicans.

**Athletics.** NCAA. **Intercollegiate:** Baseball M, basketball, cross-country, football (tackle) M, golf M, soccer W, softball W, tennis, track and field, volleyball W. **Intramural:** Badminton, basketball, bowling, cross-country, football (non-tackle), racquetball, soccer, softball, table tennis, tennis, track and field, volleyball, water polo M. **Team name:** Wildcats.

**Student services.** Adult student services, alcohol/substance abuse counseling, chaplain/spiritual director, career counseling, student employment services, financial aid counseling, health services, minority student services, personal counseling, placement for graduates, veterans' counselor. **Physically disabled:** Services for visually, speech, hearing impaired.

**Contact.** E-mail: info@admissions.acu.edu
Phone: (325) 674-2650 Toll-free number: (800) 460-6228 ext. 2650
Fax: (325) 674-2130
Mark Lavender, Director of Admissions, Abilene Christian University, ACU Box 29000, Abilene, TX 79699

## Amberton University
**Garland, Texas**
www.amberton.edu

**CB code: 6140**

- Private 4-year university affiliated with nondenominational tradition
- Commuter campus in small city
- 389 degree-seeking undergraduates: 43% part-time, 60% women, 27% African American, 3% Asian American, 6% Hispanic American
- 1,144 degree-seeking graduate students

**General.** Founded in 1971. Regionally accredited. Upper level and graduate institution designed for adult students. Must have previous college and be over 21 years old to attend. **Degrees:** 106 bachelor's awarded; master's offered. **Location:** 12 miles from downtown Dallas. **Calendar:** Four 10-week sessions. Extensive summer session. **Full-time faculty:** 15 total; 93% have terminal degrees. **Part-time faculty:** 60 total; 92% have terminal degrees.

**Basis for selection.** All students required to have previously completed college work. No first-time freshmen. Must be at least 21 years of age.

**2009-2010 Annual costs.** Tuition/fees: $6,750. Books/supplies: $500.

**Application procedures. Admission:** No deadline. No application fee. Application must be submitted on paper. Admission notification on a rolling basis. **Financial aid:** No deadline.

**Academics. Special study options:** Distance learning, independent study, weekend college. **Credit/placement by examination:** CLEP. 30 credit hours maximum toward bachelor's degree.

**Majors. Business:** General, accounting, business admin. **Liberal arts:** Arts/sciences.

**Most popular majors.** Business/marketing 90%, liberal arts 10%.

**Computing on campus.** 25 workstations in library, computer center. Online library available.

**Student services.** Adult student services, career counseling, personal counseling, placement for graduates, veterans' counselor.

**Contact.** E-mail: advisor@amberton.edu
Phone: (972) 279-6511 Fax: (972) 279-9773
Don Hebbard, Academic Dean, Amberton University, 1700 Eastgate Drive, Garland, TX 75041-5595

## Angelo State University
**San Angelo, Texas**        **CB member**
**www.angelo.edu**        **CB code: 6644**

- Public 4-year university
- Residential campus in small city
- 5,725 degree-seeking undergraduates: 15% part-time, 55% women, 8% African American, 2% Asian American, 25% Hispanic American, 1% Native American, 1% international
- 511 degree-seeking graduate students
- 92% of applicants admitted
- SAT or ACT (ACT writing optional) required
- 41% graduate within 6 years; 1% enter graduate study

**General.** Founded in 1928. Regionally accredited. **Degrees:** 791 bachelor's, 100 associate awarded; master's, professional offered. **ROTC:** Air Force. **Location:** 200 miles from Austin, 250 miles from Dallas. **Calendar:** Semester, extensive summer session. **Full-time faculty:** 246 total; 76% have terminal degrees, 17% minority, 44% women. **Part-time faculty:** 86 total; 20% have terminal degrees, 7% minority, 44% women. **Class size:** 29% < 20, 54% 20-39, 8% 40-49, 8% 50-99, less than 1% >100. **Special facilities:** Planetarium, agricultural research center, food safety and product development lab, 6,000-acre farm/ranch, natural history collections.

**Freshman class profile.** 2,920 applied, 2,674 admitted, 1,474 enrolled.

| Mid 50% test scores | | End year in good standing: | 70% |
|---|---|---|---|
| SAT critical reading: | 410-520 | Return as sophomores: | 59% |
| SAT math: | 430-540 | Out-of-state: | 1% |
| SAT writing: | 400-510 | Live on campus: | 74% |
| ACT composite: | 18-23 | Fraternities: | 3% |
| Rank in top quarter: | 31% | Sororities: | 4% |
| Rank in top tenth: | 15% | | |

**Basis for selection.** Should rank in the top half of high school class, have minimum 16 ACT or 760 SAT (exclusive of Writing). If ranked in third quartile, must have 23 ACT or 1030 SAT. If ranked in fourth quartile, must have 30 ACT or 1270 SAT. **Homeschooled:** Transcript of courses and grades required. ASU recommends that students should have completed the equivalent of a high school curriculum.

**High school preparation.** College-preparatory program recommended. 23 units recommended. Recommended units include English 4, mathematics 3, social studies 3, science 3, foreign language 2 and computer science 1.

**2010-2011 Annual costs.** Tuition/fees (projected): $6,138; $14,568 out-of-state. Room/board: $7,256. Books/supplies: $1,000.

**2008-2009 Financial aid. Need-based:** 1,209 full-time freshmen applied for aid; 925 were judged to have need; 912 of these received aid. Average need met was 46%. Average scholarship/grant was $4,966; average loan $2,891. 59% of total undergraduate aid awarded as scholarships/grants, 41% as loans/jobs. **Non-need-based:** Awarded to 1,951 full-time undergraduates, including 710 freshmen. Scholarships awarded for academics, art, athletics, leadership, music/drama, ROTC, state residency.

**Application procedures. Admission:** No deadline. $25 fee, may be waived for applicants with need. Admission notification on a rolling basis.

**Financial aid:** Priority date 4/1; no closing date. FAFSA required. Applicants notified on a rolling basis starting 4/1; must reply within 4 week(s) of notification.

**Academics. Special study options:** Combined bachelor's/graduate degree, distance learning, double major, dual enrollment of high school students, honors, independent study, internships, study abroad, teacher certification program. 4+1 programs in various fields with Texas Tech University allowing recipients of ASU bachelor's degree to earn a master's degree in related field in one year at TTU. 3-2 engineering-physics and 3-2 agriculture-education programs with Texas A&M and University of Texas El Paso. **Credit/placement by examination:** CLEP, SAT, ACT, institutional tests. Unlimited credits by examination provided student meets hours required in residence. **Support services:** Learning center, reduced course load, remedial instruction, tutoring, writing center.

**Honors college/program.** Students must have 3.25 GPA in coursework done at ASU. If enrolling from high school, must be in the top 10% of graduating class and have 27 ACT or 1200 (exclusive of Writing) SAT. Some classes are strictly honors only, but normal classes can be given honors credit by contract: student meets with professor before semester and discusses additional work necessary to qualify for honors credit.

**Majors. Agriculture:** Animal husbandry, animal sciences. **Biology:** General, biochemistry, ecology, evolutionary. **Business:** Accounting, business admin, finance, international, management information systems, marketing, real estate. **Communications:** General, journalism. **Computer sciences:** General. **Conservation:** Management/policy. **Family/consumer sciences:** Child development. **Foreign languages:** French, German, Spanish. **Health:** Athletic training, clinical lab science, nursing (RN). **History:** General. **Math:** General. **Parks/recreation:** Health/fitness. **Physical sciences:** Applied physics, chemistry, physics. **Protective services:** Criminal justice. **Psychology:** General. **Social sciences:** Political science, sociology. **Visual/performing arts:** Art, dramatic, studio arts.

**Most popular majors.** Agriculture 6%, business/marketing 23%, communications/journalism 7%, health sciences 6%, interdisciplinary studies 12%, parks/recreation 13%, psychology 7%.

**Computing on campus.** 700 workstations in dormitories, library, computer center, student center. Dormitories wired for high-speed internet access and linked to campus network. Commuter students can connect to campus network. Online course registration, online library, helpline, student web hosting, wireless network available.

**Student life. Freshman orientation:** Available, $25 fee. Preregistration for classes offered. Sessions offered several times during the summer. **Policies:** Single undergraduates with 12-60 semester credit hours of college-level work who do not live with parents are required to reside in University-owned housing. **Housing:** Coed dorms, single-sex dorms, special housing for disabled, apartments, wellness housing available. $200 nonrefundable deposit. **Activities:** Bands, campus ministries, choral groups, dance, drama, film society, international student organizations, literary magazine, music ensembles, musical theater, radio station, student government, student newspaper, TV station, Association of Mexican-American Students, Baptist student union, Black Organization Striving for Success, Block and Bridle, College Republicans, Newman Center, Nontraditional Student Organization, residence hall association, Young Democrats.

**Athletics.** NCAA. **Intercollegiate:** Baseball M, basketball, cross-country, football (tackle) M, golf W, soccer W, softball W, track and field, volleyball W. **Intramural:** Badminton, basketball, football (non-tackle), golf, racquetball, soccer, softball, swimming, table tennis, tennis, track and field, volleyball. **Team name:** Rams and Rambelles.

**Student services.** Adult student services, alcohol/substance abuse counseling, chaplain/spiritual director, career counseling, services for economically disadvantaged, student employment services, financial aid counseling, health services, minority student services, personal counseling, placement for graduates, veterans' counselor. **Physically disabled:** Services for visually, hearing impaired.

**Contact.** E-mail: admissions@angelo.edu
Phone: (325) 942-2185 Toll-free number: (800) 946-8627
Fax: (325) 942-2078
Steven Klein, Associate Vice President for Enrollment Management, Angelo State University, ASU Station #11014, San Angelo, TX 76909-1014

## Argosy University: Dallas
**Farmers Branch, Texas**
**www.argosy.edu/dallas**

- For-profit 4-year university
- Very large city
- 88 degree-seeking undergraduates

**General.** Regionally accredited. **Degrees:** 7 bachelor's awarded; master's, doctoral, professional offered. **Calendar:** Continuous. **Full-time faculty:** 16 total. **Part-time faculty:** 34 total.

**Freshman class profile.** 23 enrolled.

**Basis for selection.** Open admission.

**Academics. Credit/placement by examination:** CLEP.

**Majors. Business:** Business admin. **Liberal arts:** Arts/sciences. **Protective services:** Police science. **Psychology:** General.

**Contact.** E-mail: audadmis@argosy.edu
Phone: (214) 459-2237
Argosy University: Dallas, 5001 Lyndon B. Johnson Freeway, Heritage Square, Farmers Branch, TX 75244

## Arlington Baptist College
### Arlington, Texas
www.abconline.edu                    CB code: 6039

- Private 4-year Bible and teachers college affiliated with Baptist faith
- Commuter campus in very large city
- 153 degree-seeking undergraduates: 21% part-time, 48% women, 8% African American, 2% Asian American, 6% Hispanic American, 3% international
- 4 degree-seeking graduate students
- Application essay required

**General.** Founded in 1939. Accredited by ABHE. **Degrees:** 20 bachelor's awarded. **Location:** 10 miles from Fort Worth, 25 miles from Dallas. **Calendar:** Semester, limited summer session. **Full-time faculty:** 10 total; 10% have terminal degrees, 10% minority, 40% women. **Part-time faculty:** 10 total; 20% have terminal degrees, 10% women. **Class size:** 88% < 20, 10% 20-39, 2% 40-49.

**Freshman class profile.** 29 applied, 29 admitted, 21 enrolled.

| | | | |
|---|---|---|---|
| GPA 3.75 or higher: | 36% | End year in good standing: | 60% |
| GPA 3.0-3.49: | 24% | Return as sophomores: | 60% |
| GPA 2.0-2.99: | 36% | Out-of-state: | 17% |
| Rank in top quarter: | 38% | Live on campus: | 57% |
| Rank in top tenth: | 19% | International: | 4% |

**Basis for selection.** Open admission. Interview recommended for all; audition required for music. **Homeschooled:** Transcript of courses and grades, interview required. Advised to obtain GED.

**High school preparation.** 16 units recommended. Recommended units include English 3, mathematics 2, social studies 3, history 3 and science 1.

**2009-2010 Annual costs.** Tuition/fees: $7,340. Room/board: $4,200. Books/supplies: $750. Personal expenses: $720.

**2008-2009 Financial aid.** All financial aid based on need.

**Application procedures. Admission:** Priority date 8/1; no deadline. $15 fee, may be waived for applicants with need. Admission notification on a rolling basis. **Financial aid:** Closing date 8/15. FAFSA required. Applicants notified on a rolling basis.

**Academics. Special study options:** Distance learning, double major, dual enrollment of high school students, external degree, teacher certification program. **Credit/placement by examination:** AP, CLEP, institutional tests. 30 credit hours maximum toward bachelor's degree. **Support services:** Reduced course load, remedial instruction.

**Majors. Education:** General, elementary, English, kindergarten/preschool, middle, multi-level teacher, music, science, secondary, social studies. **Philosophy/religion:** Religion. **Psychology:** Counseling. **Theology:** Bible, missionary, pastoral counseling, religious ed, sacred music, youth ministry.

**Most popular majors.** Education 25%, theological studies 30%.

**Computing on campus.** 25 workstations in library, computer center. Wireless network available.

**Student life. Freshman orientation:** Mandatory. Preregistration for classes offered. Orientation includes placement testing. **Policies:** Religious observance required. **Housing:** Guaranteed on-campus for freshmen. Single-sex dorms, wellness housing available. $25 nonrefundable deposit. **Activities:** Campus ministries, choral groups, music ensembles, student government,

student missionary association, student preachers' fellowship, youth majors organization.

**Athletics. Intercollegiate:** Basketball M, volleyball W. **Team name:** Patriots.

**Student services.** Chaplain/spiritual director, career counseling, student employment services, financial aid counseling, personal counseling, placement for graduates, veterans' counselor.

**Contact.** E-mail: jtaylor@abconline.org
Phone: (817) 461-8741 ext. 105 Fax: (817) 274-1138
Janie Taylor, Registrar, Arlington Baptist College, 3001 West Division, Arlington, TX 76012

## Art Institute of Dallas
### Dallas, Texas
www.aid.edu                    CB code: 2680

- For-profit 4-year visual arts college
- Very large city

**General.** Regionally accredited. **Calendar:** Quarter.

**Annual costs/financial aid.** Total program costs vary by program: bachelor's programs $92,000-$98,000; associate programs $56,000-$59,000. Personal expenses: $2,880. Need-based financial aid available for full-time students.

**Contact.** Phone: (214) 692-8080
Director of Admissions, Two North Park, 8080 Park Lane, Dallas, TX 75231

## Art Institute of Houston
### Houston, Texas
www.artinstitutes.edu/houston                    CB code: 8271

- For-profit 4-year culinary school and visual arts college
- Very large city
- 2,250 degree-seeking undergraduates

**General.** Regionally accredited. **Degrees:** 200 bachelor's, 152 associate awarded. **Calendar:** Quarter. **Full-time faculty:** 61 total. **Part-time faculty:** 41 total.

**Basis for selection.** Proof of graduation from accredited high school, a Graduate Equivalency Diploma (GED), or foreign equivalent required for admissions. Applicants to Media Arts & Animation program must submit portfolio for approval by faculty committee. SAT or ACT recommended. Observes TASP guidelines. ASSET or COMPASS testing may be required. Remediation may be required if test scores fall below required ranges; some remediation available on campus.

**2009-2010 Annual costs.** Tuition for academic year based on 16 credit hours per quarter, $22,752.

**Application procedures. Admission:** No deadline. $50 fee. Admission notification on a rolling basis. **Financial aid:** Priority date 3/1; no closing date. FAFSA, institutional form required.

**Academics. Special study options:** Distance learning, honors, internships, study abroad. **Credit/placement by examination:** CLEP.

**Majors. Visual/performing arts:** Graphic design, interior design.

**Contact.** E-mail: aihadm@aii.edu
Phone: (713) 623-2040 Toll-free number: (800) 275-4244
Fax: (713) 966-2797
Justin Pond, Senior Director of Admissions, Art Institute of Houston, 1900 Yorktown, Houston, TX 77056-4115

## Austin College
### Sherman, Texas
www.austincollege.edu          CB member
                               CB code: 6016

- Private 4-year liberal arts and teachers college affiliated with Presbyterian Church (USA)
- Residential campus in small city

- 1,328 degree-seeking undergraduates: 54% women, 3% African American, 15% Asian American, 10% Hispanic American, 1% Native American, 2% international
- 26 degree-seeking graduate students
- 80% of applicants admitted
- SAT or ACT with writing, application essay required
- 74% graduate within 6 years; 44% enter graduate study

**General.** Founded in 1849. Regionally accredited. **Degrees:** 306 bachelor's awarded; master's offered. **Location:** 60 miles from Dallas. **Calendar:** 4-1-4, limited summer session. **Full-time faculty:** 91 total; 93% have terminal degrees, 8% minority, 31% women. **Part-time faculty:** 28 total; 21% have terminal degrees, 18% minority, 46% women. **Class size:** 59% < 20, 37% 20-39, less than 1% 40-49, 3% 50-99. **Special facilities:** Environmental research areas totaling 174 acres, lake recreation area, tissue culture facility for study of cellular molecular interactions of eukaryotic cells, high performance numeric and graphics computing facility for advanced scientific computing and 3-D graphics.

**Freshman class profile.** 1,750 applied, 1,394 admitted, 413 enrolled.

| Mid 50% test scores | | Rank in top quarter: | 70% |
|---|---|---|---|
| SAT critical reading: | 560-680 | Rank in top tenth: | 41% |
| SAT math: | 570-670 | End year in good standing: | 93% |
| SAT writing: | 540-650 | Return as sophomores: | 86% |
| ACT composite: | 24-28 | Out-of-state: | 8% |
| GPA 3.75 or higher: | 29% | Live on campus: | 97% |
| GPA 3.50-3.74: | 26% | International: | 1% |
| GPA 3.0-3.49: | 33% | Fraternities: | 24% |
| GPA 2.0-2.99: | 12% | Sororities: | 21% |

**Basis for selection.** Academic transcript record, test scores, recommendations, extracurricular involvement, essay important. Interview considered. Interview recommended for all; audition recommended for music, theater (required for scholarship consideration); portfolio recommended for art (required for scholarship consideration). **Homeschooled:** Transcript of courses and grades required.

**High school preparation.** College-preparatory program recommended. Required and recommended units include English 4, mathematics 3-4, social studies 2-3, science 3-4 (laboratory 2-3), foreign language 2-3, visual/performing arts 1-2 and academic electives 1.

**2010-2011 Annual costs.** Tuition/fees: $29,235. Room/board: $9,549. Books/supplies: $1,200. Personal expenses: $800.

**2009-2010 Financial aid. Need-based:** 341 full-time freshmen applied for aid; 282 were judged to have need; 282 of these received aid. Average need met was 95%. Average scholarship/grant was $21,036; average loan $4,074. 72% of total undergraduate aid awarded as scholarships/grants, 28% as loans/jobs. **Non-need-based:** Awarded to 687 full-time undergraduates, including 230 freshmen. Scholarships awarded for academics, alumni affiliation, art, leadership, music/drama, religious affiliation, state residency.

**Application procedures. Admission:** Priority date 1/15; deadline 5/1 (postmark date). $35 fee, may be waived for applicants with need, free for online applicants. Admission notification on a rolling basis beginning on or about 12/15. Must reply by 5/1. **Financial aid:** Priority date 4/1; no closing date. FAFSA required. Applicants notified on a rolling basis starting 3/1; must reply by 5/1.

**Academics. Special study options:** Double major, exchange student, honors, independent study, internships, liberal arts/career combination, student-designed major, study abroad, teacher certification program, Washington semester. 3-2 dual degree engineering program with University of Texas Dallas, Washington University in St. Louis, Columbia University, Texas A&M University. **Credit/placement by examination:** AP, CLEP, IB, institutional tests. **Support services:** Learning center, study skills assistance, tutoring.

**Majors. Area/ethnic studies:** American, Latin American. **Biology:** General, biochemistry. **Business:** General. **Communications:** General. **Computer sciences:** Computer science. **Conservation:** Environmental studies. **Foreign languages:** Classics, French, German, Latin, Spanish. **History:** General. **Math:** General. **Philosophy/religion:** Philosophy, religion. **Physical sciences:** Chemistry, physics. **Psychology:** General. **Social sciences:** Economics, international economics, international relations, political science, sociology. **Visual/performing arts:** Art.

**Most popular majors.** Biology 8%, business/marketing 13%, foreign language 8%, interdisciplinary studies 8%, psychology 15%, social sciences 20%.

**Computing on campus.** 160 workstations in dormitories, library, computer center, student center. Dormitories wired for high-speed internet access and linked to campus network. Commuter students can connect to campus network. Online library, helpline, student web hosting, wireless network available.

**Student life. Freshman orientation:** Mandatory. Preregistration for classes offered. Held the weekend prior to the first day of classes. **Housing:** Guaranteed on-campus for freshmen. Coed dorms, single-sex dorms, apartments available. Language emphasis residence, suite-style housing for upper-level students with private bedroom, common area, kitchenette. **Activities:** Bands, campus ministries, choral groups, dance, drama, international student organizations, literary magazine, music ensembles, Model UN, musical theater, student government, student newspaper, symphony orchestra, Alpha Phi Omega, Intervarsity Christian Fellowship, Black Expressions, Young Democrats, Service Station, Los Amigos, Habitat for Humanity, Activators, Amnesty International.

**Athletics.** NCAA. **Intercollegiate:** Baseball M, basketball, football (tackle) M, soccer, softball W, swimming, tennis, volleyball W. **Intramural:** Basketball, football (non-tackle), soccer, softball, volleyball. **Team name:** Roos.

**Student services.** Chaplain/spiritual director, career counseling, financial aid counseling, health services, personal counseling.

**Contact.** E-mail: admission@austincollege.edu
Phone: (903) 813-3000 Toll-free number: (800) 526-4276
Fax: (903) 813-3198
Nan Davis, Vice President for Institutional Enrollment, Austin College, 900 North Grand Avenue, Suite 6N, Sherman, TX 75090-4400

## Austin Graduate School of Theology
**Austin, Texas**
www.austingrad.edu                                   CB code: 4969

- Private two-year upper-division Bible and seminary college affiliated with Church of Christ
- Commuter campus in very large city
- Application essay required

**General.** Founded in 1917. Regionally accredited. Highly diverse ethnic and socioeconomic student body grounded in Christian faith traditions. **Degrees:** 6 bachelor's awarded; master's offered. **Location:** 80 miles from San Antonio, 150 miles from Houston. **Calendar:** Semester, limited summer session. **Full-time faculty:** 4 total; 100% have terminal degrees. **Part-time faculty:** 7 total; 71% have terminal degrees, 14% minority. **Class size:** 90% < 20, 10% 20-39.

**Student profile.** 26 degree-seeking undergraduates, 30 degree-seeking graduate students.

| Women: | 27% | Hispanic American: | 19% |
|---|---|---|---|
| African American: | 27% | Part-time: | 85% |
| Asian American: | 4% | | |

**Basis for selection.** Open admission. College transcript, application essay required. Transcript, GPA, recommendations required. High school transcript, test scores required for applicants with fewer than 35 hours. Transfer accepted as sophomores, juniors, seniors.

**2009-2010 Annual costs.** Tuition/fees: $8,250. Books/supplies: $500. Personal expenses: $1,963.

**Financial aid. Non-need-based:** Scholarships awarded for academics, leadership. **Additional information:** Generous scholarships for students taking at least 12 hours. Federal work study program available. Institutional work study program (need-based) available.

**Application procedures. Admission:** Priority date 6/1. No application fee. Application must be submitted on paper. **Financial aid:** No deadline. FAFSA, institutional form required.

**Academics. Special study options:** Dual enrollment of high school students, liberal arts/career combination. Liberal arts/career combination program in religion; combined bachelor's/graduate program in ministry. **Credit/placement by examination:** AP, CLEP. 18 credit hours maximum toward bachelor's degree.

**Majors. Theology:** Bible, theology.

**Computing on campus.** 8 workstations in library, computer center, student center. Online library available.

**Student life. Policies:** Religious observance required. **Activities:** Student government.

**Student services.** Financial aid counseling, personal counseling.

**Contact.** E-mail: admissions@austingrad.edu
Phone: (512) 476-2772 ext. 103 Toll-free number: (866) 287-4723
Fax: (512) 476-3919
Celeste Scarborough, Registrar, Austin Graduate School of Theology, 7640 Guadalupe Street, Austin, TX 78752-1333

## Baptist Missionary Association Theological Seminary
**Jacksonville, Texas**
www.bmats.edu                                        CB code: 7042

- Private 4-year Bible and seminary college affiliated with Baptist faith
- Commuter campus in large town
- 125 degree-seeking undergraduates

**General.** Founded in 1955. Regionally accredited. **Degrees:** 8 bachelor's, 4 associate awarded; master's offered. **Location:** 120 miles from Dallas. **Calendar:** Semester, limited summer session. **Full-time faculty:** 6 total. **Part-time faculty:** 4 total; 100% have terminal degrees.

**Freshman class profile.** 7 applied, 6 admitted, 6 enrolled.

**Basis for selection.** Open admission, but selective for some programs. Essay or personal statement very important. Religious commitment, interview, recommendations, school and community activities important.

**2009-2010 Annual costs.** Tuition/fees: $3,310. Room/board: $2,400.

**Application procedures. Admission:** No deadline. $35 fee.

**Academics. Special study options:** Internships. **Credit/placement by examination:** CLEP.

**Majors. Philosophy/religion:** Religion. **Theology:** Theology.

**Computing on campus.** 2 workstations in library.

**Student life. Activities:** Student government.

**Student services.** Career counseling, personal counseling.

**Contact.** E-mail: bmatsem@bmats.edu
Phone: (903) 586-2501 Fax: (903) 586-0378
Philip Attebery, Dean/Registrar, Baptist Missionary Association Theological Seminary, 1530 East Pine Street, Jacksonville, TX 75766

## Baptist University of the Americas
**San Antonio, Texas**
www.bua.edu

- Private 4-year university and Bible college affiliated with Baptist faith
- Commuter campus in very large city
- 204 degree-seeking undergraduates

**General.** Accredited by ABHE. Baptist University of the Americas trains cross-culturally students in Biblical/Theological Studies and Ministry Studies, at a higher education academic level, from a Hispanic context. **Degrees:** 27 bachelor's, 5 associate awarded. **Calendar:** Semester, limited summer session. **Full-time faculty:** 7 total. **Part-time faculty:** 3 total.

**Freshman class profile.** 54 applied, 24 admitted, 23 enrolled.

**Basis for selection.** Open admission. Observes THEA requirements.

**2009-2010 Annual costs.** Tuition/fees: $5,700. Room/board: $2,880. Books/supplies: $1,200. Personal expenses: $1,925.

**Application procedures. Admission:** No deadline. $25 fee. **Financial aid:** No deadline.

**Academics. Credit/placement by examination:** CLEP.

**Majors. Business:** Business admin. **Foreign languages:** Spanish. **Theology:** Bible, theology.

**Student life. Freshman orientation:** Available, $25 fee. **Housing:** $200 deposit. **Activities:** Campus ministries, drama, international student organizations.

**Contact.** E-mail: mranjel@bua.edu
Phone: (210) 924-4338
Mary Ranjel, Director of Admissions, Baptist University of the Americas, 8019 South Pan Am Expressway, San Antonio, TX 78224

## Baylor University
**Waco, Texas**                                      CB member
www.baylor.edu                                       CB code: 6032

- Private 4-year university affiliated with Baptist faith
- Residential campus in small city
- 12,101 degree-seeking undergraduates: 2% part-time, 59% women, 8% African American, 7% Asian American, 11% Hispanic American, 1% Native American, 2% international
- 2,456 degree-seeking graduate students
- 50% of applicants admitted
- SAT or ACT with writing, application essay required
- 70% graduate within 6 years

**General.** Founded in 1845. Regionally accredited. **Degrees:** 2,626 bachelor's awarded; master's, doctoral, professional offered. **ROTC:** Army, Air Force. **Location:** 100 miles from Dallas-Fort Worth, 100 miles from Austin. **Calendar:** Semester, extensive summer session. **Full-time faculty:** 859 total; 81% have terminal degrees, 11% minority, 38% women. **Part-time faculty:** 287 total; 8% minority, 50% women. **Class size:** 46% < 20, 37% 20-39, 8% 40-49, 7% 50-99, 2% >100. **Special facilities:** Museum of natural science, Texas collection library, Armstrong Browning library.

**Freshman class profile.** 31,440 applied, 15,699 admitted, 3,098 enrolled.

| Mid 50% test scores | | Rank in top tenth: | 40% |
|---|---|---|---|
| SAT critical reading: | 530-640 | End year in good standing: | 89% |
| SAT math: | 550-650 | Return as sophomores: | 84% |
| SAT writing: | 510-620 | Out-of-state: | 19% |
| ACT composite: | 23-29 | Live on campus: | 98% |
| Rank in top quarter: | 73% | International: | 2% |

**Basis for selection.** Competitive high school performance and competitive scores on ACT or SAT most important; above-average achievement and potential expected. Audition required for music and theater programs; interview recommended for marginal achievers; portfolio recommended for art. **Homeschooled:** Transcript of courses and grades required. If applicant graduated from home-school not officially recognized by state in which school is located, applicant must be 17 before first day of class unless GED certificate submitted prior to registration.

**High school preparation.** College-preparatory program required. Required units include English 4, mathematics 3, social studies 1, history 1, science 3 (laboratory 2) and foreign language 2.

**2010-2011 Annual costs.** Tuition/fees: $29,724. Cited cost includes room rate for community bath and 16-meal plan. Other room types are higher. Room/board: $8,331. Books/supplies: $1,398. Personal expenses: $1,890.

**2009-2010 Financial aid. Need-based:** 2,410 full-time freshmen applied for aid; 1,990 were judged to have need; 1,988 of these received aid. Average need met was 69%. Average scholarship/grant was $16,768; average loan $2,753. 62% of total undergraduate aid awarded as scholarships/grants, 38% as loans/jobs. **Non-need-based:** Awarded to 9,519 full-time undergraduates, including 2,903 freshmen. Scholarships awarded for academics, art, athletics, job skills, leadership, music/drama, ROTC.

**Application procedures. Admission:** No deadline. $50 fee, may be waived for applicants with need. Application must be submitted online. Must reply by May 1 or within 2 week(s) if notified thereafter. Notification of admission decision by 1/15 for 11/1 applications and by 3/15 for 2/15 applications; after 3/15 on space available basis. $300 enrollment deposit required by May 1. **Financial aid:** Priority date 1/15, closing date 8/15. FAFSA required. Applicants notified on a rolling basis starting 3/1; must reply by 5/1 or within 2 week(s) of notification.

**Academics.** Online support (website advising resources and tutoring)available. **Special study options:** Accelerated study, combined bachelor's/graduate degree, double major, honors, internships, student-designed major, study abroad, teacher certification program. Architecture program with Washington University, forestry with Duke University. **Credit/placement by examination:** AP, CLEP, IB, institutional tests. 60 credit hours maximum toward bachelor's degree. **Support services:** Learning center, pre-admission summer program, reduced course load, remedial instruction, study skills assistance, tutoring, writing center.

**Honors college/program.** Baylor Interdisciplinary Core: all regularly admitted students may apply, phone interview required; Honors Program: average SAT score for the last five classes 1350 (exclusive of Writing); University Scholars: no minimum SAT, current scores average above 1400 (exclusive of Writing); Great Texts: no specific requirements, students who declare a major in Great Texts are considered Honors College participants.

**Majors. Architecture:** Architecture. **Area/ethnic studies:** American, Asian, Latin American, Slavic. **Biology:** General, biochemistry, bioinformatics, exercise physiology. **Business:** General, accounting, business admin, entrepreneurial studies, fashion, finance, financial planning, human resources, insurance, international, logistics, management information systems, managerial economics, marketing, real estate, sales/distribution. **Communications:** General, digital media, journalism. **Computer sciences:** Computer science, information technology. **Conservation:** Environmental science, environmental studies, forestry. **Education:** General, early childhood, elementary, English, health occupations, mathematics, music, physical, science, social studies, special. **Engineering:** General, electrical, mechanical. **Family/consumer sciences:** General, family studies, human nutrition. **Foreign languages:** Ancient Greek, Biblical, classics, French, German, Latin, linguistics, Russian, Spanish. **Health:** Athletic training, clinical lab science, communication disorders, nursing (RN), predental, premedicine, prenursing. **History:** General. **Interdisciplinary:** Museum, neuroscience. **Liberal arts:** Humanities. **Math:** General, applied, statistics. **Parks/recreation:** Health/fitness. **Philosophy/religion:** Philosophy, religion. **Physical sciences:** Astronomy, chemistry, geology, geophysics, physics. **Psychology:** General. **Public administration:** General, social work. **Social sciences:** Anthropology, geography, international relations, political science, sociology. **Theology:** Sacred music. **Transportation:** Airline/commercial pilot. **Visual/performing arts:** Acting, art history/conservation, dramatic, fashion design, interior design, music history, music pedagogy, music performance, music theory/composition, studio arts, theater design. **Other:** Media business, Recreation.

**Most popular majors.** Biology 11%, business/marketing 22%, communications/journalism 10%, education 6%, health sciences 9%, psychology 6%, social sciences 8%.

**Computing on campus.** 1,656 workstations in dormitories, library, computer center, student center. Dormitories wired for high-speed internet access and linked to campus network. Commuter students can connect to campus network. Online course registration, online library, helpline, repair service, student web hosting, wireless network available.

**Student life. Freshman orientation:** Mandatory. Preregistration for classes offered. 10 2-day sessions primarily in June. **Policies:** All students required to participate in chapel-forum for 2 semesters. **Housing:** Guaranteed on-campus for freshmen. Single-sex dorms, special housing for disabled, apartments, wellness housing available. **Activities:** Bands, campus ministries, choral groups, dance, drama, film society, international student organizations, literary magazine, music ensembles, Model UN, musical theater, opera, radio station, student government, student newspaper, symphony orchestra, TV station, Campus Crusade for Christ, College Republicans, Young Democrats, association of black students, Hispanic student association, Asian student association, Habitat for Humanity, Alpha Phi Omega, Baylor Chamber of Commerce.

**Athletics.** NCAA. **Intercollegiate:** Baseball M, basketball, cheerleading M, cross-country, equestrian W, football (tackle) M, golf, soccer W, softball W, tennis, track and field, volleyball W. **Intramural:** Basketball, bowling, cross-country, equestrian, football (non-tackle), golf, lacrosse, racquetball, soccer, softball, swimming, table tennis, tennis, track and field, volleyball, weight lifting. **Team name:** Bears.

**Student services.** Chaplain/spiritual director, career counseling, student employment services, financial aid counseling, health services, legal services, personal counseling, placement for graduates. **Physically disabled:** Services for visually, speech, hearing impaired.

**Contact.** E-mail: admissions@baylor.edu
Phone: (254) 710-3435 Toll-free number: (800) 229-5678
Fax: (254) 710-3436
Jennifer Carron, Director of Admissions Services, Baylor University, One Bear Place #97056, Waco, TX 76798-7056

## College of Biblical Studies-Houston
**Houston, Texas**
**www.cbshouston.edu**                    CB code: 3946

▶ Private 4-year Bible college
▶ Commuter campus in very large city
▶ 326 degree-seeking undergraduates

**General.** Accredited by ABHE. Multi-denominational and multi-ethnic Christian Bible college. **Degrees:** 131 bachelor's, 18 associate awarded. **Calendar:** Trimester, limited summer session. **Full-time faculty:** 10 total. **Part-time faculty:** 43 total.

**Basis for selection.** Open admission, but selective for some programs. ASSET testing may be required for associate or baccalaureate level programs. **Homeschooled:** State high school equivalency certificate required.

**2009-2010 Annual costs.** Tuition/fees: $5,520. Books/supplies: $900. Personal expenses: $2,766.

**Application procedures. Admission:** No deadline. $40 fee. Admission notification on a rolling basis. **Financial aid:** No deadline.

**Academics. Special study options:** Accelerated study, dual enrollment of high school students, ESL, independent study. Associate degree in biblical studies taught in Spanish. **Credit/placement by examination:** CLEP, institutional tests. **Support services:** Learning center, remedial instruction.

**Majors. Theology:** Bible, preministerial. **Other:** Organizational leadership.

**Computing on campus.** 14 workstations in library.

**Student life. Freshman orientation:** Mandatory. Preregistration for classes offered. 2 sessions lasting 2 hours held week before classes begin; new students requested to attend 1 session. **Policies:** Religious observance required. **Activities:** Student government.

**Student services.** Adult student services, career counseling, financial aid counseling.

**Contact.** E-mail: cbs@cbshouston.edu
Phone: (713) 785-5995 Fax: (713) 785-5998
Director of Admission, College of Biblical Studies-Houston, 7000 Regency Square Boulevard, #110, Houston, TX 77036-3211

## College of Saint Thomas More
**Fort Worth, Texas**
**www.cstm.edu**                    CB code: 0169

▶ Private 4-year liberal arts college affiliated with Roman Catholic Church
▶ Residential campus in very large city
▶ 30 degree-seeking undergraduates
▶ 60% of applicants admitted
▶ SAT or ACT (ACT writing optional), application essay, interview required

**General.** Regionally accredited. Most classes consist of close reading of the Great Books curriculum with emphasis on reading primary sources. **Degrees:** 8 bachelor's, 2 associate awarded. **ROTC:** Army, Air Force. **Location:** 5 miles from downtown. **Calendar:** Semester, limited summer session. **Full-time faculty:** 5 total. **Part-time faculty:** 4 total. **Class size:** 100% < 20.

**Freshman class profile.** 5 applied, 3 admitted, 3 enrolled.

| Mid 50% test scores | | SAT writing: | 310-620 |
|---|---|---|---|
| SAT critical reading: | 430-770 | Live on campus: | 90% |
| SAT math: | 200-510 | | |

**Basis for selection.** Secondary school record, essay, interview, test scores important; 2 letters of recommendation required. **Homeschooled:** Transcript of courses and grades, interview, letter of recommendation (nonparent) required.

**High school preparation.** College-preparatory program recommended.

**2009-2010 Annual costs.** Tuition/fees: $12,550. Student housing includes use of private kitchen. Room only: $4,050. Books/supplies: $500. Personal expenses: $1,000.

**2008-2009 Financial aid. Non-need-based:** Scholarships awarded for academics.

**Application procedures. Admission:** No deadline. $35 fee. Application must be submitted on paper. Admission notification on a rolling basis. **Financial aid:** Closing date 7/1. FAFSA required. Applicants notified on a rolling basis starting 1/1.

**Academics.** Three inter-term courses that are part of the curriculum are presented in Rome, Greece, and Oxford, England. Rome is offered freshmen year, Greece after the sophomore year, and Oxford in the senior year. **Special study options:** Dual enrollment of high school students, study abroad. **Credit/placement by examination:** CLEP. **Support services:** Remedial instruction, study skills assistance, tutoring, writing center.

**Majors. Liberal arts:** Arts/sciences.

**Computing on campus.** 10 workstations in library, student center. Dormitories wired for high-speed internet access and linked to campus network. Online library, wireless network available.

**Student life. Freshman orientation:** Mandatory. Preregistration for classes offered. **Housing:** Guaranteed on-campus for freshmen. Apartments available. $200 fully refundable deposit. **Activities:** Student government, Chapel of Christ the Teacher, Adoration, Culture Society.

**Student services.** Alcohol/substance abuse counseling, chaplain/spiritual director, career counseling, financial aid counseling, personal counseling.

**Contact.**  E-mail: tcooper@cstm.edu
Phone: (817) 923-8459 Toll-free number: (800) 583-6489
Fax: (817) 924-3206
Travis Cooper, Registrar, College of Saint Thomas More, 3020 Lubbock Avenue, Fort Worth, TX 76109

---

## Concordia University Texas
**Austin, Texas**
www.concordia.edu                          CB code: 6127

- Private 4-year university and liberal arts college affiliated with Lutheran Church - Missouri Synod
- Commuter campus in very large city
- 1,110 degree-seeking undergraduates: 22% part-time, 58% women, 11% African American, 2% Asian American, 18% Hispanic American, 1% Native American
- 1,075 degree-seeking graduate students
- 53% of applicants admitted
- SAT or ACT (ACT writing optional) required
- 37% graduate within 6 years

**General.** Founded in 1926. Regionally accredited. **Degrees:** 235 bachelor's, 10 associate awarded; master's offered. **ROTC:** Army, Air Force. **Calendar:** Semester, extensive summer session. **Full-time faculty:** 55 total; 84% have terminal degrees, 4% minority, 33% women. **Part-time faculty:** 226 total; 56% have terminal degrees, 17% minority, 39% women. **Class size:** 80% < 20, 20% 20-39.

**Freshman class profile.** 1,023 applied, 543 admitted, 222 enrolled.

| Mid 50% test scores | | | |
|---|---|---|---|
| SAT critical reading: | 440-560 | GPA 3.0-3.49: | 35% |
| SAT math: | 450-580 | GPA 2.0-2.99: | 22% |
| SAT writing: | 420-540 | Rank in top quarter: | 50% |
| ACT composite: | 19-24 | Rank in top tenth: | 7% |
| GPA 3.75 or higher: | 24% | Return as sophomores: | 51% |
| GPA 3.50-3.74: | 19% | Out-of-state: | 5% |
| | | Live on campus: | 90% |

**Basis for selection.** School achievement record, test scores, and 2.5 GPA important. Interview recommended for academically weak.

**2009-2010 Annual costs.** Tuition/fees: $21,200. Room/board: $8,000. Books/supplies: $1,200. Personal expenses: $1,195.

**2008-2009 Financial aid. Need-based:** 60 full-time freshmen applied for aid; 47 were judged to have need; 45 of these received aid. Average need met was 89%. Average scholarship/grant was $11,481; average loan $8,926. 62% of total undergraduate aid awarded as scholarships/grants, 38% as loans/jobs. **Non-need-based:** Awarded to 124 full-time undergraduates, including 39 freshmen. Scholarships awarded for academics, alumni affiliation, leadership, music/drama, religious affiliation.

**Application procedures. Admission:** No deadline. $25 fee, may be waived for applicants with need. Admission notification on a rolling basis beginning on or about 9/15. Must reply by May 1 or within 4 week(s) if notified thereafter. Reply by August 15 if dormitory applicant. **Financial aid:** No deadline. FAFSA required. Applicants notified on a rolling basis starting 2/15; must reply within 2 week(s) of notification.

**Academics. Special study options:** Accelerated study, combined bachelor's/graduate degree, double major, independent study, liberal arts/career combination, study abroad, teacher certification program. **Credit/placement by examination:** AP, CLEP, IB, SAT, ACT, institutional tests. 15 credit hours maximum toward associate degree, 30 toward bachelor's. **Support services:** Reduced course load, remedial instruction, tutoring.

**Majors. Biology:** General. **Business:** General, business admin, training/development. **Communications:** General. **Computer sciences:** Computer science. **Conservation:** Environmental studies. **Education:** Elementary, secondary. **Health:** Health care admin. **History:** General. **Legal studies:** Prelaw. **Liberal arts:** Arts/sciences. **Math:** General. **Parks/recreation:** Exercise sciences. **Philosophy/religion:** Religion. **Protective services:** Law enforcement admin. **Social sciences:** General. **Theology:** Religious ed, sacred music. **Visual/performing arts:** Conducting, piano/organ.

**Most popular majors.** Business/marketing 41%, education 12%, parks/recreation 8%, social sciences 12%, theological studies 8%.

**Computing on campus.** 45 workstations in library, computer center. Dormitories wired for high-speed internet access and linked to campus network. Commuter students can connect to campus network. Helpline, student web hosting available.

**Student life. Freshman orientation:** Mandatory. **Housing:** Guaranteed on-campus for freshmen. Coed dorms available. $200 nonrefundable deposit, deadline 7/1. **Activities:** Concert band, campus ministries, choral groups, drama, literary magazine, music ensembles, radio station, student government, student newspaper, Sisters in Christ, Lutheran Student Fellowship, Lutheran Women's Missionary League, Pro Life, College Republicans, Pre-Sem Club (pre-seminary students), Fellowship of Christian Athletes, students active for the environment, writer's guild.

**Athletics.** NCAA. **Intercollegiate:** Baseball M, basketball, cross-country, golf, soccer, softball W, tennis, volleyball W. **Intramural:** Badminton, basketball, bowling, handball, racquetball, softball, table tennis, tennis, volleyball. **Team name:** Tornadoes.

**Student services.** Adult student services, alcohol/substance abuse counseling, chaplain/spiritual director, career counseling, student employment services, financial aid counseling, personal counseling, placement for graduates, veterans' counselor.

**Contact.**  E-mail: admissions@concordia.edu
Phone: (512) 313-4600 Toll-free number: (800) 865-4282
Fax: (512) 313-4269
Kristi Kirk, Associate Director of Admissions, Concordia University Texas, 11400 Concordia University Drive, Austin, TX 78726

---

## Criswell College
**Dallas, Texas**
www.criswell.edu                          CB code: 0794

- Private 4-year Bible and seminary college affiliated with Southern Baptist Convention
- Commuter campus in very large city

**General.** Founded in 1970. Regionally accredited. **Calendar:** Semester.

**Annual costs/financial aid.** Tuition/fees (2009-2010): $6,492. Books/supplies: $600.

**Contact.**  Phone: (214) 818-1305
Academic and Enrollment Services, 4010 Gaston Avenue, Dallas, TX 75246-1537

---

## Dallas Baptist University
**Dallas, Texas**                          CB member
www.dbu.edu                               CB code: 6159

- Private 4-year university affiliated with Baptist faith
- Commuter campus in very large city
- 3,533 degree-seeking undergraduates: 37% part-time, 59% women, 19% African American, 2% Asian American, 9% Hispanic American, 1% Native American, 8% international
- 1,867 degree-seeking graduate students
- 46% of applicants admitted
- SAT or ACT with writing, application essay required
- 47% graduate within 6 years

**General.** Founded in 1898. Regionally accredited. **Degrees:** 806 bachelor's awarded; master's, doctoral offered. **ROTC:** Army, Air Force. **Location:** 13 miles from downtown, 29 miles from Fort Worth. **Calendar:** 4-1-4, extensive summer session. **Full-time faculty:** 123 total; 72% have terminal degrees, 14% minority, 39% women. **Part-time faculty:** 409 total; 33% have terminal degrees, 8% minority, 45% women. **Class size:** 66% < 20, 30% 20-39, 2% 40-49, 2% 50-99, less than 1% >100. **Special facilities:** Corrie ten Boom collection.

**Freshman class profile.** 1,601 applied, 730 admitted, 351 enrolled.

| Mid 50% test scores | | | |
|---|---|---|---|
| SAT critical reading: | 480-640 | GPA 2.0-2.99: | 11% |
| SAT math: | 500-640 | Rank in top quarter: | 39% |
| ACT composite: | 18-22 | Rank in top tenth: | 19% |
| GPA 3.75 or higher: | 35% | Return as sophomores: | 70% |
| GPA 3.50-3.74: | 20% | Out-of-state: | 7% |
| GPA 3.0-3.49: | 34% | Live on campus: | 96% |

**Basis for selection.** All factors considered for admission, including test scores, class rank, essay and GPA. Interview recommended. **Home-schooled:** Transcript of courses and grades required. If student is not in accredited program, GED required.

**High school preparation.** College-preparatory program recommended. 16 units recommended. Recommended units include English 4, mathematics 3, social studies 3, history 2, science 2 and foreign language 2.

**2009-2010 Annual costs.** Tuition/fees: $17,490. Room/board: $5,636. Books/supplies: $1,950. Personal expenses: $1,683.

**2009-2010 Financial aid. Need-based:** 335 full-time freshmen applied for aid; 239 were judged to have need; 238 of these received aid. Average need met was 75%. Average scholarship/grant was $3,384; average loan $3,247. 50% of total undergraduate aid awarded as scholarships/grants, 50% as loans/jobs. **Non-need-based:** Awarded to 1,603 full-time undergraduates, including 324 freshmen. Scholarships awarded for academics, athletics, job skills, leadership, music/drama, religious affiliation.

**Application procedures. Admission:** Priority date 1/15; no deadline. $25 fee. Admission notification on a rolling basis. **Financial aid:** Priority date 3/6, closing date 5/1. FAFSA, institutional form required. Applicants notified on a rolling basis starting 2/1.

**Academics. Special study options:** Accelerated study, combined bachelor's/graduate degree, distance learning, double major, dual enrollment of high school students, ESL, honors, independent study, internships, study abroad, teacher certification program, Washington semester, weekend college. **Credit/placement by examination:** AP, CLEP, IB, SAT, ACT, institutional tests. Credit by examination not counted toward residency hours. Credits recorded on permanent record after student has completed minimum of 12 hours in residence. **Support services:** Learning center, pre-admission summer program, remedial instruction, study skills assistance, tutoring, writing center.

**Majors. Biology:** General. **Business:** General, accounting, business admin, finance, management information systems, managerial economics, marketing. **Communications:** General. **Computer sciences:** General, computer science. **Education:** General, early childhood, elementary, music, physical, science, secondary. **Health:** Health care admin. **History:** General. **Liberal arts:** Arts/sciences. **Math:** General. **Philosophy/religion:** Philosophy. **Protective services:** Criminal justice. **Psychology:** General. **Social sciences:** Political science, sociology. **Theology:** Bible, pastoral counseling, religious ed, sacred music. **Visual/performing arts:** Art, music theory/composition, piano/organ, voice/opera.

**Computing on campus.** 199 workstations in dormitories, library, computer center, student center. Dormitories wired for high-speed internet access and linked to campus network. Commuter students can connect to campus network. Online library, helpline, wireless network available.

**Student life. Freshman orientation:** Available. Preregistration for classes offered. **Policies:** Religious observance required. **Housing:** Single-sex dorms, special housing for disabled, apartments, wellness housing available. $100 fully refundable deposit. **Activities:** Campus ministries, choral groups, dance, drama, international student organizations, music ensembles, musical theater, opera, student government, College Republicans, Spanish-speaking students association, Chinese student association, Ministerial Alliance, Japanese student association, Korean student association.

**Athletics.** NCAA, NCCAA. **Intercollegiate:** Baseball M, cross-country, golf, soccer, tennis, track and field, volleyball W. **Intramural:** Badminton, basketball, football (non-tackle), golf M, softball, table tennis, tennis, volleyball. **Team name:** Patriots.

**Student services.** Adult student services, alcohol/substance abuse counseling, chaplain/spiritual director, career counseling, student employment services, financial aid counseling, health services, personal counseling, placement for graduates, veterans' counselor. **Physically disabled:** Services for visually, speech, hearing impaired.

**Contact.** E-mail: admiss@dbu.edu
Phone: (214) 333-5360 Toll-free number: (800) 460-1328
Fax: (214) 333-5447
Bobby Soto, Director of Undergraduate Admissions, Dallas Baptist University, 3000 Mountain Creek Parkway, Dallas, TX 75211-9299

## Dallas Christian College
**Dallas, Texas**
www.dallas.edu                                    **CB code: 0792**

- Private 4-year Bible college affiliated with nondenominational tradition
- Commuter campus in very large city
- 315 degree-seeking undergraduates
- SAT or ACT (ACT writing recommended), application essay required

**General.** Founded in 1950. Accredited by ABHE. Special program for adult, nontraditional students. **Degrees:** 51 bachelor's, 1 associate awarded. **Location:** 10 miles from downtown. **Calendar:** 4-1-4, limited summer session. **Full-time faculty:** 8 total. **Part-time faculty:** 45 total.

**Freshman class profile.** 40 enrolled.

| Mid 50% test scores | | | |
|---|---|---|---|
| SAT critical reading: | 390-500 | GPA 3.50-3.74: | 28% |
| SAT math: | 340-530 | GPA 3.0-3.49: | 41% |
| SAT writing: | 400-540 | GPA 2.0-2.99: | 20% |
| ACT composite: | 17-22 | Rank in top quarter: | 40% |
| GPA 3.75 or higher: | 11% | Rank in top tenth: | 2% |

**Basis for selection.** School record and recommendation, followed by test scores. Class rank also important. Interview recommended.

**High school preparation.** College-preparatory program recommended.

**2009-2010 Annual costs.** Tuition/fees: $10,770. Room/board: $6,500. Books/supplies: $600.

**2009-2010 Financial aid. Non-need-based:** Scholarships awarded for leadership, music/drama.

**Application procedures. Admission:** Priority date 7/1; deadline 7/15 (postmark date). $40 fee, may be waived for applicants with need. Admission notification on a rolling basis. Must reply by 8/15. **Financial aid:** Closing date 4/15. FAFSA, institutional form required. Applicants notified on a rolling basis; must reply within 2 week(s) of notification.

**Academics. Special study options:** Distance learning, double major, dual enrollment of high school students, independent study, internships, liberal arts/career combination, teacher certification program. Evening degree-seeking program for adults. **Credit/placement by examination:** AP, CLEP, IB, SAT, ACT, institutional tests. 15 credit hours maximum toward associate degree, 30 toward bachelor's. **Support services:** Reduced course load, remedial instruction, study skills assistance, tutoring.

**Majors. Business:** Business admin. **Education:** General, early childhood, elementary, English, history, multi-level teacher, music, secondary. **Interdisciplinary:** Intercultural. **Liberal arts:** Arts/sciences. **Psychology:** General. **Theology:** Bible, religious ed, sacred music, theology.

**Most popular majors.** Business/marketing 23%, education 8%, theological studies 66%.

**Computing on campus.** 16 workstations in library, student center. Dormitories wired for high-speed internet access. Commuter students can connect to campus network. Online library, helpline, wireless network available.

**Student life. Freshman orientation:** Mandatory, $100 fee. Preregistration for classes offered. Held 3 days prior to registration. **Policies:** All resident students and those taking 6 hours or more required to attend campus chapel services 2 times a week. **Housing:** Guaranteed on-campus for all undergraduates. Single-sex dorms, wellness housing available. $150 deposit, deadline 8/10. **Activities:** Pep band, campus ministries, choral groups, drama, music ensembles, student government, student newspaper.

**Athletics.** NCCAA. **Intercollegiate:** Baseball M, basketball, soccer, volleyball W. **Intramural:** Football (non-tackle), soccer, table tennis, volleyball. **Team name:** Crusaders.

**Student services.** Adult student services, chaplain/spiritual director, student employment services, financial aid counseling, personal counseling, placement for graduates.

**Contact.** E-mail: dcc@dallas.edu
Phone: (972) 241-3371 ext. 161 Toll-free number: (800) 688-1029
Fax: (972) 241-8021
Matthew Meeks, Director of Enrollment Management, Dallas Christian College, 2700 Christian Parkway, Dallas, TX 75234-7299

## DeVry University: Houston
**Houston, Texas**
www.devry.edu                                    **CB code: 4132**

◆ For-profit 4-year university
◆ Commuter campus in very large city
◆ 1,439 degree-seeking undergraduates: 45% part-time, 51% women, 33% African American, 5% Asian American, 34% Hispanic American, 1% international
◆ 249 degree-seeking graduate students

**General. Degrees:** 146 bachelor's, 54 associate awarded; master's offered. **Calendar:** Semester. **Full-time faculty:** 24 total; 33% minority, 38% women. **Part-time faculty:** 151 total; 50% minority, 44% women.

**Freshman class profile.** 269 enrolled.

**Basis for selection.** Interview, high school GPA, and test scores most important.

**High school preparation.** College-preparatory program recommended.

**2009-2010 Annual costs. Tuition/fees:** $14,160. **Books/supplies:** $1,310. **Personal expenses:** $3,574.

**Application procedures. Admission:** No deadline. $50 fee. Admission notification on a rolling basis. **Financial aid:** No deadline. Applicants notified on a rolling basis.

**Academics. Special study options:** Accelerated study, distance learning. **Credit/placement by examination:** CLEP.

**Majors. Business:** Business admin. **Computer sciences:** Networking, systems analysis. **Engineering technology:** Computer, electrical. **Other:** Technical management.

**Most popular majors.** Business/marketing 81%, computer/information sciences 14%.

**Student life. Housing:** Off-campus housing available.

**Contact.** Phone: (713) 973-3000 Fax: (713) 896-7650
DeVry University: Houston, 11125 Equity Drive, Houston, TX 77041-8217

## DeVry University: Irving
**Dallas, Texas**
www.devry.edu                                    **CB code: 6180**

◆ For-profit 4-year university
◆ Commuter campus in small city
◆ 1,712 degree-seeking undergraduates: 52% part-time, 31% women, 30% African American, 3% Asian American, 23% Hispanic American, 1% Native American
◆ 299 degree-seeking graduate students
◆ Interview required

**General.** Founded in 1969. Regionally accredited. **Degrees:** 197 bachelor's, 50 associate awarded; master's offered. **Location:** 12 miles from Dallas. **Calendar:** Semester, extensive summer session. **Full-time faculty:** 47 total; 19% minority, 34% women. **Part-time faculty:** 86 total; 33% minority, 46% women.

**Freshman class profile.** 387 enrolled.

**Basis for selection.** Applicants must have a high school diploma or equivalent or a degree from an accredited postsecondary institution, demonstrating proficiency in basic college-level skills through SAT or ACT scores or institution-administered placement examinations, and be at least 17 years of age on the first day of classes. New students may enter at beginning of any semester.

**High school preparation.** College-preparatory program recommended.

**2009-2010 Annual costs. Tuition/fees:** $14,160. **Books/supplies:** $1,310. **Personal expenses:** $3,574.

**2008-2009 Financial aid.** All financial aid based on need.

**Application procedures. Admission:** No deadline. $50 fee. Admission notification on a rolling basis. **Financial aid:** No deadline. Applicants notified on a rolling basis.

**Academics. Special study options:** Accelerated study, distance learning. **Credit/placement by examination:** CLEP, institutional tests. No more than 35% of credit toward graduation requirement accepted. **Support services:** Learning center, remedial instruction, tutoring.

**Majors. Business:** Business admin. **Computer sciences:** Networking, systems analysis. **Engineering:** Software. **Engineering technology:** Biomedical, computer, electrical. **Other:** Technical management.

**Most popular majors.** Business/marketing 58%, computer/information sciences 23%, engineering/engineering technologies 20%.

**Computing on campus.** 450 workstations in library, computer center. Online course registration, online library, helpline available.

**Student life. Freshman orientation:** Mandatory. **Housing:** Off-campus housing available. **Activities:** Association of Information Technology Professionals, campus Bible study, Christian Students Fellowship, Habitat for Humanity, Institute of Electrical and Electronics Engineers, Institute of Management Accountants, minority student union, National Society of Black Engineers, Society of Women Engineers, Telecommunications Management and Associations, Society of Hispanic Professional Engineers, gamers club.

**Athletics. Intramural:** Basketball, football (tackle) M, volleyball.

**Student services.** Career counseling, student employment services, financial aid counseling, placement for graduates, veterans' counselor. **Physically disabled:** Services for visually, hearing impaired.

**Contact.** Phone: (972) 929-5777 Toll-free number: (800) 633-3879 Fax: (972) 929-2860
Chad Williams, Director of Admissions, DeVry University: Irving, 4800 Regent Boulevard, Dallas, TX 75063-2439

## East Texas Baptist University
**Marshall, Texas**
www.etbu.edu                                    **CB code: 6187**

◆ Private 4-year university and liberal arts college affiliated with Baptist faith
◆ Residential campus in large town
◆ 1,116 degree-seeking undergraduates: 3% part-time, 51% women, 15% African American, 1% Asian American, 8% Hispanic American, 2% Native American, 1% international
◆ 53% of applicants admitted
◆ SAT or ACT (ACT writing optional) required
◆ 42% graduate within 6 years

**General.** Founded in 1912. Regionally accredited. **Degrees:** 216 bachelor's awarded. **Location:** 20 miles from Longview, 35 miles from Shreveport, Louisiana. **Calendar:** Semester, extensive summer session. **Full-time faculty:** 64 total; 89% have terminal degrees, 8% minority, 38% women. **Part-time faculty:** 36 total; 14% have terminal degrees, 8% minority, 42% women. **Class size:** 58% < 20, 34% 20-39, 8% 40-49, less than 1% 50-99. **Special facilities:** Caddo Lake international wetlands.

**Freshman class profile.** 1,038 applied, 546 admitted, 279 enrolled.

| Mid 50% test scores | | Rank in top tenth: | 13% |
|---|---|---|---|
| SAT critical reading: | 420-510 | End year in good standing: | 89% |
| SAT math: | 450-540 | Return as sophomores: | 61% |
| ACT composite: | 19-23 | Out-of-state: | 10% |
| GPA 3.75 or higher: | 18% | Live on campus: | 98% |
| GPA 3.50-3.74: | 24% | International: | 1% |
| GPA 3.0-3.49: | 38% | Fraternities: | 6% |
| GPA 2.0-2.99: | 20% | Sororities: | 15% |
| Rank in top quarter: | 45% | | |

**Basis for selection.** School achievement record and test scores most important. Evidence of good character also important. Applicants should be in top 40% of class. Interview recommended for academically deficient; audition recommended for music, speech, theater arts programs. **Learning Disabled:** Student should provide documentation of learning disability to the Student Advising and Career Development Office, which verifies documentation and assists in acquiring reasonable accommodations.

**High school preparation.** College-preparatory program recommended. 22 units recommended. Recommended units include English 4, mathematics 3, social studies 2.5, science 2 and academic electives 1. 0.5 economics, 1.5 physical education, 0.5 health education, 1 technology applications, 0.5 speech.

**2010-2011 Annual costs.** Tuition/fees: $19,550. Room/board: $5,436. Books/supplies: $892. Personal expenses: $1,448.

**2008-2009 Financial aid. Need-based:** 282 full-time freshmen applied for aid; 247 were judged to have need; 247 of these received aid. Average need met was 46%. Average scholarship/grant was $6,538; average loan $3,044. 59% of total undergraduate aid awarded as scholarships/grants, 41% as loans/jobs. **Non-need-based:** Awarded to 914 full-time undergraduates, including 289 freshmen. Scholarships awarded for academics, alumni affiliation, leadership, music/drama, religious affiliation.

**Application procedures. Admission:** $25 fee, may be waived for applicants with need. Admission notification on a rolling basis beginning on or about 9/1. **Financial aid:** Priority date 6/1; no closing date. FAFSA, institutional form required. Applicants notified on a rolling basis starting 1/1.

**Academics. Special study options:** Accelerated study, cross-registration, distance learning, double major, dual enrollment of high school students, exchange student, honors, independent study, internships, liberal arts/career combination, student-designed major, study abroad, teacher certification program, Washington semester. **Credit/placement by examination:** AP, CLEP, IB, SAT, ACT, institutional tests. ACT is used for mathematics placement. Departmental examinations administered on request upon approval of department chair. **Support services:** Reduced course load, study skills assistance, tutoring, writing center.

**Majors. Biology:** General. **Business:** General. **Communications:** General, media studies. **Education:** General, biology, chemistry, drama/dance, elementary, English, history, mathematics, music, physical, social studies, Spanish, speech. **Foreign languages:** Spanish. **Health:** Athletic training, nursing (RN). **History:** General. **Interdisciplinary:** Global studies. **Liberal arts:** Arts/sciences. **Math:** General. **Parks/recreation:** Health/fitness. **Philosophy/religion:** Religion. **Physical sciences:** Chemistry. **Protective services:** Law enforcement admin. **Psychology:** General. **Social sciences:** Political science, sociology. **Theology:** Bible, missionary, pastoral counseling, religious ed, sacred music, youth ministry. **Visual/performing arts:** Dramatic, piano/organ, voice/opera. **Other:** University studies.

**Most popular majors.** Business/marketing 13%, education 19%, English 7%, health sciences 13%, interdisciplinary studies 15%, psychology 7%, theological studies 7%.

**Computing on campus.** 200 workstations in dormitories, library, computer center, student center. Dormitories wired for high-speed internet access and linked to campus network. Commuter students can connect to campus network. Online course registration, online library, helpline, repair service, wireless network available.

**Student life. Freshman orientation:** Available. Preregistration for classes offered. 5 days of activities, lectures, seminar sessions, community service activities. **Policies:** Required chapel attendance, graded curfew, weekly clean room check. Religious observance required. **Housing:** Guaranteed on-campus for all undergraduates. Single-sex dorms, apartments, wellness housing available. $100 fully refundable deposit. **Activities:** Bands, campus ministries, choral groups, drama, international student organizations, literary magazine, music ensembles, Model UN, musical theater, radio station, student government, student newspaper, symphony orchestra, Fellowship of Christian Athletes, political awareness society, Delta Pi Theta, Pi Sigma, Sigma Sigma Epsilon, Delta Chi Rho.

**Athletics.** NCAA. **Intercollegiate:** Baseball M, basketball, cross-country, football (tackle) M, soccer, softball W, volleyball W. **Intramural:** Basketball, football (non-tackle), racquetball, soccer, softball, volleyball. **Team name:** Tigers.

**Student services.** Adult student services, chaplain/spiritual director, student employment services, financial aid counseling, health services, personal counseling, placement for graduates, veterans' counselor.

**Contact.** E-mail: admissions@etbu.edu
Phone: (903) 923-2000 Toll-free number: (800) 804-3828
Fax: (903) 923-2001
Melissa Fitts, Director of Admissions, East Texas Baptist University, 1209 North Grove, Marshall, TX 75670-1498

## Hardin-Simmons University

**Abilene, Texas**     **CB member**
**www.hsutx.edu**     **CB code: 6268**

- Private 4-year university affiliated with Baptist faith
- Residential campus in small city
- 1,882 degree-seeking undergraduates: 8% part-time, 56% women, 6% African American, 1% Asian American, 10% Hispanic American, 1% Native American, 1% international

- 399 degree-seeking graduate students
- 38% of applicants admitted
- SAT or ACT with writing required
- 50% graduate within 6 years; 39% enter graduate study

**General.** Founded in 1891. Regionally accredited. Part of 3-member consortium (with Abilene Christian University and McMurry University) comprising Abilene Intercollegiate School of Nursing. **Degrees:** 347 bachelor's awarded; master's, doctoral, professional offered. **Location:** 150 miles from Fort Worth. **Calendar:** Semester, extensive summer session. **Full-time faculty:** 136 total; 89% have terminal degrees, 2% minority, 33% women. **Part-time faculty:** 72 total; 17% have terminal degrees, 11% minority, 53% women. **Class size:** 63% < 20, 33% 20-39, 3% 40-49, less than 1% 50-99. **Special facilities:** Rare and fine book room, observatory.

**Freshman class profile.** 1,677 applied, 634 admitted, 409 enrolled.

| Mid 50% test scores | | | |
|---|---|---|---|
| SAT critical reading: | 450-560 | GPA 2.0-2.99: | 11% |
| SAT math: | 480-600 | Rank in top quarter: | 59% |
| SAT writing: | 450-570 | Rank in top tenth: | 27% |
| ACT composite: | 20-25 | End year in good standing: | 82% |
| GPA 3.75 or higher: | 48% | Return as sophomores: | 71% |
| GPA 3.50-3.74: | 16% | Out-of-state: | 5% |
| GPA 3.0-3.49: | 25% | Live on campus: | 92% |
| | | International: | 1% |

**Basis for selection.** Applicants admitted on basis of acceptable combination of test scores and prior academic record. Special cases considered individually. Non-native speakers of English require score of 550 on TOEFL, unless transferring 24 or more credits. Audition required for music program; interview recommended for special cases. Written essay, interview, and separate application required for honors program. **Homeschooled:** GED scores required only if applicant plans to apply for federal need-based financial aid. **Learning Disabled:** No special admission requirements for students with disabilities; accepted students apply to Office for Students with Disabilities.

**High school preparation.** College-preparatory program recommended. 16 units required. Required units include English 3, mathematics 2, social studies 2, science 2 and academic electives 7. Math must include algebra I and above.

**2010-2011 Annual costs.** Tuition/fees: $20,990. Tuition guarantee is only for students enrolled full-time. Room/board: $6,282. Books/supplies: $800. Personal expenses: $1,476.

**2009-2010 Financial aid. Need-based:** 401 full-time freshmen applied for aid; 306 were judged to have need; 306 of these received aid. Average need met was 81%. Average scholarship/grant was $7,301; average loan $2,889. 45% of total undergraduate aid awarded as scholarships/grants, 55% as loans/jobs. **Non-need-based:** Awarded to 1,515 full-time undergraduates, including 371 freshmen. Scholarships awarded for academics, art, job skills, leadership, music/drama, religious affiliation.

**Application procedures. Admission:** No deadline. $50 fee, may be waived for applicants with need. Admission notification on a rolling basis beginning on or about 9/1. **Financial aid:** Priority date 3/15; no closing date. FAFSA required. Applicants notified on a rolling basis starting 2/1; must reply within 2 week(s) of notification.

**Academics. Special study options:** Accelerated study, cross-registration, distance learning, double major, dual enrollment of high school students, honors, independent study, internships, New York semester, study abroad, teacher certification program, United Nations semester, Washington semester. **Credit/placement by examination:** AP, CLEP, SAT, ACT, institutional tests. 32 credit hours maximum toward bachelor's degree. Maximum 14 hours in any one discipline. **Support services:** Pre-admission summer program, reduced course load, remedial instruction, study skills assistance, tutoring, writing center.

**Majors. Agriculture:** Agronomy, animal sciences, business. **Biology:** General, Biochemistry/biophysics and molecular biology. **Business:** Accounting, business admin, finance, management information systems, management science, marketing. **Communications:** General, broadcast journalism, media studies, public relations, radio/tv. **Computer sciences:** Programming. **Conservation:** Environmental science. **Education:** Art, business, computer, drama/dance, early childhood, English, history, mathematics, music, physical, reading, science, social studies, Spanish, speech. **Foreign languages:** Spanish. **Health:** Athletic training, audiology/speech pathology, nursing (RN), predental, premedicine. **History:** General. **Legal studies:** Prelaw. **Math:** General. **Parks/recreation:** Exercise sciences, health/fitness. **Philosophy/religion:** Philosophy. **Physical sciences:** Chemistry, geology, physics. **Protective services:** Criminal justice. **Psychology:** General. **Public administration:** Social work. **Social sciences:** Economics, political science, sociology. **Theology:** Bible, missionary, preministerial, sacred music, theology, youth ministry. **Visual/performing arts:** Dramatic, graphic design, music history, music management, music performance, music theory/composition, piano/organ, stringed instruments, studio arts, voice/opera.

**Most popular majors.** Biology 9%, business/marketing 15%, communications/journalism 6%, education 17%, health sciences 12%, parks/recreation 10%, psychology 8%.

**Computing on campus.** 225 workstations in dormitories, library, computer center, student center. Dormitories wired for high-speed internet access and linked to campus network. Online library, helpline, wireless network available.

**Student life. Freshman orientation:** Available, $10 fee. Preregistration for classes offered. Held Tuesday through Sunday the week before classes begin. **Policies:** Single, undergraduate students under 21 who have not completed 60 credit hours and are not living at home required to live in residence halls. All housing is alcohol, drug and smoke-free. Religious observance required. **Housing:** Guaranteed on-campus for freshmen. Single-sex dorms, special housing for disabled, apartments available. $100 fully refundable deposit. Single, duplex housing available with priority given to families. **Activities:** Bands, campus ministries, choral groups, drama, international student organizations, literary magazine, music ensembles, Model UN, musical theater, opera, student government, student newspaper, symphony orchestra, Sigma Alpha, Student 2 Student, Tri Phi, Alphi Phi Omega, Baptist Student Ministries, Theta Alpha Zeta, Zeta Chi, Epsilon Pi Alpha, Phi Mu Alpha.

**Athletics.** NCAA. **Intercollegiate:** Baseball M, basketball, cheerleading, cross-country, football (tackle) M, golf, soccer, softball W, tennis, track and field, volleyball W. **Intramural:** Badminton, basketball, bowling, football (non-tackle), football (tackle), golf, handball, racquetball, soccer, softball, tennis, volleyball. **Team name:** Cowboys/Cowgirls.

**Student services.** Chaplain/spiritual director, career counseling, student employment services, financial aid counseling, health services, personal counseling, placement for graduates, veterans' counselor. **Physically disabled:** Services for visually, speech, hearing impaired.

**Contact.** E-mail: enroll@hsutx.edu
Phone: (325) 670-1206 Toll-free number: (877) 464-7889
Fax: (325) 671-2115
Vicki House, Director of Admissions and Recruiting, Hardin-Simmons University, PO Box 16050, Abilene, TX 79698-0001

## Houston Baptist University

| **Houston, Texas** | **CB member** |
|---|---|
| **www.hbu.edu** | **CB code: 6282** |

- Private 4-year university and liberal arts college affiliated with Baptist faith
- Commuter campus in very large city
- 2,322 degree-seeking undergraduates: 14% part-time, 65% women, 20% African American, 14% Asian American, 25% Hispanic American, 4% international
- 337 degree-seeking graduate students
- 42% of applicants admitted
- SAT or ACT (ACT writing recommended), application essay required
- 46% graduate within 6 years

**General.** Founded in 1960. Regionally accredited. Christian liberal arts university. **Degrees:** 295 bachelor's, 6 associate awarded; master's offered. **ROTC:** Army, Naval, Air Force. **Location:** 10 miles from downtown Houston. **Calendar:** Semester, extensive summer session. **Full-time faculty:** 115 total; 84% have terminal degrees, 21% minority, 49% women. **Part-time faculty:** 131 total; 40% have terminal degrees, 18% minority, 58% women. **Class size:** 63% < 20, 34% 20-39, 2% 40-49, 1% 50-99. **Special facilities:** Cultural arts center, American architecture and decorative arts museum, Bible in America museum, Southern history museum.

**Freshman class profile.** 8,119 applied, 3,431 admitted, 554 enrolled.

| Mid 50% test scores | | | |
|---|---|---|---|
| SAT critical reading: | 460-570 | Return as sophomores: | 72% |
| SAT math: | 470-590 | Out-of-state: | 4% |
| SAT writing: | 450-560 | Live on campus: | 45% |
| ACT composite: | 20-25 | International: | 3% |
| Rank in top quarter: | 51% | Fraternities: | 18% |
| Rank in top tenth: | 23% | Sororities: | 20% |

**Basis for selection.** School achievement record, test scores, recommendations, class rank, special talents, and skills most important. Audition required for music majors; portfolio required for art majors; interview recommended for academically weak students.

**High school preparation.** College-preparatory program recommended. 14 units required; 24 recommended. Required and recommended units include English 4, mathematics 3, social studies 4, history 2, science 3, foreign language 2, computer science 1, visual/performing arts 1, academic electives 3.5. 2 physical education/health, 0.5 speech.

**2010-2011 Annual costs.** Tuition/fees: $23,160. Room/board: $6,830. Books/supplies: $1,350. Personal expenses: $1,900.

**2009-2010 Financial aid. Need-based:** 464 full-time freshmen applied for aid; 412 were judged to have need; 410 of these received aid. Average need met was 85%. Average scholarship/grant was $6,228; average loan $2,703. 58% of total undergraduate aid awarded as scholarships/grants, 42% as loans/jobs. **Non-need-based:** Awarded to 1,231 full-time undergraduates, including 471 freshmen. Scholarships awarded for academics, alumni affiliation, art, athletics, music/drama, religious affiliation, ROTC.

**Application procedures. Admission:** No deadline. No application fee. Admission notification on a rolling basis. **Financial aid:** Priority date 3/1, closing date 4/15. FAFSA required. Applicants notified on a rolling basis starting 3/10.

**Academics. Special study options:** Accelerated study, combined bachelor's/graduate degree, double major, honors, internships, study abroad, teacher certification program. **Credit/placement by examination:** AP, CLEP, IB, SAT, ACT, institutional tests. CLEP credit limited to students with 63 or fewer credit hours. **Support services:** Reduced course load, remedial instruction, tutoring, writing center.

**Honors college/program.** Admission to the Honors College is a competitive process by application only. Students should have at least a 1250 SAT or 27 ACT, 3.2 GPA, two letters of recommendation (one academic, one character), leadership experience and service to the church and community. Following a review of your application by the dean and the Honors College Advisory Committee, finalists will be invited for a personal interview as part of the Honors College selection process.

**Majors. Biology:** General, molecular. **Business:** General, accounting, business admin, entrepreneurial studies, finance, information resources management, management information systems, managerial economics, marketing. **Communications:** General, media studies. **Education:** Art, early childhood, English, mathematics, middle, music, physical, science, secondary, social studies. **Family/consumer sciences:** Child development. **Foreign languages:** Biblical, French, Spanish. **Health:** Nursing (RN). **History:** General. **Interdisciplinary:** Accounting/computer science. **Math:** General. **Parks/recreation:** Exercise sciences, health/fitness. **Philosophy/religion:** Christian, philosophy. **Physical sciences:** Chemistry, physics. **Psychology:** General. **Public administration:** Policy analysis. **Social sciences:** Economics, political science, sociology. **Theology:** Pastoral counseling, sacred music. **Visual/performing arts:** Music performance, music theory/composition, studio arts.

**Most popular majors.** Biology 12%, business/marketing 37%, education 8%, psychology 6%, social sciences 6%.

**Computing on campus.** 95 workstations in dormitories, library, computer center. Dormitories wired for high-speed internet access and linked to campus network. Commuter students can connect to campus network. Online course registration, online library, helpline, repair service, wireless network available.

**Student life. Freshman orientation:** Available. Preregistration for classes offered. 2-day overnight summer orientation and registration. 2-1/2 day camp held off campus prior to start of classes. **Policies:** Spiritual Life Program graduation requirement for all undergraduate students. **Housing:** Guaranteed on-campus for freshmen. Coed dorms, single-sex dorms, special housing for disabled, apartments available. $200 partly refundable deposit. **Activities:** Bands, campus ministries, choral groups, dance, drama, international student organizations, music ensembles, opera, student government, student newspaper, symphony orchestra, Christian Life on Campus, Psi Chi, Nursing Association, Black Student Fellowship, Toastmasters, Digital Eon, Vietnamese student association, Indian student association, Sisters for the Lord, Brothers Under Christ.

**Athletics.** NCAA. **Intercollegiate:** Baseball M, basketball, cheerleading, cross-country, golf, soccer, softball W, track and field, volleyball W. **Intramural:** Badminton, basketball, bowling, football (non-tackle), softball, table tennis, volleyball. **Team name:** Huskies.

**Student services.** Adult student services, alcohol/substance abuse counseling, chaplain/spiritual director, career counseling, student employment services, financial aid counseling, health services, placement for graduates, women's services. **Physically disabled:** Services for visually, speech, hearing impaired.

**Contact.** E-mail: admissions@hbu.edu
Phone: (281) 649-3211 Toll-free number: (800) 969-3210
Fax: (281) 649-3217
Ed Borges, Director of Admissions, Houston Baptist University, 7502
Fondren Road, Houston, TX 77074-3298

## Howard Payne University
**Brownwood, Texas**
**www.hputx.edu**     **CB code: 6278**

▶ Private 4-year liberal arts and teachers college affiliated with Baptist faith
▶ Residential campus in large town
▶ 1,130 degree-seeking undergraduates: 17% part-time, 47% women, 7% African American, 1% Asian American, 16% Hispanic American, 1% Native American, 1% international
▶ 15 degree-seeking graduate students
▶ 59% of applicants admitted
▶ SAT or ACT (ACT writing optional), application essay, interview required

**General.** Founded in 1889. Regionally accredited. **Degrees:** 201 bachelor's, 4 associate awarded; master's offered. **Location:** 150 miles from Dallas, 77 miles from Abilene. **Calendar:** Semester, limited summer session. **Full-time faculty:** 78 total; 63% have terminal degrees, 1% minority, 37% women. **Part-time faculty:** 66 total; 20% have terminal degrees, 6% minority, 32% women. **Class size:** 74% < 20, 24% 20-39, 1% 40-49, less than 1% 50-99. **Special facilities:** General Douglas MacArthur Academy of Freedom, faith and life leadership center, art center, center for social justice.

**Freshman class profile.** 907 applied, 535 admitted, 218 enrolled.

| Mid 50% test scores | | | |
|---|---|---|---|
| SAT critical reading: | 410-570 | GPA 2.0-2.99: | 1% |
| SAT math: | 440-550 | Rank in top quarter: | 37% |
| ACT composite: | 18-24 | Rank in top tenth: | 16% |
| GPA 3.75 or higher: | 14% | Out-of-state: | 2% |
| GPA 3.50-3.74: | 32% | Live on campus: | 91% |
| GPA 3.0-3.49: | 53% | Fraternities: | 15% |
| | | Sororities: | 15% |

**Basis for selection.** Average GPA of 3.0 on 4.0 scale, ACT composite score of 19, or SAT 1 score of 910 (exclusive of Writing). ACT/SAT scores used to exempt students from placement tests in English, math, or reading. Interview required for academic program applicants and competitive merit scholarship; recommended for all others. Interview may be required of others by admissions committee. Audition required for music program. **Home-schooled:** Letter of recommendation (nonparent) required. **Learning Disabled:** If a student meets requirements for admission, accommodations may be initiated by Student Success Services.

**High school preparation.** College-preparatory program recommended. 16 units required. Required and recommended units include English 4, mathematics 3, social studies 2, history 2, science 3 and foreign language 2.

**2010-2011 Annual costs.** Tuition/fees (projected): $19,950. Room/board: $5,640. Books/supplies: $1,000. Personal expenses: $1,500.

**2008-2009 Financial aid.** **Need-based:** 286 full-time freshmen applied for aid; 249 were judged to have need; 249 of these received aid. Average need met was 84%. Average scholarship/grant was $10,608; average loan $3,212. 63% of total undergraduate aid awarded as scholarships/grants, 37% as loans/jobs. **Non-need-based:** Awarded to 299 full-time undergraduates, including 91 freshmen. Scholarships awarded for academics, alumni affiliation, art, music/drama.

**Application procedures.** **Admission:** Priority date 3/15; no deadline. No application fee. Admission notification on a rolling basis. **Financial aid:** Priority date 3/15; no closing date. FAFSA, institutional form required. Applicants notified on a rolling basis starting 2/1; must reply within 2 week(s) of notification.

**Academics.** **Special study options:** Accelerated study, cooperative education, distance learning, double major, dual enrollment of high school students, ESL, honors, independent study, internships, liberal arts/career combination, study abroad, teacher certification program. Extension classes in El Paso, Corpus Christi, Harlingen, Ft. Worth, Midland. **Credit/placement by examination:** AP, CLEP, SAT, ACT, institutional tests. 30 credit hours maximum toward bachelor's degree. **Support services:** Reduced course load, remedial instruction, study skills assistance, tutoring, writing center.

**Majors. Biology:** General. **Business:** General, accounting, business admin, finance, marketing. **Communications:** General, public relations. **Communications technology:** Graphics, radio/tv. **Computer sciences:** Information systems. **Education:** General, art, biology, business, chemistry, drama/ dance, elementary, English, history, mathematics, multi-level teacher, music, physical, science, secondary, social science, Spanish, speech. **Foreign languages:** Biblical, Spanish. **Health:** Athletic training, premedicine. **History:** General. **Interdisciplinary:** Intercultural. **Legal studies:** Prelaw. **Liberal arts:** Arts/sciences. **Math:** General. **Parks/recreation:** General, exercise sciences, health/fitness, sports admin. **Philosophy/religion:** Philosophy, religion. **Physical sciences:** Chemistry. **Protective services:** Police science. **Psychology:** General. **Public administration:** Social work. **Social sciences:** General, political science, sociology. **Theology:** Bible, religious ed, sacred music, theology, youth ministry. **Visual/performing arts:** Art, dramatic, music performance, piano/organ, stringed instruments, studio arts, voice/opera.

**Most popular majors.** Business/marketing 15%, communications/journalism 11%, education 15%, parks/recreation 6%, psychology 8%, social sciences 8%, theological studies 12%.

**Computing on campus.** 260 workstations in dormitories, library, computer center, student center. Dormitories wired for high-speed internet access and linked to campus network. Online library, helpline, wireless network available.

**Student life.** **Freshman orientation:** Available, $65 fee. Preregistration for classes offered. Held the weekend before fall semester classes begin. **Policies:** Religious observance required. **Housing:** Guaranteed on-campus for freshmen. Single-sex dorms, apartments, wellness housing available. $100 nonrefundable deposit, deadline 8/1. **Activities:** Bands, campus ministries, choral groups, drama, music ensembles, Model UN, opera, radio station, student government, student newspaper, symphony orchestra, student foundation, ministerial alliance, Fellowship of Christian Athletes, Students in Free Enterprise, political awareness club, social work club, Gamma Beta Phi.

**Athletics.** NCAA. **Intercollegiate:** Baseball M, basketball, cheerleading, cross-country, football (tackle) M, soccer, softball W, tennis, volleyball W. **Intramural:** Basketball, football (non-tackle), softball, table tennis, tennis, volleyball. **Team name:** Yellow Jackets.

**Student services.** Adult student services, chaplain/spiritual director, career counseling, student employment services, financial aid counseling, health services, personal counseling, placement for graduates.

**Contact.** E-mail: enroll@hputx.edu
Phone: (325) 649-8020 Toll-free number: (800) 880-4478
Fax: (325) 649-8901
Kevin Kirk, Assistant Vice President for Enrollment Management, Howard Payne University, 1000 Fisk Street, Brownwood, TX 76801-2794

## Huston-Tillotson University
**Austin, Texas**     **CB member**
**www.htu.edu**     **CB code: 6280**

▶ Private 4-year business and liberal arts college affiliated with United Church of Christ and United Methodist Church
▶ Residential campus in very large city
▶ 843 degree-seeking undergraduates: 4% part-time, 52% women, 76% African American, 13% Hispanic American, 3% international
▶ 38 degree-seeking graduate students
▶ 48% of applicants admitted
▶ SAT or ACT (ACT writing optional) required

**General.** Founded in 1876. Regionally accredited. **Degrees:** 94 bachelor's awarded. **ROTC:** Army. **Location:** Downtown. **Calendar:** Semester, extensive summer session. **Full-time faculty:** 41 total; 73% have terminal degrees, 63% minority, 58% women. **Part-time faculty:** 40 total; 22% have terminal degrees, 32% minority, 42% women. **Class size:** 63% < 20, 35% 20-39, 1% 40-49, less than 1% 50-99.

**Freshman class profile.** 1,422 applied, 686 admitted, 250 enrolled.

| Mid 50% test scores | | | |
|---|---|---|---|
| SAT critical reading: | 350-460 | GPA 2.0-2.99: | 51% |
| SAT math: | 360-460 | Rank in top quarter: | 29% |
| ACT composite: | 14-18 | Rank in top tenth: | 6% |
| GPA 3.75 or higher: | 5% | Return as sophomores: | 55% |
| GPA 3.50-3.74: | 9% | Out-of-state: | 5% |
| GPA 3.0-3.49: | 29% | Live on campus: | 91% |
| | | International: | 5% |

**Basis for selection.** School achievement record important. Test scores and interview considered.

**High school preparation.** College-preparatory program recommended. 22 units required. Required and recommended units include English 4, mathematics 3, social studies 3, science 2, foreign language 2 and computer science 1. Health, physical education recommended.

**2009-2010 Annual costs.** Tuition/fees: $11,434. Room/board: $6,690. Books/supplies: $800. Personal expenses: $2,252.

**2008-2009 Financial aid. Need-based:** 159 full-time freshmen applied for aid; 159 were judged to have need; 159 of these received aid. Average need met was 72%. Average scholarship/grant was $9,802; average loan $3,500. 60% of total undergraduate aid awarded as scholarships/grants, 40% as loans/jobs. **Non-need-based:** Awarded to 29 full-time undergraduates, including 13 freshmen. Scholarships awarded for academics, alumni affiliation, art, athletics, job skills, leadership, minority status, music/drama, religious affiliation, state residency.

**Application procedures. Admission:** Priority date 3/1; deadline 7/1. $25 fee, may be waived for applicants with need. Admission notification on a rolling basis beginning on or about 1/1. **Financial aid:** Priority date 3/15; no closing date. FAFSA, institutional form required. Applicants notified on a rolling basis starting 4/1; must reply within 4 week(s) of notification.

**Academics. Special study options:** Cooperative education, cross-registration, distance learning, double major, dual enrollment of high school students, external degree, honors, independent study, internships, liberal arts/career combination, study abroad, teacher certification program. 3-2 engineering program with Prairie View A&M University. **Credit/placement by examination:** AP, CLEP, SAT, ACT, institutional tests. 15 credit hours maximum toward bachelor's degree. **Support services:** Learning center, pre-admission summer program, remedial instruction, tutoring, writing center.

**Majors. Biology:** General. **Business:** Accounting, business admin, international, marketing. **Computer sciences:** General, computer science. **Education:** General, physical. **History:** General. **Liberal arts:** Arts/sciences. **Math:** General. **Physical sciences:** Chemistry. **Protective services:** Criminal justice. **Psychology:** General. **Social sciences:** General, political science, sociology.

**Most popular majors.** Biology 8%, business/marketing 29%, interdisciplinary studies 12%, psychology 9%, social sciences 24%.

**Computing on campus.** 400 workstations in dormitories, library, computer center, student center. Dormitories wired for high-speed internet access and linked to campus network. Commuter students can connect to campus network. Online library, helpline, wireless network available.

**Student life. Freshman orientation:** Mandatory. Preregistration for classes offered. **Housing:** Guaranteed on-campus for all undergraduates. Single-sex dorms, wellness housing available. **Activities:** Jazz band, campus ministries, choral groups, dance, drama, film society, international student organizations, literary magazine, music ensembles, Model UN, student government, NAACP student chapter, Toastmasters.

**Athletics.** NAIA. **Intercollegiate:** Baseball M, basketball, golf, soccer M, track and field, volleyball W. **Intramural:** Basketball, soccer M, softball, table tennis, volleyball. **Team name:** Rams.

**Student services.** Adult student services, career counseling, student employment services, financial aid counseling, health services, personal counseling, placement for graduates, veterans' counselor. **Physically disabled:** Services for visually, hearing impaired.

**Contact.** E-mail: slstinson@htu.edu
Phone: (512) 505-3028 Toll-free number: (877) 505-3028
Fax: (512) 505-3192
Shakitha Stinson, Director of Admission, Huston-Tillotson University, 900 Chicon Street, Austin, TX 78702-2795

## Jarvis Christian College
Hawkins, Texas
www.jarvis.edu                          CB code: 6319

- Private 4-year liberal arts and teachers college affiliated with Christian Church (Disciples of Christ)
- Residential campus in rural community
- 608 degree-seeking undergraduates: 1% part-time, 55% women

**General.** Founded in 1912. Regionally accredited. **Degrees:** 62 bachelor's awarded. **Location:** 100 miles from Dallas; 100 miles from Shreveport, Louisiana. **Calendar:** Semester, limited summer session. **Full-time faculty:** 30 total; 50% women. **Part-time faculty:** 19 total; 37% women. **Class**

**size:** 60% < 20, 37% 20-39, 3% 40-49, less than 1% >100. **Special facilities:** Observatory, natatorium, archives of black Christian church (Disciples of Christ).

**Freshman class profile.** 119 enrolled.

| | | | |
|---|---|---|---|
| GPA 3.75 or higher: | 5% | Rank in top quarter: | 6% |
| GPA 3.50-3.74: | 5% | Return as sophomores: | 71% |
| GPA 3.0-3.49: | 13% | Out-of-state: | 13% |
| GPA 2.0-2.99: | 65% | Live on campus: | 98% |

**Basis for selection.** Open admission. **Homeschooled:** State high school equivalency certificate required.

**High school preparation.** 16 units recommended. Recommended units include English 3, mathematics 2, social studies 3, science 1 and academic electives 7.

**2009-2010 Annual costs.** Tuition/fees: $8,208. Room/board: $5,078. Books/supplies: $800. Personal expenses: $950.

**2008-2009 Financial aid.** All financial aid based on need. **Additional information:** High school transcript required for scholarship consideration.

**Application procedures. Admission:** No deadline. $50 fee, may be waived for applicants with need. Admission notification on a rolling basis beginning on or about 4/1. **Financial aid:** Priority date 6/30, closing date 1/3. FAFSA required. Applicants notified on a rolling basis starting 5/1; must reply within 2 week(s) of notification.

**Academics. Special study options:** Accelerated study, combined bachelor's/graduate degree, cooperative education, cross-registration, distance learning, double major, dual enrollment of high school students, ESL, honors, internships, liberal arts/career combination, student-designed major, teacher certification program, Washington semester. **Credit/placement by examination:** AP, CLEP, IB, institutional tests. 18 credit hours maximum toward bachelor's degree. **Support services:** Learning center, reduced course load, remedial instruction, study skills assistance, tutoring, writing center.

**Majors. Biology:** General. **Business:** Business admin. **Communications:** Journalism. **Computer sciences:** General. **Education:** General, biology, business, early childhood, elementary, English, history, mathematics, middle, physical, reading, secondary, special. **Health:** Premedicine. **History:** General. **Math:** General. **Philosophy/religion:** Religion. **Physical sciences:** Chemistry. **Protective services:** Criminal justice. **Social sciences:** Sociology.

**Most popular majors.** Biology 10%, business/marketing 21%, education 27%, interdisciplinary studies 24%, social sciences 11%.

**Computing on campus.** 359 workstations in dormitories, library, computer center. Dormitories wired for high-speed internet access and linked to campus network. Commuter students can connect to campus network. Online library, helpline, repair service, wireless network available.

**Student life. Freshman orientation:** Mandatory. Preregistration for classes offered. **Policies:** Religious services available, regardless of denomination. Religious observance required. **Housing:** Guaranteed on-campus for all undergraduates. Coed dorms, single-sex dorms, special housing for disabled, apartments, wellness housing available. $100 nonrefundable deposit, deadline 8/1. Single parents housing available on limited basis. **Activities:** Bands, choral groups, music ensembles, student government, student ministers' association, United Campus Christian Fellowship, pre-law club, National Society of Black Accountants, Student National Educational Association, Students in Free Enterprise, Phi Beta Lambda English Club, college church.

**Athletics.** NAIA. **Intercollegiate:** Baseball M, basketball, cheerleading, volleyball W. **Intramural:** Baseball M, basketball, football (non-tackle), football (tackle) M, golf, soccer, softball, swimming, table tennis, tennis, volleyball, weight lifting, wrestling M. **Team name:** Bulldogs.

**Student services.** Alcohol/substance abuse counseling, chaplain/spiritual director, career counseling, services for economically disadvantaged, student employment services, financial aid counseling, health services, personal counseling, placement for graduates, veterans' counselor. **Physically disabled:** Services for visually, speech, hearing impaired.

**Contact.** E-mail: felecia_tyiska@jarvis.edu
Phone: (903) 769-5734 Fax: (903) 769-1282
Felecia Tyiska, Director of Admissions, Jarvis Christian College, PO Box 1470, Hawkins, TX 75765-1470

## Lamar University
Beaumont, Texas                         CB member
www.lamar.edu                           CB code: 6360

- Public 4-year university
- Commuter campus in small city

- 9,127 degree-seeking undergraduates: 25% part-time, 60% women, 32% African American, 4% Asian American, 8% Hispanic American, 1% international
- 4,387 degree-seeking graduate students
- 84% of applicants admitted
- SAT or ACT required
- 32% graduate within 6 years

**General.** Founded in 1923. Regionally accredited. **Degrees:** 1,219 bachelor's, 56 associate awarded; master's, doctoral offered. **Location:** 75 miles from Houston. **Calendar:** Semester, limited summer session. **Full-time faculty:** 451 total; 64% have terminal degrees, 21% minority, 43% women. **Part-time faculty:** 132 total; 27% have terminal degrees, 18% minority, 44% women. **Class size:** 34% < 20, 46% 20-39, 11% 40-49, 8% 50-99, less than 1% >100. **Special facilities:** Hazardous waste research center, city museum.

**Freshman class profile.** 5,359 applied, 4,501 admitted, 1,485 enrolled.

| Mid 50% test scores | | End year in good standing: | 82% |
|---|---|---|---|
| SAT critical reading: | 410-510 | Return as sophomores: | 66% |
| SAT math: | 420-530 | Out-of-state: | 2% |
| SAT writing: | 400-490 | Live on campus: | 44% |
| ACT composite: | 16-22 | International: | 1% |
| Rank in top quarter: | 37% | Fraternities: | 5% |
| Rank in top tenth: | 13% | Sororities: | 3% |

**Basis for selection.** Admission decision based on high school class rank, SAT scores, and completion of 14 high school units of college preparatory courses. SAT Subject Tests recommended for students with strong academic background. Interview required for early entry and of students accepted with GED tests. **Homeschooled:** Transcript of courses and grades required. Must submit SAT and meet state TASP testing requirements.

**High school preparation.** 15 units required. Required and recommended units include English 4, mathematics 3, social studies 3, science 2, foreign language 2 and academic electives 3.

**2009-2010 Annual costs.** Tuition/fees: $6,607; $14,917 out-of-state. Room/board: $6,290. Books/supplies: $2,870. Personal expenses: $4,152.

**2009-2010 Financial aid.** All financial aid based on need. 1,042 full-time freshmen applied for aid; 656 were judged to have need; 656 of these received aid. Average need met was 58%. 55% of total undergraduate aid awarded as scholarships/grants, 45% as loans/jobs.

**Application procedures. Admission:** Closing date 8/1. $25 fee. Admission notification on a rolling basis. **Financial aid:** Priority date 4/1; no closing date. FAFSA, institutional form required. Applicants notified on a rolling basis starting 4/1; must reply within 2 week(s) of notification.

**Academics. Special study options:** Accelerated study, cooperative education, distance learning, double major, dual enrollment of high school students, ESL, honors, independent study, internships, study abroad, teacher certification program. **Credit/placement by examination:** AP, CLEP, institutional tests. 15 credit hours maximum toward associate degree, 30 toward bachelor's. **Support services:** Learning center, pre-admission summer program, reduced course load, remedial instruction, study skills assistance, tutoring, writing center.

**Majors. Architecture:** Interior. **Biology:** General, marine. **Business:** General, accounting, business admin, finance, human resources, management information systems, managerial economics, marketing, office management, sales/distribution. **Communications:** General, advertising. **Computer sciences:** General. **Conservation:** General, environmental studies. **Education:** Art, Deaf/hearing impaired, early childhood, elementary, family/consumer sciences, health, mathematics, music, physical, school counseling, science, secondary, social studies, special. **Engineering:** General, chemical, civil, electrical, environmental, industrial, mechanical. **Engineering technology:** Industrial, industrial management. **Family/consumer sciences:** General, clothing/textiles, family/community services, food/nutrition. **Foreign languages:** French, Spanish. **Health:** Audiology/speech pathology, clinical lab science, nursing (RN). **History:** General. **Liberal arts:** Arts/sciences. **Math:** General, applied. **Parks/recreation:** Health/fitness. **Physical sciences:** Chemistry, geology, physics, planetary. **Protective services:** Criminal justice. **Psychology:** General. **Public administration:** Social work. **Social sciences:** Economics, political science, sociology. **Visual/performing arts:** Art, commercial/advertising art, dance, dramatic, voice/opera.

**Most popular majors.** Business/marketing 20%, engineering/engineering technologies 10%, health sciences 7%, interdisciplinary studies 17%, liberal arts 10%.

**Computing on campus.** 644 workstations in dormitories, library, computer center, student center. Dormitories wired for high-speed internet access and linked to campus network. Commuter students can connect to campus network. Online course registration, online library, helpline, repair service, student web hosting, wireless network available.

**Student life. Freshman orientation:** Available, $10 fee. Preregistration for classes offered. One-day program available June-August. **Housing:** Guaranteed on-campus for freshmen. Coed dorms, single-sex dorms, special housing for disabled, wellness housing available. $150 deposit, deadline 8/1. **Activities:** Bands, choral groups, dance, drama, film society, literary magazine, music ensembles, musical theater, opera, radio station, student government, student newspaper, symphony orchestra, TV station, Catholic student union, Church of Latter-day Saints, Episcopal center, Church of Christ student center, Wesley Foundation, Vietnamese student organization.

**Athletics.** NCAA. **Intercollegiate:** Baseball M, basketball, cross-country, golf, soccer W, tennis, track and field, volleyball W. **Intramural:** Badminton, basketball, cross-country, racquetball, soccer, softball, swimming, table tennis, tennis, track and field, volleyball, weight lifting. **Team name:** Cardinals.

**Student services.** Adult student services, career counseling, student employment services, health services, on-campus daycare, personal counseling, placement for graduates, veterans' counselor. **Physically disabled:** Services for visually, speech, hearing impaired.

**Contact.** E-mail: admissions@hal.lamar.edu
Phone: (409) 880-8888 Fax: (409) 880-8463
James Rush, Director of Academic Services, Lamar University, Box 10009, Beaumont, TX 77705

---

## LeTourneau University
### Longview, Texas
**www.letu.edu**                                           **CB code: 6365**

- Private 4-year university affiliated with nondenominational tradition
- Residential campus in small city
- 3,040 degree-seeking undergraduates: 5% part-time, 55% women, 20% African American, 1% Asian American, 7% Hispanic American, 2% international
- 287 degree-seeking graduate students
- 70% of applicants admitted
- SAT or ACT (ACT writing optional), application essay required
- 47% graduate within 6 years

**General.** Founded in 1946. Regionally accredited. Centers in Tyler, Dallas, Houston, Austin, and Bedford. **Degrees:** 719 bachelor's, 5 associate awarded; master's offered. **Location:** 120 miles from Dallas, 60 miles from Shreveport, Louisiana. **Calendar:** Semester, limited summer session. **Full-time faculty:** 70 total; 67% have terminal degrees, 10% minority, 17% women. **Part-time faculty:** 184 total; 45% have terminal degrees, 13% minority, 42% women. **Class size:** 73% < 20, 26% 20-39, 2% 40-49, less than 1% 50-99. **Special facilities:** Microprocessor and robotics laboratory, CAD laboratory, scanning electronic microscope, dynamic simulation laboratory, fleet of nine airplanes, biomedical engineering laboratory with motion analysis system.

**Freshman class profile.** 986 applied, 688 admitted, 344 enrolled.

| Mid 50% test scores | | GPA 2.0-2.99: | 8% |
|---|---|---|---|
| SAT critical reading: | 510-640 | Rank in top quarter: | 67% |
| SAT math: | 550-650 | Rank in top tenth: | 41% |
| SAT writing: | 490-620 | Return as sophomores: | 70% |
| ACT composite: | 22-29 | Out-of-state: | 45% |
| GPA 3.75 or higher: | 43% | Live on campus: | 91% |
| GPA 3.50-3.74: | 24% | International: | 4% |
| GPA 3.0-3.49: | 25% | | |

**Basis for selection.** Applicants should rank in top half of high school graduating class, have minimum ACT of 20 or minimum SAT of 950 (exclusive of Writing), and GPA of 2.5. Interview recommended. **Homeschooled:** Require SAT or ACT, transcript; recommend GED and detailed summary of curriculum used.

**High school preparation.** College-preparatory program recommended. 16 units required. Required and recommended units include English 4, mathematics 3, social studies 2, history 1, science 3 (laboratory 3), foreign language 1 and academic electives 2. 4 math (including trigonometry) recommended for engineering applicants.

**2009-2010 Annual costs.** Tuition/fees: $20,400. Room/board: $7,960. Books/supplies: $1,365. Personal expenses: $1,105.

**2009-2010 Financial aid. Non-need-based:** Scholarships awarded for academics, alumni affiliation, leadership.

**Application procedures. Admission:** Priority date 12/31; deadline 8/1. $25 fee, may be waived for applicants with need. Admission notification

8/26. Admission notification on a rolling basis. **Financial aid:** Priority date 2/1; no closing date. FAFSA required. Applicants notified on a rolling basis starting 3/1; must reply within 3 week(s) of notification.

**Academics.** Peer advisers, student resource center, CARE committee, freshman year experience course available. **Special study options:** Accelerated study, cooperative education, distance learning, double major, dual enrollment of high school students, honors, independent study, internships, study abroad, teacher certification program, weekend college. **Credit/placement by examination:** AP, CLEP, IB, SAT, ACT, institutional tests. Credit must be established by end of student's first year at school. **Support services:** Reduced course load, remedial instruction, study skills assistance, tutoring.

**Majors. Biology:** General. **Business:** General, accounting, business admin, finance, human resources, international, management information systems, marketing, operations. **Computer sciences:** General, computer science, information systems. **Education:** Business, computer, elementary, English, history, mathematics, middle, multi-level teacher, physical, science, secondary, social studies. **Engineering:** General, biomedical, computer, electrical, mechanical. **Engineering technology:** Aerospace, computer, electrical, mechanical. **Health:** Predental, premedicine, prepharmacy, preveterinary. **History:** General. **Interdisciplinary:** Math/computer science. **Legal studies:** Prelaw. **Math:** General. **Mechanic/repair:** Aircraft, aircraft powerplant. **Parks/recreation:** Exercise sciences, sports admin. **Physical sciences:** Chemistry, physical chemistry. **Psychology:** General. **Social sciences:** Political science. **Theology:** Bible. **Transportation:** Airline/commercial pilot, aviation, aviation management.

**Most popular majors.** Business/marketing 15%, education 7%, engineering/engineering technologies 34%, parks/recreation 6%, trade and industry 16%.

**Computing on campus.** 200 workstations in library, computer center. Dormitories wired for high-speed internet access and linked to campus network. Commuter students can connect to campus network. Online course registration, online library, helpline, wireless network available.

**Student life. Freshman orientation:** Mandatory, $80 fee. Preregistration for classes offered. 3-day event for students and parents held before classes start. **Policies:** Religious observance required. **Housing:** Guaranteed on-campus for all undergraduates. Single-sex dorms, special housing for disabled, apartments available. Residential societies available. **Activities:** Jazz band, campus ministries, choral groups, drama, film society, international student organizations, literary magazine, music ensembles, musical theater, student government, student newspaper, Fellowship of Christian Athletes, Student Foundation, Habitat for Humanity, summer missions, married student fellowship, student ministries, 2 CARE Council.

**Athletics.** NCAA, NCCAA. **Intercollegiate:** Baseball M, basketball, golf, soccer, softball W, tennis, volleyball W. **Intramural:** Badminton, basketball, cross-country, football (non-tackle), golf, racquetball, soccer, softball, swimming, table tennis, tennis, volleyball. **Team name:** YellowJackets.

**Student services.** Chaplain/spiritual director, career counseling, student employment services, financial aid counseling, health services, personal counseling, placement for graduates, veterans' counselor. **Physically disabled:** Services for visually, speech, hearing impaired.

**Contact.** E-mail: admissions@letu.edu
Phone: (903) 233-4300 Toll-free number: (800) 759-8811
Fax: (903) 233-4301
James Townsend, Director of Admissions, LeTourneau University, PO Box 7001, Longview, TX 75607-7001

## Lubbock Christian University
**Lubbock, Texas**
www.lcu.edu                    CB code: 6378

- Private 4-year university and liberal arts college affiliated with Church of Christ
- Commuter campus in small city
- 1,541 degree-seeking undergraduates: 17% part-time, 59% women, 6% African American, 1% Asian American, 17% Hispanic American, 1% international
- 365 degree-seeking graduate students
- 66% of applicants admitted
- SAT or ACT (ACT writing recommended) required
- 43% graduate within 6 years

**General.** Founded in 1957. Regionally accredited. **Degrees:** 387 bachelor's, 1 associate awarded; master's offered. **ROTC:** Army, Air Force. **Location:** 300 miles from Dallas; 325 miles from Albuquerque, New Mexico. **Calendar:** Semester, limited summer session. **Full-time faculty:** 85 total; 69% have terminal degrees, 5% minority, 29% women. **Part-time faculty:**

86 total; 36% have terminal degrees, 10% minority, 52% women. **Class size:** 67% < 20, 28% 20-39, 2% 40-49, 3% 50-99. **Special facilities:** 2 farms totaling 450 acres.

**Freshman class profile.** 1,044 applied, 684 admitted, 252 enrolled.

| Mid 50% test scores | | | |
|---|---|---|---|
| SAT critical reading: | 430-560 | Rank in top quarter: | 45% |
| SAT math: | 440-540 | Rank in top tenth: | 17% |
| SAT writing: | 420-540 | End year in good standing: | 83% |
| ACT composite: | 18-24 | Return as sophomores: | 67% |
| GPA 3.75 or higher: | 28% | Out-of-state: | 18% |
| GPA 3.50-3.74: | 25% | Live on campus: | 83% |
| GPA 3.0-3.49: | 37% | International: | 4% |
| GPA 2.0-2.99: | 9% | Fraternities: | 37% |
| | | Sororities: | 36% |

**Basis for selection.** Standardized test scores and secondary academic record considered. **Homeschooled:** Transcript of courses and grades required. **Learning Disabled:** Accepted applications who claim disabilities must provide evidence to Disability Coordinator.

**High school preparation.** College-preparatory program recommended. 21 units recommended. Recommended units include English 4, mathematics 3, social studies 1, history 2, science 3 (laboratory 2), foreign language 2, computer science 1, visual/performing arts 1 and academic electives 2.

**2009-2010 Annual costs.** Tuition/fees: $15,280. Room/board: $4,956. Books/supplies: $1,150. Personal expenses: $2,158.

**2008-2009 Financial aid. Need-based:** 187 full-time freshmen applied for aid; 162 were judged to have need; 162 of these received aid. Average need met was 71%. Average scholarship/grant was $9,859; average loan $3,527. 43% of total undergraduate aid awarded as scholarships/grants, 57% as loans/jobs. **Non-need-based:** Awarded to 288 full-time undergraduates, including 70 freshmen. Scholarships awarded for academics, athletics, job skills, leadership, music/drama.

**Application procedures. Admission:** Closing date 8/15 (receipt date). $25 fee, may be waived for applicants with need. Admission notification on a rolling basis. **Financial aid:** Priority date 6/1; no closing date. FAFSA, institutional form required. Applicants notified on a rolling basis starting 3/1.

**Academics.** Computer use integrated into the curriculum. **Special study options:** Distance learning, double major, ESL, honors, internships, liberal arts/career combination, student-designed major, study abroad, teacher certification program, weekend college. **Credit/placement by examination:** AP, CLEP, IB, SAT, ACT, institutional tests. 45 credit hours maximum toward bachelor's degree. **Support services:** Learning center, pre-admission summer program, reduced course load, remedial instruction, study skills assistance, tutoring, writing center.

**Majors. Agriculture:** General, animal sciences, business, plant sciences. **Biology:** General. **Business:** Accounting, business admin, finance, financial planning, information resources management, management information systems, marketing. **Communications:** General, organizational. **Computer sciences:** General. **Education:** Agricultural, art, biology, business, chemistry, computer, early childhood, elementary, English, history, mathematics, middle, multi-level teacher, music, physical, science, secondary, social studies, Spanish, special, speech. **Engineering:** General. **Family/consumer sciences:** Family systems. **Health:** Athletic training, music therapy, nursing (RN), predental, premedicine, prenursing, prepharmacy, preveterinary. **Liberal arts:** Arts/sciences, humanities. **Math:** General. **Parks/recreation:** Exercise sciences, health/fitness, sports admin. **Physical sciences:** Chemistry. **Protective services:** Law enforcement admin. **Psychology:** General. **Public administration:** Social work. **Theology:** Bible, missionary, theology, youth ministry. **Visual/performing arts:** Art, design, directing/producing, music management. **Other:** Exercise and health promotion.

**Most popular majors.** Business/marketing 29%, education 19%, health sciences 11%, parks/recreation 6%.

**Computing on campus.** 235 workstations in dormitories, library, computer center, student center. Dormitories wired for high-speed internet access and linked to campus network. Online course registration, online library, helpline, repair service, wireless network available.

**Student life. Freshman orientation:** Available, $145 fee. Preregistration for classes offered. Week-long orientation held the week before fall semester begins. **Policies:** Chapel attendance required for full-time students age 24 or under. Religious observance required. **Housing:** Guaranteed on-campus for freshmen. Single-sex dorms, special housing for disabled, apartments, wellness housing available. $90 nonrefundable deposit, deadline 8/15. **Activities:** Bands, campus ministries, choral groups, drama, music ensembles, musical theater, student government, student newspaper, Best Friends, Missions Club, Fellowship of Christian Athletes, Students in Free Enterprise, Social Work Outreach Association, social clubs, Organization of Latin American Students.

**Athletics.** NAIA. **Intercollegiate:** Baseball M, basketball, cross-country, golf, softball W, track and field, volleyball W. **Intramural:** Badminton, basketball, bowling, football (non-tackle), soccer, softball, table tennis, tennis, volleyball. **Team name:** Chaparrals.

**Student services.** Adult student services, alcohol/substance abuse counseling, chaplain/spiritual director, career counseling, student employment services, financial aid counseling, health services, personal counseling, placement for graduates, veterans' counselor.

**Contact.** E-mail: admissions@lcu.edu
Phone: (806) 720-7151 Toll-free number: (800) 933-7601 ext. 7151
Fax: (806) 720-7162
Charlie Webb, Director of Admissions, Lubbock Christian University, 5601 19th Street, Lubbock, TX 79407

## McMurry University
### Abilene, Texas
### www.mcm.edu
**CB member**
**CB code: 6402**

- Private 4-year university and liberal arts college affiliated with United Methodist Church
- Residential campus in small city
- 1,396 degree-seeking undergraduates: 13% part-time, 51% women, 16% African American, 1% Asian American, 15% Hispanic American, 1% Native American, 1% international
- 57% of applicants admitted
- SAT or ACT (ACT writing recommended), application essay required
- 39% graduate within 6 years; 27% enter graduate study

**General.** Founded in 1923. Regionally accredited. Three-week May term available; additional off-campus extension at Dyess Air Force Base; part of 3-member consortium providing collegiate nursing education in Texas. **Degrees:** 257 bachelor's awarded. **Location:** 155 miles from Fort Worth, 220 miles from Austin. **Calendar:** Semester, extensive summer session. **Full-time faculty:** 78 total; 78% have terminal degrees, 36% women. **Part-time faculty:** 68 total; 19% have terminal degrees, 50% women. **Class size:** 67% < 20, 31% 20-39, 1% 40-49, 1% 50-99. **Special facilities:** Buffalo Gap historical village.

**Freshman class profile.** 1,574 applied, 896 admitted, 320 enrolled.

| Mid 50% test scores | | Rank in top quarter: | 36% |
|---|---|---|---|
| SAT critical reading: | 410-540 | Rank in top tenth: | 15% |
| SAT math: | 440-550 | End year in good standing: | 74% |
| ACT composite: | 17-24 | Return as sophomores: | 55% |
| GPA 3.75 or higher: | 26% | Out-of-state: | 3% |
| GPA 3.50-3.74: | 16% | Live on campus: | 88% |
| GPA 3.0-3.49: | 30% | International: | 1% |
| GPA 2.0-2.99: | 27% | | |

**Basis for selection.** Applicants evaluated on basis of ACT or SAT scores, high school rank and GPA, academic preparation, and extracurricular activities; character considered. Interview recommended for all; audition required for music, theater programs; portfolio required for art; interview required for admission to Honors Program. **Learning Disabled:** Appropriate documentation required for students seeking special accommodations.

**High school preparation.** College-preparatory program recommended. 14 units required; 16 recommended. Required and recommended units include English 4, mathematics 3, social studies 4, science 3 and foreign language 2. 2 units of foreign language strongly recommended; those who enroll with fewer than 2 units required to take 8 hours of foreign language.

**2009-2010 Annual costs.** Tuition/fees: $19,205. Room/board: $6,757. Books/supplies: $1,200. Personal expenses: $1,827.

**2009-2010 Financial aid.** **Need-based:** 304 full-time freshmen applied for aid; 272 were judged to have need; 270 of these received aid. Average need met was 86%. Average scholarship/grant was $11,759; average loan $3,390. 70% of total undergraduate aid awarded as scholarships/grants, 30% as loans/jobs. **Non-need-based:** Awarded to 726 full-time undergraduates, including 187 freshmen. Scholarships awarded for academics, alumni affiliation, art, music/drama, religious affiliation.

**Application procedures.** **Admission:** Priority date 3/15; deadline 8/15 (receipt date). $20 fee, may be waived for applicants with need. Admission notification on a rolling basis beginning on or about 9/1. Must reply by May 1 or within 2 week(s) if notified thereafter. **Financial aid:** Priority date 3/15; no closing date. FAFSA required. Applicants notified on a rolling basis starting 2/1; must reply within 3 week(s) of notification.

**Academics.** Students receive credit for both nontraditional and traditional courses on and off campus during 3-week May term. Opportunities for bachelor's degree after early admission to dental, medical, or veterinary school. **Special study options:** Accelerated study, combined bachelor's/graduate degree, cross-registration, double major, dual enrollment of high school students, honors, independent study, internships, liberal arts/career combination, student-designed major, teacher certification program. **Credit/placement by examination:** CLEP, IB, SAT, ACT, institutional tests. 45 credit hours maximum toward bachelor's degree. With departmental approval, examinations may be given for credit in areas not covered by AP or CLEP. **Support services:** Learning center, reduced course load, remedial instruction, study skills assistance, tutoring, writing center.

**Majors.** **Biology:** General, biochemistry, biomedical sciences. **Business:** General, accounting, business admin, finance, management information systems, marketing. **Computer sciences:** General. **Education:** Art, biology, chemistry, computer, early childhood, elementary, English, history, mathematics, middle, physical, secondary, Spanish. **Foreign languages:** Spanish. **Health:** Athletic training, nursing (RN), prenursing. **History:** General, public archives. **Math:** General. **Parks/recreation:** Exercise sciences. **Philosophy/religion:** Christian. **Physical sciences:** Chemistry, physics. **Psychology:** General. **Social sciences:** Political science, sociology. **Visual/performing arts:** Dramatic, graphic design, studio arts. **Other:** Multi-/Interdisciplinary studies.

**Most popular majors.** Business/marketing 26%, education 24%, health sciences 12%, psychology 6%, social sciences 6%, visual/performing arts 9%.

**Computing on campus.** PC or laptop required. 248 workstations in library, computer center, student center. Dormitories wired for high-speed internet access and linked to campus network. Commuter students can connect to campus network. Online library, helpline, student web hosting, wireless network available.

**Student life. Freshman orientation:** Available, $150 fee. Preregistration for classes offered. Summer weekend orientation plus 4-day orientation before first week of classes. **Housing:** Guaranteed on-campus for all undergraduates. Coed dorms, single-sex dorms, special housing for disabled, apartments, wellness housing available. $150 partly refundable deposit, deadline 5/1. **Activities:** Bands, campus ministries, choral groups, drama, international student organizations, literary magazine, music ensembles, Model UN, musical theater, student government, student newspaper, Alpha Phi Omega, Fellowship of Christian Athletes, Religious Life, Servant Leadership, Kappa Delta Sigma, student ambassador board, Zeta Phi Beta, campus activities board.

**Athletics.** NCAA. **Intercollegiate:** Baseball M, basketball, cheerleading, cross-country, diving, football (tackle) M, golf, soccer, swimming, tennis, track and field, volleyball W. **Intramural:** Basketball, football (non-tackle), golf, racquetball, soccer, softball, tennis, volleyball.

**Student services.** Alcohol/substance abuse counseling, chaplain/spiritual director, career counseling, student employment services, financial aid counseling, health services, personal counseling, placement for graduates, veterans' counselor.

**Contact.** E-mail: admissions@mcm.edu
Phone: (325) 793-4700 Toll-free number: (800) 460-2392
Fax: (325) 793-4701
Dave Voskuil, Vice President for Enrollment Management, McMurry University, South 14th and Sayles Boulevard, Abilene, TX 79697-0001

## Midwestern State University
### Wichita Falls, Texas
### www.mwsu.edu
**CB member**
**CB code: 6408**

- Public 4-year university and liberal arts college
- Commuter campus in small city
- 5,606 degree-seeking undergraduates: 26% part-time, 58% women, 13% African American, 4% Asian American, 11% Hispanic American, 1% Native American, 7% international
- 700 degree-seeking graduate students
- 88% of applicants admitted
- SAT or ACT with writing required
- 33% graduate within 6 years

**General.** Founded in 1922. Regionally accredited. **Degrees:** 1,016 bachelor's, 44 associate awarded; master's offered. **ROTC:** Air Force. **Location:** 130 miles from Dallas-Fort Worth. **Calendar:** Semester, extensive summer session. **Full-time faculty:** 241 total; 70% have terminal degrees, 13% minority, 44% women. **Part-time faculty:** 94 total; 5% have terminal degrees, 5% minority, 57% women. **Class size:** 31% < 20, 48% 20-39, 11%

40-49, 10% 50-99, less than 1% >100. **Special facilities:** Kurzweil reading machine for the blind, greenhouse, 2 biologic study properties.

**Freshman class profile.** 2,225 applied, 1,956 admitted, 715 enrolled.

| Mid 50% test scores | | | |
|---|---|---|---|
| SAT critical reading: | 450-550 | Rank in top quarter: | 41% |
| SAT math: | 460-570 | Rank in top tenth: | 15% |
| SAT writing: | 430-540 | End year in good standing: | 52% |
| ACT composite: | 18-23 | Return as sophomores: | 78% |
| GPA 3.75 or higher: | 35% | Out-of-state: | 3% |
| GPA 3.50-3.74: | 16% | Live on campus: | 59% |
| GPA 3.0-3.49: | 28% | International: | 2% |
| GPA 2.0-2.99: | 20% | Fraternities: | 7% |
| | | Sororities: | 13% |

**Basis for selection.** For unconditional admission, students must graduate from accredited high school, meet requirements, submit official transcripts and ACT/SAT scores. Entrance exams determined by class rank. Texas public universities require THEA test score on file prior to enrollment unless student exempt. Audition required for applied music program.

**High school preparation.** College-preparatory program recommended. 15 units required. Required units include English 4, mathematics 3, science 2 and academic electives 6.

**2009-2010 Annual costs.** Tuition/fees: $6,226; $7,126 out-of-state. Room/board: $5,770. Books/supplies: $1,200. Personal expenses: $1,379.

**2009-2010 Financial aid. Need-based:** 563 full-time freshmen applied for aid; 378 were judged to have need; 375 of these received aid. Average need met was 79%. Average scholarship/grant was $7,448; average loan $5,757. 42% of total undergraduate aid awarded as scholarships/grants, 58% as loans/jobs. **Non-need-based:** Awarded to 1,382 full-time undergraduates, including 224 freshmen. Scholarships awarded for academics, alumni affiliation, art, athletics, leadership, music/drama. **Additional information:** Employees offered tuition reimbursement provided they meet stated criteria. Dependents and children of faculty and staff may receive scholarship to defer local tuition and fees.

**Application procedures. Admission:** Priority date 7/1; deadline 8/7 (receipt date). $25 fee. Admission notification on a rolling basis beginning on or about 9/1. **Financial aid:** Priority date 3/1; no closing date. FAFSA, institutional form required. Applicants notified on a rolling basis starting 4/15; must reply within 4 week(s) of notification.

**Academics. Special study options:** Combined bachelor's/graduate degree, distance learning, double major, dual enrollment of high school students, ESL, honors, independent study, internships, liberal arts/career combination, study abroad, teacher certification program. Study abroad in England, France, Spain, and Mexico. **Credit/placement by examination:** AP, CLEP, IB, SAT, ACT, institutional tests. 26 credit hours maximum toward associate degree, 60 toward bachelor's. **Support services:** Learning center, reduced course load, remedial instruction, study skills assistance, tutoring, writing center.

**Majors. Biology:** General. **Business:** General, accounting, business admin, finance, management information systems, managerial economics, marketing. **Communications:** Media studies. **Computer sciences:** General. **Conservation:** Environmental science. **Education:** Bilingual, early childhood, English, mathematics, science, social studies. **Engineering:** General, mechanical. **Engineering technology:** Manufacturing. **Foreign languages:** Spanish. **Health:** Athletic training, clinical lab science, dental hygiene, nursing (RN), predental, premedicine, prepharmacy, preveterinary, radiologic technology/medical imaging, respiratory therapy technology. **History:** General. **Interdisciplinary:** Global studies. **Legal studies:** Prelaw. **Liberal arts:** Humanities. **Math:** General. **Parks/recreation:** Exercise sciences, facilities management, health/fitness, sports admin. **Physical sciences:** General, chemistry, geology, physics. **Protective services:** Criminal justice. **Psychology:** General. **Public administration:** Social work. **Social sciences:** Economics, political science, sociology. **Visual/performing arts:** Art, dramatic, studio arts. **Other:** Mulit-/Interdisciplinary Studies, Other.

**Most popular majors.** Business/marketing 17%, education 8%, health sciences 24%, interdisciplinary studies 16%.

**Computing on campus.** 429 workstations in dormitories, library, computer center, student center. Dormitories wired for high-speed internet access and linked to campus network. Commuter students can connect to campus network. Online course registration, online library, wireless network available.

**Student life. Freshman orientation:** Mandatory. Preregistration for classes offered. Parents and family welcome to attend orientation events. **Housing:** Guaranteed on-campus for freshmen. Coed dorms, single-sex dorms, special housing for disabled, apartments, wellness housing available. $100 fully refundable deposit. Cooperative housing units for honors students and biology students. **Activities:** Bands, campus ministries, choral groups, dance,

drama, film society, international student organizations, literary magazine, music ensembles, student government, student newspaper, TV station, Methodist student foundation, Baptist student center, Student Ambassadors, black student union, organization of Hispanic students, University Democrats, College Republicans, Amnesty International.

**Athletics.** NCAA. **Intercollegiate:** Basketball, cross-country W, football (tackle) M, rowing (crew) W, soccer, softball W, tennis, volleyball W. **Intramural:** Archery, badminton, basketball, bowling, football (non-tackle), football (tackle) M, golf, soccer, softball, table tennis, tennis, volleyball. **Team name:** Mustangs.

**Student services.** Alcohol/substance abuse counseling, career counseling, student employment services, financial aid counseling, health services, personal counseling, placement for graduates, veterans' counselor. **Physically disabled:** Services for visually, speech, hearing impaired.

**Contact.** E-mail: admissions@mwsu.edu
Phone: (940) 397-4334 Toll-free number: (800) 842-1922
Fax: (940) 397-4672
Barbara Merkle, Director of Admissions, Midwestern State University, 3410 Taft Boulevard, Wichita Falls, TX 76308-2099

## Northwood University: Texas
### Cedar Hill, Texas
www.northwood.edu                                    CB code: 6499

- Private 4-year university and business college
- Residential campus in large town
- 514 degree-seeking undergraduates: 2% part-time, 47% women, 14% African American, 3% Asian American, 32% Hispanic American, 1% Native American, 9% international
- 37 degree-seeking graduate students
- 52% of applicants admitted
- SAT or ACT (ACT writing optional), application essay required
- 31% graduate within 6 years; 8% enter graduate study

**General.** Founded in 1966. Regionally accredited. Specialty university offering only business degrees in professional management; 3 residential campuses in Michigan, Florida, and Texas; 40 program centers; library center in Maine. **Degrees:** 93 bachelor's, 77 associate awarded. **Location:** 18 miles from Dallas, 28 miles from Fort Worth. **Calendar:** Semester, limited summer session. **Full-time faculty:** 22 total; 27% have terminal degrees, 18% minority, 36% women. **Part-time faculty:** 12 total; 25% have terminal degrees, 17% minority, 42% women. **Class size:** 46% < 20, 52% 20-39, 2% 40-49, less than 1% 50-99.

**Freshman class profile.** 459 applied, 237 admitted, 141 enrolled.

| Mid 50% test scores | | | |
|---|---|---|---|
| SAT critical reading: | 420-510 | GPA 2.0-2.99: | 11% |
| SAT math: | 440-560 | Rank in top quarter: | 35% |
| SAT writing: | 400-500 | Rank in top tenth: | 10% |
| ACT composite: | 17-21 | End year in good standing: | 73% |
| GPA 3.75 or higher: | 10% | Return as sophomores: | 64% |
| GPA 3.50-3.74: | 17% | Out-of-state: | 5% |
| GPA 3.0-3.49: | 62% | Live on campus: | 43% |
| | | International: | 3% |

**Basis for selection.** Minimum GPA of 2.0 and strong interest in business or related field. Test scores considered. Students with lower GPA possibly admitted on probation. Interview recommended. **Homeschooled:** Transcript of courses and grades, state high school equivalency certificate required.

**High school preparation.** College-preparatory program recommended. 17 units recommended. Recommended units include English 4, mathematics 3, social studies 3, science 3 (laboratory 2), foreign language 1 and computer science 1.

**2009-2010 Annual costs.** Tuition/fees: $18,408. Room/board: $7,590. Books/supplies: $1,581. Personal expenses: $807.

**2009-2010 Financial aid. Need-based:** 118 full-time freshmen applied for aid; 108 were judged to have need; 108 of these received aid. Average need met was 64%. Average scholarship/grant was $5,088; average loan $3,401. 58% of total undergraduate aid awarded as scholarships/grants, 42% as loans/jobs. **Non-need-based:** Awarded to 193 full-time undergraduates, including 52 freshmen. Scholarships awarded for academics, athletics, leadership, minority status, state residency.

**Application procedures. Admission:** No deadline. $25 fee, may be waived for applicants with need, free for online applicants. Admission notification on a rolling basis. **Financial aid:** No deadline. FAFSA required. Applicants notified on a rolling basis starting 3/1.

**Academics. Special study options:** Accelerated study, distance learning, double major, dual enrollment of high school students, external degree, honors, independent study, internships, student-designed major, study abroad, weekend college. **Credit/placement by examination:** AP, CLEP, IB, SAT, ACT, institutional tests. 12 credit hours maximum toward bachelor's degree. **Support services:** Learning center, reduced course load, remedial instruction, study skills assistance, tutoring, writing center.

**Majors. Business:** Accounting, business admin, marketing.

**Most popular majors.** Business/marketing 86%, communications/journalism 8%, parks/recreation 6%.

**Computing on campus.** 50 workstations in library, computer center. Dormitories wired for high-speed internet access and linked to campus network. Commuter students can connect to campus network. Online course registration, online library, helpline, student web hosting, wireless network available.

**Student life. Freshman orientation:** Mandatory, $125 fee. Preregistration for classes offered. Multiple sessions throughout the summer. **Housing:** Guaranteed on-campus for freshmen. Single-sex dorms, apartments, wellness housing available. $100 fully refundable deposit, deadline 8/1. **Activities:** Choral groups, dance, drama, literary magazine, student government, student newspaper, Christian Fellowship.

**Athletics. NAIA. Intercollegiate:** Baseball M, cross-country, golf, soccer, softball W, track and field. **Intramural:** Basketball, volleyball. **Team name:** Knights.

**Student services.** Adult student services, career counseling, student employment services, financial aid counseling, health services, personal counseling, placement for graduates.

**Contact.** E-mail: txadmit@northwood.edu
Phone: (972) 293-5400 Toll-free number: (800) 927-9663
Fax: (972) 291-3824
Sylvia Correa, Director of Admissions, Northwood University: Texas, 1114 West FM 1382, Cedar Hill, TX 75104

## Our Lady of the Lake University of San Antonio

San Antonio, Texas       CB member
www.ollusa.edu       CB code: 6550

- Private 4-year university affiliated with Roman Catholic Church
- Commuter campus in very large city
- 1,564 degree-seeking undergraduates: 26% part-time, 72% women, 8% African American, 1% Asian American, 71% Hispanic American, 1% international
- 1,033 degree-seeking graduate students
- 32% of applicants admitted
- SAT or ACT (ACT writing optional) required
- 38% graduate within 6 years

**General.** Founded in 1895. Regionally accredited. **Degrees:** 282 bachelor's awarded; master's, doctoral, professional offered. **ROTC:** Army, Air Force. **Location:** 4 miles from downtown, 80 miles from Austin. **Calendar:** Semester, limited summer session. **Full-time faculty:** 108 total; 68% have terminal degrees, 44% minority, 58% women. **Part-time faculty:** 120 total; 41% have terminal degrees, 42% minority, 41% women. **Class size:** 70% < 20, 30% 20-39. **Special facilities:** International center, international folk culture center, speech and hearing clinic, community counseling center, elementary school, child development center, center for social work research, center for women in church and society.

**Freshman class profile.** 1,232 applied, 394 admitted, 252 enrolled.

| Mid 50% test scores | | GPA 2.0-2.99: | 28% |
|---|---|---|---|
| SAT critical reading: | 390-500 | Rank in top quarter: | 39% |
| SAT math: | 410-500 | Rank in top tenth: | 13% |
| ACT composite: | 16-21 | Return as sophomores: | 59% |
| GPA 3.75 or higher: | 9% | Out-of-state: | 4% |
| GPA 3.50-3.74: | 22% | Live on campus: | 69% |
| GPA 3.0-3.49: | 41% | International: | 2% |

**Basis for selection.** High school academic record and test scores important. **Homeschooled:** Transcript of courses and grades required.

**High school preparation.** College-preparatory program recommended. 14 units required. Required units include English 4, mathematics 3, social studies 3 and science 2. 2 additional credits in English, math, social sciences, or nature sciences.

**2010-2011 Annual costs.** Tuition/fees: $21,948. Room/board: $6,838. Books/supplies: $1,200. Personal expenses: $1,850.

**2009-2010 Financial aid. Need-based:** 51% of total undergraduate aid awarded as scholarships/grants, 49% as loans/jobs. **Non-need-based:** Scholarships awarded for academics, religious affiliation.

**Application procedures. Admission:** No deadline. $25 fee, may be waived for applicants with need. Admission notification on a rolling basis. **Financial aid:** Priority date 5/1; no closing date. FAFSA, institutional form required.

**Academics. Special study options:** Accelerated study, combined bachelor's/graduate degree, cooperative education, cross-registration, distance learning, double major, dual enrollment of high school students, honors, independent study, internships, study abroad, teacher certification program, weekend college. **Credit/placement by examination:** AP, CLEP, IB, institutional tests. No limit to number of credit hours that may be awarded through CLEP or that may be counted towards bachelor's degree. **Support services:** Learning center, pre-admission summer program, reduced course load, remedial instruction, study skills assistance, tutoring.

**Majors. Biology:** General. **Business:** Accounting, business admin, human resources, marketing, nonprofit/public. **Communications:** General, broadcast journalism, journalism, public relations. **Computer sciences:** General. **Education:** Kindergarten/preschool, special, speech impaired. **Family/consumer sciences:** Business. **Foreign languages:** Spanish. **Health:** Speech pathology. **History:** General. **Interdisciplinary:** Natural sciences. **Liberal arts:** Arts/sciences. **Math:** General. **Philosophy/religion:** Philosophy, religion. **Physical sciences:** Chemistry. **Protective services:** Criminal justice. **Psychology:** General. **Public administration:** Social work. **Social sciences:** General, political science, sociology. **Visual/performing arts:** Art, dramatic.

**Most popular majors.** Business/marketing 20%, education 15%, health sciences 6%, psychology 10%, public administration/social services 11%.

**Computing on campus.** 208 workstations in dormitories, library, computer center, student center. Dormitories wired for high-speed internet access and linked to campus network. Commuter students can connect to campus network. Online course registration, online library, helpline, repair service, wireless network available.

**Student life. Freshman orientation:** Mandatory, $50 fee. Preregistration for classes offered. Overnight program, 4 times during the spring and summer. Familiarity with faculty, staff, campus, and assessment testing. Parent participation encouraged. **Housing:** Guaranteed on-campus for freshmen. Coed dorms, single-sex dorms available. $100 fully refundable deposit, deadline 8/1. **Activities:** Bands, campus ministries, choral groups, dance, drama, film society, international student organizations, literary magazine, music ensembles, musical theater, student government, student newspaper, symphony orchestra, TV station, religious organizations, black and Hispanic clubs, service clubs.

**Athletics. NAIA. Intercollegiate:** Soccer, volleyball W. **Intramural:** Basketball, football (non-tackle), golf, racquetball, soccer W, softball, swimming, tennis, volleyball M. **Team name:** Saints.

**Student services.** Adult student services, alcohol/substance abuse counseling, chaplain/spiritual director, career counseling, student employment services, financial aid counseling, health services, personal counseling, placement for graduates, veterans' counselor, women's services. **Physically disabled:** Services for visually, speech, hearing impaired.

**Contact.** E-mail: admission@lake.ollusa.edu
Phone: (210) 431-3961 Toll-free number: (800) 436-6558
Fax: (210) 431-4036
Michael Acosta, Vice President, Enrollment Management, Our Lady of the Lake University of San Antonio, 411 Southwest 24th Street, San Antonio, TX 78207-4689

## Paul Quinn College

Dallas, Texas
www.pqc.edu       CB code: 6577

- Private 4-year liberal arts college affiliated with African Methodist Episcopal Church
- Residential campus in very large city

**General.** Founded in 1872. Regionally accredited. **Location:** 12 miles from Dallas. **Calendar:** Semester.

**Annual costs/financial aid.** Books/supplies: $1,000. Personal expenses: $350.

**Contact.** Phone: (214) 302-3575
Director of Admissions, 3837 Simpson Stuart Road, Dallas, TX 75241

## Prairie View A&M University
**Prairie View, Texas**                          **CB member**
**www.pvamu.edu**                                **CB code: 6580**

- Public 4-year university
- Commuter campus in small town
- 6,712 degree-seeking undergraduates: 9% part-time, 58% women
- 1,876 degree-seeking graduate students
- 41% of applicants admitted
- SAT or ACT (ACT writing optional) required
- 35% graduate within 6 years

**General.** Founded in 1876. Regionally accredited. Historically black college. **Degrees:** 798 bachelor's awarded; master's, doctoral, professional offered. **ROTC:** Army, Naval. **Location:** 47 miles from Houston. **Calendar:** Semester, extensive summer session. **Full-time faculty:** 369 total; 78% minority, 38% women. **Part-time faculty:** 131 total; 63% minority, 56% women. **Class size:** 27% < 20, 58% 20-39, 8% 40-49, 7% 50-99, less than 1% >100. **Special facilities:** Nuclear magnetic resonance spectrometric differentiator, scanning calorimeter, high pressure liquid chromatograph, solid state engineering laboratory, computer-aided design and drafting laboratory, center for learning and teaching effectiveness, international dairy goat research center, cooperative agricultural research center, solar observatory.

**Freshman class profile.** 7,425 applied, 3,021 admitted, 1,589 enrolled.

| Mid 50% test scores | | | |
|---|---|---|---|
| SAT critical reading: | 370-460 | GPA 3.50-3.74: | 7% |
| SAT math: | 380-480 | GPA 3.0-3.49: | 31% |
| SAT writing: | 360-450 | GPA 2.0-2.99: | 59% |
| ACT composite: | 15-19 | Rank in top quarter: | 23% |
| GPA 3.75 or higher: | 2% | Rank in top tenth: | 8% |
| | | Return as sophomores: | 47% |

**Basis for selection.** Score on institution's entrance examination, personal qualities, high school GPA important. Students may be admitted conditionally if grades or test scores are below minimum requirement.

**High school preparation.** 16 units required; 18 recommended. Required and recommended units include English 4, mathematics 3-4, social studies 2, science 3, foreign language 2 and academic electives 4. Recommend 1 computer science.

**2009-2010 Annual costs.** Tuition/fees: $7,199; $15,689 out-of-state. Room/board: $7,445. Books/supplies: $1,000. Personal expenses: $1,000.

**2009-2010 Financial aid.** **Non-need-based:** Scholarships awarded for academics, athletics, ROTC.

**Application procedures.** **Admission:** Closing date 6/1 (postmark date). $25 fee, may be waived for applicants with need. Admission notification on a rolling basis. **Financial aid:** Closing date 3/15. FAFSA, institutional form required. Applicants notified by 6/1; must reply by 8/1.

**Academics.** **Special study options:** Accelerated study, combined bachelor's/graduate degree, cooperative education, cross-registration, distance learning, double major, dual enrollment of high school students, exchange student, external degree, honors, independent study, internships, liberal arts/career combination, study abroad, teacher certification program, weekend college. **Credit/placement by examination:** AP, CLEP, institutional tests. 30 credit hours maximum toward bachelor's degree. **Support services:** Learning center, pre-admission summer program, reduced course load, remedial instruction, tutoring.

**Majors.** **Agriculture:** General. **Architecture:** Architecture. **Biology:** General. **Business:** Accounting, business admin, finance, management information systems. **Communications:** General. **Computer sciences:** General. **Engineering:** Chemical, civil, computer, electrical, mechanical. **Engineering technology:** Computer, construction, drafting, electrical, industrial. **Family/consumer sciences:** Food/nutrition. **Foreign languages:** Spanish. **Health:** Clinical lab science, health services, nursing (RN). **History:** General. **Math:** General. **Parks/recreation:** Health/fitness. **Physical sciences:** Chemistry, physics. **Protective services:** Criminal justice. **Psychology:** General. **Public administration:** Social work. **Social sciences:** Political science, sociology. **Visual/performing arts:** Dramatic, music performance.

**Most popular majors.** Biology 6%, business/marketing 12%, engineering/engineering technologies 13%, health sciences 17%, interdisciplinary studies 8%, personal/culinary services 8%, security/protective services 8%.

**Computing on campus.** 500 workstations in dormitories, library, computer center, student center. Dormitories wired for high-speed internet access and linked to campus network. Commuter students can connect to campus network. Online library, helpline, wireless network available.

**Student life. Freshman orientation:** Mandatory, $60 fee. Preregistration for classes offered. 1 day for Phase 1; 3 days for Phase 2. **Housing:** Guaranteed on-campus for freshmen. Coed dorms, special housing for disabled, apartments available. $150 fully refundable deposit. **Activities:** Bands, choral groups, dance, drama, international student organizations, literary magazine, music ensembles, musical theater, radio station, student government, student newspaper, symphony orchestra, College Republicans, Spanish-speaking students association, Baptist student ministry, Chinese student association, ministerial alliance, Japanese student association, Korean student association.

**Athletics.** NAIA, NCAA. **Intercollegiate:** Baseball M, basketball, bowling W, cross-country, football (tackle) M, golf, soccer W, softball W, tennis, track and field, volleyball W. **Intramural:** Basketball, bowling W, football (tackle) M, golf, soccer W, softball, tennis, track and field, volleyball W. **Team name:** Panthers.

**Student services.** Adult student services, alcohol/substance abuse counseling, chaplain/spiritual director, career counseling, student employment services, financial aid counseling, health services, personal counseling, placement for graduates, veterans' counselor. **Physically disabled:** Services for hearing impaired.

**Contact.** E-mail: admissions@pvamu.edu
Phone: (936) 261-1000 Toll-free number: (877) 782-6830
Fax: (936) 261-1079
Mary Gooch, Assistant Director Admissions, Prairie View A&M University, PO Box 519, MS 1009, Prairie View, TX 77446-0519

## Rice University
**Houston, Texas**                               **CB member**
**www.rice.edu**                                 **CB code: 6609**

- Private 4-year university
- Residential campus in very large city
- 3,279 degree-seeking undergraduates: 1% part-time, 48% women, 7% African American, 21% Asian American, 12% Hispanic American, 9% international
- 2,277 degree-seeking graduate students
- 22% of applicants admitted
- SAT and SAT Subject Tests or ACT with writing, application essay required
- 93% graduate within 6 years

**General.** Founded in 1891. Regionally accredited. **Degrees:** 1,015 bachelor's awarded; master's, doctoral offered. **ROTC:** Army, Naval, Air Force. **Location:** 3 miles from downtown Houston. **Calendar:** Semester, limited summer session. **Full-time faculty:** 619 total; 96% have terminal degrees, 18% minority, 30% women. **Part-time faculty:** 136 total; 72% have terminal degrees, 12% minority, 35% women. **Class size:** 65% < 20, 23% 20-39, 4% 40-49, 5% 50-99, 3% >100. **Special facilities:** Art gallery, wetland center for biochemical research, arboretum, nanotechnology lab, center for study of languages and culture, civil engineering lab, concert hall with grand organ, institute for public policy, observatory, digital media center.

**Freshman class profile.** 11,172 applied, 2,495 admitted, 894 enrolled.

| Mid 50% test scores | | | |
|---|---|---|---|
| SAT critical reading: | 640-750 | Rank in top tenth: | 84% |
| SAT math: | 680-780 | End year in good standing: | 98% |
| SAT writing: | 650-740 | Return as sophomores: | 97% |
| ACT composite: | 30-34 | Out-of-state: | 46% |
| Rank in top quarter: | 94% | Live on campus: | 97% |
| | | International: | 12% |

**Basis for selection.** High school course selection and performance, test scores, teacher and counselor recommendations, extracurricular activity, and application answers/essay most important. If student submits SAT Reasoning, two SAT Subject Tests are also required (recommend subject tests be in subjects related to student's area of interest). If student submits ACT with Writing, then no SAT Subject Tests are required. Audition required for music; portfolio required for architecture. Interview recommended for all freshman applicants. **Homeschooled:** Statement describing homeschool structure and mission, letter of recommendation (nonparent) required.

**High school preparation.** College-preparatory program required. 16 units required; 20 recommended. Required and recommended units include English 4, mathematics 3-4, social studies 2, science 2-4 (laboratory 2-3), foreign language 2-4 and academic electives 3. Trigonometry (pre-calculus), physics, and chemistry required of engineering and natural science majors, although 2nd year of chemistry or biology may replace physics requirement.

**2009-2010 Annual costs.** Tuition/fees: $32,057. Room/board: $11,230. Books/supplies: $800. Personal expenses: $1,550.

**2009-2010 Financial aid. Need-based:** 606 full-time freshmen applied for aid; 370 were judged to have need; 370 of these received aid. Average need met was 100%. Average scholarship/grant was $26,850; average loan $1,333. 91% of total undergraduate aid awarded as scholarships/grants, 9% as loans/jobs. **Non-need-based:** Awarded to 930 full-time undergraduates, including 216 freshmen. Scholarships awarded for academics, art, athletics, leadership, minority status, music/drama, ROTC, state residency.

**Application procedures. Admission:** Closing date 1/2 (postmark date). $60 fee, may be waived for applicants with need. Admission notification 4/1. Must reply by May 1 or within 2 week(s) if notified thereafter. **Financial aid:** Priority date 3/1; no closing date. FAFSA, CSS PROFILE required. Applicants notified by 4/1; must reply by 5/1.

**Academics. Special study options:** Combined bachelor's/graduate degree, cross-registration, double major, dual enrollment of high school students, ESL, exchange student, honors, independent study, internships, liberal arts/career combination, student-designed major, study abroad, teacher certification program. 8-year guaranteed medical school program with Baylor College of Medicine for 14 entering freshmen. **Credit/placement by examination:** AP, CLEP, IB, institutional tests. **Support services:** Study skills assistance, tutoring, writing center.

**Majors. Architecture:** Architecture. **Area/ethnic studies:** Asian, Chicano/ Hispanic-American/Latino, German, Latin American, Slavic, women's. **Biology:** General, biochemistry, ecology, evolutionary. **Business:** Business admin. **Computer sciences:** Computer science. **Engineering:** Biomedical, chemical, civil, computer, electrical, environmental, materials, mechanical. **Foreign languages:** Ancient Greek, classics, French, German, Latin, linguistics, Slavic, Spanish. **History:** General. **Interdisciplinary:** Classical/ archaeology, cognitive science, medieval/Renaissance. **Math:** General, applied, statistics. **Parks/recreation:** Exercise sciences, sports admin. **Philosophy/ religion:** Philosophy, religion. **Physical sciences:** Astronomy, astrophysics, chemical physics, chemistry, geology, geophysics, physical chemistry, physics. **Psychology:** General. **Public administration:** Policy analysis. **Social sciences:** General, anthropology, economics, political science, sociology. **Visual/performing arts:** General, art, art history/conservation, music history, music performance, music theory/composition, studio arts.

**Most popular majors.** Biology 8%, engineering/engineering technologies 17%, English 6%, psychology 6%, social sciences 17%, visual/ performing arts 7%.

**Computing on campus.** 543 workstations in dormitories, library, computer center, student center. Dormitories wired for high-speed internet access and linked to campus network. Commuter students can connect to campus network. Online course registration, online library, helpline, student web hosting, wireless network available.

**Student life. Freshman orientation:** Mandatory, $205 fee. Held the week before start of classes. **Policies:** Academic honor code. All undergraduates are granted membership in one of 11 residential college communities and maintain that affiliation for their entire college career. Each college is self governing and designed to facilitate student and faculty networking, leadership development, pre-major advising, and social interaction. **Housing:** Guaranteed on-campus for freshmen. Coed dorms, special housing for disabled available. $100 nonrefundable deposit, deadline 5/1. **Activities:** Bands, campus ministries, choral groups, dance, drama, film society, international student organizations, literary magazine, music ensembles, Model UN, musical theater, opera, radio station, student government, student newspaper, symphony orchestra, TV station, Hispanic student association, Hillel, black student association, Young Democrats, Young Republicans, Chinese student association, Baptist student union, Catholic student center, student volunteer program.

**Athletics.** NCAA. **Intercollegiate:** Baseball M, basketball, cheerleading, cross-country, football (non-tackle) W, football (tackle) M, golf M, soccer W, swimming W, tennis, track and field, volleyball W. **Intramural:** Badminton, basketball, racquetball, soccer, softball, swimming, table tennis, tennis, track and field, volleyball. **Team name:** Owls.

**Student services.** Alcohol/substance abuse counseling, chaplain/ spiritual director, career counseling, student employment services, financial aid counseling, health services, minority student services, personal counseling, placement for graduates, women's services. **Physically disabled:** Services for visually, speech, hearing impaired.

**Contact.** E-mail: admission@rice.edu
Phone: (713) 348-7423 Toll-free number: (800) 527-6957
Fax: (713) 348-5952
Keith Todd, Director of Admission, Rice University, 6100 Main Street, Houston, TX 77251-1892

## St. Edward's University
**Austin, Texas**     **CB member**
www.gotostedwards.com     **CB code: 6619**

- Private 4-year university and liberal arts college affiliated with Roman Catholic Church
- Residential campus in very large city
- 4,339 degree-seeking undergraduates: 20% part-time, 59% women, 5% African American, 3% Asian American, 30% Hispanic American, 1% Native American, 3% international
- 899 degree-seeking graduate students
- 66% of applicants admitted
- SAT or ACT with writing, application essay required
- 66% graduate within 6 years

**General.** Founded in 1885. Regionally accredited. **Degrees:** 978 bachelor's awarded; master's offered. **ROTC:** Army, Air Force. **Location:** 80 miles from San Antonio, 180 miles from Dallas. **Calendar:** Semester, limited summer session. **Full-time faculty:** 184 total; 90% have terminal degrees, 9% minority, 45% women. **Part-time faculty:** 295 total; 52% have terminal degrees, 15% minority, 49% women. **Class size:** 50% < 20, 49% 20-39, less than 1% 40-49. **Special facilities:** Fine arts facility with photography laboratory, theater, chapel, natural sciences center, interdisciplinary research laboratory at Wild Basin Wilderness Preserve.

**Freshman class profile.** 2,981 applied, 1,970 admitted, 757 enrolled.

| Mid 50% test scores | | | |
|---|---|---|---|
| SAT critical reading: | 520-630 | Rank in top tenth: | 19% |
| SAT math: | 510-610 | End year in good standing: | 92% |
| SAT writing: | 500-610 | Return as sophomores: | 82% |
| ACT composite: | 22-27 | Out-of-state: | 8% |
| Rank in top quarter: | 54% | Live on campus: | 89% |
| | | International: | 2% |

**Basis for selection.** Holistic review process, with grades and curriculum; class rank and test scores (both preferably in top 50th percentile) most important components. Extracurricular activities, leadership and service, application essay, letters of recommendation reviewed as complement to student's academic record. **Homeschooled:** Transcript of courses and grades required. Assessment done on individual basis. **Learning Disabled:** Students may submit learning disability documentation with admission application.

**High school preparation.** College-preparatory program recommended. 14 units required; 20 recommended. Required and recommended units include English 4, mathematics 3-4, social studies 1, history 2-3, science 2-3 (laboratory 2-3), foreign language 2-3, computer science 1 and academic electives 1.

**2010-2011 Annual costs.** Tuition/fees (projected): $26,484. Room/board: $9,036. Books/supplies: $1,100. Personal expenses: $2,310.

**2009-2010 Financial aid. Need-based:** 643 full-time freshmen applied for aid; 547 were judged to have need; 546 of these received aid. Average need met was 74%. Average scholarship/grant was $13,705; average loan $3,323. 73% of total undergraduate aid awarded as scholarships/grants, 27% as loans/jobs. **Non-need-based:** Awarded to 1,942 full-time undergraduates, including 518 freshmen. Scholarships awarded for academics, art, athletics, leadership, music/drama, state residency.

**Application procedures. Admission:** Priority date 2/1; deadline 5/1 (postmark date). $45 fee, may be waived for applicants with need. Admission notification on a rolling basis beginning on or about 11/1. Must reply by May 1 or within 2 week(s) if notified thereafter. Applicants seeking scholarship consideration must apply by February 1. **Financial aid:** Priority date 3/1, closing date 4/15. FAFSA required. Applicants notified on a rolling basis starting 1/15; must reply by 5/1 or within 2 week(s) of notification.

**Academics.** Writing center, tutoring services available evenings and weekends. **Special study options:** Double major, honors, internships, study abroad, teacher certification program. **Credit/placement by examination:** AP, CLEP, IB, SAT, ACT, institutional tests. 90 credit hours maximum toward bachelor's degree. **Support services:** Learning center, pre-admission summer program, reduced course load, remedial instruction, study skills assistance, tutoring, writing center.

**Majors. Area/ethnic studies:** Latin American. **Biology:** General, biochemistry, bioinformatics. **Business:** Accounting, accounting technology, business admin, entrepreneurial studies, finance, international, marketing. **Communications:** Digital media, media studies. **Computer sciences:** General, computer science. **Conservation:** Environmental studies. **Education:** Art, biology, chemistry, drama/dance, history, mathematics, multi-level teacher, physical, social studies, Spanish. **Foreign languages:** Spanish. **History:** General. **Interdisciplinary:** Global studies. **Liberal arts:** Arts/sciences. **Math:**

General. **Parks/recreation:** Exercise sciences. **Philosophy/religion:** Philosophy. **Physical sciences:** Chemistry. **Protective services:** Criminal justice, forensics. **Psychology:** General. **Public administration:** Social work. **Social sciences:** Criminology, economics, political science, sociology. **Theology:** Religious ed, theology. **Visual/performing arts:** Art, dramatic, graphic design, photography. **Other:** Environmental chemistry.

**Most popular majors.** Business/marketing 28%, communications/journalism 12%, English 6%, psychology 11%, social sciences 8%, visual/performing arts 8%.

**Computing on campus.** 756 workstations in dormitories, library, computer center, student center. Dormitories wired for high-speed internet access and linked to campus network. Commuter students can connect to campus network. Online course registration, online library, helpline, repair service, student web hosting, wireless network available.

**Student life. Freshman orientation:** Mandatory, $150 fee. Preregistration for classes offered. 2-day sessions held 6 times during summer. **Policies:** Student organizations must receive annual university recognition through office of student life, and must also go through annual risk management training. **Housing:** Guaranteed on-campus for freshmen. Coed dorms, single-sex dorms, special housing for disabled, apartments available. $150 nonrefundable deposit, deadline 5/1. Community-style living in casitas/casas, 2 living-learning communities available. **Activities:** Campus ministries, choral groups, dance, drama, film society, international student organizations, literary magazine, music ensembles, musical theater, student government, student newspaper, symphony orchestra, TV station, Over 95 student organizations on campus.

**Athletics.** NCAA. **Intercollegiate:** Baseball M, basketball, golf, soccer, softball W, tennis, volleyball W. **Intramural:** Basketball, bowling, football (non-tackle), golf, racquetball, soccer, softball, swimming, tennis, volleyball. **Team name:** Hilltoppers.

**Student services.** Adult student services, alcohol/substance abuse counseling, chaplain/spiritual director, career counseling, student employment services, financial aid counseling, health services, personal counseling, placement for graduates, veterans' counselor. **Physically disabled:** Services for visually, speech, hearing impaired.

**Contact.** E-mail: seu.admit@stedwards.edu
Phone: (512) 448-8500 Toll-free number: (800) 555-0164
Fax: (512) 464-8877
St. Edward's University, 3001 South Congress Avenue, Austin, TX 78704-6489

## St. Mary's University
San Antonio, Texas
www.stmarytx.edu

CB member
CB code: 6637

▶ Private 4-year university affiliated with Roman Catholic Church
▶ Residential campus in very large city
▶ 2,369 degree-seeking undergraduates: 7% part-time, 60% women, 4% African American, 3% Asian American, 70% Hispanic American, 3% international
▶ 1,516 degree-seeking graduate students
▶ 76% of applicants admitted
▶ SAT or ACT (ACT writing recommended) required
▶ 56% graduate within 6 years

**General.** Founded in 1852. Regionally accredited. **Degrees:** 421 bachelor's awarded; master's, doctoral, professional offered. **ROTC:** Army, Air Force. **Location:** 5 miles from downtown. **Calendar:** Semester, limited summer session. **Full-time faculty:** 197 total; 92% have terminal degrees, 18% minority, 34% women. **Part-time faculty:** 143 total; 53% have terminal degrees, 34% minority, 43% women. **Class size:** 41% < 20, 57% 20-39, 1% 40-49, less than 1% 50-99.

**Freshman class profile.** 2,448 applied, 1,859 admitted, 531 enrolled.

| Mid 50% test scores | | | |
|---|---|---|---|
| SAT critical reading: | 470-570 | GPA 2.0-2.99: | 11% |
| SAT math: | 470-590 | Rank in top quarter: | 66% |
| SAT writing: | 460-560 | Rank in top tenth: | 33% |
| ACT composite: | 20-25 | End year in good standing: | 85% |
| GPA 3.75 or higher: | 25% | Return as sophomores: | 80% |
| GPA 3.50-3.74: | 31% | Out-of-state: | 6% |
| GPA 3.0-3.49: | 32% | Live on campus: | 84% |
| | | International: | 2% |

**Basis for selection.** Balanced consideration given to all aspects of high school performance, including selection of college-preparatory courses, GPA and grade pattern throughout high school, class rank, standardized test scores, and record of service and leadership.

**High school preparation.** College-preparatory program recommended. 16 units required; 19 recommended. Required and recommended units include English 4, mathematics 3-4, social studies 3-4, science 3-4, foreign language 2-3 and academic electives 1. Applicants to science and engineering program should complete 4 units of math and 3 units of lab science.

**2009-2010 Annual costs.** Tuition/fees: $21,876. Room/board: $7,090. Books/supplies: $1,300. Personal expenses: $3,194.

**2008-2009 Financial aid. Need-based:** 470 full-time freshmen applied for aid; 429 were judged to have need; 428 of these received aid. Average need met was 78%. Average scholarship/grant was $13,542; average loan $6,317. 59% of total undergraduate aid awarded as scholarships/grants, 41% as loans/jobs. **Non-need-based:** Awarded to 1,632 full-time undergraduates, including 483 freshmen. Scholarships awarded for academics, alumni affiliation, athletics, leadership, minority status, music/drama, ROTC, state residency.

**Application procedures. Admission:** Priority date 1/15; no deadline. $30 fee, may be waived for applicants with need, free for online applicants. Admission notification on a rolling basis beginning on or about 10/20. Must reply by May 1 or within 2 week(s) if notified thereafter. **Financial aid:** Priority date 3/31; no closing date. FAFSA required. Applicants notified on a rolling basis starting 3/1; must reply by 5/1 or within 2 week(s) of notification.

**Academics.** Writing across the curriculum program requires students in all undergraduate programs to take writing-intensive courses. **Special study options:** Combined bachelor's/graduate degree, cross-registration, distance learning, double major, dual enrollment of high school students, ESL, exchange student, honors, independent study, internships, liberal arts/career combination, study abroad, teacher certification program, Washington semester. **Credit/placement by examination:** AP, CLEP, SAT, ACT, institutional tests. 30 credit hours maximum toward bachelor's degree. **Support services:** Learning center, pre-admission summer program, reduced course load, remedial instruction, study skills assistance, tutoring, writing center.

**Majors. Biology:** General, biochemistry. **Business:** General, accounting, business admin, entrepreneurial studies, finance, human resources, international, management information systems, marketing. **Communications:** General. **Computer sciences:** General, computer science. **Education:** General. **Engineering:** Computer, electrical, industrial, science. **Engineering technology:** Industrial management. **Foreign languages:** French, Spanish. **History:** General. **Liberal arts:** Arts/sciences. **Math:** General. **Parks/recreation:** Exercise sciences. **Philosophy/religion:** Philosophy. **Physical sciences:** Chemistry, geology, physics. **Protective services:** Criminal justice. **Psychology:** General. **Social sciences:** Economics, international relations, political science, sociology. **Theology:** Theology. **Other:** Multinational organization studies.

**Most popular majors.** Biology 14%, business/marketing 27%, communications/journalism 7%, psychology 7%, security/protective services 7%, social sciences 15%.

**Computing on campus.** PC or laptop required. 100 workstations in dormitories, library, computer center, student center. Dormitories wired for high-speed internet access and linked to campus network. Commuter students can connect to campus network. Online course registration, online library, helpline, repair service, wireless network available.

**Student life. Freshman orientation:** Mandatory, $130 fee. Preregistration for classes offered. 2-day program offered twice in June and once in August. Parallel program for parents. June program offers campus accommodations for students and parents. Transfer student orientation is a 1-day program, held once in May and once in August. **Housing:** Guaranteed on-campus for freshmen. Coed dorms, single-sex dorms available. $100 nonrefundable deposit, deadline 5/1. Nontraditional residence halls for students 22 years old or above available. **Activities:** Bands, campus ministries, choral groups, dance, drama, international student organizations, literary magazine, music ensembles, musical theater, student government, student newspaper, Circle K, Amnesty International, black student union, College Democrats, Habitat for Humanity, League of United Latin American Citizens, Youth for a United World, Environmental Conservation Organization, Mexican student association, Alpha Phi Omega.

**Athletics.** NCAA. **Intercollegiate:** Baseball M, basketball, cheerleading, cross-country W, golf, soccer, softball W, tennis, volleyball W. **Intramural:** Basketball, football (tackle), racquetball, soccer, softball, table tennis, tennis, volleyball. **Team name:** Rattlers.

**Student services.** Adult student services, alcohol/substance abuse counseling, chaplain/spiritual director, career counseling, student employment services, financial aid counseling, health services, personal counseling, placement for graduates, veterans' counselor. **Physically disabled:** Services for visually, speech, hearing impaired.

**Contact.** E-mail: uadm@stmarytx.edu
Phone: (210) 436-3126 Toll-free number: (800) 367-7868
Fax: (210) 431-6742
Chadd Bridwell, Director of Admission, St. Mary's University, One Camino
Santa Maria, San Antonio, TX 78228-8503

## Sam Houston State University

| Huntsville, Texas | |
|---|---|
| | **CB member** |
| www.shsu.edu | **CB code: 6643** |

- Public 4-year university
- Residential campus in large town
- 14,569 degree-seeking undergraduates: 16% part-time, 56% women, 16% African American, 2% Asian American, 14% Hispanic American, 1% Native American, 1% international
- 2,202 degree-seeking graduate students
- 72% of applicants admitted
- SAT or ACT (ACT writing optional) required
- 44% graduate within 6 years

**General.** Founded in 1879. Regionally accredited. **Degrees:** 3,018 bachelor's awarded; master's, doctoral offered. **ROTC:** Army. **Location:** 69 miles from Houston, 170 miles from Dallas. **Calendar:** Semester, extensive summer session. **Full-time faculty:** 535 total; 69% have terminal degrees, 9% minority, 41% women. **Part-time faculty:** 16 total; 69% have terminal degrees, 6% minority, 50% women. **Class size:** 22% < 20, 52% 20-39, 12% 40-49, 11% 50-99, 3% >100. **Special facilities:** Sam Houston Memorial Museum, statue and visitors center Huntsville State Park.

**Freshman class profile.** 7,258 applied, 5,210 admitted, 2,127 enrolled.

| Mid 50% test scores | | Rank in top tenth: | 15% |
|---|---|---|---|
| SAT critical reading: | 440-540 | Return as sophomores: | 75% |
| SAT math: | 460-550 | Out-of-state: | 3% |
| ACT composite: | 18-22 | Live on campus: | 83% |
| Rank in top quarter: | 45% | International: | 1% |

**Basis for selection.** Test scores, school achievement records very important. Students graduating in top quarter of accredited high school exempt from test requirements.

**High school preparation.** College-preparatory program recommended. 22 units required; 26 recommended. Required and recommended units include English 4, mathematics 3-4, social studies 2.5-3.5, history 2.5-3.5, science 2-4 (laboratory 1), foreign language 2, computer science 1, visual/performing arts 1 and academic electives 1.

**2009-2010 Annual costs.** Tuition/fees: $6,515; $14,825 out-of-state. Room/board: $6,744. Books/supplies: $1,125. Personal expenses: $1,858.

**2008-2009 Financial aid. Need-based:** 1,529 full-time freshmen applied for aid; 1,083 were judged to have need; 968 of these received aid. Average need met was 36%. Average scholarship/grant was $1,205; average loan $215. 46% of total undergraduate aid awarded as scholarships/grants, 54% as loans/jobs. **Non-need-based:** Awarded to 1,777 full-time undergraduates, including 597 freshmen. Scholarships awarded for academics, alumni affiliation, art, athletics, job skills, leadership, music/drama, religious affiliation, ROTC, state residency.

**Application procedures. Admission:** Priority date 6/15; deadline 8/1 (postmark date). $40 fee, may be waived for applicants with need. Admission notification on a rolling basis beginning on or about 9/1. **Financial aid:** Priority date 4/1; no closing date. FAFSA, institutional form required. Applicants notified on a rolling basis starting 3/1; must reply within 4 week(s) of notification.

**Academics. Special study options:** Combined bachelor's/graduate degree, distance learning, double major, dual enrollment of high school students, ESL, honors, independent study, internships, teacher certification program. **Credit/placement by examination:** AP, CLEP, IB, SAT, ACT, institutional tests. 30 credit hours maximum toward bachelor's degree. **Support services:** Learning center, pre-admission summer program, reduced course load, remedial instruction, study skills assistance, tutoring, writing center.

**Majors. Agriculture:** General, agribusiness operations, animal sciences, horticultural science, mechanization. **Architecture:** Interior. **Biology:** General. **Business:** General, accounting, banking/financial services, business admin, fashion, finance, human resources, international, managerial economics, marketing, operations. **Communications:** Advertising, journalism, media studies, public relations, radio/tv. **Communications technology:** Animation/special effects. **Computer sciences:** General. **Conservation:** Environmental science. **Engineering technology:** Construction, drafting, electrical, industrial, manufacturing. **Family/consumer sciences:** General, food/

nutrition, institutional food production. **Foreign languages:** French, Spanish. **Health:** Health services, music therapy. **History:** General. **Interdisciplinary:** Biological/physical sciences. **Math:** General. **Parks/recreation:** Health/fitness. **Philosophy/religion:** Philosophy. **Physical sciences:** Chemistry, geology, physics. **Protective services:** Corrections, criminal justice. **Psychology:** General. **Social sciences:** Geography, political science, sociology. **Visual/performing arts:** Art, commercial/advertising art, dance, dramatic, music performance, photography, studio arts. **Other:** Academic studies, Forensic chemistry, Victim studies.

**Most popular majors.** Business/marketing 26%, interdisciplinary studies 12%, psychology 6%, security/protective services 17%, visual/performing arts 6%.

**Computing on campus.** 552 workstations in library, computer center, student center. Dormitories wired for high-speed internet access and linked to campus network. Commuter students can connect to campus network. Online course registration, online library, helpline, repair service, student web hosting, wireless network available.

**Student life. Freshman orientation:** Available, $125 fee. Preregistration for classes offered. Overnight program throughout summer and before classes commence. Parent participation. **Housing:** Guaranteed on-campus for freshmen. Coed dorms, single-sex dorms, apartments, fraternity/sorority housing available. $200 deposit. **Activities:** Bands, campus ministries, choral groups, dance, drama, international student organizations, music ensembles, musical theater, radio station, student government, student newspaper, symphony orchestra, TV station, Democratic and Republican student associations, Baptist student ministry, Church of Christ student center, Lutheran student center, Hillel, Muslim students association, student Pagan association, ROTARACT, Habitat for Humanity, Wesley Foundation.

**Athletics.** NCAA. **Intercollegiate:** Baseball M, basketball, cross-country, equestrian, football (tackle) M, golf, rifle, rodeo, soccer, softball W, tennis, track and field, volleyball W. **Intramural:** Baseball M, basketball, bowling, diving, football (tackle) M, golf, gymnastics W, handball, lacrosse M, racquetball, rugby M, soccer, softball W, swimming, tennis, volleyball, water polo. **Team name:** Bearkats.

**Student services.** Alcohol/substance abuse counseling, career counseling, student employment services, financial aid counseling, health services, legal services, minority student services, on-campus daycare, personal counseling, placement for graduates, veterans' counselor. **Physically disabled:** Services for visually impaired.

**Contact.** E-mail: admissions@shsu.edu
Phone: (936) 294-1828 Toll-free number: (866) 232-7528
Fax: (936) 294-3758
Trevor Thorn, Director of Admissions, Sam Houston State University, Box 2418, Huntsville, TX 77341-2418

## Schreiner University

| Kerrville, Texas | |
|---|---|
| | **CB member** |
| www.schreiner.edu | **CB code: 6647** |

- Private 4-year liberal arts college affiliated with Presbyterian Church (USA)
- Residential campus in large town
- 1,013 degree-seeking undergraduates: 4% part-time, 56% women, 4% African American, 22% Hispanic American, 2% Native American
- 14 degree-seeking graduate students
- 62% of applicants admitted
- SAT or ACT with writing required
- 42% graduate within 6 years

**General.** Founded in 1923. Regionally accredited. **Degrees:** 121 bachelor's, 2 associate awarded; master's offered. **Location:** 60 miles from San Antonio, 80 miles from Austin. **Calendar:** Semester, limited summer session. **Full-time faculty:** 61 total; 67% have terminal degrees, 8% minority, 48% women. **Part-time faculty:** 31 total; 19% have terminal degrees, 13% minority, 55% women. **Class size:** 49% < 20, 50% 20-39, less than 1% 40-49.

**Freshman class profile.** 991 applied, 613 admitted, 290 enrolled.

| Mid 50% test scores | | GPA 3.0-3.49: | 38% |
|---|---|---|---|
| SAT critical reading: | 440-550 | GPA 2.0-2.99: | 1% |
| SAT math: | 440-570 | Rank in top quarter: | 43% |
| SAT writing: | 420-530 | Rank in top tenth: | 16% |
| ACT composite: | 18-23 | Return as sophomores: | 68% |
| GPA 3.75 or higher: | 13% | Live on campus: | 86% |
| GPA 3.50-3.74: | 48% | International: | 1% |

**Basis for selection.** High school courses taken, grades, class rank, extracurricular activities, test scores, recommendations, interviews considered. Interview recommended for all; essay required for applicants not meeting certain admissions standards; portfolio recommended for fine arts.

**High school preparation.** College-preparatory program recommended. 24 units recommended. Recommended units include English 4, mathematics 3, social studies 2, history 2, science 3 (laboratory 2), foreign language 2, computer science 1, visual/performing arts 1 and academic electives 3.

**2009-2010 Annual costs.** Tuition/fees: $18,731. Room/board: $8,376. Books/supplies: $1,200. Personal expenses: $1,000.

**2008-2009 Financial aid. Need-based:** 242 full-time freshmen applied for aid; 191 were judged to have need; 191 of these received aid. Average need met was 75%. Average scholarship/grant was $11,815; average loan $2,978. 65% of total undergraduate aid awarded as scholarships/grants, 35% as loans/jobs. **Non-need-based:** Awarded to 258 full-time undergraduates, including 99 freshmen. Scholarships awarded for academics, art, leadership, music/drama, religious affiliation.

**Application procedures. Admission:** Priority date 5/1; deadline 8/1. $25 fee, may be waived for applicants with need. Admission notification on a rolling basis. **Financial aid:** No deadline. FAFSA required. Applicants notified on a rolling basis starting 2/15; must reply within 2 week(s) of notification.

**Academics. Special study options:** Accelerated study, double major, dual enrollment of high school students, honors, independent study, internships, liberal arts/career combination, student-designed major, study abroad, teacher certification program, weekend college. **Credit/placement by examination:** AP, CLEP, IB, SAT, ACT, institutional tests. **Support services:** Learning center, reduced course load, remedial instruction, study skills assistance, tutoring, writing center.

**Majors. Biology:** General, biochemistry. **Business:** General, accounting, business admin, finance, international, management information systems, marketing. **Education:** General, biology, early childhood, elementary, English, history, mathematics, middle, music, physical, secondary. **Engineering:** General. **History:** General. **Liberal arts:** Arts/sciences, humanities. **Math:** General. **Parks/recreation:** Exercise sciences, sports admin. **Philosophy/religion:** Religion. **Physical sciences:** Chemistry. **Psychology:** General. **Social sciences:** Political science. **Visual/performing arts:** Commercial/advertising art, dramatic, graphic design.

**Most popular majors.** Biology 14%, business/marketing 24%, interdisciplinary studies 7%, parks/recreation 18%, psychology 11%, visual/performing arts 9%.

**Computing on campus.** 103 workstations in dormitories, library, computer center, student center. Dormitories wired for high-speed internet access and linked to campus network. Commuter students can connect to campus network. Online library, helpline, repair service, student web hosting, wireless network available.

**Student life. Freshman orientation:** Mandatory. Preregistration for classes offered. Overnight program prior to start of classes. **Housing:** Guaranteed on-campus for all undergraduates. Coed dorms, special housing for disabled, apartments available. $100 nonrefundable deposit, deadline 5/1. **Activities:** Pep band, campus ministries, choral groups, dance, drama, literary magazine, music ensembles, musical theater, student government, student newspaper, symphony orchestra, community outreach program, Pre-Law Society, Celtic Cross, Episcopal-Lutheran Association, Fellowship of Christian Athletes, Young Catholic Adults, Young Republicans, Green society, Hispanic Culture Club, Asian Culture Club, Schreiner Democrats, Shades United.

**Athletics. NCAA. Intercollegiate:** Baseball M, basketball, cheerleading M, golf, soccer, softball W, tennis, volleyball W. **Intramural:** Basketball, football (non-tackle), football (tackle), golf, racquetball, soccer, swimming, table tennis, tennis, volleyball. **Team name:** Mountaineers.

**Student services.** Adult student services, chaplain/spiritual director, career counseling, student employment services, financial aid counseling, health services, personal counseling, placement for graduates. **Physically disabled:** Services for visually, speech, hearing impaired. **Learning disabled:** Comprehensive services available.

**Contact.** E-mail: admissions@schreiner.edu
Phone: (830) 792-7217 Toll-free number: (800) 343-4919
Fax: (830) 792-7226
Sandra Speed, Dean of Admissions, Schreiner University, 2100 Memorial Boulevard, Kerrville, TX 78028-5697

## Southern Methodist University

**Dallas, Texas**
www.smu.edu

**CB member**
**CB code: 6660**

- Private 4-year university affiliated with United Methodist Church
- Residential campus in large town
- 6,150 degree-seeking undergraduates: 4% part-time, 53% women, 5% African American, 6% Asian American, 8% Hispanic American, 1% Native American, 6% international
- 4,369 degree-seeking graduate students
- 53% of applicants admitted
- SAT or ACT (ACT writing optional), application essay required
- 77% graduate within 6 years

**General.** Founded in 1911. Regionally accredited. Courses are also offered at SMU-in-Legacy in Plano and SMU-in-Taos in New Mexico. **Degrees:** 1,628 bachelor's awarded; master's, doctoral, professional offered. **ROTC:** Army, Air Force. **Location:** 5 miles from downtown. **Calendar:** Semester, limited summer session. **Full-time faculty:** 660 total; 84% have terminal degrees, 17% minority, 36% women. **Part-time faculty:** 386 total; 45% have terminal degrees, 7% minority, 41% women. **Class size:** 59% < 20, 26% 20-39, 6% 40-49, 7% 50-99, 2% >100. **Special facilities:** Film/video archives, New Mexico archeological dig of 13th century Indian pueblo, institute for the study of Earth and man, seismological observatory, electron microscopy laboratory, paleontology museum, business information center.

**Freshman class profile.** 8,356 applied, 4,467 admitted, 1,329 enrolled.

| Mid 50% test scores | | | |
|---|---|---|---|
| SAT critical reading: | 560-660 | GPA 2.0-2.99: | 9% |
| SAT math: | 580-680 | Rank in top quarter: | 73% |
| SAT writing: | 560-660 | Rank in top tenth: | 43% |
| ACT composite: | 25-30 | Return as sophomores: | 88% |
| GPA 3.75 or higher: | 43% | Out-of-state: | 56% |
| GPA 3.50-3.74: | 21% | Live on campus: | 95% |
| GPA 3.0-3.49: | 27% | International: | 5% |

**Basis for selection.** GED not accepted. Students evaluated comprehensively. High school curriculum, GPA, test scores, school/community activities, recommendations, and essay important. Special talents considered. Interview recommended for all; audition required for performing arts; portfolio recommended for studio art. **Homeschooled:** SAT Subject Tests required.

**High school preparation.** 15 units required. Required and recommended units include English 4, mathematics 3-4, social studies 1-2, history 2-3, science 3-4 (laboratory 2-3) and foreign language 2-3.

**2010-2011 Annual costs.** Tuition/fees (projected): $37,230. Room/board: $12,735. Books/supplies: $800. Personal expenses: $1,600.

**2009-2010 Financial aid. Need-based:** 726 full-time freshmen applied for aid; 538 were judged to have need; 537 of these received aid. Average need met was 90%. Average scholarship/grant was $20,259; average loan $2,454. 77% of total undergraduate aid awarded as scholarships/grants, 23% as loans/jobs. **Non-need-based:** Awarded to 3,623 full-time undergraduates, including 887 freshmen. Scholarships awarded for academics, art, athletics, leadership, music/drama, religious affiliation, ROTC, state residency.

**Application procedures. Admission:** Priority date 1/15; deadline 3/15 (postmark date). $60 fee, may be waived for applicants with need. Admission notification on a rolling basis beginning on or about 12/31. **Financial aid:** Priority date 2/15; no closing date. FAFSA, CSS PROFILE required. Applicants notified on a rolling basis starting 3/15.

**Academics. Special study options:** Accelerated study, combined bachelor's/graduate degree, cooperative education, distance learning, double major, ESL, exchange student, honors, independent study, internships, student-designed major, study abroad, teacher certification program, Washington semester. **Credit/placement by examination:** AP, CLEP, IB, SAT, ACT, institutional tests. No limit on number of AP credits that may be counted toward bachelor's degree. Maximum of 8 hours of International Baccalaureate credits may be counted toward bachelor's degree. **Support services:** Learning center, pre-admission summer program, remedial instruction, study skills assistance, tutoring, writing center.

**Majors. Area/ethnic studies:** African-American, Chicano/Hispanic-American/Latino, European, German, Italian, Latin American. **Biology:** General, biochemistry. **Business:** General, accounting, business admin, finance, financial planning, management information systems, management science, marketing, organizational behavior, real estate. **Communications:** Advertising, journalism, media studies, public relations, radio/tv. **Computer sciences:** Computer science, information systems. **Conservation:** Environmental science. **Education:** Music. **Engineering:** Civil, computer, electrical, environmental, mechanical. **Engineering technology:** Industrial management. **Foreign languages:** General, French, German, Italian, Russian, Spanish. **Health:** Music therapy. **History:** General. **Interdisciplinary:** Medieval/Renaissance. **Liberal arts:** Humanities. **Math:** General, statistics. **Philosophy/religion:** Philosophy, religion. **Physical sciences:** Chemistry, geology, geophysics, physics. **Psychology:** General. **Public administration:** Policy analysis. **Social sciences:** General, anthropology, applied economics, econometrics, economics, international relations, political science, sociology. **Theology:** Preministerial. **Visual/performing arts:** Art, art history/conservation, dance, dramatic, film/cinema, music performance, music theory/composition, piano/organ, studio arts, voice/opera.

**Most popular majors.** Business/marketing 26%, communications/journalism 13%, engineering/engineering technologies 6%, psychology 6%, social sciences 17%, visual/performing arts 7%.

**Computing on campus.** 758 workstations in dormitories, library, computer center, student center. Dormitories wired for high-speed internet access and linked to campus network. Commuter students can connect to campus network. Online course registration, online library, helpline, repair service, student web hosting, wireless network available.

**Student life. Freshman orientation:** Mandatory. **Housing:** Guaranteed on-campus for freshmen. Coed dorms, apartments, fraternity/sorority housing, wellness housing available. $200 nonrefundable deposit, deadline 5/1. **Activities:** Bands, campus ministries, choral groups, dance, drama, film society, international student organizations, literary magazine, music ensembles, musical theater, opera, radio station, student government, student newspaper, symphony orchestra, over 130 groups available.

**Athletics.** NCAA. **Intercollegiate:** Basketball, cross-country W, diving, equestrian W, football (tackle) M, golf, rowing (crew) W, soccer, swimming, tennis, track and field W, volleyball W. **Intramural:** Basketball, bowling, golf, racquetball, soccer, softball, swimming, table tennis, tennis, volleyball. **Team name:** Mustangs.

**Student services.** Adult student services, alcohol/substance abuse counseling, chaplain/spiritual director, career counseling, student employment services, financial aid counseling, health services, on-campus daycare, personal counseling, placement for graduates, veterans' counselor, women's services. **Physically disabled:** Services for visually, speech, hearing impaired.

**Contact.** E-mail: ugadmission@smu.edu
Phone: (214) 768-2058 Toll-free number: (800) 323-0672
Fax: (214) 768-4880
Ron Moss, Executive Director of Enrollment Services, Southern Methodist University, PO Box 750181, Dallas, TX 75275-0181

## Southwestern Adventist University
**Keene, Texas**
www.swau.edu          CB code: 6671

- Private 4-year university and liberal arts college affiliated with Seventh-day Adventists
- Residential campus in small town
- 735 degree-seeking undergraduates: 10% part-time, 57% women, 9% African American, 5% Asian American, 26% Hispanic American, 1% Native American, 17% international
- 30 degree-seeking graduate students
- 54% of applicants admitted
- SAT or ACT (ACT writing optional) required
- 40% graduate within 6 years; 42% enter graduate study

**General.** Founded in 1893. Regionally accredited. **Degrees:** 150 bachelor's, 25 associate awarded; master's offered. **Location:** 55 miles from Dallas, 25 miles from Fort Worth. **Calendar:** Semester, limited summer session. **Full-time faculty:** 55 total; 56% have terminal degrees, 20% minority, 38% women. **Part-time faculty:** 15 total; 13% have terminal degrees, 13% minority, 53% women. **Class size:** 65% < 20, 24% 20-39, 9% 40-49, 2% 50-99, less than 1% >100. **Special facilities:** Observatory, museum of student life.

**Freshman class profile.** 659 applied, 355 admitted, 119 enrolled.

| Mid 50% test scores | | | |
|---|---|---|---|
| SAT critical reading: | 420-550 | Return as sophomores: | 65% |
| SAT math: | 420-530 | Out-of-state: | 44% |
| ACT composite: | 16-22 | Live on campus: | 35% |
| End year in good standing: | 95% | International: | 8% |

**Basis for selection.** Secondary school record, test scores important. Additional requirements for nursing and education programs. **Homeschooled:**

A state high school equivalency certificate is accepted instead of a high school diploma or GED.

**High school preparation.** College-preparatory program recommended. Recommended units include English 4, mathematics 2, social studies 2.5, science 2 and foreign language 2.

**2010-2011 Annual costs.** Tuition/fees (projected): $16,216. Room/board: $7,148. Books/supplies: $936. Personal expenses: $1,244.

**Financial aid. Non-need-based:** Scholarships awarded for academics, leadership, music/drama.

**Application procedures. Admission:** Closing date 8/31. No application fee. Admission notification on a rolling basis. **Financial aid:** Priority date 3/15; no closing date. FAFSA, institutional form required. Applicants notified on a rolling basis starting 4/15.

**Academics. Special study options:** Accelerated study, combined bachelor's/graduate degree, cross-registration, distance learning, double major, ESL, external degree, honors, independent study, internships, liberal arts/career combination, student-designed major, study abroad, teacher certification program. **Credit/placement by examination:** AP, CLEP, IB, SAT, ACT, institutional tests. **Support services:** Reduced course load, remedial instruction, tutoring, writing center.

**Majors. Biology:** General, biostatistics. **Business:** Accounting, administrative services, business admin, communications, international, management information systems, management science. **Communications:** General, broadcast journalism, journalism. **Computer sciences:** General, computer science, information systems. **Education:** Elementary, physical. **Health:** Clinical lab technology, nursing (RN). **History:** General. **Math:** General, applied. **Parks/recreation:** Health/fitness. **Philosophy/religion:** Religion. **Physical sciences:** Chemistry, theoretical physics. **Protective services:** Criminal justice. **Psychology:** General. **Social sciences:** General, international relations. **Theology:** Theology.

**Most popular majors.** Business/marketing 15%, education 14%, health sciences 12%, liberal arts 9%, psychology 12%, theological studies 7%.

**Computing on campus.** 150 workstations in library, computer center. Dormitories wired for high-speed internet access and linked to campus network. Commuter students can connect to campus network. Helpline, repair service, student web hosting, wireless network available.

**Student life. Freshman orientation:** Mandatory, $125 fee. Preregistration for classes offered. Held the week prior to fall registration. **Housing:** Guaranteed on-campus for all undergraduates. Single-sex dorms, apartments available. $100 fully refundable deposit, deadline 8/31. **Activities:** Concert band, campus ministries, choral groups, drama, international student organizations, music ensembles, musical theater, radio station, student government, student newspaper, symphony orchestra, TV station.

**Athletics. Intramural:** Badminton, basketball, football (non-tackle), gymnastics, racquetball, soccer, table tennis, tennis W, volleyball. **Team name:** Knights.

**Student services.** Adult student services, alcohol/substance abuse counseling, chaplain/spiritual director, career counseling, student employment services, financial aid counseling, health services, personal counseling, placement for graduates, veterans' counselor.

**Contact.** E-mail: admissions@swau.edu
Phone: (817) 202-6252 Toll-free number: (800) 433-2240
Fax: (817) 556-4744
Robert Gardner, Associate Academic Vice President, Southwestern Adventist University, Box 567, Keene, TX 76059

## Southwestern Assemblies of God University
**Waxahachie, Texas**
www.sagu.edu          CB code: 6669

- Private 4-year university and Bible college affiliated with Assemblies of God
- Residential campus in large town
- 1,708 degree-seeking undergraduates
- 310 graduate students
- SAT or ACT (ACT writing optional), application essay required

**General.** Founded in 1927. Regionally accredited. **Degrees:** 240 bachelor's, 63 associate awarded; master's offered. **ROTC:** Army. **Location:** 20 miles from Dallas. **Calendar:** Semester, limited summer session. **Full-time faculty:** 62 total; 53% have terminal degrees, 8% minority, 31% women.

**Part-time faculty:** 73 total; 14% have terminal degrees, 7% minority, 36% women.

### Freshman class profile.

| Mid 50% test scores | | | |
|---|---|---|---|
| | | ACT composite: | 16-23 |
| SAT critical reading: | 420-520 | Out-of-state: | 45% |
| SAT math: | 410-510 | Live on campus: | 80% |

**Basis for selection.** Minister's reference and 1 personal reference required. Interview recommended. **Learning Disabled:** Enrollment with the Achievement Center indicated.

**2009-2010 Annual costs.** Tuition/fees: $13,780. Room/board: $4,880. Books/supplies: $612. Personal expenses: $1,479.

**Application procedures. Admission:** Priority date 7/1; no deadline. $35 fee. Admission notification on a rolling basis beginning on or about 3/1. **Financial aid:** Priority date 3/1, closing date 6/1. FAFSA required. Applicants notified on a rolling basis starting 6/1; must reply within 2 week(s) of notification.

**Academics. Special study options:** Distance learning, double major, dual enrollment of high school students, external degree, independent study, internships, teacher certification program. **Credit/placement by examination:** AP, CLEP, institutional tests. 15 credit hours maximum toward associate degree, 30 toward bachelor's. **Support services:** Learning center, reduced course load, remedial instruction, tutoring.

**Majors. Business:** General, accounting, business admin, marketing. **Education:** Early childhood, elementary, English, music, reading, secondary, social studies. **Health:** Clinical pastoral counseling. **History:** General. **Philosophy/religion:** Christian. **Theology:** Bible, missionary, pastoral counseling, religious ed, sacred music, youth ministry. **Visual/performing arts:** Music performance, piano/organ, voice/opera.

**Computing on campus.** 45 workstations in dormitories, library, computer center. Dormitories wired for high-speed internet access and linked to campus network. Online library, repair service, wireless network available.

**Student life. Freshman orientation:** Mandatory. Preregistration for classes offered. **Policies:** Dress code observed. Religious observance required. **Housing:** Guaranteed on-campus for freshmen. Coed dorms, single-sex dorms, apartments available. Unmarried students 23 and under required to live in college housing unless alternative arrangements agreed to upon enrollment. **Activities:** Bands, campus ministries, choral groups, drama, music ensembles, musical theater, student government, student newspaper, prayer groups, ministry labs.

**Athletics.** NAIA, NCCAA. **Intercollegiate:** Baseball M, basketball, cheerleading, football (tackle) M, soccer M, volleyball W. **Intramural:** Basketball, football (non-tackle) W, racquetball, softball, table tennis, volleyball. **Team name:** Lions.

**Student services.** Adult student services, chaplain/spiritual director, career counseling, student employment services, financial aid counseling, health services, personal counseling, placement for graduates, veterans' counselor.

**Contact.** E-mail: admissions@sagu.edu
Phone: (972) 937-7248 Toll-free number: (888) 937-7248
Fax: (972) 923-0006
Pat Thompson, Admissions Counselor, Southwestern Assemblies of God University, 1200 Sycamore Street, Waxahachie, TX 75165

---

## Southwestern Baptist Theological Seminary
### Fort Worth, Texas
### www.swbts.edu

- Private 4-year Bible and seminary college
- Very large city
- 195 full-time, degree-seeking undergraduates
- 2,204 graduate students

**General.** Regionally accredited. **Degrees:** 16 bachelor's awarded; master's, doctoral, professional offered. **Calendar:** Semester. **Full-time faculty:** 119 total. **Part-time faculty:** 78 total.

**Basis for selection.** Commitment to Christian ministry important.

**2009-2010 Annual costs.** Tuition/fees: $6,588. All students under 20 years of age and who live more than 50 miles away are required to live in dorms and purchase 'pay-as-you-go' meal plan. Cost of dorm room $170 a month; meal plan is $1,190 per semester.

**Application procedures. Admission:** Closing date 7/15. **Financial aid:** Closing date 3/20.

**Academics. Credit/placement by examination:** CLEP.

**Majors. Liberal arts:** Humanities. **Theology:** Sacred music.

**Contact.** E-mail: admissions@swbts.edu
Phone: (800) 792-8701
Southwestern Baptist Theological Seminary, PO Box 22000, Fort Worth, TX 76122

---

## Southwestern Christian College
### Terrell, Texas
### www.swcc.edu
**CB code: 6705**

- Private 4-year Bible and liberal arts college affiliated with Church of Christ
- Residential campus in large town

**General.** Founded in 1949. Regionally accredited. **Location:** 30 miles from Dallas. **Calendar:** Semester.

**Annual costs/financial aid.** Tuition/fees (2009-2010): $6,438. Room/board: $4,388. Books/supplies: $460. Personal expenses: $400.

**Contact.** Phone: (972) 524-3341
Director of Admissions, Box 10, Terrell, TX 75160

---

## Southwestern University
### Georgetown, Texas
**CB member**
### www.southwestern.edu
**CB code: 6674**

- Private 4-year liberal arts college affiliated with United Methodist Church
- Residential campus in large town
- 1,291 degree-seeking undergraduates: 1% part-time, 63% women, 3% African American, 4% Asian American, 15% Hispanic American, 1% Native American
- 63% of applicants admitted
- SAT or ACT with writing, application essay required
- 77% graduate within 6 years; 25% enter graduate study

**General.** Founded in 1840. Regionally accredited. **Degrees:** 266 bachelor's awarded. **Location:** 28 miles from Austin. **Calendar:** Semester, limited summer session. **Full-time faculty:** 122 total; 100% have terminal degrees, 14% minority, 48% women. **Part-time faculty:** 44 total; 73% have terminal degrees, 14% minority, 48% women. **Class size:** 80% < 20, 20% 20-39, less than 1% 40-49, less than 1% 50-99.

**Freshman class profile.** 2,490 applied, 1,579 admitted, 375 enrolled.

| Mid 50% test scores | | | |
|---|---|---|---|
| | | End year in good standing: | 89% |
| SAT critical reading: | 570-680 | Return as sophomores: | 84% |
| SAT math: | 570-670 | Out-of-state: | 8% |
| ACT composite: | 25-30 | Live on campus: | 100% |
| Rank in top quarter: | 84% | Fraternities: | 30% |
| Rank in top tenth: | 49% | Sororities: | 26% |

**Basis for selection.** School record, class rank, recommendations, test scores, essay most important. Audition required for music, theater programs; portfolio required for art program.

**High school preparation.** College-preparatory program required. 17 units required; 20 recommended. Required and recommended units include English 4, mathematics 4, social studies 2-3, history 1-2, science 3-4 (laboratory 2-3), foreign language 2-3 and academic electives 1.

**2010-2011 Annual costs.** Tuition/fees: $31,360. Room/board: $9,230. Books/supplies: $1,000. Personal expenses: $900.

**2009-2010 Financial aid. Non-need-based:** Scholarships awarded for academics, art, minority status, music/drama, religious affiliation.

**Application procedures. Admission:** Closing date 2/15 (postmark date). $40 fee, may be waived for applicants with need. Admission notification 4/1. Must reply by 5/1. Applicants accepted after 2/15 if space allows. **Financial aid:** Priority date 3/1; no closing date. FAFSA required. Applicants notified on a rolling basis starting 3/1; must reply by 5/1 or within 2 week(s) of notification.

**Academics.** Students must demonstrate computer skills and grasp of major through capstone project, course, or examination prior to graduation. **Special study options:** Combined bachelor's/graduate degree, double major, honors, independent study, internships, liberal arts/career combination, New York semester, student-designed major, study abroad, teacher certification program, Washington semester. **Credit/placement by examination:** AP, CLEP, IB, institutional tests. **Support services:** Reduced course load, study skills assistance, tutoring, writing center.

**Majors. Area/ethnic studies:** American, Latin American, women's. **Biology:** General, animal behavior, biochemistry. **Business:** General, accounting. **Communications:** General, media studies. **Computer sciences:** General. **Conservation:** Environmental studies. **Education:** General, elementary, music, physical, science, social studies. **Foreign languages:** Chinese, classics, French, German, Latin, Spanish. **Health:** Athletic training. **History:** General. **Math:** General. **Philosophy/religion:** Philosophy, religion. **Physical sciences:** General, chemistry, physics. **Psychology:** General. **Social sciences:** Anthropology, economics, international relations, political science, sociology. **Visual/performing arts:** Art, art history/conservation, dramatic, music history, music performance, music theory/composition, musicology.

**Most popular majors.** Biology 11%, business/marketing 14%, communications/journalism 9%, education 6%, English 8%, psychology 9%, social sciences 14%, visual/performing arts 9%.

**Computing on campus.** 410 workstations in dormitories, library, computer center, student center. Dormitories wired for high-speed internet access and linked to campus network. Online course registration, online library, helpline, repair service, student web hosting, wireless network available.

**Student life. Freshman orientation:** Mandatory. **Housing:** Guaranteed on-campus for freshmen. Coed dorms, single-sex dorms, special housing for disabled, apartments, fraternity/sorority housing available. $500 nonrefundable deposit, deadline 5/14. **Activities:** Bands, choral groups, dance, drama, film society, literary magazine, music ensembles, musical theater, radio station, student government, student newspaper, Alpha Phi Omega, Ebony, Mexican American student association, political science society, international club, Equal Voice For Women's Perspective.

**Athletics.** NCAA. **Intercollegiate:** Baseball M, basketball, cross-country, diving, golf, lacrosse M, soccer, softball W, swimming, tennis, track and field, volleyball W. **Team name:** Bucs/Pirates.

**Student services.** Alcohol/substance abuse counseling, chaplain/spiritual director, career counseling, student employment services, financial aid counseling, health services, minority student services, personal counseling, placement for graduates. **Physically disabled:** Services for hearing impaired.

**Contact.** E-mail: admission@southwestern.edu
Phone: (512) 863-1200 Toll-free number: (800) 252-3166
Fax: (512) 863-9601
Tom Oliver, Vice President Enrollment Services, Southwestern University, 1001 East University Avenue, Georgetown, TX 78626

---

## Stephen F. Austin State University

**Nacogdoches, Texas**
**www.sfasu.edu**

**CB member**
**CB code: 6682**

- Public 4-year university
- Residential campus in large town
- 11,144 degree-seeking undergraduates: 13% part-time, 61% women, 23% African American, 1% Asian American, 10% Hispanic American, 1% Native American, 1% international
- 1,362 degree-seeking graduate students
- 73% of applicants admitted
- SAT or ACT with writing required
- 42% graduate within 6 years

**General.** Founded in 1923. Regionally accredited. **Degrees:** 1,797 bachelor's awarded; master's, doctoral offered. **ROTC:** Army. **Location:** 140 miles from Houston, 70 miles from Longview. **Calendar:** Semester, extensive summer session. **Full-time faculty:** 485 total; 74% have terminal degrees, 8% minority, 46% women. **Part-time faculty:** 172 total; 33% have terminal degrees, 6% minority, 68% women. **Class size:** 25% < 20, 53% 20-39, 11% 40-49, 8% 50-99, 2% >100. **Special facilities:** Computerized observatory; experimental forest; arboretum; beef, poultry and swine research facilities; biotechnology/environmental science research center; Stone Fort museum; agricultural pond; forest resources institute; geographic information systems lab; regional geospatial service center; early childhood research center.

**Freshman class profile.** 8,960 applied, 6,511 admitted, 2,396 enrolled.

| Mid 50% test scores | | | |
|---|---|---|---|
| SAT critical reading: | 420-530 | Rank in top quarter: | 40% |
| SAT math: | 440-540 | Rank in top tenth: | 13% |
| SAT writing: | 410-520 | Return as sophomores: | 65% |
| ACT composite: | 18-23 | Out-of-state: | 2% |
| | | Live on campus: | 90% |

**Basis for selection.** Applicants must complete prescribed high school preparation and submit official transcript and SAT or ACT scores. No minimum score required for those ranking in top quartile; those in second quartile must have composite score of 850 SAT, 18 ACT; third quartile 1050 SAT, 23 ACT; fourth quartile 1250 SAT, 28 ACT (All SAT scores exclusive of Writing). Applicants not meeting rank-in-class and test requirements reviewed on individual basis. SAT or ACT scores must be received by last day of registration for fall term admission. **Homeschooled:** Applicants individually assessed based on probability of success.

**High school preparation.** College-preparatory program required. 12 units required; 18 recommended. Required and recommended units include English 4, mathematics 3, social studies 3, science 3 and foreign language 2. 1 fine arts, 1 computer science, 1 government/economics recommended.

**2009-2010 Annual costs.** Tuition/fees: $6,732; $15,042 out-of-state. Room/board: $7,377. Books/supplies: $1,072. Personal expenses: $1,673.

**2008-2009 Financial aid. Need-based:** 1,806 full-time freshmen applied for aid; 1,409 were judged to have need; 1,382 of these received aid. Average need met was 84%. Average scholarship/grant was $3,535; average loan $3,138. 46% of total undergraduate aid awarded as scholarships/grants, 54% as loans/jobs. **Non-need-based:** Awarded to 2,129 full-time undergraduates, including 601 freshmen. Scholarships awarded for academics, alumni affiliation, athletics, leadership, music/drama, state residency.

**Application procedures. Admission:** No deadline. $35 fee, may be waived for applicants with need. Admission notification on a rolling basis beginning on or about 9/1. **Financial aid:** Priority date 4/1; no closing date. FAFSA required. Applicants notified on a rolling basis starting 4/1.

**Academics. Special study options:** Accelerated study, combined bachelor's/graduate degree, distance learning, double major, dual enrollment of high school students, honors, independent study, internships, liberal arts/career combination, student-designed major, study abroad, teacher certification program. **Credit/placement by examination:** AP, CLEP, IB, SAT, ACT, institutional tests. 32 credit hours maximum toward bachelor's degree. **Support services:** Learning center, pre-admission summer program, reduced course load, remedial instruction, study skills assistance, tutoring, writing center.

**Majors. Agriculture:** General, agribusiness operations, agronomy, animal sciences, horticultural science, horticulture, mechanization, poultry, production. **Architecture:** Interior. **Biology:** General, biochemistry. **Business:** General, accounting, business admin, fashion, finance, hospitality admin, international, managerial economics, marketing, special products marketing. **Communications:** General, journalism, radio/tv. **Computer sciences:** General, data processing, information technology. **Conservation:** Environmental science, forest management, forestry, wildlife. **Family/consumer sciences:** General, family studies, food/nutrition. **Foreign languages:** French, Spanish. **Health:** Audiology/hearing, audiology/speech pathology, health services, nursing (RN). **History:** General. **Interdisciplinary:** Gerontology. **Legal studies:** Paralegal. **Liberal arts:** Arts/sciences, humanities. **Math:** General. **Parks/recreation:** Facilities management, health/fitness. **Philosophy/religion:** Philosophy. **Physical sciences:** Chemistry, geology, physics. **Protective services:** Corrections, criminal justice, police science. **Psychology:** General. **Public administration:** General, social work. **Social sciences:** General, cartography, economics, geography, political science, sociology. **Visual/performing arts:** Art, art history/conservation, dance, dramatic. **Other:** Applied arts & sciences, Orientation & mobility.

**Most popular majors.** Business/marketing 22%, health sciences 12%, interdisciplinary studies 16%, parks/recreation 6%, visual/performing arts 8%.

**Computing on campus.** 1,000 workstations in dormitories, library, computer center, student center. Dormitories wired for high-speed internet access and linked to campus network. Commuter students can connect to campus network. Online course registration, online library, helpline, repair service, student web hosting, wireless network available.

**Student life. Freshman orientation:** Available, $135 fee. Preregistration for classes offered. Five 2-day sessions held each summer for students and parents. **Housing:** Guaranteed on-campus for freshmen. Coed dorms, single-sex dorms, special housing for disabled, apartments, fraternity/sorority housing, wellness housing available. $100 fully refundable deposit, deadline 4/9. Students must live in college housing until 60 semester hours completed. Off-campus housing permitted if student is 21 or older, married, commutes from permanent address of parent or relative, or enrolls for 8 hours or less.

**Activities:** Bands, campus ministries, choral groups, dance, drama, film society, international student organizations, literary magazine, music ensembles, musical theater, opera, radio station, student government, student newspaper, symphony orchestra, TV station, African American student association, Canterbury Episcopal student association, Campus Crusade for Christ, Jewish Student Fellowship, Habitat for Humanity, SFA Democrats, Young Republicans, social services.

**Athletics. NCAA. Intercollegiate:** Baseball M, basketball, bowling W, cross-country, football (tackle) M, golf, soccer W, softball W, tennis W, track and field, volleyball W. **Intramural:** Badminton, baseball M, basketball, cross-country, football (non-tackle), lacrosse M, racquetball, rodeo, rugby, soccer M, softball, table tennis, tennis, volleyball, water polo, wrestling M. **Team name:** Lumberjacks/Ladyjacks.

**Student services.** Adult student services, alcohol/substance abuse counseling, career counseling, student employment services, financial aid counseling, health services, legal services, minority student services, on-campus daycare, personal counseling, placement for graduates, veterans' counselor. **Physically disabled:** Services for visually, speech, hearing impaired.

**Contact.** E-mail: admissions@sfasu.edu
Phone: (936) 468-2504 Fax: (936) 468-3849
Monique Cossich, Executive Director of Enrollment Management, Stephen F. Austin State University, Box 13051, SFA Station, Nacogdoches, TX 75962-3051

---

## Sul Ross State University

| Alpine, Texas | CB member |
|---|---|
| www.sulross.edu | CB code: 6685 |

- Public 4-year university
- Residential campus in small town
- 2,167 degree-seeking undergraduates: 35% part-time, 55% women, 7% African American, 61% Hispanic American, 2% international
- 708 degree-seeking graduate students
- 97% of applicants admitted
- SAT or ACT (ACT writing optional) required

**General.** Founded in 1917. Regionally accredited. Off-campus upper-level and graduate programs also available at Rio Grande College in Del Rio, Eagle Pass, and Uvalde. **Degrees:** 364 bachelor's, 12 associate awarded; master's offered. **Location:** 140 miles from Odessa, 220 miles from El Paso. **Calendar:** Semester, limited summer session. **Full-time faculty:** 128 total; 19% minority, 34% women. **Part-time faculty:** 37 total; 14% minority, 57% women. **Class size:** 66% < 20, 30% 20-39, 2% 40-49, 2% 50-99, less than 1% >100. **Special facilities:** Center for Big Bend studies, materials characterization laboratory.

**Freshman class profile.** 956 applied, 932 admitted, 386 enrolled.

| Mid 50% test scores | | | |
|---|---|---|---|
| SAT critical reading: | 320-540 | GPA 3.0-3.49: | 30% |
| SAT math: | 320-540 | GPA 2.0-2.99: | 41% |
| SAT writing: | 350-450 | Rank in top quarter: | 13% |
| ACT composite: | 13-21 | Rank in top tenth: | 4% |
| GPA 3.75 or higher: | 11% | Out-of-state: | 3% |
| GPA 3.50-3.74: | 14% | Live on campus: | 74% |
| | | International: | 3% |

**Basis for selection.** Students must meet one of following criteria: ACT score of 20, SAT score of 800 (exclusive of Writing), or rank in top half of graduating class. Probational admission for all other applicants.

**High school preparation.** College-preparatory program recommended. 15 units required; 31 recommended. Required and recommended units include English 4, mathematics 3-4, history 1-2, science 2-4 (laboratory 2), foreign language 3, computer science 1, visual/performing arts 1, academic electives 2.5. 1 U.S. government, 1 world history/geography, 1 economics.

**2009-2010 Annual costs.** Tuition/fees: $5,302; $13,612 out-of-state. Room/board: $6,370. Books/supplies: $1,110. Personal expenses: $1,872.

**2008-2009 Financial aid. Need-based:** Average need met was 22%. Average scholarship/grant was $5,960; average loan $4,993. 32% of total undergraduate aid awarded as scholarships/grants, 68% as loans/jobs. **Non-need-based:** Scholarships awarded for academics, art, athletics, job skills, leadership, music/drama, state residency.

**Application procedures. Admission:** Priority date 3/1; no deadline. $25 fee, may be waived for applicants with need. Admission notification on a rolling basis. **Financial aid:** Priority date 3/1, closing date 4/1. FAFSA, institutional form required. Applicants notified on a rolling basis starting 5/1; must reply within 2 week(s) of notification.

**Academics. Special study options:** Distance learning, honors, internships, teacher certification program. **Credit/placement by examination:** AP, CLEP, institutional tests. 30 credit hours maximum toward bachelor's degree. **Support services:** Learning center, pre-admission summer program, reduced course load, remedial instruction, study skills assistance, tutoring, writing center.

**Majors. Agriculture:** Agribusiness operations, animal health, animal sciences, equestrian studies, food science, range science. **Biology:** General. **Business:** General, accounting, administrative services, business admin, finance, marketing, office management. **Communications:** General. **Computer sciences:** General. **Conservation:** General, management/policy, wildlife. **Education:** Elementary. **Foreign languages:** Spanish. **History:** General. **Math:** General. **Parks/recreation:** Health/fitness. **Physical sciences:** Chemistry, geology. **Protective services:** Criminal justice. **Psychology:** General. **Social sciences:** General, political science. **Visual/performing arts:** Art, dramatic.

**Most popular majors.** Health sciences 9%, interdisciplinary studies 26%, liberal arts 10%, psychology 7%, security/protective services 10%.

**Computing on campus.** 200 workstations in library, computer center. Dormitories wired for high-speed internet access and linked to campus network. Commuter students can connect to campus network. Online library, helpline, repair service, wireless network available.

**Student life. Freshman orientation:** Available, $100 fee. Preregistration for classes offered. **Housing:** Guaranteed on-campus for freshmen. Coed dorms, apartments, wellness housing available. First-year experience. **Activities:** Bands, campus ministries, choral groups, dance, drama, music ensembles, musical theater, radio station, student government, student newspaper, Wesley Foundation, Newman Club, Baptist Student Union, Fellowship of Christian Athletes, Spanish club, rodeo club, black student association, international student association, nontraditional student association.

**Athletics. NCAA. Intercollegiate:** Baseball M, basketball, cross-country, football (tackle) M, softball W, tennis, track and field, volleyball W. **Intramural:** Basketball, football (non-tackle), racquetball, soccer, softball, tennis, volleyball, water polo, weight lifting. **Team name:** Lobos.

**Student services.** Alcohol/substance abuse counseling, chaplain/spiritual director, career counseling, student employment services, financial aid counseling, health services, on-campus daycare, personal counseling, placement for graduates, veterans' counselor. **Physically disabled:** Services for visually, hearing impaired.

**Contact.** E-mail: admissions@sulross.edu
Phone: (432) 837-8050 Toll-free number: (888) 722-7778
Fax: (432) 837-8186
Gregory Schwab, Associate VP for Enrollment Management, Sul Ross State University, Box C-2, Alpine, TX 79832

---

## Tarleton State University

| Stephenville, Texas | CB member |
|---|---|
| www.tarleton.edu | CB code: 6817 |

- Public 4-year university
- Residential campus in large town
- 7,239 degree-seeking undergraduates: 19% part-time, 57% women, 6% African American, 1% Asian American, 9% Hispanic American, 1% Native American, 1% international
- 1,309 degree-seeking graduate students
- 63% of applicants admitted
- SAT or ACT (ACT writing recommended) required
- 52% graduate within 6 years

**General.** Founded in 1899. Regionally accredited. Graduate courses available at several off-campus locations within 150-mile radius. **Degrees:** 1,685 bachelor's, 24 associate awarded; master's, doctoral offered. **ROTC:** Army. **Location:** 65 miles from Fort Worth. **Calendar:** Semester, extensive summer session. **Full-time faculty:** 335 total; 69% have terminal degrees, 11% minority, 45% women. **Part-time faculty:** 272 total; 18% have terminal degrees, 11% minority, 50% women. **Class size:** 41% < 20, 48% 20-39, 5% 40-49, 5% 50-99, less than 1% >100. **Special facilities:** University farm and equine center, planetarium.

**Freshman class profile.** 3,739 applied, 2,342 admitted, 1,150 enrolled.

| Mid 50% test scores | | | |
|---|---|---|---|
| SAT critical reading: | 420-530 | Rank in top tenth: | 12% |
| SAT math: | 450-550 | Return as sophomores: | 66% |
| SAT writing: | 420-510 | Out-of-state: | 1% |
| ACT composite: | 18-23 | Live on campus: | 75% |
| Rank in top quarter: | 37% | Fraternities: | 8% |
| | | Sororities: | 7% |

**Basis for selection.** Unconditional admission requires 950 combined SAT (exclusive of Writing) or 20 ACT. Rank in top quarter of class ensures unconditional admission if student has taken 4 years English and 3 years math. **Homeschooled:** Must provide proof of curriculum completed from an agency or teacher. **Learning Disabled:** Contact Director of Disability Services for appropriate accommodation.

**High school preparation.** College-preparatory program recommended.

**2009-2010 Annual costs.** Tuition/fees: $5,565; $13,995 out-of-state. Freshmen pay additional $100 first-year experience fee, first semester only. Distance learning fee is additional $40 per credit hour. Room/board: $7,046. Books/supplies: $1,050.

**2008-2009 Financial aid. Need-based:** 1,942 full-time freshmen applied for aid; 1,897 were judged to have need; 1,819 of these received aid. Average need met was 49%. Average scholarship/grant was $2,248; average loan $1,867. 49% of total undergraduate aid awarded as scholarships/grants, 51% as loans/jobs. **Non-need-based:** Awarded to 4,689 full-time undergraduates, including 1,159 freshmen. Scholarships awarded for academics, alumni affiliation, art, athletics, leadership, music/drama, ROTC.

**Application procedures. Admission:** Priority date 3/1; no deadline. $30 fee. Admission notification on a rolling basis beginning on or about 9/1. **Financial aid:** Priority date 4/1; no closing date. FAFSA required. Applicants notified on a rolling basis starting 2/1.

**Academics. Special study options:** Accelerated study, distance learning, double major, dual enrollment of high school students, honors, internships, study abroad, teacher certification program. Specialized bachelor of applied arts and science degree for students with practical work experience in field of study; cooperative doctoral program in educational administration offered in partnership with Texas A&M University-Commerce; 2-2 engineering with Texas A&M University and University of Texas Arlington. **Credit/placement by examination:** AP, CLEP, SAT, ACT, institutional tests. Students can earn the majority of credits toward their degree by examination. **Support services:** Learning center, pre-admission summer program, reduced course load, remedial instruction, study skills assistance, tutoring, writing center.

**Majors. Agriculture:** General, agribusiness operations, agronomy, animal husbandry, animal sciences, business, economics, livestock, mechanization, ornamental horticulture, supplies. **Biology:** General, zoology. **Business:** General, accounting, business admin, finance, human resources, management information systems, marketing, office management. **Communications:** General. **Computer sciences:** General. **Conservation:** Wildlife. **Education:** Computer, science. **Engineering:** Environmental, physics. **Engineering technology:** General, industrial, manufacturing. **Family/consumer sciences:** General. **Foreign languages:** Spanish. **Health:** Clinical lab science, nursing (RN). **History:** General. **Liberal arts:** Arts/sciences. **Math:** General. **Parks/recreation:** Health/fitness. **Physical sciences:** Chemistry, geology, hydrology, physics. **Protective services:** Criminal justice. **Psychology:** General. **Public administration:** Social work. **Social sciences:** Economics, political science, sociology. **Transportation:** Airline/commercial pilot, aviation management. **Visual/performing arts:** Dramatic, music performance, studio arts.

**Most popular majors.** Agriculture 11%, business/marketing 21%, interdisciplinary studies 13%, parks/recreation 8%.

**Computing on campus.** 1,200 workstations in dormitories, library, computer center, student center. Dormitories wired for high-speed internet access and linked to campus network. Commuter students can connect to campus network. Online course registration, online library, helpline, repair service, student web hosting, wireless network available.

**Student life. Freshman orientation:** Mandatory, $100 fee. Preregistration for classes offered. Held multiple times during the summer. **Housing:** Guaranteed on-campus for freshmen. Coed dorms, single-sex dorms, apartments, wellness housing available. $100 nonrefundable deposit. **Activities:** Bands, campus ministries, choral groups, dance, drama, international student organizations, literary magazine, music ensembles, musical theater, radio station, student government, student newspaper, symphony orchestra, Los Tejanos, Chinese student association, progressive united black student organization, student social work association, Alpha Phi Omega, Circle K, Fellowship of Christian Athletes, Fellowship of Christian Cowboys, College Republicans, Young Democrats.

**Athletics.** NCAA. **Intercollegiate:** Baseball M, basketball, cheerleading, cross-country, football (tackle) M, golf W, rodeo, softball W, tennis W, track

and field, volleyball W. **Intramural:** Archery, basketball, football (non-tackle) M, football (tackle), golf, racquetball, rodeo, soccer, softball, table tennis, tennis, volleyball. **Team name:** Texans.

**Student services.** Adult student services, alcohol/substance abuse counseling, chaplain/spiritual director, career counseling, student employment services, financial aid counseling, health services, legal services, minority student services, on-campus daycare, personal counseling, placement for graduates, veterans' counselor. **Physically disabled:** Services for visually, speech, hearing impaired. **Learning disabled:** Comprehensive services available.

**Contact.** E-mail: uadm@tarleton.edu
Phone: (254) 968-9125 Toll-free number: (800) 687-8236
Fax: (254) 968-9951
Cindy Hess, Director of Admissions, Tarleton State University, Box T-0030, Stephenville, TX 76402

## Texas A&M International University

| Laredo, Texas | CB member |
|---|---|
| www.tamiu.edu | CB code: 0359 |

- Public 4-year university
- Commuter campus in small city
- 5,281 degree-seeking undergraduates: 37% part-time, 60% women, 1% African American, 1% Asian American, 94% Hispanic American, 2% international
- 986 degree-seeking graduate students
- 53% of applicants admitted
- SAT or ACT (ACT writing recommended) required
- 37% graduate within 6 years; 18% enter graduate study

**General.** Founded in 1969. Regionally accredited. **Degrees:** 723 bachelor's awarded; master's, doctoral offered. **ROTC:** Army. **Location:** 150 miles from San Antonio and Corpus Christi. **Calendar:** Semester, extensive summer session. **Full-time faculty:** 162 total; 51% have terminal degrees, 38% minority, 41% women. **Part-time faculty:** 141 total; 16% have terminal degrees, 64% minority, 48% women. **Class size:** 33% < 20, 47% 20-39, 8% 40-49, 11% 50-99, 2% >100. **Special facilities:** Planetarium.

**Freshman class profile.** 3,414 applied, 1,819 admitted, 803 enrolled.

| Mid 50% test scores | | | |
|---|---|---|---|
| SAT critical reading: | 380-490 | GPA 2.0-2.99: | 3% |
| SAT math: | 410-500 | Rank in top quarter: | 54% |
| SAT writing: | 380-480 | Rank in top tenth: | 22% |
| ACT composite: | 15-20 | End year in good standing: | 82% |
| GPA 3.75 or higher: | 27% | Return as sophomores: | 64% |
| GPA 3.50-3.74: | 42% | Out-of-state: | 1% |
| GPA 3.0-3.49: | 26% | International: | 1% |

**Basis for selection.** Students in top half of graduating class admitted with no minimum ACT or SAT score. Students in bottom half need minimum score of 860 on SAT (exclusive of Writing) or 18 on ACT.

**High school preparation.** Required and recommended units include English 4, mathematics 3, history 3, science 2, foreign language 2 and academic electives 2. 1 computer technology, 1 fine arts recommended.

**2009-2010 Annual costs.** Tuition/fees: $5,717; $14,027 out-of-state. Room/board: $6,918.

**2008-2009 Financial aid. Need-based:** 612 full-time freshmen applied for aid; 545 were judged to have need; 543 of these received aid. Average need met was 55%. Average scholarship/grant was $5,890; average loan $2,927. 65% of total undergraduate aid awarded as scholarships/grants, 35% as loans/jobs. **Non-need-based:** Awarded to 1,048 full-time undergraduates, including 237 freshmen. Scholarships awarded for academics.

**Application procedures. Admission:** Closing date 7/1 (postmark date). No application fee. Admission notification on a rolling basis beginning on or about 11/1. **Financial aid:** Priority date 3/15; no closing date. FAFSA, institutional form required. Applicants notified on a rolling basis starting 4/15; must reply within 2 week(s) of notification.

**Academics. Special study options:** Cooperative education, cross-registration, double major, dual enrollment of high school students, ESL, honors, independent study, internships, liberal arts/career combination, study abroad, teacher certification program. **Credit/placement by examination:** AP, CLEP, IB, SAT, ACT, institutional tests. 33 credit hours maximum toward bachelor's degree. **Support services:** Learning center, pre-admission summer program, reduced course load, remedial instruction, study skills assistance, tutoring, writing center.

**Majors. Area/ethnic studies:** Latin American. **Biology:** General. **Business:** Accounting, business admin, finance, management information systems, managerial economics, marketing. **Communications:** General. **Conservation:** General. **Education:** Bilingual, biology, early childhood, elementary, English, history, mathematics, reading, social studies, Spanish, special. **Foreign languages:** Spanish. **Health:** Nursing (RN), preop/surgical nursing. **History:** General. **Math:** General. **Parks/recreation:** Health/fitness. **Physical sciences:** Chemistry. **Protective services:** Criminal justice. **Psychology:** General. **Public administration:** Social work. **Social sciences:** General, political science, sociology, urban studies.

**Most popular majors.** Business/marketing 27%, interdisciplinary studies 27%, psychology 6%, security/protective services 9%.

**Computing on campus.** 200 workstations in dormitories, library, computer center. Dormitories wired for high-speed internet access and linked to campus network. Commuter students can connect to campus network. Wireless network available.

**Student life. Freshman orientation:** Mandatory, $30 fee. Preregistration for classes offered. 4 overnight sessions held June-August and 1 one-day session in August for late registrants. **Housing:** Apartments available. On-campus housing, not owned by college (private contractor) available. **Activities:** Bands, choral groups, dance, drama, literary magazine, music ensembles, student government, student newspaper, student ambassadors, Association of International Students, Tau Sigma Chi (criminal justice), High Twisters, Ballet Folklorico, student system group, student finance society.

**Athletics.** NCAA. **Intercollegiate:** Baseball M, basketball, cross-country, golf, soccer, softball W, volleyball W. **Intramural:** Baseball, basketball, soccer, table tennis, volleyball, weight lifting. **Team name:** Dust Devils.

**Student services.** Career counseling, services for economically disadvantaged, student employment services, financial aid counseling, health services, personal counseling, placement for graduates, veterans' counselor. **Physically disabled:** Services for visually, speech, hearing impaired.

**Contact.** E-mail: enroll@tamiu.edu
Phone: (956) 326-2200 Fax: (956) 326-2199
Rosa Dickinson, Director of Admissions, Texas A&M International University, 5201 University Boulevard, Laredo, TX 78041-1900

---

## Texas A&M University
### College Station, Texas
**www.tamu.edu**

CB member
CB code: 6003

- Public 4-year university
- Residential campus in small city
- 38,718 degree-seeking undergraduates: 9% part-time, 48% women, 3% African American, 5% Asian American, 14% Hispanic American, 1% Native American, 1% international·
- 9,736 degree-seeking graduate students
- 67% of applicants admitted
- SAT or ACT with writing, application essay required
- 80% graduate within 6 years

**General.** Founded in 1876. Regionally accredited. **Degrees:** 8,308 bachelor's awarded; master's, doctoral, professional offered. **ROTC:** Army, Naval, Air Force. **Location:** 90 miles from Houston, 100 miles from Austin. **Calendar:** Semester, extensive summer session. **Full-time faculty:** 2,317 total; 93% have terminal degrees, 23% minority, 30% women. **Part-time faculty:** 501 total; 68% have terminal degrees, 17% minority, 37% women. **Class size:** 22% < 20, 49% 20-39, 7% 40-49, 13% 50-99, 9% >100. **Special facilities:** Reactor, cyclotron, observatory, agriculture research property, 18-hole golf course, supercomputer center, oceanographic research vessel, Italian study center, George H. W. Bush Presidential Library and Museum.

**Freshman class profile.** 22,757 applied, 15,158 admitted, 8,071 enrolled.

| Mid 50% test scores | | Rank in top tenth: | 50% |
|---|---|---|---|
| SAT critical reading: | 530-640 | Return as sophomores: | 92% |
| SAT math: | 570-670 | Out-of-state: | 3% |
| SAT writing: | 500-620 | Live on campus: | 66% |
| ACT composite: | 24-30 | International: | 1% |
| Rank in top quarter: | 89% | | |

**Basis for selection.** Automatic admission to applicants in top 10% of Texas high school class (with completed application), as specified by state law. Strong senior year course schedule recommended. Test scores required of all applicants but not used for admission of applicants from top 10% of any Texas high school class. **Learning Disabled:** Must provide documentation from qualified professional licensed or certified to diagnose disability.

**High school preparation.** College-preparatory program required. 17.5 units required; 18.5 recommended. Required and recommended units include English 4, mathematics 3.5, social studies 2, history 1, science 3 (laboratory 2) and foreign language 2. 1 unit computer usage required.

**2009-2010 Annual costs.** Tuition/fees: $8,176; $22,609 out-of-state. Room/board: $8,039. Books/supplies: $1,278. Personal expenses: $2,223.

**2008-2009 Financial aid. Need-based:** 4,954 full-time freshmen applied for aid; 2,968 were judged to have need; 2,913 of these received aid. Average need met was 92%. Average scholarship/grant was $10,946; average loan $4,018. 63% of total undergraduate aid awarded as scholarships/grants, 37% as loans/jobs. **Non-need-based:** Awarded to 6,255 full-time undergraduates, including 1,696 freshmen. Scholarships awarded for academics, alumni affiliation, art, athletics, job skills, leadership, music/drama, religious affiliation, ROTC, state residency. **Additional information:** Short-term loans available. Out-of-state students awarded academic scholarships of $1,000 or more are eligible for waiver of out-of-state tuition.

**Application procedures. Admission:** Priority date 12/1; deadline 1/15 (receipt date). $60 fee, may be waived for applicants with need. Admission notification on a rolling basis beginning on or about 4/1. Must reply by 5/1. Housing deposit due at time of application. **Financial aid:** Priority date 3/31; no closing date. FAFSA required. Applicants notified on a rolling basis starting 3/15; must reply within 4 week(s) of notification.

**Academics.** Core curriculum requirements in foreign language and computer science may be satisfied by selected high school courses. **Special study options:** Accelerated study, combined bachelor's/graduate degree, cooperative education, distance learning, double major, dual enrollment of high school students, ESL, honors, independent study, internships, liberal arts/career combination, study abroad, teacher certification program. Exchange programs in architecture with Instituto Tecnologico y de Estudios Superiores de Monterrey, King's College London (England), University of Lancaster (England), Denmark's international study program, Ruhr University Bochum (Germany), University of Lausanne (Switzerland). **Credit/placement by examination:** AP, CLEP, IB, institutional tests. **Support services:** Learning center, pre-admission summer program, remedial instruction, tutoring, writing center.

**Majors. Agriculture:** General, agribusiness operations, agronomy, animal husbandry, animal sciences, aquaculture, business, communications, dairy, economics, farm/ranch, food science, horticultural science, horticulture, ornamental horticulture, plant protection, plant sciences, poultry, production, range science, soil science, supplies, turf management. **Architecture:** Architecture, environmental design, landscape. **Area/ethnic studies:** American. **Biology:** General, biochemistry, biomedical sciences, botany, cellular/molecular, entomology, environmental, microbiology, molecular genetics, zoology. **Business:** Accounting, finance, management science, marketing, sales/distribution, tourism promotion, tourism/travel. **Communications:** Digital media, journalism. **Computer sciences:** Computer science. **Conservation:** General, environmental science, environmental studies, forest management, forestry, management/policy, urban forestry, wildlife. **Engineering:** Aerospace, agricultural, biomedical, chemical, civil, computer, electrical, geological, industrial, mechanical, nuclear, ocean, petroleum. **Engineering technology:** General, construction, electrical, manufacturing, telecommunications. **Family/consumer sciences:** Food/nutrition. **Foreign languages:** Classics, French, German, Russian, Spanish. **Health:** Community health services, preveterinary. **History:** General. **Interdisciplinary:** Global studies. **Math:** General, applied. **Parks/recreation:** General, facilities management, health/fitness. **Philosophy/religion:** Philosophy. **Physical sciences:** Atmospheric science, chemistry, geology, geophysics, physics. **Protective services:** Forensics. **Psychology:** General. **Public administration:** Community org/advocacy. **Social sciences:** Anthropology, cartography, economics, geography, political science, sociology. **Visual/performing arts:** Dramatic.

**Most popular majors.** Agriculture 12%, biology 9%, business/marketing 18%, engineering/engineering technologies 15%, English 6%, interdisciplinary studies 8%, social sciences 7%.

**Computing on campus.** 1,840 workstations in dormitories, library, computer center, student center. Dormitories wired for high-speed internet access and linked to campus network. Commuter students can connect to campus network. Online course registration, online library, helpline, repair service, student web hosting, wireless network available.

**Student life. Freshman orientation:** Mandatory, $35 fee. Preregistration for classes offered. 2 1/2 day program throughout the summer. **Housing:** Coed dorms, single-sex dorms, special housing for disabled, apartments, fraternity/sorority housing, wellness housing available. $300 fully refundable deposit. Campus housing guaranteed to members of Corps of Cadets and recipients of major 4-year endowed academic scholarships. Freshman honors dorm available. **Activities:** Bands, campus ministries, choral groups, dance, drama, film society, literary magazine, music ensembles, musical theater, radio station, student government, student newspaper, symphony orchestra, TV station, Black awareness committee, committee for the awareness of Mexican American culture, student Y association, student conference on national affairs, social service organizations, College Republicans, Aggie Democrats, political forum, Aggies for Christ, Corps of Cadets.

**Athletics.** NCAA. **Intercollegiate:** Archery W, baseball M, basketball, cross-country, diving, equestrian W, football (tackle) M, golf, soccer W, softball W, swimming, tennis, track and field, volleyball W. **Intramural:** Archery, badminton, basketball, bowling, diving, golf, lacrosse, racquetball, rodeo, soccer, softball, squash, swimming, table tennis, track and field, volleyball. **Team name:** Aggies.

**Student services.** Alcohol/substance abuse counseling, career counseling, student employment services, financial aid counseling, health services, legal services, minority student services, on-campus daycare, personal counseling, placement for graduates, veterans' counselor, women's services. **Physically disabled:** Services for visually, speech, hearing impaired.

**Contact.** E-mail: admissions@tamu.edu
Phone: (979) 845-1060 Fax: (979) 458-1808
Scott McDonald, Director of Admissions, Texas A&M University, PO Box 30014, College Station, TX 77842-3014

## Texas A&M University-Baylor College of Dentistry
Dallas, Texas
www.bcd.tamhsc.edu                    CB code: 6059

- Public two-year upper-division health science college
- Commuter campus in very large city
- 25% of applicants admitted
- Application essay, interview required

**General.** Founded in 1905. Regionally accredited. **Degrees:** 30 bachelor's awarded; master's, doctoral, professional offered. **Articulation:** Agreement with Collin Community College District. **Calendar:** Semester. **Full-time faculty:** 122 total; 100% have terminal degrees, 12% minority, 38% women. **Part-time faculty:** 113 total; 100% have terminal degrees, 12% minority, 30% women.

**Student profile.** 61 degree-seeking undergraduates, 504 degree-seeking graduate students. 122 applied as first time-transfer students, 30 admitted, 30 enrolled. 60% transferred from two-year, 40% transferred from four-year institutions.

| Women: | 95% | Out-of-state: | 4% |
|---|---|---|---|
| Asian American: | 18% | 25 or older: | 25% |
| Hispanic American: | 16% | | |

**Basis for selection.** High school transcript, college transcript, application essay, interview required. School achievement most important. Essay, interview, and recommendations highly considered. Transfer accepted as juniors.

**2009-2010 Annual costs.** Personal expenses: $2,850.

**Financial aid. Need-based:** 61 applied for aid; 56 were judged to have need; 51 of these received aid. Average need met was 43%. 50% of total undergraduate aid awarded as scholarships/grants, 50% as loans/jobs. **Non-need-based:** Scholarships awarded for academics.

**Application procedures. Admission:** Priority date 12/31. $35 fee. **Financial aid:** FAFSA, institutional form required.

**Academics.** Participation in research activities under faculty sponsorship and annual research fellowships awarded by college offered. **Special study options:** Combined bachelor's/graduate degree, internships. **Credit/placement by examination:** CLEP.

**Majors. Health:** Dental hygiene.

**Computing on campus.** 25 workstations in library, computer center. Commuter students can connect to campus network. Online library, helpline, wireless network available.

**Student life. Housing:** Baylor Medical Center nursing dormitory housing available. **Activities:** Student government.

**Student services.** Student employment services, financial aid counseling, health services, personal counseling.

**Contact.** Phone: (214) 828-8230 Fax: (214) 828-8346
Barbara Miller, Director, Texas A&M University-Baylor College of Dentistry, PO Box 660677, Dallas, TX 75266-0677

## Texas A&M University-Commerce
Commerce, Texas                       CB member
www.tamu-commerce.edu                 CB code: 6188

- Public 4-year university
- Commuter campus in small town
- 5,194 degree-seeking undergraduates: 23% part-time, 62% women, 19% African American, 2% Asian American, 10% Hispanic American, 1% Native American, 1% international
- 3,525 degree-seeking graduate students
- 78% of applicants admitted
- SAT or ACT with writing required
- 37% graduate within 6 years; 24% enter graduate study

**General.** Founded in 1889. Regionally accredited. **Degrees:** 1,193 bachelor's awarded; master's, doctoral offered. **Location:** 60 miles from Dallas. **Calendar:** Semester, extensive summer session. **Full-time faculty:** 282 total; 67% have terminal degrees, 16% minority, 40% women. **Part-time faculty:** 220 total; 21% have terminal degrees, 11% minority, 66% women. **Class size:** 53% < 20, 33% 20-39, 6% 40-49, 7% 50-99, less than 1% >100. **Special facilities:** Instructional university farm, planetarium.

**Freshman class profile.** 2,202 applied, 1,721 admitted, 620 enrolled.

| Mid 50% test scores | | | |
|---|---|---|---|
| SAT critical reading: | 440-550 | GPA 2.0-2.99: | 34% |
| SAT math: | 450-560 | Rank in top quarter: | 39% |
| SAT writing: | 420-530 | Rank in top tenth: | 17% |
| ACT composite: | 18-24 | End year in good standing: | 47% |
| GPA 3.75 or higher: | 16% | Return as sophomores: | 67% |
| GPA 3.50-3.74: | 14% | Out-of-state: | 2% |
| GPA 3.0-3.49: | 34% | International: | 1% |

**Basis for selection.** ACT or SAT scores most important, followed by high school grades and class rank. Students admitted with 20 ACT or 920 SAT (exclusive of Writing). TASP scores may exempt student from SAT or ACT tests. If student is TASP remedial, must take TASP within first semester of enrolling. Portfolio required for advertising art program; audition recommended for music program. **Homeschooled:** Must earn GED and be at least 18 years of age.

**High school preparation.** 12 units required. Required and recommended units include English 4, mathematics 3, science 2 and foreign language 2. 2.5 hours history/social studies required.

**2009-2010 Annual costs.** Tuition/fees: $5,500; $13,840 out-of-state. Room/board: $7,090. Books/supplies: $1,400. Personal expenses: $1,830.

**2008-2009 Financial aid. Non-need-based:** Scholarships awarded for academics, art, athletics, leadership, music/drama. **Additional information:** Work-study also available for full-time students.

**Application procedures. Admission:** Closing date 8/1 (postmark date). $25 fee ($50 out-of-state). Admission notification on a rolling basis beginning on or about 10/1. High school seniors may enroll part-time before graduation with consent of high school principal if they meet requirements. **Financial aid:** Priority date 4/1; no closing date. FAFSA required. Applicants notified on a rolling basis starting 4/1; must reply within 2 week(s) of notification.

**Academics. Special study options:** Combined bachelor's/graduate degree, cooperative education, distance learning, double major, dual enrollment of high school students, external degree, honors, independent study, internships, liberal arts/career combination, study abroad, teacher certification program, weekend college. **Credit/placement by examination:** AP, CLEP, IB, SAT, ACT, institutional tests. 6 credit hours maximum toward bachelor's degree. **Support services:** Learning center, pre-admission summer program, remedial instruction, study skills assistance, tutoring, writing center.

**Majors. Agriculture:** Animal sciences, communications, economics, food science, plant sciences, soil science. **Biology:** General, cell/histology. **Business:** General, accounting, business admin, human resources, management information systems, managerial economics, marketing, office management, office/clerical, operations, public finance. **Communications:** General, advertising, broadcast journalism, digital media, journalism, public relations. **Communications technology:** Graphic/printing. **Computer sciences:** General, computer science, information systems. **Conservation:** General, environmental studies, wildlife. **Construction:** Maintenance. **Education:** Bilingual, biology, chemistry, driver/safety, early childhood, elementary, middle, multi-level teacher, physical, special. **Engineering:** Operations research. **Engineering technology:** Construction, manufacturing. **Foreign languages:** German, Spanish. **Health:** Athletic training, health care admin, medical records admin, predental, premedicine, prepharmacy, preveterinary. **History:** General. **Interdisciplinary:** Biological/physical sciences. **Legal studies:** Legal secretary, paralegal, prelaw. **Liberal arts:** Arts/sciences, library science. **Math:** General. **Parks/recreation:** Health/fitness. **Physical sciences:** Chemistry, geology, organic chemistry, physics, planetary. **Protective services:** Criminal justice, law enforcement admin. **Psychology:** General. **Public administration:** Social work. **Social sciences:** General, anthropology, criminology, economics, geography, political science, sociology. **Theology:** Preministerial. **Visual/performing arts:** General, art, arts management, ceramics, commercial photography, commercial/advertising art, design, dramatic, industrial design, metal/jewelry, music history, music pedagogy, music performance, music theory/composition, musicology, painting, photography, piano/organ, printmaking, sculpture, voice/opera.

**Most popular majors.** Business/marketing 8%, education 25%, interdisciplinary studies 33%.

**Computing on campus.** 1,500 workstations in dormitories, library, computer center, student center. Dormitories wired for high-speed internet access and linked to campus network. Commuter students can connect to campus network. Online course registration, online library, helpline, repair service, wireless network available.

**Student life. Freshman orientation:** Mandatory, $100 fee. Preregistration for classes offered. Held throughout summer; includes advising, assessment testing, and parental involvement. **Housing:** Coed dorms, single-sex dorms, special housing for disabled, apartments, fraternity/sorority housing, wellness housing available. $100 deposit, deadline 7/1. Shared freshman experience housing available. **Activities:** Bands, choral groups, dance, drama, film society, literary magazine, music ensembles, musical theater, opera, radio station, student government, student newspaper, symphony orchestra, TV station, Baptist student union, Church of Christ Bible chair, Newman Club, university Christian center, Young Democrats, association cultural de Hispanos-Americanos, Chinese student association, Muslim society, NAACP, Thai students association, Alpha Phi Omega.

**Athletics.** NCAA. **Intercollegiate:** Basketball, cross-country, football (tackle) M, golf, soccer W, track and field, volleyball W. **Intramural:** Archery, badminton, baseball M, basketball, bowling, cross-country, golf, racquetball, softball, swimming, table tennis, tennis, track and field, volleyball. **Team name:** Lions.

**Student services.** Alcohol/substance abuse counseling, chaplain/spiritual director, career counseling, student employment services, financial aid counseling, health services, legal services, on-campus daycare, personal counseling, placement for graduates, veterans' counselor. **Physically disabled:** Services for visually, speech, hearing impaired.

**Contact.** E-mail: hope_young1@tamu-commerce.edu
Phone: (903) 886-5102 Toll-free number: (888) 886-2682
Fax: (903) 468-6080
Hope Young, Director of Undergraduate Admissions, Texas A&M University-Commerce, Box 3011, Commerce, TX 75429-3011

## Texas A&M University-Corpus Christi
**Corpus Christi, Texas**      **CB member**
**www.tamucc.edu**      **CB code: 0366**

- Public 4-year university
- Commuter campus in large city
- 7,591 degree-seeking undergraduates: 23% part-time, 59% women
- 1,829 degree-seeking graduate students
- 85% of applicants admitted
- SAT or ACT required

**General.** Founded in 1947. Regionally accredited. **Degrees:** 1,405 bachelor's awarded; master's, doctoral offered. **ROTC:** Army. **Location:** 150 miles from San Antonio, 200 miles from Houston. **Calendar:** Semester, extensive summer session. **Full-time faculty:** 328 total; 81% have terminal degrees, 16% minority, 47% women. **Part-time faculty:** 200 total; 81% have terminal degrees, 24% minority, 56% women. **Class size:** 25% < 20, 51% 20-39, 8% 40-49, 13% 50-99, 2% >100. **Special facilities:** National spill control school, institute for surveying and science, center for coastal studies, center for environmental studies and services, early childhood development center, South Texas Institute for the Arts.

**Freshman class profile.** 4,744 applied, 4,015 admitted, 1,308 enrolled.

| Mid 50% test scores | | | |
|---|---|---|---|
| | | Out-of-state: | 3% |
| SAT critical reading: | 420-520 | Live on campus: | 18% |
| SAT math: | 400-520 | Fraternities: | 4% |
| ACT composite: | 19-23 | Sororities: | 5% |

**Basis for selection.** High school GPA, class rank, and course work most important. Test scores, school and community leadership activities, special talents also considered. Minimum 900 SAT (exclusive of Writing), required. Applicants not meeting minimum requirements may apply to admission committee for special consideration. Local placement exams in reading, writing and math required of all first-time freshmen.

**High school preparation.** 15 units required. Required units include English 4, mathematics 3, social studies 3, science 3 and foreign language 2.

**2009-2010 Annual costs.** Tuition/fees: $6,098; $14,408 out-of-state. Room/board: $9,250. Books/supplies: $966. Personal expenses: $1,436.

**2009-2010 Financial aid. Need-based:** 57% of total undergraduate aid awarded as scholarships/grants, 43% as loans/jobs. **Non-need-based:** Scholarships awarded for academics, art, athletics, music/drama.

**Application procedures. Admission:** Closing date 7/1 (receipt date). $20 fee. Admission notification on a rolling basis. **Financial aid:** Closing date 4/1. FAFSA, institutional form required. Applicants notified on a rolling basis starting 5/1; must reply within 2 week(s) of notification.

**Academics. Special study options:** Cooperative education, distance learning, double major, dual enrollment of high school students, ESL, honors, independent study, internships, study abroad, teacher certification program. **Credit/placement by examination:** CLEP, IB, institutional tests. DANTES, ACT, PEP accepted. **Support services:** Learning center, remedial instruction, study skills assistance, tutoring, writing center.

**Majors. Biology:** General, biomedical sciences. **Business:** General, accounting, business admin, finance, management information systems, managerial economics, marketing. **Communications:** General. **Computer sciences:** General. **Conservation:** General. **Engineering:** Mechanical. **Engineering technology:** Electrical, instrumentation, mechanical, surveying. **Foreign languages:** Spanish. **Health:** Athletic training, clinical lab science, clinical nurse specialist, health services, nurse practitioner, nursing (RN). **History:** General. **Math:** General. **Parks/recreation:** Health/fitness. **Physical sciences:** Chemistry, geology. **Protective services:** Criminal justice. **Psychology:** General. **Social sciences:** Economics, political science, sociology. **Visual/performing arts:** General, studio arts.

**Most popular majors.** Biology 9%, business/marketing 18%, communications/journalism 7%, health sciences 13%, interdisciplinary studies 15%, psychology 8%.

**Computing on campus.** 500 workstations in library, computer center. Commuter students can connect to campus network. Helpline, repair service available.

**Student life. Freshman orientation:** Available. Preregistration for classes offered. Program held various times in summer before fall entry. **Policies:** No alcohol on campus except by adult students in their own apartments. **Housing:** Guaranteed on-campus for freshmen. Coed dorms, apartments available. $150 deposit. **Activities:** Bands, choral groups, dance, drama, film society, literary magazine, music ensembles, musical theater, opera, student government, student newspaper, symphony orchestra, Baptist Student Union, Newman Club, Friends Meeting, LDS Students Association, Amigos, computer science club, African-American Cultural Society.

**Athletics.** NCAA. **Intercollegiate:** Baseball, basketball, cross-country, golf W, softball W, swimming W, tennis, track and field, volleyball W. **Intramural:** Badminton, baseball M, basketball, cross-country, golf, gymnastics, handball, racquetball, sailing, soccer, softball, swimming, table tennis, tennis, track and field, volleyball. **Team name:** Islanders.

**Student services.** Alcohol/substance abuse counseling, chaplain/spiritual director, career counseling, student employment services, financial aid counseling, health services, personal counseling, placement for graduates, veterans' counselor. **Physically disabled:** Services for visually, speech, hearing impaired.

**Contact.** E-mail: admiss@tamucc.edu
Phone: (361) 825-2624 Toll-free number: (800) 482-6822
Fax: (361) 825-5887
Christopher Fleming, Director of Admissions, Texas A&M University-Corpus Christi, 6300 Ocean Drive, Unit 5774, Corpus Christi, TX 78412-5774

## Texas A&M University-Galveston
**Galveston, Texas**      **CB member**
**www.tamug.edu**      **CB code: 6835**

- Public 4-year university and branch campus college
- Residential campus in small city
- 1,718 degree-seeking undergraduates

- 71% of applicants admitted
- SAT or ACT with writing, application essay required

**General.** Founded in 1962. Regionally accredited. Institution houses Texas Maritime Academy, 1 of 5 seacoast maritime academies in the U.S. preparing graduates for licensing as officers in the Merchant Marine. **Degrees:** 239 bachelor's awarded; master's offered. **ROTC:** Naval. **Location:** 50 miles from Houston. **Calendar:** Semester, limited summer session. **Full-time faculty:** 98 total. **Part-time faculty:** 57 total. **Class size:** 67% < 20, 23% 20-39, 4% 40-49, 4% 50-99, 2% >100. **Special facilities:** Fleet of research and training boats, 300-acre wetlands on west Galveston Bay, wetlands research center, ship bridge simulator.

**Freshman class profile.** 1,363 applied, 970 admitted, 498 enrolled.

| Mid 50% test scores | | Rank in top quarter: | 40% |
|---|---|---|---|
| SAT critical reading: | 520-580 | Rank in top tenth: | 11% |
| SAT math: | 550-560 | Out-of-state: | 14% |
| SAT writing: | 490-550 | Live on campus: | 75% |
| ACT composite: | 21-24 | | |

**Basis for selection.** School achievement record and test scores most important. Adverse circumstances, leadership, exceptional talents, course selections, and references reviewed on individual basis. **Homeschooled:** Transcript of courses and grades, letter of recommendation (nonparent) required.

**High school preparation.** 13 units required; 19 recommended. Required and recommended units include English 4, mathematics 3-4, social studies 3, science 3-4 (laboratory 2) and foreign language 3. 1 unit computer literacy required. Science courses must be selected from biology, chemistry or physics.

**2009-2010 Annual costs.** Tuition/fees: $6,818; $15,128 out-of-state. Room/board: $5,676. Books/supplies: $1,381. Personal expenses: $1,960.

**2008-2009 Financial aid. Non-need-based:** Scholarships awarded for academics, state residency.

**Application procedures. Admission:** No deadline. $45 fee, may be waived for applicants with need. Admission notification on a rolling basis. **Financial aid:** Priority date 4/1; no closing date. FAFSA required. Applicants notified on a rolling basis starting 3/15; must reply within 3 week(s) of notification.

**Academics.** All academic programs are ocean-related. USCG ship officer's license may be earned through license option program. **Special study options:** Accelerated study, combined bachelor's/graduate degree, cooperative education, double major, dual enrollment of high school students, independent study, internships, liberal arts/career combination, semester at sea, study abroad, teacher certification program. Merchant marine licensing program available with marine biology, marine science, marine transportation, and marine engineering technology degrees. **Credit/placement by examination:** AP, CLEP, IB, institutional tests. **Support services:** Learning center, pre-admission summer program, remedial instruction, study skills assistance, tutoring.

**Majors. Agriculture:** Aquaculture. **Biology:** General, aquatic, biomedical sciences, botany, marine, zoology. **Business:** Business admin, international, international finance, tourism/travel, transportation. **Conservation:** General, fisheries. **Education:** Biology, science. **Engineering:** Marine, ocean, systems. **Engineering technology:** Mechanical. **Interdisciplinary:** Biological/physical sciences. **Liberal arts:** Arts/sciences. **Parks/recreation:** General. **Physical sciences:** General, geology, hydrology, oceanography. **Transportation:** General, commercial fishing, maritime/Merchant Marine.

**Most popular majors.** Biology 31%, business/marketing 21%, engineering/engineering technologies 13%, interdisciplinary studies 7%, natural resources/environmental science 11%, trade and industry 12%.

**Computing on campus.** 130 workstations in dormitories, library, computer center. Dormitories wired for high-speed internet access and linked to campus network. Commuter students can connect to campus network. Helpline, repair service available.

**Student life. Freshman orientation:** Mandatory, $75 fee. Preregistration for classes offered. 4 days in June and August. **Housing:** Coed dorms, single-sex dorms, special housing for disabled, apartments, wellness housing available. $250 fully refundable deposit. **Activities:** Choral groups, dance, drama, literary magazine, student government, student newspaper, Circle K, Campus Crusade for Christ, emergency care team, outdoor and environmental conservation, Catholic student association, SEED (Students Encouraging Ethnic Diversity), Wesley Foundation.

**Athletics. Intercollegiate:** Rowing (crew), sailing. **Intramural:** Basketball, football (non-tackle), racquetball, soccer, softball, tennis, volleyball, water polo. **Team name:** Aggies.

**Student services.** Alcohol/substance abuse counseling, chaplain/spiritual director, career counseling, student employment services, financial aid counseling, health services, minority student services, personal counseling, placement for graduates, veterans' counselor. **Physically disabled:** Services for hearing impaired.

**Contact.** E-mail: seaaggie@tamug.edu
Phone: (409) 740-4414 Toll-free number: (877) 322-4443
Fax: (409) 740-4731
Cheryl Moon, Executive Director of Enrollment Services, Texas A&M University-Galveston, PO Box 1675, Galveston, TX 77553-1675

---

## Texas A&M University-Kingsville
**Kingsville, Texas**
www.tamuk.edu

**CB member**
**CB code: 6822**

- Public 4-year university
- Commuter campus in large town
- 6,289 degree-seeking undergraduates
- 1,946 graduate students

**General.** Founded in 1925. Regionally accredited. **Degrees:** 940 bachelor's awarded; master's, doctoral offered. **ROTC:** Army. **Location:** 40 miles from Corpus Christi, 250 miles from Houston. **Calendar:** Semester, extensive summer session. **Full-time faculty:** 270 total. **Part-time faculty:** 149 total. **Class size:** 41% < 20, 51% 20-39, 5% 40-49, 2% 50-99, less than 1% >100. **Special facilities:** Equine facilities, observatory, college-operated farms, research center for citrus, museum, venomous toxin research, greenhouses, extensive engineering facilities.

**Freshman class profile.**

| Mid 50% test scores | | Rank in top quarter: | 25% |
|---|---|---|---|
| SAT critical reading: | 410-520 | Rank in top tenth: | 15% |
| SAT math: | 410-540 | Return as sophomores: | 59% |
| ACT composite: | 16-21 | Out-of-state: | 1% |
| GPA 3.75 or higher: | 15% | Live on campus: | 60% |
| GPA 3.50-3.74: | 20% | Fraternities: | 2% |
| GPA 3.0-3.49: | 40% | Sororities: | 2% |
| GPA 2.0-2.99: | 25% | | |

**Basis for selection.** Open admission, but selective for some programs. Audition required, portfolio recommended for music program.

**High school preparation.** College-preparatory program recommended. 24 units recommended. Recommended units include English 4, mathematics 3, social studies 4, history 3, science 3, foreign language 3 and academic electives 3. One fine arts, 1 computer recommended.

**2009-2010 Annual costs.** Tuition/fees: $5,982; $14,292 out-of-state. Room/board: $5,130. Books/supplies: $614. Personal expenses: $2,108.

**Financial aid. Non-need-based:** Scholarships awarded for academics, leadership.

**Application procedures. Admission:** No deadline. $15 fee, may be waived for applicants with need. Admission notification on a rolling basis. **Financial aid:** FAFSA required. Applicants notified on a rolling basis.

**Academics. Special study options:** Combined bachelor's/graduate degree, cooperative education, distance learning, double major, dual enrollment of high school students, ESL, honors, internships, study abroad, teacher certification program. **Credit/placement by examination:** AP, CLEP. **Support services:** Remedial instruction, study skills assistance, tutoring.

**Majors. Agriculture:** Agribusiness operations, animal sciences, business, food science, plant sciences, range science. **Architecture:** Interior. **Biology:** General. **Business:** General, accounting, finance, international, management information systems, management science, managerial economics. **Communications:** General. **Conservation:** Wildlife. **Education:** General, agricultural, art, bilingual, elementary, family/consumer sciences, health, music, physical, secondary. **Engineering:** Chemical, civil, computer, electrical, mechanical, petroleum. **Engineering technology:** Industrial management. **Family/consumer sciences:** General, clothing/textiles, family studies, food/nutrition. **Foreign languages:** Spanish. **Health:** Speech pathology. **History:** General. **Math:** General. **Physical sciences:** Chemistry, geology, physics. **Psychology:** General. **Social sciences:** Political science, sociology. **Visual/performing arts:** Dramatic, interior design, studio arts.

**Student life. Freshman orientation:** Mandatory. **Housing:** Guaranteed on-campus for freshmen. Coed dorms, single-sex dorms, apartments, fraternity/sorority housing available. **Activities:** Bands, choral groups, dance, drama, international student organizations, music ensembles, musical theater, radio station, student government, student newspaper, TV station, Muslim student association, Baptist student association, black student union, La Barraca Tejana, American Society of Women Engineers, Society of Hispanic Professional Engineers, pre-law society.

**Athletics.** NCAA. **Intercollegiate:** Baseball M, basketball, cross-country, football (tackle) M, softball W, tennis, track and field, volleyball W. **Intramural:** Archery, bowling, equestrian, golf, racquetball, softball, volleyball. **Team name:** Javelinas.

**Student services.** Adult student services, alcohol/substance abuse counseling, career counseling, student employment services, financial aid counseling, health services, minority student services, on-campus daycare, personal counseling, placement for graduates, veterans' counselor, women's services. **Physically disabled:** Services for visually, speech, hearing impaired.

**Contact.** Phone: (361) 593-2315 Toll-free number: (800) 687-6000 Fax: (361) 593-2195
Bill Carter, Director of Admissions, Texas A&M University-Kingsville, MSC 105, Kingsville, TX 78363-8201

## Texas A&M University-Texarkana
**Texarkana, Texas**
**www.tamut.edu**                                        **CB code: 6206**

- Public two-year upper-division university
- Commuter campus in small city
- 99% of applicants admitted
- Test scores required

**General.** Founded in 1971. Regionally accredited. **Degrees:** 336 bachelor's awarded; master's offered. **Articulation:** Agreements with Texarkana College, Northeast Texas Community College, Panola College, Paris Junior College, Cossatot College, Rich Mountain College, University of Arkansas Community College at Hope. **Location:** 180 miles from Dallas, 145 miles from Little Rock, Arkansas. **Calendar:** Semester, limited summer session. **Full-time faculty:** 59 total; 15% minority, 41% women. **Part-time faculty:** 70 total; 11% minority, 64% women.

**Student profile.** 1,010 degree-seeking undergraduates, 568 graduate students. 347 applied as first time-transfer students, 343 admitted, 262 enrolled.

| Out-of-state: | 25% | 25 or older: | 60% |
|---|---|---|---|

**Basis for selection.** Open admission. College transcript, standardized test scores required. Minimum 2.0 GPA; must satisfy Texas Success Initiative. Transfer accepted as sophomores, juniors, seniors.

**2009-2010 Annual costs.** Tuition/fees: $4,538; $13,448 out-of-state. Books/supplies: $1,160. Personal expenses: $1,648.

**Financial aid. Non-need-based:** Scholarships awarded for academics, leadership, state residency.

**Application procedures. Admission:** Rolling admission. No application fee. **Financial aid:** Applicants notified on a rolling basis; must reply within 10 weeks of notification. Transfer students must have completed minimum of 54 semester hours of transferable college credit to apply for financial aid and notified applicants must reply within 45 days from date of award letter. Exceptions made on individual basis. April 1 financial aid deadline for scholarships.

**Academics. Special study options:** Combined bachelor's/graduate degree, cross-registration, distance learning, dual enrollment of high school students, independent study, internships, liberal arts/career combination, student-designed major, teacher certification program. **Credit/placement by examination:** AP, CLEP, IB, institutional tests. BAAS degree limits credit by exam to 18 semester credit hours. **Support services:** Tutoring, writing center.

**Majors. Biology:** General. **Business:** General, accounting, business admin, finance, human resources, international, management information systems, marketing. **Communications:** Media studies. **Computer sciences:** General. **Engineering:** Electrical. **Health:** Nursing (RN). **History:** General. **Math:** General. **Protective services:** Criminal justice. **Psychology:** General. **Social sciences:** Political science.

**Most popular majors.** Business/marketing 19%, interdisciplinary studies 42%, liberal arts 10%, psychology 7%.

**Computing on campus.** 119 workstations in library, computer center. Commuter students can connect to campus network. Online library, helpline, wireless network available.

**Student life. Activities:** Student government, student newspaper, multicultural association.

**Student services.** Career counseling, student employment services, financial aid counseling, personal counseling, placement for graduates, veterans' counselor. **Physically disabled:** Services for visually, hearing impaired.

**Contact.** E-mail: admissions@tamut.edu
Phone: (903) 223-3069 Fax: (903) 223-3140
Patricia Black, University Registrar and Director of Admissions, Texas A&M University-Texarkana, 2600 North Robinson Road, Texarkana, TX 75505-5518

## Texas Christian University
**Fort Worth, Texas**                                      **CB member**
**www.tcu.edu**                                            **CB code: 6820**

- Private 4-year university affiliated with Christian Church (Disciples of Christ)
- Residential campus in very large city
- 7,580 degree-seeking undergraduates: 4% part-time, 59% women, 5% African American, 3% Asian American, 10% Hispanic American, 1% Native American, 5% international
- 1,198 degree-seeking graduate students
- 59% of applicants admitted
- SAT or ACT (ACT writing recommended), application essay required
- 74% graduate within 6 years; 21% enter graduate study

**General.** Founded in 1873. Regionally accredited. **Degrees:** 1,677 bachelor's awarded; master's, doctoral, professional offered. **ROTC:** Army, Air Force. **Location:** 3 miles from Fort Worth, 35 miles from Dallas. **Calendar:** Semester, limited summer session. **Full-time faculty:** 523 total; 84% have terminal degrees, 12% minority, 43% women. **Part-time faculty:** 281 total; 30% have terminal degrees, 7% minority, 49% women. **Class size:** 42% < 20, 41% 20-39, 9% 40-49, 6% 50-99, 2% >100. **Special facilities:** Geological center for remote sensing, nuclear magnetic resonance facility, observatory, film library, performance complex, behavioral research institute, meteorite collection, two lab schools, speech and hearing clinic.

**Freshman class profile.** 11,953 applied, 7,083 admitted, 1,823 enrolled.

| Mid 50% test scores | | End year in good standing: | 89% |
|---|---|---|---|
| SAT critical reading: | 520-630 | Return as sophomores: | 85% |
| SAT math: | 530-650 | Out-of-state: | 27% |
| SAT writing: | 520-630 | Live on campus: | 94% |
| ACT composite: | 23-28 | International: | 4% |
| Rank in top quarter: | 61% | Fraternities: | 37% |
| Rank in top tenth: | 30% | Sororities: | 47% |

**Basis for selection.** GED not accepted. Academic credentials most important; talents, leadership potential, and applicant's determination to make difference considered. Audition, portfolio required for fine arts students; interview recommended for all. **Homeschooled:** Interview with admissions officer recommended, additional weight may be placed on SAT/ACT scores in admissions process.

**High school preparation.** College-preparatory program required. 17 units required; 20 recommended. Required and recommended units include English 4, mathematics 3-4, social studies 3-4, science 3-4, foreign language 2-4 and academic electives 2.

**2009-2010 Annual costs.** Tuition/fees: $28,298. Room/board: $9,800. Books/supplies: $1,000. Personal expenses: $1,500.

**2009-2010 Financial aid. Need-based:** 1,000 full-time freshmen applied for aid; 728 were judged to have need; 724 of these received aid. Average need met was 71%. Average scholarship/grant was $16,220; average loan $3,358. 66% of total undergraduate aid awarded as scholarships/grants, 34% as loans/jobs. **Non-need-based:** Awarded to 3,785 full-time undergraduates, including 1,018 freshmen. Scholarships awarded for academics, alumni affiliation, art, minority status, music/drama, religious affiliation, ROTC, state residency.

**Application procedures. Admission:** Closing date 2/15 (postmark date). $40 fee, may be waived for applicants with need. Admission notification 4/1. Admission notification on a rolling basis. Must reply by 5/1. **Financial aid:** Closing date 5/1. FAFSA required. Applicants notified on a rolling basis starting 3/15; must reply by 5/1 or within 2 week(s) of notification.

**Academics.** Premajor option and accompanying special academic advising for entering students unsure of major; can be used for up to 4 semesters. **Special study options:** Accelerated study, combined bachelor's/graduate degree, cross-registration, distance learning, double major, ESL, honors, independent study, internships, liberal arts/career combination, New York semester, study abroad, teacher certification program, Washington semester. Two comprehensive leadership programs offered. Leadership center, information and resources related to leadership development and training. **Credit/placement by examination:** AP, CLEP, IB, institutional tests. **Support services:** Study skills assistance, tutoring, writing center.

**Honors college/program.** Admission to Honors College is by invitation only and is separate from general university admission. Invitation normally extended to top 8% of entering students each fall. Primary metrics include strength of high school curriculum, SAT or ACT scores, high school rank (if applicable), and demonstrated commitment to leadership and/or extracurricular activities. Most honors students receive scholarship support.

**Majors. Biology:** General, biochemistry. **Business:** Accounting, actuarial science, business admin, e-commerce, entrepreneurial studies, fashion, finance, international, international finance, international marketing, management science, marketing. **Communications:** General, advertising, broadcast journalism, journalism, radio/tv. **Computer sciences:** General, information technology. **Conservation:** Environmental science. **Education:** Art, business, computer, Deaf/hearing impaired, drama/dance, early childhood, early childhood special, elementary, English, foreign languages, French, history, mathematics, middle, multi-level teacher, music, physical, reading, science, secondary, social science, social studies, Spanish, special. **Engineering:** General, electrical, mechanical. **Foreign languages:** French, German, Spanish. **Health:** Athletic training, dietetics, movement therapy, nursing (RN), premedicine, speech pathology. **History:** General. **Interdisciplinary:** Neuroscience. **Liberal arts:** Arts/sciences. **Math:** General. **Parks/recreation:** Health/fitness. **Philosophy/religion:** Philosophy, religion. **Physical sciences:** Astronomy, chemistry, geology, physics. **Protective services:** Criminal justice. **Psychology:** General. **Public administration:** Social work. **Social sciences:** Anthropology, economics, geography, international economics, international relations, political science, sociology. **Theology:** Sacred music. **Visual/performing arts:** Acting, art history/conservation, ballet, ceramics, dance, directing/producing, dramatic, film/cinema, graphic design, interior design, music pedagogy, music performance, music theory/composition, musical theater, painting, photography, piano/organ, printmaking, sculpture, stringed instruments, studio arts, theater design, voice/opera. **Other:** Child development, Modern dance, Psychosocial kinesiology, Supply and value chain management, Writing.

**Most popular majors.** Business/marketing 25%, communications/journalism 19%, education 8%, health sciences 12%, social sciences 7%, visual/performing arts 7%.

**Computing on campus.** 1,300 workstations in dormitories, library, computer center, student center. Dormitories wired for high-speed internet access and linked to campus network. Commuter students can connect to campus network. Online course registration, online library, helpline, repair service, wireless network available.

**Student life. Freshman orientation:** Mandatory. Preregistration for classes offered. 10 sessions in June and August, parents encouraged to attend. **Housing:** Guaranteed on-campus for freshmen. Coed dorms, single-sex dorms, apartments, fraternity/sorority housing, wellness housing available. $250 partly refundable deposit, deadline 5/1. Designated rooms available for ADA needs. **Activities:** Bands, campus ministries, choral groups, dance, drama, international student organizations, literary magazine, music ensembles, Model UN, musical theater, opera, radio station, student government, student newspaper, TV station, over 200 social, religious, service, academic, and preprofessional organizations.

**Athletics.** NCAA. **Intercollegiate:** Baseball M, basketball, cross-country, diving, equestrian W, football (tackle) M, golf, rifle W, soccer W, swimming, tennis, track and field, volleyball W. **Team name:** Horned Frogs.

**Student services.** Adult student services, alcohol/substance abuse counseling, chaplain/spiritual director, career counseling, student employment services, financial aid counseling, health services, minority student services, personal counseling, placement for graduates, veterans' counselor, women's services. **Physically disabled:** Services for visually, speech, hearing impaired.

**Contact.** E-mail: frogmail@tcu.edu
Phone: (817) 257-7490 Toll-free number: (800) 828-3764
Fax: (817) 257-7268
Raymond Brown, Dean of Admissions, Texas Christian University, TCU Box 297013, Fort Worth, TX 76129

---

## Texas College
### Tyler, Texas
**www.texascollege.edu**                     CB code: 6821

- Private 4-year liberal arts college affiliated with Christian Methodist Episcopal Church
- Residential campus in small city

---

- 936 degree-seeking undergraduates: 3% part-time, 45% women, 83% African American, 12% Hispanic American, 1% international
- 28 degree-seeking graduate students

**General.** Founded in 1894. Regionally accredited. Charter member college of the United Negro College Fund. **Degrees:** 93 bachelor's, 3 associate awarded. **Location:** 90 miles from Dallas, 100 miles from Shreveport, Louisiana. **Calendar:** Semester, limited summer session. **Full-time faculty:** 34 total; 35% have terminal degrees, 76% minority, 41% women. **Part-time faculty:** 17 total; 24% have terminal degrees, 76% minority, 47% women. **Class size:** 60% < 20, 17% 20-39, 6% 40-49, 15% 50-99, 1% >100.

**Freshman class profile.** 224 enrolled.

| | | | |
|---|---|---|---|
| GPA 3.75 or higher: | 5% | GPA 2.0-2.99: | 53% |
| GPA 3.50-3.74: | 12% | Return as sophomores: | 49% |
| GPA 3.0-3.49: | 23% | | |

**Basis for selection.** Open admission. SAT/ACT recommended for scholarships and placement. **Homeschooled:** Must submit notarized copy of home school transcript showing date of graduation and course requirements that meet state graduation requirements as approved by the Texas Board of Education. **Learning Disabled:** Students requiring special assistance should provide documentation of disability to the Records/Registrar's Office and the need for assistance to the Office of Academic Affairs.

**High school preparation.** 16 units required. Required units include English 4, mathematics 2, social studies 2, science 2 and academic electives 6.

**2009-2010 Annual costs.** Tuition/fees: $9,490. Room/board: $6,600. Books/supplies: $2,300. Personal expenses: $1,500.

**2008-2009 Financial aid. Need-based:** 202 full-time freshmen applied for aid; 199 were judged to have need; 195 of these received aid. Average need met was 93%. Average scholarship/grant was $6,931; average loan $2,763. 66% of total undergraduate aid awarded as scholarships/grants, 34% as loans/jobs. **Non-need-based:** Awarded to 99 full-time undergraduates, including 55 freshmen. Scholarships awarded for academics, athletics, leadership, music/drama.

**Application procedures. Admission:** No deadline. $20 fee, may be waived for applicants with need. Admission notification on a rolling basis. **Financial aid:** Priority date 6/1; no closing date. FAFSA, institutional form required. Applicants notified on a rolling basis starting 4/15.

**Academics. Special study options:** Accelerated study, distance learning, double major, dual enrollment of high school students, independent study, internships, teacher certification program. **Credit/placement by examination:** CLEP, institutional tests. 32 credit hours maximum toward bachelor's degree. **Support services:** Learning center, reduced course load, remedial instruction, study skills assistance, tutoring.

**Majors. Biology:** General. **Business:** Business admin. **Computer sciences:** General. **Education:** Art, biology, elementary, history, mathematics, middle, music, physical. **History:** General. **Liberal arts:** Arts/sciences. **Math:** General. **Parks/recreation:** Health/fitness. **Philosophy/religion:** Religion. **Protective services:** Law enforcement admin. **Public administration:** Social work. **Social sciences:** Political science, sociology. **Visual/performing arts:** Studio arts.

**Most popular majors.** Biology 12%, business/marketing 56%, health sciences 15%.

**Computing on campus.** 200 workstations in dormitories, library, computer center. Dormitories wired for high-speed internet access and linked to campus network. Commuter students can connect to campus network. Online library, helpline, repair service, student web hosting, wireless network available.

**Student life. Freshman orientation:** Mandatory. Preregistration for classes offered. Held 2-3 days prior to first day of classes each semester. **Policies:** Students required to attend chapel weekly. Religious observance required. **Housing:** Guaranteed on-campus for freshmen. Single-sex dorms, wellness housing available. $150 nonrefundable deposit. **Activities:** Bands, choral groups, dance, music ensembles, student government, Young Adults for Christ, Fellowship of Christian Athletes, pre-alumni council, Omega Psi Phi, Delta Sigma Theta, Alpha Kappa Alpha.

**Athletics.** NAIA. **Intercollegiate:** Baseball M, basketball, cheerleading, football (tackle) M, soccer, softball W, track and field, volleyball W. **Intramural:** Basketball, football (non-tackle), soccer, softball W, volleyball W. **Team name:** Steers.

**Student services.** Adult student services, alcohol/substance abuse counseling, chaplain/spiritual director, career counseling, student employment services, financial aid counseling, health services, personal counseling.

**Contact.** E-mail: jroberts@texascollege.edu
Phone: (903) 593-8311 ext. 2297 Toll-free number: (800) 306-6299
Fax: (903) 526-7879
John Roberts, Registrar/Director of Admissions, Texas College, 2404 North Grand Avenue, Tyler, TX 75712-4500

## Texas Lutheran University
Seguin, Texas        CB member
www.tlu.edu        CB code: 6823

- Private 4-year university and liberal arts college affiliated with Evangelical Lutheran Church in America
- Residential campus in large town
- 1,350 degree-seeking undergraduates: 3% part-time, 52% women, 10% African American, 1% Asian American, 23% Hispanic American, 1% international
- 66% of applicants admitted
- SAT or ACT (ACT writing optional), application essay required
- 49% graduate within 6 years

**General.** Founded in 1891. Regionally accredited. **Degrees:** 266 bachelor's awarded. **ROTC:** Army, Air Force. **Location:** 30 miles from San Antonio, 55 miles from Austin. **Calendar:** Semester, limited summer session. **Full-time faculty:** 68 total; 79% have terminal degrees, 13% minority, 41% women. **Part-time faculty:** 66 total; 35% have terminal degrees, 14% minority, 52% women. **Class size:** 55% < 20, 41% 20-39, 2% 40-49, 1% 50-99. **Special facilities:** Biology field station, Mexican-American study center, life enrichment center, geological museum, center for servant leadership.

**Freshman class profile.** 1,070 applied, 711 admitted, 346 enrolled.

| Mid 50% test scores | | | |
|---|---|---|---|
| SAT critical reading: | 440-550 | Rank in top quarter: | 52% |
| SAT math: | 460-570 | Rank in top tenth: | 22% |
| SAT writing: | 420-530 | End year in good standing: | 88% |
| ACT composite: | 18-23 | Return as sophomores: | 67% |
| GPA 3.75 or higher: | 38% | Out-of-state: | 3% |
| GPA 3.50-3.74: | 16% | Live on campus: | 87% |
| GPA 3.0-3.49: | 25% | International: | 1% |
| GPA 2.0-2.99: | 20% | | |

**Basis for selection.** Quality of academic curriculum pursued and class rank most important. Academic record and test scores also important. Interview recommended. **Homeschooled:** Transcript of courses and grades, letter of recommendation (nonparent) required. Greater emphasis placed on SAT or ACT scores.

**High school preparation.** College-preparatory program recommended. 17 units required; 23 recommended. Required and recommended units include English 4, mathematics 3-4, social studies 3-4, history 2, science 3-4 (laboratory 2), foreign language 2-3, computer science 1 and academic electives 1.

**2009-2010 Annual costs.** Tuition/fees: $21,910. Room/board: $6,870. Books/supplies: $740. Personal expenses: $1,100.

**2009-2010 Financial aid. Need-based:** 316 full-time freshmen applied for aid; 284 were judged to have need; 284 of these received aid. Average need met was 42%. Average scholarship/grant was $15,693; average loan $4,122. 63% of total undergraduate aid awarded as scholarships/grants, 37% as loans/jobs. **Non-need-based:** Awarded to 348 full-time undergraduates, including 85 freshmen. Scholarships awarded for academics, alumni affiliation, leadership, music/drama, religious affiliation.

**Application procedures. Admission:** Priority date 5/1; deadline 8/1 (postmark date). $25 fee, may be waived for applicants with need. Admission notification on a rolling basis beginning on or about 10/1. **Financial aid:** Priority date 3/1; no closing date. FAFSA required. Applicants notified on a rolling basis starting 3/1; must reply within 6 week(s) of notification.

**Academics. Special study options:** Combined bachelor's/graduate degree, double major, dual enrollment of high school students, exchange student, honors, independent study, internships, liberal arts/career combination, study abroad, teacher certification program, Washington semester. International studies curriculum, dual BS program in applied science and engineering in conjunction with Texas state institutions. **Credit/placement by examination:** AP, CLEP, IB, institutional tests. 30 credit hours maximum toward bachelor's degree. **Support services:** Study skills assistance, tutoring, writing center.

**Majors. Biology:** General, molecular. **Business:** General, accounting, business admin. **Communications:** General. **Computer sciences:** General, computer science, information systems. **Education:** Elementary, English, history, mathematics, middle, multi-level teacher, music, physical, reading, social

studies. **Foreign languages:** Spanish. **Health:** Athletic training. **History:** General, public archives. **Math:** General. **Parks/recreation:** Exercise sciences, health/fitness, sports admin. **Philosophy/religion:** Philosophy. **Physical sciences:** Chemistry, physics. **Psychology:** General. **Social sciences:** Economics, political science, sociology. **Theology:** Preministerial, youth ministry. **Visual/performing arts:** General, art, dramatic, music history, music performance. **Other:** Pre-engineering/applied science.

**Most popular majors.** Biology 8%, business/marketing 31%, education 8%, parks/recreation 16%.

**Computing on campus.** 222 workstations in dormitories, library, computer center, student center. Dormitories wired for high-speed internet access and linked to campus network. Commuter students can connect to campus network. Online library, helpline, wireless network available.

**Student life. Freshman orientation:** Mandatory. Preregistration for classes offered. Held 2 days prior to start of fall semester. **Housing:** Guaranteed on-campus for freshmen. Coed dorms, single-sex dorms, apartments available. $200 fully refundable deposit, deadline 8/1. **Activities:** Bands, campus ministries, choral groups, dance, drama, international student organizations, literary magazine, music ensembles, musical theater, student government, student newspaper, symphony orchestra, black student union, Mexican American student association, Young Democrats, College Republicans, Fellowship of Christian Athletes, Students Make a Difference, Lutheran student movement, Canterbury, Catholic student organization.

**Athletics.** NCAA. **Intercollegiate:** Baseball M, basketball, cross-country W, football (tackle) M, golf, soccer, softball W, tennis, track and field W, volleyball W. **Intramural:** Basketball, bowling, football (non-tackle), handball, racquetball, softball, swimming, tennis, volleyball. **Team name:** Bulldogs.

**Student services.** Alcohol/substance abuse counseling, chaplain/spiritual director, career counseling, student employment services, financial aid counseling, health services, personal counseling, placement for graduates, veterans' counselor.

**Contact.** E-mail: admissions@tlu.edu
Phone: (830) 372-8050 Toll-free number: (800) 771-8521
Fax: (830) 372-8096
Dale Gaubatz, Director of Admissions, Texas Lutheran University, 1000 West Court Street, Seguin, TX 78155-5999

## Texas Southern University
Houston, Texas        CB member
www.tsu.edu        CB code: 6824

- Public 4-year university
- Commuter campus in very large city
- 7,258 degree-seeking undergraduates: 19% part-time, 57% women, 89% African American, 2% Asian American, 4% Hispanic American, 3% international
- 2,136 degree-seeking graduate students
- 26% of applicants admitted

**General.** Founded in 1947. Regionally accredited. **Degrees:** 920 bachelor's awarded; master's, doctoral, professional offered. **ROTC:** Army. **Location:** 2 miles from downtown. **Calendar:** Semester, extensive summer session. **Full-time faculty:** 377 total; 86% minority, 47% women. **Part-time faculty:** 232 total; 93% minority, 47% women. **Class size:** 33% < 20, 40% 20-39, 14% 40-49, 11% 50-99, 1% >100. **Special facilities:** University museum.

**Freshman class profile.** 7,922 applied, 2,063 admitted, 1,173 enrolled.

| Mid 50% test scores | | | |
|---|---|---|---|
| SAT critical reading: | 330-440 | Rank in top quarter: | 22% |
| SAT math: | 360-450 | Rank in top tenth: | 6% |
| SAT writing: | 340-430 | End year in good standing: | 42% |
| ACT composite: | 14-18 | Return as sophomores: | 67% |
| GPA 3.75 or higher: | 4% | Out-of-state: | 18% |
| GPA 3.50-3.74: | 5% | International: | 2% |
| GPA 3.0-3.49: | 22% | Fraternities: | 3% |
| GPA 2.0-2.99: | 58% | Sororities: | 1% |

**Basis for selection.** Special requirements for pharmacy, law, accounting, marketing, and computer science programs. For selective programs high school achievement, interview, essay important; test scores, individual abilities, high school activities considered.

**High school preparation.** College-preparatory program recommended. Recommended units include English 4, mathematics 3, social studies 4, science 2, foreign language 2 and academic electives 6.

**2009-2010 Annual costs.** Tuition/fees: $7,080; $15,390 out-of-state. Books/supplies: $1,343. Personal expenses: $2,266.

**2008-2009 Financial aid.** All financial aid based on need.

**Application procedures. Admission:** Priority date 7/31; deadline 8/15 (postmark date). $42 fee, may be waived for applicants with need. Admission notification on a rolling basis. Must reply by 7/31. **Financial aid:** Priority date 5/1; no closing date. FAFSA required. Applicants notified on a rolling basis starting 6/1.

**Academics. Special study options:** Cooperative education, distance learning, double major, ESL, honors, internships, teacher certification program, weekend college. **Credit/placement by examination:** CLEP, SAT, ACT, institutional tests. **Support services:** Learning center, pre-admission summer program, remedial instruction, study skills assistance, tutoring.

**Majors. Biology:** General. **Business:** Accounting, banking/financial services, business admin, management information systems, marketing, operations. **Communications:** General, journalism, radio/tv. **Communications technology:** Recording arts. **Computer sciences:** General. **Conservation:** Environmental studies. **Education:** Health, physical. **Engineering technology:** Civil, electrical, industrial. **Family/consumer sciences:** General, child development, food/nutrition. **Foreign languages:** French, Spanish. **Health:** Clinical lab science, dietetics, environmental health, health care admin, health services, medical records admin, nursing (RN), prepharmacy, respiratory therapy technology. **History:** General. **Math:** General. **Parks/recreation:** Health/fitness. **Physical sciences:** Chemistry, physics. **Protective services:** Law enforcement admin. **Psychology:** General. **Public administration:** General, social work. **Social sciences:** Economics, political science, sociology. **Transportation:** Aviation, aviation management. **Visual/performing arts:** Dramatic, fashion design, studio arts.

**Most popular majors.** Biology 8%, business/marketing 24%, communications/journalism 6%, health sciences 14%, security/protective services 7%.

**Computing on campus.** 500 workstations in library, computer center, student center. Dormitories wired for high-speed internet access and linked to campus network. Online course registration, online library, wireless network available.

**Student life. Freshman orientation:** Mandatory. Preregistration for classes offered. Two-day orientation held every semester during registration week. First-time freshmen and transfer students participate in seminars, meet with academic advisors, complete course selection/registration, and take placement test. **Housing:** Guaranteed on-campus for freshmen. Single-sex dorms, apartments available. $300 deposit, deadline 6/1. **Activities:** Bands, choral groups, drama, film society, music ensembles, musical theater, opera, radio station, student government, student newspaper, symphony orchestra, TV station, Alpha Phi Omega, Campus Crusade for Christ, health information management association, sociology club, political science club, student psychological club, NAACP.

**Athletics.** NCAA. **Intercollegiate:** Baseball M, basketball, bowling W, cross-country, football (tackle) M, golf, soccer W, softball W, tennis, track and field, volleyball W. **Intramural:** Basketball, bowling W, cheerleading, softball W, tennis, track and field, volleyball W. **Team name:** Tigers.

**Student services.** Alcohol/substance abuse counseling, chaplain/spiritual director, career counseling, student employment services, financial aid counseling, health services, on-campus daycare, personal counseling, placement for graduates, veterans' counselor. **Physically disabled:** Services for speech impaired.

**Contact.** E-mail: admissions@tsu.edu
Phone: (713) 313-7472 Toll-free number: (866) 878-4968
Fax: (713) 313-7851
Brian Armstrong, Director of Recruitment and Retention, Texas Southern University, 3100 Cleburne Street, Houston, TX 77004

## Texas State University: San Marcos

San Marcos, Texas

www.txstate.edu

CB member
CB code: 6667

- Public 4-year university
- Commuter campus in large town
- 26,002 degree-seeking undergraduates: 18% part-time, 55% women, 6% African American, 2% Asian American, 24% Hispanic American, 1% Native American, 1% international
- 4,195 degree-seeking graduate students
- 76% of applicants admitted
- SAT or ACT with writing, application essay required
- 56% graduate within 6 years; 21% enter graduate study

**General.** Founded in 1899. Regionally accredited. **Degrees:** 5,256 bachelor's awarded; master's, doctoral, professional offered. **ROTC:** Army, Air Force. **Location:** 30 miles from Austin, 49 miles from San Antonio. **Calendar:** Semester, extensive summer session. **Full-time faculty:** 1,017 total; 72% have terminal degrees, 20% minority, 45% women. **Part-time faculty:** 454 total; 30% have terminal degrees, 12% minority, 52% women. **Class size:** 18% < 20, 55% 20-39, 9% 40-49, 11% 50-99, 7% >100. **Special facilities:** Southwestern writers collection (original manuscripts), observatory, archaeological forensic lab, clean room for microchip production, sound recording studio, ranch.

**Freshman class profile.** 12,172 applied, 9,211 admitted, 3,667 enrolled.

| Mid 50% test scores | | | |
|---|---|---|---|
| SAT critical reading: | 480-570 | Rank in top tenth: | 14% |
| SAT math: | 490-590 | End year in good standing: | 76% |
| SAT writing: | 460-550 | Return as sophomores: | 79% |
| ACT composite: | 21-25 | Out-of-state: | 2% |
| Rank in top quarter: | 52% | Live on campus: | 89% |

**Basis for selection.** Applicants who rank in top 10% of high school class have no minimum test score requirements. Otherwise score requirements are as follows: rank in next 15%, 920 SAT or 20 ACT; rank in second quarter, 1010 SAT, 22 ACT; rank in third quarter, 1180 SAT, 26 ACT; rank in bottom quarter, 1270 SAT, 29 ACT. (SAT scores exclusive of Writing). SAT Subject Tests required for placement in certain higher level courses, but not used in the admissions decision. Audition required for music program. **Homeschooled:** Transcript of courses and grades required. Minimum 26 ACT or 1180 SAT (exclusive of Writing) and admissions essay.

**High school preparation.** College-preparatory program required. 24 units required; 26 recommended. Required and recommended units include English 4, mathematics 3-4, social studies 3.5, science 3-4 (laboratory 2), foreign language 2-3, computer science 1, visual/performing arts 1, academic electives 3.5. 1.5 physical education, 0.5 economics, 0.5 speech required, 0.5 health education required.

**2009-2010 Annual costs.** Tuition/fees: $7,482; $15,792 out-of-state. Room/board: $6,392. Books/supplies: $1,050. Personal expenses: $2,670.

**2009-2010 Financial aid. Need-based:** 2,745 full-time freshmen applied for aid; 1,910 were judged to have need; 1,835 of these received aid. Average need met was 71%. Average scholarship/grant was $7,663; average loan $3,573. 50% of total undergraduate aid awarded as scholarships/grants, 50% as loans/jobs. **Non-need-based:** Awarded to 2,275 full-time undergraduates, including 913 freshmen. Scholarships awarded for academics, art, athletics, leadership, music/drama, ROTC, state residency. **Additional information:** To be eligible for the Bobcat Promise program you must be an entering first-time freshmen (transfer students are not eligible), be a Texas resident, have a family adjusted gross income of $25,000 or less, be enrolled full-time and complete at least 30 credit hours during each academic year (fall and spring semester), and submit a completed FAFSA no later than April 1.

**Application procedures. Admission:** Closing date 5/1 (receipt date). $60 fee, may be waived for applicants with need. Admission notification on a rolling basis beginning on or about 9/1. Application deadlines for McCoy College of Business and the Department of Communication Design are March 15th for fall and October 15th for spring admissions. **Financial aid:** Priority date 4/1; no closing date. FAFSA required. Applicants notified on a rolling basis starting 5/1; must reply within 3 week(s) of notification.

**Academics. Special study options:** Accelerated study, combined bachelor's/graduate degree, distance learning, double major, dual enrollment of high school students, ESL, exchange student, honors, independent study, internships, study abroad, teacher certification program, Washington semester, weekend college. **Credit/placement by examination:** AP, CLEP, IB, institutional tests. Credit hours earned by exam do not count as credit earned in residence, and 25% of course work must be completed in residence. **Support services:** Learning center, remedial instruction, study skills assistance, tutoring, writing center.

**Majors. Agriculture:** General, agribusiness operations, animal sciences. **Architecture:** Urban/community planning. **Area/ethnic studies:** American, Asian, European, Near/Middle Eastern. **Biology:** General, animal physiology, aquatic, biochemistry, botany, microbiology, wildlife, zoology. **Business:** Accounting, business admin, fashion, finance, management information systems, managerial economics, marketing. **Communications:** Advertising, journalism, media studies, public relations, radio/tv. **Communications technology:** Desktop publishing, recording arts. **Computer sciences:** General. **Conservation:** Environmental science, water/wetlands/marine. **Engineering:** Electrical, industrial, manufacturing. **Engineering technology:** General, construction, industrial, manufacturing. **Family/consumer sciences:** General, family studies, food/nutrition. **Foreign languages:** French, German, Spanish. **Health:** Athletic training, audiology/speech pathology, clinical lab science, health care admin, health services, medical radiologic technology/radiation therapy, medical records admin, nursing (RN), respiratory therapy technology. **History:** General. **Interdisciplinary:** Biological/ physical sciences, global studies. **Math:** General, applied. **Parks/ recreation:** Facilities management, health/fitness, sports admin. **Philosophy/ religion:** Philosophy. **Physical sciences:** Chemistry, physics. **Protective services:** Corrections, criminal justice, police science. **Psychology:** General. **Public administration:** General, social work. **Social sciences:** Anthropology, cartography, economics, geography, international relations, political science, sociology. **Visual/performing arts:** Art, dance, dramatic, graphic design, interior design, jazz, music performance, photography, studio arts. **Other:** Interdisciplinary Studies in Education.

**Most popular majors.** Business/marketing 21%, communications/ journalism 6%, English 6%, interdisciplinary studies 13%, parks/recreation 7%, social sciences 7%, visual/performing arts 7%.

**Computing on campus.** 1,792 workstations in dormitories, library, computer center, student center. Dormitories wired for high-speed internet access and linked to campus network. Commuter students can connect to campus network. Online course registration, helpline, repair service, student web hosting, wireless network available.

**Student life. Freshman orientation:** Mandatory, $60 fee. Preregistration for classes offered. 2-day program combined with welcome week prior to start of semester. **Policies:** All unmarried students under 21 with fewer than 56 credit hours must live in university housing. **Housing:** Guaranteed on-campus for freshmen. Coed dorms, single-sex dorms, apartments, fraternity/ sorority housing available. $300 partly refundable deposit. **Activities:** Bands, campus ministries, choral groups, dance, drama, film society, international student organizations, literary magazine, music ensembles, Model UN, musical theater, opera, radio station, student government, student newspaper, symphony orchestra, nearly 300 social, service, religious, political, and professional organizations.

**Athletics.** NCAA. **Intercollegiate:** Baseball M, basketball, cheerleading, cross-country, football (tackle) M, golf, soccer W, softball W, tennis W, track and field, volleyball W. **Intramural:** Basketball, bowling, football (non-tackle), golf, racquetball, soccer, softball, tennis, volleyball. **Team name:** Bobcats.

**Student services.** Adult student services, alcohol/substance abuse counseling, chaplain/spiritual director, career counseling, student employment services, financial aid counseling, health services, legal services, minority student services, personal counseling, placement for graduates, veterans' counselor. **Physically disabled:** Services for visually, speech, hearing impaired.

**Contact.** E-mail: admissions@txstate.edu
Phone: (512) 245-2364 Fax: (512) 245-8044
Stephanie Anderson, Director of Admissions, Texas State University: San Marcos, 429 North Guadalupe Street, San Marcos, TX 78666-5709

---

## Texas Tech University

**Lubbock, Texas**                              **CB member**
**www.ttu.edu**                                 **CB code: 6827**

- Public 4-year university
- Commuter campus in small city
- 24,236 degree-seeking undergraduates: 9% part-time, 44% women, 5% African American, 3% Asian American, 14% Hispanic American, 1% Native American, 3% international
- 5,228 degree-seeking graduate students
- 68% of applicants admitted
- SAT or ACT (ACT writing optional) required
- 60% graduate within 6 years

**General.** Founded in 1923. Regionally accredited. **Degrees:** 4,692 bachelor's awarded; master's, doctoral, professional offered. **ROTC:** Army, Air Force. **Location:** 348 miles from Dallas, 321 miles from Albuquerque, New Mexico. **Calendar:** Semester, extensive summer session. **Full-time faculty:** 1,042 total; 20% minority, 36% women. **Part-time faculty:** 103 total; 11% minority, 50% women. **Special facilities:** Museum, national ranching heritage center, special collections library, archaeological dig/state park, international cultural center, international textile research center, science research laboratory, arid and semi-arid land studies center, seismological observatory, child development research center, institutes for environmental and human health, Vietnam center, planetarium, wind energy program.

**Freshman class profile.** 16,541 applied, 11,242 admitted, 4,586 enrolled.

| Mid 50% test scores | | | |
|---|---|---|---|
| SAT critical reading: | 480-580 | Rank in top quarter: | 53% |
| SAT math: | 510-620 | Rank in top tenth: | 21% |
| SAT writing: | 470-570 | Return as sophomores: | 81% |
| ACT composite: | 21-26 | Out-of-state: | 5% |
| | | International: | 2% |

**Basis for selection.** Class rank and test scores considered first, and students meeting the following score requirements (exclusive of Writing) eligible for unconditional admission: class rank in top 10%, no minimum test scores; rank in next 15%, with 1140 SAT or 25 ACT; rank in second quarter, with 1230 SAT or 28 ACT; rank in lower half, with 1270 SAT or 29 ACT. (SAT scores exclusive of Writing.) Applicants who do not meet assured admission criteria will have records reviewed in holistic manner. Auditions and portfolios required for admission to some programs.

**High school preparation.** College-preparatory program recommended. 11 units required. Required units include English 4, mathematics 3, science 2 (laboratory 2) and foreign language 2.

**2009-2010 Annual costs.** Tuition/fees: $7,485; $15,795 out-of-state. Students from adjacent counties in New Mexico and Oklahoma pay in-state tuition rates; students from all other counties in New Mexico and Oklahoma pay reduced out-of-state tuition rates. Room/board: $7,527. Books/supplies: $100. Personal expenses: $1,890.

**2008-2009 Financial aid. Need-based:** 3,117 full-time freshmen applied for aid; 1,802 were judged to have need; 1,779 of these received aid. Average need met was 49%. Average scholarship/grant was $6,984; average loan $3,144. 45% of total undergraduate aid awarded as scholarships/grants, 55% as loans/jobs. **Non-need-based:** Awarded to 3,372 full-time undergraduates, including 1,142 freshmen. Scholarships awarded for academics, art, athletics, job skills, leadership, music/drama, ROTC.

**Application procedures. Admission:** Closing date 5/1 (receipt date). $50 fee, may be waived for applicants with need. Admission notification on a rolling basis. **Financial aid:** Priority date 4/15; no closing date. FAFSA required. Applicants notified on a rolling basis; must reply within 2 week(s) of notification.

**Academics. Special study options:** Accelerated study, combined bachelor's/ graduate degree, cooperative education, distance learning, double major, dual enrollment of high school students, ESL, external degree, honors, independent study, internships, semester at sea, student-designed major, study abroad, teacher certification program. **Credit/placement by examination:** AP, CLEP, IB, SAT, ACT, institutional tests. **Support services:** Learning center, pre-admission summer program, remedial instruction, study skills assistance, tutoring, writing center.

**Honors college/program.** Requires separate application, minimum 1200 SAT (exclusive of Writing) or 26 ACT, or top 10% class rank, essays, 2 teacher recommendations. 317 freshmen admitted. Average SAT score: 1299; total enrollment 883. Two tracks offered to students: nondegree program working with all colleges and majors to provide honors academic, co-curricular and social program; and interdisciplinary degree program for bachelor of arts degree in natural history and humanities or Honors Arts and Letters.

**Majors. Agriculture:** General, agronomy, animal sciences, business, communications, economics, food science, horticulture, range science. **Architecture:** Architecture, interior, landscape. **Area/ethnic studies:** Latin American, Russian/Slavic. **Biology:** General, biochemistry, biological/molecular, microbiology, zoology. **Business:** General, accounting, business admin, fashion, finance, hotel/motel admin, international, management information systems, marketing. **Communications:** Advertising, journalism, photojournalism, public relations, radio/tv. **Computer sciences:** General. **Conservation:** General, fisheries, wildlife. **Engineering:** General, chemical, civil, computer, construction, electrical, environmental, industrial, mechanical, petroleum, physics. **Engineering technology:** General, architectural, electrical, mechanical. **Family/consumer sciences:** General, child development, clothing/ textiles, family resources, family studies, family systems, family/ community services, food/nutrition. **Foreign languages:** Classics, French, German, Spanish. **Health:** Dietetics, health services. **History:** General. **Interdisciplinary:** Biological/physical sciences. **Liberal arts:** Arts/sciences. **Math:** General. **Parks/recreation:** Health/fitness. **Philosophy/religion:** Philosophy. **Physical sciences:** Chemistry, geology, geophysics, physics. **Psychology:** General. **Public administration:** Social work. **Social sciences:** Anthropology, economics, geography, political science, sociology. **Visual/ performing arts:** Acting, art, art history/conservation, dance, dramatic, fashion design, graphic design, music performance, music theory/composition, studio arts, theater design. **Other:** Energy commerce.

**Most popular majors.** Business/marketing 25%, communications/ journalism 6%, engineering/engineering technologies 11%, family/ consumer sciences 9%, social sciences 6%.

**Computing on campus.** 3,000 workstations in dormitories, library, computer center, student center. Dormitories wired for high-speed internet access and linked to campus network. Commuter students can connect to campus network. Online course registration, online library, helpline, repair service, student web hosting, wireless network available.

**Student life. Freshman orientation:** Mandatory, $150 fee. Preregistration for classes offered. Three-day sessions held in January, May, June, July. One-day sessions held only for transfer students only in May and July. **Policies:** Freshmen required to live on campus. **Housing:** Guaranteed on-campus for freshmen. Coed dorms, single-sex dorms, special housing for disabled, apartments, wellness housing available. $50 nonrefundable deposit, deadline 5/1. Special interest housing: honors, intensive study, learning communities. **Activities:** Bands, campus ministries, choral groups, drama, international student organizations, literary magazine, music ensembles, musical theater, student government, student newspaper, symphony orchestra, College Republicans, Wesley Foundation, black student association, Hispanic law student association, Alpha Phi Omega, women's service organization, University Democrats, Campus Crusade for Christ.

**Athletics.** NCAA. **Intercollegiate:** Baseball M, basketball, cross-country, football (tackle) M, golf, soccer W, softball W, tennis, track and field, volleyball W. **Intramural:** Badminton, baseball, basketball, bowling, football (non-tackle), golf, racquetball, soccer, softball, swimming, table tennis, tennis, volleyball, weight lifting M. **Team name:** Red Raiders/ Lady Raiders.

**Student services.** Alcohol/substance abuse counseling, career counseling, student employment services, financial aid counseling, health services, legal services, personal counseling, placement for graduates, veterans' counselor. **Physically disabled:** Services for visually, speech, hearing impaired. **Learning disabled:** Comprehensive services available.

**Contact.** E-mail: admissions@ttu.edu
Phone: (806) 742-1480 Fax: (806) 742-0062
Ethan Logan, Managing Director of Undergraduate Recruitment and Admissions, Texas Tech University, Box 45005, Lubbock, TX 79409-5005

## Texas Tech University Health Sciences Center
**Lubbock, Texas**
**www.ttuhsc.edu**                                    **CB code: 3423**

- Public two-year upper-division university
- Commuter campus in small city
- Application essay required

**General.** Founded in 1969. Regionally accredited. **Degrees:** 544 bachelor's awarded; master's, doctoral, professional offered. **Calendar:** Semester, limited summer session. **Full-time faculty:** 855 total; 69% have terminal degrees, 16% minority, 44% women. **Part-time faculty:** 73 total; 75% have terminal degrees, 12% minority, 29% women. **Class size:** 58% < 20, 30% 20-39, 4% 40-49, 6% 50-99, 2% >100.

**Student profile.** 682 degree-seeking undergraduates, 2,568 degree-seeking graduate students.

| | | | |
|---|---|---|---|
| Women: | 83% | Part-time: | 10% |
| African American: | 10% | Out-of-state: | 5% |
| Asian American: | 5% | 25 or older: | 38% |
| Hispanic American: | 16% | | |

**Basis for selection.** College transcript, application essay required. Transfer accepted as juniors.

**2009-2010 Annual costs.** Tuition/fees: $4,500; $12,810 out-of-state. Reported costs are for Allied Health Sciences and School of Nursing. Books/supplies: $1,119. Personal expenses: $3,651.

**Financial aid. Non-need-based:** Scholarships awarded for academics.

**Application procedures. Admission:** $40 fee. **Financial aid:** No deadline. Applicants notified on a rolling basis.

**Academics. Special study options:** Combined bachelor's/graduate degree, distance learning. **Credit/placement by examination:** CLEP.

**Majors. Health:** Clinical lab science, communication disorders, health care admin, health services, nursing (RN).

**Computing on campus.** PC or laptop required. 160 workstations in library. Commuter students can connect to campus network. Online library, wireless network available.

**Student services. Physically disabled:** Services for visually, speech, hearing impaired.

**Contact.** Phone: (806) 743-2300
Texas Tech University Health Sciences Center, 3601 Fourth Street, Lubbock, TX 79430

## Texas Wesleyan University
**Fort Worth, Texas**
**www.txwes.edu**                                    **CB code: 6828**

- Private 4-year university affiliated with United Methodist Church
- Commuter campus in large city
- 1,509 degree-seeking undergraduates: 23% part-time, 67% women, 20% African American, 2% Asian American, 23% Hispanic American, 1% Native American, 2% international
- 1,525 degree-seeking graduate students
- 61% of applicants admitted
- SAT or ACT (ACT writing optional) required
- 31% graduate within 6 years

**General.** Founded in 1890. Regionally accredited. **Degrees:** 313 bachelor's awarded; master's, doctoral offered. **ROTC:** Army, Air Force. **Location:** 2 miles from downtown. **Calendar:** Semester, limited summer session. **Full-time faculty:** 155 total; 12% minority, 49% women. **Part-time faculty:** 111 total; 7% minority, 49% women. **Class size:** 68% < 20, 32% 20-39.

**Freshman class profile.** 631 applied, 388 admitted, 188 enrolled.

| Mid 50% test scores | | Rank in top quarter: | 48% |
|---|---|---|---|
| SAT critical reading: | 440-530 | Rank in top tenth: | 18% |
| SAT math: | 440-530 | End year in good standing: | 76% |
| SAT writing: | 420-520 | Return as sophomores: | 65% |
| ACT composite: | 18-22 | Out-of-state: | 6% |
| GPA 3.50-3.74: | 46% | Live on campus: | 50% |
| GPA 3.0-3.49: | 30% | International: | 3% |
| GPA 2.0-2.99: | 24% | | |

**Basis for selection.** Regular freshmen admission requires minimum 2.5 high school GPA, 19 ACT or 920 SAT combined score (exclusive of Writing), top 50% ranking in senior class. **Homeschooled:** Transcript of courses and grades required.

**High school preparation.** College-preparatory program recommended. 20 units recommended. Recommended units include English 4, mathematics 4, social studies 3, science 3, foreign language 1 and academic electives 7.

**2009-2010 Annual costs.** Tuition/fees: $17,760. Room/board: $6,656. Books/supplies: $1,020. Personal expenses: $1,935.

**2008-2009 Financial aid.** All financial aid based on need.

**Application procedures. Admission:** No deadline. $25 fee, may be waived for applicants with need. Admission notification on a rolling basis. **Financial aid:** Priority date 3/15; no closing date. FAFSA required. Applicants notified on a rolling basis starting 3/15.

**Academics. Special study options:** Accelerated study, combined bachelor's/graduate degree, distance learning, double major, dual enrollment of high school students, ESL, exchange student, independent study, internships, liberal arts/career combination, study abroad, teacher certification program, weekend college. **Credit/placement by examination:** AP, CLEP, institutional tests. 30 credit hours maximum toward bachelor's degree. **Support services:** Learning center, pre-admission summer program, reduced course load, remedial instruction, study skills assistance, tutoring, writing center.

**Majors. Biology:** General, biochemistry. **Business:** Accounting, business admin, finance, international marketing, management information systems, management science, marketing, office technology. **Communications:** General, journalism, public relations, radio/tv. **Computer sciences:** General, computer science, information systems. **Education:** General, bilingual, biology, business, chemistry, early childhood, elementary, English, history, mathematics, multi-level teacher, music, physical, reading, science, secondary, social science, social studies, Spanish. **Foreign languages:** Spanish. **Health:** Athletic training, predental, premedicine. **History:** General. **Legal studies:** Paralegal, prelaw. **Math:** General. **Parks/recreation:** Facilities management, health/fitness. **Philosophy/religion:** Religion. **Physical sciences:** Chemistry. **Psychology:** General. **Social sciences:** General, political science. **Theology:** Religious ed. **Visual/performing arts:** General, art, dramatic. **Other:** Criminal justice, English, theatre arts, Liberal studies, Music, with sacred music emphasis.

**Computing on campus.** 306 workstations in library, computer center. Dormitories wired for high-speed internet access and linked to campus network. Online library, wireless network available.

**Student life. Freshman orientation:** Mandatory. Preregistration for classes offered. **Policies:** Resident chaplain on staff. **Housing:** Coed dorms, single-sex dorms, apartments, fraternity/sorority housing, wellness housing available. $150 partly refundable deposit. **Activities:** Bands, choral groups, dance, drama, international student organizations, literary magazine, music ensembles, musical theater, opera, student government, student newspaper, Methodist and Baptist student unions, Student Foundation, Alpha Phi Omega, Fellowship of Christian Athletes.

**Athletics.** NAIA. **Intercollegiate:** Baseball M, basketball, golf M, soccer, softball W, table tennis M, volleyball W. **Intramural:** Badminton, basketball, bowling, diving, golf M, soccer, softball, swimming, table tennis, tennis W, volleyball. **Team name:** Rams.

**Student services.** Adult student services, alcohol/substance abuse counseling, chaplain/spiritual director, career counseling, student employment services, financial aid counseling, health services, personal counseling, placement for graduates, veterans' counselor.

**Contact.** E-mail: admission@txwes.edu
Phone: (817) 531-4422 Toll-free number: (800) 580-8980
Fax: (817) 531-7515
Holly Kiser, Director of Freshman Admissions, Texas Wesleyan University, 1201 Wesleyan Street, Fort Worth, TX 76105-1536

## Texas Woman's University

**Denton, Texas**
**www.twu.edu**

**CB member**
**CB code: 6826**

- Public 4-year university
- Residential campus in small city
- 7,685 degree-seeking undergraduates: 31% part-time, 92% women, 21% African American, 8% Asian American, 19% Hispanic American, 1% Native American, 2% international
- 5,039 degree-seeking graduate students
- 84% of applicants admitted
- SAT or ACT (ACT writing optional) required
- 44% graduate within 6 years

**General.** Founded in 1901. Regionally accredited. **Degrees:** 1,573 bachelor's awarded; master's, doctoral, professional offered. **ROTC:** Army, Air Force. **Location:** 35 miles from Dallas and Fort Worth. **Calendar:** Semester, extensive summer session. **Full-time faculty:** 306 total; 17% minority, 71% women. **Part-time faculty:** 443 total; 13% minority, 74% women. **Class size:** 42% < 20, 44% 20-39, 7% 40-49, 6% 50-99, 1% >100. **Special facilities:** Art collection, Little Chapel-in-the-Woods, Texas Women's Hall of Fame, Texas First Ladies historic costume collection, woman's collection, Women Airforce Service Pilots memorabilia, botanical gardens, Gertrude Gibson Guest House, collection of children's book art, cookbook collection.

**Freshman class profile.** 2,382 applied, 2,010 admitted, 742 enrolled.

| Mid 50% test scores | | | |
|---|---|---|---|
| SAT critical reading: | 440-550 | Rank in top quarter: | 50% |
| SAT math: | 450-560 | Rank in top tenth: | 21% |
| ACT composite: | 19-24 | Return as sophomores: | 75% |
| GPA 3.75 or higher: | 15% | Out-of-state: | 1% |
| GPA 3.50-3.74: | 16% | Live on campus: | 77% |
| GPA 3.0-3.49: | 37% | International: | 1% |
| GPA 2.0-2.99: | 32% | Sororities: | 3% |

**Basis for selection.** School achievement record and test scores most important: Texas Academic Skills Program, SAT of 950 (exclusive of Writing) or ACT of 20. Interview and audition required for drama and music programs; interview required and portfolio recommended for art program.

**High school preparation.** 22 units required. Required units include English 4, mathematics 3, social studies 2, science 2 and academic electives 11.

**2009-2010 Annual costs.** Tuition/fees: $6,660; $15,000 out-of-state. Room/board: $5,932. Books/supplies: $960. Personal expenses: $1,890.

**Application procedures. Admission:** Priority date 2/1; deadline 7/1 (receipt date). $30 fee, may be waived for applicants with need. Admission notification on a rolling basis beginning on or about 3/1. **Financial aid:** Priority date 4/1; no closing date. FAFSA, institutional form required. Applicants notified on a rolling basis starting 3/1; must reply within 2 week(s) of notification.

**Academics. Special study options:** Accelerated study, combined bachelor's/graduate degree, cooperative education, cross-registration, distance learning, double major, dual enrollment of high school students, honors, independent study, internships, liberal arts/career combination, study abroad, teacher certification program, weekend college. **Credit/placement by examination:** AP, CLEP, SAT, ACT, institutional tests. 30 credit hours maximum toward bachelor's degree. **Support services:** Learning center, pre-admission summer program, reduced course load, remedial instruction, study skills assistance, tutoring, writing center.

**Majors. Biology:** General, biochemistry, zoology. **Business:** Accounting, administrative services, business admin, fashion, finance, marketing. **Computer sciences:** General. **Family/consumer sciences:** General, child development, family studies, food/nutrition. **Health:** Clinical lab science, dental hygiene, dietetics, health services, music therapy, nursing (RN). **History:** General. **Interdisciplinary:** Nutrition sciences. **Legal studies:** Paralegal. **Math:** General. **Parks/recreation:** Health/fitness. **Physical sciences:** Chemistry. **Protective services:** Criminal justice. **Psychology:** General. **Public administration:** Social work. **Social sciences:** Political science, sociology. **Visual/performing arts:** Art, dance, dramatic, fashion design. **Other:** Interdisciplinary studies.

**Most popular majors.** Business/marketing 6%, family/consumer sciences 6%, health sciences 37%, interdisciplinary studies 13%, liberal arts 12%, psychology 6%.

**Computing on campus.** 1,000 workstations in dormitories, library, computer center, student center. Dormitories linked to campus network. Commuter students can connect to campus network. Online course registration, helpline available.

**Student life. Freshman orientation:** Mandatory, $25 fee. Preregistration for classes offered. Two-day event. **Housing:** Guaranteed on-campus for all undergraduates. Coed dorms, single-sex dorms, special housing for disabled, apartments, cooperative housing, fraternity/sorority housing, wellness housing available. $125 partly refundable deposit. Family housing, honors students housing. **Activities:** Jazz band, campus ministries, choral groups, dance, drama, international student organizations, music ensembles, musical theater, opera, student government, student newspaper, Alpha Theta Omega, LULAC, multicultural African organization, NAACP, Alpha Kappa Alpha Sorority, Delta Sigma Theta Sorority, Zeta Phi Beta Sorority, Golden Key international honor society.

**Athletics.** NCAA. **Intercollegiate:** Basketball W, gymnastics W, soccer W, softball W, volleyball W. **Intramural:** Basketball, football (non-tackle), golf, racquetball, soccer, softball, swimming, table tennis M, tennis, volleyball, weight lifting. **Team name:** Pioneers.

**Student services.** Adult student services, alcohol/substance abuse counseling, career counseling, student employment services, financial aid counseling, health services, minority student services, personal counseling, placement for graduates, veterans' counselor, women's services. **Physically disabled:** Services for visually, speech, hearing impaired.

**Contact.** E-mail: admissions@twu.edu
Phone: (940) 898-3188 Toll-free number: (866) 809-6130
Fax: (940) 898-3081
Erma Nieto-Brecht, Director of Admissions, Texas Woman's University, Box 425589, Denton, TX 76204-5589

## Trinity University

**San Antonio, Texas**
**www.trinity.edu**

**CB member**
**CB code: 6831**

- Private 4-year liberal arts college affiliated with Presbyterian Church (USA)
- Residential campus in very large city
- 2,458 degree-seeking undergraduates: 1% part-time, 54% women, 4% African American, 7% Asian American, 11% Hispanic American, 1% Native American, 7% international
- 204 degree-seeking graduate students
- 59% of applicants admitted
- SAT or ACT (ACT writing optional), application essay required
- 79% graduate within 6 years

**General.** Founded in 1869. Regionally accredited. **Degrees:** 558 bachelor's awarded; master's offered. **ROTC:** Air Force. **Location:** 3 miles from downtown. **Calendar:** Semester, limited summer session. **Full-time faculty:** 243 total; 100% have terminal degrees, 12% minority, 38% women.

**Part-time faculty:** 83 total. **Class size:** 61% < 20, 35% 20-39, 2% 40-49, 1% 50-99, less than 1% >100.

**Freshman class profile.** 4,209 applied, 2,489 admitted, 642 enrolled.

| Mid 50% test scores | | Rank in top quarter: | 86% |
|---|---|---|---|
| SAT critical reading: | 590-700 | Rank in top tenth: | 55% |
| SAT math: | 610-690 | End year in good standing: | 94% |
| ACT composite: | 27-31 | Return as sophomores: | 89% |
| GPA 3.75 or higher: | 37% | Out-of-state: | 30% |
| GPA 3.50-3.74: | 28% | Live on campus: | 100% |
| GPA 3.0-3.49: | 27% | International: | 9% |
| GPA 2.0-2.99: | 8% | | |

**Basis for selection.** GPA, high school rank, test scores, essay, interview, recommendations, extracurricular involvement, and achievement important. **Homeschooled:** At least 3 SAT Subject Tests recommended, including natural science and foreign language.

**High school preparation.** 15 units required; 19 recommended. Required and recommended units include English 4, mathematics 3, social studies 3, science 3 (laboratory 2-3), foreign language 2-3 and academic electives 3.

**2009-2010 Annual costs.** Tuition/fees: $29,317. Room/board: $8,895. Books/supplies: $950. Personal expenses: $1,050.

**2009-2010 Financial aid. Need-based:** 407 full-time freshmen applied for aid; 285 were judged to have need; 285 of these received aid. Average need met was 94%. Average scholarship/grant was $19,259; average loan $5,491. 70% of total undergraduate aid awarded as scholarships/grants, 30% as loans/jobs. **Non-need-based:** Awarded to 1,247 full-time undergraduates, including 363 freshmen. Scholarships awarded for academics, leadership, music/drama.

**Application procedures. Admission:** Closing date 2/1 (postmark date). $50 fee, may be waived for applicants with need, free for online applicants. Admission notification 4/1. Must reply by 5/1. **Financial aid:** Priority date 2/15, closing date 4/1. FAFSA required. Applicants notified by 4/1; must reply by 5/1 or within 3 week(s) of notification.

**Academics. Special study options:** Accelerated study, combined bachelor's/graduate degree, double major, honors, independent study, internships, liberal arts/career combination, New York semester, semester at sea, student-designed major, study abroad, teacher certification program, United Nations semester, urban semester, Washington semester. **Credit/placement by examination:** AP, CLEP, IB, institutional tests. 36 credit hours maximum toward bachelor's degree. **Support services:** Writing center.

**Majors. Area/ethnic studies:** Asian, European, Latin American. **Biology:** General, biochemistry. **Business:** Accounting, business admin, finance, international, management science, marketing. **Communications:** General. **Computer sciences:** General. **Education:** Elementary. **Engineering:** Science. **Foreign languages:** Chinese, classics, French, German, Russian, Spanish. **History:** General. **Math:** General. **Philosophy/religion:** Philosophy, religion. **Physical sciences:** Chemistry, geology, physics. **Psychology:** General. **Social sciences:** Anthropology, economics, political science, sociology, urban studies. **Visual/performing arts:** Art, art history/conservation, dramatic, music performance, music theory/composition, theater design, voice/opera.

**Most popular majors.** Biology 6%, business/marketing 28%, communications/journalism 7%, English 7%, social sciences 16%, visual/performing arts 7%.

**Computing on campus.** 400 workstations in library, computer center, student center. Dormitories wired for high-speed internet access and linked to campus network. Commuter students can connect to campus network. Online course registration, online library, helpline, student web hosting, wireless network available.

**Student life. Freshman orientation:** Available. **Housing:** Guaranteed on-campus for freshmen. Coed dorms, wellness housing available. $500 nonrefundable deposit, deadline 5/1. **Activities:** Bands, campus ministries, choral groups, dance, drama, film society, literary magazine, music ensembles, Model UN, musical theater, opera, radio station, student government, student newspaper, symphony orchestra, TV station, Phi Beta Kappa, academic honor societies, activities council, Young Democrats, Young Republicans, association of student representatives, Alpha Phi Omega, religious organizations, minority student organizations, Trinity Multicultural Network.

**Athletics.** NCAA. **Intercollegiate:** Baseball M, basketball, cross-country, diving, football (tackle) M, golf, soccer, softball W, swimming, tennis, track and field, volleyball W. **Intramural:** Basketball, cross-country, football (non-tackle), racquetball, soccer, softball, swimming, table tennis, tennis, volleyball, wrestling. **Team name:** Tigers.

**Student services.** Chaplain/spiritual director, career counseling, student employment services, financial aid counseling, health services, personal counseling, placement for graduates, veterans' counselor. **Physically disabled:** Services for visually, hearing impaired.

**Contact.** E-mail: admissions@trinity.edu
Phone: (210) 999-7207 Toll-free number: (800) 874-6489
Fax: (210) 999-8164
Christopher Ellertson, Dean of Admissions and Financial Aid, Trinity University, One Trinity Place, San Antonio, TX 78212-7200

## University of Dallas
**Irving, Texas**  CB member
**www.udallas.edu**  CB code: 6868

▸ Private 4-year university and liberal arts college affiliated with Roman Catholic Church
▸ Residential campus in small city
▸ 1,297 degree-seeking undergraduates: 1% part-time, 51% women, 1% African American, 5% Asian American, 15% Hispanic American, 3% international
▸ 1,489 degree-seeking graduate students
▸ 92% of applicants admitted
▸ SAT or ACT with writing, application essay required
▸ 73% graduate within 6 years; 37% enter graduate study

**General.** Founded in 1956. Regionally accredited. Campus in Marino, Italy. **Degrees:** 255 bachelor's awarded; master's, doctoral offered. **ROTC:** Army, Air Force. **Location:** 5 miles from Dallas. **Calendar:** Semester, limited summer session. **Full-time faculty:** 124 total; 93% have terminal degrees, 6% minority, 30% women. **Part-time faculty:** 108 total; 32% have terminal degrees, 10% minority, 32% women. **Class size:** 49% < 20, 45% 20-39, 3% 40-49, 2% 50-99, less than 1% >100.

**Freshman class profile.** 1,056 applied, 972 admitted, 320 enrolled.

| Mid 50% test scores | | GPA 2.0-2.99: | 8% |
|---|---|---|---|
| SAT critical reading: | 560-700 | Rank in top quarter: | 58% |
| SAT math: | 530-650 | Rank in top tenth: | 36% |
| SAT writing: | 540-670 | End year in good standing: | 92% |
| ACT composite: | 23-30 | Return as sophomores: | 82% |
| GPA 3.75 or higher: | 48% | Out-of-state: | 55% |
| GPA 3.50-3.74: | 22% | Live on campus: | 89% |
| GPA 3.0-3.49: | 22% | International: | 2% |

**Basis for selection.** Sufficient academic preparation and ability required along with evidence of good character. Critical writing and composition skills important. Interview recommended for academically marginal; audition recommended for theater program; portfolio recommended for art program. **Homeschooled:** Transcript of courses and grades required. Transcript must be from a recognized, accredited consortium or association; or a comprehensive syllabi (including list of books used, laboratory work done, and narrative description or experiential learning) is required.

**High school preparation.** College-preparatory program recommended. Recommended units include English 4, mathematics 4, social studies 4, history 4, science 3 (laboratory 3), foreign language 2, visual/performing arts 2 and academic electives 4.

**2009-2010 Annual costs.** Tuition/fees: $26,294. Room/board: $8,220. Books/supplies: $1,700. Personal expenses: $2,000.

**2008-2009 Financial aid. Need-based:** 256 full-time freshmen applied for aid; 209 were judged to have need; 209 of these received aid. Average need met was 79%. Average scholarship/grant was $16,393; average loan $3,865. 82% of total undergraduate aid awarded as scholarships/grants, 18% as loans/jobs. **Non-need-based:** Awarded to 484 full-time undergraduates, including 144 freshmen. Scholarships awarded for academics, alumni affiliation, art, leadership, music/drama.

**Application procedures. Admission:** Priority date 1/15; deadline 3/1 (postmark date). $40 fee, may be waived for applicants with need. Admission notification on a rolling basis beginning on or about 2/1. Must reply by May 1 or within 4 week(s) if notified thereafter. Two early action deadlines: November 1 and December 1. Notification is 3-4 weeks later. **Financial aid:** Priority date 3/1, closing date 7/1. FAFSA required. Applicants notified on a rolling basis starting 3/1; must reply by 5/1 or within 2 week(s) of notification.

**Academics. Special study options:** Combined bachelor's/graduate degree, double major, dual enrollment of high school students, independent study, internships, liberal arts/career combination, student-designed major, study abroad, teacher certification program. Intensive honors chemistry summer program for entering freshmen. **Credit/placement by examination:**

AP, CLEP, IB, institutional tests. 32 credit hours maximum toward bachelor's degree. **Support services:** Pre-admission summer program, reduced course load, tutoring, writing center.

**Majors. Biology:** General, biochemistry. **Business:** Business admin. **Education:** General, elementary. **Foreign languages:** Classics, French, German, Spanish. **History:** General. **Math:** General. **Philosophy/religion:** Philosophy. **Physical sciences:** Chemistry, physics. **Psychology:** General. **Social sciences:** Economics, political science. **Theology:** Preministerial, theology. **Visual/performing arts:** Art history/conservation, ceramics, dramatic, painting, printmaking, sculpture.

**Most popular majors.** Biology 11%, business/marketing 11%, English 17%, foreign language 7%, history 9%, psychology 7%, social sciences 11%, theological studies 8%, visual/performing arts 8%.

**Computing on campus.** 125 workstations in library, computer center, student center. Dormitories wired for high-speed internet access and linked to campus network. Commuter students can connect to campus network. Online library, helpline, wireless network available.

**Student life. Freshman orientation:** Mandatory. One-day program prior to fall semester. **Housing:** Guaranteed on-campus for freshmen. Single-sex dorms, apartments available. $150 nonrefundable deposit, deadline 6/1. **Activities:** Campus ministries, choral groups, dance, drama, film society, international student organizations, literary magazine, music ensembles, musical theater, radio station, student government, student newspaper, Best Buddies, Society of St. Vincent de Paul, Alpha Phi Omega, Crusaders for Life, Asian student organization, Latin American student association.

**Athletics.** NCAA. **Intercollegiate:** Baseball M, basketball, cross-country, golf M, lacrosse, soccer, softball W, track and field, volleyball W. **Intramural:** Basketball M, football (non-tackle), soccer, softball, volleyball. **Team name:** Crusaders.

**Student services.** Chaplain/spiritual director, career counseling, student employment services, financial aid counseling, health services, personal counseling, placement for graduates. **Physically disabled:** Services for visually impaired.

**Contact.** E-mail: ugadmis@udallas.edu
Phone: (972) 721-5266 Toll-free number: (800) 628-6999
Fax: (972) 721-5017
John Plotts, Associate Provost and Dean of Enrollment, University of Dallas, 1845 East Northgate Drive, Irving, TX 75062-4736

## University of Houston

Houston, Texas
www.uh.edu

CB member
CB code: 6870

- Public 4-year university
- Commuter campus in very large city
- 28,056 degree-seeking undergraduates: 26% part-time, 50% women, 15% African American, 22% Asian American, 24% Hispanic American, 4% international
- 7,702 degree-seeking graduate students
- 70% of applicants admitted
- SAT or ACT (ACT writing optional) required
- 41% graduate within 6 years

**General.** Founded in 1927. Regionally accredited. Research university with highly diverse student population. **Degrees:** 4,874 bachelor's awarded; master's, doctoral, professional offered. **ROTC:** Army, Naval, Air Force. **Location:** 3 miles from downtown. **Calendar:** Semester, extensive summer session. **Full-time faculty:** 1,256 total; 88% have terminal degrees, 23% minority, 36% women. **Part-time faculty:** 524 total; 49% have terminal degrees, 21% minority, 37% women. **Class size:** 30% < 20, 38% 20-39, 9% 40-49, 14% 50-99, 9% >100. **Special facilities:** Theater complex, observatory, opera house, university center, wellness center.

**Freshman class profile.** 11,393 applied, 7,941 admitted, 3,295 enrolled.

| Mid 50% test scores | | | |
|---|---|---|---|
| SAT critical reading: | 470-570 | Rank in top tenth: | 24% |
| SAT math: | 500-620 | End year in good standing: | 77% |
| ACT composite: | 20-25 | Return as sophomores: | 79% |
| GPA 3.75 or higher: | 30% | Out-of-state: | 3% |
| GPA 3.50-3.74: | 18% | Live on campus: | 27% |
| GPA 3.0-3.49: | 36% | International: | 4% |
| GPA 2.0-2.99: | 16% | Fraternities: | 2% |
| Rank in top quarter: | 60% | Sororities: | 3% |

**Basis for selection.** Freshmen applicants ranked in top 10% of class are automatically accepted. Applicants in the top 11-25% with minimum score of 1000 SAT (exclusive of Writing) or 21 ACT will be admitted. Applicants in the top 25-50% with minimum score of 1100 SAT (exclusive of Writing) or 24 in ACT will be admitted. All other applicants individually reviewed. Audition and application required for music, theater, and dance programs; essay recommended for honors college and individual review. Portfolio suggested for architecture program. **Homeschooled:** Transcript of courses and grades, state high school equivalency certificate required. Must submit minimum SAT score of 1180 (exclusive of Writing) or a 26 composite score on the ACT and transcript (can be created by parent). In order to qualify for financial aid, must pass GED exam. **Learning Disabled:** Intake appointment with counselor scheduled upon receipt of required documentation of limitations due to disability.

**High school preparation.** College-preparatory program recommended. Recommended units include English 4, mathematics 3, social studies 3, science 2 and foreign language 2.

**2009-2010 Annual costs.** Tuition/fees: $8,496; $16,806 out-of-state. Room/board: $7,164. Books/supplies: $1,100. Personal expenses: $2,624.

**2009-2010 Financial aid. Need-based:** 2,364 full-time freshmen applied for aid; 1,913 were judged to have need; 1,857 of these received aid. Average need met was 83%. Average scholarship/grant was $9,424; average loan $4,870. 47% of total undergraduate aid awarded as scholarships/grants, 53% as loans/jobs. **Non-need-based:** Awarded to 845 full-time undergraduates, including 347 freshmen. Scholarships awarded for academics, alumni affiliation, art, athletics, job skills, leadership, music/drama, ROTC, state residency.

**Application procedures. Admission:** Priority date 1/15; deadline 4/1 (postmark date). $50 fee ($50 out-of-state), may be waived for applicants with need. Admission notification on a rolling basis. **Financial aid:** Priority date 4/1; no closing date. FAFSA required. Applicants notified on a rolling basis starting 5/1.

**Academics. Special study options:** Accelerated study, combined bachelor's/graduate degree, cooperative education, cross-registration, distance learning, double major, dual enrollment of high school students, ESL, exchange student, honors, independent study, internships, study abroad, teacher certification program, Washington semester, weekend college. Academic enrichment programs, certification programs and affiliated studies. **Credit/placement by examination:** AP, CLEP, IB, institutional tests. **Support services:** Learning center, reduced course load, remedial instruction, study skills assistance, tutoring, writing center.

**Honors college/program.** All students encouraged to apply. High school and/or academic record, extracurricular activities, test scores, and essay of each applicant considered. No specific requirements for admission, however the average honors student is in top 10 percent of high school class with SAT score of 1270 (exclusive of Writing).

**Majors. Architecture:** Architecture, environmental design, interior. **Area/ethnic studies:** German, Russian/Slavic. **Biology:** General, biochemistry, biophysics. **Business:** Accounting, communications, entrepreneurial studies, finance, human resources, management information systems, managerial economics, marketing, merchandising, operations, organizational behavior, personal/financial services, sales/distribution, statistics. **Communications:** General, journalism, public relations, radio/tv. **Computer sciences:** General, information systems, systems analysis. **Education:** Health, physical, trade/industrial. **Engineering:** Chemical, civil, computer, electrical, mechanical. **Engineering technology:** Architectural, civil, construction, electrical, industrial, industrial management, manufacturing. **Family/consumer sciences:** General, business, family studies, food/nutrition. **Foreign languages:** Classics, French, German, Italian, Latin, Spanish. **Health:** Audiology/speech pathology, clinical lab science, communication disorders, kinesiotherapy, nuclear medical technology, optician, prepharmacy. **History:** General. **Math:** General, applied. **Parks/recreation:** Exercise sciences, health/fitness, sports admin. **Philosophy/religion:** Philosophy. **Physical sciences:** Chemistry, geology, geophysics, physics, planetary. **Psychology:** General. **Social sciences:** Anthropology, economics, political science, sociology, urban studies. **Visual/performing arts:** Art, art history/conservation, ceramics, commercial/advertising art, dance, dramatic, graphic design, industrial design, interior design, metal/jewelry, music performance, music theory/composition, painting, photography, printmaking, sculpture, studio arts.

**Most popular majors.** Biology 6%, business/marketing 30%, communications/journalism 6%, engineering/engineering technologies 7%, interdisciplinary studies 6%, psychology 8%, social sciences 8%.

**Computing on campus.** 1,350 workstations in dormitories, library, computer center, student center. Dormitories wired for high-speed internet access and linked to campus network. Commuter students can connect to campus network. Online course registration, online library, helpline, repair service, student web hosting, wireless network available.

**Student life. Freshman orientation:** Mandatory, $120 fee. Preregistration for classes offered. Two-day conferences include advising, phone registration, placement testing, textbook orders. Held late spring and through the summer. **Housing:** Coed dorms, special housing for disabled, apartments, fraternity/sorority housing available. $300 partly refundable deposit. **Activities:** Bands, campus ministries, choral groups, dance, drama, film society, international student organizations, literary magazine, music ensembles, musical theater, opera, radio station, student government, student newspaper, symphony orchestra, TV station, Asian student association, Hispanic student association, Habitat for Humanity, Hillel, College Republicans/Democrats, NAACP, Green Party, Indian student association, Muslim students association, Bahai student association.

**Athletics.** NCAA. **Intercollegiate:** Baseball M, basketball, cross-country, diving W, football (tackle) M, golf M, soccer W, softball W, swimming W, tennis W, track and field, volleyball W. **Intramural:** Badminton, basketball, bowling, cross-country, football (non-tackle), golf, racquetball, soccer, softball, swimming, table tennis, tennis, track and field, volleyball. **Team name:** Cougars.

**Student services.** Adult student services, chaplain/spiritual director, career counseling, student employment services, financial aid counseling, health services, on-campus daycare, personal counseling, placement for graduates, veterans' counselor, women's services. **Physically disabled:** Services for visually, speech, hearing impaired.

**Contact.** E-mail: admissions@uh.edu
Phone: (713) 743-1010 Fax: (713) 743-9633
Djuana Young, Executive Director of Admissions, University of Houston, Welcome Center, Houston, TX 77204-2023

---

## University of Houston-Clear Lake
**Houston, Texas**
www.uhcl.edu

CB member
CB code: 6916

♦ Public two-year upper-division university
♦ Commuter campus in very large city
♦ 76% of applicants admitted

**General.** Founded in 1971. Regionally accredited. Upper level university for undergraduates. Located 3 miles from NASA. **Degrees:** 1,217 bachelor's awarded; master's, professional offered. **Articulation:** Agreements with all community colleges in Houston metropolitan area, Houston CC, Lone Star CC, San Jacinto College, Galveston College, Alvin CC, Lee College, College of the Mainland, Wharton County Junior College. **Location:** 21 miles from Houston. **Calendar:** Semester, limited summer session. **Full-time faculty:** 220 total; 86% have terminal degrees, 23% minority, 43% women. **Part-time faculty:** 305 total; 41% have terminal degrees, 20% minority, 59% women. **Class size:** 43% < 20, 41% 20-39, 5% 40-49, 10% 50-99.

**Student profile.** 4,104 degree-seeking undergraduates, 3,329 degree-seeking graduate students. 2,005 applied as first time-transfer students, 1,529 admitted, 1,202 enrolled. 82% entered as juniors, 18% entered as seniors.

| | | | |
|---|---|---|---|
| Women: | 69% | Live on campus: | 3% |
| Part-time: | 51% | 25 or older: | 41% |

**Basis for selection.** College transcript required. Students with 54 hours of credit with grades 2.0 or better (exclusive of remedial or development or repeated courses) from regionally accredited institution will be admitted. Students must also have completed college algebra or higher mathematics course and have passing scores on THEA. Students must be eligible to return to last institution attended. Transfer accepted as juniors, seniors.

**2009-2010 Annual costs.** Tuition/fees: $5,798; $15,038 out-of-state. Room only: $10,828. Books/supplies: $1,024.

**Financial aid. Non-need-based:** Scholarships awarded for state residency.

**Application procedures. Admission:** Deadline 8/1. $35 fee. **Financial aid:** Applicants notified on a rolling basis starting 5/15; must reply within 4 weeks of notification. FAFSA, institutional form required.

**Academics. Special study options:** Combined bachelor's/graduate degree, cooperative education, distance learning, double major, dual enrollment of high school students, independent study, internships, student-designed major, study abroad, teacher certification program, weekend college. **Credit/placement by examination:** AP, CLEP. 18 credit hours maximum toward bachelor's degree. No more than 3 hours in history and government may be earned through CLEP.

**Majors. Biology:** General. **Business:** General, accounting, business admin, finance, management information systems, marketing. **Communications:**

General. **Computer sciences:** General, computer science. **Conservation:** General, environmental science, environmental studies. **Education:** General. **Engineering:** Computer. **Health:** Health care admin, health services admin. **History:** General. **Interdisciplinary:** Behavioral sciences, math/computer science. **Legal studies:** Prelaw. **Liberal arts:** Arts/sciences, humanities. **Math:** General. **Parks/recreation:** Health/fitness. **Physical sciences:** Chemistry, physics. **Psychology:** General. **Public administration:** Policy analysis, social work. **Social sciences:** Anthropology, criminology, geography, political science, sociology. **Visual/performing arts:** Art. **Other:** Young children with disabilities.

**Most popular majors.** Business/marketing 29%, interdisciplinary studies 22%, psychology 8%.

**Computing on campus.** 715 workstations in library, computer center, student center. Commuter students can connect to campus network. Online library, helpline, wireless network available.

**Student life. Housing:** Limited apartments on campus. **Activities:** Film society, international student organizations, literary magazine, student government, student newspaper, Black student association, Chinese Christian student fellowship, Hispanic Advancement in Culture and Education, student organization for Native American studies, student council for exceptional children, clinical psychology club, Muslim student association.

**Student services.** Alcohol/substance abuse counseling, career counseling, student employment services, financial aid counseling, health services, minority student services, personal counseling, placement for graduates, veterans' counselor, women's services. **Physically disabled:** Services for visually, speech, hearing impaired.

**Contact.** E-mail: admissions@uhcl.edu
Phone: (281) 283-2500 Fax: (281) 283-2522
Rauchelle Jones, Director of Admissions, University of Houston-Clear Lake, 2700 Bay Area Boulevard, Houston, TX 77058-1098

---

## University of Houston-Downtown
**Houston, Texas**
www.uhd.edu

CB member
CB code: 6922

♦ Public 4-year university
♦ Commuter campus in very large city
♦ 12,517 degree-seeking undergraduates: 51% part-time, 62% women, 29% African American, 10% Asian American, 37% Hispanic American, 2% international
♦ 163 degree-seeking graduate students

**General.** Founded in 1974. Regionally accredited. Distance education locations in the surrounding area at these locations: Katy (Cinco Ranch), The Woodlands, Kingwood, and Cypress. **Degrees:** 2,213 bachelor's awarded; master's offered. **ROTC:** Army, Air Force. **Location:** Downtown Houston. **Calendar:** Semester, limited summer session. **Full-time faculty:** 316 total; 81% have terminal degrees, 32% minority, 49% women. **Part-time faculty:** 278 total; 32% have terminal degrees, 40% minority, 48% women. **Class size:** 26% < 20, 58% 20-39, 11% 40-49, 5% 50-99, less than 1% >100.

**Freshman class profile.** 2,442 applied, 2,434 admitted, 1,071 enrolled.

| | | | |
|---|---|---|---|
| Return as sophomores: | 61% | Fraternities: | 1% |
| Out-of-state: | 2% | Sororities: | 1% |
| International: | 2% | | |

**Basis for selection.** Open admission. **Homeschooled:** Transcript of courses and grades required.

**High school preparation.** College-preparatory program recommended. 27.5 units recommended. Recommended units include English 4, mathematics 3, social studies 1.5, history 2, science 3, foreign language 3, computer science 1, visual/performing arts 1 and academic electives 1. 8 units recommended in economics, health education, physical education and speech.

**2009-2010 Annual costs.** Tuition/fees: $5,232; $13,542 out-of-state. Books/supplies: $1,076. Personal expenses: $3,800.

**2009-2010 Financial aid. Need-based:** 570 full-time freshmen applied for aid; 563 were judged to have need; 563 of these received aid. Average need met was 65%. Average scholarship/grant was $8,153; average loan $3,203. 43% of total undergraduate aid awarded as scholarships/grants, 57% as loans/jobs. **Non-need-based:** Awarded to 120 full-time undergraduates, including 83 freshmen. Scholarships awarded for academics, leadership.

**Application procedures. Admission:** Closing date 6/1 (postmark date). $35 fee, may be waived for applicants with need. Application must be submitted online. Notified within 3-5 business days after all items received.

**Financial aid:** Priority date 4/1; no closing date. FAFSA required. Applicants notified on a rolling basis starting 4/15; must reply within 4 week(s) of notification.

**Academics. Special study options:** Cooperative education, distance learning, dual enrollment of high school students, ESL, honors, independent study, internships, study abroad, teacher certification program, weekend college. **Credit/placement by examination:** AP, CLEP, institutional tests. 24 credit hours maximum toward bachelor's degree. **Support services:** Learning center, reduced course load, remedial instruction, study skills assistance, tutoring, writing center.

**Majors. Biology:** General, microbiology. **Business:** General, accounting, business admin, finance, insurance, international, management information systems, marketing, purchasing. **Computer sciences:** General. **Engineering technology:** Civil, computer, industrial safety, mechanical, occupational safety. **Foreign languages:** Spanish. **History:** General. **Interdisciplinary:** Biological/physical sciences. **Liberal arts:** Arts/sciences, humanities. **Math:** General, applied. **Philosophy/religion:** Philosophy. **Physical sciences:** Chemistry. **Protective services:** Criminal justice. **Psychology:** General. **Public administration:** Social work. **Social sciences:** General, political science, sociology. **Visual/performing arts:** General. **Other:** Industrial chemistry.

**Most popular majors.** Business/marketing 40%, interdisciplinary studies 10%, liberal arts 18%, psychology 7%, security/protective services 7%.

**Computing on campus.** 1,650 workstations in library, computer center, student center. Commuter students can connect to campus network. Online course registration, online library, helpline, student web hosting, wireless network available.

**Student life. Freshman orientation:** Mandatory, $80 fee. Preregistration for classes offered. 2-day program for students and parents; testing and enrollment support offered. Held throughout summer, May-July. **Policies:** Students must have at least a 2.5 GPA to be an officer in student organizations and at least 2.0 GPA to be a member. **Activities:** Jazz band, campus ministries, drama, international student organizations, literary magazine, Model UN, student government, student newspaper, black student alliance, UHD Students for Bill White, India & Pakistan student association.

**Athletics. Intramural:** Badminton, basketball, bowling, football (nontackle), soccer, softball, tennis, volleyball, weight lifting. **Team name:** Gator.

**Student services.** Alcohol/substance abuse counseling, career counseling, student employment services, financial aid counseling, health services, legal services, personal counseling, placement for graduates, veterans' counselor. **Physically disabled:** Services for visually, hearing impaired.

**Contact.** E-mail: uhdadmit@uhd.edu
Phone: (713) 221-8522 Fax: (713) 221-8157
Jose Cantu, Director of Admissions and Recruitment, University of Houston-Downtown, One Main Street, Suite 350-S, Houston, TX 77002

## University of Houston-Victoria
### Victoria, Texas
### www.uhv.edu
### CB code: 6917

- Public two-year upper-division university
- Commuter campus in small city
- 76% of applicants admitted
- Test scores required

**General.** Founded in 1973. Regionally accredited. **Degrees:** 490 bachelor's awarded; master's offered. **Articulation:** Agreements with Bee County College, Victoria College, Wharton County Junior College, Blinn College. **Location:** 100 miles from Houston and San Antonio. **Calendar:** Semester, limited summer session. **Full-time faculty:** 106 total; 92% have terminal degrees, 38% minority, 45% women. **Part-time faculty:** 70 total; 31% have terminal degrees, 20% minority, 64% women. **Class size:** 36% < 20, 43% 20-39, 10% 40-49, 11% 50-99.

**Student profile.** 1,779 degree-seeking undergraduates, 1,780 degree-seeking graduate students. 820 applied as first time-transfer students, 624 admitted, 395 enrolled. 90% entered as juniors, 10% entered as seniors.

| Women: | 70% | International: | 2% |
|---|---|---|---|
| African American: | 12% | Part-time: | 62% |
| Asian American: | 7% | Out-of-state: | 1% |
| Hispanic American: | 21% | 25 or older: | 65% |
| Native American: | 1% | | |

**Basis for selection.** College transcript, standardized test scores required. Minimum of 54 semester hours in non-remedial college-level coursework from an institution accredited by one of the recognized regional accrediting associations is required for unconditional admission. Student must have earned minimum 2.0 (A-4.0) GPA and have passed all parts (reading, writing and mathematics) of TASP/THEA exam. Transfer accepted as sophomores, juniors, seniors.

**2009-2010 Annual costs.** Tuition/fees: $5,400; $13,710 out-of-state. Books/supplies: $1,100. Personal expenses: $2,028.

**Financial aid. Non-need-based:** Scholarships awarded for academics, athletics, leadership, state residency. **Additional information:** Short-term loans available at registration.

**Application procedures. Admission:** Rolling admission. No application fee. Application must be submitted online. **Financial aid:** No deadline. Applicants notified on a rolling basis; must reply within 3 weeks of notification. FAFSA required.

**Academics.** Online course support. **Special study options:** Distance learning, double major, honors, independent study, internships, study abroad, teacher certification program. **Credit/placement by examination:** CLEP.

**Majors. Biology:** General. **Business:** General, accounting, business admin, marketing. **Communications:** General. **Computer sciences:** General, information systems. **Education:** General. **Health:** Nursing (RN). **History:** General. **Math:** General. **Protective services:** Law enforcement admin. **Psychology:** General.

**Most popular majors.** Biology 7%, business/marketing 15%, education 29%, health sciences 15%, interdisciplinary studies 10%, psychology 10%.

**Computing on campus.** 250 workstations in library, computer center, student center. Commuter students can connect to campus network. Online course registration, online library, helpline, repair service, wireless network available.

**Student life. Activities:** International student organizations, student government.

**Athletics.** NAIA. **Intercollegiate:** Baseball M, softball W. **Team name:** Jaguares.

**Student services.** Career counseling, student employment services, financial aid counseling, placement for graduates, veterans' counselor. **Physically disabled:** Services for visually, hearing impaired.

**Contact.** E-mail: admission@uhv.edu
Phone: (361) 570-4110 Toll-free number: (877) 970-4848 ext. 110
Fax: (361) 570-4114
Linda Parr, Admision Officer, University of Houston-Victoria, 3007 North Ben Wilson, Victoria, TX 77901-4450

## University of Mary Hardin-Baylor
### Belton, Texas
### www.umhb.edu
### CB member
### CB code: 6396

- Private 4-year university affiliated with Baptist faith
- Residential campus in large town
- 2,547 degree-seeking undergraduates: 10% part-time, 61% women, 13% African American, 2% Asian American, 14% Hispanic American, 1% international
- 221 degree-seeking graduate students
- 42% of applicants admitted
- SAT or ACT with writing required
- 51% graduate within 6 years

**General.** Founded in 1845. Regionally accredited. **Degrees:** 579 bachelor's awarded; master's, professional offered. **ROTC:** Army, Air Force. **Location:** 60 miles from Austin. **Calendar:** Semester, limited summer session. **Full-time faculty:** 133 total; 67% have terminal degrees, 12% minority, 56% women. **Part-time faculty:** 90 total; 36% have terminal degrees, 10% minority, 53% women. **Class size:** 54% < 20, 39% 20-39, 5% 40-49, 2% 50-99, less than 1% >100.

**Freshman class profile.** 5,766 applied, 2,450 admitted, 598 enrolled.

| Mid 50% test scores | | ACT composite: | 20-26 |
|---|---|---|---|
| SAT critical reading: | 470-590 | Return as sophomores: | 65% |
| SAT math: | 480-590 | Out-of-state: | 1% |
| SAT writing: | 450-570 | Live on campus: | 90% |

**Basis for selection.** School achievement record and test scores important. Must either rank in top 10% of graduating class; rank in the top half of class and score 950 SAT or 20 ACT; or rank in lower half of class and score 990 SAT or 21 ACT (all SAT scores exclusive of Writing). Academically deficient students may be accepted on individual basis by approval of admissions committee. Interview recommended for academically marginal; audition recommended for music. **Homeschooled:** Transcript of courses and grades required. Admission based on ACT or SAT test scores.

**High school preparation.** College-preparatory program recommended. 24 units required. Required units include English 4, mathematics 3, social studies 3.5, science 3 and foreign language 2.

**2010-2011 Annual costs.** Tuition/fees: $21,700. Room/board: $5,570. Books/supplies: $1,200. Personal expenses: $1,702.

**2009-2010 Financial aid. Need-based:** 602 full-time freshmen applied for aid; 522 were judged to have need; 522 of these received aid. Average need met was 67%. Average scholarship/grant was $8,932; average loan $3,315. 68% of total undergraduate aid awarded as scholarships/grants, 32% as loans/jobs. **Non-need-based:** Awarded to 563 full-time undergraduates, including 270 freshmen. Scholarships awarded for academics, art, leadership, music/drama, religious affiliation, ROTC.

**Application procedures. Admission:** No deadline. $35 fee, may be waived for applicants with need. Admission notification on a rolling basis. Must reply by May 1 or within 2 week(s) if notified thereafter. **Financial aid:** Priority date 3/1; no closing date. FAFSA required. Applicants notified on a rolling basis starting 2/1; must reply within 2 week(s) of notification.

**Academics. Special study options:** Accelerated study, combined bachelor's/graduate degree, double major, dual enrollment of high school students, ESL, honors, independent study, internships, student-designed major, study abroad, teacher certification program. Servicemember Opportunity Colleges (SOC) programs, military degree completion programs, tuition exchange program with other participating universities. **Credit/placement by examination:** AP, CLEP, IB, institutional tests. 31 credit hours maximum toward bachelor's degree. No more than one-fourth of total credit hours required for degree may be earned through credit by examination. **Support services:** Learning center, reduced course load, remedial instruction, study skills assistance, tutoring.

**Majors. Area/ethnic studies:** American. **Biology:** Biomedical sciences. **Business:** General, accounting, business admin, finance, management information systems, marketing. **Communications:** General, public relations. **Computer sciences:** General, computer graphics, computer science, information systems. **Education:** Elementary, English, mathematics, music, physical, science, social studies, special, speech. **Foreign languages:** Spanish. **Health:** Athletic training, clinical lab science, nursing (RN). **History:** General. **Math:** General. **Parks/recreation:** Sports admin. **Philosophy/religion:** Christian. **Physical sciences:** Chemistry. **Protective services:** Law enforcement admin. **Psychology:** General. **Public administration:** Social work. **Social sciences:** Political science, sociology. **Theology:** Bible, pastoral counseling, sacred music, theology. **Visual/performing arts:** Dramatic, music performance, music theory/composition, studio arts.

**Most popular majors.** Business/marketing 17%, education 13%, health sciences 17%, liberal arts 6%, psychology 9%, visual/performing arts 6%.

**Computing on campus.** 275 workstations in dormitories, library, computer center, student center. Dormitories wired for high-speed internet access and linked to campus network. Online course registration, online library, helpline, wireless network available.

**Student life. Freshman orientation:** Available, $30 fee. Preregistration for classes offered. One-day orientation in summer for students and parents. Full-week orientation for students only before start of classes. **Policies:** Religious observance required. **Housing:** Guaranteed on-campus for freshmen. Single-sex dorms, special housing for disabled, apartments, wellness housing available. $300 partly refundable deposit. **Activities:** Bands, campus ministries, choral groups, drama, international student organizations, literary magazine, music ensembles, musical theater, opera, student government, student newspaper, symphony orchestra, Catholic student organization, College Democrats, College Republicans, Crusaders for Christ, Fellowship of Christian Athletes, Focus (community-wide worship), Habitat for Humanity.

**Athletics.** NCAA. **Intercollegiate:** Baseball M, basketball, football (tackle) M, golf, soccer, softball W, tennis, volleyball W. **Intramural:** Basketball, football (non-tackle), golf, soccer, softball, table tennis, volleyball, weight lifting. **Team name:** Crusaders.

**Student services.** Alcohol/substance abuse counseling, chaplain/spiritual director, career counseling, student employment services, financial aid counseling, health services, personal counseling, placement for graduates, veterans' counselor. **Physically disabled:** Services for visually, speech, hearing impaired.

**Contact.** E-mail: admissions@umhb.edu
Phone: (254) 295-4520 Toll-free number: (800) 727-8642 ext. 4520
Fax: (254) 295-5049
Brent Burks, Director of Admissions and Recruiting, University of Mary Hardin-Baylor, 900 College Street, Belton, TX 76513

## University of North Texas

Denton, Texas
www.unt.edu

CB member
CB code: 6481

- Public 4-year university
- Residential campus in small city
- 28,474 degree-seeking undergraduates: 22% part-time, 54% women, 14% African American, 6% Asian American, 14% Hispanic American, 1% Native American, 2% international
- 2,004 degree-seeking graduate students
- 64% of applicants admitted
- SAT or ACT (ACT writing recommended) required
- 47% graduate within 6 years

**General.** Founded in 1890. Regionally accredited. **Degrees:** 5,830 bachelor's awarded; master's, doctoral, professional offered. **ROTC:** Army, Air Force. **Location:** 35 miles from Dallas and Fort Worth. **Calendar:** Semester, extensive summer session. **Full-time faculty:** 1,018 total; 82% have terminal degrees, 26% minority, 39% women. **Part-time faculty:** 487 total; 6% have terminal degrees, 17% minority, 60% women. **Class size:** 29% < 20, 42% 20-39, 10% 40-49, 10% 50-99, 9% >100. **Special facilities:** Laser, observatory, accelerators, environmental science facility, planetarium.

**Freshman class profile.** 12,883 applied, 8,218 admitted, 3,327 enrolled.

| Mid 50% test scores | | | |
|---|---|---|---|
| SAT critical reading: | 480-590 | Return as sophomores: | 76% |
| SAT math: | 490-600 | Out-of-state: | 3% |
| ACT composite: | 20-25 | Live on campus: | 83% |
| Rank in top quarter: | 51% | International: | 2% |
| Rank in top tenth: | 21% | Fraternities: | 10% |
| End year in good standing: | 81% | Sororities: | 9% |

**Basis for selection.** It is recommended that students apply well in advance of stated application deadlines. School achievement record most important. Test score minimums vary with class rank: top 10% no minimum. High school students may be admitted on an individual basis after completion of the junior year of high school. Must rank in the top quarter of their class, have strong B average, 3 units of English and 2 units each of solid mathematics, social sciences and natural sciences, minimum SAT score of 1180 (exclusive of Writing) or ACT composite of 26, letters from high school counselor or principal recommending early admission, letter from parents or guardians stating approval, and interview with Office of Admissions. Audition required for music program. **Homeschooled:** Statement describing homeschool structure and mission, transcript of courses and grades required. An interview, essay and letters of recommendation may be required after a review of the application.

**High school preparation.** College-preparatory program recommended. 22 units required. Required units include English 4, mathematics 3, social studies 2, history 2, science 3, foreign language 2 and academic electives 3. 0.5 health, 1.5 physical education, 0.5-1 computer sciences, 1 fine arts recommended.

**2009-2010 Annual costs.** Tuition/fees: $7,301; $15,611 out-of-state. Room/board: $6,535. Books/supplies: $1,250. Personal expenses: $1,240.

**2009-2010 Financial aid. Need-based:** 2,534 full-time freshmen applied for aid; 1,777 were judged to have need; 1,751 of these received aid. Average need met was 85%. Average scholarship/grant was $7,243; average loan $3,475. 41% of total undergraduate aid awarded as scholarships/grants, 59% as loans/jobs. **Non-need-based:** Awarded to 4,479 full-time undergraduates, including 1,142 freshmen.

**Application procedures. Admission:** Priority date 3/1; deadline 8/1 (postmark date). $40 fee, may be waived for applicants with need. Application must be submitted online. Admission notification on a rolling basis beginning on or about 10/15. **Financial aid:** Priority date 4/15; no closing date. FAFSA required. Applicants notified on a rolling basis starting 4/1.

**Academics. Special study options:** Accelerated study, combined bachelor's/graduate degree, cooperative education, cross-registration, distance learning, double major, dual enrollment of high school students, ESL, exchange student, external degree, honors, independent study, internships, study abroad, teacher certification program, weekend college. **Credit/placement by examination:** AP, CLEP, IB, institutional tests. **Support services:** Learning center, pre-admission summer program, remedial instruction, study skills assistance, tutoring, writing center.

**Majors. Architecture:** Interior. **Biology:** General, biochemistry. **Business:** General, accounting, banking/financial services, e-commerce, fashion, financial planning, hospitality admin, insurance, logistics, management information systems, managerial economics, marketing, operations, organizational behavior, real estate, sales/distribution, special products marketing. **Communications:** Broadcast journalism, journalism, radio/tv. **Computer sciences:** General, information systems. **Engineering:** Computer, electrical, materials science, mechanical. **Engineering technology:** Construction, electrical, manufacturing, mechanical. **Family/consumer sciences:** Family studies. **Foreign languages:** French, German, Spanish. **Health:** Audiology/speech pathology, clinical lab science, cytotechnology, health services, vocational rehab counseling. **History:** General. **Interdisciplinary:** Behavioral sciences, gerontology, global studies. **Math:** General. **Parks/recreation:** Facilities management, health/fitness. **Philosophy/religion:** Philosophy. **Physical sciences:** Chemistry, physics. **Protective services:** Criminal justice. **Psychology:** General. **Public administration:** General, social work. **Science technology:** Nuclear power. **Social sciences:** General, anthropology, economics, geography, political science, sociology. **Visual/performing arts:** Art, art history/conservation, commercial/advertising art, dance, dramatic, fashion design, jazz, music history, music performance, music theory/composition, studio arts. **Other:** Applied technology and performance improvement, Engineering physics, Rehabilitation studies.

**Most popular majors.** Business/marketing 21%, communications/journalism 6%, interdisciplinary studies 17%, social sciences 11%, visual/performing arts 8%.

**Computing on campus.** 735 workstations in dormitories, library, computer center, student center. Dormitories wired for high-speed internet access and linked to campus network. Commuter students can connect to campus network. Online course registration, online library, helpline, student web hosting, wireless network available.

**Student life. Freshman orientation:** Mandatory, $144 fee. Preregistration for classes offered. Nine sessions during June and July; includes overnight stay in one of the resident halls. **Housing:** Guaranteed on-campus for freshmen. Coed dorms, single-sex dorms, special housing for disabled, apartments, cooperative housing, fraternity/sorority housing, wellness housing available. $400 fully refundable deposit. **Activities:** Bands, campus ministries, choral groups, dance, drama, film society, international student organizations, literary magazine, music ensembles, musical theater, opera, radio station, student government, student newspaper, symphony orchestra, TV station, honorary societies; religious, ethnic, and social service organizations.

**Athletics.** NCAA. **Intercollegiate:** Basketball, cross-country, diving W, football (tackle) M, golf, soccer W, softball, swimming W, tennis W, track and field, volleyball W. **Intramural:** Basketball, bowling, football (non-tackle), golf, racquetball, soccer, softball, table tennis, tennis, volleyball. **Team name:** Mean Green.

**Student services.** Adult student services, alcohol/substance abuse counseling, career counseling, student employment services, financial aid counseling, health services, legal services, minority student services, personal counseling, placement for graduates, veterans' counselor, women's services. **Physically disabled:** Services for visually, speech, hearing impaired.

**Contact.** E-mail: undergrad@unt.edu
Phone: (940) 565-2681 Toll-free number: (800) 868-8211
Fax: (940) 565-2408
Rebecca Lothringer, Director of Admissions, University of North Texas, 1401 West Prairie, Suite 309, Denton, TX 76203-5017

## University of St. Thomas
**Houston, Texas**
www.stthom.edu

**CB member**
**CB code: 6880**

- Private 4-year university and liberal arts college affiliated with Roman Catholic Church
- Commuter campus in very large city
- 1,668 degree-seeking undergraduates: 22% part-time, 59% women, 5% African American, 12% Asian American, 34% Hispanic American, 1% Native American, 4% international
- 1,006 degree-seeking graduate students
- 80% of applicants admitted
- SAT or ACT with writing required
- 47% graduate within 6 years

**General.** Founded in 1947. Regionally accredited. **Degrees:** 305 bachelor's awarded; master's, doctoral offered. **ROTC:** Army, Air Force. **Location:** 3 miles from downtown. **Calendar:** Semester, limited summer session. **Full-time faculty:** 125 total; 92% have terminal degrees, 14% minority, 33% women. **Part-time faculty:** 137 total; 56% have terminal degrees, 18% minority, 50% women. **Class size:** 57% < 20, 43% 20-39, less than 1% 40-49. **Special facilities:** Chapel of St. Basil, archaeology gallery.

**Freshman class profile.** 866 applied, 692 admitted, 287 enrolled.

| Mid 50% test scores | | | |
|---|---|---|---|
| SAT critical reading: | 510-620 | GPA 2.0-2.99: | 18% |
| SAT math: | 510-630 | Rank in top quarter: | 58% |
| SAT writing: | 500-600 | Rank in top tenth: | 28% |
| ACT composite: | 23-27 | End year in good standing: | 80% |
| GPA 3.75 or higher: | 24% | Return as sophomores: | 70% |
| GPA 3.50-3.74: | 23% | Out-of-state: | 5% |
| GPA 3.0-3.49: | 35% | Live on campus: | 43% |
| | | International: | 4% |

**Basis for selection.** School achievement record, test scores, and graded essay most important. Cumulative high school GPA of 2.5 or higher in a minimum of 18 college preparatory units required, as well as minimum 1020 SAT (exclusive of Writing) or 22 ACT. High school class rank in the upper 50% required, if ranking available. Audition required for applied music, drama, voice programs; portfolio required for art program.

**High school preparation.** College-preparatory program recommended. 18 units required. Required units include English 4, mathematics 3, social studies 2, history 1, science 3 (laboratory 2), foreign language 2 and academic electives 3.

**2009-2010 Annual costs.** Tuition/fees: $21,830. Room/board: $7,700.

**2009-2010 Financial aid. Need-based:** 228 full-time freshmen applied for aid; 185 were judged to have need; 184 of these received aid. Average need met was 71%. Average scholarship/grant was $13,259; average loan $3,478. 64% of total undergraduate aid awarded as scholarships/grants, 36% as loans/jobs. **Non-need-based:** Awarded to 388 full-time undergraduates, including 110 freshmen. Scholarships awarded for academics, athletics.

**Application procedures. Admission:** Closing date 5/1. $25 fee, may be waived for applicants with need. Admission notification on a rolling basis beginning on or about 11/15. Must reply by May 1 or within 2 week(s) if notified thereafter. **Financial aid:** No deadline. FAFSA required. Applicants notified on a rolling basis starting 3/22; must reply within 2 week(s) of notification.

**Academics. Special study options:** Accelerated study, combined bachelor's/graduate degree, distance learning, double major, dual enrollment of high school students, honors, independent study, internships, liberal arts/career combination, student-designed major, study abroad, teacher certification program, weekend college. **Credit/placement by examination:** AP, CLEP, IB, SAT, ACT, institutional tests. 30 credit hours maximum toward bachelor's degree. Validation of credit by examination contingent upon completion of at least 24 semester hours in residence at institution. **Support services:** Learning center, reduced course load, remedial instruction, study skills assistance, tutoring, writing center.

**Majors. Biology:** General, biochemistry, bioinformatics. **Business:** Accounting, business admin, finance, marketing. **Communications:** General. **Conservation:** Environmental science, environmental studies. **Education:** General, elementary, music, secondary. **Foreign languages:** French, Spanish. **History:** General. **Liberal arts:** Arts/sciences. **Math:** General. **Philosophy/religion:** Philosophy. **Physical sciences:** Chemistry. **Psychology:** General. **Social sciences:** International economic development, international relations, political science. **Theology:** Pastoral counseling, theology. **Visual/performing arts:** Dramatic, studio arts.

**Most popular majors.** Biology 7%, business/marketing 24%, communications/journalism 6%, education 7%, liberal arts 19%, psychology 7%, social sciences 6%.

**Computing on campus.** 340 workstations in dormitories, library, computer center. Dormitories wired for high-speed internet access. Online course registration, online library, helpline, wireless network available.

**Student life. Freshman orientation:** Available. Preregistration for classes offered. Held in August and January. **Housing:** Coed dorms, apartments available. $300 fully refundable deposit. Pets allowed in dorm rooms. **Activities:** Jazz band, campus ministries, choral groups, dance, drama, international student organizations, literary magazine, music ensembles, musical theater, student government, student newspaper, Al-Nadi Cultural Society, black student union, Chinese student association, Defense for Darfur, Fairy Godmother Project, Vietnamese student association, American Red Cross, Bilingual Education Organization, Celts for Life.

**Athletics.** NAIA. **Intercollegiate:** Basketball M, soccer M, volleyball W. **Intramural:** Basketball, bowling, football (non-tackle), racquetball, table tennis, tennis, volleyball. **Team name:** Celts.

**Student services.** Adult student services, chaplain/spiritual director, career counseling, student employment services, financial aid counseling, health services, personal counseling, placement for graduates, veterans' counselor.

**Contact.** E-mail: admissions@stthom.edu
Phone: (713) 525-3500 Toll-free number: (800) 856-8565
Fax: (713) 525-3558
Lee Holm, Director of Admissions, University of St. Thomas, 3800 Montrose Boulevard, Houston, TX 77006-4626

---

## University of Texas at Arlington
**Arlington, Texas**      **CB member**
**www.uta.edu**      **CB code: 6013**

- Public 4-year university
- Commuter campus in large city
- 20,885 degree-seeking undergraduates: 33% part-time, 54% women, 16% African American, 12% Asian American, 19% Hispanic American, 1% Native American, 4% international
- 6,380 degree-seeking graduate students
- 74% of applicants admitted
- SAT or ACT with writing required
- 43% graduate within 6 years

**General.** Founded in 1895. Regionally accredited. **Degrees:** 3,999 bachelor's awarded; master's, doctoral offered. **ROTC:** Army, Air Force. **Location:** 15 miles from Dallas and Fort Worth. **Calendar:** 4-1-4-1 January and May terms. Extensive summer session. **Full-time faculty:** 823 total; less than 1% have terminal degrees, 23% minority, 36% women. **Part-time faculty:** 328 total; 16% have terminal degrees, 11% minority, 48% women. **Class size:** 27% < 20, 40% 20-39, 7% 40-49, 19% 50-99, 7% >100. **Special facilities:** Robotics center, observatory, planetarium, maps collection, minority cultures collection, cartographic history library, library of Texana and Mexican War material, 3 art galleries, Nursing Smart Hospital, Mavericks Activities Center, studio art center, civil engineering research lab building, workforce development center, amphibian and reptile diversity research center.

**Freshman class profile.** 6,784 applied, 4,990 admitted, 2,319 enrolled.

| Mid 50% test scores | | Return as sophomores: | 68% |
|---|---|---|---|
| SAT critical reading: | 460-580 | Out-of-state: | 3% |
| SAT math: | 490-610 | Live on campus: | 59% |
| ACT composite: | 20-25 | International: | 2% |
| Rank in top quarter: | 66% | Fraternities: | 11% |
| Rank in top tenth: | 24% | Sororities: | 7% |
| End year in good standing: | 78% | | |

**Basis for selection.** GED not accepted. Admission based on test scores and high school rank. Fourth quarter of high school class must be approved by director of admissions or associate director. SAT or ACT math scores used for placement of students majoring in architecture, engineering, biology, biochemistry, chemistry, math, physics, and for students in the bachelor's geology or bachelor's psychology program. Interview recommended for academically weak; audition recommended for music; portfolio recommended for art, architecture programs. **Homeschooled:** Transcript of courses and grades, letter of recommendation (nonparent) required.

**High school preparation.** College-preparatory program required. 20 units required. Required and recommended units include English 4, mathematics 3-4, social studies 3-4, science 3, foreign language 2-3 and academic electives 5. 1 computing proficiency, 1 fine arts, 1 music/theater art, 1.5 physical education, .5 health recommended.

**2009-2010 Annual costs.** Tuition/fees: $8,186; $16,496 out-of-state. Room/board: $6,147. Books/supplies: $908. Personal expenses: $1,490.

**2009-2010 Financial aid.** **Need-based:** 1,891 full-time freshmen applied for aid; 1,563 were judged to have need; 1,563 of these received aid. Average need met was 73%. Average scholarship/grant was $8,077; average loan $3,248. 51% of total undergraduate aid awarded as scholarships/grants, 49% as loans/jobs. **Non-need-based:** Awarded to 2,833 full-time undergraduates, including 994 freshmen. Scholarships awarded for academics, art, athletics, leadership, music/drama, ROTC. **Additional information:** Free tuition to eligible students whose household income is $65,000 or less through the Maverick Promise program.

**Application procedures.** **Admission:** Priority date 6/1; no deadline. $35 fee ($50 out-of-state), may be waived for applicants with need. Notified 3-7 days after application completed. **Financial aid:** Priority date 5/15; no closing date. FAFSA required. Applicants notified on a rolling basis starting 4/1; must reply within 3 week(s) of notification.

**Academics.** **Special study options:** Combined bachelor's/graduate degree, cross-registration, distance learning, double major, dual enrollment of high school students, ESL, exchange student, honors, independent study, internships, student-designed major, study abroad, teacher certification program. **Credit/placement by examination:** AP, CLEP, IB, institutional tests. Credit by exam does not count as credit earned in residence. **Support services:** Learning center, reduced course load, remedial instruction, study skills assistance, tutoring, writing center.

**Majors.** **Architecture:** Architecture, interior. **Biology:** General, biochemistry, microbiology. **Business:** Accounting, banking/financial services, business admin, international, management information systems, managerial economics, marketing, real estate. **Communications:** Advertising, digital media, journalism, public relations, radio/tv. **Computer sciences:** Computer science, **Engineering:** General, aerospace, civil, computer, electrical, industrial, mechanical, software. **Family/consumer sciences:** Child development. **Foreign languages:** General, French, German, Russian, Spanish. **Health:** Athletic training, clinical lab science, nursing (RN). **History:** General. **Math:** General. **Parks/recreation:** Health/fitness. **Philosophy/religion:** Philosophy. **Physical sciences:** Chemistry, geology, physics. **Protective services:** Criminal justice. **Psychology:** General. **Public administration:** Social work. **Social sciences:** Anthropology, economics, political science, sociology. **Visual/performing arts:** Art, art history/conservation, dramatic, music performance, studio arts. **Other:** Geoinformation, Multi-Interdisciplinary studies.

**Most popular majors.** Biology 8%, business/marketing 23%, communications/journalism 6%, engineering/engineering technologies 6%, health sciences 8%, interdisciplinary studies 15%.

**Computing on campus.** 1,000 workstations in dormitories, library, computer center, student center. Dormitories wired for high-speed internet access and linked to campus network. Commuter students can connect to campus network. Online course registration, online library, helpline, student web hosting, wireless network available.

**Student life.** **Freshman orientation:** Mandatory. Preregistration for classes offered. One-and-a-half-day sessions held in June, July, August. Students stay in residence halls. **Housing:** Coed dorms, single-sex dorms, apartments, fraternity/sorority housing available. $350 partly refundable deposit. Priority given to students with dependent children. **Activities:** Bands, campus ministries, choral groups, dance, drama, film society, international student organizations, literary magazine, music ensembles, opera, radio station, student government, student newspaper, symphony orchestra, University Democrats, association of Mexican American students, Vietnamese student association, Wesley Foundation, Mavericks for Christ, Business Beta Gamma Sigma, College Republicans, Business Delta Sigma Pi.

**Athletics.** NCAA. **Intercollegiate:** Baseball M, basketball, cross-country, golf M, softball W, tennis, track and field, volleyball W. **Intramural:** Badminton, basketball, bowling, golf, racquetball, soccer, softball, table tennis, tennis, track and field, volleyball. **Team name:** Mavericks.

**Student services.** Alcohol/substance abuse counseling, chaplain/spiritual director, career counseling, services for economically disadvantaged, student employment services, financial aid counseling, health services, legal services, minority student services, on-campus daycare, personal counseling, placement for graduates, veterans' counselor. **Physically disabled:** Services for visually, hearing impaired.

**Contact.** E-mail: admissions@uta.edu
Phone: (817) 272-6287 Fax: (817) 272-3435
Hans Gatterdam, Executive Director of Admissions, Records and Registration, University of Texas at Arlington, Box 19111, Arlington, TX 76019

---

## University of Texas at Austin
**Austin, Texas**      **CB member**
**www.utexas.edu**      **CB code: 6882**

- Public 4-year university
- Commuter campus in very large city
- 37,464 degree-seeking undergraduates: 6% part-time, 51% women, 5% African American, 18% Asian American, 19% Hispanic American, 4% international
- 12,824 degree-seeking graduate students
- 45% of applicants admitted
- SAT or ACT with writing, application essay required
- 81% graduate within 6 years

**General.** Founded in 1883. Regionally accredited. **Degrees:** 8,747 bachelor's awarded; master's, doctoral, professional offered. **ROTC:** Army, Naval, Air Force. **Location:** 70 miles from San Antonio, 163 miles from Houston. **Calendar:** Semester, extensive summer session. **Full-time faculty:** 2,770 total; 88% have terminal degrees, 20% minority, 37% women. **Part-time faculty:** 269 total; 67% have terminal degrees, 14% minority, 43% women. **Class size:** 36% < 20, 34% 20-39, 6% 40-49, 15% 50-99, 9% >100. **Special facilities:** Humanities and scientific research centers, observatory, marine science institute, fusion reactor, presidential library and museum, performing arts center, museum of natural history, museum of art.

**Freshman class profile.** 31,362 applied, 14,213 admitted, 7,243 enrolled.

| Mid 50% test scores | | | |
|---|---|---|---|
| SAT critical reading: | 530-660 | Return as sophomores: | 93% |
| SAT math: | 570-700 | Out-of-state: | 8% |
| SAT writing: | 530-660 | Live on campus: | 64% |
| ACT composite: | 24-30 | International: | 3% |
| Rank in top quarter: | 94% | Fraternities: | 14% |
| Rank in top tenth: | 77% | Sororities: | 15% |

**Basis for selection.** Applicants from top 10% of class from accredited Texas high school automatically admitted with completed application, but available seats limited to 75% of first-time in college cohort. Off-campus coordinated admission program for Texans who complete all required high school units and apply immediately upon high school graduation, but are not otherwise eligible for regular admission. Audition required, interview recommended for music program; interview recommended for art, liberal arts honors program.

**High school preparation.** College-preparatory program recommended. 20.5 units required; 22.5 recommended. Required and recommended units include English 4, mathematics 3-4, social studies 3.5, science 3, foreign language 2-3, academic electives 4.5. .5 fine arts elective strongly recommended. Economics .5 recommended.

**2009-2010 Annual costs.** Tuition/fees: $8,930; $30,006 out-of-state. Room/board: $9,602. Books/supplies: $860. Personal expenses: $2,472.

**2009-2010 Financial aid. Need-based:** 5,477 full-time freshmen applied for aid; 3,475 were judged to have need; 3,474 of these received aid. Average need met was 85%. Average scholarship/grant was $9,453; average loan $3,001. 62% of total undergraduate aid awarded as scholarships/grants, 38% as loans/jobs. **Non-need-based:** Awarded to 6,086 full-time undergraduates, including 2,653 freshmen. Scholarships awarded for academics, art, athletics, leadership, music/drama, ROTC, state residency. **Additional information:** In general, Texas resident students from families earning less than $40,000 will be awarded grant/scholarship aid (from federal, state, institutional and private sources) to cover tuition costs.

**Application procedures. Admission:** Closing date 12/1 (receipt date). $60 fee, may be waived for applicants with need. Admission notification 4/1. Admission notification on a rolling basis. Must reply by May 1 or within 2 week(s) if notified thereafter. **Financial aid:** Priority date 3/31; no closing date. FAFSA required. Applicants notified on a rolling basis starting 3/15.

**Academics. Special study options:** Accelerated study, combined bachelor's/graduate degree, cooperative education, distance learning, double major, dual enrollment of high school students, ESL, honors, independent study, internships, liberal arts/career combination, student-designed major, study abroad, teacher certification program, Washington semester. **Credit/placement by examination:** AP, CLEP, IB, institutional tests. **Support services:** Learning center, reduced course load, remedial instruction, study skills assistance, tutoring, writing center.

**Majors. Architecture:** Architecture. **Area/ethnic studies:** American, Asian, European, Latin American, Near/Middle Eastern, Russian/Slavic, women's. **Biology:** General, biochemistry. **Business:** General, accounting, business admin, finance, logistics, management information systems, marketing. **Communications:** General, advertising, journalism, public relations, radio/tv. **Communications technology:** Recording arts. **Computer sciences:** General. **Engineering:** Aerospace, architectural, biomedical, chemical, civil, electrical, mechanical, petroleum. **Family/consumer sciences:** General, clothing/textiles, family studies, food/nutrition. **Foreign languages:** Ancient Greek, Arabic, classics, Czech, East Asian, French, German, Hebrew, Italian, Latin, linguistics, Persian, Portuguese, Russian, Scandinavian, Semitic, Spanish, Turkish. **Health:** Athletic training, clinical lab science, communication disorders, health services, nursing (RN). **History:** General. **Interdisciplinary:** Ancient studies, biological/physical sciences, math/computer science. **Liberal arts:** Arts/sciences, humanities. **Math:** General. **Parks/recreation:** Health/fitness, sports admin. **Philosophy/religion:** Islamic, Judaic, philosophy, religion. **Physical sciences:** Astronomy, chemistry, geology, geophysics, hydrology, physics. **Psychology:** General. **Public administration:** Social work. **Social sciences:** Anthropology, archaeology, economics, geography,

political science, sociology, urban studies. **Visual/performing arts:** General, art, art history/conservation, dance, design, dramatic, interior design, jazz, music history, music management, music performance, music theory/composition, studio arts. **Other:** Geosystems engineering and hydrogeology, Youth and community studies.

**Most popular majors.** Biology 8%, business/marketing 12%, communications/journalism 14%, engineering/engineering technologies 11%, social sciences 13%.

**Computing on campus.** 500 workstations in dormitories, library, computer center, student center. Dormitories wired for high-speed internet access and linked to campus network. Commuter students can connect to campus network. Online course registration, online library, helpline, repair service, student web hosting, wireless network available.

**Student life. Freshman orientation:** Available, $105 fee. **Housing:** Coed dorms, single-sex dorms, apartments available. $300 fully refundable deposit. Honors residence, living-learning centers available for first-time freshmen. **Activities:** Bands, campus ministries, choral groups, dance, drama, film society, international student organizations, literary magazine, music ensembles, musical theater, opera, radio station, student government, student newspaper, symphony orchestra, TV station, variety of religious, political, ethnic, and social service organizations.

**Athletics.** NCAA. **Intercollegiate:** Baseball M, basketball, cross-country, diving, football (tackle) M, golf, rowing (crew) W, soccer W, softball W, swimming, tennis, track and field, volleyball W. **Intramural:** Badminton, basketball, bowling, football (non-tackle), golf, handball, racquetball, soccer, softball, squash, swimming, table tennis, tennis, track and field, volleyball, weight lifting. **Team name:** Longhorns.

**Student services.** Adult student services, alcohol/substance abuse counseling, career counseling, services for economically disadvantaged, student employment services, financial aid counseling, health services, legal services, minority student services, on-campus daycare, personal counseling, placement for graduates, veterans' counselor, women's services. **Physically disabled:** Services for visually, speech, hearing impaired. **Learning disabled:** Comprehensive services available.

**Contact.** Phone: (512) 475-7399 Fax: (512) 475-7478 Kedra Ishop, Vice Provost and Director of Admissions, University of Texas at Austin, PO Box 8058, Austin, TX 78713-8058

## University of Texas at Brownsville - Texas Southmost College

| Brownsville, Texas | CB member |
|---|---|
| www.utb.edu | CB code: 6825 |

- Public 4-year university and community college
- Commuter campus in small city
- 10,145 degree-seeking undergraduates
- 849 graduate students

**General.** Founded in 1977. Regionally accredited. **Degrees:** 961 bachelor's, 865 associate awarded; master's, doctoral offered. **ROTC:** Army. **Location:** 150 miles from Corpus Christi. **Calendar:** Semester, extensive summer session. **Full-time faculty:** 384 total. **Part-time faculty:** 247 total. **Class size:** 64% < 20, 30% 20-39, 2% 40-49, 4% 50-99, less than 1% >100.

**Freshman class profile.** 3,526 applied, 3,526 admitted, 2,060 enrolled.

| | | | |
|---|---|---|---|
| GPA 3.75 or higher: | 11% | Rank in top quarter: | 27% |
| GPA 3.50-3.74: | 6% | Rank in top tenth: | 10% |
| GPA 3.0-3.49: | 17% | Out-of-state: | 1% |
| GPA 2.0-2.99: | 45% | Live on campus: | 1% |

**Basis for selection.** Open admission, but selective for some programs. Special requirements for nursing and allied health programs.

**High school preparation.** College-preparatory program recommended.

**2009-2010 Annual costs.** Tuition/fees: $5,498; $13,808 out-of-state. Books/supplies: $646. Personal expenses: $2,651.

**2008-2009 Financial aid. Need-based:** 1,191 full-time freshmen applied for aid; 1,118 were judged to have need; 1,117 of these received aid. Average need met was 64%. Average scholarship/grant was $6,259; average loan $2,991. 61% of total undergraduate aid awarded as scholarships/grants, 39% as loans/jobs. **Non-need-based:** Awarded to 3,287 full-time undergraduates, including 1,098 freshmen. Scholarships awarded for academics, alumni affiliation, art, athletics, minority status, music/drama, state residency.

**Application procedures. Admission:** Priority date 3/1; deadline 7/1 (receipt date). No application fee. Admission notification on a rolling basis.

**Financial aid:** Priority date 3/1, closing date 8/15. FAFSA required. Applicants notified on a rolling basis; must reply by 7/1 or within 12 week(s) of notification.

**Academics. Special study options:** Cooperative education, cross-registration, distance learning, double major, dual enrollment of high school students, ESL, independent study, internships, liberal arts/career combination, study abroad, teacher certification program. **Credit/placement by examination:** AP, CLEP, IB, institutional tests. **Support services:** Learning center, pre-admission summer program, reduced course load, remedial instruction, study skills assistance, tutoring, writing center.

**Majors. Biology:** General. **Business:** General, accounting, business admin, entrepreneurial studies, finance, international, marketing. **Communications:** General. **Computer sciences:** General, information systems. **Conservation:** Environmental science. **Engineering:** Physics. **Engineering technology:** Electrical, industrial, manufacturing, mechanical. **Foreign languages:** Spanish, translation. **Health:** Health services, nursing (RN). **History:** General. **Liberal arts:** Arts/sciences. **Math:** General. **Parks/recreation:** Health/fitness. **Physical sciences:** Chemistry, physics. **Protective services:** Corrections, criminal justice, law enforcement admin. **Psychology:** General. **Public administration:** General. **Social sciences:** Political science, sociology. **Visual/performing arts:** Art.

**Most popular majors.** Biology 6%, business/marketing 16%, interdisciplinary studies 27%, parks/recreation 6%, security/protective services 9%.

**Computing on campus.** 650 workstations in dormitories, library, computer center. Dormitories wired for high-speed internet access and linked to campus network. Commuter students can connect to campus network. Online course registration, online library, helpline, repair service, student web hosting, wireless network available.

**Student life. Freshman orientation:** Mandatory, $50 fee. Preregistration for classes offered. **Housing:** Coed dorms, wellness housing available. **Activities:** Jazz band, campus ministries, choral groups, dance, international student organizations, music ensembles, student government, student newspaper.

**Athletics.** NAIA. **Intercollegiate:** Baseball M, golf, soccer, volleyball W. **Team name:** Scorpions.

**Student services.** Adult student services, career counseling, services for economically disadvantaged, student employment services, financial aid counseling, health services, minority student services, on-campus daycare, personal counseling, placement for graduates, veterans' counselor. **Physically disabled:** Services for visually, speech, hearing impaired.

**Contact.** E-mail: admissions@utb.edu
Phone: (956) 882-8295 Toll-free number: (800) 850-0160
Fax: (956) 882-7810
Rene Villarreal, Director of Admissions, University of Texas at Brownsville - Texas Southmost College, 80 Fort Brown, Brownsville, TX 78520

---

## University of Texas at Dallas

**Richardson, Texas**  **CB member**
**www.utdallas.edu**  **CB code: 6897**

- Public 4-year university
- Commuter campus in very large city
- 9,634 degree-seeking undergraduates: 25% part-time, 45% women, 7% African American, 22% Asian American, 12% Hispanic American, 1% Native American, 4% international
- 5,479 degree-seeking graduate students
- 52% of applicants admitted
- SAT or ACT (ACT writing optional) required
- 63% graduate within 6 years

**General.** Founded in 1969. Regionally accredited. Established internships in industrial practice positions with over 200 advanced technology firms located near the university. **Degrees:** 2,292 bachelor's awarded; master's, doctoral, professional offered. **ROTC:** Army, Air Force. **Location:** 18 miles from downtown Dallas. **Calendar:** Semester, extensive summer session. **Full-time faculty:** 533 total; 92% have terminal degrees, 27% minority, 27% women. **Part-time faculty:** 261 total; 56% have terminal degrees, 13% minority, 46% women. **Class size:** 30% < 20, 34% 20-39, 11% 40-49, 19% 50-99, 6% >100. **Special facilities:** Geological information library, history of aviation library, rare book library, philatelic research library, center for communications disorders, Holocaust collection, translation library.

**Freshman class profile.** 5,554 applied, 2,870 admitted, 1,343 enrolled.

| Mid 50% test scores | | | |
|---|---|---|---|
| SAT critical reading: | 520-660 | Rank in top quarter: | 70% |
| SAT math: | 560-690 | Rank in top tenth: | 36% |
| SAT writing: | 500-620 | End year in good standing: | 86% |
| ACT composite: | 24-30 | Return as sophomores: | 84% |
| GPA 3.75 or higher: | 34% | Out-of-state: | 5% |
| GPA 3.50-3.74: | 30% | Live on campus: | 65% |
| GPA 3.0-3.49: | 32% | International: | 2% |
| GPA 2.0-2.99: | 4% | Fraternities: | 7% |
| | | Sororities: | 7% |

**Basis for selection.** 1200 SAT (exclusive of Writing) or 26 ACT, rank in top 15% of class, completion of required high school course work required for assured admission. All others reviewed for admission. In-state high school students finishing in top 10% of class automatically admitted to state public universities. Texas Higher Education Assessment test required for some based on high school performance.

**High school preparation.** College-preparatory program required. 18 units required; 24 recommended. Required and recommended units include English 4, mathematics 3.5-4, social studies 3-4, science 3 (laboratory 3), foreign language 2-3, computer science 1, visual/performing arts .5-1, academic electives 1.5-2.5. 0.5 health, 1.5 physical education recommended.

**2009-2010 Annual costs.** Tuition/fees: $10,340; $23,730 out-of-state. Tuition costs reflect guaranteed tuition rate for 2009-2010 incoming class. Room/board: $7,733. Books/supplies: $1,200. Personal expenses: $1,929.

**2008-2009 Financial aid. Need-based:** 712 full-time freshmen applied for aid; 496 were judged to have need; 478 of these received aid. Average need met was 68%. Average scholarship/grant was $8,016; average loan $3,208. 48% of total undergraduate aid awarded as scholarships/grants, 52% as loans/jobs. **Non-need-based:** Awarded to 1,614 full-time undergraduates, including 402 freshmen. Scholarships awarded for academics.

**Application procedures. Admission:** Closing date 7/1 (postmark date). $50 fee, may be waived for applicants with need. Admission notification on a rolling basis. **Financial aid:** Priority date 3/31, closing date 4/12. FAFSA required. Applicants notified on a rolling basis starting 3/1; must reply within 2 week(s) of notification.

**Academics. Special study options:** Accelerated study, combined bachelor's/graduate degree, cooperative education, cross-registration, distance learning, double major, dual enrollment of high school students, honors, independent study, internships, student-designed major, study abroad, teacher certification program, Washington semester, weekend college. 3-2 engineering and 2-2 transfer programs. **Credit/placement by examination:** AP, CLEP, IB, institutional tests. 30 credit hours maximum toward bachelor's degree. No limit on lower-level courses, 6 hours limit on upper-level courses. SAT Subject Tests in Math Levels I and II accepted for advanced placement. **Support services:** Learning center, pre-admission summer program, reduced course load, remedial instruction, study skills assistance, tutoring, writing center.

**Majors. Area/ethnic studies:** American, women's. **Biology:** General, biochemistry, molecular. **Business:** General, accounting, actuarial science, finance. **Communications:** Digital media. **Computer sciences:** General. **Engineering:** Computer, electrical, mechanical, software. **Foreign languages:** Comparative lit. **Health:** Audiology/speech pathology. **History:** General. **Interdisciplinary:** Cognitive science, neuroscience. **Liberal arts:** Arts/sciences. **Math:** General, applied, statistics. **Physical sciences:** Chemistry, geology, physics. **Psychology:** General. **Public administration:** General. **Social sciences:** Criminology, economics, geography, political science, sociology. **Visual/performing arts:** General, studio arts. **Other:** Interdisciplinary studies.

**Most popular majors.** Biology 8%, business/marketing 32%, engineering/engineering technologies 6%, interdisciplinary studies 13%, psychology 10%, social sciences 8%, visual/performing arts 7%.

**Computing on campus.** 630 workstations in library, computer center. Dormitories wired for high-speed internet access and linked to campus network. Commuter students can connect to campus network. Online course registration, online library, helpline, wireless network available.

**Student life. Freshman orientation:** Mandatory, $100 fee. Preregistration for classes offered. Family 1-day sessions and student 2-day sessions held in April, July and August. **Housing:** Coed dorms, apartments available. $100 partly refundable deposit, deadline 6/30. Pets allowed in dorm rooms. Living-learning communities for freshmen. **Activities:** Bands, choral groups, dance, drama, film society, international student organizations, literary magazine, music ensembles, musical theater, radio station, student government, student newspaper, symphony orchestra, TV station, College Republicans, University Democrats, black student alliance, Friendship Association of Chinese Students and Scholars, LULAC, Christians on Campus, Muslim student association, Habitat for Humanity, world aid organization, Alpha Phi Omega (service fraternity).

**Athletics.** NCAA. **Intercollegiate:** Baseball M, basketball, cross-country, golf, soccer, softball W, tennis, volleyball W. **Intramural:** Basketball, cheerleading, football (non-tackle), volleyball. **Team name:** Comets.

**Student services.** Alcohol/substance abuse counseling, career counseling, student employment services, financial aid counseling, health services, legal services, minority student services, on-campus daycare, personal counseling, placement for graduates, veterans' counselor, women's services. **Physically disabled:** Services for visually, speech, hearing impaired.

**Contact.** E-mail: interest@utdallas.edu
Phone: (972) 883-2270 Toll-free number: (800) 889-2443
Fax: (972) 883-2599
Curt Eley, VP of Enrollment Management, University of Texas at Dallas, Office of Enrollment Services, Richardson, TX 75083-0688

## University of Texas at El Paso

| El Paso, Texas | CB member |
|---|---|
| www.utep.edu | CB code: 6829 |

- Public 4-year university
- Commuter campus in very large city
- 17,110 degree-seeking undergraduates: 33% part-time, 55% women, 3% African American, 1% Asian American, 80% Hispanic American, 7% international
- 3,319 degree-seeking graduate students
- 99% of applicants admitted
- 32% graduate within 6 years

**General.** Founded in 1913. Regionally accredited. Bilingual community, programs, and student body. Located within 100 yards of Mexico. **Degrees:** 2,969 bachelor's awarded; master's, doctoral offered. **ROTC:** Army, Air Force. **Calendar:** Semester, extensive summer session. **Full-time faculty:** 695 total; 36% minority, 39% women. **Part-time faculty:** 463 total; 48% minority, 48% women. **Class size:** 35% < 20, 47% 20-39, 7% 40-49, 8% 50-99, 3% >100. **Special facilities:** Solar energy facility.

**Freshman class profile.** 5,809 applied, 5,742 admitted, 2,516 enrolled.

| Mid 50% test scores | | | |
|---|---|---|---|
| SAT critical reading: | 390-500 | Rank in top quarter: | 43% |
| SAT math: | 420-530 | Rank in top tenth: | 20% |
| ACT composite: | 16-21 | Return as sophomores: | 71% |
| GPA 3.75 or higher: | 7% | Out-of-state: | 2% |
| GPA 3.50-3.74: | 17% | International: | 4% |
| GPA 3.0-3.49: | 45% | | |
| GPA 2.0-2.99: | 27% | | |

**Basis for selection.** Minimum GED score of 45, or top half of high school class with 20 ACT or 920 SAT (exclusive of Writing). Provisional admission for in-state residents not meeting these criteria. For students in top quarter of high school class, any score acceptable. SAT or ACT, when required, may be used for counseling. Credit may be given for selected SAT Subject Tests.

**High school preparation.** College-preparatory program required. 21 units recommended. Recommended units include English 4, mathematics 3, social studies 2, history 2, science 3 and foreign language 2. 1 additional math for science and engineering majors.

**2009-2010 Annual costs.** Tuition/fees: $6,224; $14,534 out-of-state. Mexican citizens who show need may qualify for in-state tuition. Reported room-only cost based on double-occupancy apartment at $500 per month for nine months. Optional a la carte meal plan. Room only: $4,500.

**2008-2009 Financial aid. Need-based:** 1,641 full-time freshmen applied for aid; 1,338 were judged to have need; 1,324 of these received aid. Average need met was 81%. Average scholarship/grant was $8,218; average loan $4,033. 42% of total undergraduate aid awarded as scholarships/grants, 58% as loans/jobs. **Non-need-based:** Awarded to 1,728 full-time undergraduates, including 390 freshmen. Scholarships awarded for academics, alumni affiliation, art, athletics, job skills, leadership, minority status, music/drama, religious affiliation, ROTC, state residency. **Additional information:** Emergency loans available.

**Application procedures. Admission:** Priority date 5/1; deadline 7/31 (postmark date). No application fee. Admission notification on a rolling basis. Notification of early action applicants when admission file is complete. **Financial aid:** Closing date 3/15. FAFSA, institutional form required. Applicants notified by 6/30; must reply within 2 week(s) of notification.

**Academics. Special study options:** Accelerated study, combined bachelor's/graduate degree, cooperative education, cross-registration, distance learning, double major, dual enrollment of high school students, ESL, exchange student, honors, independent study, internships, study abroad, teacher certification program, weekend college. **Credit/placement by examination:** AP, CLEP, IB, institutional tests. **Support services:** Learning center, pre-admission summer program, reduced course load, remedial instruction, study skills assistance, tutoring, writing center.

**Majors. Area/ethnic studies:** Chicano/Hispanic-American/Latino, Latin American. **Biology:** General, microbiology. **Business:** General, accounting, business admin, finance, management information systems, managerial economics, marketing, operations. **Communications:** General, advertising, digital media, journalism, media studies, public relations. **Computer sciences:** General. **Conservation:** Environmental science. **Engineering:** Civil, electrical, industrial, mechanical, metallurgical. **Foreign languages:** Comparative lit, French, linguistics, Spanish. **Health:** Clinical lab science, health services, nursing (RN). **History:** General. **Math:** General, applied. **Parks/recreation:** Health/fitness. **Philosophy/religion:** Philosophy. **Physical sciences:** Chemistry, geology, geophysics, physics. **Protective services:** Criminal justice. **Psychology:** General. **Public administration:** Social work. **Social sciences:** Anthropology, political science, sociology. **Visual/performing arts:** Art, art history/conservation, ceramics, dance, dramatic, drawing, graphic design, metal/jewelry, music management, music performance, music theory/composition, painting, piano/organ, printmaking, sculpture, studio arts, voice/opera.

**Most popular majors.** Biology 6%, business/marketing 18%, engineering/engineering technologies 8%, health sciences 10%, interdisciplinary studies 24%.

**Computing on campus.** 2,500 workstations in library, computer center, student center. Dormitories wired for high-speed internet access. Commuter students can connect to campus network. Online course registration, online library, helpline, repair service, student web hosting, wireless network available.

**Student life. Freshman orientation:** Available. Preregistration for classes offered. 3-5 day program. **Housing:** Special housing for disabled, apartments available. **Activities:** Bands, choral groups, dance, drama, film society, literary magazine, music ensembles, musical theater, opera, radio station, student government, student newspaper, symphony orchestra, black student coalition, Mexican student organizations, Society of Hispanic Professional Engineers.

**Athletics.** NCAA. **Intercollegiate:** Basketball, cross-country, football (tackle) M, golf, rifle, soccer W, softball W, tennis, track and field, volleyball W. **Intramural:** Badminton, baseball M, basketball, bowling, fencing, football (tackle) M, golf, gymnastics, handball, racquetball, skiing, soccer, softball, squash, swimming, table tennis, tennis, track and field, volleyball, water polo, wrestling M. **Team name:** Miners.

**Student services.** Alcohol/substance abuse counseling, chaplain/spiritual director, career counseling, student employment services, financial aid counseling, health services, on-campus daycare, personal counseling, placement for graduates, veterans' counselor, women's services. **Physically disabled:** Services for visually, speech, hearing impaired.

**Contact.** E-mail: futureminer@utep.edu
Phone: (915) 747-5890 Fax: (915) 747-8893
Luisa Havens, Director of Admissions, University of Texas at El Paso, 500 West University Avenue, El Paso, TX 79968-0510

## University of Texas at San Antonio

| San Antonio, Texas | CB member |
|---|---|
| www.utsa.edu | CB code: 6919 |

- Public 4-year university
- Commuter campus in very large city
- 24,883 degree-seeking undergraduates: 21% part-time, 50% women, 9% African American, 7% Asian American, 44% Hispanic American, 2% international
- 3,892 degree-seeking graduate students
- 87% of applicants admitted
- SAT or ACT with writing required

**General.** Founded in 1969. Regionally accredited. Second campus in downtown area. **Degrees:** 3,806 bachelor's awarded; master's, doctoral offered. **ROTC:** Army, Air Force. **Location:** 15 miles from downtown. **Calendar:** Semester, limited summer session. **Full-time faculty:** 966 total; 72% have terminal degrees, 37% minority, 43% women. **Part-time faculty:** 255 total; 54% have terminal degrees, 31% minority, 48% women. **Class size:** 25% < 20, 43% 20-39, 10% 40-49, 14% 50-99, 8% >100. **Special facilities:** Institute of Texan cultures, center for archaeological research, neuroscience research center, center for water research, center for lasers and materials science, center for economic development, culture and policy institute, institute for music research, center for professional excellence.

**Freshman class profile.** 11,993 applied, 10,426 admitted, 4,883 enrolled.

| Mid 50% test scores | | Return as sophomores: | 56% |
|---|---|---|---|
| SAT critical reading: | 450-560 | Out-of-state: | 1% |
| SAT math: | 470-580 | Live on campus: | 43% |
| SAT writing: | 430-540 | International: | 2% |
| ACT composite: | 19-24 | Fraternities: | 2% |
| Rank in top quarter: | 38% | Sororities: | 1% |
| Rank in top tenth: | 10% | | |

**Basis for selection.** Texas residents who graduate in top 10% of high school graduating class admitted, regardless of ACT or SAT scores. Those not in top 10% must meet appropriate ACT or SAT scores based on class rank. If test score/rank criteria not met, additional factors may be taken into consideration. Out-of-state applicants must graduate in top half of graduating class in-addition to meeting corresponding ACT or SAT score requirements. **Homeschooled:** Conditional admissions decision based on SAT score over 1020 (exclusive of Writing) plus high school educational record (courses taken and grades earned) signed and dated by person responsible for conducting educational program. Upon high school graduation, final high school record indicating graduation date signed and dated by responsible educator must be submitted.

**High school preparation.** College-preparatory program recommended. 16.5 units recommended. Recommended units include English 4, mathematics 3, social studies 3.5, science 3, foreign language 2 and visual/performing arts 1. 1 or more fine arts recommended.

**2009-2010 Annual costs.** Tuition/fees: $7,527; $15,837 out-of-state. Room/board: $8,937. Books/supplies: $1,000. Personal expenses: $1,750.

**2008-2009 Financial aid. Need-based:** 3,699 full-time freshmen applied for aid; 2,496 were judged to have need; 2,381 of these received aid. Average need met was 61%. Average scholarship/grant was $7,089; average loan $3,187. 47% of total undergraduate aid awarded as scholarships/grants, 53% as loans/jobs. **Non-need-based:** Awarded to 3,003 full-time undergraduates, including 1,130 freshmen. Scholarships awarded for academics, alumni affiliation, art, athletics, job skills, leadership, music/drama, ROTC, state residency.

**Application procedures. Admission:** Priority date 5/1; deadline 7/1 (receipt date). $40 fee, may be waived for applicants with need. Admission notification 9/1. Admission notification on a rolling basis. **Financial aid:** Priority date 3/31; no closing date. FAFSA, institutional form required. Applicants notified on a rolling basis starting 4/1; must reply within 4 week(s) of notification.

**Academics.** Freshman Initiative includes learning communities and freshman seminar program, enhancing academic services for new students in order to increase retention and success in college. **Special study options:** Accelerated study, cooperative education, distance learning, double major, dual enrollment of high school students, ESL, exchange student, honors, independent study, internships, study abroad, teacher certification program. 2-2 programs with Alamo Community College District, Southwest Texas Junior College, Laredo Junior College, Victoria College, Del Mar College, Coastal Bend Community College, Austin Community College; telecampus agreement with UT System. **Credit/placement by examination:** AP, CLEP, institutional tests. Some departments have limits on number of credits earned by examination. **Support services:** Learning center, pre-admission summer program, remedial instruction, study skills assistance, tutoring, writing center.

**Majors. Architecture:** Architecture, interior. **Area/ethnic studies:** American, Chicano/Hispanic-American/Latino, women's. **Biology:** General. **Business:** General, accounting, actuarial science, business admin, finance, human resources, international, management information systems, management science, managerial economics, marketing, operations, real estate, sales/distribution, tourism/travel. **Communications:** General, media studies, public relations. **Computer sciences:** General, security. **Conservation:** Environmental science. **Construction:** Site management. **Engineering:** Civil, electrical, mechanical. **Foreign languages:** Classics, French, German, Spanish. **Health:** Clinical lab science, health services. **History:** General. **Interdisciplinary:** Biological/physical sciences. **Liberal arts:** Humanities. **Math:** General, statistics. **Parks/recreation:** Health/fitness. **Philosophy/religion:** Philosophy. **Physical sciences:** General, chemistry, geology, physics. **Protective services:** Criminal justice. **Psychology:** General. **Social sciences:** Anthropology, geography, political science, sociology. **Visual/performing arts:** Art, art history/conservation, music management, music performance, music theory/composition, studio arts. **Other:** Multi/Interdisciplinary studies, Social sciences.

**Most popular majors.** Biology 10%, business/marketing 28%, interdisciplinary studies 12%, psychology 7%, social sciences 7%.

**Computing on campus.** 550 workstations in dormitories, library, computer center, student center. Dormitories wired for high-speed internet access and linked to campus network. Commuter students can connect to campus network. Online course registration, online library, helpline, repair service, student web hosting, wireless network available.

**Student life. Freshman orientation:** Mandatory, $60 fee. Preregistration for classes offered. One-day sessions held throughout the year; optional 2-day camp held in August. **Housing:** Coed dorms, special housing for disabled, apartments available. $200 nonrefundable deposit. **Activities:** Bands, campus ministries, choral groups, dance, drama, international student organizations, literary magazine, music ensembles, opera, student government, student newspaper, symphony orchestra, IDS student association, pre-med society, Golden Key national honor society, Intervarsity Christian Fellowship, S/B Alpha Chi national honor society, Catholic student association, Mortar Board national college senior honor society, Texas Association of Chicanos in Higher Education.

**Athletics.** NCAA. **Intercollegiate:** Baseball M, basketball, cross-country, golf, soccer W, softball W, tennis, track and field, volleyball W. **Intramural:** Badminton, basketball, bowling, football (non-tackle), golf, racquetball, soccer, softball, table tennis, tennis, volleyball, weight lifting. **Team name:** Roadrunners.

**Student services.** Career counseling, student employment services, financial aid counseling, health services, personal counseling, placement for graduates, veterans' counselor. **Physically disabled:** Services for visually, speech, hearing impaired.

**Contact.** E-mail: prospects@utsa.edu
Phone: (210) 458-8000 Toll-free number: (800) 669-0919
Fax: (210) 458-2001
George Norton, Director of Admissions, University of Texas at San Antonio, One UTSA Circle, San Antonio, TX 78249-0617

---

## University of Texas at Tyler
**Tyler, Texas**  CB member
**www.uttyler.edu**  CB code: 0389

- Public 4-year university
- Commuter campus in small city
- 5,035 degree-seeking undergraduates: 23% part-time, 58% women, 10% African American, 2% Asian American, 8% Hispanic American, 1% Native American, 1% international
- 902 degree-seeking graduate students
- 86% of applicants admitted
- SAT or ACT (ACT writing recommended) required
- 35% graduate within 6 years

**General.** Founded in 1971. Regionally accredited. Off-campus sites at Palestine and Longview. Internet courses and telecampus available. **Degrees:** 1,187 bachelor's awarded; master's, doctoral offered. **Location:** 80 miles from Dallas. **Calendar:** Semester, limited summer session. **Full-time faculty:** 261 total; 75% have terminal degrees, 12% minority, 47% women. **Part-time faculty:** 126 total; 29% have terminal degrees, 5% minority, 52% women. **Class size:** 33% < 20, 45% 20-39, 10% 40-49, 10% 50-99, 2% >100. **Special facilities:** Desktop manufacturing lab, computer-based virtual lab instruments.

**Freshman class profile.** 1,568 applied, 1,347 admitted, 596 enrolled.

| Mid 50% test scores | | GPA 2.0-2.99: | 16% |
|---|---|---|---|
| SAT critical reading: | 460-580 | Rank in top quarter: | 56% |
| SAT math: | 490-590 | Rank in top tenth: | 19% |
| ACT composite: | 20-25 | Out-of-state: | 2% |
| GPA 3.75 or higher: | 22% | Fraternities: | 1% |
| GPA 3.50-3.74: | 21% | Sororities: | 4% |
| GPA 3.0-3.49: | 40% | | |

**Basis for selection.** Top 10% accepted automatically, others admitted based on ACT/SAT scores and high school preparation.

**High school preparation.** College-preparatory program recommended. Required and recommended units include English 4, mathematics 3-4, social studies 3, science 3 (laboratory 3) and foreign language 2. Math requirement must be algebra I and higher. 4 mathematics recommended for science, engineering, and other technical fields.

**2009-2010 Annual costs.** Tuition/fees: $6,042; $14,472 out-of-state. Room/board: $8,016. Books/supplies: $900. Personal expenses: $1,148.

**2008-2009 Financial aid. Need-based:** 414 full-time freshmen applied for aid; 287 were judged to have need; 282 of these received aid. Average need met was 58%. Average scholarship/grant was $7,496; average loan $2,256. 42% of total undergraduate aid awarded as scholarships/grants, 58% as loans/jobs. **Non-need-based:** Awarded to 466 full-time undergraduates, including 142 freshmen. Scholarships awarded for academics, art, music/drama. **Additional information:** Apply early for all programs.

**Application procedures. Admission:** No deadline. $25 fee, may be waived for applicants with need. Admission notification on a rolling basis beginning on or about 9/1. Must reply by May 1 or within 4 week(s) if notified thereafter. **Financial aid:** Priority date 4/1; no closing date. FAFSA, institutional form required. Applicants notified on a rolling basis starting 4/15; must reply within 2 week(s) of notification.

**Academics. Special study options:** Cooperative education, distance learning, double major, honors, independent study, internships, student-designed major, study abroad, teacher certification program. **Credit/placement by examination:** AP, CLEP, IB, SAT, ACT, institutional tests. AP, CLEP and International Baccalaureate awarded transfer credit with no maximum limit. **Support services:** Learning center, remedial instruction, study skills assistance, tutoring, writing center.

**Honors college/program.** Admission Committee typically looks at students with minimum 28 ACT composite score or minimum 1860 SAT combined score, and 3.5 or higher high school GPA.

**Majors. Biology:** General. **Business:** Accounting, business admin, construction management, finance, managerial economics, marketing, sales/distribution, training/development. **Communications:** Journalism. **Computer sciences:** General. **Engineering:** Civil, electrical, mechanical. **Engineering technology:** General, industrial, occupational safety. **Foreign languages:** General, Spanish. **Health:** Clinical lab science, community health services, nursing (RN). **History:** General. **Math:** General. **Parks/recreation:** Health/fitness. **Physical sciences:** Chemistry. **Protective services:** Criminal justice. **Psychology:** General. **Social sciences:** Political science, sociology. **Visual/performing arts:** Art.

**Most popular majors.** Business/marketing 23%, engineering/engineering technologies 7%, English 6%, health sciences 19%, interdisciplinary studies 15%, parks/recreation 6%, psychology 7%.

**Computing on campus.** 175 workstations in dormitories, library, computer center, student center. Dormitories wired for high-speed internet access and linked to campus network. Commuter students can connect to campus network. Online course registration, online library, wireless network available.

**Student life. Freshman orientation:** Mandatory, $35 fee. Preregistration for classes offered. One-day orientation in summer for students and parents. **Housing:** Coed dorms available. **Activities:** Bands, campus ministries, choral groups, international student organizations, literary magazine, music ensembles, Model UN, musical theater, opera, student government, student newspaper, Bible study fellowship, University Democrats, Nurses Christian Fellowship, Wesley Foundation Student Fellowship, Baptist student ministry, Patriots Special Olympics Texas Volunteers (Patriots SOTX), University Mothers Against Drunk Driving (UMADD), Indian student association.

**Athletics.** NCAA. **Intercollegiate:** Baseball M, basketball, cheerleading, cross-country, golf, soccer, softball W, tennis, track and field, volleyball W. **Intramural:** Baseball M, basketball, bowling, football (non-tackle), football (tackle), golf, racquetball, soccer, softball, table tennis, tennis, volleyball. **Team name:** Patriots.

**Student services.** Adult student services, alcohol/substance abuse counseling, career counseling, student employment services, financial aid counseling, health services, personal counseling, veterans' counselor. **Physically disabled:** Services for visually, speech, hearing impaired.

**Contact.** E-mail: admissions@mail.uttyl.edu
Phone: (903) 566-7202 Toll-free number: (800) 888-9537
Fax: (903) 566-7068
Sarah Bowdin, Director of Admissions, University of Texas at Tyler, 3900 University Boulevard, Tyler, TX 75799

## University of Texas Health Science Center at Houston
Houston, Texas
www.uth.tmc.edu                               CB code: 6888

- Public two-year upper-division university and health science college
- Commuter campus in very large city
- Interview required

**General.** Founded in 1972. Regionally accredited. Located in the Texas Medical Center. **Degrees:** 240 bachelor's awarded; master's, doctoral, professional offered. **Location:** 5 miles from downtown. **Calendar:** Semester, limited summer session. **Full-time faculty:** 925 total. **Part-time faculty:** 275 total.

**Student profile.** 462 degree-seeking undergraduates, 3,507 graduate students. 70% entered as juniors.

**Basis for selection.** College transcript, interview required. Applicants must submit official transcript from all previous institutions. Application closing dates, admissions policies vary by program. Dental hygiene application closing date: December 31. Minimum number of credits: 28. Nursing application closing date: January 1. Minimum number of credits: 60. Transfer accepted as sophomores, juniors.

**2009-2010 Annual costs.** Tuition/fees: $6,222; $23,286 out-of-state. Costs may vary by program. Books/supplies: $1,050.

**Financial aid.** All financial aid based on need.

**Application procedures. Admission:** Deadline 12/31. $30 fee. **Financial aid:** FAFSA, institutional form required.

**Academics.** Upper division bachelor's program for nursing, with accelerated RN-master's program. **Special study options:** Accelerated study, combined bachelor's/graduate degree, distance learning. **Credit/placement by examination:** AP, CLEP. All CLEP must appear on college transcript with credit hours and grade.

**Majors. Health:** Dental hygiene, nursing (RN).

**Computing on campus.** PC or laptop required. Helpline available.

**Student life. Housing:** Apartments available. University operates apartment complex as only student housing available. Complex located approximately 1 mile from campus. **Activities:** Student government.

**Student services.** Adult student services, alcohol/substance abuse counseling, financial aid counseling, health services, on-campus daycare, personal counseling. **Physically disabled:** Services for visually, hearing impaired.

**Contact.** E-mail: admissions@uth.tmc.edu
Phone: (713) 500-3361 Fax: (713) 500-3356
Carrie Streeter, Associate Registrar, University of Texas Health Science Center at Houston, Box 20036, Houston, TX 77225

## University of Texas Health Science Center at San Antonio
San Antonio, Texas
www.uthscsa.edu                               CB code: 6908

- Public two-year upper-division university and health science college
- Commuter campus in very large city

**General.** Founded in 1969. Regionally accredited. Located in South Texas Medical Center. **Degrees:** 349 bachelor's awarded; master's, doctoral, professional offered. **Location:** 10 miles from downtown. **Calendar:** Semester, limited summer session. **Full-time faculty:** 1,154 total. **Part-time faculty:** 355 total.

**Student profile.** 854 degree-seeking undergraduates, 2,369 graduate students. 99% entered as juniors, 1% entered as seniors.

**Basis for selection.** High school transcript, college transcript required. Admission varies with each program. In many cases, academic records and interview required. Application closing and priority dates vary with each program. Transfer accepted as juniors.

**2009-2010 Annual costs.** Tuition/fees: $6,483; $16,651 out-of-state. Tuition and fees vary by program. Reported costs are for nursing program. Books/supplies: $850. Personal expenses: $1,100.

**Financial aid. Additional information:** Students strongly advised to provide parental information on need analysis form regardless of dependency status.

**Application procedures. Admission:** $45 fee. Application must be submitted online. Application fees vary from $10 to $55 depending on program. **Financial aid:** FAFSA, institutional form required.

**Academics. Special study options:** Combined bachelor's/graduate degree, cross-registration, distance learning, internships. PharmD program with University of Texas-Austin; joint degree Health Professions program with University of Texas-San Antonio. **Credit/placement by examination:** CLEP, institutional tests.

**Majors. Health:** Clinical lab science, dental hygiene, dental lab technology, nursing (RN), physician assistant, respiratory therapy technology.

**Computing on campus.** 50 workstations in library. Commuter students can connect to campus network. Helpline, wireless network available.

**Student life. Activities:** Student government, student newspaper, Texas Association of Mexican-American Medical Students, Latin-American Nursing Student Association, Diversified Dental Students.

**Athletics. Intramural:** Baseball M, basketball, softball, tennis, volleyball.

**Student services.** Adult student services, alcohol/substance abuse counseling, financial aid counseling, health services, personal counseling, veterans' counselor.

**Contact.** E-mail: registrars@uthscsa.edu
Phone: (210) 567-2621 Fax: (210) 567-2685
Amy McGilvray, Registrar, University of Texas Health Science Center at San Antonio, 7703 Floyd Curl Drive, San Antonio, TX 78229-3900

## University of Texas Medical Branch at Galveston
**Galveston, Texas**
www.utmb.edu                          CB code: 6887

▶ Public two-year upper-division health science and nursing college
▶ Commuter campus in small city

**General.** Founded in 1881. Regionally accredited. **Degrees:** 251 bachelor's awarded; master's, doctoral, professional offered. **Location:** 50 miles from Houston. **Calendar:** Semester, limited summer session.

**Student profile.** 492 degree-seeking undergraduates, 1,862 degree-seeking graduate students.

| | | | |
|---|---|---|---|
| Women: | 80% | International: | 2% |
| African American: | 18% | Part-time: | 36% |
| Asian American: | 18% | Out-of-state: | 1% |
| Hispanic American: | 14% | 25 or older: | 65% |
| Native American: | 1% | | |

**Basis for selection.** College transcript required. Students with 60 hours from accredited college or university considered. Nonresident enrollment limited by legislature to not more than 10% of any class. Transfer decisions based on competitive comparison of transcripts, allied health experience, departmental testing, and personal interviews. Specific prerequisites and application closing dates vary by program. Transfer accepted as juniors, seniors.

**2009-2010 Annual costs.** Tuition/fees: $5,652; $14,082 out-of-state. Costs reported are for Allied Health Sciences program. Tuition and fees vary for other programs.

**Financial aid. Non-need-based:** Scholarships awarded for academics, minority status, state residency.

**Application procedures. Admission:** $50 fee. Application must be submitted online. Application closing dates vary with school and program. **Financial aid:** FAFSA required.

**Academics. Special study options:** Distance learning, independent study, internships. **Credit/placement by examination:** CLEP, IB. 30 credit hours maximum toward bachelor's degree.

**Majors. Health:** Clinical lab science, nursing (RN), respiratory therapy technology.

**Computing on campus.** Dormitories wired for high-speed internet access and linked to campus network. Commuter students can connect to campus network. Online library, helpline, repair service, wireless network available.

**Student life. Housing:** Coed dorms, apartments, fraternity/sorority housing available. $200 fully refundable deposit. **Activities:** Campus ministries, international student organizations, student government, Wesley Foundation, Newman Center, sports clubs, Christian Medical and Dental Society, Jewish student and faculty organization, multicultural awareness council, student national medical association, Texas Association of Latin American Medical Students.

**Athletics. Intramural:** Basketball, football (non-tackle), soccer, softball, volleyball.

**Student services.** Alcohol/substance abuse counseling, chaplain/spiritual director, career counseling, student employment services, financial aid counseling, health services, legal services, on-campus daycare, personal counseling, veterans' counselor, women's services. **Physically disabled:** Services for visually, speech, hearing impaired.

**Contact.** E-mail: enrollment.services@utmb.edu
Phone: (409) 772-1215 Fax: (409) 772-4466
University of Texas Medical Branch at Galveston, 301 University Boulevard, Galveston, TX 77555-1305

## University of Texas of the Permian Basin
**Odessa, Texas**                          CB member
www.utpb.edu                          CB code: 0448

▶ Public 4-year university
▶ Commuter campus in small city
▶ 2,600 degree-seeking undergraduates: 26% part-time, 59% women, 5% African American, 1% Asian American, 43% Hispanic American, 1% Native American, 1% international
▶ 669 degree-seeking graduate students
▶ 85% of applicants admitted
▶ SAT or ACT (ACT writing optional) required
▶ 31% graduate within 6 years

**General.** Founded in 1969. Regionally accredited. **Degrees:** 596 bachelor's awarded; master's offered. **Location:** 150 miles from Lubbock, 350 miles from Dallas. **Calendar:** Semester, extensive summer session. **Full-time faculty:** 119 total; 82% have terminal degrees, 24% minority, 50% women. **Part-time faculty:** 101 total; 23% have terminal degrees, 16% minority, 54% women. **Class size:** 35% < 20, 47% 20-39, 6% 40-49, 11% 50-99, less than 1% >100.

**Freshman class profile.** 884 applied, 747 admitted, 398 enrolled.

| Mid 50% test scores | | Rank in top tenth: | 23% |
|---|---|---|---|
| SAT critical reading: | 450-540 | Return as sophomores: | 62% |
| SAT math: | 460-560 | Out-of-state: | 3% |
| ACT composite: | 19-23 | Live on campus: | 48% |
| Rank in top quarter: | 53% | | |

**Basis for selection.** Secondary school record, class rank, test scores important. Foreign students whose native language is not English must take TOEFL. Requirement may be waived for non-English speakers transferring from a U.S. college or high school. Essay not required but considered if provided. **Homeschooled:** No additional requirements. Home-schooled students reviewed on an individual basis. **Learning Disabled:** No special requirements but must meet minimum admission standards.

**High school preparation.** College-preparatory program recommended. 24 units required. Required units include English 4, mathematics 3, social studies 3.5, science 3 (laboratory 3), foreign language 2, computer science 1, visual/performing arts 1, academic electives 3.5.

**2009-2010 Annual costs.** Tuition/fees: $5,599; $13,909 out-of-state. New Mexico residents living in areas contiguous to Texas border pay in-district rate. Books/supplies: $910. Personal expenses: $1,832.

**2008-2009 Financial aid. Need-based:** 231 full-time freshmen applied for aid; 157 were judged to have need; 157 of these received aid. Average need met was 24%. Average scholarship/grant was $6,516; average loan $1,979. 53% of total undergraduate aid awarded as scholarships/grants, 47% as loans/jobs. **Non-need-based:** Awarded to 1,194 full-time undergraduates, including 317 freshmen. Scholarships awarded for academics, alumni affiliation, art, athletics, leadership, music/drama.

**Application procedures. Admission:** Closing date 7/15 (postmark date). No application fee. Admission notification on a rolling basis. **Financial aid:** Priority date 3/1; no closing date. FAFSA required. Applicants notified on a rolling basis starting 3/15.

**Academics. Special study options:** Distance learning, double major, dual enrollment of high school students, ESL, honors, independent study, internships, study abroad, teacher certification program. **Credit/placement by examination:** CLEP, SAT, ACT, institutional tests. 28 credit hours maximum toward bachelor's degree. Credit/placement awarded on AP or CLEP exams, special exams administered by School of Business. **Support services:** Learning center, remedial instruction, study skills assistance, tutoring, writing center.

**Majors. Biology:** General. **Business:** Accounting, business admin, finance, managerial economics, marketing. **Communications:** General. **Computer sciences:** General, information systems. **Conservation:** Environmental science. **Engineering:** Mechanical. **Engineering technology:** Industrial. **Family/consumer sciences:** Family studies. **Foreign languages:** Spanish. **Health:** Athletic training. **History:** General. **Liberal arts:** Humanities. **Math:** General. **Parks/recreation:** Health/fitness. **Physical sciences:** Chemistry, geology. **Protective services:** Criminal justice. **Psychology:** General. **Public**

administration: Social work. **Social sciences:** Criminology, political science, sociology. **Visual/performing arts:** Art. **Other:** Multidisciplinary studies.

**Most popular majors.** Biology 6%, business/marketing 23%, family/consumer sciences 12%, history 6%, parks/recreation 8%, psychology 10%, social sciences 9%.

**Computing on campus.** 170 workstations in dormitories, library, computer center. Dormitories wired for high-speed internet access and linked to campus network. Commuter students can connect to campus network. Online course registration, online library, helpline, wireless network available.

**Student life. Freshman orientation:** Mandatory, $75 fee. Preregistration for classes offered. Choice of three separate 3-day sessions in June, July, August, includes some meals and lodging for out-of-town students; 1-day orientation in January for students entering in Spring; 1-day express orientation in August available. **Housing:** Coed dorms, apartments available. $200 fully refundable deposit, deadline 7/15. Family housing units. **Activities:** Bands, campus ministries, choral groups, dance, drama, international student organizations, literary magazine, music ensembles, student government, student newspaper, symphony orchestra, Baptist student ministries, black leadership conference, Catholic student organization, Falcons for Christ, Campus Crusade for Christ, College Republicans.

**Athletics.** NCAA. **Intercollegiate:** Baseball M, basketball, cheerleading, cross-country, soccer, softball W, swimming, volleyball W. **Intramural:** Basketball, football (non-tackle), racquetball, tennis, volleyball. **Team name:** Falcons.

**Student services.** Adult student services, alcohol/substance abuse counseling, career counseling, services for economically disadvantaged, student employment services, financial aid counseling, health services, minority student services, personal counseling.

**Contact.** E-mail: admissions@utpb.edu
Phone: (432) 552-2605 Toll-free number: (866) 552-8872
Fax: (432) 552-3605
Scott Smiley, Director of Admissions, University of Texas of the Permian Basin, 4901 East University, Odessa, TX 79762

## University of Texas Southwestern Medical Center at Dallas
**Dallas, Texas**
www.utsouthwestern.edu                    CB code: 0273

▸ Public two-year upper-division university and health science college
▸ Commuter campus in very large city
▸ 41% of applicants admitted
▸ Application essay required

**General.** Founded in 1943. Regionally accredited. Four teaching hospitals adjoin campus. **Degrees:** 43 bachelor's awarded; master's, doctoral, professional offered. **Articulation:** Agreements with Dallas County Community College District, Collin County Community College, Tarrant County College District. **Location:** 3 miles from downtown. **Calendar:** Semester, limited summer session. **Full-time faculty:** 1,539 total. **Part-time faculty:** 425 total. **Class size:** 88% < 20, 12% 20-39.

**Student profile.** 90 degree-seeking undergraduates, 2,344 degree-seeking graduate students. 91 applied as first time-transfer students, 37 admitted, 28 enrolled. 92% entered as juniors, 8% entered as seniors.

| | | | |
|---|---|---|---|
| Women: | 78% | Out-of-state: | 8% |
| Part-time: | 14% | 25 or older: | 47% |

**Basis for selection.** College transcript, application essay required. Application closing dates vary by program. No limit on transferable credits. Students must complete prescribed professional curriculum and be Texas Core Curriculum complete. Transfer accepted as juniors, seniors.

**2009-2010 Annual costs.** Tuition/fees: $4,408; $12,838 out-of-state. Tuition and fees are based on UT Southwestern School of Health Professions. Books/supplies: $821.

**Application procedures. Admission:** Rolling admission. $10 fee. **Financial aid:** Priority date 3/1. Applicants notified on a rolling basis starting 4/1; must reply within 3 weeks of notification.

**Academics. Special study options:** Cross-registration, distance learning, independent study, internships. **Credit/placement by examination:** CLEP, institutional tests. Credit granted in English, government and history via advanced standing exams. Cannot exceed 3 semester hours in each subject.

**Majors. Health:** Clinical lab science, dietetics, orthotics/prosthetics.

**Computing on campus.** 150 workstations in library, computer center. Commuter students can connect to campus network. Online library, helpline available.

**Student life. Activities:** Student Dietetic Association, student membership in American Physical Therapy Association, American Academy of Physician Assistants, American Dietetic Association, American Society for Medical Technology, National Rehabilitation Association, American Society of Allied Health Professions.

**Athletics. Intramural:** Basketball, golf, softball, table tennis, tennis, volleyball.

**Student services.** Career counseling, financial aid counseling, health services, personal counseling, placement for graduates, veterans' counselor.

**Contact.** E-mail: admissions@utsouthwestern.edu
Phone: (214) 648-5617 Fax: (214) 648-3289
Anne McLane, Associate Director of Admissions, University of Texas Southwestern Medical Center at Dallas, 5323 Harry Hines Boulevard, Dallas, TX 75390-9162

## University of Texas: Pan American
**Edinburg, Texas**                         CB member
www.utpa.edu                               CB code: 6570

▸ Public 4-year university
▸ Commuter campus in small city
▸ 15,705 degree-seeking undergraduates: 25% part-time, 56% women, 1% African American, 1% Asian American, 90% Hispanic American, 3% international
▸ 2,316 degree-seeking graduate students
▸ 68% of applicants admitted
▸ SAT or ACT (ACT writing optional) required
▸ 36% graduate within 6 years

**General.** Founded in 1927. Regionally accredited. Hispanic-serving institution. **Degrees:** 2,660 bachelor's awarded; master's, doctoral offered. **ROTC:** Army. **Location:** 250 miles from San Antonio, 300 miles from Austin. **Calendar:** Semester, extensive summer session. **Full-time faculty:** 653 total; 81% have terminal degrees, 43% minority, 38% women. **Part-time faculty:** 162 total; 62% have terminal degrees, 60% minority, 45% women. **Class size:** 17% < 20, 53% 20-39, 10% 40-49, 19% 50-99, 2% >100. **Special facilities:** Coastal studies laboratory on South Padre Island.

**Freshman class profile.** 6,531 applied, 4,433 admitted, 2,882 enrolled.

| Mid 50% test scores | | Rank in top quarter: | 45% |
|---|---|---|---|
| SAT critical reading: | 410-510 | Rank in top tenth: | 17% |
| SAT math: | 430-530 | Return as sophomores: | 74% |
| SAT writing: | 400-500 | Out-of-state: | 2% |
| ACT composite: | 17-21 | | |

**Basis for selection.** For regular admission, rank in top quartile of class or acceptable ACT/SAT scores required. Students who do not meet criteria for admission placed in PEP (Provisional Enrollment Program). **Home-schooled:** Students graduating from a private or home school required to file completed Texas Private High School Certification with transcript.

**High school preparation.** 24 units required. Required units include English 4, mathematics 3, social studies 3.5, science 3, foreign language 2, academic electives 3.5, .5 economics, 1 fine arts, .5 speech, 1 technology. Algebra 2 required of business and engineering majors. Geometry, trigonometry, chemistry, and physics required of engineering majors.

**2009-2010 Annual costs.** Tuition/fees: $5,425; $13,735 out-of-state. Mexican citizens may be eligible for in-state tuition rates. Room/board: $5,294. Books/supplies: $1,000.

**2008-2009 Financial aid. Need-based:** 2,148 full-time freshmen applied for aid; 2,064 were judged to have need; 2,064 of these received aid. Average need met was 76%. Average scholarship/grant was $9,769; average loan $2,295. 70% of total undergraduate aid awarded as scholarships/grants, 30% as loans/jobs. **Non-need-based:** Awarded to 525 full-time undergraduates, including 102 freshmen. Scholarships awarded for academics, alumni affiliation, art, athletics, leadership.

**Application procedures. Admission:** Priority date 2/1; deadline 8/11 (receipt date). No application fee. Admission notification on a rolling basis.

**Financial aid:** Priority date 4/1; no closing date. FAFSA required. Applicants notified on a rolling basis starting 3/15; must reply within 2 week(s) of notification.

**Academics. Special study options:** Accelerated study, combined bachelor's/graduate degree, cooperative education, distance learning, double major, dual enrollment of high school students, ESL, exchange student, honors, independent study, internships, study abroad, teacher certification program, weekend college. Concurrent enrollment (high school students taking limited number of college classes either on campus or through distance learning). **Credit/placement by examination:** AP, CLEP, IB, institutional tests. 45 credit hours maximum toward bachelor's degree. **Support services:** Learning center, pre-admission summer program, remedial instruction, study skills assistance, tutoring, writing center.

**Majors. Area/ethnic studies:** American, Chicano/Hispanic-American/Latino. **Biology:** General. **Business:** Accounting, business admin, finance, international, management information systems, marketing. **Communications:** General, journalism. **Computer sciences:** General, computer science. **Conservation:** Environmental science. **Engineering:** Computer, electrical, industrial, manufacturing, mechanical. **Foreign languages:** French, Spanish. **Health:** Audiology/speech pathology, clinical lab science, dietetics, health services, nursing (RN), physician assistant, substance abuse counseling, vocational rehab counseling. **History:** General. **Legal studies:** Prelaw. **Math:** General. **Parks/recreation:** Health/fitness. **Philosophy/religion:** Philosophy. **Physical sciences:** Chemistry, physics. **Protective services:** Law enforcement admin. **Psychology:** General. **Public administration:** Social work. **Social sciences:** General, anthropology, economics, political science, sociology. **Visual/performing arts:** Dance, dramatic, music performance, studio arts. **Other:** Applied arts and sciences, Rehabilitation services-deaf studies.

**Most popular majors.** Biology 7%, business/marketing 18%, English 6%, health sciences 12%, interdisciplinary studies 14%.

**Computing on campus.** 900 workstations in dormitories, library, computer center. Dormitories wired for high-speed internet access and linked to campus network. Commuter students can connect to campus network. Online course registration, online library, helpline, student web hosting, wireless network available.

**Student life. Freshman orientation:** Mandatory, $15 fee. Preregistration for classes offered. Several 1-day sessions held prior to beginning of semester. **Housing:** Coed dorms, single-sex dorms, apartments available. $75 fully refundable deposit, deadline 7/1. **Activities:** Bands, campus ministries, choral groups, dance, drama, international student organizations, music ensembles, musical theater, student government, student newspaper, symphony orchestra, Episcopal Canterbury Association, Latter-day Saints student association, Baha'i association, Baptist student union, Campus Crusade for Christ, Fellowship of Christian Athletes, Asian American students association, Society of Hispanic Professional Engineers.

**Athletics.** NCAA. **Intercollegiate:** Baseball M, basketball, cross-country, golf, tennis, track and field, volleyball W. **Intramural:** Badminton, basketball, bowling, cheerleading, football (non-tackle), golf, racquetball, soccer, softball, tennis, volleyball. **Team name:** Broncs/Lady Broncs.

**Student services.** Alcohol/substance abuse counseling, career counseling, services for economically disadvantaged, student employment services, financial aid counseling, health services, on-campus daycare, personal counseling, placement for graduates, veterans' counselor, women's services. **Physically disabled:** Services for visually, speech, hearing impaired.

**Contact.** E-mail: admissions@utpa.edu
Phone: (956) 381-2999 Toll-free number: (866) 441-8872
Fax: (956) 381-2212
Magdalena Hinojosa, Dean of Admissions & Enrollment Services, University of Texas: Pan American, 1201 West University Drive, Edinburg, TX 78539-2999

## University of the Incarnate Word

**San Antonio, Texas**  **CB member**
**www.uiw.edu**  **CB code: 6303**

- Private 4-year university and liberal arts college affiliated with Roman Catholic Church
- Commuter campus in very large city
- 5,197 degree-seeking undergraduates: 35% part-time, 65% women, 7% African American, 3% Asian American, 57% Hispanic American, 3% international
- 1,537 degree-seeking graduate students
- 66% of applicants admitted
- SAT or ACT (ACT writing optional) required
- 42% graduate within 6 years

**General.** Founded in 1881. Regionally accredited. Off-campus courses available in the San Antonio, Corpus Christi and Phoenix areas, as well as online. Two international campuses in Mexico, China. **Degrees:** 893 bachelor's, 7 associate awarded; master's, doctoral, professional offered. **ROTC:** Army, Air Force. **Location:** 5 miles from downtown. **Calendar:** Semester, extensive summer session. **Full-time faculty:** 219 total; 79% have terminal degrees, 30% minority, 54% women. **Part-time faculty:** 349 total; 14% have terminal degrees, 39% minority, 57% women. **Class size:** 55% < 20, 43% 20-39, 1% 40-49, less than 1% 50-99.

**Freshman class profile.** 3,519 applied, 2,311 admitted, 744 enrolled.

| Mid 50% test scores | | | |
|---|---|---|---|
| SAT critical reading: | 430-550 | Rank in top quarter: | 52% |
| SAT math: | 440-560 | Rank in top tenth: | 23% |
| SAT writing: | 420-530 | Return as sophomores: | 67% |
| ACT composite: | 18-23 | Out-of-state: | 3% |
| GPA 3.75 or higher: | 28% | Live on campus: | 63% |
| GPA 3.50-3.74: | 32% | International: | 3% |
| GPA 3.0-3.49: | 32% | Fraternities: | 9% |
| GPA 2.0-2.99: | 7% | Sororities: | 10% |

**Basis for selection.** Test scores and school achievement record most important. Rolling policy for submission of test scores. Interview recommended for students with weaker academic record. **Homeschooled:** Statement describing homeschool structure and mission, transcript of courses and grades required. Required to submit copy of SAT or ACT exam scores. Interview, letters of recommendation, assessment testing may be required.

**High school preparation.** College-preparatory program required. 16 units required; 18 recommended. Required and recommended units include English 4, mathematics 3-4, social studies 3-4, science 3, foreign language 2 and visual/performing arts 1.

**2010-2011 Annual costs.** Tuition/fees: $21,890. Room/board: $9,220. Books/supplies: $1,200. Personal expenses: $1,620.

**2009-2010 Financial aid. Need-based:** 637 full-time freshmen applied for aid; 574 were judged to have need; 574 of these received aid. Average need met was 66%. Average scholarship/grant was $13,345; average loan $3,372. 55% of total undergraduate aid awarded as scholarships/grants, 45% as loans/jobs. **Non-need-based:** Awarded to 2,142 full-time undergraduates, including 626 freshmen. Scholarships awarded for academics, alumni affiliation, art, athletics, leadership, music/drama, religious affiliation, ROTC, state residency. **Additional information:** Students encouraged to pursue outside scholarship programs.

**Application procedures. Admission:** Priority date 2/1; no deadline. $20 fee, may be waived for applicants with need. Admission notification on a rolling basis. Must reply by May 1 or within 4 week(s) if notified thereafter. Notification approximately 2 weeks following submission. **Financial aid:** Priority date 4/1; no closing date. FAFSA, institutional form required. Applicants notified on a rolling basis starting 2/15; must reply within 2 week(s) of notification.

**Academics.** Combined baccalaureate/master's in communication arts. **Special study options:** Accelerated study, combined bachelor's/graduate degree, cross-registration, distance learning, double major, dual enrollment of high school students, ESL, honors, independent study, internships, student-designed major, study abroad, teacher certification program, weekend college. **Credit/placement by examination:** AP, CLEP, SAT, ACT, institutional tests. 30 credit hours maximum toward bachelor's degree. **Support services:** Learning center, reduced course load, remedial instruction, study skills assistance, tutoring, writing center.

**Honors college/program.** Incoming freshmen should submit an application, have a minimum high school GPA of 3.5, and combined SAT score (Verbal, Math and Writing) of 1800 and/or a 27 composite ACT score. Applicants also need an essay, teacher recommendation, and interview. Students enroll in advanced courses, participate in one mission trip, a travel or study abroad experience, additional professional development experiences, and complete a senior project.

**Majors. Biology:** General, biochemistry, vision science. **Business:** Accounting, banking/financial services, business admin, human resources, international, management information systems, managerial economics, marketing, organizational behavior, sales/distribution. **Communications:** General, journalism, media studies, radio/tv. **Communications technology:** Animation/special effects. **Computer sciences:** Networking. **Conservation:** Environmental science. **Education:** Elementary, music, physical. **Engineering technology:** Industrial management. **Family/consumer sciences:** Apparel marketing, child development. **Foreign languages:** Spanish. **Health:** Athletic training, music therapy, nuclear medical technology, nursing (RN). **History:** General. **Interdisciplinary:** Intercultural, nutrition sciences. **Liberal arts:** Arts/sciences. **Math:** General. **Parks/recreation:** Exercise sciences, sports admin. **Philosophy/religion:** Philosophy, religion. **Physical sciences:** Chemistry, meteorology. **Psychology:** General. **Social sciences:** International relations, political science, sociology. **Visual/performing arts:** Art, art history/ conservation, dramatic, fashion design, graphic design, interior design, music management. **Other:** Educational leadership and administration.

**Most popular majors.** Business/marketing 43%, education 8%, health sciences 10%, liberal arts 6%, psychology 6%, visual/performing arts 7%.

**Computing on campus.** PC or laptop required. 180 workstations in library, computer center. Dormitories wired for high-speed internet access and linked to campus network. Commuter students can connect to campus network. Online course registration, online library, helpline, repair service, wireless network available.

**Student life. Freshman orientation:** Mandatory, $200 fee. Preregistration for classes offered. Overnight program for out-of-towners and 1-day session for local students. Parents encouraged to participate. **Housing:** Coed dorms, single-sex dorms, special housing for disabled, apartments available. $225 fully refundable deposit, deadline 5/1. **Activities:** Jazz band, campus ministries, choral groups, dance, drama, international student organizations, literary magazine, music ensembles, musical theater, radio station, student government, student newspaper, symphony orchestra, TV station, Society of Leadership and Success, pre-pharmacy association, Alpha Sigma Alpha, Lambda Chi Alpha, Hispanic student association, Alpha Phi Omega, ethics club, Christian Pharmacy Fellowship International.

**Athletics.** NCAA. **Intercollegiate:** Baseball M, basketball, cross-country, diving, football (tackle) M, golf, soccer, softball W, swimming, tennis, track and field, volleyball W. **Intramural:** Basketball, football (non-tackle), racquetball, soccer, softball, tennis, volleyball, water polo. **Team name:** Cardinals.

**Student services.** Adult student services, alcohol/substance abuse counseling, chaplain/spiritual director, career counseling, services for economically disadvantaged, student employment services, financial aid counseling, health services, personal counseling, veterans' counselor. **Physically disabled:** Services for visually, speech, hearing impaired. **Learning disabled:** Comprehensive services available.

**Contact.** E-mail: admis@uiwtx.edu
Phone: (210) 829-6005 Toll-free number: (800) 749-9673
Fax: (210) 829-3921
Andrea Cyterski-Acosta, Dean of Enrollment, University of the Incarnate Word, 4301 Broadway, San Antonio, TX 78209-6397

---

## Wayland Baptist University

**Plainview, Texas**  CB member
**www.wbu.edu**  CB code: 6930

- Private 4-year university and liberal arts college affiliated with Southern Baptist Convention
- Residential campus in large town
- 862 degree-seeking undergraduates: 13% part-time, 53% women, 6% African American, 1% Asian American, 23% Hispanic American, 1% Native American, 3% international
- 269 degree-seeking graduate students
- 99% of applicants admitted
- SAT or ACT (ACT writing optional) required
- 42% graduate within 6 years

**General.** Founded in 1908. Regionally accredited. Off-campus sites in Amarillo, Lubbock, San Antonio, Wichita Falls, Alaska, Arizona, Hawaii, Oklahoma, New Mexico. **Degrees:** 144 bachelor's, 1 associate awarded; master's offered. **ROTC:** Army, Air Force. **Location:** 50 miles from Lubbock, 70 miles from Amarillo. **Calendar:** Semester, limited summer session. **Full-time faculty:** 85 total; 76% have terminal degrees, 5% minority, 32% women. **Part-time faculty:** 33 total; 15% have terminal degrees, 3% minority, 36% women. **Class size:** 82% < 20, 18% 20-39, less than 1% 50-99. **Special facilities:** Museum of the Llano Estacado.

**Freshman class profile.** 351 applied, 347 admitted, 219 enrolled.

| Mid 50% test scores | | | |
|---|---|---|---|
| SAT critical reading: | 410-540 | Rank in top quarter: | 40% |
| SAT math: | 430-570 | Rank in top tenth: | 18% |
| SAT writing: | 420-550 | Return as sophomores: | 62% |
| ACT composite: | 18-23 | Out-of-state: | 14% |
| GPA 3.75 or higher: | 40% | Live on campus: | 74% |
| GPA 3.50-3.74: | 13% | International: | 3% |
| GPA 3.0-3.49: | 26% | Fraternities: | 2% |
| GPA 2.0-2.99: | 20% | Sororities: | 1% |

**Basis for selection.** Regular freshman admission based on combination of class rank and on either the ACT composite or SAT score. Interview, audition recommended for music and theater.

**High school preparation.** 9 units required. Required and recommended units include English 3, mathematics 2-3, social studies 2 and science 2-3.

**2009-2010 Annual costs.** Tuition/fees: $12,740. Room/board: $3,864. Books/supplies: $1,248. Personal expenses: $1,820.

**2009-2010 Financial aid. Need-based:** Average need met was 74%. Average scholarship/grant was $9,472; average loan $3,038. 64% of total undergraduate aid awarded as scholarships/grants, 36% as loans/jobs. **Non-need-based:** Scholarships awarded for academics, alumni affiliation, art, athletics, job skills, leadership, minority status, music/drama, religious affiliation, state residency.

**Application procedures. Admission:** Priority date 8/1; no deadline. $35 fee. Admission notification on a rolling basis beginning on or about 3/1. **Financial aid:** Priority date 5/1; no closing date. FAFSA, institutional form required. Applicants notified on a rolling basis starting 2/15; must reply within 3 week(s) of notification.

**Academics. Special study options:** Accelerated study, distance learning, double major, dual enrollment of high school students, external degree, honors, internships, study abroad, teacher certification program. **Credit/ placement by examination:** AP, CLEP, IB, SAT, ACT, institutional tests. 30 credit hours maximum toward bachelor's degree. **Support services:** Learning center, reduced course load, remedial instruction, study skills assistance, tutoring, writing center.

**Majors. Biology:** General, molecular. **Business:** Business admin. **Communications:** General, media studies. **Education:** Business, elementary, English, middle, multi-level teacher, music, physical, science, social studies, technology/industrial arts, trade/industrial. **Foreign languages:** Spanish. **Health:** Nursing (RN). **History:** General. **Legal studies:** Prelaw. **Math:** General. **Parks/recreation:** Facilities management, sports admin. **Philosophy/ religion:** Christian. **Physical sciences:** General, chemistry. **Protective services:** Law enforcement admin. **Psychology:** General. **Public administration:** Human services. **Social sciences:** Sociology, U.S. government. **Theology:** Religious ed, sacred music. **Visual/performing arts:** Art, dramatic, music performance.

**Most popular majors.** Biology 8%, business/marketing 23%, education 22%, English 6%, philosophy/religious studies 6%, security/protective services 7%, visual/performing arts 6%.

**Computing on campus.** 231 workstations in library, computer center. Dormitories wired for high-speed internet access and linked to campus network. Commuter students can connect to campus network. Online library, helpline, wireless network available.

**Student life. Freshman orientation:** Mandatory, $15 fee. Preregistration for classes offered. Entry seminar course designed to help students succeed academically, socially, and spiritually. Taken during initial term of enrollment. **Policies:** Religious observance required. **Housing:** Guaranteed on-campus for freshmen. Single-sex dorms, apartments available. $100 fully refundable deposit. **Activities:** Bands, campus ministries, choral groups, drama, music ensembles, musical theater, radio station, student government, student newspaper, TV station, Over 20 religious, service, and special interest organizations available.

**Athletics.** NAIA. **Intercollegiate:** Baseball M, basketball, cheerleading, cross-country, golf, soccer, track and field, volleyball W. **Intramural:** Basketball, football (non-tackle), softball, volleyball. **Team name:** Pioneers, Flying Queens.

**Student services.** Chaplain/spiritual director, career counseling, student employment services, financial aid counseling, health services, personal counseling, placement for graduates.

**Contact.** E-mail: admityou@wbu.edu
Phone: (806) 291-3500 Toll-free number: (800) 588-1928
Fax: (806) 291-1960
Debbie Stennett, Director of Admissions, Wayland Baptist University, 1900 West Seventh Street, CMB #712, Plainview, TX 79072

---

## West Texas A&M University

**Canyon, Texas**  CB member
**www.wtamu.edu**  CB code: 6938

- Public 4-year university
- Residential campus in large town
- 6,214 degree-seeking undergraduates: 22% part-time, 55% women

- 1,489 degree-seeking graduate students
- 73% of applicants admitted
- SAT or ACT (ACT writing optional) required

**General.** Founded in 1909. Regionally accredited. **Degrees:** 1,198 bachelor's awarded; master's, doctoral offered. **Location:** 17 miles from Amarillo. **Calendar:** Semester, limited summer session. **Full-time faculty:** 271 total; 73% have terminal degrees, 11% minority, 42% women. **Part-time faculty:** 144 total; 17% have terminal degrees, 9% minority, 50% women. **Class size:** 32% < 20, 50% 20-39, 7% 40-49, 11% 50-99, less than 1% >100. **Special facilities:** 24,000-acre farm and ranch, alternative energy institute, historical museum, event center.

**Freshman class profile.** 3,581 applied, 2,612 admitted, 1,162 enrolled.

| Mid 50% test scores | | | |
|---|---|---|---|
| SAT critical reading: | 440-580 | Rank in top quarter: | 49% |
| SAT math: | 440-560 | Rank in top tenth: | 15% |
| ACT composite: | 18-23 | Out-of-state: | 8% |
| | | Live on campus: | 82% |

**Basis for selection.** Freshman applicants must be in top half of graduating class, have minimum 950 SAT (exclusive of Writing) or 20 ACT, or attend a summer provisional term. Texas Success Initiative Testing required of all incoming students before entrance. Audition required for music program; portfolio recommended for art, theater programs.

**High school preparation.** 24 units required. Required and recommended units include English 4, mathematics 3, social studies 3.5, science 3 and foreign language 2.

**2009-2010 Annual costs.** Tuition/fees: $5,732; $14,042 out-of-state. Out-of-district students from border counties pay in-state tuition. Tuition reduction plan available to students from border states. Room/board: $5,898. Books/supplies: $900. Personal expenses: $1,668.

**2008-2009 Financial aid.** **Need-based:** 49% of total undergraduate aid awarded as scholarships/grants, 51% as loans/jobs. **Non-need-based:** Scholarships awarded for academics, art, athletics, leadership, music/drama, state residency. **Additional information:** Scholarship deadline February 1.

**Application procedures.** **Admission:** Priority date 7/20; no deadline. $25 fee, may be waived for applicants with need. Admission notification on a rolling basis. **Financial aid:** Priority date 4/15; no closing date. FAFSA required. Applicants notified on a rolling basis starting 3/1; must reply within 2 week(s) of notification.

**Academics. Special study options:** Combined bachelor's/graduate degree, cooperative education, distance learning, double major, ESL, honors, independent study, internships, liberal arts/career combination, study abroad, teacher certification program, Washington semester. **Credit/placement by examination:** AP, CLEP, IB, institutional tests. Only 6 of a student's last 30 hours can come from CLEP. **Support services:** Learning center, remedial instruction, study skills assistance, tutoring, writing center.

**Majors. Agriculture:** General, agribusiness operations, agronomy, animal sciences, business, communications, equestrian studies, plant protection. **Biology:** General, biotechnology, wildlife. **Business:** General, accounting, business admin, finance, management information systems, managerial economics, marketing. **Communications:** Advertising, broadcast journalism, journalism. **Computer sciences:** Computer science. **Conservation:** Environmental science. **Engineering:** Mechanical. **Engineering technology:** Industrial. **Foreign languages:** Spanish. **Health:** Athletic training, clinical lab science, communication disorders, music therapy, nursing (RN). **History:** General. **Legal studies:** Prelaw. **Math:** General. **Parks/recreation:** Health/fitness. **Physical sciences:** Chemistry, geology, physics. **Protective services:** Law enforcement admin. **Psychology:** General. **Public administration:** General, social work. **Social sciences:** General, economics, geography, political science, sociology. **Visual/performing arts:** Art, dance, dramatic, graphic design, music performance, music theory/composition, studio arts. **Other:** Interdisciplinary studies.

**Most popular majors.** Agriculture 6%, business/marketing 15%, health sciences 10%, interdisciplinary studies 15%, liberal arts 15%.

**Computing on campus.** 1,800 workstations in dormitories, library, computer center, student center. Dormitories wired for high-speed internet access and linked to campus network. Commuter students can connect to campus network. Online course registration, online library, helpline, student web hosting, wireless network available.

**Student life. Freshman orientation:** Available, $50 fee. Preregistration for classes offered. 2-day summer orientation and preregistration and 3-day orientation before school starts. **Policies:** Students with fewer than 60 semester hours accumulated, enrolled in 9 or more semester hours, and under 21 on first day of class each semester required to live in university residence halls. **Housing:** Guaranteed on-campus for all undergraduates. Coed dorms,

single-sex dorms, special housing for disabled, fraternity/sorority housing available. $100 fully refundable deposit. Honors hall available. **Activities:** Bands, campus ministries, choral groups, dance, drama, international student organizations, literary magazine, music ensembles, musical theater, opera, radio station, student government, student newspaper, symphony orchestra, Chinese student association, Hispanic association, agriculture organizations, Students in Free Enterprise, pre-professional organizations, Black students association, College Republicans, Catholic student association.

**Athletics.** NCAA. **Intercollegiate:** Baseball M, basketball, cross-country, equestrian W, football (tackle) M, golf, soccer, softball W, volleyball W. **Intramural:** Archery, badminton, basketball, bowling, football (non-tackle), golf, racquetball, rodeo, soccer, softball, swimming, table tennis, tennis, volleyball. **Team name:** Buffaloes.

**Student services.** Alcohol/substance abuse counseling, career counseling, services for economically disadvantaged, student employment services, financial aid counseling, health services, on-campus daycare, personal counseling, placement for graduates, veterans' counselor. **Physically disabled:** Services for visually, speech, hearing impaired.

**Contact.** E-mail: admissions@mail.wtamu.edu
Phone: (806) 651-2020 Toll-free number: (800) 999-8268
Fax: (806) 651-5285
Shawn Thomas, Director of Admissions, West Texas A&M University, 2501 Fourth Avenue, WTAMU Box 60907, Canyon, TX 79016-0001

## Wiley College
**Marshall, Texas**      CB member
www.wileyc.edu      CB code: 6940

- Private 4-year liberal arts college affiliated with United Methodist Church
- Residential campus in large town
- 1,237 degree-seeking undergraduates

**General.** Founded in 1873. Regionally accredited. **Degrees:** 172 bachelor's awarded. **Location:** 40 miles from Shreveport, Louisiana, 150 miles from Dallas. **Calendar:** Semester, extensive summer session. **Full-time faculty:** 56 total. **Part-time faculty:** 24 total. **Class size:** 60% < 20, 35% 20-39, 3% 40-49, 2% 50-99. **Special facilities:** Nature trail.

**Freshman class profile.** 1,811 applied, 411 admitted, 312 enrolled.

| Mid 50% test scores | | | |
|---|---|---|---|
| SAT critical reading: | 320-430 | Rank in top quarter: | 15% |
| SAT math: | 320-430 | Rank in top tenth: | 3% |
| ACT composite: | 13-17 | Out-of-state: | 38% |
| | | Live on campus: | 90% |

**Basis for selection.** Open admission, but selective for some programs.

**High school preparation.** 16 units recommended. Recommended units include English 4, mathematics 2, social studies 2, science 2 and academic electives 6.

**2009-2010 Annual costs.** Tuition/fees: $9,970. Reported tuition includes cost of books. Room/board: $5,620. Books/supplies: $1,320. Personal expenses: $1,002.

**Financial aid.** All financial aid based on need.

**Application procedures. Admission:** No deadline. $25 fee. Admission notification on a rolling basis. **Financial aid:** No deadline. FAFSA, institutional form required. Applicants notified on a rolling basis.

**Academics. Special study options:** Accelerated study, cross-registration, distance learning, double major, dual enrollment of high school students, honors, independent study, internships, liberal arts/career combination, study abroad, teacher certification program, weekend college. **Credit/placement by examination:** AP, CLEP, institutional tests. **Support services:** Learning center, reduced course load, remedial instruction, study skills assistance, tutoring.

**Majors. Biology:** General. **Business:** Accounting, business admin, operations. **Communications:** Journalism. **Computer sciences:** Computer science. **Education:** Elementary, physical, secondary. **History:** General. **Math:** General. **Physical sciences:** Chemistry. **Protective services:** Law enforcement admin. **Social sciences:** Sociology.

**Most popular majors.** Business/marketing 66%, education 6%.

**Computing on campus.** 177 workstations in dormitories, library, computer center. Dormitories wired for high-speed internet access and linked to campus network. Commuter students can connect to campus network. Online course registration, online library, helpline, wireless network available.

**Student life. Freshman orientation:** Mandatory. Preregistration for classes offered. **Policies:** Religious observance required. **Housing:** Single-sex dorms, wellness housing available. $50 deposit. **Activities:** Choral groups, drama, music ensembles, radio station, student government, student newspaper, national service fraternity, interdenominational student movement, religion majors club.

**Athletics.** NAIA. **Intercollegiate:** Baseball M, basketball, cross-country, softball W, track and field, volleyball W. **Intramural:** Baseball M, basketball, cheerleading, softball, table tennis, tennis, track and field, volleyball, weight lifting M. **Team name:** Wildcats.

**Student services.** Adult student services, chaplain/spiritual director, career counseling, services for economically disadvantaged, student employment services, financial aid counseling, health services, personal counseling, placement for graduates, veterans' counselor.

**Contact.**  E-mail: admissions@wileyc.edu
Phone: (903) 927-3311 Toll-free number: (800) 658-6889
Fax: (903) 927-3366
Alvena Jones, Director of Admissions and Recruitment, Wiley College, 711 Wiley Avenue, Marshall, TX 75670

# Utah

## Argosy University: Salt Lake City
**Draper, Utah**
www.argosy.edu/saltlakecity

▶ For-profit 4-year university
▶ Small city
▶ 66 degree-seeking undergraduates

**General. Calendar:** Continuous. **Full-time faculty:** 4 total.

**Freshman class profile.** 14 enrolled.

**Basis for selection.** Open admission.

**Academics. Credit/placement by examination:** CLEP.

**Majors. Business:** Business admin. **Liberal arts:** Arts/sciences. **Protective services:** Criminal justice. **Psychology:** General.

**Contact.** Phone: (601) 601-5000 Toll-free number: (888) 639-4756 Argosy University: Salt Lake City, 121 Election Road, Suite 300, Draper, UT 84020

## Brigham Young University
**Provo, Utah**  **CB member**
www.byu.edu  **CB code: 4019**

▶ Private 4-year university affiliated with Church of Jesus Christ of Latter-day Saints
▶ Residential campus in small city
▶ 30,745 degree-seeking undergraduates: 9% part-time, 49% women, 4% Asian American, 4% Hispanic American, 3% international
▶ 3,385 degree-seeking graduate students
▶ 69% of applicants admitted
▶ SAT or ACT (ACT writing recommended), application essay, interview required
▶ 77% graduate within 6 years

**General.** Founded in 1875. Regionally accredited. Additional educational center in Salt Lake City. **Degrees:** 6,864 bachelor's awarded; master's, doctoral, professional offered. **ROTC:** Army, Air Force. **Location:** 45 miles from Salt Lake City. **Calendar:** Semester, limited summer session. **Full-time faculty:** 1,283 total; 86% have terminal degrees, 5% minority, 21% women. **Part-time faculty:** 403 total; 29% have terminal degrees, 7% minority, 63% women. **Class size:** 47% < 20, 36% 20-39, 5% 40-49, 8% 50-99, 3% >100. **Special facilities:** Aquatic ecology laboratory, science and anthropological museums, veterinary pathology laboratory, fine arts museum, reading and writing laboratories, math and language computer laboratories, supercomputer.

**Freshman class profile.** 10,212 applied, 7,049 admitted, 5,421 enrolled.

| Mid 50% test scores | | | |
|---|---|---|---|
| SAT critical reading: | 560-670 | | |
| SAT math: | 570-680 | | |
| ACT composite: | 25-30 | | |
| GPA 3.75 or higher: | 62% | | |
| GPA 3.50-3.74: | 24% | | |
| GPA 3.0-3.49: | 13% | | |
| GPA 2.0-2.99: | | | 1% |
| Rank in top quarter: | | | 83% |
| Rank in top tenth: | | | 51% |
| Return as sophomores: | | | 84% |
| Out-of-state: | | | 66% |
| Live on campus: | | | 79% |
| International: | | | 2% |

**Basis for selection.** School achievement record, test scores, endorsements and recommendations important. Students must maintain ideals and standards in harmony with The Church of Jesus Christ of Latter-Day Saints. Interview is ecclesiastical. **Learning Disabled:** Untimed ACT accepted.

**High school preparation.** College-preparatory program recommended. Required and recommended units include English 4, mathematics 3-4, history 2, science 2-3 (laboratory 2-3), foreign language 2-4, computer science 1 and visual/performing arts 1. 2 units of literature/writing required.

**2010-2011 Annual costs.** Tuition/fees (projected): $4,420. Tuition is $8,840 for nonmembers of The Church of Jesus Christ of Latter-day Saints.

Undergraduate per-credit-hour charge $454 for nonmembers. Room/board: $7,120. Books/supplies: $1,000. Personal expenses: $2,140.

**2008-2009 Financial aid. Need-based:** 1,988 full-time freshmen applied for aid; 1,212 were judged to have need; 1,057 of these received aid. Average need met was 40%. Average scholarship/grant was $3,922; average loan $3,269. 64% of total undergraduate aid awarded as scholarships/grants, 36% as loans/jobs. **Non-need-based:** Awarded to 13,809 full-time undergraduates, including 2,749 freshmen. Scholarships awarded for academics, art, athletics, leadership, minority status, music/drama, religious affiliation, ROTC, state residency. **Additional information:** Students notified of scholarships on or about April 20.

**Application procedures. Admission:** Closing date 2/1 (receipt date). $30 fee, may be waived for applicants with need. Admission notification on a rolling basis. **Financial aid:** Priority date 4/15; no closing date. FAFSA required. Applicants notified on a rolling basis starting 5/1.

**Academics. Special study options:** Accelerated study, combined bachelor's/graduate degree, cooperative education, cross-registration, distance learning, double major, ESL, external degree, honors, independent study, internships, liberal arts/career combination, study abroad, teacher certification program, Washington semester. **Credit/placement by examination:** AP, CLEP, IB, ACT, institutional tests. **Support services:** Learning center, pre-admission summer program, reduced course load, remedial instruction, study skills assistance, tutoring, writing center.

**Majors. Agriculture:** Crop production, food processing, food science, landscaping. **Area/ethnic studies:** American, Asian, European, German, Latin American. **Biology:** General, biochemistry, bioinformatics, biophysics, biostatistics, biotechnology, botany, conservation, exercise physiology, microbiology, molecular, physiology, wildlife. **Business:** General, accounting, actuarial science, business admin, construction management, entrepreneurial studies, finance, financial planning, information resources management, logistics, management information systems, managerial economics, marketing, organizational behavior, statistics. **Communications:** General, advertising, journalism. **Communications technology:** Animation/special effects. **Computer sciences:** Computer science, information technology. **Conservation:** Environmental science, wildlife. **Education:** Biology, chemistry, drama/dance, early childhood, elementary, English, family/consumer sciences, French, German, health, history, Latin, mathematics, music, physical, physics, science, social science, Spanish, special, technology/industrial arts. **Engineering:** Chemical, civil, computer, electrical, manufacturing, mechanical. **Family/consumer sciences:** General, facilities/event planning, family studies, family systems. **Foreign languages:** General, ancient Greek, Arabic, Biblical, Chinese, classics, comparative lit, French, German, Germanic, Italian, Japanese, Korean, Latin, linguistics, Portuguese, Russian, Spanish, translation. **Health:** Athletic training, audiology/speech pathology, clinical lab science, dietetics, nursing (RN), public health ed, recreational therapy. **History:** General. **Interdisciplinary:** Biological/physical sciences, neuroscience, nutrition sciences. **Liberal arts:** Humanities. **Math:** General, statistics. **Parks/recreation:** General, health/fitness. **Philosophy/religion:** Philosophy. **Physical sciences:** Applied physics, astronomy, chemistry, geology, hydrology, physics. **Psychology:** General. **Public administration:** Social work. **Social sciences:** Anthropology, archaeology, cartography, economics, geography, international relations, political science, sociology. **Visual/performing arts:** Acting, art, art history/conservation, ballet, dance, design, dramatic, film/cinema, graphic design, illustration, industrial design, jazz, music history, music performance, music theory/composition, musical theater, photography, piano/organ, stringed instruments, studio arts, voice/opera. **Other:** Earth and space science teacher education, Family history; genealogy, Geography: urban, rural, and environmental planning emphasis, Integrative biology, Media music studies.

**Most popular majors.** Biology 10%, business/marketing 15%, education 9%, engineering/engineering technologies 6%, family/consumer sciences 7%, foreign language 6%, social sciences 9%, visual/performing arts 6%.

**Computing on campus.** 2,000 workstations in dormitories, library, computer center, student center. Dormitories wired for high-speed internet access and linked to campus network. Commuter students can connect to campus network. Online course registration, online library, helpline, repair service, student web hosting, wireless network available.

**Student life. Freshman orientation:** Available. Preregistration for classes offered. **Policies:** Honor code enforced. Religious observance required. **Housing:** Single-sex dorms, special housing for disabled, apartments, wellness housing available. $100 fully refundable deposit. Language houses available. **Activities:** Bands, choral groups, dance, drama, film society, literary magazine, music ensembles, musical theater, opera, radio station, student government, student newspaper, symphony orchestra, TV station, College Republicans, College Democrats, African American club, black student union, Latin American student association, international student association, Intercollegiate Knights, Circle-K International, Southeast Asian club, Baptist student union.

**Athletics.** NCAA. **Intercollegiate:** Baseball M, basketball, cheerleading, cross-country, diving, football (tackle) M, golf, gymnastics W, soccer W, softball W, swimming, tennis, track and field, volleyball. **Intramural:** Badminton, basketball, football (non-tackle), football (tackle), golf, racquetball, soccer, softball, tennis, volleyball, water polo, wrestling M. **Team name:** Cougars.

**Student services.** Chaplain/spiritual director, career counseling, services for economically disadvantaged, student employment services, financial aid counseling, health services, minority student services, personal counseling, placement for graduates, veterans' counselor, women's services. **Physically disabled:** Services for visually, speech, hearing impaired.

**Contact.** E-mail: admissions@byu.edu
Phone: (801) 422-2507 Fax: (801) 422-0005
Tom Gourley, Director of Admissions, Brigham Young University, A-41ASB, BYU, Provo, UT 84602

## DeVry University: Sandy
### Sandy, Utah

- For-profit 4-year business and technical college
- Small city
- 98 degree-seeking undergraduates: 54% part-time, 34% women, 1% African American, 4% Asian American, 5% Hispanic American, 1% international
- 49 degree-seeking graduate students

**General.** Regionally accredited. **Degrees:** 11 bachelor's awarded; master's offered. **Calendar:** Semester. **Part-time faculty:** 19 total; 5% minority, 37% women.

**Freshman class profile.** 16 enrolled.

**Basis for selection.** Applicants must have high school diploma or equivalent, or degree from accredited post-secondary institution, demonstrate proficiency in basic college-level skills through SAT or ACT scores or institution-administered placement examinations, and be at least 17 years of age. DeVry-administered admissions test required if SAT or ACT test scores are not submitted.

**High school preparation.** College-preparatory program recommended.

**2009-2010 Annual costs.** Tuition/fees: $14,160. Books/supplies: $1,310. Personal expenses: $3,574.

**2008-2009 Financial aid. Non-need-based:** Scholarships awarded for academics.

**Application procedures. Admission:** No deadline. $50 fee. Admission notification on a rolling basis. **Financial aid:** No deadline. FAFSA required. Applicants notified on a rolling basis.

**Academics. Special study options:** Accelerated study, distance learning. **Credit/placement by examination:** CLEP.

**Majors. Business:** Business admin. **Computer sciences:** Networking, systems analysis. **Other:** Technical management.

**Contact.** DeVry University: Sandy, 9350 South 150 East, Suite 420, Sandy, UT 84070

## Dixie State College of Utah
### St. George, Utah
new.dixie.edu                                    CB code: 4283

- Public 4-year liberal arts college
- Commuter campus in small city
- 6,484 degree-seeking undergraduates: 32% part-time, 52% women

**General.** Founded in 1911. Regionally accredited. **Degrees:** 213 bachelor's, 778 associate awarded. **ROTC:** Army. **Location:** 305 miles from Salt Lake City, 121 miles from Las Vegas. **Calendar:** Semester, limited summer session. **Full-time faculty:** 143 total; 34% have terminal degrees, 8% minority, 45% women. **Part-time faculty:** 318 total; 4% have terminal degrees, 1% minority, 51% women. **Class size:** 31% < 20, 54% 20-39, 11% 40-49, 4% 50-99.

**Freshman class profile.** 4,215 applied, 2,774 admitted, 1,741 enrolled.

| Mid 50% test scores | | | |
|---|---|---|---|
| SAT critical reading: | 400-500 | GPA 3.0-3.49: | 29% |
| SAT math: | 380-520 | GPA 2.0-2.99: | 35% |
| SAT writing: | 360-470 | Rank in top quarter: | 24% |
| ACT composite: | 18-23 | Rank in top tenth: | 7% |
| GPA 3.75 or higher: | 16% | End year in good standing: | 73% |
| GPA 3.50-3.74: | 17% | Return as sophomores: | 57% |
| | | Out-of-state: | 13% |

**Basis for selection.** Open admission, but selective for some programs. Some health occupation programs have prerequisites. Applicants for bachelor's degrees in elementary education, business administration, and nursing must have associate degree or advance standing. **Homeschooled:** Letter of recommendation (nonparent) required. Copy of formal letter of release from high school counselor or secondary school district that states the student is no longer required to attend secondary school required. Statement from student certifying that they have completed the equivalent of a high school diploma required.

**High school preparation.** College-preparatory program recommended. 16 units recommended. Recommended units include English 4, mathematics 4, history 3, science 2 (laboratory 1) and foreign language 2. One computer literacy unit recommended.

**2009-2010 Annual costs.** Tuition/fees: $3,145; $10,897 out-of-state. Room/board: $3,548. Books/supplies: $1,150. Personal expenses: $4,896.

**2008-2009 Financial aid. Need-based:** 67% of total undergraduate aid awarded as scholarships/grants, 33% as loans/jobs. **Non-need-based:** Scholarships awarded for academics, alumni affiliation, art, athletics, leadership, minority status, music/drama, religious affiliation. **Additional information:** SunFirst Bank Scholarship for communications students; Daniels Fund Scholarship for non-traditional students based on need.

**Application procedures. Admission:** Priority date 2/15; no deadline. $35 fee. Admission notification on a rolling basis. Students who have received approval for early release from high school must provide copy of formal letter or release from high school counselor, as well as written authorization from parent or legal guardian. **Financial aid:** Priority date 3/1, closing date 5/1. FAFSA required. Applicants notified on a rolling basis starting 3/1; must reply within 2 week(s) of notification.

**Academics.** Bachelor's and master's degree course work from Utah's 4-year universities presented over distance-learning media and on-campus instruction. Four-year programs in business administration, computer technology, communications media, elementary education, biology, English and nursing offered on campus. **Special study options:** Accelerated study, cooperative education, distance learning, double major, dual enrollment of high school students, ESL, honors, independent study, internships, student-designed major, study abroad, teacher certification program. **Credit/placement by examination:** AP, CLEP. 30 credit hours maximum toward associate degree, 30 toward bachelor's. **Support services:** Learning center, remedial instruction, study skills assistance, tutoring, writing center.

**Majors. Biology:** General. **Business:** Accounting, business admin. **Communications:** General. **Computer sciences:** General. **Education:** Biology, elementary, English, science. **Health:** Dental hygiene, nursing (RN). **Transportation:** Aviation management. **Other:** Integrated studies.

**Most popular majors.** Biology 7%, business/marketing 36%, communications/journalism 12%, computer/information sciences 10%, education 17%, English 10%, health sciences 7%.

**Computing on campus.** 400 workstations in dormitories, library, computer center, student center. Dormitories wired for high-speed internet access and linked to campus network. Commuter students can connect to campus network. Online course registration, online library, helpline, repair service, wireless network available.

**Student life. Freshman orientation:** Mandatory. Preregistration for classes offered. All-day sessions offered on Mondays and Tuesdays from the 2nd week of June to the 1st week of August. **Policies:** Stringent drug and alcohol policies. **Housing:** Coed dorms, single-sex dorms, apartments, wellness housing available. $75 fully refundable deposit. **Activities:** Bands, campus ministries, choral groups, dance, drama, international student organizations, literary magazine, music ensembles, musical theater, radio station, student government, student newspaper, symphony orchestra, TV station, Native American student association, Polynesian cultural club, black student association, Hispanic student association, diversity club, LDS student association, campus Christian connection, Phi Beta Lambda, College Democrats, College Republicans.

**Athletics.** NCAA. **Intercollegiate:** Baseball M, basketball, football (tackle) M, golf M, soccer, softball W, tennis W, volleyball W. **Intramural:** Basketball, football (non-tackle), soccer, table tennis, tennis M. **Team name:** Red Storm.

**Student services.** Adult student services, alcohol/substance abuse counseling, career counseling, services for economically disadvantaged, student employment services, financial aid counseling, health services, minority student services, personal counseling, placement for graduates, veterans' counselor. **Physically disabled:** Services for visually, speech, hearing impaired.

**Contact.** E-mail: Admit@dixie.edu
Phone: (435) 652-7590 Fax: (435) 656-4005
Brandon Boulter, Director of Admissions, Dixie State College of Utah, 225 South 700 East, St. George, UT 84770-3876

## Independence University
### Salt Lake City, Utah
### www.independence.edu

- For-profit 4-year health science college
- Commuter campus in small city
- 1,282 full-time, degree-seeking undergraduates

**General.** Founded in 1975. Accredited by DETC. Primarily serves home-study students. **Degrees:** 39 bachelor's, 111 associate awarded; master's offered. **Calendar:** Continuous. **Full-time faculty:** 10 total. **Part-time faculty:** 100 total.

**Basis for selection.** Open admission.

**2009-2010 Annual costs.** Tuition/fees: $9,900. Books/supplies: $1,250.

**Financial aid. Additional information:** Financial aid available for resident students only, not correspondence students.

**Application procedures. Admission:** No deadline. $50 fee. Admission notification on a rolling basis. **Financial aid:** No deadline. FAFSA required.

**Academics. Special study options:** Distance learning, liberal arts/career combination. **Credit/placement by examination:** CLEP. 30 credit hours maximum toward associate degree, 30 toward bachelor's. **Support services:** Tutoring.

**Majors. Business:** General, accounting, marketing. **Health:** Health care admin.

**Most popular majors.** Business/marketing 11%, health sciences 89%.

**Student life. Activities:** Student newspaper.

**Student services.** Adult student services.

**Contact.** E-mail: admissns@cchs.edu
Phone: (800) 972-5149 Toll-free number: (800) 972-5149
Independence University, 5295 South Commerce Drive Suite G-50, Salt Lake City, UT 84107

## ITT Technical Institute: Murray
### Murray, Utah
### www.itt-tech.edu          CB code: 3601

- For-profit 4-year technical college
- Commuter campus in small city

**General.** Founded in 1984. Accredited by ACICS. **Location:** 10 miles from Salt Lake City. **Calendar:** Quarter.

**Contact.** Phone: (801) 263-3313
Director of Recruitment, 920 West LeVoy Drive, Murray, UT 84123

## Neumont University
### South Jordan, Utah
### www.neumont.edu          CB code: 4516

- For-profit 4-year engineering and technical college
- Residential campus in very large city
- 232 degree-seeking undergraduates: 6% women
- 8 degree-seeking graduate students
- 94% of applicants admitted
- SAT or ACT (ACT writing optional), application essay required

**General.** Accredited by ACICS. **Degrees:** 95 bachelor's awarded; master's offered. **Location:** 20 miles from Salt Lake City. **Calendar:** Quarter,

extensive summer session. **Full-time faculty:** 11 total. **Part-time faculty:** 25 total.

**Freshman class profile.** 366 applied, 344 admitted, 171 enrolled.

| | | | |
|---|---|---|---|
| GPA 3.75 or higher: | 13% | Return as sophomores: | 66% |
| GPA 3.50-3.74: | 17% | Out-of-state: | 73% |
| GPA 3.0-3.49: | 30% | Live on campus: | 50% |
| GPA 2.0-2.99: | 39% | | |

**Basis for selection.** Strong work ethic, accomplishments, aptitude most important. **Homeschooled:** State high school equivalency certificate required.

**2010-2011 Annual costs.** Tuition/fees (projected): $30,300. Room only: $5,700.

**Application procedures. Admission:** No deadline. $35 fee, may be waived for applicants with need. Application must be submitted online. Admission notification on a rolling basis. **Financial aid:** No deadline.

**Academics. Special study options:** Accelerated study, internships. **Credit/placement by examination:** AP, CLEP. **Support services:** Remedial instruction, study skills assistance, tutoring.

**Majors. Business:** Entrepreneurial studies, management information systems. **Computer sciences:** Computer science, information technology.

**Computing on campus.** PC or laptop required. Commuter students can connect to campus network. Online library, helpline, repair service, student web hosting, wireless network available.

**Student life. Freshman orientation:** Mandatory. Preregistration for classes offered. **Housing:** Guaranteed on-campus for all undergraduates. Apartments available. $350 nonrefundable deposit, deadline 8/1. **Activities:** Student government.

**Student services.** Career counseling, financial aid counseling, placement for graduates.

**Contact.** E-mail: admissions@neumont.edu
Phone: (801) 302-2800 Toll-free number: (888) 638-6668
Fax: (801) 302-2880
Charlie Parker, Dean of Admissions, Neumont University, 10701 South River Front Parkway, Suite 300, South Jordan, UT 84095

## Southern Utah University
### Cedar City, Utah          CB member
### www.suu.edu          CB code: 4092

- Public 4-year university
- Residential campus in large town
- 5,797 degree-seeking undergraduates: 12% part-time, 56% women, 1% African American, 2% Asian American, 4% Hispanic American, 2% Native American, 2% international
- 837 degree-seeking graduate students
- 81% of applicants admitted
- SAT or ACT (ACT writing optional) required
- 43% graduate within 6 years

**General.** Founded in 1897. Regionally accredited. **Degrees:** 909 bachelor's, 323 associate awarded; master's offered. **ROTC:** Army. **Location:** 265 miles from Salt Lake City, 160 miles from Las Vegas. **Calendar:** Semester, extensive summer session. **Full-time faculty:** 216 total; 76% have terminal degrees, 12% minority, 29% women. **Part-time faculty:** 110 total; 28% have terminal degrees, 18% minority, 51% women. **Class size:** 40% < 20, 45% 20-39, 6% 40-49, 8% 50-99, 2% >100. **Special facilities:** Natural life museum, observatory, Shakespearean theater.

**Freshman class profile.** 3,274 applied, 2,662 admitted, 1,316 enrolled.

| Mid 50% test scores | | | |
|---|---|---|---|
| SAT critical reading: | 450-580 | Rank in top quarter: | 51% |
| SAT math: | 450-570 | Rank in top tenth: | 26% |
| ACT composite: | 19-25 | Return as sophomores: | 62% |
| GPA 3.75 or higher: | 33% | Out-of-state: | 18% |
| GPA 3.50-3.74: | 19% | Live on campus: | 41% |
| GPA 3.0-3.49: | 30% | International: | 2% |
| GPA 2.0-2.99: | 17% | Fraternities: | 4% |
| | | Sororities: | 4% |

**Basis for selection.** Admission based on GPA and ACT/SAT scores.

**High school preparation.** College-preparatory program recommended. Recommended units include English 4, mathematics 3, social studies 3, science 3 (laboratory 1) and foreign language 2. 1 unit of social studies must be U.S. history and government; 2 math units must be elementary algebra or above; English units should have a composition and literature emphasis.

**2009-2010 Annual costs.** Tuition/fees: $4,269; $12,847 out-of-state. Room/board: $5,300. Books/supplies: $1,500. Personal expenses: $2,400.

**2008-2009 Financial aid. Need-based:** 795 full-time freshmen applied for aid; 615 were judged to have need; 614 of these received aid. Average need met was 63%. Average scholarship/grant was $4,922; average loan $3,015. 46% of total undergraduate aid awarded as scholarships/grants, 54% as loans/jobs. **Non-need-based:** Awarded to 3,181 full-time undergraduates, including 1,088 freshmen. Scholarships awarded for academics, alumni affiliation, art, athletics, job skills, leadership, minority status, music/drama, state residency.

**Application procedures. Admission:** Closing date 8/1. $40 fee. Admission notification on a rolling basis. **Financial aid:** No deadline. FAFSA required. Applicants notified on a rolling basis starting 11/1.

**Academics. Special study options:** Combined bachelor's/graduate degree, cooperative education, distance learning, double major, ESL, honors, independent study, internships, liberal arts/career combination, teacher certification program, weekend college. **Credit/placement by examination:** AP, CLEP, ACT. 25 credit hours maximum toward associate degree, 25 toward bachelor's. **Support services:** Learning center, pre-admission summer program, reduced course load, remedial instruction, study skills assistance, tutoring, writing center.

**Majors. Agriculture:** General, business. **Biology:** General. **Business:** Accounting, business admin, finance, hospitality admin, management information systems, managerial economics, marketing. **Communications:** General. **Computer sciences:** General, computer science. **Conservation:** Forestry. **Construction:** Site management. **Education:** General, art, biology, business, chemistry, drama/dance, elementary, English, family/consumer sciences, foreign languages, French, German, history, learning disabled, mathematics, music, physical, science, secondary, social science, Spanish, special, speech, technology/industrial arts, trade/industrial. **Engineering:** General, science. **Engineering technology:** General. **Family/consumer sciences:** General, human nutrition. **Foreign languages:** French, German. **Health:** Athletic training, nursing (RN), premedicine, prepharmacy, preveterinary. **History:** General. **Legal studies:** Prelaw. **Math:** General. **Parks/recreation:** General. **Philosophy/religion:** Philosophy. **Physical sciences:** Geology. **Protective services:** Police science. **Psychology:** General. **Social sciences:** General, economics, political science, sociology. **Visual/performing arts:** Art, commercial/advertising art, dance, dramatic, music performance, studio arts. **Other:** Pre-medical technology.

**Most popular majors.** Biology 8%, business/marketing 15%, communications/journalism 6%, education 20%, health sciences 9%, psychology 7%, security/protective services 6%, social sciences 6%.

**Computing on campus.** 300 workstations in dormitories, library, computer center. Dormitories wired for high-speed internet access and linked to campus network. Commuter students can connect to campus network. Online library, helpline, wireless network available.

**Student life. Freshman orientation:** Mandatory. Preregistration for classes offered. One-day program held throughout summer. Parents welcome and encouraged to attend. **Housing:** Coed dorms, single-sex dorms, special housing for disabled, apartments, fraternity/sorority housing available. $100 fully refundable deposit. **Activities:** Bands, choral groups, dance, drama, literary magazine, music ensembles, musical theater, opera, radio station, student government, student newspaper, symphony orchestra, TV station, intercultural club, LDSSA, Newman Club, Campus Christian Fellowship, College Republicans, College Democrats.

**Athletics.** NAIA, NCAA. **Intercollegiate:** Badminton, baseball M, basketball, cross-country, football (tackle) M, golf M, gymnastics W, rodeo, soccer W, softball W, tennis W, track and field. **Intramural:** Badminton, basketball, golf, soccer, tennis, volleyball. **Team name:** Thunderbirds.

**Student services.** Career counseling, student employment services, health services, minority student services, personal counseling, placement for graduates, veterans' counselor. **Physically disabled:** Services for speech impaired.

**Contact.** E-mail: adminfo@suu.edu
Phone: (435) 586-7740 Fax: (435) 865-8223
Stephen Allen, Director of Admissions, Southern Utah University, 351 West Center Street, Cedar City, UT 84720

## Stevens-Henager College: Logan
Logan, Utah
www.stevenshenager.edu

- For-profit 4-year business and technical college
- Large town
- 275 full-time, degree-seeking undergraduates

**General.** Accredited by ACCSC. **Degrees:** 22 bachelor's, 21 associate awarded. **Calendar:** Continuous.

**Basis for selection.** Open admission.

**Application procedures. Admission:** No deadline. Admission notification on a rolling basis.

**Academics. Credit/placement by examination:** CLEP.

**Majors. Business:** Accounting, business admin. **Computer sciences:** Computer science. **Health:** Health care admin.

**Contact.** Phone: (435) 713-4777
Stevens-Henager College: Logan, 755 South Highway 89-91, Logan, UT 84321

## Stevens-Henager College: Murray
Salt Lake City, Utah
www.stevenshenager.edu

- For-profit 4-year business and health science college
- Commuter campus in large town

**General.** Accredited by ACCSCT. **Location:** 5 Miles from Salt Lake City. **Calendar:** Continuous.

**Annual costs/financial aid.** Tuition for academic year varies by program from $15,000 - $16,500.

**Contact.** Phone: (800) 622-2640
Admissions Director, 383 West Vine Street, Salt Lake City, UT 84123

## Stevens-Henager College: Ogden
Ogden, Utah
www.stevenshenager.edu                    CB code: 4751

- For-profit 4-year liberal arts college
- Commuter campus in small city

**General.** Accredited by ACCSCT. **Location:** 35 miles from Salt Lake City. **Calendar:** Continuous.

**Annual costs/financial aid.** Tuition and fees vary by program. Personal expenses: $4,000.

**Contact.** Phone: (801) 394-7791
Director of Admissions, 1890 South 1350 West, Ogden, UT 84401

## Stevens-Henager College: Orem
Orem, Utah
www.stevenshenager.edu

- For-profit 4-year business and health science college
- Large city

**General.** Founded in 1891. Accredited by ACCSCT. **Location:** 35 miles from Salt Lake City. **Calendar:** Continuous.

**Annual costs/financial aid.** Personal expenses: $2,123.

**Contact.** Phone: (801) 375-5455
Director of Admissions, 1476 South Sand Hill Road, Orem, UT 84058

## University of Utah
Salt Lake City, Utah                       CB member
www.utah.edu                               CB code: 4853

- Public 4-year university
- Commuter campus in very large city

- 20,983 degree-seeking undergraduates: 29% part-time, 45% women, 1% African American, 6% Asian American, 5% Hispanic American, 1% Native American, 3% international
- 7,135 degree-seeking graduate students
- 80% of applicants admitted
- ACT (writing optional) required
- 58% graduate within 6 years

**General.** Founded in 1850. Regionally accredited. **Degrees:** 4,896 bachelor's awarded; master's, doctoral, professional offered. **ROTC:** Army, Naval, Air Force. **Location:** 2 miles from downtown. **Calendar:** Semester, limited summer session. **Full-time faculty:** 1,269 total; 82% have terminal degrees, 11% minority, 40% women. **Part-time faculty:** 620 total; 25% have terminal degrees, 7% minority, 44% women. **Class size:** 43% < 20, 35% 20-39, 6% 40-49, 11% 50-99, 4% >100. **Special facilities:** Arboretum, fine arts museum, natural history museum; architecture exhibition hall, Olympic Cauldron Park, cancer research institute.

**Freshman class profile.** 7,890 applied, 6,318 admitted, 2,688 enrolled.

| Mid 50% test scores | | | |
|---|---|---|---|
| SAT critical reading: | 490-630 | Rank in top quarter: | 48% |
| SAT math: | 500-630 | Rank in top tenth: | 23% |
| SAT writing: | 480-600 | End year in good standing: | 93% |
| ACT composite: | 21-27 | Return as sophomores: | 85% |
| GPA 3.75 or higher: | 36% | Out-of-state: | 20% |
| GPA 3.50-3.74: | 22% | Live on campus: | 40% |
| GPA 3.0-3.49: | 31% | International: | 3% |
| GPA 2.0-2.99: | 10% | Fraternities: | 4% |
| | | Sororities: | 9% |

**Basis for selection.** High school course requirements, admissions index using high school GPA and test scores important. Recommendations and extracurricular activities considered. Audition required for dance, drama, music programs; portfolio required for art program. **Homeschooled:** Transcript of courses and grades, state high school equivalency certificate required. 23 ACT or 1060 SAT (exclusive of Writing), score of 550 on each of the sub-sections of the GED required. Students who graduate from non-accredited high school with test score in upper quartile (25 ACT, 1140 SAT), with no individual score below freshman class average, will not be required to take GED. **Learning Disabled:** Disclosure of learning disabilities not required; Center for Disability Services assists students with disabilities in the admission process.

**High school preparation.** College-preparatory program required. 16 units required. Required units include English 4, mathematics 2, history 1, science 3 (laboratory 1), foreign language 2 and academic electives 4. 4 units from at least 2 of the following: history, English, math beyond algebra, laboratory science, foreign language, social science, fine arts.

**2009-2010 Annual costs.** Tuition/fees: $5,746; $18,136 out-of-state. Room/board: $6,240. Books/supplies: $1,080. Personal expenses: $2,790.

**2009-2010 Financial aid. Need-based:** 1,345 full-time freshmen applied for aid; 980 were judged to have need; 966 of these received aid. Average need met was 55%. Average scholarship/grant was $6,070; average loan $4,261. 40% of total undergraduate aid awarded as scholarships/grants, 60% as loans/jobs. **Non-need-based:** Awarded to 1,017 full-time undergraduates, including 302 freshmen. Scholarships awarded for academics, alumni affiliation, art, athletics, leadership, minority status, music/drama, ROTC, state residency.

**Application procedures. Admission:** Priority date 12/15; deadline 4/1 (postmark date). $45 fee, may be waived for applicants with need. Admission notification on a rolling basis. A student with exceptional scholastic achievement (high school GPA of 3.50 or above, ACT composite of at least 25) through their junior year may be considered for early admission. **Financial aid:** Priority date 4/1; no closing date. FAFSA, institutional form required. Applicants notified on a rolling basis starting 4/15; must reply within 6 week(s) of notification.

**Academics. Special study options:** Accelerated study, combined bachelor's/graduate degree, cooperative education, cross-registration, distance learning, double major, dual enrollment of high school students, ESL, exchange student, honors, independent study, internships, liberal arts/career combination, student-designed major, study abroad, teacher certification program, Washington semester. **Credit/placement by examination:** AP, CLEP, IB, SAT, ACT, institutional tests. 32 credit hours maximum toward bachelor's degree. **Support services:** Learning center, pre-admission summer program, reduced course load, remedial instruction, study skills assistance, tutoring, writing center.

**Honors college/program.** Entering freshmen are accepted based on their Admissions Index which must be 120 or above and 3.5 cumulative GPA; transfer and continuing students accepted based on cumulative 3.5 GPA. No deadline for admisson to program.

**Majors. Architecture:** Architecture. **Area/ethnic studies:** Asian, Near/Middle Eastern, women's. **Biology:** General, cell/histology. **Business:** General, accounting, business admin, entrepreneurial studies, finance, management information systems, marketing. **Communications:** General, media studies. **Computer sciences:** Computer science. **Conservation:** Environmental science, environmental studies. **Education:** General, elementary, social science, special. **Engineering:** General, biomedical, chemical, civil, computer, electrical, geological, materials, mechanical, metallurgical, mining. **Family/consumer sciences:** Consumer economics, family studies. **Foreign languages:** Arabic, Chinese, classics, comparative lit, French, German, Hebrew, Japanese, linguistics, Persian, Russian, Spanish, Turkish. **Health:** Athletic training, audiology/speech pathology, clinical lab science, health services, nursing (RN), occupational therapy assistant, predental, premedicine, prenursing, prepharmacy, public health ed. **History:** General. **Interdisciplinary:** Global studies. **Legal studies:** Prelaw. **Liberal arts:** Humanities. **Math:** General. **Parks/recreation:** General, exercise sciences, health/fitness. **Philosophy/religion:** Philosophy. **Physical sciences:** General, chemistry, geology, geophysics, meteorology, physics. **Psychology:** General. **Public administration:** Social work. **Social sciences:** General, anthropology, economics, geography, political science, sociology, urban studies. **Visual/performing arts:** General, art, art history/conservation, ballet, dance, dramatic, film/cinema. **Other:** Health teaching.

**Most popular majors.** Business/marketing 13%, communications/journalism 8%, engineering/engineering technologies 7%, health sciences 7%, social sciences 17%, visual/performing arts 6%.

**Computing on campus.** 8,800 workstations in dormitories, library, computer center, student center. Dormitories wired for high-speed internet access and linked to campus network. Commuter students can connect to campus network. Online course registration, online library, helpline, repair service, student web hosting, wireless network available.

**Student life. Freshman orientation:** Mandatory. Preregistration for classes offered. One-day, 2-day, and 4-day programs offered before fall semester. Late orientations offered in August and mini-orientations held the first day of class. Some orientation options have fees. **Housing:** Coed dorms, special housing for disabled, apartments, fraternity/sorority housing available. $200 partly refundable deposit, deadline 3/28. Limited visitation, 24-hour quiet housing available. **Activities:** Bands, campus ministries, choral groups, dance, drama, film society, international student organizations, literary magazine, music ensembles, Model UN, musical theater, opera, radio station, student government, student newspaper, symphony orchestra, TV station, political and religious groups, ethnic clubs, outdoor clubs, community service organization.

**Athletics.** NCAA. **Intercollegiate:** Baseball M, basketball, cheerleading, cross-country W, diving, football (tackle) M, golf M, gymnastics W, skiing, soccer W, softball W, swimming, tennis, track and field W, volleyball W. **Intramural:** Badminton, basketball, field hockey, football (non-tackle) M, racquetball, soccer, softball, squash, tennis, volleyball. **Team name:** Utes.

**Student services.** Adult student services, alcohol/substance abuse counseling, chaplain/spiritual director, career counseling, student employment services, financial aid counseling, health services, minority student services, on-campus daycare, personal counseling, placement for graduates, veterans' counselor, women's services. **Physically disabled:** Services for visually, speech, hearing impaired.

**Contact.** E-mail: admissions@sa.utah.edu
Phone: (801) 581-7281 Fax: (801) 585-7864
Timothy Ebner, Associate Vice President of Enrollment Management, University of Utah, 201 South 1460 East, Room 250 S, Salt Lake City, UT 84112-9057

---

### Utah State University
**Logan, Utah**     **CB member**
**www.usu.edu**     **CB code: 4857**

- Public 4-year university
- Residential campus in small city
- 13,652 degree-seeking undergraduates: 16% part-time, 49% women, 1% African American, 2% Asian American, 3% Hispanic American, 1% Native American, 4% international
- 1,712 degree-seeking graduate students
- 98% of applicants admitted
- SAT or ACT (ACT writing optional) required
- 53% graduate within 6 years

**General.** Founded in 1888. Regionally accredited. **Degrees:** 2,968 bachelor's, 18 associate awarded; master's, doctoral, professional offered. **ROTC:** Army, Air Force. **Location:** 80 miles from Salt Lake City. **Calendar:** Semester, extensive summer session. **Full-time faculty:** 744 total; 86% have terminal degrees, 6% minority, 32% women. **Part-time faculty:** 201 total; 6% minority, 53% women. **Class size:** 34% < 20, 42% 20-39, 7% 40-49, 11% 50-99, 6% >100. **Special facilities:** Agricultural experiment stations, water research laboratory, space shuttle experiments, forestry research facility, botanical gardens, teaching greenhouse, research park, laboratory school, off-campus theater performance lab, anthropology museum.

**Freshman class profile.** 6,438 applied, 6,289 admitted, 2,839 enrolled.

| Mid 50% test scores | | GPA 2.0-2.99: | 12% |
|---|---|---|---|
| SAT critical reading: | 470-630 | Rank in top quarter: | 49% |
| SAT math: | 460-630 | Rank in top tenth: | 24% |
| ACT composite: | 21-27 | Out-of-state: | 22% |
| GPA 3.75 or higher: | 41% | International: | 2% |
| GPA 3.50-3.74: | 21% | Fraternities: | 2% |
| GPA 3.0-3.49: | 26% | Sororities: | 2% |

**Basis for selection.** High school record, test scores most important. Audition required for music; portfolio required for art. **Homeschooled:** Early entry policy applies: junior equivalent, letters of approval. **Learning Disabled:** Recent documentation/diagnosis required for special consideration.

**High school preparation.** College-preparatory program required. Required and recommended units include English 4, mathematics 3, history 1, science 3 (laboratory 1), foreign language 2 and academic electives 4. Some social studies electives required.

**2009-2010 Annual costs.** Tuition/fees: $4,828; $13,802 out-of-state. Room/board: $4,900. Books/supplies: $1,150. Personal expenses: $2,100.

**2009-2010 Financial aid. Non-need-based:** Scholarships awarded for academics, alumni affiliation, art, athletics, leadership, minority status, music/drama, religious affiliation, ROTC.

**Application procedures. Admission:** Priority date 4/1; no deadline. $40 fee. Admission notification on a rolling basis. **Financial aid:** No deadline. FAFSA required. Applicants notified on a rolling basis starting 4/1; must reply within 4 week(s) of notification.

**Academics. Special study options:** Accelerated study, cooperative education, cross-registration, distance learning, double major, dual enrollment of high school students, ESL, exchange student, honors, independent study, internships, liberal arts/career combination, student-designed major, study abroad, teacher certification program, weekend college. **Credit/placement by examination:** AP, CLEP, IB, SAT, ACT, institutional tests. 16 credits of lower division course work per language. **Support services:** Learning center, pre-admission summer program, reduced course load, remedial instruction, study skills assistance, tutoring, writing center.

**Majors. Agriculture:** Agronomy, animal sciences, business, dairy, economics, equipment technology, food science, horticultural science, ornamental horticulture, range science, soil science. **Architecture:** Landscape. **Area/ethnic studies:** American, Asian. **Biology:** General, botany, ecology, entomology, zoology. **Business:** General, accounting, administrative services, business admin, fashion, finance, human resources, marketing, operations. **Communications:** Journalism. **Computer sciences:** General, information systems. **Conservation:** Forestry, wildlife. **Education:** Agricultural, biology, business, chemistry, early childhood, elementary, family/consumer sciences, health, mathematics, multi-level teacher, music, physical, physics, sales/marketing, science, secondary, social studies, special, technology/industrial arts, voc/tech. **Engineering:** General, aerospace, agricultural, civil, computer, electrical, environmental, mechanical. **Engineering technology:** Electrical. **Family/consumer sciences:** Clothing/textiles, family studies, food/nutrition, housing. **Foreign languages:** French, German, Spanish. **Health:** Audiology/speech pathology, clinical lab science, music therapy, predental, premedicine, preveterinary. **History:** General. **Legal studies:** Prelaw. **Liberal arts:** Arts/sciences. **Math:** General, statistics. **Mechanic/repair:** Aircraft. **Parks/recreation:** General, facilities management. **Philosophy/religion:** Philosophy. **Physical sciences:** Chemistry, geology, hydrology, physics. **Psychology:** General. **Public administration:** Social work. **Social sciences:** Anthropology, economics, geography, political science, sociology. **Visual/performing arts:** Art, dance, dramatic, interior design.

**Most popular majors.** Business/marketing 17%, education 18%, engineering/engineering technologies 8%, social sciences 6%.

**Computing on campus.** 910 workstations in dormitories, library, computer center, student center. Dormitories wired for high-speed internet access and linked to campus network. Commuter students can connect to campus network. Online course registration, helpline, repair service, student web hosting, wireless network available.

**Student life. Freshman orientation:** Mandatory, $25 fee. Preregistration for classes offered. Half-day, 1-, 2- and 4-day sessions available in June and July. **Housing:** Coed dorms, single-sex dorms, special housing for disabled, apartments, fraternity/sorority housing, wellness housing available. $150 partly refundable deposit, deadline 3/15. Mobile home park available. **Activities:**

Bands, campus ministries, choral groups, dance, drama, film society, international student organizations, music ensembles, musical theater, opera, radio station, student government, student newspaper, symphony orchestra, TV station, Latter-Day Saints, Catholic, Lutheran, Baptist student organizations; Crusade for Christ; Christian Fellowship; black student union; Hispanic student union; Native American student union; Polynesian student union; Asian American student union.

**Athletics. NCAA. Intercollegiate:** Basketball, cross-country, football (tackle) M, golf M, gymnastics W, soccer W, softball W, tennis, track and field, volleyball W. **Intramural:** Badminton, basketball, cross-country, football (non-tackle), golf, racquetball, soccer, softball, table tennis, tennis, triathlon, volleyball. **Team name:** Aggies.

**Student services.** Adult student services, alcohol/substance abuse counseling, career counseling, student employment services, financial aid counseling, health services, minority student services, on-campus daycare, personal counseling, placement for graduates, veterans' counselor, women's services. **Physically disabled:** Services for visually, speech, hearing impaired.

**Contact.** E-mail: admit@usu.edu
Phone: (435) 797-1079 Toll-free number: (800) 488-8108
Fax: (435) 797-3708
Jenn Putnam, Director of Admissions, Utah State University, 0160 Old Main Hill, Logan, UT 84322-0160

---

## Utah Valley University
**Orem, Utah**
www.uvu.edu

CB member
CB code: 4870

- Public 4-year university and technical college
- Commuter campus in small city
- 24,061 degree-seeking undergraduates: 40% part-time, 42% women, 1% African American, 3% Asian American, 6% Hispanic American, 1% Native American, 1% international
- 47 degree-seeking graduate students

**General.** Founded in 1941. Regionally accredited. **Degrees:** 1,772 bachelor's, 1,651 associate awarded; master's offered. **ROTC:** Army, Air Force. **Location:** 45 miles from Salt Lake City. **Calendar:** Semester, limited summer session. **Full-time faculty:** 476 total; 58% have terminal degrees, 8% minority, 34% women. **Part-time faculty:** 1,064 total; 6% minority, 31% women. **Class size:** 34% < 20, 52% 20-39, 5% 40-49, 9% 50-99, less than 1% >100. **Special facilities:** Provo airport campus.

**Freshman class profile.** 5,795 applied, 5,795 admitted, 3,971 enrolled.

| Mid 50% test scores | | GPA 2.0-2.99: | 29% |
|---|---|---|---|
| SAT critical reading: | 420-540 | Rank in top quarter: | 27% |
| SAT math: | 420-550 | Rank in top tenth: | 10% |
| ACT composite: | 18-24 | End year in good standing: | 83% |
| GPA 3.75 or higher: | 20% | Return as sophomores: | 60% |
| GPA 3.50-3.74: | 20% | Out-of-state: | 12% |
| GPA 3.0-3.49: | 29% | International: | 1% |

**Basis for selection.** Open admission. All students under 21 must complete ACT/SAT prior to registration for placement. **Homeschooled:** State high school equivalency certificate required. **Learning Disabled:** Students with learning disabilities may apply for reasonable accommodations and assistance through the Accessibility Services Department.

**2009-2010 Annual costs.** Tuition/fees: $4,048; $11,888 out-of-state. Books/supplies: $1,692. Personal expenses: $3,326.

**2009-2010 Financial aid. Need-based:** 1,561 full-time freshmen applied for aid; 1,397 were judged to have need; 1,321 of these received aid. Average need met was 46%. Average scholarship/grant was $4,532; average loan $3,263. 34% of total undergraduate aid awarded as scholarships/grants, 66% as loans/jobs. **Non-need-based:** Awarded to 1,187 full-time undergraduates, including 438 freshmen. Scholarships awarded for academics, alumni affiliation, art, athletics, job skills, leadership, minority status, music/drama, religious affiliation, ROTC, state residency.

**Application procedures. Admission:** Closing date 8/15. $35 fee, may be waived for applicants with need. Admission notification on a rolling basis beginning on or about 1/1. **Financial aid:** Priority date 5/1; no closing date. FAFSA, institutional form required. Applicants notified on a rolling basis starting 5/15; must reply within 2 week(s) of notification.

**Academics. Special study options:** Cooperative education, distance learning, double major, dual enrollment of high school students, ESL, honors, independent study, internships, student-designed major, study abroad, teacher certification program, weekend college. Evening school, internet programs.

**Credit/placement by examination:** AP, CLEP, IB, institutional tests. 16 credit hours maximum toward associate degree, 16 toward bachelor's. No more than 25% of credits applied toward associate degree, diploma, or certificate may be awarded through challenge credit. **Support services:** Learning center, reduced course load, remedial instruction, study skills assistance, tutoring, writing center.

**Majors. Biology:** General, biotechnology. **Business:** Accounting, business admin, hospitality admin, operations. **Communications:** General. **Computer sciences:** General, computer science, data processing, web page design. **Education:** Biology, business, chemistry, drama/dance, early childhood, elementary, English, health, history, kindergarten/preschool, mathematics, music, physical, science, Spanish. **Foreign languages:** American Sign Language, Spanish. **Health:** Community health, nursing (RN). **History:** General. **Legal studies:** Paralegal. **Math:** General. **Parks/recreation:** Health/fitness. **Philosophy/religion:** Philosophy. **Physical sciences:** Chemistry, physics. **Protective services:** Fire services admin, forensics, law enforcement admin. **Psychology:** General. **Social sciences:** Economics, political science. **Transportation:** Airline/commercial pilot. **Visual/performing arts:** Dance, design, dramatic.

**Most popular majors.** Business/marketing 26%, computer/information sciences 7%, education 14%, psychology 12%, trade and industry 9%.

**Computing on campus.** 1,000 workstations in library, computer center, student center. Commuter students can connect to campus network. Online course registration, online library, helpline, repair service, wireless network available.

**Student life. Freshman orientation:** Mandatory. **Activities:** Bands, choral groups, dance, drama, film society, international student organizations, literary magazine, music ensembles, musical theater, student government, student newspaper, symphony orchestra, TV station, Baptist student union, black student union, German club, international student council, Japan club, Latin American club, Latter-Day Saint student association, multi-cultural voices, Native Sun, Russian club.

**Athletics.** NCAA. **Intercollegiate:** Baseball M, basketball, cross-country, golf, soccer W, softball W, track and field, volleyball W, wrestling M. **Intramural:** Football (tackle). **Team name:** Wolverines.

**Student services.** Adult student services, alcohol/substance abuse counseling, career counseling, services for economically disadvantaged, student employment services, financial aid counseling, health services, legal services, minority student services, on-campus daycare, personal counseling, placement for graduates, veterans' counselor, women's services. **Physically disabled:** Services for visually, speech, hearing impaired.

**Contact.** E-mail: admissions@uvu.edu
Phone: (801) 863-8466 Fax: (801) 225-4677
Liz Childs, Director of Admissions, Utah Valley University, 800 West University Parkway, Orem, UT 84058-5999

## Weber State University
Ogden, Utah     CB member
www.weber.edu     CB code: 4941

- Public 4-year university
- Commuter campus in small city
- 17,342 degree-seeking undergraduates

**General.** Founded in 1889. Regionally accredited. **Degrees:** 1,872 bachelor's, 1,851 associate awarded; master's offered. **ROTC:** Army, Naval, Air Force. **Location:** 35 miles from Salt Lake City. **Calendar:** Semester, extensive summer session. **Full-time faculty:** 481 total. **Part-time faculty:** 385 total. **Class size:** 58% < 20, 34% 20-39, 3% 40-49, 4% 50-99, less than 1% >100. **Special facilities:** Museum of natural history, planetarium, aerospace technology center.

### Freshman class profile.

| Mid 50% test scores | | GPA 2.0-2.99: | 28% |
|---|---|---|---|
| ACT composite: | 18-24 | Out-of-state: | 2% |
| GPA 3.75 or higher: | 21% | Live on campus: | 4% |
| GPA 3.50-3.74: | 17% | Fraternities: | 1% |
| GPA 3.0-3.49: | 29% | Sororities: | 1% |

**Basis for selection.** Open admission, but selective for some programs. Special requirements for nursing, dental health, health professions.

**High school preparation.** College-preparatory program recommended. 15 units recommended. Recommended units include English 4, mathematics 2, history 1, science 2, foreign language 2 and academic electives 4. 4 additional courses recommended, at least 2 of which should be from the

following: history, English, math beyond algebra, laboratory science, fine arts and computer science.

**2009-2010 Annual costs.** Tuition/fees: $4,088; $11,555 out-of-state. Room/board: $6,634. Books/supplies: $1,200. Personal expenses: $2,892.

**2008-2009 Financial aid.** All financial aid based on need.

**Application procedures. Admission:** Closing date 8/21. $30 fee. Admission notification on a rolling basis. **Financial aid:** Priority date 3/1; no closing date. FAFSA, institutional form required. Applicants notified on a rolling basis starting 3/15; must reply within 2 week(s) of notification.

**Academics.** Students apply for upper-division courses in junior year. **Special study options:** Accelerated study, cooperative education, distance learning, double major, dual enrollment of high school students, ESL, exchange student, external degree, honors, independent study, internships, New York semester, semester at sea, student-designed major, study abroad, teacher certification program, United Nations semester, Washington semester. First-year experience. **Credit/placement by examination:** AP, CLEP, IB, institutional tests. 30 credit hours maximum toward bachelor's degree. **Support services:** Learning center, pre-admission summer program, reduced course load, remedial instruction, study skills assistance, tutoring, writing center.

**Majors. Area/ethnic studies:** African-American, Chicano/Hispanic-American/Latino, Native American. **Biology:** Bacteriology, botany, zoology. **Business:** Accounting, administrative services, business admin, finance, human resources, logistics, management information systems, managerial economics, marketing, office management. **Communications:** Broadcast journalism, journalism, public relations. **Computer sciences:** General, computer science, information systems, networking. **Construction:** Maintenance. **Education:** Art, bilingual, biology, business, chemistry, drama/dance, early childhood, elementary, English, French, German, history, mathematics, music, physical, physics, science, secondary, social science, social studies, Spanish. **Engineering technology:** Electrical. **Family/consumer sciences:** Family studies. **Foreign languages:** French, German, Spanish. **Health:** Athletic training, clinical lab science, dental hygiene, health care admin, medical radiologic technology/radiation therapy, nuclear medical technology, nursing (RN), respiratory therapy technology, sonography. **History:** General. **Interdisciplinary:** Gerontology. **Liberal arts:** Arts/sciences. **Math:** General, applied. **Military:** General. **Parks/recreation:** Exercise sciences, health/fitness. **Physical sciences:** Chemistry, geology, physics. **Protective services:** Corrections, criminal justice, police science. **Psychology:** General. **Public administration:** Social work. **Social sciences:** Economics, geography, political science, sociology. **Visual/performing arts:** General, art, commercial/advertising art, dance, design, dramatic, music performance, photography, piano/organ, studio arts, voice/opera.

**Most popular majors.** Business/marketing 18%, education 11%, health sciences 21%, security/protective services 6%.

**Computing on campus.** 558 workstations in dormitories, library, computer center, student center. Dormitories wired for high-speed internet access and linked to campus network. Commuter students can connect to campus network. Online course registration, online library, helpline, repair service, student web hosting, wireless network available.

**Student life. Freshman orientation:** Available. Preregistration for classes offered. Student and parent orientations offered by appointment. **Housing:** Single-sex dorms, special housing for disabled, apartments, wellness housing available. $175 partly refundable deposit, deadline 8/1. **Activities:** Bands, choral groups, dance, drama, film society, literary magazine, music ensembles, musical theater, opera, radio station, student government, student newspaper, symphony orchestra, TV station, Latter-Day Saint student association, Newman center, Black Scholars United, international student association, physically challenged student association.

**Athletics.** NCAA. **Intercollegiate:** Basketball, cross-country, football (tackle) M, golf, soccer W, tennis, track and field, volleyball W. **Intramural:** Baseball M, basketball, bowling, racquetball, soccer, softball, tennis, track and field, volleyball. **Team name:** Wildcats.

**Student services.** Adult student services, alcohol/substance abuse counseling, chaplain/spiritual director, career counseling, services for economically disadvantaged, student employment services, financial aid counseling, health services, legal services, minority student services, on-campus daycare, personal counseling, placement for graduates, veterans' counselor, women's services. **Physically disabled:** Services for visually, speech, hearing impaired.

**Contact.** E-mail: admissions@weber.edu
Phone: (801) 626-6744 Toll-free number: (800) 848-7770
Fax: (801) 626-6747
Christopher Rivera, Director of Admissions, Weber State University, 1137 University Circle, Ogden, UT 84408-1137

## Western Governors University
### Salt Lake City, Utah
### www.wgu.edu

♦ Private 4-year virtual university
♦ Very large city
♦ 12,025 degree-seeking undergraduates: 59% women
♦ 4,190 degree-seeking graduate students
♦ Interview required

**General.** Candidate for regional accreditation.; also accredited by DETC. Programs are online-only. Degrees awarded after students demonstrate competency (through tests and assignments) in all required subjects and are not based on credit hours. **Degrees:** 679 bachelor's awarded; master's offered. **Calendar:** Continuous, extensive summer session. **Full-time faculty:** 246 total; 22% minority, 67% women. **Part-time faculty:** 4 total; 75% women.

**Basis for selection.** Open admission.

**High school preparation.** College-preparatory program recommended.

**2009-2010 Annual costs.** Tuition/fees: $5,870. Tuition is based on 2 six month terms. BSN program tuition is $6,500.

**Financial aid.** All financial aid based on need.

**Application procedures. Admission:** No deadline. $65 fee, may be waived for applicants with need. Application must be submitted online. Admission notification on a rolling basis. **Financial aid:** FAFSA required.

**Academics.** All students have access to online communities that contain learning resources and academic mentors in their field of study. Academic model is competency-based; there are no classes, but there are a number of texts, interactive learning resources, webinars, etc., available for all courses of study. **Special study options:** Accelerated study, combined bachelor's/graduate degree, distance learning, teacher certification program. **Credit/placement by examination:** CLEP. **Support services:** Learning center, tutoring.

**Majors. Business:** Accounting, business admin, finance, human resources, management information systems, marketing. **Computer sciences:** General, information technology, LAN/WAN management, security, system admin. **Education:** Biology, chemistry, elementary, kindergarten/preschool, mathematics, science, secondary, social science, special. **Health:** Medical informatics, nursing (RN).

**Computing on campus.** PC or laptop required. Helpline available.

**Student life. Freshman orientation:** Mandatory.

**Student services.** Adult student services, career counseling, services for economically disadvantaged, financial aid counseling, personal counseling, veterans' counselor.

**Contact.** E-mail: info@wgu.edu
Phone: (801) 274-3280 Toll-free number: (866) 225-5948
Fax: (801) 274-3305
Eddie Rios, Director of Enrollment, Western Governors University, 4001 South 700 East, Suite 700, Salt Lake City, UT 84107

## Westminster College
### Salt Lake City, Utah
### www.westminstercollege.edu                 CB code: 4948

♦ Private 4-year liberal arts college
♦ Commuter campus in very large city
♦ 2,141 degree-seeking undergraduates: 6% part-time, 56% women, 1% African American, 3% Asian American, 6% Hispanic American, 1% Native American, 2% international
♦ 853 degree-seeking graduate students
♦ 82% of applicants admitted
♦ SAT or ACT (ACT writing recommended), application essay required
♦ 56% graduate within 6 years; 9% enter graduate study

**General.** Founded in 1875. Regionally accredited. Curriculum combines professional and liberal arts study. **Degrees:** 419 bachelor's awarded; master's offered. **ROTC:** Army, Naval, Air Force. **Location:** 6 miles from downtown. **Calendar:** 4-1-4, limited summer session. **Full-time faculty:** 136 total; 73% have terminal degrees, 2% minority, 47% women. **Part-time faculty:** 191 total; 30% have terminal degrees, 4% minority, 53% women.

**Class size:** 59% < 20, 40% 20-39, 2% 40-49. **Special facilities:** Meade Lx200 telescope, elevated soccer/lacrosse field.

**Freshman class profile.** 1,625 applied, 1,329 admitted, 469 enrolled.

| Mid 50% test scores | | Rank in top quarter: | 60% |
|---|---|---|---|
| SAT critical reading: | 510-620 | Rank in top tenth: | 29% |
| SAT math: | 500-630 | End year in good standing: | 91% |
| ACT composite: | 22-27 | Return as sophomores: | 76% |
| GPA 3.75 or higher: | 36% | Out-of-state: | 41% |
| GPA 3.50-3.74: | 22% | Live on campus: | 68% |
| GPA 3.0-3.49: | 29% | International: | 3% |
| GPA 2.0-2.99: | 13% | | |

**Basis for selection.** Academic performance and GPA important. Interviews recommended.

**High school preparation.** College-preparatory program recommended. Required and recommended units include English 4, mathematics 2-3, social studies 2, history 1, science 3, foreign language 2-3 and academic electives 2-3.

**2009-2010 Annual costs.** Tuition/fees: $24,996. Room/board: $7,006. Books/supplies: $1,000. Personal expenses: $1,300.

**2009-2010 Financial aid. Need-based:** 343 full-time freshmen applied for aid; 278 were judged to have need; 278 of these received aid. Average need met was 89%. Average scholarship/grant was $15,732; average loan $4,171. 63% of total undergraduate aid awarded as scholarships/grants, 37% as loans/jobs. **Non-need-based:** Awarded to 801 full-time undergraduates, including 212 freshmen. Scholarships awarded for academics, alumni affiliation, art, athletics, leadership, minority status, music/drama, religious affiliation.

**Application procedures. Admission:** No deadline. $40 fee, may be waived for applicants with need. Admission notification on a rolling basis beginning on or about 9/1. Must reply by May 1 or within 3 week(s) if notified thereafter. **Financial aid:** Priority date 4/15; no closing date. FAFSA required. Applicants notified on a rolling basis starting 3/1; must reply within 3 week(s) of notification.

**Academics. Special study options:** Accelerated study, combined bachelor's/graduate degree, cooperative education, distance learning, double major, dual enrollment of high school students, ESL, honors, independent study, internships, liberal arts/career combination, semester at sea, student-designed major, study abroad, teacher certification program, weekend college. **Credit/placement by examination:** AP, CLEP, IB, SAT, ACT, institutional tests. 40 credit hours maximum toward bachelor's degree. **Support services:** Remedial instruction, study skills assistance, tutoring, writing center.

**Majors. Biology:** General. **Business:** General, accounting, business admin, entrepreneurial studies, finance, human resources, information resources management, international, management information systems, management science, managerial economics, marketing. **Communications:** General. **Computer sciences:** Computer science. **Conservation:** Environmental studies. **Education:** General, early childhood, elementary, secondary, special. **Health:** Nursing (RN). **History:** General. **Interdisciplinary:** Neuroscience. **Math:** General. **Philosophy/religion:** Philosophy. **Physical sciences:** Chemistry, physics. **Protective services:** Criminal justice. **Psychology:** General. **Social sciences:** General, economics, political science, sociology. **Transportation:** Aviation, aviation management. **Visual/performing arts:** Art, arts management.

**Most popular majors.** Business/marketing 32%, health sciences 20%, social sciences 7%.

**Computing on campus.** 412 workstations in dormitories, library, computer center, student center. Dormitories wired for high-speed internet access and linked to campus network. Commuter students can connect to campus network. Online course registration, online library, helpline, student web hosting, wireless network available.

**Student life. Freshman orientation:** Mandatory. Preregistration for classes offered. **Housing:** Guaranteed on-campus for freshmen. Coed dorms, single-sex dorms, apartments available. $200 nonrefundable deposit, deadline 6/1. **Activities:** Jazz band, campus ministries, choral groups, dance, drama, film society, international student organizations, literary magazine, music ensembles, musical theater, student government, student newspaper, symphony orchestra, College Democrats, College Republicans, Habitat for Humanity, Earth Effort, Latter-day Saint student association, Native American club, volunteer club, pride club.

**Athletics.** NAIA. **Intercollegiate:** Basketball, cross-country, golf, lacrosse, skiing, soccer, volleyball W. **Intramural:** Basketball, football (nontackle), volleyball. **Team name:** Griffins.

**Student services.** Alcohol/substance abuse counseling, chaplain/ spiritual director, career counseling, student employment services, financial aid counseling, health services, minority student services, personal counseling, placement for graduates, veterans' counselor, women's services. **Physically disabled:** Services for visually, speech, hearing impaired.

**Contact.** E-mail: admission@westminstercollege.edu
Phone: (801) 832-2200 Toll-free number: (800) 748-4753
Fax: (801) 832-3101
Louis Levy, Director of Undergraduate Admissions, Westminster College, 1840 South 1300 East, Salt Lake City, UT 84105

# Vermont

## Bennington College

**Bennington, Vermont**
www.bennington.edu

CB member
CB code: 3080

- Private 4-year liberal arts college
- Residential campus in large town
- 664 degree-seeking undergraduates: 1% part-time, 67% women, 2% African American, 2% Asian American, 2% Hispanic American, 6% international
- 144 degree-seeking graduate students
- 66% of applicants admitted
- Application essay required
- 58% graduate within 6 years

**General.** Founded in 1932. Regionally accredited. **Degrees:** 117 bachelor's awarded; master's offered. **Location:** 40 miles from Albany, New York; 150 miles from Boston. **Calendar:** Semester. **Full-time faculty:** 62 total; 73% have terminal degrees, 10% minority, 48% women. **Part-time faculty:** 32 total; 50% have terminal degrees, 19% minority, 44% women. **Class size:** 79% < 20, 21% 20-39, less than 1% >100. **Special facilities:** Observatory, greenhouse, digital arts lab, architecture, drawing, painting, printmaking, and sculpture studios, ceramics studio and kilns, color and black-and-white photography darkrooms, film and video editing studio, fully equipped professional theaters, scripts library, dance studios and archives, electronic music and sound recording studios, music practice rooms, music library.

**Freshman class profile.** 1,054 applied, 696 admitted, 197 enrolled.

| Mid 50% test scores | | | |
|---|---|---|---|
| SAT critical reading: | 620-720 | GPA 2.0-2.99: | 14% |
| SAT math: | 560-640 | Rank in top quarter: | 63% |
| SAT writing: | 610-710 | Rank in top tenth: | 31% |
| ACT composite: | 26-31 | End year in good standing: | 79% |
| GPA 3.75 or higher: | 35% | Return as sophomores: | 90% |
| GPA 3.50-3.74: | 23% | Out-of-state: | 96% |
| GPA 3.0-3.49: | 27% | Live on campus: | 100% |
| | | International: | 7% |

**Basis for selection.** Strength of academic record and extracurricular activities, quality of ideas expressed in application, and recommendations important. Interviews strongly encouraged. Supplemental materials welcome. **Homeschooled:** Statement describing homeschool structure and mission, state high school equivalency certificate, letter of recommendation (nonparent) required. Documentation of academic work, course descriptions, reading list required. SAT/ACT strongly encouraged.

**High school preparation.** College-preparatory program recommended. 21 units recommended. Recommended units include English 4, mathematics 4, social studies 4, history 4, science 3 and foreign language 2.

**2010-2011 Annual costs.** Tuition/fees: $41,350. Room/board: $11,550.

**2009-2010 Financial aid. Need-based:** 154 full-time freshmen applied for aid; 142 were judged to have need; 139 of these received aid. Average need met was 81%. Average scholarship/grant was $29,549; average loan $2,797. 81% of total undergraduate aid awarded as scholarships/grants, 19% as loans/jobs. **Non-need-based:** Awarded to 94 full-time undergraduates, including 41 freshmen. Scholarships awarded for academics. **Additional information:** All applicants for undergraduate admission considered for scholarships based on quality of overall application.

**Application procedures. Admission:** Closing date 1/3 (postmark date). $60 fee, may be waived for applicants with need. Admission notification 4/1. Must reply by May 1 or within 2 week(s) if notified thereafter. **Financial aid:** Priority date 2/1, closing date 2/15. FAFSA, institutional form required. CSS PROFILE required of early decision applicants only. Applicants notified by 4/1; must reply by 5/1 or within 2 week(s) of notification.

**Academics.** Internships and field work required. **Special study options:** Accelerated study, combined bachelor's/graduate degree, cross-registration, double major, ESL, independent study, internships, student-designed major, study abroad, teacher certification program. Annual 7-week winter internship/field work period; Postbaccalaureate program in preparation for medical or allied health school graduate programs. **Credit/placement by examination:** AP, CLEP, IB. **Support services:** Reduced course load, study skills assistance, tutoring, writing center.

**Majors. Architecture:** Architecture. **Area/ethnic studies:** American, Asian, European, gay/lesbian, Latin American, women's. **Biology:** General, botany, cellular/molecular, ecology, environmental, evolutionary, zoology. **Communications:** Journalism. **Communications technology:** Animation/special effects. **Computer sciences:** General, computer science. **Conservation:** Environmental science, environmental studies. **Education:** General, early childhood, elementary, middle, secondary. **Family/consumer sciences:** Child development. **Foreign languages:** General, Chinese, French, Germanic, Italian, Japanese, Spanish. **Health:** Premedicine. **History:** General, American, European. **Interdisciplinary:** Biological/physical sciences, global studies, math/computer science, peace/conflict. **Legal studies:** Prelaw. **Liberal arts:** Arts/sciences, humanities. **Math:** General. **Philosophy/religion:** Judaic, philosophy. **Physical sciences:** General, astronomy, chemistry, physics. **Psychology:** General, social. **Social sciences:** General, anthropology, international relations, political science, sociology, U.S. government. **Visual/performing arts:** General, acting, art history/conservation, ceramics, cinematography, dance, design, directing/producing, dramatic, drawing, film/cinema, jazz, multimedia, music history, music performance, music theory/composition, musicology, painting, photography, piano/organ, play/screenwriting, printmaking, sculpture, stringed instruments, studio arts, theater design, theater history, voice/opera. **Other:** Communication and media studies, Foreign languages, literatures, and linguistics.

**Most popular majors.** English 14%, foreign language 8%, social sciences 9%, visual/performing arts 47%.

**Computing on campus.** 100 workstations in library, computer center, student center. Dormitories wired for high-speed internet access and linked to campus network. Commuter students can connect to campus network. Online library, helpline, repair service, student web hosting, wireless network available.

**Student life. Freshman orientation:** Available. Preregistration for classes offered. 6-day program held prior to start of classes. Students may also participate in pre-orientation service or camping trips. **Housing:** Guaranteed on-campus for all undergraduates. Coed dorms, cooperative housing available. **Activities:** Choral groups, dance, drama, international student organizations, literary magazine, music ensembles, musical theater, radio station, student government, student newspaper, Students for Social Justice, Environmental Initiatives Committee, Interfaith Council, Community Outreach and Action, Bennington Debate Association, Cupcakes for a Cause, International Fellowship.

**Athletics. Intramural:** Archery, badminton, basketball, bowling, cross-country, equestrian, golf, skiing, soccer, softball, swimming, table tennis, tennis, volleyball, weight lifting.

**Student services.** Alcohol/substance abuse counseling, career counseling, student employment services, financial aid counseling, health services, minority student services, personal counseling, placement for graduates, women's services. **Physically disabled:** Services for hearing impaired.

**Contact.** E-mail: admissions@bennington.edu
Phone: (802) 440-4312 Toll-free number: (800) 833-6845
Fax: (802) 440-4320
Ken Himmelman, Dean of Admissions and Financial Aid, Bennington College, One College Drive, Bennington, VT 05201-6003

## Burlington College

**Burlington, Vermont**
www.burlington.edu

CB code: 1119

- Private 4-year visual arts and liberal arts college
- Commuter campus in small city
- 169 degree-seeking undergraduates: 29% part-time, 45% women, 2% African American, 2% Asian American, 2% Hispanic American, 1% international
- 83% of applicants admitted
- Application essay required
- 40% graduate within 6 years; 42% enter graduate study

**General.** Founded in 1972. Regionally accredited. **Degrees:** 38 bachelor's, 4 associate awarded. **Location:** 90 miles from Montreal, 160 miles from Boston. **Calendar:** Semester, limited summer session. **Full-time faculty:** 6 total; 33% have terminal degrees, 67% women. **Part-time faculty:** 55 total; 26% have terminal degrees, 56% women. **Class size:** 99% < 20, 1% 20-39. **Special facilities:** Film and video editing labs, photography darkroom, college-operated gallery.

**Freshman class profile.** 126 applied, 104 admitted, 24 enrolled.

| | | | |
|---|---|---|---|
| End year in good standing: | 78% | Live on campus: | 50% |
| Return as sophomores: | 60% | International: | 5% |
| Out-of-state: | 57% | | |

**Basis for selection.** Essay and interview very important, followed by recommendations, GPA, and test scores. Writing samples required for distance learning independent degree program. 2 letters of recommendation required for all. **Homeschooled:** Portfolio style transcripts accepted.

**High school preparation.** College-preparatory program recommended. 24 units recommended. Recommended units include English 4, mathematics 3, social studies 4, history 3, science 3 (laboratory 2), foreign language 2 and academic electives 4.

**2009-2010 Annual costs.** Tuition/fees: $20,424. Room only: $6,250. Books/supplies: $990. Personal expenses: $1,800.

**2009-2010 Financial aid. Need-based:** Average need met was 49%. Average scholarship/grant was $9,321; average loan $3,730. 37% of total undergraduate aid awarded as scholarships/grants, 63% as loans/jobs. **Non-need-based:** Scholarships awarded for academics, leadership.

**Application procedures. Admission:** Priority date 5/1; deadline 8/15 (postmark date). $50 fee, may be waived for applicants with need. Admission notification on a rolling basis. Must reply by May 1 or within 2 week(s) if notified thereafter. **Financial aid:** No deadline. FAFSA required. Applicants notified on a rolling basis starting 3/15.

**Academics. Special study options:** Cross-registration, distance learning, double major, dual enrollment of high school students, external degree, independent study, internships, liberal arts/career combination, student-designed major, study abroad. **Credit/placement by examination:** AP, CLEP, IB, institutional tests. 45 credit hours maximum toward associate degree, 90 toward bachelor's. **Support services:** Reduced course load, study skills assistance, tutoring, writing center.

**Majors. Area/ethnic studies:** Latin American. **Legal studies:** General. **Psychology:** General. **Public administration:** Human services. **Visual/performing arts:** Film/cinema, photography, studio arts. **Other:** Documentary studies, Gender studies, Individualized major/multi/Interdisciplinary studies, Transpersonal psychology, Writing and literature.

**Computing on campus.** 20 workstations in library, computer center, student center. Dormitories wired for high-speed internet access. Commuter students can connect to campus network. Online library, wireless network available.

**Student life. Freshman orientation:** Mandatory, $150 fee. Preregistration for classes offered. **Policies:** Full-time, first-year students from outside the greater-Burlington area have priority for housing. **Housing:** Apartments, cooperative housing available. $500 fully refundable deposit. **Activities:** Film society, literary magazine, student government, student newspaper, civic engagement institute, community garden.

**Student services.** Career counseling, financial aid counseling, legal services, personal counseling.

**Contact.** E-mail: admissions@burlington.edu
Phone: (802) 862-9616 ext. 104 Toll-free number: (800) 862-9616 ext. 104
Fax: (802) 660-4331
Gillian McMahon, Admissions Director, Burlington College, 95 North Avenue, Burlington, VT 05401

## Castleton State College
**Castleton, Vermont**
www.castleton.edu

**CB member**
**CB code: 3765**

- Public 4-year liberal arts college
- Residential campus in small town
- 1,965 degree-seeking undergraduates: 8% part-time, 53% women, 1% African American, 1% Asian American, 2% Hispanic American, 1% Native American, 1% international
- 70 degree-seeking graduate students
- 71% of applicants admitted
- SAT or ACT with writing, application essay required
- 50% graduate within 6 years

**General.** Founded in 1787. Regionally accredited. **Degrees:** 331 bachelor's, 49 associate awarded; master's offered. **ROTC:** Army. **Location:** 12 miles from Rutland. **Calendar:** Semester, limited summer session. **Full-time faculty:** 90 total; 96% have terminal degrees, 7% minority, 44% women.

**Part-time faculty:** 132 total; 24% have terminal degrees, 43% women. **Class size:** 73% < 20, 25% 20-39, less than 1% 40-49, 1% 50-99, less than 1% >100. **Special facilities:** Medical society museum, outdoor classroom.

**Freshman class profile.** 2,338 applied, 1,657 admitted, 515 enrolled.

| Mid 50% test scores | | GPA 2.0-2.99: | 53% |
|---|---|---|---|
| SAT critical reading: | 430-530 | Rank in top quarter: | 22% |
| SAT math: | 430-540 | Rank in top tenth: | 5% |
| SAT writing: | 420-520 | Return as sophomores: | 69% |
| ACT composite: | 11-22 | Out-of-state: | 37% |
| GPA 3.75 or higher: | 6% | Live on campus: | 88% |
| GPA 3.50-3.74: | 9% | International: | 1% |
| GPA 3.0-3.49: | 32% | | |

**Basis for selection.** School achievement record, test scores, essay, recommendations, class rank very important. Interview recommended for all; audition recommended for music.

**High school preparation.** College-preparatory program required. 14 units required; 16 recommended. Required and recommended units include English 4, mathematics 3-4, social studies 3-4, history 3, science 3-4 (laboratory 2) and foreign language 2.

**2009-2010 Annual costs.** Tuition/fees: $8,820; $18,060 out-of-state. New England Board of Higher Education rate for students from other New England states: 150% of Vermont resident tuition. Available to degree candidates in academic areas not offered by educational institutions in their home states. Room/board: $7,808. Books/supplies: $800. Personal expenses: $600.

**2008-2009 Financial aid. Non-need-based:** Scholarships awarded for academics, alumni affiliation, art, leadership, music/drama, state residency.

**Application procedures. Admission:** No deadline. $35 fee, may be waived for applicants with need. Admission notification on a rolling basis beginning on or about 12/1. **Financial aid:** Priority date 2/15; no closing date. FAFSA required. Applicants notified on a rolling basis starting 1/1; must reply by 5/1 or within 2 week(s) of notification.

**Academics. Special study options:** Combined bachelor's/graduate degree, cooperative education, cross-registration, double major, dual enrollment of high school students, honors, independent study, internships, liberal arts/career combination, student-designed major, study abroad, teacher certification program. 5-year MBA with Clarkson University, 7-year physical therapy with Sage Graduate School, 6-year occupational therapy with Sage Graduate School. **Credit/placement by examination:** AP, CLEP, SAT, ACT, institutional tests. 30 credit hours maximum toward associate degree, 60 toward bachelor's. **Support services:** Learning center, reduced course load, remedial instruction, study skills assistance, tutoring, writing center.

**Majors. Biology:** General. **Business:** General, accounting, business admin, management science, marketing. **Communications:** Digital media, journalism, media studies. **Computer sciences:** General. **Conservation:** Environmental science. **Education:** Art, biology, chemistry, drama/dance, elementary, English, foreign languages, history, mathematics, middle, music, physical, physics, science, secondary, social science, social studies, Spanish. **Foreign languages:** Spanish. **Health:** Athletic training, nursing (RN). **History:** General. **Interdisciplinary:** Biological/physical sciences, math/computer science, natural sciences. **Math:** General, statistics. **Parks/recreation:** Exercise sciences, health/fitness, sports admin. **Philosophy/religion:** Philosophy. **Physical sciences:** Geology. **Protective services:** Criminal justice. **Psychology:** General. **Public administration:** Social work. **Social sciences:** General, criminology, sociology. **Visual/performing arts:** General, art, dramatic.

**Most popular majors.** Business/marketing 21%, communications/journalism 6%, interdisciplinary studies 9%, mathematics 8%, parks/recreation 10%, psychology 7%, visual/performing arts 8%.

**Computing on campus.** 225 workstations in dormitories, library, computer center. Dormitories wired for high-speed internet access and linked to campus network. Commuter students can connect to campus network. Repair service, wireless network available.

**Student life. Freshman orientation:** Mandatory. Preregistration for classes offered. 2 and a half day program. **Housing:** Guaranteed on-campus for freshmen. Coed dorms available. $100 nonrefundable deposit, deadline 5/1. **Activities:** Bands, choral groups, dance, drama, literary magazine, music ensembles, musical theater, radio station, student government, student newspaper, TV station, Christian fellowships, political discussion group, Spanish club, social issues club, community service club, women's issues group.

**Athletics.** NCAA. **Intercollegiate:** Baseball M, basketball, cross-country, field hockey W, football (tackle) M, golf M, ice hockey, lacrosse, skiing, soccer, softball W, tennis, volleyball W. **Intramural:** Basketball, football (non-tackle), racquetball, soccer M, softball, swimming, table tennis, tennis, volleyball, water polo. **Team name:** Spartans.

**Student services.** Adult student services, alcohol/substance abuse counseling, career counseling, services for economically disadvantaged, student employment services, financial aid counseling, health services, personal counseling, placement for graduates, women's services.

**Contact.** E-mail: info@castleton.edu
Phone: (802) 468-1213 Toll-free number: (800) 639-8521
Fax: (802) 468-1476
Maurice Ouimet, Dean of Enrollment, Castleton State College, Seminary Street, Castleton, VT 05735

## Champlain College
**Burlington, Vermont**
**www.champlain.edu**
**CB member**
**CB code: 3291**

- Private 4-year liberal arts and career college
- Residential campus in small city
- 1,993 degree-seeking undergraduates: 3% part-time, 40% women, 1% African American, 2% Asian American, 1% Hispanic American
- 279 degree-seeking graduate students
- 78% of applicants admitted
- SAT or ACT (ACT writing optional), application essay required
- 70% graduate within 6 years; 13% enter graduate study

**General.** Founded in 1878. Regionally accredited. **Degrees:** 505 bachelor's awarded; master's offered. **ROTC:** Army. **Location:** 200 miles from Boston, 90 miles from Montreal. **Calendar:** Semester, extensive summer session. **Full-time faculty:** 90 total; 52% have terminal degrees, 2% minority, 33% women. **Part-time faculty:** 244 total; 23% have terminal degrees, 2% minority, 45% women. **Class size:** 60% < 20, 40% 20-39.

**Freshman class profile.** 2,929 applied, 2,270 admitted, 545 enrolled.

| Mid 50% test scores | | | |
|---|---|---|---|
| SAT critical reading: | 510-610 | GPA 2.0-2.99: | 45% |
| SAT math: | 510-600 | Rank in top quarter: | 27% |
| ACT composite: | 21-26 | Rank in top tenth: | 7% |
| GPA 3.75 or higher: | 8% | End year in good standing: | 72% |
| GPA 3.50-3.74: | 7% | Return as sophomores: | 72% |
| GPA 3.0-3.49: | 39% | Out-of-state: | 77% |
| | | Live on campus: | 90% |

**Basis for selection.** GPA, level of difficulty of high school curriculum, essay, interview, counselor recommendations most important. Waiting list for Radiography and Electronic Gaming and Interactive Design programs only. Interview strongly recommended. **Homeschooled:** GED or 2 SAT Subject Tests required.

**High school preparation.** College-preparatory program recommended. 20 units required. Required and recommended units include English 4, mathematics 3-4, social studies 2, history 4, science 3-4 (laboratory 2-3), foreign language 2 and academic electives 4.

**2010-2011 Annual costs.** Tuition/fees: $27,180. Room/board: $12,130. Books/supplies: $600. Personal expenses: $600.

**2009-2010 Financial aid. Need-based:** 435 full-time freshmen applied for aid; 353 were judged to have need; 353 of these received aid. Average need met was 76%. Average scholarship/grant was $8,197; average loan $4,178. 56% of total undergraduate aid awarded as scholarships/grants, 44% as loans/jobs. **Non-need-based:** Awarded to 584 full-time undergraduates, including 263 freshmen. Scholarships awarded for academics, leadership.

**Application procedures. Admission:** Closing date 1/31 (postmark date). $50 fee, may be waived for applicants with need, free for online applicants. Admission notification on a rolling basis beginning on or about 12/15. Must reply by 5/1. Housing deposit refundable prior to 5/1 only. **Financial aid:** Closing date 3/1. FAFSA required. Applicants notified by 3/19; must reply by 5/1.

**Academics.** 96% of majors include required internship. **Special study options:** Cooperative education, cross-registration, distance learning, double major, independent study, internships, liberal arts/career combination, study abroad, teacher certification program. Clinical internships at Fletcher Allen Medical Center. **Credit/placement by examination:** AP, CLEP, IB, institutional tests. 75 credit hours maximum toward bachelor's degree. **Support services:** Reduced course load, study skills assistance, tutoring, writing center.

**Majors. Business:** General, accounting, accounting/business management, accounting/finance, business admin, communications, e-commerce, hospitality admin, hospitality/recreation, hotel/motel admin, human resources, international, marketing, organizational behavior, restaurant/food services, small business admin, tourism promotion, tourism/travel, travel services. **Communications:** Digital media, journalism, media studies, organizational, public relations. **Communications technology:** Animation/special effects, graphics. **Computer sciences:** General, computer forensics, computer graphics, computer science, information systems, LAN/WAN management, networking, security, system admin, systems analysis, web page design, webmaster. **Education:** General, early childhood, elementary, kindergarten/preschool, middle, secondary. **Engineering:** Software. **Family/consumer sciences:** Family/community services. **Legal studies:** Paralegal, prelaw. **Liberal arts:** Arts/sciences. **Personal/culinary services:** Restaurant/catering. **Protective services:** Criminal justice, forensics, law enforcement admin, security management, security services. **Psychology:** General. **Public administration:** Human services, social work. **Visual/performing arts:** Cinematography, design, graphic design, multimedia.

**Most popular majors.** Business/marketing 36%, communications/journalism 8%, computer/information sciences 20%, education 7%, security/protective services 6%, visual/performing arts 10%.

**Computing on campus.** 260 workstations in library, computer center, student center. Dormitories wired for high-speed internet access and linked to campus network. Commuter students can connect to campus network. Online course registration, online library, helpline, wireless network available.

**Student life. Freshman orientation:** Available, $60 fee. Preregistration for classes offered. 3-day program. **Policies:** No alcohol permitted on campus. **Housing:** Guaranteed on-campus for freshmen. Coed dorms, wellness housing available. $400 nonrefundable deposit, deadline 5/1. **Activities:** Choral groups, dance, drama, international student organizations, literary magazine, musical theater, radio station, student government, student newspaper, cultural diversity committee, GET REAL community service, outing club, Champlain Heritage Society, Reader's Exchange, flash animation club, Intercollegiate Writers Exchange.

**Athletics. Intramural:** Basketball, bowling, golf, ice hockey, skiing, soccer, volleyball.

**Student services.** Adult student services, alcohol/substance abuse counseling, career counseling, student employment services, financial aid counseling, health services, minority student services, personal counseling, placement for graduates. **Physically disabled:** Services for visually, hearing impaired.

**Contact.** E-mail: admission@champlain.edu
Phone: (802) 860-2727 Toll-free number: (800) 570-5858
Fax: (802) 860-2767
Ian Mortimer, Director of Admission, Champlain College, 163 South Willard Street, Burlington, VT 05402-0670

## College of St. Joseph in Vermont
**Rutland, Vermont**
**www.csj.edu**
**CB member**
**CB code: 3297**

- Private 4-year liberal arts and teachers college affiliated with Roman Catholic Church
- Residential campus in large town
- 211 degree-seeking undergraduates: 17% part-time, 62% women, 6% African American, 1% Hispanic American, 1% Native American
- 143 degree-seeking graduate students
- 78% of applicants admitted
- SAT or ACT (ACT writing optional), application essay required
- 38% graduate within 6 years

**General.** Founded in 1950. Regionally accredited. **Degrees:** 41 bachelor's, 9 associate awarded; master's offered. **Location:** 70 miles from Burlington; 100 miles from Albany, NY. **Calendar:** Semester, extensive summer session. **Full-time faculty:** 11 total; 64% have terminal degrees, 9% minority, 27% women. **Part-time faculty:** 53 total; 17% have terminal degrees, 4% minority, 47% women. **Class size:** 97% < 20, 3% 20-39.

**Freshman class profile.** 143 applied, 112 admitted, 48 enrolled.

| Mid 50% test scores | | | |
|---|---|---|---|
| SAT critical reading: | 340-520 | GPA 2.0-2.99: | 60% |
| SAT math: | 360-520 | Rank in top quarter: | 9% |
| SAT writing: | 370-520 | End year in good standing: | 77% |
| ACT composite: | 17-21 | Return as sophomores: | 74% |
| GPA 3.0-3.49: | 40% | Out-of-state: | 33% |
| | | Live on campus: | 71% |

**Basis for selection.** Admissions based on course selection, 2.0 GPA in college preparatory courses, 2 academic letters of recommendation, essay, and ACT/SAT. Extracurricular activities considered. GED accepted only for students over 22. Interview recommended. **Homeschooled:** Transcript of courses and grades, interview, letter of recommendation (nonparent) required.

**High school preparation.** College-preparatory program recommended. 16 units required. Required and recommended units include English 4, mathematics 3, history 3, science 2 (laboratory 3), foreign language 2 and academic electives 5.

**2009-2010 Annual costs.** Tuition/fees: $17,550. Room/board: $8,350. Books/supplies: $1,000. Personal expenses: $1,350.

**2009-2010 Financial aid. Need-based:** 44 full-time freshmen applied for aid; 42 were judged to have need; 42 of these received aid. Average need met was 75%. Average scholarship/grant was $14,111; average loan $3,900. 53% of total undergraduate aid awarded as scholarships/grants, 47% as loans/jobs. **Non-need-based:** Awarded to 13 full-time undergraduates, including 3 freshmen. Scholarships awarded for academics, alumni affiliation.

**Application procedures. Admission:** Priority date 3/1; no deadline. $25 fee, may be waived for applicants with need. Admission notification on a rolling basis. Must reply by May 1 or within 2 week(s) if notified thereafter. **Financial aid:** Priority date 3/1; no closing date. FAFSA required. Applicants notified on a rolling basis starting 3/15.

**Academics.** Experiential educational options including internships available. **Special study options:** Accelerated study, double major, dual enrollment of high school students, independent study, internships, liberal arts/career combination, teacher certification program. **Credit/placement by examination:** AP, CLEP, IB, SAT, ACT, institutional tests. 12 credit hours maximum toward associate degree, 12 toward bachelor's. **Support services:** Learning center, reduced course load, study skills assistance, tutoring, writing center.

**Majors. Business:** Accounting, business admin, operations. **Education:** Elementary, English, history, multi-level teacher, secondary, social studies. **Health:** Radiologic technology/medical imaging, substance abuse counseling. **History:** General. **Interdisciplinary:** Behavioral sciences. **Liberal arts:** Arts/sciences. **Parks/recreation:** Sports admin. **Protective services:** Law enforcement admin. **Psychology:** General. **Other:** Child and family services, Professional studies - health sciences.

**Most popular majors.** Business/marketing 54%, education 15%, liberal arts 7%, psychology 20%.

**Computing on campus.** 30 workstations in library, computer center, student center. Dormitories wired for high-speed internet access and linked to campus network. Commuter students can connect to campus network. Online library, repair service, wireless network available.

**Student life. Freshman orientation:** Mandatory, $125 fee. Preregistration for classes offered. 5-day orientation before upperclassmen move into dorms. **Housing:** Guaranteed on-campus for all undergraduates. Single-sex dorms available. $200 nonrefundable deposit, deadline 5/1. Some single rooms available and graduate housing available. **Activities:** Campus ministries, choral groups, dance, literary magazine, student government, student ambassadors, human services club, education club, honor societies.

**Athletics.** NAIA. **Intercollegiate:** Basketball, cross-country, soccer. **Intramural:** Baseball M, basketball, soccer, softball. **Team name:** Fighting Saints.

**Student services.** Adult student services, alcohol/substance abuse counseling, chaplain/spiritual director, career counseling, services for economically disadvantaged, student employment services, financial aid counseling, personal counseling, placement for graduates, veterans' counselor. **Physically disabled:** Services for visually, speech, hearing impaired.

**Contact.** E-mail: admissions@csj.edu
Phone: (802) 773-5900 ext. 3286 Toll-free number: (877) 270-9998
Fax: (802) 776-5258
Susan Englese, Dean of Admissions, College of St. Joseph in Vermont, 71 Clement Road, Rutland, VT 05701-3899

---

## Goddard College
**Plainfield, Vermont**
**www.goddard.edu**                              CB code: 3416

- Private 4-year liberal arts college
- Commuter campus in rural community
- 275 degree-seeking undergraduates
- 67% of applicants admitted
- Application essay, interview required

**General.** Founded in 1938. Regionally accredited. **Degrees:** 99 bachelor's awarded; master's offered. **Location:** 10 miles from Montpelier, 45 miles from Burlington. **Calendar:** Semester. **Full-time faculty:** 7 total. **Part-time faculty:** 133 total.

---

**Freshman class profile.** 12 applied, 8 admitted, 8 enrolled.

**Basis for selection.** Academic potential, maturity, ability to work independently, personal statement, interview most important; additional writing sample may be needed. Portfolios recommended when appropriate. **Home-schooled:** State high school equivalency certificate required. GED recommended.

**2009-2010 Annual costs.** Annual tuition for distance learning Bachelor of Arts is $12,344, for Bachelor of Arts in Writing $13,424. Students attend one week on campus each semester; room and board is $1,120. Books/supplies: $600.

**2008-2009 Financial aid. Non-need-based:** Scholarships awarded for academics, art, job skills, leadership, music/drama, state residency.

**Application procedures. Admission:** $40 fee, may be waived for applicants with need. Admission notification on a rolling basis. **Financial aid:** No deadline. FAFSA required. Applicants notified on a rolling basis starting 4/15; must reply within 4 week(s) of notification.

**Academics.** Written evaluations replace grades. Individually designed majors at bachelor's and master's levels. Students design programs of study in collaboration with faculty mentor. Students on campus for 8 days at beginning of each semester and then work from home following study plan designed in collaboration with advisor. **Special study options:** Distance learning, external degree, independent study, internships, student-designed major, study abroad, teacher certification program. Guided-independent study programs convenient for working adults; students required to be on site twice a year for eight days each time. Students design their own curriculum in collaboration with faculty and spend the rest of the semester studying at home or elsewhere. MFA in Creative Writing and MFA in Interdisciplinary Arts offered in Port Townsend, WA as well as Plainfield, VT. **Credit/placement by examination:** AP, CLEP, IB. 30 credit hours maximum toward bachelor's degree. **Support services:** Study skills assistance.

**Majors. Area/ethnic studies:** African-American, American, European, gay/lesbian, Latin American, Native American, Near/Middle Eastern, women's. **Business:** Business admin. **Conservation:** Environmental studies. **Education:** General, art, early childhood, elementary, English, foundations, history, middle, secondary, social studies. **Health:** Aromatherapy, community health, community health services, environmental health, health services, herbalism, movement therapy, polarity therapy, public health ed, Reiki, somatic bodywork. **History:** General. **Liberal arts:** Arts/sciences, humanities.

**Computing on campus.** PC or laptop required. 100 workstations in library, computer center, student center. Dormitories wired for high-speed internet access and linked to campus network. Commuter students can connect to campus network. Online library, helpline, wireless network available.

**Student life. Freshman orientation:** Mandatory, $125 fee. Held day before registration. **Policies:** Dogs are not allowed on campus, with the exception of service dogs. **Housing:** Coed dorms, wellness housing available. $250 nonrefundable deposit. Housing available 8 days per semester. **Activities:** Radio station, student government.

**Student services.** Financial aid counseling.

**Contact.** E-mail: admissions@goddard.edu
Phone: (802) 454-8311 ext. 243 Toll-free number: (800) 906-8312
Fax: (802) 454-1029
Lucinda Garthwaite, Special Assistant to the President, Goddard College, Goddard College Admissions, Plainfield, VT 05667

---

## Green Mountain College
**Poultney, Vermont**                            **CB member**
**www.greenmtn.edu**                             **CB code: 3418**

- Private 4-year liberal arts college affiliated with United Methodist Church
- Residential campus in small town
- 746 degree-seeking undergraduates: 2% part-time, 54% women, 3% African American, 1% Asian American, 3% Hispanic American, 1% Native American
- 97 degree-seeking graduate students
- 62% of applicants admitted
- Application essay required

**General.** Founded in 1834. Regionally accredited. **Degrees:** 158 bachelor's awarded; master's offered. **Location:** 20 miles from Rutland, 35 miles from Killington. **Calendar:** Differs by program, limited summer session. **Full-time faculty:** 49 total; 90% have terminal degrees, 4% minority, 29%

women. **Part-time faculty:** 33 total; 24% have terminal degrees, 46% women. **Class size:** 54% < 20, 46% 20-39. **Special facilities:** Student-operated organically managed farm, ropes course, 80-acre nature preserve, collection of Welsh artifacts and literature, collection of early American decoration, art collection.

**Freshman class profile.** 1,496 applied, 923 admitted, 221 enrolled.

| Mid 50% test scores | | End year in good standing: | 90% |
|---|---|---|---|
| SAT critical reading: | 490-610 | Return as sophomores: | 70% |
| SAT math: | 460-570 | Out-of-state: | 92% |
| SAT writing: | 480-600 | Live on campus: | 99% |

**Basis for selection.** Academic achievement, recommendations, interview, essay, test scores or Insight portfolio submission, personal statement, school and community activities important. Tests are required for homeschooled students, students with a GED, and students attending high schools outside of the US. Interview recommended; audition recommended for theater or music; portfolio recommended for art. **Homeschooled:** Statement describing homeschool structure and mission, transcript of courses and grades, state high school equivalency certificate, letter of recommendation (nonparent) required. Applicants advised to develop thorough portfolio of all work completed. Students highly encouraged to interview on campus.

**High school preparation.** College-preparatory program recommended. 21 units required. Required and recommended units include English 4, mathematics 3-4, social studies 3, history 1-2, science 3-4 (laboratory 2), foreign language 2-3 and academic electives 5.

**2009-2010 Annual costs.** Tuition/fees: $26,900. Room/board: $9,670. Books/supplies: $1,100. Personal expenses: $590.

**2009-2010 Financial aid. Need-based:** 191 full-time freshmen applied for aid; 168 were judged to have need; 168 of these received aid. Average need met was 67%. Average scholarship/grant was $16,516; average loan $3,110. 66% of total undergraduate aid awarded as scholarships/grants, 34% as loans/jobs. **Non-need-based:** Awarded to 159 full-time undergraduates, including 58 freshmen. Scholarships awarded for academics, alumni affiliation, art, leadership, minority status, music/drama, religious affiliation. **Additional information:** Service/recognition awards available to all students.

**Application procedures. Admission:** Priority date 3/1; no deadline. $30 fee, may be waived for applicants with need, free for online applicants. Admission notification on a rolling basis beginning on or about 9/1. Must reply by May 1 or within 2 week(s) if notified thereafter. **Financial aid:** Priority date 3/1; no closing date. FAFSA required. CSS PROFILE is recommended to receive an earlier financial aid package. Applicants notified on a rolling basis starting 11/1; must reply by 5/1 or within 3 week(s) of notification.

**Academics.** A 37-credit general education program that uses sustainability as the organizing theme. **Special study options:** Accelerated study, double major, ESL, exchange student, honors, independent study, internships, liberal arts/career combination, student-designed major, study abroad, teacher certification program. Exchange programs at Aberystwyth University (Wales), Hannam University (Korea), Nogoya University (Japan). Credit granted for programs of National Outdoor Leadership School. Member of Eco-League Consortium; students can spend up to 2 semesters at one of 5 other schools: Alaska Pacific University, Antioch University, College of the Atlantic, Northand College, Prescott College. **Credit/placement by examination:** AP, CLEP, IB, SAT, ACT. **Support services:** Learning center, pre-admission summer program, reduced course load, remedial instruction, study skills assistance, tutoring, writing center.

**Majors. Biology:** General. **Business:** Business admin, hospitality admin, hospitality/recreation, resort management. **Communications:** General, journalism. **Conservation:** General, environmental studies, management/policy. **Education:** Art, elementary, English, middle, secondary, social studies, special. **History:** General. **Liberal arts:** Arts/sciences. **Parks/recreation:** General, facilities management. **Philosophy/religion:** Philosophy. **Psychology:** General. **Social sciences:** Anthropology, sociology. **Visual/performing arts:** Art, studio arts. **Other:** Environmental Management.

**Most popular majors.** Business/marketing 17%, education 8%, English 8%, interdisciplinary studies 7%, liberal arts 8%, natural resources/environmental science 12%, parks/recreation 6%, psychology 9%, social sciences 7%, visual/performing arts 6%.

**Computing on campus.** 60 workstations in dormitories, library, computer center, student center. Dormitories wired for high-speed internet access and linked to campus network. Commuter students can connect to campus network. Online course registration, online library, helpline, wireless network available.

**Student life. Freshman orientation:** Mandatory, $100 fee. Preregistration for classes offered. Orientation held week before classes begin in August and January. Students also may opt to come to campus on specified

days during summer. **Housing:** Guaranteed on-campus for all undergraduates. Coed dorms, wellness housing available. **Activities:** Bands, choral groups, drama, film society, literary magazine, music ensembles, radio station, student government, student newspaper, outdoor adventure programs, Poultney Partners Mentoring Program, environmental volunteer and research groups, African American Culture Club, diversity club, UNICEF.

**Athletics.** NCAA. **Intercollegiate:** Basketball, cross-country, golf M, lacrosse, skiing, soccer, softball W, tennis, volleyball W. **Intramural:** Basketball, football (non-tackle), skiing, soccer, softball, table tennis, tennis, volleyball. **Team name:** Eagles.

**Student services.** Alcohol/substance abuse counseling, chaplain/spiritual director, career counseling, student employment services, financial aid counseling, health services, personal counseling, placement for graduates.

**Contact.** E-mail: admiss@greenmtn.edu
Phone: (802) 287-8207 Toll-free number: (800) 776-6675
Fax: (802) 287-8099
Sandra Bartholomew, Dean of Enrollment Management, Green Mountain College, One Brennan Circle, Poultney, VT 05764

## Johnson State College

| Johnson, Vermont | CB member |
|---|---|
| www.jsc.edu | CB code: 3766 |

- Public 4-year liberal arts college
- Residential campus in small town
- 1,672 degree-seeking undergraduates: 28% part-time, 61% women, 2% African American, 1% Asian American, 2% Hispanic American, 1% Native American
- 200 degree-seeking graduate students
- SAT or ACT (ACT writing optional), application essay required

**General.** Founded in 1828. Regionally accredited. Special tuition rate for New England residents who apply to selected fields of study. **Degrees:** 297 bachelor's, 13 associate awarded; master's offered. **ROTC:** Army. **Location:** 50 miles from Burlington, 90 miles from Montreal. **Calendar:** Semester, limited summer session. **Full-time faculty:** 53 total; 79% have terminal degrees, 4% minority, 36% women. **Part-time faculty:** 86 total; 22% have terminal degrees, 6% minority, 54% women. **Class size:** 74% < 20, 26% 20-39. **Special facilities:** 1,000-acre nature preserve, visual arts center, human performance laboratory, interactive multimedia math, science laboratory, recording studio, community service learning center, Vermont interactive television site, snowboard park.

**Freshman class profile.**

| Mid 50% test scores | | Return as sophomores: | 68% |
|---|---|---|---|
| SAT critical reading: | 430-550 | Out-of-state: | 29% |
| SAT math: | 430-550 | Live on campus: | 90% |
| ACT composite: | 20-28 | | |

**Basis for selection.** High school transcript, GPA, SAT/ACT, class rank, recommendations, and essay important. Tests not required with GED. Interview recommended. **Homeschooled:** Transcript of courses and grades, state high school equivalency certificate, letter of recommendation (nonparent) required. Applicants encouraged to complete GED or other state certified achievement test to demonstrate aptitude.

**High school preparation.** 9 units required; 15 recommended. Required and recommended units include English 4, mathematics 3-4, social studies 2, history 2, science 2-3 (laboratory 1-2) and foreign language 1. Math units must include algebra I, geometry and algebra II.

**2009-2010 Annual costs.** Tuition/fees: $8,716; $17,956 out-of-state. New England Board of Higher Education rate for students from other New England states: 150% of Vermont resident tuition. Available to degree candidates in academic areas not offered by educational institutions in their home states. Room/board: $7,809. Books/supplies: $1,000. Personal expenses: $650.

**2009-2010 Financial aid. Need-based:** 277 full-time freshmen applied for aid; 232 were judged to have need; 232 of these received aid. Average need met was 88%. Average scholarship/grant was $6,151; average loan $3,583. 35% of total undergraduate aid awarded as scholarships/grants, 65% as loans/jobs. **Non-need-based:** Awarded to 31 full-time undergraduates, including 16 freshmen. Scholarships awarded for academics, alumni affiliation, art, leadership, music/drama, state residency.

**Application procedures. Admission:** Priority date 3/1; no deadline. $35 fee, may be waived for applicants with need, free for online applicants. Admission notification on a rolling basis beginning on or about 12/1. Must reply by May 1 or within 2 week(s) if notified thereafter. **Financial aid:**

Priority date 3/1; no closing date. FAFSA required. Applicants notified on a rolling basis starting 4/1; must reply within 3 week(s) of notification.

**Academics.** Transition program for students who show potential academic success but may be unprepared academically and/or socially. **Special study options:** Accelerated study, cross-registration, distance learning, double major, dual enrollment of high school students, ESL, exchange student, external degree, independent study, internships, study abroad, teacher certification program. **Credit/placement by examination:** AP, CLEP, IB, institutional tests. **Support services:** Learning center, pre-admission summer program, reduced course load, remedial instruction, study skills assistance, tutoring, writing center.

**Majors. Biology:** General, cell/histology, molecular. **Business:** General, business admin, hospitality admin, tourism/travel. **Communications:** Journalism. **Conservation:** General, environmental studies, management/policy. **Education:** General, art, biology, drama/dance, elementary, English, history, mathematics, middle, multi-level teacher, music, physical, science, secondary, social science, social studies. **Foreign languages:** Comparative lit. **Health:** Athletic training, premedicine. **History:** General. **Liberal arts:** Arts/sciences. **Math:** General. **Parks/recreation:** General, exercise sciences, health/fitness, sports admin. **Psychology:** General. **Social sciences:** General, anthropology, political science, sociology. **Visual/performing arts:** General, art, dance, dramatic, jazz, music history, music performance, music theory/composition, musical theater, piano/organ, studio arts, theater design, voice/opera. **Other:** Wellness and alternative medicine.

**Most popular majors.** Business/marketing 17%, education 9%, English 6%, liberal arts 20%, psychology 16%, visual/performing arts 11%.

**Computing on campus.** 131 workstations in library, computer center. Dormitories wired for high-speed internet access and linked to campus network. Commuter students can connect to campus network. Online course registration, online library, helpline, wireless network available.

**Student life. Freshman orientation:** Mandatory, $189 fee. Preregistration for classes offered. Held prior to start of semester. **Housing:** Guaranteed on-campus for all undergraduates. Coed dorms, apartments, wellness housing available. $300 nonrefundable deposit, deadline 5/1. **Activities:** Bands, choral groups, dance, drama, film society, international student organizations, literary magazine, music ensembles, musical theater, radio station, student government, student newspaper, behavioral science club, Christian fellowship club, diversity committee, political awareness club, Little Brother/Little Sister, Habitat for Humanity, Native American club, Students Enriching and Responding Through Volunteer Efforts, Earth awareness club.

**Athletics.** NCAA. **Intercollegiate:** Basketball, cross-country, golf M, lacrosse M, soccer, softball W, tennis, volleyball W. **Intramural:** Badminton, basketball, bowling, cross-country, golf, lacrosse, racquetball, rugby, soccer, softball, swimming, table tennis, tennis, volleyball, water polo, weight lifting. **Team name:** Badgers.

**Student services.** Adult student services, alcohol/substance abuse counseling, career counseling, services for economically disadvantaged, student employment services, financial aid counseling, health services, on-campus daycare, personal counseling, placement for graduates, women's services. **Physically disabled:** Services for visually, hearing impaired.

**Contact.** E-mail: jscadmissions@jsc.edu
Phone: (802) 635-1219 Toll-free number: (800) 635-2356
Fax: (802) 635-1230
Penny Howrigan, Associate Dean of Enrollment Services, Johnson State College, 337 College Hill, Johnson, VT 05656

## Lyndon State College
### Lyndonville, Vermont
www.lyndonstate.edu          **CB code: 3767**

- Public 4-year liberal arts and teachers college
- Residential campus in small town
- 1,500 degree-seeking undergraduates
- 20 graduate students
- Application essay, interview required

**General.** Founded in 1911. Regionally accredited. **Degrees:** 183 bachelor's, 22 associate awarded; master's offered. **ROTC:** Air Force. **Location:** 10 miles from St. Johnsbury, 85 miles from Burlington. **Calendar:** Semester, limited summer session. **Full-time faculty:** 58 total; 91% have terminal degrees, 40% women. **Part-time faculty:** 109 total; 43% have terminal degrees, 2% minority, 44% women. **Class size:** 75% < 20, 25% 20-39, less than 1% 40-49. **Special facilities:** Meteorology laboratory and observation deck, ropes course, rock climbing wall, ski resorts, force plate, music production studio.

## Freshman class profile.

| Mid 50% test scores | | | |
|---|---|---|---|
| SAT critical reading: | 400-510 | ACT composite: | 18-21 |
| SAT math: | 400-510 | Out-of-state: | 58% |
| SAT writing: | 400-500 | Live on campus: | 65% |

**Basis for selection.** School record, GPA, recommendations and optional test scores most important. SAT or ACT recommended. **Homeschooled:** Transcript of courses and grades, interview, letter of recommendation (non-parent) required. **Learning Disabled:** Students must meet with learning specialist and provide documentation of disability.

**High school preparation.** College-preparatory program recommended. Required and recommended units include English 4, mathematics 3-4, social studies 2, history 1, science 2-4 (laboratory 2) and foreign language 2. Physics and pre-calc for meteorology and computer science recommended.

**2009-2010 Annual costs.** Tuition/fees: $8,820; $18,060 out-of-state. New England Board of Higher Education rate for students from other New England states: 150% of Vermont resident tuition. Available to degree candidates in academic areas not offered by educational institutions in their home states. Room/board: $7,808. Books/supplies: $600. Personal expenses: $900.

**2008-2009 Financial aid. Non-need-based:** Scholarships awarded for academics, leadership.

**Application procedures. Admission:** Priority date 5/1; no deadline. $37 fee, may be waived for applicants with need. Admission notification on a rolling basis beginning on or about 11/1. Must reply by May 1 or within 2 week(s) if notified thereafter. **Financial aid:** Priority date 2/1; no closing date. FAFSA required. Applicants notified on a rolling basis starting 4/1; must reply within 2 week(s) of notification.

**Academics. Special study options:** Combined bachelor's/graduate degree, cooperative education, distance learning, double major, dual enrollment of high school students, ESL, internships, liberal arts/career combination, student-designed major, study abroad, teacher certification program. **Credit/placement by examination:** AP, CLEP, IB, institutional tests. 60 credit hours maximum toward bachelor's degree. **Support services:** Learning center, reduced course load, remedial instruction, study skills assistance, tutoring, writing center.

**Majors. Business:** Accounting, accounting/business management, accounting/finance, business admin, entrepreneurial studies, finance, marketing, resort management, small business admin. **Communications:** General, broadcast journalism, journalism, media studies, photojournalism, radio/tv. **Communications technology:** General. **Computer sciences:** General. **Conservation:** Environmental science. **Education:** General, early childhood, elementary, English, physical, science, social science, special. **Health:** Athletic training, prenursing. **Interdisciplinary:** Biological/physical sciences, global studies, natural sciences. **Liberal arts:** Arts/sciences. **Math:** General. **Parks/recreation:** Exercise sciences, facilities management, health/fitness, sports admin. **Philosophy/religion:** Philosophy. **Physical sciences:** Atmospheric science, meteorology. **Psychology:** General. **Public administration:** Human services. **Social sciences:** General. **Visual/performing arts:** General, commercial/advertising art, design, digital art, graphic design, illustration, music management, music performance. **Other:** English: journalism and writing, Exercise science, Meteorology: military track, Mountain recreation management, Music business and industry, Philosophy and film, Sustainability studies.

**Most popular majors.** Business/marketing 13%, communications/journalism 7%, communication technologies 11%, parks/recreation 13%, physical sciences 10%, psychology 7%, public administration/social services 14%, visual/performing arts 7%.

**Computing on campus.** 50 workstations in library, computer center. Dormitories wired for high-speed internet access and linked to campus network. Commuter students can connect to campus network. Online course registration, online library, helpline, repair service, wireless network available.

**Student life. Freshman orientation:** Mandatory. Preregistration for classes offered. **Policies:** Unmarried students under 23 must live on-campus for 2 consecutive years (1 year requirement for sophomore-level transfers) unless residing with parents within 45-mile commuting distance. Exceptions made on case-by-case basis. **Housing:** Guaranteed on-campus for freshmen. Coed dorms, single-sex dorms, special housing for disabled, wellness housing available. $100 deposit, deadline 5/1. **Activities:** Jazz band, choral groups, dance, drama, literary magazine, music ensembles, radio station, student government, student newspaper, symphony orchestra, TV station, American Meteorological Society (student chapter), community service learning group, alternative spring break.

**Athletics.** NAIA, NCAA. **Intercollegiate:** Baseball M, basketball, cross-country, ice hockey, soccer, softball W, tennis. **Intramural:** Basketball, cross-country, handball, ice hockey, lacrosse, racquetball, rugby, soccer, softball, squash, swimming, table tennis, tennis, track and field, volleyball, water polo M, weight lifting. **Team name:** Hornets.

**Student services.** Alcohol/substance abuse counseling, career counseling, student employment services, financial aid counseling, health services, personal counseling, placement for graduates, veterans' counselor. **Physically disabled:** Services for visually, hearing impaired.

**Contact.** E-mail: admissions@lyndonstate.edu
Phone: (802) 626-6413 Toll-free number: (800) 225-1998
Fax: (802) 626-6335
Patricia Krahnke, Dean of Admissions/Marketing, Lyndon State College, 1001 College Road, Lyndonville, VT 05851

## Marlboro College
**Marlboro, Vermont**
**www.marlboro.edu**
CB member
CB code: 3509

- Private 4-year liberal arts college
- Residential campus in rural community
- 311 degree-seeking undergraduates: 1% part-time, 48% women
- 71% of applicants admitted
- Application essay required
- 65% graduate within 6 years

**General.** Founded in 1946. Regionally accredited. **Degrees:** 75 bachelor's awarded; master's offered. **Location:** 12 miles from Brattleboro; 70 miles from Albany, NY. **Calendar:** Semester. **Full-time faculty:** 39 total; 87% have terminal degrees, 5% minority, 36% women. **Part-time faculty:** 7 total; 86% have terminal degrees, 14% women. **Class size:** 99% < 20, 1% 20-39. **Special facilities:** Aviary, observatory, darkroom, theater 3/4 round, robotics lab, DNA lab, nature preserve, organic campus farm.

**Freshman class profile.** 401 applied, 284 admitted, 64 enrolled.

| Mid 50% test scores | | | |
|---|---|---|---|
| SAT critical reading: | 590-690 | GPA 3.0-3.49: | 26% |
| SAT math: | 510-650 | GPA 2.0-2.99: | 25% |
| SAT writing: | 640-720 | Rank in top quarter: | 60% |
| ACT composite: | 24-32 | Rank in top tenth: | 40% |
| GPA 3.75 or higher: | 27% | Return as sophomores: | 75% |
| GPA 3.50-3.74: | 22% | Out-of-state: | 90% |
| | | Live on campus: | 98% |

**Basis for selection.** Academic ability, intellectual potential, writing skills, demonstrated leadership qualities, and potential to offer contribution to college community most important. Interview may be required at discretion of admission committee. **Homeschooled:** Statement describing homeschool structure and mission, letter of recommendation (nonparent) required. Provide documentation of home school curriculum and projects. List of textbooks preferred. Writing sample required. **Learning Disabled:** Additional documentation may be required.

**High school preparation.** College-preparatory program recommended. 23 units recommended. Recommended units include English 4, mathematics 3, social studies 3, history 3, science 3 (laboratory 1), foreign language 3 and academic electives 3. Advanced electives in area of interest and in performing and/or visual arts also recommended.

**2010-2011 Annual costs.** Tuition/fees: $35,120. Room/board: $9,420. Books/supplies: $1,000. Personal expenses: $150.

**2009-2010 Financial aid. Need-based:** Average need met was 88%. Average scholarship/grant was $14,746; average loan $3,500. 75% of total undergraduate aid awarded as scholarships/grants, 25% as loans/jobs. **Non-need-based:** Scholarships awarded for academics, leadership.

**Application procedures. Admission:** Priority date 3/1; no deadline. $50 fee, may be waived for applicants with need. Admission notification on a rolling basis beginning on or about 12/15. Must reply by May 1 or within 2 week(s) if notified thereafter. **Financial aid:** Closing date 3/1. FAFSA required. Applicants notified on a rolling basis starting 3/15; must reply by 5/1 or within 2 week(s) of notification.

**Academics.** Students self-design field of study, often interdisciplinary in nature. They work closely with faculty to determine concentration and have formal review in senior year by internal and external faculty. **Special study options:** Double major, dual enrollment of high school students, independent study, internships, student-designed major, study abroad. World Studies Program: opportunity to integrate study-abroad experience and/or internship in undergraduate course of study. **Credit/placement by examination:** AP, CLEP, IB, institutional tests. **Support services:** Learning center, reduced course load, study skills assistance, tutoring, writing center.

**Majors. Area/ethnic studies:** American, Asian, Central/Eastern European, East Asian, European, Latin American, Near/Middle Eastern, Russian/

Slavic, South Asian, Southeast Asian, Western European. **Biology:** General, biochemistry, botany, cell/histology, ecology, genetics, molecular, plant physiology. **Computer sciences:** General, computer science. **Conservation:** General, environmental studies. **Foreign languages:** General, comparative lit, linguistics, Spanish, translation. **History:** General. **Interdisciplinary:** Biological/physical sciences, global studies, math/computer science, peace/conflict. **Legal studies:** Prelaw. **Liberal arts:** Arts/sciences. **Math:** General. **Philosophy/religion:** Philosophy, religion. **Physical sciences:** Astronomy, chemistry, organic chemistry, physics, theoretical physics. **Psychology:** General. **Social sciences:** General, anthropology, economics, political science, sociology. **Visual/performing arts:** General, art, art history/conservation, ceramics, cinematography, dance, dramatic, drawing, film/cinema, music history, painting, photography, play/screenwriting, sculpture, studio arts, theater design, theater history.

**Most popular majors.** Area/ethnic studies 8%, biology 7%, English 25%, social sciences 19%, visual/performing arts 23%.

**Computing on campus.** 45 workstations in dormitories, library, computer center. Dormitories wired for high-speed internet access and linked to campus network. Commuter students can connect to campus network. Online course registration, online library, helpline, student web hosting, wireless network available.

**Student life. Freshman orientation:** Mandatory. 5-day program in late August; optional pre-orientation outdoor trips held the week prior to on-campus orientation and student enrollment. **Policies:** Self-governing community based on old-fashioned, historical New England-style town meeting. Students, faculty, and staff have equal vote. Elected community court enforces bylaws. **Housing:** Guaranteed on-campus for freshmen. Coed dorms, single-sex dorms, apartments, wellness housing available. $400 nonrefundable deposit, deadline 5/1. **Activities:** Dance, drama, film society, literary magazine, music ensembles, musical theater, student government, student newspaper, Amnesty International, animal rights, gay/lesbian and bisexual group, committee on environmental quality, fire and safety commission.

**Athletics. Intercollegiate:** Soccer. **Intramural:** Basketball, fencing, soccer, softball, swimming, table tennis, volleyball.

**Student services.** Alcohol/substance abuse counseling, career counseling, financial aid counseling, health services, personal counseling. **Physically disabled:** Services for visually impaired.

**Contact.** E-mail: admissions@marlboro.edu
Phone: (802) 258-9236 Toll-free number: (800) 343-0049
Fax: (802) 451-7555
Nicole Curvin, Dean of Admission, Marlboro College, PO Box A, Marlboro, VT 05344-0300

## Middlebury College
**Middlebury, Vermont**
**www.middlebury.edu**
CB member
CB code: 3526

- Private 4-year liberal arts college
- Residential campus in small town
- 2,455 degree-seeking undergraduates: 1% part-time, 51% women, 4% African American, 9% Asian American, 5% Hispanic American, 10% international
- 20% of applicants admitted
- SAT or ACT (ACT writing optional), application essay required
- 92% graduate within 6 years

**General.** Founded in 1800. Regionally accredited. Affiliated with Monterey Institute of International Studies. **Degrees:** 639 bachelor's awarded; master's, doctoral offered. **ROTC:** Army. **Location:** 200 miles from Boston, 250 miles from New York City. **Calendar:** 4-1-4, limited summer session. **Full-time faculty:** 260 total; 95% have terminal degrees, 11% minority, 41% women. **Part-time faculty:** 51 total; 82% have terminal degrees, 2% minority, 43% women. **Class size:** 69% < 20, 24% 20-39, 5% 40-49, 3% 50-99. **Special facilities:** Observatory, fine arts center, downhill and cross country ski areas, interactive language laboratories, 18-hole golf course.

**Freshman class profile.** 6,904 applied, 1,413 admitted, 603 enrolled.

| Mid 50% test scores | | | |
|---|---|---|---|
| SAT critical reading: | 640-730 | Rank in top tenth: | 87% |
| SAT math: | 650-740 | Return as sophomores: | 97% |
| SAT writing: | 650-740 | Out-of-state: | 95% |
| ACT composite: | 30-33 | Live on campus: | 100% |
| Rank in top quarter: | 94% | International: | 10% |

**Basis for selection.** School record most important (including course selection and course load), followed by class rank, extracurricular activities, letters of recommendation, and test scores. ACT or SAT or 3 SAT Subject Tests required.

**High school preparation.** College-preparatory program recommended. Recommended units include English 4, mathematics 4, social studies 3, science 3 (laboratory 3) and foreign language 4. Music, art, or drama recommended.

**2010-2011 Annual costs.** Comprehensive fee: $52,500. Books/supplies: $750. Personal expenses: $1,000.

**2008-2009 Financial aid.** All financial aid based on need. 336 full-time freshmen applied for aid; 249 were judged to have need; 249 of these received aid. Average need met was 100%. Average scholarship/grant was $34,362; average loan $2,782. 88% of total undergraduate aid awarded as scholarships/grants, 12% as loans/jobs. **Additional information:** College maintains need-blind admissions policy and meets full demonstrated financial need of students who qualify for admission, to degree resources permit.

**Application procedures.** Admission: Closing date 1/1 (postmark date). $65 fee, may be waived for applicants with need. Admission notification 4/1. Must reply by 5/1. **Financial aid:** Priority date 11/1, closing date 2/1. FAFSA, CSS PROFILE required. Applicants notified by 4/1; must reply by 5/1.

**Academics. Special study options:** Accelerated study, double major, exchange student, honors, independent study, internships, semester at sea, student-designed major, study abroad, teacher certification program, Washington semester. Williams College-Mystic Seaport Program in American Maritime Studies, Oxford University summer program, independent scholar program, exchange programs with Berea College and Swarthmore College, 3-year international major. **Credit/placement by examination:** AP, CLEP, IB, institutional tests. **Support services:** Learning center, pre-admission summer program, reduced course load, study skills assistance, tutoring, writing center.

**Majors. Area/ethnic studies:** African, American, Central/Eastern European, East Asian, European, Latin American, Near/Middle Eastern, Russian/Slavic, Southeast Asian, women's. **Biology:** General, biochemistry, molecular. **Computer sciences:** Computer science. **Conservation:** Environmental studies. **Foreign languages:** Chinese, classics, French, German, Italian, Japanese, Russian, Spanish. **History:** General. **Interdisciplinary:** Neuroscience. **Liberal arts:** Arts/sciences. **Math:** General. **Philosophy/religion:** Philosophy, religion. **Physical sciences:** Chemistry, geology, physics. **Psychology:** General. **Social sciences:** Economics, geography, international relations, political science, sociology. **Visual/performing arts:** Art history/conservation, cinematography, dance, dramatic, studio arts.

**Most popular majors.** Area/ethnic studies 10%, English 8%, foreign language 10%, social sciences 28%, visual/performing arts 9%.

**Computing on campus.** 494 workstations in dormitories, library, computer center, student center. Dormitories wired for high-speed internet access and linked to campus network. Commuter students can connect to campus network. Online course registration, online library, helpline, repair service, student web hosting, wireless network available.

**Student life. Freshman orientation:** Mandatory. Elective portion of orientation carries cost of $150. **Housing:** Guaranteed on-campus for all undergraduates. Coed dorms, special housing for disabled, apartments, wellness housing available. $200 deposit, deadline 5/1. Multicultural, environmental, foreign language, and 5 social houses available. Commons System organizes residence halls into 5 groups, each with own budget, government, faculty, and staff associates. **Activities:** Jazz band, choral groups, dance, drama, film society, international student organizations, literary magazine, music ensembles, musical theater, radio station, student government, student newspaper, symphony orchestra, African-American Alliance, Alianza Latinoamerica y Caribena, Asian students organization, environmental quality, Hillel, gay/lesbian/bisexual alliance, mountain club, volunteer service program, women's organization.

**Athletics.** NCAA. **Intercollegiate:** Baseball M, basketball, cross-country, diving, field hockey W, football (tackle) M, golf, ice hockey, lacrosse, skiing, soccer, softball W, squash W, swimming, tennis, track and field, volleyball W. **Intramural:** Badminton, basketball, cross-country, diving, football (non-tackle), golf, ice hockey, lacrosse, skiing, soccer, softball, squash W, swimming, table tennis, tennis, triathlon, volleyball. **Team name:** Panthers.

**Student services.** Alcohol/substance abuse counseling, chaplain/spiritual director, career counseling, student employment services, financial aid counseling, health services, minority student services, personal counseling, placement for graduates, women's services. **Physically disabled:** Services for visually impaired, speech, hearing impaired.

**Contact.** E-mail: admissions@middlebury.edu
Phone: (802) 443-3000 Fax: (802) 443-0258
Robert Clagett, Dean of Admissions, Middlebury College, The Emma Willard House, Middlebury, VT 05753-6002

---

## Norwich University
**Northfield, Vermont**
www.norwich.edu

CB member
CB code: 3669

- Private 4-year university and military college
- Residential campus in small town
- 2,120 degree-seeking undergraduates: 2% part-time, 28% women, 3% African American, 2% Asian American, 5% Hispanic American, 2% international
- 1,273 degree-seeking graduate students
- SAT or ACT (ACT writing optional) required

**General.** Founded in 1819. Regionally accredited. Adult programs are self-designed, individually-mentored programs. Both military and civilian students accepted. **Degrees:** 374 bachelor's awarded; master's offered. **ROTC:** Army, Naval, Air Force. **Location:** 50 miles from Burlington, 180 miles from Boston. **Calendar:** Semester, limited summer session. **Full-time faculty:** 125 total. **Part-time faculty:** 137 total. **Special facilities:** Museum.

**Freshman class profile.**

| Mid 50% test scores | | | |
|---|---|---|---|
| SAT critical reading: | 470-600 | Out-of-state: | 80% |
| SAT math: | 480-600 | Live on campus: | 98% |
| ACT composite: | 19-24 | International: | 2% |

**Basis for selection.** High school record, recommendations, activities, honors, awards, test scores important. Class rank considered and is criterion for financial aid.

**High school preparation.** 18 units recommended. Recommended units include English 4, mathematics 3, social studies 2, science 1 and foreign language 2.

**2010-2011 Annual costs.** Tuition/fees: $28,738. Room/board: $9,958. Books/supplies: $1,000. Personal expenses: $1,500.

**Financial aid. Non-need-based:** Scholarships awarded for academics, leadership, music/drama, ROTC. **Additional information:** Winners of ROTC scholarships receive full room and board; must maintain 2.75 GPA. Renewable up to 4 years.

**Application procedures.** Admission: Priority date 5/1; no deadline. $35 fee, may be waived for applicants with need. Admission notification on a rolling basis beginning on or about 11/30. Must reply by May 1 or within 3 week(s) if notified thereafter. **Financial aid:** Priority date 3/1; no closing date. FAFSA, institutional form, CSS PROFILE required. Applicants notified on a rolling basis starting 12/15.

**Academics. Special study options:** Accelerated study, combined bachelor's/graduate degree, distance learning, double major, ESL, external degree, honors, independent study, internships, liberal arts/career combination, student-designed major, study abroad, teacher certification program. **Credit/placement by examination:** AP, CLEP, IB, institutional tests. 12 credit hours maximum toward bachelor's degree. **Support services:** Learning center, pre-admission summer program, reduced course load, remedial instruction, tutoring.

**Majors. Architecture:** Architecture. **Biology:** General, biochemistry, biomedical sciences. **Business:** Accounting, business admin. **Communications:** General. **Computer sciences:** Computer science, security. **Conservation:** General. **Education:** Physical. **Engineering:** Civil, electrical, environmental, mechanical. **Foreign languages:** Spanish. **Health:** Athletic training. **History:** General. **Interdisciplinary:** Peace/conflict. **Liberal arts:** Arts/sciences. **Math:** General. **Parks/recreation:** Health/fitness, sports admin. **Physical sciences:** Chemistry, geology, physics. **Protective services:** Criminal justice. **Psychology:** General. **Social sciences:** Economics, international relations, political science.

**Most popular majors.** Architecture 7%, business/marketing 8%, engineering/engineering technologies 9%, health sciences 17%, history 8%, legal studies 24%, social sciences 8%.

**Computing on campus.** 150 workstations in library, computer center. Dormitories linked to campus network. Commuter students can connect to campus network. Online library, helpline, repair service, wireless network available.

**Student life. Freshman orientation:** Available, $10 fee. Preregistration for classes offered. Held Wednesday-Sunday; includes 1-day cruise dinner. **Policies:** ROTC participants must live in dormitories. **Housing:** Guaranteed on-campus for freshmen. Coed dorms available. $250 deposit, deadline 5/1. **Activities:** Bands, choral groups, drama, international student organizations, literary magazine, music ensembles, musical theater, radio station, student government, student newspaper, symphony orchestra, Arnold Air Society, Special Operations Company Association of the United States Army, volunteer organization, Christian Fellowship, ambulance rescue squad, Young Republicans, Square and Compass.

**Athletics.** NCAA. **Intercollegiate:** Baseball M, basketball, cross-country, diving, football (tackle) M, golf, ice hockey, lacrosse, rifle, rugby, soccer, softball W, swimming, wrestling M. **Intramural:** Basketball, cross-country, fencing, football (tackle) M, ice hockey, lacrosse M, racquetball, skiing, soccer, softball, tennis, track and field, volleyball. **Team name:** Cadets.

**Student services.** Adult student services, chaplain/spiritual director, career counseling, student employment services, financial aid counseling, health services, personal counseling, placement for graduates, veterans' counselor.

**Contact.** E-mail: nuadm@norwich.edu
Phone: (802) 485-2002 Toll-free number: (800) 468-6679
Fax: (802) 485-2032
Karen McGrath, Dean of Enrollment, Norwich University, 158 Harmon Drive, Northfield, VT 05663

## St. Michael's College
**Colchester, Vermont**
**www.smcvt.edu**

**CB member**
**CB code: 3757**

- Private 4-year liberal arts college affiliated with Roman Catholic Church
- Residential campus in small city
- 1,915 degree-seeking undergraduates: 1% part-time, 52% women, 1% African American, 1% Asian American, 2% Hispanic American, 2% international
- 278 degree-seeking graduate students
- 81% of applicants admitted
- SAT or ACT with writing, application essay required
- 76% graduate within 6 years; 21% enter graduate study

**General.** Founded in 1904. Regionally accredited. **Degrees:** 508 bachelor's awarded; master's offered. **ROTC:** Army, Air Force. **Location:** 3 miles from Burlington; 95 miles from Montreal, Canada. **Calendar:** Semester, limited summer session. **Full-time faculty:** 151 total; 85% have terminal degrees, 8% minority, 44% women. **Part-time faculty:** 63 total; 49% have terminal degrees, 5% minority, 54% women. **Class size:** 56% < 20, 42% 20-39, less than 1% 40-49, 2% 50-99. **Special facilities:** Observatory, art gallery.

**Freshman class profile.** 3,228 applied, 2,613 admitted, 475 enrolled.

| Mid 50% test scores | | GPA 2.0-2.99: | 24% |
|---|---|---|---|
| SAT critical reading: | 520-630 | Rank in top quarter: | 54% |
| SAT math: | 520-620 | Rank in top tenth: | 24% |
| SAT writing: | 510-620 | End year in good standing: | 94% |
| ACT composite: | 22-27 | Return as sophomores: | 89% |
| GPA 3.75 or higher: | 36% | Out-of-state: | 86% |
| GPA 3.50-3.74: | 18% | Live on campus: | 99% |
| GPA 3.0-3.49: | 22% | International: | 1% |

**Basis for selection.** Curriculum, high school performance, test scores, application essay, recommendations, and activities important. SAT Subject Tests or college-administered language placement tests required. **Homeschooled:** Statement describing homeschool structure and mission, transcript of courses and grades, state high school equivalency certificate required. SAT/ACT take on additional emphasis.

**High school preparation.** College-preparatory program required. 16 units required; 20 recommended. Required and recommended units include English 4, mathematics 3-4, social studies 3-4, science 3-4 (laboratory 2-3) and foreign language 3-4. Physics, math, chemistry, biology emphasized for science applicants. History courses fulfill social studies requirement.

**2010-2011 Annual costs.** Tuition/fees: $34,845. Room/board: $8,685. Books/supplies: $1,200. Personal expenses: $450.

**2009-2010 Financial aid. Need-based:** 388 full-time freshmen applied for aid; 317 were judged to have need; 317 of these received aid. Average need met was 81%. Average scholarship/grant was $17,779; average loan $4,846. 66% of total undergraduate aid awarded as scholarships/grants, 34% as loans/jobs. **Non-need-based:** Awarded to 709 full-time undergraduates, including 194 freshmen. Scholarships awarded for academics, athletics, ROTC.

**Application procedures. Admission:** Priority date 11/1; deadline 2/1 (postmark date). $50 fee, may be waived for applicants with need. Admission notification 4/1. Must reply by May 1 or within 2 week(s) if notified thereafter. Second Early Action deadline 12/1, notification 2/1. **Financial**

**aid:** Priority date 2/15; no closing date. FAFSA required. Applicants notified on a rolling basis starting 2/1; must reply by 5/1 or within 2 week(s) of notification.

**Academics.** All students must achieve second-language proficiency. **Special study options:** Combined bachelor's/graduate degree, cross-registration, distance learning, double major, dual enrollment of high school students, ESL, honors, independent study, internships, liberal arts/career combination, semester at sea, student-designed major, study abroad, teacher certification program, Washington semester. 3-2 engineering with University of Vermont and Clarkson University, 4-1 MBA with Clarkson University, international exchange student program, Pre-Pharmacy Duel Degree (BS, D.Pharm.) with Albany College of Pharmacy and Health Sciences. **Credit/placement by examination:** AP, CLEP, IB, institutional tests. 30 credit hours maximum toward bachelor's degree. **Support services:** Learning center, reduced course load, study skills assistance, tutoring, writing center.

**Majors. Area/ethnic studies:** American. **Biology:** General, biochemistry. **Business:** Accounting, business admin. **Communications:** Journalism. **Computer sciences:** Computer science, information systems. **Conservation:** Environmental science. **Education:** Art, elementary. **Engineering:** General. **Foreign languages:** General, classics, French, Latin, Spanish. **History:** General. **Math:** General. **Philosophy/religion:** Philosophy, religion. **Physical sciences:** General, chemistry, physics. **Psychology:** General. **Social sciences:** Anthropology, economics, political science, sociology. **Visual/performing arts:** Art, dramatic, studio arts. **Other:** Gender studies.

**Most popular majors.** Biology 9%, business/marketing 23%, communications/journalism 6%, English 8%, psychology 13%, social sciences 14%.

**Computing on campus.** 375 workstations in dormitories, library, computer center, student center. Dormitories wired for high-speed internet access and linked to campus network. Commuter students can connect to campus network. Online course registration, online library, helpline, student web hosting, wireless network available.

**Student life. Freshman orientation:** Mandatory. Preregistration for classes offered. One-day academic orientation held in July. Off-campus weekend experience during summer offered to all new students. **Policies:** Limited number of parking permits available for first-time, first-year students during spring semester. **Housing:** Guaranteed on-campus for all undergraduates. Coed dorms, single-sex dorms, special housing for disabled, apartments, wellness housing available. $500 nonrefundable deposit, deadline 5/1. Ambassador Housing Program allows American students to live with international students. **Activities:** Bands, campus ministries, choral groups, dance, drama, literary magazine, music ensembles, musical theater, radio station, student government, student newspaper, fire and rescue club, mobilization of volunteer efforts, Martin Luther King society, diversity coalition, environmental club, Alianza Society, Student Global AIDS Campaign, peace and justice club, Common Ground, Founders Society.

**Athletics.** NCAA. **Intercollegiate:** Baseball M, basketball, cross-country, diving, field hockey W, golf M, ice hockey, lacrosse, skiing, soccer, softball W, swimming, tennis, volleyball W. **Intramural:** Basketball, football (nontackle), ice hockey, racquetball, soccer, softball, squash, table tennis, volleyball. **Team name:** Purple Knights.

**Student services.** Alcohol/substance abuse counseling, chaplain/spiritual director, career counseling, student employment services, financial aid counseling, health services, minority student services, on-campus daycare, personal counseling, placement for graduates, veterans' counselor, women's services. **Physically disabled:** Services for visually, speech, hearing impaired.

**Contact.** E-mail: admission@smcvt.edu
Phone: (802) 654-3000 Toll-free number: (800) 762-8000
Fax: (802) 654-2906
Jacqueline Murphy, Director of Admissions, St. Michael's College, One Winooski Park, Colchester, VT 05439

## Southern Vermont College
**Bennington, Vermont**
**www.svc.edu**

**CB member**
**CB code: 3796**

- Private 4-year liberal arts college
- Residential campus in large town
- 477 degree-seeking undergraduates: 10% part-time, 64% women, 7% African American, 2% Asian American, 2% Hispanic American, 1% international
- 85% of applicants admitted
- SAT or ACT (ACT writing optional), application essay required
- 42% graduate within 6 years

**General.** Founded in 1926. Regionally accredited. **Degrees:** 42 bachelor's, 32 associate awarded. **Location:** 40 miles from Albany, NY; 90 miles from Springfield, MA. **Calendar:** Semester, limited summer session. **Full-time faculty:** 24 total; 29% have terminal degrees. **Part-time faculty:** 31 total; 6% have terminal degrees. **Class size:** 71% < 20, 29% 20-39. **Special facilities:** 25 miles of trails, 2 natural ponds, 27-room Edwardian mansion.

**Freshman class profile.** 383 applied, 326 admitted, 125 enrolled.

| Mid 50% test scores | | | |
|---|---|---|---|
| SAT critical reading: | 420-500 | GPA 2.0-2.99: | 67% |
| SAT math: | 400-500 | Rank in top quarter: | 4% |
| ACT composite: | 15-21 | End year in good standing: | 88% |
| GPA 3.50-3.74: | 2% | Return as sophomores: | 65% |
| GPA 3.0-3.49: | 30% | Out-of-state: | 75% |
| | | Live on campus: | 92% |

**Basis for selection.** Potential for academic achievement most important. Test scores, interview, personal references important. Admissions criteria not intended as absolute cut-offs, but students failing to meet these standards must demonstrate potential for academic success in other ways. Interview strongly recommended. **Homeschooled:** Statement describing home-school structure and mission, transcript of courses and grades, interview required. **Learning Disabled:** Documentation of learning disabilities required.

**High school preparation.** College-preparatory program recommended. Required and recommended units include English 4, mathematics 3, social studies 4, history 4, science 3, foreign language 2 and academic electives 4.

**2009-2010 Annual costs.** Tuition/fees: $18,880. Health insurance, if applicable, $650 per year. Room/board: $8,840.

**2009-2010 Financial aid. Non-need-based:** Scholarships awarded for academics, leadership.

**Application procedures. Admission:** No deadline. $30 fee, may be waived for applicants with need, free for online applicants. Admission notification on a rolling basis beginning on or about 12/1. Must reply by May 1 or within 2 week(s) if notified thereafter. **Financial aid:** No deadline. FAFSA required. Applicants notified on a rolling basis.

**Academics.** Students receive free walk-in tutoring, individualized tutoring, study group sessions, workshops for skill review, proofreading, and note-taking. Disabilities Support Program available. **Special study options:** Combined bachelor's/graduate degree, cross-registration, double major, independent study, internships, liberal arts/career combination, student-designed major, study abroad. **Credit/placement by examination:** CLEP, SAT, ACT. **Support services:** Learning center, reduced course load, remedial instruction, study skills assistance, tutoring, writing center.

**Majors. Business:** Business admin, entrepreneurial studies, nonprofit/public. **Communications:** General. **Health:** Nursing (RN), radiologic technology/medical imaging. **Legal studies:** Prelaw. **Liberal arts:** Arts/sciences. **Parks/recreation:** Sports admin. **Protective services:** Police science. **Psychology:** General. **Other:** History and politics, Liberal arts/management.

**Most popular majors.** Business/marketing 15%, health sciences 13%, psychology 24%, science technologies 28%, security/protective services 7%.

**Computing on campus.** 43 workstations in library, computer center. Dormitories wired for high-speed internet access and linked to campus network. Commuter students can connect to campus network. Online course registration, online library, repair service, student web hosting, wireless network available.

**Student life. Freshman orientation:** Mandatory. 3-day experience held with 3-part theme: academics, student life, outdoor recreation. **Housing:** Guaranteed on-campus for freshmen. Coed dorms, wellness housing available. $200 nonrefundable deposit. **Activities:** Drama, international student organizations, literary magazine, student government, student newspaper, criminal justice club, Everyone's Earth, community action program.

**Athletics.** NCAA. **Intercollegiate:** Baseball M, basketball, cross-country, soccer, softball W, volleyball. **Intramural:** Basketball, ice hockey, skiing, soccer, tennis, volleyball. **Team name:** Mountaineers.

**Student services.** Adult student services, alcohol/substance abuse counseling, career counseling, student employment services, financial aid counseling, health services, personal counseling, placement for graduates. **Physically disabled:** Services for visually, hearing impaired.

**Contact.** E-mail: admissions@svc.edu
Phone: (802) 447-6304 Fax: (802) 447-6313
Grant Thatcher, Director of Admissions, Southern Vermont College, 982 Mansion Drive, Bennington, VT 05201-6002

---

## Sterling College
**Craftsbury Common, Vermont**
www.sterlingcollege.edu

CB member
CB code: 3752

- Private 4-year liberal arts college
- Residential campus in rural community
- 108 degree-seeking undergraduates: 7% part-time, 46% women
- 79% of applicants admitted
- Application essay required
- 36% graduate within 6 years; 22% enter graduate study

**General.** Founded in 1958. Regionally accredited. Member of National Work Colleges Consortium. Special accreditation through Association of Experiential Educators. **Degrees:** 26 bachelor's awarded. **Location:** 40 miles from Montpelier, 70 miles from Burlington. **Calendar:** Semester, extensive summer session. **Full-time faculty:** 9 total; 22% have terminal degrees, 56% women. **Part-time faculty:** 15 total; 40% have terminal degrees, 40% women. **Class size:** 100% < 20. **Special facilities:** Managed woodlots, livestock farm, cross-country ski trails, back-country recreation, solar and wind powered barns, organic gardens, greenhouse, 32-foot climbing wall, low and high ropes challenge course, sugar house, 300-acre educational swamp (boreal forest and muskeg).

**Freshman class profile.** 94 applied, 74 admitted, 26 enrolled.

| End year in good standing: | 100% | Out-of-state: | 77% |
|---|---|---|---|
| Return as sophomores: | 67% | Live on campus: | 95% |

**Basis for selection.** Demonstrated interest in programs via activities and essay, motivation, interview/campus visit, academic record, letters of recommendation important. Admissions interview/campus visit highly recommended. **Homeschooled:** Transcript of courses and grades required. Portfolio of educational and life experience may be submitted in lieu of diploma or equivalency. Students must meet homeschool requirements for their particular state of residence.

**High school preparation.** College-preparatory program recommended. Required and recommended units include English 4, mathematics 3-4, social studies 2, history 2, science 2-3 (laboratory 2-3) and foreign language 2.

**2009-2010 Annual costs.** Tuition/fees: $23,621. Students receive $1600 tuition and book credit in exchange for work done on campus. Room/board: $7,554. Books/supplies: $900. Personal expenses: $700.

**2008-2009 Financial aid. Need-based:** 24 full-time freshmen applied for aid; 22 were judged to have need; 22 of these received aid. Average need met was 65%. Average scholarship/grant was $15,694; average loan $3,000. 63% of total undergraduate aid awarded as scholarships/grants, 37% as loans/jobs. **Non-need-based:** Awarded to 11 full-time undergraduates, including 1 freshmen. Scholarships awarded for academics, leadership, state residency.

**Application procedures. Admission:** Priority date 2/15; deadline 4/1 (postmark date). $35 fee, may be waived for applicants with need. Admission notification on a rolling basis. Must reply by May 1 or within 2 week(s) if notified thereafter. **Financial aid:** Priority date 3/15; no closing date. FAFSA, institutional form required. Applicants notified on a rolling basis starting 2/1; must reply by 5/1 or within 2 week(s) of notification.

**Academics. Special study options:** Double major, dual enrollment of high school students, exchange student, independent study, internships, student-designed major, study abroad. 2-week Global Field Studies. **Credit/placement by examination:** CLEP, IB, institutional tests. Credit for life experience and credit by exam evaluated on a case-by-case basis. **Support services:** Learning center, reduced course load, remedial instruction, study skills assistance, tutoring, writing center.

**Majors. Agriculture:** General. **Biology:** Conservation, ecology, environmental, wildlife. **Conservation:** General, environmental studies, water/wetlands/marine, wildlife. **Education:** Curriculum. **Liberal arts:** Arts/sciences. **Parks/recreation:** General. **Other:** Environmental humanities, Natural history, Northern studies.

**Computing on campus.** 20 workstations in library, computer center, student center. Dormitories wired for high-speed internet access and linked to campus network. Commuter students can connect to campus network. Online library, helpline, repair service, wireless network available.

**Student life. Freshman orientation:** Mandatory. **Housing:** Guaranteed on-campus for all undergraduates. Coed dorms, apartments, wellness housing available. Pets allowed in dorm rooms. **Activities:** Choral groups, drama, film society, literary magazine, music ensembles, student government.

**Student services.** Adult student services, alcohol/substance abuse counseling, career counseling, student employment services, financial aid counseling, health services, personal counseling, placement for graduates, veterans' counselor.

**Contact.** E-mail: admissions@sterlingcollege.edu
Phone: (802) 586-7711 ext. 100 Toll-free number: (800) 648-3591 ext. 100
Fax: (802) 586-2596
Lynne Birdsall, Director of Admissions, Sterling College, PO Box 72, Craftsbury Common, VT 05827-0072

## University of Vermont
**Burlington, Vermont**  **CB member**
**www.uvm.edu**  **CB code: 3920**

- Public 4-year university
- Residential campus in large town
- 10,371 degree-seeking undergraduates: 3% part-time, 56% women, 1% African American, 2% Asian American, 2% Hispanic American, 1% international
- 1,976 degree-seeking graduate students
- 71% of applicants admitted
- SAT or ACT with writing, application essay required
- 73% graduate within 6 years; 25% enter graduate study

**General.** Founded in 1791. Regionally accredited. **Degrees:** 2,215 bachelor's awarded; master's, doctoral, professional offered. **ROTC:** Army. **Location:** 225 miles from Boston, 100 miles from Montreal. **Calendar:** Semester, extensive summer session. **Full-time faculty:** 597 total; 86% have terminal degrees, 15% minority, 41% women. **Part-time faculty:** 155 total; 39% have terminal degrees, 3% minority, 58% women. **Class size:** 46% < 20, 34% 20-39, 7% 40-49, 7% 50-99, 6% >100. **Special facilities:** Horse farm, dairy farm, geology museum, natural areas, science center, research vessel on Lake Champlain, ecosystem science laboratory on Lake Champlain, art and anthropology museum, maple research facility.

**Freshman class profile.** 22,365 applied, 15,856 admitted, 2,619 enrolled.

| Mid 50% test scores | | Rank in top tenth: | 29% |
|---|---|---|---|
| SAT critical reading: | 540-640 | End year in good standing: | 91% |
| SAT math: | 550-640 | Return as sophomores: | 85% |
| SAT writing: | 540-640 | Out-of-state: | 75% |
| ACT composite: | 24-28 | Live on campus: | 98% |
| Rank in top quarter: | 66% | International: | 1% |

**Basis for selection.** School achievement record of primary importance; test scores also important. Essay, extracurricular activities considered. Letter of recommendation required. Special consideration to Vermont residents, children of alumni, minority students, and foreign students. Informational interview recommended. Music applicants must present audition tape or CD. **Homeschooled:** Transcript of courses and grades, state high school equivalency certificate, letter of recommendation (nonparent) required. Applicants must provide proof of completion of minimum entrance requirements and completion of GED.

**High school preparation.** College-preparatory program required. 16 units required. Required units include English 4, mathematics 3, social studies 3, science 2 (laboratory 1) and foreign language 2. Additional mathematics and/or science units required in engineering, business, health science programs.

**2009-2010 Annual costs.** Tuition/fees: $13,554; $31,410 out-of-state. Room/board: $8,996. Books/supplies: $1,050. Personal expenses: $1,274.

**2008-2009 Financial aid. Need-based:** 1,834 full-time freshmen applied for aid; 1,401 were judged to have need; 1,399 of these received aid. Average need met was 82%. Average scholarship/grant was $14,108; average loan $5,696. 71% of total undergraduate aid awarded as scholarships/grants, 29% as loans/jobs. **Non-need-based:** Awarded to 2,402 full-time undergraduates, including 937 freshmen. Scholarships awarded for academics, art, athletics, ROTC.

**Application procedures. Admission:** Closing date 1/15 (postmark date). $55 fee, may be waived for applicants with need. Admission notification 3/31. Must reply by May 1 or within 3 week(s) if notified thereafter. Wait-list admits have 2 days to reply. Early action candidates may have final decision deferred until completion of fall semester review. **Financial aid:** Priority date 2/10; no closing date. FAFSA required. Applicants notified on a rolling basis starting 3/15; must reply within 4 week(s) of notification.

**Academics. Special study options:** Combined bachelor's/graduate degree, cooperative education, cross-registration, distance learning, double major, dual enrollment of high school students, exchange student, honors, independent study, internships, liberal arts/career combination, student-designed major, study abroad, teacher certification program, Washington semester. Evening university option available in several programs, limited ESL available. **Credit/placement by examination:** CLEP, IB, institutional tests. Half of major and half of minor requirements must be completed in residence. **Support services:** Learning center, pre-admission summer program, reduced course load, study skills assistance, tutoring, writing center.

**Honors college/program.** Admissions based on excellent SAT and/or ACT scores, class rank, challenging course work, and ability to overcome obstacles; about 100 admitted each year.

**Majors. Agriculture:** General, agronomy, animal sciences, horticultural science. **Area/ethnic studies:** Asian, Canadian, European, Italian, Latin American, Russian/Slavic, women's. **Biology:** General, biochemistry, botany, microbiology, molecular, wildlife, zoology. **Business:** Business admin, entrepreneurial studies. **Communications:** Public relations. **Computer sciences:** Computer science, systems analysis. **Conservation:** General, environmental science, environmental studies, forestry. **Education:** General, art, early childhood, early childhood special, elementary, English, family/consumer sciences, foreign languages, mathematics, middle, music, physical, science, secondary, social studies. **Engineering:** General, civil, electrical, environmental, industrial, mechanical. **Family/consumer sciences:** Family studies. **Foreign languages:** Ancient Greek, Chinese, classics, French, German, Japanese, Latin, Russian, Spanish. **Health:** Athletic training, clinical lab science, communication disorders, dietetics, medical radiologic technology/radiation therapy, nuclear medical technology, nursing (RN). **History:** General. **Interdisciplinary:** Global studies, nutrition sciences. **Liberal arts:** Arts/sciences. **Math:** General, statistics. **Parks/recreation:** Exercise sciences, facilities management. **Philosophy/religion:** Philosophy, religion. **Physical sciences:** Chemistry, geology, physics. **Psychology:** General. **Public administration:** Social work. **Social sciences:** Anthropology, economics, geography, international economic development, political science, sociology. **Visual/performing arts:** Art history/conservation, dramatic, film/cinema, music performance, studio arts.

**Most popular majors.** Biology 6%, business/marketing 11%, education 8%, English 7%, health sciences 6%, natural resources/environmental science 7%, psychology 8%, social sciences 16%.

**Computing on campus.** 685 workstations in dormitories, library, computer center, student center. Dormitories wired for high-speed internet access and linked to campus network. Commuter students can connect to campus network. Online course registration, online library, helpline, repair service, wireless network available.

**Student life. Freshman orientation:** Mandatory. Preregistration for classes offered. 2-day sessions held at various times in June; additional session held prior to start of term in August. **Policies:** Student code of conduct. **Housing:** Guaranteed on-campus for freshmen. Coed dorms, apartments, fraternity/sorority housing, wellness housing available. **Activities:** Bands, campus ministries, choral groups, dance, drama, film society, international student organizations, literary magazine, music ensembles, musical theater, radio station, student government, student newspaper, symphony orchestra, TV station, Hillel, black student union, Asian American student union, gay/lesbian/bisexual/transgender alliance, Alianza Latina, Catholic center, Volunteers in Action, Vermont student environmental program.

**Athletics.** NCAA. **Intercollegiate:** Basketball, cross-country, diving W, field hockey W, ice hockey, lacrosse, skiing, soccer, swimming W, track and field. **Intramural:** Badminton, basketball, bowling, cheerleading, equestrian, fencing, football (non-tackle), ice hockey, racquetball, rowing (crew), soccer, softball, table tennis, tennis, volleyball, water polo. **Team name:** Catamounts.

**Student services.** Alcohol/substance abuse counseling, chaplain/spiritual director, career counseling, services for economically disadvantaged, student employment services, financial aid counseling, health services, minority student services, on-campus daycare, personal counseling, placement for graduates, veterans' counselor, women's services. **Physically disabled:** Services for visually, speech, hearing impaired. **Learning disabled:** Comprehensive services available.

**Contact.** E-mail: admissions@uvm.edu
Phone: (802) 656-3370 Fax: (802) 656-8611
Beth Wiser, Director of Admissions, University of Vermont, 194 South Prospect Street, Burlington, VT 05401-3596

## Vermont Technical College
**Randolph Center, Vermont**  **CB member**
**www.vtc.edu**  **CB code: 3941**

- Public 4-year technical college
- Residential campus in small town

- 1,515 degree-seeking undergraduates: 17% part-time, 42% women, 1% African American, 1% Asian American, 1% Hispanic American
- 63% of applicants admitted
- 63% graduate within 6 years

**General.** Founded in 1866. Regionally accredited. **Degrees:** 83 bachelor's, 337 associate awarded. **ROTC:** Army. **Location:** 20 miles from Montpelier, 50 miles from Burlington. **Calendar:** Semester, limited summer session. **Full-time faculty:** 85 total; 24% have terminal degrees, 4% minority, 45% women. **Part-time faculty:** 111 total; 13% have terminal degrees, 60% women. **Class size:** 64% < 20, 34% 20-39, 2% 40-49, less than 1% 50-99. **Special facilities:** 500-acre farmstead and orchard, lighted ski hill.

**Freshman class profile.** 844 applied, 534 admitted, 254 enrolled.

| Mid 50% test scores | | | |
|---|---|---|---|
| SAT critical reading: | 420-540 | GPA 2.0-2.99: | 39% |
| SAT math: | 450-540 | Rank in top quarter: | 15% |
| SAT writing: | 390-510 | Rank in top tenth: | 4% |
| GPA 3.75 or higher: | 9% | End year in good standing: | 71% |
| GPA 3.50-3.74: | 10% | Return as sophomores: | 72% |
| GPA 3.0-3.49: | 39% | Out-of-state: | 17% |
| | | Live on campus: | 75% |

**Basis for selection.** School achievement record most important, followed by test scores, recommendations, and recommended interview. Veterinary technology, dental hygiene, and nursing programs highly selective. Entrance exam required for nursing applicants. SAT or ACT not required of nursing applicants or non-traditional students. Accuplacer may be used in place of SAT/ACT. Interview and essay required for veterinary applicants. **Homeschooled:** Statement describing homeschool structure and mission required. Students may attend Vermont Academy of Science and Technology to obtain diploma and first year of college simultaneously.

**High school preparation.** 16 units required. Required and recommended units include English 4, mathematics 3-4, social studies 2, history 2, science 2-3 (laboratory 1-2), foreign language 2 and academic electives 2.

**2009-2010 Annual costs.** Tuition/fees: $10,684; $19,743 out-of-state. New England Board of Higher Education rate for students from other New England states: 150% of Vermont resident tuition. Available to degree candidates in academic areas not offered by educational institutions in their home states. Room/board: $7,809. Books/supplies: $1,000. Personal expenses: $650.

**2008-2009 Financial aid. Need-based:** 260 full-time freshmen applied for aid; 222 were judged to have need; 220 of these received aid. Average need met was 68%. Average scholarship/grant was $5,420; average loan $3,310. 34% of total undergraduate aid awarded as scholarships/grants, 66% as loans/jobs. **Non-need-based:** Awarded to 57 full-time undergraduates, including 35 freshmen. Scholarships awarded for academics.

**Application procedures. Admission:** Priority date 3/1; no deadline. $38 fee, may be waived for applicants with need. Admission notification on a rolling basis beginning on or about 12/15. Must reply by May 1 or within 4 week(s) if notified thereafter. Nursing, Dental Hygiene and Veterinary Technology applicants may not defer their acceptance. **Financial aid:** Priority date 3/1; no closing date. FAFSA required. Applicants notified on a rolling basis starting 3/15; must reply within 2 week(s) of notification.

**Academics.** 3-year preparatory program options for students planning engineering programs. **Special study options:** Distance learning, double major, dual enrollment of high school students, ESL, honors, independent study, internships. Vermont Academy of Science and Technology program combines senior year of high school and first year of college. **Credit/placement by examination:** CLEP, institutional tests. 36 credit hours maximum toward associate degree, 60 toward bachelor's. **Support services:** Learning center, pre-admission summer program, reduced course load, remedial instruction, study skills assistance, tutoring, writing center.

**Majors. Agriculture:** General, dairy husbandry, equestrian studies, equine science. **Business:** General, business admin. **Computer sciences:** General, information technology, programming. **Construction:** Maintenance. **Engineering technology:** Architectural, computer, construction, electrical. **Health:** Dental hygiene. **Other:** Sustainable design and technology/green technology.

**Most popular majors.** Business/marketing 34%, engineering/ engineering technologies 61%.

**Computing on campus.** 250 workstations in dormitories, library, computer center. Dormitories wired for high-speed internet access and linked to campus network. Commuter students can connect to campus network. Online library, helpline, repair service, student web hosting, wireless network available.

**Student life. Freshman orientation:** Mandatory, $100 fee. Preregistration for classes offered. Held 2 days prior to start of classes. **Housing:** Coed dorms, special housing for disabled, wellness housing available. $100 deposit, deadline 6/1. Williston Campus has townhouse style residence halls. **Activities:** International student organizations, radio station, student government, student newspaper, TV station, national student chapters of: American Institute of Architects, American Society of Civil Engineers, Institute of Electrical and Electronic Engineers, Society of Manufacturing Engineers, Society of Women Engineers, National Association of Veterinary Technicians, Women Issues Christian Fellowship, Phi Theta Kappa, Tau Alpha Pi.

**Athletics.** NAIA, USCAA. **Intercollegiate:** Baseball M, basketball, cross-country, golf, soccer, softball W. **Intramural:** Basketball, football (non-tackle), golf, racquetball, skiing, soccer, softball, swimming, table tennis, tennis, volleyball, water polo. **Team name:** Knights.

**Student services.** Alcohol/substance abuse counseling, career counseling, services for economically disadvantaged, student employment services, financial aid counseling, health services, minority student services, personal counseling, placement for graduates, veterans' counselor, women's services. **Physically disabled:** Services for visually, hearing impaired.

**Contact.** E-mail: admissions@vtc.edu
Phone: (802) 728-1244 Toll-free number: (800) 442-8821
Fax: (802) 728-1390
Dwight Cross, Assistant Dean of Enrollment, Vermont Technical College, PO Box 500, Randolph Center, VT 05061-0500

# Virginia

## Argosy University: Washington D.C.
### Arlington, Virginia
### www.argosy.edu/washingtondc

- For-profit 4-year university
- Very large city
- 78 degree-seeking undergraduates

**General.** Regionally accredited. **Degrees:** 9 bachelor's awarded; master's, doctoral, professional offered. **Calendar:** Continuous. **Full-time faculty:** 32 total. **Part-time faculty:** 9 total.

**Freshman class profile.** 17 enrolled.

**Basis for selection.** Open admission.

**Academics. Credit/placement by examination:** CLEP.

**Majors. Business:** Business admin. **Liberal arts:** Arts/sciences. **Protective services:** Police science. **Psychology:** General.

**Contact.** E-mail: auwadmissions@argosy.edu
Phone: (703) 526-5800 Toll-free number: (866) 703-2777
Argosy University: Washington D.C., 1550 Wilson Boulevard, Suite 600, Arlington, VA 22209

## Art Institute of Washington
### Arlington, Virginia
### www.aiw.artinstitutes.edu          CB code: 3836

- For-profit 4-year culinary school and visual arts college
- Commuter campus in small city

**General.** Regionally accredited. **Location:** One mile from Washington, DC. **Calendar:** Quarter.

**Annual costs/financial aid.** Need-based financial aid available to part-time students.

**Contact.** Phone: (703) 358-9550
Director of Admissions, 1820 North Fort Myer Drive, Arlington, VA 22209-1802

## Averett University
### Danville, Virginia          CB member
### www.averett.edu          CB code: 5017

- Private 4-year university and liberal arts college
- Residential campus in small city
- 846 degree-seeking undergraduates: 6% part-time, 48% women, 31% African American, 1% Asian American, 3% Hispanic American, 1% Native American, 5% international
- 25 degree-seeking graduate students
- 91% of applicants admitted
- SAT or ACT (ACT writing optional) required
- 47% graduate within 6 years

**General.** Founded in 1859. Regionally accredited. **Degrees:** 147 bachelor's awarded; master's offered. **Location:** 45 miles from Greensboro, North Carolina, 150 miles from Richmond. **Calendar:** Semester, limited summer session. **Full-time faculty:** 47 total; 66% have terminal degrees, 4% minority, 45% women. **Part-time faculty:** 47 total; 26% have terminal degrees, 4% minority, 55% women. **Class size:** 76% < 20, 24% 20-39. **Special facilities:** 100-acre equestrian center, flight center.

**Freshman class profile.** 1,181 applied, 1,078 admitted, 254 enrolled.

| Mid 50% test scores | | | |
|---|---|---|---|
| SAT critical reading: | 410-510 | Rank in top quarter: | 22% |
| SAT math: | 420-530 | Rank in top tenth: | 9% |
| ACT composite: | 17-21 | End year in good standing: | 92% |
| GPA 3.75 or higher: | 11% | Return as sophomores: | 50% |
| GPA 3.50-3.74: | 8% | Out-of-state: | 47% |
| GPA 3.0-3.49: | 27% | Live on campus: | 80% |
| GPA 2.0-2.99: | 53% | Fraternities: | 13% |
| | | Sororities: | 7% |

**Basis for selection.** Rigor of secondary school record and GPA very important; standardized test scores important. Recommendations, essay, interview, extracurricular activities, talent/ability/alumni/ae relation, volunteer work, work experience and level of interest all considered. Auditions required for music program; portfolios for art recommended. Essay recommended. **Homeschooled:** Transcript of courses and grades, state high school equivalency certificate required. **Learning Disabled:** Documentation of neuropsychological or comprehensive psychoeducational evaluation required for access to learning disabled services. Minimum SAT requirements may be waived.

**High school preparation.** College-preparatory program required. 16 units required; 25 recommended. Required and recommended units include English 4, mathematics 3-4, social studies 3-4, history 3, science 3-4 (laboratory 3), foreign language 3, computer science 2, visual/performing arts 1 and academic electives 3.

**2009-2010 Annual costs.** Tuition/fees: $22,112. Room/board: $7,930. Books/supplies: $900. Personal expenses: $1,400.

**2008-2009 Financial aid. Need-based:** 217 full-time freshmen applied for aid; 194 were judged to have need; 192 of these received aid. Average need met was 70%. Average scholarship/grant was $10,545; average loan $3,926. 66% of total undergraduate aid awarded as scholarships/grants, 34% as loans/jobs. **Non-need-based:** Awarded to 243 full-time undergraduates, including 70 freshmen. Scholarships awarded for academics, alumni affiliation, art, leadership, minority status, music/drama, state residency.

**Application procedures. Admission:** Priority date 5/1; deadline 7/15 (receipt date). No application fee. Admission notification on a rolling basis. Must reply by May 1 or within 2 week(s) if notified thereafter. Deferred admission is up to 1 year. **Financial aid:** Priority date 4/1; no closing date. FAFSA required. Applicants notified on a rolling basis starting 2/15; must reply within 2 week(s) of notification.

**Academics. Special study options:** Accelerated study, cooperative education, cross-registration, double major, dual enrollment of high school students, exchange student, honors, independent study, internships, student-designed major, study abroad, teacher certification program, Washington semester. Undergraduates may take graduate level classes. **Credit/placement by examination:** AP, CLEP, SAT, ACT, institutional tests. 27 credit hours maximum toward associate degree, 90 toward bachelor's. **Support services:** Learning center, reduced course load, remedial instruction, study skills assistance, tutoring, writing center.

**Majors. Agriculture:** Equestrian studies. **Biology:** General, ecology. **Business:** Accounting, business admin, finance, management science, marketing. **Communications:** Journalism. **Computer sciences:** Information systems. **Conservation:** Environmental science. **Education:** Art, biology, chemistry, English, health, mathematics, multi-level teacher, social studies. **Health:** Athletic training, clinical lab science, medical radiologic technology/radiation therapy, premedicine. **History:** General. **Interdisciplinary:** Biological/physical sciences. **Legal studies:** Prelaw. **Liberal arts:** Arts/sciences. **Math:** General. **Parks/recreation:** Health/fitness, sports admin. **Philosophy/religion:** Religion. **Physical sciences:** Chemistry. **Protective services:** Law enforcement admin. **Psychology:** Clinical, cognitive, industrial, psychobiology. **Social sciences:** Political science, sociology. **Transportation:** Airline/commercial pilot, aviation, aviation management. **Visual/performing arts:** Art, dramatic, theater history. **Other:** Criminal justice/aerospace management, Wellness/sports medicine.

**Most popular majors.** Business/marketing 10%, computer/information sciences 6%, education 15%, health sciences 8%, liberal arts 9%, parks/recreation 14%, security/protective services 9%.

**Computing on campus.** 150 workstations in library, computer center, student center. Dormitories wired for high-speed internet access. Online course registration, online library, helpline, student web hosting, wireless network available.

**Student life. Freshman orientation:** Mandatory, $50 fee. Preregistration for classes offered. 11-day orientation; begins on Saturday and lasts until classes start. **Policies:** No alcohol on campus, no smoking in dorms. **Housing:** Guaranteed on-campus for all undergraduates. Coed dorms, single-sex dorms, apartments available. $400 deposit, deadline 5/1. Coed housing by floor or suite. **Activities:** Campus ministries, choral groups, drama, international student organizations, literary magazine, Model UN, musical theater, student government, student newspaper, Alpha Beta Rho, Brothers and Sisters in Christ, campus activities board, Christian Student Union, Fellowship of Christian Athletes, multicultural student association, Phi Sigma Sigma, Phi Kappa Phi.

**Athletics. NCAA. Intercollegiate:** Baseball M, basketball, cross-country, equestrian, football (tackle) M, golf M, soccer, softball W, tennis, volleyball W. **Intramural:** Basketball, cheerleading, football (non-tackle) M, softball. **Team name:** Cougars.

**Student services.** Adult student services, alcohol/substance abuse counseling, career counseling, student employment services, financial aid counseling, personal counseling, placement for graduates, veterans' counselor. **Physically disabled:** Services for visually, speech, hearing impaired.

**Contact.** E-mail: admit@averett.edu
Phone: (434) 791-4996 Toll-free number: (800) 283-7388
Fax: (434) 797-2784
Kathie Tune, Dean of Admissions, Averett University, 420 West Main Street, Danville, VA 24541

## Bluefield College
**Bluefield, Virginia**
**www.bluefield.edu**                **CB code: 5063**

- Private 4-year liberal arts and teachers college affiliated with Baptist faith
- Residential campus in small town
- 722 degree-seeking undergraduates: 11% part-time, 60% women, 20% African American, 1% Asian American, 2% Hispanic American, 1% international
- 48% of applicants admitted
- SAT or ACT (ACT writing optional) required
- 38% graduate within 6 years; 13% enter graduate study

**General.** Founded in 1920. Regionally accredited. **Degrees:** 286 bachelor's awarded. **Location:** 90 miles from Roanoke. **Calendar:** Semester, limited summer session. **Full-time faculty:** 37 total; 65% have terminal degrees, 3% minority, 40% women. **Part-time faculty:** 59 total; 42% have terminal degrees, 5% minority, 39% women. **Class size:** 87% < 20, 13% 20-39.

**Freshman class profile.** 685 applied, 328 admitted, 126 enrolled.

| Mid 50% test scores | | End year in good standing: | 80% |
|---|---|---|---|
| SAT critical reading: | 420-520 | Return as sophomores: | 70% |
| SAT math: | 420-530 | Out-of-state: | 19% |
| ACT composite: | 17-20 | Live on campus: | 67% |
| GPA 3.75 or higher: | 23% | International: | 2% |
| GPA 3.50-3.74: | 14% | Fraternities: | 7% |
| GPA 3.0-3.49: | 30% | Sororities: | 10% |
| GPA 2.0-2.99: | 33% | | |

**Basis for selection.** Students must have minimum 2.0 GPA, 18 ACT or 860 (Critical Reading + Math) SAT. **Homeschooled:** Must supply written description and transcript of curriculum.

**High school preparation.** 22 units required. Required units include English 4, mathematics 3, social studies 3, science 3 (laboratory 1) and academic electives 6. 2 units of health and physical education; 1 unit of fine arts.

**2010-2011 Annual costs.** Tuition/fees (projected): $18,800. Room/board: $7,150. Books/supplies: $1,200. Personal expenses: $1,500.

**2009-2010 Financial aid. Need-based:** Average need met was 79%. Average scholarship/grant was $13,663; average loan $3,855. 50% of total undergraduate aid awarded as scholarships/grants, 50% as loans/jobs. **Non-need-based:** Scholarships awarded for academics, alumni affiliation, art, athletics, music/drama, religious affiliation, state residency.

**Application procedures. Admission:** Closing date 8/1 (postmark date). $30 fee, may be waived for applicants with need, free for online applicants. Admission notification on a rolling basis beginning on or about 9/1. Must reply by May 1 or within 3 week(s) if notified thereafter. **Financial aid:** Priority date 3/15; no closing date. FAFSA required. Applicants notified on a rolling basis starting 3/1; must reply within 3 week(s) of notification.

**Academics. Special study options:** Accelerated study, double major, honors, internships, liberal arts/career combination, study abroad, teacher certification program. **Credit/placement by examination:** AP, CLEP, IB, SAT,

ACT, institutional tests. 30 credit hours maximum toward bachelor's degree. **Support services:** Learning center, reduced course load, remedial instruction, study skills assistance, tutoring, writing center.

**Majors. Biology:** General, exercise physiology. **Business:** Business admin. **Communications:** General. **Communications technology:** Graphics. **Computer sciences:** Information technology. **Education:** General, art, biology, business, chemistry, elementary, English, health, history, mathematics, middle, multi-level teacher, music, physical, reading, secondary, social studies. **History:** General. **Interdisciplinary:** Behavioral sciences. **Liberal arts:** Arts/sciences. **Math:** General. **Parks/recreation:** Exercise sciences. **Philosophy/religion:** Christian. **Physical sciences:** Chemistry. **Protective services:** Forensics, law enforcement admin, police science. **Psychology:** General. **Social sciences:** General. **Theology:** Bible, preministerial, sacred music, theology, youth ministry. **Visual/performing arts:** Art, design, dramatic, music performance, piano/organ, voice/opera.

**Most popular majors.** Business/marketing 41%, psychology 27%, security/protective services 14%.

**Computing on campus.** 100 workstations in dormitories, library, computer center, student center. Dormitories wired for high-speed internet access and linked to campus network. Commuter students can connect to campus network. Online library, wireless network available.

**Student life. Freshman orientation:** Available. Preregistration for classes offered. Held in June or July. **Policies:** Weekly convocation attendance required. Limited visitation hours in dormitories. Religious observance required. **Housing:** Guaranteed on-campus for freshmen. Coed dorms, single-sex dorms, apartments, wellness housing available. $100 fully refundable deposit. **Activities:** Bands, campus ministries, choral groups, drama, film society, literary magazine, music ensembles, musical theater, opera, student government, student newspaper, Fellowship of Christian Athletes, Alpha Delta, Phi Mu Delta, Kappa Psi Omicron, Sigma Alpha Alpha, Bonner Leaders.

**Athletics. NAIA. Intercollegiate:** Baseball M, basketball, cross-country, golf M, soccer, softball W, tennis, volleyball W. **Intramural:** Badminton, basketball, bowling, football (non-tackle), softball, table tennis, tennis, volleyball. **Team name:** Rams.

**Student services.** Adult student services, chaplain/spiritual director, career counseling, financial aid counseling, health services, personal counseling, placement for graduates, veterans' counselor.

**Contact.** E-mail: admissions@bluefield.edu
Phone: (276) 326-4231 Toll-free number: (800) 872-0175
Fax: (276) 326-4395
Robert Shippey, Vice President for Enrollment Management, Bluefield College, 3000 College Drive, Bluefield, VA 24605

## Bridgewater College
**Bridgewater, Virginia**                **CB member**
**www.bridgewater.edu**                **CB code: 5069**

- Private 4-year liberal arts college affiliated with Church of the Brethren
- Residential campus in small town
- 1,575 degree-seeking undergraduates: 1% part-time, 59% women, 7% African American, 1% Asian American, 2% Hispanic American, 1% international
- 86% of applicants admitted
- SAT or ACT (ACT writing optional) required
- 57% graduate within 6 years

**General.** Founded in 1880. Regionally accredited. **Degrees:** 289 bachelor's awarded. **Location:** 8 miles from Harrisonburg, 130 miles from Washington, DC. **Calendar:** 4-1-4, limited summer session. **Full-time faculty:** 101 total; 79% have terminal degrees, 4% minority, 40% women. **Part-time faculty:** 35 total; 23% have terminal degrees, 6% minority, 69% women. **Class size:** 54% < 20, 44% 20-39, 2% 40-49, less than 1% 50-99. **Special facilities:** Museum of the Shenandoah Valley and Church of the Brethren; 75-acre equestrian center for equestrian competitions and boarding of College- and student-owned horses.

**Freshman class profile.** 3,186 applied, 2,726 admitted, 497 enrolled.

| Mid 50% test scores | | GPA 3.0-3.49: | 42% |
|---|---|---|---|
| SAT critical reading: | 450-550 | GPA 2.0-2.99: | 17% |
| SAT math: | 460-560 | Rank in top quarter: | 47% |
| SAT writing: | 430-550 | Rank in top tenth: | 20% |
| ACT composite: | 18-23 | Return as sophomores: | 74% |
| GPA 3.75 or higher: | 26% | Out-of-state: | 20% |
| GPA 3.50-3.74: | 15% | Live on campus: | 92% |

**Basis for selection.** High school GPA most important, followed by test scores and letters of recommendation. Prefer applicants in top half of high school class. Consider those in bottom half with strong compensating qualities. Interview required for some, recommended for all. **Homeschooled:** GED required for students applying for Title IV financial aid.

**High school preparation.** College-preparatory program recommended. 15 units required; 22 recommended. Required and recommended units include English 4, mathematics 3-4, science 2-4 (laboratory 2), foreign language 3 and academic electives 4. Social studies and history: 2 required, 3 recommended.

**2010-2011 Annual costs.** Tuition/fees: $25,500. Room/board: $10,350. Books/supplies: $1,100. Personal expenses: $1,080.

**2009-2010 Financial aid. Need-based:** 461 full-time freshmen applied for aid; 408 were judged to have need; 408 of these received aid. Average need met was 79%. Average scholarship/grant was $17,512; average loan $4,315. 73% of total undergraduate aid awarded as scholarships/grants, 27% as loans/jobs. **Non-need-based:** Awarded to 1,525 full-time undergraduates, including 488 freshmen. Scholarships awarded for academics, music/drama, religious affiliation.

**Application procedures. Admission:** No deadline. $30 fee, may be waived for applicants with need, free for online applicants. Admission notification on a rolling basis beginning on or about 9/1. Must reply by May 1 or within 2 week(s) if notified thereafter. **Financial aid:** Priority date 3/1; no closing date. FAFSA required. Applicants notified on a rolling basis starting 3/16; must reply within 2 week(s) of notification.

**Academics. Special study options:** Combined bachelor's/graduate degree, double major, honors, independent study, internships, liberal arts/career combination, study abroad, teacher certification program, Washington semester. 3-2 engineering with George Washington University (BA/BA) and 3-2 engineering with Virginia Tech (BA/BA), 3-2 nursing with Vanderbilt University (BA/MN), 3-4 physical therapy with Shenandoah University (BA/DPT), 3-4 veterinary medicine with Virginia Tech (BA/DVM). **Credit/placement by examination:** AP, CLEP, IB, institutional tests. **Support services:** Reduced course load, study skills assistance, tutoring, writing center.

**Majors. Biology:** General. **Business:** Business admin, management information systems. **Communications:** Media studies. **Computer sciences:** Computer science. **Conservation:** Environmental science. **Education:** Physical. **Family/consumer sciences:** General, food/nutrition. **Foreign languages:** French, Spanish. **Health:** Athletic training, clinical lab science. **History:** General. **Liberal arts:** Arts/sciences. **Math:** General. **Parks/recreation:** Health/fitness. **Physical sciences:** Chemistry, physics. **Psychology:** General. **Social sciences:** Economics, international relations, political science, sociology. **Visual/performing arts:** Music history, studio arts. **Other:** Applied physics, History and political science, Philosophy and religion.

**Most popular majors.** Biology 12%, business/marketing 17%, communications/journalism 6%, education 10%, family/consumer sciences 6%, parks/recreation 8%, psychology 8%, social sciences 10%.

**Computing on campus.** 193 workstations in library. Dormitories wired for high-speed internet access and linked to campus network. Commuter students can connect to campus network. Online course registration, online library, helpline, repair service, student web hosting, wireless network available.

**Student life. Freshman orientation:** Mandatory. Preregistration for classes offered. 2 spring 2-day sessions. One-day, summer program offered for students unable to attend a spring session. Further orientation activities 2 days preceding classes. Parents included in spring and summer orientations. **Policies:** Alcoholic beverages not permitted on campus. Co-ed visitation hours. Smoking and other tobacco products permitted only in designated areas. Unmarried students under age 23 must live on campus unless living with parents or legal guardians. The parents'/guardians' principal residence must be in Augusta, Highland, Page, Rockingham or Shenandoah counties. **Housing:** Guaranteed on-campus for all undergraduates. Coed dorms, single-sex dorms, special housing for disabled, apartments, wellness housing available. Honor Housing. **Activities:** Bands, campus ministries, choral groups, dance, drama, international student organizations, literary magazine, music ensembles, musical theater, radio station, student government, student newspaper, Believers Strongly United, Brethren Student Movement, Campus Crusade for Christ, Catholic Campus Ministry, College Republicans, Young Democrats, Black Student Association, Fellowship of Christian Athletes, Habitat for Humanity, Student Anti-Genocide Coalition.

**Athletics.** NCAA. **Intercollegiate:** Baseball M, basketball, cross-country, equestrian, field hockey W, football (tackle) M, golf M, lacrosse W, soccer, softball W, swimming W, tennis, track and field, volleyball W. **Intramural:** Badminton, basketball, bowling, football (non-tackle), golf, racquetball, soccer, softball, table tennis, tennis, volleyball. **Team name:** Eagles.

**Student services.** Chaplain/spiritual director, career counseling, student employment services, financial aid counseling, health services, minority student services, personal counseling, placement for graduates. **Physically disabled:** Services for visually impaired.

**Contact.** E-mail: admissions@bridgewater.edu
Phone: (540) 828-5375 Toll-free number: (800) 759-8328
Fax: (540) 828-5481
Linda Stout, Director of Enrollment Operations, Bridgewater College, 402 East College Street, Bridgewater, VA 22812-1599

## Catholic Distance University
### Hamilton, Virginia
### www.cdu.edu

❧ Private two-year upper-division virtual university
❧ Rural community

**General.** Accredited by DETC. **Calendar:** Differs by program.

**Annual costs/financial aid.** Tuition/fees (2009-2010): $380.

**Contact.** Phone: (540) 338-2700 ext. 710
Director of Admissions, 120 East Colonial Highway, Hamilton, VA 20158-9012

## Christendom College
### Front Royal, Virginia
### www.christendom.edu          CB code: 5691

❧ Private 4-year liberal arts college affiliated with Roman Catholic Church
❧ Residential campus in large town
❧ 390 degree-seeking undergraduates: 1% part-time, 52% women, 4% international
❧ 60 degree-seeking graduate students
❧ 86% of applicants admitted
❧ SAT or ACT (ACT writing optional), application essay required
❧ 62% graduate within 6 years

**General.** Founded in 1977. Regionally accredited. **Degrees:** 93 bachelor's awarded; master's offered. **Location:** 70 miles from Washington, DC. **Calendar:** Semester, limited summer session. **Full-time faculty:** 20 total. **Part-time faculty:** 21 total.

**Freshman class profile.** 243 applied, 208 admitted, 91 enrolled.

| Mid 50% test scores | | | |
|---|---|---|---|
| SAT critical reading: | 590-670 | GPA 2.0-2.99: | 5% |
| SAT math: | 520-630 | Rank in top quarter: | 63% |
| SAT writing: | 580-660 | Rank in top tenth: | 40% |
| ACT composite: | 23-28 | End year in good standing: | 92% |
| GPA 3.75 or higher: | 35% | Return as sophomores: | 77% |
| GPA 3.50-3.74: | 35% | Out-of-state: | 85% |
| GPA 3.0-3.49: | 25% | Live on campus: | 98% |

**Basis for selection.** Secondary school record, essay, test scores, class rank, GPA, recommendations important. Applicants can present additional material and explain scores, evaluations, etc. which they believe do not adequately reflect their abilities. Interview recommended. **Homeschooled:** Transcript forms required (available from college).

**High school preparation.** 14 units recommended. Recommended units include English 4, mathematics 2, social studies 1, history 2, science 2, foreign language 2 and academic electives 1.

**2010-2011 Annual costs.** Tuition/fees: $19,668. Room/board: $7,506. Books/supplies: $500. Personal expenses: $300.

**2009-2010 Financial aid. Need-based:** 49 full-time freshmen applied for aid; 40 were judged to have need; 40 of these received aid. Average need met was 90%. Average scholarship/grant was $5,770; average loan $5,500. 47% of total undergraduate aid awarded as scholarships/grants, 53% as loans/jobs. **Non-need-based:** Awarded to 150 full-time undergraduates, including 36 freshmen. Scholarships awarded for academics, alumni affiliation. **Additional information:** Christendom accepts no direct federal aid, nor does it participate in indirect programs of federal aid.

**Application procedures. Admission:** Priority date 3/1; no deadline. $25 fee. Admission notification on a rolling basis. **Financial aid:** Priority date

4/1, closing date 6/1. Institutional form required. Applicants notified on a rolling basis starting 2/1; must reply within 4 week(s) of notification.

**Academics. Special study options:** Double major, honors, independent study, internships, study abroad. Junior semester in Rome. **Credit/ placement by examination:** AP, CLEP, institutional tests. **Support services:** Pre-admission summer program, reduced course load, writing center.

**Majors. Foreign languages:** Classics. **History:** General. **Philosophy/ religion:** Philosophy. **Social sciences:** Political science.

**Computing on campus.** 70 workstations in library. Online course registration available.

**Student life. Freshman orientation:** Mandatory. Preregistration for classes offered. Orientation held weekend before school starts. **Policies:** Although no student is required to participate, college encourages religious activities. **Housing:** Guaranteed on-campus for all undergraduates. Single-sex dorms, wellness housing available. $250 deposit, deadline 3/15. **Activities:** Campus ministries, choral groups, dance, drama, film society, literary magazine, musical theater, student government, student newspaper, Legion of Mary, Shield of Roses, St. Genesius Society, Holy Rood Guild, College Republicans, works of mercy group.

**Athletics.** USCAA. **Intercollegiate:** Baseball M, basketball, golf, rugby M, soccer, volleyball W. **Intramural:** Basketball, boxing M, cross-country, fencing, football (non-tackle), golf, handball, racquetball, skiing, soccer, softball, table tennis, tennis, volleyball. **Team name:** Crusaders.

**Student services.** Chaplain/spiritual director, career counseling, financial aid counseling, health services, personal counseling, placement for graduates.

**Contact.** E-mail: admissions@christendom.edu
Phone: (540) 636-2900 Toll-free number: (800) 877-5456
Fax: (540) 636-1655
Thomas McFadden, Director of Admissions, Christendom College, 134 Christendom Drive, Front Royal, VA 22630

## Christopher Newport University

**Newport News, Virginia**
www.cnu.edu

**CB member**
**CB code: 5128**

- Public 4-year university and liberal arts college
- Residential campus in small city
- 4,771 degree-seeking undergraduates: 3% part-time, 56% women, 8% African American, 3% Asian American, 3% Hispanic American, 1% Native American
- 150 degree-seeking graduate students
- 60% of applicants admitted
- 58% graduate within 6 years

**General.** Founded in 1960. Regionally accredited. **Degrees:** 955 bachelor's awarded; master's offered. **ROTC:** Army. **Location:** 20 miles from Norfolk, 70 miles from Richmond. **Calendar:** Semester, limited summer session. **Full-time faculty:** 236 total; 86% have terminal degrees, 11% minority, 45% women. **Part-time faculty:** 93 total; 28% have terminal degrees, 10% minority, 38% women. **Class size:** 23% < 20, 60% 20-39, 9% 40-49, 7% 50-99, less than 1% >100. **Special facilities:** Mariner's museum, center for the arts.

**Freshman class profile.** 7,317 applied, 4,422 admitted, 1,213 enrolled.

| Mid 50% test scores | | | |
|---|---|---|---|
| SAT critical reading: | 560-640 | **GPA 2.0-2.99:** | 1% |
| SAT math: | 560-640 | **Rank in top quarter:** | 57% |
| ACT composite: | 22-27 | **Rank in top tenth:** | 19% |
| **GPA 3.75 or higher:** | 33% | **End year in good standing:** | 87% |
| **GPA 3.50-3.74:** | 36% | **Return as sophomores:** | 80% |
| **GPA 3.0-3.49:** | 30% | **Out-of-state:** | 9% |
| | | **Live on campus:** | 94% |

**Basis for selection.** Minimum 3.0 GPA, rank in top half of class. Type of diploma and difficulty of classes taken and application essays are considered. Freshman applicants who have achieved a 3.50 GPA (on a 4.00 scale) and have pursued a rigorous curriculum, may apply to the University without submitting a standardized test score (ACT or SAT). Test optional applicants will be reviewed for the strength of the curriculum and recommendations. Audition required for music; interview recommended for marginal; portfolio recommended for art. **Homeschooled:** Applicants should submit copy of high school transcript and descriptions, along with ACT or SAT score.

**High school preparation.** College-preparatory program required. 23 units required. Required and recommended units include English 4, mathematics 4, history 3-4, science 3-4, foreign language 3-4 and academic electives 4.

**2009-2010 Annual costs.** Tuition/fees: $8,050; $15,992 out-of-state. Room/ board: $9,040. Books/supplies: $988. Personal expenses: $1,848.

**2009-2010 Financial aid. Need-based:** 893 full-time freshmen applied for aid; 492 were judged to have need; 483 of these received aid. Average need met was 75%. Average scholarship/grant was $5,779; average loan $3,242. 52% of total undergraduate aid awarded as scholarships/grants, 48% as loans/jobs. **Non-need-based:** Awarded to 877 full-time undergraduates, including 446 freshmen. Scholarships awarded for academics, art, leadership, music/drama, ROTC, state residency.

**Application procedures. Admission:** Priority date 12/1; deadline 3/1 (receipt date). $45 fee, may be waived for applicants with need. Admission notification on a rolling basis beginning on or about 12/1. Must reply by May 1 or within 2 week(s) if notified thereafter. **Financial aid:** Priority date 3/1; no closing date. FAFSA required. Applicants notified on a rolling basis starting 2/21; must reply within 3 week(s) of notification.

**Academics.** Special programs for Leadership, Honors, Service/Learning and freshman learning communities. **Special study options:** Cross-registration, double major, dual enrollment of high school students, honors, independent study, internships, student-designed major, study abroad. Member of Virginia Tidewater Consortium, Freshman Learning Communities, Service Learning Opportunities. **Credit/placement by examination:** AP, CLEP, IB, institutional tests. **Support services:** Study skills assistance, tutoring, writing center.

**Majors. Area/ethnic studies:** American. **Biology:** General. **Business:** Accounting, business admin, finance, managerial economics, marketing. **Communications:** General. **Computer sciences:** Computer science, information systems. **Conservation:** Environmental studies. **Engineering:** Computer. **Foreign languages:** Classics, French, German, Spanish. **History:** General. **Math:** General. **Philosophy/religion:** Philosophy. **Physical sciences:** Chemistry, physics. **Psychology:** General. **Public administration:** Social work. **Social sciences:** Political science, sociology. **Visual/performing arts:** Dramatic, music performance, studio arts. **Other:** Interdisciplinary studies.

**Most popular majors.** Biology 12%, business/marketing 19%, communications/journalism 11%, English 7%, history 7%, psychology 10%, social sciences 16%, visual/performing arts 7%.

**Computing on campus.** 330 workstations in dormitories, library, computer center, student center. Dormitories wired for high-speed internet access and linked to campus network. Commuter students can connect to campus network. Online course registration, online library, helpline, student web hosting, wireless network available.

**Student life. Freshman orientation:** Mandatory, $250 fee. Preregistration for classes offered. 2 programs required: 1.5-day program with overnight stay in residence halls, offered June-July, and welcome week program prior to start of classes in fall. **Policies:** Alcohol not permitted in residence halls; 1st and 2nd year students required to live on campus unless they reside with their parents or legal guardians in Gloucester, Hampton, Isle of Wight, James City County, Matthews County, Newport News, Poquoson, Williamsburg or York County (of Virginia). **Housing:** Guaranteed on-campus for freshmen. Coed dorms, apartments, fraternity/sorority housing available. $250 partly refundable deposit, deadline 5/1. Learning communities available. **Activities:** Bands, campus ministries, choral groups, dance, drama, film society, international student organizations, literary magazine, music ensembles, Model UN, musical theater, opera, radio station, student government, student newspaper, symphony orchestra, TV station, Baptist Student Union, Intervarsity Christian Fellowship, Lutheran student association, honor societies, Young Life.

**Athletics.** NCAA. **Intercollegiate:** Baseball M, basketball, cheerleading, cross-country, field hockey W, football (tackle) M, golf M, lacrosse, sailing, soccer, softball W, tennis, track and field, volleyball W. **Intramural:** Badminton, basketball, football (non-tackle) M, soccer, softball, volleyball. **Team name:** Captains.

**Student services.** Chaplain/spiritual director, career counseling, student employment services, financial aid counseling, health services, minority student services, personal counseling, placement for graduates, veterans' counselor. **Physically disabled:** Services for visually, speech, hearing impaired.

**Contact.** E-mail: admit@cnu.edu
Phone: (757) 594-7015 Toll-free number: (800) 333-4268
Fax: (757) 594-7333
Patricia Patten, Dean of Admissions, Christopher Newport University, 1 University Place, Newport News, VA 23606-2998

## College of William and Mary
**Williamsburg, Virginia**
**www.wm.edu**

**CB member**
**CB code: 5115**

- Public 4-year university
- Residential campus in large town
- 5,790 degree-seeking undergraduates: 1% part-time, 54% women, 7% African American, 8% Asian American, 7% Hispanic American, 1% Native American, 3% international
- 1,992 degree-seeking graduate students
- 34% of applicants admitted
- SAT or ACT (ACT writing optional), application essay required
- 91% graduate within 6 years

**General.** Founded in 1693. Regionally accredited. **Degrees:** 1,461 bachelor's awarded; master's, doctoral, professional offered. **ROTC:** Army. **Location:** 50 miles from Richmond, 50 miles from Norfolk. **Calendar:** Semester, limited summer session. **Full-time faculty:** 630 total. **Part-time faculty:** 175 total. **Special facilities:** Observatory, continuous beam accelerator, 3 interdisciplinary centers in humanities, international studies, writing resources, marine science institute, materials processes research center, public policy research center.

**Freshman class profile.** 12,109 applied, 4,058 admitted, 1,395 enrolled.

| Mid 50% test scores | | Rank in top quarter: | 98% |
|---|---|---|---|
| SAT critical reading: | 620-730 | Rank in top tenth: | 79% |
| SAT math: | 620-720 | Return as sophomores: | 94% |
| SAT writing: | 610-710 | Out-of-state: | 35% |
| ACT composite: | 27-32 | Live on campus: | 100% |
| GPA 3.75 or higher: | 78% | International: | 4% |
| GPA 3.50-3.74: | 16% | Fraternities: | 16% |
| GPA 3.0-3.49: | 5% | Sororities: | 18% |
| GPA 2.0-2.99: | 1% | | |

**Basis for selection.** Primary importance is placed on the academic record, including in-class achievement, rigor of curriculum and standardized testing. Extracurricular involvements, writing samples, recommendations, talents and abilities also receive consideration. Preference is given to Virginia residents. Children of alumni receive special consideration.

**High school preparation.** College-preparatory program recommended. Recommended units include English 4, mathematics 4, social studies 4, science 4 (laboratory 3) and foreign language 4.

**2009-2010 Annual costs.** Tuition/fees: $10,800; $30,592 out-of-state. Room/board: $8,382.

**Application procedures. Admission:** Closing date 1/1 (postmark date). $60 fee, may be waived for applicants with need. Admission notification 4/1. Must reply by 5/1.

**Academics. Special study options:** Accelerated study, combined bachelor's/graduate degree, double major, dual enrollment of high school students, honors, independent study, internships, student-designed major, study abroad, teacher certification program, Washington semester. **Credit/placement by examination:** AP, CLEP, IB, institutional tests. **Support services:** Preadmission summer program, reduced course load, study skills assistance, tutoring, writing center.

**Majors. Area/ethnic studies:** African-American, American, women's. **Biology:** General. **Business:** Business admin. **Computer sciences:** General. **Conservation:** Environmental studies. **Foreign languages:** Chinese, classics, French, German, linguistics, Spanish. **History:** General. **Interdisciplinary:** Medieval/Renaissance, neuroscience. **Math:** General. **Parks/recreation:** Exercise sciences. **Philosophy/religion:** Philosophy, religion. **Physical sciences:** Chemistry, geology, physics. **Psychology:** General. **Public administration:** Policy analysis. **Social sciences:** Anthropology, economics, international relations, political science, sociology. **Visual/performing arts:** Art, dramatic. **Other:** Literary and cultural studies.

**Most popular majors.** Business/marketing 12%, English 8%, history 8%, interdisciplinary studies 10%, psychology 9%, social sciences 23%.

**Computing on campus.** PC or laptop required. 350 workstations in dormitories, library, computer center, student center. Dormitories wired for high-speed internet access and linked to campus network. Commuter students can connect to campus network. Online course registration, online library, helpline, repair service, student web hosting, wireless network available.

**Student life. Freshman orientation:** Mandatory, $154 fee. Preregistration for classes offered. 5-day program immediately preceding fall semester.

**Policies:** All students pledge to uphold the Honor Code. Freshman students are required to live on campus. **Housing:** Guaranteed on-campus for freshmen. Coed dorms, special housing for disabled, apartments, fraternity/sorority housing, wellness housing available. $200 nonrefundable deposit, deadline 5/1. International Studies Hall, Eco-House, Community Scholars House, Africana House, Multicultural Unit, 8 Language Houses (Arabic, Chinese, French, German, Italian, Japanese, Russian, Spanish). **Activities:** Bands, campus ministries, choral groups, dance, drama, film society, international student organizations, literary magazine, music ensembles, Model UN, musical theater, opera, radio station, student government, student newspaper, symphony orchestra, TV station, AIDS Tanzania, Asian Student Council, Black Student Organization, College Partnership for Kids, College Republicans, Global Village Project, Hispanic Cultural Organization, Student Environmental Action Coalition, Ultimate Frisbee, Young Democrats.

**Athletics.** NCAA. **Intercollegiate:** Baseball M, basketball, cross-country, diving, field hockey W, football (tackle) M, golf, gymnastics, lacrosse W, soccer, swimming, tennis, track and field, volleyball W. **Intramural:** Basketball, bowling, football (non-tackle), golf, racquetball, soccer, softball, table tennis, tennis, volleyball, weight lifting. **Team name:** Tribe.

**Student services.** Alcohol/substance abuse counseling, career counseling, student employment services, financial aid counseling, health services, legal services, minority student services, on-campus daycare, personal counseling, placement for graduates. **Physically disabled:** Services for visually, hearing impaired.

**Contact.** E-mail: admission@wm.edu
Phone: (757) 221-4223 Fax: (757) 221-1242
Henry Broaddus, Dean of Admission, College of William and Mary, PO Box 8795, Williamsburg, VA 23187-8795

## DeVry University: Arlington
**Arlington, Virginia**
**www.devry.edu**

**CB code: 3813**

- For-profit 4-year university
- Commuter campus in very large city
- 698 degree-seeking undergraduates: 41% part-time, 27% women, 51% African American, 4% Asian American, 12% Hispanic American
- 135 degree-seeking graduate students
- Interview required
- 28% graduate within 6 years

**General. Degrees:** 58 bachelor's, 4 associate awarded; master's offered. **Calendar:** Semester, extensive summer session. **Full-time faculty:** 16 total; 44% minority, 38% women. **Part-time faculty:** 125 total; less than 1% have terminal degrees, 43% minority, 39% women.

**Basis for selection.** Applicant must have high school diploma or equivalent, degree from an accredited postsecondary institution, or submit acceptable test scores and be at least 17 years of age. CPT also accepted.

**High school preparation.** Required units include mathematics 1. Math unit must be algebra or higher.

**2009-2010 Annual costs.** Tuition/fees: $14,160. Books/supplies: $1,300. Personal expenses: $3,152.

**2008-2009 Financial aid.** All financial aid based on need.

**Application procedures. Admission:** No deadline. $50 fee. Admission notification on a rolling basis. **Financial aid:** No deadline. FAFSA required. Applicants notified on a rolling basis.

**Academics. Special study options:** Accelerated study, cooperative education, distance learning. **Credit/placement by examination:** CLEP. **Support services:** Learning center, remedial instruction, tutoring.

**Majors. Business:** Business admin. **Computer sciences:** Networking, systems analysis, web page design. **Engineering:** Software. **Engineering technology:** Computer. **Other:** Technical management.

**Most popular majors.** Business/marketing 53%, computer/information sciences 16%, engineering/engineering technologies 31%.

**Computing on campus.** Online course registration, online library, helpline available.

**Student life. Freshman orientation:** Mandatory. **Activities:** Linux users' group.

**Athletics. Intramural:** Basketball, volleyball.

**Student services.** Career counseling, student employment services, financial aid counseling, placement for graduates, veterans' counselor. **Physically disabled:** Services for visually, hearing impaired.

**Contact.** E-mail: admissions@crys.devry.edu
Phone: (703) 414-4100 Toll-free number: (866) 338-7932
Fax: (703) 414-4040
Bob Pavlovics, Director of Admissions, DeVry University: Arlington, 2450 Crystal Drive, Arlington, VA 22202

## Eastern Mennonite University
**Harrisonburg, Virginia** — CB member
**www.emu.edu** — CB code: 5181

- Private 4-year university and liberal arts college affiliated with Mennonite Church
- Residential campus in large town
- 1,028 degree-seeking undergraduates: 18% part-time, 65% women, 7% African American, 1% Asian American, 4% Hispanic American, 2% international
- 326 degree-seeking graduate students
- 43% of applicants admitted
- SAT or ACT with writing required
- 62% graduate within 6 years

**General.** Founded in 1917. Regionally accredited. **Degrees:** 332 bachelor's, 1 associate awarded; master's offered. **Location:** 110 miles from Richmond, 110 miles from Washington, DC. **Calendar:** Semester, limited summer session. **Full-time faculty:** 97 total; 3% minority, 46% women. **Part-time faculty:** 85 total; 6% minority, 51% women. **Class size:** 69% < 20, 27% 20-39, 3% 40-49, 1% 50-99. **Special facilities:** Museum of natural history, arboretum, student-run coffee shop.

**Freshman class profile.** 769 applied, 330 admitted, 219 enrolled.

| Mid 50% test scores | | GPA 3.50-3.74: | 14% |
|---|---|---|---|
| SAT critical reading: | 460-600 | GPA 3.0-3.49: | 31% |
| SAT math: | 470-620 | GPA 2.0-2.99: | 19% |
| SAT writing: | 450-600 | Return as sophomores: | 77% |
| ACT composite: | 22-28 | Out-of-state: | 47% |
| GPA 3.75 or higher: | 36% | Live on campus: | 88% |

**Basis for selection.** 2.2 high school GPA required. SAT score of 920 (exclusive of Writing) or ACT minimum composite score of 20 required. Conditional admission possible for motivated applicants who fail to reach minimum admissions requirements. Interviews recommended. **Home-schooled:** Detailed record of coursework completed for grades 9-12, SAT or ACT required. **Learning Disabled:** Interview recommended for learning disabled; meet with academic support center personnel.

**High school preparation.** College-preparatory program recommended. 21 units recommended. Recommended units include English 4, mathematics 3, social studies 3, science 3 (laboratory 3), foreign language 2 and academic electives 6.

**2010-2011 Annual costs.** Tuition/fees (projected): $24,320. Room/board: $7,650. Books/supplies: $1,000. Personal expenses: $920.

**2009-2010 Financial aid. Non-need-based:** Scholarships awarded for academics, alumni affiliation, art, leadership, religious affiliation, state residency.

**Application procedures. Admission:** No deadline. $25 fee, may be waived for applicants with need. Admission notification on a rolling basis. **Financial aid:** Priority date 3/1; no closing date. FAFSA required. Applicants notified on a rolling basis starting 3/1; must reply within 4 week(s) of notification.

**Academics.** Missions programs available. Cross-cultural education component required in 3-week or 3-month assignments to locations around the world. **Special study options:** Distance learning, double major, ESL, honors, independent study, internships, liberal arts/career combination, study abroad, teacher certification program, Washington semester. **Credit/placement by examination:** AP, CLEP, IB, SAT, ACT, institutional tests. **Support services:** Learning center, reduced course load, remedial instruction, study skills assistance, tutoring, writing center.

**Majors. Biology:** General, biochemistry. **Business:** Accounting, business admin, international, organizational behavior. **Communications:** General, digital media. **Computer sciences:** Computer science. **Conservation:** Environmental science. **Education:** Physical. **Foreign languages:** French, Spanish. **Health:** Clinical lab science, nursing (RN), predental, premedicine, preveterinary. **History:** General. **Interdisciplinary:** Peace/conflict. **Liberal arts:** Arts/sciences. **Math:** General. **Parks/recreation:** Sports admin. **Physical**

**sciences:** Chemistry. **Psychology:** General. **Public administration:** Social work. **Social sciences:** General, economics, international economic development, sociology. **Theology:** Bible, preministerial, theology. **Visual/performing arts:** Art, dramatic, photography. **Other:** Camping, recreation, and outdoor ministries, Congregational and youth ministries, Philosophy and theology.

**Most popular majors.** Business/marketing 23%, education 7%, health sciences 27%, public administration/social services 6%.

**Computing on campus.** 100 workstations in library, computer center, student center. Dormitories wired for high-speed internet access and linked to campus network. Commuter students can connect to campus network. Online library, helpline, student web hosting, wireless network available.

**Student life. Freshman orientation:** Mandatory. Preregistration for classes offered. One-week orientation begins 5 days before fall semester. **Policies:** Alcohol and drug use by students prohibited. Chapel attendance expected. Students must sign and adhere to Community Lifestyle Commitment. Emphasis on justice and peacemaking. **Housing:** Guaranteed on-campus for freshmen. Coed dorms, single-sex dorms, special housing for disabled, apartments, wellness housing available. Intentional communities available. **Activities:** Bands, campus ministries, choral groups, dance, drama, film society, international student organizations, literary magazine, music ensembles, musical theater, student government, student newspaper, symphony orchestra, Young People's Christian Association, Peace Fellowship, Black student union, Latino student alliance, Earth Keepers, Social Work is People, A Safe Place, Alpha Omega Steppers For Christ.

**Athletics.** NCAA. **Intercollegiate:** Baseball M, basketball, cross-country, field hockey W, soccer, softball W, track and field, volleyball. **Intramural:** Basketball, football (tackle) M, golf, soccer, table tennis, tennis, volleyball. **Team name:** Royals.

**Student services.** Adult student services, alcohol/substance abuse counseling, chaplain/spiritual director, career counseling, student employment services, financial aid counseling, health services, minority student services, personal counseling, placement for graduates. **Physically disabled:** Services for visually, speech, hearing impaired.

**Contact.** E-mail: admiss@emu.edu
Phone: (540) 432-4118 Toll-free number: (800) 368-2665
Fax: (540) 432-4444
Stephanie Shafer, Director of Admissions, Eastern Mennonite University, 1200 Park Road, Harrisonburg, VA 22802-2462

## ECPI College of Technology: Virginia Beach
**Virginia Beach, Virginia**
**www.ecpi.edu** — CB code: 7140

- For-profit 4-year health science and technical college
- Commuter campus in very large city
- 6,200 degree-seeking undergraduates
- Interview required

**General.** Founded in 1966. Regionally accredited. **Degrees:** 45 bachelor's, 1,745 associate awarded. **Calendar:** Continuous, extensive summer session. **Full-time faculty:** 300 total. **Part-time faculty:** 200 total. **Class size:** 80% < 20, 20% 20-39.

**Basis for selection.** Requirements include interview and program specific admissions test. No special considerations given. SAT or ACT recommended. **Learning Disabled:** Consideration may be given on case-by-case basis.

**High school preparation.** Recommended units include English 4, mathematics 2, social studies 2, history 2 and science 2.

**2009-2010 Annual costs.** Tuition/fees: $12,500. Personal expenses: $1,710.

**Financial aid. Non-need-based:** Scholarships awarded for academics.

**Application procedures. Admission:** No deadline. $75 fee. Admission notification on a rolling basis. **Financial aid:** No deadline. Institutional form required. Applicants notified on a rolling basis.

**Academics. Special study options:** Accelerated study, cooperative education, distance learning, double major, dual enrollment of high school students, external degree, honors, independent study, internships, study abroad, weekend college. **Credit/placement by examination:** AP, CLEP, ACT, institutional tests. 18 credit hours maximum toward associate degree, 33 toward bachelor's. **Support services:** Learning center, remedial instruction, study skills assistance, tutoring, writing center.

**Majors. Computer sciences:** General.

**Computing on campus.** 2,800 workstations in library, computer center, student center. Commuter students can connect to campus network. Online course registration, online library, helpline, wireless network available.

**Student life. Freshman orientation:** Mandatory. Preregistration for classes offered. Half-day orientation held day prior to each term start. **Housing:** Wellness housing available. Student housing assistance provided at Virginia Beach campus. **Activities:** Student government, student newspaper, student electronic technicians association, information technology exchange, accounting society, International Association of Administrative Professionals, Phi Theta Kappa.

**Student services.** Adult student services, alcohol/substance abuse counseling, career counseling, services for economically disadvantaged, student employment services, financial aid counseling, personal counseling, placement for graduates, veterans' counselor.

**Contact.** Phone: (757) 671-7171 Toll-free number: (800) 986-1200
Fax: (757) 671-8661
David Preece, Director of Admissions, ECPI College of Technology: Virginia Beach, 5555 Greenwich Road, Suite 300, Virginia Beach, VA 23462-6542

---

## Emory & Henry College
**Emory, Virginia**
www.ehc.edu

CB member
CB code: 5185

- Private 4-year liberal arts college affiliated with United Methodist Church
- Residential campus in rural community
- 918 degree-seeking undergraduates: 2% part-time, 46% women, 8% African American, 1% Hispanic American, 1% Native American, 1% international
- 30 degree-seeking graduate students
- 70% of applicants admitted
- SAT or ACT (ACT writing recommended) required
- 57% graduate within 6 years

**General.** Founded in 1836. Regionally accredited. Partnership with Barter Theatre (state theater of Virginia), extensive Lyceum/cultural program, annual ScienceFest. **Degrees:** 192 bachelor's awarded; master's offered. **Location:** 25 miles from Bristol. **Calendar:** Semester, limited summer session. **Full-time faculty:** 75 total; 85% have terminal degrees, 5% minority, 41% women. **Part-time faculty:** 56 total; 11% have terminal degrees, 45% women. **Class size:** 75% < 20, 24% 20-39, less than 1% 40-49. **Special facilities:** Observatory, 1912 art depot, outdoor leadership center, disc golf course, golf course.

**Freshman class profile.** 1,328 applied, 932 admitted, 291 enrolled.

| Mid 50% test scores | | | |
|---|---|---|---|
| SAT critical reading: | 450-570 | GPA 2.0-2.99: | 21% |
| SAT math: | 460-570 | Rank in top quarter: | 43% |
| SAT writing: | 430-550 | Rank in top tenth: | 20% |
| ACT composite: | 18-25 | Return as sophomores: | 71% |
| GPA 3.75 or higher: | 29% | Out-of-state: | 43% |
| GPA 3.50-3.74: | 18% | Live on campus: | 94% |
| GPA 3.0-3.49: | 31% | International: | 1% |

**Basis for selection.** School achievement record, test scores, involvement in extracurricular and community activities, class rank, recommendations used. Audition required for preprofessional degrees in acting, directing, musical theater, and design/production. Auditions required for performance and teacher preparation tracks within music program. Portfolio recommended for art program.

**High school preparation.** College-preparatory program required. 15 units required. Required units include English 4, mathematics 3, social studies 2, science 2 (laboratory 2), foreign language 2 and visual/performing arts 1. 1 fine arts recommended.

**2009-2010 Annual costs.** Tuition/fees: $24,880. Room/board: $8,300. Books/supplies: $800. Personal expenses: $1,000.

**2009-2010 Financial aid. Need-based:** 265 full-time freshmen applied for aid; 231 were judged to have need; 230 of these received aid. Average need met was 90%. Average scholarship/grant was $22,287; average loan $3,375. 79% of total undergraduate aid awarded as scholarships/grants, 21% as loans/jobs. **Non-need-based:** Awarded to 318 full-time undergraduates, including 125 freshmen. Scholarships awarded for academics, art, music/

---

drama, religious affiliation, state residency. **Additional information:** Virginia residents eligible for additional in-state tuition grants.

**Application procedures. Admission:** Priority date 3/1; no deadline. Admission notification on a rolling basis beginning on or about 1/1. Must reply by May 1 or within 4 week(s) if notified thereafter. **Financial aid:** Priority date 4/15; no closing date. FAFSA required. Applicants notified on a rolling basis starting 3/1; must reply by 6/15.

**Academics. Special study options:** Combined bachelor's/graduate degree, cooperative education, distance learning, double major, dual enrollment of high school students, honors, independent study, internships, liberal arts/career combination, student-designed major, study abroad, teacher certification program. **Credit/placement by examination:** AP, CLEP, IB, SAT, ACT, institutional tests. **Support services:** Learning center, pre-admission summer program, reduced course load, study skills assistance, tutoring, writing center.

**Majors. Area/ethnic studies:** East Asian, European, French, Near/Middle Eastern, Spanish/Iberian. **Biology:** General. **Business:** Accounting, business admin, international. **Communications:** Media studies. **Computer sciences:** General, computer science. **Conservation:** Environmental science, environmental studies. **Education:** Art, biology, business, chemistry, English, French, mathematics, music, physical, Spanish. **Foreign languages:** French, Spanish. **Health:** Athletic training, prepharmacy, preveterinary. **History:** General, public archives. **Legal studies:** Prelaw. **Math:** General. **Parks/recreation:** Health/fitness, sports admin. **Philosophy/religion:** Philosophy, religion. **Physical sciences:** Chemistry, physics. **Psychology:** General. **Public administration:** Community org/advocacy. **Social sciences:** Anthropology, economics, geography, political science, sociology, U.S. government. **Visual/performing arts:** Acting, art, directing/producing, dramatic, graphic design, music performance, musical theater. **Other:** Pre-health.

**Most popular majors.** Biology 9%, business/marketing 13%, communications/journalism 7%, education 8%, physical sciences 6%, psychology 8%, social sciences 15%, visual/performing arts 9%.

**Computing on campus.** 250 workstations in dormitories, library, computer center, student center. Dormitories wired for high-speed internet access and linked to campus network. Commuter students can connect to campus network. Online library, helpline, wireless network available.

**Student life. Freshman orientation:** Mandatory. Preregistration for classes offered. Orientation occurs before registration. Students participate in community service activity and attend fine arts event following weekend as part of extended orientation. **Housing:** Guaranteed on-campus for all undergraduates. Coed dorms, single-sex dorms, special housing for disabled, wellness housing available. $400 fully refundable deposit, deadline 8/1. **Activities:** Pep band, campus ministries, choral groups, drama, international student organizations, literary magazine, music ensembles, musical theater, radio station, student government, student newspaper, TV station, Young Democrats, Young Republicans, Libertarians, Alpha Phi Omega, Fellowship of Christian Athletes, outdoor leadership program, Habitat for Humanity, Campus Christian Fellowship, multicultural student association.

**Athletics.** NCAA. **Intercollegiate:** Baseball M, basketball, cheerleading M, cross-country, football (tackle) M, golf M, soccer, softball W, swimming W, tennis, volleyball W. **Intramural:** Badminton, basketball, football (nontackle), golf, racquetball, soccer, softball, swimming, table tennis, tennis, volleyball. **Team name:** Wasps.

**Student services.** Alcohol/substance abuse counseling, chaplain/spiritual director, career counseling, student employment services, financial aid counseling, health services, on-campus daycare, personal counseling, placement for graduates, veterans' counselor. **Physically disabled:** Services for visually, hearing impaired. **Learning disabled:** Comprehensive services available.

**Contact.** E-mail: ehadmiss@ehc.edu
Phone: (276) 944-6133 Toll-free number: (800) 848-5494
Fax: (276) 944-6935
David Hawsey, Vice President of Enrollment Management, Emory & Henry College, Box 10, Emory, VA 24327

---

## Ferrum College
**Ferrum, Virginia**
www.ferrum.edu

CB member
CB code: 5213

- Private 4-year liberal arts college affiliated with United Methodist Church
- Residential campus in rural community
- 1,424 degree-seeking undergraduates: 3% part-time, 49% women, 31% African American, 1% Asian American, 3% Hispanic American, 1% Native American, 1% international

◆ 80% of applicants admitted
◆ SAT or ACT (ACT writing optional) required
◆ 35% graduate within 6 years

**General.** Founded in 1913. Regionally accredited. **Degrees:** 205 bachelor's awarded. **Location:** 35 miles from Roanoke, 65 miles from Greensboro, North Carolina. **Calendar:** Semester, limited summer session. **Full-time faculty:** 69 total; 70% have terminal degrees, 10% minority, 44% women. **Part-time faculty:** 40 total; 38% have terminal degrees, 5% minority, 60% women. **Class size:** 60% < 20, 40% 20-39, less than 1% 40-49. **Special facilities:** Farm museum, state center for Blue Ridge folklore, forest and agricultural acreage used as outdoor labs in science, high and low ropes courses, dinner theater.

**Freshman class profile.** 2,427 applied, 1,932 admitted, 546 enrolled.

| Mid 50% test scores | | | |
|---|---|---|---|
| SAT critical reading: | 390-500 | GPA 3.0-3.49: | 21% |
| SAT math: | 400-490 | GPA 2.0-2.99: | 62% |
| ACT composite: | 16-21 | Rank in top quarter: | 18% |
| GPA 3.75 or higher: | 4% | Rank in top tenth: | 4% |
| GPA 3.50-3.74: | 9% | Return as sophomores: | 51% |

**Basis for selection.** High school record most important, followed by test scores, counselor recommendations, areas of intended college study, and extracurricular activities. Essay and interview recommended. **Home-schooled:** Transcript of courses and grades required. **Learning Disabled:** Submit current disability documentation to Director of Disability Services.

**High school preparation.** College-preparatory program recommended. 22 units required; 24 recommended. Required and recommended units include English 4, mathematics 3, social studies 3, science 2 (laboratory 1), foreign language 2 and academic electives 2.

**2009-2010 Annual costs.** Tuition/fees: $23,565. Room/board: $7,630. Books/supplies: $900. Personal expenses: $1,300.

**2008-2009 Financial aid.** **Need-based:** 575 full-time freshmen applied for aid; 517 were judged to have need; 517 of these received aid. Average need met was 74%. Average scholarship/grant was $6,191; average loan $3,204. 88% of total undergraduate aid awarded as scholarships/grants, 12% as loans/jobs. **Non-need-based:** Awarded to 1,261 full-time undergraduates, including 547 freshmen. Scholarships awarded for academics, leadership, religious affiliation, state residency.

**Application procedures.** **Admission:** $25 fee, may be waived for applicants with need. Admission notification on a rolling basis beginning on or about 9/16. Must reply by May 1 or within 4 week(s) if notified thereafter. Must reply no later than 30 days after receiving official acceptance letter. **Financial aid:** Priority date 3/1; no closing date. FAFSA required. Applicants notified on a rolling basis starting 1/10.

**Academics.** Field experiences and internships emphasized. Academic services/support available fall and spring academic semesters. **Special study options:** Double major, dual enrollment of high school students, exchange student, honors, independent study, internships, liberal arts/career combination, student-designed major, study abroad, teacher certification program. **Credit/placement by examination:** AP, CLEP, IB, institutional tests. 12 credit hours maximum toward bachelor's degree. **Support services:** Learning center, pre-admission summer program, reduced course load, remedial instruction, study skills assistance, tutoring, writing center.

**Majors.** **Agriculture:** Business, horticultural science. **Biology:** General. **Business:** Accounting, business admin, finance, management information systems, marketing. **Computer sciences:** Information systems. **Conservation:** Environmental science. **Education:** General. **Foreign languages:** Russian, Spanish. **Health:** Clinical lab science, health services. **History:** General. **Liberal arts:** Arts/sciences. **Math:** General. **Parks/recreation:** General, health/fitness, sports admin. **Philosophy/religion:** Philosophy, religion. **Physical sciences:** Chemistry. **Protective services:** Criminal justice. **Psychology:** General. **Public administration:** Social work. **Social sciences:** General, international relations, political science. **Visual/performing arts:** General, art, dramatic.

**Most popular majors.** Business/marketing 14%, health sciences 31%, liberal arts 10%, security/protective services 6%.

**Computing on campus.** PC or laptop required. 600 workstations in dormitories, library, computer center, student center. Dormitories wired for high-speed internet access and linked to campus network. Commuter students can connect to campus network. Online course registration, online library, helpline, repair service, student web hosting, wireless network available.

**Student life. Freshman orientation:** Mandatory. Preregistration for classes offered. 2-day student orientation held immediately prior to fall semester.

**Policies:** All housing substance-free; no alcohol or tobacco products allowed. **Housing:** Guaranteed on-campus for all undergraduates. Coed dorms, single-sex dorms, special housing for disabled, apartments, wellness housing available. **Activities:** Bands, campus ministries, choral groups, dance, drama, international student organizations, literary magazine, music ensembles, Model UN, musical theater, radio station, student government, student newspaper, Environmental Action Coalition, Big Buddy/Little Buddy, African American student association, Bonner Scholars, Student Christian Fellowship, Kappa Delta Chi, Habitat for Humanity, Colleges Against Cancer, Alpha Phi Omega.

**Athletics.** NCAA. **Intercollegiate:** Baseball M, basketball, cheerleading, cross-country, football (tackle) M, golf M, lacrosse W, soccer, softball W, tennis, volleyball W. **Intramural:** Basketball, bowling, football (non-tackle), racquetball, soccer, softball, swimming, table tennis, tennis, volleyball. **Team name:** Panthers.

**Student services.** Adult student services, alcohol/substance abuse counseling, chaplain/spiritual director, career counseling, student employment services, financial aid counseling, health services, minority student services, personal counseling, placement for graduates, veterans' counselor.

**Contact.** E-mail: admissions@ferrum.edu
Phone: (540) 365-4290 Toll-free number: (800) 868-9797
Fax: (540) 365-4266
Gilda Woods, Director of Admissions, Ferrum College, Spilman-Daniel House, Ferrum, VA 24088

## George Mason University
**Fairfax, Virginia**
www.gmu.edu

CB member
CB code: 5827

◆ Public 4-year university
◆ Residential campus in large town
◆ 19,130 degree-seeking undergraduates: 21% part-time, 53% women, 8% African American, 16% Asian American, 9% Hispanic American, 3% international
◆ 10,513 degree-seeking graduate students
◆ 63% of applicants admitted
◆ Application essay required
◆ 63% graduate within 6 years

**General.** Founded in 1972. Regionally accredited. **Degrees:** 4,009 bachelor's awarded; master's, doctoral, professional offered. **ROTC:** Army, Air Force. **Location:** 21 miles from Washington, DC. **Calendar:** Semester, extensive summer session. **Full-time faculty:** 1,128 total; 91% have terminal degrees, 17% minority, 41% women. **Part-time faculty:** 1,072 total; 17% minority, 49% women. **Class size:** 28% < 20, 43% 20-39, 12% 40-49, 14% 50-99, 4% >100. **Special facilities:** Center for the arts, astronomy observatory, Smithsonian conservation and research center, library of congress federal theater project collection.

**Freshman class profile.** 13,732 applied, 8,691 admitted, 2,656 enrolled.

| Mid 50% test scores | | | |
|---|---|---|---|
| SAT critical reading: | 510-620 | Rank in top quarter: | 56% |
| SAT math: | 520-630 | Rank in top tenth: | 20% |
| ACT composite: | 23-27 | End year in good standing: | 80% |
| GPA 3.75 or higher: | 28% | Return as sophomores: | 85% |
| GPA 3.50-3.74: | 26% | Out-of-state: | 21% |
| GPA 3.0-3.49: | 44% | Live on campus: | 70% |
| GPA 2.0-2.99: | 2% | International: | 2% |

**Basis for selection.** Test scores, class rank, academic record with emphasis on courses taken, and GPA are most important. Special talents and abilities and counselor recommendations are also important. SAT and SAT Subject Tests or ACT recommended. Writing tests are not used in the admissions process. It is recommended that students submit standardized test scores (SAT or ACT), however, option availlable for admission without submitting test scores. Candidates should submit academic credentials that exhibit the following: A minimum GPA of 3.5; strong performance in a challenging academic curriculum; estimated class rank in the top 20 percent of high school class; and evidence of strong leadership skills. Audition required for dance and music applicants. Portfolio required for art and visual technology BFA applicants.

**High school preparation.** College-preparatory program required. 18 units required; 23 recommended. Required and recommended units include English 4, mathematics 3-4, social studies 3-4, science 3-4 (laboratory 3-4), foreign language 2-3 and academic electives 3-5. Additional mathematics and science units required for engineering, mathematics, and computer science applicants.

**2009-2010 Annual costs.** Tuition/fees: $8,024; $24,008 out-of-state. Room/board: $7,700. Books/supplies: $900. Personal expenses: $1,440.

**2009-2010 Financial aid. Need-based:** 1,948 full-time freshmen applied for aid; 1,224 were judged to have need; 1,191 of these received aid. Average need met was 74%. Average scholarship/grant was $7,157; average loan $3,528. 47% of total undergraduate aid awarded as scholarships/grants, 53% as loans/jobs. **Non-need-based:** Awarded to 1,672 full-time undergraduates, including 535 freshmen. Scholarships awarded for academics, athletics, minority status, music/drama, ROTC, state residency.

**Application procedures. Admission:** Priority date 12/1; deadline 1/15 (postmark date). $75 fee, may be waived for applicants with need. Admission notification 4/1. Must reply by May 1 or within 3 week(s) if notified thereafter. **Financial aid:** Priority date 3/1; no closing date. FAFSA required. Applicants notified by 4/1; Applicants notified on a rolling basis starting 4/1; must reply within 3 week(s) of notification.

**Academics. Special study options:** Accelerated study, combined bachelor's/graduate degree, cooperative education, cross-registration, distance learning, double major, dual enrollment of high school students, ESL, exchange student, external degree, honors, independent study, internships, liberal arts/career combination, student-designed major, study abroad, teacher certification program. **Credit/placement by examination:** AP, CLEP, IB, institutional tests. 30 credit hours maximum toward bachelor's degree. **Support services:** Learning center, reduced course load, study skills assistance, tutoring, writing center.

**Majors. Area/ethnic studies:** Latin American, Russian/Slavic. **Biology:** General. **Business:** Accounting, business admin, finance, marketing. **Communications:** General. **Communications technology:** Animation/special effects. **Computer sciences:** General. **Education:** Health, physical. **Engineering:** Civil, computer, electrical, systems. **Foreign languages:** General. **Health:** Athletic training, clinical lab science, community health, nursing (RN). **History:** General. **Interdisciplinary:** Math/computer science, neuroscience, peace/conflict. **Liberal arts:** Arts/sciences. **Math:** General. **Philosophy/religion:** Philosophy, religion. **Physical sciences:** Astronomy, chemistry, geology, physics. **Protective services:** Police science. **Psychology:** General. **Public administration:** General, social work. **Social sciences:** Anthropology, economics, geography, international relations, sociology. **Visual/performing arts:** General, art, cinematography, dance, dramatic, music performance. **Other:** Bioinformatics management, Global and environmental change, Health science, Information technology, Integrative studies, Tourism and events management.

**Most popular majors.** Business/marketing 22%, engineering/engineering technologies 8%, English 9%, health sciences 9%, psychology 7%, social sciences 14%, visual/performing arts 6%.

**Computing on campus.** 1,437 workstations in dormitories, library, computer center, student center. Dormitories wired for high-speed internet access and linked to campus network. Commuter students can connect to campus network. Online course registration, online library, helpline, repair service, student web hosting, wireless network available.

**Student life. Freshman orientation:** Mandatory, $180 fee. 2-day comprehensive overnight program. Transfer orientation occurs from June through July and students are given a half or full day option. **Housing:** Guaranteed on-campus for freshmen. Coed dorms, special housing for disabled, apartments, wellness housing available. $300 nonrefundable deposit, deadline 5/1. Townhouses available. **Activities:** Bands, campus ministries, choral groups, dance, drama, film society, international student organizations, literary magazine, music ensembles, Model UN, musical theater, opera, radio station, student government, student newspaper, symphony orchestra, TV station, Campus Crusade for Christ, Catholic Campus Ministry, Afghan Student Union, Hillel-Jewish Student Association, Muslim Student Association, African Student Association, GMU Lending Hands, Uganda HELP, Circle K International, Mason Community Outreach.

**Athletics.** NCAA. **Intercollegiate:** Baseball M, basketball, cheerleading, cross-country, diving, golf M, lacrosse W, rowing (crew) W, soccer, softball W, swimming, tennis, track and field, volleyball, wrestling M. **Intramural:** Basketball, cricket, football (non-tackle), golf, soccer, softball, swimming, table tennis, tennis, track and field, volleyball. **Team name:** Patriots.

**Student services.** Adult student services, alcohol/substance abuse counseling, chaplain/spiritual director, career counseling, services for economically disadvantaged, student employment services, financial aid counseling, health services, minority student services, on-campus daycare, personal counseling, placement for graduates, veterans' counselor, women's services. **Physically disabled:** Services for visually, speech, hearing impaired.

**Contact.** E-mail: admissions@gmu.edu
Phone: (703) 993-2400 Fax: (703) 993-4622
Andrew Flagel, Dean, Admissions/Associate Vice President, Enrollment Development, Admissions, George Mason University, 4400 University Drive, MSN 3A4, Fairfax, VA 22030-4444

## Hampden-Sydney College

**Hampden-Sydney, Virginia**
**www.hsc.edu**

CB member
CB code: 5291

- Private 4-year liberal arts college for men affiliated with Presbyterian Church (USA)
- Residential campus in rural community
- 1,068 degree-seeking undergraduates
- 56% of applicants admitted
- SAT or ACT with writing, application essay required
- 66% graduate within 6 years; 47% enter graduate study

**General.** Founded in 1776. Regionally accredited. **Degrees:** 228 bachelor's awarded. **ROTC:** Army. **Location:** 60 miles from Richmond, 69 miles from Charlottesville. **Calendar:** Semester, limited summer session. **Full-time faculty:** 98 total; 87% have terminal degrees, 7% minority, 26% women. **Part-time faculty:** 21 total; 62% have terminal degrees, 10% minority, 43% women. **Class size:** 70% < 20, 30% 20-39. **Special facilities:** International communications center, observatory, college operated museum, Athlete Hall of Fame museum, hiking trails.

**Freshman class profile.** 2,270 applied, 1,272 admitted, 295 enrolled.

| Mid 50% test scores | | | |
|---|---|---|---|
| SAT critical reading: | 500-600 | Rank in top quarter: | 35% |
| SAT math: | 500-610 | Rank in top tenth: | 15% |
| SAT writing: | 460-580 | End year in good standing: | 96% |
| ACT composite: | 20-26 | Return as sophomores: | 77% |
| GPA 3.75 or higher: | 19% | Out-of-state: | 36% |
| GPA 3.50-3.74: | 14% | Live on campus: | 100% |
| GPA 3.0-3.49: | 36% | International: | 2% |
| GPA 2.0-2.99: | 31% | Fraternities: | 34% |

**Basis for selection.** High school academic record, recommendations, test scores, extracurricular activities, essay most important. SAT Subject Tests recommended. SAT Subject Test in Math Level 1 recommended. Interview recommended. **Homeschooled:** Letter of recommendation (nonparent) required. Curriculum statement required.

**High school preparation.** College-preparatory program recommended. 16 units required. Required and recommended units include English 4, mathematics 3-4, social studies 1, history 1, science 2-3 (laboratory 1), foreign language 2-3 and academic electives 3.

**2009-2010 Annual costs.** Tuition/fees: $30,688. Room/board: $9,690. Books/supplies: $1,200. Personal expenses: $1,100.

**2009-2010 Financial aid. Need-based:** 232 full-time freshmen applied for aid; 171 were judged to have need; 171 of these received aid. Average need met was 81%. Average scholarship/grant was $19,751; average loan $3,876. 74% of total undergraduate aid awarded as scholarships/grants, 26% as loans/jobs. **Non-need-based:** Awarded to 575 full-time undergraduates, including 158 freshmen. Scholarships awarded for academics, leadership, minority status, religious affiliation, ROTC, state residency.

**Application procedures. Admission:** Closing date 3/1 (postmark date). $30 fee, may be waived for applicants with need, free for online applicants. Admission notification 4/15. Must reply by 5/1. **Financial aid:** Priority date 11/15, closing date 5/1. FAFSA, CSS PROFILE required. Applicants notified by 3/15; must reply by 5/1 or within 2 week(s) of notification.

**Academics.** Public service concentration for men interested in government involves classwork and internship followed by paper presented and defended publicly. **Special study options:** Combined bachelor's/graduate degree, cooperative education, cross-registration, double major, dual enrollment of high school students, exchange student, honors, independent study, internships, semester at sea, study abroad, Washington semester. Appalachian semester, junior year exchange program with members of Virginia consortium. **Credit/placement by examination:** AP, CLEP, IB, SAT, ACT, institutional tests. **Support services:** Reduced course load, study skills assistance, tutoring, writing center.

**Majors. Biology:** General, biochemistry, biophysics. **Business:** Managerial economics. **Computer sciences:** Computer science. **Foreign languages:** Ancient Greek, classics, French, German, Latin, Spanish. **History:** General. **Interdisciplinary:** Math/computer science. **Liberal arts:** Humanities. **Math:** General, applied. **Philosophy/religion:** Philosophy, religion. **Physical sciences:** Chemistry, physics. **Psychology:** General. **Social sciences:** Econometrics, economics, international relations, political science. **Visual/performing arts:** Studio arts.

**Most popular majors.** Biology 8%, business/marketing 15%, history 21%, psychology 6%, social sciences 25%.

**Computing on campus.** 98 workstations in dormitories, library, computer center. Dormitories wired for high-speed internet access and linked to campus network. Commuter students can connect to campus network. Online course registration, online library, helpline, repair service, wireless network available.

**Student life. Freshman orientation:** Mandatory, $150 fee. Preregistration for classes offered. 4-day program before start of classes. **Policies:** All entering freshman participate in a presentation and discussion regarding the HSC Honor Code. **Housing:** Guaranteed on-campus for all undergraduates. Apartments, fraternity/sorority housing available. $300 deposit, deadline 5/1. **Activities:** Pep band, campus ministries, choral groups, drama, international student organizations, literary magazine, music ensembles, radio station, student government, student newspaper, Inter-Varsity Christian Fellowship, Republican Society, volunteer fire department, Good Men and Good Citizens (community service), Student Environmental Action Coalition, museum board, Fellowship of Christian Athletes, Minority Student Union, Young Democrats.

**Athletics.** NCAA. **Intercollegiate:** Baseball M, basketball M, cross-country M, football (tackle) M, golf M, lacrosse M, soccer M, tennis M. **Intramural:** Basketball M, racquetball M, rugby M, soccer M, softball M, volleyball M. **Team name:** Tigers.

**Student services.** Alcohol/substance abuse counseling, chaplain/spiritual director, career counseling, student employment services, financial aid counseling, health services, minority student services, personal counseling, placement for graduates.

**Contact.** E-mail: hsapp@hsc.edu
Phone: (434) 223-6120 Toll-free number: (800) 755-0733
Fax: (434) 223-6346
Jason Ferguson, Director of Admissions, Hampden-Sydney College, Box 667, Hampden-Sydney, VA 23943

---

## Hampton University

**Hampton, Virginia**
**www.hamptonu.edu**

**CB member**
**CB code: 5292**

- Private 4-year university
- Residential campus in small city
- 4,495 degree-seeking undergraduates: 6% part-time, 63% women, 96% African American, 1% Hispanic American, 1% international
- 655 degree-seeking graduate students
- 56% of applicants admitted
- SAT or ACT (ACT writing optional), application essay required
- 53% graduate within 6 years; 34% enter graduate study

**General.** Founded in 1868. Regionally accredited. **Degrees:** 855 bachelor's awarded; master's, doctoral, professional offered. **ROTC:** Army, Naval. **Location:** 10 miles from Norfolk. **Calendar:** Semester, extensive summer session. **Full-time faculty:** 358 total; 78% have terminal degrees, 78% minority, 47% women. **Part-time faculty:** 70 total; 21% have terminal degrees, 63% minority, 66% women. **Class size:** 51% < 20, 38% 20-39, 7% 40-49, 4% 50-99, less than 1% >100. **Special facilities:** African American literature and history collection, university archives, North American Indian, African, Oceanic and Black American art collections, proton therapy institute; medical research, atmospheric sciences with satellites in earth's orbit.

**Freshman class profile.** 7,482 applied, 4,201 admitted, 1,000 enrolled.

| Mid 50% test scores | | End year in good standing: | 79% |
|---|---|---|---|
| SAT critical reading: | 480-610 | Return as sophomores: | 79% |
| SAT math: | 480-570 | Out-of-state: | 68% |
| ACT composite: | 16-28 | Live on campus: | 71% |
| GPA 3.75 or higher: | 10% | International: | 1% |
| GPA 3.50-3.74: | 15% | Fraternities: | 5% |
| GPA 3.0-3.49: | 47% | Sororities: | 4% |
| GPA 2.0-2.99: | 27% | | |

**Basis for selection.** Academic record, rank in top half of graduating class, personal references, intended major, test scores and personal statement important. Extracurricular activities, essay, school recommendation considered. Audition required for music. **Homeschooled:** Transcript of courses and grades required. Must present secondary school record if it exists, GED test scores, verification by state/regional official, SAT or ACT results.

**High school preparation.** College-preparatory program recommended. 17 units required. Required and recommended units include English 4, mathematics 3, social studies 2, science 2 (laboratory 2), foreign language 2 and academic electives 6. One chemistry, biology with lab, algebra I and II, geometry required.

**2009-2010 Annual costs.** Tuition/fees: $17,212. Room/board: $7,664. Books/supplies: $1,025. Personal expenses: $1,423.

**2009-2010 Financial aid. Need-based:** 701 full-time freshmen applied for aid; 604 were judged to have need; 535 of these received aid. Average need met was 43%. Average scholarship/grant was $1,992; average loan $1,500. 42% of total undergraduate aid awarded as scholarships/grants, 58% as loans/jobs. **Non-need-based:** Scholarships awarded for academics, athletics, leadership, music/drama, ROTC.

**Application procedures. Admission:** Priority date 12/1; deadline 3/1 (postmark date). $35 fee. Admission notification on a rolling basis beginning on or about 12/15. Must reply by 5/1. **Financial aid:** Priority date 3/1; no closing date. FAFSA required. Applicants notified on a rolling basis starting 3/1; must reply within 2 week(s) of notification.

**Academics.** Students who have completed one semester with minimum 3.2 GPA may apply to honors program. Academic skills workshops held throughout year available for all students. Students may take courses at other Tidewater consortium schools. **Special study options:** Accelerated study, combined bachelor's/graduate degree, cooperative education, cross-registration, distance learning, double major, dual enrollment of high school students, honors, independent study, internships, study abroad, teacher certification program. Grad level programs for undergraduates, coop programs in arts, business, education, engineering, social/behavioral science. **Credit/placement by examination:** AP, CLEP, IB, SAT, ACT, institutional tests. 30 credit hours maximum toward bachelor's degree. **Support services:** Learning center, pre-admission summer program, reduced course load, remedial instruction, tutoring, writing center.

**Majors. Architecture:** Architecture. **Biology:** General, marine, molecular. **Business:** Accounting, banking/financial services, business admin, finance, management information systems, managerial economics, marketing. **Communications:** Advertising, broadcast journalism, journalism, media studies, public relations. **Computer sciences:** General, computer science, networking. **Conservation:** Environmental science. **Education:** General, health, physical, special. **Engineering:** General, chemical, computer, electrical. **Foreign languages:** Spanish. **Health:** Audiology/speech pathology, communication disorders, nursing (RN). **History:** General. **Legal studies:** Paralegal, pre-law. **Liberal arts:** Arts/sciences. **Math:** General. **Parks/recreation:** General, facilities management, sports admin. **Physical sciences:** Chemistry, physics. **Protective services:** Fire services admin, law enforcement admin. **Psychology:** General. **Social sciences:** Political science, sociology. **Theology:** Theology. **Transportation:** Aviation management. **Visual/performing arts:** Art, commercial/advertising art, dramatic, music performance.

**Most popular majors.** Biology 6%, business/marketing 27%, communications/journalism 10%, health sciences 18%, psychology 13%, social sciences 6%.

**Computing on campus.** 1,500 workstations in dormitories, library, computer center, student center. Dormitories wired for high-speed internet access and linked to campus network. Commuter students can connect to campus network. Online course registration, online library, helpline, repair service, student web hosting, wireless network available.

**Student life. Freshman orientation:** Mandatory. Preregistration for classes offered. One-week orientation held in August. **Housing:** Guaranteed on-campus for freshmen. Coed dorms, single-sex dorms, wellness housing available. $500 deposit, deadline 5/1. **Activities:** Bands, campus ministries, choral groups, dance, drama, international student organizations, music ensembles, musical theater, opera, radio station, student government, student newspaper, symphony orchestra, TV station, Christian student association, Big Brothers/Big Sisters, political science/pre-law club, Women in Communications, Muslim student fellowship, service learning and leadership organizations, National Leadership of Black Journalists.

**Athletics.** NCAA. **Intercollegiate:** Basketball, bowling W, cheerleading M, cross-country, football (tackle) M, golf, sailing, softball W, tennis, track and field, volleyball W. **Intramural:** Basketball, bowling W, softball W, swimming. **Team name:** Pirates.

**Student services.** Chaplain/spiritual director, career counseling, services for economically disadvantaged, student employment services, financial aid counseling, health services, on-campus daycare, personal counseling, placement for graduates, veterans' counselor. **Physically disabled:** Services for visually, speech, hearing impaired.

**Contact.** E-mail: admit@hamptonu.edu
Phone: (757) 727-5328 Toll-free number: (800) 624-3328
Fax: (757) 727-5095
Angela Boyd, Director of Admissions, Hampton University, Office of Admissions, Hampton, VA 23668

## Hollins University
### Roanoke, Virginia
www.hollins.edu

CB member
CB code: 5294

- Private 4-year university and liberal arts college for women
- Residential campus in small city
- 775 degree-seeking undergraduates: 3% part-time, 100% women, 8% African American, 2% Asian American, 4% Hispanic American, 1% Native American, 4% international
- 236 degree-seeking graduate students
- 90% of applicants admitted
- SAT or ACT (ACT writing optional), application essay required
- 65% graduate within 6 years

**General.** Founded in 1842. Regionally accredited. **Degrees:** 178 bachelor's awarded; master's offered. **Location:** 175 miles from Richmond, 250 miles from Washington, DC. **Calendar:** 4-1-4, limited summer session. **Full-time faculty:** 72 total; 97% have terminal degrees, 10% minority, 46% women. **Part-time faculty:** 26 total; 50% have terminal degrees, 4% minority, 65% women. **Class size:** 86% < 20, 13% 20-39, 1% 40-49. **Special facilities:** Electron microscope facilities, EEG and biofeedback equipment, research facilities for chromatography, spectrophotometry, electrochemistry, gas kinetics, centrifugation.

**Freshman class profile.** 693 applied, 625 admitted, 198 enrolled.

| Mid 50% test scores | | GPA 2.0-2.99: | 10% |
|---|---|---|---|
| SAT critical reading: | 510-660 | Rank in top quarter: | 55% |
| SAT math: | 450-570 | Rank in top tenth: | 23% |
| SAT writing: | 500-620 | Return as sophomores: | 76% |
| ACT composite: | 22-28 | Out-of-state: | 48% |
| GPA 3.75 or higher: | 34% | Live on campus: | 89% |
| GPA 3.50-3.74: | 16% | International: | 4% |
| GPA 3.0-3.49: | 40% | | |

**Basis for selection.** School achievement record, school recommendation, and test scores very important. Essay, talent/ability important. Interview, class rank, character, alumni relation, extracurricular activities, volunteer work, work experience considered. Interview recommended. **Homeschooled:** Applicants encouraged to take 3 SAT Subject Tests.

**High school preparation.** College-preparatory program recommended. 16 units required. Required units include English 4, mathematics 3, social studies 3, science 3 and foreign language 3.

**2010-2011 Annual costs.** Tuition/fees: $29,485. Room/board: $10,200. Books/supplies: $800. Personal expenses: $850.

**2009-2010 Financial aid. Need-based:** 179 full-time freshmen applied for aid; 156 were judged to have need; 156 of these received aid. Average need met was 90%. Average scholarship/grant was $17,236; average loan $6,768. 65% of total undergraduate aid awarded as scholarships/grants, 35% as loans/jobs. **Non-need-based:** Awarded to 485 full-time undergraduates, including 161 freshmen. Scholarships awarded for academics, alumni affiliation, art, leadership, music/drama, state residency.

**Application procedures. Admission:** Priority date 2/1; no deadline. $35 fee, may be waived for applicants with need. Admission notification on a rolling basis beginning on or about 12/15. Must reply by May 1 or within 2 week(s) if notified thereafter. **Financial aid:** Priority date 2/15; no closing date. FAFSA required. Applicants notified on a rolling basis starting 3/1; must reply by 5/1.

**Academics. Special study options:** Accelerated study, combined bachelor's/graduate degree, cooperative education, cross-registration, double major, dual enrollment of high school students, exchange student, independent study, internships, liberal arts/career combination, student-designed major, study abroad, teacher certification program. **Credit/placement by examination:** AP, CLEP, IB, institutional tests. **Support services:** Tutoring, writing center.

**Majors. Area/ethnic studies:** Women's. **Biology:** General, environmental. **Business:** General. **Communications:** General. **Conservation:** Environmental studies. **Foreign languages:** Classics, French, German, Spanish. **History:** General. **Interdisciplinary:** Global studies. **Math:** General. **Philosophy/religion:** Philosophy, religion. **Physical sciences:** Chemistry, physics. **Psychology:** General. **Social sciences:** Economics, political science, sociology. **Visual/performing arts:** Art history/conservation, dance, dramatic, studio arts.

**Most popular majors.** Biology 7%, business/marketing 8%, communications/journalism 7%, English 19%, psychology 11%, social sciences 14%, visual/performing arts 16%.

**Computing on campus.** 100 workstations in dormitories, library, computer center, student center. Dormitories wired for high-speed internet access and linked to campus network. Commuter students can connect to campus network. Online course registration, online library, helpline, wireless network available.

**Student life. Freshman orientation:** Mandatory. 5-day program includes mini-classes and community service. **Housing:** Guaranteed on-campus for all undergraduates. Special housing for disabled, apartments, wellness housing available. $400 nonrefundable deposit. **Activities:** Campus ministries, choral groups, dance, drama, film society, international student organizations, literary magazine, music ensembles, Model UN, musical theater, student government, student newspaper, TV station, religious life association, Black student alliance, College Democrats, College Republicans, Colleges Against Cancer, Student Health Advisory Board, Students Helping Achieve Rewarding Experiences, Mujeres Unidas, Circle K.

**Athletics.** NCAA. **Intercollegiate:** Basketball W, equestrian W, field hockey W, golf W, lacrosse W, soccer W, swimming W, tennis W, volleyball W.

**Student services.** Adult student services, alcohol/substance abuse counseling, chaplain/spiritual director, career counseling, student employment services, financial aid counseling, health services, minority student services, personal counseling, placement for graduates, women's services. **Physically disabled:** Services for visually, hearing impaired.

**Contact.** E-mail: huadm@hollins.edu
Phone: (540) 362-6401 Toll-free number: (800) 456-9595
Fax: (540) 362-6218
Rebecca Eckstein, Dean of Admissions, Hollins University, PO Box 9707, Roanoke, VA 24020-1707

## ITT Technical Institute: Chantilly
### Chantilly, Virginia
CB code: 4086

- For-profit 4-year technical college
- Commuter campus in large town

**General.** Accredited by ACICS. **Calendar:** Quarter.

**Contact.** Phone: (703) 263-2541
Director of Recruitment, 14420 Albemarle Point Place, Chantilly, VA 20151

## ITT Technical Institute: Norfolk
### Norfolk, Virginia
www.itt-tech.edu
CB code: 2737

- For-profit 4-year technical college
- Commuter campus in large city

**General.** Accredited by ACICS. **Location:** 81 miles from Richmond, 145 miles from Washington, DC. **Calendar:** Quarter.

**Contact.** Phone: (757) 466-1260
Director of Recruitment, 863 Glenrock Road, Norfolk, VA 23502

## ITT Technical Institute: Richmond
### Richmond, Virginia
www.itt-tech.edu
CB code: 2748

- For-profit 4-year technical college
- Commuter campus in small city

**General.** Accredited by ACICS. **Location:** 98 miles from Washington, DC. **Calendar:** Quarter.

**Contact.** Phone: (804) 330-4992
Director of Recruitment, 300 Gateway Centre Parkway, Richmond, VA 23235

## ITT Technical Institute: Springfield
### Springfield, Virginia

- For-profit 4-year technical college
- Commuter campus in large town

**General.** Accredited by ACICS. **Calendar:** Quarter.

**Contact.** Phone: (703) 440-9535
Director of Recruitment, 7300 Boston Boulevard, Springfield, VA 22153

## James Madison University
**Harrisonburg, Virginia**                    CB member
**www.jmu.edu**                                CB code: 5392

- Public 4-year university
- Residential campus in large town
- 16,979 degree-seeking undergraduates: 3% part-time, 60% women, 4% African American, 5% Asian American, 3% Hispanic American, 1% international
- 1,334 degree-seeking graduate students
- 61% of applicants admitted
- SAT or ACT (ACT writing optional) required
- 81% graduate within 6 years; 27% enter graduate study

**General.** Founded in 1908. Regionally accredited. **Degrees:** 3,630 bachelor's awarded; master's, doctoral, professional offered. **ROTC:** Army, Air Force. **Location:** 123 miles from Washington, DC. **Calendar:** Semester, extensive summer session. **Full-time faculty:** 906 total; 78% have terminal degrees, 8% minority, 46% women. **Part-time faculty:** 434 total; 25% have terminal degrees, 4% minority, 53% women. **Class size:** 29% < 20, 49% 20-39, 7% 40-49, 11% 50-99, 3% >100. **Special facilities:** Arboretum, observatory, planetarium, mineral museum, science on a sphere (SOS).

**Freshman class profile.** 20,963 applied, 12,872 admitted, 3,952 enrolled.

| Mid 50% test scores | | | |
|---|---|---|---|
| SAT critical reading: | 520-610 | Rank in top tenth: | 28% |
| SAT math: | 530-630 | End year in good standing: | 91% |
| ACT composite: | 22-27 | Return as sophomores: | 92% |
| GPA 3.75 or higher: | 47% | Out-of-state: | 33% |
| GPA 3.50-3.74: | 30% | Live on campus: | 99% |
| GPA 3.0-3.49: | 21% | International: | 1% |
| GPA 2.0-2.99: | 2% | Fraternities: | 6% |
| Rank in top quarter: | 72% | Sororities: | 6% |

**Basis for selection.** Rigor of high school curriculum, as shown by the quantity and quality of courses, most important. Class rank or GPA, test scores, extracurricular activities, special skills or talents important. Counselor recommendation considered. Applicants with solid achievement in 5 or more academic courses in each of 4 years of high school have decided advantage in admissions process. Audition required for dance, music, theater programs; portfolio and interview required for art. Nursing, justice studies, media arts and design, political science, psychology, and social work students must apply to their applicable departments in addition to applying for undergraduate admission. **Homeschooled:** Statement describing homeschool structure and mission required.

**High school preparation.** College-preparatory program required. Required and recommended units include English 4, mathematics 4, social studies 3-4, science 3-4 (laboratory 3-4) and foreign language 2-3. 3 of same foreign language recommended, or 2 of one language and 2 of another. Social studies may include units in history. History and social studies "units required" and "units recommended" are combined for the two subjects.

**2009-2010 Annual costs.** Tuition/fees: $7,244; $19,376 out-of-state. Room/board: $7,690. Books/supplies: $876. Personal expenses: $1,854.

**2009-2010 Financial aid. Need-based:** 3,106 full-time freshmen applied for aid; 1,562 were judged to have need; 1,292 of these received aid. Average need met was 44%. Average scholarship/grant was $7,029; average loan $3,673. 52% of total undergraduate aid awarded as scholarships/grants, 48% as loans/jobs. **Non-need-based:** Awarded to 797 full-time undergraduates, including 216 freshmen. Scholarships awarded for academics, alumni affiliation, art, athletics, leadership, minority status, music/drama, state residency.

**Application procedures. Admission:** Priority date 11/1; deadline 1/15 (postmark date). $50 fee, may be waived for applicants with need. Admission notification 4/1. Must reply by 5/1. **Financial aid:** Priority date 3/1; no closing date. FAFSA required. Applicants notified on a rolling basis starting 4/1; must reply within 4 week(s) of notification.

**Academics. Special study options:** Accelerated study, combined bachelor's/graduate degree, distance learning, double major, ESL, honors, independent study, internships, study abroad, teacher certification program, Washington semester. Continuing education programs offered on campus. **Credit/placement by examination:** AP, CLEP, IB, institutional tests. Students enrolled in the BIS program earn up to 30 credits toward their bachelor's

degrees through non-traditional means, such as prior learning experience and CLEP exams. Eight non-traditional credits, considered earned credits, the remainder treated as transfer credits when calculating the minimum credits earned at the university in order to obtain a degree from JMU. **Support services:** Learning center, study skills assistance, tutoring, writing center.

**Majors. Biology:** General, biotechnology. **Business:** Accounting, business admin, finance, hospitality admin, international, managerial economics, marketing. **Communications:** General. **Computer sciences:** General, information systems. **Engineering:** General. **Family/consumer sciences:** Food/nutrition. **Foreign languages:** General. **Health:** Athletic training, community health services, health care admin, nursing (RN), speech pathology. **History:** General. **Interdisciplinary:** Science/society, systems science. **Liberal arts:** Arts/sciences. **Math:** General. **Parks/recreation:** Health/fitness. **Physical sciences:** Chemistry, geology, physics. **Psychology:** General. **Public administration:** General, social work. **Social sciences:** General, anthropology, economics, geography, international relations, political science, sociology. **Visual/performing arts:** Art, art history/conservation, dramatic, music performance. **Other:** Justice studies, Philosophy and religion, Quantitative finance.

**Most popular majors.** Business/marketing 21%, communications/journalism 9%, health sciences 13%, liberal arts 6%, psychology 6%, social sciences 9%, visual/performing arts 6%.

**Computing on campus.** 1,583 workstations in dormitories, library, computer center, student center. Dormitories wired for high-speed internet access and linked to campus network. Commuter students can connect to campus network. Online course registration, online library, helpline, repair service, student web hosting, wireless network available.

**Student life. Freshman orientation:** Mandatory, $175 fee. Preregistration for classes offered. One-day orientation in June or July, plus 5-day program in August prior to the beginning of classes. **Housing:** Guaranteed on-campus for freshmen. Coed dorms, special housing for disabled, apartments, fraternity/sorority housing, wellness housing available. Fraternities located off campus. **Activities:** Bands, campus ministries, choral groups, dance, drama, film society, international student organizations, literary magazine, music ensembles, musical theater, opera, radio station, student government, student newspaper, symphony orchestra, 298 student organizations and clubs.

**Athletics.** NCAA. **Intercollegiate:** Baseball M, basketball, cheerleading, cross-country W, diving W, field hockey W, football (tackle) M, golf, lacrosse W, soccer, softball W, swimming W, tennis, track and field W, volleyball W. **Intramural:** Basketball, bowling, football (non-tackle), golf, racquetball, soccer, softball, table tennis, tennis, volleyball. **Team name:** Dukes.

**Student services.** Adult student services, alcohol/substance abuse counseling, chaplain/spiritual director, career counseling, student employment services, financial aid counseling, health services, minority student services, personal counseling, placement for graduates. **Physically disabled:** Services for visually, speech, hearing impaired.

**Contact.** E-mail: admissions@jmu.edu
Phone: (540) 568-5681 Fax: (540) 568-3332
Michael Walsh, Director of Admissions, James Madison University, Sonner Hall, MSC 0101, Harrisonburg, VA 22807

## Jefferson College of Health Sciences
**Roanoke, Virginia**
**www.jchs.edu**                               CB code: 5099

- Private 4-year health science and nursing college
- Commuter campus in large city
- 880 degree-seeking undergraduates: 29% part-time, 85% women, 11% African American, 1% Asian American, 1% Hispanic American
- 148 degree-seeking graduate students
- 44% of applicants admitted
- SAT or ACT (ACT writing recommended) required
- 71% graduate within 6 years; 21% enter graduate study

**General.** Founded in 1982. Regionally accredited. Access to educational seminars broadcast live by American Hospital Association, Hospital Satellite network, and other networks. One of 50 demonstration centers nationwide for interactive video in nursing education. As part of the Carilion system, JCHS has access to Carilion Clinic resources, including the medical library. **Degrees:** 114 bachelor's, 161 associate awarded; master's offered. **Calendar:** Semester, limited summer session. **Full-time faculty:** 71 total; 52% have terminal degrees, 1% minority, 63% women. **Part-time faculty:** 45 total; 11% have terminal degrees, 60% women. **Class size:** 58% < 20, 39% 20-39, 3% 40-49.

**Freshman class profile.** 528 applied, 234 admitted, 92 enrolled.

| Mid 50% test scores | | | |
|---|---|---|---|
| SAT critical reading: | 420-530 | GPA 3.0-3.49: | 42% |
| SAT math: | 430-510 | GPA 2.0-2.99: | 24% |
| SAT writing: | 430-500 | End year in good standing: | 79% |
| ACT composite: | 18-23 | Return as sophomores: | 68% |
| GPA 3.75 or higher: | 20% | Out-of-state: | 5% |
| GPA 3.50-3.74: | 14% | Live on campus: | 49% |

**Basis for selection.** Certification required for some programs. Emergency health sciences program requires emergency medical technician ambulance certification prior to entering program. SAT/ACT test scores are not required if applicant has been out of high school for three years or more.

**High school preparation.** 16 units required. Required and recommended units include English 4, mathematics 2-3 and science 2-4.

**2009-2010 Annual costs.** Tuition/fees: $17,740. Room/board: $7,010. Books/supplies: $1,200. Personal expenses: $2,576.

**2008-2009 Financial aid. Need-based:** Average need met was 43%. Average scholarship/grant was $4,033; average loan $7,171. 17% of total undergraduate aid awarded as scholarships/grants, 83% as loans/jobs. **Non-need-based:** Scholarships awarded for academics.

**Application procedures. Admission:** No deadline. $35 fee, may be waived for applicants with need, free for online applicants. Admission notification on a rolling basis. Must reply by May 1 or within 2 week(s) if notified thereafter. **Financial aid:** No deadline. FAFSA, institutional form required. Applicants notified on a rolling basis; must reply within 2 week(s) of notification.

**Academics. Special study options:** Accelerated study, cross-registration, distance learning, double major, dual enrollment of high school students, independent study, internships, liberal arts/career combination. **Credit/placement by examination:** AP, CLEP, IB, SAT, ACT, institutional tests. Maximum of 18 credit hours may be satisfied by CLEP/DANTES examinations. **Support services:** Learning center, pre-admission summer program, study skills assistance, tutoring, writing center.

**Majors. Biology:** Biomedical sciences. **Health:** Athletic training, EMT paramedic, health care admin, nursing (RN), premedicine, prenursing, prepharmacy. **Parks/recreation:** Exercise sciences. **Psychology:** Medical.

**Most popular majors.** Biology 12%, health sciences 88%.

**Computing on campus.** 56 workstations in library, computer center, student center. Dormitories wired for high-speed internet access. Online library, helpline, repair service available.

**Student life. Freshman orientation:** Mandatory. Preregistration for classes offered. One-day orientation held multiple times during summer. **Housing:** Coed dorms available. $250 nonrefundable deposit. **Activities:** Campus ministries, choral groups, student government, student newspaper, student nurse association, student occupational therapy association, student physical therapy assistant assembly, Good Samaritan Club, Habitat for Humanity, Hands of Healing.

**Athletics. Team name:** Blue Healers.

**Student services.** Adult student services, career counseling, student employment services, financial aid counseling, health services, personal counseling, placement for graduates. **Physically disabled:** Services for visually impaired.

**Contact.** E-mail: cijom1@jchs.edu
Phone: (540) 985-8483 Toll-free number: (888) 985-8483
Fax: (540) 985-9773
Judith McKeon, Director of Admissions, Jefferson College of Health Sciences, Box 13186, Roanoke, VA 24031-3186

---

## Liberty University
**Lynchburg, Virginia**
www.liberty.edu

CB member
CB code: 5385

- Private 4-year university affiliated with Baptist faith
- Residential campus in small city
- 28,243 degree-seeking undergraduates: 35% part-time, 54% women, 14% African American, 1% Asian American, 3% Hispanic American, 2% international
- 17,101 degree-seeking graduate students
- SAT or ACT (ACT writing optional), application essay required

**General.** Founded in 1971. Regionally accredited. **Degrees:** 3,519 bachelor's, 294 associate awarded; master's, doctoral, professional offered. **ROTC:** Army, Air Force. **Location:** 120 miles from Richmond, 150 miles from Raleigh, North Carolina. **Calendar:** Semester, limited summer session. **Full-time faculty:** 439 total. **Part-time faculty:** 1,023 total. **Class size:** 36% < 20, 50% 20-39, 3% 40-49, 6% 50-99, 5% >100. **Special facilities:** Snow-flex ski slope, ice rink, running and hiking trails, paintball fields, indoor soccer complex.

**Freshman class profile.**

| Mid 50% test scores | | | |
|---|---|---|---|
| SAT critical reading: | 430-570 | GPA 2.0-2.99: | 33% |
| SAT math: | 430-550 | Rank in top quarter: | 23% |
| ACT composite: | 18-24 | Rank in top tenth: | 5% |
| GPA 3.75 or higher: | 23% | Out-of-state: | 60% |
| GPA 3.50-3.74: | 14% | Live on campus: | 90% |
| GPA 3.0-3.49: | 29% | International: | 2% |

**Basis for selection.** Secondary school record, standardized test scores, and essay most important. Applicants who fail to meet the minimum required GPA may be admitted on academic warning status and will be limited to 13 semester hours of coursework. TOEFL required for international students.

**High school preparation.** College-preparatory program required. 17 units recommended. Recommended units include English 4, mathematics 3, social studies 2, science 2 (laboratory 2), foreign language 2 and academic electives 4.

**2010-2011 Annual costs.** Tuition/fees (projected): $17,202. Room/board: $5,996. Books/supplies: $1,400. Personal expenses: $1,000.

**2009-2010 Financial aid. Non-need-based:** Scholarships awarded for academics, alumni affiliation, athletics, leadership, music/drama, religious affiliation, ROTC, state residency.

**Application procedures. Admission:** Priority date 6/30; no deadline. $40 fee, may be waived for applicants with need. Admission notification on a rolling basis. Must reply by May 1 or within 2 week(s) if notified thereafter. **Financial aid:** Closing date 3/1. FAFSA required. Applicants notified on a rolling basis starting 3/15; must reply within 3 week(s) of notification.

**Academics. Special study options:** Accelerated study, cooperative education, distance learning, double major, dual enrollment of high school students, ESL, external degree, honors, independent study, internships, student-designed major, teacher certification program, weekend college. Associate school of the Institute of Holy Land Studies in Jerusalem. **Credit/placement by examination:** AP, CLEP, IB, SAT, ACT, institutional tests. 30 credit hours maximum toward bachelor's degree. **Support services:** Learning center, reduced course load, remedial instruction, study skills assistance, tutoring.

**Majors. Biology:** General, biochemistry. **Business:** General, accounting, management information systems. **Communications:** General. **Computer sciences:** General, web page design. **Education:** ESL. **Engineering:** Computer, electrical, industrial, software, systems. **Family/consumer sciences:** General, clothing/textiles. **Foreign languages:** Spanish. **Health:** Athletic training, community health, nursing (RN), public health ed. **History:** General. **Liberal arts:** Arts/sciences. **Math:** General. **Parks/recreation:** Exercise sciences, health/fitness, sports admin. **Philosophy/religion:** Philosophy, religion. **Protective services:** Criminal justice. **Psychology:** General. **Social sciences:** General, political science. **Theology:** Bible, missionary, pastoral counseling, sacred music, youth ministry. **Transportation:** Aviation. **Visual/performing arts:** Design, dramatic.

**Most popular majors.** Business/marketing 16%, health sciences 6%, interdisciplinary studies 18%, philosophy/religious studies 19%, psychology 12%.

**Computing on campus.** 406 workstations in library, computer center, student center. Dormitories wired for high-speed internet access and linked to campus network. Commuter students can connect to campus network. Online course registration, online library, helpline, repair service, wireless network available.

**Student life. Freshman orientation:** Mandatory. Preregistration for classes offered. **Policies:** All students involved in Christian or community service. **Housing:** Guaranteed on-campus for all undergraduates. Single-sex dorms, special housing for disabled, apartments, wellness housing available. $250 nonrefundable deposit. Students required to live on campus unless living with parents, over age 21, or married. **Activities:** Bands, campus ministries, choral groups, drama, literary magazine, music ensembles, musical theater, radio station, student government, student newspaper, symphony orchestra, TV station, Circle K, Youthquest, Light Ministries, Fellowship of Christian Athletes, Students Teaching Elementary School, College Republicans, Campus SERVE.

**Athletics.** NCAA. **Intercollegiate:** Baseball M, basketball, cheerleading, cross-country, football (tackle) M, golf M, soccer, softball W, tennis, track and field, volleyball W. **Intramural:** Basketball, football (non-tackle), soccer, softball, tennis, volleyball. **Team name:** Flames.

**Student services.** Chaplain/spiritual director, career counseling, student employment services, financial aid counseling, health services, minority student services, personal counseling, placement for graduates, veterans' counselor, women's services. **Physically disabled:** Services for hearing impaired.

**Contact.** E-mail: admissions@liberty.edu
Phone: (434) 582-5985 Toll-free number: (800) 543-5317
Fax: (800) 542-2311
Tim Rees, Director of Residential Admissions, Liberty University, 1971 University Boulevard, Lynchburg, VA 24502

---

## Longwood University

**Farmville, Virginia** — CB member
**www.longwood.edu** — CB code: 5368

- Public 4-year university
- Residential campus in small town
- 4,021 degree-seeking undergraduates: 5% part-time, 66% women, 6% African American, 1% Asian American, 2% Hispanic American, 1% Native American
- 362 degree-seeking graduate students
- 70% of applicants admitted
- SAT or ACT (ACT writing optional), application essay required
- 58% graduate within 6 years

**General.** Founded in 1839. Regionally accredited. **Degrees:** 761 bachelor's awarded; master's offered. **ROTC:** Army. **Location:** 65 miles from Richmond, 60 miles from Charlottesville. **Calendar:** Semester, limited summer session. **Full-time faculty:** 207 total; 79% have terminal degrees, 7% minority, 48% women. **Part-time faculty:** 72 total; 31% have terminal degrees, 14% minority, 64% women. **Class size:** 44% < 20, 50% 20-39, 5% 40-49, 1% 50-99. **Special facilities:** Golf course, rock climbing wall, flora collection, visual arts center, greenhouse.

**Freshman class profile.** 4,301 applied, 2,995 admitted, 1,010 enrolled.

| Mid 50% test scores | | | |
|---|---|---|---|
| SAT critical reading: | 480-560 | GPA 2.0-2.99: | 18% |
| SAT math: | 480-560 | Rank in top quarter: | 40% |
| ACT composite: | 20-24 | Rank in top tenth: | 12% |
| GPA 3.75 or higher: | 16% | Return as sophomores: | 78% |
| GPA 3.50-3.74: | 17% | Out-of-state: | 4% |
| GPA 3.0-3.49: | 49% | Live on campus: | 98% |
| | | International: | 1% |

**Basis for selection.** Rank in top half of class, combined SAT score (exclusive of Writing) of 1000 minimum and GPA of 2.7 minimum in college preparatory courses required. Extracurricular activities and recommendations also considered. Early Action consideration, applicants must have 3.0 GPA and 1000 on SAT (exclusive of Writing). Modern language majors required to take SAT subject test in intended language of study for placement. Audition required for music. **Homeschooled:** Statement describing homeschool structure and mission, letter of recommendation (nonparent) required. Applications reviewed on case-by-case basis.

**High school preparation.** College-preparatory program required. 24 units required. Required and recommended units include English 4, mathematics 3-4, social studies 2, history 2, science 3-4 (laboratory 2-3), foreign language 2-4 and visual/performing arts 1.

**2009-2010 Annual costs.** Tuition/fees: $8,925; $17,835 out-of-state. Required laptop computer for first-year students $1,700. Capital Outlay Fee for out of state students pay an additional $390 in required fees. Room/board: $7,596. Books/supplies: $800. Personal expenses: $1,200.

**2008-2009 Financial aid. Need-based:** 755 full-time freshmen applied for aid; 440 were judged to have need; 435 of these received aid. Average need met was 80%. Average scholarship/grant was $5,580; average loan $727. 52% of total undergraduate aid awarded as scholarships/grants, 48% as loans/jobs. **Non-need-based:** Awarded to 417 full-time undergraduates, including 97 freshmen. Scholarships awarded for academics, alumni affiliation, art, athletics, leadership, music/drama, ROTC, state residency.

**Application procedures. Admission:** Priority date 3/1; no deadline. $40 fee, may be waived for applicants with need. Admission notification on a rolling basis beginning on or about 1/15. Must reply by May 1 or within 1 week(s) if notified thereafter. **Financial aid:** Priority date 3/1; no closing date. FAFSA required. Applicants notified on a rolling basis starting 4/1; must reply within 4 week(s) of notification.

**Academics. Special study options:** Accelerated study, combined bachelor's/graduate degree, cross-registration, distance learning, double major, dual enrollment of high school students, honors, independent study, internships, study abroad, teacher certification program. Summer field programs in archaeology and botany. **Credit/placement by examination:** AP, CLEP, IB, institutional tests. **Support services:** Learning center, reduced course load, study skills assistance, tutoring, writing center.

**Honors college/program.** Students must have at least a 1200 on the SAT (combined Critical Reading and Math only) and at least a 3.5 GPA to be considered for the Cormier Honors College. About 40-50 freshman admitted each year.

**Majors. Biology:** General. **Business:** General, accounting, business admin, finance, management information systems, management science, marketing, retailing. **Communications:** General. **Computer sciences:** General, computer science. **Education:** General, art, biology, business, chemistry, early childhood, elementary, English, French, German, health, history, mathematics, middle, multi-level teacher, music, physical, physics, science, social studies, Spanish, special, speech impaired. **Foreign languages:** French, German, Spanish. **Health:** Athletic training, nursing (RN), predental, premedicine, prepharmacy, preveterinary, recreational therapy. **History:** General, public archives. **Legal studies:** Prelaw. **Liberal arts:** Arts/sciences. **Math:** General. **Parks/recreation:** Exercise sciences, health/fitness. **Physical sciences:** Chemistry, physics. **Protective services:** Criminal justice. **Psychology:** General. **Public administration:** Social work. **Social sciences:** Anthropology, criminology, economics, political science, sociology. **Visual/performing arts:** General, art, art history/conservation, commercial/advertising art, dramatic, music performance, studio arts.

**Most popular majors.** Business/marketing 17%, communications/journalism 7%, history 7%, liberal arts 22%, parks/recreation 6%, social sciences 9%, visual/performing arts 6%.

**Computing on campus.** PC or laptop required. 197 workstations in dormitories, library, computer center, student center. Dormitories wired for high-speed internet access and linked to campus network. Commuter students can connect to campus network. Online course registration, online library, helpline, repair service, student web hosting, wireless network available.

**Student life. Freshman orientation:** Mandatory, $150 fee. Preregistration for classes offered. One-day orientation held during spring and summer. **Housing:** Guaranteed on-campus for freshmen. Coed dorms, single-sex dorms, special housing for disabled, apartments, fraternity/sorority housing, wellness housing available. $400 nonrefundable deposit, deadline 5/1. **Activities:** Bands, campus ministries, choral groups, dance, drama, international student organizations, literary magazine, music ensembles, radio station, student government, student newspaper, College Democrats, unity alliance, interfraternity council, Habitat for Humanity, Alpha Phi Omega, Students Educating for Active Leadership, College Republicans, Peer Helpers, Big Sibling Program.

**Athletics.** NCAA. **Intercollegiate:** Baseball M, basketball, cheerleading, cross-country, field hockey W, golf, soccer, softball W, tennis. **Intramural:** Basketball, bowling, football (non-tackle), soccer, softball, tennis, volleyball. **Team name:** Lancers.

**Student services.** Adult student services, alcohol/substance abuse counseling, career counseling, student employment services, financial aid counseling, health services, minority student services, personal counseling, placement for graduates, women's services. **Physically disabled:** Services for visually, speech, hearing impaired.

**Contact.** E-mail: admissions@longwood.edu
Phone: (434) 395-2060 Toll-free number: (800) 281-4677 ext. 2
Fax: (434) 395-2332
Robert Chonko, Dean of Admissions, Longwood University, 201 High Street, Farmville, VA 23909-1898

---

## Lynchburg College

**Lynchburg, Virginia** — CB member
**www.lynchburg.edu** — CB code: 5372

- Private 4-year liberal arts college affiliated with Christian Church (Disciples of Christ)
- Residential campus in small city
- 2,165 degree-seeking undergraduates: 3% part-time, 60% women, 8% African American, 1% Asian American, 2% Hispanic American, 1% Native American
- 269 degree-seeking graduate students
- 66% of applicants admitted
- SAT or ACT (ACT writing optional) required
- 63% graduate within 6 years

**General.** Founded in 1903. Regionally accredited. **Degrees:** 406 bachelor's awarded; master's offered. **Location:** 180 miles from Washington, DC, 50 miles from Roanoke. **Calendar:** Semester, extensive summer session. **Full-time faculty:** 155 total; 74% have terminal degrees, 7% minority, 50% women. **Part-time faculty:** 104 total; 34% have terminal degrees, 6% minority, 51% women. **Class size:** 59% < 20, 41% 20-39, less than 1% 40-49, less than 1% 50-99. **Special facilities:** Nature study center, center for media development, geographic information system labs, forensic cadaver lab, astronomical observatory, fine arts gallery.

**Freshman class profile.** 4,571 applied, 3,011 admitted, 593 enrolled.

| Mid 50% test scores | | | |
|---|---|---|---|
| SAT critical reading: | 460-560 | GPA 2.0-2.99: | 37% |
| SAT math: | 460-570 | Rank in top quarter: | 40% |
| SAT writing: | 450-550 | Rank in top tenth: | 12% |
| ACT composite: | 19-24 | End year in good standing: | 81% |
| GPA 3.75 or higher: | 15% | Return as sophomores: | 72% |
| GPA 3.50-3.74: | 15% | Out-of-state: | 40% |
| GPA 3.0-3.49: | 33% | Live on campus: | 91% |

**Basis for selection.** School record, test scores, school and community involvement, recommendation, academic quality of secondary school attended, essay, interview important. Audition recommended for music, theater arts programs; portfolio recommended for studio art. Essay or personal statement strongly encouraged, but not formally required. **Learning Disabled:** Documentation must be received no later than 45 days prior to the first day of class.

**High school preparation.** College-preparatory program required. 16 units required; 20 recommended. Required and recommended units include English 4, mathematics 3-4, social studies 2, history 2, science 3-4 (laboratory 2), foreign language 2-3 and academic electives 1.

**2010-2011 Annual costs.** Tuition/fees: $29,905. Room/board: $8,020. Books/supplies: $750. Personal expenses: $800.

**2009-2010 Financial aid. Need-based:** 512 full-time freshmen applied for aid; 420 were judged to have need; 420 of these received aid. Average need met was 83%. Average scholarship/grant was $18,465; average loan $3,126. 73% of total undergraduate aid awarded as scholarships/grants, 27% as loans/jobs. **Non-need-based:** Awarded to 763 full-time undergraduates, including 205 freshmen. Scholarships awarded for academics, leadership, music/drama, religious affiliation.

**Application procedures. Admission:** No deadline. $30 fee, may be waived for applicants with need, free for online applicants. Admission notification on a rolling basis beginning on or about 9/1. Must reply by May 1 or within 2 week(s) if notified thereafter. **Financial aid:** Priority date 3/1; no closing date. FAFSA required. Applicants notified on a rolling basis starting 3/5; must reply by 5/1 or within 2 week(s) of notification.

**Academics. Special study options:** Accelerated study, combined bachelor's/graduate degree, cross-registration, double major, dual enrollment of high school students, honors, independent study, internships, study abroad, teacher certification program. **Credit/placement by examination:** AP, CLEP, IB, institutional tests. **Support services:** Study skills assistance, tutoring, writing center.

**Majors. Biology:** General, exercise physiology. **Business:** Accounting, business admin, international, marketing. **Communications:** General. **Computer sciences:** General. **Conservation:** Environmental science. **Education:** Elementary, health, physical. **Foreign languages:** French, Spanish. **Health:** Athletic training, nursing (RN). **History:** General. **Math:** General. **Parks/recreation:** Health/fitness, sports admin. **Philosophy/religion:** Philosophy, religion. **Physical sciences:** Chemistry, physics. **Psychology:** General. **Social sciences:** Economics, international relations, political science, sociology. **Visual/performing arts:** Art, dramatic.

**Most popular majors.** Biology 9%, business/marketing 11%, communications/journalism 11%, education 12%, health sciences 14%, psychology 6%, social sciences 8%, visual/performing arts 6%.

**Computing on campus.** Dormitories wired for high-speed internet access and linked to campus network. Online library, repair service, wireless network available.

**Student life. Freshman orientation:** Mandatory. Preregistration for classes offered. Held during summer for fall semester students and in January for spring semester students. Separate but concurrent orientation programs available to parents and other guests of new students. **Policies:** Honor system promoted and adhered to. **Housing:** Guaranteed on-campus for all undergraduates. Coed dorms, single-sex dorms, special housing for disabled, apartments, fraternity/sorority housing, wellness housing available. $200 nonrefundable deposit, deadline 5/1. College-owned townhomes, houses, and special interest houses available. **Activities:** Bands, campus ministries, choral groups,

dance, drama, film society, international student organizations, literary magazine, music ensembles, Model UN, musical theater, student government, student newspaper, symphony orchestra, over 50 clubs and organizations.

**Athletics.** NCAA. **Intercollegiate:** Baseball M, basketball, cheerleading M, cross-country, equestrian, field hockey W, golf M, lacrosse, soccer, softball W, tennis, track and field, volleyball W. **Intramural:** Basketball, field hockey W, football (non-tackle), lacrosse M, soccer, softball, volleyball. **Team name:** Hornets.

**Student services.** Adult student services, chaplain/spiritual director, career counseling, student employment services, financial aid counseling, health services, minority student services, personal counseling. **Physically disabled:** Services for visually, hearing impaired.

**Contact.** E-mail: admissions@lynchburg.edu
Phone: (434) 544-8300 Toll-free number: (800) 426-8101 ext. 8300
Fax: (434) 544-8653
Sharon Walters-Bower, Director of Admissions, Lynchburg College, 1501 Lakeside Drive, Lynchburg, VA 24501-3199

---

## Mary Baldwin College
Staunton, Virginia
www.mbc.edu

**CB member**
**CB code: 5397**

- Private 4-year liberal arts college for women affiliated with Presbyterian Church (USA)
- Residential campus in large town
- 1,363 degree-seeking undergraduates: 27% part-time, 90% women, 18% African American, 2% Asian American, 4% Hispanic American, 1% international
- 258 graduate students
- 62% of applicants admitted
- SAT or ACT (ACT writing optional), interview required
- 45% graduate within 6 years; 25% enter graduate study

**General.** Founded in 1842. Regionally accredited. Bachelor's degree available for younger women (13-15) in program for exceptionally gifted. Adult degree program available on main campus and at several satellite campuses throughout Virginia. Men admitted to adult program. The Virginia Women's Institute for Leadership program. **Degrees:** 256 bachelor's awarded; master's offered. **ROTC:** Army, Naval, Air Force. **Location:** 100 miles from Richmond, 150 miles from Washington, DC. **Calendar:** 4-1-4, limited summer session. **Full-time faculty:** 76 total; 99% have terminal degrees, 10% minority, 53% women. **Part-time faculty:** 60 total; 22% minority, 62% women. **Class size:** 61% < 20, 39% 20-39, less than 1% 50-99. **Special facilities:** Electron microscope, gas chromatoscope.

**Freshman class profile.** 2,147 applied, 1,332 admitted, 227 enrolled.

| Mid 50% test scores | | | |
|---|---|---|---|
| SAT critical reading: | 460-600 | GPA 2.0-2.99: | 34% |
| SAT math: | 430-560 | Rank in top quarter: | 39% |
| SAT writing: | 430-580 | Rank in top tenth: | 13% |
| ACT composite: | 18-23 | End year in good standing: | 87% |
| GPA 3.75 or higher: | 25% | Return as sophomores: | 65% |
| GPA 3.50-3.74: | 15% | Out-of-state: | 29% |
| GPA 3.0-3.49: | 26% | Live on campus: | 91% |
| | | International: | 1% |

**Basis for selection.** School achievement record most important; test scores, involvement in school or civic groups also important; recommendations considered; 3.0 GPA recommended. Portfolio recommended for art majors.

**High school preparation.** Required and recommended units include English 4, mathematics 3, social studies 3, science 2 (laboratory 1), foreign language 2-3 and academic electives 2. Higher requirements for Virginia Women's Institute for Leadership.

**2009-2010 Annual costs.** Tuition/fees: $24,585. Room/board: $7,770. Books/supplies: $900. Personal expenses: $915.

**2008-2009 Financial aid. Non-need-based:** Scholarships awarded for academics, leadership, state residency.

**Application procedures. Admission:** No deadline. $35 fee, may be waived for applicants with need. Admission notification on a rolling basis beginning on or about 9/1. Regular admission notification within 48 hours of receipt of all necessary materials. It is recommended for International Students to get applications in by June 1 to allow time to get a visa. **Financial aid:** Priority date 5/15; no closing date. FAFSA required. Applicants notified on a rolling basis starting 2/1; must reply by 5/1.

**Academics.** Students complete requirements in experiential education, international education, women's studies. May term offers opportunity for individualized programming, externships, study abroad. Institute combines academics, physical training and leadership development in rigorous 4-year bachelor's program. **Special study options:** Accelerated study, combined bachelor's/graduate degree, cooperative education, cross-registration, distance learning, double major, dual enrollment of high school students, ESL, exchange student, external degree, honors, independent study, internships, liberal arts/career combination, semester at sea, student-designed major, study abroad, teacher certification program. Summer exchange program with Doshisha Women's College in Kyoto, Japan. **Credit/placement by examination:** AP, CLEP, IB, institutional tests. 25% of required credits may be counted toward bachelor's degree. **Support services:** Learning center, reduced course load, study skills assistance, tutoring, writing center.

**Honors college/program.** Minimum SAT score of 1150 (exclusive of Writing) or ACT score of 25, minimum 3.5 high school GPA, essay, interview required for admission. About 36 freshmen admitted.

**Majors. Area/ethnic studies:** Asian. **Biology:** General. **Business:** Business admin. **Communications:** General. **Computer sciences:** General. **Foreign languages:** French, Spanish. **Health:** Clinical lab science, health care admin. **History:** General. **Math:** General, applied. **Philosophy/religion:** Philosophy, religion. **Physical sciences:** Chemistry, physics. **Psychology:** General. **Social sciences:** Economics, international relations, political science, sociology. **Visual/performing arts:** Art, arts management, dramatic.

**Most popular majors.** Business/marketing 15%, communications/journalism 6%, history 14%, psychology 11%, social sciences 15%, visual/performing arts 15%.

**Computing on campus.** 244 workstations in dormitories, library, computer center. Dormitories wired for high-speed internet access and linked to campus network. Commuter students can connect to campus network. Online course registration, online library, helpline, repair service, wireless network available.

**Student life. Freshman orientation:** Mandatory. Preregistration for classes offered. **Policies:** College prohibits drinking under age 21. Honor code observed. Working dogs (to aid the handicaped) are allowed in dorm rooms. **Housing:** Guaranteed on-campus for all undergraduates. Apartments, wellness housing available. $300 partly refundable deposit. **Activities:** Marching band, choral groups, dance, drama, film society, literary magazine, music ensembles, musical theater, radio station, student government, student newspaper, TV station, Circle K, Habitat for Humanity, College Republicans, College Democrats, Black Student Alliance, Latinas Unidas, Christian Student Union, Campus Crusade for Christ, Anointed Voices of Praise Gospel Choir.

**Athletics.** NCAA. **Intercollegiate:** Basketball W, cross-country W, field hockey W, soccer W, softball W, swimming W, tennis W, volleyball W. **Team name:** Squirrels.

**Student services.** Adult student services, chaplain/spiritual director, career counseling, student employment services, health services, minority student services, personal counseling, placement for graduates, women's services. **Physically disabled:** Services for visually, hearing impaired.

**Contact.** E-mail: admit@mbc.edu
Phone: (540) 887-7019 Toll-free number: (800) 468-2262
Fax: (540) 887-7279
Andrew Modlin, Executive Director of Enrollment Management, Mary Baldwin College, Office of Admissions, Staunton, VA 24401

---

## Marymount University

**Arlington, Virginia**
**www.marymount.edu**

CB member
CB code: 5405

- Private 4-year university affiliated with Roman Catholic Church
- Residential campus in small city
- 2,194 degree-seeking undergraduates: 14% part-time, 72% women, 15% African American, 8% Asian American, 13% Hispanic American, 9% international
- 1,217 degree-seeking graduate students
- 83% of applicants admitted
- SAT or ACT (ACT writing optional) required
- 48% graduate within 6 years

**General.** Founded in 1950. Regionally accredited. Courses taught in three sites: Marymount's main campus, the Ballston Center in Arlington, VA, and Reston Center in Reston, VA. **Degrees:** 570 bachelor's, 1 associate awarded; master's, professional offered. **ROTC:** Army. **Location:** 7 miles from Washington, DC. **Calendar:** Semester, extensive summer session. **Full-time faculty:** 139 total; 87% have terminal degrees, 4% minority, 70% women.

**Part-time faculty:** 178 total; 50% have terminal degrees, 5% minority, 60% women. **Class size:** 49% < 20, 47% 20-39, 3% 40-49, less than 1% 50-99.

**Freshman class profile.** 1,809 applied, 1,495 admitted, 390 enrolled.

| Mid 50% test scores | | | |
|---|---|---|---|
| SAT critical reading: | 440-540 | Rank in top quarter: | 34% |
| SAT math: | 420-530 | Rank in top tenth: | 9% |
| SAT writing: | 430-540 | Return as sophomores: | 70% |
| ACT composite: | 18-22 | Out-of-state: | 45% |
| GPA 3.75 or higher: | 9% | Live on campus: | 61% |
| GPA 3.50-3.74: | 10% | International: | 5% |
| GPA 3.0-3.49: | 36% | | |

And GPA 2.0-2.99: 45%, Rank in top quarter: 34%.

**Basis for selection.** GPA in academic courses and test scores most important. Class rank, recommendations from guidance counselors and teachers also important. Essay, interview recommended.

**High school preparation.** College-preparatory program required. 15 units required. Required and recommended units include English 4, mathematics 3, social studies 3, science 2 and foreign language 3.

**2010-2011 Annual costs.** Tuition/fees: $23,426. Room/board: $10,325. Books/supplies: $800. Personal expenses: $900.

**2009-2010 Financial aid. Need-based:** 322 full-time freshmen applied for aid; 260 were judged to have need; 258 of these received aid. Average need met was 73%. Average scholarship/grant was $5,295; average loan $3,525. 47% of total undergraduate aid awarded as scholarships/grants, 53% as loans/jobs. **Non-need-based:** Awarded to 1,281 full-time undergraduates, including 363 freshmen. Scholarships awarded for academics, alumni affiliation, leadership, ROTC, state residency.

**Application procedures. Admission:** Priority date 4/1; no deadline. $40 fee, may be waived for applicants with need. Admission notification on a rolling basis. Must reply by May 1 or within 3 week(s) if notified thereafter. **Financial aid:** Priority date 3/1; no closing date. FAFSA required. Applicants notified on a rolling basis starting 3/15; must reply within 2 week(s) of notification.

**Academics.** All undergraduates complete internship before graduation. **Special study options:** Accelerated study, combined bachelor's/graduate degree, cross-registration, distance learning, double major, ESL, honors, independent study, internships, student-designed major, study abroad, teacher certification program. Member of the Consortium of Universities of the Washington DC metropolitan area. **Credit/placement by examination:** AP, CLEP, IB, institutional tests. 30 credit hours maximum toward bachelor's degree. Credit for prior work/life experience available through Portfolio Assessment and Credit by Examination program. **Support services:** Learning center, reduced course load, tutoring.

**Honors college/program.** Admission competitive and limited to 20 students each year. Minimum high school or college GPA of 3.5, minimum composite SAT score of 1200 (exclusive of Writing) or ACT score of 26, minimum TOEFL score of 617 (paper), 260 (computer), or 105 (internet) for international students, and strong background in English composition and literature.

**Majors. Biology:** General, cellular/molecular. **Business:** Business admin, fashion, human resources. **Communications:** General. **Computer sciences:** Information systems. **Health:** Nursing (RN). **History:** General. **Legal studies:** Paralegal. **Liberal arts:** Arts/sciences. **Math:** General. **Parks/recreation:** Exercise sciences. **Philosophy/religion:** Philosophy, religion. **Protective services:** Criminal justice. **Psychology:** General. **Social sciences:** Criminology, economics, political science, sociology. **Visual/performing arts:** Fashion design, graphic design, interior design, studio arts.

**Most popular majors.** Business/marketing 16%, health sciences 26%, liberal arts 6%, psychology 8%, social sciences 9%, visual/performing arts 15%.

**Computing on campus.** 270 workstations in dormitories, library, computer center. Dormitories wired for high-speed internet access and linked to campus network. Commuter students can connect to campus network. Online course registration, online library, helpline, wireless network available.

**Student life. Freshman orientation:** Mandatory. Preregistration for classes offered. 3 weekend sessions in summer. **Housing:** Guaranteed on-campus for freshmen. Coed dorms, single-sex dorms available. $300 nonrefundable deposit, deadline 5/1. **Activities:** Campus ministries, choral groups, dance, drama, international student organizations, literary magazine, student government, student newspaper, Black Student Alliance, College Democrats/College Republicans, Global Charity Project, Latino Student Association, Muslim Student Association, Students in Free Enterprise.

**Athletics.** NCAA. **Intercollegiate:** Basketball, cross-country, golf M, lacrosse, soccer, swimming, volleyball W. **Intramural:** Basketball, football (non-tackle), golf M, soccer, softball, swimming, volleyball, water polo, weight lifting. **Team name:** Saints.

**Student services.** Alcohol/substance abuse counseling, chaplain/spiritual director, career counseling, student employment services, financial aid counseling, health services, personal counseling. **Physically disabled:** Services for visually, speech, hearing impaired.

**Contact.** E-mail: admissions@marymount.edu
Phone: (703) 284-1500 Toll-free number: (800) 548-7638
Fax: (703) 522-0349
Chris Domes, Vice President for Enrollment and Student Services, Marymount University, 2807 North Glebe Road, Arlington, VA 22207-4299

## National College: Roanoke Valley
### Roanoke, Virginia
### www.national-college.edu
**CB code: 5502**

- For-profit 4-year business college
- Commuter campus in large city
- 805 degree-seeking undergraduates
- Interview required

**General.** Founded in 1886. Accredited by ACICS. **Degrees:** 31 bachelor's, 95 associate awarded; master's offered. **Calendar:** Quarter, limited summer session. **Full-time faculty:** 14 total. **Part-time faculty:** 52 total.

**Basis for selection.** Open admission.

**2009-2010 Annual costs.** Tuition/fees: $10,080.

**Financial aid.** All financial aid based on need.

**Application procedures. Admission:** Closing date 9/1 (receipt date). $30 fee, may be waived for applicants with need. Admission notification on a rolling basis. **Financial aid:** No deadline. FAFSA required. Applicants notified on a rolling basis.

**Academics. Special study options:** Double major, internships. **Credit/placement by examination:** CLEP, institutional tests. **Support services:** Tutoring.

**Majors. Business:** Accounting, business admin.

**Computing on campus.** 35 workstations in library, computer center.

**Student life. Freshman orientation:** Mandatory. Preregistration for classes offered. **Housing:** Coed dorms available. Hotel accommodations available. **Activities:** Student government.

**Student services.** Career counseling, financial aid counseling, placement for graduates.

**Contact.** Phone: (540) 986-1800 Fax: (540) 444-4198
Larry Steele, Vice President of Admissions, National College: Roanoke Valley, PO Box 6400, Roanoke, VA 24017-0400

## Norfolk State University
### Norfolk, Virginia
### www.nsu.edu
**CB member**
**CB code: 5864**

- Public 4-year university
- Commuter campus in small city
- 6,102 degree-seeking undergraduates: 15% part-time, 63% women, 88% African American, 1% Asian American, 1% Hispanic American, 1% international
- 774 degree-seeking graduate students
- 63% of applicants admitted
- SAT or ACT (ACT writing optional) required

**General.** Founded in 1935. Regionally accredited. **Degrees:** 777 bachelor's, 60 associate awarded; master's, doctoral offered. **ROTC:** Army, Naval. **Location:** 5 miles from downtown. **Calendar:** Semester, extensive summer session. **Full-time faculty:** 270 total. **Part-time faculty:** 105 total. **Special facilities:** Planetarium, crystal laboratory, laser laboratory, nuclear magnetic resonance laboratory, institute for service learning, literacy center for entrepreneurial studies, center for materials research, institute for minorities in applied sciences, assistive technology laboratory.

**Freshman class profile.** 5,187 applied, 3,290 admitted, 1,205 enrolled.

| Mid 50% test scores | | | |
|---|---|---|---|
| SAT critical reading: | 400-470 | Rank in top quarter: | 17% |
| SAT math: | 400-470 | Rank in top tenth: | 10% |
| ACT composite: | 17-20 | Return as sophomores: | 70% |
| GPA 3.75 or higher: | 4% | Out-of-state: | 29% |
| GPA 3.50-3.74: | 5% | Live on campus: | 77% |
| GPA 3.0-3.49: | 24% | Fraternities: | 10% |
| GPA 2.0-2.99: | 66% | Sororities: | 10% |

**Basis for selection.** Combination of academic preparation, aptitude, achievements, and motivation predict a reasonable probability of success are most important. Interview recommended for electronics, engineering, nursing programs; audition recommended for music; portfolio recommended for art. **Homeschooled:** Transcript of courses and grades required.

**High school preparation.** 22 units required. Required units include English 4, mathematics 3, history 3, science 3 and academic electives 9. 2 science required for nursing applicants: 1 chemistry, 1 biology, 2 high school math (1 algebra), 2 science required for business applicants. 1 geometry, 2 algebra recommended for mathematics applicants. 2 mathematics must include algebra for computer science applicants.

**2009-2010 Annual costs.** Tuition/fees: $5,872; $17,931 out-of-state. Room/board: $7,329. Books/supplies: $1,000. Personal expenses: $1,400.

**2009-2010 Financial aid. Non-need-based:** Scholarships awarded for academics, alumni affiliation, athletics, leadership, music/drama, ROTC, state residency.

**Application procedures. Admission:** Closing date 5/31 (postmark date). $25 fee, may be waived for applicants with need. Admission notification on a rolling basis. Must reply by May 1 or within 2 week(s) if notified thereafter. **Financial aid:** Priority date 5/31; no closing date. FAFSA required. Applicants notified on a rolling basis starting 4/1; must reply within 2 week(s) of notification.

**Academics. Special study options:** Combined bachelor's/graduate degree, cooperative education, cross-registration, distance learning, double major, dual enrollment of high school students, ESL, honors, independent study, internships, liberal arts/career combination, teacher certification program. **Credit/placement by examination:** AP, CLEP, SAT, ACT, institutional tests. No limit on number of credits university will accept, as long as student passes exam and has departmental approval. **Support services:** Learning center, reduced course load, study skills assistance, tutoring, writing center.

**Majors. Biology:** General. **Business:** General, accounting, hospitality admin. **Communications:** Journalism, media studies. **Computer sciences:** General. **Education:** Business, kindergarten/preschool, special, trade/industrial. **Engineering:** Electrical. **Engineering technology:** CAD/CADD, computer, construction, electrical. **Health:** Clinical lab science, health care admin, medical records admin, nursing (RN). **History:** General. **Math:** General. **Parks/recreation:** Exercise sciences. **Physical sciences:** Chemistry, optics, physics. **Psychology:** General. **Public administration:** Social work. **Social sciences:** Political science, sociology. **Visual/performing arts:** Art.

**Computing on campus.** 948 workstations in dormitories, library, computer center. Dormitories linked to campus network. Online library, helpline available.

**Student life. Freshman orientation:** Mandatory. Preregistration for classes offered. Held during June, July and August. **Housing:** Single-sex dorms, special housing for disabled, wellness housing available. $300 nonrefundable deposit, deadline 5/31. **Activities:** Bands, choral groups, dance, drama, music ensembles, radio station, student government, student newspaper, symphony orchestra, TV station, Beta Psi Club, Omega Psi Phi, Alpha Kappa Alpha, Delta Sigma Theta, Alpha Delta Mu, Young Democrats, Young Republicans, Alpha Phi Alpha, Kappa Alpha Psi.

**Athletics.** NCAA. **Intercollegiate:** Baseball M, basketball, bowling W, cross-country, football (tackle) M, softball W, tennis, track and field, volleyball W. **Intramural:** Basketball, bowling, cheerleading, football (non-tackle) M, soccer M, softball, swimming, table tennis, tennis, volleyball. **Team name:** Spartans.

**Student services.** Adult student services, alcohol/substance abuse counseling, chaplain/spiritual director, career counseling, student employment services, financial aid counseling, health services, on-campus daycare, personal counseling, placement for graduates, veterans' counselor, women's services. **Physically disabled:** Services for visually, speech, hearing impaired.

**Contact.** E-mail: admissions@nsu.edu
Phone: (757) 823-8396 Fax: (757) 823-2078
James Smith, Director of Admissions, Norfolk State University, 700 Park Avenue, Norfolk, VA 23504

## Old Dominion University

**Norfolk, Virginia**
**www.odu.edu**

CB member
CB code: 5126

- Public 4-year university
- Commuter campus in small city
- 17,819 degree-seeking undergraduates: 23% part-time, 55% women, 24% African American, 5% Asian American, 4% Hispanic American, 1% Native American, 1% international
- 4,193 degree-seeking graduate students
- 72% of applicants admitted
- SAT or ACT (ACT writing optional) required
- 50% graduate within 6 years

**General.** Founded in 1930. Regionally accredited. 4 regional Centers of Higher Education, distance learning network TELETECHNET, includes more than 40 sites across Virginia, Georgia, Illinois, Arizona, Washington, the Bahamas and the District of Columbia, along with U.S. Navy ships at sea. **Degrees:** 2,955 bachelor's awarded; master's, doctoral offered. **ROTC:** Army, Naval. **Location:** 2 miles from downtown, 200 miles from Washington, DC. **Calendar:** Semester, extensive summer session. **Full-time faculty:** 696 total; 79% have terminal degrees, 22% minority, 42% women. **Part-time faculty:** 461 total; 14% minority, 57% women. **Class size:** 35% < 20, 43% 20-39, 9% 40-49, 8% 50-99, 5% >100. **Special facilities:** Student art gallery, centers for urban research/service, economic education and child study centers, laser optics lab, planetarium, robotics lab, sub-/super-sonic wind tunnels, marine science research vessel, random wave pool.

**Freshman class profile.** 9,878 applied, 7,125 admitted, 2,755 enrolled.

| Mid 50% test scores | | | |
|---|---|---|---|
| SAT critical reading: | 480-570 | Rank in top quarter: | 39% |
| SAT math: | 480-580 | Rank in top tenth: | 11% |
| SAT writing: | 460-560 | End year in good standing: | 79% |
| ACT composite: | 18-23 | Return as sophomores: | 80% |
| GPA 3.75 or higher: | 14% | Out-of-state: | 8% |
| GPA 3.50-3.74: | 17% | Live on campus: | 72% |
| GPA 3.0-3.49: | 46% | International: | 1% |
| GPA 2.0-2.99: | 23% | Fraternities: | 7% |
| | | Sororities: | 9% |

**Basis for selection.** Students who submit acceptable GPA and SAT/ACT scores are admitted. Those who do not meet acceptable GPA or SAT scores are reviewed by admissions committee. Committee looks at grades in core curriculum courses, student essay, student activity, resume/letters of recommendation, high school attended, IB and AP courses taken, etc. Audition required for music; portfolio required for art. **Homeschooled:** Scores from SAT or ACT must be submitted. GED not required. Students not attending program that requires regular curriculum review and submission of test scores to local school board must submit Stanford 9 results. **Learning Disabled:** Documentation of disabilities must be submitted before receiving services from Office of Disability Services.

**High school preparation.** College-preparatory program recommended. 16 units required. Required units include English 4, mathematics 3, social studies 3, science 3 and foreign language 3.

**2009-2010 Annual costs.** Tuition/fees: $7,318; $19,768 out-of-state. Room/board: $7,868. Books/supplies: $1,000. Personal expenses: $1,875.

**2009-2010 Financial aid.** **Need-based:** 2,186 full-time freshmen applied for aid; 1,819 were judged to have need; 1,659 of these received aid. Average need met was 78%. Average scholarship/grant was $5,103; average loan $3,220. 53% of total undergraduate aid awarded as scholarships/grants, 47% as loans/jobs. **Non-need-based:** Awarded to 2,602 full-time undergraduates, including 897 freshmen. Scholarships awarded for academics, alumni affiliation, art, athletics, leadership, music/drama, ROTC, state residency.

**Application procedures.** **Admission:** Priority date 12/1; deadline 2/1 (postmark date). $50 fee, may be waived for applicants with need. Admission notification on a rolling basis beginning on or about 1/15. Students are required to submit following: $50 application fee, high school transcripts, application, SAT or ACT scores, 1-3 letters of recommendation, one essay, one student activity resume. **Financial aid:** Priority date 2/15, closing date 3/15. FAFSA required. Applicants notified on a rolling basis starting 2/1; must reply within 2 week(s) of notification.

**Academics.** Guaranteed work or internship experience for credit in all fields of study. **Special study options:** Accelerated study, combined bachelor's/graduate degree, cooperative education, cross-registration, distance learning, double major, dual enrollment of high school students, ESL, exchange student, honors, independent study, internships, liberal arts/career combination, student-designed major, study abroad, teacher certification program, weekend college. Experiential learning. **Credit/placement by examination:** AP, CLEP, IB, institutional tests. 60 credit hours maximum toward

bachelor's degree. Credit hours earned for assessment of prior learning outside of the college classroom not to exceed 60. Work life credits awarded through certification or department evaluations. Essay required to receive CLEP credit in Analysis and Interpretation of Literature. **Support services:** Learning center, reduced course load, study skills assistance, tutoring, writing center.

**Majors. Area/ethnic studies:** African-American, Asian, women's. **Biology:** General, biochemistry, marine. **Business:** Accounting, business admin, finance, international, management information systems, managerial economics, marketing. **Communications:** General. **Computer sciences:** General. **Education:** Art, biology, chemistry, drama/dance, English, foreign languages, French, geography, German, history, mathematics, music, physical, physics, sales/marketing, Spanish, technology/industrial arts. **Engineering:** Civil, computer, electrical, environmental, mechanical. **Engineering technology:** General, civil, computer, electrical, mechanical, nuclear. **Foreign languages:** General, French, German, Spanish. **Health:** Audiology/speech pathology, clinical lab science, community health services, cytotechnology, dental hygiene, environmental health, health services, nuclear medical technology, nursing (RN), ophthalmic technology. **History:** General. **Math:** General. **Parks/recreation:** Exercise sciences, facilities management, sports admin. **Philosophy/religion:** Philosophy. **Physical sciences:** Chemistry, geology, oceanography, physics. **Psychology:** General. **Social sciences:** Criminology, economics, geography, international relations, political science, sociology. **Visual/performing arts:** Acting, art, art history/conservation, dance, dramatic, graphic design, music performance, studio arts. **Other:** Interdisciplinary studies, Maritime and supply chain management.

**Most popular majors.** Business/marketing 19%, communications/journalism 6%, education 8%, engineering/engineering technologies 10%, health sciences 16%, interdisciplinary studies 6%, psychology 6%, social sciences 11%.

**Computing on campus.** 2,035 workstations in library, computer center, student center. Dormitories wired for high-speed internet access and linked to campus network. Commuter students can connect to campus network. Online course registration, online library, helpline, repair service, wireless network available.

**Student life. Freshman orientation:** Mandatory, $110 fee. Preregistration for classes offered. **Policies:** All student sponsored dances are restricted to ODU students only. Students must agree to hazing policy and can agree to FERPA when they sign up on-line for their organizations. **Housing:** Coed dorms, special housing for disabled, apartments available. $250 partly refundable deposit, deadline 5/1. **Activities:** Bands, choral groups, dance, drama, international student organizations, music ensembles, Model UN, musical theater, radio station, student government, student newspaper, TV station, College Democrats, College Republicans, Baptist Student Union, Black Student Alliance, African Caribbean Association, Catholic Campus Ministry, Latino Student Alliance, Colleges Against Cancer, ODU Out, Circle K.

**Athletics.** NCAA. **Intercollegiate:** Baseball M, basketball, diving, field hockey W, football (tackle) M, golf, lacrosse W, rowing (crew) W, sailing, soccer, tennis, wrestling M. **Intramural:** Badminton, basketball, bowling, cross-country, football (non-tackle), golf, racquetball, sailing, soccer, softball, table tennis, tennis, volleyball. **Team name:** Monarchs.

**Student services.** Adult student services, alcohol/substance abuse counseling, chaplain/spiritual director, career counseling, services for economically disadvantaged, student employment services, financial aid counseling, health services, minority student services, on-campus daycare, personal counseling, placement for graduates, veterans' counselor, women's services. **Physically disabled:** Services for visually, speech, hearing impaired. **Learning disabled:** Comprehensive services available.

**Contact.** E-mail: admit@odu.edu
Phone: (757) 683-3685 Toll-free number: (800) 348-7926
Fax: (757) 683-3255
Lakeisha Phelps, Director of Admissions, Old Dominion University, 108 Rollins Hall, 5215 Hampton Boulevard, Norfolk, VA 23529

## Patrick Henry College

**Purcellville, Virginia**
**www.phc.edu**

CB code: 2804

- Private 4-year liberal arts college affiliated with non-denominational Christian
- Residential campus in small town
- 331 degree-seeking undergraduates: 9% part-time, 47% women
- SAT or ACT (ACT writing optional), application essay, interview required

**General.** Regionally accredited; also accredited by TRACS. **Degrees:** 62 bachelor's awarded. **Location:** 50 miles from Washington, DC. **Calendar:**

Semester, limited summer session. **Full-time faculty:** 21 total; 95% have terminal degrees, 10% women. **Part-time faculty:** 24 total; 25% have terminal degrees, 21% women. **Class size:** 75% < 20, 25% 20-39.

### Freshman class profile.

| Mid 50% test scores | | | |
|---|---|---|---|
| SAT critical reading: | 620-730 | GPA 3.50-3.74: | 19% |
| SAT math: | 550-650 | GPA 3.0-3.49: | 11% |
| SAT writing: | 590-700 | GPA 2.0-2.99: | 4% |
| ACT composite: | 26-31 | End year in good standing: | 94% |
| GPA 3.75 or higher: | 66% | Return as sophomores: | 83% |

**Basis for selection.** School record, GPA, recommendations, test scores, essay, interview, character, and religious commitment very important. Reading List.

**High school preparation.** College-preparatory program required. 18 units required. Required and recommended units include English 4, mathematics 3, history 2, science 2 (laboratory 2), foreign language 1 and academic electives 5. 1 course of government is required.

**2009-2010 Annual costs.** Tuition/fees: $20,030. Room/board: $8,000. Books/supplies: $1,000. Personal expenses: $1,000.

**2008-2009 Financial aid. Non-need-based:** Scholarships awarded for academics, leadership, music/drama.

**Application procedures. Admission:** Priority date 11/1; deadline 6/15 (postmark date). $40 fee, may be waived for applicants with need. Admission notification on a rolling basis beginning on or about 10/1. Must reply by 7/1. **Financial aid:** Priority date 2/1, closing date 6/15. Institutional form required. Required for students seeking need-based aid. Applicants notified on a rolling basis starting 4/1; must reply by 5/1.

**Academics. Special study options:** Distance learning, internships, liberal arts/career combination. **Credit/placement by examination:** AP, CLEP, IB, institutional tests. Credits from the Program on Non-Collegiate Sponsored Instruction, Dantes Subject Standardized Tests, and International Baccalaureate are evaluated on a case by case basis. **Support services:** Reduced course load, tutoring.

**Majors. Communications:** Journalism. **History:** General. **Liberal arts:** Arts/sciences. **Social sciences:** Political science.

**Computing on campus.** PC or laptop required. 6 workstations in library. Dormitories wired for high-speed internet access and linked to campus network. Commuter students can connect to campus network. Online course registration, online library, helpline, student web hosting, wireless network available.

**Student life. Freshman orientation:** Mandatory. Held for four days prior to beginning of fall classes. **Policies:** Students are accountable to public legal standards, to Biblical standards, and to the College's community standards. We have a redemptive approach to discipline. Religious observance required. **Housing:** Guaranteed on-campus for freshmen. Single-sex dorms available. $250 fully refundable deposit, deadline 7/1. **Activities:** Concert band, campus ministries, choral groups, drama, film society, literary magazine, music ensembles, Model UN, student government, student newspaper, Streaming Media Film, College Republicans, College Democrats, Alexis de Tocqueville Society, Sans Frontieres, Libertas Society.

**Athletics. Intercollegiate:** Basketball, soccer. **Intramural:** Football (non-tackle) M, football (tackle) M, softball W, tennis, volleyball. **Team name:** The Sentinels.

**Student services.** Chaplain/spiritual director, career counseling, financial aid counseling, personal counseling. **Physically disabled:** Services for visually impaired.

**Contact.** E-mail: admissions@phc.edu
Phone: (888) 338-1776 ext. 8881 Fax: (540) 441-8119
Patrick Henry College, Ten Patrick Henry Circle, Purcellville, VA 20132-3197

## Potomac College
**Herndon, Virginia**
**www.potomac.edu**

- For-profit 4-year business college
- Residential campus in large town
- 75 undergraduates

**General. Degrees:** 8 bachelor's, 2 associate awarded. **Location:** 30 miles from Washington, DC. **Calendar:** Continuous, extensive summer session. **Full-time faculty:** 2 total. **Part-time faculty:** 4 total.

**Basis for selection.** Open admission.

**2009-2010 Annual costs.** Upper division tuition and fees vary.

**Application procedures. Admission:** No deadline. $15 fee, may be waived for applicants with need. Admission notification on a rolling basis.

**Academics. Special study options:** Accelerated study, independent study. **Credit/placement by examination:** CLEP, institutional tests.

**Majors. Business:** Business admin. **Computer sciences:** General, information technology.

**Computing on campus.** 16 workstations in library, computer center. Wireless network available.

**Student life. Freshman orientation:** Mandatory. Preregistration for classes offered.

**Contact.** Phone: (703) 709-5875 Fax: (703) 709-8972
Marcus Palmore, Admissions Director, Potomac College, 1029 Herndon Parkway, Herndon, VA 20170

## Radford University
**Radford, Virginia**
**www.radford.edu**
CB member
CB code: 5565

- Public 4-year university
- Residential campus in large town
- 7,736 degree-seeking undergraduates: 4% part-time, 57% women, 6% African American, 2% Asian American, 3% Hispanic American, 1% international
- 960 degree-seeking graduate students
- 71% of applicants admitted
- SAT or ACT (ACT writing optional) required
- 60% graduate within 6 years; 22% enter graduate study

**General. Founded** in 1910. Regionally accredited. **Degrees:** 1,762 bachelor's awarded; master's, doctoral offered. **ROTC:** Army. **Location:** 36 miles from Roanoke. **Calendar:** Semester, limited summer session. **Full-time faculty:** 387 total; 83% have terminal degrees, 10% minority, 47% women. **Part-time faculty:** 140 total; 28% have terminal degrees, 4% minority, 62% women. **Class size:** 33% < 20, 49% 20-39, 12% 40-49, 6% 50-99, less than 1% >100. **Special facilities:** Center for visual and performing arts.

**Freshman class profile.** 6,166 applied, 4,384 admitted, 1,447 enrolled.

| Mid 50% test scores | | | |
|---|---|---|---|
| SAT critical reading: | 460-550 | GPA 2.0-2.99: | 34% |
| SAT math: | 460-550 | Rank in top quarter: | 25% |
| ACT composite: | 19-23 | Rank in top tenth: | 9% |
| GPA 3.75 or higher: | 10% | Return as sophomores: | 78% |
| GPA 3.50-3.74: | 11% | Out-of-state: | 7% |
| GPA 3.0-3.49: | 45% | Live on campus: | 96% |
| | | International: | 1% |

**Basis for selection.** High school records, including grades, strength of academic program, and performance trend: standardized test scores, optional student essay, and evidence of interest and motivation as indicated in supplied materials. **Homeschooled:** SAT subject tests in Math and English recommended. If curriculum is not supported by a recognized homeschool organization, the student may need to supply course descriptions (including text book information, where appropriate.).

**High school preparation.** College-preparatory program recommended. 24 units recommended. Recommended units include English 4, mathematics 4, social studies 2, history 2, science 4 (laboratory 3), foreign language 3 and academic electives 5. Pre-nursing students should complete units in both biology and chemistry.

**2009-2010 Annual costs.** Tuition/fees: $6,904; $16,568 out-of-state. Room/board: $6,970. Books/supplies: $1,100. Personal expenses: $1,900.

**2008-2009 Financial aid. Need-based:** 1,217 full-time freshmen applied for aid; 689 were judged to have need; 649 of these received aid. Average need met was 79%. Average scholarship/grant was $7,635; average loan $2,733. 53% of total undergraduate aid awarded as scholarships/grants, 47% as loans/jobs. **Non-need-based:** Awarded to 739 full-time undergraduates, including 155 freshmen. Scholarships awarded for academics, alumni affiliation, art, athletics, leadership, music/drama, ROTC. **Additional information:** Student's need and grades considered. Top consideration given to those with greatest need and who apply by deadline.

**Application procedures. Admission:** Closing date 2/1 (postmark date). $50 fee, may be waived for applicants with need. Admission notification 4/1. Must reply by 5/1. **Financial aid:** Priority date 3/1; no closing date. FAFSA required. Applicants notified on a rolling basis starting 4/15; must reply within 4 week(s) of notification.

**Academics.** The Learning Assistance and Resource Center provides all Radford University undergraduate and graduate students academic support services in content-specific matter, writing, and general study skills. **Special study options:** Accelerated study, cross-registration, distance learning, double major, dual enrollment of high school students, honors, independent study, internships, student-designed major, study abroad, teacher certification program. **Credit/placement by examination:** AP, CLEP, IB. **Support services:** Learning center, study skills assistance, tutoring, writing center.

**Majors. Biology:** General. **Business:** Accounting, business admin, finance, marketing. **Communications:** General, journalism. **Computer sciences:** Computer science, information systems. **Education:** Health, physical. **Family/consumer sciences:** Food/nutrition. **Foreign languages:** General. **Health:** Nursing (RN). **History:** General. **Math:** General. **Parks/recreation:** General. **Physical sciences:** Chemistry, geology, physics. **Protective services:** Criminal justice. **Psychology:** General. **Public administration:** Social work. **Social sciences:** General, anthropology, economics, geography, political science, sociology. **Visual/performing arts:** Art, dance, design, dramatic, studio arts.

**Most popular majors.** Business/marketing 19%, communications/journalism 10%, education 7%, health sciences 7%, interdisciplinary studies 11%, security/protective services 6%, social sciences 6%, visual/performing arts 9%.

**Computing on campus.** 772 workstations in dormitories, library, computer center, student center. Dormitories wired for high-speed internet access and linked to campus network. Commuter students can connect to campus network. Online course registration, online library, helpline, repair service, student web hosting, wireless network available.

**Student life. Freshman orientation:** Available, $275 fee. Preregistration for classes offered. 5 2-day sessions in June or August. **Policies:** Honor code enforced. **Housing:** Guaranteed on-campus for freshmen. Coed dorms, special housing for disabled, apartments, wellness housing available. $200 nonrefundable deposit, deadline 5/1. **Activities:** Bands, campus ministries, choral groups, dance, drama, international student organizations, literary magazine, music ensembles, musical theater, radio station, student government, student newspaper, TV station, College Republicans, Young Democrats, International Student Advisory Council, Habitat for Humanity, American Red Cross, Campus Crusade for Christ, NAACP, La Sociedad de Hispanica, Diversity Awareness Programs, Hillel.

**Athletics.** NCAA. **Intercollegiate:** Baseball M, basketball, cross-country, diving W, field hockey W, golf, soccer, softball W, swimming W, tennis, track and field, volleyball W. **Intramural:** Basketball, bowling, cross-country, football (non-tackle), racquetball, soccer, softball, table tennis, tennis, volleyball, weight lifting. **Team name:** Highlanders.

**Student services.** Adult student services, alcohol/substance abuse counseling, chaplain/spiritual director, career counseling, services for economically disadvantaged, student employment services, financial aid counseling, health services, minority student services, personal counseling, placement for graduates, veterans' counselor, women's services. **Physically disabled:** Services for visually, speech, hearing impaired.

**Contact.** E-mail: admissions@radford.edu
Phone: (540) 831-5371 Fax: (540) 831-5038
Steven Nape, Vice Provost for Enrollment Management, Radford University, 115 Martin Hall, Radford, VA 24142

---

## Randolph College
**Lynchburg, Virginia**
www.randolphcollege.edu

**CB member**
**CB code: 5567**

- Private 4-year liberal arts college affiliated with United Methodist Church
- Residential campus in small city
- 470 degree-seeking undergraduates: 1% part-time, 73% women
- 12 degree-seeking graduate students
- 81% of applicants admitted
- SAT or ACT (ACT writing optional), application essay required
- 64% graduate within 6 years; 30% enter graduate study

---

**General.** Founded in 1891. Regionally accredited. **Degrees:** 140 bachelor's awarded; master's offered. **Location:** 60 miles from Roanoke and Charlottesville. **Calendar:** Semester, limited summer session. **Full-time faculty:** 64 total; 94% have terminal degrees, 9% minority, 55% women. **Part-time faculty:** 22 total; 46% have terminal degrees, 64% women. **Class size:** 88% < 20, 12% 20-39. **Special facilities:** Observatory, 3 nature preserves, botanical garden, 100-acre equestrian center, museum of American art, science and mathematics resource center, learning resources center, writing lab, new artificial turf field and track facility.

**Freshman class profile.** 1,068 applied, 865 admitted, 135 enrolled.

| Mid 50% test scores | | | |
|---|---|---|---|
| SAT critical reading: | 500-620 | GPA 2.0-2.99: | 10% |
| SAT math: | 500-600 | Rank in top quarter: | 53% |
| ACT composite: | 21-29 | Rank in top tenth: | 25% |
| GPA 3.75 or higher: | 36% | Return as sophomores: | 70% |
| GPA 3.50-3.74: | 17% | Out-of-state: | 56% |
| GPA 3.0-3.49: | 37% | Live on campus: | 97% |
| | | International: | 7% |

**Basis for selection.** Rigor of high school curriculum and achievement most important, followed by teacher and counselor recommendations, test scores, activities, personal achievement. International students may submit SAT or ACT in lieu of TOEFL. Interview recommended. Essay submission may be essay written on topic of applicant's choice, copy of graded essay written by applicant in 11th or 12th grade, or SAT/ACT writing component. **Learning Disabled:** Submit documentation to Director of the Learning Resources Center, who will work in consultation with Office of the Dean of the College and faculty to determine reasonable and appropriate accommodations.

**High school preparation.** College-preparatory program required. 16 units required. Required and recommended units include English 4, mathematics 3, history 2, science 2 (laboratory 2), foreign language 3-4 and academic electives 1-2. 3 years of one foreign language recommended, but applicants may offer 2 units of each of 2 languages instead. Student must have successfully completed or be enrolled in algebra II senior year in order for application to be considered.

**2010-2011 Annual costs.** Tuition/fees: $29,254. Room/board: $9,995. Books/supplies: $800. Personal expenses: $1,000.

**2009-2010 Financial aid. Need-based:** 118 full-time freshmen applied for aid; 102 were judged to have need; 102 of these received aid. Average need met was 77%. Average scholarship/grant was $17,863; average loan $4,461. 69% of total undergraduate aid awarded as scholarships/grants, 31% as loans/jobs. **Non-need-based:** Awarded to 189 full-time undergraduates, including 54 freshmen. Scholarships awarded for academics, alumni affiliation, art, leadership, minority status, music/drama, religious affiliation, state residency.

**Application procedures. Admission:** Priority date 12/1; deadline 4/1 (postmark date). $50 fee, may be waived for applicants with need. Admission notification 4/15. Must reply by May 1 or within 2 week(s) if notified thereafter. Randolph College has three application deadlines: December 1, Early Action I for priority consideration for presidential scholarships; February 1, Early Action II and FAFSA priority deadline April 1, Regular deadline. **Financial aid:** Priority date 3/1; no closing date. FAFSA required. Applicants notified on a rolling basis starting 3/1; must reply by 5/1 or within 2 week(s) of notification.

**Academics.** Honor system includes self-scheduled examinations. **Special study options:** Accelerated study, combined bachelor's/graduate degree, cross-registration, double major, dual enrollment of high school students, exchange student, honors, independent study, internships, liberal arts/career combination, student-designed major, study abroad, teacher certification program, Washington semester. 7-college exchange with Washington and Lee University, Hollins University, Hampden-Sydney College, Mary Baldwin College, Sweet Briar College, Randolph-Macon College; junior year abroad program at University of Reading, England; affiliate abroad programs in Greece, France, Denmark, Japan, Italy, Ireland, Mexico, Spain; assistance with non-affiliated abroad programs; Marine Biological Laboratory Semester in Environmental Science; American Culture program (1-semester program including study on-site at key locations in and near Virginia), Tri-College Consortium with Lynchburg College and Sweet Briar College. **Credit/placement by examination:** AP, CLEP, IB, SAT, ACT, institutional tests. Applicants with scores at or above 50th percentile awarded credit for CLEP subject examinations in subject areas offered by college. However, subject tests in foreign languages granted credit only if they represent achievement beyond that of previous high school or college preparation. **Support services:** Learning center, reduced course load, study skills assistance, tutoring, writing center.

**Majors. Biology:** General. **Business:** General. **Communications:** General. **Conservation:** Environmental studies. **Engineering:** Physics. **Foreign languages:** Ancient Greek, classics, French, Latin, Spanish. **Health:** Health services. **History:** General. **Interdisciplinary:** Global studies, museum. **Math:**

General. **Philosophy/religion:** Philosophy, religion. **Physical sciences:** Chemistry, physics. **Psychology:** General. **Social sciences:** Economics, political science, sociology. **Visual/performing arts:** Art history/conservation, dance, dramatic, music history, music performance, music theory/composition, studio arts.

**Most popular majors.** Biology 8%, English 8%, foreign language 6%, history 8%, psychology 7%, social sciences 28%, visual/performing arts 9%.

**Computing on campus.** 155 workstations in dormitories, library, computer center, student center. Dormitories wired for high-speed internet access and linked to campus network. Commuter students can connect to campus network. Online course registration, online library, helpline, student web hosting, wireless network available.

**Student life. Freshman orientation:** Mandatory, $150 fee. Preregistration for classes offered. 2-day summer sessions as well as program prior to the start of fall and spring classes. Sessions include advising, and activities designed to acquaint students with the campus, the community, and each other. **Policies:** The Honor code is fundamental to the conduct and governance of the College. **Housing:** Guaranteed on-campus for all undergraduates. Coed dorms, single-sex dorms, wellness housing available. $300 non-refundable deposit, deadline 5/1. **Activities:** Pep band, campus ministries, choral groups, dance, drama, film society, international student organizations, literary magazine, music ensembles, Model UN, radio station, student government, student newspaper, Young Democrats, College Republicans, Amnesty International, Club Asia, Catholic Students Association, Black Students Alliance, Circle K, Pan World Club.

**Athletics.** NCAA. **Intercollegiate:** Basketball, cross-country, equestrian, lacrosse, soccer, softball W, tennis, volleyball W. **Intramural:** Basketball, softball, table tennis, tennis, volleyball. **Team name:** Wildcats.

**Student services.** Adult student services, alcohol/substance abuse counseling, chaplain/spiritual director, career counseling, student employment services, financial aid counseling, health services, minority student services, personal counseling, placement for graduates, women's services. **Physically disabled:** Services for visually, hearing impaired.

**Contact.** E-mail: admissions@randolphcollege.edu
Phone: (434) 947-8100 Toll-free number: (800) 745-7692
Fax: (434) 947-8996
Dean of Admissions and Student Financial Services, Randolph College, 2500 Rivermont Avenue, Lynchburg, VA 24503-1555

## Randolph-Macon College

**Ashland, Virginia**    **CB member**
**www.rmc.edu**    **CB code: 5566**

- Private 4-year liberal arts college affiliated with United Methodist Church
- Residential campus in small town
- 1,227 degree-seeking undergraduates: 1% part-time, 53% women, 11% African American, 2% Asian American, 2% Hispanic American, 1% Native American, 2% international
- 58% of applicants admitted
- SAT or ACT (ACT writing recommended), application essay required
- 63% graduate within 6 years; 41% enter graduate study

**General.** Founded in 1830. Regionally accredited. **Degrees:** 202 bachelor's awarded. **ROTC:** Army. **Location:** 15 miles from Richmond, 90 miles from Washington, DC. **Calendar:** 4-1-4, limited summer session. **Full-time faculty:** 92 total; 97% have terminal degrees, 5% minority, 42% women. **Part-time faculty:** 51 total; 37% have terminal degrees, 8% minority, 47% women. **Class size:** 67% < 20, 33% 20-39. **Special facilities:** Observatory with 12-inch reflecting telescope and 3-meter radio telescope, 6 historic buildings, greenhouse.

**Freshman class profile.** 4,308 applied, 2,507 admitted, 362 enrolled.

| Mid 50% test scores | | | |
|---|---|---|---|
| SAT critical reading: | 490-580 | Rank in top quarter: | 40% |
| SAT math: | 490-580 | Rank in top tenth: | 16% |
| SAT writing: | 480-580 | End year in good standing: | 87% |
| GPA 3.75 or higher: | 19% | Return as sophomores: | 76% |
| GPA 3.50-3.74: | 17% | Out-of-state: | 32% |
| GPA 3.0-3.49: | 35% | Live on campus: | 95% |
| GPA 2.0-2.99: | 29% | International: | 2% |

**Basis for selection.** School achievement record, class rank, and test scores most important. Personal recommendations, leadership skills and participation considered. Interview recommended. **Homeschooled:** Statement describing homeschool structure and mission, transcript of courses and grades, letter of recommendation (nonparent) required. **Learning Disabled:** Students with learning disabilities encouraged to meet with director of disability support services.

**High school preparation.** College-preparatory program required. 16 units required; 22 recommended. Required and recommended units include English 4, mathematics 3-4, social studies 2-3, history 1, science 3-4 (laboratory 2-4), foreign language 2-4 and academic electives 1-2.

**2010-2011 Annual costs.** Tuition/fees: $30,608. Room/board: $9,326. Books/supplies: $1,000. Personal expenses: $720.

**2009-2010 Financial aid. Need-based:** 301 full-time freshmen applied for aid; 246 were judged to have need; 246 of these received aid. Average need met was 80%. Average scholarship/grant was $18,530; average loan $4,573. 73% of total undergraduate aid awarded as scholarships/grants, 27% as loans/jobs. **Non-need-based:** Awarded to 550 full-time undergraduates, including 161 freshmen. Scholarships awarded for academics, alumni affiliation, minority status, religious affiliation, state residency.

**Application procedures. Admission:** Priority date 2/1; deadline 3/1 (postmark date). $30 fee, may be waived for applicants with need, free for online applicants. Admission notification 4/1. Must reply by May 1 or within 2 week(s) if notified thereafter. Applications accepted after March 1 on space-available basis. **Financial aid:** Priority date 3/1, closing date 2/15. FAFSA required. Applicants notified by 3/15; must reply by 5/1 or within 2 week(s) of notification.

**Academics.** Comprehensive liberal arts core curriculum. All students must complete an internship, study abroad, or original research project for graduation. Interdisciplinary First-Year Experience for all freshmen. **Special study options:** Accelerated study, combined bachelor's/graduate degree, cross-registration, double major, dual enrollment of high school students, exchange student, honors, independent study, internships, liberal arts/career combination, study abroad, teacher certification program, United Nations semester, Washington semester. Member of Seven College consortium, 3-2 program in engineering with Columbia University and University of Virginia, 3-2 in forestry with Duke University, 4-1 in accounting with Virginia Commonwealth University. **Credit/placement by examination:** AP, CLEP, IB, institutional tests. 75 credit hours maximum toward bachelor's degree. At least one-half major course of study must be completed at Randolph-Macon College. **Support services:** Learning center, reduced course load, study skills assistance, tutoring, writing center.

**Majors. Area/ethnic studies:** Women's. **Biology:** General. **Business:** Accounting, managerial economics. **Computer sciences:** General. **Conservation:** Environmental studies. **Foreign languages:** Ancient Greek, classics, French, German, Latin, Spanish. **History:** General. **Interdisciplinary:** Global studies. **Math:** General. **Philosophy/religion:** Philosophy, religion. **Physical sciences:** Chemistry, physics. **Psychology:** General. **Social sciences:** Economics, political science, sociology. **Visual/performing arts:** Art history/conservation, arts management, dramatic, studio arts.

**Most popular majors.** Biology 7%, business/marketing 8%, history 12%, philosophy/religious studies 6%, psychology 7%, social sciences 34%, visual/performing arts 8%.

**Computing on campus.** 350 workstations in library, computer center, student center. Dormitories wired for high-speed internet access and linked to campus network. Commuter students can connect to campus network. Online course registration, online library, helpline, repair service, student web hosting, wireless network available.

**Student life. Freshman orientation:** Mandatory, $100 fee. Preregistration for classes offered. 4-day program held for students and parents prior to start of fall classes. **Housing:** Guaranteed on-campus for all undergraduates. Coed dorms, single-sex dorms, special housing for disabled, apartments, fraternity/sorority housing, wellness housing available. Honors house, special interest housing available. **Activities:** Bands, choral groups, dance, drama, film society, literary magazine, musical theater, radio station, student government, student newspaper, TV station, over 100 clubs and organizations.

**Athletics.** NCAA. **Intercollegiate:** Baseball M, basketball, field hockey W, football (tackle) M, golf M, lacrosse, soccer, softball W, swimming W, tennis, volleyball W. **Intramural:** Basketball, football (non-tackle), lacrosse, racquetball, rugby, soccer, softball, table tennis, tennis, volleyball. **Team name:** Yellow Jackets.

**Student services.** Alcohol/substance abuse counseling, chaplain/spiritual director, career counseling, student employment services, financial aid counseling, health services, minority student services, personal counseling, placement for graduates, women's services. **Physically disabled:** Services for visually, speech, hearing impaired.

**Contact.** E-mail: admissions@rmc.edu
Phone: (804) 752-7305 Toll-free number: (800) 888-1762
Fax: (804) 752-4707
David Lesesne, Dean of Admissions and Financial Aid, Randolph-Macon College, PO Box 5005, Ashland, VA 23005-5505

## Regent University
**Virginia Beach, Virginia**
**www.regent.edu**                                    CB code: 4452

- Private 4-year university affiliated with interdenominational tradition
- Commuter campus in large city
- 1,874 degree-seeking undergraduates: 44% part-time, 66% women, 26% African American, 2% Asian American, 6% Hispanic American, 1% Native American, 1% international
- 2,741 degree-seeking graduate students
- 64% of applicants admitted
- SAT or ACT (ACT writing optional), application essay required

**General.** Founded in 1977. Regionally accredited. **Degrees:** 175 bachelor's, 1 associate awarded; master's, doctoral, professional offered. **ROTC:** Army. **Location:** 8 miles from Norfolk. **Calendar:** Semester, extensive summer session. **Full-time faculty:** 178 total; 85% have terminal degrees, 18% minority, 32% women. **Part-time faculty:** 378 total; 56% have terminal degrees, 16% minority, 46% women. **Class size:** 55% < 20, 45% 20-39. **Special facilities:** Communication and performing arts center, The Founders Inn and Spa.

**Freshman class profile.** 223 applied, 143 admitted, 106 enrolled.

| Mid 50% test scores | | | |
|---|---|---|---|
| SAT critical reading: | 460-600 | GPA 3.0-3.49: | 20% |
| SAT math: | 420-580 | GPA 2.0-2.99: | 50% |
| SAT writing: | 450-570 | End year in good standing: | 84% |
| ACT composite: | 16-22 | Return as sophomores: | 75% |
| GPA 3.75 or higher: | 13% | Out-of-state: | 62% |
| GPA 3.50-3.74: | 14% | Live on campus: | 11% |
| | | International: | 1% |

**Basis for selection.** GPA, test scores, response to an essay question all required along with application. **Homeschooled:** Transcript of courses and grades required.

**High school preparation.** Recommended units include English 4, mathematics 3, social studies 3, science 3 and foreign language 3.

**2009-2010 Annual costs.** Tuition/fees: $13,950. Room only: $5,625. Books/supplies: $598. Personal expenses: $6,606.

**2009-2010 Financial aid. Need-based:** Average need met was 26%. Average scholarship/grant was $6,013; average loan $3,461. 54% of total undergraduate aid awarded as scholarships/grants, 46% as loans/jobs. **Non-need-based:** Scholarships awarded for academics, alumni affiliation, leadership.

**Application procedures. Admission:** Closing date 5/1 (receipt date). $50 fee. Admission notification on a rolling basis. Must reply by 5/1. **Financial aid:** Priority date 3/15; no closing date. FAFSA, institutional form required. Applicants notified on a rolling basis starting 3/1; must reply within 2 week(s) of notification.

**Academics. Special study options:** Combined bachelor's/graduate degree, distance learning, double major, dual enrollment of high school students, internships, study abroad, teacher certification program, Washington semester. **Credit/placement by examination:** AP, CLEP, IB. 30 credit hours maximum toward bachelor's degree. **Support services:** Remedial instruction, study skills assistance, tutoring, writing center.

**Majors. Business:** Accounting, business admin, international, organizational behavior. **Communications:** General, journalism. **Communications technology:** Animation/special effects. **Computer sciences:** Information technology. **Education:** General. **History:** General. **Math:** General. **Philosophy/religion:** Religion. **Psychology:** General. **Social sciences:** Political science. **Theology:** Bible. **Visual/performing arts:** Cinematography, theater arts management. **Other:** Christian ministry.

**Most popular majors.** Business/marketing 29%, communications/journalism 17%, interdisciplinary studies 9%, philosophy/religious studies 11%, psychology 30%.

**Computing on campus.** 130 workstations in library, computer center, student center. Dormitories wired for high-speed internet access and linked to campus network. Online course registration, online library, helpline, wireless network available.

**Student life. Freshman orientation:** Mandatory. Preregistration for classes offered. **Housing:** Apartments available. $350 deposit, deadline 5/1. **Activities:** Concert band, campus ministries, choral groups, dance, drama, international student organizations, student government, student newspaper, Association of Black Psychologists, College Republicans, Undergraduate Student Advisory Council, Newman Club, Regent Students for Life, Students in Free Enterprise, Student Alumni Association, Student Advisory Leadership Team.

**Athletics. Intramural:** Basketball, soccer, volleyball.

**Student services.** Chaplain/spiritual director, career counseling, financial aid counseling.

**Contact.** E-mail: admissions@regent.edu
Phone: (757) 352-4127 Toll-free number: (800) 373-5504
Fax: (757) 352-4381
Ken Baker, Director of Admissions, Regent University, 1000 Regent University Drive, Virginia Beach, VA 23464-9800

## Roanoke College
**Salem, Virginia**                                    **CB member**
**www.roanoke.edu**                                    **CB code: 5571**

- Private 4-year liberal arts college affiliated with Evangelical Lutheran Church in America
- Residential campus in large town
- 1,978 degree-seeking undergraduates: 3% part-time, 56% women, 4% African American, 1% Asian American, 3% Hispanic American, 1% Native American, 1% international
- 68% of applicants admitted
- SAT or ACT (ACT writing optional) required
- 64% graduate within 6 years; 20% enter graduate study

**General.** Founded in 1842. Regionally accredited. **Degrees:** 450 bachelor's awarded. **Location:** 7 miles from Roanoke. **Calendar:** Semester, extensive summer session. **Full-time faculty:** 166 total; 82% have terminal degrees, 9% minority, 48% women. **Part-time faculty:** 42 total; 26% have terminal degrees, 2% minority, 43% women. **Class size:** 54% < 20, 46% 20-39. **Special facilities:** Fine arts center with 3 galleries, multimedia classrooms, greenhouse, nuclear magnetic resonance equipment, center for community research, center for church and society, center for learning and teaching.

**Freshman class profile.** 4,169 applied, 2,853 admitted, 560 enrolled.

| Mid 50% test scores | | | |
|---|---|---|---|
| SAT critical reading: | 500-600 | Rank in top quarter: | 47% |
| SAT math: | 490-590 | Rank in top tenth: | 21% |
| SAT writing: | 490-590 | Return as sophomores: | 77% |
| GPA 3.75 or higher: | 23% | Out-of-state: | 51% |
| GPA 3.50-3.74: | 16% | Live on campus: | 90% |
| GPA 3.0-3.49: | 35% | International: | 1% |
| GPA 2.0-2.99: | 26% | Fraternities: | 13% |
| | | Sororities: | 13% |

**Basis for selection.** School achievement record and class rank most important. Essay, interview recommended for all; audition recommended for music; portfolio recommended for graphic arts. **Homeschooled:** Transcript of courses and grades required. **Learning Disabled:** Documentation of learning disability needed for special services after enrollment.

**High school preparation.** College-preparatory program recommended. 18 units required. Required and recommended units include English 4, mathematics 3, social studies 2, science 2 (laboratory 2), foreign language 4 and academic electives 5. Mathematics must include Algebra II.

**2010-2011 Annual costs.** Tuition/fees: $31,214. Room/board: $10,308. Books/supplies: $1,000. Personal expenses: $1,000.

**2009-2010 Financial aid. Need-based:** 482 full-time freshmen applied for aid; 410 were judged to have need; 410 of these received aid. Average need met was 86%. Average scholarship/grant was $20,634; average loan $3,941. 68% of total undergraduate aid awarded as scholarships/grants, 32% as loans/jobs. **Non-need-based:** Awarded to 1,883 full-time undergraduates, including 542 freshmen. Scholarships awarded for academics, minority status, music/drama, religious affiliation.

**Application procedures. Admission:** Closing date 3/15 (postmark date). $33 fee, may be waived for applicants with need, free for online applicants. Admission notification 4/1. Must reply by May 1 or within 2 week(s) if notified thereafter. **Financial aid:** Priority date 3/1; no closing date. FAFSA

Four-Year Colleges

required. Applicants notified on a rolling basis starting 11/1; must reply within 2 week(s) of notification.

**Academics. Special study options:** Accelerated study, combined bachelor's/graduate degree, cross-registration, double major, dual enrollment of high school students, ESL, honors, independent study, internships, liberal arts/career combination, study abroad, teacher certification program, Washington semester. **Credit/placement by examination:** AP, CLEP, IB, institutional tests. 27 credit hours maximum toward bachelor's degree. **Support services:** Learning center, reduced course load, study skills assistance, tutoring, writing center.

**Majors. Biology:** General, biochemistry. **Business:** Business admin. **Computer sciences:** General, computer science, information systems. **Conservation:** Environmental science, management/policy. **Education:** Physical. **Foreign languages:** French, Spanish. **Health:** Athletic training, clinical lab science. **History:** General. **Math:** General. **Parks/recreation:** Health/fitness. **Philosophy/religion:** Philosophy, religion. **Physical sciences:** Chemistry, physics. **Protective services:** Criminal justice. **Psychology:** General. **Social sciences:** Economics, international relations, political science, sociology. **Theology:** Theology. **Visual/performing arts:** Art, art history/conservation, dramatic.

**Most popular majors.** Biology 7%, business/marketing 23%, English 9%, history 8%, psychology 10%, social sciences 17%, visual/performing arts 6%.

**Computing on campus.** 185 workstations in library, computer center, student center. Dormitories wired for high-speed internet access and linked to campus network. Commuter students can connect to campus network. Online course registration, online library, helpline, repair service, student web hosting, wireless network available.

**Student life. Freshman orientation:** Mandatory, $125 fee. Preregistration for classes offered. **Housing:** Guaranteed on-campus for freshmen. Coed dorms, single-sex dorms, apartments, fraternity/sorority housing, wellness housing available. $300 deposit, deadline 5/1. **Activities:** Bands, campus ministries, choral groups, dance, drama, film society, international student organizations, literary magazine, music ensembles, Model UN, musical theater, radio station, student government, student newspaper, Alpha Phi Omega, Earthbound, Fellowship of Christian Athletes, Habitat for Humanity, Lutheran Student Movement, Baptist Student Union, Shades of Maroon, Inter-Varsity.

**Athletics.** NCAA. **Intercollegiate:** Baseball M, basketball, cross-country, field hockey W, golf M, lacrosse, soccer, softball W, tennis, track and field, volleyball W. **Intramural:** Badminton, baseball M, basketball, field hockey W, football (non-tackle), golf W, racquetball, soccer, softball, table tennis, tennis, volleyball. **Team name:** Maroons.

**Student services.** Adult student services, alcohol/substance abuse counseling, chaplain/spiritual director, career counseling, student employment services, financial aid counseling, health services, minority student services, personal counseling, placement for graduates.

**Contact.** E-mail: admissions@roanoke.edu
Phone: (540) 375-2270 Toll-free number: (800) 388-2276
Fax: (540) 375-2267
Brenda Poggendorf, Vice President of Enrollment Management, Roanoke College, 221 College Lane, Salem, VA 24153-3794

## St. Paul's College
**Lawrenceville, Virginia**
**www.saintpauls.edu**
CB code: 5604

- Private 4-year liberal arts college affiliated with Episcopal Church
- Residential campus in small town
- 584 degree-seeking undergraduates: 3% part-time, 50% women, 97% African American, 1% Hispanic American
- 99% of applicants admitted
- SAT or ACT (ACT writing optional), application essay required

**General.** Founded in 1888. Regionally accredited. **Degrees:** 101 bachelor's awarded. **ROTC:** Army. **Location:** 80 miles from Richmond. **Calendar:** Semester, limited summer session. **Full-time faculty:** 28 total; 43% have terminal degrees, 75% minority, 39% women. **Part-time faculty:** 18 total; 100% have terminal degrees, 94% minority, 61% women. **Class size:** 73% < 20, 20% 20-39, 6% 40-49, less than 1% 50-99, less than 1% >100.

**Freshman class profile.** 403 applied, 398 admitted, 157 enrolled.

| Mid 50% test scores | | | |
|---|---|---|---|
| SAT critical reading: | 250-420 | GPA 3.0-3.49: | 3% |
| SAT math: | 320-420 | GPA 2.0-2.99: | 53% |
| SAT writing: | 330-420 | Return as sophomores: | 39% |
| ACT composite: | 13-16 | Out-of-state: | 1% |
| GPA 3.50-3.74: | 1% | Live on campus: | 94% |
| | | International: | 1% |

**Basis for selection.** School achievement record most important. School recommendations considered. Rank in top half of class important. 3.0 GPA recommended. Interview recommended.

**High school preparation.** Required units include English 4, mathematics 2, social studies 2, science 2 and foreign language 1.

**2009-2010 Annual costs.** Tuition/fees: $13,210. Room/board: $6,640. Books/supplies: $1,500. Personal expenses: $2,730.

**2008-2009 Financial aid. Need-based:** 201 full-time freshmen applied for aid; 196 were judged to have need; 186 of these received aid. Average need met was 55%. Average scholarship/grant was $4,009; average loan $997. 36% of total undergraduate aid awarded as scholarships/grants, 64% as loans/jobs. **Non-need-based:** Awarded to 245 full-time undergraduates, including 55 freshmen. Scholarships awarded for academics, alumni affiliation, athletics.

**Application procedures. Admission:** No deadline. $20 fee, may be waived for applicants with need. Must reply by May 1 or within 2 week(s) if notified thereafter. **Financial aid:** No deadline. FAFSA required. Applicants notified on a rolling basis starting 1/15; must reply by 7/1 or within 4 week(s) of notification.

**Academics. Special study options:** Accelerated study, double major, honors, independent study, internships, liberal arts/career combination, teacher certification program. Organizational Management Program for adults 25 and older. **Credit/placement by examination:** AP, CLEP, institutional tests. 24 credit hours maximum toward bachelor's degree. **Support services:** Learning center, pre-admission summer program, reduced course load, remedial instruction, tutoring.

**Majors. Biology:** General, marine. **Business:** Accounting, administrative services, business admin, management information systems, operations. **Computer sciences:** General. **Conservation:** General. **Education:** Business. **Math:** General. **Philosophy/religion:** Philosophy, religion. **Protective services:** Criminal justice. **Social sciences:** General, political science, sociology.

**Most popular majors.** Business/marketing 71%, security/protective services 11%, social sciences 6%.

**Computing on campus.** 100 workstations in dormitories, library, computer center, student center. Dormitories wired for high-speed internet access and linked to campus network. Commuter students can connect to campus network. Helpline, repair service, wireless network available.

**Student life. Freshman orientation:** Mandatory. Preregistration for classes offered. **Housing:** Single-sex dorms available. $50 nonrefundable deposit. **Activities:** Campus ministries, choral groups, student government, Altar Guild, veterans club, Canterbury club, NAACP, single parent support system.

**Athletics.** NCAA. **Intercollegiate:** Baseball M, basketball, bowling, cross-country, football (tackle) M, golf, softball W, tennis, track and field, volleyball W. **Intramural:** Basketball, softball, volleyball. **Team name:** Tigers.

**Student services.** Adult student services, career counseling, student employment services, financial aid counseling, health services, on-campus daycare, personal counseling, placement for graduates, veterans' counselor.

**Contact.** E-mail: admissions@saintpauls.edu
Phone: (434) 848-3111 Toll-free number: (800) 678-7071
Fax: (434) 848-1846
Rosemary Lewis, Director of Admissions, St. Paul's College, 115 College Drive, Lawrenceville, VA 23868

## Sanford-Brown College: Vienna
**Vienna, Virginia**
**www.gibbsva.edu**
CB code: 5655

- For-profit 4-year business and technical college
- Large city

**General.** Accredited by ACICS. **Calendar:** Quarter.

**Contact.** Phone: (703) 556-8888
1980 Gallows Road, Vienna, VA 22182

## Shenandoah University
**Winchester, Virginia**
www.su.edu

CB member
CB code: 5613

- Private 4-year university affiliated with United Methodist Church
- Residential campus in small city
- 1,717 degree-seeking undergraduates: 3% part-time, 56% women, 12% African American, 2% Asian American, 3% Hispanic American, 3% international
- 1,619 degree-seeking graduate students
- 84% of applicants admitted
- SAT or ACT (ACT writing optional) required
- 47% graduate within 6 years

**General.** Founded in 1875. Regionally accredited. **Degrees:** 362 bachelor's awarded; master's, doctoral, professional offered. **Location:** 100 miles from Baltimore, 75 miles from Washington, DC. **Calendar:** Semester, limited summer session. **Full-time faculty:** 211 total; 77% have terminal degrees, 12% minority, 52% women. **Part-time faculty:** 175 total; 34% have terminal degrees, 12% minority, 64% women. **Class size:** 78% < 20, 19% 20-39, 2% 40-49, less than 1% 50-99, less than 1% >100. **Special facilities:** Arts and media centers, conservatory, recording studio.

**Freshman class profile.** 1,466 applied, 1,236 admitted, 425 enrolled.

| Mid 50% test scores | | | |
|---|---|---|---|
| SAT critical reading: | 440-570 | GPA 3.0-3.49: | 27% |
| SAT math: | 440-560 | GPA 2.0-2.99: | 39% |
| ACT composite: | 18-23 | Return as sophomores: | 70% |
| GPA 3.75 or higher: | 24% | Out-of-state: | 37% |
| GPA 3.50-3.74: | 10% | Live on campus: | 91% |
| | | International: | 2% |

**Basis for selection.** Applicants evaluated on basis of GPA and standardized test scores along with recommendation. Audition required for Conservatory applicants. Nursing applicants must take ATI Test of Essential Academic Skills. In-house English proficiency tests administered. Interview recommended for all; audition required for dance, music, and theater programs. **Homeschooled:** Transcript of courses and grades, letter of recommendation (nonparent) required. May request GED score. Applicants must submit written documentation of local school district approval of the homeschool arrangement if available.

**High school preparation.** College-preparatory program recommended. 15 units required. Required units include English 4, mathematics 3, social studies 2, science 2 (laboratory 1) and foreign language 2.

**2010-2011 Annual costs.** Tuition/fees: $25,080. Room/board: $8,870. Books/supplies: $1,000. Personal expenses: $1,500.

**2009-2010 Financial aid. Need-based:** 345 full-time freshmen applied for aid; 345 were judged to have need; 345 of these received aid. Average need met was 85%. Average scholarship/grant was $8,500; average loan $3,500. 44% of total undergraduate aid awarded as scholarships/grants, 56% as loans/jobs. **Non-need-based:** Awarded to 1,158 full-time undergraduates, including 363 freshmen. Scholarships awarded for academics, job skills, leadership, music/drama, religious affiliation, state residency. **Additional information:** Emergency Grant Fund available for books, meals, tuition and fees.

**Application procedures. Admission:** Priority date 3/1; deadline 8/20 (receipt date). $30 fee, may be waived for applicants with need. Admission notification on a rolling basis beginning on or about 10/1. Must reply by May 1 or within 2 week(s) if notified thereafter. **Financial aid:** Closing date 3/15. FAFSA required. Applicants notified on a rolling basis starting 3/15; must reply within 2 week(s) of notification.

**Academics. Special study options:** Accelerated study, combined bachelor's/graduate degree, distance learning, double major, dual enrollment of high school students, ESL, internships, study abroad, teacher certification program, weekend college. **Credit/placement by examination:** AP, CLEP, IB, SAT, ACT, institutional tests. AP placement grade may be higher for exams taken in student's major. CEEB, CLEP, academic department exams used. **Support services:** Learning center, reduced course load, remedial instruction, study skills assistance, tutoring, writing center.

**Majors. Area/ethnic studies:** American. **Biology:** General. **Business:** Business admin. **Communications:** General. **Conservation:** Environmental studies. **Education:** Drama/dance, music, physical. **Foreign languages:** Spanish. **Health:** Music therapy, nursing (RN), respiratory therapy technology. **History:** General. **Liberal arts:** Arts/sciences. **Math:** General. **Philosophy/religion:** Religion. **Physical sciences:** Chemistry. **Protective services:** Law enforcement admin. **Psychology:** General. **Public administration:** General. **Social sciences:** Sociology. **Visual/performing arts:** General, acting, arts management, dance, dramatic, music performance, music theory/

composition, piano/organ, theater design. **Other:** Dramatic/theatre arts and stagecraft.

**Most popular majors.** Biology 6%, business/marketing 13%, education 7%, health sciences 31%, visual/performing arts 22%.

**Computing on campus.** 120 workstations in dormitories, library, computer center, student center. Dormitories wired for high-speed internet access and linked to campus network. Commuter students can connect to campus network. Online course registration, online library, helpline, repair service, wireless network available.

**Student life. Freshman orientation:** Mandatory. Preregistration for classes offered. One week; the week before start of classes. Also, one-day student/family Summer Freshman Orientation sessions offered four times in June/July. **Policies:** All first and second year undergraduate students required to live in on-campus housing. **Housing:** Guaranteed on-campus for freshmen. Coed dorms, special housing for disabled, wellness housing available. $100 nonrefundable deposit, deadline 4/15. **Activities:** Bands, choral groups, dance, drama, literary magazine, music ensembles, musical theater, opera, student government, student newspaper, symphony orchestra, TV station, Circle K, Alpha Chi Honor Society, Alpha Lambda Delta Freshman Honor Society, nursing honor society, Christian Pharmacists Fellowship International, International Students Association, College Democrats, Campus Crusade for Christ, Amnesty International, Rotaract.

**Athletics.** NCAA. **Intercollegiate:** Baseball M, basketball, cross-country, field hockey W, football (tackle) M, golf M, lacrosse, soccer, softball W, tennis, track and field. **Team name:** Hornets.

**Student services.** Adult student services, alcohol/substance abuse counseling, chaplain/spiritual director, career counseling, student employment services, financial aid counseling, health services, minority student services, personal counseling, placement for graduates, veterans' counselor. **Physically disabled:** Services for visually, speech, hearing impaired.

**Contact.** E-mail: admit@su.edu
Phone: (540) 665-4581 Toll-free number: (800) 432-2266
Fax: (540) 665-4627
David Anthony, Dean of Admissions, Shenandoah University, 1460 University Drive, Winchester, VA 22601-5195

## Southern Virginia University
**Buena Vista, Virginia**
www.svu.edu

CB member
CB code: 5625

- Private 4-year liberal arts college affiliated with Church of Jesus Christ of Latter-day Saints
- Residential campus in small town
- 638 degree-seeking undergraduates: 53% women, 5% African American, 3% Asian American, 3% Hispanic American, 2% international
- 95% of applicants admitted
- SAT or ACT (ACT writing optional) required

**General. Degrees:** 84 bachelor's awarded. **ROTC:** Army. **Location:** 60 miles from Roanoke, 60 miles from Charlottesville. **Calendar:** Semester, extensive summer session. **Full-time faculty:** 36 total; 81% have terminal degrees, 8% minority, 44% women. **Part-time faculty:** 33 total; 18% have terminal degrees, 33% women. **Class size:** 69% < 20, 30% 20-39, less than 1% 50-99, less than 1% >100.

**Freshman class profile.** 573 applied, 546 admitted, 217 enrolled.

| Mid 50% test scores | | | |
|---|---|---|---|
| SAT critical reading: | 460-560 | GPA 2.0-2.99: | 34% |
| SAT math: | 450-580 | Rank in top quarter: | 37% |
| SAT writing: | 430-540 | Rank in top tenth: | 14% |
| ACT composite: | 19-26 | End year in good standing: | 87% |
| GPA 3.75 or higher: | 22% | Return as sophomores: | 43% |
| GPA 3.50-3.74: | 15% | Out-of-state: | 86% |
| GPA 3.0-3.49: | 28% | Live on campus: | 91% |

**Basis for selection.** GPA, test scores, interview, religious affiliation or commitment all important. **Homeschooled:** Transcript of courses and grades required.

**High school preparation.** College-preparatory program recommended. Recommended units include English 4, mathematics 2, social studies 2, history 2, science 2 (laboratory 2), foreign language 2, computer science 1, visual/performing arts 1 and academic electives 1.

**2010-2011 Annual costs.** Tuition/fees (projected): $17,500. Room/board: $6,000. Books/supplies: $1,000. Personal expenses: $400.

**2008-2009 Financial aid. Need-based:** 192 full-time freshmen applied for aid; 157 were judged to have need; 157 of these received aid. Average need met was 61%. Average scholarship/grant was $8,151; average loan $2,852. 62% of total undergraduate aid awarded as scholarships/grants, 38% as loans/jobs. **Non-need-based:** Awarded to 308 full-time undergraduates, including 140 freshmen. Scholarships awarded for academics, art, athletics, leadership, music/drama, ROTC.

**Application procedures. Admission:** Closing date 8/31. $35 fee, may be waived for applicants with need. Admission notification on a rolling basis beginning on or about 10/1. **Financial aid:** Priority date 5/1; no closing date. FAFSA required. Applicants notified on a rolling basis starting 3/1; must reply by 5/1 or within 3 week(s) of notification.

**Academics. Special study options:** Accelerated study, double major, independent study, internships, liberal arts/career combination, study abroad. **Credit/placement by examination:** AP, CLEP, IB, SAT, ACT, institutional tests. **Support services:** Learning center, remedial instruction, study skills assistance, tutoring.

**Majors. Biology:** General. **Business:** Business admin. **Computer sciences:** General. **Family/consumer sciences:** Family systems. **Foreign languages:** Spanish. **History:** General. **Liberal arts:** Arts/sciences. **Philosophy/religion:** Philosophy. **Visual/performing arts:** Art, dramatic.

**Most popular majors.** Business/marketing 26%, English 11%, family/consumer sciences 7%, history 7%, liberal arts 16%, parks/recreation 6%, philosophy/religious studies 7%, visual/performing arts 16%.

**Computing on campus.** 43 workstations in library, computer center. Dormitories wired for high-speed internet access and linked to campus network. Commuter students can connect to campus network. Online course registration, online library, helpline, repair service, wireless network available.

**Student life. Freshman orientation:** Mandatory. Preregistration for classes offered. **Policies:** Students are responsible for familiarizing themselves with and abiding by the honor code, the dress and grooming standards, and the residential living policies. Most housing is wheelchair accessible. **Housing:** Guaranteed on-campus for freshmen. Single-sex dorms, apartments, wellness housing available. $250 fully refundable deposit, deadline 5/1. **Activities:** Bands, campus ministries, choral groups, dance, drama, international student organizations, literary magazine, music ensembles, musical theater, student government, student newspaper, symphony orchestra.

**Athletics.** NAIA, USCAA. **Intercollegiate:** Baseball M, basketball, cheerleading, cross-country, football (tackle) M, golf, soccer, softball W, tennis, track and field, volleyball W, wrestling M. **Team name:** Knights.

**Student services.** Chaplain/spiritual director, career counseling, financial aid counseling, health services, personal counseling.

**Contact.** E-mail: admissions@svu.edu
Phone: (540) 261-2756 Toll-free number: (800) 229-8420
Fax: (540) 264-8559
Brett Garcia, Dean of Admissions, Southern Virginia University, One University Hill Drive, Buena Vista, VA 24416-3097

### Stratford University: Falls Church
**Falls Church, Virginia**
www.stratford.edu
CB code: 3778

- For-profit 4-year university and career college
- Commuter campus in small city

**General.** Accredited by ACICS. **Location:** 12 Miles from the District of Columbia. **Calendar:** Quarter.

**Contact.** Phone: (703) 821-8570
Director of Admissions, 7777 Leesburg Pike, Falls Church, VA 22043

### Stratford University: Woodbridge
**Woodbridge, Virginia**
www.stratford.edu

- For-profit 4-year university
- Large town
- 631 degree-seeking undergraduates
- 83% of applicants admitted

**General.** Accredited by ACICS. **Degrees:** 376 bachelor's, 201 associate awarded; master's offered. **Calendar:** Quarter. **Full-time faculty:** 44 total. **Part-time faculty:** 128 total.

**Freshman class profile.** 174 applied, 144 admitted, 101 enrolled.

**Academics. Credit/placement by examination:** CLEP.

**Majors. Business:** Accounting, business admin. **Computer sciences:** Computer forensics, information systems. **Health:** Nursing admin. **Personal/culinary services:** General, restaurant/catering.

**Contact.** E-mail: admissions@stratford.edu
Phone: (703) 897-1982 Toll-free number: (888) 546-1250
Susan Merritt, Director of Admissions, Stratford University: Woodbridge, 13576 Minnieville Road, Woodbridge, VA 22192

### Sweet Briar College
**Sweet Briar, Virginia**
www.sbc.edu
CB member
CB code: 5634

- Private 4-year liberal arts college for women
- Residential campus in rural community
- 611 degree-seeking undergraduates: 1% part-time, 100% women, 4% African American, 1% Asian American, 4% Hispanic American, 2% international
- 11 degree-seeking graduate students
- 82% of applicants admitted
- SAT or ACT (ACT writing optional), application essay required
- 60% graduate within 6 years; 30% enter graduate study

**General.** Founded in 1901. Regionally accredited. **Degrees:** 133 bachelor's awarded; master's offered. **Location:** 12 miles from Lynchburg, 166 miles from Washington, DC. **Calendar:** Semester, limited summer session. **Full-time faculty:** 76 total; 95% have terminal degrees, 8% minority, 50% women. **Part-time faculty:** 31 total; 6% minority, 48% women. **Class size:** 91% < 20, 9% 20-39. **Special facilities:** Indoor and outdoor riding facilities, three nature sanctuaries, art barn, college-run nursery school and kindergarten for student teaching, observatory, environmental education and nature center.

**Freshman class profile.** 572 applied, 471 admitted, 157 enrolled.

| Mid 50% test scores | | | |
|---|---|---|---|
| SAT critical reading: | 480-630 | GPA 2.0-2.99: | 24% |
| SAT math: | 460-520 | Rank in top quarter: | 45% |
| SAT writing: | 480-620 | Rank in top tenth: | 22% |
| ACT composite: | 20-27 | End year in good standing: | 80% |
| GPA 3.75 or higher: | 20% | Return as sophomores: | 78% |
| GPA 3.50-3.74: | 22% | Out-of-state: | 56% |
| GPA 3.0-3.49: | 34% | Live on campus: | 93% |
| | | International: | 3% |

**Basis for selection.** High school curriculum and grades are of primary importance, followed by school and teacher recommendations, test scores, and writing ability as demonstrated by essay or personal statement. Interview, extracurricular activities, and personal characteristics are also considered. **Learning Disabled:** Applicant must submit written request for accommodated admissions review to Office of Admissions and enclose appropriate documentation with request.

**High school preparation.** College-preparatory program required. 16 units required; 20 recommended. Required and recommended units include English 4, mathematics 3-4, social studies 3-4, science 3-4 (laboratory 2-3) and foreign language 2-4.

**2010-2011 Annual costs.** Tuition/fees: $30,195. Room/board: $10,780. Books/supplies: $900. Personal expenses: $1,250.

**2008-2009 Financial aid. Need-based:** 146 full-time freshmen applied for aid; 146 were judged to have need; 144 of these received aid. Average need met was 31%. Average scholarship/grant was $17,084; average loan $4,179. 74% of total undergraduate aid awarded as scholarships/grants, 26% as loans/jobs. **Non-need-based:** Awarded to 496 full-time undergraduates, including 128 freshmen. Scholarships awarded for academics, art, leadership, music/drama, state residency.

**Application procedures. Admission:** Closing date 2/1 (postmark date). $40 fee, may be waived for applicants with need. Admission notification on a rolling basis. Must reply by 5/1. **Financial aid:** Priority date 2/15; no closing date. FAFSA required. Applicants notified on a rolling basis starting 3/1; must reply by 5/1.

**Academics.** General Education Program: students complete requirements that involve communication and quantitative reasoning skills; rationale for broad liberal arts background; emphasis on internships; regular progress self-assessments. Summer research program provides opportunities for high-level work with faculty. **Special study options:** Accelerated study, combined bachelor's/graduate degree, cross-registration, double major, dual enrollment of high school students, exchange student, honors, independent study, internships, liberal arts/career combination, student-designed major, study abroad, teacher certification program, Washington semester. **Credit/placement by examination:** AP, CLEP, IB, institutional tests. Exemption from 1 or more of degree requirements and/or admission to advanced courses may be granted on basis of Advanced Placement Exams, International Baccalaureate Program, transfer credit, or, in some cases, placement tests taken at college. **Support services:** Learning center, study skills assistance, tutoring, writing center.

**Majors. Area/ethnic studies:** German, Italian. **Biology:** General. **Business:** General. **Conservation:** Environmental science, environmental studies. **Engineering:** Science. **Engineering technology:** Industrial management. **Foreign languages:** General, classics, French, German, Spanish. **History:** General. **Liberal arts:** Arts/sciences. **Math:** General. **Philosophy/religion:** Philosophy, religion. **Physical sciences:** Chemistry, physics, theoretical physics. **Psychology:** General. **Social sciences:** Anthropology, archaeology, economics, international relations, political science, sociology. **Visual/performing arts:** Art history/conservation, dance, dramatic, studio arts. **Other:** Biochemistry and molecular biology, Multi/interdisciplinary studies.

**Computing on campus.** 117 workstations in library, computer center. Dormitories wired for high-speed internet access and linked to campus network. Commuter students can connect to campus network. Online course registration, online library, helpline, repair service, student web hosting, wireless network available.

**Student life. Freshman orientation:** Mandatory. Preregistration for classes offered. Begins on a Saturday in August through the following Thursday, which is the official beginning of classes. **Policies:** Self-governing student body; honor system observed. **Housing:** Guaranteed on-campus for all undergraduates. Wellness housing available. **Activities:** Campus ministries, choral groups, dance, drama, film society, literary magazine, music ensembles, musical theater, radio station, student government, student newspaper, symphony orchestra, TV station, Campus Christian Fellowship, campus spirituality coalition, College Republicans, College Democrats, Circle K, Habitat for Humanity, student environmental organization, Vixen PAWS, Newman Club.

**Athletics.** NCAA. **Intercollegiate:** Field hockey W, lacrosse W, soccer W, softball W, swimming W, tennis W, volleyball W. **Team name:** Vixens.

**Student services.** Alcohol/substance abuse counseling, chaplain/spiritual director, career counseling, student employment services, financial aid counseling, health services, personal counseling, placement for graduates, women's services. **Physically disabled:** Services for hearing impaired.

**Contact.** E-mail: admissions@sbc.edu
Phone: (434) 381-6142 Toll-free number: (800) 381-6142
Fax: (434) 381-6152
Ken Huus, Dean of Admissions, Sweet Briar College, PO Box 1052, Sweet Briar, VA 24595-1502

---

## University of Management and Technology
### Arlington, Virginia
### www.umtweb.edu

▶ For-profit 4-year business and engineering college
▶ Very large city
▶ 2,491 degree-seeking undergraduates

**General.** Accredited by DETC. **Degrees:** 384 bachelor's, 97 associate awarded; master's offered. **Calendar:** Continuous, extensive summer session. **Full-time faculty:** 26 total.

**Freshman class profile.** 650 applied, 475 admitted, 413 enrolled.

**Basis for selection.** Open admission, but selective for some programs.

**Application procedures. Admission:** $30 fee, may be waived for applicants with need. Application must be submitted online. Admission notification on a rolling basis.

**Academics. Special study options:** Accelerated study, combined bachelor's/graduate degree, distance learning, independent study. **Credit/placement by examination:** CLEP. 45 credit hours maximum toward associate degree, 90 toward bachelor's.

**Majors. Business:** General, business admin, international marketing, market research, marketing. **Computer sciences:** General, computer science,

information systems, information technology, LAN/WAN management, networking, security, systems analysis, web page design, webmaster.

**Computing on campus.** PC or laptop required.

**Contact.** E-mail: admissions@umtweb.edu
Phone: (703) 516-0035 Fax: (703) 516-0985
University of Management and Technology, 1901 N Fort Myer Drive/Suite 700, Arlington, VA 22209

---

## University of Mary Washington
### Fredericksburg, Virginia
### www.umw.edu
**CB member**
**CB code: 5398**

▶ Public 4-year university and liberal arts college
▶ Residential campus in small city
▶ 4,258 degree-seeking undergraduates: 12% part-time, 65% women, 5% African American, 5% Asian American, 4% Hispanic American
▶ 788 degree-seeking graduate students
▶ 74% of applicants admitted
▶ SAT or ACT (ACT writing optional), application essay required
▶ 72% graduate within 6 years; 24% enter graduate study

**General.** Founded in 1908. Regionally accredited. Stafford location offering bachelor's degree-completion program and master's degrees. **Degrees:** 928 bachelor's awarded; master's offered. **ROTC:** Army. **Location:** 50 miles from Richmond, 50 miles from Washington, DC. **Calendar:** Semester, limited summer session. **Full-time faculty:** 242 total; 90% have terminal degrees, 13% minority, 48% women. **Part-time faculty:** 128 total; 39% have terminal degrees, 9% minority, 56% women. **Class size:** 42% < 20, 51% 20-39, 4% 40-49, 4% 50-99. **Special facilities:** Center for historic preservation, James Monroe museum and memorial library, Gari Melchers home and studio, center for Asian studies, multicultural center.

**Freshman class profile.** 4,761 applied, 3,541 admitted, 963 enrolled.

| Mid 50% test scores | | | |
|---|---|---|---|
| SAT critical reading: | 540-650 | GPA 3.0-3.49: | 37% |
| SAT math: | 520-620 | GPA 2.0-2.99: | 6% |
| SAT writing: | 530-630 | End year in good standing: | 96% |
| ACT composite: | 24-28 | Return as sophomores: | 83% |
| GPA 3.75 or higher: | 36% | Out-of-state: | 20% |
| GPA 3.50-3.74: | 21% | Live on campus: | 93% |
| | | International: | 1% |

**Basis for selection.** Rigor of high school program most important, followed by GPA, standardized test scores, activities, essays, recommendations. Music majors encouraged to audition. **Homeschooled:** Transcript of courses and grades required. Students are advised to take 3 SAT Subject Tests to demonstrate abilities in core curriculum.

**High school preparation.** College-preparatory program recommended. 15 units required; 20 recommended. Required and recommended units include English 4, mathematics 3-4, social studies 2, history 1-2, science 3-4 (laboratory 3-4) and foreign language 2-4.

**2009-2010 Annual costs.** Tuition/fees: $7,112; $18,840 out-of-state. Room/board: $8,316.

**2008-2009 Financial aid. Need-based:** 576 full-time freshmen applied for aid; 221 were judged to have need; 221 of these received aid. Average need met was 53%. Average scholarship/grant was $6,360; average loan $3,170. 45% of total undergraduate aid awarded as scholarships/grants, 55% as loans/jobs. **Non-need-based:** Awarded to 631 full-time undergraduates, including 223 freshmen. Scholarships awarded for academics, alumni affiliation, art, leadership, music/drama, state residency.

**Application procedures. Admission:** Priority date 1/15; deadline 2/1 (postmark date). $50 fee, may be waived for applicants with need. Admission notification 4/1. Admission notification on a rolling basis. Must reply by 5/1. Applicants for regular admission with superior qualifications and who complete the application by 1/15 are eligible for Honors Admission (early notification, non-binding). **Financial aid:** Priority date 3/1, closing date 5/31. FAFSA, institutional form required. Applicants notified by 4/15; must reply by 5/1 or within 2 week(s) of notification.

**Academics.** College provides grants for undergraduate research program enabling students to work individually with faculty members. **Special study options:** Accelerated study, combined bachelor's/graduate degree, distance learning, double major, independent study, internships, semester at sea, student-designed major, study abroad, teacher certification program, Washington semester. **Credit/placement by examination:** AP, CLEP, IB, institutional tests. Credit from CLEP scores applicable to adult degree; limited to to BA/BS degree program. **Support services:** Pre-admission summer program, study skills assistance, tutoring, writing center.

**Majors. Area/ethnic studies:** American. **Biology:** General. **Business:** Business admin. **Computer sciences:** General. **Foreign languages:** General, classics. **History:** General. **Interdisciplinary:** Historic preservation. **Liberal arts:** Arts/sciences. **Math:** General. **Philosophy/religion:** Philosophy, religion. **Physical sciences:** Chemistry, physics. **Psychology:** General. **Social sciences:** Anthropology, economics, geography, international relations, political science, sociology. **Visual/performing arts:** General, art history/conservation. **Other:** Environmental sciences and geology.

**Most popular majors.** Biology 6%, business/marketing 13%, English 10%, history 6%, interdisciplinary studies 10%, liberal arts 7%, psychology 12%, social sciences 16%, visual/performing arts 6%.

**Computing on campus.** 350 workstations in library, computer center, student center. Dormitories wired for high-speed internet access and linked to campus network. Commuter students can connect to campus network. Online course registration, online library, helpline, repair service, wireless network available.

**Student life. Freshman orientation:** Mandatory. Preregistration for classes offered. 5-day freshmen/transfer orientation held in August prior to start of classes. **Policies:** Honor system. **Housing:** Guaranteed on-campus for freshmen. Coed dorms, single-sex dorms, special housing for disabled, apartments, wellness housing available. $250 nonrefundable deposit, deadline 5/1. **Activities:** Bands, campus ministries, choral groups, dance, drama, film society, international student organizations, literary magazine, music ensembles, Model UN, musical theater, opera, radio station, student government, student newspaper, symphony orchestra, Amnesty International, Baptist Student Union, Catholic Student Union, Hillel, Hispanic student association, Asian student association, Young Democrats, Campus Christian Community, College Republicans.

**Athletics.** NCAA. **Intercollegiate:** Baseball M, basketball, cross-country, equestrian, field hockey W, lacrosse, rowing (crew), soccer, softball W, swimming, tennis, track and field, volleyball W. **Intramural:** Badminton, basketball, bowling, football (non-tackle), golf, handball, soccer, softball, volleyball, water polo. **Team name:** Eagles.

**Student services.** Adult student services, chaplain/spiritual director, career counseling, services for economically disadvantaged, student employment services, financial aid counseling, health services, minority student services, personal counseling, placement for graduates, veterans' counselor, women's services. **Physically disabled:** Services for visually, speech, hearing impaired.

**Contact.** E-mail: admit@umw.edu
Phone: (540) 654-2000 Toll-free number: (800) 468-5614
Fax: (540) 654-1857
Martin Wilder, Dean of Enrollment and Student Services, University of Mary Washington, 1301 College Avenue, Fredericksburg, VA 22401-5300

---

## University of Richmond
**University of Richmond, Virginia**
**www.richmond.edu**

CB member
CB code: 5569

- Private 4-year university and liberal arts college
- Residential campus in very large city
- 2,826 degree-seeking undergraduates: 1% part-time, 53% women, 8% African American, 5% Asian American, 4% Hispanic American, 5% international
- 584 degree-seeking graduate students
- 39% of applicants admitted
- SAT or ACT (ACT writing optional), application essay required
- 87% graduate within 6 years

**General.** Founded in 1830. Regionally accredited. **Degrees:** 796 bachelor's, 11 associate awarded; master's, professional offered. **ROTC:** Army. **Location:** 6 miles from Richmond, 100 miles from Washington, DC. **Calendar:** Semester, limited summer session. **Full-time faculty:** 322 total; 84% have terminal degrees, 12% minority, 41% women. **Part-time faculty:** 45 total; 62% have terminal degrees, 4% minority, 58% women. **Class size:** 66% < 20, 34% 20-39, less than 1% 40-49. **Special facilities:** Greenhouse, electron microscope, radionuclide complex, print study center, natural sciences museum, neuroscience research laboratory, music technology laboratory, art technology laboratory, foundry, herbarium, computer connection to the Jefferson Lab's particle accelerator.

**Freshman class profile.** 7,880 applied, 3,093 admitted, 918 enrolled.

| Mid 50% test scores | | | |
|---|---|---|---|
| SAT critical reading: | 580-670 | 'Rank in top quarter: | 87% |
| SAT math: | 590-680 | Rank in top tenth: | 58% |
| SAT writing: | 580-690 | Return as sophomores: | 92% |
| ACT composite: | 26-30 | Out-of-state: | 79% |
| | | International: | 6% |

**Basis for selection.** High school transcript, test scores, essay, GPA, character/personal qualities and letter of reference. Campus visits recommended; interviews not offered. SAT Subject Tests in foreign languages may be used for placement, but not required. January SAT and SAT Subject Test date and February ACT test date are last acceptable testing dates for fall admission. Character statement required. **Homeschooled:** Statement describing homeschool structure and mission, interview required. Applicant must submit narrative description of home schooling environment. 2 SAT Subject Tests in history and natural science strongly recommended.

**High school preparation.** College-preparatory program recommended. 16 units required; 20 recommended. Required and recommended units include English 4, mathematics 3-4, history 2-4, science 2-4 (laboratory 2-4) and foreign language 2-4.

**2010-2011 Annual costs.** Tuition/fees: $41,610. Room/board: $8,810. Books/supplies: $1,050.

**2009-2010 Financial aid. Need-based:** 603 full-time freshmen applied for aid; 486 were judged to have need; 486 of these received aid. Average need met was 100%. Average scholarship/grant was $33,712; average loan $2,930. 93% of total undergraduate aid awarded as scholarships/grants, 7% as loans/jobs. **Non-need-based:** Scholarships awarded for academics, art, athletics, leadership, minority status, music/drama, ROTC. **Additional information:** VA residents whose family income is $40,000 or less and who qualify for need-based aid will receive grant assistance equal to full tuition, room and board. Early decision: Financial aid package estimated using historical data; applicant still required to submit all financial aid forms.

**Application procedures. Admission:** Closing date 1/15 (postmark date). $50 fee, may be waived for applicants with need. Admission notification 4/1. Admission notification on a rolling basis. Must reply by May 1 or within 2 week(s) if notified thereafter. **Financial aid:** Closing date 2/15. FAFSA, institutional form required. Prior year federal tax return. Applicants notified by 4/1; must reply within 4 week(s) of notification.

**Academics. Special study options:** Accelerated study, cross-registration, distance learning, double major, ESL, exchange student, external degree, honors, independent study, internships, student-designed major, study abroad, teacher certification program, Washington semester. 86 different study abroad programs in over 30 different countries. **Credit/placement by examination:** AP, CLEP, IB, institutional tests. 30 credit hours maximum toward bachelor's degree. School of Continuing Studies follows different guidelines and credit granting procedures. **Support services:** Learning center, study skills assistance, tutoring, writing center.

**Majors. Area/ethnic studies:** African, American, Asian, European, German, Latin American, Russian/Slavic, women's. **Biology:** General, molecular biochemistry. **Business:** Accounting, business admin, human resources, organizational behavior. **Communications:** Journalism. **Computer sciences:** General, information technology. **Conservation:** Environmental studies. **Foreign languages:** Ancient Greek, French, Latin, Spanish. **History:** General. **Interdisciplinary:** Ancient studies, cognitive science. **Liberal arts:** Humanities. **Math:** General. **Philosophy/religion:** Philosophy, religion. **Physical sciences:** Chemistry, physics. **Protective services:** Criminal justice. **Psychology:** General. **Public administration:** Human services. **Social sciences:** Anthropology, economics, international economics, international relations, political science, sociology. **Visual/performing arts:** Art history/conservation, dramatic, studio arts. **Other:** Mathematical Economics.

**Most popular majors.** Business/marketing 29%, English 8%, foreign language 7%, psychology 6%, social sciences 17%.

**Computing on campus.** 900 workstations in dormitories, library, computer center, student center. Dormitories wired for high-speed internet access and linked to campus network. Commuter students can connect to campus network. Online course registration, online library, helpline, repair service, student web hosting, wireless network available.

**Student life. Freshman orientation:** Mandatory. 3 days before upperclassmen arrive in the fall. **Policies:** Undergraduate students become members of residential colleges: Richmond College (men) and Westhampton College (women). Classes and extracurricular activities co-educational. Separate student governments, honor/judicial councils and deans. **Housing:** Coed dorms, single-sex dorms, special housing for disabled, apartments, wellness housing available. $300 nonrefundable deposit, deadline 5/1. **Activities:** Bands, campus ministries, choral groups, dance, drama, film society, international student organizations, literary magazine, music ensembles, Model UN, musical theater, radio station, student government, student newspaper, symphony orchestra, over 200 organizations.

**Athletics.** NCAA. **Intercollegiate:** Baseball M, basketball, cross-country, diving W, field hockey W, football (tackle) M, golf, lacrosse W, soccer, swimming W, tennis, track and field. **Intramural:** Basketball, golf, racquetball, soccer, softball, squash, swimming, synchronized swimming W, table tennis, tennis, volleyball, water polo M, wrestling M. **Team name:** Spiders.

**Student services.** Alcohol/substance abuse counseling, chaplain/spiritual director, career counseling, student employment services, financial aid counseling, health services, minority student services, personal counseling, placement for graduates, veterans' counselor. **Physically disabled:** Services for visually, speech, hearing impaired.

**Contact.** E-mail: admissions@richmond.edu
Phone: (804) 289-8640 Toll-free number: (800) 700-1662
Fax: (804) 287-6003
Pamela Spence, Dean of Admissions, University of Richmond, 28 Westhampton Way, University of Richmond, VA 23173

---

## University of Virginia
**Charlottesville, Virginia**　　　　　　　　**CB member**
**www.virginia.edu**　　　　　　　　　　　**CB code: 5820**

- Public 4-year university
- Residential campus in small city
- 14,225 degree-seeking undergraduates: 3% part-time, 56% women, 8% African American, 12% Asian American, 5% Hispanic American, 5% international
- 6,739 degree-seeking graduate students
- 32% of applicants admitted
- SAT or ACT with writing, application essay required
- 93% graduate within 6 years

**General.** Founded in 1819. Regionally accredited. **Degrees:** 3,560 bachelor's awarded; master's, doctoral, professional offered. **ROTC:** Army, Naval, Air Force. **Location:** 70 miles from Richmond, 120 miles from Washington, DC. **Calendar:** Semester, extensive summer session. **Full-time faculty:** 1,220 total; 92% have terminal degrees, 12% minority, 33% women. **Part-time faculty:** 104 total; 61% have terminal degrees, 8% minority, 44% women. **Class size:** 52% < 20, 26% 20-39, 7% 40-49, 9% 50-99, 6% >100. **Special facilities:** Observatory, center for biological timing, experimental farm, art museum.

**Freshman class profile.** 21,108 applied, 6,768 admitted, 3,246 enrolled.

| Mid 50% test scores | | | |
|---|---|---|---|
| SAT critical reading: | 600-710 | GPA 2.0-2.99: | 1% |
| SAT math: | 630-730 | Rank in top quarter: | 97% |
| SAT writing: | 610-710 | Rank in top tenth: | 89% |
| ACT composite: | 27-32 | End year in good standing: | 97% |
| GPA 3.75 or higher: | 89% | Return as sophomores: | 97% |
| GPA 3.50-3.74: | 7% | Out-of-state: | 28% |
| GPA 3.0-3.49: | 3% | Live on campus: | 100% |
| | | International: | 6% |

**Basis for selection.** School achievement record, class rank, test scores most important. Extracurricular activities and interests, quality of writing, recommendation also important. Special consideration for minorities, children of alumni, and in-state students. School diploma may be waived for especially qualified applicants. Following international tests accepted: International Baccalaureate, German Abitur, British AICE, French Baccalaureate, Swiss Federal Maturity Certificate. SAT Subject Tests recommended. Two SAT subject tests of the student's choosing are strongly recommended.

**High school preparation.** College-preparatory program required. 16 units required. Required and recommended units include English 4, mathematics 4-5, social studies 1-4, science 2-4 and foreign language 2-5. 3 units of science (1 chemistry, 1 physics) required if applying to the School of Engineering and Applied Science.

**2009-2010 Annual costs.** Tuition/fees: $9,672; $31,230 out-of-state. Room/board: $8,290.

**2009-2010 Financial aid. Non-need-based:** Scholarships awarded for academics, athletics, leadership, minority status, music/drama, state residency.

**Application procedures. Admission:** Closing date 1/1 (receipt date). $60 fee, may be waived for applicants with need. Admission notification 4/1. Must reply by May 1 or within 2 week(s) if notified thereafter. Deferred admission maximum postponement is one year. **Financial aid:** Priority date 3/1; no closing date. FAFSA, institutional form required. Applicants notified by 4/1; must reply by 5/1.

**Academics. Special study options:** Accelerated study, combined bachelor's/graduate degree, cooperative education, double major, ESL, exchange student, honors, independent study, internships, liberal arts/career combination, semester at sea, student-designed major, study abroad, teacher certification program. Jefferson, Echols, Rodman, and College Science Scholar programs for highest-achieving high school students. January Term. **Credit/placement by examination:** AP, CLEP, IB, institutional tests. 60 credit hours maximum toward bachelor's degree. **Support services:** Learning center, pre-admission summer program, reduced course load, study skills assistance, tutoring, writing center.

**Majors. Architecture:** Architecture, history/criticism, urban/community planning. **Area/ethnic studies:** African-American, Latin American. **Biology:** General. **Business:** General. **Computer sciences:** General. **Conservation:** Environmental science. **Engineering:** General, aerospace, biomedical, chemical, civil, computer, electrical, mechanical, systems. **Foreign languages:** Classics, comparative lit, French, German, Italian, Slavic, Spanish. **Health:** Audiology/speech pathology, nursing (RN). **History:** General. **Liberal arts:** Arts/sciences. **Math:** General. **Parks/recreation:** Exercise sciences. **Philosophy/religion:** Philosophy, religion. **Physical sciences:** Astronomy, chemistry, physics. **Psychology:** General. **Social sciences:** Anthropology, economics, international relations, political science, sociology. **Visual/performing arts:** Art, dramatic.

**Most popular majors.** Biology 6%, business/marketing 7%, engineering/engineering technologies 9%, English 6%, history 7%, liberal arts 7%, psychology 7%, social sciences 21%.

**Computing on campus.** Dormitories wired for high-speed internet access and linked to campus network. Commuter students can connect to campus network. Online course registration, online library, helpline, repair service, student web hosting, wireless network available.

**Student life. Freshman orientation:** Mandatory, $200 fee. Preregistration for classes offered. 2-day program held in July; August session held for international students. **Housing:** Guaranteed on-campus for freshmen. Coed dorms, apartments, fraternity/sorority housing available. 5 residential colleges available. **Activities:** Bands, choral groups, dance, drama, film society, international student organizations, literary magazine, music ensembles, Model UN, musical theater, opera, radio station, student government, student newspaper, symphony orchestra, TV station, community service group, Black Student Alliance, general clubs and religious organizations, political organizations, service fraternities and sororities, debating union.

**Athletics.** NCAA. **Intercollegiate:** Baseball M, basketball, cross-country, diving, field hockey W, football (tackle) M, golf, lacrosse, rowing (crew) W, soccer, softball W, swimming, tennis, track and field, volleyball W, wrestling M. **Intramural:** Basketball, field hockey W, football (non-tackle), golf, racquetball, rowing (crew), soccer, softball, tennis, volleyball, water polo. **Team name:** Cavaliers.

**Student services.** Alcohol/substance abuse counseling, career counseling, student employment services, financial aid counseling, health services, legal services, minority student services, on-campus daycare, personal counseling, placement for graduates, veterans' counselor, women's services. **Physically disabled:** Services for visually, speech, hearing impaired.

**Contact.** E-mail: undergradadmission@virginia.edu
Phone: (434) 982-3200 Fax: (434) 924-3587
Gregory Roberts, Dean of Admission, University of Virginia, Box 400160, Charlottesville, VA 22904-4160

---

## University of Virginia's College at Wise
**Wise, Virginia**　　　　　　　　　　　**CB member**
**www.uvawise.edu**　　　　　　　　　　**CB code: 5124**

- Public 4-year liberal arts college
- Commuter campus in small town
- 1,627 degree-seeking undergraduates: 9% part-time, 47% women, 11% African American, 1% Asian American, 2% Hispanic American
- 89% of applicants admitted
- SAT or ACT (ACT writing recommended) required
- 46% graduate within 6 years

**General.** Founded in 1954. Regionally accredited. **Degrees:** 287 bachelor's awarded. **Location:** 60 miles from Bristol. **Calendar:** Semester, limited summer session. **Full-time faculty:** 93 total; 70% have terminal degrees, 5% minority, 40% women. **Part-time faculty:** 77 total. **Class size:** 60% < 20, 35% 20-39, 3% 40-49, less than 1% 50-99, less than 1% >100. **Special facilities:** Observatory, scanning electron microscope, oral communication center, nursing assessment stations.

**Freshman class profile.** 1,068 applied, 952 admitted, 406 enrolled.

| Mid 50% test scores | | | |
|---|---|---|---|
| SAT critical reading: | 420-530 | GPA 2.0-2.99: | 33% |
| SAT math: | 420-530 | Rank in top quarter: | 38% |
| SAT writing: | 410-510 | Rank in top tenth: | 12% |
| ACT composite: | 16-22 | Return as sophomores: | 65% |
| GPA 3.75 or higher: | 19% | Out-of-state: | 6% |
| GPA 3.50-3.74: | 15% | Live on campus: | 75% |
| GPA 3.0-3.49: | 32% | Fraternities: | 5% |
| | | Sororities: | 2% |

**Basis for selection.** Applications reviewed on rolling basis. Emphasis given to academic courses and grades earned in those courses. Interview required for marginal applicants.

**High school preparation.** 18 units required. Required units include English 4, mathematics 3, social studies 1, history 1, science 2 (laboratory 2), foreign language 2 and academic electives 5. 1 American history, 1 world history required.

**2010-2011 Annual costs.** Tuition/fees (projected): $6,748; $18,876 out-of-state. Room/board: $7,323. Books/supplies: $756. Personal expenses: $1,182.

**2008-2009 Financial aid. Need-based:** 349 full-time freshmen applied for aid; 272 were judged to have need; 272 of these received aid. Average need met was 94%. Average scholarship/grant was $5,837; average loan $2,180. 65% of total undergraduate aid awarded as scholarships/grants, 35% as loans/jobs. **Non-need-based:** Awarded to 1,032 full-time undergraduates, including 391 freshmen. Scholarships awarded for academics, alumni affiliation, art, athletics, job skills, leadership, music/drama, religious affiliation, state residency.

**Application procedures. Admission:** Priority date 12/1; deadline 8/15 (postmark date). $25 fee, may be waived for applicants with need. Admission notification 8/20. Admission notification on a rolling basis. Must reply by May 1 or within 2 week(s) if notified thereafter. Early action notification on a rolling basis. **Financial aid:** Priority date 4/1; no closing date. FAFSA required. Applicants notified on a rolling basis starting 2/15; must reply within 4 week(s) of notification.

**Academics. Special study options:** Accelerated study, cooperative education, distance learning, double major, dual enrollment of high school students, honors, independent study, internships, liberal arts/career combination, student-designed major, study abroad, teacher certification program. **Credit/placement by examination:** AP, CLEP, IB, institutional tests. **Support services:** Learning center, reduced course load, remedial instruction, study skills assistance, tutoring, writing center.

**Majors. Biology:** General. **Business:** Accounting, business admin, management information systems. **Communications:** General. **Computer sciences:** Computer science. **Conservation:** Environmental studies. **Engineering technology:** Software. **Foreign languages:** General, French, Spanish. **Health:** Clinical lab science, nursing (RN). **History:** General. **Liberal arts:** Arts/sciences. **Math:** General. **Physical sciences:** Chemistry. **Protective services:** Criminal justice. **Psychology:** General. **Public administration:** General. **Social sciences:** Economics, political science, sociology. **Visual/performing arts:** Art, dramatic.

**Most popular majors.** Biology 6%, business/marketing 23%, history 10%, liberal arts 16%, psychology 8%, social sciences 14%.

**Computing on campus.** 300 workstations in dormitories, library, computer center. Dormitories wired for high-speed internet access and linked to campus network. Commuter students can connect to campus network. Helpline, repair service, student web hosting available.

**Student life. Freshman orientation:** Mandatory, $45 fee. Preregistration for classes offered. 2-day program held for students and parents. Dormitory space available (free for students, $35 per night for parents). **Housing:** Coed dorms, single-sex dorms, special housing for disabled, apartments available. $150 deposit, deadline 5/1. **Activities:** Concert band, choral groups, dance, drama, international student organizations, literary magazine, music ensembles, musical theater, radio station, student government, student newspaper, TV station, Young Republicans, Young Democrats, multicultural alliance, honors societies, professional organizations, student activities board, Baptist Student Union, Wesley Foundation.

**Athletics.** NAIA. **Intercollegiate:** Baseball M, basketball, cross-country, football (tackle) M, golf M, softball W, tennis, track and field, volleyball W. **Intramural:** Badminton, basketball, football (non-tackle), racquetball, soccer, softball, table tennis, tennis, volleyball, water polo. **Team name:** Cavaliers.

**Student services.** Alcohol/substance abuse counseling, chaplain/spiritual director, career counseling, services for economically disadvantaged, student employment services, financial aid counseling, health services, minority student services, personal counseling, placement for graduates. **Physically disabled:** Services for visually, speech, hearing impaired.

**Contact.** E-mail: admissions@uvawise.edu
Phone: (276) 328-0102 Toll-free number: (888) 282-9324
Fax: (276) 328-0251
Russell Necessary, Vice Chancellor of Enrollment Management, University of Virginia's College at Wise, 1 College Avenue, Wise, VA 24293-4412

## Virginia Baptist College
### Fredericksburg, Virginia
### www.vbc.edu

- Private 4-year Bible college
- Large city
- 84 degree-seeking undergraduates
- Application essay required

**General.** Regionally accredited; also accredited by TRACS. **Degrees:** 4 bachelor's, 2 associate awarded; master's offered. **Location:** 60 miles from Washington, DC. **Calendar:** Semester, limited summer session. **Full-time faculty:** 2 total. **Part-time faculty:** 23 total.

**Basis for selection.** Application reviewed by admissions to determine acceptance.

**2009-2010 Annual costs.** Tuition/fees: $3,780. Books/supplies: $400.

**Application procedures. Admission:** No deadline. $25 fee, may be waived for applicants with need.

**Academics. Credit/placement by examination:** CLEP, institutional tests.

**Majors. Other:** Ministry.

**Contact.** E-mail: office@vbc.edu
Phone: (540) 785-5440
Wayne Scott, Director of Admissions, Virginia Baptist College, 4105 Plank Road, Fredericksburg, VA 22407

## Virginia Commonwealth University
### Richmond, Virginia
### www.vcu.edu
**CB member**
**CB code: 5570**

- Public 4-year university
- Commuter campus in small city
- 21,500 degree-seeking undergraduates: 12% part-time, 57% women, 20% African American, 12% Asian American, 4% Hispanic American, 1% Native American, 3% international
- 7,363 degree-seeking graduate students
- 59% of applicants admitted
- SAT or ACT (ACT writing optional) required
- 51% graduate within 6 years

**General.** Founded in 1838. Regionally accredited. **Degrees:** 3,726 bachelor's awarded; master's, doctoral, professional offered. **ROTC:** Army. **Location:** 100 miles from Washington, DC. **Calendar:** Semester, extensive summer session. **Full-time faculty:** 1,919 total; 20% minority, 42% women. **Part-time faculty:** 1,128 total; 15% minority, 50% women. **Class size:** 38% < 20, 38% 20-39, 8% 40-49, 8% 50-99, 8% >100.

**Freshman class profile.** 16,915 applied, 10,055 admitted, 3,665 enrolled.

| Mid 50% test scores | | | |
|---|---|---|---|
| SAT critical reading: | 490-600 | GPA 2.0-2.99: | 16% |
| SAT math: | 490-590 | Rank in top quarter: | 47% |
| SAT writing: | 480-580 | Rank in top tenth: | 16% |
| ACT composite: | 20-25 | End year in good standing: | 86% |
| GPA 3.75 or higher: | 22% | Return as sophomores: | 84% |
| GPA 3.50-3.74: | 18% | Out-of-state: | 9% |
| GPA 3.0-3.49: | 44% | Live on campus: | 79% |
| | | International: | 2% |

**Basis for selection.** Strength of the high school transcript, grades and test scores important. Some programs review additional material such as art portfolios or auditions. **Homeschooled:** Transcript of courses and grades required.

**High school preparation.** College-preparatory program recommended. 20 units required; 24 recommended. Required and recommended units include English 4, mathematics 3-4, social studies 1, history 2-3, science 3-4 (laboratory 1), foreign language 2-3, visual/performing arts 1 and academic electives 5.

**2009-2010 Annual costs.** Tuition/fees: $7,117; $20,341 out-of-state. Room/board: $8,335.

**2008-2009 Financial aid. Need-based:** 2,274 full-time freshmen applied for aid; 1,723 were judged to have need; 1,723 of these received aid. Average need met was 58%. Average scholarship/grant was $5,344; average loan $3,427. 36% of total undergraduate aid awarded as scholarships/grants, 64% as loans/jobs. **Non-need-based:** Awarded to 3,888 full-time undergraduates, including 1,334 freshmen. Scholarships awarded for academics, alumni affiliation, art, athletics, leadership, music/drama.

**Application procedures. Admission:** Closing date 1/15. $40 fee, may be waived for applicants with need. Admission notification on a rolling basis beginning on or about 12/1. Must reply by May 1 or within 4 week(s) if notified thereafter. Deadline for freshmen applying for guaranteed admission to the School of Medicine is 11/15. **Financial aid:** Priority date 3/1; no closing date. FAFSA required. Applicants notified by 4/1; Applicants notified on a rolling basis starting 4/1; must reply within 2 week(s) of notification.

**Academics. Special study options:** Accelerated study, combined bachelor's/graduate degree, cooperative education, distance learning, double major, dual enrollment of high school students, ESL, exchange student, honors, independent study, internships, liberal arts/career combination, student-designed major, study abroad, teacher certification program. **Credit/placement by examination:** AP, CLEP, IB, institutional tests. **Support services:** Learning center, reduced course load, study skills assistance, tutoring, writing center.

**Honors college/program.** Entering students with combined SAT scores of at least 1910 who rank in the upper 15% of their graduating class and have a 3.5 or higher unweighted high school GPA or are the recipients of a VCU Presidential Scholarship are eligible.

**Majors. Area/ethnic studies:** African-American, women's. **Biology:** General, bioinformatics. **Business:** General, accounting, managerial economics, marketing. **Communications:** Media studies. **Computer sciences:** General, information systems. **Conservation:** Environmental studies. **Education:** Art, health. **Engineering:** Biomedical, chemical, computer, electrical, mechanical. **Foreign languages:** General. **Health:** Clinical lab science, dental hygiene, nursing (RN), radiologic technology/medical imaging. **History:** General. **Interdisciplinary:** Biological/physical sciences, global studies. **Math:** General. **Parks/recreation:** General. **Philosophy/religion:** Philosophy, religion. **Physical sciences:** Chemistry, physics. **Protective services:** Emergency management/homeland security, forensics, law enforcement admin. **Psychology:** General. **Public administration:** Social work. **Social sciences:** Anthropology, political science, sociology, urban studies. **Visual/performing arts:** Art history/conservation, cinematography, crafts, dance, dramatic, fashion design, graphic design, illustration, interior design, music performance, painting, photography, sculpture. **Other:** Financial technology, Kinetic imaging.

**Most popular majors.** Business/marketing 14%, health sciences 11%, psychology 9%, security/protective services 8%, visual/performing arts 13%.

**Computing on campus.** PC or laptop required. 1,733 workstations in dormitories, library, computer center, student center. Dormitories wired for high-speed internet access and linked to campus network. Commuter students can connect to campus network. Online course registration, online library, helpline, repair service, student web hosting, wireless network available.

**Student life. Freshman orientation:** Mandatory, $40 fee. Preregistration for classes offered. **Housing:** Coed dorms, special housing for disabled, apartments available. $250 fully refundable deposit, deadline 6/1. **Activities:** Pep band, choral groups, dance, drama, international student organizations, literary magazine, musical theater, radio station, student government, student newspaper, symphony orchestra, TV station, Alternative Spring Break, Alpha Phi Omega Service Fraternity, Intervarsity Christian Fellowship, Muslim students association, Reformed University Fellowship, College Republicans, Young Democrats, Tiranga Indian National Dance, Filipino Americans Coming Together, Black Caucus.

**Athletics.** NAIA, NCAA. **Intercollegiate:** Baseball M, basketball, cross-country, field hockey W, golf M, soccer, tennis, track and field, volleyball W. **Intramural:** Badminton, basketball, football (non-tackle), racquetball, soccer, softball, table tennis, tennis, volleyball. **Team name:** Rams.

**Student services.** Adult student services, alcohol/substance abuse counseling, career counseling, student employment services, financial aid counseling, health services, on-campus daycare, personal counseling, placement for graduates, veterans' counselor. **Physically disabled:** Services for visually, speech, hearing impaired.

**Contact.** E-mail: ugrad@vcu.edu
Phone: (804) 828-1222 Toll-free number: (800) 841-3638
Fax: (804) 828-1899
Sybil Halloran, Director of Admissions, Virginia Commonwealth University, Box 842526, Richmond, VA 23284-2526

## Virginia Intermont College
**Bristol, Virginia**
www.vic.edu                    CB code: 5857

- Private 4-year liberal arts and teachers college affiliated with Baptist faith
- Residential campus in small city
- 577 degree-seeking undergraduates
- 46% of applicants admitted
- SAT or ACT (ACT writing recommended) required
- 30% graduate within 6 years; 1.6% enter graduate study

**General.** Founded in 1884. Regionally accredited. Evening and weekend college available for working adults; limited majors available. **Degrees:** 131 bachelor's, 1 associate awarded. **Location:** 144 miles from Roanoke, 114 miles from Knoxville, Tennessee. **Calendar:** Semester, limited summer session. **Full-time faculty:** 39 total; 80% have terminal degrees, 5% minority, 44% women. **Part-time faculty:** 42 total; 40% have terminal degrees, 2% minority, 57% women. **Class size:** 93% < 20, 7% 20-39, less than 1% 40-49. **Special facilities:** 120-acre riding center with 2 indoor riding arenas.

**Freshman class profile.** 2,485 applied, 1,136 admitted, 132 enrolled.

| Mid 50% test scores | | | |
|---|---|---|---|
| SAT critical reading: | 360-640 | GPA 3.0-3.49: | 31% |
| SAT math: | 370-580 | GPA 2.0-2.99: | 42% |
| ACT composite: | 11-27 | Rank in top quarter: | 24% |
| GPA 3.75 or higher: | 14% | Rank in top tenth: | 7% |
| GPA 3.50-3.74: | 13% | End year in good standing: | 96% |
| | | Return as sophomores: | 60% |

**Basis for selection.** School achievement record, SAT or ACT scores, school and community activities important. Essay, interview recommended for all; audition recommended for equine studies, performing arts; portfolio recommended for art, photography. **Homeschooled:** Statement describing homeschool structure and mission, transcript of courses and grades, state high school equivalency certificate required. **Learning Disabled:** Students admitted conditionally, restricted to 12 credit hours in first semester.

**High school preparation.** College-preparatory program recommended. 16 units required. Required units include English 4, mathematics 2, social studies 2, science 2 (laboratory 1) and academic electives 5.

**2010-2011 Annual costs.** Tuition/fees (projected): $24,300. Room/board: $7,500. Books/supplies: $1,200. Personal expenses: $3,000.

**2008-2009 Financial aid. Need-based:** 82 full-time freshmen applied for aid; 74 were judged to have need; 74 of these received aid. Average need met was 67%. Average scholarship/grant was $12,818; average loan $3,791. 49% of total undergraduate aid awarded as scholarships/grants, 51% as loans/jobs. **Non-need-based:** Awarded to 95 full-time undergraduates, including 26 freshmen. Scholarships awarded for art, athletics, music/drama, religious affiliation, state residency.

**Application procedures. Admission:** No deadline. $25 fee, may be waived for applicants with need. Admission notification on a rolling basis. **Financial aid:** Priority date 3/1, closing date 6/1. FAFSA required. Applicants notified on a rolling basis starting 2/15; must reply within 3 week(s) of notification.

**Academics. Special study options:** Accelerated study, cross-registration, distance learning, double major, dual enrollment of high school students, honors, independent study, internships, teacher certification program. **Credit/placement by examination:** AP, CLEP, IB, institutional tests. No maximums for prior work or credit by examination; no cumulative restrictions imposed upon hours earned toward elective credits. Students must complete at least one half of major and take minimum of 25% of classes at school to meet minimum residency requirement. **Support services:** Learning center, reduced course load, study skills assistance, tutoring, writing center.

**Majors. Agriculture:** Equestrian studies. **Biology:** General. **Business:** Business admin, international, marketing. **Conservation:** Environmental studies. **Education:** General, art, biology, elementary, English, physical, secondary, social studies, special. **Health:** Premedicine, preveterinary. **History:** General. **Legal studies:** General, paralegal, prelaw. **Parks/recreation:** Health/fitness, sports admin. **Philosophy/religion:** Religion. **Protective services:** Law enforcement admin. **Psychology:** General. **Public administration:** Social work. **Social sciences:** Political science. **Visual/performing arts:** Art, dance, dramatic, photography.

**Most popular majors.** Agriculture 9%, business/marketing 21%, interdisciplinary studies 27%, parks/recreation 6%, visual/performing arts 20%.

**Computing on campus.** 100 workstations in dormitories, library, computer center. Dormitories wired for high-speed internet access and linked to campus network. Commuter students can connect to campus network. On-line course registration, online library, helpline, wireless network available.

**Student life. Freshman orientation:** Mandatory. Preregistration for classes offered. **Policies:** Alcohol and tobacco use prohibited on campus. No open flame items or cooking appliances other than microwave ovens. (Juniors and seniors may live off campus, but all other students under 21 years of age not living with parents must live on campus.). **Housing:** Guaranteed on-campus for all undergraduates. Coed dorms, single-sex dorms, apartments, wellness housing available. $200 partly refundable deposit. **Activities:** Campus ministries, choral groups, drama, international student organizations, music ensembles, musical theater, student government, Christian student union, Cardinal Key, social work action group, Fellowship of Christian Athletes, Alpha Phi Omega.

**Athletics.** NAIA. **Intercollegiate:** Baseball M, basketball, cheerleading M, equestrian, golf M, soccer M, softball W, volleyball W. **Intramural:** Basketball, bowling, football (non-tackle), golf, softball, table tennis, volleyball. **Team name:** Cobras.

**Student services.** Adult student services, alcohol/substance abuse counseling, chaplain/spiritual director, career counseling, student employment services, financial aid counseling, health services, minority student services, personal counseling, placement for graduates. **Physically disabled:** Services for visually, hearing impaired.

**Contact.** E-mail: viadmit@vic.edu
Phone: (276) 466-7856 Toll-free number: (800) 451-1842
Fax: (276) 466-7855
Beth Shumaker, Vice President of Enrollment, Virginia Intermont College, 1013 Moore Street, Bristol, VA 24201

## Virginia Military Institute
**Lexington, Virginia**  CB member
**www.vmi.edu**  CB code: 5858

- Public 4-year liberal arts and military college
- Residential campus in small town
- 1,500 degree-seeking undergraduates: 8% women, 6% African American, 4% Asian American, 4% Hispanic American, 2% international
- 56% of applicants admitted
- SAT or ACT (ACT writing optional) required
- 74% graduate within 6 years

**General.** Founded in 1839. Regionally accredited. Mandatory ROTC classes and optional commissioning in the Army, Air Force, Navy, or Marines. **Degrees:** 290 bachelor's awarded. **ROTC:** Army, Naval, Air Force. **Location:** 55 miles from Roanoke, 140 miles from Richmond. **Calendar:** Semester, limited summer session. **Full-time faculty:** 122 total; 96% have terminal degrees, 8% minority, 18% women. **Part-time faculty:** 50 total; 38% have terminal degrees, 10% minority, 30% women. **Class size:** 71% < 20, 29% 20-39. **Special facilities:** Historical museums, research library, observatory, particle accelerator.

**Freshman class profile.** 1,598 applied, 889 admitted, 455 enrolled.

| Mid 50% test scores | | GPA 2.0-2.99: | 17% |
|---|---|---|---|
| SAT critical reading: | 520-610 | Rank in top quarter: | 39% |
| SAT math: | 530-610 | Rank in top tenth: | 2% |
| SAT writing: | 480-580 | Return as sophomores: | 84% |
| ACT composite: | 22-27 | Out-of-state: | 44% |
| GPA 3.75 or higher: | 24% | Live on campus: | 100% |
| GPA 3.50-3.74: | 20% | International: | 2% |
| GPA 3.0-3.49: | 39% | | |

**Basis for selection.** GED not accepted. Admissions based on secondary school record, class rank, standardized test scores, character, and personal qualities. Interview, extracurricular activities, state residency, minority status, and volunteer work also important. **Homeschooled:** Require transcript with list of texts used or group affiliation.

**High school preparation.** College-preparatory program required. 16 units required; 19 recommended. Required and recommended units include English 4, mathematics 3-4, social studies 2, history 1, science 3-4 (laboratory 3-4) and foreign language 3-4.

**2010-2011 Annual costs.** Tuition/fees (projected): $11,190; $28,738 out-of-state. Room/board: $6,792.

**2008-2009 Financial aid. Need-based:** 297 full-time freshmen applied for aid; 198 were judged to have need; 192 of these received aid. Average need met was 89.5%. Average scholarship/grant was $9,600; average loan

$4,130. 80% of total undergraduate aid awarded as scholarships/grants, 20% as loans/jobs. **Non-need-based:** Awarded to 475 full-time undergraduates, including 139 freshmen. Scholarships awarded for academics, alumni affiliation, athletics, leadership.

**Application procedures. Admission:** Closing date 2/1 (postmark date). $40 fee, may be waived for applicants with need. Admission notification on a rolling basis beginning on or about 1/1. Must reply by 5/1. Must reply by May 1 or within 2 week(s) if notified thereafter. **Financial aid:** Priority date 3/1, closing date 3/1. FAFSA, institutional form required. Applicants notified on a rolling basis starting 3/1; must reply by 5/1.

**Academics. Special study options:** Double major, exchange student, honors, independent study, internships, study abroad, teacher certification program. Summer Transition program: Optional for incoming freshmen. **Credit/placement by examination:** AP, CLEP, IB, institutional tests. No policy, but it is unlikely any student would receive more than 36 hours credit. **Support services:** Learning center, pre-admission summer program, study skills assistance, tutoring, writing center.

**Majors. Biology:** General. **Computer sciences:** Computer science. **Engineering:** Civil, electrical, mechanical. **Foreign languages:** General. **History:** General. **Interdisciplinary:** Global studies. **Math:** General. **Physical sciences:** Chemistry, physics. **Psychology:** General. **Social sciences:** Economics.

**Most popular majors.** Biology 6%, engineering/engineering technologies 26%, English 6%, history 15%, physical sciences 6%, psychology 11%, social sciences 27%.

**Computing on campus.** PC or laptop required. 200 workstations in library, computer center. Dormitories wired for high-speed internet access and linked to campus network. Online course registration, online library, helpline, repair service, wireless network available.

**Student life. Freshman orientation:** Mandatory. 8 days before beginning of fall classes. Optional month-long summer orientation program coincides with summer academic session, and participants can complete 1 freshman course. **Policies:** Student-run honor system integral part of institution. **Housing:** Guaranteed on-campus for all undergraduates. Barracks house 3-5 students per room. **Activities:** Bands, choral groups, drama, literary magazine, music ensembles, musical theater, student government, student newspaper, more than 50 clubs and student organizations available.

**Athletics.** NCAA. **Intercollegiate:** Baseball M, basketball M, cross-country, diving M, football (tackle) M, golf M, lacrosse M, rifle M, soccer, swimming, tennis M, track and field, wrestling M. **Intramural:** Basketball, football (non-tackle), soccer, softball. **Team name:** Keydets.

**Student services.** Alcohol/substance abuse counseling, chaplain/spiritual director, career counseling, student employment services, financial aid counseling, health services, personal counseling, placement for graduates.

**Contact.** E-mail: admissions@vmi.edu
Phone: (540) 464-7211 Toll-free number: (800) 767-4207
Fax: (540) 464-7746
Col. Vernon Beitzel, Director of Admissions, Virginia Military Institute, VMI Office of Admissions, Lexington, VA 24450-9967

## Virginia Polytechnic Institute and State University
**Blacksburg, Virginia**  CB member
**www.vt.edu**  CB code: 5859

- Public 4-year university
- Residential campus in large town
- 23,461 degree-seeking undergraduates: 2% part-time, 43% women, 4% African American, 8% Asian American, 3% Hispanic American, 2% international
- 7,276 degree-seeking graduate students
- 67% of applicants admitted
- SAT or ACT with writing required
- 80% graduate within 6 years

**General.** Founded in 1872. Regionally accredited. Option of enrolling as member of cadet corps. **Degrees:** 5,307 bachelor's, 51 associate awarded; master's, doctoral, professional offered. **ROTC:** Army, Naval, Air Force. **Location:** 38 miles from Roanoke. **Calendar:** Semester, limited summer session. **Full-time faculty:** 1,364 total; 90% have terminal degrees, 17% minority, 32% women. **Part-time faculty:** 224 total; 8% minority, 42% women. **Class size:** 24% < 20, 44% 20-39, 11% 40-49, 12% 50-99, 9%

>100. **Special facilities:** Natural history, geology and art museums, observatory, wind tunnel, Black cultural center, digital music center, robotics laboratory, multimedia laboratory, media center, women's center, math emporium, advanced communications/information technology center, teaching forest.

**Freshman class profile.** 21,053 applied, 14,040 admitted, 5,050 enrolled.

| Mid 50% test scores | | GPA 2.0-2.99: | 1% |
| --- | --- | --- | --- |
| SAT critical reading: | 540-640 | Rank in top quarter: | 85% |
| SAT math: | 570-670 | Rank in top tenth: | 44% |
| SAT writing: | 540-630 | Return as sophomores: | 91% |
| GPA 3.75 or higher: | 64% | Out-of-state: | 27% |
| GPA 3.50-3.74: | 25% | Live on campus: | 91% |
| GPA 3.0-3.49: | 10% | International: | 2% |

**Basis for selection.** High school course work, grades, test scores most important. Prospective students encouraged to pursue rigorous preparatory course of study through senior year. Students from other than accredited schools must take, in addition to SAT (including mandatory Writing component) or ACT (including Writing component), SAT Subject Tests in Math (Level Ic or IIc) and second area of study to be chosen by applicant. SAT Subject Tests may not be required if student has dual-enrollment or AP credit. Audition required for music. **Homeschooled:** Transcript of courses and grades required. Must submit standardized test scores; statement describing homeschool structure and mission recommended but not required.

**High school preparation.** 18 units required. Required and recommended units include English 4, mathematics 3-4, social studies 1, history 1, science 2-3 (laboratory 2), foreign language 3 and academic electives 4. Preference given to applicants with mathematics beyond Algebra II. 4 mathematics required for general engineering, biochemistry, chemistry, computer science, math, physics and statistics. 3 science including physics required for engineering and recommended for all science-related majors.

**2009-2010 Annual costs.** Tuition/fees: $8,605; $21,488 out-of-state. Room/board: $5,824. Books/supplies: $1,080. Personal expenses: $1,700.

**2008-2009 Financial aid. Need-based:** 3,837 full-time freshmen applied for aid; 2,245 were judged to have need; 1,992 of these received aid. Average need met was 63%. Average scholarship/grant was $6,653; average loan $3,837. 54% of total undergraduate aid awarded as scholarships/grants, 46% as loans/jobs. **Non-need-based:** Awarded to 3,941 full-time undergraduates, including 1,210 freshmen. Scholarships awarded for academics, art, athletics, leadership, minority status, music/drama, ROTC, state residency.

**Application procedures. Admission:** Closing date 1/15 (postmark date). $50 fee, may be waived for applicants with need. Admission notification 4/1. Must reply by 5/1. $400 matriculation deposit required. **Financial aid:** Priority date 3/1; no closing date. FAFSA required. Must reply by 5/1 or within 4 week(s) of notification.

**Academics. Special study options:** Accelerated study, combined bachelor's/graduate degree, cooperative education, distance learning, double major, dual enrollment of high school students, ESL, honors, independent study, internships, study abroad, teacher certification program, Washington semester. **Credit/placement by examination:** AP, CLEP, IB, institutional tests. 12 credit hours maximum toward associate degree, 12 toward bachelor's. **Support services:** Learning center, pre-admission summer program, study skills assistance, tutoring, writing center.

**Majors. Agriculture:** General, agronomy, animal sciences, dairy, economics, food science, horticultural science. **Architecture:** Architecture, landscape. **Biology:** General, biochemistry. **Business:** Accounting, business admin, construction management, finance, hospitality admin, management science, managerial economics, marketing. **Communications:** General. **Computer sciences:** General. **Conservation:** Environmental science, environmental studies, forestry. **Education:** Secondary. **Engineering:** Aerospace, agricultural, chemical, civil, computer, construction, electrical, industrial, materials, mechanical, mechanics, mining. **Family/consumer sciences:** Business, family studies, food/nutrition. **Foreign languages:** General. **History:** General. **Interdisciplinary:** Science/society. **Liberal arts:** Arts/sciences. **Math:** General, statistics. **Philosophy/religion:** Philosophy. **Physical sciences:** Chemistry, geology, physics. **Psychology:** General. **Public administration:** Policy analysis. **Social sciences:** Economics, geography, international relations, political science, sociology. **Visual/performing arts:** Art, dramatic, industrial design, interior design. **Other:** Biomedical and veterinary sciences.

**Most popular majors.** Biology 7%, business/marketing 22%, engineering/engineering technologies 20%, family/consumer sciences 8%, social sciences 9%.

**Computing on campus.** PC or laptop required. 1,000 workstations in library, computer center. Dormitories wired for high-speed internet access and linked to campus network. Commuter students can connect to campus network. Online course registration, online library, helpline, repair service, student web hosting, wireless network available.

**Student life. Freshman orientation:** Available, $140 fee. Preregistration for classes offered. Day and a half long program held in July. **Policies:** Freshmen required to live on campus, unless living with parents or close relatives, married, veteran, or at least 21 years old. Honor system in force. **Housing:** Guaranteed on-campus for freshmen. Coed dorms, single-sex dorms, special housing for disabled, fraternity/sorority housing, wellness housing available. Cadets live in cadet residence halls. Foreign language hall and academic success hall available. **Activities:** Bands, choral groups, dance, drama, literary magazine, music ensembles, musical theater, radio station, student government, student newspaper, 400 clubs and organizations available.

**Athletics.** NCAA. **Intercollegiate:** Baseball M, basketball, cheerleading, cross-country, diving, football (tackle) M, golf M, lacrosse W, soccer, softball W, swimming, tennis, track and field, volleyball W, wrestling M. **Intramural:** Basketball, bowling, football (non-tackle), golf, racquetball, soccer, softball, squash, swimming, table tennis, tennis, volleyball, water polo. **Team name:** Hokies.

**Student services.** Alcohol/substance abuse counseling, chaplain/spiritual director, career counseling, student employment services, financial aid counseling, health services, legal services, minority student services, personal counseling, placement for graduates, veterans' counselor, women's services. **Physically disabled:** Services for visually, hearing impaired.

**Contact.** E-mail: vtadmiss@vt.edu
Phone: (540) 231-6267 Fax: (540) 231-3242
Mildred Johnson, Director of Undergraduate Admissions, Virginia Polytechnic Institute and State University, 201 Burruss Hall, Blacksburg, VA 24061-0202

---

## Virginia State University
**Petersburg, Virginia**      **CB member**
**www.vsu.edu**      **CB code: 5860**

▶ Public 4-year university
▶ Residential campus in large town
▶ 4,775 degree-seeking undergraduates: 5% part-time, 62% women, 93% African American, 1% Hispanic American
▶ 416 degree-seeking graduate students
▶ 67% of applicants admitted
▶ SAT or ACT (ACT writing optional) required
▶ 40% graduate within 6 years

**General.** Founded in 1882. Regionally accredited. **Degrees:** 609 bachelor's, 8 associate awarded; master's, doctoral offered. **ROTC:** Army. **Location:** 25 miles from Richmond. **Calendar:** Semester, limited summer session. **Full-time faculty:** 210 total; 73% minority, 44% women. **Part-time faculty:** 103 total; 81% minority, 52% women. **Class size:** 37% < 20, 44% 20-39, 9% 40-49, 10% 50-99, less than 1% >100.

**Freshman class profile.** 6,341 applied, 4,225 admitted, 1,204 enrolled.

| Mid 50% test scores | | GPA 3.0-3.49: | 24% |
| --- | --- | --- | --- |
| SAT critical reading: | 400-480 | GPA 2.0-2.99: | 66% |
| SAT math: | 390-470 | Rank in top quarter: | 24% |
| SAT writing: | 380-460 | Rank in top tenth: | 7% |
| ACT composite: | 18-21 | Return as sophomores: | 67% |
| GPA 3.75 or higher: | 4% | Out-of-state: | 40% |
| GPA 3.50-3.74: | 6% | Live on campus: | 95% |

**Basis for selection.** School achievement record most important; recommendation required. Essay recommended for all; audition required for music; portfolio recommended for art.

**High school preparation.** 11 units required. Required and recommended units include English 4, mathematics 3, social studies 2, science 2 (laboratory 1) and foreign language 2. Mathematics requirement must include algebra I.

**2009-2010 Annual costs.** Tuition/fees: $6,174; $14,236 out-of-state. Out of state students pay an additional fee. Room/board: $8,050. Books/supplies: $900. Personal expenses: $775.

**2008-2009 Financial aid. Non-need-based:** Scholarships awarded for academics, alumni affiliation, art, athletics, job skills, leadership, music/drama, religious affiliation, ROTC. **Additional information:** Strongly recommend that students apply for scholarship assistance through federal, state, local and private agencies.

**Application procedures. Admission:** Priority date 3/31; deadline 5/1 (postmark date). $25 fee, may be waived for applicants with need. Admission notification on a rolling basis. Must reply by May 1 or within 2 week(s) if notified thereafter. **Financial aid:** Priority date 3/31, closing date 5/1. FAFSA, institutional form required. Applicants notified on a rolling basis starting 5/1; must reply within 2 week(s) of notification.

**Academics. Special study options:** Cooperative education, double major, dual enrollment of high school students, exchange student, honors, independent study, internships, teacher certification program. **Credit/placement by examination:** AP, CLEP, institutional tests. 12 credit hours maximum toward bachelor's degree. **Support services:** Study skills assistance, tutoring, writing center.

**Majors. Agriculture:** General. **Biology:** General. **Business:** Accounting, business admin, hospitality admin, managerial economics, marketing. **Communications:** Media studies. **Computer sciences:** Computer science, information technology. **Education:** Business, physical, trade/industrial. **Engineering:** Computer, manufacturing. **Engineering technology:** General, electrical, mechanical. **Family/consumer sciences:** Communication. **History:** General. **Liberal arts:** Arts/sciences. **Math:** General. **Physical sciences:** Chemistry, physics. **Protective services:** Criminal justice. **Psychology:** General. **Public administration:** General, social work. **Social sciences:** Political science, sociology. **Visual/performing arts:** General, music performance.

**Most popular majors.** Business/marketing 20%, communications/journalism 9%, computer/information sciences 7%, education 12%, interdisciplinary studies 8%, psychology 9%, security/protective services 10%.

**Computing on campus.** 750 workstations in dormitories, library, student center. Dormitories wired for high-speed internet access and linked to campus network. Commuter students can connect to campus network. Online course registration, online library, helpline, repair service available.

**Student life. Freshman orientation:** Mandatory, $75 fee. Preregistration for classes offered. Two-day orientation held at various times in the summer. **Housing:** Guaranteed on-campus for freshmen. Coed dorms, single-sex dorms, apartments, wellness housing available. $150 deposit. **Activities:** Bands, campus ministries, choral groups, dance, drama, literary magazine, music ensembles, radio station, student government, student newspaper, TV station, NAACP, Black Students Against Drugs, Muslim student organization, peer mediators, Betterment of Brothers and Sisters, Caribbean students association, Institute for Leadership Development.

**Athletics. NCAA. Intercollegiate:** Baseball M, basketball, bowling W, cheerleading, cross-country, football (tackle) M, golf, softball W, tennis, track and field, volleyball W. **Intramural:** Basketball, football (tackle) M, swimming, table tennis, tennis, track and field, volleyball W. **Team name:** Trojans.

**Student services.** Alcohol/substance abuse counseling, chaplain/spiritual director, career counseling, services for economically disadvantaged, student employment services, financial aid counseling, health services, personal counseling, placement for graduates, veterans' counselor. **Physically disabled:** Services for visually, hearing impaired.

**Contact.** E-mail: admiss@vsu.edu
Phone: (804) 524-5902 Toll-free number: (800) 871-7611
Fax: (804) 524-5055
Irene Logan, Director of Admissions, Virginia State University, One Hayden Drive, Petersburg, VA 23806

## Virginia Union University
**Richmond, Virginia**    CB member
www.vuu.edu                CB code: 5862

- Private 4-year university and liberal arts college affiliated with Baptist faith
- Residential campus in small city
- 1,210 degree-seeking undergraduates
- 81% of applicants admitted
- SAT or ACT (ACT writing recommended) required

**General.** Founded in 1865. Regionally accredited. **Degrees:** 141 bachelor's awarded; master's, professional offered. **ROTC:** Army. **Location:** 90 miles from Norfolk, 100 miles from Washington, DC. **Calendar:** Semester, limited summer session. **Full-time faculty:** 64 total. **Part-time faculty:** 34 total. **Special facilities:** Police academy, learning resource center.

**Freshman class profile.** 5,260 applied, 4,257 admitted, 602 enrolled.

| Mid 50% test scores | | | |
|---|---|---|---|
| SAT critical reading: | 350-420 | GPA 3.0-3.49: | 8% |
| SAT math: | 320-410 | GPA 2.0-2.99: | 70% |
| ACT composite: | 13-17 | Rank in top quarter: | 12% |
| GPA 3.75 or higher: | 2% | Rank in top tenth: | 4% |
| GPA 3.50-3.74: | 2% | Out-of-state: | 46% |
| | | Live on campus: | 79% |

**Basis for selection.** Secondary school record, test scores, extracurricular activities most important. Essay, interview, and talent or ability also important. Essay recommended for all. Interview recommended for academically weak. Audition required for band, choir, music, university players.

**High school preparation.** 16 units required. Required units include English 4, mathematics 3, social studies 2, science 2, foreign language 2 and academic electives 3.

**2009-2010 Annual costs.** Tuition/fees: $13,934. Room/board: $6,506. Books/supplies: $1,080. Personal expenses: $1,750.

**2009-2010 Financial aid. Non-need-based:** Scholarships awarded for academics, athletics, ROTC, state residency.

**Application procedures. Admission:** Priority date 6/30; no deadline. $25 fee, may be waived for applicants with need. Admission notification on a rolling basis. **Financial aid:** Priority date 4/27; no closing date. FAFSA required. Applicants notified on a rolling basis starting 5/1; must reply within 2 week(s) of notification.

**Academics. Special study options:** Cooperative education, honors, independent study, internships, liberal arts/career combination, teacher certification program, weekend college. **Credit/placement by examination:** AP, CLEP, IB, institutional tests. 18 credit hours maximum toward bachelor's degree. **Support services:** Learning center, reduced course load, remedial instruction, tutoring, writing center.

**Majors. Biology:** General. **Business:** Accounting, business admin, finance, management information systems, sales/distribution. **Communications:** Journalism. **Computer sciences:** General. **Education:** Multi-level teacher. **History:** General. **Interdisciplinary:** Natural sciences. **Math:** General. **Philosophy/religion:** Religion. **Physical sciences:** Chemistry. **Psychology:** General. **Public administration:** Social work. **Social sciences:** Political science, sociology. **Visual/performing arts:** Art, dramatic, music theory/composition, piano/organ, voice/opera.

**Most popular majors.** Business/marketing 14%, education 9%, psychology 8%, social sciences 11%, theological studies 42%.

**Computing on campus.** PC or laptop required. 148 workstations in library, computer center. Dormitories linked to campus network. Online course registration, wireless network available.

**Student life. Freshman orientation:** Mandatory. Preregistration for classes offered. **Housing:** Coed dorms, single-sex dorms available. $250 deposit, deadline 7/1. **Activities:** Bands, campus ministries, choral groups, dance, drama, music ensembles, musical theater, opera, student government, student newspaper, social work club, sociology club, student education association, Ministers Alliance.

**Athletics. NCAA. Intercollegiate:** Basketball, bowling W, cross-country, football (tackle) M, golf, softball W, tennis, track and field, volleyball W. **Intramural:** Basketball, football (non-tackle) M, softball, table tennis. **Team name:** Panthers.

**Student services.** Career counseling, student employment services, health services, personal counseling, placement for graduates.

**Contact.** E-mail: admissions@vuu.edu
Phone: (804) 342-3570 Toll-free number: (800) 368-3227
Fax: (804) 342-3511
Sandra Williamson, Office of Enrollment, Virginia Union University, 1500 North Lombardy Street, Richmond, VA 23220

## Virginia University of Lynchburg
**Lynchburg, Virginia**
www.vul.edu

- Private 4-year liberal arts and seminary college
- Commuter campus in small city
- 228 degree-seeking undergraduates: 56% part-time, 59% women
- 84 degree-seeking graduate students
- 66% graduate within 6 years

**General.** Regionally accredited; also accredited by TRACS. **Degrees:** 76 bachelor's, 16 associate awarded; master's, doctoral offered. **Calendar:** Semester, limited summer session. **Full-time faculty:** 10 total; 100% have terminal degrees, 100% minority, 40% women. **Part-time faculty:** 72 total; 49% have terminal degrees, 90% minority, 42% women.

**Basis for selection.** Open admission. **Homeschooled:** Transcript of courses and grades, state high school equivalency certificate required.

**2009-2010 Annual costs.** Tuition/fees: $5,300. Books/supplies: $650.

**Application procedures. Admission:** No deadline. $25 fee, may be waived for applicants with need. Application must be submitted on paper. Admission notification on a rolling basis.

**Academics. Special study options:** Distance learning, external degree. **Credit/placement by examination:** AP, CLEP, IB, institutional tests. **Support services:** Learning center, reduced course load, remedial instruction, study skills assistance, tutoring, writing center.

**Majors. Business:** Business admin, management science. **Philosophy/religion:** Religion. **Social sciences:** Sociology.

**Computing on campus.** 10 workstations in library, computer center. Dormitories wired for high-speed internet access and linked to campus network. Commuter students can connect to campus network. Online library, helpline, wireless network available.

**Student life. Freshman orientation:** Mandatory. Preregistration for classes offered. **Housing:** Coed dorms available. $100 partly refundable deposit. **Activities:** Campus ministries, choral groups, student government.

**Athletics. Intramural:** Basketball.

**Student services.** Adult student services, chaplain/spiritual director, career counseling, financial aid counseling, health services, personal counseling, veterans' counselor.

**Contact.** E-mail: cglass@vul.edu
Phone: (434) 528-5276 ext. 106 Fax: (434) 528-4257
Cheryl Glass, Director of Admissions, Virginia University of Lynchburg, 2058 Garfield Avenue, Lynchburg, VA 24501-6417

## Virginia Wesleyan College
**Norfolk, Virginia**
**www.vwc.edu**

**CB member**
**CB code: 5867**

- Private 4-year liberal arts college affiliated with United Methodist Church
- Residential campus in large city
- 1,300 degree-seeking undergraduates: 12% part-time, 62% women, 21% African American, 2% Asian American, 4% Hispanic American, 1% international
- 75% of applicants admitted
- SAT or ACT (ACT writing optional), application essay required
- 44% graduate within 6 years; 32% enter graduate study

**General.** Founded in 1961. Regionally accredited. **Degrees:** 270 bachelor's awarded. **ROTC:** Army. **Location:** 8 miles from downtown. **Calendar:** 4-1-4, limited summer session. **Full-time faculty:** 84 total; 89% have terminal degrees, 10% minority, 40% women. **Part-time faculty:** 58 total; 10% have terminal degrees, 9% minority, 59% women. **Class size:** 75% < 20, 25% 20-39. **Special facilities:** Research vessel, center for sacred music, greenhouse, center for the study of religious freedom, rock climbing wall.

**Freshman class profile.** 1,372 applied, 1,033 admitted, 319 enrolled.

| Mid 50% test scores | | | |
|---|---|---|---|
| SAT critical reading: | 440-530 | GPA 2.0-2.99: | 45% |
| SAT math: | 440-540 | Rank in top quarter: | 34% |
| SAT writing: | 430-520 | Rank in top tenth: | 10% |
| ACT composite: | 18-23 | End year in good standing: | 90% |
| GPA 3.75 or higher: | 14% | Return as sophomores: | 69% |
| GPA 3.50-3.74: | 14% | Out-of-state: | 26% |
| GPA 3.0-3.49: | 26% | Live on campus: | 80% |

**Basis for selection.** Above average grades in solid college-preparatory curriculum, SAT scores, campus interview, personal statement, extracurricular activities important. **Homeschooled:** Transcript of courses and grades required. **Learning Disabled:** Interview with student disabilities coordinator, appropriate documentation dated within past 3-5 years.

**High school preparation.** College-preparatory program recommended. 12 units required; 16 recommended. Required and recommended units include English 4, mathematics 3, history 1, science 2 (laboratory 2), foreign language 2, computer science 1 and academic electives 4.

**2009-2010 Annual costs.** Tuition/fees: $27,476. Room/board: $7,696. Books/supplies: $1,000. Personal expenses: $1,800.

**2008-2009 Financial aid. Need-based:** 308 full-time freshmen applied for aid; 256 were judged to have need; 252 of these received aid. Average need met was 86%. Average scholarship/grant was $15,330; average loan $5,828. 63% of total undergraduate aid awarded as scholarships/grants, 37% as loans/jobs. **Non-need-based:** Awarded to 386 full-time undergraduates, including 124 freshmen. Scholarships awarded for academics, alumni affiliation, leadership, religious affiliation, ROTC, state residency.

**Application procedures. Admission:** Priority date 3/1; no deadline. $40 fee, may be waived for applicants with need. Admission notification on a rolling basis beginning on or about 9/15. Must reply by May 1 or within 2 week(s) if notified thereafter. **Financial aid:** Priority date 3/1; no closing date. FAFSA required. Applicants notified on a rolling basis starting 2/15; must reply by 5/1 or within 2 week(s) of notification.

**Academics. Special study options:** Accelerated study, cross-registration, distance learning, double major, honors, independent study, internships, liberal arts/career combination, student-designed major, study abroad, teacher certification program. Alternative teacher certification program; living and learning communities; distance learning/hybrid courses offerings. **Credit/placement by examination:** AP, CLEP, IB, institutional tests. 30 credit hours maximum toward bachelor's degree. **Support services:** Learning center, reduced course load, remedial instruction, study skills assistance, tutoring, writing center.

**Majors. Area/ethnic studies:** Women's. **Biology:** General. **Business:** Business admin. **Communications:** General. **Computer sciences:** Computer science. **Conservation:** Environmental studies. **Education:** Art. **Foreign languages:** General, French, German, Spanish. **Health:** Predental, premedicine, prepharmacy, preveterinary. **History:** General. **Interdisciplinary:** Global studies, math/computer science, natural sciences. **Liberal arts:** Arts/sciences, humanities. **Math:** General. **Parks/recreation:** General. **Philosophy/religion:** Philosophy, religion. **Physical sciences:** Chemistry. **Protective services:** Criminal justice. **Psychology:** General. **Public administration:** Human services. **Social sciences:** General, international relations, political science, sociology. **Visual/performing arts:** Art, dramatic, theater history.

**Most popular majors.** Business/marketing 18%, communications/journalism 9%, education 7%, interdisciplinary studies 6%, parks/recreation 7%, psychology 6%, security/protective services 10%, social sciences 15%.

**Computing on campus.** 118 workstations in library, computer center, student center. Dormitories wired for high-speed internet access and linked to campus network. Online course registration, online library, helpline, repair service, student web hosting, wireless network available.

**Student life. Freshman orientation:** Mandatory, $225 fee. Preregistration for classes offered. 2-day event scheduled twice in July; multi-day academic-related orientation in August. **Policies:** Virginia State Alcohol and Drug Laws enforced. **Housing:** Guaranteed on-campus for freshmen. Coed dorms, single-sex dorms, special housing for disabled, apartments, fraternity/sorority housing, wellness housing available. $300 nonrefundable deposit, deadline 5/1. If campus housing is full and student cannot commute, Residential Life will locate nearby off-campus housing. **Activities:** Campus ministries, choral groups, dance, drama, international student organizations, literary magazine, Model UN, musical theater, radio station, student government, student newspaper, Political Science Association, Habitat for Humanity, Black student Union, Holy Fire, Honors & Scholars, Campus Kaleidoscope, SALSA, Activities Council.

**Athletics.** NCAA. **Intercollegiate:** Baseball M, basketball, cheerleading M, cross-country, field hockey W, golf M, lacrosse, soccer, softball W, tennis, track and field, volleyball W. **Intramural:** Basketball, field hockey W, football (non-tackle), racquetball, soccer, table tennis, volleyball. **Team name:** Marlins.

**Student services.** Adult student services, alcohol/substance abuse counseling, chaplain/spiritual director, career counseling, student employment services, financial aid counseling, health services, minority student services, personal counseling, veterans' counselor, women's services. **Physically disabled:** Services for visually, hearing impaired.

**Contact.** E-mail: admissions@vwc.edu
Phone: (757) 455-3208 Toll-free number: (800) 737-8684
Fax: (757) 461-5238
Richard Hinshaw, Vice President for Enrollment Management and Dean of Admissions, Virginia Wesleyan College, 1584 Wesleyan Drive, Norfolk, VA 23502-5599

## Washington and Lee University
Lexington, Virginia
www.wlu.edu

CB member
CB code: 5887

- Private 4-year university and liberal arts college
- Residential campus in small town
- 1,757 degree-seeking undergraduates: 50% women, 4% African American, 4% Asian American, 2% Hispanic American, 5% international
- 393 degree-seeking graduate students
- 19% of applicants admitted
- SAT or ACT with writing, SAT Subject Tests, application essay required
- 91% graduate within 6 years; 23% enter graduate study

**General.** Founded in 1749. Regionally accredited. **Degrees:** 430 bachelor's awarded; master's, professional offered. **ROTC:** Army. **Location:** 50 miles from Roanoke, 60 miles from Charlottesville. **Calendar:** 4-4-1. **Full-time faculty:** 225 total; 96% have terminal degrees, 9% minority, 36% women. **Part-time faculty:** 56 total; 52% have terminal degrees, 4% minority, 27% women. **Class size:** 72% < 20, 28% 20-39, less than 1% 40-49, less than 1% 50-99. **Special facilities:** Asian export pottery center, Asian art pavilion, performing arts center, university special collections, multimedia center, archaeology museum.

**Freshman class profile.** 6,222 applied, 1,181 admitted, 472 enrolled.

| Mid 50% test scores | | End year in good standing: | 96% |
|---|---|---|---|
| SAT critical reading: | 660-740 | Return as sophomores: | 94% |
| SAT math: | 660-730 | Out-of-state: | 86% |
| SAT writing: | 650-730 | Live on campus: | 100% |
| ACT composite: | 29-32 | International: | 6% |
| Rank in top quarter: | 94% | Fraternities: | 79% |
| Rank in top tenth: | 81% | Sororities: | 79% |

**Basis for selection.** School achievement record most important, followed closely by test scores, school and community activities, recommendations and personal qualities. Special consideration given to children of alumni and applicants from minorities and low-income families. 2 unrelated SAT Subject Tests required. Interview recommended. **Homeschooled:** Recommend taking 5 SAT Subject Tests in unrelated fields, interview with admissions officer. Require documentation of reading lists and syllabi.

**High school preparation.** College-preparatory program recommended. 17 units required. Required and recommended units include English 4, mathematics 3-4, social studies 1, history 1-2, science 1-3 (laboratory 1), foreign language 3-4 and academic electives 4.

**2010-2011 Annual costs.** Tuition/fees: $40,387. Room/board: $10,243. Books/supplies: $1,700. Personal expenses: $1,890.

**2009-2010 Financial aid. Need-based:** 282 full-time freshmen applied for aid; 220 were judged to have need; 220 of these received aid. Average need met was 99%. Average scholarship/grant was $30,451; average loan $2,948. 91% of total undergraduate aid awarded as scholarships/grants, 9% as loans/jobs. **Non-need-based:** Awarded to 582 full-time undergraduates, including 178 freshmen. Scholarships awarded for academics.

**Application procedures. Admission:** Priority date 11/16; deadline 1/15 (postmark date). $50 fee, may be waived for applicants with need. Admission notification 4/1. Must reply by 5/1. **Financial aid:** Priority date 2/1, closing date 3/1. FAFSA, CSS PROFILE required. Applicants notified by 4/1; must reply by 5/1.

**Academics. Special study options:** Combined bachelor's/graduate degree, double major, exchange student, honors, independent study, internships, liberal arts/career combination, New York semester, semester at sea, student-designed major, study abroad, teacher certification program, Washington semester. Member Seven College Consortium, professional ethics seminars in business, law, medicine, journalism. **Credit/placement by examination:** AP, CLEP, IB, SAT, ACT, institutional tests. **Support services:** Study skills assistance, tutoring, writing center.

**Majors. Area/ethnic studies:** East Asian, Russian/Slavic. **Biology:** General, biochemistry. **Business:** Accounting, business admin. **Communications:** Journalism. **Computer sciences:** General. **Conservation:** Environmental science. **Engineering:** Chemical, physics. **Foreign languages:** General, classics, East Asian, French, German, Romance, Spanish. **History:** General. **Interdisciplinary:** Medieval/Renaissance, neuroscience. **Math:** General. **Philosophy/religion:** Philosophy, religion. **Physical sciences:** Chemistry, geology, physics. **Psychology:** General. **Public administration:** Policy analysis. **Social sciences:** Anthropology, archaeology, economics, political science, sociology. **Visual/performing arts:** Art history/conservation, dramatic, studio arts.

**Most popular majors.** Biology 6%, business/marketing 21%, communications/journalism 6%, English 6%, foreign language 10%, history 8%, social sciences 20%.

**Computing on campus.** 300 workstations in dormitories, library, computer center, student center. Dormitories wired for high-speed internet access and linked to campus network. Commuter students can connect to campus network. Online course registration, online library, helpline, repair service, wireless network available.

**Student life. Freshman orientation:** Mandatory. Preregistration for classes offered. 4 days prior to beginning of fall term. **Policies:** Student-run honor system, observed with single sanction. **Housing:** Guaranteed on-campus for freshmen. Coed dorms, special housing for disabled, apartments, fraternity/sorority housing, wellness housing available. $150 nonrefundable deposit, deadline 5/1. Outing Club House, Spanish House, Chavis House available. **Activities:** Bands, campus ministries, choral groups, dance, drama, film society, international student organizations, literary magazine, music ensembles, Model UN, radio station, student government, student newspaper, symphony orchestra, TV station, Alpha Phi Omega, Young Life, Generals Fellowship, Multicultural Student Association, Hillel, Habitat for Humanity, Americans for Informed Democracy, Baptist Student Union, Catholic Campus Ministry, Campus Kitchen.

**Athletics.** NCAA. **Intercollegiate:** Baseball M, basketball, cross-country, equestrian W, field hockey W, football (tackle) M, golf M, lacrosse, soccer, swimming, tennis, track and field, volleyball W, wrestling M. **Intramural:** Badminton, basketball, football (non-tackle), soccer, softball, swimming, table tennis, tennis, volleyball, water polo, wrestling M. **Team name:** Generals.

**Student services.** Alcohol/substance abuse counseling, chaplain/spiritual director, career counseling, student employment services, financial aid counseling, health services, minority student services, personal counseling, placement for graduates. **Physically disabled:** Services for visually, hearing impaired.

**Contact.** E-mail: admissions@wlu.edu
Phone: (540) 458-8710 Fax: (540) 458-8062
William Hartog, Dean of Admissions and Financial Aid, Washington and Lee University, 204 West Washington Street, Lexington, VA 24450-2116

## World College
Virginia Beach, Virginia
www.cie-wc.edu

CB code: 3970

- For-profit 4-year technical college
- Large city
- 486 degree-seeking undergraduates

**General.** Accredited by DETC. Affiliated with Cleveland Institute of Electronics. **Degrees:** 26 bachelor's awarded. **Calendar:** Continuous. **Full-time faculty:** 6 total. **Part-time faculty:** 75 total.

**Basis for selection.** Open admission, but selective for some programs.

**2010-2011 Annual costs.** Tuition/fees: $3,770. Books/supplies: $1,600.

**Application procedures. Admission:** No deadline. No application fee. Admission notification on a rolling basis.

**Academics. Special study options:** Accelerated study, distance learning, independent study. **Credit/placement by examination:** CLEP.

**Majors. Computer sciences:** Security. **Engineering technology:** Electrical.

**Computing on campus.** PC or laptop required.

**Contact.** E-mail: instruct@cie-wc.edu
Phone: (800) 696-7532 Toll-free number: (800) 696-7532
World College, Lake Shore Plaza, 5193 Shore Drive, Suite 105, Virginia Beach, VA 23455-2500

# Washington

## Antioch University Seattle
Seattle, Washington
www.antiochsea.edu
CB code: 3070

▶ Private two-year upper-division university and liberal arts college
▶ Commuter campus in very large city
▶ Application essay, interview required

**General.** Founded in 1976. Regionally accredited. Individualized degree programs offered on both graduate and undergraduate levels. **Degrees:** 60 bachelor's awarded; master's, professional offered. **Calendar:** Quarter, extensive summer session. **Full-time faculty:** 40 total. **Part-time faculty:** 30 total.

**Student profile.** 238 degree-seeking undergraduates, 721 graduate students.

**Basis for selection.** High school transcript, college transcript, application essay, interview required. Transfer accepted as juniors, seniors.

**2009-2010 Annual costs.** Tuition/fees: $22,440. For BA with Teacher Prep program, $20,925 per year, $465 per credit hour. Books/supplies: $972. Personal expenses: $555.

**Financial aid. Need-based:** Average need met was 2%. 54% of total undergraduate aid awarded as scholarships/grants, 46% as loans/jobs. **Non-need-based:** Awarded to 2 undergraduates.

**Application procedures. Admission:** Rolling admission. $50 fee, may be waived for applicants with need. **Financial aid:** Applicants notified on a rolling basis starting 3/15; must reply within 2 weeks of notification. FAFSA required.

**Academics.** Bachelor's program is a completion program only. Students generally transfer in with at least 90 credits. **Special study options:** Accelerated study, cross-registration, dual enrollment of high school students, independent study, student-designed major, study abroad, teacher certification program, weekend college. **Credit/placement by examination:** CLEP.

**Majors. Liberal arts:** Arts/sciences.

**Computing on campus.** 16 workstations in library, computer center. Commuter students can connect to campus network. Online library, wireless network available.

**Student life. Activities:** Literary magazine, student government, student newspaper.

**Student services.** Career counseling, financial aid counseling, personal counseling, veterans' counselor. **Physically disabled:** Services for visually impaired.

**Contact.** E-mail: admissions@antiochsea.edu
Phone: (206) 441-5352 ext. 5201 Toll-free number: (888) 268-4477
Fax: (206) 268-4242
Doug Arnold, Director of Admissions, Antioch University Seattle, 2326 Sixth Avenue, Seattle, WA 98121-1814

## Argosy University: Seattle
Seattle, Washington
www.argosy.edu/seattle

▶ For-profit 4-year university
▶ Very large city
▶ 73 degree-seeking undergraduates

**General.** Regionally accredited. **Degrees:** 5 bachelor's awarded; master's, doctoral, professional offered. **Calendar:** Continuous. **Full-time faculty:** 12 total. **Part-time faculty:** 32 total.

**Freshman class profile.** 4 enrolled.

**Basis for selection.** Open admission.

**Academics. Credit/placement by examination:** CLEP.

**Majors. Business:** Business admin. **Liberal arts:** Arts/sciences. **Protective services:** Police science. **Psychology:** General.

**Contact.** E-mail: ausadmissions@argosy.edu
Phone: (206) 393-3516 Toll-free number: (888) 283-2777
Argosy University: Seattle, 2601-A Elliott Avenue, Seattle, WA 98121

## Art Institute of Seattle
Seattle, Washington
www.ais.edu
CB code: 4805

▶ For-profit 4-year visual arts and technical college
▶ Commuter campus in very large city
▶ 2,202 degree-seeking undergraduates: 32% part-time, 48% women
▶ Application essay, interview required

**General.** Founded in 1982. Regionally accredited. **Degrees:** 161 bachelor's, 302 associate awarded. **Location:** Downtown. **Calendar:** Quarter, extensive summer session. **Full-time faculty:** 59 total; 22% have terminal degrees, 8% minority, 32% women. **Part-time faculty:** 81 total; 10% have terminal degrees, 21% minority, 40% women. **Class size:** 45% < 20, 54% 20-39, 1% 40-49. **Special facilities:** Gallery with rotating art/design shows.

**Freshman class profile.**

| | | | |
|---|---|---|---|
| Out-of-state: | 37% | Live on campus: | 20% |

**Basis for selection.** Open admission, but selective for some programs. Secondary school record, essay, interview most important; recommendations, academic records, test scores required. Some programs require a portfolio. **Learning Disabled:** Admissions notifies counselors of students who disclose learning disabilities and special needs. Counselor determines eligibility.

**2009-2010 Annual costs.** Tuition/fees: $21,195. Room only: $11,136. Books/supplies: $975. Personal expenses: $2,265.

**2009-2010 Financial aid. Non-need-based:** Scholarships awarded for academics, art.

**Application procedures. Admission:** No deadline. $50 fee. Admission notification on a rolling basis. **Financial aid:** Priority date 4/15; no closing date. FAFSA required. Applicants notified on a rolling basis; must reply within 4 week(s) of notification.

**Academics. Special study options:** Distance learning, ESL, independent study, internships, study abroad. **Credit/placement by examination:** AP, CLEP, IB, institutional tests. 6 credit hours maximum toward associate degree, 6 toward bachelor's. Course waived by proficiency exam; credit does not count toward degree. **Support services:** Learning center, reduced course load, remedial instruction, study skills assistance, tutoring.

**Majors. Computer sciences:** Game design, web page design. **Visual/performing arts:** General, cinematography, fashion design, graphic design, interior design.

**Computing on campus.** 494 workstations in library, computer center, student center. Dormitories wired for high-speed internet access. Online course registration, online library, helpline, student web hosting, wireless network available.

**Student life. Freshman orientation:** Available. Preregistration for classes offered. 1- to 4-day program held 1 week before start of the quarter. **Housing:** Guaranteed on-campus for all undergraduates. Coed dorms available. $200 deposit. AIS housing located 1 mile from campus. Students share 1 bedroom and studio apartments in secured apartment complexes. **Activities:** Student government, student newspaper.

**Athletics. Intramural:** Soccer, softball.

**Student services.** Adult student services, career counseling, student employment services, financial aid counseling, personal counseling, placement for graduates, veterans' counselor. **Physically disabled:** Services for visually, speech, hearing impaired.

**Contact.** E-mail: aisadm@aii.edu
Phone: (206) 448-6600 Toll-free number: (800) 275-2471
Fax: (206) 269-0275
Brian Cicero, Director of Admissions, Art Institute of Seattle, 2323 Elliott Avenue, Seattle, WA 98121-1622

## Bastyr University
### Kenmore, Washington
www.bastyr.edu                    CB code: 0181

♦ Private two-year upper-division university and health science college
♦ Commuter campus in small city
♦ Application essay required

**General.** Founded in 1978. Regionally accredited. **Degrees:** 92 bachelor's awarded; master's, professional offered. **Location:** 16 miles from Seattle. **Calendar:** Quarter, limited summer session. **Full-time faculty:** 46 total; 78% have terminal degrees, 17% minority, 59% women. **Part-time faculty:** 81 total; 86% have terminal degrees, 15% minority, 59% women. **Special facilities:** Whole-foods vegetarian cafeteria, research institute and laboratory, natural health sciences library and bookstore, medicinal herb and culinary garden, reflexology path.

**Student profile.** 173 degree-seeking undergraduates, 734 degree-seeking graduate students. 100% entered as juniors. 75% transferred from two-year, 25% transferred from four-year institutions.

| | | | |
|---|---|---|---|
| Women: | 84% | Live on campus: | 5% |
| Part-time: | 17% | 25 or older: | 63% |
| Out-of-state: | 52% | | |

**Basis for selection.** College transcript, application essay required. Transfer accepted as juniors, seniors.

**2009-2010 Annual costs.** Tuition/fees: $20,790. Room only: $4,100. Books/supplies: $1,125.

**Financial aid. Need-based:** 189 applied for aid; 178 were judged to have need; 178 of these received aid. Average need met was 50%. 10% of total undergraduate aid awarded as scholarships/grants, 90% as loans/jobs. **Non-need-based:** Awarded to 10 undergraduates. Scholarships awarded for academics.

**Application procedures. Admission:** Priority date 3/15. $60 fee. **Financial aid:** No deadline. Applicants notified on a rolling basis; must reply within 3 weeks of notification. FAFSA, institutional form required.

**Academics. Special study options:** Double major, internships. Selected tracks within major. **Credit/placement by examination:** AP, CLEP.

**Majors. Health:** Acupuncture, Chinese medicine/herbology, herbalism. **Interdisciplinary:** Nutrition sciences. **Parks/recreation:** Exercise sciences. **Psychology:** General.

**Most popular majors.** Health sciences 92%.

**Computing on campus.** 72 workstations in library, computer center. Dormitories wired for high-speed internet access and linked to campus network. Online library, helpline, wireless network available.

**Student life. Housing:** Coed dorms, wellness housing available. Eco-friendly LEED-certified student housing village on campus, **Activities:** Choral groups, international student organizations, student government, Student Physicians for Social Responsibility, Herbal Ways, nature cure club, Africana student association, Christian Fellowship, pediatrics club, student nutrition association, tai chi club, yoga club, Voice for Queer Natural Health.

**Athletics. Intramural:** Basketball, soccer.

**Student services.** Career counseling, financial aid counseling, health services, on-campus daycare, personal counseling, placement for graduates. **Physically disabled:** Services for visually impaired.

**Contact.** E-mail: admissions@bastyr.edu
Phone: (425) 602-3330 Fax: (425) 602-3090
Ted Olsen, Director of Admissions, Bastyr University, 14500 Juanita Drive, NE, Kenmore, WA 98028

## Central Washington University
### Ellensburg, Washington
www.cwu.edu
CB member
CB code: 4044

♦ Public 4-year university
♦ Residential campus in large town

**General.** Founded in 1890. Regionally accredited. **Location:** 105 miles from Seattle. **Calendar:** Quarter.

**Annual costs/financial aid.** Tuition/fees (2009-2010): $6,418; $16,684 out-of-state. Room/board: $8,460. Books/supplies: $924. Personal expenses: $1,683. Need-based financial aid available to full-time and part-time students.

**Contact.** Phone: (509) 963-1211
Director of Admissions, 400 East University Way, Ellensburg, WA 98926-7463

## City University of Seattle
### Bellevue, Washington
www.cityu.edu                    CB code: 4042

♦ Private two-year upper-division university
♦ Commuter campus in very large city

**General.** Founded in 1973. Regionally accredited. University maintains satellite sites in Renton, Everett, North Seattle, Tacoma, and Vancouver, Washington; Victoria, Vancouver, Edmonton, and Calgary, Canada; Trencin and Bratislava, Slovakia; Prague, Czech Republic; Sofia and Pratvetz, Bulgaria; Athens, Greece; Zurich, Switzerland; and Beijing, China; partnership in Queensland, Australia. **Degrees:** 525 bachelor's, 49 associate awarded; master's offered. **Location:** 12 miles from Seattle. **Calendar:** Quarter, extensive summer session. **Full-time faculty:** 62 total; 32% have terminal degrees, 44% women. **Part-time faculty:** 983 total; 14% have terminal degrees, 56% women. **Class size:** 95% < 20, 5% 20-39.

**Student profile.** 1,180 degree-seeking undergraduates, 1,565 degree-seeking graduate students.

| | | | |
|---|---|---|---|
| Women: | 56% | International: | 4% |
| African American: | 5% | Part-time: | 41% |
| Asian American: | 4% | Out-of-state: | 15% |
| Hispanic American: | 2% | 25 or older: | 81% |
| Native American: | 1% | | |

**Basis for selection.** Open admission. High school transcript, college transcript required. Based on course content equivalency and grade point average. Transfer accepted as sophomores, juniors, seniors.

**2009-2010 Annual costs.** Tuition/fees: $15,615. Books/supplies: $860.

**Financial aid. Non-need-based:** Scholarships awarded for academics. **Additional information:** All degree programs approved for veteran's administration education benefits.

**Application procedures. Admission:** Rolling admission. $50 fee. **Financial aid:** FAFSA, institutional form required.

**Academics.** Online tutoring service available to all registered students at all times. **Special study options:** Accelerated study, distance learning, double major, dual enrollment of high school students, ESL, external degree, internships, student-designed major, study abroad, teacher certification program, weekend college. **Credit/placement by examination:** CLEP, IB. 45 credit hours maximum toward associate degree, 90 toward bachelor's. **Support services:** Reduced course load, tutoring.

**Majors. Business:** Accounting, business admin, international, management information systems, marketing. **Communications:** General. **Computer sciences:** Programming. **Education:** Elementary, middle, special. **Liberal arts:** Arts/sciences. **Psychology:** General.

**Most popular majors.** Business/marketing 64%, computer/information sciences 11%, education 15%.

**Computing on campus.** PC or laptop required. 150 workstations in library, computer center. Commuter students can connect to campus network. Online course registration, online library, helpline, wireless network available.

**Student services.** Adult student services, career counseling, financial aid counseling, personal counseling, veterans' counselor. **Physically disabled:** Services for visually, hearing impaired.

**Contact.** E-mail: info@cityu.edu
Phone: (425) 637-1010 Toll-free number: (888) 422-4898
Fax: (425) 709-5361
Melissa Mecham, Vice President Admissions/Student Affairs, City University of Seattle, 11900 NE First Street, Bellevue, WA 98005

## Cornish College of the Arts
**Seattle, Washington**
www.cornish.edu
CB code: 0058

▶ Private 4-year visual arts and performing arts college
▶ Commuter campus in very large city
▶ 775 degree-seeking undergraduates
▶ 67% of applicants admitted
▶ Application essay required

**General.** Founded in 1914. Regionally accredited. **Degrees:** 164 bachelor's awarded. **Calendar:** Semester, limited summer session. **Full-time faculty:** 59 total. **Part-time faculty:** 104 total. **Class size:** 87% < 20, 13% 20-39. **Special facilities:** Electronic music laboratory, experimental books laboratory, music listening center, costumemaking facilities, video editing facilities.

**Freshman class profile.** 1,099 applied, 740 admitted, 277 enrolled.

**Basis for selection.** Portfolio (for visual artists) or audition (for performing artists), academic achievement history, creative ability, and artistic goals considered. SAT or ACT recommended. Interview recommended for all; audition required for dance, music, theater; portfolio required for art, design, performance production. Alternative audition and portfolio arrangements for long-distance applicants. **Homeschooled:** Transcript of courses and grades, state high school equivalency certificate required.

**High school preparation.** Required and recommended units include English 4, mathematics 2-4, social studies 3, science 2-4 (laboratory 1) and foreign language 2.

**2009-2010 Annual costs.** Tuition/fees: $27,400. Design majors required to have laptop computer and Adobe software, estimated cost $3,000. Room/board: $9,500. Books/supplies: $1,800.

**2009-2010 Financial aid. Non-need-based:** Scholarships awarded for academics.

**Application procedures. Admission:** Priority date 3/1; deadline 8/15 (receipt date). $35 fee, may be waived for applicants with need. Admission notification on a rolling basis beginning on or about 1/1. Must reply by May 1 or within 2 week(s) if notified thereafter. **Financial aid:** Priority date 3/1; no closing date. FAFSA, institutional form required. Applicants notified on a rolling basis starting 4/15; must reply by 5/1 or within 2 week(s) of notification.

**Academics. Special study options:** Cooperative education, independent study, internships, study abroad. **Credit/placement by examination:** AP, CLEP, institutional tests. 30 credit hours maximum toward bachelor's degree. A total of 30 credits through a combination of prior work experience and credit by exam allowed. **Support services:** Remedial instruction, study skills assistance, tutoring, writing center.

**Majors. Visual/performing arts:** General, acting, art, cinematography, commercial/advertising art, dance, design, directing/producing, dramatic, drawing, graphic design, illustration, interior design, jazz, music performance, music theory/composition, painting, photography, piano/organ, play/screenwriting, printmaking, sculpture, stringed instruments, studio arts, theater design, voice/opera.

**Computing on campus.** 91 workstations in library, computer center, student center. Online library, helpline, wireless network available.

**Student life. Freshman orientation:** Mandatory, $175 fee. Preregistration for classes offered. Begins one week before class starts each fall. Students will meet the Chair of their department and register for classes. **Activities:** Bands, choral groups, dance, drama, film society, literary magazine, music ensembles, musical theater, opera, student government, student newspaper, art history club, Birds and Whistles, Black student alliance, bowling club, digital illustration club, Inform the Misinformed Campaign/Corporate Watchdogs, movie club, Salt and Light (Bible study), sports/intramural club.

**Student services.** Adult student services, alcohol/substance abuse counseling, career counseling, student employment services, financial aid counseling, personal counseling, placement for graduates. **Physically disabled:** Services for visually impaired.

**Contact.** E-mail: admissions@cornish.edu
Phone: (206) 726-5016 Toll-free number: (800) 726-2787
Fax: (206) 720-1011
Sharron Starling, Director of Admissions, Cornish College of the Arts, 1000 Lenora Street, Seattle, WA 98121

## DeVry University: Federal Way
**Federal Way, Washington**
www.devry.edu
CB code: 3696

▶ For-profit 4-year university
▶ Commuter campus in large city
▶ 672 degree-seeking undergraduates: 37% part-time, 29% women, 11% African American, 8% Asian American, 9% Hispanic American, 1% Native American
▶ 153 degree-seeking graduate students
▶ Interview required
▶ 32% graduate within 6 years

**General. Degrees:** 124 bachelor's, 5 associate awarded; master's offered. **ROTC:** Army. **Calendar:** Semester, extensive summer session. **Full-time faculty:** 19 total; 32% minority, 16% women. **Part-time faculty:** 60 total; 2% minority, 43% women.

**Freshman class profile.** 131 enrolled.

**Basis for selection.** Applicants must have high school diploma or equivalent, or a degree from an accredited postsecondary institution. Must demonstrate proficiency in basic college level skills through test scores and/or institutionally-administered placement exams, and be at least 17 years of age on the first day of classes. New students may enter at the beginning of any semester. CPT also accepted.

**High school preparation.** College-preparatory program recommended. Required units include mathematics 1. Math unit must be algebra or higher.

**2009-2010 Annual costs.** Tuition/fees: $14,800. Books/supplies: $1,310. Personal expenses: $3,574.

**2008-2009 Financial aid.** All financial aid based on need.

**Application procedures. Admission:** No deadline. $50 fee. Admission notification on a rolling basis. **Financial aid:** No deadline. FAFSA required. Applicants notified on a rolling basis.

**Academics. Special study options:** Accelerated study, distance learning. **Credit/placement by examination:** CLEP. **Support services:** Learning center, remedial instruction, tutoring.

**Majors. Business:** General, business admin. **Computer sciences:** Game design, information technology, networking, security, systems analysis, web page design. **Engineering:** Software. **Engineering technology:** Biomedical, computer, electrical. **Other:** Technical management.

**Most popular majors.** Business/marketing 45%, computer/information sciences 24%, engineering/engineering technologies 31%.

**Computing on campus.** 335 workstations in library, computer center. Online course registration, online library, helpline available.

**Student life. Freshman orientation:** Mandatory. **Housing:** Private apartments, student-plan housing, private rooms. **Activities:** Student government, student newspaper, alternative sports, business & technology club, gaming, robotics, Institution of Electrical and Electronic Engineers, network gaming.

**Student services.** Career counseling, student employment services, financial aid counseling, placement for graduates, veterans' counselor. **Physically disabled:** Services for visually, hearing impaired.

**Contact.** E-mail: admissions@sea.devry.edu
Phone: (253) 943-2810 Toll-free number: (877) 923-3879
Fax: (253) 943-3291
Fred Pressel, Director of Admissions, DeVry University: Federal Way, 3600 South 344th Way, Federal Way, WA 98001-9558

## DigiPen Institute of Technology
**Redmond, Washington**
www.digipen.edu
CB code: 4138

▶ For-profit 4-year visual arts and engineering college
▶ Residential campus in large town
▶ 839 degree-seeking undergraduates
▶ 51 graduate students
▶ 33% of applicants admitted
▶ Application essay required

**General.** Accredited by ACCSC. Comprised of two campuses: main campus and the art campus. **Degrees:** 129 bachelor's awarded; master's offered. **Location:** 20 miles from downtown Seattle. **Calendar:** Semester, limited summer session. **Full-time faculty:** 43 total; 21% women. **Part-time faculty:** 29 total; 21% women. **Class size:** 40% < 20, 41% 20-39, 10% 40-49, 8% 50-99, less than 1% >100.

**Freshman class profile.** 423 applied, 138 admitted, 137 enrolled.

| Mid 50% test scores | | SAT writing: | 490-600 |
|---|---|---|---|
| SAT critical reading: | 530-640 | ACT composite: | 24-29 |
| SAT math: | 540-670 | Out-of-state: | 46% |

**Basis for selection.** Applicants must submit official transcripts, test scores, recommendation letters, a personal statement, and an art portfolio when applying to the animation program. Non-native English speakers must provide a minimum TOEFL iBT score of 80 or other pre-approved proof of having English proficiency. Applicants who have already graduated from high school and have at least one year of full-time college experience are not required to submit SAT/ACT scores. Portfolios of 15-20 pieces of artwork required for BA/BFA program applicants. Supplemental pieces required for Game Design degrees. **Homeschooled:** Transcript of courses and grades, state high school equivalency certificate required. In addition to standard application materials, applicants from the state of Washington should submit detailed transcript that provides course titles, brief description of each course's content, grade or performance assessment for each course, details concerning duration of study, and expected graduation date. Out-of-state applicants should submit transcript from nationally recognized homeschool program or detailed transcript (as described above for Washington residents) and passing GED scores. Other proof of high school equivalence will be considered on a case-by-case basis by admissions office. **Learning Disabled:** Students desiring special needs should contact the Disability Support Services Coordinator to self-identify and arrange for appropriate accommodations.

**High school preparation.** College-preparatory program recommended. Recommended units include English 4, mathematics 4, science 4, computer science 1 and visual/performing arts 1. Applicants for the BA/BFA programs are recommended to take as many art classes as possible and BS applicants are encouraged to take classes in computer science and physics.

**2009-2010 Annual costs.** Full-time tuition for academic year (based on 20 hours per term), $19,040; required fees, $160; per-credit-hour charge, $476. Full-time tuition for non-resident aliens for academic year (based on 20 hours per term), $24,840; per-credit-hour charge, $621. Books/supplies: $972.

**2008-2009 Financial aid.** **Non-need-based:** Scholarships awarded for job skills, leadership, minority status. **Additional information:** Many aid programs are on a first-come, first-served basis.

**Application procedures.** **Admission:** Priority date 2/1; no deadline. $35 fee, may be waived for applicants with need. Admission notification on a rolling basis. Applicants must respond by the date listed on their individual acceptance letters. **Financial aid:** Priority date 4/15; no closing date. FAFSA, institutional form required. Applicants notified on a rolling basis starting 1/1; must reply within 4 week(s) of notification.

**Academics.** **Special study options:** Accelerated study, independent study, internships. **Credit/placement by examination:** AP, CLEP, IB, institutional tests. **Support services:** Reduced course load, study skills assistance, tutoring.

**Majors. Communications technology:** Animation/special effects. **Computer sciences:** Programming. **Engineering:** Computer. **Visual/performing arts:** Design, multimedia.

**Most popular majors.** Communication technologies 24%, computer/information sciences 72%.

**Computing on campus.** PC or laptop required. Online course registration, online library, helpline, student web hosting, wireless network available.

**Student life. Freshman orientation:** Mandatory. Preregistration for classes offered. 3-4 day orientation held week before classes begin. **Housing:** All housing is off campus. Most students live in co-ed situations with 2-4 students in an apartment; housing options near campus. Most students relocate to Redmond, WA. DigiPen offers resources for acquiring housing and finding roommates. **Activities:** International student organizations, music ensembles, student government.

**Student services.** Career counseling, student employment services, financial aid counseling, personal counseling, veterans' counselor. **Physically disabled:** Services for hearing impaired.

**Contact.** E-mail: admissions@digipen.edu
Phone: (425) 558-0299 Toll-free number: (866) 478-5236
Fax: (425) 558-0378
Angela Kugler, Director of Admissions, DigiPen Institute of Technology, 5001-150th Avenue Northeast, Redmond, WA 98052

## Eastern Washington University
**Cheney, Washington** — CB member
**www.ewu.edu** — CB code: 4301

- Public 4-year university
- Commuter campus in large town
- 9,919 degree-seeking undergraduates: 13% part-time, 55% women, 4% African American, 4% Asian American, 9% Hispanic American, 2% Native American, 2% international
- 1,383 degree-seeking graduate students
- 82% of applicants admitted
- SAT or ACT with writing required
- 48% graduate within 6 years

**General.** Founded in 1882. Regionally accredited. **Degrees:** 1,845 bachelor's awarded; master's, professional offered. **ROTC:** Army. **Location:** 17 miles from Spokane, 200 miles from Seattle. **Calendar:** Quarter, extensive summer session. **Full-time faculty:** 412 total; 97% have terminal degrees, 11% minority, 45% women. **Part-time faculty:** 207 total; 8% minority, 56% women. **Class size:** 32% < 20, 46% 20-39, 10% 40-49, 11% 50-99, less than 1% >100. **Special facilities:** Planetarium, 17,000-acre national wildlife refuge, on-campus elementary school, anthropology museum, laboratory for ecological studies, photography and print gallery, children's center, English language institute, state crime lab.

**Freshman class profile.** 3,728 applied, 3,069 admitted, 1,469 enrolled.

| Mid 50% test scores | | GPA 3.0-3.49: | 36% |
|---|---|---|---|
| SAT critical reading: | 420-530 | GPA 2.0-2.99: | 36% |
| SAT math: | 430-540 | Return as sophomores: | 72% |
| SAT writing: | 410-520 | Out-of-state: | 7% |
| ACT composite: | 17-23 | Live on campus: | 66% |
| GPA 3.75 or higher: | 13% | International: | 1% |
| GPA 3.50-3.74: | 15% | | |

**Basis for selection.** Admission based on index combining GPA, test scores and requisite high school core curriculum. Essay and special review considered for applicants who do not meet these standards. Limited number enrolled below index and core requirements. Letters of recommendation from teachers and/or counselors encouraged. Interview or essay required for returning adult applicants and high school students below admission index. **Homeschooled:** Must show evidence of completing required core courses.

**High school preparation.** College-preparatory program required. 15 units required. Required units include English 4, mathematics 3, social studies 3, science 2 (laboratory 1), foreign language 2 and visual/performing arts 1. Math requirement includes algebra, geometry, and trigonometry or advanced algebra. One year fine arts or core elective required. Foreign language requirement includes 2 years in 1 foreign language (American Sign Language accepted).

**2009-2010 Annual costs.** Tuition/fees: $5,872; $14,599 out-of-state. Room/board: $7,073. Books/supplies: $1,305. Personal expenses: $2,163.

**2008-2009 Financial aid.** **Need-based:** 1,203 full-time freshmen applied for aid; 831 were judged to have need; 814 of these received aid. Average need met was 91%. Average scholarship/grant was $6,041; average loan $2,266. 48% of total undergraduate aid awarded as scholarships/grants, 52% as loans/jobs. **Non-need-based:** Awarded to 1,347 full-time undergraduates, including 421 freshmen. Scholarships awarded for academics, alumni affiliation, athletics, ROTC, state residency. **Additional information:** The High Demand Scholarship program helps low income students pursue "high demand" careers.

**Application procedures.** **Admission:** Priority date 3/1; deadline 8/15. $50 fee, may be waived for applicants with need. Admission notification on a rolling basis beginning on or about 11/1. Must reply by May 1 or within 4 week(s) if notified thereafter. Application deadline is 10 days prior to start of quarter. **Financial aid:** Priority date 2/15; no closing date. FAFSA required. Applicants notified on a rolling basis starting 4/1; must reply within 4 week(s) of notification.

**Academics.** Extensive internship opportunities available. **Special study options:** Distance learning, double major, ESL, honors, independent study, internships, student-designed major, study abroad, teacher certification program. Nursing consortium with Washington State University, Whitworth College, Gonzaga University. Dual degree program: Master's of Social Work

(EWU) and Law (Gonzaga). **Credit/placement by examination:** AP, CLEP, IB, SAT, ACT, institutional tests. 45 credit hours maximum toward bachelor's degree. **Support services:** Learning center, pre-admission summer program, remedial instruction, study skills assistance, tutoring, writing center.

**Majors. Architecture:** Urban/community planning. **Area/ethnic studies:** Women's. **Biology:** General. **Business:** Accounting, business admin, finance, management information systems, managerial economics, marketing. **Communications:** General, journalism. **Communications technology:** Graphics. **Computer sciences:** General. **Conservation:** Environmental science. **Education:** Art, biology, business, chemistry, early childhood, early childhood special, English, French, health, mathematics, music, physics, reading, science, social studies, Spanish, special. **Engineering:** Electrical. **Engineering technology:** Computer, mechanical. **Family/consumer sciences:** Child development. **Foreign languages:** French, Spanish. **Health:** Athletic training, community health services, dental hygiene, health care admin, nursing (RN), public health ed, recreational therapy, speech pathology. **History:** General. **Liberal arts:** Humanities. **Math:** General. **Military:** General. **Parks/recreation:** General, exercise sciences, facilities management, health/fitness. **Philosophy/religion:** Philosophy. **Physical sciences:** Chemistry, geology, physics. **Psychology:** General, developmental. **Public administration:** Social work. **Social sciences:** Anthropology, criminology, economics, geography, international relations, political science, sociology. **Visual/performing arts:** Art history/conservation, cinematography, dramatic, graphic design, studio arts. **Other:** Interdisciplinary studies, Technology.

**Most popular majors.** Business/marketing 23%, education 11%, health sciences 9%, interdisciplinary studies 7%, psychology 6%, social sciences 9%.

**Computing on campus.** 226 workstations in dormitories, library, computer center, student center. Dormitories wired for high-speed internet access and linked to campus network. Commuter students can connect to campus network. Online course registration, online library, helpline, student web hosting, wireless network available.

**Student life. Freshman orientation:** Available. Preregistration for classes offered. One-day sessions in summer plus a 3-day program prior to start of classes with advising, student activities, enrollment services. **Policies:** Student conduct code, academic integrity policy, alcohol/substance use and abuse policy. **Housing:** Coed dorms, special housing for disabled, apartments, fraternity/sorority housing, wellness housing available. $250 nonrefundable deposit, deadline 5/1. **Activities:** Bands, campus ministries, choral groups, dance, drama, film society, international student organizations, literary magazine, music ensembles, Model UN, musical theater, radio station, student government, student newspaper, symphony orchestra, Native American student association; Chinese student association; R.A.I.C.E.S. (Reconociendo A La Identidad con Educacion y Sociedad); Black Student Union; United Ministries; international affairs club; Mind, Body, and Soul; Eastern Environmental; debate club.

**Athletics.** NCAA. **Intercollegiate:** Basketball, cheerleading, cross-country, football (tackle) M, golf W, soccer W, tennis, track and field, volleyball W. **Intramural:** Badminton, basketball, bowling, cross-country, football (tackle), golf, racquetball, soccer, softball, tennis, triathlon, volleyball. **Team name:** Eagles.

**Student services.** Alcohol/substance abuse counseling, career counseling, student employment services, financial aid counseling, health services, minority student services, on-campus daycare, personal counseling, placement for graduates, veterans' counselor, women's services. **Physically disabled:** Services for visually, speech, hearing impaired.

**Contact.** E-mail: admissions@mail.ewu.edu
Phone: (509) 359-2397 Fax: (509) 359-6692
Shannon Carr, Director of Admissions, Eastern Washington University, 101 Sutton Hall, Cheney, WA 99004-2447

---

**Evergreen State College**
Olympia, Washington          CB member
www.evergreen.edu            CB code: 4292

- Public 4-year liberal arts college
- Commuter campus in small city
- 4,385 degree-seeking undergraduates: 6% part-time, 54% women, 5% African American, 5% Asian American, 5% Hispanic American, 4% Native American, 1% international
- 327 degree-seeking graduate students
- 95% of applicants admitted
- SAT or ACT (ACT writing optional) required
- 63% graduate within 6 years; 75% enter graduate study

**General.** Founded in 1967. Regionally accredited. **Degrees:** 1,086 bachelor's awarded; master's offered. **Location:** 6 miles from downtown, 60 miles from Seattle. **Calendar:** Quarter, limited summer session. **Class size:** 36% < 20, 40% 20-39, 16% 40-49, 8% 50-99. **Special facilities:** Organic farm and community gardens, Longhouse Education and Cultural Center, animation and design studio, ceramics studio, metal shop, wood shop, photography studios and darkrooms, 3,000 feet of waterfront property on Puget Sound.

**Freshman class profile.** 1,769 applied, 1,687 admitted, 578 enrolled.

| Mid 50% test scores | | | |
|---|---|---|---|
| SAT critical reading: | 500-640 | GPA 3.0-3.49: | 36% |
| SAT math: | 460-590 | GPA 2.0-2.99: | 46% |
| SAT writing: | 480-600 | Rank in top quarter: | 29% |
| ACT composite: | 20-26 | Rank in top tenth: | 12% |
| GPA 3.75 or higher: | 8% | Return as sophomores: | 72% |
| GPA 3.50-3.74: | 9% | Out-of-state: | 43% |
| | | Live on campus: | 80% |

**Basis for selection.** School achievement record, test scores, strength of curriculum taken in high school, personal statement, and understanding of interdisciplinary study. Official TOEFL test scores are required for most students whose native language is not English. Essay recommended. Interviews optional (by appointment for non-residents.). **Homeschooled:** Transcript of courses and grades required.

**High school preparation.** College-preparatory program required. 15 units required. Required units include English 4, mathematics 3, social studies 3, science 2 (laboratory 1), foreign language 2 and academic electives 1. One fine, visual, or performing arts elective or other college prep elective from the areas above required.

**2009-2010 Annual costs.** Tuition/fees: $5,959; $16,987 out-of-state. Room/board: $8,052. Books/supplies: $924. Personal expenses: $1,941.

**2008-2009 Financial aid. Need-based:** 449 full-time freshmen applied for aid; 324 were judged to have need; 311 of these received aid. Average need met was 83%. Average scholarship/grant was $6,783; average loan $3,280. 47% of total undergraduate aid awarded as scholarships/grants, 53% as loans/jobs. **Non-need-based:** Awarded to 531 full-time undergraduates, including 245 freshmen. Scholarships awarded for academics, art, athletics, state residency. **Additional information:** Application deadline for merit and cultural diversity scholarships February 1. Minority students may apply for tuition and fee waiver scholarships; amount of award equal to in-state tuition and fees. Discount waiver for employees. To meet priority deadline for required financial aid forms, official results of FAFSA must be received by March 15.

**Application procedures. Admission:** Priority date 3/1; no deadline. $50 fee, may be waived for applicants with need. Admission notification on a rolling basis beginning on or about 11/1. Must reply by May 1 or within 4 week(s) if notified thereafter. **Financial aid:** Priority date 3/15; no closing date. FAFSA, institutional form required. Applicants notified on a rolling basis starting 4/1; must reply within 8 week(s) of notification.

**Academics. Special study options:** Accelerated study, double major, exchange student, independent study, internships, semester at sea, student-designed major, study abroad, teacher certification program, weekend college. **Credit/placement by examination:** AP, CLEP, IB. 135 credit hours maximum toward bachelor's degree. **Support services:** Learning center, reduced course load, study skills assistance, tutoring, writing center.

**Majors. Agriculture:** General. **Area/ethnic studies:** Native American. **Biology:** General. **Business:** Business admin. **Communications:** General, journalism. **Computer sciences:** General. **Conservation:** General, environmental science, environmental studies. **Education:** General. **Foreign languages:** General, classics, linguistics. **Health:** Health services. **History:** General. **Interdisciplinary:** Biological/physical sciences, global studies, intercultural, natural sciences. **Liberal arts:** Arts/sciences, humanities. **Math:** Probability. **Philosophy/religion:** Philosophy, religion. **Physical sciences:** General. **Psychology:** General. **Public administration:** General. **Social sciences:** General, political science, sociology. **Visual/performing arts:** General, art, cinematography, dramatic, film/cinema, multimedia, studio arts.

**Most popular majors.** Interdisciplinary studies 12%, liberal arts 88%.

**Computing on campus.** 375 workstations in dormitories, library, computer center. Dormitories wired for high-speed internet access and linked to campus network. Commuter students can connect to campus network. Online course registration, online library, helpline, student web hosting, wireless network available.

**Student life. Freshman orientation:** Mandatory. Preregistration for classes offered. Week-long orientation offers academic and social events to familiarize students with teaching, learning, and resources at campus. **Housing:** Guaranteed on-campus for freshmen. Coed dorms, special housing for disabled, apartments, wellness housing available. $250 fully refundable deposit, deadline 7/15. Freshmen halls, freshmen quiet, community action, sustainability, apartment-style quiet available. **Activities:** Pep band, choral groups, dance, drama, film society, literary magazine, music ensembles, Model UN, radio station, student government, student newspaper, Developing Ecological Agricultural Practices (DEAP), Evergreen Queer Alliance (EQA), Women of Color Coalition, Common Bread, Movimento Estudiantil Chicano(a) de Aztlan (MEChA), Women's Resource Center, Students at Evergreen for Ecological Design (SEED), Geoduck Union.

**Athletics.** NAIA. **Intercollegiate:** Basketball, cross-country, soccer, track and field, volleyball W. **Intramural:** Badminton, basketball, soccer, softball, tennis. **Team name:** Geoducks.

**Student services.** Adult student services, alcohol/substance abuse counseling, career counseling, services for economically disadvantaged, student employment services, financial aid counseling, health services, minority student services, on-campus daycare, personal counseling, placement for graduates, veterans' counselor, women's services. **Physically disabled:** Services for visually, speech, hearing impaired.

**Contact.** E-mail: admissions@evergreen.edu
Phone: (360) 867-6170 Fax: (360) 867-5114
Doug Scrima, Director of Admissions, Evergreen State College, 2700 Evergreen Parkway NW, Olympia, WA 98505

## Faith Evangelical Seminary
**Tacoma, Washington**
**www.faithseminary.edu**

▶ Private 4-year seminary college
▶ Large city
▶ 89 degree-seeking undergraduates

**General.** Regionally accredited; also accredited by TRACS. **Degrees:** 75 bachelor's awarded; master's, doctoral, professional offered. **Calendar:** Quarter, limited summer session. **Full-time faculty:** 10 total. **Part-time faculty:** 5 total.

**Freshman class profile.** 15 enrolled.

**Basis for selection.** Open admission, but selective for some programs.

**2009-2010 Annual costs.** Tuition/fees: $6,285.

**Application procedures. Admission:** No deadline. $40 fee. **Financial aid:** Closing date 8/15.

**Academics. Credit/placement by examination:** CLEP.

**Majors. Philosophy/religion:** Religion. **Theology:** Theology.

**Contact.** E-mail: admissions@faithseminary.edu
Phone: (888) 777-7675 ext. 21
Eric Rice, Director of Admissions, Faith Evangelical Seminary, 3504 North Pearl Street, Tacoma, WA 98407

## Gonzaga University
**Spokane, Washington**                                    **CB member**
**www.gonzaga.edu**                                        **CB code: 4330**

▶ Private 4-year university and liberal arts college affiliated with Roman Catholic Church
▶ Residential campus in large city
▶ 4,655 degree-seeking undergraduates: 2% part-time, 53% women, 1% African American, 5% Asian American, 5% Hispanic American, 1% Native American, 2% international
▶ 2,720 degree-seeking graduate students
▶ 78% of applicants admitted
▶ SAT or ACT (ACT writing optional), application essay required
▶ 82% graduate within 6 years

**General.** Founded in 1887. Regionally accredited. **Degrees:** 1,002 bachelor's awarded; master's, doctoral, professional offered. **ROTC:** Army. **Location:** 300 miles from Seattle. **Calendar:** Semester, extensive summer session. **Full-time faculty:** 387 total; 84% have terminal degrees, 14% minority, 40% women. **Part-time faculty:** 334 total. **Class size:** 46% < 20, 49% 20-39, 4% 40-49, 1% 50-99. **Special facilities:** 2 electron microscopes.

**Freshman class profile.** 5,042 applied, 3,952 admitted, 1,239 enrolled.

| Mid 50% test scores | | | |
|---|---|---|---|
| SAT critical reading: | 530-640 | Rank in top quarter: | 72% |
| SAT math: | 550-650 | Rank in top tenth: | 38% |
| ACT composite: | 24-29 | End year in good standing: | 95% |
| GPA 3.75 or higher: | 46% | Return as sophomores: | 92% |
| GPA 3.50-3.74: | 24% | Out-of-state: | 51% |
| GPA 3.0-3.49: | 27% | Live on campus: | 95% |
| GPA 2.0-2.99: | 3% | International: | 1% |

**Basis for selection.** GED not accepted. Academic achievement, scholastic aptitude, personal characteristics important. GPA below 3.0 reevaluated to include only grades in academic subjects. Course content and test scores important. Interview recommended for all; audition recommended for music. **Homeschooled:** Test scores, interview by admissions representative required.

**High school preparation.** College-preparatory program required. Required and recommended units include English 4, mathematics 3-4, social studies 2-3, history 2-3, science 3-4 (laboratory 3-4), foreign language 3-4 and academic electives 3. Algebra, geometry, trigonometry required of engineering applicants. Of 6 additional electives 4 must be from subjects mentioned and the arts.

**2009-2010 Annual costs.** Tuition/fees: $29,675. Room/board: $7,976. Books/supplies: $1,000. Personal expenses: $1,700.

**2008-2009 Financial aid. Need-based:** 869 full-time freshmen applied for aid; 596 were judged to have need; 596 of these received aid. Average need met was 87%. Average scholarship/grant was $13,457; average loan $4,305. 68% of total undergraduate aid awarded as scholarships/grants, 32% as loans/jobs. **Non-need-based:** Awarded to 2,863 full-time undergraduates, including 723 freshmen. Scholarships awarded for academics, alumni affiliation, athletics, leadership, minority status, music/drama, ROTC.

**Application procedures. Admission:** Closing date 2/1 (postmark date). $50 fee, may be waived for applicants with need. Admission notification 3/15. Must reply by 5/1. **Financial aid:** Priority date 2/1, closing date 6/30. FAFSA required. Applicants notified on a rolling basis starting 3/1; must reply by 5/1 or within 3 week(s) of notification.

**Academics. Special study options:** Accelerated study, combined bachelor's/graduate degree, double major, ESL, exchange student, honors, independent study, internships, semester at sea, study abroad, teacher certification program, Washington semester, weekend college. **Credit/placement by examination:** AP, CLEP, IB, SAT, ACT. 32 credit hours maximum toward bachelor's degree. **Support services:** Pre-admission summer program, study skills assistance, writing center.

**Majors. Area/ethnic studies:** Asian, European, Latin American, women's. **Biology:** General, biochemistry. **Business:** Accounting, banking/financial services, business admin, international, management information systems, managerial economics. **Communications:** Broadcast journalism, journalism, public relations. **Computer sciences:** Computer science. **Education:** Music, physical, special. **Engineering:** General, civil, computer, electrical, mechanical. **Foreign languages:** Comparative lit, French, Italian, Spanish. **Health:** Preop/surgical nursing. **History:** General. **Liberal arts:** Arts/sciences. **Math:** General. **Parks/recreation:** Sports admin. **Philosophy/religion:** Philosophy, religion. **Physical sciences:** Chemistry, physics. **Protective services:** Criminal justice. **Psychology:** General. **Social sciences:** Economics, international relations, political science, sociology. **Visual/performing arts:** Dramatic, music performance, studio arts.

**Most popular majors.** Business/marketing 27%, communications/journalism 11%, engineering/engineering technologies 9%, psychology 8%, social sciences 10%.

**Computing on campus.** 560 workstations in library, computer center. Dormitories wired for high-speed internet access and linked to campus network. Commuter students can connect to campus network. Online course registration, online library, helpline, repair service, student web hosting, wireless network available.

**Student life. Freshman orientation:** Mandatory, $60 fee. Preregistration for classes offered. **Housing:** Guaranteed on-campus for freshmen. Coed dorms, single-sex dorms, special housing for disabled, apartments, wellness housing available. $200 fully refundable deposit, deadline 5/1. International students, freshmen and sophomores under 21 must live on campus, unless living at home. **Activities:** Bands, campus ministries, choral groups, dance, drama, international student organizations, literary magazine, music ensembles, radio station, student government, student newspaper, symphony orchestra, TV station, 102 student clubs and service organizations.

**Athletics.** NCAA. **Intercollegiate:** Baseball M, basketball, cross-country, golf, rowing (crew), soccer, tennis, track and field, volleyball W. **Intramural:** Badminton, basketball, racquetball, soccer, softball, tennis, volleyball, weight lifting, wrestling M. **Team name:** Bulldogs.

**Student services.** Adult student services, alcohol/substance abuse counseling, chaplain/spiritual director, career counseling, student employment services, financial aid counseling, health services, minority student services, personal counseling, veterans' counselor. **Physically disabled:** Services for visually, speech, hearing impaired.

**Contact.** E-mail: mcculloh@gu.gonzaga.edu
Phone: (509) 313-6572 Toll-free number: (800) 322-2584
Fax: (509) 313-5780
Julie McCulloh, Dean of Admissions, Gonzaga University, 502 East Boone Avenue, Spokane, WA 99258-0001

## Heritage University
### Toppenish, Washington
www.heritage.edu                    CB code: 4344

- Private 4-year liberal arts and teachers college affiliated with interdenominational tradition
- Commuter campus in small town

**General.** Founded in 1982. Regionally accredited. **Location:** 165 miles from Seattle, 20 miles from Yakima. **Calendar:** Semester.

**Annual costs/financial aid.** Tuition/fees (2009-2010): $14,010. Books/supplies: $1,155. Personal expenses: $2,984. Need-based financial aid available to full-time and part-time students.

**Contact.** Phone: (509) 865-8508
Director of Admissions, 3240 Fort Road, Toppenish, WA 98948-9599

## International Academy of Design and Technology: Seattle
### Seattle, Washington
www.iadtseattle.com

- For-profit 4-year university
- Very large city

**General.** Accredited by ACICS. **Calendar:** Quarter.

**Annual costs/financial aid.** Tuition/fees (2009-2010): $17,350.

**Contact.** Phone: (888) 424-8111
Director of Admissions, 645 Andover Park West, Seattle, WA 98188

## ITT Technical Institute: Everett
### Everett, Washington
www.itt-tech.edu                    CB code: 2697

- For-profit 4-year technical college
- Commuter campus in large town

**General.** Accredited by ACICS. **Calendar:** Quarter.

**Contact.** Phone: (425) 485-0303
Director of Recruitment, 1615 75th Street, S.W., Everett, WA 98203

## ITT Technical Institute: Seattle
### Seattle, Washington
www.itt-tech.edu                    CB code: 3599

- For-profit 4-year technical college
- Commuter campus in very large city

**General.** Founded in 1932. Accredited by ACICS. **Location:** 12 miles from downtown. **Calendar:** Quarter.

**Contact.** Phone: (206) 244-3300
Director of Recruitment, 12720 Gateway Drive, Suite 100, Seattle, WA 98168

## ITT Technical Institute: Spokane
### Spokane Valley, Washington
www.itt-tech.edu                    CB code: 7027

- For-profit 4-year technical college
- Commuter campus in small city

**General.** Accredited by ACICS. **Location:** 5 miles from downtown. **Calendar:** Quarter.

**Contact.** Phone: (509) 926-2900
Director of Recruitment, 13518 East Indiana Avenue, Spokane Valley, WA 99216

## Northwest College of Art
### Poulsbo, Washington
www.nca.edu                    CB code: 2432

- For-profit 4-year visual arts college
- Commuter campus in large town
- 108 full-time, degree-seeking undergraduates
- Application essay, interview required

**General.** Founded in 1982. Accredited by ACCSC. **Degrees:** 27 bachelor's awarded. **Location:** 30 miles from Seattle, 60 miles from Tacoma. **Calendar:** Semester, extensive summer session. **Part-time faculty:** 15 total; 27% have terminal degrees, 40% women. **Class size:** 98% < 20, 2% 20-39.

**Basis for selection.** Requirements include minimum 2.5 GPA, 2 interviews, 3 letters of recommendation, 2-3 page typed essay, portfolio. TOEFL test required for international students from non-English speaking countries. SAT required for students with a GED. Portfolio required and a second essay is required if your grade point is below 2.0. **Homeschooled:** GED required except when homeschool programs show proof of school or program accreditation.

**2010-2011 Annual costs.** Tuition/fees (projected): $17,350. Books/supplies: $3,000.

**Financial aid. Non-need-based:** Scholarships awarded for academics, art, state residency.

**Application procedures. Admission:** No deadline. $50 fee. Admission notification on a rolling basis. **Financial aid:** Priority date 3/1, closing date 6/1. FAFSA required. Applicants notified on a rolling basis.

**Academics. Special study options:** Double major, internships. **Credit/placement by examination:** AP, CLEP.

**Majors. Visual/performing arts:** Design, studio arts.

**Computing on campus.** PC or laptop required. Wireless network available.

**Student life. Freshman orientation:** Mandatory, $15 fee. Preregistration for classes offered.

**Student services.** Adult student services, career counseling, student employment services, financial aid counseling, personal counseling, placement for graduates.

**Contact.** E-mail: admissions@nca.edu
Phone: (360) 779-9993 Toll-free number: (800) 769-2787
Fax: (360) 779-9933
Kim Perigard, Northwest College of Art, Northwest College of Art, 16301 Creative Drive NE, Poulsbo, WA 98370-8651

## Northwest University
### Kirkland, Washington
www.northwestu.edu          CB member          CB code: 4541

- Private 4-year university and liberal arts college affiliated with Assemblies of God
- Residential campus in small city
- 1,046 degree-seeking undergraduates: 7% part-time, 61% women
- 237 degree-seeking graduate students
- 74% of applicants admitted
- SAT or ACT (ACT writing optional), application essay required

**General.** Founded in 1934. Regionally accredited. **Degrees:** 409 bachelor's, 9 associate awarded; master's, professional offered. **ROTC:** Army. **Location:** 10 miles from Seattle. **Calendar:** Semester, limited summer session. **Full-time faculty:** 61 total; 64% have terminal degrees, 8% minority, 38% women. **Part-time faculty:** 62 total; 6% have terminal degrees, 3% minority, 64% women. **Class size:** 63% < 20, 32% 20-39, 3% 40-49, 3% 50-99.

**Freshman class profile.** 469 applied, 348 admitted, 167 enrolled.

| Mid 50% test scores | | | |
|---|---|---|---|
| SAT critical reading: | 440-580 | GPA 3.75 or higher: | 23% |
| SAT math: | 430-570 | GPA 3.50-3.74: | 19% |
| SAT writing: | 450-560 | GPA 3.0-3.49: | 31% |
| ACT composite: | 17-24 | GPA 2.0-2.99: | 26% |
| | | Out-of-state: | 18% |

**Basis for selection.** Entire application reviewed: includes essay, references, transcript, SAT or ACT. GPA of 2.3 required: those with GPA below 2.3 but greater than 2.0 admitted on academic probation if space available. TOEFL (minimum score 500) required for non-native speakers of English. Audition recommended for music and drama scholarships. **Learning Disabled:** Interview with Director of Student Success.

**High school preparation.** 16 units recommended. Recommended units include English 4, mathematics 3, social studies 2, history 2, science 2, foreign language 2 and academic electives 3.

**2009-2010 Annual costs.** Tuition/fees: $21,994. Room/board: $6,724. Books/supplies: $1,000. Personal expenses: $1,650.

**2008-2009 Financial aid.** **Need-based:** 164 full-time freshmen applied for aid; 135 were judged to have need; 135 of these received aid. Average need met was 74%. Average scholarship/grant was $12,453; average loan $3,252. 59% of total undergraduate aid awarded as scholarships/grants, 41% as loans/jobs. **Non-need-based:** Awarded to 282 full-time undergraduates, including 68 freshmen. Scholarships awarded for academics, art, athletics, leadership, music/drama, religious affiliation.

**Application procedures.** **Admission:** Priority date 3/1; deadline 8/1 (postmark date). $30 fee, may be waived for applicants with need. Admission notification on a rolling basis beginning on or about 10/1. **Financial aid:** Priority date 3/1, closing date 8/1. FAFSA, institutional form required. Applicants notified by 3/31; Applicants notified on a rolling basis starting 3/3; must reply within 4 week(s) of notification.

**Academics.** **Special study options:** Accelerated study, double major, dual enrollment of high school students, ESL, independent study, internships, student-designed major, study abroad, teacher certification program, Washington semester. **Credit/placement by examination:** AP, CLEP, IB, SAT, ACT, institutional tests. 30 credit hours maximum toward associate degree, 30 toward bachelor's. **Support services:** Learning center, reduced course load, remedial instruction, study skills assistance, tutoring, writing center.

**Majors. Biology:** General. **Business:** Business admin. **Communications:** General, media studies, organizational. **Conservation:** Environmental science. **Education:** Elementary, middle, secondary. **Health:** Nursing (RN), premedicine. **History:** General. **Math:** General. **Philosophy/religion:** Philosophy. **Psychology:** General. **Social sciences:** Political science. **Theology:** Bible, missionary, pastoral counseling, sacred music, theology, youth ministry. **Other:** Communications/drama.

**Computing on campus.** 135 workstations in dormitories, library, computer center, student center. Dormitories wired for high-speed internet access and linked to campus network. Commuter students can connect to campus network. Online course registration, online library, helpline, repair service, student web hosting, wireless network available.

**Student life. Freshman orientation:** Mandatory. Held end of August, one week before start of classes. **Policies:** Religious observance required. **Housing:** Guaranteed on-campus for all undergraduates. Single-sex dorms, apartments available. $300 fully refundable deposit, deadline 5/1. **Activities:** Bands, choral groups, drama, music ensembles, musical theater, radio station, student government, student newspaper, community outreach groups, Psi Chi Honor Society (psychology), Association of International Students, Environmental Stewardship Club, Students in Free Enterprise.

**Athletics.** NAIA, NCCAA. **Intercollegiate:** Basketball, cross-country, soccer, track and field, volleyball W. **Intramural:** Football (non-tackle). **Team name:** Eagles.

**Student services.** Adult student services, alcohol/substance abuse counseling, chaplain/spiritual director, career counseling, student employment services, financial aid counseling, health services, personal counseling, veterans' counselor. **Physically disabled:** Services for visually impaired.

**Contact.** E-mail: admissions@northwestu.edu
Phone: (425) 889-5231 Toll-free number: (800) 669-3781
Fax: (425) 889-5224
Rose-mary Smith, Assistant Vice President, Enrollment, Northwest University, 5520 108th Avenue, NE, Kirkland, WA 98083-0579

## Pacific Lutheran University
Tacoma, Washington
www.plu.edu

CB member
CB code: 4597

- Private 4-year university affiliated with Evangelical Lutheran Church in America
- Residential campus in large city
- 3,305 degree-seeking undergraduates
- 78% of applicants admitted
- SAT or ACT (ACT writing optional), application essay required

**General.** Founded in 1890. Regionally accredited. **Degrees:** 763 bachelor's awarded; master's offered. **ROTC:** Army. **Location:** 7 miles from Tacoma, 30 miles from Seattle. **Calendar:** 4-1-4, extensive summer session. **Full-time faculty:** 276 total. **Part-time faculty:** 15 total. **Class size:** 28% < 20, 66% 20-39, 4% 40-49, 2% 50-99, less than 1% >100. **Special facilities:** Herbarium, invertebrate and vertebrate museums, greenhouse, field station and boat equipped for studies of Puget Sound, Scandinavian cultural center, observatory, performing arts center.

**Freshman class profile.** 2,571 applied, 2,014 admitted, 716 enrolled.

| Mid 50% test scores | | | |
|---|---|---|---|
| SAT critical reading: | 480-610 | GPA 3.0-3.49: | 23% |
| SAT math: | 500-610 | GPA 2.0-2.99: | 10% |
| SAT writing: | 470-590 | Rank in top quarter: | 66% |
| ACT composite: | 23-28 | Rank in top tenth: | 32% |
| GPA 3.75 or higher: | 45% | Out-of-state: | 29% |
| GPA 3.50-3.74: | 22% | Live on campus: | 90% |

**Basis for selection.** Grades, test scores, essay, recommendations, service, leadership. Admission on rolling basis until class is full. Interview recommended for borderline, exceptional; audition required for music, forensics, theater; portfolio recommended for art. **Homeschooled:** Must provide proof of high-school equivalency.

**High school preparation.** College-preparatory program required. 17 units recommended. Required and recommended units include English 4, mathematics 2-3, social studies 2, science 2 (laboratory 2), foreign language 2, visual/performing arts 1 and academic electives 3. Computer science, speech, debate, music also recommended. 2 years visual or performing arts recommended.

**2009-2010 Annual costs.** Tuition/fees: $28,100. Room/board: $8,600. Books/supplies: $924. Personal expenses: $2,094.

**2009-2010 Financial aid.** **Non-need-based:** Scholarships awarded for academics, alumni affiliation, art, leadership, music/drama, religious affiliation, ROTC.

**Application procedures.** **Admission:** Priority date 2/1; no deadline. $40 fee, may be waived for applicants with need, free for online applicants. Admission notification on a rolling basis beginning on or about 10/1. Must reply by May 1 or within 2 week(s) if notified thereafter. Housing deposit is refundable only through May 1. **Financial aid:** Priority date 1/31; no closing date. FAFSA required. Applicants notified on a rolling basis starting 3/15; must reply by 5/1 or within 4 week(s) of notification.

**Academics.** Freshman year program includes topic-oriented writing and critical conversation classes. **Special study options:** Combined bachelor's/graduate degree, cooperative education, cross-registration, double major, dual enrollment of high school students, ESL, exchange student, honors, independent study, internships, liberal arts/career combination, student-designed major, study abroad, teacher certification program. **Credit/placement by examination:** AP, CLEP, IB, institutional tests. 30 credit hours maximum toward bachelor's degree. **Support services:** Pre-admission summer program, reduced course load, study skills assistance, tutoring, writing center.

**Majors. Area/ethnic studies:** Scandinavian, women's. **Biology:** General. **Business:** Business admin. **Communications:** General. **Computer sciences:** Computer science. **Conservation:** Environmental science. **Education:** Elementary, secondary. **Engineering:** Computer, science. **Foreign languages:** Chinese, classics, French, German, Norwegian, Spanish. **Health:** Nursing (RN). **History:** General. **Interdisciplinary:** Global studies. **Math:** General. **Parks/recreation:** General, health/fitness. **Philosophy/religion:** Philosophy, religion. **Physical sciences:** Chemistry, geology, physics. **Psychology:** General. **Public administration:** Social work. **Social sciences:** Anthropology, economics, political science, sociology. **Visual/performing arts:** Art, studio arts, theater arts management.

**Most popular majors.** Biology 8%, business/marketing 14%, communications/journalism 6%, education 7%, English 6%, health sciences 10%, psychology 6%, social sciences 11%.

**Computing on campus.** 250 workstations in library, student center. Dormitories wired for high-speed internet access and linked to campus network. Commuter students can connect to campus network. Helpline, student web hosting available.

**Student life. Freshman orientation:** Available. Preregistration for classes offered. **Policies:** All single, full-time students must live in university housing, unless student lives at home with parent or legal guardian, is 20 years of age or older on or before a specific college-designated date, or has achieved junior status. **Housing:** Guaranteed on-campus for all undergraduates. Coed dorms, single-sex dorms, special housing for disabled, apartments available. $200 deposit, deadline 5/1. **Activities:** Bands, campus ministries, choral groups, dance, drama, film society, international student organizations, literary magazine, music ensembles, musical theater, opera, radio station, student government, student newspaper, symphony orchestra, TV station, Intervarsity Christian Fellowship, Advocates for Social Justice, Asian & Pacific Islanders club, B.L.A.C.K. at PLU, environmental action, Puentes, social work organization, Amnesty International, Habitat for Humanity, Young Life.

**Athletics.** NCAA. **Intercollegiate:** Baseball M, basketball, cheerleading, cross-country, football (tackle) M, golf, rowing (crew), soccer, softball W, swimming, tennis, track and field, volleyball W. **Intramural:** Badminton, basketball, bowling, cross-country, football (non-tackle), golf, handball, racquetball, soccer, softball, squash, table tennis, tennis, track and field, volleyball. **Team name:** Lutes.

**Student services.** Adult student services, chaplain/spiritual director, career counseling, student employment services, financial aid counseling, health services, minority student services, personal counseling, placement for graduates, veterans' counselor, women's services. **Physically disabled:** Services for visually, speech, hearing impaired.

**Contact.** E-mail: admission@plu.edu
Phone: (253) 535-7151 Toll-free number: (800) 274-6758
Fax: (253) 536-5136
Karl Stumo, Vice President of Admissions, Pacific Lutheran University, Office of Admissions, Tacoma, WA 98447-0003

---

## Saint Martin's University
**Lacey, Washington**
www.stmartin.edu
**CB member**
**CB code: 4674**

- Private 4-year university affiliated with Roman Catholic Church
- Residential campus in large town
- 1,298 degree-seeking undergraduates: 19% part-time, 55% women, 8% African American, 10% Asian American, 9% Hispanic American, 2% Native American, 6% international
- 328 degree-seeking graduate students
- 78% of applicants admitted
- SAT or ACT with writing, application essay required
- 55% graduate within 6 years

**General.** Founded in 1895. Regionally accredited. Saint Martin's Abbey, located on campus, is the home of the Benedictine monks. **Degrees:** 343 bachelor's awarded; master's offered. **ROTC:** Army, Air Force. **Location:** 3 miles from Olympia, 60 miles from Seattle. **Calendar:** Semester, limited summer session. **Full-time faculty:** 78 total; 78% have terminal degrees, 13% minority, 36% women. **Part-time faculty:** 114 total; 23% have terminal degrees, 10% minority, 44% women. **Class size:** 62% < 20, 26% 20-39, 5% 40-49, 4% 50-99, 1% >100.

**Freshman class profile.** 734 applied, 575 admitted, 180 enrolled.

| Mid 50% test scores | | | |
|---|---|---|---|
| SAT critical reading: | 430-550 | GPA 3.0-3.49: | 30% |
| SAT math: | 440-560 | GPA 2.0-2.99: | 30% |
| SAT writing: | 410-530 | Rank in top quarter: | 50% |
| ACT composite: | 16-24 | Rank in top tenth: | 19% |
| GPA 3.75 or higher: | 18% | Return as sophomores: | 71% |
| GPA 3.50-3.74: | 22% | Out-of-state: | 24% |
| | | Live on campus: | 77% |

**Basis for selection.** School achievement record most important. Test scores important. 3.0 GPA required for regular admittance. Interview recommended. **Homeschooled:** Statement describing homeschool structure and mission, transcript of courses and grades required. **Learning Disabled:** Students with disabilities initiate contact with the Office of Disability Support Services.

**High school preparation.** College-preparatory program recommended. 18 units recommended. Recommended units include English 4, mathematics 3, social studies 2, science 3 (laboratory 1), foreign language 2 and academic electives 3.

---

**2010-2011 Annual costs.** Tuition/fees (projected): $26,677. Room/board: $8,660. Books/supplies: $1,000. Personal expenses: $1,000.

**2008-2009 Financial aid. Need-based:** 164 full-time freshmen applied for aid; 148 were judged to have need; 148 of these received aid. Average need met was 81%. Average scholarship/grant was $16,664; average loan $2,746. 60% of total undergraduate aid awarded as scholarships/grants, 40% as loans/jobs. **Non-need-based:** Awarded to 315 full-time undergraduates, including 83 freshmen. Scholarships awarded for academics, alumni affiliation, art, athletics, leadership, minority status, music/drama, religious affiliation, ROTC, state residency.

**Application procedures. Admission:** Priority date 3/1; no deadline. $35 fee, may be waived for applicants with need. Admission notification on a rolling basis beginning on or about 10/1. Must reply by May 1 or within 3 week(s) if notified thereafter. **Financial aid:** Priority date 3/1; no closing date. FAFSA required. Applicants notified on a rolling basis starting 2/15.

**Academics. Special study options:** Combined bachelor's/graduate degree, distance learning, double major, ESL, exchange student, independent study, internships, study abroad, teacher certification program, Washington semester. **Credit/placement by examination:** AP, CLEP, IB, institutional tests. 32 credit hours maximum toward associate degree, 64 toward bachelor's. **Support services:** Learning center, pre-admission summer program, reduced course load, remedial instruction, study skills assistance, tutoring, writing center.

**Majors. Biology:** General. **Business:** Accounting, business admin. **Computer sciences:** Computer science. **Education:** Elementary, special. **Engineering:** Civil, mechanical. **Health:** Predental, premedicine, prepharmacy, preveterinary. **History:** General. **Liberal arts:** Humanities. **Math:** General. **Philosophy/religion:** Philosophy, religion. **Physical sciences:** Chemistry. **Protective services:** Criminal justice. **Psychology:** General. **Public administration:** Community org/advocacy. **Social sciences:** Political science, sociology. **Visual/performing arts:** Dramatic.

**Most popular majors.** Biology 6%, business/marketing 32%, education 10%, engineering/engineering technologies 8%, psychology 15%, security/protective services 8%, social sciences 7%.

**Computing on campus.** 80 workstations in library, computer center. Dormitories wired for high-speed internet access and linked to campus network. Commuter students can connect to campus network. Online library, helpline, repair service, student web hosting, wireless network available.

**Student life. Freshman orientation:** Mandatory, $150 fee. Preregistration for classes offered. Freshmen orientation program begins on the Thursday before school starts in the fall. **Policies:** Alcohol possession, consumption, possession by means of consumption (if under the age of 21) and the sale of alcoholic beverages is prohibited in or around University-owned or University-controlled property. **Housing:** Guaranteed on-campus for freshmen. Coed dorms, special housing for disabled, apartments available. $200 fully refundable deposit, deadline 7/1. **Activities:** Bands, campus ministries, choral groups, dance, drama, international student organizations, Model UN, musical theater, student government, student newspaper, Circle K, Hawaiian club, international club, non-traditional students group, social action club, College Republicans, Gay/Straight Alliance, Young Democrats, Saint for Life.

**Athletics.** NCAA. **Intercollegiate:** Baseball M, basketball, cross-country, golf, soccer, softball W, track and field, volleyball W. **Intramural:** Basketball, bowling, football (non-tackle), soccer, softball, tennis, volleyball. **Team name:** Saints.

**Student services.** Adult student services, alcohol/substance abuse counseling, chaplain/spiritual director, career counseling, financial aid counseling, health services, personal counseling, veterans' counselor. **Physically disabled:** Services for visually, hearing impaired.

**Contact.** E-mail: admissions@stmartin.edu
Phone: (360) 438-4596 Toll-free number: (800) 368-8803
Fax: (360) 412-6189
Eric Pedersen, Dean, Enrollment and Financial Aid, Saint Martin's University, 5300 Pacific Avenue SE, Lacey, WA 98503-7500

---

## Seattle Pacific University
**Seattle, Washington**
www.spu.edu
**CB member**
**CB code: 4694**

- Private 4-year university affiliated with Free Methodist Church of North America
- Residential campus in very large city
- 3,001 degree-seeking undergraduates: 4% part-time, 67% women, 3% African American, 9% Asian American, 4% Hispanic American, 1% Native American, 1% international

♦ 944 degree-seeking graduate students
♦ 93% of applicants admitted
♦ Application essay required
♦ 64% graduate within 6 years

**General.** Founded in 1891. Regionally accredited. **Degrees:** 780 bachelor's awarded; master's, doctoral offered. **ROTC:** Army, Naval, Air Force. **Location:** 3 miles from downtown. **Calendar:** Quarter, limited summer session. **Full-time faculty:** 191 total; 86% have terminal degrees, 8% minority, 41% women. **Part-time faculty:** 160 total; 9% have terminal degrees, 6% minority, 56% women. **Class size:** 47% < 20, 40% 20-39, 8% 40-49, 4% 50-99, less than 1% >100. **Special facilities:** 2 island campuses used for biological studies.

**Freshman class profile.** 1,973 applied, 1,830 admitted, 682 enrolled.

| Mid 50% test scores | | | |
|---|---|---|---|
| SAT critical reading: | 500-630 | GPA 3.0-3.49: | 33% |
| SAT math: | 490-620 | GPA 2.0-2.99: | 8% |
| SAT writing: | 500-590 | Return as sophomores: | 87% |
| ACT composite: | 21-28 | Out-of-state: | 43% |
| GPA 3.75 or higher: | 41% | Live on campus: | 94% |
| GPA 3.50-3.74: | 18% | International: | 1% |

**Basis for selection.** Admission decisions based primarily based on grades, grade trend, test scores, essays, letters of recommendation and extracurricular activities. Audition required for music, performing art workshop; portfolio required for fine art scholarship. **Homeschooled:** Copy of reading list and information regarding the curriculum used in homeschool program. **Learning Disabled:** Contact Disability Support Services in the Center for Learning to make arrangements for an interview to determine the level of assistance needed. Students required to provide documentation of the nature of the disability.

**High school preparation.** College-preparatory program recommended. Required units include English 4, mathematics 3, history 2, science 3 and foreign language 3.

**2010-2011 Annual costs.** Tuition/fees: $28,965. Room/board: $8,817. Books/supplies: $942. Personal expenses: $1,869.

**2009-2010 Financial aid.** **Need-based:** 596 full-time freshmen applied for aid; 505 were judged to have need; 505 of these received aid. Average need met was 83%. Average scholarship/grant was $23,290; average loan $5,033. 63% of total undergraduate aid awarded as scholarships/grants, 37% as loans/jobs. **Non-need-based:** Awarded to 772 full-time undergraduates, including 156 freshmen. Scholarships awarded for academics, alumni affiliation, art, athletics, leadership, minority status, music/drama, religious affiliation, ROTC.

**Application procedures.** **Admission:** Closing date 2/1 (postmark date). $45 fee, may be waived for applicants with need. Admission notification 3/1. Admission notification on a rolling basis. Must reply by May 1 or within 2 week(s) if notified thereafter. **Financial aid:** Priority date 2/1; no closing date. FAFSA required. Applicants notified on a rolling basis starting 3/11; must reply by 5/1 or within 30 week(s) of notification.

**Academics.** **Special study options:** Distance learning, double major, exchange student, external degree, honors, independent study, internships, liberal arts/career combination, student-designed major, study abroad, teacher certification program, Washington semester. **Credit/placement by examination:** AP, CLEP, IB, SAT, ACT, institutional tests. 45 credit hours maximum toward bachelor's degree. **Support services:** Learning center, reduced course load, remedial instruction, study skills assistance, tutoring, writing center.

**Majors.** **Area/ethnic studies:** European, Latin American. **Biology:** General, biochemistry. **Business:** Accounting. **Communications:** General. **Computer sciences:** Computer science. **Education:** Art, English, mathematics, music, science, social science, special. **Engineering:** Computer, electrical, science. **Family/consumer sciences:** Clothing/textiles, food/nutrition. **Foreign languages:** Classics, French, German, Latin, Russian, Spanish. **Health:** Nursing (RN). **History:** General. **Legal studies:** Prelaw. **Liberal arts:** Arts/sciences. **Math:** General, computational. **Parks/recreation:** Exercise sciences. **Philosophy/religion:** Philosophy. **Physical sciences:** Chemistry, physics. **Psychology:** General. **Social sciences:** Economics, political science, sociology. **Theology:** Religious ed. **Visual/performing arts:** General, art, dramatic, interior design. **Other:** Global development studies.

**Most popular majors.** Biology 7%, business/marketing 15%, communications/journalism 7%, family/consumer sciences 8%, health sciences 9%, psychology 7%, social sciences 10%, visual/performing arts 8%.

**Computing on campus.** 475 workstations in dormitories, library, computer center, student center. Dormitories wired for high-speed internet access and linked to campus network. Commuter students can connect to campus network. Online course registration, online library, helpline, repair service, wireless network available.

**Student life.** **Freshman orientation:** Mandatory. Preregistration for classes offered. **Policies:** Religious observance required. **Housing:** Coed dorms, special housing for disabled, apartments available. $300 fully refundable deposit, deadline 6/1. **Activities:** Bands, campus ministries, choral groups, drama, literary magazine, music ensembles, musical theater, radio station, student government, student newspaper, symphony orchestra, more than 25 clubs and organizations.

**Athletics.** NCAA. **Intercollegiate:** Basketball, cross-country, gymnastics W, rowing (crew), soccer, track and field, volleyball W. **Intramural:** Badminton, basketball, bowling, cross-country, football (tackle) M, golf, skiing, soccer, softball, swimming, table tennis, tennis, track and field, volleyball, wrestling M. **Team name:** Falcons.

**Student services.** Adult student services, chaplain/spiritual director, career counseling, student employment services, financial aid counseling, health services, minority student services, personal counseling, placement for graduates, veterans' counselor. **Physically disabled:** Services for visually, hearing impaired.

**Contact.** E-mail: admissions@spu.edu
Phone: (206) 281-2021 Toll-free number: (800) 366-3344
Fax: (206) 281-2669
Jobe Korb-Nice, Director of Undergraduate Admissions, Seattle Pacific University, 3307 Third Avenue West, Suite 115, Seattle, WA 98119-1997

## Seattle University

Seattle, Washington
www.seattleu.edu

CB member
CB code: 4695

♦ Private 4-year university affiliated with Roman Catholic Church
♦ Residential campus in very large city
♦ 4,267 degree-seeking undergraduates: 5% part-time, 60% women, 5% African American, 19% Asian American, 8% Hispanic American, 1% Native American, 10% international
♦ 3,412 degree-seeking graduate students
♦ 66% of applicants admitted
♦ SAT or ACT (ACT writing optional) required
♦ 73% graduate within 6 years

**General.** Founded in 1891. Regionally accredited. Courses also offered at Bellevue Campus. **Degrees:** 1,062 bachelor's awarded; master's, doctoral, professional offered. **ROTC:** Army, Naval, Air Force. **Location:** One mile from downtown. **Calendar:** Quarter, extensive summer session. **Full-time faculty:** 435 total; 79% have terminal degrees, 8% minority, 46% women. **Part-time faculty:** 243 total; 16% have terminal degrees, 3% minority, 53% women. **Class size:** 53% < 20, 46% 20-39, less than 1% 40-49, 1% 50-99. **Special facilities:** Design center (where engineering students work with major companies in the area), observatory.

**Freshman class profile.** 5,578 applied, 3,692 admitted, 734 enrolled.

| Mid 50% test scores | | | |
|---|---|---|---|
| SAT critical reading: | 520-640 | GPA 2.0-2.99: | 4% |
| SAT math: | 520-640 | Rank in top quarter: | 61% |
| SAT writing: | 510-620 | Rank in top tenth: | 30% |
| ACT composite: | 23-29 | Return as sophomores: | 90% |
| GPA 3.75 or higher: | 38% | Out-of-state: | 51% |
| GPA 3.50-3.74: | 24% | Live on campus: | 87% |
| GPA 3.0-3.49: | 34% | International: | 4% |

**Basis for selection.** 2.75 GPA minimum, higher for some programs. Secondary school record, recommendations, test scores most important. Essay, school, community activities also important. Applicants must submit one test with writing component. ACT writing component is required if applicant does not submit SAT Reasoning scores.

**High school preparation.** College-preparatory program required. 16 units required. Required units include English 4, mathematics 3, social studies 2, history 1, science 2 (laboratory 2), foreign language 2 and academic electives 2.

**2009-2010 Annual costs.** Tuition/fees: $29,340. $200 enrollment deposit, $95 matriculation fee required. $95 per-credit-hour charge for credit by examination. $95 per-credit-hour charge for validation of field experience. Room/board: $8,805. Books/supplies: $945. Personal expenses: $1,878.

**2009-2010 Financial aid.** **Need-based:** 662 full-time freshmen applied for aid; 500 were judged to have need; 498 of these received aid. Average need met was 77%. Average scholarship/grant was $16,022; average loan $4,363. 67% of total undergraduate aid awarded as scholarships/grants, 33% as loans/jobs. **Non-need-based:** Awarded to 608 full-time undergraduates, including 96 freshmen. Scholarships awarded for academics, alumni affiliation, athletics, leadership, minority status, music/drama, ROTC, state residency.

**Application procedures. Admission:** Priority date 1/15; no deadline. $50 fee, may be waived for applicants with need. Admission notification on a rolling basis beginning on or about 2/6. Must reply by May 1 or within 4 week(s) if notified thereafter. **Financial aid:** Priority date 2/1; no closing date. FAFSA required. Applicants notified on a rolling basis starting 3/21; must reply by 5/1 or within 2 week(s) of notification.

**Academics. Special study options:** Cooperative education, cross-registration, double major, honors, independent study, internships, liberal arts/career combination, student-designed major, study abroad. **Credit/ placement by examination:** AP, CLEP, IB, institutional tests. 45 credit hours maximum toward bachelor's degree. Special arrangements for nursing majors who take NLN exams. 50 credits maximum. **Support services:** Learning center, pre-admission summer program, reduced course load, study skills assistance, tutoring, writing center.

**Majors. Area/ethnic studies:** Asian, women's. **Biology:** General, biochemistry. **Business:** General, accounting, business admin, e-commerce, finance, international, managerial economics, marketing. **Communications:** Journalism, media studies, public relations. **Computer sciences:** Computer science. **Conservation:** General. **Engineering:** Civil, electrical, mechanical. **Foreign languages:** General, French, Spanish. **Health:** Clinical lab science, medical records admin, nurse practitioner, nursing (RN), public health nursing, sonography. **History:** General. **Interdisciplinary:** Global studies. **Liberal arts:** Arts/sciences, humanities. **Math:** General. **Philosophy/ religion:** Philosophy, religion. **Physical sciences:** General, chemistry, physics. **Protective services:** Criminal justice, criminalistics. **Psychology:** General. **Public administration:** General, social work. **Social sciences:** Economics, political science, sociology. **Visual/performing arts:** General, art history/ conservation, dramatic.

**Most popular majors.** Business/marketing 23%, communications/ journalism 6%, health sciences 15%, liberal arts 7%, psychology 6%, social sciences 7%.

**Computing on campus.** 467 workstations in dormitories, library, computer center, student center. Dormitories wired for high-speed internet access and linked to campus network. Commuter students can connect to campus network. Online course registration, helpline, student web hosting, wireless network available.

**Student life. Freshman orientation:** Mandatory. Preregistration for classes offered. 3 days prior to start of classes. **Housing:** Guaranteed on-campus for freshmen. Coed dorms, apartments available. $300 nonrefundable deposit, deadline 5/1. Single-gender floors available. **Activities:** Bands, campus ministries, choral groups, drama, international student organizations, literary magazine, music ensembles, radio station, student government, student newspaper, 65 clubs available.

**Athletics.** NCAA. **Intercollegiate:** Baseball M, basketball, cross-country, golf, soccer, softball W, swimming, tennis, track and field, volleyball W. **Intramural:** Basketball, football (non-tackle), soccer, softball, tennis, volleyball. **Team name:** Redhawks.

**Student services.** Adult student services, alcohol/substance abuse counseling, chaplain/spiritual director, career counseling, student employment services, financial aid counseling, health services, minority student services, personal counseling, placement for graduates, veterans' counselor, women's services. **Physically disabled:** Services for visually, speech, hearing impaired.

**Contact.** E-mail: admissions@seattleu.edu
Phone: (206) 296-2000 Toll-free number: (800) 426-7123
Fax: (206) 296-5656
Melore Nielsen, Dean of Admissions, Seattle University, 901 12th Avenue, Seattle, WA 98122-4340

## Trinity Lutheran College
**Everett, Washington**
www.tlc.edu                          CB code: 4408

- Private 4-year Bible and liberal arts college affiliated with Lutheran Church
- Residential campus in small city
- 119 degree-seeking undergraduates
- SAT or ACT (ACT writing optional) required

**General.** Founded in 1944. Regionally accredited. All students participate in off-campus service learning practicums. **Degrees:** 21 bachelor's awarded. **Location:** 30 miles from Seattle. **Calendar:** 4-1-4. **Full-time faculty:** 13

total. **Part-time faculty:** 18 total. **Special facilities:** Children, youth and family resource center; preschool and Christian school.

**Freshman class profile.**

| Mid 50% test scores | ACT composite: | 20-23 |
|---|---|---|

**Basis for selection.** High school GPA, test scores, one recommendation. Interview considered. **Homeschooled:** Statement describing homeschool structure and mission, transcript of courses and grades, letter of recommendation (nonparent) required.

**High school preparation.** Recommended units include English 3, mathematics 2, history 2, science 2 and foreign language 1.

**2009-2010 Annual costs.** Tuition/fees: $19,425. Lunch-only meal plan (5 days per week) for academic year, $900. Room only: $6,570. Books/ supplies: $924. Personal expenses: $1,818.

**2009-2010 Financial aid. Non-need-based:** Scholarships awarded for academics, alumni affiliation, art, leadership, music/drama.

**Application procedures. Admission:** Priority date 3/1; no deadline. $30 fee, may be waived for applicants with need, free for online applicants. Admission notification on a rolling basis beginning on or about 10/1. Must reply by May 1 or within 2 week(s) if notified thereafter. **Financial aid:** Priority date 3/1; no closing date. FAFSA, institutional form required. Applicants notified on a rolling basis starting 3/15; must reply within 2 week(s) of notification.

**Academics. Special study options:** Combined bachelor's/graduate degree, cooperative education, dual enrollment of high school students, independent study, internships, liberal arts/career combination, student-designed major, study abroad, urban semester. Study trips to Holy Lands, Italy, Greece, Africa. **Credit/placement by examination:** AP, CLEP, IB, institutional tests. 8 credit hours maximum toward associate degree, 8 toward bachelor's. **Support services:** Reduced course load, remedial instruction, study skills assistance, tutoring, writing center.

**Majors. Business:** Business admin, nonprofit/public. **Communications:** Media studies. **Education:** Early childhood, elementary. **Philosophy/ religion:** Christian, religion. **Psychology:** General. **Public administration:** Social work. **Theology:** Bible, missionary, sacred music, theology, youth ministry.

**Computing on campus.** 15 workstations in dormitories, library, computer center, student center. Dormitories wired for high-speed internet access and linked to campus network. Commuter students can connect to campus network. Online library, helpline, wireless network available.

**Student life. Freshman orientation:** Mandatory. Preregistration for classes offered. 3-day session held before classes begin. **Housing:** Guaranteed on-campus for all undergraduates. Single-sex dorms, special housing for disabled, apartments, wellness housing available. $75 partly refundable deposit, deadline 5/1. **Activities:** Choral groups, drama, music ensembles, musical theater, student government, student newspaper, Student learning practicums, Global Concerns Mission, Worship Commission, Environmental Commission.

**Athletics. Intramural:** Basketball, football (non-tackle), soccer, softball, table tennis, tennis, volleyball. **Team name:** Eagles.

**Student services.** Adult student services, chaplain/spiritual director, career counseling, student employment services, financial aid counseling, health services, personal counseling, placement for graduates. **Physically disabled:** Services for visually impaired.

**Contact.** E-mail: admissions@tlc.edu
Phone: (425) 249-4800 Toll-free number: (800) 843-5659
Fax: (425) 249-4801
Pamela Renn, Director of Enrollment, Trinity Lutheran College, 2802 Wetmore Avenue, Everett, WA 98201

## University of Puget Sound
**Tacoma, Washington**                    CB member
www.pugetsound.edu                        CB code: 4067

- Private 4-year liberal arts college
- Residential campus in small city
- 2,596 degree-seeking undergraduates: 1% part-time, 59% women, 3% African American, 10% Asian American, 4% Hispanic American, 2% Native American, 1% international
- 274 degree-seeking graduate students
- 63% of applicants admitted

▶ SAT or ACT (ACT writing recommended), application essay required

▶ 78% graduate within 6 years; 18% enter graduate study

**General.** Founded in 1888. Regionally accredited. **Degrees:** 598 bachelor's awarded; master's, professional offered. **ROTC:** Army. **Location:** 35 miles from Seattle, 28 miles from Olympia. **Calendar:** Semester, limited summer session. **Full-time faculty:** 226 total; 87% have terminal degrees, 7% minority, 46% women. **Part-time faculty:** 51 total; 47% have terminal degrees, 6% minority, 53% women. **Class size:** 55% < 20, 43% 20-39, 2% 40-49, less than 1% 50-99. **Special facilities:** Natural history museum, arboretum, x-ray laboratory, electron microscope lab, observatory, concert hall, sculpture building, greenhouse, sedimentology lab, rock and mineral collection, exercise science lab, physiology labs.

**Freshman class profile.** 5,588 applied, 3,526 admitted, 721 enrolled.

| Mid 50% test scores | | Rank in top quarter: | 62% |
|---|---|---|---|
| SAT critical reading: | 570-680 | Rank in top tenth: | 15% |
| SAT math: | 560-680 | End year in good standing: | 96% |
| ACT composite: | 25-32 | Return as sophomores: | 86% |
| GPA 3.75 or higher: | 32% | Out-of-state: | 76% |
| GPA 3.50-3.74: | 24% | Live on campus: | 98% |
| GPA 3.0-3.49: | 35% | International: | 1% |
| GPA 2.0-2.99: | 9% | | |

**Basis for selection.** High school record most important followed by academic GPA. Writing ability as demonstrated through the essay and short answer questions. Recommendations and activities important. If applicants have taken both SAT and ACT, they should submit all scores. Interview recommended for all; audition required for music; portfolio recommended for art; audition recommended for theater. **Homeschooled:** Applicants should show work in writing, critical reading, mathematics, history; and social, physical, and natural sciences. Foreign language recommended.

**High school preparation.** College-preparatory program recommended. 19 units recommended. Recommended units include English 4, mathematics 4, social studies 3, history 3, science 4 (laboratory 4), foreign language 3 and visual/performing arts 1. One fine, visual or performing art recommended.

**2010-2011 Annual costs.** Tuition/fees: $37,225. Room/board: $9,650. Books/supplies: $1,000. Personal expenses: $1,800.

**2009-2010 Financial aid. Need-based:** 551 full-time freshmen applied for aid; 465 were judged to have need; 465 of these received aid. Average need met was 85%. Average scholarship/grant was $23,361; average loan $4,785. 70% of total undergraduate aid awarded as scholarships/grants, 30% as loans/jobs. **Non-need-based:** Awarded to 730 full-time undergraduates, including 205 freshmen. Scholarships awarded for academics, alumni affiliation, art, leadership, music/drama, religious affiliation. **Additional information:** Cooperative education allows qualified upperclassmen to alternate semesters of full-time study and full-time work.

**Application procedures. Admission:** Closing date 1/15 (postmark date). $50 fee, may be waived for applicants with need. Admission notification 4/1. Must reply by May 1 or within 2 week(s) if notified thereafter. **Financial aid:** Priority date 2/1; no closing date. FAFSA required. Students applying for Early Decision must complete the CSS PROFILE for notification of need-based financial aid eligibility. Applicants notified on a rolling basis starting 3/15; must reply by 5/1 or within 2 week(s) of notification.

**Academics.** All students complete core curriculum, including courses in writing and rhetoric, scholarly and creative inquiry, fine arts, humanistic, mathematical, natural scientific and social scientific approaches, and a connections course intended to develop an understanding of the interrelationship of fields of knowledge. **Special study options:** Combined bachelor's/graduate degree, cooperative education, double major, dual enrollment of high school students, honors, independent study, internships, student-designed major, study abroad, teacher certification program. Institution also offers community service opportunities, forensics & debate, diversity & leadership training, multiple speaker/lecturer programs, year of study in Asia, 3-2 engineering program, business leadership program. **Credit/placement by examination:** AP, CLEP, IB, institutional tests. **Support services:** Learning center, reduced course load, study skills assistance, tutoring, writing center.

**Majors. Area/ethnic studies:** Asian. **Biology:** General, biochemistry, cellular/molecular. **Business:** Business admin. **Communications:** General. **Computer sciences:** General, computer science. **Education:** Music. **Foreign languages:** Classics, French, German, Spanish. **History:** General. **Interdisciplinary:** Natural sciences, science/society. **Math:** General. **Parks/recreation:** Exercise sciences. **Philosophy/religion:** Philosophy, religion. **Physical sciences:** Chemistry, geology, physics. **Psychology:** General. **Social sciences:** Economics, international economics, political science, sociology. **Visual/performing arts:** Art, dramatic, music management, music performance.

**Most popular majors.** Biology 8%, business/marketing 16%, English 9%, foreign language 9%, psychology 6%, social sciences 22%, visual/performing arts 8%.

**Computing on campus.** 324 workstations in dormitories, library, computer center, student center. Dormitories wired for high-speed internet access and linked to campus network. Commuter students can connect to campus network. Online course registration, online library, helpline, repair service, student web hosting, wireless network available.

**Student life. Freshman orientation:** Available. 9-day introduction to academic life and campus community. **Housing:** Guaranteed on-campus for freshmen. Coed dorms, single-sex dorms, special housing for disabled, fraternity/sorority housing, wellness housing available. $300 nonrefundable deposit, deadline 5/1. 56 university-owned homes on campus. **Activities:** Bands, campus ministries, choral groups, dance, drama, film society, international student organizations, literary magazine, music ensembles, Model UN, musical theater, opera, radio station, student government, student newspaper, symphony orchestra, Black student union, Hui-o-Hawaii, Circle K, Jewish student organization, Bisexuals, Gays, Lesbians, and Allies for Diversity, Pacific American student union, Students for Peace and Justice, First Nations, Habitat for Humanity, film and theatre society.

**Athletics.** NCAA. **Intercollegiate:** Baseball M, basketball, cheerleading, cross-country, football (tackle) M, golf, lacrosse W, rowing (crew), soccer, softball W, swimming, tennis, track and field, volleyball W. **Intramural:** Basketball, football (non-tackle), soccer, softball, tennis, volleyball. **Team name:** Loggers.

**Student services.** Alcohol/substance abuse counseling, chaplain/spiritual director, career counseling, services for economically disadvantaged, student employment services, financial aid counseling, health services, legal services, minority student services, personal counseling, placement for graduates. **Physically disabled:** Services for visually, speech, hearing impaired.

**Contact.** E-mail: admission@pugetsound.edu
Phone: (253) 879-3211 Toll-free number: (800) 396-7191
Fax: (253) 879-3993
George Mills, Vice President for Enrollment, University of Puget Sound, 1500 North Warner Street, Tacoma, WA 98416-1062

---

## University of Washington
**Seattle, Washington**
**www.washington.edu**
CB member
CB code: 4854

▶ Public 4-year university

▶ Residential campus in very large city

▶ 30,554 degree-seeking undergraduates: 8% part-time, 50% women, 3% African American, 28% Asian American, 6% Hispanic American, 1% Native American, 6% international

▶ 13,225 degree-seeking graduate students

▶ 58% of applicants admitted

▶ SAT or ACT with writing, application essay required

▶ 81% graduate within 6 years

**General.** Founded in 1861. Regionally accredited. **Degrees:** 6,952 bachelor's awarded; master's, doctoral, professional offered. **ROTC:** Army, Naval, Air Force. **Location:** 5 miles from downtown. **Calendar:** Quarter, extensive summer session. **Full-time faculty:** 3,046 total; 21% minority, 37% women. **Part-time faculty:** 706 total; 18% minority, 50% women. **Class size:** 33% < 20, 39% 20-39, 10% 40-49, 10% 50-99, 8% >100. **Special facilities:** Arboretum, observatory, anthropological museum, applied physics laboratory, planetarium.

**Freshman class profile.** 21,268 applied, 12,264 admitted, 5,338 enrolled.

| Mid 50% test scores | | Rank in top quarter: | 97% |
|---|---|---|---|
| SAT critical reading: | 530-650 | Rank in top tenth: | 86% |
| SAT math: | 570-680 | Return as sophomores: | 93% |
| SAT writing: | 530-640 | Out-of-state: | 16% |
| ACT composite: | 24-30 | Live on campus: | 63% |
| GPA 3.75 or higher: | 55% | International: | 9% |
| GPA 3.50-3.74: | 30% | Fraternities: | 10% |
| GPA 3.0-3.49: | 14% | Sororities: | 9% |
| GPA 2.0-2.99: | 1% | | |

**Basis for selection.** Applicants evaluated and ranked on completion of core subject requirements, grades and test scores and supplemental factors including personal statement, completion of substantial number of courses beyond minimum, grades in college-preparatory courses, enrollment in AP or honors courses, cultural diversity and documented evidence of exceptional artistic talent. Auditions required for admission to performing arts programs. Application interviews not available, only informational appointments. **Homeschooled:** Each applicant is reviewed case-by-case. To confirm successful completion of certain core subject requirements or levels, applicants may be asked to provide additional documentation or placement testing information. **Learning Disabled:** Applicants with documented disabilities not expected to disclose them at time of application, but welcome do so in the applicant's own written materials, or via relevant documentation or letters. Students encouraged to first speak with an admissions counselor.

**High school preparation.** 15 units required; 20 recommended. Required and recommended units include English 4, mathematics 3-4, social studies 3-4, history 1, science 2-3 (laboratory 1-3), foreign language 2-3, computer science 1, visual/performing arts .5-1. One semester (.5) elective from required subjects list and .5 fine arts course.

**2009-2010 Annual costs.** Tuition/fees: $7,692; $24,367 out-of-state. Required fees include mandatory intramural bond fee of $105. Room/board: $8,949. Books/supplies: $1,008. Personal expenses: $2,265.

**2009-2010 Financial aid. Non-need-based:** Scholarships awarded for academics, alumni affiliation, art, athletics, leadership, music/drama, ROTC. **Additional information:** Tuition not due until third week of term.

**Application procedures. Admission:** Priority date 12/1; deadline 1/15 (postmark date). $60 fee, may be waived for applicants with need. Admission notification 4/15. Admission notification on a rolling basis. Must reply by 5/1. Applications accepted after closing date on space-available basis. **Financial aid:** Priority date 2/28; no closing date. FAFSA required. Applicants notified by 3/31; must reply within 3 week(s) of notification.

**Academics. Special study options:** Combined bachelor's/graduate degree, cooperative education, distance learning, double major, ESL, exchange student, honors, independent study, internships, student-designed major, study abroad, teacher certification program, Washington semester. Quarter at Friday Harbor Laboratories, San Juan Islands. **Credit/placement by examination:** AP, CLEP, IB, institutional tests. 90 credit hours maximum toward bachelor's degree. **Support services:** Learning center, pre-admission summer program, reduced course load, remedial instruction, study skills assistance, tutoring, writing center.

**Majors. Architecture:** Architecture, landscape, urban/community planning. **Area/ethnic studies:** African, African-American, Asian, Asian-American, Canadian, Central/Eastern European, Chicano/Hispanic-American/Latino, Chinese, European, French, German, Italian, Japanese, Korean, Latin American, Native American, Near/Middle Eastern, Russian/Slavic, Scandinavian, Slavic, South Asian, Southeast Asian, women's. **Biology:** General, bacteriology, biochemistry, botany, ecology, marine, microbiology, zoology. **Business:** Accounting, business admin, construction management, finance, human resources, international, management information systems, organizational behavior. **Communications:** General. **Computer sciences:** General, computer science, information systems, information technology. **Conservation:** General, fisheries, forest resources, forestry, wildlife. **Education:** Music. **Engineering:** General, aerospace, biomedical, ceramic, chemical, civil, computer, electrical, environmental, forest, industrial, materials, materials science, mechanical, metallurgical. **Foreign languages:** Ancient Greek, Arabic, Chinese, classics, comparative lit, Danish, East Asian, French, German, Germanic, Hebrew, Italian, Japanese, Korean, Latin, linguistics, Norwegian, Russian, Scandinavian, South Asian, Southeast Asian, Spanish, Swedish, Turkish, Ukrainian. **Health:** Audiology/speech pathology, clinical lab science, dental hygiene, environmental health, nursing (RN), orthotics/prosthetics, physician assistant. **History:** General. **Interdisciplinary:** Peace/conflict. **Liberal arts:** Arts/sciences. **Math:** General, applied. **Philosophy/religion:** Judaic, philosophy, religion. **Physical sciences:** Astronomy, astrophysics, atmospheric science, chemistry, geology, oceanography, physics, planetary. **Psychology:** General. **Public administration:** Social work. **Social sciences:** General, anthropology, economics, geography, international relations, political science, sociology. **Visual/performing arts:** Art, art history/conservation, ceramics, commercial/advertising art, dance, dramatic, fiber arts, industrial design, metal/jewelry, music history, music performance, music theory/composition, musicology, painting, photography, piano/organ, printmaking, sculpture, stringed instruments, voice/opera.

**Most popular majors.** Biology 10%, business/marketing 11%, engineering/engineering technologies 9%, social sciences 17%.

**Computing on campus.** 2,000 workstations in dormitories, library, computer center, student center. Dormitories wired for high-speed internet access and linked to campus network. Commuter students can connect to campus network. Online course registration, online library, helpline, repair service, student web hosting, wireless network available.

**Student life. Freshman orientation:** Mandatory, $250 fee. Preregistration for classes offered. Advising and registration throughout the summer.

**Housing:** Guaranteed on-campus for freshmen. Coed dorms, special housing for disabled, apartments, cooperative housing, fraternity/sorority housing, wellness housing available. $500 nonrefundable deposit, deadline 5/1. Special interest houses available. **Activities:** Bands, campus ministries, choral groups, dance, drama, film society, international student organizations, literary magazine, music ensembles, Model UN, musical theater, opera, radio station, student government, student newspaper, symphony orchestra, TV station, over 500 student organizations.

**Athletics.** NCAA. **Intercollegiate:** Baseball M, basketball, cheerleading, cross-country, football (tackle) M, golf, gymnastics W, rowing (crew), soccer, softball W, swimming, tennis, track and field, volleyball W. **Intramural:** Basketball, bowling, football (non-tackle), racquetball, rowing (crew), soccer, softball, swimming, tennis, volleyball. **Team name:** Huskies.

**Student services.** Alcohol/substance abuse counseling, career counseling, services for economically disadvantaged, student employment services, financial aid counseling, health services, legal services, minority student services, on-campus daycare, personal counseling, placement for graduates, veterans' counselor, women's services. **Physically disabled:** Services for visually, speech, hearing impaired.

**Contact.** Phone: (206) 543-9686 Fax: (206) 685-3655
Philip Ballinger, Director of Admissions, University of Washington, 1410 Northeast Campus Parkway, Box 355852, Seattle, WA 98195-5852

## University of Washington Bothell
**Bothell, Washington**
www.uwb.edu    **CB code: 4467**

- Public 4-year university
- Commuter campus in large town
- 2,329 degree-seeking undergraduates: 33% part-time, 55% women, 4% African American, 24% Asian American, 6% Hispanic American, 1% Native American, 2% international
- 440 degree-seeking graduate students
- 77% of applicants admitted
- SAT or ACT (ACT writing optional), application essay required

**General. Degrees:** 557 bachelor's awarded; master's offered. **ROTC:** Army, Naval, Air Force. **Location:** 20 miles from Seattle. **Calendar:** Quarter, limited summer session. **Full-time faculty:** 96 total; 86% have terminal degrees, 21% minority, 45% women. **Part-time faculty:** 49 total; 29% have terminal degrees, 10% minority, 45% women. **Class size:** 23% < 20, 46% 20-39, 27% 40-49, 4% 50-99. **Special facilities:** 58 acres of wetlands.

**Freshman class profile.** 1,200 applied; 921 admitted, 309 enrolled.

| Mid 50% test scores | | | |
|---|---|---|---|
| SAT critical reading: | 430-560 | GPA 3.0-3.49: | 53% |
| SAT math: | 480-600 | GPA 2.0-2.99: | 26% |
| SAT writing: | 430-540 | End year in good standing: | 88% |
| ACT composite: | 18-24 | Return as sophomores: | 77% |
| GPA 3.75 or higher: | 8% | Out-of-state: | 3% |
| GPA 3.50-3.74: | 13% | Live on campus: | 8% |
| | | International: | 3% |

**Basis for selection.** GPA, test scores, academic rigor, essays most important. Non-resident alien applicants must report scores from TOEFL or the International English Language Testing System (IELTS). SAT essay component used for admission for the Business program only. **Homeschooled:** Transcript of courses and grades required.

**High school preparation.** College-preparatory program required. Required units include English 4, mathematics 3, social studies 3, science 2 (laboratory 2), foreign language 2 and visual/performing arts 1.

**2009-2010 Annual costs.** Tuition/fees: $7,575; $24,250 out-of-state.

**2009-2010 Financial aid. Need-based:** 195 full-time freshmen applied for aid; 135 were judged to have need; 126 of these received aid. Average need met was 78%. Average scholarship/grant was $9,900; average loan $4,300. 54% of total undergraduate aid awarded as scholarships/grants, 46% as loans/jobs. **Non-need-based:** Awarded to 22 full-time undergraduates, including 5 freshmen.

**Application procedures. Admission:** Priority date 1/15; no deadline. $60 fee, may be waived for applicants with need. Admission notification on a rolling basis beginning on or about 11/1. Must reply by May 1 or within 3 week(s) if notified thereafter. **Financial aid:** Priority date 2/28; no closing date. FAFSA required. Applicants notified by 4/1; must reply within 3 week(s) of notification.

**Academics. Special study options:** Combined bachelor's/graduate degree, cross-registration, double major, dual enrollment of high school students, independent study, internships, student-designed major, study abroad, teacher certification program. **Credit/placement by examination:** AP, CLEP, IB, institutional tests. **Support services:** Learning center, pre-admission summer program, reduced course load, study skills assistance, writing center.

**Majors. Area/ethnic studies:** American. **Biology:** General. **Business:** Accounting, business admin. **Communications:** Media studies. **Computer sciences:** General, applications programming, information systems, systems analysis. **Conservation:** Environmental science, environmental studies. **Education:** General. **Engineering:** Electrical. **Health:** Nursing (RN). **Interdisciplinary:** Global studies, science/society. **Liberal arts:** Humanities. **Philosophy/religion:** Ethics. **Psychology:** Community. **Visual/performing arts:** Art. **Other:** Interdisciplinary arts.

**Most popular majors.** Business/marketing 34%, computer/information sciences 8%, health sciences 21%, interdisciplinary studies 37%.

**Computing on campus.** 850 workstations in library, computer center. Dormitories wired for high-speed internet access. Commuter students can connect to campus network. Online course registration, online library, helpline, student web hosting, wireless network available.

**Student life. Freshman orientation:** Mandatory. **Housing:** Apartments available. $50 nonrefundable deposit. **Activities:** Marching band, international student organizations, student government, student newspaper, African American student union, Chinese culture club, Christians in Action, entrepreneur's network, Gay/Straight Alliance, Human Equality and Rights Everywhere, intercultural club, Policy Information and Networking Group, Still I Rise Organization, Woman and Leadership Development.

**Athletics. Intramural:** Basketball, football (non-tackle), soccer, softball, tennis, volleyball. **Team name:** Huskies.

**Student services.** Career counseling, student employment services, financial aid counseling, personal counseling, veterans' counselor. **Physically disabled:** Services for visually, speech, hearing impaired. **Learning disabled:** Comprehensive services available.

**Contact.** E-mail: admissions@uwb.edu
Phone: (425) 352-5000 Toll-free number: (800) 736-6650
Fax: (425) 352-5455
Jill Orcutt, Director of Admission, University of Washington Bothell, 18115 Campus Way NE, Bothell, WA 98011-8246

---

## University of Washington Tacoma
**Tacoma, Washington**                               CB member
**www.tacoma.washington.edu**                        CB code: 4445

- Public 4-year university and branch campus college
- Commuter campus in small city
- 2,530 degree-seeking undergraduates: 21% part-time, 57% women, 8% African American, 17% Asian American, 7% Hispanic American, 1% Native American, 1% international
- 542 degree-seeking graduate students
- 82% of applicants admitted
- SAT or ACT (ACT writing optional), application essay required

**General.** Regionally accredited. **Degrees:** 746 bachelor's awarded; master's offered. **Calendar:** Quarter, limited summer session. **Full-time faculty:** 135 total; 95% have terminal degrees, 54% women. **Part-time faculty:** 52 total; 67% have terminal degrees, 56% women. **Class size:** 29% < 20, 52% 20-39, 14% 40-49, 4% 50-99.

**Freshman class profile.** 688 applied, 563 admitted, 211 enrolled.

| Mid 50% test scores | | | |
|---|---|---|---|
| SAT critical reading: | 430-550 | GPA 3.50-3.74: | 19% |
| SAT math: | 460-570 | GPA 3.0-3.49: | 44% |
| SAT writing: | 440-540 | GPA 2.0-2.99: | 22% |
| ACT composite: | 18-24 | End year in good standing: | 79% |
| GPA 3.75 or higher: | 15% | Return as sophomores: | 68% |
| | | Out-of-state: | 2% |

**Basis for selection.** Admissions based on school achievement record, including quality of test scores, fullness of application including essay and involvement. **Homeschooled:** Transcript of courses and grades required.

**High school preparation.** College-preparatory program required. 16 units required. Required units include English 4, mathematics 3, social studies 3, science 2 (laboratory 1), foreign language 2, visual/performing arts .5, academic electives 0.5.

---

**2009-2010 Annual costs.** Tuition/fees: $7,575; $24,250 out-of-state. Books/supplies: $1,035. Personal expenses: $2,265.

**Financial aid. Non-need-based:** Scholarships awarded for academics.

**Application procedures. Admission:** $60 fee, may be waived for applicants with need. Application must be submitted online. Admission notification on a rolling basis beginning on or about 11/1. Must reply by May 1 or within 2 week(s) if notified thereafter.

**Academics. Special study options:** Cross-registration, double major, dual enrollment of high school students, honors, independent study, internships, semester at sea, student-designed major, study abroad, teacher certification program. **Credit/placement by examination:** AP, CLEP, IB, SAT, institutional tests. 90 credit hours maximum toward bachelor's degree. **Support services:** Learning center, pre-admission summer program, remedial instruction, study skills assistance, tutoring, writing center.

**Majors. Area/ethnic studies:** American, Asian, Chicano/Hispanic-American/Latino. **Business:** General, accounting, business admin, finance, international, marketing. **Communications:** General. **Computer sciences:** General, security, systems analysis. **Conservation:** Environmental science, environmental studies. **Health:** Nursing (RN), nursing admin. **Interdisciplinary:** Intercultural. **Liberal arts:** Arts/sciences. **Psychology:** General. **Public administration:** Social work. **Social sciences:** International relations, political science, urban studies. **Other:** Ethnic, gender and labor studies, Politics and values, Self and society.

**Most popular majors.** Business/marketing 24%, computer/information sciences 7%, health sciences 8%, interdisciplinary studies 49%.

**Computing on campus.** 138 workstations in library, computer center, student center. Dormitories wired for high-speed internet access. Commuter students can connect to campus network. Online course registration, online library, helpline, student web hosting, wireless network available.

**Student life. Freshman orientation:** Mandatory. Preregistration for classes offered. **Housing:** Special housing for disabled, apartments available. $150 nonrefundable deposit, deadline 6/1. **Activities:** Campus ministries, dance, international student organizations, literary magazine, student government, student newspaper.

**Athletics. Team name:** Huskies.

**Student services.** Alcohol/substance abuse counseling, career counseling, student employment services, financial aid counseling, minority student services, personal counseling, veterans' counselor. **Physically disabled:** Services for visually, speech, hearing impaired.

**Contact.** E-mail: uwtinfo@u.washington.edu
Phone: (253) 692-4400 Toll-free number: (800) 736-7750
Fax: (253) 692-4414
Bobbe Miller-Murray, Director of Admission, University of Washington Tacoma, Campus Box 358400, Tacoma, WA 98402-3100

---

## Walla Walla University
**College Place, Washington**
**www.wallawalla.edu**                               CB code: 4940

- Private 4-year university and liberal arts college affiliated with Seventh-day Adventists
- Residential campus in large town
- 1,570 degree-seeking undergraduates: 7% part-time, 51% women, 4% African American, 7% Asian American, 10% Hispanic American, 1% Native American, 1% international
- 238 degree-seeking graduate students
- 98% of applicants admitted
- SAT or ACT (ACT writing optional) required
- 48% graduate within 6 years

**General.** Founded in 1892. Regionally accredited. Branch campus in Portland, Oregon, for final two years of nursing program. Summer biology courses offered at marine research facility near Anacortes. Graduate social work program in Billings and Missoula, Montana. **Degrees:** 305 bachelor's, 6 associate awarded; master's offered. **Location:** 270 miles from Seattle, 250 miles from Portland, Oregon. **Calendar:** Quarter, extensive summer session. **Full-time faculty:** 117 total; 71% have terminal degrees, 5% minority, 36% women. **Part-time faculty:** 88 total; 19% have terminal degrees, 9% minority, 58% women. **Class size:** 63% < 20, 28% 20-39, 5% 40-49, 4% 50-99, less than 1% >100. **Special facilities:** Marine biological research facility, observatory.

**Freshman class profile.** 505 applied, 496 admitted, 311 enrolled.

| Mid 50% test scores | | Rank in top quarter: | 5% |
|---|---|---|---|
| ACT composite: | 21-27 | Rank in top tenth: | 2% |
| GPA 3.75 or higher: | 35% | Return as sophomores: | 78% |
| GPA 3.50-3.74: | 19% | Out-of-state: | 61% |
| GPA 3.0-3.49: | 25% | Live on campus: | 90% |
| GPA 2.0-2.99: | 13% | International: | 2% |

**Basis for selection.** Must have a combined 2.0 high school GPA. If entering with GED must have an average score of 500 or higher and each test must be 450 or higher. Official TOEFL scores required for prospective students whose first language is not English. ACT recommended. Audition recommended. **Homeschooled:** May be admitted by acceptable score on ACT test, GED test, or transcript from accredited home school organization.

**High school preparation.** College-preparatory program recommended. 11 units required; 16 recommended. Required and recommended units include English 4, mathematics 3-4, social studies 1, history 2, science 2-3 (laboratory 2) and foreign language 2. Mathematics units must be algebra and geometry. 2 laboratory units recommended.

**2009-2010 Annual costs.** Tuition/fees: $22,794. Room/board: $4,710. Books/supplies: $1,068. Personal expenses: $1,836.

**2008-2009 Financial aid. Non-need-based:** Scholarships awarded for academics, leadership, music/drama.

**Application procedures. Admission:** No deadline. $40 fee, may be waived for applicants with need. Admission notification on a rolling basis beginning on or about 9/26. **Financial aid:** Priority date 4/30; no closing date. FAFSA, institutional form required. Applicants notified on a rolling basis starting 3/15.

**Academics. Special study options:** Combined bachelor's/graduate degree, cooperative education, distance learning, double major, honors, independent study, internships, liberal arts/career combination, study abroad, teacher certification program. **Credit/placement by examination:** AP, CLEP, IB, SAT, ACT, institutional tests. 12 credit hours maximum toward associate degree, 24 toward bachelor's. **Support services:** Learning center, preadmission summer program, reduced course load, remedial instruction, study skills assistance, tutoring, writing center.

**Majors. Biology:** General, biochemistry, biophysics. **Business:** Accounting, business admin, finance, human resources, international, management science. **Communications:** General, journalism, media studies. **Communications technology:** Graphic/printing. **Computer sciences:** General, computer graphics, computer science, data processing, information systems. **Education:** General, business, elementary, music, physical, special, voc/tech. **Engineering:** General, biomedical, civil, computer, electrical, mechanical. **Foreign languages:** French, German, Spanish. **Health:** Nursing (RN). **History:** General. **Liberal arts:** Arts/sciences. **Math:** General. **Mechanic/repair:** Automotive. **Philosophy/religion:** Religion. **Physical sciences:** Chemistry, physics. **Psychology:** General. **Public administration:** Social work. **Social sciences:** Sociology. **Theology:** Theology. **Visual/performing arts:** Art, music performance.

**Most popular majors.** Business/marketing 19%, education 6%, engineering/engineering technologies 12%, health sciences 18%.

**Computing on campus.** 105 workstations in dormitories, library, computer center. Dormitories wired for high-speed internet access and linked to campus network. Commuter students can connect to campus network. Online course registration, online library, helpline, repair service, student web hosting, wireless network available.

**Student life. Freshman orientation:** Mandatory. Preregistration for classes offered. Held during week before classes begin. **Policies:** Chapel requirement once a week; worship policy for resident students. Religious observance required. **Housing:** Guaranteed on-campus for all undergraduates. Single-sex dorms, special housing for disabled, apartments, wellness housing available. **Activities:** Bands, campus ministries, choral groups, drama, international student organizations, literary magazine, music ensembles, radio station, student government, student newspaper, symphony orchestra, TV station, student entrepreneur group, student missionary groups, drama, foreign student organizations, academic department clubs, service clubs, music groups.

**Athletics.** NCCAA. **Intercollegiate:** Basketball, golf, ice hockey M, soccer M, softball W, volleyball. **Intramural:** Badminton, basketball, football (non-tackle), racquetball, soccer, softball, table tennis, tennis, volleyball. **Team name:** Wolves.

**Student services.** Chaplain/spiritual director, career counseling, student employment services, financial aid counseling, health services, minority student services, on-campus daycare, personal counseling, placement for graduates, veterans' counselor. **Physically disabled:** Services for visually, speech, hearing impaired.

**Contact.** E-mail: info@wallawalla.edu
Phone: (509) 527-2615 Toll-free number: (800) 541-8900
Fax: (509) 527-2397
Dallas Weis, Director for Admissions/International Student Advisor, Walla Walla University, 204 South College Avenue, College Place, WA 99324-3000

## Washington State University
**Pullman, Washington**   CB member
www.wsu.edu   CB code: 4705

- Public 4-year university
- Residential campus in large town
- 21,312 degree-seeking undergraduates: 13% part-time, 52% women, 2% African American, 6% Asian American, 7% Hispanic American, 1% Native American, 3% international
- 4,002 degree-seeking graduate students
- 76% of applicants admitted
- SAT or ACT (ACT writing optional) required
- 69% graduate within 6 years; 38% enter graduate study

**General.** Founded in 1890. Regionally accredited. Regional campuses in Spokane, Tri-Cities, Vancouver, and online degree programs. **Degrees:** 4,907 bachelor's awarded; master's, doctoral, professional offered. **ROTC:** Army, Naval, Air Force. **Location:** 80 miles from Spokane. **Calendar:** Semester, extensive summer session. **Full-time faculty:** 1,151 total; 90% have terminal degrees, 14% minority, 39% women. **Part-time faculty:** 475 total; 51% have terminal degrees, 8% minority, 47% women. **Class size:** 39% < 20, 33% 20-39, 8% 40-49, 12% 50-99, 8% >100. **Special facilities:** Anthropology museum, art museum, creamery, ecological reserve, geological collections, historic textiles and costume collection, entomological collection, natural history museum, observatory, planetarium, herbarium and mycological herbarium, soil monolith collection, veterinary anatomy teaching museum, laboratory for atmospheric research, laboratory for biotechnology and bioanalysis, electron microscopy center, environmental research center, geoanalytical laboratory, nuclear radiation center, social and economic sciences research center, state of Washington water research center, center for spectroscopy, music recording studio, center for teaching, learning and technology, vet teaching hospital.

**Freshman class profile.** 12,478 applied, 9,489 admitted, 3,668 enrolled.

| Mid 50% test scores | | Rank in top quarter: | 55% |
|---|---|---|---|
| SAT critical reading: | 480-590 | Rank in top tenth: | 30% |
| SAT math: | 490-610 | End year in good standing: | 88% |
| SAT writing: | 460-570 | Return as sophomores: | 84% |
| ACT composite: | 21-26 | Out-of-state: | 11% |
| GPA 3.75 or higher: | 21% | Live on campus: | 99% |
| GPA 3.50-3.74: | 24% | International: | 2% |
| GPA 3.0-3.49: | 42% | Fraternities: | 24% |
| GPA 2.0-2.99: | 13% | Sororities: | 27% |

**Basis for selection.** Combination of high school GPA and SAT or ACT scores, completion of required course work, and personal statement. Special circumstances, community activities, recommendations considered in some cases. Assured admission for Washington State high school students ranked among top 10% of their high school class or who have at least a 3.5 GPA. An appeal process is available for those denied admission. **Homeschooled:** Transcript of courses and grades required. An academic resume (homeschool transcript) should provide documentation of all subjects studied, and detailed proof that home-based instruction fulfills core requirements. Resume must include signature of parent or guardian responsible for the student's curriculum. **Learning Disabled:** Upon acceptance a student can opt to notify Disability Services of desire to have assistance with disability.

**High school preparation.** College-preparatory program recommended. 15 units required; 16 recommended. Required and recommended units include English 4, mathematics 3-4, social studies 3, science 2 (laboratory 2) and foreign language 2. 1 unit of fine, visual, or performing arts, or 1 additional unit of academic elective. English: 4 years, including at least 3 of composition and literature. Mathematics: must include 1 year each of algebra I, geometry, and advanced algebra. Science: 2 years lab sciences, at least 1 must be algebra-based biology, chemistry, or physics. World Language: 2 years of a single world language, Native American language, or American Sign Language.

**2009-2010 Annual costs.** Tuition/fees: $8,489; $19,565 out-of-state. Room/board: $9,330. Books/supplies: $936. Personal expenses: $2,108.

**2008-2009 Financial aid. Need-based:** 2,642 full-time freshmen applied for aid; 1,624 were judged to have need; 1,619 of these received aid. Average need met was 77%. Average scholarship/grant was $6,890; average loan $3,268. 57% of total undergraduate aid awarded as scholarships/grants, 43% as loans/jobs. **Non-need-based:** Awarded to 4,804 full-time undergraduates, including 1,990 freshmen. Scholarships awarded for academics, alumni affiliation, art, athletics, job skills, leadership, minority status, music/drama, religious affiliation, ROTC, state residency.

**Application procedures. Admission:** Priority date 1/31; no deadline. $50 fee, may be waived for applicants with need. Admission notification on a rolling basis beginning on or about 11/1. Must reply by May 1 or within 2 week(s) if notified thereafter. Applications accepted after May 1 and later, if space is still available. **Financial aid:** Priority date 2/15; no closing date. FAFSA required. Applicants notified on a rolling basis starting 4/15.

**Academics. Special study options:** Accelerated study, combined bachelor's/graduate degree, cross-registration, distance learning, double major, dual enrollment of high school students, ESL, exchange student, external degree, honors, independent study, internships, liberal arts/career combination, semester at sea, student-designed major, study abroad, teacher certification program. **Credit/placement by examination:** AP, CLEP, IB, SAT, ACT, institutional tests. **Support services:** Learning center, pre-admission summer program, reduced course load, study skills assistance, tutoring, writing center.

**Honors college/program.** Acceptance into the Honors College is competitive, spaces are limited. Selection based on GPA and SAT/ACT scores, essay responses, strength of high school or college coursework, Running Start credits, AP/IB programs, honors courses, 2 letters of recommendation, one from a math or science teacher and one from an English teacher, and overall motivation, organizational skills, and a desire for challenge.

**Majors. Agriculture:** General, agronomy, animal sciences, business, business technology, communications, crop production, economics, horticultural science, mechanization, plant protection, plant sciences, products processing, soil science. **Architecture:** Architecture, landscape. **Area/ethnic studies:** American, Asian, women's. **Biology:** General, biochemistry, biomedical sciences, genetics, microbiology, molecular genetics, zoology. **Business:** General, accounting, business admin, construction management, entrepreneurial studies, finance, hospitality admin, international, management information systems, marketing, operations, real estate. **Communications:** Digital media, media studies. **Computer sciences:** General, computer science. **Conservation:** General, environmental science, wildlife. **Education:** General, agricultural, bilingual, biology, chemistry, early childhood, elementary, English, ESL, family/consumer sciences, foreign languages, French, German, health, history, kindergarten/preschool, mathematics, multi-level teacher, music, physical, physics, reading, science, secondary, social studies, Spanish, special. **Engineering:** Biomedical, chemical, civil, computer, electrical, manufacturing, materials, mechanical. **Family/consumer sciences:** General, clothing/textiles, family studies, food/nutrition, human nutrition. **Foreign languages:** General, French, linguistics, Spanish. **Health:** Athletic training, audiology/speech pathology, nursing (RN), premedicine. **History:** General. **Interdisciplinary:** Biological/physical sciences, neuroscience. **Liberal arts:** Arts/sciences, humanities. **Math:** General, applied. **Parks/recreation:** Exercise sciences, sports admin. **Philosophy/religion:** Philosophy, religion. **Physical sciences:** General, chemistry, geology, physics. **Protective services:** Law enforcement admin. **Psychology:** General. **Public administration:** Policy analysis. **Social sciences:** General, anthropology, economics, political science, sociology. **Visual/performing arts:** Interior design, music performance, music theory/composition, studio arts. **Other:** Comparative ethnic studies, Electronic media and culture.

**Most popular majors.** Business/marketing 17%, communications/journalism 9%, engineering/engineering technologies 7%, health sciences 9%, psychology 6%, social sciences 15%.

**Computing on campus.** 2,500 workstations in dormitories, library, computer center, student center. Dormitories wired for high-speed internet access and linked to campus network. Commuter students can connect to campus network. Online course registration, online library, helpline, student web hosting, wireless network available.

**Student life. Freshman orientation:** Mandatory, $227 fee. Preregistration for classes offered. Three-day (two-day for transfer students) orientation and registration program offered to new students and their families throughout the year depending on enrolled semester start date. **Policies:** Single undergraduate freshmen under 20 required to live on campus. **Housing:** Guaranteed on-campus for freshmen. Coed dorms, single-sex dorms, special housing for disabled, apartments, fraternity/sorority housing, wellness housing available. $550 partly refundable deposit, deadline 6/1. Freshman Focus living/learning communities. **Activities:** Bands, campus ministries, choral groups, dance, drama, film society, international student organizations, literary magazine, music ensembles, Model UN, musical theater, opera, radio station, student government, student newspaper, symphony orchestra, TV station, over 200 clubs and special interest groups.

**Athletics.** NCAA. **Intercollegiate:** Baseball M, basketball, cheerleading, cross-country, football (tackle) M, golf, rowing (crew) W, soccer W, swimming W, tennis W, track and field, volleyball W. **Intramural:** Badminton,

basketball, football (non-tackle), golf, racquetball, soccer, softball, tennis, volleyball. **Team name:** Cougars.

**Student services.** Adult student services, alcohol/substance abuse counseling, career counseling, services for economically disadvantaged, student employment services, financial aid counseling, health services, legal services, minority student services, on-campus daycare, personal counseling, placement for graduates, veterans' counselor, women's services. **Physically disabled:** Services for visually, speech, hearing impaired.

**Contact.** E-mail: admiss2@wsu.edu
Phone: (509) 335-5586 Toll-free number: (888) 468-6978
Fax: (509) 335-4902
Wendy Peterson, Director of Admissions, Washington State University, 370 Lighty Student Services Bldg, Pullman, WA 99164-1067

## Western Washington University
**Bellingham, Washington**  — CB member
www.wwu.edu — CB code: 4947

- Public 4-year university
- Residential campus in small city
- 13,249 degree-seeking undergraduates: 7% part-time, 55% women, 3% African American, 9% Asian American, 5% Hispanic American, 3% Native American, 1% international
- 1,179 graduate students
- 73% of applicants admitted
- SAT or ACT (ACT writing optional), application essay required
- 69% graduate within 6 years

**General.** Founded in 1893. Regionally accredited. **Degrees:** 3,102 bachelor's awarded; master's offered. **Location:** 90 miles from Seattle. **Calendar:** Quarter, extensive summer session. **Full-time faculty:** 498 total; 85% have terminal degrees, 15% minority, 43% women. **Part-time faculty:** 232 total; 41% have terminal degrees, 12% minority, 55% women. **Class size:** 36% < 20, 46% 20-39, 5% 40-49, 10% 50-99, 3% >100. **Special facilities:** Wind tunnel, electron microscope, neutron generator laboratory, planetarium, air pollution laboratory, motor vehicle research laboratory, electronic music studio, 11-acre recreational park on lake, marine laboratory, integrated laboratory network.

**Freshman class profile.** 9,620 applied, 6,990 admitted, 2,688 enrolled.

| Mid 50% test scores | | | |
|---|---|---|---|
| SAT critical reading: | 500-620 | GPA 3.0-3.49: | 42% |
| SAT math: | 510-610 | GPA 2.0-2.99: | 5% |
| SAT writing: | 490-590 | Rank in top quarter: | 58% |
| ACT composite: | 21-27 | Rank in top tenth: | 24% |
| GPA 3.75 or higher: | 24% | Return as sophomores: | 84% |
| GPA 3.50-3.74: | 29% | Out-of-state: | 9% |
| | | Live on campus: | 92% |

**Basis for selection.** Academic achievement most significant factor. Curriculum rigor (level and difficulty of courses), grade trends, school, community activities, special talent, multicultural experience, personal circumstances considered. All students encouraged to take courses beyond minimums. Consideration given to motivation, achievements outside of classroom, multicultural experience, and attributes that will enhance institution's learning community. Audition recommended for music; portfolio required for art.

**High school preparation.** College-preparatory program required. 16 units required. Required units include English 4, mathematics 3, social studies 3, science 2 (laboratory 1), foreign language 2, visual/performing arts .5, academic electives 0.5. Mathematics requirement includes 1 geometry and 2 algebra. Sciences include 1 algebra-based chemistry or physics. Foreign language should be in 1 language. .5 fine arts and .5 academic elective required.

**2009-2010 Annual costs.** Tuition/fees: $6,159; $17,190 out-of-state. Room/board: $8,394. Books/supplies: $924. Personal expenses: $1,854.

**2009-2010 Financial aid. Need-based:** 2,032 full-time freshmen applied for aid; 1,151 were judged to have need; 1,106 of these received aid. Average need met was 88%. Average scholarship/grant was $7,779; average loan $3,521. 52% of total undergraduate aid awarded as scholarships/grants, 48% as loans/jobs. **Non-need-based:** Awarded to 409 full-time undergraduates, including 105 freshmen. Scholarships awarded for academics, alumni affiliation, art, athletics, job skills, leadership, minority status, music/drama, state residency. **Additional information:** Short-term student loans ranging from $100 to $1,000 available on a quarterly basis.

**Application procedures. Admission:** Closing date 3/1 (postmark date). $50 fee, may be waived for applicants with need. Admission notification on a rolling basis beginning on or about 11/1. Must reply by May 1 or within 2 week(s) if notified thereafter. **Financial aid:** Priority date 2/15; no closing date. FAFSA required. Applicants notified on a rolling basis starting 3/20; must reply within 3 week(s) of notification.

**Academics. Special study options:** Distance learning, double major, ESL, exchange student, honors, independent study, internships, student-designed major, study abroad, teacher certification program. **Credit/placement by examination:** AP, CLEP, IB, institutional tests. 135 credit hours maximum toward bachelor's degree. **Support services:** Learning center, study skills assistance, tutoring, writing center.

**Majors. Area/ethnic studies:** American, Canadian, East Asian. **Biology:** General, biochemistry, botany, cell/histology, cellular/molecular, ecology, evolutionary, marine, zoology. **Business:** Accounting, business admin, finance, human resources, international, management information systems, marketing, operations. **Communications:** General, journalism. **Computer sciences:** General. **Conservation:** Environmental science, environmental studies. **Education:** Art, biology, chemistry, drama/dance, elementary, English, German, history, mathematics, music, physical, science, social science, social studies, Spanish, special, speech, technology/industrial arts. **Engineering technology:** Electrical, industrial, manufacturing, plastics. **Family/consumer sciences:** Child development. **Foreign languages:** General, French, German, linguistics, Spanish. **Health:** Audiology/speech pathology, community health services. **History:** General. **Interdisciplinary:** Accounting/computer science, biological/physical sciences. **Liberal arts:** Humanities. **Math:** General, applied. **Parks/recreation:** General, health/fitness. **Philosophy/religion:** Philosophy. **Physical sciences:** Chemistry, geology, geophysics, physics. **Psychology:** General, developmental. **Public administration:** Human services. **Social sciences:** Anthropology, archaeology, economics, geography, political science, sociology. **Visual/performing arts:** General, art, art history/conservation, ceramics, commercial/advertising art, dance, design, dramatic, drawing, fiber arts, graphic design, industrial design, multimedia, music history, music performance, music theory/composition, painting, photography, printmaking, sculpture.

**Most popular majors.** Business/marketing 15%, communications/journalism 6%, English 6%, psychology 6%, social sciences 13%, visual/performing arts 7%.

**Computing on campus.** 2,479 workstations in dormitories, library, computer center, student center. Dormitories wired for high-speed internet access and linked to campus network. Commuter students can connect to campus network. Online course registration, online library, helpline, repair service, student web hosting, wireless network available.

**Student life. Freshman orientation:** Available. Preregistration for classes offered. 6 programs offered for students and family members, early-mid August. Program 1-2 days, based on housing needs. **Housing:** Coed dorms, special housing for disabled, apartments, wellness housing available. $200 partly refundable deposit, deadline 6/15. Multicultural floors, honors, quiet floors, freshman interest groups available. **Activities:** Bands, campus ministries, choral groups, dance, drama, film society, international student organizations, literary magazine, music ensembles, musical theater, opera, radio station, student government, student newspaper, symphony orchestra, TV station, Campus Christian Fellowship, veteran's outreach center, volunteer services and resources, international student club, The Inn (nondenominational), ethnic student center, Mecha, Circle K, American Red Cross chapter.

**Athletics.** NCAA. **Intercollegiate:** Basketball, cross-country, football (tackle) M, golf, rowing (crew), soccer, softball W, track and field, volleyball W. **Intramural:** Basketball, football (non-tackle), golf, racquetball, soccer, softball, table tennis, tennis, volleyball. **Team name:** Vikings.

**Student services.** Adult student services, alcohol/substance abuse counseling, chaplain/spiritual director, career counseling, student employment services, financial aid counseling, health services, minority student services, on-campus daycare, personal counseling, placement for graduates, veterans' counselor. **Physically disabled:** Services for visually, speech, hearing impaired.

**Contact.** E-mail: admit@wwu.edu
Phone: (360) 650-3440 Fax: (360) 650-7369
Karen Copetas, Director of Admissions and Enrollment Planning, Western Washington University, 516 High Street, Bellingham, WA 98225-9009

---

## Whitman College
**Walla Walla, Washington**
www.whitman.edu

**CB member**
**CB code: 4951**

- Private 4-year liberal arts college
- Residential campus in large town
- 1,491 degree-seeking undergraduates: 1% part-time, 58% women, 2% African American, 11% Asian American, 6% Hispanic American, 1% Native American, 2% international

- 44% of applicants admitted
- SAT or ACT with writing, application essay required
- 89% graduate within 6 years

**General.** Founded in 1883. Regionally accredited. **Degrees:** 340 bachelor's awarded. **Location:** 150 miles from Spokane, 235 miles from Portland, Oregon. **Calendar:** Semester. **Full-time faculty:** 130 total; 95% have terminal degrees, 17% minority, 44% women. **Part-time faculty:** 56 total; 61% have terminal degrees, 4% minority, 45% women. **Class size:** 67% < 20, 30% 20-39, 1% 40-49, less than 1% 50-99. **Special facilities:** Asian art collection, natural history museum, planetarium, 2 electron microscopes, outdoor observatory, rock-climbing walls, outdoor sculpture walk, organic garden.

**Freshman class profile.** 3,290 applied, 1,442 admitted, 396 enrolled.

| Mid 50% test scores | | | |
|---|---|---|---|
| SAT critical reading: | 630-730 | Rank in top tenth: | 67% |
| SAT math: | 610-700 | End year in good standing: | 99% |
| SAT writing: | 610-710 | Return as sophomores: | 93% |
| GPA 3.75 or higher: | 66% | Out-of-state: | 38% |
| GPA 3.50-3.74: | 23% | Live on campus: | 100% |
| GPA 3.0-3.49: | 10% | International: | 2% |
| GPA 2.0-2.99: | 1% | Fraternities: | 42% |
| Rank in top quarter: | 90% | Sororities: | 25% |

**Basis for selection.** Scholastic record, quality of written expression, and level of motivation are very important. Evidence of talent, imagination, creativity, leadership, responsibility, and maturity are also considered. Writing for all students. TOEFL, ELPT, or APIEL accepted as language proficiency exams. Interview recommended.

**High school preparation.** College-preparatory program recommended. 16 units recommended. Recommended units include English 4, mathematics 4, social studies 2, history 2, science 3 (laboratory 2), foreign language 2 and visual/performing arts 1.

**2010-2011 Annual costs.** Tuition/fees: $38,770. Room/board: $9,720. Books/supplies: $1,400.

**2009-2010 Financial aid. Need-based:** 282 full-time freshmen applied for aid; 194 were judged to have need; 194 of these received aid. Average need met was 94%. Average scholarship/grant was $24,003; average loan $4,145. 81% of total undergraduate aid awarded as scholarships/grants, 19% as loans/jobs. **Non-need-based:** Scholarships awarded for academics, art, leadership, minority status, music/drama, religious affiliation, state residency.

**Application procedures. Admission:** Closing date 1/15 (postmark date). $50 fee, may be waived for applicants with need. Admission notification 4/1. Must reply by May 1 or within 2 week(s) if notified thereafter. **Financial aid:** Priority date 11/15, closing date 2/1. FAFSA, CSS PROFILE required. Applicants notified on a rolling basis starting 12/22; must reply within 2 week(s) of notification.

**Academics. Special study options:** Accelerated study, combined bachelor's/graduate degree, cooperative education, cross-registration, double major, dual enrollment of high school students, exchange student, honors, independent study, liberal arts/career combination, student-designed major, study abroad, urban semester, Washington semester. Study abroad opportunities in over 20 countries; Whitman-In-China allows recent graduates to spend a year teaching English in one of 3 Chinese universities; 3-2 engineering and computer science programs with California Institute of Technology, Columbia University (NY), Duke University (NC), Washington University (MO) and University of Washington; 3-2 oceanography and biology or geology program with University of Washington; 3-3 law program with Columbia University; 3-2 program with Monterey Institute of International Studies; 4-1 program with Bank Street College of Education; undergraduate research conference; semester in the West field study. **Credit/placement by examination:** AP, CLEP, IB, institutional tests. 30 credit hours maximum toward bachelor's degree. **Support services:** Learning center, reduced course load, study skills assistance, tutoring, writing center.

**Majors. Area/ethnic studies:** Asian, Latin American. **Biology:** General, Biochemistry/biophysics and molecular biology. **Conservation:** Environmental studies. **Foreign languages:** Classics, French, German, Spanish. **History:** General. **Math:** General. **Philosophy/religion:** Philosophy, religion. **Physical sciences:** Astronomy, chemistry, geology, physics. **Psychology:** General. **Social sciences:** Anthropology, economics, political science, sociology. **Visual/performing arts:** Art history/conservation, dramatic, film/cinema, studio arts. **Other:** Race and ethnic studies.

**Most popular majors.** Biology 14%, English 6%, philosophy/religious studies 8%, physical sciences 9%, psychology 9%, social sciences 20%, visual/performing arts 11%.

**Computing on campus.** 410 workstations in dormitories, library, computer center, student center. Dormitories wired for high-speed internet access and linked to campus network. Commuter students can connect to campus network. Online library, helpline, student web hosting, wireless network available.

**Student life. Freshman orientation:** Available. Preregistration for classes offered. **Housing:** Guaranteed on-campus for freshmen. Coed dorms, single-sex dorms, apartments, fraternity/sorority housing available. $300 nonrefundable deposit, deadline 5/1. German, French, Spanish, Japanese language houses. Asian Studies, multi-ethnic, environmental, fine arts, community service, writing, global awareness houses available, college-owned rentals. **Activities:** Bands, campus ministries, choral groups, dance, drama, film society, international student organizations, literary magazine, music ensembles, Model UN, musical theater, radio station, student government, student newspaper, symphony orchestra, multi-ethnic cultural association, many religious groups, community service, political organizations, environmental groups, sexual-assault prevention educators.

**Athletics.** NCAA. **Intercollegiate:** Baseball M, basketball, cross-country, golf, soccer, swimming, tennis, volleyball W. **Intramural:** Basketball, bowling, football (non-tackle), soccer, tennis, triathlon, volleyball. **Team name:** Missionaries.

**Student services.** Alcohol/substance abuse counseling, chaplain/spiritual director, career counseling, student employment services, financial aid counseling, health services, minority student services, on-campus daycare, personal counseling, placement for graduates, veterans' counselor, women's services. **Physically disabled:** Services for visually, speech, hearing impaired.

**Contact.** E-mail: admission@whitman.edu
Phone: (509) 527-5176 Toll-free number: (877) 462-9448
Fax: (509) 527-4967
Tony Cabasco, Dean of Admission and Financial Aid, Whitman College, 345 Boyer Avenue, Walla Walla, WA 99362-2046

## Whitworth University
**Spokane, Washington**      **CB member**
**www.whitworth.edu**      **CB code: 4953**

- Private 4-year liberal arts college affiliated with Presbyterian Church (USA)
- Residential campus in large city
- 2,413 degree-seeking undergraduates: 5% part-time, 58% women, 2% African American, 4% Asian American, 3% Hispanic American, 1% Native American, 1% international
- 267 degree-seeking graduate students
- 53% of applicants admitted
- Application essay required
- 73% graduate within 6 years

**General.** Founded in 1890. Regionally accredited. **Degrees:** 546 bachelor's awarded; master's offered. **ROTC:** Army. **Location:** 6 miles from downtown, 280 miles from Seattle. **Calendar:** 4-1-4, limited summer session. **Full-time faculty:** 127 total; 76% have terminal degrees, 8% minority, 41% women. **Part-time faculty:** 170 total; 11% minority. **Class size:** 58% < 20, 35% 20-39, 4% 40-49, 2% 50-99, less than 1% >100.

**Freshman class profile.** 5,862 applied, 3,129 admitted, 555 enrolled.

| Mid 50% test scores | | | |
|---|---|---|---|
| SAT critical reading: | 540-650 | GPA 3.0-3.49: | 19% |
| SAT math: | 540-630 | GPA 2.0-2.99: | 5% |
| SAT writing: | 530-630 | End year in good standing: | 90% |
| ACT composite: | 24-29 | Return as sophomores: | 87% |
| GPA 3.75 or higher: | 52% | Out-of-state: | 45% |
| GPA 3.50-3.74: | 24% | Live on campus: | 96% |
| | | International: | 1% |

**Basis for selection.** School achievement, extracurricular activities, recommendations most important. SAT or ACT recommended. Interview recommended.

**High school preparation.** College-preparatory program recommended. 18 units recommended. Recommended units include English 4, mathematics 3, social studies 3, history 3, science 3 (laboratory 2) and foreign language 2.

**2009-2010 Annual costs.** Tuition/fees: $28,650. Room/board: $8,120. Books/supplies: $960. Personal expenses: $1,609.

**2009-2010 Financial aid. Need-based:** 484 full-time freshmen applied for aid; 427 were judged to have need; 426 of these received aid. Average need met was 86%. Average scholarship/grant was $19,575; average loan

$4,243. 66% of total undergraduate aid awarded as scholarships/grants, 34% as loans/jobs. **Non-need-based:** Awarded to 672 full-time undergraduates, including 167 freshmen. Scholarships awarded for academics, art, music/drama, ROTC.

**Application procedures. Admission:** Closing date 3/1 (postmark date). No application fee. Admission notification on a rolling basis beginning on or about 12/20. Must reply by 5/1. **Financial aid:** Priority date 3/1; no closing date. FAFSA required. Applicants notified on a rolling basis starting 3/1; must reply by 5/1 or within 4 week(s) of notification.

**Academics. Special study options:** Accelerated study, cross-registration, distance learning, double major, dual enrollment of high school students, ESL, exchange student, independent study, internships, student-designed major, study abroad, teacher certification program, Washington semester. 3-2 engineering programs. **Credit/placement by examination:** AP, CLEP, IB, SAT, ACT, institutional tests. 32 credit hours maximum toward bachelor's degree. **Support services:** Learning center, reduced course load, study skills assistance, tutoring, writing center.

**Majors. Area/ethnic studies:** American. **Biology:** General, biophysics. **Business:** Accounting, business admin, international, marketing. **Communications:** General, journalism. **Computer sciences:** General, computer science. **Education:** General, biology, chemistry, elementary, ESL, French, history, mathematics, middle, multi-level teacher, music, physical, physics, secondary, Spanish, special, speech. **Engineering:** General. **Foreign languages:** French, Spanish. **Health:** Athletic training, nursing (RN). **History:** General. **Interdisciplinary:** Biological/physical sciences, peace/conflict. **Liberal arts:** Arts/sciences. **Math:** General, applied. **Parks/recreation:** Health/fitness. **Philosophy/religion:** Philosophy. **Physical sciences:** Applied physics, chemistry, physics. **Psychology:** General. **Social sciences:** General, economics, international relations, political science, sociology. **Theology:** Theology. **Visual/performing arts:** General, art, jazz, music performance, piano/organ, theater history, voice/opera.

**Most popular majors.** Business/marketing 16%, communications/journalism 6%, education 9%, health sciences 7%, psychology 6%, social sciences 9%, visual/performing arts 6%.

**Computing on campus.** 175 workstations in library, computer center, student center. Dormitories wired for high-speed internet access and linked to campus network. Commuter students can connect to campus network. Online course registration, online library, helpline, repair service available.

**Student life. Freshman orientation:** Mandatory. Preregistration for classes offered. **Housing:** Guaranteed on-campus for freshmen. Coed dorms, single-sex dorms, special housing for disabled, apartments available. $100 partly refundable deposit, deadline 5/1. **Activities:** Bands, campus ministries, choral groups, dance, drama, international student organizations, literary magazine, music ensembles, Model UN, musical theater, radio station, student government, student newspaper, symphony orchestra, Black Student Union, Fellowship of Christian Athletes, international club, Hawaiian club, political activist club, Native American club, Amnesty International, Habitat for Humanity, Asian American club, Circle-K International.

**Athletics.** NCAA. **Intercollegiate:** Baseball M, basketball, cross-country, football (tackle) M, golf, soccer, softball W, swimming, tennis, track and field, volleyball W. **Intramural:** Basketball, soccer, softball, table tennis, tennis, volleyball. **Team name:** Pirates.

**Student services.** Adult student services, chaplain/spiritual director, career counseling, student employment services, financial aid counseling, health services, minority student services, personal counseling, placement for graduates, veterans' counselor. **Physically disabled:** Services for visually, speech, hearing impaired.

**Contact.** E-mail: admissions@whitworth.edu
Phone: (509) 777-4786 Toll-free number: (800) 533-4668
Fax: (509) 777-3758
Fred Pfursich, Vice President, Admissions and Financial Aid, Whitworth University, 300 West Hawthorne Road, Spokane, WA 99251-0002

# West Virginia

## Alderson-Broaddus College

**Philippi, West Virginia**                                    **CB member**
**www.ab.edu**                                                 **CB code: 5005**

▶ Private 4-year liberal arts college affiliated with American Baptist Churches in the USA

▶ Residential campus in small town

▶ 582 degree-seeking undergraduates: 3% part-time, 66% women, 4% African American, 1% Asian American, 2% Hispanic American, 3% international

▶ 119 degree-seeking graduate students

▶ 74% of applicants admitted

▶ SAT and SAT Subject Tests or ACT (ACT writing optional) required

▶ 39% graduate within 6 years; 14% enter graduate study

**General.** Founded in 1871. Regionally accredited. **Degrees:** 124 bachelor's, 22 associate awarded; master's offered. **Location:** 100 miles from Charleston, 125 miles from Pittsburgh. **Calendar:** Semester, limited summer session. **Full-time faculty:** 60 total; 47% have terminal degrees, 13% minority, 58% women. **Part-time faculty:** 15 total; 13% have terminal degrees, 47% women. **Class size:** 79% < 20, 19% 20-39, less than 1% 40-49, 2% 50-99. **Special facilities:** Gross anatomy laboratory, hydro-therapy pool, simulation lab.

**Freshman class profile.** 597 applied, 441 admitted, 162 enrolled.

| Mid 50% test scores | | GPA 2.0-2.99: | 28% |
|---|---|---|---|
| SAT critical reading: | 440-530 | Rank in top quarter: | 41% |
| SAT math: | 420-510 | Rank in top tenth: | 21% |
| SAT writing: | 430-500 | End year in good standing: | 85% |
| ACT composite: | 19-23 | Return as sophomores: | 71% |
| GPA 3.75 or higher: | 25% | Out-of-state: | 18% |
| GPA 3.50-3.74: | 10% | Live on campus: | 77% |
| GPA 3.0-3.49: | 37% | International: | 1% |

**Basis for selection.** High school record, rank in top half of class, test scores, interview very important. Physician's assistant and nursing applicants should have strong background in science. Interview required for physician's assistant applicants, recommended for all others. Audition required for music.

**High school preparation.** College-preparatory program recommended. 11 units required; 14 recommended. Required and recommended units include English 4, mathematics 3, social studies 1-3, science 3 (laboratory 1-3) and foreign language 1.

**2009-2010 Annual costs.** Tuition/fees: $21,654. Room/board: $7,002. Books/supplies: $800. Personal expenses: $1,500.

**2009-2010 Financial aid. Need-based:** 161 full-time freshmen applied for aid; 153 were judged to have need; 152 of these received aid. Average need met was 85%. Average scholarship/grant was $17,914; average loan $4,450. 63% of total undergraduate aid awarded as scholarships/grants, 37% as loans/jobs. **Non-need-based:** Awarded to 137 full-time undergraduates, including 46 freshmen. Scholarships awarded for academics, athletics, music/drama.

**Application procedures. Admission:** No deadline. $25 fee, may be waived for applicants with need. Admission notification on a rolling basis. **Financial aid:** Priority date 3/1; no closing date. FAFSA required. Applicants notified on a rolling basis starting 2/15; must reply within 2 week(s) of notification.

**Academics. Special study options:** Accelerated study, double major, honors, independent study, internships, liberal arts/career combination, study abroad, teacher certification program. Business department offers on-line certificate program. **Credit/placement by examination:** AP, CLEP, SAT, ACT, institutional tests. 40 credit hours maximum toward associate degree, 60 toward bachelor's. **Support services:** Learning center, reduced course load, remedial instruction, study skills assistance, tutoring.

**Majors. Biology:** General. **Business:** Accounting, business admin, human resources, marketing, nonprofit/public. **Communications:** General. **Computer sciences:** Computer science. **Conservation:** Environmental science.

**Education:** Elementary, music, physical, secondary. **Family/consumer sciences:** Family systems. **Health:** Athletic training, health services, medical radiologic technology/radiation therapy, nursing (RN), recreational therapy. **History:** General. **Liberal arts:** Arts/sciences. **Math:** Applied. **Parks/recreation:** Facilities management, sports admin. **Philosophy/religion:** Christian. **Physical sciences:** Chemistry. **Psychology:** General. **Social sciences:** Criminology, political science. **Visual/performing arts:** Music performance, studio arts. **Other:** Natural science.

**Most popular majors.** Biology 8%, business/marketing 11%, education 10%, health sciences 48%.

**Computing on campus.** 100 workstations in dormitories, library, student center. Dormitories wired for high-speed internet access and linked to campus network. Commuter students can connect to campus network. Online library, helpline, student web hosting, wireless network available.

**Student life. Freshman orientation:** Available. Preregistration for classes offered. Held Saturday prior to start of fall classes. **Policies:** Participation in campus activities stressed. Voluntary weekly chapel service offered. **Housing:** Guaranteed on-campus for all undergraduates. Coed dorms, single-sex dorms, special housing for disabled, apartments, wellness housing available. $100 fully refundable deposit. **Activities:** Bands, campus ministries, choral groups, drama, literary magazine, music ensembles, musical theater, radio station, student government, student newspaper, TV station, Collegiate 4-H, ambassadors club, College Players, Baptist campus ministries, Students in Free Enterprise, Students Learning in Community Education, mission team, outdoor club.

**Athletics.** NCAA. **Intercollegiate:** Baseball M, basketball, cross-country, soccer, softball W, track and field, volleyball W. **Intramural:** Basketball, bowling, football (non-tackle), golf, racquetball, soccer, softball W, table tennis, tennis, volleyball. **Team name:** Battlers.

**Student services.** Adult student services, alcohol/substance abuse counseling, chaplain/spiritual director, career counseling, financial aid counseling, health services, personal counseling, placement for graduates, veterans' counselor. **Physically disabled:** Services for visually, hearing impaired.

**Contact.** E-mail: admissions@ab.edu
Phone: (304) 457-6256 Toll-free number: (800) 263-1549
Fax: (304) 457-6239
Kimberly Klaus, Director of Admissions, Alderson-Broaddus College, 101 College Hill Drive, Philippi, WV 26416

## American Public University System

**Charles Town, West Virginia**
**www.apus.edu**

▶ For-profit 4-year virtual university

▶ Small town

▶ 47,258 degree-seeking undergraduates

▶ 13,757 graduate students

**General.** Accredited by DETC. Regionally and nationally accredited online institution serving military and public service communities through the American Military University and American Public University. **Degrees:** 1,138 bachelor's, 214 associate awarded; master's offered. **Location:** Online university. **Calendar:** Continuous, extensive summer session. **Full-time faculty:** 225 total. **Part-time faculty:** 610 total.

**Freshman class profile.** 2,565 enrolled.

**Basis for selection.** Open admission.

**2009-2010 Annual costs.** Tuition/fees: $7,500. Distance learning only. Personal expenses: $1,920.

**Financial aid. Additional information:** Students should complete a Federal Student Aid Intent Form and register for classes at least 37 days prior to start to allow sufficient time for financial aid process.

**Application procedures. Admission:** No deadline. No application fee. Application must be submitted online. Admission notification on a rolling basis. **Financial aid:** No deadline. FAFSA, institutional form required. Applicants notified on a rolling basis; must reply within 14 week(s) of notification.

**Academics. Credit/placement by examination:** CLEP. **Support services:** Remedial instruction, study skills assistance, tutoring.

**Majors. Area/ethnic studies:** African, Asian, Near/Middle Eastern. **Business:** Business admin, hospitality admin, marketing, transportation. **Computer sciences:** General, information technology, security. **Conservation:**

Environmental studies. **Family/consumer sciences:** Child development, family studies. **History:** General. **Interdisciplinary:** Global studies. **Legal studies:** General. **Military:** General. **Parks/recreation:** Sports admin. **Philosophy/religion:** Philosophy, religion. **Protective services:** Correctional facilities, fire safety technology, fire services admin, law enforcement admin, security management. **Psychology:** General. **Social sciences:** International relations, political science, sociology. **Transportation:** Aviation.

**Most popular majors.** Business/marketing 20%, computer/information sciences 9%, interdisciplinary studies 15%, security/protective services 27%, social sciences 6%.

**Computing on campus.** PC or laptop required. Online library available.

**Student life. Freshman orientation:** Mandatory. Preregistration for classes offered.

**Contact.** E-mail: info@apus.edu
Phone: (877) 777-9081 Toll-free number: (877) 777-9081
Terry Grant, Associate Vice President, Enrollment Management, American Public University System, 111 West Congress Street, Charles Town, WV 25414

## Appalachian Bible College
### Bradley, West Virginia
**www.abc.edu**                                   CB code: 7305

◗ Private 4-year Bible college affiliated with nondenominational tradition
◗ Residential campus in rural community
◗ 258 degree-seeking undergraduates
◗ 15 graduate students
◗ 77% of applicants admitted
◗ SAT or ACT (ACT writing optional), application essay required

**General.** Founded in 1950. Regionally accredited; also accredited by ABHE. **Degrees:** 39 bachelor's, 10 associate awarded; master's offered. **Location:** 5 miles from Beckley. **Calendar:** Semester, limited summer session. **Full-time faculty:** 21 total. **Part-time faculty:** 6 total.

**Freshman class profile.** 112 applied, 86 admitted, 67 enrolled.

| Mid 50% test scores | | ACT composite: | 19-26 |
|---|---|---|---|
| SAT critical reading: | 440-610 | Out-of-state: | 64% |
| SAT math: | 430-580 | Live on campus: | 89% |

**Basis for selection.** Profession of Jesus Christ as Savior, essential agreement with doctrinal statement of college, approved character very important. Minimum 2.0 GPA, test scores, achievement and potential in English also considered. If no scores are submitted, student must test on first available test date after enrollment and must take developmental English. Interview recommended. **Homeschooled:** Must provide accurate record of curriculum used, subjects studied, grades earned for grade levels 9-12.

**High school preparation.** Recommended units include English 4, mathematics 3, social studies 3, history 3, science 3, foreign language 1 and academic electives 4.

**2009-2010 Annual costs.** Tuition/fees: $10,390. Room/board: $5,400. Books/supplies: $900. Personal expenses: $1,208.

**2008-2009 Financial aid.** All financial aid based on need.

**Application procedures. Admission:** No deadline. $35 fee, may be waived for applicants with need. Admission notification on a rolling basis. **Financial aid:** Closing date 6/15. FAFSA, institutional form required. Applicants notified on a rolling basis starting 6/15; must reply by 8/1 or within 4 week(s) of notification.

**Academics. Special study options:** Cooperative education, dual enrollment of high school students, independent study, internships, teacher certification program. **Credit/placement by examination:** AP, CLEP, SAT, ACT, institutional tests. 29 credit hours maximum toward bachelor's degree. **Support services:** Reduced course load, remedial instruction, study skills assistance, tutoring.

**Majors. Theology:** Bible.

**Computing on campus.** 10 workstations in library. Dormitories wired for high-speed internet access and linked to campus network. Commuter students can connect to campus network. Online library, repair service available.

**Student life. Freshman orientation:** Mandatory. Preregistration for classes offered. Held for 3 days immediately prior to beginning of semester. **Policies:** Chapel held three times a week. Annual Spiritual Life Conference,

Distinguished Christian Lecture Series, Bible and missions conferences. Religious observance required. **Housing:** Single-sex dorms, apartments, wellness housing available. $25 nonrefundable deposit. **Activities:** Choral groups, drama, music ensembles, student government, student newspaper.

**Athletics.** NCCAA. **Intercollegiate:** Basketball, soccer M, volleyball W. **Intramural:** Basketball, soccer M, table tennis, tennis, volleyball. **Team name:** Warriors.

**Student services.** Career counseling, financial aid counseling, health services, personal counseling, placement for graduates, veterans' counselor.

**Contact.** E-mail: admissions@abc.edu
Phone: (304) 877-6428 Toll-free number: (800) 678-9222
Fax: (304) 877-5082
Scott Ross, Director of Admissions, Appalachian Bible College, PO Box ABC, Bradley, WV 25818-1353

## Bethany College
### Bethany, West Virginia
                                                  CB member
**www.bethanywv.edu**                             CB code: 5060

◗ Private 4-year liberal arts college affiliated with Christian Church (Disciples of Christ)
◗ Residential campus in rural community
◗ 822 degree-seeking undergraduates: 1% part-time, 47% women, 10% African American, 1% Asian American, 2% Hispanic American, 1% international
◗ 78% of applicants admitted
◗ SAT or ACT (ACT writing optional), application essay required
◗ 69% graduate within 6 years; 45% enter graduate study

**General.** Founded in 1840. Regionally accredited. **Degrees:** 141 bachelor's awarded. **Location:** 14 miles from Wheeling, 40 miles from Pittsburgh. **Calendar:** 4-1-4. **Full-time faculty:** 49 total; 80% have terminal degrees, 10% minority, 33% women. **Part-time faculty:** 31 total; 16% have terminal degrees, 6% minority, 71% women. **Class size:** 73% < 20, 23% 20-39, 3% 40-49, less than 1% 50-99, less than 1% >100.

**Freshman class profile.** 1,378 applied, 1,076 admitted, 284 enrolled.

| | | | |
|---|---|---|---|
| GPA 3.75 or higher: | 13% | Return as sophomores: | 63% |
| GPA 3.50-3.74: | 10% | Live on campus: | 98% |
| GPA 3.0-3.49: | 23% | International: | 1% |
| GPA 2.0-2.99: | 48% | Fraternities: | 29% |
| End year in good standing: | 75% | Sororities: | 44% |

**Basis for selection.** Rank in top half of graduating class, test scores, interview, activities, and recommendations important. Interviews strongly recommended, but not required. **Homeschooled:** Statement describing homeschool structure and mission required. **Learning Disabled:** Students with learning disabilities must apply by February 15 for priority consideration in limited-enrollment learning disabled program. Students should submit official diagnosis of learning disability after acceptance.

**High school preparation.** College-preparatory program recommended. 15 units required. Required and recommended units include English 4, mathematics 3, social studies 3, science 3 (laboratory 1), foreign language 2 and academic electives 2.

**2009-2010 Annual costs.** Tuition/fees: $21,465. Room/board: $8,700. Books/supplies: $1,300. Personal expenses: $1,300.

**2008-2009 Financial aid. Need-based:** 261 full-time freshmen applied for aid; 237 were judged to have need; 237 of these received aid. Average need met was 81%. Average scholarship/grant was $14,960; average loan $5,108. 69% of total undergraduate aid awarded as scholarships/grants, 31% as loans/jobs. **Non-need-based:** Awarded to 77 full-time undergraduates, including 30 freshmen. **Additional information:** Scholarships available for travel program.

**Application procedures. Admission:** Priority date 4/1; no deadline. No application fee. Admission notification on a rolling basis beginning on or about 10/1. **Financial aid:** Priority date 3/1; no closing date. FAFSA required. Applicants notified on a rolling basis starting 3/1; must reply within 2 week(s) of notification.

**Academics. Special study options:** Accelerated study, combined bachelor's/graduate degree, distance learning, double major, dual enrollment of high school students, ESL, independent study, internships, liberal arts/career combination, student-designed major, study abroad, teacher certification program, United Nations semester, Washington semester. **Credit/placement by examination:** AP, CLEP, IB, SAT, ACT, institutional tests. 80 credit hours maximum toward bachelor's degree. **Support services:** Learning center, pre-admission summer program, remedial instruction, study skills assistance, tutoring, writing center.

**Majors. Agriculture:** Equestrian studies. **Biology:** General, biochemistry. **Business:** General, accounting, finance, international, international finance. **Communications:** General, advertising, broadcast journalism, journalism, public relations, radio/tv. **Communications technology:** Graphics. **Computer sciences:** General, computer science. **Conservation:** Environmental studies. **Education:** General, art, biology, chemistry, elementary, English, foreign languages, French, German, history, learning disabled, mathematics, multi-level teacher, multiple handicapped, physical, secondary, social studies, Spanish, special. **Foreign languages:** French, German, Spanish. **History:** General. **Interdisciplinary:** Biological/physical sciences, global studies, math/computer science. **Math:** General. **Parks/recreation:** Health/fitness, sports admin. **Philosophy/religion:** Philosophy, religion. **Physical sciences:** Chemistry, physics. **Psychology:** General. **Public administration:** Social work. **Social sciences:** Economics, international relations, political science. **Visual/performing arts:** General, art, design, dramatic, studio arts.

**Most popular majors.** Biology 7%, communications/journalism 12%, education 18%, parks/recreation 7%, psychology 15%, social sciences 10%.

**Computing on campus.** 145 workstations in dormitories, library, computer center, student center. Dormitories wired for high-speed internet access and linked to campus network. Commuter students can connect to campus network. Online library, helpline, repair service, student web hosting, wireless network available.

**Student life. Freshman orientation:** Mandatory, $125 fee. Preregistration for classes offered. Held prior to start of fall classes. **Housing:** Guaranteed on-campus for all undergraduates. Coed dorms, single-sex dorms, special housing for disabled, apartments, fraternity/sorority housing, wellness housing available. **Activities:** Bands, campus ministries, choral groups, dance, drama, film society, international student organizations, literary magazine, music ensembles, Model UN, musical theater, radio station, student government, student newspaper, TV station, community service organization, ecumenical religious organization, multicultural students club, advertising club, social work club, Amnesty International, Coalition for Christian Outreach, Circle K, equestrian club.

**Athletics.** NCAA. **Intercollegiate:** Baseball M, basketball, cross-country, diving, football (tackle) M, golf, soccer, softball W, swimming, tennis, track and field, volleyball W. **Intramural:** Basketball, football (non-tackle) M, handball, racquetball, soccer, softball, swimming, tennis, volleyball. **Team name:** Bison.

**Student services.** Alcohol/substance abuse counseling, chaplain/spiritual director, career counseling, student employment services, financial aid counseling, health services, minority student services, personal counseling, placement for graduates, veterans' counselor, women's services. **Physically disabled:** Services for visually, speech, hearing impaired. **Learning disabled:** Comprehensive services available.

**Contact.** E-mail: kdayich@bethanywv.edu
Phone: (304) 829-7611 Toll-free number: (800) 922-7611
Fax: (304) 829-7142
Karina Dayich, Director of Admission, Bethany College, Office of Admission, Bethany, WV 26032-0428

## Bluefield State College
### Bluefield, West Virginia
www.bluefieldstate.edu                    CB code: 5064

- Public 4-year liberal arts and technical college
- Commuter campus in large town
- 1,868 degree-seeking undergraduates: 15% part-time, 60% women, 13% African American, 1% Hispanic American, 3% international
- 79% of applicants admitted
- SAT or ACT (ACT writing optional) required

**General.** Founded in 1895. Regionally accredited. Off-campus locations in Lewisburg, Welch, and Beckley. **Degrees:** 227 bachelor's, 95 associate awarded. **Location:** 100 miles from Charleston; 100 miles from Roanoke, Virginia. **Calendar:** Semester, limited summer session. **Full-time faculty:** 79 total; 54% have terminal degrees, 11% minority, 44% women. **Part-time faculty:** 70 total; 10% have terminal degrees, 59% women. **Class size:** 46% < 20, 47% 20-39, 6% 40-49, 1% 50-99. **Special facilities:** Instructional technology center.

**Freshman class profile.** 546 applied, 434 admitted, 319 enrolled.

| Mid 50% test scores | | | |
|---|---|---|---|
| SAT critical reading: | 400-500 | GPA 2.0-2.99: | 26% |
| SAT math: | 380-530 | Return as sophomores: | 61% |
| ACT composite: | 16-21 | Out-of-state: | 10% |
| GPA 3.75 or higher: | 22% | International: | 1% |
| GPA 3.50-3.74: | 14% | Fraternities: | 1% |
| GPA 3.0-3.49: | 36% | Sororities: | 1% |

**Basis for selection.** 2.5 GPA, college preparatory program, test scores required for applicants to health, teacher education, humanities, social science and business administration programs. High school requirements not necessary for associate's program.

**High school preparation.** College-preparatory program recommended. 17 units required. Required units include English 4, mathematics 4, social studies 3, science 3 (laboratory 2), foreign language 2 and visual/performing arts 1.

**2009-2010 Annual costs.** Tuition/fees: $4,596; $9,000 out-of-state. Tuition for students residing in border counties is $6,288. Books/supplies: $1,600. Personal expenses: $2,840.

**2009-2010 Financial aid. Need-based:** 265 full-time freshmen applied for aid; 230 were judged to have need; 230 of these received aid. Average need met was 70%. Average scholarship/grant was $3,500; average loan $3,600. 58% of total undergraduate aid awarded as scholarships/grants, 42% as loans/jobs. **Non-need-based:** Awarded to 521 full-time undergraduates, including 164 freshmen. Scholarships awarded for academics, alumni affiliation, art, athletics, job skills, leadership, minority status, state residency.

**Application procedures. Admission:** No deadline. No application fee. Admission notification on a rolling basis beginning on or about 8/1. **Financial aid:** Priority date 3/1; no closing date. FAFSA, institutional form required. Applicants notified on a rolling basis starting 5/1.

**Academics. Special study options:** Distance learning, double major, dual enrollment of high school students, honors, independent study, internships, teacher certification program. **Credit/placement by examination:** AP, CLEP, IB, ACT, institutional tests. **Support services:** Learning center, pre-admission summer program, reduced course load, remedial instruction, study skills assistance, tutoring, writing center.

**Majors. Business:** Accounting, business admin. **Computer sciences:** General. **Education:** Elementary. **Engineering technology:** Architectural, civil, electrical, mechanical, mining. **Health:** Nursing (RN), radiologic technology/medical imaging. **Interdisciplinary:** Biological/physical sciences. **Liberal arts:** Arts/sciences, humanities. **Protective services:** Criminal justice. **Social sciences:** General.

**Most popular majors.** Business/marketing 13%, education 12%, engineering/engineering technologies 15%, health sciences 11%, liberal arts 23%, security/protective services 10%, social sciences 9%.

**Computing on campus.** 370 workstations in library, computer center. Online library, helpline, student web hosting, wireless network available.

**Student life. Freshman orientation:** Available. Preregistration for classes offered. One day in July or August. **Activities:** Choral groups, drama, international student organizations, Model UN, radio station, student government, student newspaper, Minorities on the Move, student nurses association.

**Athletics.** NCAA. **Intercollegiate:** Baseball M, basketball, cheerleading, cross-country, golf M, softball W, tennis, volleyball W. **Intramural:** Badminton, basketball, bowling, football (non-tackle) M, golf, racquetball, softball, swimming, table tennis, tennis, volleyball. **Team name:** Big Blues.

**Student services.** Career counseling, student employment services, financial aid counseling, health services, minority student services, personal counseling, placement for graduates, veterans' counselor. **Physically disabled:** Services for visually, speech, hearing impaired.

**Contact.** E-mail: bscadmit@bluefieldstate.edu
Phone: (304) 327-4065 Toll-free number: (800) 654-7798
Fax: (304) 325-7747
Kenny Mandeville, Director of Admissions, Bluefield State College, 219 Rock Street, Bluefield, WV 24701

## Concord University
### Athens, West Virginia                    CB member
www.concord.edu                    CB code: 5120

- Public 4-year university and liberal arts college
- Residential campus in small town

◗ 2,634 degree-seeking undergraduates: 11% part-time, 58% women

◗ 135 degree-seeking graduate students

◗ 60% of applicants admitted

◗ SAT or ACT (ACT writing optional) required

**General.** Founded in 1872. Regionally accredited. **Degrees:** 351 bachelor's, 2 associate awarded; master's offered. **Location:** 5 miles from Princeton, 80 miles from Charleston. **Calendar:** Semester, extensive summer session. **Full-time faculty:** 117 total; 63% have terminal degrees, 38% women. **Part-time faculty:** 89 total; 15% have terminal degrees, 60% women. **Class size:** 60% < 20, 32% 20-39, 5% 40-49, 3% 50-99, less than 1% >100. **Special facilities:** Southern West Virginia technology center.

**Freshman class profile.** 2,102 applied, 1,258 admitted, 611 enrolled.

| Mid 50% test scores | | | |
|---|---|---|---|
| SAT critical reading: | 420-520 | GPA 3.50-3.74: | 17% |
| SAT math: | 430-530 | GPA 3.0-3.49: | 29% |
| SAT writing: | 310-610 | GPA 2.0-2.99: | 27% |
| ACT composite: | 18-23 | Rank in top quarter: | 43% |
| GPA 3.75 or higher: | 25% | Rank in top tenth: | 18% |

**Basis for selection.** 2.0 GPA and 870 SAT (exclusive of Writing) or 18 ACT required. **Homeschooled:** Statement describing homeschool structure and mission, transcript of courses and grades required.

**High school preparation.** Required units include English 4, mathematics 3, social studies 2, history 1, science 1 (laboratory 2). Math courses must include algebra I and another higher level course. Social science requirement includes 1 US history.

**2009-2010 Annual costs.** Tuition/fees: $4,974; $11,050 out-of-state. Room/board: $6,766. Books/supplies: $1,500. Personal expenses: $2,169.

**2008-2009 Financial aid. Need-based:** 43% of total undergraduate aid awarded as scholarships/grants, 57% as loans/jobs. **Non-need-based:** Scholarships awarded for academics, alumni affiliation, art, athletics, job skills, leadership, minority status, music/drama, state residency. **Additional information:** March 1 priority deadline for state forms. April 15 priority deadline for FAFSA.

**Application procedures. Admission:** No deadline. No application fee. Admission notification on a rolling basis beginning on or about 9/1. **Financial aid:** FAFSA, institutional form required. Applicants notified on a rolling basis starting 3/1; must reply within 2 week(s) of notification.

**Academics. Special study options:** Cooperative education, distance learning, double major, dual enrollment of high school students, ESL, honors, internships, liberal arts/career combination, student-designed major, study abroad, teacher certification program. English as a second language program for foreign students, mentoring programs for pre-law and pre-med students. **Credit/placement by examination:** AP, CLEP, SAT, ACT, institutional tests. **Support services:** Learning center, reduced course load, remedial instruction, study skills assistance, tutoring, writing center.

**Majors. Biology:** General, genetics. **Business:** General, accounting, business admin, finance, hospitality admin, hospitality/recreation, hotel/motel admin, human resources, managerial economics, marketing, resort management, restaurant/food services, tourism promotion, tourism/travel. **Communications:** General, advertising, broadcast journalism, journalism, public relations. **Computer sciences:** General, computer science. **Education:** General, art, biology, business, chemistry, early childhood, elementary, English, health, learning disabled, mathematics, mentally handicapped, music, physical, science, social studies, speech. **Health:** Athletic training, clinical lab science, predental, premedicine, prepharmacy, preveterinary. **History:** General. **Interdisciplinary:** Global studies. **Legal studies:** Prelaw. **Liberal arts:** Arts/sciences, library science. **Math:** General. **Parks/recreation:** General, facilities management, health/fitness, sports admin. **Physical sciences:** Chemistry, geology. **Psychology:** General. **Public administration:** General, social work. **Social sciences:** Geography, political science, sociology. **Visual/performing arts:** Art, commercial/advertising art, dramatic, graphic design, studio arts.

**Most popular majors.** Biology 9%, business/marketing 21%, education 19%, liberal arts 7%, public administration/social services 6%, social sciences 8%.

**Computing on campus.** 250 workstations in dormitories, library, computer center, student center. Dormitories wired for high-speed internet access and linked to campus network. Commuter students can connect to campus network. Online course registration, online library, helpline, wireless network available.

**Student life. Freshman orientation:** Mandatory, $40 fee. Preregistration for classes offered. **Housing:** Guaranteed on-campus for freshmen. Coed dorms, single-sex dorms, special housing for disabled, apartments, fraternity/sorority housing, wellness housing available. $50 deposit. **Activities:** Bands, campus ministries, choral groups, dance, drama, film society, international student organizations, literary magazine, music ensembles, radio station, student government, student newspaper, TV station, over 50 clubs and organizations.

**Athletics.** NCAA. **Intercollegiate:** Baseball M, basketball, cross-country, football (tackle) M, golf, soccer, softball W, tennis, track and field, volleyball W. **Intramural:** Archery, badminton, basketball, bowling, football (tackle) M, golf, handball, racquetball, soccer W, softball, swimming, tennis, track and field, volleyball, water polo. **Team name:** Mountain Lions.

**Student services.** Career counseling, student employment services, financial aid counseling, health services, on-campus daycare, personal counseling, placement for graduates, veterans' counselor. **Learning disabled:** Comprehensive services available.

**Contact.** E-mail: admissions@concord.edu
Phone: (304) 384-5248 Toll-free number: (888) 384-5249
Fax: (304) 384-3218
Kent Gamble, Director of Enrollment, Concord University, PO Box 1000, Athens, WV 24712-1000

---

## Davis and Elkins College
**Elkins, West Virginia**  **CB member**
**www.davisandelkins.edu**  **CB code: 5151**

◗ Private 4-year liberal arts college affiliated with Presbyterian Church (USA)

◗ Residential campus in small town

◗ 648 degree-seeking undergraduates: 4% part-time, 60% women, 4% African American, 1% Hispanic American, 1% Native American, 6% international

◗ 68% of applicants admitted

◗ SAT or ACT (ACT writing optional) required

◗ 49% graduate within 6 years; 13% enter graduate study

**General.** Founded in 1904. Regionally accredited. **Degrees:** 75 bachelor's, 51 associate awarded. **Location:** 130 miles from Pittsburgh; 200 miles from Washington, DC. **Calendar:** 4-1-4, extensive summer session. **Full-time faculty:** 40 total; 88% have terminal degrees, 12% minority, 50% women. **Part-time faculty:** 31 total; 16% have terminal degrees, 48% women. **Class size:** 70% < 20, 29% 20-39, 2% 50-99. **Special facilities:** Pearl S. Buck collection, observatory, greenhouse, planetarium, 8 buildings on the national historic registry.

**Freshman class profile.** 1,141 applied, 775 admitted, 235 enrolled.

| Mid 50% test scores | | | |
|---|---|---|---|
| SAT critical reading: | 410-540 | Rank in top quarter: | 29% |
| SAT math: | 420-550 | Rank in top tenth: | 16% |
| SAT writing: | 420-550 | End year in good standing: | 68% |
| ACT composite: | 17-22 | Return as sophomores: | 57% |
| GPA 3.75 or higher: | 17% | Out-of-state: | 43% |
| GPA 3.50-3.74: | 9% | Live on campus: | 54% |
| GPA 3.0-3.49: | 31% | International: | 7% |
| GPA 2.0-2.99: | 40% | Fraternities: | 2% |
| | | Sororities: | 5% |

**Basis for selection.** Admission based on school achievement record, 2.0 GPA, test scores, and extracurricular activities. Recommended interview also important. Essay, academic/personal recommendations recommended for all applicants; audition required for musicians and theater students; portfolio required for art students. **Homeschooled:** Transcript of courses and grades required. **Learning Disabled:** Must complete a separate application for the Supported Learning Program.

**High school preparation.** College-preparatory program recommended. 15 units required. Required and recommended units include English 4, mathematics 3-4, social studies 3-4, science 3-4 (laboratory 1-2), foreign language 1-2 and academic electives 4. Math units must include Algebra I or Algebra II, and Geometry.

**2009-2010 Annual costs.** Tuition/fees: $19,800. Room/board: $7,450. Books/supplies: $1,200. Personal expenses: $1,500.

**2009-2010 Financial aid. Need-based:** Average need met was 85%. Average scholarship/grant was $4,406; average loan $3,289. 72% of total undergraduate aid awarded as scholarships/grants, 28% as loans/jobs. **Non-need-based:** Scholarships awarded for academics, alumni affiliation, art, athletics, leadership, minority status, music/drama, religious affiliation.

**Application procedures. Admission:** Priority date 5/1; no deadline. No application fee. Admission notification on a rolling basis beginning on or about 9/30. **Financial aid:** Priority date 3/1; no closing date. FAFSA required. Applicants notified on a rolling basis starting 5/1; must reply within 2 week(s) of notification.

**Academics. Special study options:** Combined bachelor's/graduate degree, cooperative education, cross-registration, distance learning, double major, dual enrollment of high school students, external degree, honors, independent study, internships, liberal arts/career combination, student-designed major, study abroad, teacher certification program, Washington semester. **Credit/placement by examination:** AP, CLEP, IB, institutional tests. **Support services:** Learning center, reduced course load, remedial instruction, study skills assistance, tutoring, writing center.

**Majors. Biology:** General. **Business:** Accounting, business admin, hospitality admin, international, international marketing, management information systems, marketing. **Computer sciences:** Computer science, information systems. **Conservation:** Environmental science. **Education:** Business, drama/dance, elementary, mathematics, music, physical. **Foreign languages:** Spanish. **History:** General. **Math:** General. **Parks/recreation:** General, exercise sciences, sports admin. **Philosophy/religion:** Religion. **Physical sciences:** Chemistry. **Psychology:** General. **Social sciences:** Criminology, economics, political science, sociology. **Theology:** Religious ed. **Visual/performing arts:** Dramatic, theater design. **Other:** Biology and environmental sciences, Pre-forestry.

**Most popular majors.** Business/marketing 22%, education 16%, English 8%, history 7%, parks/recreation 11%, psychology 9%, social sciences 20%.

**Computing on campus.** 81 workstations in library, computer center, student center. Dormitories wired for high-speed internet access and linked to campus network. Commuter students can connect to campus network. Helpline, repair service, wireless network available.

**Student life. Freshman orientation:** Mandatory. Preregistration for classes offered. **Housing:** Guaranteed on-campus for all undergraduates. Coed dorms, single-sex dorms, fraternity/sorority housing, wellness housing available. **Activities:** Bands, choral groups, drama, international student organizations, literary magazine, music ensembles, musical theater, radio station, student government, student newspaper, Alpha Phi Omega, Appalachian music and dance, Green Works.

**Athletics. NCAA. Intercollegiate:** Baseball M, basketball, cross-country, golf M, skiing, soccer, softball W, tennis, volleyball W. **Intramural:** Basketball, soccer, volleyball. **Team name:** Senators.

**Student services.** Alcohol/substance abuse counseling, chaplain/spiritual director, career counseling, student employment services, financial aid counseling, health services, personal counseling, placement for graduates, veterans' counselor. **Learning disabled:** Comprehensive services available.

**Contact.** E-mail: admiss@davisandelkins.edu
Phone: (304) 637-1230 Toll-free number: (800) 624-3157 ext. 1230
Fax: (304) 637-1800
Kevin Wilson, Vice President for Enrollment Management, Davis and Elkins College, 100 Campus Drive, Elkins, WV 26241-3996

---

## Fairmont State University
**Fairmont, West Virginia**
**www.fairmontstate.edu**      CB code: 5211

- Public 4-year university
- Commuter campus in large town
- 4,170 degree-seeking undergraduates: 12% part-time, 55% women, 4% African American, 1% Asian American, 1% Hispanic American, 1% international
- 332 degree-seeking graduate students
- 88% of applicants admitted
- SAT or ACT required
- 39% graduate within 6 years; 23% enter graduate study

**General.** Founded in 1865. Regionally accredited. **Degrees:** 645 bachelor's, 107 associate awarded; master's offered. **ROTC:** Army, Air Force. **Location:** 90 miles from Pittsburgh. **Calendar:** Semester, limited summer session. **Full-time faculty:** 165 total; 72% have terminal degrees, 9% minority, 47% women. **Part-time faculty:** 169 total; 32% have terminal degrees, 8% minority, 56% women. **Class size:** 48% < 20, 42% 20-39, 3% 40-49, 6% 50-99, 2% >100. **Special facilities:** Student life center, folk-life center.

**Freshman class profile.** 3,072 applied, 2,703 admitted, 784 enrolled.

| Mid 50% test scores | | | |
|---|---|---|---|
| SAT critical reading: | 410-530 | Rank in top tenth: | 9% |
| SAT math: | 420-540 | End year in good standing: | 86% |
| ACT composite: | 18-23 | Return as sophomores: | 65% |
| GPA 3.75 or higher: | 11% | Out-of-state: | 10% |
| GPA 3.50-3.74: | 16% | Live on campus: | 51% |
| GPA 3.0-3.49: | 34% | International: | 3% |
| GPA 2.0-2.99: | 38% | Fraternities: | 3% |
| Rank in top quarter: | 30% | Sororities: | 2% |

**Basis for selection.** 2.5 GPA and 17 ACT or 830 SAT (exclusive of Writing) required for bachelor's programs. For associate degree programs, SAT or ACT required for placement but not admission. **Homeschooled:** GED required.

**High school preparation.** 24 units required; 26 recommended. Required and recommended units include English 4, mathematics 3, social studies 2, history 1, science 3 (laboratory 2), foreign language 2 and academic electives 11. 1 unit U.S. history required. Math must include algebra and at least 1 higher unit. 2 units lab science required for biology, chemistry, and physics majors.

**2009-2010 Annual costs.** Tuition/fees: $4,952; $10,684 out-of-state. Room/board: $6,683. Books/supplies: $1,000. Personal expenses: $1,500.

**2008-2009 Financial aid.** All financial aid based on need.

**Application procedures. Admission:** Priority date 3/1; deadline 8/15 (postmark date). No application fee. Admission notification on a rolling basis beginning on or about 10/1. **Financial aid:** Closing date 3/1. FAFSA required. Applicants notified on a rolling basis starting 4/1; must reply within 2 week(s) of notification.

**Academics. Special study options:** Cooperative education, distance learning, double major, dual enrollment of high school students, ESL, exchange student, honors, internships, liberal arts/career combination, study abroad, teacher certification program, Washington semester, weekend college. **Credit/placement by examination:** AP, CLEP, IB, institutional tests. 28 credit hours maximum toward bachelor's degree. **Support services:** Learning center, reduced course load, remedial instruction, study skills assistance, tutoring.

**Majors. Biology:** General. **Business:** General, accounting, banking/financial services, business admin, management information systems, management science, office management. **Communications:** General. **Communications technology:** Graphic/printing. **Computer sciences:** General, computer science. **Education:** General, art, biology, business, chemistry, early childhood, elementary, emotionally handicapped, English, family/consumer sciences, gifted/talented, history, mathematics, mentally handicapped, middle, music, physical, physics, science, secondary, social studies, speech, technology/industrial arts, trade/industrial. **Engineering technology:** Aerospace, architectural, civil, construction, drafting, electrical, mechanical, occupational safety. **Family/consumer sciences:** General. **Foreign languages:** French, Spanish. **Health:** Health care admin, nursing (RN). **History:** General. **Math:** General. **Parks/recreation:** Exercise sciences, health/fitness. **Physical sciences:** Chemistry. **Protective services:** Criminal justice, forensics, law enforcement admin. **Psychology:** General. **Social sciences:** Political science, sociology. **Transportation:** Aviation, aviation management. **Visual/performing arts:** Commercial/advertising art, dramatic.

**Most popular majors.** Business/marketing 24%, education 20%, engineering/engineering technologies 9%, liberal arts 7%, psychology 8%, security/protective services 9%.

**Computing on campus.** 950 workstations in dormitories, library, computer center, student center. Dormitories wired for high-speed internet access and linked to campus network. Commuter students can connect to campus network. Online library, helpline, student web hosting, wireless network available.

**Student life. Freshman orientation:** Available. Preregistration for classes offered. Held 2 days in fall, one day in spring. **Policies:** Alcohol not allowed. **Housing:** Guaranteed on-campus for freshmen. Coed dorms, single-sex dorms, apartments available. $200 fully refundable deposit, deadline 6/15. **Activities:** Bands, campus ministries, choral groups, dance, drama, international student organizations, literary magazine, music ensembles, musical theater, student government, student newspaper, symphony orchestra, black student union, Circle K, disabled students society, society of non-traditional students.

**Athletics. NCAA. Intercollegiate:** Baseball M, basketball, cheerleading M, cross-country, football (tackle) M, golf, softball W, swimming, tennis, volleyball W. **Intramural:** Archery, badminton W, basketball, bowling, cross-country, field hockey W, football (tackle) M, golf, gymnastics, racquetball, softball, swimming, table tennis, tennis, track and field, volleyball, wrestling M. **Team name:** Falcons.

**Student services.** Adult student services, career counseling, student employment services, financial aid counseling, health services, on-campus daycare, personal counseling, placement for graduates, veterans' counselor. **Physically disabled:** Services for visually, hearing impaired.

**Contact.** E-mail: admit@fairmontstate.edu
Phone: (304) 367-4892 Toll-free number: (800) 641-5678
Fax: (304) 367-4789
Steve Leadman, Executive Director of Enrollment Services, Fairmont State University, 1201 Locust Avenue, Fairmont, WV 26554-2470

## Glenville State College
**Glenville, West Virginia**
www.glenville.edu

**CB member**
**CB code: 5254**

- Public 4-year liberal arts and teachers college
- Commuter campus in rural community
- 1,191 degree-seeking undergraduates: 4% part-time, 48% women, 9% African American, 1% Hispanic American, 1% Native American
- 100% of applicants admitted
- SAT or ACT (ACT writing optional) required
- 39% graduate within 6 years

**General.** Founded in 1872. Regionally accredited. **Degrees:** 174 bachelor's, 31 associate awarded. **Location:** 87 miles from Charleston, 86 miles from Morgantown. **Calendar:** Semester, limited summer session. **Full-time faculty:** 61 total; 52% have terminal degrees, 3% minority. **Part-time faculty:** 41 total; 5% have terminal degrees, 2% minority. **Class size:** 55% < 20, 40% 20-39, 3% 40-49, less than 1% 50-99.

**Freshman class profile.** 927 applied, 926 admitted, 325 enrolled.

| Mid 50% test scores | | | |
|---|---|---|---|
| SAT critical reading: | 370-480 | Rank in top quarter: | 30% |
| SAT math: | 370-470 | Rank in top tenth: | 12% |
| ACT composite: | 17-22 | End year in good standing: | 55% |
| GPA 3.75 or higher: | 10% | Return as sophomores: | 55% |
| GPA 3.50-3.74: | 10% | Out-of-state: | 15% |
| GPA 3.0-3.49: | 31% | Live on campus: | 69% |
| GPA 2.0-2.99: | 41% | | |

**Basis for selection.** Students must have graduated from accredited high school with 2.0 GPA or 18 ACT/860 SAT (exclusive of Writing). Associate degree programs open to all students who have graduated from high school or hold a GED. Students who want to pursue bachelor's degree, but do not meet the requirements may enter 2-year program and later transfer into bachelor's degree program. Audition required for music education only. **Homeschooled:** GED required. **Learning Disabled:** Students must provide documentation of their disability to the disabilities coordinator to receive services.

**High school preparation.** 28 units required. Required units include English 4, mathematics 4, social studies 3, science 3 (laboratory 3), foreign language 2, visual/performing arts 1 and academic electives 15. 3 math units must be algebra I or higher. Social studies should include US history. English should include courses in grammar, composition, and literature.

**2009-2010 Annual costs.** Tuition/fees: $4,888; $11,702 out-of-state. Tuition for students residing in border counties is $8,064. Room/board: $6,660. Books/supplies: $1,000. Personal expenses: $2,140.

**2008-2009 Financial aid.** **Need-based:** 288 full-time freshmen applied for aid; 252 were judged to have need; 251 of these received aid. Average need met was 72%. Average scholarship/grant was $4,859; average loan $3,096. 73% of total undergraduate aid awarded as scholarships/grants, 27% as loans/jobs. **Non-need-based:** Awarded to 519 full-time undergraduates, including 181 freshmen. Scholarships awarded for academics, athletics, music/drama, state residency.

**Application procedures.** **Admission:** No deadline. $10 fee, may be waived for applicants with need. Admission notification on a rolling basis. **Financial aid:** Priority date 2/1; no closing date. FAFSA required. Applicants notified on a rolling basis starting 3/1; must reply within 3 week(s) of notification.

**Academics.** Students can receive credit for employment, military, and/or life experience in Regents Bachelor of Arts program (designed for nontraditional students). **Special study options:** Combined bachelor's/graduate degree, distance learning, double major, dual enrollment of high school students, internships, student-designed major, study abroad, teacher certification program, Washington semester. **Credit/placement by examination:** AP, CLEP, SAT, ACT, institutional tests. Unlimited number of hours of credit may be

counted for degree. **Support services:** Remedial instruction, study skills assistance, tutoring, writing center.

**Majors. Biology:** General. **Business:** General, business admin. **Conservation:** Management/policy. **Education:** Elementary, kindergarten/preschool, secondary, special. **History:** General. **Physical sciences:** Chemistry. **Social sciences:** General. **Visual/performing arts:** Music performance. **Other:** Multi/Interdisciplinary studies.

**Most popular majors.** Business/marketing 20%, education 24%, liberal arts 9%, natural resources/environmental science 12%, social sciences 22%.

**Computing on campus.** 183 workstations in library, computer center, student center. Dormitories wired for high-speed internet access and linked to campus network. Commuter students can connect to campus network. Online course registration, online library, helpline, repair service, wireless network available.

**Student life. Freshman orientation:** Mandatory, $100 fee. Preregistration for classes offered. **Policies:** All unmarried students who have earned less than 58 credit hours required to reside on campus. Alcoholic beverages and controlled substances not permitted on campus. All students required to adhere to Student Code of Conduct. Community service required of student organizations. **Housing:** Guaranteed on-campus for freshmen. Single-sex dorms, special housing for disabled, apartments, wellness housing available. $75 partly refundable deposit, deadline 4/1. **Activities:** Bands, choral groups, drama, literary magazine, music ensembles, student government, student newspaper, Fellowship of Christian Athletes, environmental organization, students in free enterprise, Student National Education Association, student athlete advisory committee, student awareness organization, Music Educators National Conference, Kappa Delta Pi.

**Athletics.** NCAA. **Intercollegiate:** Basketball, cross-country, football (tackle) M, golf, softball W, track and field, volleyball W. **Intramural:** Basketball, fencing, football (non-tackle), softball, table tennis, tennis, volleyball, weight lifting, wrestling. **Team name:** Pioneers.

**Student services.** Adult student services, alcohol/substance abuse counseling, career counseling, services for economically disadvantaged, student employment services, financial aid counseling, health services, personal counseling, placement for graduates, veterans' counselor. **Physically disabled:** Services for visually, speech, hearing impaired.

**Contact.** E-mail: admissions@glenville.edu
Phone: (304) 462-4128 Toll-free number: (800) 924-2010
Fax: (304) 462-8619
Donald Chapman, Vice President for Enrollment Services, Glenville State College, Office of Enrollment Services, Glenville, WV 26351-1292

## Marshall University
**Huntington, West Virginia**
www.marshall.edu

**CB member**
**CB code: 5396**

- Public 4-year university
- Commuter campus in small city
- 9,051 degree-seeking undergraduates: 12% part-time, 56% women, 6% African American, 1% Asian American, 1% Hispanic American, 1% international
- 3,393 degree-seeking graduate students
- 86% of applicants admitted
- SAT or ACT (ACT writing optional) required
- 44% graduate within 6 years

**General.** Founded in 1837. Regionally accredited. **Degrees:** 1,402 bachelor's, 111 associate awarded; master's, doctoral, professional offered. **ROTC:** Army. **Location:** 126 miles from Lexington, KY; 160 miles from Columbus, OH. **Calendar:** Semester, limited summer session. **Full-time faculty:** 478 total; 80% have terminal degrees, 13% minority, 41% women. **Part-time faculty:** 269 total; 7% have terminal degrees, 4% minority, 52% women. **Class size:** 40% < 20, 49% 20-39, 6% 40-49, 5% 50-99, less than 1% >100. **Special facilities:** Confederate history collection, superconducting nuclear magnetic resonance spectrometer.

**Freshman class profile.** 2,577 applied, 2,208 admitted, 1,882 enrolled.

| Mid 50% test scores | | | |
|---|---|---|---|
| SAT critical reading: | 440-500 | GPA 3.50-3.74: | 16% |
| SAT math: | 430-550 | GPA 3.0-3.49: | 27% |
| SAT writing: | 430-550 | GPA 2.0-2.99: | 27% |
| ACT composite: | 19-25 | Return as sophomores: | 71% |
| GPA 3.75 or higher: | 28% | Out-of-state: | 25% |
| | | International: | 1% |

**Basis for selection.** Full admission requires 2.0 GPA and 19 ACT/910 SAT (exclusive of Writing). Conditional admission granted with below 2.0

GPA or the above scores, on a limited, first-come, first-served basis. Programs and colleges may have different requirements for admissions. Audition required for music majors; interview recommended for academically weak, learning disabled; portfolio recommended. **Homeschooled:** Applicants should apply early and have home schooling well documented.

**High school preparation.** College-preparatory program required. 20 units required. Required units include English 4, mathematics 4, social studies 3, science 3 (laboratory 3), foreign language 2 and visual/performing arts 1.

**2009-2010 Annual costs.** Tuition/fees: $5,236; $12,482 out-of-state. Tuition for students residing in border counties is $8,668. Room/board: $7,556. Books/supplies: $1,100. Personal expenses: $2,230.

**2009-2010 Financial aid. Need-based:** 1,207 full-time freshmen applied for aid; 898 were judged to have need; 887 of these received aid. Average need met was 55%. Average scholarship/grant was $6,635; average loan $5,651. 40% of total undergraduate aid awarded as scholarships/grants, 60% as loans/jobs. **Non-need-based:** Awarded to 3,333 full-time undergraduates, including 857 freshmen. Scholarships awarded for academics, art, athletics, minority status, music/drama, ROTC, state residency.

**Application procedures. Admission:** No deadline. $30 fee, may be waived for applicants with need. Admission notification on a rolling basis beginning on or about 9/1. **Financial aid:** Priority date 3/1; no closing date. FAFSA required. Applicants notified on a rolling basis starting 5/1; must reply within 2 week(s) of notification.

**Academics. Special study options:** Accelerated study, combined bachelor's/graduate degree, cooperative education, cross-registration, distance learning, double major, dual enrollment of high school students, ESL, exchange student, honors, independent study, internships, study abroad, teacher certification program, Washington semester. 2-2 preengineering program, 3-2 program in forestry with Duke University. **Credit/placement by examination:** AP, CLEP, IB, SAT, ACT, institutional tests. **Support services:** Learning center, pre-admission summer program, reduced course load, remedial instruction, study skills assistance, tutoring, writing center.

**Majors. Biology:** General. **Business:** Accounting, business admin, finance, international, management information systems, managerial economics, marketing. **Communications:** Journalism. **Computer sciences:** General. **Conservation:** Environmental science. **Education:** Elementary, kindergarten/preschool, physical, school counseling, secondary. **Engineering:** General. **Engineering technology:** Occupational safety. **Family/consumer sciences:** General. **Foreign languages:** General. **Health:** Athletic training, clinical lab science, cytotechnology, dietetics, nursing (RN), radiologic technology/medical imaging, respiratory therapy technology, speech pathology. **History:** General. **Interdisciplinary:** Systems science. **Liberal arts:** Humanities. **Math:** General. **Parks/recreation:** Exercise sciences, facilities management. **Physical sciences:** Chemistry, geology, physics. **Protective services:** Criminal justice. **Psychology:** General. **Public administration:** Social work. **Social sciences:** Economics, geography, international relations, political science, sociology. **Other:** Adult and continuing education administration.

**Most popular majors.** Biology 6%, business/marketing 18%, education 18%, health sciences 9%, liberal arts 17%, psychology 6%.

**Computing on campus.** 1,461 workstations in dormitories, library, computer center, student center. Dormitories wired for high-speed internet access and linked to campus network. Commuter students can connect to campus network. Online course registration, online library, helpline, student web hosting available.

**Student life. Freshman orientation:** Available. Preregistration for classes offered. One-day programs in June, July, August. **Housing:** Guaranteed on-campus for freshmen. Coed dorms, single-sex dorms, special housing for disabled available. $200 deposit, deadline 5/15. **Activities:** Bands, campus ministries, choral groups, dance, drama, international student organizations, literary magazine, music ensembles, Model UN, musical theater, opera, radio station, student government, student newspaper, symphony orchestra, TV station, black united students, College Republicans, Lambda Society, Habitat for Humanity, student organization for alumni relations.

**Athletics.** NCAA. **Intercollegiate:** Baseball M, basketball, cross-country, football (tackle) M, golf, soccer, softball W, swimming W, tennis W, track and field, volleyball W. **Intramural:** Basketball, bowling, football (tackle), golf, racquetball, soccer, softball, swimming, tennis, track and field, volleyball. **Team name:** Thundering Herd.

**Student services.** Adult student services, alcohol/substance abuse counseling, chaplain/spiritual director, career counseling, student employment services, health services, minority student services, on-campus daycare, personal counseling, placement for graduates, veterans' counselor, women's services. **Physically disabled:** Services for visually, speech, hearing impaired.

**Contact.** E-mail: admissions@marshall.edu
Phone: (304) 696-3160 Toll-free number: (800) 642-3499
Fax: (304) 696-3135
Tammy Johnson, Director of Admissions, Marshall University, One John Marshall Drive, Huntington, WV 25755

## Mountain State University
**Beckley, West Virginia**　　　　　　　　　**CB member**
**www.mountainstate.edu**　　　　　　　　**CB code: 5054**

▸ Private 4-year university and health science college
▸ Commuter campus in large town
▸ 5,137 degree-seeking undergraduates: 28% part-time, 67% women, 15% African American, 2% Asian American, 2% Hispanic American, 1% Native American, 5% international
▸ 708 degree-seeking graduate students

**General.** Founded in 1933. Regionally accredited. **Degrees:** 669 bachelor's, 174 associate awarded; master's, doctoral offered. **Location:** 55 miles from Charleston; 125 miles from Roanoke, Virginia. **Calendar:** Semester, limited summer session. **Full-time faculty:** 97 total; 29% have terminal degrees, 75% minority, 71% women. **Part-time faculty:** 335 total; 21% have terminal degrees, 57% minority, 52% women. **Class size:** 66% < 20, 32% 20-39, 1% 40-49, less than 1% 50-99. **Special facilities:** YMCA, medicinal botanical garden, greenhouse.

**Freshman class profile.** 1,780 applied, 1,780 admitted, 762 enrolled.

| Mid 50% test scores | | Rank in top tenth: | 2% |
|---|---|---|---|
| ACT composite: | 17-23 | End year in good standing: | 40% |
| GPA 3.75 or higher: | 5% | Return as sophomores: | 38% |
| GPA 3.50-3.74: | 8% | Out-of-state: | 39% |
| GPA 3.0-3.49: | 27% | Live on campus: | 6% |
| GPA 2.0-2.99: | 43% | International: | 1% |
| Rank in top quarter: | 14% | Fraternities: | 1% |

**Basis for selection.** Open admission, but selective for some programs. Special requirements for health science programs. ACT/SAT scores required for nursing and physician's assistant programs. **Homeschooled:** Official academic records required.

**High school preparation.** College-preparatory program recommended. 15 units recommended. Recommended units include English 4, mathematics 2, social studies 3, history 2, science 2 (laboratory 2).

**2010-2011 Annual costs.** Tuition/fees (projected): $8,700. Certain undergraduate programs require additional costs. Per-credit-hour costs vary: $300 for Organizational Leadership; $310 for Medical Assisting, Online Criminal Justice, Online Business and Accounting, and Online General Education; $320 for Online Administration of Criminal Justice, Online Medical Assisting, and Online Organizational Leadership; $330 for Culinary Arts, Diagnostic Medical Sonography, Engineering, Occupational Therapy Assistant, Physical Therapy Assistant, and Radiologic Technology; $350 for Nursing; $430 for Online Diagnostic Medical Sonography. Room/board: $6,116. Books/supplies: $1,300. Personal expenses: $3,000.

**2008-2009 Financial aid. Need-based:** 210 full-time freshmen applied for aid; 195 were judged to have need; 195 of these received aid. Average need met was 39%. Average scholarship/grant was $3,916; average loan $2,982. 40% of total undergraduate aid awarded as scholarships/grants, 60% as loans/jobs. **Non-need-based:** Awarded to 107 full-time undergraduates, including 15 freshmen. Scholarships awarded for academics, alumni affiliation, athletics, leadership, minority status, state residency.

**Application procedures. Admission:** No deadline. $25 fee, may be waived for applicants with need. Admission notification on a rolling basis. **Financial aid:** Priority date 3/1; no closing date. FAFSA required. Applicants notified on a rolling basis starting 4/1.

**Academics. Special study options:** Accelerated study, combined bachelor's/graduate degree, cooperative education, cross-registration, distance learning, double major, dual enrollment of high school students, ESL, honors, independent study, internships, liberal arts/career combination, student-designed major, weekend college. Degree completion program, credit for prior learning (challenge exam and portfolio assessment). **Credit/placement by examination:** AP, CLEP, IB, institutional tests. 32 credit hours maximum toward associate degree, 64 toward bachelor's. CLEP, DANTES and Challenge exams available. **Support services:** Learning center, reduced course load, remedial instruction, study skills assistance, tutoring, writing center.

**Majors. Biology:** General. **Business:** Accounting, business admin, nonprofit/public. **Computer sciences:** Computer science, information technology. **Health:** Health services, nursing (RN), sonography. **Legal studies:** General. **Personal/**

culinary services: Chef training. **Philosophy/religion:** Religion. **Protective services:** Criminal justice, forensics. **Psychology:** General. **Public administration:** Social work. **Transportation:** Aviation management. **Visual/performing arts:** Graphic design. **Other:** Interdisciplinary/liberal studies.

**Most popular majors.** Health sciences 37%, liberal arts 6%, security/protective services 11%.

**Computing on campus.** 207 workstations in library, computer center. Dormitories wired for high-speed internet access and linked to campus network. Commuter students can connect to campus network. Online course registration, online library, helpline, student web hosting, wireless network available.

**Student life. Freshman orientation:** Mandatory. Preregistration for classes offered. One-day orientation held in June and August for Health Sciences, Arts and Sciences, and Business and Technology. **Housing:** Guaranteed on-campus for freshmen. Coed dorms, wellness housing available. $150 nonrefundable deposit. Handicapped-accessible dorms, off-campus housing for athletes available. **Activities:** Pep band, campus ministries, choral groups, drama, international student organizations, literary magazine, music ensembles, student government, student newspaper, Christian volunteers, criminal justice club, forensic investigation association, student nurses association, Student in Free Enterprise, student social work organization, Campus Crusade for Christ, culinary club, student radiologic technologist association.

**Athletics.** NAIA. **Intercollegiate:** Basketball M, cheerleading M, cross-country, soccer, track and field, volleyball W. **Intramural:** Basketball M, soccer, volleyball W. **Team name:** Cougars.

**Student services.** Adult student services, alcohol/substance abuse counseling, career counseling, student employment services, financial aid counseling, health services, personal counseling, placement for graduates, veterans' counselor.

**Contact.** E-mail: gomsu@mountainstate.edu
Phone: (304) 929-1433 Toll-free number: (800) 766-6067
Fax: (304) 253-3463
Tammy Toney, Director of the Admissions Process, Mountain State University, 609 South Kanawha Street, Beckley, WV 25802-9003

## Ohio Valley University
### Vienna, West Virginia
www.ovu.edu                           CB code: 5519

- Private 4-year university and liberal arts college affiliated with Church of Christ
- Residential campus in small city
- 444 degree-seeking undergraduates: 7% part-time, 52% women, 5% African American, 4% Hispanic American, 7% international
- 22 degree-seeking graduate students
- 57% of applicants admitted
- SAT or ACT (ACT writing optional) required
- 55% graduate within 6 years

**General.** Founded in 1960. Regionally accredited. **Degrees:** 92 bachelor's, 20 associate awarded; master's offered. **Location:** 95 miles from Columbus, 120 miles from Pittsburgh. **Calendar:** Semester, limited summer session. **Full-time faculty:** 23 total; 56% have terminal degrees, 4% minority, 26% women. **Part-time faculty:** 52 total; 15% have terminal degrees, 42% women. **Class size:** 79% < 20, 21% 20-39.

**Freshman class profile.** 437 applied, 251 admitted, 125 enrolled.

| Mid 50% test scores | | GPA 2.0-2.99: | 39% |
|---|---|---|---|
| SAT critical reading: | 430-510 | Rank in top quarter: | 26% |
| SAT math: | 440-500 | Rank in top tenth: | 16% |
| SAT writing: | 430-540 | End year in good standing: | 91% |
| ACT composite: | 19-24 | Return as sophomores: | 66% |
| GPA 3.75 or higher: | 14% | Out-of-state: | 12% |
| GPA 3.50-3.74: | 10% | Live on campus: | 90% |
| GPA 3.0-3.49: | 31% | International: | 5% |

**Basis for selection.** School achievement record, test scores and reference considered. Essay, interview recommended.

**High school preparation.** 12 units recommended. Recommended units include English 3, mathematics 3, social studies 2, history 1, science 3 (laboratory 1).

**2009-2010 Annual costs.** Tuition/fees: $17,200. Room/board: $6,676. Books/supplies: $1,000. Personal expenses: $800.

**2009-2010 Financial aid. Need-based:** 80 full-time freshmen applied for aid; 67 were judged to have need; 67 of these received aid. Average need met was 69%. Average scholarship/grant was $10,326; average loan $3,281. 51% of total undergraduate aid awarded as scholarships/grants, 49% as loans/jobs. **Non-need-based:** Scholarships awarded for academics, alumni affiliation, athletics, job skills, leadership, music/drama.

**Application procedures. Admission:** No deadline. $20 fee, may be waived for applicants with need. Admission notification on a rolling basis. **Financial aid:** Priority date 2/15; no closing date. FAFSA required. Applicants notified on a rolling basis starting 3/15; must reply within 4 week(s) of notification.

**Academics.** Bible course required of full-time students each semester. **Special study options:** Cooperative education, double major, dual enrollment of high school students, ESL, honors, independent study, internships, student-designed major, study abroad, teacher certification program, Washington semester, weekend college. Degree completion programs and special certifications. **Credit/placement by examination:** AP, CLEP, IB, SAT, ACT, institutional tests. 30 credit hours maximum toward associate degree, 30 toward bachelor's. Challenge course testing. **Support services:** Learning center, pre-admission summer program, reduced course load, remedial instruction, study skills assistance, tutoring.

**Majors. Business:** Accounting, business admin, human resources, nonprofit/public. **Computer sciences:** Information technology. **Education:** General, elementary, English, mathematics, multi-level teacher, physical, science, secondary, social studies. **Liberal arts:** Arts/sciences. **Philosophy/religion:** Religion. **Psychology:** General. **Theology:** Bible.

**Most popular majors.** Business/marketing 53%, education 17%, psychology 13%, theological studies 8%.

**Computing on campus.** 44 workstations in dormitories, library, computer center. Dormitories wired for high-speed internet access and linked to campus network. Commuter students can connect to campus network. Online library, repair service, wireless network available.

**Student life. Freshman orientation:** Mandatory. Preregistration for classes offered. **Policies:** Chapel/assembly attendance required 3 times a week. Religious observance required. **Housing:** Guaranteed on-campus for all undergraduates. Single-sex dorms, apartments, wellness housing available. $150 deposit, deadline 8/20. **Activities:** Bands, choral groups, drama, literary magazine, music ensembles, musical theater, student government, student newspaper, symphony orchestra, prospective ministers and prospective missionaries clubs, women's club, Diversity at the University club.

**Athletics.** NCAA. **Intercollegiate:** Baseball M, basketball, cross-country, golf, soccer, softball W, volleyball W. **Intramural:** Basketball, bowling, cross-country, football (non-tackle), soccer, softball, table tennis, track and field, volleyball. **Team name:** Fighting Scots.

**Student services.** Adult student services, alcohol/substance abuse counseling, chaplain/spiritual director, career counseling, student employment services, financial aid counseling, health services, minority student services, personal counseling, placement for graduates.

**Contact.** E-mail: admissions@ovu.edu
Phone: (304) 865-6200 Toll-free number: (877) 446-8668
Fax: (304) 865-6175
Amy Bortell, Director of Admissions, Ohio Valley University, One Campus View Drive, Vienna, WV 26105

## Salem International University
### Salem, West Virginia
www.salemu.edu                           CB code: 5608

- For-profit 4-year university and liberal arts college
- Residential campus in rural community
- 442 degree-seeking undergraduates
- 251 graduate students

**General.** Founded in 1888. Regionally accredited. **Degrees:** 28 bachelor's, 3 associate awarded; master's offered. **Location:** 12 miles from Clarksburg, 125 miles from Pittsburgh. **Calendar:** Semester, limited summer session. **Full-time faculty:** 13 total; 46% have terminal degrees, 8% minority, 23% women. **Part-time faculty:** 3 total; 67% women. **Class size:** 77% < 20, 17% 20-39, 6% 40-49.

**Freshman class profile.**

| Out-of-state: | 46% | Fraternities: | 5% |
|---|---|---|---|
| Live on campus: | 90% | Sororities: | 8% |

**Basis for selection.** Open admission. School achievement record, test scores, counselor recommendations most important. Essay, interview recommended. **Homeschooled:** State high school equivalency certificate required.

**High school preparation.** 16 units recommended. Recommended units include English 4, mathematics 2, social studies 3, science 2 and foreign language 2.

**2009-2010 Annual costs.** Books/supplies: $660. Personal expenses: $320.

**2008-2009 Financial aid. Non-need-based:** Scholarships awarded for academics.

**Application procedures. Admission:** No deadline. $25 fee, may be waived for applicants with need. Admission notification on a rolling basis. **Financial aid:** Priority date 4/15; no closing date. FAFSA required. Applicants notified on a rolling basis starting 2/15; must reply within 4 week(s) of notification.

**Academics.** In keeping with college's mission to foster global awareness, all students required to complete international core curriculum. **Special study options:** Accelerated study, distance learning, double major, dual enrollment of high school students, independent study, internships, liberal arts/career combination, student-designed major, study abroad, teacher certification program, Washington semester. **Credit/placement by examination:** AP, CLEP, IB, institutional tests. 24 credit hours maximum toward bachelor's degree. **Support services:** Learning center, reduced course load, remedial instruction, study skills assistance, tutoring, writing center.

**Majors. Biology:** General. **Business:** Business admin. **Computer sciences:** General, computer science. **Education:** General, multi-level teacher, secondary. **Liberal arts:** Arts/sciences. **Protective services:** Criminal justice.

**Most popular majors.** Business/marketing 44%, computer/information sciences 26%, liberal arts 13%.

**Computing on campus.** 50 workstations in library, computer center. Dormitories wired for high-speed internet access and linked to campus network. Commuter students can connect to campus network. Online library, helpline, wireless network available.

**Student life. Freshman orientation:** Available, $30 fee. Preregistration for classes offered. Program includes introduction to international aspects of college. Special orientation for international students with U.S. life-skills training. **Policies:** Unless local resident, freshmen and sophomores required to live on-campus. **Housing:** Guaranteed on-campus for all undergraduates. Coed dorms, single-sex dorms, wellness housing available. $50 fully refundable deposit. Private rooms subject to availability. **Activities:** Choral groups, international student organizations, student government, student newspaper, Gamma Beta Phi honor society, Alpha Phi Omega fraternity service organization, Campus Crusade for Christ, Rainbow Alliance, international woman's alliance, Christian Student Fellowship, Indian student association, Chinese student association.

**Athletics.** NCAA. **Intercollegiate:** Baseball M, basketball, golf, soccer, softball W, tennis M, volleyball W, water polo. **Intramural:** Basketball, football (non-tackle), racquetball, skiing M, soccer, swimming, table tennis, tennis, volleyball. **Team name:** Tigers.

**Student services.** Services for economically disadvantaged, financial aid counseling.

**Contact.** E-mail: admissions@salemu.edu
Phone: (888) 235-5024 Toll-free number: (888) 235-5024
Fax: (304) 326-1592
Gina Cossey, Vice Presdent, Recruiting and Marketing, Salem International University, 223 West Main Street, Salem, WV 26426

---

## Shepherd University

**Shepherdstown, West Virginia**
www.shepherd.edu

**CB member**
**CB code: 5615**

- Public 4-year university
- Commuter campus in small town
- 3,676 degree-seeking undergraduates: 10% part-time, 58% women, 5% African American, 2% Asian American, 2% Hispanic American
- 154 degree-seeking graduate students
- 94% of applicants admitted
- SAT or ACT (ACT writing optional) required
- 44% graduate within 6 years; 38% enter graduate study

**General.** Founded in 1871. Regionally accredited. **Degrees:** 662 bachelor's awarded; master's offered. **ROTC:** Air Force. **Location:** 8 miles from Martinsburg; 70 miles from Washington, DC. **Calendar:** Semester, extensive summer session. **Full-time faculty:** 124 total; 76% have terminal degrees, 17% minority, 43% women. **Part-time faculty:** 210 total; 31% have terminal degrees, 12% minority, 49% women. **Class size:** 40% < 20, 56% 20-39, 2% 40-49, 1% 50-99. **Special facilities:** Creative arts center with computer-controlled theater, recital hall with concert grand piano, recording studio, nursery school, 3 theaters, Civil War center, observatory, legislative studies center, nursing building, creative arts center.

**Freshman class profile.** 1,768 applied, 1,657 admitted, 796 enrolled.

| Mid 50% test scores | | | |
|---|---|---|---|
| SAT critical reading: | 450-560 | GPA 3.0-3.49: | 27% |
| SAT math: | 450-550 | GPA 2.0-2.99: | 34% |
| ACT composite: | 20-24 | End year in good standing: | 65% |
| GPA 3.75 or higher: | 22% | Return as sophomores: | 66% |
| GPA 3.50-3.74: | 15% | Out-of-state: | 38% |
| | | Live on campus: | 39% |

**Basis for selection.** 2.0 GPA and 19 ACT/910 SAT (exclusive of Writing) required. Essays and recommendations optional but important. Interview required for honors program and nursing applicants; recommended for others. Audition required for music; portfolio required for art majors. **Homeschooled:** Portfolio of completed work required.

**High school preparation.** College-preparatory program recommended. 21 units required. Required units include English 4, mathematics 4, social studies 3, history 1, science 3 (laboratory 3), foreign language 2, visual/performing arts 1 and academic electives 6. History unit must include US history; science unit must include biology. All science courses must be college preparatory laboratory sciences.

**2009-2010 Annual costs.** Tuition/fees: $5,234; $13,574 out-of-state. Room/board: $7,228. Books/supplies: $1,100. Personal expenses: $1,000.

**2008-2009 Financial aid. Need-based:** 621 full-time freshmen applied for aid; 364 were judged to have need; 352 of these received aid. Average need met was 91%. Average scholarship/grant was $4,306; average loan $3,383. 45% of total undergraduate aid awarded as scholarships/grants, 55% as loans/jobs. **Non-need-based:** Awarded to 1,242 full-time undergraduates, including 354 freshmen. Scholarships awarded for academics, art, athletics, job skills, leadership, minority status, music/drama, state residency.

**Application procedures. Admission:** Priority date 2/1; no deadline. $45 fee, may be waived for applicants with need. Admission notification on a rolling basis beginning on or about 9/1. Must reply by May 1 or within 3 week(s) if notified thereafter. **Financial aid:** Priority date 3/1; no closing date. FAFSA required. Applicants notified on a rolling basis starting 3/15; must reply within 3 week(s) of notification.

**Academics. Special study options:** Cooperative education, double major, honors, independent study, internships, liberal arts/career combination, study abroad, teacher certification program, Washington semester. **Credit/placement by examination:** AP, CLEP, IB, SAT, ACT, institutional tests. 32 credit hours maximum toward bachelor's degree. No limit for students pursuing Regents' Bachelor of Arts degree. **Support services:** Learning center, remedial instruction, study skills assistance, tutoring, writing center.

**Majors. Biology:** General. **Business:** Accounting, business admin. **Communications:** General. **Computer sciences:** General, applications programming. **Conservation:** General, environmental studies. **Education:** Elementary, secondary. **Family/consumer sciences:** General. **Foreign languages:** Spanish. **Health:** Nursing (RN). **History:** General. **Math:** General. **Parks/recreation:** General. **Physical sciences:** Chemistry. **Psychology:** General. **Public administration:** Social work. **Social sciences:** Economics, political science, sociology. **Visual/performing arts:** Art.

**Most popular majors.** Business/marketing 18%, education 15%, health sciences 8%, liberal arts 14%, parks/recreation 7%, visual/performing arts 8%.

**Computing on campus.** 370 workstations in library, computer center, student center. Dormitories wired for high-speed internet access and linked to campus network. Commuter students can connect to campus network. Online course registration, helpline, student web hosting, wireless network available.

**Student life. Freshman orientation:** Mandatory, $75 fee. Preregistration for classes offered. 2-day sessions held in June and July for students and parents. August orientation conducted on the Thursday and/or Friday and Saturday prior to the first day of classes. **Housing:** Guaranteed on-campus for all undergraduates. Coed dorms, apartments, wellness housing available. $200 partly refundable deposit, deadline 6/1. Honors housing available. **Activities:** Bands, campus ministries, choral groups, dance, drama, international student organizations, literary magazine, music ensembles, musical theater, radio station, student government, student newspaper, symphony orchestra, College Republicans, College Democrats, Christians in Action,

NAACP, United Brothers, Shepherd Greens, Allies, Sistaz, student community services.

**Athletics.** NCAA. **Intercollegiate:** Baseball M, basketball, football (tackle) M, golf M, lacrosse W, soccer, softball W, tennis, volleyball W. **Intramural:** Basketball, bowling, football (non-tackle), racquetball, soccer, softball, swimming, table tennis, tennis, volleyball, water polo, weight lifting, wrestling. **Team name:** Rams.

**Student services.** Adult student services, alcohol/substance abuse counseling, career counseling, student employment services, financial aid counseling, health services, minority student services, personal counseling, placement for graduates, veterans' counselor. **Physically disabled:** Services for visually, speech, hearing impaired.

**Contact.** E-mail: admissions@shepherd.edu
Phone: (304) 876-5212 Toll-free number: (800) 344-5231 ext. 5212
Fax: (304) 876-5165
Randall Friend, Director of Admissions, Shepherd University, PO Box 5000, Shepherdstown, WV 25443-5000

## University of Charleston
**Charleston, West Virginia**
**www.ucwv.edu**

CB member
CB code: 5419

- Private 4-year university and liberal arts college
- Residential campus in small city
- 1,006 degree-seeking undergraduates: 2% part-time, 59% women, 8% African American, 1% Asian American, 1% Hispanic American, 10% international
- 384 degree-seeking graduate students
- 79% of applicants admitted
- SAT or ACT (ACT writing optional) required
- 44% graduate within 6 years

**General.** Founded in 1888. Regionally accredited. **Degrees:** 175 bachelor's, 36 associate awarded; master's, professional offered. **ROTC:** Army. **Location:** 200 miles from Pittsburgh; 200 miles from Charlotte, North Carolina. **Calendar:** Semester, limited summer session. **Full-time faculty:** 86 total; 59% have terminal degrees, 10% minority, 62% women. **Part-time faculty:** 34 total; 35% have terminal degrees, 53% women. **Class size:** 70% < 20, 29% 20-39, less than 1% 40-49, less than 1% 50-99. **Special facilities:** Sports medicine clinic, clinics at nearby hospital, entrepreneurship center.

**Freshman class profile.** 1,225 applied, 970 admitted, 273 enrolled.

| Mid 50% test scores | | | | |
|---|---|---|---|---|
| SAT critical reading: | 440-530 | Rank in top quarter: | 44% |
| SAT math: | 430-520 | Rank in top tenth: | 20% |
| ACT composite: | 19-24 | Return as sophomores: | 57% |
| GPA 3.75 or higher: | 29% | Out-of-state: | 46% |
| GPA 3.50-3.74: | 10% | Live on campus: | 74% |
| GPA 3.0-3.49: | 28% | | |
| GPA 2.0-2.99: | 32% | | |

**Basis for selection.** School achievement record and courses taken most important. Test scores, school recommendation, school and community activities, class rank, and interview also considered. GPA recomputed to reflect performance in academic subjects only. Essay, interview, portfolio recommended for all; audition required for music. **Homeschooled:** If part of diploma-granting organization, list of coursework completed and level of performance required. Otherwise, detailed portfolio required and essay, 3 letters of reference, on-campus interview recommended. **Learning Disabled:** Documentation from professional within last 2 years required.

**High school preparation.** College-preparatory program recommended. 16 units recommended. Recommended units include English 4, mathematics 3, social studies 3, history 2, science 3 and foreign language 1. Chemistry, algebra required for 4-year nursing program.

**2009-2010 Annual costs.** Tuition/fees: $24,000. Tuition for pharmacy students: $25,224. Room/board: $8,700. Books/supplies: $1,500. Personal expenses: $250.

**2008-2009 Financial aid. Need-based:** 292 full-time freshmen applied for aid; 256 were judged to have need; 256 of these received aid. Average need met was 84%. Average scholarship/grant was $5,310; average loan $7,110. 70% of total undergraduate aid awarded as scholarships/grants, 30% as loans/jobs. **Non-need-based:** Awarded to 850 full-time undergraduates, including 270 freshmen. Scholarships awarded for academics, alumni affiliation, athletics, leadership, music/drama, ROTC.

**Application procedures. Admission:** No deadline. $25 fee, may be waived for applicants with need, free for online applicants. Admission notification on a rolling basis. For most health science programs, application deadline is January 15, early decision recommended. **Financial aid:** Priority date 3/1; no closing date. FAFSA required. Applicants notified on a rolling basis starting 3/1.

**Academics.** Students can fulfill course requirements at their own pace. **Special study options:** Combined bachelor's/graduate degree, double major, ESL, independent study, internships, liberal arts/career combination, study abroad. **Credit/placement by examination:** AP, CLEP, IB, SAT, ACT, institutional tests. 30 credit hours maximum toward associate degree, 60 toward bachelor's. **Support services:** Learning center, reduced course load, remedial instruction, study skills assistance, tutoring, writing center.

**Majors. Biology:** General. **Business:** Accounting, business admin, finance. **Communications:** Media studies. **Education:** General, biology, elementary, English, health, physical, science, secondary, social studies, special. **Health:** Athletic training, nursing (RN), predental, premedicine, prepharmacy, preveterinary, radiologic technology/medical imaging. **History:** General. **Parks/recreation:** Sports admin. **Physical sciences:** Chemistry. **Psychology:** General. **Public administration:** Policy analysis. **Social sciences:** Political science. **Visual/performing arts:** Art, interior design.

**Most popular majors.** Biology 15%, business/marketing 22%, education 6%, health sciences 18%, parks/recreation 6%, social sciences 6%, visual/performing arts 7%.

**Computing on campus.** 65 workstations in dormitories, library, computer center, student center. Dormitories wired for high-speed internet access and linked to campus network. Commuter students can connect to campus network. Online library, helpline, student web hosting, wireless network available.

**Student life. Freshman orientation:** Mandatory. Preregistration for classes offered. **Policies:** On-campus housing required for dependent freshmen and sophomores not living with parents or legal guardian in local area. **Housing:** Guaranteed on-campus for freshmen. Coed dorms, special housing for disabled, apartments available. $100 fully refundable deposit. Single rooms and suites available. **Activities:** Pep band, campus ministries, choral groups, dance, drama, international student organizations, music ensembles, Model UN, student government, student newspaper, honorary fraternities, Fellowship Christian Athletes, Young Republicans, College Democrats.

**Athletics.** NCAA. **Intercollegiate:** Baseball M, basketball, cheerleading, cross-country, football (tackle) M, golf M, rowing (crew) W, soccer, softball W, tennis, track and field W, volleyball W. **Intramural:** Basketball, bowling, football (non-tackle) M, tennis, volleyball. **Team name:** Golden Eagles.

**Student services.** Career counseling, student employment services, financial aid counseling, personal counseling, placement for graduates.

**Contact.** E-mail: admissions@ucwv.edu
Phone: (304) 357-4750 Toll-free number: (800) 995-4682
Fax: (304) 357-4781
Alan Liebrecht, Vice President for Enrollment, University of Charleston, 2300 MacCorkle Avenue, SE, Charleston, WV 25304

## West Liberty University
**West Liberty, West Virginia**
**www.westliberty.edu**

CB code: 5901

- Public 4-year university
- Residential campus in rural community
- 2,399 degree-seeking undergraduates: 6% part-time, 56% women
- 48 graduate students
- 79% of applicants admitted
- SAT or ACT with writing required
- 47% graduate within 6 years

**General.** Founded in 1837. Regionally accredited. **Degrees:** 357 bachelor's, 32 associate awarded; master's offered. **ROTC:** Army. **Location:** 10 miles from Wheeling, 50 miles from Pittsburgh. **Calendar:** Semester, limited summer session. **Full-time faculty:** 114 total; 49% have terminal degrees, 5% minority, 42% women. **Part-time faculty:** 88 total; 58% women. **Class size:** 45% < 20, 47% 20-39, 7% 40-49, less than 1% 50-99. **Special facilities:** Media arts center, rare book room, rare sheet music collection.

**Freshman class profile.** 1,773 applied, 1,392 admitted, 578 enrolled.

| Mid 50% test scores | | | |
|---|---|---|---|
| SAT critical reading: | 390-490 | Rank in top quarter: | 30% |
| SAT math: | 380-490 | Rank in top tenth: | 10% |
| SAT writing: | 350-470 | Return as sophomores: | 67% |
| ACT composite: | 17-23 | Out-of-state: | 32% |
| GPA 3.75 or higher: | 15% | Live on campus: | 83% |
| GPA 3.50-3.74: | 14% | International: | 1% |
| GPA 3.0-3.49: | 32% | Fraternities: | 2% |
| GPA 2.0-2.99: | 39% | Sororities: | 2% |

**Basis for selection.** 2.0 GPA or 17 ACT or 810 SAT (exclusive of Writing) required. Audition required for music education; portfolio recommended for art.

**High school preparation.** College-preparatory program required. 15 units required. Required and recommended units include English 4, mathematics 3, social studies 2, history 1, science 3 (laboratory 2) and foreign language 2. Math must be algebra I and higher. Social science must include American history.

**2009-2010 Annual costs.** Tuition/fees: $4,880; $11,950 out-of-state. Tuition for students residing in border counties is $9,560. Room/board: $6,870. Books/supplies: $1,300. Personal expenses: $1,682.

**2009-2010 Financial aid. Need-based:** Average scholarship/grant was $5,034; average loan $3,598. 51% of total undergraduate aid awarded as scholarships/grants, 49% as loans/jobs. **Non-need-based:** Scholarships awarded for academics, alumni affiliation, art, athletics, music/drama, state residency. **Additional information:** Non-need based student employment available at food service, college union, bookstore, and tutoring office. Resident assistant and campus security jobs also available.

**Application procedures. Admission:** No deadline. No application fee. Admission notification on a rolling basis beginning on or about 9/1. **Financial aid:** Priority date 3/1; no closing date. FAFSA required. Applicants notified on a rolling basis starting 3/1; must reply within 2 week(s) of notification.

**Academics.** Freshman experience course available. **Special study options:** Accelerated study, distance learning, double major, dual enrollment of high school students, external degree, honors, independent study, internships, liberal arts/career combination, student-designed major, study abroad, teacher certification program, Washington semester. **Credit/placement by examination:** AP, CLEP, SAT, ACT, institutional tests. **Support services:** Reduced course load, remedial instruction, tutoring.

**Majors. Biology:** General, bacteriology, biotechnology. **Business:** General, accounting, banking/financial services, business admin, managerial economics, tourism promotion, tourism/travel. **Communications:** General. **Computer sciences:** Information systems. **Education:** Art, biology, chemistry, early childhood, elementary, English, health, mathematics, mentally handicapped, music, physical, science, secondary, social science, special. **Health:** Clinical lab science, dental hygiene. **History:** General. **Liberal arts:** Arts/sciences. **Math:** General. **Parks/recreation:** Exercise sciences. **Physical sciences:** Chemistry. **Protective services:** Criminal justice. **Psychology:** General. **Social sciences:** General, political science, sociology. **Visual/performing arts:** Commercial/advertising art.

**Most popular majors.** Business/marketing 23%, education 22%, health sciences 15%, liberal arts 8%, security/protective services 7%.

**Computing on campus.** 300 workstations in dormitories, library, computer center, student center. Dormitories wired for high-speed internet access and linked to campus network. Commuter students can connect to campus network. Online course registration, helpline, repair service available.

**Student life. Freshman orientation:** Mandatory, $30 fee. Preregistration for classes offered. Held Friday through Sunday before first day of classes. **Housing:** Guaranteed on-campus for all undergraduates. Coed dorms, single-sex dorms, special housing for disabled, apartments, fraternity/sorority housing available. $100 fully refundable deposit, deadline 6/1. Honors residence for students who meet criteria. **Activities:** Bands, campus ministries, choral groups, dance, drama, international student organizations, literary magazine, music ensembles, musical theater, radio station, student government, student newspaper, TV station, Amnesty International, Students for Life, B-Pride, Electric Square, non-traditional student support group, Students in Free Enterprise, Students for Unity and Understanding.

**Athletics.** NCAA. **Intercollegiate:** Baseball M, basketball, cross-country, football (tackle) M, golf, softball W, tennis, track and field, volleyball W, wrestling M. **Intramural:** Basketball, golf, handball M, racquetball, softball, table tennis, tennis, volleyball. **Team name:** Hilltoppers.

**Student services.** Alcohol/substance abuse counseling, chaplain/spiritual director, career counseling, student employment services, financial aid counseling, health services, minority student services, personal counseling, placement for graduates, veterans' counselor. **Physically disabled:** Services for visually, hearing impaired.

**Contact.** E-mail: wladmsn1@wlsc.edu
Phone: (304) 336-8076 Toll-free number: (800) 732-6204
Fax: (304) 336-8403
Brenda King, Director of Admissions & Recruitment, West Liberty University, PO Box 295, West Liberty, WV 26074-0295

---

## West Virginia State University

| | |
|---|---|
| Institute, West Virginia | CB member |
| www.wvstateu.edu | CB code: 5903 |

- Public 4-year liberal arts and teachers college
- Commuter campus in small town
- 2,525 degree-seeking undergraduates: 31% part-time, 57% women
- 49 graduate students
- 100% of applicants admitted
- SAT or ACT with writing required

**General.** Founded in 1891. Regionally accredited. **Degrees:** 374 bachelor's awarded; master's offered. **ROTC:** Army. **Location:** 8 miles from Charleston. **Calendar:** Semester, limited summer session. **Full-time faculty:** 118 total. **Part-time faculty:** 83 total.

**Freshman class profile.** 1,651 applied, 1,651 admitted, 372 enrolled.

| Mid 50% test scores | | | |
|---|---|---|---|
| SAT critical reading: | 370-450 | ACT composite: | 16-21 |
| SAT math: | 310-430 | Return as sophomores: | 63% |
| SAT writing: | 310-440 | Out-of-state: | 21% |

**Basis for selection.** School achievement record and test scores considered. Interview recommended for academically weak applicants to regents bachelor of arts programs. **Homeschooled:** Must provide detailed description of homeschool curriculum.

**High school preparation.** 14 units required. Required units include English 4, mathematics 2, social studies 3, science 3 (laboratory 2) and foreign language 2.

**2009-2010 Annual costs.** Tuition/fees: $4,644; $10,884 out-of-state. Room/board: $6,070. Books/supplies: $948. Personal expenses: $2,951.

**Financial aid. Non-need-based:** Scholarships awarded for academics, athletics, ROTC, state residency.

**Application procedures. Admission:** No deadline. No application fee. Admission notification on a rolling basis. **Financial aid:** Priority date 3/1, closing date 6/15. FAFSA required. Applicants notified on a rolling basis starting 2/15; must reply within 2 week(s) of notification.

**Academics. Special study options:** Cooperative education, cross-registration, distance learning, double major, dual enrollment of high school students, external degree, honors, internships, teacher certification program, weekend college. Nontraditional life experience degree program. **Credit/placement by examination:** CLEP, IB, institutional tests. **Support services:** Learning center, reduced course load, remedial instruction, study skills assistance, tutoring.

**Majors. Biology:** General. **Business:** General, accounting, banking/financial services, business admin. **Communications:** General. **Computer sciences:** Computer science. **Education:** General, art, early childhood, elementary, English, gifted/talented, health, mathematics, mentally handicapped, middle, music, physical, science, secondary, social studies, special. **Health:** Recreational therapy. **History:** General. **Liberal arts:** Arts/sciences. **Math:** General, applied. **Parks/recreation:** Facilities management. **Physical sciences:** Chemistry, physics. **Protective services:** Criminal justice, police science. **Psychology:** General. **Public administration:** Social work. **Social sciences:** Economics, political science, sociology. **Visual/performing arts:** Ceramics, commercial/advertising art, drawing, fiber arts, painting, photography, printmaking, sculpture, studio arts.

**Most popular majors.** Business/marketing 17%, communications/journalism 13%, education 15%, liberal arts 21%, security/protective services 8%.

**Computing on campus.** 200 workstations in dormitories, library, computer center, student center. Dormitories linked to campus network. Commuter students can connect to campus network. Helpline available.

**Student life. Freshman orientation:** Mandatory. Preregistration for classes offered. **Housing:** Guaranteed on-campus for freshmen. Single-sex dorms, apartments available. **Activities:** Bands, choral groups, drama, film society, literary magazine, music ensembles, radio station, student government, student newspaper, TV station, DNA science club, pre-alumni club, College Students for Christ, NAACP, access awareness council, Fellowship for Christian Athletes, poetry workshop.

**Athletics.** NCAA. **Intercollegiate:** Baseball M, basketball, football (tackle) M, golf, softball W, tennis, track and field, volleyball W. **Intramural:** Basketball, bowling, football (tackle) M, softball, swimming, tennis, volleyball. **Team name:** Yellow Jackets.

**Student services.** Career counseling, student employment services, health services, on-campus daycare, personal counseling, placement for graduates, veterans' counselor. **Physically disabled:** Services for visually, speech, hearing impaired.

**Contact.** E-mail: admission@wvstateu.edu
Phone: (304) 766-3221 Toll-free number: (800) 987-2112
Fax: (304) 766-4104
Trina Sweeney, Director, West Virginia State University, Campus Box 197, Institute, WV 25112-1000

---

## West Virginia University
**Morgantown, West Virginia**

**CB member**
**CB code: 5904**

www.wvu.edu

▶ Public 4-year university
▶ Residential campus in small city
▶ 21,720 degree-seeking undergraduates: 7% part-time, 45% women
▶ 7,178 degree-seeking graduate students
▶ 88% of applicants admitted
▶ SAT or ACT with writing required
▶ 56% graduate within 6 years

**General.** Founded in 1867. Regionally accredited. Regional centers at Charleston, Clarksburg, Parkersburg, Potomac State College in Keyser, Shepherdstown, WVU Institute of Technology, and West Liberty. Health Sciences Center operates division in Charleston. **Degrees:** 3,892 bachelor's awarded; master's, doctoral, professional offered. **ROTC:** Army, Air Force. **Location:** 70 miles from Pittsburgh, 200 miles from Baltimore. **Calendar:** Semester, extensive summer session. **Full-time faculty:** 935 total; 80% have terminal degrees, 13% minority, 39% women. **Part-time faculty:** 300 total; 32% have terminal degrees, 4% minority, 55% women. **Class size:** 33% < 20, 38% 20-39, 10% 40-49, 11% 50-99, 8% >100. **Special facilities:** Personal rapid transit system, arboretum, planetarium, herbarium, pharmacy museum, 2 art galleries, 7 experimental farms, 3 forests, software development center, mineral and energy resources museum, black culture and research center.

**Freshman class profile.** 14,229 applied, 12,496 admitted, 4,589 enrolled.

| Mid 50% test scores | | | | |
|---|---|---|---|---|
| SAT critical reading: | 460-560 | Rank in top quarter: | 45% |
| SAT math: | 480-580 | Rank in top tenth: | 19% |
| ACT composite: | 21-26 | Return as sophomores: | 80% |
| GPA 3.75 or higher: | 26% | Out-of-state: | 51% |
| GPA 3.50-3.74: | 15% | Live on campus: | 84% |
| GPA 3.0-3.49: | 32% | Fraternities: | 7% |
| GPA 2.0-2.99: | 27% | Sororities: | 7% |

**Basis for selection.** GPA and SAT/ACT scores most important. 2.0 GPA and 910 SAT (exclusive of Writing) or 19 ACT required of state residents. 2.5 GPA and 990 SAT or 21 ACT required of nonresidents. Applicants with high GPA, high test scores, or special talents (athletics or the arts) who do not meet all admissions criteria may be considered on individual basis. Up to 5% of each incoming class may be admitted under this special policy. Interview required for dental hygiene; audition required for drama, music; portfolio required for art. Essay required for some programs. **Home-schooled:** Typed manuscript of completed courses required, including content of courses, measurement of student assessment, grades, and number of credits earned for each course. Description should be separated by year of study and be signed by the person who administrated the curriculum.

**High school preparation.** 17 units required. Required units include English 4, mathematics 4, social studies 3, science 3 (laboratory 3), foreign language 2 and visual/performing arts 1.

**2009-2010 Annual costs.** Tuition/fees: $5,304; $16,402 out-of-state. Room/board: $7,770. Books/supplies: $1,160. Personal expenses: $970.

**2009-2010 Financial aid.** **Need-based:** 3,765 full-time freshmen applied for aid; 2,937 were judged to have need; 2,052 of these received aid.

Average need met was 72%. Average scholarship/grant was $5,384; average loan $3,804. 49% of total undergraduate aid awarded as scholarships/grants, 51% as loans/jobs. **Non-need-based:** Awarded to 10,808 full-time undergraduates, including 2,905 freshmen. Scholarships awarded for academics, alumni affiliation, art, athletics, job skills, leadership, minority status, music/drama, state residency. **Additional information:** February 1 closing date for freshman scholarships.

**Application procedures.** **Admission:** Priority date 3/1; deadline 8/1. $25 fee ($40 out-of-state), may be waived for applicants with need. Admission notification on a rolling basis beginning on or about 9/15. **Financial aid:** Closing date 3/1. FAFSA required. Applicants notified on a rolling basis starting 3/15; must reply within 4 week(s) of notification.

**Academics.** **Special study options:** Accelerated study, combined bachelor's/graduate degree, cooperative education, distance learning, double major, ESL, exchange student, external degree, honors, independent study, internships, semester at sea, student-designed major, study abroad, teacher certification program, Washington semester. **Credit/placement by examination:** AP, CLEP, IB, SAT, ACT, institutional tests. 38 credit hours maximum toward bachelor's degree. **Support services:** Learning center, pre-admission summer program, reduced course load, remedial instruction, study skills assistance, tutoring, writing center.

**Majors.** **Agriculture:** Agronomy, animal sciences, business, economics, horticultural science, plant sciences, soil science. **Architecture:** Landscape. **Biology:** General, biochemistry, exercise physiology. **Business:** Accounting, business admin, finance, management information systems, managerial economics, marketing. **Communications:** General, advertising, broadcast journalism, journalism, media studies, public relations. **Computer sciences:** Computer science. **Conservation:** Forest management, wildlife, wood science. **Education:** Agricultural, physical. **Engineering:** Aerospace, chemical, civil, computer, electrical, industrial, mechanical, mining, petroleum. **Family/consumer sciences:** General, child development, clothing/textiles, family/community services, food/nutrition. **Foreign languages:** General. **Health:** Athletic training, audiology/speech pathology, clinical lab science, dental hygiene, nursing (RN), prenursing, prepharmacy. **History:** General. **Liberal arts:** Arts/sciences. **Math:** General. **Parks/recreation:** Exercise sciences, facilities management, health/fitness, sports admin. **Philosophy/religion:** Philosophy. **Physical sciences:** Chemistry, geology, physics. **Protective services:** Criminalistics, forensics. **Psychology:** General. **Public administration:** Social work. **Social sciences:** Economics, geography, political science, sociology. **Visual/performing arts:** General, art, art history/conservation, design, dramatic, theater history. **Other:** Biometric systems, Multidisciplinary.

**Most popular majors.** Biology 6%, business/marketing 13%, communications/journalism 10%, engineering/engineering technologies 9%, health sciences 9%, interdisciplinary studies 8%, liberal arts 6%, social sciences 8%.

**Computing on campus.** 2,500 workstations in dormitories, library, computer center, student center. Dormitories wired for high-speed internet access and linked to campus network. Commuter students can connect to campus network. Online course registration, online library, helpline, repair service, student web hosting, wireless network available.

**Student life.** **Freshman orientation:** Available, $45 fee. Preregistration for classes offered. Held during summer; several options ranging in length and fees. **Policies:** Anti-hazing, affirmative action and nondiscrimination policies. Mandatory freshmen housing program places faculty residence hall leaders adjacent to residence halls. **Housing:** Guaranteed on-campus for freshmen. Coed dorms, single-sex dorms, special housing for disabled, apartments, fraternity/sorority housing, wellness housing available. $200 partly refundable deposit, deadline 5/1. Special interest floors available. **Activities:** Bands, campus ministries, choral groups, dance, drama, international student organizations, literary magazine, music ensembles, musical theater, radio station, student government, student newspaper, symphony orchestra, TV station, Sierra student coalition, Hillel House, Zeta Delat Phi, Circle K, Campus Crusade for Christ, College Republicans, Muslim student association.

**Athletics.** NCAA. **Intercollegiate:** Baseball M, basketball, cross-country W, diving, football (tackle) M, gymnastics W, rifle, rowing (crew) W, soccer, swimming, tennis W, track and field W, volleyball W, wrestling M. **Intramural:** Badminton, basketball, bowling, football (non-tackle), racquetball, soccer, tennis W, volleyball. **Team name:** Mountaineers.

**Student services.** Adult student services, alcohol/substance abuse counseling, chaplain/spiritual director, career counseling, services for economically disadvantaged, student employment services, financial aid counseling, health services, legal services, minority student services, on-campus daycare, personal counseling, placement for graduates, veterans' counselor, women's services. **Physically disabled:** Services for visually, speech, hearing impaired.

**Contact.** E-mail: go2wvu@mail.wvu.edu
Phone: (304) 293-2121 Toll-free number: (800) 344-9881
Fax: (304) 293-3080
Marlynn Potts, Director of Admissions and Records, West Virginia University, Admissions and Records Office, Morgantown, WV 26506-6009

## West Virginia University at Parkersburg
**Parkersburg, West Virginia**                   **CB member**
**www.wvup.edu**                               **CB code: 5932**

▶ Public 4-year community college
▶ Commuter campus in large town
▶ 3,649 degree-seeking undergraduates

**General.** Founded in 1971. Regionally accredited. **Degrees:** 188 bachelor's, 367 associate awarded. **Location:** 80 miles from Charleston; 110 miles from Columbus, Ohio. **Calendar:** Semester, limited summer session. **Full-time faculty:** 88 total; 16% have terminal degrees, 3% minority, 52% women. **Part-time faculty:** 163 total; 4% have terminal degrees, 1% minority, 45% women. **Class size:** 56% < 20, 40% 20-39, 2% 40-49, 1% 50-99.

**Freshman class profile.**

| Mid 50% test scores | | GPA 3.0-3.49: | 30% |
|---|---|---|---|
| ACT composite: | 16-21 | GPA 2.0-2.99: | 46% |
| GPA 3.75 or higher: | 8% | Out-of-state: | 1% |
| GPA 3.50-3.74: | 9% | | |

**Basis for selection.** Open admission, but selective for some programs. Special requirements for nursing, surgical technology, paramedic science and bachelor's degree programs. SAT or ACT (ACT preferred) required but not used in admission decisions. Interview required for nursing program.

**High school preparation.** 16 units recommended. Recommended units include English 4, mathematics 3, social studies 4, science 3 (laboratory 2). Social studies recommendations may be fulfilled with history units.

**2009-2010 Annual costs.** Tuition/fees: $2,076; $7,347 out-of-state. Books/supplies: $1,000. Personal expenses: $1,400.

**2009-2010 Financial aid. Non-need-based:** Scholarships awarded for academics, leadership, state residency.

**Application procedures. Admission:** No deadline. No application fee. Admission notification on a rolling basis. **Financial aid:** Priority date 3/1; no closing date. FAFSA required. Applicants notified on a rolling basis; must reply within 2 week(s) of notification.

**Academics. Special study options:** Combined bachelor's/graduate degree, cooperative education, cross-registration, distance learning, dual enrollment of high school students, ESL, external degree, honors, independent study, internships, teacher certification program, weekend college. **Credit/placement by examination:** AP, CLEP, IB, institutional tests. **Support services:** Learning center, reduced course load, remedial instruction, study skills assistance, tutoring.

**Majors. Business:** Business admin. **Education:** Elementary. **Engineering technology:** Industrial management. **Protective services:** Criminal justice.

**Most popular majors.** Business/marketing 19%, education 20%, liberal arts 56%.

**Computing on campus.** 435 workstations in library, computer center. Online course registration, online library, helpline, wireless network available.

**Student life. Freshman orientation:** Mandatory. Preregistration for classes offered. **Activities:** Choral groups, drama, literary magazine, music ensembles, musical theater, student government, student newspaper, reading association, environmental action group, multicultural awareness coalition, psychology club, Campus Christian Fellowship, criminal justice organization, Spark (community volunteers), student nursing association, American Welding Society.

**Athletics. Intramural:** Basketball, bowling, golf, softball, table tennis, volleyball. **Team name:** Riverhawks.

**Student services.** Adult student services, career counseling, services for economically disadvantaged, student employment services, financial aid counseling, on-campus daycare, personal counseling, placement for graduates, veterans' counselor. **Physically disabled:** Services for visually, speech, hearing impaired.

---

**Contact.** E-mail: info@mail.wvup.edu
Phone: (304) 424-8220 Fax: (304) 424-8332
Christine Post, Assistant Dean for Enrollment Management, West Virginia University at Parkersburg, 300 Campus Drive, Parkersburg, WV 26104-8647

## West Virginia University Institute of Technology
**Montgomery, West Virginia**
**www.wvutech.edu**                            **CB code: 5902**

▶ Public 4-year engineering college
▶ Commuter campus in small town
▶ 1,244 degree-seeking undergraduates
▶ 63% of applicants admitted
▶ SAT or ACT with writing required

**General.** Founded in 1895. Regionally accredited. **Degrees:** 193 bachelor's awarded; master's offered. **ROTC:** Army. **Location:** 30 miles from Charleston. **Calendar:** Semester, limited summer session. **Full-time faculty:** 84 total. **Part-time faculty:** 33 total. **Class size:** 64% < 20, 31% 20-39, 3% 40-49, 2% 50-99, less than 1% >100. **Special facilities:** Hiking trail.

**Freshman class profile.** 1,115 applied, 697 admitted, 291 enrolled.

| Mid 50% test scores | | SAT writing: | 340-530 |
|---|---|---|---|
| SAT critical reading: | 300-530 | ACT composite: | 14-23 |
| SAT math: | 470-510 | Live on campus: | 23% |

**Basis for selection.** 20 GPA and 18 ACT or 870 SAT (exclusive of Writing) required. Engineering applicants must have 19 ACT math. For associate degree programs, SAT/ACT required for placement but not admission. Residual ACT tests given on-site as needed for placement. Interview recommended for engineering. **Homeschooled:** Students may be required to take GED exam.

**High school preparation.** 17 units required. Required and recommended units include English 4, mathematics 2, social studies 3, history 3, science 2 (laboratory 2). 2 algebra, 1 plane geometry, 1 advanced math required of engineering majors. 1 algebra, 1 chemistry, 1 biology required of dental hygiene majors. 2 laboratory sciences, including chemistry, 2 higher mathematics required for nursing program.

**2009-2010 Annual costs.** Tuition/fees: $5,164; $13,264 out-of-state. Room/board: $7,607. Books/supplies: $800. Personal expenses: $1,600.

**Financial aid. Additional information:** Room and board may be deferred for up to 60 days. First 50% due in 30 days.

**Application procedures. Admission:** No deadline. No application fee. Admission notification on a rolling basis. Must reply by May 1 or within 2 week(s) if notified thereafter. **Financial aid:** Closing date 3/1. FAFSA required. Applicants notified on a rolling basis; must reply within 3 week(s) of notification.

**Academics. Special study options:** Combined bachelor's/graduate degree, cooperative education, distance learning, double major, dual enrollment of high school students, external degree, internships, liberal arts/career combination, student-designed major. Cooperative programs in engineering and business. **Credit/placement by examination:** CLEP, institutional tests. 90 credit hours maximum toward bachelor's degree. **Support services:** Learning center, pre-admission summer program, reduced course load, remedial instruction, tutoring.

**Majors. Biology:** General. **Business:** General, business admin. **Computer sciences:** General, computer science, programming. **Education:** Physical. **Engineering:** Chemical, civil, electrical, mechanical. **History:** General. **Math:** General. **Physical sciences:** Chemistry.

**Computing on campus.** 400 workstations in dormitories, library, computer center, student center. Dormitories wired for high-speed internet access and linked to campus network. Online library, helpline, wireless network available.

**Student life. Freshman orientation:** Available. Preregistration for classes offered. **Housing:** Guaranteed on-campus for all undergraduates. Coed dorms, single-sex dorms, fraternity/sorority housing available. $100 deposit. **Activities:** Marching band, campus ministries, drama, music ensembles, student government, student newspaper, Christian student union, Alpha Phi Omega service fraternity.

**Athletics. NCAA. Intercollegiate:** Baseball M, basketball, football (tackle) M, golf M, soccer, softball W, volleyball W, wrestling M. **Intramural:** Basketball, cross-country, softball, volleyball. **Team name:** Golden Bears.

**Student services.** Adult student services, career counseling, student employment services, financial aid counseling, health services, personal counseling, placement for graduates, veterans' counselor. **Physically disabled:** Services for speech impaired.

**Contact.** E-mail: admissions@wvutech.edu
Phone: (304) 442-3167 Toll-free number: (888) 554-8324
Fax: (304) 442-3097
Carl Gerbasi, Director of Admissions, West Virginia University Institute of Technology, 405 Fayette Pike, Montgomery, WV 25136-2436

## West Virginia Wesleyan College
**Buckhannon, West Virginia**
www.wvwc.edu                                        CB code: 5905

- Private 4-year liberal arts college affiliated with United Methodist Church
- Residential campus in small town
- 1,341 degree-seeking undergraduates: 2% part-time, 54% women, 8% African American, 1% Asian American, 3% Hispanic American, 1% Native American, 4% international
- 53 degree-seeking graduate students
- 81% of applicants admitted
- SAT or ACT (ACT writing optional) required
- 53% graduate within 6 years; 26% enter graduate study

**General.** Founded in 1890. Regionally accredited. **Degrees:** 229 bachelor's awarded; master's offered. **Location:** 115 miles from Charleston, 135 miles from Pittsburgh. **Calendar:** Semester, limited summer session. **Full-time faculty:** 75 total; 76% have terminal degrees, 1% minority, 44% women. **Part-time faculty:** 81 total; 26% have terminal degrees, 2% minority, 57% women. **Class size:** 52% < 20, 44% 20-39, 3% 40-49, less than 1% 50-99. **Special facilities:** Planetarium, botany museum, herbarium, greenhouse, performing arts center, research center.

**Freshman class profile.** 1,353 applied, 1,096 admitted, 399 enrolled.

| Mid 50% test scores | | | |
|---|---|---|---|
| SAT critical reading: | 420-540 | GPA 2.0-2.99: | 28% |
| SAT math: | 440-570 | Rank in top quarter: | 59% |
| SAT writing: | 420-540 | Rank in top tenth: | 28% |
| ACT composite: | 19-25 | End year in good standing: | 74% |
| GPA 3.75 or higher: | 29% | Return as sophomores: | 75% |
| GPA 3.50-3.74: | 18% | Out-of-state: | 44% |
| GPA 3.0-3.49: | 24% | Live on campus: | 91% |
| | | International: | 3% |

**Basis for selection.** School achievement record and test scores required. Essay, interview recommended for all; audition recommended for drama, music; portfolio recommended for art. **Homeschooled:** Transcript of courses and grades, state high school equivalency certificate required.

**High school preparation.** College-preparatory program recommended. 15 units recommended. Recommended units include English 4, mathematics 2, social studies 2, history 2, science 2 (laboratory 2), foreign language 1, computer science 1 and visual/performing arts 1.

**2009-2010 Annual costs.** Tuition/fees: $22,880. Room/board: $6,800. Books/supplies: $2,500. Personal expenses: $2,500.

**2009-2010 Financial aid. Non-need-based:** Scholarships awarded for academics, alumni affiliation, art, athletics, leadership, music/drama, religious affiliation, state residency.

**Application procedures. Admission:** Priority date 3/1; no deadline. $35 fee, may be waived for applicants with need, free for online applicants. Admission notification on a rolling basis beginning on or about 9/15. Must reply by May 1 or within 4 week(s) if notified thereafter. **Financial aid:** Priority date 3/1; no closing date. FAFSA required. Applicants notified on a rolling basis starting 3/15; must reply within 4 week(s) of notification.

**Academics. Special study options:** Combined bachelor's/graduate degree, double major, ESL, exchange student, honors, independent study, internships, liberal arts/career combination, New York semester, student-designed major, study abroad, teacher certification program, Washington semester. **Credit/placement by examination:** AP, CLEP, IB, SAT, ACT, institutional tests. **Support services:** Learning center, reduced course load, remedial instruction, study skills assistance, tutoring, writing center.

**Majors. Biology:** General. **Business:** Accounting, business admin, finance, international, managerial economics, marketing. **Communications:** General, public relations. **Computer sciences:** General, computer science, information systems. **Conservation:** Environmental science. **Education:** General, art, biology, chemistry, elementary, English, health, history, kindergarten/preschool, learning disabled, mathematics, music, physical, science, secondary,

social studies, special. **Engineering:** General. **Health:** Athletic training, nursing (RN), predental, premedicine, prepharmacy, preveterinary. **History:** General. **Legal studies:** Prelaw. **Math:** General. **Parks/recreation:** Exercise sciences, health/fitness. **Philosophy/religion:** Philosophy, religion. **Physical sciences:** Chemistry, physics. **Protective services:** Law enforcement admin. **Psychology:** General. **Social sciences:** Economics, international relations, political science, sociology. **Theology:** Religious ed. **Visual/performing arts:** Art, arts management, ceramics, dramatic, drawing, graphic design, painting, studio arts, theater arts management.

**Most popular majors.** Biology 7%, business/marketing 20%, education 13%, English 6%, parks/recreation 10%, physical sciences 6%, psychology 10%.

**Computing on campus.** PC or laptop required. Dormitories wired for high-speed internet access and linked to campus network. Commuter students can connect to campus network. Online library, helpline, repair service, wireless network available.

**Student life. Freshman orientation:** Mandatory, $200 fee. Preregistration for classes offered. Held weekend before fall class registration; provides programs for new students and parents. **Policies:** Full-time students required to live on campus unless married, living with parents, or have received written permission from the Housing Committee to live off campus. **Housing:** Guaranteed on-campus for all undergraduates. Coed dorms, single-sex dorms, special housing for disabled, apartments, fraternity/sorority housing, wellness housing available. $200 deposit. **Activities:** Bands, campus ministries, choral groups, dance, drama, international student organizations, literary magazine, music ensembles, musical theater, radio station, student government, student newspaper, TV station, Christian life council, Fellowship of Christian Athletes, Alpha Phi Omega service fraternity, black student union, College Republicans, Young Democrats, green club, Wesleyan service corps.

**Athletics.** NCAA. **Intercollegiate:** Baseball M, basketball, cross-country, football (tackle) M, golf, soccer, softball W, swimming, tennis, track and field, volleyball W. **Intramural:** Basketball, football (non-tackle), racquetball, softball, table tennis, volleyball, water polo M. **Team name:** Bobcats.

**Student services.** Alcohol/substance abuse counseling, chaplain/spiritual director, career counseling, financial aid counseling, health services, minority student services, personal counseling, placement for graduates. **Physically disabled:** Services for visually, speech, hearing impaired.

**Contact.** E-mail: admission@wvwc.edu
Phone: (304) 473-8510 Toll-free number: (800) 722-9933
Fax: (304) 473-8108
John Waltz, Director of Admission, West Virginia Wesleyan College, 59 College Avenue, Buckhannon, WV 26201-2998

## Wheeling Jesuit University
**Wheeling, West Virginia**                          CB member
www.wju.edu                                         CB code: 5906

- Private 4-year university and liberal arts college affiliated with Roman Catholic Church
- Residential campus in small city
- 1,001 degree-seeking undergraduates: 10% part-time, 59% women, 2% African American, 1% Asian American, 2% Hispanic American, 3% international
- 275 degree-seeking graduate students
- 74% of applicants admitted
- SAT or ACT (ACT writing optional) required
- 55% graduate within 6 years

**General.** Founded in 1954. Regionally accredited. **Degrees:** 143 bachelor's awarded; master's, professional offered. **Location:** 55 miles from Pittsburgh; 125 miles from Columbus, Ohio. **Calendar:** Semester, limited summer session. **Full-time faculty:** 72 total; 65% have terminal degrees, 10% minority, 43% women. **Part-time faculty:** 73 total; 30% have terminal degrees, 47% women. **Class size:** 66% < 20, 33% 20-39, less than 1% 40-49. **Special facilities:** NASA Classroom of the Future.

**Freshman class profile.** 1,299 applied, 966 admitted, 264 enrolled.

| Mid 50% test scores | | | |
|---|---|---|---|
| SAT critical reading: | 470-560 | GPA 2.0-2.99: | 21% |
| SAT math: | 460-560 | Rank in top quarter: | 50% |
| ACT composite: | 20-25 | Rank in top tenth: | 22% |
| GPA 3.75 or higher: | 33% | End year in good standing: | 85% |
| GPA 3.50-3.74: | 19% | Return as sophomores: | 77% |
| GPA 3.0-3.49: | 27% | Out-of-state: | 60% |
| | | Live on campus: | 92% |

**Basis for selection.** High school GPA, quality of courses taken, and test scores most important. Some exception made to minimum when warranted by high school record. Personal recommendations and extracurricular activities important. In-state and out-of-state applicants treated equally. Interview, essay recommended. **Learning Disabled:** Students need to submit written documentation of disability.

**High school preparation.** 15 units required. Required and recommended units include English 4, mathematics 2, social studies 2, history 2, science 1 (laboratory 1), foreign language 2 and academic electives 6. Applicants for programs in natural sciences should have 1 biology and 1 chemistry. Applicants preparing for future study in physical therapy doctorate program should have 3 years of college preparatory math and 3 years of lab science, including physics.

**2009-2010 Annual costs.** Tuition/fees: $24,630. Required fees include $200 "new student fee" charged only to freshmen. Room/board: $8,524. Books/supplies: $1,000. Personal expenses: $600.

**2009-2010 Financial aid. Need-based:** 256 full-time freshmen applied for aid; 221 were judged to have need; 221 of these received aid. Average need met was 89%. Average scholarship/grant was $7,436; average loan $4,401. 45% of total undergraduate aid awarded as scholarships/grants, 55% as loans/jobs. **Non-need-based:** Awarded to 891 full-time undergraduates, including 280 freshmen. Scholarships awarded for academics, alumni affiliation, athletics, leadership, music/drama.

**Application procedures. Admission:** No deadline. $25 fee, may be waived for applicants with need, free for online applicants. Admission notification on a rolling basis beginning on or about 9/1. Must reply by May 1 or within 2 week(s) if notified thereafter. **Financial aid:** Priority date 2/15; no closing date. FAFSA required. Applicants notified on a rolling basis starting 3/15; must reply within 2 week(s) of notification.

**Academics. Special study options:** Combined bachelor's/graduate degree, distance learning, double major, ESL, honors, independent study, internships, liberal arts/career combination, semester at sea, student-designed major, study abroad, teacher certification program, United Nations semester, Washington semester. **Credit/placement by examination:** AP, CLEP, SAT, ACT. 30 credit hours maximum toward bachelor's degree. **Support services:** Learning center, remedial instruction, study skills assistance, tutoring, writing center.

**Majors. Biology:** General. **Business:** Accounting, business admin, international. **Computer sciences:** Computer science. **Education:** Science. **Foreign languages:** French, Spanish. **Health:** Health care admin, nuclear medical technology, nursing (RN), respiratory therapy technology. **History:** General. **Liberal arts:** Arts/sciences. **Math:** General. **Philosophy/religion:** Philosophy. **Physical sciences:** Chemistry, physics. **Protective services:** Criminal justice. **Psychology:** General. **Social sciences:** International relations, political science. **Theology:** Theology. **Other:** Political and economic philosophy.

**Most popular majors.** Business/marketing 15%, health sciences 24%, physical sciences 10%, psychology 14%, social sciences 13%.

**Computing on campus.** 243 workstations in dormitories, library, computer center, student center. Dormitories wired for high-speed internet access and linked to campus network. Commuter students can connect to campus network. Online library, helpline, wireless network available.

**Student life. Freshman orientation:** Mandatory. Preregistration for classes offered. 3-day orientation held prior to beginning of fall semester. **Housing:** Guaranteed on-campus for all undergraduates. Coed dorms, single-sex dorms, special housing for disabled, apartments, cooperative housing, wellness housing available. $100 fully refundable deposit. **Activities:** Pep band, campus ministries, choral groups, dance, drama, international student organizations, literary magazine, musical theater, radio station, student government, student newspaper, TV station, social service outreach organization, academic clubs, leadership development group.

**Athletics.** NCAA. **Intercollegiate:** Baseball M, basketball, cheerleading, cross-country, golf, lacrosse M, soccer, softball W, swimming, track and field, volleyball W. **Intramural:** Basketball, soccer, softball, tennis, volleyball. **Team name:** Cardinals.

**Student services.** Adult student services, alcohol/substance abuse counseling, chaplain/spiritual director, career counseling, student employment services, financial aid counseling, health services, minority student services, personal counseling, placement for graduates, veterans' counselor. **Physically disabled:** Services for visually, hearing impaired.

**Contact.** E-mail: admiss@wju.edu
Phone: (304) 243-2359 Toll-free number: (800) 624-6992
Fax: (304) 243-2397
Becky Forney, Dean of Enrollment Management, Wheeling Jesuit University, 316 Washington Avenue, Wheeling, WV 26003-6295

# Wisconsin

## Alverno College
**Milwaukee, Wisconsin**
**www.alverno.edu**
**CB member**
**CB code: 1012**

- Private 4-year liberal arts college for women affiliated with Roman Catholic Church
- Commuter campus in very large city
- 2,307 degree-seeking undergraduates: 26% part-time, 100% women, 18% African American, 5% Asian American, 13% Hispanic American, 1% Native American, 1% international
- 291 degree-seeking graduate students
- 85% of applicants admitted
- SAT or ACT (ACT writing optional), application essay required
- 38% graduate within 6 years; 11% enter graduate study

**General.** Founded in 1887. Regionally accredited. **Degrees:** 321 bachelor's, 6 associate awarded; master's offered. **ROTC:** Army, Air Force. **Location:** 5 miles from downtown. **Calendar:** Semester, limited summer session. **Full-time faculty:** 118 total; 92% have terminal degrees, 9% minority, 75% women. **Part-time faculty:** 137 total; 61% have terminal degrees, 10% minority, 82% women. **Class size:** 46% < 20, 53% 20-39, less than 1% 40-49, less than 1% >100. **Special facilities:** Multimedia productions facility, independent science research areas, native prairie, clinical nursing resource center.

**Freshman class profile.** 525 applied, 446 admitted, 244 enrolled.

| Mid 50% test scores | | | |
|---|---|---|---|
| ACT composite: | 17-22 | Return as sophomores: | 73% |
| GPA 3.75 or higher: | 9% | Out-of-state: | 7% |
| GPA 3.50-3.74: | 12% | Live on campus: | 28% |
| GPA 3.0-3.49: | 27% | Sororities: | 2% |

| | |
|---|---|
| GPA 2.0-2.99: | 46% |

**Basis for selection.** Admissions based on review of transcripts, GPA, academic units, standardized tests, essay, and Communication Placement Assessment results. Audition required for music therapy; portfolio required for studio art. **Homeschooled:** Letter of recommendation (nonparent) required. Portfolio of work required.

**High school preparation.** College-preparatory program required. 17 units required. Required and recommended units include English 4, mathematics 3, social studies 3, science 3, foreign language 2 and academic electives 4.

**2009-2010 Annual costs.** Tuition/fees: $19,074. Tuition and fees may vary by program. Room/board: $6,504. Books/supplies: $1,050. Personal expenses: $1,760.

**2009-2010 Financial aid.** **Need-based:** 224 full-time freshmen applied for aid; 202 were judged to have need; 202 of these received aid. Average scholarship/grant was $13,044; average loan $2,903. 68% of total undergraduate aid awarded as scholarships/grants, 32% as loans/jobs. **Non-need-based:** Awarded to 1,331 full-time undergraduates, including 208 freshmen. Scholarships awarded for academics, alumni affiliation, leadership.

**Application procedures.** **Admission:** No deadline. $20 fee, may be waived for applicants with need, free for online applicants. Admission notification on a rolling basis beginning on or about 9/1. Must reply by May 1 or within 2 week(s) if notified thereafter. **Financial aid:** Priority date 3/15; no closing date. FAFSA, institutional form required. Applicants notified on a rolling basis starting 3/15; must reply within 2 week(s) of notification.

**Academics.** Required internships in all majors provide research opportunities through federal government, local organizations and businesses. Students in every major area spend from 8 to 12 hours per week for one semester in field internship. Students also have opportunities to do service learning through individual courses. Degrees with honor awarded based on outstanding achievement and application of learning in service to others. **Special study options:** Double major, independent study, internships, semester at sea, student-designed major, study abroad, teacher certification program, Washington semester, weekend college. **Credit/placement by examination:** AP, CLEP, IB, institutional tests. Each student's background and experience are looked at on an individual basis by the department faculty. **Support services:** Learning center, pre-admission summer program, reduced course load, remedial instruction, study skills assistance, tutoring, writing center.

**Majors. Biology:** General, molecular. **Business:** Business admin, international, operations. **Communications:** General. **Computer sciences:** General. **Conservation:** Environmental science. **Education:** General, art, elementary, English, middle, music, science, social studies. **Health:** Art therapy, music therapy, nursing (RN). **History:** General. **Liberal arts:** Arts/sciences, **Math:** General. **Philosophy/religion:** Philosophy, religion. **Physical sciences:** Chemistry. **Psychology:** General. **Public administration:** Community org/advocacy. **Social sciences:** General, international relations, political science, sociology. **Visual/performing arts:** Art. **Other:** Communication management and technology, Interactive media design, Multi/Interdisciplinary studies.

**Most popular majors.** Business/marketing 19%, communications/journalism 7%, education 9%, health sciences 37%, psychology 8%.

**Computing on campus.** 580 workstations in dormitories, library, computer center. Dormitories wired for high-speed internet access and linked to campus network. Commuter students can connect to campus network. Online library, student web hosting, wireless network available.

**Student life. Freshman orientation:** Mandatory. Preregistration for classes offered. Overnight program held during the summer. **Housing:** $100 nonrefundable deposit. Smoke-free, semi-apartment living within residence halls available to older students. **Activities:** Campus ministries, choral groups, dance, drama, international student organizations, literary magazine, music ensembles, student government, student newspaper, College Democrats, College Republicans, Student Education Organization, Association for Women in Communications, Circle K, Hispanic Women of Alverno, Pre-professional Women of Alverno, Student Nurses Association, Students in Free Enterprise, Women of Asian Ethnicity.

**Athletics.** NCAA. **Intercollegiate:** Basketball W, cross-country W, soccer W, softball W, tennis W, volleyball W. **Intramural:** Basketball W, volleyball W. **Team name:** Alverno Inferno.

**Student services.** Adult student services, chaplain/spiritual director, career counseling, financial aid counseling, health services, on-campus daycare, personal counseling. **Physically disabled:** Services for visually, speech, hearing impaired.

**Contact.** E-mail: admissions@alverno.edu
Phone: (414) 382-6101 Toll-free number: (800) 933-3401
Fax: (414) 382-6055
Dianna Gaebler, Executive Director of Admissions, Alverno College, 3400 South 43rd Street, Milwaukee, WI 53234-3922

## Bellin College
**Green Bay, Wisconsin**
**www.bellincollege.edu**
**CB code: 1046**

- Private 4-year nursing college
- Commuter campus in small city

**General.** Founded in 1909. Regionally accredited. **Location:** 120 miles from Milwaukee. **Calendar:** Semester.

**Annual costs/financial aid.** Tuition/fees (2009-2010): $18,278. Books/supplies: $875. Personal expenses: $665. Need-based financial aid available to full-time and part-time students.

**Contact.** Phone: (920) 433-6650
Director of Admissions, 3201 Eaton Road, Green Bay, WI 54322

## Beloit College
**Beloit, Wisconsin**
**www.beloit.edu**
**CB member**
**CB code: 1059**

- Private 4-year liberal arts college
- Residential campus in large town
- 1,323 degree-seeking undergraduates: 1% part-time, 57% women, 4% African American, 3% Asian American, 4% Hispanic American, 1% Native American, 6% international
- 73% of applicants admitted
- SAT or ACT (ACT writing optional), application essay required
- 84% graduate within 6 years

**General.** Founded in 1846. Regionally accredited. **Degrees:** 282 bachelor's awarded. **Location:** 60 miles from Madison, 90 miles from Chicago. **Calendar:** Semester, limited summer session. **Full-time faculty:** 94% have terminal degrees, 11% minority, 49% women. **Part-time faculty:** 111 total. **Class size:** 70% < 20, 29% 20-39, less than 1% 40-49, less than 1% 50-99. **Special facilities:** LEED-certified science center, anthropology museum, art museum, observatory, 2 nature preserves, social science research laboratory, immunology laboratory, 2 electron microscopes, superconducting NMR, ICAP spectrometer, marketing research center, center for entrepreneurial leadership.

**Freshman class profile.** 1,962 applied, 1,429 admitted, 332 enrolled.

| Mid 50% test scores | | GPA 2.0-2.99: | 19% |
|---|---|---|---|
| SAT critical reading: | 580-710 | Rank in top quarter: | 69% |
| SAT math: | 560-670 | Rank in top tenth: | 32% |
| ACT composite: | 24-32 | Return as sophomores: | 90% |
| GPA 3.75 or higher: | 22% | Out-of-state: | 79% |
| GPA 3.50-3.74: | 22% | Live on campus: | 100% |
| GPA 3.0-3.49: | 37% | International: | 9% |

**Basis for selection.** Rigor of high school curriculum and high school record most important. Test scores, recommendations, essays, interviews, and extracurricular activities also very important. Interview recommended. **Homeschooled:** Letter of recommendation (nonparent) required.

**High school preparation.** College-preparatory program required. Recommended units include English 4, mathematics 4, social studies 4, science 3 and foreign language 2.

**2009-2010 Annual costs.** Tuition/fees: $33,418. Room/board: $6,830. Books/supplies: $500. Personal expenses: $900.

**2009-2010 Financial aid.** **Need-based:** 258 full-time freshmen applied for aid; 215 were judged to have need; 215 of these received aid. Average need met was 95%. Average scholarship/grant was $23,727; average loan $2,833. 69% of total undergraduate aid awarded as scholarships/grants, 31% as loans/jobs. **Non-need-based:** Awarded to 350 full-time undergraduates, including 98 freshmen. Scholarships awarded for academics, leadership, minority status, music/drama.

**Application procedures.** **Admission:** Priority date 1/15; no deadline. $35 fee, may be waived for applicants with need. Admission notification on a rolling basis beginning on or about 2/15. Must reply by May 1 or within 2 week(s) if notified thereafter. **Financial aid:** Closing date 3/1. FAFSA, institutional form required. Applicants notified on a rolling basis starting 4/1; must reply by 5/1 or within 2 week(s) of notification.

**Academics.** Heavy emphasis placed on international education, interdisciplinary study, and experiential learning. **Special study options:** Combined bachelor's/graduate degree, double major, ESL, exchange student, independent study, internships, liberal arts/career combination, student-designed major, study abroad, teacher certification program, urban semester, Washington semester. Field schools in archeology and geology, Center for Language Studies, intensive summer foreign language program, reserved admission to Medical College of Wisconsin. 3-2 programs in engineering, nursing, and forestry. **Credit/placement by examination:** AP, CLEP, IB. 32 credit hours maximum toward bachelor's degree. **Support services:** Learning center, study skills assistance, tutoring, writing center.

**Majors.** **Area/ethnic studies:** Women's. **Biology:** General, biochemistry, cellular/molecular, environmental, molecular. **Business:** Business admin, managerial economics. **Computer sciences:** Computer science. **Conservation:** Environmental science, forestry. **Education:** General, art, science. **Engineering:** General. **Foreign languages:** General, classics, comparative lit, East Asian, French, German, Russian, Spanish. **Health:** Nursing (RN). **History:** General. **Interdisciplinary:** Science/society. **Liberal arts:** Arts/sciences. **Math:** General. **Philosophy/religion:** Philosophy, religion. **Physical sciences:** Chemistry, geology, physics. **Psychology:** General. **Social sciences:** Anthropology, economics, international relations, political science, sociology. **Visual/performing arts:** Art history/conservation, dance, dramatic. **Other:** Health and Society.

**Computing on campus.** 300 workstations in dormitories, library, computer center, student center. Dormitories wired for high-speed internet access and linked to campus network. Commuter students can connect to campus network. Helpline, student web hosting, wireless network available.

**Student life.** **Freshman orientation:** Mandatory. Preregistration for classes offered. Held 10 days prior to fall semester. **Housing:** Guaranteed on-campus for all undergraduates. Coed dorms, single-sex dorms, apartments, cooperative housing, fraternity/sorority housing, wellness housing available. Residence hall system is student managed. Special-interest housing available to students that have completed at least one semester. **Activities:** Jazz band, campus ministries, choral groups, dance, drama, film society, international student organizations, literary magazine, music ensembles, musical theater, radio station, student government, student newspaper, symphony orchestra, TV station, volunteer community tutoring service, women's center program, gay alliance, Young Republicans, Young Democrats, science fiction and fantasy association, Voces Latinas, black students united.

**Athletics.** NCAA. **Intercollegiate:** Baseball M, basketball, cross-country, diving, football (tackle) M, soccer, softball W, swimming, tennis, track and field, volleyball W. **Intramural:** Basketball, fencing, handball, ice hockey M, racquetball, rugby M, sailing, soccer, softball, swimming, tennis, volleyball, water polo. **Team name:** Bucs.

**Student services.** Chaplain/spiritual director, career counseling, services for economically disadvantaged, student employment services, financial aid counseling, health services, minority student services, on-campus daycare, personal counseling, placement for graduates, women's services. **Physically disabled:** Services for visually, hearing impaired.

**Contact.** E-mail: admiss@beloit.edu
Phone: (608) 363-2500 Toll-free number: (800) 923-5648
Fax: (608) 363-2075
Nancy Benedict, Vice President of Enrollment Services, Beloit College, 700 College Street, Beloit, WI 53511-5595

## Cardinal Stritch University
**Milwaukee, Wisconsin**
**www.stritch.edu**          CB code: 1100

▶ Private 4-year university affiliated with Roman Catholic Church
▶ Commuter campus in very large city
▶ 3,046 degree-seeking undergraduates
▶ 41% of applicants admitted
▶ SAT or ACT (ACT writing optional), application essay required

**General.** Founded in 1937. Regionally accredited. **Degrees:** 548 bachelor's, 190 associate awarded; master's, doctoral offered. **Location:** 7 miles from downtown, 85 miles from Chicago. **Calendar:** Semester, limited summer session. **Full-time faculty:** 103 total. **Part-time faculty:** 350 total. **Class size:** 97% < 20, 3% 20-39, less than 1% 40-49, less than 1% 50-99.

**Freshman class profile.** 1,033 applied, 421 admitted, 172 enrolled.

| Mid 50% test scores | | ACT composite: | 18-26 |
|---|---|---|---|
| SAT critical reading: | 450-530 | Out-of-state: | 20% |
| SAT math: | 460-520 | Live on campus: | 63% |

**Basis for selection.** Admissions based on 2.0 GPA, 20 ACT or 840 SAT (exclusive of Writing). Interview, activities, and recommendations considered. Conditional admission available to applicants not meeting all admissions criteria. Institutional tests used for admission of academically weak students. Interview recommended for all; portfolio recommended for art; audition recommended for music and theatre.

**High school preparation.** College-preparatory program recommended. 16 units required; 18 recommended. Required and recommended units include English 4, mathematics 2-3, social studies 1, history 1, science 2-3, foreign language 2 and academic electives 4.

**2009-2010 Annual costs.** Tuition/fees: $21,790. Room/board: $6,500. Books/supplies: $500. Personal expenses: $1,200.

**Financial aid. Non-need-based:** Scholarships awarded for academics, art, athletics, music/drama.

**Application procedures. Admission:** Priority date 4/1; no deadline. $25 fee, may be waived for applicants with need, free for online applicants. Admission notification on a rolling basis beginning on or about 9/1. **Financial aid:** Priority date 4/15; no closing date. FAFSA, institutional form required. Applicants notified on a rolling basis starting 3/1; must reply within 3 week(s) of notification.

**Academics. Special study options:** Accelerated study, distance learning, double major, exchange student, independent study, internships, student-designed major, study abroad, teacher certification program. **Credit/placement by examination:** AP, CLEP, IB, institutional tests. 30 credit hours maximum toward associate degree, 60 toward bachelor's. **Support services:** Learning center, reduced course load, remedial instruction, study skills assistance, tutoring, writing center.

**Majors. Biology:** General. **Business:** General, accounting, business admin, international, management information systems. **Communications:** General. **Computer sciences:** Computer science. **Education:** General, special. **Foreign languages:** Spanish. **Health:** Nursing (RN). **History:** General. **Interdisciplinary:** Math/computer science. **Legal studies:** Prelaw. **Math:** General. **Parks/recreation:** Sports admin. **Philosophy/religion:** Religion. **Physical sciences:** Chemistry. **Psychology:** General. **Social sciences:** General, political science, sociology. **Theology:** Pastoral counseling, youth ministry. **Visual/performing arts:** Art, commercial/advertising art, dramatic, music performance, photography, studio arts.

**Most popular majors.** Business/marketing 75%, education 6%.

**Computing on campus.** 236 workstations in dormitories, library, computer center, student center. Dormitories wired for high-speed internet access and linked to campus network. Commuter students can connect to campus network. Online library, helpline, wireless network available.

**Student life. Freshman orientation:** Mandatory. Preregistration for classes offered. Week-long program held prior to start of classes. **Housing:** Coed dorms available. $50 fully refundable deposit. **Activities:** Bands, campus ministries, choral groups, dance, drama, literary magazine, music ensembles, Model UN, musical theater, radio station, student government, student newspaper, students for political awareness, multicultural committee, Asian club, black student union, united Latino organization, Fellowship of Christian Students, service corps, peer helpers.

**Athletics.** NAIA. **Intercollegiate:** Baseball M, basketball, cross-country, soccer, softball W, volleyball. **Intramural:** Basketball, volleyball. **Team name:** Wolves.

**Student services.** Adult student services, alcohol/substance abuse counseling, chaplain/spiritual director, career counseling, student employment services, financial aid counseling, health services, personal counseling, placement for graduates, veterans' counselor. **Physically disabled:** Services for hearing impaired.

**Contact.** E-mail: admityou@stritch.edu
Phone: (414) 410-4040 Toll-free number: (800) 347-8822 ext. 4040
Fax: (414) 410-4058
Kirk Messer, Director of Admission, Cardinal Stritch University, 6801 North Yates Road, Box 516, Milwaukee, WI 53217-7516

## Carroll University
**Waukesha, Wisconsin**
**www.carrollu.edu**
**CB code: 1101**

- Private 4-year liberal arts college affiliated with Presbyterian Church (USA)
- Residential campus in small city
- 3,050 degree-seeking undergraduates: 15% part-time, 66% women, 2% African American, 1% Asian American, 4% Hispanic American, 2% international
- 219 degree-seeking graduate students
- 73% of applicants admitted
- SAT or ACT (ACT writing optional) required
- 67% graduate within 6 years

**General.** Founded in 1846. Regionally accredited. **Degrees:** 549 bachelor's awarded; master's, professional offered. **ROTC:** Army, Air Force. **Location:** 15 miles from Milwaukee. **Calendar:** Semester, extensive summer session. **Full-time faculty:** 118 total; 68% have terminal degrees, 4% minority, 52% women. **Part-time faculty:** 203 total; 14% have terminal degrees, 65% women. **Class size:** 60% < 20, 36% 20-39, 2% 40-49, 2% 50-99, less than 1% >100. **Special facilities:** Scientific study and conservancy, class 1 trout stream, wetland and upland habitats.

**Freshman class profile.** 2,906 applied, 2,113 admitted, 742 enrolled.

| Mid 50% test scores | | | |
|---|---|---|---|
| **ACT composite:** | 20-25 | **Rank in top tenth:** | 18% |
| **GPA 3.75 or higher:** | 22% | **End year in good standing:** | 71% |
| **GPA 3.50-3.74:** | 22% | **Return as sophomores:** | 77% |
| **GPA 3.0-3.49:** | 34% | **Out-of-state:** | 24% |
| **GPA 2.0-2.99:** | 22% | **Live on campus:** | 86% |
| **Rank in top quarter:** | 50% | **Fraternities:** | 4% |
| | | **Sororities:** | 9% |

**Basis for selection.** School achievement record most important, followed by test scores. Recommendations, essay, interview considered. Essay, interview recommended for all; audition recommended for music, theater; portfolio recommended for art. **Homeschooled:** Transcript of courses and grades required.

**High school preparation.** College-preparatory program recommended. 17 units recommended. Recommended units include English 4, mathematics 4, social studies 3, history 3, science 3 (laboratory 2).

**2009-2010 Annual costs.** Tuition/fees: $22,937. Room/board: $7,023. Books/supplies: $1,120. Personal expenses: $1,363.

**2009-2010 Financial aid. Need-based:** 650 full-time freshmen applied for aid; 517 were judged to have need; 517 of these received aid. Average need met was 100%. Average scholarship/grant was $14,644; average loan $2,122. 70% of total undergraduate aid awarded as scholarships/grants, 30% as loans/jobs. **Non-need-based:** Awarded to 2,239 full-time undergraduates, including 629 freshmen. Scholarships awarded for academics, alumni affiliation, art, leadership, music/drama, ROTC.

**Application procedures. Admission:** Priority date 3/15; no deadline. No application fee. Admission notification on a rolling basis beginning on or about 8/1. **Financial aid:** No deadline. FAFSA required. Applicants notified on a rolling basis starting 2/15; must reply by 5/1 or within 2 week(s) of notification.

**Academics.** Education majors must maintain 2.75 GPA in major and teaching minors. Nursing students must maintain 2.75 GPA. Six majors available for pre-physical therapy programs. **Special study options:** Combined bachelor's/graduate degree, distance learning, double major, exchange student, honors, independent study, internships, liberal arts/career combination, student-designed major, study abroad, teacher certification program, United Nations semester, Washington semester. **Credit/placement by examination:** AP, CLEP, IB, institutional tests. 24 credit hours maximum toward bachelor's degree. **Support services:** Learning center, pre-admission summer program, reduced course load, remedial instruction, study skills assistance, tutoring, writing center.

**Majors. Area/ethnic studies:** European. **Biology:** General, animal behavior, biochemistry. **Business:** Accounting, actuarial science, business admin, finance, human resources, management information systems, marketing, organizational behavior, small business admin. **Communications:** General, journalism, organizational, public relations. **Communications technology:** Graphics, printing management. **Computer sciences:** General, information systems. **Conservation:** General, environmental science. **Education:** General, art, biology, chemistry, early childhood, elementary, English, foreign languages, geography, health, history, mathematics, middle, music, physical, psychology, science, social science, social studies, Spanish. **Engineering:** Physics, software. **Foreign languages:** Spanish. **Health:** Athletic training, clinical lab science, nursing (RN), predental, premedicine, prepharmacy, preveterinary, public health ed, radiologic technology/medical imaging. **History:** General, European. **Interdisciplinary:** Global studies. **Math:** General, applied. **Parks/recreation:** Exercise sciences, facilities management, health/fitness. **Philosophy/religion:** Religion. **Physical sciences:** Applied physics, chemistry. **Protective services:** Criminal justice, forensics. **Psychology:** General. **Social sciences:** Political science, sociology. **Visual/performing arts:** Art, commercial/advertising art, dramatic, photography, studio arts. **Other:** Philosophy, politics, and economics.

**Most popular majors.** Biology 9%, business/marketing 14%, education 12%, health sciences 22%, psychology 11%.

**Computing on campus.** 250 workstations in dormitories, library, computer center, student center. Dormitories wired for high-speed internet access and linked to campus network. Commuter students can connect to campus network. Online library, helpline, student web hosting, wireless network available.

**Student life. Freshman orientation:** Mandatory, $140 fee. Preregistration for classes offered. **Housing:** Guaranteed on-campus for freshmen. Coed dorms, single-sex dorms, apartments available. $200 nonrefundable deposit. **Activities:** Bands, campus ministries, choral groups, dance, drama, international student organizations, literary magazine, music ensembles, radio station, student government, student newspaper, Bible study group, Intervarsity Christian Fellowship, Fellowship of Christian Athletes, black student union, Queers & Allies, Questions & Answers, international experience club, Latin American student organization, University Republicans, College Democrats.

**Athletics.** NCAA. **Intercollegiate:** Baseball M, basketball, cross-country, football (tackle) M, golf, soccer, swimming, tennis, track and field, volleyball W. **Intramural:** Basketball, bowling, cheerleading, football (non-tackle), soccer, tennis, volleyball. **Team name:** Pioneers.

**Student services.** Adult student services, chaplain/spiritual director, career counseling, student employment services, financial aid counseling, health services, minority student services, personal counseling, placement for graduates. **Physically disabled:** Services for visually, hearing impaired.

**Contact.** E-mail: info@carrollu.edu
Phone: (262) 524-7220 Toll-free number: (800) 227-7655
Fax: (262) 951-3037
Jim Wiseman, Vice President for Enrollment, Carroll University, 100 North East Avenue, Waukesha, WI 53186-9988

## Carthage College
**Kenosha, Wisconsin**
**www.carthage.edu**
**CB member**
**CB code: 1103**

- Private 4-year liberal arts college affiliated with Evangelical Lutheran Church in America
- Residential campus in small city
- 2,648 degree-seeking undergraduates
- 75% of applicants admitted
- SAT or ACT (ACT writing optional) required

**General.** Founded in 1847. Regionally accredited. **Degrees:** 512 bachelor's awarded; master's offered. **ROTC:** Army, Air Force. **Location:** 60 miles from Chicago, 30 miles from Milwaukee. **Calendar:** 4-1-4, limited summer session. **Full-time faculty:** 150 total. **Part-time faculty:** 95 total. **Class size:** 54% < 20, 45% 20-39, 1% 40-49. **Special facilities:** Planetarium, paleontology institute, center for children's literature, undergraduate science research laboratory, computer/mathematics research laboratory, greenhouse, arboretum, Audubon sanctuary, geographic information systems (GIS) lab, 24-hour cyber-cafe.

**Freshman class profile.** 6,338 applied, 4,757 admitted, 722 enrolled.

| Mid 50% test scores | | | |
|---|---|---|---|
| SAT critical reading: | 490-600 | GPA 3.50-3.74: | 18% |
| SAT math: | 500-600 | GPA 3.0-3.49: | 29% |
| ACT composite: | 21-26 | GPA 2.0-2.99: | 31% |
| GPA 3.75 or higher: | 22% | Out-of-state: | 72% |

**Basis for selection.** High school GPA (calculated based on academic courses) and test scores most important. Interview recommended; audition recommended for music and theater. **Homeschooled:** Transcript of courses and grades required.

**High school preparation.** 18 units recommended. Recommended units include English 4, mathematics 3, social studies 3, science 3 (laboratory 2), foreign language 2 and academic electives 3.

**2009-2010 Annual costs.** Tuition/fees: $28,250. Room/board: $7,750. Books/supplies: $1,200. Personal expenses: $1,500.

**2009-2010 Financial aid. Non-need-based:** Scholarships awarded for academics, alumni affiliation, art, leadership, minority status, music/drama, religious affiliation.

**Application procedures. Admission:** Priority date 12/11; no deadline. $35 fee, may be waived for applicants with need. Admission notification on a rolling basis. Must reply by May 1 or within 2 week(s) if notified thereafter. **Financial aid:** Priority date 2/15; no closing date. FAFSA required. Applicants notified on a rolling basis starting 3/1.

**Academics.** All students take 2-course combination of oral and written communication skills and cross-cultural studies. Students must also complete symposium and senior thesis. **Special study options:** Accelerated study, combined bachelor's/graduate degree, cross-registration, double major, dual enrollment of high school students, honors, independent study, internships, liberal arts/career combination, student-designed major, study abroad, teacher certification program, Washington semester. **Credit/placement by examination:** AP, CLEP, IB, institutional tests. 32 credit hours maximum toward bachelor's degree. **Support services:** Pre-admission summer program, reduced course load, study skills assistance, tutoring, writing center.

**Majors. Area/ethnic studies:** Asian. **Biology:** General. **Business:** Accounting, business admin, management information systems, marketing. **Communications:** Public relations. **Communications technology:** Graphics. **Computer sciences:** Computer science. **Conservation:** Environmental science. **Education:** Elementary, physical, special. **Foreign languages:** Classics, French, German, Spanish. **Health:** Athletic training. **History:** General. **Interdisciplinary:** Neuroscience. **Liberal arts:** Humanities. **Math:** General. **Parks/recreation:** Exercise sciences. **Philosophy/religion:** Philosophy, religion. **Physical sciences:** Chemistry, physics. **Protective services:** Correctional facilities, police science. **Psychology:** General. **Public administration:** Social work. **Social sciences:** General, economics, geography, international economics, political science, sociology. **Visual/performing arts:** Art history/conservation, dramatic, studio arts, theater design. **Other:** Communications and media studies.

**Most popular majors.** Business/marketing 23%, education 9%, social sciences 7%, visual/performing arts 7%.

**Computing on campus.** 275 workstations in dormitories, library, computer center, student center. Dormitories wired for high-speed internet access and linked to campus network. Commuter students can connect to campus network. Online library, helpline, repair service, student web hosting, wireless network available.

**Student life. Freshman orientation:** Mandatory. Preregistration for classes offered. Held a few days immediately prior to start of classes. **Housing:** Guaranteed on-campus for freshmen. Coed dorms, single-sex dorms, apartments, fraternity/sorority housing, wellness housing available. $300 deposit, deadline 5/1. **Activities:** Bands, campus ministries, choral groups, dance, drama, film society, international student organizations, literary magazine, music ensembles, Model UN, musical theater, opera, radio station, student government, student newspaper, symphony orchestra, black student union, international friendship society, United Women of Color, Christian Fellowship, Latinos Unidos, Circle K International, College Republicans, Young Democrats.

**Athletics.** NCAA. **Intercollegiate:** Baseball M, basketball, cross-country, football (tackle) M, golf, lacrosse, soccer, softball W, swimming, tennis, track and field, volleyball, water polo W. **Intramural:** Basketball, football (non-tackle), racquetball, soccer, softball, volleyball. **Team name:** Red Men, Lady Reds.

**Student services.** Adult student services, alcohol/substance abuse counseling, chaplain/spiritual director, career counseling, student employment services, financial aid counseling, health services, personal counseling, placement for graduates, veterans' counselor.

**Contact.** E-mail: admissions@carthage.edu
Phone: (262) 551-6000 Toll-free number: (800) 351-4058
Fax: (262) 551-5762
Bradley Andrews, Vice President for Enrollment and Student Life, Carthage College, 2001 Alford Park Drive, Kenosha, WI 53140-1994

---

## Columbia College of Nursing
### Milwaukee, Wisconsin
www.ccon.edu                                      CB code: 3409

- Private 4-year nursing college
- Commuter campus in very large city

**General.** Founded in 1901. Regionally accredited. **Location:** 90 miles from Chicago, 70 miles from Madison. **Calendar:** Semester.

**Annual costs/financial aid.** Tuition/fees (2009-2010): $21,050. Room/board: $5,600. Books/supplies: $734. Personal expenses: $1,234. Need-based financial aid available to full-time and part-time students.

**Contact.** Phone: (414) 256-1219
Dean of Enrollment, Mount Mary College, Mount Mary College Enrollment Office, Milwaukee, WI 53222-4597

---

## Concordia University Wisconsin
### Mequon, Wisconsin
www.cuw.edu                                      CB code: 1139

- Private 4-year university and liberal arts college affiliated with Lutheran Church - Missouri Synod
- Residential campus in large town
- 3,790 degree-seeking undergraduates: 39% part-time, 65% women, 14% African American, 1% Asian American, 2% Hispanic American, 1% Native American, 1% international
- 2,908 degree-seeking graduate students
- 64% of applicants admitted
- ACT (writing optional) required
- 58% graduate within 6 years

**General.** Founded in 1881. Regionally accredited. **Degrees:** 523 bachelor's, 22 associate awarded; master's, doctoral, professional offered. **Location:** 15 miles from Milwaukee. **Calendar:** 4-1-4, limited summer session. **Full-time faculty:** 109 total; 68% have terminal degrees, 4% minority, 45% women. **Part-time faculty:** 150 total; 15% have terminal degrees, 7% minority, 61% women. **Class size:** 51% < 20, 44% 20-39, 3% 40-49, 2% 50-99. **Special facilities:** Access to Lake Michigan.

**Freshman class profile.** 2,538 applied, 1,616 admitted, 471 enrolled.

| Mid 50% test scores | | | |
|---|---|---|---|
| ACT composite: | 19-25 | Rank in top quarter: | 23% |
| GPA 3.75 or higher: | 23% | Rank in top tenth: | 15% |
| GPA 3.50-3.74: | 17% | Return as sophomores: | 83% |
| GPA 3.0-3.49: | 32% | Out-of-state: | 29% |
| GPA 2.0-2.99: | 26% | Live on campus: | 88% |
| | | International: | 1% |

**Basis for selection.** School achievement record and test scores important. Essay, interview recommended; audition recommended for music.

**High school preparation.** College-preparatory program recommended. 16 units required. Required and recommended units include English 3-4, mathematics 2-3, social studies 2, science 2, foreign language 2 and academic electives 5. Two liberal arts required.

**2009-2010 Annual costs.** Tuition/fees: $20,990. Room/board: $7,990. Books/supplies: $1,100. Personal expenses: $1,950.

**2009-2010 Financial aid. Need-based:** 444 full-time freshmen applied for aid; 376 were judged to have need; 376 of these received aid. Average need met was 80%. Average scholarship/grant was $13,226; average loan $4,972. 59% of total undergraduate aid awarded as scholarships/grants, 41%

as loans/jobs. **Non-need-based:** Scholarships awarded for academics, minority status, music/drama, religious affiliation.

**Application procedures. Admission:** Priority date 5/1; deadline 8/15. $35 fee, may be waived for applicants with need, free for online applicants. Admission notification on a rolling basis beginning on or about 10/15. **Financial aid:** Priority date 4/1; no closing date. FAFSA required. Applicants notified on a rolling basis starting 2/15; must reply within 3 week(s) of notification.

**Academics. Special study options:** Accelerated study, combined bachelor's/ graduate degree, cross-registration, distance learning, double major, dual enrollment of high school students, ESL, exchange student, independent study, internships, liberal arts/career combination, student-designed major, study abroad, teacher certification program, weekend college. Cooperative programs with Cardinal Stritch University, Marquette University, and Milwaukee Institute of Art and Design. **Credit/placement by examination:** AP, CLEP, IB, ACT, institutional tests. 15 credit hours maximum toward associate degree, 30 toward bachelor's. **Support services:** Learning center, reduced course load, remedial instruction, tutoring, writing center.

**Majors. Biology:** General, exercise physiology. **Business:** General, accounting, actuarial science, business admin, finance, international finance, marketing. **Communications:** General, broadcast journalism, digital media, media studies. **Computer sciences:** General. **Conservation:** Environmental studies. **Education:** General, art, biology, business, early childhood, elementary, English, health, history, kindergarten/preschool, mathematics, middle, multi-level teacher, music, physical, science, secondary, social science, social studies, Spanish. **Foreign languages:** Biblical, German, Spanish. **Health:** Athletic training, clinical/medical social work, health services, medical radiologic technology/radiation therapy, nursing (RN). **History:** General. **Legal studies:** Prelaw. **Liberal arts:** Arts/sciences, humanities. **Math:** General. **Philosophy/religion:** Religion. **Protective services:** Criminal justice. **Psychology:** General. **Public administration:** Social work. **Social sciences:** Economics. **Theology:** Bible, missionary, pastoral counseling, preministerial, religious ed, sacred music, theology, youth ministry. **Visual/ performing arts:** Art, commercial/advertising art, graphic design, illustration, interior design, music performance, photography, piano/organ. **Other:** Business communication, Rehabilitative science.

**Most popular majors.** Biology 6%, business/marketing 37%, education 12%, health sciences 17%, security/protective services 7%.

**Computing on campus.** 200 workstations in dormitories, library, computer center, student center. Dormitories wired for high-speed internet access and linked to campus network. Commuter students can connect to campus network. Online library, helpline, repair service available.

**Student life. Freshman orientation:** Available. Preregistration for classes offered. Held before start of fall semester, includes sessions for parents. **Policies:** Lutheran church services available every Sunday. Chapel services held daily. **Housing:** Single-sex dorms, wellness housing available. $160 deposit, deadline 4/15. **Activities:** Bands, campus ministries, choral groups, dance, drama, international student organizations, music ensembles, musical theater, radio station, student government, student newspaper, Jeremiah Project, Servant Events.

**Athletics.** NCAA. **Intercollegiate:** Baseball M, basketball, cross-country, football (tackle) M, golf, soccer, softball W, tennis, track and field, volleyball, wrestling M. **Intramural:** Basketball, soccer, softball, table tennis, tennis, volleyball. **Team name:** Falcons.

**Student services.** Adult student services, alcohol/substance abuse counseling, chaplain/spiritual director, career counseling, student employment services, financial aid counseling, health services, minority student services, personal counseling, placement for graduates, veterans' counselor. **Physically disabled:** Services for hearing impaired.

**Contact.** E-mail: admission@cuw.edu
Phone: (262) 243-5700 Toll-free number: (888) 628-9472
Fax: (262) 243-4545
Kenneth Gaschk, Vice President of Enrollment Services, Concordia University Wisconsin, 12800 North Lake Shore Drive, Mequon, WI 53097

## DeVry University: Milwaukee
### Milwaukee, Wisconsin
www.devry.edu

- For-profit 4-year university
- Commuter campus in very large city
- 128 degree-seeking undergraduates: 73% part-time, 51% women, 48% African American, 6% Asian American, 8% Hispanic American, 1% Native American

- 85 degree-seeking graduate students
- Interview required

**General. Degrees:** 14 bachelor's awarded; master's offered. **Calendar:** Semester. **Full-time faculty:** 1 total; 100% women. **Part-time faculty:** 28 total; 36% minority, 46% women.

**Basis for selection.** Interview important.

**2009-2010 Annual costs.** Tuition/fees: $14,160. Books/supplies: $1,300. Personal expenses: $3,270.

**2008-2009 Financial aid. Non-need-based:** Scholarships awarded for academics.

**Application procedures. Admission:** No deadline. $50 fee. Admission notification on a rolling basis. **Financial aid:** No deadline. FAFSA required. Applicants notified on a rolling basis.

**Academics. Special study options:** Accelerated study, distance learning. **Credit/placement by examination:** CLEP.

**Majors. Business:** Business admin. **Computer sciences:** General, systems analysis. **Other:** Technical management.

**Most popular majors.** Business/marketing 86%, communication technologies 14%.

**Contact.** Phone: (414) 278-7677
DeVry University: Milwaukee, 100 East Wisconsin Avenue, Suite 2550, Milwaukee, WI 53202

## Edgewood College
### Madison, Wisconsin
www.edgewood.edu

CB member
CB code: 1202

- Private 4-year liberal arts college affiliated with Roman Catholic Church
- Commuter campus in small city
- 1,779 degree-seeking undergraduates: 16% part-time, 71% women, 4% African American, 2% Asian American, 4% Hispanic American, 1% Native American, 2% international
- 484 degree-seeking graduate students
- 72% of applicants admitted
- SAT or ACT (ACT writing optional), application essay required
- 52% graduate within 6 years

**General.** Founded in 1927. Regionally accredited. **Degrees:** 436 bachelor's awarded; master's, professional offered. **ROTC:** Army. **Location:** 82 miles from Milwaukee, 140 miles from Chicago. **Calendar:** Semester, limited summer session. **Full-time faculty:** 108 total; 89% have terminal degrees, 9% minority, 51% women. **Part-time faculty:** 197 total; 39% have terminal degrees, 10% minority, 51% women. **Class size:** 77% < 20, 21% 20-39, less than 1% 40-49, less than 1% 50-99. **Special facilities:** Science center, biological research station, nursery school.

**Freshman class profile.** 1,210 applied, 876 admitted, 287 enrolled.

| Mid 50% test scores | | | |
|---|---|---|---|
| SAT critical reading: | 440-570 | GPA 2.0-2.99: | 25% |
| SAT math: | 430-580 | Rank in top quarter: | 36% |
| ACT composite: | 20-25 | Rank in top tenth: | 12% |
| GPA 3.75 or higher: | 19% | Return as sophomores: | 76% |
| GPA 3.50-3.74: | 17% | Out-of-state: | 9% |
| GPA 3.0-3.49: | 39% | Live on campus: | 83% |

**Basis for selection.** High school transcript and test scores most important.

**High school preparation.** College-preparatory program recommended. Required units include English 4, mathematics 2, social studies 2, history 1, science 2 (laboratory 1) and foreign language 2.

**2009-2010 Annual costs.** Tuition/fees: $21,042. Room/board: $7,101. Books/supplies: $800. Personal expenses: $2,300.

**2008-2009 Financial aid. Need-based:** 263 full-time freshmen applied for aid; 226 were judged to have need; 226 of these received aid. Average need met was 81%. Average scholarship/grant was $12,232; average loan $3,774. 48% of total undergraduate aid awarded as scholarships/grants, 52% as loans/jobs. **Non-need-based:** Awarded to 345 full-time undergraduates,

including 91 freshmen. Scholarships awarded for academics, alumni affiliation, art, leadership, music/drama, religious affiliation. **Additional information:** Auditions required for music scholarships; portfolios required for fine arts scholarships; essays required for many institutional scholarships.

**Application procedures. Admission:** Priority date 3/1; deadline 8/14 (receipt date). $25 fee, may be waived for applicants with need. Admission notification on a rolling basis beginning on or about 9/15. **Financial aid:** Priority date 3/1; no closing date. FAFSA, institutional form required. Applicants notified on a rolling basis starting 3/15.

**Academics. Special study options:** Accelerated study, double major, dual enrollment of high school students, honors, independent study, internships, liberal arts/career combination, student-designed major, study abroad, teacher certification program. **Credit/placement by examination:** AP, CLEP, IB, ACT, institutional tests. 30 credit hours maximum toward associate degree, 60 toward bachelor's. **Support services:** Learning center, reduced course load, remedial instruction, study skills assistance, tutoring, writing center.

**Majors. Biology:** General. **Business:** General, accounting, business admin, management information systems. **Communications:** General. **Computer sciences:** General. **Education:** Art, biology, business, chemistry, computer, drama/dance, early childhood, early childhood special, elementary, English, French, mathematics, music, science, Spanish, special. **Foreign languages:** French, Spanish. **Health:** Art therapy, cytotechnology, nursing (RN). **History:** General. **Interdisciplinary:** Natural sciences. **Math:** General. **Philosophy/religion:** Religion. **Physical sciences:** Chemistry. **Protective services:** Criminal justice. **Psychology:** General. **Social sciences:** General, economics, international relations, political science, sociology. **Theology:** Religious ed. **Visual/performing arts:** General, art, graphic design.

**Most popular majors.** Business/marketing 26%, communications/journalism 6%, education 13%, health sciences 18%, psychology 10%, social sciences 7%.

**Computing on campus.** 100 workstations in dormitories, library, computer center, student center. Dormitories wired for high-speed internet access and linked to campus network. Commuter students can connect to campus network. Online course registration, online library, helpline available.

**Student life. Freshman orientation:** Available. Preregistration for classes offered. 3-day program held in fall. **Housing:** Coed dorms, single-sex dorms, special housing for disabled available. $150 fully refundable deposit. **Activities:** Bands, campus ministries, choral groups, dance, drama, international student organizations, literary magazine, music ensembles, musical theater, student government, student newspaper, symphony orchestra, student business association, student nurse association, Amnesty International, Habitat for Humanity.

**Athletics.** NCAA. **Intercollegiate:** Baseball M, basketball, cross-country, golf, soccer, softball W, tennis, volleyball W. **Intramural:** Basketball, bowling, diving, skiing, softball, swimming, table tennis, volleyball, weight lifting. **Team name:** Eagles.

**Student services.** Chaplain/spiritual director, career counseling, student employment services, financial aid counseling, health services, minority student services, personal counseling, placement for graduates, veterans' counselor.

**Contact.** E-mail: admissions@edgewood.edu
Phone: (608) 663-2294 Toll-free number: (800) 444-4861 ext. 2294
Fax: (608) 663-2214
Christine Benedict, Director of Undergraduate Admissions, Edgewood College, 1000 Edgewood College Drive, Madison, WI 53711-1997

## Herzing University
**Madison, Wisconsin**
**www.herzing.edu/madison**          CB code: 0388

- For-profit 3-year business and career college
- Commuter campus in small city
- 964 degree-seeking undergraduates
- Interview required

**General.** Founded in 1948. Regionally accredited. **Degrees:** 80 bachelor's, 105 associate awarded. **Location:** 90 miles from Milwaukee, 150 miles from Chicago. **Calendar:** Continuous, extensive summer session. **Full-time faculty:** 27 total. **Part-time faculty:** 21 total.

**Basis for selection.** Open admission, but selective for some programs. Interview and placement test required prior to acceptance. Application process varies by program. **Homeschooled:** State high school equivalency certificate required. **Learning Disabled:** Must provide documentation to admissions advisor prior to starting classes.

**2009-2010 Annual costs.** Tuition/fees: $11,300. Tuition is $365 per credit hour for most on-campus courses; $405 for on-line courses. Book use included in tuition. Personal expenses: $3,213.

**Application procedures. Admission:** No deadline. No application fee. Application must be submitted on paper. Admission notification on a rolling basis. **Financial aid:** No deadline. FAFSA, institutional form required. Applicants notified on a rolling basis.

**Academics.** Bachelors degree may be acquired in 3 years, associate degree in 1 year, 8 months. **Special study options:** Combined bachelor's/graduate degree, cooperative education, distance learning, honors, independent study, internships, liberal arts/career combination, study abroad, weekend college. **Credit/placement by examination:** AP, CLEP, institutional tests. **Support services:** Learning center, reduced course load, remedial instruction, study skills assistance, tutoring, writing center.

**Majors. BACHELOR'S. Business:** Accounting, accounting/business management, accounting/finance, business admin, finance, human resources, office management, office technology, office/clerical. **Communications technology:** Animation/special effects. **Computer sciences:** General, applications programming, computer graphics, computer science, game design, information systems, information technology, LAN/WAN management, networking, programming. **Engineering:** Software. **Engineering technology:** Architectural drafting, CAD/CADD, civil, civil drafting, computer, computer hardware, computer systems, drafting, electrical, electrical drafting, mechanical drafting, software, telecommunications. **Health:** Facilities admin, health care admin, medical records admin, medical records technology, office admin, ward supervisor. **Legal studies:** General. **Mechanic/repair:** Communications systems, computer, electronics/electrical, industrial electronics. **Protective services:** Emergency management/homeland security. **Visual/performing arts:** Graphic design. **Other:** Electronics engineering technology. **ASSOCIATE. Business:** Accounting/business management, business admin, office management, office technology, office/clerical. **Communications technology:** Animation/special effects. **Computer sciences:** General, applications programming, computer graphics, computer science, information systems, information technology, LAN/WAN management, networking, programming. **Engineering:** Software. **Engineering technology:** Architectural drafting, CAD/CADD, civil, civil drafting, computer, computer hardware, computer systems, drafting, electrical, electrical drafting, mechanical drafting, software, telecommunications. **Health:** Insurance coding, insurance specialist, medical records admin, nursing (RN), office admin, office assistant, office computer specialist, receptionist. **Legal studies:** General, paralegal. **Mechanic/repair:** Communications systems, computer, electronics/electrical, industrial electronics. **Visual/performing arts:** Graphic design. **Other:** Electronics engineering technology.

**Computing on campus.** 450 workstations in library, computer center, student center. Commuter students can connect to campus network. Online library, helpline, repair service, wireless network available.

**Student life. Freshman orientation:** Mandatory. **Activities:** Student government, student newspaper.

**Student services.** Adult student services, career counseling, student employment services, financial aid counseling, personal counseling, placement for graduates. **Physically disabled:** Services for visually, speech, hearing impaired.

**Contact.** E-mail: info@msn.herzing.edu
Phone: (608) 249-6611 Toll-free number: (800) 582-1227
Fax: (608) 249-8593
Matthew Schneider, Director of Admissions, Herzing University, 5218 East Terrace Drive, Madison, WI 53718

## ITT Technical Institute: Green Bay
**Green Bay, Wisconsin**
**www.itt-tech.edu**

- For-profit 4-year technical college
- Small city

**General.** Accredited by ACICS. **Calendar:** Trimester.

**Contact.** Phone: (920) 662-9000
Director of Recruitment, 470 Security Boulevard, Green Bay, WI 54313

## ITT Technical Institute: Greenfield
**Greenfield, Wisconsin**
**www.itt-tech.edu**          CB code: 2706

- For-profit 4-year technical college
- Commuter campus in large town

**General.** Accredited by ACICS. **Calendar:** Quarter.

**Contact.** Phone: (414) 282-9494
Director of Recruitment, 6300 West Layton Avenue, Greenfield, WI 53220-4612

## Lakeland College
### Sheboygan, Wisconsin
www.lakeland.edu                    CB code: 1393

- Private 4-year liberal arts college affiliated with United Church of Christ
- Residential campus in small city
- 2,790 degree-seeking undergraduates
- 91% of applicants admitted
- SAT or ACT (ACT writing recommended) required

**General.** Founded in 1862. Regionally accredited. Evening, online, and graduate classes offered for nontraditional students at 7 in-state sites. Associate program available at Tokyo, Japan campus. **Degrees:** 582 bachelor's, 35 associate awarded; master's offered. **Location:** 60 miles from Milwaukee, 60 miles from Green Bay. **Calendar:** 4-4-1. Limited summer session. **Full-time faculty:** 57 total. **Part-time faculty:** 325 total. **Class size:** 69% < 20, 30% 20-39, 1% 40-49.

**Freshman class profile.** 687 applied, 628 admitted, 150 enrolled.

| Mid 50% test scores | | Rank in top quarter: | 24% |
|---|---|---|---|
| ACT composite: | 18-23 | Rank in top tenth: | 8% |
| GPA 3.75 or higher: | 10% | Out-of-state: | 15% |
| GPA 3.50-3.74: | 9% | Live on campus: | 90% |
| GPA 3.0-3.49: | 29% | Fraternities: | 3% |
| GPA 2.0-2.99: | 49% | Sororities: | 3% |

**Basis for selection.** Applicants with 19 ACT, 2.0 GPA and rank in the top half of class admitted. Essays are recommended. **Homeschooled:** Transcript of courses and grades, state high school equivalency certificate required.

**High school preparation.** Recommended units include English 4, mathematics 2, social studies 2, history 2, science 2, foreign language 2 and academic electives 2.

**2009-2010 Annual costs.** Tuition/fees: $18,970. Room/board: $6,588. Books/supplies: $900. Personal expenses: $750.

**2009-2010 Financial aid. Non-need-based:** Scholarships awarded for academics.

**Application procedures. Admission:** No deadline. $20 fee, may be waived for applicants with need. Admission notification on a rolling basis. **Financial aid:** Priority date 3/31, closing date 7/1. FAFSA, institutional form required. Applicants notified on a rolling basis starting 2/1; must reply within 2 week(s) of notification.

**Academics.** Applicants whose test scores reflect weakness in basic skills must take basic skills courses in freshman year. **Special study options:** Combined bachelor's/graduate degree, cooperative education, distance learning, double major, dual enrollment of high school students, ESL, honors, independent study, internships, liberal arts/career combination, study abroad, teacher certification program. Engineering program with University of Wisconsin-Madison, nursing program with Bellin College of Nursing. **Credit/placement by examination:** AP, CLEP, IB, institutional tests. 30 credit hours maximum toward bachelor's degree. **Support services:** Learning center, reduced course load, remedial instruction, study skills assistance, tutoring, writing center.

**Majors. Biology:** General, biochemistry. **Business:** Accounting, business admin, international, marketing, nonprofit/public, resort management. **Computer sciences:** Computer science. **Education:** Elementary, kindergarten/preschool, middle, secondary. **Foreign languages:** German, Spanish. **History:** General. **Math:** General. **Philosophy/religion:** Religion. **Physical sciences:** Chemistry. **Protective services:** Law enforcement admin. **Psychology:** General. **Social sciences:** Sociology. **Visual/performing arts:** Art.

**Most popular majors.** Business/marketing 68%, computer/information sciences 19%, education 11%.

**Computing on campus.** 218 workstations in dormitories, library, computer center, student center. Dormitories wired for high-speed internet access and linked to campus network. Commuter students can connect to campus network. Online course registration, online library, helpline, wireless network available.

**Student life. Freshman orientation:** Mandatory. Preregistration for classes offered. **Housing:** Guaranteed on-campus for freshmen. Coed dorms, single-sex dorms, special housing for disabled, apartments available. $50 deposit. Honor apartments and apartments for students with senior standing available. **Activities:** Concert band, choral groups, drama, international student organizations, music ensembles, student government, student newspaper, campus activities board, black student union, Mortar Board, global students association, business fraternity, Inter-Greek Council.

**Athletics.** NCAA. **Intercollegiate:** Baseball M, basketball, cross-country, football (tackle) M, golf, soccer, softball W, tennis, track and field, volleyball W, wrestling M. **Team name:** Muskies.

**Student services.** Alcohol/substance abuse counseling, chaplain/spiritual director, career counseling, services for economically disadvantaged, student employment services, financial aid counseling, health services, on-campus daycare, personal counseling, placement for graduates, veterans' counselor. **Physically disabled:** Services for visually impaired.

**Contact.** E-mail: admissions@lakeland.edu
Phone: (920) 565-1217 Toll-free number: (800) 242-3347
Fax: (920) 565-1206
Nick Spaeth, Lakeland College, Box 359, Sheboygan, WI 53082-0359

## Lawrence University
### Appleton, Wisconsin
www.lawrence.edu          CB member   CB code: 1398

- Private 4-year music and liberal arts college
- Residential campus in small city
- 1,433 degree-seeking undergraduates: 2% part-time, 54% women, 3% African American, 3% Asian American, 2% Hispanic American, 8% international
- 69% of applicants admitted
- Application essay required
- 76% graduate within 6 years; 18% enter graduate study

**General.** Founded in 1847. Regionally accredited. **Degrees:** 320 bachelor's awarded. **Location:** 100 miles from Milwaukee, 30 miles from Green Bay. **Calendar:** Trimester. **Full-time faculty:** 157 total; 89% have terminal degrees, 12% minority, 38% women. **Part-time faculty:** 32 total; 25% have terminal degrees, 9% minority, 44% women. **Class size:** 75% < 20, 20% 20-39, 2% 40-49, 2% 50-99, less than 1% >100. **Special facilities:** Laser physics laboratory, 250 MHz nuclear magnetic resonance spectrometer, physics/computational graphics laboratory, lakefront retreat center.

**Freshman class profile.** 2,516 applied, 1,739 admitted, 352 enrolled.

| Mid 50% test scores | | GPA 2.0-2.99: | 6% |
|---|---|---|---|
| SAT critical reading: | 590-730 | Rank in top quarter: | 70% |
| SAT math: | 600-710 | Rank in top tenth: | 38% |
| SAT writing: | 590-680 | Return as sophomores: | 92% |
| ACT composite: | 27-31 | Out-of-state: | 65% |
| GPA 3.75 or higher: | 49% | Live on campus: | 99% |
| GPA 3.50-3.74: | 22% | International: | 7% |
| GPA 3.0-3.49: | 23% | | |

**Basis for selection.** GED not accepted. Strength of curriculum, school achievement record most important. Recommendations, out-of-class activities, test scores considered. Music applicants judged on musicianship, teacher's recommendations, and academic ability. Interview recommended for all; portfolio recommended for studio art; audition required for conservatory of music study. **Homeschooled:** Require some standardized test results, evidence of coursework completed and level of performance, letters of recommendation, and GED if applicable.

**High school preparation.** College-preparatory program recommended. 16 units required. Required and recommended units include English 4, mathematics 3, social studies 2, history 2, science 3 and foreign language 2. Strong musical preparation required of music applicants.

**2009-2010 Annual costs.** Tuition/fees: $34,596. Room/board: $7,053. Books/supplies: $750. Personal expenses: $900.

**2009-2010 Financial aid. Need-based:** 286 full-time freshmen applied for aid; 230 were judged to have need; 230 of these received aid. Average need met was 95%. Average scholarship/grant was $20,960; average loan $4,460. 75% of total undergraduate aid awarded as scholarships/grants, 25% as loans/jobs. **Non-need-based:** Awarded to 416 full-time undergraduates, including 104 freshmen. Scholarships awarded for academics, alumni affiliation, minority status, music/drama. **Additional information:** The first $1,000 (aggregate) of independently-sponsored scholarships received by a needy student will reduce student's loan or work-study commitment. Half of scholarships in excess of $1,000 will offset loan or work-study and the other half will reduce institutional need-based grant funding.

**Application procedures. Admission:** Closing date 1/15 (postmark date). $40 fee, may be waived for applicants with need. Admission notification 4/1. Must reply by 5/1. **Financial aid:** Priority date 3/1; no closing date. FAFSA, institutional form required. Applicants notified on a rolling basis starting 3/1; must reply by 5/1 or within 2 week(s) of notification.

**Academics.** As an adjunct to a major, students may pursue 1 interdisciplinary area of study: biomedical ethics, international studies, neuroscience or cognitive science. **Special study options:** Combined bachelor's/graduate degree, double major, independent study, internships, semester at sea, student-designed major, study abroad, teacher certification program, urban semester, Washington semester. Study abroad programs in 27 countries; marine biology term, Oak Ridge science semester; urban semester in Chicago; Newberry Library Program in humanities; environmental studies and forestry programs with Duke University; occupational therapy program with Washington University, St. Louis. **Credit/placement by examination:** AP, CLEP, IB, institutional tests. 30 credit hours maximum toward bachelor's degree. Course credit awarded for scores of at least 5 on International Baccalaureate examinations. **Support services:** Learning center, reduced course load, study skills assistance, tutoring, writing center.

**Majors. Area/ethnic studies:** Chinese, East Asian, Japanese, Russian/Slavic. **Biology:** General, biochemistry. **Computer sciences:** General. **Conservation:** Environmental studies. **Education:** Music. **Foreign languages:** Ancient Greek, Chinese, classics, East Asian, French, German, Japanese, Latin, linguistics, Russian, Spanish. **History:** General. **Interdisciplinary:** Cognitive science, global studies, math/computer science, natural sciences, neuroscience. **Math:** General. **Philosophy/religion:** Philosophy, religion. **Physical sciences:** Chemistry, geology, physics. **Psychology:** General. **Social sciences:** Anthropology, economics, political science. **Visual/performing arts:** Art, art history/conservation, dramatic, music performance, music theory/composition, studio arts.

**Most popular majors.** Biology 9%, English 8%, foreign language 8%, interdisciplinary studies 6%, physical sciences 8%, psychology 10%, social sciences 13%, visual/performing arts 23%.

**Computing on campus.** 354 workstations in dormitories, library, computer center. Dormitories wired for high-speed internet access and linked to campus network. Commuter students can connect to campus network. Online course registration, online library, helpline, repair service, wireless network available.

**Student life. Freshman orientation:** Mandatory. Preregistration for classes offered. Held 5 days prior to start of fall classes. **Policies:** Honor code in effect. **Housing:** Guaranteed on-campus for all undergraduates. Coed dorms, single-sex dorms, special housing for disabled, apartments, wellness housing available. Apartment-style units available to upperclass students. All single students required to live on-campus for 4 years. **Activities:** Bands, campus ministries, choral groups, dance, drama, film society, international student organizations, literary magazine, music ensembles, musical theater, opera, radio station, student government, student newspaper, symphony orchestra, Chavurah, Christian fellowship, black organization of students, Latin American student organization, social service groups, political and academic clubs, professional sororities and fraternities.

**Athletics.** NCAA. **Intercollegiate:** Baseball M, basketball, cross-country, diving, fencing, football (tackle) M, golf M, ice hockey M, soccer, softball W, swimming, tennis, track and field, volleyball W. **Intramural:** Badminton, basketball, bowling, fencing, football (non-tackle), golf, handball, racquetball, soccer, softball, squash, table tennis, tennis, volleyball, water polo. **Team name:** Vikings.

**Student services.** Alcohol/substance abuse counseling, career counseling, student employment services, financial aid counseling, health services, minority student services, personal counseling, placement for graduates. **Physically disabled:** Services for visually, speech, hearing impaired.

**Contact.** E-mail: excel@lawrence.edu
Phone: (920) 832-6500 Toll-free number: (800) 227-0982
Fax: (920) 832-6782
Steven Syverson, Vice President for Enrollment Management, Lawrence University, Box 599, Appleton, WI 54912-0599

## Maranatha Baptist Bible College
**Watertown, Wisconsin**
www.mbbc.edu                    CB code: 2732

- Private 4-year Bible college affiliated with Baptist faith
- Residential campus in large town

- 773 degree-seeking undergraduates: 5% part-time, 57% women, 1% African American, 1% Asian American, 1% Hispanic American
- 53 degree-seeking graduate students
- 51% of applicants admitted
- SAT or ACT (ACT writing optional), application essay required
- 48% graduate within 6 years; 18% enter graduate study

**General.** Founded in 1968. Regionally accredited. **Degrees:** 147 bachelor's, 14 associate awarded; master's offered. **ROTC:** Army, Air Force. **Location:** 45 miles from Milwaukee, 38 miles from Madison. **Calendar:** Semester, limited summer session. **Full-time faculty:** 42 total; 36% have terminal degrees, 7% minority, 33% women. **Part-time faculty:** 33 total; 12% have terminal degrees, 3% minority, 39% women. **Class size:** 62% < 20, 27% 20-39, 4% 40-49, 6% 50-99, 2% >100.

**Freshman class profile.** 406 applied, 207 admitted, 198 enrolled.

| Mid 50% test scores | | | |
|---|---|---|---|
| SAT critical reading: | 500-620 | End year in good standing: | 91% |
| SAT math: | 430-590 | Return as sophomores: | 68% |
| ACT composite: | 20-26 | Out-of-state: | 75% |
| | | Live on campus: | 76% |

**Basis for selection.** Recommendations, religious commitment most important. Secondary school record, test scores, character also important. Class rank, essay considered. At-risk students placed on admissions probation. Audition required for fine arts.

**High school preparation.** College-preparatory program recommended. 18 units recommended. Recommended units include English 4, mathematics 3, social studies 3, history 3, science 3 and foreign language 2. Two units of physical education and one unit of word processing recommended.

**2009-2010 Annual costs.** Tuition/fees: $11,000. Room/board: $5,990.

**2009-2010 Financial aid. Non-need-based:** Scholarships awarded for academics.

**Application procedures. Admission:** No deadline. $50 fee. Admission notification on a rolling basis. **Financial aid:** Priority date 3/1; no closing date. FAFSA required. Applicants notified on a rolling basis starting 2/1; must reply within 2 week(s) of notification.

**Academics.** Hands-on ministerial work available. **Special study options:** Distance learning, double major, independent study, internships, liberal arts/career combination, study abroad, teacher certification program. **Credit/placement by examination:** AP, CLEP, ACT, institutional tests. 12 credit hours maximum toward associate degree, 12 toward bachelor's. Only 6 credits may be counted in any one field of study. **Support services:** Reduced course load, remedial instruction, study skills assistance, tutoring, writing center.

**Majors. Biology:** General. **Business:** Accounting/business management, business admin, marketing, office management. **Education:** General, biology, business, early childhood, elementary, English, history, mathematics, music, physical, science, secondary, social studies. **Health:** Nursing (RN). **Liberal arts:** Humanities. **Theology:** Bible, missionary, pastoral counseling, sacred music, youth ministry. **Visual/performing arts:** Music pedagogy, music performance, piano/organ.

**Most popular majors.** Business/marketing 20%, education 22%, health sciences 15%, liberal arts 18%, theological studies 22%.

**Computing on campus.** 120 workstations in dormitories, library, computer center. Dormitories wired for high-speed internet access and linked to campus network. Online library, repair service, student web hosting, wireless network available.

**Student life. Freshman orientation:** Mandatory. Preregistration for classes offered. Held Saturday through Monday before classes begin. **Policies:** Religious observance required. **Housing:** Guaranteed on-campus for all undergraduates. Single-sex dorms, wellness housing available. $175 nonrefundable deposit. **Activities:** Bands, campus ministries, choral groups, drama, music ensembles, musical theater, student government, symphony orchestra.

**Athletics.** NCAA, NCCAA. **Intercollegiate:** Baseball M, basketball, cross-country, football (tackle) M, soccer, softball W, volleyball W, wrestling M. **Intramural:** Basketball, soccer W, volleyball. **Team name:** Crusaders.

**Student services.** Chaplain/spiritual director, career counseling, financial aid counseling, health services, on-campus daycare, personal counseling, placement for graduates, veterans' counselor.

**Contact.** E-mail: admissions@mbbc.edu
Phone: (920) 261-9300 Toll-free number: (800) 611-1947
Fax: (920) 261-9109
James Harrison, Director of Admissions, Maranatha Baptist Bible College, 745 West Main Street, Watertown, WI 53094

## Marian University
### Fond du Lac, Wisconsin
### www.marianuniversity.edu
CB member
CB code: 1443

- Private 4-year university and liberal arts college affiliated with Roman Catholic Church
- Residential campus in large town
- 1,935 degree-seeking undergraduates: 23% part-time, 73% women, 7% African American, 2% Asian American, 3% Hispanic American, 1% Native American, 1% international
- 669 degree-seeking graduate students
- 83% of applicants admitted
- SAT or ACT (ACT writing optional) required
- 41% graduate within 6 years; 13% enter graduate study

**General.** Founded in 1936. Regionally accredited. Offsite center for law enforcement training facilities in Appleton, WI. **Degrees:** 385 bachelor's awarded; master's, doctoral offered. **ROTC:** Army. **Location:** 60 miles from Milwaukee, 65 miles from Green Bay. **Calendar:** Semester, extensive summer session. **Full-time faculty:** 84 total; 60% have terminal degrees, 5% minority, 57% women. **Part-time faculty:** 202 total; 9% have terminal degrees, 7% minority, 55% women. **Class size:** 66% < 20, 29% 20-39, 3% 40-49, 2% 50-99.

**Freshman class profile.** 1,016 applied, 844 admitted, 319 enrolled.

| Mid 50% test scores | | | |
|---|---|---|---|
| ACT composite: | 18-22 | Rank in top tenth: | 8% |
| GPA 3.75 or higher: | 7% | Return as sophomores: | 75% |
| GPA 3.50-3.74: | 11% | Out-of-state: | 9% |
| GPA 3.0-3.49: | 31% | Live on campus: | 76% |
| GPA 2.0-2.99: | 46% | International: | 1% |
| Rank in top quarter: | 31% | Fraternities: | 4% |
| | | Sororities: | 6% |

**Basis for selection.** School achievement record most important, followed by test scores. Applicants must meet 2 of following 3 criteria: 2.0 GPA, top half of class, 18 ACT. Special admissions procedures required for nursing and education divisions. If admission criteria not met, students may be admitted on provisional basis. Interview, audition recommended.

**High school preparation.** College-preparatory program required. Required and recommended units include English 4, mathematics 2-3, history 1, science 1-2 (laboratory 1) and foreign language 2. Biology and chemistry prerequisite for nursing program.

**2009-2010 Annual costs.** Tuition/fees: $20,900. Room/board: $5,640. Books/supplies: $700. Personal expenses: $1,420.

**2008-2009 Financial aid. Need-based:** 283 full-time freshmen applied for aid; 260 were judged to have need; 260 of these received aid. Average need met was 89%. Average scholarship/grant was $11,291; average loan $5,264. 58% of total undergraduate aid awarded as scholarships/grants, 42% as loans/jobs. **Non-need-based:** Awarded to 1,116 full-time undergraduates, including 258 freshmen. Scholarships awarded for academics, ROTC, state residency.

**Application procedures. Admission:** Priority date 4/1; no deadline. $20 fee, may be waived for applicants with need. Admission notification on a rolling basis. Must reply by May 1 or within 4 week(s) if notified thereafter. **Financial aid:** Priority date 3/1; no closing date. FAFSA, institutional form required. Applicants notified on a rolling basis starting 3/1; must reply within 4 week(s) of notification.

**Academics. Special study options:** Accelerated study, combined bachelor's/graduate degree, cooperative education, distance learning, double major, dual enrollment of high school students, honors, independent study, internships, liberal arts/career combination, student-designed major, study abroad, teacher certification program. Accelerated programs for adults in business, nursing, operation management, radiologic technology, organizational communication, administration of justice. **Credit/placement by examination:** AP, CLEP, IB, institutional tests. 30 credit hours maximum toward bachelor's degree. Writing sample required for placement and counseling. **Support services:** Learning center, pre-admission summer program, reduced course load, remedial instruction, study skills assistance, tutoring, writing center.

**Honors college/program.** Unrestricted admissions with 25 ACT, 3.5 GPA, positive recommendation, application essay.

**Majors. Biology:** General. **Business:** General, accounting, business admin, finance, human resources, marketing, operations. **Communications:** General, organizational. **Computer sciences:** Information technology. **Education:** Art, early childhood, elementary, English, music, science, secondary, social studies, Spanish. **Foreign languages:** Spanish. **Health:** Cytotechnology, health care admin, nursing (RN), radiologic technology/medical imaging. **History:** General. **Liberal arts:** Arts/sciences. **Math:** General. **Parks/recreation:** Sports admin. **Philosophy/religion:** Religion. **Physical sciences:** Chemistry. **Protective services:** Emergency management/homeland security, forensics, police science. **Psychology:** General. **Public administration:** Human services, social work. **Social sciences:** Political science. **Visual/performing arts:** Graphic design, music management, studio arts.

**Most popular majors.** Business/marketing 24%, education 9%, health sciences 39%, security/protective services 13%.

**Computing on campus.** 400 workstations in library, computer center, student center. Dormitories wired for high-speed internet access and linked to campus network. Commuter students can connect to campus network. Online course registration, online library, helpline, repair service, wireless network available.

**Student life. Freshman orientation:** Mandatory. Preregistration for classes offered. **Policies:** Emphasis on community volunteer activity. Service transcript available for graduates. **Housing:** Guaranteed on-campus for all undergraduates. Coed dorms, special housing for disabled, apartments, fraternity/sorority housing, wellness housing available. $100 nonrefundable deposit. Townhouses, penthouses and residential suites available. **Activities:** Bands, campus ministries, choral groups, dance, drama, international student organizations, literary magazine, music ensembles, Model UN, student government, student newspaper, symphony orchestra, environmental club, social justice committee, African American student union, Association Latina, math and science association.

**Athletics.** NCAA. **Intercollegiate:** Baseball M, basketball, cross-country, golf, ice hockey, soccer, softball W, tennis, volleyball W. **Intramural:** Badminton, basketball, bowling, football (non-tackle) M, skiing, softball M, tennis, volleyball. **Team name:** Sabres.

**Student services.** Adult student services, alcohol/substance abuse counseling, chaplain/spiritual director, career counseling, services for economically disadvantaged, student employment services, financial aid counseling, health services, minority student services, on-campus daycare, personal counseling, placement for graduates, women's services. **Physically disabled:** Services for visually, speech, hearing impaired.

**Contact.** E-mail: admissions@marianuniversity.edu
Phone: (920) 923-7650 Toll-free number: (800) 262-7426
Fax: (920) 923-8755
Stacey Akey, Vice President for Enrollment and Marketing, Marian University, 45 South National Avenue, Fond du Lac, WI 54935-4699

## Marquette University
### Milwaukee, Wisconsin
### www.marquette.edu
CB member
CB code: 1448

- Private 4-year university affiliated with Roman Catholic Church
- Residential campus in very large city
- 7,857 degree-seeking undergraduates: 3% part-time, 53% women, 5% African American, 4% Asian American, 6% Hispanic American, 2% international
- 3,485 degree-seeking graduate students
- 66% of applicants admitted
- SAT or ACT (ACT writing recommended), application essay required
- 80% graduate within 6 years

**General.** Founded in 1881. Regionally accredited. **Degrees:** 1,703 bachelor's awarded; master's, doctoral, professional offered. **ROTC:** Army, Naval, Air Force. **Location:** Downtown. **Calendar:** Semester, extensive summer session. **Full-time faculty:** 620 total. **Part-time faculty:** 470 total. **Class size:** 39% < 20, 42% 20-39, 8% 40-49, 7% 50-99, 4% >100. **Special facilities:** 15th century St. Joan of Arc chapel.

**Freshman class profile.** 17,825 applied, 11,682 admitted, 1,952 enrolled.

| Mid 50% test scores | | | |
|---|---|---|---|
| SAT critical reading: | 540-640 | Rank in top quarter: | 65% |
| SAT math: | 540-660 | Rank in top tenth: | 33% |
| SAT writing: | 530-640 | Return as sophomores: | 89% |
| ACT composite: | 24-29 | Out-of-state: | 64% |
| | | International: | 1% |

**Basis for selection.** High school course selection, trend of performance, test scores and class rank most important. Essay, leadership, community service and extracurricular activities considered. **Homeschooled:** Provide detailed list of curriculum and bibliography. Personal interview may be required.

**High school preparation.** 16 units required; 22 recommended. Required and recommended units include English 4, mathematics 2-4, social studies 2-3, science 2-3 (laboratory 2-3), foreign language 2 and academic electives 2-5. Algebra, geometry, and intermediate algebra required for arts & sciences, business administration and health sciences. Algebra and geometry required for nursing. 3 years of science recommended for premedical, predental and science majors. Students interested in international business strongly urged to complete 4 units of single foreign language.

**2009-2010 Annual costs.** Tuition/fees: $29,096. Required fees include cost of UPASS, which allows unlimited use of Milwaukee County Bus System. Room/board: $9,680. Books/supplies: $900. Personal expenses: $1,350.

**2009-2010 Financial aid. Non-need-based:** Scholarships awarded for academics, athletics, leadership, music/drama, ROTC.

**Application procedures. Admission:** Closing date 12/1 (postmark date). $30 fee, may be waived for applicants with need, free for online applicants. Admission notification on a rolling basis. Must reply by May 1 or within 2 week(s) if notified thereafter. **Financial aid:** Priority date 2/1; no closing date. FAFSA required. Applicants notified on a rolling basis starting 3/20; must reply by 5/1 or within 3 week(s) of notification.

**Academics. Special study options:** Accelerated study, combined bachelor's/graduate degree, cooperative education, cross-registration, double major, dual enrollment of high school students, honors, internships, student-designed major, study abroad, teacher certification program, Washington semester, weekend college. **Credit/placement by examination:** AP, CLEP, IB, institutional tests. 30 credit hours maximum toward bachelor's degree. **Support services:** Learning center, pre-admission summer program, reduced course load, study skills assistance, tutoring, writing center.

**Majors. Area/ethnic studies:** African-American, women's. **Biology:** General, biochemistry, molecular. **Business:** Accounting, accounting technology, business admin, e-commerce, finance, human resources, international, management information systems, managerial economics, marketing. **Communications:** General, advertising, broadcast journalism, journalism, media studies, public relations. **Computer sciences:** Computer science, information systems. **Education:** Elementary, English, foreign languages, mathematics, middle, science, secondary, social science, social studies. **Engineering:** General, biomedical, civil, computer, construction, electrical, environmental, manufacturing, mechanical. **Foreign languages:** Classics, French, German, Spanish. **Health:** Athletic training, audiology/speech pathology, clinical lab technology, nursing (RN), predental, premedicine. **History:** General. **Interdisciplinary:** Global studies, intercultural, math/computer science. **Legal studies:** Prelaw. **Math:** General, computational, statistics. **Parks/recreation:** Exercise sciences. **Philosophy/religion:** Philosophy, religion. **Physical sciences:** Chemistry, physics. **Psychology:** General. **Social sciences:** General, anthropology, criminology, economics, international relations, political science, sociology. **Visual/performing arts:** Dramatic.

**Most popular majors.** Biology 7%, business/marketing 26%, communications/journalism 10%, education 6%, engineering/engineering technologies 9%, health sciences 12%, social sciences 9%.

**Computing on campus.** 1,200 workstations in dormitories, library, computer center, student center. Dormitories wired for high-speed internet access and linked to campus network. Commuter students can connect to campus network. Online course registration, online library, helpline, student web hosting, wireless network available.

**Student life. Freshman orientation:** Available. Preregistration for classes offered. 4-day session held week before classes begin; June program also available. **Policies:** Written policies in effect concerning racial and sexual harassment, alcohol, drugs and safety. **Housing:** Guaranteed on-campus for freshmen. Coed dorms, single-sex dorms, special housing for disabled, apartments, cooperative housing, fraternity/sorority housing, wellness housing available. $200 nonrefundable deposit, deadline 5/1. Special housing for engineering, nursing, and honor students. **Activities:** Bands, campus ministries, choral groups, dance, drama, international student organizations, literary magazine, music ensembles, Model UN, musical theater, opera, radio station, student government, student newspaper, symphony orchestra, TV station, JUSTICE, College Republicans, College Democrats, Campus Crusade for Christ, Intervarsity, Latin American student organization.

**Athletics.** NCAA. **Intercollegiate:** Basketball, cheerleading, cross-country, golf M, soccer, tennis, track and field, volleyball W. **Intramural:** Badminton, basketball, football (tackle), golf, racquetball, soccer, softball, squash, tennis, track and field, volleyball, water polo, weight lifting. **Team name:** Golden Eagles.

**Student services.** Adult student services, alcohol/substance abuse counseling, chaplain/spiritual director, career counseling, services for economically disadvantaged, student employment services, financial aid counseling,

health services, minority student services, on-campus daycare, personal counseling, placement for graduates. **Physically disabled:** Services for visually, speech, hearing impaired.

**Contact.** E-mail: admissions@marquette.edu
Phone: (414) 288-7302 Toll-free number: (800) 222-6544
Fax: (414) 288-3764
Robert Blust, Dean of Undergraduate Admissions, Marquette University, PO Box 1881, Milwaukee, WI 53201-1881

## Milwaukee Institute of Art & Design
### Milwaukee, Wisconsin
**www.miad.edu** **CB code: 1506**

- Private 4-year visual arts college
- Commuter campus in very large city

**General.** Founded in 1974. Regionally accredited. **Location:** 90 miles from Chicago. **Calendar:** Semester.

**Annual costs/financial aid.** Tuition/fees (2009-2010): $26,050. Room/board: $7,700. Books/supplies: $1,828. Personal expenses: $1,624. Need-based financial aid available to full-time and part-time students.

**Contact.** Phone: (414) 291-8070
Director of Admissions, 273 East Erie Street, Milwaukee, WI 53202

## Milwaukee School of Engineering
### Milwaukee, Wisconsin **CB member**
**www.msoe.edu** **CB code: 1476**

- Private 4-year university
- Residential campus in very large city
- 2,438 degree-seeking undergraduates: 8% part-time, 19% women, 3% African American, 3% Asian American, 3% Hispanic American, 1% Native American, 3% international
- 210 degree-seeking graduate students
- 67% of applicants admitted
- SAT or ACT (ACT writing optional) required
- 55% graduate within 6 years; 9% enter graduate study

**General.** Founded in 1903. Regionally accredited. **Degrees:** 361 bachelor's awarded; master's offered. **ROTC:** Army, Naval, Air Force. **Location:** 72 miles from Chicago. **Calendar:** Quarter, limited summer session. **Full-time faculty:** 132 total; 73% have terminal degrees, 10% minority, 26% women. **Part-time faculty:** 119 total; 28% have terminal degrees, 13% minority, 31% women. **Class size:** 41% < 20, 59% 20-39. **Special facilities:** Museum, teaching and research laboratories for fluid power motion control, construction engineering, energy systems, renewable energy, rapid prototyping, software development, health and wellness fitness facility, indoor ice hockey arena.

**Freshman class profile.** 2,126 applied, 1,427 admitted, 534 enrolled.

| Mid 50% test scores | | End year in good standing: | 74% |
|---|---|---|---|
| SAT critical reading: | 500-640 | Return as sophomores: | 75% |
| SAT math: | 530-590 | Out-of-state: | 37% |
| ACT composite: | 24-29 | Live on campus: | 79% |
| GPA 3.75 or higher: | 36% | International: | 1% |
| GPA 3.50-3.74: | 23% | Fraternities: | 4% |
| GPA 3.0-3.49: | 34% | Sororities: | 8% |
| GPA 2.0-2.99: | 7% | | |

**Basis for selection.** Admissions based on secondary school record and standardized test scores. **Homeschooled:** Transcript of courses and grades required. **Learning Disabled:** Untimed standardized tests required.

**High school preparation.** College-preparatory program recommended. 10 units required. Required and recommended units include English 4, mathematics 4, science 2 (laboratory 2). For business and technical communication, math units should include 1 algebra. For biomedical engineering, science units should include 1 biological science.

**2010-2011 Annual costs.** Tuition/fees (projected): $29,520. Room/board: $7,431. Books/supplies: $1,500. Personal expenses: $2,640.

**2008-2009 Financial aid. Need-based:** 581 full-time freshmen applied for aid; 509 were judged to have need; 506 of these received aid. Average need met was 70%. Average scholarship/grant was $15,572; average loan $2,473. 66% of total undergraduate aid awarded as scholarships/grants, 34%

as loans/jobs. **Non-need-based:** Awarded to 547 full-time undergraduates, including 155 freshmen. Scholarships awarded for academics, ROTC.

**Application procedures. Admission:** Priority date 2/1; no deadline. $25 fee, may be waived for applicants with need, free for online applicants. Admission notification on a rolling basis beginning on or about 10/1. **Financial aid:** Priority date 3/15; no closing date. FAFSA required. Applicants notified on a rolling basis starting 3/1; must reply within 2 week(s) of notification.

**Academics.** Average of 600 hours of laboratory experience for each program. **Special study options:** Accelerated study, combined bachelor's/graduate degree, distance learning, double major, dual enrollment of high school students, ESL, internships, study abroad. Bachelor of Science in business, mechanical engineering, and in electrical engineering with Lubeck University of Applied Sciences, Germany; exchange program with Czech Technical University, bachelor's or master's option in an engineering discipline and master's in environmental engineering. **Credit/placement by examination:** AP, CLEP, IB, SAT, ACT. **Support services:** Learning center, pre-admission summer program, reduced course load, study skills assistance, tutoring, writing center.

**Majors. Business:** General, business admin, construction management, international, management information systems. **Communications:** General. **Engineering:** General, architectural, biomedical, computer, electrical, industrial, mechanical, software. **Engineering technology:** Electrical, mechanical. **Health:** Nursing (RN). **Other:** Biomolecular Engineering.

**Most popular majors.** Business/marketing 17%, engineering/engineering technologies 74%, health sciences 8%.

**Computing on campus.** PC or laptop required. 150 workstations in dormitories, library, computer center, student center. Dormitories wired for high-speed internet access and linked to campus network. Commuter students can connect to campus network. Online course registration, online library, helpline, repair service, student web hosting, wireless network available.

**Student life. Freshman orientation:** Available. Preregistration for classes offered. 3-4 day program prior to start of classes. **Policies:** Smoke-free campus and residential facilities. **Housing:** Guaranteed on-campus for all undergraduates. Coed dorms, special housing for disabled, wellness housing available. $75 fully refundable deposit, deadline 6/1. **Activities:** Bands, campus ministries, dance, drama, international student organizations, literary magazine, radio station, student government, symphony orchestra, residence hall association, Circle-K, Society of Hispanic Professional Engineers, National Society of Black Engineers, National Student Nurses Association, campus volunteer services, Mont Pelleriu Colloquium.

**Athletics.** NCAA. **Intercollegiate:** Baseball M, basketball, cheerleading, cross-country, golf, ice hockey M, rowing (crew) M, soccer, softball W, tennis, track and field, volleyball, wrestling M. **Intramural:** Basketball, football (non-tackle), soccer, softball, volleyball. **Team name:** Raiders.

**Student services.** Alcohol/substance abuse counseling, career counseling, services for economically disadvantaged, student employment services, financial aid counseling, health services, personal counseling, placement for graduates, veterans' counselor, women's services. **Physically disabled:** Services for visually, speech, hearing impaired. **Learning disabled:** Comprehensive services available.

**Contact.** E-mail: explore@msoe.edu
Phone: (414) 277-6763 Toll-free number: (800) 332-6763
Fax: (414) 277-7475
Dana Grennier, Director, Admission, Milwaukee School of Engineering, 1025 North Broadway, Milwaukee, WI 53202-3109

## Mount Mary College
**Milwaukee, Wisconsin**
www.mtmary.edu                    CB code: 1490

- Private 4-year liberal arts college for women affiliated with Roman Catholic Church
- Commuter campus in very large city
- 1,253 degree-seeking undergraduates: 27% part-time, 98% women
- 460 degree-seeking graduate students
- 50% of applicants admitted
- SAT or ACT (ACT writing optional) required
- 40% graduate within 6 years

**General.** Founded in 1913. Regionally accredited. Open to all faiths. Small number of men admitted as part-time non-degree-seeking students and for joint nursing students with Columbia College of Nursing. **Degrees:** 232 bachelor's awarded; master's offered. **ROTC:** Army, Naval. **Location:** 7

miles from downtown. **Calendar:** Semester, limited summer session. **Full-time faculty:** 67 total; 61% have terminal degrees, 85% women. **Part-time faculty:** 140 total; 24% have terminal degrees, 77% women. **Class size:** 81% < 20, 17% 20-39, less than 1% 40-49, less than 1% 50-99. **Special facilities:** Historic costume collection, labyrinth.

**Freshman class profile.** 808 applied, 404 admitted, 161 enrolled.

| Mid 50% test scores | | Rank in top tenth: | 16% |
|---|---|---|---|
| ACT composite: | 16-22 | End year in good standing: | 82% |
| GPA 3.75 or higher: | 6% | Return as sophomores: | 68% |
| GPA 3.50-3.74: | 10% | Out-of-state: | 1% |
| GPA 3.0-3.49: | 35% | Live on campus: | 64% |
| GPA 2.0-2.99: | 47% | International: | 1% |
| Rank in top quarter: | 41% | | |

**Basis for selection.** Academic record, test scores and supplemental information reviewed. Class rank, core curriculum, test scores and GPA important. Interview recommended and essay required for students who do not meet direct admission requirements. **Homeschooled:** Transcript of courses and grades required. **Learning Disabled:** Students encouraged to talk with Disabilities Coordinator at least one semester prior to enrollment to determine if reasonable accommodations can be made.

**High school preparation.** College-preparatory program recommended. 16 units required. Required and recommended units include English 4, mathematics 2-3, social studies 2, history 2, science 2 (laboratory 2), foreign language 2 and academic electives 2.

**2010-2011 Annual costs.** Tuition/fees: $21,668. Room/board: $7,498. Books/supplies: $1,260.

**2009-2010 Financial aid. Need-based:** 150 full-time freshmen applied for aid; 145 were judged to have need; 145 of these received aid. Average need met was 78%. Average scholarship/grant was $16,781; average loan $3,451. 53% of total undergraduate aid awarded as scholarships/grants, 47% as loans/jobs. **Non-need-based:** Awarded to 156 full-time undergraduates, including 27 freshmen. Scholarships awarded for academics, alumni affiliation, art, leadership, music/drama.

**Application procedures. Admission:** No deadline. $25 fee, may be waived for applicants with need, free for online applicants. Admission notification on a rolling basis beginning on or about 9/15. **Financial aid:** Priority date 3/1; no closing date. FAFSA required. Applicants notified on a rolling basis starting 3/1; must reply within 2 week(s) of notification.

**Academics. Special study options:** Accelerated study, combined bachelor's/graduate degree, double major, honors, independent study, internships, liberal arts/career combination, student-designed major, study abroad, teacher certification program. **Credit/placement by examination:** AP, CLEP, IB, ACT, institutional tests. Maximum of 24 credits earned through a combination of credit exams, credit from life experience, directed and independent study. **Support services:** Learning center, reduced course load, remedial instruction, study skills assistance, tutoring.

**Majors. Biology:** General. **Business:** Accounting, business admin, fashion, marketing. **Communications:** General, public relations. **Education:** General, art, biology, business, chemistry, early childhood, elementary, English, foreign languages, history, mathematics, music, science, secondary, social studies, Spanish. **Foreign languages:** Spanish. **Health:** Art therapy, dietetics, medical radiologic technology/radiation therapy, nursing (RN), predental, premedicine, preveterinary, sonography. **History:** General. **Interdisciplinary:** Behavioral sciences, biological/physical sciences. **Legal studies:** Prelaw. **Math:** General. **Philosophy/religion:** Philosophy, religion. **Physical sciences:** Chemistry. **Protective services:** Criminal justice. **Psychology:** General. **Public administration:** Social work. **Social sciences:** General, international relations. **Theology:** Religious ed. **Visual/performing arts:** Art, commercial/advertising art, fashion design, interior design.

**Most popular majors.** Business/marketing 17%, health sciences 33%, psychology 6%, visual/performing arts 16%.

**Computing on campus.** 320 workstations in dormitories, library, computer center, student center. Dormitories wired for high-speed internet access and linked to campus network. Commuter students can connect to campus network. Online course registration, online library, helpline, wireless network available.

**Student life. Freshman orientation:** Mandatory. Preregistration for classes offered. **Policies:** No overnight male visitation. **Housing:** Guaranteed on-campus for freshmen. $100 nonrefundable deposit, deadline 5/1. **Activities:** Campus ministries, choral groups, dance, international student organizations, literary magazine, music ensembles, Model UN, student government, student newspaper, commuter council, hall council, gospel choir, programming and activities council, department-affiliated clubs.

**Athletics.** NCAA. **Intercollegiate:** Basketball W, cross-country W, soccer W, softball W, tennis W, volleyball W. **Intramural:** Basketball W, bowling W, cross-country W, golf W, skiing W, soccer W, swimming W, tennis W, track and field W, volleyball W. **Team name:** Blue Angels.

**Student services.** Adult student services, chaplain/spiritual director, career counseling, services for economically disadvantaged, student employment services, financial aid counseling, minority student services, on-campus daycare, personal counseling. **Physically disabled:** Services for visually, hearing impaired.

**Contact.** E-mail: admiss@mtmary.edu
Phone: (414) 256-1219 Toll-free number: (800) 321-6265
Fax: (414) 256-0180
Amy Dobson, Dean of Enrollment, Mount Mary College, 2900 North Menomonee River Parkway, Milwaukee, WI 53222-4597

## Northland Baptist Bible College
### Dunbar, Wisconsin
### www.ni.edu

- Private 4-year university and Bible college affiliated with Independent Baptist
- Rural community

**General.** Regionally accredited. **Location:** 1.5 hours north of Green Bay, Wisconsin. **Calendar:** Semester.

**Annual costs/financial aid.** Tuition/fees (2009-2010): $11,480. Room/board: $5,160. Books/supplies: $600. Personal expenses: $1,800.

**Contact.** Phone: (715) 324-6900 ext. 3100
Director of Admissions, W10085 Pike Plains Road, Dunbar, WI 54119

## Northland College
### Ashland, Wisconsin                      CB member
### www.northland.edu                       CB code: 1561

- Private 4-year liberal arts college affiliated with United Church of Christ
- Residential campus in small town
- 587 degree-seeking undergraduates: 4% part-time, 55% women, 1% Asian American, 2% Hispanic American, 3% Native American, 3% international
- 10 graduate students
- 79% of applicants admitted
- SAT or ACT (ACT writing optional), application essay required
- 61% graduate within 6 years

**General.** Founded in 1892. Regionally accredited. **Degrees:** 132 bachelor's awarded. **Location:** 65 miles from Duluth, MN. **Calendar:** 4-1-4, limited summer session. **Full-time faculty:** 39 total; 82% have terminal degrees, 10% minority, 31% women. **Part-time faculty:** 35 total; 11% have terminal degrees, 11% minority, 46% women. **Class size:** 61% < 20, 39% 20-39. **Special facilities:** Field stations for natural science courses, atmospheric and environmental satellite links.

**Freshman class profile.** 582 applied, 457 admitted, 136 enrolled.

| Mid 50% test scores | | Rank in top quarter: | 48% |
|---|---|---|---|
| SAT critical reading: | 510-670 | Rank in top tenth: | 25% |
| SAT math: | 500-640 | End year in good standing: | 78% |
| ACT composite: | 20-27 | Return as sophomores: | 68% |
| GPA 3.75 or higher: | 27% | Out-of-state: | 58% |
| GPA 3.50-3.74: | 20% | Live on campus: | 99% |
| GPA 3.0-3.49: | 26% | International: | 1% |
| GPA 2.0-2.99: | 24% | | |

**Basis for selection.** High school curriculum evaluation, class rank, guidance counselor recommendation, GPA, and test scores considered. Audition, portfolio recommended; interview required for borderline applicants. **Learning Disabled:** Strongly recommend students contact disabilities coordinator.

**High school preparation.** College-preparatory program recommended. 18 units required; 21 recommended. Required and recommended units include English 4, mathematics 3, social studies 3, science 3 (laboratory 2), foreign language 2 and academic electives 3-4.

**2009-2010 Annual costs.** Tuition/fees: $24,021. Room/board: $6,765. Books/supplies: $800. Personal expenses: $1,650.

**2009-2010 Financial aid. Need-based:** 126 full-time freshmen applied for aid; 118 were judged to have need; 118 of these received aid. Average need met was 92%. Average scholarship/grant was $15,867; average loan $4,028. 74% of total undergraduate aid awarded as scholarships/grants, 26% as loans/jobs. **Non-need-based:** Awarded to 92 full-time undergraduates, including 17 freshmen. Scholarships awarded for academics, alumni affiliation, art, job skills, leadership, minority status, music/drama, religious affiliation, state residency. **Additional information:** $500 grant available to students to help offset travel costs.

**Application procedures. Admission:** Priority date 12/1; no deadline. No application fee. Admission notification on a rolling basis beginning on or about 9/1. Must reply by May 1 or within 2 week(s) if notified thereafter. **Financial aid:** Priority date 3/15; no closing date. FAFSA required. Applicants notified on a rolling basis starting 3/1; must reply by 5/1 or within 4 week(s) of notification.

**Academics. Special study options:** Double major, exchange student, independent study, internships, student-designed major, study abroad, teacher certification program. 3-2 cooperative degree programs in engineering with Michigan Technological University and Washington University. Member of the Ecoleague exchange consortium with Alaska Pacific University, Green Mountain College, Prescott College, and College of the Atlantic. **Credit/placement by examination:** AP, CLEP, IB, SAT, ACT, institutional tests. 30 credit hours maximum toward bachelor's degree. **Support services:** Remedial instruction, tutoring.

**Majors. Area/ethnic studies:** Native American. **Biology:** General. **Business:** Business admin. **Conservation:** General, environmental studies. **Education:** Mathematics, multi-level teacher, science, social studies. **Engineering:** General. **Liberal arts:** Humanities. **Math:** General. **Public administration:** Community org/advocacy. **Social sciences:** Sociology. **Visual/performing arts:** Art. **Other:** Environmental geosciences, Humanity and nature studies, Multi/Interdisciplinary studies, Outdoor education, Outdoor Eeucation, Writing.

**Most popular majors.** Biology 9%, business/marketing 6%, education 19%, English 9%, health sciences 9%, natural resources/environmental science 6%, philosophy/religious studies 6%, physical sciences 9%, psychology 6%, visual/performing arts 6%.

**Computing on campus.** 125 workstations in dormitories, library, computer center, student center. Dormitories wired for high-speed internet access and linked to campus network. Commuter students can connect to campus network. Online course registration, online library, repair service, wireless network available.

**Student life. Freshman orientation:** Mandatory. Preregistration for classes offered. Outdoor orientation or North County orientation available. **Policies:** Training and certification available in ethical leadership and active citizenship. **Housing:** Guaranteed on-campus for freshmen. Coed dorms, single-sex dorms, special housing for disabled, apartments, cooperative housing, wellness housing available. $100 nonrefundable deposit, deadline 5/1. **Activities:** Bands, campus ministries, choral groups, dance, drama, international student organizations, literary magazine, music ensembles, radio station, student government, student newspaper, symphony orchestra, environmental institute, communications commission, volunteer program, environmental council, Native American student association, eco-visionary program, community bike shop, LGBT Alliance, community gardens.

**Athletics.** NCAA. **Intercollegiate:** Baseball M, basketball, cross-country, ice hockey M, soccer, softball W, volleyball W. **Intramural:** Archery, badminton, basketball, football (non-tackle), skiing W, soccer, softball, table tennis, volleyball. **Team name:** Lumberjacks, Lumberjills.

**Student services.** Adult student services, alcohol/substance abuse counseling, chaplain/spiritual director, career counseling, services for economically disadvantaged, student employment services, financial aid counseling, health services, minority student services, personal counseling, placement for graduates, women's services. **Physically disabled:** Services for visually, hearing impaired.

**Contact.** E-mail: admit@northland.edu
Phone: (715) 682-1224 Toll-free number: (800) 753-1840
Fax: (715) 682-1258
Ralph Stewart, Director of Admission, Northland College, 1411 Ellis Avenue, Ashland, WI 54806-3999

## Ripon College
### Ripon, Wisconsin                        CB member
### www.ripon.edu                           CB code: 1664

- Private 4-year liberal arts college
- Residential campus in small town

◆ 1,038 degree-seeking undergraduates: 1% part-time, 51% women, 1% African American, 1% Asian American, 3% Hispanic American, 1% Native American, 3% international

◆ 79% of applicants admitted

◆ SAT or ACT (ACT writing optional), application essay required

◆ 76% graduate within 6 years; 33% enter graduate study

**General.** Founded in 1851. Regionally accredited. **Degrees:** 192 bachelor's awarded. **ROTC:** Army. **Location:** 80 miles from Milwaukee, 80 miles from Madison. **Calendar:** Semester. **Full-time faculty:** 60 total; 90% have terminal degrees, 8% minority, 43% women. **Part-time faculty:** 32 total; 53% have terminal degrees, 34% women. **Class size:** 59% < 20, 37% 20-39, 2% 40-49, 2% 50-99. **Special facilities:** Woodland preservation area with outdoor classroom.

**Freshman class profile.** 1,064 applied, 845 admitted, 249 enrolled.

| Mid 50% test scores | | Rank in top tenth: | 28% |
|---|---|---|---|
| SAT critical reading: | 490-640 | End year in good standing: | 94% |
| SAT math: | 500-640 | Return as sophomores: | 83% |
| ACT composite: | 22-27 | Out-of-state: | 28% |
| GPA 3.75 or higher: | 27% | Live on campus: | 98% |
| GPA 3.50-3.74: | 22% | International: | 5% |
| GPA 3.0-3.49: | 33% | Fraternities: | 23% |
| GPA 2.0-2.99: | 18% | Sororities: | 12% |
| Rank in top quarter: | 61% | | |

**Basis for selection.** School achievement record, interview, class rank, test scores, recommendations, extracurricular or community activities important. **Homeschooled:** Transcript of courses and grades required.

**High school preparation.** College-preparatory program recommended. 17 units required. Required and recommended units include English 4, mathematics 2-4, social studies 2-4, science 2-4 and foreign language 2. Math must include 1 algebra and geometry. 7 units chosen from additional units in math, science, social science, foreign language.

**2009-2010 Annual costs.** Tuition/fees: $25,445. Room/board: $7,270. Books/supplies: $1,000. Personal expenses: $800.

**2009-2010 Financial aid. Need-based:** 228 full-time freshmen applied for aid; 202 were judged to have need; 202 of these received aid. Average need met was 92%. Average scholarship/grant was $19,198; average loan $4,002. 74% of total undergraduate aid awarded as scholarships/grants, 26% as loans/jobs. **Non-need-based:** Awarded to 891 full-time undergraduates, including 66 freshmen. Scholarships awarded for academics, alumni affiliation, art, leadership, minority status, music/drama, religious affiliation, ROTC, state residency.

**Application procedures. Admission:** Priority date 3/15; no deadline. $30 fee, may be waived for applicants with need. Admission notification on a rolling basis beginning on or about 9/15. Must reply by May 1 or within 2 week(s) if notified thereafter. **Financial aid:** Priority date 3/1; no closing date. FAFSA required. Applicants notified on a rolling basis starting 3/1; must reply within 2 week(s) of notification.

**Academics. Special study options:** Accelerated study, combined bachelor's/graduate degree, double major, exchange student, internships, student-designed major, study abroad, teacher certification program, urban semester, Washington semester. Domestic and international off-campus study programs. **Credit/placement by examination:** AP, CLEP, IB. Amount of credit and placement for AP exams subject to departmental approval. **Support services:** Learning center, study skills assistance, tutoring.

**Majors. Area/ethnic studies:** Latin American, women's. **Biology:** General, biochemistry. **Business:** Business admin. **Communications:** General. **Computer sciences:** Computer science. **Conservation:** Environmental studies. **Education:** General. **Foreign languages:** General, classics, French, German, Spanish. **Health:** Predental, premedicine, prenursing, prepharmacy, preveterinary. **History:** General. **Interdisciplinary:** Biopsychology, global studies. **Legal studies:** Prelaw. **Math:** General. **Parks/recreation:** Exercise sciences. **Philosophy/religion:** Philosophy, religion. **Physical sciences:** General, chemistry, physics. **Psychology:** General. **Social sciences:** Anthropology, economics, political science, sociology. **Visual/performing arts:** Art, art history/conservation, dramatic.

**Most popular majors.** Biology 6%, business/marketing 15%, education 7%, history 10%, psychology 11%, social sciences 16%, visual/performing arts 7%.

**Computing on campus.** 150 workstations in dormitories, library, computer center. Dormitories wired for high-speed internet access and linked to campus network. Commuter students can connect to campus network. Helpline, student web hosting available.

**Student life. Freshman orientation:** Mandatory, $45 fee. Preregistration for classes offered. 2-day overnight orientation held in late June for students and family. **Housing:** Guaranteed on-campus for all undergraduates. Coed dorms, single-sex dorms, fraternity/sorority housing, wellness housing available. $200 nonrefundable deposit, deadline 8/15. **Activities:** Bands, campus ministries, choral groups, dance, drama, film society, international student organizations, literary magazine, music ensembles, musical theater, radio station, student government, student newspaper, symphony orchestra, Christian Fellowship, Big Brother/Big Sister, multicultural club, romance language club, environmental group, Feminists for Equality, College Democrats, College Republicans.

**Athletics.** NCAA. **Intercollegiate:** Baseball M, basketball, cross-country, diving, football (tackle) M, golf, soccer, softball W, swimming, tennis, track and field, volleyball W. **Intramural:** Basketball, bowling, fencing, football (non-tackle), golf, racquetball, soccer, softball, table tennis, tennis, volleyball, water polo. **Team name:** Red Hawks.

**Student services.** Career counseling, student employment services, financial aid counseling, health services, personal counseling, placement for graduates.

**Contact.** E-mail: adminfo@ripon.edu
Phone: (920) 748-8114 Toll-free number: (800) 947-4766
Fax: (920) 748-8335
Leigh Mlodzik, Director of Admission, Ripon College, 300 Seward Street, Ripon, WI 54971-0248

## St. Norbert College
**De Pere, Wisconsin**  CB member
www.snc.edu  CB code: 1706

◆ Private 4-year liberal arts college affiliated with Roman Catholic Church

◆ Residential campus in large town

◆ 2,060 degree-seeking undergraduates: 2% part-time, 58% women, 1% African American, 1% Asian American, 1% Hispanic American, 1% Native American, 4% international

◆ 38 degree-seeking graduate students

◆ 83% of applicants admitted

◆ SAT or ACT (ACT writing optional) required

◆ 70% graduate within 6 years; 19% enter graduate study

**General.** Founded in 1898. Regionally accredited. **Degrees:** 424 bachelor's awarded; master's offered. **ROTC:** Army. **Location:** 5 miles from Green Bay. **Calendar:** Semester, limited summer session. **Full-time faculty:** 134 total; 87% have terminal degrees, 7% minority, 43% women. **Part-time faculty:** 48 total; 38% have terminal degrees, 2% minority, 40% women. **Class size:** 45% < 20, 54% 20-39, less than 1% 40-49, less than 1% 50-99. **Special facilities:** Marina, on-campus hotel and conference center, fine and performing arts centers, center for international education, peace and justice center, center for leadership and service, children's center, women's center, men's center, survey center, center for Norbertine studies.

**Freshman class profile.** 2,024 applied, 1,686 admitted, 545 enrolled.

| Mid 50% test scores | | Rank in top tenth: | 24% |
|---|---|---|---|
| ACT composite: | 21-26 | End year in good standing: | 86% |
| GPA 3.75 or higher: | 31% | Return as sophomores: | 81% |
| GPA 3.50-3.74: | 19% | Out-of-state: | 27% |
| GPA 3.0-3.49: | 31% | Live on campus: | 98% |
| GPA 2.0-2.99: | 19% | International: | 4% |
| Rank in top quarter: | 53% | | |

**Basis for selection.** High school record, rigor of courses, and grades earned important. Preference given to students successfully completing challenging courses. Counselor and teacher recommendations, community service considered. Students not in college preparatory programs may be offered admission if test results, class rank, and grades demonstrate aptitude for college work. Essay, interview recommended for all; audition recommended for music. **Learning Disabled:** Students should submit documentation of specific disability to receive proper level of support from institution.

**High school preparation.** College-preparatory program recommended. 16 units recommended. Recommended units include English 4, mathematics 3, social studies 2, history 2, science 3 (laboratory 3) and foreign language 2. As many college-prep elective units as possible.

**2009-2010 Annual costs.** Tuition/fees: $26,972. Room/board: $7,052. Books/supplies: $900. Personal expenses: $750.

**2008-2009 Financial aid. Need-based:** 449 full-time freshmen applied for aid; 366 were judged to have need; 366 of these received aid. Average need met was 98%. Average scholarship/grant was $18,460; average loan $3,440. 59% of total undergraduate aid awarded as scholarships/grants, 41% as loans/jobs. **Non-need-based:** Awarded to 657 full-time undergraduates, including 159 freshmen. Scholarships awarded for academics, art, leadership, minority status, music/drama, ROTC, state residency.

**Application procedures. Admission:** Priority date 4/1; no deadline. $25 fee, may be waived for applicants with need. Admission notification on a rolling basis beginning on or about 10/1. Must reply by May 1 or within 3 week(s) if notified thereafter. **Financial aid:** Priority date 3/1; no closing date. FAFSA required. Applicants notified on a rolling basis starting 3/15; must reply within 2 week(s) of notification.

**Academics.** Study abroad strongly supported, and students are allowed to apply all of their financial aid to their study abroad program costs; student/faculty collaborative research. **Special study options:** Distance learning, double major, ESL, honors, independent study, internships, student-designed major, study abroad, teacher certification program, Washington semester. Foundation for International Education (London) Internship. **Credit/placement by examination:** AP, CLEP, IB, institutional tests. **Support services:** Learning center, reduced course load, remedial instruction, study skills assistance, tutoring, writing center.

**Majors. Biology:** General, biochemistry. **Business:** General, accounting, business admin, finance, human resources, international, management information systems, marketing. **Communications:** General, media studies. **Computer sciences:** Computer graphics, computer science. **Conservation:** Environmental science. **Education:** Early childhood, elementary, music. **Foreign languages:** French, German, Spanish. **Health:** Predental, premedicine, prenursing, prepharmacy, preveterinary. **History:** General. **Interdisciplinary:** Biological/physical sciences. **Legal studies:** Prelaw. **Liberal arts:** Humanities. **Math:** General. **Philosophy/religion:** Philosophy, religion. **Physical sciences:** Chemistry, geology, physics. **Psychology:** General. **Social sciences:** Economics, international relations, political science, sociology. **Theology:** Religious ed. **Visual/performing arts:** Art, commercial/advertising art, dramatic, graphic design.

**Most popular majors.** Biology 6%, business/marketing 26%, communications/journalism 11%, education 16%, social sciences 11%.

**Computing on campus.** 271 workstations in dormitories, library, computer center, student center. Dormitories wired for high-speed internet access and linked to campus network. Commuter students can connect to campus network. Online course registration, online library, helpline, repair service, wireless network available.

**Student life. Freshman orientation:** Mandatory. Preregistration for classes offered. 2-day summer program for students and parents. **Housing:** Guaranteed on-campus for all undergraduates. Coed dorms, single-sex dorms, special housing for disabled, apartments, wellness housing available. $100 nonrefundable deposit, deadline 5/1. Townhouses and college-owned houses near campus available. **Activities:** Bands, campus ministries, choral groups, drama, film society, international student organizations, literary magazine, music ensembles, musical theater, radio station, student government, student newspaper, TV station, ballroom club, Beyond Borders, Campus Crusade for Christ, College Democrats and Republicans, environmental club, Graphos, Habitat for Humanity, pre-health science club, Rainbow Alliance, Students in Free Enterprise.

**Athletics.** NCAA. **Intercollegiate:** Baseball M, basketball, cross-country, football (tackle) M, golf, ice hockey, soccer, softball W, tennis, track and field, volleyball W. **Intramural:** Badminton, basketball, football (non-tackle), racquetball, volleyball. **Team name:** Green Knights.

**Student services.** Alcohol/substance abuse counseling, chaplain/spiritual director, career counseling, student employment services, financial aid counseling, health services, minority student services, on-campus daycare, personal counseling, placement for graduates, veterans' counselor, women's services. **Physically disabled:** Services for visually, speech, hearing impaired.

**Contact.** E-mail: admit@snc.edu
Phone: (920) 403-3005 Toll-free number: (800) 236-4878
Fax: (920) 403-4072
Bridget O'Connor, Enrollment Management and Communications, St. Norbert College, 100 Grant Street, De Pere, WI 54115-2099

---

## Sanford-Brown College: Milwaukee
**West Allis, Wisconsin**
**www.sbcmilwaukee.com**

▶ For-profit 4-year business and health science college
▶ Commuter campus in small city

---

**General.** Accredited by ACICS. **Calendar:** Continuous.

**Annual costs/financial aid.** Criminal Justice Associate and Bachelor degree $3750 per term (12 credits), Business Associate and Bachelor degree $3250 per term (12 credits), Medical Assistant Associate degree $3250 per term (12 credits), Medical Assistant diploma program $2750 per term (12 credits), Medical Coding and Billing diploma program $2750 per term (12 credits).

**Contact.** Phone: (414) 771-2200
6737 West Washington Street, Suite 2355, West Allis, WI 53214

---

## Silver Lake College
**Manitowoc, Wisconsin**
**www.sl.edu**                                    **CB code: 1300**

▶ Private 4-year business and liberal arts college affiliated with Roman Catholic Church
▶ Commuter campus in large town
▶ 339 degree-seeking undergraduates: 48% part-time, 72% women, 4% African American, 1% Asian American, 1% Hispanic American, 4% Native American, 1% international
▶ 100 degree-seeking graduate students
▶ 74% of applicants admitted
▶ SAT or ACT (ACT writing optional) required
▶ 48% graduate within 6 years

**General.** Founded in 1935. Regionally accredited. **Degrees:** 114 bachelor's awarded; master's offered. **Location:** 80 miles from Milwaukee, 30 miles from Green Bay. **Calendar:** Semester, extensive summer session. **Full-time faculty:** 41 total; 46% have terminal degrees. **Part-time faculty:** 5 total; 20% have terminal degrees. **Class size:** 98% < 20, 2% 20-39. **Special facilities:** Nature preserve.

**Freshman class profile.** 152 applied, 112 admitted, 30 enrolled.

| Mid 50% test scores | | | |
|---|---|---|---|
| ACT composite: | 16-23 | Rank in top quarter: | 17% |
| GPA 3.75 or higher: | 21% | Rank in top tenth: | 4% |
| GPA 3.50-3.74: | 3% | End year in good standing: | 73% |
| GPA 3.0-3.49: | 17% | Return as sophomores: | 61% |
| GPA 2.0-2.99: | 49% | Out-of-state: | 13% |

**Basis for selection.** Admission based on formula of GPA x ACT x 10. Those below 300 will be denied admission, 301-449 granted provisional admission, and 450 and above accepted. Audition required, interview recommended for music; portfolio, interview recommended for art. **Home-schooled:** Transcript of courses and grades required. **Learning Disabled:** IEP should be submitted to Director of Learning Resources.

**High school preparation.** 21 units required. Required and recommended units include English 4, mathematics 2, social studies 2, history 2, science 2 (laboratory 2), foreign language 1 and academic electives 8.

**2009-2010 Annual costs.** Tuition/fees: $20,540. Room/board: $8,300. Books/supplies: $1,050. Personal expenses: $1,200.

**2009-2010 Financial aid. Need-based:** 30 full-time freshmen applied for aid; 29 were judged to have need; 29 of these received aid. Average need met was 77%. Average scholarship/grant was $8,835; average loan $3,478. 50% of total undergraduate aid awarded as scholarships/grants, 50% as loans/jobs. **Non-need-based:** Awarded to 108 full-time undergraduates, including 28 freshmen. Scholarships awarded for academics, art, athletics, leadership, music/drama, religious affiliation, state residency.

**Application procedures. Admission:** Priority date 8/1; no deadline. $50 fee, may be waived for applicants with need. Admission notification on a rolling basis beginning on or about 9/1. **Financial aid:** Priority date 3/15; no closing date. FAFSA required. Applicants notified on a rolling basis starting 3/15.

**Academics. Special study options:** Accelerated study, combined bachelor's/graduate degree, distance learning, double major, dual enrollment of high school students, independent study, internships, liberal arts/career combination, student-designed major, teacher certification program. **Credit/placement by examination:** AP, CLEP, IB, SAT, ACT, institutional tests. 30 credit hours maximum toward associate degree, 60 toward bachelor's. **Support services:** Learning center, reduced course load, remedial instruction, study skills assistance, tutoring.

**Majors. Biology:** General. **Business:** Accounting, business admin, human resources. **Computer sciences:** Computer science, information systems. **Education:** Art, early childhood, elementary, learning disabled, mentally handicapped, music. **Health:** Nursing (RN). **History:** General. **Math:** General. **Psychology:** General. **Public administration:** General. **Theology:** Theology. **Visual/performing arts:** Art.

**Most popular majors.** Business/marketing 44%, education 21%, health sciences 7%, psychology 16%.

**Computing on campus.** 70 workstations in dormitories, library, computer center. Commuter students can connect to campus network. Online course registration, online library, wireless network available.

**Student life. Freshman orientation:** Mandatory. Preregistration for classes offered. **Housing:** Guaranteed on-campus for all undergraduates. Coed dorms, wellness housing available. $100 nonrefundable deposit, deadline 8/1. **Activities:** Jazz band, campus ministries, choral groups, dance, literary magazine, music ensembles, student government, student newspaper, psychology student organization, Music Educators National Conference, Society of Human Resource Management, Students of Wisconsin Early Childhood Association, Student Council for Exceptional Children, Student Wisconsin Education Association, Wisconsin Art Education Association/National Art Education Association, campus ministry.

**Athletics. USCAA. Intercollegiate:** Basketball, cross-country, golf. **Intramural:** Football (non-tackle), table tennis, volleyball. **Team name:** Lakers.

**Student services.** Adult student services, alcohol/substance abuse counseling, chaplain/spiritual director, career counseling, student employment services, financial aid counseling, health services, personal counseling, placement for graduates.

**Contact.** E-mail: admslc@silver.sl.edu
Phone: (920) 686-6175 Toll-free number: (800) 236-4752 ext. 175
Fax: (920) 686-6322
Perry White, Vice President of External Relations & Admissions, Silver Lake College, 2406 South Alverno Road, Manitowoc, WI 54220-9319

## University of Wisconsin-Eau Claire
Eau Claire, Wisconsin
www.uwec.edu                                          CB code: 1913

- Public 4-year university
- Residential campus in small city
- 10,384 degree-seeking undergraduates: 6% part-time, 59% women, 1% African American, 3% Asian American, 1% Hispanic American, 1% Native American, 1% international
- 484 degree-seeking graduate students
- 67% of applicants admitted
- SAT or ACT (ACT writing optional) required
- 65% graduate within 6 years; 10% enter graduate study

**General.** Founded in 1916. Regionally accredited. **Degrees:** 1,876 bachelor's, 7 associate awarded; master's offered. **ROTC:** Army. **Location:** 90 miles from Minneapolis-St. Paul. **Calendar:** Semester, extensive summer session. **Full-time faculty:** 410 total; 81% have terminal degrees, 11% minority, 46% women. **Part-time faculty:** 95 total; 30% have terminal degrees, 5% minority, 68% women. **Class size:** 25% < 20, 52% 20-39, 10% 40-49, 10% 50-99, 3% >100. **Special facilities:** Bird museum, human development center, planetarium, natural preserve, ropes course, material sciences center, clinical simulation skills Lab, 200 kev transmission electron microscope, x-ray photoelectron spectroscopy system, scanning tunneling microscope, scanning electron microscope with energy dispersive x-ray microanalysis, x-ray fluorescence spectrometer, x-ray diffractometer, high resolution inductively coupled plasma mass spectrometer.

**Freshman class profile.** 7,414 applied, 4,993 admitted, 2,013 enrolled.

| Mid 50% test scores | | | |
|---|---|---|---|
| SAT critical reading: | 520-640 | Rank in top tenth: | 29% |
| SAT math: | 520-670 | End year in good standing: | 88% |
| SAT writing: | 490-620 | Return as sophomores: | 84% |
| ACT composite: | 23-26 | Out-of-state: | 27% |
| Rank in top quarter: | 61% | Live on campus: | 91% |
| | | International: | 1% |

**Basis for selection.** Applicants must present required combination of rank and test scores. Special consideration to disadvantaged, veterans, and minority applicants. Applicants with rank in top 50% or 23 ACT given first priority. Some applicants not admitted to fall semester may be considered for the following spring semester. Wisconsin residents required to take ACT; non-residents may submit SAT. Audition required for music programs.

**High school preparation.** College-preparatory program required. 17 units required. Required units include English 4, mathematics 3, social studies 3, science 3, foreign language 2 and academic electives 2. 3 units English must be composition and/or literature. 1 social studies unit must be world or US history.

**2009-2010 Annual costs.** Tuition/fees: $6,633; $14,206 out-of-state. Minnesota reciprocity tuition: $239 per credit hour. Room/board: $5,630. Books/supplies: $460. Personal expenses: $1,800.

**2008-2009 Financial aid. Need-based:** 1,574 full-time freshmen applied for aid; 840 were judged to have need; 834 of these received aid. Average need met was 92%. Average scholarship/grant was $5,603; average loan $3,881. 37% of total undergraduate aid awarded as scholarships/grants, 63% as loans/jobs. **Non-need-based:** Awarded to 909 full-time undergraduates, including 353 freshmen. Scholarships awarded for academics, art, leadership, minority status, music/drama, state residency.

**Application procedures. Admission:** Priority date 12/1; no deadline. $44 fee, may be waived for applicants with need. Admission notification on a rolling basis beginning on or about 9/15. Closing and priority dates vary. **Financial aid:** Priority date 4/15; no closing date. FAFSA required. Applicants notified on a rolling basis starting 4/15.

**Academics.** Baccalaureate degree includes service-learning requirement, freshman seminars, capstone courses, internships in most majors, and opportunities for students to collaborate with faculty on research and scholarly projects. **Special study options:** Accelerated study, cooperative education, cross-registration, distance learning, double major, dual enrollment of high school students, ESL, exchange student, external degree, honors, independent study, internships, student-designed major, study abroad, teacher certification program. Program with University of Wisconsin-Stout in early childhood education. **Credit/placement by examination:** CLEP, IB, ACT, institutional tests. 15 credit hours maximum toward associate degree, 30 toward bachelor's. **Support services:** Learning center, pre-admission summer program, reduced course load, remedial instruction, study skills assistance, tutoring, writing center.

**Majors. Area/ethnic studies:** Latin American, Native American, women's. **Biology:** General, molecular. **Business:** Accounting, business admin, finance, information resources management, marketing. **Communications:** General, journalism, media studies. **Computer sciences:** General. **Education:** Elementary, science, social studies, special. **Foreign languages:** French, Germanic, Spanish. **Health:** Athletic training, communication disorders, community health, health care admin, nursing (RN). **History:** General. **Liberal arts:** Arts/sciences. **Math:** General. **Parks/recreation:** Exercise sciences. **Philosophy/religion:** Philosophy, religion. **Physical sciences:** Chemistry, geology, physics. **Protective services:** Criminal justice. **Psychology:** General. **Public administration:** Social work. **Social sciences:** Economics, geography, political science, sociology. **Visual/performing arts:** Art, dramatic. **Other:** Chemistry with business emphasis, Physics-math teacher education.

**Most popular majors.** Biology 6%, business/marketing 23%, communications/journalism 8%, education 8%, health sciences 11%, security/protective services 7%, social sciences 6%, visual/performing arts 6%.

**Computing on campus.** 1,150 workstations in dormitories, library, computer center, student center. Dormitories wired for high-speed internet access and linked to campus network. Commuter students can connect to campus network. Online course registration, online library, helpline, wireless network available.

**Student life. Freshman orientation:** Mandatory, $100 fee. Preregistration for classes offered. One-day session. **Housing:** Guaranteed on-campus for freshmen. Coed dorms, single-sex dorms, apartments available. $75 fully refundable deposit. **Activities:** Bands, campus ministries, choral groups, dance, drama, film society, international student organizations, literary magazine, music ensembles, Model UN, musical theater, opera, radio station, student government, student newspaper, symphony orchestra, TV station, College Republicans, College Democrats, Newman Student Association, ecumenical religious center student association, Alpha Phi Omega service fraternity, Mortar Board, Black student organization, Native American student organization, Hmong student association.

**Athletics. NCAA. Intercollegiate:** Basketball, cross-country, diving, football (tackle) M, golf, gymnastics W, ice hockey, soccer W, softball W, swimming, tennis, track and field, volleyball W, wrestling M. **Intramural:** Badminton, basketball, football (non-tackle), racquetball, soccer M, softball M, tennis, volleyball. **Team name:** Blugolds.

**Student services.** Adult student services, alcohol/substance abuse counseling, chaplain/spiritual director, career counseling, services for economically disadvantaged, student employment services, financial aid counseling, health services, legal services, minority student services, on-campus daycare, personal counseling, placement for graduates, veterans' counselor, women's services. **Physically disabled:** Services for visually, speech, hearing impaired.

**Contact.** E-mail: admissions@uwec.edu
Phone: (715) 836-5415 Fax: (715) 836-2409
Kristina Anderson, Executive Director, Enrollment Services & Admissions, University of Wisconsin-Eau Claire, 112 Schofield Hall, Eau Claire, WI 54701

## University of Wisconsin-Green Bay
**Green Bay, Wisconsin**                    **CB member**
**www.uwgb.edu**                             **CB code: 1859**

- Public 4-year university and liberal arts college
- Residential campus in small city
- 6,068 degree-seeking undergraduates: 18% part-time, 64% women, 1% African American, 3% Asian American, 1% Hispanic American, 2% Native American, 1% international
- 144 degree-seeking graduate students
- 70% of applicants admitted
- SAT or ACT (ACT writing optional) required
- 52% graduate within 6 years; 20% enter graduate study

**General.** Founded in 1965. Regionally accredited. **Degrees:** 971 bachelor's, 4 associate awarded; master's offered. **ROTC:** Army. **Location:** 80 miles from Milwaukee. **Calendar:** Semester, limited summer session. **Full-time faculty:** 189 total; 85% have terminal degrees, 15% minority, 46% women. **Part-time faculty:** 141 total; 21% have terminal degrees, 4% minority, 57% women. **Class size:** 26% < 20, 42% 20-39, 18% 40-49, 9% 50-99, 4% >100. **Special facilities:** Natural history museum, herbarium, 290-acre arboretum, performing arts center.

**Freshman class profile.** 3,563 applied, 2,487 admitted, 1,046 enrolled.

| Mid 50% test scores | | Return as sophomores: | 75% |
|---|---|---|---|
| ACT composite: | 20-24 | Out-of-state: | 5% |
| GPA 3.75 or higher: | 14% | Live on campus: | 74% |
| GPA 3.50-3.74: | 18% | International: | 1% |
| GPA 3.0-3.49: | 40% | Fraternities: | 1% |
| GPA 2.0-2.99: | 28% | Sororities: | 1% |
| End year in good standing: | 80% | | |

**Basis for selection.** 17 ACT, 2.25 GPA and extracurricular or community involvement important. Priority given to students with 23 ACT or 3.25 GPA. Students not meeting standard admission requirements may be considered on individual basis. ACT reports should be supplied prior to receiving admission. Interview may be requested of borderline applicants; audition required for music. **Homeschooled:** Transcript of courses and grades required.

**High school preparation.** College-preparatory program required. 17 units required; 19 recommended. Required and recommended units include English 4, mathematics 3, social studies 3, science 3 (laboratory 1), foreign language 2 and academic electives 4. Math must include algebra or more advanced course. 2 of the 4 required academic electives must be from English, math, science, social studies, or foreign language.

**2009-2010 Annual costs.** Tuition/fees: $6,814; $14,387 out-of-state. Minnesota reciprocity tuition: $239 per-credit-hour. Room/board: $5,300. Books/supplies: $800. Personal expenses: $1,960.

**2009-2010 Financial aid. Need-based:** 917 full-time freshmen applied for aid; 672 were judged to have need; 642 of these received aid. Average need met was 85%. Average scholarship/grant was $6,046; average loan $4,302. 45% of total undergraduate aid awarded as scholarships/grants, 55% as loans/jobs. **Non-need-based:** Awarded to 1,264 full-time undergraduates, including 287 freshmen. Scholarships awarded for academics, art, athletics, leadership, minority status, music/drama. **Additional information:** Auditions required for music and theater scholarships. Tuition is waived for children of Wisconsin soldiers and policemen who were slain in the line of duty. Tuition is also waived for all veterans.

**Application procedures. Admission:** Priority date 4/15; no deadline. $44 fee, may be waived for applicants with need. Admission notification on a rolling basis beginning on or about 9/15. **Financial aid:** Priority date 4/1; no closing date. FAFSA required. Applicants notified on a rolling basis starting 1/1; must reply within 3 week(s) of notification.

**Academics.** Teacher certification available in conjunction with bachelor's degree. **Special study options:** Combined bachelor's/graduate degree, distance learning, double major, dual enrollment of high school students, exchange student, external degree, independent study, internships, liberal arts/career combination, student-designed major, study abroad, teacher certification program. **Credit/placement by examination:** AP, CLEP, IB, ACT, institutional tests. 47 credit hours maximum toward associate degree, 93 toward

bachelor's. **Support services:** Pre-admission summer program, reduced course load, remedial instruction, study skills assistance, tutoring, writing center.

**Majors. Area/ethnic studies:** Native American, women's. **Biology:** General. **Business:** Accounting, business admin. **Communications:** General. **Computer sciences:** Computer science, information systems. **Conservation:** Environmental science, environmental studies. **Education:** Elementary. **Foreign languages:** French, German, Spanish. **Health:** Nursing (RN). **History:** General. **Interdisciplinary:** Biological/physical sciences. **Liberal arts:** Arts/sciences, humanities. **Math:** General. **Philosophy/religion:** Philosophy. **Physical sciences:** Chemistry, physics. **Psychology:** General. **Public administration:** General, social work. **Social sciences:** Economics, political science, sociology, urban studies. **Visual/performing arts:** General, art, dramatic.

**Most popular majors.** Biology 10%, business/marketing 17%, communications/journalism 6%, education 6%, psychology 17%, social sciences 6%, visual/performing arts 7%.

**Computing on campus.** 600 workstations in dormitories, library, computer center, student center. Dormitories wired for high-speed internet access and linked to campus network. Commuter students can connect to campus network. Online course registration, online library, helpline, repair service, wireless network available.

**Student life. Freshman orientation:** Available, $200 fee. Preregistration for classes offered. Held the week before fall classes begin. **Housing:** Coed dorms, apartments, wellness housing available. $225 fully refundable deposit. Suite-style apartments with private bathrooms. **Activities:** Bands, choral groups, dance, drama, film society, international student organizations, literary magazine, music ensembles, Model UN, musical theater, radio station, student government, student newspaper, TV station, College Republicans, College Democrats, Habitat for Humanity, Circle K, Ten Percent Society, Athletes in Action, American Marketing Association, psychology and human development club, student government association, Wisconsin Education Assocation Council.

**Athletics.** NCAA. **Intercollegiate:** Basketball, cheerleading, cross-country, diving, golf, skiing, soccer, softball W, swimming, tennis, volleyball W. **Intramural:** Basketball, football (non-tackle), golf, racquetball, soccer, softball, tennis, volleyball. **Team name:** Phoenix.

**Student services.** Adult student services, alcohol/substance abuse counseling, career counseling, student employment services, financial aid counseling, health services, minority student services, personal counseling, placement for graduates, veterans' counselor. **Physically disabled:** Services for visually, hearing impaired.

**Contact.** E-mail: admissions@uwgb.edu
Phone: (920) 465-2111 Fax: (920) 465-5754
Pam Harvey-Jacobs, Director of Admissions, University of Wisconsin-Green Bay, 2420 Nicolet Drive, Green Bay, WI 54311-7001

## University of Wisconsin-La Crosse
**La Crosse, Wisconsin**                    **CB member**
**www.uwlax.edu**                            **CB code: 1914**

- Public 4-year university
- Residential campus in small city
- 8,493 degree-seeking undergraduates: 4% part-time, 58% women, 1% African American, 3% Asian American, 2% Hispanic American, 2% international
- 1,016 degree-seeking graduate students
- 69% of applicants admitted
- SAT or ACT (ACT writing optional) required
- 70% graduate within 6 years

**General.** Founded in 1909. Regionally accredited. **Degrees:** 1,626 bachelor's, 2 associate awarded; master's, doctoral offered. **ROTC:** Army. **Location:** 140 miles from Madison, 160 miles from Minneapolis-St. Paul. **Calendar:** Semester, limited summer session. **Full-time faculty:** 376 total; 75% have terminal degrees, 15% minority, 43% women. **Part-time faculty:** 153 total; 19% have terminal degrees, 6% minority, 58% women. **Class size:** 42% < 20, 45% 20-39, 5% 40-49, 6% 50-99, less than 1% >100. **Special facilities:** Greenhouse, planetarium, nuclear radiation laboratory, river studies center, archaeology center.

**Freshman class profile.** 6,504 applied, 4,492 admitted, 1,778 enrolled.

| Mid 50% test scores | | | |
|---|---|---|---|
| ACT composite: | 23-27 | Out-of-state: | 17% |
| Rank in top quarter: | 79% | Live on campus: | 94% |
| Rank in top tenth: | 30% | International: | 3% |
| End year in good standing: | 77% | Fraternities: | 1% |
| Return as sophomores: | 86% | Sororities: | 1% |

**Basis for selection.** Applicants should rank in top 25% of class with 23 ACT (or rank in top 30% with 26 ACT), and complete rigorous college prep curriculum. Optional interviews may be considered. Auditions may be required for some scholarships. Portfolios and essays may be included with application and will be considered. **Homeschooled:** Interview may be required. **Learning Disabled:** Information regarding learning disability may be considered in admission decision.

**High school preparation.** College-preparatory program required. 17 units required; 23 recommended. Required and recommended units include English 4, mathematics 3-4, social studies 3-4, science 3-4 (laboratory 2-3), foreign language 3 and academic electives 4.

**2009-2010 Annual costs.** Tuition/fees: $7,509; $15,082 out-of-state. Minnesota reciprocity tuition: $268 per-credit-hour. Room/board: $5,630. Books/supplies: $300. Personal expenses: $2,000.

**2008-2009 Financial aid.** **Need-based:** 1,331 full-time freshmen applied for aid; 736 were judged to have need; 695 of these received aid. Average need met was 76%. Average scholarship/grant was $5,784; average loan $3,048. 41% of total undergraduate aid awarded as scholarships/grants, 59% as loans/jobs. **Non-need-based:** Awarded to 425 full-time undergraduates, including 139 freshmen. Scholarships awarded for academics, art, athletics, leadership, music/drama.

**Application procedures.** **Admission:** Priority date 2/1; no deadline. $44 fee, may be waived for applicants with need. Admission notification on a rolling basis beginning on or about 9/15. **Financial aid:** Priority date 3/15; no closing date. FAFSA required. Applicants notified on a rolling basis starting 4/1.

**Academics.** **Special study options:** Cooperative education, cross-registration, distance learning, double major, dual enrollment of high school students, ESL, honors, independent study, internships, liberal arts/career combination, study abroad, teacher certification program. **Credit/placement by examination:** AP, CLEP, IB, SAT, ACT, institutional tests. 16 credit hours maximum toward associate degree, 32 toward bachelor's. **Support services:** Learning center, pre-admission summer program, reduced course load, remedial instruction, study skills assistance, tutoring, writing center.

**Majors.** **Biology:** General, biochemistry, microbiology. **Business:** Accounting, business admin, finance, international, management information systems, marketing. **Communications:** General. **Computer sciences:** General. **Education:** Elementary, health, science, social studies. **Foreign languages:** French, German, Spanish. **Health:** Athletic training, clinical lab science, community health, nuclear medical technology, physician assistant, recreational therapy. **History:** General. **Math:** General. **Parks/recreation:** Exercise sciences, facilities management. **Philosophy/religion:** Philosophy. **Physical sciences:** Chemistry, physics. **Psychology:** General. **Social sciences:** Archaeology, economics, geography, political science, sociology. **Visual/performing arts:** Art, dramatic.

**Most popular majors.** Biology 11%, business/marketing 23%, communications/journalism 6%, education 15%, health sciences 8%, psychology 8%, social sciences 10%.

**Computing on campus.** 600 workstations in dormitories, library, computer center, student center. Dormitories wired for high-speed internet access and linked to campus network. Commuter students can connect to campus network. Online course registration, online library, helpline, wireless network available.

**Student life.** **Freshman orientation:** Available, $60 fee. Preregistration for classes offered. Held week prior to classes. **Housing:** Coed dorms, wellness housing available. $75 fully refundable deposit, deadline 5/1. First Year Experience housing available. **Activities:** Bands, choral groups, drama, international student organizations, music ensembles, radio station, student government, student newspaper, symphony orchestra, Black Students Unity, Native American Council, Hispanic student organization, Asian association, Amnesty International, Newman Club, hall councils, Intervarsity Christian Fellowship, Campus Crusade.

**Athletics.** NAIA, NCAA. **Intercollegiate:** Baseball M, basketball, cross-country, diving, football (tackle) M, gymnastics W, soccer W, softball W, swimming, tennis, track and field, volleyball W, wrestling M. **Intramural:** Badminton, basketball, football (non-tackle), golf M, racquetball, soccer, softball, tennis, volleyball. **Team name:** Eagles.

**Student services.** Adult student services, alcohol/substance abuse counseling, chaplain/spiritual director, career counseling, services for economically disadvantaged, student employment services, financial aid counseling, health services, legal services, minority student services, on-campus daycare, personal counseling, placement for graduates, veterans' counselor, women's services. **Physically disabled:** Services for visually, speech, hearing impaired.

**Contact.** E-mail: admissions@uwlax.edu
Phone: (608) 785-8939 Fax: (608) 785-8940
Kathryn Kiefer, Associate Director of Admissions, University of Wisconsin-La Crosse, 1725 State Street, Cleary Center, La Crosse, WI 54601

---

## University of Wisconsin-Madison
**Madison, Wisconsin**   CB member
**www.wisc.edu**   CB code: 1846

- Public 4-year university
- Residential campus in small city
- 28,690 degree-seeking undergraduates: 4% part-time, 52% women, 3% African American, 6% Asian American, 4% Hispanic American, 1% Native American, 5% international
- 11,756 degree-seeking graduate students
- 57% of applicants admitted
- SAT or ACT with writing, application essay required
- 82% graduate within 6 years

**General.** Founded in 1849. Regionally accredited. **Degrees:** 6,637 bachelor's awarded; master's, doctoral, professional offered. **ROTC:** Army, Naval, Air Force. **Location:** 90 miles from Milwaukee, 150 miles from Chicago. **Calendar:** Semester, extensive summer session. **Full-time faculty:** 2,397 total; 91% have terminal degrees, 16% minority, 36% women. **Part-time faculty:** 441 total; 68% have terminal degrees, 10% minority, 48% women. **Class size:** 44% < 20, 32% 20-39, 6% 40-49, 9% 50-99, 10% >100. **Special facilities:** Teaching nuclear reactor, observatory, botanical gardens, arboretum, museums.

**Freshman class profile.** 24,855 applied, 14,228 admitted, 5,680 enrolled.

| Mid 50% test scores | | | |
|---|---|---|---|
| SAT critical reading: | 550-670 | Rank in top quarter: | 91% |
| SAT math: | 620-720 | Rank in top tenth: | 57% |
| SAT writing: | 570-670 | Return as sophomores: | 94% |
| ACT composite: | 26-30 | Out-of-state: | 36% |
| GPA 3.75 or higher: | 55% | Live on campus: | 88% |
| GPA 3.50-3.74: | 22% | International: | 5% |
| GPA 3.0-3.49: | 19% | Fraternities: | 9% |
| GPA 2.0-2.99: | 4% | Sororities: | 8% |

**Basis for selection.** Secondary school record including level of challenge relative to high school offerings, evidence of either increasing or consistent level of academic challenge and performance, course grades, class rank, ACT or SAT test scores important. Application statement/essay, recommendations, extracurricular activities and personal characteristics also considered. Audition required for music; portfolio recommended for fine arts.

**High school preparation.** College-preparatory program required. 17 units required; 20 recommended. Required and recommended units include English 4, mathematics 3-4, social studies 3-4, science 3-4, foreign language 2-4 and academic electives 2. Math units must include 1 each algebra and geometry, plus 1 year advanced math. Computer science or statistics will not fulfill math requirement. Applicants strongly advised to present academic credentials well in excess of minimum units.

**2009-2010 Annual costs.** Tuition/fees: $8,310; $23,059 out-of-state. Minnesota reciprocity tuition: $380 per-credit-hour. Room/board: $8,040. Books/supplies: $1,040. Personal expenses: $2,310.

**2008-2009 Financial aid.** **Need-based:** 3,577 full-time freshmen applied for aid; 1,861 were judged to have need; 1,840 of these received aid. Average need met was 77%. Average scholarship/grant was $3,840; average loan $4,117. 40% of total undergraduate aid awarded as scholarships/grants, 60% as loans/jobs. **Non-need-based:** Awarded to 7,892 full-time undergraduates, including 2,473 freshmen. Scholarships awarded for academics, alumni affiliation, art, athletics, job skills, leadership, minority status, music/drama, religious affiliation, ROTC, state residency.

**Application procedures.** **Admission:** Closing date 2/1 (postmark date). $44 fee, may be waived for applicants with need. Admission notification on a rolling basis beginning on or about 10/1. Must reply by May 1 or within 3 week(s) if notified thereafter. **Financial aid:** No deadline. FAFSA, institutional form required. Applicants notified on a rolling basis starting 4/1; must reply within 9 week(s) of notification.

**Academics. Special study options:** Accelerated study, combined bachelor's/graduate degree, cooperative education, distance learning, double major, dual enrollment of high school students, ESL, honors, independent study, internships, liberal arts/career combination, student-designed major, study abroad, teacher certification program. **Credit/placement by examination:** AP, CLEP, IB, institutional tests. **Support services:** Learning center, pre-admission summer program, reduced course load, remedial instruction, study skills assistance, tutoring, writing center.

**Majors. Agriculture:** Agronomy, animal sciences, business, communications, dairy, economics, food science, horticultural science, poultry, soil science. **Area/ethnic studies:** African-American, Asian, Latin American, Scandinavian, South Asian, women's. **Biology:** General, bacteriology, biochemistry, botany, conservation, entomology, genetics, microbiology, molecular, pharmacology/toxicology, plant pathology, zoology. **Business:** General, accounting, actuarial science, business admin, finance, insurance, international, management information systems, marketing, operations, real estate. **Communications:** General, journalism. **Computer sciences:** General. **Conservation:** Forest sciences, wildlife. **Education:** Agricultural, art, elementary, family/consumer sciences, music, social studies, special. **Engineering:** Agricultural, biomedical, chemical, civil, computer, electrical, geological, industrial, marine, materials, mechanical, mechanics, nuclear, physics. **Family/consumer sciences:** General, clothing/textiles, communication, consumer economics, family studies, merchandising. **Foreign languages:** Ancient Greek, Chinese, classics, comparative lit, French, Germanic, Hebrew, Italian, Japanese, Latin, linguistics, Polish, Portuguese, Romance, Russian, Spanish. **Health:** Audiology/speech pathology, clinical lab science, communication disorders, nursing (RN), physician assistant, vocational rehab counseling. **History:** General, science/technology. **Interdisciplinary:** Behavioral sciences, global studies. **Legal studies:** General. **Math:** General, applied, statistics. **Parks/recreation:** Exercise sciences, facilities management. **Philosophy/religion:** Philosophy, religion. **Physical sciences:** Astronomy, astrophysics, atmospheric science, chemistry, geology, geophysics, physics, planetary. **Protective services:** Criminal justice. **Psychology:** General. **Public administration:** Social work. **Social sciences:** Anthropology, cartography, economics, geography, political science, sociology. **Visual/performing arts:** Art, art history/conservation, ceramics, cinematography, commercial/advertising art, conducting, dance, design, dramatic, fashion design, fiber arts, film/cinema, interior design, jazz, metal/jewelry, music history, music performance, music theory/composition, painting, piano/organ, printmaking, sculpture, theater design, voice/opera.

**Most popular majors.** Biology 13%, business/marketing 10%, communications/journalism 6%, engineering/engineering technologies 9%, social sciences 14%.

**Computing on campus.** 3,350 workstations in dormitories, library, computer center, student center. Dormitories wired for high-speed internet access and linked to campus network. Commuter students can connect to campus network. Online course registration, online library, helpline, repair service, student web hosting, wireless network available.

**Student life. Freshman orientation:** Mandatory, $150 fee. Preregistration for classes offered. Held in the summer. **Housing:** Coed dorms, single-sex dorms, apartments, cooperative housing, fraternity/sorority housing, wellness housing available. $250 partly refundable deposit. Residential learning communities available. **Activities:** Bands, choral groups, dance, drama, film society, international student organizations, literary magazine, music ensembles, musical theater, opera, radio station, student government, student newspaper, symphony orchestra, TV station.

**Athletics.** NCAA. **Intercollegiate:** Basketball, cheerleading, cross-country, football (tackle) M, golf, ice hockey, rowing (crew), soccer, softball W, swimming, tennis, track and field, volleyball W, wrestling M. **Team name:** Badgers.

**Student services.** Adult student services, alcohol/substance abuse counseling, career counseling, services for economically disadvantaged, student employment services, financial aid counseling, health services, minority student services, personal counseling, placement for graduates, veterans' counselor, women's services. **Physically disabled:** Services for visually, speech, hearing impaired.

**Contact.** E-mail: onwisconsin@admissions.wisc.edu
Phone: (608) 262-3961 Fax: (608) 262-7706
Tom Reason, Director of Admissions, University of Wisconsin-Madison, Armory & Gymnasium, Madison, WI 53706-1481

## University of Wisconsin-Milwaukee

**Milwaukee, Wisconsin**      **CB member**
**www.uwm.edu**      **CB code: 1473**

- Public 4-year university
- Commuter campus in very large city

- 23,553 degree-seeking undergraduates: 12% part-time, 50% women
- 4,772 degree-seeking graduate students
- 77% of applicants admitted
- SAT or ACT (ACT writing optional) required

**General.** Founded in 1956. Regionally accredited. **Degrees:** 3,617 bachelor's awarded; master's, doctoral, professional offered. **ROTC:** Army, Air Force. **Location:** 90 miles from Chicago. **Calendar:** Semester, extensive summer session. **Full-time faculty:** 1,050 total; 24% minority, 45% women. **Part-time faculty:** 557 total; 16% minority, 56% women. **Class size:** 35% < 20, 43% 20-39, 6% 40-49, 9% 50-99, 8% >100. **Special facilities:** Planetarium, geological museum, American Geological Society Collection.

**Freshman class profile.** 11,469 applied, 8,841 admitted, 4,100 enrolled.

| Mid 50% test scores | | | |
|---|---|---|---|
| SAT critical reading: | 470-600 | GPA 3.0-3.49: | 35% |
| SAT math: | 490-620 | GPA 2.0-2.99: | 43% |
| SAT writing: | 450-590 | Rank in top quarter: | 26% |
| ACT composite: | 19-24 | Rank in top tenth: | 7% |
| GPA 3.75 or higher: | 8% | Return as sophomores: | 73% |
| GPA 3.50-3.74: | 13% | Out-of-state: | 3% |
| | | Live on campus: | 60% |

**Basis for selection.** Academic record and class rank in top half important. If applicant ranks in lower half of class, 21 ACT required. Additional requirements for architecture. Students who do not meet standard admission requirements may apply through Academic Opportunity Program Office. Some applicants must take placement tests in chemistry and/or foreign language. Audition required for dance, music, theater.

**High school preparation.** College-preparatory program required. 17 units required; 20 recommended. Required and recommended units include English 4, mathematics 3-4, social studies 3, science 3 (laboratory 1), foreign language 2 and academic electives 2. Math includes algebra, geometry, and beyond.

**2009-2010 Annual costs.** Tuition/fees: $7,702; $17,431 out-of-state. Minnesota reciprocity tuition: $368 per credit hour. Room/board: $7,890. Books/supplies: $950. Personal expenses: $1,600.

**2009-2010 Financial aid. Need-based:** 3,346 full-time freshmen applied for aid; 2,649 were judged to have need; 2,516 of these received aid. Average need met was 48%. Average scholarship/grant was $7,270; average loan $3,605. 48% of total undergraduate aid awarded as scholarships/grants, 52% as loans/jobs. **Non-need-based:** Awarded to 1,351 full-time undergraduates, including 436 freshmen. Scholarships awarded for academics, art, athletics.

**Application procedures. Admission:** Closing date 7/1. $44 fee, may be waived for applicants with need. Admission notification on a rolling basis beginning on or about 9/15. **Financial aid:** Priority date 3/1; no closing date. FAFSA required. Applicants notified on a rolling basis starting 3/1; must reply within 2 week(s) of notification.

**Academics. Special study options:** Accelerated study, cooperative education, cross-registration, distance learning, double major, dual enrollment of high school students, ESL, external degree, honors, independent study, internships, liberal arts/career combination, student-designed major, study abroad, teacher certification program, United Nations semester, Washington semester. **Credit/placement by examination:** AP, CLEP, institutional tests. **Support services:** Learning center, pre-admission summer program, reduced course load, remedial instruction, tutoring, writing center.

**Majors. Architecture:** Architecture. **Area/ethnic studies:** African-American, women's. **Biology:** General, biochemistry, conservation, microbiology. **Business:** Accounting, actuarial science, finance, human resources, management information systems, marketing, operations, real estate, training/development. **Communications:** General, journalism, media studies. **Computer sciences:** General, computer science. **Conservation:** Environmental science. **Education:** General, art, music. **Engineering:** Civil, computer, electrical, manufacturing, materials, mechanical. **Foreign languages:** Classics, comparative lit, French, German, Hebrew, Italian, linguistics, Russian, Spanish. **Health:** Clinical lab science, communication disorders, facilities admin, nursing (RN), predental, premedicine, prepharmacy, preveterinary, recreational therapy. **History:** General. **Interdisciplinary:** Global studies. **Legal studies:** Prelaw. **Math:** General, applied. **Parks/recreation:** General, exercise sciences. **Philosophy/religion:** Judaic, philosophy, religion. **Physical sciences:** Atmospheric physics, chemistry, geology, physics. **Protective services:** Criminal justice. **Psychology:** General. **Public administration:** Social work. **Social sciences:** General, anthropology, economics, geography, political science, sociology, urban studies. **Visual/performing arts:** Art, art history/conservation, dance, dramatic, film/cinema, multimedia.

**Most popular majors.** Business/marketing 26%, communications/journalism 7%, education 9%, health sciences 9%, social sciences 7%, visual/performing arts 8%.

**Computing on campus.** 1,255 workstations in dormitories, library, computer center, student center. Dormitories wired for high-speed internet access and linked to campus network. Commuter students can connect to campus network. Online course registration, online library, helpline, repair service, student web hosting, wireless network available.

**Student life. Housing:** Coed dorms, special housing for disabled, apartments available. $300 partly refundable deposit. **Activities:** Bands, choral groups, dance, drama, film society, literary magazine, music ensembles, musical theater, radio station, student government, student newspaper, symphony orchestra.

**Athletics.** NCAA. **Intercollegiate:** Baseball M, basketball, cross-country, diving, soccer, swimming, tennis, track and field, volleyball. **Intramural:** Badminton, baseball M, basketball, bowling, diving, fencing, football (tackle) M, golf, handball, racquetball, rugby, sailing, skiing, soccer, softball, swimming, tennis, volleyball, water polo, wrestling M. **Team name:** Panthers.

**Student services.** Adult student services, career counseling, student employment services, health services, on-campus daycare, personal counseling, placement for graduates, veterans' counselor. **Physically disabled:** Services for visually, speech, hearing impaired.

**Contact.** E-mail: uwmlook@uwm.edu
Phone: (414) 229-2222 Fax: (414) 229-6940
Beth Weckmueller, Executive Director of Enrollment Services and Registrar, University of Wisconsin-Milwaukee, Box 749, Milwaukee, WI 53201

## University of Wisconsin-Oshkosh
**Oshkosh, Wisconsin**  CB member
**www.uwosh.edu**  CB code: 1916

- Public 4-year university
- Residential campus in small city
- 10,425 degree-seeking undergraduates: 12% part-time, 58% women, 2% African American, 3% Asian American, 2% Hispanic American, 1% Native American, 1% international
- 1,021 degree-seeking graduate students
- 85% of applicants admitted
- ACT (writing optional) required
- 52% graduate within 6 years

**General.** Founded in 1871. Regionally accredited. **Degrees:** 1,837 bachelor's awarded; master's offered. **ROTC:** Army. **Location:** 90 miles from Milwaukee. **Calendar:** Semester, limited summer session. **Full-time faculty:** 386 total; 81% have terminal degrees, 10% minority, 45% women. **Part-time faculty:** 213 total; 24% have terminal degrees, 5% minority, 63% women. **Class size:** 35% < 20, 53% 20-39, 3% 40-49, 6% 50-99, 3% >100. **Special facilities:** Planetarium.

**Freshman class profile.** 4,901 applied, 4,172 admitted, 1,897 enrolled.

| Mid 50% test scores | | Rank in top tenth: | 10% |
|---|---|---|---|
| ACT composite: | 20-24 | End year in good standing: | 85% |
| GPA 3.75 or higher: | 13% | Return as sophomores: | 75% |
| GPA 3.50-3.74: | 16% | Out-of-state: | 2% |
| GPA 3.0-3.49: | 45% | Live on campus: | 84% |
| GPA 2.0-2.99: | 26% | Fraternities: | 6% |
| Rank in top quarter: | 37% | Sororities: | 5% |

**Basis for selection.** Students must rank in top half of high school class or have 22 ACT if rank is in third quartile. Out-of-state applicants may submit SAT scores. Interview recommended for all; audition required for music.

**High school preparation.** College-preparatory program required. 17 units required. Required and recommended units include English 4, mathematics 3-4, social studies 3, science 3-4 (laboratory 3-4), foreign language 2 and academic electives 4. Social studies must include 1 history.

**2009-2010 Annual costs.** Tuition/fees: $6,349; $13,922 out-of-state. Minnesota reciprocity tuition: $239 per credit hour. Room/board: $5,864. Books/supplies: $500. Personal expenses: $1,000.

**2008-2009 Financial aid. Non-need-based:** Scholarships awarded for academics, alumni affiliation, art, leadership, minority status, music/drama, state residency.

**Application procedures. Admission:** No deadline. $44 fee, may be waived for applicants with need. Admission notification on a rolling basis. **Financial aid:** Priority date 3/15; no closing date. FAFSA required. Applicants notified on a rolling basis starting 4/15; must reply within 2 week(s) of notification.

**Academics. Special study options:** Accelerated study, cooperative education, cross-registration, distance learning, double major, dual enrollment of high school students, ESL, exchange student, honors, independent study, internships, liberal arts/career combination, student-designed major, study abroad, teacher certification program, weekend college. **Credit/placement by examination:** CLEP, IB, institutional tests. 32 credit hours maximum toward bachelor's degree. **Support services:** Learning center, preadmission summer program, reduced course load, study skills assistance, tutoring, writing center.

**Majors. Biology:** General, bacteriology. **Business:** Accounting, finance, human resources, management information systems, operations. **Communications:** General, broadcast journalism, journalism. **Computer sciences:** Computer science. **Education:** Elementary, emotionally handicapped, learning disabled, mentally handicapped, music, physical, science, secondary, social science, special. **Foreign languages:** French, German, Spanish. **Health:** Clinical lab technology, nursing (RN), predental, premedicine, prepharmacy, preveterinary. **History:** General. **Legal studies:** Prelaw. **Liberal arts:** Arts/sciences. **Math:** General. **Philosophy/religion:** Philosophy, religion. **Physical sciences:** Chemistry, geology, physics. **Psychology:** General. **Public administration:** Human services, social work. **Social sciences:** Anthropology, economics, geography, political science, sociology, urban studies. **Visual/performing arts:** Art, cinematography, dramatic, studio arts.

**Most popular majors.** Business/marketing 19%, communications/journalism 8%, education 17%, health sciences 12%, social sciences 8%.

**Computing on campus.** 475 workstations in dormitories, library, computer center, student center. Dormitories wired for high-speed internet access and linked to campus network. Commuter students can connect to campus network. Online course registration, helpline, wireless network available.

**Student life. Freshman orientation:** Available. Preregistration for classes offered. **Housing:** Guaranteed on-campus for freshmen. Coed dorms, single-sex dorms, fraternity/sorority housing, wellness housing available. $125 deposit, deadline 6/15. Select group of freshmen take part in residential college experience with more individualized instruction. **Activities:** Bands, campus ministries, choral groups, dance, drama, film society, literary magazine, music ensembles, Model UN, musical theater, opera, radio station, student government, student newspaper, symphony orchestra, TV station, black student union, Asian student association, American Indian student association, Hispanic Cultures United, InterVarsity Christian Fellowship, Athletes in Action, community involvement program, Habitat for Humanity.

**Athletics.** NCAA. **Intercollegiate:** Baseball M, basketball, cross-country, diving, football (tackle) M, golf W, gymnastics W, rifle, soccer, softball W, swimming, tennis, track and field, volleyball W, wrestling M. **Intramural:** Basketball, racquetball, skiing, soccer, softball, volleyball. **Team name:** Titans.

**Student services.** Adult student services, alcohol/substance abuse counseling, career counseling, services for economically disadvantaged, student employment services, financial aid counseling, health services, minority student services, on-campus daycare, personal counseling, placement for graduates, veterans' counselor, women's services. **Physically disabled:** Services for visually, speech, hearing impaired.

**Contact.** E-mail: oshadmuw@uwosh.edu
Phone: (920) 424-0202 Fax: (920) 424-1098
Jill Endries, Director of Admissions, University of Wisconsin-Oshkosh, 800 Algoma Boulevard, Oshkosh, WI 54901-8602

## University of Wisconsin-Parkside
**Kenosha, Wisconsin**  CB member
**www.uwp.edu**  CB code: 1860

- Public 4-year university
- Commuter campus in small city
- 4,826 degree-seeking undergraduates: 24% part-time, 55% women, 11% African American, 3% Asian American, 9% Hispanic American
- 120 degree-seeking graduate students
- 63% of applicants admitted

**General.** Founded in 1968. Regionally accredited. **Degrees:** 643 bachelor's awarded; master's offered. **ROTC:** Army. **Location:** 30 miles from Milwaukee, 60 miles from Chicago. **Calendar:** Semester, extensive summer session. **Full-time faculty:** 175 total; 78% have terminal degrees, 26% minority, 47% women. **Part-time faculty:** 106 total; 34% have terminal degrees, 10% minority, 46% women. **Class size:** 46% < 20, 39% 20-39, 7% 40-49, 8% 50-99, less than 1% >100. **Special facilities:** Communication arts building.

**Freshman class profile.** 2,287 applied, 1,452 admitted, 890 enrolled.

| Mid 50% test scores | | Return as sophomores: | 64% |
| --- | --- | --- | --- |
| ACT composite: | 18-23 | Out-of-state: | 8% |
| Rank in top quarter: | 29% | Live on campus: | 41% |
| Rank in top tenth: | 11% | International: | 1% |

**Basis for selection.** Rank in top half of class with specified distribution of high school units required for standard admission. Conditional admissions may be granted to applicants in top 65% of class or with 18 ACT. Test scores also used for placement in English and math courses. Audition required for theater, recommended for music; portfolio recommended for art.

**High school preparation.** College-preparatory program required. 17 units required; 20 recommended. Required and recommended units include English 4, mathematics 3-4, social studies 3-4, science 3-4 (laboratory 1-2), foreign language 2 and academic electives 4-7.

**2009-2010 Annual costs.** Tuition/fees: $6,348; $13,922 out-of-state. Minnesota Reciprocity tuition: $239 per credit hour. Room/board: $5,750. Books/supplies: $904. Personal expenses: $1,670.

**2008-2009 Financial aid.** **Need-based:** 663 full-time freshmen applied for aid; 523 were judged to have need; 500 of these received aid. Average scholarship/grant was $6,932. 55% of total undergraduate aid awarded as scholarships/grants, 45% as loans/jobs. **Non-need-based:** Awarded to 421 full-time undergraduates, including 106 freshmen. Scholarships awarded for academics, art, athletics, minority status, music/drama, state residency.

**Application procedures.** **Admission:** Priority date 3/1; deadline 8/1 (postmark date). $44 fee, may be waived for applicants with need. Admission notification on a rolling basis beginning on or about 9/15. **Financial aid:** Priority date 3/15; no closing date. FAFSA required. Applicants notified on a rolling basis starting 4/1; must reply within 2 week(s) of notification.

**Academics.** **Special study options:** Accelerated study, combined bachelor's/graduate degree, distance learning, double major, dual enrollment of high school students, exchange student, honors, independent study, internships, liberal arts/career combination, study abroad, teacher certification program, weekend college. Cooperative nursing program with University of Wisconsin-Milwaukee. **Credit/placement by examination:** AP, CLEP, IB, SAT, ACT, institutional tests. 30 credit hours maximum toward bachelor's degree. Retroactive credit policy for foreign language study. **Support services:** Learning center, reduced course load, remedial instruction, study skills assistance, tutoring, writing center.

**Majors.** **Area/ethnic studies:** French, German. **Biology:** General, molecular. **Business:** General, accounting, business admin, finance, human resources, management information systems. **Communications:** General. **Computer sciences:** Computer science. **Foreign languages:** French, German, Spanish. **Health:** Predental, premedicine, preveterinary. **History:** General. **Interdisciplinary:** Math/computer science. **Legal studies:** Prelaw. **Liberal arts:** Arts/sciences. **Math:** General. **Parks/recreation:** Sports admin. **Philosophy/religion:** Philosophy. **Physical sciences:** Chemistry, geology, physics. **Protective services:** Criminal justice. **Psychology:** General. **Social sciences:** Economics, geography, political science, sociology. **Visual/performing arts:** Art, dramatic.

**Most popular majors.** Biology 7%, business/marketing 22%, communications/journalism 7%, English 6%, parks/recreation 7%, psychology 7%, security/protective services 12%, social sciences 9%, visual/performing arts 8%.

**Computing on campus.** 225 workstations in dormitories, library, computer center, student center. Dormitories wired for high-speed internet access and linked to campus network. Commuter students can connect to campus network. Online course registration, online library, helpline, student web hosting, wireless network available.

**Student life.** **Freshman orientation:** Mandatory, $52 fee. Preregistration for classes offered. Day-long session offered several times throughout summer. **Housing:** Coed dorms, special housing for disabled, apartments, wellness housing available. $50 fully refundable deposit. **Activities:** Bands, choral groups, dance, drama, international student organizations, literary magazine, music ensembles, musical theater, radio station, student government, student newspaper, symphony orchestra, Campus Crusade for Christ, Intervarsity Christian Fellowship, ethnic organization, Amnesty International, black student union, activities board.

**Athletics.** NCAA. **Intercollegiate:** Baseball M, basketball, cross-country, golf M, soccer, softball W, track and field, volleyball W, wrestling M. **Intramural:** Basketball, racquetball, soccer, softball, table tennis, tennis, volleyball. **Team name:** Rangers.

**Student services.** Adult student services, alcohol/substance abuse counseling, career counseling, services for economically disadvantaged, student employment services, financial aid counseling, health services, minority student services, on-campus daycare, personal counseling, placement for graduates, veterans' counselor, women's services. **Physically disabled:** Services for visually, speech, hearing impaired.

**Contact.** E-mail: admissions@uwp.edu
Phone: (262) 595-2355 Fax: (262) 595-2008
DeAnn Possehl, Executive Director of Enrollment Management, University of Wisconsin-Parkside, PO Box 2000, Kenosha, WI 53141-2000

## University of Wisconsin-Platteville
**Platteville, Wisconsin**      **CB member**
**www.uwplatt.edu**      **CB code: 1917**

- Public 4-year university
- Residential campus in large town
- 6,770 degree-seeking undergraduates: 8% part-time, 36% women, 2% African American, 1% Asian American, 1% Hispanic American, 1% Native American
- 653 degree-seeking graduate students
- 80% of applicants admitted
- SAT or ACT (ACT writing optional) required

**General.** Founded in 1866. Regionally accredited. **Degrees:** 1,031 bachelor's, 2 associate awarded; master's offered. **ROTC:** Army. **Location:** 25 miles from Dubuque, IA; 75 miles from Madison. **Calendar:** Semester, limited summer session. **Full-time faculty:** 290 total. **Part-time faculty:** 85 total. **Class size:** 26% < 20, 57% 20-39, 12% 40-49, 3% 50-99, 2% >100. **Special facilities:** Pioneer farm, nature trail, disc golf course, campus micro-brewery.

**Freshman class profile.** 3,661 applied, 2,936 admitted, 1,895 enrolled.

| Mid 50% test scores | | Out-of-state: | 20% |
| --- | --- | --- | --- |
| ACT composite: | 20-25 | Live on campus: | 92% |
| Rank in top quarter: | 34% | Fraternities: | 3% |
| Rank in top tenth: | 9% | Sororities: | 3% |
| Return as sophomores: | 74% | | |

**Basis for selection.** School record, class rank, and test scores most important. Audition required for music scholarships. **Homeschooled:** Transcript of courses and grades required.

**High school preparation.** College-preparatory program required. 17 units required. Required units include English 4, mathematics 3, social studies 3, science 3 (laboratory 2) and academic electives 4. 3 units natural science (2 from biology, chemistry, or physics); 3 units algebra I, geometry, algebra II, or higher required.

**2009-2010 Annual costs.** Tuition/fees: $6,314; $13,887 out-of-state. Minnesota reciprocity tuition: $239 per credit hour. Tri-State Initiative offers Illinois and Iowa students discounted out-of-state rate for select majors. Room/board: $5,916. Books/supplies: $300. Personal expenses: $1,170.

**Financial aid.** All financial aid based on need.

**Application procedures.** **Admission:** Priority date 1/1; no deadline. $44 fee, may be waived for applicants with need. Admission notification on a rolling basis. **Financial aid:** Priority date 3/15; no closing date. FAFSA required. Applicants notified on a rolling basis starting 6/1; must reply within 2 week(s) of notification.

**Academics.** **Special study options:** Combined bachelor's/graduate degree, cooperative education, distance learning, double major, dual enrollment of high school students, ESL, exchange student, external degree, honors, independent study, internships, liberal arts/career combination, student-designed major, study abroad, teacher certification program. Physical activity, physical education, international education, ethnic and gender study. **Credit/placement by examination:** AP, CLEP, institutional tests. 30 credit hours maximum toward bachelor's degree. **Support services:** Learning center, study skills assistance, tutoring, writing center.

**Majors.** **Agriculture:** Agribusiness operations, agronomy, animal sciences, economics. **Biology:** General. **Business:** General, accounting, business admin, entrepreneurial studies, finance, human resources, investments/securities, organizational behavior. **Communications:** General. **Computer sciences:** Computer science. **Conservation:** General. **Construction:** Maintenance. **Education:** Agricultural, art, biology, chemistry, early childhood, elementary, English, German, history, mathematics, science, social science, social studies, Spanish, speech, technology/industrial arts, voc/tech. **Engineering:** Civil, electrical, mechanical, physics. **Foreign languages:** German, Spanish. **History:** General. **Math:** General. **Parks/recreation:** Health/fitness. **Philosophy/religion:** Philosophy. **Physical sciences:** Chemistry.

**Protective services:** Law enforcement admin. **Psychology:** General. **Social sciences:** General, economics, geography, political science, sociology. **Visual/performing arts:** Art, commercial/advertising art, dramatic. **Other:** Criminal Justice Forensic Investigations.

**Most popular majors.** Agriculture 7%, biology 6%, business/marketing 16%, education 9%, engineering/engineering technologies 30%, security/protective services 9%.

**Computing on campus.** 483 workstations in dormitories, library, computer center, student center. Dormitories wired for high-speed internet access and linked to campus network. Commuter students can connect to campus network. Online course registration, online library, helpline, repair service, student web hosting available.

**Student life. Freshman orientation:** Available. Preregistration for classes offered. **Housing:** Guaranteed on-campus for freshmen. Coed dorms, single-sex dorms, special housing for disabled, apartments available. $100 partly refundable deposit. **Activities:** Bands, campus ministries, choral groups, drama, international student organizations, literary magazine, music ensembles, musical theater, radio station, student government, student newspaper, symphony orchestra, TV station, black student union, ASIA student group, Hmong club, inter-tribal council, Young Democrats, College Republicans, Circle K.

**Athletics.** NCAA. **Intercollegiate:** Baseball M, basketball, cross-country, football (tackle) M, golf W, soccer, softball W, track and field, volleyball W, wrestling M. **Intramural:** Basketball, bowling, football (tackle), racquetball, soccer, softball, tennis, volleyball, water polo. **Team name:** Pioneers.

**Student services.** Adult student services, alcohol/substance abuse counseling, chaplain/spiritual director, career counseling, student employment services, financial aid counseling, health services, minority student services, on-campus daycare, personal counseling, placement for graduates, veterans' counselor, women's services. **Physically disabled:** Services for visually, speech, hearing impaired.

**Contact.** E-mail: admit@uwplatt.edu
Phone: (608) 342-1125 Toll-free number: (800) 362-5515
Fax: (608) 342-1122
Angela Udelhofen, Dean of Admissions and Enrollment Management, University of Wisconsin-Platteville, One University Plaza, Platteville, WI 53818

## University of Wisconsin-River Falls
**River Falls, Wisconsin**
**www.uwrf.edu**                                    **CB code: 1918**

- Public 4-year university and liberal arts college
- Residential campus in large town
- 6,044 degree-seeking undergraduates: 5% part-time, 59% women, 1% African American, 2% Asian American, 1% Hispanic American, 1% international
- 506 degree-seeking graduate students
- 76% of applicants admitted
- SAT or ACT (ACT writing optional), application essay required
- 55% graduate within 6 years

**General.** Founded in 1874. Regionally accredited. **Degrees:** 1,075 bachelor's awarded; master's offered. **ROTC:** Army. **Location:** 30 miles from Minneapolis-St. Paul. **Calendar:** Semester, limited summer session. **Full-time faculty:** 236 total; 72% have terminal degrees, 8% minority, 39% women. **Part-time faculty:** 112 total; 16% have terminal degrees, 5% minority, 54% women. **Class size:** 37% < 20, 47% 20-39, 10% 40-49, 5% 50-99, less than 1% >100. **Special facilities:** 2 laboratory farms, 20-inch reflecting telescope, USDA-approved food science laboratory, computerized greenhouse, 42-foot rapelling and climbing wall, indoor track and field house, ice arena, electron microscope, observatory, education regional archive collection.

**Freshman class profile.** 3,358 applied, 2,566 admitted, 1,336 enrolled.

| Mid 50% test scores | | | |
|---|---|---|---|
| SAT critical reading: | 440-520 | Rank in top quarter: | 35% |
| SAT math: | 470-590 | Rank in top tenth: | 12% |
| SAT writing: | 430-560 | Return as sophomores: | 75% |
| ACT composite: | 20-24 | Out-of-state: | 48% |
| GPA 3.75 or higher: | 17% | Live on campus: | 90% |
| GPA 3.50-3.74: | 18% | International: | 1% |
| GPA 3.0-3.49: | 41% | Fraternities: | 2% |
| GPA 2.0-2.99: | 23% | Sororities: | 1% |

**Basis for selection.** Rank in top 40% of class with 18 ACT, or rank in top 60% with 22 ACT required. Minority student applications given special

consideration. Elementary Education and Animal Science applicants must rank in the top 40% of class with 24 ACT.

**High school preparation.** College-preparatory program required. 17 units required; 22 recommended. Required and recommended units include English 4, mathematics 3-4, social studies 3-4, science 3-4 (laboratory 1), foreign language 2 and academic electives 4. Vocational agriculture units also recommended for applicants to College of Agriculture. Wisconsin residents who receive GED must also complete Wisconsin high school equivalency diploma.

**2009-2010 Annual costs.** Tuition/fees: $6,390; $13,963 out-of-state. Minnesota reciprocity tuition: $239 per credit hour. Room/board: $5,330. Books/supplies: $330. Personal expenses: $1,900.

**2009-2010 Financial aid.** All financial aid based on need. 38% of total undergraduate aid awarded as scholarships/grants, 62% as loans/jobs.

**Application procedures. Admission:** Priority date 2/1; no deadline. $44 fee, may be waived for applicants with need. Admission notification on a rolling basis beginning on or about 9/15. **Financial aid:** Priority date 3/15; no closing date. FAFSA required. Applicants notified on a rolling basis starting 4/15.

**Academics. Special study options:** Combined bachelor's/graduate degree, cross-registration, distance learning, double major, dual enrollment of high school students, ESL, exchange student, external degree, honors, independent study, internships, liberal arts/career combination, study abroad, teacher certification program. **Credit/placement by examination:** AP, CLEP, IB, institutional tests. 27 credit hours maximum toward bachelor's degree. Placement in English, foreign languages, and math based on university system placement exams. **Support services:** Learning center, reduced course load, remedial instruction, study skills assistance, tutoring, writing center.

**Majors. Agriculture:** General, agronomy, animal sciences, business, crop production, dairy, dairy husbandry, equestrian studies, equine science, equipment technology, food science, greenhouse operations, horticultural science, horticulture, landscaping, products processing, soil science. **Biology:** General, biochemistry, biotechnology. **Business:** Accounting, business admin. **Communications:** General, journalism. **Computer sciences:** General. **Conservation:** General, environmental science, management/policy. **Education:** Agricultural, art, elementary, ESL, music, physical, speech impaired. **Foreign languages:** French, German, Spanish. **Health:** Communication disorders. **History:** General. **Interdisciplinary:** Biological/physical sciences, global studies. **Math:** General. **Physical sciences:** Chemistry, geology, organic chemistry, physics, planetary, polymer chemistry. **Psychology:** General. **Public administration:** Social work. **Social sciences:** General, economics, geography, political science, sociology. **Visual/performing arts:** Art, studio arts.

**Most popular majors.** Agriculture 14%, biology 7%, business/marketing 15%, communications/journalism 13%, education 14%, social sciences 6%.

**Computing on campus.** 700 workstations in dormitories, library, computer center, student center. Dormitories wired for high-speed internet access and linked to campus network. Commuter students can connect to campus network. Online course registration, online library, helpline, repair service, student web hosting, wireless network available.

**Student life. Freshman orientation:** Mandatory. Preregistration for classes offered. Held weekend prior to classes starting. **Policies:** Freshmen and sophomores must live in residence halls unless they reside with parents. **Housing:** Guaranteed on-campus for freshmen. Coed dorms, single-sex dorms, special housing for disabled available. $125 partly refundable deposit, deadline 6/1. **Activities:** Bands, campus ministries, choral groups, dance, drama, international student organizations, literary magazine, music ensembles, Model UN, musical theater, radio station, student government, student newspaper, symphony orchestra, TV station, African American Alliance, Hispanic Student Coalition, Native American Council, Hmong student association, Habitat for Humanity, Fellowship of Christian Athletes, Young Democrats, Young Republicans, Young Life, Intervarsity Christian Fellowship.

**Athletics.** NCAA. **Intercollegiate:** Basketball, cross-country, diving, football (tackle) M, golf W, ice hockey, soccer W, softball W, swimming, tennis W, track and field, volleyball W. **Intramural:** Badminton, basketball, bowling, cheerleading, football (non-tackle), golf, handball, ice hockey, racquetball, softball, swimming, tennis, volleyball, water polo. **Team name:** Falcons.

**Student services.** Adult student services, alcohol/substance abuse counseling, chaplain/spiritual director, career counseling, services for economically disadvantaged, student employment services, financial aid counseling, health services, minority student services, on-campus daycare, personal counseling, placement for graduates, veterans' counselor, women's services. **Physically disabled:** Services for visually, speech, hearing impaired.

**Contact.** E-mail: admit@uwrf.edu
Phone: (715) 425-3500 Fax: (715) 425-0676
Mark Meydam, Director of Admission, University of Wisconsin-River
Falls, 410 South 3rd Street, River Falls, WI 54022-5001

## University of Wisconsin-Stevens Point

| Stevens Point, Wisconsin | CB member |
|---|---|
| www.uwsp.edu | CB code: 1919 |

- Public 4-year university
- Residential campus in large town
- 8,610 degree-seeking undergraduates: 5% part-time, 52% women, 1% African American, 3% Asian American, 1% Hispanic American, 1% Native American, 2% international
- 207 degree-seeking graduate students
- 73% of applicants admitted
- SAT or ACT (ACT writing optional) required
- 61% graduate within 6 years; 15% enter graduate study

**General.** Founded in 1894. Regionally accredited. **Degrees:** 1,613 bachelor's, 19 associate awarded; master's, doctoral offered. **ROTC:** Army. **Location:** 110 miles from Madison, 240 miles from Chicago. **Calendar:** Semester, extensive summer session. **Full-time faculty:** 398 total; 78% have terminal degrees, 5% minority, 41% women. **Part-time faculty:** 75 total; 35% have terminal degrees, 5% minority, 65% women. **Special facilities:** Natural history museum, planetarium and observatory, nature preserve, Foucault pendulum, electron microscope, 1,000-acre natural resources summer camp, fire science center, multicultural center.

**Freshman class profile.** 5,178 applied, 3,767 admitted, 1,640 enrolled.

| Mid 50% test scores | | GPA 2.0-2.99: | 13% |
|---|---|---|---|
| SAT critical reading: | 440-610 | Rank in top quarter: | 47% |
| SAT math: | 460-610 | Rank in top tenth: | 15% |
| SAT writing: | 440-640 | Return as sophomores: | 78% |
| ACT composite: | 21-25 | Out-of-state: | 9% |
| GPA 3.75 or higher: | 22% | Live on campus: | 88% |
| GPA 3.50-3.74: | 22% | International: | 2% |
| GPA 3.0-3.49: | 43% | | |

**Basis for selection.** Applicants must rank in top 25% of class, or have 21 ACT/990 SAT (exclusive of Writing) and rank in top 50% of class, or have 3.25 GPA. Campus visit recommended.

**High school preparation.** College-preparatory program required. 17 units required; 22 recommended. Required and recommended units include English 4, mathematics 3-4, social studies 3-4, science 3-4 and foreign language 4. Additional 2 units from English, math, social sciences, sciences, or foreign language and 2 units from above areas or fine arts, computer science, or other academic areas.

**2009-2010 Annual costs.** Tuition/fees: $6,532; $14,105 out-of-state. Minnesota reciprocity tuition: $239 per credit hour. Room/board: $5,612. Books/supplies: $500. Personal expenses: $1,718.

**2008-2009 Financial aid.** **Need-based:** 1,262 full-time freshmen applied for aid; 781 were judged to have need; 735 of these received aid. Average need met was 76%. Average scholarship/grant was $5,386; average loan $3,777. 39% of total undergraduate aid awarded as scholarships/grants, 61% as loans/jobs. **Non-need-based:** Awarded to 1,114 full-time undergraduates, including 200 freshmen. Scholarships awarded for academics, alumni affiliation, art, music/drama, ROTC. **Additional information:** Tuition discounts offered to qualified residents from other states.

**Application procedures.** **Admission:** No deadline. $44 fee, may be waived for applicants with need. Admission notification on a rolling basis beginning on or about 9/15. **Financial aid:** Priority date 5/15, closing date 6/15. FAFSA required. Applicants notified on a rolling basis starting 5/1; must reply within 4 week(s) of notification.

**Academics.** **Special study options:** Accelerated study, cooperative education, distance learning, double major, dual enrollment of high school students, ESL, independent study, internships, student-designed major, study abroad, teacher certification program. Cooperative program with University of Wisconsin: Eau Claire and St. Joseph's Hospital; collaborative degree program with University of Wisconsin-Marshfield, University of Wisconsin-Marathon and University of Wisconsin-Marinette. **Credit/placement by examination:** AP, CLEP, IB, institutional tests. 16 credit hours maximum toward associate degree, 32 toward bachelor's. **Support services:** Learning center, pre-admission summer program, reduced course load, remedial instruction, study skills assistance, tutoring, writing center.

**Majors.** **Agriculture:** Soil science. **Architecture:** Interior. **Biology:** General. **Business:** Accounting, business admin. **Communications:** General. **Computer sciences:** General, web page design. **Conservation:** General, fisheries, forestry, water/wetlands/marine, wildlife, wood science. **Education:** Early childhood, elementary, family/consumer sciences, music, physical, secondary. **Foreign languages:** French, German, Spanish. **Health:** Athletic training, audiology/speech pathology, clinical lab science. **History:** General. **Interdisciplinary:** Biological/physical sciences. **Liberal arts:** Arts/sciences. **Math:** General. **Parks/recreation:** Health/fitness. **Philosophy/religion:** Philosophy. **Physical sciences:** Chemistry, physics. **Psychology:** General. **Public administration:** General. **Social sciences:** General, economics, geography, political science, sociology. **Visual/performing arts:** General, art, arts management, dance, dramatic, interior design, music history, music performance.

**Most popular majors.** Biology 7%, business/marketing 8%, communications/journalism 6%, education 12%, natural resources/environmental science 13%, psychology 6%, social sciences 14%, visual/performing arts 6%.

**Computing on campus.** 634 workstations in dormitories, library, computer center, student center. Dormitories wired for high-speed internet access and linked to campus network. Commuter students can connect to campus network. Online course registration, online library, helpline, student web hosting, wireless network available.

**Student life.** **Freshman orientation:** Mandatory, $45 fee. **Policies:** Non-smoking policy for all campus buildings. **Housing:** Coed dorms, single-sex dorms, wellness housing available. $125 partly refundable deposit. **Activities:** Bands, campus ministries, choral groups, dance, drama, film society, international student organizations, literary magazine, music ensembles, Model UN, musical theater, radio station, student government, student newspaper, symphony orchestra, TV station, American Indians Reaching for Opportunities, black student union, College Republicans, College Democrats, Lutheran Collegians, Association for Community Tasks, Newman Catholic student association, Habitat for Humanity, gay-straight alliance.

**Athletics.** NCAA. **Intercollegiate:** Baseball M, basketball, cross-country, diving, football (tackle) M, golf W, ice hockey, soccer W, softball W, swimming, tennis W, track and field, volleyball W, wrestling M. **Intramural:** Badminton, basketball, football (non-tackle), football (tackle) M, golf, ice hockey, racquetball, soccer, softball, tennis, volleyball. **Team name:** Pointers.

**Student services.** Adult student services, alcohol/substance abuse counseling, career counseling, services for economically disadvantaged, student employment services, financial aid counseling, health services, minority student services, on-campus daycare, personal counseling, placement for graduates, veterans' counselor, women's services. **Physically disabled:** Services for visually, speech, hearing impaired.

**Contact.** E-mail: admiss@uwsp.edu
Phone: (715) 346-2441 Fax: (715) 346-3296
Catherine Glennon, Director of Admissions, University of
Wisconsin-Stevens Point, Student Services Center, Stevens Point, WI
54481

## University of Wisconsin-Stout

| Menomonie, Wisconsin | |
|---|---|
| www.uwstout.edu | CB code: 1740 |

- Public 4-year university
- Residential campus in large town
- 7,893 degree-seeking undergraduates: 14% part-time, 48% women, 1% African American, 3% Asian American, 1% Hispanic American, 1% Native American, 1% international
- 770 degree-seeking graduate students
- 77% of applicants admitted
- SAT or ACT (ACT writing optional) required
- 54% graduate within 6 years

**General.** Founded in 1891. Regionally accredited. **Degrees:** 1,488 bachelor's awarded; master's offered. **ROTC:** Army, Air Force. **Location:** 60 miles from Minneapolis-St. Paul. **Calendar:** 4-1-4, limited summer session. **Full-time faculty:** 346 total; 80% have terminal degrees, 13% minority, 41% women. **Part-time faculty:** 68 total; 32% have terminal degrees, 2% minority, 54% women. **Class size:** 35% < 20, 57% 20-39, 4% 40-49, 4% 50-99, 1% >100. **Special facilities:** Teleproduction center, technology transfer institute, vocational rehabilitation institute.

**Freshman class profile.** 3,817 applied, 2,930 admitted, 1,526 enrolled.

| Mid 50% test scores | | Out-of-state: | 34% |
|---|---|---|---|
| ACT composite: | 19-23 | Live on campus: | 95% |
| Rank in top quarter: | 26% | International: | 1% |
| Rank in top tenth: | 7% | Fraternities: | 5% |
| Return as sophomores: | 71% | Sororities: | 12% |

**Basis for selection.** Rank in top half of class or 22 ACT required. Limited enrollment in all programs. Applied science and manufacturing engineering require upper 40% of class or 22 ACT along with 22 ACT math. **Learning Disabled:** Current IEP may be submitted with application.

**High school preparation.** College-preparatory program required. Required and recommended units include English 4, mathematics 3, social studies 3, science 3, foreign language 2 and academic electives 4. Electives in English, math, social sciences, and sciences, technology business, fine art, family & consumer education, sciences.

**2009-2010 Annual costs.** Tuition/fees: $7,821; $15,566 out-of-state. Laptop computer included in the cost of tuition. Minnesota reciprocity tuition: $263 per-credit-hour. Room/board: $5,336. Books/supplies: $356. Personal expenses: $1,882.

**2009-2010 Financial aid. Need-based:** 1,262 full-time freshmen applied for aid; 822 were judged to have need; 812 of these received aid. Average need met was 90%. Average scholarship/grant was $5,689; average loan $3,403. 40% of total undergraduate aid awarded as scholarships/grants, 60% as loans/jobs. **Non-need-based:** Awarded to 680 full-time undergraduates, including 221 freshmen. Scholarships awarded for academics.

**Application procedures. Admission:** Priority date 1/1; no deadline. $44 fee, may be waived for applicants with need. Admission notification on a rolling basis beginning on or about 9/15. Early application recommended. Art-graphic design deadline of 11/1; not all qualified applicants will be admitted. **Financial aid:** Priority date 3/15; no closing date. FAFSA required. Applicants notified on a rolling basis starting 4/1; must reply within 4 week(s) of notification.

**Academics. Special study options:** Accelerated study, cooperative education, cross-registration, distance learning, double major, dual enrollment of high school students, exchange student, external degree, honors, independent study, internships, study abroad, teacher certification program. **Credit/placement by examination:** AP, CLEP, IB, ACT, institutional tests. **Support services:** Learning center, pre-admission summer program, reduced course load, remedial instruction, study skills assistance, tutoring, writing center.

**Majors. Business:** Business admin, customer service, golf management, hospitality admin, operations, real estate, sales/distribution. **Communications technology:** Printing management. **Computer sciences:** Game design, information technology, networking. **Education:** Art, early childhood, family/consumer sciences, mentally handicapped, sales/marketing, science, special, technology/industrial arts, voc/tech. **Engineering:** Computer, manufacturing, polymer. **Engineering technology:** General, construction. **Family/consumer sciences:** Clothing/textiles, family studies, institutional food production. **Health:** Dietetics, vocational rehab counseling. **Math:** Applied. **Psychology:** General. **Visual/performing arts:** Art, studio arts. **Other:** Applied Science, Packaging, Sustainable Management, Technology and Science Education.

**Most popular majors.** Business/marketing 47%, education 10%, engineering/engineering technologies 10%, family/consumer sciences 7%, visual/performing arts 9%.

**Computing on campus.** 590 workstations in dormitories, library, computer center, student center. Dormitories wired for high-speed internet access and linked to campus network. Commuter students can connect to campus network. Online course registration, helpline, repair service, student web hosting, wireless network available.

**Student life. Freshman orientation:** Available. 1-day program with additional activities held the week before classes begin. **Housing:** Guaranteed on-campus for freshmen. Coed dorms, special housing for disabled, apartments, wellness housing available. $125 partly refundable deposit. **Activities:** Bands, campus ministries, choral groups, dance, drama, film society, international student organizations, literary magazine, music ensembles, Model UN, musical theater, radio station, student government, student newspaper, black student union, Hmong student organization, Lutheran student fellowship, College Democrats, College Republicans, Chi Alpha Christians in Action, single parent association, Club Los Hispanos.

**Athletics.** NCAA. **Intercollegiate:** Baseball M, basketball, cross-country, football (tackle) M, gymnastics W, ice hockey M, soccer W, softball W, tennis W, track and field, volleyball W. **Intramural:** Baseball M, basketball, golf, ice hockey, racquetball, soccer, softball, volleyball. **Team name:** Blue Devils.

**Student services.** Chaplain/spiritual director, career counseling, student employment services, health services, on-campus daycare, personal counseling, placement for graduates, veterans' counselor. **Physically disabled:** Services for visually, speech, hearing impaired.

**Contact.** E-mail: admissions@uwstout.edu
Phone: (715) 232-1411 Toll-free number: (800) 447-8688
Fax: (715) 232-1667
Pam Holsinger-Fuchs, Executive Director of Enrollment Services,
University of Wisconsin-Stout, 1 Clocktower Plaza, Menomonie, WI 54751

## University of Wisconsin-Superior
**Superior, Wisconsin**
**www.uwsuper.edu** **CB code: 1920**

- Public 4-year university and liberal arts college
- Commuter campus in small city
- 2,515 degree-seeking undergraduates: 18% part-time, 57% women, 2% African American, 1% Asian American, 1% Hispanic American, 3% Native American, 6% international
- 209 degree-seeking graduate students
- 68% of applicants admitted
- SAT or ACT (ACT writing optional) required
- 41% graduate within 6 years

**General.** Founded in 1893. Regionally accredited. **Degrees:** 438 bachelor's, 10 associate awarded; master's offered. **ROTC:** Air Force. **Location:** 2 miles from Duluth, Minnesota, 150 miles from Minneapolis-St. Paul. **Calendar:** Semester, limited summer session. **Full-time faculty:** 112 total; 73% have terminal degrees, 10% minority, 46% women. **Part-time faculty:** 56 total; 20% have terminal degrees, 9% minority, 48% women. **Class size:** 55% < 20, 39% 20-39, 2% 40-49, 3% 50-99, less than 1% >100. **Special facilities:** Observatory, wetlands, research vessel on Lake Superior.

**Freshman class profile.** 965 applied, 655 admitted, 369 enrolled.

| Mid 50% test scores | | Out-of-state: | 41% |
|---|---|---|---|
| ACT composite: | 19-24 | Live on campus: | 60% |
| Rank in top quarter: | 33% | International: | 10% |
| Rank in top tenth: | 11% | Sororities: | 5% |
| Return as sophomores: | 72% | | |

**Basis for selection.** Admissions based on secondary school record and class rank. Standardized test scores also important. Essay, audition, portfolio, interview recommended. **Homeschooled:** Statement describing home-school structure and mission, transcript of courses and grades required.

**High school preparation.** College-preparatory program required. 17 units required. Required and recommended units include English 4, mathematics 3-4, social studies 3-4, science 3-4, foreign language 2 and academic electives 4.

**2009-2010 Annual costs.** Tuition/fees: $6,736; $14,309 out-of-state. Minnesota reciprocity tuition: $239 per-credit-hour. Room/board: $5,485. Books/supplies: $860. Personal expenses: $1,890.

**2009-2010 Financial aid. Need-based:** 259 full-time freshmen applied for aid; 198 were judged to have need; 197 of these received aid. Average scholarship/grant was $6,160; average loan $2,870. 49% of total undergraduate aid awarded as scholarships/grants, 51% as loans/jobs. **Non-need-based:** Awarded to 324 full-time undergraduates, including 98 freshmen. Scholarships awarded for academics, alumni affiliation, art, leadership, minority status, music/drama, ROTC, state residency. **Additional information:** Tuition Assistance Program (TAP) available to non-resident students on limited basis.

**Application procedures. Admission:** Priority date 4/1; no deadline. $44 fee, may be waived for applicants with need. Admission notification on a rolling basis beginning on or about 10/1. Must reply by May 1 or within 4 week(s) if notified thereafter. **Financial aid:** Priority date 4/1; no closing date. FAFSA required. Applicants notified on a rolling basis starting 3/15; must reply by 5/1 or within 4 week(s) of notification.

**Academics.** Post-bachelor's certificates offered in early childhood education, counseling, and secondary education. Post-master's certificate offered in library science. **Special study options:** Combined bachelor's/graduate degree, cooperative education, cross-registration, distance learning, double major, dual enrollment of high school students, ESL, exchange student, external degree, independent study, internships, liberal arts/career combination, student-designed major, study abroad, teacher certification program. Engineering with University of Wisconsin-Madison and Michigan Technological University, Forestry with Michigan Technological University. **Credit/placement by examination:** AP, CLEP, IB, ACT, institutional tests. 32 credit hours maximum toward associate degree, 32 toward bachelor's. **Support services:** Learning center, pre-admission summer program, reduced course load, remedial instruction, study skills assistance, tutoring, writing center.

**Majors. Biology:** General, aquatic, botany, cell/histology, ecology, environmental, molecular. **Business:** General, accounting, business admin, finance, international, management information systems, marketing. **Communications:** General, broadcast journalism, journalism, media studies. **Computer sciences:** Computer science. **Education:** Art, biology, chemistry, elementary, English, history, mathematics, multi-level teacher, music, physical, science, social science, social studies. **Health:** Art therapy. **History:** General. **Interdisciplinary:** Biological/physical sciences. **Legal studies:** General, prelaw. **Liberal arts:** Arts/sciences. **Math:** General. **Physical sciences:** Chemistry. **Protective services:** Criminal justice, police science. **Psychology:** General. **Public administration:** General, policy analysis, social work. **Social sciences:** General, economics, political science, sociology. **Transportation:** General. **Visual/performing arts:** General, art, art history/conservation, dramatic, music performance, studio arts.

**Most popular majors.** Biology 7%, business/marketing 18%, communications/journalism 9%, education 15%, interdisciplinary studies 9%, psychology 6%, public administration/social services 6%, social sciences 9%, visual/performing arts 6%.

**Computing on campus.** 343 workstations in dormitories, library, computer center, student center. Dormitories wired for high-speed internet access and linked to campus network. Commuter students can connect to campus network. Online course registration, online library, helpline, repair service, student web hosting, wireless network available.

**Student life. Freshman orientation:** Mandatory, $100 fee. Preregistration for classes offered. Sessions held in spring and summer; 2 1/2 day program just prior to classes beginning. **Housing:** Guaranteed on-campus for freshmen. Coed dorms, single-sex dorms, special housing for disabled, wellness housing available. $200 partly refundable deposit, deadline 7/1. Suites available in nontraditional residence halls for married students. Single parents have access to student residences. **Activities:** Bands, campus ministries, choral groups, dance, drama, international student organizations, music ensembles, radio station, student government, student newspaper, symphony orchestra, TV station, criminal justice association, black student union, College Democrats, social work student association, College Republicans, intervarsity Christian fellowship, World Student Association.

**Athletics.** NCAA. **Intercollegiate:** Baseball M, basketball, cross-country, golf W, ice hockey, soccer, softball W, track and field, volleyball W. **Intramural:** Badminton, basketball, bowling, cheerleading, football (non-tackle), golf, ice hockey, racquetball, rifle, skiing, soccer, softball, swimming, table tennis, tennis, volleyball. **Team name:** Yellowjackets.

**Student services.** Adult student services, alcohol/substance abuse counseling, chaplain/spiritual director, career counseling, services for economically disadvantaged, student employment services, financial aid counseling, health services, minority student services, on-campus daycare, personal counseling, placement for graduates, veterans' counselor, women's services. **Physically disabled:** Services for visually, hearing impaired.

**Contact.** E-mail: admissions@uwsuper.edu
Phone: (715) 394-8230 Fax: (715) 394-8407
Tonya Roth, Director of Admission, University of Wisconsin-Superior, Belknap and Catlin, PO Box 2000, Superior, WI 54880

## University of Wisconsin-Whitewater
**Whitewater, Wisconsin**
www.uww.edu                                    CB code: 1921

▶ Public 4-year university
▶ Residential campus in large town
▶ 9,652 degree-seeking undergraduates

**General.** Founded in 1868. Regionally accredited. **Degrees:** 1,740 bachelor's, 9 associate awarded; master's offered. **ROTC:** Army, Air Force. **Location:** 40 miles from Madison, 50 miles from Milwaukee. **Calendar:** Semester, extensive summer session. **Full-time faculty:** 383 total; 84% have terminal degrees, 19% minority, 44% women. **Part-time faculty:** 121 total; 35% have terminal degrees, 9% minority, 49% women. **Class size:** 42% < 20, 45% 20-39, 7% 40-49, 5% 50-99, less than 1% >100. **Special facilities:** Observatory, nature preserve and recreation area, weather station.

### Freshman class profile.

| Mid 50% test scores | | | |
|---|---|---|---|
| SAT critical reading: | 470-610 | GPA 2.0-2.99: | 30% |
| SAT math: | 480-600 | Rank in top quarter: | 31% |
| ACT composite: | 20-24 | Rank in top tenth: | 9% |
| GPA 3.75 or higher: | 11% | Out-of-state: | 7% |
| GPA 3.50-3.74: | 15% | Live on campus: | 90% |
| GPA 3.0-3.49: | 44% | Fraternities: | 7% |
| | | Sororities: | 6% |

**Basis for selection.** College prep curriculum and rank in top 40% of high school class important. SAT or ACT recommended. Audition required for music; portfolio recommended for art. **Homeschooled:** Transcript of courses and grades required. **Learning Disabled:** Disability should be referenced in essay and include review by Center for Students with Disabilities. Medical documentation may be requested.

**High school preparation.** 17 units required; 20 recommended. Required and recommended units include English 4, mathematics 3-4, social studies 3-4, science 3-4 (laboratory 1), foreign language 2 and academic electives 4.

**2009-2010 Annual costs.** Tuition/fees: $6,496; $14,069 out-of-state. Minnesota reciprocity tuition: $239 per credit hour. Room/board: $4,928. Books/supplies: $170. Personal expenses: $400.

**2009-2010 Financial aid. Non-need-based:** Scholarships awarded for academics, alumni affiliation, art, leadership, minority status, music/drama, ROTC, state residency.

**Application procedures. Admission:** Priority date 12/1; deadline 5/1 (postmark date). $44 fee, may be waived for applicants with need. Admission notification on a rolling basis beginning on or about 9/15. **Financial aid:** Priority date 3/15; no closing date. FAFSA required. Applicants notified on a rolling basis starting 4/1; must reply within 3 week(s) of notification.

**Academics. Special study options:** Accelerated study, combined bachelor's/graduate degree, cooperative education, cross-registration, distance learning, double major, dual enrollment of high school students, ESL, exchange student, external degree, honors, independent study, internships, liberal arts/career combination, student-designed major, study abroad, teacher certification program, weekend college. **Credit/placement by examination:** AP, CLEP, IB, SAT, ACT, institutional tests. 30 credit hours maximum toward associate degree, 60 toward bachelor's. **Support services:** Learning center, pre-admission summer program, reduced course load, remedial instruction, study skills assistance, tutoring, writing center.

**Majors. Area/ethnic studies:** Women's. **Biology:** General. **Business:** General, accounting, business admin, finance, human resources, managerial economics, marketing, nonprofit/public, office/clerical, operations. **Communications:** General, broadcast journalism, journalism. **Computer sciences:** General, information technology, systems analysis, web page design. **Education:** General, art, biology, business, chemistry, computer, drama/dance, early childhood, elementary, English, French, German, history, learning disabled, mathematics, music, physical, sales/marketing, science, secondary, social science, social studies, Spanish, special, speech. **Engineering technology:** Occupational safety. **Foreign languages:** French, German, Spanish. **Health:** Speech pathology. **History:** General. **Interdisciplinary:** Global studies. **Legal studies:** Prelaw. **Liberal arts:** Arts/sciences. **Math:** General. **Physical sciences:** Chemistry, physics. **Psychology:** General. **Public administration:** General, policy analysis, social work. **Social sciences:** General, economics, geography, political science, sociology. **Visual/performing arts:** Art, art history/conservation, dance, dramatic, music theory/composition, theater arts management, theater history. **Other:** Integrated Science/Business.

**Most popular majors.** Business/marketing 28%, communications/journalism 10%, education 17%, public administration/social services 6%, social sciences 9%.

**Computing on campus.** 1,373 workstations in dormitories, library, computer center, student center. Dormitories wired for high-speed internet access and linked to campus network. Commuter students can connect to campus network. Online course registration, online library, helpline, repair service, student web hosting, wireless network available.

**Student life. Freshman orientation:** Mandatory, $75 fee. Preregistration for classes offered. Full-day program held in summer. **Housing:** Guaranteed on-campus for freshmen. Coed dorms, single-sex dorms, special housing for disabled, wellness housing available. $125 fully refundable deposit. **Activities:** Bands, choral groups, dance, drama, literary magazine, music ensembles, musical theater, opera, radio station, student government, student newspaper, symphony orchestra, TV station, Campus Crusade for Christ, Diamond Way Buddhist, College Democrats, College Republicans, Arabic club, black student union, Adopt-A-School Program, America Reads.

**Athletics.** NCAA. **Intercollegiate:** Baseball M, basketball, bowling W, cross-country, diving, football (tackle) M, golf W, gymnastics W, soccer, softball W, swimming, tennis, track and field, volleyball W, wrestling M. **Intramural:** Badminton, basketball, bowling, football (non-tackle), golf, racquetball, soccer, softball, table tennis, tennis, volleyball. **Team name:** Warhawks.

**Student services.** Adult student services, alcohol/substance abuse counseling, chaplain/spiritual director, career counseling, services for economically disadvantaged, student employment services, financial aid counseling, health services, legal services, minority student services, on-campus daycare, personal counseling, placement for graduates, veterans' counselor, women's services. **Physically disabled:** Services for visually, speech, hearing impaired. **Learning disabled:** Comprehensive services available.

**Contact.** E-mail: uwwadmit@uww.edu
Phone: (262) 472-1440 Fax: (262) 472-1515
Stephen McKellips, Director of Admissions, University of Wisconsin-Whitewater, 800 West Main Street, Whitewater, WI 53190-1790

## Viterbo University
**La Crosse, Wisconsin**
**www.viterbo.edu**
**CB member**
**CB code: 1878**

◆ Private 4-year university and liberal arts college affiliated with Roman Catholic Church
◆ Residential campus in small city
◆ 2,109 degree-seeking undergraduates
◆ 87% of applicants admitted
◆ ACT (writing optional) required

**General.** Founded in 1890. Regionally accredited. **Degrees:** 420 bachelor's, 10 associate awarded; master's offered. **ROTC:** Army. **Location:** 150 miles from Minneapolis-St. Paul, 150 miles from Madison. **Calendar:** Semester, limited summer session. **Full-time faculty:** 112 total. **Part-time faculty:** 171 total. **Class size:** 64% < 20, 34% 20-39, 1% 40-49, 1% 50-99. **Special facilities:** Center for ethics, science and technology; fine arts center; center for recreation and education in conjunction with Boys and Girls Club of America.

**Freshman class profile.** 1,463 applied, 1,272 admitted, 417 enrolled.

| Mid 50% test scores | | GPA 2.0-2.99: | 26% |
|---|---|---|---|
| ACT composite: | 20-25 | Rank in top quarter: | 39% |
| GPA 3.75 or higher: | 26% | Rank in top tenth: | 14% |
| GPA 3.50-3.74: | 15% | Out-of-state: | 25% |
| GPA 3.0-3.49: | 32% | Live on campus: | 93% |

**Basis for selection.** High school GPA and ACT score most important, then placement testing. Auditions and portfolio reviews required for students applying to School of Fine Arts (music, theater, art, dance). Interview required for students not meeting admission requirements. **Homeschooled:** Transcript of courses and grades required. **Learning Disabled:** All students encouraged to file ADA petition for reasonable accommodations, preferably 8 weeks prior to start of classes.

**High school preparation.** College-preparatory program recommended. 16 units required; 19 recommended. Required and recommended units include English 3-4, mathematics 2, social studies 2, history 2, science 2 (laboratory 2), foreign language 2 and academic electives 5. Chemistry required for nursing, dietetics, natural sciences, allied health preprofessional students. Portfolios or auditions required for fine arts students.

**2009-2010 Annual costs.** Tuition/fees: $20,160. Additional fees for some fine arts, dietetics, science courses, and nursing clinicals. Room/board: $6,710. Books/supplies: $850. Personal expenses: $1,800.

**Financial aid. Non-need-based:** Scholarships awarded for academics, alumni affiliation, art, athletics, leadership, minority status, music/drama, ROTC.

**Application procedures. Admission:** Priority date 8/1; no deadline. $25 fee, may be waived for applicants with need, free for online applicants. Admission notification on a rolling basis. Must reply by May 1 or within 2 week(s) if notified thereafter. **Financial aid:** Priority date 3/15; no closing date. FAFSA, institutional form required. Applicants notified on a rolling basis starting 4/1; must reply within 3 week(s) of notification.

**Academics.** Learning Center offers individual and small group tutoring in all subject areas daily. Library services available daily, on weekends and evenings. **Special study options:** Accelerated study, combined bachelor's/graduate degree, cross-registration, distance learning, double major, dual enrollment of high school students, honors, independent study, internships, liberal arts/career combination, student-designed major, study abroad, teacher

certification program, urban semester, Washington semester, weekend college. Weekend college is primarily for students at master's level. **Credit/placement by examination:** AP, CLEP, IB, ACT, institutional tests. 30 credit hours maximum toward bachelor's degree. 16 hours awarded for military services. **Support services:** Learning center, reduced course load, remedial instruction, study skills assistance, tutoring, writing center.

**Majors. Biology:** General, biochemistry. **Business:** Accounting, business admin, management information systems, marketing. **Communications:** Organizational. **Computer sciences:** General. **Education:** Art, biology, business, chemistry, drama/dance, elementary, English, mathematics, music, science, secondary, social studies, Spanish, technology/industrial arts. **Foreign languages:** Spanish. **Health:** Clinical lab technology, dietetics, nursing (RN). **Interdisciplinary:** Biological/physical sciences, natural sciences. **Liberal arts:** Arts/sciences. **Math:** General. **Parks/recreation:** Exercise sciences, sports admin. **Philosophy/religion:** Philosophy, religion. **Physical sciences:** Chemistry. **Protective services:** Criminal justice. **Psychology:** General. **Public administration:** Social work. **Social sciences:** General, sociology. **Visual/performing arts:** General, art, arts management, design, dramatic, graphic design, music pedagogy, music performance, studio arts. **Other:** English and theatre arts, Individualized learning, Ministry, Organizational management, Religious studies/philosophy.

**Most popular majors.** Business/marketing 21%, education 10%, health sciences 37%, interdisciplinary studies 8%, visual/performing arts 6%.

**Computing on campus.** 396 workstations in dormitories, library, computer center, student center. Dormitories wired for high-speed internet access and linked to campus network. Commuter students can connect to campus network. Online course registration, online library, helpline, wireless network available.

**Student life. Freshman orientation:** Mandatory. Preregistration for classes offered. One-day program offered 4 times in the summer for incoming freshmen and parents. **Policies:** Standards of conduct, sexual harassment code, anti-hazing initiation policy, academic honesty policy, academic due process, campus security policy, residence hall terms and conditions, alcohol and drug policy, student event policies. **Housing:** Guaranteed on-campus for freshmen. Coed dorms, apartments, wellness housing available. $100 fully refundable deposit, deadline 8/1. **Activities:** Pep band, campus ministries, choral groups, dance, drama, international student organizations, literary magazine, music ensembles, musical theater, opera, student government, student newspaper, Connect, Students in Free Enterprise, Circle K, student nurses association, education club, Sigma Pi Delta, CREW, Global Rhythms, psychology club.

**Athletics.** NAIA. **Intercollegiate:** Baseball M, basketball, bowling, cross-country, golf, soccer, softball W, volleyball W. **Intramural:** Badminton, basketball, bowling, cross-country, football (non-tackle), golf, handball, racquetball, rugby M, skiing, soccer, softball, table tennis, tennis, volleyball. **Team name:** V-Hawks.

**Student services.** Adult student services, alcohol/substance abuse counseling, chaplain/spiritual director, career counseling, services for economically disadvantaged, student employment services, financial aid counseling, health services, personal counseling, placement for graduates, veterans' counselor, women's services. **Physically disabled:** Services for visually, hearing impaired.

**Contact.** E-mail: admission@viterbo.edu
Phone: (608) 796-3010 Toll-free number: (800) 848-3726
Fax: (608) 796-3020
Roland Nelson, Vice President for Enrollment, Viterbo University, 900 Viterbo Drive, La Crosse, WI 54601-8804

## Wisconsin Lutheran College
**Milwaukee, Wisconsin**
**www.wlc.edu**
**CB code: 1513**

◆ Private 4-year liberal arts college affiliated with Wisconsin Evangelical Lutheran Synod
◆ Residential campus in very large city
◆ 743 degree-seeking undergraduates
◆ 73% of applicants admitted
◆ SAT or ACT (ACT writing optional) required

**General.** Founded in 1973. Regionally accredited. **Degrees:** 135 bachelor's awarded. **ROTC:** Army, Naval, Air Force. **Calendar:** Semester, limited summer session. **Full-time faculty:** 60 total; 67% have terminal degrees, 33% women. **Part-time faculty:** 31 total. **Class size:** 73% < 20, 25% 20-39, less than 1% 40-49, less than 1% 50-99.

**Freshman class profile.** 693 applied, 506 admitted, 202 enrolled.

| Mid 50% test scores | | | | |
|---|---|---|---|---|
| SAT critical reading: | 490-590 | GPA 3.0-3.49: | 38% |
| SAT math: | 470-650 | GPA 2.0-2.99: | 21% |
| ACT composite: | 19-27 | Rank in top quarter: | 43% |
| GPA 3.75 or higher: | 25% | Rank in top tenth: | 18% |
| GPA 3.50-3.74: | 16% | Out-of-state: | 25% |
| | | Live on campus: | 92% |

**Basis for selection.** ACT, GPA, high school rank considered. Interview recommended for some; audition required for music scholarships.

**High school preparation.** College-preparatory program recommended. 16 units required; 20 recommended. Required and recommended units include English 4, mathematics 3-4, history 2, science 2-3 (laboratory 1-2), foreign language 2-4 and academic electives 3. Mathematics or science majors should complete 4 units of mathematics and 3-4 units of appropriate science courses.

**2009-2010 Annual costs.** Tuition/fees: $21,180. Room/board: $7,700. Books/supplies: $700. Personal expenses: $1,510.

**2009-2010 Financial aid. Non-need-based:** Scholarships awarded for academics, art, leadership, music/drama.

**Application procedures. Admission:** Priority date 3/1; no deadline. $20 fee, may be waived for applicants with need, free for online applicants. Admission notification on a rolling basis beginning on or about 9/1. Must reply by May 1 or within 2 week(s) if notified thereafter. **Financial aid:** Priority date 3/1; no closing date. FAFSA, institutional form required. Applicants notified on a rolling basis starting 3/15; must reply within 2 week(s) of notification.

**Academics.** Special graduation requirements include freshman seminar. **Special study options:** Double major, dual enrollment of high school students, ESL, independent study, internships, student-designed major, study abroad, teacher certification program. **Credit/placement by examination:** AP, CLEP, SAT, ACT, institutional tests. **Support services:** Learning center, reduced course load, study skills assistance, tutoring, writing center.

**Majors. Area/ethnic studies:** Chinese. **Biology:** General, biochemistry. **Business:** Business admin. **Communications:** General. **Conservation:** Environmental science, environmental studies. **Education:** General, early childhood, elementary, secondary. **Foreign languages:** German, Spanish. **Health:** Nursing (RN). **History:** General. **Math:** General. **Parks/recreation:** Exercise sciences. **Philosophy/religion:** Philosophy. **Physical sciences:** Chemistry. **Psychology:** General. **Public administration:** Human services. **Social sciences:** General. **Theology:** Theology. **Visual/performing arts:** Art, dramatic, graphic design. **Other:** Interdisciplinary studies.

**Most popular majors.** Biology 8%, business/marketing 12%, communications/journalism 23%, education 11%, psychology 13%, visual/performing arts 13%.

**Computing on campus.** 100 workstations in dormitories, library, computer center, student center. Dormitories wired for high-speed internet access and linked to campus network. Commuter students can connect to campus network. Online course registration, online library, helpline, repair service, wireless network available.

**Student life. Freshman orientation:** Mandatory. Preregistration for classes offered. 2-day program held over the weekend before start of fall semester. **Policies:** Drug-free, alcohol-free campus. Smoking permitted ouside only. **Housing:** Guaranteed on-campus for all undergraduates. Single-sex dorms, apartments available. $100 fully refundable deposit, deadline 5/1. All traditional age, unmarried students less than 5 years out of high school must live in college housing. Upperclassmen eligible for college apartments. **Activities:** Bands, campus ministries, choral groups, dance, drama, international student organizations, music ensembles, student government, student newspaper.

**Athletics.** NCAA. **Intercollegiate:** Baseball M, basketball, cross-country, football (tackle) M, golf, soccer, softball W, tennis, track and field, volleyball W. **Intramural:** Volleyball. **Team name:** Warriors.

**Student services.** Adult student services, chaplain/spiritual director, career counseling, student employment services, financial aid counseling, health services, minority student services, personal counseling, placement for graduates. **Physically disabled:** Services for visually, hearing impaired.

**Contact.** E-mail: admissions@wlc.edu
Phone: (414) 443-8811 Fax: (414) 443-8547
Craig Swiontek, Director of Admissions, Wisconsin Lutheran College, 8800 West Bluemound Road, Milwaukee, WI 53226-4699

# Wyoming

## University of Wyoming
**Laramie, Wyoming**      **CB member**
www.uwyo.edu      **CB code: 4855**

▶ Public 4-year university

▶ Residential campus in large town

▶ 9,586 degree-seeking undergraduates: 15% part-time, 53% women, 1% African American, 1% Asian American, 4% Hispanic American, 1% Native American, 3% international

▶ 2,315 degree-seeking graduate students

▶ 96% of applicants admitted

▶ SAT or ACT (ACT writing optional) required

▶ 53% graduate within 6 years

**General.** Founded in 1886. Regionally accredited. Undergraduate and graduate degree programs offered in Casper. Extension classes available in off-campus locations throughout the state. Online classes offered nationally. **Degrees:** 1,747 bachelor's awarded; master's, doctoral, professional offered. **ROTC:** Army, Air Force. **Location:** 45 miles from Cheyenne, 130 miles from Denver. **Calendar:** Semester, extensive summer session. **Full-time faculty:** 730 total; 85% have terminal degrees, 9% minority, 36% women. **Part-time faculty:** 53 total; 45% have terminal degrees, 8% minority, 53% women. **Class size:** 39% < 20, 44% 20-39, 8% 40-49, 5% 50-99, 4% >100. **Special facilities:** Museums (art, geological, anthropology, entomology), range herbarium, Rocky Mountain Herbarium/mycological herbarium, spatial data and visualization center, botany conservatory, zoological center, learning resource center, meteorological station, Grand Teton National Park research center, planetarium, veterinary laboratory, materials characterization lab, biological research facility, on-site elementary school, infrared telescope observatory, survey research center, institute of environment/ natural resources, fishery and wildlife research unit, American heritage center, insect galleries.

**Freshman class profile.** 3,709 applied, 3,557 admitted, 1,594 enrolled.

| Mid 50% test scores | | | |
|---|---|---|---|
| SAT critical reading: | 480-600 | Rank in top quarter: | 49% |
| SAT math: | 490-620 | Rank in top tenth: | 22% |
| ACT composite: | 21-27 | End year in good standing: | 72% |
| GPA 3.75 or higher: | 31% | Return as sophomores: | 72% |
| GPA 3.50-3.74: | 20% | Out-of-state: | 47% |
| GPA 3.0-3.49: | 31% | Live on campus: | 87% |
| GPA 2.0-2.99: | 18% | International: | 2% |

**Basis for selection.** GPA, ACT or SAT scores and completion of 13 required units in pre-college curriculum most important. Test scores not required for non-degree-seeking students or for students over the age of 21. **Homeschooled:** Credit evaluation form completed by homeschool instructor required. **Learning Disabled:** Must apply and present documentation of disability.

**High school preparation.** College-preparatory program required. 13 units required; 19 recommended. Required and recommended units include English 4, mathematics 3-4, science 3-4 (laboratory 3) and foreign language 2. 3 cultural context electives required: behavioral or social sciences; visual or performing arts; humanities or foreign languages.

**2010-2011 Annual costs.** Tuition/fees: $3,927; $12,237 out-of-state. International students must pay an additional $40 fee per semester. Room/board: $8,360. Books/supplies: $1,200. Personal expenses: $2,200.

**2008-2009 Financial aid. Need-based:** 1,273 full-time freshmen applied for aid; 744 were judged to have need; 728 of these received aid. Average need met was 34%. Average scholarship/grant was $3,550; average loan $2,772. 44% of total undergraduate aid awarded as scholarships/grants, 56% as loans/jobs. **Non-need-based:** Awarded to 4,065 full-time undergraduates, including 1,222 freshmen. Scholarships awarded for academics, alumni affiliation, art, athletics, leadership, minority status, music/drama, religious affiliation, ROTC, state residency.

**Application procedures. Admission:** Priority date 3/1; deadline 8/10 (postmark date). $40 fee, may be waived for applicants with need. Admission notification on a rolling basis. Early application recommended for students seeking financial aid and university housing preferences. **Financial aid:** Priority date 3/1; no closing date. FAFSA required. Applicants notified on a rolling basis starting 3/15; must reply within 3 week(s) of notification.

**Academics.** Remedial instruction offered on campus through Laramie County Community College. **Special study options:** Accelerated study, distance learning, double major, ESL, exchange student, external degree, honors, independent study, internships, semester at sea, student-designed major, study abroad, Washington semester. **Credit/placement by examination:** AP, CLEP, IB, SAT, ACT, institutional tests. Unlimited hours of credit examination may be counted toward a bachelor's degree. Individual departments may also allow additional tests on case-by-case basis. **Support services:** Learning center, pre-admission summer program, reduced course load, study skills assistance, tutoring, writing center.

**Majors. Agriculture:** General, agribusiness operations, animal sciences, communications, range science. **Area/ethnic studies:** American, women's. **Biology:** General, botany, microbiology, molecular, physiology, wildlife, zoology. **Business:** Accounting, business admin, finance, management science, managerial economics, marketing. **Communications:** General, journalism. **Computer sciences:** Computer science. **Conservation:** Environmental studies. **Education:** Agricultural, elementary, music, physical, secondary, special, technology/industrial arts, trade/industrial. **Engineering:** Architectural, chemical, civil, computer, electrical, mechanical, petroleum, systems. **Family/consumer sciences:** General. **Foreign languages:** French, German, Russian, Spanish. **Health:** Audiology/speech pathology, dental hygiene, health services, nursing (RN). **History:** General. **Liberal arts:** Humanities. **Math:** General, statistics. **Parks/recreation:** Exercise sciences. **Philosophy/religion:** Philosophy, religion. **Physical sciences:** General, astronomy, astrophysics, chemistry, geology, physics. **Protective services:** Criminal justice. **Psychology:** General. **Public administration:** Social work. **Social sciences:** General, anthropology, geography, international relations, political science, sociology. **Visual/performing arts:** Art, dramatic, music performance. **Other:** Agroecology, Elementary and special education, Environmental geology/geohydrology, Mathematics/science.

**Most popular majors.** Biology 7%, business/marketing 14%, education 14%, engineering/engineering technologies 10%, health sciences 9%, social sciences 8%.

**Computing on campus.** 885 workstations in dormitories, library, computer center, student center. Dormitories wired for high-speed internet access and linked to campus network. Commuter students can connect to campus network. Online course registration, online library, helpline, student web hosting, wireless network available.

**Student life. Freshman orientation:** Available, $60 fee. Preregistration for classes offered. 8 2-day sessions in June. **Policies:** New freshmen subject to live-in policy. **Housing:** Guaranteed on-campus for all undergraduates. Coed dorms, special housing for disabled, apartments, fraternity/sorority housing available. $100 partly refundable deposit. **Activities:** Bands, campus ministries, choral groups, dance, drama, international student organizations, literary magazine, music ensembles, Model UN, musical theater, opera, radio station, student government, student newspaper, symphony orchestra, TV station, black student leaders, local church organizations, College Republicans, Rocky Mountain Democrats, Fellowship of Christian Athletes, Amnesty International, lesbian/gay/bisexual/transgendered association, Movimiento Estudiantil Chicanos de Atzlan, student health advisory council.

**Athletics.** NCAA. **Intercollegiate:** Basketball, cross-country, diving, football (tackle) M, golf, soccer W, swimming, tennis W, track and field, volleyball W, wrestling M. **Intramural:** Badminton, basketball, bowling, football (non-tackle), golf, racquetball, soccer, softball, swimming, table tennis, tennis, track and field, volleyball, water polo, wrestling M. **Team name:** Cowboys, Cowgirls.

**Student services.** Adult student services, alcohol/substance abuse counseling, career counseling, services for economically disadvantaged, student employment services, financial aid counseling, health services, legal services, minority student services, on-campus daycare, personal counseling, placement for graduates, veterans' counselor, women's services. **Physically disabled:** Services for visually, speech, hearing impaired. **Learning disabled:** Comprehensive services available.

**Contact.** E-mail: why-wyo@uwyo.edu
Phone: (307) 766-5160 Toll-free number: (800) 342-5996
Fax: (307) 766-4042
Noah Buckley, Director of Admissions, University of Wyoming, 1000 East University Avenue/Department 3435, Laramie, WY 82071

# Guam

**Student services.** Alcohol/substance abuse counseling, career counseling, services for economically disadvantaged, student employment services, financial aid counseling, health services, personal counseling, placement for graduates, veterans' counselor. **Physically disabled:** Services for visually, speech, hearing impaired.

**Contact.** E-mail: admitme@uguam.uog.edu
Phone: (671) 735-2201 Fax: (671) 735-2203
Remedios Cristobal, Registrar, University of Guam, UOG Station, Mangilao, GU 96923

## University of Guam
Mangilao, Guam
www.uog.edu                                    CB code: 0959

- Public 4-year university
- Commuter campus in large town
- 3,211 degree-seeking undergraduates: 22% part-time, 60% women, 92% Asian American, 1% Hispanic American, 1% international
- 248 degree-seeking graduate students

**General.** Founded in 1952. Regionally accredited. **Degrees:** 302 bachelor's, 6 associate awarded; master's offered. **ROTC:** Army. **Calendar:** Semester, limited summer session. **Full-time faculty:** 182 total; 50% minority, 42% women. **Part-time faculty:** 76 total; 83% minority, 67% women. **Class size:** 45% < 20, 49% 20-39, 3% 40-49, 2% 50-99, less than 1% >100. **Special facilities:** Planetarium, marine lab, Pacific and Micronesian library resources.

**Freshman class profile.** 619 enrolled.

| | | | |
|---|---|---|---|
| GPA 3.75 or higher: | 14% | Rank in top tenth: | 19% |
| GPA 3.50-3.74: | 3% | End year in good standing: | 65% |
| GPA 3.0-3.49: | 27% | Return as sophomores: | 67% |
| GPA 2.0-2.99: | 44% | Out-of-state: | 1% |
| Rank in top quarter: | 44% | Live on campus: | 3% |

**Basis for selection.** Open admission, but selective for some programs. Nursing students required to complete certain science, math, and English high school courses. **Homeschooled:** State high school equivalency certificate required. **Learning Disabled:** UOG will reasonably accommodate individuals with disabilities. Students expected to make timely requests for special accommodation.

**2009-2010 Annual costs.** Tuition/fees: $6,150; $17,410 out-of-state. Room/board: $9,102. Books/supplies: $4,570. Personal expenses: $5,540.

**Application procedures. Admission:** Priority date 6/1; deadline 8/20 (receipt date). $49 fee. Admission notification on a rolling basis. **Financial aid:** Priority date 4/15; no closing date. FAFSA required. Applicants notified on a rolling basis starting 6/1; must reply within 2 week(s) of notification.

**Academics. Special study options:** Accelerated study, double major, dual enrollment of high school students, ESL, exchange student, honors, internships, study abroad, teacher certification program. **Credit/placement by examination:** AP, CLEP, IB, institutional tests. **Support services:** Reduced course load, remedial instruction, study skills assistance, tutoring, writing center.

**Majors. Agriculture:** General. **Area/ethnic studies:** East Asian, Japanese. **Biology:** General. **Business:** Accounting, business admin. **Communications:** General. **Computer sciences:** General, computer science. **Education:** Bilingual, biology, chemistry, early childhood, elementary, English, mathematics, physical, secondary, social studies, special. **Family/consumer sciences:** General. **Health:** Health services, nursing (RN). **History:** General. **Math:** General. **Philosophy/religion:** Philosophy. **Physical sciences:** Chemistry. **Protective services:** Criminal justice. **Psychology:** General. **Public administration:** General, social work. **Social sciences:** Anthropology, economics, political science, sociology. **Visual/performing arts:** Art. **Other:** Interdisciplinary arts and sciences.

**Computing on campus.** 412 workstations in dormitories, library, computer center, student center. Dormitories wired for high-speed internet access and linked to campus network. Commuter students can connect to campus network. Online library, wireless network available.

**Student life. Freshman orientation:** Available. Preregistration for classes offered. Held one week before semester begins and includes campus tour; students receive results of English and math placement tests, academic advising, and orientation of support services. **Housing:** Coed dorms available. $100 partly refundable deposit, deadline 8/7. **Activities:** Concert band, campus ministries, choral groups, dance, drama, musical theater, student government, student newspaper.

**Athletics. Intramural:** Basketball M, softball, table tennis, volleyball. **Team name:** Tritons.

# Virgin Islands, U.S.

## University of the Virgin Islands
St. Thomas, Virgin Islands, U.S.                    CB member
www.uvi.edu                                          CB code: 0879

- Public 4-year university
- Commuter campus in small city
- 2,308 degree-seeking undergraduates: 33% part-time, 74% women, 76% African American, 7% Hispanic American, 7% international
- 152 degree-seeking graduate students
- 70% of applicants admitted
- SAT or ACT (ACT writing optional) required
- 32% graduate within 6 years

**General.** Founded in 1962. Regionally accredited. Additional campus on St. Croix. **Degrees:** 210 bachelor's, 77 associate awarded; master's offered. **ROTC:** Army. **Location:** 45 miles from San Juan, Puerto Rico. **Calendar:** Semester, limited summer session. **Full-time faculty:** 110 total; 67% have terminal degrees, 54% minority, 43% women. **Part-time faculty:** 122 total; 18% have terminal degrees, 80% minority, 57% women. **Class size:** 71% < 20, 28% 20-39, less than 1% 40-49, less than 1% 50-99. **Special facilities:** Amphitheater, Caribbean collection, African art collection.

**Freshman class profile.** 1,162 applied, 809 admitted, 475 enrolled.

| Mid 50% test scores | | | |
|---|---|---|---|
| SAT critical reading: | 350-440 | GPA 2.0-2.99: | 67% |
| SAT math: | 310-420 | Rank in top quarter: | 33% |
| SAT writing: | 350-450 | Rank in top tenth: | 10% |
| ACT composite: | 14-17 | End year in good standing: | 82% |
| GPA 3.75 or higher: | 4% | Return as sophomores: | 75% |
| GPA 3.50-3.74: | 5% | Out-of-state: | 3% |
| GPA 3.0-3.49: | 20% | International: | 5% |

**Basis for selection.** Secondary school record important in admission decisions. Students must have a minimum 2.0 GPA. Nursing Aptitude Test required of nursing applicants.

**High school preparation.** 11 units required. Required units include English 4, mathematics 2, social studies 2, science 2 and foreign language 1.

**2009-2010 Annual costs.** Tuition/fees: $4,100; $11,300 out-of-state. Room/board: $8,420. Books/supplies: $1,650. Personal expenses: $1,980.

**2008-2009 Financial aid. Need-based:** 409 full-time freshmen applied for aid; 358 were judged to have need; 341 of these received aid. Average scholarship/grant was $4,105; average loan $2,875. 67% of total undergraduate aid awarded as scholarships/grants, 33% as loans/jobs. **Non-need-based:** Awarded to 61 full-time undergraduates, including 23 freshmen. Scholarships awarded for academics, art, athletics.

**Application procedures. Admission:** Priority date 2/1; deadline 4/30 (postmark date). $30 fee. Admission notification on a rolling basis. Must reply by 6/30. **Financial aid:** Closing date 3/1. FAFSA required. Applicants notified on a rolling basis starting 4/1; must reply within 2 week(s) of notification.

**Academics. Special study options:** Combined bachelor's/graduate degree, distance learning, exchange student, external degree, honors, independent study, internships. **Credit/placement by examination:** AP, CLEP, SAT, ACT, institutional tests. **Support services:** Learning center, pre-admission summer program, reduced course load, remedial instruction, study skills assistance, tutoring, writing center.

**Majors. Biology:** General, marine. **Business:** Accounting, business admin. **Computer sciences:** Computer science. **Education:** Elementary, music. **Health:** Nursing (RN). **Liberal arts:** Arts/sciences. **Math:** General. **Physical sciences:** Chemistry. **Protective services:** Police science. **Psychology:** General. **Social sciences:** General.

**Most popular majors.** Biology 11%, business/marketing 44%, education 6%, English 7%, health sciences 9%, psychology 10%.

**Computing on campus.** 300 workstations in library, computer center, student center. Dormitories wired for high-speed internet access and linked to campus network. Commuter students can connect to campus network. Online course registration, online library, helpline, wireless network available.

**Student life. Freshman orientation:** Mandatory, $90 fee. One-week orientation activities held on both campuses. **Housing:** Single-sex dorms available. $100 partly refundable deposit, deadline 6/1. **Activities:** Jazz band, choral groups, drama, literary magazine, music ensembles, student government, student newspaper, political clubs, President's club, Future Business Leaders of America, explorer's club, Virgin Islands student association, British Virgin Islands student association, Baptist student union, environment association, Health Educators.

**Athletics.** NCAA. **Intercollegiate:** Basketball, cross-country, tennis, volleyball. **Intramural:** Archery, badminton, basketball, fencing, golf, gymnastics, racquetball, softball, swimming, table tennis, tennis, track and field, volleyball. **Team name:** Bucs.

**Student services.** Career counseling, student employment services, financial aid counseling, health services, personal counseling, placement for graduates. **Physically disabled:** Services for visually, speech, hearing impaired.

**Contact.** E-mail: admissions@uvi.edu
Phone: (340) 693-1150 Fax: (340) 693-1155
Judith Edwin, Vice Provost for Access and Enrollment Management, University of the Virgin Islands, No. 2 John Brewers Bay, St. Thomas, VI 00802-9990

# Northern Mariana Islands

## Northern Marianas College
### Saipan, Northern Mariana Islands
www.nmcnet.edu                                    CB code: 0781

◗ Public two-year upper-division community and liberal arts college
◗ Commuter campus in large town

**General.** Founded in 1981. Regionally accredited. **Location:** 150 miles from Guam, 3,000 miles from Hawaii. **Calendar:** Semester.

**Annual costs/financial aid.** Books/supplies: $1,500. Personal expenses: $900.

**Contact.** Phone: (670) 234-3690 ext. 1528
Director of Admissions and Records, PO Box 501250, Saipan, MP 96950

# Canada

## McGill University
### Montreal, Canada                              CB member
www.mcgill.ca                                     CB code: 0935

◗ Public 4-year university
◗ Commuter campus in very large city

**General.** Founded in 1821. **Location:** Main campus located at the foot of Mount Royal, in the heart of downtown Montreal. The Macdonald campus is situated on the western tip of the island of Montreal, in Saint Anne de Bellevue. **Calendar:** Semester.

**Annual costs/financial aid.** Costs reported in Canadian dollars. Full-time tuition for Quebec residents $1,968, for other Canadian students $5,500, for international students $13,965 to $23,000 depending on program. Required fees start at $1,500 and range upward depending on program. Room and board expenses range from $9,444 to $13,594. Per-credit-hour charges for Quebec residents $66, for other Canadian students $183, for international students $466 to $767 depending on program. Compulsory health insurance for international students $639 (single), $1,794 (dependent), and $3,408 (family). Books and supplies $1,000; other expenses estimated at $2,000. Public transit system $37 per month. Need-based financial aid available for full-time students.

**Contact.** Phone: (514) 398-3910
Director, Admissions and Recruitment, 845 Sherbrooke Street West, Montreal, CN H3A-2T5

## Memorial University of Newfoundland
### St. John's, Newfoundland, Canada             CB member
www.mun.ca                                        CB code: 0885

◗ Public 4-year university
◗ Commuter campus in small city

**General.** Founded in 1925. Additional campus (Sir Wilfred Grenfell College) in Corner Brook, Newfoundland; campus in Harlow, England. **Location:** Located in St. John's. **Calendar:** Trimester, limited summer session. **Full-time faculty:** 1,151 total. **Part-time faculty:** 45 total. **Special facilities:** Center for cold ocean resources engineering, botanical gardens, archaeology unit, ocean sciences center, flume tank, center for fisheries innovation, marine simulator.

**Basis for selection.** Open admission, but selective for some programs. GED not accepted. School achievement in a university preparatory high school program most important. Non-native speakers of English must submit TOEFL, Michigan Test of English Proficiency (minimum score of 85), or other acceptable test, unless graduating from English-language high school. Interviews, auditions, and essay required of music, theater, and visual arts majors. Portfolio required of visual arts majors.

**High school preparation.** 16 units required. Required units include English 3, mathematics 3, social studies 1, science 2, foreign language 1 and academic electives 6.

**2009-2010 Annual costs.** Annual tuition for Canadian students, $2,550; non-Canadians, $8,800. Required fees, $205; room and board, $6,450 for academic year. Costs reported in Canadian dollars. Books/supplies: $700.

**Application procedures. Admission:** Closing date 3/1 (receipt date). $40 fee. Admission notification on a rolling basis beginning on or about 4/30. Application fee $40 for in-province residents, $80 for out-of-province and international students. Housing deposit $500. Costs in Canadian dollars. **Financial aid:** Priority date 3/15; no closing date.

**Academics.** 3-year diplomas in fisheries and nautical science available from Marine Institute. **Special study options:** Accelerated study, cooperative education, distance learning, double major, ESL, exchange student, honors, internships, liberal arts/career combination, study abroad, teacher certification program. **Credit/placement by examination:** CLEP, IB. **Support services:** Learning center, reduced course load, remedial instruction, study skills assistance, tutoring, writing center.

**Majors. Area/ethnic studies:** Canadian, regional, Russian/Slavic, women's. **Biology:** General, bacteriology, biochemistry, cell/histology, ecology, entomology, marine, parasitology. **Business:** Business admin, marketing. **Computer sciences:** General, computer science. **Conservation:** General, environmental studies, forestry. **Education:** General, adult/continuing, bilingual, biology, chemistry, curriculum, early childhood, elementary, French, history, music, physical, physics, reading, science, secondary, social science, social studies, special. **Engineering:** General, civil, electrical, marine, mechanical, ocean. **Foreign languages:** Classics, French, German, linguistics, Spanish. **Health:** Preop/surgical nursing. **History:** General. **Interdisciplinary:** Math/computer science, medieval/Renaissance, neuroscience, nutrition sciences. **Liberal arts:** Arts/sciences, humanities. **Math:** General, applied, statistics. **Parks/recreation:** General, facilities management. **Philosophy/religion:** Philosophy, religion. **Physical sciences:** Chemistry, geology, oceanography, physics. **Psychology:** General. **Social sciences:** Anthropology, archaeology, demography, economics, geography, political science, sociology. **Visual/performing arts:** General, dramatic, music history, music performance, music theory/composition, studio arts, theater design.

**Most popular majors.** Biology 6%, business/marketing 12%, education 21%, engineering/engineering technologies 6%, health sciences 11%, science technologies 7%.

**Computing on campus.** 850 workstations in dormitories, library, computer center. Dormitories wired for high-speed internet access and linked to campus network. Commuter students can connect to campus network. Online course registration, online library, helpline, repair service, student web hosting, wireless network available.

**Student life. Freshman orientation:** Mandatory. Held a few days prior to start of classes. **Housing:** Coed dorms, single-sex dorms, special housing for disabled, apartments available. $500 nonrefundable deposit, deadline 5/31. **Activities:** Bands, choral groups, dance, drama, international student organizations, literary magazine, music ensembles, musical theater, radio station, student government, student newspaper, symphony orchestra.

**Athletics. Intercollegiate:** Basketball, cross-country, diving, fencing, field hockey W, soccer, swimming, volleyball. **Intramural:** Badminton, basketball, boxing, cheerleading, cross-country, diving, fencing, field hockey W, ice hockey M, judo, racquetball, rifle, soccer, softball, squash, swimming, table tennis, tennis, volleyball, water polo, weight lifting M, wrestling. **Team name:** Seahawks.

**Student services.** Chaplain/spiritual director, career counseling, student employment services, health services, on-campus daycare, personal counseling, placement for graduates, women's services. **Physically disabled:** Services for visually, speech, hearing impaired.

**Contact.** E-mail: admissions@mun.ca
Phone: (709) 737-4431 Fax: (709) 737-4893
Glenn Collins, Registrar, Memorial University of Newfoundland, Memorial University of Newfoundland, Admissions Office-Arts and Admin. Bldg, St. John's, Newfoundland, Canada, CN A1C-S7

---

## Simon Fraser University

**Burnaby, Canada**
www.sfu.ca

**CB member**
**CB code: 0999**

- Public 4-year university
- Commuter campus in very large city
- 21,150 degree-seeking undergraduates: 48% part-time, 54% women
- 3,452 degree-seeking graduate students
- 77% of applicants admitted
- 66% graduate within 6 years

**General.** Founded in 1965. Regionally accredited. Harbour Centre campus in downtown Vancouver; Surrey campus in Surrey, British Columbia. **Degrees:** 4,160 bachelor's awarded; master's, doctoral offered. **Location:** 9 miles from Vancouver, British Columbia; 130 miles from Seattle, Washington. **Calendar:** Trimester, extensive summer session. **Full-time faculty:** 931 total; 89% have terminal degrees, 33% women. **Part-time faculty:** 11 total; 73% have terminal degrees, 64% women. **Class size:** 29% < 20, 34% 20-39, 5% 40-49, 16% 50-99, 16% >100. **Special facilities:** Climbing wall, child care facility, hyperbaric chamber, underwater laboratory, combative room, apiary, archaeology museum.

**Freshman class profile.** 10,170 applied, 7,817 admitted, 3,401 enrolled.

**Return as sophomores:** 81% **Out-of-state:** 9%

**Basis for selection.** GED not accepted. Senior academic courses, test scores, and advanced academic course work (International Baccalaureate, Advanced Placement, honors, etc.). Successful applicants normally have

GPA of 2.80 or above (3.00 for programs in the Faculty of Business Administration) and SAT score of 1550 or higher (ACT 22). Academic background, GPA, and test scores most important. Canadian residents not required to submit SAT or ACT. Audition/interview may be required for school of contemporary arts. Applicants may submit personal information profile and at least one letter of reference. **Homeschooled:** Transcript of courses and grades required. Applicants must meet state high school graduation requirements.

**High school preparation.** 13 units required. Required units include English 4, mathematics 3, social studies 1, history 1, science 2 and foreign language 2.

**2009-2010 Annual costs.** Undergraduate tuition and required fees (most degree programs), Canadian citizens and permanent residents: $4,988; non-Canadian citizens: $1,4990. Standard double-occupancy on-campus room: $4,590; board (19 meals per week): $2,700. Freshman students are housed in single rooms. Figures, which cover expenses for full academic year, are in Canadian dollars. Books/supplies: $700.

**2008-2009 Financial aid. Need-based:** 11% of total undergraduate aid awarded as scholarships/grants, 89% as loans/jobs. **Non-need-based:** Scholarships awarded for academics, alumni affiliation, art, athletics, leadership, music/drama, state residency.

**Application procedures. Admission:** Priority date 2/28; deadline 4/30 (receipt date). $45 fee ($100 out-of-state). Application must be submitted online. Admission notification 6/30. Admission notification on a rolling basis. Must reply by May 1 or within 3 week(s) if notified thereafter. Application fee of $100 (Canadian) if academic records originate outside of Canada. **Financial aid:** Priority date 6/1, closing date 11/15. FAFSA, institutional form required. Applicants notified on a rolling basis.

**Academics. Special study options:** Cooperative education, distance learning, double major, exchange student, honors, independent study, study abroad, teacher certification program. Dual degree program with Zhejiang University in China. **Credit/placement by examination:** CLEP, IB. 60 credit hours maximum toward bachelor's degree. **Support services:** Learning center, study skills assistance, writing center.

**Majors. Area/ethnic studies:** Canadian, women's. **Biology:** General, biochemistry, molecular. **Business:** Accounting/business management, actuarial science, business admin, entrepreneurial studies, finance, management information systems, management science, marketing. **Communications:** General, digital media. **Computer sciences:** General, information systems, programming. **Conservation:** General, environmental science, environmental studies. **Education:** General. **Engineering:** Science. **Foreign languages:** French, linguistics. **Health:** International public health. **History:** General. **Interdisciplinary:** Cognitive science, math/computer science, systems science. **Liberal arts:** Arts/sciences. **Math:** General, applied, statistics. **Parks/recreation:** Exercise sciences. **Philosophy/religion:** Philosophy. **Physical sciences:** Chemical physics, chemistry, geology, physics, planetary, theoretical physics. **Psychology:** General. **Social sciences:** Anthropology, archaeology, criminology, economics, geography, political science, sociology. **Visual/performing arts:** General, cinematography, dance, design, dramatic.

**Most popular majors.** Business/marketing 13%, communications/journalism 6%, education 10%, liberal arts 6%, social sciences 21%.

**Computing on campus.** 900 workstations in library, computer center, student center. Dormitories wired for high-speed internet access. Commuter students can connect to campus network. Online course registration, helpline, repair service, student web hosting, wireless network available.

**Student life. Freshman orientation:** Available, $20 fee. Depending on type of program, 1 or 2 days. **Housing:** Coed dorms, single-sex dorms, special housing for disabled, apartments available. $450 nonrefundable deposit. **Activities:** Dance, drama, film society, international student organizations, radio station, student government, student newspaper, First Nations student center, center for students with disabilities, crisis line, public interest research group, women's center, interfaith center, harassment resolution office, Canadian Federation of Students, student society.

**Athletics. NCAA. Intercollegiate:** Basketball, cross-country, diving, field hockey W, football (tackle) M, golf M, soccer, softball W, swimming, track and field, volleyball W, wrestling. **Intramural:** Badminton, basketball, football (non-tackle), soccer, softball, tennis, volleyball. **Team name:** The Clan.

**Student services.** Alcohol/substance abuse counseling, chaplain/spiritual director, career counseling, financial aid counseling, health services, legal services, minority student services, on-campus daycare, personal counseling, women's services. **Physically disabled:** Services for visually, speech, hearing impaired.

**Contact.** E-mail: undergraduate-admissions@sfu.ca
Phone: (778) 782-3397 Fax: (778) 782-4969
Louise Legris, Director of Admission, Simon Fraser University, 8888
University Drive, Burnaby, CN

## University of Alberta
**Edmonton, Canada**
**www.ualberta.ca**

**CB member**
**CB code: 0963**

- Public 4-year university
- Commuter campus in very large city
- 28,149 degree-seeking undergraduates
- 7,131 graduate students
- 58% of applicants admitted

**General.** Founded in 1906. Regionally accredited. Campus Saint-Jean is
the French-speaking element within the university and offers degree programs in education, science, and the arts, with graduate programs in education (MEd) and Canadian Studies (MA). **Degrees:** 5,747 bachelor's awarded;
master's, doctoral, professional offered. **Location:** 180 miles from Calgary.
**Calendar:** Semester, extensive summer session. **Full-time faculty:** 3,744
total. **Special facilities:** Center for the arts, museums, research library system, botanical gardens, research farm, agricultural research stations, professional development center, nanotechnology institute, heart institute, diabe-
tes institute.

**Freshman class profile.** 10,296 applied, 5,991 admitted, 4,761 enrolled.

**Basis for selection.** GED not accepted. Admission based on completion
of 5 appropriate Grade 12 subjects (faculty/program specific), including English. Applicant must present competitive average for admission, with minimum grade of 50% in each subject (based on 50% passing grade). Competitive averages range from 70-85%. SAT or ACT, SAT Subject Tests
recommended. Auditions, portfolios, letters of intent/essays, or interviews
required for several programs.

**High school preparation.** 3 units required. Required and recommended
units include English 3, mathematics 3, social studies 3, history 3, science 3
(laboratory 3), foreign language 3 and academic electives 3. Specific course
requirements vary by program.

**2009-2010 Annual costs.** Full-time undergraduate tuition and required
fees (most degree programs): Canadian citizens and permanent residents,
$6,300; non-Canadian citizens, $18,651; standard double-occupancy on-
campus room, $2,624; board (19 meals per week), $2,730. Figures, which
cover the academic year (2 terms at 15 credits per term), are in Canadian
dollars. Books/supplies: $1,000. Personal expenses: $1,000.

**2008-2009 Financial aid. Additional information:** American students
may apply U.S. federal aid and student loans toward university tuition, but
must apply for that aid in U.S. prior to attending university.

**Application procedures. Admission:** Priority date 3/1; deadline 5/1 (postmark date). $115 fee. Admission notification on a rolling basis beginning on
or about 12/1. Must reply by 8/15. Early Admission conditional on completion of admission criteria and maintaining competitive average. **Financial
aid:** Closing date 5/1. Institutional form required. Applicants notified on a
rolling basis; must reply by 8/15.

**Academics. Special study options:** Combined bachelor's/graduate degree, cooperative education, distance learning, double major, ESL, exchange student, honors, internships, student-designed major, study abroad,
teacher certification program. **Credit/placement by examination:** CLEP,
IB. **Support services:** Learning center, pre-admission summer program, reduced course load, remedial instruction, study skills assistance, tutoring,
writing center.

**Majors. Agriculture:** General, animal sciences, business, crop production,
economics, food science, horticultural science. **Area/ethnic studies:** African, Central/Eastern European, East Asian, Latin American, Near/Middle
Eastern, Scandinavian, Southeast Asian, women's. **Biology:** General, animal physiology, biochemistry, bioinformatics, botany, cell/histology, environmental, microbiology, molecular genetics, neurobiology/physiology, pharmacology, physiology, plant molecular, zoology. **Business:** General, accounting,
actuarial science, business admin, communications, entrepreneurial studies,
finance, human resources, international, international finance, management
information systems, marketing, operations, organizational behavior, retailing, sales/distribution. **Computer sciences:** Computer science, programming. **Conservation:** General, forestry, wildlife. **Education:** Agricultural,
art, biology, comparative, computer, drama/dance, early childhood, English,
ESL, foreign languages, French, mathematics, middle, music, physical, physics, science, social studies, special, trade/industrial. **Engineering:** General,

chemical, civil, computer, electrical, materials, mechanical, mechanics, mining, petroleum, physics, software. **Family/consumer sciences:** Clothing/
textiles, family/community services, food/nutrition. **Foreign languages:** General, Chinese, classics, French, German, Italian, Japanese, Latin, linguistics,
modern Greek, Romance, Scandinavian, Spanish. **Health:** Athletic training,
clinical lab technology, dental hygiene, hematology, nursing (RN), occupational therapy assistant, predental, premedicine, preop/surgical nursing, prepharmacy, preveterinary. **History:** General. **Legal studies:** General. **Math:**
General, computational, statistics. **Parks/recreation:** General, exercise sciences, sports admin. **Philosophy/religion:** Philosophy, religion. **Physical
sciences:** Atmospheric science, chemistry, physics. **Protective services:** Criminal justice. **Psychology:** General. **Social sciences:** Anthropology, criminology, economics, geography, international relations, political science, sociology. **Visual/performing arts:** Dramatic, film/cinema, metal/jewelry, music
history, music theory/composition, printmaking, studio arts, theater design.

**Computing on campus.** 1,300 workstations in dormitories, library, computer center, student center. Dormitories wired for high-speed internet access and linked to campus network. Commuter students can connect to campus network. Online course registration, online library, helpline, wireless
network available.

**Student life. Freshman orientation:** Available. Preregistration for classes
offered. Two-day program includes peer advice presentations and campus
tour. **Housing:** Guaranteed on-campus for freshmen. Coed dorms, single-
sex dorms, special housing for disabled, apartments, fraternity/sorority housing available. $175 deposit. **Activities:** Bands, campus ministries, choral
groups, dance, drama, film society, international student organizations, literary magazine, music ensembles, Model UN, musical theater, opera, radio
station, student government, student newspaper, symphony orchestra, more
than 300 clubs available.

**Athletics. Intercollegiate:** Basketball, cross-country, field hockey W, football (tackle) M, golf, gymnastics, ice hockey, rugby W, soccer, swimming,
tennis, track and field, volleyball, wrestling. **Intramural:** Archery M, badminton, baseball, basketball, bowling, cross-country, diving, football (non-
tackle) M, football (tackle) M, golf, gymnastics, ice hockey, judo, racquetball, rugby, skiing, soccer, softball, squash, swimming, table tennis, tennis,
track and field, triathlon, volleyball, water polo, wrestling. **Team name:**
Golden Bears, Pandas.

**Student services.** Adult student services, alcohol/substance abuse counseling, chaplain/spiritual director, career counseling, services for economically disadvantaged, student employment services, financial aid counseling,
health services, legal services, minority student services, on-campus daycare, personal counseling, placement for graduates, women's services. **Physically disabled:** Services for visually, speech, hearing impaired. **Learning
disabled:** Comprehensive services available.

**Contact.** Phone: (780) 492-3113 Fax: (780) 492-7172
Pat Dalton, Associate Registrar and Director of Enrollment Management,
University of Alberta, Administration Building, Room 120, Edmonton, CN
T6G 2-M7

## University of British Columbia
**Vancouver, Canada**
**www.ubc.ca**

**CB member**
**CB code: 0965**

- Public 4-year university
- Commuter campus in very large city
- 28,817 degree-seeking undergraduates: 26% part-time, 53% women
- 15,154 graduate students
- 53% of applicants admitted
- 77% graduate within 6 years

**General.** Founded in 1915. UBC comprises 18 faculties, 14 schools and 3
colleges across two major campuses (UBC Vancouver & UBC Okanagan)
and two satellite campuses. Undergraduate students may study abroad at
any one of 190 partner institutions in 41 countries. **Degrees:** 5,740 bachelor's awarded; master's, professional offered. **Location:** 6 miles from downtown Vancouver (Vancouver campus), 5 miles from downtown Kelowna
(Okanagan campus). **Calendar:** Semester, limited summer session. **Full-
time faculty:** 2,530 total; 99% have terminal degrees, 14% minority, 33%
women. **Class size:** 23% < 20, 31% 20-39, 12% 40-49, 17% 50-99, 17%
>100. **Special facilities:** Museum of anthropology, museum of biodiversity,
museum of geological sciences, botany collection and herbarium, botanical
garden, Japanese garden, two astronomical observatories, performing arts
center, global issues center, winter sports center (venue for events of the
2010 Olympic Winter Games), world's largest cyclotron.

**Freshman class profile.** 23,102 applied, 12,285 admitted, 6,225 enrolled.

**Basis for selection.** GED not accepted. Academic averages most important. Minimum requirement is strong B+ average; for science and engineering-based programs, strong A average likely to be required. Evaluation of those from American curriculum made on best 8 academic courses from junior and senior years. All applicants, regardless of citizenship and schooling, must meet the university's English language admission standard. Applicants schooled outside Canada encouraged to submit a broader admission package (including personal statement, references, and special academic and extracurricular achievements). Applicants must also meet specific program requirements. Applications encouraged from students completing enriched secondary school programs such as International Baccalaureate (IB), Advanced Placement (AP), General Certificate of Education (GCE), and French Baccalaureate. Generous first-year credit offered to students with high academic achievement in these programs. Standardized achievement test results must be submitted by applicants following US curriculum. (Exceptions may be granted for countries where tests are not available.) Competitive score for SAT is 1600. Competitive score for ACT is 26 + 8 writing. Interviews generally not required. Exceptions at UBC Vancouver are applications to School of Music (interview, audition, and/or portfolio required) and School of Business (supplemental application demonstrating documented leadership and accomplishment required). At UBC Okanagan application to Fine Arts program requires portfolio and letter of intent.

**High school preparation.** College-preparatory program required. 19 units required. Required units include English 4, mathematics 3 and academic electives 12.

**2009-2010 Annual costs.** Tuition for international students (those who are not Canadian citizens or permanent residents) is $677 per credit for most undergraduate programs; examples of full-time tuition costs include 30-credit Arts program, $20,306, and 35-credit Engineering program, $23,690. Tuition for Canadian citizens is $148 per credit for most programs. Although student fees vary according to program, they are generally $725 to $857; fees cover extended health and dental insurance, as well as a local public-transit pass. On-campus room and board expenses average $7,000. Amounts shown are in Canadian dollars and are for academic year. Books/supplies: $2,000.

**2008-2009 Financial aid. Non-need-based:** Scholarships awarded for academics, athletics. **Additional information:** Need-based financial aid from public funds is available only to Canadian citizens or permanent residents of Canada. Need-based financial aid for international students is limited.

**Application procedures. Admission:** Closing date 2/28 (receipt date). $60 fee ($100 out-of-state). Admission notification on a rolling basis beginning on or about 1/30. Students applying for on-campus student housing must accept offer of academic admission by June 1 in order to retain offer of housing placement. Housing deposit ($700 Canadian) is due at time of accepting housing offer. Students not required to accept admission offers by May 1. Supporting documents should be submitted as soon as possible, in order to secure a timely admissions decision. Admitted students may request deferment of offer of admission for up to one year. Requests for deferment must be received by July 15, or within 30 days of offer, whichever is later. **Financial aid:** Closing date 2/15. Institutional form required. Applicants notified by 4/14.

**Academics.** Several cross-disciplinary options available in first-year study. Undergraduate students encouraged to engage in research projects supported by annual Undergraduate Research Conference. **Special study options:** Combined bachelor's/graduate degree, cooperative education, cross-registration, distance learning, double major, dual enrollment of high school students, ESL, exchange student, honors, internships, liberal arts/career combination, student-designed major, study abroad, teacher certification program. **Credit/placement by examination:** CLEP, IB. **Support services:** Learning center, pre-admission summer program, reduced course load, study skills assistance, tutoring, writing center.

**Majors. Agriculture:** General, agronomy, animal sciences, aquaculture, economics, food processing, food science, horticultural science, plant sciences, soil science. **Architecture:** Environmental design. **Area/ethnic studies:** Asian, Canadian, Central/Eastern European, Chicano/Hispanic-American/Latino, East Asian, European, German, Italian, Latin American, Russian/Slavic, Slavic, South Asian, Southeast Asian, Western European, women's. **Biology:** General, anatomy, animal physiology, bacteriology, biochemistry, biophysics, biotechnology, cell/histology, conservation, ecology, environmental, epidemiology, evolutionary, genetics, molecular, molecular biochemistry, pathology, pharmacology/toxicology, physiology, reproductive, zoology. **Business:** General, accounting, business admin, finance, human resources, international, international finance, international marketing, investments/securities, labor relations, management information systems, management science, managerial economics, marketing, operations, real estate, transportation. **Computer sciences:** General, a.i./robotics, computer science. **Conservation:** General, economics, environmental science, environmental studies, forest management, forest resources, forest sciences, forestry, management/policy, wood science. **Education:** General, elementary, middle, multi-level teacher, Native American, physical, secondary. **Engineering:** General, biomedical, chemical, civil, computer, electrical, environmental, forest, geological, materials, materials science, mechanical, mechanics, metallurgical, mining, operations research, physics, software. **Family/consumer sciences:** General,

family/community services, food/nutrition, human nutrition. **Foreign languages:** Chinese, classics, French, German, Germanic, Italian, Japanese, Korean, Latin, linguistics, Native American, Portuguese, Romance, Slavic, South Asian, Spanish, Urdu. **Health:** Athletic training, clinical lab assistant, community health, dental hygiene, nurse midwife, nursing (RN), occupational health, preveterinary. **History:** General. **Interdisciplinary:** Ancient studies, biological/physical sciences, classical/archaeology, cognitive science, medieval/Renaissance, neuroscience, nutrition sciences. **Legal studies:** General. **Math:** General, applied, statistics. **Parks/recreation:** Exercise sciences, facilities management, health/fitness, sports admin. **Philosophy/religion:** Philosophy, religion. **Physical sciences:** Astronomy, atmospheric science, chemistry, geology, geophysics, oceanography, physics, planetary, theoretical physics. **Psychology:** General. **Public administration:** Social work. **Science technology:** Biological. **Social sciences:** Anthropology, archaeology, Canadian government, economics, geography, international relations, political science, sociology. **Transportation:** General. **Visual/performing arts:** General, art, art history/conservation, cinematography, conducting, dramatic, film/cinema, music history, music performance, music theory/composition, musicology, piano/organ, stringed instruments, theater arts management, theater design, voice/opera.

**Computing on campus.** Dormitories wired for high-speed internet access and linked to campus network. Commuter students can connect to campus network. Online course registration, online library, helpline, repair service, wireless network available.

**Student life. Freshman orientation:** Available. Preregistration for classes offered. 3 different orientation programs: GALA International Orientation (3-day event held during week before start of winter term); Parents Orientation (on Sunday before start of term); IMAGINE UBC (Vancouver) and CREATE (UBC Okanagan), official welcome and orientation experience on first day of winter term. **Housing:** Guaranteed on-campus for freshmen. Coed dorms, single-sex dorms, apartments, fraternity/sorority housing available. $700 partly refundable deposit. Cultural houses in partnership with universities in Japan, Korea, and Mexico available. **Activities:** Bands, choral groups, dance, drama, film society, international student organizations, literary magazine, music ensembles, Model UN, musical theater, opera, radio station, student government, student newspaper, symphony orchestra, TV station, over 250 clubs, societies, and other groups.

**Athletics.** NAIA. **Intercollegiate:** Baseball M, basketball, cross-country, equestrian, field hockey, football (tackle) M, golf, ice hockey, rowing (crew), rugby, skiing, soccer, swimming, track and field, volleyball. **Intramural:** Badminton, basketball, cheerleading, cross-country, football (non-tackle), ice hockey, judo, racquetball, skiing, soccer, softball, squash, swimming, tennis, triathlon, volleyball, water polo, wrestling M. **Team name:** Thunderbirds.

**Student services.** Alcohol/substance abuse counseling, career counseling, student employment services, financial aid counseling, health services, minority student services, on-campus daycare, personal counseling, placement for graduates, women's services. **Physically disabled:** Services for visually, speech, hearing impaired.

**Contact.** Phone: (604) 822-8999 Toll-free number: (877) 272-1422 Fax: (604) 822-9858
Denise Lauritano, Assistant Registrar, International Undergraduate Admissions, University of British Columbia, 2016 - 1874 East Mall, Vancouver, CN

---

## University of Manitoba
**Winnipeg, Canada**                                    **CB member**
**www.umanitoba.ca**                                    **CB code: 0973**

- Public 4-year university
- Commuter campus in very large city
- 22,640 degree-seeking undergraduates

**General.** Founded in 1877. **Degrees:** 4,811 bachelor's awarded; master's, doctoral, professional offered. **Location:** 10 miles from downtown Winnipeg. **Calendar:** Semester, limited summer session. **Full-time faculty:** 1,700 total. **Part-time faculty:** 1,600 total. **Special facilities:** Planetarium, astronomical observatory, farm education center.

**Basis for selection.** Open admission, but selective for some programs. **Homeschooled:** State high school equivalency certificate required.

**High school preparation.** 30 units required.

**2009-2010 Annual costs.** Full-time tuition for international students varies according to program of study. Academic year undergraduate tuition in arts & sciences, $10,319; required fees, $471; room and board ranges from $4,669 to $7,759. Costs reported in Canadian dollars.

**Application procedures. Admission:** $90 fee.

**Academics. Special study options:** Combined bachelor's/graduate degree, cooperative education, distance learning, double major, ESL, honors, independent study, internships, liberal arts/career combination, study abroad, teacher certification program, weekend college. **Credit/placement by examination:** CLEP, IB. 30 credit hours maximum toward bachelor's degree. **Support services:** Learning center, reduced course load, study skills assistance, tutoring.

**Majors. Agriculture:** General, agribusiness operations, agronomy, animal health, animal nutrition, animal sciences, business, dairy, economics, farm/ranch, food science, horticultural science, ornamental horticulture, plant breeding, plant protection, plant sciences, poultry, soil science. **Architecture:** Environmental design. **Area/ethnic studies:** Asian, Canadian, Central/Eastern European, Latin American, Near/Middle Eastern, Russian/Slavic, women's. **Biology:** Bacteriology, biochemistry, botany, cell/histology, ecology, entomology, genetics, molecular, pathology, pharmacology, plant pathology, plant physiology, zoology. **Business:** Accounting, actuarial science, business admin, finance, international, labor relations, market research. **Computer sciences:** General, computer science, data processing, information systems, programming, systems analysis. **Conservation:** General, environmental studies. **Education:** General, adult ed admin, business, curriculum, early childhood, elementary, ESL, family/consumer sciences, foundations, instructional media, leadership, middle, multi-level teacher, music, physical, secondary, special, technology/industrial arts. **Engineering:** General, agricultural, civil, computer, electrical, materials science, mechanical. **Family/consumer sciences:** General, clothing/textiles, family/community services, food/nutrition. **Foreign languages:** Biblical, classics, comparative lit, French, German, Hebrew, Italian, linguistics, modern Greek, Russian, Spanish. **Health:** Athletic training, dental hygiene, nursing (RN), occupational therapy, physical therapy. **History:** General. **Interdisciplinary:** Behavioral sciences, gerontology, global studies, math/computer science, medieval/Renaissance, nutrition sciences. **Legal studies:** General. **Math:** General, applied, statistics. **Parks/recreation:** General, exercise sciences, health/fitness, sports admin. **Philosophy/religion:** Judaic, philosophy, religion. **Physical sciences:** Astronomy, chemistry, geology, physics. **Psychology:** General, clinical, counseling, educational. **Public administration:** General, social work. **Social sciences:** Anthropology, criminology, economics, geography, political science, sociology. **Visual/performing arts:** Art, art history/conservation, commercial/advertising art, dramatic, film/cinema, interior design, music history, music performance, music theory/composition, piano/organ, studio arts, theater history, voice/opera.

**Computing on campus.** 392 workstations in library, computer center. Commuter students can connect to campus network. Online course registration, online library, helpline, repair service, student web hosting, wireless network available.

**Student life. Freshman orientation:** Mandatory. **Housing:** Coed dorms available. **Activities:** Bands, choral groups, dance, drama, music ensembles, musical theater, radio station, student government, student newspaper, symphony orchestra.

**Athletics. Intercollegiate:** Basketball, cheerleading, cross-country, diving, field hockey W, football (tackle) M, ice hockey, skiing, soccer, swimming, synchronized swimming W, tennis, track and field, volleyball, weight lifting M, wrestling. **Intramural:** Archery, basketball, cross-country, diving, field hockey W, football (non-tackle) M, handball, ice hockey, judo M, racquetball, soccer, squash, swimming, tennis, volleyball. **Team name:** Bisons.

**Student services.** Adult student services, alcohol/substance abuse counseling, chaplain/spiritual director, career counseling, student employment services, financial aid counseling, health services, legal services, on-campus daycare, personal counseling, placement for graduates. **Physically disabled:** Services for visually, speech, hearing impaired.

**Contact.** E-mail: admissions@umanitoba.ca
Phone: (204) 474-8808 Fax: (204) 474-7554
Iris Reece-Tougas, Director of Admissions, University of Manitoba, 424 University Centre, Winnipeg, CN R3T 2-N2

## University of Toronto
Toronto, Canada
www.utoronto.ca/       CB member

- Public 4-year university
- Commuter campus in very large city
- SAT or ACT with writing, SAT Subject Tests, application essay required

**General. Location:** 95 miles from Buffalo, NY. **Calendar:** Semester, limited summer session. **Full-time faculty:** 2,719 total. **Part-time faculty:** 288 total. **Special facilities:** Greenhouses, observatory, university-operated art galleries and theaters, teaching hospitals, 150-acre farm.

**Basis for selection.** Typically, applicants who are competitive for admission to the University of Toronto are among the top third of their class. Only those applicants who have attained a high level of academic achievement in these qualifications and who present credits to satisfy any prerequisites of specific courses or programs in which they intend to enroll will be admitted. The Faculty of Arts and Science St. George campus, University of Toronto Mississauga, University of Toronto Scarborough, the Faculty of Music, and the Faculty of Physical Education and Health/Kinesiology will consider applications from students in the USA and other countries who have completed or who are completing 12th grade in an accredited high school; such applicants must present high scores in SAT Reasoning or ACT examinations including the Writing Test component and at least three SAT Subject Tests or AP/IB subjects appropriate to their proposed area of study. Scores below 500 in any part of the SAT Reasoning or SAT Subject Tests are not acceptable. Many programs require higher scores. Students seeking admission to science or business/commerce programs are strongly advised to complete AP Calculus (AB or BC) or IB Mathematics (HL or SL or Math Methods with Calculus option). Student profiles required for some programs. **Homeschooled:** Statement describing homeschool structure and mission, transcript of courses and grades required. Application should include course outlines, textbooks and method of evaluation used, samples of written work, relevant details of any independent evaluations or assessments; results of standardized tests may also be considered. **Learning Disabled:** Students can send a letter with supporting documentation.

**2009-2010 Annual costs.** Costs reported in Canadian dollars: full-time tuition, $19,404; required fees, $1,500; room and board, $10,000. Books/supplies: $1,000.

**Financial aid.** All financial aid based on need.

**Application procedures. Admission:** Closing date 3/1 (receipt date). $105 fee. Admission notification 5/1. Admission notification on a rolling basis. Must reply by 5/28. Application deadlines vary by program.

**Academics. Special study options:** Combined bachelor's/graduate degree, cooperative education, double major, ESL, exchange student, honors, independent study, internships, student-designed major, study abroad, teacher certification program. **Credit/placement by examination:** AP, CLEP, IB, SAT, ACT, institutional tests. **Support services:** Learning center, preadmission summer program, reduced course load, study skills assistance, tutoring, writing center.

**Majors. Architecture:** Architecture, environmental design, history/criticism, urban/community planning. **Area/ethnic studies:** African, African-American, American, Asian, Canadian, Caribbean, Central/Eastern European, Chinese, East Asian, European, French, gay/lesbian, German, Italian, Latin American, Native American, Near/Middle Eastern, Polish, Russian/Slavic, Slavic, Spanish/Iberian, Ukraine, women's. **Biology:** General, animal physiology, biochemistry, Biochemistry/biophysics and molecular biology, bioinformatics, biophysics, biotechnology, botany, cellular/anatomical, conservation, ecology, environmental, genetics, molecular, molecular biochemistry, molecular biophysics, molecular pharmacology, pharmacology, pharmacology/toxicology, toxicology, zoology. **Business:** General. **Communications:** General, digital media, health, journalism, media studies. **Communications technology:** General. **Computer sciences:** General, a.i./robotics, computer science, information systems, information technology, programming, systems analysis. **Conservation:** General, environmental science, environmental studies, forestry. **Education:** General, elementary, middle, multi-level teacher, secondary. **Engineering:** General, aerospace, agricultural, biomedical, chemical, civil, computer, environmental, industrial, materials, mechanical, physics, science. **Foreign languages:** Ancient Greek, Biblical, Celtic, classics, Czech, French, German, Germanic, Hebrew, Italian, Latin, linguistics, Polish, Portuguese, Russian, Serbo-Croatian, Slavic, Slovak, South Asian, Southeast Asian, Spanish, Ukrainian. **Health:** EMT paramedic, ethics, pharmaceutical sciences, predental, premedicine, prepharmacy. **History:** General, European, science/technology. **Interdisciplinary:** Accounting/computer science, ancient studies, behavioral sciences, biological/physical sciences, classical/archaeology, cognitive science, global studies, intercultural, math/computer science, medieval/Renaissance, neuroscience, nutrition sciences, peace/conflict. **Legal studies:** Prelaw. **Liberal arts:** Arts/sciences, humanities. **Math:** General, probability, statistics. **Parks/recreation:** Exercise sciences, health/fitness. **Philosophy/religion:** Buddhist, Christian, ethics, Judaic, logic, philosophy, religion. **Physical sciences:** General, applied physics, astronomy, astrophysics, chemistry, forensic chemistry, paleontology, physics, planetary. **Psychology:** General, forensic. **Social sciences:** Anthropology, archaeology, Canadian government, criminology, economics, geography, international economic development, international economics, international relations, physical anthropology, political science, sociology, U.S. government, urban studies. **Theology:** Religious ed, theology. **Visual/performing arts:** General, art, art history/conservation, dramatic, film/cinema, jazz, music history, music performance, music theory/composition, stringed instruments, studio arts, voice/opera. **Other:** Estonian studies.

**Computing on campus.** Dormitories wired for high-speed internet access and linked to campus network. Commuter students can connect to campus network. Online course registration, online library, helpline, repair service, student web hosting, wireless network available.

**Student life. Freshman orientation:** Available. Usually held the week before classes begin. Cost varies. **Housing:** Guaranteed on-campus for freshmen. Coed dorms, single-sex dorms, special housing for disabled, apartments, cooperative housing, wellness housing available. $600 nonrefundable deposit, deadline 6/15. **Activities:** Bands, campus ministries, choral groups, dance, drama, film society, international student organizations, literary magazine, music ensembles, Model UN, musical theater, opera, radio station, student government, student newspaper, symphony orchestra, TV station.

**Athletics. Intercollegiate:** Badminton, baseball M, basketball, cross-country, fencing, field hockey W, football (non-tackle) M, football (tackle) M, golf, ice hockey, lacrosse, rowing (crew), rugby M, skiing, soccer, softball W, swimming, synchronized swimming W, tennis, track and field, volleyball, water polo, wrestling M. **Intramural:** Badminton, baseball M, basketball, cross-country, fencing, field hockey W, football (non-tackle) M, football (tackle) M, golf, ice hockey, lacrosse, rowing (crew) M, rugby M, skiing, soccer, softball W, swimming, tennis, track and field, volleyball, water polo, wrestling M. **Team name:** Varsity Blues.

**Student services.** Adult student services, alcohol/substance abuse counseling, chaplain/spiritual director, career counseling, services for economically disadvantaged, student employment services, financial aid counseling, health services, legal services, minority student services, on-campus daycare, personal counseling, placement for graduates, women's services. **Physically disabled:** Services for visually, speech, hearing impaired. **Learning disabled:** Comprehensive services available.

**Contact.** E-mail: admissions.help@utoronto.ca
Phone: (416) 978-2190 Fax: (416) 978-7022
Merike Remmel, Director of Admissions, University of Toronto, 172 St. George Street, Toronto, CN

## University of Waterloo
**Waterloo, Canada**      **CB member**
**www.uwaterloo.ca**      **CB code: 0996**

- Public 4-year university
- Residential campus in small city
- 22,118 degree-seeking undergraduates
- 3,350 graduate students
- 57% of applicants admitted
- SAT or ACT with writing, application essay, interview required
- 77% graduate within 6 years

**General.** Regionally accredited. Four affiliated university colleges: Conrad Grebel College (Mennonite), St. Jerome's University (Catholic), St. Paul's University (United), and Renison University (Anglican). Each college is coed and open to students of all religious/non-religious backgrounds. **Degrees:** 4,717 bachelor's awarded; master's, doctoral offered. **Location:** 62 miles from Toronto. **Calendar:** Trimester, limited summer session. **Full-time faculty:** 951 total; 93% have terminal degrees, 25% women. **Part-time faculty:** 694 total; 24% women. **Special facilities:** Museum and archive of games, dinosaur museum, observatory, greenhouses, optometry clinic, museum of vision science, real time lab, center for education in mathematics and computing,.

**Freshman class profile.** 38,698 applied, 21,908 admitted, 6,970 enrolled.

| | | | |
|---|---|---|---|
| GPA 3.75 or higher: | 5% | End year in good standing: | 75% |
| GPA 3.50-3.74: | 21% | Return as sophomores: | 88% |
| GPA 3.0-3.49: | 55% | Out-of-state: | 8% |
| GPA 2.0-2.99: | 19% | Live on campus: | 73% |

**Basis for selection.** GED not accepted. All applicants are encouraged to complete the Admission Information Form (AIF) to augment their application and to explain any extenuating circumstances that may have affected their past academic performance. Minimum SAT combined Critical Reading and Math score is normally 1100 for all faculties. SAT Writing component is evaluated on an individual basis. Faculty of Arts and Faculty of Environment require a minimum score of 600 on the Critical Reading component. Minimum ACT comprehensive score is normally 26 for all faculties. Faculty of Arts and Faculty of Environment require a minimum score of 26 on the English component. Selected accounting and financial management applicants will be invited to write the Accounting and Financial Management Admission Assessment. Selected architecture applicants will be invited for interview, writing exercise, and discussion of their portfolios. Social work applicants will need letter of reference and personal statement that confirm sufficient practical experience and personal suitability. **Home-schooled:** Transcript of courses and grades, state high school equivalency certificate required. Admissions office prefers that home-schooled applicants complete their final year of pre-university studies at a traditional (accredited) high school.

**High school preparation.** Admission requirements vary by program.

**2009-2010 Annual costs.** Undergraduates pay $21,000 to $32,300 for the academic year (depending upon academic program) for full-time tuition, books, supplies. On-campus housing and meals cost between $7,600 and $10,000 (depending upon specific accommodations). All figures are in Canadian dollars.

**2008-2009 Financial aid.** All financial aid based on need. **Additional information:** Students who are not Province of Ontario (Canada) residents as defined by the Ontario Student Assistance Program (OSAP) should apply for financial aid in their home states/countries.

**Application procedures. Admission:** Closing date 3/31 (postmark date). $110 fee. Admission notification 5/17. Admission notification on a rolling basis. Must reply by 5/28. **Financial aid:** Closing date 6/15. Institutional form required. Applicants notified by 5/28; must reply by 5/28.

**Academics.** Waterloo is home to the world's largest co-operative education program, with some 3,500 employers around the world. **Special study options:** Combined bachelor's/graduate degree, cooperative education, cross-registration, distance learning, double major, ESL, exchange student, honors, independent study, study abroad. **Credit/placement by examination:** CLEP, IB. **Support services:** Study skills assistance, tutoring, writing center.

**Majors. Architecture:** Architecture, urban/community planning. **Area/ethnic studies:** Central/Eastern European, East Asian, French, Italian, Latin American, Russian/Slavic, women's. **Biology:** General, biochemistry, bioinformatics, biomedical sciences, biotechnology. **Business:** General, accounting, actuarial science, business admin, finance, human resources, information resources management, international, investments/securities, tourism/travel. **Communications:** General, digital media. **Conservation:** Environmental science, environmental studies, management/policy. **Education:** French, mathematics. **Engineering:** Chemical, civil, computer, electrical, environmental, geological, mechanical, operations research, software, systems. **Family/consumer sciences:** Work/family studies. **Foreign languages:** German. **Health:** Health services, premedicine, prepharmacy, recreational therapy. **History:** General. **Interdisciplinary:** Accounting/computer science, biological/physical sciences, classical/archaeology, cognitive science, cultural resource management, gerontology, global studies, medieval/Renaissance, peace/conflict, science/society. **Liberal arts:** Arts/sciences. **Math:** General, applied, computational, statistics. **Parks/recreation:** General, exercise sciences. **Philosophy/religion:** Judaic, philosophy, religion. **Physical sciences:** General, chemistry, geology, physics, theoretical physics. **Psychology:** General. **Public administration:** Social work. **Social sciences:** Anthropology, criminology, economics, geography, international economic development, political science, sociology. **Theology:** Sacred music. **Transportation:** Airline/commercial pilot. **Visual/performing arts:** General, dramatic, studio arts. **Other:** Combinatorics and optimization.

**Computing on campus.** Dormitories wired for high-speed internet access and linked to campus network. Commuter students can connect to campus network. Online course registration, online library, helpline, repair service, wireless network available.

**Student life. Freshman orientation:** Available, $100 fee. 3-day program. **Housing:** Guaranteed on-campus for freshmen. Coed dorms, special housing for disabled, apartments available. $500 nonrefundable deposit, deadline 5/28. Living-learning communities allow students to live in small groups, with all students in a given community enrolled in the same academic program. **Activities:** Bands, campus ministries, choral groups, dance, drama, film society, international student organizations, literary magazine, music ensembles, Model UN, musical theater, opera, radio station, student government, student newspaper, symphony orchestra, Aboriginal Students Association, Association of Caribbean Students, University Association of New Democrats, Chinese Drama Club, Hindu Students Association, Konnichiwa Japan, Latin American Student Association, Polish Students Association, World Vision Club, International Health Development Association.

**Athletics. Intercollegiate:** Badminton, baseball M, basketball, cheerleading, cross-country, field hockey W, football (tackle) M, golf, ice hockey, rugby, skiing, soccer, squash M, swimming, tennis, track and field, volleyball. **Intramural:** Badminton, baseball, basketball, cricket, football (non-tackle), soccer, softball, volleyball. **Team name:** Warriors.

**Student services.** Alcohol/substance abuse counseling, chaplain/spiritual director, career counseling, student employment services, financial aid counseling, health services, legal services, on-campus daycare, personal counseling. **Physically disabled:** Services for visually, speech, hearing impaired. **Learning disabled:** Comprehensive services available.

**Contact.** E-mail: myapplication@uwaterloo.ca
Phone: (519) 888-4567 ext. 33106 Toll-free
number: (519) 888-4567 ext. 33107 Fax: (519) 746-2882
Nancy Weiner, Associate Registrar, University of Waterloo, Ontario Universities Application Centre, Guelph, CN

# Egypt

## American University in Cairo

Cairo, Egypt
www.aucegypt.edu

CB member
CB code: 0903

- Private 4-year university
- Commuter campus in very large city
- 5,055 degree-seeking undergraduates: 9% part-time, 51% women
- 1,148 degree-seeking graduate students
- 56% of applicants admitted
- Application essay required
- 82% graduate within 6 years

**General.** Founded in 1919. Regionally accredited. Language of instruction is English; 75% of degree-seeking students must be of Egyptian nationality. **Degrees:** 778 bachelor's awarded; master's offered. **Location:** 40 kilometers from downtown. **Calendar:** Semester, extensive summer session. **Full-time faculty:** 394 total; 69% have terminal degrees, 48% women. **Part-time faculty:** 324 total; 60% have terminal degrees, 50% women. **Class size:** 57% < 20, 36% 20-39, 6% 40-49, less than 1% 50-99.

**Freshman class profile.** 2,686 applied, 1,505 admitted, 1,222 enrolled.

| Mid 50% test scores | | | |
|---|---|---|---|
| SAT critical reading: | 410-520 | GPA 3.50-3.74: | 16% |
| SAT math: | 530-640 | GPA 3.0-3.49: | 35% |
| SAT writing: | 500-580 | GPA 2.0-2.99: | 26% |
| GPA 3.75 or higher: | 23% | Return as sophomores: | 94% |

**Basis for selection.** Applicants from the United States expected to have completed college preparatory (academic) high school program and to submit minimum SAT score of 1350. Arab students must take Thanawiya 'Amma, with minimum score of 75% required. CE/GCSE/IGCSE certificates will also be considered for admission. SAT Subject Tests required for applicants who have graduated from American-style high schools with less than 3 semesters in residence. TOEFL/English placements are required for all students. **Homeschooled:** Statement describing homeschool structure and mission, transcript of courses and grades, state high school equivalency certificate required.

**High school preparation.** Recommended units include English 3, mathematics 3, social studies 3, science 2 and foreign language 2. One unit fine arts recommended.

**2009-2010 Annual costs.** Undergraduates pay $6,720 to $14,861 per semester (depending upon academic program) for full-time tuition, books, supplies; on-campus housing (no meals included), $1,700 to $2,100 (depending upon accommodations). All figures are in U.S. dollars.

**2008-2009 Financial aid. Need-based:** 634 full-time freshmen applied for aid; 492 were judged to have need; 375 of these received aid. **Non-need-based:** Scholarships awarded for academics, art, athletics, leadership, music/drama, state residency.

**Application procedures. Admission:** Priority date 3/2; deadline 5/15 (receipt date). $45 fee. Admission notification on a rolling basis beginning on or about 7/20. **Financial aid:** Closing date 5/15. Institutional form required. Applicants notified by 8/15.

**Academics. Special study options:** Double major, ESL, independent study, liberal arts/career combination, study abroad. **Credit/placement by examination:** CLEP, IB, SAT, institutional tests. **Support services:** Learning center, reduced course load, remedial instruction, study skills assistance, writing center.

**Majors. Area/ethnic studies:** Near/Middle Eastern. **Biology:** General. **Business:** Accounting, actuarial science, business admin. **Communications:** Journalism, media studies. **Computer sciences:** General. **Engineering:** Architectural, computer, construction, electrical, mechanical, petroleum. **Foreign languages:** Arabic, comparative lit. **History:** General, Asian. **Math:** General. **Philosophy/religion:** Philosophy. **Physical sciences:** Chemistry, physics. **Psychology:** General. **Social sciences:** Anthropology, archaeology, economics, political science, sociology. **Visual/performing arts:** Art, dramatic.

**Most popular majors.** Business/marketing 37%, communications/journalism 20%, engineering/engineering technologies 16%, social sciences 14%.

**Computing on campus.** 687 workstations in dormitories, library, computer center. Dormitories wired for high-speed internet access and linked to campus network. Commuter students can connect to campus network. Online course registration, online library, helpline, repair service, wireless network available.

**Student life. Freshman orientation:** Available. Held in August for 3 days. **Policies:** Non-smoking campus. **Housing:** Single-sex dorms, apartments available. $300 nonrefundable deposit, deadline 9/1. **Activities:** Choral groups, dance, drama, film society, international student organizations, literary magazine, music ensembles, Model UN, radio station, student government, student newspaper, African students association, community service society, Model United Nations, Model Arab League.

**Athletics. Intercollegiate:** Basketball, boxing M, fencing, football (tackle), gymnastics, handball, judo, rowing (crew), rugby M, soccer, squash, swimming, table tennis, tennis, track and field, volleyball, water polo M, wrestling M. **Intramural:** Basketball, football (tackle), soccer, swimming, table tennis, tennis, volleyball, weight lifting M.

**Student services.** Adult student services, career counseling, student employment services, financial aid counseling, health services, on-campus daycare, personal counseling, placement for graduates. **Physically disabled:** Services for visually, hearing impaired.

**Contact.** E-mail: aucegypt@aucnyo.edu
Phone: (212) 730-8800 ext. 223 Fax: (212) 730-1600
Ghada Hazem, Director of Admissions, American University in Cairo, 420 Fifth Avenue, Third Floor, New York, NY 10018-2729

# France

## Parsons Paris School of Design

Paris, France
www.parsons-paris.com

CB member

- Private 4-year visual arts and business college
- Commuter campus in very large city
- 100 degree-seeking undergraduates
- 76% of applicants admitted
- Application essay, interview required

**General.** While the legal structure of the school is that of an independent organization, the academic program of Parsons Paris is coordinated with that of Parsons The New School for Design in New York. **Degrees:** 14 bachelor's awarded. **Calendar:** Semester, limited summer session. **Full-time faculty:** 1 total. **Part-time faculty:** 94 total; 54% women.

**Freshman class profile.** 156 applied, 119 admitted, 60 enrolled.

| | | | |
|---|---|---|---|
| Out-of-state: | 100% | Live on campus: | 5% |

**Basis for selection.** A large part of the Admissions Committee's decision is based upon evaluation of the portfolio and home exam. A prospective student's potential for artistic achievement is one of the most important criteria in evaluating candidates for admission. Portfolio of art work and home assignment.

**2010-2011 Annual costs.** Tuition/fees (projected): $35,095. Books/supplies: $2,050.

**Application procedures. Admission:** Priority date 3/1; deadline 7/1. $60 fee. Application must be submitted online. Must reply by May 1 or within 2 week(s) if notified thereafter. **Financial aid:** Closing date 5/1.

**Academics. Special study options:** Accelerated study, ESL, independent study, internships, study abroad. **Credit/placement by examination:** AP, CLEP, IB. 18 credit hours maximum toward bachelor's degree. **Support services:** Pre-admission summer program, writing center.

**Majors. Visual/performing arts:** Design, fashion design, illustration, photography, studio arts.

**Computing on campus.** PC or laptop required. 40 workstations in computer center. Wireless network available.

**Student life. Freshman orientation:** Mandatory. **Housing:** Coed dorms available.

**Student services.** Career counseling.

**Contact.** E-mail: admissions@parsons-paris.com
Phone: (33) 145-774017
Sara Krauskopf, Director of Admissions and Student Life, Parsons Paris School of Design, 14 rue Letellier, Paris, FR

# Germany

## University of Karlsruhe
**Karlsruhe, Germany**    **CB member**
**www.university-karlsruhe.de**    **CB code: 3592**

▸ Public 3-year university
▸ Small city

**General. Calendar:** Semester.

**Contact.** Phone: (721) 608-7880
Admissions Director, Schlossplatz 19, Karlsruhe, GE

# Guatemala

## Universidad del Valle de Guatemala
**Guatemala City, Guatemala**    **CB member**
**www.uvg.edu.gt**    **CB code: 3875**

▸ Private 5-year university
▸ Commuter campus in very large city
▸ 2,923 degree-seeking undergraduates: 35% part-time, 51% women
▸ Interview required

**General. Calendar:** Semester. **Full-time faculty:** 54 total. **Part-time faculty:** 426 total.

**Basis for selection.** Open admission, but selective for some programs and for out-of-state students.

**Financial aid.** All financial aid based on need.

**Application procedures. Admission:** Closing date 1/16. $55 fee. Application must be submitted on paper. Admission notification on a rolling basis.

**Academics. Special study options:** Combined bachelor's/graduate degree, exchange student, teacher certification program, weekend college. **Credit/placement by examination:** CLEP, IB.

**Majors. Agriculture:** General, food processing. **Computer sciences:** General. **Education:** General. **Engineering:** Agricultural, chemical, civil, computer, electrical, forest, industrial, mechanical, mechanics. **History:** General. **Math:** General. **Psychology:** General. **Social sciences:** Anthropology, archaeology, sociology.

**Computing on campus.** Commuter students can connect to campus network. Student web hosting, wireless network available.

**Student life. Activities:** Concert band, choral groups, music ensembles, student government.

**Student services.** Career counseling, services for economically disadvantaged, financial aid counseling.

**Contact.** E-mail: info@uvg.edu.gt
Phone: (2) 364-0336 ext. 451
Eugenia Rosales, Secretaria General, Universidad del Valle de Guatemala, 18 Avenida 11-95 zona 15, Vista Hermosa III, Guatemala City, GT

# Lebanon

## American University of Beirut
**Beirut, Lebanon**    **CB member**
**www.aub.edu.lb**    **CB code: 0902**

▸ Private 4-year university
▸ Commuter campus in very large city
▸ 6,248 degree-seeking undergraduates: 2% part-time, 48% women
▸ 1,066 degree-seeking graduate students
▸ 60% of applicants admitted
▸ SAT required
▸ 83% graduate within 6 years; 17% enter graduate study

**General.** Regionally accredited. Most students are from the Arab world. **Degrees:** 1,388 bachelor's awarded; master's, doctoral, professional offered. **Location:** In Beirut City. **Calendar:** Semester, extensive summer session. **Full-time faculty:** 457 total; 89% have terminal degrees, 39% women. **Part-time faculty:** 260 total; 52% have terminal degrees, 44% women. **Class size:** 29% < 20, 57% 20-39, 4% 40-49, 6% 50-99, 3% >100. **Special facilities:** Archaeological museum, geological museum, rare biological collection.

**Freshman class profile.** 3,995 applied, 2,378 admitted, 1,463 enrolled.

| Mid 50% test scores | | | |
|---|---|---|---|
| SAT critical reading: | 430-530 | GPA 2.0-2.99: | 34% |
| SAT math: | 570-680 | Rank in top quarter: | 64% |
| SAT writing: | 450-560 | Rank in top tenth: | 36% |
| GPA 3.75 or higher: | 12% | End year in good standing: | 91% |
| GPA 3.50-3.74: | 14% | Return as sophomores: | 94% |
| GPA 3.0-3.49: | 33% | Live on campus: | 21% |

**Basis for selection.** Admission based on composite scores: 50% SAT (25% verbal, 25% math) and 50% standardized school grades. Holders of Lebanese, French, and International Baccalaureate, among other regional governmental secondary diplomas, will be admitted directly into the sophomore class. SAT must be taken before January of the year preceding admissions. **Homeschooled:** State high school equivalency certificate required. Most applicants must take 3 SAT Subject Tests.

**2009-2010 Annual costs.** Tuition/fees: $13,073. Room only: $2,924. Books/supplies: $300. Personal expenses: $100.

**2008-2009 Financial aid. Need-based:** Average scholarship/grant was $3,131. 83% of total undergraduate aid awarded as scholarships/grants, 17% as loans/jobs. **Non-need-based:** Scholarships awarded for academics.

**Application procedures. Admission:** Priority date 11/30; deadline 1/15 (receipt date). $50 fee. Admission notification on a rolling basis beginning on or about 4/30. Must reply by 6/30. Early action applicants must have a minimum SAT and must have been in top 40th percentile of their class for the past two years. **Financial aid:** Closing date 2/2. Institutional form required. Applicants notified by 6/15.

**Academics. Special study options:** Cross-registration, double major, ESL, exchange student, honors, independent study, internships, liberal arts/career combination, study abroad, teacher certification program. **Credit/placement by examination:** AP, CLEP, IB, SAT, institutional tests. **Support services:** Learning center, remedial instruction, study skills assistance, tutoring, writing center.

**Majors. Agriculture:** General, food science, landscaping. **Architecture:** Architecture. **Biology:** General. **Computer sciences:** Computer science. **Education:** Elementary. **Engineering:** Chemical, civil, construction, mechanical. **Foreign languages:** Arabic. **Health:** Environmental health, nursing (RN).

History: General. **Math:** General, statistics. **Philosophy/religion:** Philosophy. **Physical sciences:** Chemistry, geology, physics. **Psychology:** General. **Public administration:** General. **Social sciences:** Archaeology, economics. **Visual/performing arts:** Graphic design. **Other:** Art history, Business administration, general, Computer and communications engineering.

**Most popular majors.** Agriculture 6%, biology 11%, business/marketing 31%, engineering/engineering technologies 15%, social sciences 7%.

**Computing on campus.** 1,478 workstations in dormitories, library, computer center, student center. Dormitories wired for high-speed internet access and linked to campus network. Commuter students can connect to campus network. Online course registration, online library, helpline, repair service, student web hosting, wireless network available.

**Student life. Freshman orientation:** Mandatory. Preregistration for classes offered. Week-long program held in September, one week before classes begin. **Policies:** Student code of conduct; violations may be of an academic or non-academic nature. Designated smoking areas. **Housing:** Guaranteed on-campus for freshmen. Single-sex dorms, wellness housing available. $150 fully refundable deposit, deadline 8/17. **Activities:** Choral groups, dance, drama, film society, international student organizations, music ensembles, Model UN, student government, student newspaper, Palestinian cultural club, Syrian cultural club, Jordanian cultural club, Saudi cultural club, Lebanese Armenian heritage club, Lebanese Red Cross club, human rights and peace club, women's rights club, debate club.

**Athletics. Intercollegiate:** Basketball, cross-country, handball, rugby M, skiing, soccer, squash, swimming, table tennis, tennis, track and field, triathlon, volleyball, water polo M. **Intramural:** Basketball, cross-country, handball, racquetball, soccer, squash, swimming, table tennis, tennis, volleyball, weight lifting.

**Student services.** Alcohol/substance abuse counseling, career counseling, student employment services, financial aid counseling, health services, personal counseling, placement for graduates. **Physically disabled:** Services for visually, hearing impaired.

**Contact.** E-mail: admissions@aub.edu.lb
Phone: (961) 137-4374 ext. 2590 Fax: (961) 175-0775
Salim Kanaan, Director of Admissions, American University of Beirut, PO Box 11-0236, Beirut, LB

# Mexico

## Instituto Tecnologico Autonomo de Mexico

| Mexico City, Mexico | CB member |
| www.itam.mx | CB code: 7144 |

- Private 4-year business and engineering college
- Residential campus in very large city
- 4,647 degree-seeking undergraduates

**General. Degrees:** 4,647 bachelor's awarded; master's offered. **Calendar:** Semester, limited summer session. **Full-time faculty:** 476 total. **Part-time faculty:** 454 total.

**Basis for selection.** Open admission. High school records and admission test mandatory. **Homeschooled:** Complete high school diploma, minimum GPA, and admission test.

**2009-2010 Annual costs.** Undergraduates pay approximately 129,151 Mexican pesos for academic year.

**Application procedures. Admission:** No deadline. $54 fee, may be waived for applicants with need. Application must be submitted on paper. Admission notification on a rolling basis.

**Academics. Special study options:** Combined bachelor's/graduate degree, double major, ESL, exchange student, liberal arts/career combination, study abroad. **Credit/placement by examination:** AP, CLEP, IB, institutional tests. **Support services:** Study skills assistance, tutoring, writing center.

**Majors. Business:** Accounting, accounting/business management, actuarial science, business admin. **Communications:** Digital media. **Communications technology:** Computer typography. **Computer sciences:** General. **Engineering:** Computer. **Engineering technology:** General. **Interdisciplinary:** Science/society. **Legal studies:** General, prelaw. **Math:** Applied. **Social sciences:** Economics, international relations, political science.

**Computing on campus.** 140 workstations in library, computer center. Commuter students can connect to campus network. Online library, wireless network available.

**Student life. Freshman orientation:** Available. **Activities:** Concert band, choral groups, dance, drama, international student organizations, literary magazine, music ensembles, Model UN, radio station, student government, student newspaper.

**Athletics. Intercollegiate:** Baseball M, basketball, soccer, volleyball. **Team name:** Dragones.

**Student services.** Student employment services, health services, legal services.

**Contact.** E-mail: admisiones@itam.mx
Phone: (5) 556-284156 Toll-free number: (55) 018-00000 ext. 4826
Fax: (5) 554-904655
Cynthia Figueroa, Director of Admissions, Instituto Tecnologico Autonomo de Mexico, Rio Hondo 1, Colonia Progreso Tizapan, Mexico City, MX

## Instituto Tecnologico y de Estudios Superiores de Occidente

| Tlaquepaque, Mexico | CB member |
| www.iteso.mx | CB code: 7145 |

- Private 4-year business and engineering college affiliated with Roman Catholic Church
- Commuter campus in very large city

**General. Location:** In metropolitan Guadalajara. **Calendar:** Semester, extensive summer session.

**Basis for selection.** Open admission, but selective for some programs.

**2009-2010 Annual costs.** Tuition ranges from 880 to 904 Mexican pesos per credit hour.

**Academics. Special study options:** Combined bachelor's/graduate degree, ESL, exchange student, liberal arts/career combination. **Credit/placement by examination:** CLEP.

**Majors. Architecture:** Architecture. **Business:** Accounting, business admin, international, labor relations, marketing. **Communications:** Digital media, media studies, organizational, radio/tv. **Computer sciences:** Information technology. **Education:** General, multicultural, statistics. **Engineering technology:** Civil, computer systems, electrical, environmental, industrial, mechanical, telecommunications. **Legal studies:** General. **Philosophy/religion:** Philosophy. **Psychology:** General. **Public administration:** General. **Visual/performing arts:** Design, fashion design, graphic design, industrial design, interior design.

**Computing on campus.** Repair service, wireless network available.

**Student life. Activities:** Choral groups, dance, drama, literary magazine, music ensembles, student newspaper.

**Contact.** E-mail: admision@iteso.mx
Phone: (52) 333-6693535 Toll-free number: (01) 800-7149092
Fax: (52) 333-1342956
Alfonso Aldrete Saldivar, Chief of the Admission Office, Instituto Tecnologico y de Estudios Superiores de Occidente, AP 31-175, Zapopan, MX 45090

## Universidad Anahuac

| Huixquilucan, Mexico | CB member |
| www.anahuac.mx | CB code: 7146 |

- Private 6-year university and career college affiliated with Roman Catholic Church
- Commuter campus in small city
- SAT, interview required

**General.** Founded in 1964. **Calendar:** Semester, limited summer session. **Full-time faculty:** 191 total. **Part-time faculty:** 770 total.

**Basis for selection.** GED not accepted. Admission decisions based on careful consideration of all factors, not on numerical factors alone.

**High school preparation.** College-preparatory program required. 13 units required. Required units include English 2, mathematics 2, social studies 1, history 2, science 2, foreign language 3 and academic electives 1.

**2009-2010 Annual costs.** Books/supplies: $200. Personal expenses: $550.

**2009-2010 Financial aid.** All financial aid based on need.

**Application procedures. Admission:** Closing date 7/31. $99 fee. Application must be submitted on paper. Must reply by 7/31. **Financial aid:** Priority date 7/20; no closing date. Institutional form required. Applicants notified on a rolling basis starting 8/13; must reply within 2 week(s) of notification.

**Academics. Special study options:** Cooperative education, double major, ESL, exchange student, study abroad, teacher certification program. **Credit/placement by examination:** CLEP, institutional tests. **Support services:** Learning center, pre-admission summer program, reduced course load, remedial instruction, study skills assistance, tutoring.

**Majors. Architecture:** Architecture. **Business:** Accounting, actuarial science, business admin, international, international marketing, tourism/travel. **Communications:** General, advertising, public relations. **Communications technology:** General. **Computer sciences:** Data processing, information systems. **Engineering:** Civil, electrical, mechanics, systems. **Engineering technology:** Electrical, industrial management. **Family/consumer sciences:** General. **Legal studies:** General. **Personal/culinary services:** General, culinary arts. **Psychology:** General. **Social sciences:** Economics.

**Computing on campus.** 500 workstations in library, computer center, student center. Online course registration, online library, helpline, wireless network available.

**Student life. Freshman orientation:** Available. **Housing:** Host families provide housing for international and out-of-state students. **Activities:** Bands, campus ministries, choral groups, dance, drama, music ensembles, musical theater, opera, radio station, student government, student newspaper, Anahuac Challenge, Anahuac for Mexico, Anahuac Social Action, Anahuac Social Foundation, Center for Integral Community Development, Perpetual Adoration Society, Red Cross, Youth Weekend Mission Program.

**Athletics. Intercollegiate:** Baseball M, basketball M, cheerleading M, diving, judo, soccer, swimming, tennis, volleyball. **Intramural:** Cheerleading W, diving, judo, soccer, swimming, tennis, volleyball. **Team name:** Leones.

**Student services.** Chaplain/spiritual director, career counseling, financial aid counseling, health services, personal counseling, placement for graduates.

**Contact.** E-mail: pbertha@anahuac.mx
Phone: (555) 627-0210 ext. 8458 Toll-free number: (800) 508-9800
Fax: (555) 596-1938
Bertha Perez Vera, Director of Admissions, Universidad Anahuac, Av. Lomas Anahuac #46., Huixquilucan, MX

---

## Universidad Autonoma de Aguascalientes

| | |
|---|---|
| Aguascalientes, Mexico | CB member |
| www.uaa.mx | CB code: 7147 |

- Public 4-year university
- Residential campus in very large city

**General.** Founded in 1974. Regionally accredited. **Location:** 319 miles from Mexico City. **Calendar:** Semester, limited summer session. **Full-time faculty:** 413 total. **Part-time faculty:** 1,142 total.

**Basis for selection.** School achievement record, test scores most important.

**Financial aid.** All financial aid based on need.

**Application procedures. Admission:** Priority date 6/16; deadline 6/20. Admission notification on a rolling basis beginning on or about 7/12.

**Academics. Special study options:** Combined bachelor's/graduate degree, ESL, exchange student, liberal arts/career combination, weekend college. **Credit/placement by examination:** AP, CLEP. **Support services:** Tutoring.

**Majors. Agriculture:** General, animal sciences, food science. **Architecture:** Architecture, urban/community planning. **Biology:** General, ecology. **Business:** General, business admin, financial planning, tourism promotion,

tourism/travel. **Communications:** Broadcast journalism. **Computer sciences:** General, computer science. **Education:** General, business, English, evaluation, foreign languages, health, school counseling. **Engineering:** Agricultural, civil, computer, textile. **Foreign languages:** Spanish. **Health:** Dental assistant, medical assistant, nursing (RN), ophthalmic lab technology, optician, pharmacy assistant, preveterinary, veterinary technology/assistant. **History:** General. **Legal studies:** General. **Liberal arts:** Arts/sciences. **Math:** General, applied. **Philosophy/religion:** Philosophy. **Psychology:** General. **Public administration:** Social work. **Social sciences:** Economics, political science, sociology, urban studies. **Visual/performing arts:** Commercial/advertising art, design, fashion design, fiber arts, industrial design.

**Computing on campus.** 49 workstations in library, computer center, student center. Commuter students can connect to campus network. Online course registration, online library available.

**Student life. Freshman orientation:** Mandatory. **Activities:** Concert band, choral groups, drama, musical theater, radio station, student government, student newspaper, TV station.

**Athletics. Intramural:** Baseball M, basketball, soccer M, swimming, tennis, volleyball. **Team name:** Gallos.

**Student services.** Alcohol/substance abuse counseling, career counseling, student employment services, health services, legal services, personal counseling, placement for graduates.

**Contact.** E-mail: merangel@correo.uaa.mx
Phone: (449) 910-7422 Toll-free number: (449) 910-7400 ext. 136
Fax: (449) 910-7423
Maria Esther Jimenez, Jefe de Departamento de Control Escolar, Universidad Autonoma de Aguascalientes, Av. Universidad No. 940, Aguascalientes, MX

---

## Universidad Autonoma de Coahuila

| | |
|---|---|
| Saltillo, Mexico | CB member |
| www.uadec.mx | CB code: 7148 |

- Public 4-year university
- Commuter campus in very large city
- 31,450 undergraduates

**General. Calendar:** Semester.

**Freshman class profile.** 22,225 applied, 10,913 admitted, 10,200 enrolled.

**Basis for selection.** Open admission. **Homeschooled:** Statement describing homeschool structure and mission, transcript of courses and grades, state high school equivalency certificate required.

**High school preparation.** College-preparatory program required.

**2009-2010 Annual costs.** Books/supplies: $80.

**Financial aid.** All financial aid based on need.

**Application procedures. Admission:** Closing date 5/22 (postmark date). $23 fee, may be waived for applicants with need. Admission notification 8/1. Admission notification on a rolling basis. **Financial aid:** No deadline. Institutional form, CSS PROFILE required.

**Academics. Special study options:** Accelerated study, combined bachelor's/graduate degree, cooperative education, cross-registration, distance learning, double major, ESL, exchange student, independent study, study abroad, urban semester. **Credit/placement by examination:** CLEP. **Support services:** Learning center, pre-admission summer program, reduced course load, remedial instruction, study skills assistance, tutoring, writing center.

**Majors. Architecture:** Architecture. **Business:** Accounting, business admin, human resources. **Communications technology:** General. **Computer sciences:** Systems analysis. **Education:** General. **Engineering:** Mechanical, mechanics, metallurgical, mining. **Engineering technology:** Electrical, industrial management. **Health:** Nursing (RN). **Math:** Applied. **Physical sciences:** Chemistry. **Psychology:** General. **Public administration:** General. **Social sciences:** Economics, political science, sociology. **Visual/performing arts:** Commercial/advertising art, music theory/composition, piano/organ, voice/opera.

**Computing on campus.** 60 workstations in library, computer center. Commuter students can connect to campus network. Online library, helpline, student web hosting, wireless network available.

**Student life. Freshman orientation:** Mandatory. Preregistration for classes offered. **Housing:** Cooperative housing available. $23 nonrefundable deposit. **Activities:** Concert band, choral groups, dance, drama, literary magazine, music ensembles, musical theater, student newspaper.

**Athletics. Intercollegiate:** Baseball, basketball, boxing, cheerleading, football (tackle), gymnastics, judo, soccer, softball, tennis, triathlon, volleyball, weight lifting, wrestling. **Intramural:** Baseball, basketball, boxing, cheerleading, football (tackle), gymnastics, judo, soccer, softball, tennis, triathlon, volleyball, weight lifting, wrestling. **Team name:** Wolves (Lobos).

**Student services.** Alcohol/substance abuse counseling, career counseling, services for economically disadvantaged, student employment services, health services, legal services, minority student services, personal counseling, placement for graduates. **Physically disabled:** Services for visually, speech, hearing impaired.

**Contact.** E-mail: armandoesparza@edu.uadec.mx
Phone: (844) 438-1651 ext. 1655 Fax: (844) 438-1651
Armando Zatarayn, Director of Admissions, Universidad Autonoma de Coahuila, Blvd. V. Carranza y Gonzalez Lobo, Saltillo, MX

---

### Universidad de Monterrey
**San Pedro Garza Garcia, Mexico**
**www.udem.edu.mx**                                    **CB member**

- Private 4-year university affiliated with Roman Catholic Church
- Residential campus in very large city

**General. Calendar:** Semester.

**Contact.** Phone: (81) 821-51010
Dean of Admissions, Avenida Ignacio Morones Prieto, 4500 Pte., San Pedro Garza Garcia, NL, MX 66238

---

# Republic of Korea

---

### Yonsei University
**Seoul, Republic of Korea**                           **CB member**
**www.yonsei.ac.kr/eng/**                              **CB code: 9893**

- Private 4-year university
- Commuter campus in very large city
- 25,353 degree-seeking undergraduates
- 8,867 graduate students
- Application essay, interview required

**General. ROTC:** Army. **Calendar:** Semester, limited summer session. **Full-time faculty:** 1,725 total. **Part-time faculty:** 2,137 total.

#### Freshman class profile.

| Mid 50% test scores | | | |
|---|---|---|---|
| SAT critical reading: | 640-750 | SAT math: | 720-790 |
| | | SAT writing: | 660-730 |

**Basis for selection.** Admission based on two stages: (1) high school and junior high school academic performance, foreign language proficiency certification, teachers' recommendations, personal statement, and other application information; (2) candidates selected from 1st stage in admission process will proceed to interview, and each candidate will be scored for interview evaluation. Final admission granted to top scoring candidates based on combined scores from 1st and 2nd rounds of selection process. **Homeschooled:** State high school equivalency certificate required.

**2009-2010 Annual costs.** Academic year charges: $6,400 (tuition), $1,200 (on-campus room/board); books and miscellaneous expenses, $1,200. All costs reported in U.S. dollars.

**Application procedures. Admission:** Closing date 5/15 (postmark date). $200 fee.

**Academics. Special study options:** Accelerated study, combined bachelor's/graduate degree, cooperative education, cross-registration, double major, dual

enrollment of high school students, study abroad, teacher certification program. **Credit/placement by examination:** CLEP, institutional tests. **Support services:** Learning center, pre-admission summer program, study skills assistance, tutoring, writing center.

**Majors. Architecture:** Architecture, urban/community planning. **Biology:** General, biochemistry. **Business:** General. **Communications:** Media studies. **Computer sciences:** General, information technology. **Education:** General. **Engineering:** Ceramic, chemical, civil, computer, electrical, metallurgical. **Engineering technology:** Electrical. **Foreign languages:** Chinese, French, German, Korean, Russian. **Health:** Nursing (RN), predental, premedicine. **History:** General. **Legal studies:** General. **Liberal arts:** Library science. **Math:** General, statistics. **Philosophy/religion:** Philosophy. **Physical sciences:** Chemistry. **Psychology:** General. **Public administration:** General. **Social sciences:** Economics. **Theology:** Theology.

**Computing on campus.** 1,050 workstations in dormitories, library, computer center, student center. Dormitories wired for high-speed internet access. Commuter students can connect to campus network. Online course registration, online library, helpline, repair service, student web hosting, wireless network available.

**Student life. Freshman orientation:** Available. **Housing:** Coed dorms available. **Activities:** Bands, campus ministries, choral groups, dance, drama, film society, international student organizations, literary magazine, music ensembles, Model UN, musical theater, opera, radio station, student government, student newspaper, symphony orchestra, TV station.

**Student services.** Chaplain/spiritual director, career counseling, services for economically disadvantaged, student employment services, financial aid counseling, health services, minority student services, personal counseling, placement for graduates, women's services. **Physically disabled:** Services for visually, speech, hearing impaired. **Learning disabled:** Comprehensive services available.

**Contact.** E-mail: ysadms@yonsei.ac.kr
Phone: (822) 212-34131 Fax: (822) 364-2364
Eun-kyung Kim, Admissions Officer, Yonsei University, 262 Seongsanno, Seodaemun-gu, Seoul, KR

---

# Singapore

---

### Singapore Management University
**Singapore, Singapore**                               **CB member**
**www.smu.edu.sg**                                     **CB code: 3873**

- Private 4-year university
- Very large city

**General. Calendar:** Semester.

**Annual costs/financial aid.** Full tuition and fees for Law and non-Law programs are $28,800 (Singapore dollars) per year. Successfully enrolled students are eligible for tuition grant offered by Singapore government that provides qualified students with a subsidy worth on average 50% of full tuition and fees. Subsidized tuition and fees for international students admitted into a non-Law program are $13,700 (Singapore dollars) per year; $15,080 (Singapore dollars) per year for Law program. Students who opt for this tuition grant will be bonded to work in any Singapore-registered company for three years upon graduation.

**Contact.** Phone: (65) 682-80305
Director of Undergraduate Admissions, 81 Victoria Street, Singapore, SG 25975

# Switzerland

## Franklin College: Switzerland

**Lugano, Switzerland**      **CB member**
**www.fc.edu**      **CB code: 0922**

- Private 4-year liberal arts college
- Residential campus in small city
- 433 degree-seeking undergraduates: 2% part-time, 65% women
- 70% of applicants admitted
- SAT or ACT with writing, application essay required
- 44% graduate within 6 years

**General.** Founded in 1969. Regionally accredited. Undergraduate degree programs accredited in United States and Switzerland. Classes taught in English. Students from 60 nations. **Degrees:** 61 bachelor's, 6 associate awarded. **Location:** 60 miles from Milan, Italy; 80 miles from Lucerne. **Calendar:** Semester, extensive summer session. **Full-time faculty:** 25 total; 76% have terminal degrees, 36% women. **Part-time faculty:** 25 total; 32% have terminal degrees, 56% women. **Class size:** 69% < 20, 31% 20-39.

**Freshman class profile.** 547 applied, 385 admitted, 112 enrolled.

| Mid 50% test scores | | | |
|---|---|---|---|
| SAT critical reading: | 550-660 | GPA 3.50-3.74: | 20% |
| SAT math: | 500-630 | GPA 3.0-3.49: | 33% |
| SAT writing: | 550-640 | GPA 2.0-2.99: | 30% |
| ACT composite: | 23-28 | End year in good standing: | 94% |
| GPA 3.75 or higher: | 17% | Return as sophomores: | 66% |
| | | Live on campus: | 100% |

**Basis for selection.** High school academic record, recommendations, extracurricular participation most important. Essay, test scores, interview also important. TOEFL or IELTS required for students whose first language is not English. SAT Subject Tests recommended. Essay and personal statement required. Interview recommended for all. **Homeschooled:** Statement describing homeschool structure and mission, letter of recommendation (nonparent) required.

**High school preparation.** College-preparatory program required. 19 units recommended. Recommended units include English 4, mathematics 3, social studies 1, history 3, science 3, foreign language 3 and academic electives 2. Electives include computer science, art, music.

**2009-2010 Annual costs.** Tuition/fees: $34,400. Room/board: $11,500. Books/supplies: $1,500. Personal expenses: $1,450.

**2008-2009 Financial aid.** All financial aid based on need.

**Application procedures. Admission:** Priority date 3/15; no deadline. $90 fee. Admission notification on a rolling basis beginning on or about 12/15. Must reply by May 1 or within 2 week(s) if notified thereafter. **Financial aid:** Priority date 2/15, closing date 4/15. FAFSA, institutional form required. CSS PROFILE preferred. Applicants notified on a rolling basis starting 2/15; must reply by 5/1 or within 3 week(s) of notification.

**Academics.** 2-week credit-bearing academic travel program required each semester. **Special study options:** Double major, ESL, exchange student, honors, independent study, internships, semester at sea, study abroad, Washington semester. Sophomore and junior year abroad programs with cooperating colleges/universities. **Credit/placement by examination:** CLEP, IB, institutional tests. 15 credit hours maximum toward associate degree, 30 toward bachelor's. **Support services:** Learning center, reduced course load, study skills assistance, tutoring, writing center.

**Majors. Business:** International finance. **Communications:** Media studies. **Conservation:** Environmental science. **Foreign languages:** General, French, Italian. **History:** General. **Social sciences:** International economics, international relations. **Visual/performing arts:** General, art history/conservation. **Other:** Creative writing and literature, French studies, International management.

**Most popular majors.** Business/marketing 24%, communications/journalism 14%, interdisciplinary studies 10%, liberal arts 6%, natural resources/environmental science 6%, social sciences 31%.

**Computing on campus.** 119 workstations in library, computer center, student center. Dormitories wired for high-speed internet access and linked to campus network. Commuter students can connect to campus network. Online library, helpline, repair service, student web hosting, wireless network available.

**Student life. Freshman orientation:** Mandatory, $360 fee. **Policies:** All students required to live in on-campus housing their first year. **Housing:** Guaranteed on-campus for freshmen. Coed dorms, single-sex dorms, apartments, wellness housing available. $360 partly refundable deposit, deadline 6/15. College-owned and leased apartments on and adjacent to campus and in Lugano; freshmen and sophomores must live in college housing. **Activities:** Dance, drama, literary magazine, student government, student newspaper, international business club, language clubs, international relations club, cultural and ethnic clubs, Amnesty International, literary society, service learning club, honor society, performing arts club, media club.

**Athletics. Intramural:** Basketball, soccer, tennis, volleyball. **Team name:** Falcons.

**Student services.** Alcohol/substance abuse counseling, career counseling, student employment services, financial aid counseling, health services, personal counseling, placement for graduates, women's services.

**Contact.** E-mail: info@fc.edu
Phone: (212) 922-9650 Fax: (212) 922-9870
Karen Ballard, Dean of Admissions, Franklin College: Switzerland, 420 Lexington Avenue, Suite 2746, New York, NY 10170

# United Arab Emirates

## American University in Dubai

**Dubai, United Arab Emirates**      **CB member**
**www.aud.edu**      **CB code: 2688**

- Private 4-year university
- Commuter campus in very large city
- 2,444 degree-seeking undergraduates: 19% part-time, 46% women
- 135 degree-seeking graduate students
- 96% of applicants admitted
- Application essay required

**General.** Regionally accredited. **Degrees:** 392 bachelor's awarded; master's offered. **Calendar:** Semester, extensive summer session. **Full-time faculty:** 101 total; 28% women. **Part-time faculty:** 56 total.

**Freshman class profile.** 885 applied, 847 admitted, 387 enrolled.

**Basis for selection.** GED not accepted. Students can take math placement test or submit acceptable SAT score. All engineering applicants must take SAT; combined score of 1090 (exclusive of Writing) required for admission to the program. **Learning Disabled:** Student should declare disability upon applying. Student services provides support on a case by case basis.

**2009-2010 Annual costs.** Tuition/fees: $17,224. Room only: $4,626. Books/supplies: $600.

**2009-2010 Financial aid. Non-need-based:** Scholarships awarded for academics, athletics.

**Application procedures. Admission:** Closing date 8/20. $55 fee. Application must be submitted on paper. Admission notification on a rolling basis. Applications reviewed on a rolling basis. Students will be notified of their admissions status within two weeks after applying.

**Academics. Special study options:** Combined bachelor's/graduate degree, double major, ESL, internships, study abroad. **Credit/placement by examination:** AP, CLEP, IB, SAT, institutional tests. **Support services:** Preadmission summer program, reduced course load, remedial instruction, study skills assistance, tutoring, writing center.

**Majors. Architecture:** Architecture. **Business:** General, accounting, banking/financial services, e-commerce, management science, marketing. **Communications:** Media studies. **Communications technology:** Graphics. **Computer sciences:** Information technology. **Engineering:** Civil, computer,

Four-Year Colleges

electrical. **Visual/performing arts:** Commercial/advertising art, graphic design, illustration, interior design, photography.

**Computing on campus.** 65 workstations in library, computer center. Dormitories wired for high-speed internet access. Commuter students can connect to campus network. Online library, helpline, repair service, wireless network available.

**Student life. Freshman orientation:** Mandatory. **Policies:** Dress code; no alcohol and no drugs on campus. **Housing:** Single-sex dorms, special housing for disabled, wellness housing available. $680 nonrefundable deposit, deadline 6/2. **Activities:** Dance, drama, international student organizations, student government, student newspaper, African cultural club, Egyptian cultural club, Indian cultural club, Khaleej student association, Lebanese student association, Palestinian student association, Pakistani student association, Syrian and Islamic awareness club.

**Athletics. Intercollegiate:** Basketball, soccer, swimming, tennis, track and field, volleyball. **Intramural:** Soccer, table tennis, volleyball, water polo.

**Student services.** Alcohol/substance abuse counseling, career counseling, student employment services, health services, on-campus daycare, personal counseling, placement for graduates. **Physically disabled:** Services for visually, speech, hearing impaired.

**Contact.** E-mail: admissions@aud.edu
Phone: (4) 399-9000 Fax: (4) 399-8899
Carol Maalouf, Director of Admissions, American University in Dubai, PO Box 28282, Dubai, AE

# United Kingdom

## Richmond, The American International University in London
**Richmond-upon-Thames, United Kingdom**    CB member
**www.richmond.ac.uk**    CB code: 0823

- Private 4-year university and liberal arts college
- Residential campus in very large city
- 803 degree-seeking undergraduates
- Application essay required

**General.** Founded in 1972. Regionally accredited. International student body with over 100 countries represented. Students spend their first two years on the Richmond Hill campus and the second two on the Kensington campus in London. Richmond also has study centers in Florence and Rome. Richmond degrees are accredited in the both the US and the UK. **Degrees:** 156 bachelor's awarded; master's offered. **Location:** Richmond upon Thames campus on the outskirts of London; Kensington campus in central London. **Calendar:** Semester, extensive summer session. **Full-time faculty:** 43 total. **Part-time faculty:** 51 total. **Class size:** 68% < 20, 32% 20-39, less than 1% 40-49. **Special facilities:** Richmond Hill campus is next to Richmond Park, the largest of the Royal Parks and Europe's largest urban walled park; Kensington campus is close to some of London's pre-eminent museums.

### Freshman class profile.

Out-of-state:    100%    **Live on campus:**    86%

**Basis for selection.** Open admission, but selective for some programs. School achievement record most important. Letters of recommendation and personal statement considered. SAT/ACT scores also considered but not required.

**High school preparation.** College-preparatory program recommended. 19 units required. Required and recommended units include English 4, mathematics 3-4, social studies 1, history 1, science 3-4 (laboratory 1), foreign language 2-3, computer science 1, visual/performing arts 1 and academic electives 2-4.

**2010-2011 Annual costs.** Tuition/fees: $27,000. Room/board: $13,100. Books/supplies: $576. Personal expenses: $7,157.

**2009-2010 Financial aid. Need-based:** 54% of total undergraduate aid awarded as scholarships/grants, 46% as loans/jobs. **Non-need-based:** Scholarships awarded for academics. **Additional information:** U.S. government loan programs available for eligible U.S. citizens/students.

**Application procedures. Admission:** Priority date 3/1; no deadline. $50 fee, may be waived for applicants with need. Admission notification on a rolling basis. Must reply by May 1 or within 4 week(s) if notified thereafter. **Financial aid:** Priority date 3/15, closing date 8/1. FAFSA required. Applicants notified on a rolling basis starting 3/1; must reply by 5/1 or within 4 week(s) of notification.

**Academics.** English language development programs for non-native English speakers. **Special study options:** Combined bachelor's/graduate degree, cross-registration, double major, ESL, independent study, internships, liberal arts/career combination, study abroad. **Credit/placement by examination:** AP, CLEP, IB, institutional tests. **Support services:** Reduced course load, remedial instruction, study skills assistance, tutoring, writing center.

**Majors. Business:** Finance, international, marketing. **Communications:** Journalism, media studies. **History:** General. **Psychology:** General. **Social sciences:** Economics, international relations, political science. **Visual/performing arts:** Design, studio arts.

**Most popular majors.** Business/marketing 35%, communications/journalism 20%, computer/information sciences 9%, psychology 6%, social sciences 18%, visual/performing arts 6%.

**Computing on campus.** 333 workstations in dormitories, library, computer center, student center. Dormitories wired for high-speed internet access and linked to campus network. Commuter students can connect to campus network. Online course registration, online library, helpline, student web hosting, wireless network available.

**Student life. Freshman orientation:** Mandatory. Preregistration for classes offered. **Housing:** Guaranteed on-campus for all undergraduates. Coed dorms, single-sex dorms, special housing for disabled, apartments, wellness housing available. $1,000 nonrefundable deposit, deadline 5/1. **Activities:** Bands, choral groups, dance, drama, film society, international student organizations, literary magazine, music ensembles, Model UN, musical theater, student government, student newspaper, Community Outreach Club, Amnesty International, Pan-African Club, Middle Eastern Society, Literary Society, International Night, Student Ambassadors, Kuwaiti United, History/Politics Society, Royal United Services Institute for Defense and Security Studies (RUSI for Richmond University).

**Athletics. Team name:** Roebucks.

**Student services.** Alcohol/substance abuse counseling, career counseling, student employment services, financial aid counseling, health services, minority student services, personal counseling, placement for graduates.

**Contact.** E-mail: us_admissions@richmond.ac.uk
Phone: (617) 450-5617 Fax: (617) 450-5601
Nicholas Atkinson, Director of U.S. Admissions, Richmond, The American International University in London, 343 Congress Street, Suite 3100, Boston, MA 02210-1214

# Two-year colleges

## Alabama

### Alabama Southern Community College
**Monroeville, Alabama**
www.ascc.edu                    CB code: 1644

▸ Public 2-year community and junior college
▸ Commuter campus in small town

**General.** Founded in 1965. Regionally accredited. Institution has 3 campuses and 3 centers. **Enrollment:** 1,431 degree-seeking undergraduates. **Degrees:** 168 associate awarded. **Location:** 85 miles from Mobile. **Calendar:** Semester, extensive summer session. **Full-time faculty:** 45 total. **Part-time faculty:** 70 total. **Special facilities:** Nature trail.

**Basis for selection.** Open admission.

**2009-2010 Annual costs.** Tuition/fees: $2,700; $4,830 out-of-state. Per-credit charge: $71 in-state; $142 out-of-state. Books/supplies: $750.

**Application procedures. Admission:** No deadline. No application fee. Admission notification on a rolling basis. **Financial aid:** Priority date 7/15; no closing date. FAFSA required. Applicants notified on a rolling basis; must reply within 4 week(s) of notification.

**Academics. Special study options:** Accelerated study, dual enrollment of high school students, honors, independent study. Degrees in allied health available through University of Alabama at Birmingham, registered nurse program through Jefferson Davis State Junior College. **Credit/placement by examination:** CLEP, institutional tests. 30 credit hours maximum toward associate degree. **Support services:** GED preparation and test center, learning center, pre-admission summer program, reduced course load, remedial instruction, tutoring.

**Majors. Business:** General, administrative services. **Computer sciences:** General. **Engineering:** Electrical. **Engineering technology:** Electrical. **Health:** Licensed practical nurse, nursing (RN), nursing assistant. **Liberal arts:** Arts/sciences. **Mechanic/repair:** Electronics/electrical, industrial. **Personal/culinary services:** Cosmetic. **Protective services:** Firefighting.

**Computing on campus.** 9 workstations in library, computer center.

**Student life. Freshman orientation:** Mandatory. Preregistration for classes offered. **Activities:** Bands, choral groups, student government, student newspaper, Baptist student union,. Circle K, ethnic student society, Phi Theta Kappa, Phi Beta Lambda, Baptist campus ministry, Students in Free Enterprise.

**Athletics.** NJCAA. **Intercollegiate:** Baseball M, basketball M. **Intramural:** Basketball M, softball, table tennis, tennis, volleyball. **Team name:** Eagles.

**Student services.** Adult student services, career counseling, personal counseling, placement for graduates, veterans' counselor.

**Contact.** Phone: (251) 575-3156 Fax: (251) 575-5238 Jana Horton, Alabama Southern Community College, Box 2000, Monroeville, AL 36461

### Bevill State Community College
**Jasper, Alabama**
www.bscc.edu                    CB code: 0723

▸ Public 2-year community college
▸ Commuter campus in small town

**General.** Founded in 1969. Regionally accredited. Additional campuses in Fayette, Hamilton, and Sumiton. Learning site in Carrollton. **Enrollment:** 4,376 degree-seeking undergraduates; 172 non-degree-seeking students. **Degrees:** 472 associate awarded. **Location:** 25 miles from Birmingham. **Calendar:** Semester, limited summer session. **Full-time faculty:** 121 total. **Part-time faculty:** 182 total. **Special facilities:** Observatory, simulated underground mine, museum. **Partnerships:** Formal partnerships with 3M, Alabama Power, McWane Cast Iron Pipe Co.

**Student profile.** Among degree-seeking undergraduates, 44% enrolled in a transfer program, 54% enrolled in a vocational program, 1% already have a bachelor's degree or higher, 1,185 enrolled as first-time, first-year students, 1,966 transferred in from other institutions.

| | | | |
|---|---|---|---|
| Part-time: | 42% | Live on campus: | 1% |
| Women: | 64% | | |

**Transfer out. Colleges most students transferred to 2009:** University of Alabama, Auburn University, University of North Alabama, University of Alabama Birmingham, University of Montevallo.

**Basis for selection.** Open admission, but selective for some programs. Admission to nursing programs competitive and limited. High school diploma not required in some technical programs. COMPASS required for placement unless applicant has 480 SAT verbal and 526 SAT math, or 20 ACT. **Adult students:** COMPASS placement testing required unless student is senior citizen or non-award seeking major taking classes for vocational reasons. **Homeschooled:** Transcript of courses and grades required. 16 ACT required.

**2009-2010 Annual costs.** Tuition/fees: $2,730; $4,860 out-of-state. Per-credit charge: $71 in-state; $142 out-of-state. Room only: $1,350. Books/supplies: $1,200. Personal expenses: $6,450.

**2008-2009 Financial aid. Need-based:** Need-based aid available for part-time students. **Non-need-based:** Scholarships awarded for academics, athletics, leadership, music/drama.

**Application procedures. Admission:** No deadline. No application fee. Admission notification on a rolling basis beginning on or about 7/1. **Financial aid:** Priority date 5/1; no closing date. FAFSA required. Applicants notified on a rolling basis starting 7/1.

**Academics. Special study options:** Accelerated study, cooperative education, distance learning, dual enrollment of high school students, ESL, honors, weekend college. License preparation in nursing, paramedic, physical therapy, real estate. **Credit/placement by examination:** CLEP, institutional tests. Only 25% of program credits can be awarded through nontraditional means. **Support services:** GED preparation and test center, learning center, reduced course load, remedial instruction, tutoring, writing center.

**Majors. Business:** Administrative services. **Computer sciences:** General, computer science. **Construction:** Electrician. **Engineering technology:** Drafting, heat/ac/refrig. **Family/consumer sciences:** Child care. **Health:** EMT paramedic, nursing (RN). **Legal studies:** Paralegal. **Liberal arts:** Arts/sciences. **Mechanic/repair:** Industrial electronics. **Personal/culinary services:** Cosmetic. **Production:** Tool and die.

**Computing on campus.** 1,200 workstations in library, computer center, student center. Commuter students can connect to campus network. Online course registration, online library, helpline, wireless network available.

**Student life. Freshman orientation:** Mandatory, $30 fee. Preregistration for classes offered. **Housing:** Coed dorms, wellness housing available. Housing for student athletes available. **Activities:** Bands, campus ministries, choral groups, dance, drama, music ensembles, student government, student newspaper, Cross Seekers, Circle K, College Democrats, College Republicans, Phi Theta Kappa.

**Athletics.** NJCAA. **Intercollegiate:** Baseball M, basketball, cheerleading, cross-country W, softball W, volleyball W. **Intramural:** Basketball, bowling, boxing, football (non-tackle), softball, table tennis. **Team name:** Bears.

**Student services.** Chaplain/spiritual director, career counseling, services for economically disadvantaged, student employment services, financial aid counseling, on-campus daycare, placement for graduates. **Physically disabled:** Services for visually, speech, hearing impaired. **Transfer:** Transfer adviser, college fairs on campus for students transferring to 4-year colleges.

**Contact.** Phone: (205) 387-0511 ext. 5726 Toll-free number: (800) 648-3271 ext. 5400 Fax: (205) 648-3311
Melissa Stowe, Assistant to the Dean of Student Services, Bevill State Community College, 1411 Indiana Avenue, Jasper, AL 35501

## Bishop State Community College
### Mobile, Alabama
www.bishop.edu     CB code: 1517

- Public 2-year community college
- Commuter campus in small city

**General.** Founded in 1963. Regionally accredited. 4 off-campus sites for technical and health-related programs. **Enrollment:** 2,958 degree-seeking undergraduates. **Degrees:** 274 associate awarded. **ROTC:** Army, Air Force. **Calendar:** Semester, limited summer session. **Full-time faculty:** 98 total. **Part-time faculty:** 84 total. **Partnerships:** Training for business and industry, JTPA Assessment Center, formal partnership with Mobile County public school system.

**Basis for selection.** Open admission.

**2009-2010 Annual costs.** Tuition/fees: $2,700; $4,830 out-of-state. Per-credit charge: $71 in-state; $142 out-of-state. Books/supplies: $700. Personal expenses: $1,033.

**Financial aid. Non-need-based:** Scholarships awarded for academics, athletics.

**Application procedures. Admission:** No deadline. No application fee. Admission notification on a rolling basis. **Financial aid:** Priority date 4/1; no closing date. FAFSA, institutional form required. Applicants notified on a rolling basis; must reply within 2 week(s) of notification.

**Academics.** Students must complete 112 credit hours for graduation from technical programs. **Special study options:** Accelerated study, cooperative education, cross-registration, dual enrollment of high school students, honors, internships, weekend college. Degree programs available in allied health through University of Alabama at Birmingham. License preparation in nursing. **Credit/placement by examination:** CLEP. **Support services:** Learning center, pre-admission summer program, reduced course load, remedial instruction, tutoring.

**Majors. Business:** Accounting, administrative services, business admin. **Computer sciences:** General. **Education:** General. **Engineering technology:** Civil, drafting. **Health:** Medical records technology, nursing (RN), physical therapy assistant. **Liberal arts:** Arts/sciences. **Mechanic/repair:** Electronics/electrical. **Personal/culinary services:** Culinary arts, mortuary science. **Protective services:** Fire services admin, law enforcement admin.

**Computing on campus.** 71 workstations in library, computer center.

**Student life. Freshman orientation:** Available. **Activities:** Bands, choral groups, dance, drama, music ensembles, radio station, student government, student newspaper, social service organization, Baptist student union, Young Democrats.

**Athletics.** NJCAA. **Intercollegiate:** Baseball M, basketball, softball W. **Team name:** Wildcats.

**Student services.** Adult student services, career counseling, student employment services, health services, on-campus daycare, personal counseling, placement for graduates, veterans' counselor. **Physically disabled:** Services for visually, speech, hearing impaired. **Transfer:** Transfer adviser for students transferring to 4-year colleges.

**Contact.** Phone: (251) 405-7000 Fax: (251) 438-5403
Wanda Daniels, Director of Admissions, Bishop State Community College, 351 North Broad Street, Mobile, AL 36603-5898

## Calhoun Community College
### Decatur, Alabama     CB member
www.calhoun.edu     CB code: 1356

- Public 2-year community and junior college
- Commuter campus in small city

**General.** Founded in 1963. Regionally accredited. Satellite campus at Research Park in Huntsville. **Enrollment:** 9,800 degree-seeking undergraduates. **Degrees:** 787 associate awarded. **Location:** 20 miles from Huntsville. **Calendar:** Semester, limited summer session. **Full-time faculty:** 129 total. **Part-time faculty:** 289 total. **Partnerships:** Formal partnership with Boeing.

**Transfer out. Colleges most students transferred to 2009:** Athens State University, University of North Alabama, Wallace State Community College, Auburn University, University of Alabama.

**Basis for selection.** Open admission, but selective for some programs. SAT/ACT scores used for placement. Students from unaccredited high schools required to have 16 ACT or 790 SAT (exclusive of Writing). Selective admission to nursing program. Portfolio recommended for art majors. **Home-schooled:** 16 ACT/790 SAT (exclusive of Writing), successful completion of GED or high school graduation examination required.

**High school preparation.** 26 units recommended. Recommended units include English 4, mathematics 4, social studies 4, science 4, foreign language 2 and academic electives 10. In-state high school graduates must pass state high school competency examination.

**2009-2010 Annual costs.** Tuition/fees: $2,850; $4,980 out-of-state. Per-credit charge: $71 in-state; $142 out-of-state. Books/supplies: $1,500. Personal expenses: $1,000.

**Financial aid. Need-based:** Work-study available for part-time students. **Non-need-based:** Scholarships awarded for academics.

**Application procedures. Admission:** No deadline. No application fee. Admission notification on a rolling basis. **Financial aid:** Priority date 5/1; no closing date. FAFSA, institutional form required. Applicants notified on a rolling basis starting 7/1; must reply within 2 week(s) of notification.

**Academics.** Numerous courses available online. **Special study options:** Accelerated study, distance learning, dual enrollment of high school students, liberal arts/career combination, weekend college. License preparation in dental hygiene, nursing, paramedic, real estate. **Credit/placement by examination:** AP, CLEP, institutional tests. 30 credit hours maximum toward associate degree. AP Exam credit limited to 18 semester hours. **Support services:** GED preparation and test center, reduced course load, remedial instruction, tutoring, writing center.

**Majors. Agriculture:** General. **Biology:** General. **Business:** Accounting, business admin. **Communications technology:** General, photo/film/video. **Computer sciences:** General, applications programming, computer graphics, programming. **Construction:** Electrician. **Education:** General, secondary. **Engineering technology:** Aerospace, drafting, heat/ac/refrig. **Family/consumer sciences:** Child care, child development. **Health:** Cytogenetics, dental assistant, EMT paramedic, nursing (RN), predental, premedicine, prenursing, prepharmacy, preveterinary. **History:** General. **Legal studies:** Paralegal, prelaw. **Liberal arts:** Arts/sciences. **Math:** General. **Mechanic/repair:** Heating/ac/refrig. **Parks/recreation:** Health/fitness. **Physical sciences:** Chemistry. **Production:** Machine tool, tool and die. **Social sciences:** General. **Transportation:** Aviation. **Visual/performing arts:** Commercial/advertising art, photography, theater arts management. **Other:** Family financial planning and counseling, Missile and munitions technology, Music industry communications.

**Most popular majors.** Business/marketing 20%, health sciences 43%, legal studies 9%, liberal arts 13%.

**Computing on campus.** 166 workstations in library, student center. Commuter students can connect to campus network. Online course registration, online library, wireless network available.

**Student life. Freshman orientation:** Mandatory. Preregistration for classes offered. Class held the first semester of attendance. **Activities:** Jazz band, campus ministries, choral groups, drama, music ensembles, student government, student newspaper, TV station, BACCHUS/SADD, black students alliance club, criminal justice club, Native American club, Phi Theta Kappa, allied health students association, the Centurians.

**Athletics.** NJCAA. **Intercollegiate:** Baseball M, softball W. **Team name:** Warhawks.

**Student services.** Career counseling, financial aid counseling, minority student services, on-campus daycare, veterans' counselor. **Transfer:** Transfer adviser, college fairs on campus for students transferring to 4-year colleges.

**Contact.** E-mail: sjl@calhoun.edu
Phone: (256) 306-2593 Toll-free number: (800) 626-3628
Fax: (256) 306-2941
Rob Steinmetz, Associate Dean of Enrollment Management, Calhoun Community College, Box 2216, Decatur, AL 35609-2216

## Central Alabama Community College
**Childersburg, Alabama**
www.cacc.cc.al.us                    CB code: 0715

- Public 2-year community college
- Commuter campus in large town

**General.** Founded in 1965. Regionally accredited. 2 campuses: Childersburg, predominantly for technical courses, and Alexander City, predominantly for transfer courses. 1 instructional site in Talladega. **Enrollment:** 2,444 degree-seeking undergraduates. **Degrees:** 283 associate awarded. **Calendar:** Semester, extensive summer session. **Full-time faculty:** 60 total. **Part-time faculty:** 70 total. **Class size:** 59% < 20, 37% 20-39, 3% 40-49, 1% 50-99, less than 1% >100. **Special facilities:** Wildlife museum, wellness center, pioneer village.

**Student profile.** Among degree-seeking undergraduates, 63% enrolled in a transfer program, 37% enrolled in a vocational program.

Out-of-state:              1%       25 or older:            39%

**Basis for selection.** Open admission, but selective for some programs. Graduates of non-accredited high schools and certain nursing applicants may be required to take SAT or ACT.

**2009-2010 Annual costs.** Tuition/fees: $2,700; $4,830 out-of-state. Per-credit charge: $71 in-state; $142 out-of-state. Books/supplies: $800. Personal expenses: $500.

**2009-2010 Financial aid. Need-based:** 77% of total undergraduate aid awarded as scholarships/grants, 23% as loans/jobs. **Non-need-based:** Scholarships awarded for academics, athletics, state residency.

**Application procedures. Admission:** Closing date 8/21. No application fee. Admission notification on a rolling basis. **Financial aid:** Priority date 7/15; no closing date. FAFSA, institutional form required. Applicants notified on a rolling basis.

**Academics. Special study options:** Cooperative education, dual enrollment of high school students, independent study. Bachelor's degree programs available on campus. **Credit/placement by examination:** CLEP, institutional tests. 48 credit hours maximum toward associate degree. **Support services:** GED preparation and test center, learning center, remedial instruction, study skills assistance, tutoring.

**Majors. Agriculture:** Business. **Business:** General, administrative services, business admin, management information systems. **Computer sciences:** General. **Education:** General. **Engineering:** General. **Engineering technology:** Drafting, electrical. **Health:** Clinical lab science, EMT paramedic, health services, medical assistant, medical radiologic technology/ radiation therapy, medical records technology, occupational therapy assistant, physical therapy assistant, respiratory therapy technology. **Liberal arts:** Arts/sciences. **Protective services:** Criminal justice, firefighting, police science.

**Computing on campus.** 45 workstations in library, computer center, student center. Online course registration available.

**Student life. Freshman orientation:** Mandatory. **Activities:** Jazz band, choral groups, dance, drama, radio station, student government.

**Athletics.** NJCAA. **Intercollegiate:** Baseball M, golf M, softball W, tennis, volleyball W. **Team name:** Trojans.

**Student services.** Career counseling, financial aid counseling, personal counseling, veterans' counselor. **Transfer:** Pre-admission transcript evaluation for new students. Transfer adviser, college fairs on campus for students transferring to 4-year colleges.

**Contact.** Phone: (256) 215-4255 Toll-free number: (800) 643-2657 Amanda Harkins, Dean of Students, Central Alabama Community College, 34091 US Highway 280 South, Childersburg, AL 35044

## Chattahoochee Valley Community College
**Phenix City, Alabama**
www.cv.edu                    CB code: 1187

- Public 2-year community college
- Commuter campus in small city

**General.** Founded in 1974. Regionally accredited. **Enrollment:** 1,907 degree-seeking undergraduates. **Degrees:** 152 associate awarded. **ROTC:** Army.

**Location:** 5 miles from Columbus, GA. **Calendar:** Semester, extensive summer session. **Full-time faculty:** 31 total. **Part-time faculty:** 98 total.

**Student profile.**

Part-time:              30%      **Women:**              67%

**Transfer out. Colleges most students transferred to 2009:** Columbus State University, Auburn University, Columbus Technical College, Southern Union State Community College, Troy State University.

**Basis for selection.** Open admission, but selective for some programs. COMPASS placement exam waived for students submitting appropriate ACT/ SAT scores. Additional requirements for health occupation programs. **Homeschooled:** State high school equivalency certificate required. Program must be accreditated by state or federal department of education.

**2009-2010 Annual costs.** Tuition/fees: $2,940; $5,070 out-of-state. Per-credit charge: $71 in-state; $142 out-of-state. Books/supplies: $1,000. Personal expenses: $750.

**2008-2009 Financial aid. Need-based:** Need-based aid available for part-time students. Work-study available nights, weekends and for part-time students. **Non-need-based:** Scholarships awarded for academics, art, athletics, leadership, music/drama.

**Application procedures. Admission:** Priority date 7/15; no deadline. No application fee. Application must be submitted on paper. Admission notification on a rolling basis. **Financial aid:** Priority date 7/1; no closing date. FAFSA required. Applicants notified on a rolling basis; must reply within 1 week(s) of notification.

**Academics. Special study options:** Accelerated study, distance learning, dual enrollment of high school students, ESL, honors, independent study, liberal arts/career combination. License preparation in nursing. **Credit/ placement by examination:** CLEP, institutional tests. 18 credit hours maximum toward associate degree. **Support services:** GED preparation and test center, learning center, reduced course load, remedial instruction, tutoring.

**Majors. Biology:** General. **Business:** Accounting, administrative services, business admin. **Computer sciences:** General, data processing. **Education:** Business, elementary, physical, secondary. **Engineering:** General. **Health:** Medical records technology, nursing (RN). **Liberal arts:** Arts/sciences. **Math:** General. **Parks/recreation:** Health/fitness. **Physical sciences:** Chemistry, physics. **Protective services:** Criminal justice, firefighting. **Visual/ performing arts:** Art history/conservation, dramatic.

**Computing on campus.** 150 workstations in library, computer center. Online library available.

**Student life. Freshman orientation:** Available. Preregistration for classes offered. **Activities:** Choral groups, drama, music ensembles, musical theater, student government, student newspaper.

**Athletics.** NJCAA. **Intercollegiate:** Baseball M, basketball, softball W. **Team name:** Pirates.

**Student services.** Adult student services, career counseling, personal counseling, placement for graduates, veterans' counselor. **Physically disabled:** Services for visually, hearing impaired.

**Contact.** Phone: (334) 291-4900 ext. 4929 Fax: (334) 291-4994 David Hodge, Dean of Student and Administrative Services, Chattahoochee Valley Community College, 2602 College Drive, Phenix City, AL 36869

## Community College of the Air Force
**Maxwell-Gunter AFB, Alabama**                    CB member
www.au.af.mil/au/ccaf                              CB code: 1175

- Public 2-year community and technical college
- Commuter campus in small city

**General.** Founded in 1972. Regionally accredited. **Location:** 160 miles from Atlanta, 90 miles from Birmingham. **Calendar:** Continuous.

**Annual costs/financial aid.** Students pay no tuition or fees.

**Contact.** Phone: (334) 953-2794 Director of Enrollment Management, 100 South Turner Boulevard, Maxwell-Gunter AFB, AL 36114-3011

## Enterprise-Ozark Community College
**Enterprise, Alabama**
www.escc.edu                        CB code: 1213

◗ Public 2-year community college
◗ Commuter campus in large town

**General.** Founded in 1963. Regionally accredited. Courses offered at Enterprise, Ozark, Fort Rucker, Mobile, Albertville, and Andalusia. **Enrollment:** 2,753 undergraduates. **Degrees:** 294 associate awarded. **Location:** 25 miles from Dothan, 85 miles from Montgomery. **Calendar:** Semester, limited summer session. **Full-time faculty:** 66 total; 32% women. **Part-time faculty:** 104 total; 23% women.

**Transfer out. Colleges most students transferred to 2009:** Troy University, Auburn University, University of Alabama.

**Basis for selection.** Open admission. **Homeschooled:** If sponsoring organization is not accredited, then the student must either take Alabama High School Exit Exam and pass all five parts or take the ACT scoring at least a 16.

**High school preparation.** 28 units recommended. Recommended units include English 4, mathematics 4, social studies 4 and science 4.

**2009-2010 Annual costs.** Tuition/fees: $2,700; $4,830 out-of-state. Per-credit charge: $71 in-state; $142 out-of-state. Books/supplies: $1,000. Personal expenses: $500.

**Financial aid. Need-based:** Work-study available for part-time students. **Non-need-based:** Scholarships awarded for academics, art, athletics, leadership, music/drama, state residency.

**Application procedures. Admission:** No deadline. No application fee. Admission notification on a rolling basis. **Financial aid:** Priority date 6/15; no closing date. FAFSA, institutional form required. Applicants notified on a rolling basis starting 7/1; must reply within 2 week(s) of notification.

**Academics.** Federal Aviation Administration certified Aviation Maintenance Technology program. **Special study options:** Distance learning, dual enrollment of high school students, ESL, honors, internships, weekend college. License preparation in aviation, paramedic. **Credit/placement by examination:** AP, CLEP, institutional tests. 30 credit hours maximum toward associate degree. **Support services:** GED preparation and test center, learning center, remedial instruction, tutoring.

**Majors. Business:** Administrative services, business admin, management information systems, office management, real estate. **Computer sciences:** General. **Health:** EMT paramedic, medical assistant, medical records technology. **Legal studies:** Paralegal. **Liberal arts:** Arts/sciences. **Mechanic/repair:** Aircraft, avionics.

**Computing on campus.** Commuter students can connect to campus network. Online course registration, helpline available.

**Student life. Freshman orientation:** Mandatory, $10 fee. Preregistration for classes offered. **Activities:** Concert band, campus ministries, choral groups, dance, drama, music ensembles, student government, student newspaper, community band, concert choir.

**Athletics.** NJCAA. **Intercollegiate:** Baseball M, basketball, softball W. **Team name:** Boll Weevils.

**Student services.** Adult student services, career counseling, student employment services, financial aid counseling, on-campus daycare, personal counseling, placement for graduates, veterans' counselor, women's services. **Physically disabled:** Services for visually, speech, hearing impaired. **Transfer:** Transfer adviser, college fairs on campus for students transferring to 4-year colleges.

**Contact.** E-mail: gdeas@escc.edu
Phone: (334) 347-2623 ext. 2234 Fax: (334) 347-5569
M. Gary Deas, Associate Dean of Students/Registrar, Enterprise-Ozark Community College, Box 1300, Enterprise, AL 36331

## Faulkner State Community College
**Bay Minette, Alabama**
www.faulknerstate.edu               CB code: 1939

◗ Public 2-year community college
◗ Commuter campus in large town

**General.** Founded in 1965. Regionally accredited. Branch campuses in Fairhope and Gulf Shores. **Enrollment:** 3,976 degree-seeking undergraduates. **Degrees:** 352 associate awarded. **Location:** 35 miles from Mobile. **Calendar:** Semester, extensive summer session. **Full-time faculty:** 68 total. **Part-time faculty:** 136 total.

**Transfer out. Colleges most students transferred to 2009:** University of Alabama, Auburn University, University of South Alabama.

**Basis for selection.** Open admission, but selective for some programs. Students applying for dental assisting program must take and pass Health Occupations Aptitude exam. Audition recommended for music majors, portfolio for art majors. **Homeschooled:** If school is non-accredited, 16 ACT or GED required.

**2009-2010 Annual costs.** Tuition/fees: $2,790; $4,920 out-of-state. Per-credit charge: $71 in-state; $142 out-of-state. Room/board: $4,800. Books/supplies: $450. Personal expenses: $800.

**Application procedures. Admission:** No deadline. No application fee. Admission notification on a rolling basis. **Financial aid:** Priority date 7/1; no closing date. FAFSA, institutional form required. Applicants notified on a rolling basis starting 8/1.

**Academics. Special study options:** Accelerated study, cooperative education, distance learning, double major, dual enrollment of high school students, honors, independent study, internships. **Credit/placement by examination:** CLEP. 20 credit hours maximum toward associate degree. **Support services:** GED preparation and test center, learning center, remedial instruction, tutoring.

**Majors. Agriculture:** General, business, landscaping. **Biology:** General. **Business:** Administrative services, business admin, finance, hospitality admin, office technology. **Communications:** Journalism. **Computer sciences:** General, computer graphics, systems analysis. **Conservation:** Forestry. **Education:** Business, early childhood, elementary, physical. **Engineering technology:** Hazardous materials. **Family/consumer sciences:** General. **Health:** Clinical lab science, clinical lab technology, dental assistant, EMT paramedic, medical secretary, predental, premedicine, prenursing, prepharmacy, preveterinary. **Legal studies:** Court reporting, legal secretary, paralegal. **Liberal arts:** Arts/sciences. **Math:** General. **Parks/recreation:** Facilities management. **Personal/culinary services:** Culinary arts. **Physical sciences:** Chemistry. **Social sciences:** General. **Visual/performing arts:** General, art, commercial/advertising art, studio arts.

**Computing on campus.** 16 workstations in library, computer center.

**Student life. Freshman orientation:** Available. **Housing:** Single-sex dorms available. $35 deposit. **Activities:** Jazz band, choral groups, drama, music ensembles, student government, student newspaper, pow-wow leadership, Phi Beta Lambda, Baptist campus ministries, Phi Theta Kappa, Psi Beta, association of computational machinery.

**Athletics.** NJCAA. **Intercollegiate:** Baseball M, basketball, cheerleading, golf, softball W, tennis, volleyball. **Intramural:** Basketball M, bowling, racquetball, softball, volleyball W. **Team name:** Sun Chiefs.

**Student services.** Career counseling, student employment services, health services, personal counseling, placement for graduates, veterans' counselor. **Physically disabled:** Services for visually impaired. **Transfer:** Transfer adviser for students transferring to 4-year colleges.

**Contact.** Phone: (251) 580-2111 Toll-free number: (800) 231-3752
Fax: (251) 580-2285
Betty Sheffield, Director of Admissions, Faulkner State Community
College, 1900 Highway 31 South, Bay Minette, AL 36507

## Gadsden State Community College
**Gadsden, Alabama**
www.gadsdenstate.edu                CB code: 1262

◗ Public 2-year community and technical college
◗ Commuter campus in small city

**General.** Founded in 1985. Regionally accredited. Off-campus sites include Ayers Campus, McClellan Campus and Cherokee County Center. **Enrollment:** 6,494 degree-seeking undergraduates; 423 non-degree-seeking students. **Degrees:** 448 associate awarded. **ROTC:** Army. **Location:** 60 miles from Birmingham. **Calendar:** Semester, extensive summer session. **Full-time faculty:** 153 total. **Part-time faculty:** 190 total. **Special facilities:** Advanced technology center, language institute, aquaculture education, cadaver lab.

**Student profile.** Among degree-seeking undergraduates, 74% enrolled in a transfer program, 26% enrolled in a vocational program, 4,497 enrolled as first-time, first-year students.

| | | | |
|---|---|---|---|
| Part-time: | 37% | 25 or older: | 30% |
| Out-of-state: | 2% | Live on campus: | 4% |
| Women: | 61% | | |

**Transfer out. Colleges most students transferred to 2009:** Jacksonville State University, Auburn University, University of Alabama, University of Alabama at Birmingham, University of Alabama at Huntsville.

**Basis for selection.** Open admission, but selective for some programs. Special requirements for health-related programs. Career Program Assessment Test required for some programs. Interview recommended for computer technology, court reporting, and most health science majors. **Homeschooled:** Transcript of courses and grades required. 16 ACT or 790 SAT required.

**High school preparation.** 27 units recommended. Recommended units include English 4, mathematics 4, social studies 4, science 4 (laboratory 2) and academic electives 9. Electives must include .5 unit computer, .5 unit of fine arts.

**2009-2010 Annual costs.** Tuition/fees: $2,700; $4,830 out-of-state. Per-credit charge: $71 in-state; $142 out-of-state. Room/board: $3,200. Books/supplies: $800. Personal expenses: $825.

**2008-2009 Financial aid. Need-based:** Need-based aid available for part-time students. Work-study available for part-time students. **Non-need-based:** Scholarships awarded for academics, alumni affiliation, art, athletics, job skills, leadership, minority status, music/drama, state residency.

**Application procedures. Admission:** No deadline. No application fee. Admission notification on a rolling basis. **Financial aid:** Priority date 4/15; no closing date. FAFSA, institutional form required. Applicants notified on a rolling basis starting 6/10.

**Academics. Special study options:** Accelerated study, cooperative education, cross-registration, distance learning, dual enrollment of high school students, ESL, honors, independent study, internships, weekend college. License preparation in nursing, paramedic, radiology. **Credit/placement by examination:** CLEP, institutional tests. 20 credit hours maximum toward associate degree. **Support services:** GED preparation and test center, remedial instruction, study skills assistance, tutoring, writing center.

**Majors. Agriculture:** General. **Area/ethnic studies:** American. **Biology:** General. **Business:** Accounting technology, administrative services, business admin, sales/distribution. **Communications:** General. **Communications technology:** General, graphics. **Computer sciences:** General, computer science, information systems, information technology, LAN/WAN management, networking, programming. **Conservation:** Forestry. **Education:** General, early childhood, elementary, kindergarten/preschool, mathematics. **Engineering:** General. **Engineering technology:** Civil, civil drafting, computer systems, electrical, heat/ac/refrig, industrial, mechanical, mechanical drafting, telecommunications. **Family/consumer sciences:** Child development. **Health:** Clinical lab assistant, clinical lab technology, EMT paramedic, medical radiologic technology/radiation therapy, medical records technology, nursing (RN), predental, premedicine, prenursing, prepharmacy, preveterinary, substance abuse counseling. **History:** General. **Legal studies:** Court reporting, paralegal, prelaw. **Liberal arts:** Arts/sciences. **Math:** General. **Mechanic/repair:** Electronics/electrical, heating/ac/refrig, industrial. **Parks/recreation:** Health/fitness. **Philosophy/religion:** Religion. **Physical sciences:** Chemistry. **Protective services:** Law enforcement admin. **Psychology:** General. **Social sciences:** Sociology. **Visual/performing arts:** Art.

**Computing on campus.** 250 workstations in dormitories, library, computer center, student center. Dormitories wired for high-speed internet access. Online course registration, online library available.

**Student life. Freshman orientation:** Mandatory, $90 fee. Preregistration for classes offered. **Housing:** Coed dorms, wellness housing available. $200 fully refundable deposit. **Activities:** Bands, campus ministries, choral groups, dance, drama, international student organizations, music ensembles, student government, Circle-K, international club, Baptist student union, Phi Beta Lambda.

**Athletics.** NJCAA. **Intercollegiate:** Baseball M, basketball, cross-country W, softball W, tennis M, volleyball W. **Team name:** Cardinals.

**Student services.** Adult student services, career counseling, services for economically disadvantaged, student employment services, financial aid counseling, personal counseling, placement for graduates, veterans' counselor. **Physically disabled:** Services for visually, speech, hearing impaired. **Transfer:** Pre-admission transcript evaluation for new students. Transfer adviser, college fairs on campus for students transferring to 4-year colleges.

**Contact.** Phone: (256) 549-8210 Toll-free number: (800) 226-5563 Fax: (256) 549-8205
Teresa Rhea, Associate Dean of Student Services and Registrar, Gadsden State Community College, 1001 George Wallace Drive, Gadsden, AL 35902-0227

## George C. Wallace Community College at Dothan
### Dothan, Alabama
www.wallace.edu                                         CB code: 1264

- Public 2-year community college
- Commuter campus in small city

**General.** Founded in 1949. Regionally accredited. Additional campuses in Eufaula and Ft. Rucker. **Enrollment:** 4,655 degree-seeking undergraduates. **Degrees:** 446 associate awarded. **Calendar:** Semester, extensive summer session. **Full-time faculty:** 132 total. **Part-time faculty:** 122 total.

**Student profile.**

| | | | |
|---|---|---|---|
| Out-of-state: | 4% | 25 or older: | 43% |

**Transfer out. Colleges most students transferred to 2009:** University of Alabama, Auburn University, University of Alabama at Birmingham.

**Basis for selection.** Open admission, but selective for some programs. Additional requirements for allied health and nursing programs. National League for Nursing examination required for nursing applicants. Interview required of nursing majors.

**2009-2010 Annual costs.** Tuition/fees: $2,700; $4,830 out-of-state. Per-credit charge: $71 in-state; $142 out-of-state. Books/supplies: $1,900. Personal expenses: $666.

**Financial aid. Need-based:** Work-study available for part-time students. **Non-need-based:** Scholarships awarded for academics, athletics, leadership.

**Application procedures. Admission:** No deadline. No application fee. Admission notification on a rolling basis. **Financial aid:** Priority date 5/1; no closing date. FAFSA required. Applicants notified on a rolling basis.

**Academics. Special study options:** Accelerated study, cooperative education, cross-registration, distance learning, dual enrollment of high school students, ESL, honors. License preparation in nursing, paramedic, physical therapy, radiology. **Credit/placement by examination:** AP, CLEP, institutional tests. 48 credit hours maximum toward associate degree. **Support services:** GED preparation and test center, learning center, pre-admission summer program, remedial instruction, study skills assistance, tutoring.

**Majors. Business:** Administrative services. **Computer sciences:** General. **Construction:** Electrician. **Engineering technology:** Drafting. **Health:** EMT paramedic, medical assistant, medical radiologic technology/radiation therapy, respiratory therapy technology. **Liberal arts:** Arts/sciences. **Mechanic/repair:** Electronics/electrical.

**Student life. Freshman orientation:** Mandatory. Preregistration for classes offered. **Activities:** Jazz band, choral groups, drama, music ensembles, student government, student newspaper, Association of Student Practical Nursing, Diplomats, Elite club, National Vocational-Technical Honor Society, Phi Theta Kappa, Phi Beta Lambda, Respiratory Therapy Association for Better Breathing.

**Athletics.** NJCAA. **Intercollegiate:** Baseball M, softball W. **Team name:** Govs (M), Lady Govs (W).

**Student services.** Adult student services, career counseling, services for economically disadvantaged, student employment services, financial aid counseling, personal counseling, placement for graduates, veterans' counselor. **Learning disabled:** Comprehensive services available. **Transfer:** Transfer adviser, college fairs on campus for students transferring to 4-year colleges.

**Contact.** Phone: (334) 983-3521 Toll-free number: (800) 543-2426 Fax: (334) 983-6066
Keith Saulsberry, George C. Wallace Community College at Dothan, 1141 Wallace Drive, Dothan, AL 36303-0943

## George C. Wallace State Community College at Selma
### Selma, Alabama
www.wccs.edu                                            CB code: 3146

- Public 2-year community and technical college
- Commuter campus in large town

**General.** Founded in 1963. Regionally accredited. **Enrollment:** 1,937 degree-seeking undergraduates. **Degrees:** 272 associate awarded. **Location:** 50 miles from Montgomery, 90 miles from Birmingham. **Calendar:** Semester, extensive summer session. **Full-time faculty:** 50 total. **Part-time faculty:** 56 total.

**Basis for selection.** Open admission, but selective for some programs. Generic/mobility (RN) nursing candidates need 20 ACT. Practical (LPN) nursing candidates need 18 ACT, or 41 on the Nursing Entrance Test.

**2009-2010 Annual costs.** Tuition/fees: $2,700; $4,830 out-of-state. Per-credit charge: $71 in-state; $142 out-of-state. Books/supplies: $690. Personal expenses: $976.

**2008-2009 Financial aid. Non-need-based:** Scholarships awarded for academics, athletics.

**Application procedures. Admission:** Priority date 8/21; no deadline. No application fee. Admission notification on a rolling basis. **Financial aid:** Priority date 6/1; no closing date. FAFSA required. Applicants notified on a rolling basis starting 6/15.

**Academics. Special study options:** Accelerated study, double major, dual enrollment of high school students. **Credit/placement by examination:** CLEP, institutional tests. 30 credit hours maximum toward associate degree. **Support services:** GED preparation and test center, learning center, reduced course load, remedial instruction, study skills assistance, tutoring.

**Majors. Business:** Administrative services, business admin. **Computer sciences:** General. **Engineering technology:** Drafting. **Health:** Nursing (RN). **Liberal arts:** Arts/sciences. **Mechanic/repair:** General.

**Student life. Freshman orientation:** Available. Preregistration for classes offered. **Activities:** Student government, Baptist student union, Phi Theta Kappa, Fellowship of Christian Athletes.

**Athletics.** NJCAA. **Intercollegiate:** Baseball M, basketball, softball W. **Intramural:** Baseball M, basketball, softball. **Team name:** Patriots.

**Student services.** Career counseling, student employment services, personal counseling, placement for graduates, veterans' counselor. **Physically disabled:** Services for visually, speech, hearing impaired. **Transfer:** Transfer adviser, college fairs on campus for students transferring to 4-year colleges.

**Contact.** Phone: (334) 876-9295 Fax: (334) 876-9300
Donitha Griffin, Dean of Students, George C. Wallace State Community College at Selma, PO Box 2530, Selma, AL 36702-2530

## Jefferson Davis Community College
**Brewton, Alabama**
www.jdcc.edu    CB code: 1355

- Public 2-year nursing and community college
- Commuter campus in small town

**General.** Founded in 1965. Regionally accredited. **Enrollment:** 1,292 degree-seeking undergraduates; 143 non-degree-seeking students. **Degrees:** 122 associate awarded. **Location:** 60 miles from Pensacola, Florida. **Calendar:** Semester, limited summer session. **Full-time faculty:** 41 total. **Part-time faculty:** 38 total. **Class size:** 63% < 20, 37% 20-39. **Special facilities:** Museum, golf course, telecommunications center.

**Student profile.** Among degree-seeking undergraduates, 450 enrolled as first-time, first-year students.

| | | | |
|---|---|---|---|
| Part-time: | 48% | Hispanic American: | 1% |
| Out-of-state: | 8% | Native American: | 4% |
| Women: | 58% | 25 or older: | 48% |
| African American: | 34% | Live on campus: | 6% |
| Asian American: | 1% | | |

**Basis for selection.** Open admission, but selective for some programs. Special admissions requirements for nursing program. **Homeschooled:** 16 ACT required.

**High school preparation.** 24 units recommended. Recommended units include English 4, mathematics 4, social studies 4, science 4 and academic electives 8.

**2009-2010 Annual costs.** Tuition/fees: $2,700; $4,830 out-of-state. Per-credit charge: $71 in-state; $142 out-of-state. Room only: $1,866. Books/supplies: $800. Personal expenses: $400.

**2008-2009 Financial aid. Need-based:** Need-based aid available for part-time students. Work-study available nights and for part-time students. **Non-need-based:** Scholarships awarded for academics, athletics, leadership.

**Application procedures. Admission:** No deadline. No application fee. Admission notification on a rolling basis. **Financial aid:** Priority date 5/8; no closing date. FAFSA required. Applicants notified on a rolling basis; must reply within 2 week(s) of notification.

**Academics. Special study options:** Cooperative education, distance learning, dual enrollment of high school students, ESL, honors, independent study. Bachelor's degree programs available on campus. License preparation in nursing, paramedic. **Credit/placement by examination:** AP, CLEP. **Support services:** GED preparation and test center, learning center, remedial instruction, study skills assistance, tutoring.

**Majors. Business:** Administrative services. **Engineering technology:** Drafting. **Health:** Nursing (RN). **Liberal arts:** Arts/sciences.

**Most popular majors.** Health sciences 34%, liberal arts 60%.

**Computing on campus.** 420 workstations in library, computer center. Dormitories wired for high-speed internet access. Online course registration, helpline, wireless network available.

**Student life. Freshman orientation:** Mandatory. Preregistration for classes offered. Held during summer. **Housing:** Coed dorms, wellness housing available. $150 partly refundable deposit. **Activities:** Campus ministries, student government, student newspaper, Baptist student union, Phi Theta Kappa, Phi Beta Lambda, Psi Beta.

**Athletics.** NJCAA. **Intercollegiate:** Baseball M, basketball M, softball W, volleyball W. **Team name:** Warhawks.

**Student services.** Adult student services, chaplain/spiritual director, career counseling, services for economically disadvantaged, financial aid counseling, personal counseling, veterans' counselor. **Physically disabled:** Services for visually impaired. **Transfer:** Pre-admission transcript evaluation for new students. Transfer adviser, college fairs on campus for students transferring to 4-year colleges.

**Contact.** Phone: (251) 809-1594 Fax: (251) 809-1593
Robin Sessions, Registrar, Jefferson Davis Community College, PO Box 958, Brewton, AL 36427

## Jefferson State Community College
**Birmingham, Alabama**
www.jeffstateonline.com    CB code: 1352

- Public 2-year community college
- Commuter campus in very large city

**General.** Founded in 1963. Regionally accredited. **Enrollment:** 7,098 degree-seeking undergraduates; 1,450 non-degree-seeking students. **Degrees:** 619 associate awarded. **ROTC:** Army, Air Force. **Location:** 12 miles from downtown. **Calendar:** Semester, extensive summer session. **Full-time faculty:** 146 total; 18% have terminal degrees, 22% minority, 70% women. **Part-time faculty:** 295 total; 15% have terminal degrees, 21% minority, 53% women. **Class size:** 49% < 20, 44% 20-39, 7% 40-49, less than 1% 50-99. **Special facilities:** Learning success center, nature trail.

**Student profile.** Among degree-seeking undergraduates, 49% enrolled in a transfer program, 51% enrolled in a vocational program, 1,538 enrolled as first-time, first-year students, 793 transferred in from other institutions.

| | | | |
|---|---|---|---|
| Part-time: | 57% | Asian American: | 2% |
| Out-of-state: | 4% | Hispanic American: | 2% |
| Women: | 61% | International: | 1% |
| African American: | 20% | 25 or older: | 45% |

**Transfer out. Colleges most students transferred to 2009:** University of Alabama at Birmingham, University of Alabama, Auburn University.

**Basis for selection.** Open admission, but selective for some programs. Special requirements for allied health programs. Students registering for 5 or more hours of credit must take ACT ASSET or ACT COMPASS for placement. Exemptions given for students who have completed college level math or English courses, or students who have equivalent ACT scores. Applicants from non-accredited high schools admitted with high school diploma and 16 ACT or equivalent SAT. **Homeschooled:** Must have 16 ACT or pass Alabama Public High School Graduation Exam.

**High school preparation.** Recommended units include English 4, mathematics 4, social studies 2, science 3 and foreign language 2.

**2010-2011 Annual costs.** Tuition/fees (projected): $3,480; $6,030 out-of-state. Per-credit charge: $85 in-state; $170 out-of-state. Books/supplies: $1,500. Personal expenses: $4,336.

**2009-2010 Financial aid. Need-based:** Need-based aid available for part-time students. Work-study available nights and for part-time students. **Non-need-based:** Scholarships awarded for academics, art, athletics, leadership, music/drama. **Additional information:** Any Alabama resident over age 60 may attend classes tuition free, on a space available basis.

**Application procedures. Admission:** No deadline. No application fee. Admission notification on a rolling basis. **Financial aid:** Priority date 5/1; no closing date. FAFSA, institutional form required. Applicants notified on a rolling basis starting 6/1.

**Academics. Special study options:** Accelerated study, distance learning, dual enrollment of high school students, ESL, honors, independent study, internships. License preparation in nursing, paramedic, radiology, real estate. **Credit/placement by examination:** AP, CLEP, IB, institutional tests. 20 credit hours maximum toward associate degree. **Support services:** GED preparation and test center, learning center, reduced course load, remedial instruction, study skills assistance, tutoring.

**Majors. Agriculture:** Business. **Business:** General, accounting technology, administrative services, banking/financial services, hospitality admin. **Communications technology:** Radio/tv. **Computer sciences:** General. **Engineering technology:** General, construction, manufacturing. **Family/consumer sciences:** Child care. **Health:** Clinical lab technology, EMT paramedic, medical radiologic technology/radiation therapy, nursing (RN), physical therapy assistant, veterinary technology/assistant. **Liberal arts:** Arts/sciences. **Personal/culinary services:** Mortuary science. **Protective services:** Fire services admin, police science.

**Most popular majors.** Business/marketing 12%, health sciences 45%, liberal arts 27%.

**Computing on campus.** 295 workstations in library, computer center. Commuter students can connect to campus network. Online course registration, online library, helpline available.

**Student life. Freshman orientation:** Available. Preregistration for classes offered. **Activities:** Campus ministries, choral groups, drama, literary magazine, music ensembles, musical theater, radio station, student government, student newspaper, senior adult student club, African American society, BACCHUS, Students in Free Enterprise, ambassadors.

**Athletics.** NJCAA. **Intercollegiate:** Baseball M, softball W. **Intramural:** Basketball, football (non-tackle), softball, volleyball. **Team name:** Pioneers.

**Student services.** Adult student services, career counseling, student employment services, financial aid counseling, placement for graduates, veterans' counselor, women's services. **Physically disabled:** Services for visually, speech, hearing impaired. **Transfer:** Transfer adviser, college fairs on campus for students transferring to 4-year colleges.

**Contact.** E-mail: help@jeffstateonline.com
Phone: (205) 856-7704 Toll-free number: (800) 239-5900
Fax: (205) 856-6070
Lillian Owens, Director, Admissions & Retention, Jefferson State Community College, 2601 Carson Road, Birmingham, AL 35215-3098

## Lawson State Community College
**Birmingham, Alabama**
www.lawsonstate.edu
CB member
CB code: 1933

- Public 2-year community college
- Commuter campus in small city

**General.** Founded in 1949. Regionally accredited. **Enrollment:** 4,354 degree-seeking undergraduates. **Degrees:** 233 associate awarded. **Calendar:** Semester, limited summer session. **Full-time faculty:** 100 total. **Part-time faculty:** 132 total. **Class size:** 100% >100.

**Student profile.** Among degree-seeking undergraduates, 1,305 transferred in from other institutions.

| Out-of-state: | 1% | Live on campus: | 2% |

**Transfer out. Colleges most students transferred to 2009:** Miles College, University of Alabama at Birmingham, Alabama A&M University, Alabama State University, Jefferson State Community College.

**Basis for selection.** Open admission, but selective for some programs. Advanced placement option for licensed practical nurses (LPN) and nursing

education. Nursing students must pass nursing entrance exam or have 20 ACT or comparable SAT.

**2009-2010 Annual costs.** Tuition/fees: $3,000; $5,130 out-of-state. Per-credit charge: $71 in-state; $142 out-of-state. Room/board: $2,000. Books/supplies: $1,680. Personal expenses: $3,500.

**2009-2010 Financial aid.** All financial aid based on need. 97% of total undergraduate aid awarded as scholarships/grants, 3% as loans/jobs. Need-based aid available for part-time students. Work-study available nights and for part-time students.

**Application procedures. Admission:** No deadline. No application fee. Admission notification on a rolling basis. **Financial aid:** Priority date 6/1; no closing date. FAFSA required. Applicants notified on a rolling basis starting 8/1; must reply within 2 week(s) of notification.

**Academics. Special study options:** Accelerated study, double major, dual enrollment of high school students, internships, liberal arts/career combination, student-designed major. License preparation in dental hygiene, nursing, real estate. **Credit/placement by examination:** AP, CLEP, institutional tests. **Support services:** GED preparation and test center, learning center, reduced course load, remedial instruction, tutoring.

**Majors. Business:** Accounting, administrative services, business admin, office management, office technology, operations. **Computer sciences:** Computer science. **Construction:** General. **Engineering:** Electrical. **Engineering technology:** Architectural, automotive, construction, drafting, electrical, mechanical drafting. **Health:** Medical secretary, nursing (RN). **Legal studies:** Legal secretary, prelaw. **Liberal arts:** Arts/sciences. **Mechanic/repair:** Auto body. **Protective services:** Criminal justice. **Public administration:** Social work.

**Most popular majors.** Business/marketing 20%, computer/information sciences 10%, engineering/engineering technologies 8%, health sciences 16%, liberal arts 35%.

**Computing on campus.** 462 workstations in dormitories, library, computer center, student center. Dormitories linked to campus network. Online course registration, online library available.

**Student life. Freshman orientation:** Mandatory. Preregistration for classes offered. **Housing:** Coed dorms available. **Activities:** Jazz band, choral groups, dance, drama, music ensembles, radio station, student government, scholars bowl team, Sophist club.

**Athletics.** NJCAA. **Intercollegiate:** Baseball M, basketball, volleyball W. **Intramural:** Baseball M, basketball. **Team name:** Cougars.

**Student services.** Adult student services, career counseling, services for economically disadvantaged, student employment services, financial aid counseling, health services, on-campus daycare, personal counseling, placement for graduates, veterans' counselor. **Physically disabled:** Services for hearing impaired. **Transfer:** College fairs on campus for students transferring to 4-year colleges.

**Contact.** E-mail: jshelley@lawsonstate.edu
Phone: (205) 929-6309 Fax: (205) 923-7106
Jeff Shelley, Director of Admissions, Lawson State Community College, 3060 Wilson Road SW, Birmingham, AL 35221-1717

## Lurleen B. Wallace Community College
**Andalusia, Alabama**
www.lbwcc.edu
CB code: 1429

- Public 2-year community college
- Commuter campus in small town

**General.** Founded in 1969. Regionally accredited. Additional campuses in Opp, Greenville, Luverne. **Enrollment:** 1,700 degree-seeking undergraduates. **Degrees:** 210 associate awarded. **Location:** 90 miles from Montgomery. **Calendar:** Semester, limited summer session. **Full-time faculty:** 51 total. **Part-time faculty:** 45 total. **Special facilities:** Nature trail.

**Student profile.** Among degree-seeking undergraduates, 220 transferred in from other institutions.

**Transfer out. Colleges most students transferred to 2009:** Troy University, Auburn University, Auburn University in Montgomery.

**Basis for selection.** Open admission. COMPASS required for placement unless student scores 20 ACT math and English. **Homeschooled:** 16 ACT required. **Learning Disabled:** Students with disabilities encouraged to meet with ADA coordinator.

**High school preparation.** College-preparatory program recommended. 24 units required. Required units include English 4, mathematics 4, social studies 4, science 4, computer science .5, visual/performing arts .5, academic electives 5.5.

**2009-2010 Annual costs.** Tuition/fees: $2,700; $4,830 out-of-state. Per-credit charge: $71 in-state; $142 out-of-state. Books/supplies: $450. Personal expenses: $600.

**2008-2009 Financial aid.** **Non-need-based:** Scholarships awarded for academics, art, athletics, leadership, music/drama.

**Application procedures.** **Admission:** No deadline. No application fee. Application must be submitted on paper. Admission notification on a rolling basis. **Financial aid:** Priority date 5/1; no closing date. Applicants notified on a rolling basis starting 7/1; must reply within 2 week(s) of notification.

**Academics.** **Special study options:** Accelerated study, cooperative education, dual enrollment of high school students, honors. License preparation in paramedic. **Credit/placement by examination:** CLEP, institutional tests. 30 credit hours maximum toward associate degree. **Support services:** GED preparation and test center, learning center, reduced course load, remedial instruction, tutoring.

**Majors.** **Business:** Administrative services. **Computer sciences:** General. **Conservation:** Forest resources. **Engineering technology:** Drafting. **Health:** EMT paramedic, nursing (RN), sonography. **Liberal arts:** Arts/sciences. **Mechanic/repair:** Industrial electronics.

**Most popular majors.** Health sciences 20%, liberal arts 58%.

**Computing on campus.** 50 workstations in computer center.

**Student life.** **Freshman orientation:** Mandatory, $10 fee. Offered as a hybrid course: half on-campus activities; half on-line. Students meet with advisers and register for classes. **Activities:** Jazz band, choral groups, drama, music ensembles, musical theater, student government, student newspaper, Collegiate Civitan club, Adult Re-entry Club.

**Athletics.** NJCAA. **Intercollegiate:** Baseball M, basketball, softball W. **Team name:** Saints.

**Student services.** Career counseling, services for economically disadvantaged, student employment services, personal counseling, placement for graduates, veterans' counselor. **Transfer:** Transfer adviser for students transferring to 4-year colleges.

**Contact.** Phone: (334) 222-6591 ext. 273 Fax: (334) 881-2201
Mackie Stephens, Director of Admissions, Lurleen B. Wallace Community College, Box 1418, Andalusia, AL 36420-1418

## Marion Military Institute
**Marion, Alabama**
**www.marionmilitary.edu**                          CB code: 1447

- Public 2-year junior and military college
- Residential campus in small town

**General.** Founded in 1842. Regionally accredited. **Location:** 70 miles from Birmingham, 52 miles from Tuscaloosa. **Calendar:** Semester.

**Annual costs/financial aid.** Tuition/fees (2009-2010): $8,570; $14,570 out-of-state. Required fees include one-time uniform fee of $1,850 and accident insurance of $150 per academic year. Room/board: $3,450. Need-based financial aid available to full-time and part-time students.

**Contact.** Phone: (334) 683-2305
Director of Enrollment Management, 1101 Washington Street, Marion, AL 36756-0420

## Northeast Alabama Community College
**Rainsville, Alabama**
**www.nacc.edu**                          CB code: 1576

- Public 2-year community college
- Commuter campus in rural community

**General.** Founded in 1963. Regionally accredited. **Enrollment:** 2,100 degree-seeking undergraduates. **Degrees:** 337 associate awarded. **Location:** 55 miles from Huntsville, 110 miles from Birmingham. **Calendar:** Semester, extensive summer session. **Full-time faculty:** 47 total. **Special facilities:** Community theater, lakeside walking trail.

**Transfer out.** **Colleges most students transferred to 2009:** Jacksonville State University, University of Alabama at Huntsville, Athens State University, University of Alabama, Auburn University.

**Basis for selection.** Open admission, but selective for some programs. **Homeschooled:** Transcript of courses and grades required. 16 ACT required. **Learning Disabled:** Students who may require accommodations encouraged to communicate with Disability Services.

**High school preparation.** 24 units recommended. Recommended units include English 4, mathematics 4, social studies 2, history 2, science 4 (laboratory 2), foreign language 2, computer science .5, academic electives 3.5.

**2009-2010 Annual costs.** Tuition/fees: $2,850; $4,980 out-of-state. Per-credit charge: $71 in-state; $142 out-of-state. Personal expenses: $1,500.

**Financial aid.** **Need-based:** Need-based aid available for part-time students. Work-study available for part-time students. **Non-need-based:** Scholarships awarded for academics, art, leadership, minority status, music/drama.

**Application procedures.** **Admission:** No deadline. No application fee. Admission notification on a rolling basis. **Financial aid:** No deadline. FAFSA required. Applicants notified on a rolling basis.

**Academics.** **Special study options:** Accelerated study, distance learning, dual enrollment of high school students, ESL. 2-year degree programs in allied health available requiring 1 year study at Wallace State Community College at Hanceville. Bachelor's degree programs available on campus. License preparation in dental hygiene, nursing, paramedic. **Credit/placement by examination:** AP, CLEP, institutional tests. 16 credit hours maximum toward associate degree. **Support services:** GED preparation and test center, learning center, remedial instruction, study skills assistance, tutoring, writing center.

**Majors.** **Business:** General, administrative services, business admin, office management. **Computer sciences:** General, computer science. **Engineering technology:** CAD/CADD, electrical. **Health:** EMT paramedic, medical assistant, nursing (RN), office admin, office assistant. **Legal studies:** Paralegal. **Liberal arts:** Arts/sciences. **Mechanic/repair:** Computer, electronics/electrical, industrial, industrial electronics. **Production:** Machine tool, welding. **Protective services:** Law enforcement admin, police science.

**Computing on campus.** 475 workstations in library, computer center. Commuter students can connect to campus network. Online course registration, online library, helpline, wireless network available.

**Student life.** **Freshman orientation:** Mandatory. Preregistration for classes offered. Groups of 100 meet for an afternoon. **Activities:** Bands, campus ministries, choral groups, dance, drama, literary magazine, music ensembles, musical theater, student government.

**Athletics.** **Intramural:** Basketball. **Team name:** Mustangs.

**Student services.** Career counseling, student employment services, financial aid counseling, personal counseling, veterans' counselor. **Physically disabled:** Services for visually, speech, hearing impaired. **Transfer:** Pre-admission transcript evaluation for new students. Transfer adviser, college fairs on campus for students transferring to 4-year colleges.

**Contact.** E-mail: niblettt@nacc.edu
Phone: (256) 228-6001 ext. 222 Fax: (256) 638-6043
Tonie Niblett, Dean of Student Services, Northeast Alabama Community College, Admissions Office, NACC, Rainsville, AL 35986-0159

## Northwest-Shoals Community College
**Muscle Shoals, Alabama**
**www.nwscc.edu**                          CB code: 0188

- Public 2-year community and technical college
- Commuter campus in large town

**General.** Founded in 1966. Regionally accredited. Two campuses: Phil Campbell and Muscle Shoals. **Enrollment:** 3,908 degree-seeking undergraduates; 623 non-degree-seeking students. **Degrees:** 245 associate awarded. **Location:** 120 miles from Birmingham; 134 miles from Memphis, Tennessee. **Calendar:** Semester, extensive summer session. **Full-time faculty:** 91 total; 8% have terminal degrees, 8% minority, 54% women. **Part-time faculty:** 148 total; 3% have terminal degrees, 9% minority, 54% women.

**Student profile.** Among degree-seeking undergraduates, 41% enrolled in a transfer program, 33% enrolled in a vocational program, 1,107 enrolled as first-time, first-year students.

| | | | |
|---|---|---|---|
| Part-time: | 38% | Hispanic American: | 2% |
| Out-of-state: | 2% | Native American: | 1% |
| Women: | 60% | 25 or older: | 29% |
| African American: | 11% | Live on campus: | 7% |
| Asian American: | 1% | | |

**Transfer out. Colleges most students transferred to 2009:** University of North Alabama, University of Alabama, Athens State University, University of Alabama at Huntsville.

**Basis for selection.** Open admission, but selective for some programs. Additional requirements for health occupation programs. **Homeschooled:** Equivalent number of required units for graduation and 16 ACT or 790 SAT (exclusive of Writing) required.

**High school preparation.** 22 units recommended. Recommended units include English 4, mathematics 2, social studies 3 and science 4.

**2009-2010 Annual costs.** Tuition/fees: $2,880; $5,010 out-of-state. Per-credit charge: $71 in-state; $142 out-of-state. Room only: $1,600. Books/supplies: $1,300.

**2008-2009 Financial aid. Need-based:** 54% of total undergraduate aid awarded as scholarships/grants, 46% as loans/jobs. Need-based aid available for part-time students. Work-study available nights and for part-time students. **Non-need-based:** Scholarships awarded for academics, art, athletics, leadership, minority status, music/drama.

**Application procedures. Admission:** No deadline. No application fee. Admission notification on a rolling basis. **Financial aid:** Priority date 4/1, closing date 8/1. FAFSA, institutional form required. Applicants notified on a rolling basis; must reply within 2 week(s) of notification.

**Academics. Special study options:** Accelerated study, cooperative education, cross-registration, distance learning, dual enrollment of high school students, honors, independent study, internships, liberal arts/career combination. License preparation in nursing, paramedic. **Credit/placement by examination:** AP, CLEP, institutional tests. 30 credit hours maximum toward associate degree. **Support services:** GED preparation and test center, learning center, pre-admission summer program, remedial instruction, tutoring.

**Majors. Agriculture:** Business. **Business:** Accounting technology, administrative services. **Computer sciences:** General, applications programming, information systems, information technology, programming. **Conservation:** Environmental studies, forestry. **Engineering technology:** Drafting, environmental. **Health:** EMT paramedic, nursing (RN). **Liberal arts:** Arts/sciences. **Protective services:** Police science.

**Most popular majors.** Business/marketing 7%, health sciences 26%, interdisciplinary studies 6%, liberal arts 48%.

**Computing on campus.** 710 workstations in library, computer center, student center. Online course registration, online library, helpline, repair service, wireless network available.

**Student life. Freshman orientation:** Mandatory, $10 fee. Preregistration for classes offered. Program includes components for developing research skills and good study habits. Occupational students also receive orientation to work ethics and workplace readiness. **Housing:** Coed dorms, wellness housing available. $75 fully refundable deposit. **Activities:** Bands, campus ministries, choral groups, music ensembles, student government, Phi Theta Kappa, Ambassadors, Fellowship of Christian Athletes, Music Educators National Conference, student government association, college bowl team, science club, American Society of Heating, Refrigerating and Air Conditioning Engineers.

**Athletics.** NJCAA. **Intercollegiate:** Baseball M, basketball, cheerleading, softball W, volleyball W. **Intramural:** Basketball, table tennis. **Team name:** Patriots.

**Student services.** Career counseling, student employment services, financial aid counseling, on-campus daycare, personal counseling, placement for graduates, veterans' counselor. **Physically disabled:** Services for visually, speech, hearing impaired. **Transfer:** Pre-admission transcript evaluation for new students. Transfer adviser, college fairs on campus for students transferring to 4-year colleges.

**Contact.** Phone: (256) 331-5363 Fax: (256) 331-5366
Karen Berryhill, Vice President for Student Development Services, Northwest-Shoals Community College, PO Box 2545, Muscle Shoals, AL 35662

## Prince Institute of Professional Studies
**Montgomery, Alabama**
www.princeinstitute.edu
**CB code: 3450**

- For-profit 2-year technical and career college
- Commuter campus in large city
- Interview required

**General.** Accredited by ACICS. **Enrollment:** 96 undergraduates. **Degrees:** 1 associate awarded. **Calendar:** Quarter, limited summer session. **Full-time faculty:** 10 total. **Part-time faculty:** 5 total.

**Basis for selection.** Open admission.

**2009-2010 Annual costs.** Tuition/fees: $8,095. Books/supplies: $2,000. Personal expenses: $1,674.

**2009-2010 Financial aid.** All financial aid based on need. Need-based aid available for part-time students.

**Application procedures. Admission:** No deadline. $125 fee. Applications must be received before class start. **Financial aid:** No deadline. FAFSA required.

**Academics. Special study options:** Distance learning. **Credit/placement by examination:** CLEP.

**Majors. Computer sciences:** Information systems. **Health:** Medical transcription. **Legal studies:** Court reporting.

**Student life. Freshman orientation:** Available. Preregistration for classes offered.

**Contact.** E-mail: shill@princeinstitute.edu
Phone: (334) 271-1670 ext. 209 Toll-free number: (877) 853-5569
Fax: (334) 271-1671
Sherry Hill, Admissions Director, Prince Institute of Professional Studies, 7735 Atlanta Highway, Montgomery, AL 36117-4231

## Remington College: Mobile
**Mobile, Alabama**
www.remingtoncollege.edu
**CB code: 3157**

- For-profit 2-year career college
- Commuter campus in large city

**General.** Accredited by ACCSC. **Enrollment:** 150 degree-seeking undergraduates. **Degrees:** 60 associate awarded. **Calendar:** Quarter, extensive summer session. **Full-time faculty:** 40 total. **Part-time faculty:** 20 total.

**Basis for selection.** Open admission. **Homeschooled:** Transcript of courses and grades, state high school equivalency certificate required.

**2009-2010 Annual costs.** Associate degree program annual tuition $39,900 plus $50 fees. 8-month diploma program full tuition $13,900 plus $50 fees. Tuition includes textbooks and supplies.

**2008-2009 Financial aid.** All financial aid based on need. Work-study available nights.

**Application procedures. Admission:** No deadline. $50 fee. **Financial aid:** FAFSA required.

**Academics. Special study options:** Cooperative education, distance learning, honors, liberal arts/career combination. **Credit/placement by examination:** CLEP. **Support services:** Tutoring.

**Majors. Computer sciences:** System admin. **Protective services:** Law enforcement admin. **Other:** Computer and network administration, Electronics and computer technology.

**Computing on campus.** PC or laptop required. Online library, helpline, repair service, wireless network available.

**Student life. Freshman orientation:** Mandatory. Preregistration for classes offered. Held the week before class for 2 1/2 hours.

**Student services.** Career counseling, financial aid counseling, placement for graduates. **Transfer:** Pre-admission transcript evaluation for new students.

**Contact.** Phone: (251) 343-8200 Toll-free number: (800) 866-0850
Fax: (251) 343-8200
Angela Wisdom, Director of Admissions, Remington College: Mobile, 828
Downtowner Loop West, Mobile, AL 36609-5404

## Shelton State Community College
### Tuscaloosa, Alabama
**www.sheltonstate.edu**       CB code: 3338

- Public 2-year community and technical college
- Commuter campus in small city

**General.** Founded in 1963. Regionally accredited. Designated as Alabama's Community College of the Fine Arts; includes C.A. Fredd campus, a Historically Black College. **Enrollment:** 5,834 degree-seeking undergraduates. **Degrees:** 247 associate awarded. **ROTC:** Army, Air Force. **Location:** 60 miles from Birmingham. **Calendar:** Semester, extensive summer session. **Full-time faculty:** 82 total. **Part-time faculty:** 207 total. **Class size:** 42% < 20, 48% 20-39, 10% 40-49, less than 1% 50-99. **Special facilities:** Observatories, wellness center, community theatre.

**Student profile.**

| | | | |
|---|---|---|---|
| Out-of-state: | 5% | 25 or older: | 32% |

**Transfer out. Colleges most students transferred to 2009:** University of Alabama, Auburn University, Stillman College, University of Alabama at Birmingham.

**Basis for selection.** Open admission. COMPASS test required of all first-time freshmen for placement unless students submit ACT.

**2009-2010 Annual costs.** Tuition/fees: $2,700; $4,830 out-of-state. Per-credit charge: $71 in-state; $142 out-of-state. Books/supplies: $750. Personal expenses: $200.

**Financial aid.** All financial aid based on need. Need-based aid available for part-time students. Work-study available nights.

**Application procedures. Admission:** No deadline. No application fee. Admission notification on a rolling basis. **Financial aid:** Priority date 6/30; no closing date. FAFSA required. Applicants notified on a rolling basis starting 7/30.

**Academics. Special study options:** Accelerated study, distance learning, double major, dual enrollment of high school students, honors, liberal arts/career combination. License preparation in nursing, real estate. **Credit/placement by examination:** AP, CLEP, IB, institutional tests. 20 credit hours maximum toward associate degree. **Support services:** GED preparation and test center, learning center, reduced course load, remedial instruction, study skills assistance, tutoring.

**Majors. Architecture:** Technology. **Business:** Administrative services. **Construction:** Electrician. **Education:** General, music, secondary. **Engineering:** General. **Engineering technology:** Drafting, heat/ac/refrig. **Health:** Nursing (RN), respiratory therapy technology. **Liberal arts:** Arts/sciences. **Math:** General. **Mechanic/repair:** Industrial electronics. **Production:** General, tool and die. **Public administration:** Social work. **Visual/performing arts:** Studio arts.

**Most popular majors.** Business/marketing 25%, health sciences 26%, liberal arts 33%, trade and industry 11%.

**Computing on campus.** 300 workstations in library, computer center. Commuter students can connect to campus network. Online course registration, wireless network available.

**Student life. Freshman orientation:** Mandatory. Preregistration for classes offered. **Activities:** Jazz band, choral groups, dance, drama, music ensembles, musical theater, student government, student newspaper, Phi Theta Kappa, Circle K.

**Athletics.** NJCAA. **Intercollegiate:** Baseball M, basketball, cheerleading, soccer W, softball W. **Team name:** Buccaneers.

**Student services.** Career counseling, student employment services, financial aid counseling, personal counseling, placement for graduates, veterans' counselor. **Transfer:** College fairs on campus for students transferring to 4-year colleges.

**Contact.** E-mail: admissions@sheltonstate.edu
Phone: (205) 391-2214 Fax: (205) 391-3910
Tommy Taylor, Dean of Student Services, Shelton State Community College, 9500 Old Greensboro Road, Tuscaloosa, AL 35405-8522

## Snead State Community College
### Boaz, Alabama
**www.snead.edu**       CB code: 1721

- Public 2-year community college
- Commuter campus in small town

**General.** Founded in 1898. Regionally accredited. Upper-level courses offered on campus through Athens State University and distance learning. **Enrollment:** 2,483 degree-seeking undergraduates. **Degrees:** 248 associate awarded. **Location:** 65 miles from Birmingham. **Calendar:** Semester, extensive summer session. **Full-time faculty:** 35 total. **Part-time faculty:** 80 total. **Special facilities:** Museum, state diagnostic lab. **Partnerships:** Partnership with Marshall County Tech Prep Consortium (grant writer and fiscal agent for eight secondary schools).

**Student profile.**

| | | | |
|---|---|---|---|
| Out-of-state: | 2% | Live on campus: | 4% |
| 25 or older: | 33% | | |

**Transfer out. Colleges most students transferred to 2009:** Jacksonville State University, Auburn University, University of Alabama, University of Alabama at Birmingham, University of Alabama in Huntsville.

**Basis for selection.** Open admission, but selective for some programs. Nursing students must submit application package. 16 ACT or equivalent SAT required for high school graduates from non-accredited schools and for those receiving occupational diplomas.

**High school preparation.** 24 units recommended. Recommended units include English 4, mathematics 4, social studies 4, science 4, foreign language 2 and academic electives 8. Half unit fine arts, 1/2 computer applications, 5 1/2 electives recommended.

**2009-2010 Annual costs.** Tuition/fees: $2,820; $4,950 out-of-state. Per-credit charge: $71 in-state; $142 out-of-state. Room/board: $3,190. Books/supplies: $1,050. Personal expenses: $1,200.

**Financial aid. Need-based:** Need-based aid available for part-time students. Work-study available nights and for part-time students. **Non-need-based:** Scholarships awarded for academics, alumni affiliation, art, athletics, leadership, music/drama.

**Application procedures. Admission:** Closing date 8/14 (postmark date). No application fee. Application must be submitted on paper. Admission notification on a rolling basis. **Financial aid:** Closing date 4/15. FAFSA required. Applicants notified on a rolling basis starting 4/15.

**Academics. Special study options:** Accelerated study, distance learning, dual enrollment of high school students, independent study, internships, student-designed major. **Credit/placement by examination:** CLEP, institutional tests. 20 credit hours maximum toward associate degree. **Support services:** GED preparation and test center, learning center, remedial instruction, study skills assistance, tutoring, writing center.

**Majors. Business:** Administrative services. **Computer sciences:** General. **Engineering:** General. **Engineering technology:** General. **Family/consumer sciences:** Child care. **Health:** Nursing (RN). **Liberal arts:** Arts/sciences. **Personal/culinary services:** Cosmetic.

**Computing on campus.** 350 workstations in library, computer center, student center. Online course registration, online library available.

**Student life. Freshman orientation:** Available, $94 fee. Preregistration for classes offered. Orientation offered on 2 consecutive Fridays or Saturdays. **Housing:** Coed dorms available. $25 deposit. **Activities:** Jazz band, choral groups, music ensembles, student government, student newspaper, Baptist campus ministry, Ambassadors, agricultural organization, Phi Beta Lambda, Phi Theta Kappa, student government association, College Republicans, Civitans.

**Athletics.** NJCAA. **Intercollegiate:** Baseball M, basketball, softball W, tennis W. **Intramural:** Basketball, softball, table tennis, volleyball. **Team name:** Parsons.

**Student services.** Chaplain/spiritual director, career counseling, services for economically disadvantaged, student employment services, financial aid counseling, personal counseling, placement for graduates, veterans' counselor. **Physically disabled:** Services for visually, speech, hearing impaired. **Transfer:** Pre-admission transcript evaluation for new students. Transfer center, transfer adviser, college fairs on campus for students transferring to 4-year colleges.

**Contact.** Phone: (256) 593-5120 ext. 207 Fax: (256) 593-7180
Amanda Harbison, Admissions and Records Director, Snead State
Community College, PO Box 734, Boaz, AL 35957-0734

## Southern Union State Community College
**Wadley, Alabama**
**www.suscc.edu**                                     **CB code: 1728**

▶ Public 2-year community and technical college
▶ Commuter campus in small city

**General.** Founded in 1963. Regionally accredited. Additional campuses in
Opelika and Valley. **Enrollment:** 5,000 degree-seeking undergraduates. **Degrees:** 489 associate awarded. **Location:** 90 miles from Atlanta, 90 miles
from Birmingham. **Calendar:** Semester, extensive summer session. **Full-
time faculty:** 85 total. **Part-time faculty:** 240 total.

**Student profile.**

| | | | |
|---|---|---|---|
| Out-of-state: | 20% | Live on campus: | 4% |
| 25 or older: | 25% | | |

**Basis for selection.** Open admission, but selective for some programs.
Criteria for some health sciences programs include test scores.

**2009-2010 Annual costs.** Tuition/fees: $2,700; $4,830 out-of-state. Per-
credit charge: $71 in-state; $142 out-of-state. Room/board: $3,200. Books/
supplies: $400. Personal expenses: $1,100.

**2009-2010 Financial aid. Need-based:** Need-based aid available for part-
time students.

**Application procedures. Admission:** No deadline. No application fee.
Admission notification on a rolling basis. **Financial aid:** Priority date 4/1;
no closing date. FAFSA required. Applicants notified on a rolling basis.

**Academics. Special study options:** Accelerated study, distance learning,
dual enrollment of high school students. License preparation in nursing,
paramedic, radiology. **Credit/placement by examination:** CLEP. **Support
services:** GED preparation and test center, remedial instruction, tutoring.

**Majors. Biology:** General. **Business:** Accounting, office management. **Communications:** General. **Computer sciences:** General. **Construction:** Carpentry. **Education:** Physical. **Engineering technology:** Drafting. **Health:**
EMT paramedic, insurance coding, nursing (RN), radiologic technology/
medical imaging. **Mechanic/repair:** Heating/ac/refrig. **Physical sciences:**
Chemistry. **Social sciences:** General.

**Student life. Freshman orientation:** Available. Preregistration for classes
offered. Held during June and July. **Housing:** Single-sex dorms, wellness
housing available. **Activities:** Campus ministries, choral groups, dance, drama,
musical theater, student government, student newspaper, association of radiologic students, global environmental organization of students, music club,
letterman's club, National Student Nurses' Association, Phi Beta Lambda,
Phi Theta Kappa, Southern Union Players.

**Athletics.** NJCAA. **Intercollegiate:** Baseball M, basketball, cheerleading,
cross-country, softball W, volleyball W. **Team name:** Bison.

**Student services.** Adult student services, career counseling, financial
aid counseling.

**Contact.** E-mail: cstringfellow@suscc.edu
Phone: (256) 395-2211 Fax: (256) 395-2215
Catherine Stringfellow, Registrar, Southern Union State Community
College, 750 Roberts Street, Wadley, AL 36276

## Virginia College at Mobile
**Mobile, Alabama**
**www.vc.edu/mobile**

▶ For-profit 2-year technical college
▶ Commuter campus in large city

**General.** Accredited by ACICS. **Calendar:** Continuous.

**Annual costs/financial aid.** Students taking 13-16 hours pay an average of $4,630 per quarter, fees included.

**Contact.** Phone: (251) 343-7227
Director of Admissions, 2970 Cottage Hill Road, Mobile, AL 36606

## Virginia College at Montgomery
**Montgomery, Alabama**
**www.vc.edu**

▶ For-profit 2-year health science and career college
▶ Large city

**General.** Regionally accredited. **Calendar:** Quarter.

**Annual costs/financial aid.** Students taking 13-16 hours pay an average of $4,630 per quarter, fees included.

**Contact.** Phone: (334) 277-3390
6200 Atlanta Highway, Montgomery, AL 36117

## Wallace State Community College at Hanceville
**Hanceville, Alabama**
**www.wallacestate.edu**                               **CB code: 0528**

▶ Public 2-year health science and community college
▶ Commuter campus in rural community

**General.** Founded in 1966. Regionally accredited. **Enrollment:** 3,100 full-
time, degree-seeking students. **Degrees:** 765 associate awarded. **Location:**
35 miles from Birmingham, 50 miles from Huntsville. **Calendar:** Semester,
limited summer session. **Full-time faculty:** 125 total. **Part-time faculty:**
150 total. **Special facilities:** Extensive genealogy collection, recording studio, nature trail, college-operated museum.

**Transfer out. Colleges most students transferred to 2009:** Athens State
College, University of Alabama, University of Alabama in Huntsville, University of Alabama at Birmingham, Auburn University.

**Basis for selection.** Open admission, but selective for some programs.
ACT required of applicants to certain allied health programs. National League
for Nursing, Pre-Nursing and Guidance Examination required for nursing
applicants. Interview recommended for health program applicants; auditions recommended for music education majors.

**2009-2010 Annual costs.** Tuition/fees: $2,700; $4,830 out-of-state. Per-
credit charge: $71 in-state; $142 out-of-state. Room only: $1,650. Books/
supplies: $700. Personal expenses: $2,650.

**Financial aid.** All financial aid based on need. Need-based aid available
for part-time students. Work-study available nights.

**Application procedures. Admission:** No deadline. No application fee.
Admission notification on a rolling basis beginning on or about 7/15. **Financial aid:** Priority date 5/1; no closing date. FAFSA required. Applicants
notified on a rolling basis starting 7/15; must reply within 2 week(s) of
notification.

**Academics. Special study options:** Accelerated study, cooperative education, distance learning, double major, dual enrollment of high school students, internships, weekend college. Bachelor's degree programs available
on campus. License preparation in aviation, dental hygiene, nursing, occupational therapy, paramedic, physical therapy, radiology, real estate. **Credit/
placement by examination:** AP, CLEP, institutional tests. 26 credit hours
maximum toward associate degree. **Support services:** GED preparation and
test center, learning center, reduced course load, remedial instruction, study
skills assistance, tutoring.

**Majors. Agriculture:** Agribusiness operations. **Business:** General, accounting, banking/financial services, fashion, insurance, labor relations, office management, office/clerical, sales/distribution. **Computer sciences:** Data processing, programming. **Education:** General. **Engineering:** General, electrical.
**Engineering technology:** Drafting. **Family/consumer sciences:** Child care,
food/nutrition, institutional food production. **Health:** Athletic training, clinical lab technology, dental assistant, dental hygiene, EMT paramedic, health
services, medical assistant, medical radiologic technology/radiation therapy,
medical records technology, nursing (RN), occupational therapy assistant,
physical therapy assistant, respiratory therapy technology, sonography, substance abuse counseling. **Legal studies:** Legal secretary, paralegal, prelaw.
**Liberal arts:** Arts/sciences. **Mechanic/repair:** Auto body, automotive, diesel, electronics/electrical, heating/ac/refrig. **Parks/recreation:** Facilities management. **Production:** Woodworking. **Protective services:** Police science.
**Visual/performing arts:** Art, fashion design, interior design.

**Most popular majors.** Business/marketing 6%, health sciences 61%, liberal arts 17%.

**Computing on campus.** 65 workstations in library, computer center. Commuter students can connect to campus network. Online course registration, online library, helpline, wireless network available.

**Student life. Freshman orientation:** Available. Preregistration for classes offered. **Housing:** Single-sex dorms, wellness housing available. $200 deposit. **Activities:** Bands, choral groups, drama, music ensembles, student government, student newspaper, Baptist campus ministry.

**Athletics.** NJCAA. **Intercollegiate:** Baseball M, basketball, cross-country, golf M, soccer M, softball W, track and field M, volleyball. **Intramural:** Badminton, basketball, softball, tennis, track and field, volleyball. **Team name:** Lions.

**Student services.** Chaplain/spiritual director, career counseling, student employment services, financial aid counseling, placement for graduates, veterans' counselor. **Physically disabled:** Services for visually, speech, hearing impaired. **Transfer:** Transfer adviser, college fairs on campus for students transferring to 4-year colleges.

**Contact.** Phone: (256) 352-8236 Toll-free number: (866) 350-9722 Fax: (256) 352-8129
Linda Sperling, Director of Admissions/Registrar, Wallace State Community College at Hanceville, PO Box 2000, Hanceville, AL 35077-2000

# Alaska

## Ilisagvik College
**Barrow, Alaska**
www.ilisagvik.cc                    CB code: 0469

♦ Public 2-year Tribal Community College
♦ Commuter campus in rural community

**General. Enrollment:** 94 degree-seeking undergraduates; 132 non-degree-seeking students. **Degrees:** 4 associate awarded. **Location:** 500 miles from Fairbanks. **Calendar:** Semester, limited summer session. **Full-time faculty:** 12 total; 25% minority, 33% women. **Part-time faculty:** 19 total; 42% minority, 63% women.

**Student profile.** Among degree-seeking undergraduates, 7% enrolled in a transfer program, 9% enrolled in a vocational program, 17 enrolled as first-time, first-year students, 5 transferred in from other institutions.

| | | | |
|---|---|---|---|
| Part-time: | 56% | Asian American: | 4% |
| Women: | 70% | Native American: | 85% |
| African American: | 1% | | |

**Basis for selection.** Open admission.

**2009-2010 Annual costs.** Tuition/fees: $2,820; $4,020 out-of-state. Per-credit charge: $100 in-state; $150 out-of-state. Room/board: $10,650. Books/supplies: $800. Personal expenses: $2,730.

**2008-2009 Financial aid. Need-based:** 77% of total undergraduate aid awarded as scholarships/grants, 23% as loans/jobs.

**Application procedures. Admission:** No deadline. No application fee. Application must be submitted on paper. Admission notification on a rolling basis. **Financial aid:** No deadline.

**Academics.** Many Inupiat Eskimo traditional courses offered. **Special study options:** Double major, dual enrollment of high school students, ESL, independent study. **Credit/placement by examination:** CLEP. 12 credit hours maximum toward associate degree. **Support services:** GED preparation and test center, remedial instruction, tutoring.

**Majors. Area/ethnic studies:** Native American. **Business:** Accounting, business admin, management science, office management. **Health:** Health services.

**Most popular majors.** Business/marketing 75%, computer/information sciences 25%.

**Computing on campus.** Commuter students can connect to campus network. Helpline, wireless network available.

**Student life. Freshman orientation:** Available. **Housing:** Coed dorms, apartments available. **Activities:** Student government.

**Student services.** Financial aid counseling, personal counseling.

**Contact.** E-mail: dararath.cahoon@ilisagvik.cc
Phone: (907) 852-1763 Toll-free number: (800) 478-7337 ext. 1763
Fax: (907) 852-1784
Dararath Cahoon, Registrar, Ilisagvik College, 100 Stevenson Road, Barrow, AK 99723

## Prince William Sound Community College
**Valdez, Alaska**
www.pwscc.edu                    CB code: 4636

♦ Public 2-year community college
♦ Commuter campus in small town

**General.** Founded in 1978. Regionally accredited. Service area of 44,000 square miles. Full schedule of courses plus live video and audio conferencing for students in remote areas. Off-campus centers at Cordova and Glennallen offer credit-bearing courses. **Enrollment:** 170 degree-seeking undergraduates. **Degrees:** 15 associate awarded. **Location:** 300 miles from Anchorage. **Calendar:** Semester, limited summer session. **Full-time faculty:** 8 total. **Part-time faculty:** 50 total. **Class size:** 94% < 20, 5% 20-39, less than 1% 40-49, less than 1% 50-99, less than 1% >100. **Special facilities:** Alaska native museum.

**Transfer out. Colleges most students transferred to 2009:** University of Alaska-Anchorage.

**Basis for selection.** Open admission. **Homeschooled:** Statement describing homeschool structure and mission required.

**2009-2010 Annual costs.** Tuition/fees: $4,170. Per-credit charge: $122. Room only: $4,970. Books/supplies: $600.

**Financial aid. Need-based:** Need-based aid available for part-time students. **Non-need-based:** Scholarships awarded for state residency.

**Application procedures. Admission:** No deadline. $25 fee. Application must be submitted on paper. Admission notification on a rolling basis. **Financial aid:** Priority date 6/30; no closing date. FAFSA required. Applicants notified on a rolling basis.

**Academics. Special study options:** Distance learning, double major, dual enrollment of high school students, ESL, external degree, honors, independent study, internships. Bachelor's degree programs available on campus. **Credit/placement by examination:** CLEP, IB, institutional tests. **Support services:** GED preparation and test center, learning center, reduced course load, remedial instruction, study skills assistance, tutoring.

**Majors. Business:** Office management. **Engineering technology:** Electrical. **Liberal arts:** Arts/sciences.

**Computing on campus.** 50 workstations in dormitories, library, computer center. Online library, helpline available.

**Student life. Freshman orientation:** Available. Preregistration for classes offered. **Housing:** Coed dorms, apartments, wellness housing available. $200 deposit. **Activities:** Drama, film society, student government.

**Student services.** Adult student services, career counseling, financial aid counseling, veterans' counselor. **Transfer:** Transfer adviser, college fairs on campus for students transferring to 4-year colleges.

**Contact.** E-mail: sfoster@pwscc.edu
Phone: (907) 834-1632 Toll-free number: (800) 478-8800
Fax: (907) 834-1635
Shannon Foster, Director of Admissions and Records, Prince William Sound Community College, Box 97, Valdez, AK 99686

# Arizona

Two-Year Colleges

## Anthem College
### Phoenix, Arizona
www.hightechinstitute.edu       CB code: 3170

- For-profit 2-year technical college
- Commuter campus in very large city
- Interview required

**General.** Accredited by ACICS, ACCSC. **Enrollment:** 2,500 degree-seeking undergraduates. **Degrees:** 87 bachelor's, 1,129 associate awarded. **Calendar:** Continuous, extensive summer session. **Full-time faculty:** 55 total.

**Basis for selection.** Open admission. **Homeschooled:** Transcript of courses and grades, state high school equivalency certificate, interview required.

**2009-2010 Annual costs.** Costs for diploma programs range from $12,150 to $25,850. Fees, books, uniforms and tools included. Personal expenses: $205.

**Financial aid.** All financial aid based on need.

**Application procedures. Admission:** No deadline. $50 fee. Application must be submitted on paper. Admission notification on a rolling basis. **Financial aid:** No deadline.

**Academics. Special study options:** Distance learning. Bachelor's degree programs available on campus. **Credit/placement by examination:** CLEP, institutional tests. **Support services:** GED preparation, study skills assistance, tutoring.

**Majors. Business:** Business admin. **Computer sciences:** Security, web page design. **Engineering:** General, electrical. **Engineering technology:** Drafting. **Health:** Insurance specialist, office computer specialist. **Protective services:** Police science.

**Most popular majors.** Computer/information sciences 73%, health sciences 27%.

**Computing on campus.** 2 workstations in library, computer center. Commuter students can connect to campus network. Online course registration, online library, helpline available.

**Student life. Freshman orientation:** Mandatory.

**Student services.** Financial aid counseling, placement for graduates. **Transfer:** Pre-admission transcript evaluation for new students.

**Contact.** Phone: (602) 279-9700 Toll-free number: (800) 832-4011 Fax: (602) 279-2999
Todd Rash, Director of Marketing, Anthem College, 1515 East Indian School Road, Phoenix, AZ 85014-4901

## Arizona Automotive Institute
### Glendale, Arizona
www.aai.edu       CB code: 2127

- For-profit 2-year technical college
- Commuter campus in small city

**General.** Founded in 1967. Accredited by ACCSC. **Enrollment:** 1,200 undergraduates. **Degrees:** 266 associate awarded. **Location:** 3 miles from Phoenix. **Calendar:** Quarter, extensive summer session. **Full-time faculty:** 25 total. **Part-time faculty:** 5 total.

**Student profile.**

| | | | |
|---|---|---|---|
| Out-of-state: | 36% | 25 or older: | 25% |

**Basis for selection.** Open admission. Interview highly recommended.

**2009-2010 Annual costs.** Total cost of associate degree program is $27,412 including tuition, books, uniforms, supplies, tools. Cost of diploma is $18,308.

**Application procedures. Admission:** No deadline. $100 fee. Admission notification on a rolling basis. **Financial aid:** No deadline. FAFSA, institutional form required. Applicants notified on a rolling basis.

**Academics. Special study options:** Double major. **Credit/placement by examination:** CLEP. **Support services:** Tutoring.

**Majors. Mechanic/repair:** Automotive, diesel.

**Computing on campus.** 15 workstations in computer center.

**Student life. Freshman orientation:** Available. Preregistration for classes offered. **Housing:** Apartments available.

**Athletics. Intramural:** Basketball M, bowling, football (tackle) M, softball, volleyball.

**Student services.** Career counseling, student employment services, personal counseling, placement for graduates, veterans' counselor.

**Contact.** E-mail: info@azautoinst.com
Phone: (623) 934-7273 Toll-free number: (800) 528-0717
Fax: (623) 930-4948
Deborah Armstrong, Director of Admissions, Arizona Automotive Institute, 6829 North 46th Avenue, Glendale, AZ 85301

## Arizona Western College
### Yuma, Arizona
www.azwestern.edu       CB member    CB code: 4013

- Public 2-year community college
- Commuter campus in small city

**General.** Founded in 1963. Regionally accredited. Satellite sites in Parker, San Luis-Somerton, Wellton. Campus shared with Northern Arizona University, which offers completion of bachelor's, master's and doctoral programs. **Enrollment:** 7,269 degree-seeking undergraduates; 715 non-degree-seeking students. **Degrees:** 590 associate awarded. **Location:** 7 miles from Yuma. **Calendar:** Semester, limited summer session. **Full-time faculty:** 111 total. **Part-time faculty:** 299 total. **Class size:** 54% < 20, 45% 20-39, less than 1% 40-49, less than 1% 50-99, less than 1% >100. **Partnerships:** Formal partnerships with Yuma Educational Consortium and Yuma Regional Medical Center.

**Student profile.** Among degree-seeking undergraduates, 65% enrolled in a transfer program, 25% enrolled in a vocational program, 157 enrolled as first-time, first-year students, 179 transferred in from other institutions.

| | | | |
|---|---|---|---|
| Part-time: | 64% | Hispanic American: | 58% |
| Out-of-state: | 14% | Native American: | 1% |
| Women: | 58% | International: | 11% |
| African American: | 3% | 25 or older: | 31% |
| Asian American: | 2% | | |

**Transfer out.** 21% of students enrolled in the transfer program go on to 4-year colleges. **Colleges most students transferred to 2009:** Northern Arizona University at Yuma, Arizona State University, University of Arizona.

**Basis for selection.** Open admission, but selective for some programs. Special requirements for students under age 18, international students, undergraduate exchange program, Colorado River Consortium, nursing program, massage therapy program, radiologic technology program. **Homeschooled:** Admissions decision dependent upon one or more of the following: placement test scores, academic history, current course enrollment, instructor approval. **Learning Disabled:** Proof of disability written by specialist must be submitted to Coordinator of Services for Students with Disabilities at least 8 weeks before start of classes to ensure accommodations by the first day of class.

**High school preparation.** College-preparatory program recommended.

**2009-2010 Annual costs.** Tuition/fees: $1,800; $6,360 out-of-state. Per-credit charge: $60 in-state; $212 out-of-state. Room/board: $5,140. Books/supplies: $1,343. Personal expenses: $2,962.

**2009-2010 Financial aid. Need-based:** Need-based aid available for part-time students. Work-study available nights, weekends and for part-time students. **Non-need-based:** Scholarships awarded for academics, athletics.

**Application procedures. Admission:** No deadline. No application fee. Admission notification on a rolling basis. **Financial aid:** Priority date 4/1; no closing date. FAFSA, institutional form required. Applicants notified on a rolling basis starting 5/1.

**Academics. Special study options:** Accelerated study, cooperative education, distance learning, dual enrollment of high school students, ESL, honors, independent study, internships, study abroad, teacher certification program, weekend college. License preparation in nursing, occupational therapy, paramedic, radiology. **Credit/placement by examination:** AP, CLEP, IB, institutional tests. 24 credit hours maximum toward associate degree. **Support services:** GED preparation, learning center, reduced course load, remedial instruction, study skills assistance, tutoring, writing center.

**Majors. Agriculture:** General, plant sciences. **Biology:** General. **Business:** General, business admin, hospitality admin, management science, marketing, office management. **Communications:** General, radio/tv. **Communications technology:** Radio/tv. **Computer sciences:** General, computer graphics, data entry. **Conservation:** Environmental science. **Education:** General, secondary. **Engineering:** General. **Engineering technology:** CAD/CADD, industrial, water quality. **Family/consumer sciences:** General, child development. **Foreign languages:** Spanish. **Health:** EMT paramedic, health services, massage therapy, nursing (RN), nursing admin, radiologic technology/medical imaging. **History:** General. **Math:** General. **Mechanic/repair:** Automotive, electronics/electrical, heating/ac/refrig. **Parks/recreation:** Health/fitness. **Personal/culinary services:** Restaurant/catering. **Philosophy/religion:** Philosophy. **Physical sciences:** Chemistry, oceanography, physics. **Production:** Welding. **Protective services:** Firefighting, law enforcement admin, police science. **Public administration:** Human services. **Social sciences:** General, political science. **Visual/performing arts:** Dramatic, multimedia, studio arts.

**Most popular majors.** Business/marketing 15%, health sciences 14%, liberal arts 35%, security/protective services 8%.

**Computing on campus.** 270 workstations in dormitories, library, computer center, student center. Dormitories wired for high-speed internet access and linked to campus network. Commuter students can connect to campus network. Online course registration, online library, helpline, repair service, student web hosting, wireless network available.

**Student life. Freshman orientation:** Available. Preregistration for classes offered. **Housing:** Coed dorms, single-sex dorms, special housing for disabled, wellness housing available. $100 fully refundable deposit. **Activities:** Bands, choral groups, dance, drama, international student organizations, literary magazine, music ensembles, radio station, student government, student newspaper, TV station, AACHE, Phi Theta Kappa, Native American club, Hispanic students club.

**Athletics.** NJCAA. **Intercollegiate:** Baseball M, basketball, football (tackle) M, soccer M, softball W, volleyball W. **Team name:** Matadors.

**Student services.** Adult student services, career counseling, services for economically disadvantaged, student employment services, financial aid counseling, health services, minority student services, on-campus daycare, personal counseling, placement for graduates, veterans' counselor, women's services. **Physically disabled:** Services for visually, speech, hearing impaired. **Transfer:** Pre-admission transcript evaluation for new students. Transfer center, transfer adviser, college fairs on campus for students transferring to 4-year colleges.

**Contact.** E-mail: amy.pignatore@azwestern.edu
Phone: (928) 317-6000 Toll-free number: (888) 293-0392
Fax: (928) 344-7543
Amy Pignatore, Director of Admissions/Registrar, Arizona Western College, PO Box 929, Yuma, AZ 85366-0929

## Brookline College: Phoenix
**Phoenix, Arizona**
**www.brooklinecollege.edu**          CB code: 2188

▶ For-profit 2-year career college
▶ Commuter campus in very large city
▶ Interview required

**General.** Accredited by ACICS. Additional campuses in Tempe, Tucson, and Albuquerque. **Enrollment:** 1,186 degree-seeking undergraduates. **Degrees:** 16 bachelor's, 106 associate awarded. **Calendar:** Continuous, extensive summer session. **Full-time faculty:** 46 total; 13% have terminal degrees, 35% minority, 80% women. **Part-time faculty:** 23 total; 4% have terminal degrees, 17% minority, 83% women.

**Student profile.**

| | | | |
|---|---|---|---|
| Women: | 86% | 25 or older: | 56% |

**Basis for selection.** Open admission, but selective for some programs. Must be 18 years of age or 17 years 6 months with parent or legal guardian consent. Must be citizen of the US or eligible non-citizen as classified by

Department of Homeland Security. **Homeschooled:** Letter of Attestation required.

**2010-2011 Annual costs.** Tuition/fees (projected): $13,000. Tuition shown is an average, actual tuition and fees may vary by program. $100 Technology fee per pay period for programs taken online. Personal expenses: $6,120.

**Financial aid.** All financial aid based on need.

**Application procedures. Admission:** No deadline. No application fee. Admission notification on a rolling basis. **Financial aid:** No deadline. FAFSA, institutional form required.

**Academics. Special study options:** Accelerated study, distance learning. Bachelor's degree programs available on campus. License preparation in nursing. **Credit/placement by examination:** CLEP, institutional tests. **Support services:** GED preparation and test center, learning center, tutoring.

**Majors. Business:** Accounting, business admin. **Health:** Health care admin, nursing (RN). **Legal studies:** Paralegal. **Protective services:** Law enforcement admin.

**Most popular majors.** Business/marketing 20%, health sciences 74%, legal studies 6%.

**Computing on campus.** 240 workstations in library, computer center. Commuter students can connect to campus network. Online library available.

**Student life. Freshman orientation:** Mandatory.

**Student services.** Career counseling, services for economically disadvantaged, financial aid counseling, placement for graduates. **Transfer:** Pre-admission transcript evaluation for new students.

**Contact.** E-mail: wdavidson@brooklinecollege.edu
Phone: (602) 242-6265 Toll-free number: (800) 793-2428
Fax: (602) 973-2572
Wendy Davidson, Vice President of Admissions, Brookline College: Phoenix, 2445 West Dunlap Avenue, Suite 100, Phoenix, AZ 85021-5820

## Brookline College: Tempe
**Tempe, Arizona**
**www.brooklinecollege.edu**          CB code: 3455

▶ For-profit 2-year branch campus and career college
▶ Commuter campus in very large city
▶ Interview required

**General.** Accredited by ACICS. Additional campuses in Phoenix, Tucson, and Albuquerque. **Enrollment:** 301 degree-seeking undergraduates. **Degrees:** 9 associate awarded. **Calendar:** Continuous, extensive summer session. **Full-time faculty:** 9 total; 22% have terminal degrees, 33% minority, 56% women. **Part-time faculty:** 12 total; 17% have terminal degrees, 33% minority, 83% women.

**Student profile.**

| | | | |
|---|---|---|---|
| Women: | 83% | 25 or older: | 52% |

**Basis for selection.** Open admission, but selective for some programs. Must be 18 years of age or 17 years 6 months with parent or legal guardian consent. Must be US citizen or eligible non-citizen as classified by Department of Homeland Security. **Homeschooled:** Letter of Attestation required.

**2010-2011 Annual costs.** Tuition/fees (projected): $13,000. Tuition shown is an average, actual tuition and fees may vary by program. Personal expenses: $6,120.

**Financial aid.** All financial aid based on need.

**Application procedures. Admission:** No deadline. No application fee. Admission notification on a rolling basis. **Financial aid:** No deadline. FAFSA, institutional form required.

**Academics. Special study options:** Accelerated study, distance learning. **Credit/placement by examination:** CLEP, institutional tests. **Support services:** GED preparation and test center, learning center, tutoring.

**Majors. Business:** Business admin. **Health:** Health care admin. **Legal studies:** Paralegal. **Protective services:** Law enforcement admin.

**Most popular majors.** Business/marketing 45%, health sciences 10%, legal studies 45%.

**Computing on campus.** 240 workstations in library, computer center. Commuter students can connect to campus network. Online library available.

**Student life. Freshman orientation:** Mandatory.

**Student services.** Career counseling, services for economically disadvantaged, financial aid counseling, placement for graduates. **Transfer:** Pre-admission transcript evaluation for new students.

**Contact.** E-mail: wdavidson@brooklinecollege.edu
Phone: (480) 545-8755 Toll-free number: (888) 886-2428
Fax: (480) 926-1371
Wendy Davidson, Vice President of Admissions, Brookline College: Tempe, 1140-1150 South Priest Drive, Tempe, AZ 85281-5240

## Brookline College: Tucson
**Tucson, Arizona**
**www.brooklinecollege.edu**　　　　**CB code: 3454**

- For-profit 2-year branch campus and career college
- Commuter campus in very large city
- Interview required

**General.** Accredited by ACICS. Additional campuses in Phoenix, Tempe, and Albuquerque. **Enrollment:** 598 degree-seeking undergraduates. **Degrees:** 24 associate awarded. **Calendar:** Continuous, extensive summer session. **Full-time faculty:** 18 total; 11% have terminal degrees, 22% minority, 56% women. **Part-time faculty:** 8 total; 12% minority, 62% women.

**Student profile.**

| | | | |
|---|---|---|---|
| Women: | 75% | 25 or older: | 50% |

**Basis for selection.** Open admission, but selective for some programs. Must be 18 years of age or 17 years 6 months with parent or legal guardian consent. Must be US citizen or eligible non-citizen as classified by Department of Homeland Security. **Homeschooled:** Letter of Attestation required.

**2010-2011 Annual costs.** Tuition/fees (projected): $13,000. Tuition shown is an average, actual tuition and fees may vary by program. Personal expenses: $6,120.

**Financial aid.** All financial aid based on need. Need-based aid available for part-time students.

**Application procedures. Admission:** No deadline. No application fee. Admission notification on a rolling basis. **Financial aid:** No deadline. FAFSA, institutional form required.

**Academics. Special study options:** Accelerated study, distance learning. **Credit/placement by examination:** CLEP, institutional tests. **Support services:** GED preparation and test center, learning center, tutoring.

**Majors. Business:** Business admin. **Legal studies:** Paralegal. **Protective services:** Law enforcement admin.

**Most popular majors.** Business/marketing 37%, health sciences 21%, legal studies 42%.

**Computing on campus.** 240 workstations in library, computer center. Commuter students can connect to campus network. Online library available.

**Student life. Freshman orientation:** Mandatory.

**Student services.** Career counseling, services for economically disadvantaged, financial aid counseling, placement for graduates. **Transfer:** Pre-admission transcript evaluation for new students.

**Contact.** E-mail: wdavidson@brooklinecollege.edu
Phone: (520) 748-9799 Toll-free number: (888) 292-2428
Fax: (520) 748-9355
Wendy Davidson, Vice President of Admissions, Brookline College: Tucson, 5441 East 22nd Street, Suite 125, Tucson, AZ 85711-5444

## Bryman School
**Phoenix, Arizona**
**www.brymanschool.edu**　　　　**CB code: 3040**

- For-profit 2-year health science college
- Very large city

**General.** Accredited by ACCSC. **Enrollment:** 1,100 degree-seeking undergraduates. **Degrees:** 102 associate awarded. **Calendar:** Continuous. **Full-time faculty:** 60 total.

**Basis for selection.** Open admission. Wonderlic exam required for placement.

**2009-2010 Annual costs.** Diploma programs range from $10,750 to $21,950 ($9,050 to $19,850 for agency) and $22,950 to $26,250 for degree ($18,100 to $22,000 for agency). Registration fee of $50.00. Books/supplies: $642. Personal expenses: $3,360.

**Application procedures. Admission:** No deadline. No application fee. Admission notification on a rolling basis.

**Academics. Credit/placement by examination:** CLEP.

**Majors. Health:** Insurance coding, insurance specialist.

**Student life. Freshman orientation:** Mandatory.

**Contact.** Phone: (602) 274-4300 Toll-free number: (800) 987-0110
Cecilia Gomez, Director of Admissions, Bryman School, 2250 West Peoria Ave, Phoenix, AZ 85029-4919

## Central Arizona College
**Coolidge, Arizona**
**www.centralaz.edu/**　　　　**CB code: 4122**

- Public 2-year community college
- Commuter campus in rural community

**General.** Founded in 1962. Regionally accredited. **Enrollment:** 5,282 degree-seeking undergraduates; 1,513 non-degree-seeking students. **Degrees:** 317 associate awarded. **Location:** 45 miles from Phoenix, 60 miles from Tucson. **Calendar:** Semester, limited summer session. **Full-time faculty:** 100 total. **Part-time faculty:** 362 total. **Special facilities:** Observatory. **Partnerships:** Formal partnership with CAVIT.

**Student profile.** Among degree-seeking undergraduates, 1,723 enrolled as first-time, first-year students.

| | | | |
|---|---|---|---|
| Part-time: | 67% | Hispanic American: | 26% |
| Out-of-state: | 2% | Native American: | 5% |
| Women: | 59% | 25 or older: | 65% |
| African American: | 8% | Live on campus: | 4% |
| Asian American: | 2% | | |

**Transfer out. Colleges most students transferred to 2009:** Arizona State University, Northern Arizona University, University of Arizona.

**Basis for selection.** Open admission, but selective for some programs. Special requirements for nursing programs. **Learning Disabled:** Student must register disability and present appropriate documentation.

**2009-2010 Annual costs.** Tuition/fees: $1,736; $7,728 out-of-state. Per-credit charge: $62 in-state; $120 out-of-state. Room/board: $4,900. Books/supplies: $1,300. Personal expenses: $3,000.

**Financial aid. Need-based:** Need-based aid available for part-time students. Work-study available nights, weekends and for part-time students.

**Application procedures. Admission:** No deadline. No application fee. Admission notification on a rolling basis. **Financial aid:** Priority date 5/1, closing date 7/15. FAFSA required. Must reply within 3 week(s) of notification.

**Academics. Special study options:** Distance learning, dual enrollment of high school students, ESL, honors, independent study, liberal arts/career combination. Bachelor's degree programs available on campus. License preparation in nursing, radiology, real estate. **Credit/placement by examination:** CLEP, institutional tests. 30 credit hours maximum toward associate degree. **Support services:** GED preparation and test center, learning center, pre-admission summer program, reduced course load, remedial instruction, study skills assistance, tutoring, writing center.

**Majors. Agriculture:** Business. **Biology:** General. **Business:** General, accounting, accounting technology, administrative services, business admin, hospitality/recreation, marketing, office technology. **Communications:** Journalism. **Computer sciences:** General, applications programming, data processing, programming. **Education:** General, early childhood, elementary, multi-level teacher, special. **Engineering:** General, civil, manufacturing, mechanical, mechanics. **Engineering technology:** Electrical, industrial management. **Family/consumer sciences:** Child development, family studies.

**Health:** Clinical nutrition, dietetic technician, EMT paramedic, massage therapy, medical assistant, medical secretary, medical transcription, nursing (RN), pharmacy assistant, preveterinary. **Interdisciplinary:** Biological/physical sciences. **Liberal arts:** Arts/sciences, humanities. **Math:** General. **Mechanic/repair:** Automotive, diesel, industrial. **Parks/recreation:** Exercise sciences. **Personal/culinary services:** Culinary arts. **Physical sciences:** Chemistry. **Protective services:** Corrections, criminal justice, fire safety technology, fire services admin. **Psychology:** General. **Social sciences:** General, criminology. **Visual/performing arts:** General, art, dramatic.

**Computing on campus.** 500 workstations in dormitories, library, computer center. Dormitories wired for high-speed internet access. Commuter students can connect to campus network. Online course registration, online library, helpline, wireless network available.

**Student life. Freshman orientation:** Available. Preregistration for classes offered. **Policies:** Student code of conduct must be followed. **Housing:** Coed dorms, special housing for disabled, wellness housing available. $100 fully refundable deposit. **Activities:** Bands, choral groups, drama, international student organizations, music ensembles, student government, student newspaper, Phi Theta, Kappa/Lamba, art club, Playmasters, Campus Crusade For Christ, Native American club, rodeo club, Student Nurses Association of Arizona.

**Athletics.** NJCAA. **Intercollegiate:** Baseball M, basketball, cross-country, rodeo, softball W, track and field. **Team name:** Vaqueros.

**Student services.** Adult student services, alcohol/substance abuse counseling, career counseling, student employment services, financial aid counseling, on-campus daycare, personal counseling. **Physically disabled:** Services for visually, hearing impaired. **Transfer:** Re-entry adviser, pre-admission transcript evaluation for new students. Transfer center, transfer adviser, college fairs on campus for students transferring to 4-year colleges.

**Contact.** E-mail: Admissions@centralaz.edu
Phone: (520) 494-5260 Toll-free number: (800) 237-9814
Fax: (520) 494-5083
James Moore, Director of Admission and Records, Central Arizona College, Admissions Office, Coolidge, AZ 85128-9030

## Chandler-Gilbert Community College: Pecos
**Chandler, Arizona**
www.cgc.maricopa.edu                    CB code: 0535

▶ Public 2-year community college
▶ Commuter campus in small city

**General.** Regionally accredited. Additional campuses in Sun Lakes and Williams. **Enrollment:** 4,127 degree-seeking undergraduates; 6,282 non-degree-seeking students. **Degrees:** 395 associate awarded. **Location:** 20 miles from Phoenix. **Calendar:** Semester, limited summer session. **Full-time faculty:** 125 total. **Part-time faculty:** 350 total. **Class size:** 44% < 20, 47% 20-39, 9% 40-49, less than 1% 50-99.

**Student profile.** Among degree-seeking undergraduates, 76% enrolled in a transfer program, 18% enrolled in a vocational program, 1% already have a bachelor's degree or higher, 1,392 enrolled as first-time, first-year students.

| | | | |
|---|---|---|---|
| Part-time: | 62% | Hispanic American: | 18% |
| Out-of-state: | 5% | Native American: | 2% |
| Women: | 56% | International: | 1% |
| African American: | 5% | 25 or older: | 28% |
| Asian American: | 5% | Live on campus: | 2% |

**Transfer out.** Colleges most students transferred to 2009: Arziona State University, Northern Arizona University, University of Arizona.

**Basis for selection.** Open admission.

**2009-2010 Annual costs.** Tuition/fees: $2,145; $8,595 out-of-state. Per-credit charge: $71 in-state; $286 out-of-state. Books/supplies: $1,064. Personal expenses: $4,878.

**2009-2010 Financial aid. Need-based:** Work-study available nights, weekends and for part-time students.

**Application procedures. Admission:** No deadline. No application fee.

**Academics. Special study options:** Distance learning, dual enrollment of high school students, ESL, honors, independent study, teacher certification program, weekend college. License preparation in aviation, nursing. **Credit/placement by examination:** AP, CLEP, IB, institutional tests. 30 credit

hours maximum toward associate degree. **Support services:** Learning center, reduced course load, remedial instruction, study skills assistance, tutoring, writing center.

**Majors. Business:** General, accounting, nonprofit/public, office technology, retailing. **Computer sciences:** General, computer science, data entry, information technology, networking, system admin, vendor certification. **Education:** Elementary. **Health:** Clinical nutrition, dietetic technician, massage therapy, nursing assistant. **Transportation:** Aviation. **Visual/performing arts:** Music management. **Other:** Automated manufacturing systems.

**Most popular majors.** Computer/information sciences 7%, education 10%, history 7%, liberal arts 63%, physical sciences 9%.

**Computing on campus.** 150 workstations in library, computer center. Commuter students can connect to campus network. Online course registration, online library, wireless network available.

**Student life. Freshman orientation:** Mandatory. Preregistration for classes offered. One-day sessions held at beginning of term; choice of weekend day and weeknight evening. **Housing:** Coed dorms available. Student housing for CGCC students available on-campus only at Williams campus in cooperation with Arizona State University Polytechnic. CGCC students attending any of the college's campuses can apply for student housing at the Williams campus. **Activities:** Bands, choral groups, dance, drama, music ensembles, musical theater, student government, political science organization, Christians in Action, Latter Day Saints student association, intercultural exchange club, Wall Street club, Phi Theta Kappa, black student union, Hispanic student organization.

**Athletics.** NJCAA. **Intercollegiate:** Baseball M, basketball, golf, soccer, softball W, volleyball W. **Team name:** Coyotes.

**Student services.** Adult student services, alcohol/substance abuse counseling, career counseling, services for economically disadvantaged, student employment services, financial aid counseling, personal counseling, placement for graduates, veterans' counselor. **Physically disabled:** Services for visually, speech, hearing impaired. **Transfer:** Pre-admission transcript evaluation for new students. Transfer center, transfer adviser, college fairs on campus for students transferring to 4-year colleges.

**Contact.** Phone: (480) 732-7320
Douglas Bullock, Dean Enrollment Services, Chandler-Gilbert Community College: Pecos, 2626 East Pecos Road, Chandler, AZ 85225

## Chandler-Gilbert Community College: Sun Lakes Education Center
**Sun Lakes, Arizona**
www.cgc.maricopa.edu                    CB code: 3826

▶ Public 2-year community college
▶ Commuter campus in small town

**General.** Regionally accredited. **Location:** 25 miles from Phoenix. **Calendar:** Semester.

**Annual costs/financial aid.** Tuition/fees (2009-2010): $2,145; $8,595 out-of-state. Books/supplies: $1,064. Personal expenses: $4,878.

**Contact.** Phone: (480) 857-5500
Supervisor of Admissions Records and Registration, 25105 South Alma School Road, Sun Lakes, AZ 85248-7158

## Chandler-Gilbert Community College: Williams Campus
**Mesa, Arizona**
www.cgc.maricopa.edu                    CB code: 3827

▶ Public 2-year community college
▶ Commuter campus in large city

**General.** Regionally accredited. **Location:** 33 miles from Phoenix. **Calendar:** Semester.

**Annual costs/financial aid.** Tuition/fees (2009-2010): $2,145; $8,595 out-of-state. Books/supplies: $1,064. Personal expenses: $4,878.

**Contact.** Phone: (480) 732-7320
Supervisor of Admissions, Records and Registration, 2626 East Pecos Road, Chandler, AZ 85225-2499

## Cochise College
**Douglas, Arizona**  CB member
**www.cochise.edu**  CB code: 4097

- Public 2-year community college
- Commuter campus in large town

**General.** Founded in 1962. Regionally accredited. Courses offered at 2 campuses; 4 extended learning centers located in 2 counties and online. **Enrollment:** 3,512 degree-seeking undergraduates; 1,261 non-degree-seeking students. **Degrees:** 995 associate awarded. **Location:** 120 miles from Tucson. **Calendar:** Semester, limited summer session. **Full-time faculty:** 93 total; 4% have terminal degrees, 16% minority, 43% women. **Part-time faculty:** 227 total; 7% have terminal degrees, 20% minority, 50% women. **Class size:** 78% < 20, 21% 20-39, less than 1% 40-49, less than 1% 50-99. **Special facilities:** Asian art collection, college airport.

**Student profile.** Among degree-seeking undergraduates, 32% enrolled in a transfer program, 68% enrolled in a vocational program, 1% already have a bachelor's degree or higher, 820 enrolled as first-time, first-year students, 1,152 transferred in from other institutions.

| | | | |
|---|---|---|---|
| Part-time: | 69% | Hispanic American: | 44% |
| Out-of-state: | 9% | Native American: | 1% |
| Women: | 60% | 25 or older: | 49% |
| African American: | 5% | Live on campus: | 3% |
| Asian American: | 3% | | |

**Transfer out.** 60% of students enrolled in the transfer program go on to 4-year colleges. **Colleges most students transferred to 2009:** University of Arizona, University of Maryland-University College, University of Phoenix, Central Texas College, Wayland Baptist University-External Campus.

**Basis for selection.** Open admission, but selective for some programs. Nursing program requires additional application and satisfactory score on HESI Entrance Exam. Flight program requires additional application, and in-person interview.

**2009-2010 Annual costs.** Tuition/fees: $1,630; $8,770 out-of-state. Per-credit charge: $52 in-state; $290 out-of-state. Room/board: $4,600. Books/supplies: $1,000. Personal expenses: $1,350.

**2008-2009 Financial aid. Need-based:** 220 full-time freshmen applied for aid; 192 were judged to have need; 190 of these received aid. Average scholarship/grant was $3,355; average loan $2,665. 76% of total undergraduate aid awarded as scholarships/grants, 24% as loans/jobs. Need-based aid available for part-time students. Work-study available for part-time students. **Non-need-based:** Awarded to 180 full-time undergraduates, including 53 freshmen. Scholarships awarded for academics, athletics.

**Application procedures. Admission:** No deadline. No application fee. Admission notification on a rolling basis. **Financial aid:** Closing date 4/15. FAFSA, institutional form required. Applicants notified on a rolling basis starting 6/15; must reply within 2 week(s) of notification.

**Academics. Special study options:** Distance learning, dual enrollment of high school students, ESL, honors, independent study, internships. License preparation in aviation, nursing, paramedic, real estate. **Credit/placement by examination:** AP, CLEP, institutional tests. 30 credit hours maximum toward associate degree. Student must complete at least one course in residence before credit may be granted for CLEP/DANTES. **Support services:** GED preparation and test center, learning center, pre-admission summer program, reduced course load, remedial instruction, study skills assistance, tutoring, writing center.

**Majors. Agriculture:** Business. **Biology:** General. **Business:** Administrative services, business admin, hospitality admin, logistics. **Communications:** General, journalism. **Computer sciences:** Computer science, data processing, information systems, networking, programming, security. **Construction:** General. **Education:** Art, biology, chemistry, early childhood, English, foreign languages, history, mathematics, music, physical. **Engineering:** General, manufacturing. **Engineering technology:** Electrical. **Family/consumer sciences:** Family studies. **Foreign languages:** General, sign language interpretation, translation. **Health:** EMT paramedic, health services, nursing (RN). **History:** General. **Liberal arts:** Humanities. **Math:** General. **Mechanic/repair:** Aircraft, automotive, avionics. **Military:** General. **Parks/recreation:** Health/fitness. **Personal/culinary services:** Chef training. **Philosophy/religion:** Philosophy. **Physical sciences:** Chemistry, physics. **Production:** Welding. **Protective services:** Fire safety technology, police science. **Psychology:** General. **Public administration:** Human services, social work. **Social sciences:** Anthropology, economics, geography, political science, sociology. **Transportation:** Airline/commercial pilot. **Visual/performing arts:** General, art.

**Most popular majors.** Liberal arts 14%, military 62%.

**Computing on campus.** 571 workstations in dormitories, library, computer center, student center. Dormitories wired for high-speed internet access. Online course registration, online library, helpline, repair service, wireless network available.

**Student life. Freshman orientation:** Available. Preregistration for classes offered. **Housing:** Coed dorms, special housing for disabled, apartments available. $100 partly refundable deposit. **Activities:** Choral groups, drama, film society, literary magazine, music ensembles, student government, student newspaper, animal science club, Armed Forces communications and electronics association, Cineaste Circle film club, math and computer sciences club, Phi Theta Kappa, pre-pharmacy club, social concerns club, Spanish club.

**Athletics.** NJCAA. **Intercollegiate:** Baseball M, basketball, rodeo, soccer W. **Team name:** Apaches.

**Student services.** Career counseling, student employment services, financial aid counseling, health services, personal counseling, placement for graduates, veterans' counselor. **Physically disabled:** Services for visually, speech, hearing impaired. **Transfer:** Pre-admission transcript evaluation for new students. Transfer adviser, college fairs on campus for students transferring to 4-year colleges.

**Contact.** E-mail: admissions@cochise.edu
Phone: (520) 515-5412 Toll-free number: (800) 593-9567
Fax: (520) 515-5452
Debbie Quick, Director of Admissions, Cochise College, 901 North Colombo Avenue, Sierra Vista, AZ 85635

## Coconino County Community College
**Flagstaff, Arizona**  CB member
**www.coconino.edu**  CB code: 1712

- Public 2-year community college
- Commuter campus in small city

**General.** Regionally accredited. **Enrollment:** 2,742 degree-seeking undergraduates. **Degrees:** 156 associate awarded. **ROTC:** Army, Air Force. **Location:** 140 miles from Phoenix. **Calendar:** Semester, limited summer session. **Full-time faculty:** 38 total; 55% women. **Part-time faculty:** 220 total; 52% women. **Special facilities:** Community garden, wind turbine, green building, telescope.

**Student profile.** Among degree-seeking undergraduates, 55% enrolled in a transfer program, 17% enrolled in a vocational program, 4% already have a bachelor's degree or higher, 128 transferred in from other institutions.

| | | | |
|---|---|---|---|
| Out-of-state: | 7% | Hispanic American: | 9% |
| African American: | 2% | Native American: | 27% |
| Asian American: | 1% | 25 or older: | 42% |

**Transfer out.** 47% of students enrolled in the transfer program go on to 4-year colleges. **Colleges most students transferred to 2009:** Northern Arizona University, Arizona State University, University of Arizona.

**Basis for selection.** Open admission, but selective for some programs. Special requirements for nursing program.

**2009-2010 Annual costs.** Tuition/fees: $1,800; $6,000 out-of-state. Per-credit charge: $75 in-state; $250 out-of-state. Books/supplies: $1,004. Personal expenses: $1,593.

**2008-2009 Financial aid. Need-based:** 21% of total undergraduate aid awarded as scholarships/grants, 79% as loans/jobs.

**Application procedures. Admission:** No deadline. No application fee. Application must be submitted on paper. Admission notification on a rolling basis. **Financial aid:** Priority date 4/15, closing date 6/30.

**Academics.** Writing center, learning center and tutoring available. **Special study options:** Distance learning, dual enrollment of high school students, honors, internships. License preparation in nursing, paramedic, real estate. **Credit/placement by examination:** CLEP. **Support services:** GED preparation and test center, learning center, remedial instruction, study skills assistance, tutoring, writing center.

**Majors. Architecture:** Technology. **Business:** General, accounting, business admin, construction management, finance, hospitality admin, marketing. **Computer sciences:** System admin. **Conservation:** Environmental science. **Construction:** Carpentry. **Education:** General, early childhood, elementary. **Engineering:** General. **Engineering technology:** Architectural drafting, CAD/CADD, computer systems, construction, software, solar energy. **Health:** Medical secretary, nursing assistant. **Interdisciplinary:** Biological/physical sciences. **Legal studies:** Paralegal. **Protective services:** Criminal justice, firefighting. **Psychology:** General. **Public administration:** Social work. **Social sciences:** Anthropology, sociology. **Visual/performing arts:** Art. **Other:** Colorado plateau studies.

**Most popular majors.** Health sciences 7%, liberal arts 52%, security/protective services 8%.

**Computing on campus.** 100 workstations in library, computer center, student center. Online course registration, online library, helpline available.

**Student life. Freshman orientation:** Available. Preregistration for classes offered. **Activities:** Dance, literary magazine, music ensembles, symphony orchestra.

**Athletics. Team name:** Comets.

**Student services.** Adult student services, career counseling, financial aid counseling, on-campus daycare, veterans' counselor. **Physically disabled:** Services for visually, speech, hearing impaired. **Transfer:** Pre-admission transcript evaluation for new students. Transfer adviser, college fairs on campus for students transferring to 4-year colleges.

**Contact.** E-mail: admissions&registration@coconino.edu
Phone: (928) 527-1222 ext. 4299 Toll-free
number: (800) 350-7122 ext. 4299 Fax: (928) 226-4110
Liz Gallegos, Registrar/Director for Admissions, Coconino County Community College, 2800 South Lone Tree Road, Flagstaff, AZ 86001

## Dine College
**Tsaile, Arizona**
www.dinecollege.edu
**CB member**
**CB code: 4550**

- Public 2-year community college
- Residential campus in rural community

**General.** Founded in 1968. Regionally accredited. The first tribally controlled community college in the United States; chartered by the Navajo Nation. **Enrollment:** 600 full-time, degree-seeking students. **Degrees:** 172 associate awarded. **Location:** 55 miles from Window Rock. **Calendar:** Semester, limited summer session. **Full-time faculty:** 61 total; 43% women. **Part-time faculty:** 73 total; 48% women. **Special facilities:** Museum.

**Student profile.**

| | | | |
|---|---|---|---|
| Out-of-state: | 15% | Live on campus: | 20% |
| 25 or older: | 49% | | |

**Transfer out. Colleges most students transferred to 2009:** Northern Arizona University, Arizona State University, Fort Lewis College, University of Arizona, University of New Mexico.

**Basis for selection.** Open admission. **Homeschooled:** Statement describing homeschool structure and mission, transcript of courses and grades, state high school equivalency certificate required.

**2009-2010 Annual costs.** Tuition/fees: $850. Room/board: $4,472. Books/supplies: $950. Personal expenses: $2,500.

**2008-2009 Financial aid.** All financial aid based on need. Need-based aid available for part-time students.

**Application procedures. Admission:** No deadline. $20 fee. Application must be submitted on paper. Admission notification on a rolling basis. **Financial aid:** Priority date 4/15; no closing date. FAFSA, institutional form required. Applicants notified on a rolling basis starting 5/1; must reply within 4 week(s) of notification.

**Academics. Special study options:** Cooperative education, distance learning, double major, independent study. **Credit/placement by examination:** CLEP, institutional tests. 12 credit hours maximum toward associate degree. **Support services:** Learning center, pre-admission summer program, remedial instruction, tutoring.

**Majors. Area/ethnic studies:** Native American. **Biology:** General. **Business:** Administrative services, business admin, office/clerical. **Computer sciences:** General, computer science. **Conservation:** Environmental science. **Education:** General. **Foreign languages:** Native American. **Health:** Public health ed. **Liberal arts:** Arts/sciences. **Psychology:** General. **Social sciences:** General. **Visual/performing arts:** Studio arts. **Other:** Pre-engineering.

**Computing on campus.** 104 workstations in dormitories, library, computer center, student center. Dormitories wired for high-speed internet access and linked to campus network. Online library, helpline, repair service, wireless network available.

**Student life. Freshman orientation:** Available. Preregistration for classes offered. **Housing:** Coed dorms, single-sex dorms, wellness housing available. **Activities:** Student government, Red Dawn Indian club.

**Athletics.** NJCAA. **Intercollegiate:** Archery, cross-country, rodeo. **Intramural:** Archery, cross-country, rodeo. **Team name:** Warrior.

**Student services.** Alcohol/substance abuse counseling, career counseling, personal counseling, veterans' counselor. **Transfer:** Pre-admission transcript evaluation for new students. Transfer adviser, college fairs on campus for students transferring to 4-year colleges.

**Contact.** Phone: (928) 724-6630 Fax: (928) 724-3349
Louise Litzin, Registrar, Dine College, Box 67, Tsaile, AZ 86556

## Eastern Arizona College
**Thatcher, Arizona**
www.eac.edu
**CB code: 4297**

- Public 2-year community college
- Commuter campus in large town

**General.** Founded in 1888. Regionally accredited. Near archaeological sites. Several continuing education centers within 165 miles of campus. **Enrollment:** 4,470 degree-seeking undergraduates; 2,771 non-degree-seeking students. **Degrees:** 302 associate awarded. **Location:** 160 miles from Phoenix, 130 miles from Tucson. **Calendar:** Semester, limited summer session. **Full-time faculty:** 88 total; 16% have terminal degrees, 12% minority, 32% women. **Part-time faculty:** 188 total; 7% have terminal degrees, 13% minority, 55% women. **Class size:** 67% < 20, 27% 20-39, 2% 40-49, 3% 50-99, less than 1% >100. **Special facilities:** Observatory, golf course, wilderness area. **Partnerships:** Formal partnerships with local high schools allow high school students to obtain degrees in areas such as office technology and drafting.

**Student profile.** Among degree-seeking undergraduates, 1,463 enrolled as first-time, first-year students, 58 transferred in from other institutions.

| | | | |
|---|---|---|---|
| Part-time: | 55% | Hispanic American: | 21% |
| Out-of-state: | 4% | Native American: | 9% |
| Women: | 57% | International: | 1% |
| African American: | 3% | 25 or older: | 56% |
| Asian American: | 2% | Live on campus: | 6% |

**Basis for selection.** Open admission, but selective for some programs. Special requirements for nursing and several paramedical programs.

**High school preparation.** 15 units recommended. Recommended units include English 4, mathematics 4, social studies 1, history 1, science 3 (laboratory 3) and foreign language 2.

**2009-2010 Annual costs.** Tuition/fees: $1,520; $8,120 out-of-state. Per-credit charge: $65 in-state; $140 out-of-state. Room/board: $4,795. Books/supplies: $800. Personal expenses: $1,722.

**2009-2010 Financial aid. Need-based:** Average need met was 37%. Average scholarship/grant was $5,012. 94% of total undergraduate aid awarded as scholarships/grants, 6% as loans/jobs. Need-based aid available for part-time students. Work-study available nights, weekends and for part-time students. **Non-need-based:** Scholarships awarded for academics, art, athletics, leadership, music/drama, state residency. **Additional information:** Limited number of tuition waivers for New Mexico residents. Unlimited number of waivers for those meeting WUE requirements.

**Application procedures. Admission:** No deadline. No application fee. Admission notification on a rolling basis. **Financial aid:** Priority date 3/1; no closing date. FAFSA, institutional form required. Applicants notified on a rolling basis starting 3/15.

**Academics. Special study options:** Cooperative education, distance learning, double major, dual enrollment of high school students, independent study. Bachelor's degree programs available on campus. License preparation in nursing, paramedic. **Credit/placement by examination:** CLEP, IB, institutional tests. 48 credit hours maximum toward associate degree. **Support services:** GED preparation and test center, learning center, reduced course load, remedial instruction, study skills assistance, tutoring, writing center.

**Majors. Agriculture:** Agribusiness operations. **Biology:** General, environmental, wildlife. **Business:** Administrative services, business admin, entrepreneurial studies, office technology. **Computer sciences:** Information systems, system admin. **Conservation:** Forestry. **Education:** Art, business, elementary, secondary, technology/industrial arts. **Engineering technology:** Civil, drafting, mining. **Foreign languages:** General. **Health:** EMT paramedic, nursing (RN), pharmacy assistant, premedicine, prepharmacy. **History:** General. **Legal studies:** Prelaw. **Liberal arts:** Arts/sciences. **Math:**

General. **Mechanic/repair:** Automotive. **Parks/recreation:** Health/fitness. **Personal/culinary services:** Cosmetic. **Physical sciences:** Chemistry, geology, physics. **Protective services:** Law enforcement admin, police science. **Psychology:** General. **Social sciences:** Anthropology, political science, sociology. **Visual/performing arts:** Art, commercial/advertising art, dramatic, studio arts.

**Most popular majors.** Business/marketing 6%, health sciences 16%, liberal arts 53%, visual/performing arts 8%.

**Computing on campus.** 564 workstations in library, computer center. Dormitories wired for high-speed internet access and linked to campus network. Online course registration, online library, wireless network available.

**Student life. Freshman orientation:** Available. Preregistration for classes offered. Half-day session given the week prior to beginning of classes each semester and weekly during summer months. **Housing:** Single-sex dorms, wellness housing available. $150 fully refundable deposit. **Activities:** Bands, choral groups, dance, drama, literary magazine, music ensembles, musical theater, student government, symphony orchestra, Latter-Day-Saints student association, Newman club, drama club, Hispanic Leaders, Intertribal club, Phi Theta Kappa, Spanish Club, Gila Force, Rowdy Reptiles.

**Athletics.** NJCAA. **Intercollegiate:** Baseball M, basketball, football (tackle) M, golf M, softball W, tennis W, volleyball W. **Intramural:** Basketball, soccer, swimming, tennis, volleyball. **Team name:** Gila Monsters.

**Student services.** Adult student services, alcohol/substance abuse counseling, career counseling, services for economically disadvantaged, student employment services, financial aid counseling, minority student services, personal counseling, placement for graduates, veterans' counselor, women's services. **Physically disabled:** Services for visually, speech, hearing impaired. **Transfer:** Re-entry adviser, pre-admission transcript evaluation for new students. Transfer adviser, college fairs on campus for students transferring to 4-year colleges.

**Contact.** E-mail: admissions@eac.edu
Phone: (928) 428-8272 Toll-free number: (800) 678-3808 ext. 8272
Fax: (928) 428-2578
Erik Lehmann, Admissions Counselor, Eastern Arizona College, 615 North Stadium Avenue, Thatcher, AZ 85552-0769

## Estrella Mountain Community College
Avondale, Arizona
www.estrellamountain.edu          CB code: 3810

- Public 2-year community college
- Commuter campus in small city

**General.** Regionally accredited. **Enrollment:** 3,390 degree-seeking undergraduates; 2,968 non-degree-seeking students. **Degrees:** 540 associate awarded. **ROTC:** Air Force. **Location:** 15 miles from Phoenix. **Calendar:** Semester, limited summer session.

**Student profile.** Among degree-seeking undergraduates, 920 enrolled as first-time, first-year students.

| Part-time: | 71% | Women: | 63% |
|---|---|---|---|

**Transfer out. Colleges most students transferred to 2009:** Arizona State University.

**Basis for selection.** Open admission.

**2009-2010 Annual costs.** Tuition/fees: $2,145; $8,985 out-of-state. Per-credit charge: $71 in-state; $286 out-of-state. Books/supplies: $1,104. Personal expenses: $2,718.

**2008-2009 Financial aid. Need-based:** Need-based aid available for part-time students. Work-study available nights and for part-time students. **Non-need-based:** Scholarships awarded for leadership.

**Application procedures. Admission:** No deadline. No application fee. **Financial aid:** Priority date 4/1; no closing date. Applicants notified on a rolling basis starting 4/15.

**Academics. Special study options:** Accelerated study, dual enrollment of high school students, ESL, honors, independent study, weekend college. **Credit/placement by examination:** CLEP, IB. 30 credit hours maximum toward associate degree. **Support services:** GED test center, learning center, pre-admission summer program, reduced course load, remedial instruction, study skills assistance, tutoring, writing center.

**Majors. Business:** Business admin, hotel/motel admin, organizational behavior. **Computer sciences:** Applications programming, data entry, LAN/

WAN management, vendor certification. **Education:** General, secondary, teacher assistance. **Health:** Speech-language pathology assistant. **Liberal arts:** Arts/sciences. **Personal/culinary services:** Chef training, culinary arts. **Protective services:** Criminal justice. **Psychology:** General. **Public administration:** Social work.

**Computing on campus.** 185 workstations in library, computer center. Online course registration, online library, helpline, wireless network available.

**Student life. Freshman orientation:** Available. Preregistration for classes offered. **Activities:** Student government.

**Student services.** Adult student services, alcohol/substance abuse counseling, career counseling, financial aid counseling, personal counseling, veterans' counselor. **Physically disabled:** Services for visually, speech, hearing impaired. **Transfer:** Pre-admission transcript evaluation for new students. College fairs on campus for students transferring to 4-year colleges.

**Contact.** E-mail: frank.amparo@estrellamountain.edu
Phone: (623) 935-8000 Fax: (623) 935-8870
Frank Amparo, Director of Admission and Records, Estrella Mountain Community College, 3000 North Dysart Road, Avondale, AZ 85392

## Everest College: Phoenix
Phoenix, Arizona
www.everestcollegephoenix.edu          CB code: 2172

- For-profit 2-year junior and technical college
- Commuter campus in very large city
- Interview required

**General.** Founded in 1982. Regionally accredited. **Enrollment:** 5,342 degree-seeking undergraduates. **Degrees:** 47 bachelor's, 225 associate awarded. **Location:** 10 miles from downtown. **Calendar:** Quarter, extensive summer session. **Full-time faculty:** 441 total. **Part-time faculty:** 28 total.

**Student profile.**

| Out-of-state: | 5% | 25 or older: | 65% |
|---|---|---|---|

**Transfer out. Colleges most students transferred to 2009:** Arizona State University, Northern Arizona University, University of Phoenix.

**Basis for selection.** Open admission, but selective for some programs. Interview very important for selective programs.

**2009-2010 Annual costs.** Full-time tuition is $15,024 for associate and bachelor degree students, except for nursing which is $21,654. Diploma program tuition averages $12,310 for entire certificate program. Books/supplies: $930.

**Application procedures. Admission:** No deadline. No application fee. Admission notification on a rolling basis. **Financial aid:** No deadline. FAFSA required. Applicants notified on a rolling basis.

**Academics. Special study options:** Cooperative education, distance learning, independent study, internships, weekend college. Bachelor's degree programs available on campus. License preparation in nursing. **Credit/ placement by examination:** AP, CLEP, institutional tests. 68 credit hours maximum toward associate degree, 136 toward bachelor's. **Support services:** Reduced course load, remedial instruction, study skills assistance, tutoring.

**Majors. Business:** Accounting, business admin, office management. **Health:** Nursing (RN). **Legal studies:** Paralegal. **Protective services:** Criminal justice.

**Most popular majors.** Business/marketing 7%, legal studies 28%, security/protective services 65%.

**Computing on campus.** 120 workstations in library, computer center. Commuter students can connect to campus network. Online course registration, online library, helpline, wireless network available.

**Student life. Freshman orientation:** Mandatory.

**Student services.** Adult student services, career counseling, student employment services, financial aid counseling, personal counseling, placement for graduates, veterans' counselor. **Transfer:** Re-entry adviser, pre-admission transcript evaluation for new students. Transfer adviser for students transferring to 4-year colleges.

**Contact.** E-mail: smilgram@cci.edu
Phone: (602) 942-4141 Toll-free number: (888) 741-4271
Fax: (602) 943-0960
Stacey Milgram, Director of Admissions, Everest College: Phoenix, 10400 North 25th Avenue Suite 190, Phoenix, AZ 85021

## GateWay Community College
### Phoenix, Arizona
www.gatewaycc.edu                    CB code: 0455

◗ Public 2-year community and technical college
◗ Commuter campus in very large city

**General.** Founded in 1968. Regionally accredited. **Enrollment:** 7,076 degree-seeking undergraduates. **Degrees:** 560 associate awarded. **ROTC:** Army, Naval, Air Force. **Calendar:** Semester, extensive summer session. **Full-time faculty:** 98 total; 18% minority. **Part-time faculty:** 270 total. **Partnerships:** Formal partnerships with Johnson Control, Toyota, Honda, Nissan, Banner Health.

**Student profile.** Among degree-seeking undergraduates, 15% enrolled in a transfer program, 85% enrolled in a vocational program. Of all enrolled students, 5% already have a bachelor's degree or higher.

Out-of-state:               5%       25 or older:              80%

**Transfer out.** 1% of students enrolled in the transfer program go on to 4-year colleges. **Colleges most students transferred to 2009:** Arizona State Unversity, Northern Arizona University, University of Arizona.

**Basis for selection.** Open admission, but selective for some programs. Special requirements for nursing and some allied health programs. General Aptitude Test Battery required of health science applicants.

**2009-2010 Annual costs.** Tuition/fees: $2,145; $8,085 out-of-state. Per-credit charge: $71 in-state; $269 out-of-state.

**2008-2009 Financial aid. Need-based:** Need-based aid available for part-time students. Work-study available nights, weekends and for part-time students. **Non-need-based:** Scholarships awarded for athletics.

**Application procedures. Admission:** No deadline. No application fee. Admission notification on a rolling basis. **Financial aid:** Priority date 4/15; no closing date. FAFSA, institutional form required. Applicants notified on a rolling basis; must reply within 4 week(s) of notification.

**Academics. Special study options:** Accelerated study, cooperative education, cross-registration, distance learning, double major, dual enrollment of high school students, ESL, external degree, honors, independent study, internships, liberal arts/career combination, study abroad. License preparation in nursing, physical therapy, radiology. **Credit/placement by examination:** AP, CLEP, IB, institutional tests. 30 credit hours maximum toward associate degree. **Support services:** Learning center, reduced course load, remedial instruction, study skills assistance, tutoring, writing center.

**Majors. Business:** General, accounting, administrative services, banking/financial services, international, office management. **Computer sciences:** General, information systems, LAN/WAN management, networking, system admin, systems analysis. **Construction:** Carpentry, electrician, maintenance, masonry, pipefitting, power transmission. **Engineering:** General, aerospace. **Engineering technology:** Aerospace, hazardous materials, manufacturing, occupational safety, water quality. **Health:** Health care admin, medical radiologic technology/radiation therapy, medical transcription, nuclear medical technology, nursing (RN), physical therapy assistant, respiratory therapy technology, sonography, surgical technology. **Legal studies:** Court reporting. **Liberal arts:** Arts/sciences. **Mechanic/repair:** Automotive, electronics/electrical, heating/ac/refrig. **Social sciences:** Sociology.

**Most popular majors.** Health sciences 67%, liberal arts 23%, trade and industry 6%.

**Computing on campus.** 100 workstations in library, computer center, student center. Commuter students can connect to campus network. Online course registration, online library, helpline, wireless network available.

**Student life. Freshman orientation:** Mandatory. Preregistration for classes offered. **Activities:** Film society, student government, student newspaper, MEHCA, Indian Tribal club, single parents association, women's club, health sciences club, business club.

**Athletics.** NJCAA. **Intercollegiate:** Cross-country, golf, soccer M, softball W, tennis. **Team name:** Geckos.

**Student services.** Adult student services, alcohol/substance abuse counseling, career counseling, services for economically disadvantaged, student employment services, financial aid counseling, minority student services, on-campus daycare, personal counseling, placement for graduates, veterans' counselor, women's services. **Physically disabled:** Services for visually, speech, hearing impaired. **Learning disabled:** Comprehensive services available. **Transfer:** Re-entry adviser, pre-admission transcript evaluation for new students. Transfer center, transfer adviser, college fairs on campus for students transferring to 4-year colleges.

**Contact.** E-mail: brenda.starck@gwmail.maricopa.edu
Phone: (602) 286-8200 Fax: (602) 286-8072
Brenda Starck, Supervisor Registration and Records, GateWay Community College, 108 North 40th Street, Phoenix, AZ 85034

## Glendale Community College
### Glendale, Arizona
www.gccaz.edu                    CB code: 4338

◗ Public 2-year community college
◗ Commuter campus in small city

**General.** Founded in 1965. Regionally accredited. Additional campus in Peoria. **Enrollment:** 8,438 degree-seeking undergraduates; 11,405 non-degree-seeking students. **Degrees:** 1,076 associate awarded. **Location:** 17 miles from Phoenix. **Calendar:** Semester, extensive summer session. **Full-time faculty:** 244 total; 17% minority, 51% women. **Part-time faculty:** 813 total; 30% minority, 46% women. **Class size:** 42% < 20, 54% 20-39, 3% 40-49, less than 1% 50-99, less than 1% >100. **Special facilities:** Performing arts center, high-technology centers, international student center. **Partnerships:** Formal partnerships with General Motors, Ford, Chrysler, Best Western, and John Deere.

**Student profile.** Among degree-seeking undergraduates, 43% enrolled in a transfer program, 6% already have a bachelor's degree or higher.

| | | | |
|---|---|---|---|
| Part-time: | 59% | Asian American: | 4% |
| Out-of-state: | 5% | Hispanic American: | 24% |
| Women: | 55% | Native American: | 2% |
| African American: | 6% | 25 or older: | 34% |

**Transfer out. Colleges most students transferred to 2009:** Arizona State University, Arizona State University West, University of Arizona, Grand Canyon University.

**Basis for selection.** Open admission, but selective for some programs. Special requirements for nursing, basic emergency medical technology, General Motors and Ford automotive programs, international students. **Home-schooled:** If under 18, special admissions required.

**2009-2010 Annual costs.** Tuition/fees: $2,145; $9,375 out-of-state. Per-credit charge: $7 in-state; $312 out-of-state. Books/supplies: $1,000. Personal expenses: $2,988.

**2008-2009 Financial aid. Need-based:** 52% of total undergraduate aid awarded as scholarships/grants, 48% as loans/jobs. Need-based aid available for part-time students. Work-study available nights, weekends and for part-time students.

**Application procedures. Admission:** No deadline. No application fee. Admission notification on a rolling basis. **Financial aid:** Priority date 4/30, closing date 7/31. FAFSA required. Applicants notified on a rolling basis starting 5/1.

**Academics. Special study options:** Cooperative education, distance learning, dual enrollment of high school students, ESL, honors, independent study, internships, weekend college. ACE Plus (Achieving College Education), high school bridge program, intensive English program. License preparation in nursing, paramedic. **Credit/placement by examination:** AP, CLEP, IB, institutional tests. 30 credit hours maximum toward associate degree. **Support services:** GED preparation and test center, learning center, remedial instruction, study skills assistance, tutoring, writing center.

**Majors. Biology:** Biotechnology. **Business:** General, accounting, accounting technology, administrative services, marketing, real estate. **Communications:** Public relations. **Communications technology:** Recording arts. **Computer sciences:** General, data entry, networking, security, systems analysis, web page design. **Education:** Early childhood, trade/industrial. **Engineering technology:** CAD/CADD, energy systems. **Family/consumer sciences:** Family/community services. **Health:** EMT paramedic, nursing (RN). **Interdisciplinary:** Behavioral sciences. **Mechanic/repair:** Automotive. **Parks/recreation:** Exercise sciences. **Protective services:** Criminal justice, firefighting. **Visual/performing arts:** Cinematography, graphic design, music management. **Other:** Emergency Management.

**Most popular majors.** Business/marketing 10%, health sciences 13%, liberal arts 49%, physical sciences 9%.

**Computing on campus.** 1,500 workstations in library, computer center, student center. Commuter students can connect to campus network. Online course registration, online library, helpline, student web hosting, wireless network available.

**Student life. Freshman orientation:** Available. Preregistration for classes offered. **Activities:** Bands, choral groups, dance, drama, literary magazine, music ensembles, musical theater, opera, student government, student newspaper.

**Athletics.** NJCAA. **Intercollegiate:** Baseball M, basketball, cheerleading, cross-country, football (tackle) M, golf M, soccer, softball W, tennis, track and field, volleyball W. **Team name:** Gauchos.

**Student services.** Adult student services, chaplain/spiritual director, career counseling, student employment services, financial aid counseling, minority student services, on-campus daycare, veterans' counselor. **Physically disabled:** Services for visually, speech, hearing impaired. **Transfer:** Transfer adviser, college fairs on campus for students transferring to 4-year colleges.

**Contact.** E-mail: admissions.recruitment@gcmail.maricopa.edu
Phone: (623) 845-3333 Fax: (623) 845-3060
Mary Blackwell, Dean, Enrollment Services, Glendale Community College, 6000 West Olive Avenue, Glendale, AZ 85302

## Golf Academy of America: Phoenix
Scottsdale, Arizona
www.golfacademy.edu                      CB code: 3460

- For-profit 2-year college of golf course management
- Small city

**General.** Accredited by ACICS. **Calendar:** Semester.

**Annual costs/financial aid.** Books/supplies: $700. Personal expenses: $2,862.

**Contact.** Phone: (480) 905-9288
7373 North Scottsdale Road, Suite B-100, Scottsdale, AZ 85253

## Kaplan College: Phoenix
Phoenix, Arizona
www.kc-phoenix.com                        CB code: 3052

- For-profit 2-year technical college
- Residential campus in very large city
- Interview required

**General.** Accredited by ACICS, ACCSC. **Enrollment:** 824 degree-seeking undergraduates. **Degrees:** 82 associate awarded. **Calendar:** Continuous. **Full-time faculty:** 14 total. **Part-time faculty:** 13 total.

**Basis for selection.** Open admission, but selective for some programs. Wonderlic entrance exam required for placement.

**Application procedures. Admission:** No deadline. $25 fee. **Financial aid:** No deadline.

**Academics. Credit/placement by examination:** CLEP. **Support services:** Learning center, tutoring.

**Majors. Health:** Respiratory therapy technology.

**Student life. Freshman orientation:** Mandatory, $20 fee.

**Contact.** E-mail: mcrance@kaplan.edu
Phone: (602) 548-1955 ext. 1366 Toll-free
number: (877) 548-1955 ext. 1366 Fax: (602) 548-1956
Jim Lillard, Director of Admissions, Kaplan College: Phoenix, 13610 North Black Canyon Highway, Suite 104, Phoenix, AZ 85029

## Lamson College
Tempe, Arizona
www.lamsoncollege.com                     CB code: 1899

- For-profit 2-year junior and technical college
- Commuter campus in very large city
- Interview required

**General.** Founded in 1889. Accredited by ACICS. **Enrollment:** 643 full-time, degree-seeking students. **Degrees:** 27 associate awarded. **Calendar:** Quarter, extensive summer session.

**Basis for selection.** Open admission.

**2009-2010 Annual costs.** Per-credit-hour charges vary according to program: $250 to $271; cost of books and supplies ranges from $995 to $3,000, depending on program of study.

**Financial aid. Need-based:** Need-based aid available for part-time students.

**Application procedures. Admission:** No deadline. $30 fee. Application must be submitted on paper. Admission notification on a rolling basis. **Financial aid:** No deadline. FAFSA required. Applicants notified on a rolling basis.

**Academics. Special study options:** Independent study, internships. **Credit/placement by examination:** CLEP. **Support services:** Learning center, tutoring.

**Majors. Business:** Accounting, business admin. **Health:** Medical assistant. **Legal studies:** Paralegal.

**Computing on campus.** 73 workstations in library, computer center.

**Student life. Freshman orientation:** Mandatory.

**Student services.** Career counseling, student employment services, financial aid counseling, placement for graduates, veterans' counselor. **Transfer:** Pre-admission transcript evaluation for new students.

**Contact.** E-mail: lamsonadmissions@gryphoncolleges.edu
Phone: (480) 898-7000 Toll-free number: (800) 898-7017
Fax: (480) 967-6645
Jeff Bing, Director of Admission, Lamson College, 1126 North Scottsdale Road, Suite 17, Tempe, AZ 85281-1700

## Mesa Community College
Mesa, Arizona
www.mc.maricopa.edu                       CB code: 4513

- Public 2-year community college
- Commuter campus in very large city

**General.** Founded in 1965. Regionally accredited. **Enrollment:** 8,475 full-time, degree-seeking students. **Degrees:** 1,640 associate awarded. **ROTC:** Army, Naval, Air Force. **Location:** 12 miles from Phoenix. **Calendar:** Semester, extensive summer session. **Full-time faculty:** 345 total. **Part-time faculty:** 730 total.

**Basis for selection.** Open admission, but selective for some programs. General education requirements and 2.5 GPA required for nursing, mortuary science, and fire academy programs.

**2010-2011 Annual costs.** Tuition/fees (projected): $2,160; $8,610 out-of-state. Per-credit charge: $71 in-state; $286 out-of-state. Books/supplies: $500.

**Financial aid. Non-need-based:** Scholarships awarded for academics, athletics. **Additional information:** Awards available for Maricopa County residents.

**Application procedures. Admission:** No deadline. No application fee. Admission notification on a rolling basis. Diploma or GED required for applicants under 18. **Financial aid:** Priority date 5/1; no closing date. Institutional form required. Applicants notified on a rolling basis starting 7/1.

**Academics.** Associate of General Studies degree allows students to take half of credits in required courses, and dictate own program of electives. **Special study options:** Cooperative education, cross-registration, distance learning, dual enrollment of high school students, ESL, exchange student, honors, independent study, internships, liberal arts/career combination, student-designed major, study abroad, teacher certification program, weekend college. License preparation in dental hygiene, nursing, real estate. **Credit/placement by examination:** CLEP, IB, institutional tests. 30 credit hours maximum toward associate degree. **Support services:** GED preparation and test center, learning center, remedial instruction, study skills assistance, tutoring, writing center.

**Honors college/program.** 3.5 GPA required.

**Majors. Agriculture:** Agribusiness operations, horticulture, landscaping. **Biology:** Anatomy. **Business:** Accounting, business admin, fashion, marketing, office management, office/clerical. **Communications:** Journalism. **Computer sciences:** General, applications programming, computer science, networking. **Education:** Teacher assistance. **Engineering:** General. **Engineering technology:** Architectural. **Family/consumer sciences:** Clothing/textiles, food/nutrition. **Health:** Nursing (RN). **Liberal arts:** Arts/sciences, humanities, library assistant. **Math:** General, applied. **Personal/culinary services:** General. **Philosophy/religion:** Philosophy, religion. **Physical sciences:** General, astronomy, chemistry, organic chemistry, physics, planetary. **Psychology:** General. **Visual/performing arts:** Interior design.

**Computing on campus.** 1,000 workstations in library, computer center, student center. Commuter students can connect to campus network. Online course registration, online library, helpline, repair service, student web hosting, wireless network available.

**Student life. Freshman orientation:** Available. **Housing:** Housing available at Williams campus. **Activities:** Jazz band, choral groups, dance, drama, international student organizations, music ensembles, Model UN, musical theater, opera, student government, student newspaper.

**Athletics.** NJCAA. **Intercollegiate:** Baseball M, basketball, cross-country, football (tackle) M, golf, gymnastics W, soccer, softball W, swimming M, track and field, volleyball W, wrestling M. **Intramural:** Basketball, bowling, cross-country, football (tackle) M, softball, track and field, volleyball, wrestling M. **Team name:** Thunderbirds.

**Student services.** Adult student services, alcohol/substance abuse counseling, career counseling, services for economically disadvantaged, student employment services, financial aid counseling, legal services, on-campus daycare, personal counseling, placement for graduates, veterans' counselor. **Physically disabled:** Services for visually, speech, hearing impaired. **Transfer:** Transfer adviser for students transferring to 4-year colleges.

**Contact.** E-mail: admissions@mc.maricopa.edu
Phone: (480) 461-7000 Fax: (480) 461-7805
Director of Admissions, Mesa Community College, 1833 West Southern Avenue, Mesa, AZ 85202

## Mohave Community College
### Kingman, Arizona
### www.mohave.edu
CB code: 0443

- Public 2-year community college
- Commuter campus in small city

**General.** Founded in 1971. Regionally accredited. **Enrollment:** 6,010 degree-seeking undergraduates. **Degrees:** 325 associate awarded. **Location:** 200 miles from Phoenix, 100 miles from Las Vegas. **Calendar:** Semester, limited summer session. **Full-time faculty:** 63 total. **Part-time faculty:** 345 total.

**Transfer out. Colleges most students transferred to 2009:** Northern Arizona University, University of Arizona, Arizona State University.

**Basis for selection.** Open admission, but selective for some programs. Special requirements for nursing, dental hygiene and EMT/paramedic programs.

**2009-2010 Annual costs.** Tuition/fees: $2,020; $4,516 out-of-state. Per-credit charge: $64 in-state; $192 out-of-state.

**2009-2010 Financial aid. Need-based:** Need-based aid available for part-time students. Work-study available nights and for part-time students.

**Application procedures. Admission:** No deadline. No application fee. **Financial aid:** Priority date 4/15; no closing date. FAFSA, institutional form required. Applicants notified on a rolling basis starting 5/1; must reply within 2 week(s) of notification.

**Academics. Special study options:** Distance learning, dual enrollment of high school students, ESL, independent study, internships, liberal arts/career combination, student-designed major. License preparation in dental hygiene, nursing, paramedic, physical therapy. **Credit/placement by examination:** CLEP, IB, institutional tests. 20 credit hours maximum toward associate degree. **Support services:** GED preparation and test center, learning center, reduced course load, remedial instruction, study skills assistance, tutoring.

**Majors. Business:** Administrative services, business admin. **Computer sciences:** General. **Education:** General. **Health:** Dental hygiene, nursing (RN), pharmacy assistant, physical therapy assistant, surgical technology. **Legal**

studies: Paralegal. **Liberal arts:** Arts/sciences. **Mechanic/repair:** Automotive, heating/ac/refrig. **Protective services:** Firefighting, police science. **Other:** Chemical dependency therapy.

**Computing on campus.** 300 workstations in library, computer center. Commuter students can connect to campus network. Online course registration, online library, helpline, wireless network available.

**Student life. Freshman orientation:** Available. Preregistration for classes offered. **Activities:** Dance, drama, music ensembles, musical theater, student government.

**Student services.** Adult student services, career counseling, student employment services, financial aid counseling, veterans' counselor. **Physically disabled:** Services for visually, speech, hearing impaired. **Transfer:** Transfer adviser for students transferring to 4-year colleges.

**Contact.** E-mail: johwil@mohave.edu
Phone: (928) 757-0847 Toll-free number: (866) 664-2832
Fax: (928) 757-0808
John Wilson, Registrar, Mohave Community College, 1971 Jagerson Avenue, Kingman, AZ 86409

## Northland Pioneer College
### Holbrook, Arizona
### www.npc.edu
CB code: 0325

- Public 2-year community and technical college
- Commuter campus in small town

**General.** Founded in 1973. Regionally accredited. 10 locations in Navajo and Apache Counties. **Enrollment:** 1,684 degree-seeking undergraduates; 2,952 non-degree-seeking students. **Degrees:** 159 associate awarded. **Location:** 200 miles from Phoenix, 90 miles from Flagstaff. **Calendar:** Semester, limited summer session. **Full-time faculty:** 85 total; 12% have terminal degrees. **Part-time faculty:** 260 total.

**Student profile.** Among degree-seeking undergraduates, 492 enrolled as first-time, first-year students.

| | | | |
|---|---|---|---|
| Part-time: | 70% | Asian American: | 1% |
| Out-of-state: | 1% | Hispanic American: | 6% |
| Women: | 71% | Native American: | 38% |
| African American: | 1% | 25 or older: | 69% |

**Transfer out. Colleges most students transferred to 2009:** Northern Arizona University, University of Arizona, Arizona State University, Western New Mexico University, Brigham Young University.

**Basis for selection.** Open admission, but selective for some programs. Students under 18 must have satisfactory placement test score. Special requirements for nursing and cosmetology.

**2009-2010 Annual costs.** Tuition/fees: $1,595; $7,535 out-of-state. Per-credit charge: $52 in-state; $85 out-of-state. Books/supplies: $1,200. Personal expenses: $3,260.

**2009-2010 Financial aid. Need-based:** Need-based aid available for part-time students. Work-study available nights, weekends and for part-time students. **Non-need-based:** Scholarships awarded for academics, art, job skills, leadership, minority status, music/drama, state residency.

**Application procedures. Admission:** No deadline. No application fee. Admission notification on a rolling basis. **Financial aid:** Priority date 6/1; no closing date. FAFSA, institutional form required. Applicants notified on a rolling basis starting 5/15; must reply within 2 week(s) of notification.

**Academics. Special study options:** Cooperative education, distance learning, dual enrollment of high school students, honors, independent study, internships, liberal arts/career combination. License preparation in nursing, paramedic, real estate. **Credit/placement by examination:** CLEP, IB, institutional tests. 52 credit hours maximum toward associate degree. **Support services:** GED preparation and test center, learning center, remedial instruction, study skills assistance, tutoring, writing center.

**Majors. Agriculture:** Turf management. **Business:** General, accounting, administrative services, business admin. **Communications technology:** General. **Computer sciences:** General, computer graphics, data processing, networking. **Construction:** General, carpentry, electrician, plumbing. **Education:** General, early childhood, elementary. **Engineering technology:** Electrical. **Family/consumer sciences:** Child care. **Health:** EMT paramedic, medical assistant, medical transcription, nursing (RN). **Interdisciplinary:** Biological/physical sciences. **Liberal arts:** Arts/sciences, library assistant. **Mechanic/repair:** Automotive, heating/ac/refrig, industrial. **Parks/recreation:** General. **Personal/culinary services:** Cosmetic. **Production:** Welding. **Protective**

**services:** Criminal justice, firefighting. **Transportation:** Heavy/earthmoving equipment. **Other:** Power plant operations.

**Most popular majors.** Business/marketing 13%, education 9%, health sciences 22%.

**Computing on campus.** 140 workstations in library, computer center. Commuter students can connect to campus network. Online course registration, online library, helpline, wireless network available.

**Student life. Freshman orientation:** Available. Preregistration for classes offered. **Activities:** Jazz band, choral groups, dance, drama, literary magazine, music ensembles, musical theater, student government, symphony orchestra, National Honor Society, Phi Theta Kappa.

**Student services.** Adult student services, career counseling, services for economically disadvantaged, student employment services, financial aid counseling, placement for graduates, veterans' counselor. **Physically disabled:** Services for visually, hearing impaired. **Transfer:** Pre-admission transcript evaluation for new students. Transfer adviser, college fairs on campus for students transferring to 4-year colleges.

**Contact.** E-mail: admissions@npc.edu
Phone: (928) 536-6257 Toll-free number: (800) 266-7845
Fax: (928) 524-7612
Jake Hinton-Rivera, Director of Enrollment Services, Northland Pioneer College, PO Box 610, Holbrook, AZ 86025-0610

## Paradise Valley Community College

Phoenix, Arizona — CB member
www.pvc.maricopa.edu — CB code: 2179

- Public 2-year community college
- Commuter campus in very large city

**General.** Founded in 1985. Regionally accredited. **Enrollment:** 3,790 degree-seeking undergraduates. **Degrees:** 450 associate awarded. **ROTC:** Army. **Calendar:** Semester, limited summer session. **Full-time faculty:** 98 total; 22% minority, 52% women. **Part-time faculty:** 444 total. **Special facilities:** Studio theater, performing arts center.

**Student profile.** Among degree-seeking undergraduates, 40% enrolled in a transfer program, 40% enrolled in a vocational program, 8% already have a bachelor's degree or higher.

| Out-of-state: | 3% | 25 or older: | 50% |
|---|---|---|---|

**Transfer out. Colleges most students transferred to 2009:** Arizona State University, Arizona State University West, Northern Arizona University, University of Arizona.

**Basis for selection.** Open admission.

**2009-2010 Annual costs.** Tuition/fees: $2,160; $8,610 out-of-state. Per-credit charge: $71 in-state; $286 out-of-state. Books/supplies: $1,200. Personal expenses: $2,805.

**2008-2009 Financial aid. Need-based:** 35% of total undergraduate aid awarded as scholarships/grants, 65% as loans/jobs. Need-based aid available for part-time students.

**Application procedures. Admission:** No deadline. No application fee. Admission notification on a rolling basis. **Financial aid:** No deadline. FAFSA required. Applicants notified on a rolling basis starting 6/1.

**Academics. Special study options:** Accelerated study, cooperative education, cross-registration, distance learning, dual enrollment of high school students, ESL, honors, independent study, internships, teacher certification program, weekend college. License preparation in nursing, paramedic. **Credit/placement by examination:** AP, CLEP, institutional tests. 30 credit hours maximum toward associate degree. **Support services:** Learning center, remedial instruction, study skills assistance, tutoring, writing center.

**Majors. Business:** General, accounting, administrative services, international, office technology, office/clerical, organizational behavior. **Computer sciences:** General, word processing. **Education:** Instructional media. **Engineering technology:** Hazardous materials. **Liberal arts:** Arts/sciences. **Visual/performing arts:** Music.

**Computing on campus.** 600 workstations in library, computer center, student center. Commuter students can connect to campus network. Online course registration, helpline, wireless network available.

**Student life. Freshman orientation:** Mandatory. **Activities:** Jazz band, choral groups, dance, drama, international student organizations, literary magazine, music ensembles, musical theater, opera, student government, student

newspaper, Phi Theta Kappa, student Christian association, human service club, Returning Adults to Education, environmental club, Latter Day Saints student association, recreational outdoor club.

**Athletics.** NJCAA. **Intercollegiate:** Baseball M, cross-country, golf, soccer, softball W, tennis, track and field. **Team name:** Pumas.

**Student services.** Adult student services, alcohol/substance abuse counseling, career counseling, student employment services, financial aid counseling, minority student services, on-campus daycare, personal counseling, placement for graduates, veterans' counselor, women's services. **Physically disabled:** Services for visually, speech, hearing impaired. **Transfer:** Transfer adviser, college fairs on campus for students transferring to 4-year colleges.

**Contact.** Phone: (602) 787-7020 Fax: (602) 787-6625
Shirley Green, Associate Dean Student Services, Paradise Valley Community College, 18401 North 32nd Street, Phoenix, AZ 85032

## Paralegal Institute

Glendale, Arizona
www.theparalegalinstitute.edu — CB code: 3888

- For-profit 2-year virtual career college
- Very large city

**General.** Accredited by DETC. **Enrollment:** 350 degree-seeking undergraduates. **Degrees:** 30 associate awarded. **Calendar:** Continuous, extensive summer session. **Full-time faculty:** 2 total. **Part-time faculty:** 3 total.

**Student profile.** Among degree-seeking undergraduates, 159 transferred in from other institutions.

**Basis for selection.** Open admission.

**2010-2011 Annual costs.** Per-credit charge: $150. Diploma programs are $4,600; associate degree programs are $9,000.

**Application procedures. Admission:** No deadline. No application fee. Application must be submitted on paper.

**Academics. Special study options:** Distance learning. **Credit/placement by examination:** CLEP.

**Majors. Legal studies:** Paralegal.

**Student life. Freshman orientation:** Available. Preregistration for classes offered.

**Student services. Transfer:** Pre-admission transcript evaluation for new students.

**Contact.** E-mail: kscheib@theparalegalinstitute.edu
Phone: (602) 212-0501 Toll-free number: (800) 354-1254
Fax: (602) 212-0502
Keith Scheib, Director of Adminssions, Paralegal Institute, 18275 North 59th Avenue, Suite 186 Building N, Glendale, AZ 85308

## Penn Foster College

Scottsdale, Arizona
www.pennfostercollege.edu — CB code: 7313

- For-profit 2-year virtual college
- Commuter campus in small city

**General.** Founded in 1975. Accredited by DETC. All courses offered via distance learning. **Enrollment:** 32,887 undergraduates. **Degrees:** 209 associate awarded. **Calendar:** Continuous. **Full-time faculty:** 21 total. **Part-time faculty:** 58 total.

**Basis for selection.** Open admission. **Homeschooled:** Copy of completion document from a school or copy of standardized tests required. **Learning Disabled:** Evidence of disability recommended so that accommodations can be made.

**2009-2010 Annual costs.** Average cost for a four-semester full associate degree program: $3,920.

**Application procedures. Admission:** No deadline. $75 fee. Admission notification on a rolling basis.

**Academics.** Students allowed 12 months to complete semester (15-20 credit hours). **Special study options:** Distance learning, external degree, independent study. Bachelor's degree programs available on campus. **Credit/ placement by examination:** CLEP. **Support services:** Remedial instruction, tutoring.

**Majors. Business:** General, accounting, finance, hospitality admin, marketing. **Computer sciences:** General. **Education:** Early childhood. **Engineering technology:** Civil, electrical, industrial, mechanical. **Health:** Medical records technology. **Legal studies:** Paralegal. **Protective services:** Police science.

**Student life. Freshman orientation:** Mandatory.

**Student services.** Veterans' counselor. **Transfer:** Pre-admission transcript evaluation for new students.

**Contact.** E-mail: info@pennfoster.edu
Phone: (800) 275-4410 Toll-free number: (800) 275-4410
Linda Smith, Manager, DP Services, Penn Foster College, 14300 North Northsight Boulevard, Suite 111, Scottsdale, AZ 85260

## Phoenix College
Phoenix, Arizona
www.pc.maricopa.edu                               CB code: 4606

- Public 2-year community college
- Commuter campus in very large city

**General.** Founded in 1920. Regionally accredited. **Enrollment:** 2,496 full-time, degree-seeking students. **Degrees:** 729 associate awarded. **ROTC:** Army, Air Force. **Calendar:** Semester, limited summer session. **Full-time faculty:** 145 total. **Part-time faculty:** 419 total. **Class size:** 63% < 20, 35% 20-39, 1% 40-49, 1% 50-99, less than 1% >100.

**Student profile.**

Out-of-state:            2%        **25 or older:**        51%

**Basis for selection.** Open admission, but selective for some programs. ASSET, COMPASS and Celsa test scores used for placement.

**2009-2010 Annual costs.** Tuition/fees: $2,160; $9,390 out-of-state. Per-credit charge: $71 in-state; $312 out-of-state. Books/supplies: $700. Personal expenses: $3,654.

**Financial aid. Need-based:** Work-study available weekends.

**Application procedures. Admission:** No deadline. No application fee. Admission notification on a rolling basis. **Financial aid:** Priority date 6/30; no closing date. FAFSA required. Applicants notified on a rolling basis starting 5/1.

**Academics. Special study options:** Cooperative education, cross-registration, distance learning, dual enrollment of high school students, ESL, honors, independent study, internships, liberal arts/career combination, study abroad. License preparation in nursing. **Credit/placement by examination:** CLEP, institutional tests. 30 credit hours maximum toward associate degree. **Support services:** GED test center, learning center, reduced course load, remedial instruction, study skills assistance, tutoring.

**Honors college/program.** Requires 3.0 GPA.

**Majors. Architecture:** Interior. **Business:** General, accounting, banking/ financial services, business admin, management information systems, management science, marketing, tourism promotion, tourism/travel. **Communications:** General. **Computer sciences:** General, computer graphics, information systems. **Education:** General, family/consumer sciences. **Engineering:** General, software. **Engineering technology:** Civil. **Family/consumer sciences:** General, child care, institutional food production. **Foreign languages:** Sign language interpretation. **Health:** Clinical lab science, dental assistant, dental hygiene, EMT paramedic, medical records technology, medical transcription, nursing (RN), premedicine. **Legal studies:** Legal secretary, paralegal. **Liberal arts:** Arts/sciences. **Physical sciences:** Chemistry. **Protective services:** Firefighting, police science. **Visual/performing arts:** Art, commercial/ advertising art, interior design.

**Computing on campus.** Online course registration, online library, helpline, wireless network available.

**Student life. Freshman orientation:** Available. Preregistration for classes offered. **Activities:** Bands, choral groups, dance, drama, music ensembles, musical theater, opera, student newspaper, symphony orchestra, TV station.

**Athletics.** NJCAA. **Intercollegiate:** Baseball M, basketball, cross-country, football (tackle) M, golf M, soccer M, softball W, tennis, track and field, volleyball W. **Team name:** PC Bears.

**Student services.** Adult student services, career counseling, services for economically disadvantaged, student employment services, legal services, on-campus daycare, personal counseling, placement for graduates, veterans' counselor. **Physically disabled:** Services for visually, speech, hearing impaired. **Transfer:** Re-entry adviser, pre-admission transcript evaluation for new students. Transfer adviser, college fairs on campus for students transferring to 4-year colleges.

**Contact.** E-mail: info@pcmail.maricopa.edu
Phone: (602) 285-7502 Fax: (602) 285-7813
Kathy French, Director of Admissions and Records, Phoenix College, 1202 West Thomas Road, Phoenix, AZ 85013

## Pima Community College
Tucson, Arizona                                    CB member
www.pima.edu                                       CB code: 4623

- Public 2-year community and technical college
- Commuter campus in very large city

**General.** Founded in 1966. Regionally accredited. 6 campuses, distance education/online courses available. **Enrollment:** 35,880 undergraduates. **Degrees:** 2,232 associate awarded. **ROTC:** Army, Naval, Air Force. **Location:** 120 miles from Phoenix. **Calendar:** Semester, extensive summer session. **Full-time faculty:** 330 total; 19% minority, 59% women. **Part-time faculty:** 1,223 total; 18% minority, 54% women. **Special facilities:** Arts center, public safety institute.

**Student profile.** 70% enrolled in a transfer program, 30% enrolled in a vocational program, 6% already have a bachelor's degree or higher.

| | | | |
|---|---|---|---|
| African American: | 4% | Native American: | 3% |
| Asian American: | 3% | International: | 1% |
| Hispanic American: | 29% | 25 or older: | 43% |

**Transfer out.** 33% of students enrolled in the transfer program go on to 4-year colleges. **Colleges most students transferred to 2009:** University of Arizona, Arizona State University, Northern Arizona University, University of Phoenix.

**Basis for selection.** Open admission, but selective for some programs. Special requirements for programs in the health related professions, such as nursing.

**2009-2010 Annual costs.** Tuition/fees: $1,685; $7,910 out-of-state. Per-credit charge: $52 in-state; $87 out-of-state. Books/supplies: $2,000. Personal expenses: $2,520.

**Financial aid. Need-based:** Need-based aid available for part-time students. **Non-need-based:** Scholarships awarded for academics, alumni affiliation, art, athletics, minority status, music/drama.

**Application procedures. Admission:** No deadline. No application fee. Admission notification on a rolling basis. **Financial aid:** Priority date 3/15; no closing date. FAFSA required. Applicants notified on a rolling basis starting 7/1; must reply within 2 week(s) of notification.

**Academics.** Upward Bound programs available. **Special study options:** Accelerated study, cooperative education, distance learning, double major, dual enrollment of high school students, ESL, honors, independent study, internships, student-designed major, teacher certification program, weekend college. Bachelor's degree programs available on campus. License preparation in dental hygiene, nursing, radiology. **Credit/placement by examination:** AP, CLEP, IB, institutional tests. 30 credit hours maximum toward associate degree. **Support services:** GED preparation and test center, learning center, pre-admission summer program, remedial instruction, study skills assistance, tutoring.

**Majors. Area/ethnic studies:** Native American. **Business:** Accounting, administrative services, business admin, fashion, hospitality admin, international, tourism/travel. **Communications:** Digital media, radio/tv. **Communications technology:** Animation/special effects, graphics. **Computer sciences:** General, networking, systems analysis. **Construction:** Maintenance. **Education:** General, adult/continuing, early childhood. **Engineering technology:** Architectural drafting, computer, construction, environmental, laser/ optical. **Family/consumer sciences:** Child development. **Foreign languages:** Sign language interpretation. **Health:** Clinical lab technology, dental hygiene, dental lab technology, EMT paramedic, histologic assistant, massage therapy, medical records admin, medical records technology, nursing (RN), pharmacy assistant, radiologic technology/medical imaging, respiratory therapy technology, substance abuse counseling, veterinary technology/assistant. **Legal studies:** Paralegal. **Liberal arts:** Arts/sciences. **Mechanic/repair:** Aircraft powerplant, automotive, industrial electronics. **Personal/culinary services:** Restaurant/catering. **Production:** Machine shop technology, welding. **Protective services:** Criminal justice, firefighting, police science. **Social**

**sciences:** Anthropology, archaeology, political science, sociology. **Visual/performing arts:** General, art, design, dramatic.

**Most popular majors.** Business/marketing 12%, health sciences 17%, liberal arts 53%.

**Computing on campus.** 3,000 workstations in library, computer center. Commuter students can connect to campus network. Online course registration, online library, helpline, wireless network available.

**Student life. Freshman orientation:** Mandatory. Orientation programs based on majors. **Activities:** Bands, choral groups, dance, drama, literary magazine, music ensembles, student government, student newspaper, TV station.

**Athletics.** NJCAA. **Intercollegiate:** Baseball M, basketball, cross-country, football (tackle) M, golf, soccer, softball W, tennis, track and field, volleyball W. **Intramural:** Badminton, baseball M, basketball, cross-country, football (non-tackle) M, golf, racquetball, tennis, track and field, volleyball. **Team name:** Aztecs.

**Student services.** Career counseling, student employment services, financial aid counseling, health services, minority student services, on-campus daycare, personal counseling, placement for graduates, veterans' counselor. **Physically disabled:** Services for visually, speech, hearing impaired. **Transfer:** Transfer adviser, college fairs on campus for students transferring to 4-year colleges.

**Contact.** E-mail: coadmit@pima.edu
Phone: (520) 206-4643 Toll-free number: (800) 860-7462
Fax: (520) 206-4790
Michael Tulino, Director and Registrar, Pima Community College, 4905B East Broadway, Tucson, AZ 85709-1120

## Refrigeration School
Phoenix, Arizona
www.rsiaz.edu                                        CB code: 2888

- For-profit 2-year technical college
- Very large city
- Interview required

**General.** Accredited by ACCSC. **Enrollment:** 170 full-time, degree-seeking students. **Degrees:** 25 associate awarded. **Calendar:** 3, 6 or 8 month programs. **Full-time faculty:** 12 total. **Part-time faculty:** 14 total.

**Basis for selection.** Open admission. **Homeschooled:** State high school equivalency certificate required.

**2009-2010 Annual costs.** Costs of entire programs range from $6,500 to $22,862; includes books, fees and supplies.

**Application procedures. Admission:** No deadline. No application fee.

**Academics. Credit/placement by examination:** CLEP. **Support services:** Tutoring.

**Majors. Engineering technology:** Energy systems. **Mechanic/repair:** Heating/ac/refrig.

**Computing on campus.** 4 workstations in library.

**Contact.** Phone: (602) 275-7133 Toll-free number: (877) 477-4669
Fax: (602) 267-4805
Mary Simmons, Admissions Director, Refrigeration School, 4210 East Washington Street, Phoenix, AZ 85034-1816

## Rio Salado College
Tempe, Arizona                                       CB member
www.riosalado.edu                                    CB code: 0997

- Public 2-year virtual community college
- Commuter campus in very large city

**General.** Founded in 1978. Regionally accredited. Access to libraries at Arizona State University and 10 Maricopa County community colleges. **Enrollment:** 1,223 degree-seeking undergraduates. **Degrees:** 490 associate awarded. **Location:** 120 miles from Tucson, 10 miles from Phoenix. **Calendar:** Semester, extensive summer session. **Full-time faculty:** 31 total. **Part-time faculty:** 1,048 total. **Special facilities:** Public radio stations.

**Student profile.**

| Out-of-state: | 5% | **25 or older:** | 49% |

**Transfer out. Colleges most students transferred to 2009:** Arizona State University, University of Arizona, Northern Arizona University.

**Basis for selection.** Open admission, but selective for some programs. Dental hygiene program has GPA requirements.

**2009-2010 Annual costs.** Tuition/fees: $2,160; $9,390 out-of-state. Per-credit charge: $71 in-state; $312 out-of-state. Books/supplies: $1,024. Personal expenses: $2,616.

**2008-2009 Financial aid.** All financial aid based on need. Need-based aid available for part-time students.

**Application procedures. Admission:** No deadline. No application fee. Admission notification on a rolling basis. **Financial aid:** Priority date 6/30; no closing date. FAFSA, institutional form required. Applicants notified on a rolling basis starting 6/30.

**Academics.** Agreement with Army allows military personnel to take Internet courses. Online clinical dental assisting program offered. **Special study options:** Accelerated study, cooperative education, cross-registration, distance learning, double major, dual enrollment of high school students, ESL, honors, independent study, internships, liberal arts/career combination, weekend college. License preparation in dental hygiene, nursing. **Credit/placement by examination:** AP, CLEP, institutional tests. 30 credit hours maximum toward associate degree. **Support services:** GED preparation, learning center, remedial instruction, study skills assistance, tutoring, writing center.

**Majors. Business:** General, accounting, banking/financial services, business admin, international, office management. **Computer sciences:** General. **Engineering technology:** Water quality. **Health:** Dental hygiene, nursing assistant, substance abuse counseling. **Protective services:** Law enforcement admin. **Public administration:** General.

**Computing on campus.** 500 workstations in library, computer center. Commuter students can connect to campus network. Online course registration, online library, helpline, wireless network available.

**Student life. Freshman orientation:** Available. Online orientation materials available. **Activities:** Radio station, TV station, Phi Theta Kappa.

**Student services.** Adult student services, career counseling, student employment services, financial aid counseling, personal counseling, veterans' counselor. **Physically disabled:** Services for visually, speech, hearing impaired. **Transfer:** Re-entry adviser, pre-admission transcript evaluation for new students. Transfer adviser for students transferring to 4-year colleges.

**Contact.** E-mail: admissions@email.rio.maricopa.edu
Phone: (480) 517-8150 Toll-free number: (800) 729-1197
Fax: (480) 517-8199
Ruby Miller, Associate Dean, Student Enrollment Services, Rio Salado College, 2323 West 14th Street, Tempe, AZ 85281

## Scottsdale Community College
Scottsdale, Arizona
www.scottsdalecc.edu                                 CB code: 4755

- Public 2-year community college
- Commuter campus in small city

**General.** Founded in 1969. Regionally accredited. **Enrollment:** 4,267 degree-seeking undergraduates. **Degrees:** 903 associate awarded. **Location:** 10 miles from Tempe. **Calendar:** Semester, limited summer session. **Full-time faculty:** 168 total; 27% have terminal degrees, 14% minority, 51% women. **Part-time faculty:** 471 total; 8% have terminal degrees, 10% minority, 50% women. **Class size:** 45% < 20, 52% 20-39, 2% 40-49, 1% 50-99, less than 1% >100. **Special facilities:** Student-operated restaurant associated with school of culinary arts.

**Student profile.** Among degree-seeking undergraduates, 39% enrolled in a transfer program, 11% already have a bachelor's degree or higher.

| Out-of-state: | 6% | **25 or older:** | 38% |

**Basis for selection.** Open admission.

**High school preparation.** 16 units recommended. Recommended units include English 4, mathematics 4, social studies 2, history 1, science 3 and foreign language 2.

**2009-2010 Annual costs.** Tuition/fees: $2,160; $9,390 out-of-state. Per-credit charge: $71 in-state; $312 out-of-state. Books/supplies: $1,200. Personal expenses: $5,544.

**2008-2009 Financial aid. Non-need-based:** Scholarships awarded for academics, athletics. **Additional information:** Athletic scholarships offered in rodeo. All athletic scholarships limited to county residents.

**Application procedures. Admission:** No deadline. No application fee. Admission notification on a rolling basis. **Financial aid:** Priority date 6/30; no closing date. FAFSA, institutional form required. Applicants notified on a rolling basis starting 4/1; must reply by 7/15 or within 3 week(s) of notification.

**Academics. Special study options:** Cooperative education, cross-registration, distance learning, dual enrollment of high school students, ESL, honors, internships, study abroad, teacher certification program. **Credit/placement by examination:** AP, CLEP, institutional tests. 52 credit hours maximum toward associate degree. **Support services:** Learning center, remedial instruction, tutoring, writing center.

**Majors. Agriculture:** Equestrian studies. **Architecture:** Environmental design. **Area/ethnic studies:** Native American. **Business:** General, accounting, administrative services, fashion, hospitality admin, international, management information systems, retailing. **Communications:** Public relations. **Communications technology:** Radio/tv. **Computer sciences:** General, information systems. **Construction:** Building inspection. **Education:** Early childhood. **Engineering technology:** Architectural drafting. **Family/consumer sciences:** Child care. **Health:** EMT paramedic, medical radiologic technology/radiation therapy, nursing (RN). **Liberal arts:** Arts/sciences. **Parks/recreation:** General. **Personal/culinary services:** Culinary arts. **Physical sciences:** General. **Protective services:** Criminal justice, firefighting, law enforcement admin. **Visual/performing arts:** General, cinematography, dance, dramatic, interior design, studio arts.

**Most popular majors.** Business/marketing 13%, health sciences 18%, liberal arts 40%, visual/performing arts 14%.

**Computing on campus.** 998 workstations in library, computer center, student center. Commuter students can connect to campus network. Online course registration, online library, helpline, repair service, wireless network available.

**Student life. Freshman orientation:** Available. Preregistration for classes offered. **Activities:** Bands, choral groups, dance, drama, international student organizations, music ensembles, student government, student newspaper, symphony orchestra, TV station, American Indian honor society, black student union, Latino student association, green club, GLBT-straight alliance, Rotoract, advocacy group, student leadership club.

**Athletics.** NAIA, NJCAA. **Intercollegiate:** Baseball M, basketball, cross-country, football (tackle) M, golf M, soccer M, softball W, tennis, track and field, volleyball W. **Intramural:** Baseball M. **Team name:** Artichokes.

**Student services.** Alcohol/substance abuse counseling, career counseling, student employment services, financial aid counseling, personal counseling, veterans' counselor. **Physically disabled:** Services for visually, speech, hearing impaired. **Transfer:** Transfer adviser, college fairs on campus for students transferring to 4-year colleges.

**Contact.** E-mail: admissions@sccmail.maricopa.edu
Phone: (480) 423-6100 Fax: (480) 423-6200
Fran Watkins, Director of Admissions and Records, Scottsdale Community College, 9000 East Chaparral Road, Scottsdale, AZ 85256-2626

## Scottsdale Culinary Institute
### Scottsdale, Arizona
www.scichefs.com                                       CB code: 3028

- For-profit 2-year culinary school and technical college
- Commuter campus in large city
- Application essay, interview required

**General.** Accredited by ACCSC. **Enrollment:** 1,275 degree-seeking undergraduates. **Degrees:** 50 bachelor's, 540 associate awarded. **Location:** 2 miles from downtown. **Calendar:** Continuous. **Full-time faculty:** 40 total. **Part-time faculty:** 32 total.

**Student profile.**

| | | | |
|---|---|---|---|
| Out-of-state: | 55% | 25 or older: | 60% |

**Basis for selection.** Open admission.

**2009-2010 Annual costs.** Tuition and fees vary by degree and by program. Total costs of programs (includes fees and books): certificate programs start at $21,350; Associate degree programs start at $35,100; Bachelor's degree programs start at $61,400. Personal expenses: $2,275.

**Application procedures. Admission:** No deadline. $95 fee. Admission notification on a rolling basis.

**Academics. Special study options:** Distance learning, internships. **Credit/placement by examination:** CLEP. **Support services:** Learning center, remedial instruction, tutoring.

**Majors. Personal/culinary services:** Culinary arts.

**Student life. Freshman orientation:** Mandatory.

**Student services.** Alcohol/substance abuse counseling, career counseling, financial aid counseling, placement for graduates.

**Contact.** E-mail: sciadmissions@scichefs.com
Phone: (480) 990-3773 Toll-free number: (800) 848-2433
Fax: (480) 990-0351
Christopher Tolbert, Vice President of Admissions, Scottsdale Culinary Institute, 8100 East Camelback Road, Suite 1001, Scottsdale, AZ 85251

## South Mountain Community College
### Phoenix, Arizona                                    CB member
www.smc.maricopa.edu                                   CB code: 4734

- Public 2-year community college
- Commuter campus in very large city

**General.** Founded in 1979. Regionally accredited. **Location:** 8 miles from downtown Phoenix. **Calendar:** Semester.

**Annual costs/financial aid.** Tuition/fees (2009-2010): $2,160; $8,610 out-of-state. Books/supplies: $760. Personal expenses: $1,250. Need-based financial aid available to full-time and part-time students.

**Contact.** Phone: (602) 243-8123
Associate Dean of Student Services, 7050 South 24th Street, Phoenix, AZ 85042

## Tohono O'odham Community College
### Sells, Arizona
www.tocc.cc.az.us

- Public 2-year community college
- Commuter campus in rural community

**General. Enrollment:** 25 full-time, degree-seeking students. **Degrees:** 4 associate awarded. **Location:** 60 miles from Tucson. **Calendar:** Semester, limited summer session. **Full-time faculty:** 14 total; 21% have terminal degrees. **Part-time faculty:** 15 total. **Class size:** 98% < 20, 2% 20-39.

**Basis for selection.** Open admission. **Homeschooled:** Transcript of courses and grades, state high school equivalency certificate required.

**2009-2010 Annual costs.** Books/supplies: $750.

**2008-2009 Financial aid.** All financial aid based on need. Need-based aid available for part-time students. Work-study available for part-time students.

**Application procedures. Admission:** No deadline. No application fee. **Financial aid:** No deadline. FAFSA, institutional form required. Applicants notified on a rolling basis.

**Academics. Special study options:** Distance learning, dual enrollment of high school students, independent study. **Credit/placement by examination:** CLEP. **Support services:** GED preparation, learning center, remedial instruction, study skills assistance, tutoring, writing center.

**Majors. Agriculture:** Production. **Business:** Business admin. **Computer sciences:** System admin. **Construction:** Carpentry, electrician, painting, plumbing, site management. **Education:** Early childhood special, elementary. **Liberal arts:** Arts/sciences. **Social sciences:** General.

**Most popular majors.** Business/marketing 17%, education 33%, interdisciplinary studies 33%, public administration/social services 17%.

**Student life. Freshman orientation:** Mandatory. Preregistration for classes offered. Orientation class offers information on student services and academic support services. **Activities:** Student government.

**Student services.** Adult student services, career counseling, student employment services, financial aid counseling, personal counseling, placement for graduates. **Transfer:** Re-entry adviser, pre-admission transcript evaluation for new students. College fairs on campus for students transferring to 4-year colleges.

**Contact.** E-mail: lluna@tocc.cc.az.us
Phone: (520) 383-8401 ext. 35 Fax: (520) 383-0029
Leslie Luna, Registrar, Tohono O'odham Community College, PO Box 3129, Sells, AZ 85634-3129

## Universal Technical Institute
### Avondale, Arizona
www.uti.edu                    CB code: 2504

- For-profit 2-year technical college
- Commuter campus in small city

**General.** Founded in 1965. Accredited by ACCSC. **Enrollment:** 2,108 full-time, degree-seeking students. **Degrees:** 1,646 associate awarded. **Location:** 17 miles from Phoenix, 11 miles from Glendale. **Calendar:** Continuous, extensive summer session. **Full-time faculty:** 75 total.

**Basis for selection.** Open admission. **Homeschooled:** Must pass the Wonderlic Scholastic Level Exam. **Learning Disabled:** Students seeking accommodations must provide copy of IEP from high school and/or medical documentation. They must also complete paperwork requesting the accommodation and meet with the School Counselor or Student Services Director prior to starting school.

**2009-2010 Annual costs.** Tuition/fees: $16,015. Tuition varies by program and by campus.

**Application procedures. Admission:** No deadline. No application fee. Admission notification on a rolling basis. **Financial aid:** No deadline. FAFSA required.

**Academics. Special study options:** Accelerated study. **Credit/placement by examination:** CLEP. **Support services:** Tutoring.

**Majors. Mechanic/repair:** Automotive, diesel.

**Computing on campus.** 9 workstations in library.

**Student life. Freshman orientation:** Mandatory.

**Student services.** Career counseling, services for economically disadvantaged, student employment services, financial aid counseling, veterans' counselor. **Physically disabled:** Services for hearing impaired.

**Contact.** E-mail: info@uticorp.com
Phone: (623) 245-4600 Toll-free number: (800) 859-1202
Fax: (602) 245-4601
Campus Admissions Director, Universal Technical Institute, 10695 West Pierce Street, Avondale, AZ 85323

## Yavapai College
### Prescott, Arizona
www.yc.edu                    CB code: 4996

- Public 2-year community college
- Commuter campus in large town

**General.** Founded in 1966. Regionally accredited. **Location:** 100 miles from Phoenix. **Calendar:** Semester.

**Annual costs/financial aid.** Tuition/fees (2009-2010): $1,740; $8,410 out-of-state. Room/board: $5,170. Books/supplies: $1,000. Personal expenses: $1,900. Need-based financial aid available to full-time and part-time students.

**Contact.** Phone: (928) 445-7300 ext. 2148
Registrar, 1100 East Sheldon Street, Prescott, AZ 86301

# Arkansas

## Arkansas Northeastern College
**Blytheville, Arkansas**
www.anc.edu                                    CB code: 1267

▶ Public 2-year community college
▶ Commuter campus in small town

**General.** Founded in 1974. Regionally accredited. **Enrollment:** 1,340 degree-seeking undergraduates. **Degrees:** 200 associate awarded. **Location:** 65 miles from Memphis, Tennessee. **Calendar:** Semester, limited summer session. **Full-time faculty:** 78 total. **Part-time faculty:** 95 total. **Class size:** 66% < 20, 32% 20-39, less than 1% 40-49, 1% 50-99. **Partnerships:** Formal partnership with Tech Prep for business and technical courses.

**Student profile.**

Out-of-state:          18%        25 or older:          50%

**Transfer out. Colleges most students transferred to 2009:** Arkansas State University, Southeast Missouri State University.

**Basis for selection.** Open admission, but selective for some programs. Entrance exam required for LPN and RN programs.

**High school preparation.** Recommended units include English 4, mathematics 4, social studies 1, history 2, science 3 (laboratory 3).

**2009-2010 Annual costs.** Tuition/fees: $1,780; $2,080 out-of-district; $3,580 out-of-state. Per-credit charge: $52 in-district; $62 out-of-district; $112 out-of-state. Books/supplies: $1,446. Personal expenses: $4,847.

**2009-2010 Financial aid. Need-based:** Need-based aid available for part-time students. Work-study available for part-time students. **Non-need-based:** Scholarships awarded for academics, art, minority status, music/drama, state residency.

**Application procedures. Admission:** No deadline. No application fee. Admission notification on a rolling basis. **Financial aid:** Priority date 4/15; no closing date. FAFSA, institutional form required. Applicants notified on a rolling basis starting 5/1; must reply within 2 week(s) of notification.

**Academics. Special study options:** Distance learning, double major, dual enrollment of high school students. Bachelor's degree programs available on campus. License preparation in nursing, paramedic. **Credit/placement by examination:** CLEP, institutional tests. 15 credit hours maximum toward associate degree. Placement tests required for algebra and English composition. **Support services:** GED preparation and test center, learning center, reduced course load, remedial instruction, study skills assistance, tutoring, writing center.

**Majors. Agriculture:** Food science, horticulture. **Business:** General, administrative services, management information systems. **Education:** Middle. **Engineering technology:** Metallurgical. **Health:** Nursing (RN). **Liberal arts:** Arts/sciences. **Mechanic/repair:** Industrial. **Protective services:** Police science.

**Most popular majors.** Business/marketing 12%, education 8%, health sciences 12%, liberal arts 58%.

**Computing on campus.** 400 workstations in library, computer center. Commuter students can connect to campus network. Online library available.

**Student life. Freshman orientation:** Available. Preregistration for classes offered. **Activities:** Choral groups, music ensembles, Cultural Diversity Association, Baptist College Ministry, Adult Student Association.

**Student services.** Adult student services, career counseling, services for economically disadvantaged, student employment services, financial aid counseling, on-campus daycare, personal counseling, placement for graduates, veterans' counselor. **Physically disabled:** Services for visually, speech, hearing impaired. **Transfer:** Pre-admission transcript evaluation for new students. Transfer adviser, college fairs on campus for students transferring to 4-year colleges.

**Contact.** Phone: (870) 762-1020 ext. 1103 Fax: (870) 763-1654 Laura Yarbrough, Registrar, Arkansas Northeastern College, Box 1109, Blytheville, AR 72316-1109

## Arkansas State University: Beebe
**Beebe, Arkansas**
www.asub.edu                                    CB code: 0782

▶ Public 2-year community college
▶ Commuter campus in small town

**General.** Founded in 1927. Regionally accredited. Approved as Serviceman's Opportunity College. **Enrollment:** 3,663 degree-seeking undergraduates; 828 non-degree-seeking students. **Degrees:** 576 associate awarded. **ROTC:** Army. **Location:** 35 miles from Little Rock. **Calendar:** Semester, extensive summer session. **Class size:** 56% < 20, 43% 20-39, 1% 40-49.

**Student profile.** Among degree-seeking undergraduates, 68% enrolled in a transfer program, 32% enrolled in a vocational program, 1,047 enrolled as first-time, first-year students, 461 transferred in from other institutions.

Part-time:          30%        Women:          62%

**Basis for selection.** Open admission.

**High school preparation.** College-preparatory program recommended. 15 units recommended. Recommended units include English 3, mathematics 1, social studies 2 and science 2.

**2009-2010 Annual costs.** Tuition/fees: $2,670; $4,350 out-of-state. Per-credit charge: $78 in-state; $134 out-of-state. Room/board: $3,150. Books/supplies: $1,000. Personal expenses: $2,500.

**2008-2009 Financial aid. Need-based:** Need-based aid available for part-time students. Work-study available nights, weekends and for part-time students. **Non-need-based:** Scholarships awarded for academics, leadership, music/drama.

**Application procedures. Admission:** No deadline. No application fee. Admission notification on a rolling basis. **Financial aid:** Priority date 6/1; no closing date. FAFSA, institutional form required. Applicants notified on a rolling basis starting 6/1; must reply within 2 week(s) of notification.

**Academics. Special study options:** Accelerated study, double major, dual enrollment of high school students, honors, independent study, internships. Bachelor's degree programs available on campus. License preparation in nursing, paramedic. **Credit/placement by examination:** AP, CLEP. 30 credit hours maximum toward associate degree. **Support services:** Learning center, reduced course load, remedial instruction, tutoring.

**Majors. Agriculture:** Business. **Business:** General, hospitality admin, management information systems. **Education:** Early childhood, multi-level teacher. **Engineering technology:** Computer systems, drafting, electrical. **Health:** Clinical lab technology, EMT paramedic, health services, pharmacy assistant, veterinary technology/assistant. **Liberal arts:** Arts/sciences. **Mechanic/repair:** Industrial. **Production:** Welding. **Protective services:** Forensics, law enforcement admin, police science. **Other:** Agriculture equipment technology, Creative arts enterprise.

**Most popular majors.** Business/marketing 12%, engineering/engineering technologies 6%, health sciences 16%, liberal arts 52%, security/protective services 6%, trade and industry 7%.

**Computing on campus.** Dormitories linked to campus network. Online course registration, online library, wireless network available.

**Student life. Freshman orientation:** Mandatory. Preregistration for classes offered. **Housing:** Single-sex dorms available. $75 partly refundable deposit. **Activities:** Campus ministries, choral groups, drama, international student organizations, student government, Gamma Beta Phi, Phi Beta Lambda, Student Advisory Board, Leadership Council.

**Athletics. Intramural:** Archery, badminton, basketball, bowling, football (non-tackle), golf, racquetball, softball, table tennis, tennis, track and field, volleyball.

**Student services.** Career counseling, services for economically disadvantaged, financial aid counseling, personal counseling, placement for graduates, veterans' counselor. **Learning disabled:** Comprehensive services available. **Transfer:** Transfer adviser, college fairs on campus for students transferring to 4-year colleges.

**Contact.** E-mail: rahayes@asub.edu
Phone: (501) 882-8860 Toll-free number: (800) 632-9985
Fax: (501) 882-8895
Robin Hayes, Director of Admissions, Arkansas State University: Beebe, PO Box 1000, Beebe, AR 72012-1000

## Arkansas State University: Mountain Home
### Mountain Home, Arkansas
### www.asumh.edu                                    CB code: 6057

♦ Public 2-year community and technical college
♦ Commuter campus in large town

**General. Enrollment:** 1,437 degree-seeking undergraduates; 80 non-degree-seeking students. **Degrees:** 159 associate awarded. **ROTC:** Army. **Location:** 130 miles from Little Rock. **Calendar:** Semester, limited summer session. **Full-time faculty:** 44 total; 27% have terminal degrees, 4% minority, 57% women. **Part-time faculty:** 25 total; 12% have terminal degrees, 48% women. **Class size:** 61% < 20, 39% 20-39.

**Student profile.** Among degree-seeking undergraduates, 25% enrolled in a transfer program, 3% enrolled in a vocational program, 2% already have a bachelor's degree or higher, 350 enrolled as first-time, first-year students, 125 transferred in from other institutions.

| | | | |
|---|---|---|---|
| Part-time: | 36% | Hispanic American: | 1% |
| Out-of-state: | 7% | Native American: | 1% |
| Women: | 63% | 25 or older: | 38% |
| Asian American: | 1% | | |

**Transfer out. Colleges most students transferred to 2009:** Arkansas State University-Jonesboro, University of Central Arkansas-Conway, University of Arkansas-Fayetteville.

**Basis for selection.** Open admission, but selective for some programs. Additional requirements for practical nursing, respiratory care, and phlebotomy programs. **Homeschooled:** Statement describing homeschool structure and mission, transcript of courses and grades, state high school equivalency certificate required. **Learning Disabled:** Students with learning disabilities must document them with disability coordinator.

**High school preparation.** College-preparatory program recommended. Recommended units include English 4, mathematics 4, social studies 3 and science 4.

**2009-2010 Annual costs.** Tuition/fees: $2,760; $4,410 out-of-state. Per-credit charge: $77 in-state; $132 out-of-state. Books/supplies: $1,250. Personal expenses: $3,055.

**2008-2009 Financial aid. Need-based:** 84% of total undergraduate aid awarded as scholarships/grants, 16% as loans/jobs. Need-based aid available for part-time students. **Non-need-based:** Scholarships awarded for academics, alumni affiliation, state residency.

**Application procedures. Admission:** Closing date 8/15 (receipt date). No application fee. Application must be submitted on paper. Admission notification on a rolling basis. **Financial aid:** Priority date 7/1; no closing date. FAFSA, institutional form required. Applicants notified on a rolling basis starting 5/1; must reply within 2 week(s) of notification.

**Academics. Special study options:** Combined bachelor's/graduate degree, cooperative education, distance learning, dual enrollment of high school students, ESL, honors, independent study, liberal arts/career combination. License preparation in funeral sciences, practical nursing, respiratory care, and paramedic tech. Bachelor's degree programs available on campus. License preparation in nursing, paramedic. **Credit/placement by examination:** CLEP. 15 credit hours maximum toward associate degree, 15 toward bachelor's. **Support services:** GED preparation and test center, learning center, remedial instruction, study skills assistance, tutoring, writing center.

**Majors. Business:** Administrative services. **Computer sciences:** Information systems. **Education:** Middle. **Health:** EMT paramedic, respiratory therapy technology. **Liberal arts:** Arts/sciences. **Personal/culinary services:** Mortuary science. **Production:** Welding. **Protective services:** Forensics, law enforcement admin.

**Most popular majors.** Computer/information sciences 9%, education 14%, liberal arts 58%, personal/culinary services 8%.

**Computing on campus.** 90 workstations in library, computer center, student center. Commuter students can connect to campus network. Online course registration, online library, helpline, wireless network available.

**Student life. Freshman orientation:** Available. Preregistration for classes offered. **Activities:** Campus ministries, choral groups, drama, literary magazine, student government, Circle K, criminal justice club, mortuary science club, student ambassadors, student practical nurses association, Phi Beta Lambda, Phi Delta Kappa, Phi Theta Kappa, Rotaract.

**Student services.** Adult student services, chaplain/spiritual director, career counseling, financial aid counseling, veterans' counselor. **Physically disabled:** Services for visually, hearing impaired. **Transfer:** Pre-admission transcript evaluation for new students. College fairs on campus for students transferring to 4-year colleges.

**Contact.** E-mail: rblagg@asumh.edu
Phone: (870) 508-6104 Fax: (870) 508-6287
Rosalyn Blagg, Assistant Vice Chancellor for Enrollment, Arkansas State University: Mountain Home, 1600 South College Street, Mountain Home, AR 72653

## Arkansas State University: Newport
### Newport, Arkansas
### www.asun.edu

♦ Public 2-year community and liberal arts college
♦ Commuter campus in small town

**General. Enrollment:** 1,562 degree-seeking undergraduates. **Degrees:** 101 associate awarded. **Location:** 100 miles from Little Rock. **Calendar:** Semester, limited summer session. **Full-time faculty:** 73 total. **Part-time faculty:** 30 total.

**Transfer out. Colleges most students transferred to 2009:** University of Central Arkansas.

**Basis for selection.** Open admission. **Homeschooled:** Transcript of courses and grades required.

**2009-2010 Annual costs.** Tuition/fees: $2,400; $3,930 out-of-state. Per-credit charge: $75 in-state; $126 out-of-state.

**Application procedures. Admission:** No deadline. No application fee. Admission notification on a rolling basis. **Financial aid:** Priority date 5/1; no closing date.

**Academics. Special study options:** Cooperative education, distance learning, dual enrollment of high school students, independent study, internships, liberal arts/career combination, study abroad, teacher certification program. License preparation in nursing. **Credit/placement by examination:** AP, CLEP, institutional tests. 30 credit hours maximum toward associate degree. **Support services:** GED preparation and test center, learning center, remedial instruction, study skills assistance, tutoring.

**Majors. Business:** General, management information systems. **Education:** Middle. **Engineering technology:** Computer. **Health:** EMT paramedic. **Liberal arts:** Arts/sciences.

**Computing on campus.** Commuter students can connect to campus network. Online course registration, online library, helpline, repair service, wireless network available.

**Student life. Activities:** Drama, student government.

**Student services. Transfer:** Re-entry adviser, pre-admission transcript evaluation for new students. Transfer adviser, college fairs on campus for students transferring to 4-year colleges.

**Contact.** E-mail: tbyrd@asun.edu
Phone: (870) 512-7800 Toll-free number: (800) 976-1676
Fax: (870) 512-7825
Tara Byrd, Registrar/Director of Admissions, Arkansas State University: Newport, 7648 Victory Boulevard, Newport, AR 72112

## Black River Technical College
### Pocahontas, Arkansas
### www.blackrivertech.edu                              CB code: 3879

♦ Public 2-year technical college
♦ Large town
♦ SAT or ACT (ACT writing optional) required

**General. Regionally accredited. Enrollment:** 1,904 degree-seeking undergraduates. **Degrees:** 236 associate awarded. **Calendar:** Semester, limited summer session. **Full-time faculty:** 63 total. **Part-time faculty:** 57 total.

**Basis for selection.** High school transcript and standardized test scores most important. **Homeschooled:** Transcript of courses and grades required.

**2009-2010 Annual costs.** Tuition/fees: $2,190; $5,550 out-of-state. Per-credit charge: $70 in-state; $182 out-of-state.

**Application procedures. Admission:** No deadline. No application fee. **Financial aid:** Priority date 4/1, closing date 6/30.

**Academics. Special study options:** Distance learning, dual enrollment of high school students, independent study, weekend college. License preparation in aviation, nursing, paramedic. **Credit/placement by examination:** AP, CLEP, SAT, ACT. **Support services:** GED preparation and test center, learning center, remedial instruction, tutoring.

**Majors. Business:** Accounting, business admin, management information systems. **Education:** Early childhood, elementary. **Protective services:** Criminal justice. **Social sciences:** Economics. **Visual/performing arts:** Art.

**Computing on campus.** Commuter students can connect to campus network. Online course registration, online library, helpline, wireless network available.

**Student life. Freshman orientation:** Mandatory. **Activities:** Choral groups, music ensembles.

**Contact.** E-mail: rachel.koons@blackrivertech.edu
Phone: (870) 248-4000 Fax: (870) 248-4100
Mary Anderson, Academic Advisor, Black River Technical College, Highway 304 East, Pocahontas, AR 72455

## Cossatot Community College of the University of Arkansas
De Queen, Arkansas
www.cccua.edu                    CB code: 3613

- Public 2-year community college
- Commuter campus in small town

**General.** Regionally accredited. Off-campus sites located in Nashville and Ashdown. **Enrollment:** 1,486 degree-seeking undergraduates. **Degrees:** 86 associate awarded. **Location:** 60 miles from Texarkana. **Calendar:** Semester, limited summer session. **Full-time faculty:** 33 total. **Part-time faculty:** 50 total. **Class size:** 69% < 20, 31% 20-39. **Partnerships:** Secondary Vocational Center for local high schools.

**Student profile.**

Out-of-state:          2%      25 or older:          38%

**Transfer out. Colleges most students transferred to 2009:** Henderson State University, Texas A&M - Texarkana, Arkansas Tech University, University of Central Arkansas, Southern Arkansas University.

**Basis for selection.** Open admission, but selective for some programs. Admission to Nursing programs are based upon test scores and previous course grades.

**High school preparation.** 22 units required. Required units include English 4, mathematics 4, social studies 2, history 1, science 3 (laboratory 2), foreign language 1 and academic electives 5.

**2009-2010 Annual costs.** Tuition/fees: $1,840; $2,140 out-of-district; $4,900 out-of-state. Per-credit charge: $48 in-district; $58 out-of-district; $150 out-of-state. Residents of bordering out-of-state counties may qualify for in-state tuition. Books/supplies: $1,400. Personal expenses: $1,658.

**2008-2009 Financial aid. Need-based:** Need-based aid available for part-time students. Work-study available nights and for part-time students. **Additional information:** Active or honorably discharged military and their dependents receive tuition discounts.

**Application procedures. Admission:** No deadline. $25 fee. Admission notification on a rolling basis. **Financial aid:** Priority date 5/1; no closing date. FAFSA, institutional form required. Applicants notified on a rolling basis starting 3/1.

**Academics. Special study options:** Combined bachelor's/graduate degree, cooperative education, distance learning, double major, dual enrollment of high school students, ESL, exchange student, independent study, internships, liberal arts/career combination, student-designed major. Bachelor's degree programs available on campus. License preparation in nursing. **Credit/placement by examination:** AP, CLEP, institutional tests. 15 credit hours maximum toward associate degree. **Support services:** GED

preparation and test center, learning center, remedial instruction, study skills assistance, tutoring.

**Majors. Business:** General, management information systems. **Construction:** Carpentry. **Education:** Elementary, middle. **Family/consumer sciences:** Child care. **Health:** Medical assistant, nursing (RN). **Liberal arts:** Arts/sciences. **Mechanic/repair:** Automotive. **Protective services:** Forensics, law enforcement admin.

**Most popular majors.** Business/marketing 23%, liberal arts 68%.

**Computing on campus.** 95 workstations in library, computer center. Commuter students can connect to campus network. Online course registration, online library, helpline, wireless network available.

**Student life. Freshman orientation:** Available. Preregistration for classes offered. Course offered each semester. **Activities:** Student government, student newspaper, Baptist Collegiate Ministry, Phi Theta Kappa, Journalism Club, Arkansas Licensed Practical Nursing Association, Amnesty International, SkillsUSA.

**Student services.** Adult student services, alcohol/substance abuse counseling, career counseling, services for economically disadvantaged, student employment services, financial aid counseling, minority student services, on-campus daycare, personal counseling, placement for graduates, veterans' counselor. **Physically disabled:** Services for visually, speech, hearing impaired. **Transfer:** Pre-admission transcript evaluation for new students. Transfer adviser, college fairs on campus for students transferring to 4-year colleges.

**Contact.** E-mail: ncowling@cccua.edu
Phone: (870) 584-4471 Toll-free number: (800) 844-4471
Fax: (870) 642-8766
Brenda Morris, Director of Institutional Research and Registrar, Cossatot Community College of the University of Arkansas, 183 Highway 399, De Queen, AR 71832

## Crowley's Ridge College
Paragould, Arkansas
www.crowleysridgecollege.edu          CB code: 6131

- Private 2-year junior college affiliated with Church of Christ
- Commuter campus in large town

**General.** Regionally accredited. **Enrollment:** 138 degree-seeking undergraduates. **Degrees:** 24 associate awarded. **Location:** 23 miles from Jonesboro. **Calendar:** Semester, limited summer session. **Full-time faculty:** 9 total. **Part-time faculty:** 11 total.

**Transfer out. Colleges most students transferred to 2009:** Arkansas State University, Williams Baptist College, Harding University, Freed-Hardeman University.

**Basis for selection.** Open admission. Placement in freshman composition and algebra determined by ACT and ASSET scores. Development courses required for students with ACT score under 19.

**2009-2010 Annual costs.** Tuition/fees: $8,710. Per-credit charge: $255. Room/board: $5,500. Books/supplies: $550.

**2009-2010 Financial aid. Need-based:** Work-study available nights and weekends. **Non-need-based:** Scholarships awarded for academics, leadership, music/drama.

**Application procedures. Admission:** No deadline. No application fee. Admission notification on a rolling basis. **Financial aid:** No deadline. FAFSA required.

**Academics. Special study options:** Dual enrollment of high school students, independent study. **Credit/placement by examination:** CLEP. 34 credit hours maximum toward associate degree. **Support services:** Remedial instruction, study skills assistance, tutoring.

**Majors. Education:** General. **Liberal arts:** Arts/sciences. **Philosophy/religion:** Religion.

**Computing on campus.** 15 workstations in dormitories, library, computer center. Dormitories linked to campus network.

**Student life. Freshman orientation:** Available. Preregistration for classes offered. Takes place second week of August. **Policies:** Chapel attendance required. **Housing:** Guaranteed on-campus for all undergraduates. Single-sex dorms available. $100 deposit. **Activities:** Choral groups, music ensembles, student government.

**Athletics. Intercollegiate:** Baseball M, basketball, volleyball W. **Intramural:** Baseball M, basketball M, softball W, volleyball W. **Team name:** Pioneers.

**Student services.** Chaplain/spiritual director, financial aid counseling. **Transfer:** Pre-admission transcript evaluation for new students. College fairs on campus for students transferring to 4-year colleges.

**Contact.** E-mail: njoneshill@crc.edu
Phone: (870) 236-6901 ext. 14 Toll-free number: (800) 264-1096
Fax: (870) 236-7748
Nancy Joneshill, Admissions Director, Crowley's Ridge College, 100 College Drive, Paragould, AR 72450

## East Arkansas Community College
### Forrest City, Arkansas
www.eacc.edu                                    CB code: 0847

◆ Public 2-year community college
◆ Commuter campus in large town

**General.** Founded in 1973. Regionally accredited. **Enrollment:** 1,303 degree-seeking undergraduates; 227 non-degree-seeking students. **Degrees:** 117 associate awarded. **Location:** 40 miles from Memphis, Tennessee. **Calendar:** Semester, limited summer session. **Full-time faculty:** 38 total; 13% have terminal degrees, 8% minority, 58% women. **Part-time faculty:** 51 total; 16% minority, 61% women.

**Student profile.** Among degree-seeking undergraduates, 346 enrolled as first-time, first-year students, 67 transferred in from other institutions.

| | | | |
|---|---|---|---|
| Part-time: | 36% | Women: | 68% |
| Out-of-state: | 1% | 25 or older: | 47% |

**Transfer out. Colleges most students transferred to 2009:** Arkansas State University.

**Basis for selection.** Open admission, but selective for some programs. ASSET may be substituted for ACT or SAT for placement. Interview required of Allied Health majors. **Homeschooled:** Transcript of courses and grades, state high school equivalency certificate required.

**2009-2010 Annual costs.** Tuition/fees: $2,040; $2,280 out-of-district; $2,700 out-of-state. Per-credit charge: $60 in-district; $68 out-of-district; $82 out-of-state. Books/supplies: $1,200. Personal expenses: $1,000.

**Financial aid.** All financial aid based on need. Need-based aid available for part-time students.

**Application procedures. Admission:** No deadline. No application fee. Admission notification on a rolling basis. **Financial aid:** Priority date 3/1, closing date 7/1. FAFSA required. Applicants notified on a rolling basis starting 5/15; must reply within 2 week(s) of notification.

**Academics. Special study options:** Cooperative education, distance learning, dual enrollment of high school students, honors, internships, liberal arts/career combination. License preparation in nursing, paramedic, radiology. **Credit/placement by examination:** AP, CLEP, institutional tests. 12 credit hours maximum toward associate degree. **Support services:** Learning center, remedial instruction, tutoring.

**Majors. Agriculture:** General. **Business:** Administrative services, business admin, finance, management information systems. **Computer sciences:** Web page design. **Education:** Middle, multi-level teacher. **Engineering technology:** CAD/CADD, environmental, manufacturing. **Family/consumer sciences:** Child care. **Health:** EMT paramedic, medical assistant, medical radiologic technology/radiation therapy, nursing (RN), occupational therapy assistant. **Mechanic/repair:** Industrial. **Protective services:** Police science.

**Most popular majors.** Business/marketing 18%, education 6%, health sciences 27%, liberal arts 38%, security/protective services 7%.

**Computing on campus.** 35 workstations in library, computer center. Commuter students can connect to campus network.

**Student life. Freshman orientation:** Available. Preregistration for classes offered. **Activities:** Choral groups, student government, student newspaper.

**Athletics. Intramural:** Basketball, softball, tennis, volleyball.

**Student services.** Career counseling, student employment services, health services, personal counseling, placement for graduates, veterans' counselor.

**Physically disabled:** Services for visually, hearing impaired. **Transfer:** Transfer adviser, college fairs on campus for students transferring to 4-year colleges.

**Contact.** E-mail: dadams@eacc.edu
Phone: (870) 633-4480 ext. 300 Toll-free number: (877) 797-3222
Fax: (870) 633-3840
DeAnna Adams, Director of Enrollment Management/Institutional Research, East Arkansas Community College, 1700 Newcastle Road, Forrest City, AR 72335-9598

## Mid-South Community College
### West Memphis, Arkansas
www.midsouthcc.edu                              CB code: 3880

◆ Public 2-year community and junior college
◆ Commuter campus in large town

**General.** Regionally accredited. **Enrollment:** 1,567 degree-seeking undergraduates. **Degrees:** 76 associate awarded. **Location:** 8 miles from Memphis, Tennessee. **Calendar:** Semester, limited summer session. **Full-time faculty:** 23 total. **Part-time faculty:** 105 total. **Class size:** 77% < 20, 23% 20-39.

**Student profile.**

| | | | |
|---|---|---|---|
| Out-of-state: | 10% | 25 or older: | 53% |

**Transfer out. Colleges most students transferred to 2009:** Arkansas State University, University of Memphis.

**Basis for selection.** Open admission. **Homeschooled:** Transcript of courses and grades required.

**2009-2010 Annual costs.** Tuition/fees: $2,120; $2,570 out-of-district; $4,370 out-of-state. Per-credit charge: $60 in-district; $75 out-of-district; $135 out-of-state. Books/supplies: $1,000. Personal expenses: $5,500.

**2008-2009 Financial aid. Need-based:** Need-based aid available for part-time students. Work-study available nights and for part-time students. **Non-need-based:** Scholarships awarded for academics, state residency.

**Application procedures. Admission:** No deadline. No application fee. Application must be submitted on paper. Admission notification on a rolling basis. **Financial aid:** No deadline. FAFSA, institutional form required. Applicants notified on a rolling basis starting 6/1; must reply within 2 week(s) of notification.

**Academics. Special study options:** Cooperative education, distance learning, dual enrollment of high school students, liberal arts/career combination. Bachelor's degree programs available on campus. **Credit/placement by examination:** AP, CLEP, institutional tests. 18 credit hours maximum toward associate degree. **Support services:** GED preparation and test center, learning center, reduced course load, remedial instruction, study skills assistance, tutoring, writing center.

**Majors. Agriculture:** General. **Business:** Office technology. **Computer sciences:** General. **Education:** Middle. **Liberal arts:** Arts/sciences. **Protective services:** Forensics, law enforcement admin.

**Computing on campus.** 250 workstations in library, computer center, student center. Commuter students can connect to campus network. Online course registration, online library available.

**Student life. Freshman orientation:** Available. Preregistration for classes offered. **Activities:** Jazz band, choral groups, student newspaper, TV station.

**Student services.** Adult student services, career counseling, services for economically disadvantaged, student employment services, financial aid counseling, minority student services, veterans' counselor. **Physically disabled:** Services for visually, speech, hearing impaired. **Transfer:** Transfer adviser, college fairs on campus for students transferring to 4-year colleges.

**Contact.** E-mail: admission@midsouthcc.edu
Phone: (870) 733-6728 Fax: (870) 733-6719
Jeremy Reece, Director of Admissions and Recruiting, Mid-South Community College, 2000 West Broadway, West Memphis, AR 72301

## National Park Community College
### Hot Springs, Arkansas
www.npcc.edu                                    CB code: 6243

◆ Public 2-year liberal arts and technical college
◆ Commuter campus in large town

**General.** Founded in 1973. Regionally accredited. Located in the Hot Springs National Park. **Enrollment:** 3,257 degree-seeking undergraduates; 613 non-degree-seeking students. **Degrees:** 379 associate awarded. **Location:** 53 miles from Little Rock. **Calendar:** Semester, extensive summer session. **Full-time faculty:** 62 total. **Part-time faculty:** 142 total. **Class size:** 63% < 20, 37% 20-39, less than 1% 40-49, less than 1% 50-99.

**Student profile.** Among degree-seeking undergraduates, 60% enrolled in a transfer program, 40% enrolled in a vocational program, 5% already have a bachelor's degree or higher, 626 enrolled as first-time, first-year students.

| | | | |
|---|---|---|---|
| Part-time: | 44% | Women: | 63% |
| Out-of-state: | 1% | 25 or older: | 56% |

**Transfer out.** 30% of students enrolled in the transfer program go on to 4-year colleges. **Colleges most students transferred to 2009:** Henderson State University, Arkadelphia-University of Arkansas, University of Arkansas-Little Rock, University of Arkansas-Fayetteville.

**Basis for selection.** Open admission, but selective for some programs. Limited admission to allied health programs and nursing. Interview required for some health-related majors. **Homeschooled:** State Mandated Notification to High School to be Home-Schooled.

**High school preparation.** College-preparatory program recommended. 18 units recommended. Recommended units include English 4, mathematics 4, social studies 3, history 2, science 3 (laboratory 3) and foreign language 2.

**2009-2010 Annual costs.** Tuition/fees: $2,075; $2,375 out-of-district; $4,145 out-of-state. Per-credit charge: $65 in-district; $75 out-of-district; $134 out-of-state. Books/supplies: $700. Personal expenses: $1,420.

**Financial aid. Need-based:** Need-based aid available for part-time students. Work-study available nights, weekends and for part-time students. **Non-need-based:** Scholarships awarded for academics, minority status, music/drama, state residency.

**Application procedures. Admission:** No deadline. No application fee. Application must be submitted online. Admission notification on a rolling basis beginning on or about 3/1. **Financial aid:** Priority date 7/1; no closing date. FAFSA, institutional form required. Applicants notified on a rolling basis starting 3/1.

**Academics. Special study options:** Cooperative education, cross-registration, distance learning, double major, dual enrollment of high school students, honors, independent study, internships, liberal arts/career combination, student-designed major. Bachelor's degree programs available on campus. License preparation in aviation, nursing, paramedic, radiology, real estate. **Credit/placement by examination:** AP, CLEP, institutional tests. 18 credit hours maximum toward associate degree. **Support services:** Learning center, reduced course load, remedial instruction, study skills assistance, tutoring, writing center.

**Majors. Business:** Accounting, hospitality admin, hospitality/recreation, office management, office technology. **Computer sciences:** General, applications programming, computer graphics. **Engineering technology:** Electrical. **Health:** Clinical lab technology, EMT paramedic, medical assistant, medical radiologic technology/radiation therapy, medical records technology, medical secretary, nursing (RN). **Liberal arts:** Arts/sciences. **Parks/recreation:** General. **Visual/performing arts:** Commercial/advertising art.

**Computing on campus.** 470 workstations in library, computer center, student center. Online library available.

**Student life. Freshman orientation:** Mandatory. Preregistration for classes offered. 2-day orientation, held one week prior to beginning of classes. **Activities:** Choral groups, dance, literary magazine, music ensembles, student government, student newspaper, Baptist Student Union, Black Awareness, Association for Barrier Awareness.

**Athletics. Intramural:** Baseball, basketball, bowling, skin diving, softball, table tennis, tennis, volleyball.

**Student services.** Adult student services, career counseling, services for economically disadvantaged, student employment services, financial aid counseling, health services, personal counseling, placement for graduates, veterans' counselor. **Physically disabled:** Services for visually, speech, hearing impaired. **Learning disabled:** Comprehensive services available. **Transfer:** Pre-admission transcript evaluation for new students. Transfer adviser, college fairs on campus for students transferring to 4-year colleges.

**Contact.** E-mail: admissions@npcc.edu
Phone: (501) 760-4222 ext. 4231 Toll-free number: (800) 761-1825
Fax: (501) 760-4100
Holly Garrett, Director of Admissions, National Park Community College, 101 College Drive, Hot Springs, AR 71913

## North Arkansas College
**Harrison, Arkansas**
www.northark.edu                                CB code: 1423

▶ Public 2-year community and technical college
▶ Commuter campus in large town

**General.** Founded in 1974. Regionally accredited. **Enrollment:** 2,107 degree-seeking undergraduates; 322 non-degree-seeking students. **Degrees:** 221 associate awarded. **Location:** 75 miles from Fayetteville. **Calendar:** Semester, limited summer session. **Full-time faculty:** 66 total; 9% have terminal degrees, 52% women. **Part-time faculty:** 89 total; 1% minority, 55% women. **Class size:** 59% < 20, 39% 20-39, 1% 40-49, 1% 50-99. **Special facilities:** Community health resource center, lyric theater.

**Student profile.** Among degree-seeking undergraduates, 43% enrolled in a transfer program, 52% enrolled in a vocational program, 1% already have a bachelor's degree or higher, 578 enrolled as first-time, first-year students, 235 transferred in from other institutions.

| | | | |
|---|---|---|---|
| Part-time: | 30% | Asian American: | 1% |
| Out-of-state: | 2% | Hispanic American: | 2% |
| Women: | 61% | Native American: | 1% |
| African American: | 1% | 25 or older: | 44% |

**Transfer out.** 35% of students enrolled in the transfer program go on to 4-year colleges. **Colleges most students transferred to 2009:** Arkansas Tech University, University of Arkansas, University of Central Arkansas, Franklin University, Ozark Technical Community College.

**Basis for selection.** Open admission, but selective for some programs. Allied health programs require separate application. Regarding CLEP examinations, to receive college credit, a student must score at the 50th percentile or higher, based on national norms, and may not have earned college credit nor have ever been enrolled in the course for which he/she is writing the test.

**High school preparation.** College-preparatory program required. 14 units recommended. Recommended units include English 4, mathematics 4, social studies 1, history 2, science 3 (laboratory 3).

**2009-2010 Annual costs.** Tuition/fees: $1,800; $2,460 out-of-district; $4,590 out-of-state. Per-credit charge: $60 in-district; $82 out-of-district; $153 out-of-state. Residents of contiguous Missouri counties (Barry, Stone, Taney, Ozark) pay $102 per credit hour and $3,060 full-time tuition. Books/supplies: $954. Personal expenses: $2,054.

**2008-2009 Financial aid. Need-based:** Need-based aid available for part-time students. Work-study available nights and for part-time students. **Non-need-based:** Scholarships awarded for academics, athletics, state residency.

**Application procedures. Admission:** No deadline. No application fee. Application must be submitted on paper. Admission notification on a rolling basis. **Financial aid:** Priority date 5/1; no closing date. FAFSA, institutional form required. Applicants notified on a rolling basis starting 5/1.

**Academics. Special study options:** Distance learning, dual enrollment of high school students, ESL, honors, independent study, internships, student-designed major. Bachelor's degree programs available on campus. License preparation in nursing, paramedic, radiology, real estate. **Credit/placement by examination:** AP, CLEP, institutional tests. 20 credit hours maximum toward associate degree. Only one-third of the credit hours for a degree can be from Advanced Placement, CLEP, the College Now Program, Challenge Test, various other examinations, or independent studies. Credit for Advanced Placement, CLEP, or Professional Certification Examinations will not be posted to an academic record until the student has successfully completed at least 12 semester credit hours of work. **Support services:** GED preparation and test center, learning center, pre-admission summer program, remedial instruction, study skills assistance, tutoring, writing center.

**Majors. Agriculture:** General. **Business:** General. **Computer sciences:** General. **Education:** Multi-level teacher. **Engineering technology:** Biomedical, electrical. **Health:** Clinical lab technology, EMT paramedic, medical radiologic technology/radiation therapy, nursing (RN), surgical technology. **Liberal arts:** Arts/sciences. **Protective services:** Forensics, law enforcement admin. **Other:** General Technology.

**Most popular majors.** Business/marketing 13%, computer/information sciences 10%, health sciences 30%, liberal arts 41%.

**Computing on campus.** 250 workstations in library, computer center. Online course registration, online library, wireless network available.

**Student life. Freshman orientation:** Available. Preregistration for classes offered. **Activities:** Drama, literary magazine, student government, Baptist

Student Union, Future Farmers of America, Health Occupations Students of America, Phi Beta Lambda, Phi Theta Kappa, Pioneer Hands club, Rad Tech club, Skills USA, student nurses association.

**Athletics.** NJCAA. **Intercollegiate:** Baseball M, basketball, cheerleading M, rodeo, softball W. **Intramural:** Archery, badminton, basketball, football (non-tackle) M, golf, racquetball, softball, table tennis, tennis, volleyball, weight lifting. **Team name:** Pioneers.

**Student services.** Adult student services, alcohol/substance abuse counseling, career counseling, services for economically disadvantaged, student employment services, financial aid counseling, placement for graduates, veterans' counselor. **Physically disabled:** Services for visually, speech, hearing impaired. **Transfer:** Pre-admission transcript evaluation for new students. Transfer adviser, college fairs on campus for students transferring to 4-year colleges.

**Contact.** E-mail: charlam@northark.edu
Phone: (870) 391-3505 Toll-free number: (800) 679-6622
Fax: (870) 391-3339
Charla Jennings, Director of Enrollment Services, North Arkansas College, 1515 Pioneer Drive, Harrison, AR 72601

## Northwest Arkansas Community College
### Bentonville, Arkansas
www.nwacc.edu                                    CB code: 7101

▶ Public 2-year community college
▶ Commuter campus in small city

**General.** Regionally accredited. **Enrollment:** 6,188 degree-seeking undergraduates; 1,818 non-degree-seeking students. **Degrees:** 503 associate awarded. **ROTC:** Army, Air Force. **Location:** 30 miles from Fayetteville. **Calendar:** Semester, extensive summer session. **Full-time faculty:** 121 total; 31% have terminal degrees, 8% minority, 60% women. **Part-time faculty:** 328 total; 8% have terminal degrees, 11% minority, 52% women. **Class size:** 42% < 20, 57% 20-39, less than 1% 40-49.

**Student profile.** Among degree-seeking undergraduates, 1,275 enrolled as first-time, first-year students, 1,044 transferred in from other institutions.

| | | | |
|---|---|---|---|
| Part-time: | 56% | Hispanic American: | 12% |
| Out-of-state: | 2% | Native American: | 2% |
| Women: | 60% | International: | 1% |
| African American: | 2% | 25 or older: | 47% |
| Asian American: | 3% | | |

**Transfer out. Colleges most students transferred to 2009:** University of Arkansas, John Brown University.

**Basis for selection.** Open admission, but selective for some programs. Additional requirements for nursing, physical therapy, respiratory therapy, emergency medical technician/paramedic programs.

**High school preparation.** College-preparatory program recommended. 22 units recommended. Recommended units include English 4, mathematics 4, social studies 3, science 3 (laboratory 2), foreign language 2 and academic electives 4.

**2010-2011 Annual costs.** Tuition/fees (projected): $2,493; $3,603 out-of-district; $4,863 out-of-state. Per-credit charge: $66 in-district; $103 out-of-district; $145 out-of-state. Books/supplies: $1,000. Personal expenses: $2,250.

**Financial aid. Need-based:** Need-based aid available for part-time students. Work-study available nights, weekends and for part-time students. **Non-need-based:** Scholarships awarded for academics, leadership, music/drama, state residency.

**Application procedures. Admission:** No deadline. $10 fee. Admission notification on a rolling basis. **Financial aid:** Priority date 4/1; no closing date. FAFSA, institutional form required. Applicants notified on a rolling basis starting 4/1; must reply within 2 week(s) of notification.

**Academics. Special study options:** Distance learning, double major, dual enrollment of high school students, ESL, honors, independent study, internships, liberal arts/career combination, teacher certification program, weekend college. License preparation in nursing, paramedic, physical therapy. **Credit/placement by examination:** AP, CLEP. 15 credit hours maximum toward associate degree. **Support services:** GED preparation and test center, learning center, remedial instruction, study skills assistance, tutoring, writing center.

**Majors. Agriculture:** General. **Business:** Accounting, administrative services, banking/financial services, business admin. **Computer sciences:** General, LAN/WAN management, programming, webmaster. **Education:** Early childhood, middle. **Engineering:** Environmental. **Engineering technology:** Drafting, electrical, environmental. **Family/consumer sciences:** Child care. **Health:** EMT paramedic, nursing (RN), physical therapy assistant, respiratory therapy technology. **Legal studies:** Paralegal. **Liberal arts:** Arts/sciences. **Protective services:** Criminal justice, emergency management/homeland security, firefighting, forensics, law enforcement admin. **Transportation:** Aviation. **Visual/performing arts:** Commercial/advertising art.

**Most popular majors.** Education 6%, health sciences 20%, liberal arts 59%.

**Computing on campus.** 125 workstations in library, computer center, student center. Commuter students can connect to campus network. Online course registration, online library, wireless network available.

**Student life. Freshman orientation:** Available. Preregistration for classes offered. **Activities:** Jazz band, choral groups, drama, literary magazine, music ensembles, musical theater, student government, student newspaper, symphony orchestra.

**Athletics. Intramural:** Archery, basketball, bowling, golf, soccer, softball, table tennis, volleyball.

**Student services.** Adult student services, alcohol/substance abuse counseling, career counseling, financial aid counseling, personal counseling, placement for graduates, veterans' counselor. **Transfer:** Transfer center, transfer adviser, college fairs on campus for students transferring to 4-year colleges.

**Contact.** E-mail: askregistration@nwacc.edu
Phone: (479) 619-4398 Toll-free number: (800) 995-6922
Fax: (479) 619-2229
Todd Kitchen, Director of Admissions, Northwest Arkansas Community College, One College Drive, Bentonville, AR 72712

## Ouachita Technical College
### Malvern, Arkansas
www.otcweb.edu                                    CB code: 3619

▶ Public 2-year community and technical college
▶ Commuter campus in small town

**General.** Regionally accredited. **Enrollment:** 837 degree-seeking undergraduates; 773 non-degree-seeking students. **Degrees:** 90 associate awarded. **ROTC:** Army. **Location:** 45 miles from Little Rock. **Calendar:** Semester, limited summer session. **Full-time faculty:** 35 total. **Part-time faculty:** 67 total.

**Student profile.** Among degree-seeking undergraduates, 34% enrolled in a transfer program, 64% enrolled in a vocational program, 170 enrolled as first-time, first-year students, 76 transferred in from other institutions.

| | | | |
|---|---|---|---|
| Part-time: | 35% | Hispanic American: | 2% |
| Out-of-state: | 1% | Native American: | 1% |
| Women: | 66% | International: | 1% |
| African American: | 16% | 25 or older: | 28% |
| Asian American: | 1% | | |

**Transfer out. Colleges most students transferred to 2009:** Henderson State University, University of Central Arkansas.

**Basis for selection.** Open admission, but selective for some programs. Admission to practical nursing, registered nursing, and cosmetology programs based on test scores.

**2009-2010 Annual costs.** Tuition/fees: $2,240; $4,010 out-of-state. Per-credit charge: $59 in-state; $118 out-of-state. Books/supplies: $904. Personal expenses: $1,202.

**2008-2009 Financial aid. Need-based:** 69% of total undergraduate aid awarded as scholarships/grants, 31% as loans/jobs. Need-based aid available for part-time students. Work-study available nights.

**Application procedures. Admission:** No deadline. No application fee. **Financial aid:** Closing date 6/30. FAFSA required. Applicants notified on a rolling basis starting 7/1; must reply within 6 week(s) of notification.

**Academics.** Associate of Arts in General Education and Associate of Applied Science in Criminal Justice offered online. **Special study options:** Distance learning, dual enrollment of high school students, independent study, internships, liberal arts/career combination. License preparation in nursing.

Two-Year Colleges

**Credit/placement by examination:** AP, CLEP, institutional tests. **Support services:** GED preparation and test center, learning center, remedial instruction, study skills assistance, tutoring.

**Majors. Business:** General, business admin. **Computer sciences:** General. **Education:** Early childhood. **Family/consumer sciences:** Child care. **Health:** Nursing (RN). **Liberal arts:** Arts/sciences. **Production:** General. **Protective services:** Criminal justice, forensics.

**Most popular majors.** Business/marketing 18%, computer/information sciences 13%, family/consumer sciences 8%, liberal arts 42%, trade and industry 13%.

**Computing on campus.** 150 workstations in library, computer center. Online library, helpline, wireless network available.

**Student life. Freshman orientation:** Mandatory. Preregistration for classes offered. Mandatory orientation can be completed online. Optional orientation offered on-campus. **Activities:** Student government.

**Student services.** Adult student services, alcohol/substance abuse counseling, chaplain/spiritual director, career counseling, services for economically disadvantaged, student employment services, financial aid counseling, personal counseling, placement for graduates, veterans' counselor. **Physically disabled:** Services for visually, speech, hearing impaired. **Transfer:** Pre-admission transcript evaluation for new students. College fairs on campus for students transferring to 4-year colleges.

**Contact.** E-mail: info@otcweb.edu
Phone: (501) 337-5000 ext. 1118 Fax: (501) 337-9382
Linda Johnson, Registrar, Ouachita Technical College, One College Circle, Malvern, AR 72104

## Ozarka College
**Melbourne, Arkansas**
www.ozarka.edu                                    **CB code: 3621**

▶ Public 2-year community and technical college
▶ Commuter campus in rural community

**General.** Regionally accredited. **Enrollment:** 1,291 degree-seeking undergraduates. **Degrees:** 142 associate awarded. **Location:** 125 miles from Little Rock, 160 miles from Memphis, Tennessee. **Calendar:** Semester, limited summer session. **Full-time faculty:** 37 total. **Part-time faculty:** 50 total.

**Transfer out. Colleges most students transferred to 2009:** Arkansas State University, Lyon College, University of Arkansas, University of Central Arkansas, Williams Baptist College.

**Basis for selection.** Open admission, but selective for some programs. Admission to licensed practical nursing, Registered Nursing, and culinary arts programs based on test scores, and/or essay, interview. **Adult students:** ACT/ASSET/COMPASS/SAT are accepted for placement in math and English. **Homeschooled:** Transcript of courses and grades required.

**2009-2010 Annual costs.** Tuition/fees: $2,620; $5,560 out-of-state. Per-credit charge: $70 in-state; $168 out-of-state. Books/supplies: $800. Personal expenses: $1,800.

**2009-2010 Financial aid. Need-based:** Need-based aid available for part-time students.

**Application procedures. Admission:** No deadline. No application fee. Admission notification on a rolling basis. **Financial aid:** No deadline. FAFSA required. Applicants notified on a rolling basis; must reply within 2 week(s) of notification.

**Academics. Special study options:** Combined bachelor's/graduate degree, cooperative education, distance learning, dual enrollment of high school students, liberal arts/career combination. Bachelor's degree programs available on campus. License preparation in nursing. **Credit/placement by examination:** AP, CLEP, institutional tests. 36 credit hours maximum toward associate degree. **Support services:** GED preparation and test center, learning center, remedial instruction, study skills assistance, tutoring.

**Majors. Business:** Business admin, information resources management. **Education:** General, elementary, middle. **Engineering technology:** General. **Health:** Licensed practical nurse, medical transcription. **Liberal arts:** Arts/sciences. **Mechanic/repair:** Automotive. **Personal/culinary services:** Culinary arts. **Protective services:** Law enforcement admin.

**Computing on campus.** 175 workstations in library, computer center. Commuter students can connect to campus network. Online course registration, helpline, wireless network available.

**Student life. Freshman orientation:** Mandatory. **Activities:** Student government.

**Athletics. Team name:** Eagles.

**Student services.** Chaplain/spiritual director, career counseling, services for economically disadvantaged, financial aid counseling, on-campus daycare, veterans' counselor, women's services. **Transfer:** Pre-admission transcript evaluation for new students. College fairs on campus for students transferring to 4-year colleges.

**Contact.** E-mail: zwilkerson@ozarka.edu
Phone: (870) 368-2028 Toll-free number: (800) 821-4335 ext. 2028
Fax: (870) 368-2091
Zeda Wilkerson, Director of Admissions, Ozarka College, 218 College Drive, Melbourne, AR 72556-0010

## Phillips Community College of the University of Arkansas
**Helena, Arkansas**
www.pccua.edu                                    **CB code: 6583**

▶ Public 2-year community college
▶ Commuter campus in large town

**General.** Founded in 1965. Regionally accredited. Campuses in Helena, Phillips County, as well as Stuttgart and DeWitt in Arkansas County. **Enrollment:** 1,285 degree-seeking undergraduates; 253 non-degree-seeking students. **Degrees:** 207 associate awarded. **Location:** 117 miles from Little Rock. **Calendar:** Semester, limited summer session. **Full-time faculty:** 78 total; 4% have terminal degrees, 17% minority, 73% women. **Part-time faculty:** 54 total; 28% minority, 70% women. **Class size:** 90% < 20, 9% 20-39, less than 1% 40-49, less than 1% 50-99. **Special facilities:** Performing arts center.

**Student profile.** Among degree-seeking undergraduates, 32% enrolled in a transfer program, 52% enrolled in a vocational program, 248 enrolled as first-time, first-year students, 248 transferred in from other institutions.

| | | | |
|---|---|---|---|
| Part-time: | 36% | Asian American: | 1% |
| Out-of-state: | 3% | Hispanic American: | 2% |
| Women: | 74% | 25 or older: | 49% |
| African American: | 47% | | |

**Basis for selection.** Open admission, but selective for some programs. Additional requirements for nursing program. Interview required of applicants with no high school transcript or test scores. **Adult students:** ASSET or COMPASS test required for students taking English or math. **Homeschooled:** Transcript of courses and grades, state high school equivalency certificate required.

**2009-2010 Annual costs.** Tuition/fees: $2,030; $2,300 out-of-district; $3,440 out-of-state. Per-credit charge: $55 in-district; $64 out-of-district; $102 out-of-state. Books/supplies: $1,200. Personal expenses: $3,660.

**2008-2009 Financial aid.** All financial aid based on need. 185 full-time freshmen applied for aid; 185 were judged to have need; 185 of these received aid. Average scholarship/grant was $2,616; average loan $3,203. 77% of total undergraduate aid awarded as scholarships/grants, 23% as loans/jobs. Need-based aid available for part-time students. Work-study available nights and for part-time students. **Additional information:** Tuition waivers are given to firefighters and law enforcement officers.

**Application procedures. Admission:** No deadline. No application fee. Admission notification on a rolling basis. **Financial aid:** Priority date 4/1, closing date 6/30. FAFSA required. Applicants notified on a rolling basis starting 4/1; must reply within 2 week(s) of notification.

**Academics. Special study options:** Distance learning, dual enrollment of high school students, honors, independent study, internships, weekend college. Bachelor's degree programs available on campus. License preparation in nursing. **Credit/placement by examination:** CLEP, institutional tests. 30 credit hours maximum toward associate degree. **Support services:** GED preparation and test center, learning center, remedial instruction, study skills assistance, tutoring.

**Majors. Biology:** General. **Business:** General, business admin, office technology. **Communications technology:** Graphic/printing. **Computer sciences:** Computer science, information technology, LAN/WAN management. **Education:** General, early childhood, elementary. **Engineering:** General. **Engineering technology:** Biomedical, drafting, manufacturing. **Health:** Nursing (RN), phlebotomy. **Legal studies:** Prelaw. **Liberal arts:** Arts/sciences.

**Math:** General. **Mechanic/repair:** Industrial. **Physical sciences:** Chemistry, physics. **Psychology:** General. **Social sciences:** General. **Visual/performing arts:** Printmaking.

**Most popular majors.** Business/marketing 12%, computer/information sciences 9%, education 20%, health sciences 13%, liberal arts 36%.

**Computing on campus.** 275 workstations in library, computer center. Commuter students can connect to campus network. Online course registration, wireless network available.

**Student life. Freshman orientation:** Available. Preregistration for classes offered. **Activities:** Choral groups, dance, drama, musical theater, Baptist Collegiate Ministries, Phi Theta Kappa, Arkansas Licensed Practical Nurses Association, National Student Nurses Association, Young Democrats, Book Club.

**Athletics. Intramural:** Archery, badminton, basketball, football (non-tackle) M, golf, soccer, softball, table tennis, tennis, volleyball.

**Student services.** Adult student services, career counseling, services for economically disadvantaged, student employment services, financial aid counseling, personal counseling, placement for graduates, veterans' counselor. **Physically disabled:** Services for visually, hearing impaired. **Transfer:** Transfer adviser, college fairs on campus for students transferring to 4-year colleges.

**Contact.** E-mail: lboone@pccua.edu
Phone: (870) 338-6474 ext. 1336 Fax: (870) 338-7542
Lynn Boone, Vice Chancellor for Student Services/Registrar, Phillips Community College of the University of Arkansas, 1000 Campus Drive, Helena, AR 72342

## Pulaski Technical College
**North Little Rock, Arkansas**
**www.pulaskitech.edu** CB code: 3622

- Public 2-year community and technical college
- Commuter campus in small city

**General.** Regionally accredited. **Enrollment:** 9,187 degree-seeking undergraduates. **Degrees:** 530 associate awarded. **Location:** 4 miles from Little Rock. **Calendar:** Semester, extensive summer session. **Full-time faculty:** 153 total. **Part-time faculty:** 320 total. **Class size:** 55% < 20, 45% 20-39.

**Student profile.**

Out-of-state: 1% 25 or older: 59%

**Transfer out. Colleges most students transferred to 2009:** University of Arkansas at Little Rock, University of Central Arkansas.

**Basis for selection.** Open admission, but selective for some programs. Additional requirements for dental assisting, practical nursing, respiratory therapy, occupational therapy assistant and military technology programs. **Adult students:** COMPASS or ACT scores may be used for placement.

**2009-2010 Annual costs.** Tuition/fees: $2,790; $4,320 out-of-state. Per-credit charge: $80 in-state; $131 out-of-state. Books/supplies: $1,200. Personal expenses: $2,732.

**2009-2010 Financial aid. Need-based:** Need-based aid available for part-time students. Work-study available for part-time students.

**Application procedures. Admission:** No deadline. No application fee. Admission notification on a rolling basis. **Financial aid:** Closing date 5/15. FAFSA, institutional form required. Applicants notified on a rolling basis starting 5/1; must reply within 2 week(s) of notification.

**Academics. Special study options:** Cooperative education, distance learning, double major, dual enrollment of high school students, external degree, internships, liberal arts/career combination, weekend college. License preparation in aviation, dental hygiene, nursing, occupational therapy. **Credit/placement by examination:** AP, CLEP, institutional tests. **Support services:** Learning center, pre-admission summer program, remedial instruction, study skills assistance, tutoring.

**Majors. Business:** General, hospitality admin, management information systems. **Construction:** General. **Education:** Early childhood. **Engineering technology:** Drafting, environmental, industrial, manufacturing. **Family/consumer sciences:** Child care. **Health:** Occupational therapy assistant, respiratory therapy technology. **Legal studies:** Paralegal. **Liberal arts:** Arts/sciences. **Mechanic/repair:** Aircraft powerplant, electronics/electrical, heating/ac/refrig. **Military:** General. **Personal/culinary services:** Chef training.

**Protective services:** Forensics, law enforcement admin. **Transportation:** Airline/commercial pilot. **Other:** General technologies.

**Most popular majors.** Business/marketing 13%, liberal arts 69%.

**Computing on campus.** 281 workstations in library, computer center, student center. Commuter students can connect to campus network. Online course registration, online library, helpline, wireless network available.

**Student life. Freshman orientation:** Available. Preregistration for classes offered. Online orientation is ongoing. **Activities:** Campus ministries, choral groups, literary magazine, student government, Metro student ministries, Culture Shock, philosophy club, Student Ambassadors, Phi Theta Kappa, College Democrats, Fusion, Phi Beta Lambda.

**Student services.** Adult student services, career counseling, services for economically disadvantaged, student employment services, financial aid counseling, minority student services, personal counseling, veterans' counselor. **Physically disabled:** Services for visually, hearing impaired. **Learning disabled:** Comprehensive services available. **Transfer:** Transfer adviser, college fairs on campus for students transferring to 4-year colleges.

**Contact.** E-mail: admissions@pulaskitech.edu
Phone: (501) 812-2231 Fax: (501) 812-2316
Clark Atkins, Director of Admissions, Pulaski Technical College, 3000 West Scenic Drive, North Little Rock, AR 72118-3347

## Remington College: Little Rock
**Little Rock, Arkansas**
**www.remingtoncollege.edu**

- For-profit 2-year technical college
- Commuter campus in very large city

**General.** Accredited by ACCSCT. **Calendar:** Quarter.

**Annual costs/financial aid.** Costs of entire programs leading to diploma, associate degree, and bachelor's degree range from $13,950 to $39,950; include books and supplies.

**Contact.** Phone: (501) 312-0007
Director of Admissions, 19 Remington Drive, Little Rock, AR 72204

## Rich Mountain Community College
**Mena, Arkansas**
**www.rmcc.edu** CB code: 0226

- Public 2-year community college
- Commuter campus in small town

**General.** Founded in 1983. Regionally accredited. **Enrollment:** 638 degree-seeking undergraduates. **Degrees:** 58 associate awarded. **Location:** 85 miles from Fort Smith, 80 miles from Hot Springs. **Calendar:** Semester, limited summer session. **Full-time faculty:** 20 total. **Part-time faculty:** 58 total.

**Student profile.**

Out-of-state: 25% 25 or older: 51%

**Transfer out. Colleges most students transferred to 2009:** Henderson State University, Arkansas Tech University, Westark College, Cossatot Community College.

**Basis for selection.** Open admission, but selective for some programs. Limited admission to licensed practical nurse program.

**High school preparation.** 18 units recommended. Recommended units include English 4, mathematics 3, social studies 2 and science 4.

**2009-2010 Annual costs.** Tuition/fees: $1,620; $2,010 out-of-district; $5,190 out-of-state. Per-credit charge: $51 in-district; $64 out-of-district; $170 out-of-state. Books/supplies: $1,000. Personal expenses: $2,974.

**2008-2009 Financial aid. Need-based:** Need-based aid available for part-time students. Work-study available for part-time students. **Non-need-based:** Scholarships awarded for academics.

**Application procedures. Admission:** No deadline. No application fee. Admission notification on a rolling basis. **Financial aid:** Priority date 7/1; no closing date. FAFSA, institutional form required. Applicants notified on a rolling basis starting 6/1; must reply within 2 week(s) of notification.

**Academics.** MBA, masters in education leadership offered on campus by Henderson State University. **Special study options:** Cooperative education, distance learning, dual enrollment of high school students, external degree, internships, student-designed major. Bachelor's degree programs available on campus. License preparation in nursing. **Credit/placement by examination:** AP, CLEP, institutional tests. 30 credit hours maximum toward associate degree. **Support services:** GED preparation and test center, pre-admission summer program, remedial instruction, study skills assistance, tutoring.

**Majors. Agriculture:** General. **Business:** Administrative services, business admin, management information systems. **Computer sciences:** General, information systems, LAN/WAN management, programming, systems analysis. **Education:** General. **Engineering technology:** Computer hardware. **Liberal arts:** Arts/sciences. **Production:** Machine tool.

**Most popular majors.** Business/marketing 17%, liberal arts 78%.

**Computing on campus.** 73 workstations in library, computer center. Commuter students can connect to campus network.

**Student life. Freshman orientation:** Available. Preregistration for classes offered. **Activities:** Radio station, student government, TV station, Baptist student union.

**Student services.** Adult student services, career counseling, services for economically disadvantaged, financial aid counseling, personal counseling, veterans' counselor. **Physically disabled:** Services for visually, hearing impaired. **Transfer:** Pre-admission transcript evaluation for new students. Transfer adviser, college fairs on campus for students transferring to 4-year colleges.

**Contact.** Phone: (479) 394-7622 ext. 1440 Fax: (479) 394-2760 Tammy Young, Director of Admissions, Rich Mountain Community College, 1100 College Drive, Mena, AR 71953

## South Arkansas Community College
### El Dorado, Arkansas
www.southark.edu                        CB code: 1550

▶ Public 2-year community and junior college
▶ Commuter campus in large town

**General.** Founded in 1975. Regionally accredited. **Enrollment:** 1,526 degree-seeking undergraduates. **Degrees:** 110 associate awarded. **Location:** 115 miles from Little Rock. **Calendar:** Semester, limited summer session. **Full-time faculty:** 62 total. **Part-time faculty:** 53 total. **Class size:** 54% < 20, 44% 20-39, 1% 40-49, less than 1% 50-99.

**Transfer out. Colleges most students transferred to 2009:** Southern Arkansas University, Louisiana Tech, University of Arkansas at Monticello.

**Basis for selection.** Open admission. **Homeschooled:** Transcript of courses and grades, state high school equivalency certificate required.

**High school preparation.** Recommended units include English 4, mathematics 3, social studies 3 and science 4.

**2009-2010 Annual costs.** Tuition/fees: $2,240; $2,480 out-of-district; $4,370 out-of-state. Per-credit charge: $68 in-district; $76 out-of-district; $139 out-of-state. $25 lab fee for most courses. Books/supplies: $600. Personal expenses: $550.

**2008-2009 Financial aid. Need-based:** Need-based aid available for part-time students.

**Application procedures. Admission:** Priority date 7/31; no deadline. No application fee. Admission notification on a rolling basis. **Financial aid:** Closing date 8/1. FAFSA, institutional form required. Applicants notified on a rolling basis starting 7/1; must reply within 2 week(s) of notification.

**Academics. Special study options:** Distance learning, dual enrollment of high school students, liberal arts/career combination. License preparation in nursing, occupational therapy, paramedic, physical therapy, radiology, real estate. **Credit/placement by examination:** AP, CLEP, IB, institutional tests. 30 credit hours maximum toward associate degree. **Support services:** GED preparation and test center, learning center, reduced course load, remedial instruction, study skills assistance, tutoring.

**Majors. Business:** General, administrative services, business admin. **Communications:** Digital media. **Communications technology:** Desktop publishing. **Computer sciences:** General, applications programming, computer

graphics, computer science, information technology, programming. **Conservation:** General. **Education:** General, secondary. **Family/consumer sciences:** Child care. **Health:** Clinical lab technology, EMT paramedic, medical radiologic technology/radiation therapy, nursing (RN), occupational therapy assistant, physical therapy assistant, radiologic technology/medical imaging. **Liberal arts:** Arts/sciences. **Mechanic/repair:** Automotive, industrial. **Protective services:** Police science. **Visual/performing arts:** Commercial/advertising art.

**Computing on campus.** 250 workstations in library, computer center, student center. Online course registration, student web hosting available.

**Student life. Freshman orientation:** Available. Preregistration for classes offered. **Activities:** Choral groups, literary magazine, Phi Beta Lambda, Phi Theta Kappa, student leadership group.

**Student services.** Adult student services, career counseling, services for economically disadvantaged, student employment services, financial aid counseling, personal counseling, placement for graduates, veterans' counselor. **Physically disabled:** Services for visually, hearing impaired. **Transfer:** Transfer adviser, college fairs on campus for students transferring to 4-year colleges.

**Contact.** E-mail: registrar@southark.edu
Phone: (870) 862-8131 Toll-free number: (800) 955-2289
Fax: (870) 864-7137
Dean Inman, Dean of Enrollment Services, South Arkansas Community College, Box 7010, El Dorado, AR 71731-7010

## Southeast Arkansas College
### Pine Bluff, Arkansas
www.seark.edu                           CB code: 3624

▶ Public 2-year community and technical college
▶ Commuter campus in small city

**General.** Regionally accredited. **Enrollment:** 1,688 degree-seeking undergraduates; 295 non-degree-seeking students. **Degrees:** 165 associate awarded. **Location:** 42 miles from Little Rock. **Calendar:** Semester, limited summer session. **Full-time faculty:** 56 total; 4% have terminal degrees, 34% women. **Part-time faculty:** 76 total; 4% have terminal degrees, 57% women. **Class size:** 71% < 20, 29% 20-39.

**Student profile.** Among degree-seeking undergraduates, 74% enrolled in a vocational program, 343 enrolled as first-time, first-year students, 38 transferred in from other institutions.

| Part-time: | 37% | Women: | 70% |
|---|---|---|---|

**Transfer out. Colleges most students transferred to 2009:** University of Arkansas at Pine Bluff, University of Arkansas at Monticello, University of Arkansas at Little Rock.

**Basis for selection.** Open admission, but selective for some programs. Additional requirements for some health programs. ACT, ASSET or COMPASS required for placement. **Learning Disabled:** Learning disability must be officially documented.

**High school preparation.** Recommended units include English 4, mathematics 6, social studies 2, history 2, science 5 and foreign language 2.

**2009-2010 Annual costs.** Tuition/fees: $2,290; $4,330 out-of-state. Per-credit charge: $68 in-state; $136 out-of-state. Books/supplies: $800. Personal expenses: $3,400.

**2008-2009 Financial aid. Need-based:** 76% of total undergraduate aid awarded as scholarships/grants, 24% as loans/jobs. Need-based aid available for part-time students. Work-study available nights and for part-time students. **Non-need-based:** Scholarships awarded for academics, leadership, state residency.

**Application procedures. Admission:** No deadline. No application fee. **Financial aid:** Priority date 6/1; no closing date. FAFSA required. Applicants notified on a rolling basis starting 5/1; must reply within 2 week(s) of notification.

**Academics. Special study options:** Distance learning, dual enrollment of high school students, independent study, internships. License preparation in nursing, paramedic, radiology, real estate. **Credit/placement by examination:** AP, CLEP. 15 credit hours maximum toward associate degree. Credit awarded through challenge exams. **Support services:** Learning center, remedial instruction, study skills assistance, tutoring.

**Majors. Biology:** Biotechnology. **Business:** General, management information systems. **Computer sciences:** Networking. **Engineering technology:**

Drafting. **Health:** EMT paramedic, medical radiologic technology/radiation therapy, nursing (RN), respiratory therapy technology, surgical technology. **Legal studies:** Paralegal. **Liberal arts:** Arts/sciences. **Mechanic/repair:** Electronics/electrical, industrial, industrial electronics. **Protective services:** Criminal justice, firefighting, forensics, law enforcement admin. **Other:** Emergency administration and management.

**Most popular majors.** Business/marketing 12%, computer/information sciences 10%, health sciences 25%, liberal arts 23%, security/protective services 16%.

**Computing on campus.** 100 workstations in library, computer center. Commuter students can connect to campus network. Wireless network available.

**Student life. Freshman orientation:** Available. Preregistration for classes offered. 1-hour program held one weekday morning and one weekday evening before start of classes. **Activities:** Campus ministries, student government, symphony orchestra.

**Student services.** Adult student services, alcohol/substance abuse counseling, career counseling, services for economically disadvantaged, student employment services, financial aid counseling, personal counseling, placement for graduates, veterans' counselor. **Physically disabled:** Services for visually, speech, hearing impaired. **Learning disabled:** Comprehensive services available. **Transfer:** Pre-admission transcript evaluation for new students. College fairs on campus for students transferring to 4-year colleges.

**Contact.**  E-mail: bdunn@seark.edu
Phone: (870) 543-5908 Fax: (870) 543-5956
Barbara Dunn, Admissions and Enrollment Management Coordinator, Southeast Arkansas College, 1900 Hazel Street, Pine Bluff, AR 71603

## Southern Arkansas University Tech
**Camden, Arkansas**
www.sautech.edu                          CB code: 6704

▶ Public 2-year community and technical college
▶ Commuter campus in large town

**General.** Founded in 1967. Regionally accredited. **Enrollment:** 981 degree-seeking undergraduates. **Degrees:** 123 associate awarded. **Location:** 90 miles from Little Rock. **Calendar:** Semester, limited summer session. **Full-time faculty:** 29 total; 3% have terminal degrees, 7% minority, 48% women. **Part-time faculty:** 75 total; 4% have terminal degrees, 8% minority, 43% women. **Class size:** 61% < 20, 34% 20-39, 5% 40-49, less than 1% 50-99. **Special facilities:** Fire training academy, environmental science academy, law enforcement academy, career academy, business and industry center. **Partnerships:** Formal partnerships with area businesses/industries and high schools.

**Student profile.** Among degree-seeking undergraduates, 251 enrolled as first-time, first-year students.

| | | | |
|---|---|---|---|
| Out-of-state: | 2% | Live on campus: | 2% |
| 25 or older: | 28% | | |

**Transfer out. Colleges most students transferred to 2009:** Southern Arkansas University, Henderson State University, University of Arkansas at Monticello, University of Central Arkansas, South Arkansas Community College.

**Basis for selection.** Open admission, but selective for some programs. Additional application and testing for nursing program. **Homeschooled:** State high school equivalency certificate required. Applicants must take the GED test.

**High school preparation.** College-preparatory program recommended. 23 units recommended. Recommended units include English 4, mathematics 4, social studies 2, history 2, science 3, foreign language 2 and academic electives 6.

**2009-2010 Annual costs. Tuition/fees:** $3,180; $4,500 out-of-state. Per-credit charge: $85 in-state; $129 out-of-state. Books/supplies: $1,400. Personal expenses: $4,500.

**2008-2009 Financial aid. Need-based:** Need-based aid available for part-time students. Work-study available nights, weekends and for part-time students. **Non-need-based:** Scholarships awarded for academics, state residency.

**Application procedures. Admission:** Priority date 4/15; deadline 6/1 (postmark date). No application fee. Admission notification on a rolling

basis. **Financial aid:** Priority date 6/1; no closing date. FAFSA required. Applicants notified on a rolling basis starting 5/1.

**Academics. Special study options:** Distance learning, double major, dual enrollment of high school students, honors, independent study, internships. Articulation agreements for Nursing Assistant and Practical Nursing programs. Bachelor's degree programs available on campus. License preparation in aviation, nursing. **Credit/placement by examination:** AP, CLEP, institutional tests. 15 credit hours maximum toward associate degree. **Support services:** GED preparation and test center, learning center, pre-admission summer program, remedial instruction, study skills assistance, tutoring, writing center.

**Majors. Business:** Business admin, office management. **Computer sciences:** Computer science, networking, programming, web page design. **Education:** Multi-level teacher. **Engineering technology:** Computer systems, environmental, industrial. **Mechanic/repair:** Aircraft powerplant. **Protective services:** Fire services admin, firefighting. **Other:** Technology.

**Most popular majors.** Business/marketing 18%, computer/information sciences 18%, education 13%, engineering/engineering technologies 29%, liberal arts 10%.

**Computing on campus.** 250 workstations in library, computer center. Dormitories wired for high-speed internet access and linked to campus network. Commuter students can connect to campus network. Online course registration, online library, helpline, repair service, wireless network available.

**Student life. Freshman orientation:** Mandatory. Preregistration for classes offered. 4 one-days program in late July or early August depending on number of students. **Housing:** Apartments available. $100 partly refundable deposit, deadline 7/15. Off-campus housing is available. **Activities:** Campus ministries, radio station, TV station, student government, multi-cultural club, aviation club, multimedia graphics, audio/video, computer club, electronics club, Phi Beta Lambda, Phi Theta Kappa, SAU Tech Ambassadors, allied health student club.

**Athletics. Intramural:** Basketball, football (non-tackle), soccer, softball, tennis, volleyball, weight lifting. **Team name:** Varmits.

**Student services.** Adult student services, chaplain/spiritual director, career counseling, services for economically disadvantaged, student employment services, financial aid counseling, on-campus daycare, personal counseling, placement for graduates, veterans' counselor. **Physically disabled:** Services for visually, speech, hearing impaired. **Transfer:** Re-entry adviser, pre-admission transcript evaluation for new students. Transfer center, transfer adviser, college fairs on campus for students transferring to 4-year colleges.

**Contact.**  E-mail: bellis@sautech.edu
Phone: (870) 574-4558 Fax: (870) 574-4478
Patricia Sindle, Director, Enrollment Services, Southern Arkansas University Tech, PO Box 3499, Camden, AR 71711-1599

## University of Arkansas Community College at Morrilton
**Morrilton, Arkansas**
www.uaccm.edu                          CB code: 3881

▶ Public 2-year community college
▶ Commuter campus in small town

**General.** Regionally accredited. **Enrollment:** 2,375 degree-seeking undergraduates; 46 non-degree-seeking students. **Degrees:** 231 associate awarded. **Location:** 26 miles from Russellville. **Calendar:** Semester, limited summer session. **Full-time faculty:** 59 total; 3% have terminal degrees, 51% women. **Part-time faculty:** 41 total; 12% have terminal degrees, 7% minority, 61% women. **Class size:** 50% < 20, 50% 20-39.

**Student profile.** Among degree-seeking undergraduates, 30% enrolled in a transfer program, 70% enrolled in a vocational program, 1% already have a bachelor's degree or higher, 765 enrolled as first-time, first-year students, 268 transferred in from other institutions.

| | | | |
|---|---|---|---|
| Part-time: | 32% | Hispanic American: | 4% |
| Women: | 58% | Native American: | 4% |
| African American: | 9% | 25 or older: | 36% |
| Asian American: | 1% | | |

**Transfer out.** 8% of students enrolled in the transfer program go on to 4-year colleges. **Colleges most students transferred to 2009:** University of Central Arkansas, Arkansas Tech University, University of Arkansas at Fayetteville, University of Arkansas at Little Rock.

**Basis for selection.** ASSET or COMPASS test scores required for placement. **Homeschooled:** Transcript of courses and grades required.

**2009-2010 Annual costs.** Tuition/fees: $2,640; $2,850 out-of-district; $3,900 out-of-state. Per-credit charge: $70 in-district; $77 out-of-district; $112 out-of-state. Books/supplies: $900. Personal expenses: $2,500.

**2008-2009 Financial aid. Need-based:** 476 full-time freshmen applied for aid; 413 were judged to have need; 387 of these received aid. Average need met was 46%. Average scholarship/grant was $2,895; average loan $2,264. 67% of total undergraduate aid awarded as scholarships/grants, 33% as loans/jobs. Need-based aid available for part-time students. Work-study available nights and for part-time students. **Non-need-based:** Awarded to 671 full-time undergraduates, including 183 freshmen. Scholarships awarded for academics, leadership, state residency.

**Application procedures. Admission:** No deadline. No application fee. Admission notification on a rolling basis. **Financial aid:** Priority date 7/1; no closing date. FAFSA, institutional form, CSS PROFILE required. Applicants notified by 4/15.

**Academics. Special study options:** Cooperative education, distance learning, dual enrollment of high school students, internships, liberal arts/career combination. License preparation in nursing. **Credit/placement by examination:** AP, CLEP, ACT, institutional tests. 30 credit hours maximum toward associate degree. **Support services:** GED preparation and test center, learning center, reduced course load, remedial instruction, study skills assistance, tutoring, writing center.

**Majors. Business:** General. **Engineering technology:** Computer systems, drafting, petroleum, surveying. **Family/consumer sciences:** Child development. **Health:** Nursing (RN). **Liberal arts:** Arts/sciences. **Mechanic/repair:** Auto body, automotive, heating/ac/refrig. **Protective services:** Forensics, law enforcement admin. **Visual/performing arts:** Commercial/advertising art.

**Most popular majors.** Engineering/engineering technologies 25%, health sciences 8%, liberal arts 53%, trade and industry 6%.

**Computing on campus.** Commuter students can connect to campus network. Wireless network available.

**Student life. Freshman orientation:** Mandatory. Preregistration for classes offered. Two day orientation activities held the first two days before classes start for the fall and spring semesters. **Activities:** Choral groups, drama, music ensembles, student government, student newspaper.

**Athletics. Intramural:** Basketball, football (non-tackle), table tennis, volleyball. **Team name:** Timberwolves.

**Student services.** Career counseling, student employment services, financial aid counseling, on-campus daycare, placement for graduates, veterans' counselor. **Physically disabled:** Services for visually, speech, hearing impaired. **Transfer:** College fairs on campus for students transferring to 4-year colleges.

**Contact.** E-mail: adm@uaccm.edu
Phone: (501) 977-2053 Toll-free number: (800) 264-1094
Fax: (501) 977-2123
Susan Dewey, Director of Admissions, University of Arkansas Community College at Morrilton, 1537 University Boulevard, Morrilton, AR 72110

## University of Arkansas: Community College at Batesville
**Batesville, Arkansas**
www.uaccb.edu                    CB code: 3628

- Public 2-year community college
- Commuter campus in small town

**General.** Regionally accredited. **Enrollment:** 1,547 degree-seeking undergraduates. **Degrees:** 167 associate awarded. **Location:** 90 miles from Little Rock. **Calendar:** Semester, limited summer session. **Full-time faculty:** 50 total; 10% have terminal degrees, 4% minority, 64% women. **Part-time faculty:** 57 total; 4% minority, 58% women.

**Student profile.** Among degree-seeking undergraduates, 132 transferred in from other institutions.

**Transfer out. Colleges most students transferred to 2009:** Lyon College, Arkansas State University, University of Arkansas, University of Central Arkansas, Arkansas Tech University.

**Basis for selection.** Open admission, but selective for some programs. Admission to nursing program based on GPA in prerequisite courses and a

nursing entrance exam. **Homeschooled:** Transcript of courses and grades required.

**2009-2010 Annual costs.** Tuition/fees: $2,210; $2,570 out-of-district; $4,190 out-of-state. Per-credit charge: $54 in-district; $66 out-of-district; $120 out-of-state. Books/supplies: $1,000. Personal expenses: $2,100.

**Financial aid.** All financial aid based on need. Work-study available nights, weekends and for part-time students.

**Application procedures. Admission:** No deadline. No application fee. Application must be submitted on paper. Admission notification on a rolling basis. **Financial aid:** No deadline. FAFSA required. Applicants notified on a rolling basis starting 3/1; must reply within 2 week(s) of notification.

**Academics. Special study options:** Cooperative education, distance learning, dual enrollment of high school students, ESL, independent study, internships, liberal arts/career combination, weekend college. Bachelor's degree programs available on campus. License preparation in paramedic. **Credit/placement by examination:** AP, CLEP, institutional tests. **Support services:** GED preparation and test center, remedial instruction, study skills assistance, tutoring.

**Majors. Business:** General, accounting, administrative services, business admin. **Computer sciences:** General. **Education:** Early childhood. **Health:** EMT paramedic, nursing (RN). **Liberal arts:** Arts/sciences. **Mechanic/repair:** General, aircraft, electronics/electrical, industrial. **Protective services:** Criminal justice.

**Most popular majors.** Business/marketing 14%, health sciences 37%, liberal arts 38%.

**Computing on campus.** 25 workstations in library, computer center. Online course registration available.

**Student life. Freshman orientation:** Available. Preregistration for classes offered. **Activities:** Student government, Baptist Collegiate Ministry, Young Democrats, College Republicans.

**Student services.** Adult student services, career counseling, services for economically disadvantaged, student employment services, financial aid counseling, personal counseling, veterans' counselor. **Physically disabled:** Services for visually, speech, hearing impaired. **Transfer:** College fairs on campus for students transferring to 4-year colleges.

**Contact.** E-mail: casey.bromley@uaccb.edu
Phone: (870) 612-2000 Toll-free number: (800) 508-7878
Fax: (870) 793-4988
Randy Scaggs, Director of Enrollment Services, University of Arkansas: Community College at Batesville, Box 3350, Batesville, AR 72503

## University of Arkansas: Community College at Hope
**Hope, Arkansas**
www.uacch.edu                    CB code: 3629

- Public 2-year community and technical college
- Commuter campus in small town

**General.** Regionally accredited. **Enrollment:** 1,358 degree-seeking undergraduates. **Degrees:** 128 associate awarded. **Location:** 30 miles from Texarkana. **Calendar:** Semester, limited summer session. **Full-time faculty:** 38 total; 5% have terminal degrees, 8% minority, 45% women. **Part-time faculty:** 23 total; 48% women.

**Basis for selection.** Open admission, but selective for some programs. Additional requirements for nursing, funeral services, respiratory therapy programs.

**High school preparation.** 15 units recommended. Recommended units include English 4, mathematics 3, social studies 1, history 2, science 3 and academic electives 2.

**2009-2010 Annual costs.** Tuition/fees: $1,790; $1,940 out-of-district; $3,620 out-of-state. Per-credit charge: $54 in-district; $59 out-of-district; $115 out-of-state. Books/supplies: $900. Personal expenses: $500.

**2008-2009 Financial aid. Need-based:** Need-based aid available for part-time students. Work-study available nights and for part-time students. **Non-need-based:** Scholarships awarded for academics.

**Application procedures. Admission:** No deadline. No application fee. Admission notification on a rolling basis. **Financial aid:** Closing date 7/6.

FAFSA, institutional form required. Applicants notified on a rolling basis starting 1/1; must reply within 4 week(s) of notification.

**Academics.** **Special study options:** Distance learning, double major, dual enrollment of high school students, ESL, independent study, liberal arts/ career combination. Bachelor's degree programs available on campus. License preparation in nursing, paramedic. **Credit/placement by examination:** AP, CLEP, institutional tests. **Support services:** GED test center, remedial instruction, study skills assistance, tutoring.

**Majors.** **Agriculture:** General. **Business:** General. **Education:** Middle. **Family/consumer sciences:** Child care. **Health:** Respiratory therapy technology. **Legal studies:** Paralegal. **Liberal arts:** Arts/sciences. **Personal/ culinary services:** Mortuary science. **Protective services:** Forensics, law enforcement admin, police science.

**Most popular majors.** Business/marketing 7%, health sciences 9%, legal studies 6%, liberal arts 62%, personal/culinary services 7%.

**Computing on campus.** 20 workstations in library. Commuter students can connect to campus network. Online course registration, online library, helpline, wireless network available.

**Student life.** **Freshman orientation:** Available. **Activities:** Jazz band, choral groups, drama, music ensembles, student government, student newspaper.

**Student services.** Adult student services, alcohol/substance abuse counseling, chaplain/spiritual director, career counseling, services for economically disadvantaged, student employment services, financial aid counseling, personal counseling, placement for graduates, veterans' counselor. **Physically disabled:** Services for visually, speech, hearing impaired. **Transfer:** Pre-admission transcript evaluation for new students. College fairs on campus for students transferring to 4-year colleges.

**Contact.**  E-mail: diana.syata@uacch.edu
Phone: (870) 777-5722 Fax: (870) 722-6630
Judy Anderson, Director for Enrollment Services, University of Arkansas: Community College at Hope, 2500 South Main, Hope, AR 71802-0140

# California

## Allan Hancock College
Santa Maria, California
www.hancockcollege.edu

CB code: 4002

▶ Public 2-year community college
▶ Commuter campus in small city

**General.** Founded in 1920. Regionally accredited. **Enrollment:** 5,330 degree-seeking undergraduates; 5,295 non-degree-seeking students. **Degrees:** 988 associate awarded. **Location:** 70 miles from Santa Barbara, 175 miles from Los Angeles. **Calendar:** Semester, extensive summer session. **Full-time faculty:** 158 total. **Part-time faculty:** 450 total.

**Student profile.** Among degree-seeking undergraduates, 92% enrolled in a transfer program, 47% enrolled in a vocational program, 7% already have a bachelor's degree or higher, 1,217 enrolled as first-time, first-year students.

| | | | |
|---|---|---|---|
| Part-time: | 67% | Hispanic American: | 37% |
| Women: | 54% | Native American: | 2% |
| African American: | 3% | International: | 2% |
| Asian American: | 5% | | |

**Transfer out. Colleges most students transferred to 2009:** California Polytechnic State University, San Luis Obispo; UC Santa Barbara, CSU, San Diego; CSU, Northridge; CSU, Fresno.

**Basis for selection.** Open admission, but selective for some programs. Special requirements for allied health and drama programs. Students required to make separate application for admission to nursing, drama, police academy programs. Interviews required for allied health applicants. Auditions required for drama applicants. **Adult students:** SAT/ACT scores not required.

**2009-2010 Annual costs.** Tuition/fees: $824; $6,524 out-of-state. Per-credit charge: $26 in-state; $216 out-of-state. Books/supplies: $1,422. Personal expenses: $2,924.

**Financial aid.** All financial aid based on need. Need-based aid available for part-time students. Work-study available for part-time students.

**Application procedures. Admission:** No deadline. No application fee. Admission notification on a rolling basis. **Financial aid:** Priority date 5/1; no closing date. FAFSA required. Applicants notified on a rolling basis starting 6/1.

**Academics. Special study options:** Accelerated study, cooperative education, distance learning, double major, dual enrollment of high school students, ESL, honors, independent study, internships, liberal arts/career combination, study abroad, weekend college. Bachelor's degree programs available on campus. License preparation in dental hygiene, nursing, paramedic, real estate. **Credit/placement by examination:** AP, CLEP, institutional tests. 30 credit hours maximum toward associate degree. **Support services:** GED preparation and test center, learning center, reduced course load, remedial instruction, study skills assistance, tutoring, writing center.

**Majors. Agriculture:** Agribusiness operations. **Architecture:** Technology. **Biology:** General. **Business:** General, accounting, administrative services, business admin, international marketing, management information systems, management science, office technology, office/clerical. **Communications technology:** Animation/special effects, graphic/printing, graphics, photo/film/video. **Computer sciences:** General, computer science, information technology. **Conservation:** Environmental studies. **Education:** Early childhood, elementary, physical. **Engineering:** General. **Engineering technology:** General, architectural, civil, electrical, electromechanical, environmental, robotics. **Family/consumer sciences:** General, fashion consultant, housing. **Foreign languages:** Spanish. **Health:** Dental assistant, health services, licensed practical nurse, medical assistant, medical records admin, medical records technology, nursing (RN), physical therapy assistant. **Legal studies:** Legal secretary. **Liberal arts:** Arts/sciences. **Math:** General, computational. **Mechanic/repair:** General, auto body, automotive, diesel, electronics/electrical. **Parks/recreation:** General. **Personal/culinary services:** Chef training, cosmetic. **Physical sciences:** Chemistry, physics. **Protective services:** Fire safety technology. **Psychology:** General. **Public administration:** Human services. **Social sciences:** General, international relations. **Visual/performing arts:** Art, commercial photography, commercial/advertising art, dance, design, fashion design, film/cinema, interior design, photography.

**Most popular majors.** Health sciences 9%, liberal arts 58%, security/protective services 12%.

**Computing on campus.** 180 workstations in library, computer center. Online library, wireless network available.

**Student life. Freshman orientation:** Available. **Activities:** Bands, choral groups, dance, drama, film society, literary magazine, music ensembles, musical theater, student government, student newspaper.

**Athletics. Intercollegiate:** Baseball M, basketball, cross-country, football (tackle) M, golf, soccer, softball W, tennis, track and field, volleyball W. **Team name:** Bulldogs.

**Student services.** Adult student services, career counseling, services for economically disadvantaged, student employment services, health services, on-campus daycare, personal counseling, placement for graduates, veterans' counselor. **Physically disabled:** Services for visually, hearing impaired. **Transfer:** Pre-admission transcript evaluation for new students. Transfer center, transfer adviser, college fairs on campus for students transferring to 4-year colleges.

**Contact.** Phone: (805) 922-6966 ext. 3248 Fax: (805) 922-3477 Adela Esquivel-Swinson, Director, Admissions and Records, Allan Hancock College, 800 South College Drive, Santa Maria, CA 93454-6399

## American Academy of Dramatic Arts: West
Los Angeles, California
www.aada.org

CB code: 7024

▶ Private 2-year performing arts college
▶ Commuter campus in very large city
▶ Application essay, interview required

**General.** Founded in 1974. Regionally accredited. **Enrollment:** 155 degree-seeking undergraduates. **Degrees:** 12 associate awarded. **Calendar:** Semester, limited summer session. **Full-time faculty:** 8 total. **Part-time faculty:** 13 total; 23% minority. **Class size:** 93% < 20, 7% 20-39. **Special facilities:** Performance theater.

**Student profile.**

| | | | |
|---|---|---|---|
| Out-of-state: | 25% | 25 or older: | 20% |

**Basis for selection.** Open admission, but selective for some programs. Each candidate evaluated individually; consideration based on dramatic ability and potential, academic qualifications and readiness, in terms of maturity and motivation. Auditions required.

**2009-2010 Annual costs.** Tuition/fees: $28,000. Books/supplies: $600.

**2008-2009 Financial aid. Non-need-based:** Scholarships awarded for academics, music/drama.

**Application procedures. Admission:** Priority date 3/1; deadline 7/25. $50 fee. Admission notification on a rolling basis. SAT or ACT recommended for applicants attending directly from high school. **Financial aid:** Priority date 7/1; no closing date. Institutional form required. Applicants notified on a rolling basis starting 6/1; must reply within 3 week(s) of notification.

**Academics.** Select group of students invited to return for additional year of study and performance after graduation in repertory situation. **Special study options:** Cross-registration, exchange student. Students may study 1 year in each of 2 campuses (NY and CA). **Credit/placement by examination:** AP, CLEP. **Support services:** Pre-admission summer program, tutoring, writing center.

**Majors. Visual/performing arts:** Acting.

**Computing on campus.** 10 workstations in computer center.

**Student life. Freshman orientation:** Mandatory. **Activities:** Student government.

**Student services.** Alcohol/substance abuse counseling, career counseling, financial aid counseling, personal counseling, veterans' counselor.

**Contact.** E-mail: khigginbotham@ca.aada.org
Phone: (323) 464-2777 ext. 103 Toll-free number: (800) 222-2867
Fax: (323) 464-1250
Karen Higginbotham, Director of Admissions, American Academy of Dramatic Arts: West, 1336 N. La Brea Avenue, Los Angeles, CA 90028

## American River College
Sacramento, California
www.arc.losrios.edu                    CB code: 4004

- Public 2-year community college
- Commuter campus in large city

**General.** Founded in 1955. Regionally accredited. **Enrollment:** 40,144 undergraduates. **Degrees:** 1,881 associate awarded. **Location:** 10 miles from downtown. **Calendar:** Semester, limited summer session. **Full-time faculty:** 380 total. **Part-time faculty:** 605 total.

**Basis for selection.** Open admission, but selective for some programs. Limited admission to nursing program. **Homeschooled:** Transcript of courses and grades, interview, letter of recommendation (nonparent) required.

**2009-2010 Annual costs.** Tuition/fees: $812; $6,512 out-of-state. Per-credit charge: $26 in-state; $216 out-of-state. Books/supplies: $1,638. Personal expenses: $2,826.

**Financial aid.** All financial aid based on need. Need-based aid available for part-time students.

**Application procedures. Admission:** No deadline. No application fee in-state; $181 out-of-state. Application must be submitted online. Admission notification on a rolling basis beginning on or about 7/1. **Financial aid:** Priority date 3/2; no closing date. FAFSA required. Applicants notified on a rolling basis starting 7/1; must reply within 2 week(s) of notification.

**Academics. Special study options:** Accelerated study, cooperative education, cross-registration, distance learning, ESL, honors, independent study, internships, liberal arts/career combination, study abroad, weekend college. **Credit/placement by examination:** AP, CLEP, IB. 15 credit hours maximum toward associate degree. **Support services:** Learning center, pre-admission summer program, reduced course load, remedial instruction, study skills assistance, tutoring, writing center.

**Majors. Architecture:** Landscape. **Business:** Accounting, administrative services, fashion, hospitality/recreation, management information systems, office/clerical, real estate. **Communications:** Journalism. **Communications technology:** Graphic/printing. **Computer sciences:** General, database management, networking, programming. **Conservation:** General. **Education:** Teacher assistance. **Engineering technology:** General, biomedical, drafting, electrical, GIS. **Family/consumer sciences:** General, child care, institutional food production. **Health:** Health services, nursing (RN), respiratory therapy technology. **Interdisciplinary:** Biological/physical sciences, gerontology. **Legal studies:** Paralegal. **Liberal arts:** Arts/sciences. **Mechanic/repair:** Automotive. **Parks/recreation:** General. **Personal/culinary services:** Culinary arts, mortuary science, restaurant/catering. **Protective services:** Fire safety technology, police science. **Visual/performing arts:** Dramatic, interior design.

**Computing on campus.** Online course registration, helpline available.

**Student life. Freshman orientation:** Available. **Activities:** Bands, choral groups, dance, drama, international student organizations, literary magazine, music ensembles, Model UN, musical theater, student government, student newspaper, symphony orchestra.

**Athletics. Intercollegiate:** Baseball M, basketball, cross-country, football (tackle) M, golf, soccer, softball W, swimming, tennis, track and field, volleyball W, water polo M. **Team name:** Beavers.

**Student services.** Adult student services, career counseling, services for economically disadvantaged, student employment services, financial aid counseling, health services, minority student services, on-campus daycare, personal counseling, placement for graduates, veterans' counselor. **Physically disabled:** Services for visually, speech, hearing impaired. **Learning disabled:** Comprehensive services available. **Transfer:** Transfer center, transfer adviser for students transferring to 4-year colleges.

**Contact.** Phone: (916) 484-8261 Fax: (916) 484-8864
Robin Neal, Dean of Enrollment Services, American River College, 4700 College Oak Drive, Sacramento, CA 95841

## Antelope Valley College
Lancaster, California
www.avc.edu                    CB code: 4005

- Public 2-year community college
- Commuter campus in large city

**General.** Founded in 1929. Regionally accredited. CSU Bakersfield extension office on campus. **Enrollment:** 12,069 degree-seeking undergraduates. **Degrees:** 847 associate awarded. **Location:** 50 miles from Los Angeles. **Calendar:** Semester, extensive summer session. **Full-time faculty:** 183 total. **Part-time faculty:** 397 total. **Class size:** 27% < 20, 63% 20-39, 6% 40-49, 3% 50-99, less than 1% >100. **Partnerships:** Formal partnerships with Lockheed Martin Corporation, Boeing Corporation.

**Transfer out. Colleges most students transferred to 2009:** California State University: Northridge, California State University: Bakersfield, University of California: Los Angeles.

**Basis for selection.** Open admission, but selective for some programs. Limited enrollment for nursing programs.

**2009-2010 Annual costs.** Tuition/fees: $782; $6,482 out-of-state. Per-credit charge: $26 in-state; $216 out-of-state. Books/supplies: $1,638. Personal expenses: $3,096.

**Financial aid. Need-based:** Need-based aid available for part-time students. Work-study available for part-time students.

**Application procedures. Admission:** No deadline. No application fee in-state; $175 out-of-state. Admission notification on a rolling basis. **Financial aid:** Priority date 3/2; no closing date. FAFSA, institutional form required. Applicants notified on a rolling basis starting 7/15; must reply within 2 week(s) of notification.

**Academics. Special study options:** Accelerated study, cooperative education, distance learning, double major, dual enrollment of high school students, ESL, honors, independent study, internships, study abroad, teacher certification program, weekend college. Bachelor's degree programs available on campus. License preparation in aviation, nursing, real estate. **Credit/placement by examination:** AP, CLEP, institutional tests. Maximum of 4 courses allowed. **Support services:** Learning center, reduced course load, remedial instruction, study skills assistance, tutoring, writing center.

**Majors. Agriculture:** Landscaping, ornamental horticulture. **Biology:** General. **Business:** General, administrative services, business admin, real estate. **Communications technology:** Graphic/printing. **Computer sciences:** General, computer graphics, computer science, data processing, information systems, programming. **Education:** Teacher assistance. **Engineering:** General. **Engineering technology:** Aerospace, construction, drafting. **Family/consumer sciences:** General, child care, child development, clothing/textiles, communication, family resources, food/nutrition, home furnishings. **Foreign languages:** American Sign Language. **Health:** Medical assistant, medical secretary, nursing (RN), office assistant. **Liberal arts:** Arts/sciences. **Math:** General. **Mechanic/repair:** Aircraft, auto body, automotive, electronics/electrical. **Parks/recreation:** Health/fitness. **Production:** Welding. **Protective services:** Fire safety technology. **Visual/performing arts:** General, cinematography, interior design, multimedia, photography.

**Computing on campus.** 300 workstations in library, computer center, student center. Online course registration, online library available.

**Student life. Freshman orientation:** Available. Preregistration for classes offered. Online orientation available. **Activities:** Bands, choral groups, dance, drama, music ensembles, Model UN, musical theater, student government, student newspaper, symphony orchestra.

**Athletics.** NCAA. **Intercollegiate:** Baseball M, basketball, cheerleading, cross-country, football (tackle) M, golf, soccer W, softball W, track and field, volleyball W. **Team name:** Marauders.

**Student services.** Adult student services, career counseling, services for economically disadvantaged, student employment services, financial aid counseling, health services, minority student services, on-campus daycare, personal counseling, veterans' counselor. **Physically disabled:** Services for visually, speech, hearing impaired. **Learning disabled:** Comprehensive services available. **Transfer:** Re-entry adviser for new students. Transfer center, transfer adviser, college fairs on campus for students transferring to 4-year colleges.

**Contact.** E-mail: registration@avc.edu
Phone: (661) 722-6300 ext. 6504 Fax: (661) 722-6531
LaDonna Trimble, Dean of Enrollment Services, Antelope Valley College, 3041 West Avenue K, Lancaster, CA 93536-5426

## Art Institute of California: Los Angeles
Santa Monica, California
www.artinstitutes.edu/losangeles                    CB code: 2490

- For-profit 2-year visual arts college
- Commuter campus in small city
- Application essay, interview required

Two-Year Colleges

**General.** Accredited by ACICS. **Enrollment:** 2,159 degree-seeking undergraduates. **Degrees:** 329 bachelor's, 105 associate awarded. **Calendar:** Continuous. **Full-time faculty:** 64 total. **Part-time faculty:** 63 total. **Class size:** 57% < 20, 43% 20-39.

**Basis for selection.** High school record and general appropriateness of educational background to specific program applied for most important. Portfolio, interview, standardized test scores also important. SAT or ACT recommended.

**2009-2010 Annual costs.** Tuition/fees: $24,244. Per-credit charge: $503. Apartment-style housing: $2,994/quarter for 2-bedroom. Books/supplies: $1,822.

**2009-2010 Financial aid. Need-based:** Need-based aid available for part-time students. Work-study available nights, weekends and for part-time students. **Non-need-based:** Scholarships awarded for academics.

**Application procedures. Admission:** No deadline. $50 fee. Admission notification on a rolling basis. **Financial aid:** No deadline. FAFSA required. Applicants notified on a rolling basis.

**Academics. Special study options:** Independent study, internships, study abroad. Bachelor's degree programs available on campus. **Credit/placement by examination:** AP, CLEP, SAT, ACT, institutional tests. **Support services:** Reduced course load, tutoring, writing center.

**Majors. Computer sciences:** Computer graphics, web page design. **Personal/culinary services:** Chef training, culinary arts, food prep. **Visual/performing arts:** Cinematography, commercial/advertising art, design, graphic design.

**Computing on campus.** 250 workstations in library, computer center. Student web hosting available.

**Student life. Freshman orientation:** Mandatory. Preregistration for classes offered. One day program before start of quarter. **Housing:** Guaranteed on-campus for all undergraduates. Apartments available. $250 deposit. **Activities:** Literary magazine, gay, lesbian, straight alliance.

**Athletics. Intramural:** Basketball, softball, volleyball.

**Student services.** Alcohol/substance abuse counseling, career counseling, student employment services, financial aid counseling, personal counseling, placement for graduates.

**Contact.** E-mail: ailaadm@aii.edu
Phone: (310) 752-4700 Toll-free number: (888) 646-4610
Fax: (310) 752-4708
Paul Sallenbach, Director of Admissions, Art Institute of California: Los Angeles, 2900 31st Street, Santa Monica, CA 90405-3035

## Art Institute of California: Sunnyvale
Sunnyvale, California
www.artinstitutes.edu/sunnyvale

- For-profit 2-year technical college
- Residential campus in very large city

**General.** Regionally accredited; also accredited by ACICS. Campus of Brooks College: Long Beach. **Enrollment:** 545 degree-seeking undergraduates. **Location:** 45 miles south of San Francisco. **Calendar:** Quarter, extensive summer session. **Full-time faculty:** 11 total. **Part-time faculty:** 15 total.

**Basis for selection.** Open admission. We have the Accuplacer placement system for English and Math. Students can use acceptable ACT or SAT scores to waive this test. **Homeschooled:** Transcript of courses and grades, state high school equivalency certificate required.

**2009-2010 Annual costs.** Tuition/fees: $24,194. Per-credit charge: $503. Room only: $7,200. Books/supplies: $3,088.

**Application procedures. Admission:** Priority date 10/8; deadline 10/8 (receipt date). $50 fee. Application must be submitted on paper.

**Academics. Special study options:** Bachelor's degree programs available on campus. **Credit/placement by examination:** CLEP, SAT, ACT.

**Majors. Computer sciences:** Web page design. **Personal/culinary services:** Chef training. **Visual/performing arts:** Graphic design.

**Contact.** Phone: (408) 962-6400
Liane Soohoo, Director of Admissions, Art Institute of California: Sunnyvale, 1120 Kifer Road, Sunnyvale, CA 94086

## Bakersfield College
Bakersfield, California
www.bakersfieldcollege.edu                CB code: 4015

- Public 2-year community college
- Commuter campus in small city

**General.** Founded in 1913. Regionally accredited. **Enrollment:** 17,945 undergraduates. **Degrees:** 993 associate awarded. **Location:** 114 miles from Los Angeles. **Calendar:** Semester, limited summer session. **Full-time faculty:** 249 total. **Part-time faculty:** 257 total. **Special facilities:** Planetarium.

**Basis for selection.** Open admission, but selective for some programs. Nursing and other allied health programs have additional admission requirements including required coursework.

**2009-2010 Annual costs.** Tuition/fees: $818; $6,848 out-of-state. Per-credit charge: $26 in-state; $227 out-of-state. Books/supplies: $1,638. Personal expenses: $2,150.

**Application procedures. Admission:** No deadline. No application fee. **Financial aid:** Priority date 3/2, closing date 6/30. FAFSA required. Applicants notified on a rolling basis starting 6/1; must reply within 2 week(s) of notification.

**Academics. Special study options:** Double major, dual enrollment of high school students. **Credit/placement by examination:** CLEP, institutional tests. 12 credit hours maximum toward associate degree. **Support services:** Learning center, pre-admission summer program, reduced course load, remedial instruction, tutoring.

**Majors. Agriculture:** Agribusiness operations, animal sciences, horticulture, ornamental horticulture. **Biology:** General, bacteriology. **Business:** Accounting, administrative services, business admin, management information systems, office technology, office/clerical, real estate. **Communications:** Broadcast journalism, journalism. **Communications technology:** General, graphic/printing. **Computer sciences:** Applications programming, data processing. **Conservation:** Forestry. **Construction:** Carpentry, masonry, pipefitting, power transmission. **Engineering technology:** Aerospace, drafting. **Family/consumer sciences:** General, food/nutrition, institutional food production. **Foreign languages:** German, Spanish. **Health:** Dental assistant, EMT paramedic, licensed practical nurse, medical radiologic technology/radiation therapy, nursing (RN), predental, premedicine, prepharmacy, preveterinary. **History:** General. **Legal studies:** Prelaw. **Liberal arts:** Arts/sciences. **Math:** General. **Mechanic/repair:** Automotive. **Parks/recreation:** General. **Personal/culinary services:** Culinary arts. **Philosophy/religion:** Philosophy. **Physical sciences:** Chemistry, geology, physics. **Production:** Woodworking. **Protective services:** Fire safety technology, police science. **Psychology:** General. **Social sciences:** Anthropology, criminology, economics, geography, political science, sociology. **Visual/performing arts:** Interior design, photography.

**Student life. Activities:** Bands, choral groups, dance, drama, literary magazine, music ensembles, radio station, student government, student newspaper.

**Athletics. Intercollegiate:** Baseball M, basketball, cross-country, diving, football (tackle) M, golf M, softball W, swimming, tennis, track and field, volleyball W, wrestling M. **Team name:** Renegades.

**Student services.** Career counseling, student employment services, health services, on-campus daycare. **Physically disabled:** Services for visually, speech, hearing impaired.

**Contact.** Phone: (661) 395-4301
Sue Vaughn, Director of Enrollment Services, Bakersfield College, 1801 Panorama Drive, Bakersfield, CA 93305

## Barstow Community College
Barstow, California
www.barstow.edu                CB code: 4020

- Public 2-year community college
- Commuter campus in large town

**General.** Founded in 1959. Regionally accredited. **Enrollment:** 5,087 undergraduates. **Degrees:** 342 associate awarded. **Location:** 70 miles from San Bernardino. **Calendar:** Semester, limited summer session. **Full-time faculty:** 35 total. **Part-time faculty:** 70 total.

## Student profile.

| | | | |
|---|---|---|---|
| Out-of-state: | 10% | **25 or older:** | 43% |

**Basis for selection.** Open admission.

**2009-2010 Annual costs.** Tuition/fees: $780; $6,120 out-of-state. Per-credit charge: $26 in-state; $204 out-of-state.

**2008-2009 Financial aid.** All financial aid based on need. 96% of total undergraduate aid awarded as scholarships/grants, 4% as loans/jobs. Need-based aid available for part-time students. Work-study available for part-time students.

**Application procedures. Admission:** No deadline. No application fee. Admission notification on a rolling basis. **Financial aid:** Closing date 6/17. FAFSA required. Applicants notified on a rolling basis starting 7/1.

**Academics. Special study options:** Accelerated study, cooperative education, distance learning, double major, dual enrollment of high school students, ESL, independent study, liberal arts/career combination. **Credit/placement by examination:** AP, CLEP, institutional tests. 30 credit hours maximum toward associate degree. **Support services:** Learning center, reduced course load, remedial instruction, study skills assistance, tutoring.

**Majors. Biology:** General. **Business:** General, accounting, office management, office/clerical. **Computer sciences:** General, applications programming, programming. **Education:** General, elementary, teacher assistance. **Engineering technology:** Automotive, construction. **Family/consumer sciences:** Child care. **Health:** Medical assistant. **Liberal arts:** Arts/sciences. **Math:** General. **Production:** Welding. **Protective services:** Fire safety technology, police science. **Social sciences:** General.

**Computing on campus.** 40 workstations in library, computer center. Online course registration, online library, wireless network available.

**Student life. Freshman orientation:** Available. Preregistration for classes offered. **Activities:** Bands, choral groups, dance, drama, music ensembles, musical theater, student government, Christian Club, Alpha Gamma Sigma, Phi Theta Kappa.

**Athletics.** NJCAA. **Intercollegiate:** Baseball M, basketball M, cross-country, softball W. **Intramural:** Badminton, baseball M, basketball, bowling, soccer, softball, swimming, tennis, volleyball. **Team name:** Vikings.

**Student services.** Adult student services, career counseling, services for economically disadvantaged, student employment services, financial aid counseling, personal counseling, placement for graduates, veterans' counselor. **Physically disabled:** Services for visually, speech, hearing impaired. **Transfer:** Pre-admission transcript evaluation for new students. Transfer center, transfer adviser, college fairs on campus for students transferring to 4-year colleges.

**Contact.** E-mail: admit@barstow.edu
Phone: (760) 252-2411 ext. 7236 Fax: (760) 252-6754
Heather Caldon, Admissions, Records and Financial Aid Manager, Barstow Community College, 2700 Barstow Road, Barstow, CA 92311-9984

## Berkeley City College
### Berkeley, California
### www.berkeleycitycollege.edu          CB code: 7711

- Public 2-year community college
- Commuter campus in small city

**General.** Founded in 1974. Regionally accredited. **Enrollment:** 7,300 undergraduates. **Degrees:** 96 associate awarded. **Location:** 15 miles from San Francisco. **Calendar:** Semester, limited summer session. **Full-time faculty:** 49 total. **Part-time faculty:** 137 total.

**Basis for selection.** Open admission.

**2009-2010 Annual costs.** Tuition/fees: $814; $6,514 out-of-state. Per-credit charge: $26 in-state; $216 out-of-state. Books/supplies: $1,450. Personal expenses: $2,600.

**Financial aid.** All financial aid based on need. Need-based aid available for part-time students. Work-study available for part-time students.

**Application procedures. Admission:** No deadline. No application fee. Admission notification on a rolling basis. **Financial aid:** No deadline. Applicants notified on a rolling basis.

**Academics. Special study options:** Accelerated study, cooperative education, cross-registration, distance learning, dual enrollment of high school students, ESL, honors, independent study, internships, liberal arts/career combination, study abroad, weekend college. **Credit/placement by examination:** CLEP, institutional tests. 6 credit hours maximum toward associate degree. **Support services:** Learning center, reduced course load, remedial instruction, study skills assistance, tutoring, writing center.

**Majors. Biology:** Biotechnology. **Business:** Business admin, office/clerical, small business admin. **Communications technology:** General. **Computer sciences:** General. **Foreign languages:** Sign language interpretation. **Liberal arts:** Arts/sciences, humanities. **Science technology:** Biological. **Social sciences:** General. **Visual/performing arts:** Art. **Other:** Multimedia arts.

**Computing on campus.** Commuter students can connect to campus network. Online course registration, online library, wireless network available.

**Student life. Freshman orientation:** Mandatory. Preregistration for classes offered. **Housing:** Berkeley City College students can apply for UC Berkeley off-campus coops if they intend to transfer. **Activities:** Choral groups, dance, film society, international student organizations, literary magazine, student government, Phi Theta Kappa, Spanish Club, X Club, Bahai Club, Black Students Union, Global Studies Club, Associated Students of Berkeley City College, Digital Arts Club, Milvia Street Literary Magazine, Film Club.

**Student services.** Adult student services, career counseling, services for economically disadvantaged, student employment services, financial aid counseling, minority student services, personal counseling, veterans' counselor. **Physically disabled:** Services for visually, speech, hearing impaired. **Learning disabled:** Comprehensive services available. **Transfer:** Transfer center, transfer adviser, college fairs on campus for students transferring to 4-year colleges.

**Contact.** Phone: (510) 981-2805 Fax: (510) 841-7333
Loretta Newsom, Admissions and Records Specialist, Berkeley City College, 2050 Center Street, Berkeley, CA 94704

## Bryan College: Los Angeles
### Los Angeles, California
### www.bryancollege.edu

- For-profit 2-year virtual technical and career college
- Commuter campus in very large city

**General.** Regionally accredited; also accredited by ACICS. **Enrollment:** 615 degree-seeking undergraduates. **Degrees:** 2 associate awarded. **Location:** Downtown. **Calendar:** Quarter, extensive summer session. **Full-time faculty:** 28 total; 89% women. **Part-time faculty:** 10 total; 50% women.

**Basis for selection.** Open admission, but selective for some programs. **Homeschooled:** State high school equivalency certificate required.

**2010-2011 Annual costs.** Tuition/fees: $19,200.

**Application procedures. Admission:** No deadline. $25 fee. Admission notification on a rolling basis.

**Academics. Special study options:** Distance learning. **Credit/placement by examination:** CLEP. **Support services:** Learning center, remedial instruction, study skills assistance, tutoring.

**Majors. Legal studies:** Court reporting. **Other:** Advanced health and fitness training.

**Computing on campus.** PC or laptop required. Commuter students can connect to campus network. Online course registration, online library, helpline, repair service, wireless network available.

**Student life. Freshman orientation:** Mandatory.

**Student services.** Adult student services, alcohol/substance abuse counseling, career counseling, student employment services, financial aid counseling, health services, legal services, personal counseling, placement for graduates.

**Contact.** E-mail: info@bryancollege.edu
Phone: (877) 484-8850 Fax: (213) 483-3936
Mark Evans, Director of Admissions, Bryan College: Los Angeles, 3580 Wilshire Boulevard, Suite 400, Los Angeles, CA 90010

## Bryan College: Sacramento
### Gold River, California
### www.bryancollege.com

- For-profit 2-year technical college
- Very large city
- Interview required

**General.** Accredited by ACCSC. **Enrollment:** 164 degree-seeking undergraduates. **Degrees:** 114 associate awarded. **Location:** 10 miles from downtown Sacramento. **Calendar:** Continuous, limited summer session. **Full-time faculty:** 25 total. **Part-time faculty:** 10 total.

**Basis for selection.** Interview, interest important.

**2010-2011 Annual costs.** Tuition/fees (projected): $12,000. Books and supplies included in tuition cost.

**Application procedures. Admission:** No deadline. $35 fee. **Financial aid:** No deadline.

**Academics. Special study options:** Massage therapy students get hands-on experience in public massage clinic. Personal training students work with fitness professionals to gain field experience. **Credit/placement by examination:** CLEP.

**Majors. Biology:** Exercise physiology. **Health:** Massage therapy. **Legal studies:** Court reporting.

**Contact.** E-mail: admissions@bryancollege.com
Phone: (916) 649-2400 Toll-free number: (866) 649-2400
Fax: (916) 641-8649
Jordan Farmer, Director of Admissions, Bryan College: Sacramento, 2317 Gold Meadow Way, Gold River, CA 95670

## Butte College
**Oroville, California**
**www.butte.edu**                          **CB code: 4226**

- Public 2-year community college
- Commuter campus in small city

**General.** Founded in 1966. Regionally accredited. **Enrollment:** 14,417 undergraduates. **Degrees:** 1,076 associate awarded. **Location:** 100 miles from Sacramento. **Calendar:** Semester, extensive summer session. **Full-time faculty:** 130 total. **Part-time faculty:** 470 total. **Special facilities:** 900-acre wild game refuge, nature trails.

**Basis for selection.** Open admission, but selective for some programs. Nursing, allied health programs have special requirements. Interviews required for allied health applicants.

**2009-2010 Annual costs.** Tuition/fees: $960; $6,660 out-of-state. Per-credit charge: $26 in-state; $216 out-of-state. Books/supplies: $700. Personal expenses: $1,954.

**Application procedures. Admission:** No deadline. No application fee. Admission notification on a rolling basis. **Financial aid:** Priority date 5/1; no closing date. FAFSA required. Applicants notified on a rolling basis starting 8/1.

**Academics. Special study options:** Cooperative education, cross-registration, distance learning, double major, dual enrollment of high school students, ESL, honors, independent study, study abroad. License preparation in nursing, paramedic, real estate. **Credit/placement by examination:** CLEP, institutional tests. 9 credit hours maximum toward associate degree. **Support services:** Learning center, remedial instruction, study skills assistance, tutoring.

**Majors. Agriculture:** Agronomy, animal sciences, business, horticulture, ornamental horticulture. **Business:** General, accounting, administrative services, business admin, fashion, management information systems, marketing, office technology, real estate, tourism promotion. **Communications:** Broadcast journalism, journalism. **Communications technology:** General, graphic/printing. **Computer sciences:** General, applications programming, networking. **Construction:** Maintenance. **Education:** General, bilingual, early childhood, physical. **Engineering technology:** Civil, construction, drafting, electrical. **Family/consumer sciences:** General, child care. **Health:** Cardiovascular technology, EMT paramedic, licensed practical nurse, medical assistant, medical secretary, nursing (RN), respiratory therapy technology, substance abuse counseling. **Legal studies:** Court reporting, legal secretary, paralegal, prelaw. **Liberal arts:** Arts/sciences. **Math:** General. **Mechanic/repair:** Automotive. **Parks/recreation:** Facilities management. **Personal/culinary services:** Cosmetic. **Production:** Welding. **Protective services:** Fire safety technology, police science. **Social sciences:** General. **Visual/performing arts:** Ceramics, commercial photography, commercial/advertising art, fashion design, photography, studio arts.

**Computing on campus.** 200 workstations in library, computer center. Wireless network available.

**Student life. Activities:** Bands, drama, film society, music ensembles, radio station, student government, student newspaper, symphony orchestra, TV station.

**Athletics.** NJCAA. **Intercollegiate:** Baseball M, basketball, cross-country, field hockey W, football (tackle) M, golf, soccer, softball W, tennis, track and field, volleyball W. **Team name:** Roadrunners.

**Student services.** Adult student services, career counseling, student employment services, health services, on-campus daycare, personal counseling, placement for graduates, veterans' counselor. **Physically disabled:** Services for visually, speech, hearing impaired. **Transfer:** Re-entry adviser for new students. Transfer center, transfer adviser for students transferring to 4-year colleges.

**Contact.** E-mail: admissions@butte.edu
Phone: (530) 895-2361 Fax: (530) 895-2411
Clinton Slaughter, Director of Admissions and Records, Butte College, 3536 Butte Campus Drive, Oroville, CA 95965

## Cabrillo College
**Aptos, California**
**www.cabrillo.edu**                          **CB code: 4084**

- Public 2-year community college
- Commuter campus in large town

**General.** Founded in 1959. Regionally accredited. A signatory of the American College and University Presidents Climate Commitment to reduce emissions of greenhouse gases. **Enrollment:** 4,751 full-time, degree-seeking students. **Degrees:** 787 associate awarded. **Location:** 25 miles from San Jose. **Calendar:** Semester, extensive summer session. **Full-time faculty:** 217 total; 22% have terminal degrees. **Part-time faculty:** 403 total. **Special facilities:** Observatory, planetarium, horticulture garden.

**Student profile.**

| | | | |
|---|---|---|---|
| Out-of-state: | 2% | 25 or older: | 52% |

**Transfer out. Colleges most students transferred to 2009:** University of California-Santa Cruz, San Jose State University, California State University-Monterey Bay.

**Basis for selection.** Open admission, but selective for some programs. Special prerequisite requirements for nursing, dental hygiene, and radiologic technology. International applicants have special admission requirements.

**2009-2010 Annual costs.** Tuition/fees: $826; $6,646 out-of-state. Per-credit charge: $26 in-state; $220 out-of-state. Books/supplies: $1,566. Personal expenses: $2,754.

**2008-2009 Financial aid. Need-based:** Need-based aid available for part-time students.

**Application procedures. Admission:** No deadline. No application fee. Admission notification on a rolling basis beginning on or about 6/1. **Financial aid:** No deadline. FAFSA, institutional form required. Applicants notified on a rolling basis starting 7/31; must reply within 3 week(s) of notification.

**Academics. Special study options:** Cooperative education, distance learning, dual enrollment of high school students, honors, independent study, internships, liberal arts/career combination, study abroad. License preparation in dental hygiene, nursing, radiology. **Credit/placement by examination:** AP, CLEP, institutional tests. **Support services:** Learning center, pre-admission summer program, reduced course load, remedial instruction, study skills assistance, tutoring, writing center.

**Majors. Agriculture:** Ornamental horticulture. **Area/ethnic studies:** Asian. **Biology:** General. **Business:** General, accounting, banking/financial services, business admin, construction management, entrepreneurial studies, office technology, real estate. **Communications:** Journalism. **Computer sciences:** General, data processing. **Engineering technology:** Hazardous materials, solar energy. **Family/consumer sciences:** General, child care. **Foreign languages:** General, French, German, Italian, Japanese, Spanish. **Health:** Dental hygiene, licensed practical nurse, medical assistant, medical radiologic technology/radiation therapy, nursing (RN). **History:** General. **Liberal arts:** Arts/sciences, library assistant. **Math:** General. **Mechanic/repair:** Industrial. **Physical sciences:** Chemistry, physics. **Protective services:** Firefighting, police science. **Psychology:** General. **Social sciences:** General, anthropology, economics, geography, political science, sociology. **Visual/performing arts:** General, art, dance, studio arts.

**Computing on campus.** 350 workstations in library, computer center, student center. Online course registration, wireless network available.

**Student life. Freshman orientation:** Available. Preregistration for classes offered. **Activities:** Bands, choral groups, dance, drama, music ensembles, musical theater, student government, student newspaper, various clubs, literacy, recreational, cultural and/or ethnic organizations.

**Athletics. Intercollegiate:** Baseball M, basketball, cross-country, diving, football (tackle) M, golf M, soccer M, softball W, swimming, tennis, track and field, volleyball W, water polo M. **Team name:** Seahawks.

**Student services.** Adult student services, career counseling, services for economically disadvantaged, student employment services, financial aid counseling, health services, personal counseling, placement for graduates, veterans' counselor. **Physically disabled:** Services for visually, speech, hearing impaired. **Transfer:** Transfer center, transfer adviser for students transferring to 4-year colleges.

**Contact.** Phone: (831) 479-6201 Fax: (831) 479-5782
Nan McAden, Director of Admissions and Records, Cabrillo College, 6500 Soquel Drive, Aptos, CA 95003

## California Christian College
### Fresno, California
### www.calchristiancollege.org

- Private 2-year Bible college
- Large city

**General.** Regionally accredited; also accredited by TRACS. **Enrollment:** 25 degree-seeking undergraduates. **Degrees:** 2 bachelor's, 4 associate awarded. **Calendar:** Semester. **Full-time faculty:** 2 total. **Part-time faculty:** 10 total.

**2009-2010 Annual costs.** Tuition/fees: $8,950. Per-credit charge: $285. Room/board: $4,050.

**Academics. Credit/placement by examination:** CLEP.

**Majors. Other:** Bible and Christian Ministry.

**Contact.** E-mail: cccadmissions@sbcglobal.net
Mallory Breshears, Admissions, California Christian College, 4881 East University Avenue, Fresno, CA 93703

## California Culinary Academy
### San Francisco, California
### www.caculinary.edu                    CB code: 2209

- For-profit 2-year culinary school and career college
- Commuter campus in very large city
- Interview required

**General.** Founded in 1977. Accredited by ACCSC. All programs offered sanctioned by Le Cordon Bleu. **Enrollment:** 775 degree-seeking undergraduates. **Degrees:** 374 associate awarded. **Location:** Downtown. **Calendar:** Continuous. **Full-time faculty:** 29 total. **Part-time faculty:** 14 total. **Special facilities:** Student-staffed public restaurant, mixology lab, gaming room, professional production kitchens, demonstration kitchens, pastry kitchens, confisseries, butchery lab, culinary library.

**Basis for selection.** Open admission. The school has an open enrollment policy but the student needs to complete an interview with an admissions representative, pass a short entrance exam, have a High School diploma or equivalent before starting school. Wonderlic testing required for all programs.

**2009-2010 Annual costs.** Tuition/fees: $37,285. Tuition quoted is for 12 months.

**Application procedures. Admission:** No deadline. $50 fee. Admission notification on a rolling basis. **Financial aid:** No deadline. FAFSA required. Applicants notified on a rolling basis; must reply within 1 week(s) of notification.

**Academics. Special study options:** Internships. **Credit/placement by examination:** CLEP. **Support services:** Study skills assistance, tutoring.

**Majors. Personal/culinary services:** Culinary arts, restaurant/catering.

**Computing on campus.** Student web hosting, wireless network available.

**Student life. Freshman orientation:** Mandatory. **Housing:** Coed dorms available. $600 fully refundable deposit. **Activities:** Brewing arts association, Cuisine Des Femmes, Asian food club, baking and pastry arts club, dinner club, wine club.

**Student services.** Career counseling, student employment services, financial aid counseling, placement for graduates. **Transfer:** Re-entry adviser, pre-admission transcript evaluation for new students.

**Contact.** E-mail: admissions@caculinary.edu
Phone: (415) 771-3500 Toll-free number: (800) 229-2433
Fax: (415) 621-5625
Jose Saez, Director of Admissions, California Culinary Academy, 350 Rhode Island, San Francisco, CA 94103

## California School of Culinary Arts
### Pasadena, California
### www.chefs.edu/los-angeles/#

- For-profit 2-year culinary school
- Commuter campus in very large city
- Interview required

**General.** Accredited by ACICS. Le Cordon Bleu college. **Enrollment:** 1,355 degree-seeking undergraduates. **Degrees:** 603 associate awarded. **Location:** 15 miles from downtown Los Angeles. **Calendar:** Continuous, extensive summer session. **Full-time faculty:** 80 total; 1% have terminal degrees, 30% minority, 38% women. **Part-time faculty:** 11 total; 36% minority, 54% women. **Special facilities:** Fine-dining restaurant and casual cafe where students gain practical work experience.

**Basis for selection.** Open admission. High school diploma/GED, entrance examination required. Students whose first language is not English are required to submit evidence of English Proficiency. This may be done by submitting a TOEFL test score of 500 or higher (for the CPT version, a score of 150 or higher). Entrance Test is required by state agency for diploma programs. Wonderlic SLE Exam used to comply with these regulations. **Learning Disabled:** Students requesting special needs and services required to submit Application for Auxiliary Aid request. Application must include supporting documentation as evidence of disability.

**2009-2010 Annual costs.** Diploma programs vary in cost. Associate of Occupational Studies in culinary arts program tuition: $43,950, fees $2,800. Associate of Occupational Studies in hospitality/restaurant management tuition: $31,000, fees $3,470. Associate of Occupational Studies in patisserie and baking program tuition: $35,750, fees $ 2,760. Books/supplies: $1,500. Personal expenses: $1,347.

**2008-2009 Financial aid. Need-based:** Need-based aid available for part-time students. Work-study available nights and weekends.

**Application procedures. Admission:** No deadline. $75 fee. Admission notification on a rolling basis. **Financial aid:** No deadline. FAFSA required. Applicants notified on a rolling basis.

**Academics. Credit/placement by examination:** AP, CLEP. **Support services:** Learning center, study skills assistance, tutoring.

**Majors. Personal/culinary services:** Chef training, restaurant/catering.

**Computing on campus.** 40 workstations in library, computer center, student center. Commuter students can connect to campus network. Online library available.

**Student life. Freshman orientation:** Mandatory. Preregistration for classes offered. **Activities:** Student newspaper.

**Student services.** Adult student services, career counseling, financial aid counseling, placement for graduates. **Transfer:** Re-entry adviser, pre-admission transcript evaluation for new students.

**Contact.** E-mail: admissionsinfo@csca.edu
Phone: (626) 229-1300 Toll-free number: (888) 900-2433
Fax: (626) 403-4835
Robert Woy, Vice President of Admissions, California School of Culinary Arts, 530 East Colorado Boulevard, Pasadena, CA 91101

## Canada College
### Redwood City, California
### www.canadacollege.edu                    CB code: 4109

- Public 2-year community college
- Commuter campus in small city

**General.** Founded in 1968. Regionally accredited. **Enrollment:** 7,287 undergraduates. **Degrees:** 220 associate awarded. **Location:** 20 miles from San Francisco. **Calendar:** Semester, limited summer session. **Full-time faculty:** 65 total. **Part-time faculty:** 182 total.

**Transfer out. Colleges most students transferred to 2009:** San Francisco State, San Jose State, College of Notre de Namur, California State University-East Bay.

**Basis for selection.** Open admission, but selective for some programs. Special admission to radiologic technology programs.

**2009-2010 Annual costs.** Tuition/fees: $798; $6,528 out-of-state. Per-credit charge: $26 in-state; $217 out-of-state. Books/supplies: $1,260. Personal expenses: $2,376.

**Application procedures. Admission:** No deadline. No application fee. Admission notification on a rolling basis. **Financial aid:** Priority date 5/1; no closing date. FAFSA required. Applicants notified on a rolling basis starting 7/15; must reply within 2 week(s) of notification.

**Academics. Special study options:** Cooperative education, cross-registration, distance learning, double major, dual enrollment of high school students, ESL, independent study, internships, study abroad. Bachelor's degree programs available on campus. **Credit/placement by examination:** AP, CLEP, IB, institutional tests. 12 credit hours maximum toward associate degree. **Support services:** Learning center, reduced course load, remedial instruction, study skills assistance, tutoring, writing center.

**Majors. Biology:** General. **Business:** General, accounting, administrative services, banking/financial services, business admin, fashion, management information systems, management science, office technology, office/clerical, tourism/travel. **Communications:** Journalism. **Computer sciences:** General, applications programming, programming. **Education:** Early childhood. **Engineering technology:** Computer hardware. **Family/consumer sciences:** General, child care. **Foreign languages:** French, Spanish. **Health:** Medical radiologic technology/radiation therapy, ophthalmic lab technology. **History:** General. **Legal studies:** Paralegal. **Liberal arts:** Arts/sciences. **Math:** General. **Philosophy/religion:** Philosophy. **Physical sciences:** Chemistry, physics. **Psychology:** General. **Public administration:** Human services. **Social sciences:** General, anthropology, geography, political science. **Visual/performing arts:** Art, dramatic, interior design, multimedia.

**Computing on campus.** 300 workstations in library, computer center. Online course registration, wireless network available.

**Student life. Freshman orientation:** Available. Preregistration for classes offered. **Activities:** Concert band, choral groups, dance, drama, music ensembles, student government, symphony orchestra, Latin American club, Rotarians, international student club, black student union.

**Athletics.** NJCAA. **Intercollegiate:** Baseball M, basketball M, golf M, soccer, tennis M. **Team name:** Colts.

**Student services.** Adult student services, career counseling, health services, personal counseling, veterans' counselor. **Physically disabled:** Services for visually, hearing impaired. **Transfer:** Transfer center, transfer adviser, college fairs on campus for students transferring to 4-year colleges.

**Contact.** Phone: (650) 306-3226 Fax: (650) 306-3113
Ruth Miller, Assistant Registrar, Canada College, 4200 Farm Hill Boulevard, Redwood City, CA 94061

## Cerritos College
**Norwalk, California**      **CB member**
www.cerritos.edu      **CB code: 4083**

- Public 2-year community college
- Commuter campus in large city

**General.** Founded in 1955. Regionally accredited. **Enrollment:** 25,000 undergraduates. **Degrees:** 1,391 associate awarded. **Location:** 15 miles from Los Angeles. **Calendar:** Semester, limited summer session. **Full-time faculty:** 290 total. **Part-time faculty:** 590 total. **Special facilities:** Health occupations lab.

**Basis for selection.** Open admission, but selective for some programs. Limited admissions to nursing program.

**2009-2010 Annual costs.** Tuition/fees: $832; $6,532 out-of-state. Per-credit charge: $26 in-state; $216 out-of-state. Books/supplies: $1,566. Personal expenses: $2,772.

**Application procedures. Admission:** No deadline. No application fee. Admission notification on a rolling basis. **Financial aid:** Priority date 5/8; no closing date. FAFSA required. Applicants notified on a rolling basis; must reply within 2 week(s) of notification.

**Academics. Special study options:** Cooperative education, distance learning, dual enrollment of high school students, honors. Bachelor's degree programs available on campus. License preparation in dental hygiene, nursing, physical therapy. **Credit/placement by examination:** CLEP, institutional tests. 12 credit hours maximum toward associate degree. **Support services:** Learning center, remedial instruction, tutoring.

**Majors. Agriculture:** Ornamental horticulture. **Area/ethnic studies:** Chicano/Hispanic-American/Latino. **Biology:** General, bacteriology, biomedical sciences, botany, zoology. **Business:** General, accounting, administrative services, banking/financial services, business admin, human resources, logistics, office management, office/clerical, real estate. **Communications:** Journalism. **Computer sciences:** General, applications programming, data processing, programming, systems analysis. **Conservation:** Wildlife. **Education:** Bilingual, early childhood, special, teacher assistance. **Engineering technology:** Drafting, electrical, manufacturing, plastics, robotics. **Family/consumer sciences:** General, clothing/textiles, institutional food production. **Foreign languages:** French, German, Spanish. **Health:** Dental assistant, dental hygiene, licensed practical nurse, medical assistant, medical records technology, nursing (RN), physical therapy assistant. **History:** General. **Legal studies:** Court reporting, paralegal. **Math:** General. **Mechanic/repair:** General, auto body, electronics/electrical. **Parks/recreation:** General. **Philosophy/religion:** Philosophy. **Physical sciences:** Chemistry, geology, physics, planetary. **Protective services:** Police science. **Psychology:** General. **Social sciences:** Anthropology, economics, geography, political science, sociology. **Visual/performing arts:** Art, dramatic, interior design, photography.

**Computing on campus.** 100 workstations in computer center.

**Student life. Activities:** Bands, choral groups, dance, drama, film society, literary magazine, music ensembles, musical theater, radio station, student government, student newspaper, symphony orchestra, Ahora, Indian club, Vietnamese club, Black Student Union.

**Athletics.** NJCAA. **Intercollegiate:** Baseball M, basketball, cross-country, diving, football (tackle) M, golf M, soccer M, softball W, swimming, tennis, track and field, volleyball W, water polo M, wrestling M. **Team name:** Falcons.

**Student services.** Adult student services, career counseling, financial aid counseling, health services, on-campus daycare, personal counseling, veterans' counselor, women's services. **Physically disabled:** Services for visually, speech, hearing impaired. **Transfer:** Transfer adviser, college fairs on campus for students transferring to 4-year colleges.

**Contact.** Phone: (562) 860-2451 ext. 2211 Fax: (562) 860-9680
Stephanie Murguia, Dean, Admissions and Records, Cerritos College, 11110 Alondra Boulevard, Norwalk, CA 90650

## Cerro Coso Community College
**Ridgecrest, California**
www.cerrocoso.edu      **CB code: 4027**

- Public 2-year community college
- Commuter campus in large town

**General.** Founded in 1973. Regionally accredited. **Enrollment:** 5,506 undergraduates. **Degrees:** 194 associate awarded. **Location:** 120 miles from Bakersfield. **Calendar:** Semester, limited summer session. **Full-time faculty:** 55 total; 27% have terminal degrees. **Part-time faculty:** 140 total. **Class size:** 44% < 20, 52% 20-39, 3% 40-49, 1% 50-99. **Special facilities:** Nature preserve, sculpture garden.

**Student profile.**

| | | | |
|---|---|---|---|
| Out-of-state: | 2% | 25 or older: | 63% |

**Basis for selection.** Open admission. Interview required of nursing majors.

**2009-2010 Annual costs.** Tuition/fees: $780; $6,810 out-of-state. Per-credit charge: $26 in-state; $227 out-of-state. Books/supplies: $1,638. Personal expenses: $2,150.

**Financial aid. Need-based:** Need-based aid available for part-time students. Work-study available nights and for part-time students.

**Application procedures. Admission:** No deadline. No application fee. Admission notification on a rolling basis. **Financial aid:** Priority date 5/15;

no closing date. FAFSA required. Applicants notified on a rolling basis starting 6/1; must reply within 2 week(s) of notification.

**Academics. Special study options:** Cooperative education, distance learning, double major, dual enrollment of high school students, ESL, honors, independent study, internships, study abroad. License preparation in nursing. **Credit/placement by examination:** AP, CLEP. 30 credit hours maximum toward associate degree. **Support services:** GED preparation and test center, learning center, remedial instruction, study skills assistance, tutoring.

**Majors. Business:** General, administrative services, business admin, office management, office technology, office/clerical. **Computer sciences:** General. **Education:** Early childhood. **Engineering technology:** General, drafting, electrical. **Family/consumer sciences:** Child care. **Health:** Licensed practical nurse. **Interdisciplinary:** Biological/physical sciences. **Liberal arts:** Arts/sciences. **Mechanic/repair:** Auto body, heating/ac/refrig. **Parks/recreation:** Facilities management. **Physical sciences:** General. **Protective services:** Fire safety technology, police science. **Social sciences:** General. **Visual/performing arts:** Art.

**Most popular majors.** Business/marketing 18%, computer/information sciences 6%, health sciences 6%, liberal arts 52%, social sciences 13%.

**Computing on campus.** Online course registration, online library available.

**Student life. Freshman orientation:** Available. One week before class starts. **Activities:** Bands, choral groups, drama, literary magazine, student government, student newspaper, symphony orchestra.

**Athletics. Intercollegiate:** Baseball M, basketball W. **Team name:** Coyotes.

**Student services.** Career counseling, student employment services, financial aid counseling, on-campus daycare, personal counseling, placement for graduates, veterans' counselor. **Physically disabled:** Services for visually, speech, hearing impaired. **Learning disabled:** Comprehensive services available. **Transfer:** Transfer adviser, college fairs on campus for students transferring to 4-year colleges.

**Contact.** E-mail: jboard@cerrocoso.edu
Phone: (760) 384-6357 Fax: (760) 384-6377
Dave Cornell, Director of Admission and Records, Cerro Coso Community College, 3000 College Heights Boulevard, Ridgecrest, CA 93555-7777

## Chabot College
### Hayward, California
### www.chabotcollege.edu
**CB code: 4725**

- Public 2-year community college
- Commuter campus in large city

**General.** Founded in 1961. Regionally accredited. **Enrollment:** 9,091 degree-seeking undergraduates; 5,778 non-degree-seeking students. **Degrees:** 706 associate awarded. **ROTC:** Army, Air Force. **Location:** 30 miles from San Francisco, 15 miles from Berkeley. **Calendar:** Semester, extensive summer session. **Full-time faculty:** 184 total; 28% minority. **Part-time faculty:** 338 total; 28% minority. **Special facilities:** Planetarium.

**Student profile.** Among degree-seeking undergraduates, 10% already have a bachelor's degree or higher, 1,907 enrolled as first-time, first-year students.

| | | | |
|---|---|---|---|
| Part-time: | 63% | Women: | 55% |
| Out-of-state: | 1% | 25 or older: | 45% |

**Transfer out. Colleges most students transferred to 2009:** CSU: East Bay, San Jose State University, UC: Berkeley, San Francisco State University, UC: Davis.

**Basis for selection.** Open admission. Special requirements for nursing, dental hygiene, and paramedic programs.

**2009-2010 Annual costs.** Tuition/fees: $808; $6,508 out-of-state. Per-credit charge: $26 in-state; $216 out-of-state. Books/supplies: $1,638. Personal expenses: $2,772.

**Financial aid. Need-based:** Work-study available nights, weekends and for part-time students. **Additional information:** Tuition and/or fee waivers for low-income students.

**Application procedures. Admission:** No deadline. No application fee. Admission notification on a rolling basis. Early action available for local

high school students only. **Financial aid:** Priority date 8/1; no closing date. FAFSA, institutional form required. Applicants notified on a rolling basis.

**Academics. Special study options:** Cooperative education, cross-registration, distance learning, double major, dual enrollment of high school students, ESL, independent study, internships, liberal arts/career combination, student-designed major, study abroad, weekend college. License preparation in dental hygiene, nursing, real estate. **Credit/placement by examination:** CLEP, institutional tests. 15 credit hours maximum toward associate degree. English and math tests required for placement. **Support services:** Learning center, pre-admission summer program, reduced course load, remedial instruction, study skills assistance, tutoring, writing center.

**Majors. Biology:** General. **Business:** General, accounting, administrative services, banking/financial services, logistics, management information systems, management science, office management, office technology, office/clerical, real estate, sales/distribution, tourism/travel. **Communications:** Broadcast journalism, journalism. **Communications technology:** General, radio/tv. **Computer sciences:** General, applications programming, computer science, data processing, information systems, programming. **Construction:** Maintenance, power transmission. **Education:** Early childhood, teacher assistance. **Engineering:** General. **Engineering technology:** Architectural, civil, drafting, electrical, surveying. **Family/consumer sciences:** Child care, clothing/textiles. **Foreign languages:** French, German, Italian, Portuguese, Spanish. **Health:** Clinical lab technology, dental hygiene, medical assistant, medical records admin, medical records technology, nursing (RN), predental, premedicine, prepharmacy, preveterinary. **History:** General. **Legal studies:** Court reporting, legal secretary, prelaw. **Liberal arts:** Arts/sciences, library assistant. **Math:** General. **Mechanic/repair:** Auto body, automotive, electronics/electrical. **Parks/recreation:** General. **Personal/culinary services:** General. **Philosophy/religion:** Philosophy. **Physical sciences:** Physics. **Production:** Welding. **Protective services:** Firefighting, police science. **Psychology:** General. **Social sciences:** General, criminology, geography, political science, sociology. **Transportation:** Aviation, flight attendant. **Visual/performing arts:** Art, ceramics, commercial/advertising art, dance, dramatic, drawing, music performance, painting, photography, sculpture, studio arts.

**Most popular majors.** Business/marketing 10%, health sciences 15%, liberal arts 50%.

**Computing on campus.** Online course registration, wireless network available.

**Student life. Freshman orientation:** Available. Preregistration for classes offered. Introduction to college experience, programs, services, and registration process. **Activities:** Bands, choral groups, drama, film society, literary magazine, musical theater, radio station, student government, student newspaper, TV station, various religious, political, ethnic, and social service organizations.

**Athletics.** NJCAA. **Intercollegiate:** Baseball M, basketball, cross-country, football (tackle) M, golf M, soccer, softball W, swimming, tennis, track and field, volleyball W, water polo W, wrestling M. **Intramural:** Archery, badminton, basketball, bowling, handball, racquetball, soccer, softball, table tennis, tennis, volleyball. **Team name:** Gladiators.

**Student services.** Adult student services, career counseling, student employment services, on-campus daycare, personal counseling, placement for graduates. **Physically disabled:** Services for visually, speech, hearing impaired. **Transfer:** Re-entry adviser for new students. Transfer center, college fairs on campus for students transferring to 4-year colleges.

**Contact.** E-mail: jyoung@chabotcollege.edu
Phone: (510) 723-6700 Fax: (510) 723-7510
Judy Young, Director of Admissions & Records, Chabot College, 25555 Hesperian Boulevard, Hayward, CA 94545

## Chaffey College
### Rancho Cucamonga, California
### www.chaffey.edu
**CB code: 4046**

- Public 2-year community college
- Commuter campus in small city

**General.** Founded in 1883. Regionally accredited. **Enrollment:** 20,893 undergraduates. **Degrees:** 1,292 associate awarded. **Location:** 50 miles from Los Angeles. **Calendar:** Semester, limited summer session. **Special facilities:** Nature preserve, natural history collection, planetarium, 2 swimming pools, children's center.

**Transfer out. Colleges most students transferred to 2009:** CSU San Bernardino, California State Polytechnic University: Pomona, CSU Fullerton, University of LaVerne, Loma Linda University.

**Basis for selection.** Open admission. Assessment testing is recommended.

**2009-2010 Annual costs.** Tuition/fees: $814; $6,514 out-of-state. Per-credit charge: $26 in-state; $216 out-of-state. Books/supplies: $1,638. Personal expenses: $3,096.

**Financial aid. Need-based:** Need-based aid available for part-time students. Work-study available for part-time students. **Non-need-based:** Scholarships awarded for academics. **Additional information:** State of California Board of Governors fee waivers to qualified state residents. Criteria for eligibility: households which receive public assistance, meet state's low income guidelines, and demonstrate need as defined by Title IV programs.

**Application procedures. Admission:** No deadline. No application fee. Admission notification on a rolling basis. **Financial aid:** No deadline. FAFSA required. Applicants notified on a rolling basis starting 7/15; must reply within 2 week(s) of notification.

**Academics. Special study options:** Accelerated study, cooperative education, dual enrollment of high school students, ESL, honors, independent study, internships, liberal arts/career combination, study abroad, weekend college. License preparation in aviation, nursing. **Credit/placement by examination:** CLEP, institutional tests. **Support services:** GED preparation, learning center, remedial instruction, tutoring, writing center.

**Majors. Biology:** General. **Business:** Accounting, administrative services, business admin, fashion, office management, sales/distribution. **Communications:** General, broadcast journalism. **Computer sciences:** General, applications programming. **Conservation:** Environmental studies. **Education:** General, early childhood, physical. **Engineering:** General. **Engineering technology:** Architectural, drafting. **Family/consumer sciences:** General, child care. **Foreign languages:** French, German, Spanish. **Health:** Dental assistant, medical radiologic technology/radiation therapy, nursing (RN). **History:** General. **Interdisciplinary:** Gerontology, science/society. **Liberal arts:** Arts/sciences. **Math:** General. **Mechanic/repair:** Aircraft, auto body, automotive, electronics/electrical. **Philosophy/religion:** Philosophy, religion. **Physical sciences:** Chemistry, geology, physics, planetary. **Psychology:** General. **Social sciences:** General, anthropology, economics, geography, political science, sociology. **Visual/performing arts:** Art, commercial/advertising art, dance, design, dramatic, fashion design, graphic design, interior design, multimedia, photography, studio arts.

**Computing on campus.** 950 workstations in library, computer center. Repair service available.

**Student life. Freshman orientation:** Mandatory. 3-hour session covers registration procedures, fees, financial aid, programs and services, counseling, course descriptions. **Activities:** Bands, choral groups, dance, drama, film society, music ensembles, Model UN, musical theater, student government, student newspaper, multicultural organizations, Vietnamese club, MECHA, Alpha Gamma Sigma, Black Student Union, ski club, religious organizations, French club, German club, Spanish club, Lambda.

**Athletics. Intercollegiate:** Baseball M, basketball, diving, football (tackle) M, softball W, swimming, volleyball W, water polo M. **Team name:** Panthers.

**Student services.** Alcohol/substance abuse counseling, career counseling, services for economically disadvantaged, student employment services, financial aid counseling, health services, on-campus daycare, personal counseling, veterans' counselor. **Physically disabled:** Services for visually, speech, hearing impaired. **Transfer:** Pre-admission transcript evaluation for new students. Transfer center, transfer adviser, college fairs on campus for students transferring to 4-year colleges.

**Contact.** Phone: (909) 652-6600 Fax: (909) 652-6006
Cecilia Carrera, Director of Admissions, Chaffey College, 5885 Haven Avenue, Rancho Cucamonga, CA 91701-3002

## Citrus College
**Glendora, California**
www.citruscollege.edu          CB code: 4051

- Public 2-year community college
- Commuter campus in large town

**General.** Founded in 1915. Regionally accredited. **Enrollment:** 12,769 undergraduates. **Degrees:** 849 associate awarded. **Location:** 25 miles from Los Angeles. **Calendar:** Semester, limited summer session. **Full-time faculty:** 172 total. **Part-time faculty:** 284 total. **Special facilities:** Performing arts center, golf driving range.

**Student profile.**

| Out-of-state: | 3% | 25 or older: | 29% |

**Basis for selection.** Open admission.

**2009-2010 Annual costs.** Tuition/fees: $814; $6,484 out-of-state. Per-credit charge: $26 in-state; $215 out-of-state. Books/supplies: $1,638. Personal expenses: $2,772.

**2009-2010 Financial aid. Need-based:** Need-based aid available for part-time students. Work-study available nights, weekends and for part-time students.

**Application procedures. Admission:** No deadline. No application fee. Application must be submitted online. Admission notification on a rolling basis. **Financial aid:** Priority date 3/1; no closing date. FAFSA required. Applicants notified on a rolling basis; must reply within 2 week(s) of notification.

**Academics. Special study options:** Cooperative education, distance learning, double major, dual enrollment of high school students, ESL, honors, independent study, study abroad. License preparation in nursing. **Credit/placement by examination:** AP, CLEP, IB. 30 credit hours maximum toward associate degree. **Support services:** Learning center, remedial instruction, tutoring.

**Majors. Biology:** Botany, zoology. **Business:** General, management information systems, office management, office/clerical. **Computer sciences:** General, data processing. **Conservation:** Forestry. **Engineering:** General. **Engineering technology:** Drafting. **Foreign languages:** French, German, Japanese, Spanish. **Health:** Dental assistant, licensed practical nurse, medical assistant. **Interdisciplinary:** Biological/physical sciences. **Liberal arts:** Arts/sciences, library assistant. **Math:** General. **Mechanic/repair:** Automotive, diesel, electronics/electrical, heating/ac/refrig. **Parks/recreation:** Health/fitness. **Personal/culinary services:** Cosmetic. **Physical sciences:** Chemistry, physics. **Protective services:** Criminal justice, law enforcement admin. **Psychology:** General. **Social sciences:** General. **Visual/performing arts:** Art, photography, studio arts.

**Most popular majors.** Business/marketing 17%, English 6%, interdisciplinary studies 15%, liberal arts 13%, social sciences 33%, visual/performing arts 9%.

**Computing on campus.** 1,100 workstations in library, computer center. Online course registration available.

**Student life. Freshman orientation:** Available. **Activities:** Jazz band, dance, drama, literary magazine, music ensembles, musical theater, student government, student newspaper, African American Student Alliance, European Heritage Club, Get Real Christian Fellowship, International Students Club, Latinos Unidos Student Association, Latter Day Saints Students Association, Natives of the Americas Student Association, Students United for Societal Change.

**Athletics. Intercollegiate:** Baseball M, basketball, cross-country, football (tackle) M, golf, soccer, softball W, swimming, tennis, track and field, volleyball W, water polo. **Team name:** Owls.

**Student services.** Career counseling, services for economically disadvantaged, student employment services, financial aid counseling, health services, legal services, minority student services, on-campus daycare, personal counseling, placement for graduates, veterans' counselor. **Physically disabled:** Services for visually, speech, hearing impaired.

**Contact.** E-mail: admissions@citruscollege.edu
Phone: (626) 914-8511 Fax: (626) 914-8613
Lois Papner, Dean of Admissions, Citrus College, 1000 West Foothill Boulevard, Glendora, CA 91741-1899

## City College of San Francisco
**San Francisco, California**          CB member
www.ccsf.edu          CB code: 4052

- Public 2-year community college
- Commuter campus in very large city

**General.** Founded in 1935. Regionally accredited. **Enrollment:** 25,421 degree-seeking undergraduates; 10,092 non-degree-seeking students. **Degrees:** 1,126 associate awarded. **ROTC:** Army. **Location:** Downtown. **Calendar:** Semester, extensive summer session. **Full-time faculty:** 741 total; 39% minority. **Part-time faculty:** 1,184 total; 34% minority. **Special facilities:** Observatory.

**Student profile.** Among degree-seeking undergraduates, 75% enrolled in a transfer program, 25% enrolled in a vocational program, 24% already have a bachelor's degree or higher, 3,461 enrolled as first-time, first-year students, 3,505 transferred in from other institutions.

| | | | |
|---|---|---|---|
| Part-time: | 63% | Asian American: | 33% |
| Out-of-state: | 5% | Hispanic American: | 14% |
| Women: | 52% | International: | 4% |
| African American: | 8% | 25 or older: | 65% |

**Transfer out. Colleges most students transferred to 2009:** San Francisco State University, California State University: East Bay, San Jose State University, University of California: Berkeley, University of California: Davis.

**Basis for selection.** Open admission, but selective for some programs. If applicant lacks high school diploma or equivalent, must be 18 or older and demonstrate ability to benefit. Program for registered nursing and a few other programs have a competitive/ special admissions process. All students entering the credit program are tested for placement into English or ESL and mathematics courses. **Adult students:** SAT/ACT scores not required. Credit programs require placement tests in English or ESL and mathematics. Free noncredit classes require placement tests depending on intended course of study.

**2009-2010 Annual costs.** Tuition/fees: $802; $6,172 out-of-state. Per-credit charge: $26 in-state; $205 out-of-state. Books/supplies: $1,638. Personal expenses: $2,664.

**Financial aid. Need-based:** Work-study available nights, weekends and for part-time students. **Additional information:** Board of Governor fee waiver for low income students.

**Application procedures. Admission:** No deadline. No application fee. Admission notification on a rolling basis. **Financial aid:** Priority date 3/1; no closing date. FAFSA required. Applicants notified on a rolling basis starting 7/1.

**Academics.** Free, noncredit classes offered in some subjects. Working Adults Degree Program. Bookloan program for low-income students. Intercollegiate Speech and Debate. Learning assistance, diversity, and student success programs. **Special study options:** Accelerated study, distance learning, dual enrollment of high school students, ESL, honors, independent study, internships, liberal arts/career combination, study abroad, weekend college. Credit is available for service-learning. License preparation in dental hygiene, nursing, paramedic, radiology. **Credit/placement by examination:** CLEP, institutional tests. 45 credit hours maximum toward associate degree. Various limitations and stipulations on credit by examination. **Support services:** GED preparation and test center, learning center, pre-admission summer program, remedial instruction, study skills assistance, tutoring, writing center.

**Majors. Agriculture:** Floriculture, landscaping, nursery operations, ornamental horticulture. **Architecture:** Environmental design, interior. **Biology:** General. **Business:** Accounting, administrative services, business admin, fashion, hospitality/recreation, human resources, management information systems, marketing, office technology, office/clerical, operations, real estate, tourism promotion, tourism/travel. **Communications:** Journalism. **Communications technology:** General, graphic/printing. **Computer sciences:** General, computer science. **Construction:** Site management. **Education:** Teacher assistance. **Engineering:** General, mechanical. **Engineering technology:** General, mechanical. **Family/consumer sciences:** Child development. **Health:** Clinical lab science, dental assistant, EMT paramedic, medical assistant, medical radiologic technology/radiation therapy, medical records admin, medical records technology, medical secretary, nursing (RN), office admin, office assistant, physician assistant, ward clerk. **Legal studies:** Legal secretary, paralegal. **Liberal arts:** Library assistant. **Mechanic/repair:** Aircraft. **Personal/culinary services:** Chef training, restaurant/catering. **Physical sciences:** Chemistry. **Protective services:** Fire safety technology, police science. **Transportation:** Aviation. **Visual/performing arts:** Cinematography, graphic design, interior design, photography, printmaking.

**Computing on campus.** 750 workstations in library, computer center, student center. Commuter students can connect to campus network. Online course registration, online library, helpline, wireless network available.

**Student life. Freshman orientation:** Mandatory. **Activities:** Jazz band, choral groups, dance, drama, film society, literary magazine, music ensembles, musical theater, opera, radio station, student government, student newspaper, symphony orchestra, TV station, City College Press Club, Cartoon Illustration and Art, La Raza Unida, Chinese Culture Club, Christian Fellowship Club, Le Cercle Francais, African American Changing Times, LBGTstr8 Alliance, Students Linking Education and Activism, Women of Color Organization.

**Athletics.** NJCAA. **Intercollegiate:** Badminton W, baseball M, basketball, cheerleading, cross-country, football (tackle) M, judo W, soccer, softball W, tennis, track and field, volleyball W. **Intramural:** Archery, badminton, baseball, basketball, cheerleading, fencing, football (non-tackle), golf,

gymnastics, judo, racquetball, soccer, swimming, tennis, volleyball, weight lifting. **Team name:** Rams.

**Student services.** Adult student services, alcohol/substance abuse counseling, career counseling, services for economically disadvantaged, student employment services, financial aid counseling, health services, minority student services, on-campus daycare, personal counseling, placement for graduates, veterans' counselor, women's services. **Physically disabled:** Services for visually, speech, hearing impaired. **Transfer:** Transfer center, transfer adviser, college fairs on campus for students transferring to 4-year colleges.

**Contact.** E-mail: admits@ccsf.edu
Phone: (415) 239-3285 Fax: (415) 239-3936
MaryLou Leyba-Frank, Dean of Admissions and Records, City College of San Francisco, Office of Admissions and Records E-107, San Francisco, CA 94112

## Coastline Community College
**Fountain Valley, California** — **CB member**
www.coastline.edu — **CB code: 0933**

- Public 2-year community college
- Commuter campus in small city

**General.** Founded in 1976. Regionally accredited. Classes held at community-based sites during the daytime, evenings, weekends, and through extensive distance learning education. **Enrollment:** 14,011 undergraduates. **Degrees:** 1,980 associate awarded. **Location:** 30 miles from Los Angeles. **Calendar:** Semester, limited summer session. **Full-time faculty:** 43 total. **Part-time faculty:** 215 total. **Class size:** 45% < 20, 40% 20-39, 6% 40-49, 6% 50-99, 2% >100. **Special facilities:** Workplace preparation center.

**Student profile.**

| | | | |
|---|---|---|---|
| Out-of-state: | 1% | 25 or older: | 73% |

**Transfer out. Colleges most students transferred to 2009:** California State University: Long Beach, University of California: Irvine, California State University: Fullerton, National University.

**Basis for selection.** Open admission. If submitted, SAT/ACT used for placement and counseling, in lieu of college administered English and math tests.

**2009-2010 Annual costs.** Tuition/fees: $806; $6,506 out-of-state. Per-credit charge: $26 in-state; $216 out-of-state. Students who attend one of the three main learning centers are required to pay for a parking decal: Fall/Spring semester $10; Summer $5. Books/supplies: $1,566. Personal expenses: $3,024.

**2008-2009 Financial aid.** All financial aid based on need. Need-based aid available for part-time students. **Additional information:** Board of Governor's Grant: statewide fee waiver program for students or dependents receiving HFOL/TANF, SSI, General Relief, or whose income meets set standards or who are considered eligible through Federal needs analysis.

**Application procedures. Admission:** No deadline. No application fee. Admission notification on a rolling basis. **Financial aid:** Priority date 3/2; no closing date. FAFSA, institutional form required. Applicants notified on a rolling basis starting 8/1; must reply within 2 week(s) of notification.

**Academics. Special study options:** Accelerated study, cooperative education, distance learning, dual enrollment of high school students, ESL, independent study, liberal arts/career combination, study abroad, weekend college. Midnight college via telecourse delivery. License preparation in physical therapy, real estate. **Credit/placement by examination:** AP, CLEP. 30 credit hours maximum toward associate degree. **Support services:** GED preparation, reduced course load, remedial instruction, tutoring.

**Majors. Business:** General, accounting, business admin, entrepreneurial studies, management science, office technology, real estate. **Computer sciences:** General. **Liberal arts:** Arts/sciences. **Mechanic/repair:** Electronics/electrical.

**Computing on campus.** 100 workstations in computer center.

**Student life. Freshman orientation:** Available. Preregistration for classes offered. **Activities:** Choral groups, dance, student government.

**Student services.** Career counseling, services for economically disadvantaged, student employment services, financial aid counseling, health services, personal counseling, veterans' counselor. **Physically disabled:** Services for hearing impaired. **Transfer:** Transfer center, transfer adviser, college fairs on campus for students transferring to 4-year colleges.

**Contact.** E-mail: jmcdonald@cccd.edu
Phone: (714) 241-6176 Fax: (714) 241-6288
Jennifer McDonald, Director of Admissions and Records, Coastline Community College, 11460 Warner Avenue, Fountain Valley, CA 92708

## Coleman College: San Marcos
### San Marcos, California
### www.coleman.edu

▶ For-profit 2-year technical college
▶ Commuter campus in small city

**General.** Accredited by ACICS. Branch campus of Coleman College, La Mesa. **Enrollment:** 49 degree-seeking undergraduates. **Degrees:** 50 associate awarded. **Calendar:** Continuous. **Full-time faculty:** 6 total. **Part-time faculty:** 12 total.

**2009-2010 Annual costs.** Per-credit charge: $290. 13-month associate degree program in computer information science: $31,320. Bachelor degree program in computer information science: $52,200. Effective September 1, 2009. Costs vary depending on program.

**Academics. Credit/placement by examination:** CLEP.

**Majors. Biology:** Bioinformatics. **Computer sciences:** Programming. **Visual/performing arts:** Graphic design.

**Contact.** Phone: (760) 747-3990
Coleman College: San Marcos, 1284 West San Marcos Boulevard, Suite 110, San Marcos, CA 92069

## College of Alameda
### Alameda, California
### www.alameda.peralta.edu          CB code: 4118

▶ Public 2-year community college
▶ Commuter campus in small city

**General.** Founded in 1970. Regionally accredited. **Enrollment:** 7,632 undergraduates. **Degrees:** 146 associate awarded. **Calendar:** Semester, limited summer session. **Full-time faculty:** 70 total; 17% have terminal degrees, 43% minority.

**Student profile.**

Out-of-state:          2%     25 or older:          44%

**Basis for selection.** Open admission.

**High school preparation.** College-preparatory program recommended.

**2009-2010 Annual costs.** Tuition/fees: $784; $6,484 out-of-state. Per-credit charge: $26 in-state; $216 out-of-state. Books/supplies: $1,566. Personal expenses: $3,024.

**Application procedures. Admission:** No deadline. No application fee. Admission notification on a rolling basis. **Financial aid:** Priority date 3/2; no closing date. FAFSA required. Applicants notified on a rolling basis starting 7/1; must reply within 2 week(s) of notification.

**Academics. Special study options:** Cooperative education, cross-registration, dual enrollment of high school students, honors, independent study, liberal arts/career combination. License preparation in aviation. **Credit/placement by examination:** CLEP, institutional tests. **Support services:** Learning center, remedial instruction, tutoring.

**Majors. Area/ethnic studies:** African-American. **Biology:** General. **Business:** General, accounting, administrative services, business admin, entrepreneurial studies, fashion, marketing, office/clerical. **Education:** Teacher assistance. **Foreign languages:** Spanish. **Health:** Dental assistant, health aide. **History:** General. **Liberal arts:** Arts/sciences. **Math:** General. **Mechanic/repair:** Aircraft. **Philosophy/religion:** Philosophy. **Psychology:** General. **Social sciences:** General, anthropology, economics, geography, political science, sociology, urban studies. **Transportation:** Aviation management. **Visual/performing arts:** General, studio arts.

**Computing on campus.** Online course registration available.

**Student life. Freshman orientation:** Available. **Activities:** Jazz band, choral groups, dance, drama, student government, student newspaper.

**Athletics. Intercollegiate:** Basketball, bowling, cross-country M, fencing, golf, soccer M, tennis, track and field, volleyball. **Intramural:** Golf, sailing, softball W. **Team name:** COUGARS.

**Student services.** Adult student services, career counseling, services for economically disadvantaged, student employment services, health services, on-campus daycare, personal counseling, placement for graduates, veterans' counselor. **Physically disabled:** Services for visually, speech, hearing impaired. **Transfer:** Transfer adviser, college fairs on campus for students transferring to 4-year colleges.

**Contact.** E-mail: admissions@peralta.edu
Phone: (510) 748-2228 Fax: (510) 748-5227
Kelly Compton, Vice President of Student Services, College of Alameda, 555 Ralph Appezzato Memorial Parkway, Alameda, CA 94501

## College of Marin: Kentfield
### Kentfield, California
### www.marin.edu          CB code: 4061

▶ Public 2-year community college
▶ Commuter campus in small town

**General.** Founded in 1926. Regionally accredited. Additional campus at Indian Valley - Novato, CA. **Enrollment:** 7,460 undergraduates. **Degrees:** 249 associate awarded. **Location:** 15 miles from San Francisco. **Calendar:** Semester. **Full-time faculty:** 135 total. **Part-time faculty:** 160 total.

**Transfer out. Colleges most students transferred to 2009:** University of California: Berkeley, San Francisco State, University of California: Davis.

**Basis for selection.** Open admission. Limited admissions to nursing programs. **Adult students:** SAT/ACT scores not required.

**2009-2010 Annual costs.** Tuition/fees: $816; $6,516 out-of-state. Per-credit charge: $26 in-state; $216 out-of-state. Books/supplies: $1,638. Personal expenses: $3,096.

**Financial aid.** All financial aid based on need. Need-based aid available for part-time students.

**Application procedures. Admission:** No deadline. No application fee. Admission notification on a rolling basis. **Financial aid:** Priority date 3/1; no closing date. FAFSA required. Applicants notified on a rolling basis starting 5/15.

**Academics. Special study options:** Distance learning, ESL. **Credit/placement by examination:** CLEP, institutional tests. **Support services:** GED preparation, remedial instruction, study skills assistance, tutoring, writing center.

**Majors. Agriculture:** Landscaping, nursery operations. **Architecture:** Environmental design. **Biology:** General, environmental. **Business:** General, accounting, business admin, real estate. **Communications:** Media studies. **Computer sciences:** General, computer science, web page design. **Foreign languages:** General, French, Spanish. **Health:** Dental assistant, medical assistant, nursing (RN). **History:** General. **Legal studies:** Court reporting. **Liberal arts:** Arts/sciences. **Math:** General. **Mechanic/repair:** Auto body. **Physical sciences:** General, chemistry, physics. **Psychology:** General. **Social sciences:** General, geography. **Visual/performing arts:** Dance, dramatic, studio arts.

**Computing on campus.** Online course registration available.

**Student life. Activities:** Concert band, choral groups, dance, drama, student government, student newspaper.

**Athletics. Intercollegiate:** Baseball M, basketball, cross-country, diving, soccer, softball, squash, tennis, track and field.

**Student services.** Career counseling, services for economically disadvantaged, on-campus daycare, personal counseling. **Transfer:** Transfer center, transfer adviser, college fairs on campus for students transferring to 4-year colleges.

**Contact.** Phone: (415) 485-9412
Robert Balestreri, Dean of Enrollment Services, College of Marin: Kentfield, 835 College Avenue, Kentfield, CA 94904

## College of San Mateo
### San Mateo, California
### www.collegeofsanmateo.edu          CB code: 4070

▶ Public 2-year community college
▶ Commuter campus in small city

**General.** Founded in 1922. Regionally accredited. **Enrollment:** 11,723 undergraduates. **Degrees:** 415 associate awarded. **ROTC:** Army, Air Force. **Location:** 15 miles from San Francisco. **Calendar:** Semester, limited summer session. **Full-time faculty:** 350 total. **Part-time faculty:** 200 total. **Special facilities:** Planetarium.

**Student profile.**

| | | | |
|---|---|---|---|
| Out-of-state: | 2% | 25 or older: | 51% |

**Basis for selection.** Open admission, but selective for some programs. Nursing program has separate requirements.

**2009-2010 Annual costs.** Tuition/fees: $816; $6,546 out-of-state. Per-credit charge: $26 in-state; $217 out-of-state. Books/supplies: $1,638. Personal expenses: $2,772.

**Application procedures. Admission:** No deadline. No application fee. Admission notification on a rolling basis. Completion of CSM Placement tests for English, reading and mathematics recommended prior to counseling session. **Financial aid:** Priority date 3/2; no closing date. FAFSA, institutional form required. Applicants notified on a rolling basis starting 6/15.

**Academics. Special study options:** Cooperative education, cross-registration, distance learning, double major, dual enrollment of high school students, ESL, honors, independent study, liberal arts/career combination, study abroad, weekend college. License preparation in dental hygiene, nursing, real estate. **Credit/placement by examination:** AP, CLEP, IB, institutional tests. 12 credit hours maximum toward associate degree. **Support services:** Learning center, reduced course load, remedial instruction, study skills assistance, tutoring, writing center.

**Majors. Agriculture:** Horticulture, ornamental horticulture. **Biology:** General, biomedical sciences. **Business:** General, accounting, entrepreneurial studies, fashion, logistics, management information systems, office/clerical, real estate. **Communications:** Advertising, broadcast journalism. **Communications technology:** General. **Computer sciences:** General, web page design. **Construction:** Pipefitting. **Engineering:** General. **Engineering technology:** Drafting, electrical. **Foreign languages:** French, German, Spanish. **Health:** Dental assistant, medical assistant, nursing (RN), substance abuse counseling. **Legal studies:** Legal secretary. **Liberal arts:** Arts/sciences. **Math:** General. **Mechanic/repair:** Aircraft, heating/ac/refrig. **Personal/culinary services:** General. **Physical sciences:** Chemistry, geology, physics. **Protective services:** Fire safety technology. **Social sciences:** General. **Transportation:** Airline/commercial pilot, aviation. **Visual/performing arts:** Cinematography, commercial/advertising art, painting, photography, studio arts.

**Computing on campus.** 150 workstations in library, computer center, student center. Online course registration, wireless network available.

**Student life. Freshman orientation:** Available. **Activities:** Bands, choral groups, dance, literary magazine, radio station, student government, student newspaper, symphony orchestra, TV station, Asian student union, Christian Fellowship, ethnic studies society, international students union, Latin American student organization, Arts in Recovery, Ballet Folklorico de CSM, Earth Preservation Committee, Peace Action, Unity Among Brothers.

**Athletics.** NCAA. **Intercollegiate:** Baseball M, basketball W, cross-country, football (tackle) M, softball W, swimming, tennis W, track and field, water polo. **Team name:** Bulldogs.

**Student services.** Adult student services, alcohol/substance abuse counseling, career counseling, services for economically disadvantaged, student employment services, financial aid counseling, health services, minority student services, on-campus daycare, personal counseling, veterans' counselor. **Physically disabled:** Services for visually, speech, hearing impaired. **Learning disabled:** Comprehensive services available. **Transfer:** Pre-admission transcript evaluation for new students. Transfer center, transfer adviser, college fairs on campus for students transferring to 4-year colleges.

**Contact.** E-mail: villarealh@smccd.net
Phone: (650) 574-6165 Fax: (650) 574-6506
Henry Villareal, Dean of Admissions and Records, College of San Mateo, 1700 West Hillsdale Boulevard, San Mateo, CA 94402-3784

## College of the Canyons
**Santa Clarita, California**
www.canyons.edu                                    CB code: 4117

▶ Public 2-year community college
▶ Commuter campus in large city

**General.** Founded in 1967. Regionally accredited. **Enrollment:** 5,040 full-time, degree-seeking students. **Degrees:** 1,024 associate awarded. **Location:** 36 miles from Los Angeles. **Calendar:** Semester, extensive summer

session. **Full-time faculty:** 191 total. **Part-time faculty:** 496 total. **Class size:** 26% < 20, 62% 20-39, 9% 40-49, 1% 50-99, less than 1% >100. **Special facilities:** Performing arts center, proscenium performing arts stage, experimental "black box" theater, university center for access to upper-division and graduate programs.

**Student profile.** Among full-time, degree-seeking students, 71% enrolled in a transfer program, 6% enrolled in a vocational program, 10% already have a bachelor's degree or higher, 1,019 enrolled as first-time, first-year students.

| | | | |
|---|---|---|---|
| Out-of-state: | 2% | Native American: | 1% |
| African American: | 5% | International: | 1% |
| Asian American: | 10% | 25 or older: | 31% |
| Hispanic American: | 26% | | |

**Transfer out.** Colleges most students transferred to 2009: California State University: Northridge, University of California: Los Angeles, San Diego State University, California State University: Long Beach, University of California: Santa Barbara.

**Basis for selection.** Open admission, but selective for some programs. Limited admission to nursing program. Nursing applicant selections are made using both multi-criteria screening and random screening. **Homeschooled:** Transcript of courses and grades required. Per state guidelines, students must be associated with program approved through Los Angeles County, or must be taught by person holding California teaching credential, or must hold a current private school affidavit filed with the State Superintendent of Public Instruction.

**2009-2010 Annual costs.** Tuition/fees: $808; $5,788 out-of-state. Per-credit charge: $26 in-state; $192 out-of-state. Books/supplies: $1,638. Personal expenses: $2,772.

**2008-2009 Financial aid. Need-based:** 70% of total undergraduate aid awarded as scholarships/grants, 30% as loans/jobs. Need-based aid available for part-time students. Work-study available nights, weekends and for part-time students. **Non-need-based:** Scholarships awarded for academics, alumni affiliation, art, leadership, minority status, music/drama, state residency.

**Application procedures. Admission:** No deadline. No application fee. Admission notification on a rolling basis. **Financial aid:** Closing date 3/2. FAFSA required. Applicants notified on a rolling basis starting 6/1; must reply within 4 week(s) of notification.

**Academics. Special study options:** Accelerated study, cooperative education, distance learning, dual enrollment of high school students, ESL, honors, independent study, internships, liberal arts/career combination, study abroad, weekend college. Bachelor's degree programs available on campus. License preparation in nursing, real estate. **Credit/placement by examination:** AP, CLEP, institutional tests. 18 credit hours maximum toward associate degree. Applicants must take institutional English, ESL, chemistry, and mathematics placement tests. **Support services:** GED preparation, learning center, remedial instruction, study skills assistance, tutoring.

**Majors. Agriculture:** Landscaping. **Business:** Accounting, administrative services, business admin, hospitality admin, hotel/motel admin, real estate, sales/distribution, small business admin. **Communications:** Digital media, journalism, radio/tv. **Communications technology:** Animation/special effects. **Computer sciences:** Computer science, networking. **Construction:** Site management. **Engineering:** General. **Engineering technology:** Architectural drafting, manufacturing, surveying, water quality. **Family/consumer sciences:** Child development. **Foreign languages:** French, sign language interpretation, Spanish. **Health:** Nursing (RN). **Interdisciplinary:** Biological/physical sciences. **Legal studies:** Paralegal. **Liberal arts:** Arts/sciences, humanities, library assistant. **Math:** General. **Mechanic/repair:** Automotive. **Parks/recreation:** General, health/fitness. **Personal/culinary services:** Restaurant/catering. **Production:** Welding. **Protective services:** Firefighting, police science. **Psychology:** General. **Social sciences:** General, sociology. **Visual/performing arts:** Art, cinematography, dramatic, graphic design, interior design, multimedia, photography. **Other:** History, Mathematics & sciences, Music: performance/guitar.

**Most popular majors.** Business/marketing 11%, health sciences 15%, interdisciplinary studies 8%, liberal arts 42%, security/protective services 6%.

**Computing on campus.** 1,750 workstations in library, computer center, student center. Online course registration, online library, helpline, wireless network available.

**Student life. Freshman orientation:** Mandatory. **Activities:** Jazz band, choral groups, dance, drama, literary magazine, music ensembles, Model UN, musical theater, student government, symphony orchestra, Club MESA, Students for Sustainability, Future Educators Club, Political Science Club,

Speech & Debate Society, National Student Nurses Association, Biology Club, Bible Talk, Grace on Campus, Latter-day Saints Student Association.

**Athletics. Intercollegiate:** Baseball M, basketball, cross-country, football (tackle) M, golf, soccer, softball W, swimming, track and field, volleyball W. **Team name:** Cougars.

**Student services.** Adult student services, career counseling, services for economically disadvantaged, student employment services, financial aid counseling, health services, on-campus daycare, personal counseling, placement for graduates, veterans' counselor, women's services. **Physically disabled:** Services for visually, speech, hearing impaired. **Learning disabled:** Comprehensive services available. **Transfer:** Re-entry adviser, pre-admission transcript evaluation for new students. Transfer center, transfer adviser, college fairs on campus for students transferring to 4-year colleges.

**Contact.** E-mail: jasmine.ruys@canyons.edu
Phone: (661) 362-3280 Fax: (661) 259-8302
Jasmine Ruys, Director, Admissions, Records and Online Services, College of the Canyons, 26455 Rockwell Canyon Road, Santa Clarita, CA 91355

## College of the Desert
**Palm Desert, California** — CB member
www.collegeofthedesert.edu — CB code: 4085

▶ Public 2-year community college
▶ Commuter campus in small city

**General.** Founded in 1958. Regionally accredited. **Enrollment:** 12,213 undergraduates. **Degrees:** 543 associate awarded. **Location:** 20 miles from Palm Springs, 120 miles from Los Angeles. **Calendar:** Semester, limited summer session. **Full-time faculty:** 106 total; 23% have terminal degrees, 17% minority, 47% women. **Part-time faculty:** 307 total; 16% have terminal degrees, 22% minority, 47% women. **Special facilities:** Performing arts center, golf institute, public safety academy.

**Student profile.**

| | | | |
|---|---|---|---|
| Out-of-state: | 3% | 25 or older: | 40% |

**Basis for selection.** Open admission, but selective for some programs. Separate application requirements for nursing and golf management and public safety academy. Interviews required for nursing/allied health majors. **Adult students:** SAT/ACT scores not required. **Learning Disabled:** Participation is voluntary. Interested students must meet with the appropriate Disabled Students Programs and Services counselor to apply for these programs.

**2009-2010 Annual costs.** Tuition/fees: $810; $6,000 out-of-state. Per-credit charge: $26 in-state; $199 out-of-state. Books/supplies: $1,638. Personal expenses: $3,096.

**2008-2009 Financial aid.** All financial aid based on need. 93% of total undergraduate aid awarded as scholarships/grants, 7% as loans/jobs. Need-based aid available for part-time students. Work-study available weekends and for part-time students.

**Application procedures. Admission:** Priority date 5/6; deadline 9/8 (receipt date). No application fee. Application must be submitted online. Admission notification on a rolling basis. **Financial aid:** Priority date 3/2; no closing date. FAFSA required. Applicants notified on a rolling basis starting 7/1.

**Academics. Special study options:** Cooperative education, distance learning, double major, dual enrollment of high school students, ESL, honors, independent study, liberal arts/career combination. License preparation in nursing. **Credit/placement by examination:** CLEP, institutional tests. **Support services:** GED preparation and test center, learning center, remedial instruction, study skills assistance, tutoring, writing center.

**Majors. Agriculture:** Business, ornamental horticulture, plant sciences, turf management. **Architecture:** Technology. **Biology:** General. **Business:** Business admin, construction management, golf management, hotel/motel admin, managerial economics, office management, restaurant/food services. **Communications:** General, journalism, media studies, organizational. **Computer sciences:** General, computer science. **Conservation:** General, environmental science, environmental studies. **Engineering technology:** Architectural, architectural drafting, drafting, heat/ac/refrig. **Family/consumer sciences:** Child care, food/nutrition, human nutrition. **Foreign languages:** French, German, Italian, Spanish. **Health:** Dietetic technician, licensed practical nurse, nursing (RN). **History:** General. **Interdisciplinary:** Biological/physical sciences. **Liberal arts:** Arts/sciences. **Math:** General. **Mechanic/repair:** Heating/ac/refrig. **Parks/recreation:** General, facilities management.

**Personal/culinary services:** Restaurant/catering. **Philosophy/religion:** Philosophy. **Physical sciences:** Chemistry, geology, physics. **Protective services:** Fire safety technology, law enforcement admin. **Psychology:** General. **Social sciences:** General, anthropology, economics, geography, political science, sociology. **Visual/performing arts:** Acting, art, art history/conservation, dance, dramatic, drawing, graphic design, painting, photography, printmaking, studio arts, theater history.

**Most popular majors.** Business/marketing 12%, health sciences 22%, liberal arts 40%.

**Computing on campus.** 125 workstations in library, computer center, student center. Online course registration, online library, wireless network available.

**Student life. Freshman orientation:** Mandatory. **Activities:** Choral groups, dance, drama, international student organizations, music ensembles, musical theater, opera, student government, student newspaper.

**Athletics. Intercollegiate:** Baseball M, basketball, cheerleading, cross-country, fencing, football (tackle) M, golf, soccer, softball W, tennis, volleyball W. **Team name:** Roadrunners.

**Student services.** Adult student services, career counseling, services for economically disadvantaged, financial aid counseling, health services, minority student services, on-campus daycare, personal counseling, placement for graduates, veterans' counselor. **Physically disabled:** Services for visually, speech, hearing impaired. **Learning disabled:** Comprehensive services available. **Transfer:** Re-entry adviser, pre-admission transcript evaluation for new students. Transfer center, transfer adviser, college fairs on campus for students transferring to 4-year colleges.

**Contact.** Phone: (760) 773-2516 Fax: (760) 862-1379
John Loera, Dean of Enrollment Services, College of the Desert, 43-500 Monterey Avenue, Palm Desert, CA 92260

## College of the Redwoods
**Eureka, California**
www.redwoods.edu — CB code: 4100

▶ Public 2-year community college
▶ Commuter campus in large town

**General.** Founded in 1964. Regionally accredited. Centers at Fort Bragg and Crescent City; instructional sites in Hoopa, Klamath, downtown Eureka, and Arcata. **Enrollment:** 8,614 degree-seeking undergraduates. **Degrees:** 364 associate awarded. **Location:** 275 miles from San Francisco. **Calendar:** Semester, limited summer session. **Full-time faculty:** 87 total; 22% minority, 44% women. **Part-time faculty:** 325 total; 29% minority, 52% women. **Class size:** 53% < 20, 44% 20-39, 1% 40-49, 2% 50-99, less than 1% >100. **Special facilities:** Observatory, fish hatchery, organic farm, fine woodworking shop.

**Student profile.** Among degree-seeking undergraduates, 3,235 enrolled as first-time, first-year students.

| | | | |
|---|---|---|---|
| Part-time: | 55% | 25 or older: | 43% |
| Out-of-state: | 4% | Live on campus: | 1% |
| Women: | 56% | | |

**Transfer out. Colleges most students transferred to 2009:** Humboldt State University, California State University: Chico.

**Basis for selection.** Open admission, but selective for some programs. Admission for nursing applicants based on school record and test scores. **Homeschooled:** Must submit a copy of affidavit filed with County Office of Education.

**2009-2010 Annual costs.** Tuition/fees: $804; $7,584 out-of-state. Per-credit charge: $26 in-state; $252 out-of-state. Room/board: $6,558. Books/supplies: $1,566. Personal expenses: $1,476.

**2009-2010 Financial aid. Need-based:** Need-based aid available for part-time students. Work-study available for part-time students.

**Application procedures. Admission:** Priority date 8/13; no deadline. No application fee. Admission notification on a rolling basis. **Financial aid:** Priority date 4/15; no closing date. FAFSA, institutional form required. Applicants notified on a rolling basis starting 5/1; must reply within 6 week(s) of notification.

**Academics. Special study options:** Cooperative education, cross-registration, distance learning, double major, dual enrollment of high school students, ESL, honors, independent study, teacher certification program. License preparation in nursing. **Credit/placement by examination:** CLEP, institutional tests. **Support services:** GED preparation and test center, learning center, pre-admission summer program, remedial instruction, tutoring, writing center.

**Majors. Agriculture:** Agribusiness operations, animal sciences, plant sciences. **Business:** General, administrative services, hospitality admin, managerial economics, office technology, real estate. **Communications:** Journalism. **Computer sciences:** General. **Conservation:** Fisheries, forestry. **Construction:** Maintenance. **Education:** Early childhood. **Engineering:** Electrical. **Engineering technology:** Construction, drafting. **Legal studies:** Legal secretary, paralegal. **Liberal arts:** Arts/sciences. **Physical sciences:** Planetary. **Protective services:** Law enforcement admin. **Visual/performing arts:** Commercial/advertising art.

**Most popular majors.** Health sciences 21%, liberal arts 62%.

**Computing on campus.** 578 workstations in dormitories, library, computer center, student center. Dormitories wired for high-speed internet access. Online course registration, online library available.

**Student life. Freshman orientation:** Available. Preregistration for classes offered. **Housing:** Coed dorms available. Limited housing also available for police academy students. **Activities:** Jazz band, choral groups, dance, student government, student newspaper, Native American club, international students club, apologetics club, Bible study, Latter-day Saints club, veterans club, EOPS club.

**Athletics. Intercollegiate:** Baseball M, basketball, cross-country, football (tackle) M, golf M, soccer W, track and field, volleyball W. **Intramural:** Badminton, bowling, diving, golf, gymnastics, soccer, volleyball, water polo. **Team name:** Corsairs.

**Student services.** Career counseling, services for economically disadvantaged, student employment services, financial aid counseling, health services, on-campus daycare, personal counseling, placement for graduates, veterans' counselor. **Physically disabled:** Services for visually, speech, hearing impaired. **Transfer:** Transfer center, transfer adviser, college fairs on campus for students transferring to 4-year colleges.

**Contact.** E-mail: admissions@redwoods.edu
Phone: (707) 476-4200 Toll-free number: (800) 641-0400
Fax: (707) 476-4406
Kathy Goodlive, Manager, Admissions and Records, College of the Redwoods, 7351 Tompkins Hill Road, Eureka, CA 95501-9300

## College of the Sequoias
### Visalia, California
### www.cos.edu
**CB code: 4071**

- Public 2-year community college
- Commuter campus in small city

**General.** Founded in 1925. Regionally accredited. Broad range of two year transfer, vocational, and basic skill programs offered. **Enrollment:** 6,568 degree-seeking undergraduates; 6,069 non-degree-seeking students. **Degrees:** 734 associate awarded. **ROTC:** Air Force. **Location:** 45 miles from Fresno. **Calendar:** Semester, limited summer session. **Full-time faculty:** 173 total. **Part-time faculty:** 270 total. **Class size:** 33% < 20, 54% 20-39, 5% 40-49, 3% 50-99, 5% >100. **Special facilities:** Self-sufficient farm.

**Student profile.** Among degree-seeking undergraduates, 83% enrolled in a transfer program, 15% enrolled in a vocational program, 1,661 enrolled as first-time, first-year students.

| | | | |
|---|---|---|---|
| Part-time: | 56% | Asian American: | 4% |
| Out-of-state: | 3% | Hispanic American: | 27% |
| Women: | 58% | Native American: | 1% |
| African American: | 2% | 25 or older: | 39% |

**Transfer out. Colleges most students transferred to 2009:** California State University: Fresno, California State University: Bakersfield, California Polytechnic State University: San Luis Obispo, California State University: Long Beach, California State University: Davis.

**Basis for selection.** Open admission, but selective for some programs. Limited admission to nursing program. Interviews required for work program, nursing majors. Auditions required for music majors.

**High school preparation.** College-preparatory program recommended.

**2009-2010 Annual costs.** Tuition/fees: $841; $7,531 out-of-state. Per-credit charge: $26 in-state; $249 out-of-state. Books/supplies: $1,566. Personal expenses: $3,024.

**2008-2009 Financial aid. Need-based:** 97% of total undergraduate aid awarded as scholarships/grants, 3% as loans/jobs.

**Application procedures. Admission:** No deadline. No application fee. Admission notification on a rolling basis. **Financial aid:** Priority date 3/2; no closing date. FAFSA, institutional form required. Applicants notified on a rolling basis starting 6/1; must reply within 2 week(s) of notification.

**Academics. Special study options:** Distance learning, dual enrollment of high school students, ESL, honors, independent study, internships, student-designed major, study abroad, weekend college. License preparation in nursing, paramedic, physical therapy. **Credit/placement by examination:** CLEP, institutional tests. 12 credit hours maximum toward associate degree. **Support services:** Learning center, pre-admission summer program, reduced course load, remedial instruction, study skills assistance, tutoring, writing center.

**Majors. Agriculture:** Agribusiness operations, landscaping, ornamental horticulture. **Business:** General, accounting, administrative services, management information systems, office/clerical, real estate, sales/distribution. **Communications:** General, journalism. **Computer sciences:** Computer science. **Construction:** Carpentry, maintenance. **Education:** Physical. **Engineering:** General. **Engineering technology:** Architectural, construction, drafting, electrical, industrial, manufacturing. **Family/consumer sciences:** General, child care. **Foreign languages:** General, French. **Health:** Nursing (RN). **Interdisciplinary:** Biological/physical sciences. **Legal studies:** Paralegal. **Liberal arts:** Arts/sciences. **Math:** General. **Mechanic/repair:** Electronics/electrical. **Parks/recreation:** Facilities management. **Personal/culinary services:** Cosmetic. **Protective services:** Fire safety technology, law enforcement admin. **Public administration:** Human services. **Social sciences:** General. **Visual/performing arts:** Art, commercial/advertising art, dramatic, multimedia, studio arts, theater design.

**Most popular majors.** Business/marketing 6%, health sciences 22%, liberal arts 48%.

**Computing on campus.** 325 workstations in library, computer center. Online course registration, helpline, wireless network available.

**Student life. Freshman orientation:** Available. Preregistration for classes offered. Both online and in person. In person classes are held just before the beginning of each semester. **Activities:** Bands, choral groups, dance, drama, music ensembles, musical theater, student government, student newspaper, symphony orchestra.

**Athletics. Intercollegiate:** Baseball M, basketball, cross-country, diving, football (tackle) M, golf, soccer W, softball W, swimming, tennis, track and field, volleyball W. **Team name:** Giants.

**Student services.** Adult student services, alcohol/substance abuse counseling, career counseling, services for economically disadvantaged, student employment services, financial aid counseling, health services, minority student services, personal counseling, placement for graduates, veterans' counselor. **Physically disabled:** Services for visually, speech, hearing impaired. **Learning disabled:** Comprehensive services available. **Transfer:** Transfer adviser, college fairs on campus for students transferring to 4-year colleges.

**Contact.** Phone: (559) 730-3727 Fax: (559) 730-3894
Tamara Ravalin, Dean of Student Services, College of the Sequoias, 915 South Mooney Boulevard, Visalia, CA 93277

## College of the Siskiyous
### Weed, California
### www.siskiyous.edu
**CB code: 4087**

- Public 2-year community and junior college
- Commuter campus in small town

**General.** Founded in 1957. Regionally accredited. **Enrollment:** 3,352 undergraduates. **Degrees:** 188 associate awarded. **Location:** 285 miles from San Francisco, 80 miles from Medford, Oregon. **Calendar:** Semester, limited summer session. **Full-time faculty:** 50 total; 16% have terminal degrees, 10% minority, 36% women. **Part-time faculty:** 150 total; 8% have terminal degrees, 10% minority, 36% women. **Class size:** 57% < 20, 35% 20-39, 3% 40-49, 4% 50-99, less than 1% >100. **Special facilities:** Fire science burn tower and flashover unit, welding lab, emergency services training center, distance learning center.

**Student profile.**

| | | | |
|---|---|---|---|
| Out-of-state: | 27% | Live on campus: | 14% |
| 25 or older: | 39% | | |

**Transfer out. Colleges most students transferred to 2009:** California State University: Chico, Southern Oregon University, University of California: Davis, Simpson University, Humboldt State University.

**Basis for selection.** Open admission, but selective for some programs. **Adult students:** SAT/ACT scores not required. SAT/ACT scores not required if out of high school 1 year(s) or more.

**2009-2010 Annual costs.** Tuition/fees: $810; $6,780 out-of-state. Per-credit charge: $26 in-state; $225 out-of-state. Oregon residents with inter-state exchange program: $42 per unit (no enrollment fee). Room/board: $7,984. Books/supplies: $1,638. Personal expenses: $2,500.

**2008-2009 Financial aid.** All financial aid based on need. Need-based aid available for part-time students. Work-study available nights, weekends and for part-time students.

**Application procedures. Admission:** No deadline. No application fee. **Financial aid:** Priority date 4/30; no closing date. FAFSA required. Applicants notified on a rolling basis starting 6/1; must reply within 2 week(s) of notification.

**Academics. Special study options:** Cooperative education, distance learning, dual enrollment of high school students, ESL, exchange student, independent study, internships, liberal arts/career combination, student-designed major, study abroad. Bachelor's degree programs available on campus. License preparation in nursing, paramedic. **Credit/placement by examination:** AP, CLEP, institutional tests. 48 credit hours maximum toward associate degree. **Support services:** GED preparation, learning center, pre-admission summer program, reduced course load, remedial instruction, study skills assistance, tutoring, writing center.

**Majors. Biology:** General. **Business:** General, accounting, accounting technology, administrative services, business admin, management information systems, office management, office/clerical. **Communications:** General, broadcast journalism, digital media, media studies, radio/tv. **Communications technology:** General, graphics, radio/tv. **Computer sciences:** General, applications programming, computer science, programming. **Education:** General, early childhood, early childhood special. **Engineering:** General. **Family/consumer sciences:** Child care, child development, family studies, family/community services. **Foreign languages:** Spanish. **Health:** EMT paramedic, licensed practical nurse, nursing (RN), predental, premedicine, prenursing, prepharmacy, preveterinary, substance abuse counseling. **History:** General. **Interdisciplinary:** Accounting/computer science, behavioral sciences, biological/physical sciences, natural sciences. **Legal studies:** Prelaw. **Liberal arts:** Arts/sciences, humanities. **Math:** General. **Parks/recreation:** Health/fitness. **Philosophy/religion:** Philosophy. **Physical sciences:** General, chemistry, geology, physics. **Production:** Welding. **Protective services:** Criminal justice, fire safety technology, fire services admin, firefighting, law enforcement admin, police science. **Psychology:** General. **Public administration:** Human services. **Social sciences:** General, anthropology. **Visual/performing arts:** General, acting, art, digital art, directing/producing, dramatic, graphic design, music performance, studio arts, theater arts management, voice/opera. **Other:** Alcohol and drug studies.

**Most popular majors.** Liberal arts 89%, security/protective services 9%.

**Computing on campus.** 260 workstations in dormitories, library, computer center. Dormitories wired for high-speed internet access and linked to campus network. Commuter students can connect to campus network. Online course registration, online library, helpline, repair service, wireless network available.

**Student life. Freshman orientation:** Available. Preregistration for classes offered. Held three months prior to the start of the semester. **Housing:** Guaranteed on-campus for freshmen. Coed dorms, wellness housing available. $100 fully refundable deposit. **Activities:** Bands, choral groups, dance, drama, international student organizations, music ensembles, musical theater, student government, student newspaper, symphony orchestra, TV station, Latino Student Union, Black Student Union, Phi Theta Kappa honor society, intercultural club, American Indian Alliance, intervarsity club, speech club, chess club, disabled student aliance, speech and forensics club.

**Athletics. Intercollegiate:** Baseball M, basketball, cross-country, football (tackle) M, skiing, softball W, track and field, volleyball W. **Intramural:** Badminton, basketball, bowling, boxing, golf, skiing, softball, tennis, volleyball. **Team name:** Eagles.

**Student services.** Adult student services, alcohol/substance abuse counseling, career counseling, services for economically disadvantaged, student employment services, financial aid counseling, health services, legal services, on-campus daycare, personal counseling, veterans' counselor. **Physically disabled:** Services for visually, speech, hearing impaired. **Learning disabled:** Comprehensive services available. **Transfer:** Re-entry adviser, pre-admission transcript evaluation for new students. Transfer center, transfer adviser, college fairs on campus for students transferring to 4-year colleges.

**Contact.** E-mail: registration@siskiyous.edu
Phone: (530) 938-5555 Toll-free number: (888) 397-4339
Fax: (530) 938-5367
Teresa Winkelman, Director of Admissions & Records, College of the Siskiyous, 800 College Avenue, Weed, CA 96094-2899

## Columbia College
### Sonora, California
www.gocolumbia.edu — CB code: 4108

- Public 2-year community college
- Commuter campus in small town

**General.** Founded in 1968. Regionally accredited. **Enrollment:** 4,302 undergraduates. **Degrees:** 172 associate awarded. **Location:** 150 miles from Sacramento. **Calendar:** Semester, limited summer session. **Full-time faculty:** 45 total. **Part-time faculty:** 80 total. **Special facilities:** Jogging/fitness trail, arboretum, astronomy dome, seismograph, on-campus fire house.

**Basis for selection.** Open admission. Institution uses own assessment test for placement only.

**2009-2010 Annual costs.** Tuition/fees: $826; $6,526 out-of-state. Per-credit charge: $26 in-state; $216 out-of-state. Books/supplies: $1,638. Personal expenses: $2,514.

**2009-2010 Financial aid. Need-based:** Need-based aid available for part-time students. **Non-need-based:** Scholarships awarded for academics.

**Application procedures. Admission:** No deadline. No application fee. Admission notification on a rolling basis. Matriculation procedures required before new or returning students may register. Early application assures accommodation to new student priority registration periods. **Financial aid:** Priority date 3/2; no closing date. FAFSA, institutional form required. Applicants notified on a rolling basis starting 6/15; must reply within 2 week(s) of notification.

**Academics. Special study options:** Cooperative education, distance learning, double major, ESL, independent study, internships, liberal arts/career combination. License preparation in paramedic. **Credit/placement by examination:** AP, CLEP, institutional tests. 12 credit hours maximum toward associate degree. **Support services:** GED preparation and test center, learning center, remedial instruction, study skills assistance, tutoring, writing center.

**Majors. Biology:** General. **Business:** General, administrative services, business admin, hospitality admin. **Computer sciences:** General, programming. **Conservation:** General, forest technology, forestry, management/policy. **Family/consumer sciences:** Child development. **Interdisciplinary:** Natural sciences. **Liberal arts:** Arts/sciences. **Math:** General. **Mechanic/repair:** Automotive. **Parks/recreation:** Health/fitness. **Personal/culinary services:** Culinary arts. **Physical sciences:** Chemistry, physics, planetary. **Protective services:** Fire safety technology. **Social sciences:** General. **Visual/performing arts:** Art, photography.

**Computing on campus.** 60 workstations in library, computer center, student center. Online course registration, online library, wireless network available.

**Student life. Freshman orientation:** Mandatory. 1-hour session prior to registration. **Housing:** Coed dorms, special housing for disabled, apartments available. **Activities:** Bands, choral groups, dance, drama, music ensembles, student government, student newspaper, symphony orchestra.

**Athletics. Intercollegiate:** Basketball M, volleyball W. **Team name:** Claim Jumpers.

**Student services.** Adult student services, alcohol/substance abuse counseling, career counseling, services for economically disadvantaged, student employment services, financial aid counseling, health services, on-campus daycare, personal counseling, placement for graduates, veterans' counselor. **Physically disabled:** Services for visually, speech, hearing impaired. **Transfer:** Re-entry adviser for new students. Transfer center, transfer adviser, college fairs on campus for students transferring to 4-year colleges.

**Contact.** Phone: (209) 588-5231 Fax: (209) 588-5337
Kathy Smith, Director of Admissions and Records, Columbia College, 11600 Columbia College Drive, Sonora, CA 95370

## Concorde Career College: Garden Grove
### Garden Grove, California
www.concorde.edu

- For-profit 2-year health science and technical college
- Small city

**General.** Regionally accredited; also accredited by ACCSC. **Enrollment:** 148 degree-seeking undergraduates. **Degrees:** 113 associate awarded. **Calendar:** Continuous. **Full-time faculty:** 40 total.

**Basis for selection.** Open admission, but selective for some programs.

**2009-2010 Annual costs.** Prices effective on or after September 1, 2009. Medical Assisting: $12,876. Dental Assisting: $12,609. Insurance Coding Specialist: $12,644. Vocational Nursing (Days): $32,481. Vocational Nursing (Weekend): $33,576. Respiratory Therapy (A.S.): $37,482. Prices include: Uniforms, Health Screen, Registration fee, Books, and Tax.

**Academics.** Credit/placement by examination: CLEP.

**Majors. Health:** Respiratory therapy technology.

**Contact.** E-mail: agueco@concorde.edu
Phone: (714) 703-1900
Cary Kaplan, Director of Admissions, Concorde Career College: Garden Grove, 12951 Euclid Street, #101, Garden Grove, CA 92840

## Concorde Career College: North Hollywood
North Hollywood, California
www.concorde.edu

- For-profit 2-year health science college
- Large city

**General.** Accredited by ACCSC. **Enrollment:** 160 degree-seeking undergraduates. **Degrees:** 90 associate awarded. **Calendar:** Continuous. **Full-time faculty:** 35 total. **Part-time faculty:** 15 total.

**Basis for selection.** Institutional exam scores important. CPAT, Wonderlic used.

**2009-2010 Annual costs.** Costs vary by program from $8,000 to $40,000.

**Application procedures. Admission:** No deadline. No application fee. Admission notification on a rolling basis.

**Academics.** Credit/placement by examination: CLEP.

**Majors. Health:** Respiratory therapy technology.

**Contact.** Phone: (818) 766-8151 Toll-free number: (800) 464-1212
Fax: (818) 766-1587
Concorde Career College: North Hollywood, 12412 Victory Boulevard, North Hollywood, CA 91606

## Concorde Career College: San Bernardino
San Bernardino, California
www.concorde.edu

- For-profit 2-year technical college
- Small city

**General.** Regionally accredited; also accredited by ACCSC. **Enrollment:** 796 degree-seeking undergraduates. **Degrees:** 100 associate awarded. **Calendar:** Continuous. **Full-time faculty:** 52 total. **Part-time faculty:** 15 total.

**2009-2010 Annual costs.** Prices effective on or after September 1, 2009. Medical Assistant: $13,455. Dental Assistant: $13,567. Medical Administrative Assistant: $13,443. Vocational Nursing (Days): $28,452. Vocational Nursing (Night Class): $29,872. Respiratory Therapy: $41,208. Surgical Technology: $23,159. Prices include: Uniforms, Health Screen, Registration fee, Books, and Tax.

**Application procedures. Financial aid:** Closing date 3/2.

**Academics.** Credit/placement by examination: CLEP.

**Majors. Health:** Respiratory therapy technology.

**Contact.** Concorde Career College: San Bernardino, 201 East Airport Dr., San Bernardino, CA 92408

## Concorde Career College: San Diego
San Diego, California
www.concorde.edu

- For-profit 2-year health science and nursing college
- Very large city

**General.** Regionally accredited; also accredited by ACCSC. **Enrollment:** 649 degree-seeking undergraduates. **Degrees:** 36 associate awarded. **Calendar:** Differs by program. **Full-time faculty:** 83 total. **Part-time faculty:** 3 total.

**Basis for selection.** Open admission. **Homeschooled:** Transcript of courses and grades required.

**2009-2010 Annual costs.** Prices effective on or after September 1, 2009. Medical Assistant: $13,575. Dental Assistant: $13,780. Insurance Billing Specialist: $13,497. Vocational Nursing: $30,651. Massage Therapy: $13,911. Surgical Technology: $25,523. Respiratory Therapy (A.S.): $37,787. Prices include: Uniforms, Health Screen, Registration fee, Books, and Tax.

**Application procedures. Admission:** No deadline. $100 fee.

**Academics.** Credit/placement by examination: CLEP.

**Majors. Health:** Respiratory therapy assistant.

**Contact.** E-mail: creese@concorde.edu
Lauren Freeman, Director of Admissions, Concorde Career College: San Diego, 4393 Imperial Avenue, San Diego, CA 92113

## Contra Costa College
San Pablo, California
www.contracosta.edu     CB code: 4943

- Public 2-year community college
- Commuter campus in large town

**General.** Founded in 1948. Regionally accredited. Middle College High School on-campus. 100% pass rate on NCLEX for nursing program graduates. **Enrollment:** 8,995 undergraduates. **Degrees:** 425 associate awarded. **ROTC:** Naval. **Location:** 20 miles from San Francisco. **Calendar:** Semester, limited summer session. **Full-time faculty:** 110 total. **Part-time faculty:** 225 total. **Special facilities:** Center for scientific excellence.

**Transfer out. Colleges most students transferred to 2009:** California State University: East Bay, California State University: San Francisco, University of California: Davis, San Jose State University, University of California: Berkeley.

**Basis for selection.** Open admission.

**High school preparation.** College-preparatory program recommended.

**2009-2010 Annual costs.** Tuition/fees: $782; $6,302 out-of-state. Per-credit charge: $26 in-state; $210 out-of-state.

**Application procedures. Admission:** No deadline. No application fee. Admission notification on a rolling basis. **Financial aid:** Priority date 3/2; no closing date. FAFSA required. Applicants notified on a rolling basis; must reply within 2 week(s) of notification.

**Academics. Special study options:** Cross-registration, dual enrollment of high school students, honors, independent study. License preparation in nursing, paramedic, radiology, real estate. **Credit/placement by examination:** CLEP, institutional tests. 12 credit hours maximum toward associate degree. **Support services:** Learning center, remedial instruction, tutoring.

**Majors. Area/ethnic studies:** African-American, Chicano/Hispanic-American/Latino. **Biology:** General. **Business:** Administrative services, office/clerical, real estate. **Computer sciences:** General, applications programming. **Education:** Bilingual, teacher assistance. **Engineering:** General. **Engineering technology:** Architectural, drafting. **Family/consumer sciences:** Institutional food production. **Health:** Dental assistant, medical assistant, nursing (RN). **History:** General. **Liberal arts:** Arts/sciences. **Math:** General. **Mechanic/repair:** Auto body. **Personal/culinary services:** Cosmetic. **Physical sciences:** Chemistry, physics. **Protective services:** Police science. **Psychology:** General. **Social sciences:** Geography, sociology. **Visual/performing arts:** Dramatic, interior design.

**Most popular majors.** Business/marketing 11%, health sciences 20%, liberal arts 48%.

**Student life. Activities:** Jazz band, choral groups, dance, drama, international student organizations, literary magazine, music ensembles, musical theater, student government, student newspaper, TV station.

**Athletics.** NAIA, NCAA, NJCAA. **Intercollegiate:** Baseball M, basketball, football (tackle) M, tennis, track and field. **Team name:** Comets.

**Student services.** Adult student services, alcohol/substance abuse counseling, career counseling, student employment services, financial aid counseling, health services, minority student services, on-campus daycare, personal counseling, veterans' counselor, women's services. **Transfer:** Re-entry adviser for new students. Transfer center, transfer adviser, college fairs on campus for students transferring to 4-year colleges.

**Contact.** Phone: (510) 235-7800 ext. 4210 Fax: (510) 236-6768
Mikeal Aldaco, Director of Admissions and Records, Contra Costa College, 2600 Mission Bell Drive, San Pablo, CA 94806

## Copper Mountain College
### Joshua Tree, California
### www.cmccd.edu
CB code: 3889

- Public 2-year community college
- Commuter campus in small town

**General.** Regionally accredited. **Enrollment:** 2,329 undergraduates. **Degrees:** 142 associate awarded. **Location:** 120 miles from Los Angeles, 45 miles from Palm Springs. **Calendar:** Semester, limited summer session. **Full-time faculty:** 40 total. **Part-time faculty:** 115 total.

**Transfer out. Colleges most students transferred to 2009:** California State University: San Bernardino.

**Basis for selection.** Open admission. Limited admission to some allied health programs. **Adult students:** Accuplacer assessment tests required.

**2009-2010 Annual costs.** Tuition/fees: $782; $6,482 out-of-state. Per-credit charge: $26 in-state; $216 out-of-state. Books/supplies: $1,566. Personal expenses: $2,520.

**2008-2009 Financial aid. Need-based:** Need-based aid available for part-time students.

**Application procedures. Admission:** No deadline. No application fee. Application must be submitted online. Admission notification on a rolling basis. **Financial aid:** Priority date 3/2; no closing date. FAFSA required.

**Academics. Special study options:** Distance learning, dual enrollment of high school students, ESL, independent study, study abroad. License preparation in nursing, paramedic. **Credit/placement by examination:** AP, CLEP, institutional tests. **Support services:** GED preparation and test center, remedial instruction, study skills assistance, tutoring.

**Majors. Business:** Business admin. **Communications:** General. **Computer sciences:** General, computer science. **Foreign languages:** Spanish. **Health:** Licensed practical nurse. **History:** General. **Liberal arts:** Arts/sciences. **Math:** General. **Mechanic/repair:** Automotive. **Philosophy/religion:** Philosophy. **Protective services:** Fire safety technology, law enforcement admin. **Psychology:** General. **Social sciences:** General, anthropology, economics, political science. **Visual/performing arts:** Art.

**Computing on campus.** 40 workstations in library, computer center.

**Student life. Freshman orientation:** Mandatory. Preregistration for classes offered. 1.5 hour group orientation offered about 16 times prior to each semester. **Activities:** Literary magazine, student government, student newspaper.

**Student services.** Adult student services, career counseling, services for economically disadvantaged, student employment services, financial aid counseling, veterans' counselor. **Physically disabled:** Services for visually, speech, hearing impaired. **Transfer:** Pre-admission transcript evaluation for new students. Transfer center, transfer adviser, college fairs on campus for students transferring to 4-year colleges.

**Contact.** Phone: (760) 366-3791 ext. 4232 Toll-free number: (866) 366-3791 ext. 4232 Fax: (760) 366-5257
Gregory Brown, Vice President of Student Services, Copper Mountain College, 6162 Rotary Way, Joshua Tree, CA 92252

## Cosumnes River College
### Sacramento, California
### www.crc.losrios.edu
CB code: 4121

- Public 2-year junior college
- Commuter campus in large city

**General.** Founded in 1970. Regionally accredited. Classes offered at Folsom Lake Center, El Dorado Center and Folsom Prison. **Enrollment:** 16,235 undergraduates. **Degrees:** 583 associate awarded. **Location:** 12 miles from downtown. **Calendar:** Semester, limited summer session. **Full-time faculty:** 175 total. **Part-time faculty:** 200 total.

**Basis for selection.** Open admission.

**2009-2010 Annual costs.** Tuition/fees: $812; $6,512 out-of-state. Per-credit charge: $26 in-state; $216 out-of-state. Books/supplies: $1,638. Personal expenses: $2,826.

**Application procedures. Admission:** No deadline. No application fee. Admission notification on a rolling basis beginning on or about 3/1. First-time students encouraged to participate in orientation and matriculation sessions. English and mathematics tests for placement recommended. **Financial aid:** Priority date 5/1; no closing date. FAFSA required. Applicants notified on a rolling basis starting 7/20; must reply within 4 week(s) of notification.

**Academics. Special study options:** Cooperative education, distance learning, double major, dual enrollment of high school students, ESL, honors, independent study, internships, study abroad. **Credit/placement by examination:** CLEP. 15 credit hours maximum toward associate degree. **Support services:** Learning center, reduced course load, remedial instruction, tutoring.

**Majors. Agriculture:** Animal sciences, business, equestrian studies, horticultural science, plant sciences. **Architecture:** Environmental design, interior, landscape. **Area/ethnic studies:** American, women's. **Business:** General, accounting, business admin, entrepreneurial studies, finance, real estate. **Communications:** Advertising, broadcast journalism, journalism, public relations. **Communications technology:** General. **Computer sciences:** Information systems, programming. **Construction:** Maintenance. **Education:** Early childhood. **Engineering technology:** Drafting. **Health:** Medical assistant, medical records technology. **Interdisciplinary:** Gerontology. **Liberal arts:** Arts/sciences. **Protective services:** Fire safety technology, law enforcement admin. **Social sciences:** Sociology. **Visual/performing arts:** Art, art history/conservation, cinematography, commercial photography, dramatic, interior design, photography, studio arts.

**Most popular majors.** Business/marketing 8%, health sciences 6%, liberal arts 52%, trade and industry 6%.

**Student life. Activities:** Bands, choral groups, drama, radio station, student government, student newspaper, TV station, African-American Students Association, Hispanic/Latino Scholars, Asian American Club, Christian Club, earth club.

**Athletics. Intercollegiate:** Baseball M, basketball, soccer, softball W, tennis, track and field, volleyball W. **Intramural:** Badminton, bowling, fencing, golf, racquetball, skiing, swimming, tennis, track and field, volleyball.

**Student services.** Adult student services, career counseling, student employment services, health services, on-campus daycare, personal counseling, placement for graduates, veterans' counselor. **Physically disabled:** Services for hearing impaired. **Transfer:** Transfer adviser for students transferring to 4-year colleges.

**Contact.** Phone: (916) 691-7410 Fax: (916) 691-7467
Celia Esposito-Noy, Vice President, Student Services and Enrollment Management, Cosumnes River College, 8401 Center Parkway, Sacramento, CA 95823

## Crafton Hills College
### Yucaipa, California
### www.craftonhills.edu
CB code: 4126

- Public 2-year community college
- Commuter campus in large town

**General.** Founded in 1972. Regionally accredited. Located in southern California, on rolling hills above the Yucaipa Valley, Crafton Hills College offers majors in the liberal arts and sciences, career and technical studies. **Enrollment:** 6,703 undergraduates. **Degrees:** 326 associate awarded. **Location:** 17 miles from San Bernardino, 40 miles from Ontario. **Calendar:** Semester, limited summer session. **Full-time faculty:** 58 total. **Part-time faculty:** 160 total. **Special facilities:** Walking trails, child care services for preschool-aged children.

**Basis for selection.** Open admission.

**2009-2010 Annual costs.** Tuition/fees: $808; $6,628 out-of-state. Per-credit charge: $26 in-state; $220 out-of-state. Books/supplies: $1,566. Personal expenses: $1,800.

**Financial aid.** All financial aid based on need. Need-based aid available for part-time students. Work-study available nights and for part-time students.

**Application procedures. Admission:** No deadline. No application fee. Application must be submitted online. Admission notification on a rolling basis. Students under 18 admitted with special permission. **Financial aid:** Priority date 4/15, closing date 6/2. FAFSA, institutional form required. Applicants notified on a rolling basis starting 7/31; must reply within 2 week(s) of notification.

**Academics. Special study options:** Cooperative education, cross-registration, distance learning, double major, dual enrollment of high school students, honors, study abroad. License preparation in paramedic, radiology. **Credit/placement by examination:** CLEP, institutional tests. 36 credit hours maximum toward associate degree. **Support services:** Learning center, remedial instruction, study skills assistance, tutoring.

**Majors. Biology:** General, bacteriology. **Business:** Administrative services, business admin, marketing, office/clerical. **Computer sciences:** General, programming. **Education:** Early childhood, health occupations. **Foreign languages:** General, French, Spanish. **Health:** EMT paramedic, medical radiologic technology/radiation therapy, respiratory therapy technology. **History:** General. **Liberal arts:** Arts/sciences. **Math:** General. **Physical sciences:** Chemistry, geology, physics. **Protective services:** Firefighting, law enforcement admin. **Psychology:** General. **Social sciences:** General, anthropology, economics, geography, political science, sociology. **Visual/performing arts:** Art, dramatic.

**Most popular majors.** Health sciences 16%, interdisciplinary studies 48%, public administration/social services 7%, social sciences 6%.

**Computing on campus.** 172 workstations in library, computer center.

**Student life. Freshman orientation:** Available. **Activities:** Jazz band, drama, music ensembles, musical theater, student government, student newspaper.

**Athletics. Intercollegiate:** Golf, tennis, volleyball, weight lifting.

**Student services.** Career counseling, student employment services, health services, on-campus daycare, personal counseling, placement for graduates, veterans' counselor. **Physically disabled:** Services for visually, speech, hearing impaired. **Transfer:** Pre-admission transcript evaluation for new students. Transfer center, transfer adviser, college fairs on campus for students transferring to 4-year colleges.

**Contact.** E-mail: admissions@craftonhills.edu
Phone: (909) 389-3372 Fax: (909) 389-9141
Joe Cabrales, Dean, Student Services, Crafton Hills College, 11711 Sand Canyon Road, Yucaipa, CA 92399-1799

## Cuesta College
### San Luis Obispo, California
www.cuesta.org                              CB code: 4101

- Public 2-year community college
- Commuter campus in large town

**General.** Founded in 1964. Regionally accredited. Additional North County Campus in Paso Robles and South County Center(s) in Arroyo Grande and Nipomo. **Enrollment:** 12,911 undergraduates. **Degrees:** 712 associate awarded. **Location:** 200 miles from Los Angeles, 6 miles from San Luis Obispo. **Calendar:** Semester, extensive summer session. **Full-time faculty:** 145 total. **Part-time faculty:** 315 total. **Special facilities:** Adobe museum (Chumash Indian).

**Student profile.**

| | | | |
|---|---|---|---|
| Out-of-state: | 3% | 25 or older: | 33% |

**Transfer out. Colleges most students transferred to 2009:** California Polytechnic State University: San Luis Obispo, CSU: Chico, San Francisco State University, California State Polytechnic University: Pomona.

**Basis for selection.** Open admission, but selective for some programs. Nursing program requires critical thinking and math assessments. Prerequisite courses evaluated. **Learning Disabled:** No special admission but must be assessed and qualified to receive services.

**2009-2010 Annual costs.** Tuition/fees: $846; $6,516 out-of-state. Per-credit charge: $26 in-state; $215 out-of-state. Books/supplies: $1,638. Personal expenses: $2,664.

**Financial aid. Need-based:** Work-study available for part-time students.

**Application procedures. Admission:** No deadline. No application fee. Admission notification on a rolling basis. **Financial aid:** Priority date 3/2; no closing date. FAFSA required. Applicants notified on a rolling basis starting 4/15.

**Academics. Special study options:** Cooperative education, distance learning, double major, ESL, honors, independent study, student-designed major, study abroad, weekend college. Bachelor's degree programs available on campus. **Credit/placement by examination:** CLEP, institutional tests. 12 credit hours maximum toward associate degree. **Support services:** Learning center, remedial instruction, study skills assistance, tutoring, writing center.

**Majors. Biology:** General. **Business:** General, real estate. **Communications:** General, broadcast journalism, journalism. **Computer sciences:** Computer science. **Education:** Art, early childhood, mathematics, physical, special. **Engineering:** Electrical. **Health:** Nursing (RN). **Liberal arts:** Arts/sciences, library assistant. **Math:** General. **Mechanic/repair:** Auto body. **Physical sciences:** Chemistry, physics. **Protective services:** Law enforcement admin. **Visual/performing arts:** Interior design.

**Computing on campus.** 300 workstations in library, computer center, student center. Online course registration, online library available.

**Student life. Freshman orientation:** Available. **Activities:** Jazz band, choral groups, dance, drama, music ensembles, musical theater, radio station, student government, student newspaper, TV station, Alpha Gamma Sigma (honor society).

**Athletics. Intercollegiate:** Baseball M, basketball, cross-country, diving, soccer W, softball W, swimming, tennis W, track and field, volleyball W, water polo, wrestling M.

**Student services.** Adult student services, career counseling, student employment services, financial aid counseling, health services, legal services, on-campus daycare, personal counseling, veterans' counselor. **Physically disabled:** Services for visually, speech, hearing impaired. **Transfer:** Re-entry adviser for new students. Transfer center, transfer adviser, college fairs on campus for students transferring to 4-year colleges.

**Contact.** E-mail: admit@bass.cuesta.cc.ca.us
Phone: (805) 546-3140 Fax: (805) 546-3975
Joy Chambers, Director of Admissions and Records, Cuesta College, Box 8106, San Luis Obispo, CA 93403

## Cuyamaca College
### El Cajon, California
www.cuyamaca.net                            CB code: 4252

- Public 2-year community college
- Small city

**General.** Founded in 1978. Regionally accredited. **Enrollment:** 9,230 undergraduates. **Degrees:** 360 associate awarded. **ROTC:** Army, Air Force. **Location:** 18 miles from San Diego. **Calendar:** Semester, limited summer session. **Full-time faculty:** 89 total. **Part-time faculty:** 292 total. **Special facilities:** Automotive technology facility, water gardens, child care facility, museum.

**Transfer out. Colleges most students transferred to 2009:** San Diego State University, National University.

**Basis for selection.** Open admission.

**2009-2010 Annual costs.** Tuition/fees: $820; $6,520 out-of-state. Per-credit charge: $26 in-state; $216 out-of-state. Books/supplies: $1,500. Personal expenses: $1,700.

**2008-2009 Financial aid. Need-based:** Work-study available nights, weekends and for part-time students.

**Application procedures. Admission:** No deadline. No application fee in-state; $163 out-of-state. Admission notification on a rolling basis. **Financial aid:** Priority date 3/2; no closing date. FAFSA required. Applicants notified on a rolling basis; must reply within 2 week(s) of notification.

**Academics. Special study options:** Cooperative education, cross-registration, distance learning, double major, dual enrollment of high school students, ESL, honors, independent study, internships, study abroad, weekend college. License preparation in real estate. **Credit/placement by examination:** AP, CLEP, institutional tests. **Support services:** Remedial instruction, tutoring.

**Majors. Agriculture:** Ornamental horticulture. **Business:** Accounting, business admin, real estate. **Engineering technology:** Architectural, computer systems, drafting, electrical, surveying. **Family/consumer sciences:** Child care. **Liberal arts:** Arts/sciences.

**Most popular majors.** Business/marketing 15%, computer/information sciences 6%, education 7%, liberal arts 48%.

**Computing on campus.** Online course registration available.

**Student life. Freshman orientation:** Available. **Activities:** Dance, student government, student newspaper, African American student union, Christian club, Cuyamaca College Spanish club, MECHA, Phi Theta Kappa.

**Athletics. Intercollegiate:** Basketball, cross-country, golf M, soccer, tennis W, track and field, volleyball W. **Team name:** Coyotes.

**Student services.** Adult student services, career counseling, student employment services, financial aid counseling, health services, on-campus daycare, personal counseling, veterans' counselor. **Physically disabled:** Services for visually, speech, hearing impaired. **Transfer:** Pre-admission transcript evaluation for new students. Transfer center, transfer adviser, college fairs on campus for students transferring to 4-year colleges.

**Contact.** Phone: (619) 660-4275 Fax: (619) 660-4575
Susan Topham, Admissions Director, Cuyamaca College, 900 Rancho San Diego Parkway, El Cajon, CA 92019-4304

## Cypress College
**Cypress, California**
**www.cypresscollege.edu**                  **CB code: 4104**

◗   Public 2-year community college
◗   Commuter campus in small city

**General.** Founded in 1966. Regionally accredited. **Enrollment:** 16,670 undergraduates. **Degrees:** 879 associate awarded. **Location:** 30 miles from Los Angeles. **Calendar:** Semester, limited summer session. **Full-time faculty:** 190 total. **Part-time faculty:** 220 total.

**Student profile.**

Out-of-state:               5%        25 or older:               44%

**Transfer out. Colleges most students transferred to 2009:** CSU Fullerton, CSU Long Beach.

**Basis for selection.** Open admission. College administered English and math placement exams.

**High school preparation.** College-preparatory program required.

**2009-2010 Annual costs.** Tuition/fees: $812; $6,512 out-of-state. Per-credit charge: $26 in-state; $216 out-of-state. Books/supplies: $1,386. Personal expenses: $1,898.

**Application procedures. Admission:** No deadline. No application fee. Admission notification on a rolling basis. **Financial aid:** Priority date 5/31; no closing date. FAFSA required. Applicants notified on a rolling basis starting 8/1; must reply within 2 week(s) of notification.

**Academics. Special study options:** Distance learning, dual enrollment of high school students, ESL, honors, independent study, internships, liberal arts/career combination, study abroad. License preparation in aviation, dental hygiene, nursing, real estate. **Credit/placement by examination:** CLEP, institutional tests. 12 credit hours maximum toward associate degree. **Support services:** Learning center, reduced course load, remedial instruction, study skills assistance, tutoring, writing center.

**Majors. Area/ethnic studies:** Asian, Latin American. **Business:** General, accounting, administrative services, business admin, hospitality/recreation, management information systems, management science, office technology, office/clerical, tourism promotion. **Communications:** Journalism. **Computer sciences:** General, data processing, information systems. **Education:** General, elementary, physical, secondary, technology/industrial arts. **Engineering:** General. **Family/consumer sciences:** Institutional food production. **Foreign languages:** French, German, Spanish. **Health:** Dental assistant, dental hygiene, dental lab technology, health services, medical assistant, medical radiologic technology/radiation therapy, medical records admin, medical records technology, nursing (RN), predental, premedicine, prepharmacy, preveterinary. **History:** General. **Legal studies:** Court reporting. **Liberal arts:** Arts/sciences. **Math:** General. **Mechanic/repair:** Aircraft, auto body, automotive, electronics/electrical, heating/ac/refrig. **Personal/culinary services:** Culinary arts, mortuary science. **Philosophy/religion:** Philosophy. **Physical sciences:** Chemistry, geology, physics. **Psychology:** General. **Public administration:** Human services. **Social sciences:** Anthropology, economics, geography, political science, sociology. **Transportation:** Airline/

commercial pilot, aviation, aviation management, flight attendant. **Visual/performing arts:** General, art, commercial/advertising art, dance, dramatic, music performance, theater design.

**Computing on campus.** 800 workstations in library, computer center, student center.

**Student life. Freshman orientation:** Available. **Activities:** Bands, choral groups, dance, drama, literary magazine, music ensembles, musical theater, student government, student newspaper.

**Athletics.** NJCAA. **Intercollegiate:** Baseball M, basketball, diving, golf, soccer, softball W, swimming, tennis, volleyball W, water polo, wrestling M. **Intramural:** Badminton, baseball M, basketball, softball, volleyball. **Team name:** Chargers.

**Student services.** Career counseling, student employment services, health services, on-campus daycare, personal counseling, veterans' counselor. **Physically disabled:** Services for visually, speech, hearing impaired. **Transfer:** Re-entry adviser, pre-admission transcript evaluation for new students. Transfer center, transfer adviser, college fairs on campus for students transferring to 4-year colleges.

**Contact.** E-mail: admissions@cypresscollege.edu
Phone: (714) 484-7346 Fax: (714) 484-7446
Dave Wassenaar, Dean of Admissions and Records, Cypress College, 9200 Valley View Street, Cypress, CA 90630

## De Anza College
**Cupertino, California**
**www.deanza.edu**                  **CB code: 4286**

◗   Public 2-year community college
◗   Commuter campus in large town

**General.** Founded in 1967. Regionally accredited. **Enrollment:** 24,000 undergraduates. **Degrees:** 1,195 associate awarded. **ROTC:** Army, Air Force. **Location:** 5 miles from San Jose, 40 miles from San Francisco. **Calendar:** Quarter, extensive summer session. **Full-time faculty:** 300 total. **Part-time faculty:** 540 total. **Special facilities:** Planetarium, California history center, environmental studies area, advanced technology center, art museum, performing arts facility.

**Transfer out. Colleges most students transferred to 2009:** University of California: Davis, San Jose State, San Francisco State, University of California: Berkeley, University of California: Santa Cruz.

**Basis for selection.** Open admission, but selective for some programs. Limited admission for nursing and physical therapist assistant applicants.

**2009-2010 Annual costs.** Tuition/fees: $855; $6,345 out-of-state. Per-credit charge: $17 in-state; $139 out-of-state. Books/supplies: $1,728. Personal expenses: $2,826.

**Financial aid.** All financial aid based on need. Need-based aid available for part-time students.

**Application procedures. Admission:** No deadline. No application fee. Admission notification on a rolling basis. **Financial aid:** No deadline. FAFSA required. Applicants notified on a rolling basis starting 5/15; must reply within 2 week(s) of notification.

**Academics. Special study options:** Cooperative education, cross-registration, distance learning, dual enrollment of high school students, ESL, honors, independent study, internships, study abroad, weekend college. License preparation in nursing. **Credit/placement by examination:** AP, CLEP, institutional tests. 45 credit hours maximum toward associate degree. **Support services:** Learning center, pre-admission summer program, remedial instruction, tutoring.

**Majors. Area/ethnic studies:** African-American, Asian-American, Chicano/Hispanic-American/Latino, Latin American, Native American. **Biology:** General. **Business:** Accounting, administrative services, business admin, marketing, purchasing, real estate, taxation. **Communications:** General. **Computer sciences:** General, applications programming, computer science, programming, systems analysis. **Education:** Early childhood. **Engineering:** General, computer, electrical, mechanical. **Engineering technology:** Drafting. **Foreign languages:** French, German, Spanish. **Health:** Medical assistant, nursing (RN). **History:** General. **Legal studies:** Paralegal. **Liberal arts:** Arts/sciences. **Math:** General. **Philosophy/religion:** Philosophy. **Physical sciences:** Astronomy, chemistry, geology, physics. **Protective services:** Law enforcement admin, security services. **Psychology:** General. **Science technology:** Biological. **Social sciences:** Anthropology, economics, geography, political science, sociology. **Visual/performing arts:** Art, art history/

conservation, ceramics, cinematography, commercial/advertising art, painting, photography, printmaking, sculpture.

**Computing on campus.** 300 workstations in library, computer center, student center. Online course registration available.

**Student life. Freshman orientation:** Available. Two day counseling course for new, incoming students. **Activities:** Bands, choral groups, dance, drama, literary magazine, music ensembles, student government, student newspaper, symphony orchestra, TV station.

**Athletics. Intercollegiate:** Baseball M, basketball, cross-country, diving, football (tackle) M, golf, soccer, softball W, swimming, tennis, track and field, volleyball, water polo M. **Intramural:** Badminton, baseball M, basketball, bowling, fencing, gymnastics, racquetball, soccer W, swimming, tennis, volleyball. **Team name:** Dons.

**Student services.** Adult student services, alcohol/substance abuse counseling, career counseling, services for economically disadvantaged, student employment services, financial aid counseling, health services, legal services, minority student services, on-campus daycare, personal counseling, placement for graduates, veterans' counselor. **Physically disabled:** Services for visually, speech, hearing impaired. **Transfer:** Re-entry adviser for new students. Transfer center, transfer adviser, college fairs on campus for students transferring to 4-year colleges.

**Contact.** E-mail: webreg@fhda.edu
Phone: (408) 864-5300 Fax: (408) 864-8329
Dean of Admissions and Records, De Anza College, 21250 Stevens Creek Boulevard, Cupertino, CA 95014

---

## Deep Springs College
### Dyer, Nevada
**www.deepsprings.edu**  CB code: 4281

- Private 2-year liberal arts college for men
- Residential campus in rural community
- SAT or ACT (ACT writing optional), application essay, interview required

**General.** Founded in 1917. Regionally accredited. All-male liberal arts college located on a cattle-ranch and alfalfa farm in California's High Desert. Electrical pioneer L.L. Nunn founded the school in 1917 on the three pillars of academics, labor, and self-governance in order to help young men prepare themselves for lives of service to humanity. **Enrollment:** 24 degree-seeking undergraduates. **Degrees:** 13 associate awarded. **Location:** 45 miles from Bishop. **Calendar:** Continuous, limited summer session. **Full-time faculty:** 4 total; 75% have terminal degrees, 25% minority, 25% women. **Part-time faculty:** 12 total; 100% have terminal degrees, 8% minority, 17% women. **Class size:** 100% < 20. **Special facilities:** Student-operated 2,600-acre cattle and alfalfa ranch, dairy.

**Student profile.** Among degree-seeking undergraduates, 1 transferred in from other institutions.

**Out-of-state:** 100%  **Live on campus:** 100%

**Transfer out.** 100% of students enrolled in the transfer program go on to 4-year colleges. **Colleges most students transferred to 2009:** Brown University, University of Chicago, Bard College, Northwestern, Stanford University.

**Basis for selection.** Essays most important. School achievement record, interview, extracurricular activities, and recommendations strongly considered. Admissions process created and run by student committee. SAT Subject Tests recommended. International students who cannot take SAT or who have taken equivalent standardized test evaluated on case-by-case basis. 2-round application process: in first round, 3 essays are required. If accepted into second round, additional 4 essays and 3- to 4-day campus visit and interview required.

**2009-2010 Annual costs.** All students receive full scholarship covering tuition, room, and board valued at $50,000. Books/supplies: $1,000.

**2008-2009 Financial aid. Need-based:** Work-study available nights and weekends. **Non-need-based:** Scholarships awarded for academics.

**Application procedures. Admission:** Closing date 11/15 (postmark date). No application fee. Application must be submitted on paper. Admission notification 4/15. Must reply by 5/1. Approximately 40 applicants invited to complete part II of application process between January and March. Includes a 3-day campus visit, interview, and writing 3 additional essays. Foreign students and those with economic hardship may be exempt from

visit upon request. Financial aid available for students with economic hardship to visit college for second round interviews. **Financial aid:** No deadline.

**Academics.** Students required to take 3 classes: composition, public speaking, and summer seminar (interdisciplinary course broadly oriented around questions of political theory). Regular curriculum includes courses in humanities, social sciences and natural sciences. **Special study options:** Independent study. **Credit/placement by examination:** CLEP.

**Majors. Liberal arts:** Arts/sciences.

**Computing on campus.** 7 workstations in library, computer center. Online library, helpline, repair service available.

**Student life. Freshman orientation:** Mandatory. **Policies:** All students work on jobs running college or ranch. Student committees organize all community events as well as handle admissions, faculty hiring, public relations, and review/reinvitation process. Students also self-govern, managing community issues and each other's conduct. Student-formulated isolation and drug/alcohol policies: drugs prohibited, students prohibited from leaving valley during term, guests prohibited from visiting. **Housing:** Guaranteed on-campus for all undergraduates. Special housing for disabled available. Pets allowed in dorm rooms. **Activities:** Jazz band, campus ministries, choral groups, dance, drama, literary magazine, music ensembles, musical theater, student government, student newspaper.

**Athletics. Intramural:** Basketball M, boxing M, cross-country M, equestrian M, football (non-tackle) M, football (tackle) M, rifle M, rodeo M, skiing M, soccer M, swimming M, table tennis M, track and field M, volleyball M, weight lifting M, wrestling M.

**Student services.** Career counseling, health services, personal counseling, placement for graduates. **Transfer:** Transfer center, transfer adviser for students transferring to 4-year colleges.

**Contact.** E-mail: apcom@deepsprings.edu
Phone: (760) 872-2000 Fax: (760) 874-7077
Noam Finkelstein, Chair, Applications Committee, Deep Springs College, Applications Committee, Dyer, NV 89010-9803

---

## Diablo Valley College
### Pleasant Hill, California
**www.dvc.edu**  CB code: 4295

- Public 2-year community college
- Commuter campus in large town

**General.** Founded in 1948. Regionally accredited. College for Kids available on-campus which provides enrichment activities for fourth through ninth graders. **Enrollment:** 9,228 degree-seeking undergraduates. **Degrees:** 621 associate awarded. **ROTC:** Army, Naval. **Location:** 25 miles from San Francisco. **Calendar:** Semester, extensive summer session. **Full-time faculty:** 255 total; 36% minority, 54% women. **Part-time faculty:** 551 total; 38% minority, 52% women. **Class size:** 21% < 20, 60% 20-39, 15% 40-49, 3% 50-99, less than 1% >100. **Special facilities:** Student-run restaurant and bakery, observatory, planetarium, three art collections, duck pond. **Partnerships:** Formal partnerships with Wells Fargo, Chevron, Pacific Bell, City of San Ramon, Contra Costa/Tri-Valley Telecommunication Incubator.

**Student profile.** Among degree-seeking undergraduates, 52% enrolled in a transfer program, 15% enrolled in a vocational program, 11,553 transferred in from other institutions.

**Transfer out.** 53% of students enrolled in the transfer program go on to 4-year colleges. **Colleges most students transferred to 2009:** University of California: Berkeley, San Francisco State, University of California: East Bay, California State University: Sacramento, University of California: Davis.

**Basis for selection.** Open admission. **Adult students:** SAT/ACT scores not required. **Homeschooled:** Applicants must supply a copy of their private school affidavit.

**2009-2010 Annual costs.** Tuition/fees: $780; $6,030 out-of-state. Per-credit charge: $26 in-state; $201 out-of-state. Books/supplies: $1,332. Personal expenses: $2,430.

**2008-2009 Financial aid. Need-based:** 90% of total undergraduate aid awarded as scholarships/grants, 10% as loans/jobs. Need-based aid available for part-time students.

**Application procedures. Admission:** Priority date 4/1; no deadline. No application fee. Admission notification on a rolling basis beginning on or about 4/1. **Financial aid:** Priority date 3/2, closing date 5/1. FAFSA, institutional form required. Applicants notified on a rolling basis starting 6/1; must reply within 2 week(s) of notification.

**Academics.** The college offers a comprehensive educational program that includes courses in general education, transfer, vocational, basic skills, and life-long learning. These courses are offered in flexible formats that include different hours, days, term length, and a variety of instructional delivery methods (classroom and on-line). **Special study options:** Accelerated study, cooperative education, cross-registration, distance learning, dual enrollment of high school students, ESL, honors, independent study, internships, liberal arts/career combination, study abroad, weekend college. Study abroad programs in Florence, Italy; Salamanca, Spain; Capetown, South Africa; Ghana; and London, England. License preparation in dental hygiene. **Credit/placement by examination:** AP, CLEP, institutional tests. **Support services:** Learning center, pre-admission summer program, reduced course load, remedial instruction, study skills assistance, tutoring, writing center.

**Majors. Architecture:** Technology. **Business:** Business admin. **Communications:** Digital media. **Communications technology:** General. **Computer sciences:** General, computer science, networking. **Education:** Early childhood, physical, special. **Engineering technology:** Electrical. **Health:** Athletic training. **Math:** General. **Psychology:** General. **Social sciences:** Geography, political science. **Visual/performing arts:** Digital art, theater design. **Other:** Energy Systems, Interdisciplinary studies, Library Technology, Physical Education - Fitness Instruction/Personal Trainer.

**Most popular majors.** Interdisciplinary studies 84%.

**Computing on campus.** 1,000 workstations in library, computer center, student center. Commuter students can connect to campus network. Online course registration, online library, helpline, repair service, student web hosting, wireless network available.

**Student life. Freshman orientation:** Mandatory. **Policies:** No smoking except in the quad. **Activities:** Bands, choral groups, dance, drama, film society, international student organizations, literary magazine, music ensembles, musical theater, student government, student newspaper, symphony orchestra, TV station, Alpha Gamma Sigma, Asian student union, DVC Republicans, DVC Democrats, Black student union, Latino students' alliance, Muslim student association, Christians on Campus, Greater China Cultural Association, Taiwan Discovery Club.

**Athletics.** NJCAA. **Intercollegiate:** Baseball M, basketball, cross-country, football (tackle) M, soccer W, softball W, swimming, tennis, track and field, volleyball W, water polo. **Team name:** Vikings.

**Student services.** Adult student services, career counseling, services for economically disadvantaged, student employment services, financial aid counseling, on-campus daycare, personal counseling, placement for graduates, veterans' counselor, women's services. **Physically disabled:** Services for visually, speech, hearing impaired. **Learning disabled:** Comprehensive services available. **Transfer:** Re-entry adviser for new students. Transfer center, transfer adviser, college fairs on campus for students transferring to 4-year colleges.

**Contact.** E-mail: informationcenter@dvc.edu
Phone: (925) 685-1310 Fax: (925) 609-8085
Ileana Dorn, Director of Admissions and Records, Diablo Valley College, 321 Golf Club Road, Pleasant Hill, CA 94523-1529

## East Los Angeles College

**Monterey Park, California**  |  **CB member**
**www.elac.edu**  |  **CB code: 4296**

▶ Public 2-year community college
▶ Commuter campus in very large city

**General.** Founded in 1945. Regionally accredited. **Enrollment:** 12,473 degree-seeking undergraduates; 17,676 non-degree-seeking students. **Degrees:** 1,303 associate awarded. **Location:** 7 miles from Los Angeles. **Calendar:** Semester, limited summer session. **Full-time faculty:** 212 total; 50% minority. **Part-time faculty:** 816 total; 46% minority. **Class size:** 58% < 20, 25% 20-39, 11% 40-49, 6% 50-99.

**Student profile.** Among degree-seeking undergraduates, 33% enrolled in a transfer program, 34% enrolled in a vocational program, 6% already have a bachelor's degree or higher, 2,485 enrolled as first-time, first-year students.

| | | | |
|---|---|---|---|
| **Part-time:** | 66% | **Hispanic American:** | 48% |
| **Out-of-state:** | 1% | **Native American:** | 1% |
| **Women:** | 59% | **International:** | 9% |
| **African American:** | 2% | **25 or older:** | 36% |
| **Asian American:** | 10% | | |

**Transfer out. Colleges most students transferred to 2009:** California State University: Los Angeles, California State Polytechnic University: Pomona, California State University: Long Beach, California State University: Dominguez Hills, University of California: Los Angeles.

**Basis for selection.** Open admission, but selective for some programs. Limited admission to nursing and allied health associate programs. Institution uses Assessment Placement Test for English and mathematics placement. Interview required for some nursing, respiratory technology majors.

**2009-2010 Annual costs.** Tuition/fees: $802; $6,442 out-of-state. Per-credit charge: $26 in-state; $214 out-of-state. Books/supplies: $1,638. Personal expenses: $3,096.

**2008-2009 Financial aid.** All financial aid based on need. Need-based aid available for part-time students. Work-study available nights, weekends and for part-time students. **Additional information:** Need-based enrollment fee waivers available through a state aid program.

**Application procedures. Admission:** No deadline. No application fee. **Financial aid:** Closing date 3/2. FAFSA required.

**Academics. Special study options:** Accelerated study, cooperative education, cross-registration, distance learning, double major, dual enrollment of high school students, ESL, honors, independent study, internships, study abroad, weekend college. Program for Adult College Education (PACE), ITV (Instructional Television) and Saturday classes. License preparation in nursing. **Credit/placement by examination:** CLEP. 15 credit hours maximum toward associate degree. **Support services:** GED preparation, learning center, pre-admission summer program, reduced course load, remedial instruction, study skills assistance, tutoring, writing center.

**Majors. Architecture:** Landscape, urban/community planning. **Area/ethnic studies:** African-American. **Business:** Accounting, administrative services, business admin, international marketing, managerial economics, office technology, office/clerical, real estate, sales/distribution. **Communications:** Journalism. **Communications technology:** Animation/special effects, desktop publishing. **Computer sciences:** General, programming. **Engineering:** General, architectural, civil, electrical, mechanics. **Engineering technology:** Architectural. **Family/consumer sciences:** Child development. **Health:** Community health, electrocardiograph technology, medical assistant, nursing (RN), respiratory therapy technology. **History:** General. **Legal studies:** Legal secretary. **Liberal arts:** Arts/sciences. **Math:** General. **Mechanic/repair:** Automotive. **Parks/recreation:** Health/fitness. **Philosophy/religion:** Philosophy. **Physical sciences:** Chemistry, geology, physics. **Protective services:** Firefighting, police science. **Psychology:** General. **Social sciences:** General, anthropology, economics, geography, political science, sociology. **Visual/performing arts:** Art, dramatic, photography. **Other:** Electron microscopy.

**Most popular majors.** Health sciences 6%, liberal arts 60%, security/protective services 10%.

**Computing on campus.** 1,597 workstations in library, computer center, student center. Online course registration, online library, helpline, wireless network available.

**Student life. Freshman orientation:** Available. **Policies:** All Student Life activities conform to Title V, LACCD regulations, LACCD Board Rules, Roberts rules of order, and CA Brown Act. **Activities:** Bands, campus ministries, dance, drama, international student organizations, music ensembles, musical theater, student government, student newspaper, Associated Students Union, engineering club, French club, Asia club, Chicanos for Creative Medicine, MESA, American Society of Engineers and Architects.

**Athletics.** NJCAA. **Intercollegiate:** Badminton W, baseball M, basketball, cheerleading M, cross-country, football (tackle) M, soccer, softball W, track and field, volleyball W, wrestling M. **Team name:** Huskies.

**Student services.** Adult student services, alcohol/substance abuse counseling, career counseling, services for economically disadvantaged, student employment services, financial aid counseling, health services, minority student services, on-campus daycare, personal counseling, placement for graduates, veterans' counselor, women's services. **Physically disabled:** Services for visually, hearing impaired. **Transfer:** Pre-admission transcript evaluation for new students. Transfer center, transfer adviser, college fairs on campus for students transferring to 4-year colleges.

**Contact.** Phone: (323) 265-8712 Fax: (323) 265-8688
Jeremy Allred, Dean of Admissions, East Los Angeles College, 1301
Avenida Cesar Chavez, Monterey Park, CA 91754

## El Camino College
### Torrance, California
www.elcamino.edu                               CB code: 4302

- Public 2-year community and junior college
- Commuter campus in very large city

**General.** Founded in 1947. Regionally accredited. **Enrollment:** 26,398
undergraduates. **Degrees:** 1,133 associate awarded. **Location:** 15 miles from
Los Angeles. **Calendar:** Semester, limited summer session. **Full-time faculty:** 336 total; 53% women. **Part-time faculty:** 673 total; 51% women.
**Special facilities:** Anthropology museum, planetarium, conference center,
computer/media center, child development center.

**Student profile.** 12% enrolled in a transfer program, 22% enrolled in a
vocational program, 7% already have a bachelor's degree or higher.

Out-of-state:                    1%      **25 or older:**                    36%

**Transfer out. Colleges most students transferred to 2009:** California
State University: Long Beach, California State University: Dominguez Hills,
California State University: Fullerton, University of California: Los Angeles.

**Basis for selection.** Open admission. Allied health programs require
completion of preparatory courses (anatomy, microbiology, college-level English and mathematics). Interview required for nursing, honors program,
x-ray technician, respiratory care majors. **Adult students:** SAT/ACT scores
not required. **Homeschooled:** Statement describing homeschool structure
and mission, transcript of courses and grades, state high school equivalency
certificate, letter of recommendation (nonparent) required. Home school must
be registered with state of California. **Learning Disabled:** Contact Special
Resources Center and provide evidence of a learning disability.

**2009-2010 Annual costs.** Tuition/fees: $815; $6,515 out-of-state. Per-credit charge: $26 in-state; $216 out-of-state. Books/supplies: $1,638. Personal expenses: $2,664.

**2008-2009 Financial aid. Need-based:** 86% of total undergraduate aid
awarded as scholarships/grants, 14% as loans/jobs. Need-based aid available for part-time students. Work-study available for part-time students. **Non-need-based:** Scholarships awarded for academics, art, athletics, leadership,
music/drama. **Additional information:** Students may apply for Pell grants
until June 30.

**Application procedures. Admission:** No deadline. No application fee.
Application must be submitted online. Admission notification on a rolling
basis beginning on or about 8/20. **Financial aid:** Priority date 3/2, closing
date 6/30. FAFSA, institutional form required. Applicants notified on a rolling basis starting 7/15.

**Academics. Special study options:** Cooperative education, cross-registration, distance learning, double major, dual enrollment of high school
students, ESL, honors, independent study, liberal arts/career combination,
study abroad, weekend college. License preparation in nursing, paramedic,
radiology. **Credit/placement by examination:** CLEP, IB, institutional tests.
15 credit hours maximum toward associate degree. **Support services:** Learning center, remedial instruction, study skills assistance, tutoring, writing center.

**Majors. Agriculture:** Ornamental horticulture. **Area/ethnic studies:** African-American, American, Asian-American, Chicano/Hispanic-American/Latino,
Native American. **Biology:** General, botany, zoology. **Business:** General,
administrative services, business admin, office management, real estate, sales/
distribution. **Communications:** Journalism. **Communications technology:**
General. **Computer sciences:** General, computer science. **Construction:**
Maintenance. **Education:** Early childhood. **Engineering:** General. **Engineering technology:** Architectural, construction, drafting. **Family/
consumer sciences:** General. **Foreign languages:** French, German, Japanese, Spanish. **Health:** Licensed practical nurse, medical radiologic technology/
radiation therapy, nursing (RN), predental, premedicine, prepharmacy, respiratory
therapy technology. **History:** General. **Legal studies:** Paralegal. **Math:** General. **Mechanic/repair:** Auto body, automotive, electronics/electrical, heating/
ac/refrig. **Parks/recreation:** Health/fitness. **Personal/culinary services:** Cosmetic. **Philosophy/religion:** Philosophy. **Physical sciences:** Astronomy,
chemistry, geology, physics. **Protective services:** Fire safety technology,
law enforcement admin, police science. **Psychology:** General. **Social sciences:** Anthropology, economics, geography, political science, sociology.
**Visual/performing arts:** Art, dance, dramatic, photography, studio arts.

**Most popular majors.** Business/marketing 13%, health sciences 11%,
liberal arts 37%, social sciences 6%.

**Computing on campus.** 150 workstations in library, computer center.
Online course registration, wireless network available.

**Student life. Freshman orientation:** Available. **Activities:** Bands, choral
groups, dance, drama, literary magazine, music ensembles, musical theater,
student government, student newspaper, symphony orchestra, Alpha Gamma
Sigma, anthropology club, environmental club, Gay-Straight Alliance, Iota
Kappa Chi (Nursing), Puente Club, Veterans Club, Muslim Students Association, Native American Club, Tailor Made (Fashion Design).

**Athletics.** NJCAA. **Intercollegiate:** Badminton W, baseball M, basketball, cross-country, football (tackle) M, golf M, soccer, softball W, swimming, tennis, track and field, volleyball, water polo. **Team name:** Warriors.

**Student services.** Adult student services, career counseling, services for
economically disadvantaged, student employment services, financial aid counseling, health services, on-campus daycare, personal counseling, placement
for graduates, veterans' counselor. **Physically disabled:** Services for visually, speech, hearing impaired. **Transfer:** Re-entry adviser, pre-admission
transcript evaluation for new students. Transfer center, transfer adviser, college fairs on campus for students transferring to 4-year colleges.

**Contact.** E-mail: admissionshelp@elcamino.edu
Phone: (310) 660-3414 Fax: (310) 660-3818
Bill Mulrooney, Director of Admissions and Records, El Camino College,
16007 Crenshaw Boulevard, Torrance, CA 90506

## El Camino College: Compton Center
### Compton, California                         CB member
www.compton.edu                               CB code: 4078

- Public 2-year community college
- Commuter campus in small city

**General.** Founded in 1927. Regionally accredited. **Enrollment:** 3,200 degree-seeking undergraduates. **Degrees:** 102 associate awarded. **Location:** 25 miles
from Los Angeles. **Calendar:** Semester, limited summer session. **Full-time
faculty:** 83 total. **Part-time faculty:** 176 total.

**Transfer out. Colleges most students transferred to 2009:** California
State University: Dominguez Hills.

**Basis for selection.** Open admission, but selective for some programs
and for out-of-state students. If under 18, applicant must have graduated
from high school and passed the California High School Certificate of Proficiency test. Selective admission to nursing programs.

**2009-2010 Annual costs.** Tuition/fees: $781; $6,481 out-of-state. Per-credit charge: $26 in-state; $216 out-of-state. Books/supplies: $1,566. Personal expenses: $2,556.

**Application procedures. Admission:** No deadline. No application fee.
Admission notification on a rolling basis. **Financial aid:** Closing date 5/15.
FAFSA required. Applicants notified on a rolling basis starting 5/15.

**Academics. Special study options:** Accelerated study, cooperative education, cross-registration, dual enrollment of high school students, honors.
**Credit/placement by examination:** CLEP, institutional tests. 12 credit hours
maximum toward associate degree. **Support services:** Learning center, reduced course load, remedial instruction, tutoring.

**Majors. Area/ethnic studies:** Women's. **Biology:** General, bacteriology,
botany. **Business:** Accounting, administrative services, banking/financial services, business admin, entrepreneurial studies, management information systems, office technology, office/clerical, real estate. **Communications:** Journalism. **Communications technology:** Graphics. **Computer sciences:** General,
applications programming, data processing. **Education:** Bilingual, physical,
special, teacher assistance. **Engineering:** Computer. **Engineering technology:** Construction, drafting, electrical. **Family/consumer sciences:** General, child care, clothing/textiles. **Foreign languages:** French, German, Spanish. **Health:** EMT paramedic, licensed practical nurse, medical assistant,
medical radiologic technology/radiation therapy, nursing (RN), premedicine, preop/surgical nursing, respiratory therapy technology. **History:** General. **Legal studies:** Paralegal. **Liberal arts:** Arts/sciences. **Math:** General.
**Mechanic/repair:** General, auto body, automotive, small engine. **Parks/
recreation:** General. **Personal/culinary services:** Cosmetic. **Philosophy/
religion:** Philosophy. **Physical sciences:** Astronomy, chemistry, geology,
physics. **Production:** Woodworking. **Protective services:** Firefighting, police science. **Psychology:** General. **Social sciences:** General, geography,
political science, sociology. **Visual/performing arts:** Art, commercial/
advertising art, dance, dramatic.

**Computing on campus.** 35 workstations in computer center.

**Student life. Activities:** Bands, choral groups, dance, drama, music ensembles, musical theater, student government, student newspaper, TV station, Christian club, Moslem student association.

**Athletics. Intercollegiate:** Baseball M, basketball, cross-country, football (tackle) M, tennis M, track and field. **Intramural:** Basketball, tennis. **Team name:** Tartars.

**Student services.** Career counseling, student employment services, on-campus daycare, personal counseling, placement for graduates, veterans' counselor. **Physically disabled:** Services for visually, speech, hearing impaired. **Transfer:** Transfer adviser, college fairs on campus for students transferring to 4-year colleges.

**Contact.** E-mail: info@compton.edu
Phone: (310) 900-1600 ext. 2043 Fax: (310) 900-1695
Gerald Sequeira, Director of Admission and Records, El Camino College: Compton Center, 1111 East Artesia Boulevard, Compton, CA 90221

## Empire College
### Santa Rosa, California
### www.empcol.edu
### CB code: 4275

- For-profit 2-year business college
- Commuter campus in small city
- Interview required

**General.** Accredited by ACICS. **Enrollment:** 119 degree-seeking undergraduates; 149 non-degree-seeking students. **Degrees:** 82 associate awarded. **Location:** 55 miles from San Francisco. **Calendar:** Continuous. **Full-time faculty:** 24 total; 62% women. **Part-time faculty:** 12 total; 58% women. **Special facilities:** Law library.

**Student profile.** Among degree-seeking undergraduates, 2% enrolled in a transfer program, 10% enrolled in a vocational program, 1% already have a bachelor's degree or higher, 119 enrolled as first-time, first-year students.

| | | | |
|---|---|---|---|
| Women: | 73% | Hispanic American: | 22% |
| African American: | 1% | Native American: | 1% |
| Asian American: | 3% | 25 or older: | 60% |

**Transfer out. Colleges most students transferred to 2009:** Santa Rosa Junior College.

**Basis for selection.** Open admission. Scholastic Level Exam (SLE) administered during admission process. Some programs also have typing speed requirement for entrance.

**High school preparation.** College-preparatory program required.

**2009-2010 Annual costs.** Tuition/fees: $9,000. Books/supplies: $2,200. Personal expenses: $350.

**2009-2010 Financial aid.** All financial aid based on need.

**Application procedures. Admission:** No deadline. $75 fee. Admission notification on a rolling basis. No fall term, ongoing 5-week application/entry. **Financial aid:** No deadline. FAFSA required. Applicants notified on a rolling basis.

**Academics. Special study options:** Accelerated study, double major, internships. **Credit/placement by examination:** CLEP. **Support services:** Tutoring.

**Majors. Business:** Accounting, administrative services. **Computer sciences:** Information systems. **Health:** Medical secretary. **Legal studies:** Paralegal.

**Computing on campus.** 600 workstations in library, computer center. Online library, student web hosting, wireless network available.

**Student life. Freshman orientation:** Mandatory. Preregistration for classes offered. **Activities:** Student newspaper.

**Student services.** Career counseling, student employment services, financial aid counseling, placement for graduates. **Transfer:** Re-entry adviser, pre-admission transcript evaluation for new students.

**Contact.** E-mail: dstraub@empirecollege.com
Phone: (707) 546-4000 ext. 238 Fax: (707) 546-4058
Dahnja Straub, Director of Admissions, Empire College, 3035 Cleveland Avenue, Santa Rosa, CA 95403-2100

## Evergreen Valley College
### San Jose, California
### www.evc.edu
### CB code: 4273

- Public 2-year community and junior college
- Commuter campus in very large city

**General.** Founded in 1975. Regionally accredited. **Enrollment:** 11,807 undergraduates. **Degrees:** 392 associate awarded. **Location:** 7 miles from downtown. **Calendar:** Semester, extensive summer session. **Full-time faculty:** 127 total; 32% have terminal degrees. **Part-time faculty:** 203 total. **Special facilities:** Hiking trails, parks, observatory, natural habitat, cross-country course.

**Transfer out. Colleges most students transferred to 2009:** San Jose State.

**Basis for selection.** Open admission, but selective for some programs. Limited admission for nursing and criminal justice programs. **Homeschooled:** Interview required. Must complete form R-42 and state affidavit.

**2009-2010 Annual costs.** Tuition/fees: $826; $6,556 out-of-state. Per-credit charge: $26 in-state; $217 out-of-state. Books/supplies: $1,566. Personal expenses: $3,024.

**Application procedures. Admission:** No deadline. No application fee. Admission notification on a rolling basis. **Financial aid:** Priority date 5/31; no closing date. FAFSA required. Applicants notified on a rolling basis.

**Academics. Special study options:** Accelerated study, cooperative education, cross-registration, distance learning, double major, dual enrollment of high school students, ESL, honors, independent study, internships, liberal arts/career combination, weekend college. License preparation in nursing; paramedic. **Credit/placement by examination:** AP, CLEP, institutional tests. 12 credit hours maximum toward associate degree. Assessment testing as prescribed by California law required for placement in English and mathematics. **Support services:** Learning center, reduced course load, remedial instruction, study skills assistance, tutoring, writing center.

**Majors. Business:** Administrative services, fashion, management information systems, office technology, office/clerical. **Computer sciences:** General, applications programming. **Engineering technology:** Drafting. **Health:** Nursing (RN). **Liberal arts:** Arts/sciences. **Protective services:** Police science. **Visual/performing arts:** Commercial/advertising art.

**Computing on campus.** 800 workstations in library, computer center, student center.

**Student life. Freshman orientation:** Mandatory. Preregistration for classes offered. **Activities:** Choral groups, dance, drama, literary magazine, music ensembles, musical theater, student government, student newspaper, Black Students Union, ASPIRE, Enlace, AFFIRM.

**Athletics.** NJCAA. **Intercollegiate:** Soccer, track and field, volleyball W, wrestling M. **Intramural:** Basketball, football (non-tackle) M. **Team name:** Hawks.

**Student services.** Alcohol/substance abuse counseling, career counseling, services for economically disadvantaged, student employment services, financial aid counseling, health services, minority student services, on-campus daycare, personal counseling, veterans' counselor. **Physically disabled:** Services for visually, speech, hearing impaired. **Transfer:** Transfer center, transfer adviser, college fairs on campus for students transferring to 4-year colleges.

**Contact.** E-mail: lynn.gulkin@evc.edu
Phone: (408) 270-6441 Fax: (408) 223-9351
Octavio Cruz, Dean of Enrollment Services, Evergreen Valley College, 3095 Yerba Buena Road, San Jose, CA 95135

## Fashion Careers College
### San Diego, California
### www.fashioncareerscollege.com
### CB code: 3494

- Private 2-year business college
- Commuter campus in very large city
- Application essay, interview required

**General.** Accredited by ACICS. **Enrollment:** 79 degree-seeking undergraduates. **Degrees:** 33 associate awarded. **Calendar:** Quarter. **Part-time faculty:** 10 total; 100% women.

**Basis for selection.** Exam score, essay, interview important. Wonderlic test used for admission.

**2009-2010 Annual costs.** Tuition/fees: $20,425.

**Application procedures. Admission:** No deadline. $25 fee. Admission notification on a rolling basis. **Financial aid:** No deadline. FAFSA required.

**Academics. Credit/placement by examination:** CLEP.

**Majors. Business:** Fashion. **Visual/performing arts:** Fashion design.

**Most popular majors.** Business/marketing 50%, visual/performing arts 50%.

**Computing on campus.** 23 workstations in computer center. Repair service available.

**Student life. Freshman orientation:** Mandatory. Held 1 week before classes start.

**Student services.** Career counseling, financial aid counseling, placement for graduates.

**Contact.** E-mail: info@fashioncareerscollege.com
Phone: (619) 275-4700 Toll-free number: (888) 322-2999
Fax: (619) 275-0635
Kathleen Hammond, Director of Admission, Fashion Careers College, 1923 Morena Boulevard, San Diego, CA 92110

## Fashion Institute of Design and Merchandising: Los Angeles
**Los Angeles, California**
www.fidm.edu

CB member
CB code: 4457

- For-profit 2-year visual arts and business college
- Commuter campus in very large city
- Application essay, interview required

**General.** Founded in 1969. Regionally accredited. Branch campuses in Orange County, San Francisco and San Diego. **Enrollment:** 4,562 degree-seeking undergraduates. **Degrees:** 98 bachelor's, 2,100 associate awarded. **Calendar:** Quarter, extensive summer session. **Full-time faculty:** 60 total; 23% minority, 57% women. **Part-time faculty:** 232 total; 16% minority, 62% women. **Class size:** 77% < 20, 23% 20-39. **Special facilities:** Hollywood costume collection, costume study collection and museum, textile museum, fragrance bottle collection, fashion library.

**Student profile.**

| | | | |
|---|---|---|---|
| Out-of-state: | 35% | 25 or older: | 32% |

**Basis for selection.** High school transcripts, standardized test scores, references, portfolio or admissions project, essays, and evidence of interest in major area through work experience, high school preparation, or extracurricular activities considered. In addition to transcript evaluation, SAT and/or ACT scores are considered to determine if additional testing is required. SAT or ACT recommended. Portfolio or admissions project required. Out-of-state applicants interviewed by telephone. Projects are required of all students. International students are not required to interview. **Homeschooled:** Statement describing homeschool structure and mission, interview required. Admissions or standardized testing required.

**High school preparation.** College-preparatory program recommended.

**2009-2010 Annual costs.** Tuition/fees: $20,685. Tuition and fees may vary depending on program. Books/supplies: $2,160. Personal expenses: $2,142.

**Financial aid. Need-based:** Work-study available for part-time students. **Non-need-based:** Scholarships awarded for academics. **Additional information:** Tuition/fee expenses may be reduced by applying for admission by December 31 of year before student plans to attend.

**Application procedures. Admission:** No deadline. $225 fee ($375 out-of-state). Admission notification on a rolling basis. **Financial aid:** Priority date 3/1; no closing date. FAFSA, institutional form required. Applicants notified on a rolling basis starting 3/15; must reply within 3 week(s) of notification.

**Academics.** Faculty and staff come from related industries. Project-oriented courses give students hands-on experience. **Special study options:** Distance learning, ESL, exchange student, independent study, internships, study abroad, weekend college. **Credit/placement by examination:** AP, CLEP, IB, institutional tests. 45 credit hours maximum toward associate

degree, 45 toward bachelor's. **Support services:** Learning center, reduced course load, remedial instruction, study skills assistance, tutoring, writing center.

**Majors. Business:** Fashion, marketing, merchandising, operations, retailing, sales/distribution. **Family/consumer sciences:** Apparel marketing, clothing/textiles, fashion consultant, merchandising, textile manufacture, textile science. **Visual/performing arts:** Design, digital art, fashion design, fiber arts, graphic design, interior design, metal/jewelry, multimedia, theater design.

**Most popular majors.** Visual/performing arts 12%.

**Computing on campus.** 400 workstations in library, computer center, student center. Commuter students can connect to campus network. Online course registration, online library, helpline, wireless network available.

**Student life. Freshman orientation:** Mandatory. Preregistration for classes offered. **Activities:** International student organizations, student government, student newspaper, honor society, international club, design council, ASID, Phi Theta Kappa.

**Student services.** Adult student services, alcohol/substance abuse counseling, career counseling, student employment services, financial aid counseling, personal counseling, placement for graduates, women's services. **Physically disabled:** Services for visually, hearing impaired. **Transfer:** Pre-admission transcript evaluation for new students. Transfer center, transfer adviser for students transferring to 4-year colleges.

**Contact.** E-mail: admissionsdirector@fidm.edu
Phone: (213) 624-1200 Toll-free number: (800) 624-1200
Fax: (213) 624-4799
Susan Aronson, Executive Director of Admissions, Fashion Institute of Design and Merchandising: Los Angeles, 919 South Grand Avenue, Los Angeles, CA 90015-1421

## Fashion Institute of Design and Merchandising: San Diego
**San Diego, California**
www.fidm.edu

CB code: 2949

- For-profit 2-year visual arts and business college
- Commuter campus in very large city
- Application essay, interview required

**General.** Regionally accredited. Other campuses in Los Angeles, Orange County, and San Francisco. **Enrollment:** 305 degree-seeking undergraduates. **Degrees:** 53 associate awarded. **Calendar:** Quarter, extensive summer session. **Full-time faculty:** 3 total; 67% women. **Part-time faculty:** 24 total; 29% minority, 88% women. **Class size:** 77% < 20, 23% 20-39. **Special facilities:** Hollywood costume study collection and museum, textile museum, historical Annette Green fragrance bottle collection, fashion library.

**Basis for selection.** High school transcripts, standardized test scores, references, portfolio or admissions project, essays and evidence of interest in major through work experience, high school preparation, or extracurricular activities considered. In addition to transcript evaluation, SAT and/or ACT scores are considered to determine if additional testing is required. SAT or ACT recommended. Portfolio or admissions project required of all applicants. Out-of-state applicants are interviewed by telephone. International students are not required to interview. **Homeschooled:** Transcript of courses and grades, state high school equivalency certificate, interview required. Admissions or standardized testing required.

**High school preparation.** College-preparatory program recommended.

**2009-2010 Annual costs.** Tuition/fees: $20,685. Tuition and fees vary by program. Books/supplies: $2,160. Personal expenses: $2,142.

**Financial aid. Need-based:** Work-study available for part-time students. **Non-need-based:** Scholarships awarded for academics.

**Application procedures. Admission:** No deadline. $225 fee ($375 out-of-state). Admission notification on a rolling basis. **Financial aid:** No deadline. FAFSA, institutional form required. Applicants notified on a rolling basis; must reply within 3 week(s) of notification.

**Academics.** Faculty and staff are recruited from industry. Project-oriented courses provide hands-on learning experiences. **Special study options:** Distance learning, ESL, exchange student, independent study, internships, study abroad, weekend college. **Credit/placement by examination:** AP, CLEP, IB, institutional tests. 15 credit hours maximum toward associate degree. **Support services:** Learning center, reduced course load, remedial instruction, study skills assistance, tutoring, writing center.

**Majors. Business:** Fashion, marketing. **Family/consumer sciences:** Apparel marketing, clothing/textiles, fashion consultant, merchandising, textile manufacture, textile science. **Visual/performing arts:** Design, fashion design, fiber arts, graphic design.

**Computing on campus.** 35 workstations in library, computer center, student center. Commuter students can connect to campus network. Online course registration, online library, helpline, wireless network available.

**Student life. Freshman orientation:** Mandatory. Preregistration for classes offered. **Activities:** International student organizations, honor students society, alumni association, ASID student chapter, Design Council, Phi Theta Kappa, student activities committee.

**Student services.** Adult student services, alcohol/substance abuse counseling, career counseling, student employment services, financial aid counseling, personal counseling, placement for graduates, women's services. **Physically disabled:** Services for visually, hearing impaired. **Transfer:** Pre-admission transcript evaluation for new students. Transfer center, transfer adviser for students transferring to 4-year colleges.

**Contact.** E-mail: admissionsdirector@fidm.edu
Phone: (619) 235-2049 Toll-free number: (800) 243-3436
Fax: (619) 232-4322
Susan Aronson, Executive Director of Admissions, Fashion Institute of Design and Merchandising: San Diego, 350 Tenth Avenue, Third Floor, San Diego, CA 92101

---

## Fashion Institute of Design and Merchandising: San Francisco
**San Francisco, California**
**www.fidm.edu**                         CB code: 4988

▶ For-profit 2-year visual arts and business college
▶ Commuter campus in very large city
▶ Application essay, interview required

**General.** Founded in 1969. Regionally accredited. Other campuses in Los Angeles, Orange County, and San Diego. **Enrollment:** 1,031 degree-seeking undergraduates. **Degrees:** 371 associate awarded. **Calendar:** Quarter, extensive summer session. **Full-time faculty:** 13 total; 8% minority, 69% women. **Part-time faculty:** 57 total; 18% minority, 68% women. **Class size:** 77% < 20, 23% 20-39. **Special facilities:** Acces to Hollywood costume collection, costume study collection and museum, textiles museum, Annette Green fragrance bottle collection, fashion library.

**Basis for selection.** Recommendations and application essay very important. Rigor of secondary school record and academic GPA important. In addition to transcript, SAT and/or ACT scores are considered to determine if additional testing is required. SAT or ACT recommended. Portfolio or admissions project is required of all candidates. Out-of-state applicants are interviewed by telephone. International students are not required to interview. **Homeschooled:** Statement describing homeschool structure and mission, interview required.

**High school preparation.** College-preparatory program recommended. High school transcripts, standardized test scores, references, portfolio or admissions project, essays, and evidence of interest in major through work experience, high school preparation, or extracurricular activities accepted.

**2009-2010 Annual costs.** Tuition/fees: $20,685. Tuition and fees vary by program. Books/supplies: $2,160. Personal expenses: $2,142.

**Financial aid. Need-based:** Work-study available for part-time students. **Non-need-based:** Scholarships awarded for academics.

**Application procedures. Admission:** No deadline. $225 fee ($375 out-of-state). Admission notification on a rolling basis. **Financial aid:** No deadline. FAFSA, institutional form required. Applicants notified on a rolling basis starting 3/15; must reply within 3 week(s) of notification.

**Academics.** Faculty and staff are recruited from industry. Project oriented courses provide hands-on learning experiences. **Special study options:** Distance learning, ESL, exchange student, independent study, internships, study abroad, weekend college. **Credit/placement by examination:** AP, CLEP, IB, institutional tests. 45 credit hours maximum toward associate degree, 45 toward bachelor's. **Support services:** Learning center, reduced course load, remedial instruction, study skills assistance, tutoring, writing center.

**Majors. Business:** Fashion. **Computer sciences:** Computer graphics, webmaster. **Family/consumer sciences:** Apparel marketing, clothing/textiles, fashion consultant, merchandising, textile manufacture, textile science. **Visual/performing arts:** Design, digital art, fashion design, fiber arts, graphic design, interior design, metal/jewelry, multimedia, theater design.

**Most popular majors.** Business/marketing 36%, visual/performing arts 64%.

**Computing on campus.** 130 workstations in library, computer center, student center. Commuter students can connect to campus network. Online course registration, online library, helpline, wireless network available.

**Student life. Freshman orientation:** Mandatory. Preregistration for classes offered. **Activities:** International student organizations, student government, student newspaper, honor society, international club, design council, ASID student chapter, Phi Theta Kappa.

**Student services.** Adult student services, alcohol/substance abuse counseling, career counseling, student employment services, financial aid counseling, personal counseling, placement for graduates, women's services. **Physically disabled:** Services for visually, hearing impaired. **Transfer:** Pre-admission transcript evaluation for new students. Transfer center, transfer adviser for students transferring to 4-year colleges.

**Contact.** E-mail: admissionsdirector@fidm.edu
Phone: (415) 675-5200 Toll-free number: (800) 422-3436
Fax: (415) 394-9700
Sheryl Badalamente, Director of Admissions, Fashion Institute of Design and Merchandising: San Francisco, 55 Stockton Street, San Francisco, CA 94108-5805

---

## Feather River College
**Quincy, California**
**www.frc.edu**                         CB code: 4318

▶ Public 2-year community and liberal arts college
▶ Commuter campus in small town

**General.** Founded in 1968. Regionally accredited. **Enrollment:** 781 degree-seeking undergraduates. **Degrees:** 132 associate awarded. **Location:** 150 miles from Sacramento, 80 miles from Reno, Nevada. **Calendar:** Semester, limited summer session. **Full-time faculty:** 26 total; 42% women. **Part-time faculty:** 80 total; 6% minority, 49% women. **Class size:** 56% < 20, 38% 20-39, 4% 40-49, 2% 50-99. **Special facilities:** Fish hatchery, horse boarding and training facility, state wildlife preserve.

**Student profile.** Among degree-seeking undergraduates, 390 enrolled as first-time, first-year students, 143 transferred in from other institutions.

| | | | |
|---|---|---|---|
| African American: | 18% | Native American: | 3% |
| Asian American: | 3% | International: | 1% |
| Hispanic American: | 10% | | |

**Transfer out. Colleges most students transferred to 2009:** CSU: Chico, Humboldt State University, University of Nevada: Reno, California Polytechnic State University: San Luis Obispo.

**Basis for selection.** Open admission.

**2009-2010 Annual costs.** Tuition/fees: $859; $6,559 out-of-state. Per-credit charge: $26 in-state; $216 out-of-state. Room/board: $7,824. Books/supplies: $1,638. Personal expenses: $2,250.

**2008-2009 Financial aid.** All financial aid based on need. 63% of total undergraduate aid awarded as scholarships/grants, 37% as loans/jobs. Need-based aid available for part-time students. Work-study available nights, weekends and for part-time students.

**Application procedures. Admission:** No deadline. No application fee. **Financial aid:** Priority date 3/2; no closing date. FAFSA required. Applicants notified on a rolling basis starting 4/1; must reply within 3 week(s) of notification.

**Academics.** General education/core courses are offered that satisfy all lower division requirements of California State University, University of California, and University of Nevada system. **Special study options:** Cooperative education, cross-registration, distance learning, double major, dual enrollment of high school students, ESL, honors, independent study, liberal arts/career combination. License preparation in nursing, paramedic. **Credit/placement by examination:** AP, CLEP, institutional tests. 12 credit hours maximum toward associate degree. **Support services:** GED preparation and test center, learning center, reduced course load, remedial instruction, study skills assistance, tutoring.

**Majors. Agriculture:** General, equine science. **Biology:** General. **Business:** General, administrative services. **Conservation:** General, environmental studies, forestry, wildlife. **Family/consumer sciences:** Food/nutrition. **Health:** Licensed practical nurse. **History:** General. **Liberal arts:** Arts/sciences, humanities. **Math:** General. **Parks/recreation:** General, health/

fitness. **Physical sciences:** General. **Protective services:** Police science. **Social sciences:** General. **Visual/performing arts:** General.

**Most popular majors.** Agriculture 11%, liberal arts 61%, parks/recreation 10%.

**Computing on campus.** 120 workstations in dormitories, library, computer center, student center. Dormitories wired for high-speed internet access. Online course registration, online library, wireless network available.

**Student life. Freshman orientation:** Mandatory. Online orientation available. **Housing:** Apartments available. **Activities:** Student government, Phi Theta Kappa.

**Athletics.** NJCAA. **Intercollegiate:** Baseball M, basketball, football (tackle) M, rodeo, soccer, softball W, volleyball W. **Intramural:** Volleyball W. **Team name:** Golden Eagles.

**Student services.** Adult student services, career counseling, services for economically disadvantaged, student employment services, financial aid counseling, health services, on-campus daycare, personal counseling, placement for graduates, veterans' counselor. **Physically disabled:** Services for visually, speech, hearing impaired. **Transfer:** Re-entry adviser, pre-admission transcript evaluation for new students. Transfer center, transfer adviser, college fairs on campus for students transferring to 4-year colleges.

**Contact.** Phone: (530) 283-0202 ext. 600 Toll-free number: (800) 442-9799 ext. 600 Fax: (530) 283-9961 Tama Bolton, Registrar, Feather River College, 570 Golden Eagle Avenue, Quincy, CA 95971

---

## Folsom Lake College
### Folsom, California
### www.flc.losrios.edu
### CB code: 4462

- Public 2-year community college
- Commuter campus in small city

**General.** Regionally accredited. **Enrollment:** 9,456 undergraduates. **Degrees:** 641 associate awarded. **Location:** 25 miles from Sacramento. **Calendar:** Semester, limited summer session. **Full-time faculty:** 109 total. **Part-time faculty:** 186 total. **Special facilities:** Observatory; regional visual and performing arts center.

**Transfer out. Colleges most students transferred to 2009:** California State University: Sacramento, University of California: Davis.

**Basis for selection.** Open admission. **Adult students:** SAT/ACT scores not required.

**2009-2010 Annual costs.** Tuition/fees: $812; $6,512 out-of-state. Per-credit charge: $26 in-state; $216 out-of-state. Books/supplies: $1,638. Personal expenses: $2,826.

**Application procedures. Admission:** No deadline. No application fee.

**Academics. Special study options:** Distance learning, ESL, internships, study abroad. **Credit/placement by examination:** AP, CLEP, institutional tests. **Support services:** Remedial instruction, study skills assistance, tutoring, writing center.

**Majors. Area/ethnic studies:** American, women's. **Biology:** General. **Business:** General, accounting, administrative services, management science, marketing, real estate, small business admin. **Communications:** Organizational. **Computer sciences:** General. **Education:** Early childhood. **Family/consumer sciences:** Aging, family studies. **Interdisciplinary:** Biological/physical sciences, gerontology. **Liberal arts:** Arts/sciences. **Math:** General. **Physical sciences:** Geology. **Protective services:** Firefighting, law enforcement admin. **Psychology:** General. **Public administration:** Human services. **Social sciences:** General. **Visual/performing arts:** Art, art history/conservation.

**Computing on campus.** 1,300 workstations in library, computer center. Online course registration, online library, wireless network available.

**Student life. Freshman orientation:** Available. **Activities:** Bands, choral groups, dance, drama, international student organizations, literary magazine, music ensembles, student government, student newspaper.

**Athletics. Intercollegiate:** Golf, tennis. **Team name:** Falcons.

---

**Student services.** Services for economically disadvantaged, financial aid counseling, health services, veterans' counselor. **Physically disabled:** Services for visually, speech, hearing impaired. **Learning disabled:** Comprehensive services available. **Transfer:** Transfer center, transfer adviser, college fairs on campus for students transferring to 4-year colleges.

**Contact.** Phone: (916) 608-6500 Fax: (916) 608-6569 Christine Wurzer, Admissions and Records Supervisor, Folsom Lake College, 10 College Parkway, Folsom, CA 95630

---

## Foothill College
### Los Altos Hills, California
### www.foothill.edu
### CB code: 4315

- Public 2-year community college
- Commuter campus in large town

**General.** Founded in 1958. Regionally accredited. **Enrollment:** 19,107 undergraduates. **Degrees:** 488 associate awarded. **ROTC:** Army, Naval, Air Force. **Location:** 40 miles from San Francisco. **Calendar:** Quarter, limited summer session. **Full-time faculty:** 206 total; 58% women. **Special facilities:** Center for innovation, Japanese cultural center, observatory, bamboo garden, dental health clinic, travel careers computer lab, math center.

**Student profile.** 24% already have a bachelor's degree or higher, 3,385 transferred in from other institutions.

**Transfer out. Colleges most students transferred to 2009:** San Jose State, University of California: Berkeley, University of California: Santa Cruz, University of California: Los Angeles, University of California: Davis.

**Basis for selection.** Open admission, but selective for some programs. Allied health programs have special prerequisites: using point system to rank required college-level and general education classes, top 20-40 students selected for admission. Must be 2-year transfer.

**2009-2010 Annual costs.** Tuition/fees: $808; $6,298 out-of-state. Per-credit charge: $17 in-state; $139 out-of-state. Books/supplies: $1,656. Personal expenses: $2,754.

**Financial aid.** All financial aid based on need. Need-based aid available for part-time students.

**Application procedures. Admission:** No deadline. No application fee. Admission notification on a rolling basis. **Financial aid:** Priority date 3/30; no closing date. FAFSA, institutional form required. Applicants notified on a rolling basis; must reply within 2 week(s) of notification.

**Academics.** NASA Ames Research Center internships available. **Special study options:** Cooperative education, cross-registration, distance learning, ESL, exchange student, honors, independent study, internships, liberal arts/career combination, study abroad, weekend college. Bachelor's degree programs available on campus. License preparation in dental hygiene, paramedic, radiology, real estate. **Credit/placement by examination:** AP, CLEP, institutional tests. 20 credit hours maximum toward associate degree. **Support services:** Learning center, remedial instruction, study skills assistance, tutoring, writing center.

**Honors college/program.** Continuing students should have minimum 3.3 cumulative GPA in 10 or more units completed at Foothill College. New students must have minimum 3.5 cumulative high school GPA or SAT total of at least 2100 or Enhanced ACT Composite of 26 or minimum 3.3 cumulative GPA in 10 or more units completed at another accredited college or university. Minimum AP English score of 3 or 2, minimum score on assessment test of ENGL Reading 93 and ENGL Writing 111 or completion of English 1A with a grade of B or better. Letter of recommendation and personal statement required.

**Majors. Agriculture:** Landscaping, nursery operations, ornamental horticulture. **Area/ethnic studies:** American, women's. **Biology:** General, bioinformatics, biotechnology. **Business:** Accounting, business admin, international, office technology, real estate, tourism promotion. **Communications:** General, broadcast journalism, media studies, radio/tv. **Computer sciences:** General, computer graphics, computer science, database management, information technology, LAN/WAN management, programming. **Construction:** Electrician. **Education:** Early childhood. **Engineering:** General, software. **Engineering technology:** Biomedical, electrical. **Family/consumer sciences:** Child development. **Foreign languages:** Chinese, French, Japanese, linguistics, Spanish. **Health:** Athletic training, dental assistant, dental hygiene, medical radiologic technology/radiation therapy, pharmacy assistant, physician assistant, predental, premedicine, prepharmacy, preveterinary, radiologic technology/medical imaging, respiratory therapy assistant, respiratory therapy technology, sonography, veterinary technology/assistant. **History:** General. **Interdisciplinary:** Intercultural. **Legal studies:** Prelaw. **Liberal**

arts: Arts/sciences, library assistant. **Math:** General. **Mechanic/repair:** Aircraft. **Philosophy/religion:** Philosophy. **Physical sciences:** Chemistry, geology, physics. **Psychology:** General. **Science technology:** Biological. **Social sciences:** General, anthropology, economics, geography, political science, sociology. **Visual/performing arts:** Art, art history/conservation, commercial/advertising art, dramatic, photography, studio arts, theater design. **Other:** Informatics, Viticulture & enology.

**Computing on campus.** 200 workstations in library, computer center, student center. Commuter students can connect to campus network. Online course registration, online library, wireless network available.

**Student life. Freshman orientation:** Available. **Activities:** Bands, choral groups, dance, drama, film society, music ensembles, musical theater, radio station, student government, student newspaper, symphony orchestra, TV station, 32 different multicultural/ethnic campus clubs.

**Athletics. Intercollegiate:** Basketball, diving, football (tackle) M, golf, soccer, softball W, swimming, tennis, volleyball W, water polo W. **Intramural:** Basketball, cheerleading, football (non-tackle), soccer, softball, volleyball. **Team name:** Owls.

**Student services.** Adult student services, alcohol/substance abuse counseling, career counseling, services for economically disadvantaged, student employment services, financial aid counseling, health services, legal services, minority student services, personal counseling, placement for graduates, veterans' counselor. **Physically disabled:** Services for visually, speech, hearing impaired. **Transfer:** Transfer adviser, college fairs on campus for students transferring to 4-year colleges.

**Contact.** Phone: (650) 949-7325 Fax: (650) 949-7048
Laureen Balducci, Dean Counseling and Matriculation, Foothill College, 12345 El Monte Road, Los Altos Hills, CA 94022

## Fremont College
**Cerritos, California**
www.fremont.edu                                    CB code: 3007

⬧ For-profit 2-year health science and career college
⬧ Commuter campus in very large city
⬧ Application essay, interview required

**General.** Accredited by ACCSC. Year-round program with starts every 5 weeks. **Enrollment:** 243 degree-seeking undergraduates. **Degrees:** 70 associate awarded. **Location:** 20 miles from Los Angeles. **Calendar:** Continuous. **Full-time faculty:** 2 total. **Part-time faculty:** 10 total. **Class size:** 58% < 20, 42% 20-39.

**Basis for selection.** Open admission, but selective for some programs. High school diploma or GED and successful completion of CPAt required. **Homeschooled:** State high school equivalency certificate required.

**2009-2010 Annual costs.** Paralegal: $24,200. Sports therapy: $21,800. Massage Therapy: $15,200.

**2008-2009 Financial aid.** All financial aid based on need.

**Application procedures. Admission:** No deadline. $85 fee. **Financial aid:** FAFSA, institutional form required.

**Academics. Special study options:** Accelerated study. **Credit/placement by examination:** CLEP. **Support services:** Tutoring.

**Majors. Business:** General. **Legal studies:** Paralegal. **Parks/recreation:** Exercise sciences.

**Computing on campus.** PC or laptop required. 30 workstations in library, computer center.

**Student life. Freshman orientation:** Available. Preregistration for classes offered.

**Student services.** Financial aid counseling, placement for graduates. **Transfer:** Pre-admission transcript evaluation for new students.

**Contact.** E-mail: leads@fremont.edu
Phone: (562) 809-5100 Toll-free number: (877) 344-2345
Fax: (562) 809-7100
Brian Watson, Admissions Director, Fremont College, 18000 Studebaker Road, 900A, Cerritos, CA 90703-5342

## Fresno City College
**Fresno, California**                              CB member
www.fresnocitycollege.edu                          CB code: 4311

⬧ Public 2-year community and liberal arts college
⬧ Commuter campus in large city

**General.** Founded in 1910. Regionally accredited. **Enrollment:** 25,574 undergraduates. **Degrees:** 1,442 associate awarded. **ROTC:** Army, Air Force. **Location:** 185 miles from San Francisco. **Calendar:** Semester, extensive summer session. **Full-time faculty:** 309 total; 29% minority, 47% women. **Part-time faculty:** 742 total; 22% minority, 43% women. **Class size:** 28% < 20, 59% 20-39, 7% 40-49, 4% 50-99, 3% >100. **Special facilities:** Anthropology museum, greenhouse and koi pond, high-tech laboratory for disabled students.

**Student profile.**

| Out-of-state: | 2% | 25 or older: | 39% |
|---|---|---|---|

**Transfer out. Colleges most students transferred to 2009:** California State University: Fresno, University of Phoenix, National University, Fresno Pacific University.

**Basis for selection.** Open admission, but selective for some programs. Limited admission to allied health programs, police academy, and apprenticeship programs.

**2009-2010 Annual costs.** Tuition/fees: $814; $6,514 out-of-state. Per-credit charge: $26 in-state; $216 out-of-state. Books/supplies: $1,400. Personal expenses: $2,472.

**2008-2009 Financial aid.** All financial aid based on need. 86% of total undergraduate aid awarded as scholarships/grants, 14% as loans/jobs. Need-based aid available for part-time students. Work-study available for part-time students. **Additional information:** Board of Governors Grant Program to offset enrollment fees based on untaxed income, low income, or calculated need. Students qualifying for program also automatically exempt from health fees. March 2 application deadline for California grants.

**Application procedures. Admission:** No deadline. No application fee. Application must be submitted online. Admission notification on a rolling basis. **Financial aid:** Priority date 4/15, closing date 6/30. FAFSA required. Applicants notified on a rolling basis starting 4/1.

**Academics. Special study options:** Accelerated study, cross-registration, distance learning, double major, dual enrollment of high school students, ESL, honors, independent study, internships, study abroad, weekend college. License preparation in dental hygiene, nursing, radiology, real estate. **Credit/placement by examination:** CLEP, institutional tests. 48 credit hours maximum toward associate degree. **Support services:** Learning center, pre-admission summer program, reduced course load, remedial instruction, study skills assistance, tutoring, writing center.

**Majors. Agriculture:** General, food science. **Area/ethnic studies:** African-American, Chicano/Hispanic-American/Latino, Native American, women's. **Business:** General, accounting, administrative services, banking/financial services, business admin, fashion, insurance, office/clerical, purchasing, real estate. **Communications:** General, journalism. **Communications technology:** Graphic/printing. **Computer sciences:** General, computer science, data processing, information systems, programming. **Conservation:** General. **Construction:** Carpentry, electrician, maintenance, pipefitting, power transmission. **Education:** Bilingual, early childhood, multi-level teacher. **Engineering:** General. **Engineering technology:** Drafting. **Family/consumer sciences:** General, child care, clothing/textiles, food/nutrition, institutional food production. **Foreign languages:** General, Spanish. **Health:** Clinical lab technology, dental hygiene, medical assistant, medical radiologic technology/radiation therapy, medical records technology, medical secretary, medical transcription, nursing (RN), radiologic technology/medical imaging, respiratory therapy technology, substance abuse counseling. **History:** General. **Interdisciplinary:** Biological/physical sciences. **Legal studies:** Legal secretary, paralegal. **Liberal arts:** Arts/sciences, library assistant. **Math:** General. **Mechanic/repair:** General, auto body, automotive, electronics/electrical, heating/ac/refrig, industrial. **Parks/recreation:** General, facilities management. **Physical sciences:** Chemistry. **Protective services:** Corrections, firefighting, law enforcement admin, police science. **Psychology:** General. **Public administration:** General, social work. **Social sciences:** General, anthropology, criminology, geography, sociology. **Transportation:** General. **Visual/performing arts:** General, art, crafts, dance, dramatic, music management, photography, piano/organ, printmaking, theater design, voice/opera.

**Most popular majors.** Health sciences 30%, liberal arts 55%.

**Computing on campus.** 400 workstations in library, computer center. Commuter students can connect to campus network. Online course registration, online library, wireless network available.

**Student life. Freshman orientation:** Available. **Activities:** Bands, choral groups, dance, drama, film society, international student organizations, literary magazine, music ensembles, musical theater, student government, student newspaper, symphony orchestra, TV station, Christian Athletes in Acting, MECHA, Pan American Association, Alpha Gamma Sigma, Phi Theta Kappa.

**Athletics. NJCAA. Intercollegiate:** Badminton, baseball M, basketball, cheerleading, cross-country, football (tackle) M, golf, soccer, softball W, tennis, track and field, volleyball W, wrestling M. **Intramural:** Basketball, football (non-tackle), soccer, softball, table tennis, volleyball, weight lifting. **Team name:** Rams.

**Student services.** Adult student services, career counseling, services for economically disadvantaged, student employment services, financial aid counseling, health services, minority student services, on-campus daycare, personal counseling, placement for graduates, veterans' counselor. **Physically disabled:** Services for visually, speech, hearing impaired. **Transfer:** Transfer center, transfer adviser, college fairs on campus for students transferring to 4-year colleges.

**Contact.** E-mail: info@scccd.com
Phone: (559) 442-4600 Toll-free number: (866) 245-3276
Fax: (559) 237-4232
John Cummings, District Dean of Admissions, Records and Institutional Research, Fresno City College, 1101 East University Avenue, Fresno, CA 93741

## Fullerton College
### Fullerton, California
### www.fullcoll.edu
CB code: 4314

- Public 2-year community and technical college
- Commuter campus in small city
- SAT or ACT required

**General.** Founded in 1913. Regionally accredited. **Enrollment:** 24,135 undergraduates. **Degrees:** 1,144 associate awarded. **ROTC:** Naval. **Location:** 35 miles from Los Angeles. **Calendar:** Semester, extensive summer session. **Full-time faculty:** 315 total. **Part-time faculty:** 480 total.

**Basis for selection.** Open admission. College-administered English, reading, and math exams used for placement.

**2009-2010 Annual costs.** Tuition/fees: $812; $6,512 out-of-state. Per-credit charge: $26 in-state; $216 out-of-state. Books/supplies: $1,638. Personal expenses: $3,096.

**Application procedures. Admission:** No deadline. No application fee. Admission notification on a rolling basis. **Financial aid:** No deadline. FAFSA required. Applicants notified on a rolling basis.

**Academics. Special study options:** Distance learning, double major, dual enrollment of high school students, ESL, honors, independent study, internships, study abroad. License preparation in real estate. **Credit/placement by examination:** CLEP, institutional tests. 15 credit hours maximum toward associate degree. **Support services:** Learning center, remedial instruction, study skills assistance, tutoring, writing center.

**Majors. Agriculture:** Horticulture, nursery operations. **Architecture:** Landscape. **Area/ethnic studies:** Latin American. **Biology:** General, bacteriology, zoology. **Business:** Accounting, administrative services, business admin, fashion, international, management information systems, purchasing, real estate, tourism promotion. **Communications:** General, broadcast journalism, journalism. **Communications technology:** Graphic/printing. **Computer sciences:** General, applications programming, data processing. **Conservation:** General, fisheries, forestry. **Construction:** Carpentry, maintenance. **Education:** Business, trade/industrial. **Engineering:** General. **Engineering technology:** Drafting, electrical. **Family/consumer sciences:** General, child care, family studies. **Foreign languages:** General. **Health:** Clinical lab science, prenursing. **History:** General. **Legal studies:** Legal secretary, paralegal. **Liberal arts:** Arts/sciences, library assistant. **Math:** General. **Mechanic/repair:** Auto body. **Parks/recreation:** General. **Personal/culinary services:** Cosmetic. **Philosophy/religion:** Philosophy. **Physical sciences:** Astronomy, chemistry, geology, physics. **Protective services:** Police science. **Psychology:** General. **Social sciences:** Anthropology, economics, geography, political science, sociology. **Visual/performing arts:** General, art, commercial/advertising art, dance, design, dramatic, fashion design.

**Computing on campus.** 400 workstations in library, computer center. Online course registration, helpline, wireless network available.

**Student life. Activities:** Bands, choral groups, dance, drama, film society, literary magazine, music ensembles, musical theater, radio station, student government, student newspaper, symphony orchestra, TV station, volunteer bureau, Movimiento Estudiantil Chicano de Aztlan.

**Athletics. Intercollegiate:** Badminton, baseball M, basketball, cross-country, diving, football (tackle) M, golf M, gymnastics, soccer, softball W, swimming, tennis, track and field, volleyball, water polo M. **Team name:** Hornets.

**Student services.** Adult student services, career counseling, student employment services, health services, on-campus daycare, personal counseling, placement for graduates, veterans' counselor. **Physically disabled:** Services for visually, speech, hearing impaired. **Transfer:** Transfer adviser for students transferring to 4-year colleges.

**Contact.** E-mail: admissions@fullcoll.edu
Phone: (714) 992-7568
Albert Abutin, Dean, Admissions and Records, Fullerton College, 321 East Chapman Avenue, Fullerton, CA 92832-2095

## Gavilan College
### Gilroy, California
### www.gavilan.edu
CB code: 4678

- Public 2-year community college
- Large town

**General.** Founded in 1919. Regionally accredited. **Enrollment:** 9,333 undergraduates. **Degrees:** 287 associate awarded. **Location:** 35 miles from San Jose. **Calendar:** Semester, limited summer session. **Full-time faculty:** 71 total; 11% have terminal degrees. **Part-time faculty:** 116 total; 3% have terminal degrees. **Special facilities:** Golf course, hiking trails.

**Transfer out. Colleges most students transferred to 2009:** San Jose State, California State University: Monterey Bay, University of California: Santa Cruz.

**Basis for selection.** Open admission.

**2009-2010 Annual costs.** Tuition/fees: $822; $6,642 out-of-state. Per-credit charge: $26 in-state; $220 out-of-state. Books/supplies: $1,332. Personal expenses: $2,430.

**Application procedures. Admission:** No deadline. No application fee. Application must be submitted on paper. Admission notification on a rolling basis. **Financial aid:** Priority date 6/30; no closing date. FAFSA required. Applicants notified on a rolling basis starting 7/15; must reply within 2 week(s) of notification.

**Academics. Special study options:** Distance learning, dual enrollment of high school students, ESL, honors, independent study, internships, liberal arts/career combination, study abroad. License preparation in aviation, nursing. **Credit/placement by examination:** AP, CLEP, institutional tests. **Support services:** Learning center, reduced course load, remedial instruction, study skills assistance, tutoring, writing center.

**Majors. Biology:** General, ecology. **Business:** General. **Communications:** General, journalism. **Computer sciences:** General, computer graphics. **Foreign languages:** Spanish. **Health:** Nursing (RN). **History:** General. **Liberal arts:** Arts/sciences. **Math:** General. **Mechanic/repair:** Aircraft. **Personal/culinary services:** Cosmetic. **Philosophy/religion:** Philosophy. **Physical sciences:** Astronomy, chemistry, geology. **Protective services:** Corrections. **Psychology:** General. **Social sciences:** General, anthropology, economics, geography, political science, sociology. **Visual/performing arts:** Art, art history/conservation, dramatic, music performance, studio arts, theater design.

**Most popular majors.** Education 6%, health sciences 18%, liberal arts 61%, security/protective services 6%.

**Computing on campus.** 600 workstations in library, computer center. Wireless network available.

**Student life. Freshman orientation:** Mandatory. **Activities:** Choral groups, drama, literary magazine, music ensembles, musical theater, student government, student newspaper, symphony orchestra, TV station.

**Athletics. Intercollegiate:** Baseball M, basketball, football (tackle) M, golf, soccer W, softball W, tennis, volleyball W. **Team name:** Rams.

**Student services.** Adult student services, career counseling, services for economically disadvantaged, financial aid counseling, health services, on-campus daycare, personal counseling, veterans' counselor. **Physically disabled:** Services for visually, speech, hearing impaired. **Learning disabled:**

Comprehensive services available. **Transfer:** Transfer center, transfer adviser, college fairs on campus for students transferring to 4-year colleges.

**Contact.** Phone: (408) 848-4735 Fax: (408) 848-4940
Joy Parker, Director of Admissions and Records, Gavilan College, 5055 Santa Teresa Boulevard, Gilroy, CA 95020

## Glendale Community College
**Glendale, California**
www.glendale.edu                    CB code: 4327

- Public 2-year community college
- Commuter campus in small city

**General.** Founded in 1927. Regionally accredited. **Enrollment:** 23,449 undergraduates. **Degrees:** 680 associate awarded. **Location:** 10 miles from Los Angeles. **Calendar:** Semester, extensive summer session. **Full-time faculty:** 253 total; 26% minority, 51% women. **Part-time faculty:** 519 total; 22% minority, 50% women. **Class size:** 24% < 20, 57% 20-39, 13% 40-49, 5% 50-99, less than 1% >100. **Special facilities:** Science center with planetarium, Baja California (Mexico) field station.

**Student profile.** 71% enrolled in a transfer program, 7% enrolled in a vocational program, 9% already have a bachelor's degree or higher, 2,073 enrolled as first-time, first-year students, 776 transferred in from other institutions.

| | | | |
|---|---|---|---|
| African American: | 2% | International: | 22% |
| Asian American: | 8% | 25 or older: | 45% |
| Hispanic American: | 20% | | |

**Transfer out. Colleges most students transferred to 2009:** California State University: Northridge, University of California: Los Angeles, California State University: Los Angeles, University of Southern California.

**Basis for selection.** Open admission, but selective for some programs. Nursing program has special requirements.

**2009-2010 Annual costs.** Tuition/fees: $813; $6,243 out-of-state. Per-credit charge: $26 in-state; $207 out-of-state. Books/supplies: $1,638. Personal expenses: $2,550.

**2008-2009 Financial aid.** All financial aid based on need. Need-based aid available for part-time students. Work-study available nights, weekends and for part-time students.

**Application procedures. Admission:** Priority date 4/15; no deadline. No application fee. Admission notification on a rolling basis. **Financial aid:** Priority date 4/15; no closing date. FAFSA, institutional form required. Applicants notified on a rolling basis starting 6/15; must reply within 2 week(s) of notification.

**Academics. Special study options:** Cooperative education, distance learning, dual enrollment of high school students, ESL, honors, independent study, internships, study abroad. License preparation in aviation, nursing, real estate. **Credit/placement by examination:** AP, CLEP, institutional tests. 12 credit hours maximum toward associate degree. **Support services:** GED preparation and test center, learning center, remedial instruction, study skills assistance, tutoring, writing center.

**Honors college/program.** Scholars program admits academically accomplished students and offers priority transfer opportunites at UCLA, USC, Pepperdine, and others.

**Majors. Biology:** General. **Business:** General, accounting, administrative services, hospitality/recreation, office management, real estate. **Communications:** Broadcast journalism, journalism. **Computer sciences:** General. **Education:** Early childhood, multi-level teacher. **Engineering technology:** Drafting. **Family/consumer sciences:** General, child care, clothing/textiles, food/nutrition. **Foreign languages:** General, French, Spanish. **Health:** Licensed practical nurse, medical assistant, medical secretary, nursing (RN). **History:** General. **Interdisciplinary:** Biological/physical sciences. **Legal studies:** Legal secretary, paralegal. **Liberal arts:** Arts/sciences, humanities. **Math:** General. **Mechanic/repair:** Aircraft. **Parks/recreation:** General. **Personal/culinary services:** Culinary arts. **Philosophy/religion:** Philosophy. **Physical sciences:** Chemistry, physics. **Protective services:** Fire safety technology, law enforcement admin, police science. **Psychology:** General. **Social sciences:** General, anthropology, economics, sociology. **Visual/performing arts:** General, commercial/advertising art, dance, theater design.

**Most popular majors.** Business/marketing 11%, health sciences 20%, liberal arts 49%.

**Computing on campus.** 1,000 workstations in library, computer center. Online course registration, helpline, repair service, wireless network available.

**Student life. Freshman orientation:** Available. **Activities:** Bands, choral groups, dance, drama, international student organizations, literary magazine, music ensembles, Model UN, musical theater, radio station, student government, student newspaper, TV station, International Student Association, Armenian Student Association, Korean Christian Club, Organization of Latin for Higher Education, Association of Latin American Students.

**Athletics. Intercollegiate:** Baseball M, basketball, cross-country, football (tackle) M, soccer M, tennis, track and field, volleyball W. **Team name:** Vaqueros.

**Student services.** Adult student services, career counseling, services for economically disadvantaged, student employment services, financial aid counseling, health services, on-campus daycare, personal counseling, placement for graduates, veterans' counselor. **Physically disabled:** Services for visually, speech, hearing impaired. **Learning disabled:** Comprehensive services available. **Transfer:** Re-entry adviser for new students. Transfer center, transfer adviser, college fairs on campus for students transferring to 4-year colleges.

**Contact.** E-mail: info@glendale.edu
Phone: (818) 240-1000 ext. 5901 Fax: (818) 549-9436
Sharon Combs, Dean of Admissions and Records, Glendale Community College, 1500 North Verdugo Road, Glendale, CA 91208-2809

## Golden West College
**Huntington Beach, California**
www.goldenwestcollege.edu            CB code: 4339

- Public 2-year community college
- Commuter campus in small city

**General.** Founded in 1966. Regionally accredited. **Enrollment:** 8,235 degree-seeking undergraduates. **Degrees:** 877 associate awarded. **Location:** 40 miles from Los Angeles. **Calendar:** Semester, extensive summer session. **Full-time faculty:** 144 total. **Part-time faculty:** 311 total. **Special facilities:** Outdoor amphitheatre, California native garden.

**Transfer out. Colleges most students transferred to 2009:** California State University: Long Beach, California State University: Dominguez Hills, California State University: Fullerton, University of California: Irvine, University of California: Los Angeles.

**Basis for selection.** Open admission, but selective for some programs. Any student at least 18 years of age eligible for admission. Limited admission to police academy and nursing program. Nursing applicants accepted on basis of prerequisite courses completed and GPA. SAT or ACT scores can be used for counseling and placement in lieu of institutional placement exams.

**2009-2010 Annual costs.** Tuition/fees: $812; $6,512 out-of-state. Per-credit charge: $26 in-state; $216 out-of-state. Parking fee is $30 per semester. Books/supplies: $810. Personal expenses: $1,530.

**2009-2010 Financial aid. Non-need-based:** Scholarships awarded for academics.

**Application procedures. Admission:** Priority date 4/1; no deadline. No application fee. Admission notification on a rolling basis. **Financial aid:** Priority date 6/1; no closing date. FAFSA, institutional form required. Applicants notified on a rolling basis starting 7/1; must reply within 3 week(s) of notification.

**Academics. Special study options:** Accelerated study, cooperative education, cross-registration, distance learning, double major, dual enrollment of high school students, ESL, honors, independent study, study abroad, weekend college. License preparation in nursing, real estate. **Credit/placement by examination:** CLEP, institutional tests. 6 credit hours maximum toward associate degree. **Support services:** Learning center, pre-admission summer program, remedial instruction, tutoring, writing center.

**Majors. Agriculture:** Horticultural science. **Biology:** General. **Business:** General, accounting, administrative services, business admin, office management, office technology, office/clerical, real estate, sales/distribution. **Communications:** Broadcast journalism, journalism, public relations. **Computer sciences:** General. **Education:** Physical. **Engineering technology:** Architectural, drafting. **Foreign languages:** General, French, German, sign language interpretation, Spanish. **Health:** Nursing (RN), predental, premedicine, prepharmacy, preveterinary. **History:** General. **Interdisciplinary:** Biological/physical sciences. **Legal studies:** Legal secretary, prelaw. **Liberal arts: Arts/sciences. **Math:** General. **Mechanic/repair:** Auto body, automotive, diesel. **Personal/culinary services:** Cosmetic. **Philosophy/religion:** Philosophy. **Physical sciences:** Astronomy, chemistry, geology. **Protective services:** Criminal justice, law enforcement admin. **Psychology:** General. **Social sciences:** General, anthropology, economics, political science, sociology. **Visual/performing arts:** Art, commercial/advertising art, dance, dramatic, music performance, music theory/composition, photography, studio arts.

**Computing on campus.** Online course registration, online library, wireless network available.

**Student life. Freshman orientation:** Mandatory. Preregistration for classes offered. Program held prior to enrollment. **Activities:** Bands, choral groups, dance, drama, film society, international student organizations, literary magazine, music ensembles, musical theater, radio station, student government, student newspaper, symphony orchestra, TV station, honor society, student nurses organization, cosmetology club, French club, Circle K, Women of Action.

**Athletics.** NJCAA. **Intercollegiate:** Baseball M, basketball, cross-country, football (tackle) M, golf M, soccer, softball W, swimming, tennis, track and field, volleyball, water polo M, wrestling M. **Team name:** Rustlers.

**Student services.** Adult student services, career counseling, services for economically disadvantaged, student employment services, health services, on-campus daycare, personal counseling, placement for graduates, veterans' counselor. **Physically disabled:** Services for visually, speech, hearing impaired. **Transfer:** Transfer center, transfer adviser, college fairs on campus for students transferring to 4-year colleges.

**Contact.** Phone: (714) 895-8306 Fax: (714) 895-8960
Shirley Donnelly, Director Enrollment Services, Golden West College, 15744 Golden West Street, Box 2748, Huntington Beach, CA 92647-2748

## Golf Academy of America: San Diego
### Carlsbad, California
www.golfacademy.edu                        CB code: 3495

▶ For-profit 2-year college of golf course management
▶ Small city

**General.** Accredited by ACICS. **Enrollment:** 274 degree-seeking undergraduates. **Degrees:** 162 associate awarded. **Calendar:** Semester. **Full-time faculty:** 7 total.

**2009-2010 Annual costs.** Tuition/fees: $15,050.

**Academics. Credit/placement by examination:** CLEP.

**Majors. Parks/recreation:** Facilities management.

**Contact.** E-mail: sdga@sdgagolf.com
Phone: (760) 734-1208 Toll-free number: (800) 342-7342
Golf Academy of America: San Diego, 1950 Camino Vida Roble, Suite 125, Carlsbad, CA 92008

## Grossmont College
### El Cajon, California
www.grossmont.edu                          CB code: 4334

▶ Public 2-year community college
▶ Commuter campus in small city

**General.** Founded in 1961. Regionally accredited. **Enrollment:** 20,371 undergraduates. **Degrees:** 1,171 associate awarded. **Location:** 25 miles from San Diego. **Calendar:** Semester, extensive summer session. **Full-time faculty:** 262 total. **Part-time faculty:** 821 total.

**Transfer out. Colleges most students transferred to 2009:** San Diego State University.

**Basis for selection.** Open admission, but selective for some programs. Limited admission to health professions programs.

**2009-2010 Annual costs.** Tuition/fees: $810; $6,510 out-of-state. Per-credit charge: $26 in-state; $216 out-of-state. Books/supplies: $1,500. Personal expenses: $2,000.

**2008-2009 Financial aid.** All financial aid based on need. Need-based aid available for part-time students. Work-study available nights, weekends and for part-time students.

**Application procedures. Admission:** Priority date 8/21; no deadline. No application fee. Admission notification on a rolling basis. **Financial aid:** Closing date 6/30. FAFSA required. Applicants notified on a rolling basis starting 7/15; must reply within 2 week(s) of notification.

**Academics. Special study options:** Accelerated study, cross-registration, distance learning, double major, dual enrollment of high school students, ESL, independent study, internships, student-designed major, study abroad. License preparation in nursing. **Credit/placement by examination:** AP, CLEP. Students may earn a maximum of 18 units on the CLEP general examinations. **Support services:** Learning center, reduced course load, remedial instruction, tutoring, writing center.

**Majors. Area/ethnic studies:** Native American. **Biology:** General. **Business:** General, administrative services, business admin, executive assistant, hospitality admin, international, management science, marketing, sales/distribution, tourism promotion, tourism/travel. **Communications:** General, broadcast journalism, digital media, journalism. **Computer sciences:** General, applications programming, computer science, LAN/WAN management, programming, webmaster. **Family/consumer sciences:** Child care, child development. **Foreign languages:** American Sign Language, Arabic, French, German, Japanese, Russian, Spanish. **Health:** Athletic training, cardiovascular technology, nursing (RN), occupational therapy assistant, respiratory therapy technology, speech-language pathology assistant. **History:** General. **Liberal arts:** Arts/sciences. **Math:** General. **Parks/recreation:** Exercise sciences. **Personal/culinary services:** Baking, culinary arts, restaurant/catering. **Philosophy/religion:** Philosophy. **Physical sciences:** Chemistry, geology, physics. **Protective services:** Corrections, forensics, police science, security services. **Social sciences:** Economics, geography, political science. **Visual/performing arts:** Acting, art history/conservation, ceramics, cinematography, dance, digital art, drawing, jazz, musical theater, painting, photography, sculpture, theater design. **Other:** Orthopedic technology.

**Computing on campus.** 500 workstations in library, computer center. Online course registration, wireless network available.

**Student life. Freshman orientation:** Available. **Activities:** Bands, choral groups, dance, drama, music ensembles, musical theater, radio station, student government, student newspaper, symphony orchestra.

**Athletics. Intercollegiate:** Baseball M, basketball, football (tackle) M, soccer W, softball W, swimming, tennis, volleyball, water polo. **Team name:** Griffins.

**Student services.** Adult student services, alcohol/substance abuse counseling, career counseling, services for economically disadvantaged, student employment services, financial aid counseling, health services, on-campus daycare, personal counseling, placement for graduates. **Physically disabled:** Services for visually, speech, hearing impaired. **Transfer:** Transfer center, transfer adviser, college fairs on campus for students transferring to 4-year colleges.

**Contact.** Phone: (619) 644-7186 Fax: (619) 644-7933
Grossmont College, 8800 Grossmont College Drive, El Cajon, CA 92020

## Hartnell College
### Salinas, California
www.hartnell.edu                           CB code: 4340

▶ Public 2-year community college
▶ Commuter campus in small city

**General.** Founded in 1920. Regionally accredited. **Enrollment:** 11,503 undergraduates. **Degrees:** 499 associate awarded. **Location:** 110 miles from San Francisco, 65 miles from San Jose. **Calendar:** Semester, limited summer session. **Full-time faculty:** 92 total. **Part-time faculty:** 233 total.

**Basis for selection.** Open admission, but selective for some programs. Limited admission to nursing programs and animal health technology. Interview required for nursing, physician's assistant, animal health technician majors.

**2009-2010 Annual costs.** Tuition/fees: $788; $6,578 out-of-state. Per-credit charge: $26 in-state; $219 out-of-state. Books/supplies: $1,638. Personal expenses: $3,096.

**Application procedures. Admission:** No deadline. No application fee. Admission notification on a rolling basis. **Financial aid:** Priority date 8/1; no closing date. FAFSA required. Applicants notified on a rolling basis.

**Academics. Special study options:** Cooperative education. **Credit/placement by examination:** CLEP. **Support services:** Learning center, remedial instruction, tutoring.

**Majors. Agriculture:** General, agribusiness operations. **Biology:** General. **Business:** Administrative services, banking/financial services, business admin, real estate. **Communications:** Digital media. **Computer sciences:** Information technology, programming, system admin, web page design. **Construction:** Site management. **Education:** Teacher assistance. **Engineering:** General. **Engineering technology:** General, drafting, hazardous materials, mechanical, water quality. **Family/consumer sciences:** Child development. **Health:** Clinical lab technology, dental hygiene, nursing (RN), physician assistant, substance abuse counseling, veterinary technology/assistant. **History:** General. **Liberal arts:** Arts/sciences. **Math:** General. **Mechanic/repair:** Auto body, automotive, diesel, electronics/electrical. **Physical sciences:** Chemistry, geology, physics. **Protective services:** Corrections, firefighting, law enforcement admin. **Psychology:** General. **Social sciences:** General. **Visual/performing arts:** Art, dramatic, photography.

**Student life. Activities:** Bands, choral groups, drama, music ensembles, musical theater, student government, student newspaper.

**Athletics. Intercollegiate:** Baseball M, basketball, cross-country M, football (tackle) M, soccer M.

**Student services.** Career counseling, student employment services, personal counseling, placement for graduates.

**Contact.** Phone: (831) 755-6711 Fax: (831) 759-6014
Mary Dominguez, Director of Enrollment Services, Hartnell College, 411 Central Avenue, Salinas, CA 93901

## Heald College: Concord
**Concord, California**
www.heald.edu                    CB code: 0235

- For-profit 2-year business and technical college
- Commuter campus in small city
- Interview required

**General.** Founded in 1863. Regionally accredited. **Enrollment:** 1,250 degree-seeking undergraduates. **Degrees:** 420 associate awarded. **Location:** 25 miles from San Francisco. **Calendar:** Quarter. **Full-time faculty:** 21 total. **Part-time faculty:** 32 total.

**Basis for selection.** Open admission, but selective for some programs. Institutional admissions examination required. Institutionally designed test used for admissions.

**2009-2010 Annual costs.** Full time students on 2-year plan pay $3,060 per quarter for 4 quarters ($12,240 per year). Books/supplies: $1,500.

**Financial aid.** All financial aid based on need. Need-based aid available for part-time students. Work-study available nights, weekends and for part-time students.

**Application procedures. Admission:** No deadline. No application fee. Admission notification on a rolling basis. **Financial aid:** No deadline. FAFSA required. Applicants notified on a rolling basis.

**Academics. Special study options:** Cooperative education, distance learning, internships. **Credit/placement by examination:** CLEP. **Support services:** GED preparation, learning center, remedial instruction, study skills assistance, tutoring.

**Majors. Business:** Business admin. **Health:** Dental assistant, office admin.

**Computing on campus.** Online library available.

**Student life. Freshman orientation:** Mandatory.

**Student services.** Financial aid counseling, placement for graduates, veterans' counselor.

**Contact.** E-mail: info@heald.edu
Phone: (925) 288-5800 Toll-free number: (800) 755-3550
Fax: (925) 288-5896
Michael Dean, Admissions Director, Heald College: Concord, 5130 Commercial Circle, Concord, CA 94520

## Heald College: Fresno
**Fresno, California**
www.heald.edu                    CB code: 2119

- For-profit 2-year business and technical college
- Commuter campus in small city
- Interview required

**General.** Founded in 1863. Regionally accredited. **Enrollment:** 1,300 degree-seeking undergraduates. **Degrees:** 391 associate awarded. **Location:** 200 miles from San Francisco. **Calendar:** Quarter. **Full-time faculty:** 35 total. **Part-time faculty:** 30 total. **Class size:** 46% < 20, 54% 20-39.

**Transfer out. Colleges most students transferred to 2009:** California State University: Fresno, Fresno City College, National University.

**Basis for selection.** COMPASS entrance exam. **Homeschooled:** Interview required.

**2009-2010 Annual costs.** Full time students on 2-year plan pay $3,060 per quarter for 4 quarters ($12,240 per year). Books/supplies: $1,500.

**Application procedures. Admission:** No deadline. No application fee. Admission notification on a rolling basis. **Financial aid:** No deadline. FAFSA required. Applicants notified on a rolling basis.

**Academics. Special study options:** Liberal arts/career combination. **Credit/placement by examination:** CLEP. **Support services:** GED preparation, learning center, reduced course load, study skills assistance, tutoring.

**Majors. Business:** Accounting, business admin, management information systems, office technology, office/clerical. **Computer sciences:** Data processing. **Legal studies:** Legal secretary.

**Student life. Freshman orientation:** Mandatory.

**Student services.** Adult student services, career counseling, student employment services, placement for graduates.

**Contact.** E-mail: info@heald.edu
Phone: (559) 438-4222 Toll-free number: (800) 755-3550
Fax: (559) 438-0948
Tina Mathis, Admissions Director, Heald College: Fresno, 255 West Bullard Avenue, Fresno, CA 93704-1706

## Heald College: Hayward
**Hayward, California**
www.heald.edu                    CB code: 7106

- For-profit 2-year technical and career college
- Commuter campus in small city

**General.** Regionally accredited. **Enrollment:** 953 degree-seeking undergraduates. **Degrees:** 332 associate awarded. **Location:** 20 miles from San Francisco, 40 miles from San Jose. **Calendar:** Quarter. **Full-time faculty:** 33 total. **Part-time faculty:** 28 total.

**Basis for selection.** Open admission. Admission based on high school diploma/GED equivalent, entrance placement assessment, recommendation of admissions adviser.

**2009-2010 Annual costs.** Full time students on 2-year plan pay $3,060 per quarter for 4 quarters ($12,240 per year). Books/supplies: $1,500.

**Financial aid.** All financial aid based on need. Need-based aid available for part-time students. Work-study available nights, weekends and for part-time students.

**Application procedures. Admission:** No deadline. No application fee. **Financial aid:** No deadline. FAFSA required.

**Academics. Special study options:** Cooperative education, internships. **Credit/placement by examination:** CLEP. Math and English placement by COMPASS exam. **Support services:** GED preparation, learning center, remedial instruction, study skills assistance, tutoring.

**Majors. Business:** Accounting, business admin, construction management, sales/distribution. **Computer sciences:** Security, system admin. **Health:** Dental assistant, insurance coding, medical assistant, office admin, pharmacy assistant. **Legal studies:** Paralegal. **Protective services:** Law enforcement admin.

**Computing on campus.** 630 workstations in library, computer center. Online library available.

**Student life. Freshman orientation:** Available.

**Student services.** Career counseling, student employment services, financial aid counseling, placement for graduates.

**Contact.** Phone: (510) 783-2100 Toll-free number: (800) 755-3550
Fax: (510) 783-3287
Cheryl Valente, Admissions Director, Heald College: Hayward, 25500 Industrial Boulevard, Hayward, CA 94545

## Heald College: Rancho Cordova
### Rancho Cordova, California
www.heald.edu

CB code: 7105

- For-profit 2-year technical college
- Commuter campus in large city
- Interview required

**General.** Regionally accredited. **Enrollment:** 850 degree-seeking undergraduates. **Degrees:** 250 associate awarded. **Calendar:** Quarter. **Full-time faculty:** 30 total. **Part-time faculty:** 15 total.

**Student profile.** Among degree-seeking undergraduates, 100% enrolled in a vocational program.

**Basis for selection.** Institutional admissions test and interview very important.

**2009-2010 Annual costs.** Full time students on 2-year plan pay $3,060 per quarter for 4 quarters ($12,240 per year). Books/supplies: $1,800.

**Financial aid.** All financial aid based on need. Need-based aid available for part-time students. Work-study available nights, weekends and for part-time students.

**Application procedures. Admission:** No deadline. No application fee. **Financial aid:** No deadline. FAFSA required.

**Academics. Special study options:** Cooperative education, internships. **Credit/placement by examination:** CLEP. **Support services:** Learning center, remedial instruction, study skills assistance, tutoring.

**Majors. Business:** Accounting, hospitality admin, office technology. **Computer sciences:** Networking. **Health:** Medical secretary. **Legal studies:** Legal secretary.

**Computing on campus.** 450 workstations in library, computer center. Online library available.

**Student services.** Career counseling, student employment services, financial aid counseling, placement for graduates.

**Contact.** E-mail: info@heald.edu
Phone: (916) 414-2700 Toll-free number: (800) 884-323
Fax: (916) 414-2675
Cindi Stevens, Director of Admissions, Heald College: Rancho Cordova, 2910 Prospect Park Drive, Rancho Cordova, CA 95670

## Heald College: Roseville
### Roseville, California
www.heald.edu

CB code: 4145

- For-profit 2-year career college
- Commuter campus in small city
- Interview required

**General.** Regionally accredited. **Enrollment:** 1,020 degree-seeking undergraduates. **Degrees:** 152 associate awarded. **Calendar:** Quarter. **Full-time faculty:** 8 total. **Part-time faculty:** 50 total. **Class size:** 66% < 20, 34% 20-39. **Special facilities:** Pharmacy tech lab, medical lab.

**Basis for selection.** Open admission. Institutional placement assessment, interview considered.

**2010-2011 Annual costs.** Students completing program in 6 quarters are charged $4,080 per quarter. Students completing program longer than 6 quarters are charged $3,060 per quarter.

**Financial aid.** All financial aid based on need. Need-based aid available for part-time students. Work-study available nights, weekends and for part-time students.

**Application procedures. Admission:** No deadline. No application fee. Application must be submitted on paper. Admission notification on a rolling basis. **Financial aid:** No deadline. FAFSA required.

**Academics. Special study options:** Cooperative education, internships. **Credit/placement by examination:** CLEP. **Support services:** GED preparation, learning center, reduced course load, remedial instruction, study skills assistance, tutoring.

**Majors. Business:** Accounting, business admin. **Computer sciences:** Security, system admin. **Construction:** Site management. **Health:** Health services, medical assistant, office admin, pharmacy assistant. **Legal studies:** Paralegal. **Protective services:** Corrections, law enforcement admin.

**Computing on campus.** Online library available.

**Student life. Freshman orientation:** Mandatory. **Activities:** Phi Theta Kappa, National Technical Honor Society.

**Student services.** Adult student services, career counseling, student employment services, financial aid counseling, placement for graduates, veterans' counselor.

**Contact.** E-mail: rosevilleinfo@heald.edu
Phone: (916) 789-8600 Toll-free number: (800) 755-3550
Fax: (916) 789-8616
Vickie McDougal, Director of Admissions, Heald College: Roseville, 7 Sierra Gate Plaza, Roseville, CA 95678

## Heald College: Salinas
### Salinas, California
www.heald.edu

CB code: 7107

- For-profit 2-year business college
- Commuter campus in small city
- Interview required

**General.** Regionally accredited. **Enrollment:** 1,000 degree-seeking undergraduates. **Degrees:** 134 associate awarded. **Location:** 62 miles from San Jose. **Calendar:** Quarter. **Full-time faculty:** 20 total. **Part-time faculty:** 33 total.

**Basis for selection.** Entrance placement assessment, interview important.

**2010-2011 Annual costs.** Full-time students on a 2-year plan pay $4,080 per quarter for 4 quarters ($16,320 per year). Books/supplies: $1,500. Personal expenses: $3,024.

**Financial aid.** All financial aid based on need. Need-based aid available for part-time students. Work-study available nights, weekends and for part-time students.

**Application procedures. Admission:** No deadline. No application fee. **Financial aid:** No deadline. FAFSA required.

**Academics. Special study options:** Cooperative education, internships. **Credit/placement by examination:** CLEP. **Support services:** Learning center, remedial instruction, study skills assistance, tutoring.

**Majors. Business:** General, accounting, administrative services. **Health:** Medical secretary. **Protective services:** Law enforcement admin.

**Computing on campus.** Online library available.

**Student services.** Career counseling, student employment services, financial aid counseling, placement for graduates.

**Contact.** Phone: (831) 443-1700 Toll-free number: (800) 755-3550
Fax: (831) 444-4600
Daniel Ujueta, Admissions Director, Heald College: Salinas, 1450 North Main Street, Salinas, CA 93906

## Heald College: San Francisco
### San Francisco, California
www.heald.edu

CB code: 7109

- For-profit 2-year business college
- Commuter campus in very large city
- Interview required

**General.** Regionally accredited. **Enrollment:** 800 degree-seeking undergraduates. **Degrees:** 240 associate awarded. **Calendar:** Quarter. **Full-time faculty:** 15 total. **Part-time faculty:** 25 total.

**Basis for selection.** Admission based on high school diploma/GED equivalent, entrance placement assessment, recommendation of admissions adviser.

**2009-2010 Annual costs.** Full time students on 2-year plan pay $3,060 per quarter for 4 quarters ($12,240 per year). Books/supplies: $1,500.

**Financial aid.** All financial aid based on need. Need-based aid available for part-time students. Work-study available nights, weekends and for part-time students.

**Application procedures. Admission:** No deadline. No application fee. **Financial aid:** No deadline. FAFSA required.

**Academics. Special study options:** Cooperative education, internships. **Credit/placement by examination:** CLEP. **Support services:** Learning center, remedial instruction, study skills assistance, tutoring.

**Majors. Business:** Business admin. **Engineering technology:** Computer. **Health:** Medical secretary.

**Computing on campus.** Online library available.

**Student services.** Career counseling, student employment services, financial aid counseling, placement for graduates.

**Contact.** Phone: (415) 808-3000 Toll-free number: (800) 755-3550 Fax: (418) 808-3005
Edward Lubin, Admissions Director, Heald College: San Francisco, 350 Mission Street, San Francisco, CA 94105

## Heald College: San Jose
**Milpitas, California**
**www.heald.edu**                                  CB code: 0405

- For-profit 2-year business college
- Commuter campus in very large city
- Interview required

**General.** Founded in 1863. Regionally accredited. **Enrollment:** 1,119 degree-seeking undergraduates. **Degrees:** 226 associate awarded. **Location:** 45 miles from San Francisco. **Calendar:** Quarter. **Full-time faculty:** 23 total. **Part-time faculty:** 16 total.

**Basis for selection.** Institutional admissions test and personal interview most important.

**2009-2010 Annual costs.** Full time students on 2-year plan pay $3,060 per quarter for 4 quarters ($12,240 per year). Books/supplies: $1,500.

**Financial aid.** All financial aid based on need. Need-based aid available for part-time students. Work-study available nights, weekends and for part-time students.

**Application procedures. Admission:** No deadline. No application fee. Admission notification on a rolling basis. **Financial aid:** No deadline. FAFSA required. Applicants notified on a rolling basis starting 6/15; must reply within 2 week(s) of notification.

**Academics. Special study options:** Internships. **Credit/placement by examination:** CLEP, institutional tests. 45 credit hours maximum toward associate degree. **Support services:** Learning center, reduced course load, remedial instruction, tutoring.

**Majors. Business:** Accounting, business admin, office management. **Health:** Office admin. **Legal studies:** Legal secretary.

**Computing on campus.** Online library available.

**Student services.** Career counseling, student employment services, financial aid counseling, placement for graduates.

**Contact.** E-mail: sanjoseinfo@heald.edu
Phone: (408) 934-4900 Toll-free number: (800) 755-3550
Fax: (415) 934-7777
Clarence Hardiman, Director of Admissions, Heald College: San Jose, 341 Great Mall Parkway, Milpitas, CA 95035

## Heald College: Stockton
**Stockton, California**
**www.heald.edu**                                  CB code: 7108

- For-profit 2-year career college
- Large city

**General.** Regionally accredited. **Enrollment:** 913 degree-seeking undergraduates. **Degrees:** 245 associate awarded. **Calendar:** Quarter. **Full-time faculty:** 34 total. **Part-time faculty:** 40 total.

**Basis for selection.** Open admission. Interview, entrance placement assessment considered.

**2009-2010 Annual costs.** Full time students on 2-year plan pay $3,060 per quarter for 4 quarters ($12,240 per year). Books/supplies: $1,500.

**Financial aid. Need-based:** Work-study available for part-time students.

**Application procedures. Admission:** No deadline. No application fee. **Financial aid:** No deadline. FAFSA required.

**Academics. Special study options:** Accelerated study, internships. **Credit/placement by examination:** CLEP, institutional tests. **Support services:** GED preparation, learning center, reduced course load, study skills assistance, tutoring.

**Majors. Business:** Accounting, office technology. **Computer sciences:** Data entry, vendor certification. **Health:** Dental assistant, medical assistant, office assistant. **Legal studies:** Paralegal. **Protective services:** Law enforcement admin. **Other:** Construction management, Medical insurance billing and coding.

**Computing on campus.** 347 workstations in library.

**Student life. Freshman orientation:** Mandatory. Held every quarter on the Thursday before each start date.

**Student services.** Career counseling, services for economically disadvantaged, student employment services, financial aid counseling, placement for graduates, veterans' counselor.

**Contact.** Phone: (209) 473-5200 Toll-free number: (800) 755-3550 Fax: (209) 477-2739
Hola Motuapuaka, Director of Admissions, Heald College: Stockton, 1605 East March Lane, Stockton, CA 95210

## Imperial Valley College
**Imperial, California**                            CB member
**www.imperial.edu**                               CB code: 4358

- Public 2-year community college
- Commuter campus in large town

**General.** Founded in 1922. Regionally accredited. **Enrollment:** 3,866 full-time, degree-seeking students. **Degrees:** 468 associate awarded. **Location:** 6 miles from El Centro. **Calendar:** Semester, limited summer session. **Full-time faculty:** 118 total; 25% have terminal degrees, 22% minority, 41% women. **Part-time faculty:** 187 total; 4% have terminal degrees, 58% minority, 36% women.

**Student profile.**

| | | | |
|---|---|---|---|
| Out-of-state: | 2% | 25 or older: | 33% |

**Transfer out. Colleges most students transferred to 2009:** San Diego State University, California State Polytechnic University: Pomona, California State University: San Marcos, California State University: San Bernadino, California State University: Long Beach.

**Basis for selection.** Open admission, but selective for some programs. Limited admission for nursing programs. **Adult students:** SAT/ACT scores not required.

**2009-2010 Annual costs.** Tuition/fees: $810; $6,510 out-of-state. Per-credit charge: $26 in-state; $216 out-of-state. Books/supplies: $1,422. Personal expenses: $2,862.

**2008-2009 Financial aid. Need-based:** 95% of total undergraduate aid awarded as scholarships/grants, 5% as loans/jobs. Need-based aid available for part-time students.

**Application procedures. Admission:** No deadline. No application fee. Application must be submitted online. Admission notification on a rolling basis. **Financial aid:** Priority date 3/2, closing date 6/30. FAFSA required. Applicants notified on a rolling basis.

**Academics. Special study options:** Accelerated study, distance learning, double major, dual enrollment of high school students, ESL, liberal arts/career combination. License preparation in nursing, paramedic. **Credit/placement by examination:** AP, CLEP, institutional tests. 25 credit hours maximum toward associate degree. **Support services:** GED test center, learning center, reduced course load, remedial instruction, study skills assistance, tutoring, writing center.

**Majors. Agriculture:** General, business. **Biology:** General. **Business:** Accounting technology, administrative services, banking/financial services, business admin, marketing, office technology, office/clerical. **Communications:** General, journalism. **Computer sciences:** General, computer science, web page design. **Education:** Early childhood, elementary. **Engineering:** General. **Engineering technology:** Heat/ac/refrig, water quality. **Family/consumer sciences:** Child development. **Foreign languages:** General, American Sign Language, Arabic, French, Spanish. **Health:** EMT paramedic, licensed practical nurse, nursing (RN), substance abuse counseling. **History:** General. **Interdisciplinary:** Behavioral sciences, biological/physical sciences. **Legal studies:** Paralegal. **Liberal arts:** Arts/sciences, humanities. **Math:** General. **Mechanic/repair:** General, auto body, automotive, heating/ac/refrig. **Parks/recreation:** Health/fitness. **Physical sciences:** General. **Production:** Welding. **Protective services:** Corrections, firefighting, law enforcement admin. **Psychology:** General. **Social sciences:** General, anthropology. **Visual/performing arts:** Art. **Other:** Disability services technician.

**Most popular majors.** Business/marketing 13%, health sciences 16%, liberal arts 27%, psychology 10%, security/protective services 6%, social sciences 15%.

**Computing on campus.** 90 workstations in library, computer center. Commuter students can connect to campus network. Online course registration, online library, helpline, wireless network available.

**Student life. Freshman orientation:** Available. Preregistration for classes offered. First-Step one day program offered to entering Freshmen including orientation, program college fair, campus tour, and priority registration. **Policies:** Smoke free campus. **Activities:** Jazz band, choral groups, music ensembles, student government, student newspaper, Christian club, Movimiento Estudiantil Chicano de Aztlan, Upward Bound club, French club, Spirit club, adventure club, agriculture club, business club, educational talent search club, Lamplighter's club.

**Athletics.** NJCAA. **Intercollegiate:** Baseball M, basketball, cheerleading, cross-country W, soccer, softball W, tennis, volleyball W. **Team name:** Arabs.

**Student services.** Adult student services, alcohol/substance abuse counseling, career counseling, services for economically disadvantaged, student employment services, financial aid counseling, health services, on-campus daycare, personal counseling, veterans' counselor. **Physically disabled:** Services for visually, speech, hearing impaired. **Learning disabled:** Comprehensive services available. **Transfer:** Pre-admission transcript evaluation for new students. Transfer center, transfer adviser, college fairs on campus for students transferring to 4-year colleges.

**Contact.** Phone: (760) 352-8320 Fax: (760) 355-2663
Gloria Carmona, Director of Admissions & Records, Imperial Valley College, Box 158, Imperial, CA 92251-0158

## Irvine Valley College
**Irvine, California**
**www.ivc.edu**   CB code: 3356

- Public 2-year community college
- Commuter campus in small city

**General.** Regionally accredited. **Enrollment:** 15,710 undergraduates. **Degrees:** 433 associate awarded. **ROTC:** Air Force. **Location:** 50 miles from Los Angeles. **Calendar:** Semester, extensive summer session. **Full-time faculty:** 117 total. **Part-time faculty:** 597 total. **Special facilities:** Dance studio, Microsoft Office user specialist testing site, telescope, performing arts center.

**Transfer out. Colleges most students transferred to 2009:** University of California: Irvine, California State University: Fullerton.

**Basis for selection.** Open admission.

**2009-2010 Annual costs.** Tuition/fees: $814; $6,514 out-of-state. Per-credit charge: $26 in-state; $216 out-of-state. Books/supplies: $1,638. Personal expenses: $2,826.

**2008-2009 Financial aid.** All financial aid based on need. Need-based aid available for part-time students. Work-study available nights and for part-time students.

**Application procedures. Admission:** No deadline. No application fee. Admission notification on a rolling basis. **Financial aid:** No deadline. FAFSA, institutional form required. Applicants notified on a rolling basis starting 4/30.

**Academics. Special study options:** Accelerated study, cooperative education, cross-registration, distance learning, double major, dual enrollment

of high school students, ESL, honors, independent study, internships, study abroad, weekend college. **Credit/placement by examination:** CLEP, institutional tests. 12 credit hours maximum toward associate degree. Minimum 2.0 GPA in at least 12 units completed at IVC required to enroll in credit by examination. **Support services:** Learning center, remedial instruction, study skills assistance, tutoring, writing center.

**Majors. Area/ethnic studies:** Women's. **Biology:** General, ecology. **Business:** General, accounting, business admin, office management, office technology, real estate. **Communications:** Advertising. **Computer sciences:** General, applications programming, networking, programming, systems analysis. **Conservation:** General. **Education:** Early childhood, physical. **Engineering technology:** Drafting, electrical, manufacturing. **Foreign languages:** French, Spanish. **History:** General. **Liberal arts:** Arts/sciences. **Math:** General. **Parks/recreation:** Health/fitness. **Philosophy/religion:** Philosophy. **Physical sciences:** Chemistry, geology. **Protective services:** Law enforcement admin, police science. **Psychology:** General. **Social sciences:** Anthropology, economics, geography, political science, sociology. **Visual/performing arts:** General, art, dance, dramatic, photography, studio arts, theater design.

**Most popular majors.** Business/marketing 9%, liberal arts 77%.

**Computing on campus.** 250 workstations in library, computer center. Commuter students can connect to campus network. Online course registration, online library, helpline available.

**Student life. Freshman orientation:** Mandatory. **Housing:** Homestay referral for international students. **Activities:** Bands, choral groups, dance, drama, literary magazine, music ensembles, musical theater, student government, student newspaper, symphony orchestra, administration of justice club, Phi Theta Kappa honor society, Muslim Student Association, biology society, dance club, geology club, health sciences society, journalism club, Phi Theta Kappa, Psi Beta.

**Athletics. Intercollegiate:** Badminton W, baseball M, basketball, cross-country, golf, soccer, softball W, tennis, volleyball. **Intramural:** Basketball, soccer, tennis, volleyball. **Team name:** Lasers.

**Student services.** Adult student services, career counseling, services for economically disadvantaged, student employment services, financial aid counseling, health services, on-campus daycare, personal counseling, placement for graduates, veterans' counselor, women's services. **Physically disabled:** Services for visually, speech, hearing impaired. **Transfer:** Re-entry adviser for new students. Transfer center, transfer adviser, college fairs on campus for students transferring to 4-year colleges.

**Contact.** E-mail: admissions@ivc.edu
Phone: (949) 451-5461 Fax: (949) 451-5443
Arleen Elseroad, Director of Admissions, Records & Enrollment Services, Irvine Valley College, 5500 Irvine Center Drive, Irvine, CA 92618-4399

## Kaplan College: Palm Springs
**Palm Springs, California**
**www.mariccollege.edu**

- For-profit 2-year health science and technical college
- Commuter campus in large town

**General.** Accredited by ACCSC. **Enrollment:** 780 degree-seeking undergraduates. **Degrees:** 21 associate awarded. **Calendar:** Continuous. **Full-time faculty:** 14 total. **Part-time faculty:** 15 total.

**2009-2010 Annual costs.** Tuition varies by program from $13,368 (fees $95) to $33,264 (fees $170).

**Application procedures. Admission:** $25 fee.

**Academics. Credit/placement by examination:** CLEP.

**Majors. Legal studies:** Paralegal.

**Student life. Freshman orientation:** Available, $20 fee.

**Contact.** Phone: (760) 327-4562
Brian Mendenhall, Director of Admissions, Kaplan College: Palm Springs, 2475 East Tahquitz Canyon Way, Palm Springs, CA 92262

## Kaplan College: Panorama City
**Panorama City, California**
**www.panorama-city.kaplancollege.com/**   CB code: 3541

- For-profit 2-year junior and technical college
- Commuter campus in very large city
- Interview required

**General.** Accredited by ACICS. **Enrollment:** 45 degree-seeking undergraduates. **Degrees:** 20 associate awarded. **Location:** 15 miles from Los Angeles. **Calendar:** Continuous. **Full-time faculty:** 7 total. **Part-time faculty:** 7 total. **Class size:** 76% < 20, 24% 20-39.

**Basis for selection.** Open admission. **Homeschooled:** Interview required.

**2009-2010 Annual costs.** Tuition varies by program from $13,090 (fees $45) to $30,205 (fees $45).

**Financial aid.** All financial aid based on need. Work-study available nights.

**Application procedures. Admission:** No deadline. No application fee. Application must be submitted on paper. **Financial aid:** No deadline. FAFSA, institutional form required.

**Academics. Special study options:** Internships, liberal arts/career combination. **Credit/placement by examination:** AP, CLEP. **Support services:** Learning center, study skills assistance, tutoring.

**Majors. Business:** Accounting, accounting technology, accounting/business management, business admin, office management. **Computer sciences:** Information technology, LAN/WAN management, system admin. **Legal studies:** Court reporting, paralegal.

**Most popular majors.** Business/marketing 17%, computer/information sciences 35%, legal studies 46%.

**Computing on campus.** 20 workstations in library, computer center. Online library available.

**Student life. Freshman orientation:** Mandatory. **Activities:** Student newspaper.

**Student services.** Career counseling, student employment services, financial aid counseling, placement for graduates.

**Contact.** E-mail: ehacker@kaplan.edu
Phone: (818) 672-3000 Toll-free number: (800) 206-0095
Fax: (818) 672-8919
Carol Kersting, Director of Admissions, Kaplan College: Panorama City, 14355 Roscoe Boulevard, Panorama City, CA 91402

## Kaplan College: Sacramento
Sacramento, California
www.mariccollege.edu

- For-profit 2-year business and technical college
- Commuter campus in large city

**General.** Accredited by ACICS. **Enrollment:** 799 degree-seeking undergraduates. **Degrees:** 45 associate awarded. **Calendar:** Continuous. **Full-time faculty:** 11 total. **Part-time faculty:** 29 total.

**Basis for selection.** Open admission.

**2009-2010 Annual costs.** Tuition varies by program from $12,130 (fees $1,664) to $25,200 (fees $2,305).

**Application procedures. Admission:** No deadline. $25 fee.

**Academics. Credit/placement by examination:** CLEP.

**Majors. Legal studies:** Paralegal.

**Student life. Freshman orientation:** Available, $20 fee.

**Contact.** E-mail: admissions@mariccollege.edu
Phone: (916) 649-8168
Carol Johnson, Director of Admissions, Kaplan College: Sacramento, 4330 Watt Avenue, Suite 400, Sacramento, CA 95821

## Kaplan College: Salida
Salida, California
www.mariccollege.edu

- For-profit 2-year health science and technical college
- Commuter campus in small city
- Interview required

**General.** Accredited by ACCSC. **Enrollment:** 2,298 degree-seeking undergraduates. **Degrees:** 150 associate awarded. **Calendar:** Continuous. **Full-time faculty:** 20 total. **Part-time faculty:** 35 total.

**Basis for selection.** Open admission. **Homeschooled:** Transcript of courses and grades required.

**2009-2010 Annual costs.** Tuition varies by program from $12,475 (fees $1,100) to $37,651 (fees $6,329).

**Application procedures. Admission:** No deadline. $25 fee. Application must be submitted on paper.

**Academics. Credit/placement by examination:** CLEP.

**Majors. Health:** Respiratory therapy assistant, surgical technology.

**Most popular majors.** Health sciences 64%.

**Computing on campus.** 90 workstations in computer center.

**Student life. Freshman orientation:** Mandatory, $20 fee.

**Student services.** Adult student services, career counseling, financial aid counseling, placement for graduates, veterans' counselor.

**Contact.** E-mail: wtriplett@mariccollege.edu
Phone: (209) 543-7000
Doug Stucker, Director of Admissions, Kaplan College: Salida, 5172 Kiernan Court, Salida, CA 95368

## Kaplan College: San Diego
San Diego, California
www.mariccollege.edu                    CB code: 3064

- For-profit 2-year business and health science college
- Commuter campus in very large city

**General.** Accredited by ACCSC. **Enrollment:** 1,418 degree-seeking undergraduates. **Degrees:** 177 associate awarded. **Calendar:** Continuous. **Full-time faculty:** 57 total. **Part-time faculty:** 43 total.

**2009-2010 Annual costs.** Cost of full programs: associate degree programs $28,250, diploma programs $14,320, including fees and books. Personal expenses: $2,925.

**Application procedures. Admission:** $25 fee.

**Academics. Credit/placement by examination:** AP, CLEP.

**Student life. Freshman orientation:** Available, $20 fee.

**Contact.** Phone: (858) 279-4500 Toll-free number: (800) 400-8232
Fax: (858) 279-4885
Christopher Drozd, Director of Admissions, Kaplan College: San Diego, 9055 Balboa Avenue, San Diego, CA 92123

## Kaplan College: Vista
Vista, California
www.mariccollege.edu

- For-profit 2-year technical college
- Commuter campus in small city

**General.** Accredited by ACCSC. **Enrollment:** 1,338 degree-seeking undergraduates. **Degrees:** 20 associate awarded. **Calendar:** Continuous. **Full-time faculty:** 19 total. **Part-time faculty:** 43 total.

**Basis for selection.** Institutional entrance exam important. High school diploma/GED required for some programs. Timed institutional examination administered onsite.

**2009-2010 Annual costs.** Tuition/fees: $13,363. Diploma program costs range from $4,567-$31,174. Associate degree program Criminal Justice $27,596.

**Application procedures. Admission:** No deadline. $25 fee.

**Academics. Credit/placement by examination:** CLEP.

**Majors. Computer sciences:** LAN/WAN management. **Legal studies:** Paralegal. **Protective services:** Criminal justice.

**Student life. Freshman orientation:** Available, $20 fee.

**Contact.** Phone: (760) 630-1555 Fax: (760) 630-1656
Renee Codner, Director of Admissions, Kaplan College: Vista, 2022
University Drive, Vista, CA 92083

## Lake Tahoe Community College
### South Lake Tahoe, California
www.ltcc.edu                                          CB code: 4420

- Public 2-year community college
- Commuter campus in large town

**General.** Founded in 1975. Regionally accredited. The wooded 164-acre campus is located in the Sierra Nevada mountains near the south shore of Lake Tahoe. **Enrollment:** 1,415 degree-seeking undergraduates. **Degrees:** 160 associate awarded. **Location:** 55 miles from Reno, Nevada, 110 miles from Sacramento. **Calendar:** Quarter, limited summer session. **Full-time faculty:** 44 total; 50% women. **Part-time faculty:** 175 total.

**Transfer out. Colleges most students transferred to 2009:** California State University, University of California, University of Nevada: Reno.

**Basis for selection.** Open admission. Open admission policy for students who are at least 18 or have graduated from high school. Special admission criteria apply to international students. **Learning Disabled:** Assistance is available through the Disability Resource Center.

**2010-2011 Annual costs.** Tuition/fees (projected): $777; $6,852 out-of-state. Per-credit charge: $17 in-state; $152 out-of-state. Books/supplies: $1,566. Personal expenses: $3,024.

**Application procedures. Admission:** No deadline. No application fee. Application must be submitted online. Admission notification on a rolling basis. **Financial aid:** Priority date 5/1; no closing date. FAFSA required. Applicants notified on a rolling basis starting 7/1; must reply within 2 week(s) of notification.

**Academics. Special study options:** Cooperative education, distance learning, double major, ESL, internships, study abroad. License preparation in dental hygiene, real estate. **Credit/placement by examination:** CLEP, institutional tests. 4 credit hours maximum toward associate degree. **Support services:** GED preparation, learning center, remedial instruction, study skills assistance, tutoring, writing center.

**Majors. Business:** General, accounting, administrative services, entrepreneurial studies, finance, marketing, office/clerical. **Education:** Early childhood. **Foreign languages:** Spanish. **Health:** Medical assistant, medical records admin, substance abuse counseling. **Interdisciplinary:** Natural sciences. **Liberal arts:** Arts/sciences, humanities. **Math:** General. **Parks/recreation:** Health/fitness. **Personal/culinary services:** Culinary arts. **Protective services:** Firefighting, law enforcement admin. **Psychology:** General. **Social sciences:** General, anthropology, sociology. **Visual/performing arts:** Art, dance, dramatic, studio arts. **Other:** Wilderness education.

**Computing on campus.** 155 workstations in library, computer center, student center. Online course registration, online library, wireless network available.

**Student life. Freshman orientation:** Available. **Activities:** Choral groups, dance, drama, music ensembles, musical theater, student government, Alpha Gamma Sigma, associated student council, international club.

**Student services.** Adult student services, career counseling, services for economically disadvantaged, student employment services, financial aid counseling, minority student services, on-campus daycare, personal counseling, placement for graduates, veterans' counselor. **Physically disabled:** Services for visually, speech, hearing impaired. **Learning disabled:** Comprehensive services available. **Transfer:** Transfer center, transfer adviser, college fairs on campus for students transferring to 4-year colleges.

**Contact.** E-mail: admissions@ltcc.edu
Phone: (530) 541-4660 ext. 211 Fax: (530) 542-1781
Cheri Jones, Director of Admissions & Records, Lake Tahoe Community College, One College Drive, South Lake Tahoe, CA 96150-4524

## Laney College
### Oakland, California
www.laney.peralta.edu                                 CB code: 4406

- Public 2-year community college
- Commuter campus in large city

**General.** Founded in 1953. Regionally accredited. Vocational programs include programs with PGE and a solar program with UC Lawrence Laboratories. **Enrollment:** 14,541 undergraduates. **Degrees:** 488 associate awarded. **Location:** 10 miles from San Francisco. **Calendar:** Semester, extensive summer session. **Full-time faculty:** 122 total. **Part-time faculty:** 364 total. **Special facilities:** CAD laboratory.

**Student profile.**

| | | | |
|---|---|---|---|
| Out-of-state: | 2% | **25 or older:** | 61% |

**Transfer out. Colleges most students transferred to 2009:** California State University: East Bay, San Francisco State, University of California: Berkeley.

**Basis for selection.** Open admission.

**2009-2010 Annual costs.** Tuition/fees: $814; $6,514 out-of-state. Per-credit charge: $26 in-state; $216 out-of-state. Books/supplies: $1,638. Personal expenses: $3,096.

**2008-2009 Financial aid. Need-based:** 96% of total undergraduate aid awarded as scholarships/grants, 4% as loans/jobs.

**Application procedures. Admission:** No deadline. No application fee. Admission notification on a rolling basis. **Financial aid:** Priority date 4/1; no closing date. FAFSA, institutional form required. Applicants notified on a rolling basis; must reply within 2 week(s) of notification.

**Academics. Special study options:** Cooperative education, distance learning, dual enrollment of high school students, ESL, honors, independent study, liberal arts/career combination, weekend college. **Credit/placement by examination:** CLEP, institutional tests. **Support services:** Learning center, remedial instruction, study skills assistance, tutoring.

**Majors. Area/ethnic studies:** African-American, Asian, Latin American. **Business:** General, accounting, administrative services, banking/financial services, management information systems, office technology, office/clerical, operations, sales/distribution. **Communications:** Broadcast journalism, journalism. **Communications technology:** General, graphic/printing. **Computer sciences:** General, information systems. **Construction:** Carpentry, maintenance. **Education:** General. **Engineering technology:** Architectural. **Interdisciplinary:** Biological/physical sciences. **Liberal arts:** Arts/sciences. **Math:** General. **Mechanic/repair:** Heating/ac/refrig. **Personal/culinary services:** Cosmetic, culinary arts. **Production:** Woodworking. **Social sciences:** General. **Visual/performing arts:** Art, ceramics, commercial/advertising art, dance, design, dramatic.

**Computing on campus.** 400 workstations in library, computer center, student center. Online course registration, online library available.

**Student life. Freshman orientation:** Mandatory. Preregistration for classes offered. **Activities:** Pep band, dance, drama, literary magazine, musical theater, student government, student newspaper, TV station.

**Athletics. Intercollegiate:** Badminton W, baseball M, basketball M, football (tackle) M, softball W, swimming, track and field W, volleyball W, water polo W. **Team name:** Eagles.

**Student services.** Adult student services, career counseling, services for economically disadvantaged, student employment services, financial aid counseling, health services, minority student services, on-campus daycare, personal counseling, placement for graduates. **Physically disabled:** Services for visually, speech, hearing impaired. **Transfer:** Re-entry adviser for new students. Transfer center, transfer adviser, college fairs on campus for students transferring to 4-year colleges.

**Contact.** E-mail: admissions@peralta.edu
Phone: (510) 464-3121 Fax: (510) 464-3240
Howard Perdue, Director of Admissions and Records, Laney College, 900 Fallon Street, Oakland, CA 94607

## Las Positas College
### Livermore, California
www.laspositascollege.edu                             CB code: 6507

- Public 2-year community college
- Commuter campus in small city

**General.** Founded in 1991. Regionally accredited. **Enrollment:** 9,691 undergraduates. **Degrees:** 492 associate awarded. **Location:** 43 miles from San Francsico, 39 miles from San Jose. **Calendar:** Semester, limited summer session. **Full-time faculty:** 101 total. **Part-time faculty:** 250 total.

**Transfer out. Colleges most students transferred to 2009:** California State University: East Bay.

**Basis for selection.** Open admission. High school diploma or GED required for student under 18 years.

**2009-2010 Annual costs.** Tuition/fees: $810; $6,510 out-of-state. Per-credit charge: $26 in-state; $216 out-of-state. Books/supplies: $1,566. Personal expenses: $2,664.

**Application procedures. Admission:** No deadline. No application fee. Admission notification on a rolling basis. **Financial aid:** Priority date 5/1; no closing date. Institutional form required. Applicants notified on a rolling basis starting 7/1; must reply within 2 week(s) of notification.

**Academics. Special study options:** Accelerated study, distance learning, dual enrollment of high school students, ESL, honors, independent study, internships, student-designed major. **Credit/placement by examination:** CLEP. **Support services:** Learning center, remedial instruction, tutoring.

**Computing on campus.** 285 workstations in library, computer center.

**Student life. Freshman orientation:** Available. **Activities:** Jazz band, choral groups, dance, drama, international student organizations, literary magazine, music ensembles, musical theater, student government, student newspaper.

**Athletics. Intercollegiate:** Basketball, cross-country, soccer. **Intramural:** Basketball, bowling, fencing, handball M, racquetball, skin diving, soccer, swimming, volleyball. **Team name:** Hawks.

**Student services.** Adult student services, career counseling, student employment services, financial aid counseling, health services, personal counseling, veterans' counselor. **Physically disabled:** Services for visually, speech, hearing impaired. **Learning disabled:** Comprehensive services available. **Transfer:** Transfer center, transfer adviser, college fairs on campus for students transferring to 4-year colleges.

**Contact.** Phone: (925) 424-1000 Fax: (925) 443-0742
Sylvia Rodriguez, Registrar, Las Positas College, 3033 Collier Canyon Road, Livermore, CA 94551

## Lassen Community College
**Susanville, California**
www.lassencollege.edu      **CB code: 4383**

- Public 2-year community college
- Small town

**General.** Founded in 1925. Regionally accredited. **Enrollment:** 2,345 undergraduates. **Degrees:** 172 associate awarded. **Location:** 100 miles from Chico, 84 miles from Reno, Nevada. **Calendar:** Semester, limited summer session. **Full-time faculty:** 35 total. **Part-time faculty:** 68 total.

**Student profile.**

| | | | |
|---|---|---|---|
| Out-of-state: | 7% | Live on campus: | 3% |

**Basis for selection.** Open admission, but selective for some programs. Limited admission to nursing program.

**2009-2010 Annual costs.** Tuition/fees: $796; $6,496 out-of-state. Per-credit charge: $26 in-state; $216 out-of-state. Nevada residents pay $42 per-credit-hour with good neighbor policy. Room/board: $5,490. Books/supplies: $1,638. Personal expenses: $2,250.

**2008-2009 Financial aid. Additional information:** Board of Governors Grant: low-income California residents can have registration fees waived.

**Application procedures. Admission:** No deadline. No application fee. Admission notification on a rolling basis. Institutional placement tests recommended. **Financial aid:** Priority date 7/1; no closing date. FAFSA required. Applicants notified on a rolling basis starting 7/1; must reply within 2 week(s) of notification.

**Academics.** Gunsmithing and summer NRA programs offered. **Special study options:** Cooperative education, distance learning, dual enrollment of high school students, honors, independent study, internships. **Credit/placement by examination:** AP, CLEP, institutional tests. 15 credit hours maximum toward associate degree. **Support services:** Learning center, pre-admission summer program, reduced course load, remedial instruction, tutoring.

**Majors. Business:** General, accounting, administrative services, business admin, management information systems, office technology, office/clerical,

real estate. **Communications:** Journalism. **Computer sciences:** General, applications programming. **Construction:** Maintenance. **Education:** General, early childhood, physical. **Health:** Nursing (RN), nursing assistant. **Interdisciplinary:** Biological/physical sciences. **Liberal arts:** Arts/sciences. **Math:** General. **Mechanic/repair:** Auto body, automotive. **Protective services:** Corrections, law enforcement admin, police science. **Social sciences:** General. **Visual/performing arts:** Art.

**Computing on campus.** 40 workstations in computer center.

**Student life. Housing:** Coed dorms available. **Activities:** Choral groups, drama, film society, student government, student newspaper, over 20 student organizations and clubs.

**Athletics.** NJCAA. **Intercollegiate:** Baseball M, basketball, cross-country, golf, rifle, softball W, track and field, volleyball W, wrestling M. **Intramural:** Skiing.

**Student services.** Career counseling, health services, on-campus daycare, personal counseling, veterans' counselor. **Physically disabled:** Services for visually, speech, hearing impaired. **Transfer:** Transfer adviser, college fairs on campus for students transferring to 4-year colleges.

**Contact.** Phone: (530) 251-8808 Fax: (530) 257-8964
Registrar and Admissions Director, Lassen Community College, Box 3000, Susanville, CA 96130

## Long Beach City College
**Long Beach, California**
www.lbcc.edu      **CB code: 4388**

- Public 2-year community college
- Commuter campus in large city

**General.** Founded in 1927. Regionally accredited. **Enrollment:** 31,275 undergraduates. **Degrees:** 968 associate awarded. **Location:** 20 miles from downtown Los Angeles. **Calendar:** Semester, limited summer session. **Full-time faculty:** 356 total. **Part-time faculty:** 623 total. **Class size:** 35% < 20, 47% 20-39, 10% 40-49, 7% 50-99, 1% >100.

**Student profile.**

| | | | |
|---|---|---|---|
| Out-of-state: | 1% | 25 or older: | 51% |

**Transfer out. Colleges most students transferred to 2009:** California State University: Long Beach, California State University: Dominguez Hills, California State University: Fullerton, University of California: Irvine.

**Basis for selection.** Open admission.

**2009-2010 Annual costs.** Tuition/fees: $808; $6,508 out-of-state. Per-credit charge: $26 in-state; $216 out-of-state. Books/supplies: $1,638. Personal expenses: $3,096.

**Financial aid.** All financial aid based on need. Need-based aid available for part-time students. Work-study available for part-time students.

**Application procedures. Admission:** No deadline. No application fee. Admission notification on a rolling basis. **Financial aid:** Priority date 5/6; no closing date. FAFSA, institutional form required. Applicants notified on a rolling basis starting 7/6; must reply within 2 week(s) of notification.

**Academics. Special study options:** Accelerated study, cooperative education, cross-registration, distance learning, dual enrollment of high school students, ESL, honors, independent study, internships, liberal arts/career combination, study abroad, weekend college. License preparation in aviation, nursing, radiology, real estate. **Credit/placement by examination:** AP, CLEP, IB, institutional tests. 40 credit hours maximum toward associate degree. Students must first complete 12 units in residence. **Support services:** GED preparation, learning center, pre-admission summer program, remedial instruction, study skills assistance, tutoring, writing center.

**Majors. Agriculture:** Ornamental horticulture. **Biology:** General. **Business:** General, accounting, administrative services, business admin, fashion, hotel/motel admin, office technology, office/clerical, real estate, restaurant/food services, sales/distribution, tourism promotion, tourism/travel. **Communications:** Advertising, broadcast journalism, journalism, public relations, publishing. **Communications technology:** General, desktop publishing, graphic/printing. **Computer sciences:** Applications programming, data processing, word processing. **Construction:** Carpentry. **Education:** Teacher assistance. **Engineering:** General. **Engineering technology:** Architectural, architectural drafting, drafting, heat/ac/rcfrig. **Family/consumer sciences:** General, child care, child development, consumer economics, family resources, institutional food production. **Foreign languages:** General, Spanish. **Health:** Dietetic technician, licensed practical nurse, medical assistant, medical radiologic technology/radiation therapy, nursing (RN). **Legal studies:** Legal secretary. **Liberal arts:** Arts/sciences. **Math:** General. **Mechanic/repair:** General, aircraft powerplant, alternative fuel vehicle, auto body, automotive, diesel, electronics/electrical. **Parks/recreation:** Health/fitness. **Personal/culinary services:** Baking, culinary arts, restaurant/catering. **Physical sciences:** General. **Production:** Cabinetmaking/millwright, machine shop technology, machine tool, welding. **Protective services:** Fire safety technology, law enforcement admin. **Public administration:** General, human services. **Social sciences:** General. **Transportation:** Aviation. **Visual/performing arts:** Art, commercial photography, commercial/advertising art, dance, design, dramatic, drawing, fashion design, film/cinema, interior design, multimedia, printmaking, sculpture, theater design.

**Most popular majors.** Business/marketing 7%, health sciences 19%, liberal arts 44%, security/protective services 7%.

**Computing on campus.** 500 workstations in library, computer center, student center. Online course registration, online library, helpline, wireless network available.

**Student life. Freshman orientation:** Available. Preregistration for classes offered. **Activities:** Bands, campus ministries, choral groups, dance, drama, international student organizations, literary magazine, music ensembles, musical theater, radio station, student government, student newspaper, symphony orchestra, TV station, College Republicans, Students for a Democratic Society.

**Athletics.** NJCAA. **Intercollegiate:** Baseball M, basketball, cross-country, football (tackle) M, golf, soccer, softball W, swimming, tennis, track and field, volleyball, water polo. **Intramural:** Archery, badminton, basketball, bowling, golf, racquetball, soccer, softball, swimming, table tennis, tennis, track and field, volleyball, wrestling M. **Team name:** Vikings.

**Student services.** Career counseling, student employment services, health services, on-campus daycare, personal counseling, veterans' counselor. **Physically disabled:** Services for visually, speech, hearing impaired. **Transfer:** Re-entry adviser for new students. Transfer center, transfer adviser, college fairs on campus for students transferring to 4-year colleges.

**Contact.** Phone: (562) 938-4139 Fax: (562) 938-4858
Ross Miyashiro, Dean of Admissions and Records, Long Beach City College, 4901 East Carson Street, Long Beach, CA 90808

## Los Angeles City College
### Los Angeles, California
### www.lacitycollege.edu
**CB code: 4391**

- Public 2-year community college
- Very large city

**General.** Founded in 1929. Regionally accredited. **Enrollment:** 17,636 undergraduates. **Degrees:** 662 associate awarded. **ROTC:** Army, Naval, Air Force. **Location:** 5 miles from downtown. **Calendar:** Semester, limited summer session. **Full-time faculty:** 179 total; 41% minority. **Part-time faculty:** 430 total; 27% minority.

**Basis for selection.** Open admission. Auditions required of theater academy, music majors.

**2009-2010 Annual costs.** Tuition/fees: $802; $6,442 out-of-state. Per-credit charge: $26 in-state; $214 out-of-state. Books/supplies: $1,638. Personal expenses: $3,096.

**2008-2009 Financial aid.** All financial aid based on need. Need-based aid available for part-time students. **Additional information:** Fee waivers available for public assistance and Social Security insurance recipients; fee credits available for low income families.

**Application procedures. Admission:** Closing date 9/1. No application fee. Admission notification on a rolling basis beginning on or about 4/30. **Financial aid:** Priority date 3/2; no closing date. FAFSA required. Applicants notified by 7/6; Applicants notified on a rolling basis starting 7/6; must reply within 2 week(s) of notification.

**Academics. Special study options:** Accelerated study, cooperative education, cross-registration, distance learning, dual enrollment of high school students, ESL, honors, independent study. License preparation in dental hygiene, nursing, radiology. **Credit/placement by examination:** CLEP, institutional tests. 15 credit hours maximum toward associate degree. **Support services:** Learning center, remedial instruction, tutoring.

**Majors. Area/ethnic studies:** African-American, Asian-American. **Biology:** General. **Business:** Accounting, administrative services, banking/financial services, business admin, entrepreneurial studies, management information systems, office technology, office/clerical, real estate, tourism promotion, tourism/travel. **Communications:** Advertising, broadcast journalism, journalism, public relations. **Communications technology:** General. **Computer sciences:** General, applications programming. **Engineering:** General, software. **Engineering technology:** Biomedical, drafting, electrical. **Family/consumer sciences:** General, child care. **Foreign languages:** Chinese, French, German, Italian, Japanese, Spanish. **Health:** Dental lab technology, health services, medical radiologic technology/radiation therapy, medical records technology, medical secretary. **Legal studies:** Legal secretary, paralegal. **Liberal arts:** Arts/sciences. **Math:** General. **Mechanic/repair:** Electronics/electrical. **Physical sciences:** Chemistry, physics. **Protective services:** Police science. **Psychology:** General. **Visual/performing arts:** Art, cinematography, commercial/advertising art, dramatic, film/cinema, photography.

**Computing on campus.** 200 workstations in library, computer center.

**Student life. Activities:** Bands, choral groups, dance, drama, film society, literary magazine, music ensembles, musical theater, radio station, student government, student newspaper, TV station, religious, political, ethnic, and foreign student clubs.

**Athletics.** NJCAA. **Intercollegiate:** Baseball M, basketball M, cross-country, track and field. **Team name:** CUBS.

**Student services.** Career counseling, student employment services, health services, on-campus daycare, personal counseling, veterans' counselor. **Physically disabled:** Services for visually, speech, hearing impaired. **Transfer:** Transfer adviser, college fairs on campus for students transferring to 4-year colleges.

**Contact.** Phone: (323) 953-4381 Fax: (323) 953-4013
William Marmolejo, Dean of Admissions, Los Angeles City College, 855 North Vermont Avenue, Los Angeles, CA 90029-3589

## Los Angeles County College of Nursing and Allied Health
### Los Angeles, California
### www.ladhs.org/wps/portal/CollegeOfNursing/

- Public 2-year nursing and community college
- Commuter campus in very large city

**General.** Clinical component of studies undertaken in cooperation with Los Angeles County Department of Health Services medical centers. Applicants must be residents of the County of Los Angeles. **Enrollment:** 325 degree-seeking undergraduates. **Degrees:** 100 associate awarded. **Location:** 2 miles from Los Angeles. **Calendar:** Semester, limited summer session. **Full-time faculty:** 40 total.

**Student profile.** Among degree-seeking undergraduates, 97% enrolled in a vocational program, 15% already have a bachelor's degree or higher.

**Basis for selection.** Admissions criteria include high school diploma or equivalency, prior college experience, California Achievement Test. Geographical residency in Los Angeles County required. Point system applied when there are more qualified applicants than openings. **Learning Disabled:** Must submit documentation to obtain accommodations.

**High school preparation.** College-preparatory program recommended. Recommended units include English 3, mathematics 3, social studies 2, history 1, science 3 (laboratory 2), foreign language 2, computer science 1 and academic electives 2.

**2010-2011 Annual costs.** Tuition/fees: $4,925. Per-credit charge: $240. Books/supplies: $1,419.

**Application procedures. Admission:** Closing date 3/1 (receipt date). $5 fee. Application must be submitted on paper. Admission notification 6/1.

**Academics. Special study options:** License preparation in nursing. **Credit/placement by examination:** CLEP, institutional tests. **Support services:** Reduced course load, tutoring.

**Majors. Health:** Nursing (RN).

**Computing on campus.** 20 workstations in library, computer center.

**Student life. Freshman orientation:** Mandatory. Preregistration for classes offered. **Activities:** Student government.

**Student services.** Financial aid counseling. **Transfer:** Pre-admission transcript evaluation for new students.

**Contact.** Phone: (323) 226-4911 Fax: (323) 226-6343
Maria Caballero, Dean, Administrative and Student Services, Los Angeles
County College of Nursing and Allied Health, 1237 North Mission Road,
Los Angeles, CA 90033-1084

## Los Angeles Harbor College
**Wilmington, California**
www.lahc.edu                                    **CB code: 4395**

- Public 2-year community college
- Commuter campus in small city

**General.** Founded in 1949. Regionally accredited. **Enrollment:** 10,626
undergraduates. **Degrees:** 510 associate awarded. **Location:** 15 miles from
downtown. **Calendar:** Semester, limited summer session. **Full-time faculty:** 114 total; 46% minority, 57% women. **Part-time faculty:** 395 total;
46% minority, 50% women. **Special facilities:** Observatory, nature museum.

**Transfer out. Colleges most students transferred to 2009:** California
State University: Long Beach, California State University: Dominguez Hills.

**Basis for selection.** Open admission.

**High school preparation.** 10 units recommended. Recommended units
include English 4, mathematics 3, science 2 (laboratory 1). Nursing program requires high school diploma with chemistry and algebra, or college
equivalent.

**2009-2010 Annual costs.** Tuition/fees: $802; $6,442 out-of-state. Per-
credit charge: $26 in-state; $214 out-of-state. Books/supplies: $1,638. Personal expenses: $3,096.

**2009-2010 Financial aid.** All financial aid based on need. 4% of total
undergraduate aid awarded as scholarships/grants, 96% as loans/jobs. Need-based aid available for part-time students. Work-study available nights, weekends and for part-time students.

**Application procedures. Admission:** Closing date 9/9. No application
fee. Admission notification on a rolling basis. High school students accepted on part-time basis. **Financial aid:** Priority date 3/2; no closing date.
FAFSA, institutional form required. Applicants notified on a rolling basis;
must reply within 2 week(s) of notification.

**Academics. Special study options:** Accelerated study, cooperative education, cross-registration, distance learning, double major, dual enrollment
of high school students, ESL, honors, independent study, liberal arts/career
combination, study abroad, weekend college. License preparation in nursing, paramedic, physical therapy, real estate. **Credit/placement by examination:** AP, CLEP, IB, institutional tests. **Support services:** GED preparation, learning center, remedial instruction, study skills assistance, tutoring,
writing center.

**Majors. Architecture:** Technology. **Business:** General, accounting, administrative services, business admin, management information systems, office
management, office technology, office/clerical, real estate. **Computer sciences:** General, applications programming, data entry, information systems.
**Engineering:** Electrical. **Engineering technology:** Architectural, computer
systems, drafting, electrical. **Family/consumer sciences:** Child care. **Health:**
Medical secretary, nursing (RN). **Legal studies:** Legal secretary. **Liberal
arts:** Arts/sciences, library science. **Mechanic/repair:** Automotive, electronics/
electrical. **Protective services:** Firefighting, police science. **Psychology:** General. **Visual/performing arts:** Art, interior design.

**Most popular majors.** Health sciences 21%, liberal arts 67%.

**Computing on campus.** 660 workstations in library, computer center,
student center. Commuter students can connect to campus network. Online
course registration, online library, wireless network available.

**Student life. Activities:** Bands, choral groups, dance, drama, literary magazine, music ensembles, musical theater, student government, student newspaper, TV station, Equal Opportunity Program Student Association.

**Athletics.** NJCAA. **Intercollegiate:** Baseball M, basketball, football (tackle)
M, soccer, volleyball W. **Team name:** Seahawks.

**Student services.** Adult student services, career counseling, student employment services, health services, legal services, on-campus daycare, personal counseling, placement for graduates, veterans' counselor. **Physically
disabled:** Services for visually, speech, hearing impaired. **Transfer:** Transfer center, transfer adviser, college fairs on campus for students transferring
to 4-year colleges.

**Contact.** Phone: (310) 233-5090 Fax: (310) 233-4223
David Ching, Dean of Admissions and Records, Los Angeles Harbor
College, 1111 Figueroa Place, Wilmington, CA 90744-2397

## Los Angeles Mission College
**Sylmar, California**
www.lamission.edu                               **CB code: 4404**

- Public 2-year community college
- Large town

**General.** Founded in 1974. Regionally accredited. College serves nontraditional student body. **Enrollment:** 10,740 undergraduates. **Degrees:** 404
associate awarded. **ROTC:** Army, Air Force. **Location:** 20 miles from Los
Angeles. **Calendar:** Semester, limited summer session. **Full-time faculty:**
60 total. **Part-time faculty:** 305 total.

**Basis for selection.** Open admission.

**2009-2010 Annual costs.** Tuition/fees: $802; $6,442 out-of-state. Per-credit charge: $26 in-state; $214 out-of-state. Books/supplies: $1,638. Personal expenses: $3,096.

**2008-2009 Financial aid. Additional information:** Board of Governors
Grant available to those in receipt of AFDC, Social Security Insurance, or
General Relief. If not in receipt of program, may qualify based on income.

**Application procedures. Admission:** Priority date 4/20; no deadline.
No application fee. Admission notification on a rolling basis. **Financial aid:**
Priority date 8/1; no closing date. FAFSA required. Applicants notified on a
rolling basis starting 8/15.

**Academics.** Bilingual instruction available. **Special study options:** Accelerated study, cooperative education, dual enrollment of high school students, independent study. **Credit/placement by examination:** CLEP, institutional tests. 15 credit hours maximum toward associate degree. **Support
services:** Learning center, remedial instruction, tutoring.

**Majors. Business:** Accounting, administrative services, business admin,
management science, market research, office management, office/clerical,
real estate. **Computer sciences:** General. **Education:** Teacher assistance.
**Family/consumer sciences:** Clothing/textiles, food/nutrition, institutional food
production. **Foreign languages:** Spanish. **Legal studies:** Paralegal. **Liberal
arts:** Arts/sciences. **Math:** General. **Mechanic/repair:** Electronics/
electrical. **Personal/culinary services:** Culinary arts. **Philosophy/religion:**
Philosophy. **Protective services:** Criminal justice. **Psychology:** General. **Visual/
performing arts:** Art, interior design.

**Computing on campus.** 10 workstations in library.

**Student life. Activities:** Choral groups, drama, student government.

**Athletics. Intercollegiate:** Baseball M, cross-country, golf M, soccer M.

**Student services.** Career counseling, on-campus daycare, personal counseling, placement for graduates, veterans' counselor. **Physically disabled:**
Services for speech, hearing impaired.

**Contact.** Phone: (818) 364-7661
Joe Ramirez, Vice President, Los Angeles Mission College, 13356 Eldridge
Avenue, Sylmar, CA 91342-3245

## Los Angeles Pierce College
**Woodland Hills, California**                   **CB member**
www.piercecollege.edu                            **CB code: 4398**

- Public 2-year community college
- Commuter campus in very large city

**General.** Founded in 1947. Regionally accredited. **Enrollment:** 22,133
undergraduates. **Degrees:** 933 associate awarded. **Location:** 27 miles from
downtown. **Calendar:** Semester, extensive summer session. **Full-time faculty:** 173 total. **Part-time faculty:** 533 total. **Special facilities:** Braille nature trail, life science museum, nature center, weather station, working farm,
botanical garden.

**Transfer out. Colleges most students transferred to 2009:** California
State University: Northridge, University of California: Los Angeles.

**Basis for selection.** Open admission, but selective for some programs.
Limited admission to nursing and animal health technology programs. All
students required to take English and math placement tests prior to course
registration.

**2009-2010 Annual costs.** Tuition/fees: $802; $6,442 out-of-state. Per-credit charge: $26 in-state; $214 out-of-state. International Students are charged additional fees: $35 Application Fee + $25 SEVIS Processing Fee. Books/supplies: $1,638. Personal expenses: $3,096.

**2009-2010 Financial aid.** All financial aid based on need. Need-based aid available for part-time students. Work-study available nights and weekends.

**Application procedures. Admission:** Closing date 9/10 (receipt date). No application fee. Admission notification on a rolling basis. **Financial aid:** Priority date 3/2; no closing date. FAFSA, institutional form required. Applicants notified on a rolling basis starting 8/1.

**Academics. Special study options:** Accelerated study, cooperative education, distance learning, dual enrollment of high school students, ESL, honors, student-designed major, study abroad. **Credit/placement by examination:** CLEP, institutional tests. 15 credit hours maximum toward associate degree. **Support services:** GED preparation, learning center, pre-admission summer program, remedial instruction, study skills assistance, tutoring, writing center.

**Majors. Agriculture:** Animal health, animal sciences, business, equestrian studies, equine science, greenhouse operations, horticultural science, horticulture, landscaping, ornamental horticulture. **Architecture:** Technology. **Area/ethnic studies:** Latin American. **Business:** General, accounting, business admin, management science, marketing. **Communications:** Journalism, photojournalism. **Computer sciences:** General, applications programming, computer science, data processing, programming. **Conservation:** Management/policy. **Education:** Early childhood, kindergarten/preschool. **Engineering:** General. **Engineering technology:** Construction, drafting, electrical. **Foreign languages:** French, Italian, sign language interpretation, Spanish. **Health:** Nursing (RN), preveterinary, substance abuse counseling, veterinary technology/assistant. **Liberal arts:** Arts/sciences. **Mechanic/repair:** Auto body, automotive. **Social sciences:** Criminology. **Visual/performing arts:** Commercial/advertising art, dramatic, industrial design, studio arts, theater design.

**Computing on campus.** Commuter students can connect to campus network. Online course registration, online library, repair service available.

**Student life. Freshman orientation:** Available. Preregistration for classes offered. **Activities:** Bands, choral groups, dance, drama, international student organizations, literary magazine, music ensembles, musical theater, student government, student newspaper, symphony orchestra, Bible Fellowship, Alpha Gamma Sigma honor society, Phi Theta Kappa honor society, Phi Beta Lambda business association, Hillel, Union of African American Students, Muslim students association.

**Athletics. Intercollegiate:** Baseball M, basketball, cheerleading, diving, football (tackle) M, soccer W, softball W, swimming, tennis M, volleyball. **Team name:** Brahmas.

**Student services.** Adult student services, career counseling, services for economically disadvantaged, student employment services, financial aid counseling, health services, on-campus daycare, personal counseling, placement for graduates, veterans' counselor. **Physically disabled:** Services for visually, speech, hearing impaired. **Learning disabled:** Comprehensive services available. **Transfer:** Transfer center, transfer adviser, college fairs on campus for students transferring to 4-year colleges.

**Contact.** E-mail: pierceinfo@piercecollege.edu
Phone: (818) 719-6404 Fax: (818) 716-1087
Marco De La Garza, Dean of Admissions and Records, Los Angeles Pierce College, 6201 Winnetka Avenue, Woodland Hills, CA 91371

## Los Angeles Southwest College
### Los Angeles, California
### www.lasc.edu
CB code: 4409

- Public 2-year community college
- Commuter campus in very large city

**General.** Founded in 1967. Regionally accredited. **Enrollment:** 7,585 undergraduates. **Degrees:** 374 associate awarded. **Calendar:** Semester, limited summer session. **Full-time faculty:** 47 total. **Part-time faculty:** 227 total. **Special facilities:** Career services center.

**Transfer out. Colleges most students transferred to 2009:** Cal State University: Dominguez Hills, Los Angeles, Long Beach, Northridge, UCLA.

**Basis for selection.** Open admission, but selective for some programs. Limited admission to nursing and allied health programs.

**2009-2010 Annual costs.** Tuition/fees: $802; $6,442 out-of-state. Per-credit charge: $26 in-state; $214 out-of-state. Books/supplies: $1,638. Personal expenses: $3,096.

**Financial aid. Need-based:** Need-based aid available for part-time students. **Additional information:** Board of Governors Enrollment Fee Waiver available to students receiving AFDC, SSI/SSP, or General Assistance. May also qualify on basis of income.

**Application procedures. Admission:** No deadline. No application fee. Late registration allowed through third week of classes, if permitted by instructor. **Financial aid:** No deadline. FAFSA required. Applicants notified on a rolling basis; must reply within 2 week(s) of notification.

**Academics. Special study options:** Accelerated study, cooperative education, cross-registration, double major, dual enrollment of high school students, ESL, honors, independent study, liberal arts/career combination, study abroad, weekend college. **Credit/placement by examination:** CLEP, institutional tests. 15 credit hours maximum toward associate degree. **Support services:** Learning center, reduced course load, remedial instruction, tutoring.

**Majors. Area/ethnic studies:** African-American. **Biology:** General, molecular. **Business:** General, accounting, administrative services, banking/financial services, business admin, insurance, management information systems, office technology, office/clerical, real estate. **Communications:** Advertising, journalism. **Communications technology:** General. **Computer sciences:** General, applications programming, computer graphics, computer science, programming. **Education:** General, early childhood, foreign languages, mathematics, music, teacher assistance. **Engineering:** General, electrical. **Engineering technology:** Drafting, electrical. **Family/consumer sciences:** Child care. **Foreign languages:** General, French, Spanish. **Health:** Clinical lab technology, nursing (RN), respiratory therapy technology. **History:** General. **Legal studies:** Paralegal. **Liberal arts:** Arts/sciences. **Math:** General. **Parks/recreation:** General. **Philosophy/religion:** Philosophy. **Physical sciences:** Chemistry, geology, physics. **Psychology:** General. **Social sciences:** Geography, political science, sociology. **Visual/performing arts:** Art, art history/conservation, commercial/advertising art, dramatic, fashion design, photography.

**Computing on campus.** Helpline, repair service available.

**Student life. Freshman orientation:** Available. **Activities:** Bands, choral groups, dance, drama, literary magazine, musical theater, student government, student newspaper.

**Athletics. NJCAA. Intercollegiate:** Basketball M, cross-country, football (tackle) M, tennis W, track and field. **Intramural:** Baseball M, basketball, bowling, golf, softball, tennis, track and field, volleyball. **Team name:** Cougars.

**Student services.** Career counseling, student employment services, on-campus daycare, personal counseling, placement for graduates. **Transfer:** Transfer adviser for students transferring to 4-year colleges.

**Contact.** Phone: (323) 241-5321
Deborah Odom, Admissions and Records Supervisor, Los Angeles Southwest College, 1600 West Imperial Highway, Los Angeles, CA 90047-4899

## Los Angeles Trade and Technical College
### Los Angeles, California
### www.lattc.edu
CB code: 4400

- Public 2-year community and technical college
- Commuter campus in very large city

**General.** Founded in 1925. Regionally accredited. Specialized culinary arts program; fashion, cosmetology, nursing programs. **Enrollment:** 15,477 undergraduates. **Degrees:** 389 associate awarded. **Calendar:** Semester, limited summer session. **Full-time faculty:** 147 total. **Part-time faculty:** 294 total. **Class size:** 46% < 20, 38% 20-39, 9% 40-49, 4% 50-99, 4% >100.

**Student profile.**

| | | | |
|---|---|---|---|
| Out-of-state: | 8% | 25 or older: | 60% |

**Transfer out. Colleges most students transferred to 2009:** University of California: Los Angeles, California State University: Los Angeles, California State University: Dominguez Hills, University of Southern California.

**Basis for selection.** Open admission. Limited admission to nursing program. Portfolio recommended of commercial art majors.

**2009-2010 Annual costs.** Tuition/fees: $802; $6,442 out-of-state. Per-credit charge: $26 in-state; $214 out-of-state. Books/supplies: $1,638. Personal expenses: $3,096.

**Financial aid.** All financial aid based on need. Need-based aid available for part-time students. Work-study available nights, weekends and for part-time students.

**Application procedures. Admission:** No deadline. No application fee. Admission notification on a rolling basis. **Financial aid:** Priority date 5/1; no closing date. FAFSA required. Applicants notified on a rolling basis.

**Academics. Special study options:** Accelerated study, cooperative education, distance learning, dual enrollment of high school students, ESL, independent study, liberal arts/career combination, study abroad, weekend college. License preparation in nursing. **Credit/placement by examination:** CLEP, institutional tests. 15 credit hours maximum toward associate degree. **Support services:** GED preparation, learning center, pre-admission summer program, reduced course load, remedial instruction, study skills assistance, tutoring, writing center.

**Majors. Business:** General, accounting, administrative services, business admin, entrepreneurial studies, fashion, hospitality/recreation, labor relations, office/clerical, real estate. **Communications:** Journalism. **Communications technology:** General, graphic/printing. **Computer sciences:** General, computer science. **Construction:** Carpentry, electrician, maintenance, pipefitting, power transmission. **Engineering:** General. **Engineering technology:** Architectural, drafting, electrical. **Family/consumer sciences:** Clothing/textiles, institutional food production. **Health:** Health services, licensed practical nurse. **Liberal arts:** Arts/sciences. **Mechanic/repair:** Auto body, diesel, electronics/electrical, heating/ac/refrig. **Personal/culinary services:** Culinary arts. **Public administration:** Community org/advocacy. **Visual/performing arts:** Commercial/advertising art, fashion design, photography.

**Most popular majors.** Computer/information sciences 11%, health sciences 11%, liberal arts 34%, trade and industry 30%, visual/performing arts 8%.

**Computing on campus.** 550 workstations in library, computer center. Commuter students can connect to campus network. Online course registration, wireless network available.

**Student life. Freshman orientation:** Available. **Activities:** Dance, student government, student newspaper, political organizations.

**Athletics.** NJCAA. **Intercollegiate:** Basketball, cross-country, tennis, track and field. **Intramural:** Golf, swimming. **Team name:** Beaver.

**Student services.** Adult student services, career counseling, services for economically disadvantaged, student employment services, financial aid counseling, health services, minority student services, on-campus daycare, personal counseling, placement for graduates, veterans' counselor. **Physically disabled:** Services for visually, speech, hearing impaired. **Transfer:** Transfer adviser, college fairs on campus for students transferring to 4-year colleges.

**Contact.** Phone: (213) 763-7000
Ester Usaha, Registrar, Los Angeles Trade and Technical College, 400 West Washington Boulevard, Los Angeles, CA 90015-4181

## Los Angeles Valley College
**Valley Glen, California**
**www.lavc.edu**                    **CB code: 5546**

- Public 2-year community college
- Commuter campus in very large city

**General.** Founded in 1949. Regionally accredited. **Enrollment:** 19,619 undergraduates. **Degrees:** 892 associate awarded. **Location:** 15 miles from downtown. **Calendar:** Semester, limited summer session. **Full-time faculty:** 154 total. **Part-time faculty:** 420 total. **Special facilities:** Planetarium.

**Student profile.**

| | | | |
|---|---|---|---|
| Out-of-state: | 2% | 25 or older: | 69% |

**Basis for selection.** Open admission, but selective for some programs. Registered nursing program has competitive admission based on points accumulated for prerequisite courses, grades, and placement test scores. Institutional placement tests required of all students.

**2009-2010 Annual costs.** Tuition/fees: $804; $6,444 out-of-state. Per-credit charge: $26 in-state; $214 out-of-state. Books/supplies: $1,638. Personal expenses: $3,096.

**2009-2010 Financial aid.** All financial aid based on need. Need-based aid available for part-time students.

**Application procedures. Admission:** No deadline. No application fee. Admission notification on a rolling basis. **Financial aid:** Priority date 3/2, closing date 5/1. FAFSA required. Applicants notified on a rolling basis.

**Academics. Special study options:** Cooperative education, dual enrollment of high school students, honors, independent study. License preparation in nursing, paramedic. **Credit/placement by examination:** AP, CLEP, IB, institutional tests. 15 credit hours maximum toward associate degree. **Support services:** Learning center, remedial instruction, study skills assistance, tutoring, writing center.

**Majors. Area/ethnic studies:** American. **Biology:** General. **Business:** General, administrative services, fashion, hospitality/recreation, management information systems, office technology, office/clerical. **Communications:** Broadcast journalism, journalism. **Computer sciences:** Applications programming, data processing. **Engineering technology:** Electrical. **Family/consumer sciences:** General. **Foreign languages:** French, German, Italian, Spanish. **Health:** Nursing (RN), respiratory therapy technology. **History:** General. **Liberal arts:** Arts/sciences. **Math:** General. **Parks/recreation:** General. **Philosophy/religion:** Philosophy. **Physical sciences:** Chemistry, geology, physics, planetary. **Protective services:** Police science. **Psychology:** General. **Social sciences:** Economics, geography, political science, sociology. **Visual/performing arts:** Art, art history/conservation, commercial/advertising art.

**Computing on campus.** 300 workstations in library, computer center, student center. Online course registration, wireless network available.

**Student life. Freshman orientation:** Available. Preregistration for classes offered. **Activities:** Bands, choral groups, dance, drama, film society, literary magazine, music ensembles, musical theater, radio station, student government, student newspaper, symphony orchestra.

**Athletics.** NJCAA. **Intercollegiate:** Baseball M, basketball, cross-country, diving, football (tackle) M, soccer W, softball W, swimming, track and field, water polo M. **Team name:** Monarchs.

**Student services.** Career counseling, student employment services, health services, on-campus daycare, personal counseling, placement for graduates, veterans' counselor. **Physically disabled:** Services for visually, speech, hearing impaired. **Learning disabled:** Comprehensive services available. **Transfer:** Transfer adviser, college fairs on campus for students transferring to 4-year colleges.

**Contact.** E-mail: trudgej@lavc.edu
Phone: (818) 947-2553 Fax: (818) 947-2501
Florentino Manzano, Dean of Enrollment Management, Los Angeles Valley College, 5800 Fulton Avenue, Valley Glen, CA 91401-4096

## Los Medanos College
**Pittsburg, California**
**www.losmedanos.edu**                    **CB code: 4396**

- Public 2-year community college
- Commuter campus in small city

**General.** Founded in 1973. Regionally accredited. **Enrollment:** 11,062 undergraduates. **Degrees:** 399 associate awarded. **Location:** 45 miles from San Francisco. **Calendar:** Semester. **Full-time faculty:** 110 total. **Part-time faculty:** 288 total.

**Student profile.**

| | | | |
|---|---|---|---|
| Out-of-state: | 1% | 25 or older: | 53% |

**Basis for selection.** Open admission.

**2009-2010 Annual costs.** Tuition/fees: $790; $6,310 out-of-state. Per-credit charge: $26 in-state; $210 out-of-state. Books/supplies: $1,566. Personal expenses: $2,664.

**Application procedures. Admission:** No deadline. Admission notification on a rolling basis. **Financial aid:** Priority date 3/2; no closing date. FAFSA required. Applicants notified on a rolling basis starting 7/1; must reply within 2 week(s) of notification.

**Academics. Special study options:** Cooperative education, cross-registration, independent study, study abroad. **Credit/placement by examination:** CLEP, institutional tests. 20 credit hours maximum toward associate degree. **Support services:** Learning center, remedial instruction, tutoring.

**Majors. Biology:** General. **Business:** Accounting, entrepreneurial studies, labor relations, office management, real estate, tourism promotion. **Communications:** Journalism. **Family/consumer sciences:** Child care. **Health:** EMT paramedic, nursing (RN). **Liberal arts:** Arts/sciences. **Math:** General. **Mechanic/repair:** Electronics/electrical, small engine. **Physical sciences:** Chemistry. **Protective services:** Firefighting. **Psychology:** General. **Social sciences:** Anthropology, sociology. **Visual/performing arts:** Commercial/advertising art, music performance, studio arts.

**Most popular majors.** Business/marketing 7%, health sciences 18%, liberal arts 60%.

**Computing on campus.** 150 workstations in computer center.

**Student life. Activities:** Bands, choral groups, drama, music ensembles, student government, student newspaper.

**Athletics. Intercollegiate:** Baseball M, basketball, football (tackle) M, soccer M, softball W, volleyball W. **Intramural:** Basketball, softball, tennis.

**Student services.** Career counseling, student employment services, on-campus daycare, personal counseling, placement for graduates. **Physically disabled:** Services for visually, speech, hearing impaired. **Transfer:** Transfer adviser, college fairs on campus for students transferring to 4-year colleges.

**Contact.** Phone: (925) 439-2181 ext. 7500 Fax: (925) 427-6351
Robin Armour, Director of Admissions and Records, Los Medanos College, 2700 East Leland Road, Pittsburg, CA 94565

---

## Marymount College

**Rancho Palos Verdes, California**  **CB member**
**www.marymountpv.edu**  **CB code: 4515**

- Private 2-year junior and liberal arts college affiliated with Roman Catholic Church
- Residential campus in large town

**General.** Founded in 1933. Regionally accredited. **Enrollment:** 561 degree-seeking undergraduates. **Degrees:** 140 associate awarded. **Location:** 30 miles from Los Angeles. **Calendar:** Semester, limited summer session. **Full-time faculty:** 26 total; 65% have terminal degrees, 8% minority, 42% women. **Part-time faculty:** 36 total; 31% have terminal degrees, 19% minority, 56% women. **Class size:** 64% < 20, 35% 20-39, less than 1% 40-49.

**Student profile.** Among degree-seeking undergraduates, 301 enrolled as first-time, first-year students, 46 transferred in from other institutions.

| | | | |
|---|---|---|---|
| Part-time: | 1% | Women: | 51% |
| Out-of-state: | 10% | Live on campus: | 57% |

**Transfer out. Colleges most students transferred to 2009:** University of Southern California, Loyola Marymount University, University of California, California State University, Chapman University.

**Basis for selection.** High school record, quality of academic preparation, recommendations, student's personal statement, standardized test scores all considered. SAT or ACT recommended. ACCUPLACER used for placement. Interview and essay recommended. **Homeschooled:** Transcript of courses and grades, letter of recommendation (nonparent) required. General syllabus of all coursework completed or private tutoring received, statement explaining why family chose home schooling and its advantages and disadvantages required. SAT or ACT scores and state H.S. equivalency certificate recommended.

**High school preparation.** College-preparatory program recommended. 14 units recommended. Recommended units include English 4, mathematics 3, social studies 2, science 2 (laboratory 1) and foreign language 2.

**2009-2010 Annual costs.** Tuition/fees: $24,422. Per-credit charge: $825. Room/board: $10,600. Books/supplies: $1,638. Personal expenses: $2,250.

**2009-2010 Financial aid. Need-based:** 71% of total undergraduate aid awarded as scholarships/grants, 29% as loans/jobs. **Non-need-based:** Scholarships awarded for academics.

**Application procedures. Admission:** Priority date 3/2; no deadline. $40 fee, may be waived for applicants with need. Admission notification on a rolling basis beginning on or about 12/1. Must reply by May 1 or within 4 week(s) if notified thereafter. **Financial aid:** Priority date 3/1; no closing date. FAFSA required. Applicants notified on a rolling basis starting 2/1; must reply by 5/1 or within 4 week(s) of notification.

**Academics. Special study options:** Cooperative education, dual enrollment of high school students, ESL, honors, independent study, internships, study abroad, urban semester, weekend college. Bachelor's degree programs available on campus. **Credit/placement by examination:** AP, CLEP,

IB, institutional tests. 15 credit hours maximum toward associate degree. **Support services:** Learning center, pre-admission summer program, reduced course load, remedial instruction, study skills assistance, tutoring.

**Honors college/program.** Admitted students are reviewed by the Honors faculty for Honors consideration. Average GPA is 3.3; SAT or ACT scores highly recommended. Approximately 30 students admitted each year. Students may earn their way into the Honors program based on academic success in their first year of college. Honors courses are designated each year. Successful Honors students may join Phi Theta Kappa Honor Society; graduates may secure PTK scholarships upon transfer.

**Majors. Liberal arts:** Arts/sciences.

**Most popular majors.** Business/marketing 7%, communications/journalism 12%, liberal arts 42%, psychology 12%.

**Computing on campus.** 77 workstations in library, computer center. Dormitories wired for high-speed internet access and linked to campus network. Commuter students can connect to campus network. Online library, helpline, repair service, wireless network available.

**Student life. Freshman orientation:** Mandatory, $150 fee. Preregistration for classes offered. **Housing:** Single-sex dorms, special housing for disabled, apartments available. $400 partly refundable deposit, deadline 7/1. Housing available through volunteers in the community. **Activities:** Campus ministries, choral groups, dance, drama, international student organizations, music ensembles, musical theater, radio station, student government, volunteer club, philosophy discussion club, pre-med club, student integrity council, Phi Theta Kappa, Latinos Unidos, Black Student Union, International Peers, Jewish club, campus ministry leadership team.

**Athletics.** NJCAA. **Intercollegiate:** Soccer. **Intramural:** Basketball, football (non-tackle), golf, softball. **Team name:** Mariners.

**Student services.** Adult student services, alcohol/substance abuse counseling, chaplain/spiritual director, career counseling, student employment services, financial aid counseling, health services, personal counseling. **Physically disabled:** Services for visually, hearing impaired. **Transfer:** Pre-admission transcript evaluation for new students. Transfer center, transfer adviser, college fairs on campus for students transferring to 4-year colleges.

**Contact.** E-mail: admissions@marymountpv.edu
Phone: (310) 377-5501 ext. 311 Fax: (310) 265-0962
Barbara Layne, Dean of Enrollment Management, Marymount College, 30800 Palos Verdes Drive East, Rancho Palos Verdes, CA 90275-6299

---

## Mendocino College

**Ukiah, California**
**www.mendocino.edu**  **CB code: 4517**

- Public 2-year community college
- Commuter campus in large town

**General.** Founded in 1973. Regionally accredited. **Enrollment:** 2,358 degree-seeking undergraduates; 2,405 non-degree-seeking students. **Degrees:** 332 associate awarded. **Location:** 60 miles from Santa Rosa, 110 miles from San Francisco. **Calendar:** Semester, limited summer session. **Full-time faculty:** 50 total; 18% have terminal degrees, 4% minority, 46% women. **Part-time faculty:** 255 total; 7% minority, 55% women. **Class size:** 59% < 20, 37% 20-39, 2% 40-49, 1% 50-99, less than 1% >100. **Special facilities:** Gallery and theater complex, point arena field station, oceanography, environmental chemistry, marine ecology, coastal geology.

**Student profile.** Among degree-seeking undergraduates, 61% enrolled in a transfer program, 16% enrolled in a vocational program, 15% already have a bachelor's degree or higher, 521 enrolled as first-time, first-year students, 10 transferred in from other institutions.

| | | | |
|---|---|---|---|
| Part-time: | 57% | Hispanic American: | 17% |
| Out-of-state: | 5% | Native American: | 5% |
| Women: | 62% | International: | 1% |
| African American: | 2% | 25 or older: | 60% |
| Asian American: | 2% | | |

**Transfer out.** 40% of students enrolled in the transfer program go on to 4-year colleges. **Colleges most students transferred to 2009:** Sonoma State University, University of California.

**Basis for selection.** Open admission. Open admission.

**2009-2010 Annual costs.** Tuition/fees: $800; $6,500 out-of-state. Per-credit charge: $26 in-state; $216 out-of-state. Books/supplies: $1,638. Personal expenses: $3,096.

**2008-2009 Financial aid. Need-based:** 178 full-time freshmen applied for aid; 178 were judged to have need; 178 of these received aid. Average need met was 100%. Average scholarship/grant was $1,735; average loan $1,678. 81% of total undergraduate aid awarded as scholarships/grants, 19% as loans/jobs. Need-based aid available for part-time students. Work-study available nights and for part-time students. **Non-need-based:** Awarded to 83 full-time undergraduates, including 19 freshmen. Scholarships awarded for academics, leadership, music/drama, state residency.

**Application procedures. Admission:** Priority date 5/1; no deadline. No application fee. Admission notification on a rolling basis beginning on or about 7/1. **Financial aid:** Priority date 5/31; no closing date. FAFSA required. Applicants notified on a rolling basis starting 7/1; must reply within 2 week(s) of notification.

**Academics. Special study options:** Distance learning, double major, dual enrollment of high school students, ESL, independent study, internships, student-designed major. License preparation in nursing, paramedic, real estate. **Credit/placement by examination:** AP, CLEP, institutional tests. 12 credit hours maximum toward associate degree. **Support services:** GED test center, learning center, pre-admission summer program, remedial instruction, study skills assistance, tutoring.

**Majors. Agriculture:** Plant sciences. **Biology:** General. **Business:** General, accounting, administrative services, business admin, entrepreneurial studies. **Communications:** General. **Computer sciences:** General. **Foreign languages:** French, Spanish. **Health:** Substance abuse counseling. **Liberal arts:** Arts/sciences. **Math:** General. **Mechanic/repair:** Auto body, electronics/electrical. **Parks/recreation:** Sports admin. **Protective services:** Law enforcement admin. **Psychology:** General. **Public administration:** Human services. **Social sciences:** General. **Visual/performing arts:** Art, dramatic.

**Most popular majors.** Business/marketing 18%, family/consumer sciences 7%, health sciences 8%, liberal arts 38%, psychology 6%.

**Computing on campus.** 144 workstations in library, computer center, student center. Commuter students can connect to campus network. Online course registration, online library, wireless network available.

**Student life. Freshman orientation:** Available. Preregistration for classes offered. Orientation held before and during first week of class. **Activities:** Bands, choral groups, dance, drama, film society, music ensembles, musical theater, radio station, student government, symphony orchestra.

**Athletics.** NJCAA. **Intercollegiate:** Baseball M, basketball, cheerleading M, football (tackle) M, soccer, softball W, volleyball W. **Intramural:** Basketball, bowling, softball, volleyball. **Team name:** Eagles.

**Student services.** Adult student services, career counseling, services for economically disadvantaged, student employment services, financial aid counseling, on-campus daycare, personal counseling, placement for graduates, veterans' counselor, women's services. **Physically disabled:** Services for visually, speech, hearing impaired. **Transfer:** Transfer center, transfer adviser, college fairs on campus for students transferring to 4-year colleges.

**Contact.** E-mail: webaccess@mendocino.edu
Phone: (707) 468-3101 Fax: (707) 468-3120
Kristie Anderson, Director of Admissions and Records, Mendocino College, 1000 Hensley Creek/Box 3000, Ukiah, CA 95482

---

## Merced College
### Merced, California
### www.mccd.edu
**CB code: 4500**

❖ Public 2-year community college
❖ Commuter campus in small city

**General.** Founded in 1962. Regionally accredited. Off-campus centers at Los Banos. **Enrollment:** 14,922 undergraduates. **Degrees:** 386 associate awarded. **Location:** 50 miles from Fresno. **Calendar:** Semester, limited summer session. **Full-time faculty:** 120 total. **Part-time faculty:** 479 total.

**Transfer out. Colleges most students transferred to 2009:** CSU Stanislaus, CSU Fresno, UC Davis.

**Basis for selection.** Open admission. Institutional placement tests used.

**2009-2010 Annual costs.** Tuition/fees: $814; $6,514 out-of-state. Per-credit charge: $26 in-state; $216 out-of-state. Books/supplies: $1,638. Personal expenses: $3,096.

**2008-2009 Financial aid. Non-need-based:** Scholarships awarded for academics.

---

**Application procedures. Admission:** No deadline. No application fee. Application must be submitted on paper. Admission notification on a rolling basis. Must reply by May 1 or within 4 week(s) if notified thereafter. **Financial aid:** Priority date 6/1; no closing date. FAFSA required. Applicants notified on a rolling basis starting 1/2; must reply within 3 week(s) of notification.

**Academics. Special study options:** Cooperative education, distance learning, dual enrollment of high school students, honors, internships, study abroad. License preparation in nursing, paramedic, radiology, real estate. **Credit/placement by examination:** AP, CLEP, institutional tests. 12 credit hours maximum toward associate degree. **Support services:** Learning center, pre-admission summer program, remedial instruction, tutoring.

**Majors. Agriculture:** General, agronomy, animal sciences, business, horticulture, ornamental horticulture, soil science. **Biology:** General. **Business:** General, accounting, administrative services, business admin, merchandising, real estate. **Communications:** General, journalism. **Computer sciences:** General, information systems. **Education:** Early childhood. **Engineering:** General. **Engineering technology:** Drafting, electrical. **Family/consumer sciences:** General, child development, family studies. **Foreign languages:** French, German, Spanish. **Health:** Health services, licensed practical nurse, medical radiologic technology/radiation therapy, medical secretary, nursing (RN), office admin, substance abuse counseling. **History:** General. **Legal studies:** Legal secretary. **Liberal arts:** Arts/sciences. **Math:** General. **Mechanic/repair:** Auto body, diesel, electronics/electrical, heating/ac/refrig, industrial. **Parks/recreation:** Health/fitness. **Philosophy/religion:** Philosophy. **Physical sciences:** General, chemistry, geology, physics. **Production:** Welding. **Protective services:** Firefighting, police science. **Psychology:** General. **Public administration:** Human services, social work. **Social sciences:** General, anthropology, archaeology, physical anthropology. **Visual/performing arts:** General, art history/conservation, dramatic, photography.

**Computing on campus.** 400 workstations in library, computer center. Commuter students can connect to campus network. Online library, helpline available.

**Student life. Freshman orientation:** Available. **Activities:** Bands, choral groups, dance, drama, international student organizations, music ensembles, musical theater, student government, student newspaper, symphony orchestra, black student union, Movimiento Estudiantil Chicano de Aztlan, intervarsity Christian group, Rotaract.

**Athletics.** NJCAA. **Intercollegiate:** Baseball M, basketball, cheerleading M, cross-country, diving, football (tackle) M, golf, softball W, swimming, track and field, volleyball W, water polo. **Team name:** Blue Devils.

**Student services.** Alcohol/substance abuse counseling, career counseling, services for economically disadvantaged, student employment services, financial aid counseling, health services, on-campus daycare, personal counseling, placement for graduates, veterans' counselor. **Physically disabled:** Services for visually, speech, hearing impaired. **Transfer:** Transfer center, transfer adviser, college fairs on campus for students transferring to 4-year colleges.

**Contact.** Phone: (209) 384-6187 Fax: (209) 384-6339
Everett Lovelace, Dean of Student Services, Merced College, Lesher Student Services Building, floor 2, Merced, CA 95348

---

## Merritt College
### Oakland, California
### www.merritt.edu
**CB code: 4502**

❖ Public 2-year community college
❖ Large city

**General.** Founded in 1953. Regionally accredited. **Enrollment:** 7,797 undergraduates. **Degrees:** 306 associate awarded. **Location:** 15 miles from San Francisco. **Calendar:** Semester, extensive summer session. **Full-time faculty:** 90 total. **Part-time faculty:** 215 total. **Special facilities:** Anthropology museum, landscape/horticulture complex.

**Student profile.**

| | | | |
|---|---|---|---|
| **Out-of-state:** | 5% | **25 or older:** | 60% |

**Basis for selection.** Open admission.

**2009-2010 Annual costs.** Tuition/fees: $784; $6,484 out-of-state. Per-credit charge: $26 in-state; $216 out-of-state. Books/supplies: $1,450. Personal expenses: $2,600.

**Financial aid. Need-based:** Need-based aid available for part-time students.

**Application procedures. Admission:** No deadline. No application fee. Admission notification on a rolling basis. **Financial aid:** Priority date 4/1, closing date 6/30. FAFSA, institutional form required. Applicants notified on a rolling basis starting 6/1.

**Academics. Special study options:** Cooperative education, cross-registration, distance learning, dual enrollment of high school students, honors, independent study. **Credit/placement by examination:** CLEP, institutional tests. 15 credit hours maximum toward associate degree. **Support services:** Learning center, pre-admission summer program, reduced course load, remedial instruction, tutoring.

**Majors. Agriculture:** Horticultural science, landscaping. **Area/ethnic studies:** African-American. **Business:** General, real estate. **Computer sciences:** General. **Education:** General, business, early childhood. **Engineering:** Electrical. **Family/consumer sciences:** Child care, family/community services. **Foreign languages:** French, Spanish. **Health:** Licensed practical nurse, medical radiologic technology/radiation therapy, nursing (RN). **Legal studies:** Paralegal. **Liberal arts:** Arts/sciences. **Math:** General. **Parks/recreation:** General. **Public administration:** Community org/advocacy. **Social sciences:** General.

**Computing on campus.** 200 workstations in library, computer center, student center.

**Student life. Activities:** Choral groups, dance, student government, student newspaper, Merritt Christian Fellowship, LaRaza Student Union, Native American Association, Black Student Union, Asian Student Union, Ecology Action Club, Disabled Students Coalition.

**Athletics. Intercollegiate:** Basketball, cross-country, track and field. **Intramural:** Badminton, golf, tennis, volleyball.

**Student services.** Adult student services, career counseling, student employment services, health services, on-campus daycare, personal counseling, placement for graduates, veterans' counselor. **Physically disabled:** Services for visually, speech, hearing impaired. **Transfer:** Transfer adviser, college fairs on campus for students transferring to 4-year colleges.

**Contact.** E-mail: admissions@peralta.edu
Phone: (510) 436-2487
Howard Perdue, Dean of Admissions and Records, Merritt College, 12500 Campus Drive, Oakland, CA 94619

---

## MiraCosta College
### Oceanside, California
### www.miracosta.edu
**CB code: 4582**

◗ Public 2-year community college
◗ Commuter campus in large city

**General.** Founded in 1934. Regionally accredited. **Enrollment:** 9,115 degree-seeking undergraduates; 4,161 non-degree-seeking students. **Degrees:** 528 associate awarded. **ROTC:** Army, Air Force. **Location:** 35 miles from San Diego. **Calendar:** Semester, limited summer session. **Full-time faculty:** 132 total; 29% minority, 52% women. **Part-time faculty:** 389 total; 17% minority, 60% women. **Class size:** 22% < 20, 68% 20-39, 10% 40-49, less than 1% 50-99, less than 1% >100. **Special facilities:** Bioprocessing training facility, music recording studios, radiation protection technology. **Partnerships:** Formal partnerships with Cisco Academy.

**Student profile.** Among degree-seeking undergraduates, 56% enrolled in a transfer program, 8% enrolled in a vocational program, 11% already have a bachelor's degree or higher, 1,821 enrolled as first-time, first-year students.

| | | | |
|---|---|---|---|
| Part-time: | 60% | Asian American: | 8% |
| Out-of-state: | 1% | Hispanic American: | 22% |
| Women: | 55% | Native American: | 1% |
| African American: | 5% | International: | 1% |

**Transfer out.** 33% of students enrolled in the transfer program go on to 4-year colleges. **Colleges most students transferred to 2009:** San Diego State University, Cal State: San Marcos, University of California: San Diego.

**Basis for selection.** Open admission, but selective for some programs. Must be either 18 yrs of age or high school graduate. High school students require principal and parental permission with grade level limitations. Nursing programs require special application with course and GPA requirements. Locally administered tests may be used for placement and counseling.

**2009-2010 Annual costs.** Tuition/fees: $824; $6,524 out-of-state. Per-credit charge: $26 in-state; $216 out-of-state.

**2008-2009 Financial aid. Need-based:** 11% of total undergraduate aid awarded as scholarships/grants, 89% as loans/jobs. Need-based aid available for part-time students. Work-study available nights and for part-time students. **Additional information:** Waiver of in-state fees for eligible low-income students.

**Application procedures. Admission:** No deadline. No application fee. Admission notification on a rolling basis. **Financial aid:** Priority date 4/10; no closing date. FAFSA, institutional form required. Applicants notified on a rolling basis; must reply within 4 week(s) of notification.

**Academics. Special study options:** Accelerated study, cooperative education, distance learning, double major, dual enrollment of high school students, ESL, honors, independent study, internships, liberal arts/career combination, student-designed major, study abroad, teacher certification program, weekend study. Study abroad programs in Japan, Mexico, Costa Rica and several countries in Europe. License preparation in nursing, real estate. **Credit/placement by examination:** AP, CLEP, IB, institutional tests. 15 credit hours maximum toward associate degree. **Support services:** GED preparation and test center, learning center, pre-admission summer program, reduced course load, remedial instruction, study skills assistance, tutoring, writing center.

**Honors college/program.** Students wanting to study at the honors level contract for an honors option in designated courses.

**Majors. Agriculture:** Business, floriculture, landscaping, nursery operations, turf management. **Architecture:** Landscape. **Biology:** General. **Business:** Accounting, administrative services, business admin, hospitality admin, office management, office/clerical, real estate, tourism/travel. **Communications:** General. **Computer sciences:** General, computer graphics, computer science, LAN/WAN management, programming. **Education:** Early childhood. **Engineering technology:** Drafting. **Family/consumer sciences:** Child care. **Foreign languages:** General, French, German, Japanese, Spanish. **Health:** Licensed practical nurse, premedicine, preveterinary. **History:** General. **Interdisciplinary:** Behavioral sciences, gerontology. **Legal studies:** Prelaw. **Liberal arts:** Arts/sciences. **Math:** General. **Mechanic/repair:** Auto body, automotive. **Personal/culinary services:** Cosmetic. **Philosophy/religion:** Philosophy. **Physical sciences:** Chemistry, geology, physics. **Protective services:** Police science. **Psychology:** General. **Science technology:** Biological. **Social sciences:** General, economics, geography, political science, sociology. **Visual/performing arts:** Art, art history/conservation, commercial/advertising art, dance, dramatic, theater design.

**Most popular majors.** Business/marketing 19%, communications/journalism 6%, communication technologies 19%, health sciences 9%, liberal arts 16%, security/protective services 6%, social sciences 12%.

**Computing on campus.** 1,000 workstations in library, computer center, student center. Online course registration, online library, student web hosting available.

**Student life. Freshman orientation:** Available. One-hour session offered 14 times prior to classes each semester, online orientations offered 24/7. **Activities:** Bands, choral groups, dance, drama, international student organizations, music ensembles, musical theater, student government, student newspaper, symphony orchestra, MECHA/Latina organization, Black Student Union, Chinese Club, Phi Theta Kappa, Non-Partisan Political Discussion Group, Single Parents on Campus, Japanese Club, Allied Health Club.

**Athletics. Intercollegiate:** Basketball, soccer. **Intramural:** Basketball, soccer, softball, tennis, volleyball. **Team name:** Spartans.

**Student services.** Alcohol/substance abuse counseling, career counseling, services for economically disadvantaged, student employment services, financial aid counseling, health services, personal counseling, veterans' counselor. **Physically disabled:** Services for visually, speech, hearing impaired. **Learning disabled:** Comprehensive services available. **Transfer:** Transfer center, transfer adviser, college fairs on campus for students transferring to 4-year colleges.

**Contact.** E-mail: admissions@miracosta.edu
Phone: (760) 795-6620 Toll-free number: (888) 201-8480
Fax: (760) 795-6626
Alicia Terry, Director of Admissions and Records, MiraCosta College, One Barnard Drive, Oceanside, CA 92056-3899

---

## Mission College
### Santa Clara, California
### www.missioncollege.org
**CB code: 7587**

◗ Public 2-year community college
◗ Small city

**General.** Founded in 1975. Regionally accredited. **Enrollment:** 12,900 undergraduates. **Degrees:** 604 associate awarded. **ROTC:** Naval, Air Force. **Location:** 8 miles from San Jose. **Calendar:** Semester, limited summer session. **Full-time faculty:** 146 total. **Part-time faculty:** 189 total.

**Transfer out. Colleges most students transferred to 2009:** San Jose State.

**Basis for selection.** Open admission. Limited admission to vocational nursing and allied health. Interviews required of nursing, psychiatric technician majors.

**2009-2010 Annual costs.** Tuition/fees: $838; $6,808 out-of-state. Per-credit charge: $26 in-state; $225 out-of-state. Books/supplies: $2,388. Personal expenses: $3,096.

**Application procedures. Admission:** No deadline. No application fee. Admission notification on a rolling basis. **Financial aid:** Priority date 5/1; no closing date. Applicants notified on a rolling basis starting 8/1; must reply within 2 week(s) of notification.

**Academics. Special study options:** Cooperative education, dual enrollment of high school students, honors, independent study, weekend college. Bachelor's degree programs available on campus. **Credit/placement by examination:** CLEP, institutional tests. 12 credit hours maximum toward associate degree. **Support services:** Learning center, remedial instruction, tutoring.

**Majors. Agriculture:** Food science. **Biology:** General. **Business:** General, accounting, administrative services, banking/financial services, business admin, management information systems, management science, office management, office/clerical, real estate. **Communications technology:** Graphic/printing. **Computer sciences:** Applications programming, computer science, information systems. **Engineering:** General. **Engineering technology:** Drafting. **Health:** Health services, licensed practical nurse, nursing (RN). **Liberal arts:** Arts/sciences. **Math:** General. **Physical sciences:** Chemistry, physics. **Protective services:** Fire safety technology. **Social sciences:** General. **Visual/performing arts:** Art, commercial/advertising art.

**Student life. Freshman orientation:** Available. **Activities:** Bands, music ensembles, musical theater, TV station.

**Athletics. Intercollegiate:** Baseball M, basketball W, soccer M, softball W, tennis. **Team name:** Saints.

**Student services.** Adult student services, career counseling, student employment services, health services, on-campus daycare, personal counseling, placement for graduates, veterans' counselor. **Transfer:** Transfer center, transfer adviser, college fairs on campus for students transferring to 4-year colleges.

**Contact.** Phone: (408) 988-2200 Fax: (408) 980-8980
Paulette Lino, Director of Admissions, Mission College, 3000 Mission College Boulevard, Santa Clara, CA 95054-1897

## Modesto Junior College
Modesto, California
www.mjc.edu
CB code: 4486

- Public 2-year community college
- Commuter campus in small city

**General.** Founded in 1921. Regionally accredited. **Enrollment:** 19,522 undergraduates. **Degrees:** 1,262 associate awarded. **Location:** 90 miles from San Francisco. **Calendar:** Semester, limited summer session. **Full-time faculty:** 218 total. **Part-time faculty:** 147 total. **Special facilities:** Natural history museum.

**Transfer out. Colleges most students transferred to 2009:** California State University: Stanislaus, California State University: Fresno, California State University: Sacramento, University of California: Davis, University of California: San Diego.

**Basis for selection.** Open admission. Limited admission offered to nursing (RN), dental assisting, medical assisting, and related majors. Selective admission to fire academy.

**High school preparation.** Certain programs require specific courses.

**2009-2010 Annual costs.** Tuition/fees: $826; $6,526 out-of-state. Per-credit charge: $26 in-state; $216 out-of-state. Books/supplies: $1,638. Personal expenses: $2,514.

**2009-2010 Financial aid.** All financial aid based on need. Need-based aid available for part-time students. Work-study available nights, weekends

and for part-time students. **Additional information:** Modesto Junior College scholarship priority deadline 12/15.

**Application procedures. Admission:** No deadline. No application fee. Admission notification on a rolling basis. **Financial aid:** Priority date 3/2; no closing date. FAFSA, institutional form required. Applicants notified on a rolling basis starting 5/1; must reply within 2 week(s) of notification.

**Academics. Special study options:** Cooperative education, distance learning, double major, dual enrollment of high school students, ESL, honors, independent study, internships, liberal arts/career combination, study abroad, weekend college. License preparation in nursing, real estate. **Credit/placement by examination:** AP, CLEP, institutional tests. 30 credit hours maximum toward associate degree. **Support services:** GED preparation, learning center, pre-admission summer program, remedial instruction, study skills assistance, tutoring, writing center.

**Majors. Agriculture:** Agronomy, animal breeding, animal sciences, business, dairy, food science, landscaping, ornamental horticulture, plant sciences, poultry, soil science, supplies. **Architecture:** Landscape, urban/community planning. **Business:** General, accounting, administrative services, business admin, fashion, finance, management information systems, marketing, real estate. **Communications:** General, broadcast journalism, journalism. **Communications technology:** Graphic/printing. **Computer sciences:** General, computer graphics, computer science, programming. **Conservation:** General, forestry, wildlife. **Construction:** Electrician, maintenance, pipefitting. **Engineering:** General, electrical. **Engineering technology:** Architectural, drafting. **Family/consumer sciences:** General, child care, clothing/textiles, family/community services, food/nutrition. **Foreign languages:** General, Spanish. **Health:** Dental assistant, medical assistant, nursing (RN), respiratory therapy technology. **Mechanic/repair:** General, auto body, automotive, electronics/electrical, heating/ac/refrig. **Parks/recreation:** General, health/fitness. **Personal/culinary services:** Culinary arts. **Protective services:** Firefighting, law enforcement admin. **Public administration:** Human services. **Social sciences:** General. **Visual/performing arts:** General, art, cinematography, commercial photography, commercial/advertising art, dramatic, fashion design, interior design, photography, studio arts.

**Computing on campus.** 137 workstations in library, computer center, student center. Commuter students can connect to campus network. Online course registration available.

**Student life. Freshman orientation:** Available. One hour, held during registration. **Activities:** Bands, choral groups, dance, drama, film society, international student organizations, music ensembles, musical theater, opera, radio station, student government, student newspaper, symphony orchestra, TV station, Christian Collegiate Fellowship, Able-Disabled Association, foreign, ethnic, minority student and women re-entry clubs, Young Farmers.

**Athletics. Intercollegiate:** Baseball M, basketball, cross-country, diving, football (tackle) M, golf, soccer, softball W, swimming, tennis, track and field, volleyball W, water polo, wrestling M. **Team name:** Pirates.

**Student services.** Adult student services, career counseling, services for economically disadvantaged, student employment services, financial aid counseling, health services, minority student services, on-campus daycare, personal counseling, placement for graduates, veterans' counselor. **Physically disabled:** Services for visually, speech, hearing impaired. **Learning disabled:** Comprehensive services available. **Transfer:** Re-entry adviser for new students. Transfer center, transfer adviser, college fairs on campus for students transferring to 4-year colleges.

**Contact.** Phone: (209) 575-6013 Fax: (209) 575-6859
Therese Agostini, Dean of Matriculation, Admissions, and Records, Modesto Junior College, 435 College Avenue, Modesto, CA 95350-5800

## Monterey Peninsula College
Monterey, California
www.mpc.edu
CB code: 4490

- Public 2-year community college
- Commuter campus in large town

**General.** Founded in 1947. Regionally accredited. **Enrollment:** 12,992 undergraduates. **Degrees:** 370 associate awarded. **Location:** 120 miles from San Francisco. **Calendar:** Semester, limited summer session. **Full-time faculty:** 113 total. **Part-time faculty:** 271 total.

**Basis for selection.** Open admission. Additional requirements, including interview, for dental assistant, nursing, administrative justice and police academy programs.

**2009-2010 Annual costs.** Tuition/fees: $844; $6,544 out-of-state. Per-credit charge: $26 in-state; $216 out-of-state. Books/supplies: $1,638. Personal expenses: $2,790.

**Financial aid. Need-based:** Need-based aid available for part-time students.

**Application procedures. Admission:** No deadline. No application fee. Admission notification on a rolling basis. **Financial aid:** Closing date 6/30. FAFSA, institutional form required. Applicants notified on a rolling basis starting 6/1.

**Academics. Special study options:** Cooperative education, cross-registration, distance learning, double major, dual enrollment of high school students, ESL, independent study, weekend college. **Credit/placement by examination:** CLEP, institutional tests. 30 credit hours maximum toward associate degree. **Support services:** Learning center, remedial instruction, tutoring.

**Majors. Agriculture:** Ornamental horticulture. **Area/ethnic studies:** Women's. **Biology:** General. **Business:** General, accounting, business admin, hospitality admin, hospitality/recreation, international, office/clerical, real estate. **Communications:** General. **Computer sciences:** General, data processing, LAN/WAN management, programming, web page design, word processing. **Engineering technology:** Drafting. **Family/consumer sciences:** General, child development, clothing/textiles, family/community services, fashion consultant, institutional food production. **Foreign languages:** General. **Health:** Dental assistant, medical assistant, nursing (RN), predental, premedicine, prepharmacy, preveterinary. **History:** General. **Liberal arts:** Arts/sciences. **Math:** General. **Philosophy/religion:** Philosophy. **Physical sciences:** Chemistry, physics. **Protective services:** Fire safety technology, law enforcement admin. **Psychology:** General. **Social sciences:** Anthropology, economics, political science, sociology. **Visual/performing arts:** Acting, art, art history/conservation, ceramics, dance, directing/producing, dramatic, drawing, graphic design, interior design, metal/jewelry, painting, photography, printmaking, sculpture, studio arts.

**Student life. Activities:** Bands, choral groups, dance, drama, music ensembles, musical theater, opera, student government.

**Athletics.** NJCAA. **Intercollegiate:** Baseball M, basketball, cross-country, football (tackle) M, golf, softball W, swimming, tennis W, track and field, volleyball W. **Team name:** Lobos.

**Student services.** Career counseling, student employment services, health services, on-campus daycare, personal counseling. **Physically disabled:** Services for visually, speech, hearing impaired. **Transfer:** Transfer center, transfer adviser, college fairs on campus for students transferring to 4-year colleges.

**Contact.** Phone: (831) 646-4002 Fax: (831) 646-4015
Vera Coleman, Director of Admissions and Records, Monterey Peninsula College, 980 Fremont Street, Monterey, CA 93940-4799

## Moorpark College
### Moorpark, California
www.moorparkcollege.edu **CB code: 4512**

▶ Public 2-year community college
▶ Commuter campus in small city

**General.** Founded in 1963. Regionally accredited. **Enrollment:** 9,599 degree-seeking undergraduates. **Degrees:** 1,250 associate awarded. **Location:** 50 miles from Los Angeles. **Calendar:** Semester, limited summer session. **Full-time faculty:** 172 total. **Part-time faculty:** 395 total. **Class size:** 25% 20-39, 50% 40-49, 25% 50-99. **Special facilities:** Exotic animal compound and teaching zoo, observatory.

**Student profile.**

Out-of-state: 1%    25 or older: 74%

**Transfer out. Colleges most students transferred to 2009:** California State University, University of Southern California, University of California: Los Angeles, UC Santa Barbara.

**Basis for selection.** Open admission. Limited admission to nursing program, exotic animal training management program, radiologic technology.

**2009-2010 Annual costs.** Tuition/fees: $824; $6,494 out-of-state. Per-credit charge: $26 in-state; $215 out-of-state. Books/supplies: $1,638. Personal expenses: $3,096.

**Application procedures. Admission:** Priority date 7/30; no deadline. No application fee. Admission notification on a rolling basis. **Financial aid:** Priority date 5/14; no closing date. FAFSA required. Applicants notified on a rolling basis starting 6/15; must reply within 2 week(s) of notification.

**Academics. Special study options:** Accelerated study, cooperative education, distance learning, honors, independent study, internships, study abroad.

License preparation in nursing, paramedic, radiology. **Credit/placement by examination:** AP, CLEP. 12 credit hours maximum toward associate degree. **Support services:** Learning center, remedial instruction, study skills assistance, tutoring, writing center.

**Majors. Agriculture:** Animal sciences. **Biology:** General. **Business:** Accounting, administrative services, business admin, management information systems, office management, real estate. **Communications:** General, broadcast journalism. **Communications technology:** General, graphic/printing. **Computer sciences:** General, applications programming, information systems. **Engineering technology:** Electrical. **Family/consumer sciences:** General, child care, family studies. **Health:** Medical radiologic technology/radiation therapy, nursing (RN). **Liberal arts:** Arts/sciences. **Math:** General. **Physical sciences:** Chemistry, geology, physics. **Protective services:** Police science. **Social sciences:** General. **Visual/performing arts:** General, cinematography, commercial/advertising art, dramatic, interior design, photography, studio arts.

**Most popular majors.** Agriculture 8%, health sciences 9%, liberal arts 66%.

**Computing on campus.** 400 workstations in library, computer center. Online course registration, online library, helpline, wireless network available.

**Student life. Freshman orientation:** Available. Online orientation. **Activities:** Bands, choral groups, dance, drama, international student organizations, literary magazine, music ensembles, Model UN, musical theater, opera, student government, student newspaper, symphony orchestra, TV station, Alpha Gamma Sigma, Muslim Student Association.

**Athletics. Intercollegiate:** Baseball M, basketball, cheerleading M, cross-country, football (tackle) M, softball W, track and field, volleyball. **Team name:** Raiders.

**Student services.** Career counseling, services for economically disadvantaged, student employment services, financial aid counseling, health services, on-campus daycare, personal counseling, veterans' counselor. **Physically disabled:** Services for visually, speech, hearing impaired. **Transfer:** Transfer center, transfer adviser, college fairs on campus for students transferring to 4-year colleges.

**Contact.** E-mail: mcadmissions@vcccd.net
Phone: (805) 378-1429 Fax: (805) 378-1499
Katherine Colborn, Registrar, Moorpark College, 7075 Campus Road, Moorpark, CA 93021

## Mount San Antonio College
### Walnut, California
www.mtsac.edu **CB code: 4494**

▶ Public 2-year community college
▶ Commuter campus in small city

**General.** Founded in 1946. Regionally accredited. **Enrollment:** 38,563 undergraduates. **Degrees:** 2,107 associate awarded. **ROTC:** Air Force. **Location:** 30 miles from Los Angeles. **Calendar:** Semester, extensive summer session. **Full-time faculty:** 419 total. **Part-time faculty:** 860 total. **Special facilities:** Planetarium, wildlife sanctuary.

**Transfer out. Colleges most students transferred to 2009:** California State Polytechnic University: Pomona, California State University: Los Angeles, California State University: Fullerton.

**Basis for selection.** Open admission.

**2009-2010 Annual costs.** Tuition/fees: $836; $6,536 out-of-state. Per-credit charge: $26 in-state; $216 out-of-state. Books/supplies: $1,638. Personal expenses: $3,838.

**Financial aid.** All financial aid based on need. Need-based aid available for part-time students.

**Application procedures. Admission:** No deadline. No application fee. Admission notification on a rolling basis. **Financial aid:** Closing date 3/2. FAFSA, institutional form required. Applicants notified on a rolling basis starting 6/1; must reply within 4 week(s) of notification.

**Academics. Special study options:** Cooperative education, cross-registration, distance learning, dual enrollment of high school students, ESL, honors, internships, study abroad, teacher certification program, weekend college. License preparation in aviation, nursing, paramedic, radiology, real estate. **Credit/placement by examination:** CLEP. 12 credit hours maximum toward associate degree. **Support services:** GED preparation, learning center, pre-admission summer program, remedial instruction, study skills assistance, tutoring, writing center.

**Majors. Agriculture:** Animal sciences, business, horticulture. **Biology:** General, marine. **Business:** General, accounting, administrative services, banking/financial services, business admin, entrepreneurial studies, fashion, office/clerical, real estate. **Communications:** Advertising, broadcast journalism, journalism. **Communications technology:** General. **Computer sciences:** Data processing. **Conservation:** General, forestry. **Engineering:** General. **Engineering technology:** Architectural, drafting, electrical. **Family/consumer sciences:** General, clothing/textiles. **Foreign languages:** Sign language interpretation. **Health:** EMT paramedic, health services, medical radiologic technology/radiation therapy, medical secretary, nursing (RN), respiratory therapy technology. **Legal studies:** Paralegal. **Liberal arts:** Arts/sciences. **Mechanic/repair:** Aircraft, electronics/electrical, heating/ac/refrig. **Parks/recreation:** General, facilities management. **Protective services:** Firefighting, police science. **Transportation:** Air traffic control, aviation, flight attendant. **Visual/performing arts:** Design, interior design, photography.

**Computing on campus.** 600 workstations in library, computer center, student center. Commuter students can connect to campus network. Online course registration, helpline available.

**Student life. Freshman orientation:** Mandatory. Preregistration for classes offered. **Activities:** Bands, choral groups, dance, drama, film society, literary magazine, music ensembles, musical theater, radio station, student government, student newspaper, symphony orchestra, TV station, Asian student association, Chinese club, Black student alliance, Indo-Pak club, Democratic club, Republican club, sign language club, MECHA, Muslim student association.

**Athletics. Intercollegiate:** Badminton W, baseball M, basketball, cross-country, diving, football (tackle) M, golf, soccer, softball W, swimming, tennis, track and field, volleyball, water polo, wrestling M. **Team name:** Mounties.

**Student services.** Adult student services, alcohol/substance abuse counseling, career counseling, services for economically disadvantaged, student employment services, financial aid counseling, health services, minority student services, on-campus daycare, personal counseling, placement for graduates, veterans' counselor. **Physically disabled:** Services for visually, speech, hearing impaired. **Transfer:** Re-entry adviser, pre-admission transcript evaluation for new students. Transfer center, transfer adviser, college fairs on campus for students transferring to 4-year colleges.

**Contact.** Phone: (909) 594-5611 ext. 4415 Fax: (909) 468-4068
George Bradshaw, Director of Admissions and Records, Mount San Antonio College, 1100 North Grand Avenue, Walnut, CA 91789

## Mount San Jacinto College
San Jacinto, California
www.msjc.edu                    CB code: 4501

▶ Public 2-year community college
▶ Commuter campus in small city

**General.** Founded in 1962. Regionally accredited. **Enrollment:** 18,532 undergraduates. **Degrees:** 1,515 associate awarded. **Location:** 35 miles from Riverside, 45 miles from Palm Springs. **Calendar:** Semester, limited summer session. **Full-time faculty:** 134 total. **Part-time faculty:** 622 total. **Class size:** 38% < 20, 54% 20-39, 7% 40-49, less than 1% 50-99.

**Transfer out. Colleges most students transferred to 2009:** California State University: San Bernardino, University of California: Riverside, California State University: San Marcos, San Diego State University, Azusa Pacific University.

**Basis for selection.** Open admission, but selective for some programs. Special requirements for nursing and diagnostic medical sonography programs and for concurrently enrolled high school students.

**2009-2010 Annual costs.** Tuition/fees: $780; $6,210 out-of-state. Per-credit charge: $26 in-state; $207 out-of-state. Books/supplies: $1,566. Personal expenses: $3,024.

**Financial aid. Need-based:** Need-based aid available for part-time students. Work-study available nights and for part-time students. **Non-need-based:** Scholarships awarded for academics, music/drama. **Additional information:** Board of Governors Grant Program for state residents to defray cost of enrollment fees.

**Application procedures. Admission:** Closing date 12/18 (receipt date). No application fee. Admission notification on a rolling basis beginning on or about 4/24. **Financial aid:** Priority date 3/2; no closing date. FAFSA, institutional form required. Applicants notified on a rolling basis starting 5/1; must reply within 3 week(s) of notification.

**Academics. Special study options:** Cross-registration, distance learning, double major, dual enrollment of high school students, ESL, honors, independent study, internships, study abroad, weekend college. License preparation in nursing, paramedic, real estate. **Credit/placement by examination:** AP, CLEP, institutional tests. 12 credit hours maximum toward associate degree. **Support services:** Learning center, reduced course load, remedial instruction, study skills assistance, tutoring, writing center.

**Majors. Agriculture:** Turf management. **Business:** Business admin, real estate. **Computer sciences:** General. **Education:** Early childhood, physical. **Health:** Nursing (RN), substance abuse counseling. **Interdisciplinary:** Behavioral sciences. **Liberal arts:** Arts/sciences. **Math:** General. **Mechanic/repair:** Automotive. **Protective services:** Police science. **Social sciences:** General. **Visual/performing arts:** Art, dance, dramatic, photography.

**Computing on campus.** 120 workstations in library, computer center. Commuter students can connect to campus network. Online course registration, online library, helpline, wireless network available.

**Student life. Freshman orientation:** Mandatory. 2-hour orientation; online or group session. **Activities:** Bands, dance, drama, international student organizations, musical theater, radio station, student government.

**Athletics.** NAIA, NCAA. **Intercollegiate:** Baseball M, basketball, football (tackle) M, golf, soccer W, softball W, tennis, volleyball W. **Intramural:** Cheerleading, weight lifting. **Team name:** Eagles.

**Student services.** Adult student services, career counseling, services for economically disadvantaged, student employment services, financial aid counseling, minority student services, on-campus daycare, veterans' counselor. **Physically disabled:** Services for visually, speech, hearing impaired. **Learning disabled:** Comprehensive services available. **Transfer:** Pre-admission transcript evaluation for new students. Transfer center, transfer adviser, college fairs on campus for students transferring to 4-year colleges.

**Contact.** E-mail: enrollsvcs@msjc.edu
Phone: (951) 487-3215 Fax: (951) 654-6738
Susan Loomis, Director, Enrollment Services, Mount San Jacinto College, 1499 North State Street, San Jacinto, CA 92583

## MTI College
Sacramento, California
www.mticollege.edu                CB code: 3543

▶ For-profit 2-year business and technical college
▶ Commuter campus in large city
▶ Interview required

**General.** Regionally accredited. **Enrollment:** 300 degree-seeking undergraduates. **Degrees:** 93 associate awarded. **Calendar:** Continuous, extensive summer session. **Full-time faculty:** 12 total. **Part-time faculty:** 56 total.

**Transfer out. Colleges most students transferred to 2009:** University of Phoenix, Golden Gate University.

**Basis for selection.** Interview, talent, ability, character and personal qualities important.

**2009-2010 Annual costs.** Tuition/fees: $11,245. Books/supplies: $1,386. Personal expenses: $322.

**Financial aid. Need-based:** Work-study available nights.

**Application procedures. Admission:** No deadline. $50 fee. Admission notification on a rolling basis.

**Academics. Special study options:** Cooperative education, distance learning, internships, liberal arts/career combination. **Credit/placement by examination:** CLEP, institutional tests. **Support services:** Learning center, reduced course load, remedial instruction, study skills assistance, tutoring.

**Majors. Business:** Business admin. **Computer sciences:** System admin, systems analysis. **Legal studies:** Paralegal.

**Most popular majors.** Business/marketing 9%, computer/information sciences 27%, legal studies 64%.

**Computing on campus.** 300 workstations in library, computer center.

Two-Year Colleges

**Student life. Freshman orientation:** Mandatory.

**Student services.** Adult student services, career counseling, financial aid counseling, placement for graduates, veterans' counselor. **Transfer:** Pre-admission transcript evaluation for new students. College fairs on campus for students transferring to 4-year colleges.

**Contact.** E-mail: webmaster@mticollege.edu
Phone: (916) 339-1500 Fax: (916) 339-0305
Eric Patterson, Director of Admissions, MTI College, 5221 Madison Avenue, Sacramento, CA 95841

## Napa Valley College
### Napa, California
### www.napavalley.edu
**CB code: 4530**

▶ Public 2-year community college
▶ Commuter campus in small city

**General.** Founded in 1940. Regionally accredited. **Enrollment:** 7,780 undergraduates. **Degrees:** 615 associate awarded. **Location:** 50 miles from San Francisco. **Calendar:** Semester, limited summer session. **Full-time faculty:** 110 total. **Part-time faculty:** 297 total. **Special facilities:** Nature preserve, working vineyard, telecommunications laboratory.

**Basis for selection.** Open admission, but selective for some programs. Special admission requirements for health occupations programs and athletic program applicants.

**2009-2010 Annual costs.** Tuition/fees: $808; $6,508 out-of-state. Per-credit charge: $26 in-state; $216 out-of-state. Books/supplies: $1,638. Personal expenses: $3,096.

**Application procedures. Admission:** No deadline. No application fee. Admission notification on a rolling basis. College-administered placement tests recommended for students enrolling in English or mathematics. **Financial aid:** Closing date 5/29. FAFSA required. Applicants notified on a rolling basis starting 6/1; must reply within 3 week(s) of notification.

**Academics.** Culinary arts program available. **Special study options:** Cooperative education, distance learning, double major, dual enrollment of high school students, ESL, honors, independent study, internships, study abroad, weekend college. Exchange program with Tafe College, Tasmania. **Credit/placement by examination:** CLEP, institutional tests. 12 credit hours maximum toward associate degree. **Support services:** Learning center, remedial instruction, tutoring, writing center.

**Majors. Agriculture:** General. **Business:** General, accounting, administrative services, real estate. **Communications technology:** General. **Computer sciences:** General. **Conservation:** Wildlife. **Education:** General, early childhood. **Engineering technology:** Biomedical, drafting, electrical. **Health:** Health services, licensed practical nurse, nursing (RN), respiratory therapy technology. **Legal studies:** Paralegal. **Liberal arts:** Arts/sciences. **Protective services:** Police science. **Social sciences:** General.

**Computing on campus.** 30 workstations in library, computer center.

**Student life. Activities:** Bands, choral groups, dance, drama, music ensembles, musical theater, student government, student newspaper, symphony orchestra, various religious, ethnic, social service, and special interest organizations including International Student Club, Amnesty International, Hispano-Americano Club.

**Athletics.** NJCAA. **Intercollegiate:** Baseball M, basketball, diving, golf, soccer M, softball W, swimming, tennis, volleyball W. **Intramural:** Volleyball. **Team name:** Storm.

**Student services.** Adult student services, career counseling, student employment services, on-campus daycare, personal counseling, veterans' counselor. **Physically disabled:** Services for visually, speech, hearing impaired. **Transfer:** Re-entry adviser for new students. Transfer center, transfer adviser, college fairs on campus for students transferring to 4-year colleges.

**Contact.** Phone: (707) 253-3000 Fax: (707) 253-3064
Javier Urena, Director of Admissions, Napa Valley College, 2277 Napa-Vallejo Highway, Napa, CA 94558

## National Polytechnic College of Science
### San Diego, California
### www.natpoly.edu
**CB code: 1243**

▶ Private 2-year health science and maritime college
▶ Commuter campus in large city

**General.** Founded in 1969. Regionally accredited. **Enrollment:** 185 degree-seeking undergraduates. **Degrees:** 23 associate awarded. **Calendar:** Continuous. **Full-time faculty:** 10 total. **Part-time faculty:** 10 total.

**Basis for selection.** Open admission. Must be medically approved to dive. Applicants who do not have high school diploma or GED must prove their ability to benefit from program. Students expected to have mechanical aptitude and, if possible, experience in construction-related field. Interviews recommended.

**2009-2010 Annual costs.** Associate degree program charge (covering 12 months), $28,612; per-credit-hour charge, $311. Academic year is comprised of 30 weeks (36 quarter credits), with courses offered in five-week sessions. Undergraduate courses are scheduled, typically, for eight to ten hours per day (two days each week, five-week period). Some courses require basic supplies (e.g., wet suit, fins, weights, work boots) that are not covered by tuition; additional cost of these supplies could amount to $800 or more.

**Financial aid. Additional information:** Work-study programs available.

**Application procedures. Admission:** No deadline. $60 fee. Admission notification on a rolling basis. **Financial aid:** No deadline. FAFSA, institutional form required. Applicants notified on a rolling basis; must reply within 3 week(s) of notification.

**Academics.** Special programs prepare students for work as underwater welders, diver medical technicians, and topside/underwater nondestructive testing/inspection personnel. **Credit/placement by examination:** CLEP, institutional tests. 20 credit hours maximum toward associate degree. **Support services:** Remedial instruction, tutoring.

**Majors. Construction:** General. **Health:** Medical records technology, substance abuse counseling. **Protective services:** Emergency management/homeland security. **Transportation:** Diver. **Other:** Hyperbaric medical technology.

**Student services.** Career counseling, student employment services, personal counseling, placement for graduates, veterans' counselor. **Transfer:** Transfer adviser for students transferring to 4-year colleges.

**Contact.** E-mail: moreinfo@natpoly.edu
Phone: (858) 309-3510 Fax: (858) 309-3510
Shelly Mitchell, Director of Admissions, National Polytechnic College of Science, 3580 Aero Court, San Diego, CA 92123

## Ohlone College
### Fremont, California
### www.ohlone.edu
**CB code: 4579**

▶ Public 2-year community college
▶ Commuter campus in large city

**General.** Founded in 1966. Regionally accredited. **Enrollment:** 10,909 undergraduates. **Degrees:** 426 associate awarded. **ROTC:** Air Force. **Location:** 15 miles from San Jose, 40 miles from San Francisco. **Calendar:** Semester, extensive summer session. **Full-time faculty:** 140 total. **Part-time faculty:** 340 total. **Class size:** 54% < 20, 40% 20-39, 2% 40-49, 2% 50-99, less than 1% >100. **Special facilities:** Fine and performing arts center, business and technology center, Newark center for health sciences and technology. **Partnerships:** Formal partnerships with Sun Microsystems, Metatec Inc., Washington Hospital, Fremont Unified School District, Newark Unified School District.

**Student profile.**

| | | | |
|---|---|---|---|
| Out-of-state: | 1% | 25 or older: | 45% |

**Transfer out. Colleges most students transferred to 2009:** California State University: East Bay, San Jose State University, University of California: Berkeley, University of California: Davis, San Francisco State University.

**Basis for selection.** Open admission. Nursing, respiratory therapy and physical therapy assisting programs require basic competence in reading comprehension and English skills, basic knowledge of related sciences. All candidates who achieve minimum standards selected by lottery. High school diploma or equivalent not required if applicant is 18 years of age or older.

**High school preparation.** Nursing and physical therapy assisting programs require anatomy and physiology. Respiratory therapy program requires algebra and physics.

**2009-2010 Annual costs.** Tuition/fees: $834; $6,534 out-of-state. Per-credit charge: $26 in-state; $216 out-of-state. Books/supplies: $810. Personal expenses: $2,616.

**Financial aid. Need-based:** Need-based aid available for part-time students. Work-study available for part-time students. **Non-need-based:** Scholarships awarded for academics.

**Application procedures. Admission:** No deadline. No application fee. **Financial aid:** Priority date 7/1; no closing date. FAFSA, institutional form required. Applicants notified on a rolling basis starting 7/30; must reply within 2 week(s) of notification.

**Academics. Special study options:** Cooperative education, cross-registration, distance learning, double major, dual enrollment of high school students, ESL, independent study, internships, liberal arts/career combination, study abroad, weekend college. License preparation in nursing, physical therapy. **Credit/placement by examination:** AP, CLEP, IB, institutional tests. 10 credit hours maximum toward associate degree. **Support services:** Learning center, pre-admission summer program, reduced course load, remedial instruction, study skills assistance, tutoring, writing center.

**Majors. Biology:** General. **Business:** General, accounting, administrative services, business admin, marketing, office management, office technology, office/clerical, real estate, receptionist, small business admin. **Communications:** Broadcast journalism, digital media, journalism. **Communications technology:** Desktop publishing. **Computer sciences:** Computer graphics, information systems, LAN/WAN management, programming, system admin. **Education:** Early childhood. **Engineering technology:** CAD/CADD, electrical, electromechanical. **Family/consumer sciences:** Child care, food/nutrition, institutional food production. **Foreign languages:** American Sign Language. **Health:** Medical assistant, nursing (RN), physical therapy assistant, respiratory therapy technology. **Interdisciplinary:** Biological/physical sciences, natural sciences. **Liberal arts:** Arts/sciences. **Mechanic/repair:** Electronics/electrical. **Protective services:** Law enforcement admin. **Social sciences:** General. **Visual/performing arts:** Commercial/advertising art, graphic design, interior design, multimedia, studio arts, theater design.

**Most popular majors.** Biological/life sciences 21%, business/marketing 10%, health sciences 18%, liberal arts 38%.

**Computing on campus.** 450 workstations in library, computer center. Commuter students can connect to campus network. Online course registration, online library, helpline, wireless network available.

**Student life. Freshman orientation:** Mandatory. **Activities:** Bands, choral groups, dance, drama, literary magazine, music ensembles, musical theater, radio station, student government, student newspaper, symphony orchestra, TV station, Abundant Life Christian Fellowship, Afghan Students Association, Asian Pacific Islanders Club, Chinese Culture Club, Muslim Student Association, Alpha Gamma Sigma Honor Society, Ohlone Women Engineers and Physical Scientists, Theater and Dance Alliance.

**Athletics. Intercollegiate:** Baseball M, basketball, soccer, softball W, swimming, tennis, volleyball, water polo. **Team name:** Renegades.

**Student services.** Adult student services, career counseling, services for economically disadvantaged, student employment services, financial aid counseling, health services, on-campus daycare, personal counseling, placement for graduates, veterans' counselor. **Physically disabled:** Services for visually, hearing impaired. **Transfer:** Pre-admission transcript evaluation for new students. Transfer center, transfer adviser, college fairs on campus for students transferring to 4-year colleges.

**Contact.** E-mail: admissions@ohlone.edu
Phone: (510) 659-6100 Fax: (510) 659-7231
Christopher Williamson, Interim Director of Admissions and Records, Ohlone College, 43600 Mission Boulevard, Fremont, CA 94539-0390

---

## Orange Coast College
Costa Mesa, California
www.orangecoastcollege.edu          CB code: 4584

- Public 2-year community college
- Commuter campus in small city

**General.** Founded in 1947. Regionally accredited. **Enrollment:** 23,399 degree-seeking undergraduates; 1,343 non-degree-seeking students. **Degrees:** 1,446 associate awarded. **Location:** 40 miles from Los Angeles. **Calendar:** Semester, extensive summer session. **Full-time faculty:** 286 total; 24% minority, 48% women. **Part-time faculty:** 495 total; 27% minority, 56% women. **Class size:** 28% < 20, 51% 20-39, 11% 40-49, 7% 50-99, 4% >100. **Special facilities:** Planetarium, plastination lab, sailing academy, international center.

**Student profile.** Among degree-seeking undergraduates, 5,255 enrolled as first-time, first-year students.

| | | | |
|---|---|---|---|
| Part-time: | 59% | Hispanic American: | 19% |
| Out-of-state: | 3% | Native American: | 1% |
| Women: | 49% | International: | 3% |
| African American: | 2% | 25 or older: | 32% |
| Asian American: | 24% | | |

**Transfer out. Colleges most students transferred to 2009:** University of California: Irvine, California State University: Fullerton, California State University: Long Beach.

**Basis for selection.** Open admission. **Homeschooled:** Transcript of courses and grades required.

**2009-2010 Annual costs.** Tuition/fees: $812; $6,512 out-of-state. Per-credit charge: $26 in-state; $216 out-of-state. Books/supplies: $1,638. Personal expenses: $3,096.

**2008-2009 Financial aid. Need-based:** 1,146 full-time freshmen applied for aid; 1,131 were judged to have need; 1,127 of these received aid. Average need met was 33%. Average scholarship/grant was $3,858; average loan $2,972. 82% of total undergraduate aid awarded as scholarships/grants, 18% as loans/jobs. Need-based aid available for part-time students. Work-study available for part-time students. **Non-need-based:** Awarded to 4 full-time undergraduates, including 4 freshmen. Scholarships awarded for academics.

**Application procedures. Admission:** No deadline. No application fee. Admission notification on a rolling basis. Admission opens January for summer and fall semester, September for spring semester; dates establish registration priority. **Financial aid:** Priority date 3/2, closing date 5/25. FAFSA, institutional form required. Applicants notified on a rolling basis; must reply within 2 week(s) of notification.

**Academics.** Student Success Center (individual tutoring, drop-in tutoring, online tutoring, and study skills assistance) and Math Center available. **Special study options:** Cooperative education, cross-registration, distance learning, ESL, honors, independent study, internships, liberal arts/career combination, student-designed major, study abroad, weekend college. License preparation in aviation, dental hygiene, paramedic, radiology, real estate. **Credit/placement by examination:** AP, CLEP, institutional tests. 12 credit hours maximum toward associate degree. **Support services:** Learning center, pre-admission summer program, reduced course load, remedial instruction, study skills assistance, tutoring, writing center.

**Honors college/program.** Students complete a minimum of 18 units in honors courses for program certification.

**Majors. Agriculture:** Ornamental horticulture. **Architecture:** Technology. **Biology:** General, ecology. **Business:** General, accounting, administrative services, fashion, hospitality/recreation, international, management information systems, office technology, office/clerical, real estate, sales/distribution, selling, travel services. **Communications:** Advertising, journalism, media studies. **Computer sciences:** General, computer graphics, data entry, information systems, programming. **Construction:** General, maintenance, pipefitting, power transmission. **Education:** Drama/dance, early childhood, kindergarten/preschool, music. **Engineering:** General. **Engineering technology:** Architectural, CAD/CADD, drafting, electrical, heat/ac/refrig, mechanical drafting. **Family/consumer sciences:** General, child care, clothing/textiles, food/nutrition, institutional food production. **Foreign languages:** French, German, Italian, Japanese, Spanish. **Health:** Athletic training, cardiovascular technology, dental assistant, dietetic technician, electroencephalograph technology, medical assistant, medical radiologic technology/radiation therapy, medical records technology, radiologic technology/medical imaging, respiratory therapy technology, sonography, speech-language pathology assistant. **History:** General. **Interdisciplinary:** Natural sciences. **Liberal arts:** Arts/sciences, humanities. **Math:** General. **Mechanic/repair:** Aircraft, avionics, electronics/electrical, heating/ac/refrig. **Parks/recreation:** Health/fitness, sports admin. **Personal/culinary services:** Baking, culinary arts, restaurant/catering. **Philosophy/religion:** Philosophy, religion. **Physical sciences:** Astronomy, chemistry, geology, physics. **Production:** Machine tool. **Psychology:** General. **Social sciences:** General, anthropology, economics, geography, political science, sociology. **Transportation:** Airline/commercial pilot, aviation, flight attendant. **Visual/performing arts:** Art, cinematography, commercial photography, commercial/advertising art, dance, dramatic, fashion design, film/cinema, interior design, music management, photography, studio arts.

**Computing on campus.** 1,500 workstations in library, computer center, student center. Online course registration, online library, helpline, wireless network available.

**Student life. Freshman orientation:** Mandatory. 3-hour sessions given year round. **Activities:** Bands, choral groups, dance, drama, film society, international student organizations, literary magazine, music ensembles, Model UN, musical theater, student government, student newspaper, symphony orchestra, Buddhists Crusade for Christ, Christian Fellowship, COPTIC, Hillel.

**Athletics. Intercollegiate:** Baseball M, basketball, cheerleading, cross-country, diving, football (tackle) M, golf M, rowing (crew), soccer, softball W, swimming, tennis, track and field, volleyball, water polo. **Team name:** Pirates.

**Student services.** Adult student services, alcohol/substance abuse counseling, career counseling, services for economically disadvantaged, student employment services, financial aid counseling, health services, minority student services, on-campus daycare, personal counseling, placement for graduates, veterans' counselor. **Physically disabled:** Services for visually, speech, hearing impaired. **Learning disabled:** Comprehensive services available. **Transfer:** Re-entry adviser for new students. Transfer center, transfer adviser, college fairs on campus for students transferring to 4-year colleges.

**Contact.** E-mail: campustours@occ.cccd.edu
Phone: (714) 432-5072
Efren Galvan, Director of Admissions & Records, Orange Coast College, 2701 Fairview Road, Costa Mesa, CA 92628-5005

## Oxnard College
### Oxnard, California
www.oxnardcollege.edu                    CB code: 4591

- Public 2-year community college
- Commuter campus in small city

**General.** Founded in 1975. Regionally accredited. **Enrollment:** 8,129 undergraduates. **Degrees:** 519 associate awarded. **Location:** 60 miles from Los Angeles. **Calendar:** Semester, limited summer session. **Full-time faculty:** 96 total. **Part-time faculty:** 186 total. **Special facilities:** Marine education center.

**Basis for selection.** Open admission.

**2009-2010 Annual costs.** Tuition/fees: $824; $6,494 out-of-state. Per-credit charge: $26 in-state; $215 out-of-state. Books/supplies: $1,638. Personal expenses: $3,096.

**Application procedures. Admission:** No deadline. No application fee. Admission notification on a rolling basis. **Financial aid:** Closing date 3/2. FAFSA required. Applicants notified on a rolling basis; must reply within 2 week(s) of notification.

**Academics. Special study options:** Accelerated study, cross-registration, distance learning, dual enrollment of high school students, independent study, study abroad. First 2 years of bilingual (English-Spanish) teacher preparatory program. **Credit/placement by examination:** CLEP, institutional tests. 12 credit hours maximum toward associate degree. **Support services:** Learning center, remedial instruction, tutoring.

**Majors. Biology:** General, marine. **Business:** Accounting, administrative services, business admin, hotel/motel admin. **Communications:** Digital media, journalism, public relations, radio/tv. **Computer sciences:** General, information technology, networking, web page design. **Engineering technology:** Hazardous materials, heat/ac/refrig. **Family/consumer sciences:** Child development. **Foreign languages:** Sign language interpretation, Spanish. **Health:** Dental hygiene, medical records technology, substance abuse counseling. **History:** General. **Interdisciplinary:** Biological/physical sciences. **Legal studies:** Paralegal. **Liberal arts:** Arts/sciences, humanities. **Math:** General. **Mechanic/repair:** Auto body, automotive, electronics/electrical. **Personal/culinary services:** Culinary arts, restaurant/catering. **Philosophy/religion:** Philosophy. **Protective services:** Firefighting. **Psychology:** General. **Public administration:** Human services. **Social sciences:** Anthropology, economics, political science, sociology. **Visual/performing arts:** Art, drawing, sculpture.

**Most popular majors.** Business/marketing 13%, liberal arts 63%, security/protective services 6%.

**Computing on campus.** 57 workstations in library. Online course registration available.

**Student life. Freshman orientation:** Available. **Activities:** Jazz band, choral groups, drama, student government, student newspaper, TV station, Hispanic club, EconoBus club, Asian-American club, math club, MECha, Condor christian club, Chemistry Club, Art Underground.

**Athletics. Intercollegiate:** Baseball M, basketball, cross-country, soccer, softball W, track and field, volleyball W. **Team name:** Condors.

**Student services.** Career counseling, services for economically disadvantaged, student employment services, financial aid counseling, health services, on-campus daycare, personal counseling, veterans' counselor. **Physically disabled:** Services for visually, speech, hearing impaired. **Transfer:** Transfer center, transfer adviser, college fairs on campus for students transferring to 4-year colleges.

**Contact.** E-mail: ocadmissions@vcccd.edu
Phone: (805) 986-5810 Fax: (805) 986-5943
Susan Cabral, Director of Admissions, Oxnard College, 4000 South Rose Avenue, Oxnard, CA 93033

## Palo Verde College
### Blythe, California
www.paloverde.edu                    CB code: 4603

- Public 2-year community college
- Commuter campus in large town

**General.** Founded in 1947. Regionally accredited. **Enrollment:** 1,672 degree-seeking undergraduates. **Degrees:** 154 associate awarded. **Location:** 160 miles from Riverside. **Calendar:** Semester, limited summer session. **Full-time faculty:** 40 total; 15% have terminal degrees, 40% minority, 35% women. **Part-time faculty:** 96 total; 3% have terminal degrees, 18% minority, 45% women.

**Transfer out. Colleges most students transferred to 2009:** Coastline Community College, College of the Desert, Mohave Community College, Fresno Pacific College, Riverside Community College.

**Basis for selection.** Open admission, but selective for some programs. Limited admission to nursing program.

**2009-2010 Annual costs.** Tuition/fees: $780; $6,480 out-of-state. Per-credit charge: $26 in-state; $216 out-of-state. Books/supplies: $1,638. Personal expenses: $2,000.

**2008-2009 Financial aid.** All financial aid based on need. 98% of total undergraduate aid awarded as scholarships/grants, 2% as loans/jobs. Need-based aid available for part-time students. Work-study available nights and for part-time students.

**Application procedures. Admission:** Closing date 8/28. No application fee. Application must be submitted online. Admission notification on a rolling basis. SAT or ACT recommended for placement. **Financial aid:** No deadline. FAFSA, institutional form required. Applicants notified on a rolling basis starting 7/1; must reply within 4 week(s) of notification.

**Academics. Special study options:** Cooperative education, distance learning, dual enrollment of high school students, ESL, independent study. **Credit/placement by examination:** AP, CLEP, institutional tests. 12 credit hours maximum toward associate degree. **Support services:** GED test center, learning center, remedial instruction, study skills assistance, tutoring, writing center.

**Majors. Business:** Accounting, business admin, office/clerical. **Computer sciences:** General. **Construction:** General. **Family/consumer sciences:** Child development. **History:** General. **Liberal arts:** Arts/sciences. **Mechanic/repair:** Automotive. **Protective services:** Firefighting, law enforcement admin.

**Most popular majors.** Business/marketing 49%, liberal arts 38%, social sciences 6%.

**Computing on campus.** 125 workstations in library, computer center.

**Student life. Freshman orientation:** Mandatory. Preregistration for classes offered. **Activities:** Literary magazine, student government.

**Athletics. Intramural:** Soccer.

**Student services.** Career counseling, services for economically disadvantaged, student employment services, financial aid counseling, personal counseling, placement for graduates. **Physically disabled:** Services for visually, speech, hearing impaired. **Transfer:** Transfer center, transfer adviser, college fairs on campus for students transferring to 4-year colleges.

**Contact.** E-mail: mwalnoha@paloverde.edu
Phone: (760) 921-5500
Melinda Walnoha, Registrar, Palo Verde College, One College Drive, Blythe, CA 92225

## Palomar College
**San Marcos, California** CB member
www.palomar.edu CB code: 4602

◆ Public 2-year community college
◆ Commuter campus in large town

**General.** Founded in 1946. Regionally accredited. Off-campus sites located throughout North County area. **Enrollment:** 28,182 undergraduates. **Degrees:** 1,620 associate awarded. **Location:** 40 miles from San Diego. **Calendar:** Semester, extensive summer session. **Full-time faculty:** 306 total. **Part-time faculty:** 1,050 total. **Special facilities:** Arboretum, observatory.

**Basis for selection.** Open admission, but selective for some programs. ASSET mathematics and English tests required for nursing applicants. **Adult students:** SAT/ACT scores not required.

**2009-2010 Annual costs.** Tuition/fees: $824; $6,524 out-of-state. Per-credit charge: $26 in-state; $216 out-of-state. Books/supplies: $648. Personal expenses: $1,620.

**Financial aid.** All financial aid based on need. Need-based aid available for part-time students. Work-study available nights and for part-time students.

**Application procedures. Admission:** Priority date 6/9; no deadline. No application fee. Application deadlines for nursing program April 1 for fall semester, November 1 for spring semester. **Financial aid:** Priority date 4/1; no closing date. FAFSA, institutional form required. Applicants notified on a rolling basis starting 6/1.

**Academics. Special study options:** Cooperative education, distance learning, dual enrollment of high school students, ESL, internships, liberal arts/career combination, study abroad, weekend college. **Credit/placement by examination:** AP, CLEP, institutional tests. 15 credit hours maximum toward associate degree. **Support services:** Learning center, pre-admission summer program, reduced course load, remedial instruction, tutoring, writing center.

**Majors. Biology:** General, zoology. **Business:** General, accounting, administrative services, banking/financial services, business admin, fashion, international, management science, office/clerical, operations, real estate, tourism promotion. **Communications:** Advertising, journalism. **Communications technology:** General, graphic/printing. **Computer sciences:** General, computer science, information systems. **Construction:** Carpentry, maintenance, masonry, pipefitting, power transmission. **Education:** Early childhood. **Engineering:** General. **Engineering technology:** Drafting, surveying. **Family/consumer sciences:** Child care, institutional food production. **Foreign languages:** Sign language interpretation. **Health:** Dental assistant, EMT paramedic, medical assistant, medical records admin, medical secretary, nursing (RN). **Legal studies:** Legal secretary, paralegal. **Liberal arts:** Arts/sciences, library assistant. **Math:** General. **Mechanic/repair:** General, auto body, diesel, electronics/electrical. **Parks/recreation:** General, facilities management, health/fitness. **Physical sciences:** Astronomy, chemistry, geology. **Production:** Woodworking. **Protective services:** Firefighting, law enforcement admin, police science, security services. **Public administration:** General. **Social sciences:** Archaeology, economics. **Transportation:** Aviation. **Visual/performing arts:** Art, ceramics, commercial/advertising art, crafts, dance, dramatic, fashion design, film/cinema, interior design, metal/jewelry, painting, photography, printmaking, sculpture.

**Most popular majors.** Health sciences 6%, liberal arts 61%, social sciences 7%, trade and industry 6%.

**Computing on campus.** 922 workstations in library, computer center, student center. Online course registration, online library, wireless network available.

**Student life. Freshman orientation:** Available. **Activities:** Bands, choral groups, dance, drama, literary magazine, music ensembles, musical theater, radio station, student government, student newspaper, symphony orchestra, TV station.

**Athletics.** NJCAA. **Intercollegiate:** Baseball M, basketball, football (tackle) M, golf M, soccer, softball W, swimming, tennis, volleyball, water polo M, wrestling M. **Intramural:** Volleyball W. **Team name:** Comets.

**Student services.** Career counseling, student employment services, financial aid counseling, health services, on-campus daycare, personal counseling, placement for graduates, veterans' counselor. **Physically disabled:** Services for visually, speech, hearing impaired. **Transfer:** Transfer center, transfer adviser, college fairs on campus for students transferring to 4-year colleges.

**Contact.** E-mail: admissions@palomar.edu
Phone: (760) 744-1150 ext. 2164 Fax: (760) 761-3536
Herman Lee, Director of Enrollment Services, Palomar College, 1140 West Mission Road, San Marcos, CA 92069-1487

## Pasadena City College
**Pasadena, California**
www.pasadena.edu CB code: 4604

◆ Public 2-year community college
◆ Commuter campus in small city

**General.** Founded in 1924. Regionally accredited. **Enrollment:** 29,638 undergraduates. **Degrees:** 1,687 associate awarded. **Location:** 10 miles from downtown Los Angeles. **Calendar:** Semester, limited summer session. **Full-time faculty:** 320 total; 30% have terminal degrees. **Part-time faculty:** 740 total; 14% have terminal degrees. **Class size:** 6% < 20, 66% 20-39, 25% 40-49, 2% 50-99, 1% >100. **Special facilities:** Observatory.

**Student profile.**

| | | | |
|---|---|---|---|
| Out-of-state: | 3% | 25 or older: | 36% |

**Transfer out. Colleges most students transferred to 2009:** California State University: Los Angeles, Long Beach, Northridge; California State Polytechnic Institute: Pomona.

**Basis for selection.** Open admission, but selective for some programs. Admission to RN, LVN, dental hygiene programs based on test scores, interview, high school record; minimum 2.0 high school GPA required. School and College Ability Tests, SAT, ACT, or California Achievement Test scores used for admission to some programs. Interview required of dental hygiene majors. Audition required of music majors.

**2009-2010 Annual costs.** Tuition/fees: $808; $6,508 out-of-state. Per-credit charge: $26 in-state; $216 out-of-state. Books/supplies: $1,638. Personal expenses: $3,780.

**Financial aid.** All financial aid based on need.

**Application procedures. Admission:** Closing date 8/11. No application fee. Admission notification on a rolling basis beginning on or about 3/1. **Financial aid:** Priority date 5/13; no closing date. FAFSA required. Applicants notified on a rolling basis starting 6/1; must reply within 2 week(s) of notification.

**Academics. Special study options:** Accelerated study, distance learning, dual enrollment of high school students, honors, independent study, internships, liberal arts/career combination, study abroad. **Credit/placement by examination:** CLEP, institutional tests. 12 credit hours maximum toward associate degree. **Support services:** Learning center, pre-admission summer program, reduced course load, remedial instruction, study skills assistance, tutoring, writing center.

**Majors. Biology:** General. **Business:** General, accounting, administrative services, banking/financial services, entrepreneurial studies, fashion, hospitality/recreation, management information systems, office/clerical, real estate, sales/distribution, tourism promotion. **Communications:** General, broadcast journalism, journalism. **Communications technology:** General. **Computer sciences:** Applications programming, data processing, programming. **Construction:** Carpentry, maintenance. **Education:** Early childhood. **Engineering technology:** Drafting. **Health:** Clinical lab technology, dental assistant, dental hygiene, dental lab technology, licensed practical nurse, medical assistant, medical radiologic technology/radiation therapy, medical secretary, nursing (RN), speech-language pathology assistant. **Legal studies:** Legal secretary, paralegal. **Liberal arts:** Arts/sciences, library assistant. **Mechanic/repair:** Auto body. **Parks/recreation:** General. **Protective services:** Firefighting, police science. **Psychology:** General. **Social sciences:** General. **Visual/performing arts:** Ceramics, commercial photography, commercial/advertising art, crafts, drawing, painting, printmaking, sculpture, studio arts.

**Computing on campus.** 300 workstations in computer center, student center.

**Student life. Freshman orientation:** Available. **Activities:** Bands, choral groups, dance, drama, film society, literary magazine, music ensembles, musical theater, radio station, student government, student newspaper, symphony orchestra, TV station, wide variety of religious, political, ethnic, and social service organizations.

**Athletics. Intercollegiate:** Badminton W, baseball M, basketball, cross-country, football (tackle) M, soccer, softball W, swimming, tennis W, track and field, volleyball W, water polo W. **Team name:** Lancers.

**Student services.** Career counseling, student employment services, health services, personal counseling, placement for graduates. **Physically disabled:** Services for visually, speech, hearing impaired. **Transfer:** Transfer center, transfer adviser, college fairs on campus for students transferring to 4-year colleges.

**Contact.** Phone: (626) 578-7396 Fax: (626) 585-7912
Margaret Ramey, Associate Dean of Admissions and Records, Pasadena City College, 1570 East Colorado Boulevard, Pasadena, CA 91106

## Platt College: Los Angeles
### Alhambra, California
### www.plattcollege.edu                    CB code: 3014

- For-profit 2-year visual arts and technical college
- Commuter campus in very large city
- Application essay, interview required

**General.** Accredited by ACCSC. **Enrollment:** 211 degree-seeking undergraduates. **Degrees:** 19 bachelor's, 51 associate awarded. **Location:** 10 miles from dowtown Los Angeles. **Calendar:** Continuous. **Full-time faculty:** 25 total. **Class size:** 85% < 20, 15% 20-39.

**Transfer out. Colleges most students transferred to 2009:** University of LaVerne, University of Phoenix.

**Basis for selection.** Must score at least 126 on CPAT for admissions. Multimedia program requires degree. MCSE program requires computer background. **Learning Disabled:** Students with learning disabilities allowed 30 extra minutes on CPAT examination.

**2009-2010 Annual costs.** Cost varies by program. Associate degree cost ranges from $24,915 to $34,955. Bachelor's degree cost ranges from $69,930 to $73,930.

**Financial aid. Need-based:** Need-based aid available for part-time students. Work-study available nights.

**Application procedures. Admission:** No deadline. $75 fee. Admission notification on a rolling basis. **Financial aid:** Priority date 3/2; no closing date. FAFSA, institutional form required. Applicants notified on a rolling basis starting 1/1.

**Academics. Special study options:** Accelerated study, cooperative education, internships. **Credit/placement by examination:** CLEP, institutional tests. 48 credit hours maximum toward associate degree. **Support services:** Tutoring.

**Majors. Computer sciences:** General, computer graphics. **Visual/performing arts:** General, commercial/advertising art.

**Computing on campus.** 60 workstations in library.

**Student life. Freshman orientation:** Mandatory. Preregistration for classes offered. 2-hour program on or around first day of classes.

**Student services.** Adult student services, career counseling, student employment services, financial aid counseling, placement for graduates. **Transfer:** Re-entry adviser, pre-admission transcript evaluation for new students. Transfer adviser for students transferring to 4-year colleges.

**Contact.** Phone: (626) 300-5444 Toll-free number: (866) 752-8852 Fax: (626) 300-3978
Teresa Moore, Director of Admissions, Platt College: Los Angeles, 1000 South Fremont Avenue A9W, Alhambra, CA 91803

## Porterville College
### Porterville, California
### www.portervillecollege.edu              CB code: 4608

- Public 2-year community college
- Commuter campus in large town

**General.** Founded in 1927. Regionally accredited. **Enrollment:** 4,471 undergraduates. **Degrees:** 251 associate awarded. **Location:** 75 miles from Fresno, 50 miles from Bakersfield. **Calendar:** Semester, limited summer session. **Full-time faculty:** 80 total. **Part-time faculty:** 1,510 total. **Special facilities:** Anthropology library.

**Basis for selection.** Open admission.

**2009-2010 Annual costs.** Tuition/fees: $814; $6,844 out-of-state. Per-credit charge: $26 in-state; $227 out-of-state. Books/supplies: $1,656. Personal expenses: $1,800.

**Application procedures. Admission:** No deadline. No application fee. Admission notification on a rolling basis. **Financial aid:** Priority date 3/1; no closing date. FAFSA required. Applicants notified on a rolling basis; must reply within 2 week(s) of notification.

**Academics. Special study options:** Double major, dual enrollment of high school students. **Credit/placement by examination:** CLEP, institutional tests. 30 credit hours maximum toward associate degree. **Support services:** Learning center, reduced course load, remedial instruction, tutoring.

**Majors. Biology:** General. **Business:** General, administrative services, banking/financial services, business admin, office/clerical, real estate. **Computer sciences:** General. **Construction:** Carpentry. **Education:** General. **Engineering technology:** Drafting. **Family/consumer sciences:** Child care. **Health:** Licensed practical nurse. **Interdisciplinary:** Biological/physical sciences. **Liberal arts:** Arts/sciences. **Math:** General. **Mechanic/repair:** Auto body. **Physical sciences:** Chemistry. **Protective services:** Police science. **Social sciences:** General, criminology. **Visual/performing arts:** General, commercial/advertising art, studio arts.

**Computing on campus.** 25 workstations in library, computer center.

**Student life. Activities:** Choral groups, drama, music ensembles, musical theater, student government, Mexican-American Student Association.

**Athletics.** NJCAA. **Intercollegiate:** Baseball M, basketball, tennis, volleyball W. **Team name:** Pirates.

**Student services.** Career counseling, student employment services, health services, on-campus daycare, personal counseling, placement for graduates, veterans' counselor. **Physically disabled:** Services for visually, speech, hearing impaired. **Transfer:** Transfer adviser for students transferring to 4-year colleges.

**Contact.** Phone: (209) 791-2220 Fax: (209) 784-4779
Virginia Gurrola, Vice President Student Services and Enrollment, Porterville College, 100 East College Avenue, Porterville, CA 93257

## Professional Golfers Career College
### Temecula, California
### www.golfcollege.edu                     CB code: 3548

- For-profit 2-year golf academy
- Commuter campus in small city

**General.** Accredited by ACICS. **Enrollment:** 130 degree-seeking undergraduates. **Degrees:** 217 associate awarded. **Location:** 60 miles from San Diego. **Calendar:** Semester. **Full-time faculty:** 6 total; 33% have terminal degrees. **Part-time faculty:** 18 total; 11% women. **Special facilities:** Pro shop, video studio.

**Basis for selection.** Open admission. Handicap of 20 or below, 3 letters of personal character reference, 1 letter of recommendation attesting to golf ability required. **Homeschooled:** Transcript of courses and grades, letter of recommendation (nonparent) required.

**2009-2010 Annual costs.** Tuition $5,590/semester for domestic students and $5,890/semester for international students; program lasts 4 semesters. Books/supplies: $200.

**Application procedures. Admission:** No deadline. $75 fee. Application must be submitted on paper. Admission notification on a rolling basis. **Financial aid:** No deadline.

**Academics. Credit/placement by examination:** CLEP.

**Majors. Parks/recreation:** Facilities management.

**Computing on campus.** Online library, wireless network available.

**Student life. Freshman orientation:** Mandatory. **Housing:** Single-sex dorms, apartments, wellness housing available. $700 nonrefundable deposit.

**Student services.** Alcohol/substance abuse counseling, career counseling, financial aid counseling, personal counseling, placement for graduates, veterans' counselor.

Two-Year Colleges

Two-Year Colleges

**Contact.** E-mail: admin@progolfed.com
Phone: (951) 719-2994 Toll-free number: (800) 877-4380
Fax: (951) 719-1643
Mark Bland, Admissions Director, Professional Golfers Career College, 26109 Ynez Road, Temecula, CA 92591

## Reedley College
Reedley, California
www.reedleycollege.edu    CB code: 4655

- Public 2-year community college
- Commuter campus in large town

**General.** Founded in 1926. Regionally accredited. Courses also offered at community campus sites in Madera, Clovis, Sanger, Easton, Selma, Kerman, Oakhurst, Parlier, Fowler, Orange Cove, Dinuba, Kingsburg, and Sunnyside. **Enrollment:** 15,234 undergraduates. **Degrees:** 696 associate awarded. **Location:** 25 miles from Fresno. **Calendar:** Semester, extensive summer session. **Full-time faculty:** 80 total. **Part-time faculty:** 190 total.

**Student profile.**

| 25 or older: | 35% | Live on campus: | 4% |
|---|---|---|---|

**Transfer out. Colleges most students transferred to 2009:** California State University: Fresno, California State University: Long Beach.

**Basis for selection.** Open admission. **Homeschooled:** If under 18, a letter from parent required.

**2009-2010 Annual costs.** Tuition/fees: $814; $6,514 out-of-state. Per-credit charge: $26 in-state; $216 out-of-state. Room/board: $5,504. Books/supplies: $1,566. Personal expenses: $2,600.

**2008-2009 Financial aid.** All financial aid based on need. Need-based aid available for part-time students. Work-study available for part-time students. **Additional information:** Board of Governors fee waiver available for low-income students. Book voucher available for EOPS students.

**Application procedures. Admission:** No deadline. No application fee. Admission notification on a rolling basis. **Financial aid:** Priority date 3/2; no closing date. FAFSA required. Applicants notified on a rolling basis starting 3/2; must reply within 3 week(s) of notification.

**Academics. Special study options:** Cooperative education, cross-registration, distance learning, double major, dual enrollment of high school students, ESL, honors, independent study, study abroad, weekend college. License preparation in aviation, dental hygiene. **Credit/placement by examination:** AP, CLEP. 48 credit hours maximum toward associate degree. **Support services:** Learning center, pre-admission summer program, reduced course load, remedial instruction, study skills assistance, tutoring, writing center.

**Majors. Agriculture:** Business, plant sciences. **Biology:** General. **Business:** Accounting. **Computer sciences:** General, computer science, information systems. **Conservation:** Forestry. **Education:** Early childhood, physical. **Foreign languages:** General. **Health:** Dental assistant. **Liberal arts:** Arts/sciences. **Math:** General. **Social sciences:** General. **Visual/performing arts:** Art, dramatic.

**Most popular majors.** Interdisciplinary studies 80%.

**Computing on campus.** 140 workstations in dormitories, library, computer center. Dormitories wired for high-speed internet access and linked to campus network. Commuter students can connect to campus network. Online course registration, online library available.

**Student life. Freshman orientation:** Available. Preregistration for classes offered. **Housing:** Single-sex dorms available. $125 deposit. **Activities:** Bands, choral groups, drama, music ensembles, musical theater, student government, student newspaper, symphony orchestra.

**Athletics.** NJCAA. **Intercollegiate:** Baseball M, basketball, equestrian, football (tackle) M, golf, softball W, tennis, track and field, volleyball W. **Team name:** Tigers.

**Student services.** Adult student services, alcohol/substance abuse counseling, career counseling, services for economically disadvantaged, student employment services, financial aid counseling, health services, minority student services, on-campus daycare, personal counseling, placement for graduates, veterans' counselor, women's services. **Physically disabled:** Services for visually, speech, hearing impaired. **Transfer:** Transfer adviser, college fairs on campus for students transferring to 4-year colleges.

**Contact.** Phone: (559) 638-0323 Fax: (559) 638-5040
Leticia Alvarez, Admissions and Records Manager, Reedley College, 995 North Reed Avenue, Reedley, CA 93654

## Rio Hondo College
Whittier, California
www.riohondo.edu    CB code: 4663

- Public 2-year community college
- Commuter campus in small city

**General.** Founded in 1960. Regionally accredited. **Enrollment:** 11,561 degree-seeking undergraduates; 4,065 non-degree-seeking students. **Degrees:** 833 associate awarded. **Location:** 15 miles from Los Angeles. **Calendar:** Semester, extensive summer session. **Full-time faculty:** 200 total; 43% minority, 52% women. **Part-time faculty:** 334 total; 41% minority, 47% women. **Special facilities:** Observatory, nature preserve.

**Student profile.** Among degree-seeking undergraduates, 2,524 enrolled as first-time, first-year students.

| Part-time: | 44% | Women: | 50% |
|---|---|---|---|
| Out-of-state: | 4% | | |

**Transfer out. Colleges most students transferred to 2009:** Cal State Los Angeles, Cal State Long Beach, Cal State Fullerton, Cal State Polytech, University of California-Los Angeles.

**Basis for selection.** Open admission, but selective for some programs. Nursing program has special requirements. **Learning Disabled:** Disabled Services Program available to students with disabilities.

**2009-2010 Annual costs.** Tuition/fees: $803; $6,293 out-of-state. Per-credit charge: $26 in-state; $209 out-of-state. Books/supplies: $1,566. Personal expenses: $3,024.

**2008-2009 Financial aid. Need-based:** Need-based aid available for part-time students.

**Application procedures. Admission:** No deadline. No application fee. Admission notification on a rolling basis. **Financial aid:** Priority date 7/15; no closing date. FAFSA required. Applicants notified on a rolling basis.

**Academics. Special study options:** Distance learning, dual enrollment of high school students, ESL, honors, independent study, study abroad, weekend college. **Credit/placement by examination:** CLEP, institutional tests. 12 credit hours maximum toward associate degree. **Support services:** Learning center, pre-admission summer program, remedial instruction, tutoring, writing center.

**Majors. Architecture:** Environmental design. **Area/ethnic studies:** Chicano/Hispanic-American/Latino. **Business:** Accounting. **Communications:** Journalism, media studies. **Communications technology:** General, graphic/printing. **Computer sciences:** General. **Engineering technology:** Drafting. **Health:** Health services, licensed practical nurse, nursing (RN). **Liberal arts:** Arts/sciences, library assistant. **Mechanic/repair:** Auto body, automotive. **Protective services:** Fire safety technology, police science. **Social sciences:** Geography. **Visual/performing arts:** General, commercial/advertising art, dance, dramatic, photography.

**Most popular majors.** Business/marketing 12%, education 7%, health sciences 14%, interdisciplinary studies 42%, public administration/social services 19%.

**Computing on campus.** Online course registration, wireless network available.

**Student life. Freshman orientation:** Available. **Activities:** Jazz band, choral groups, dance, drama, film society, literary magazine, music ensembles, musical theater, radio station, student government, student newspaper, TV station.

**Athletics.** NJCAA. **Intercollegiate:** Baseball M, basketball, cross-country, golf, soccer, softball W, swimming, tennis, track and field, volleyball W, water polo, wrestling M. **Team name:** Roadrunners.

**Student services.** Career counseling, student employment services, financial aid counseling, health services, on-campus daycare, personal counseling, veterans' counselor. **Physically disabled:** Services for visually, speech, hearing impaired. **Transfer:** Transfer center, transfer adviser, college fairs on campus for students transferring to 4-year colleges.

**Contact.** Phone: (562) 908-3415 Fax: (562) 692-8318
Judy Pearson, Director of Admissions and Records, Rio Hondo College, 3600 Workman Mill Road, Whittier, CA 90601-1699

## Riverside Community College
**Riverside, California**  **CB member**
www.rcc.edu  **CB code: 4658**

- Public 2-year community college
- Commuter campus in large city

**General.** Founded in 1916. Regionally accredited. **Enrollment:** 37,254 undergraduates. **Degrees:** 2,513 associate awarded. **ROTC:** Army, Naval, Air Force. **Location:** 60 miles from Los Angeles. **Calendar:** Semester, limited summer session. **Full-time faculty:** 347 total; 22% minority. **Part-time faculty:** 1,072 total; 30% minority. **Class size:** 49% < 20, 44% 20-39, 4% 40-49, 2% 50-99, less than 1% >100. **Special facilities:** Planetarium.

**Student profile.**

Out-of-state: 1%  25 or older: 36%

**Transfer out. Colleges most students transferred to 2009:** University of California: Riverside, California State University: San Bernardino.

**Basis for selection.** Open admission. Limited admission to nursing program.

**2009-2010 Annual costs.** Tuition/fees: $814; $6,244 out-of-state. Per-credit charge: $26 in-state; $207 out-of-state. Books/supplies: $1,638. Personal expenses: $2,826.

**2008-2009 Financial aid. Need-based:** Need-based aid available for part-time students. Work-study available nights, weekends and for part-time students. **Non-need-based:** Scholarships awarded for academics, alumni affiliation, art, leadership, minority status, music/drama, state residency.

**Application procedures. Admission:** No deadline. No application fee. Admission notification on a rolling basis. **Financial aid:** Priority date 3/1; no closing date. FAFSA, institutional form required. Applicants notified on a rolling basis starting 7/1.

**Academics.** Honor Society (Alpha Gamma Sigma) for freshmen with 3.0 GPA. **Special study options:** Cooperative education, distance learning, double major, dual enrollment of high school students, ESL, honors, internships, study abroad, weekend college. License preparation in nursing. **Credit/placement by examination:** CLEP, institutional tests. 30 credit hours maximum toward associate degree. **Support services:** GED preparation, learning center, remedial instruction, study skills assistance, tutoring, writing center.

**Majors. Business:** General, accounting, administrative services, business admin, marketing, office technology, real estate. **Communications technology:** Graphic/printing. **Computer sciences:** General, programming. **Construction:** Maintenance. **Education:** Early childhood. **Engineering:** General. **Engineering technology:** Construction, drafting, electrical. **Family/consumer sciences:** General, food/nutrition. **Foreign languages:** Sign language interpretation. **Health:** Dental lab technology, licensed practical nurse, medical assistant, medical secretary, medical transcription, nursing (RN). **Legal studies:** Legal secretary. **Mechanic/repair:** General, auto body, automotive, heating/ac/refrig. **Personal/culinary services:** Cosmetic. **Protective services:** Fire safety technology. **Public administration:** Human services. **Social sciences:** Cartography. **Visual/performing arts:** Commercial/advertising art, photography.

**Most popular majors.** Health sciences 11%, interdisciplinary studies 35%, liberal arts 46%.

**Computing on campus.** 200 workstations in library, computer center. Online course registration, online library, helpline, repair service, wireless network available.

**Student life. Freshman orientation:** Available. **Housing:** No dormitories are available. **Activities:** Bands, choral groups, dance, drama, international student organizations, literary magazine, music ensembles, Model UN, musical theater, student government, student newspaper, TV station, College Democrats, MECHA, Latter-day Saints student association, multicultural advisory council, African American student union.

**Athletics. Intercollegiate:** Baseball M, basketball, cross-country, diving, football (tackle) M, golf, soccer, softball W, swimming, tennis, track and field, volleyball W, water polo. **Intramural:** Badminton, baseball M, basketball, bowling, golf, racquetball, soccer, tennis, volleyball. **Team name:** Tigers.

**Student services.** Adult student services, career counseling, services for economically disadvantaged, student employment services, financial aid counseling, health services, on-campus daycare, personal counseling, placement for graduates, veterans' counselor. **Physically disabled:** Services for visually, speech, hearing impaired. **Transfer:** Transfer center, transfer adviser, college fairs on campus for students transferring to 4-year colleges.

**Contact.** E-mail: webmstr@rcc.edu
Phone: (951) 222-8600 Fax: (951) 222-8028
Lorraine Anderson, District Dean, Admissions and Records, Riverside Community College, 4800 Magnolia Avenue, Riverside, CA 92506

## Sacramento City College
**Sacramento, California**
www.scc.losrios.edu  **CB code: 4670**

- Public 2-year community college
- Commuter campus in large city

**General.** Founded in 1916. Regionally accredited. **Enrollment:** 26,412 undergraduates. **Degrees:** 1,257 associate awarded. **ROTC:** Army, Naval, Air Force. **Location:** 75 miles from San Francisco. **Calendar:** Semester, extensive summer session. **Full-time faculty:** 290 total. **Part-time faculty:** 140 total. **Special facilities:** Observatory.

**Student profile.**

Out-of-state: 5%  25 or older: 68%

**Basis for selection.** Open admission.

**2009-2010 Annual costs.** Tuition/fees: $812; $6,512 out-of-state. Per-credit charge: $26 in-state; $216 out-of-state. Books/supplies: $1,638. Personal expenses: $2,826.

**Financial aid. Need-based:** Need-based aid available for part-time students. Work-study available nights, weekends and for part-time students.

**Application procedures. Admission:** Priority date 7/28; no deadline. No application fee. Admission notification on a rolling basis. **Financial aid:** Priority date 3/2; no closing date. FAFSA required. Applicants notified on a rolling basis starting 7/1; must reply within 2 week(s) of notification.

**Academics. Special study options:** Accelerated study, cooperative education, cross-registration, distance learning, double major, dual enrollment of high school students, ESL, honors, independent study, internships, study abroad, weekend college. License preparation in aviation, dental hygiene, nursing, physical therapy, real estate. **Credit/placement by examination:** CLEP, institutional tests. 15 credit hours maximum toward associate degree. **Support services:** Learning center, remedial instruction, study skills assistance, tutoring, writing center.

**Majors. Area/ethnic studies:** Women's. **Business:** General, accounting, administrative services, international marketing, management information systems, office/clerical, real estate. **Communications:** Journalism. **Communications technology:** Graphic/printing. **Computer sciences:** General. **Education:** Bilingual, special. **Engineering technology:** Drafting. **Family/consumer sciences:** General, child care, clothing/textiles, family/community services. **Health:** Dental assistant, dental hygiene, licensed practical nurse, medical secretary, nursing (RN), occupational therapy assistant, physical therapy assistant. **Legal studies:** Legal secretary. **Liberal arts:** Arts/sciences, library assistant. **Math:** General. **Mechanic/repair:** Aircraft, electronics/electrical, heating/ac/refrig. **Personal/culinary services:** Cosmetic. **Protective services:** Corrections, police science. **Social sciences:** General. **Visual/performing arts:** General, commercial photography, dramatic, music management, studio arts.

**Computing on campus.** 350 workstations in library, computer center. Online course registration available.

**Student life. Freshman orientation:** Available. **Activities:** Bands, choral groups, dance, drama, literary magazine, music ensembles, musical theater, student government, student newspaper, minority groups, professional associations, Bible club, gay and lesbian student alliance, special interest groups.

**Athletics. Intercollegiate:** Baseball M, basketball, cross-country, football (tackle) M, golf W, soccer W, softball W, swimming, tennis, track and field, volleyball W, water polo W, wrestling M. **Intramural:** Badminton, baseball M, basketball, bowling, boxing M, fencing, football (tackle) M, golf, handball, racquetball, softball, swimming, table tennis, tennis, volleyball. **Team name:** Panthers.

**Student services.** Adult student services, career counseling, services for economically disadvantaged, student employment services, financial aid counseling, health services, on-campus daycare, personal counseling, placement for graduates, veterans' counselor. **Physically disabled:** Services for visually, speech, hearing impaired. **Transfer:** Transfer center, transfer adviser, college fairs on campus for students transferring to 4-year colleges.

**Contact.** E-mail: sccaeinfo@scc.losrios.edu
Phone: (916) 558-2351 Fax: (916) 558-2190
Catherine Fites, Dean of Enrollment and Student Services, Sacramento City College, 3835 Freeport Boulevard, Sacramento, CA 95822

## Saddleback College
### Mission Viejo, California
### www.saddleback.edu
**CB code: 4747**

- Public 2-year community college
- Commuter campus in small city

**General.** Founded in 1967. Regionally accredited. **Enrollment:** 28,104 undergraduates. **Degrees:** 1,004 associate awarded. **Location:** 55 miles from Los Angeles and San Diego. **Calendar:** Semester, limited summer session. **Full-time faculty:** 223 total. **Part-time faculty:** 509 total. **Special facilities:** Solar observatory, outdoor environmental laboratory, golf driving range, computer/technology centers, greenhouse.

**Basis for selection.** Open admission, but selective for some programs. Nursing candidates must complete core curriculum with 2.5 GPA or better before screening process. SAT/ACT recommended for placement and counseling.

**High school preparation.** 10 units recommended. Recommended units include English 3, mathematics 2, social studies 3 and science 2.

**2009-2010 Annual costs.** Tuition/fees: $814; $6,514 out-of-state. Per-credit charge: $26 in-state; $216 out-of-state. Books/supplies: $1,638. Personal expenses: $2,826.

**2008-2009 Financial aid.** All financial aid based on need. Need-based aid available for part-time students. Work-study available for part-time students.

**Application procedures. Admission:** No deadline. No application fee. Admission notification on a rolling basis. **Financial aid:** Closing date 6/30. FAFSA required. Applicants notified on a rolling basis starting 4/1.

**Academics. Special study options:** Cooperative education, cross-registration, distance learning, double major, dual enrollment of high school students, ESL, honors, independent study, internships, student-designed major, study abroad, weekend college. License preparation in nursing, paramedic, real estate. **Credit/placement by examination:** AP, CLEP, institutional tests. 30 credit hours maximum toward associate degree. **Support services:** Learning center, pre-admission summer program, reduced course load, remedial instruction, study skills assistance, tutoring, writing center.

**Honors college/program.** Overall GPA of 3.25 in all academic work required.

**Majors. Agriculture:** Ornamental horticulture. **Area/ethnic studies:** Women's. **Biology:** General. **Business:** General, accounting, administrative services, business admin, fashion, marketing, office management, real estate, tourism/travel. **Communications:** Broadcast journalism, journalism. **Computer sciences:** General, computer science, programming. **Conservation:** General, environmental studies. **Education:** Early childhood, family/consumer sciences, mathematics, music, physical, social science. **Engineering:** General. **Engineering technology:** Drafting. **Family/consumer sciences:** General, food/nutrition. **Foreign languages:** General, sign language interpretation. **Health:** Medical assistant, nursing (RN), surgical technology. **History:** General. **Interdisciplinary:** Natural sciences. **Legal studies:** Legal secretary, paralegal. **Liberal arts:** Arts/sciences. **Math:** General. **Parks/recreation:** Health/fitness. **Philosophy/religion:** Philosophy. **Physical sciences:** Astronomy, chemistry, geology, physics. **Psychology:** General. **Social sciences:** General, anthropology, economics, geography, international relations, political science, sociology. **Visual/performing arts:** Art, commercial photography, commercial/advertising art, dance, design, dramatic, fashion design, interior design, photography, studio arts.

**Most popular majors.** Business/marketing 13%, health sciences 11%, liberal arts 42%.

**Computing on campus.** 1,030 workstations in library, computer center, student center. Commuter students can connect to campus network. Online course registration, online library, wireless network available.

**Student life. Activities:** Bands, choral groups, dance, drama, literary magazine, music ensembles, musical theater, radio station, student government, student newspaper, symphony orchestra, TV station, Democratic Club, Republican Club, Christian Club, Black United Students, Hillel, Gay and Lesbian Club, Amnesty International, Muslim Student Union, environmental awareness, sign language club.

**Athletics.** NJCAA. **Intercollegiate:** Baseball M, basketball, cheerleading M, cross-country, diving, football (tackle) M, golf, soccer W, softball W, swimming, tennis, track and field, volleyball W, water polo. **Team name:** Gauchos.

**Student services.** Adult student services, alcohol/substance abuse counseling, career counseling, services for economically disadvantaged, student employment services, health services, on-campus daycare, personal counseling, placement for graduates, veterans' counselor, women's services. **Physically disabled:** Services for visually, speech, hearing impaired. **Transfer:** Re-entry adviser for new students. Transfer center, transfer adviser, college fairs on campus for students transferring to 4-year colleges.

**Contact.** E-mail: scadmissions@saddleback.edu
Phone: (949) 582-4555 Fax: (949) 347-8315
Jane Rosenkrans, Director, Admissions, Records and Enrollment Services, Saddleback College, 28000 Marguerite Parkway, Mission Viejo, CA 92692

## Sage College
### Moreno Valley, California
### www.sagecollege.edu

- For-profit 2-year technical college
- Commuter campus in large city

**General.** Accredited by ACICS. **Enrollment:** 258 full-time, degree-seeking students. **Degrees:** 1 associate awarded. **Calendar:** Quarter. **Full-time faculty:** 13 total. **Part-time faculty:** 15 total.

**Basis for selection.** Satisfactory performance on institutional examination required. **Homeschooled:** State high school equivalency certificate required.

**2009-2010 Annual costs.** Tuition/fees: $8,455. Books/supplies: $800.

**Application procedures. Admission:** No deadline. $100 fee. Admission notification on a rolling basis.

**Academics. Credit/placement by examination:** CLEP.

**Majors. Legal studies:** Court reporting, paralegal.

**Student life. Freshman orientation:** Mandatory.

**Student services.** Career counseling, financial aid counseling, placement for graduates.

**Contact.** E-mail: admissions@sagecollege.edu
Phone: (951) 781-2727
Lauren Somma, Executive Director, Sage College, 12125 Day Street, Building L, Moreno Valley, CA 92557-6720

## Salvation Army College for Officer Training at Crestmont
### Rancho Palos Verdes, California
### www.crestmont.edu
**CB code: 3890**

- Private 2-year seminary college
- Residential campus in small city

**General.** Regionally accredited. Christian education for Salvation Army officer candidates and others. Officers ordained ministers who manage human service programs and ministries in western US and overseas. Require applicants to have at least 1 year membership in local corps (church). Admissions inquiries should be directed to local Salvation Army community centers. **Enrollment:** 71 degree-seeking undergraduates. **Degrees:** 16 associate awarded. **Calendar:** Semester. **Full-time faculty:** 24 total. **Part-time faculty:** 6 total. **Special facilities:** Salvation Army museum.

**Basis for selection.** Open admission. High school diploma, Salvation Army officer candidate status required.

**2009-2010 Annual costs.** Tuition/fees: $5,265. Tuition includes on-campus room and board. Books/supplies: $750.

**Application procedures. Admission:** No deadline. No application fee.

**Academics. Credit/placement by examination:** CLEP.

**Majors. Theology:** Missionary.

**Student life. Housing:** Housing for both students and families.

**Contact.** Phone: (310) 377-0481
Major, John Brackenbury, Director of Admissions, Salvation Army College for Officer Training at Crestmont, 30840 Hawthorne Boulevard, Rancho Palos Verdes, CA 90275

## San Bernardino Valley College
### San Bernardino, California
www.valleycollege.edu                    CB code: 4679

◗ Public 2-year community college
◗ Small city

**General.** Founded in 1926. Regionally accredited. **Enrollment:** 14,435 undergraduates. **Degrees:** 699 associate awarded. **Location:** 60 miles from Los Angeles. **Calendar:** Semester, limited summer session. **Full-time faculty:** 161 total. **Part-time faculty:** 391 total. **Special facilities:** Planetarium.

**Basis for selection.** Open admission, but selective for some programs. Special requirements for nursing program. **Homeschooled:** Transcript of courses and grades required.

**2009-2010 Annual costs.** Tuition/fees: $826; $6,646 out-of-state. Per-credit charge: $26 in-state; $220 out-of-state. Books/supplies: $1,638. Personal expenses: $2,000.

**Application procedures. Admission:** No deadline. No application fee. **Financial aid:** Priority date 5/25; no closing date. Applicants notified on a rolling basis starting 5/1; must reply within 2 week(s) of notification.

**Academics. Special study options:** Cooperative education, cross-registration, distance learning, double major, dual enrollment of high school students, ESL, honors, independent study, internships, liberal arts/career combination, weekend college. Service Members Opportunity College. **Credit/placement by examination:** AP, CLEP, institutional tests. **Support services:** GED preparation, learning center, pre-admission summer program, reduced course load, remedial instruction, study skills assistance, tutoring, writing center.

**Majors. Biology:** General. **Business:** Accounting, business admin, real estate. **Communications:** General. **Computer sciences:** Computer science, systems analysis. **Engineering technology:** Electrical. **Liberal arts:** Arts/sciences, library assistant. **Math:** General. **Mechanic/repair:** Automotive, diesel, electronics/electrical, heating/ac/refrig. **Physical sciences:** Astronomy, chemistry, geology, physics. **Protective services:** Law enforcement admin. **Psychology:** General. **Public administration:** Social work. **Social sciences:** Geography. **Transportation:** Aviation management. **Visual/performing arts:** Commercial/advertising art.

**Computing on campus.** 180 workstations in library, computer center, student center.

**Student life. Freshman orientation:** Available. **Activities:** Choral groups, drama, literary magazine, music ensembles, musical theater, radio station, student government, student newspaper, TV station, Campus Crusade for Christ, Newman Club, Baptist Student Union, Movimiento Estudiantil Chicano de Aztlan, Black Student Union, Young Democrats, Young Republicans.

**Athletics.** NCAA. **Intercollegiate:** Baseball M, basketball, cross-country, football (tackle) M, soccer, softball W, track and field, volleyball W. **Team name:** Wolverines.

**Student services.** Adult student services, career counseling, services for economically disadvantaged, student employment services, financial aid counseling, health services, on-campus daycare, personal counseling, placement for graduates, veterans' counselor. **Physically disabled:** Services for visually, speech, hearing impaired. **Transfer:** Pre-admission transcript evaluation for new students.

**Contact.** E-mail: admissions@valleycollege.edu
Phone: (909) 384-4401
Dan Angelo, Associate Dean of Enrollment, San Bernardino Valley College, 701 South Mount Vernon Avenue, San Bernardino, CA 92410

## San Diego City College
### San Diego, California
www.sdccd.edu                    CB code: 4681

◗ Public 2-year community and junior college
◗ Commuter campus in very large city

**General.** Founded in 1914. Regionally accredited. **Enrollment:** 9,956 degree-seeking undergraduates. **Degrees:** 667 associate awarded. **ROTC:** Army, Air Force. **Location:** Downtown. **Calendar:** Semester, extensive summer session. **Full-time faculty:** 159 total; 87% minority. **Part-time faculty:** 561 total; 26% minority. **Special facilities:** Computerized independent study and learning laboratories, vocational training centers.

**Student profile.** Among degree-seeking undergraduates, 3% enrolled in a vocational program, 8% already have a bachelor's degree or higher, 9,956 transferred in from other institutions.

**Out-of-state:**          6%     **25 or older:**          50%

**Basis for selection.** Open admission. High school students seeking college admission must submit an approved application certified by parents, principal, registrar, and/or school district official.

**2009-2010 Annual costs.** Tuition/fees: $814; $6,514 out-of-state. Per-credit charge: $26 in-state; $216 out-of-state. Books/supplies: $1,638. Personal expenses: $3,096.

**2008-2009 Financial aid.** All financial aid based on need. Need-based aid available for part-time students. Work-study available for part-time students.

**Application procedures. Admission:** No deadline. No application fee. **Financial aid:** Priority date 4/15; no closing date. FAFSA required. Applicants notified on a rolling basis starting 7/1; must reply within 4 week(s) of notification.

**Academics. Special study options:** Accelerated study, cooperative education, cross-registration, double major, dual enrollment of high school students, honors, independent study, internships, liberal arts/career combination, student-designed major, study abroad, teacher certification program, weekend college. **Credit/placement by examination:** AP, CLEP, institutional tests. 15 credit hours maximum toward associate degree. **Support services:** Learning center, pre-admission summer program, reduced course load, remedial instruction, study skills assistance, tutoring, writing center.

**Majors. Area/ethnic studies:** African, African-American, Latin American. **Biology:** General. **Business:** General, accounting, administrative services, business admin, labor relations, management information systems, management science, office technology, office/clerical, operations, purchasing, real estate, tourism promotion. **Communications:** Broadcast journalism. **Communications technology:** General. **Computer sciences:** General, applications programming, data entry, data processing, information systems, systems analysis. **Construction:** Pipefitting, power transmission. **Education:** Bilingual. **Engineering:** General. **Engineering technology:** Drafting, electrical, manufacturing. **Family/consumer sciences:** Child care. **Foreign languages:** General, French, Italian, Spanish. **Health:** Nursing (RN), substance abuse counseling. **History:** General. **Interdisciplinary:** Behavioral sciences. **Legal studies:** Paralegal, prelaw. **Liberal arts:** Arts/sciences. **Math:** General, applied. **Mechanic/repair:** Heating/ac/refrig. **Parks/recreation:** Health/fitness. **Philosophy/religion:** Philosophy. **Physical sciences:** Chemistry, geology, physics. **Psychology:** General. **Science technology:** Biological. **Social sciences:** General, anthropology, geography, political science. **Visual/performing arts:** General, art history/conservation, commercial/advertising art, dramatic, photography, studio arts.

**Most popular majors.** Business/marketing 8%, health sciences 8%, interdisciplinary studies 9%, liberal arts 40%.

**Computing on campus.** 150 workstations in library, computer center, student center. Online course registration, online library, helpline, repair service available.

**Student life. Freshman orientation:** Available. **Activities:** Jazz band, choral groups, dance, drama, film society, musical theater, radio station, student government, student newspaper, symphony orchestra, TV station, Arabic club, Italian club, MECHA, National Society of Black Engineers, Society of Hispanic Professional Engineers, California Coalition Against Poverty, students for labor and solidarity, lesbian, gay, bisexual and transsexual student union.

**Athletics. Intercollegiate:** Baseball, basketball M, cross-country, football (tackle) M, golf, soccer, softball W, tennis, track and field, volleyball. **Intramural:** Archery, badminton, baseball M, basketball, bowling, racquetball, soccer, tennis, track and field, volleyball, weight lifting. **Team name:** Knights.

**Student services.** Adult student services, career counseling, student employment services, health services, on-campus daycare, personal counseling, placement for graduates, veterans' counselor. **Physically disabled:** Services for visually, speech, hearing impaired. **Transfer:** Pre-admission transcript evaluation for new students. Transfer center, transfer adviser, college fairs on campus for students transferring to 4-year colleges.

**Contact.** Phone: (619) 388-3475 Fax: (619) 388-3505
Lou Humphries, Student Services Supervisor II, San Diego City College, 1313 Park Boulevard, San Diego, CA 92101-4787

## San Diego Mesa College
San Diego, California      **CB member**
www.sdmesa.edu      **CB code: 4735**

- Public 2-year community college
- Commuter campus in very large city

**General.** Founded in 1964. Regionally accredited. **Enrollment:** 22,423 undergraduates. **Degrees:** 915 associate awarded. **Calendar:** Semester, limited summer session. **Full-time faculty:** 320 total. **Part-time faculty:** 599 total. **Special facilities:** Anthropology museum.

**Student profile.**

Out-of-state:      1%      25 or older:      43%

**Transfer out.** Colleges most students transferred to 2009: San Diego State University, University of California: San Diego.

**Basis for selection.** Open admission. Students without high school diploma or equivalent admitted provisionally. **Learning Disabled:** Disabled Student Service Program (DSPS) available.

**2009-2010 Annual costs.** Tuition/fees: $814; $6,514 out-of-state. Per-credit charge: $26 in-state; $216 out-of-state. Books/supplies: $1,422. Personal expenses: $1,584.

**Application procedures. Admission:** No deadline. No application fee. Admission notification on a rolling basis. Applications not accepted by mail. **Financial aid:** Priority date 3/2; no closing date. FAFSA required. Applicants notified on a rolling basis starting 6/15; must reply within 3 week(s) of notification.

**Academics. Special study options:** Accelerated study, distance learning, double major, dual enrollment of high school students, honors, independent study, internships, liberal arts/career combination, student-designed major, study abroad, teacher certification program. License preparation in dental hygiene, physical therapy, radiology, real estate. **Credit/placement by examination:** CLEP, institutional tests. 15 credit hours maximum toward associate degree. Institutional test required for placement and counseling. **Support services:** Learning center, reduced course load, remedial instruction, study skills assistance, tutoring.

**Majors. Agriculture:** Animal health. **Architecture:** Landscape. **Area/ethnic studies:** African, African-American, Chicano/Hispanic-American/Latino. **Biology:** General. **Business:** General, accounting, business admin, fashion, hotel/motel admin, real estate, tourism/travel. **Computer sciences:** Programming, web page design. **Education:** Physical, sales/marketing, speech. **Engineering:** General. **Engineering technology:** Construction, water quality. **Family/consumer sciences:** Child development. **Foreign languages:** American Sign Language, French, Spanish. **Health:** Dental assistant, dental lab technology, medical assistant, medical radiologic technology/radiation therapy, physical therapy assistant. **Liberal arts:** Arts/sciences. **Math:** General. **Personal/culinary services:** Culinary arts. **Philosophy/religion:** Philosophy. **Physical sciences:** Chemistry, physics. **Psychology:** General. **Social sciences:** General, anthropology, sociology. **Visual/performing arts:** Art, dramatic, interior design, studio arts.

**Most popular majors.** Business/marketing 10%, liberal arts 20%.

**Computing on campus.** Commuter students can connect to campus network. Online library available.

**Student life. Freshman orientation:** Available. **Activities:** Concert band, choral groups, dance, drama, music ensembles, student government, student newspaper.

**Athletics. Intercollegiate:** Badminton W, baseball M, basketball, cross-country, diving, football (tackle) M, soccer, softball W, swimming, tennis, track and field, volleyball, water polo. **Team name:** Olympians.

**Student services.** Adult student services, career counseling, health services, on-campus daycare, personal counseling, placement for graduates, veterans' counselor. **Physically disabled:** Services for visually, speech, hearing impaired. **Transfer:** Transfer center, transfer adviser, college fairs on campus for students transferring to 4-year colleges.

**Contact.** E-mail: csawyer@sdccd.edu
Phone: (619) 388-2682 Fax: (619) 388-2960
Ivonne Alvarez, Director of Admissions and Records, San Diego Mesa College, 7250 Mesa College Drive, San Diego, CA 92111

## San Diego Miramar College
San Diego, California
www.miramarcollege.net      **CB code: 4728**

- Public 2-year community college
- Commuter campus in very large city

**General.** Founded in 1969. Regionally accredited. **Enrollment:** 11,637 undergraduates. **Degrees:** 547 associate awarded. **Location:** 9 miles from downtown. **Calendar:** Semester, limited summer session. **Full-time faculty:** 91 total.

**Student profile.**

Out-of-state:      1%      25 or older:      45%

**Basis for selection.** Open admission.

**2009-2010 Annual costs.** Tuition/fees: $814; $6,514 out-of-state. Per-credit charge: $26 in-state; $216 out-of-state. Books/supplies: $1,638. Personal expenses: $3,096.

**2008-2009 Financial aid. Need-based:** Need-based aid available for part-time students. Work-study available for part-time students. **Additional information:** Private scholarships available.

**Application procedures. Admission:** No deadline. No application fee. Admission notification on a rolling basis. **Financial aid:** Priority date 3/2; no closing date. FAFSA required. Applicants notified on a rolling basis; must reply within 3 week(s) of notification.

**Academics. Special study options:** Accelerated study, cross-registration, distance learning, dual enrollment of high school students, honors, independent study, weekend college. **Credit/placement by examination:** CLEP. 15 credit hours maximum toward associate degree. Institutional placement tests required. **Support services:** Learning center, remedial instruction, study skills assistance, tutoring.

**Majors. Biology:** General. **Business:** Administrative services, business admin, marketing, office/clerical. **Communications:** General. **Computer sciences:** General. **Education:** Early childhood. **Family/consumer sciences:** Family studies. **Legal studies:** Paralegal. **Liberal arts:** Humanities. **Math:** General. **Mechanic/repair:** Aircraft, automotive, diesel, heavy equipment. **Parks/recreation:** Health/fitness. **Physical sciences:** Chemistry, physics. **Protective services:** Corrections, firefighting, law enforcement admin. **Psychology:** General. **Social sciences:** General. **Visual/performing arts:** Studio arts. **Other:** Art/visual studies, Aviation operations-professional pilot, Business management-mortgage brokerage and banking, Military studies, Occupational/technical studies, Pre-engineering studies, World language studies.

**Most popular majors.** Business/marketing 14%, legal studies 6%, liberal arts 29%, security/protective services 30%.

**Computing on campus.** 10 workstations in library, computer center.

**Student life. Activities:** Student government, student newspaper, Amnesty International, Child Development Professionals, Filipino American Association, Latin American club, Miramar Associated Gaming Imagination Club (MAGIC), parent student advisory board, Phi Theta Kappa.

**Athletics. Team name:** Jets.

**Student services.** Career counseling, services for economically disadvantaged, health services, on-campus daycare, personal counseling, veterans' counselor. **Physically disabled:** Services for visually, hearing impaired. **Transfer:** Transfer adviser, college fairs on campus for students transferring to 4-year colleges.

**Contact.** E-mail: dstack@sdccd.edu
Phone: (619) 388-7844 Fax: (619) 388-7915
Dana Stack, Student Services Supervisor II, San Diego Miramar College, 10440 Black Mountain Road, San Diego, CA 92126-2999

## San Joaquin Delta College
Stockton, California
www.deltacollege.edu      **CB code: 4706**

- Public 2-year community college
- Commuter campus in large city

**General.** Founded in 1935. Regionally accredited. 14 off-campus sites located in service district, including the new Mountain House Center in South San Joaquin County. **Enrollment:** 7,927 full-time, degree-seeking students.

**Degrees:** 2,086 associate awarded. **Location:** 45 miles from Sacramento. **Calendar:** Semester, extensive summer session. **Full-time faculty:** 236 total. **Part-time faculty:** 335 total. **Class size:** 48% <20, 40% 20-39, 7% 40-49, 5% 50-99, less than 1% >100. **Special facilities:** Planetarium, electron microscopy laboratory, farm laboratory, natural resources laboratory, 3 theaters. **Partnerships:** Nissan, General Motors, Caterpillar.

**Transfer out. Colleges most students transferred to 2009:** California State University: Stanislaus, California State University: Sacramento, University of the Pacific, California State Polytechnic University, University of California: Davis.

**Basis for selection.** Open admission, but selective for some programs. Limited admission to registered nursing, psychiatric technician, licensed vocational nursing, radiological technician, and police academy programs.

**2009-2010 Annual costs.** Tuition/fees: $782; $6,482 out-of-state. Per-credit charge: $26 in-state; $216 out-of-state. Books/supplies: $1,566. Personal expenses: $3,024.

**2008-2009 Financial aid. Need-based:** Need-based aid available for part-time students. Work-study available nights, weekends and for part-time students. **Non-need-based:** Scholarships awarded for academics, athletics. **Additional information:** Enrollment fee waivers available for low-income California residents.

**Application procedures. Admission:** No deadline. No application fee. Admission notification on a rolling basis beginning on or about 6/5. **Financial aid:** Closing date 6/30. FAFSA, institutional form required. Applicants notified on a rolling basis starting 5/1; must reply within 3 week(s) of notification.

**Academics. Special study options:** Cooperative education, distance learning, dual enrollment of high school students, ESL, internships, liberal arts/career combination, study abroad, weekend college. License preparation in nursing, real estate. **Credit/placement by examination:** AP, CLEP, IB, institutional tests. 15 credit hours maximum toward associate degree. All students taking more than one course must take ASSET or COMPASS for placement. AP and CLEP credit granted after 12 semester hours in residence completed. **Support services:** GED preparation, learning center, reduced course load, remedial instruction, study skills assistance, tutoring, writing center.

**Majors. Agriculture:** Agribusiness operations, agronomy, animal sciences, business, economics, food science, horticulture, ornamental horticulture, plant protection, plant sciences, soil science. **Architecture:** Landscape. **Biology:** General, botany, zoology. **Business:** General, accounting, administrative services, business admin, fashion, management information systems, managerial economics, office technology, office/clerical, real estate. **Communications:** Broadcast journalism, journalism. **Communications technology:** Graphic/printing. **Computer sciences:** General, computer science, data processing, database management, programming. **Conservation:** General, wildlife. **Construction:** Carpentry, maintenance, power transmission. **Engineering:** General, architectural. **Engineering technology:** Architectural, drafting, electrical, software. **Family/consumer sciences:** General, child care, food/nutrition, institutional food production. **Foreign languages:** French, German, Spanish. **Health:** EMT paramedic, medical radiologic technology/radiation therapy, mental health services, nursing (RN). **Interdisciplinary:** Natural sciences. **Legal studies:** Prelaw. **Liberal arts:** Arts/sciences. **Math:** General. **Mechanic/repair:** Heavy equipment, locksmithing. **Personal/culinary services:** Culinary arts. **Physical sciences:** Astronomy, chemistry, geology, physics. **Production:** Woodworking. **Protective services:** Fire safety technology, police science. **Psychology:** General. **Public administration:** General. **Social sciences:** General, anthropology. **Visual/performing arts:** General, crafts, fashion design, interior design, photography, studio arts.

**Most popular majors.** Business/marketing 9%, health sciences 8%, interdisciplinary studies 7%, liberal arts 62%.

**Computing on campus.** 220 workstations in library, computer center. Commuter students can connect to campus network. Online course registration, online library, helpline, wireless network available.

**Student life. Freshman orientation:** Available. **Activities:** Bands, choral groups, dance, drama, literary magazine, music ensembles, musical theater, radio station, student government, student newspaper, symphony orchestra, African-American Student Union, Movimiento Estudiantil Chicano de Aztlan, Vietnamese and Asian student clubs, International Student Association.

**Athletics.** NJCAA. **Intercollegiate:** Baseball M, basketball, cross-country, diving, football (tackle) M, golf M, soccer, softball W, swimming, tennis, track and field, volleyball W, water polo, wrestling M. **Intramural:** Baseball M, basketball, bowling, diving, fencing, golf, softball, swimming, tennis, track and field, volleyball. **Team name:** Mustangs.

**Student services.** Adult student services, alcohol/substance abuse counseling, career counseling, services for economically disadvantaged, student employment services, financial aid counseling, health services, legal services, minority student services, on-campus daycare, personal counseling, placement for graduates, veterans' counselor. **Physically disabled:** Services for visually, hearing impaired. **Transfer:** Re-entry adviser for new students. Transfer center, transfer adviser, college fairs on campus for students transferring to 4-year colleges.

**Contact.** Phone: (209) 954-5635 Fax: (209) 954-5644
Catherine Mooney, Registrar, San Joaquin Delta College, 5151 Pacific Avenue, Stockton, CA 95207-6370

## San Joaquin Valley College
### Visalia, California
www.sjvc.edu                                   CB code: 2052

- For-profit 2-year junior college
- Commuter campus in small city
- Application essay, interview required

**General.** Regionally accredited. Additional campuses in Bakersfield, Fresno, Modesto, Rancho Cordova, and Rancho Cucamonga. Aviation campus located in Fresno. **Enrollment:** 1,000 degree-seeking undergraduates. **Degrees:** 427 associate awarded. **Calendar:** Semester, extensive summer session. **Full-time faculty:** 50 total. **Part-time faculty:** 20 total.

**Student profile.** Among degree-seeking undergraduates, 100% enrolled in a vocational program.

**Basis for selection.** Open admission, but selective for some programs. Selective admission to allied health programs. Various programs use either Accuplacer or Wonderlick for placement. ACCUPLACER for placement in Math and English.

**2009-2010 Annual costs.** Tuition/fees: $12,450. Costs may vary by program, annual tuition includes textbooks and supplies.

**Application procedures. Admission:** No deadline. No application fee. Admission notification on a rolling basis. **Financial aid:** No deadline. FAFSA, institutional form required.

**Academics. Special study options:** Independent study, internships, liberal arts/career combination. License preparation in aviation, dental hygiene, nursing. **Credit/placement by examination:** CLEP. **Support services:** Learning center, remedial instruction, study skills assistance, tutoring.

**Majors. Business:** Business admin, construction management, human resources. **Computer sciences:** Computer support specialist. **Health:** Dental assistant, dental hygiene, EMT paramedic, health care admin, insurance coding, licensed practical nurse, massage therapy, medical assistant, medical records admin, medical secretary, nursing (RN), office assistant, pharmacy assistant, physician assistant, respiratory therapy technology, surgical technology, veterinary technology/assistant. **Mechanic/repair:** Aircraft, heating/ac/refrig. **Protective services:** Corrections.

**Computing on campus.** 100 workstations in library, computer center.

**Student life. Freshman orientation:** Mandatory. Preregistration for classes offered. Full day on Friday prior to start of classes, continues through first week. **Activities:** Student government, student newspaper.

**Student services.** Adult student services, career counseling, services for economically disadvantaged, student employment services, financial aid counseling, personal counseling, placement for graduates. **Transfer:** Pre-admission transcript evaluation for new students.

**Contact.** Phone: (559) 651-2500 Fax: (559) 651-0574
Susie Topjian, Enrollment Services Director, San Joaquin Valley College, 8400 West Mineral King Avenue, Visalia, CA 93291-9283

## San Jose City College
### San Jose, California
www.sjcc.edu                                   CB code: 4686

- Public 2-year community college
- Commuter campus in very large city

**General.** Founded in 1921. Regionally accredited. **Enrollment:** 12,156 undergraduates. **Degrees:** 333 associate awarded. **Location:** 55 miles from San Francisco. **Calendar:** Semester, limited summer session. **Full-time faculty:** 170 total. **Part-time faculty:** 230 total. **Partnerships:** Formal partnerships with Intel (Manufacturing Technology program), Laser Electro-Optics

Manufacturing Association (Laser Technology program), IntelSemiconductor (Mask Design Technology program).

**Transfer out. Colleges most students transferred to 2009:** San Jose State University, California State University: East Bay.

**Basis for selection.** Open admission.

**2009-2010 Annual costs.** Tuition/fees: $824; $6,554 out-of-state. Per-credit charge: $26 in-state; $217 out-of-state. Books/supplies: $1,638. Personal expenses: $3,096.

**2009-2010 Financial aid.** All financial aid based on need. **Additional information:** Board of Governors Grant (fee waivers) available to all qualified applicants.

**Application procedures. Admission:** No deadline. No application fee. **Financial aid:** Closing date 6/30. FAFSA required. Applicants notified on a rolling basis; must reply within 4 week(s) of notification.

**Academics. Special study options:** Accelerated study, cooperative education, dual enrollment of high school students, honors, independent study, weekend college. License preparation in real estate. **Credit/placement by examination:** CLEP, IB, institutional tests. 30 credit hours maximum toward associate degree. **Support services:** Learning center, pre-admission summer program, reduced course load, remedial instruction, tutoring.

**Majors. Business:** Accounting, administrative services, banking/financial services, entrepreneurial studies, labor studies, marketing, office technology, office/clerical, real estate. **Communications technology:** General. **Computer sciences:** General, applications programming, data entry, networking, programming. **Construction:** General, power transmission. **Education:** Early childhood. **Engineering technology:** Drafting, electrical, heat/ac/refrig, laser/optical. **Health:** Dental assistant, substance abuse counseling. **Liberal arts:** Arts/sciences. **Mechanic/repair:** Electronics/electrical, heating/ac/refrig. **Personal/culinary services:** Cosmetic, hair styling. **Production:** Machine tool. **Protective services:** Law enforcement admin. **Psychology:** General. **Social sciences:** General. **Visual/performing arts:** Studio arts.

**Computing on campus.** 250 workstations in library, computer center. Commuter students can connect to campus network. Online course registration available.

**Student life. Freshman orientation:** Available. **Activities:** Bands, choral groups, dance, drama, music ensembles, musical theater, radio station, student government, student newspaper, symphony orchestra.

**Athletics. Intercollegiate:** Baseball M, basketball, cross-country, football (tackle) M, golf M, softball W, track and field, volleyball W. **Team name:** Jaguars.

**Student services.** Career counseling, services for economically disadvantaged, student employment services, health services, minority student services, on-campus daycare, personal counseling, veterans' counselor. **Physically disabled:** Services for visually, speech, hearing impaired. **Transfer:** Transfer center, transfer adviser, college fairs on campus for students transferring to 4-year colleges.

**Contact.** Phone: (408) 288-3700 Fax: (408) 298-1935
Carlo Santos, Director of Admissions and Records, San Jose City College, 2100 Moorpark Avenue, San Jose, CA 95128-2798

## Santa Ana College
**Santa Ana, California**
**www.sac.edu**                                    **CB code: 4689**

- Public 2-year community college
- Commuter campus in large city

**General.** Founded in 1915. Regionally accredited. **Enrollment:** 10,536 degree-seeking undergraduates. **Degrees:** 1,294 associate awarded. **Location:** 40 miles from Los Angeles. **Calendar:** Semester, extensive summer session. **Full-time faculty:** 243 total; 40% minority, 59% women. **Part-time faculty:** 986 total; 28% minority, 39% women. **Class size:** 26% < 20, 31% 20-39, 20% 40-49, 22% 50-99, 2% >100. **Special facilities:** Planetarium, 2 art galleries, digital media center/digital incubator.

**Student profile.** Among degree-seeking undergraduates, 4,981 enrolled as first-time, first-year students, 2,067 transferred in from other institutions.

| African American: | 3% | Native American: | 1% |
|---|---|---|---|
| Asian American: | 16% | 25 or older: | 34% |
| Hispanic American: | 59% | | |

**Transfer out. Colleges most students transferred to 2009:** California State University: Fullerton, California State University: Long Beach, California State University: Irvine, California State University: Los Angeles.

**Basis for selection.** Open admission. All students 18 years and older who can benefit from instruction are admitted. **Adult students:** SAT/ACT scores not required.

**2009-2010 Annual costs.** Tuition/fees: $808; $6,508 out-of-state. Per-credit charge: $26 in-state; $216 out-of-state. Books/supplies: $1,500. Personal expenses: $2,928.

**2008-2009 Financial aid. Need-based:** 474 full-time freshmen applied for aid; 469 were judged to have need; 463 of these received aid. Average need met was 46%. Average scholarship/grant was $4,459; average loan $1,724. 82% of total undergraduate aid awarded as scholarships/grants, 18% as loans/jobs.

**Application procedures. Admission:** Priority date 4/1; no deadline. No application fee. Admission notification on a rolling basis. **Financial aid:** Priority date 6/30; no closing date. FAFSA required. Applicants notified on a rolling basis starting 6/1; must reply within 2 week(s) of notification.

**Academics. Special study options:** Cooperative education, distance learning, double major, dual enrollment of high school students, ESL, honors, independent study, internships, liberal arts/career combination, study abroad, weekend college. **Credit/placement by examination:** AP, CLEP, institutional tests. 30 credit hours maximum toward associate degree. **Support services:** GED preparation, learning center, pre-admission summer program, reduced course load, remedial instruction, study skills assistance, tutoring.

**Majors. Area/ethnic studies:** African-American, Chicano/Hispanic-American/Latino, women's. **Biology:** General. **Business:** Accounting, business admin, entrepreneurial studies, fashion, insurance, international, management science, marketing. **Communications:** General, advertising, broadcast journalism, journalism. **Computer sciences:** General, computer science, data processing. **Education:** Early childhood. **Engineering:** General. **Engineering technology:** Drafting. **Family/consumer sciences:** Family/community services, food/nutrition. **Foreign languages:** General. **Health:** Medical assistant, nursing (RN), occupational therapy assistant, pharmacy assistant. **History:** General. **Legal studies:** Paralegal. **Liberal arts:** Arts/sciences, library assistant. **Math:** General. **Mechanic/repair:** Automotive, diesel. **Parks/recreation:** Exercise sciences. **Philosophy/religion:** Philosophy. **Physical sciences:** Chemistry, geology, physics. **Production:** Welding. **Protective services:** Fire safety technology, fire services admin, firefighting, police science. **Psychology:** General. **Social sciences:** General, anthropology, economics, geography, political science, sociology. **Visual/performing arts:** General, commercial/advertising art, dance, dramatic, fashion design, photography.

**Most popular majors.** Business/marketing 9%, health sciences 14%, liberal arts 54%, security/protective services 7%.

**Computing on campus.** 66 workstations in library, computer center. Online course registration, wireless network available.

**Student life. Freshman orientation:** Available. **Activities:** Bands, choral groups, dance, drama, international student organizations, literary magazine, music ensembles, musical theater, radio station, student government, student newspaper, TV station.

**Athletics.** NJCAA. **Intercollegiate:** Baseball M, basketball, cross-country, football (tackle) M, soccer, softball W, track and field, volleyball, water polo, wrestling M. **Team name:** Dons.

**Student services.** Adult student services, alcohol/substance abuse counseling, career counseling, services for economically disadvantaged, student employment services, financial aid counseling, health services, minority student services, on-campus daycare, personal counseling, veterans' counselor, women's services. **Physically disabled:** Services for visually, speech, hearing impaired. **Transfer:** Re-entry adviser, pre-admission transcript evaluation for new students. Transfer center, transfer adviser, college fairs on campus for students transferring to 4-year colleges.

**Contact.** E-mail: adm_records@sac.edu
Phone: (714) 564-6042 Fax: (714) 564-6455
Mark Liang, Interim Director, Admissions and Records, Santa Ana College, 1530 West 17th Street, Santa Ana, CA 92706

## Santa Barbara Business College
**Santa Barbara, California**
**www.sbbcollege.edu**

- For-profit 2-year junior and career college
- Small city
- Interview required

**General.** Accredited by ACICS. Campuses located in Santa Barbara, Ventura, Santa Maria, Bakersfield, Palm Desert, and On-Line. **Enrollment:** 80 degree-seeking undergraduates. **Degrees:** 54 associate awarded. **Location:** 90 miles from Los Angeles. **Calendar:** Terms begin every 10 weeks. **Full-time faculty:** 5 total. **Part-time faculty:** 10 total.

**Basis for selection.** Admission decisions based on Wonderlic assessment and interview to determine interest and motivation of prospective student. **Homeschooled:** Transcript of courses and grades required. Need to take ATB proctored test if unable to supply an official transcript.

**2009-2010 Annual costs.** Costs for full programs as follows: medical assistant diploma: $20,940; medical assistant associate degree: $34,371; business administration associate degree: $35,216; business administration diploma: $21,226; massage therapy: $12,721; fitness trainer: $11,636; criminal justice associate degree: $35,511; paralegal diploma: $22,792; paralegal associate degree program: $34,871; pharmacy technician diploma: $21,814; pharmacy technician associate degree: $31,738; medical office systems diploma: $20,718. Tuition, fees, books, supplies, equipment included in program costs.

**Application procedures. Admission:** No deadline. $25 fee. **Financial aid:** No deadline. FAFSA required. Applicants notified on a rolling basis.

**Academics. Special study options:** License preparation in nursing. **Credit/placement by examination:** CLEP. **Support services:** Remedial instruction, study skills assistance, tutoring. .

**Majors. Business:** General. **Health:** Office assistant, pharmacy assistant. **Legal studies:** Paralegal. **Protective services:** Criminal justice.

**Computing on campus.** Online library available.

**Student life. Freshman orientation:** Mandatory.

**Contact.** Phone: (805) 967-9677 Fax: (805) 967-4248
Holly Ortiz, Director of Admissions, Santa Barbara Business College, 506 Chapala Street, Santa Barbara, CA 93101

## Santa Barbara Business College: Bakersfield
### Bakersfield, California
### www.sbbcollege.edu

- For-profit 2-year junior and career college
- Commuter campus in large city
- Interview required

**General.** Accredited by ACICS. Campuses located in Santa Barbara, Ventura, Santa Maria, Bakersfield, Palm Desert, and On-Line. **Enrollment:** 483 degree-seeking undergraduates. **Degrees:** 92 associate awarded. **Calendar:** Terms begin every 10 weeks. **Full-time faculty:** 10 total. **Part-time faculty:** 20 total.

**Basis for selection.** Admissions decisions based on Wonderlic assessment and interview to determine interest and motivation of prospective student. **Homeschooled:** Transcript of courses and grades required. Need to take ATB proctored test if unable to supply an official transcript.

**2009-2010 Annual costs.** Costs for full programs: medical office systems diploma, $20,860; medical assistant diploma, $20,651; medical assistant associate degree, $34,760; business administration associate degree, $35,118; criminal justice associate degree, $32,730; network systems administration diploma, $21,823; network systems administration associate degree, $31,958; paralegal diploma for students with 2 or 4-year degree in field, $22,756; paralegal associate degree, $34,777; pharmacy technician diploma, $21,656; pharmacy technician associate degree, $31,572; vocational nursing, $30,108; fitness trainer, $11,543; massage therapy, $12,620. Tuition, fees, books, supplies, equipment included in program costs.

**Application procedures. Admission:** No deadline. $25 fee. **Financial aid:** FAFSA required. Applicants notified on a rolling basis.

**Academics. Special study options:** License preparation in nursing. **Credit/placement by examination:** CLEP. **Support services:** GED preparation, remedial instruction, study skills assistance, tutoring.

**Majors. Business:** General. **Computer sciences:** LAN/WAN management. **Health:** Office assistant, pharmacy assistant. **Legal studies:** Paralegal. **Protective services:** Criminal justice.

**Computing on campus.** Online library available.

**Student life. Freshman orientation:** Mandatory.

**Contact.** Phone: (866) 749-7222
Holly Ortiz, Director of Admissions, Santa Barbara Business College: Bakersfield, 5300 California Avenue, Bakersfield, CA 93304

## Santa Barbara Business College: Palm Desert
### Palm Desert, California
### www.sbbcollege.edu

- For-profit 2-year junior and career college
- Small city
- Interview required

**General.** Regionally accredited; also accredited by ACICS. Campuses also located in Bakersfield, Ventura, Santa Barbara, Santa Maria and on-line. **Enrollment:** 183 degree-seeking undergraduates. **Calendar:** Continuous. Every 5 weeks. **Part-time faculty:** 12 total.

**Basis for selection.** Open admission.

**2009-2010 Annual costs.** Costs for full programs as follows: medical assistant diploma: $20,940; medical assistant associate degree: $34,371; business administration associate degree: $35,216; business administration diploma: $21,226; massage therapy: $12,721; fitness trainer: $11,636; criminal justice associate degree: $35,511; paralegal diploma: $22,792; paralegal associate degree program: $34,871; pharmacy technician diploma: $21,814; pharmacy technician associate degree: $31,738; medical office systems diploma: $20,718. Tuition, fees, books, supplies, equipment included in program costs.

**Application procedures. Financial aid:** No deadline.

**Academics. Credit/placement by examination:** CLEP.

**Majors. Business:** Business admin. **Health:** Medical assistant. **Legal studies:** Paralegal. **Protective services:** Criminal justice.

**Contact.** E-mail: hollyo@sbbcollege.edu
Phone: (866) 749-7222
Holly Ortiz, Director of Admissions, Santa Barbara Business College: Palm Desert, 75-030 Gerald Ford Drive, Building 2, Palm Desert, CA 92211

## Santa Barbara Business College: Santa Maria
### Santa Maria, California
### www.sbbcollege.edu

- For-profit 2-year junior and career college
- Small city
- Interview required

**General.** Accredited by ACICS. Campuses located in Santa Barbara, Ventura, Santa Maria, Bakersfield, Palm Desert, and On-Line. **Enrollment:** 296 degree-seeking undergraduates. **Degrees:** 60 associate awarded. **Location:** Located on Central Coast, halfway between Los Angeles and San Francisco. **Calendar:** Quarter. Terms begin every 10 weeks. **Full-time faculty:** 8 total. **Part-time faculty:** 12 total.

**Basis for selection.** Open admission, but selective for some programs. Admissions decisions based on Wonderlic assessment and interview to determine interest and motivation of prospective student. **Homeschooled:** Transcript of courses and grades required. Need to take ATB proctored test if unable to supply an official transcript.

**2009-2010 Annual costs.** Costs for full programs as follows: medical assistant diploma: $20,940; medical assistant associate degree: $34,371; business administration associate degree: $35,216; business administration diploma: $21,226; massage therapy: $12,721; fitness trainer: $11,636; criminal justice associate degree: $35,511; paralegal diploma: $22,792; paralegal associate degree program: $34,871; pharmacy technician diploma: $21,814; pharmacy technician associate degree: $31,738; medical office systems diploma: $20,718. Tuition, fees, books, supplies, equipment included in program costs.

**Application procedures. Admission:** No deadline. $25 fee. **Financial aid:** No deadline. FAFSA required. Applicants notified on a rolling basis.

**Academics. Special study options:** License preparation in nursing. **Credit/placement by examination:** CLEP. **Support services:** Remedial instruction, study skills assistance, tutoring.

**Majors. Business:** General. **Health:** Office assistant, pharmacy assistant. **Legal studies:** Paralegal. **Protective services:** Criminal justice.

**Computing on campus.** Online library available.

**Student life. Freshman orientation:** Mandatory.

**Student services.** Career counseling, placement for graduates.

**Contact.** Phone: (866) 749-7222 Toll-free number: (866) 749-7222 Fax: (805) 346-1862
Holly Ortiz, Director of Admissions, Santa Barbara Business College: Santa Maria, 303 East Plaza Drive, Santa Maria, CA 93454

## Santa Barbara Business College: Ventura
**Ventura, California**
**www.sbbcollege.edu**

- For-profit 2-year junior and career college
- Commuter campus in small city
- Interview required

**General.** Accredited by ACICS. Campuses located in Santa Barbara, Ventura, Santa Maria, Bakersfield, Palm Desert, and On-Line. **Enrollment:** 180 degree-seeking undergraduates. **Degrees:** 43 associate awarded. **Location:** 40 miles from Los Angeles. **Calendar:** Quarter. Terms begin every 10 weeks. **Full-time faculty:** 4 total. **Part-time faculty:** 27 total.

**Basis for selection.** Admission decisions based on Wonderlic assessment and interview to determine interest and motivation of prospective student. Wonderlic Basic Skills Test required. **Homeschooled:** Transcript of courses and grades required. Need to take ATB proctored test if unable to supply an official transcript.

**2009-2010 Annual costs.** Costs for full programs as follows: medical assistant diploma, $20,753; medical assistant associate degree, $34,832; business administration associate degree, $35,103; criminal justice associate degree, $32,747; paralegal diploma for students with 2 or 4-year degree in field, $22,791; paralegal associate degree, $34,809; fitness trainer, $11,753; massage therapy, $12,697; legal office system, $19,133. Tuition, fees, books, supplies, equipment included in program costs.

**Application procedures. Admission:** No deadline. $25 fee. **Financial aid:** No deadline. FAFSA required. Applicants notified on a rolling basis.

**Academics. Credit/placement by examination:** CLEP. **Support services:** GED preparation, learning center, remedial instruction, study skills assistance, tutoring.

**Majors. Business:** Business admin. **Health:** Office assistant. **Legal studies:** Paralegal. **Protective services:** Criminal justice.

**Computing on campus.** Online library available.

**Student life. Freshman orientation:** Mandatory.

**Contact.** Phone: (866) 749-7222 Fax: (805) 339-2994
Holly Ortiz, Director of Admissions, Santa Barbara Business College: Ventura, 4839 Market Street, Ventura, CA 93003

## Santa Barbara City College
**Santa Barbara, California**
**www.sbcc.edu**                    CB code: 4690

- Public 2-year community college
- Commuter campus in small city

**General.** Founded in 1908. Regionally accredited. **Enrollment:** 20,448 undergraduates. **Degrees:** 1,196 associate awarded. **Location:** 90 miles from Los Angeles. **Calendar:** Semester, limited summer session. **Full-time faculty:** 266 total; 20% minority, 54% women. **Part-time faculty:** 553 total; 18% minority, 58% women. **Class size:** 18% < 20, 65% 20-39, 10% 40-49, 4% 50-99, 2% >100.

**Student profile.**

Out-of-state:          7%     25 or older:          25%

**Transfer out. Colleges most students transferred to 2009:** University of California: Santa Barbara, California State University: Northridge, San Francisco State University, San Diego State University, University of California: Los Angeles.

**Basis for selection.** Open admission, but selective for some programs. Special requirements for hotel/restaurant/culinary, nursing, radiography, early childhood education, cosmetology, marine diving technology programs. Criteria vary by program. Interview required of nursing, hotel and restaurant management, marine technology majors. Audition required of some music and theater majors. **Adult students:** English assessment test required for placement.

**2009-2010 Annual costs.** Tuition/fees: $866; $6,566 out-of-state. Per-credit charge: $26 in-state; $216 out-of-state. Books/supplies: $1,566. Personal expenses: $3,024.

**2009-2010 Financial aid. Need-based:** Need-based aid available for part-time students. **Additional information:** California residents may qualify for Board of Governor's Financial Assistance Program, which will allow institutions to waive enrollment fee.

**Application procedures. Admission:** Priority date 2/1; deadline 8/21 (receipt date). No application fee. Admission notification on a rolling basis beginning on or about 3/1. **Financial aid:** No deadline. FAFSA required. Applicants notified on a rolling basis starting 5/1; must reply within 2 week(s) of notification.

**Academics. Special study options:** Cooperative education, cross-registration, distance learning, double major, dual enrollment of high school students, ESL, honors, independent study, internships, study abroad. License preparation in nursing, paramedic, radiology, real estate. **Credit/placement by examination:** AP, CLEP, IB, institutional tests. 12 credit hours maximum toward associate degree. **Support services:** Learning center, pre-admission summer program, reduced course load, remedial instruction, study skills assistance, tutoring, writing center.

**Majors. Agriculture:** Horticulture, landscaping, ornamental horticulture. **Area/ethnic studies:** African-American, Chicano/Hispanic-American/Latino, Native American. **Biology:** General. **Business:** General, accounting, accounting technology, administrative services, banking/financial services, business admin, finance, hospitality/recreation, international, marketing, office management, real estate, sales/distribution, selling, small business admin. **Communications:** General, digital media. **Communications technology:** General, computer typography. **Computer sciences:** General, computer science, data processing. **Conservation:** Environmental studies. **Education:** Early childhood, kindergarten/preschool, physical. **Engineering:** General, computer, marine. **Engineering technology:** General, automotive, biomedical, computer, drafting, electrical. **Family/consumer sciences:** Child care, institutional food production. **Foreign languages:** French, Spanish. **Health:** Athletic training, licensed practical nurse, medical radiologic technology/radiation therapy, nursing (RN), recreational therapy, sonography, substance abuse counseling. **History:** General. **Legal studies:** General. **Liberal arts:** Arts/sciences. **Math:** General. **Mechanic/repair:** Automotive, electronics/electrical. **Parks/recreation:** General, exercise sciences, health/fitness. **Personal/culinary services:** Cosmetic, culinary arts, institutional food service. **Philosophy/religion:** Philosophy. **Physical sciences:** Chemistry, geology, physics. **Protective services:** Law enforcement admin. **Psychology:** General. **Public administration:** General. **Science technology:** Biological. **Social sciences:** Anthropology, economics, geography, political science, sociology. **Transportation:** Diver. **Visual/performing arts:** Art, art history/conservation, commercial/advertising art, dramatic, film/cinema, interior design, multimedia, studio arts, theater design.

**Most popular majors.** Health sciences 9%, liberal arts 63%.

**Computing on campus.** 1,399 workstations in library, computer center, student center. Commuter students can connect to campus network. Online library, helpline, wireless network available.

**Student life. Freshman orientation:** Mandatory. Preregistration for classes offered. 2-hour on-campus or on-line orientation. **Activities:** Bands, choral groups, dance, drama, literary magazine, music ensembles, musical theater, student government, student newspaper, symphony orchestra, Black Student Union, College Republicans, EOPS, Hillel Club, Latter Day Saint Student Association, Phi Theta Kappa, Shodo Japanese Calligraphy Club, Special Abilities Club, Students Left Alliance Party, Student Sustainability Club, Vaquero Christian Fellowship.

**Athletics. Intercollegiate:** Baseball M, basketball, cross-country, football (tackle) M, golf, soccer, softball W, tennis, track and field, volleyball. **Team name:** Vaqueros.

**Student services.** Adult student services, alcohol/substance abuse counseling, career counseling, services for economically disadvantaged, student employment services, financial aid counseling, health services, minority student services, on-campus daycare, personal counseling, placement for graduates, veterans' counselor, women's services. **Physically disabled:** Services for visually, speech, hearing impaired. **Learning disabled:** Comprehensive services available. **Transfer:** Transfer center, transfer adviser, college fairs on campus for students transferring to 4-year colleges.

**Contact.** E-mail: admissions@sbcc.edu
Phone: (805) 965-0581 ext. 2200 Fax: (805) 963-7222
Allison Curtis, Director of Admissions and Records, Santa Barbara City College, 721 Cliff Drive, Santa Barbara, CA 93109-2394

## Santa Monica College
### Santa Monica, California — CB member
### www.smc.edu — CB code: 4691

- Public 2-year community college
- Commuter campus in small city

**General.** Founded in 1929. Regionally accredited. Off-campus program at Santa Monica College of Design. **Enrollment:** 31,211 degree-seeking undergraduates; 1,116 non-degree-seeking students. **Degrees:** 1,329 associate awarded. **Location:** 18 miles from Los Angeles. **Calendar:** Semester, extensive summer session. **Full-time faculty:** 318 total; 32% minority, 58% women. **Part-time faculty:** 1,114 total; 22% minority, 54% women. **Special facilities:** Planetarium, photo gallery, humanities center, entertainment technology academy. **Partnerships:** Formal partnerships with DreamWorks, Disney Channel, Sony, 20th Century Fox, and other entertainment industry leaders (for Academy of Entertainment Technology students).

**Student profile.** Among degree-seeking undergraduates, 6,501 enrolled as first-time, first-year students.

| | | | |
|---|---|---|---|
| Part-time: | 63% | Hispanic American: | 25% |
| Women: | 55% | International: | 9% |
| African American: | 10% | 25 or older: | 39% |
| Asian American: | 13% | | |

**Transfer out. Colleges most students transferred to 2009:** University of California at Los Angeles, California State University-Northridge, University of Southern California.

**Basis for selection.** Open admission, but selective for some programs. Music, theater arts, entertainment technology are competitive with various requirements. Nursing program has course requirements for admission. Audition and portfolio required for music, theater arts.

**2009-2010 Annual costs.** Tuition/fees: $826; $6,526 out-of-state. Per-credit charge: $26 in-state; $216 out-of-state. Books/supplies: $1,566. Personal expenses: $2,664.

**2008-2009 Financial aid. Need-based:** Need-based aid available for part-time students.

**Application procedures. Admission:** No deadline. No application fee. Admission notification on a rolling basis. **Financial aid:** No deadline. FAFSA, institutional form required. Applicants notified on a rolling basis starting 7/1; must reply within 2 week(s) of notification.

**Academics. Special study options:** Accelerated study, cooperative education, distance learning, dual enrollment of high school students, ESL, honors, independent study, internships, study abroad, weekend college. License preparation in nursing. **Credit/placement by examination:** AP, CLEP, institutional tests. 30 credit hours maximum toward associate degree. Math and English placement tests required for some students. **Support services:** Learning center, pre-admission summer program, remedial instruction, study skills assistance, tutoring, writing center.

**Majors. Business:** General, accounting, business admin, entrepreneurial studies, office/clerical, real estate. **Communications:** Journalism. **Communications technology: Computer sciences:** Data processing, information systems, programming. **Construction:** Maintenance. **Engineering technology:** Architectural, drafting, electrical. **Family/consumer sciences:** General. **History:** General. **Liberal arts:** Arts/sciences. **Mechanic/repair:** Auto body. **Parks/recreation:** General. **Physical sciences:** Chemistry, geology, physics. **Protective services:** Firefighting, law enforcement admin, police science. **Social sciences:** General, political science. **Visual/performing arts:** Commercial photography, commercial/advertising art, dance, dramatic, photography, studio arts.

**Computing on campus.** 600 workstations in library, computer center, student center. Commuter students can connect to campus network. Helpline available.

**Student life. Freshman orientation:** Mandatory. **Activities:** Concert band, choral groups, dance, drama, literary magazine, music ensembles, musical theater, opera, radio station, student government, student newspaper.

**Athletics.** NJCAA. **Intercollegiate:** Basketball, cross-country M, diving, football (tackle) M, swimming, tennis, track and field, volleyball, water polo M. **Intramural:** Badminton. **Team name:** Corsairs.

**Student services.** Adult student services, career counseling, services for economically disadvantaged, student employment services, financial aid counseling, health services, minority student services, on-campus daycare, personal counseling, placement for graduates, veterans' counselor. **Physically disabled:** Services for visually, speech, hearing impaired. **Learning disabled:** Comprehensive services available. **Transfer:** Transfer center, transfer adviser, college fairs on campus for students transferring to 4-year colleges.

**Contact.** Phone: (310) 434-4380 Fax: (310) 434-3645
Kiersten Elliott, Associate Dean of Enrollment Services, Santa Monica College, 1900 Pico Boulevard, Santa Monica, CA 90405-1628

## Santa Rosa Junior College
### Santa Rosa, California
### www.santarosa.edu — CB code: 4692

- Public 2-year community college
- Commuter campus in small city

**General.** Founded in 1918. Regionally accredited. **Enrollment:** 25,319 undergraduates. **Degrees:** 1,194 associate awarded. **Location:** 55 miles from San Francisco. **Calendar:** Semester, extensive summer session. **Full-time faculty:** 305 total; 15% have terminal degrees, 15% minority, 59% women. **Part-time faculty:** 1,116 total; 9% have terminal degrees, 9% minority, 60% women. **Special facilities:** Native American art museum, college farm, summer repertory theater, planetarium, culinary cafe.

**Student profile.** 1,559 transferred in from other institutions.

| | | | |
|---|---|---|---|
| Out-of-state: | 2% | 25 or older: | 51% |

**Transfer out. Colleges most students transferred to 2009:** Sonoma State University, San Francisco State University, University of California: Davis, California State University: Sacramento, University of California: Berkeley.

**Basis for selection.** Open admission, but selective for some programs. Audition recommended of music performance, some physical education, some communications majors.

**2009-2010 Annual costs.** Tuition/fees: $814; $6,514 out-of-state. Per-credit charge: $26 in-state; $216 out-of-state. Books/supplies: $1,638. Personal expenses: $3,096.

**2009-2010 Financial aid. Need-based:** 77% of total undergraduate aid awarded as scholarships/grants, 23% as loans/jobs. Need-based aid available for part-time students. Work-study available nights and for part-time students. **Non-need-based:** Scholarships awarded for academics, art, leadership, music/drama, state residency. **Additional information:** California's Board of Governors Program provides fee waivers for applicants with need.

**Application procedures. Admission:** No deadline. No application fee. **Financial aid:** Priority date 3/1; no closing date. FAFSA required. Applicants notified on a rolling basis starting 4/15.

**Academics. Special study options:** Cooperative education, cross-registration, distance learning, double major, dual enrollment of high school students, ESL, independent study, internships, liberal arts/career combination, study abroad, weekend college. License preparation in dental hygiene, nursing, paramedic, radiology, real estate. **Credit/placement by examination:** AP, CLEP, IB, institutional tests. 15 credit hours maximum toward associate degree. Credit will be granted to any student who satisfactorily passes an exam approved or conducted by proper authorities of the college. Such credit may be granted only to a student who is registered at the college and in good standing and only for a course listed in the College Catalog. **Support services:** GED preparation and test center, learning center, pre-admission summer program, reduced course load, remedial instruction, study skills assistance, tutoring.

**Majors. Agriculture:** Agribusiness operations, equestrian studies, equine science. **Area/ethnic studies:** Latin American. **Biology:** General, physiology. **Business:** Business admin. **Computer sciences:** Computer science. **Conservation:** General, environmental studies. **Education:** General, early childhood. **Engineering:** General. **Engineering technology:** Civil, electrical. **Foreign languages:** American Sign Language, Spanish. **Health:** Dental assistant, dental hygiene, EMT paramedic, licensed practical nurse, medical radiologic technology/radiation therapy, mental health services, nursing (RN), nursing assistant, pharmacy assistant. **History:** General. **Interdisciplinary:** Natural sciences. **Liberal arts:** Arts/sciences. **Math:** General. **Parks/recreation:** General. **Philosophy/religion:** Philosophy. **Physical sciences:** Chemistry, physics. **Protective services:** Firefighting, police science. **Psychology:** General. **Social sciences:** Anthropology, economics, geography, political science, sociology. **Visual/performing arts:** Art, commercial/advertising art, dramatic, fashion design.

**Most popular majors.** Health sciences 16%, interdisciplinary studies 47%, social sciences 19%.

**Computing on campus.** 1,900 workstations in library, computer center. Commuter students can connect to campus network. Online course registration, wireless network available.

**Student life. Freshman orientation:** Available. Preregistration for classes offered. Year round drop-in orientation. Online orientation. **Activities:** Jazz band, choral groups, dance, drama, film society, international student organizations, music ensembles, musical theater, student government, student newspaper, symphony orchestra.

**Athletics. Intercollegiate:** Badminton W, baseball M, basketball, cross-country, diving, football (tackle) M, golf M, soccer, softball W, swimming, tennis, track and field, volleyball W, water polo, wrestling M. **Team name:** Bear Cubs.

**Student services.** Adult student services, career counseling, services for economically disadvantaged, student employment services, financial aid counseling, health services, on-campus daycare, personal counseling, placement for graduates, veterans' counselor. **Physically disabled:** Services for visually, speech, hearing impaired. **Transfer:** Re-entry adviser, pre-admission transcript evaluation for new students. Transfer center, transfer adviser, college fairs on campus for students transferring to 4-year colleges.

**Contact.** E-mail: admininfo@santarosa.edu
Phone: (707) 527-4685 Toll-free number: (800) 564-7752
Fax: (707) 527-4798
Diane Traversi, Director of Enrollment Services, Santa Rosa Junior College, 1501 Mendocino Avenue, Santa Rosa, CA 95401-4395

## Santiago Canyon College
### Orange, California
www.sccollege.edu                                    CB code: 2830

▶ Public 2-year community college
▶ Commuter campus in small city

**General.** Regionally accredited. **Enrollment:** 5,555 degree-seeking undergraduates. **Degrees:** 595 associate awarded. **Location:** 30 miles from Los Angeles. **Calendar:** Semester, extensive summer session. **Full-time faculty:** 112 total; 32% minority, 67% women. **Part-time faculty:** 350 total; 27% minority, 42% women. **Class size:** 13% < 20, 31% 20-39, 24% 40-49, 30% 50-99, 2% >100.

**Student profile.** Among degree-seeking undergraduates, 3,035 enrolled as first-time, first-year students, 1,082 transferred in from other institutions.

**Transfer out. Colleges most students transferred to 2009:** California State University: Fullerton, California State University: Long Beach, Chapman University, University of California: Irvine, University of California: Riverside.

**Basis for selection.** Open admission. **Adult students:** SAT/ACT scores not required. Placement tests for English, math, reading, and chemistry. **Homeschooled:** Statement describing homeschool structure and mission required. Must show private school affidavit confirmation from the California Department of Education.

**2009-2010 Annual costs.** Tuition/fees: $808; $6,508 out-of-state. Per-credit charge: $26 in-state; $216 out-of-state. Books/supplies: $1,500. Personal expenses: $2,300.

**2008-2009 Financial aid.** All financial aid based on need. 177 full-time freshmen applied for aid; 150 were judged to have need; 147 of these received aid. Average need met was 43%. Average scholarship/grant was $3,120; average loan $2,116. 73% of total undergraduate aid awarded as scholarships/grants, 27% as loans/jobs. Need-based aid available for part-time students.

**Application procedures. Admission:** No application fee. **Financial aid:** Priority date 7/1; no closing date. FAFSA, institutional form required. Applicants notified on a rolling basis starting 6/1.

**Academics. Special study options:** Accelerated study, cooperative education, distance learning, double major, dual enrollment of high school students, ESL, honors, weekend college. License preparation in real estate. **Credit/placement by examination:** CLEP, institutional tests. **Support services:** GED preparation and test center, learning center, remedial instruction, study skills assistance, tutoring, writing center.

**Majors. Biology:** General. **Business:** Accounting, business admin, managerial economics, marketing, selling, tourism/travel. **Communications:** General. **Communications technology:** Graphics, photo/film/video. **Computer**

**sciences:** Computer science, information systems, web page design. **Construction:** Carpentry, electrician. **Engineering:** General. **Engineering technology:** Drafting. **Family/consumer sciences:** General. **Foreign languages:** General, American Sign Language, French, Italian, Spanish. **Health:** Medical assistant. **History:** General. **Legal studies:** Paralegal. **Liberal arts:** Arts/sciences, library assistant. **Math:** General. **Mechanic/repair:** Automotive. **Personal/culinary services:** Cosmetic. **Philosophy/religion:** Philosophy. **Physical sciences:** Chemistry, geology, hydrology, physics. **Protective services:** Fire safety technology. **Psychology:** General. **Social sciences:** General, anthropology, economics, geography, political science, sociology. **Visual/performing arts:** Art, commercial/advertising art, crafts, dance, fashion design, metal/jewelry.

**Most popular majors.** Liberal arts 81%.

**Computing on campus.** Online course registration, wireless network available.

**Student life. Freshman orientation:** Available. **Activities:** Bands, choral groups, dance, drama, music ensembles, student government, student newspaper, TV station.

**Athletics. Intercollegiate:** Cross-country, golf, soccer, track and field. **Intramural:** Softball, track and field. **Team name:** Hawks.

**Student services.** Adult student services, alcohol/substance abuse counseling, career counseling, services for economically disadvantaged, student employment services, financial aid counseling, health services, minority student services, on-campus daycare, personal counseling, veterans' counselor, women's services. **Physically disabled:** Services for visually, speech, hearing impaired. **Learning disabled:** Comprehensive services available. **Transfer:** Re-entry adviser, pre-admission transcript evaluation for new students. Transfer center, transfer adviser, college fairs on campus for students transferring to 4-year colleges.

**Contact.** E-mail: admissions@sccollege.edu
Phone: (714) 628-4901 Fax: (714) 628-4723
Linda Miskovic, Associate Dean of Admissions, Santiago Canyon College, 8045 East Chapman Avenue, Orange, CA 92869

## Shasta College
### Redding, California
www.shastacollege.edu                                CB code: 4696

▶ Public 2-year community and junior college
▶ Commuter campus in small city

**General.** Founded in 1948. Regionally accredited. **Enrollment:** 13,034 undergraduates. **Degrees:** 683 associate awarded. **Location:** 160 miles from Sacramento. **Calendar:** Semester, extensive summer session. **Full-time faculty:** 114 total; 12% minority, 39% women. **Part-time faculty:** 308 total; 8% minority, 55% women. **Class size:** 41% < 20, 53% 20-39, 3% 40-49, 2% 50-99, less than 1% >100. **Special facilities:** Early childhood education center lab school, college farm.

**Student profile.**

| | | | |
|---|---|---|---|
| Out-of-state: | 1% | Live on campus: | 1% |
| 25 or older: | 49% | | |

**Transfer out. Colleges most students transferred to 2009:** California State University: Chico, California State University: Sacramento, Humboldt State University, Simpson University, National University.

**Basis for selection.** Open admission, but selective for some programs. Applicants to the nursing and dental hygiene programs must have a high school diploma and complete a series of courses as outlined in college catalog. In addition, nursing program applicants must take the National League for Nursing examination.

**2009-2010 Annual costs.** Tuition/fees: $855; $6,645 out-of-state. Per-credit charge: $26 in-state; $219 out-of-state. Room only: $2,610. Books/supplies: $1,638. Personal expenses: $2,000.

**2008-2009 Financial aid.** All financial aid based on need. 74% of total undergraduate aid awarded as scholarships/grants, 26% as loans/jobs. Need-based aid available for part-time students.

**Application procedures. Admission:** No deadline. No application fee. Admission notification on a rolling basis. **Financial aid:** Priority date 3/2; no closing date. FAFSA, institutional form required. Applicants notified on a rolling basis starting 7/1.

**Academics.** On-campus programs leading to bachelor's degree from California State University: Chico offered. **Special study options:** Cooperative

Two-Year Colleges

education, distance learning, double major, dual enrollment of high school students, ESL, honors, independent study, internships, liberal arts/career combination, study abroad, weekend college. Bachelor's degree programs available on campus. License preparation in dental hygiene, nursing, paramedic, real estate. **Credit/placement by examination:** AP, CLEP, institutional tests. 12 credit hours maximum toward associate degree. **Support services:** GED preparation, learning center, reduced course load, remedial instruction, study skills assistance, tutoring, writing center.

**Majors. Agriculture:** General, agribusiness operations, business, equestrian studies, ornamental horticulture. **Biology:** General. **Business:** General, accounting, administrative services, business admin, entrepreneurial studies, executive assistant, hotel/motel admin, management information systems, office management, office technology, office/clerical, restaurant/food services, sales/distribution. **Communications:** General, journalism. **Computer sciences:** General, data processing, networking. **Construction:** General. **Education:** Early childhood, elementary, science. **Engineering:** General. **Engineering technology:** Architectural drafting, civil, construction, electrical. **Family/consumer sciences:** General, child care, child development, family studies, institutional food production. **Foreign languages:** General. **Health:** Dental hygiene, EMT paramedic, health services, nursing (RN). **Interdisciplinary:** Behavioral sciences, intercultural, natural sciences. **Legal studies:** Legal secretary, paralegal. **Liberal arts:** Humanities. **Math:** General. **Mechanic/repair:** Automotive, diesel. **Parks/recreation:** Health/fitness. **Personal/culinary services:** Chef training, culinary arts, restaurant/catering. **Physical sciences:** General, atmospheric science, climatology, geology, oceanography. **Production:** Welding. **Protective services:** Criminal justice, fire safety technology, fire services admin, firefighting, law enforcement admin, police science. **Public administration:** Human services. **Social sciences:** General. **Visual/performing arts:** Art, commercial/advertising art, dramatic, studio arts. **Other:** Earth system science, Industrial technologies, Wildland fire reconnaissance.

**Most popular majors.** Business/marketing 8%, health sciences 11%, liberal arts 56%.

**Computing on campus.** 191 workstations in library, computer center. Dormitories wired for high-speed internet access and linked to campus network. Commuter students can connect to campus network. Online course registration, online library, helpline, wireless network available.

**Student life. Freshman orientation:** Mandatory. Preregistration for classes offered. **Housing:** Single-sex dorms available. **Activities:** Bands, choral groups, dance, drama, international student organizations, music ensembles, musical theater, student government, student newspaper, symphony orchestra, Agriculture/Natural Resources Leaders Club, Amigos Unidos Club, Early Childhood Educators Network, Intercultural Club, Intervarsity Christian Fellowship, NATIVE (Native American Tradition in Valued Education) Club, Rotaract, science club, sustainability club, Veterans Organization.

**Athletics.** NJCAA. **Intercollegiate:** Baseball M, basketball, cross-country, football (tackle) M, golf M, soccer, softball W, swimming, tennis, track and field, volleyball W, wrestling M. **Team name:** Knights.

**Student services.** Career counseling, services for economically disadvantaged, student employment services, financial aid counseling, health services, on-campus daycare, personal counseling, veterans' counselor. **Physically disabled:** Services for visually, speech, hearing impaired. **Transfer:** Transfer center, transfer adviser, college fairs on campus for students transferring to 4-year colleges.

**Contact.** E-mail: Admissions@shastacollege.edu
Phone: (530) 242-7650 Fax: (530) 225-4995
Kevin O'Rorke, Dean, Enrollment Services, Shasta College, Box 496006, Redding, CA 96049-6006

## Sierra College
### Rocklin, California
www.sierracollege.edu                    CB code: 4697

▶ Public 2-year community college
▶ Commuter campus in small city

**General.** Founded in 1914. Regionally accredited. **Enrollment:** 21,373 undergraduates. **Degrees:** 2,284 associate awarded. **Location:** 25 miles from Sacramento. **Calendar:** Semester, extensive summer session. **Full-time faculty:** 219 total. **Part-time faculty:** 752 total. **Special facilities:** Nature trail, planetarium, science museum displays, learning resource center, cross-country trail.

**Student profile.**

| | | | |
|---|---|---|---|
| Out-of-state: | 1% | Live on campus: | 1% |

**Transfer out. Colleges most students transferred to 2009:** California State University: Sacramento, University of California: Davis, California State University: Chico, University of California: Berkeley, San Francisco State University.

**Basis for selection.** Open admission, but selective for some programs.

**2009-2010 Annual costs.** Tuition/fees: $836; $6,536 out-of-state. Per-credit charge: $26 in-state; $216 out-of-state. Room/board: $6,700. Books/supplies: $2,222. Personal expenses: $1,800.

**2009-2010 Financial aid. Need-based:** 68% of total undergraduate aid awarded as scholarships/grants, 32% as loans/jobs. Need-based aid available for part-time students. Work-study available nights, weekends and for part-time students.

**Application procedures. Admission:** No deadline. No application fee. Application must be submitted online. Applicants notified within 4 working days. **Financial aid:** Priority date 3/2; no closing date. FAFSA required. Applicants notified on a rolling basis starting 5/15.

**Academics. Special study options:** Cross-registration, distance learning, double major, dual enrollment of high school students, ESL, honors, independent study, internships, study abroad, weekend college. License preparation in nursing, real estate. **Credit/placement by examination:** AP, CLEP, institutional tests. 15 credit hours maximum toward associate degree. **Support services:** Learning center, remedial instruction, study skills assistance, tutoring, writing center.

**Majors. Agriculture:** General, animal husbandry, equestrian studies, horticulture. **Biology:** General. **Business:** General, accounting, administrative services, business admin, real estate, sales/distribution, small business admin. **Communications:** Digital media. **Computer sciences:** Data entry, information technology, networking, programming, system admin, web page design, webmaster. **Construction:** Carpentry. **Education:** Early childhood. **Engineering:** General. **Engineering technology:** Architectural drafting, mechanical drafting. **Family/consumer sciences:** General, child care. **Foreign languages:** American Sign Language. **Health:** Nursing (RN). **History:** General. **Liberal arts:** Arts/sciences, library assistant. **Math:** General. **Mechanic/repair:** Automotive, electronics/electrical. **Parks/recreation:** Health/fitness. **Philosophy/religion:** Philosophy. **Physical sciences:** Chemistry, geology, physics. **Production:** Woodworking. **Protective services:** Criminal justice, fire safety technology, firefighting, police science, security services. **Psychology:** General. **Social sciences:** General. **Visual/performing arts:** Art, dramatic, music performance, photography, studio arts.

**Most popular majors.** Business/marketing 11%, liberal arts 44%, security/protective services 6%, social sciences 8%.

**Computing on campus.** 300 workstations in dormitories, library, computer center. Dormitories wired for high-speed internet access and linked to campus network. Commuter students can connect to campus network. Online course registration, online library, helpline, wireless network available.

**Student life. Freshman orientation:** Mandatory. **Housing:** Coed dorms available. $250 fully refundable deposit. **Activities:** Concert band, choral groups, drama, international student organizations, music ensembles, student government, student newspaper, symphony orchestra, Persian Cultural Club, Rainbow Alliance, Contemporary Arts Club, Veteran Students Alliance, Environmentally Concerned Students, Freethinkers, Intervarsity Christian Fellowship, Law Club, Circle K International.

**Athletics. Intercollegiate:** Baseball M, basketball, cross-country W, diving, football (tackle) M, golf, soccer W, softball W, swimming, tennis, volleyball W, water polo W, wrestling M. **Intramural:** Archery, badminton, basketball, cheerleading W, football (non-tackle), golf, softball, tennis, volleyball. **Team name:** Wolverines.

**Student services.** Adult student services, alcohol/substance abuse counseling, career counseling, services for economically disadvantaged, student employment services, financial aid counseling, health services, on-campus daycare, personal counseling, veterans' counselor. **Physically disabled:** Services for visually, speech, hearing impaired. **Transfer:** Pre-admission transcript evaluation for new students. Transfer center, transfer adviser, college fairs on campus for students transferring to 4-year colleges.

**Contact.** Phone: (916) 660-7340 Toll-free number: (800) 242-4004
Fax: (916) 630-4500
Gail Modder, Admissions and Records Program Manager, Sierra College, 5000 Rocklin Road, Rocklin, CA 95677

## Skyline College
### San Bruno, California
www.skylinecollege.edu                    CB code: 4746

▶ Public 2-year community college
▶ Commuter campus in small city

**General.** Founded in 1969. Regionally accredited. **Enrollment:** 2,929 degree-seeking undergraduates; 7,677 non-degree-seeking students. **Degrees:** 517 associate awarded. **Location:** 15 miles from San Francisco. **Calendar:** Semester, limited summer session. **Full-time faculty:** 105 total. **Part-time faculty:** 200 total.

**Student profile.** Among degree-seeking undergraduates, 19% enrolled in a transfer program, 10% enrolled in a vocational program, 15% already have a bachelor's degree or higher, 1,978 transferred in from other institutions.

| | | | |
|---|---|---|---|
| Part-time: | 70% | Women: | 53% |
| Out-of-state: | 1% | 25 or older: | 49% |

**Transfer out. Colleges most students transferred to 2009:** San Francisco State University, San Jose State University, California State University: East Bay, UC Berkeley.

**Basis for selection.** Open admission, but selective for some programs. Supplemental application must be submitted to automotive technology, cosmetology, and respiratory therapy programs. Selection is made by the department. Concurrent enrollment students must submit a high school permission form. SAT/ACT may be substituted for institutional placement tests. Interview required of respiratory therapy majors. Essay required of full-time international student applicants. **Adult students:** Assessment test required to determine placement for math and English courses. **Home-schooled:** State high school equivalency certificate required. **Learning Disabled:** Students may request a skills assessment for best placement in courses.

**High school preparation.** College-preparatory program recommended.

**2009-2010 Annual costs.** Tuition/fees: $842; $6,572 out-of-state. Per-credit charge: $26 in-state; $217 out-of-state. Books/supplies: $1,638. Personal expenses: $2,772.

**Financial aid. Need-based:** Need-based aid available for part-time students.

**Application procedures. Admission:** No deadline. No application fee. Application must be submitted online. Admission notification on a rolling basis. **Financial aid:** Priority date 5/2; no closing date. FAFSA, institutional form required. Applicants notified on a rolling basis starting 5/1; must reply within 2 week(s) of notification.

**Academics. Special study options:** Cooperative education, cross-registration, distance learning, double major, dual enrollment of high school students, ESL, honors, independent study, liberal arts/career combination, study abroad, weekend college. License preparation in paramedic, real estate. **Credit/placement by examination:** AP, CLEP, institutional tests. 12 credit hours maximum toward associate degree. **Support services:** Learning center, remedial instruction, study skills assistance, tutoring, writing center.

**Majors. Business:** Accounting, administrative services, business admin, hospitality admin, management information systems, office/clerical. **Communications technology:** General. **Computer sciences:** General, computer science, data processing, information systems, webmaster. **Education:** Early childhood. **Family/consumer sciences:** General, business. **Foreign languages:** Spanish. **Health:** Medical secretary, medical transcription, respiratory therapy technology, surgical technology. **Interdisciplinary:** Global studies. **Legal studies:** Legal secretary, paralegal. **Liberal arts:** Arts/sciences. **Math:** General. **Mechanic/repair:** Automotive. **Personal/culinary services:** Cosmetic. **Protective services:** Law enforcement admin. **Psychology:** General. **Science technology:** Biological. **Visual/performing arts:** General, art, dance.

**Most popular majors.** Business/marketing 13%, health sciences 11%, liberal arts 53%.

**Computing on campus.** 220 workstations in library, computer center, student center. Online course registration, helpline, repair service, wireless network available.

**Student life. Freshman orientation:** Available. Preregistration for classes offered. **Activities:** Bands, choral groups, dance, literary magazine, student government, student newspaper.

**Athletics.** NJCAA. **Intercollegiate:** Baseball M, basketball M, cross-country, soccer M, softball W, track and field, volleyball W, wrestling M. **Team name:** Trojans.

**Student services.** Adult student services, career counseling, services for economically disadvantaged, student employment services, financial aid counseling, health services, minority student services, on-campus daycare, personal counseling, veterans' counselor, women's services. **Physically disabled:** Services for visually, speech, hearing impaired. **Transfer:** Transfer

center, transfer adviser, college fairs on campus for students transferring to 4-year colleges.

**Contact.** E-mail: skyadmissions@smccd.edu
Phone: (650) 738-4252 Fax: (650) 738-4200
Sherri Hancock, Dean of Enrollment Services, Skyline College, 3300 College Drive, San Bruno, CA 94066-1662

## Solano Community College
### Fairfield, California
www.solano.edu                                     CB code: 4930

- Public 2-year community college
- Commuter campus in small city

**General.** Founded in 1945. Regionally accredited. Classes offered in Vallejo and Vacaville. **Enrollment:** 4,700 degree-seeking undergraduates. **Degrees:** 971 associate awarded. **ROTC:** Air Force. **Location:** 11 miles from Vallejo. **Calendar:** Semester, extensive summer session. **Full-time faculty:** 174 total. **Part-time faculty:** 285 total.

**Basis for selection.** Open admission, but selective for some programs. Special requirements for nursing program.

**2009-2010 Annual costs.** Tuition/fees: $816; $6,516 out-of-state. Per-credit charge: $26 in-state; $216 out-of-state. Books/supplies: $1,712. Personal expenses: $2,800.

**Application procedures. Admission:** No deadline. No application fee. Admission notification on a rolling basis. **Financial aid:** Priority date 3/1; no closing date. FAFSA required. Applicants notified on a rolling basis starting 7/1.

**Academics. Special study options:** Cooperative education, cross-registration, distance learning, double major, dual enrollment of high school students, ESL, honors, independent study, internships, study abroad, weekend college. **Credit/placement by examination:** AP, CLEP, institutional tests. 15 credit hours maximum toward associate degree. **Support services:** Reduced course load, remedial instruction, tutoring, writing center.

**Majors. Agriculture:** Landscaping, ornamental horticulture. **Area/ethnic studies:** African-American, Asian-American, Chicano/Hispanic-American/Latino, Native American. **Biology:** General. **Business:** Accounting, administrative services, banking/financial services, business admin, office management, real estate. **Communications:** General, journalism. **Computer sciences:** General, programming. **Education:** Early childhood. **Engineering technology:** Aerospace, drafting, electrical, water quality. **Family/consumer sciences:** General. **Foreign languages:** General, French, German, Spanish. **Health:** Medical secretary, nursing (RN). **History:** General. **Interdisciplinary:** Biological/physical sciences. **Legal studies:** Legal secretary. **Liberal arts:** Arts/sciences. **Math:** General. **Mechanic/repair:** Aircraft, appliance, auto body, computer. **Parks/recreation:** Health/fitness, sports admin. **Personal/culinary services:** Cosmetic. **Physical sciences:** Chemistry, physics. **Production:** Welding. **Protective services:** Firefighting, police science. **Psychology:** General. **Public administration:** Human services. **Science technology:** Biological. **Social sciences:** General, international relations, political science. **Visual/performing arts:** Commercial photography, commercial/advertising art, dramatic, drawing, interior design, painting, sculpture, studio arts.

**Computing on campus.** 240 workstations in library, computer center.

**Student life. Freshman orientation:** Available. **Activities:** Bands, choral groups, drama, musical theater, student government, student newspaper, symphony orchestra, Black Student Union, women's change, veterans organization, Sierra club, student nurses, Filipino club, Democratic club, Mathematics, Engineering & Science Achievement club, Asian-Pacific Islander club.

**Athletics. Intercollegiate:** Baseball M, basketball, cross-country, diving, football (tackle) M, soccer W, softball W, swimming, track and field, volleyball W, water polo M. **Intramural:** Table tennis, tennis. **Team name:** Falcons.

**Student services.** Career counseling, student employment services, financial aid counseling, health services, on-campus daycare, personal counseling, placement for graduates, veterans' counselor. **Physically disabled:** Services for visually, speech, hearing impaired. **Transfer:** Transfer center for students transferring to 4-year colleges.

**Contact.** E-mail: admissions@solano.edu
Phone: (707) 864-7171 Fax: (707) 864-7175
Barbara Fountain, Dean, Admissions and Records, Solano Community College, 4000 Suisun Valley Road, Fairfield, CA 94534-3197

## South Coast College
### Orange, California
### www.southcoastcollege.com

◗ For-profit 2-year business and career college
◗ Small city

**General.** Accredited by ACICS. **Enrollment:** 389 degree-seeking undergraduates. **Degrees:** 17 associate awarded. **Location:** 20 miles from Los Angeles. **Calendar:** Quarter, extensive summer session. **Full-time faculty:** 20 total. **Part-time faculty:** 25 total. **Special facilities:** Computer training center.

**Basis for selection.** Open admission, but selective for some programs.

**2009-2010 Annual costs.** Tuition/fees: $9,450. Registration fee: $99. Program cost: $1,050/month (Day), $787.5/month (Night). Books/supplies: $700.

**Application procedures. Admission:** Closing date 3/31. $99 fee.

**Academics. Credit/placement by examination:** CLEP.

**Majors. Health:** Medical transcription. **Legal studies:** Paralegal.

**Contact.** E-mail: requestinfo@southcoastcollege.com
Phone: (714) 867-5009 Toll-free number: (800) 337-8366
Kevin Magner, Dean of Admissions and Marketing, South Coast College, 2011 West Chapman Avenue, Orange, CA 92868

## Southwestern College
### Chula Vista, California
### www.swccd.edu
**CB member**
**CB code: 4726**

◗ Public 2-year community college
◗ Commuter campus in small city

**General.** Founded in 1961. Regionally accredited. Medical occupation programs accredited by the National League for Nursing Accrediting Commission Inc. (NLNAC). **Enrollment:** 23,283 undergraduates. **Degrees:** 1,152 associate awarded. **Location:** 10 miles from San Diego. **Calendar:** Semester, extensive summer session. **Full-time faculty:** 80 total. **Part-time faculty:** 120 total. **Class size:** 36% < 20, 49% 20-39, 13% 40-49, 3% 50-99.

**Transfer out. Colleges most students transferred to 2009:** San Diego State University, University of California: San Diego.

**Basis for selection.** Open admission, but selective for some programs. Limited admission to nursing and dental hygiene programs.

**2009-2010 Annual costs.** Tuition/fees: $824; $6,524 out-of-state. Per-credit charge: $26 in-state; $216 out-of-state. Books/supplies: $1,638. Personal expenses: $2,772.

**Financial aid. Need-based:** Need-based aid available for part-time students. Work-study available nights, weekends and for part-time students.

**Application procedures. Admission:** No deadline. No application fee. Admission notification on a rolling basis. **Financial aid:** Closing date 3/2. FAFSA required. Applicants notified on a rolling basis starting 7/1.

**Academics.** Broad offerings of online and traditional courses. Online credit and non-credit courses available. **Special study options:** Cooperative education, cross-registration, distance learning, double major, dual enrollment of high school students, ESL, honors, independent study, internships, study abroad, weekend college. License preparation in dental hygiene, nursing, paramedic, real estate. **Credit/placement by examination:** AP, CLEP, IB, institutional tests. 15 credit hours maximum toward associate degree. In-house placement test required for some. **Support services:** Learning center, pre-admission summer program, remedial instruction, study skills assistance, tutoring, writing center.

**Majors. Agriculture:** Floriculture, greenhouse operations, landscaping, nursery operations, ornamental horticulture, turf management. **Architecture:** Landscape, technology. **Area/ethnic studies:** African-American, American, Asian-American, Chicano/Hispanic-American/Latino, women's. **Biology:** General, biotechnology. **Business:** Accounting, business admin, construction management, entrepreneurial studies, finance, financial planning, international, market research, office management, office/clerical, real estate, tourism promotion, tourism/travel. **Communications:** General, broadcast journalism, journalism. **Communications technology:** General, radio/tv, recording arts. **Computer sciences:** General, applications programming, computer science, information systems, information technology, networking, programming, web

page design, webmaster. **Conservation:** Environmental studies. **Construction:** Building inspection, maintenance. **Education:** General, early childhood, elementary, kindergarten/preschool, physical. **Engineering:** General. **Engineering technology:** CAD/CADD, computer, drafting, occupational safety, telecommunications. **Family/consumer sciences:** Child care, child development. **Foreign languages:** French, Spanish. **Health:** Clinical lab technology, dental hygiene, EMT paramedic, insurance coding, licensed practical nurse, medical records admin, medical records technology, medical transcription, nursing (RN), prenursing, surgical technology. **History:** General. **Legal studies:** General, legal secretary, paralegal. **Liberal arts:** Arts/sciences, humanities. **Math:** General. **Mechanic/repair:** Automotive, electronics/electrical, small engine. **Parks/recreation:** General, health/fitness. **Philosophy/religion:** Philosophy. **Physical sciences:** Astronomy, chemistry, geology, physics. **Protective services:** Criminal justice, firefighting, forensics, law enforcement admin. **Psychology:** General. **Public administration:** Social work. **Social sciences:** Anthropology, economics, geography, political science, sociology. **Visual/performing arts:** Art, cinematography, dance, dramatic, graphic design, photography.

**Computing on campus.** 1,360 workstations in library, computer center. Online course registration, online library, helpline, student web hosting, wireless network available.

**Student life. Freshman orientation:** Available. Preregistration for classes offered. **Activities:** Jazz band, choral groups, dance, drama, literary magazine, music ensembles, musical theater, student government, student newspaper, over 40 student clubs and organizations available.

**Athletics. Intercollegiate:** Baseball M, basketball, cross-country, football (tackle) M, soccer, softball W, tennis, track and field, volleyball W, water polo. **Team name:** Jaguars.

**Student services.** Career counseling, services for economically disadvantaged, student employment services, financial aid counseling, health services, legal services, on-campus daycare, personal counseling, veterans' counselor, women's services. **Physically disabled:** Services for visually, speech, hearing impaired. **Transfer:** Pre-admission transcript evaluation for new students. Transfer center, transfer adviser, college fairs on campus for students transferring to 4-year colleges.

**Contact.** E-mail: admissions@swccd.edu
Phone: (619) 421-6700 ext. 5215 Fax: (619) 482-6489
Mia McClellan, Dean, Student Services, Southwestern College, 900 Otay Lakes Road, Chula Vista, CA 91910-7297

## Taft College
### Taft, California
### www.taftcollege.edu
**CB code: 4820**

◗ Public 2-year community college
◗ Commuter campus in small town

**General.** Founded in 1922. Regionally accredited. **Enrollment:** 13,247 undergraduates. **Degrees:** 146 associate awarded. **Location:** 35 miles from Bakersfield. **Calendar:** Semester, limited summer session. **Full-time faculty:** 40 total. **Part-time faculty:** 55 total.

**Transfer out. Colleges most students transferred to 2009:** California State University: Bakersfield, California State University: Fresno, California Polytechnic State University: San Luis Obispo, University of La Verne.

**Basis for selection.** Open admission. **Adult students:** SAT/ACT scores not required.

**2009-2010 Annual costs.** Tuition/fees: $780; $6,480 out-of-state. Per-credit charge: $26 in-state; $216 out-of-state. Room/board: $3,824.

**2008-2009 Financial aid. Need-based:** 96% of total undergraduate aid awarded as scholarships/grants, 4% as loans/jobs. Need-based aid available for part-time students. Work-study available nights and for part-time students. **Non-need-based:** Scholarships awarded for academics.

**Application procedures. Admission:** No deadline. No application fee. Admission notification on a rolling basis. **Financial aid:** No deadline. FAFSA, institutional form required. Applicants notified on a rolling basis; must reply within 4 week(s) of notification.

**Academics. Special study options:** Distance learning, double major, ESL, independent study. License preparation in dental hygiene, paramedic. **Credit/placement by examination:** AP, CLEP, institutional tests. 12 credit hours maximum toward associate degree. **Support services:** GED preparation and test center, learning center, pre-admission summer program, reduced course load, remedial instruction, study skills assistance, tutoring.

**Majors. Business:** General, accounting, administrative services, business admin, management information systems, office/clerical. **Communications:** Journalism. **Computer sciences:** General, computer science, information systems. **Education:** General, early childhood, physical, social science. **Engineering technology:** Automotive, CAD/CADD, electrical, petroleum. **Health:** Dental hygiene. **Legal studies:** Court reporting. **Liberal arts:** Arts/sciences. **Math:** General. **Mechanic/repair:** Automotive, industrial. **Physical sciences:** General. **Protective services:** Corrections, criminal justice. **Social sciences:** General. **Visual/performing arts:** Art. **Other:** Direct support education, Energy technician, Journalism, Life science, Recreation.

**Computing on campus.** 121 workstations in dormitories, library, computer center, student center. Dormitories wired for high-speed internet access. Online course registration, online library, helpline, wireless network available.

**Student life. Freshman orientation:** Available. Offered online or by video. **Housing:** Single-sex dorms, special housing for disabled available. $125 fully refundable deposit. **Activities:** Drama, student government, student newspaper, International club, Rotary club, MECHA club, Best Buddies.

**Athletics.** NJCAA. **Intercollegiate:** Baseball M, basketball W, soccer, softball W, volleyball W. **Team name:** Cougars.

**Student services.** Adult student services, career counseling, services for economically disadvantaged, student employment services, financial aid counseling, minority student services, on-campus daycare, personal counseling, veterans' counselor. **Physically disabled:** Services for visually, speech, hearing impaired. **Learning disabled:** Comprehensive services available. **Transfer:** Re-entry adviser for new students. Transfer center, transfer adviser, college fairs on campus for students transferring to 4-year colleges.

**Contact.** E-mail: hrussell@taft.org
Phone: (661) 763-7741 Toll-free number: (800) 379-6784
Fax: (661) 763-7758
Brian McKee, Registrar and Director of Admissions, Taft College, 29 Emmons Park Drive, Taft, CA 93268

## Trinity Life Bible College
### Sacramento, California
### www.tlbc.edu

- Private 2-year Bible college
- Very large city

**General.** Regionally accredited; also accredited by TRACS. **Enrollment:** 235 degree-seeking undergraduates. **Degrees:** 7 bachelor's, 29 associate awarded. **Calendar:** Quarter. **Full-time faculty:** 5 total. **Part-time faculty:** 33 total.

**Basis for selection.** Must have expressed personal experience of Christian conversion.

**2009-2010 Annual costs.** Tuition/fees: $9,255. Per-credit charge: $199.

**Application procedures. Admission:** Closing date 8/15.

**Academics. Special study options:** Bachelor's degree programs available on campus. **Credit/placement by examination:** CLEP.

**Majors. Philosophy/religion:** Christian. **Theology:** Preministerial.

**Contact.** Phone: (916) 348-4689
Kathy Clarke, Director of Records, Trinity Life Bible College, 5225 Hillsdale Boulevard, Sacramento, CA 95842

## Ventura College
### Ventura, California
### www.venturacollege.edu
**CB code: 4931**

- Public 2-year community college
- Commuter campus in small city

**General.** Founded in 1925. Regionally accredited. **Enrollment:** 14,754 undergraduates. **Degrees:** 1,093 associate awarded. **Location:** 60 miles from downtown Los Angeles. **Calendar:** Semester, limited summer session. **Full-time faculty:** 136 total. **Part-time faculty:** 386 total.

**Basis for selection.** Open admission, but selective for some programs. Limited admission to nursing program.

**2009-2010 Annual costs.** Tuition/fees: $822; $6,492 out-of-state. Per-credit charge: $26 in-state; $215 out-of-state. Books/supplies: $1,638. Personal expenses: $3,096.

**Financial aid. Need-based:** Need-based aid available for part-time students.

**Application procedures. Admission:** No deadline. No application fee. Admission notification on a rolling basis. **Financial aid:** Priority date 3/2; no closing date. FAFSA required. Applicants notified on a rolling basis.

**Academics. Special study options:** Cross-registration, distance learning, dual enrollment of high school students, ESL, independent study, study abroad. **Credit/placement by examination:** AP, CLEP, institutional tests. 12 credit hours maximum toward associate degree. **Support services:** Learning center, reduced course load, remedial instruction, tutoring.

**Majors. Agriculture:** Plant sciences. **Biology:** General. **Business:** General, accounting, administrative services, business admin, fashion, office management, office/clerical. **Computer sciences:** General. **Conservation:** General. **Construction:** Maintenance. **Education:** Early childhood. **Engineering:** General. **Engineering technology:** Architectural, drafting, water quality. **Family/consumer sciences:** General, child development. **Health:** EMT paramedic, medical secretary, nursing (RN). **Mechanic/repair:** Automotive. **Production:** Welding. **Protective services:** Criminal justice. **Social sciences:** International relations. **Visual/performing arts:** Ceramics, commercial/advertising art, dramatic, fashion design, photography, studio arts.

**Computing on campus.** Online course registration available.

**Student life. Freshman orientation:** Available. **Housing:** Student housing available off-campus at nearby apartments. **Activities:** Jazz band, choral groups, dance, drama, international student organizations, music ensembles, student government, student newspaper, religious, ethnic, political, special interest organizations, international student club.

**Athletics. Intercollegiate:** Baseball M, basketball, cheerleading, cross-country, diving, football (tackle) M, golf M, softball W, swimming, tennis, track and field, volleyball M, water polo M. **Team name:** Pirates.

**Student services.** Adult student services, career counseling, services for economically disadvantaged, student employment services, health services, on-campus daycare, personal counseling, placement for graduates, veterans' counselor. **Physically disabled:** Services for visually, hearing impaired. **Learning disabled:** Comprehensive services available. **Transfer:** Transfer center, transfer adviser, college fairs on campus for students transferring to 4-year colleges.

**Contact.** Phone: (805) 654-6457 Fax: (805) 654-6357
Susan Bricker, Registrar, Ventura College, 4667 Telegraph Road, Ventura, CA 93003

## Victor Valley College
### Victorville, California
### www.vvc.edu
**CB code: 4932**

- Public 2-year community college
- Small city

**General.** Founded in 1960. Regionally accredited. **Enrollment:** 5,955 degree-seeking undergraduates. **Degrees:** 995 associate awarded. **Location:** 38 from San Bernardino. **Calendar:** Semester, limited summer session. **Full-time faculty:** 132 total. **Part-time faculty:** 389 total. **Class size:** 18% < 20, 67% 20-39, 10% 40-49, 4% 50-99, less than 1% >100. **Special facilities:** Planetarium, mock archaeological dig site.

**Student profile.** Among degree-seeking undergraduates, 357 transferred in from other institutions.

| Out-of-state: | 2% | 25 or older: | 35% |

**Transfer out. Colleges most students transferred to 2009:** California State University: San Bernardino.

**Basis for selection. Open admission**, but selective for some programs. **Adult students:** SAT/ACT scores not required. **Homeschooled:** Must complete concurrent enrollment form with parent signature.

**2009-2010 Annual costs.** Tuition/fees: $790; $6,490 out-of-state. Per-credit charge: $26 in-state; $216 out-of-state. Nevada residents may qualify for tuition reduction program as part of Good Neighbor policy. Books/supplies: $1,566. Personal expenses: $3,024.

**Financial aid. Need-based:** Need-based aid available for part-time students. Work-study available for part-time students. **Additional information:** Board of Governors grant pays enrollment fee in full for low-income students.

**Application procedures. Admission:** No deadline. No application fee. Admission notification on a rolling basis. **Financial aid:** Priority date 3/2; no closing date. FAFSA, institutional form, CSS PROFILE required. Applicants notified on a rolling basis starting 8/1; must reply within 4 week(s) of notification.

**Academics. Special study options:** Accelerated study, cooperative education, cross-registration, distance learning, double major, dual enrollment of high school students, ESL, honors, independent study, internships, semester at sea, study abroad, weekend college. License preparation in nursing, paramedic. **Credit/placement by examination:** CLEP, institutional tests. 32 credit hours maximum toward associate degree. **Support services:** Learning center, pre-admission summer program, reduced course load, remedial instruction, study skills assistance, tutoring, writing center.

**Majors. Agriculture:** Ornamental horticulture. **Business:** General, administrative services, business admin, real estate. **Construction:** Carpentry. **Health:** EMT paramedic, medical assistant, nursing (RN), respiratory therapy technology. **Liberal arts:** Arts/sciences. **Math:** General. **Mechanic/repair:** Automotive, electronics/electrical, industrial electronics. **Production:** Welding. **Protective services:** Fire safety technology, law enforcement admin. **Visual/performing arts:** Art.

**Most popular majors.** Business/marketing 12%, health sciences 9%, interdisciplinary studies 18%, liberal arts 48%.

**Computing on campus.** 350 workstations in computer center, student center. Online course registration, online library, helpline available.

**Student life. Freshman orientation:** Available. **Activities:** Concert band, campus ministries, choral groups, dance, drama, music ensembles, Model UN, musical theater, student government, student newspaper.

**Athletics.** NJCAA. **Intercollegiate:** Baseball M, basketball, cross-country, football (tackle) M, golf M, soccer, softball W, tennis, track and field, volleyball W, wrestling M. **Team name:** Rams.

**Student services.** Career counseling, services for economically disadvantaged, student employment services, financial aid counseling, health services, on-campus daycare, personal counseling, placement for graduates, veterans' counselor. **Physically disabled:** Services for visually, speech, hearing impaired. **Transfer:** Re-entry adviser, pre-admission transcript evaluation for new students. College fairs on campus for students transferring to 4-year colleges.

**Contact.** E-mail: moong@vvc.edu
Phone: (760) 245-4271 ext. 2373 Fax: (760) 843-7707
Greta Moon, Director, Admissions and Records, Victor Valley College, 18422 Bear Valley Road, Victorville, CA 92392-5850

## West Hills College: Coalinga
Coalinga, California
www.westhillscollege.com          CB code: 4056

- Public 2-year community college
- Commuter campus in small town

**General.** Founded in 1932. Regionally accredited. 2 campuses in district: West Hills College-Coalinga, West Hills College-Lemore. **Enrollment:** 2,786 undergraduates. **Degrees:** 205 associate awarded. **Location:** 60 miles from Fresno. **Calendar:** Semester, limited summer session. **Full-time faculty:** 47 total; 11% minority, 49% women. **Part-time faculty:** 85 total; 20% minority, 42% women. **Class size:** 10% < 20, 90% 20-39.

**Student profile.**

Out-of-state:          15%     25 or older:          48%

**Transfer out. Colleges most students transferred to 2009:** California State University: Fresno, California Polytechnic University, Univeristy of Phoenix, Fresno Pacific University.

**Basis for selection.** Open admission. K-12 students admitted with parental permission and principal of the educational institution recommendation as special admit students. **Adult students:** SAT/ACT scores not required. **Homeschooled:** Students must petition President of College in writing for admittance.

**2009-2010 Annual costs.** Tuition/fees: $780; $6,480 out-of-state. Per-credit charge: $26 in-state; $216 out-of-state. Additional $250 refundable deposit for room and board plan. Room/board: $5,321. Books/supplies: $1,400.

**Financial aid. Need-based:** Need-based aid available for part-time students.

**Application procedures. Admission:** No deadline. No application fee. Application must be submitted online. Admission notification on a rolling basis. **Financial aid:** Priority date 3/2; no closing date. FAFSA required. Applicants notified on a rolling basis starting 6/1.

**Academics. Special study options:** Cooperative education, distance learning, dual enrollment of high school students, ESL, honors, independent study, study abroad. **Credit/placement by examination:** AP, CLEP, institutional tests. 15 credit hours maximum toward associate degree. **Support services:** GED preparation, learning center, reduced course load, remedial instruction, tutoring.

**Majors. Agriculture:** General, animal sciences, business. **Business:** General, accounting, administrative services, business admin, management information systems, office technology, office/clerical. **Computer sciences:** General, applications programming. **Education:** Early childhood. **Health:** Health services. **Liberal arts:** Arts/sciences. **Protective services:** Police science. **Psychology:** General. **Social sciences:** General, criminology, geography. **Visual/performing arts:** Art, commercial/advertising art, studio arts.

**Most popular majors.** Business/marketing 9%, health sciences 7%, liberal arts 65%.

**Computing on campus.** 40 workstations in dormitories, library, computer center. Dormitories wired for high-speed internet access. Online course registration, helpline available.

**Student life. Freshman orientation:** Mandatory. Preregistration for classes offered. **Housing:** Single-sex dorms, wellness housing available. $500 fully refundable deposit. **Activities:** Dance, drama, musical theater, student government.

**Athletics.** NJCAA. **Intercollegiate:** Baseball M, basketball M, cross-country M, football (tackle) M, rodeo, softball W, volleyball W. **Team name:** Falcons.

**Student services.** Adult student services, career counseling, services for economically disadvantaged, student employment services, on-campus daycare, personal counseling, veterans' counselor. **Physically disabled:** Services for visually, speech, hearing impaired. **Transfer:** Pre-admission transcript evaluation for new students. Transfer center, transfer adviser, college fairs on campus for students transferring to 4-year colleges.

**Contact.** E-mail: sandradagnino@whccd.edu
Phone: (559) 934-2302 Toll-free number: (800) 266-1114
Fax: (559) 935-2788
Darlene Georgatos, Director of District Enrollment, West Hills College: Coalinga, 300 Cherry Lane, Coalinga, CA 93210

## West Hills College: Lemoore
Lemoore, California
www.westhillscollege.com

- Public 2-year community college
- Large town

**General.** Candidate for regional accreditation. 2 campuses in district: West Hills College Coalinga and West Hills College Lemoore. **Enrollment:** 3,833 undergraduates. **Degrees:** 328 associate awarded. **Location:** 20 miles from Fresno. **Calendar:** Semester, extensive summer session. **Full-time faculty:** 47 total; 23% minority, 45% women. **Part-time faculty:** 104 total; 24% minority, 44% women. **Class size:** 4% < 20, 96% 20-39.

**Student profile.**

Out-of-state:          15%     25 or older:          48%

**Transfer out. Colleges most students transferred to 2009:** California State University Fresno, California State University Bakersfield, California State University Chico.

**Basis for selection.** Open admission. K-12 students admitted with parental and principal of the educational institution recommendation as special admit students required. **Adult students:** SAT/ACT scores not required. **Homeschooled:** Statement describing homeschool structure and mission required. Parent or guardian must petition the President of West Hills College Lemoore in writing.

**2009-2010 Annual costs.** Tuition/fees: $780; $6,480 out-of-state. Per-credit charge: $26 in-state; $216 out-of-state. Room/board: $5,576. Books/supplies: $1,500.

**Application procedures. Admission:** No deadline. No application fee. Application must be submitted online. Admission notification on a rolling basis.

**Academics. Special study options:** Cooperative education, distance learning, dual enrollment of high school students, ESL, honors, independent study. **Credit/placement by examination:** AP, CLEP, institutional tests. 15 credit hours maximum toward associate degree. **Support services:** GED preparation, learning center, reduced course load, remedial instruction, tutoring.

**Majors. Biology:** General. **Business:** General, business admin. **Computer sciences:** General. **Engineering:** General. **Liberal arts:** Arts/sciences, humanities. **Math:** General. **Personal/culinary services:** Restaurant/catering. **Protective services:** Law enforcement admin. **Psychology:** General. **Social sciences:** General.

**Most popular majors.** Business/marketing 12%, health sciences 8%, liberal arts 54%, security/protective services 13%.

**Computing on campus.** 60 workstations in library, computer center. Online course registration available.

**Student life. Freshman orientation:** Mandatory. Preregistration for classes offered. **Activities:** Student government, student newspaper.

**Athletics.** NJCAA. **Intercollegiate:** Golf, soccer, wrestling M. **Team name:** Golden Eagles.

**Student services.** Adult student services, career counseling, services for economically disadvantaged, student employment services, on-campus daycare, personal counseling, veterans' counselor. **Physically disabled:** Services for visually, speech, hearing impaired. **Learning disabled:** Comprehensive services available. **Transfer:** Pre-admission transcript evaluation for new students. Transfer center, transfer adviser, college fairs on campus for students transferring to 4-year colleges.

**Contact.** E-mail: admissions@westhillscollege.com
Phone: (559) 925-3317 Toll-free number: (800) 266-1114
Fax: (559) 925-3837
Darlene Georgatos, Director of District Enrollment, West Hills College: Lemoore, 555 College Avenue, Lemoore, CA 93245

## West Los Angeles College
Culver City, California
www.wlac.edu                                           CB code: 4964

- Public 2-year community college
- Commuter campus in large town

**General.** Founded in 1968. Regionally accredited. **Enrollment:** 11,440 undergraduates. **Degrees:** 393 associate awarded. **Location:** 10 miles from Civic Center. **Calendar:** Semester, limited summer session. **Full-time faculty:** 70 total. **Part-time faculty:** 325 total.

**Student profile.**

| Out-of-state: | 1% | 25 or older: | 74% |

**Basis for selection.** Open admission.

**2009-2010 Annual costs.** Tuition/fees: $802; $6,442 out-of-state. Per-credit charge: $26 in-state; $214 out-of-state. Books/supplies: $1,638. Personal expenses: $3,096.

**2009-2010 Financial aid.** All financial aid based on need. Need-based aid available for part-time students. Work-study available for part-time students. **Additional information:** California residents may qualify for Board of Governors Grant Program.

**Application procedures. Admission:** No deadline. No application fee. Admission notification on a rolling basis. **Financial aid:** No deadline. FAFSA required. Applicants notified on a rolling basis; must reply within 4 week(s) of notification.

**Academics. Special study options:** Accelerated study, cooperative education, distance learning, dual enrollment of high school students, ESL, honors, independent study, internships, student-designed major, study abroad, weekend college. License preparation in aviation, dental hygiene, nursing, paramedic, real estate. **Credit/placement by examination:** CLEP, institutional tests. 15 credit hours maximum toward associate degree. **Support

services:** GED preparation, learning center, reduced course load, remedial instruction, study skills assistance, tutoring, writing center.

**Majors. Biology:** General. **Business:** General, accounting, administrative services, business admin, real estate. **Engineering:** General. **Foreign languages:** French, Spanish. **Health:** Dental hygiene. **History:** General. **Legal studies:** Paralegal. **Liberal arts:** Arts/sciences. **Mechanic/repair:** Aircraft. **Parks/recreation:** Health/fitness. **Philosophy/religion:** Philosophy. **Physical sciences:** Chemistry, geology, physics. **Psychology:** General. **Social sciences:** Anthropology, economics, geography, political science, sociology. **Visual/performing arts:** Art, ceramics.

**Computing on campus.** Commuter students can connect to campus network. Online course registration, online library, wireless network available.

**Student life. Freshman orientation:** Available. 2 hour session prior to start of each semester. **Activities:** Bands, choral groups, dance, drama, film society, student government, student newspaper, TV station.

**Athletics. Intercollegiate:** Baseball M, basketball, cross-country, football (tackle) M, track and field. **Team name:** Oilers.

**Student services.** Adult student services, career counseling, services for economically disadvantaged, student employment services, financial aid counseling, health services, on-campus daycare, personal counseling, placement for graduates, veterans' counselor. **Physically disabled:** Services for visually, speech, hearing impaired.

**Contact.** Phone: (310) 287-4501
Michael Goltermann, Dean, West Los Angeles College, 9000 Overland Avenue, Culver City, CA 90230

## West Valley College
Saratoga, California
www.westvalley.edu                                     CB code: 4958

- Public 2-year community college
- Large town

**General.** Founded in 1963. Regionally accredited. **Enrollment:** 12,233 undergraduates. **Degrees:** 632 associate awarded. **ROTC:** Army, Air Force. **Location:** 13 miles from downtown San Jose. **Calendar:** Semester, limited summer session. **Full-time faculty:** 176 total. **Part-time faculty:** 486 total. **Special facilities:** Planetarium, wireless campus center.

**Transfer out. Colleges most students transferred to 2009:** University of California: Davis, San Jose State University.

**Basis for selection.** Open admission.

**2009-2010 Annual costs.** Tuition/fees: $850; $6,280 out-of-state. Per-credit charge: $26 in-state; $207 out-of-state. Books/supplies: $2,388. Personal expenses: $3,096.

**Financial aid.** All financial aid based on need. Need-based aid available for part-time students.

**Application procedures. Admission:** Priority date 4/21; no deadline. No application fee. Admission notification on a rolling basis. **Financial aid:** Priority date 5/31; no closing date. FAFSA required. Applicants notified on a rolling basis starting 7/1.

**Academics. Special study options:** Distance learning, double major, dual enrollment of high school students, ESL, honors, independent study, teacher certification program. **Credit/placement by examination:** CLEP, institutional tests. 12 credit hours maximum toward associate degree. **Support services:** Learning center, pre-admission summer program, remedial instruction, study skills assistance, tutoring, writing center.

**Majors. Architecture:** Landscape. **Area/ethnic studies:** Women's. **Biology:** General. **Business:** General, accounting, administrative services, business admin, fashion, office management, office technology, office/clerical, real estate. **Computer sciences:** General, programming. **Construction:** Maintenance. **Education:** Early childhood. **Engineering:** General. **Engineering technology:** Drafting, electrical. **Family/consumer sciences:** Child care. **Foreign languages:** General. **Health:** Medical assistant. **History:** General. **Legal studies:** Court reporting, paralegal. **Liberal arts:** Arts/sciences. **Math:** General. **Parks/recreation:** Facilities management. **Physical sciences:** Chemistry, geology, physics. **Protective services:** Criminal justice. **Psychology:** General. **Social sciences:** General, sociology. **Visual/performing arts:** Art, dramatic, fashion design, interior design.

**Computing on campus.** 150 workstations in library, computer center. Commuter students can connect to campus network. Online course registration, online library, wireless network available.

**Student life. Freshman orientation:** Available. **Activities:** Bands, choral groups, drama, music ensembles, student government, student newspaper, symphony orchestra, TV station, Vietnamese student association, Unlimited Horizons (handicapped), Descendants of Africa, Latin American student association, Alpha Gamma Sigma, Latter-Day Saints, fashion design, Puente, JC Ministries (Christian).

**Athletics. Intercollegiate:** Baseball M, basketball, cross-country, field hockey W, football (tackle) M, gymnastics W, soccer M, softball W, swimming, tennis, track and field, volleyball, water polo M, wrestling M. **Intramural:** Badminton, basketball, bowling, swimming, tennis, volleyball. **Team name:** Vikings.

**Student services.** Adult student services, career counseling, student employment services, health services, on-campus daycare, personal counseling, veterans' counselor. **Physically disabled:** Services for visually, speech, hearing impaired. **Transfer:** Re-entry adviser for new students. Transfer center, transfer adviser, college fairs on campus for students transferring to 4-year colleges.

**Contact.** Phone: (408) 741-2001 Fax: (408) 867-5033
Barbara Ogilvie, Director of Admissions, West Valley College, 14000 Fruitvale Avenue, Saratoga, CA 95070-5698

## Western Career College: Antioch
Antioch, California
www.westerncollege.edu                    CB code: 3033

- For-profit 2-year technical college
- Commuter campus in small city

**General.** Regionally accredited. **Enrollment:** 338 degree-seeking undergraduates. **Degrees:** 41 associate awarded. **Calendar:** Continuous. **Full-time faculty:** 16 total. **Part-time faculty:** 10 total.

**Basis for selection.** Open admission, but selective for some programs. CPAT results important.

**2009-2010 Annual costs.** ASHS: tuition $11,748, fees $1,439; CJD: tuition $24,825, fees $2,326; DA: tuition $18,440, fees $314; DAD: tuition $30,188, fees $1,753; HIT: tuition $16,596, fees $1,306; HITD: tuition $28,344, fees $2,745; MA: tuition $16,596, fees $411; MAD: tuition $28,344, fees $1,850; MT: tuition $15,213, fees $631; MTD: tuition $26,961, fees $2,070; PTD: tuition $24,825, fees $1,825; VN: tuition $42,770, fees $1,552; VND: tuition $50,246, fees $2,498. Registration fee $100.

**Application procedures. Admission:** No deadline. $100 fee. Admission notification on a rolling basis. **Financial aid:** No deadline.

**Academics. Special study options:** Accelerated study, distance learning. License preparation in nursing. **Credit/placement by examination:** CLEP.

**Majors. Health:** Licensed practical nurse, massage therapy, medical assistant, medical records technology, pharmacy assistant. **Protective services:** Law enforcement admin.

**Contact.** Phone: (925) 522-7777
Jeremy McReady, Director of Admissions, Western Career College: Antioch, 2157 Country Hills Drive, Antioch, CA 94531

## Western Career College: Citrus Heights
Citrus Heights, California
www.westerncollege.edu

- For-profit 2-year health science and technical college
- Very large city

**General.** Regionally accredited. **Enrollment:** 372 degree-seeking undergraduates. **Degrees:** 86 associate awarded. **Calendar:** Continuous. **Full-time faculty:** 19 total. **Part-time faculty:** 15 total.

**2009-2010 Annual costs.** ASHS: tuition $11,748, fees $1,439; CJD: tuition $24,825, fees $2,326; DA: tuition $18,440, fees $314; DAD: tuition $30,188, fees $1,753; HCA: tuition $16,596, fees $796; HCAD: tuition $28,344, fees $2,235; HIT: tuition $16,596, fees $1,306; HITD: tuition $28,344, fees $2,745; MA: tuition $16,596, fees $411; MAD: tuition $28,344, fees $1,850; PTD: tuition $24,825, fees $1,825; ST: tuition $33,866, fees $1,216; STD: tuition $41,342, fees $2,159; UT: tuition $40,796, fees $990; UTD: tuition $48,272, fees $1,933; VTD: tuition $30,156, fees $1,995. Registration fee $100.

**Academics. Credit/placement by examination:** CLEP.

**Majors. Health:** Dental assistant, health care admin, massage therapy, office assistant, pharmacy assistant, sonography, surgical technology, veterinary technology/assistant. **Protective services:** Law enforcement admin.

**Contact.** Western Career College: Citrus Heights, 7301 Greenback Lane, Suite A, Citrus Heights, CA 95621

## Western Career College: Pleasant Hill
Pleasant Hill, California
www.westerncollege.com                    CB code: 2922

- For-profit 2-year health science and technical college
- Commuter campus in small city

**General.** Regionally accredited. **Enrollment:** 163 degree-seeking undergraduates. **Degrees:** 69 associate awarded. **Calendar:** Continuous. **Full-time faculty:** 11 total. **Part-time faculty:** 53 total.

**Basis for selection.** CPAT examination important.

**2009-2010 Annual costs.** ASHS: tuition $11,748, fees $1,439; CJD: tuition $24,825, fees $2,326; DA: tuition $18,440, fees $314; DAD: tuition $30,188, fees $1,753; GD: tuition $20,745, fees $382; GDD: tuition $29,289, fees $1,384; HCA: tuition $16,596, fees $796; HCAD: tuition $28,344, fees $2,235; HIT: tuition $16,596, fees $1,306; HITD: tuition $28,344, fees $2,745; MA: tuition $16,596, fees $411; MAD: tuition $28,344, fees $1,850; MT: tuition $15,213, fees $631; MTD: tuition $26,961, fees $2,070; PTD: tuition $24,825, fees $1,825; RTD: tuition $46,500, fees $3,192; VTD: tuition $30,156, fees $1,995. Registration fee $100.

**Application procedures. Admission:** No deadline. $100 fee. Admission notification on a rolling basis. **Financial aid:** No deadline. Applicants notified on a rolling basis.

**Academics. Credit/placement by examination:** CLEP.

**Majors. Health:** Dental assistant, medical assistant.

**Contact.** Phone: (925) 609-6650 Toll-free number: (800) 584-4520 Fax: (925) 609-6666
Lashon Wells, Admissions Director/Executive Director, Western Career College: Pleasant Hill, 380 Civic Drive, Suite 300, Pleasant Hill, CA 94523

## Western Career College: Sacramento
Sacramento, California
www.westerncollege.edu                    CB code: 2917

- For-profit 2-year health science and technical college
- Commuter campus in large city

**General.** Regionally accredited. **Enrollment:** 433 full-time, degree-seeking students. **Degrees:** 433 associate awarded. **Calendar:** Continuous. **Full-time faculty:** 19 total. **Part-time faculty:** 53 total.

**2009-2010 Annual costs.** Tuition/fees: $13,930. Per-credit charge: $461. $356 per credit for general education. Books/supplies: $448. Personal expenses: $1,686.

**Academics. Credit/placement by examination:** CLEP.

**Majors. Health:** Dental assistant, health care admin, licensed practical nurse, massage therapy, medical assistant, medical records technology, nursing (RN), pharmacy assistant, veterinary technology/assistant.

**Contact.** E-mail: info@westerncollege.edu
Phone: (800) 321-2386 Toll-free number: (800) 321-2386
Mary Langley, Director of Admissions, Western Career College: Sacramento, 7801 Folsom Blvd #210, Sacramento, CA 95826

## Western Career College: San Jose
San Jose, California
www.svcollege.com

- For-profit 2-year technical college
- Commuter campus in very large city

**General.** Regionally accredited. **Enrollment:** 379 degree-seeking undergraduates. **Degrees:** 102 associate awarded. **Calendar:** Continuous. **Full-time faculty:** 35 total. **Part-time faculty:** 10 total.

**Basis for selection.** Open admission, but selective for some programs. Limited admission to dental programs.

**2009-2010 Annual costs.** ADD: tuition $16,596, fees $546; ADD-AS: tuition $25,140, fees $1,548; ASHS: tuition $11,748, fees $1,439; CJD: tuition $24,825, fees $2,326; DA: tuition $18,440, fees $314; DAD: tuition $30,188, fees $1,753; DAD-PreDH: tuition $41,212, fees $2,313; DH: tuition $53,070, fees $1,397; GD: tuition $20,745, fees $382; GDD: tuition $29,289, fees $1,384; HIT: tuition $16,596, fees $1,306; HITD: tuition $28,344, fees $2,745; MA: tuition $16,596, fees $411; MAD: tuition $28,344, fees $1,850; MT: tuition $15,213, fees $631; MTD: tuition $26,961, fees $2,070; PTD: tuition $24,825, fees $1,825; ST: tuition $33,866, fees $1,216; STD: tuition $41,342, fees $2,159; VTD: tuition $30,156, fees $1,995; VN: tuition $42,770, fees $1,552; VND: tuition $50,246, fees $2,498; VND-PreRN: tuition $62,910, fees $3,837. Registration fee $100.

**Application procedures. Admission:** No deadline. $75 fee. Admission notification on a rolling basis.

**Academics. Credit/placement by examination:** CLEP.

**Majors. Computer sciences:** Computer graphics. **Engineering technology:** Architectural drafting. **Health:** Dental assistant, dental hygiene, massage therapy, medical assistant, medical records technology, pharmacy assistant, surgical technology, veterinary technology/assistant.

**Contact.** Phone: (408) 360-0840 Fax: (408) 360-0848
Indy Decroos, Admissions Director, Western Career College: San Jose, 6201 San Ignacio Avenue, San Jose, CA 95119

## Western Career College: San Leandro
San Leandro, California
www.westerncollege.edu                     CB code: 2918

- For-profit 2-year health science and technical college
- Commuter campus in small city
- Interview required

**General.** Regionally accredited. **Enrollment:** 173 degree-seeking undergraduates; 543 non-degree-seeking students. **Degrees:** 63 associate awarded. **Location:** 10 miles from Oakland. **Calendar:** Continuous. **Full-time faculty:** 37 total. **Part-time faculty:** 20 total. **Special facilities:** Labs.

**Student profile.** Among degree-seeking undergraduates, 100% enrolled in a vocational program.

**Basis for selection.** Open admission, but selective for some programs. CPAT score, interest important. CPAT required.

**2009-2010 Annual costs.** All programs require $100 registration fee. Associate in Criminal Justice (60 weeks): tuition, $24,825; books and uniform, $2,326. Associate in Pharmacy Technology (60 to 80 weeks): tuition, $24,825; books and uniform, $1,825. Associate in Veterinary Technology (86 weeks): tuition, $30,156; books and uniform, $1,995. Students in certificate programs have option to continue and complete associate degree. Dental Assisting certificate (42 weeks): tuition, $18,440; books and uniform, $314. Health Care Administration Certificate (36 weeks): tuition, $16,596; books and uniform, $796. Certificate in Health Information Technology (36 weeks): tuition, $16,596; books and uniform, $1,306. Certificate in Medical Assisting (36 to 50 weeks): tuition, $16,596; books and uniform, $411. Certificate in Massage Therapy (34 weeks): tuition, $15,213; books, uniform and supplies, $1,026. Certificate in Vocational Nursing (67 weeks): tuition, $42,770; books, uniform and supplies, $1,676.

**Application procedures. Admission:** No deadline. $100 fee. Admission notification on a rolling basis. **Financial aid:** No deadline. Applicants notified on a rolling basis.

**Academics. Special study options:** Distance learning. **Credit/placement by examination:** CLEP. **Support services:** Study skills assistance, tutoring.

**Majors. Health:** Licensed practical nurse, medical secretary, pharmacy assistant, veterinary technology/assistant.

**Computing on campus.** 55 workstations in library, computer center. Online library available.

**Student life. Activities:** Student newspaper.

**Contact.** Phone: (510) 276-3888 Toll-free number: (800) 584-4553 Fax: (510) 276-3653
Tiffany Rhodes, Director of Admissions, Western Career College: San Leandro, 1555 East 14th Street Suite 500, San Leandro, CA 94578

## Western Career College: Stockton
Stockton, California
www.westerncollege.edu

- For-profit 2-year technical and career college
- Small city

**General.** Regionally accredited. **Enrollment:** 160 degree-seeking undergraduates. **Degrees:** 114 associate awarded. **Location:** 40 miles from Sacramento. **Calendar:** Continuous. **Full-time faculty:** 14 total. **Part-time faculty:** 7 total.

**Basis for selection.** Admissions decisions are based upon high school diploma (GED or ATB) formal interview with applicant, a completed application and a passing score on an entrance exam.

**2009-2010 Annual costs.** All programs require $100 registration fee. Associate in Criminal Justice (60 weeks): tuition, $24,066; books and uniform, $2,052. Associate in Pharmacy Technology (60 to 80 weeks): tuition, $24,066; books and uniform, $1,779. Associate in Veterinary Technology (86 weeks): tuition, $29,253; books and uniform, $1,760. Associate in Health Science (30 weeks): tuition, $11,385; books and uniform, $1,248. Certificate in Medical assisting (36 weeks): tuition, $16,092; books and uniform, $387. Certificate in Health Care Administration (36 weeks): tuition, $16,092; books and uniform, $704. Certificate in Massage Therapy (34 weeks): tuition, $14,751; books and uniform, $819.

**Application procedures. Admission:** No deadline. $100 fee.

**Academics. Special study options:** Accelerated study. Bachelor's degree programs available on campus. **Credit/placement by examination:** CLEP. **Support services:** Learning center, tutoring.

**Majors. Health:** Health care admin, massage therapy, medical assistant, pharmacy assistant, veterinary technology/assistant. **Protective services:** Police science.

**Computing on campus.** 25 workstations in library, computer center. Online library available.

**Student life. Freshman orientation:** Mandatory. **Activities:** Student newspaper.

**Contact.** Anna Meli, Assistant Director of Admissions, Western Career College: Stockton, 1313 West Robinhood Drive Suite B, Stockton, CA 95207

## Westwood College: Los Angeles
Los Angeles, California
www.westwood.edu/locations/california/los-angeles-campus

- For-profit 2-year technical college
- Very large city

**General.** Accredited by ACICS. **Enrollment:** 1,060 degree-seeking undergraduates. **Degrees:** 500 bachelor's, 115 associate awarded; master's offered. **Calendar:** 10-week terms throughout year. **Full-time faculty:** 12 total. **Part-time faculty:** 47 total.

**Basis for selection.** Open admission. Accuplacer required.

**2009-2010 Annual costs.** Tuition/fees: $15,273. Per-credit charge: $559. Books/supplies: $1,720. Personal expenses: $3,121.

**Application procedures. Admission:** No deadline. $100 fee. Admission notification on a rolling basis. **Financial aid:** FAFSA required. Applicants notified on a rolling basis.

**Academics. Credit/placement by examination:** CLEP.

**Majors. Business:** Fashion. **Computer sciences:** Programming. **Engineering:** Computer. **Visual/performing arts:** Fashion design, graphic design.

**Contact.** Phone: (213) 739-9999
Brian Willingham, Director of Admissions, Westwood College: Los Angeles, 3250 Wilshire Boulevard, Suite 400, Los Angeles, CA 90010

## WyoTech: Fremont
### Fremont, California
### www.wyotech.edu                    CB code: 3030

- For-profit 2-year technical college
- Small city
- Interview required

**General.** Accredited by ACCSC. **Enrollment:** 1,489 degree-seeking undergraduates. **Degrees:** 88 associate awarded. **Calendar:** Continuous. **Full-time faculty:** 84 total.

**Basis for selection.** Satisfactory performance on state-mandated entrance exam required.

**2010-2011 Annual costs.** Tuition ranges from $16,500 to $34,890 depending on program. Tuition includes books, uniforms, training materials, and supplies. A set of tools will be loaned at no additional charge. Additional $500 materials fee. On-line service fee $200 for AOS Degree programs.

**Application procedures. Admission:** No deadline. No application fee. **Financial aid:** FAFSA required.

**Academics. Credit/placement by examination:** CLEP. **Support services:** Learning center.

**Majors. Mechanic/repair:** General, heating/ac/refrig.

**Contact.** Phone: (510) 490-6900 Toll-free number: (800) 248-8585 Fax: (510) 490-8599
Sophy Son, Director of Admissions, WyoTech: Fremont, 200 Whitney Place, Fremont, CA 94539

## WyoTech: Long Beach
### Long Beach, California
### www.wyotech.edu/campus/long_beach      CB code: 3162

- For-profit 2-year health science and technical college
- Commuter campus in large city

**General.** Accredited by ACCSC. **Enrollment:** 3,723 degree-seeking undergraduates. **Calendar:** Continuous. **Full-time faculty:** 63 total. **Part-time faculty:** 11 total.

**Basis for selection.** Open admission. Institutional placement assessment examination, interview important.

**2009-2010 Annual costs.** Costs vary by program. Full program costs: automotive $23,900, electrical $18,400, HVAC $15,900, IET $23,700, medical assistant $14,000, plumbing $17,400.

**Application procedures. Admission:** No deadline. No application fee. Application fee varies by program. **Financial aid:** Closing date 6/30.

**Academics. Credit/placement by examination:** CLEP.

**Majors. Construction:** Electrician.

**Contact.** Phone: (562) 624-9530 Toll-free number: (888) 741-4271 Fax: (562) 437-8111
Christopher Adams, Director of Admissions, WyoTech: Long Beach, 2161 Technology Place, Long Beach, CA 90810

## Yuba Community College District
### Marysville, California
### www.yccd.edu                       CB code: 4994

- Public 2-year community college
- Commuter campus in small city

**General.** Founded in 1927. Regionally accredited. **Enrollment:** 2,864 full-time, degree-seeking students. **Degrees:** 672 associate awarded. **Location:** 56 miles from Sacramento. **Calendar:** Semester, limited summer session. **Full-time faculty:** 135 total. **Part-time faculty:** 375 total. **Special facilities:** Veterinary technical training clinic, manufacturing technology facilities (factory), measurement science/scale repair training facilities. **Partnerships:** Formal partnerships with numerous local businesses.

**Transfer out.** Colleges most students transferred to 2009: California State University: Sacramento, California State University: Chico, University of California: Davis.

**Basis for selection.** Open admission, but selective for some programs. Limited admission to allied health programs. CPT tests recommended for counseling.

**2009-2010 Annual costs.** Tuition/fees: $792; $6,492 out-of-state. Per-credit charge: $26 in-state; $216 out-of-state. Books/supplies: $1,566. Personal expenses: $3,024.

**Financial aid. Need-based:** Need-based aid available for part-time students. Work-study available for part-time students. **Non-need-based:** Scholarships awarded for academics, athletics, job skills, minority status, music/drama. **Additional information:** Tuition fee waiver based on Board of Governors Grant.

**Application procedures. Admission:** No deadline. No application fee. Application must be submitted online. Admission notification on a rolling basis beginning on or about 6/1. **Financial aid:** Closing date 3/1. FAFSA required. Applicants notified on a rolling basis starting 4/1.

**Academics. Special study options:** Cooperative education, distance learning, ESL. License preparation in nursing, radiology. **Credit/placement by examination:** AP, CLEP, institutional tests. **Support services:** Learning center, remedial instruction, tutoring.

**Majors. Agriculture:** Business, landscaping, mechanization, ornamental horticulture. **Business:** Accounting, administrative services, business admin, entrepreneurial studies, human resources, taxation. **Communications:** Journalism, media studies. **Computer sciences:** General, computer science. **Education:** Early childhood, physical. **Engineering technology:** Electrical, water quality. **Family/consumer sciences:** Family/community services. **Health:** Medical radiologic technology/radiation therapy, medical transcription, nursing (RN), substance abuse counseling, veterinary technology/assistant. **History:** General. **Liberal arts:** Arts/sciences. **Math:** General. **Mechanic/repair:** General, automotive, electronics/electrical. **Personal/culinary services:** Cosmetology. **Production:** General, sheet metal. **Protective services:** Criminal justice, fire safety technology, police science. **Social sciences:** General. **Visual/performing arts:** Art, dramatic, photography, studio arts.

**Computing on campus.** 300 workstations in library. Online course registration, online library, wireless network available.

**Student life. Freshman orientation:** Available. **Activities:** Bands, choral groups, drama, music ensembles, musical theater, student government, student newspaper, symphony orchestra, AD Nursing Students Association, Care Club, EOP&S Club DECA/Marketing Club, Christian Students Association, Green Society, Future Teachers of America, Speech Team, Photography Guild, Veterinary Technicians Association.

**Athletics. Intercollegiate:** Baseball M, basketball, cross-country, football (tackle) M, soccer, softball W, tennis, track and field, volleyball W. **Team name:** 49'ers.

**Student services.** Adult student services, career counseling, services for economically disadvantaged, student employment services, financial aid counseling, health services, minority student services, on-campus daycare, personal counseling, placement for graduates, veterans' counselor, women's services. **Physically disabled:** Services for visually, speech, hearing impaired. **Transfer:** Transfer adviser, college fairs on campus for students transferring to 4-year colleges.

**Contact.** E-mail: kpope@yccd.edu
Phone: (530) 741-6720 Fax: (530) 741-6872
Kendyl Magnuson, Director, Admissions and Enrollment Services, Yuba Community College District, 2088 North Beale Road, Marysville, CA 95901

# Colorado

## Aims Community College
**Greeley, Colorado**      **CB member**
**www.aims.edu**      **CB code: 4204**

▶ Public 2-year community college
▶ Commuter campus in small city

**General.** Founded in 1967. Regionally accredited. **Enrollment:** 4,041 degree-seeking undergraduates. **Degrees:** 545 associate awarded. **ROTC:** Air Force. **Location:** 55 miles from Denver. **Calendar:** Semester, extensive summer session. **Full-time faculty:** 89 total. **Part-time faculty:** 308 total.

**Student profile.**

Out-of-state: 2%    25 or older: 80%

**Basis for selection.** Open admission, but selective for some programs. Special requirements for radiologic technology, police academy and biofeedback programs based on test scores. All students must meet assessment requirement by taking computerized placement test, submitting ACT/SAT scores or showing proof of previous college experience. Interview required of radiologic technology, police academy, biofeedback majors.

**2009-2010 Annual costs.** Tuition/fees: $2,265; $3,135 out-of-district; $12,045 out-of-state. Per-credit charge: $60 in-district; $89 out-of-district; $386 out-of-state. Books/supplies: $600. Personal expenses: $450.

**Application procedures. Admission:** No deadline. No application fee. Admission notification on a rolling basis. **Financial aid:** Priority date 4/15; no closing date. FAFSA required. Applicants notified on a rolling basis starting 6/1.

**Academics. Special study options:** Cooperative education, double major, dual enrollment of high school students, independent study, internships, weekend college. **Credit/placement by examination:** AP, CLEP, institutional tests. 48 credit hours maximum toward associate degree. **Support services:** Learning center, remedial instruction, tutoring.

**Majors. Agriculture:** General, supplies. **Business:** Accounting, administrative services, management information systems, marketing. **Communications technology:** Graphic/printing. **Engineering technology:** Electrical. **Family/consumer sciences:** Child care. **Health:** Medical radiologic technology/radiation therapy. **Liberal arts:** Arts/sciences. **Mechanic/repair:** Auto body. **Protective services:** Fire safety technology, law enforcement admin. **Transportation:** Aviation.

**Computing on campus.** 500 workstations in computer center, student center.

**Student life. Activities:** Concert band, dance, drama, literary magazine, musical theater, student government, student newspaper.

**Athletics. Intramural:** Basketball, volleyball.

**Student services.** Career counseling, student employment services, on-campus daycare, placement for graduates, veterans' counselor. **Physically disabled:** Services for visually, speech, hearing impaired. **Transfer:** Transfer adviser, college fairs on campus for students transferring to 4-year colleges.

**Contact.** E-mail: admissions.records@aims.edu
Phone: (970) 339-6404 Toll-free number: (800) 301-5388
Stuart Thomas, Director of Admissions, Aims Community College, 5401 West 20th Street, Greeley, CO 80632

## Anthem College
**Aurora, Colorado**
**www.cambridgecollege.com**      **CB code: 3201**

▶ For-profit 2-year technical college
▶ Commuter campus in small city
▶ Interview required

**General.** Accredited by ACCSC. **Enrollment:** 600 degree-seeking undergraduates. **Degrees:** 66 associate awarded. **Calendar:** Continuous, extensive summer session. **Full-time faculty:** 35 total.

**Basis for selection.** Interview most important. Entrance exam required for students out of high school more than 6 months.

**2009-2010 Annual costs.** Tuition for associate degree programs $22,950 to $24,500 depending on program; tuition for diploma programs $12,450 to $23,850.

**Financial aid.** All financial aid based on need.

**Application procedures. Admission:** No deadline. $50 fee ($150 out-of-state). Admission notification on a rolling basis. **Financial aid:** No deadline. FAFSA, institutional form required. Applicants notified on a rolling basis.

**Academics. Special study options:** License preparation in radiology. **Credit/placement by examination:** CLEP. **Support services:** GED preparation.

**Majors. Computer sciences:** General. **Health:** Massage therapy, medical assistant, radiologic technology/medical imaging, surgical technology.

**Student life. Freshman orientation:** Mandatory.

**Student services.** Adult student services, career counseling, student employment services, financial aid counseling, placement for graduates.

**Contact.** Phone: (720) 859-7900 Toll-free number: (800) 322-4132
Fax: (303) 338-9701
Belinda Rogers, Director of Admissions, Anthem College, 350 Blackhawk Street, Aurora, CO 80011

## Arapahoe Community College
**Littleton, Colorado**
**www.arapahoe.edu**      **CB code: 4014**

▶ Public 2-year community college
▶ Commuter campus in large town

**General.** Founded in 1965. Regionally accredited. **Enrollment:** 8,226 degree-seeking undergraduates. **Degrees:** 497 associate awarded. **ROTC:** Army, Air Force. **Location:** 10 miles from Denver. **Calendar:** Semester, limited summer session. **Full-time faculty:** 100 total; 3% minority, 67% women. **Part-time faculty:** 351 total; 7% minority, 55% women. **Class size:** 67% < 20, 33% 20-39, less than 1% 40-49, less than 1% 50-99. **Partnerships:** Formal partnerships with National Cable Telecommunications Institute, Swedish Medical Center, Porter Adventist Hospital, Skyridge Medical Center.

**Student profile.** Among degree-seeking undergraduates, 607 transferred in from other institutions.

Out-of-state: 5%    25 or older: 57%

**Transfer out. Colleges most students transferred to 2009:** University of Colorado at Denver, Colorado State University, University of Northern Colorado, Colorado School of Mines, Adams State College.

**Basis for selection.** Open admission, but selective for some programs. Allied health, nursing, automotive, legal assistant, and law enforcement programs require interviews and/or test scores.

**2009-2010 Annual costs.** Tuition/fees: $2,811; $11,979 out-of-state. Per-credit charge: $88 in-state; $394 out-of-state. In-state tuition based upon assumption of Colorado Opportunity Fund waiver of $68 per-credit-hour. Books/supplies: $850.

**2008-2009 Financial aid. Need-based:** 47% of total undergraduate aid awarded as scholarships/grants, 53% as loans/jobs. Need-based aid available for part-time students. Work-study available nights, weekends and for part-time students. **Non-need-based:** Scholarships awarded for academics, leadership, state residency.

**Application procedures. Admission:** No deadline. No application fee. Admission notification on a rolling basis. Closing date for nursing applicants February 4. **Financial aid:** Priority date 5/1; no closing date. FAFSA, institutional form required. Applicants notified on a rolling basis starting 5/1; must reply within 3 week(s) of notification.

**Academics. Special study options:** Accelerated study, cooperative education, distance learning, double major, dual enrollment of high school students, ESL, independent study, internships. License preparation in nursing, occupational therapy, paramedic, physical therapy, real estate. **Credit/placement by examination:** AP, CLEP, IB, institutional tests. No more than half of required credit can be fulfilled through credit for prior learning. **Support services:** GED preparation and test center, learning center, preadmission summer program, reduced course load, remedial instruction, study skills assistance, tutoring, writing center.

**Majors. Business:** Accounting technology, administrative services, banking/financial services, hospitality admin, international, management information systems, marketing, office management, selling. **Communications technology:** General. **Computer sciences:** Data entry, LAN/WAN management, networking, web page design. **Construction:** General, building inspection. **Engineering technology:** General, architectural, computer, electrical, manufacturing. **Family/consumer sciences:** Child development. **Health:** Clinical lab technology, medical records technology, nursing (RN), occupational therapy assistant, office admin, physical therapy assistant. **Legal studies:** Paralegal. **Liberal arts:** Arts/sciences. **Mechanic/repair:** Automotive. **Parks/recreation:** Health/fitness. **Personal/culinary services:** Mortuary science. **Protective services:** Law enforcement admin. **Visual/performing arts:** Graphic design, interior design.

**Most popular majors.** Health sciences 26%, liberal arts 40%, personal/culinary services 7%, visual/performing arts 9%.

**Computing on campus.** 110 workstations in library, computer center, student center. Commuter students can connect to campus network. Online course registration, online library, helpline, wireless network available.

**Student life. Freshman orientation:** Mandatory. Preregistration for classes offered. **Activities:** Bands, choral groups, international student organizations, literary magazine, music ensembles, student government, student newspaper, Phi Theta Kappa, diversity council, Ron Paul society.

**Athletics. Team name:** Coyotes.

**Student services.** Adult student services, career counseling, services for economically disadvantaged, student employment services, financial aid counseling, minority student services, on-campus daycare, placement for graduates, veterans' counselor. **Physically disabled:** Services for visually, speech, hearing impaired. **Learning disabled:** Comprehensive services available. **Transfer:** Pre-admission transcript evaluation for new students. Transfer adviser, college fairs on campus for students transferring to 4-year colleges.

**Contact.** E-mail: admissions@arapahoe.edu
Phone: (303) 797-5621 Fax: (303) 797-5970
Darcy Briggs, Registrar-Director of Enrollment Services, Arapahoe Community College, PO Box 9002, Littleton, CO 80160-9002

## Bel-Rea Institute of Animal Technology
### Denver, Colorado
### www.bel-rea.com                                    CB code: 0928

- For-profit 2-year technical college
- Commuter campus in very large city

**General.** Accredited by ACCSC. **Enrollment:** 630 degree-seeking undergraduates. **Degrees:** 196 associate awarded. **Calendar:** Continuous. **Full-time faculty:** 25 total. **Part-time faculty:** 5 total.

**Transfer out. Colleges most students transferred to 2009:** University of Denver.

**Basis for selection.** Interview most important, followed by school achievement record. Recommendations considered. Minimum 2.5 GPA or GED required. Applicants with below 2.5 GPA or without GED must take entrance exam.

**High school preparation.** As much science and math as possible recommended. Algebra and chemistry recommended.

**2009-2010 Annual costs.** Tuition for full associate program $24,250. Books/supplies: $1,500. Personal expenses: $1,100.

**Financial aid.** All financial aid based on need.

**Application procedures. Admission:** No deadline. No application fee. Admission notification on a rolling basis. **Financial aid:** Priority date 8/31; no closing date. FAFSA required. Applicants notified on a rolling basis starting 8/15.

**Academics.** Students intern at college-affiliated emergency veterinary hospital. **Special study options:** Internships. **Credit/placement by examination:** CLEP. **Support services:** Reduced course load, study skills assistance, tutoring.

**Majors. Health:** Veterinary technology/assistant.

**Computing on campus.** PC or laptop required. 20 workstations in student center.

**Student life. Freshman orientation:** Available. **Activities:** Student government.

**Student services.** Career counseling, student employment services, personal counseling, placement for graduates, veterans' counselor.

**Contact.** E-mail: kaufman@bel-rea.com
Phone: (303) 751-8700 Toll-free number: (800) 950-8001
Fax: (303) 751-9969
Paulette Kaufman, Director, Bel-Rea Institute of Animal Technology, 1681 South Dayton Street, Denver, CO 80247

## Boulder College of Massage Therapy
### Boulder, Colorado
### www.bcmt.org

- Private 2-year health science college
- Residential campus in small city
- Application essay, interview required

**General.** Accredited by ACCSC. **Enrollment:** 165 degree-seeking undergraduates. **Degrees:** 30 associate awarded. **Location:** 30 miles from Denver. **Calendar:** Quarter, extensive summer session. **Full-time faculty:** 2 total. **Part-time faculty:** 38 total; 10% have terminal degrees. **Class size:** 97% < 20, 3% 20-39. **Special facilities:** Student massage therapy clinic, wellness bookstore, spa classroom.

**Basis for selection.** Open admission, but selective for some programs. Health history form required.

**2009-2010 Annual costs.** Program costs range from $13,700-$17,500.

**Financial aid.** All financial aid based on need. Need-based aid available for part-time students.

**Application procedures. Admission:** No deadline. $75 fee, may be waived for applicants with need. Application must be submitted on paper. Admission notification on a rolling basis. **Financial aid:** No deadline. FAFSA required.

**Academics. Special study options:** Honors, internships. **Credit/placement by examination:** CLEP. **Support services:** Learning center, reduced course load, study skills assistance, tutoring.

**Majors. Health:** Massage therapy.

**Computing on campus.** 10 workstations in library, computer center. Online library, wireless network available.

**Student life. Freshman orientation:** Mandatory. Preregistration for classes offered. Held Monday prior to start of quarter. **Activities:** Student government.

**Student services.** Adult student services, alcohol/substance abuse counseling, career counseling, services for economically disadvantaged, student employment services, financial aid counseling, personal counseling, placement for graduates, veterans' counselor. **Physically disabled:** Services for visually, speech, hearing impaired.

**Contact.** E-mail: admissions@bcmt.org
Phone: (303) 530-2100 Toll-free number: (800) 442-5131
Fax: (303) 530-2204
Director of Marketing and Admissions, Boulder College of Massage Therapy, 6255 Longbow Drive, Boulder, CO 80301

## CollegeAmerica: Denver
### Denver, Colorado
### www.collegeamerica.com

- For-profit 2-year technical college
- Commuter campus in very large city
- Application essay, interview required

**General.** Accredited by ACCSC. **Enrollment:** 645 degree-seeking undergraduates. **Degrees:** 21 bachelor's, 51 associate awarded. **Calendar:** Continuous, extensive summer session. **Full-time faculty:** 8 total; 12% have terminal degrees, 25% minority, 50% women. **Part-time faculty:** 35 total. **Class size:** 91% < 20, 9% 20-39.

Two-Year Colleges

**Basis for selection.** Open admission. **Homeschooled:** Transcript of courses and grades, state high school equivalency certificate required.

**2009-2010 Annual costs.** Tuition, fees, books, and supplies: $37,500 for associate degree programs; $66,100 for bachelor's degree programs. Books/supplies: $101. Personal expenses: $1,000.

**2009-2010 Financial aid.** All financial aid based on need.

**Application procedures. Admission:** No deadline. $50 fee, may be waived for applicants with need. Application must be submitted on paper. Admission notification on a rolling basis. **Financial aid:** No deadline. FAFSA, institutional form required. Applicants notified on a rolling basis; must reply within 4 week(s) of notification.

**Academics. Special study options:** Accelerated study, distance learning. Bachelor's degree programs available on campus. License preparation in radiology. **Credit/placement by examination:** AP, CLEP. **Support services:** Tutoring.

**Majors. Business:** Accounting/business management, business admin. **Computer sciences:** Computer graphics, networking, programming. **Health:** Health services.

**Most popular majors.** Business/marketing 10%, computer/information sciences 10%, health sciences 80%.

**Computing on campus.** 50 workstations in library, computer center. Commuter students can connect to campus network. Online course registration, online library, repair service, wireless network available.

**Student life. Freshman orientation:** Mandatory.

**Student services.** Career counseling, services for economically disadvantaged, student employment services, financial aid counseling, placement for graduates.

**Contact.** Phone: (303) 691-9756 Toll-free number: (800) 977-5455 Jaclyn Haack, Director of Admissions, CollegeAmerica: Denver, 1385 South Colorado Boulevard, 5th Floor, Denver, CO 80222-1912

## Colorado Mountain College
### Glenwood Springs, Colorado
www.coloradomtn.edu                          CB code: 4112

▶ Public 2-year community and liberal arts college
▶ Residential campus in small town

**General.** Founded in 1965. Regionally accredited. Total of 12 campuses. Three residential campuses are Alpine Campus in Steamboat Springs, Spring Valley Campus in Glenwood Springs, and Timberline Campus in Leadville. Commuter campuses in Aspen, Summit, Vail-Eagle Valley in Edwards, Rifle, Breckinridge, Buena Vista. **Enrollment:** 5,095 degree-seeking undergraduates. **Degrees:** 351 associate awarded. **Location:** 160 miles from Denver. **Calendar:** Semester, limited summer session. **Full-time faculty:** 80 total. **Part-time faculty:** 270 total. **Special facilities:** Outdoor education center, farm for veterinarian technician program, hot springs, climbing wall, ice wall, community theater.

**Student profile.**

| Out-of-state: | 10% | 25 or older: | 68% |
|---|---|---|---|

**Transfer out. Colleges most students transferred to 2009:** University of Colorado-Boulder, Colorado State University, Mesa State University, Western State College, Fort Lewis College.

**Basis for selection.** Open admission, but selective for some programs. Special requirements for nursing applicants. Testing requirements for veterinary technology, photography, outdoor recreation leadership, culinary arts, paramedic, and ski area operations.

**2009-2010 Annual costs.** Tuition/fees: $1,550; $2,450 out-of-district; $7,250 out-of-state. Per-credit charge: $45 in-district; $75 out-of-district; $235 out-of-state. Room/board: $7,400. Books/supplies: $650. Personal expenses: $2,050.

**2008-2009 Financial aid.** All financial aid based on need. Need-based aid available for part-time students. Work-study available nights, weekends and for part-time students.

**Application procedures. Admission:** No deadline. No application fee. Application must be submitted on paper. Admission notification on a rolling basis. **Financial aid:** Priority date 3/31; no closing date. FAFSA required.

Applicants notified on a rolling basis starting 5/15; must reply within 4 week(s) of notification.

**Academics. Special study options:** Distance learning, dual enrollment of high school students, independent study, internships, liberal arts/career combination, study abroad. License preparation in nursing. **Credit/placement by examination:** AP, CLEP, IB, institutional tests. 30 credit hours maximum toward associate degree. Also recognize and accept exam results for DANTES, Excelsior, Institutional Challenge Exams, and credit for life experiences. **Support services:** GED preparation and test center, learning center, reduced course load, remedial instruction, study skills assistance, tutoring.

**Majors. Agriculture:** Animal health, food processing, food science, soil science. **Biology:** General. **Business:** General, accounting, business admin, hospitality admin, hotel/motel admin, management information systems, real estate, resort management. **Communications:** Photojournalism. **Communications technology:** Animation/special effects, graphic/printing, graphics, photo/film/video. **Computer sciences:** General, applications programming, computer graphics, information technology, networking, programming. **Conservation:** General, forestry, management/policy. **Education:** General, bilingual. **Engineering:** General, mechanical. **Health:** Nursing (RN), prenursing, veterinary technology/assistant. **Interdisciplinary:** Accounting/computer science, biological/physical sciences, natural sciences, science/society. **Legal studies:** Prelaw. **Liberal arts:** Arts/sciences. **Math:** General. **Parks/recreation:** General, facilities management. **Personal/culinary services:** General, chef training, culinary arts, food prep, restaurant/catering. **Physical sciences:** Chemistry, geology. **Protective services:** Criminal justice, firefighting. **Social sciences:** General. **Visual/performing arts:** General, art, commercial photography, commercial/advertising art, design, dramatic, graphic design, photography.

**Computing on campus.** 30 workstations in dormitories, library, computer center, student center. Dormitories wired for high-speed internet access and linked to campus network. Online library, helpline, wireless network available.

**Student life. Freshman orientation:** Available. Preregistration for classes offered. Fee charged for some orientation activities. **Policies:** All students living on-campus must follow housing policies. **Housing:** Guaranteed on-campus for freshmen. Coed dorms, special housing for disabled, wellness housing available. $300 partly refundable deposit, deadline 7/1. **Activities:** Dance, drama, musical theater, student government, student newspaper.

**Athletics.** NJCAA. **Intercollegiate:** Skiing, soccer. **Intramural:** Basketball, cross-country, skiing, soccer, softball, volleyball. **Team name:** Eagles.

**Student services.** Adult student services, career counseling, student employment services, financial aid counseling, health services, personal counseling, placement for graduates, veterans' counselor. **Physically disabled:** Services for visually, speech, hearing impaired. **Transfer:** Transfer center, transfer adviser, college fairs on campus for students transferring to 4-year colleges.

**Contact.** E-mail: joinus@coloradomtn.edu
Phone: (970) 947-8327 Toll-free number: (800) 621-8559 ext. 8327
Fax: (970) 947-8324
Bill Sommers, Director of Pre-Enrollment Services, Collegewide, Colorado Mountain College, 831 Grand Avenue, Glenwood Springs, CO 81601

## Colorado Northwestern Community College
### Rangely, Colorado
www.cncc.edu                                CB code: 4665

▶ Public 2-year community college
▶ Residential campus in rural community

**General.** Founded in 1962. Regionally accredited. Courses also offered at campus in Craig and 3 off-campus sites in Meeker, Hayden, Oak Creek. **Enrollment:** 748 degree-seeking undergraduates; 584 non-degree-seeking students. **Degrees:** 106 associate awarded. **Location:** 300 miles from Denver, 90 miles from Grand Junction. **Calendar:** Semester, limited summer session. **Full-time faculty:** 34 total. **Part-time faculty:** 69 total. **Class size:** 90% < 20, 10% 20-39. **Special facilities:** Flight simulator, firearms training simulator, cadaver lab.

**Student profile.** Among degree-seeking undergraduates, 51% enrolled in a transfer program, 49% enrolled in a vocational program, 223 enrolled as first-time, first-year students.

| | | | |
|---|---|---|---|
| Part-time: | 42% | Hispanic American: | 9% |
| Out-of-state: | 20% | Native American: | 1% |
| Women: | 66% | 25 or older: | 37% |
| African American: | 6% | Live on campus: | 32% |
| Asian American: | 2% | | |

**Transfer out. Colleges most students transferred to 2009:** University of Northern Colorado, Colorado State University, Mesa State College.

**Basis for selection.** Open admission, but selective for some programs. Selective admissions to dental hygiene and nursing. Both programs have application deadline and pre-requisite requirements. Interview required of dental hygiene majors.

**High school preparation.** Biological science and/or chemistry required for dental hygiene. Math/science desirable for aviation technology and aviation maintenance.

**2009-2010 Annual costs.** Tuition/fees: $2,875; $5,676 out-of-state. Per-credit charge: $88 in-state; $182 out-of-state. In-state tuition based upon assumption of Colorado Opportunity Fund waiver of $68 per-credit-hour. Room/board: $5,868. Books/supplies: $1,000. Personal expenses: $1,650.

**2008-2009 Financial aid. Need-based:** Need-based aid available for part-time students. Work-study available nights, weekends and for part-time students. **Non-need-based:** Scholarships awarded for academics, athletics, state residency.

**Application procedures. Admission:** No deadline. No application fee. Admission notification on a rolling basis. Application closing date for dental hygiene program 2/15. **Financial aid:** Priority date 5/1; no closing date. FAFSA, institutional form required. Applicants notified on a rolling basis starting 5/15; must reply within 4 week(s) of notification.

**Academics. Special study options:** Distance learning, dual enrollment of high school students, independent study, internships, student-designed major. Bachelor's degree programs available on campus. License preparation in aviation, dental hygiene, nursing. **Credit/placement by examination:** AP, CLEP, institutional tests. 30 credit hours maximum toward associate degree. **Support services:** GED preparation and test center, learning center, remedial instruction, study skills assistance, tutoring, writing center.

**Majors. Agriculture:** Equestrian studies. **Business:** Accounting technology, banking/financial services, entrepreneurial studies, management information systems, office management. **Construction:** Power transmission. **Engineering technology:** Civil, energy systems, GIS, instrumentation, petroleum. **Family/consumer sciences:** Child care. **Health:** Dental hygiene, EMT paramedic, nursing (RN). **Legal studies:** Paralegal. **Liberal arts:** Arts/sciences. **Mechanic/repair:** Aircraft. **Protective services:** Law enforcement admin. **Transportation:** Aviation.

**Most popular majors.** Business/marketing 7%, health sciences 48%, liberal arts 39%, trade and industry 6%.

**Computing on campus.** 54 workstations in dormitories, library, computer center. Dormitories wired for high-speed internet access and linked to campus network. Online course registration, online library, wireless network available.

**Student life. Freshman orientation:** Mandatory, $45 fee. Preregistration for classes offered. 2 sessions in July, one in August. **Housing:** Guaranteed on-campus for freshmen. Coed dorms, special housing for disabled available. $100 deposit. **Activities:** Choral groups, drama, music ensembles, musical theater, student government, student newspaper.

**Athletics.** NJCAA. **Intercollegiate:** Baseball M, basketball, softball W, volleyball W. **Intramural:** Basketball, football (non-tackle), golf, racquetball, soccer, softball, table tennis, volleyball. **Team name:** Spartans.

**Student services.** Adult student services, alcohol/substance abuse counseling, career counseling, student employment services, financial aid counseling, personal counseling, placement for graduates, veterans' counselor. **Physically disabled:** Services for visually, hearing impaired. **Transfer:** Pre-admission transcript evaluation for new students. Transfer adviser, college fairs on campus for students transferring to 4-year colleges.

**Contact.** E-mail: lisa.lefevre@cncc.edu
Phone: (970) 675-3218 Toll-free number: (800) 562-1105
Fax: (970) 975-3343
Tresa England, Director of Student Services/Registrar, Colorado Northwestern Community College, 500 Kennedy Drive, Rangely, CO 81648

## Colorado School of Healing Arts
**Lakewood, Colorado**
**www.csha.net**

◆ For-profit 2-year career college
◆ Commuter campus in small city
◆ Application essay, interview required

**General.** Accredited by ACCSC. **Enrollment:** 200 degree-seeking undergraduates. **Degrees:** 35 associate awarded. **Location:** 7 miles from Denver. **Calendar:** Quarter, extensive summer session. **Part-time faculty:** 34 total. **Class size:** 79% < 20, 21% 20-39.

**Basis for selection.** Open admission. **Homeschooled:** Interview required.

**2009-2010 Annual costs.** Tuition/fees: $12,379. Per-credit charge: $166. Books, massage table package, materials fees, and insurance are included in required fees. Books/supplies: $1,249. Personal expenses: $300.

**2008-2009 Financial aid.** All financial aid based on need. Need-based aid available for part-time students.

**Application procedures. Admission:** No deadline. $50 fee. Application must be submitted on paper. Admission notification on a rolling basis. **Financial aid:** No deadline. FAFSA required.

**Academics. Special study options:** Accelerated study. **Credit/placement by examination:** CLEP. **Support services:** Learning center, tutoring.

**Majors. Health:** Massage therapy.

**Computing on campus.** 2 workstations in library.

**Student life. Freshman orientation:** Mandatory. Preregistration for classes offered. Four-hour program held prior to start of quarter.

**Student services.** Career counseling, financial aid counseling.

**Contact.** E-mail: tiffany@csha.net
Phone: (303) 986-2320 Toll-free number: (800) 233-7114
Fax: (303) 980-6594
Patty Higginbotham, Admissions Representative, Colorado School of Healing Arts, 7655 West Mississippi Avenue, Suite 100, Lakewood, CO 80226

## Colorado School of Trades
**Lakewood, Colorado**
**www.schooloftrades.com**          CB code: 3211

◆ For-profit 2-year technical college
◆ Small city

**General.** Accredited by ACCSC. **Enrollment:** 148 degree-seeking undergraduates. **Degrees:** 106 associate awarded. **Calendar:** Continuous. **Full-time faculty:** 10 total. **Part-time faculty:** 3 total.

**Basis for selection.** Open admission.

**2010-2011 Annual costs.** For gunsmithing program: tuition, $18,900; tools $3,000; miscellaneous $161.

**Application procedures. Admission:** No deadline. $25 fee. Admission notification on a rolling basis. **Financial aid:** FAFSA, institutional form required.

**Academics. Credit/placement by examination:** CLEP.

**Majors. Education:** Trade/industrial. **Mechanic/repair:** General.

**Computing on campus.** 4 workstations in computer center.

**Contact.** Phone: (303) 233-4697 ext. 45 Toll-free number: (800) 234-4594 ext. 45 Fax: (303) 233-4723
Sunny Duvont-Holt, Director of Admissions, Colorado School of Trades, 1575 Hoyt Street, Lakewood, CO 80215-2945

## Community College of Aurora
Aurora, Colorado
www.ccaurora.edu                          CB code: 0969

♦ Public 2-year community college
♦ Commuter campus in large city

**General.** Founded in 1983. Regionally accredited. **Enrollment:** 6,358 undergraduates. **Degrees:** 356 associate awarded. **Calendar:** Semester, extensive summer session. **Full-time faculty:** 42 total. **Part-time faculty:** 300 total.

**Student profile.**

| | | | |
|---|---|---|---|
| Out-of-state: | 3% | Live on campus: | 2% |
| 25 or older: | 60% | | |

**Transfer out. Colleges most students transferred to 2009:** Metropolitan State University, University of Colorado Denver, Colorado State University, University of Northern Colorado.

**Basis for selection.** Open admission.

**2009-2010 Annual costs.** Tuition/fees: $2,805; $11,973 out-of-state. Per-credit charge: $88 in-state; $394 out-of-state. In-state tuition based upon assumption of Colorado Opportunity Fund waiver of $68 per-credit-hour. Books/supplies: $400.

**Financial aid. Need-based:** Need-based aid available for part-time students. Work-study available nights and for part-time students.

**Application procedures. Admission:** No deadline. No application fee. Admission notification on a rolling basis. **Financial aid:** Priority date 6/1; no closing date. FAFSA, institutional form required. Applicants notified on a rolling basis starting 7/15.

**Academics. Special study options:** Cooperative education, cross-registration, distance learning, ESL, internships, study abroad, weekend college. License preparation in paramedic. **Credit/placement by examination:** CLEP, IB. 30 credit hours maximum toward associate degree. **Support services:** GED preparation, learning center, remedial instruction, tutoring.

**Majors. Business:** General, accounting, administrative services, banking/financial services, business admin, management information systems, marketing, office technology, sales/distribution. **Communications technology:** Graphic/printing. **Computer sciences:** General, information systems. **Construction:** Carpentry, power transmission. **Education:** Early childhood. **Engineering technology:** Drafting, electrical. **Family/consumer sciences:** Child care. **Health:** Medical secretary. **Legal studies:** Legal secretary, paralegal. **Mechanic/repair:** Heating/ac/refrig. **Personal/culinary services:** Culinary arts. **Protective services:** Criminal justice, law enforcement admin.

**Computing on campus.** 210 workstations in dormitories, library, computer center, student center. Dormitories wired for high-speed internet access and linked to campus network. Commuter students can connect to campus network. Online course registration, online library, repair service available.

**Student life. Freshman orientation:** Available. Preregistration for classes offered. **Housing:** Guaranteed on-campus for freshmen. Coed dorms available. $150 deposit. **Activities:** Dance, drama, music ensembles, musical theater, student government, student newspaper, black student alliance, Lazos Culturales, Phi Theta Kappa, Phi Alpha Omega, Campus Crusade for Christ.

**Athletics. Intramural:** Basketball, softball, tennis, volleyball.

**Student services.** Career counseling, student employment services, financial aid counseling, personal counseling, veterans' counselor. **Physically disabled:** Services for visually, speech, hearing impaired. **Transfer:** Transfer adviser, college fairs on campus for students transferring to 4-year colleges.

**Contact.** Phone: (303) 360-4700 Fax: (303) 361-7432
Kristen Cusack, Registrar, Community College of Aurora, 16000 East CentreTech Parkway, Aurora, CO 80011-9036

## Community College of Denver
Denver, Colorado
www.ccd.edu                               CB code: 4137

♦ Public 2-year community college
♦ Commuter campus in very large city

**General.** Founded in 1970. Regionally accredited. Library, student center and physical education facilities shared with Metropolitan State College at Denver and University of Colorado/Health Sciences Center at Denver. **Enrollment:** 5,257 degree-seeking undergraduates; 2,993 non-degree-seeking students. **Degrees:** 432 associate awarded. **ROTC:** Army, Air Force. **Calendar:** Semester, limited summer session. **Full-time faculty:** 80 total; 20% minority, 64% women. **Part-time faculty:** 314 total; 24% minority, 56% women. **Class size:** 52% < 20, 48% 20-39.

**Student profile.** Among degree-seeking undergraduates, 1,518 enrolled as first-time, first-year students, 868 transferred in from other institutions.

| | | | |
|---|---|---|---|
| Part-time: | 68% | Hispanic American: | 27% |
| Women: | 62% | Native American: | 1% |
| African American: | 16% | International: | 6% |
| Asian American: | 6% | 25 or older: | 42% |

**Transfer out. Colleges most students transferred to 2009:** Metropolitan State College of Denver, University of Colorado at Denver.

**Basis for selection.** Open admission, but selective for some programs. Special requirements for health occupations and computer information systems programs.

**2009-2010 Annual costs.** Tuition/fees: $3,194; $12,362 out-of-state. Per-credit charge: $88 in-state; $394 out-of-state. In-state tuition based upon assumption of Colorado Opportunity Fund waiver of $68 per-credit-hour. Books/supplies: $1,749. Personal expenses: $3,402.

**2008-2009 Financial aid. Need-based:** 58% of total undergraduate aid awarded as scholarships/grants, 42% as loans/jobs. Need-based aid available for part-time students. **Non-need-based:** Scholarships awarded for academics, leadership, state residency.

**Application procedures. Admission:** Priority date 8/1; no deadline. No application fee. Admission notification on a rolling basis. **Financial aid:** Priority date 3/1; no closing date. FAFSA, institutional form required. Applicants notified on a rolling basis.

**Academics. Special study options:** Accelerated study, cooperative education, cross-registration, distance learning, double major, dual enrollment of high school students, ESL, external degree, honors, independent study, internships. **Credit/placement by examination:** AP, CLEP, institutional tests. 45 credit hours maximum toward associate degree. **Support services:** GED preparation and test center, learning center, pre-admission summer program, reduced course load, remedial instruction, study skills assistance, tutoring, writing center.

**Majors. Biology:** Biomedical sciences. **Business:** Accounting technology, administrative services, business admin, management information systems. **Computer sciences:** General, applications programming. **Education:** Teacher assistance. **Engineering technology:** Drafting, heat/ac/refrig. **Family/consumer sciences:** Child development. **Health:** Dental hygiene, electroencephalograph technology, health aide, nursing (RN), radiologic technology/medical imaging, veterinary technology/assistant. **Legal studies:** Paralegal. **Liberal arts:** Arts/sciences. **Parks/recreation:** General, health/fitness. **Production:** Welding. **Protective services:** Security services. **Public administration:** Human services. **Visual/performing arts:** Graphic design.

**Most popular majors.** Health sciences 44%, liberal arts 44%.

**Computing on campus.** 1,032 workstations in library, computer center, student center. Commuter students can connect to campus network. Online course registration available.

**Student life. Freshman orientation:** Mandatory. **Housing:** Dormitory housing available at Lowry campus through cooperative agreement. **Activities:** Choral groups, international student organizations, student government, student newspaper, Mexican-American student organization, African-American student organization, Amnesty International, nursing club.

**Student services.** Adult student services, career counseling, services for economically disadvantaged, student employment services, financial aid counseling, health services, legal services, minority student services, on-campus daycare, personal counseling, placement for graduates, veterans' counselor, women's services. **Physically disabled:** Services for visually, hearing impaired. **Transfer:** Re-entry adviser, pre-admission transcript evaluation for new students. Transfer center, transfer adviser, college fairs on campus for students transferring to 4-year colleges.

**Contact.** E-mail: enrollment_services@ccd.edu
Phone: (303) 556-2420 Fax: (303) 556-2431
Michael Rusk, Dean of Students, Community College of Denver, Campus Box 201, PO Box 173363, Denver, CO 80217-3363

## Concorde Career College: Aurora
### Aurora, Colorado
### www.concorde.edu/denver

- For-profit 2-year health science college
- Large city

**General.** Accredited by ACCSCT. **Calendar:** Continuous.

**Contact.** Phone: (303) 861-1151
Director of Admissions, 111 North Havana Street, Aurora, CO 80010

## Denver Academy of Court Reporting
### Denver, Colorado
### www.dacr.org                          CB code: 3561

- For-profit 2-year college of court reporting
- Large city
- Interview required

**General.** Accredited by ACICS. **Enrollment:** 152 degree-seeking undergraduates. **Degrees:** 10 associate awarded. **Calendar:** Quarter, extensive summer session. **Full-time faculty:** 10 total. **Part-time faculty:** 10 total.

**Basis for selection.** Open admission. Must meet with an admissions representative, tour the facility, and inspect the equipment used in the training program.

**2009-2010 Annual costs.** Day program tuition $2,300 per quarter, evening program $2,200 per quarter. $150 enrollment fee. $190 per quarter technology fee. Books/supplies: $450.

**Application procedures. Admission:** No deadline. $175 fee.

**Academics. Special study options:** Internships. **Credit/placement by examination:** CLEP.

**Majors. Legal studies:** Court reporting.

**Computing on campus.** Online library, wireless network available.

**Student life. Freshman orientation:** Mandatory.

**Student services. Transfer:** Pre-admission transcript evaluation for new students.

**Contact.** E-mail: info@dacr.org
Phone: (303) 427-5292 Fax: (303) 427-5383
Susan Williford, Director of Admissions, Denver Academy of Court Reporting, 9051 Harlan Street, Unit #20, Westminster, CO 80031

## Everest College: Aurora
### Aurora, Colorado
### www.cci.edu                           CB code: 3568

- For-profit 2-year branch campus and technical college
- Commuter campus in large city

**General.** Accredited by ACICS. **Location:** 15 miles from Denver. **Calendar:** Continuous.

**Annual costs/financial aid.** $366 per credit hour for all linear programs; estimated cost per term for books: $370-$500, varies by program. Books/supplies: $900. Need-based financial aid available to full-time and part-time students.

**Contact.** Phone: (303) 745-6244
Director of Admissions, 14280 East Jewell Suite 100, Aurora, CO 80012

## Everest College: Colorado Springs
### Colorado Springs, Colorado
### www.cci.edu                           CB code: 0934

- For-profit 2-year business and junior college
- Commuter campus in large city

**General.** Founded in 1897. Accredited by ACICS. **Location:** 70 miles from Denver. **Calendar:** Quarter.

**Annual costs/financial aid.** Accounting, Business Administration, Computers: $350 per credit hour. Business Accounting, Criminal Justice, Paralegal: $348 per credit hour. Diploma programs: Medical Assisting, $14,225; Medical Administrative Assistant: $14,085; Massage Therapy: $14,428; Dental Assisting: $13,150. Cost includes books, uniforms, materials. No additional fees. Books/supplies: $1,025. Need-based financial aid available to full-time and part-time students.

**Contact.** Phone: (719) 638-6580
Director of Admissions, 1815 Jet Wing Drive, Colorado Springs, CO 80916

## Everest College: Denver
### Denver, Colorado
### www.cci.edu                           CB code: 0349

- For-profit 2-year junior college
- Commuter campus in very large city

**General.** Founded in 1895. Accredited by ACICS. **Location:** 7 miles from downtown. **Calendar:** Quarter.

**Contact.** Phone: (303) 457-2757
Director of Admissions, 9065 Grant Street, Denver, CO 80229

## Front Range Community College
### Westminster, Colorado
### www.frontrange.edu                     CB code: 4119

- Public 2-year community college
- Commuter campus in large city

**General.** Founded in 1968. Regionally accredited. Additional campuses in Brighton, Boulder County, Larimer County. **Enrollment:** 12,857 degree-seeking undergraduates; 2,838 non-degree-seeking students. **Degrees:** 1,010 associate awarded. **ROTC:** Army, Air Force. **Location:** 12 miles from Denver. **Calendar:** Semester, limited summer session. **Full-time faculty:** 201 total; 59% women. **Part-time faculty:** 802 total. **Class size:** 45% < 20, 54% 20-39, less than 1% 40-49. **Special facilities:** Observatories, city/college libraries. **Partnerships:** Formal partnerships with local workforce centers for career training or retraining.

**Student profile.** Among degree-seeking undergraduates, 67% enrolled in a transfer program, 33% enrolled in a vocational program, 2% already have a bachelor's degree or higher, 3,358 enrolled as first-time, first-year students, 544 transferred in from other institutions.

| | | | |
|---|---|---|---|
| Part-time: | 62% | Hispanic American: | 12% |
| Out-of-state: | 7% | Native American: | 1% |
| Women: | 58% | International: | 2% |
| African American: | 2% | 25 or older: | 39% |
| Asian American: | 4% | | |

**Transfer out. Colleges most students transferred to 2009:** Colorado State University, University of Colorado at Boulder, Metropolitan State College, University of Northern Colorado, University of Colorado at Denver Health Sciences.

**Basis for selection.** Open admission.

**High school preparation.** 13 units recommended. Recommended units include English 4, mathematics 3, history 3, science 2 (laboratory 1).

**2009-2010 Annual costs.** Tuition/fees: $2,893; $12,061 out-of-state. Per-credit charge: $88 in-state; $394 out-of-state. In-state tuition based upon assumption of Colorado Opportunity Fund waiver of $68 per-credit-hour. Books/supplies: $1,198.

**2008-2009 Financial aid. Need-based:** 41% of total undergraduate aid awarded as scholarships/grants, 59% as loans/jobs. Need-based aid available for part-time students. Work-study available nights, weekends and for part-time students. **Non-need-based:** Scholarships awarded for academics, job skills, leadership, ROTC, state residency.

**Application procedures. Admission:** No deadline. No application fee. Admission notification on a rolling basis. **Financial aid:** Priority date 5/1; no closing date. FAFSA, institutional form required. Applicants notified on a rolling basis starting 7/1; must reply within 3 week(s) of notification.

**Academics. Special study options:** Cooperative education, cross-registration, distance learning, double major, dual enrollment of high school students, ESL, honors, independent study, internships, liberal arts/career combination, study abroad, teacher certification program, weekend college. License preparation in dental hygiene, nursing, paramedic. **Credit/placement**

**by examination:** AP, CLEP, institutional tests. 30 credit hours maximum toward associate degree. **Support services:** GED preparation and test center, learning center, remedial instruction, study skills assistance, tutoring.

**Majors. Agriculture:** Animal health, horticulture. **Business:** Accounting technology, business admin, hospitality admin, management information systems, office management. **Communications technology:** Animation/special effects. **Conservation:** Wildlife. **Construction:** Masonry. **Engineering technology:** Architectural, CAD/CADD, electrical, heat/ac/refrig, manufacturing. **Family/consumer sciences:** Child care. **Foreign languages:** Sign language interpretation. **Health:** Dietician assistant, EMT paramedic, medical records technology, nursing (RN), office assistant, veterinary technology/assistant. **Legal studies:** Paralegal. **Liberal arts:** Arts/sciences. **Mechanic/repair:** Automotive. **Production:** Machine shop technology, welding. **Visual/performing arts:** Interior design. **Other:** Applied technology.

**Most popular majors.** Business/marketing 8%, health sciences 23%, liberal arts 57%.

**Computing on campus.** 233 workstations in library, computer center. Commuter students can connect to campus network. Online course registration, helpline, wireless network available.

**Student life. Freshman orientation:** Available. Preregistration for classes offered. **Activities:** Dance, drama, student government, student newspaper, interpreters for the deaf, gay/straight alliance, pharmacy tech club, dance club, ski/snowboard club, Phi Theta Kappa, horticulture club, student vet tech association, Latino club, science club.

**Student services.** Adult student services, career counseling, services for economically disadvantaged, student employment services, financial aid counseling, minority student services, on-campus daycare, personal counseling, veterans' counselor, women's services. **Physically disabled:** Services for visually, speech, hearing impaired. **Transfer:** Transfer center, college fairs on campus for students transferring to 4-year colleges.

**Contact.** Phone: (303) 404-5414 Fax: (303) 404-5150
Yolonda Espinoza, Registrar, Front Range Community College, 3645 West 112th Avenue, Westminster, CO 80031

## Institute of Business & Medical Careers
**Fort Collins, Colorado**
www.ibmc.edu                                    CB code: 3566

- For-profit 2-year technical college
- Residential campus in small city
- Application essay, interview required

**General.** Accredited by ACICS. Additional campuses in Greeley and Cheyenne, WY. **Enrollment:** 324 degree-seeking undergraduates. **Degrees:** 180 associate awarded. **Location:** 60 miles from Denver; 45 miles from Cheyenne, WY. **Calendar:** Continuous. **Full-time faculty:** 20 total; 15% minority, 85% women. **Part-time faculty:** 55 total; 6% minority, 73% women.

**Student profile.** Among degree-seeking undergraduates, 100% enrolled in a vocational program. 10% already have a bachelor's degree or higher.

**Transfer out. Colleges most students transferred to 2009:** Colorado Christian University, Front Range Community College, Aims Community College.

**Basis for selection.** Open admission, but selective for some programs. Institutional entrance exam required for placement. **Homeschooled:** State high school equivalency certificate required.

**2009-2010 Annual costs.** Cost of Medical Assisting program (96 credits) is $28,000. Credit requirements for other programs range from 52 to 106 credits, or $15,600 to $31,800 at $300 per credit hour. Books/supplies: $1,400.

**Application procedures. Admission:** No deadline. $75 fee. Admission notification on a rolling basis.

**Academics. Credit/placement by examination:** AP, CLEP, institutional tests. Up to 50% of total progam credits may be obtained through transfer or test out. **Support services:** Learning center, reduced course load, study skills assistance, tutoring.

**Majors. Business:** Business admin.

**Computing on campus.** 10 workstations in library, student center. Commuter students can connect to campus network. Wireless network available.

**Student life. Freshman orientation:** Available.

**Student services.** Career counseling, student employment services, financial aid counseling, placement for graduates. **Transfer:** Pre-admission transcript evaluation for new students.

**Contact.** E-mail: info@ibmc.edu
Phone: (970) 223-2669 Toll-free number: (800) 495-2669
Karla Alpers, Registrar, Institute of Business & Medical Careers, 3842 South Mason Street, Fort Collins, CO 80525

## IntelliTec College
**Colorado Springs, Colorado**
www.intelliteccollege.com                        CB code: 2500

- For-profit 2-year technical college
- Commuter campus in large city

**General.** Founded in 1965. Accredited by ACCSCT. **Location:** 68 miles from Denver. **Calendar:** 6-week cycle.

**Annual costs/financial aid.** HVAC - Refrigeration Technician, $24,177; Computer and Network Systems, $24,969; Automotive Technician, $24,822; Architectural Drafting, $21,828; Mechanical Drafting, $22,122. Books/supplies: $1,200. Need-based financial aid available to full-time and part-time students.

**Contact.** Phone: (719) 632-7626
Director of Admissions, 2315 East Pikes Peak Avenue, Colorado Springs, CO 80909

## IntelliTec College: Grand Junction
**Grand Junction, Colorado**
www.intelliteccollege.edu                         CB code: 2489

- For-profit 2-year technical college
- Commuter campus in small city

**General.** Accredited by ACCSCT. **Location:** 250 miles from Denver, 300 miles from Salt Lake City. **Calendar:** Continuous.

**Annual costs/financial aid.** Tuition is $215 per credit hour for all programs. Number of credits required for completion varies by program. Total cost for some programs include: Medical Assistant, $19,565; Massage Therapist, $15,695; Architectural/Structural Drafting, $23,650. Books/supplies: $1,500. Need-based financial aid available for full-time students.

**Contact.** Phone: (970) 245-8101
Director of Admissions, 772 Horizon Drive, Grand Junction, CO 81506

## Kaplan College: Denver
**Thornton, Colorado**
www.kaplancollege.com

- For-profit 2-year technical and career college
- Very large city

**General.** Accredited by ACCSC. **Enrollment:** 368 degree-seeking undergraduates. **Degrees:** 27 associate awarded. **Calendar:** Quarter, extensive summer session. **Full-time faculty:** 6 total. **Part-time faculty:** 31 total.

**Basis for selection.** Open admission, but selective for some programs.

**2009-2010 Annual costs.** Tuition varies by program from $13,913 to $33,818, including fees and books.

**Application procedures. Admission:** No deadline. $25 fee. **Financial aid:** FAFSA required.

**Academics.** Paralegal program is ABA certified. **Special study options:** Accelerated study, independent study. **Credit/placement by examination:** CLEP. **Support services:** GED preparation, learning center, study skills assistance, tutoring.

**Majors. Legal studies:** Paralegal. **Protective services:** Law enforcement admin.

**Computing on campus.** 50 workstations in library, computer center.

**Student life. Freshman orientation:** Mandatory, $20 fee. Preregistration for classes offered.

**Student services.** Alcohol/substance abuse counseling, personal counseling, women's services.

**Contact.** Phone: (303) 295-0550 Toll-free number: (800) 848-0550 Fax: (303) 295-0102
Renee Keddington, Director of Admissions, Kaplan College: Denver, 500 East 84th Avenue, Suite W-200, Thornton, CO 80229

## Lamar Community College
### Lamar, Colorado
www.lamarcc.edu                    CB code: 4382

- Public 2-year community college
- Commuter campus in large town

**General.** Founded in 1937. Regionally accredited. **Enrollment:** 611 degree-seeking undergraduates. **Degrees:** 136 associate awarded. **Location:** 117 miles from Pueblo. **Calendar:** Semester, limited summer session. **Full-time faculty:** 24 total. **Part-time faculty:** 34 total.

**Student profile.**

| | | | |
|---|---|---|---|
| Out-of-state: | 10% | Live on campus: | 50% |
| 25 or older: | 75% | | |

**Basis for selection.** Open admission, but selective for some programs. Admission criteria for horse training management based on riding skills; admission to nursing based on specific prerequisite course grades. Interview required of horse training and management, practical nursing majors.

**2009-2010 Annual costs.** Tuition/fees: $2,863; $5,844 out-of-state. Per-credit charge: $88 in-state; $182 out-of-state. In-state tuition based upon assumption of Colorado Opportunity Fund waiver of $68 per-credit-hour. Room/board: $5,190. Books/supplies: $1,163. Personal expenses: $420.

**Financial aid. Need-based:** Need-based aid available for part-time students.

**Application procedures. Admission:** No application fee. Admission notification on a rolling basis. Applicants to horse training and management and LPN nursing program encouraged to apply early. **Financial aid:** Priority date 4/1; no closing date. FAFSA, institutional form required. Applicants notified on a rolling basis starting 7/1.

**Academics. Special study options:** Cooperative education, distance learning, dual enrollment of high school students, ESL, independent study, internships, student-designed major. **Credit/placement by examination:** CLEP, institutional tests. 16 credit hours maximum toward associate degree. **Support services:** GED preparation and test center, learning center, pre-admission summer program, remedial instruction, tutoring.

**Majors. Agriculture:** Agronomy, animal sciences, business, equestrian studies, range science. **Biology:** General. **Business:** General, accounting, administrative services, banking/financial services, business admin, office management. **Communications:** General. **Computer sciences:** Computer science, information systems. **Education:** General. **Family/consumer sciences:** Child care. **Health:** Medical secretary, predental, prepharmacy, preveterinary. **History:** General. **Legal studies:** Legal secretary, prelaw. **Liberal arts:** Arts/sciences. **Math:** General. **Psychology:** General. **Public administration:** Social work. **Social sciences:** General. **Visual/performing arts:** Art.

**Computing on campus.** 65 workstations in dormitories, library, computer center. Online course registration, online library, wireless network available.

**Student life. Freshman orientation:** Available. Preregistration for classes offered. **Policies:** All single freshmen under age 21 not living with parent, guardian, or relatives must live in dormitory. **Housing:** Guaranteed on-campus for freshmen. Coed dorms, single-sex dorms available. **Activities:** International student organizations, student government, Christian athletes, horse and rodeo club, Kosmetiques, LPN association, Phi Beta Lambda, nontraditional students club.

**Athletics.** NJCAA. **Intercollegiate:** Baseball M, basketball M, volleyball W. **Intramural:** Bowling, golf, softball, tennis, volleyball. **Team name:** Lopes.

**Student services.** Career counseling, student employment services, health services, personal counseling. **Transfer:** Transfer adviser, college fairs on campus for students transferring to 4-year colleges.

**Contact.** E-mail: admissions@lamarcc.edu
Phone: (719) 336-1590
Chad DeBono, Vice President of Student Services, Lamar Community College, 2401 South Main Street, Lamar, CO 81052-3999

## Lincoln College of Technology: Denver
### Denver, Colorado
www.dadc.com                    CB code: 3133

- For-profit 2-year technical college
- Very large city

**General.** Accredited by ACCSCT. **Calendar:** Continuous.

**Annual costs/financial aid.** Cost of complete 2-year associate degree program is $30,000. Books/supplies: $360. Personal expenses: $1,967.

**Contact.** Phone: (303) 722-5724
Director of Admissions, 460 South Lipan Street, Denver, CO 80223-9366

## Morgan Community College
### Fort Morgan, Colorado
www.morgancc.edu                    CB code: 0444

- Public 2-year community college
- Commuter campus in large town

**General.** Founded in 1967. Regionally accredited. **Enrollment:** 1,671 undergraduates. **Degrees:** 178 associate awarded. **Location:** 81 miles from Denver. **Calendar:** Semester, limited summer session. **Full-time faculty:** 35 total. **Part-time faculty:** 123 total. **Class size:** 69% < 20, 31% 20-39.

**Student profile.**

| | | | |
|---|---|---|---|
| Out-of-state: | 3% | 25 or older: | 46% |

**Basis for selection.** Open admission, but selective for some programs. Special requirements for physical therapist assistant, occupational therapy assistant, and nursing programs. Interview required of allied health majors.

**2009-2010 Annual costs.** Tuition/fees: $2,819; $11,987 out-of-state. Per-credit charge: $88 in-state; $394 out-of-state. In-state tuition based upon assumption of Colorado Opportunity Fund waiver of $68 per-credit-hour. Books/supplies: $675.

**2009-2010 Financial aid. Need-based:** Need-based aid available for part-time students. Work-study available nights, weekends and for part-time students.

**Application procedures. Admission:** No deadline. No application fee. Admission notification on a rolling basis. **Financial aid:** Priority date 6/1; no closing date. FAFSA required. Applicants notified on a rolling basis.

**Academics. Special study options:** Distance learning, double major, dual enrollment of high school students, ESL, independent study, internships, liberal arts/career combination, student-designed major, teacher certification program, weekend college. License preparation in nursing, real estate. **Credit/placement by examination:** AP, CLEP, institutional tests. 31 credit hours maximum toward associate degree. **Support services:** GED preparation and test center, learning center, reduced course load, remedial instruction, study skills assistance, tutoring.

**Majors. Business:** General, accounting. **Computer sciences:** Webmaster. **Education:** General. **Health:** Nursing (RN), occupational therapy assistant, physical therapy assistant. **Interdisciplinary:** Biological/physical sciences. **Liberal arts:** Arts/sciences. **Mechanic/repair:** Auto body, automotive. **Visual/performing arts:** Art. **Other:** Agricultural business planning and financial records.

**Computing on campus.** 50 workstations in library, computer center, student center. Commuter students can connect to campus network. Online course registration available.

**Student life. Activities:** Student newspaper, TV station, occupational therapy association, vocational industrial collusion association, Phi Theta Kappa, science club, history club, student nursing association, Phi Beta Lambda, health occupation student organization, physical therapy association.

**Student services.** Career counseling. **Transfer:** Pre-admission transcript evaluation for new students.

**Contact.** Phone: (970) 542-3156 Fax: (970) 542-3114
Dan Marler, Director of Guidance and Placement, Morgan Community College, 920 Barlow Road, Fort Morgan, CO 80701

## Northeastern Junior College
Sterling, Colorado
www.njc.edu                    CB code: 4537

- Public 2-year community and junior college
- Commuter campus in large town

**General.** Founded in 1941. Regionally accredited. **Enrollment:** 1,282 degree-seeking undergraduates; 537 non-degree-seeking students. **Degrees:** 205 associate awarded. **Location:** 125 miles from Denver. **Calendar:** Semester, limited summer session. **Full-time faculty:** 53 total; 4% have terminal degrees, 2% minority, 57% women. **Part-time faculty:** 62 total; 2% have terminal degrees, 76% women. **Class size:** 78% < 20, 21% 20-39, less than 1% 40-49, less than 1% 50-99, less than 1% >100. **Special facilities:** Equine center, greenhouse, college farm.

**Student profile.** Among degree-seeking undergraduates, 410 enrolled as first-time, first-year students, 50 transferred in from other institutions.

| | | | |
|---|---|---|---|
| Part-time: | 26% | Hispanic American: | 9% |
| Out-of-state: | 7% | Native American: | 1% |
| Women: | 55% | 25 or older: | 24% |
| African American: | 8% | Live on campus: | 48% |
| Asian American: | 1% | | |

**Transfer out. Colleges most students transferred to 2009:** Colorado State University, University of Northern Colorado, University of Colorado, University of Wyoming, Oklahoma State University.

**Basis for selection.** Open admission, but selective for some programs. Qualifications for programs with limited space, such as licensed practical nursing program, set individually by department. SAT or ACT required for some technical vocational programs. Assessment required by AC-CUPLACER, minimum ACT or SAT scores in subject areas, or proof of previous successful college experience. Cooperative admission program with Colorado State University. **Adult students:** ACCUPLACER required. **Homeschooled:** Transcript of courses and grades, state high school equivalency certificate required. **Learning Disabled:** IEP required.

**2009-2010 Annual costs.** Tuition/fees: $3,244; $10,046 out-of-state. Per-credit charge: $88 in-state; $315 out-of-state. In-state tuition based upon assumption of Colorado Opportunity Fund waiver of $68 per-credit-hour. Room/board: $5,654. Books/supplies: $1,749. Personal expenses: $3,402.

**2008-2009 Financial aid. Need-based:** 54% of total undergraduate aid awarded as scholarships/grants, 46% as loans/jobs. Need-based aid available for part-time students. **Non-need-based:** Scholarships awarded for academics, alumni affiliation, art, athletics, job skills, leadership, music/drama, state residency. **Additional information:** Need-based financial aid available to part-time students taking 6 credits or more per semester.

**Application procedures. Admission:** No deadline. No application fee. Admission notification on a rolling basis. **Financial aid:** Priority date 3/1; no closing date. FAFSA, institutional form required. Applicants notified on a rolling basis starting 4/15; must reply within 3 week(s) of notification.

**Academics. Special study options:** Accelerated study, cooperative education, cross-registration, distance learning, double major, dual enrollment of high school students, ESL, exchange student, honors, independent study, internships, liberal arts/career combination, student-designed major, study abroad, teacher certification program, weekend college. Bachelor's degree programs available on campus. License preparation in nursing. **Credit/placement by examination:** AP, CLEP, IB, SAT, ACT, institutional tests. 45 credit hours maximum toward associate degree. **Support services:** GED preparation and test center, learning center, remedial instruction, study skills assistance, tutoring.

**Majors. Agriculture:** Agribusiness operations, farm/ranch, horticulture, mechanization, ornamental horticulture, production. **Business:** Accounting technology, management information systems. **Education:** Early childhood. **Family/consumer sciences:** Child development. **Health:** EMT paramedic, nursing (RN). **Liberal arts:** Arts/sciences. **Mechanic/repair:** Automotive, diesel. **Protective services:** Law enforcement admin. **Other:** Wind technology.

**Most popular majors.** Agriculture 12%, health sciences 19%, liberal arts 54%, personal/culinary services 6%.

**Computing on campus.** 302 workstations in library, computer center, student center. Dormitories wired for high-speed internet access. Online course registration, helpline, student web hosting available.

**Student life. Freshman orientation:** Mandatory. Preregistration for classes offered. **Policies:** No drugs, alcohol, or smoking on campus. **Housing:** Coed dorms, single-sex dorms available. $125 fully refundable deposit. Honors house available. **Activities:** Jazz band, campus ministries, choral groups, dance, drama, literary magazine, music ensembles, student government, student newspaper, campus Christian fellowship.

**Athletics.** NJCAA. **Intercollegiate:** Baseball M, basketball, rodeo, volleyball W. **Intramural:** Basketball, cheerleading W, football (non-tackle) M, tennis, volleyball. **Team name:** Plainswomen, Plainsmen.

**Student services.** Adult student services, alcohol/substance abuse counseling, career counseling, student employment services, financial aid counseling, health services, personal counseling. **Physically disabled:** Services for visually, speech, hearing impaired. **Transfer:** Pre-admission transcript evaluation for new students. Transfer adviser, college fairs on campus for students transferring to 4-year colleges.

**Contact.** E-mail: admissions@njc.edu
Phone: (970) 521-7000 Toll-free number: (800) 626-4367
Fax: (970) 521-6715
Andy Long, Director of Admissions, Northeastern Junior College, 100 College Avenue, Sterling, CO 80751

## Otero Junior College
La Junta, Colorado
www.ojc.edu                    CB code: 4588

- Public 2-year community and junior college
- Commuter campus in small town

**General.** Founded in 1941. Regionally accredited. **Enrollment:** 800 full-time, degree-seeking students. **Degrees:** 145 associate awarded. **Location:** 60 miles from Pueblo, 100 miles from Colorado Springs. **Calendar:** Semester, limited summer session. **Full-time faculty:** 33 total. **Part-time faculty:** 24 total. **Class size:** 74% < 20, 21% 20-39, 2% 40-49, 3% 50-99. **Special facilities:** Koshare Indian kiva museum.

**Student profile.**

| | | | |
|---|---|---|---|
| Out-of-state: | 7% | Live on campus: | 10% |
| 25 or older: | 33% | | |

**Basis for selection.** Open admission, but selective for some programs. Special admission requirements for nursing program.

**2009-2010 Annual costs.** Tuition/fees: $2,855; $5,656 out-of-state. Per-credit charge: $88 in-state; $182 out-of-state. In-state tuition based upon assumption of Colorado Opportunity Fund waiver of $68 per-credit-hour. Room/board: $5,172. Books/supplies: $1,100. Personal expenses: $2,500.

**2009-2010 Financial aid. Need-based:** Need-based aid available for part-time students. Work-study available nights, weekends and for part-time students. **Non-need-based:** Scholarships awarded for academics, athletics, state residency.

**Application procedures. Admission:** No deadline. No application fee. Admission notification on a rolling basis. **Financial aid:** Priority date 4/15; no closing date. FAFSA required. Applicants notified on a rolling basis starting 4/15; must reply within 2 week(s) of notification.

**Academics. Special study options:** Dual enrollment of high school students. Bachelor's degree programs available on campus. **Credit/placement by examination:** AP, CLEP, institutional tests. 30 credit hours maximum toward associate degree. **Support services:** GED preparation and test center, learning center, reduced course load, remedial instruction, study skills assistance, tutoring.

**Majors. Biology:** General. **Business:** Administrative services, business admin. **Computer sciences:** General. **Education:** General, early childhood, elementary, secondary, teacher assistance. **Health:** Medical secretary, nursing (RN), pharmacy assistant, predental, premedicine, prepharmacy, preveterinary, veterinary technology/assistant. **History:** General. **Legal studies:** Legal secretary, prelaw. **Liberal arts:** Arts/sciences. **Math:** General. **Physical sciences:** Chemistry. **Psychology:** General. **Social sciences:** Political science. **Visual/performing arts:** Dramatic.

**Computing on campus.** 100 workstations in library, computer center, student center. Dormitories wired for high-speed internet access. Wireless network available.

**Student life. Freshman orientation:** Available. Preregistration for classes offered. **Housing:** Single-sex dorms available. **Activities:** Dance, drama, student government.

**Athletics.** NJCAA. **Intercollegiate:** Baseball M, basketball, golf, soccer M, softball W, volleyball W. **Intramural:** Basketball, volleyball. **Team name:** Rattlers.

**Student services.** Career counseling, student employment services, on-campus daycare, personal counseling, placement for graduates, veterans' counselor. **Physically disabled:** Services for visually, hearing impaired. **Transfer:** Pre-admission transcript evaluation for new students. Transfer adviser, college fairs on campus for students transferring to 4-year colleges.

**Contact.** E-mail: jan.schiro@ojc.edu
Phone: (719) 384-6831 Fax: (719) 384-6933
Jan Schiro, Admissions Coordinator, Otero Junior College, 1802 Colorado Avenue, La Junta, CO 81050

## Pikes Peak Community College
### Colorado Springs, Colorado
www.ppcc.edu                              CB code: 4291

- Public 2-year community college
- Commuter campus in large city

**General.** Founded in 1967. Regionally accredited. **Enrollment:** 11,510 degree-seeking undergraduates. **Degrees:** 821 associate awarded. **Location:** 70 miles from Denver. **Calendar:** Semester, extensive summer session. **Full-time faculty:** 158 total. **Part-time faculty:** 508 total. **Class size:** 59% < 20, 41% 20-39, less than 1% 40-49, less than 1% 50-99, less than 1% >100. **Partnerships:** Formal partnership with Cheyenne Mountain Zoo.

**Student profile.**

| | | | |
|---|---|---|---|
| Out-of-state: | 17% | 25 or older: | 49% |

**Transfer out. Colleges most students transferred to 2009:** University of Colorado at Colorado Springs, Colorado State University-Pueblo.

**Basis for selection.** Open admission.

**High school preparation.** College-preparatory program recommended.

**2009-2010 Annual costs.** Tuition/fees: $2,897; $12,065 out-of-state. Per-credit charge: $88 in-state; $394 out-of-state. In-state tuition based upon assumption of Colorado Opportunity Fund waiver of $68 per-credit-hour. Books/supplies: $1,163. Personal expenses: $2,547.

**Financial aid. Need-based:** Need-based aid available for part-time students. Work-study available nights and for part-time students.

**Application procedures. Admission:** No deadline. No application fee. Admission notification on a rolling basis. **Financial aid:** Priority date 7/1; no closing date. FAFSA required. Applicants notified on a rolling basis starting 8/1; must reply within 2 week(s) of notification.

**Academics. Special study options:** Cooperative education, distance learning, double major, dual enrollment of high school students, ESL, external degree, independent study, internships, study abroad, weekend college. License preparation in nursing, paramedic, radiology, real estate. **Credit/placement by examination:** CLEP, IB, institutional tests. Students may receive up to 75% of total credits for all types of prior learning (testing, work and/or life experience). **Support services:** GED test center, learning center, remedial instruction, study skills assistance, tutoring, writing center.

**Majors. Biology:** General. **Business:** General, accounting, accounting technology, business admin, executive assistant, financial planning, international, management information systems, marketing. **Communications technology:** Graphics, radio/tv. **Computer sciences:** General, computer science, LAN/WAN management, networking. **Conservation:** Management/policy. **Construction:** Maintenance. **Engineering technology:** Architectural, CAD/CADD, drafting, electrical, robotics. **Family/consumer sciences:** Child development. **Foreign languages:** General, sign language interpretation. **Health:** Dental assistant, EMT paramedic, mental health services, nursing (RN), office admin, premedicine. **History:** General. **Legal studies:** Paralegal. **Liberal arts:** Arts/sciences, humanities. **Math:** General. **Mechanic/repair:** Auto body, automotive. **Personal/culinary services:** Culinary arts. **Philosophy/religion:** Philosophy. **Physical sciences:** Chemistry, geology, physics. **Production:** Machine shop technology, welding. **Protective services:** Emergency management/homeland security, fire safety technology, firefighting, law enforcement admin. **Social sciences:** Anthropology, geography, political science, sociology. **Visual/performing arts:** Dance, dramatic, interior design, music, studio arts.

**Most popular majors.** Health sciences 11%, liberal arts 53%, security/protective services 13%.

**Computing on campus.** 180 workstations in library, computer center. Commuter students can connect to campus network. Online course registration, helpline, wireless network available.

**Student life. Freshman orientation:** Available. **Policies:** Dormitory housing available through agreement with the University of Colorado at Colorado Springs. **Activities:** Choral groups, dance, drama, radio station, student government, student newspaper, Phi Theta Kappa.

**Athletics. Team name:** Aardvarks.

**Student services.** Adult student services, alcohol/substance abuse counseling, career counseling, services for economically disadvantaged, student employment services, financial aid counseling, on-campus daycare, personal counseling, placement for graduates, veterans' counselor. **Physically disabled:** Services for visually, speech, hearing impaired. **Learning disabled:** Comprehensive services available. **Transfer:** Re-entry adviser, pre-admission transcript evaluation for new students. Transfer adviser, college fairs on campus for students transferring to 4-year colleges.

**Contact.** E-mail: admissions@ppcc.edu
Phone: (719) 502-3000 Toll-free number: (800) 456-6847
Admissions, Pikes Peak Community College, 5675 South Academy Boulevard, Colorado Springs, CO 80906-5498

## Pueblo Community College
### Pueblo, Colorado
www.pueblocc.edu                           CB code: 4634

- Public 2-year community college
- Commuter campus in small city

**General.** Founded in 1933. Regionally accredited. **Enrollment:** 5,484 degree-seeking undergraduates; 1,044 non-degree-seeking students. **Degrees:** 478 associate awarded. **Location:** 50 miles from Colorado Springs, 100 miles from Denver. **Calendar:** Semester, extensive summer session. **Full-time faculty:** 99 total; 5% have terminal degrees, 17% minority, 64% women. **Part-time faculty:** 9 total. **Class size:** 73% < 20, 26% 20-39, less than 1% 40-49, 1% 50-99. **Special facilities:** Advanced technology center.

**Student profile.** Among degree-seeking undergraduates, 48% enrolled in a transfer program, 52% enrolled in a vocational program, 1% already have a bachelor's degree or higher, 1,414 enrolled as first-time, first-year students, 410 transferred in from other institutions.

| | | | |
|---|---|---|---|
| Part-time: | 55% | Women: | 62% |
| Out-of-state: | 1% | 25 or older: | 51% |

**Transfer out.** 30% of students enrolled in the transfer program go on to 4-year colleges. **Colleges most students transferred to 2009:** Colorado State University: Pueblo.

**Basis for selection.** Open admission, but selective for some programs. Admission to health programs based on GPA, high school courses, test scores. ACT required of dental hygiene applicants; score report by May 1. Assessment testing required for all entering degree- and certificate-seeking students, unless ACT/SAT scores or transcripts showing successful completion of college-level English and math courses provided. Interview required of allied health majors.

**2009-2010 Annual costs.** Tuition/fees: $2,992; $12,160 out-of-state. Per-credit charge: $88 in-state; $394 out-of-state. In-state tuition based upon assumption of Colorado Opportunity Fund waiver of $68 per-credit-hour. Books/supplies: $1,749.

**2008-2009 Financial aid. Need-based:** 480 full-time freshmen applied for aid; 405 were judged to have need; 388 of these received aid. Average need met was 50%. Average scholarship/grant was $3,000; average loan $2,000. 61% of total undergraduate aid awarded as scholarships/grants, 39% as loans/jobs. Need-based aid available for part-time students. Work-study available for part-time students. **Non-need-based:** Awarded to 91 full-time undergraduates, including 41 freshmen. Scholarships awarded for academics, art, job skills, leadership, music/drama.

**Application procedures. Admission:** Priority date 8/1; no deadline. No application fee. Admission notification on a rolling basis. Foreign applicants must show evidence of resources sufficient to cover tuition/fees for full academic year before acceptance. Application closing date for allied health programs: 4/1. **Financial aid:** Priority date 3/15; no closing date. FAFSA required. Applicants notified on a rolling basis starting 4/1.

**Academics. Special study options:** Accelerated study, cooperative education, distance learning, double major, dual enrollment of high school students, ESL, honors, independent study, internships, liberal arts/career combination, weekend college. License preparation in aviation, dental hygiene, nursing, occupational therapy, paramedic, physical therapy, radiology, real estate. **Credit/placement by examination:** AP, CLEP, institutional tests. All but 15 hour residence requirement for certificate or associate degree may be from credit for prior learning. **Support services:** GED preparation and test center, learning center, reduced course load, remedial instruction, study skills assistance, tutoring, writing center.

**Majors. Agriculture:** Business technology, farm/ranch, supplies. **Business:** Accounting technology, administrative services, business admin, entrepreneurial studies, hospitality/recreation, office technology, small business admin. **Communications technology:** General, animation/special effects. **Computer sciences:** General, web page design. **Construction:** Carpentry. **Engineering technology:** General, electrical, energy systems. **Family/consumer sciences:** Child development. **Health:** Dental assistant, dental hygiene, EMT paramedic, nursing (RN), occupational therapy assistant, physical therapy assistant, radiologic technology/medical imaging, respiratory therapy technology, sonography. **Liberal arts:** Arts/sciences, library assistant. **Mechanic/repair:** Aircraft, auto body, automotive. **Personal/culinary services:** Cosmetic. **Production:** Machine shop technology, welding. **Protective services:** Firefighting, law enforcement admin. **Other:** Applied technology, Wildland firefighter, Young farmer.

**Most popular majors.** Business/marketing 8%, family/consumer sciences 6%, health sciences 37%, liberal arts 39%.

**Computing on campus.** Commuter students can connect to campus network. Online course registration, online library, helpline, wireless network available.

**Student life. Freshman orientation:** Available. **Activities:** Choral groups, dance, drama, student government, student newspaper, TV station.

**Athletics. Team name:** Panthers.

**Student services.** Adult student services, career counseling, financial aid counseling, health services, personal counseling, placement for graduates. **Physically disabled:** Services for visually, speech, hearing impaired. **Transfer:** Transfer center, transfer adviser, college fairs on campus for students transferring to 4-year colleges.

**Contact.** E-mail: admissions@pueblocc.edu
Phone: (719) 549-3010 Toll-free number: (888) 642-6017
Fax: (719) 549-3012
Maija Kurtz, Director of Admissions and Records, Pueblo Community College, 900 West Orman Avenue, Pueblo, CO 81004-1499

## Red Rocks Community College
### Lakewood, Colorado
**www.rrcc.edu**      CB code: 4130

- Public 2-year community college
- Commuter campus in small city

**General.** Founded in 1969. Regionally accredited. **Enrollment:** 7,179 degree-seeking undergraduates; 1,926 non-degree-seeking students. **Degrees:** 448 associate awarded. **ROTC:** Army, Air Force. **Location:** 10 miles from Denver. **Calendar:** Semester, extensive summer session. **Full-time faculty:** 79 total; 10% have terminal degrees, 5% minority, 60% women. **Part-time faculty:** 429 total; 8% minority, 45% women. **Class size:** 59% < 20, 41% 20-39, less than 1% 40-49. **Partnerships:** Formal partnerships with Coors, Microsoft, Apple, Oracle.

**Student profile.** Among degree-seeking undergraduates, 1,858 enrolled as first-time, first-year students, 860 transferred in from other institutions.

| | | | |
|---|---|---|---|
| Part-time: | 63% | Asian American: | 3% |
| Out-of-state: | 4% | Hispanic American: | 12% |
| Women: | 49% | Native American: | 2% |
| African American: | 2% | 25 or older: | 51% |

**Transfer out. Colleges most students transferred to 2009:** Metropolitan State College of Denver, University of Colorado, Regis University, Colorado School of Mines, Colorado State University.

**Basis for selection.** Open admission.

**2009-2010 Annual costs.** Tuition/fees: $2,946; $12,114 out-of-state. Per-credit charge: $88 in-state; $394 out-of-state. In-state tuition based upon assumption of Colorado Opportunity Fund waiver of $68 per-credit-hour. Books/supplies: $1,698. Personal expenses: $2,853.

**2008-2009 Financial aid. Need-based:** Need-based aid available for part-time students. Work-study available nights, weekends and for part-time students.

**Application procedures. Admission:** No deadline. No application fee. Admission notification on a rolling basis. **Financial aid:** Priority date 4/1; no closing date. FAFSA, institutional form required. Applicants notified on a rolling basis starting 6/1; must reply within 2 week(s) of notification.

**Academics.** Students in advanced ESL classes may begin some college-level courses early. Scholarships offered for outstanding ESL performance when funds are available. **Special study options:** Accelerated study, cross-registration, distance learning, dual enrollment of high school students, ESL, honors, independent study, internships, liberal arts/career combination, teacher certification program, weekend college. License preparation in paramedic, radiology, real estate. **Credit/placement by examination:** AP, CLEP, IB, institutional tests. 45 credit hours maximum toward associate degree. **Support services:** GED preparation and test center, learning center, reduced course load, remedial instruction, study skills assistance, tutoring, writing center.

**Majors. Biology:** General, biotechnology. **Business:** Accounting technology, business admin, management information systems, office technology, real estate. **Computer sciences:** Webmaster. **Conservation:** Forest technology. **Construction:** General, carpentry, electrician, plumbing. **Education:** Teacher assistance. **Engineering technology:** Drafting, energy systems, heat/ac/refrig, industrial, manufacturing. **Family/consumer sciences:** Child development. **Foreign languages:** French, German, Spanish. **Health:** EMT paramedic, nursing (RN), office admin, radiologic technology/medical imaging, sonography. **Liberal arts:** Arts/sciences. **Mechanic/repair:** Auto body, automotive. **Personal/culinary services:** Chef training, cosmetic, manicurist. **Production:** Machine shop technology, welding, woodworking. **Protective services:** Emergency management/homeland security, fire safety technology, law enforcement admin. **Visual/performing arts:** Cinematography, photography, theater design. **Other:** Applied technology.

**Most popular majors.** Health sciences 13%, liberal arts 58%, security/protective services 8%, trade and industry 8%.

**Computing on campus.** 175 workstations in library, computer center, student center. Online course registration, online library, helpline, wireless network available.

**Student life. Freshman orientation:** Available. **Activities:** Campus ministries, dance, drama, film society, international student organizations, literary magazine, music ensembles, musical theater, student government.

**Student services.** Adult student services, career counseling, student employment services, health services, on-campus daycare, personal counseling, placement for graduates, veterans' counselor. **Physically disabled:** Services for visually, speech, hearing impaired. **Transfer:** Transfer adviser, college fairs on campus for students transferring to 4-year colleges.

**Contact.** E-mail: admissions@rrcc.edu
Phone: (303) 914-6348 Fax: (303) 989-6919
Dean Rathe, Director of Enrollment Services, Red Rocks Community College, 13300 West Sixth Avenue, Lakewood, CO 80228-1255

## Redstone College
### Broomfield, Colorado
**www.redstonecollege.com**      CB code: 2230

- For-profit 2-year technical college
- Commuter campus in small city

**General.** Accredited by ACCSC. **Enrollment:** 581 degree-seeking undergraduates. **Degrees:** 236 associate awarded. **Location:** 15 miles from Denver and Boulder. **Calendar:** Continuous. **Full-time faculty:** 24 total. **Part-time faculty:** 20 total.

**Basis for selection.** Open admission.

**2009-2010 Annual costs.** Tuition for entire associate degree ranges from $32,000 to $38,000 depending on program.

**2009-2010 Financial aid.** All financial aid based on need.

**Application procedures. Admission:** No deadline. $100 fee. Admission notification on a rolling basis. **Financial aid:** No deadline. FAFSA required. Applicants notified on a rolling basis; must reply within 2 week(s) of notification.

**Academics. Special study options:** License preparation in aviation. **Credit/placement by examination:** CLEP. **Support services:** Learning center, tutoring.

**Majors. Mechanic/repair:** Aircraft, electronics/electrical.

**Computing on campus.** 8 workstations in computer center.

**Student life. Housing:** Apartments available.

**Student services.** Career counseling, student employment services, placement for graduates, veterans' counselor.

**Contact.** Phone: (303) 466-1714 Toll-free number: (800) 460-0592
Fax: (303) 469-3797
Cate Clark, Director of Admissions, Redstone College, 10851 West 120th
Avenue, Broomfield, CO 80021-3401

## Remington College: Colorado Springs
### Colorado Springs, Colorado
www.remingtoncollege.edu                CB code: 3565

- For-profit 2-year technical college
- Commuter campus in very large city
- Interview required

**General.** Accredited by ACICS. **Enrollment:** 121 degree-seeking undergraduates. **Degrees:** 11 bachelor's, 13 associate awarded. **Location:** 60 miles
from Denver. **Calendar:** Quarter, extensive summer session. **Full-time faculty:** 5 total; 20% minority, 60% women. **Part-time faculty:** 15 total; 20%
have terminal degrees, 20% minority, 40% women. **Class size:** 100% < 20.

**Student profile.** Among degree-seeking undergraduates, 106 enrolled as
first-time, first-year students.

Women:                77%        25 or older:        59%

**Basis for selection.** Open admission, but selective for some programs.
Non-GED or high school program applicants required to pass Wonderlic
assessment.

**2009-2010 Annual costs.** Cost of entire program leading to diploma,
associate, and bachelor's degrees ranges from $14,450 to $39,950; includes
books and supplies.

**2009-2010 Financial aid.** All financial aid based on need. Need-based
aid available for part-time students.

**Application procedures. Admission:** No deadline. $50 fee. Admission
notification on a rolling basis. **Financial aid:** No deadline. FAFSA required.
Applicants notified on a rolling basis; must reply within 3 week(s) of notification.

**Academics. Special study options:** Accelerated study, distance learning.
Bachelor's degree programs available on campus. **Credit/placement by examination:** AP, CLEP. **Support services:** GED preparation, tutoring.

**Majors. Protective services:** Criminal justice.

**Computing on campus.** 34 workstations in library, computer center.
Online library, helpline, repair service available.

**Student life. Freshman orientation:** Mandatory. Preregistration for classes
offered.

**Student services.** Alcohol/substance abuse counseling, career counseling, student employment services, financial aid counseling, personal counseling, placement for graduates, veterans' counselor. **Transfer:** Pre-
admission transcript evaluation for new students.

**Contact.** E-mail: jennifer.granado@remingtoncollege.edu
Phone: (719) 532-1234 ext. 221 Toll-free number: (866) 717-0013
Fax: (719) 264-1234
Larry Schafer, Director of Recruitment, Remington College: Colorado
Springs, 6050 Erin Park Drive, Colorado Springs, CO 80918

## Trinidad State Junior College
### Trinidad, Colorado
www.trinidadstate.edu                CB code: 4821

- Public 2-year community and junior college
- Commuter campus in small town

**General.** Founded in 1925. Regionally accredited. **Enrollment:** 1,740 degree-
seeking undergraduates. **Degrees:** 202 associate awarded. **Location:** 90 miles
from Pueblo. **Calendar:** Semester, limited summer session. **Full-time faculty:** 59 total; 5% have terminal degrees, 58% women. **Part-time faculty:**
117 total; 5% have terminal degrees, 58% women. **Class size:** 93% < 20,
6% 20-39, less than 1% 40-49, less than 1% 50-99. **Special facilities:** Museum of anthropology and geology, gunsmithing laboratory, gun range.

**Student profile.**

| Out-of-state: | 15% | Live on campus: | 22% |
| 25 or older: | 43% | | |

**Transfer out. Colleges most students transferred to 2009:** Colorado
State University, Pueblo, Adams State College, Colorado State University,
Northern Colorado University.

**Basis for selection.** Open admission, but selective for some programs.
Special requirements for nursing program. Interview recommended for nursing majors. **Adult students:** ACT/SAT or ACCUPLACER required for placement.

**2009-2010 Annual costs.** Tuition/fees: $3,054; $5,855 out-of-state. Per-
credit charge: $88 in-state; $182 out-of-state. In-state tuition based upon
assumption of Colorado Opportunity Fund waiver of $68 per-credit-hour.
Room/board: $4,874. Books/supplies: $800. Personal expenses: $972.

**2008-2009 Financial aid. Need-based:** Need-based aid available for part-
time students. Work-study available nights and for part-time students. **Non-
need-based:** Scholarships awarded for academics, athletics, state residency.

**Application procedures. Admission:** No deadline. No application fee.
Admission notification on a rolling basis. **Financial aid:** Priority date 5/1;
no closing date. FAFSA, institutional form required. Applicants notified on
a rolling basis starting 6/15.

**Academics. Special study options:** Accelerated study, combined bachelor's/
graduate degree, cooperative education, distance learning, double major, dual
enrollment of high school students, ESL, independent study, liberal arts/
career combination. Bachelor's degree programs available on campus. License preparation in nursing, paramedic. **Credit/placement by examination:** AP, CLEP, institutional tests. 45 credit hours maximum toward associate
degree. **Support services:** GED preparation and test center, learning center,
pre-admission summer program, reduced course load, remedial instruction,
study skills assistance, tutoring, writing center.

**Majors. Biology:** General. **Business:** General, accounting, business admin.
**Communications:** Advertising, journalism. **Computer sciences:** General,
computer science, programming, word processing. **Conservation:** General,
fisheries. **Education:** General, physical, social studies. **Engineering:** General. **Engineering technology:** Civil, construction, drafting, manufacturing,
occupational safety. **Family/consumer sciences:** Child care. **Foreign languages:** Spanish. **Health:** Massage therapy. **Legal studies:** Prelaw. **Liberal
arts:** Arts/sciences. **Math:** General. **Mechanic/repair:** Auto body, automotive, diesel, gunsmithing. **Parks/recreation:** Health/fitness. **Personal/
culinary services:** Cosmetic. **Philosophy/religion:** Philosophy. **Physical sciences:** Chemistry. **Production:** Welding. **Protective services:** Criminal justice,
law enforcement admin, police science. **Psychology:** General. **Social sciences:** Criminology. **Transportation:** General. **Visual/performing arts:** Com-
mercial/advertising art.

**Most popular majors.** Health sciences 30%, liberal arts 45%.

**Computing on campus.** 260 workstations in dormitories, library, student center. Dormitories wired for high-speed internet access and linked to
campus network. Online course registration, helpline, repair service, wireless network available.

**Student life. Freshman orientation:** Available. Preregistration for classes
offered. **Housing:** Guaranteed on-campus for all undergraduates. Single-sex
dorms available. $150 partly refundable deposit. **Activities:** Pep band, cam-
pus ministries, choral groups, drama, student government, student newspaper, TV station, MECHA, black student alliance.

**Athletics.** NJCAA. **Intercollegiate:** Baseball M, basketball M, golf M,
softball W, volleyball W. **Intramural:** Baseball M, basketball, rifle, softball, table tennis, tennis, volleyball. **Team name:** Trojans.

**Student services.** Adult student services, alcohol/substance abuse counseling, career counseling, student employment services, financial aid counseling, personal counseling, placement for graduates, veterans' counselor.
**Physically disabled:** Services for visually, speech, hearing impaired. **Transfer:** Transfer adviser, college fairs on campus for students transferring to
4-year colleges.

**Contact.** E-mail: nicole.janssen@trinidadstate.edu
Phone: (719) 846-5621 Toll-free number: (800) 621-8752
Fax: (719) 846-5620
Sandra Veltri, Vice President of Student and Academic Affairs, Trinidad
State Junior College, 600 Prospect Street, Trinidad, CO 81082

# Connecticut

## Asnuntuck Community College

**Enfield, Connecticut**
www.acc.commnet.edu

CB member
CB code: 3656

◆ Public 2-year community and technical college
◆ Commuter campus in large town

**General.** Founded in 1972. Regionally accredited. **Enrollment:** 1,213 degree-seeking undergraduates; 595 non-degree-seeking students. **Degrees:** 164 associate awarded. **Location:** 15 miles from Hartford; 10 miles from Springfield, Massachusetts. **Calendar:** Semester, extensive summer session. **Full-time faculty:** 25 total. **Part-time faculty:** 90 total. **Class size:** 47% < 20, 52% 20-39, less than 1% 40-49.

**Student profile.** Among degree-seeking undergraduates, 49% enrolled in a transfer program, 51% enrolled in a vocational program, 328 enrolled as first-time, first-year students.

| | | | |
|---|---|---|---|
| Part-time: | 46% | Women: | 56% |
| Out-of-state: | 4% | 25 or older: | 45% |

**Transfer out. Colleges most students transferred to 2009:** Eastern Connecticut State University, Central Connecticut State University, University of Connecticut, Western New England College.

**Basis for selection.** Open admission. Applicants should present evidence of graduation from an approved secondary school or should have been awarded a state high school diploma or its equivalent (GED), or be qualified under the provision of Board Policy 5.1.5 for Home Schooled Students. Special waivers may be granted to applicants who demonstrate the ability to perform academically at the college level. **Homeschooled:** Transcript of courses and grades required.

**High school preparation.** College-preparatory program recommended.

**2009-2010 Annual costs.** Tuition/fees: $3,200; $9,560 out-of-state. Per-credit charge: $118 in-state; $354 out-of-state. Books/supplies: $1,200. Personal expenses: $1,392.

**2008-2009 Financial aid.** All financial aid based on need. Need-based aid available for part-time students. Work-study available nights, weekends and for part-time students.

**Application procedures. Admission:** No deadline. $20 fee, may be waived for applicants with need. Admission notification on a rolling basis. **Financial aid:** Priority date 6/1; no closing date. FAFSA, institutional form required. Applicants notified on a rolling basis starting 7/1; must reply within 2 week(s) of notification.

**Academics.** On-line tutoring available. **Special study options:** Combined bachelor's/graduate degree, cooperative education, cross-registration, distance learning, double major, dual enrollment of high school students, independent study, internships, liberal arts/career combination, weekend college. License preparation in paramedic, real estate. **Credit/placement by examination:** CLEP, institutional tests. 48 credit hours maximum toward associate degree. **Support services:** Learning center, remedial instruction, study skills assistance, tutoring.

**Majors. Business:** Accounting, business admin, office technology. **Communications technology:** General, radio/tv. **Computer sciences:** General. **Education:** Early childhood. **Engineering:** Science. **Engineering technology:** Industrial, manufacturing. **Family/consumer sciences:** Child care. **Health:** Mental health services. **Liberal arts:** Arts/sciences. **Production:** Machine tool, welding. **Protective services:** Police science. **Public administration:** Human services.

**Most popular majors.** Business/marketing 31%, family/consumer sciences 7%, liberal arts 47%, security/protective services 7%.

**Computing on campus.** 111 workstations in library, computer center. Online course registration, online library, wireless network available.

**Student life. Freshman orientation:** Available. **Activities:** Drama, literary magazine, radio station, student government, TV station, human services club, Phi Theta Kappa.

**Student services.** Career counseling, student employment services, financial aid counseling, minority student services, on-campus daycare, personal counseling, placement for graduates, veterans' counselor. **Physically disabled:** Services for visually, speech, hearing impaired. **Transfer:** Pre-admission transcript evaluation for new students. Transfer adviser, college fairs on campus for students transferring to 4-year colleges.

**Contact.** E-mail: tstjames@acc.commnet.edu
Phone: (860) 253-3000 ext. 3010 Toll-free number: (800) 501-3967
Fax: (860) 253-3014
Timothy St. James, Director of Admissions and Marketing, Asnuntuck Community College, 170 Elm Street, Enfield, CT 06082

## Capital Community College

**Hartford, Connecticut**
www.ccc.commnet.edu

CB code: 3421

◆ Public 2-year community and technical college
◆ Commuter campus in small city

**General.** Founded in 1946. Regionally accredited. **Enrollment:** 3,748 degree-seeking undergraduates; 532 non-degree-seeking students. **Degrees:** 361 associate awarded. **ROTC:** Army, Naval, Air Force. **Calendar:** Semester, limited summer session. **Full-time faculty:** 69 total. **Part-time faculty:** 178 total. **Special facilities:** Math development center, computerized English as a Second Language lab, interactive videodisc instruction for nursing students, learning/writing center. **Partnerships:** Formal partnerships with high schools for Tech Prep program.

**Student profile.** Among degree-seeking undergraduates, 706 enrolled as first-time, first-year students.

| | | | |
|---|---|---|---|
| Part-time: | 68% | 25 or older: | 57% |
| Women: | 73% | | |

**Transfer out. Colleges most students transferred to 2009:** University of Connecticut, Central Connecticut State University, University of Hartford, Eastern Connecticut State University.

**Basis for selection.** Open admission, but selective for some programs. SAT scores used to satisfy admission criteria for nursing, physical therapist assistant, and radiologic technology programs.

**High school preparation.** Algebra, biology, and chemistry required for nursing program. Physical therapy assistant, radiologic technology, and pre-nursing programs also have specific course requirements. Paramedic program has specific educational and training requirements.

**2009-2010 Annual costs.** Tuition/fees: $3,200; $9,560 out-of-state. Per-credit charge: $118 in-state; $354 out-of-state. Books/supplies: $850. Personal expenses: $1,965.

**Financial aid.** All financial aid based on need. Need-based aid available for part-time students. Work-study available nights, weekends and for part-time students.

**Application procedures. Admission:** No deadline. $20 fee, may be waived for applicants with need. Admission notification on a rolling basis. **Financial aid:** Closing date 7/15. FAFSA required. Applicants notified on a rolling basis starting 7/15; must reply within 2 week(s) of notification.

**Academics. Special study options:** Accelerated study, cross-registration, distance learning, double major, dual enrollment of high school students, ESL, independent study, internships, liberal arts/career combination, weekend college. Interdisciplinary summer program with Smith College. License preparation in nursing, paramedic, radiology. **Credit/placement by examination:** AP, CLEP, institutional tests. **Support services:** GED preparation, learning center, pre-admission summer program, remedial instruction, study skills assistance, tutoring, writing center.

**Majors. Business:** Accounting, administrative services, business admin. **Computer sciences:** General. **Education:** Early childhood. **Engineering:** Electrical. **Engineering technology:** Architectural. **Health:** EMT paramedic, medical assistant, medical radiologic technology/radiation therapy, mental health services, nursing (RN), physical therapy assistant. **Liberal arts:** Arts/sciences, library assistant. **Protective services:** Fire safety technology.

**Most popular majors.** Business/marketing 18%, health sciences 40%, liberal arts 26%, public administration/social services 6%.

**Computing on campus.** 500 workstations in library, computer center, student center. Commuter students can connect to campus network. Online course registration, online library, wireless network available.

**Student life. Freshman orientation:** Available. Preregistration for classes offered. 3-days, held prior to start of semester. **Policies:** Policies against drugs and alcohol, violence, weapons, and sexual harassment on campus. **Activities:** Choral groups, dance, drama, literary magazine, radio station, student government, TV station, Latin American students association, senior renewal club, early childhood club, pre-professional club, Phi Theta Kappa, nursing club, black student union, student senate.

**Student services.** Adult student services, chaplain/spiritual director, career counseling, services for economically disadvantaged, student employment services, financial aid counseling, minority student services, on-campus daycare, personal counseling, placement for graduates, veterans' counselor, women's services. **Physically disabled:** Services for visually, speech, hearing impaired. **Learning disabled:** Comprehensive services available. **Transfer:** College fairs on campus for students transferring to 4-year colleges.

**Contact.** E-mail: mball-davis@ccc.commnet.edu
Phone: (860) 906-5126 Toll-free number: (800) 894-6126
Marsha Ball-Davis, Director of Admissions, Capital Community College, 950 Main Street, Hartford, CT 06103-1207

---

### Gateway Community College
**New Haven, Connecticut**     **CB member**
**www.gwcc.commnet.edu**     **CB code: 3425**

- Public 2-year community college
- Commuter campus in small city

**General.** Founded in 1992. Regionally accredited. **Enrollment:** 5,764 degree-seeking undergraduates; 1,083 non-degree-seeking students. **Degrees:** 523 associate awarded. **Location:** 75 miles from New York City, 130 miles from Boston. **Calendar:** Semester, limited summer session. **Full-time faculty:** 86 total; 17% have terminal degrees, 19% minority, 56% women. **Part-time faculty:** 321 total; 18% minority, 55% women. **Class size:** 24% < 20, 71% 20-39, 4% 40-49, less than 1% 50-99. **Special facilities:** Early childhood learning center, day care center, student operated cafe, student art museum.

**Student profile.** Among degree-seeking undergraduates, 3% enrolled in a transfer program, 56% enrolled in a vocational program, 1% already have a bachelor's degree or higher, 1,431 enrolled as first-time, first-year students.

| | | | |
|---|---|---|---|
| Part-time: | 58% | Asian American: | 3% |
| Out-of-state: | 1% | Hispanic American: | 14% |
| Women: | 59% | International: | 2% |
| African American: | 22% | 25 or older: | 32% |

**Transfer out. Colleges most students transferred to 2009:** Southern Connecticut State University, University of New Haven, Quinnipiac College.

**Basis for selection.** Open admission, but selective for some programs. Special requirements for radiology, nursing, nuclear medicine technology, diagnostic medical sonography, drug and alcohol rehabilitation counselor. Interview required of radiology, drug and alcohol counseling, nuclear medicine technology, diagnostic medical sonography, nursing majors. **Homeschooled:** Transcript of courses and grades required.

**2009-2010 Annual costs.** Tuition/fees: $3,200; $9,560 out-of-state. Per-credit charge: $118 in-state; $354 out-of-state. Books/supplies: $1,200. Personal expenses: $1,100.

**Financial aid.** All financial aid based on need. Need-based aid available for part-time students. Work-study available nights, weekends and for part-time students.

**Application procedures. Admission:** Priority date 6/1; deadline 9/1. $20 fee, may be waived for applicants with need. Admission notification on a rolling basis beginning on or about 2/1. **Financial aid:** No deadline. FAFSA, institutional form required. Applicants notified on a rolling basis; must reply within 2 week(s) of notification.

**Academics. Special study options:** Accelerated study, cross-registration, distance learning, dual enrollment of high school students, ESL, independent study, internships, liberal arts/career combination, weekend college. License preparation in nursing, radiology. **Credit/placement by examination:** AP, CLEP, institutional tests. 30 credit hours maximum toward associate degree. **Support services:** GED preparation, learning center, pre-admission summer program, reduced course load, remedial instruction, study skills assistance, tutoring, writing center.

**Majors. Business:** Accounting, administrative services, business admin, fashion, hotel/motel admin, office/clerical, restaurant/food services, sales/distribution. **Computer sciences:** Computer science, data processing, information systems, networking, programming, word processing. **Conservation:** General, environmental science. **Education:** Early childhood, special.

**Engineering:** Science. **Engineering technology:** Biomedical, electrical, manufacturing. **Family/consumer sciences:** Aging, food/nutrition, institutional food production. **Health:** Medical radiologic technology/radiation therapy, medical secretary, nuclear medical technology, nursing (RN), pharmacy assistant, sonography, substance abuse counseling. **Legal studies:** Legal secretary. **Liberal arts:** Arts/sciences. **Math:** General. **Mechanic/repair:** General, automotive. **Parks/recreation:** Sports admin. **Personal/culinary services:** Chef training, food prep, restaurant/catering. **Protective services:** Fire services admin. **Visual/performing arts:** Graphic design, studio arts.

**Most popular majors.** Business/marketing 10%, engineering/engineering technologies 11%, family/consumer sciences 8%, health sciences 25%, liberal arts 44%.

**Computing on campus.** 650 workstations in library, computer center, student center. Online library, helpline, wireless network available.

**Student life. Freshman orientation:** Available. **Activities:** Choral groups, drama, international student organizations, literary magazine, music ensembles, student government, student newspaper, Spanish-American club, math/science club, Phi Theta Kappa, art club, athletic club, veteran's club, biology club, Theater Goers, black student union.

**Athletics.** NJCAA. **Intercollegiate:** Baseball M, basketball. **Team name:** Ravens.

**Student services.** Adult student services, career counseling, student employment services, financial aid counseling, health services, on-campus daycare, personal counseling, placement for graduates, veterans' counselor, women's services. **Physically disabled:** Services for visually, speech, hearing impaired. **Transfer:** Transfer adviser for students transferring to 4-year colleges.

**Contact.** E-mail: kshea@gwcc.commnet.edu
Phone: (203) 285-2010 Toll-free number: (800) 390-7723
Fax: (203) 285-2018
Shea Kim, Director of Admissions, Gateway Community College, 60 Sargent Drive, New Haven, CT 06511-5970

---

### Goodwin College
**East Hartford, Connecticut**
**www.goodwin.edu**     **CB member**

- Private 2-year health science and career college
- Commuter campus in small city

**General. Enrollment:** 2,052 degree-seeking undergraduates; 31 non-degree-seeking students. **Degrees:** 218 associate awarded. **Location:** 5 miles from Hartford. **Calendar:** Semester, extensive summer session. **Full-time faculty:** 25 total; 24% have terminal degrees, 20% minority, 76% women. **Part-time faculty:** 49 total.

**Student profile.** Among degree-seeking undergraduates, 387 enrolled as first-time, first-year students, 355 transferred in from other institutions.

| | | | |
|---|---|---|---|
| Part-time: | 75% | Women: | 86% |

**Transfer out. Colleges most students transferred to 2009:** Manchester Community College, Capital Community College, University of Connecticut, Central Connecticut State University, Tunxis Community College.

**Basis for selection.** Open admission, but selective for some programs. Applicants to nursing, respiratory therapist, and histology technician programs must have successfully completed prerequisite courses prior to application and submit completed application to program desired. Interviews may be required for some programs. **Homeschooled:** State high school equivalency certificate required.

**2009-2010 Annual costs.** Tuition/fees: $17,600. Per-credit charge: $530.

**2008-2009 Financial aid.** All financial aid based on need. 41% of total undergraduate aid awarded as scholarships/grants, 59% as loans/jobs. Need-based aid available for part-time students. Work-study available nights and for part-time students.

**Application procedures. Admission:** No deadline. $50 fee, may be waived for applicants with need. Admission notification on a rolling basis. **Financial aid:** No deadline. FAFSA required. Applicants notified on a rolling basis starting 8/1.

**Academics. Special study options:** Cooperative education, distance learning, double major, ESL, internships, weekend college. Bachelor's degree programs available on campus. License preparation in nursing, paramedic. **Credit/placement by examination:** AP, CLEP, institutional tests. 30 credit hours maximum toward associate degree, 30 toward bachelor's. **Support**

**services:** Learning center, pre-admission summer program, reduced course load, remedial instruction, study skills assistance, tutoring, writing center.

**Majors. Business:** General, administrative services, business admin, entrepreneurial studies, human resources, international, nonprofit/public. **Conservation:** Environmental studies. **Education:** Early childhood, teacher assistance. **Family/consumer sciences:** Child care, child development. **Health:** Health services, medical assistant, nursing (RN), office admin, office assistant, respiratory therapy technology. **Protective services:** Emergency management/homeland security. **Public administration:** Human services, youth services.

**Most popular majors.** Health sciences 77%.

**Computing on campus.** 100 workstations in library, computer center, student center. Commuter students can connect to campus network. Online library, helpline, repair service, wireless network available.

**Student life. Freshman orientation:** Mandatory. Preregistration for classes offered. **Activities:** Student government, student newspaper.

**Student services.** Adult student services, career counseling, student employment services, financial aid counseling, personal counseling, placement for graduates, veterans' counselor. **Physically disabled:** Services for visually impaired. **Transfer:** Re-entry adviser, pre-admission transcript evaluation for new students.

**Contact.** E-mail: dnoonan@goodwin.edu
Phone: (860) 727-6902 Toll-free number: (800) 889-3282
Fax: (860) 291-9550
Daniel Noonan, Director of Enrollment, Goodwin College, One Riverside Drive, East Hartford, CT 06118

## Housatonic Community College
**Bridgeport, Connecticut**   CB member
**www.hcc.commnet.edu**   CB code: 3446

- Public 2-year community college
- Commuter campus in small city

**General.** Founded in 1966. Regionally accredited. **Enrollment:** 1,880 full-time, degree-seeking students. **Degrees:** 397 associate awarded. **Location:** 60 miles from Hartford, 60 miles from New York City. **Calendar:** Semester, extensive summer session. **Full-time faculty:** 73 total. **Part-time faculty:** 220 total. **Class size:** 45% < 20, 53% 20-39, 2% 40-49, less than 1% 50-99.

**Basis for selection.** Open admission, but selective for some programs. Special requirements for clinical lab science, physical therapist assistant, occupational therapy assistant, nursing programs. Interview required of allied health, computer program majors.

**2009-2010 Annual costs.** Tuition/fees: $3,200; $9,560 out-of-state. Per-credit charge: $118 in-state; $354 out-of-state. Books/supplies: $700.

**2008-2009 Financial aid.** All financial aid based on need. Need-based aid available for part-time students.

**Application procedures. Admission:** No deadline. $20 fee, may be waived for applicants with need. Admission notification on a rolling basis. Application period ends one week after start of classes. **Financial aid:** Priority date 11/1, closing date 5/1. FAFSA required. Applicants notified on a rolling basis starting 6/1.

**Academics. Special study options:** Cooperative education, distance learning, double major, dual enrollment of high school students, ESL, honors, independent study, internships, weekend college. **Credit/placement by examination:** CLEP, institutional tests. 30 credit hours maximum toward associate degree. New Jersey Basic Skills Placement Test and/or ACCUPLACER used for advising and placement. **Support services:** GED preparation, learning center, reduced course load, remedial instruction, study skills assistance, tutoring, writing center.

**Majors. Business:** General, accounting, administrative services, business admin. **Computer sciences:** General. **Education:** Early childhood. **Family/consumer sciences:** Child care. **Health:** Mental health services, nursing (RN), physical therapy assistant, substance abuse counseling. **Liberal arts:** Arts/sciences. **Mechanic/repair:** Aircraft. **Protective services:** Police science. **Public administration:** Human services. **Visual/performing arts:** Commercial/advertising art, studio arts.

**Computing on campus.** 140 workstations in library, computer center.

**Student life. Freshman orientation:** Available. Preregistration for classes offered. **Activities:** Drama, literary magazine, student government, student newspaper.

**Student services.** Adult student services, career counseling, services for economically disadvantaged, student employment services, financial aid counseling, health services, on-campus daycare, personal counseling, placement for graduates, veterans' counselor. **Transfer:** Transfer adviser, college fairs on campus for students transferring to 4-year colleges.

**Contact.** Phone: (203) 332-5100 Fax: (203) 332-5123
Deloris Curtis, Director of Admissions, Housatonic Community College, 900 Lafayette Boulevard, Bridgeport, CT 06604-4704

## Lincoln College of New England: Briarwood
**Southington, Connecticut**
**www.briarwood.edu**   CB code: 3121

- For-profit 2-year junior college
- Commuter campus in large town
- Application essay required

**General.** Founded in 1966. Regionally accredited. **Enrollment:** 772 degree-seeking undergraduates. **Degrees:** 10 bachelor's, 89 associate awarded. **Location:** 19 miles from Hartford. **Calendar:** Semester, limited summer session. **Full-time faculty:** 25 total. **Part-time faculty:** 60 total.

**Student profile.**

| | | | |
|---|---|---|---|
| Out-of-state: | 6% | Live on campus: | 19% |
| 25 or older: | 41% | | |

**Transfer out. Colleges most students transferred to 2009:** Central Connecticut State University, Saint Joseph College, Quinnipiac College, Teikyo Post University, University of New Haven, University of Connecticut.

**Basis for selection.** Open admission, but selective for some programs. 8-hour observation and interview required for Occupational Therapy Assistant program. Interview, essay and 2 letters of recommendation required for Dental Hygiene program.

**High school preparation.** For occupational therapy assistant program, 2 math, 2 science (including 1 biological science) required.

**2009-2010 Annual costs.** Tuition/fees: $18,490. Per-credit charge: $590. Room only: $4,200. Books/supplies: $1,000. Personal expenses: $2,400.

**Financial aid. Need-based:** Need-based aid available for part-time students. Work-study available nights, weekends and for part-time students. **Non-need-based:** Scholarships awarded for academics, alumni affiliation, leadership.

**Application procedures. Admission:** No deadline. $30 fee, may be waived for applicants with need. Admission notification on a rolling basis beginning on or about 9/15. **Financial aid:** Priority date 4/30; no closing date. FAFSA required. Applicants notified on a rolling basis starting 3/15; must reply within 2 week(s) of notification.

**Academics. Special study options:** Double major, ESL, independent study, internships, liberal arts/career combination, weekend college. Bachelor's degree programs available on campus. **Credit/placement by examination:** AP, CLEP, institutional tests. 29 credit hours maximum toward associate degree. **Support services:** Learning center, pre-admission summer program, reduced course load, remedial instruction, study skills assistance, tutoring, writing center.

**Majors. Business:** General, accounting, administrative services, business admin, fashion, office technology, tourism/travel. **Communications:** General, broadcast journalism. **Family/consumer sciences:** Child care. **Health:** Dental assistant, dietetics, medical assistant, medical records technology, medical secretary, occupational therapy assistant. **Legal studies:** Legal secretary, paralegal. **Liberal arts:** Arts/sciences. **Personal/culinary services:** Mortuary science. **Protective services:** Criminal justice.

**Computing on campus.** 66 workstations in library, computer center. Dormitories wired for high-speed internet access.

**Student life. Freshman orientation:** Mandatory. **Housing:** Coed dorms, apartments, wellness housing available. $100 deposit. Townhouse apartments with kitchens available. **Activities:** Choral groups, radio station, student government, psychology honor society, allied health club.

**Athletics.** NJCAA. **Intramural:** Basketball M.

**Student services.** Career counseling, student employment services, financial aid counseling, health services, personal counseling, placement for graduates, veterans' counselor. **Physically disabled:** Services for visually, hearing impaired. **Transfer:** Pre-admission transcript evaluation for new students. Transfer adviser, college fairs on campus for students transferring to 4-year colleges.

**Contact.** E-mail: admis@briarwood.edu
Phone: (860) 628-4751 ext. 108 Toll-free number: (800) 952-2444 ext. 108
Fax: (860) 628-6444
Anthony Reich, Dean of Administration, Lincoln College of New England: Briarwood, 2279 Mount Vernon Road, Southington, CT 06489-1057

## Lincoln College of New England: Suffield
**Suffield, Connecticut**
http://lincolncollegene.edu    CB code: 3615

- For-profit 2-year culinary school and business college
- Residential campus in small town
- Application essay, interview required

**General.** Regionally accredited. Transfer to sister schools in Switzerland or Australia possible for second year. Students can complete degree program in 18-month accelerated format. Cost of attendance includes 6-month paid internship. **Enrollment:** 102 degree-seeking undergraduates. **Degrees:** 34 associate awarded. **Location:** 50 miles from Hartford. **Calendar:** Continuous, limited summer session. **Full-time faculty:** 7 total. **Part-time faculty:** 7 total. **Class size:** 95% < 20, 5% 20-39.

**Student profile.**

| | | | |
|---|---|---|---|
| Out-of-state: | 90% | Live on campus: | 90% |
| 25 or older: | 40% | | |

**Transfer out. Colleges most students transferred to 2009:** University Center Cesar Ritz (Switzerland), Institut Hotelier Cesar Ritz (Switzerland).

**Basis for selection.** Recommendations and interview important. Visa required for international students.

**2009-2010 Annual costs.** Tuition/fees: $14,648. Culinary student pay an extra $943 for cutlery and tools. Room/board: $5,808.

**Financial aid. Need-based:** Need-based aid available for part-time students. Work-study available nights, weekends and for part-time students. **Non-need-based:** Scholarships awarded for academics.

**Application procedures. Admission:** Priority date 1/15; no deadline. $40 fee, may be waived for applicants with need. Admission notification on a rolling basis. **Financial aid:** No deadline. Applicants notified on a rolling basis starting 1/1.

**Academics. Special study options:** Accelerated study, cooperative education, internships, liberal arts/career combination, study abroad. **Credit/placement by examination:** AP, CLEP, institutional tests. 18 credit hours maximum toward associate degree. **Support services:** Learning center, remedial instruction, study skills assistance, tutoring, writing center.

**Majors. Business:** Hospitality admin. **Personal/culinary services:** Culinary arts.

**Computing on campus.** 38 workstations in dormitories, library, computer center, student center. Dormitories wired for high-speed internet access and linked to campus network. Online library, helpline, wireless network available.

**Student life. Freshman orientation:** Mandatory. Preregistration for classes offered. Half of the first week devoted to orientation. **Housing:** Guaranteed on-campus for freshmen. Coed dorms, wellness housing available. $500 deposit. **Activities:** Film society, student government, Ritz Guild.

**Athletics. Intramural:** Basketball, soccer, table tennis, tennis, volleyball, weight lifting.

**Student services.** Adult student services, alcohol/substance abuse counseling, career counseling, student employment services, financial aid counseling, health services, placement for graduates. **Transfer:** Pre-admission transcript evaluation for new students.

**Contact.** E-mail: admissions@lincolncollegene.edu
Phone: (860) 668-3515 ext. 228 Toll-free number: (800) 955-0809
Fax: (860) 668-7369
Director of Admissions, Lincoln College of New England: Suffield, 1760 Mapleton Avenue, Suffield, CT 06078

## Manchester Community College
**Manchester, Connecticut**    CB member
www.mcc.commnet.edu    CB code: 3544

- Public 2-year community college
- Commuter campus in small city

**General.** Founded in 1963. Regionally accredited. **Enrollment:** 6,502 degree-seeking undergraduates; 864 non-degree-seeking students. **Degrees:** 706 associate awarded. **Location:** 8 miles from Hartford. **Calendar:** Semester, extensive summer session. **Full-time faculty:** 105 total; 19% minority, 60% women. **Part-time faculty:** 375 total; 28% minority, 53% women. **Class size:** 23% < 20, 71% 20-39, 6% 40-49.

**Student profile.** Among degree-seeking undergraduates, 1,745 enrolled as first-time, first-year students, 877 transferred in from other institutions.

| | | | |
|---|---|---|---|
| Part-time: | 49% | Hispanic American: | 13% |
| Women: | 51% | International: | 1% |
| African American: | 13% | 25 or older: | 31% |
| Asian American: | 3% | | |

**Transfer out. Colleges most students transferred to 2009:** Central Connecticut State University, University of Connecticut, Eastern Connecticut State University.

**Basis for selection.** Open admission, but selective for some programs. Interview required of allied health, drug and alcohol rehabilitation counselor majors.

**High school preparation.** 2 units math and 1 unit laboratory science required of allied health applicants.

**2009-2010 Annual costs.** Tuition/fees: $3,200; $9,560 out-of-state. Per-credit charge: $118 in-state; $354 out-of-state. Books/supplies: $800. Personal expenses: $3,032.

**2009-2010 Financial aid. Need-based:** Need-based aid available for part-time students.

**Application procedures. Admission:** No deadline. $20 fee, may be waived for applicants with need. Admission notification on a rolling basis beginning on or about 5/1. **Financial aid:** Priority date 5/15; no closing date. FAFSA required. Applicants notified on a rolling basis starting 5/1; must reply within 2 week(s) of notification.

**Academics. Special study options:** Cooperative education, cross-registration, distance learning, double major, dual enrollment of high school students, ESL, independent study, internships, semester at sea, student-designed major, weekend college. License preparation in occupational therapy, paramedic. **Credit/placement by examination:** AP, CLEP, SAT, ACT, institutional tests. 45 credit hours maximum toward associate degree. **Support services:** Learning center, reduced course load, remedial instruction, study skills assistance, tutoring, writing center.

**Majors. Area/ethnic studies:** Women's. **Business:** Accounting, administrative services, business admin, hospitality/recreation, management information systems. **Communications:** Digital media, journalism. **Computer sciences:** Data entry, information systems, networking. **Education:** Early childhood, teacher assistance. **Engineering:** Science. **Engineering technology:** Manufacturing. **Family/consumer sciences:** Institutional food production. **Health:** Clinical lab technology, occupational therapy assistant, pharmacy assistant, physical therapy assistant, respiratory therapy technology, substance abuse counseling, surgical technology. **Legal studies:** Paralegal. **Liberal arts:** Arts/sciences. **Parks/recreation:** Exercise sciences. **Public administration:** Community org/advocacy. **Visual/performing arts:** Commercial/advertising art.

**Most popular majors.** Business/marketing 14%, education 11%, family/consumer sciences 15%, health sciences 11%, legal studies 7%, security/protective services 35%.

**Computing on campus.** 310 workstations in library, computer center. Online course registration, online library, wireless network available.

**Student life. Freshman orientation:** Available. **Activities:** Choral groups, dance, drama, student government, student newspaper, student organization of Latinos, African American Males Achieving Excellence, Muslim student association, Spanish club, political union, PRIDE, Phi Theta Kappa, Veterans Empowering Themselves to Succeed.

**Athletics.** NJCAA. **Intercollegiate:** Baseball M, basketball W, soccer, softball W. **Team name:** Cougars.

**Student services.** Adult student services, career counseling, student employment services, health services, on-campus daycare, personal counseling, placement for graduates, veterans' counselor. **Physically disabled:** Services for visually, speech, hearing impaired. **Transfer:** Transfer adviser, college fairs on campus for students transferring to 4-year colleges.

**Contact.** Phone: (860) 512-3210 Fax: (860) 512-3221
Peter Harris, Director of Admissions, Manchester Community College, Great Path PO Box 1046, MS 12, Manchester, CT 06040-1046

## Middlesex Community College
**Middletown, Connecticut**
www.mxcc.commnet.edu
**CB member**
**CB code: 3551**

- Public 2-year community college
- Commuter campus in large town

**General.** Founded in 1966. **Enrollment:** 2,233 degree-seeking undergraduates; 681 non-degree-seeking students. **Degrees:** 236 associate awarded. **Location:** 20 miles from Hartford and New Haven. **Calendar:** Semester, limited summer session. **Full-time faculty:** 43 total; 12% minority, 49% women. **Part-time faculty:** 122 total; 8% minority, 66% women. **Class size:** 24% < 20, 76% 20-39. **Special facilities:** Nature trails, art gallery.

**Student profile.** Among degree-seeking undergraduates, 49% enrolled in a transfer program, 51% enrolled in a vocational program, 604 enrolled as first-time, first-year students, 279 transferred in from other institutions.

| | | | |
|---|---|---|---|
| Part-time: | 49% | Asian American: | 2% |
| Out-of-state: | 1% | Hispanic American: | 14% |
| Women: | 58% | 25 or older: | 65% |
| African American: | 9% | | |

**Transfer out.** 55% of students enrolled in the transfer program go on to 4-year colleges.

**Basis for selection.** Open admission, but selective for some programs. Special requirements for radiology technician, broadcast communications, human services, and drug and alcohol rehabilitation counselor programs. Interview recommended of mental health, radiology, drug and alcohol counseling program majors.

**High school preparation.** College-preparatory program recommended.

**2009-2010 Annual costs.** Tuition/fees: $3,200; $9,560 out-of-state. Per-credit charge: $118 in-state; $354 out-of-state. Out-of-state tuition includes fees. Books/supplies: $1,000. Personal expenses: $1,925.

**Financial aid.** All financial aid based on need. Need-based aid available for part-time students. Work-study available for part-time students. **Additional information:** Tuition and/or fee waiver for veterans.

**Application procedures. Admission:** Priority date 7/1; deadline 8/1 (postmark date). $20 fee, may be waived for applicants with need. Admission notification on a rolling basis beginning on or about 1/1. **Financial aid:** Priority date 6/1; no closing date. FAFSA, institutional form required. Applicants notified on a rolling basis starting 7/1; must reply within 2 week(s) of notification.

**Academics. Special study options:** Cross-registration, dual enrollment of high school students, ESL, independent study, internships, student-designed major. License preparation in radiology. **Credit/placement by examination:** CLEP, institutional tests. 48 credit hours maximum toward associate degree. **Support services:** Pre-admission summer program, reduced course load, remedial instruction, tutoring.

**Majors. Business:** Accounting, administrative services, business admin, marketing. **Communications:** General, broadcast journalism. **Computer sciences:** Information systems. **Conservation:** General. **Education:** Early childhood. **Health:** Medical radiologic technology/radiation therapy, medical secretary, ophthalmic lab technology, optician, substance abuse counseling. **Legal studies:** Legal secretary. **Liberal arts:** Arts/sciences. **Public administration:** Human services. **Visual/performing arts:** Metal/jewelry, studio arts.

**Most popular majors.** Business/marketing 30%, health sciences 25%, liberal arts 35%.

**Computing on campus.** Online library, helpline available.

**Student life. Freshman orientation:** Available. Preregistration for classes offered. **Activities:** Drama, international student organizations, literary magazine, student government, student newspaper, Student Senate, poetry club, national scholastic honor society, student guild, computer club, Minority Opportunities in Education club, art club, human services organization.

**Student services.** Career counseling, student employment services, financial aid counseling, minority student services, on-campus daycare, personal counseling, placement for graduates, veterans' counselor. **Physically disabled:** Services for visually, hearing impaired. **Transfer:** Transfer adviser, college fairs on campus for students transferring to 4-year colleges.

**Contact.** E-mail: mshabazz@mxcc.commnet.edu
Phone: (860) 343-5719 Toll-free number: (800) 818-5501
Fax: (860) 344-7488
Mensimah Shabazz, Director of Admissions, Middlesex Community College, 100 Training Hill Road, Middletown, CT 06457-4889

## Naugatuck Valley Community College
**Waterbury, Connecticut**
www.nvcc.commnet.edu
**CB member**
**CB code: 3550**

- Public 2-year community and technical college
- Commuter campus in small city

**General.** Founded in 1992. Regionally accredited. **Enrollment:** 5,766 degree-seeking undergraduates; 959 non-degree-seeking students. **Degrees:** 510 associate awarded. **Location:** 32 miles from Hartford. **Calendar:** Semester, limited summer session. **Full-time faculty:** 107 total; 11% minority, 57% women. **Part-time faculty:** 334 total. **Class size:** 82% < 20, 16% 20-39, 1% 40-49. **Special facilities:** Fine arts center, 2 theaters, music and dance studios, video studios, rehearsal rooms, fire sprinkler laboratory, automotive center, greenhouse laboratory, observatory, arboretum, nature trail. **Partnerships:** Formal partnership with Disney.

**Student profile.** Among degree-seeking undergraduates, 43% enrolled in a transfer program, 57% enrolled in a vocational program, 2% already have a bachelor's degree or higher, 1,339 enrolled as first-time, first-year students, 521 transferred in from other institutions.

| | | | |
|---|---|---|---|
| Part-time: | 54% | 25 or older: | 37% |
| Women: | 59% | | |

**Transfer out.** 12% of students enrolled in the transfer program go on to 4-year colleges. **Colleges most students transferred to 2009:** Western Connecticut State University, Southern Connecticut State University, Central Connecticut State University, University of Connecticut, Post University.

**Basis for selection.** Open admission, but selective for some programs. Admission to nursing, physical therapy assistant, radiology, respiratory care programs based on school achievement, recommendations, test scores, maturity of student, motivation. Levels of English Proficiency (LOEP) used for ESL population. Interview required of physical therapy majors. Audition recommended of music majors. Portfolio recommended of art majors. **Homeschooled:** Statement describing homeschool structure and mission, interview required. Placement test and interview required.

**High school preparation.** Recommended units include English 4, mathematics 3, social studies 2, history 2 and science 1. Most allied health programs require high school algebra, biology, chemistry. Engineering technologies require 2 years algebra, 1 year laboratory science (preferably physics or chemistry), and computer literacy.

**2009-2010 Annual costs.** Tuition/fees: $3,200; $9,560 out-of-state. Per-credit charge: $118 in-state; $354 out-of-state. Non-resident fees $1,064. Books/supplies: $1,400. Personal expenses: $1,507.

**2008-2009 Financial aid.** All financial aid based on need. Need-based aid available for part-time students. Work-study available for part-time students.

**Application procedures. Admission:** Priority date 6/1; no deadline. $20 fee, may be waived for applicants with need. Admission notification on a rolling basis beginning on or about 9/1. **Financial aid:** Priority date 4/1; no closing date. FAFSA required. Applicants notified on a rolling basis starting 6/1.

**Academics.** Composition, technical writing, literature, computer information systems, math, business law, psychology, astronomy, biology and criminal justice courses available through distance learning. **Special study options:** Cooperative education, cross-registration, distance learning, double major, dual enrollment of high school students, ESL, independent study, internships, study abroad. License preparation in aviation, nursing, physical therapy, radiology, real estate. **Credit/placement by examination:** AP, CLEP, institutional tests. 45 credit hours maximum toward associate degree. **Support services:** Learning center, reduced course load, remedial instruction, study skills assistance, tutoring, writing center.

**Majors. Agriculture:** Horticulture. **Business:** Accounting technology, administrative services, banking/financial services, business admin, merchandising. **Computer sciences:** General, networking, web page design. **Engineering technology:** General, CAD/CADD, electrical, energy systems, environmental, industrial management, manufacturing, mechanical, quality control. **Family/consumer sciences:** Child development, facilities/event planning, institutional food production. **Health:** Medical radiologic technology/radiation therapy, mental health services, nursing (RN), physical therapy assistant, respiratory therapy technology, substance abuse counseling. **Legal studies:** Legal secretary, paralegal. **Liberal arts:** Arts/sciences. **Mechanic/repair:** Automotive. **Protective services:** Fire safety technology, police science. **Psychology:** General. **Public administration:** Human services, social work. **Transportation:** Aviation. **Visual/performing arts:** Art, dance, dramatic, multimedia.

**Most popular majors.** Business/marketing 15%, health sciences 25%, liberal arts 25%, security/protective services 6%.

**Computing on campus.** 1,100 workstations in library, computer center. Commuter students can connect to campus network. Online course registration, online library, helpline, repair service, wireless network available.

**Student life. Freshman orientation:** Available. Preregistration for classes offered. **Activities:** Bands, choral groups, dance, drama, literary magazine, music ensembles, musical theater, opera, student government, student newspaper, symphony orchestra, black student union, Hispanic student union, human services club, Phi Theta Kappa, Alpha Beta Gamma, agro-bio club, student nurses clubs, book club.

**Student services.** Adult student services, career counseling, student employment services, financial aid counseling, health services, personal counseling, placement for graduates, veterans' counselor. **Physically disabled:** Services for visually, speech, hearing impaired. **Learning disabled:** Comprehensive services available. **Transfer:** Pre-admission transcript evaluation for new students. Transfer adviser, college fairs on campus for students transferring to 4-year colleges.

**Contact.** E-mail: nvcc@nvcc.commnet.edu
Phone: (203) 575-8054 Fax: (203) 596-8766
Linda Stango, Director of Admissions, Naugatuck Valley Community College, 750 Chase Parkway, Waterbury, CT 06708-3089

## Northwestern Connecticut Community College
**Winsted, Connecticut** — **CB member**
www.nwcc.commnet.edu — **CB code: 3652**

◗ Public 2-year community and technical college
◗ Commuter campus in large town

**General.** Founded in 1965. Regionally accredited. **Enrollment:** 1,254 degree-seeking undergraduates; 457 non-degree-seeking students. **Degrees:** 113 associate awarded. **Location:** 25 miles from Hartford, 25 miles from Waterbury. **Calendar:** Semester, limited summer session. **Full-time faculty:** 28 total. **Part-time faculty:** 102 total. **Special facilities:** Computer graphics multimedia laboratory.

**Student profile.** Among degree-seeking undergraduates, 312 enrolled as first-time, first-year students.

Part-time: 53% Women: 67%

**Basis for selection.** Open admission, but selective for some programs. Special requirements for drug and alcohol rehabilitation counseling, adventure education, physical therapy assistant, dialysis patient care programs.

**2009-2010 Annual costs.** Tuition/fees: $3,200; $9,560 out-of-state. Per-credit charge: $118 in-state; $354 out-of-state. Books/supplies: $600. Personal expenses: $1,000.

**Application procedures. Admission:** No deadline. $20 fee, may be waived for applicants with need. Admission notification on a rolling basis. **Financial aid:** Priority date 6/1; no closing date. FAFSA required. Applicants notified on a rolling basis starting 6/1.

**Academics.** Career education for the deaf program offers full range of services and participation in all majors by deaf and hearing impaired students. Interpreting major prepares hearing students for National Registry test for interpreters for the deaf. **Special study options:** Cooperative education, cross-registration, distance learning, double major, dual enrollment of high school students, ESL, independent study, internships. **Credit/placement by examination:** AP, CLEP, institutional tests. 48 credit hours maximum toward associate degree. **Support services:** Learning center, reduced course load, remedial instruction, tutoring.

**Majors. Business:** Accounting, banking/financial services, business admin, hospitality admin, marketing. **Communications technology:** Animation/special effects, graphics. **Computer sciences:** Systems analysis. **Education:** Early childhood. **Engineering technology:** General, industrial. **Foreign languages:** Sign language interpretation. **Health:** Health services, medical assistant, physical therapy assistant, recreational therapy, veterinary technology/assistant. **Liberal arts:** Arts/sciences. **Protective services:** Law enforcement admin. **Public administration:** Human services.

**Student life. Freshman orientation:** Available. **Housing:** Dormitory for hearing impaired and interpreting students available in Winsted. **Activities:** Literary magazine, student government, student newspaper, Spectrum, community service club, Signs of Our Times.

**Student services.** Career counseling, student employment services, on-campus daycare, personal counseling, veterans' counselor. **Physically disabled:** Services for hearing impaired. **Transfer:** Transfer adviser, college fairs on campus for students transferring to 4-year colleges.

**Contact.** E-mail: dmartineau@nwcc.commnet.edu
Phone: (860) 738-6330 Fax: (860) 379-4465
Beverly Chrzan, Director of Admissions, Northwestern Connecticut Community College, Park Place East, Winsted, CT 06098

## Norwalk Community College
**Norwalk, Connecticut**
www.ncc.commnet.edu — **CB code: 3677**

◗ Public 2-year community and technical college
◗ Commuter campus in small city

**General.** Founded in 1961. Regionally accredited. Non-credit courses offered through continuing education department. Lifetime Learners Institute for senior citizens. **Enrollment:** 4,829 degree-seeking undergraduates. **Degrees:** 468 associate awarded. **Location:** 45 miles from New York City. **Calendar:** Semester, extensive summer session. **Full-time faculty:** 100 total. **Part-time faculty:** 250 total. **Special facilities:** Theater, rotating art and cultural exhibits, culinary arts facility, early childhood education lab/preschool.

**Student profile.**

Out-of-state: 1% 25 or older: 52%

**Basis for selection.** Open admission, but selective for some programs. Special requirements for nursing, legal assistant, respiratory care programs.

**High school preparation.** Recommended units include English 4, mathematics 3 and science 2. Chemistry, biology and algebra required for nursing and respiratory therapy applicants. Nursing applicants must have taken chemistry within past 5 years.

**2009-2010 Annual costs.** Tuition/fees: $3,200; $9,560 out-of-state. Per-credit charge: $118 in-state; $354 out-of-state. New England Regional Student Program: $177 per credit hour plus fees. Books/supplies: $1,200. Personal expenses: $1,751.

**Financial aid. Need-based:** Need-based aid available for part-time students. Work-study available for part-time students. **Non-need-based:** Scholarships awarded for academics, alumni affiliation.

**Application procedures. Admission:** No deadline. $20 fee, may be waived for applicants with need. Admission notification on a rolling basis. Applicants to nursing program should apply by February 1. **Financial aid:** Priority date 7/1; no closing date. FAFSA, institutional form required. Applicants notified on a rolling basis starting 7/1; must reply within 2 week(s) of notification.

**Academics.** Special 10-week sessions with longer class hours per day let students finish courses more quickly during fall and spring. **Special study options:** Cooperative education, cross-registration, double major, dual enrollment of high school students, ESL, honors, internships, liberal arts/career combination, weekend college. Early childhood education credential training program. License preparation in nursing, paramedic, real estate. **Credit/placement by examination:** AP, CLEP, IB, institutional tests. 45 credit hours maximum toward associate degree. **Support services:** Learning center, pre-admission summer program, reduced course load, remedial instruction, study skills assistance, tutoring, writing center.

**Majors. Business:** Accounting, business admin, finance, hospitality admin, management information systems, marketing, office management, office technology. **Communications:** Journalism. **Communications technology:** General. **Computer sciences:** General, applications programming, data processing, information systems, programming, systems analysis. **Education:** Early childhood. **Engineering:** General, architectural, science. **Engineering technology:** Architectural, construction. **Health:** Nursing (RN), recreational therapy, respiratory therapy technology. **Legal studies:** Legal secretary, paralegal. **Liberal arts:** Arts/sciences. **Math:** General. **Parks/recreation:** General. **Protective services:** Fire safety technology, fire services admin, law enforcement admin. **Public administration:** Human services. **Visual/performing arts:** Art, commercial/advertising art, studio arts.

**Computing on campus.** 90 workstations in library, computer center, student center. Commuter students can connect to campus network. Online library, helpline available.

**Student life. Freshman orientation:** Available. One-day orientation for new students before start of semester. **Activities:** Choral groups, drama, international student organizations, literary magazine, student government, student newspaper, TV station, African culture club, Hay Motivo, Phi Theta Kappa, legal assistants club, early childhood education club, French club, Haitian student association, criminal justice club.

**Student services.** Adult student services, career counseling, services for economically disadvantaged, student employment services, financial aid counseling, on-campus daycare, placement for graduates, veterans' counselor, women's services. **Physically disabled:** Services for visually, speech, hearing impaired. **Transfer:** Re-entry adviser, pre-admission transcript evaluation for new students. Transfer adviser, college fairs on campus for students transferring to 4-year colleges.

**Contact.** E-mail: admissions@ncc.commnet.edu
Phone: (203) 857-7060 Fax: (203) 857-3335
Kimberlee Csapo-Ebert, Director of Enrollment Management, Norwalk Community College, 188 Richards Avenue, Norwalk, CT 06854-1655

## Quinebaug Valley Community College
**Danielson, Connecticut**      **CB member**
**www.qvcc.commnet.edu**      **CB code: 3716**

- Public 2-year community and technical college
- Commuter campus in large town

**General.** Founded in 1971. Regionally accredited. Smaller center in downtown Willimantic. **Enrollment:** 1,873 degree-seeking undergraduates; 237 non-degree-seeking students. **Degrees:** 169 associate awarded. **Location:** 50 miles from Hartford, 25 miles from Providence, Rhode Island. **Calendar:** Semester, limited summer session. **Full-time faculty:** 29 total; 17% have terminal degrees, 10% minority, 55% women. **Part-time faculty:** 117 total; 8% have terminal degrees, 7% minority, 55% women. **Class size:** 30% < 20, 70% 20-39. **Special facilities:** Art museum, plastics laboratory.

**Student profile.** Among degree-seeking undergraduates, 493 enrolled as first-time, first-year students, 234 transferred in from other institutions.

| | | | |
|---|---|---|---|
| Part-time: | 60% | Asian American: | 1% |
| Out-of-state: | 1% | Hispanic American: | 11% |
| Women: | 66% | 25 or older: | 42% |
| African American: | 2% | | |

**Transfer out. Colleges most students transferred to 2009:** Eastern Connecticut State University, University of Connecticut, Worcester State College.

**Basis for selection.** Open admission. Interview recommended. **Learning Disabled:** Meeting with Coordinator of Learning Disability Services recommended.

**2009-2010 Annual costs.** Tuition/fees: $3,200; $9,560 out-of-state. Per-credit charge: $118 in-state; $354 out-of-state. Books/supplies: $1,300. Personal expenses: $1,200.

**2009-2010 Financial aid.** All financial aid based on need. 96% of total undergraduate aid awarded as scholarships/grants, 4% as loans/jobs. Need-based aid available for part-time students. Work-study available nights and for part-time students.

**Application procedures. Admission:** No deadline. $20 fee, may be waived for applicants with need. Admission notification on a rolling basis. **Financial aid:** Closing date 10/1. FAFSA required. Applicants notified on a rolling basis starting 5/1.

**Academics. Special study options:** Distance learning, double major, dual enrollment of high school students, ESL, independent study, internships. License preparation in real estate. **Credit/placement by examination:** CLEP, institutional tests. 30 credit hours maximum toward associate degree. **Support services:** Learning center, pre-admission summer program, reduced

course load, remedial instruction, study skills assistance, tutoring, writing center.

**Majors. Business:** Accounting, administrative services, business admin, office technology. **Computer sciences:** General. **Construction:** General. **Education:** Early childhood. **Engineering:** Polymer. **Engineering technology:** Biomedical, CAD/CADD, construction, plastics. **Health:** Community health services, medical assistant. **Liberal arts:** Arts/sciences. **Public administration:** Human services. **Visual/performing arts:** Graphic design, photography, studio arts.

**Most popular majors.** Business/marketing 9%, liberal arts 40%, public administration/social services 33%.

**Computing on campus.** 115 workstations in library, computer center. Commuter students can connect to campus network. Online course registration, online library, helpline, wireless network available.

**Student life. Freshman orientation:** Available. **Activities:** Student government, medical assisting association, Phi Theta Kappa, Alpha Beta Gamma.

**Student services.** Adult student services, career counseling, student employment services, financial aid counseling, minority student services, on-campus daycare, placement for graduates, veterans' counselor. **Physically disabled:** Services for visually, speech, hearing impaired. **Transfer:** Re-entry adviser, pre-admission transcript evaluation for new students. Transfer adviser, college fairs on campus for students transferring to 4-year colleges.

**Contact.** E-mail: admissions@qvcc.commnet.edu
Phone: (860) 412-7380 Fax: (860) 774-7768
Maria Angelos, Director of Admissions, Quinebaug Valley Community College, 742 Upper Maple Street, Danielson, CT 06239-1440

## St. Vincent's College
**Bridgeport, Connecticut**
**www.stvincentscollege.edu**      **CB code: 3789**

- Private 2-year health science and junior college
- Commuter campus in small city
- SAT or ACT with writing, application essay required

**General.** Regionally accredited. Majority of students are adult learners. Nursing and radiography programs highly competitive; pre-programs available. **Enrollment:** 50 full-time, degree-seeking students. **Degrees:** 71 associate awarded. **Location:** 55 miles from New York City. **Calendar:** Semester, limited summer session. **Full-time faculty:** 12 total. **Part-time faculty:** 32 total.

**Transfer out. Colleges most students transferred to 2009:** Southern Connecticut State University.

**Basis for selection.** High school record and GPA most important, followed by character, talents, work and volunteer experience. **Adult students:** SAT/ACT scores not required if out of high school 1 year(s) or more. **Homeschooled:** Transcript of courses and grades, letter of recommendation (nonparent) required.

**High school preparation.** College-preparatory program required. 16 units required. Required units include English 4, mathematics 2, social studies 2, science 2 and academic electives 6.

**2009-2010 Annual costs.** Tuition/fees: $13,126. Per-credit charge: $396. Books/supplies: $1,400.

**Application procedures. Admission:** Priority date 5/1; deadline 8/1 (receipt date). $50 fee, may be waived for applicants with need. Admission notification on a rolling basis beginning on or about 10/1.

**Academics. Special study options:** Distance learning, internships. License preparation in nursing, radiology. **Credit/placement by examination:** AP, CLEP, institutional tests. 18 credit hours maximum toward associate degree. **Support services:** Learning center, pre-admission summer program, reduced course load, remedial instruction, study skills assistance, tutoring, writing center.

**Majors. Health:** Cardiovascular technology, medical assistant, nursing (RN), radiologic technology/medical imaging.

**Computing on campus.** 40 workstations in computer center, student center. Commuter students can connect to campus network. Online library, wireless network available.

**Student life. Freshman orientation:** Mandatory. Held each spring and fall. **Activities:** Student government, student newspaper.

**Student services.** Alcohol/substance abuse counseling, chaplain/ spiritual director, career counseling, student employment services, financial aid counseling, health services, personal counseling.

**Contact.** E-mail: admissions@stvincentscollege.edu
Phone: (203) 576-5513 Fax: (203) 576-5318
Joseph Marrone, Admissions Director, St. Vincent's College, 2800 Main Street, Bridgeport, CT 06606

## Three Rivers Community College

**Norwich, Connecticut**
www.trcc.commnet.edu

**CB member**
**CB code: 3558**

- Public 2-year community and liberal arts college
- Commuter campus in large town

**General.** Founded in 1969. Regionally accredited. **Enrollment:** 4,186 degree-seeking undergraduates; 375 non-degree-seeking students. **Degrees:** 370 associate awarded. **Location:** 45 miles from Hartford. **Calendar:** Semester, limited summer session. **Full-time faculty:** 77 total; 9% have terminal degrees, 10% minority, 52% women. **Part-time faculty:** 156 total; 2% have terminal degrees, 8% minority, 48% women. **Special facilities:** Nuclear reactor simulator.

**Student profile.** Among degree-seeking undergraduates, 14% enrolled in a transfer program, 6% already have a bachelor's degree or higher, 1,019 enrolled as first-time, first-year students.

| | | | |
|---|---|---|---|
| Part-time: | 64% | Asian American: | 4% |
| Out-of-state: | 1% | Hispanic American: | 11% |
| Women: | 59% | Native American: | 1% |
| African American: | 7% | 25 or older: | 45% |

**Transfer out. Colleges most students transferred to 2009:** Eastern Connecticut State University, University of Connecticut, Central Connecticut State University, Southern Illinois University, Sacred Heart University.

**Basis for selection.** Open admission, but selective for some programs. Selective admission for nursing program based on successful performance on ATI-TEAS Exam, completion of prerequisite courses, and 2.7 GPA. **Adult students:** Basic skills placement tests in math and English required unless student has completed college level math and English course. **Home-schooled:** Student may take Ability to Benefit Test if standard documentation requirements are not met.

**High school preparation.** College-preparatory program recommended. One unit chemistry, biology, and algebra required for nursing program.

**2009-2010 Annual costs.** Tuition/fees: $3,200; $9,560 out-of-state. Per-credit charge: $118 in-state; $354 out-of-state. Out-of-state required fees $1,064. New England state students pay $4,248 for tuition and $542 for fees. Books/supplies: $1,200. Personal expenses: $1,304.

**2008-2009 Financial aid.** All financial aid based on need. Average need met was 50%. Average scholarship/grant was $3,378; average loan $3,376. 83% of total undergraduate aid awarded as scholarships/grants, 17% as loans/jobs. Need-based aid available for part-time students. Work-study available nights, weekends and for part-time students.

**Application procedures. Admission:** No deadline. $20 fee, may be waived for applicants with need. Admission notification on a rolling basis beginning on or about 3/30. **Financial aid:** Priority date 7/15; no closing date. FAFSA required. Applicants notified on a rolling basis; must reply within 2 week(s) of notification.

**Academics. Special study options:** Cooperative education, cross-registration, distance learning, double major, dual enrollment of high school students, ESL, independent study, internships, liberal arts/career combination, study abroad. License preparation in nursing. **Credit/placement by examination:** AP, CLEP, institutional tests. 45 credit hours maximum toward associate degree. **Support services:** Learning center, remedial instruction, study skills assistance, tutoring, writing center.

**Majors. Architecture:** Technology. **Business:** Accounting, banking/financial services, business admin, construction management, hospitality admin, office technology, restaurant/food services, tourism/travel. **Communications:** Public relations. **Computer sciences:** General, applications programming, information systems. **Conservation:** Environmental science. **Education:** Early childhood, special. **Engineering technology:** General, architectural, CAD/CADD, civil, drafting, electrical, environmental, hazardous materials, laser/optical, manufacturing, nuclear, water quality. **Family/consumer sciences:** Family studies. **Health:** Nursing (RN). **Interdisciplinary:** Accounting/computer science. **Liberal arts:** Arts/sciences, library

assistant. **Personal/culinary services:** Food service, restaurant/catering. **Physical sciences:** General. **Protective services:** Criminal justice, fire safety technology, law enforcement admin, police science. **Public administration:** Human services. **Science technology:** Nuclear power. **Transportation:** Aviation.

**Most popular majors.** Business/marketing 17%, engineering/engineering technologies 11%, liberal arts 39%.

**Computing on campus.** 300 workstations in library, computer center, student center. Online course registration, online library, helpline, wireless network available.

**Student life. Freshman orientation:** Available. **Policies:** Student government controls student activity fees. **Activities:** Drama, literary magazine, student government, student newspaper, Spanish-American association, Afro-American association, student chapters of professional organizations, gay-straight alliance, volunteer club, golf club, student nurses association, environmentalists club, senior student ambassadors, veterans organization.

**Student services.** Career counseling, student employment services, financial aid counseling, on-campus daycare. **Physically disabled:** Services for visually, hearing impaired. **Transfer:** Re-entry adviser for new students. Transfer adviser, college fairs on campus for students transferring to 4-year colleges.

**Contact.** E-mail: admissions@trcc.commnet.edu
Phone: (860) 383-5260
Dan Zaneski, Director of Admissions, Three Rivers Community College, 574 New London Turnpike, Norwich, CT 06360-6598

## Tunxis Community College

**Farmington, Connecticut**
www.tunxis.commnet.edu

**CB member**
**CB code: 3897**

- Public 2-year community college
- Commuter campus in large town

**General.** Founded in 1970. Regionally accredited. **Enrollment:** 3,560 degree-seeking undergraduates; 936 non-degree-seeking students. **Degrees:** 420 associate awarded. **ROTC:** Army, Naval, Air Force. **Location:** 15 miles from Hartford. **Calendar:** Semester, limited summer session. **Full-time faculty:** 61 total. **Part-time faculty:** 186 total. **Class size:** 29% < 20, 70% 20-39, less than 1% 40-49. **Special facilities:** Early childhood center, art gallery.

**Student profile.** Among degree-seeking undergraduates, 60% enrolled in a transfer program, 40% enrolled in a vocational program, 8% already have a bachelor's degree or higher, 846 enrolled as first-time, first-year students.

| | | | |
|---|---|---|---|
| Part-time: | 51% | Asian American: | 3% |
| Out-of-state: | 1% | Hispanic American: | 13% |
| Women: | 59% | 25 or older: | 38% |
| African American: | 5% | | |

**Transfer out.** 33% of students enrolled in the transfer program go on to 4-year colleges. **Colleges most students transferred to 2009:** Central Connecticut State University, Charter Oak College, St. Joseph College, University of Connecticut.

**Basis for selection.** Open admission, but selective for some programs. Special requirements for dental hygiene, drug and alcohol rehabilitation counselor, physical therapist assistant, technological studies: television operations option, dental assisting, criminal justice command institute: supervisory leadership programs, and correction pre-service certification. ESL placement test required of non-native English speakers. Interview required of dental hygiene, drug and alcohol rehabilitation counselor majors. **Home-schooled:** Interview required. Placement test (ACCUPLACER) required. **Learning Disabled:** Contact Academic Support Center prior to placement testing if accommodations are necessary.

**High school preparation.** College-preparatory program recommended.

**2009-2010 Annual costs.** Tuition/fees: $3,200; $9,560 out-of-state. Per-credit charge: $118 in-state; $354 out-of-state. Out-of-state required fees: $1,064. Books/supplies: $420. Personal expenses: $1,210.

**2008-2009 Financial aid. Need-based:** Need-based aid available for part-time students. Work-study available nights, weekends and for part-time students. **Non-need-based:** Scholarships awarded for academics, leadership. **Additional information:** Financial aid available to all students showing need. Part-time students encouraged to apply.

**Application procedures. Admission:** No deadline. $20 fee, may be waived for applicants with need. Admission notification on a rolling basis. Dental hygiene program closing date 1/1, notification by 3/1. **Financial**

**aid:** Priority date 6/1; no closing date. FAFSA required. Applicants notified on a rolling basis starting 3/1.

**Academics. Special study options:** Cross-registration, distance learning, double major, dual enrollment of high school students, ESL, independent study, internships, liberal arts/career combination. License preparation in dental hygiene, physical therapy. **Credit/placement by examination:** CLEP, institutional tests. 30 credit hours maximum toward associate degree. **Support services:** Learning center, pre-admission summer program, reduced course load, remedial instruction, tutoring.

**Majors. Business:** Accounting, administrative services, business admin, fashion, finance, office/clerical. **Computer sciences:** Applications programming, computer graphics. **Education:** Early childhood. **Engineering:** Science. **Engineering technology:** Manufacturing. **Health:** Dental hygiene, medical secretary, substance abuse counseling. **Legal studies:** Legal secretary. **Liberal arts:** Arts/sciences. **Public administration:** Human services. **Visual/performing arts:** General, commercial/advertising art.

**Computing on campus.** 200 workstations in library, computer center. Commuter students can connect to campus network. Wireless network available.

**Student life. Freshman orientation:** Available. Preregistration for classes offered. Held once a week during the month before start of classes. **Activities:** Jazz band, literary magazine, student government, student newspaper, minority student alliance, human services club, criminal justice club, dental hygiene group.

**Student services.** Career counseling, student employment services, financial aid counseling, health services, minority student services, on-campus daycare, personal counseling, placement for graduates. **Physically disabled:** Services for visually impaired. **Transfer:** Transfer adviser, college fairs on campus for students transferring to 4-year colleges.

**Contact.** E-mail: tx-admissions@txcc.commnet.edu
Phone: (860) 255-3555 Fax: (860) 255-3559
Peter McCluskey, Director of Admissions, Tunxis Community College, 271 Scott Swamp Road, Farmington, CT 06032-3187

# Delaware

## Delaware College of Art and Design
### Wilmington, Delaware
www.dcad.edu      CB code: 5161

▶ Private 2-year visual arts college
▶ Residential campus in large city

**General.** Regionally accredited. **Enrollment:** 226 degree-seeking undergraduates. **Degrees:** 71 associate awarded. **Calendar:** Semester, limited summer session. **Full-time faculty:** 7 total; 86% have terminal degrees, 29% women. **Part-time faculty:** 20 total. **Class size:** 86% < 20, 14% 20-39.

**Student profile.** Among degree-seeking undergraduates, 126 enrolled as first-time, first-year students, 2 transferred in from other institutions.

| | | | |
|---|---|---|---|
| Part-time: | 8% | Hispanic American: | 7% |
| Out-of-state: | 54% | International: | 2% |
| Women: | 60% | 25 or older: | 8% |
| African American: | 19% | Live on campus: | 61% |
| Asian American: | 3% | | |

**Transfer out.** 68% of students enrolled in the transfer program go on to 4-year colleges.

**Basis for selection.** High school record considered. Art Portfolio required. **Adult students:** SAT/ACT scores not required. **Homeschooled:** Transcript of courses and grades, state high school equivalency certificate required.

**High school preparation.** College-preparatory program recommended. Recommended units include English 4, mathematics 3, social studies 4, history 2, science 3, foreign language 2, computer science 2 and visual/performing arts 4.

**2009-2010 Annual costs.** Tuition/fees: $18,140. Room only: $6,700.

**Application procedures. Admission:** Priority date 3/1; no deadline. $40 fee, may be waived for applicants with need. Admission notification on a rolling basis. Must reply by May 1 or within 2 week(s) if notified thereafter.

**Academics. Credit/placement by examination:** AP, CLEP, institutional tests. **Support services:** Remedial instruction, tutoring.

**Majors. Communications technology:** Animation/special effects. **Visual/performing arts:** Graphic design, illustration, interior design, photography, studio arts.

**Computing on campus.** Dormitories wired for high-speed internet access. Wireless network available.

**Student life. Freshman orientation:** Mandatory. **Housing:** Coed dorms, apartments available. $350 nonrefundable deposit, deadline 5/1. Apartment-style housing with full kitchen/living room, semi-furnished. **Activities:** Film society.

**Student services.** Financial aid counseling.

**Contact.** E-mail: admissions@dcad.edu
Phone: (302) 622-8867 ext. 118 Fax: (302) 622-8870
Elizabeth Gatti, Director of Admissions, Delaware College of Art and Design, 600 North Market Street, Wilmington, DE 19801

## Delaware Technical and Community College: Owens
### Georgetown, Delaware
www.dtcc.edu      CB code: 5169

▶ Public 2-year community and technical college
▶ Commuter campus in small town

**General.** Founded in 1967. Regionally accredited. **Enrollment:** 4,170 degree-seeking undergraduates; 511 non-degree-seeking students. **Degrees:** 413 associate awarded. **Location:** 80 miles from Wilmington. **Calendar:** Semester, limited summer session. **Full-time faculty:** 117 total. **Part-time faculty:** 201 total. **Class size:** 62% < 20, 38% 20-39, less than 1% 50-99. **Special facilities:** Treasures of the Sea Maritime exhibit.

**Student profile.** Among degree-seeking undergraduates, 766 enrolled as first-time, first-year students.

| | | | |
|---|---|---|---|
| Part-time: | 46% | Women: | 65% |

**Basis for selection.** Open admission, but selective for some programs.

**2009-2010 Annual costs.** Tuition/fees: $2,763; $6,471 out-of-state. Per-credit charge: $103 in-state; $258 out-of-state. Books/supplies: $1,500. Personal expenses: $200.

**Financial aid.** All financial aid based on need. Need-based aid available for part-time students. Work-study available for part-time students.

**Application procedures. Admission:** No deadline. $10 fee, may be waived for applicants with need. Admission notification on a rolling basis. **Financial aid:** Priority date 6/15; no closing date. FAFSA required. Applicants notified on a rolling basis; must reply within 2 week(s) of notification.

**Academics. Special study options:** Distance learning, double major, dual enrollment of high school students, ESL, internships, study abroad. License preparation in nursing, occupational therapy, physical therapy, radiology, real estate. **Credit/placement by examination:** AP, CLEP, institutional tests. **Support services:** GED preparation and test center, learning center, pre-admission summer program, remedial instruction, study skills assistance, tutoring, writing center.

**Majors. Agriculture:** Business, horticulture, poultry, production, turf management. **Biology:** General. **Business:** General, accounting, construction management, e-commerce, entrepreneurial studies, management information systems, marketing, office management, office technology. **Computer sciences:** General. **Education:** Early childhood, elementary, kindergarten/preschool, mathematics, middle, multi-level teacher. **Engineering technology:** Aerospace, architectural, civil, computer systems, drafting, electrical, mechanical drafting, nuclear, surveying, water quality. **Health:** Clinical lab assistant, EMT paramedic, medical assistant, nursing (RN), occupational therapy assistant, physical therapy assistant, radiologic technology/medical imaging, respiratory therapy assistant, sonography, veterinary technology/assistant. **Legal studies:** Legal secretary. **Mechanic/repair:** Automotive, heating/ac/refrig. **Protective services:** Law enforcement admin, police science. **Public administration:** Human services. **Science technology:** Biological. **Visual/performing arts:** Music.

**Most popular majors.** Business/marketing 24%, education 9%, engineering/engineering technologies 11%, health sciences 28%, public administration/social services 7%, security/protective services 6%.

**Computing on campus.** 728 workstations in library, computer center, student center. Commuter students can connect to campus network. Online course registration, online library, helpline, wireless network available.

**Student life. Freshman orientation:** Available. **Activities:** Radio station, student government, student newspaper.

**Athletics.** NJCAA. **Intercollegiate:** Baseball M, golf M. **Team name:** Road Runners.

**Student services.** Adult student services, career counseling, student employment services, financial aid counseling, personal counseling, placement for graduates, veterans' counselor. **Physically disabled:** Services for visually, hearing impaired. **Transfer:** Transfer adviser for students transferring to 4-year colleges.

**Contact.** E-mail: g-admissions@dtcc.edu
Phone: (302) 856-5400 Fax: (302) 855-5961
Claire MacDonald, Admissions Coordinator, Delaware Technical and Community College: Owens, PO Box 610, Georgetown, DE 19947

## Delaware Technical and Community College: Stanton/Wilmington
### Newark, Delaware
www.dtcc.edu      CB code: 5154

▶ Public 2-year community and technical college
▶ Commuter campus in small city

**General.** Founded in 1967. Regionally accredited. Multi-location institution. **Enrollment:** 6,894 degree-seeking undergraduates; 432 non-degree-seeking students. **Degrees:** 558 associate awarded. **ROTC:** Air Force. **Location:** 30 miles from Philadelphia. **Calendar:** Semester, limited summer session. **Full-time faculty:** 178 total. **Part-time faculty:** 353 total. **Class size:** 68% < 20, 31% 20-39, less than 1% 40-49, less than 1% 50-99.

**Student profile.** Among degree-seeking undergraduates, 1,403 enrolled as first-time, first-year students.

| Part-time: | 56% | **Women:** | 59% |
|---|---|---|---|

**Basis for selection.** Open admission, but selective for some programs. Admission to health technologies program restricted to state residents. Restricted admission to Allied Health, Nursing, and Culinary Arts programs.

**2009-2010 Annual costs.** Tuition/fees: $2,763; $6,471 out-of-state. Per-credit charge: $103 in-state; $258 out-of-state. Books/supplies: $1,500. Personal expenses: $200.

**Financial aid.** All financial aid based on need. Need-based aid available for part-time students. Work-study available for part-time students.

**Application procedures. Admission:** No deadline. $10 fee, may be waived for applicants with need. Admission notification on a rolling basis. **Financial aid:** Priority date 6/15; no closing date. FAFSA required. Applicants notified on a rolling basis; must reply within 2 week(s) of notification.

**Academics. Special study options:** Distance learning, double major, dual enrollment of high school students, ESL, internships, study abroad. License preparation in dental hygiene, nursing, occupational therapy, paramedic, physical therapy, radiology. **Credit/placement by examination:** AP, CLEP, institutional tests. **Support services:** GED preparation and test center, learning center, pre-admission summer program, remedial instruction, study skills assistance, tutoring, writing center.

**Majors. Agriculture:** Business. **Biology:** General. **Business:** General, accounting, banking/financial services, business admin, construction management, customer service, hotel/motel admin, management information systems, management science, marketing, office management, office technology. **Computer sciences:** General, networking. **Education:** Early childhood, elementary, kindergarten/preschool, mathematics, middle, multi-level teacher. **Engineering:** Operations research. **Engineering technology:** Architectural, CAD/CADD, civil drafting, computer, drafting, electrical, heat/ac/refrig, industrial management, manufacturing, mechanical, nuclear, surveying. **Health:** Cardiovascular technology, dental hygiene, electrocardiograph technology, EMT ambulance attendant, EMT paramedic, histologic technology, medical assistant, nuclear medical technology, nursing (RN), occupational therapy assistant, physical therapy assistant, radiologic technology/medical imaging, respiratory therapy assistant, sonography, substance abuse counseling. **Mechanic/repair:** Automotive. **Parks/recreation:** Exercise sciences. **Personal/culinary services:** Chef training, restaurant/catering. **Protective services:** Fire safety technology, fire services admin, firefighting, law enforcement admin, police science. **Public administration:** Human services. **Science technology:** Biological, chemical. **Visual/performing arts:** Music. **Other:** Science technologies.

**Most popular majors.** Business/marketing 19%, engineering/engineering technologies 8%, health sciences 49%, security/protective services 6%.

**Computing on campus.** 1,139 workstations in library, computer center. Commuter students can connect to campus network. Online course registration, online library, helpline, wireless network available.

**Student life. Freshman orientation:** Available. **Activities:** Student government, student newspaper.

**Athletics.** NJCAA. **Intercollegiate:** Basketball, soccer M, softball W. **Intramural:** Basketball, football (tackle), softball W, volleyball. **Team name:** Spirit.

**Student services.** Adult student services, career counseling, student employment services, financial aid counseling, health services, personal counseling, placement for graduates, veterans' counselor, women's services. **Physically disabled:** Services for visually, speech, hearing impaired. **Transfer:** Transfer adviser for students transferring to 4-year colleges.

**Contact.** E-mail: s-admissions@dtcc.edu
Phone: (302) 454-3954 Fax: (302) 453-3084
Rebecca Bailey-Bell, Admissions Representative, Delaware Technical and Community College: Stanton/Wilmington, 400 Stanton-Christiana Road, Newark, DE 19713

---

## Delaware Technical and Community College: Terry

Dover, Delaware — **CB member**
www.dtcc.edu — **CB code: 5201**

- Public 2-year community and technical college
- Commuter campus in large town

**General.** Founded in 1972. Regionally accredited. **Enrollment:** 3,214 degree-seeking undergraduates; 150 non-degree-seeking students. **Degrees:** 272 associate awarded. **Location:** 90 miles from Baltimore, 75 miles from Philadelphia. **Calendar:** Semester, limited summer session. **Full-time faculty:** 81 total. **Part-time faculty:** 160 total. **Class size:** 69% < 20, 31% 20-39.

**Student profile.** Among degree-seeking undergraduates, 687 enrolled as first-time, first-year students.

| Part-time: | 53% | **Women:** | 67% |
|---|---|---|---|

**Basis for selection.** Open admission, but selective for some programs. Special requirements for health/nursing programs.

**2009-2010 Annual costs.** Tuition/fees: $2,763; $6,471 out-of-state. Per-credit charge: $103 in-state; $258 out-of-state. Books/supplies: $1,500. Personal expenses: $200.

**Financial aid.** All financial aid based on need. Need-based aid available for part-time students. Work-study available for part-time students.

**Application procedures. Admission:** No deadline. $10 fee, may be waived for applicants with need. Admission notification on a rolling basis. **Financial aid:** Priority date 6/15; no closing date. FAFSA required. Applicants notified on a rolling basis starting 7/1; must reply within 2 week(s) of notification.

**Academics. Special study options:** Distance learning, double major, dual enrollment of high school students, ESL, internships, study abroad. License preparation in nursing, paramedic. **Credit/placement by examination:** AP, CLEP, institutional tests. **Support services:** GED preparation and test center, learning center, pre-admission summer program, remedial instruction, study skills assistance, tutoring, writing center.

**Majors. Agriculture:** Business. **Business:** General, accounting, business admin, construction management, e-commerce, entrepreneurial studies, hotel/motel admin, human resources, management information systems, marketing, office management, office technology. **Communications:** Digital media. **Computer sciences:** General, networking. **Education:** Bilingual, early childhood, elementary, kindergarten/preschool, mathematics, middle, multi-level teacher. **Engineering technology:** Architectural, biomedical, civil, computer, computer systems, drafting, electrical, electromechanical. **Health:** EMT paramedic, medical assistant, nursing (RN), substance abuse counseling. **Legal studies:** Legal secretary. **Personal/culinary services:** Chef training. **Protective services:** Law enforcement admin, police science. **Public administration:** Human services. **Visual/performing arts:** Commercial/advertising art, interior design, photography. **Other:** EMT management.

**Most popular majors.** Business/marketing 15%, education 7%, engineering/engineering technologies 6%, health sciences 32%, public administration/social services 10%, security/protective services 7%, visual/performing arts 12%.

**Computing on campus.** 423 workstations in library, computer center. Commuter students can connect to campus network. Online course registration, online library, helpline available.

**Student life. Freshman orientation:** Available. **Activities:** Student government, student newspaper.

**Athletics.** NJCAA. **Intercollegiate:** Lacrosse M, soccer, softball W. **Team name:** Hawks.

**Student services.** Adult student services, career counseling, student employment services, financial aid counseling, personal counseling, placement for graduates, veterans' counselor. **Physically disabled:** Services for visually, hearing impaired. **Transfer:** Transfer adviser for students transferring to 4-year colleges.

**Contact.** E-mail: t-admissions@dtcc.edu
Phone: (302) 857-1020 Fax: (302) 739-6169
Maria Harris, Admissions Coordinator, Delaware Technical and Community College: Terry, 100 Campus Drive, Dover, DE 19901

Two-Year Colleges

# Florida

## Angley College
### Deland, Florida
### www.angley.edu

- For-profit 2-year technical and career college
- Commuter campus in small city
- Interview required

**General.** Accredited by ACICS. **Enrollment:** 251 degree-seeking undergraduates. **Degrees:** 3 associate awarded. **Location:** 30 miles from Orlando. **Calendar:** Quarter, extensive summer session. **Full-time faculty:** 8 total; 50% have terminal degrees, 50% minority, 75% women. **Part-time faculty:** 21 total; 48% have terminal degrees, 52% minority, 76% women. **Class size:** 83% < 20, 17% 20-39. **Special facilities:** Play care center for students on campus. **Partnerships:** Formal partnerships with local hospitals, clinics and local businesses.

**Student profile.** Among degree-seeking undergraduates, 10% enrolled in a transfer program, 90% enrolled in a vocational program, 251 enrolled as first-time, first-year students, 15 transferred in from other institutions.

| | | | |
|---|---|---|---|
| Out-of-state: | 15% | 25 or older: | 75% |
| Women: | 89% | | |

**Transfer out.** 8% of students enrolled in the transfer program go on to 4-year colleges.

**Basis for selection.** Completion of high school with standard high school diploma, successful completion of college-administered admission test, and results of interview (in person or via telephone) with admissions officer important. **Homeschooled:** State high school equivalency certificate required.

**2009-2010 Annual costs.** Tuition/fees: $15,900. Per-credit charge: $323. Textbooks included in program cost. Books/supplies: $1,350.

**2008-2009 Financial aid. Need-based:** 76% of total undergraduate aid awarded as scholarships/grants, 24% as loans/jobs.

**Application procedures. Admission:** No deadline. $100 fee. Admission notification on a rolling basis.

**Academics. Special study options:** Accelerated study, cooperative education, distance learning, double major, independent study, internships, weekend college. Bachelor's degree programs available on campus. License preparation in aviation. **Credit/placement by examination:** AP, CLEP, institutional tests. 22.5 credit hours maximum toward associate degree, 45 toward bachelor's. **Support services:** Learning center, remedial instruction, study skills assistance, tutoring.

**Majors. Business:** Business admin. **Health:** Massage therapy, medical assistant, office assistant.

**Most popular majors.** Business/marketing 10%, health sciences 90%.

**Computing on campus.** 25 workstations in library, computer center. Online library, wireless network available.

**Student life. Freshman orientation:** Mandatory. Preregistration for classes offered. Held Saturday before each class start; lasts approximately 2 hours. **Activities:** Student government.

**Student services.** Adult student services, alcohol/substance abuse counseling, career counseling, financial aid counseling, on-campus daycare, personal counseling, placement for graduates, veterans' counselor. **Transfer:** Pre-admission transcript evaluation for new students.

**Contact.** E-mail: admissions@angley.edu
Phone: (386) 740-1215 Toll-free number: (866) 639-1215
Fax: (386) 740-2077
Anthony Jenkins, Director of Admissions, Angley College, 1700 Woodland Boulevard, Deland, FL 32720-4289

## ATI Career Training Center: Ft. Lauderdale
### Ft. Lauderdale, Florida
### www.aticareertraining.edu          CB code: 2945

- For-profit 2-year technical college
- Small city

**General.** Accredited by ACCSCT. **Calendar:** Continuous.

**Annual costs/financial aid.** Full program costs: $25,440 for electronics, $13,800 for medical assistant technician, $10,500 for medical administration assisting technology; $21,400 for Network Administration. Costs include all tuition, fees and supplies.

**Contact.** Phone: (954) 973-4760
2890 NW 62nd Street, Fort Lauderdale, FL 33309-9731

## ATI Career Training Center: Oakland Park
### Oakland Park, Florida
### www.aticareertraining.edu          CB code: 3182

- For-profit 2-year technical college
- Very large city

**General.** Accredited by ACCSC. **Enrollment:** 940 degree-seeking undergraduates. **Degrees:** 155 associate awarded. **Calendar:** Continuous. **Full-time faculty:** 10 total.

**Student profile.** Among degree-seeking undergraduates, 100% enrolled in a vocational program, 940 enrolled as first-time, first-year students.

**Basis for selection.** Open admission. GED not accepted.

**2009-2010 Annual costs.** Tuition and fees entire AC/refrigeration program $22,500 (diploma program $19,822); for entire automotive service technician program $26,980 (diploma program $24,740); for entire business administration technology program $16,280; for entire electronic systems technician $14,000.

**Application procedures. Admission:** $100 fee, may be waived for applicants with need.

**Academics. Credit/placement by examination:** CLEP.

**Majors. Mechanic/repair:** Automotive, heating/ac/refrig.

**Contact.** E-mail: lead130@atienterprises.edu
Phone: (954) 563-5899 Fax: (954) 568-0874
Kertney Thompson, Executive Director, ATI Career Training Center: Oakland Park, 3501 NW 9th Avenue, Oakland Park, FL 33309

## ATI College of Health
### Miami, Florida
### www.aticareertraining.edu          CB code: 3183

- For-profit 2-year health science and technical college
- Commuter campus in very large city

**General.** Accredited by ACCSC. **Enrollment:** 1,119 degree-seeking undergraduates. **Degrees:** 1,550 associate awarded. **Calendar:** Semester. **Full-time faculty:** 48 total; 54% have terminal degrees, 52% minority, 60% women. **Part-time faculty:** 42 total; 48% have terminal degrees, 48% minority, 52% women. **Class size:** 100% 20-39.

**Student profile.** Among degree-seeking undergraduates, 25% enrolled in a transfer program, 12% enrolled in a vocational program, 770 enrolled as first-time, first-year students, 20 transferred in from other institutions.

**Transfer out.** 12% of students enrolled in the transfer program go on to 4-year colleges.

**Basis for selection.** Open admission, but selective for some programs. Respiratory therapist program requires HOBET. Evaluation exam required.

**2009-2010 Annual costs.** $44,520 tuition for diagnostic ultrasound program and respiratory therapist program; $31,102 for dental and health information technology. Personal expenses: $2,064.

**Financial aid.** All financial aid based on need. Need-based aid available for part-time students.

**Application procedures. Admission:** No deadline. $100 fee. Admission notification on a rolling basis. **Financial aid:** No deadline. FAFSA, institutional form, CSS PROFILE required. Applicants notified on a rolling basis.

**Academics. Credit/placement by examination:** CLEP, institutional tests. **Support services:** Learning center, study skills assistance, tutoring.

**Majors. Health:** Cardiovascular technology, respiratory therapy technology.

**Computing on campus.** 75 workstations in library, computer center.

**Student life. Freshman orientation:** Available. Held the Saturday before the class start, about 4 hours.

**Student services.** Career counseling, student employment services, financial aid counseling, placement for graduates.

**Contact.** E-mail: ekranidis@atienterprises.edu
Phone: (305) 628-1000 Fax: (305) 628-1461
Elias Kranidis, Director of Admissions, ATI College of Health, 1395 NW 167th Street, Miami, FL 33169-5745

## Brevard Community College
**Cocoa, Florida**
www.brevardcc.edu

**CB member**
**CB code: 5073**

- Public 2-year community college
- Commuter campus in large town

**General.** Founded in 1960. Regionally accredited. Campuses in Cocoa, Melbourne, Palm Bay, Titusville. Aerospace technology courses taught at the Kennedy Space Center. **Enrollment:** 16,723 degree-seeking undergraduates; 1,130 non-degree-seeking students. **Degrees:** 2,244 associate awarded. **ROTC:** Army, Air Force. **Location:** 50 miles from Orlando. **Calendar:** Semester, extensive summer session. **Full-time faculty:** 215 total; 20% have terminal degrees, 11% minority, 60% women. **Part-time faculty:** 822 total; 9% minority, 51% women. **Class size:** 44% < 20, 56% 20-39, less than 1% 40-49, less than 1% 50-99. **Special facilities:** Planetarium, observatory, playhouse, performing arts center, multicultural center.

**Student profile.** Among degree-seeking undergraduates, 73% enrolled in a transfer program, 27% enrolled in a vocational program, 10% already have a bachelor's degree or higher, 2,881 enrolled as first-time, first-year students, 501 transferred in from other institutions.

| | | | |
|---|---|---|---|
| Part-time: | 58% | Hispanic American: | 7% |
| Out-of-state: | 2% | Native American: | 1% |
| Women: | 57% | International: | 1% |
| African American: | 12% | 25 or older: | 34% |
| Asian American: | 3% | | |

**Transfer out.** 75% of students enrolled in the transfer program go on to 4-year colleges. **Colleges most students transferred to 2009:** University of Central Florida.

**Basis for selection.** Open admission, but selective for some programs. Additional application and requirements for health science, law enforcement and corrections programs. CPT required for admission but scores not used. SAT or ACT may be submitted instead of CPT. California Achievement Tests, Stanford Test of Academic Skills, Test of Adult Basic Education required for health program applicants. **Homeschooled:** Affidavit of home school completion required. **Learning Disabled:** Students may self-disclose with Office for Students with Disabilities.

**High school preparation.** Standard high school or equivalent required for degree seeking students. College prep courses required for students testing below college proficiency.

**2009-2010 Annual costs.** Tuition/fees: $2,685; $9,675 out-of-state. Books/supplies: $800. Personal expenses: $1,224.

**2008-2009 Financial aid. Need-based:** Need-based aid available for part-time students. **Non-need-based:** Scholarships awarded for academics, athletics.

**Application procedures. Admission:** No deadline. $30 fee, may be waived for applicants with need. Admission notification on a rolling basis. **Financial aid:** Priority date 4/15, closing date 6/30. FAFSA required. Applicants notified on a rolling basis starting 6/1; must reply within 2 week(s) of notification.

**Academics. Special study options:** Accelerated study, cooperative education, cross-registration, distance learning, double major, dual enrollment

of high school students, ESL, honors, independent study, internships, study abroad, teacher certification program, weekend college. Bachelor's degree programs available on campus. License preparation in dental hygiene, nursing, paramedic, radiology, real estate. **Credit/placement by examination:** AP, CLEP, IB, institutional tests. 45 credit hours maximum toward associate degree. **Support services:** Learning center, reduced course load, remedial instruction, study skills assistance, tutoring, writing center.

**Majors. Business:** Administrative services, business admin, management information systems, office management. **Computer sciences:** Programming, systems analysis. **Education:** Early childhood. **Engineering:** General, computer. **Engineering technology:** Drafting, electrical. **Health:** Clinical lab technology, dental hygiene, EMT paramedic, medical radiologic technology/radiation therapy, nursing (RN). **Legal studies:** Court reporting, legal secretary, paralegal. **Protective services:** Firefighting, police science. **Visual/performing arts:** Commercial/advertising art.

**Computing on campus.** 1,800 workstations in library, computer center, student center. Commuter students can connect to campus network. Online course registration, online library, helpline, student web hosting, wireless network available.

**Student life. Freshman orientation:** Mandatory. **Activities:** Bands, choral groups, dance, drama, international student organizations, literary magazine, music ensembles, musical theater, student government, TV station, Student Nurses Association of Florida, Phi Theta Kappa, African American Student Association, Phi Mu Alpha.

**Athletics.** NJCAA. **Intercollegiate:** Baseball M, basketball, golf M, softball W, volleyball W. **Team name:** Titans.

**Student services.** Adult student services, career counseling, services for economically disadvantaged, student employment services, financial aid counseling, minority student services, on-campus daycare, veterans' counselor. **Physically disabled:** Services for visually, speech, hearing impaired. **Learning disabled:** Comprehensive services available. **Transfer:** College fairs on campus for students transferring to 4-year colleges.

**Contact.** E-mail: Registrar@brevardcc.edu
Phone: (321) 632-1111 Toll-free number: (888) 747-2802
Fax: (321) 433-7357
Michelle Loufek, Associate Director, Collegewide Admissions, Brevard Community College, 1519 Clearlake Road, Cocoa, FL 32922-9987

## Broward College
**Fort Lauderdale, Florida**
www.broward.edu

**CB member**
**CB code: 5074**

- Public 2-year community college
- Commuter campus in small city

**General.** Founded in 1959. Regionally accredited. Multilocation institution (3 main campuses and 6 centers as well as 4 overseas centers). **Enrollment:** 32,727 degree-seeking undergraduates; 4,633 non-degree-seeking students. **Degrees:** 3,893 associate awarded. **ROTC:** Army, Air Force. **Location:** 20 miles from Miami. **Calendar:** Semester, extensive summer session. **Full-time faculty:** 419 total; 32% minority, 53% women. **Part-time faculty:** 1,180 total; 28% minority, 48% women. **Class size:** 39% < 20, 58% 20-39, 1% 40-49, less than 1% 50-99, less than 1% >100. **Special facilities:** Concert hall, planetarium, golf course.

**Student profile.** Among degree-seeking undergraduates, 6,320 enrolled as first-time, first-year students, 1,172 transferred in from other institutions.

| | | | |
|---|---|---|---|
| Part-time: | 61% | Asian American: | 4% |
| Out-of-state: | 5% | Hispanic American: | 31% |
| Women: | 59% | International: | 4% |
| African American: | 31% | 25 or older: | 32% |

**Transfer out. Colleges most students transferred to 2009:** Florida Atlantic University, Florida International University.

**Basis for selection.** Open admission, but selective for some programs. Limited access and baccalaureate programs require secondary application process. **Homeschooled:** Statement describing homeschool structure and mission required.

**High school preparation.** Required units include English 4, mathematics 3, science 2 and foreign language 2.

**2009-2010 Annual costs.** Tuition/fees: $2,518; $9,081 out-of-state. Books/supplies: $1,200. Personal expenses: $1,755.

**2008-2009 Financial aid. Need-based:** 73% of total undergraduate aid awarded as scholarships/grants, 27% as loans/jobs. Need-based aid available for part-time students. Work-study available nights, weekends and for part-time students. **Non-need-based:** Scholarships awarded for academics, athletics, leadership, state residency.

**Application procedures. Admission:** No deadline. $35 fee, may be waived for applicants with need. Admission notification on a rolling basis beginning on or about 2/15. **Financial aid:** Priority date 4/15; no closing date. FAFSA, institutional form required. Applicants notified on a rolling basis starting 6/1.

**Academics. Special study options:** Accelerated study, cooperative education, distance learning, dual enrollment of high school students, ESL, exchange student, honors, independent study, internships, study abroad, teacher certification program, weekend college. Bachelor's degree programs available on campus. License preparation in aviation, dental hygiene, nursing, paramedic, physical therapy, radiology, real estate. **Credit/placement by examination:** AP, CLEP, IB, institutional tests. 30 credit hours maximum toward associate degree. **Support services:** Learning center, pre-admission summer program, reduced course load, remedial instruction, study skills assistance, tutoring, writing center.

**Majors. Architecture:** Landscape. **Biology:** General. **Business:** General, accounting, business admin, finance, hospitality admin, international, international marketing, management science, office/clerical, tourism/travel. **Communications:** Broadcast journalism, journalism. **Computer sciences:** General, computer graphics, computer science, data processing, information systems, programming, systems analysis. **Conservation:** Environmental science. **Education:** General, early childhood, elementary, mathematics, music, science, special. **Engineering:** General, civil, computer, electrical, software. **Engineering technology:** Civil. **Family/consumer sciences:** Child care, food/nutrition. **Foreign languages:** General. **Health:** Athletic training, cardiovascular technology, clinical lab assistant, clinical lab technology, dental hygiene, EMT paramedic, health care admin, medical radiologic technology/radiation therapy, medical records admin, nuclear medical technology, nursing (RN), ophthalmic lab technology, physical therapy assistant, predental, premedicine, prenursing, prepharmacy, preveterinary, recreational therapy, respiratory therapy technology, sonography. **History:** General. **Legal studies:** Court reporting, legal secretary, paralegal, prelaw. **Liberal arts:** Arts/sciences. **Math:** General. **Mechanic/repair:** Automotive. **Parks/recreation:** General. **Personal/culinary services:** General. **Philosophy/religion:** Religion. **Physical sciences:** Chemistry, physics. **Protective services:** Criminal justice, firefighting, security services. **Psychology:** General. **Public administration:** Social work. **Social sciences:** Anthropology, economics, geography, political science, sociology. **Transportation:** Aviation, aviation management. **Visual/performing arts:** Art, dramatic, interior design, music history.

**Computing on campus.** 4,162 workstations in library, computer center, student center. Commuter students can connect to campus network. Online course registration, online library, helpline, wireless network available.

**Student life. Freshman orientation:** Available. Preregistration for classes offered. **Activities:** Bands, choral groups, dance, drama, international student organizations, literary magazine, music ensembles, musical theater, opera, student government, student newspaper, symphony orchestra, Phi Theta Kappa, Phi Beta Lambda, African American student union, American Institute of Architecture Students, Catholic club, chess club, HIV peer educators, film club, French club.

**Athletics.** NJCAA. **Intercollegiate:** Baseball M, basketball, softball W, tennis W, volleyball W. **Team name:** Seahawks.

**Student services.** Adult student services, alcohol/substance abuse counseling, career counseling, student employment services, financial aid counseling, health services, on-campus daycare, personal counseling, placement for graduates, veterans' counselor, women's services. **Physically disabled:** Services for visually, speech, hearing impaired. **Transfer:** College fairs on campus for students transferring to 4-year colleges.

**Contact.** Phone: (954) 201-7541 Fax: (954) 201-7466
Willie Alexander, Associate Vice President for Student Affairs and Registrar, Broward College, 225 East Las Olas Boulevard, Fort Lauderdale, FL 33301

## Brown Mackie College: Miami
**Miami, Florida**
**www.brownmackie.edu**

- For-profit 2-year business and career college
- Commuter campus in very large city

**General.** Accredited by ACICS. **Enrollment:** 960 degree-seeking undergraduates. **Degrees:** 210 associate awarded. **Location:** Downtown. **Calendar:** Quarter, extensive summer session. **Full-time faculty:** 15 total. **Part-time faculty:** 32 total.

**Student profile.** Among degree-seeking undergraduates, 100% enrolled in a transfer program, 2% already have a bachelor's degree or higher.

**Basis for selection.** Open admission. **Homeschooled:** Transcript of courses and grades, state high school equivalency certificate, interview required.

**2009-2010 Annual costs.** Tuition, which varies according to area of study, is $336 per credit hour for most programs leading to a degree.

**Application procedures. Admission:** No application fee. Admission notification on a rolling basis.

**Academics. Special study options:** Double major, independent study, internships, liberal arts/career combination. Bachelor's degree programs available on campus. **Credit/placement by examination:** CLEP, institutional tests. **Support services:** Learning center, remedial instruction, study skills assistance, tutoring.

**Majors. Business:** Accounting, business admin. **Engineering technology:** Software. **Health:** Medical secretary. **Legal studies:** Paralegal. **Protective services:** Law enforcement admin.

**Computing on campus.** 300 workstations in library, computer center, student center. Commuter students can connect to campus network. Online library, wireless network available.

**Student life. Freshman orientation:** Mandatory. **Activities:** Student newspaper.

**Athletics. Team name:** The Lions.

**Student services.** Adult student services, alcohol/substance abuse counseling, career counseling, student employment services, financial aid counseling, personal counseling, placement for graduates, veterans' counselor. **Transfer:** Re-entry adviser, pre-admission transcript evaluation for new students. Transfer adviser, college fairs on campus for students transferring to 4-year colleges.

**Contact.** E-mail: bmmiadm@brownmackie.edu
Phone: (305) 341-6600 Toll-free number: (866) 505-0335
Fax: (305) 341-6649
Campbell Rey, Associate Director of Admissions, Brown Mackie College: Miami, One Herald Plaza, Miami, FL 33132

## Central Florida College
**Winter Park, Florida**
**www.centralfloridacollege.edu**

- For-profit 2-year technical college
- Very large city
- Interview required

**General.** Accredited by ACCSC. **Enrollment:** 500 degree-seeking undergraduates. **Degrees:** 108 associate awarded. **Calendar:** Continuous, extensive summer session. **Full-time faculty:** 18 total. **Part-time faculty:** 20 total.

**Basis for selection.** Open admission.

**Financial aid.** All financial aid based on need.

**Application procedures. Admission:** No deadline. $50 fee. Admission notification on a rolling basis. **Financial aid:** No deadline. FAFSA required.

**Academics. Special study options:** Distance learning, liberal arts/career combination. **Credit/placement by examination:** CLEP. **Support services:** Study skills assistance.

**Majors. Business:** Accounting, business admin. **Health:** Insurance specialist, medical assistant, medical records technology. **Personal/culinary services:** Cosmetic. **Protective services:** Police science.

**Most popular majors.** Business/marketing 13%, health sciences 80%.

**Computing on campus.** 64 workstations in library, computer center. Online library available.

**Contact.** E-mail: admissions@centralfloridacollege.edu
Phone: (407) 843-3984
Bill Poulmear, Director, Central Florida College, 1573 West Fairbanks Avenue, Winter Park, FL 32789

## Central Florida Community College
**Ocala, Florida**
www.cf.edu                    CB code: 5127

- Public 2-year community college
- Commuter campus in small city

**General.** Founded in 1957. Regionally accredited. **Enrollment:** 7,830 degree-seeking undergraduates; 514 non-degree-seeking students. **Degrees:** 557 associate awarded. **Location:** 72 miles from Orlando. **Calendar:** Semester, extensive summer session. **Full-time faculty:** 125 total. **Part-time faculty:** 512 total. **Special facilities:** Art museum. **Partnerships:** Formal partnership with Emergency One Corporation.

**Student profile.** Among degree-seeking undergraduates, 1,896 enrolled as first-time, first-year students.

| | | | |
|---|---|---|---|
| Part-time: | 62% | Women: | 62% |
| Out-of-state: | 1% | 25 or older: | 34% |

**Transfer out. Colleges most students transferred to 2009:** University of Florida, University of Central Florida, Florida State University.

**Basis for selection.** Open admission, but selective for some programs. Special requirements for registered nursing, dental assisting, physical therapy assistant, child care, criminal justice, practical nursing, surgical technology programs.

**High school preparation.** Recommended units include English 4, mathematics 3, social studies 3 and science 3.

**2009-2010 Annual costs.** Tuition/fees: $2,587; $9,728 out-of-state. Books/supplies: $1,230. Personal expenses: $3,386.

**2008-2009 Financial aid. Need-based:** Need-based aid available for part-time students. **Non-need-based:** Scholarships awarded for academics, athletics, minority status, music/drama, state residency.

**Application procedures. Admission:** $20 fee, may be waived for applicants with need. Application must be submitted on paper. Admission notification on a rolling basis. **Financial aid:** No deadline. FAFSA required.

**Academics. Special study options:** Accelerated study, cooperative education, distance learning, dual enrollment of high school students, ESL, honors, independent study, internships, liberal arts/career combination, teacher certification program. Bachelor's degrees available through on-campus University Center. Corporate training available through CFCC Institute. Bachelor's degree programs available on campus. License preparation in real estate. **Credit/placement by examination:** AP, CLEP, IB, institutional tests. 21 credit hours maximum toward associate degree. ACT, SAT, CPT are authorized placement tests for community colleges in Florida. **Support services:** GED preparation and test center, learning center, pre-admission summer program, reduced course load, remedial instruction, study skills assistance, tutoring, writing center.

**Majors. Agriculture:** Equestrian studies, horticulture, landscaping. **Business:** Accounting, accounting technology, business admin, executive assistant, restaurant/food services. **Computer sciences:** System admin. **Education:** Early childhood, elementary. **Engineering technology:** Architectural drafting. **Health:** EMT paramedic, licensed practical nurse, medical records technology, nursing (RN), physical therapy assistant. **Legal studies:** Paralegal. **Liberal arts:** Arts/sciences. **Mechanic/repair:** Automotive. **Personal/culinary services:** Chef training. **Protective services:** Fire safety technology, law enforcement admin. **Public administration:** Human services.

**Most popular majors.** Business/marketing 6%, health sciences 14%, liberal arts 75%.

**Computing on campus.** 2,200 workstations in library, computer center, student center. Online library, helpline available.

**Student life. Freshman orientation:** Mandatory. Preregistration for classes offered. Program held prior to beginning of term; also available online. **Housing:** College Square Student Residence Center owned and operated by Central Florida Community College Foundation near campus. **Activities:** Bands, campus ministries, choral groups, dance, drama, literary magazine, music ensembles, musical theater, student government, student newspaper, symphony orchestra, Afro-student union, Hispanic club, Phi Theta Kappa, Community of Scholars, Brain Bowl, Phi Beta Lambda, gay/straight alliance, peer educators.

**Athletics.** NJCAA. **Intercollegiate:** Baseball M, basketball, softball W, tennis W. **Team name:** Patriots.

**Student services.** Adult student services, career counseling, services for economically disadvantaged, student employment services, financial aid counseling, on-campus daycare, personal counseling, placement for graduates, veterans' counselor. **Physically disabled:** Services for visually, speech, hearing impaired. **Transfer:** Transfer adviser, college fairs on campus for students transferring to 4-year colleges.

**Contact.** Phone: (352) 873-5801 Fax: (352) 873-5875
Lyn Powell, Director of Admissions, Central Florida Community College, 3001 SW College Road, Ocala, FL 34474-4415

## City College: Casselberry
**Casselberry, Florida**

- For-profit 2-year career college
- Large town
- Interview required

**General.** Accredited by ACICS. **Enrollment:** 267 degree-seeking undergraduates. **Degrees:** 43 associate awarded. **Calendar:** Quarter, extensive summer session. **Full-time faculty:** 4 total. **Part-time faculty:** 26 total.

**Basis for selection.** Open admission.

**2009-2010 Annual costs.** Tuition/fees: $10,575. Per-credit charge: $235.

**Application procedures. Admission:** No deadline. $25 fee. **Financial aid:** No deadline.

**Academics. Credit/placement by examination:** CLEP.

**Majors. Business:** Business admin, marketing. **Computer sciences:** General. **Health:** Health services. **Protective services:** Security management.

**Contact.** Phone: (407) 831-8466 Fax: (407) 831-1147
I Cruz, Director of Admissions, City College: Casselberry, 853 State Road 436, Suite 200, Casselberry, FL 32707-5353

## City College: Gainesville
**Gainesville, Florida**
www.citycollege.edu                    CB code: 3579

- For-profit 2-year business and health science college
- Small city

**General.** Accredited by ACICS. **Enrollment:** 406 degree-seeking undergraduates. **Degrees:** 8 bachelor's, 68 associate awarded. **Calendar:** Continuous.

**Basis for selection.** Open admission.

**2009-2010 Annual costs.** Tuition/fees: $11,295. Per-credit charge: $235. Books/supplies: $1,377. Personal expenses: $5,688.

**Academics. Credit/placement by examination:** CLEP.

**Majors. Business:** Business admin. **Computer sciences:** General. **Legal studies:** General.

**Contact.** E-mail: kbowden@citycollege.edu
Phone: (352) 335-4000 Fax: (352) 335-4303
Kim Bowden, Director of Admissions, City College: Gainesville, 2400 SW 13th Street, Gainesville, FL 32608

## City College: Miami
**Miami, Florida**
www.citycollege.edu                    CB code: 3580

- For-profit 2-year business and health science college
- Large city

**General.** Accredited by ACICS. **Enrollment:** 270 degree-seeking undergraduates. **Degrees:** 18 bachelor's, 59 associate awarded. **Calendar:** Continuous. **Full-time faculty:** 4 total. **Part-time faculty:** 25 total.

**Basis for selection.** TABE is required. SAT or ACT considered if submitted.

**2009-2010 Annual costs.** Tuition/fees: $13,680.

**Financial aid.** All financial aid based on need. Need-based aid available for part-time students.

**Application procedures. Admission:** No deadline. $25 fee. Admission notification on a rolling basis. **Financial aid:** No deadline. FAFSA, institutional form required. Applicants notified on a rolling basis.

**Academics. Credit/placement by examination:** CLEP.

**Majors. Business:** Business admin.

**Contact.** E-mail: sespath@citycollege.edu
Phone: (305) 666-9242 Fax: (305) 666-9243
Anna Hernandez, Director of Admissions, City College: Miami, 9300 South Dadeland Boulevard, Miami, FL 33156

## College of Business and Technology: Flagler
**Miami, Florida**
**www.cbt.edu**

- For-profit 2-year junior and technical college
- Commuter campus in very large city
- Interview required

**General.** Accredited by ACICS. **Enrollment:** 150 degree-seeking undergraduates. **Degrees:** 8 associate awarded. **Calendar:** Semester. **Full-time faculty:** 8 total. **Part-time faculty:** 12 total.

**Student profile.** Among degree-seeking undergraduates, 10% enrolled in a transfer program, 60% enrolled in a vocational program, 20 transferred in from other institutions.

**Transfer out.** 70% of students enrolled in the transfer program go on to 4-year colleges. **Colleges most students transferred to 2009:** Jones College, Carlos Albizu University.

**Basis for selection.** Open admission. **Homeschooled:** Transcript of courses and grades required.

**2009-2010 Annual costs.** Tuition/fees: $14,904. Per-credit charge: $414. Books/supplies: $1,350.

**Financial aid.** All financial aid based on need. Need-based aid available for part-time students. Work-study available nights and for part-time students.

**Application procedures. Admission:** No deadline. $25 fee. **Financial aid:** No deadline. FAFSA required.

**Academics. Special study options:** Distance learning, ESL. **Credit/placement by examination:** CLEP. **Support services:** Tutoring.

**Majors. Business:** Accounting, business admin. **Computer sciences:** Networking, web page design. **Health:** Medical assistant, office admin. **Mechanic/repair:** Heating/ac/refrig.

**Computing on campus.** PC or laptop required. 100 workstations in library. Online library, repair service, wireless network available.

**Student life. Freshman orientation:** Mandatory.

**Student services.** Career counseling, student employment services, financial aid counseling.

**Contact.** E-mail: admissions@cbt.edu
Phone: (305) 273-4499 ext. 2-204 Fax: (305) 485-4411
Ivet Torres, Director of Admission, College of Business and Technology: Flagler, 8230 West Flagler Street, Miami, FL 33144

## College of Business and Technology: Hialeah
**Hialeah, Florida**
**www.cbt.edu**

- For-profit 2-year business and technical college
- Small city

**General.** Accredited by ACICS. **Calendar:** Continuous.

**Annual costs/financial aid.** Tuition/fees (2009-2010): $12,960.

**Contact.** Phone: (786) 693-8842
Admissions Director, 935 West 49th Street Suite 203, Hialeah, FL 33012-3436

## College of Business and Technology: Kendall
**Miami, Florida**
**www.cbt.edu**

- For-profit 2-year health science and junior college
- Very large city

**General.** Accredited by ACICS. **Enrollment:** 105 degree-seeking undergraduates. **Degrees:** 14 associate awarded. **Calendar:** Semester. **Full-time faculty:** 8 total. **Part-time faculty:** 6 total.

**Basis for selection.** Open admission.

**2009-2010 Annual costs.** Tuition/fees: $12,960. Per-credit charge: $360.

**Academics. Credit/placement by examination:** CLEP.

**Majors. Business:** Accounting, business admin. **Computer sciences:** LAN/WAN management. **Health:** Medical assistant, office admin. **Mechanic/repair:** Heating/ac/refrig. **Visual/performing arts:** Graphic design.

**Contact.** E-mail: admissions@cbt.edu
Phone: (305) 273-4499
Ivet Torres, Director of Admissions, College of Business and Technology: Kendall, 8991 SW 107 Avenue, Miami, FL 33176

## Daytona State College
**Daytona Beach, Florida**
**www.daytonastate.edu**                    **CB code: 5159**

- Public 2-year community and technical college
- Commuter campus in large city

**General.** Founded in 1958. Regionally accredited. **Enrollment:** 15,205 degree-seeking undergraduates; 2,574 non-degree-seeking students. **Degrees:** 34 bachelor's, 1,601 associate awarded. **ROTC:** Army, Air Force. **Location:** 90 miles from Jacksonville, 65 miles from Orlando. **Calendar:** Semester, limited summer session. **Full-time faculty:** 316 total; 83% have terminal degrees, 17% minority, 51% women. **Part-time faculty:** 753 total; 44% have terminal degrees, 18% minority, 50% women. **Special facilities:** Museum of photography.

**Student profile.** Among degree-seeking undergraduates, 2,654 enrolled as first-time, first-year students.

| | | | |
|---|---|---|---|
| Part-time: | 53% | Asian American: | 2% |
| Out-of-state: | 19% | Hispanic American: | 10% |
| Women: | 61% | Native American: | 1% |
| African American: | 17% | 25 or older: | 40% |

**Transfer out.** 75% of students enrolled in the transfer program go on to 4-year colleges. **Colleges most students transferred to 2009:** University of Central Florida.

**Basis for selection.** Open admission, but selective for some programs. Special requirements for limited access programs including Bachelor's degree program.

**2009-2010 Annual costs.** Tuition/fees: $2,624; $9,942 out-of-state. Books/supplies: $800. Personal expenses: $3,400.

**2008-2009 Financial aid. Need-based:** Need-based aid available for part-time students. Work-study available for part-time students. **Non-need-based:** Scholarships awarded for athletics, leadership, music/drama.

**Application procedures. Admission:** No deadline. No application fee. Admission notification on a rolling basis. **Financial aid:** No deadline. FAFSA required. Applicants notified on a rolling basis starting 2/15.

**Academics. Special study options:** Cooperative education, distance learning, dual enrollment of high school students, ESL, honors, independent study, internships, liberal arts/career combination, study abroad, teacher certification program, weekend college. Bachelor's degree programs available on campus. License preparation in dental hygiene, nursing, occupational therapy, paramedic, physical therapy, radiology. **Credit/placement by examination:** AP, CLEP, IB, institutional tests. 45 credit hours maximum toward associate degree, 45 toward bachelor's. **Support services:** GED preparation and test center, learning center, pre-admission summer program, remedial instruction, study skills assistance, tutoring, writing center.

**Majors. Agriculture:** Turf management. **Architecture:** Interior. **Biology:** General, botany, marine, microbiology, zoology. **Business:** Accounting, accounting technology, banking/financial services, business admin, executive assistant, hospitality admin, management information systems, marketing, operations. **Communications technology:** Photo/film/video. **Computer sciences:** General, applications programming, systems analysis. **Construction:** Electrician, plumbing. **Education:** General, Deaf/hearing impaired. **Engineering:** General, computer. **Engineering technology:** Aerospace, architectural, automotive, civil, computer systems, construction, drafting, electrical, manufacturing. **Health:** Clinical lab technology, dental hygiene, EMT paramedic, medical radiologic technology/radiation therapy, medical records technology, mental health services, nursing (RN), occupational therapy assistant, physical therapy assistant, respiratory therapy technology, veterinary technology/assistant. **Legal studies:** Paralegal. **Liberal arts:** Arts/sciences. **Math:** General, statistics. **Mechanic/repair:** Automotive. **Personal/culinary services:** Restaurant/catering. **Philosophy/religion:** Philosophy. **Physical sciences:** General, astronomy, chemistry, meteorology. **Protective services:** Fire safety technology, law enforcement admin. **Psychology:** General. **Public administration:** Human services, social work. **Social sciences:** Economics, geography, political science, sociology. **Visual/performing arts:** General, acting, art, commercial/advertising art, dance, graphic design, interior design, photography, studio arts. **Other:** Computer/Info tech services administration and management.

**Most popular majors.** Health sciences 18%, liberal arts 65%.

**Computing on campus.** 3,577 workstations in library, computer center, student center. Online course registration, online library, helpline, wireless network available.

**Student life. Freshman orientation:** Mandatory. Preregistration for classes offered. **Housing:** Assistance in locating off-campus housing available to international students. **Activities:** Bands, campus ministries, choral groups, dance, drama, international student organizations, music ensembles, musical theater, opera, student government, student newspaper, symphony orchestra, TV station, Baptist Campus ministries, Campus Crusade for Christ, Black Student Nurses Association, Global Friends, human services paraprofessional organization, African American student union.

**Athletics.** NJCAA. **Intercollegiate:** Baseball M, basketball, golf W, softball W, swimming. **Intramural:** Basketball, football (tackle), soccer, swimming, table tennis, tennis, volleyball, weight lifting. **Team name:** Falcons.

**Student services.** Adult student services, alcohol/substance abuse counseling, career counseling, student employment services, financial aid counseling, minority student services, on-campus daycare, personal counseling, placement for graduates, veterans' counselor, women's services. **Physically disabled:** Services for visually, speech, hearing impaired. **Transfer:** Transfer adviser, college fairs on campus for students transferring to 4-year colleges.

**Contact.** E-mail: admissions@daytonastate.edu
Phone: (386) 506-3000 ext. 3059 Fax: (386) 506-4489
Karen Sanders, Director of Admissions, Daytona State College, Daytona State College Admissions Office, Daytona Beach, FL 32114-2811

## Florida Career College: Hialeah
Hialeah, Florida
www.careercollege.edu

▸ For-profit 2-year junior and technical college
▸ Commuter campus in very large city

**General.** Accredited by ACICS. **Calendar:** Quarter.

**Annual costs/financial aid.** Tuition varies by length of program and is $445 per credit hour; which leads to certificate, associate or bachelor degree. Books/supplies: $1,000.

**Contact.** Phone: (305) 825-3231
Director of Admissions, 3750 West 18th Avenue, Hialeah, FL 33012

## Florida Career College: Miami
Miami, Florida
www.careercollege.edu                    CB code: 3581

▸ For-profit 2-year business and technical college
▸ Large city

**General.** Accredited by ACICS. **Calendar:** Continuous.

**Annual costs/financial aid.** Tuition varies by length of program and is $445 per credit hour; which leads to certificate, associate or bachelor degree.

**Contact.** Phone: (305) 553-6065
Director of Admission, 1321 SW 107 Avenue, Suite 201B, Miami, FL 3317-521

## Florida Career College: Pembroke Pines
Pembroke Pines, Florida
www.careercollege.edu

▸ For-profit 2-year business and technical college
▸ Small city

**General.** Accredited by ACICS. **Calendar:** Continuous.

**Annual costs/financial aid.** Tuition varies by length of program and is $445 per credit hour; which leads to certificate, associate or bachelor degree.

**Contact.** Phone: (954) 965-7272
Director of Admission, 7891 Pines Boulevard, Pembroke Pines, FL 33024

## Florida Career College: West Palm Beach
West Palm Beach, Florida

▸ For-profit 2-year technical college
▸ Commuter campus in small city

**General.** Accredited by ACICS. **Calendar:** Continuous.

**Annual costs/financial aid.** Tuition varies by length of program and is $445 per credit hour; which leads to certificate, associate or bachelor degree.

**Contact.** Phone: (561) 689-0550
Director of Admissions, 6065 Okeechobee Boulevard West, West Palm Beach, FL 33417

## Florida College of Natural Health: Bradenton
Bradenton, Florida
www.fcnh.com                              CB code: 5024

▸ For-profit 2-year health science and career college
▸ Commuter campus in small city

**General.** Accredited by ACCSCT. **Location:** 40 miles from Tampa. **Calendar:** Continuous.

**Annual costs/financial aid.** Tuition/fees (2009-2010): $21,697. Non-degree programs from $4,870 to $11,379 for tuition, plus $850 for books and supplies. Books/supplies: $2,250. Personal expenses: $4,620. Need-based financial aid available for full-time students.

**Contact.** Phone: (941) 744-1244
Admissions, 616 67th Street Circle East, Bradenton, FL 34208

## Florida College of Natural Health: Maitland
Maitland, Florida
www.fcnh.com                              CB code: 5239

▸ For-profit 2-year health science and junior college
▸ Large town

**General.** Accredited by ACCSCT. **Calendar:** Continuous.

**Annual costs/financial aid.** Tuition/fees (2009-2010): $21,697. Non-degree programs from $4,870 to $11,379 for tuition, plus $850 for books and supplies. Books/supplies: $2,250. Personal expenses: $2,464. Need-based financial aid available for full-time students.

**Contact.** Phone: (407) 261-0319
Director of Marketing, 2600 Lake Lucien Drive; Suite 240, Maitland, FL 32751

## Florida College of Natural Health: Miami
**Miami, Florida**
www.fcnh.com                                CB code: 5231

- For-profit 2-year branch campus and community college
- Very large city
- SAT or ACT (ACT writing optional) required

**General.** Accredited by ACCSC. **Enrollment:** 321 undergraduates. **Degrees:** 35 associate awarded. **Calendar:** Continuous. **Full-time faculty:** 8 total. **Part-time faculty:** 3 total.

**Basis for selection.** Entrance exams and secondary school record considered. Must take OLSAT if SAT or ACT not submitted.

**2009-2010 Annual costs.** Tuition/fees: $21,697. Non-degree programs from $4,870 to $11,379 for tuition, plus $850 for books and supplies. Books/supplies: $2,250. Personal expenses: $2,464.

**Financial aid.** All financial aid based on need.

**Application procedures. Admission:** No deadline. No application fee. Admission notification on a rolling basis. **Financial aid:** No deadline. FAFSA required. Applicants notified on a rolling basis.

**Academics. Credit/placement by examination:** CLEP.

**Majors. Health:** Massage therapy.

**Contact.**  E-mail: miami@fcnh.com
Phone: (305) 597-9599 Toll-free number: (800) 599-9599
Fax: (305) 597-9110
Florida College of Natural Health: Miami, 7925 Northwest 12th Street, Suite 201, Miami, FL 33126

## Florida College of Natural Health: Pompano Beach
**Pompano Beach, Florida**
www.fcnh.com                                CB code: 5238

- For-profit 2-year junior college
- Very large city

**General.** Accredited by ACCSCT. **Calendar:** Continuous.

**Annual costs/financial aid.** Tuition/fees (2009-2010): $21,697. Non-degree programs from $4,870 to $11,379 for tuition, plus $850 for books and supplies. Books/supplies: $2,250. Need-based financial aid available for full-time students.

**Contact.**  Phone: (954) 975-6400
Chief Operating Officer, 2001 West Sample Road, Suite 100, Pompano Beach, FL 33064

## Florida Keys Community College
**Key West, Florida**
www.fkcc.edu                                CB code: 5236

- Public 2-year nursing and community college
- Commuter campus in large town

**General.** Founded in 1965. Regionally accredited. 2-year AA and AS programs offered at the main campus in Key West, Coral Shores and Marathon branch campuses. **Enrollment:** 1,407 undergraduates. **Degrees:** 160 associate awarded. **Location:** 154 miles from Miami. **Calendar:** Semester, limited summer session. **Full-time faculty:** 25 total. **Part-time faculty:** 110 total. **Special facilities:** Fine arts center and theater, marine propulsion technology center, welding lab, aquatic center, diving program underwater education complex, ceramics studio.

**Student profile.**

| | | | |
|---|---|---|---|
| Out-of-state: | 2% | 25 or older: | 55% |

**Transfer out. Colleges most students transferred to 2009:** University of Central Florida, Florida International University, University of Florida, Florida State University, St. Leo's College.

**Basis for selection.** Open admission, but selective for some programs. Special application, placement examination, physical examination, and interview required for nursing technology applicants. Admission based on objective points system.

**High school preparation.** College-preparatory program recommended. Recommended units include English 4, mathematics 3, social studies 3 and science 3.

**2009-2010 Annual costs.** Tuition/fees: $2,677; $9,401 out-of-state. Books/supplies: $2,300. Personal expenses: $1,000.

**Financial aid. Need-based:** Need-based aid available for part-time students. Work-study available for part-time students. **Non-need-based:** Scholarships awarded for academics, art, leadership, minority status.

**Application procedures. Admission:** No deadline. $20 fee. Admission notification on a rolling basis. **Financial aid:** Priority date 5/1; no closing date. FAFSA, institutional form required. Applicants notified on a rolling basis starting 6/15; must reply within 2 week(s) of notification.

**Academics. Special study options:** Distance learning, double major, dual enrollment of high school students, ESL, independent study, semester at sea, teacher certification program. Bachelor's degree programs available on campus. License preparation in nursing, paramedic, real estate. **Credit/placement by examination:** CLEP, IB, institutional tests. 45 credit hours maximum toward associate degree. Students taking Florida College Entry Level Placement Test prior to registering do not need SAT or ACT. **Support services:** Learning center, reduced course load, remedial instruction, tutoring.

**Majors. Biology:** Marine. **Business:** Business admin. **Computer sciences:** General, programming. **Health:** Nursing (RN). **Interdisciplinary:** Marine science. **Mechanic/repair:** Marine. **Public administration:** General. **Transportation:** Diver, maritime/Merchant Marine.

**Computing on campus.** 25 workstations in library, computer center.

**Student life. Freshman orientation:** Available. Preregistration for classes offered. **Activities:** Choral groups, student government, student newspaper, nurses pinning club, Florida nurses student association, Mud-Pi ceramics club, Phi Theta Kappa, cyber league, photo guild club, wreckers club, propmasters club.

**Athletics. Team name:** Wreckers.

**Student services.** Adult student services, career counseling, student employment services, financial aid counseling, placement for graduates, veterans' counselor. **Physically disabled:** Services for visually, speech, hearing impaired. **Transfer:** Pre-admission transcript evaluation for new students. Transfer adviser, college fairs on campus for students transferring to 4-year colleges.

**Contact.**  E-mail: cheryl.malsheimer@fkcc.edu
Phone: (305) 809-3188 Fax: (305) 292-5155
Cheryl Malsheimer, Director of Enrollment Services, Florida Keys Community College, 5901 College Road, Key West, FL 33040

## Florida National College
**Hialeah, Florida**
www.fnc.edu                                 CB code: 2057

- For-profit 2-year junior college
- Commuter campus in very large city
- Interview required

**General.** Regionally accredited. **Enrollment:** 2,744 degree-seeking undergraduates; 36 non-degree-seeking students. **Degrees:** 323 associate awarded. **Location:** 12 miles from Miami. **Calendar:** Semester. **Full-time faculty:** 35 total; 40% have terminal degrees, 40% women. **Part-time faculty:** 43 total; 37% have terminal degrees, 60% women. **Class size:** 100% 20-39.

**Student profile.** Among degree-seeking undergraduates, 677 enrolled as first-time, first-year students.

| | | | |
|---|---|---|---|
| Part-time: | 27% | 25 or older: | 65% |
| Women: | 68% | | |

**Transfer out.** 24% of students enrolled in the transfer program go on to 4-year colleges. **Colleges most students transferred to 2009:** Nova Southeastern University, Florida International University, American Intercontinental University, Miami Institute of Psychology, Carlos Albizu University.

**Basis for selection.** Open admission.

**2010-2011 Annual costs.** Tuition/fees: $17,100. Per-credit charge: $525. Books/supplies: $1,000.

**2008-2009 Financial aid.** All financial aid based on need. 616 full-time freshmen applied for aid; 609 were judged to have need; 609 of these received aid. Need-based aid available for part-time students.

**Application procedures. Admission:** No deadline. No application fee. Admission notification on a rolling basis. **Financial aid:** No deadline. FAFSA, institutional form required.

**Academics. Special study options:** Cooperative education, distance learning, dual enrollment of high school students, ESL, student-designed major. Bachelor's degree programs available on campus. License preparation in nursing, radiology. **Credit/placement by examination:** AP, CLEP, institutional tests. 9 credit hours maximum toward associate degree. **Support services:** GED preparation, reduced course load, remedial instruction, tutoring.

**Majors. Business:** Accounting, business admin, hospitality admin, tourism promotion, tourism/travel. **Computer sciences:** General, programming, system admin, web page design. **Education:** General. **Health:** Dental hygiene, dental lab technology, health services admin, medical assistant, medical secretary, radiologic technology/medical imaging, respiratory therapy technology, sonography. **Legal studies:** Paralegal. **Protective services:** Criminal justice. **Public administration:** General. **Other:** Medical laboratory technology, Paralegal/studies.

**Most popular majors.** Business/marketing 24%, computer/information sciences 6%, health sciences 50%, legal studies 6%, public administration/social services 12%.

**Student life. Freshman orientation:** Mandatory. **Activities:** Student government, student newspaper.

**Student services.** Career counseling, student employment services, financial aid counseling, placement for graduates.

**Contact.** E-mail: admissions@fnc.edu
Phone: (305) 821-3333 Fax: (305) 362-0595
Guillermo Araya, Admissions Coodinator, Florida National College, 4425 West 20th Avenue, Hialeah, FL 33012

---

## Florida State College at Jacksonville
### Jacksonville, Florida
**www.fscj.edu**

**CB code: 5232**

▸ Public 2-year junior college
▸ Commuter campus in very large city

**General.** Founded in 1963. Regionally accredited. 4 campus locations, 6 center sites, 1 online campus. **Enrollment:** 20,135 degree-seeking undergraduates; 7,758 non-degree-seeking students. **Degrees:** 4 bachelor's, 3,206 associate awarded. **ROTC:** Army, Naval. **Location:** Downtown. **Calendar:** Semester, extensive summer session. **Full-time faculty:** 375 total; 20% have terminal degrees, 17% minority, 59% women. **Part-time faculty:** 780 total; 14% have terminal degrees, 24% minority, 51% women. **Class size:** 51% < 20, 49% 20-39, less than 1% 40-49, less than 1% 50-99. **Special facilities:** Performing arts theater, criminal justice center, advanced technology center. **Partnerships:** Formal partnerships with Florida Construction Institute, Florida Home Builders Association, Navy Contracts, GM/ASEP contracts for non-credit (Education-To-Go), NE Florida Credit Union Association, Aviation Professional/Pilot Contract, Cisco Agreement with 2 schools in midwest.

**Student profile.** Among degree-seeking undergraduates, 68% enrolled in a transfer program, 32% enrolled in a vocational program, 1% already have a bachelor's degree or higher, 3,685 enrolled as first-time, first-year students, 1,324 transferred in from other institutions.

| | | | |
|---|---|---|---|
| **Part-time:** | 61% | **Women:** | 61% |
| **Out-of-state:** | 2% | **25 or older:** | 43% |

**Transfer out. Colleges most students transferred to 2009:** University of North Florida, Jacksonville University, University of Florida, Florida State University, Central Florida University.

**Basis for selection.** Open admission, but selective for some programs. Special requirements for some associate of science programs. Additional program application may be required. SAT/ACT, or CPT test required for placement. **Homeschooled:** Transcript of courses and grades required. Home school letter form required. **Learning Disabled:** Medical documentation required.

**High school preparation.** 24 units recommended. Recommended units include English 4, mathematics 3, social studies 3, science 3 (laboratory 2), foreign language 2 and academic electives 9. One algebra strongly recommended. Social studies should be .5 U.S. government, .5 economics, 1 U.S. history, 1 world history.

**2009-2010 Annual costs.** Tuition/fees: $2,511; $9,703 out-of-state. Books/supplies: $900. Personal expenses: $812.

**2009-2010 Financial aid. Need-based:** Need-based aid available for part-time students. Work-study available nights, weekends and for part-time students. **Non-need-based:** Scholarships awarded for academics, alumni affiliation, art, athletics, job skills, leadership, minority status, music/drama.

**Application procedures. Admission:** Priority date 8/1; no deadline. $15 fee. Admission notification on a rolling basis. **Financial aid:** Priority date 8/1; no closing date. FAFSA, institutional form required.

**Academics. Special study options:** Accelerated study, cooperative education, cross-registration, distance learning, double major, dual enrollment of high school students, ESL, exchange student, external degree, honors, independent study, internships, liberal arts/career combination, study abroad, teacher certification program, weekend college. Bachelor's degree programs available on campus. License preparation in aviation, dental hygiene, nursing, paramedic, physical therapy, radiology, real estate. **Credit/placement by examination:** AP, CLEP, institutional tests. 45 credit hours maximum toward associate degree. **Support services:** GED preparation and test center, learning center, reduced course load, remedial instruction, study skills assistance, tutoring.

**Majors. Architecture:** Environmental design, interior. **Biology:** Biomedical sciences. **Business:** Accounting, administrative services, banking/financial services, business admin, fashion, financial planning, hospitality admin, insurance, management information systems, office management, office technology, sales/distribution, tourism/travel. **Communications technology:** Graphic/printing. **Computer sciences:** General, applications programming, computer graphics, data processing, information systems, networking, programming, systems analysis. **Construction:** Maintenance. **Education:** Elementary. **Engineering:** General, civil, computer. **Engineering technology:** Architectural, biomedical, civil, construction, drafting, electrical. **Family/consumer sciences:** Clothing/textiles. **Foreign languages:** Sign language interpretation. **Health:** Clinical lab technology, dental hygiene, EMT paramedic, medical radiologic technology/radiation therapy, medical records technology, medical secretary, nursing (RN), physical therapy assistant, respiratory therapy technology, sonography, substance abuse counseling. **Legal studies:** Paralegal. **Mechanic/repair:** Automotive. **Military:** General. **Personal/culinary services:** Culinary arts, mortuary science. **Protective services:** Criminal justice, fire safety technology, fire services admin, firefighting, law enforcement admin. **Public administration:** Human services. **Transportation:** Air traffic control, aviation, aviation management. **Visual/performing arts:** General, cinematography, commercial/advertising art, design, dramatic, interior design, theater design.

**Most popular majors.** Health sciences 17%, liberal arts 73%.

**Computing on campus.** 2,500 workstations in library, computer center, student center. Commuter students can connect to campus network. Online course registration, online library, helpline, repair service, student web hosting, wireless network available.

**Student life. Freshman orientation:** Mandatory. Preregistration for classes offered. **Housing:** Housing assistance available to qualified Talent Grant students. **Activities:** Bands, choral groups, dance, drama, international student organizations, literary magazine, music ensembles, musical theater, radio station, student government, student newspaper, TV station, Baptist Campus Ministries, Phi Theta Kappa, Community Service Club, Gospel and Concert Chorale, Spanish Club.

**Athletics.** NJCAA. **Intercollegiate:** Baseball M, basketball, softball W, tennis W, volleyball W. **Intramural:** Badminton, basketball, bowling, football (non-tackle), golf, soccer, softball, table tennis, tennis, volleyball. **Team name:** Stars.

**Student services.** Adult student services, career counseling, services for economically disadvantaged, student employment services, financial aid counseling, minority student services, on-campus daycare, personal counseling, placement for graduates, veterans' counselor, women's services. **Physically disabled:** Services for visually, speech, hearing impaired. **Transfer:** Transfer adviser, college fairs on campus for students transferring to 4-year colleges.

**Contact.** E-mail: justask@fscj.edu
Phone: (904) 359-5433 Fax: (904) 632-5105
Rosalind Harris, Director of Admissions, Florida State College at Jacksonville, 501 West State Street, Jacksonville, FL 32202

## Florida Technical College: Auburndale
### Lakeland, Florida
### www.flatech.edu
### CB code: 3432

- For-profit 2-year business and junior college
- Large town

**General.** Accredited by ACICS. **Calendar:** Continuous.

**Annual costs/financial aid.** Need-based financial aid available to full-time and part-time students.

**Contact.** Phone: (863) 967-8822
School Director, 4715 South Florida Avenue, Lakeland, FL 33813

## Florida Technical College: Deland
### Deland, Florida
### www.flatech.edu
### CB code: 3589

- For-profit 2-year junior and technical college
- Small city

**General.** Accredited by ACICS. **Location:** 30 miles from Orlando, 20 miles from Daytona Beach. **Calendar:** Quarter.

**Annual costs/financial aid.** Need-based financial aid available to full-time and part-time students.

**Contact.** Phone: (386) 734-3303
Director of Admissions, 1199 South Woodland Boulevard, Deland, FL 32720

## Florida Technical College: Jacksonville
### Jacksonville, Florida
### www.flatech.edu
### CB code: 3590

- For-profit 2-year technical college
- Very large city

**General.** Accredited by ACICS. **Calendar:** Continuous.

**Contact.** Phone: (904) 724-2229
Campus Director, 8711 Lone Star Road, Jacksonville, FL 32211

## Florida Technical College: Orlando
### Orlando, Florida
### www.flatech.edu
### CB code: 3588

- For-profit 2-year junior and technical college
- Commuter campus in large city

**General.** Accredited by ACICS. **Location:** 13 miles from downtown. **Calendar:** Continuous.

**Annual costs/financial aid.** Need-based financial aid available to full-time and part-time students.

**Contact.** Phone: (407) 447-7300
Director, 12689 Challenger Parkway, #130, Orlando, FL 32826-2707

## Golf Academy of America: Orlando
### Altamonte Springs, Florida
### www.golfacademy.edu

- For-profit 2-year community college
- Large town

**General.** Accredited by ACICS. **Calendar:** Semester.

**Annual costs/financial aid.** Books/supplies: $700.

**Contact.** Phone: (480) 905-9288
7373 North Scottsdale Road, Suite B-100, Scottsdale, AZ 85253

## Gulf Coast College
### Tampa, Florida
### www.gulfcoastcollege.edu
### CB code: 3448

- For-profit 2-year technical and career college
- Commuter campus in large city
- Interview required

**General.** Accredited by ACICS. **Enrollment:** 119 degree-seeking undergraduates. **Degrees:** 9 associate awarded. **Location:** 13 miles from Tampa. **Calendar:** Quarter, extensive summer session. **Full-time faculty:** 17 total. **Part-time faculty:** 13 total.

**Transfer out. Colleges most students transferred to 2009:** Hillsborough Community College.

**Basis for selection.** Open admission, but selective for some programs. Nursing applicants must pass standardized tests for admission (HESI). **Homeschooled:** State high school equivalency certificate required.

**2009-2010 Annual costs.** Tuition and fees vary by program. Books/supplies: $1,200. Personal expenses: $1,863.

**Application procedures. Admission:** No deadline. $50 fee. Admission notification on a rolling basis.

**Academics. Special study options:** Independent study. License preparation in nursing. **Credit/placement by examination:** CLEP. **Support services:** Learning center, remedial instruction, study skills assistance, tutoring, writing center.

**Majors. Business:** Business admin. **Computer sciences:** General.

**Computing on campus.** 50 workstations in library, computer center. Online library, wireless network available.

**Student life. Freshman orientation:** Mandatory.

**Student services.** Adult student services, career counseling, financial aid counseling, placement for graduates, veterans' counselor.

**Contact.** Phone: (813) 620-1446 Fax: (813) 620-1641
Tonya Chestnut, Director of Admissions, Gulf Coast College, 3910 U.S. Highway 301 North, Suite 200, Tampa, FL 33619-1290

## Gulf Coast Community College
### Panama City, Florida
### www.gulfcoast.edu
### CB code: 5271

- Public 2-year community college
- Commuter campus in small city

**General.** Founded in 1957. Regionally accredited. **Enrollment:** 4,757 degree-seeking undergraduates; 1,421 non-degree-seeking students. **Degrees:** 899 associate awarded. **Location:** 100 miles from Tallahassee, 100 miles from Pensacola. **Calendar:** Semester, limited summer session. **Full-time faculty:** 116 total; 14% have terminal degrees, 10% minority, 61% women. **Part-time faculty:** 318 total; 2% have terminal degrees, 12% minority, 52% women. **Partnerships:** Formal partnerships with local businesses.

**Student profile.** Among degree-seeking undergraduates, 1,047 enrolled as first-time, first-year students.

| | | | |
|---|---|---|---|
| Part-time: | 56% | Women: | 57% |
| Out-of-state: | 6% | 25 or older: | 42% |

**Transfer out. Colleges most students transferred to 2009:** Florida State University, University of Florida, University of Central Florida, University of West Florida.

**Basis for selection.** Open admission, but selective for some programs. Admission to health science programs determined through high school transcripts, placement test performance and other admissions criteria. Interview required of allied health applicants. Audition recommended for music majors. **Homeschooled:** Home School Affidavit must be submitted with parent's signature and notarized.

**High school preparation.** 13 units recommended. Recommended units include English 4, mathematics 3, social studies 3 and science 3.

**2009-2010 Annual costs.** Tuition/fees: $2,439; $9,151 out-of-state. Books/supplies: $800. Personal expenses: $1,500.

**Financial aid. Need-based:** Need-based aid available for part-time students. Work-study available nights, weekends and for part-time students. **Non-need-based:** Scholarships awarded for academics, athletics, job skills, leadership, minority status, music/drama, state residency.

**Application procedures. Admission:** No deadline. $20 fee. Admission notification on a rolling basis. Application deadline for nursing program February 28; dental hygiene April 1; EMT and paramedic June 1; radiography May 15; physical therapist assistant April 1; surgical technology October 21. **Financial aid:** Priority date 5/15, closing date 7/1. FAFSA required. Applicants notified on a rolling basis starting 7/1.

**Academics. Special study options:** Accelerated study, cooperative education, distance learning, dual enrollment of high school students, ESL, honors, independent study, internships, teacher certification program, weekend college. License preparation in dental hygiene, nursing, paramedic, physical therapy, radiology, real estate. **Credit/placement by examination:** AP, CLEP, IB, institutional tests. 45 credit hours maximum toward associate degree. **Support services:** GED preparation, learning center, reduced course load, remedial instruction, study skills assistance, tutoring.

**Majors. Agriculture:** General, landscaping, ornamental horticulture. **Area/ethnic studies:** Women's. **Biology:** General, entomology, marine. **Business:** Accounting, business admin, e-commerce, hospitality admin, office/clerical. **Communications:** General, advertising, broadcast journalism, journalism. **Computer sciences:** General, a.i./robotics, applications programming, computer science, information technology, networking, programming, systems analysis, web page design. **Conservation:** Forestry. **Education:** Biology, business, chemistry, early childhood, elementary, health, mathematics, middle, physical, physics, science, special. **Engineering:** General, electrical. **Engineering technology:** Architectural, civil, construction, drafting, electrical. **Foreign languages:** General. **Health:** Chiropractic assistant, clinical lab science, clinical nutrition, dental hygiene, EMT paramedic, health services, medical radiologic technology/radiation therapy, medical records admin, nursing (RN), occupational therapy assistant, optician, physical therapy assistant, predental, premedicine, prepharmacy, preveterinary, radiologic technology/medical imaging, respiratory therapy assistant, sonography. **History:** General. **Interdisciplinary:** Natural sciences. **Legal studies:** General, paralegal, prelaw. **Liberal arts:** Arts/sciences. **Math:** General. **Parks/recreation:** General, health/fitness, sports admin. **Personal/culinary services:** Culinary arts. **Philosophy/religion:** Philosophy, religion. **Physical sciences:** Atmospheric science, chemistry, geology, oceanography, physics. **Protective services:** Criminal justice, firefighting, forensics, law enforcement admin. **Psychology:** General. **Public administration:** Social work. **Social sciences:** Anthropology, archaeology, economics, political science, sociology. **Visual/performing arts:** Art, dramatic.

**Computing on campus.** 560 workstations in library, computer center. Commuter students can connect to campus network. Online course registration, online library, helpline, wireless network available.

**Student life. Freshman orientation:** Available. Preregistration for classes offered. Orientation programs also available on the Internet. **Activities:** Bands, campus ministries, choral groups, dance, drama, international student organizations, literary magazine, music ensembles, musical theater, radio station, student government, student newspaper, African American Student Association, Baptist Collegiate Ministries, Muslim Student Association, Gay Straight Alliance, Veterans Association, Florida Nurses Student Association, Rotaract, World Philosophy and Religion Association, Phi Theta Kappa.

**Athletics.** NJCAA. **Intercollegiate:** Baseball M, basketball, softball W, volleyball W. **Intramural:** Basketball. **Team name:** Commodores.

**Student services.** Adult student services, career counseling, services for economically disadvantaged, student employment services, financial aid counseling, minority student services, personal counseling, veterans' counselor, women's services. **Physically disabled:** Services for visually, speech, hearing impaired. **Learning disabled:** Comprehensive services available. **Transfer:** Pre-admission transcript evaluation for new students. Transfer adviser, college fairs on campus for students transferring to 4-year colleges.

**Contact.** Phone: (850) 872-3892 Toll-free number: (800) 311-3685 Fax: (850) 913-3308
Sharon Todd, Director of Enrollment Services, Gulf Coast Community College, 5230 West US Highway 98, Panama City, FL 32401

## Herzing University
**Winter Park, Florida**
**www.herzing.edu**
**CB code: 3438**

- For-profit 2-year business and health science college
- Commuter campus in very large city
- Interview required

**General.** Regionally accredited. **Enrollment:** 355 degree-seeking undergraduates. **Degrees:** 13 bachelor's, 41 associate awarded. **Calendar:** Semester, extensive summer session. **Full-time faculty:** 15 total. **Part-time faculty:** 10 total.

**Basis for selection.** Open admission, but selective for some programs. Entrance test and evaluation for all applicants.

**2009-2010 Annual costs.** Tuition/fees: $12,700. Per-credit charge: $395. Reported annual tuition is representative. Actual costs vary by program.

**Application procedures. Admission:** No deadline. No application fee. Admission notification on a rolling basis.

**Academics. Special study options:** Distance learning. Bachelor's degree programs available on campus. **Credit/placement by examination:** AP, CLEP, IB, institutional tests. 52 credit hours maximum toward associate degree, 97 toward bachelor's. **Support services:** Reduced course load, remedial instruction, study skills assistance, tutoring.

**Majors. Business:** General, business admin. **Computer sciences:** Information technology, LAN/WAN management, programming. **Health:** Insurance coding, insurance specialist, nursing (RN). **Legal studies:** Paralegal.

**Computing on campus.** 120 workstations in library, computer center. Online library, wireless network available.

**Student life. Freshman orientation:** Mandatory. Preregistration for classes offered.

**Student services.** Adult student services, student employment services, financial aid counseling. **Transfer:** Pre-admission transcript evaluation for new students.

**Contact.** E-mail: info@orl.herzing.edu
Phone: (407) 478-0500 Toll-free number: (800) 574-4446
Fax: (401) 418-0501
Tessie Uranga, Director of Admissions, Herzing University, 1595 South Semoran Boulevard, Suite 1501, Winter Park, FL 32792-5509

## High-Tech Institute
**Orlando, Florida**
**www.hightechinstitute.edu**

- For-profit 2-year health science and technical college
- Commuter campus in large city

**General.** Accredited by ACCSCT. **Calendar:** Continuous.

**Contact.** Phone: (407) 893-7400
Admissions Director, 3710 Maguire Boulevard, Orlando, FL 32803

## Hillsborough Community College
**Tampa, Florida**
**www.hccfl.edu**
**CB member**
**CB code: 5304**

- Public 2-year community college
- Commuter campus in large city

**General.** Founded in 1968. Regionally accredited. **Enrollment:** 21,175 degree-seeking undergraduates; 5,789 non-degree-seeking students. **Degrees:** 2,453 associate awarded. **ROTC:** Army. **Calendar:** Semester, limited summer session. **Full-time faculty:** 282 total; 25% have terminal degrees, 21% minority, 55% women. **Part-time faculty:** 986 total; 9% have terminal degrees, 23% minority, 47% women. **Class size:** 19% < 20, 80% 20-39, 1% 40-49, less than 1% 50-99. **Special facilities:** Environmental study centers (English Creek, Cockroach Bay, Upper Tampa Bay Park), Florida studies center.

**Student profile.** Among degree-seeking undergraduates, 69% enrolled in a transfer program, 31% enrolled in a vocational program, 4,513 enrolled as first-time, first-year students, 695 transferred in from other institutions.

| | | | |
|---|---|---|---|
| Part-time: | 55% | Asian American: | 4% |
| Out-of-state: | 4% | Hispanic American: | 23% |
| Women: | 56% | International: | 3% |
| African American: | 20% | 25 or older: | 35% |

**Transfer out.** Colleges most students transferred to 2009: University of South Florida, University of Central Florida, University of Florida, Florida State University, Florida Gulf Coast University.

**Basis for selection.** Open admission, but selective for some programs. Limited access to certain health programs. Degree-seeking students must provide assessment/placement scores from CPT, FCELPT, ACT, or SAT prior to registering for classes. Test scores may be no more than two years old. **Homeschooled:** Signed affidavit affirming completion required. **Learning Disabled:** Students should contact Coordinator of Services for students with disabilities to discuss documentation guidelines at least 1 month prior to semester.

**High school preparation.** 24 units recommended. Recommended units include English 4, mathematics 3, science 3, foreign language 2 and academic electives 8.

**2009-2010 Annual costs.** Tuition/fees: $2,621; $9,550 out-of-state. Books/supplies: $1,950. Personal expenses: $2,676.

**2008-2009 Financial aid. Need-based:** 88% of total undergraduate aid awarded as scholarships/grants, 12% as loans/jobs. Need-based aid available for part-time students. Work-study available nights, weekends and for part-time students. **Non-need-based:** Scholarships awarded for academics, art, athletics, minority status, music/drama.

**Application procedures. Admission:** No deadline. $20 fee, may be waived for applicants with need. Admission notification on a rolling basis. **Financial aid:** Priority date 5/15, closing date 6/30. FAFSA, institutional form required. Applicants notified on a rolling basis.

**Academics. Special study options:** Accelerated study, cross-registration, distance learning, double major, dual enrollment of high school students, ESL, honors, independent study, internships, liberal arts/career combination, study abroad, teacher certification program, weekend college. License preparation in dental hygiene, nursing, paramedic. **Credit/placement by examination:** AP, CLEP, IB, institutional tests. Approval required. **Support services:** GED preparation, learning center, remedial instruction, study skills assistance, tutoring, writing center.

**Majors. Agriculture:** Aquaculture, landscaping. **Business:** Accounting technology, business admin, executive assistant, hospitality admin, management information systems, operations, restaurant/food services. **Computer sciences:** Applications programming, systems analysis. **Education:** Deaf/hearing impaired. **Engineering technology:** Architectural, computer systems, electrical, manufacturing. **Family/consumer sciences:** Child care. **Health:** Dental hygiene, dietician assistant, EMT paramedic, medical radiologic technology/radiation therapy, mental health services, nuclear medical technology, nursing (RN), optician, optometric assistant, respiratory therapy technology, sonography, veterinary technology/assistant. **Legal studies:** Paralegal. **Liberal arts:** Arts/sciences. **Personal/culinary services:** Restaurant/catering. **Protective services:** Fire safety technology, law enforcement admin. **Visual/performing arts:** Cinematography. **Other:** Computer/information technology services administration and management, Environmental control technologies / technicians.

**Most popular majors.** Health sciences 15%, liberal arts 78%.

**Computing on campus.** 2,014 workstations in library, computer center, student center. Dormitories wired for high-speed internet access. Commuter students can connect to campus network. Online course registration, online library, helpline, wireless network available.

**Student life. Freshman orientation:** Mandatory. Preregistration for classes offered. Held 2 hours prior to registration. **Housing:** Apartments available. **Activities:** Bands, choral groups, dance, drama, literary magazine, music ensembles, radio station, student government, student newspaper, African-American student union, American Sign Language club, aquaculture club, Arete club, Association of Professional Scholastic Opticians, College Republicans, computer club, Democrats, dive club.

**Athletics.** NJCAA. **Intercollegiate:** Baseball M, basketball, softball W, tennis W, volleyball W. **Team name:** Hawks.

**Student services.** Career counseling, services for economically disadvantaged, student employment services, financial aid counseling, on-campus daycare. **Physically disabled:** Services for visually, speech, hearing impaired. **Learning disabled:** Comprehensive services available. **Transfer:** Transfer center, transfer adviser, college fairs on campus for students transferring to 4-year colleges.

**Contact.** E-mail: eolmo2@hccfl.edu
Phone: (813) 253-7032 Toll-free number: (866) 253-7077
Fax: (813) 253-7196
Edwin Olmo, Enrollment and Student Success Officer, Hillsborough Community College, Box 31127, Tampa, FL 33631-3127

---

## Indian River State College
**Fort Pierce, Florida**     CB member
**www.irsc.edu**     CB code: 5322

- Public 2-year community college
- Commuter campus in small city

**General.** Founded in 1960. Regionally accredited. Branch campuses in Vero Beach, Stuart, Okeechobee, Port St. Lucie; Criminal Justice Academy, Marine Center in Fort Pierce. **Enrollment:** 9,517 degree-seeking undergraduates; 6,663 non-degree-seeking students. **Degrees:** 34 bachelor's, 1,731 associate awarded. **Location:** 65 miles from West Palm Beach. **Calendar:** Semester, limited summer session. **Full-time faculty:** 201 total; 30% have terminal degrees, 19% minority, 59% women. **Part-time faculty:** 778 total; 8% have terminal degrees, 18% minority, 56% women. **Special facilities:** Olympic-size pool complex, fine arts center, planetarium.

**Student profile.** Among degree-seeking undergraduates, 2,126 enrolled as first-time, first-year students, 1,715 transferred in from other institutions.

| | | | |
|---|---|---|---|
| Part-time: | 58% | Women: | 61% |
| Out-of-state: | 2% | 25 or older: | 44% |

**Transfer out. Colleges most students transferred to 2009:** University of Central Florida, University of South Florida, University of Florida, Florida State University, Florida Atlantic University.

**Basis for selection.** Open admission, but selective for some programs. Testing and academic records determine admission to health science programs.

**High school preparation.** 24 units recommended. Recommended units include English 4, mathematics 3, social studies 3, history 2, science 3, foreign language 2 and academic electives 7.

**2009-2010 Annual costs.** Tuition/fees: $2,543; $9,471 out-of-state.

**2008-2009 Financial aid. Need-based:** 80% of total undergraduate aid awarded as scholarships/grants, 20% as loans/jobs. Need-based aid available for part-time students. Work-study available for part-time students. **Non-need-based:** Scholarships awarded for academics, athletics, minority status, music/drama, state residency.

**Application procedures. Admission:** No deadline. No application fee. Admission notification on a rolling basis. **Financial aid:** Priority date 7/18; no closing date. FAFSA, institutional form required. Applicants notified on a rolling basis starting 5/15.

**Academics. Special study options:** Accelerated study, distance learning, dual enrollment of high school students, ESL, honors, teacher certification program, weekend college. License preparation in dental hygiene, nursing, paramedic, physical therapy, radiology, real estate. **Credit/placement by examination:** CLEP, IB, institutional tests. 45 credit hours maximum toward associate degree. Degree-seeking students must achieve state-designated cutoff scores on placement test to enter college-level programs, or complete sequence of developmental courses. **Support services:** GED preparation and test center, learning center, pre-admission summer program, reduced course load, remedial instruction, study skills assistance, tutoring.

**Majors. Agriculture:** Business technology, turf management. **Biology:** General. **Business:** Accounting, administrative services, business admin, hospitality admin, management information systems, office management, sales/distribution. **Communications:** Public relations. **Communications technology:** Graphic/printing. **Computer sciences:** General, applications programming, computer graphics, information technology, programming, systems analysis, web page design. **Conservation:** Environmental studies. **Education:** General, early childhood, elementary, secondary. **Engineering:** General. **Engineering technology:** Architectural drafting, civil, construction, electrical. **Foreign languages:** General. **Health:** Clinical lab technology, dental hygiene, dental lab technology, EMT paramedic, medical radiologic technology/radiation therapy, medical records admin, medical records technology, medical transcription, nursing (RN), physical therapy assistant, predental, premedicine, prepharmacy, preveterinary, respiratory therapy technology. **History:** General. **Legal studies:** Legal secretary, paralegal, prelaw. **Liberal arts:** Arts/sciences, library assistant. **Math:** General. **Mechanic/repair:** Automotive, heating/ac/refrig. **Personal/culinary services:** Restaurant/catering. **Philosophy/religion:** Philosophy. **Physical sciences:** Chemistry, physics. **Protective services:** Criminal justice, fire safety technology. **Psychology:** General. **Public administration:** Human services. **Social sciences:** Anthropology, economics, political science, sociology. **Visual/performing arts:** Art, commercial/advertising art, dance, dramatic, interior design.

**Computing on campus.** Online course registration, online library available.

**Student life. Freshman orientation:** Available. **Housing:** Apartments available. **Activities:** Bands, choral groups, dance, drama, international student organizations, literary magazine, music ensembles, musical theater, radio station, student government, symphony orchestra, Distributive Education Clubs of America, Vocational International Clubs of America, cultural exchange club, human services club, ambassador club, Bacchus club, Phi Beta Lambda.

**Athletics.** NJCAA. **Intercollegiate:** Baseball M, basketball, cheerleading W, diving, softball W, swimming, volleyball W. **Team name:** Pioneers.

**Student services.** Alcohol/substance abuse counseling, career counseling, services for economically disadvantaged, student employment services, financial aid counseling, health services, minority student services, on-campus daycare, placement for graduates, veterans' counselor, women's services. **Physically disabled:** Services for visually, speech, hearing impaired. **Transfer:** Transfer adviser, college fairs on campus for students transferring to 4-year colleges.

**Contact.** Phone: (772) 462-4740 Toll-free number: (866) 866-4722 Fax: (772) 462-4699
Karen Chapdelaine, Director of Admissions, Indian River State College, 3209 Virginia Avenue, Fort Pierce, FL 34981-5596

## Keiser Career College: Greenacres
### Greenacres, Florida

- For-profit 2-year business and health science college
- Commuter campus in small city

**General.** Accredited by ACCSCT. **Calendar:** Continuous.

**Contact.** Phone: (561) 433-2330
6812 Forest Hill Boulevard, Greenacres, FL 33413

## Keiser Career College: Miami Lakes
### Miami Lakes, Florida

- For-profit 2-year business and health science college
- Commuter campus in large town

**General.** Accredited by ACCSCT. **Calendar:** Continuous.

**Contact.** Phone: (305) 820-5003
17395 NW 59th Avenue, Miami Lakes, FL 33015

## Keiser University
### Ft. Lauderdale, Florida
### www.keiseruniversity.edu          CB code: 7004

- For-profit 2-year business and health science college
- Commuter campus in large city

**General.** Founded in 1977. Regionally accredited. **Location:** 35 miles from Miami. **Calendar:** Semester.

**Annual costs/financial aid.** Need-based financial aid available to full-time and part-time students.

**Contact.** Phone: (954) 776-4456
Central Admissions, 1500 Northwest 49th Street, Fort Lauderdale, FL 33309

## Key College
### Dania Beach, Florida
### www.keycollege.edu          CB code: 3577

- For-profit 2-year business and technical college
- Commuter campus in very large city
- Interview required

**General.** Accredited by ACICS. **Enrollment:** 158 degree-seeking undergraduates. **Degrees:** 10 associate awarded. **Calendar:** Quarter, extensive summer session. **Full-time faculty:** 7 total. **Part-time faculty:** 7 total.

**Student profile.**

| | | | |
|---|---|---|---|
| Out-of-state: | 6% | 25 or older: | 72% |

**Basis for selection.** Admissions based on entrance exam and school record. SAT or ACT recommended. CPAT, SAT or ACT required. **Home-schooled:** State high school equivalency certificate required.

**2009-2010 Annual costs.** Tuition/fees: $10,110. Books/supplies: $900. Personal expenses: $3,186.

**Financial aid. Additional information:** Federal Supplemental Educational Opportunities Grant (FSEOG), PELL grant, ACG, FFEL (federal loan program) available; direct loans offered.

**Application procedures. Admission:** No deadline. $35 fee. Application must be submitted on paper. Admission notification on a rolling basis. **Financial aid:** No deadline.

**Academics. Credit/placement by examination:** CLEP, institutional tests. **Support services:** Remedial instruction, study skills assistance.

**Majors. Engineering technology:** Drafting. **Health:** Medical secretary. **Legal studies:** Court reporting, paralegal.

**Most popular majors.** Engineering/engineering technologies 27%, health sciences 9%, legal studies 64%.

**Computing on campus.** 65 workstations in library, computer center.

**Student life. Freshman orientation:** Mandatory. Held one week prior to beginning of classes for approximately 3 hours. **Activities:** Student newspaper.

**Student services.** Career counseling, financial aid counseling, personal counseling, veterans' counselor.

**Contact.** E-mail: admissions@keycollege.edu
Phone: (954) 923-4440 Toll-free number: (800) 581-8292
Fax: (954) 923-9226
Cindy Ruccolo, Admissions Specialist, Key College, 225 East Dania Beach Boulevard, Dania Beach, FL 33004-3046

## Lake City Community College
### Lake City, Florida          CB member
### www.lakecitycc.edu          CB code: 5377

- Public 2-year community college
- Commuter campus in large town

**General.** Founded in 1947. Regionally accredited. **Enrollment:** 3,070 degree-seeking undergraduates; 117 non-degree-seeking students. **Degrees:** 370 associate awarded. **Location:** 60 miles from Jacksonville, 45 miles from Gainesville. **Calendar:** Semester, limited summer session. **Full-time faculty:** 64 total. **Part-time faculty:** 79 total. **Class size:** 61% < 20, 37% 20-39, less than 1% 40-49, 1% 50-99. **Special facilities:** Performing arts center, arboretum. **Partnerships:** Formal partnership with The Employ Florida Banner Center for Logistics & Distribution.

**Student profile.** Among degree-seeking undergraduates, 59% enrolled in a transfer program, 42% enrolled in a vocational program, 2% already have a bachelor's degree or higher, 822 enrolled as first-time, first-year students.

| | | | |
|---|---|---|---|
| Part-time: | 59% | Asian American: | 1% |
| Out-of-state: | 3% | Hispanic American: | 2% |
| Women: | 67% | 25 or older: | 37% |
| African American: | 12% | | |

**Transfer out. Colleges most students transferred to 2009:** University of Florida, Florida State University, University of North Florida.

**Basis for selection.** Open admission, but selective for some programs. Limited admission to allied health and golf course management programs. Interview recommended for most allied health programs and all golf course operations programs.

**High school preparation.** College-preparatory program recommended. 13 units recommended. Recommended units include English 4, mathematics 3, social studies 3 and science 3.

**2009-2010 Annual costs.** Tuition/fees: $2,448; $9,571 out-of-state. Books/supplies: $1,000.

**Financial aid. Need-based:** Need-based aid available for part-time students. Work-study available for part-time students. **Non-need-based:** Scholarships awarded for academics.

**Application procedures. Admission:** Priority date 8/1; no deadline. $15 fee. Application must be submitted on paper. Admission notification on a rolling basis. Some technical programs reach maximum enrollment and are closed prior to August 1. **Financial aid:** Priority date 6/1; no closing date. FAFSA, institutional form required. Applicants notified on a rolling basis starting 6/1; must reply within 2 week(s) of notification.

**Academics. Special study options:** Accelerated study, cooperative education, distance learning, dual enrollment of high school students, exchange student, independent study, internships, teacher certification program, weekend college. Bachelor's degree programs available on campus. License preparation in nursing, paramedic, physical therapy. **Credit/placement by examination:** CLEP, IB, institutional tests. 30 credit hours maximum toward associate degree. **Support services:** GED preparation and test center, learning center, reduced course load, remedial instruction, study skills assistance, tutoring.

**Majors. Agriculture:** Landscaping. **Business:** Business admin, office management, office/clerical. **Computer sciences:** General, information systems, programming. **Education:** Early childhood. **Health:** EMT paramedic, nursing (RN), physical therapy assistant. **Liberal arts:** Arts/sciences. **Parks/recreation:** Facilities management. **Protective services:** Criminal justice. **Social sciences:** Criminology. **Visual/performing arts:** Graphic design.

**Most popular majors.** Health sciences 24%, liberal arts 71%.

**Computing on campus.** 320 workstations in library, computer center, student center. Online course registration, online library, wireless network available.

**Student life. Freshman orientation:** Available. **Activities:** Bands, choral groups, dance, drama, literary magazine, music ensembles, student government, TV station, Florida Turf Grass Association, Florida Student Nurses Association, Phi Theta Kappa, medical lab technology club, physical therapy assistant club, Practical Nurses Association.

**Athletics. Intramural:** Basketball, football (non-tackle), soccer. **Team name:** Timberwolves.

**Student services.** Alcohol/substance abuse counseling, career counseling, student employment services, financial aid counseling, personal counseling, veterans' counselor. **Physically disabled:** Services for visually, speech, hearing impaired. **Transfer:** Transfer adviser, college fairs on campus for students transferring to 4-year colleges.

**Contact.** E-mail: admissions@lakecitycc.edu
Phone: (386) 754-4287 Fax: (386) 754-4787
Sandra Johnston, Director Enrollment Management, Lake City Community College, 149 SE College Place, Lake City, FL 32025-8703

## Lake-Sumter Community College
**Leesburg, Florida**
**www.lscc.edu**                              CB code: 5376

◆  Public 2-year community college
◆  Commuter campus in small city

**General.** Founded in 1962. Regionally accredited. **Enrollment:** 3,756 degree-seeking undergraduates; 806 non-degree-seeking students. **Degrees:** 532 associate awarded. **Location:** 35 miles from Orlando. **Calendar:** Semester, limited summer session. **Full-time faculty:** 74 total; 19% have terminal degrees, 5% minority, 68% women. **Part-time faculty:** 263 total; 16% have terminal degrees, 9% minority, 60% women. **Class size:** 41% < 20, 57% 20-39, 1% 40-49, less than 1% 50-99. **Special facilities:** Wellness facilities.

**Student profile.** Among degree-seeking undergraduates, 78% enrolled in a transfer program, 22% enrolled in a vocational program, 795 enrolled as first-time, first-year students, 392 transferred in from other institutions.

| Part-time: | 62% | Women: | 64% |
| Out-of-state: | 1% | 25 or older: | 31% |

**Transfer out. Colleges most students transferred to 2009:** University of Central Florida, University of Florida, Florida State University, University of South Florida.

**Basis for selection.** Open admission, but selective for some programs. Special requirements for nursing program. **Homeschooled:** In lieu of a high school diploma or GED, a home-schooled affidavit will be accepted.

**2009-2010 Annual costs.** Tuition/fees: $2,556; $9,627 out-of-state. Books/supplies: $1,000. Personal expenses: $2,582.

**2009-2010 Financial aid. Need-based:** Average scholarship/grant was $1,998. Need-based aid available for part-time students. Work-study available nights and for part-time students. **Non-need-based:** Scholarships awarded for academics, athletics, minority status, state residency.

**Application procedures. Admission:** No deadline. $25 fee. Application must be submitted on paper. Admission notification on a rolling basis. **Financial aid:** Priority date 6/1; no closing date. FAFSA, institutional form required. Applicants notified on a rolling basis starting 7/1.

**Academics. Special study options:** Cooperative education, distance learning, dual enrollment of high school students, independent study, liberal arts/career combination, teacher certification program. Bachelor's degree programs available on campus. License preparation in nursing, real estate. **Credit/placement by examination:** AP, CLEP, institutional tests. 45 credit hours maximum toward associate degree. **Support services:** Learning center, reduced course load, remedial instruction, study skills assistance, tutoring, writing center.

**Majors. Business:** Business admin, executive assistant. **Computer sciences:** Applications programming, systems analysis. **Education:** Early childhood. **Engineering technology:** Computer systems, electrical. **Health:** EMT paramedic, medical records technology, nursing (RN). **Legal studies:** Paralegal. **Liberal arts:** Arts/sciences. **Parks/recreation:** Sports admin. **Protective services:** Fire safety technology, firefighting, law enforcement admin. **Visual/performing arts:** Commercial/advertising art. **Other:** Sports medicine.

**Most popular majors.** Health sciences 15%, liberal arts 77%.

**Computing on campus.** 779 workstations in library, computer center, student center. Commuter students can connect to campus network. Online course registration, online library, wireless network available.

**Student life. Freshman orientation:** Mandatory. Both day and evening sessions are scheduled as well as online orientation. **Activities:** Bands, campus ministries, choral groups, drama, literary magazine, music ensembles, student government, student newspaper, symphony orchestra, College Democrats, College Republicans, environmental society, Fellowship of Christian Athletes, Health Explorers, Spanish club.

**Athletics. NJCAA. Intercollegiate:** Baseball M, softball W, volleyball W. **Intramural:** Basketball, football (non-tackle), table tennis, volleyball. **Team name:** Lakers.

**Student services.** Adult student services, career counseling, services for economically disadvantaged, student employment services, financial aid counseling, minority student services, personal counseling, placement for graduates, veterans' counselor, women's services. **Physically disabled:** Services for visually, speech, hearing impaired. **Transfer:** Pre-admission transcript evaluation for new students. Transfer adviser, college fairs on campus for students transferring to 4-year colleges.

**Contact.** E-mail: admissinquiry@lscc.edu
Phone: (352) 323-3665 Fax: (352) 365-3553
Mark Swearingen, Director, Admissions/ Registrar, Lake-Sumter Community College, 9501 U.S. Highway 441, Leesburg, FL 34788-8751

## Le Cordon Bleu College of Culinary Arts: Miami
**Hollywood, Florida**
**www.miamiculinary.com**

◆  For-profit 2-year culinary school
◆  Small city

**General.** Accredited by ACCSCT. **Calendar:** Continuous.

**Contact.** Phone: (954) 438-8882
3221 Enterprise Way, Miramar, FL 33025

## Lincoln College of Technology: West Palm Beach
**West Palm Beach, Florida**
**www.newenglandtech.com**                    CB code: 0529

◆  For-profit 2-year technical college
◆  Commuter campus in small city

**General.** Founded in 1982. Accredited by ACICS. **Location:** 75 miles from Miami. **Calendar:** Quarter.

**Annual costs/financial aid.** Need-based financial aid available for full-time students.

**Contact.** Phone: (561) 842-8324
Admissions Director, 2410 Metrocentre Boulevard, West Palm Beach, FL 33407

## Miami Dade College

Miami, Florida  CB member
www.mdc.edu/main/  CB code: 5458

▶ Public 2-year community college
▶ Commuter campus in very large city

**General.** Founded in 1959. Regionally accredited. Multilocation institution consisting of campuses and outreach centers. **Enrollment:** 51,369 degree-seeking undergraduates; 7,751 non-degree-seeking students. **Degrees:** 192 bachelor's, 7,563 associate awarded. **ROTC:** Army, Air Force. **Calendar:** Semester, limited summer session. **Full-time faculty:** 662 total; 27% have terminal degrees, 61% minority, 52% women. **Part-time faculty:** 1,548 total; 15% have terminal degrees, 67% minority, 49% women. **Class size:** 16% < 20, 70% 20-39, 13% 40-49, less than 1% 50-99, less than 1% >100. **Special facilities:** Environmental demonstration center, bilingual center, greenhouse, fire science tower, fire science burn building, emerging technologies center of the Americas, center for the environment, horticulture center, firearms demonstration lab, earth science museum, studio theater, human patient simulator lab, flight simulator lab, child care labs. **Partnerships:** Formal partnerships with Florida Power and Light.

**Student profile.** Among degree-seeking undergraduates, 72% enrolled in a transfer program, 28% enrolled in a vocational program, 1% already have a bachelor's degree or higher, 11,613 enrolled as first-time, first-year students, 1,370 transferred in from other institutions.

| | | | |
|---|---|---|---|
| Part-time: | 59% | Women: | 60% |
| Out-of-state: | 6% | 25 or older: | 37% |

**Transfer out.** 80% of students enrolled in the transfer program go on to 4-year colleges. **Colleges most students transferred to 2009:** Florida International University.

**Basis for selection.** Open admission, but selective for some programs. Special requirements for visual and performing arts, honors, allied health, bachelor's in education, bachelor of applied science with major in public safety management, and bachelor's in nursing. Audition required of performing arts majors. Portfolio required of visual arts majors. **Learning Disabled:** The Office of ACCESS (Disability Services) provides, arranges and coordinates accommodations for students with documented disabilities.

**High school preparation.** 24 units recommended. 18 credits with a 3-year high school option or 24 credits with a 4-year high school option.

**2009-2010 Annual costs.** Tuition/fees: $2,585; $9,377 out-of-state. Books/supplies: $1,800. Personal expenses: $2,400.

**2008-2009 Financial aid. Need-based:** 6,149 full-time freshmen applied for aid; 6,098 were judged to have need; 5,996 of these received aid. Average need met was 67%. Average scholarship/grant was $2,925; average loan $973. 80% of total undergraduate aid awarded as scholarships/grants, 20% as loans/jobs. Need-based aid available for part-time students. Work-study available nights, weekends and for part-time students. **Non-need-based:** Awarded to 1,321 full-time undergraduates, including 630 freshmen. Scholarships awarded for academics, art, athletics, music/drama, state residency.

**Application procedures. Admission:** No deadline. $20 fee. Admission notification on a rolling basis. **Financial aid:** Priority date 3/15, closing date 6/30. FAFSA required. Applicants notified on a rolling basis starting 5/15.

**Academics. Special study options:** Accelerated study, cooperative education, cross-registration, distance learning, dual enrollment of high school students, ESL, honors, independent study, internships, study abroad, teacher certification program, weekend college. Bachelor's degree programs available on campus. License preparation in aviation, dental hygiene, nursing, paramedic, physical therapy, radiology, real estate. **Credit/placement by examination:** AP, CLEP, IB, institutional tests. 45 credit hours maximum toward associate degree, 45 toward bachelor's. **Support services:** GED preparation, learning center, reduced course load, remedial instruction, study skills assistance, tutoring, writing center.

**Majors. Agriculture:** Agribusiness operations, landscaping. **Architecture:** Technology. **Area/ethnic studies:** American, Asian, Latin American. **Biology:** General, biotechnology. **Business:** Accounting, administrative services, banking/financial services, business admin, management science, office management, office/clerical, real estate, tourism promotion, tourism/travel. **Communications:** Broadcast journalism, journalism. **Communications technology:** General, animation/special effects, graphic/printing, graphics, radio/tv. **Computer sciences:** General, applications programming, information systems, information technology, web page design. **Conservation:** Environmental science, forestry. **Construction:** Maintenance. **Education:** Early childhood, elementary, mathematics, physical, science, secondary, special,

technology/industrial arts. **Engineering:** Architectural, civil, electrical. **Engineering technology:** Architectural, civil, electrical, electrical drafting. **Family/consumer sciences:** Child development, food/nutrition. **Foreign languages:** General, sign language interpretation, translation. **Health:** Clinical lab technology, dental hygiene, EMT paramedic, histologic technology, medical assistant, medical radiologic technology/radiation therapy, medical records admin, medical secretary, midwifery, nursing (RN), optician, physician assistant, predental, premedicine, prepharmacy, preveterinary, respiratory therapy technology, veterinary technology/assistant. **History:** General. **Legal studies:** Court reporting, legal secretary, paralegal, prelaw. **Liberal arts:** Arts/sciences. **Math:** General. **Mechanic/repair:** Heating/ac/refrig, industrial. **Parks/recreation:** Exercise sciences. **Personal/culinary services:** Mortuary science. **Philosophy/religion:** Philosophy, religion. **Physical sciences:** Atmospheric science, chemistry, geology, physics. **Protective services:** Criminal justice, fire services admin. **Psychology:** General. **Public administration:** General, human services, social work. **Social sciences:** Anthropology, economics, international relations, political science, sociology. **Transportation:** Aviation, aviation management. **Visual/performing arts:** Cinematography, commercial/advertising art, dance, dramatic, studio arts.

**Most popular majors.** Health sciences 12%, liberal arts 79%.

**Computing on campus.** 8,000 workstations in library, computer center. Commuter students can connect to campus network. Online course registration, online library, helpline, wireless network available.

**Student life. Freshman orientation:** Available. **Activities:** Bands, campus ministries, choral groups, dance, drama, film society, international student organizations, literary magazine, music ensembles, Model UN, musical theater, radio station, student government, student newspaper, TV station, Newman Club, Chabad Jewish Student Union, African Student Union, Phi Beta Lambda, Phi Theta Kappa, Spirit of Faith, Haitian Boukan Club, Catholic Ministries, Miami Dade Students for Peace.

**Athletics.** NJCAA. **Intercollegiate:** Baseball M, basketball, softball W, volleyball W. **Intramural:** Basketball, soccer, softball, table tennis, tennis. **Team name:** Sharks.

**Student services.** Adult student services, career counseling, services for economically disadvantaged, student employment services, financial aid counseling, on-campus daycare, personal counseling, placement for graduates, veterans' counselor. **Physically disabled:** Services for visually, speech, hearing impaired. **Transfer:** Transfer center, transfer adviser, college fairs on campus for students transferring to 4-year colleges.

**Contact.** Phone: (305) 237-2222 Fax: (305) 237-2964
Dulce Beltran, College Director, Admissions and Registration Services, Miami Dade College, 11011 SW 104th Street, Miami, FL 33176-3393

## North Florida Community College

Madison, Florida
www.nfcc.edu  CB code: 5503

▶ Public 2-year community college
▶ Commuter campus in rural community

**General.** Founded in 1958. Regionally accredited. **Enrollment:** 925 degree-seeking undergraduates. **Degrees:** 176 associate awarded. **Location:** 56 miles from Tallahassee. **Calendar:** Semester, limited summer session. **Full-time faculty:** 27 total; 22% have terminal degrees. **Part-time faculty:** 1 total. **Special facilities:** Nature center.

**Transfer out. Colleges most students transferred to 2009:** Florida State University, Florida A&M University, Valdosta State University, University of Florida.

**Basis for selection.** Open admission, but selective for some programs. Limited enrollment for nursing, criminal justice, EMT. Background checks completed by Florida Department of Law Enforcement. Florida College Entry-Level Placement Tests required for all students. Students with satisfactory ACT or SAT scores are exempt from taking FCELPT. **Home-schooled:** Statement describing homeschool structure and mission required. Submit affidavit stating that home education complies with Florida law. **Learning Disabled:** Disabilities must have documentation.

**High school preparation.** 24 units recommended. Recommended units include English 4, mathematics 4, social studies 3, science 2 (laboratory 1) and foreign language 2. Algebra 1 recommended.

**2009-2010 Annual costs.** Tuition/fees: $2,406; $9,240 out-of-state. Books/supplies: $500. Personal expenses: $475.

**2008-2009 Financial aid.** All financial aid based on need. Need-based aid available for part-time students. Work-study available nights, weekends and for part-time students.

**Application procedures. Admission:** Priority date 7/1; no deadline. $20 fee, may be waived for applicants with need. Application must be submitted on paper. Admission notification on a rolling basis. **Financial aid:** Priority date 5/15; no closing date. FAFSA required. Applicants notified on a rolling basis starting 6/20; must reply within 2 week(s) of notification.

**Academics. Special study options:** Accelerated study, distance learning, dual enrollment of high school students, independent study, teacher certification program. Bachelor's degree programs available on campus. License preparation in nursing, paramedic, real estate. **Credit/placement by examination:** AP, CLEP, IB, institutional tests. 45 credit hours maximum toward associate degree. **Support services:** GED preparation and test center, reduced course load, remedial instruction, study skills assistance, tutoring, writing center.

**Majors. Health:** Nursing assistant. **Liberal arts:** Arts/sciences.

**Computing on campus.** 65 workstations in library, computer center, student center. Online course registration, online library, wireless network available.

**Student life. Freshman orientation:** Available. **Activities:** Jazz band, choral groups, drama, music ensembles, musical theater, student government, student newspaper, environmental awareness group, African-American Association, veterans club, ASL.

**Athletics.** NJCAA. **Intercollegiate:** Baseball M, basketball W, softball W. **Team name:** Sentinels.

**Student services.** Adult student services, career counseling, student employment services, health services, personal counseling, placement for graduates, veterans' counselor. **Physically disabled:** Services for hearing impaired. **Transfer:** Pre-admission transcript evaluation for new students. Transfer adviser, college fairs on campus for students transferring to 4-year colleges.

**Contact.** Phone: (850) 973-1622 Toll-free number: (866) 937-6322 Fax: (850) 973-1697
Mary Wheeler, Dean of Enrollment Services, North Florida Community College, 325 NW Turner Davis Drive, Madison, FL 32340

## North Florida Institute: Orange Park
### Orange Park, Florida

▶ For-profit 2-year business and health science college
▶ Large city

**General.** Accredited by ACICS. **Calendar:** Differs by program.

**Contact.** Phone: (904) 269-7086
560 Wells Road, Orange Park, FL 32073

## Orlando Culinary Academy
### Orlando, Florida
www.orlandoculinary.com

▶ For-profit 2-year culinary school
▶ Very large city

**General.** Accredited by ACICS. **Location:** Downtown. **Calendar:** Continuous.

**Contact.** Phone: (407) 888-4000
8511 Commodity Circle, Suite 100, Orlando, FL 32819

## Palm Beach Community College
### Lake Worth, Florida
www.pbcc.edu

CB member
CB code: 5531

▶ Public 2-year community college
▶ Commuter campus in large town

**General.** Founded in 1933. Regionally accredited. Multilocation institution with 4 campuses, numerous other locations throughout service area. **Enrollment:** 21,774 degree-seeking undergraduates; 6,243 non-degree-seeking students. **Degrees:** 2,168 associate awarded. **Location:** 30 miles from Fort Lauderdale. **Calendar:** Semester, limited summer session. **Full-time faculty:** 250 total; 24% have terminal degrees, 28% minority, 57% women. **Part-time faculty:** 1,451 total; 27% minority, 49% women. **Special facilities:** Performing arts centers at 3 campuses.

**Student profile.** Among degree-seeking undergraduates, 77% enrolled in a transfer program, 23% enrolled in a vocational program, 4,259 enrolled as first-time, first-year students, 1,020 transferred in from other institutions.

| | | | |
|---|---|---|---|
| Part-time: | 57% | Asian American: | 3% |
| Out-of-state: | 6% | Hispanic American: | 20% |
| Women: | 58% | International: | 2% |
| African American: | 25% | 25 or older: | 40% |

**Transfer out. Colleges most students transferred to 2009:** Florida Atlantic University, University of Florida, Florida State University, University of South Florida.

**Basis for selection.** Open admission, but selective for some programs. Special requirements for dental, nursing, dietetic, occupational therapy assistant programs. Admission to paramedic, radiography, respiratory care programs based on test scores and GPA. SAT or ACT required for admission to nursing and dental programs. CPT, SAT or ACT used for placement for all incoming freshmen. Interview required for nursing, dental, radiography, respiratory care, paramedic majors. Audition required of music majors. **Home-schooled:** Home education program affidavit required.

**High school preparation.** Special requirements for health program applicants.

**2009-2010 Annual costs.** Tuition/fees: $2,475; $8,980 out-of-state. Books/supplies: $1,000. Personal expenses: $400.

**2009-2010 Financial aid. Need-based:** 75% of total undergraduate aid awarded as scholarships/grants, 25% as loans/jobs. Work-study available nights, weekends and for part-time students. **Non-need-based:** Scholarships awarded for academics, alumni affiliation, athletics, leadership, state residency.

**Application procedures. Admission:** Closing date 8/23. $20 fee. Admission notification on a rolling basis beginning on or about 3/1. **Financial aid:** Priority date 7/1; no closing date. FAFSA, institutional form required. Applicants notified on a rolling basis; must reply within 2 week(s) of notification.

**Academics.** Center for Personalized Instruction offers full assistance in all academic areas for students. **Special study options:** Cooperative education, distance learning, double major, dual enrollment of high school students, ESL, honors, independent study, internships, study abroad, weekend college. Bachelor's degree programs available on campus. License preparation in aviation, dental hygiene, nursing, paramedic, radiology, real estate. **Credit/placement by examination:** AP, CLEP, IB, institutional tests. 45 credit hours maximum toward associate degree. **Support services:** Learning center, pre-admission summer program, reduced course load, remedial instruction, study skills assistance, tutoring, writing center.

**Majors. Agriculture:** Ornamental horticulture. **Architecture:** Interior. **Biology:** General, zoology. **Business:** General, accounting, business admin, finance, hospitality admin, management information systems, marketing, sales/distribution. **Communications:** Broadcast journalism, journalism. **Communications technology:** Graphic/printing. **Computer sciences:** General, applications programming, information systems, programming, systems analysis. **Construction:** Maintenance. **Education:** Art, early childhood, elementary, health, health occupations, music, physical, sales/marketing, science, secondary, social science, voc/tech. **Engineering:** General, electrical. **Engineering technology:** Construction, drafting, electrical, industrial management, surveying. **Family/consumer sciences:** General, child care. **Health:** Clinical lab technology, dental hygiene, dietetics, EMT paramedic, health services, massage therapy, medical radiologic technology/radiation therapy, nursing (RN), occupational therapy assistant, premedicine, respiratory therapy technology. **History:** General. **Interdisciplinary:** Biological/physical sciences. **Legal studies:** Paralegal. **Liberal arts:** Arts/sciences. **Math:** General. **Mechanic/repair:** Automotive, marine. **Parks/recreation:** General, health/fitness. **Philosophy/religion:** Philosophy. **Physical sciences:** Chemistry, physics. **Protective services:** Fire services admin, firefighting. **Psychology:** General. **Public administration:** Human services, social work. **Social sciences:** General, anthropology, geography, international relations, political science, sociology. **Transportation:** Aviation. **Visual/performing arts:** General, art history/conservation, cinematography, commercial/advertising art, dance, dramatic, interior design, jazz, photography, studio arts.

**Most popular majors.** Biological/life sciences 10%, health sciences 10%, liberal arts 75%.

**Computing on campus.** 1,500 workstations in library, computer center. Online course registration, online library, helpline, wireless network available.

**Student life. Freshman orientation:** Mandatory. Preregistration for classes offered. **Activities:** Bands, choral groups, dance, drama, literary magazine, music ensembles, musical theater, student government, student newspaper, black student union, Students for International Understanding, ASPIRA, Christian Fellowship, Community Earth, Kiskeya Club.

**Athletics.** NJCAA. **Intercollegiate:** Baseball M, basketball, softball W, volleyball W. **Intramural:** Basketball, softball, volleyball. **Team name:** Panthers.

**Student services.** Adult student services, alcohol/substance abuse counseling, career counseling, student employment services, financial aid counseling, minority student services, personal counseling, placement for graduates, veterans' counselor. **Physically disabled:** Services for visually, speech, hearing impaired. **Transfer:** Transfer adviser, college fairs on campus for students transferring to 4-year colleges.

**Contact.** E-mail: muellere@pbcc.edu
Phone: (561) 868-3300 Fax: (561) 868-3584
Edward Mueller, District Registrar, Palm Beach Community College, 4200 Congress Avenue, Lake Worth, FL 33461

## Pasco-Hernando Community College
**New Port Richey, Florida**
www.phcc.edu                        CB code: 5562

- Public 2-year community college
- Commuter campus in large town

**General.** Founded in 1972. Regionally accredited. District covers counties of Pasco and Hernando; 4 college locations. Distance learning courses are offered for a variety of courses. **Enrollment:** 9,186 degree-seeking undergraduates. **Degrees:** 585 associate awarded. **ROTC:** Army, Naval. **Location:** 35 miles from Tampa. **Calendar:** Semester, limited summer session. **Full-time faculty:** 104 total. **Part-time faculty:** 271 total.

**Transfer out. Colleges most students transferred to 2009:** University of South Florida, St. Leo University, University of Florida, University of Central Florida, St. Petersburg College.

**Basis for selection.** Open admission, but selective for some programs. Special requirements for law enforcement, registered nursing, practical nursing, radiography, paramedic, dental hygiene, dental assisting. **Learning Disabled:** Appropriate documentation to Office of Disabilities Services required.

**2009-2010 Annual costs.** Tuition/fees: $2,419; $9,272 out-of-state. Books/supplies: $1,200. Personal expenses: $1,571.

**Financial aid. Need-based:** Need-based aid available for part-time students. Work-study available nights, weekends and for part-time students. **Non-need-based:** Scholarships awarded for academics, athletics, minority status. **Additional information:** Childcare assistance grants available to eligible students.

**Application procedures. Admission:** No deadline. $25 fee. Admission notification on a rolling basis. **Financial aid:** No deadline. FAFSA required. Applicants notified on a rolling basis.

**Academics. Special study options:** Accelerated study, combined bachelor's/graduate degree, cross-registration, distance learning, double major, dual enrollment of high school students, external degree, honors, independent study, internships, liberal arts/career combination, study abroad, teacher certification program, weekend college. Bachelor's degree programs available on campus. License preparation in dental hygiene, nursing, paramedic, radiology. **Credit/placement by examination:** CLEP, IB, institutional tests. 45 credit hours maximum toward associate degree. **Support services:** GED preparation and test center, learning center, reduced course load, remedial instruction, study skills assistance, tutoring, writing center.

**Majors. Business:** Administrative services, business admin, e-commerce, marketing. **Computer sciences:** Information technology, networking, programming, security, systems analysis. **Health:** Dental hygiene, nursing (RN), radiologic technology/medical imaging. **Legal studies:** Paralegal. **Liberal arts:** Arts/sciences. **Protective services:** Law enforcement admin. **Public administration:** Human services.

**Computing on campus.** Online course registration, online library, wireless network available.

**Student life. Freshman orientation:** Mandatory. 3- or 4-hour program held on variety of days and nights. **Activities:** Choral groups, drama, literary magazine, music ensembles, student government, 3D-developing, drafters & designers club, Campus Crusade for Christ, Earth awareness organization, Legal Eagles club, Men of Excellence, nursing club, veterans club, science club, human services club.

**Athletics.** NJCAA. **Intercollegiate:** Baseball M, basketball M, softball W, volleyball W. **Team name:** Conquistadors.

**Student services.** Career counseling, services for economically disadvantaged, financial aid counseling, minority student services, on-campus daycare, personal counseling, placement for graduates, veterans' counselor. **Physically disabled:** Services for visually, speech, hearing impaired. **Transfer:** College fairs on campus for students transferring to 4-year colleges.

**Contact.** E-mail: bullard@phcc.edu
Phone: (727) 816-3261 Toll-free number: (877) 879-7422
Fax: (727) 816-3389
Debra Bullard, Director of Admissions and Student Records, Pasco-Hernando Community College, 10230 Ridge Road, New Port Richey, FL 34654-5199

## Pensacola Junior College
**Pensacola, Florida**                    CB member
www.pjc.edu                          CB code: 5535

- Public 2-year community college
- Commuter campus in small city

**General.** Founded in 1948. Regionally accredited. Additional campuses: Milton, Warrington, Downtown Center, South Santa Rosa Campus. **Enrollment:** 7,857 degree-seeking undergraduates. **Degrees:** 1,604 associate awarded. **ROTC:** Army. **Location:** 60 miles from Mobile, Alabama. **Calendar:** Semester, extensive summer session. **Full-time faculty:** 217 total. **Part-time faculty:** 549 total. **Special facilities:** Science and space theater.

**Student profile.**

| | | | |
|---|---|---|---|
| Out-of-state: | 2% | 25 or older: | 50% |

**Basis for selection.** Open admission, but selective for some programs. Special requirements for health programs. Florida Entry Level Placement Test must be taken for admission; student may submit SAT or ACT in its place. Scores used for placement only. **Homeschooled:** State high school equivalency certificate required.

**High school preparation.** 24 units recommended. Recommended units include English 4, mathematics 3, social studies 3, science 3, foreign language 2 and academic electives 11. College preparatory program required for associate of arts program: 13 academic units including 4 English, 3 science, 3 mathematics, and 3 social science.

**2009-2010 Annual costs.** Tuition/fees: $2,522; $9,510 out-of-state. Books/supplies: $1,100. Personal expenses: $1,170.

**Financial aid. Non-need-based:** Scholarships awarded for academics, athletics, state residency.

**Application procedures. Admission:** No deadline. $30 fee. Admission notification on a rolling basis. **Financial aid:** Priority date 4/1; no closing date. FAFSA, institutional form required. Applicants notified on a rolling basis starting 7/1; must reply within 2 week(s) of notification.

**Academics. Special study options:** Accelerated study, cooperative education, cross-registration, distance learning, double major, dual enrollment of high school students, ESL, honors, independent study, internships, study abroad, weekend college. License preparation in dental hygiene, nursing, paramedic, radiology. **Credit/placement by examination:** AP, CLEP, IB, institutional tests. 39 credit hours maximum toward associate degree. **Support services:** GED preparation and test center, learning center, reduced course load, remedial instruction, study skills assistance, tutoring, writing center.

**Majors. Agriculture:** General, ornamental horticulture. **Biology:** General, biochemistry, botany, zoology. **Business:** General, accounting, administrative services, banking/financial services, business admin, hospitality/recreation, management information systems, management science, office management. **Communications:** General, journalism. **Communications technology:** General. **Computer sciences:** General, computer science, information systems, programming. **Conservation:** Forest resources, forestry, management/policy. **Construction:** Maintenance. **Education:** General, art, early childhood, elementary, music, physical, special. **Engineering:** General, civil, computer, electrical. **Engineering technology:** Civil, construction, electrical, hazardous materials, manufacturing. **Family/consumer sciences:** Advocacy, child care, food/nutrition, institutional food production. **Health:** Dental hygiene, EMT paramedic, health care admin, medical radiologic technology/radiation therapy, medical records admin, nursing (RN), physical therapy assistant, predental, premedicine, prenursing, prepharmacy, preveterinary, sonography. **History:** General. **Legal studies:** Legal secretary, paralegal, prelaw. **Liberal arts:** Arts/sciences. **Math:** General. **Mechanic/repair:** Automotive. **Personal/culinary services:** Culinary arts. **Philosophy/religion:** Philosophy, religion. **Physical sciences:** Chemistry, geology, physics. **Protective services:** Firefighting, law enforcement admin. **Psychology:** General. **Science technology:** Chemical. **Social sciences:** Sociology. **Visual/performing arts:** Art, commercial/advertising art, dramatic.

**Computing on campus.** 1,500 workstations in library, computer center. Online course registration, wireless network available.

**Student life. Freshman orientation:** Mandatory. **Activities:** Bands, campus ministries, choral groups, dance, drama, international student organizations, literary magazine, music ensembles, musical theater, student government, student newspaper, symphony orchestra, TV station, Florida African-American Student Association, Wesley Foundation, Phi Theta Kappa, Campus Activities Board, Students for Multi-Cultural Society.

**Athletics.** NJCAA. **Intercollegiate:** Baseball M, basketball, cheerleading, softball W, volleyball W. **Intramural:** Archery, badminton, basketball, bowling, racquetball, skin diving, soccer, softball W, table tennis, tennis, volleyball, water polo, weight lifting. **Team name:** Pirates.

**Student services.** Adult student services, alcohol/substance abuse counseling, chaplain/spiritual director, career counseling, services for economically disadvantaged, student employment services, financial aid counseling, health services, minority student services, on-campus daycare, personal counseling, placement for graduates, veterans' counselor, women's services. **Physically disabled:** Services for visually, speech, hearing impaired. **Transfer:** Pre-admission transcript evaluation for new students. Transfer adviser, college fairs on campus for students transferring to 4-year colleges.

**Contact.** Phone: (850) 484-1601 Toll-free number: (888) 897-3605 Fax: (850) 484-1829
Martha Caughey, Director Admissions and Registrar, Pensacola Junior College, 1000 College Boulevard, Pensacola, FL 32504-8998

---

## Polk State College
### Winter Haven, Florida
### www.polk.edu
**CB member**
**CB code: 5548**

◆ Public 2-year community college
◆ Commuter campus in large town

**General.** Founded in 1963. Regionally accredited. Branch campus in Lakeland shared with University of South Florida. **Enrollment:** 7,968 degree-seeking undergraduates; 1,469 non-degree-seeking students. **Degrees:** 962 associate awarded. **ROTC:** Army. **Location:** 60 miles from Tampa, 60 miles from Orlando. **Calendar:** Semester, extensive summer session. **Full-time faculty:** 154 total; 14% have terminal degrees, 18% minority, 58% women. **Part-time faculty:** 356 total; 2% have terminal degrees, 18% minority, 50% women. **Class size:** 40% < 20, 59% 20-39, less than 1% 40-49, less than 1% 50-99.

**Student profile.** Among degree-seeking undergraduates, 66% enrolled in a transfer program, 34% enrolled in a vocational program, 1,479 enrolled as first-time, first-year students, 338 transferred in from other institutions.

| | | | |
|---|---|---|---|
| Part-time: | 63% | Asian American: | 3% |
| Out-of-state: | 1% | Hispanic American: | 13% |
| Women: | 63% | International: | 1% |
| African American: | 16% | 25 or older: | 34% |

**Transfer out.** Colleges most students transferred to 2009: University of South Florida, University of Central Florida, University of Florida, Florida State University.

**Basis for selection.** Open admission, but selective for some programs. Limited access to nursing, radiology, physical therapy assistant, occupational therapy assistant, respiratory therapy, paramedic programs, cardiovascular tech, medical sonography. Audition recommended for theater, music majors. Portfolio recommended for graphic arts majors. **Homeschooled:** Adheres to FLDOE policy and Florida state statute: affidavit signed by guardian attesting to home school applicant completion required in place of high school diploma. **Learning Disabled:** Students needing classroom accommodations must provide documentation as required.

**High school preparation.** Recommended units include English 4, mathematics 4, social studies 3, science 3 and foreign language 2.

**2009-2010 Annual costs.** Tuition/fees: $2,585; $9,596 out-of-state. Books/supplies: $1,100. Personal expenses: $2,600.

**Financial aid. Need-based:** Need-based aid available for part-time students. Work-study available nights, weekends and for part-time students. **Non-need-based:** Scholarships awarded for academics, athletics, leadership, state residency.

**Application procedures. Admission:** No deadline. $20 fee, may be waived for applicants with need. Admission notification on a rolling basis. **Financial aid:** Priority date 5/15; no closing date. FAFSA required. Applicants notified on a rolling basis.

**Academics. Special study options:** Accelerated study, cross-registration, distance learning, double major, dual enrollment of high school students, ESL, honors, independent study, internships. License preparation in nursing, occupational therapy, paramedic, physical therapy, radiology. **Credit/placement by examination:** AP, CLEP, IB. 45 credit hours maximum toward associate degree. **Support services:** Learning center, reduced course load, remedial instruction, study skills assistance, tutoring.

**Honors college/program.** High school graduates with 3.5 GPA may apply for honors program and designated courses.

**Majors. Business:** Accounting, administrative services, banking/financial services, business admin, marketing, office management, office/clerical. **Computer sciences:** General, computer graphics, information systems, programming. **Construction:** Power transmission. **Education:** General. **Engineering technology:** Electrical. **Family/consumer sciences:** Child care. **Health:** Cardiovascular technology, EMT paramedic, medical records admin, medical records technology, nursing (RN), occupational therapy assistant, physical therapy assistant, respiratory therapy technology, sonography. **Liberal arts:** Arts/sciences. **Mechanic/repair:** Computer. **Protective services:** Criminal justice, firefighting, police science. **Visual/performing arts:** Cinematography. **Other:** Supply Chain Management.

**Most popular majors.** Health sciences 21%, liberal arts 70%.

**Computing on campus.** 775 workstations in library, computer center, student center. Online course registration available.

**Student life. Freshman orientation:** Available. Preregistration for classes offered. **Activities:** Bands, choral groups, drama, music ensembles, musical theater, student government.

**Athletics.** NJCAA. **Intercollegiate:** Baseball M, basketball M, soccer W, softball W, volleyball W. **Intramural:** Basketball, bowling, football (nontackle), table tennis, volleyball. **Team name:** Vikings.

**Student services.** Adult student services, career counseling, services for economically disadvantaged, student employment services, financial aid counseling, personal counseling. **Physically disabled:** Services for visually, speech, hearing impaired. **Transfer:** Re-entry adviser for new students. Transfer adviser, college fairs on campus for students transferring to 4-year colleges.

**Contact.** E-mail: studentservices@polk.edu
Phone: (863) 297-1010 ext. 5225 Fax: (863) 297-1060
Kathy Bucklew, Registrar, Polk State College, 999 Avenue H NE, Winter Haven, FL 33881-4299

---

## Professional Golfers Career College: Orlando
### Winter Garden, Florida
### www.golfcollege.edu

◆ For-profit 2-year branch campus college
◆ Commuter campus in very large city

**General.** Accredited by ACICS. **Enrollment:** 185 degree-seeking undergraduates. **Degrees:** 101 associate awarded. **Location:** 16 miles from Orlando. **Calendar:** Semester. **Full-time faculty:** 3 total. **Part-time faculty:** 12 total. **Special facilities:** Pro shop, video studio.

**Basis for selection.** Character/personal qualities and level of applicant's interest very important. **Homeschooled:** Letter of recommendation (nonparent) required.

**2009-2010 Annual costs.** Tuition/fees: $5,590.

**Application procedures. Admission:** No deadline. $75 fee. Application must be submitted on paper. Admission notification on a rolling basis.

**Academics. Credit/placement by examination:** CLEP, institutional tests.

**Majors. Parks/recreation:** Facilities management.

**Computing on campus.** 12 workstations in computer center. Online library available.

**Student life. Freshman orientation:** Mandatory.

**Student services.** Alcohol/substance abuse counseling, career counseling, financial aid counseling, personal counseling, placement for graduates, veterans' counselor.

**Contact.** E-mail: admin@golfcollege.edu
Phone: (866) 407-7422 Toll-free number: (866) 407-7422
Fax: (407) 905-2241
David Wood, Admissions Director, Professional Golfers Career College:
Orlando, PO Box 892319, Temecula, CA 92589-2319

## Saint Johns River Community College
### Palatka, Florida
www.sjrcc.edu                                    CB code: 5641

▶ Public 2-year community college
▶ Commuter campus in large town

**General.** Founded in 1957. Regionally accredited. **Enrollment:** 5,826 undergraduates. **Degrees:** 661 associate awarded. **Location:** 55 miles from Jacksonville and Daytona Beach. **Calendar:** Trimester, limited summer session. **Full-time faculty:** 114 total. **Part-time faculty:** 162 total.

**Basis for selection.** Open admission, but selective for some programs. Interview, audition, and portfolio required of applicants to Florida School of Arts program.

**High school preparation.** 24 units recommended. Recommended units include English 4, mathematics 3, social studies 3 and science 3.

**2009-2010 Annual costs.** Tuition/fees: $2,550; $9,585 out-of-state. Books/supplies: $752. Personal expenses: $87.

**2008-2009 Financial aid. Need-based:** Need-based aid available for part-time students.

**Application procedures. Admission:** Priority date 7/15; no deadline. $30 fee. Admission notification on a rolling basis. **Financial aid:** Priority date 5/15; no closing date. FAFSA required. Applicants notified on a rolling basis.

**Academics. Special study options:** Dual enrollment of high school students. **Credit/placement by examination:** AP, CLEP. 45 credit hours maximum toward associate degree. **Support services:** Remedial instruction, tutoring.

**Majors. Business:** Accounting, accounting technology, administrative services, business admin. **Computer sciences:** Programming, systems analysis. **Engineering technology:** Electrical. **Health:** EMT paramedic. **Liberal arts:** Arts/sciences. **Protective services:** Fire safety technology. **Visual/performing arts:** General.

**Student life. Activities:** Student government, student newspaper, Black Student Union, Circle-K, Compass Club, future educators, Phi Beta Lamba, Mathematical Association of America.

**Athletics.** NJCAA. **Intercollegiate:** Baseball M, basketball M, softball W. **Intramural:** Table tennis.

**Student services.** Career counseling, personal counseling, placement for graduates, veterans' counselor. **Physically disabled:** Services for speech impaired.

**Contact.** Phone: (386) 312-4030 Fax: (386) 312-4048
O'Neal Williams, Admission and Records, Saint Johns River Community College, 5001 St. Johns Avenue, Palatka, FL 32177-3897

## St. Petersburg College
### St. Petersburg, Florida                     CB member
www.spcollege.edu                                CB code: 5606

▶ Public 2-year community college
▶ Commuter campus in large city

**General.** Founded in 1927. Regionally accredited. Campuses include Clearwater, Seminole, St. Petersburg, Tarpon Springs. Health education center in Pinellas Park. Criminal justice/computer complex in St. Petersburg. Corporate training and Cisco at the Epicenter. Downtown and midtown centers. **Enrollment:** 20,964 degree-seeking undergraduates; 8,318 non-degree-seeking students. **Degrees:** 709 bachelor's, 2,978 associate awarded. **Location:** 20 miles from Tampa. **Calendar:** Semester, extensive summer session. **Full-time faculty:** 309 total; 37% have terminal degrees, 15% minority, 56% women. **Part-time faculty:** 1,425 total; 24% minority, 49% women. **Special facilities:** Observatory, planetarium, firing range, college-operated museums, nature preserves.

**Student profile.** Among degree-seeking undergraduates, 4,665 enrolled as first-time, first-year students.

| | | | |
|---|---|---|---|
| Part-time: | 64% | Asian American: | 3% |
| Out-of-state: | 4% | Hispanic American: | 6% |
| Women: | 61% | International: | 1% |
| African American: | 12% | 25 or older: | 46% |

**Basis for selection.** Open admission, but selective for some programs. Limited enrollment to health-related programs. Florida CPT required for all degree-seeking students. Interview recommended for allied health applicants. **Homeschooled:** Transcript of courses and grades, state high school equivalency certificate required.

**2009-2010 Annual costs.** Tuition/fees: $2,614; $9,491 out-of-state. Books/supplies: $1,600. Personal expenses: $3,612.

**Financial aid. Need-based:** Need-based aid available for part-time students. Work-study available nights, weekends and for part-time students. **Non-need-based:** Scholarships awarded for academics, art, athletics, minority status, music/drama.

**Application procedures. Admission:** No deadline. $40 fee. Admission notification on a rolling basis. **Financial aid:** Priority date 4/15; no closing date. FAFSA required. Applicants notified on a rolling basis starting 5/15; must reply within 2 week(s) of notification.

**Academics. Special study options:** Accelerated study, cooperative education, cross-registration, distance learning, dual enrollment of high school students, ESL, exchange student, honors, independent study, internships, liberal arts/career combination, study abroad, teacher certification program, weekend college. 2-year associate degree program in business and computer science for deaf students. Bachelor's degree programs available on campus. License preparation in dental hygiene, nursing, paramedic, physical therapy, radiology. **Credit/placement by examination:** AP, CLEP, IB, institutional tests. 45 credit hours maximum toward associate degree, 45 toward bachelor's. Florida CPT required for placement. **Support services:** GED preparation, learning center, reduced course load, remedial instruction, study skills assistance, tutoring.

**Majors. Business:** Accounting technology, banking/financial services, business admin, hospitality admin, marketing. **Computer sciences:** General, networking, programming, system admin, web page design, webmaster. **Education:** Early childhood. **Engineering technology:** General, architectural drafting, computer, drafting, electrical, industrial. **Foreign languages:** Sign language interpretation. **Health:** Clinical lab technology, dental hygiene, EMT paramedic, maternal/child health nursing, medical records admin, nursing (RN), physical therapy assistant, radiologic technology/medical imaging, respiratory therapy technology, substance abuse counseling, veterinary technology/assistant. **Interdisciplinary:** Natural sciences. **Legal studies:** Paralegal. **Liberal arts:** Arts/sciences. **Mechanic/repair:** Aircraft. **Parks/recreation:** General. **Personal/culinary services:** Mortuary science. **Protective services:** Fire safety technology, firefighting, forensics, law enforcement admin, security services. **Public administration:** Human services. **Visual/performing arts:** Photography.

**Most popular majors.** Health sciences 19%, liberal arts 72%.

**Computing on campus.** 4,011 workstations in library, computer center, student center. Commuter students can connect to campus network. Online course registration, online library, helpline, student web hosting, wireless network available.

**Student life. Freshman orientation:** Mandatory. Preregistration for classes offered. **Activities:** Jazz band, choral groups, dance, drama, film society, international student organizations, music ensembles, student government, student newspaper, Phi Theta Kappa, Harambee black culture club, ethics club, math and science club, American Sign Language club, Rotary club, College Deomocrats, College Republicans, digital artists in motion, hospitality club.

**Athletics.** NJCAA. **Intercollegiate:** Baseball M, basketball, softball W, tennis W, volleyball W. **Team name:** Titans.

**Student services.** Career counseling, services for economically disadvantaged, student employment services, financial aid counseling, health services, minority student services, personal counseling, placement for graduates, veterans' counselor, women's services. **Physically disabled:** Services for visually, speech, hearing impaired. **Transfer:** College fairs on campus for students transferring to 4-year colleges.

**Contact.** Phone: (727) 341-4772
Susan Fell, Director of Admissions and Records, St. Petersburg College, Box 13489, St. Petersburg, FL 33733-3489

## Sanford-Brown Institute: Jacksonville
**Jacksonville, Florida**
**www.sbjacksonville.com**

- For-profit 2-year health science college
- Commuter campus in large city
- Application essay, interview required

**General.** Accredited by ACICS. **Enrollment:** 783 degree-seeking undergraduates. **Degrees:** 271 associate awarded. **Calendar:** Continuous. **Full-time faculty:** 23 total. **Part-time faculty:** 30 total.

**Basis for selection.** Open admission, but selective for some programs. **Homeschooled:** Statement describing homeschool structure and mission, transcript of courses and grades, state high school equivalency certificate, interview, letter of recommendation (nonparent) required.

**Application procedures. Admission:** No deadline. $25 fee. Admission notification on a rolling basis.

**Academics. Credit/placement by examination:** CLEP. **Support services:** Learning center, reduced course load, study skills assistance, tutoring.

**Majors. Health:** Cardiovascular technology.

**Computing on campus.** 60 workstations in library, computer center, student center. Commuter students can connect to campus network.

**Student life. Freshman orientation:** Mandatory. Preregistration for classes offered.

**Student services.** Adult student services, career counseling, student employment services, financial aid counseling, health services, personal counseling, placement for graduates. **Physically disabled:** Services for speech, hearing impaired.

**Contact.** Phone: (904) 363-6221
Deborah King, Director of Admissions, Sanford-Brown Institute: Jacksonville, 10255 Fortune Parkway, Suite 501, Jacksonville, FL 32256

## Sanford-Brown Institute: Tampa
**Tampa, Florida**
**www.sbtampa.com**

- For-profit 2-year health science and community college
- Large city

**General.** Accredited by ACICS. **Calendar:** Continuous.

**Contact.** Phone: (813) 621-0072
Director of Admissions, 5701 East Hillsboro Avenue, Tampa, FL 33610

## Santa Fe College
**Gainesville, Florida**                   **CB member**
**www.sfcollege.edu**                      **CB code: 5653**

- Public 2-year community college
- Commuter campus in small city

**General.** Founded in 1965. Regionally accredited. Branch campuses located in Gainesville, Starke, Archer, Keystone Heights, and Alachua. **Enrollment:** 13,606 degree-seeking undergraduates; 1,190 non-degree-seeking students. **Degrees:** 2,767 associate awarded. **ROTC:** Army, Air Force. **Location:** 80 miles from Jacksonville, 110 miles from Orlando. **Calendar:** Semester, extensive summer session. **Full-time faculty:** 254 total; 25% have terminal degrees, 15% minority, 59% women. **Part-time faculty:** 567 total; 13% have terminal degrees, 14% minority, 50% women. **Class size:** 32% < 20, 67% 20-39, less than 1% 40-49. **Special facilities:** Teaching zoo, planetarium, rock cycle garden, laboratory pre-school.

**Student profile.** Among degree-seeking undergraduates, 66% enrolled in a transfer program, 23% enrolled in a vocational program, 2,684 enrolled as first-time, first-year students.

| | | | |
|---|---|---|---|
| Part-time: | 54% | Asian American: | 3% |
| Out-of-state: | 2% | Hispanic American: | 11% |
| Women: | 53% | International: | 2% |
| African American: | 14% | 25 or older: | 29% |

**Basis for selection.** Open admission, but selective for some programs. Computerized placement tests, SAT or ACT required for placement.

**High school preparation.** Recommended units include foreign language 2.

**2009-2010 Annual costs.** Tuition/fees: $2,537; $9,495 out-of-state. Books/supplies: $700. Personal expenses: $1,008.

**Financial aid. Need-based:** Need-based aid available for part-time students. **Non-need-based:** Scholarships awarded for academics, art, athletics, leadership, minority status, music/drama, state residency.

**Application procedures. Admission:** No deadline. No application fee. Application must be submitted online. Admission notification on a rolling basis. High school diploma not required of applicants to most vocational programs. **Financial aid:** Priority date 3/15, closing date 6/30. FAFSA required. Applicants notified by 8/1.

**Academics. Special study options:** Cooperative education, cross-registration, distance learning, dual enrollment of high school students, ESL, honors, independent study, internships, study abroad, teacher certification program, weekend college. Bachelor's degree programs available on campus. License preparation in aviation, dental hygiene, nursing, paramedic, radiology, real estate. **Credit/placement by examination:** AP, CLEP, IB, institutional tests. 30 credit hours maximum toward associate degree. **Support services:** GED preparation, learning center, remedial instruction, tutoring, writing center.

**Majors. Biology:** Biomedical sciences. **Business:** Administrative services, business admin, office technology, office/clerical. **Computer sciences:** LAN/WAN management, web page design, webmaster. **Construction:** Maintenance. **Education:** Early childhood. **Engineering technology:** Automotive, biomedical, CAD/CADD, construction. **Health:** Cardiovascular technology, dental hygiene, EMT paramedic, medical radiologic technology/radiation therapy, medical secretary, nuclear medical technology, nursing (RN), radiologic technology/medical imaging, respiratory therapy technology. **Legal studies:** Legal secretary, paralegal. **Liberal arts:** Arts/sciences. **Physical sciences:** Astronomy, chemistry. **Protective services:** Firefighting, police science. **Social sciences:** Anthropology. **Transportation:** Airline/commercial pilot. **Visual/performing arts:** Graphic design. **Other:** Zoo Animal Technology.

**Most popular majors.** Health sciences 9%, liberal arts 83%.

**Computing on campus.** Commuter students can connect to campus network. Online course registration, helpline, repair service available.

**Student life. Freshman orientation:** Available. **Policies:** Students expected to abide by student conduct code. **Activities:** Jazz band, choral groups, dance, drama, international student organizations, literary magazine, music ensembles, Model UN, musical theater, student government, student newspaper, Campus Advent, Christians on Campus, black student union, Hispanic organization of Latino activities, international student cultural association, Democratic Saints, Republican club, Students for Environmental Harmony, Phi Theta Kappa, Circle K International.

**Athletics.** NJCAA. **Intercollegiate:** Baseball M, basketball, softball W. **Intramural:** Basketball, football (non-tackle), golf, racquetball, soccer, volleyball, weight lifting. **Team name:** Saints.

**Student services.** Adult student services, alcohol/substance abuse counseling, career counseling, services for economically disadvantaged, student employment services, financial aid counseling, health services, legal services, minority student services, on-campus daycare, personal counseling, placement for graduates, veterans' counselor, women's services. **Physically disabled:** Services for visually, speech, hearing impaired. **Transfer:** Transfer adviser, college fairs on campus for students transferring to 4-year colleges.

**Contact.** E-mail: admission@sfcollege.edu
Phone: (352) 395-7322 Fax: (352) 395-7300
Michael Hutley, Associate Registrar, Santa Fe College, 3000 NW 83rd Street, R-112, Gainesville, FL 32606-6210

## Seminole Community College
**Sanford, Florida**
**www.scc-fl.edu**                          **CB code: 5662**

- Public 2-year Seminole State College is offering a new Bachelor of Applied Science degree (B.A.S.) in Interior Design.
- Commuter campus in large town

**General.** Founded in 1965. Regionally accredited. **Enrollment:** 14,505 degree-seeking undergraduates; 1,912 non-degree-seeking students. **Degrees:** 1,714 associate awarded. **Location:** 21 miles from Orlando. **Calendar:** Semester, limited summer session. **Full-time faculty:** 189 total; 17% have terminal degrees, 18% minority, 62% women. **Part-time faculty:** 534 total; 20% minority, 52% women. **Class size:** 15% < 20, 82% 20-39, 2% 40-49, less than 1% 50-99, less than 1% >100. **Special facilities:** Planetarium. **Partnerships:** Formal partnerships with Siemens/Stromberg, local businesses.

**Student profile.** Among degree-seeking undergraduates, 2,935 enrolled as first-time, first-year students.

| | | | |
|---|---|---|---|
| Part-time: | 52% | Women: | 59% |
| Out-of-state: | 3% | 25 or older: | 48% |

**Basis for selection.** Open admission, but selective for some programs. Limited access to associate of science degrees including nursing, physical therapy, and respiratory care. Interview recommended for respiratory therapy, nursing, and physical therapy majors. **Homeschooled:** Transcript of courses and grades required. Affidavit of home school completion required.

**High school preparation.** 24 units required. Required units include English 4, mathematics 4, social studies 3, science 3 and academic electives 10.

**2009-2010 Annual costs.** Tuition/fees: $2,636; $9,640 out-of-state. Books/supplies: $1,200. Personal expenses: $900.

**2008-2009 Financial aid. Need-based:** 43% of total undergraduate aid awarded as scholarships/grants, 57% as loans/jobs. Need-based aid available for part-time students. Work-study available for part-time students. **Non-need-based:** Scholarships awarded for academics, art, athletics, leadership, minority status, music/drama, state residency.

**Application procedures. Admission:** Closing date 9/21 (postmark date). No application fee. Admission notification on a rolling basis beginning on or about 9/1. **Financial aid:** Priority date 7/1; no closing date. FAFSA required. Applicants notified on a rolling basis starting 4/1.

**Academics. Special study options:** Accelerated study, cooperative education, cross-registration, distance learning, dual enrollment of high school students, ESL, honors, independent study, study abroad, teacher certification program, weekend college. **Credit/placement by examination:** AP, CLEP, IB, institutional tests. 45 credit hours maximum toward associate degree. **Support services:** GED preparation and test center, learning center, reduced course load, remedial instruction, study skills assistance, tutoring.

**Majors. Architecture:** Interior. **Business:** Accounting technology, administrative services, banking/financial services, business admin, office management. **Communications:** General. **Communications technology:** General. **Computer sciences:** General, applications programming, computer graphics, computer science, data processing, information systems, networking, programming, systems analysis. **Education:** Kindergarten/preschool. **Engineering:** Electrical, software. **Engineering technology:** Architectural, construction, electrical. **Family/consumer sciences:** Child care. **Health:** EMT paramedic, medical secretary, nursing (RN), physical therapy assistant, respiratory therapy technology. **Legal studies:** Legal secretary, paralegal. **Liberal arts:** Arts/sciences. **Mechanic/repair:** Automotive. **Protective services:** Fire safety technology, firefighting, law enforcement admin. **Visual/performing arts:** Commercial/advertising art, interior design.

**Most popular majors.** Health sciences 14%, liberal arts 73%.

**Computing on campus.** 100 workstations in library, computer center. Commuter students can connect to campus network. Online course registration, online library, student web hosting, wireless network available.

**Student life. Freshman orientation:** Mandatory. Preregistration for classes offered. **Activities:** Bands, choral groups, drama, film society, international student organizations, literary magazine, music ensembles, musical theater, student government, student newspaper, symphony orchestra, African American cultural forum, College Republicans, disabled student association, Hispanic student associations, Muslim student association, Unity Organization, Fellowship of Christian Athletes, Campus Crusade for Christ, Intervarsity Christian Fellowship, Sigma Phi Gamma.

**Athletics.** NJCAA. **Intercollegiate:** Baseball M, golf W, softball W. **Team name:** Raider.

**Student services.** Adult student services, alcohol/substance abuse counseling, career counseling, services for economically disadvantaged, student employment services, financial aid counseling, minority student services, personal counseling, placement for graduates, veterans' counselor. **Physically disabled:** Services for visually, speech, hearing impaired. **Transfer:** Transfer adviser for students transferring to 4-year colleges.

**Contact.** E-mail: admissions@scc-fl.edu
Phone: (407) 708-2580 Fax: (407) 708-2395
Pamela Mennechey, Director of Admissions, Seminole Community College, 100 Weldon Boulevard, Sanford, FL 32773-6199

## South Florida Community College
Avon Park, Florida | **CB member**
www.southflorida.edu | **CB code: 5666**

▶ Public 2-year community and technical college
▶ Commuter campus in small town

**General.** Founded in 1965. Regionally accredited. **Enrollment:** 2,441 degree-seeking undergraduates; 461 non-degree-seeking students. **Degrees:** 267 associate awarded. **ROTC:** Army. **Location:** 90 miles from Orlando. **Calendar:** Semester, limited summer session. **Full-time faculty:** 63 total; 22% have terminal degrees, 8% minority, 54% women. **Part-time faculty:** 154 total; 4% have terminal degrees, 16% minority, 52% women. **Class size:** 59% < 20, 41% 20-39, less than 1% 40-49. **Special facilities:** Museum of Florida Art and Culture, nature walk.

**Student profile.** Among degree-seeking undergraduates, 64% enrolled in a transfer program, 36% enrolled in a vocational program, 783 enrolled as first-time, first-year students, 128 transferred in from other institutions.

| | | | |
|---|---|---|---|
| Part-time: | 60% | 25 or older: | 27% |
| Out-of-state: | 3% | Live on campus: | 2% |
| Women: | 62% | | |

**Basis for selection.** Open admission, but selective for some programs. Some programs have test and prerequisite requirements. Interview recommended for selected programs. **Homeschooled:** Students must meet with registrar prior to admission. **Learning Disabled:** Recommend students seek assistance from campus disabilities specialist.

**High school preparation.** College-preparatory program recommended. 24 units recommended. Recommended units include English 4, mathematics 4, social studies 1, history 2, science 3 (laboratory 2), visual/performing arts 1 and academic electives 9.

**2009-2010 Annual costs.** Tuition/fees: $2,561; $9,667 out-of-state. Books/supplies: $947. Personal expenses: $1,082.

**2008-2009 Financial aid. Need-based:** 92% of total undergraduate aid awarded as scholarships/grants, 8% as loans/jobs. Need-based aid available for part-time students. Work-study available for part-time students. **Non-need-based:** Scholarships awarded for academics, athletics, leadership, minority status, music/drama, state residency.

**Application procedures. Admission:** No deadline. No application fee. Admission notification on a rolling basis. **Financial aid:** Priority date 4/15; no closing date. FAFSA required. Applicants notified on a rolling basis starting 4/1.

**Academics. Special study options:** Accelerated study, cooperative education, distance learning, double major, dual enrollment of high school students, ESL, external degree, honors, independent study, internships, teacher certification program. Bachelor's degree programs available on campus. License preparation in dental hygiene, nursing, paramedic, radiology. **Credit/placement by examination:** AP, CLEP, IB, institutional tests. 30 credit hours maximum toward associate degree. **Support services:** GED preparation and test center, learning center, reduced course load, remedial instruction, study skills assistance, tutoring, writing center.

**Majors. Agriculture:** General, agribusiness operations, ornamental horticulture. **Business:** Accounting, administrative services, business admin, hospitality admin. **Computer sciences:** LAN/WAN management, programming. **Construction:** General, power transmission. **Education:** Teacher assistance. **Engineering technology:** Biomedical, computer hardware, drafting, electrical, industrial. **Family/consumer sciences:** Child care. **Health:** Dental hygiene, EMT paramedic, medical secretary, nursing (RN), radiologic technology/medical imaging. **Liberal arts:** Arts/sciences. **Protective services:** Firefighting, law enforcement admin.

**Most popular majors.** Health sciences 17%, liberal arts 76%.

**Computing on campus.** 100 workstations in library, computer center, student center. Online course registration, online library, wireless network available.

**Student life. Freshman orientation:** Mandatory. Preregistration for classes offered. Online video with review quiz. **Housing:** Coed dorms, wellness housing available. **Activities:** Campus ministries, dance, drama, international student organizations, music ensembles, student government, student newspaper, Adventist social club, African American association.

**Two-Year Colleges**

**Athletics.** NJCAA. **Intercollegiate:** Softball W, volleyball W. **Intramural:** Baseball M. **Team name:** Panthers.

**Student services.** Adult student services, career counseling, services for economically disadvantaged, student employment services, financial aid counseling, minority student services, personal counseling, placement for graduates, veterans' counselor, women's services. **Physically disabled:** Services for visually, speech, hearing impaired. **Transfer:** Transfer adviser, college fairs on campus for students transferring to 4-year colleges.

**Contact.** E-mail: deborah.fuschetti@southflorida.edu
Phone: (863) 453-6661 ext. 7405 Fax: (863) 453-2365
Deborah Fuschetti, Registrar, South Florida Community College, 600 West College Drive, Avon Park, FL 33825

## Southwest Florida College
**Ft. Myers, Florida**
**www.swfc.edu**                                    **CB code: 3445**

- Private 2-year career college
- Commuter campus in large city

**General.** Accredited by ACICS. Learning site in Estero. **Enrollment:** 1,810 degree-seeking undergraduates; 27 non-degree-seeking students. **Degrees:** 53 bachelor's, 414 associate awarded. **Location:** 130 miles from Tampa. **Calendar:** Quarter, extensive summer session. **Full-time faculty:** 44 total; 9% have terminal degrees, 11% minority, 59% women. **Part-time faculty:** 133 total; 8% have terminal degrees, 21% minority, 57% women. **Class size:** 64% < 20, 36% 20-39.

**Student profile.** Among degree-seeking undergraduates, 456 enrolled as first-time, first-year students, 289 transferred in from other institutions.

| | | | |
|---|---|---|---|
| Part-time: | 16% | 25 or older: | 60% |
| Women: | 73% | | |

**Basis for selection.** Open admission, but selective for some programs. Surgical Technology requires an interview with the Program Manager prior to acceptance; students placing extraordinarily low on placement assessment may not be accepted. Interviews required for some programs.

**2009-2010 Annual costs.** Tuition/fees: $14,175. Per-credit charge: $290. Required fees do not include lab or online fees.

**Financial aid. Need-based:** Need-based aid available for part-time students. Work-study available nights, weekends and for part-time students.

**Application procedures. Admission:** No deadline. $25 fee. Application must be submitted on paper. Admission notification on a rolling basis. **Financial aid:** No deadline. FAFSA required. Applicants notified on a rolling basis.

**Academics.** Online academic assistance availabe to students enrolled in online courses. **Special study options:** Accelerated study, cooperative education, distance learning, double major, internships, liberal arts/career combination, teacher certification program. Bachelor's degree programs available on campus. **Credit/placement by examination:** AP, CLEP, institutional tests. 24 credit hours maximum toward associate degree, 48 toward bachelor's. **Support services:** Learning center, reduced course load, remedial instruction, study skills assistance, tutoring, writing center.

**Majors. Business:** Accounting, marketing. **Communications technology:** Animation/special effects. **Computer sciences:** Information technology, networking, programming, web page design. **Education:** Early childhood. **Engineering:** Computer. **Engineering technology:** Drafting. **Health:** Massage therapy, medical assistant, medical records technology, surgical technology. **Legal studies:** Paralegal. **Protective services:** Law enforcement admin. **Visual/performing arts:** Interior design.

**Most popular majors.** Business/marketing 12%, education 6%, engineering/engineering technologies 9%, health sciences 32%, security/protective services 13%, visual/performing arts 22%.

**Computing on campus.** 195 workstations in library, computer center, student center. Commuter students can connect to campus network. Online library, repair service, wireless network available.

**Student life. Freshman orientation:** Mandatory. Preregistration for classes offered. Held the week before classes begin and lasts 1-2 hours. **Activities:** Student newspaper.

**Student services.** Adult student services, career counseling, services for economically disadvantaged, student employment services, financial aid counseling, placement for graduates. **Physically disabled:** Services for visually, speech, hearing impaired. **Learning disabled:** Comprehensive services available. **Transfer:** Re-entry adviser, pre-admission transcript evaluation for new students.

**Contact.** E-mail: kreynolds@swfc.edu
Phone: (239) 939-4766 Toll-free number: (877) 493-5147
Fax: (239) 936-4040
Ken Reynolds, Regional Vice President of Enrollment Management, Southwest Florida College, 1685 Medical Lane, Ft. Myers, FL 33907-1108

## Southwest Florida College: Tampa
**Tampa, Florida**
**www.swfc.edu**

- Private 2-year branch campus and junior college
- Commuter campus in very large city

**General.** Accredited by ACICS. **Location:** 15 miles from downtown. **Calendar:** Quarter.

**Contact.** Phone: (813) 630-4401
Vice President of Admissions, 3910 Riga Boulevard, Tampa, FL 33619

## Stenotype Institute: Jacksonville
**Jacksonville, Florida**
**www.thestenotypeinstitute.com**

- For-profit 2-year business and community college
- Very large city

**General.** Accredited by ACICS. **Calendar:** Continuous.

**Contact.** Phone: (904) 398-4141
Director of Admissions, 3563 Phillips Highway, Building E, #501, Jacksonville, FL 32207

## Stenotype Institute: Orlando
**Orlando, Florida**

- For-profit 2-year technical college
- Very large city

**General.** Accredited by ACICS. **Calendar:** Semester.

**Contact.** Phone: (407) 816-5573
1636 West Oakridge Road, Orlando, FL 32809

## Tallahassee Community College
**Tallahassee, Florida**                          **CB member**
**www.tcc.fl.edu**                                 **CB code: 5794**

- Public 2-year community college
- Commuter campus in small city

**General.** Founded in 1965. Regionally accredited. **Enrollment:** 13,127 degree-seeking undergraduates; 1,399 non-degree-seeking students. **Degrees:** 2,351 associate awarded. **ROTC:** Army, Naval, Air Force. **Location:** 230 miles from Tampa, 200 miles from Pensacola. **Calendar:** Semester, extensive summer session. **Full-time faculty:** 184 total. **Part-time faculty:** 658 total. **Class size:** 20% < 20, 60% 20-39, 15% 40-49, 6% 50-99.

**Student profile.** Among degree-seeking undergraduates, 3,328 enrolled as first-time, first-year students.

| | | | |
|---|---|---|---|
| Part-time: | 44% | Hispanic American: | 7% |
| Women: | 55% | International: | 1% |
| African American: | 34% | 25 or older: | 25% |
| Asian American: | 2% | | |

**Transfer out. Colleges most students transferred to 2009:** Florida State University.

**Basis for selection.** Open admission, but selective for some programs. Special requirements for nursing, dental hygiene, emergency medical technology, radiologic technology and respiratory therapy programs. Each program requires specific course prerequisites or test scores or required GPA in addition to letters of recommendation. **Homeschooled:** Present affidavit verifying completion of high school requirements. **Learning Disabled:** If service or accommodations are needed, documentation required.

**2009-2010 Annual costs.** Tuition/fees: $2,220; $7,836 out-of-state. Books/supplies: $800. Personal expenses: $1,800.

**2008-2009 Financial aid. Need-based:** Need-based aid available for part-time students. **Non-need-based:** Scholarships awarded for academics, art, athletics, leadership, music/drama, state residency.

**Application procedures. Admission:** Closing date 8/1 (receipt date). No application fee. Admission notification on a rolling basis. Separate application procedure for health programs. **Financial aid:** Priority date 5/1; no closing date. FAFSA, institutional form required. Applicants notified on a rolling basis starting 5/15.

**Academics. Special study options:** Cooperative education, cross-registration, distance learning, double major, dual enrollment of high school students, ESL, honors, independent study, liberal arts/career combination, study abroad. Bachelor's degree programs available on campus. License preparation in dental hygiene, nursing, paramedic, real estate. **Credit/placement by examination:** AP, CLEP, IB, institutional tests. 45 credit hours maximum toward associate degree. **Support services:** GED preparation, learning center, pre-admission summer program, reduced course load, remedial instruction, study skills assistance, tutoring, writing center.

**Majors. Business:** General, accounting, administrative services, banking/financial services, business admin, management information systems, sales/distribution. **Computer sciences:** Computer graphics, networking, programming. **Construction:** Maintenance. **Education:** Early childhood, health. **Engineering:** General, civil, software. **Engineering technology:** Civil, construction, drafting, industrial management. **Health:** Dental hygiene, EMT paramedic, medical radiologic technology/radiation therapy, nursing (RN), respiratory therapy technology. **Legal studies:** Paralegal. **Liberal arts:** Arts/sciences. **Parks/recreation:** Facilities management. **Protective services:** Criminal justice, law enforcement admin. **Public administration:** General. **Social sciences:** General. **Visual/performing arts:** General, commercial/advertising art, film/cinema.

**Most popular majors.** Health sciences 6%, liberal arts 88%.

**Computing on campus.** 1,733 workstations in library, computer center, student center. Commuter students can connect to campus network. Online course registration, online library, helpline, wireless network available.

**Student life. Freshman orientation:** Mandatory. Preregistration for classes offered. All-day event held few days prior to start of term; includes small group meetings and advising. Online orientation also available. **Activities:** Bands, campus ministries, choral groups, dance, drama, international student organizations, literary magazine, music ensembles, musical theater, student government, student newspaper, TV station, Phi Theta Kappa, Black Student Union, Returning Adults Valuing Education, Future Educators of America, students interested in legal careers, College Democrats, BACCHUS, student environmental action coalition.

**Athletics.** NJCAA. **Intercollegiate:** Baseball M, basketball, softball W. **Intramural:** Basketball, golf, soccer, softball, table tennis, tennis. **Team name:** Eagles.

**Student services.** Adult student services, career counseling, services for economically disadvantaged, financial aid counseling, minority student services, on-campus daycare, personal counseling, placement for graduates, veterans' counselor. **Physically disabled:** Services for visually, speech, hearing impaired. **Transfer:** Transfer adviser, college fairs on campus for students transferring to 4-year colleges.

**Contact.** E-mail: enrollment@tcc.fl.edu
Phone: (850) 201-8555 Fax: (850) 201-8474
Sheri Rowland, Dean, Enrollment Services, Tallahassee Community College, 444 Appleyard Drive, Tallahassee, FL 32304

## Valencia Community College
**Orlando, Florida**
www.valenciacc.edu

**CB member**
**CB code: 5869**

- Public 2-year community college
- Commuter campus in very large city

**General.** Founded in 1967. Regionally accredited. **Enrollment:** 31,845 degree-seeking undergraduates; 7,163 non-degree-seeking students. **Degrees:** 5,146 associate awarded. **ROTC:** Army, Air Force. **Location:** 90 miles from Tampa, 145 miles from Jacksonville. **Calendar:** Semester, extensive summer session. **Full-time faculty:** 434 total; 23% have terminal degrees, 21% minority, 57% women. **Part-time faculty:** 1,058 total; 13% have terminal degrees, 26% minority, 51% women. **Class size:** 16% < 20, 83% 20-39, less than 1% 40-49, less than 1% 50-99, less than 1% >100.

**Student profile.** Among degree-seeking undergraduates, 21% enrolled in a transfer program, 79% enrolled in a vocational program, 7,272 enrolled as first-time, first-year students, 1,191 transferred in from other institutions.

| | | | |
|---|---|---|---|
| Part-time: | 49% | Asian American: | 5% |
| Out-of-state: | 3% | Hispanic American: | 28% |
| Women: | 56% | International: | 2% |
| African American: | 17% | 25 or older: | 27% |

**Transfer out.** 45% of students enrolled in the transfer program go on to 4-year colleges. **Colleges most students transferred to 2009:** University of Central Florida, University of Florida.

**Basis for selection.** Open admission, but selective for some programs. Special requirements for criminal justice, associate of arts, dance transfer plan, film production technology, and health science programs. **Home-schooled:** Homeschool diplomas accepted with official Homeschool Verification Affidavit.

**High school preparation.** College-preparatory program recommended. Recommended units include English 4, mathematics 3, social studies 3 and science 3.

**2009-2010 Annual costs.** Tuition/fees: $2,621; $9,926 out-of-state. Books/supplies: $1,109. Personal expenses: $7,983.

**2009-2010 Financial aid. Need-based:** Need-based aid available for part-time students. Work-study available nights and for part-time students.

**Application procedures. Admission:** Closing date 8/1 (postmark date). $35 fee. Admission notification on a rolling basis beginning on or about 3/31. **Financial aid:** Closing date 3/15. FAFSA required. Applicants notified on a rolling basis starting 4/2; must reply within 2 week(s) of notification.

**Academics. Special study options:** Combined bachelor's/graduate degree, cooperative education, distance learning, double major, dual enrollment of high school students, ESL, honors, independent study, internships, student-designed major, study abroad, weekend college. License preparation in dental hygiene, nursing, paramedic, physical therapy, radiology, real estate. **Credit/placement by examination:** CLEP, IB, institutional tests. 45 credit hours maximum toward associate degree. Less than 75 percent of a program's hours may be met with credit by examination and/or other acceleration mechanisms. **Support services:** Learning center, remedial instruction, study skills assistance, tutoring, writing center.

**Majors. Agriculture:** Horticultural science, landscaping. **Architecture:** Technology. **Business:** Accounting, accounting technology, business admin, entrepreneurial studies, hospitality admin, human resources, management information systems, marketing, real estate, restaurant/food services, small business admin. **Communications:** Digital media, public relations. **Computer sciences:** General, computer science, information technology, programming, systems analysis, webmaster. **Construction:** General. **Engineering:** General. **Engineering technology:** General, CAD/CADD, civil, drafting, electrical. **Family/consumer sciences:** Institutional food production. **Health:** Cardiovascular technology, dental hygiene, EMT paramedic, insurance coding, medical records admin, medical records technology, medical secretary, nursing (RN), radiologic technology/medical imaging, respiratory therapy assistant, respiratory therapy technology, sonography. **Legal studies:** Paralegal. **Liberal arts:** Arts/sciences. **Personal/culinary services:** Baking, culinary arts, restaurant/catering. **Protective services:** Fire safety technology, law enforcement admin, police science. **Visual/performing arts:** Dance, graphic design, theater design.

**Most popular majors.** Health sciences 10%, liberal arts 78%.

**Computing on campus.** 2,500 workstations in library, computer center, student center. Commuter students can connect to campus network. Online course registration, online library, helpline, wireless network available.

**Student life. Freshman orientation:** Mandatory. Preregistration for classes offered. 2-hour program. **Activities:** Bands, choral groups, dance, drama, international student organizations, literary magazine, music ensembles, musical theater, student government, student newspaper, symphony orchestra, African American cultural society, Brain Bowl, Latin American student organization, student nurses association, volunteer club, Phi Beta Lambda, Earth club, Muslim student organization, black high achievers club.

**Student services.** Career counseling, student employment services, financial aid counseling, health services, personal counseling, placement for graduates, veterans' counselor. **Physically disabled:** Services for visually, hearing impaired. **Transfer:** College fairs on campus for students transferring to 4-year colleges.

**Contact.** Phone: (407) 582-1507 Fax: (407) 582-1403
Renee Simpson, Director of Admissions and Records, Valencia Community College, PO Box 3028, Orlando, FL 32802-3028

Two-Year Colleges

## Virginia College at Pensacola
**Pensacola, Florida**
**www.vc.edu/pensacola**

▶ For-profit 2-year business and health science college
▶ Commuter campus in small city

**General.** Accredited by ACICS. **Calendar:** Quarter.

**Contact.** Phone: (850) 436-8444
Director of Admissions, 19 West Garden Street, Pensacola, FL 32502

# Georgia

## Abraham Baldwin Agricultural College
**Tifton, Georgia**     **CB member**
www.abac.edu     **CB code: 5001**

- Public 2-year agricultural and community college
- Commuter campus in large town

**General.** Founded in 1924. Regionally accredited. **Enrollment:** 3,298 degree-seeking undergraduates. **Degrees:** 4 bachelor's, 481 associate awarded. **Location:** 100 miles from Macon, 50 miles from Albany. **Calendar:** Semester. **Full-time faculty:** 98 total. **Part-time faculty:** 54 total. **Class size:** 25% < 20, 65% 20-39, 9% 40-49, less than 1% 50-99. **Special facilities:** 200-acre farm.

**Student profile.**

| | | | |
|---|---|---|---|
| Out-of-state: | 3% | Live on campus: | 32% |
| 25 or older: | 20% | | |

**Basis for selection.** 1.8 GPA, 330 SAT verbal and 310 SAT math or 12 ACT English and 14 ACT math necessary to obtain required Freshman Index of 1830. College-preparatory program not required for students pursuing AAS degree. Interview recommended for nursing majors.

**High school preparation.** College-preparatory program recommended. 16 units required. Required units include English 4, mathematics 4, social studies 3, science 3 (laboratory 2) and foreign language 2.

**2009-2010 Annual costs.** Tuition/fees: $3,196; $10,178 out-of-state. Room/board: $6,320. Books/supplies: $775. Personal expenses: $1,500.

**Application procedures. Admission:** Closing date 8/1. $20 fee, may be waived for applicants with need. Admission notification on a rolling basis. **Financial aid:** Priority date 5/1; no closing date. FAFSA, institutional form required. Applicants notified on a rolling basis starting 5/15; must reply within 2 week(s) of notification.

**Academics. Special study options:** Accelerated study, distance learning, double major, dual enrollment of high school students, external degree, honors, independent study, internships, study abroad. **Credit/placement by examination:** CLEP, institutional tests. **Support services:** Learning center, remedial instruction, tutoring, writing center.

**Majors. Agriculture:** Animal sciences, business, ornamental horticulture, plant sciences, poultry, turf management. **Biology:** General. **Business:** Accounting, business admin, fashion, hospitality admin, office technology, office/clerical. **Communications:** General, journalism, media studies. **Computer sciences:** General, applications programming, computer science, data processing, information technology, web page design. **Conservation:** Forest management, forest technology, forestry, wildlife. **Education:** General, early childhood. **Engineering:** General, agricultural. **Family/consumer sciences:** General, child care. **Foreign languages:** General. **Health:** Athletic training, dental hygiene, medical records technology, predental, premedicine, prepharmacy. **History:** General. **Legal studies:** Prelaw. **Liberal arts:** Arts/sciences. **Math:** General. **Parks/recreation:** Facilities management, health/fitness. **Physical sciences:** Chemistry, physics. **Protective services:** Police science. **Psychology:** General. **Public administration:** Human services. **Social sciences:** General, sociology. **Visual/performing arts:** General, studio arts.

**Most popular majors.** Agriculture 10%, health sciences 20%, liberal arts 59%.

**Computing on campus.** 100 workstations in library. Dormitories wired for high-speed internet access. Commuter students can connect to campus network. Online course registration, wireless network available.

**Student life. Freshman orientation:** Mandatory, $40 fee. **Housing:** Coed dorms, apartments available. $235 nonrefundable deposit. **Activities:** Bands, campus ministries, choral groups, drama, literary magazine, radio station, student government, student newspaper.

**Athletics.** NJCAA. **Intercollegiate:** Baseball M, golf M, rodeo, soccer W, softball W, tennis, volleyball W. **Intramural:** Badminton W, basketball, bowling, football (non-tackle) M, softball, tennis, volleyball.

**Student services.** Adult student services, career counseling, student employment services, health services, personal counseling, placement for graduates, veterans' counselor. **Transfer:** Transfer adviser, college fairs on campus for students transferring to 4-year colleges.

**Contact.** E-mail: admissions@abac.edu
Phone: (229) 391-5004 Toll-free number: (800) 733-3653
Fax: (229) 391-5002
Debra McCrary, Director of Admissions and Registrar, Abraham Baldwin Agricultural College, ABAC 4, 2802 Moore Highway, Tifton, GA 31793-2601

## Albany Technical College
**Albany, Georgia**
www.albanytech.edu     **CB code: 3921**

- Public 2-year technical college
- Commuter campus in small city

**General.** Regionally accredited. Hands-on environment. **Enrollment:** 3,671 degree-seeking undergraduates; 291 non-degree-seeking students. **Degrees:** 110 associate awarded. **Location:** 225 miles from Atlanta. **Calendar:** Quarter, extensive summer session. **Full-time faculty:** 91 total.

**Student profile.** Among degree-seeking undergraduates, 841 enrolled as first-time, first-year students.

| | | | |
|---|---|---|---|
| Part-time: | 32% | African American: | 73% |
| Women: | 58% | 25 or older: | 62% |

**Transfer out. Colleges most students transferred to 2009:** Albany State University.

**Basis for selection.** Open admission, but selective for some programs. Limited admission to health technology programs. ACT or SAT may be accepted in lieu of COMPASS or ASSET for placement.

**High school preparation.** College-preparatory program recommended. 22 units recommended. Recommended units include English 4, mathematics 3, social studies 3, science 3, foreign language 1 and academic electives 3. 4 tech prep, 1 health science recommended.

**2009-2010 Annual costs.** Tuition/fees: $2,043; $3,843 out-of-state. Per-credit charge: $40 in-state; $80 out-of-state. Books/supplies: $1,260.

**2009-2010 Financial aid. Need-based:** Need-based aid available for part-time students. Work-study available nights and for part-time students. **Non-need-based:** Scholarships awarded for academics, state residency.

**Application procedures. Admission:** No deadline. $15 fee, may be waived for applicants with need. Admission notification on a rolling basis beginning on or about 8/1. **Financial aid:** No deadline. FAFSA required. Applicants notified on a rolling basis starting 5/1.

**Academics. Special study options:** Distance learning, dual enrollment of high school students, weekend college. License preparation in nursing, paramedic, radiology. **Credit/placement by examination:** CLEP, institutional tests. **Support services:** GED preparation and test center, remedial instruction, tutoring.

**Majors. Business:** Sales/distribution. **Computer sciences:** Data processing, networking. **Conservation:** Forestry. **Construction:** Carpentry. **Education:** Early childhood. **Engineering technology:** Drafting. **Health:** Pharmacy assistant. **Mechanic/repair:** Electronics/electrical, industrial. **Personal/culinary services:** Chef training. **Protective services:** Criminal justice.

**Most popular majors.** Business/marketing 36%, computer/information sciences 16%, education 10%, health sciences 13%, security/protective services 17%, trade and industry 7%.

**Computing on campus.** Online library available.

**Student life. Freshman orientation:** Available. Preregistration for classes offered. Students contact advisor to register for classes. Advisor registers students via Internet. **Activities:** Choral groups, student government.

**Athletics. Intercollegiate:** Basketball M. **Team name:** Titans.

**Student services.** Adult student services, career counseling, services for economically disadvantaged, student employment services, financial aid counseling, on-campus daycare, personal counseling, placement for graduates, veterans' counselor. **Physically disabled:** Services for visually, speech, hearing impaired. **Transfer:** Pre-admission transcript evaluation for new students.

**Contact.** Phone: (229) 430-3520 Fax: (229) 430-6180
Director of Admissions, Albany Technical College, 1704 South Slappy
Boulevard, Albany, GA 31701-3514

## Altamaha Technical College
### Jesup, Georgia
### www.altamahatech.edu

- Public 2-year technical college
- Small town

**General.** Regionally accredited. **Enrollment:** 873 undergraduates. **Degrees:** 5 associate awarded. **Calendar:** Quarter. **Full-time faculty:** 44 total.
**Part-time faculty:** 32 total.

**Basis for selection.** Open admission.

**Academics. Credit/placement by examination:** CLEP.

**Majors. Business:** Accounting, business admin, marketing. **Computer sciences:** Computer support specialist, networking. **Education:** Early childhood. **Engineering technology:** Drafting. **Protective services:** Police science.

**Contact.** E-mail: atcadmissions@altamahatech.edu
Phone: (912) 427-1950
Altamaha Technical College, 1777 West Cherry Street, Jesup, GA 31545

## Andrew College
### Cuthbert, Georgia
### www.andrewcollege.edu          CB code: 5009

- Private 2-year junior and liberal arts college affiliated with United Methodist Church
- Residential campus in small town
- SAT or ACT (ACT writing recommended) required

**General.** Founded in 1854. Regionally accredited. **Enrollment:** 227 degree-seeking undergraduates. **Degrees:** 42 associate awarded. **Location:** 60 miles from Columbus, 40 miles from Albany. **Calendar:** Semester, limited summer session. **Full-time faculty:** 21 total. **Part-time faculty:** 5 total. **Class size:** 75% < 20, 25% 20-39.

**Student profile.**

| | | | |
|---|---|---|---|
| African American: | 46% | Hispanic American: | 5% |
| Asian American: | 1% | International: | 2% |

**Transfer out. Colleges most students transferred to 2009:** Georgia Southwestern State University, Valdosta State University, Georgia Southern University, Columbus State University, Troy State University.

**Basis for selection.** High school academic record, test scores, school and community activities important. Essay recommended. Interview required of the academically weak. Audition required of music majors. Portfolio recommended for art majors. **Homeschooled:** Transcript of courses and grades required.

**High school preparation.** 18 units recommended.

**2009-2010 Annual costs.** Tuition/fees: $11,416. Room/board: $7,170. Books/supplies: $600. Personal expenses: $1,200.

**Financial aid. Need-based:** Need-based aid available for part-time students. **Non-need-based:** Scholarships awarded for academics, art, athletics, leadership, music/drama, religious affiliation, state residency.

**Application procedures. Admission:** Priority date 6/1; deadline 8/1 (receipt date). $20 fee, may be waived for applicants with need. Admission notification on a rolling basis. **Financial aid:** Priority date 4/1, closing date 8/1. FAFSA, institutional form required. Applicants notified on a rolling basis starting 4/15.

**Academics. Special study options:** Double major, dual enrollment of high school students, ESL, honors. **Credit/placement by examination:** AP, CLEP, SAT, ACT, institutional tests. 24 credit hours maximum toward associate degree. **Support services:** Learning center, pre-admission summer program, remedial instruction, study skills assistance, tutoring.

**Majors. Agriculture:** General. **Business:** General. **Communications:** General, journalism. **Computer sciences:** Computer science. **Conservation:** Forestry. **Education:** General. **Engineering:** General. **Health:** Athletic training, predental, premedicine, prenursing, prepharmacy, preveterinary. **History:**

**General. Legal studies:** Prelaw. **Liberal arts:** Arts/sciences. **Math:** General. **Parks/recreation:** Health/fitness. **Physical sciences:** General. **Psychology:** General. **Social sciences:** General, sociology. **Visual/performing arts:** General, dramatic.

**Computing on campus.** 100 workstations in dormitories, library, computer center, student center. Dormitories wired for high-speed internet access and linked to campus network. Commuter students can connect to campus network. Online library, repair service, wireless network available.

**Student life. Freshman orientation:** Mandatory. Preregistration for classes offered. Held selected weekends during summer and beginning of fall term for 3-4 days. **Policies:** No alcohol/illegal drugs allowed on campus. **Housing:** Guaranteed on-campus for all undergraduates. Coed dorms, single-sex dorms available. **Activities:** Choral groups, drama, international student organizations, literary magazine, music ensembles, musical theater, student government, student newspaper, Baptist Student Union, Wesley Fellowship, Unity, community service group, interdenominational Christian group.

**Athletics.** NJCAA. **Intercollegiate:** Baseball M, basketball W, cross-country, golf, soccer, softball W. **Intramural:** Archery, badminton, basketball, cheerleading W, cross-country, football (non-tackle) M, golf, racquetball, soccer, softball, swimming, table tennis, tennis, volleyball, weight lifting. **Team name:** Tigers.

**Student services.** Alcohol/substance abuse counseling, chaplain/spiritual director, career counseling, services for economically disadvantaged, financial aid counseling, health services, veterans' counselor. **Transfer:** Transfer adviser, college fairs on campus for students transferring to 4-year colleges.

**Contact.** E-mail: admissions@andrewcollege.edu
Phone: (800) 664-9250 Toll-free number: (800) 664-9250
Fax: (229) 732-2176
Jason Goodner, Director of Admissions and Financial Aid, Andrew College, 501 College Street, Cuthbert, GA 39840-1395

## Ashworth College
### Norcross, Georgia
### www.ashworthcollege.edu          CB code: 3912

- For-profit 2-year community and career college
- Very large city

**General.** Accredited by DETC. **Enrollment:** 3,000 degree-seeking undergraduates. **Degrees:** 5 bachelor's, 425 associate awarded; master's offered. **Location:** 18 miles from Atlanta. **Calendar:** Continuous, extensive summer session. **Full-time faculty:** 20 total. **Part-time faculty:** 70 total.

**Transfer out. Colleges most students transferred to 2009:** Ashford University, Phoenix University.

**Basis for selection.** Open admission. **Homeschooled:** Statement describing homeschool structure and mission, transcript of courses and grades required.

**2009-2010 Annual costs.** All inclusive undergraduate program is $1200 per semester (5 courses). Students enrolling in a full program will complete 4 semesters.

**Application procedures. Admission:** No application fee.

**Academics. Special study options:** Distance learning. Bachelor's degree programs available on campus. **Credit/placement by examination:** CLEP. 15 credit hours maximum toward associate degree, 30 toward bachelor's. **Support services:** Study skills assistance, tutoring.

**Majors. Business:** Accounting, business admin, finance, human resources, marketing. **Construction:** Site management. **Education:** Early childhood. **Health:** Health care admin. **Legal studies:** Paralegal. **Protective services:** Criminal justice, security management. **Psychology:** General.

**Student services. Transfer:** Transfer adviser for students transferring to 4-year colleges.

**Contact.** E-mail: info@ashworthcollege.edu
Phone: (770) 729-8400 Toll-free number: (800) 223-4542
Fax: (770) 729-9389
Eric Ryall, Registrar, Ashworth College, 430 Technology Parkway, Norcross, GA 30092-3406

## Athens Technical College
Athens, Georgia
www.athenstech.edu                    CB code: 0462

◆ Public 2-year technical college
◆ Commuter campus in small city

**General.** Founded in 1959. Regionally accredited. **Enrollment:** 4,555 degree-seeking undergraduates; 612 non-degree-seeking students. **Degrees:** 262 associate awarded. **Location:** 65 miles from Atlanta. **Calendar:** Quarter, extensive summer session. **Full-time faculty:** 81 total. **Part-time faculty:** 208 total. **Class size:** 61% < 20, 36% 20-39, 1% 40-49, 2% 50-99.

**Student profile.** Among degree-seeking undergraduates, 793 enrolled as first-time, first-year students.

| | | | |
|---|---|---|---|
| Part-time: | 58% | Asian American: | 6% |
| Women: | 65% | Hispanic American: | 3% |
| African American: | 23% | 25 or older: | 49% |

**Transfer out. Colleges most students transferred to 2009:** University of Georgia.

**Basis for selection.** Open admission, but selective for some programs. Special requirements for radiology, respiratory therapy, nursing, physical therapy assistant, dental hygiene, surgical technology, veterinary technology dental assisting, medical assisting, practical nursing and diagnostic medical sonography. School record, recommendations, standardized test scores, essay, and interview required or recommended depending on program. ACT or SAT may be accepted in lieu of COMPASS or ASSET for placement. Interview required of radiology, respiratory therapy, nursing, physical therapy assistant, dental assisting, and dental hygiene majors. **Homeschooled:** Must provide documentation of designated home study program activities.

**High school preparation.** College-preparatory program recommended. 22 units recommended. Recommended units include English 4, mathematics 3, social studies 3, science 3, foreign language 1 and academic electives 3. 4 tech prep and 1 health science recommended.

**2009-2010 Annual costs.** Tuition/fees: $2,043; $3,843 out-of-state. Per-credit charge: $40 in-state; $80 out-of-state. Books/supplies: $800. Personal expenses: $1,000.

**2008-2009 Financial aid. Need-based:** Need-based aid available for part-time students. Work-study available for part-time students. **Non-need-based:** Scholarships awarded for academics, leadership.

**Application procedures. Admission:** Priority date 8/1; no deadline. $20 fee. Admission notification on a rolling basis. 2/1 deadline for nursing and dental hygiene; 3/1 deadline for dental assistance; 4/1 deadline for radiography, surgical technology, diagnostic medical sonography, nursing accelerated, and veterinary technology; 5/1 deadline for physical therapist assistant, practical nursing; 7/1 deadline for respiratory therapy; 8/1 deadline for medical assistance. **Financial aid:** No deadline. FAFSA required. Applicants notified on a rolling basis starting 6/15; must reply within 2 week(s) of notification.

**Academics. Special study options:** Distance learning, dual enrollment of high school students, weekend college. License preparation in real estate. **Credit/placement by examination:** CLEP, institutional tests. **Support services:** GED preparation and test center, learning center, reduced course load, remedial instruction, study skills assistance, tutoring.

**Majors. Biology:** Biotechnology. **Business:** Accounting technology, administrative services, sales/distribution, travel services. **Computer sciences:** Applications programming, data processing, networking, programming. **Education:** Early childhood. **Health:** Dental assistant, dental hygiene, nursing (RN), physical therapy assistant, radiologic technology/medical imaging, respiratory therapy technology, sonography, veterinary technology/assistant. **Legal studies:** Paralegal. **Protective services:** Law enforcement admin. **Public administration:** Social work. **Science technology:** Biological. **Visual/performing arts:** Interior design.

**Most popular majors.** Business/marketing 23%, computer/information sciences 9%, education 8%, health sciences 44%, legal studies 6%.

**Computing on campus.** 346 workstations in computer center. Commuter students can connect to campus network. Online course registration, online library, wireless network available.

**Student life. Freshman orientation:** Mandatory. Preregistration for classes offered. **Activities:** Student government.

**Student services.** Adult student services, career counseling, student employment services, financial aid counseling, personal counseling, placement for graduates, veterans' counselor. **Physically disabled:** Services for visually, speech, hearing impaired. **Transfer:** Transfer adviser for students transferring to 4-year colleges.

**Contact.** E-mail: admissions@athenstech.edu
Phone: (706) 355-5004 Fax: (706) 369-5756
Lenzy Reid, Director of Admissions, Athens Technical College, 800 US Highway 29 North, Athens, GA 30601-1500

## Atlanta Metropolitan College
Atlanta, Georgia                       CB member
www.atlm.edu                           CB code: 5725

◆ Public 2-year junior college
◆ Commuter campus in very large city

**General.** Founded in 1974. Regionally accredited. **Enrollment:** 2,663 degree-seeking undergraduates; 102 non-degree-seeking students. **Degrees:** 259 associate awarded. **Location:** 4 miles from downtown. **Calendar:** Semester, extensive summer session. **Full-time faculty:** 48 total; 42% have terminal degrees, 90% minority, 56% women. **Part-time faculty:** 105 total; 95% minority, 53% women.

**Student profile.** Among degree-seeking undergraduates, 13% enrolled in a transfer program, 615 enrolled as first-time, first-year students.

| | | | |
|---|---|---|---|
| Part-time: | 39% | Women: | 65% |
| Out-of-state: | 6% | 25 or older: | 26% |

**Transfer out.** 56% of students enrolled in the transfer program go on to 4-year colleges.

**Basis for selection.** Applicants who have followed college preparatory curriculum must have 2.0 GPA. Applicants who have followed technology/career curriculum must have 2.2 GPA. All applicants must meet immunization requirements. Applicants with 430 SAT verbal or 17 ACT English and completion of college preparatory curriculum in English exempt from taking COMPASS Placement Test in English and Reading. Applicants with 400 SAT math or 17 ACT math and completion of college preparatory curriculum in math exempt from taking COMPASS Placement Test in math. **Homeschooled:** Transcript of courses and grades required.

**High school preparation.** 16 units required. Required units include English 4, mathematics 4, social studies 1, history 2, science 3 (laboratory 2) and foreign language 2.

**2009-2010 Annual costs.** Tuition/fees: $2,728; $9,606 out-of-state. Per-credit charge: $77 in-state; $306 out-of-state. Books/supplies: $1,300.

**2008-2009 Financial aid.** All financial aid based on need. Need-based aid available for part-time students. Work-study available nights, weekends and for part-time students.

**Application procedures. Admission:** Priority date 7/15; no deadline. $20 fee. Admission notification on a rolling basis. **Financial aid:** Closing date 6/1. FAFSA required. Applicants notified on a rolling basis; must reply by 6/30.

**Academics.** Academic and technological workshops provided. Tutorial services available in math, physics, chemistry, English, reading, accounting, and general science. **Special study options:** Combined bachelor's/graduate degree, distance learning, dual enrollment of high school students, ESL, external degree, honors, independent study, study abroad, weekend college. **Credit/placement by examination:** AP, CLEP. **Support services:** Learning center, remedial instruction, study skills assistance, tutoring, writing center.

**Majors. Area/ethnic studies:** African-American. **Biology:** General. **Business:** Business admin, office management. **Communications:** General. **Computer sciences:** General, computer science. **Education:** Multi-level teacher. **Engineering technology:** General. **Foreign languages:** General. **Health:** Medical records admin. **History:** General. **Math:** General. **Parks/recreation:** Health/fitness. **Physical sciences:** Chemistry, physics. **Protective services:** Law enforcement admin. **Psychology:** General. **Public administration:** Social work. **Social sciences:** Political science. **Visual/performing arts:** Art.

**Most popular majors.** Liberal arts 94%.

**Computing on campus.** 580 workstations in library, computer center, student center. Commuter students can connect to campus network. Online course registration, online library, helpline, repair service, wireless network available.

**Student life. Freshman orientation:** Mandatory. Preregistration for classes offered. 1 daytime and 1 evening session held each semester. **Housing:**

Off-campus housing available for college athletes only. **Activities:** Choral groups, dance, drama, international student organizations, student government, student newspaper.

**Athletics.** NJCAA. **Intercollegiate:** Basketball. **Team name:** Red-Eyed Panthers.

**Student services.** Adult student services, career counseling, services for economically disadvantaged, financial aid counseling, minority student services, personal counseling, veterans' counselor. **Physically disabled:** Services for visually, speech, hearing impaired. **Learning disabled:** Comprehensive services available. **Transfer:** Pre-admission transcript evaluation for new students. College fairs on campus for students transferring to 4-year colleges.

**Contact.** E-mail: areid@atlm.edu
Phone: (404) 756-4004 Fax: (404) 756-4407
Audrey Reid, Director of Admissions, Atlanta Metropolitan College, 1630 Metropolitan Parkway, SW, Atlanta, GA 30310-4498

## Atlanta Technical College
### Atlanta, Georgia
www.atlantatech.edu          CB code: 5030

- Public 2-year community and technical college
- Commuter campus in very large city

**General.** Regionally accredited. **Enrollment:** 3,671 degree-seeking undergraduates; 291 non-degree-seeking students. **Degrees:** 110 associate awarded. **Location:** 2 miles from downtown. **Calendar:** Quarter. **Full-time faculty:** 86 total. **Part-time faculty:** 102 total.

**Student profile.** Among degree-seeking undergraduates, 841 enrolled as first-time, first-year students.

| | | | |
|---|---|---|---|
| Part-time: | 32% | African American: | 73% |
| Women: | 58% | 25 or older: | 63% |

**Basis for selection.** Open admission, but selective for some programs. Requirements vary by program for selective admission majors. ACT or SAT may be accepted in lieu of COMPASS or ASSET for placement. **Home-schooled:** Letter from superintendent's office confirming compliance with Georgia/DTAE policies and attendance and final exit exam scores from accredited national testing program required.

**High school preparation.** College-preparatory program recommended. 22 units recommended. Recommended units include English 4, mathematics 3, social studies 3, science 3, foreign language 1 and academic electives 3. 4 tech prep and 1 health science recommended.

**2009-2010 Annual costs.** Tuition/fees: $2,046; $3,846 out-of-state. Per-credit charge: $40 in-state; $80 out-of-state. Books/supplies: $1,200. Personal expenses: $900.

**2009-2010 Financial aid. Need-based:** Need-based aid available for part-time students. Work-study available nights and for part-time students.

**Application procedures. Admission:** Priority date 9/8; deadline 9/22 (receipt date). $20 fee. Admission notification on a rolling basis. **Financial aid:** Priority date 3/1; no closing date. Applicants notified on a rolling basis starting 4/15.

**Academics. Special study options:** Distance learning, dual enrollment of high school students, study abroad, weekend college. License preparation in aviation, nursing, paramedic, real estate. **Credit/placement by examination:** CLEP, IB, institutional tests. **Support services:** GED test center, learning center, tutoring.

**Majors. Computer sciences:** General. **Legal studies:** Paralegal. **Visual/performing arts:** Music.

**Most popular majors.** Business/marketing 27%, computer/information sciences 15%, education 39%, health sciences 6%, legal studies 13%.

**Computing on campus.** 55 workstations in library, computer center. Online library, wireless network available.

**Student life. Freshman orientation:** Mandatory. Preregistration for classes offered.

**Student services.** On-campus daycare.

**Contact.** E-mail: vbillups@atlantatech.edu
Phone: (404) 225-4455 Fax: (404) 225-4721
Vory Billups, Director of Admissions, Atlanta Technical College, 1560 Metropolitan Parkway, SW, Atlanta, GA 30310-4446

## Augusta Technical College
### Augusta, Georgia
www.augustatech.edu          CB code: 2620

- Public 2-year technical college
- Commuter campus in large city

**General.** Founded in 1961. Regionally accredited. Additional campuses in Thomson and Waynesboro. **Enrollment:** 4,501 degree-seeking undergraduates; 527 non-degree-seeking students. **Degrees:** 309 associate awarded. **Location:** 145 miles from Atlanta, 75 miles from Columbia, South Carolina. **Calendar:** Quarter, extensive summer session. **Full-time faculty:** 136 total. **Part-time faculty:** 240 total.

**Student profile.** Among degree-seeking undergraduates, 802 enrolled as first-time, first-year students.

| | | | |
|---|---|---|---|
| Part-time: | 48% | Asian American: | 2% |
| Women: | 61% | Hispanic American: | 2% |
| African American: | 52% | 25 or older: | 56% |

**Basis for selection.** Open admission, but selective for some programs. Competitive admission to cardiovascular technology, respiratory therapy care, occupational therapy assistant, radiologic technology, and practical nursing. These programs use combination of factors including all or some of the following: required college courses, placement exam scores, interviews, essays, and GPA. ACT or SAT may be accepted in lieu of COMPASS or ASSET for placement.

**High school preparation.** College-preparatory program recommended. 22 units recommended. Recommended units include English 4, mathematics 3, social studies 3, science 3, foreign language 1 and academic electives 3. Highly recommended that math units include algebra and trigonometry. 4 tech prep and 1 health science recommended.

**2009-2010 Annual costs.** Tuition/fees: $2,055; $3,855 out-of-state. Per-credit charge: $40 in-state; $80 out-of-state. Books/supplies: $450.

**Financial aid. Non-need-based:** Scholarships awarded for state residency.

**Application procedures. Admission:** No deadline. $20 fee, may be waived for applicants with need. Application deadlines exist for competitive healthcare programs and vary by major. **Financial aid:** No deadline. FAFSA, institutional form required. Must reply within 2 week(s) of notification.

**Academics. Special study options:** Distance learning, dual enrollment of high school students, study abroad, weekend college. **Credit/placement by examination:** CLEP, institutional tests. **Support services:** GED preparation and test center, learning center, reduced course load, remedial instruction, tutoring.

**Majors. Business:** Accounting, administrative services, sales/distribution. **Computer sciences:** Applications programming. **Engineering technology:** Electrical. **Health:** Cardiovascular technology, clinical lab technology, EMT paramedic, pharmacy assistant, respiratory therapy technology.

**Most popular majors.** Business/marketing 32%, computer/information sciences 17%, education 6%, health sciences 20%, security/protective services 10%, trade and industry 6%.

**Computing on campus.** Commuter students can connect to campus network. Online course registration, online library available.

**Student life. Freshman orientation:** Available. Preregistration for classes offered. **Activities:** Student government.

**Student services.** Career counseling, student employment services, financial aid counseling, on-campus daycare, placement for graduates, veterans' counselor. **Physically disabled:** Services for visually, speech, hearing impaired. **Transfer:** Pre-admission transcript evaluation for new students.

**Contact.** E-mail: bcrobert@augustatech.edu
Phone: (706) 771-4150 Fax: (706) 771-4034
Brian Roberts, Director of Admissions, Augusta Technical College, 3200 Augusta Tech Drive, Augusta, GA 30906

## Bainbridge College
### Bainbridge, Georgia
www.bainbridge.edu          CB code: 5062

- Public 2-year community and technical college
- Commuter campus in large town

**General.** Founded in 1973. Regionally accredited. **Enrollment:** 3,557 degree-seeking undergraduates. **Degrees:** 173 associate awarded. **Location:** 43 miles from Tallahassee, FL. **Calendar:** Semester, limited summer session. **Full-time faculty:** 73 total; 22% have terminal degrees, 11% minority, 58% women. **Part-time faculty:** 126 total; 11% have terminal degrees, 14% minority, 57% women. **Class size:** 60% < 20, 39% 20-39, less than 1% 50-99. **Special facilities:** Nature trail.

**Student profile.** Among degree-seeking undergraduates, 43% enrolled in a transfer program, 57% enrolled in a vocational program, 1% already have a bachelor's degree or higher, 944 enrolled as first-time, first-year students.

| | | | |
|---|---|---|---|
| Part-time: | 51% | Women: | 70% |
| Out-of-state: | 1% | 25 or older: | 38% |

**Transfer out.** 88% of students enrolled in the transfer program go on to 4-year colleges. **Colleges most students transferred to 2009:** Valdosta State University, Albany State University, Georgia Southwestern University.

**Basis for selection.** 330 SAT verbal/13 ACT English, 310 SAT math/14 ACT math, or 1.8 GPA required. College preparatory curriculum required for associate of arts degree-seeking students. Limited number admitted who do not meet admission standards. **Adult students:** Compass test required. **Homeschooled:** Acceptable scores on COMPASS required.

**High school preparation.** College-preparatory program recommended. 16 units required. Required units include English 4, mathematics 4, social studies 3, science 3 and foreign language 2. Tech Prep students exempt from foreign language requirement.

**2009-2010 Annual costs.** Tuition/fees: $2,886; $9,764 out-of-state. Per-credit charge: $77 in-state; $308 out-of-state. Books/supplies: $600. Personal expenses: $450.

**2008-2009 Financial aid.** All financial aid based on need. Need-based aid available for part-time students. **Additional information:** 30-day loans available for tuition and fees.

**Application procedures. Admission:** Closing date 8/10 (receipt date). No application fee. Admission notification on a rolling basis. **Financial aid:** Priority date 6/1, closing date 8/1. FAFSA, institutional form required. Applicants notified on a rolling basis starting 6/1; must reply within 2 week(s) of notification.

**Academics. Special study options:** Distance learning, double major, dual enrollment of high school students, honors, independent study, internships, study abroad, weekend college. 2-year registered nursing program. Bachelor's degree programs available on campus. License preparation in nursing, real estate. **Credit/placement by examination:** AP, CLEP, institutional tests. 18 credit hours maximum toward associate degree. **Support services:** GED preparation, learning center, reduced course load, remedial instruction, study skills assistance, tutoring.

**Majors. Business:** General, accounting, administrative services, management information systems, marketing. **Communications:** General. **Computer sciences:** General. **Construction:** Electrician. **Education:** General, early childhood, health, middle, physical, secondary. **Engineering technology:** Drafting, electrical. **Foreign languages:** General. **Health:** Nursing (RN). **History:** General. **Math:** General. **Mechanic/repair:** Industrial. **Protective services:** Law enforcement admin, police science. **Psychology:** General. **Social sciences:** Political science.

**Most popular majors.** Business/marketing 29%, liberal arts 61%.

**Computing on campus.** 295 workstations in library, computer center, student center. Online course registration, online library, wireless network available.

**Student life. Freshman orientation:** Mandatory. Preregistration for classes offered. Held prior to the semester; on-line orientation. **Activities:** Concert band, choral groups, drama, music ensembles, student government, student newspaper, Delta club, service organizations, Phi Theta Kappa, Sigma Kappa Delta.

**Athletics. Intramural:** Basketball M, football (non-tackle), softball, table tennis, tennis, volleyball. **Team name:** Panthers.

**Student services.** Adult student services, career counseling, services for economically disadvantaged, student employment services, financial aid counseling, minority student services, personal counseling, placement for graduates, veterans' counselor. **Physically disabled:** Services for visually, speech, hearing impaired. **Transfer:** Transfer adviser, college fairs on campus for students transferring to 4-year colleges.

**Contact.** E-mail: csnyder@bainbridge.edu
Phone: (229) 248-2504 Fax: (229) 248-2623
Connie Snyder, Director of Admissions and Records, Bainbridge College, 2500 East Shotwell Street, Bainbridge, GA 39818-0990

## Brown Mackie College: Atlanta
### Atlanta, Georgia

◗ For-profit 2-year business, health science and technical college
◗ Very large city

**General.** Accredited by ACICS. **Enrollment:** 650 degree-seeking undergraduates. **Degrees:** 86 associate awarded. **Calendar:** Quarter. **Full-time faculty:** 7 total. **Part-time faculty:** 7 total.

**Basis for selection.** Open admission.

**2009-2010 Annual costs.** Tuition, which varies according to area of study, is $314 per credit hour for most programs. Surgical Technology program tuition is $310 per credit hour.

**Academics. Credit/placement by examination:** CLEP.

**Majors. Business:** Accounting, business admin. **Health:** Medical assistant, occupational therapy assistant, surgical technology. **Legal studies:** Paralegal.

**Contact.** E-mail: jthee@brownmackie.edu
Phone: (770) 638-0121 Toll-free number: (888) 301-3670
Jonelle Thee, Enrollment Manager, Brown Mackie College: Atlanta, 6600 Peachtree Dunwoody NE, Atlanta, GA 30328

## Central Georgia Technical College
### Macon, Georgia
### www.cgtcollege.edu
**CB code: 1709**

◗ Public 2-year community and technical college
◗ Commuter campus in small city

**General.** Regionally accredited. **Enrollment:** 6,687 degree-seeking undergraduates; 263 non-degree-seeking students. **Degrees:** 231 associate awarded. **Location:** 80 miles from Atlanta. **Calendar:** Quarter, extensive summer session. **Full-time faculty:** 109 total. **Part-time faculty:** 375 total. **Class size:** 87% < 20, 13% 20-39, less than 1% 40-49. **Partnerships:** Formal partnerships with Cisco and local industries.

**Student profile.** Among degree-seeking undergraduates, 1,402 enrolled as first-time, first-year students.

| | | | |
|---|---|---|---|
| Part-time: | 42% | Asian American: | 1% |
| Women: | 67% | 25 or older: | 60% |
| African American: | 61% | | |

**Basis for selection.** Open admission, but selective for some programs. Requirements vary according to program of study. ACT or SAT may be accepted in lieu of COMPASS or ASSET for placement.

**High school preparation.** College-preparatory program recommended. 22 units recommended. Recommended units include English 4, mathematics 3, social studies 3, science 3, foreign language 1 and academic electives 3. 4 tech prep and 1 health science recommended.

**2009-2010 Annual costs.** Tuition/fees: $2,043; $3,843 out-of-state. Per-credit charge: $40 in-state; $80 out-of-state. Books/supplies: $750.

**2008-2009 Financial aid. Need-based:** Need-based aid available for part-time students.

**Application procedures. Admission:** $15 fee, may be waived for applicants with need. Admission notification on a rolling basis. Application closing date is one month prior to first day of attendance. **Financial aid:** Closing date 7/14. FAFSA, institutional form required.

**Academics. Special study options:** Distance learning, dual enrollment of high school students, weekend college. License preparation in dental hygiene, nursing, paramedic, radiology, real estate. **Credit/placement by examination:** CLEP, institutional tests. Dependent on approval by department/program. **Support services:** GED preparation and test center, reduced course load, remedial instruction, study skills assistance, tutoring, writing center.

**Majors. Business:** Accounting technology, administrative services, logistics, operations. **Computer sciences:** Data processing, networking, web page design. **Education:** Early childhood. **Engineering technology:** Drafting. **Health:** Clinical lab technology, dental hygiene, medical assistant. **Protective services:** Criminal justice.

**Most popular majors.** Business/marketing 28%, computer/information sciences 10%, education 8%, health sciences 33%, security/protective services 8%, trade and industry 7%.

**Computing on campus.** 400 workstations in library, computer center. Commuter students can connect to campus network. Online course registration, online library, helpline, repair service, wireless network available.

**Student life. Freshman orientation:** Mandatory. Preregistration for classes offered. Held prior to each quarterly registration period. **Activities:** Student government.

**Student services.** Adult student services, career counseling, services for economically disadvantaged, financial aid counseling, on-campus daycare, placement for graduates, veterans' counselor. **Physically disabled:** Services for visually, speech, hearing impaired. **Transfer:** College fairs on campus for students transferring to 4-year colleges.

**Contact.** E-mail: tcarter@centralgatech.edu
Phone: (478) 757-3408 Fax: (478) 757-3454
Tammy Carter, Director of Admissions, Central Georgia Technical College, 3300 Macon Tech Drive, Macon, GA 31206

## Chattahoochee Technical College
**Marietta, Georgia**
**www.chattahoocheetech.edu**                 **CB code: 5441**

◆   Public 2-year technical college
◆   Commuter campus in large city

**General.** Founded in 1961. Regionally accredited. **Enrollment:** 10,534 degree-seeking undergraduates; 857 non-degree-seeking students. **Degrees:** 476 associate awarded. **Location:** 20 miles from Atlanta. **Calendar:** Quarter, extensive summer session. **Full-time faculty:** 61 total. **Part-time faculty:** 201 total.

**Student profile.** Among degree-seeking undergraduates, 7,801 enrolled as first-time, first-year students.

| | | | |
|---|---|---|---|
| Part-time: | 52% | Hispanic American: | 3% |
| Women: | 60% | International: | 1% |
| African American: | 31% | 25 or older: | 50% |
| Asian American: | 2% | | |

**Basis for selection.** Open admission, but selective for some programs. Special requirements for allied health programs. ACT or SAT may be accepted in lieu of COMPASS or ASSET for placement.

**High school preparation.** College-preparatory program recommended. 22 units recommended. Recommended units include English 4, mathematics 3, social studies 3, science 3, foreign language 1 and academic electives 3. 4 tech prep and 1 health science recommended.

**2009-2010 Annual costs.** Tuition/fees: $2,064; $3,864 out-of-state. Per-credit charge: $40 in-state; $80 out-of-state. Books/supplies: $1,020. Personal expenses: $1,300.

**2008-2009 Financial aid. Need-based:** Need-based aid available for part-time students. Work-study available nights, weekends and for part-time students. **Non-need-based:** Scholarships awarded for state residency.

**Application procedures. Admission:** Closing date 9/8. $15 fee. Admission notification on a rolling basis. **Financial aid:** Priority date 7/15; no closing date. FAFSA, institutional form required. Applicants notified on a rolling basis starting 6/15.

**Academics. Special study options:** Distance learning, dual enrollment of high school students, weekend college. License preparation in nursing. **Credit/placement by examination:** CLEP, institutional tests. 15 credit hours maximum toward associate degree. **Support services:** Learning center, reduced course load, remedial instruction, study skills assistance, tutoring.

**Majors. Business:** General, accounting, administrative services, marketing, office management. **Computer sciences:** General, applications programming. **Engineering technology:** Electrical. **Family/consumer sciences:** Child care. **Mechanic/repair:** Automotive. **Personal/culinary services:** Culinary arts. **Protective services:** Criminal justice.

**Most popular majors.** Business/marketing 36%, communication technologies 7%, computer/information sciences 13%, education 9%, engineering/engineering technologies 10%, health sciences 6%, security/protective services 10%.

**Computing on campus.** 857 workstations in library, computer center, student center. Commuter students can connect to campus network. Online course registration, repair service available.

**Student life. Activities:** Student government.

**Student services.** Career counseling, student employment services, personal counseling, placement for graduates, veterans' counselor. **Physically disabled:** Services for visually, hearing impaired. **Transfer:** Pre-admission transcript evaluation for new students. College fairs on campus for students transferring to 4-year colleges.

**Contact.** Phone: (770) 528-4565 Fax: (770) 528-4581
John Parton, Director of Admissions, Chattahoochee Technical College, 980 South Cobb Drive, SE, Marietta, GA 30060-3300

## College of Coastal Georgia
**Brunswick, Georgia**                          **CB member**
**www.ccga.edu**                               **CB code: 5078**

◆   Public 2-year liberal arts college
◆   Commuter campus in large town

**General.** Founded in 1961. Regionally accredited. Students may take courses at Camden Center in Kingsland. **Enrollment:** 2,971 degree-seeking undergraduates; 109 non-degree-seeking students. **Degrees:** 295 associate awarded. **Location:** 70 miles from Savannah; 60 miles from Jacksonville, FL. **Calendar:** Semester, limited summer session. **Full-time faculty:** 71 total; 39% have terminal degrees, 10% minority, 54% women. **Part-time faculty:** 42 total; 21% have terminal degrees, 12% minority, 45% women. **Class size:** 21% < 20, 66% 20-39, 8% 40-49, 4% 50-99.

**Student profile.** Among degree-seeking undergraduates, 75% enrolled in a transfer program, 25% enrolled in a vocational program, 1% already have a bachelor's degree or higher, 915 enrolled as first-time, first-year students, 65 transferred in from other institutions.

| | | | |
|---|---|---|---|
| Part-time: | 51% | Women: | 69% |
| Out-of-state: | 4% | 25 or older: | 38% |

**Transfer out. Colleges most students transferred to 2009:** Armstrong Atlantic State University, Georgia Southern University.

**Basis for selection.** Open admission, but selective for some programs. Additional requirements for career associate health science programs and all bachelors programs. Tests are not required, but will be used to exempt students from placement testing. **Homeschooled:** Statement describing homeschool structure and mission, transcript of courses and grades, letter of recommendation (nonparent) required. Must take SAT or ACT and score at the average of last year's freshman class. **Learning Disabled:** Students must go through an accreditation process with system agency on learning disabilities to receive accommodations.

**High school preparation.** College-preparatory program required. 16 units recommended. Recommended units include English 4, mathematics 4, social studies 3, science 2 (laboratory 1) and foreign language 2.

**2009-2010 Annual costs.** Tuition/fees: $2,860; $10,342 out-of-state. Costs may vary among students. Books/supplies: $1,000. Personal expenses: $1,000.

**2008-2009 Financial aid. Need-based:** Need-based aid available for part-time students. Work-study available nights, weekends and for part-time students. **Non-need-based:** Scholarships awarded for academics, athletics, leadership, state residency.

**Application procedures. Admission:** Closing date 7/15 (postmark date). $20 fee, may be waived for applicants with need. Admission notification on a rolling basis. **Financial aid:** Priority date 5/1; no closing date. FAFSA required. Applicants notified on a rolling basis starting 7/1.

**Academics. Special study options:** Accelerated study, cooperative education, distance learning, dual enrollment of high school students, independent study, internships, liberal arts/career combination, study abroad, teacher certification program. Bachelor's degree programs available on campus. License preparation in real estate. **Credit/placement by examination:** AP, CLEP, IB, institutional tests. 24 credit hours maximum toward associate degree, 24 toward bachelor's. **Support services:** Learning center, reduced course load, remedial instruction, study skills assistance, tutoring.

**Majors. Agriculture:** Agribusiness operations. **Biology:** General. **Business:** Business admin. **Communications:** General. **Computer sciences:** Computer science. **Education:** General, elementary, middle, secondary, special. **Engineering:** General. **Foreign languages:** General. **Health:** Clinical lab technology, medical radiologic technology/radiation therapy, nursing (RN). **History:** General. **Legal studies:** Prelaw. **Liberal arts:** Arts/sciences. **Math:**

General. **Parks/recreation:** General. **Personal/culinary services:** Restaurant/catering. **Physical sciences:** Chemistry, physics. **Protective services:** Law enforcement admin. **Psychology:** General. **Social sciences:** Sociology. **Visual/performing arts:** Art.

**Most popular majors.** Health sciences 31%, liberal arts 60%.

**Computing on campus.** 350 workstations in library, computer center, student center. Commuter students can connect to campus network. Online course registration, online library, helpline, repair service, wireless network available.

**Student life. Freshman orientation:** Mandatory. Preregistration for classes offered. **Activities:** Campus ministries, choral groups, drama, international student organizations, literary magazine, student government, student newspaper, minority club.

**Athletics.** NJCAA. **Intercollegiate:** Basketball M, golf, tennis. **Intramural:** Basketball, bowling, cheerleading W, cross-country, football (non-tackle), softball, table tennis, volleyball. **Team name:** Mariners.

**Student services.** Adult student services, career counseling, services for economically disadvantaged, student employment services, financial aid counseling, minority student services, personal counseling, placement for graduates, veterans' counselor. **Physically disabled:** Services for visually, speech, hearing impaired. **Transfer:** College fairs on campus for students transferring to 4-year colleges.

**Contact.** E-mail: admiss@ccga.edu
Phone: (912) 279-5730 Toll-free number: (800) 675-7235
Fax: (912) 262-3072
Lisa Lesseig, Registrar/Director of Admissions, College of Coastal Georgia, 3700 Altama Avenue, Brunswick, GA 31520

## Columbus Technical College
### Columbus, Georgia
### www.columbustech.org
### CB code: 7005

- Public 2-year technical college
- Commuter campus in small city
- Interview required

**General.** Founded in 1961. Regionally accredited. **Enrollment:** 4,100 degree-seeking undergraduates; 72 non-degree-seeking students. **Degrees:** 295 associate awarded. **Location:** 110 miles from Atlanta, 86 miles from Albany. **Calendar:** Quarter, extensive summer session. **Full-time faculty:** 77 total. **Part-time faculty:** 153 total.

**Student profile.** Among degree-seeking undergraduates, 855 enrolled as first-time, first-year students.

| | | | |
|---|---|---|---|
| Part-time: | 56% | Hispanic American: | 3% |
| Women: | 68% | Native American: | 1% |
| African American: | 46% | 25 or older: | 53% |
| Asian American: | 2% | | |

**Basis for selection.** Open admission, but selective for some programs. Special requirements for health programs. ACT or SAT may be accepted in lieu of COMPASS or ASSET for placement.

**High school preparation.** College-preparatory program recommended. 22 units recommended. Recommended units include English 4, mathematics 3, social studies 3, science 3, foreign language 1 and academic electives 3. 4 tech prep and 1 health science recommended.

**2009-2010 Annual costs.** Tuition/fees: $2,043; $3,843 out-of-state. Per-credit charge: $40 in-state; $80 out-of-state. Books/supplies: $1,600. Personal expenses: $1,100.

**Financial aid. Need-based:** Need-based aid available for part-time students.

**Application procedures. Admission:** Closing date 9/16. $25 fee. Notification before registration date. **Financial aid:** No deadline. FAFSA required. Applicants notified on a rolling basis.

**Academics. Special study options:** Distance learning, dual enrollment of high school students, weekend college. License preparation in dental hygiene, nursing, paramedic, radiology, real estate. **Credit/placement by examination:** AP, CLEP. **Support services:** Learning center, remedial instruction, study skills assistance, tutoring.

**Majors. Agriculture:** Horticultural science. **Business:** Accounting, administrative services, business admin. **Education:** Early childhood. **Engineering technology:** Electrical. **Health:** Cardiovascular technology, dental hygiene, nursing (RN), surgical technology. **Mechanic/repair:** Automotive, industrial.

**Most popular majors.** Business/marketing 23%, computer/information sciences 11%, education 7%, health sciences 49%.

**Computing on campus.** 40 workstations in library, computer center. Online library available.

**Student life. Freshman orientation:** Mandatory. Preregistration for classes offered. Three-hour orientation held day before start of classes. **Activities:** Student government.

**Student services.** Career counseling, student employment services, financial aid counseling, personal counseling, placement for graduates, veterans' counselor. **Physically disabled:** Services for speech, hearing impaired.

**Contact.** Phone: (706) 649-1800 Fax: (404) 649-1885
Nicole Kennedy, Director of Admissions, Columbus Technical College, 928 Manchester Expressway, Columbus, GA 31904

## Darton College
### Albany, Georgia
### www.darton.edu
### CB member
### CB code: 5026

- Public 2-year community college
- Commuter campus in small city

**General.** Founded in 1963. Regionally accredited. **Enrollment:** 4,651 degree-seeking undergraduates; 855 non-degree-seeking students. **Degrees:** 456 associate awarded. **Location:** 175 miles from Atlanta. **Calendar:** Semester, extensive summer session. **Full-time faculty:** 112 total; 16% minority, 67% women. **Part-time faculty:** 162 total; 17% minority, 54% women. **Class size:** 56% < 20, 41% 20-39, 2% 40-49, less than 1% 50-99, less than 1% >100. **Special facilities:** 50-foot Carolina tower and climbing wall, nature trail.

**Student profile.** Among degree-seeking undergraduates, 1,239 enrolled as first-time, first-year students.

| | | | |
|---|---|---|---|
| Part-time: | 45% | 25 or older: | 49% |
| Out-of-state: | 5% | Live on campus: | 4% |
| Women: | 69% | | |

**Transfer out. Colleges most students transferred to 2009:** Georgia Southwestern State University, Albany State University, Florida State University, Valdosta State University.

**Basis for selection.** Open admission, but selective for some programs. Special requirements for nursing, diagnostic medical sonography, physical therapy, and respiratory care programs. Criminal background check required for all students. Interview, portfolios and essays considered when students do not meet minimum admission requirements but show promise. **Homeschooled:** Transcript of courses and grades required.

**High school preparation.** College-preparatory program required. 16 units required. Required units include English 4, mathematics 4, social studies 3, science 3 and foreign language 2.

**2009-2010 Annual costs.** Tuition/fees: $2,992; $9,870 out-of-state. Per-credit charge: $77 in-state; $306 out-of-state. Books/supplies: $1,100. Personal expenses: $1,200.

**2008-2009 Financial aid. Need-based:** 99% of total undergraduate aid awarded as scholarships/grants, 1% as loans/jobs. Need-based aid available for part-time students. Work-study available nights, weekends and for part-time students. **Non-need-based:** Scholarships awarded for academics, alumni affiliation, art, athletics, music/drama, state residency. **Additional information:** Auditions, portfolios, essays, extracurricular activities impact scholarship decisions.

**Application procedures. Admission:** Priority date 8/1; no deadline. $20 fee. Admission notification on a rolling basis. Applications must be received 10 days prior to registration. **Financial aid:** No deadline. FAFSA, institutional form required. Applicants notified on a rolling basis; must reply within 3 week(s) of notification.

**Academics.** Career and transfer programs available. **Special study options:** Cooperative education, cross-registration, distance learning, double major, dual enrollment of high school students, ESL, honors, independent study, liberal arts/career combination, weekend college. License preparation in dental hygiene, nursing, occupational therapy, paramedic, physical therapy. **Credit/placement by examination:** AP, CLEP, IB, institutional tests. 18 hours in residence required. **Support services:** Learning center, reduced course load, remedial instruction, study skills assistance, tutoring, writing center.

**Majors. Agriculture:** General. **Biology:** General, biomedical sciences. **Business:** Accounting, administrative services, business admin, entrepreneurial studies, office management. **Communications:** Journalism. **Computer sciences:** General, computer science, information systems, networking. **Conservation:** Environmental studies, forestry. **Education:** Art, business, early childhood, English, foreign languages, mathematics, middle, multi-level teacher, music, social science, speech. **Engineering technology:** General. **Foreign languages:** General. **Health:** Cardiovascular technology, clinical lab science, community health services, dental hygiene, EMT paramedic, histologic assistant, licensed practical nurse, medical radiologic technology/radiation therapy, medical records admin, medical records technology, mental health services, nuclear medical technology, nursing (RN), occupational therapy assistant, physical therapy assistant, predental, premedicine, prepharmacy, preveterinary, respiratory therapy assistant, respiratory therapy technology, sonography. **History:** General. **Legal studies:** Paralegal, prelaw. **Math:** General. **Parks/recreation:** General, exercise sciences, health/fitness, sports admin. **Philosophy/religion:** Philosophy. **Physical sciences:** Chemistry, physics. **Protective services:** Criminal justice, forensics. **Psychology:** General. **Public administration:** Human services, social work. **Social sciences:** Anthropology, economics, geography, political science, sociology. **Visual/performing arts:** Art, dance, dramatic. **Other:** Pre-engineering.

**Most popular majors.** Business/marketing 9%, education 12%, health sciences 52%.

**Computing on campus.** 420 workstations in library, computer center. Dormitories linked to campus network. Commuter students can connect to campus network. Online course registration, online library, helpline, wireless network available.

**Student life. Freshman orientation:** Available. Preregistration for classes offered. Held every semester, required of all students enrolled in learning support classes. **Housing:** Coed dorms available. **Activities:** Bands, choral groups, dance, drama, international student organizations, literary magazine, music ensembles, musical theater, student government, student newspaper, symphony orchestra, cultural exchange club, Democratic Independent Republican Team (DIRT).

**Athletics.** NJCAA. **Intercollegiate:** Baseball M, basketball W, golf M, soccer, softball W, swimming, wrestling M. **Intramural:** Basketball, bowling, football (non-tackle), golf, softball, table tennis, tennis, volleyball. **Team name:** Cavaliers.

**Student services.** Alcohol/substance abuse counseling, career counseling, student employment services, financial aid counseling, minority student services, personal counseling, veterans' counselor. **Physically disabled:** Services for visually, speech, hearing impaired. **Transfer:** Pre-admission transcript evaluation for new students. Transfer adviser, college fairs on campus for students transferring to 4-year colleges.

**Contact.** E-mail: info@darton.edu
Phone: (229) 317-6740 Toll-free number: (866) 775-1214
Fax: (229) 317-6607
Susan Bowen, Director of Admission, Darton College, 2400 Gillionville Road, Albany, GA 31707-3098

## DeKalb Technical College
**Clarkston, Georgia**
www.dekalbtech.edu                          **CB code: 3226**

- Public 2-year technical college
- Commuter campus in large city

**General.** Founded in 1961. Regionally accredited. Second campus located in Covington. **Enrollment:** 4,664 degree-seeking undergraduates; 78 non-degree-seeking students. **Degrees:** 266 associate awarded. **Location:** 17 miles from Atlanta. **Calendar:** Quarter, extensive summer session. **Full-time faculty:** 101 total. **Part-time faculty:** 423 total. **Class size:** 88% < 20, 12% 20-39. **Special facilities:** Conference center. **Partnerships:** Formal partnerships wtih MARTA; Fulton County Government; DeKalb, Rockdale, Newton, Morgan County Schools; Decatur City Schools.

**Student profile.** Among degree-seeking undergraduates, 942 enrolled as first-time, first-year students.

| | | | |
|---|---|---|---|
| Part-time: | 58% | Asian American: | 3% |
| Women: | 62% | Hispanic American: | 1% |
| African American: | 75% | 25 or older: | 67% |

**Transfer out. Colleges most students transferred to 2009:** Georgia State University, Southern Polytechnic State University, DeVry University, Clayton College and State University, Georgia Perimeter College.

**Basis for selection.** Open admission, but selective for some programs. Limited admission to health technologies programs. ACT or SAT may be accepted in lieu of COMPASS or ASSET for placement. Interview recommended.

**High school preparation.** College-preparatory program recommended. 22 units recommended. Recommended units include English 4, mathematics 3, social studies 3, science 3, foreign language 1 and academic electives 3. 4 tech prep and 1 health science recommended.

**2009-2010 Annual costs.** Tuition/fees: $2,091; $3,891 out-of-state. Per-credit charge: $40 in-state; $80 out-of-state. Truck driving and flight technology are higher cost programs. Books/supplies: $1,200. Personal expenses: $900.

**2009-2010 Financial aid. Need-based:** Need-based aid available for part-time students. Work-study available nights, weekends and for part-time students.

**Application procedures. Admission:** Closing date 8/22 (receipt date). $25 fee. Application must be submitted on paper. Admission notification on a rolling basis. **Financial aid:** Priority date 7/15, closing date 8/20. FAFSA required. Applicants notified on a rolling basis starting 6/1.

**Academics. Special study options:** Distance learning, dual enrollment of high school students, weekend college. License preparation in nursing, paramedic, real estate. **Credit/placement by examination:** AP, CLEP, institutional tests. 35 credit hours maximum toward associate degree. **Support services:** GED preparation and test center, learning center, reduced course load, remedial instruction, study skills assistance, tutoring.

**Majors. Business:** Accounting, business admin, marketing. **Computer sciences:** General, programming. **Engineering:** Computer, electrical. **Engineering technology:** Electrical, instrumentation. **Health:** Ophthalmic lab technology, optician. **Mechanic/repair:** Automotive.

**Most popular majors.** Business/marketing 39%, computer/information sciences 11%, education 13%, legal studies 13%, trade and industry 6%.

**Computing on campus.** 500 workstations in computer center. Online course registration, online library available.

**Student life. Freshman orientation:** Available. **Activities:** Student government, student newspaper, Delta Epsilon Chi, Collegiate Secretaries International, Noon Net-Working of New Connections, Phi Beta Lambda, Student Optical Society, Licensed Practical Nurses Association, Vocational Industrial Clubs of America, Epsilon Delta Phi Honorary Society, Phi Theta Kappa Honor Society.

**Student services.** Adult student services, career counseling, services for economically disadvantaged, student employment services, financial aid counseling, minority student services, placement for graduates, veterans' counselor, women's services. **Physically disabled:** Services for visually, speech, hearing impaired. **Transfer:** Pre-admission transcript evaluation for new students.

**Contact.** E-mail: richardt@dekalbtech.edu
Phone: (404) 297-9522 ext. 1602 Toll-free
number: (877) 780-3032 ext. 1602 Fax: (404) 294-3424
Terry Richardson, Coordinator of Admissions and Special Services, DeKalb Technical College, 495 North Indian Creek Drive, Clarkston, GA 30021-2397

## East Georgia College
**Swainsboro, Georgia**                      **CB member**
www.ega.edu                                   **CB code: 5200**

- Public 2-year community and junior college
- Commuter campus in small town

**General.** Founded in 1973. Regionally accredited. **Enrollment:** 2,754 degree-seeking undergraduates. **Degrees:** 149 associate awarded. **ROTC:** Army. **Location:** 85 miles from Savannah and Augusta. **Calendar:** Semester, limited summer session. **Full-time faculty:** 52 total; 42% have terminal degrees, 10% minority, 40% women. **Part-time faculty:** 51 total; 28% have terminal degrees, 12% minority, 45% women. **Class size:** 16% < 20, 80% 20-39, 3% 40-49, less than 1% >100. **Special facilities:** Outdoor exercise trail, fitness center, community learning center.

**Student profile.** Among degree-seeking undergraduates, 31 transferred in from other institutions.

| | | | |
|---|---|---|---|
| **Out-of-state:** | 2% | **25 or older:** | 20% |

**Transfer out. Colleges most students transferred to 2009:** Georgia Southern University.

**Basis for selection.** Graduation from accredited or approved high school or GED, 16 college prep curriculum units, COMPASS test scores, and 2.0 GPA required. **Homeschooled:** SAT/ACT, home-school portfolio, and letter of completion from primary teacher or program administrator with date of graduation required. Applicants with GED need to submit GED scores and home-school portfolio; SAT/ACT not required. COMPASS placement test may be required.

**High school preparation.** 16 units required. Required and recommended units include English 4, mathematics 4, social studies 3, science 3 and foreign language 2.

**2009-2010 Annual costs.** Tuition/fees: $2,767; $9,645 out-of-state. Per-credit charge: $77 in-state; $306 out-of-state. Books/supplies: $1,400. Personal expenses: $1,400.

**Financial aid. Need-based:** Need-based aid available for part-time students. **Non-need-based:** Scholarships awarded for academics, leadership, state residency.

**Application procedures. Admission:** No deadline. $20 fee, may be waived for applicants with need. Admission notification on a rolling basis beginning on or about 2/1. **Financial aid:** Priority date 6/1; no closing date. FAFSA, institutional form required. Applicants notified on a rolling basis starting 6/1; must reply within 2 week(s) of notification.

**Academics. Special study options:** Distance learning, double major, dual enrollment of high school students, honors, independent study, study abroad. Bachelor's degree programs available on campus. License preparation in nursing. **Credit/placement by examination:** CLEP, IB, institutional tests. 30 credit hours maximum toward associate degree. **Support services:** Learning center, reduced course load, remedial instruction, study skills assistance, tutoring, writing center.

**Majors. Agriculture:** General. **Biology:** General. **Business:** Business admin. **Computer sciences:** Computer science. **Education:** General, business, multi-level teacher. **Family/consumer sciences:** General. **Foreign languages:** Translation. **Health:** Prenursing. **History:** General. **Liberal arts:** Arts/sciences. **Math:** General. **Parks/recreation:** General, exercise sciences, health/fitness. **Physical sciences:** Chemistry, geology. **Protective services:** Criminal justice. **Psychology:** General. **Social sciences:** Anthropology, criminology, political science, sociology. **Visual/performing arts:** Art.

**Computing on campus.** 271 workstations in library, computer center, student center. Commuter students can connect to campus network. Online course registration, online library, helpline, wireless network available.

**Student life. Freshman orientation:** Mandatory. Preregistration for classes offered. Combined 1-day orientation and registration event. **Policies:** Substance-free campus. **Activities:** Campus ministries, choral groups, drama, international student organizations, literary magazine, student government, student newspaper, Afro-American union, Earth club, Students in Free Enterprise, Student Professional Association of Georgia Educators, art club, Circle K, non-traditonal club, ECHO club, nursing club, pursuit club.

**Athletics. Intercollegiate:** Baseball M, basketball, cheerleading, softball W. **Intramural:** Football (non-tackle) M, table tennis, tennis, volleyball. **Team name:** Bobcats.

**Student services.** Adult student services, alcohol/substance abuse counseling, career counseling, financial aid counseling, minority student services, personal counseling, veterans' counselor. **Physically disabled:** Services for visually, hearing impaired. **Transfer:** Pre-admission transcript evaluation for new students. Transfer adviser, college fairs on campus for students transferring to 4-year colleges.

**Contact.** E-mail: kjones@ega.edu
Phone: (478) 289-2017 Fax: (478) 289-2140
Karen Jones, Director of Admissions, East Georgia College, 131 College Circle, Swainsboro, GA 30401-2699

## Everest Institute
### Atlanta, Georgia
### www.georgia-med.com

- For-profit 2-year health science college
- Very large city

**General.** Accredited by ACCSCT. **Calendar:** Continuous.

**Contact.** Phone: (404) 327-8787
1706 Northeast Expressway, Atlanta, GA 30329

## Gainesville State College
### Gainesville, Georgia
### www.gsc.edu
**CB code: 5273**

- Public 2-year junior college
- Commuter campus in large town

**General.** Founded in 1964. Regionally accredited. **Enrollment:** 8,565 degree-seeking undergraduates. **Degrees:** 61 bachelor's, 667 associate awarded. **Location:** 45 miles from Atlanta, 40 miles from Athens. **Calendar:** Semester, extensive summer session. **Full-time faculty:** 207 total. **Part-time faculty:** 224 total. **Class size:** 21% < 20, 79% 20-39, less than 1% 40-49, less than 1% 50-99.

**Transfer out. Colleges most students transferred to 2009:** North Georgia College and State University, University of Georgia, Brenau University, Georgia State University, Georgia Institute of Technology.

**Basis for selection.** 2.0 GPA required for applicants with college prep curriculum diploma; 2.2 GPA required for applicants with technical prep curriculum diploma. SAT or ACT scores may be used for placement test screening and/or academic advising.

**High school preparation.** College-preparatory program recommended. 16 units required. Required units include English 4, mathematics 4, social studies 3, science 3 (laboratory 3) and foreign language 2.

**2009-2010 Annual costs.** Tuition/fees: $2,948; $10,430 out-of-state. Books/supplies: $630. Personal expenses: $1,000.

**2008-2009 Financial aid. Need-based:** Need-based aid available for part-time students. Work-study available nights, weekends and for part-time students. **Non-need-based:** Scholarships awarded for academics, art, leadership, music/drama.

**Application procedures. Admission:** Closing date 7/1 (postmark date). $35 fee, may be waived for applicants with need. Admission notification on a rolling basis. **Financial aid:** Closing date 6/1. FAFSA required. Applicants notified on a rolling basis starting 5/1; must reply within 2 week(s) of notification.

**Academics. Special study options:** Distance learning, dual enrollment of high school students, ESL, honors, study abroad, teacher certification program. Bachelor's degree programs available on campus. License preparation in dental hygiene, paramedic. **Credit/placement by examination:** AP, CLEP, SAT, ACT, institutional tests. 30 credit hours maximum toward associate degree. **Support services:** Learning center, remedial instruction, study skills assistance, tutoring, writing center.

**Majors. Agriculture:** General, business. **Business:** General, accounting, administrative services, business admin. **Communications:** Journalism. **Computer sciences:** General. **Conservation:** Forestry. **Education:** General, art, early childhood, elementary, mathematics, music, physical, science, secondary, social science. **Engineering:** General. **Engineering technology:** Electrical. **Family/consumer sciences:** Child care. **Health:** Dental hygiene, EMT paramedic. **History:** General. **Legal studies:** Paralegal. **Liberal arts:** Arts/sciences. **Math:** General. **Physical sciences:** Chemistry, geology, physics. **Protective services:** Criminal justice. **Psychology:** General. **Public administration:** Social work. **Social sciences:** Anthropology, political science, sociology. **Visual/performing arts:** Dramatic, music performance, studio arts.

**Computing on campus.** 1,000 workstations in library, computer center, student center. Commuter students can connect to campus network. Online course registration, online library, helpline, student web hosting, wireless network available.

**Student life. Freshman orientation:** Mandatory. Preregistration for classes offered. **Activities:** Bands, choral groups, drama, film society, international student organizations, literary magazine, music ensembles, musical theater, student government, student newspaper.

**Athletics. Intramural:** Basketball, bowling, football (non-tackle), golf, softball, tennis, volleyball.

**Student services.** Adult student services, alcohol/substance abuse counseling, career counseling, student employment services, financial aid counseling, minority student services, personal counseling, placement for graduates, veterans' counselor. **Physically disabled:** Services for visually, speech, hearing impaired. **Transfer:** Transfer adviser, college fairs on campus for students transferring to 4-year colleges.

**Contact.** E-mail: admissions@gsc.edu
Phone: (678) 717-3641 Fax: (678) 717-3643
Mack Palmour, Director of Admissions, Gainesville State College, PO Box 1358, Gainesville, GA 30503

## Georgia Highlands College
### Rome, Georgia                                    CB member
### www.highlands.edu                                CB code: 5237

- Public 2-year community and liberal arts college
- Commuter campus in large city

**General.** Founded in 1968. Regionally accredited. Classes offered at Cartersville, Marietta, Paulding, Douglasville, and Rome. **Enrollment:** 5,237 degree-seeking undergraduates. **Degrees:** 428 associate awarded. **Location:** 75 miles from Atlanta. **Calendar:** Semester, limited summer session. **Full-time faculty:** 85 total. **Part-time faculty:** 110 total. **Special facilities:** Observatory, wetlands preserve.

**Student profile.** Among degree-seeking undergraduates, 14% enrolled in a transfer program, 1,704 enrolled as first-time, first-year students, 483 transferred in from other institutions.

| Part-time: | 39% | Asian American: | 2% |
|---|---|---|---|
| Women: | 63% | Hispanic American: | 4% |
| African American: | 11% | 25 or older: | 22% |

**Transfer out. Colleges most students transferred to 2009:** Kennesaw State University, State University of West Georgia, Berry College, Shorter College, University of Georgia.

**Basis for selection.** 2.0 college prep or 2.2 technical prep GPA required. SAT or ACT required for admissions into nursing and dental hygiene programs. SAT or ACT can be used to exempt COMPASS placement examinations. **Homeschooled:** Statement describing homeschool structure and mission, transcript of courses and grades, state high school equivalency certificate required. Must submit SAT scores that are equal to or greater than last year's freshman class average and provide completed home school college prep curriculum evaluation form; portfolio required. **Learning Disabled:** Foreign language college preparatory curriculum may be waived through Georgia Board of Regents Center of Learning Disabilities.

**High school preparation.** College-preparatory program recommended. 16 units recommended. Recommended units include English 4, mathematics 4, social studies 3, science 3 (laboratory 2) and foreign language 2. College preparatory program required for students planning to transfer to 4-year school.

**2009-2010 Annual costs.** Tuition/fees: $2,644; $9,514 out-of-state. Per-credit charge: $77 in-state; $306 out-of-state. Books/supplies: $750. Personal expenses: $550.

**2008-2009 Financial aid. Need-based:** 41% of total undergraduate aid awarded as scholarships/grants, 59% as loans/jobs. Need-based aid available for part-time students. Work-study available nights and for part-time students. **Non-need-based:** Scholarships awarded for academics, art.

**Application procedures. Admission:** Priority date 7/1; no deadline. $20 fee, may be waived for applicants with need. Admission notification on a rolling basis beginning on or about 1/2. **Financial aid:** Closing date 4/1. FAFSA required. Applicants notified on a rolling basis starting 4/1; must reply within 2 week(s) of notification.

**Academics. Special study options:** Cooperative education, distance learning, double major, dual enrollment of high school students, independent study, liberal arts/career combination, study abroad. License preparation in dental hygiene, nursing. **Credit/placement by examination:** AP, CLEP, IB, SAT, ACT, institutional tests. No limit on credits awarded. **Support services:** Learning center, remedial instruction, study skills assistance, tutoring, writing center.

**Majors. Agriculture:** General. **Biology:** General. **Business:** Accounting technology, business admin, managerial economics, office management, office technology. **Communications:** General, journalism. **Computer sciences:** General. **Education:** General, multi-level teacher. **Engineering technology:** Drafting. **Foreign languages:** General. **Health:** Dental hygiene, health services, nursing (RN), physician assistant, premedicine, prenursing, prepharmacy, preveterinary, radiologic technology/medical imaging, respiratory therapy technology. **Liberal arts:** Arts/sciences. **Math:** General. **Philosophy/religion:** Philosophy. **Physical sciences:** Chemistry, geology, physics. **Protective services:** Police science. **Psychology:** General. **Public**

administration: Human services. **Social sciences:** Political science, sociology.

**Most popular majors.** Business/marketing 24%, education 17%, health sciences 32%, liberal arts 10%.

**Computing on campus.** Commuter students can connect to campus network. Online course registration, online library, helpline, repair service, wireless network available.

**Student life. Freshman orientation:** Mandatory. **Policies:** Access program tracks all student involvement in school and community activities. Transcripts available for resume use or when transferring to another institution. **Housing:** Housing available through Southern Poly Tech University for Marietta Campus. **Activities:** Literary magazine, student government, student newspaper, TV station, Baptist student union, College Bowl Team, volunteer opportunity center, black student awareness, Insiders, Phi Theta Kappa.

**Athletics. Intramural:** Archery, badminton, basketball, bowling, field hockey W, football (tackle) M, golf, sailing, skiing, soccer, softball, table tennis, tennis, volleyball, wrestling M. **Team name:** Chargers.

**Student services.** Adult student services, alcohol/substance abuse counseling, career counseling, student employment services, financial aid counseling, minority student services, personal counseling, placement for graduates, veterans' counselor. **Physically disabled:** Services for visually, speech, hearing impaired. **Transfer:** Re-entry adviser, pre-admission transcript evaluation for new students. College fairs on campus for students transferring to 4-year colleges.

**Contact.** E-mail: admitme@highlands.edu
Phone: (706) 295-6339 Toll-free number: (800) 332-2406 ext. 6339
Fax: (706) 295-6341
Todd Jones, Director of Admissions, Georgia Highlands College, 3175 Cedartown Highway, Rome, GA 30161

## Georgia Military College
### Milledgeville, Georgia
### www.gmc.cc.ga.us                                  CB code: 5249

- Public 2-year community and military college
- Commuter campus in large town

**General.** Founded in 1879. Regionally accredited. Multiple location institution. **Enrollment:** 5,854 degree-seeking undergraduates. **Degrees:** 673 associate awarded. **ROTC:** Army. **Location:** 90 miles from Atlanta, 30 miles from Macon. **Calendar:** Quarter, limited summer session. **Full-time faculty:** 107 total; 13% have terminal degrees, 13% minority, 49% women. **Part-time faculty:** 167 total; 23% have terminal degrees, 30% minority, 61% women. **Class size:** 70% < 20, 30% 20-39.

**Student profile.** Among degree-seeking undergraduates, 3,271 enrolled as first-time, first-year students.

| Part-time: | 30% | Asian American: | 2% |
|---|---|---|---|
| Out-of-state: | 9% | Hispanic American: | 3% |
| Women: | 62% | 25 or older: | 36% |
| African American: | 40% | Live on campus: | 2% |

**Basis for selection.** Open admission, but selective for some programs. ROTC applicants for early commissioning must have 920 SAT (exclusive of Writing) or 19 ACT and 2.0 GPA. Interview recommended for ROTC cadets. **Homeschooled:** Transcript of courses and grades required. List of courses completed and bibliography of textbooks and/or assigned readings required. Must submit writing sample or show successful GED completion.

**2009-2010 Annual costs.** Tuition/fees: $5,513. Per-credit charge: $105. Tuition and fees for cadet students: $12,150 with $1,150 additional for uniforms. Room/board: $5,535. Books/supplies: $675. Personal expenses: $600.

**2008-2009 Financial aid. Need-based:** Need-based aid available for part-time students. Work-study available nights and for part-time students. **Non-need-based:** Scholarships awarded for athletics, leadership, ROTC, state residency. **Additional information:** Institutional aid offered to those enrolled in Cadet Corps who reside on campus.

**Application procedures. Admission:** Priority date 8/1; deadline 9/1 (receipt date). $35 fee, may be waived for applicants with need. Admission notification on a rolling basis. August 1 closing date for cadets. Students interested in attending ROTC Basic Camp must apply by May 1. **Financial aid:** No deadline. FAFSA required. Applicants notified on a rolling basis starting 3/1.